International WHO'S WHO of

Authors

AND Writers

2008

International WHO'S WHO of   2008

Authors
AND Writers

23rd Edition

Routledge
Taylor & Francis Group

LONDON AND NEW YORK

First published 1934

© **Routledge 2007**
Haines House, 21 John Street, London, WC1N 2BP, United Kingdom
(Routledge is an imprint of the Taylor & Francis Group, an **informa** business)

Please send comments and enquiries to **worldwhoswho@informa.com**
Our complete catalogue is available at **www.routledge.com/reference**

ISBN-10: 1-85743-428-5
ISBN-13: 978-1-85743-428-6
ISSN: 1740-018X

Series Editor: Robert J. Elster
Associate Editor: Alison Neale
Assistant Editor: Amy Tyndall
Freelance Editorial Team: Annabella Gabb, Neil Higgins
Administrative Assistant: Charley McCartney

The Publishers make no representation, express or implied, with regard
to the accuracy of the information contained in this book and cannot accept
any legal responsibility for any errors or omissions that may take place.

Typeset by Data Standards Limited, Frome
Printed and bound in Great Britain by Polestar Wheatons, Exeter

FOREWORD

The 23rd edition of the INTERNATIONAL WHO'S WHO OF AUTHORS AND WRITERS provides biographical information on novelists, journalists, essayists, dramatists, poets and editors, as well as literary agents and publishers. The biographies include, where available, personal and contact details, information on career and awards, publications, and contributions to books and periodicals.

For each edition entrants are given the opportunity to make necessary amendments and additions to their biographies. Supplementary research is done by the editorial department in order to ensure that the book is as up to date as possible on publication.

In addition to the biographical information, the directory section provides details of literary awards and prizes, literary organizations and, for the first time this year, literary festivals and national libraries of the world. The introduction contains a list of abbreviations and international telephone codes. The names of entrants whose death has been reported over the past year are included in the obituary.

Readers are referred to the book's companion title in The Europa Biographical Reference Series, the INTERNATIONAL WHO'S WHO IN POETRY, for a comprehensive collection of information on the most prominent international poets.

The assistance of the individuals and organizations included in this publication in providing up-to-date material is invaluable, and the editors would like to take this opportunity to express their appreciation.

August 2007

ALPHABETIZATION AND THE TRANSCRIPTION OF NAMES

The list of names is alphabetical, with the entrants listed under their family name. If part of an entrant's family name is in parentheses, indicating that this part is not usually used, this will be ignored for the purposes of the alphabetical listing.

If an entrant's name is spelt in a variety of ways, a cross-reference is provided. An entrant who is known by a pseudonym or by an abbreviation of their name is either listed under this name or a cross-reference is provided. Multiple pseudonyms are cross-referenced where considered necessary.

Titles as part of a pseudonym, such as DJ, are ignored for the purposes of the alphabetical listing. Pseudonyms that include numbers as part of the name are listed alphabetically under the spelling of that number.

All names beginning Mc and Mac are listed as if they began Mac, e.g. McDevitt before MacDonald.

In the case of surnames beginning De, Des, Du, van or von the entries are normally found under the prefix. Names beginning St are listed as if they began Saint, e.g. St Germain before Salamun.

It should be noted that in some countries (including The People's Republic of China, The Republic of Korea, The Democratic People's Republic of Korea, Cambodia and Viet Nam) the family name is given first, followed by the given name; however, this does not affect alphabetization.

In Indonesia some people have only one name, under which their entries are alphabetized. In Thailand people often have two names, but these do not always equate to Western usage. We alphabetize the entries under the better-known name, providing the full name in the entry and cross-references where considered necessary.

Arabic names have been transliterated from the written form, rather than from pronunciation (which can vary from place to place). However, in Arabic pronunciation, when the word to which the definite article, al, is attached begins with one of certain letters called 'Sun-letters', the l of the article changes to the initial letter in question, e.g. al-shamsu (the sun) is pronounced ash-shamsu. Accordingly, where the article is attached to a name beginning with a Sun-letter, it has been rendered phonetically. Names beginning with 'Moon-letters', however, retain the l of the definite article. Names with Arabic prefixes are alphabetized after the prefix, unless requested otherwise by the entrant.

In a few cases consistency of transliteration has been sacrificed in order to avoid replacing a familiar and accepted form of a name by another which, although more accurate, would be unrecognizable.

CONTENTS

page

Abbreviations   viii

International Telephone Codes   xviii

Obituary   xx

PART ONE

Biographies   3

PART TWO

Directory

Appendix A: Literary Awards and Prizes   791

Appendix B: Literary Organizations   798

Appendix C: Literary Festivals   804

Appendix D: National Libraries   805

ABBREVIATIONS

AA	Associate in Arts
AAA	Agricultural Adjustment Administration
AAAS	American Association for the Advancement of Science
AAF	Army Air Force
AASA	Associate of the Australian Society of Accountants
AB	Aktiebolag
AB	Alberta
AB	Bachelor of Arts
ABA	American Bar Association
ABC	American Broadcasting Company
ABC	Australian Broadcasting Corporation
ABRSM	Associated Board for the Royal Schools of Music
AC	Companion of the Order of Australia
ACA	American Composers' Alliance
ACA	Associate of the Institute of Chartered Accountants
Acad.	Académie, Academy
Acad.	Académie
Acad.	Academy
ACCA	Associate of the Association of Certified Accountants
Accad.	Accademia
accred	accredited
ACIS	Associate of the Chartered Institute of Secretaries
ACLS	American Council of Learned Societies
ACM	Academy of Country Music
ACP	American College of Physicians
ACS	American Chemical Society
ACT	Australian Capital Territory
ADB	African Development Bank
ADC	Aide-de-camp
Adm.	Admiral
Admin.	Administration, Administrative, Administrator
Admin	Administration
Admin.	Administrative
Admin.	Administrator
AE	Air Efficiency Award
AERE	Atomic Energy Research Establishment
AF	Air Force
AFC	Air Force Cross
affil.	affiliated
AFL	American Federation of Labor
AFM	Air Force Medal
AFofM	American Federation of Musicians
AFTRA	American Federation of Television and Radio Artists
AG	Aktiengesellschaft (Joint Stock Company)
AGMA	American Guild of Musical Artists
Agric.	Agriculture
a.i.	ad interim
AIA	American Institute of Architects, Associate of the Institute of Actuaries
AIA	American Institute of Architects
AIA	Associate of the Institute of Actuaries
AIAA	American Institute of Aeronautics and Astronautics
AIB	Associate of the Institute of Bankers
AICC	All-India Congress Committee
AICE	Associate of the Institute of Civil Engineers
AIChE	American Institute of Chemical Engineers
AIDS	Acquired Immune Deficiency Syndrome
AIEE	American Institute of Electrical Engineers
AIME	American Institute of Mining Engineers, Associate of the Institution of Mining Engineers
AIME	American Institute of Mining Engineers
AIME	Associate of the Institution of Mining Engineers
AIMechE	Associate of the Institution of Mechanical Engineers
AIR	All-India Radio
AK	Alaska
AK	Knight of the Order of Australia
aka	also known as
Akad.	Akademie
AL	Alabama
Ala	Alabama
ALCS	Authors' Lending and Copyright Society
ALS	Associate of the Linnaean Society
Alt.	Alternate
AM	Albert Medal, Alpes Maritimes, Master of Arts, Member of the Order of Australia
AM	Albert Medal
AM	Alpes Maritimes
AM	amplitude modulation
AM	Master of Arts
AM	Member of the Order of Australia
Amb.	Ambassador
AMICE	Associate Member of the Institution of Civil Engineers
AMIEE	Associate Member of the Institution of Electrical Engineers
AMIMechE	Associate Member of the Institution of Mechanical Engineers
ANC	African National Congress
ANU	Australian National University
AO	Officer of the Order of Australia
AP	Andhra Pradesh (India)
Apdo	Apartado (Post Box)
APEC	Asia and Pacific Economic Co-operation
approx.	approximately
appt	appointment
apptd	appointed
APRA	Australian Performing Rights Association
apt	apartment
apto	apartamento
A&R	Artists and Repertoire
AR	Arkansas
ARA	Associate of the Royal Academy
ARAM	Associate of the Royal Academy of Music
ARAS	Associate of the Royal Astronomical Society
ARC	Agriculture Research Council
ARCA	Associate of the Royal College of Art
ARCM	Associate of the Royal College of Music
ARCO	Associate of the Royal College of Organists
ARCS	Associate of the Royal College of Science
ARIBA	Associate of the Royal Institute of British Architects
Ariz.	Arizona
Ark.	Arkansas
ARSA	Associate of the Royal Scottish Academy, Associate of the Royal Society of Arts
ARSA	Associate of the Royal Scottish Academy
ARSA	Associate of the Royal Society of Arts
ASCAP	American Society of Composers, Authors and Publishers
ASEAN	Association of South-East Asian Nations
ASLIB	Association of Special Libraries and Information Bureaux
ASME	American Society of Mechanical Engineers
Asoc.	Asociación
Ass.	Assembly
Asscn	Association
Assoc.	Associate
ASSR	Autonomous Soviet Socialist Republic
Asst	Assistant
ATD	Art Teacher's Diploma
ATV	Associated Television
Aug.	August
autobiog.	autobiography
Avda	Avenida (Avenue)
AZ	Arizona
b.	born
BA	Bachelor of Arts, British Airways
BA	Bachelor of Arts
BA	British Airways
BAAS	British Association for the Advancement of Science
BAC&S	British Academy of Composers and Songwriters
BAFTA	British Academy of Film and Television Arts
BAgr	Bachelor of Agriculture
BAgrSc	Bachelor of Agricultural Science
BAO	Bachelor of Obstetrics
BAOR	British Army of the Rhine
BArch	Bachelor of Architecture
Bart	Baronet
BAS	Bachelor in Agricultural Science
BASc	Bachelor of Applied Science
BASCA	British Association of Songwriters, Composers and Authors (now BAC&S)
BBA	Bachelor of Business Administration
BBC	British Broadcasting Corporation
BC	British Columbia
BCC	British Council of Churches
BCE	Bachelor of Civil Engineering
BChir	Bachelor of Surgery
BCL	Bachelor of Canon Law, Bachelor of Civil Law

BCL	Bachelor of Canon Law	CBS	Columbia Broadcasting System
BCL	Bachelor of Civil Law	CBSO	City of Birmingham Symphony Orchestra
BCom	Bachelor of Commerce	CC	Companion of the Order of Canada
BComm	Bachelor of Commerce	CChem	Chartered Chemist
BCS	Bachelor of Commercial Sciences	CCMA	Canadian Country Music Association
BD	Bachelor of Divinity	CCMI	Companion of the Chartered Management Institute (formerly CIMgt)
Bd	Board		
BDS	Bachelor of Dental Surgery	CCP	Chinese Communist Party
Bdwy	Broadway	CD	Canadian Forces Decoration, Commander Order of Distinction
BE	Bachelor of Education, Bachelor of Engineering		
BE	Bachelor of Education	CD	Canadian Forces Decoration
BE	Bachelor of Engineering	CD	Commander Order of Distinction
BEA	British European Airways	CD	compact disc
BEcons	Bachelor of Economics	Cdre	Commodore
BEd	Bachelor of Education	CD-ROM	compact disc read-only memory
Beds.	Bedfordshire	CDU	Christlich-Demokratische Union
BEE	Bachelor of Electrical Engineering	CE	Chartered Engineer, Civil Engineer
BEM	British Empire Medal	CE	Chartered Engineer
BEng	Bachelor of Engineering	CE	Civil Engineer
Berks.	Berkshire	CEAO	Communauté Economique de l'Afrique de l'Ouest
BET	Black Entertainment Television	Cen.	Central
BFA	Bachelor of Fine Arts	CEng	Chartered Engineer
BFI	British Film Institute	CENTO	Central Treaty Organization
BIM	British Institute of Management	CEO	Chief Executive Officer
biog.	biography	CERN	Conseil (now Organisation) Européen(ne) pour la Recherche Nucléaire
BIS	Bank for International Settlements		
BJ	Bachelor of Journalism	CFR	Commander of the Federal Republic of Nigeria
BL	Bachelor of Laws	CGM	Conspicuous Gallantry Medal
BLA	Bachelor of Landscape Architecture	CGT	Confédération Général du Travail
Bldg	Building	CH	Companion of Honour
BLit	Bachelor of Letters	Chair.	Chairman, Chairwoman, Chairperson
BLit	Bachelor of Literature	Chair.	Chairman
BLit(t)	Bachelor of Letters	Chair.	Chairperson
BLitt	Bachelor of Letters	Chair.	Chairwoman
BLitt	Bachelor of Literature	ChB	Bachelor of Surgery
BLL	Bachelor of Laws	CHB	Companion of Honour of Barbados
BLS	Bachelor in Library Science	Chem.	Chemistry
blvd	boulevard	ChM	Master of Surgery
BM	Bachelor of Medicine	CI	Channel Islands
BM	Bachelor of Music	CIA	Central Intelligence Agency
BMA	British Medical Association	Cia	Compagnia, Companhia (Company)
BME	Bachelor of Music Education	Cía	Compañía (Company)
BMEd	Bachelor of Music Education	CID	Criminal Investigation Department
BMI	Broadcast Music Incorporated	Cie	Compagnie (Company)
BMus	Bachelor of Music	CIE	Companion of (the Order of) the Indian Empire
Bn	Battalion	CIEE	Companion of the Institution of Electrical Engineers
BNOC	British National Oil Corporation	CIMgt	Companion of the Institute of Management (now CCMI)
BOAC	British Overseas Airways Corporation		
BP	Boîte Postale (Post Box)	C-in-C	Commander-in-Chief
BPA	Bachelor of Public Administration	CIO	Congress of Industrial Organizations
BPharm	Bachelor of Pharmacy	CIOMS	Council of International Organizations of Medical Science
BPhil	Bachelor of Philosophy	circ.	circulation
Br.	Branch	CIS	Commonwealth of Independent States
Brig.	Brigadier	CLD	Doctor of Civil Law (USA)
BS	Bachelor of Science, Bachelor of Surgery	CLit	Companion of Literature
BS	Bachelor of Science	CM	Canada Medal, Master of Surgery
BS	Bachelor of Surgery	CM	Canada Medal
BSA	Bachelor of Scientific Agriculture	CM	Master of Surgery
BSc	Bachelor of Science	CMA	Country Music Association
BSE	Bachelor of Science in Engineering (USA)	CMEA	Council for Mutual Economic Assistance
BSFA	British Science Fiction Association	CMG	Companion of (the Order of) St Michael and St George
Bt	Baronet	CNAA	Council for National Academic Awards
BTh	Bachelor of Theology	CNRS	Centre National de la Recherche Scientifique
BTI	British Theatre Institute	CO	Chamber Orchestra
Bucks.	Buckinghamshire	CO	Colorado
		CO	Commanding Officer
		Co.	Company, County
c.	circa	Co.	Company
c.	child(ren)	Co.	County
c/o	care of	COI	Central Office of Information
CA	California	Col	Colonel
CA	Chartered Accountant	Col.	Colonia, Colima (hill)
Calif.	California	Coll.	College
Cambs.	Cambridgeshire	Colo	Colorado
CAMI	Columbia Artists Management International	COMECON	Council for Mutual Economic Assistance
Cand.	Candidate, Candidature	COMESA	Common Market for Eastern and Southern Asia
Cand.	Candidate	Comm.	Commission
Cand.	Candidature	Commdg	Commanding
Cantab.	of Cambridge University	Commdr	Commander, Commandeur
Capt.	Captain	Commdr	Commander
Cards.	Cardiganshire	Commdr	Commandeur
CB	Companion of (the Order of) the Bath	Commdt	Commandant
CBC	Canadian Broadcasting Corporation	Commr	Commissioner
CBE	Commander of (the Order of) the British Empire	CON	Commander of Order of Nigeria
CBI	Confederation of British Industry	Conf.	Conference
CBIM	Companion of the British Institute of Management	Confed.	Confederation
CBiol	Chartered Biologist	Conn.	Connecticut

Contrib.	contribution, Contributor
Contrib.	contribution
Contrib.	Contributor
COO	Chief Operating Officer
Corp.	Corporate
Corpn	Corporation
Corresp.	Correspondent, Corresponding
Corresp.	Correspondent
Corresp.	Corresponding
CP	Caixa Postal (Post Box), Communist Party
CP	Caixa Postal, Case Postale, Casella Postale (Post Box)
CP	Communist Party
CPA	Certified Public Accountant
CPA	Commonwealth Parliamentary Association
CPhys	Chartered Physicist
CPP	Convention People's Party (Ghana)
CPPCC	Chinese People's Political Consultative Conference
CPSU	Communist Party of the Soviet Union
cr.	created
CRNCM	Companion of the Royal Northern College of Music
CSc	Candidate of Sciences
CSCE	Conference on Security and Co-operation in Europe
CSI	Companion of (the Order of) the Star of India
CSIRO	Commonwealth Scientific and Industrial Research Organization
CSSR	Czechoslovak Socialist Republic
CStJ	Commander of (the Order of) St John of Jerusalem
CT	Connecticut
Cttee	Committee
CUNY	City University of New York
CV	Commanditaire Vennootschap
CVO	Commander of the Royal Victorian Order
CWA	(British) Crime Writers' Association
d.	daughter(s)
DArch	Doctor of Architecture
DB	Bachelor of Divinity
DBA	Doctor of Business Administration
DBE	Dame Commander of (the Order of) the British Empire
DC	District of Columbia
DC	Distrito Central
DCE	Doctor of Civil Engineering
DCL	Doctor of Canon Law, Doctor of Civil Law
DCL	Doctor of Canon Law
DCL	Doctor of Civil Law
DCM	Distinguished Conduct Medal
DCMG	Dame Commander of (the Order of) St Michael and St George
DCnL	Doctor of Canon Law
DComm	Doctor of Commerce
DCS	Doctor of Commercial Sciences
DCT	Doctor of Christian Theology
DCVO	Dame Commander of the Royal Victorian Order
DD	Doctor of Divinity
Dd'ES	Diplôme d'études supérieures
DDR	Deutsche Demokratische Republik (German Democratic Republic)
DDS	Doctor of Dental Surgery
DE	Delaware
Dec.	December
DEcon	Doctor of Economics
DEd	Doctor of Education
DEFRA	Department for Environment, Food and Rural Affairs
Del.	Delaware, Delegate, Delegation
Del.	Delaware
Del.	Delegate
Del.	Delegation
Denbighs.	Denbighshire
DenD	Docteur en Droit
DEng	Doctor of Engineering
DenM	Docteur en Medicine
Dep.	Deputy
Dept	Department
DES	Department of Education and Science
Desig.	Designate
DèsL	Docteur ès Lettres
DèsSc	Docteur ès Sciences
Devt	Development
DF	Distrito Federal
DFA	Diploma of Fine Arts, Doctor of Fine Arts
DFA	Diploma of Fine Arts
DFA	Doctor of Fine Arts
DFC	Distinguished Flying Cross
DFM	Distinguished Flying Medal
DH	Doctor of Humanities
DHist	Doctor of History
DHL	Doctor of Hebrew Literature
DHSS	Department of Health and Social Security
DHumLitt	Doctor of Humane Letters
DIC	Diploma of Imperial College
DipAD	Diploma in Art and Design
DipAgr	Diploma in Agriculture
DipArch	Diploma in Architecture
DipEd	Diploma in Education
DipEng	Diploma in Engineering
DipMus	Diploma in Music
DipScEconSc	Diploma of Social and Economic Science
DipTh	Diploma in Theology
Dir	Director
Dist	District
DIur	Doctor of Law
DIurUtr	Doctor of both Civil and Canon Law
Div.	Division, Divisional
Div.	Division
Div.	Divisional
DJ	disc jockey
DJur	Doctor of Law
DK	Most Esteemed Family (Malaysia)
DL	Deputy Lieutenant
DLit	Doctor of Letters
DLit	Doctor of Literature
DLit(t)	Doctor of Letters, Doctor of Literature
DLitt	Doctor of Letters
DLitt	Doctor of Literature
DLS	Doctor of Library Science
DM	Doctor of Medicine (Oxford)
DM	Doctor of Music
DMA	Doctor of Musical Arts
DMD	Doctor of Dental Medicine
DME	Doctor of Musical Education
DMEd	Doctor of Musical Education
DMedSc	Doctor of Medical Science
DMilSc	Doctor of Military Science
DMinSci	Doctor of Municipal Science
DMS	Director of Medical Services
DMus	Doctor of Music
DMusEd	Doctor of Music Education
DMV	Doctor of Veterinary Medicine
DN	Distrito Nacional
DO	Doctor of Ophthalmology
DPH	Diploma in Public Health
DPhil	Doctor of Philosophy
DPM	Diploma in Psychological Medicine
DPS	Doctor of Public Service
dpto	departamento
Dr	Doctor
Dr(a)	Doctor(a)
Dr rer. nat	Doctor of Natural Sciences
Dr rer. pol	Doctor of Political Science
DrAgr	Doctor of Agriculture
DrIng	Doctor of Engineering
DrIur	Doctor of Laws
DrMed	Doctor of Medicine
DrOecPol	Doctor of Political Economy
DrOecPubl	Doctor of (Public) Economy
DrPhilNat	Doctor of Natural Philosophy
DrSc	Doctor of Sciences
DrSci	Doctor of Sciences
DrScNat	Doctor of Natural Sciences
DS	Doctor of Science
DSC	Distinguished Service Cross
DSc	Doctor of Science
DSci	Doctor of Sciences
DScS	Doctor of Social Science
DSM	Distinguished Service Medal
DSO	Companion of the Distinguished Service Order
DSocSc	Doctor of Social Science
DSocSci	Doctor of Social Science
DST	Doctor of Sacred Theology
DTech	Doctor of Technology
DTechSc	Doctor of Technical Sciences
DTechSci	Doctor of Technical Sciences
DTh	Doctor of Theology
DTheol	Doctor of Theology
DTM	Diploma in Tropical Medicine
DTM&H	Diploma in Tropical Medicine and Hygiene
DUniv	Doctor of the University
DUP	Diploma of the University of Paris
DVD	digital versatile disc
E	East, Eastern
EBRD	European Bank for Reconstruction and Development
EC	European Commission, European Community

EC	European Commission
EC	European Community
ECA	Economic Commission for Africa, Economic Co-operation Administration
ECA	Economic Commission for Africa
ECA	Economic Co-operation Administration
ECAFE	Economic Commission for Asia and the Far East
ECE	Economic Commission for Europe
ECLA	Economic Commission for Latin America
ECLAC	Economic Commission for Latin America and the Caribbean
ECO	Economic Co-operation Organization
Econ.	Economic
Econ(s)	Economic(s)
Econs	Economics
ECOSOC	Economic and Social Council
ECSC	European Coal and Steel Community
ECWA	Economic Commission for Western Asia
ED	Doctor of Engineering (USA), Efficiency Decoration
ED	Doctor of Engineering (USA)
ED	Efficiency Decoration
ed	educated
ed.	edited, editor
ed	edited
Ed.	Editor
ed.	editor
EdD	Doctor of Education
Edif.	Edificio (Building)
Edin.	Edinburgh
EdM	Master of Education
Edn	Edition
edn	edition
Educ.	Education
EEC	European Economic Community
EFTA	European Free Trade Association
e.g.	exempli gratia (for example)
eh	Ehrenhalben (Honorary)
EIB	European Investment Bank
EM	Edward Medal, Master of Engineering (USA)
EM	Edward Medal
EM	Master of Engineering (USA)
Emer.	Emerita, Emeritus
EMI	Electrical and Musical Industries
Eng	Engineering
EngD	Doctor of Engineering
ENO	English National Opera
EP	extended-play (record)
EPLF	Eritrean People's Liberation Front
ESA	European Space Agency
ESCAP	Economic and Social Commission for Asia and the Pacific
ESCWA	Economic and Social Commission for Western Asia
esq.	esquina (corner)
est.	established
etc.	et cetera
ETH	Eidgenössische Technische Hochschule (Swiss Federal Institute of Technology)
Ets	Etablissements
EU	European Union
EURATOM	European Atomic Energy Community
eV	eingetragener Verein
Exec.	Executive
Exhbn	Exhibition
Ext.	Extension
f.	founded
FAA	Fellow of the Australian Academy of Science
FAAS	Fellow of the American Association for the Advancement of Science
FAATS	Fellow of the Australian Academy of Technological Sciences
FACC	Fellow of the American College of Cardiology
FACCA	Fellow of the Association of Certified and Corporate Accountants
FACE	Fellow of the Australian College of Education
FACP	Fellow of the American College of Physicians
FACS	Fellow of the American College of Surgeons
FAHA	Fellow of the Australian Academy of the Humanities
FAIA	Fellow of the American Institute of Architects
FAIAS	Fellow of the Australian Institute of Agricultural Science
FAIM	Fellow of the Australian Institute of Management
FAO	Food and Agriculture Organization
FAS	Fellow of the Antiquarian Society
FASE	Fellow of the Antiquarian Society of Edinburgh
FASSA	Fellow of the Academy of Social Sciences of Australia
FBA	Fellow of the British Academy
FBI	Federal Bureau of Investigation
FBIM	Fellow of the British Institute of Management
FBIP	Fellow of the British Institute of Physics

FCA	Fellow of the Institute of Chartered Accountants
FCAE	Fellow of the Canadian Academy of Engineering
FCGI	Fellow of the City and Guilds of London Institute
FCIA	Fellow of the Chartered Institute of Arbitrators
FCIB	Fellow of the Chartered Institute of Bankers
FCIC	Fellow of the Chemical Institute of Canada
FCIM	Fellow of the Chartered Institute of Management
FCIS	Fellow of the Chartered Institute of Secretaries
FCMA	Fellow of the Chartered Institute of Management Accountants
FCO	Foreign and Commonwealth Office
FCSD	Fellow of the Chartered Society of Designers
FCT	Federal Capital Territory
FCWA	Fellow of the Institute of Cost and Works Accountants (now FCMA)
FDGB	Freier Deutscher Gewerkschaftsbund
FDP	Freier Demokratische Partei
Feb.	February
Fed.	Federal, Federation
Fed.	Federal
Fed.	Federation
FEng	Fellow(ship) of Engineering
FFCM	Fellow of the Faculty of Community Medicine
FFPHM	Fellow of the Faculty of Public Health Medicine
FGCM	Fellow of the Guild of Church Musicians
FGS	Fellow of the Geological Society
FGSM	Fellow of the Guildhall School of Music and Drama
FIA	Fellow of the Institute of Actuaries
FIAL	Fellow of the International Institute of Arts and Letters
FIAM	Fellow of the International Academy of Management
FIAMS	Fellow of the Indian Academy of Medical Sciences
FIAP	Fellow of the Institution of Analysts and Programmers
FIArb	Fellow of the Institute of Arbitrators
FIB	Fellow of the Institute of Bankers
FIBA	Fellow of the Institute of Banking Associations
FIBiol	Fellow of the Institute of Biologists
FICE	Fellow of the Institution of Civil Engineers
FIChemE	Fellow of the Institute of Chemical Engineers
FID	Fellow of the Institute of Directors
FIE	Fellow of the Institute of Engineers
FIEE	Fellow of the Institution of Electrical Engineers
FIEEE	Fellow of the Institute of Electrical and Electronics Engineers
FIFA	Fédération Internationale de Football Association
FIJ	Fellow of the Institute of Journalists
FilLic	Licentiate in Philosophy
FIM	Fellow of the Institute of Metallurgists
FIME	Fellow of the Institute of Mining Engineers
FIMechE	Fellow of the Institute of Mechanical Engineers
FIMI	Fellow of the Institute of the Motor Industry
FInstF	Fellow of the Institute of Fuel
FInstM	Fellow of the Institute of Marketing
FInstP	Fellow of the Institute of Physics
FInstPet	Fellow of the Institute of Petroleum
FIPM	Fellow of the Institute of Personnel Management
FIRE	Fellow of the Institution of Radio Engineers
FITD	Fellow of the Institute of Training and Development
FL	Florida
FLA	Fellow of the Library Association
Fla	Florida
FLN	Front de Libération Nationale
FLS	Fellow of the Linnaean Society
FM	frequency modulation
FMA	Florida Music Association
FMedSci	Fellow of the Academy of Medical Sciences
fmr	former
fmrly	formerly
FNI	Fellow of the National Institute of Sciences of India
FNZIA	Fellow of the New Zealand Institute of Architects
FRACP	Fellow of the Royal Australasian College of Physicians
FRACS	Fellow of the Royal Australasian College of Surgeons
FRAeS	Fellow of the Royal Aeronautical Society
FRAI	Fellow of the Royal Anthropological Institute
FRAIA	Fellow of the Royal Australian Institute of Architects
FRAIC	Fellow of the Royal Architectural Institute of Canada
FRAM	Fellow of the Royal Academy of Music
FRAS	Fellow of the Royal Asiatic Society, Fellow of the Royal Astronomical Society
FRAS	Fellow of the Royal Asiatic Society
FRAS	Fellow of the Royal Astronomical Society
FRBS	Fellow of the Royal Society of British Sculptors
FRCA	Fellow of the Royal College of Anaesthetists
FRCM	Fellow of the Royal College of Music
FRCO	Fellow of the Royal College of Organists
FRCOG	Fellow of the Royal College of Obstetricians and Gynaecologists
FRCP	Fellow of the Royal College of Physicians (UK)

ABBREVIATIONS

FRCPath	Fellow of the Royal College of Pathologists		HE	His (or Her) Excellency
FRCP(E)	Fellow of the Royal College of Physicians (Edinburgh)		Herefords.	Herefordshire
FRCPE	Fellow of the Royal College of Physicians, Edinburgh		Herts.	Hertfordshire
FRCPGlas	Fellow of the Royal College of Physicians (Glasgow)		HH	His (or Her) Highness
FRCPI	Fellow of the Royal College of Physicians of Ireland		HHD	Doctor of Humanities
FRCR	Fellow of the Royal College of Radiology		HI	Hawaii
FRCS	Fellow of the Royal College of Surgeons		HIV	human immunodeficiency virus
FRCS(E)	Fellow of the Royal College of Surgeons (Edinburgh)		HLD	Doctor of Humane Letters
FRCSE	Fellow of the Royal College of Surgeons, Edinburgh		HM	His (or Her) Majesty
FRCVS	Fellow of the Royal College of Veterinary Surgeons		HMS	His (or Her) Majesty's Ship
FREconS	Fellow of the Royal Economic Society		Hon.	Honorary, Honourable
FREng	Fellow of the Royal Academy of Engineering		Hon.	Honorary
FRES	Fellow of the Royal Entomological Society		Hon.	Honourable
FRFPS	Fellow of the Royal Faculty of Physicians and Surgeons		Hons	Honours
FRG	Federal Republic of Germany		Hosp.	Hospital
FRGS	Fellow of the Royal Geographical Society		HQ	Headquarters
FRHistS	Fellow of the Royal Historical Society		HRH	His (or Her) Royal Highness
FRHortS	Fellow of the Royal Horticultural Society		HS	Heraldry Society
FRIBA	Fellow of the Royal Institute of British Architects		HSH	His (or Her) Serene Highness
FRIC	Fellow of the Royal Institute of Chemists		HSP	Hungarian Socialist Party
FRICS	Fellow of the Royal Institute of Chartered Surveyors		HSWP	Hungarian Socialist Workers' Party
FRMetS	Fellow of the Royal Meteorological Society		Hunts.	Huntingdonshire
FRNCM	Fellow of the Royal Northern College of Music			
FRPS	Fellow of the Royal Photographic Society		IA	Iowa
FRS	Fellow of the Royal Society		Ia	Iowa
FRSA	Fellow of the Royal Society of Arts		IAAF	International Association of Athletics Federations
FRSAMD	Fellow of the Royal Scottish Academy of Music and Drama		IAEA	International Atomic Energy Agency
FRSC	Fellow of the Royal Society of Canada, Fellow of the Royal Society of Chemistry		IATA	International Air Transport Association
			IBA	Independent Broadcasting Authority
FRSC	Fellow of the Royal Society of Canada		IBRD	International Bank for Reconstruction and Development (World Bank)
FRSC	Fellow of the Royal Society of Chemistry			
FRSE	Fellow of the Royal Society of Edinburgh		ICAO	International Civil Aviation Organization
FRSL	Fellow of the Royal Society of Literature		ICC	International Chamber of Commerce
FRSM	Fellow of the Royal Society of Medicine		ICE	Institution of Civil Engineers
FRSNZ	Fellow of the Royal Society of New Zealand		ICEM	Intergovernmental Committee for European Migration
FRSS	Fellow of the Royal Statistical Society		ICFTU	International Confederation of Free Trade Unions
FRSSA	Fellow of the Royal Society of South Africa		ICI	Imperial Chemical Industries
FRTS	Fellow of the Royal Television Society		ICOM	International Council of Museums
FSA	Fellow of the Society of Antiquaries		ICRC	International Committee for the Red Cross
FSIAD	Fellow of the Society of Industrial Artists and Designers		ICS	Indian Civil Service
FTCL	Fellow of Trinity College London		ICSID	International Centre for Settlement of Investment Disputes
FTI	Fellow of the Textile Institute		ICSU	International Council of Scientific Unions
FTS	Fellow of Technological Sciences		ID	Idaho
FWAAS	Fellow of the World Academy of Arts and Sciences		Ida	Idaho
FZS	Fellow of the Zoological Society		IDA	International Development Association
			IDB	Inter-American Development Bank
GA	Georgia		i.e.	id est (that is to say)
Ga	Georgia		IEA	International Energy Agency
GATT	General Agreement on Tariffs and Trade		IEE	Institution of Electrical Engineers
GB	Great Britain		IEEE	Institution of Electrical and Electronic Engineers
GBE	Knight (or Dame) Grand Cross of (the Order of) the British Empire		IFAD	International Fund for Agricultural Development
			IFC	International Finance Corporation
GC	George Cross		IGAD	Intergovernmental Authority on Development
GCB	Knight Grand Cross of (the Order of) the Bath		IISS	International Institute for Strategic Studies
GCIE	Knight Grand Commander of (the Order of) the Indian Empire		IL	Illinois
			Ill.	Illinois
GCMG	Knight (or Dame) Grand Cross of (the Order of) St Michael and St George		ILO	International Labour Organization
			IMC	International Music Council
GCSI	Knight Grand Commander of (the Order of) the Star of India		IMCO	Inter-Governmental Maritime Consultative Organization
GCVO	Knight (or Dame) Grand Cross of the Royal Victorian Order		IMechE	Institution of Mechanical Engineers
GDR	German Democratic Republic		IMF	International Monetary Fund
Gen.	General		IMMIE	Indian Music Excellence (award)
GHQ	General Headquarters		IMO	International Maritime Organization
GLA	Greater London Authority		IN	Indiana
Glam.	Glamorganshire		Inc.	Incorporated
GLC	Greater London Council		incl.	including
Glos.	Gloucestershire		Ind.	Independent, Indiana
GM	George Medal		Ind.	Independent
GmbH	Gesellschaft mit beschränkter Haftung (Limited Liability Company)		Ind.	Indiana
			Insp.	Inspector
GMT	Greenwich Mean Time		Inst.	Institute, Institution
GOC	General Officer Commanding		Inst.	Institute
GOC-in-C	General Officer Commanding-in-Chief		Inst.	Institution
Gov.	Governor		Int.	International
Govt	Government		INTERPOL	International Criminal Police Organization
GP	General Practitioner		INTUC	Indian National Trades Union Congress
GPO	General Post Office		IOC	International Olympic Committee
Grad.	Graduate		IPC	Institute of Professional Critics
GRSM	Graduate of the Royal School of Music		IPU	Inter-Parliamentary Union
GSMD	Guildhall School of Music and Drama, London		IRCAM	Institut de Recherche et Coordination Acoustique/Musique
GSO	General Staff Officer		ISCM	International Society for Contemporary Music
			ISM	Incorporated Society of Musicians
Hants.	Hampshire		ISO	Companion of the Imperial Service Order
hc	honoris causa		ITA	Independent Television Authority
HE	His Eminence, His (or Her) Excellency		ITN	Independent Television News
HE	His Eminence		ITU	International Telecommunications Union

ITV	Independent Television
IUPAC	International Union of Pure and Applied Chemistry
IUPAP	International Union of Pure and Applied Physics
Jan.	January
JCB	Bachelor of Canon Law
JCD	Doctor of Canon Law
JD	Doctor of Jurisprudence
JMK	Johan Mangku Negara (Malaysia)
JP	Justice of the Peace
Jr	Junior
JSD	Doctor of Juristic Science
Jt	Joint
Jtly	Jointly
JuD	Doctor of Law
JUD	Juris utriusque Doctor (Doctor of both Civil and Canon Law)
JUDr	Juris utriusque Doctor (Doctor of both Civil and Canon Law), Doctor of Law
Kan.	Kansas
KBE	Knight Commander of (the Order of) the British Empire
KC	King's Counsel
KCB	Knight Commander of (the Order of) the Bath
KCIE	Knight Commander of (the Order of) the Indian Empire
KCMG	Knight Commander of (the Order of) St Michael and St George
KCSI	Knight Commander of (the Order of) the Star of India
KCVO	Knight Commander of the Royal Victorian Order
KG	Royal Knight of the Most Noble Order of the Garter
KGB	Committee of State Security (USSR)
KK	Kaien Kaisha
KLM	Koninklijke Luchtvaart Maatschappij (Royal Dutch Airlines)
km	kilometre(s)
KNZM	Knight of the New Zealand Order of Merit
KP	Knight of (the Order of) St Patrick
KS	Kansas
KStJ	Knight of (the Order of) St John of Jerusalem
Kt	Knight
KT	Knight of (the Order of) the Thistle
KY	Kentucky
Ky	Kentucky
LA	Los Angeles
LA	Louisiana
La	Louisiana
Lab.	Laboratory
LAMDA	London Academy of Music and Dramatic Art
Lancs.	Lancashire
LDP	Liberal Democratic Party
LDS	Licentiate in Dental Surgery
LEA	Local Education Authority
Legis.	Legislative
Leics.	Leicestershire
LenD	Licencié en Droit
LèsL	Licencié ès Lettres
LèsSc	Licencié ès Sciences
LG	Lady of (the Order of) the Garter
LHD	Doctor of Humane Letters
LI	Long Island
LicenDer	Licenciado en Derecho
LicenFil	Licenciado en Filosofía
LicenLet	Licenciado en Letras
LicMed	Licentiate in Medicine
Lincs.	Lincolnshire
LittD	Doctor of Letters
LLB	Bachelor of Laws
LLC	Limited Liability Company
LLD	Doctor of Laws
LLL	Licentiate of Laws
LLM	Master of Laws
LLP	Limited Liability Partnership
LM	Licentiate of Medicine, Licentiate of Midwifery
LM	Licentiate of Medicine
LM	Licentiate of Midwifery
LN	League of Nations
LP	long-playing (record)
LPh	Licentiate of Philosophy
LPO	London Philharmonic Orchestra
LRAM	Licentiate of the Royal Academy of Music
LRCP	Licentiate of the Royal College of Physicians
LRSM	Licentiate of the Royal Schools of Music
LSE	London School of Economics and Political Science
LSO	London Symphony Orchestra
Lt	Lieutenant
LTCL	Licentiate of Trinity College of Music, London
Ltd	Limited

Ltd(a)	Limited, Limitada
Ltda	Limitada
LTh	Licentiate in Theology
LVO	Lieutenant, Royal Victorian Order
LW	long wave
LWT	London Weekend Television
m.	marriage, married, metre(s)
m.	marriage
m.	married
m.	metre(s)
MA	Massachusetts
MA	Master of Arts
MAgr	Master of Agriculture (USA)
Maj.	Major
MALD	Master of Arts in Law and Diplomacy
Man.	Management, Manager, Managing, Manitoba
Man.	Management
Man.	Manager
Man.	Managing
Man.	Manitoba
MArch	Master of Architecture
Mass	Massachusetts
MAT	Master of Arts and Teaching
Math.	Mathematical, Mathematics
Math.	Mathematical
Math.	Mathematics
MB	Bachelor of Medicine
MB	Manitoba
MBA	Master of Business Administration
MBE	Member of (the Order of) the British Empire
MBS	Master of Business Studies
MC	master of ceremonies
MC	Military Cross
MCC	Marylebone Cricket Club
MCE	Master of Civil Engineering
MCh	Master of Surgery
MChD	Master of Dental Surgery
MCL	Master of Civil Law
MCom	Master of Commerce
MComm	Master of Commerce
MCP	Master of City Planning
MD	Doctor of Medicine
MD	Maryland
Md	Maryland
MD	Music Director
MDiv	Master of Divinity
MDS	Master of Dental Surgery
Me	Maine
ME	Maine
ME	Myalgic Encephalomyehtis
MEconSc	Master of Economic Sciences
MEd	Master of Education
mem.	member
MEng	Master of Engineering (Dublin)
MEngSc	Master of Engineering
MEP	Member of European Parliament
Met	Metropolitan Opera House, New York
MFA	Master of Fine Arts
Mfg	Manufacturing
Mfrs	Manufacturers
Mgr	Monseigneur, Monsignor
Mgr	Monseigneur
Mgr	Monsignor
MHRA	Modern Humanities Research Association
MHz	megahertz (megacycles)
MI	Marshall Islands
MI	Michigan
MIA	Master of International Affairs
MICE	Member of the Institution of Civil Engineers
Mich.	Michigan
MIChemE	Member of the Institution of Chemical Engineers
Middx	Middlesex
MIDI	Musical Instrument Digital Interface
MIEE	Member of the Institution of Electrical Engineers
Mil.	Military
MIMarE	Member of the Institute of Marine Engineers
MIMechE	Member of the Institution of Mechanical Engineers
MIMinE	Member of the Institution of Mining Engineers
Minn.	Minnesota
MInstT	Member of the Institute of Transport
Miss.	Mississippi
MIStructE	Member of the Institution of Structural Engineers
MIT	Massachusetts Institute of Technology
MJ	Master of Jurisprudence

MLA	Master of Landscape Architecture, Member of the Legislative Assembly
MLA	Master of Landscape Architecture
MLA	Member of the Legislative Assembly
MLA	Modern Language Association
MLC	Member of the Legislative Council
MLitt	Master of Letters
MLitt	Master of Literature
MLS	Master of Library Science
MM	Master of Music
MM	Military Medal
MME	Master of Music Education
MMEd	Master of Music Education
MMus	Master of Music
MN	Minnesota
MNOC	Movement of Non-Aligned Countries
MO	Missouri
Mo.	Missouri
MOBO	Music of Black Origin
MOH	Medical Officer of Health
Mon.	Monmouthshire
Mont.	Montana
Movt	Movement
MP	Madhya Pradesh (India), Member of Parliament
MP	Madhya Pradesh (India)
MP	Member of Parliament
MP3	MPEG-1 Audio Layer-3 (audio compression format)
MPA	Master of Public Administration (Harvard)
MPEG	Moving Picture Experts Group
MPh	Master of Philosophy (USA)
MPhil	Master of Philosophy
MPolSci	Master of Political Science
MPP	Member of Provincial Parliament (Canada)
MRAS	Member of the Royal Asiatic Society
MRC	Medical Research Council
MRCP	Member of the Royal College of Physicians
MRCP(E)	Member of the Royal College of Physicians (Edinburgh)
MRCPE	Member of the Royal College of Physicians, Edinburgh
MRCS	Member of the Royal College of Surgeons of England
MRCSE	Member of the Royal College of Surgeons, Edinburgh
MRCVS	Member of the Royal College of Veterinary Surgeons
MRI	Member of the Royal Institution
MRIA	Member of the Royal Irish Academy
MRIC	Member of the Royal Institute of Chemistry
MRP	Mouvement Républicain Populaire
MS	manuscript
MS	Master of Science, Master of Surgery
MS	Master of Science
MS	Master of Surgery
MS	Mississippi
MSA	Memphis Songwriters' Association
MSc	Master of Science
MScS	Master of Social Science
MSO	Melbourne Symphony Orchestra
MSP	Member Scottish Parliament
MT	Montana
MTh	Master of Theology
MTS	Master of Theological Studies
MTV	Music Television
MUDr	Doctor of Medicine
MusB	Bachelor of Music
MusBac	Bachelor of Music
MusD	Doctor of Music
MusDoc	Doctor of Music
MusM	Master of Music (Cambridge)
MVD	Master of Veterinary Medicine
MVO	Member of the Royal Victorian Order
MW	Master of Wine
MW	medium wave
MWA	Mystery Writers of America
N	North, Northern
NABOB	National Association of Black-Owned Broadcasters
NARAS	National Academy of Recording Arts and Sciences
NAS	National Academy of Sciences (USA)
NAS	National Academy of Songwriters
NASA	National Aeronautics and Space Administration
Nat.	National
NATO	North Atlantic Treaty Organization
Naz.	Nazionale
NB	New Brunswick
NBC	National Broadcasting Company
NC	North Carolina
ND	North Dakota
NDD	National Diploma in Design
NE	Nebraska
NE	North East
NEA	National Endowment for the Arts
Neb.	Nebraska
NEDC	National Economic Development Council
NEH	National Endowment for the Humanities
NERC	Natural Environment Research Council
Nev.	Nevada
NF	Newfoundland
NFSPS	National Federation of State Poetry Societies
NGO	non-governmental organization
NH	New Hampshire
NHK	Nippon Hoso Kyokai (Japanese broadcasting system)
NHS	National Health Service
NI	Northern Ireland
NIH	National Institutes of Health
NJ	New Jersey
NL	Newfoundland and Labrador
NM	New Mexico
NME	New Musical Express
no.	number
Northants.	Northamptonshire
Notts.	Nottinghamshire
Nov.	November
NPC	National People's Congress
nr	near
NRC	Nuclear Research Council
NRK	Norsk Rikskringkasting (Norwegian broadcasting system)
NS	Nova Scotia
NSAI	Nashville Songwriters' Association International
NSF	National Science Foundation
NSW	New South Wales
NT	Northern Territory
NT	Northwest Territories
NU	Nunavut Territory
NUJ	National Union of Journalists
NV	Naamloze Vennootschap
NV	Nevada
NW	North West
NWT	North West Territories
NY	New York (State)
NYPO	New York Philharmonic Orchestra
NYSO	New York Symphony Orchestra
NZ	New Zealand
NZIC	New Zealand Institute of Chemistry
NZSA	New Zealand Society of Authors
O	Ohio
OAPEC	Organization of Arab Petroleum Exporting Countries
OAS	Organization of American States
OAU	Organization of African Unity
OBE	Officer of (the Order of) the British Empire
OC	Officer of the Order of Canada
Oct.	October
OE	Order of Excellence (Guyana)
OECD	Organisation for Economic Co-operation and Development
OEEC	Organization for European Economic Co-operation
Of.	Oficina (Office)
OFS	Orange Free State
OH	Ohio
OHCHR	Office of the United Nations High Commissioner for Human Rights
OIC	Organization of the Islamic Conference
OJ	Order of Jamaica
OK	Oklahoma
Okla	Oklahoma
OM	Member of the Order of Merit
ON	Ontario
ON	Order of Nigeria
Ont.	Ontario
ONZ	Order of New Zealand
ONZM	Officer of the New Zealand Order of Merit
OP	Ordo Praedicatorum (Dominicans)
OPCW	Organization for the Prohibition of Chemical Weapons
OPEC	Organization of the Petroleum Exporting Countries
OPM	Office of Production Management
OQ	Officer National Order of Québec
OR	Oregon
Ore.	Oregon
Org.	Organization
ORTF	Office de Radiodiffusion-Télévision Française
OSB	Order of St Benedict
OSCE	Organization for Security and Co-operation in Europe
OST	original soundtrack
Oxon.	of Oxford University, Oxfordshire
Oxon.	of Oxford University
Oxon.	Oxfordshire

PA	Pennsylvania	q.v.	quod vide (to which refer)
Pa	Pennsylvania		
Parl.	Parliament, Parliamentary	RA	Royal Academician, Royal Academy, Royal Artillery
Parl.	Parliament	RA	Royal Academician
Parl.	Parliamentary	RA	Royal Academy
PBS	Public Broadcasting Service	RA	Royal Artillery
PC	Privy Councillor	RAAF	Royal Australian Air Force
PCC	Provincial Congress Committee	RAC	Royal Armoured Corps
PdB	Bachelor of Pedagogy	RACP	Royal Australasian College of Physicians
PdD	Doctor of Pedagogy	RADA	Royal Academy of Dramatic Art
PdM	Master of Pedagogy	RAF	Royal Air Force
PDS	Partei des Demokratischen Sozialismus	RAFVR	Royal Air Force Volunteer Reserve
PE	Prince Edward Island	RAH	Royal Albert Hall, London
PEI	Prince Edward Island	RAI	Radio Audizioni Italiane
Pembs.	Pembrokeshire	RAM	Royal Academy of Music
PEN	Poets, Playwrights, Essayists, Editors and Novelists (Club)	RAMC	Royal Army Medical Corps
Perm.	Permanent	RAOC	Royal Army Ordnance Corps
PETA	People for the Ethical Treatment of Animals	R&B	Rhythm and Blues
PF	Postfach (Post Box)	RC	Roman Catholic
PGCE	Postgraduate Certificate of Education	RCA	Radio Corporation of America, Royal Canadian Academy, Royal College of Art
PharmD	Docteur en Pharmacie		
PhB	Bachelor of Philosophy	RCA	Radio Corporation of America
PhD	Doctor of Philosophy	RCA	Royal Canadian Academy
PhDr	Doctor of Philosophy	RCA	Royal College of Art
Phila	Philadelphia	RCAF	Royal Canadian Air Force
PhL	Licentiate of Philosophy	RCM	Royal College of Music
PLA	People's Liberation Army, Port of London Authority	RCO	Royal College of Organists
PLA	People's Liberation Army	RCP	Romanian Communist Party
PLA	Port of London Authority	RCP	Royal College of Physicians
PLC	Public Limited Company	RCPI	Royal College of Physicians of Ireland
PLO	Palestine Liberation Organization	Regt	Regiment
PMB	Private Mail Bag	REME	Royal Electric and Mechanical Engineers
pnr	partner	Rep.	Representative, Represented
PO	Philharmonia Orchestra	Rep.	Representative
PO	Post Office	Rep.	Represented
PO Box	Post Office Box	Repub.	Republic
POB	Post Office Box	resgnd	resigned
POW	Prisoner of War	retd	retired
PPR	Polish Workers' Party	Rev.	Reverend
PPRA	Past President of the Royal Academy	rev. edn	revised edition
PPRNCM	Professsional Performer of the Royal Northern College of Music	RFH	Royal Festival Hall, London
		RGS	Royal Geographical Society
PQ	Province of Québec	RI	Rhode Island
PR	Puerto Rico	RIAS	Radio im Amerikanischen Sektor
PR(O)	Public Relations (Officer)	RIBA	Royal Institute of British Architects
PRA	President of the Royal Academy	RLPO	Royal Liverpool Philharmonic Orchestra
Pref.	Prefecture	RMA	Royal Military Academy
Prep.	Preparatory	RMA	Royal Musical Association
Pres.	President	RN	Royal Navy
PRI	President of the Royal Institute (of Painters in Water Colours)	RNCM	Royal Northern College of Music (formerly Royal Manchester College of Music)
PRIBA	President of the Royal Institute of British Architects	RNLI	Royal National Life-boat Institution
Prin.	Principal	RNR	Royal Naval Reserve
Priv Doz	Privat Dozent (recognized teacher not on the regular staff)	RNVR	Royal Naval Volunteer Reserve
PRO	Public Relations Officer	RNZAF	Royal New Zealand Air Force
Proc.	Proceedings	RO	Radio Orchestra
Prod.	Producer	ROC	Rock Out Censorship
Prof.	Professor	ROH	Royal Opera House, London
promo	promotional	RP	Member Royal Society of Portrait Painters
Propr	Proprietor	rpm	revolutions per minute
Prov.	Province, Provincial	RPO	Royal Philharmonic Orchestra
Prov.	Province	RPR	Rassemblement pour la République
Prov.	Provincial	RSA	Royal Scottish Academy, Royal Society of Arts
PRS	Performing Right Society	RSA	Royal Scottish Academy
PRS	President of the Royal Society	RSA	Royal Society of Arts
PRSA	President of the Royal Scottish Academy	RSAMD	Royal Scottish Academy of Music and Drama
PSM	Panglima Setia Mahkota (Malaysia)	RSC	Royal Shakespeare Company, Royal Society of Canada
pt	part	RSC	Royal Shakespeare Company
Pty	Proprietary	RSC	Royal Society of Canada
Publ.	Publication	RSDr	Doctor of Social Sciences
publ.	publication	RSFSR	Russian Soviet Federative Socialist Republic
Publr	Publisher	RSL	Royal Society of Literature
Publ(s)	Publication(s)	RSNO	Royal Scottish National Orchestra (formerly SNO)
Publs	Publications	RSO	Radio Symphony Orchestra
publs	publications	RSPB	Royal Society for Protection of Birds
Pvt.	Private	Rt Hon.	Right Honourable
PZPR	Polish United Workers' Party	Rt Rev.	Right Reverend
		RTÉ	Radio Telefís Éireann
QC	Province of Québec	RTF	Radiodiffusion-Télévision Française
QC	Queen's Counsel	RTS	Royal Television Society
QEH	Queen Elizabeth Hall, London	RVO	Royal Victorian Order
QGM	Queen's Gallantry Medal	RWS	Royal Society of Painters in Water Colours
Qld	Queensland		
QPM	Queen's Police Medal	S	South, Southern
QSO	Queen's Service Order	S.	San
QSO	Queensland Symphony Orchestra	s.	son(s)

ABBREVIATIONS

SA	Sociedad Anónima, Société Anonyme, South Africa
SA	Sociedad Anónima (Limited Company)
SA	Société Anonyme (Limited Company)
SA	South Africa
SA	South Australia
SAARC	South Asian Association for Regional Co-operation
SACEM	Société d'Auteurs, Compositeurs et Editeurs de Musique
SADC	South African Development Community
SAE	Society of Aeronautical Engineers
SAG	Screen Actors' Guild
Salop.	Shropshire
SALT	Strategic Arms Limitation Treaty
Sask.	Saskatchewan
SATB	soprano, alto, tenor, bass
SB	Bachelor of Science (USA)
SC	Senior Counsel
SC	South Carolina
SCAP	Supreme Command Allied Powers
ScB	Bachelor of Science
ScD	Doctor of Science
SD	South Dakota
SDak	South Dakota
SDLP	Social and Democratic Liberal Party
SDP	Social Democratic Party
SE	South East
SEATO	South East Asia Treaty Organization
SEC	Securities and Exchange Commission
Sec.	Secretary
Secr.	Secretariat
SED	Sozialistische Einheitspartei Deutschlands (Socialist Unity Party of the German Democratic Republic)
Sept.	September
S-et-O	Seine-et-Oise
SFWA	Science Fiction and Fantasy Writers of America
SGA	Songwriters' Guild of America
SHAEF	Supreme Headquarters Allied Expeditionary Force
SHAPE	Supreme Headquarters Allied Powers in Europe
SJ	Society of Jesus (Jesuits)
SJD	Doctor of Juristic Science
SK	Saskatchewan
SL	Sociedad Limitada
SLD	Social and Liberal Democrats
SM	Master of Science
SO	Symphony Orchestra
SOAS	School of Oriental and African Studies
Soc.	Société, Society
Soc.	Société
Soc.	Society
SOCAN	Society of Composers, Authors and Music Publishers of Canada
SOSA	State Opera of South Australia
SpA	Società per Azioni
SPD	Sozialdemokratische Partei Deutschlands
SPNM	Society for the Promotion of New Music
Sr	Senior
SRC	Science Research Council
Srl	Società a responsabilità
SSM	Seria Seta Mahkota (Malaysia)
SSR	Soviet Socialist Republic
St	Saint
Sta	Santa
Staffs.	Staffordshire
STB	Bachelor of Sacred Theology
STD	Doctor of Sacred Theology
Ste	Sainte
STL	Licentiate of Sacred Theology
STM	Master of Sacred Theology
str.	strasse
SUNY	State University of New York
Supt	Superintendent
SVSA	South West Virginia Songwriters' Association
SW	short wave
SW	South West
SWAPO	South West Africa People's Organization
TA	Territorial Army
TCL	Trinity College of Music, London
TD	Teachta Dála (mem. of the Dáil), Territorial Decoration
TD	Teachta Dála (mem. of the Dáil)
TD	Territorial Decoration
Tech.	Technical, Technology
Tech.	Technical
Tech.	Technology
Temp.	Temporary
Tenn.	Tennessee
Tex.	Texas

ThB	Bachelor of Theology
ThD	Doctor of Theology
THDr	Doctor of Theology
ThM	Master of Theology
TLS	Times Literary Supplement
TN	Tennessee
trans.	translated
Trans.	Translation, translator
Trans.	Translation
Trans.	translator
Treas.	Treasurer
TU(C)	Trades Union (Congress)
TV	television
TX	Texas
u.	utca (street)
UAE	United Arab Emirates
UAR	United Arab Republic
UCLA	University of California at Los Angeles
UDEAC	L'Union Douanière et Economique de l'Afrique Centrale
UDR	Union des Démocrates pour la République
UED	University Education Diploma
UHF	ultra-high frequency
UK	United Kingdom (of Great Britain and Northern Ireland)
UKAEA	United Kingdom Atomic Energy Authority
ul.	ulitsa (street)
UMIST	University of Manchester Institute of Science and Technology
UMNO	United Malays National Organization
UN(O)	United Nations (Organization)
UNA	United Nations Association
UNCED	United Nations Council for Education and Development
UNCHS	United Nations Centre for Human Settlements (Habitat)
UNCTAD	United Nations Conference on Trade and Development
UNDCP	United Nations International Drug Control Programme
UNDP	United Nations Development Programme
UNDRO	United Nations Disaster Relief Office
UNEF	United Nations Emergency Force
UNEP	United Nations Environment Programme
UNESCO	United Nations Educational, Scientific and Cultural Organization
UNFPA	United Nations Population Fund
UNHCR	United Nations High Commissioner for Refugees
UNICEF	United Nations International Children's Emergency Fund
UNIDO	United Nations Industrial Development Organization
UNIFEM	United Nations Development Fund for Women
UNITAR	United Nations Institute for Training and Research
Univ.	University
UNKRA	United Nations Korean Relief Administration
UNRRA	United Nations Relief and Rehabilitation Administration
UNRWA	United Nations Relief and Works Agency
UNU	United Nations University
UP	United Provinces, Uttar Pradesh (India)
UP	United Provinces
UP	Uttar Pradesh (India)
UPU	Universal Postal Union
Urb.	Urbanización (urban district)
US	United States
USA	United States of America
USAAF	United States Army Air Force
USAF	United States Air Force
USAID	United States Agency for International Development
USN	United States Navy
USNR	United States Navy Reserve
USPHS	United States Public Health Service
USS	United States Ship
USSR	Union of Soviet Socialist Republics
UT	Utah
UWI	University of the West Indies
VA	Virginia
Va	Virginia
VC	Victoria Cross
VHF	very high frequency
VI	(US) Virgin Islands
Vic.	Victoria
Vol.	Volume
vol.	volume
Vol(s)	Volume(s)
Vols	Volumes
vols	volumes
VSO	Victoria State Opera
VSO	Voluntary Service Overseas
VT	Vermont
Vt	Vermont
W	West, Western

ABBREVIATIONS

WA	Washington (State)	WNO	Welsh National Opera
WA	Western Australia	WOMAD	World of Music, Arts and Dance
Warwicks.	Warwickshire	Worcs.	Worcestershire
Wash.	Washington (State)	WRAC	Women's Royal Army Corps
WCC	World Council of Churches	WRNS	Women's Royal Naval Service
WCMD	Welsh College of Music and Drama, Cardiff	WTO	World Trade Organization
WCT	World Championship Tennis	WV	West Virginia
WEU	Western European Union	WVa	West Virginia
WFP	World Food Programme	WWF	World Wildlife Fund
WFTU	World Federation of Trade Unions	WY	Wyoming
WHO	World Health Organization	Wyo.	Wyoming
WI	Wisconsin		
Wilts.	Wiltshire	YMCA	Young Men's Christian Association
WIPO	World Intellectual Property Organization	Yorks.	Yorkshire
Wis.	Wisconsin	YT	Yukon Territory
WMO	World Meteorological Organization	YWCA	Young Women's Christian Association

INTERNATIONAL TELEPHONE CODES

To make international calls to telephone and fax numbers listed in the book, dial the international code of the country from which you are calling, followed by the appropriate code for the country you wish to call (listed below), followed by the area code (if applicable) and telephone or fax number listed in the entry.

	Country code	+ or – GMT*
Afghanistan	93	+4½
Albania	355	+1
Algeria	213	+1
Andorra	376	+1
Angola	244	+1
Antigua and Barbuda	1 268	–4
Argentina	54	–3
Armenia	374	+4
Australia	61	+8 to +10
Australian External Territories:		
Australian Antarctic Territory	672	+3 to +10
Christmas Island	61	+7
Cocos (Keeling) Islands	61	+6½
Norfolk Island	672	+11½
Austria	43	+1
Azerbaijan	994	+5
The Bahamas	1 242	–5
Bahrain	973	+3
Bangladesh	880	+6
Barbados	1 246	–4
Belarus	375	+2
Belgium	32	+1
Belize	501	–6
Benin	229	+1
Bhutan	975	+6
Bolivia	591	–4
Bosnia and Herzegovina	387	+1
Botswana	267	+2
Brazil	55	–3 to –4
Brunei	673	+8
Bulgaria	359	+2
Burkina Faso	226	0
Burundi	257	+2
Cambodia	855	+7
Cameroon	237	+1
Canada	1	–3 to –8
Cape Verde	238	–1
The Central African Republic	236	+1
Chad	235	+1
Chile	56	–4
China, People's Republic	86	+8
Special Administrative Regions:		
Hong Kong	852	+8
Macao	853	+8
China (Taiwan)	886	+8
Colombia	57	–5
The Comoros	269	+3
Congo, Democratic Republic	243	+1
Congo, Republic	242	+1
Costa Rica	506	–6
Côte d'Ivoire	225	0
Croatia	385	+1
Cuba	53	–5
Cyprus	357	+2
'Turkish Republic of Northern Cyprus'	90 392	+2
Czech Republic	420	+1
Denmark	45	+1
Danish External Territories:		
Faroe Islands	298	0
Greenland	299	–1 to –4
Djibouti	253	+3
Dominica	1 767	–4
Dominican Republic	1 809	–4
Ecuador	593	–5

	Country code	+ or – GMT*
Egypt	20	+2
El Salvador	503	–6
Equatorial Guinea	240	+1
Eritrea	291	+3
Estonia	372	+2
Ethiopia	251	+3
Fiji	679	+12
Finland	358	+2
Finnish External Territory:		
Åland Islands	358	+2
France	33	+1
French Overseas Departments:		
French Guiana	594	–3
Guadeloupe	590	–4
Martinique	596	–4
Réunion	262	+4
French Overseas Collectivité Départementale:		
Mayotte	269	+3
Overseas Collectivité Territoriale:		
Saint Pierre and Miquelon	508	–3
French Overseas Territories:		
French Polynesia	689	–9 to –10
Wallis and Futuna Islands	681	+12
French Overseas Country:		
New Caledonia	687	+11
Gabon	241	+1
Gambia	220	0
Georgia	995	+4
Germany	49	+1
Ghana	233	0
Greece	30	+2
Grenada	1 473	–4
Guatemala	502	–6
Guinea	224	0
Guinea-Bissau	245	0
Guyana	592	–4
Haiti	509	–5
Honduras	504	–6
Hungary	36	+1
Iceland	354	0
India	91	+5½
Indonesia	62	+7 to +9
Iran	98	+3½
Iraq	964	+3
Ireland	353	0
Israel	972	+2
Italy	39	+1
Jamaica	1 876	–5
Japan	81	+9
Jordan	962	+2
Kazakhstan	7	+6
Kenya	254	+3
Kiribati	686	+12 to +13
Korea, Democratic People's Republic (North Korea)	850	+9
Korea, Republic (South Korea)	82	+9
Kuwait	965	+3
Kyrgyzstan	996	+5
Laos	856	+7
Latvia	371	+2
Lebanon	961	+2
Lesotho	266	+2
Liberia	231	0
Libya	218	+1

	Country code	+ or − GMT*		Country code	+ or − GMT*
Liechtenstein	423	+1	Spain	34	+1
Lithuania	370	+2	Sri Lanka	94	+6
Luxembourg	352	+1	Sudan	249	+2
Macedonia, former Yugoslav republic	389	+1	Suriname	597	−3
Madagascar	261	+3	Swaziland	268	+2
Malawi	265	+2	Sweden	46	+1
Malaysia	60	+8	Switzerland	41	+1
Maldives	960	+5	Syria	963	+2
Mali	223	0	Tajikistan	992	+5
Malta	356	+1	Tanzania	255	+3
Marshall Islands	692	+12	Thailand	66	+7
Mauritania	222	0	Timor-Leste	670	+9
Mauritius	230	+4	Togo	228	0
Mexico	52	−6 to −7	Tonga	676	+13
Micronesia, Federated States	691	+10 to +11	Trinidad and Tobago	1 868	−4
Moldova	373	+2	Tunisia	216	+1
Monaco	377	+1	Turkey	90	+2
Mongolia	976	+7 to +9	Turkmenistan	993	+5
Morocco	212	0	Tuvalu	688	+12
Mozambique	258	+2	Uganda	256	+3
Myanmar	95	+6½	Ukraine	380	+2
Namibia	264	+2	United Arab Emirates	971	+4
Nauru	674	+12	United Kingdom	44	0
Nepal	977	+5¾	United Kingdom Crown Dependencies	44	0
Netherlands	31	+1	United Kingdom Overseas Territories:		
Netherlands Dependencies:			Anguilla	1 264	−4
Aruba	297	−4	Ascension Island	247	0
Netherlands Antilles	599	−4	Bermuda	1 441	−4
New Zealand	64	+12	British Virgin Islands	1 284	−4
New Zealand's Dependent and Associated			Cayman Islands	1 345	−5
Territories:			Diego Garcia (British Indian Ocean		
Tokelan	690	−10	Territory)	246	+5
Cook Islands	682	−10	Falkland Islands	500	−4
Niue	683	−11	Gibraltar	350	+1
Nicaragua	505	−6	Montserrat	1 664	−4
Niger	227	+1	Pitcairn Islands	872	−8
Nigeria	234	+1	Saint Helena	290	0
Norway	47	+1	Tristan da Cunha	2 897	0
Norwegian External Territory:			Turks and Caicos Islands	1 649	−5
Svalbard	47	+1	United States of America	1	−5 to −10
Oman	968	+4	United States Commonwealth Territories:		
Pakistan	92	+5	Northern Mariana Islands	1 670	+10
Palau	680	+9	Puerto Rico	1 787	−4
Palestinian Autonomous Areas	970	+2	United States External Territories:		
Panama	507	−5	American Samoa	1 684	−11
Papua New Guinea	675	+10	Guam	1 671	+10
Paraguay	595	−4	United States Virgin Islands	1 340	−4
Peru	51	−5	Uruguay	598	−3
The Philippines	63	+8	Uzbekistan	998	+5
Poland	48	+1	Vanuatu	678	+11
Portugal	351	0	Vatican City	39	+1
Qatar	974	+3	Venezuela	58	−4
Romania	40	+2	Viet Nam	84	+7
Russian Federation	7	+2 to +12	Yemen	967	+3
Rwanda	250	+2	Zambia	260	+2
Saint Christopher and Nevis	1 869	−4	Zimbabwe	263	+2
Saint Lucia	1 758	−4			
Saint Vincent and the Grenadines	1 784	−4			
Samoa	685	−11			
San Marino	378	+1			
São Tomé and Príncipe	239	0			
Saudi Arabia	966	+3			
Senegal	221	0			
Serbia and Montenegro	381	+1			
Seychelles	248	+4			
Sierra Leone	232	0			
Singapore	65	+8			
Slovakia	421	+1			
Slovenia	386	+1			
Solomon Islands	677	+11			
Somalia	252	+3			
South Africa	27	+2			

* The times listed compare the standard (winter) times in the various countries. Some countries adopt Summer (Daylight Saving) Time— i.e. +1 hour—for part of the year.

OBITUARY

Amanshauser, Gerhard	2 September 2006
Anderson, Quentin	18 February 2003
Asselineau, Roger Maurice	July 2002
Auchincloss, Kenneth	4 March 2003
Ballantyne, Sheila	2 May 2007
Barr, James	14 October 2006
Beasley, William Gerald	19 November 2006
Beasley-Murray, George Raymond	February 2000
Beck, James Henry	26 May 2007
Behr, Edward Samuel	26 May 2007
Bennett-Coverley, Hon. Louise Simone	26 July 2006
Berry, Francis	10 October 2006
Bishop, Wendy	2003
Blanch, Lesley	6 May 2007
Bonham-Carter, Victor	13 March 2007
Booms, Hans	16 April 2007
Booth, Philip	2 July 2007
Brickner, Richard Pilpel	12 May 2006
Buchheim, Lothar-Gunther	22 February 2007
Buchwald, Art	17 January 2007
Budden, Julian Medforth	28 February 2007
Burnett, John	5 November 2006
Buzo, Alexander John	16 August 2006
Castaneda, Omar	1997
Chissell, Joan Olive	31 January 2007
Chraïbi, Driss	1 April 2007
Collins, Philip Arthur William	6 May 2007
Comden, Betty	23 November 2006
Critchley, Sir Julian Michael Gordon	9 September 2000
De Guise, Elizabeth Mary Teresa (aka Isobel Chase, Elizabeth Hunter)	2005
De Regniers, Beatrice Schenk	1 March 2000
Dempster, Nigel Richard Patton	12 July 2007
Desmaris, Ovid	12 March 1998
Dibdin, Michael John	30 March 2007
Dorn, Edward (Ed) Merton	12 October 1999
Elberg, Yehuda (aka Y. L. Berg, Y. Renas)	2003
Fallaci, Oriana	15 September 2006
Fest, Joachim C.	11 September 2006
Fox, Levi	3 September 2006
Fox-Genovese, Elizabeth Ann Teresa	2 January 2007
Friedman, Milton	16 November 2006
Galliner, Peter	19 December 2006
Geertz, Clifford James	30 October 2006
Gemmell, David	28 July 2006
Gibson, Charles Edmund	1997
Glazebrook, Philip Kirkland	2 July 2007
Gray, Tony George Hugh	31 October 2004
Grealy, Lucy	18 December 2002
Guerard, Albert Joseph	2000
Halberstam, David	23 April 2007
Hamburger, Michael Peter Leopold	7 June 2007
Hamilton, Donald Bengtsson	2006
Hankinson, Alan	22 March 2007
Harris, Mark	30 May 2007
Határ, Victor Gyozo	27 November 2006
Haylock, John Mervyn	1 July 2006
Heath-Stubbs, John Francis Alexander	26 December 2006
Hempstone, Smith	19 November 2006
Henderson, Hamish Scott	8 March 2002
Hendriks, Arthur Lemière	1992
Hill, Douglas Arthur;re	21 June 2007
Hurd, Michael John	8 August 2006
Johnson, Frank Robert	15 December 2006
Jolley, Elizabeth Monica	13 February 2007
Justice, Donald	6 August 2004
Kaiser, Philip Mayer	24 May 2007
Kaplan, Jeremiah	10 August 1993
Kapuściński, Ryszard	23 January 2007
Karim, Mustai	21 September 2005
Kelly, Tim	n.a.
Kemp, Harry Vincent	1994
Kiely, Benedict	8 February 2007
King, Betty Alice	9 January 2007
Kirby, Louis Albert Francis	14 October 2006
Kofler, Gerhard	2 November 2005
Kunene, Mazisi Raymond	12 August 2006
Lanier, Sterling Edward	28 June 2007
Levy, Alan	2 April 2004
Little, Geraldine Clinton	8 March 1997
Lipset, Seymour Martin	31 December 2006
Lowbury, Edward Joseph Lister	10 July 2007
McDowell, Edwin Stewart	10 July 2007
MacKenzie, Norman Hugh	1 March 2004
McLanathan, Richard	1997
Magnusson, Magnus	7 January 2007
Mahfouz, Naguib	30 August 2006
Mala'ika, Nazik al-	20 June 2007
Martin, Robert Bernard (aka Robert Bernard)	29 November 1999
Marwick, Arthur	27 September 2006
Mathews, Nieves Hayat	2003
McEvedy, Colin Peter	1 August 2005
Melly, George Heywood	5 July 2007
Meredith, William Morris	30 May 2007
Mingay, Gordon Edmund	3 January 2006
Miyamoto, Kenji	18 July 2007
Morley, Sheridan Robert	16 February 2007
Mottram, Eric	1995
Munif, Abdelrahman	24 January 2004
Nagy, Gáspár	4 January 2007
Nassauer, Rudolf	2002
Newby, (George) Eric	20 October 2006
Norris, Leslie	6 April 2006
Oakes, Philip Barlow	18 December 2005
Oberman, Sheldon Arnold	26 March 2004
Ollard, Richard Laurence	21 January 2007
Paniker, Ayyappa	2006
Papas, William	19 June 2000
Pearce, (Ann) Philippa	22 December 2006
Pearce, Brian Louis	4 April 2006
Pearsall, Ronald	27 September 2005
Philp, (Dennis Alfred) Peter	5 February 2006
Pitt, Barrie William Edward	15 April 2006
Pocock, Tom	7 May 2007
Poirot-Delpech, Bertrand	14 November 2006
Politkovskaya, Anna	7 October 2006
Press, John Bryant	26 February 2007
Prigov, Dmitri Aleksandrovich	16 July 2007
Quintavalle, Umberto Paolo	1996
Rae, John Malcolm	16 December 2006
Rao, Raja	8 July 2006
Rifaat, Alifa	January 1996
Rorty, Richard McKay	8 June 2007
Rossner, Judith Perelman	9 August 2005
Sachtouris, Miltos	29 March 2005
Sawkins, Raymond Harold (aka Jay Bernard, Colin Forbes, Richard Raine)	23 August 2006
Schlesinger, Arthur Meier Jr	28 Februrary 2007
Scott, Nathan Alexander Jr	12 December 2006
Scott, William (Bill) Neville	22 December 2005
Sembène, Ousmane	10 June 2007
Servan-Schreiber, Jean-Jacques	7 November 2006
Sheldon, Sidney	30 January 2007
Sofola, Zulu	1995
Spillane, Frank Morrison (Mickey)	17 July 2006
Stoker, Alan (aka Alan Evans)	n.a.
Styron, William	1 November 2006
Trier Mørch, Dea	26 May 2001
Trigger, Bruce Graham	1 December 2006
Trow, George W. S.	24 November 2006
Troyat, Henri	3 March 2007
Uhnak, Dorothy	8 July 2006
Vonnegut, Kurt, Jr	11 April 2007
Wakeman, Frederic Evans	14 September 2006
Wall, Mervyn	1997
Weber, Eugen Joseph	17 May 2007
Weston, Corinne Comstock	November 2002
Wiesenthal, Simon	20 September 2005
Willett, Frank	15 June 2006
Williamson, John (Jack) Stewart	10 November 2006
Woodiwiss, Kathleen Erin	6 July 2007

Biographies

AARON, Hugh, (Max Barnet), BA; American writer; b. 30 Nov. 1924, Worcester, Mass; m. Ann Stein 1989; one s. two d. *Education:* Univ. of Chicago. *Plays:* Family Agendas, A Son's Father, A Father's Son: A Tale of Two Wars. *Publications:* Business Not as Usual 1993, When Wars Were Won 1995, It's All Chaos 1996, Letters from the Good War 1997, Films in Review 1998, Suzy, Fair Suzy 1998, Quintet 2005; as Max Barnet: Driven 1995, Go West Old Man 1996; contrib. to Sail Magazine, Wall Street Journal. *Address:* c/o Stones Point Press, 6 Henderson Lane, Cushing, ME 04563, USA (office). *E-mail:* books@stonespoint.com (office); haaron@adelphia.net (home). *Website:* www.stonespoint.com (office); www.hughaaron.com.

ABBENSETTS, Michael; British writer; b. 8 June 1938, British Guiana. *Education:* Queen's Coll., Guyana, Stanstead Coll., QC, Canada and Sir George Williams Univ., Montréal. *Career:* security attendant, Tower of London 1963–67; staff mem., Sir John Soane's Museum, London 1968–71; resident playwright, Royal Court Theatre, London 1974; Visiting Prof. of Drama, Carnegie Mellon Univ., Pittsburgh 1981; writer for radio and television. *Plays:* Sweet Talk (London 1973, New York 1974), Alterations (London and New York 1978, revised prod. London 1985), Samba (London 1980), In the Mood (London 1981), Outlaw (Leicester and London 1983), El Dorado (London 1984). *Publication:* Empire Road (novel, from TV series) 1979. *Honours:* George Devine Award 1973, Arts Council Bursary 1977, Afro-Caribbean Award 1979. *Literary Agent:* Sheil Associates, 43 Doughty Street, London, WC1N 2LF, England.

ABBS, Peter Francis, BA, DPhil; British writer, poet, editor and academic; *Professor of Creative Writing, University of Sussex;* b. 22 Feb. 1942, Cromer, Norfolk, England; m. Barbara Beazeley 1963 (divorced 2002); one s. two d. *Education:* Univ. of Bristol, Univ. of Sussex. *Career:* Lecturer in Education 1976–85, Reader 1985–99, Prof. of Creative Writing 1999–, Univ. of Sussex; founding mem. New Metaphysical Art. *Publications:* English for Diversity: A Polemic 1969, The Forms of Narrative: A Practical Guide (with John Richardson) 1970, Autobiography in Education 1974, The Black Rainbow: Essays on the Present Breakdown of Culture (ed.) 1975, Root and Blossom: Essays on the Philosophy, Practice and Politics of English Teaching 1976, Proposal for a New College (with Graham Carey) 1977, For Man and Islands (poems) 1978, Reclamations: Essays on Culture, Mass-Culture and the Curriculum 1979, Songs of a New Taliesin (poems) 1979, English Within the Arts: A Radical Alternative 1982, Living Powers: The Arts in Education (ed.) 1987, A is for Aesthetic: Essays on Creative and Aesthetic Education 1988, The Symbolic Order: A Contemporary Reader on the Arts Debate (ed.) 1989, The Forms of Poetry: A Practical Guide (with John Richardson) 1991, Icons of Time: An Experiment in Autobiography 1991, The Educational Imperative 1994, The Polemics of Imagination: Essays on Art, Culture and Society 1996, Love After Sappho (poems) 1999, Selected Poems 2001, Earth Songs: an anthology of contemporary eco-poetry 2002, Against the Flow: Education, the Arts and Postmodern Culture 2003, Viva la Vida (poems) 2005; contrib. to scholarly and literary periodicals. *Address:* c/o Graduate Research Centre in the Humanities, Arts Bldg B, University of Sussex, Falmer, Brighton, BN1 9QN, England (office). *Telephone:* (1273) 606755. *Fax:* (1273) 625972. *E-mail:* p.f.abbs@sussex.ac.uk. *Website:* www.sussex.ac.uk/education.

ABDEL-MALEK, Anouar I., DLit, PhD; Egyptian academic and writer; *Adviser, National Centre for Middle East Studies;* b. 23 Oct. 1924, Cairo; s. of Iskandar Abdel-Malek and Alice Zaki Ibrahim; m. Karin Konigseider 1961; one d. *Education:* Coll. de la Sainte Famille, British Inst., Ain Shams Univ., Cairo and Univ. de Paris-Sorbonne. *Career:* leading mem. Egyptian Nat. and Progressive Movt 1941–; official, Nat. Bank of Egypt, Cairo 1941–42, Crédit Foncier Egyptien, Cairo 1943–46; Jt Ed. Actualité, Cairo 1950–59; journalist, Le Journal d'Egypte, Cairo 1950–59; contrib. to Rose el-Yusef, Al-Magallah, Al-Masa, Cairo 1950–59; teacher of philosophy, Lycée Al-Hurriya, Cairo 1958–59; Research Asst, Ecole Pratique des Hautes Etudes, Paris 1959–60; Research Lecturer, later Research Reader, Research Prof., CNRS, Paris 1960–, Dir of Research 1970–90, Hon. Dir 1990–; Project Co-ordinator, The UN Univ., Tokyo 1976–86; Prof. of Sociology and Politics, Faculty of Int. Relations, Ristumeikan Univ., Kyoto 1989–92; Prof. Emer. of Philosophy, Ain Shams Univ. 1998–; Adviser Nat. Centre for Middle East Studies, Cairo 1990–; mem. Bd and Adviser, Centre for Asian Studies, Cairo Univ. 1994–; writer, Al-Ahram 1995; mem. exec. cttee, EEC Int. Sociological Asscn 1970–74 (vice-pres. 1974–78), Egyptian Council for Foreign Affairs 2002–, IISS, Int. Political Science Asscn, Royal Inst. for Int. Affairs, Chatham House 2007–; Visiting Prof., Univ. of Santiago, Chile 1969, Ain Shams 1975, Québec 1986, Cairo 1992; Visiting Fellow, Clare Coll., Cambridge 1985, Life Assoc. 1986–; Ed. Library of the Contemporary Orient 1989, Ideas of the New World 1991. *Publications include:* Egypte, société militaire 1962, Studies on National Culture 1967, Idéologie et renaissance nationale: l'Egypte moderne 1969, La pensée politique arabe contemporaine 1970, Sociologie de l'impérialisme 1970, La dialectique sociale 1972, The Army and National Movements 1974, Spécificité et Théorie sociale 1977, Intellectual Creativity in Endogenous Culture 1983, East Wind 1983, The Transformation of the World 1985, The Egyptian Street and Thought 1989, Creativity and the Civilizational Project 1991, Endogenous Intellectual Creativity in the Arab World 1994, Towards a Civilizational Strategy 2005, On the Origins of the Civilizational Question

2005, Along the Path Towards a New Egypt 2005, China in the Eyes of Egyptians 2006, Patriotism is the Solution 2006. *Honours:* Prix du Jury de l'Amitié Franco-Arabe, Paris 1965, Gold Medal, Nasser Higher Mil. Acad. 1976, State Prize in the Social Sciences 1996, Prize for Best Book, Cairo 2001, Gold Medal, Faculty of Econs and Political Sciences, Cairo Univ. 2003. *Address:* 48 Nehru Street, 11351 Heliopolis, Cairo, Egypt (home). *Telephone:* (2) 634-3977 (home). *Fax:* (2) 634-3977 (home). *E-mail:* anouarmalek@hotmail .com (home).

ABEL, Sam, BA, MA, PhD; American writer, editor and educator; b. 5 Oct. 1957, Norwood, MA; pnr Craig B. Palmer 1994. *Education:* Dartmouth Coll., Indiana Univ. *Career:* Assoc. Instructor, Indiana Univ., Bloomington 1981–82; Instructor, Moorhead State Univ., Moorhead, MN 1983–84, Asst Prof., DePauw Univ., Greencastle, IN 1985–90, Dartmouth Coll., Hanover, NH 1990–; book review ed., reader 1990–93, Co-Ed. 1993–, New England Theatre Journal; Consulting Ed., Theatre History Studies 1996–; consultant for OUP, Univ. of Michigan Press, Indiana Univ., Warner Bentley Theatre; dir various stage productions; mem. Asscn for Theatre in Higher Education, MLA, American Soc. for Theatre Research, Popular Culture Asscn. *Publications:* Opera in the Flesh: Sexuality in Operatic Performance 1996, Irrational Entertainment: Reflections on Opera for the Twenty-First Century 1998; contrib. articles and reviews to periodicals, journals and anthologies, including Journal of Dramatic Theory and Criticism, Journal of Popular Culture, Memory, Practice, Desire: Gay Performances, New England Theatre Journal, A Night at the Opera, Media Representation of Opera, Notable Gays and Lesbians in American Theatre History, Opera News, Terrance McNally: A Casebook, Theatre Annual: A Journal of Performance Studies, Theatre History Studies, Theatre Journal, Theatre Survey, Theatre Topics, Western European Studies. *Honours:* Dartmouth Coll. Marcus Heiman Award for the Creative and Performing Arts 1979, Burke Research Grant 1990–93, Indiana Univ. Graduate Fellow 1979–80, American Coll. Theatre Festival Regional Award for Dramatic Criticism 1980, American Coll. Theatre Festival Regional Award for Playwriting 1981, DePauw Univ. Creative Project Grant 1988, DePauw Univ. Course Development Grant 1989. *Address:* c/o New England Theatre Journal, PMB 502, 198 Tremont Street, Boston, MA 02116-4750, USA.

ABISH, Walter; American writer; b. 24 Dec. 1931, Vienna, Austria; m. Cecile Abish. *Career:* Fellow, American Acad. of Arts and Sciences; mem. PEN American Centre (exec. bd 1982–88), New York Foundation for the Arts (mem. bd of govs 1990–93). *Publications:* Duel Site 1970, Alphabetical Africa 1974, Minds Meet 1975, In the Future Perfect 1977, How German Is It 1980, 99 – The New Meaning 1990, Eclipse Fever 1993, Double Vision – A Self-Portrait 2004; contrib. to Antaeus, Conjunctions, Granta, Manuskripte, New Directions Annual, Paris Review, Partisan Review, Tri-Quarterly, Salmagundi. *Honours:* Hon. DLitt (State Univ. of NY at Oneonta) 1996; Ingram Merrill Foundation grant 1977, Nat. Endowment for the Arts Fellowships 1979, 1985, PEN-Faulkner Award 1981, Guggenheim Fellowship 1981, Deutscher Akademischer Austauschdienst Residency, Berlin 1987, John D. and Catherine T. MacArthur Foundation Fellowship 1987–92, American Acad. of Arts and Letters Medal of Merit 1991, Lila Wallace-Reader's Digest Fellowship 1992–95. *Address:* PO Box 485, Cooper Station, NY 10276, USA.

ABOULELA, Leila, MSc; Sudanese writer; b. 1964, Cairo, Egypt; m.; three c. *Education:* The Sisters' School, Khartoum, Univ. of Khartoum and LSE, England. *Career:* lived in Aberdeen, Scotland 1990–2000, currently living in Indonesia; fmr lecturer in statistics and part-time research asst in Scotland; began writing 1992; author of short stories, a novel and co-writer of a play broadcast on BBC Radio 4. *Publications:* The Translator (novel) 1999, The Museum (short story) (Caine Prize for African Writing) 2000, Coloured Lights (novel) 2001, Minaret (novel) 2005; work included in anthologies Scottish Short Stories 1996, Ahead of its Time 1998. *Address:* c/o Polygon Books, 22 George Square, Edinburgh, EH8 9LF, Scotland (office).

ABOUZEÏD, Leïla; Moroccan novelist and journalist; b. 1950, al-Ksiba, Middle Atlas Mountains. *Education:* Mohamed V Univ., Rabat, Univ. of Texas at Austin, World Press Inst., St Paul, Minn. (USA), London School of Journalism (UK). *Career:* worked as radio and TV journalist; press asst in govt ministries and Prime Minister's Office 1970s, 1983, 1991; full-time fiction writer 1992–. *Publications include:* Bid' Sanābil Khudr (articles, short stories, Few Green Wheat Stalks) 1978, 'Am al-Fil (novel, trans. as Year of the Elephant: A Moroccan Woman's Journey Toward Independence) 1983, Rujū' ilā at-Tufula (autobiog., trans. as Return to Childhood) 1993, The Last Chapter (semi-autobiog. in trans.) 2003. *Address:* c/o The American University in Cairo Press, 113 Sharia Kasr al-Aini Street, Cairo, Egypt.

ABRAHAM, Henry Julian, BA, MA, PhD; American political scientist; *James Hart Professor Emeritus in Government and Foreign Affairs, University of Virginia;* b. 25 Aug. 1921, Offenbach am Main, Germany; m. Mildred K. Kosches 1954; two s. *Education:* Kenyon Coll., Columbia Univ., Univ. of Pennsylvania. *Career:* instructor, Univ. of Pennsylvania 1949–53, Asst Prof. 1953–57, Assoc. Prof. 1957–62, Prof. of Political Science 1962–72; Henry L. and Grace Doherty Memorial Foundation Prof. in Govt and Foreign Affairs, Univ. of Virginia 1972–78, James Hart Prof. in Govt and Foreign Affairs (now

Prof. Emer.) 1978–; Visiting Lecturer and Visiting Prof. at many univs and colls in USA and abroad; Fulbright Lecturer 1959–60; American Philosophical Soc. Fellow 1960–61, 1970–71, 1979; Rockefeller Foundation Resident Scholar, Bellagio, Italy 1978; mem. American Judicature Soc., American Political Science Asscn (vice-pres. 1980–82), American Soc. for Legal History, English-Speaking Union, Int. Political Science Asscn, Nat. Asscn of Scholars, Southern Political Science Asscn. *Publications:* Elements of Democratic Government (with J. A. Corry, fourth edn) 1964, The Judicial Process: An Introductory Analysis of the Courts of the United States, England, and France 1962, The Judiciary: The Supreme Court in the Governmental Process 1965, Freedom and the Court: Civil Rights and Liberties in the United States 1967, Essentials of American National Government (with J. C. Phillips, third edn) 1971, Justices and Presidents: A Political History of Appointments to the Supreme Court 1974, American Democracy 1983, Justices, President and Senators: A History of Supreme Court Appointments from Jay to Clinton 1999; numerous chapters in books, articles, monographs and essays. *Honours:* Hon. LLD 1972, 1982, 1982, 1987; Hon. LHD 1996; Thomas Jefferson Award, Univ. of Virginia 1983, First Lifetime Achievement Award, Organized Section on Law and Courts, American Political Science Asscn 1996. *Address:* Apt 5311, 250 Pantops Mountain Road, Charlottesville, VA 22911-8704 (home); Department of Politics, 232 Cabell Hall, University of Virginia, Charlottesville, VA 22904, USA (office). *Telephone:* (434) 972-2482 (home); (434) 924-3192 (office). *Fax:* (434) 924-3359 (office).

ABRAHAMS, Peter Henry; South African novelist; b. 19 March 1919, Vrededorp, Johannesburg; m. Daphne Elizabeth Miller; three c. *Education:* Church of England mission schools and colls. *Career:* Controller, West Indian News, Jamaica 1955–64; Chair., Radio Jamaica, Kingston 1977–80. *Publications:* fiction: Song of the City 1945, Mine Boy 1946, The Path of Thunder 1948, Wild Conquest 1950, Tell Freedom 1954, A Wreath for Udomo 1956, A Night of Their Own 1965, This Island Now 1966, The View from Coyaba 1985, The Coyaba Chronicles: Reflections on the Black Experience in the Twentieth Century 2000, Oblivion 2005, End of Story 2006; short story collection: Dark Testament 1942; poetry: A Black Man Speaks of Freedom 1938. *Address:* Red Hills, PO Box 20, St Andrew, Jamaica.

ABRAHAMS, Roger David, BA, MA, PhD; American academic and writer; b. 12 June 1933, Philadelphia, Pa. *Education:* Swarthmore Coll., Columbia Univ., Univ. of Pennsylvania. *Career:* Instructor, Univ. of Texas at Austin 1960–63, Asst Prof. 1963–66, Assoc. Prof. 1966–69, Prof. of English and Anthropology 1969–79, Chair. English Dept 1974–79; Alexander H. Kenan Prof. of Humanities and Anthropology, Pitzer Coll. and Scripps Coll., Claremont, Calif. 1979–85; Prof. of Folklore and Folklife, Univ. of Pennsylvania 1985–2002 (Founder and Dir Center for Folklore and Ethnography 1998–2001), teaching graduate-level courses in Folklore and Folklife 2002–; various visiting professorships; American Folklore Soc. Fellow 1970; Nat. Humanities Inst. Fellow 1976–77; mem. American Folklore Soc. (Pres. 1978–79), Int. Soc. for Folk Narrative Research. *Publications:* Deep Down in the Jungle: Negro Narrative Folklore from the Streets of Philadelphia 1964, Anglo-American Folksong Style (with George W. Foss Jr) 1968, Positively Black 1970, Deep the Water, Shallow the Shore: Three Essays on Shantying in the West Indies 1974, Talking Black 1976, Afro-American Folk Culture: An Annotated Bibliography 1977, Between the Living and the Dead: Riddles Which Tell Stories 1980, The Man-of-Words in the West Indies 1983, Singing the Master: The Emergence of African-American Culture in the Plantation South 1992. *Honours:* Guggenheim Fellowship 1965–66, American Folklore Soc. Lifetime Achievement Award 1989.

ABRAMS, Meyer Howard, BA, MA, PhD; American writer and academic; *Professor Emeritus, Cornell University;* b. 23 July 1912, Long Branch, NJ; m. Ruth Gaynes 1937; two d. *Education:* Harvard Univ., Univ. of Cambridge, UK. *Career:* instructor in English 1938–42, Research Assoc., Psycho-Acoustic Laboratory 1942–45, Harvard Univ.; Asst Prof. Cornell Univ. 1945–47, Assoc. Prof. 1947–53, Prof. of English 1953–61, Frederic J. Whiton Prof. 1961–73, Class of 1916 Prof. 1973–83, Prof. Emer. 1983–; Visiting Lecturer at several insts of higher learning; Corresp. Fellow, British Acad.; mem. American Acad. of Arts and Sciences, American Acad. of Arts and Letters, American Asscn of Univ. Profs, American Philosophical Soc., Modern Language Asscn of America, Nat. Humanities Center Founders' Group. *Publications:* The Milk of Paradise: The Effects of Opium Visions on the Works of De Quincey, Crabbe, Francis Thompson and Coleridge 1934, The Mirror and the Lamp: Romantic Theory and the Critical Tradition 1953, A Glossary of Literary Terms 1957, Natural Supernaturalism: Tradition and Revolution in Romantic Literature 1971, The Correspondent Breeze: Essays in English Romanticism 1984, Doing Things With Texts: Essays in Criticism and Critical Theory 1989; editor: The Poetry of Pope 1954, Literature and Belief 1958, English Romantic Poets: Modern Essays in Criticism 1960, The Norton Anthology of English Literature 1962, Wordsworth: A Collection of Critical Essays 1972, William Wordsworth: Prelude 1979; contrib. to several vols. *Honours:* Rockefeller Foundation Fellowship 1946–47, Ford Foundation Fellowship 1953, Fulbright Scholarship 1954, Guggenheim Fellowships 1958, 1960, Fellow Center for Advanced Study in the Behavioral Sciences 1967, Christian Gauss Prize 1954, MLA of America James Russell Lowell Prize 1971, Visiting Fellow All Soul's Coll., Oxford 1977, American Acad. of Arts and Sciences Award in Humanistic Studies 1984, Keats-Shelley Asscn Distinguished Scholar Award 1987, American Acad. and Inst. of Arts and Letters Award 1990. *Address:* 378 Savage Farm Drive,

Ithaca, NY 14850, USA (home). *Telephone:* (607) 257-7012 (home). *E-mail:* mha5@cornell.edu (home).

ABRAMSKY, Jennifer, CBE, BA; British radio producer and editor; *Director, BBC Radio and Music;* b. 7 Oct. 1946, d. of Chimen Abramsky and the late Miriam Abramsky (née Nirenstein); m. Alasdair D. MacDuff Liddell 1976; one s. one d. *Education:* Holland Park School and Univ. of East Anglia. *Career:* joined BBC Radio as Programme Operations Asst 1969, Producer, The World at One 1973, Ed. PM 1978–81, Producer Radio Four Budget Programmes 1979–86, The World at One 1981–86, Ed. Today programme 1986–87, News and Current Affairs Radio 1987–93, est. Radio Four News FM 1991, Controller BBC Radio Five Live 1993–96, Dir Continuous News Services, BBC (including Radio Five Live, BBC News 24, BBC World, BBC News Online, Ceefax) 1996–98, Dir BBC Radio 1998–2000, BBC Radio and Music 2000–; mem. Econ. and Social Research Council 1992–96, Editorial Bd British Journalism Review 1993–; Vice-Chair. Digital Radio Devt Bureau 2002–; Dir Hampstead Theatre 2003–; mem. Bd of Govs BFI 2000–; News Int. Visiting Prof. of Broadcast Media, Exeter Coll., Oxford 2002; Radio Acad. Fellowship 1998. *Honours:* Hon. Prof. Thames Valley Univ. 1994; Hon. RAM 2002; Hon. MA (Salford) 1997; Woman of Distinction, Jewish Care 1990, Sony Radio Acad. Award 1995. *Address:* BBC, Room 2811, Broadcasting House, Portland Place, London, W1A 1AA, England. *Telephone:* (20) 7765-4561 (office).

ABRAMSON, Jill, BA; American newspaper editor; *News Managing Editor, New York Times;* b. 1954; m. Henry Griggs; two c. *Education:* Harvard Univ. *Career:* Ed.-in-Chief Legal Times, Washington, DC 1986–88; Deputy Bureau Chief and investigative reporter, Wall Street Journal 1988–97; joined New York Times 1997, Enterprise Ed., Washington Bureau 1997–99, Washington Ed. 1999–2000, Washington Bureau Chief 2000–03, News Man. Ed. 2003–. *Publications include:* Where They Are Now 1986, Strange Justice (with Jane Mayer) 1994. *Honours:* Nat. Press Club Award 1992. *Address:* New York Times, 229 W 43rd Street, New York, NY 10036, USA (office). *Telephone:* (212) 556-8000 (office). *Website:* www.nytimes.com (office).

ABSE, Dannie, DLitt, LRCP, MRCS, FRSL; British writer, poet and physician; b. 22 Sept. 1923, Cardiff, Wales; s. of Rudolph Abse and Kate Shepherd; m. Joan Mercer 1951; one s. two d. *Education:* St Illtyd's Coll. Cardiff, Univ. Coll. Cardiff, King's Coll. London and Westminster Hosp., London. *Career:* first book of poems published while still a medical student 1948; qualified as doctor 1950; Squadron-Leader RAF 1951–55; doctor in charge of chest clinic at Cen. Medical Establishment, Cleveland Street, London 1954–89; writer-in-residence, Princeton Univ., NJ, USA 1973–74; Pres. Poetry Soc. 1979–92; Fellow Welsh Acad. 1993; council mem. Royal Soc. of Literature. *Publications:* poetry: Funland and Other Poems 1973, Way Out in the Centre 1981, White Coat, Purple Coat: Collected Poems 1948–1988 1989, Remembrance of Crimes Past 1990, On the Evening Road 1994, Arcadia, One Mile 1998; editor: Voices in the Gallery 1986, The Music Lover's Literary Companion (with Joan Abse) 1989, The Hutchinson Book of Post-War British Poets 1989, Twentieth-Century Anglo-Welsh Poetry 1997, New and Collected Poems 2003; fiction: Pythagoras (a play), Ash on a Young Man's Sleeve 1954, Some Corner of an English Field 1956, O Jones, O Jones 1970, Ask the Bloody Horse 1986, There was a Young Man from Cardiff 2001, The Strange Case of Dr Simmonds and Dr Glas 2002; other: Journals from the Ant Heap 1986, Intermittent Journals 1994, A Welsh Retrospective 1997, Goodbye, Twentieth Century 2001, The Two Roads Taken 2003, The Presence (memoir) 2007; contributions: BBC and various publs in the UK and USA. *Honours:* Hon. Fellow, Univ. of Wales Coll. of Medicine 1999; Hon. DLitt (Univ. of Wales) 1989, (Glamorgan) 1997; Welsh Arts Council Literature Prize 1971, 1987, Henry Foyle Award 1964, Jewish Chronicle Award, Cholmondeley Award 1983, 1985. *Literary Agent:* PFD, Drury House, 34–43 Russell Street, London, WC2B 5HA. *Address:* 85 Hodford Road, London, NW11 8NH, England.

ABU KHALID, Fawziyya, MA; Saudi Arabian poet and essayist; *Lecturer in Sociology, King Saud University;* b. 1955, Riyadh. *Education:* American Univ. of Beirut, Lebanon, Lewis and Clark Coll., Portland, OR, USA. *Career:* taught at Women's Coll. King Saud Univ., Riyadh, now Lecturer in Sociology. *Publications:* poetry: Ila Mata Yakhtatifunaki Laylalt as-Urs (How Long Will They Keep Raping You on Your Wedding Night) 1973, Oira' a fi as-Sirr li-Tarikh as-samt al-'Arabi (Secret Reading in the History of Arab Silence) 1985, Ma' as-Sarab (Water of the Mirage) 1995; also stories for children. *Address:* c/o Department of Sociology, King Saud University, POB 2454, Riyadh 11451, Saudi Arabia.

ABU ZAYD, Layla (see Abouzeïd, Leïla)

ACAR, Özgen; Turkish journalist; b. 29 Sept. 1938, Bor; s. of Mihilmi Acar and Naciye (née Eren) Acar; m. Inci Güven 1980; one s. *Education:* Ankara Univ. *Career:* Parl. Corresp. Cumhuriyet Daily Newspaper 1960–61, Econ. Corresp. 1961–63, Diplomatic Corresp. 1963–65, 1967–72, Investigative Corresp. 1990–92, 1994–, Ed.-in-Chief Istanbul 1992–94; Corresp. Reuters, Ankara 1972–74; Bureau Chief Milliyet Daily Newspaper Athens 1980–84, Ankara 1984–86, New York 1986–88; TV and radio reporter; mem. Exec. Cttee of Int. Fed of Journalists (IFJ) 1971, Adviser 1972–78. *Publications:* numerous investigative reports. *Honours:* several journalism awards. *Address:* Cumhuriyet Newspaper, Türkocağı Cad. 39, Cağaloğlu, İstanbul 34334, Turkey. *Telephone:* (212) 5120505. *Fax:* (212) 5138595. *E-mail:* postakutusu@ cumhuriyet.com.tr. *Website:* www.cumhuriyet.com.tr.

ACCAD, Evelyne, MA, PhD; Lebanese/Swiss/American academic and writer; *Professor Emerita, University of Illinois at Urbana-Champaign*; b. 6 Oct. 1943, Beirut, Lebanon; partner, Paul Vieille. *Education:* Beirut Coll. for Women, Anderson Coll., Ball State Univ., Indiana Univ. *Career:* Prof., Univ. of Illinois at Urbana-Champaign, now Emer., mem. core faculty African Center, Women's Studies Center, Middle East Studies Program, Campus Honors Faculty 1974–; Prof. Emer., Lebanese American Univ.; teacher, Beirut Univ. Coll. 1978–84, Northwestern Univ. 1991; mem. of jury, Int. Neustadt Prize for Literature. *Publications:* Veil of Shame: The Role of Women in the Modern Fiction of North Africa and the Arab World 1978, Montjoie Palestine! or Last Year in Jerusalem 1980, L'Excisée 1982, Coquelicot du Massacre 1988, Sexuality and War: Literary Masks of the Middle East 1990, Des femmes, des hommes et la guerre: Fiction et Réalité au Proche-Orient (France-Lebanon Literary Award ADELF) 1993, Blessures des Mots 1993, Wounding Words: A Woman's Journal in Tunisia 1996, Voyages en Cancer (translated as The Wounded Breast: Intimate Journeys Through Cancer) (Prix Phénix 2001) 2000; other: four edited vols, 14 book chapters and 73 articles. *Honours:* Florence Howard Award (Hon. Mention) 1975, special recognition Illinois Arts Council Creative Writing Fellowship 1979, Fulbright Awards 1983–85, 2002, Social Science Research Council Fellowship 1988–89, Studies of Cultural Values and Ethics Program Award 1992, 1996–97, Emmanuel Robles Poetry Award, 2006. *Address:* Department of French, 2090 Foreign Languages Bldg, University of Illinois, Urbana, IL 61801 (office); 306 W Michigan, Urbana, IL 61801, USA (home). *E-mail:* e-accad@uiuc.edu (office).

ACHEBE, (Albert Chinualumogu) Chinua, BA, FRSL; Nigerian writer, poet and academic; *Charles P. Stevenson Jr Professor of Languages and Literature, Bard College*; b. 16 Nov. 1930, Ogidi, Anambra State; s. of the late Isaiah O. Achebe and Janet N. Achebe; m. Christie C. Okoli 1961; two s. two d. *Education:* Govt Coll., Umuahia and Univ. Coll., Ibadan. *Career:* Producer, Nigerian Broadcasting Corpn, Lagos 1954–58, Regional Controller, Enugu 1958–61, Dir Voice of Nigeria, Lagos 1961–66; Sr Research Fellow, Univ. of Nigeria, Nsukka 1967–72; Rockefeller Fellowship 1960–61; UNESCO Fellowship 1963; Foundation mem. Asscn of Nigerian Authors 1982–, Pres. 1981–86; mem. Gov. Council, Lagos Univ. 1966, mem. E. Cen. State Library Bd 1971–72; Founding Ed., Okike 1971–; Prof. of English, Univ. of Mass 1972–75, Univ. of Conn. 1975–76, Univ. of Nigeria, Nsukka 1976–81, Prof. Emer. 1985–; Charles P. Stevenson Jr Prof. of Languages and Literature, Bard Coll. 1991–; Pro-Chancellor and Chair. of Council, Anambra State Univ. of Tech., Enugu, Nigeria 1986–88; Regents Lecturer, UCLA 1984; Founding Ed. African Writers' Series (Heinemann) 1962–72; Dir Heinemann Educational Books (Nigeria) Ltd, Nwamife (Publishers), Enugu; mem. Tokyo Colloquium 1981; Visiting Distinguished Prof. of English, City Coll., New York 1989; Montgomery Fellow and Visiting Prof., Dartmouth Coll., Hanover 1990; Visiting Fellow, Ashby Lecturer, Clare Hall, Cambridge 1993; Scottish Arts Council Neil Gunn Int. Fellow 1975; Fellow, Ghana Asscn of Writers 1975; Goodwill Amb. (UN Population Fund) 1998–. *Publications:* fiction: Things Fall Apart 1958, No Longer at Ease 1960, The Sacrificial Egg and Other Stories (short stories) 1962, Arrow of God 1964, A Man of the People 1966, Chike and the River (juvenile) 1966, How the Leopard Got his Claws (juvenile, with John Iroaganachi) 1972, Girls at War (short stories) 1973, The Flute (juvenile) 1978, The Drum (juvenile) 1978, African Short Stories (ed., with C. L. Innes) 1984, Anthills of the Savannah 1987, The Heinemann Book of Contemporary African Short Stories (ed., with C. L. Innes) 1992, Telling Tales (contrib. to charity anthology) 2004; poetry: Beware, Soul-Brother and Other Poems 1971, Christmas in Biafra and Other Poems 1973, Don't Let him Die: An Anthology of Memorial Poems for Christopher Okigbo (ed., with Dubem Okafor) 1978, Aka Weta: An Anthology of Igbo Poetry (ed., with Obiora Udechukwu) 1982, Home and Exile 2000, Collected Poems 2004; non-fiction: Morning Yet on Creation Day (essays) 1975, The Trouble with Nigeria (essays) 1983, Hopes and Impediments: Selected Essays 1965–87 1988, Essays and Poems: Another Africa (ed., with Robert Lyons) 1998, Home and Exile (essays) 2000; contrib. to New York Review of Books, Transition, Callaloo. *Honours:* Hon. mem. American Acad. of Arts and Letters 1982; Hon. Fellow, Modern Language Asscn of America 1974; Hon. DUniv, Hon. DLitt (16 times), Hon. DHL (eight times), Hon. LLD (three times), Dr hc (Open Univ.) 1989; Margaret Wrong Memorial Prize 1959, Nigerian Nat. Trophy 1960, Jock Campbell New Statesman Award 1965, Commonwealth Poetry Prize 1972, The Lotus Prize (Afro-Asian writers) 1975, Order of the Federal Republic (Nigeria) 1979, Nigerian Nat. Merit Award 1979, Nonino Prize (Italy) 1994, Campion Medal, New York 1996, Nat. Creativity Award 1999, Friedenspreis (Germany) 2002, Man Booker Int. Prize 2007. *Literary Agent:* David Higham Associates, 5–8 Lower John Street, Golden Square, London, W1F 9HA, England. *Address:* Bard College, PO Box 41, Annandale-on-Hudson, NY 12504, USA (office). *Telephone:* (845) 758-7325 (office). *E-mail:* achebe@bard.edu (office). *Website:* www.bard.edu/academics/programs/langlit (office).

ACHOLONU, Catherine Obianuju, MA, PhD; Nigerian poet, playwright, literary critic and essayist; *Senior Special Assistant for Arts and Culture, Office of the Head of State*; b. 1950, Orlu; d. of Chief Lazarus Olumba; m.; four c. *Education:* Univ. of Düsseldorf, Germany. *Career:* teacher Alvan Ikoku Coll., Owerri 1978–; currently Sr Special Asst to the Pres., for Arts and Culture. *Plays:* Into the Heart of Biafra 1985, Trial of the Beautiful Ones 1985, The Deal and Who is the Head of State 1986. *Publications:* poetry: Nigeria in the Year 1999 1985, The Spring's Last Drop 1985; non-fiction: In the Heart of Biafra 1970, The Igbo Roots of Olaudah Equiano 1989, The Earth Unchained: A Quantum Leap in Consciousness 1989, Motherism: The Afrocentric Alternative to Feminism 1995; children's books and poems; contrib. poems and short stories to anthologies, articles and chapters to magazines and journals. *Honours:* Fulbright Scholar; numerous literary awards. *Address:* c/o Office of the Head of State, New Federal Secretariat Complex, Shehu Shagari Way, Central Area District, Abuja, Nigeria.

ACKERMAN, Diane, BA, MFA, PhD; American poet, writer and educator; b. 7 Oct. 1948, Waukegan, IL. *Education:* Boston Univ., Pennsylvania State Univ., Cornell Univ. *Career:* Teaching Asst 1971–78, Lecturer 1978, Visiting Writer 1987, Visiting Prof. 1998–2000, Cornell Univ.; Asst Prof., Univ. of Pittsburgh 1980–83; writer-in-residence, Coll. of William and Mary 1982–83, Ohio Univ. 1983, New York Univ. 1986, Columbia Univ. 1986–87; writer-in-residence 1983–86, Dir Writers' Program 1984–86, Washington Univ.; staff writer, New Yorker magazine 1988–94; Visiting Prof., Soc. for the Humanities, Cornell Univ. 1998–2000; Nat. Endowment for the Humanities Distinguished Prof. of English, Univ. of Richmond 2001. *Publications:* The Planets: A Cosmic Pastoral 1976, Wife of Light 1978, Twilight of the Tenderfoot 1980, Lady Faustus 1983, On Extended Wings 1985, Reverse Thunder 1988, A Natural History of the Senses 1990, Jaguar of Sweet Laughter: New and Selected Poems 1991, The Moon by Whale Light and Other Adventures Among Bats, Crocodilians, Penguins and Whales 1991, A Natural History of Love 1994, The Rarest of the Rare 1995, Monk Seal Hideaway 1995, A Slender Thread 1997, Bats: Shadows in the Night 1997, I Praise My Destroyer 1998, The Norton Book of Love (ed. with Jeanne Mackin) 1998, Deep Play 1999, Cultivating Delight: A Natural History of My Garden 2001; contrib. to numerous anthologies, books, newspapers, journals and magazines. *Honours:* Abbie Copps Poetry Prize 1974, Nat. Endowment for the Arts Creative Writing Fellowships 1976, 1986, Black Warrior Review Poetry Prize 1981, Pushcart Prize 1984, Acad. of American Poets Peter I. B. Lavan Award 1985, Lowell Thomas Award 1990, New York Times Book Review Notable Books of the Year 1991, 1992, and New and Noteworthy Books of the Year 1993, 1997, Wordsmith Award 1992, New York Public Library Literary Lion 1994, John Burroughs Nature Award 1997, Art of Fact Award 2000, Best American Essays Citation 2001, Guggenheim Fellowship 2003, molecule Dianeackerone, named in her honour. *Literary Agent:* William Morris Agency, 1325 Avenue of the Americas, New York, NY 10019, USA. *E-mail:* da31@cornell.edu (office).

ACKERMAN, Susan Yoder, BA; American teacher and writer; b. 2 Nov. 1945, Newport News, VA; m. Robert W. Ackerman II 1969; one s. two d. *Education:* Eastern Mennonite Coll., Coll. of William and Mary, Univ. of Virginia, Longwood Coll. and Hampton Univ. *Career:* elementary school teacher, Newport News, VA 1966–67, 1972; teacher of English as a foreign language, Lubumbashi, Zaïre 1969–70, Kongolo, Zaïre 1979–80; middle and high school French teacher, Newport News 1984–86, 1989–96; Day Care Dir, Newport News 1989–90; elementary school prin. 2000–03; Writer-in-Residence, Island Inst., Sitka, Alaska April 2000; speaker on African experiences and on writing; leader, workshops on writing children's fiction; mem. Soc. of Children's Book Writers and Illustrators. *Publications:* Copper Moons 1990, The Flying Pie and Other Stories 1996, Zane the Train 2006, Kindermusik; contrib. of educational testing material, stories and articles to periodicals, including Cricket, On the Line, With, Instructor, Story Friends, Christian Living, Purpose, Together, Live, Mothering Click, Cicada, Zootles; lyrics to CD by Do, Re, Mi, and You. *Address:* 524 Marlin Drive, Newport News, VA 23602, USA. *E-mail:* susan@ackerman.net.

ACKLIN, Jürg; Swiss psychoanalyst and writer; b. 20 Feb. 1945, Zürich; m. Claudia Acklin-Gaiser 1984 (separated); two d. one s. *Education:* Univs of Zürich and Bremen. *Career:* Leader, Literturclub, Swiss Television. *Publications:* collection of poems 1967; fiction: Michael Häuptli 1969, Alias 1971, Das Uberhandnehmen 1973, Der Aufstieg des Fesselballons 1980, Der Känguruhmann 1992, Das Tangopaar 1994, Froschgesang 1996, Der Vater 1998, Defekt 2002. *Honours:* C. F. Meyer Prize 1971, Bremer Literature Prize 1972, Zürcher Buch Prize 1997. *Address:* c/o Verlag Nagel & Kimche AG, V-Nr. 1320 506, Nordstr. 9 Postfach, 8035 Zürich, Switzerland (office).

ACKROYD, Peter, CBE, MA, FRSL; British writer; b. 5 Oct. 1949, London; s. of Graham Ackroyd and Audrey Whiteside. *Education:* St Benedict's School, Ealing, Clare Coll., Cambridge and Yale Univ., USA. *Career:* Literary Ed. The Spectator 1973–77, Jt Man. Ed. 1978–82; Chief Book Reviewer The Times 1986–; Mellon Fellow Yale Univ. *Play:* The Mystery of Charles Dickens 2000. *Television:* Charles Dickens (BBC 2), Peter Ackroyd's London (BBC 2) 2004, The Romantics (BBC 2) 2006. *Publications:* fiction: The Great Fire of London 1982, The Last Testament of Oscar Wilde (Somerset Maugham Prize 1984) 1983, Hawksmoor (Whitbread Award for Fiction 1986, Guardian Fiction Award 1986) 1985, Chatterton 1987, First Light 1989, English Music 1992, The House of Doctor Dee 1993, Dan Leno and the Limehouse Golem 1994, Milton in America 1996, The Plato Papers 1999, The Clerkenwell Tales (short stories) 2003, The Lambs of London 2004, The Fall of Troy 2006; non-fiction: Notes for a New Culture 1976, Dressing Up: Transvestism and Drag: The History of an Obsession 1979, Ezra Pound and his World 1980, T. S. Eliot (RSL W. H. Heinemann Award 1985, Whitbread Award for Biography 1985) 1984, Dickens 1990, Introduction to Dickens 1991, Blake 1995, The Life of Thomas More 1998, London: The Biography 2000, Dickens: Public Life and Private Passion 2002, The Collection 2002, Albion: The Origins of the English Imagination 2002, Illustrated London 2003, The Beginning: Voyages Through Time (juvenile) 2003, Chaucer 2004, Shakespeare: The Biography 2005, Brief Lives – Newton 2006; poetry: London Lickpenny 1973, Country Life 1978, The

Diversions of Purley 1987. *Honours:* Hon. DLitt (Univ. of Exeter), (London Guildhall), (City Univ.), (Univ. Coll., London), (Brunel Univ.) 2006. *Literary Agent:* Anthony Sheil Associates Ltd, 43 Doughty Street, London, WC1N 2LF, England. *Telephone:* (20) 7405-9351.

ACLAND, Alice (see Wignall, Anne)

ACOSTA, Devashish Donald, MFA; American writer; b. 9 Nov. 1956, New York, NY. *Education:* San Diego State Univ. *Publications:* Felicitavia: A Spiritual Journey 1997, When the Time Comes 1998, Sadvipra 2000, The Ashram 2004. *Address:* c/o Innerworld Publications, PO Box 1613, San German, PR 00683, USA.

ÁCS, Margit; Hungarian writer and editor; b. 11 June 1941, Újpest; d. of Ferenc Ács and Margit Ács (née Baracsi); m. Mátyás Domokos 1967; two s. *Education:* Loránd Eötvös Univ. *Career:* Ed. Szépirodalmi Publishing 1964–87, Magvető Publishing 1987. *Publications:* short stories: Only Air and Water 1977, Whip and Alms 1983; novels: Initiation 1979, Chance 1988, The Unsuspecting Traveller 1988. *Honours:* Füst Milán Prize 1989, József Attila Prize 1991. *Address:* c/o Magvető Könyvkiadó, 1806 Budapest, Vörösmarty tér 1 (office); Budapest 1085, Somogyi Béla u 24, Hungary (home). *Telephone:* (1) 118-5109 (office); (1) 114-3610 (home).

ADAIR, Gilbert; British novelist, poet, screenwriter and critic; b. 29 Dec. 1944, Edinburgh, Scotland. *Film screenplays:* The Territory 1982, The Dreamers 2003. *Publications:* novels: Alice Through the Needle's Eye 1984, Peter Pan and the Only Children 1987, The Holy Innocents: A Romance (Authors' Club First Novel Award 1989) 1988, Love and Death on Long Island 1990, The Death of the Author 1992, The Key to the Tower: A Novel 1997, A Closed Book 1999, The Dreamers 2003, Buenas Noches Buenos Aires 2003, The Act of Roger Murgatroyd 2006; poem: The Rape of the Cock 1991; non-fiction: Hollywood's Vietnam: From the Green Berets to Apocalypse Now (aka Vietnam on Film: From the Green Berets to Apocalypse Now) 1981, A Night at the Pictures: Ten Decades of British Film (with Nick Roddick) 1985, Myths & Memories 1986, The Postmodernist Always Rings Twice: Reflections on Culture in the 90s 1992, Flickers: An Illustrated Celebration of 100 Years of Cinema 1995, Surfing the Zeitgeist 1997, The Real Tadzio: Thomas Mann's 'Death in Venice' and the boy who inspired it 2001; editor: Movies 1999; translations: Kubrick (by Michel Ciment) 1983, John Boorman (by Michel Ciment) 1986, Letters/François Truffaut (aka François Truffaut: Correspondence 1945–1984) 1989, A Void (by Georges Perec) (Scott Moncrieff Translation Prize); contrib. to Wonder Tales: Six French Stories of Enchantment 1996. *Literary Agent:* Blake Friedmann Literary, Film & TV Agency, 122 Arlington Road, London, NW1 7HP, England. *Telephone:* (20) 7284-0408. *Fax:* (20) 7284-0442. *Website:* www.blakefriedmann.co.uk. *Address:* c/o Faber and Faber Ltd, 3 Queen Square, London, WC1N 3AU, England.

ADAIR, James Radford; American writer and editor; b. 2 Feb. 1923, Asheville, NC. *Career:* Ed., Power for Living, Free Way, Teen Power, and Counselor weekly churchpapers 1949–77; Sr Ed., Victor Books Div., Scripture Press Publications Inc., Wheaton, IL 1970–96. *Publications:* Saints Alive 1951, God's Power Within (ed.) 1961, We Found Our Way Out (ed. with Ted Miller) 1965, The Old Lighthouse 1966, The Man from Steamtown 1967, Tom Skinner: Top Man of the Lords and Other Stories (ed.) 1967, M. R. DeHaan: The Man and his Ministry 1969, Hooked on Jesus (ed.) 1971, A Greater Strength (with Jerry Jenkins) 1975, Surgeon on Safari 1976, Escape from Darkness (ed. with Ted Miller) 1982, 101 Days in the Gospels with Oswald Chambers (ed. with Harry Verploegh) 1992, 101 Days in the the Epistles with Oswald Chambers (ed. with Harry Verploegh) 1994, A New Testament Walk with Oswald Chambers (with Harry Verploegh) 1998, The Story of Scripture Press: The Whole Word for the Whole World 1998, Through the Year (with Warren W. Wiersbe) 1999, Be Quoted: From A to Z (with Warren W. Wiersbe) 2000. *Address:* 703 Webster Avenue, Wheaton, IL 60187, USA.

ADAMESTEANU, Gabriela; Romanian writer, journalist and translator; *Editor-in-Chief, 22 magazine*; b. 1942, Targu Ocna. *Career:* Ed.-in-Chief 22 magazine 1991–; mem. Romanian PEN Centre (pres.). *Publications:* Drumul egal al fiecarei zile (novel) 1975, Daruieste-ti o zi de vacanta (short stories) 1979, Vara-primavara (short stories) 1989, Obsesia politicii (interviews) 1995, Cele doua Romanii 2000, Intalnirea (novel) 2003, Dimineata pierduta (novel) 2004. *Honours:* Human Rights Watch Hellman Hammett Grant 2002, Ziarul de Iasi Nat. Award for Fiction 2004. *Address:* c/o Editura Polirom SA, Bulevardul Carol I nr. 4, etaj 4, CP 266, Iasi, Romania. *Website:* www.polirom.ro.

ADAMS, Chuck (see Tubb, Edwin Charles)

ADAMS, Daniel (see Nicole, Christopher Robin)

ADAMS, Deborah; American writer and poet; b. 22 Jan. 1956, Tennessee; m.; three c. *Education:* Univ. of Tennessee at Martin, Austin Peay Univ. *Career:* Adjunct Faculty, Nashville State Technical Inst.; mem. Appalachian Writers' Asscn, MWA, Sisters in Crime. *Publications:* fiction: All the Great Pretenders 1992, All the Crazy Winters 1992, All the Dark Disguises 1993, All the Hungry Mothers 1994, All the Deadly Beloved 1995, All the Blood Relatives 1997, All the Dirty Cowards 2000; poetry: Propriety 1976, Looking for Heroes 1984. *Address:* c/o Silver Dagger Mysteries, 325 W Walnut Street, Johnson City, TN, USA.

ADAMS, Glenda, BA, MS; Australian writer, playwright and screenwriter; b. 30 Dec. 1939, Sydney, NSW. *Education:* Univ. of Sydney, Columbia Univ.

Career: Fellow, New York State Creative Artist Programme Service 1975–76; Sr Fellow, Australia Council 1979; Fiction Fellow, NEA 1980; mem. Australian Soc. of Authors, Australian Writers' Guild, PEN American Center. *Publications:* Lies and Stories, 1976; The Hottest Night of the Century (short stories), 1979; Games of the Strong (novel), 1982; Dancing on Coral (novel), 1987; Longleg (novel), 1990; The Tempest of Clemenza (novel), 1996. Productions: Pride and Wrath (TV plays, ABC), 1993; The Monkey Trap (play, Griffin Theatre Co, Sydney), 1998. Contributions: periodicals. *Honours:* Miles Franklin Literary Award, 1987; Age Fiction Book of the Year, 1990; Australian National Book Council Award for Fiction, 1991. *Literary Agent:* Goodman Associates, 500 West End Avenue, New York, NY 10025, USA.

ADAMS, Harold, BA; American writer; b. 20 Feb. 1923, Clark, SD; m. Betty E. Skogsberg 1959 (divorced 1965); one d. *Education:* Univ. of Minnesota. *Career:* mem. Authors' Guild, MWA. *Publications:* Murder 1981, Paint the Town Red 1982, The Missing Moon 1983, The Naked Liar 1985, The Fourth Widow 1986, When Rich Men Die 1987, The Barbed Wire Noose 1987, The Man who met the Train 1988, The Man who missed the Party 1989, The Man who was taller than God 1992, A Perfectly Proper Murder 1993, A Way with Widows 1994, The Ditched Blonde 1995, The Hatchet Job 1996, The Ice Pick Artist 1997, No Badge, No Gun 1998, Lead, so I can follow 2000. *Honours:* Shamus Award, Best Private Eye Novel 1992, Minnesota Book Award, Mystery and Detective 1993. *Literary Agent:* c/o Ivy Fischer Stone, Fifi Oscard Agency Inc., 110 W 40th Street, 16th Floor, New York, NY 10018, USA. *E-mail:* ifischer@fifioscard.com.

ADAMS, Hazard Simeon, MA, PhD; American writer, poet, editor and academic; *Byron W. and Alice L. Lockwood Professor Emeritus of Humanities, University of Washington*; b. 15 Feb. 1926, Cleveland, OH; m. Diana White, 17 Sept. 1949, two s. *Education:* Princeton Univ., Univ. of Washington. *Career:* Instructor, Cornell Univ. 1952–56; Asst Prof., Univ. of Texas 1956–59; Assoc. Prof. to Prof., Michigan State Univ. 1959–64; Fulbright Lecturer, Trinity Coll., Dublin 1961–62; Prof., Univ. of California, Irvine 1964–77, 1990–94; Byron W. and Alice L. Lockwood Prof. of Humanities, Univ. of Washington 1977–97, Prof. Emer. 1997–. *Publications:* Blake and Yeats – The Contrary Vision 1955, William Blake – A Reading of the Shorter Poems 1963, The Contexts of Poetry 1963, The Horses of Instruction – A Novel 1968, The Interests of Criticism 1969, The Truth About Dragons – An Anti-Romance 1971, Lady Gregory 1973, The Academic Tribes 1976, Philosophy of the Literary Symbolic 1983, Joyce Cary's Trilogies – Pursuit of the Particular Real 1983, Antithetical Essays in Literary Criticism and Liberal Education 1990, The Book of Yeats's Poems 1990, The Book of Yeats's Vision 1995, The Farm at Richwood and Other Poems 1997, Many Pretty Toys – A Novel 1999, Home – A Novel 2001; Ed.: Poems by Robert Simeon Adams 1952, Poetry – An Introductory Anthology 1968, Fiction as Process (with Carl Hartman) 1968, William Blake – Jerusalem, Selected Poems and Prose 1970, Critical Theory Since Plato 1971, 3rd edn 2003, Critical Theory Since 1965 (with Leroy Searle) 1986, Critical Essays on William Blake 1991; contribs to numerous poetry, scholarly and critical journals. *Honours:* Guggenheim Fellowship 1974. *Address:* 3930 NE 157th Place, Lake Forest Park, WA 98155, USA (home). *Telephone:* (206) 364-4302 (home).

ADAMS, James MacGregor David; British journalist and writer; b. 22 April 1951, Newcastle upon Tyne, England; m. Rene Thatcher Riley 1990; one d. *Education:* Harrow, Neuchâtel Univ. *Publications:* The Unnatural Alliance 1984, The Financing of Terror 1986, Secret Armies 1988, Ambush (the War Between the SAS and the IRA) with Robin, Morgan and Anthony Bambridge 1988, Merchants of Death 1990, The Final Terror 1991, Bull's Eye 1992, Taking the Tunnel 1993; contribs to Sunday Times, Washington Post, Los Angeles Times, Atlantic. *Literary Agent:* Janklow & Nesbit Associates, 445 Park Avenue, New York, NY 10022, USA.

ADAMS, Joanna Z. (see Koch, Joanne Barbara)

ADAMS, Perseus, BA; South African writer, journalist, poet and teacher (retd); b. 11 March 1933, Cape Town; m. 1958. *Education:* Univ. of Cape Town. *Publications:* The Land at My Door, 1965; Grass for the Unicorn, 1975; Cries and Silences: Selected Poems, 1996. Contributions: numerous, mostly to Contrast, Cape Town. *Honours:* South Africa State Poetry Prize, 1963; Festival of Rhodesia Prize, 1970; Keats Memorial International Prize, 1971; Bridport Arts Festival Prize, 1984; Co-winner, Writing Section, Bard of the Year, 1993. *Address:* 21 Mapesbury Road, Kilburn, London NW2, England.

ADAMS, Phillip Andrew, AO, AM, FRSA; Australian writer, broadcaster and film-maker; b. 12 July 1939; m. 1st (divorced); three d.; m. 2nd Patrice Newell; one d. *Education:* Eltham High School. *Career:* columnist and critic 1956–; Chair. Film, Radio and TV Bd 1972–75; founder-mem. Australia Council 1972–75; Vic. Govt Rep. Australian Children's TV Foundation 1981–87; Pres. Vic. Council for Arts 1982–86; Chair. Australian Film Inst. 1975–80, Australian Film Comm. 1983–90, Comm. for the Future 1985–90, Nat. Australia Day Council 1992–96; mem. Bd Ausflag 1990–; mem. Cttee for the Centenary of Fed. 1994; worked with Families in Distress 1985–, Montsalvat Artists' Soc. 1986–, CARE Australia 1995–97; mem. Bd Nat. Museum of Australia 1996–97, Festival of Ideas 1999; mem. Council, Adelaide Festival 1996. *Films include:* Jack and Jill: A Postcript 1970, The Naked Bunyip 1971, The Adventures of Barry McKenzie 1972, Don's Party 1975, The Getting of Wisdom 1976, Grendel Grendel Grendel 1980, We of the Never Never 1982, Lonely Hearts 1982, Fighting Back 1983. *Radio includes:* Compere, Late Night Live (ABC). *Television includes:* Death and Destiny, Short and Sweet

(ABC), Adam's Australia (BBC), The Big Question, Face the Press (SBS). *Publications:* Adams With Added Enzymes 1970, The Unspeakable Adams 1977, More Unspeakable Adams 1979, The Uncensored Adams 1981, The Inflammable Adams 1983, Adams Versus God 1985, Harold Cazneaux: The Quiet Observer (with H. Ennis) 1994, Classic Columns 1994, The Penguin Book of Australian Jokes (with P. Newell) 1994, The Penguin Book of Jokes from Cyberspace (with P. Newell) 1995, The Big Questions (with P. Davies) 1996, The Penguin Book of More Australian Jokes 1996, Kookaburra 1996, Emperors of the Air 1997, Retreat from Tolerance? 1997, More Big Questions (with P. Davies) 1998, The Penguin Book of Schoolyard Jokes (with P. Newell) 1998, A Billion Voices 1999, The Penguin Book of All New Australian Jokes (with P. Newell) 2000, Adams Ark 2004. *Honours:* Hon. DUniv (Griffith Univ.) 1998, (Univ. of S Australia) 2004, Hon. DLitt (Edith Cowan Univ.) 2003, (Univ. of Sydney); Sr ANZAC Fellow 1981; Raymond Longford Award 1981, Australian Arts Award 1987, Australian Humanist of the Year 1987, CSICOP Award for Responsibility in Media (New York) 1996, Australian Republican of the Year 2006, Human Rights and Equal Opportunity Commission Human Rights Medal 2006. *Address:* c/o Radio National, ABC, GPO Box 9994, Sydney, NSW 2001, Australia (office). *Telephone:* (2) 9362 3971. *E-mail:* philadams@ozemail.com.au.

ADAMS, Richard George, MA, FRSA, FRSL; British novelist; b. 9 May 1920, Newbury, Berks.; s. of Dr E. G. B. Adams and Lilian Rosa Adams (née Button); m. Barbara Elizabeth Acland 1949; two d. *Education:* Bradfield Coll., Berks. and Worcester Coll., Oxford. *Career:* army service 1940–46; Home Civil Service 1948–74; Pres. Royal Soc. for the Prevention of Cruelty to Animals 1980–82; Writer-in-Residence, Univ. of Florida, 1975, Hollins Coll., Va 1976. *Publications:* Watership Down 1972, Shardik 1974, Nature Through the Seasons, The Tyger Voyage 1976, The Plague Dogs 1977 (filmed 1982), The Ship's Cat 1977, Nature Day and Night 1978, The Girl in a Swing 1980 (filmed 1988), The Unbroken Web (The Iron Wolf) 1980, Voyage Through the Antarctic 1982, Maia 1984, The Bureaucats 1985, A Nature Diary 1985, Occasional Poets: anthology (ed. and contrib.) 1986, The Legend of Te Tuna 1986, Traveller 1988, The Day Gone By (autobiog.) 1990, Tales From Watership Down 1996, The Outlandish Knight 2000, Daniel 2006. *Honours:* Carnegie Medal 1972, Guardian Award for Children's Fiction 1972, Medal of California Young Readers' Asscn 1977. *Address:* 26 Church Street, Whitchurch, Hants., RG28 7AR, England.

ADAMSON, Donald, KStJ, JP, MA, MLitt, DPhil, FRSL, FSA; British critic, biographer and historian; b. 30 March 1939, Culcheth, Cheshire, England; m. Helen Freda Griffiths 1966; two s. *Education:* Magdalen Coll., Oxford, Univ. of Paris. *Career:* Visiting Fellow Wolfson Coll., Cambridge; Fellow Chartered Inst. of Linguists. *Publications:* T. S. Eliot: A Memoir 1971, The House of Nell Gwyn (co-author) 1974, Les Romantiques Français devant la Peinture espagnole 1989, Blaise Pascal: Mathematician, Physicist, And Thinker About God 1995, Rides Round Britain, The Travel Journals of John Byng, 5th Viscount Torrington 1996, The Curriers' Company: A Modern History 2000, Pascal's Views on Mathematics and the Divine 2005; studies of Balzac's Comédie Humaine and various translations of Balzac and Maupassant. *Honours:* Chevalier, Ordre des Palmes Académiques, France 1986. *Address:* Dodmore House, The Street, Meopham, Kent, DA13 0AJ, England (office). *Telephone:* (7747) 733931 (office); (1474) 815955 (office). *Fax:* (1474) 815955 (office). *E-mail:* aimsworthy@aol.com. *Website:* www.dodmore.co.uk.

ADAMSON, Robert Harry; Australian poet, writer and publisher; b. 17 May 1943, Sydney, NSW; m. 1st Cheryl Adamson 1973; m. 2nd Juno Adamson 1989; one s. *Career:* Assoc. Ed. 1968–70, Ed. 1970–75, Asst Ed. 1975–77, New Poetry magazine, Sydney; Ed. and Dir, Prism Books, Sydney 1970–77; Founding Ed. and Dir (with Dorothy Hewett), Big Smoke Books, Sydney 1979–; Founder (with Michael Wilding), Paper Bark Press 1988–; mem. Australian Soc. of Authors, Poetry Soc. of Australia (pres. 1970–80). *Publications:* poetry: Canticles on the Skin 1970, The Rumour 1971, Swamp Riddles 1974, Theatre I–XIX 1976, Cross the Border 1977, Selected Poems 1977, Where I Come From 1979, The Law at Heart's Desire 1982, The Clean Dark 1989, Robert Adamson Selected Poems 1970–1989 1990, Waving to Hart Crane 1994, Mulberry Leaves: New and Selected Poems 1970–2001 2002, Reading the River: Selected Poems 2004; prose: Zimmer's Essay (with Bruce Hanford) 1974, Australian Writing Now (ed. with Manfred Jurgensen) 1988, Wards of the State: An Autobiographical Novella 1992, Inside Out (autobiog.) 2004; contrib. to periodicals. *Honours:* Australia Council Fellowships 1976, 1977, Grace Leven Prize for Poetry 1977, Kenneth Slessor Award 1990, Turnbull-Fox Philips Poetry Prize 1990, C. J. Dennis Prize for Poetry 1990. *Address:* PO Box 59, Brooklyn, NSW 2083, Australia.

ADCOCK, Fleur, OBE, MA, FRSL; British writer; b. 10 Feb. 1934, Papakura, New Zealand; d. of Cyril John Adcock and Irene Robinson; m. 1st Alistair Teariki Campbell 1952 (divorced 1958); two s.; m. 2nd Barry Crump 1962 (divorced 1966). *Education:* Victoria Univ. Wellington. *Career:* Asst Lecturer Univ. of Otago 1958, Asst Librarian 1959–61; with Alexander Turnbull Library 1962; with FCO 1963–79; freelance writer 1979–; Northern Arts Fellowship in Literature, Univs of Newcastle upon Tyne and Durham 1979–81; Eastern Arts Fellowship, Univ. of E Anglia 1984; writer-in-residence, Univ. of Adelaide 1986; mem. Poetry Soc. *Publications:* The Eye of the Hurricane 1964, Tigers 1967, High Tide in the Garden 1971, The Scenic Route 1974, The Inner Harbour 1979, Below Loughrigg 1979, The Oxford Book of Contemporary New Zealand Poetry (ed.) 1982, Selected Poems 1983, The Virgin and the Nightingale: Medieval Latin Poems 1983, Hotspur: A

Ballad for Music 1986, The Incident Book 1986, The Faber Book of 20th Century Women's Poetry 1987, Orient Express: Poems by Grete Tartler (trans.) 1989, Time Zones 1991, Letters from Darkness: Poems by Daniela Crasnaru (trans.) 1991, High Primas and the Archpoet (ed. and trans.) 1994, The Oxford Book of Creatures (ed. with Jacqueline Simms) 1995, Looking Back 1997, Poems 1960–2000 (Queen's Gold Medal for Poetry 2006) 2000. *Honours:* Festival of Wellington Poetry Award 1961, New Zealand State Literary Fund Award 1964, Buckland Award 1967, 1979, Jessie MacKay Award 1968, 1972, Cholmondeley Award 1976, New Zealand Nat. Book Award 1984, Arts Council Writers' Award 1988. *Address:* 14 Lincoln Road, London, N2 9DL, England. *Telephone:* (20) 8444-7881.

ADDINGTON, Larry Holbrook, BA, MA, PhD; American writer and academic; *Professor Emeritus of History, The Citadel;* b. 16 Nov. 1932, Charlotte, NC. *Education:* Univ. of North Carolina at Chapel Hill, Duke Univ. *Career:* Asst Prof., San Jose State Coll. 1962–64; Asst Prof. 1964–66, Assoc. Prof. 1966–70, Prof. 1970–94, Head of Dept 1989–94, Prof. Emeritus 1994–, of History, The Citadel; Visiting Prof., Duke Univ. 1976–77; Charter Mem. The Citadel Chapter 1974, Nat. Honor Soc.; mem. Soc. for Mil. History. *Publications:* From Moltke to Hitler: The Evolution of German Military Doctrine, 1865–1939 1966, Firepower and Maneuver: The European Inheritance in the Two World Wars 1967, Firepower and Maneuver: Historical Case Studies 1969, The Blitzkrieg Era and the German General Staff, 1865–1941 1971, The Patterns of War Since the Eighteenth Century 1984, The Patterns of War Through the Eighteenth Century 1990, America's War in Vietnam: A Short Narrative History 2000; contrib. to encyclopedias, books and scholarly journals. *Honours:* AMI Award for Best Seminal Work 1984. *Address:* 1341 New Castle Street, Charleston, SC 29407, USA (office). *E-mail:* larrya103@aol.com (office).

ADDIS, Richard James, MA; British journalist; *Assistant Editor, Financial Times;* b. 23 Aug. 1956, s. of Richard Thomas Addis and Jane Addis; m. Eunice Minogue 1983 (divorced 2000); one s. two d. *Education:* West Downs, Rugby, Downing Coll., Cambridge. *Career:* with Evening Standard 1985–89; Deputy Ed. Sunday Telegraph 1989–91; Exec. Ed. Daily Mail 1991–95; Ed. Daily Express 1995–98, The Express on Sunday 1996–98; Consultant Ed. Mail on Sunday 1998–99; Ed. The Globe and Mail, Toronto 1999–2002; Asst Ed. and Design Ed., Financial Times 2002–; apptd Hon. Gov. York Univ., Canada 2002. *Address:* Financial Times, One Southwark Bridge, London, SE1 9HL, England (office). *Telephone:* (20) 7873-3000 (office). *E-mail:* richard.addis@ft.com (office). *Website:* www.ft.com (office).

ADEBAYO, Diran; Nigerian novelist, critic and journalist; b. 1968, London. *Education:* Malvern Public School, Univ. of Oxford. *Career:* broadcaster for LWT. *Publications:* novels: Some Kind of Black 1996, My Once Upon a Time 2000; contrib. to The Guardian, Daily Mail, Daily Express, The Times. *Honours:* Saga Prize 1996. *Literary Agent:* c/o Abacus, Little, Brown & Co. (UK), Brettenham House, Lancaster Place, London, WC2E 7EN, England. *Telephone:* (20) 7911-8000. *Fax:* (20) 7911-8100. *Website:* www.timewarnerbooks.co.uk.

ADHIKARI, Santosh Kumar; Indian college administrator (retd), writer and poet; b. 24 Nov. 1923, West Bengal; m. 1948; one s. two d. *Education:* Univ. of Calcutta, Indian Inst. of Bankers, Mumbai, Indian Inst. of Management. *Career:* Prin., Staff Coll., United Bank of India, Kolkata –1983; Vidyasagar Lecturer, Univ. of Calcutta 1979; Speaker, Bengal Studies Conference, Univ. of Chicago 1990; Ed., Spark 1975–96; Founder and fmr Sec. Vidyasagar Research Centre; mem. Asiatic Soc., Akhil Bharat, Bhasa Sahitya Sammelan, PEN West Bengal Branch (Sec. 1985–87). *Publications include:* fiction: Rakta-Kamal 1967, Nirjan Shikhar 1971, Panka-Lipi 1985, Durer Desh Durer Manus 1988; poetry: Ekla Chalore 1948, Diganter Megh 1960, Anya Kono Khane 1973, Blossoms in the Dust (in English) 1980, Paari 1986; non-fiction: Vidya Sagar 1970, Santrasbad O' Bhagat Singh 1979, Vidyasagar and the Regeneration of Bengal (in English) 1980, Vidyasagarer Jiboner Seshdinguli 1985, Vidyasagarer Sikshaneeti 1987, Netaji Subhas Chandra 1990, Vidyasagar: Educator, Reformer and Humanist (in English) 1995; contrib. to All India Radio and major journals. *Honours:* hon. title of Bharat Bhasa Bhusan 1991; Prasad Puraskar for Poetry 1986. *Address:* c/o Vidyasagar Research Centre, 81 Raja Basanta Roy Road, Kolkata 700029, India. *Telephone:* (33) 24008393 (home); (33) 24660441 (home).

ADICHIE, Chimamanda Ngozi, BSc, MA; Nigerian writer; b. 1977, Abba, Anambra State. *Education:* Univ. of Nigeria, Eastern Connecticut Univ. and Johns Hopkins Univ., USA. *Career:* Fellow Princeton Univ. 2005–06. *Publications:* novels: Purple Hibiscus (Commonwealth Writers' Best First Book Award) 2004, Half of a Yellow Sun (Orange Broadband Prize for Fiction 2007) 2006; short stories: Lye, The American Embassy, My Mother The Crazy African, You in America 2001; poetry: Decisions 1997; play: For Love of Biafra 1998; contrib. to Prism International, Poetry Magazine, Posse Review, Zoetrope All-Story, Allegheny Review of Undergraduate Literature, Iowa Review, Granta, New Yorker, Virginia Quarterly Review, Conjunctions. *Honours:* International PEN/David Wong Award 2003, Hurston/Wright Legacy Award 2004, Commonwealth Writers Prize 2005. *Literary Agent:* c/o The Wylie Agency 17 Bedford Square, London, WC1B 3JA, England. *Telephone:* (20) 7908-5900. *E-mail:* mail@wylieagency.com. *Website:* www.wylieagency.com. *E-mail:* chimamanda.adichie@gmail.com (home). *Website:* www.halfofayellowsun.com.

ADICKES, Sandra, BA, MA, PhD; American academic and writer; *Professor Emerita, Winona State University*; b. 14 July 1933, New York, NY; three d. *Education:* Douglass Coll., Hunter Coll., CUNY, New York Univ. *Career:* Prof. of English 1988–98, Prof. Emerita 1998–, Winona State Univ. *Publications:* The Social Quest 1991, Legends of Good Women (novel) 1992, To Be Young Was Very Heaven: Women in New York Before the First World War 1997, The Legend of a Freedom School 2005; contrib. to reference books and journals. *Address:* 93 Renaissance Lane, New Brunswick, NJ 08901, USA. *E-mail:* s.adickes@att.net.

ADIE, Kathryn (Kate), OBE, BA; British journalist and broadcaster; b. 19 Sept. 1945, d. of Babe Dunnett (née Issit) and adopted d. of the late John Wilfrid Adie and of Maud Adie (née Fambely). *Education:* Sunderland Church High School, Univ. of Newcastle. *Career:* technician and producer BBC Radio 1969–76; reporter BBC TV South 1977–78, BBC TV News 1979–81, corresp. 1982–89, Chief News Corresp. 1989–2003, presenter, From Our Own Correspondent, BBC Radio 4; freelance journalist, broadcaster and TV presenter 2003–; Visiting Fellow, Univ. of Bournemouth 1998–. *Publications:* The Kindness of Strangers (autobiog.) 2002, Corsets to Camouflage: Women and War 2003, Nobody's Child: The Lives of Abandoned Children 2005. *Honours:* Hon. Prof., Sunderland Univ. 1995; Hon. Fellow, Royal Holloway, Univ. of London 1996; Freeman of Sunderland 1990; Hon. MA (Bath) 1987, (Newcastle) 1990; Hon. DLitt (City Univ.) 1989, (Loughborough) 1991, (Sunderland) 1993, (Robert Gordon) 1996, (Nottingham) 1998, (Nottingham Trent) 1998; Hon. MUniv (Open Univ.) 1996; Royal Television Soc. News Award 1981, 1987, Monte Carlo Int. News Award 1981, 1990, BAFTA Richard Dimbleby Award 1989. *Address:* c/o BBC TV, Wood Lane, London, W12 7RJ, England.

ADISA, Opal Palmer, BA, MA, PhD; Jamaican/American writer, poet, educator, consultant and storyteller and performer; *Professor of Literature and Creative Writing, California College of the Arts*; b. 6 Nov. 1954, Jamaica; d. of Orlando Palmer and Catherine Palmer; three c. *Education:* Hunter Coll., NY, San Francisco State Univ., Calif., Univ. of California, Berkeley. *Career:* Co-founder and fmr Artistic Dir Bay Area Children's group, Watoto Wa Kuumba; taught Caribbean and African Literature San Francisco State Univ.; now Prof. of Literature and Creative Writing, Calif. Coll. of the Arts, fmr Chair. Ethnic Studies/Cultural Diversity Program; has taught storytelling workshops in Oakland and San Francisco Unified School Dists; numerous live storytelling performances, broadcasts on TV and radio, writer-in-residences. *Exhibitions:* six black and white photographs from the Cuba series and six colour photographs from Brazil in Group Show, A Celebration of Latin Art, Health & Community, at WCRC Gallery, Oakland, Calif. 2006, Swimming with Yemanja in Brazil (mixed media), Faculty Group Show, California College of the Arts 2006, two mixed-media pieces, Inside the Teeth of Love and So This is It in travelling exhbn, Afetos Roubados No Tempo, Bahía, Brazil and in different cites throughout Brazil before travelling to S Africa 2006, four pieces in Conversations/Conversaciones: Women Collaborate, de Saisset Museum, Santa Clara Univ. 2004, Working Man (photo/poem), Art of Living Black 2004, Richmond Art Center, Calif. 2002, Juried Group Show at Pro Arts, Oakland 2002–03. *Recordings:* Fierce/Love (with Devorah Major) 1992, The Tongue is a Drum (with Devorah Major) 2002. *Publications:* Pina, The Many-Eyed Fruit (juvenile) 1985, Bake-Face and Other Guava Stories 1986, Traveling Women (poems) 1989, Tamarind and Mango Women (poems) (PEN Oakland/Josephine Miles Award), It Begins with Years (novel) 1997, Leaf-of-Life (poems) 2000, Saucy Caribbean Tales (stories CD) 2003, Until Judgment Comes (short stories) 2004, The Orishas Command the Dance (novel) 2004, Caribbean Passion (poems) 2004, Eros Muse – Poetry and Essays 2006, Sacatar Wombs – Words, Poems and Photos (chapbook) 2006, Until Judgment Comes (stories) 2007; contrib. poems, fiction and essays to anthologies and magazines, including The Caribbean Writer. *Honours:* Calif. Arts Council Master Folk Artist for Storytelling, City of Oakland Creative Artist Fellowship Award for Storytelling, Distinguished Bay Area Woman Writer Award Nat. Women's Political Caucus, Daily News Prize for Best Poems in The Caribbean Writer Univ. of the Virgin Islands, Canute A. Brodhurst Prize, Distinguished Writer for the Middle Atlantic Writers Asscn . *Address:* PO Box 10625, Oakland, CA 94610, USA. *Telephone:* (510) 383-9883. *E-mail:* opalwrites@sbcglobal.net. *Website:* www.opalwriters.com.

ADLER, Carole Schwerdtfeger, BA, MS; American writer; b. 23 Feb. 1932, Long Island, NY; m. Arnold R. Adler 1952; three s. *Education:* Hunter Coll., CUNY, Russell Sage Coll. *Career:* mem. Soc. of Children's Book Writers, Authors' Guild. *Publications:* The Magic of the Glits 1979, The Silver Coach 1979, In Our House Scott is My Brother 1980, The Cat That Was Left Behind 1981, Down By the River 1981, Shelter on Blue Barns Road 1981, Footsteps on the Stairs 1982, The Evidence That Wasn't There 1982, The Once in a While Hero 1982, Some Other Summer 1982, The Shell Lady's Daughter 1983, Get Lost Little Brother 1983, Roadside Valentine 1983, Shadows on Little Reef Bay 1984, Fly Free 1984, Binding Ties 1985, With Westie and the Tin Man 1985, Good-Bye Pink Pig 1985, Split Sisters 1986, Kiss the Clown 1986, Carly's Buck 1987, Always and Forever Friends 1988, If You Need Me 1988, Eddie's Blue Winged Dragon 1988, One Sister Too Many 1989, The Lump in the Middle 1989, Help Pink Pig! 1990, Ghost Brother 1990, Mismatched Summer 1991, A Tribe for Lexi 1991, Tuna Fish Thanksgiving 1992, Daddy's Climbing Tree 1993, Willie, the Frog Prince 1994, That Horse Whiskey 1994, Youn Hee and Me 1995, Court Yard Cat 1995, What's to be Scared of, Suki? 1996, More Than a Horse 1997, Her Blue Straw Hat 1997, Not Just A Summer Crush 1998, Winning 1999, One Unhappy Horse 2001, No Place Cat 2002, Saving Dove 2003. *Honours:* William Allen White Award 1980, Golden Kite Award 1980, American Library Asscn Best Young Adult Book 1984, Children's Book Award, Child Study Committee 1986, IRA Children's Selections 1987, 1991, ASPCA Henry Berg Award 2001. *Address:* 7041 N Cathedral Rock Place, Tucson, AZ 85718, USA.

ADLER, Laure; French journalist, historian and writer; b. 11 March 1950, Caen; m. 1st Fred Adler 1968; m. 2nd Alain Veinstein. *Career:* sec. France Culture radio station 1974, Dir 1999–2005; responsible for essays and documents, Grasset 1997; responsible for literature dept, Editions du Seuil 2005–. *Film:* actress in Des nouvelles du bon Dieu 1996. *Publications:* non-fiction: A laube du féminisme: les premières journalistes (1830–1850) 1979, Lamour à l'arsenic: Histoire de Marie Lafarge 1985, Avignon: 40 ans de festival 1987, La Vie quotidienne dans les maisons closes: 1830–1930 1990, Les femmes politiques 1993, L'année des adieux 1995, Marguerite Duras 2000, A ce soir 2001, Les Maisons closes 2002, Bis heute abend 2004, Dans les pas de Hannah Arendt 2005, Les Femmes qui lisent sont dangereuses (with Stefan Bollmann) 2006. *Address:* Editions du Seuil, 27 rue Jacob, 75006 Paris, France (office). *E-mail:* contact@seuil.com. *Website:* www.seuil.com.

ADLER, Margot Susanna, BA, MS; American journalist and broadcaster; *Correspondent, National Public Radio*; b. 16 April 1946, Little Rock, AR. *Education:* Univ. of California, Berkeley, Columbia School of Journalism, Harvard Univ. *Career:* Corresp., Nat. Public Radio 1979–; mem. Authors' Guild, American Fed. of Radio and Television Artists. *Publications:* Drawing Down the Moon: Witches, Druids, Goddess-Worshippers and Other Pagans in America Today 1979, Heretic's Heart: A Journey Through Spirit and Revolution 1997. *Honours:* Neman Fellow, Harvard Univ. 1982. *Literary Agent:* c/o Jane Rotrosen, 333 Central Park W, New York, NY 10025, USA. *Telephone:* (212) 878-1435 (office); (212) 222-6298 (home). *E-mail:* madler@npr.org.

ADLER, Renata, AB, Dd'ES, MA, JD; American writer; *Fellow of the University Professors and Visiting Professor of Journalism, Boston University*; b. 19 Oct. 1938, Milan, Italy. *Education:* Bryn Mawr Coll., Sorbonne Univ., Paris, Harvard Univ., Yale Univ. Law School. *Career:* writer-reporter, New Yorker 1962–68, 1970–82; Fellow, Trubull Coll., Yale Univ. 1969–72; Assoc. Prof. of Theatre and Cinema, Hunter Coll., CUNY 1972–73; Guggenheim Fellowship 1973–74; Woodrow Wilson and Fulbright Fellowships; fmr chief film critic The New York Times; currently Fellow of the Univ. Profs and Visiting Prof. of Journalism, Coll. of Communication, Boston Univ.; elected mem. American Acad. and Inst. of Arts and Letters 1987; mem. PEN. *Publications:* Toward a Radical Middle: Fourteen Pieces of Reporting and Criticism 1969, A Year in the Dark: Journal of a Film Critic, 1968–69 1970, Speedboat (novel) (Ernest Hemingway Prize) 1976, Pitch Dark (novel) 1983, Reckless Disregard: Westmoreland v. CBS et al: Sharon v. Time 1986, Politics and Media: Essays 1988, Gone: The Last Days of the New Yorker 1999, Private Capacity 2000, Canaries in the Mineshaft: Essays on Politics and Media 2001, Irreparable Harm: The US Supreme Court and the Decision That Made George W. Bush President 2004. *Honours:* Hon. LLD (Georgetown Univ. Law School) 1989; O. Henry Short Story Award 1974, American Acad. and Inst. of Arts and Letters Award 1976, New York Newswomen's Club Front Page Award. *Address:* c/o Department of Journalism, College of Communication, Boston University, 640 Commonwealth Avenue, Boston, MA, USA.

ADLER, Warren, BA; American writer; b. 16 Dec. 1927, New York, NY; m. Sonia Kline 1951; three s. *Education:* New York Univ., New School Univ., New York. *Career:* Ed. New York Daily News, Queens Post, Forest Hills, NY; pres. advertising and public relations agency, Washington, DC 1959–78; mem. Century Asscn, Lotos Club, PEN, Authors' Guild. *Publications:* Undertow 1974, Options 1974, Banquet Before Dawn 1976, The Henderson Equation 1976, Trans-Siberian Express 1977, The Sunset Gang 1978 (TV mini-series 1991), The Casanova Embrace 1978, Blood Ties 1979, Natural Enemies 1980, The War of the Roses 1981 (film 1989), American Quartet 1982, American Sextet 1983, Random Hearts 1984 (film 1999), Twilight Child 1989, Immaculate Deception 1991, Senator Love 1991, Private Lies 1992, The Witch of Watergate 1992, The Ties That Bind 1994, Never Too Late for Love 1996, Jackson Hole Uneasy Eden 1997, Mourning Glory 1997, Cult: A Novel of Brainwashing and Death 2002, Death of a Washington Madame 2005; TV series Fiona 2002 based on his novels. *Address:* 300 E 56th Street, New York, NY 10022, USA. *Telephone:* (212) 350-9357. *E-mail:* adlernovel@aol.com. *Website:* warrenadler.com.

ADNAN, Etel; American artist and writer; b. 24 Feb. 1925, Beirut, Lebanon. *Education:* Univ. de Paris (Sorbonne) and Univs of Berkeley and Harvard, USA. *Career:* Prof. of Aesthetics, Dominican Coll., San Rafael, CA, USA –1972; artist c 1960–, more than 30 solo exhbns in USA, Europe, Middle East; Cultural Ed. Al-Safa, Lebanon 1972–74, L'Orient-Le Jour 1974–79; mem. Poetry Center, San Francisco. *Publications include:* poetry: Moonshots 1966, Five Senses for One Death 1971, From A to Z 1982, The Indian Never Had a Horse and Other Poems 1985, The Arab Apocalypse 1989, The Spring Flowers Own and the Manifestations of the Voyage 1990, In/somnia 2002; novel: Sitt Marie Rose 1982; other: Journey to Mount Tamalpais 1986, Paris When It's Naked 1993, Of Cities and Women: Letters to Fawazz 1993, There: In the Light and the Darkness of the Self and of the Other 1995, To Write in a Foreign Language 1996, In the Heart of the Heart of Another Country 2005. *Honours:* France-Pays Arabes Prize 1978. *Address:* 35 Marie Street,

Sausalito, CA 94965, USA (home); 29 rue Madame, Paris 75006, France (home). *Telephone:* (415) 332-1458 (USA) (home); 1-45-44-33-31 (France) (home). *E-mail:* sifattal@yahoo.com (home).

ADOFF, Arnold, BA; American poet, writer and literary agent; b. 16 July 1935, New York, NY; m. Virginia Hamilton 1960; two c. *Education:* City Coll., CUNY, Columbia Univ., New School for Social Research Poetry Workshops, New York. *Career:* teacher, New York City Public Schools 1957–69; literary agent, Yellow Springs, OH 1977–; Distinguished Visiting Prof., Queens Coll., CUNY 1986–87; guest lecturer in many US venues. *Publications:* poetry: Black Is Brown Is Tan 1973, Make a Circle Keep Us In: Poems for a Good Day 1975, Big Sister Tells Me That I'm Black 1976, Tornado!: Poems 1977, Under the Early Morning Trees 1978, Where Wild Willie 1978, Eats: Poems 1979, I Am the Running Girl 1979, Friend Dog 1980, OUTside INside Poems 1981, Today We Are Brother and Sister 1981, Birds 1982, All the Colors of the Race 1982, The Cabbages are Chasing the Rabbits 1985, Sports Pages 1986, Flamboyan 1988, Greens 1988, Chocolate Dreams 1989, Hard to Be Six 1990, In for Winter, Out for Spring 1991; other: Malcolm X (biog.) 1970, MA nDA LA (picture book) 1971; editor: I Am the Darker Brother: An Anthology of Modern Poems by Negro Americans 1968, Black on Black: Commentaries by Negro Americans 1968, City in All Directions: An Anthology of Modern Poems by Black Americans 1970, Brothers and Sisters: Modern Stories by Black Americans 1970, It is the Poem Singing into Your Eyes: An Anthology of New Young Poets 1971, The Poetry of Black America: An Anthology of the 20th Century 1973, My Black Me: A Beginning Book of Black Poetry 1974, Celebrations: A New Anthology of Black American Poetry 1978; contrib. articles and reviews to periodicals. *Honours:* Child Study Asscn of America Children's Book of the Year Citations 1968, 1969, 1986, American Library Asscn Notable Book Awards 1968, 1970, 1971, 1972, 1979, School Library Journal Best Children's Book Citations 1971, 1973, Children's Book Council-Nat. Council for Social Studies Notable Children's Trade Book Citation 1974, Jane Addams Peace Asscn Special Certificate 1983, Int. Reading Asscn-Children's Book Council Children's Choice Citation 1985, Nat. Council of Teachers of English Poetry Award 1988. *Address:* Arnold Adoff Agency, PO Box 293, Yellow Springs, OH 45387, USA. *Website:* www.arnoldadoff.com.

ADONIS (see Said, Ali Ahman)

ADRIAN, Frances (see Polland, Madelaine Angela)

AFOLABI, Segun A.; Nigerian-born writer; b. 1966, Kaduna; s. of James Afolabi and Christine Afolabi. *Education:* Brighton Coll., Univ. Coll., Wales. *Career:* has lived in various countries, including the Congo, Canada, E Germany and Indonesia; fmrly worked for the BBC, London. *Publications:* Monday Morning (short story) (Caine Prize 2005) 2004, A Life Elsewhere (short stories) 2006, Goodbye Lucille (novel) 2007; contrib. to Wasafiri, The Edinburgh Review, Granta, New Welsh Review, The Interpreter's House, Dream Catcher, Salamander, Prism International, Pretext, London Magazine, The Kenyon Review, Tampa Review, Pretext, The Malahat Review, Msafiri. *Address:* c/o Jonathan Cape, 20 Vauxhall Bridge Road, London, SW1V 2SA, England. *E-mail:* capepublicity@randomhouse.co.uk.

AFRICANO, Lillian, (Nora Ashby, Lila Cook, Jessica March), BA; American writer and columnist; b. 7 June 1935, Paterson, NJ; m. (divorced); two s. one d. *Education:* Barnard Coll., Columbia Univ. Graduate School. *Career:* Arts Ed., The Villager 1971; News Ed., Penthouse/Forum 1973; columnist, New York Times Syndicate 1977, Woman's World 1980; mem. Drama Desk (vice-pres., sec.), Outer Critics' Circle, American Soc. of Journalists and Authors, Authors' Guild. *Publications:* Businessman's Guide to the Middle East, 1977; Doctor's Walking Book (co-author), 1980; Something Old, Something New, 1983; Passions, 1985; Gone From Breezy Hill (as Nora Ashby), 1985; Illusions (as Jessica March), 1988; Consenting Adults (as Lila Cook), 1988; Temptations (as Jessica March), 1989; Obsessions, 1990. Contributions: New York Times; New York News; Reader's Digest; Harper's Bazaar; Woman's Day; Woman's World; National Review; Nation. *E-mail:* author@lillianafricano.com. *Website:* www.lillianafricano.com.

AĞAOĞLU, Adalet; Turkish writer; b. 1929, Ankara; d. of Mustafa and İsmet Sümer; m. Halim Ağaoğlu 1954. *Education:* Univ. of Ankara. *Career:* worked for Türkiye Radyo Televizyon Kurumu (TRT) 1953–73; freelance writer 1973–. *Publications include:* (in Turkish) novels: Lying Down to Die 1973, The Mince Rose of My Mind 1977, A Wedding Party 1978, Summer's End 1980, Four or Five People 1984, No... 1987, Shiver of Soul 1990, Curfew (in trans.) 1997; short stories: High Tension (Sait Faik Prize) 1974, The First Sound of Silence 1978, Come On, Let's Go 1982; plays: Three Play (Prize of Turkish Language Inst.) 1956, Plays 1982, Too Far, Much Closer (Is Bankasi Grand Award for the Theatre) 1991. *Honours:* Dr hc (Ohio State Univ.) 1998; Sedat Simavi Prize, Orhan Kemal Prize, Madarali Prize, Pres. of the Turkish Repub. Grand Prize for Culture and the Arts 1995. *Address:* Piyasa Cad, Bülbül Sok, 10/5 Ceviz Apt, Büyükdere, Istanbul, Turkey. *Telephone:* (1) 1422636.

AGARD, John; Guyanan poet, children's writer and editor; b. 21 June 1949; pnr Grace Nichols. *Career:* sub-ed. and feature writer, Guyana Sunday Chronicle newspaper; moved to England 1977; touring lecturer with Commonwealth Inst.; writer-in-residence, South Bank Centre London 1993; poet-in-residence, BBC Educ. Dept 1997–98. *Publications include:* Shoot Me with Flowers 1974, Letters for Lettie and Other Stories 1979, Dig Away Two-Hole Tim 1981, Man to Pan (Casa de las Américas Prize, Cuba) 1982, I Din Do

Nuttin and Other Poems 1983, Limbo Dancer in Dark Glasses 1983, Livingroom 1983, Mangoes and Bullets: Selected and New Poems 1972-84 1985, Say it Again, Granny! 1986, Lend Me Your Wings 1987, Life Doesn't Frighten Me At All (ed.) 1989, Go Noah Go! 1990, Laughter is an Egg 1990, The Calypso Alphabet 1990, No Hickory, No Dockory, No Dock (with Grace Nichols) 1991, The Emperor's Dan-dan 1992, A Stone's Throw from Embankment: The South Bank Collection 1993, The Great Snakeskin (play for children) 1993, Grandfather's Old Bruk-a-Down Car 1994, Oriki and the Monster Who Hated Balloons 1994, The Monster Who Loved Cameras 1994, The Monster Who Loved Telephones 1994, The Monster Who Loved Toothbrushes 1994, A Caribbean Dozen (co-ed.) 1994, Poems in My Earphone (ed.) 1995, Eat a Poem, Wear a Poem 1995, Get Back, Pimple! 1996, Why is the Sky? (ed.) 1996, We Animals Would Like a Word With You (Bronze Award, Nestle Smarties Book Prize) 1996, From the Devil's Pulpit 1997, Brer Rabbit: The Great Tug-o-War 1998, Points of View with Professor Peekabo 2000, Weblines 2000, A Child's Year of Stories and Poems (with Michael Rosen and Robert Frost) 2000, Hello New: New Poems for a New Century (ed.) 2000, Come Back to Me My Boomerang (with Lydia Monks) 2001, Number Parade: Number Poems from 0–100 (with Jackie Kay, Grace Nichols, Nick Toczek and Michael Rosen) 2002, Under The Moon and Over the Sea (co-ed.) 2002, Einstein, The Girl Who Hated Maths 2002, Hello H2O 2003, Butter-Finger (with Bob Cattell), We Brits 2007; contrib. to Caribbean Poetry Now 1984, The Penguin Book of Caribbean Verse (ed.) 1986, Border Country: Poems in Progress 1991, Grandchildren of Albion 1992, The Heinemann Book of Caribbean Poetry 1992, Another Day on your Foot and I Would Have Died 1996. *Honours:* Arts Council Bursary 1989, Paul Hamlyn Award for Poetry 1997, Cholmondley Award 2004. *Address:* c/o Bloodaxe Books Ltd, Highgreen, Tarset, Northumberland NE48 1RP, England.

AGBABI, Patience; British poet; b. 1965, Nigeria. *Career:* performance poet, world-wide projects incl. Crossing Border (Netherlands), Diggante Festival (Sweden), Rough Talk Sweet Song tour (South Africa), British Council tour (Namibia), Rome Poetry Festival (Italy), Aldeburgh Festival, Soho Jazz Festival, Royal Albert Hall, Poetry International, Cheltenham Festival, London Palladium, Edinburgh Book Festival, Glastonbury Festival, Spit Lit Festival, Brixton Acad., Modern Love tour 2001, Bittersweet tour 1999–2000 (all UK); TV and radio appearances; resident poet, tattoo parlour, Flamin' 8 2000; poet-in-residence, Oxford Brookes Univ. –2001; Lecturer, Cardiff Univ. 2002. *Publications:* R.A.W. 1997, Transformatrix 2000; contrib. to anthologies including Bittersweet 1998, The Fire People 1998, Wasafiri 2000, Poetry Review 2000, Modern Love 2001. *Honours:* Excelle Literary Award for Poetry. *Literary Agent:* Renaissance One, PO Box 22004, London, SW2 5ZS, England.

AGBOLUAJE, Oladipo (Dipo), PhD; Nigerian playwright; b. UK. *Education:* Open Univ. *Career:* involved in Eclipse Writers' Lab. *Plays:* Early Morning 2003, Royal Phone 2004, Mother Courage and her Children (adaptation) 2004. *Address:* c/o Oval House Theatre, 52–54 Kennington Oval, London, SE11 5SW, England. *Website:* www.ovalhouse.com.

AGEE, Jonis, BA, MA, PhD; American writer, poet and academic; b. 31 May 1943, Omaha, NE; m. Paul McDonough; one d. *Education:* Univ. of Iowa, SUNY at Binghamton. *Career:* teacher, Coll. of St Catherine, St Paul, Minnesota 1975–95; literary consultant, Walker Arts Center, Minneapolis 1978–84; adjunct teacher, Macalester Coll., St Paul, Minnesota 1980–88; teacher and Ed., Literary Post Program for Sr Citizen Writers 1986–89; Prof., Univ. of Michigan 1995; currently Prof., Univ. of Nebraska at Lincoln; many poetry readings; mem. Literary Guild. *Publications:* Houses (chapbook) 1976, Mercury (chapbook) 1981, Two Poems 1982, Border Crossings (ed.) 1984, Stiller's Pond (ed.) 1988, Bend This Heart (short stories) 1989, Pretend We've Never Met (short stories) 1989, Sweet Eyes (novel) 1991, My Mother's Hands 1994, Strange Angels (novel) 1994, A .38 Special and a Broken Heart (short stories) 1995, South of Resurrection (novel) 1997, The Weight of Dreams 1999, Taking the Wall 1999, Acts of Love on Indigo Road: New and Selected Stories (ForeWord magazine Gold Book of the Year Award 2004) 2003, The River Wife 2007; contrib. to anthologies and periodicals. *Honours:* Minnesota State Arts Board Award 1977, NEA Fellowship 1978, Loft-McKnight Awards 1987, 1991. *Address:* 8005 West Pioneers Blvd, Denton, NE 68339 (home); 215 Andrews Hall, Department of English, University of Nebraska, Lincoln, NE 68588-0333, USA (office). *E-mail:* jagee@unl.edu (office). *Website:* www.jonisagee.com.

AGOSÍN, Marjorie, PhD; Chilean human rights activist, writer and poet; *Professor of Spanish, Wellesley College;* b. 1955, Bethesda, MD, USA. *Education:* Univ. of Georgia, Indiana Univ., Bloomington. *Career:* grew up in Chile, moved to USA aged 16 to escape military coup; currently Prof. of Spanish Wellesley Coll. *Publications:* Zones of Pain 1988, Circles of Madness: Mothers of the Plaza de Mayo 1992, Dear Anne Frank (poems), Tapestries of Hope, Threads of Love, A Cross and a Star: Memoirs of a Jewish Girl in Chile 1994, Always From Somewhere Else; some 20 vols of fiction, non-fiction, poetry and essays; contrib. articles to newspapers and magazines. *Honours:* Letras de Oro Award 1995, Latino Literature Prize 1995, Conf. of Christians and Jews Good Neighbor Award 1995, Jeanette Rankin Award 1995, UNA of Greater Boston Leadership Award for contrib. to int. understanding and human rights 1998. *Address:* c/o Wellesley College Spanish Department, Green Hall, Room 331, 106 Central Street, Wellesley, MA 02481, USA. *Telephone:* (781) 283-2425. *E-mail:* magosin@wellesley.edu.

AGRAWALA, Vasudeva Sharan, PhD, DLitt; Indian writer and academic; b. Aug. 1904. *Education:* Banaras Hindu Univ., Lucknow Univ. *Career:* Curator, Mathura Museum 1931–39, Lucknow Museum 1940–45; Supt Nat. Museum and Nat. Museum Branch of Archaeological Survey of India, New Delhi 1946–51; Prof. and Head of Dept of Art and Architecture, Coll. of Indology, Banaras Hindu Univ. 1951; fmr Pres. Museums Asscn of India and other historical asscns; Pres. All-India Prakrit Text Soc. 1964–. *Publications:* A Revised Catalogue of Mathura Museum 1950, India as Known to Panini 1953, Paninikalina Bharatavarsha 1955, Jayasi's Padamavata 1955, Kadambari: A Cultural Study 1958, Prithiviputra, or Essays on Indian Culture 1960, Sparks from the Vedic Fire 1962, The Thousand-Syllabled Speech of Vedic Symbolism, Vol. I 1963, Vidyapati's Kirtilata 1962, Matsya Purana: A Study 1963, Devi Mahatmya: Glorification of the Great Goddess 1963, Solar Symbolism of the Boar 1963, Vedic Lectures 1963, Harshacharita: A Cultural Commentary 1964, Vamana Purana: A Study 1964, Bharata Savitri, Vol. I 1957, Vol. II 1964, Chakradhvaja: The Wheel Flag of India 1964, Ancient Indian Folk-Cults 1964, Divyavadana 1965, Indian Art 1965, Heritage of Indian Art 1971. *Address:* c/o Department of Art and Architecture, College of Indology, Banaras Hindu University, Banaras 5, India.

AGUALUSA, José Eduardo; Angolan novelist and poet; b. 13 Dec. 1960, Huambo. *Education:* Instituto Superior de Agronomia, Lisbon, Portugal. *Career:* newspaper and radio journalist, journal Público; mem. União dos Escritores Angolanos. *Television:* A Hora das Cigarras (series, Antena 1, RDP Africa). *Publications:* novels: A Conjura 1989, A Feira dos Assombrados (novella) 1992, Estação das Chuvas 1996, Nação crioula (trans. as Creole) 1997, Um estranho em Goa 2000, O Ano em que Zumbi Tomou o Rio 2002, O Vendedor de Passados 2004, As Mulheres do meu Pai 2007; short stories: D. Nicolau Água-Rosada e outras estórias verdadeiras e inverosímeis 1990, Fronteiras Perdidas, contos para viajar 1999, A Substância do Amor e Outras Crónicas 2000, Estranhões e Bizarrocos 2000, O Homem que Parecia um Domingo 2002, Catálogo de Sombras 2003, Manual prático de levitação 2005, A girafa que comia estrelas 2005, Passageiros em Trânsito 2006, O filho do vento 2006; poetry: Coração dos Bosques 1980–1990 1991; non-fiction: Lisboa Africana (co-author) 1993. *Honours:* Grand Prize for Literature, Portugal 1997, Independent Foreign Fiction Prize 2007. *Address:* c/o Arcadia Books Ltd, 15–16 Nassau Street, London, W1N 7RF, England. *E-mail:* agualusa@hotlink.com.br. *Website:* www.agualusa.info.

AGUILAR, Mila D., (Clarita Roja); Philippine poet and journalist; b. 1949; m. Magtanggol Roque; one s. *Career:* worked at St Joseph' s Coll. Quezon City; twice detained under Marcos govt; was active in fighting for families of the disappeared. *Publications:* A Comrade is as Precious as a Rice Seedling (poems) 1984, Why Cage Pigeons (poems) 1984, Journey: An Autobiography in Verse (1964–1995) 1996; contrib. poems to anthologies including Pintig 1985. *Address:* c/o Philippine Center of International PEN, 531 Padre Faura, Ermita, Manila 1000, Phililppines. *E-mail:* philippinepen@yahoo.com.

AGUILAR-CARIÑO, Ma. Luisa B. (see Igloria, Luisa A.)

AGUIRRE, Eugenio, BA, MA; Mexican writer; b. 31 July 1944, México, DF; m. 1971; one s. one d. *Education:* Universidad Nacional Autónoma de México. *Career:* Lecturer, Univ. of Lawrence, KS, USA; Wabash Col., USA; Writers' Asscn of Panama; several bank and government offices, Mexico; past pres., Asociación de Escritores de México; bd mem., Sociedad General de Escritores de México; mem. Int. PEN. *Publications:* fiction: Jesucristo Perez 1973, Pajar de Imaginación 1975, El caballero de las espadas 1978, Gonzalo Guerrero 1980, El testamento del diablo 1982, En el campo 1983, Cadaver exquisito 1984, Cuentos de tierra y asfalto (short stories) 1984, El rumor que llegó del mar 1985, Pájaros de fuego 1986, La suerta de la fea 1986, Un mundo de niño lleno de mar 1986, Pasos de sangre 1988, Amor de mis amores 1988, Los siete pecados capitales (short stories) 1989, El guerrero del sur 1991, Cosas de ángeles y otros cuentos (short stories) 1992, Los niños de colores 1993, Elena o el laberinto de la lujuria 1994, El demonio me visita 1994, La fascinación de la bestia 1994, Desierto ardiente 1995, Ruiz Massieu: el mejor enemigo 1995, Cuarto cerrado 1996, El hombre baldío 1998, Los perros de Angagua (short stories) 1998, El silencio de los pequeños secretos (short stories) 1999, La lotería del deseo 2003, La fotografía del hombre colgado 2005; biographical novels: Valentín Gómez Farías 1982, Leona Vicario 1986, Victoria 2005, The Maya Cross; non-fiction: Eugenio Aguirre: De cuerpo entero (autobiog.) 1991; contrib. to Mexican and foreign publications. *Honours:* Int. Acad. of Lutece Great Silver Medal, Paris 1981. *Address:* Avenida Vasco de Quiroga, casa 4, La Campiña, Colonia La Rosita, Delegación Cuajimalpa, 05340 México DF (home); c/o Alfaguara, Avenida Universidad 767, Col. del Valle, 03100 México DF, Mexico (office). *E-mail:* aguirre_eugenio@yahoo.com (home).

AHARONI, Ada Andrée, PhD; Israeli writer, poet and educationalist; *President, International Forum for the Culture and Literature of Peace (IFLAC)*; b. 30 July 1933, Egypt; d. of Nessim Yadid and Fortunée Hemsi; m. Chaim Aharoni 26 March 1951; one s. one d. *Education:* Hebrew Univ., Jerusalem, Univ. of London. *Career:* Lecturer Dept of English, Haifa Univ. 1967–77; Sr Lecturer in Peace and Conflict Studies Technion–Israel Inst. of Tech., Haifa 1977–93; Ed. Horizon and Poetry Israel 1997–98; Pres. World Congress of Poets XIII 1992, Writers' and Poets' Asscn 1984–96, To Pave a World Beyond War Through Literature (PAVE) 1985–96, Int. Friends of Literature (IFLA) 1995–; f. IFLAC (Int. Forum for the Culture and Literature of Peace), Pres. 1999–, The Bridge: Jewish and Arab Women for Peace in the Middle East, Pres. 1978–90; Vice-Pres., Hebrew Writers' Asscn in Israel 2003–05; Ed. of Chapter of EOLSS, UNESCO Encyclopedia, on The Culture of Peace and Pres. and Dir, World Congress of Jews from Egypt 2004–06; mem. PEN, Galim Writers Asscn, Cttee Hebrew Writers' Org. *Publications include:* Poems From Israel and Other Poems 1974, From the Pyramids to Mount Carmel 1980, Love Poems 1980, The Second Exodus: A Historical Novel 1983, Shin Shalom: Poems 1984, Shin Shalom: New Poems 1986, A Green Week 1988, Metal et Violettes 1989, Selected Poems from Israel and Around the World 1992, Saul Bellow: A Mosaic 1992, Selected Poems: In My Carmel Woods 1993, Memoirs from Alexandria 1993, In the Curve of Your Palm 1994, From the Nile to the Jordan 1995, The Peace Flower 1996, Waves of Peace 1997, Peace Poems 1997, Not in Vain: An Extraordinary Life (co-author) 1998, You and I Can Change the World: New and Selected Poems 2000, Culture of Peace Poetry Anthology 2000, Women Creating a World Beyond War and Violence 2001, The Pomegranate 2002, Moznaim 2004, Muestros 2004, Chosen Verse: English and Chinese – Bilingual 2004; contributions: Poetry Nippon, Jewish Chronicle, Voices, Arc, New Society, International Poetry Review, El Shark, Poet, Galim 10 Poetry Anthology 2003; editor: various online magazines: Horizon Pave Peace; JAC: Jews from Arab Countries. *Honours:* British Council Poetry Award 1972, Haifa and Bremen Poetry Award 1975, Pres. of Israel's Literature Award, Keren Amos 1977, Bank Discount Literary Award 1979, Boston Forum Prize 1981, Haifa Culture Poetry Prize 1984, The Bemaaracha Jerusalem Poetry Grant 1987, Pennsylvania Poetry Award 1989, World Acad. of Arts and Culture, UNESCO Prize 1991, Yunus Imri Poetry Award 1992, Korean World Poetry Crown Award 1993, Shin Shalom Peace Poetry Award 1993, Int. Poetry Prize 1994, Best of the Planet Award for website 1998, 100 Global Heroines Award 1998, UNESCO Italy Poetry Contest 2003; Turkish-Atatuck Literary Award 2003. *Address:* IFLAC, POB 9934, Haifa, 34341, Israel (office); 57 Horev Street, Haifa 34343, Israel (home). *Telephone:* (4) 8243230. *Fax:* (4) 8261288. *E-mail:* ada@tx.technion.ac.il (office); ada@iflac.com (home). *Website:* www.iflac.com/horizon (office); www.iflac.com (office); www.iflac.com/ada (home); ada.up.co.il.

AHERN, Cecelia; Irish novelist; b. 1981. *Education:* Griffith Coll. Dublin. *Publications:* P.S. I Love You 2004, Where Rainbows End (Corine Award, Germany 2005) 2004, If You Could See Me Now 2005, A Place Called Here 2006; contrib. short stories to anthologies. *Honours:* Irish Post Award for Literature 2005. *Address:* c/o HarperCollins Publishers Ltd, 77–85 Fulham Palace Road, London, W6 8JB, England (office). *Website:* www.ceceliaahern.ie.

AHLBERG, Allan; British writer; b. 1938, Croydon; m. Janet Ahlberg (nèe Hall) 1969 (died 1994); one d. *Career:* primary school teacher for ten years; formed successful author/illustrator partnership with his late wife, Janet; also worked with illustrators Fritz Wegner, Andre Amstultz, Colin McNaughton, Faith Jaques, Joe Wright, Emma Chichester-Clarke. *Publications include:* juvenile: with Janet Ahlberg: The Old Joke Book 1977, The Vanishment of Thomas Tull 1977, Burglar Bill 1977, Jeremiah in the Dark Woods 1977, Cops and Robbers 1978, Each Peach Pear Plum 1978, One and Only Two Heads 1979, The Baby's Catalogue 1982, See the Rabbit 1982, Peepo 1983, Poorly Pig 1984, Yum Yum 1984, Playmates 1984, The Jolly Postman (Kate Greenaway Medal, Emil/Kurt Maschler Award) 1986, The Cinderella Show 1986, Starting School 1988, Bye Bye Baby 1989, The Bear Nobody Wanted 1992, It was a Dark and Stormy Night 1993, The Jolly Pocket Postman 1995, Janet's Last Book 1996; with Colin McNaughton: Mr and Mrs Hay the Horse 1981, Big Bad Pig 1985, Fee Fi Fo Fum 1985, Happy Worm 1985, Help! 1985; with Andre Amstultz: Master Salt the Sailor's Son 1982, Hip-hippo-ray 1984, Dinosaur Dreams 1991, The Black Cat 1993, Monkey Do! 1998; with Fritz Wegner: Woof! 1987, The Giant Baby 1994, The Better Brown Stories 1995; with other illustrators: The Adventures of Bert (with Robert Briggs) 2001, Happy Families series (with various illustrators), The Runaway Dinner (with Bruce Ingman) 2006, The Boyhood of Burglar Bill 2007; poetry: Heard it in the Playground, Please, Mrs Butler. *Honours:* Children's Book Award 1987, Blue Peter Book Award 2001, Children's Book Awards Book for Young Children 2002. *Address:* c/o Puffin Publicity, 80 Strand, London, WC2R 0RL, England.

AHLMARK, Per, BA; Swedish politician, journalist, novelist and poet; *Adviser, Elie Wiesel Foundation for Humanity*; b. 15 Jan. 1939, Stockholm; s. of Prof. Axel Ahlmark; m. 1st (divorced); one s. one d.; m. 2nd Bibi Andersson 1978 (divorced); m. 3rd Lilian Edström; one s. *Career:* Leader of Young Liberals 1960–62; columnist for Expressen 1961–95, for Dagens Nyheter 1997–; mem. Parl. 1967–78; Deputy Chair. Swedish-Israeli Friendship Org. 1970–97; mem. Council of Europe 1971–76; mem. Royal Comms. on Literature, Human Rights, etc. in the 1970s; Leader, Folkpartiet (Liberal Party) 1975–78; Deputy Prime Minister and Minister of Labour 1976–78; Deputy Chair. Martin Luther King Fund 1968–73; Chair. Swedish Film Inst. 1978–81; Founder and Deputy Chair. Swedish Comm. Against Antisemitism 1983–95; Adviser to Elie Wiesel Foundation for Humanity, New York 1987–; mem. UN Watch, Geneva 1993–; mem. Acad. Universelle des Cultures, Paris; Fellow Wissenschaftskolleg zu Berlin 1998–99. *Publications:* An Open Sore, Tyranny and the Left, many political books, essays and numerous articles, three books of poetry, one novel. *Honours:* Hon. Fellow, Hebrew Univ., Jerusalem 1992; Defender of Jerusalem Award, New York 1986. *Address:* Folkungag 61, 11622 Stockholm, Sweden.

AHLSEN, Leopold; German writer; b. 12 Jan. 1927, Munich; m. Ruth Gehwald 1964; one s. one d. *Publications:* 13 plays, 23 radio plays, 68 television plays, 7 novels. *Honours:* Gerhart Hauptmann Prize, Schiller-Förderungspreis, Goldener Bildschirm, Hörspielpreis der Kriegsblinden,

Silver Nymph of Monte Carlo, Bundesverdienstkreuz and other awards. *Address:* Waldschulstrasse 58, 81827 Munich, Germany (home). *Telephone:* (89) 4301466 (home). *Fax:* (89) 4301466 (home).

AHMAD, Datuk Shahnon, BA, MA; Malaysian writer; b. 1933, Sik, Kedah. *Education:* studied in Australia and at Univ. of Science, Penang. *Career:* Head of Islamic Centre, Univ. of Science, Penang –1996; taught literature, Dean School of Humanities, Univ. of Science, Penang –1999. *Publications:* Anjing-anjing 1964, Debu merah 1965, Terdedah 1965, Rentong (Rope of Ash) 1965, Ranjau Sepanjang Jalan (No Harvest but a Thorn) 1966, Protes 1967, Menteri 1967, Perdana 1969, Srengenge 1973, Sampah 1974, Kemelut 1977, Selasai sudah 1977, Seluang menolak Baung 1978, Penglibatan dalam puisi 1978, Gubahan novel 1979, The Third Notch and Other Stories 1980, Kesusasteraan dan etika Islam 1981, Al-syiqaq 1985, Tok Guru 1988, Ummi dan Abang Syeikhul 1992, Pongang sastera: gema karya kreatif dan kesannya terhadap khalayak 1995, Shit 1999. *Honours:* National Literary Award, 1982; Malaysian National Laureate, 1984. *Address:* c/o Universiti Sains Malaysia, Minden, 11800 Penang, Malaysia.

AHRENS, Bridget, BA, MPh, MFA; American writer; b. 9 Jan. 1958, Buffalo, NY; m. 1981; one s. one d. *Education:* SUNY, Univ. of California, Vermont Coll. *Career:* instructor in fiction and non-fiction writing, Lebanon Coll. 1990–; Assoc. Ed., AIDS and Society: An International Research and Policy Bulletin; mem. Poets and Writers. *Publications:* Our Lady of the Keyboard 1989, The Problems and Pitfalls of Writing about Sex 1989, A Woman's Place is Intuition 1990, The Art of Baking, The Politics of Love 1991, The Eye of the Needle 1991, Atlas's Revenge 1992. *Honours:* Fellowship, Vermont Council on the Arts, 1992. *Address:* c/o Lebanon College, 15 Hanover Street, Lebanon, NH 03766, USA.

AI, MFA; American poet; b. (Florence Anthony), 2 Jan. 1947, Albany, TX. *Education:* Univ. of Arizona, Univ. of California at Irvine. *Career:* currently Prof. English Dept, Oklahoma State Univ.; Vice-Pres. Native American Faculty and Staff Asscn. *Publications:* Cruelty 1973, The Killing Floor (Lamont Poetry Award 1978) 1979, Sin (Before Columbus Foundation American Book Award) 1986, Fate 1991, Temporomandibul Joint Dysfunction 1992, Greed 1993, Vice (Nat. Book Award for Poetry) 1999, Dread 2003. *Honours:* Guggenheim Foundation Fellowship 1975, NEA Award 1978, 1985. *Address:* 201C Morrill Hall, Oklahoma State University, Stillwater, OK 74078, USA (office). *E-mail:* professorai@aol.com (office).

AICHINGER, Ilse; Austrian writer; b. 1 Nov. 1921, Vienna; m. Günter Eich (died 1972). *Education:* Universität Wien. *Career:* fmrly worked with Inge Scholl at Hochschule für Gestaltung, Ulm; later worked as a reader for S. Fischer (publrs), Frankfurt and Vienna. *Publications include:* Die Grössere Hoffnung (novel) 1948, Knöpfe (radio play) 1952, Der Gefesselte (short stories) 1953, Zu keiner Stunde (dialogues) 1957, Besuch im Pfarrhaus (radio play) 1961, Wo ich wohne (stories, dialogues, poems) 1963, Eliza, Eliza (stories) 1965, Nachricht von Tag (stories) 1970, Schlechte Worter 1976, Meine Sprache und Ich Erzählungen 1978, Radio Plays, Selected Poetry and Prose by Ilse Aichinger 1983, Kleist, Moos, Fasane 1987, Collected Works (eight vols) 1991, Film und Verhängnis 2001. *Honours:* Förderungspreis des Österreichischen Staatspreises 1952, Preis der Gruppe 47 1952, Literaturpreis der Freien und Hansestadt Bremen 1954, Immermannpreis der Stadt Düsseldorf 1955, Literaturpreis der Bayerischen Akad. 1961, Nyell Sachs-Preis, Dortmund 1971, City of Vienna Literature Prize 1974, Georg Tracke Prize 1979, Petrarca Prize 1982, Belgian Europe Festival Prize 1987, Town of Solothurn Prize 1991, Joseph-Breitbach-Preis 2000. *Address:* c/o Fischer Verlag, POB 700480, 60008 Frankfurt, Germany.

AIDOO, Ama Ata; Ghanaian writer; b. Abeadzi Kyiakor, Gold Coast (now Ghana); one d. *Career:* Lecturer, Cape Coast Univ. 1970–73; Consultant Prof., Phelps-Stokes Fund Ethnic Studies Program, Washington 1974–75; consultant at univs, acads and research insts in Africa, Europe and USA; Prof. of English, Univ. of Ghana; Minister of Educ. 1982–83; Chair. African Regional Panel of the Commonwealth Writers' Prize 1990, 1991; Fellow Inst. for African Studies. *Publications include:* novels: Our Sister Killjoy or Reflections from a Black-Eyed Squint 1977, Changes: A Love Story (Commonwealth Writers Prize for the Africa region 1993) 1991; poetry: Someone Talking to Sometime 1985, Birds and Other Poems; plays: The Dilemma of a Ghost 1965, Anowa 1970, Changes: A Love Story 1991; short stories: No Sweetness Here 1970, The Eagle and The Chicken and Other Stories 1987, The Girl Who Can and Other Stories 1999; numerous contribs to magazines and journals. *Address:* PO Box 4930, Harare, Zimbabwe. *Telephone:* (4) 731901.

AINI, Lea; Israeli writer and poet; b. 1962, Tel-Aviv; d. of Yitzhak Aini. *Play:* Mi-Alma, staged by Habima Nat. Theater 2006–07. *Publications:* Diokan (poems) 1988, Keisarit Ha-Pirion Ha-Medumeh (poems) 1991, Gibborei Kayitz (short stories and novella, The Sea Horse Race) 1991, Geut Ha-Hol (novel) 1992, Tikrah Li Mi-Lemata (juvenile) 1994, Mar Arnav Mehapes Avoda (juvenile) 1994, Hei, Yuli (juvenile) 1995, Mishehi Tzerikha Lehiyot Kan (novel, Someone Must Be Here) 1995, Hetzi ve-ananas: Tamnunina (juvenile) 1996, Hardufim O Sipurim Mur'alim Al Ahava (short stories) 1997, Ashtoret (novel) 1999, Shir Ani, Shir Imma (poems for children) 2000, Anak, Malka, Ve'aman Hamischakim (novel), Sdommel (novella and short stories) 2001, The Giant, the Queen and the Master of Games (novel) 2004. *Honours:* Wertheim Prize 1988, Adler Prize 1988, Tel-Aviv Foundation Award 1994, Prime Minister's Prize 1994, 2004, Bernstein's Prize for Drama 2006. *Address:* c/o

Hakibbutz Hameuchad Publishing House Ltd, PO Box 1432, Bnei Brak, Tel-Aviv 51114, Israel. *E-mail:* iradscharss@013.net.il.

AIRA, César; Argentine novelist, essayist and dramatist; b. 23 Feb. 1949, Coronel Pringles; m.; two c. *Career:* fmr lecturer, Universidad de Buenos Aires, Universidad de Rosario. *Plays:* El mensajero 1996, Madre e hijo 1993. *Publications:* novels: Moreira 1975, Ema, la cautiva 1981, La luz argentina 1983, Las ovejas 1984, Canto Castrato 1984, Una novela china 1987, Los fantasmas 1990, El bautismo 1991, La liebre 1991, Embalse 1992, La guerra de los gimnasios 1992, La prueba 1992, El llanto 1992, El volante 1992, Cómo me hice monja 1993, El infinito 1994, La costurera y el viento 1994, Los misterios de Rosario 1994, La fuente 1995, Los dos payasos 1995, Dante y Reina, Abeja 1996, La serpiente 1997, El Mago, Cumpleaños, La villa, La pastilla de hormona, El juego de los mundos, El Sueño 1998, Las curas milagrosas del Dr Aira 1998, La mendiga 1998, El congreso de literatura 1999, Un episodio en la vida del pintor viajero 2000, Fragmento de un diario en los Alpes 2002, El tilo 2003; short stories: El vestido rosa 1984, Cecil Taylor, La trompeta de mimbre 1998; essays: Copi 1991, Nouvelles impressions du Petit Maroc 1991, Taxol: precedido de Duchamp en México y La broma 1997, Alejandra Pizarnik 1998, Las tres fechas 2001, Edward Lear 2004; non-fiction: Diccionario de autores latinoamericanos; contrib. to numerous periodicals and books world-wide. *Address:* c/o Beatriz Viterbo Editora, España 1150 (2000), Rosario, Argentina. *E-mail:* info@beatrizviterbo.com.ar. *Website:* www .beatrizviterbo.com.ar.

AITMATOV, Tchinguiz Torekulovich; Kyrgyzstani writer and diplomat-ist; *Ambassador to EU, NATO and Belgium;* b. 12 Dec. 1928, Sheker Village; s. of the late Torekul Aitmatov and of Nagima Aitmatova; m. Maria Urmatova 1974; three s. one d. *Education:* Kyrgyz Agricultural Inst. *Career:* writer 1952–; fmrly corresp. for Pravda; mem. CPSU 1959–91; First Sec. of Cinema Union of Kyrgyz SSR 1964–69, Chair. 1969–86; Chair. of Union of Writers of Kyrgyzstan 1986–; Cand. mem. Cen. Cttee of CP of Kyrgyz SSR 1969–71, mem. 1971–90; People's Writer of Kyrgyz SSR 1968; Vice-Chair. Cttee of Solidarity with Peoples of Asian and African Countries 1974–89; Deputy to USSR Supreme Soviet 1966–89; People's Deputy of the USSR 1989–91; mem. Presidential Council 1990–91; USSR (now Russian) Amb. to Luxembourg 1990–92; Kyrgyzstan Amb. to Benelux countries and France 1992–96, Amb. to Belgium, the EU, and NATO 1996–; mem. Kyrgyz Acad. of Science 1974, European Acad. of Arts, Science and Humanity 1983, World Acad. of Art and Science 1987; Chair. Issyk-Kul Forum 1986–; Chief Ed. Innostrannaya Literatura 1988–90; Rep. Euro–Atlantic Partnership Council, NATO. *Stories filmed include:* The First Teacher, Djamilya, My Poplar in a Red Kerchief, The White Steamship. *Publications include:* stories: Face to Face, Short Stories, Melody 1961, Tales of the Hills and the Steppes (Lenin Prize 1963) 1963, Stories 1967, Mother Earth and Other Stories 1989; novels: Djamilya 1959, My Poplar in a Red Kerchief 1960, Camel's Eye, The First Teacher, Farewell Gulsary, Mother Earth 1963, The White Steamship (English trans. 1972), The Lament of the Migrating Bird (English trans. 1972), The Ascent of Mount Fuji (with Muhamegjanov) 1973, Earth and Water (co-author) 1978, Works (three vols) 1978, Early Storks 1979, Stories 1979, Piebald Dog, Running Along the Sea Shore, The Day Lasts More Than a Hundred Years 1980, Executioner's Block (English trans.) 1986, The Place of the Skull, The White Cloud of Chingiz Khan 1991, A Conversation at the Foothill of Fudjiyama Mountain (with Daisaku Ikeda) 1992, The Brand of Cassandra (novel) 1994, Djamilia 1996, Tuer ne pas tuer 2005. *Honours:* Austrian State Prize for European Literature 1994, Hero of Socialist Labour 1978, State Prize in Literature 1968, 1977, 1983 and other decorations and prizes from Germany, Kyrgyzstan, India, Turkey and USA . *Address:* Toktogul str. 98, Apt 9, 720000 Bishkek, Kyrgyzstan (home); blvd Léopold III, 1110 Brussels, Belgium (office). *Telephone:* (32) 672-27-22 (home); (2) 707-41-11 (office). *Fax:* (32) 646-37-29 (home); (2) 707-45-79 (office). *E-mail:* aitmatov@infonie.be (office); natodoc@ hq.nato.int (office). *Website:* www.nato.int (office).

AKAEKE ONWUEME, Tess (see Onwueme, Osonye Tess)

AKAGAWA, Jiro; Japanese writer; b. 29 Feb. 1948, Fukuoka; m. Fumiko Serita 1973; one d. *Education:* Toho-gakuen High School. *Career:* fmr proof-reader for Japan Soc. of Mechanical Engineers; mem. Japanese Mystery Writers' Asscn 1977–. *Publications:* more than 400 works including novels: The School Festival for the Dead 1977, Ghost Train 1978, The Deduction of Tortoise-shell Holmes 1978, High School Girl with a Machine Gun 1978, The Requiem Dedicated to the Bad Wife 1980, Virgin Road 1983, Chizuko's Younger Sister 1989, The Ghost Story of the Hitokoizaka-Slope 1995. *Honours:* All Yomimono Debut Writers' Award 1976; Kadokawa Publishing Book Award 1980. *Address:* 40-16-201 Ohyama-cho, Sibuya-ku, Tokyo 151-0065, Japan.

AKAVIA, Miriam; Israeli (b. Polish) writer and translator; b. 20 Nov. 1927, Kraków, Poland; m. 1946; two d. *Education:* Univ. of Tel-Aviv, Israel. *Career:* licensed nurse; went through Holocaust in Kraków Ghetto, Plaszów and Auschwitz and later in Bergen-Belsen; arrived in Israel via Sweden 1946; worked at Jewish Agency; served as Israel's Social and Cultural Attaché in Stockholm; began publishing in 1975, describing her childhood, Holocaust and post-war experiences; translates Polish literature into Hebrew and Hebrew into Polish; Chair. Friendship and Cultural Affairs, Israel-Poland Asscn. *Publications:* An End To Childhood (novel, translated into several languages) 1975, Adolescence of Autumn 1975, The Price (stories) 1977, Ha mechir 1978, Galia and Miklosh – Severance of Relations (for young people) 1982, (in Polish)

2000, Karmi Sheli (My Own Vineyard) (novel, translated into several languages) 1984, Bus Adventure (for children) 1986, Ma Vigne A Moi 1992, Ha-Derech Ha-Aheret: Sipur Ha-Kevutza (The Other Way: The Story of a Group) (novel) 1992, Jurek and Ania 2000, Lomhullas 2000, Short Stories (translated into German and Polish) 2000, Build a House with Love 2001 (for children); contribs to various literary magazines. *Honours:* Yakir Tel-Aviv 2000; Yad Va-Shem Prize 1978, Sec Prize 1985, Korczak Prize (Germany) (1988), Gold Medal (Poland) 1991, Prime Minister's Prize (Israel) 1993, Wizo Prize (Tel-Aviv) 1998. *Address:* PO Box 53050, Tel-Aviv 61550 (office); K. Zytomir 11, Tel-Aviv, 69405 Israel (home). *Telephone:* (3) 6479833 (home). *Fax:* (3) 6479833 (home). *E-mail:* akavie@inter.net.il (home).

AKELLO, Grace; Ugandan poet, essayist and folklorist; *Minister of State, Ministry of Gender, Labour and Social Development;* b. c. 1940; m. 2nd; four s. *Education:* Makerere Univ. *Career:* fmr Deputy Ed. Viva magazine; mem. Parl. 1996–; Minister of State in Ministry of Gender, Labour and Social Devt (Entandikwa) 1999–; f. Nile Book Service; advised on setting up of Pres. Comm. to help resolve armed conflict in Teso area of Uganda, Sec., then Chair.; f. mem. Teso Devt Trust; bd mem. Christian Aid; lives in Kenya. *Publications:* My Dear Brother (poem) 1977, Iteso Thought Patterns in Tales 1975, My Barren Song (poems) 1979, Self Twice-Removed: Ugandan Woman (non-fiction) 1982, Problems Women Face (essay) 1995. *Address:* c/o Ministry of Gender, Labour and Social Development, Udyam House, Jinja Road, POB 7168, Kampala, Uganda.

AKENSON, Donald Harman, BA, MEd, PhD, DLitt, DHum, FRSA, FRSC, FRHistS; Canadian historian and academic; *Douglas Professor of Canadian and Colonial History, Queen's University;* b. 22 May 1941, Minneapolis, Minn.; s. of Donald Nels Akenson and Fern L. Harman Akenson. *Education:* Yale and Harvard Univs. *Career:* Allston Burr Sr Tutor, Dunster House, Harvard Coll. 1966–67; Assoc. Prof. of History, Queen's Univ., Kingston, Ont. 1970–74, Prof. 1974–, currently Douglas Prof. of Canadian and Colonial History; Beamish Research Prof., Inst. of Irish Studies, Univ. of Liverpool 1998–2002; Guggenheim Fellow 1984–85. *Publications:* The Irish Education Experiment 1970, The Church of Ireland: Ecclesiastical Reform and Revolution 1800–1885 1971, Education and Enmity: The Control of Schooling in Northern Ireland 1920–50 1973, The United States and Ireland 1973, A Mirror to Kathleen's Face: Education in Independent Ireland 1922–60 1975, Local Poets and Social History: James Orr, Bard of Ballycarry 1977, Between Two Revolutions: Islandmagee, Co. Antrim 1798–1920 1979, A Protestant in Purgatory: Richard Whately: Archbishop of Dublin 1981, The Irish in Ontario: A Study of Rural History 1984, Being Had: Historians, Evidence and the Irish in North America 1985, The Life and Times of Ogle Gowan 1986, Small Differences: Irish Catholics and Irish Protestants, 1815–1921 1988, Half the World from Home: Perspectives on the Irish in New Zealand 1990, Occasional Papers on the Irish in South Africa 1991, God's Peoples: Covenant and Land in South Africa, Israel and Ulster 1992, The Irish Diaspora, A Primer 1993, Conor: A Biography of Conor Cruise O'Brien 1994, If the Irish Ran the World: Montserrat 1630–1730, Surpassing Wonder: The Invention of the Bible and the Talmuds 1998, Saint Saul: A Skeleton Key to the Historical Jesus 2000, Intolerance: The E. Coli of the Human Mind 2004, An Irish History of Civilization (two vols) 2006; novels: The Lazar House Notebooks 1981, Brotherhood Week in Belfast 1984, The Orangeman: The Edgerston Audit 1987, At Face Value: The Life and Times of Eliza McCormack 1990. *Honours:* Hon. DLitt (McMaster) 1995, (Guelph) 2000; Hon. DHumLitt (Lethbridge) 1996; Hon. LLD (Regina) 2002; Chalmers Prize 1985, Landon Prize 1987, Grawemeyer World Peace Prize 1993, Molson Laureate 1996 and many other awards and distinctions. *Address:* Department of History, Queen's University, Kingston, ON, K7L 3N6, Canada (office). *Website:* www.queensu.ca/history (office).

AKHMADULINA, Isabella (Bella) Akhatovna; Russian poet; b. 10 April 1937, Moscow; d. of Ahat Akhmadulin and Nadya Akhmadulina (née Lazareva); m. 1st Yevgeniy Yevtushenko (q.v.) 1960; m. 2nd Yuriy Nagibin; m. 3rd Boris Messerer 1974; m. 4th Gennadi Mamlin. *Education:* Gorky Inst. of Literature, Moscow. *Career:* Sec. USSR (now Russian) Writers' Union 1986–91, mem. Bd Russian PEN-Centre 1989–92. *Publications:* Fire Tree 1958, The String 1962, The Rain 1963, My Ancestry 1964, Summer Leaves 1968, The Lessons of Music 1969, Fever and Other New Poems 1970, Tenerezza 1971, Poems 1975, The Dreams About Georgia 1977, The Candle 1978, The Snowstorm 1978, The Mystery 1983, The Garden 1987, The Seaboard 1991, Selected Works (vols 1–3) 1996, The Ancient Style Attracts Me 1997, Beautiful Features of My Friends 1999, and trans from Georgian. *Honours:* Hon. mem. American Acad. of Arts and Letters 1977; State Prize USSR 1989, Pushkin Prize, Russian President's Prize 1998, Alfred Tepfer Prize. *Address:* Chernyachovskogo str. 4, Apt 37, 125319 Moscow, Russia. *Telephone:* (495) 151-22-00.

AKMAKJIAN, Alan Paul, BA, MA, PhD; American educator, poet and writer; b. 18 July 1948, Highland Park, MI. *Education:* Eastern Michigan Univ., Univ. of Texas at Dallas, St John's Univ., New York, Wayne State Univ., Detroit, California State Univ., San Francisco. *Career:* teacher, California State Univ., San Francisco 1989, St John's Univ., New York 1994–95, Univ. of Texas at Dallas 1995–; instructor, Poets in the Schools, CA 1986–91; mem. Acad. of American Poets, Associated Writing Programs, MLA, PEN, Poetry Soc. of America. *Publications:* Treading Pages of Water 1992, Let the Sun Go 1992, California Picnic 1992, Grounded Angels 1993, Breaking the Silence 1994, California Picnic and Other Poems 1997; contrib. to anthologies,

journals, reviews and magazines. *Honours:* Nat. Endowment for the Arts grant 1984, California Arts Council grant 1984, St John's Univ. Fellowship 1994–95, Univ. of Texas Fellowships 1994–95, 1995–96, 1996–97, Texas Public Educational grant 1996–97. *Address:* c/o University of Texas at Dallas, PO Box 830688, Richardson, TX 75083-0688 (office); 2200 Waterview Pkwy, Apt 2134, Richardson, TX 75080, USA (home).

AKSYONOV, Vasiliy Pavlovich; Russian writer; b. 20 Aug. 1932, Kazan; s. of Pavel V. Aksyonov and Yevgeniya Ginzburg; m. 1st Kira L. Mendeleva 1957; m. 2nd Maya A. Karmen; one s. *Education:* Leningrad Medical Inst. *Career:* Physician 1956–60, Moscow Tubercular Dispensary 1960–61; professional writer 1960–; emigrated to USA 1980; mem. Union of Russian Writers, Editorial bd Yunost; citizenship restored 1990; lecturer George Mason Univ., USA 1995–. *Publications:* novels: Colleagues 1960, Starry Ticket 1961, 1970, Oranges from Morocco 1963, Time, My Friend, Time 1964, The Empty Barrels 1968, Love of Electricity 1971, My Grandpa is a Monument 1972, The Box Inside Which Something Knocks (children's book) 1976, Our Golden Ironware 1980, The Burn 1980, The Island of Crimea 1981, An Aristopheana 1981, Paper Landscape 1983, The Right to the Island 1983, Say 'Cheese' 1985, In Search of a Genre 1986, In Search of Melancholy Baby 1987, Our Garden Fronburg 1989, The Moscow Saga 1993, The Negative of a Positive Hero 1996, New Sweet Style 1998, Volteryantsy i Volteryanki (Russian Booker Prize) 2004; collected stories: Catapult 1964, Half-Way to the Moon 1966, Wish You Were Here 1969; screenplay for films: Colleagues, My Young Friend, When They Raise the Bridges, Travelling 1967, The Murmar House 1972; play: On Sale 1965; travel: An Unusual Journey 1963, Twenty-Four Hours Non-Stop 1976, The Steel Bird and Other Stories 1978; jt ed. Metropol 1979, Four Temperaments (comedy) 1979. *Address:* c/o Random House Inc., 201 East 50th Street, New York, NY 10022, USA. *Telephone:* (495) 915-45-63 (Moscow).

AKUNIN, Boris; Russian (b. Georgian) writer; b. (Grigory Shalvovich Chkhartishvili), 1956, Georgia. *Education:* Moscow State Univ. *Career:* Deputy Ed.-in-Chief Inostrannaya Literatura (magazine) –2000; Ed.-in-Chief Anthology of Japanese Literature (20 vols); Chair. Exec. Bd Pushkin Library (Soros Foundation). *Publications:* (names in translation) fiction: Azazel, Special Errands, Counsellor of State, Coronation or the Last of the Novels, Lover of Death vol one, Lover of Death vol two, Pelagia and the White Bulldog, Pelagia and the Black Monkey, Pelagia and the Red Rooster, The Winter Queen, Leviathan, Turkish Gambit, The Death of Achilles, Jack of Spades, The Decorator, The Diamond Chariot, F.M. 2006, Special Assignments 2007, Pelagia and the Black Monk 2007; non-fiction: Tales for Idiots (essays), The Writer and Suicide; contrib. to numerous reviews and criticisms, numerous translations of Japanese, American and English literature. *Address:* Poema Press Publications, Zvezdny blvd 23, 129075 Moscow, Russia (office). *Telephone:* (095) 925-42-05 (home). *E-mail:* erikavoronova@mtu-net .ru (office). *Website:* www.akunin.ru (office).

ALAGIAH, George; British journalist, broadcaster and writer; *Presenter, Six O'Clock News, British Broadcasting Corporation (BBC);* b. 22 Nov. 1955, Sri Lanka; m.; two s. *Education:* St John's Coll., Portsmouth and Univ. of Durham. *Career:* family moved to Ghana 1960; worked in print journalism for South Magazine 1982–89; joined the BBC 1989, Leading Foreign Corresp. specializing in Africa and the developing world, BBC's Africa Corresp., Johannesburg 1994–98, Presenter The World News on BBC 4 2002, Presenter BBC Six O'Clock News 2003–; has interviewed many internationally prominent figures; has contributed to The Guardian, Daily Telegraph, The Independent and Daily Express newspapers; Patron The Presswise Trust, NAZ Project, Parenting, Educ. and Support Forum, Fairtrade Foundation. *Publications:* A Passage to Africa 2001, The Day That Shook the World, A Home from Home (autobiog.) 2006. *Honours:* Critics' Award and Golden Nymph Award, Monte Carlo TV Festival 1992, Best Int. Report, Royal TV Soc. 1993, Best TV Journalist Award, Amnesty Int. 1994, One World Broadcasting Trust Award 1994, James Cameron Memorial Trust Award 1995, Bayeux Award for War Reporting 1996, Media Personality of the Year, Ethnic Minority Media Awards 1998, BAFTA Award (part of BBC Team) for coverage of Kosovo conflict 2000. *Address:* BBC, Room 1640, Television Centre, Wood Lane, London, W12 7RJ, England (office). *Telephone:* (20) 8743-8000 (office). *Fax:* (20) 8743-7882 (office). *Website:* www.bbc.co.uk (office).

ALBAHARI, David; Serbian writer; b. 1948, Pec. *Career:* Markin-Flanagan distinguished writer-in-residence, Univ. of Calgary 1995–96; mem. Federation of Jewish Communities of Yugoslavia (pres. 1991). *Publications:* novels: Sudija Dimitrijevic 1978, Cink 1988 (trans. as Tsing 1997), Kratka knjiga 1993, Snezni covek 1995, Mamac 1996 (NIN Prize; trans. as Bait 2001), Mrak 1997, Gec i Majer 1998 (trans. as Götz and Meyer 2004); other: Porodicno vreme 1978, Obicne price 1978, Opis smrti 1982 (Ivo Andric Prize), Fras u supi 1984, Jednostavnost 1988, Pelerina 1993 (Stanislav Winaver Prize), Izabrane price 1994, Words are Something Else (trans.) 1996, Neobicne price 1999. *Address:* c/o Northwestern University Press, 629 Noyes Street, Evanston, IL 60208-4210, USA (office).

ALBANY, James (see Rae, Hugh Crauford)

ALBEE, Edward Franklin, III; American playwright; b. 12 March 1928, Virginia; adopted s. of Reed Albee and Frances Cotter. *Education:* Lawrenceville and Choate Schools, Washington, Valley Forge Mil. Acad., Pa and Trinity Coll., Hartford. *Career:* Comm. Chair. Brandeis Univ. Creative Arts Awards 1983, 1984; Pres. The Edward F. Albee Foundation Inc.; Distinguished Prof., Univ. of Houston 1988–2003; mem. Dramatists Guild Council,

PEN America, The American Acad., Nat. Inst. of Arts and Letters. *Plays include:* The Zoo Story (Vernon Rice Award 1960) 1958, The Death of Bessie Smith 1959, The Sandbox 1959, Fam and Yam 1959, The American Dream (Foreign Press Asscn Award 1961) 1960, Who's Afraid of Virginia Woolf? (Drama Critics' Circle Award for Best Play) 1961–62, stage adaptation of The Ballad of the Sad Café (Carson McCuller) 1963, Tiny Alice 1964, Malcolm (from novel by James Purdy) 1965, A Delicate Balance (Pulitzer Prize 1966) 1966, Everything in the Garden (after a play by Giles Cooper) 1967, Box 1968, Quotations from Chairman Mao Tse-tung 1968, All Over 1971, Seascape (Pulitzer Prize 1975) 1974, Listening 1975, Counting the Ways 1976, The Lady from Dubuque 1977–79, Lolita (adapted from Vladimir Nabokov) 1979, The Man Who Had Three Arms 1981, Finding the Sun 1982, Marriage Play 1986–87, Three Tall Women (Pulitzer Prize 1994) 1990–91, Fragments 1993, The Play About the Baby 1996, The Goat, or, Who is Sylvia? 2000, Occupant 2001, Peter and Jerry (Act 1: Home Life, Act 2: The Zoo Story) 2004, Me, Myself and I 2007. *Honours:* Tony Awards 1963, 1996, 2002, Gold Medal, American Acad. and Inst. of Arts and Letters 1980; inducted, Theater Hall of Fame 1985, Kennedy Center Award 1996, Nat. Medal of Arts 1996, Special Tony Award for Lifetime Achievement 2005. *Address:* 14 Harrison Street, New York, NY 10013 (office); 320 Old Montauk Highway, Montauk, NY 11954, USA (office). *Telephone:* (212) 226-2020 (office). *E-mail:* albee@albeefoundation.org (office). *Website:* www.albeefoundation.org (office).

ALBERT, Bill, BA, PhD; American writer and economist; *CEO, Norfolk Coalition of Disabled People;* b. (William Gombert), 16 Dec. 1942, New York, NY, USA; s. of Matthrews Gombert and Ruth Buchman; m. 1st Ada Rapoport (divorced 1990); m. 2nd Gillian Ann Albert 1990; one s. two d. *Education:* Univ. of California, Berkeley, London School of Econs. *Career:* Reader in Econ. History, Univ. of East Anglia, Norwich, England 1968–93; CEO Norfolk Coalition of Disabled People. *Publications:* fiction: Et Rodriguez alors? 1990, Desert Blues 1994, Castle Garden 1996. *Literary Agent:* c/o Agence Littéraire Lora Fountain, 7 rue de Belfort, 75011 Paris, France.

ALBERT, Gábor; Hungarian writer and editor; b. 30 Oct. 1929; m. Zsuzsanna Marek 1954; one s. one d. *Education:* Eötvös Lorand Univ. *Career:* librarian, Széchényi Nat. Library 1955–64, Inst. of Musicology 1964–95; Ed.-in-Chief, Új Magyarország 1991–92, Magyarok Világlapja 1992–96; mem. Asscn of Hungarian Writers, Hungarian Acad. of Arts. *Publications:* Dragon and Octahedron (short stories), After Scattering (essays), Where Are Those Columns (novel), In a Shell (novel), Book of Kings (novel), Heroes of the Failures (essays), Atheist (short stories), Final Settlement of a Wedding (short stories), Stephen King's Tart Wine (essays) 1993, ...We Have Survived Him (novel) 1996, The Stone Don't Feel It (essays) 1998, I am Reading the Letters of B. Szemere (essay) 1999, The Old Dog Is About To Cast His Coat (essays) 2001, Vaults, Gargoyles, Rosettes (memoirs) 2002, In the Belly of the Fish (novel) 2002, Initiation Ceremonies (essays) 2003, Waves and the Shore (short stories) 2004; contrib. to periodicals. *Honours:* Book of the Year 1990, Attila József Award 1996, Arany János Award 2003. *Address:* Erdő u 150, 2092 Budakeszi, Hungary (home). *Telephone:* 36-23 453 438 (home). *E-mail:* albert@vivamail.hu (home). *Website:* www.albertgabor.hu.

ALBERT, Neil, BS, MA, JD; American attorney; b. 12 May 1950, Los Angeles, CA; m. Linda Kling 1979. *Education:* Univ. of Oregon, Villanova Law School. *Career:* attorney, Lancaster, PA 1976–; mem. MWA. *Publications:* The January Corpse 1991, The February Trouble 1992, Burning March 1993, Cruel April 1994, Appointment in May 1996, Tangled June 1997. *Address:* 2226 Main Street, Narvon, PA 17602, USA. *E-mail:* nalbert@epix.net.

ALBERT, Susan Wittig, (Robin Paige), BA, PhD; American writer; b. 2 Jan. 1940, Maywood, IL; m. 1st (divorced); three c.; m. 2nd William Albert 1986. *Education:* Univ. of Ill., Univ. of Calif. at Berkeley. *Career:* instructor, Univ. of San Francisco 1969–71; Asst Prof. 1972–77, Assoc. Prof. 1977–79, Assoc. Dean Graduate School 1977–79, Univ. of Texas at Austin; Dean, Sophie Newcomb Coll. 1979–81; Grad. Dean 1981–82, Prof. of English 1981–87, Vice-Pres. for Academic Affairs 1982–86, Southwest Texas State Univ.; mem. Garden Writers of America, Herb Soc. of America, MWA, Sisters in Crime, Story Circle Network (pres. and journal ed. 1997–). *Publications:* fiction: Thyme of Death 1992, Witches' Bane 1993, Hangman's Root 1994, Rosemary Remembered 1995, Rueful Death 1996, Love Lies Bleeding 1997, Chile Death 1998, Lavender Lies 1999, Mistletoe Man 2000, Bloodroot 2001, Indigo Dying 2003, A Dilly of a Death 2004, Dead Man's Bones 2004, The Tale of Hill Top Farm 2004, The Tale of Holly How 2005; co-author as Robin Paige: Death at Bishop's Keep 1994, Death at Gallow's Green 1995, Death at Daisy's Folly 1997, Death at Devil's Bridge 1998, Death at Rottingdean 1999, Death at Whitechapel 2000, Death at Epsom Downs 2001, Death at Dartmoor 2002, Death at Glamis Castle 2003, Death in Hyde Park 2004, Death at Blenheim Palace 2005; author or co-author of about 60 juvenile books; non-fiction: Stylistic and Narrative Structures in the Middle English Verse Romances 1977, The Participating Reader (co-author) 1979, Work of Her Own: How Women Create Success and Fulfillment off the Traditonal Career Track 1992, Writing from Life: Telling Your Soul's Story 1997. *Address:* PO Box 1616, Bertram, TX 78605, USA. *E-mail:* china@tstar.net (home). *Website:* www.mysterypartners.com.

ALBEVERIO-MANZONI, Solvejg Giovanna Maria; Swiss artist and writer; b. 6 Nov. 1939, Arogno; d. of Cesco Manzoni and Madi Manzoni (née Angioletti); m. Sergio Albeverio 1970; one d. *Education:* textile design, Como, Italy, Kunstgewerbeschule, Zürich, Switzerland and Statens Handverk og Kunstindustriskole, Oslo, Norway. *Career:* has given poetry readings at int. meetings at Ferrara, Italy 1987, Poesia dell'Europa latina, Fano, Italy 1987, World Conf. for Poets, Crete, Greece 1991, Sintra, Portugal 1995, The Gerard Manley Hopkins Soc. Summer School, Monasterevin, Co. Kildare, Ireland 2002. *Exhibitions include:* solo: Campione d'Italia, Bielefeld, Bochum, Berlin and Wilhelmshaven (Germany), Marseille (France), Zürich, Biasca and Bellinzona (Switzerland), Salzburg (Austria); group: Fredrikstad (Norway), New York (USA), Bielefeld, Essen (Germany), Maastricht (Netherlands) and Zürich, Ascona, Basel and Lugano (Switzerland). *Publications:* Da stanze chiuse (poetry and drawings) 1987, Il pensatore con il mantello come meteora (novel) 1990, Controcanto al chiuso (drawings, with poetry by B. M. Frabotta) 1991, Il fiore e il frutto. Triandro donna (poetry) 1993, Frange di solitudine (novel) 1994, Spiagge confinanti (poetry) 1996, All'ombra delle farfalle in fiore (drawings with poetry by Folco Portinari) 1998, La carcassa color del cielo (novel) 2001, Il castello, le autostrade, i boschi (drawings) 2001, La Ronda (novel) 2001; numerous stories, poetry and drawings in magazines, journals and anthologies. *Honours:* Premio Ascona for unpublished narrative 1987, Pro Helvetia Scholarship 1995. *Address:* Liebfrauenweg 5B, Bonn, Germany. *Telephone:* (228) 2599991.

ALBINATI, Edoardo; Italian novelist, poet and translator; b. 1956, Rome. *Career:* fmr Ed. cultural review, Nuovi Argomenti; fmr Visiting Writer Columbia Univ.; teaches at Rebibbia Penitentiary, Rome 1994–. *Publications:* Arabeschi della vita morale (novel) 1988, Il polacco lavatore dei vetri (novel) 1989, Elegie e proverbi (poems) 1989, La comunione dei beni (poems) 1995, Mare o monti (poem) 1997, Orti di guerra (novel) 1997, Maggio selvaggio (autobiog.) 1999, 19 (novel) 2000, Sintassi italiana (poems) 2001, Il ritorno 2002, Svenimenti (Premio Viareggio) 2004. *Address:* c/o Giulio Einaudi Editore SpA, Via Umberto Biancamano 2, CP 245, 10121 Turin, Italy.

ALBOM, Mitch, MA, MBA; American writer and journalist; b. 23 May 1958, Passaic, NJ; m. *Education:* Brandeis Univ., Columbia Univ. *Career:* sports columnist, Detroit Free Press newspaper 1985–; f. charities, The Dream Fund 1989, A Time to Help 1998, S.A.Y Detroit; bd mem. CATCH, Forgotten Harvest, Michigan Hospice Org. *Radio:* presenter The Mitch Albom Show, The Monday Sports Albom. *Films:* Tuesdays with Morrie (book) 1999, The Five People You Meet in Heaven 2004 (screenwriter and producer). *Plays:* has written numerous plays including off-Broadway version of Tuesdays With Morrie (co-written with Jeffrey Hatcher). *Publications:* Live Albom I 1987, Bo (with Bo Schembechler) 1989, Live Albom II 1990, Live Albom III 1992, Fab Five 1992, Live Albom IV 1995, Tuesdays with Morrie 1997, The Five People You Meet in Heaven 2003, For One More Day 2006; contrib. to Sports Illustrated, GQ, Sport, The New York Times, TV Guide, USA Today, GEO Magazine. *Honours:* APSE No. 1 Sports Columnist in the Nation, seven APSE awards for feature writing, writing awards from AP, UPI, Headliners Club, Nat. Sportswriters and Broadcasters Asscns, Nat. Hospice Organization Man of the Year 1999. *Address:* The Detroit Free Press, 600 West Fort Street, Detroit, MI 48226, USA. *Telephone:* (313) 222-6400. *E-mail:* albom@freepress.com. *Website:* www.albom.com.

ALBRIGHT, Daniel, BA, MPhil, PhD; American academic and writer; *Ernest Bernbaum Professor of Literature, Harvard University;* b. 29 Oct. 1945, Chicago, IL; m. Karin Larson 1977; one d. *Education:* Rice Univ., Yale Univ. *Career:* Asst Prof., Univ. of Virginia 1970–75, Assoc. Prof. 1975–81, Prof. 1981–87; Visiting Prof., Univ. of Munich 1986–87; Prof., Univ. of Rochester 1987–, Richard L. Turner Prof. in the Humanities 1995; now Ernest Bernbaum Prof. of Literature, Harvard Univ. *Publications:* The Myth Against Myth: A Study of Yeats' Imagination in Old Age 1972, Personality and Impersonality: Lawrence, Woolf, Mann 1978, Representation and the Imagination: Beckett, Kafka, Nabokov and Schoenberg 1981, Lyricality in English Literature 1985, Tennyson: The Muses' Tug-of-War 1986, Poetries of America: Essays in the Relation of Character to Style, by Irvin Ehrenpreis (ed.) 1988, Stravinsky: The Music-Box and the Nightingale 1989, Amerikanische Lyrik: Texte und Deutungen (ed. and co-trans.) 1989, W. B. Yeats: The Poems (ed.) 1990, Quantum Poetics: Yeats, Pound, Eliot, and the Science of Modernism 1997, Untwisting the Serpent: Modernism in Music, Literature, and the Visual Arts 2000, Berlioz's Semi-Operas: Roméo et Juliette and La Damnation de Faust 2001, Beckett and Aesthetics 2003, Modernism and Music: An Anthology of Sources 2004. *Honours:* NEA Fellowship 1973–74, Guggenheim Fellowship 1976–77. *Address:* Harvard University Department of English and American Literature and Language, Barker Center, 12 Quincy Street, Cambridge, MA 02138, USA. *E-mail:* albright@fas.harvard.edu.

ALCALÁ, Kathleen, BA, MA; American writer and editor; b. 29 Aug. 1954, Compton, CA; m. Wayne C. Roth 1979; one s. *Education:* Stanford University, University of Washington. *Career:* grantwriter, Administrator, public broadcasting, other non-profit groups, 1976–89; Board Mem., Seattle Review, 1986–; Contributing Ed., Raven Chronicles; mem. PEN West; Authors' Guild; Artist Trust; Clarion West. *Publications:* Mrs Vargas and the Dead Naturalist, 1992; Spirits of the Ordinary (novel, produced as play), 1997; The Flower in the Skull, 1998; Treasures in Heaven, 2000. *Contributions:* journals and periodicals, including: Americas Review; American Voice; Calyx; Seattle Review; Before Columbus Review; Black Ice; Chiricu; Seattle Times; Ploughshares; The Colorado Review; Hopscotch; Anthologies, including: Women and Aging; Dreams in a Minor Key: Magic Realism by Women; Mirrors Beneath the Earth; Dreamers and Desperadoes; A Writer's Journal; Cracking the Earth; Fantasmas; Norton's Anthology of Latino Literature. *Honours:* Milliman Scholar of Creative Writing, University of Washington,

1984; Artist Trust GAP Grants, 1989, 1991; Invitational Residency at Cottages at Hedgebrook; King County Fiction Publication Project, 1990; Authors' Award, Brandeis University Women's Committee, 1994; Washington State-Artist Trust Fellowship, 1996; Pacific NW Booksellers Asscn Award, 1998; Western States Book Award and Gov.'s Writng Award, 1999; Washington State Book Award, 2000. *Literary Agent:* Kim Witherspoon and Assocs, 235 E 31st Street, New York, NY 10016, USA. *Website:* www .kathleenalcala.com.

ALDERSEY-WILLIAMS, Hugh Arthur, BA, MA, FRSA; British journalist and writer; b. 17 June 1959, London, England; m. Moira Morrissey 1989; one s. *Education:* St John's Coll., Cambridge. *Career:* mem. Soc. of Authors, European Acad. of Design. *Publications:* New American Design 1988, Hollington Industrial Design 1990, King and Miranda: Poetry of the Machine 1991, World Design: Nationalism and Globalism in Design 1992, The Most Beautiful Molecule: An Adventure in Chemistry (aka The Most Beautiful Molecule: The Discovery of the Buckyball) 1994, Zoomorphic: New Animal Architecture 2003; contrib. monographs on leading designers, various book chapters, articles to The Independent, Independent on Sunday. *E-mail:* hugh@hughalderseywilliams.com. *Website:* www.hughalderseywilliams.com.

ALDERSON, Margaret (Maggie) Hanne, MA; British writer and journalist; b. 31 July 1959, London; d. of Douglas Arthur Alderson and Margaret Dura Alderson (née Mackay); m. 1st Geoffrey Francis Laurence 1991 (divorced 1996); m. 2nd Radenko Popovic 2002; one d. *Education:* St Dominic's Priory and Alleynes School, Stone, Staffs. and Univ. of St Andrews. *Career:* writer and features ed. several magazines and newspapers, including Honey, You and London Evening Standard 1983–88; Ed. ES (London Evening Standard Magazine) 1988–89, Elle 1989–92, Mode 1994–95; Deputy Ed. Cleo 1993–94; journalist and Sr Writer Sydney Morning Herald 1996–2001; mem. British Soc. of Magazine Eds. *Publications include:* Shoe Money 1998, Pants On Fire 2000, Handbag Heaven 2001, Mad About the Boy 2003; Big Night Out 2002 (co-ed.), Handbags and Gladrags 2004, Ladies' Night (co-ed.) 2005, Cents and Sensibility 2006. *Honours:* British Soc. of Magazine Eds Ed. of the Year (Colour Supplements) 1989. *Literary Agent:* Curtis Brown, 28–29 Haymarket, London, SW1Y 4SP, England. *Telephone:* (1424) 421479 (office).

ALDERSON, Sue Ann, MA; American academic; *Professor of Creative Writing, University of British Columbia*; b. 11 Sept. 1940, New York; d. of Eugene Leonard Hartley and Ruth Edith Hartley (née Schuchowsky); m. Evan Alderson 1965 (divorced); two c. *Education:* Antioch Coll., Ohio State Univ. and Univ. of Calif. at Berkeley. *Career:* English Instructor, Simon Fraser Univ., Canada 1967–71, Capilano Coll. 1973–80; Asst Prof., Univ. of British Columbia, Canada 1980–84, Assoc. Prof. of Creative Writing 1984–92, Prof. 1992– (sole instructor on writing for children); juror, Canadian Council on Children's Literary Prize 1981–83. *Publications include:* for children: Bonnie McSmithers, You're Driving Me Dithers 1974, The Finding Princess 1977, The Adventures of Prince Paul 1977, Hurry Up, Bonnie! 1977, Bonnie McSmithers Is At It Again! 1979, Anne-Marie Maginol tu me rends folle 1981, Ida and the Wool Smugglers 1987; jr fiction: Comet's Tale 1983, The Not Impossible Summer 1983, The Something in Thurlo Darby's House 1984, Maybe You Had To Be There, By Duncan 1989, Chapter One 1990, Sure as Strawberries 1992, A Ride for Martha 1993, Ten for Lots of Boxes 1995, Pond Seasons 1997, The Not Impossible Summer 1998, Wherever Bears Be 1999. *Address:* University of British Columbia, Department of Creative Writing, Buchanan E468, Vancouver, BC V6T 1Z4 (office); 4004 West 32nd Street Vancouver, BC V6S 1Z6, Canada (home). *E-mail:* salderso@interchange.ubc .ca (office). *Website:* www.ubc.ca (office).

ALDING, Peter (see Jeffries, Roderic Graeme)

ALDISS, Brian Wilson, OBE, FRSL; British writer, critic and actor; b. 18 Aug. 1925, Norfolk; m. 2nd Margaret Manson 1965 (died 1997); two s. two d. *Education:* Framlingham Coll. and West Buckland School. *Career:* fmr soldier, draughtsman, bookseller and film critic; Literary Ed. Oxford Mail 1957–69; Pres. British Science Fiction Asscn 1960–65; Jt-Pres. European Science Fiction Cttees 1976–80; Chair. John W. Campbell Memorial Award 1976–77; Chair. Cttee of Man. Soc. of Authors 1977–78; mem. Literature Advisory Panel, Arts Council 1978–80; Chair. Cultural Exchanges Cttee of Authors 1978; Judge, Booker McConnell Prize 1981; Pres. World SF 1982–84; Ed. S.F. Horizons 1964–; Vice-Pres. H.G. Wells Soc., W. Buckland School 1997–. *Opera:* Oedipus on Mars. *Plays (author):* SF Blues, Kindred Blood in Kensington Gore, Monsters of Every Day (Oxford Literary Festival) 2000, Drinks with The Spider King (Florida) 2000; acted in own productions 1985–2002. *Publications:* The Brightfount Diaries 1955, Space, Time & Nathaniel 1957, Non-Stop (Jules Verne Award 1977) 1958, The Male Response 1959, Hothouse (Hugo Award 1962) 1962, The Airs of Earth 1963, The Dark Light Years 1964, Greybeard 1964, Earthworks 1965, Best Science Fiction Stories of Brian W. Aldiss 1965, The Saliva Tree (Nebula Award) 1965, Cities and Stones: A Traveller's Jugoslavia 1966, Report on Probability A 1968, Barefoot in the Head 1969, Intangibles Inc., 1969, A Brian Aldiss Omnibus 1969, The Hand-Reared Boy 1970, The Shape of Further Things 1970, A Soldier Erect 1971, The Moment of Eclipse (British Science Fiction Asscn Award 1972) 1971, Brian Aldiss Omnibus 2 1971, Penguin Science Fiction Omnibus (ed.) 1973, Comic Inferno 1973, Billion Year Spree (III Merit Award 1976) 1973, Frankenstein Unbound (made into film directed by Roger Corman) 1973, The Eighty-Minute Hour 1974, Hell's Cartographers (ed.) 1975, Space Odysseys, Evil Earths, Science Fiction Art 1975, The Malacia

Tapestry, Galactic Empires (two vols) 1976, Last Orders, Brothers of the Head 1977, Perilous Planets 1977, A Rude Awakening 1978, Enemies of the System 1978, This World and Nearer Ones 1979, Pile 1979, New Arrivals, Old Encounters 1979, Moreau's Other Island 1980, Life in the West 1980, An Island Called Moreau 1981, Foreign Bodies 1981, Helliconia Spring 1982, Science Fiction Quiz 1983, Helliconia Summer 1983, Seasons in Flight 1984, Helliconia Winter 1985, The Pale Shadow of Science 1985, . . . And the Lurid Glare of the Comet 1986, Trillion Year Spree (Hugo Award 1987) 1986, Ruins 1987, Forgotten Life 1988, Science Fiction Blues 1988, Best SF Stories of Brian W. Aldiss 1988, Cracken at Critical 1989, A Romance of the Equator 1990, Bury My Heart at W. H. Smith's 1990, Dracula Unbound 1991, Remembrance Day 1993, A Tupolev Too Far 1993, Somewhere East of Life 1994, The Detached Retina 1995, At the Caligula Hotel (poems) 1995, The Secret of this Book 1995, Songs from the Steppes of Central Asia 1996, The Twinkling of an Eye 1998, The Squire Quartet (four vols) 1998, When the Feast is Finished 1999, White Mars 1999, Supertoys Last All Summer Long (made into Kubrick–Spielberg film A.I. 2001) 2001, The Cretan Teat 2001, Super-State 2002, Researches and Churches in Serbia 2002, The Dark Sun Rises (poems) 2002, Affairs in Hampden Ferrers 2004, Jocasta 2005, Sanity and the Lady 2005, Harm 2007; contributions: TLS, Nature. *Honours:* Hon. DLitt 2000; Ditmar Award for World's Best Contemporary Science Fiction Writer 1969, first James Blish Award for Excellence in Criticism 1977, Pilgrim Award 1978, John W. Campbell Award 1983, Kurt Lasswitz Award 1984, IAFA Distinguished Scholarship Award 1986, J. Lloyd Eaton Award 1988, Prix Utopie (France) 1999, Grand Master of Science Fiction 2000. *Address:* Hambleden, 39 St Andrew's Road, Old Headington, Oxford, OX3 9DL, England. *Telephone:* (1865) 762464. *Fax:* (1865) 744435. *E-mail:* aldiss@dial .pipex.com (office). *Website:* www.brianwaldiss.com (office).

ALDRIDGE, (Harold Edward) James; British author and journalist; b. 10 July 1918, White Hills, Vic., Australia; s. of William Thomas Aldridge and Edith Quayle Aldridge; m. Dina Mitchnik 1942; two s. *Career:* with Herald and Sun, Melbourne, Australia 1937–38, Daily Sketch and Sunday Dispatch, London 1939; with Australian Newspaper Service and North American Newspaper Alliance (as war corresp.), Finland, Norway, Middle East, Greece, USSR 1939–45; corresp. for Time and Life, Tehran 1944. *Plays:* 49th State 1947, One Last Glimpse 1981. *Publications:* Signed with Their Honour 1942, The Sea Eagle 1944, Of Many Men 1946, The Diplomat 1950, The Hunter 1951, Heroes of the Empty View 1954, Underwater Hunting for Inexperienced Englishmen 1955, I Wish He Would Not Die 1958, Gold and Sand (short stories) 1960, The Last Exile 1961, A Captive in the Land 1962, The Statesman's Game 1966, My Brother Tom 1966, The Flying 19 1966, Living Egypt (with Paul Strand) 1969, Cairo: Biography of a City 1970, A Sporting Proposition 1973, The Marvellous Mongolian 1974, Mockery in Arms 1974, The Untouchable Juli 1975, One Last Glimpse 1977, Goodbye Un-America 1979, The Broken Saddle 1982, The True Story of Lilli Stubek (Australian Children's Book of the Year 1985) 1984, The True Story of Spit Mac Phee (Guardian Children's Fiction Prize) 1985, The True Story of Lola MacKellar 1993, The Girl From the Sea 2003, The Wings of Kitty St Clair 2006. *Honours:* Rhys Memorial Award 1945, New South Wales Premier's Literary Award 1986; Lenin Peace Prize 1972. *Literary Agent:* Curtis Brown Ltd, Haymarket House, 28–29 Haymarket, London, SW1Y 4SP, England. *Telephone:* (20) 7393-4400. *Fax:* (20) 7393-4401. *E-mail:* info@curtisbrown.co.uk. *Website:* www .curtisbrown.co.uk.

ALDRIDGE, John Watson, BA; American critic and writer; b. 26 Sept. 1922, Sioux City, IA; m. 1st; five s.; m. 2nd Patricia McGuire Eby 1983. *Education:* Univ. of California at Berkeley. *Career:* Lecturer, Princeton Univ. 1953–54, Bread Loaf Writers' Conference 1966–69; Special Adviser on American Studies, American Embassy, Bonn 1972–73; book critic, MacNeil/Lehrer Report, PBS TV 1983–84; Prof. of English, Univ. of Michigan. *Publications:* After the Lost Generation 1951, In Search of Heresy 1956, The Party at Cranton 1960, Time to Murder and Create 1966, In the Country of the Young 1970, The Devil in the Fire 1972, The American Novel and the Way We Live Now 1983, Talents and Technicians 1992, Classics and Contemporaries 1992. *Honours:* Rockefeller Foundation Fellowship 1976. *Address:* c/o Department of English, University of Michigan, 435 South State Street, 3187 Angell Hall, Ann Arbor, MI 48109-1003, USA.

ALDRIDGE, Sarah (see Marchant, Anyda)

ALDUY, Dominique, MA; French newspaper executive and economist; *Director-General, Le Monde*; b. 23 Feb. 1944, Paris; d. of Maurice and Madeleine (née Colas) Daumas; m. Jean-Paul Alduy 1969; one s. two d. *Education:* Univ. of Paris, Inst. d'Etudes Politiques de Paris and Pennsylvania State Univ., USA. *Career:* in charge of local community financial studies, Ministry of Equipment 1972–76; Rep. to Secr.-Gen. for New Towns 1976–78; in charge of Habitat and Environment Comm., Comm. Gen. du Plan 1979–81; Social Policies Rep. to Cabinet of the Prime Minister 1981–83; Dir of Programmes, Caisse des Dépôts et Consignations 1983–86, Dir Devt of Deposits-Devt 1986, Pres., Dir-Gen. of Communication Devt 1986–89; Dir-Gen. Soc. Nationale de Programmes—France Régions 3 (FR3) 1989–93, apptd Dir-Gen. Film 3 production 1989; Dir-Gen. Centre Nat. d'Art et de Culture Georges Pompidou 1993–94; Dir-Gen. Le Monde newspaper 1994–, mem. Bd Dirs Le Monde and Le Monde SA 1995–; Co-Man. Cahiers du Cinéma; Pres. European Newspapers Publrs' Asscn (ENPA) 2000–04. *Honours:* Chevalier de la Légion d'Honneur. *Address:* Le Monde, 21 bis rue Claude Bernard, 75242 Paris Cedex 05 (office); 74A rue Lecourbe, 75015 Paris, France (home).

Telephone: 1-42-17-20-00 (office). *Fax:* 1-42-17-21-21 (office). *Website:* www .lemonde.fr (office).

ALEGRÍA, Claribel, BA; Salvadorean writer and poet; b. 12 May 1924, Estelí, Nicaragua; d. of Daniel and Ana Maria (née Vides) Alegría; m. Darwin J. Flakoll 1947 (died 1995); one s. three d. *Education:* George Washington Univ., DC, USA. *Career:* extensive travelling in USA, S America and Europe 1943–; writer 1943–. *Publications include:* poetry: Anillo de Silencio 1948, Acuario 1955, Huésped de mi tiempo 1961, Aprendizaje 1970, Sobrevivo (Casa de las Américas Award, Cuba) 1978, Flores del volcano 1982, Umbrales 1997; prose: Fuga de canto grande (with Darwin J. Flakoll) 1992, Death of Somoza (with Darwin J. Flakoll, title in trans.), The Sandinista Revolution (with Darwin J. Flakoll, title in trans.), They'll Never Take Me Alive (with Darwin J. Flakoll, title in trans.), Ashes of Izalco (novel, with Darwin J. Flakoll). *Honours:* Dr hc (East Connecticut State Univ.) 1998, (León) 2005; Independent Publisher Book Award 2000, Book Sense Choice 2001, Neustadt Int. Prize for Literature 2005. *Address:* Apdo Postal A-36, Managua, Nicaragua. *Telephone:* (2) 774 903. *E-mail:* claribel@ibw.com.ni.

ALEKSANDROWICZ, Piotr, MSc, MBA; Polish editor; *Editor, Rzeczpospolita;* b. 4 Oct. 1953, Warsaw. *Education:* Warsaw Tech. Univ., Warsaw Univ. and Univ. of Illinois, USA. *Career:* Ed. Rzeczpospolita (The Republic) newspaper. *Address:* Rzeczpospolita, Plac Starynkiewicza 7, 02-015, Warsaw, Poland (office). *E-mail:* p.aleksandrowicz@rzeczpospolita.pl (office). *Website:* www.rzeczpospolita.pl (office).

ALEKSIEVICH, Svetlana; Belarusian journalist and writer; b. 31 May 1948, Minsk, Ukraine. *Education:* Minsk Univ. *Career:* worked as journalist on local newspaper in early 1970s. *Publications include:* non-fiction: Aposhniya svedki. kniga nedzitsyachyh raskaza? 1985, U voyny ne zhenskoe litso (The War's Unwomanly Face) 1985, Tsinkovye mal'chiki (Zinky Boys: Soviet Voices from a Forgotten War) 1991, Zacharavannya smertsu (Enchanted with Death) 1993, Poslednie svideteli (The Last Witnesses), Charnobyl'skaya malitva (trans. as Chernobyl Prayer: A Chronicle of the Future) 1997. *Honours:* Kurt Tucholsky Prize, Swedish PEN Club, Stockholm 1996, Andrej Sinjavskij Prize, Moscow 1997, Triumph Prize 1998, European Understanding Prize for contrib. to a better understanding among European nations 1998, 'Témoin du Monde', Paris 1999, Erich Maria Remarque Peace Prize (Germany) 2001, Nat. Book Critics' Circle Award, New York 2006. *Address:* c/o Aurum Press, 25 Bedford Avenue, London, WC1B 3AT, England. *E-mail:* svett_al@hotmail.com.

ALEX, Peter (see Haining, Peter Alexander)

ALEXANDER, Brooke, BA; American art dealer and publisher; b. 26 April 1937, Los Angeles; s. of Richard H. Alexander and Marion C. Alexander; m. Carolyn Rankin 1967; two d. *Education:* Yale Univ. *Career:* f. Brooke Alexander Inc. to publish and distribute graphic art 1968, expanded co. 1975; f. Brooke Alexander Editions, opened separate gallery for graphics 1989; partner in Madrid gallery, Galería Weber, Alexander y Cobo 1991–; mem. Governing Bd Yale Univ. Art Gallery 1988–. *Address:* Brooke Alexander Editions, 59 Wooster Street, New York, NY 10012-4349, USA. *Telephone:* (212) 925-4338. *Fax:* (212) 941-9565. *E-mail:* info@baeditions.com. *Website:* www.baeditions.com.

ALEXANDER, Caroline Elizabeth, BA, PhD; American writer; b. 13 March 1956, Florida. *Education:* Florida State Univ., Univ. of Oxford, Columbia Univ. *Career:* mem. American Philological Society, RGS. *Publications:* One Dry Season: In the Footsteps of Mary Kingsley 1990, The Way to Xanadu 1994, Battle's End, Mrs Chippy's Last Expedition 1997, The Endurance 1998, The Bounty: The True Story of the Mutiny on the Bounty 2003; *Contributions:* New Yorker, Smithsonian, Independent, Sunday Telegraph Weekend Magazine. *Honours:* Mellon Fellowship, Rhodes Scholarship. *Literary Agent:* Aitken Alexander Associates Ltd, 18–21 Cavaye Place, London, SW10 9PT, England. *Telephone:* (20) 7373-8672. *Fax:* (20) 7373-6002. *E-mail:* reception@ aitkenalexander.co.uk. *Website:* www.aitkenalexander.co.uk.

ALEXANDER, Christine Anne, PhD; New Zealand academic and writer; *Professor, University of New South Wales;* b. 9 July 1949, Hastings; m. Peter Fraser Alexander 1977; one s. one d. *Education:* Univ. of Canterbury, Univ. of Cambridge. *Career:* Asst Lectureship, Univ. of Canterbury, 1972; Tutor Univ. of New South Wales, Australia 1978–83; Lecturer 1986–88, Senior Lecturer 1988–92, Assoc. Prof. 1993–97, Prof. 1998–2007, Scientia Prof. (2008–); mem. Brontë Society; Australasian Language and Literature Asscn; Australian Victorian Studies Asscn; Australian and South Pacific Asscn for Comparative Literary Studies; Cambridge Society; Jane Austen Society; Asscn for the Study of Australian Literature; Bibliographical Society of Australia and New Zealand; Society for Textual Scholarship; Society for the History of Authorship, Reading and Publishing. *Publications:* Bibliography of the Manuscripts of Charlotte Brontë 1982, The Early Writings of Charlotte Brontë 1983, An Edition of the Early Writings of Charlotte Brontë, three vols 1987–, The Art of the Brontës 1994, High Life in Verdopolis: A Tale from the Glass Town Saga 1995, The Oxford Companion to the Brontës 2003, The Child Writer from Austen to Woolf 2005, Jane Austen's Lady Susan 2005; contrib. to books and journals. *Honours:* New Zealand Postgraduate Scholarships; New Zealand University Women's Fellowship; Travel Grants; Special Research Grants; British Acad. Rose Mary Crawshay Prize, 1984; Visiting Scholarship Pembroke Coll., Cambridge 1990–91, Fellow Australian Acad. of the Humanities 1994, Australian Research Council Senior Research Fellowship

1995–97, Library Fellowship Princeton Univ. 1996, Centenary Medal for Service to Australian Soc. and the Humanities 2003. *Address:* School of English, University of New South Wales, Sydney, NSW 2052, Australia (office). *E-mail:* c.alexander@unsw.edu.au (office).

ALEXANDER, Clare; British literary agent; *Director, Aitken Alexander Associates Ltd.* *Career:* ed. with Penguin Books 1981–90; Publishing Dir Viking 1990–97; Ed.-in-Chief, Macmillan 1997–98; literary agent, later Dir Gillon Aitken Assocs (now Aitken Alexander Associates Ltd) 1998–. *Address:* Aitken Alexander Associates Ltd, 18–21 Cavaye Place, London, SW10 9PT, England (office). *Telephone:* (20) 7373-8672 (office). *Fax:* (20) 7373-6002 (office). *E-mail:* clare@aitkenalexander.co.uk (office). *Website:* www .aitkenalexander.co.uk (office).

ALEXANDER, Doris Muriel, BA, MA, PhD; American academic and writer; b. 14 Dec. 1922, Newark, NJ. *Education:* Univ. of Missouri, Univ. of Pennsylvania, New York Univ. *Career:* Instructor, Rutgers University 1950–56; Assoc. Prof., then Dept Chair, CUNY 1956–62; mem. Asscn of Literary Scholars and Critics, Eugene O'Neill Society. *Publications:* The Tempering of Eugene O'Neill 1962, Creating Characters with Charles Dickens 1991, Eugene O'Neill's Creative Struggle 1992, Creating Literature Out of Life 1996, Eugene O'Neill's Last Plays: Separating Art from Autobiography 2004; contrib. to many journals. *Honours:* Penfield Fellowship, New York University, 1946; Fulbright Prof., University of Athens, 1966–67. *Address:* San Trovaso 1116, Dorsoduro, 30123 Venice, Italy (home). *E-mail:* dalex1@tin .it (home).

ALEXANDER, Elisabeth; German poet and writer; b. 21 Aug. 1922, Linz am Rhein. *Career:* freelance writer 1970–; contributor to Feuilleton des Heidelberger Tageblatts magazine 1975–82; publs in newspapers and magazines and for radio and TV, including Frankfurter Rundschau, Basler Zeitung, Frankfurter Hefte, Badische Neueste Nachrichten, Die Zeit, Passagen, Mannheimer Morgen; Visiting Writer, Texas Tech. Univ., USA 1986; lecture tours of USA, Guest Lecturer, Goethe Inst. Amsterdam, Paris, Brussels, Montreal etc.; works translated into English, French and Chinese. *Publications include:* poetry: Bums 1971, Ich bin kein Pferd 1976, Brotkrumen 1977, Ich hänge mich ans schwarze Brette 1979, Wo bist du Trost 1980, Glückspfennig – Gedichte für das ganze Jahr 1984, Zeitflusen 1986, Die Uhr läuft rückwärts wenn der Schnee fällt 1994; novels and short stories: Die Frau, die lachte 1975, Fritte Pomm (for children) 1976, Die törichte Jungfrau 1978, Sie hätte ihre Kinder töten sollen 1982, Damengeschichte 1983, Lisas Liebe 1994, Domizil Heidelberg 1995, Bauchschuß, Am Fußende des Bettes (co-author) 2000, Werksausgabe 1. Die sieben Häute der Hanna Winter 2002; co-writer and ed. of many other works, works feature in anthologies. *Honours:* Honoured Guest, Deutschen Akad. Rom Villa Massimo 1996; Scholarship, Kunststiftung Baden-Württemberg 1979, Promotion Scholarship, Baden-Württemberg 1980, 1991, 1995, work scholarship, Rhineland-Palatinate 1984, 1987, First Prize, Poetensitz 1996, Verdienstmedaille des Landes Baden-Württemberg 1997, Scholarship, Stiftung Kulturaustausch Niederlande/ Deutschland, Amsterdam 1998. *Address:* Erwin-Rohde-Straße 22, 69120 Heidelberg, Germany. *Telephone:* (6221) 480561. *Fax:* (6221) 480561. *E-mail:* Elisabeth.Alexander@t-online.de.

ALEXANDER, Gary Roy; American writer; b. 18 Jan. 1941, Bremerton, Wash.; m. Shari 1969; three d. *Education:* Olympic Community Coll., Univ. of Washington. *Career:* mem. Mystery Writers of America. *Publications:* Pigeon Blood 1988, Unfunny Money 1989, Kiet and the Golden Peacock 1989, Kiet and the Opium War 1990, Deadly Drought 1991, Dead Dinosaurs 1994, Kiet Goes West 1992, Blood Sacrifice 1993; contrib. of many stories and travel articles in magazines. *Address:* 6709 S 238th Place, H-102, Kent, WA 98032, USA. *E-mail:* alexagr61@hotmail.com.

ALEXANDER, Helen Anne, CBE, MA, MBA; British publishing executive; *Group CEO, The Economist Group;* b. 10 Feb. 1957, d. of the late Bernard Alexander and Tania Alexander (née Benckendorff); m. Tim Suter 1985; two s. one d. *Education:* Hertford Coll. Oxford, Institut Européen d' Admin des Affaires (INSEAD), France. *Career:* mem. staff Gerald Duckworth 1978–79, Faber & Faber 1979–83; joined The Economist Group 1984, Man. Dir Economist Intelligence Unit 1993–96, Group CEO 1997–; Dir (non-exec.) Northern Foods PLC 1994–2003, British Telecom PLC 2000–2002, Centrica PLC; Trustee Tate Gallery; Gov. St Paul's Girls' School. *Honours:* Hon. Fellow Hertford Coll., Oxford. *Address:* The Economist Group, 25 St James's Street, London, SW1A 1HG, England (office). *Telephone:* (20) 7830-7000 (office). *Website:* www.economistgroup.com (office).

ALEXANDER, Meena, BA, PhD; American (b. Indian) poet, writer and academic; *Distinguished Professor of English and Women's Studies, Hunter College and the Graduate School and University Center, City University of New York;* b. 17 Feb. 1951, Allahabad, India; m. David Lelyveld 1979; one s. one d. *Education:* Univ. of Khartoum, Sudan, Univ. of Nottingham, UK. *Career:* Lecturer Univ. of Hyderabad 1977–79, Reader 1979; Asst Prof. Fordham Univ. 1980–87; Asst Prof., Hunter Coll. and the Grad. School and Univ. Center, CUNY 1987–89, Assoc. Prof. 1989–92, Prof. of English 1992–99, Distinguished Prof. of English and Women's Studies 1999–; Int. Writer-in-Residence, Arts Council of England 1995; Lila Wallace Writer-in-Residence, Asian American Renaissance, Minneapolis 1995; Poet-in-Residence, Nat. Univ. of Singapore 1999; Comm. for Poetry International, Royal Festival Hall, London 2002; mem. Modern Language Asscn, PEN American Center. *Publications:* The Poetic Self: Towards a Phenomenology of Romanticism

1979, Stone Roots (poems) 1980, House of a Thousand Doors (poems and prose) 1988, Women in Romanticism: Mary Wollstonecraft, Dorothy Wordsworth and Mary Shelley 1989, The Storm: A Poem in Five Parts 1989, Nampally Road (novel) 1991, Night-Scene: The Garden (poem) 1992, Fault Lines (memoir) 1993, River and Bridge (poems) 1995, The Shock of Arrival: Reflections on Postcolonial Experience (poems and prose) 1996, Manhattan Music (novel) 1997, Illiterate Heart (poems) 2002, Raw Silk (poems) 2004, Indian Love Poems (ed.) 2005; contribs to books, anthologies and periodicals. *Honours:* MacDowell Colony Fellow 1993, 1998, Fondation Ledig-Rowohlt residency, Château de Lavigny 2001, Rockefeller Foundation residency, Bellagio 2002; Altrusa Int. Award 1973, New York State Foundation for the Arts Poetry Award 1999, Fulbright Scholar Award, India 2002, PEN Open Book Award 2002, Martha Walsh Pulver Residency for a Poet, Yaddo 2005. *Address:* Graduate School and University Center, City University of New York, 365 Fifth Avenue, New York, NY 10016, USA (office). *Telephone:* (212) 817-8344 (office). *E-mail:* malexander@gc.cuny.edu (office); malexander217@earthlink.net (home). *Website:* www.poets.org/malex.

ALEXANDER, Phil; British editor; *Editor-in-Chief, Mojo. Career:* Man. Ed., Kerrang! –2002; Man. Ed., Q magazine 2002; currently Ed.-in-Chief, Mojo magazine. *Television:* presenter rock show, Raw Power 1990, presenter Popped In, Crashed Out (series) 1999. *Address:* MOJO, Mappin House, 4 Winsley Street, London, W1W 8HF, England (office). *E-mail:* MOJO@emap.com (office). *Website:* www.mojo4music.com.

ALEXANDER, Sue; American writer; b. 20 Aug. 1933, Tucson, AZ; m.; two s. one d. *Education:* Drake Univ., Northwestern Univ. *Career:* mem. Soc. of Children's Book Writers and Illustrators (chair. bd of dirs), Children's Literature Council of Southern California (mem. of bd), Friends of Children and Libraries, California Readers' Asscn. *Publications:* Small Plays for You and a Friend 1973, Nadir of the Streets 1975, Peacocks Are Very Special 1976, Witch, Goblin and Sometimes Ghost 1976, Small Plays for Special Days 1977, Marc the Magnificent 1978, More Witch, Goblin and Ghost Stories 1978, Seymour the Prince 1979, Finding Your First Job 1980, Whatever Happened to Uncle Albert? and Other Puzzling Plays 1980, Witch, Goblin and Ghost in the Haunted Woods 1981, Witch, Goblin and Ghost's Book of Things to Do 1982, Nadia the Willful 1983, Dear Phoebe 1984, World Famous Muriel 1984, Witch, Goblin and Ghost Are Back 1985, World Famous Muriel and the Scary Dragon 1985, America's Own Holidays 1986, Lila on the Landing 1987, There's More – Much More 1987, World Famous Muriel and the Magic Mystery 1990, Who Goes Out on Halloween? 1990, Sara's City 1995, What's Wrong Now, Millicent? 1996, One More Time, Mama 1999, Behold the Trees 2001. *Honours:* Dorothy C. McKenzie Award for distinguished contribution to the field of children's literature 1980. *E-mail:* suelalexander@earthlink.net. *Website:* www.sue-alexander.com.

ALEXIE, Sherman, BA; American poet and novelist; b. 7 Oct. 1966, Spokane, WA; m. Diane 1994; two s. *Education:* Washington State Univ., Pullman. *Career:* Spokane/Coeur d'Alene Indian; stand-up comedian, poet, songwriter, writer. *Publications:* The Business of Fancydancing (short stories and poems, also screenplay) 1991, The Lone Ranger and Tonto Fist Fight in Heaven (short stories) 1993, Old Shirts and New Skins (poems) 1993, I Would Steal Horses (poems) 1993, First Indian on the Moon (poems) 1993, Reservation Blues (novel) 1995, Water Flowing Home (poems) 1995, The Summer of Black Widows (poems) 1996, Indian Killer (novel) 1996, Smoke Signals (screenplay) 1998, The Man Who Loves Salmon (poems) 1998, The Toughest Indian in the World (short stories) 2000, One Stick Song (poems) 2000, Ten Little Indians (short stories) 2003, Flight 2007; contrib. to The Stranger, Indiana Review, New Yorker. *Honours:* PEN/Hemingway Best First Book Award 1993, Malamud short story award (with Richard Ford) 2001. *Address:* FallsApart Productions Inc., PMB 2294, 10002 Aurora Avenue N, Suite 36, Seattle, WA 98133-9334, USA. *E-mail:* fallsapart_fans@hotmail.com. *Website:* www.fallsapart.com.

ALFTAN, Maija Kyllikki; Finnish journalist; *Reporter, Helsingin Sanomat;* b. 17 Dec. 1948, Alatornio; d. of Oskar Tallgren and Henni Tallgren; m. Robert Alftan 1976; two d. *Education:* Sanoma School of Journalism, Helsinki. *Career:* reporter on Ilta-Sanomat 1969–78, Kotiliesi 1978–83; Man. Ed. Avotakka 1983–85, Kodin Kuvalehti magazine 1986–89; apptd Ed.-in-Chief Kodin Kuvalehti 1989–94; reporter, Helsingin Sanomat 1994–. *Address:* PO Box 85, 00089 Sanomat, Finland (office).

ALI, Monica; Bangladeshi/British novelist; b. 1967, Dhaka, E Pakistan (now Bangladesh); m. Simon Torrance; one s. one d. *Education:* Wadham Coll., Oxford. *Career:* family moved to Bolton, UK during civil war 1971; worked in publishing, design and branding. *Publications:* Brick Lane (WH Smith People's Choice Award for Best Debut Novel 2003, British Book Awards Newcomer of the Year 2003) 2003, Knife (short story in The Weekenders: Adventures in Calcutta) 2004, Alentejo Blue 2006. *Honours:* Granta's Best of Young British Novelists list 2003. *Literary Agent:* The Marsh Agency, 11 Dover Street, London, W1S 4LJ, England. *Telephone:* (20) 7399-2800. *Fax:* (20) 7399-2801. *Website:* www.marsh-agency.co.uk.

ALI, Tariq; Pakistani political activist and writer; b. 21 Oct. 1943, Lahore; pnr Susan Watkins; two d. one s. *Education:* Punjab Univ., Univ. of Oxford. *Career:* Editorial Dir Verso 1999–; mem. editorial bd New Left Review 1982–; mem. Fourth International. *Publications:* fiction: Redemption 1990, Shadows of the Pomegranate Tree 1992, Fear of Mirrors 1998, The Book of Saladin 1999, The Stone Woman 2000, The Illustrious Corpse 2003, A Sultan in Palermo 2005; non-fiction: The Thoughts of Chairman Harold (compiler) 1967, The New Revolutionaries: A Handbook of the International Radical Left (ed.) 1969, Pakistan: Military Rule or People's Power? 1970, The Coming British Revolution 1972, Chile: Lessons of the Coup: Which Way to Workers' Power? (with Gerry Hedley) 1974, 1968 and After: Inside the Revolution 1978, Trotsky for Beginners 1980, Can Pakistan Survive? 1983, What is Stalinism? (ed.) 1984, The Stalinist Legacy: Its Impact on Twentieth-Century World Politics (ed.) 1984, An Indian Dynasty: The Story of the Nehru-Gandhi Family 1985, Street Fighting Years: An Autobiography of the Sixties 1987, Revolution from Above: Where is the Soviet Union Going? 1988, Moscow Gold (with Howard Brenton) 1990, 1968: Marching in the Streets (with Susan Watkins) 1998, Ugly Rumours (with Howard Brenton) 1998, Masters of the Universe?: NATO's Balkan Crusade (ed.) 2000, The Clash of Fundamentalisms: Crusades, Jihads and Modernity 2002, The Clash of Fundamentalisms: Bush in Babylon: Recolonising Iraq 2003, Rough Music 2005, Pirates of the Caribbean: Axis of Hope 2006; contribs to periodicals, including London Review of Books. *Address:* c/o Verso, 6 Meard Street, London, W1F 0EG, England. *Website:* www.tariqali.org.

ALIA, Josette, (Josette de Benbrahem); French journalist; b. 25 Nov. 1929, Ferté-Bernard; d. of Jack David and Germaine David (née Legeay); m. Raouf Benbrahem 1952; one s. *Education:* Inst. d'Etudes Politiques de Paris and Univ. of Paris (Paris-Sorbonne). *Career:* journalist, Jeune Afrique 1960–62; Corresp., Le Monde newspaper 1962–67; apptd Sr Reporter, then Ed.-in-Chief, then Deputy Editorial Dir, then Editorial Dir Le Nouvel Observateur magazine 1985; Pres. Jury Prix Albert Londres. *Publications include:* La guerre de Mitterrand: La dernière grande illusion 1991, Quand le soleil était chaud (Prix des Maisons de la Presse) 1993, Étoile Bleue, Chapeaux Noirs 1999, Impossible Israel 1999, Le Pensionnat 2005. *Honours:* Echo de la Presse et de la Publicité Best Journalist Award 1980, Personality of the Year 1985, Prix Mumm 1993. *Address:* c/o Le Nouvel Observateur, 12 place de la Bourse, 75002 Paris (office); 169 rue de Rennes, 75006 Paris, France (home). *Telephone:* 1-44-88-34-33 (office); 1-45-48-96-72 (home). *E-mail:* josette.alia@nouvelobs.com (office).

ALIOTH, Gabrielle, Lic.rer.pol.; Swiss novelist; b. 21 April 1955, Basel; m. Martin Alioth. *Career:* Writer-in-Residence, Univ. of Southern California, USA 1997, California State Univ. 1997, Case Western Reserve Univ., Cleveland, OH, USA 2002, Univ. Coll., Dublin, Ireland 2005–06; Lecturer, Coll. of Design and Art, Lucere; mem. Irish del. 1996, Swiss del. 1998 at Frankfurt Book Fair; mem. PEN, AdS. *Publications:* novels: Der Narr (translated as The Fool) 1990, Wie ein kostbarer Stein (translated as Like a Precious Stone) 1994, Die Arche der Frauen (translated as Women's Arch) 1996, Die Stumme Reiterin (translated as The Silent Rider) 1998. *Honours:* Hamburg Literary Award for Best First Novel. *Literary Agent:* c/o Verlag Nagel & Kimche AG, V-Nr. 1320 506, Nordstr. 9, 8035, Zürich, Switzerland. *Telephone:* (44) 366-66-80. *Fax:* (44) 366-66-88. *E-mail:* info@nagel-kimche.ch. *Website:* www.nagel-kimche.ch. *Address:* Rosemount, Julianstown, Co. Meath, Ireland (office). *Telephone:* (41) 9829302 (office). *Fax:* (41) 9829612 (office). *E-mail:* info@gabriellealioth.com (office). *Website:* www.gabriellealioth.com.

ALKALI, Zaynab, PhD; Nigerian novelist and essayist; b. 1950, Garkida; m. Mohammed Nur Alkali (divorced); five c. *Education:* Ahmadu Bello Univ., Zaira, Bayero Univ., Kano. *Career:* fmr Asst Lecturer Bayero Univ., Kano, now Reader; Lecturer Univ. of Maiduguri 1981–83, then Sr Lecturer, Assoc. Prof. of African Literature and Creative Writing; also lectured at Madibbo Adama Coll., Yola 1983–84; fmr Ed. Ganga: A Journal of Language and Literature; fmr head of NGO for women's rights. *Publications:* The Stillborn (Asscn of Nigerian Authors' Prose Prize for Best Novel 1985) 1984, The Virtuous Woman (novel) 1987, Saltless Ash (short story), The Vagabond (short story), The Cobwebs (short story) 1990, Vultures in the Air: Voices from Northern Nigeria (ed. with Al Imfeld) 1995, The Cobwebs and Other Stories 1997, The Matriarch 2003, The House Guest 2003. *Honours:* Magiran Garkida (traditional title); Asscn of Nigerian Authors' Best Short Story of the Year Prize 1997, Merit Award for Literature Nat. Council for Women Socs 2000, Merit Award Nat. Council for Arts and Culture 2001. *Address:* c/o University of Maiduguri, POB 1069, Maiduguri, Borno State, Nigeria.

ALKHATIB, Burhan, BEng, MA; Iraqi writer, translator and engineer; b. 10 Oct. 1944, Mosaib, Babel; m. 1st 1978 (divorced 1982); m. 2nd 1988 (divorced 1994); two s. one d. *Education:* Univ. of Baghdad, Gorky Literary Inst. Moscow. *Career:* mem. Writers' Union of Sweden. *Publications:* Khutwat ila Alufq Albaid (Steps Toward a Distant Horizon) 1967, Dabab fi Addahira (Mist at Midday) 1968, Shiqqatun fi Shari' Abi Nuwas (An Apartment on Abi Nuwas Street) 1972, Ajusur Azujajiyya (Bridges of Glass) 1975, Ashari 'aljadid (A New Street) 1980, Nujum Oldhuhr (Under the Heat of Midday) 1986, Suqut Sparta (The Fall of Sparta) 1992, Layla Baghdadia (A Baghdad Night) 1993, Babel alfaiha (The Aromatic Babylon) 1995, Thalik assaif fi Iskendria (That Summer in Alexandria) 1998, Aljanain Almuglaqa (The Closed Gardens) 2000; translations of 13 books; contrib. to Arab magazines and journals. *Address:* Berg V 22 tr 3, 19631 Kungsangen, Sweden (home).

ALLABY, (John) Michael; British writer and editor; b. 18 Sept. 1933, Belper, Derbyshire, England; m. Ailsa Marthe McGregor 1957; one s. one d. *Career:* mem. Asscn of British Science Writers, New York Acad. of Sciences, Soc. of Authors. *Publications:* The Eco-Activists 1971, Who Will Eat? 1972, Robots Behind the Plow 1974, Ecology 1975, Inventing Tomorrow 1976, World

Food Resources, Actual and Potential 1977, Dictionary of the Environment 1977, 1983, 1988, 1994, Making and Managing a Smallholding 1979, Animals that Hunt 1979, Wildlife of North America 1979, The Politics of Self-Sufficency 1980, Le Foreste Tropicali 1981, A Year in the Life of a Field 1981, The Curious Cat 1982, Animal Artisans 1982, The Great Extinction 1983, The Food Chain 1984, The Greening of Mars 1984, The Oxford Dictionary of Natural History 1985, Your Child and the Computer 1985, Nine Lives 1985, 2040: Our World in the Future 1985, A Dog's Life 1986, The Woodland Trust Book of British Woodlands 1986, Ecology Facts 1986, The Concise Oxford Dictionary of Earth Sciences 1986, The Ordnance Survey Outdoor Handbook 1987, A Pony's Tale 1987, Conservation at Home 1988, Green Facts 1989, Thinking Green: An Anthology of Essential Ecological Writing 1989, Guide to Gaia 1989, Into Harmony with the Planet 1990, Living in the Greenhouse 1990, Concise Oxford Dictionary of Zoology 1991, Concise Oxford Dictionary of Botany 1992, Elements: Water 1992, Elements: Air 1993, Elements: Fire 1993, Elements: Earth 1993, Planet Earth: A Visual Factfinder 1993, The Concise Oxford Dictionary of Ecology 1994, Facing the Future 1995, How it Works: The Environment 1996, Basics of Environmental Science 1996, Dangerous Weather (six vols) 1997–98, (eight vols) 2003–04, Temperate Forests 1999, Biomes of the World (nine vols) 1999, DK Guide to Weather (Aventis Jr Prize for Science Books 2001) 2000, Plants and Plant Life (five vols) 2001, Deserts 2001, Encyclopedia of Weather and Climate 2002, Facts on File: Weather and Climate Handbook 2002, How it Works: The World's Weather 2002, Countries of the World: India 2005, A Change in the Weather 2004, Temperate Forests 2005, Tropical Forests 2006, Deserts 2006, Grasslands 2006; contrib. to newspapers and magazines. *Address:* Braehead Cottage, Tighnabruaich, Argyll PA21 2ED, Scotland. *E-mail:* mike_allaby@compuserve.com. *Website:* www.michaelallaby.com.

ALLAN, John B. (see Westlake, Donald Edwin)

ALLAN, Keith, BA, MLitt, PhD, FAHA; British academic, writer and editor; b. 27 March 1943, London; m. Wendy F. Allen 1993; two d. *Education:* Univs of Leeds and Edinburgh. *Career:* Research Assoc., Nuffield Language Devt Research Project, Dept of Child Life and Health, Univ. of Edinburgh 1967–70; Lecturer in English Language, Ahmadu Bello Univ., Zaria, Nigeria 1970–73; Lecturer in Linguistics, Univ. of Essex 1973–74, Univ. of Nairobi, Kenya 1975–77; Guest Prof. in Linguistics, Gesamthochschule, Paderborn, Germany 1975; Sr Tutor in Linguistics, Monash Univ., Australia 1978–81, Lecturer in Linguistics 1982–87, Sr Lecturer in Linguistics 1988–91, Acting Prof. and Head, Dept of Linguistics 1992–93, Reader in Linguistics 1992–; Visiting Prof. in Linguistics, Univ. of Arizona, USA 1990; Visiting Fellow, Research Centre for English and Applied Linguistics and also Clare Hall, Cambridge 2000, St Catherine's Coll., Oxford 2005; Chair. Linguistics and Philology Section, Australian Acad. of Humanities 1997–2000. *Publications:* Linguistic Meaning (two vols) 1986, Oxford International Encyclopedia of Linguistics (semantics ed.) 1991, Euphemism and Dysphemism: Language Used as Shield and Weapon (with Kate Burridge) 1991, Natural Language Semantics 2001, Encyclopedia of Languages and Linguistics (2nd edn) (semantics ed.) 2005, Forbidden Words (with Kate Burridge) 2006, The Western Classical Tradition in Linguistics 2007; contribs to reference works, scholarly books and professional journals. *Honours:* Centenary Medal for Services to Linguistics and Philology, Australian Govt. *Address:* Linguistics Program, Bldg 11, Monash University, Vic. 3800, Australia (office). *Website:* www.arts.monash .edu.au/ling/staff/allan (office).

ALLASON, Rupert William Simon; British writer and editor; b. 8 Nov. 1951, London, England; m. Nicole Van Moppes 1979 (divorced 1996); one s. one d. *Education:* Univ. of Grenoble, Univ. of London. *Career:* Ed. World Intelligence Review 1985–; MP for Torbay, Conservative Party 1987–97; mem. Special Forces Club. *Publications:* SPY! (with Richard Deacon) 1980, British Security Service Operations 1909–45 1981, A Matter of Trust: MI5 1945–72 1982, MI6: British Secret Intelligence Service Operations 1909–45 1983, The Branch: A History of the Metropolitan Police Special Branch 1983, Unreliable Witness: Espionage Myths of the Second World War 1984, GARBO (with Juan Pjujol) 1985, GCHQ: The Secret Wireless War 1986, Molehunt 1987, The Friends: Britain's Postwar Secret Intelligence Operations 1988, Games of Intelligence 1989, Seven Spies Who Changed the World 1991, Secret War: The Story of SOE 1992, The Faber Book of Espionage 1993, The Illegals 1993, Mortal Crimes 1994, The Faber Book of Treachery 1995, The Secret War for the Falklands 1997, Counterfeit Spies 1998, Crown Jewels 1998, Venona 1999, The Third Secret 2000, Mortal Crimes 2004, Mask 2005, The Guy Liddell Diaries (ed.) 2005, Historical Dictionary of British Intelligence 2005. *Honours:* Asscn of Former Intelligence Officers Lifetime Literature Achievement Award 2004. *Address:* 6 Burton Mews, London, SW1W 9EP, England. *Telephone:* (7836) 200600 (home). *Fax:* (20) 7352-1111 (office). *E-mail:* westintel@compuserve.com. *Website:* www.nigelwest.com.

ALLDRITT, Keith, BA, MA, FRSL; British academic and writer; b. 10 Dec. 1935, Wolverhampton, England; m. Joan Hardwick 1980, one s. one d. *Education:* St Catharine's Coll., Cambridge. *Career:* Prof. of English, Univ. of British Columbia, now Prof. Emeritus; mem. Arnold Bennett Soc., Soc. of Authors, D. H. Lawrence Soc., Int. Churchill Soc., MLA. *Publications:* The Making of George Orwell 1969, The Visual Imagination of D. H. Lawrence 1970, The Good Pit Man 1975, The Lover Next Door 1977, Elgar on the Journey to Hanley 1978, Poetry as Chamber Music 1978, Modernism in the Second World War 1989, Churchill the Writer: His Life as a Man of Letters 1992, The Greatest of Friends: Franklin Roosevelt and Winston Churchill 1939–45 1995. *Address:* c/o Department of English, University of British Columbia, 397 - 1873 East Mall (Buchanan Tower), Vancouver, BC V6T 1Z1, Canada.

ALLEN, Blair H., (Ghosthand), AA, BA; American writer, poet, editor and artist; *Special Feature Editor, Cerulean Press and Kent Publications*; b. 2 July 1933, Los Angeles, Calif.; m. Juanita Aguilar Raya 1968; one s. one d. *Education:* San Diego City Coll., Univ. of Washington, San Diego State Univ. *Career:* book reviewer, Los Angeles Times, 1977–78; Special Feature Ed., Cerulean Press and Kent Publs 1982–; mem. Asscn for Applied Poetry, Beyond Baroque Foundation, California State Poetry Soc., Medina Foundation, Acad. of American Poets, Poets and Writers (US). *Publications:* Televisual Poems for Bloodshot Eyeballs 1973, Malice in Blunderland 1974, N/Z 1979, The Atlantis Trilogy 1982, Dreamwish of the Magician 1983, Right Through the Silver Lined 1984 Looking Glass 1984, The Magical World of David Cole (ed.) 1984, Snow Summits in the Sun (ed.) 1988, Trapped in a Cold War Travelogue 1991, May Burning into August 1992, The Subway Poems 1993, Bonfire on the Beach, by John Brander (ed.) 1993, The Cerulean Anthology of Sci-Fi/Outer Space/Fantasy/Poetry and Prose Poems (ed.) 1995, When the Ghost of Cassandra Whispers in My Ears 1996, Ashes Ashes All Fall Down 1997, Around the World in 56 Days 1998, Thunderclouds from the Door 1999, Jabberbunglemerkeltoy 1999, The Athens Café 2000, The Day of the Jamberee Call 2001, Assembled I Stand 2002, Wine of Starlight 2002, Hour of Iced Wheels 2003, Snow Birds in Cloud Hands (ed. anthology) 2003, Trek into Yellowstone's Cascade Corner Wilderness 2003, Light in the Crossroads 2004, Shot Doves 2005, What Time Does: One Man Show (art book retrospective) 2006, Moon Hiding in the Orange Tree 2007; contribs to numerous periodicals and anthologies. *Honours:* First Prize for Poetry, Pacificus Foundation Competition 1992, Pacificus Foundation Literary Prize for Lifetime Achievement in Poetry and Story Writing 2003, various other honours and awards. *Address:* PO Box 162, Colton, CA 92324-0162, USA. *Website:* www.pe.org/directory/writer-detail.php?writer_id=14154B.

ALLEN, (Mary) Darina; Irish cookery writer; *Founder and Principal, Ballymaloe Cookery School*; b. 30 July 1948, Dublin; d. of William and Elizabeth O'Connell; m. Timothy Allen; two s. two d. *Education:* Dominican Convent, Wicklow and Dublin Coll. of Catering. *Career:* Cook at Ballymaloe House Hotel 1968–83; Founder and Prin. Ballymaloe Cookery School (with Timothy Allen) 1983; Presenter, Radio Telefís Eireann (RTE) Simply Delicious Series on TV 1989–96; featured in BBC Hot Chefs Series 1992; columnist, The Irish Examiner; responsible for setting up Ireland's first Farmers' Markets; mem. Bd BIM (Irish Sea Fisheries Bd) 1989; mem. Int. Asscn of Culinary Professionals (IACP), Eurotoques; Certified Teacher, Culinary Professional and Food Professional, IACP. *Television:* A Year at Ballymaloe Cookery School (26-part series for Carlton Food Network) 1998, Ballymaloe Cookery School (RTE) 2002; guest appearances on numerous TV shows, including judging BBC's Masterchef and Junior Masterchef, Food and Drink Show, The Holiday Programme, Wish You Were Here, Good Morning America, NBC Weekend Today Show. *Publications:* Simply Delicious (series of five titles) 1989–92, Darina Allen's Simply Delicious Recipes 1992, Simply Delicious Versatile Vegetables 1994, Irish Traditional Cooking 1995, A Year at Ballymaloe Cookery School 1997, Festive Food of Ireland 2001, Darina Allen's Simply Delicious Suppers 2001, Ballymaloe Cookery Course 2001, Healthy Gluten-Free Eating (co-author); contribs to Sainsburys Magazine, Irish Times, BBC Good Food. *Honours:* Veuve Clicquot Irish Businesswoman of the Year Award 2001. *Literary Agent:* c/o Jacqueline Korn, David Higham Associates, 5–8 Lower John Street, Golden Square, London, W1F 9HA, England. *Telephone:* (20) 7434-5900. *Fax:* (20) 7437-1072. *E-mail:* dha@ davidhigham.co.uk. *Website:* www.davidhigham.co.uk. *Address:* Ballymaloe Cookery School, Shanagarry, Middleton, Co. Cork, Ireland (office). *Telephone:* (21) 4646785 (office). *Fax:* (21) 4646909 (office). . *Website:* www.cookingisfun.ie (office).

ALLEN, Rev. Diogenes, BA, BD, MA, PhD; American academic and writer; *Professor Emeritus, Princeton Theological Seminary*; b. 17 Oct. 1932, Lexington, KY; m. Jane Mary Billing 1958, three s. one d. *Education:* Univ. of Kentucky, Princeton Univ., Univ. of Oxford, Yale Univ. *Career:* ordained, Presbyterian Church 1959; Pastor, Windham Presbyterian Church, NH 1958–61; Asst Prof. 1964–66, Assoc. Prof. 1966–67, York Univ., Toronto; Assoc. Prof. 1967–74, Prof. of Philosophy 1974–81, Chair Dept of Theology 1977–79, 1988–91, Stuart Prof. of Philosophy 1981–2002, Prof. Emeritus 2002–, Princeton Theological Seminary; ordained deacon and priest, Episcopal Church, USA 2002; currently Priest Assoc. All Saints Church, Princeton, NJ; Fellow St Deiniol's Library, Hawarden, N Wales 2003; mem. American Philosophical Asscn, American Theological Soc., American Weil Soc. (co-founder and exec. board mem.), Asscn étude pensées S. Weil, Canadian Philosophical Asscn, Leibniz Gesellschaft, Soc. of Christian Philosophers, American Acad. of Religion. *Publications:* Leibniz' Theodicy (ed.) 1966, The Reasonableness of Faith 1968, Finding Our Father (aka The Path of Perfect Love) 1974, Between Two Worlds (aka Temptation) 1977, Traces of God in a Frequently Hostile World 1981, Three Outsiders: Pascal, Kierkegaard and Simone Weil 1983, Mechanical Explanations and the Ultimate Origin of the Universe According to Leibniz 1983, Philosophy for Understanding Theology 1985, Love: Christian Romance, Marriage and Friendship 1987, Christian Relief in a Postmodern World: The Full Wealth of Conviction 1989, Quest: The Search for Meaning Through Christ 1990, Primary Reading in Philosophy for Understanding Theology (ed. with Eric Springsted) 1992, Nature, Spirit, and

Community: Issues in the Thought of Yesterday for Help Today (with Eric Springsted) 1997, Spiritual Theology 1997, Steps Along the Way 2002. *Honours:* Rhodes Scholar 1955–57, 1963–64, Rockefeller Doctoral Fellow 1962–64, Asscn of Theological Schools Research Fellowship 1975–76, Center of Theological Inquiry Research Fellowship 1985–86, 1994–95, Pew Evangelical Scholarship 1991–92, John Templeton Awards in Science and Theology 1992, 1993, and Prize for Best Courses in Science and Religion 1995. *Address:* c/o Princeton Theological Seminary, PO Box 821, Princeton, NJ 08542-0803, USA.

ALLEN, Edward Hathaway, MA, PhD; American writer and poet; b. 20 Oct. 1948, New Haven, CT. *Education:* Iowa Writers' Workshop on Poetry, Ohio Univ. *Career:* Asst Prof., Rhodes College, Memphis, TN 1989–91; mem. Acad. of American Poets, Associated Writing Programs, MLA, Poets and Writers, Writers' Guild of America. *Publications:* fiction: Straight Through the Night 1989, Mustang Sally 1992; contrib. to newspapers and periodicals.

ALLEN, John (see Perry, Ritchie)

ALLEN, Judy; British writer; b. 8 July 1941, Old Sarum, Wilts.; d. of the late Maj. Jack Turner Allen and of Janet Marion Beall. *Education:* privately. *Career:* writer 1976–; dramatized The Secret Garden (by Frances Hodgson-Burnett) for BBC Radio 5, Tom's Midnight Garden, The River. *Radio plays:* Survival, The Sailor's Return, Squatter's Rights, Unicorn Calling. *Publications include:* adult fiction: December Flower (Christopher Award, USA for TV version 1987) 1982, Bag and Baggage 1988, The Book of the Dragon, Wildlife in the Country 1995, Wildlife in the City 1999; jr fiction: Auntie Billie's Greatest Invention, Seven Weird Days at Number 31, Rainforest, What is a Wall, After All?, The Most Brilliant Trick Ever, Five Weird Days at Aunt Carly's, Frogs and Toads, Something Rare and Special 1985, Travelling Hopefully 1987, Awaiting Developments (Whitbread Children's Novel Award 1988, Friends of the Earth Earthworm Award 1989) 1988, Stones of the Moon, Lord of the Dance, Between the Moon and the Rock, Something Rare and Special, The Blue Death, The Last Green Book on Earth, The Spring on the Mountain, The Burning, Storm-Voice, The Dream Thing, Anthology for the Earth, Animals at Risk series (Eagle, Panda, Tiger, Elephant, Seal, Whale), City Farm series (The Great Pig Sprint, The Cheap Sheep Shock, The Dim Thin Ducks, The Long Loan Llama) 1990, Endangered Species series 1991–92, Between the Moon and the Rock 1992, Highfliers series (Paris Quest, Sydney Quest, Spanish Quest, Amsterdam Quest, New York Quest, Highland Quest) 1996, Up the Garden Path series (Are you a Ladybird?, Are You a Butterfly?, Are You a Bee?, Are You an Ant?, Are You a Snail?, Are You a Spider?, Are You a Dragonfly?, Are You a Grasshopper?) 1999–2002; non-fiction: The Last Green Book on Earth 1994; guide books: London Arts Guide (Best Specialist Guidebook Award, London Tourist Bd) 1984, The Guide to London by Bus and Tube 1987, London Docklands Street Atlas and Guide 1988; other: The Diary of Minnie Gorrie (abridgement for BBC Radio 4). *Honours:* Washington State Children's Choice Award 1995. *Address:* c/o Laurence Fitch Ltd, 483 Southbank House, Black Prince Road, Albert Embankment, London, SE1 7SJ; c/o Rogers, Coleridge & White, 20 Powis Mews, London, W11 1JN, England. *Telephone:* (20) 7735-8171 (Fitch); (20) 7221-3717 (Rogers, Coleridge & White). *E-mail:* contactjudyallen@beeb.net (office). *Website:* www.judyallen .co.uk (office).

ALLEN, Paula Gunn, BA, MFA, PhD; American writer, poet and university lecturer; b. 1939, Cubero, NM. *Education:* Colorado's Women's Coll., Univ. of Oregon, Univ. of New Mexico. *Career:* fmr teacher DeAnza Community Coll., Univ. of New Mexico; postdoctoral fellowships at UCLA, Univ. of California at Berkeley; fmr Assoc. Fellow Stanford Humanities Inst.; fmr lecturer Fort Lewis Coll., Durango, CO, Coll. of San Mateo, San Diego State Univ., Univ. of New Mexico at Albuquerque; fmr Dir Native American Studies Program, San Francisco State Univ.; fmr Prof. of Native American and Ethnic Studies, Univ. of California at Berkeley; Prof. of English, Creative Writing and American Indian Studies, Univ. of California at Los Angeles –1999. *Publications:* The Blind Lion 1974, Sipapu: A Cultural Perspective 1975, Coyote's Daylight Trip 1978, A Cannon Between My Knees 1981, From the Center: A Folio of Native American Art and Poetry (ed.) 1981, Shadow Country 1982, Studies of American Indian Literature: Critical Essays and Course Designs (ed.) 1983, The Woman Who Owned the Shadows 1983, The Sacred Hoop: Recovering the Feminine in American Indian Traditions (essays) 1986, Skins and Bones 1988, Spider Woman's Granddaughters: Traditional Tales and Contemporary Writing by Native American Women (ed.) 1989, Grandmothers of the Light: A Medicine Woman's Sourcebook 1991, Columbus and Beyond 1992, Voice of the Turtle 1994. *Honours:* American Book Award 1990, Ford Foundation grant, Nat. Endowment for the Arts Award. *Address:* c/o Diane Cleaver Inc., 55 Fifth Avenue, 15th Floor, New York, NY 10003, USA.

ALLEN, Roberta L.; American writer and artist; b. 6 Oct. 1945, New York; d. of Sol Allen and Jeanette Allen (née Waldner). *Education:* Fashion Inst. of Tech., New York. *Career:* Lecturer, Corcoran School of Art 1975, Kutztown State Coll., Pa 1979; Instructor in Creative Writing, Parsons School of Design 1986, The Writer's Voice 1992–97, The New School 1993–2006, School of Continuing Educ., New York Univ. 1993–2000, Columbia Univ. School of the Arts 1998–99; Tennessee Williams Fellow in Creative Writing, Univ. of the South, Sewanee, TN 1998; Fellow, Eugene Long Coll., The New School 2000. *Solo exhibitions include:* Galerie 845, Amsterdam, Netherlands 1967, John Weber Gallery, New York 1974, 1977, 1979, Galerie Maier-Hahn, Düsseldorf, Germany 1977, Galleria Primo Piano, Italy 1981, Galerie Walter Storms,

Munich, Germany 1981, PSI Museums, New York 1977, 1981, Perth Inst. of Contemporary Arts, Australia 1989, Art Resources Transfer, New York 2001, State Univ. of New York, Binghamton, NY 2001, New Arts Program, Kutztown, Pa 2001. *Publications include:* Pointless Arrows 1976, Possibilities 1977, The Traveling Woman 1986, The Daughter 1992, Pointless Acts 1976, Amazon Dream 1993, Certain People 1997, Fast Fiction 1997, The Dreaming Girl 2000, The Playful Way to Serious Writing 2002, The Playful Way to Knowing Yourself 2003. *Honours:* MacDowell Colony Residency 1971, 1972, Ossabaw Island Project Residency 1972, Creative Artists Public Service Grant 1978–79, Yaddo Residency 1983, 1987, 1993, LINE (NEA and NYS Council) Grant 1985, Virginia Center for Creative Arts Residency 1985, 1994, 2005, Artist-in-Residence Fellowship, Art Gallery of Western Australia, Perth 1989. *Address:* 5 West 16th Street, New York, NY 10011, USA. *Telephone:* (212) 675-0111. *E-mail:* roall@aol.com. *Website:* www.robertaallen.com.

ALLEN, William L.; American editor and executive; b. 28 Dec. 1940, Tyler, TX. *Education:* Georgia Tech., Louisiana State Univ. *Career:* served in US army as lieutenant late 1960s, ran several military newspapers; became freelance photographer; joined Nat. Geographic magazine 1969, Illustrations Ed. 1985–92, Sr Asst Ed., then Assoc. Ed. 1992–95; Ed.-in-Chief, Nat. Geographic Soc. 1995– (also bd mem.); bd mem. Nat. Geographic Editiorial Foundation, Nat. Space Biomedical Research Inst., Inst. of Nautical Archaeology, Teton Science School, Nat. Council of the World Wildlife Fund, Council on Foreign Relations; mem. Cosmos Club. *Honours:* Nat. Magazine Award 2000. *Address:* National Geographic, 1145 17th Street NW, Washington, DC 20036-4688, USA (office). *Website:* www.nationalgeographic.com (office).

ALLEN, Woody; American actor, writer, producer and director; b. (Allen Stewart Konigsberg), 1 Dec. 1935, Brooklyn, NY; s. of the late Martin Konigsberg and of Nettie Konigsberg (née Cherry); m. 1st Harlene Rosen (divorced); m. 2nd Louise Lasser 1966 (divorced 1969); m. 3rd Soon-Yi Previn 1997; two adopted d.; one s. with Mia Farrow. *Education:* City Coll. of New York and New York Univ. *Career:* made his debut as a performer in 1961 at the Duplex in Greenwich Village; has performed in a variety of nightclubs across the USA; produced the play Don't Drink the Water, Morosco Theater 1966, Broadhurst Theatre 1969; made his Broadway debut as Allan Felix in Play it Again, Sam, which he also wrote; during the 1950s wrote for TV performers Herb Shriner 1953, Sid Caesar 1957, Art Carney 1958–59, Jack Parr and Carol Channing, also wrote for the Tonight Show and the Gary Moore Show. *Films include:* What's New Pussycat? 1965, Casino Royale 1967, What's Up, Tiger Lily? 1967, Take the Money and Run 1969, Bananas 1971, Everything You Always Wanted to Know About Sex 1972, Play it Again, Sam 1972, Sleeper 1973, Love and Death 1976, The Front 1976, Annie Hall (Academy Awards for Best Dir and Best Writer) 1977, Interiors 1978, Manhattan 1979, Stardust Memories 1980, A Midsummer Night's Sex Comedy 1982, Zelig 1983, Broadway Danny Rose 1984, The Purple Rose of Cairo 1985, Hannah and Her Sisters 1985, Radio Days 1987, September 1987, Another Woman 1988, Oedipus Wrecks 1989, Crimes and Misdemeanors 1989, Alice 1990, Scenes from a Mall, Shadows and Fog 1991, Husbands and Wives 1992, Manhattan Murder Mystery 1993, Bullets Over Broadway 1995, Mighty Aphrodite 1995, Everybody Says I Love You 1996, Deconstructing Harry 1997, Celebrity 1998, Antz (voice only) 1998, Wild Man Blues 1998, Stuck on You 1998, Company Men 1999, Sweet and Lowdown 1999, Small Town Crooks 2000, The Curse of the Jade Scorpion 2001, Hail Sid Caesar! 2001, Hollywood Ending 2002, Anything Else 2003, Melinda and Melinda 2004, Match Point 2005, Scoop 2006. *Television:* Sounds from a Town I Love 2001. *Plays written include:* Don't Drink the Water 1966, The Floating Lightbulb 1981, Death Defying Acts (one act) 1995. *Publications:* Getting Even 1971, Without Feathers 1975, Side Effects 1980, The Complete Prose 1994, Telling Tales (contrib. to charity anthology) 2004, Mere Anarchy 2007; contribs to Playboy and New Yorker. *Honours:* Dr hc (Universitat Pompeu Fabra, Spain) 2007; D.W. Griffith Award 1996, San Sebastian Film Festival Donostia Prize 2004. *Address:* 930 Fifth Avenue, New York, NY 10021, USA.

ALLENDE, Isabel; Chilean (b. Peruvian) writer; b. 2 Aug. 1942, Lima, Peru; d. of Tomás Allende and Francisca Llona Barros; m. 1st Miguel Frias 1962; one s. one d.; m. 2nd William Gordon 1988. *Career:* journalist, Paula women's magazine 1967–74, Mampato children's magazine 1969–74, TV shows and film documentaries 1970–74, El Nacional newspaper, Caracas, Venezuela 1975–84; taught literature at Montclair State Coll., NJ 1985, Univ. of Virginia, Charlottesville 1988, Univ. of California, Berkeley 1989; Goodwill Amb. for Hans Christian Andersen Bicentenary 2004; lecture tours in USA and Europe, speech tours in univs and cols, numerous literature workshops; mem. Academia de Artes y Ciencias, Puerto Rico 1995, Academia de la Lengua, Chile 1989, American Acad. of Arts and Letters 2004. *Plays:* El Embajador 1971, La balada del medio pelo 1973, Los siete espejos 1974. *Publications:* La casa de los espíritus (novel, trans. as The House of the Spirits) 1982, La gorda de porcelana (juvenile short stories) 1983, De amor y de sombra (novel, trans. as Of Love and Shadows) 1984, Cuentos de Eva Luna (short stories, trans. as Stories of Eva Luna) 1989, El plan infinito (novel, trans. as The Infinite Plan) 1991, Paula (memoir) 1994, Afrodita (trans. as Aphrodite) 1998, Hija de la fortuna (novel, trans. as Daughter of Fortune) 1999, Retrato en sepia (novel, trans. as Portrait in Sepia) 2000, La ciudad de las bestias (juvenile novel, trans. as City of the Beasts) 2002, Mi país inventado (memoir, trans. as My Invented Country) (Latino Literacy Now Award for Best Biography 2004) 2003, El reino del dragón de oro (juvenile novel, trans. as Kingdom of the Golden Dragon) (Latino Literacy Now Award for Best Young Adult Fiction 2004) 2003, El Zorro (novel) 2005, El Bosque de los Pigmeos (juvenile novel, trans. as Forest of the Pygmies) 2005, Inés del alma mía (novel, trans. as Inés of My Soul) 2006. *Honours:* Hon. Citizen of Austin, Tex. USA 1995; Hon. Prof. of Literature, Univ. of Chile 1991; Hon. mem. Acad. of Devt and Peace, Austria 2000; Chevalier, Ordre des Arts et Lettres 1994, Condecoracion Gabriela Mistral (Chile) 1994; Hon. DLitt (New York State Univ.) 1991, (Bates Coll., USA) 1994, (Dominican Coll., USA) 1994, (Columbia Coll., USA) 1996; Hon. DHumLitt (Florida Atlantic Univ.) 1996; Dr hc (Lawrence Univ., USA) 2000, (Mills Coll., USA) 2000, (Illinois Wesleyan Univ.) 2002; Best Novel of the Year (Chile) 1983, Panorama Literario Award (Chile) 1983, Author of the Year (Germany) 1984, Book of the Year (Germany) 1984, Grand Prix d'Evasion Award (France) 1984, Point de Mire Award, Belgian Radio and TV 1984, Quality Paperback Book Club New Voice (USA) 1986, Premio Literario Colima Award (Mexico) 1986, XV Premio Internazionale I Migliori Dell'Anno (Italy) 1987, Mulheres Best Foreign Novel Award (Portugal) 1987, Quimera Libros (Chile) 1987, Book of the Year (Switzerland) 1987, Library Journal's Best Book (USA) 1988, Before Columbus Foundation Award (USA) 1988, Best Novel (Mexico) 1985, Author of the Year (Germany) 1986, Freedom to Write Pen Club (USA) 1991, XLI Bancarella Literary Award (Italy) 1993, Ind. Foreign Fiction Award (UK) 1993, Brandeis Univ. Major Book Collection Award (USA) 1993, Marin Women's Hall of Fame (USA) 1994, Feminist of the Year Award, The Feminist Majority Foundation (USA) 1994, Read About Me Literary Award (USA) 1996, Critics' Choice Award (USA) 1996, Books to Remember Award, American Library Asscn 1996, Gift of HOPE Award, HOPE Educ. and Leadership Fund (USA) 1996, Harold Washington Literary Award, City of Chicago 1996, Malaparte Award, Amici di Capri (Italy) 1998, Donna Città Di Roma Literary Award, Italy 1998, Dorothy and Lillian Gish Prize (USA) 1998, Sara Lee Frontrunner Award (USA) 1998, GEMS Women of the Year Award (USA) 1999, Donna Dell'Anno 1999 Award (Italy) 1999, Books to Remember, The New York Public Library WILLA Literary Award 2000, Excellence in Int. Literature and Arts Award (USA) 2002, The Celebration of Books Amb. Award (USA) 2002, Int. Women's Forum Award (Mexico) 2002, Nopal Award, Cal Poly Pomona (USA) 2003, Cyril Magnin Lifetime Achievement Award (USA) 2003, Premios Iberoamericano de Letrasjose Donoso (Chile) 2003, Premio Personalidad Distinguida, Universdidad del Pacifico (Chile) 2004, Commonwealth Award of Distinguished Service for Literature (USA) 2004. *Literary Agent:* Carmen Balcells, Diagonal 580, Barcelona 21, Spain. *Address:* 116 Caledonia Street, Sausalito, CA 94965, USA. *Fax:* (415) 332-4149. *Website:* www.isabelallende.com.

ALLISON, Dorothy, BA, MA; American writer and poet; b. 11 April 1949, Greenville, SC. *Education:* Florida Presbyterian College, New School for Social Research. *Career:* writer in residence Columbia Coll., Chicago 2007, Emory Coll., Atlanta (2008); mem. Authors' Guild, PEN, Writers' Union. *Publications:* Fiction: Trash, 1988; Bastard Out of Carolina, 1992; Cavedweller, 1998. Poetry: The Women Who Hate Me, 1983. Non-Fiction: Skin: Talking About Sex, Class and Literature, 1994; Two or Three Things I Know for Sure, 1995. *Honours:* Lambda Literary Awards for Best Small Press Book and Best Lesbian Book, 1989. *Address:* PO Box 136, Guerneville, CA 95446, USA. *E-mail:* rydab@aol.com (office). *Website:* www.dorothyallison.net (office).

ALLISON, John, BMus, PhD, ARCO; British editor and critic; *Editor, Opera;* b. 20 May 1965, Cape Town, S Africa; s. of David Allison and Adele Allison; m. Nicole Galgut. *Education:* Univ. of Cape Town. *Career:* fmr organist at Cape Town Cathedral; music critic for The Times; Ed. Opera magazine 2000–. *Publications:* Edward Elgar: Sacred Music 1994, Mitchell Beazley Pocket Guide to Opera 1998; contrib. to Opera News, BBC Music Magazine, Classic FM Magazine, Financial Times, London Evening Standard, The Observer, The Australian, New Grove Dictionary of Music and Musicians, The New Penguin Opera Guide, Music and Words—Essays in Honour of Andrew Porter. *Address:* Opera Magazine, 36 Black Lion Lane, London, W6 9BE, England (office). *E-mail:* editor@operamag.clara.co.uk (office). *Website:* www.opera.co.uk (office).

ALLOTT, Miriam, MA, PhD; British academic and writer; b. 16 June 1920, London, England; m. Kenneth Allott 1951 (died 1973). *Education:* Univ. of Liverpool. *Career:* Lecturer to Reader in English Literature 1948–73, Andrew Cecil Bradley Prof. of Modern English Literature 1973–81, Univ. of Liverpool; Prof. of English 1981–85, Prof. Emerita 1985–, Birkbeck Coll., Univ. of London; mem. English Asscn (exec. cttee). *Publications:* The Art of Graham Greene (with Kenneth Allott) 1951, Novelists on the Novel 1959, The Complete Poems of Matthew Arnold (ed. with Kenneth Allott) 1965, The Complete Poems of John Keats (ed.) 1970, Matthew Arnold (with R. H. Super) 1986. *Honours:* William Noble Fellowship in English Literature 1946–48, Hon. Sr Fellow Univ. of Liverpool. *Address:* c/o School of English & Humanities, Birkbeck College, University of London, Malet Street, London, WC1E 7HX, England.

ALLOUACHE, Merzak; Algerian film director and writer; b. 6 Oct. 1944, Algiers; s. of Omar Allouache and Fatma Allouache; m. Lazib Anissa 1962; one d. *Career:* worked in Nat. Inst. of Cinema, Algiers, later in Inst. of Film, Paris; after return to Algeria worked as Adviser, Ministry of Culture. *Films include:* Our Agrarian Revolution (documentary) 1973, Omar Gatlato, Les aventures d'un héros, L'homme qui regardait les fenêtres 1982, Bab El-Oued City 1994, Lumiére et Compagnie 1995, Salut Cousin! 1996, Dans la décapotable 1996, Alger–Beyrouth: Pour Mémoire 1998, Pepe Carvalho: La Solitude du Manager (TV) 1999, À bicyclette (TV) 2001, L'Autre Monde 2001, Chouchou 2003. *Publications:* Bab El-Oued (novel) 1994. *Honours:* Silver Prize, Moscow Festival; Tanit D'Or Prize, Carthage 1979. *Address:* Cité des Asphodèles, Bt D15, 183 Ben Aknoun, Algiers, Algeria. *Telephone:* 79 33 60.

ALMODÓVAR, Pedro; Spanish film director and screenwriter; b. 25 Sept. 1951, Calzada de Calatrava, Ciudad Real, Castilla La Mancha. *Career:* fronted a rock band; worked at Telefónica for ten years; started career with full-length super-8 films; made 16mm short films 1974–83. *Films as writer and director:* Film político 1974, Dos putas, o historia de amor que termina en boda 1974, El Sueño, o la estrella 1975, Homenaje 1975, La caída de Sódoma 1975, Blancor 1975, Sea caritativo 1976, Muerte en la carretera 1976, Sexo va, sexo viene 1977, Salomé 1978, ¡Folle... folle... fólleme Tim! 1978, Pepe, Luci, Bom y otras chicas del montón 1980, Laberinto de pasiones 1982, Entre tinieblas 1983, ¿Qué he hecho yo para merecer esto? 1985, Matador 1986, La ley del deseo 1987, Mujeres al borde de un ataque de nervios (Felix Award) 1988, ¡Atame! 1990, Tacones lejanos 1991, Kika 1993, La flor de mi secreto 1995, Carne trémula (Best Foreign Film Nat. Bd of Review 2006, Goya Award for Best Film, Best Director 2007, Best Foreign Film, London Film Critics' Circle Awards 2007) 2006. *Films as producer:* Laberinto de pasiones 1982, Mujeres al borde de un ataque de nervios 1988, Acción mutante 1993, Mi nombre es sombra (assoc. producer) 1996, Cuernos de espuma 1996, El Espinazo del diablo 2001, Mi vida sin mí (exec. producer) 2003, La Mala educación 2004. *Publications:* Fuego en las entrañas 1982, The Patty Diphusa Stories and Other Writings 1992. *Honours:* Asturias Prize 2006. *Address:* c/o El Deseo SA, Ruiz Perelló 15, Madrid 28028, Spain; Miramax Films, 18 E 48th Street, New York, NY 10017, USA.

ALMOG, Ruth; Israeli novelist and journalist; b. 1936, Petach Tikva; two d. *Education:* Tel-Aviv Univ. *Career:* taught in schools and Depts of Philosophy and Film, Tel-Aviv Univ.; Deputy Ed. Literary Section, Ha'aretz daily newspaper 1967–; Writer-in-Residence and Tutor in Creative Writing, Hebrew Univ. of Jerusalem; also taught creative writing at Ben-Gurion Univ., Beersheba. *Publications:* short stories: Hasdei Ha-Laila Shel Margerita 1969, Aharei Tu Bi-Shvat 1979, Nashim 1986, Tikun Omanuti (novella and stories) 1993, Kol Ha-Osher Ha-Mufraz Haze 2003; novels: Be-Eretz Gezirah 1971, Mavet Ba-Geshem 1982, Shorshei Avir (Brenner Prize 1989) 1987, Meahev Mushlam (with Esther Ettinger) 1995, Estelina Ahuvati (with Esther Ettinger) 2002; juvenile: Naphy Nasich Ha-Karnafim 1979, Gilgil 1986, Tzoanim Ba-Pardes 1986, Kadur Ha-Kesef 1986, Hasibor 1991, Ahavati Ha-Rishonah 1992, Gilgil Rotza Kelev 1998, Hamasa Sheli Im Alex (trans. as My Journey with Alex) (Yad Vashem Prize, Andersen Honor Citation) 1998, Balut Ha-pele shel Kamila 1999, Od Chibuk Echad 2003; other: Et Ha-Zar Ve-Ha-Oyev 1980, Ha-Agam Ha-pnimi 2000, All This Exaggerated Happiness 2001, Love, Nostalgia 2005. *Honours:* Yad Vashem Prize, Agnon Prize 2001, Newman Prize 2004, Prime Minister's Prize, German Gerty Spies Prize for Literature, Rheinland-Pfalz 2004. *Address:* 4 Haneriim Street, Tel-Aviv 64356, Israel (home). *Telephone:* (3) 5282451 (home). *E-mail:* ruth66@bezegint.net (home).

ALMOND, David, BA; British writer; b. 15 May 1951, Felling-on-Tyne, England; pnr; one d. *Education:* Univ. of East Anglia. *Career:* fmr teacher; Ed., Panurge magazine 1987–93. *Plays:* Wild Girl Wild Boy 2001, Skellig 2002, My Dad's a Birdman 2003. *Publications:* short story collections: Sleepless Nights 1985, A Kind of Heaven 1997, Counting Stars 2000; juvenile fiction: Skellig (Carnegie Medal 1998, Whitbread Children's Book of the Year 1998) 1998, Kit's Wilderness (Smarties Prize Silver Medal 2000) 1999, Heaven Eyes 2000, Secret Heart 2001, Where Your Wings Were 2002, The Fire-Eaters (Nestlé Smarties Prize Gold Award 2003, Whitbread Children's Book of the Year 2003) 2003, Clay 2005; picture book: Kate, the Cat and the Moon (with Stephen Lambert, illustrator) 2004. *Honours:* Michael L. Printz Award 2001, Boston Globe-Horn Book Award 2004. *Address:* Ravenside, Humshaugh, Hexham,, Northumberland, NE46 4AA (home); c/o Hodder Children's Books, Publicity Department, 338 Euston Road, London, NW1 3BH, England (office). *Telephone:* (1434) 689577. *E-mail:* dalmond@lineone.net. *Website:* www.davidalmond.com.

ALPERT, Cathryn, BA, MA, PhD; American writer; b. 4 Jan. 1952, Santa Monica, CA; m. Marco Alpert 1982; two s. three d. *Education:* Univ. of California at Los Angeles. *Career:* Asst Prof., Centre Coll. 1980–84; writer 1984–; mem. San Francisco Literary Soc. (bd dir). *Publications:* Rocket City – MacMurray and Beck 1995, Rocket City – Vintage Contemporaries 1996; contrib. to Puerto del Sol, Thema, Wittenberg Review. *Honours:* second place O. Henry Festival Short Story Contest 1989, hon. mention Raymond Carver Short Story Contest 1989, first place Amaranth Review Short Fiction Contest 1991, third place CPU Short Story Contest 1991. *Address:* 555 Bryant Street, Suite 350, Palo Alto, CA 94301, USA.

ALPHONSO-KARKALA, John B., BA, MA, PhD; Indian writer, poet and academic; b. 30 May 1923, South Kanara, Mysore State; m. Leena Anneli Hakalehto 1964, three c. *Education:* Mumbai Univ., Univ. of London, Columbia Univ. *Career:* Visiting Lecturer, City Coll., CUNY 1963; Asst Prof. 1964–65, Assoc. Prof. 1965–68, Prof. of Literature 1969–, SUNY at New Paltz; Visiting Prof., Columbia Univ. 1969–70; mem. American Oriental Soc., Asscn for Asian Studies, Int. Congress of Comparative Literature, Int. Congress of Orientalists, MLA of America. *Publications:* Indo-English Literature in the Nineteenth Century 1970, Anthology of Indian Literature (ed., aka Ages of

Rishis, Buddha, Acharyas, Bhaktas and Mahatma) 1971, Bibliography of Indo-English Literature, 1800–1966 (ed. with Leena Karkala) 1974, Comparative World Literature: Seven Essays 1974, Passions of the Nightless Night (novel) 1974, Jawaharlal Nehru: A Literary Portrait 1975, When Night Falls (poems) 1980, Vedic Vision (ed.) 1980, Joys of Jayanagara (novel) 1981, Indo-English Literature: Essays (with Leena Karkala) 1994.

ALSTON, William Payne, BM, PhD; American academic and writer; b. 29 Nov. 1921, Shreveport, LA; m. 1st Mary Frances Collins 1943 (divorced); one d.; m. 2nd Valerie Tibbetts Barnes 1963. *Education:* Centenary College, Univ. of Chicago. *Career:* Instructor 1949–52, Asst Prof. 1952–56, Assoc. Prof. 1956–61, Prof. 1961–71, Acting Chair. 1961–64, Dir of Graduate Studies 1966–71, Dept of Philosophy, Univ. of Michigan; Visiting Lecturer Harvard Univ. 1955–56; Fellow Centre for Advanced Studies in Behavioural Sciences 1965–66; Prof. of Philosophy Douglass College Rutgers Univ. 1971–76, Univ. of Illinois at Urbana-Champaign 1976–80, Syracuse Univ. 1980–2000, Prof. Emer. 2000–; Austin Fagothey Visiting Prof. of Philosophy, Santa Clara Univ. 1991; Fellow American Acad. of Arts and Sciences; mem. Soc. for Philosophy and Psychology, pres. 1976–77; American Philosophical Asscn, pres. of Central Division 1978–79; Soc. of Christian Philosophers, pres. 1978–81; American Theological Soc.; Soc. for Philosophy of Religion. *Publications:* Religious Belief and Philosophical Thought 1963, Readings in Twentieth Century Philosophy (with G. Nakhnikian) 1963, The Philosophy of Language 1964, The Problems of Philosophy: Introductory Readings (with R. B. Brandt) 1967, Divine Nature and Human Language 1989, Epistemic Justification 1989, Perceiving God 1991, The Reliability of Sense Perception 1993, A Realist Conception of Truth 1996, Illocutionary Acts and Sentence Meaning 2000, A Sensible Metaphysical Realism 2001; ed.: Philosophical Research Archives 1974–77, Faith and Philosophy 1982–90, Cornell Studies in the Philosophy of Religion 1987–; contribs to scholarly books and journals. *Honours:* DLitt Hum. hc Church Divinity School of the Pacific 1988; Chancellor's Exceptional Academic Achievement Award Syracuse University 1990. *Address:* c/o Department of Philosophy, Syracuse University, Syracuse, NY 13244, USA (office).

ALTER, Robert Bernard, BA, MA, PhD; American literary critic; *Class of 1937 Professor, University of California at Berkeley*; b. 2 April 1935, New York, NY; m. Carol Cosman 1974; three s. one d. *Education:* Columbia Coll., Harvard Univ. *Career:* instructor, Asst Prof. of English, Columbia Univ., New York 1962–66; Assoc. Prof. of Hebrew and Comparative Literature, Univ. of California, Berkeley 1967–69, Prof. of Hebrew and Comparative Literature 1969–89, Class of 1937 Prof. 1989–; mem. American Comparative Literature Asscn, Assc of Literary Scholars and Critics, Council of Scholars of the Library of Congress, American Acad. of Arts and Sciences, American Philosophical Soc. *Publications:* Rogue's Progress 1965, After the Tradition 1968, Modern Hebrew Literature 1975, Partial Magic 1975, Defenses of the Imagination 1978, Stendhal: A Biography 1979, The Art of Biblical Narrative 1981, Motives for Fiction 1984, The Art of Biblical Poetry 1985, The Invention of Hebrew Prose 1988, The Pleasures of Reading in an Ideological Age 1989, Necessary Angels 1991, The World of Biblical Literature 1992, Hebrew and Modernity 1994, Genesis: Translation and Commentary 1996, Canon and Creativity: Modern Writing and the Authority of Scripture 2000, The Five Books of Moses 2004, Imagined Cities 2005; contrib. to Commentary, New Republic, New York Times Book Review, London Review of Books, Times Literary Supplement. *Honours:* English Inst. Essay Prize 1965, Nat. Jewish Book Award for Jewish Thought 1982, Present Tense Award for Religious Thought 1986, Nat. Foundation for Jewish Culture Award for Scholarship 1995, Koret Trans. Award 2005, PEN-USA Trans. Award 2005. *Address:* 1475 Le Roy Avenue, Berkeley, CA 94708, USA (office). *Telephone:* (510) 642-6457 (office), (510) 845-2640 (home). *Fax:* (510) 841-4085 (home). *E-mail:* altcos@berkeley.edu (home).

ALTHER, Lisa, BA; American writer and academic; b. 23 July 1944, Kingsport, Tenn.; d. of John Shelton Reed and Alice Greene Reed; m. Richard Alther 1966 (divorced); one d. *Education:* Wellesley Coll., Radcliffe Coll. *Career:* editorial asst, Atheneum Publrs, New York 1967–68; freelance writer 1968–; Lecturer, St Michael's Coll., Winooski, Vt 1980–81; Prof. and Basler Chair, East Tenn. State Univ. 1999–2000. *Publications:* Kinflicks 1975, Original Sins 1980, Other Women 1984, Bedrock 1990, Birdman and the Dancer 1993, Five Minutes in Heaven 1995; contrib. to periodicals. *Literary Agent:* c/o Martha Kaplan Agency, 115 West 29th Street, New York, NY 10001, USA. *Telephone:* (423) 612-2147. *Fax:* (423) 538-8866. *E-mail:* lalther@aol.com (office).

ALTICK, Richard Daniel; American academic and writer; b. 19 Sept. 1915, Lancaster, PA; m. Helen W. Keller 1942; two d. *Education:* BA, Franklin and Marshall College, 1936; PhD, University of Pennsylvania, 1941. *Career:* Faculty, 1945, Regent's Prof. of English, 1968–82, Regent's Prof. Emeritus of English, 1982–, Ohio State University, Columbus. *Publications:* Preface to Critical Reading, 1946; The Cowden Clarkes, 1948; The Scholar Adventurers, 1950; The English Common Reader: A Social History of the Mass Reading Public, 1800–1900, 1957; The Art of Literary Research, 1963; Lives and Letters: A History of Literary Biography in England and America, 1965; Carlyle: Past and Present (ed.), 1965; Browning's Roman Murder Story (with J. F. Loucks), 1968; To Be in England, 1969; Victorian Studies in Scarlet, 1970; Browning: The Ring and the Book (ed.), 1971; Victorian People and Ideas: A Companion for the Modern Reader of Victorian Literature, 1973; The Shows of London, 1978; Paintings from Books: Art and Literature in Britain

1760–1900, 1985; Deadly Encounters: Two Victorian Sensations (in the UK as Evil Encounters), 1986; Writers, Readers and Occasions, 1989; The Presence of the Present: Topics of the Day in the Victorian Novel, 1991; Punch: The Lively Youth of a British Institution 1841–51, 1997. *Honours:* Guggenheim Fellowship, 1975. *Address:* 276 W Southington Avenue, Worthington, OH 43085, USA.

ALTON, Roger Martin; British journalist; *Editor, The Observer*; b. 20 Dec. 1947, Oxford; s. of the late Reggie Alton and of Jeanine Alton; m. (divorced); one d. *Education:* Clifton Coll., Exeter Coll., Oxford. *Career:* grad. trainee, Liverpool Post, then Gen. Reporter and Deputy Features Ed. 1969–74; Sub-Ed. News The Guardian 1974–76, Chief Sub-Ed. News 1976–81, Deputy Sports Ed. 1981–85, Arts Ed. 1985–90, Weekend Magazine Ed. 1990–93, Features Ed. 1993–96, Asst Ed. 1996–98, Ed. The Observer 1998–. *Honours:* Editor of the Year, What the Papers Say Awards 2000, GQ Editor of the Year 2005. *Address:* Office of the Editor, The Observer, 3–7 Herbal Hill, London, EC1R 5EJ, England (office). *Telephone:* (20) 7713-4744 (office). *Fax:* (20) 7873-7817 (office). *E-mail:* editor@observer.co.uk (office). *Website:* www.observer.co.uk (office).

ALUNAN, Merlie M., MA; Philippine poet; *Professor of Literature and Communication, University of the Philippines in the Visayas*; b. 1943. *Education:* Univ. of the Visayas, Cebu City, Silliman Univ. Grad. School. *Career:* Prof. of Literature and Communication Tacloban Coll., Univ. of the Philippines in the Visayas, also involved in creative writing workshops. *Publications include:* Mater Dolorosa in Two Voices (poems) (First Prize English of Home Life poetry competition), Fern Garden: Anthology of Women Writing in the South, Hearthstone Sacred Tree (poems) 1993, Kabilin: 100 Years of Negros Oriental (non-fiction) 1993, Amina Among Angels (poems) 1997. *Honours:* Palanca, Free Press, Home Life UMPIL Gawad Alagad ni Balagtas, Chancellor's Award for Excellence in Creative Work, Lillian Jerome Thornton Award for Nonfiction, Likhaan Workshop Award. *Address:* c/o University of the Philippines in the Visayas, Miagao, Iloilo 5023-A, Philippines.

ALVAREZ, Alfred (Al), BA, MA; British poet and writer; b. 5 Aug. 1929, London, England; m. 1966; two s. one d. *Education:* Oundle School, Corpus Christi Coll., Oxford. *Career:* poetry critic and Ed., Observer 1956–66; Advisory Ed., Penguin Modern European Poets 1964–76. *Publications:* The Shaping Spirit 1958, The School of Donne 1961, The New Poetry 1962, Under Pressure 1965, Beyond All This Fiddle 1968, Lost 1968, Penguin Modern Poets No. 18 1970, Apparition 1971, The Savage God 1971, Beckett 1973, Hers 1974, Autumn to Autumn and Selected Poems 1978, Hunt 1978, Life After Marriage 1982, The Biggest Game in Town 1983, Offshore 1986, Feeding the Rat 1988, Rain Forest 1988, Day of Atonement 1991, Faber Book of Modern European Poetry 1992, Night 1995, Where Did It All Go Right? 1999, Poker: Bets, Bluffs and Bad Beats 2001, New and Selected Poems 2002, The Writer's Voice 2005, Risky Business 2007; contrib. to numerous magazines and journals. *Honours:* Hon. DLitt (Univ. of East London) 1998, Hon. Fellow Corpus Christi Coll., Oxford 2001; Vachel Lindsay Prize for Poetry 1961. *Literary Agent:* Aitken Alexander Associates Ltd, 18–21 Cavaye Place, London, SW10 9PT, England. *Telephone:* (20) 7373-8672. *Fax:* (20) 7373-6002. *E-mail:* reception@aitkenalexander.co.uk. *Website:* www.aitkenalexander.co.uk.

ALVES, Miriam; Brazilian writer, poet and literary critic; b. 1952, São Paulo. *Career:* assoc. with Quilombhoge black writers group, which edits Cadernos negros anthology 1983–; employed as social worker. *Publications:* Momentos de Busca (poems) 1983, Estrelas no dedo (poems) 1985, Terramar (play), Enfim... Nos (ed, trans. as Finally... Us: Contemporary Black Brazilian Women Writers) 1995; contrib. to numerous collections of poetry and critical essays. *Address:* c/o Lynne Rienner Publishers, 1800 30th Street, Suite 314, Boulder, CO 80301, USA.

ALVI, Moniza; British poet; b. 1954, Lahore, Pakistan. *Education:* Univ. of York, Univ. of London. *Career:* school teacher; tutor at Open Coll. of the Arts and the Poetry School, London. *Publications:* poetry: Peacock Luggage (with Peter Daniels) 1992, The Country at My Shoulder 1993, A Bowl of Warm Air 1996, Carrying My Wife 2000, Souls 2002, How the Stone Found its Voice 2005; contrib. to A Dragonfly in the Sun: An Anthology of Pakistani Writing in English 1998, The Poetry Quartets: 6 2000. *Honours:* The Poetry Business Prize 1991, Cholmondeley Award 2002. *Address:* c/o Bloodaxe Books Ltd, Highgreen, Tarset, Northumberland NE48 1RP, England.

AMABILE, George, BA, MA, PhD; American academic, poet and writer; b. 29 May 1936, Jersey City, NJ. *Education:* Amherst Coll., Univ. of Minnesota, Univ. of Connecticut. *Career:* Lecturer 1963, Asst Prof. 1966–68, 1969–71, Assoc. Prof. 1972–86, Prof. of English 1987–, Univ. of Manitoba; Visiting writer-in-residence, Univ. of British Columbia 1968–69; various readings, Manitoba Theatre Centre, radio, and television; mem. League of Canadian Poets, Western Canadian Publishers' Asscn. *Publications:* Blood Ties, 1972; Open Country, 1976; Flower and Song, 1977; Ideas of Shelter, 1981; The Presence of Fire, 1982; Four of a Kind, 1994; Rumours of Paradise/Rumours of War, 1995. Contributions: many anthologies, journals and periodicals. *Honours:* Canada Council Grants, 1968, 1969, 1981, 1982, 1995, 1996; Canadian Authors' Asscn National Prize for Poetry, 1983; Third Prize, CBC National Literary Competition, 1992. *Address:* c/o University of Manitoba, Winnipeg, MB R3T 2N2, Canada. *E-mail:* gamabile@home.com.

AMADI, Elechi, BSc; Nigerian writer and fmr teacher, army officer and administrative officer; *Founder and Director, Elechi Amadi School of Creative Writing*; b. 12 May 1934, Aluu, Rivers State; s. of Chief Wonuchukwu Amadi and Enwere Amadi; m. 1st Dorah Nwonne Ohale 1957; m. 2nd Priye Iyalla 1991; four s. eight d. *Education:* Govt Coll. Umuaphia, Univ. Coll. Ibadan, Brookings Inst., USA. *Career:* worked as land surveyor 1959–60, teacher 1960–63; army officer (capt.) 1963–66, with 3rd Marine Commandos during civil war 1968–69; Prin. Asa Grammar School 1967; Perm. Sec. Rivers State Govt 1973–83, Commr of Educ. 1987–89, of Lands and Housing 1989–90; Writer-in-Residence and Lecturer, Rivers State Coll. of Educ. 1984–85, Dean of Arts 1985–86, Head Dept of Literature 1991–93; Founder and Dir Elechi Amadi School of Creative Writing 1997–; Chair. Asscn of Nigerian Authors (Rivers State Br.); Fellow, Nigerian Acad. of Educ. 2003–. *Publications:* novels: The Concubine 1966, The Great Ponds 1969, The Slave 1978, Estrangement 1986; plays: Isiburu 1973, The Road to Ibadan 1977, Dancer of Johannesburg 1978, The Woman of Calabar 2002; Sunset in Biafra (war diary) 1973; Ethics in Nigerian Culture (philosophy) 1982, Speaking and Singing (papers and poems) 2003. *Honours:* mem. Order of Fed. Repub.; Hon. DSc (Rivers State Univ. of Science and Tech. 2003; Rivers State Silver Jubilee Merit Award 1992, Ikwerre Ethnic Nationality Merit Award for Literature 1995, Rivers State Silver Jubilee Award 1992, Rivers State Productivity Award 2005. *Address:* PO Box 331, Port Harcourt (office); 7 Mbodo Road, Aluu, Kelga, Rivers State, Nigeria (home). *Telephone:* (803) 339-8036 (home). *E-mail:* amadielechi@yahoo.com (home). *Website:* www.elechiamadi.s5.com (home).

AMADIUME, Ifi, PhD; Nigerian poet, ethnographer and essayist; *Professor of Religion, Dartmouth College*; b. 1947, Kaduna. *Education:* School of Oriental and African Studies, Univ. of London, UK. *Career:* moved to UK in 1971; fmr Ed. journal, Pan-African Liberation Platform; taught African Studies, Univ. of Nigeria, SOAS; moved to USA 1993; Assoc. Prof. of Religion and African Studies, Dartmouth Coll. 1993–2000, Chair. African and African-American Studies program, Prof. of Religion 2000–. *Publications:* non-fiction: Male Daughters, Female Husbands: Gender and Sex in an African Society 1987, African Matriarchal Foundations: The Igbo Case 1987, Reinventing Africa: Matriarchy, Religion and Culture 1997, Daughters of the Goddess, Daughters of Imperialism 2000, The Politics of Memory: Truth, Healing and Social Justice (co-ed. with Abdullahi An Na'im) 2000; poetry: Passion Waves 1985, Ecstasy 1995, Circle of Love 2006, Voice Draped in Black 2006. *Address:* Department of Religion, Dartmouth College, 6036 Thornton Hall, Hanover, NH 03755, USA (office). *E-mail:* religion@dartmouth.edu (office).

AMAL, Nukila; Indonesian novelist; b. 1971, Ternate. *Education:* Bandung Tourism Acad. *Publications:* novel: Cala Ibi 2003; contrib. to Kalam. *Literary Agent:* c/o Pena Gaia Klasik, Jakarta, Indonesia Indonesia.

AMANN, Jürg, PhD; Swiss writer and dramatist; b. 2 July 1947, Winterthur. *Education:* Univs of Zürich and Berlin. *Career:* mem. Authors of Switzerland AdS, PEN. *Theatre includes:* Das Fenster, Zürich 1975, Das Ende von Venedig, Zürich 1976, Der Traum des Seiltänzers vom freien Fall, Zürich 1978, Die Korrektur, Zürich 1980, Die deutsche Nacht, St Gallen 1982, Nachgerufen, Regensburg 1984, Cologne 1995, Büchners Lenz, Staatstheater Darmstadt 1984, ÖE Vienna 1991, Gruppe 80 Vienna 2002, Ach, diese Wege sind sehr dunkel, Staatstheater Karlsruhe 1985, SE Zürich 1985, Zürich 1993, Memmingen, Graz, Stuttgart, Vienna, Bremen, Bonn, Innsbruck, Würzburg, Krefeld etc, Der Rücktritt, Schauspielhaus, Zürich 1989, Nach dem Fest, Theater Forum Stadtpark, Graz 1989, IE Teatro Due, Rome 1992, SE Zürich 1995, Zweite Liebe, Basel 1992, Liebe Frau Mermet, Ensemble Theatre, Berlin 1992, SE Zürich 1992, Jugend ohne Gott (after Horvath), Neumarkt Theater, Zürich 1993, Staatstheater Braunschweig 1994, Ich bin nicht Ihre Luise (after Nachgerufen), Theater am Sachsenring, Cologne 1995, Sit well, Edith, Zürich 1996, ÖE Vienna 1997, Ach, diese Wege sind sehr dunkel (opera, music by Roger Matscheizik), Badisches Staatstheater, Karlsruhe 1996, Reise zum Nordpol, Zürich 1997, Hotel, Sils-Maria 1997, Weil immer das Meer vor der Liebe ist. Elegie für und nach Hertha Kräftner, Vienna 2000, SE Zürich 2000, Synchronisation in Birkenwald (after Viktor E. Frankl), Odeon Theater, Vienna 2003. *Radio plays:* productions by Radio Bremen, Bayerischer Rundfunk, Südwestrundfunk, WDR, ORF, Radio DRS, RSI. *Publications:* Das Symbol Kafka 1974, Hardenberg 1978, Verirren oder das plötzliche Schweigen des Robert Walser 1978, Die Kunst des wirkungsvollen Abgangs 1979, Die Baumschule 1982, Franz Kafka 1983, Nachgerufen 1983, Ach, diese Wege sind sehr dunkel 1985, Patagonien 1985, Robert Walser 1985, Fort 1987, Aus dem Hohen Lied 1987, Nach dem Fest 1988, Tod Weidigs 1989, Der Rücktritt 1989, Der Vater der Mutter und der Vater des Vaters 1990, Der Anfang der Angst 1991, Der Lauf der Zeit 1993, Zwei oder drei Dinge 1993, Über die Jahre 1994, Und über die Liebe wäre wieder zu sprechen 1994, Robert Walser 1995, Rondo 1996, Schöne Aussicht 1997, Iphigenie oder Operation Meereswind 1998, Ikarus 1998, Golomir 1999, Kafka 2000, Am Ufer des Flusses 2001, Kein Weg nach Rom 2001, Mutter töten 2003, Sternendrift 2003, Wind und Weh 2005, Pornographische Novelle 2005, Übermalungen, Überspitzungen: Van Gogh Variationen (with Urs Amann) 2005, Zimmer zum Hof 2006. *Honours:* Ingeborg Bachmann Prize 1982, Conrad Ferdinand Meyer Prize 1983, Schiller Foundation Award 1989, Art Prize of Winterthur 1989, int. awards for radio plays 1998 1999, 2000, Schiller Prize 2001, Floriana Prize 2004. *Address:* Haus zum Spiegel, Napfgasse, 3, 8001 Zürich, Switzerland (home). *Telephone:* (44) 252-43-23 (home). *Fax:* (44) 252-43-23 (home).

AMANPOUR, Christiane, CBE, AB; British broadcasting correspondent; *Chief International Correspondent, Cable News Network (CNN)*; b. 12 Jan. 1958, London; d. of Mohammad Amanpour and Patricia Amanpour; m. James Rubin 1998; one s. *Education:* primary school in Tehran, Iran, Holy Cross Convent, UK, New Hall School, UK and Univ. of Rhode Island, USA. *Career:* radio producer/research asst, BBC Radio, London 1980–82; radio reporter, WBRU Brown Univ., USA 1981–83; electronic graphics designer, WJAR, Providence, RI 1983; Asst CNN int. assignment desk, Atlanta, GA 1983; news writer, CNN, Atlanta 1984–86; reporter/producer, CNN, New York 1987–90; Int. Corresp. CNN 1990, Sr Int. Corresp. 1994, Chief Int. Corresp. 1996–; assignments have included coverage of Gulf War 1990–91, break-up of USSR and subsequent war in Tbilisi 1991, extensive reports on conflict in Fmr Yugoslavia, Israel and Afghanistan and coverage of civil unrest and political crises in Haiti, Algeria, Somalia, Rwanda, Iran and Pakistan; Fellow, Soc. of Professional Journalists. *Honours:* several hon. degrees including Dr hc (Rhode Island); three Dupont-Columbia Awards 1986–96, nine Emmy Awards, Women, Men and Media Breakthrough Award 1991, named Woman of the Year by New York Chapter of Women in Cable and Telecommunications 1994, George Polk Award 1997, Nymphe d'Honneur, Monte Carlo Television Festival 1997, two News and Documentary Emmy Awards 1999, two George Foster Peabody Awards 1999, Univ. of Missouri Honor Award for Distinguished Service to Journalism 1999, Courage in Journalism Award, Worldfest-Houston Int. Film Festival Gold Award, Livingston Award for Young Journalists, Edward R. Murrow Award for Distinguished Achievement in Broadcast Journalism 2002, Sigma Chi Award, ranked by Forbes magazine amongst 100 Most Powerful Women (72nd) 2005, (79th) 2006. *Address:* c/o CNN International, CNN House, 19–22 Rathbone Place, London, W1P 1DF, England. *Telephone:* (20) 7637-6800.

AMBAI, PhD; Indian writer and researcher; *Director, Sound and Picture Archives for Research on Women*; b. (C. S. Lakshmi), 1944, Coimbatore, Tamil Nadu; m. Vishnu Mathur. *Education:* Jawaharlal Nehru Univ. *Career:* f. and Dir Sound and Picture Archives for Research on Women (SPARROW), Trustee. *Publications:* Andhi Malai (novel) 1966, Siragugal Muriyam (short stories) 1976, The Face Behind the Mask: Women in Tamil Literature (criticism) 1984, Veettin Moollayil Oru Samayalari (short stories) 1988, A Purple Sea: Short Stories by Ambai (in trans.) 1992; contrib. (as C. S. Lakshmi) articles and papers to Economic and Political Weekly. *Honours:* Narayanaswamy Aiyar Prize for Fiction 1961. *Address:* c/o SPARROW, B-32, Jeet Nagar, J.P. Road, Versova, Mumbai 400061, India. *Website:* www .sparrowonline.org.

AMBARTSUMOV, Yevgeniy Arshakovich, CandHistSc; Russian politician, social scientist, political analyst and journalist; *Professor, Universidad La Salle*; b. 19 Aug. 1929, Moscow; s. of Arshak Ambartsumov and Alexandra Vassilevskaia; m. Nina Ignatovskaia 1978; one s. *Education:* Moscow Inst. of Int. Relations. *Career:* with Novoye Vremya 1954–59, Problems of Peace and Socialism 1959–63; Sr Scientific Researcher, Inst. of World Econs and Int. Relations 1956–59, Head of Dept Inst. of World Int. Labour Movt 1966–69; Head of Dept, Inst. of Sociology 1969–73; Head of Dept of Politics, Inst. of Economics of World Socialist System (now Inst. of Int. Economic and Political Studies) 1973–90; Russian People's Deputy 1990–93; Chair. Foreign Affairs Cttee of Russian Supreme Soviet 1992–93; mem. State Duma (Parl.) 1993–94; mem. Presidential Council 1993–95; Amb. to Mexico, also accred to Belize 1994–99; Prof. Universidad La Salle, Mexico 1999–. *Publications include:* How Socialism Began: Russia under Lenin 1978, NEP: A Modern View 1988, Socialism: Past and Present (ed.). *Honours:* Order of Aguila Azteca con banda Mexico 1999. *Address:* Universidad La Salle, Benjamin Franklin 47, Col Condesa, Del. Cuauhtémoc, 06140 México, DF, Mexico. *Telephone:* (55) 26-14-40-79 (Mexico) (home); (495) 332-64-25 (Russia) (home).

AMBERT, Alba, BA, MEd, DEd; American writer and poet; b. 10 Oct. 1946, San Juan, PR; m. Walter McCann 1984; one d. *Education:* Univ. of Puerto Rico, Harvard Univ. *Career:* bilingual teacher, Boston Public Schools 1975–80; Asst Prof. and Dir, Bilingual Special Education Teacher Training Program, Univ. of Hartford 1980–84; Visiting Scientist, MIT 1984–85; Sr Research Scholar, Athens Coll., Greece 1985–93; writer-in-residence, Richmond Univ. 1993; mem. Authors' Guild, Writers' Union. *Publications:* fiction: Porque hay silencio 1989, A Perfect Silence 1995, The Eighth Continent and Other Stories 1997, An Inclination of Mirrors 1997; poetry: Gotas sobre el columpio 1980, The Fifth Sun 1989, Habito tu nombre 1994, At Dawn We Start Again 1997; children's books: Thunder from the Earth 1997, Why the Wild Winds Blow 1997, Face to Sky 1998. *Honours:* Ford Foundation Fellowship, 1984; Institute of Puerto Rican Literature Award, 1989; Carey McWilliams Award, 1996; Pres.'s Award, Massachusetts Asscn for Bilingual Education, 1997. *Address:* c/o Mango Publishing, PO Box 13378, London, SE27 OZN, England.

AMBROSE, David Edwin, LLB; British playwright, screenwriter and writer; b. 21 Feb. 1943, Chorley, Lancashire, England; m. Laurence Huguette Hammerli 1979. *Education:* Merton Coll., Oxford. *Career:* mem. Dramatists' Club, London. *Publications:* fiction: Seige (play, Cambridge Theatre, London) 1972, The Man Who Turned into Himself 1993, Mother of God 1995, Hollywood Lies, Superstition 1997, Coincidence 2002, A Memory of Demons 2003; many television plays and screenplays world-wide. *Honours:* Sitges Film Festival First Prize for Screenplay 1980. *Literary Agent:* William Morris Agency (UK) Ltd, 52–53 Poland Street, London, W1F 7LX, England.

AMERY, Carl (see Mayer, Christian)

AMES, Jonathan, ; American writer. *Publications:* I Pass Like Night 1989, The Extra Man 1998, What's Not to Love?: The Adventures of a Mildly Perverted Young Writer 2000, My Less Than Secret Life 2002, Wake Up, Sir! 2004; contrib. to McSweeny's, boldtype. *Address:* c/o Scribner Book Company, Simon & Schuster, 1230 Avenue of the Americas, New York, NY 10020, USA. *E-mail:* jonathanames2@aol.com. *Website:* www.jonathanames.com.

AMETTE, Jacques-Pierre, (Paul Clément); French novelist and playwright; b. 18 May 1943, Normandy. *Career:* French correspondent, New York Times, numerous French newspapers. *Plays:* Les sables mouvants 1974, Le maître-nageur 1989, Les environs de Heilbronn 1989, La Waldstein 1991, Après nous 1991, Singe 1992, Le mal du pays 1992, Passions secrètes, crimes d'avril 1993, Appassionata 1993, La clarière 1997. *Publications include:* novels: La congé 1965, Élisabeth Skerla 1966, La vie comme ça 1974, Bermuda 1977, La nuit tombante 1978, Jeunesse dans une ville normande 1981, Enquête d'hiver 1985, L'après-midi 1987, La peau du monde 1992, Province 1995, L'Homme du silence 1999, Ma vie, son oeuvre 2001, La maîtresse de Brecht (trans. as Brecht's Lover) (Prix Goncourt) 2003; other: Un voyage en province 1970, Les lumières de l'Antarctique 1973, Confessions d'un enfant gâté 1986, L'adieu à la raison 1993, Stendhal: 3 juin 1819 1994; as Paul Clément: Exit 1981, Je tue à la campagne 1982. *Honours:* Prix Roger Nimier 1986, Prix CIC du Théâtre 1992, Prix Contre-point 1997. *Address:* c/o Editions Albin Michel, 22 rue Huyghens, 75014 Paris, France. *Website:* www.albin-michel.fr.

AMICOLA, José, LèsL, PhD; Argentine academic and writer; *Professor, Universidad Nacional de la Plata;* b. 15 Feb. 1942, Buenos Aires. *Education:* Universidad de Buenos Aires, Universität Göttingen, Germany. *Career:* Prof., Universidad Nacional de la Plata 1986–; mem. Instituto Intern Literatura Iberoamericana, Pittsburgh. *Publications:* Sobre Cortázar 1969, Astrología y fascismo en la obra de Arlt 1984, Manuel Puig y la tela que atrapa al lector 1992, Dostoievski 1994, De la forma a la información 1997, Camp y postvanguardia 2000, Manuel Puig's El beso de la mujer araña (critical edn) 2002, Batalla de los géneros: Novela gótica versus novela de educación 2003, Autobiografía como Autofiguración 2007. *Honours:* Premio Banco Mercantil 1992. *Address:* Las Heras, 3794-11A, 1425 Buenos Aires, Argentina.

AMIEL, Barbara, Lady Black of Crossharbour, BA; Canadian/British journalist and writer; b. 4 Dec. 1940, Watford, Herts., UK; d. of Harold Joffre Amiel and Vera Isserles Amiel (née Barnett); m. 1st Gary Smith 1959; m. 2nd George Jonas 1974 (divorced 1979); m. 3rd David Graham 1984 (divorced 1988); m. 4th Conrad Black (now Lord Black of Crossharbour) 1992. *Education:* North London Collegiate School and Univ. of Toronto. *Career:* family moved to Canada and settled in Hamilton, Ont. 1952; joined CBC as a typist, later script asst, story ed. and TV presenter; columnist, Maclean's 1976–, The Times, UK 1986–90, The Sunday Times 1986–94, The Daily Telegraph 1994–2004; Ed. Toronto Sun 1983–85 (first female ed.), Assoc. Ed. 1985–; Vice-Pres. Editorial Hollinger Int. 1995–, Dir 1996–; mem. Bd Dirs The Spectator, Jerusalem Post, Saturday Night, Southam Inc., Hollinger Int. *Publications include:* By Person Unknown (jtly) (Mystery Writers of America Edgar Award for Best Non-Fiction 1978) 1977, Confessions (essays) (Canadian Periodical Publrs' Prize) 1980. *Honours:* Media Club of Canada Award 1976, Periodical Publishers' Asscn Award 1977, Mystery Writers of America Edgar Allan Poe Award 1978, British Press Award 1987, Women of Distinction, UK 1989. *Address:* c/o Hollinger Inc., 10 Toronto Street, Toronto, Ontario, M5C 2B7, Canada.

AMIN, Haji Khalidah Adibah; Malaysian columnist, essayist and scriptwriter; b. 19 Feb. 1936. *Education:* Univ. of Malaya. *Career:* columnist English daily newspaper 1970s. *Publications:* As I Was Passing (essays, two vols) 1976, 1978. *Honours:* Asian Journalist of the Year 1979, Southeast Asia Writer Award 1983, Esso-Gapena Award 1991. *Address:* c/o Ministry of Arts, Culture and Heritage, Menara Dato' Onn, 34th–36th Floors, POB 5–7, Putra World Trade Centre, 45 Jalan Tun Ismail, 50694 Kuala Lumpur, Malaysia.

AMĪR, Daisy al-; Iraqi short story writer, poet and novelist; b. 1935, Alexandria, Egypt. *Education:* Baghdad Univ., Inst. for Fine Arts. *Career:* Dir Iraqi Cultural Centre, Beirut 1970–85; returned to Iraq in 1985–89; spent two years in USA; returned to Beirut 1991–. *Publications include:* short story collections: Al-Balad al-Ba'īd Alladhī Tuhibb (The Distant Land She Loves) 1964, Fī Dawwāmat al-Hubb wa-al-Karāhiya (The Vortex of Love and Hate) 1978, Ala La'ihat al-Intizar (trans. as The Waiting List: An Iraqi Woman's Tales of Alienation) 1988, Amaliyyat Tajmīl li-al-Zaman (Plastic Surgery for Time) 1997; other short stories: The Eyes in the Mirror, An Andalusian Tale. *Address:* c/o Modern Middle East Literature in Translation series, University of Texas Press, POB 7819, Austin, TX 78713-7819, USA.

AMIREDJIBI, Chabua; Georgian writer, editor and politician; b. (Mzechabuk I. Amiredjibi), 18 Nov. 1921, Tbilisi; s. of Irakli Amiredjibi and Maria Nakashidze; m. Tamar Djavakhishvili 1966; four s. (one deceased) two d. *Education:* Tbilisi State Univ., A. Pushkin Tbilisi Pedagogical Inst. *Career:* as student of Tbilisi State Univ. arrested for anti-Soviet activities 1944, sentenced to 25 years' imprisonment in Gulag, released 1959; Dir Advertising-Information Bureau Goskinoprokat 1965–70; Chief Ed. Kino anthology 1970–83; Dir Mematiane documentary film studio 1983–89; mem. Parl. 1992–96; Chair. Defence Fund of Georgia 1992–96; f. PEN Centre of Georgia, Pres. 1994–97, Hon. Chair. 1998–; Publr and Ed.-in-Chief Ganakhlebuli Iveria newspaper 1999–2003; mem. Writers' Union of Georgia 1964–; mem. editorial bds of several journals and newspapers. *Screenplay:* Data Tutash-

khia 1979. *Publications:* Road (short stories) 1964, Tales for Children 1966, Data Tutashkhia (novel) 1973, Gora Mborgali (novel) 1994, King George the Excellent (novel) 2003, From the Thoughts 2007. *Honours:* Honoured Art Worker of Georgia 1987, Order of Honour 1994, Order of King Vakhtang Gorgasili (First Class) 2001; USSR State Prize 1979, Sh. Rustaveli Prize 1994. *Address:* 8/45 Tamarashvili Street, 0162 Tbilisi, Georgia (home). *E-mail:* kutsna@posta.ge (office).

AMIRSHAHI, Mahshid, MA; Iranian writer; b. 1940, Qazvin. *Education:* Univ. of Oxford. *Career:* educated in England, returned to Iran; self-exile after Islamic Revolution 1979–; Rockefeller Fellow in Middle Eastern Studies Univ. of Michigan 1990–91. *Publications:* short stories: Kusheh-ye Bonbast (The Blind Alley & Other Stories) 1966, Sar-e Bibi Khanom (Bibi Khanom's Starling & Other Stories) 1968, Badaz Ruz-e Akher (After the Last Day & Other Stories) 1969, Be-Sigheh-ye Avval Shakhas-e Mofrad (First Person Singular) 1970, An Anthology of Short Stories 1972, Tales of A Persian Teenage Girl (in trans.) 1995, Short Stories 1998; novels: Dar Hazar (At Home) 1987, Dar Safar (Away) 1995, Mothers and Daughters quartet: Abbass Khan's Wedding 1998, Dadeh Good Omen 1999, Shahrbanoo's Honey Moon 2001; other: Hezaar Bishe (miscellaneous, anthology of views, reviews and interviews in Persian, English and French) 2000. *E-mail:* mamirshahy@aol .com. *Website:* www.amirshahi.org.

AMIS, Martin Louis, BA; British writer; b. 25 Aug. 1949, Oxford; s. of the late Kingsley Amis and of Hilary Bardwell; m. 1st Antonia Phillips 1984 (divorced 1996); two s.; m. 2nd Isabel Fonseca 1998; two d. *Education:* Exeter Coll., Oxford. *Career:* Asst Ed., TLS 1971, Fiction and Poetry Ed. TLS 1974–75; Asst Literary Ed., New Statesman 1975–77, Literary Ed. 1977–79; special writer for The Observer newspaper 1980–; Prof., Centre for New Writing, Univ. of Manchester 2007–. *Publications:* fiction: The Rachel Papers (Somerset Maugham Award 1974) 1973, Dead Babies 1975, new edn as Dark Secrets 1977, Success 1978, Other People: A Mystery Story 1981, Money: A Suicide Note 1984, Einstein's Monsters (short stories) 1987, London Fields 1989, Time's Arrow, or, the Nature of the Offence 1991, God's Dice 1995, The Information 1995, Night Train 1997, Heavy Water and Other Stories 1999, Yellow Dog 2003, The Last Days of Muhammad Atta (short stories, novella, essay) 2006, House of Meetings (novella) 2006; non-fiction: My Oxford (with others) 1977, Invasion of the Space Invaders 1982, The Moronic Inferno and Other Visits to America 1986, Visiting Mrs Nabokov and Other Excursions 1993, Experience: A Memoir (James Tait Black Memorial Prize for Biography 2001) 2000, The War Against Cliché (essays and reviews 1971–2000) 2001, Koba the Dread: Laughter and Twenty Million 2002; contrib. to many publs. *Literary Agent:* Wylie Agency (UK) Ltd, 17 Bedford Square, London, WC1B 3JA, England. *Telephone:* (20) 7908-5900 (office). *Fax:* (20) 7908-5901 (office). *E-mail:* mail@wylieagency.co.uk.

AMMANITI, Niccolò; Italian writer; b. 25 Sept. 1966, Rome. *Publications:* La figlia di Siva (short story in La giungla sotto l'asfalto) 1993, Branchie! 1994, Nel nome del figlio (essays, with Massimo Ammaniti) 1995, Fango (short stories) 1996, Seratina (short story in Gioventù Cannibale, with Luisa Brancaccio) 1996, Alba tragica (short story in Tutti i denti del mostro sono perfetti) 1997, Anche il sole fa schifo 1997, Enchanted Music & Light Records (short story in Il fagiano Jonathan Livingstone, with Jaime D'Alessandro) 1998, Ti prendo e ti porto via 1999, L'amico di Jeffrey Dahmer è l'amico mio (short story in Italia odia) 2000, Io non ho paura 2001, Fa un po' male 2002, Sei il mio tesoro (short story in Crimini) 2005. *Honours:* Viareggio-Repaci Prize. *Address:* c/o Einaudi, via Biancamano 2, 10121 Turin, Italy. *Website:* www .niccoloammaniti.com.

AMOR, Anne Clark, (Anne Clark), BA; British writer; b. 4 Feb. 1933, London, England; m. 1982; one s. one d. *Education:* Birkbeck Coll., Univ. of London. *Career:* mem. Lewis Carroll Soc. (founder mem., trustee 1969–, currently Pres.), Oscar Wilde Soc. (cttee mem. 1993–). *Publications:* Beasts and Bawdy 1975, Lewis Carroll: A Biography 1979, The Real Alice 1981, Mrs Oscar Wilde: A Woman of Some Importance 1983, William Holman Hunt: The True Pre-Raphaelite 1989, Lewis Carroll: Child of the North 1995, Wonderland Come True to Alice in Lyndhurst 1996, Charles Dodgson and Alice Liddell Go to Paris 1997; editor: Letters to Skeffington Dodgson from His Father, The Carrollian; Contributions: books, periodicals, including Washington Post, Los Angeles Times, The Lady, Literary Review, Books and Bookmen, The Wildean.

ANAGNOSTAKI, Loula, LLB; Greek playwright; b. Thessaloniki; m. Yiorgos Chimonas (divorced). *Education:* Aristotle Univ., Thessaloniki. *Career:* plays staged in Italy, France, London, New York and on Cyprus TV. *Plays:* Staying Overnight (one-act play, Carolos Koun's Theatre Co. Art Theatre) 1965, The City (one-act play, Carolos Koun's Theatre Co. Art Theatre) 1965, The Parade (one-act play, Carolos Koun's Theatre Co. Art Theatre) 1965, Antonio e to menyma (Antonio or the Message) 1972, He Nike (The Victory) 1978, He Kaseta (The Cassette) 1982, Ho Ecos tou Hoplou (The Sound of the Gun) 1987, He Synanastrophe (The Gathering, Nat. Theatre of Greece) 1967, Diamantia kai Blues (Diamonds and Blues, Karezi-Kazakos theatre group) 1990, To Taxidi Makria (The Journey Far Away) 1995, The Sky is Scarlet (Contemporary Stage of the Nat. Theatre of Greece) 1998, To You Who Listen to Me (Theatre of Cyclades Street, Athens) 2003. *Address:* c/o Art Theatre Company, 25 Tzavela Str., 10681 Athens, Greece.

ANAYA, Rudolfo, MA; American author; *Professor Emeritus, University of New Mexico;* b. 30 Oct. 1937, Pastura, NM; s. of Martin Anaya and Rafaelita

Mares; m. Patricia Lawless 1966. *Education:* Albuquerque High School, Browning Business School, Univ. of New Mexico. *Career:* teacher, Albuquerque public schools 1963–70; Dir Counseling Center, Univ. of Albuquerque 1971–73; Lecturer, Univ. Anahuac, Mexico City 1974; Prof., Dept of Language and Literature, Univ. of New Mexico 1974–93, Prof. Emer. 1993–; Founder, Ed. Blue Mesa Review 1989–93; Martin Luther King, Jr/César Chávez, Rosa Parks Visiting Prof., Univ. of Michigan, Ann Arbor 1996; currently Assoc. Ed. The American Book Review; Bd Contributing Ed. The Americas Review; Advisory Ed. Great Plains Quarterly; f. PEN-NM, Teachers of English and Chicano Language Arts 1991; Founder, Pres. NM Rio Grande Writers Asscn; mem. Bd Before Columbus Foundation; mem. Nat. Asscn of Chicano Studies. *Plays:* Billy the Kid, Who Killed Don José?, Matachines, Angie, Ay, Compadre, The Farolitos of Christmas. *Publications include:* Bless Me, Ultima 1972 (Premio Quinto Sol Award 1971), Heart of Aztlan 1976, Tortuga 1979 (American Book Award, Before Columbus Foundation 1979), Cuentos: Tales from the Hispanic Southwest (trans.) 1980, The Silence of the Llano (short stories) 1982, The Legend of La Llorona 1984, The Adventures of Juan Chicaspatas (poem) 1985, A Chicano in China 1986, Lord of the Dawn, The Legend of Quetzalcoatl 1987, Alburquerque 1992 (PEN-WEST Fiction Award 1993), The Anaya Reader (anthology) 1994, Zia Summer 1995, The Farolitos of Christmas (children's fiction) 1995, Jalamanta, A Message from the Desert 1996, Rio Grande Fall 1996, Maya's Children (children's fiction) 1997, Descansos: An Interrupted Journey (with Estevan Arellano and Denise Chávez) 1997, Isis in the Heart 1998, Shaman Winter 1999, Farolitos for Abuelo (children's fiction) 1999, My Land Sings 1999, Roadrunner's Dance 2000, Elegy for Cesar Chavez 2000, The Santero's Miracle 2004; short stories in literary magazines in USA and internationally; has also ed. various collections of short stories. *Honours:* Hon. DHumLitt (Albuquerque) 1981, (Marycrest Coll.) 1984, (New England) 1992, (Calif. Lutheran Univ.) 1994, (New Hampshire) 1997; Hon. PhD (Santa Fe) 1991; Hon. DLitt (New Hampshire) 1996; recipient of numerous awards including National Endowment for the Arts Fellowship 1980, New Mexico Governor's Award for Excellence anad Achievement in Literature 1980, W. K. Kellogg Foundation Fellowship 1983–86, New Mexico Eminent Scholar Award 1989, Rockefeller Foundation Residency Bellagio, Italy 1991, Excellence in the Humanities Award, New Mexico Endowment for the Humanities 1995, Tomás Rivera Mexican American Children's Book Awards 1995, 2000, Distinguished Achievement Award, Western Literature Asscn 1997, Arizona Adult Authors Award, Arizona Library Asscn 2000, Wallace Stegner Award Center of the American West 2001, National Asscn of Chicano/Chicana Studies Scholar 2002. *Address:* Department of Language and Literature, University of New Mexico, Albuquerque, NM 87131 (office); 5324 Cañada Vista NW, Albuquerque, NM 87120-2412, USA (home). *Fax:* (505) 899-0014 (home).

ANDAHAZI, Federico; Argentine writer; b. 1963, Buenos Aires. *Publications:* Las piadosas (short story) 1995, Por encargo (short story) 1995, La trilliza (short story) (first prize Concurso de Cuento Buenos Artes Joven II) 1996, El anatomista (novel) 1997, Las piadosas (collection of short stories) 1998. *Address:* c/o Random House, 1745 Broadway, Third Floor, New York, NY 10019, USA (office).

ANDELSON, Robert V., BA, MA, PhD; American academic, writer and editor; b. 19 Feb. 1931, Los Angeles, CA; m. Bonny Orange Johnson 1964. *Education:* University of Chicago, University of Southern California. *Career:* Asst Prof. to Prof. of Philosophy Emeritus, Auburn University, 1965–92; Editorial Board, American Journal of Economics and Sociology, 1969–; Distinguished Research Fellow, American Institute for Economic Research, 1993–; corpn mem. and dir, 1999–; mem. International Union for Land-Value Taxation and Free Trade, pres., 1997–2001; Robert Schalkenbach Foundation, vice-pres., 1998–2001. *Publications:* Imputed Rights: An Essay in Christian Social Theory, 1971; Critics of Henry George (ed. and co-author), 1979; Commons Without Tragedy (ed. and co-author), 1991; From Wasteland to Promised Land (with J. M. Dawsey), 1992; Land-Value Taxation Around the World (ed. and co-author), third edn, 2000. Contributions: scholarly journals. *Honours:* Foundation for Social Research Award, 1959; Relm Foundation Award, 1967; George Washington Honor Medals, Freedoms Foundation, 1970, 1972. *Address:* 534 Cary Drive, Auburn, AL 36830, USA.

ANDERKA, Johanna; German writer; b. 12 Jan. 1933, Mährisch-Ostrau, Czechoslovakia; d. of Leo and Margarete (née Kutschera) Anderka. *Education:* Volksschule and Lyzeum (Mährisch-Ostrau and other towns in E and W Germany) and Handelsschule (Flensburg). *Career:* office and admin. work 1950–. *Publications include:* Ergebnis eines Tages 1977, Herr, halte meine Hände 1979, Heilige Zeit 1981, Über die Freude 1983, Zweierlei Dinge 1983, Für L 1986, Blaue Wolke meiner Träume 1987, Ich werfe meine Fragen aus 1989, Sprachlos mein Schrei 1991, Nachtstadt 1992, Gegen die Fermdheit gesprochen 1994, Vertauschte Gezeiten 1995, Ausgefahren d. Brucken 1997, Bewahrte Landschaft 1999, Silbenhaus 2000; Radio plays: Der Mann im Lift 1983, Beginn einer Freundschaft 1984; numerous publs in anthologies and literary journals. *Honours:* Kulturpreis für Schrifttum (Sudetendeutsche Landsmannschaft) 1988, Hafizpreis Prosa 1988, prize in GEDOK Rhein-Main-Taunus Prose competition 1990, Nikolaus-Lenau-Preis (Künstlergilde Esslingen) 1991, Ehrengabe zum Andreas-Gryphius-Preis (Lyrische Gesamtwerk) 1992, Inge-Czernik-Förderpreis für Lyrik 1995, A. Launhardt Lyrikpreis 1998. *Address:* Tannenäcker 52, 89079 Ulm, Germany. *Telephone:* (731) 42112.

ANDERSEN, Benny Allan; Danish writer and poet; b. 7 Nov. 1929, Copenhagen; m. Cynthia La Touche Andersen 1981. *Publications include:* Den Musikalske ål 1960, Kamera med Køkkenadgang 1962, Den indre bowlerhat 1964, Puderne (short stories) 1965, Portrætgalleri 1966, Tykke-Olsen m. fl. (short stories) 1968, Det Sidste Øh 1969, Her i reservatet 1971, Man burde burde 1971, Svantes viser 1972, Personlige papirer 1974, Under begge øjne 1978, Himmelspræt – eller Kunsten at komme til Verden 1979, Tiden og Storken 1985, Andre Sider 1987, Chagall og skorpiondans 1991, Denne Kommen og Gåen 1993, Verdensborger i Danmark 1995, Verden udenfor Syltetøjsglasset 1996, Samlede digte 1960–1996 (poems) 1998, Sjælen marineret 2001, Spredte digte 2005. *Honours:* Louisiana-Prisen 1964, Tildelt Carl Møllers Humoristlegat 1965, Arbejdernes Fællesorganisations Kulturpris 1965, Kritiker-Prisen 1966, Ministeriet for Kulturelle Anliggenders Forfatterpris for børne- og ungdomsbøger 1971, H.C. Andersen Legatet 1974, Boghandlernes Ærespris De Gyldne Laurbær 1975, Otto Rungs Forfatterlegat 1975, IFPIs Jubilæumspris 1980, Aarestrup Medaljen 1984, PH-Fondens Fødselsdagspris 1984, Modersmål-Selskabets Pris 1985, LOs Kulturpris 1985, Ejner Hansen Fondens Hæderspris 1985, Henri Nathansens Mindelagt 1989, BMFs Børnebogspris 1989, Kunst og Kulturhøjskolens Kulturpris 1990, Hovedstadens Oplysningsforbunds Pris 1990, Den Folkelige Sangs Pris 1991, Morten Nielsens Mindelegat 1992, Weekendavisens Litteraturpris 1994, Niels-Prisen af Niels Matthiasens Mindefond 1995, Værkets Kulturpris 1995, Dansk Forfatterforenings Jubilæumslegat 1995, Hartmann-Prisen 1996, Landsforeningen af Danske Flygtningevenners Pris 1997, Dansk AFS Interkulturpris 1998, Nordisk Populærautorunions Pris 1999, Den Gyldne Grundtvig 2000, Foreningen Nordens Hæderspris 2001, Holberg-Medaljen 2001, Blicher-prisen 2003, Krebs Skoles Pris 2004, Lumbye Prisen 2004, Poul Sørensen og fru Susanne Sørensens legat 2004. *Literary Agent:* ARTE Booking ApS, Taastrup Hovedgade 121, 2630 Taastrup, Denmark. *E-mail:* booking@artebooking.dk.

ANDERSON, Annelise Graebner, PhD; American economist; *Senior Research Fellow, Hoover Institute on War, Revolution and Peace, Stanford University*; b. 19 Nov. 1938, Oklahoma City, OK; d. of Ellmer Graebner and Dorothy Graebner (née Zilisch); m. Martin Anderson 1965. *Education:* Wellesley Coll., MA and Columbia Univ., New York. *Career:* Assoc. Ed., McKinsey and Co. Inc. 1963–65; researcher, Nixon Campaign Staff 1968–69; Project Man., Dept of Justice 1970–71; Asst Prof. of Business Admin, then Assoc. Prof., Calif. State Univ. at Hayward 1975–80; Sr Policy Advisor, Reagan Presidential Campaign and Transition, Washington, DC 1980; Assoc. Dir of Econs and Govt, Office of Man. and Budget, Washington, DC 1981–83; adviser on econ. reform to govts of Russia, Romania, and Repub. of Georgia; Sr Research Fellow, Hoover Inst. on War, Revolution and Peace, Stanford Univ., CA 1983–, Assoc. Dir 1989–90; mem. Bd Overseers RAND/UCLA Center for Soviet Studies 1987–91; fmr mem. Advisory Bd RAND Center for the Study of Immigration Policy, Gov. Wilson's Council of Econ. Advisers, Gov.'s Task Force on California Tax Reform and Reduction; mem. Nat. Science Bd 1985–90. *Publications include:* The Business of Organized Crime: A Cosa Nostra Family 1979, Illegal Aliens and Employer Sanctions: Solving the Wrong Problem 1986, Thinking About America: The United States in the 1990s (co-ed.) 1988, Political Money: Deregulating American Politics 2000, Reagan, In His Own Hand: The Writings of Ronald Reagan That Reveal His Revolutionary Vision for America (co-ed.) 2001, Free BSD: An Open Source Operating System for Your Personal Computer 2001, Reagan: A Life in Letters (co-ed.) 2003, Reagan's Path to Victory (co-ed.) 2004; numerous contribs to professional journals. *Address:* Stanford University, Hoover Institution on War, Revolution and Peace, HHMB – Room 301, Stanford, CA 94305-6010, USA (office). *Telephone:* (650) 723-3139 (office). *E-mail:* andrsn@andrsn.stanford.edu (office). *Website:* www.stanford.edu/~andrsn (office).

ANDERSON, Barbara, BSc, BA; New Zealand writer and dramatist; b. 14 April 1926; m. Neil Anderson; two s. *Education:* Univ. of Otago, Victoria Univ., Wellington. *Career:* mem. PEN New Zealand (cttee mem. 1992–94). *Publications:* Uncollected Short Stories 1985, I Think We Should Go into the Jungle (short stories) 1989, Girls High 1990, We Could Celebrate 1991, Portrait of the Artist's Wife 1992, All the Nice Girls 1993, The House Guest 1995, Proud Garments 1996, The Peacocks and Other Stories (aka Glorious Things) 1997, Beginnings (essay) 1998, Long Hot Summer 1999, The Swing Around 2002, Change of Heart 2003; several radio plays, short stories. *Honours:* John Cowie Reid Memorial Award (play) 1986, Ansett/Sunday Star Short Story Award 1988, Timaru Herald/Aoraki Short Story Award 1990, Victoria Univ. Fellowship 1991, Goodman Fielder Wattie Award 1992, Scholarship of Letters 1994. *Address:* PFD, Drury House, 34–43 Russell Street, London, WC2B 5HA, England (office). *Telephone:* (4) 385-8494 (home). *E-mail:* barbaraanderson@nettel.net.nz (home). *Website:* www.pfd.co.uk (office).

ANDERSON, Christopher (Chris), BEcons; Australian journalist; *CEO, Optus Communications*; b. 9 Dec. 1944, s. of C.F. Anderson and L.A. Anderson; m. Gabriella Douglas 1969; one s. one d. *Education:* Picton High School, NSW, Univ. of Sydney, Columbia Univ., New York. *Career:* journalist and political commentator 1962–76; Deputy Ed., later Ed., The Sun-Herald 1976–79; Deputy Ed., later Ed., The Sydney Morning Herald 1980–83, Ed.-in-Chief 1983–88; Man. Dir and Group Ed. Dir John Fairfax Ltd 1987–90, Chief Exec. 1990–91; Man. Ed. Australian Broadcasting Corpn 1993–95; Chief Exec. TV New Zealand Ltd 1995–97; CEO Optus Communications 1997–. *Address:* Optus Communications, 101 Miller Street, North Sydney, NSW 2060, Australia. *Telephone:* (2) 9342-7800. *Fax:* (2) 9342-7100.

ANDERSON, David Daniel, BS, MA, PhD; American academic, writer and editor; b. 8 June 1924, Lorain, OH; m. Patricia Ann Rittenhour 1953. *Education:* Bowling Green State Univ., Michigan State Univ. *Career:* Distinguished Univ. Prof., Dept of American Thought and Language, Michigan State Univ., East Lansing 1957–; Ed., Midwestern Miscellany Annual; Exec. Sec., Soc. for the Study of Midwestern Literature 1971–73. *Publications:* Louis Bromfield 1964, Critical Studies in American Literature 1964, Sherwood Anderson 1967, Sherwood Anderson's Winesburg, Ohio 1967, Brand Whitlock 1968, The Black Experience (ed.-in-chief) 1969, Abraham Lincoln 1970, The Literary Works of Abraham Lincoln 1970, The Dark and Tangled Path (with R. Wright) 1971, Sunshine and Smoke 1971, Robert Ingersoll 1972, Mid-America I–XIV 1974–87, Sherwood Anderson: Dimensions of his Literary Art (essays) 1976, Woodrow Wilson 1978, Sherwood Anderson: The Writer at his Craft 1979, Ignatius Donnelly 1980, William Jennings Bryan 1981, Critical Essays on Sherwood Anderson 1981, Michigan: A State Anthology 1982, Route Two, Titus, Ohio 1993, The Path in the Shadow 1998, The Durability of Raintree County 1998, Ohio in Myth, Memory and Imagination 2004. *Honours:* Hon. DLitt (Wittenburg Univ.) 1989. *Address:* c/o Department of American Thought and Language, Michigan State University, East Lansing, MI 48821, USA.

ANDERSON, Jessica; Australian novelist; b. 1916, Brisbane; m.; two c. *Education:* Brisbane Tech. Art School. *Publications:* An Ordinary Lunacy (novel) 1963, The Last Man's Head (novel) 1970, The Commandant (novel) 1975, Tirra Lirra by the River (novel) (Miles Franklin Award) 1978, The Only Daughter (novel) 1980, The Impersonators (novel) (Miles Franklin Award, NSW Premier's Award) 1980, Stories from the Warm Zone and Sydney Stories (Age Book of the Year Award) 1987, Taking Shelter (novel) 1989, One of the Wattle Birds (novel) 1994; other: plays and adaptations for radio. *Address:* c/o Penguin Group (Australia), POB 701, Hawthorn 3122, Australia.

ANDERSON, Kevin James, (Gabriel Mesta), BS; American writer and editor; b. 27 March 1962, Racine, WI; m. 1st Mary Franco Nijhuis 1983 (divorced 1987); m. 2nd Rebecca Moesta 1991; one step-s. *Education:* Univ. of Wisconsin-Madison. *Career:* Technical Writer-Ed., Lawrence Livermore Nat. Lab. 1983–96; columnist, Materials Research Soc. 1988–96; copy ed., Int. Soc. for Respiratory Protection 1989–95; mem. SFWA, Horror Writers of America. *Publications:* novels (author or co-author): Resurrection Inc 1988, Lifeline 1991, The Trinity Paradox 1991, Afterimage 1992, Assemblers of Infinity 1993, Climbing Olympus 1994, Ill Wind 1995, Blindfold 1995, Born of Elven Blood 1995, Virtual Destruction 1996, Ignition 1997, Fallout 1997, Hidden Empire 2002, Captain Nemo 2002 A Forest of Stars 2003, Horizon Storms 2004; X-Files series: Ground Zero 1995, Ruins 1996, War of the Worlds: Global Dispatches (anthology, ed.) 1996; Gamearth series: Gamearth 1989, Gameplay 1989, Game's End 1990; Star Wars series: Darksaber 1995, Dark Lords 1997, Delusions of Grandeur 1997, Diversity Alliance 1997, Jedi Bounty 1997; Star Wars: Jedi Academy trilogy: Jedi Search 1994, Dark Apprentice 1994, Champions of the Force 1994; Star Wars: Young Jedi Knights series: The Lost Ones 1995, Shadow Academy 1995, Heirs of the Force 1995, Darkest Knight 1996, Lightsabers 1996, Jedi under Siege 1996, Shards of Alderaan 1997; Star Wars anthologies (ed.): Star Wars: Tales from the Mos Eisley Cantina 1995, Star Wars: Tales from Jabba's Palace 1995, Star Wars: Tales of the Bounty Hunters 1996; Star Wars: Tales of the Jedi series: Dark Lords of the Sith 1996, Golden Age of Sith 1997; non-fiction: The Illustrated Star Wars Universe 1995, Star Wars: The Mos Eisley Cantina Pop-Up Book 1995, Star Wars: Jabba's Palace Pop-Up Book 1995; Dune series: Dune: House Atreides 1999, Dune: House Harkonnen 2000, Dune: House Corrino 2001, Dune: The Butlerian Jihad 2002, Dune: The Machine Crusade 2003, Dune: The Battle of Corrin 2004, Hunters of Dune (with Brian Herbert) 2006; contribs to anthologies and periodicals. *Honours:* Bram Stoker Award 1988. *Literary Agent:* John Silbersack, Trident Media Group LLC, 41 Madison Avenue, New York, NY 10010, USA.

ANDERSON, Michael Falconer; British writer and journalist; b. 16 Jan. 1947, Aberdeen, Scotland; m. Hildegarde Becze 1970; two s. *Career:* newspaper and magazine ed.; chief sub-ed. of a national weekly; sub-ed. of a daily newspaper; showbusiness writer; reporter; correspondent in newspapers, television and radio; mem. Soc. of Authors, NUJ. *Publications:* The Woodsmen 1986, Blood Rite 1986, The Unholy 1987, God of a Thousand Faces 1987, The Covenant 1988, Black Trinity 1989, The Clan of Golgotha Scalp 1990; numerous short stories and plays for radio and television; contrib. feature articles on subjects including travel, history, the environment and books, in newspapers and magazines worldwide.

ANDERSON, Rachel; British writer and dramatist; b. 18 March 1943, Hampton Court, Surrey, England; m. David Bradby, four c. *Publications:* Pineapple 1965, The Purple Heart Throbs: A Survey of Popular Romantic Fiction 1850–1972, 1974, Dream Lovers 1978, For the Love of Sang 1990; young children's fiction: Tim Walks 1985, The Cat's Tale 1985, Wild Goose Chase 1986, Jessy Runs Away 1988, Best Friends 1991, Jessy and the Long-Short Dress 1992, Tough as Old Boots 1991, Little Lost Fox 1992; older children's fiction: Moffatt's Road 1978, The Poacher's Son 1982, The War Orphan 1984, Little Angel Comes to Stay 1985, Renard the Fox (with David Bradby) 1986, Little Angel Bonjour 1988, French Lessons 1988, The Boy Who Laughed 1989, The Bus People 1989, Paper Faces 1991, When Mum Went to Work 1992, The Working Class 1993, Blackwater 1994, The Scavenger's Tale 1998, Warlands 2000, Moving Times Trilogy 1999–2000, This Strange New Life 2006, Red Moon 2006. *Honours:* Medical Journalists' Asscn Award, 1990;

25th Anniversary Guardian Children's Fiction Award, 1992. *Address:* c/o Oxford University Press, Great Clarendon Street, Oxford, OX2 6DP, England (office).

ANDERSON, Robert David, MA, FSA; British conductor, writer and editor; b. 20 Aug. 1927, Shillong, Assam, India; s. of Robert David Anderson and Gladys Anderson (née Clayton). *Education:* Gonville and Caius Coll., Cambridge. *Career:* Asst Ed. Record News 1954–56; Asst Master and Dir of Music Gordonstoun School 1956–62; Conductor Moray Choral Union; Asst Conductor Spoleto Festival 1962; Conductor St Bartholomew's Hosp. Choral Soc. 1965–90; Extra-Mural Lecturer, Univ. of London 1966–77; Assoc. Ed. The Musical Times 1967–85; critic, the Times 1967–72; Visiting Lecturer, City Univ. 1983–92; Co-ordinating Ed. Elgar Complete Edition 1983–2003; mem. Egypt Exploration Soc. (Hon. Sec. 1971–82), Royal Musical Asscn. *Publications:* Egyptian Antiquities in the British Museum III: Musical Instruments 1976, Wagner 1980, Egypt in 1800 (co-ed.) 1988, Wagner, in Heritage of Music III 1989, Elgar in Manuscript 1990, Elgar 1993, Music and Dance in Pharaonic Egypt in Civilisations of the Ancient Near East IV 1995, Elgar and Chivalry 2002, Baalbek, Heliopolis and Rome 2006. *Honours:* Hon. Prof. of History, State Univ. of Rostov-on-Don 2002; Hon. DMus (City Univ.) 1985; Hon. DHist (Russian State Univ. for Humanities, Moscow) 2000; Liveryman Worshipful Co. of Musicians 1977. *Address:* 54 Hornton Street, London, W8 4NT, England (home). *Telephone:* (20) 7937-5146 (home).

ANDERSON, Robert Woodruff, BA, MA; American playwright, screenwriter and novelist; b. 28 April 1917, New York, NY. *Education:* Harvard Univ. *Career:* mem. Dramatists' Guild (Pres. 1971–73), Authors' League Council, Writers' Guild of America West, American Playwrights' Theatre (mem. Bd of Trustees), Theatre Hall of Fame 1981, PEN. *Publications:* plays: Tea and Sympathy 1953, All Summer Long 1954, Silent Night Lonely Night 1959, The Days Between 1965, You Know I Can't Hear When the Water's Running 1967, I Never Sang for My Father 1968, Solitaire/Double Solitaire 1971, Free and Clear 1983; co-author: Elements of Literature 1988; fiction: After 1973, Getting Up and Going Home 1978; screenplays: Tea and Sympathy 1956, Until They Sail 1957, The Nun's Story 1959, The Sand Pebbles 1966, I Never Sang For My Father 1970, The Last Act is a Solo 1991, Absolute Strangers 1991. *Honours:* Writers' Guild Award 1970, Ace Award 1991, Michaela O'Harra Award for distinguished contribs to the Theatre and to the New Dramatists 1999. *Address:* 14 Sutton Place S, New York, NY 10022, USA.

ANDERSON-DARGATZ, Gail, BA; Canadian writer; b. 14 Nov. 1963, Kamloops, BC; m. Floyd Dargatz 1990. *Education:* Univ. of Victoria. *Career:* mem. Canadian Writers' Union. *Publications:* The Miss Hereford Stories, 1994; The Cure for Death by Lightning, 1996; The Glass Room, 1998. Contributions: periodicals. *Honours:* First Prize for Fiction, Federation of British Columbia Writers, 1988; Okanagan Short Story Award, Canadian Author and Bookman, 1992; First Prize for Fiction, CBC Radio Literary Awards, 1995; Giller Prize, 1996.

ANDIIEVSKA, Emma; Ukrainian poet, writer and artist; b. 1931, Donetsk; m. Ivan Koshelivets (died 1999). *Career:* settled in Munich, Germany after World War II; exhibited her artistic work in USA, Canada, Australia, Brazil, Ukraine; mem. PEN, Ukrainian Acad. of Arts and Sciences (Germany). *Publications include:* Poeziia (poems) 1951, Podorozh (short stories) 1955, Narodzhennia idola (poems) 1958, Ryba i rozmir (poems) 1961, Kuty opostin' (poems) 1962, Tyhry (short stories) 1962, Dzhalapita (short stories) 1962, Roman pro dobru liudyny (novel) 1973, Roman pro liudske pryznachennia (novel) (Tatiana and Omelan Antonovych Award 1984) 1982, Kavarnia (poems) 1983, Vigilii (poems) 1987, Arkkhitekturni Ansambli 1989, Znaky Tarok 1995, Mezhyrichchia 1998, Segmenty Snu 1998, Villi nad Morem 2000, Problema Holovy (short stories) 2000, Kazky (novel) 2004. *Address:* Ukrainian Academy of Arts and Sciences, c/o Embassy of Ukraine, Albrechtstr. 26, 10117 Berlin, Germany.

ANDRÉE, Alice (see Cluysenaar, Anne)

ANDRESKI, Stanislav Leonard, MSc, PhD; British/Polish writer and academic; b. 18 May 1919, Czestochowa; two s. two d. *Education:* Univ. of Poznań, Univ. of London. *Career:* mil. service in Polish Army 1937–38, 1939–42, 1943–47; Lecturer in Sociology, Rhodes Univ. 1947–53; Sr Research Fellow in Anthropology, Univ. of Manchester 1954–56; Lecturer in Econs, Acton Tech. Coll., London 1956–57; Lecturer in Man. Studies, Brunel Coll. of Tech., London 1957–60; Prof. of Social Sciences, Santiago, Chile 1960–61; Sr Research Fellow, Nigerian Inst. of Social and Economic Research, Ibadan, Nigeria 1962–64; Prof. of Sociology, Univ. of Reading 1964–84, Head of Dept 1964–82, Prof. Emer. 1984–; part-time Prof., Polish Univ. in London 1969–99, Duxx School of Business, Monterey, Mexico 1995–98, Wyższa Szkoła Języków Obcych i Ekonomii, Czestochowa, Poland 1998–2002; Visiting Prof., CUNY 1968–69, Simon Frazer Univ., Vancouver, Canada 1976–77; mem. Editorial Bd Journal of Strategic Studies; mem. Writers' Guild, Inst. of Patentees and Inventors. *Publications:* Military Organisation and Society 1954, Elements of Comparative Sociology 1964, Parasitism and Subversion: The Case of Latin America 1966, The African Predicament: A Study in Pathology of Modernisation 1968, Social Sciences as Sorcery 1972, The Prospects of a Revolution in the USA 1973, Max Weber's Insights and Errors 1984, Syphilis, Puritanism and Witch Hunts: Historical Explanations in the Light of Medicine and Psychoanalysis with a Forecast About Aids 1989, Wars, Revolutions, Dictatorships 1992, Is Marriage Doomed to Obsolescence (with Alex Robinson) 2004; editor: Herbert Spencer: Principles of Sociology 1968, Herbert Spencer:

Structure, Function and Evolution 1971, The Essential Comte 1974, Reflections on Inequality 1975, Max Weber on Capitalism, Bureaucracy and Religion 1984; contribs approximately 90 articles in learned journals, including British Journal of Sociology, Japanese Journal of Sociology, Science Journal, European Journal of Sociology, Encounter. *Address:* Farriers, Village Green, Upper Basildon, Berks. RG8 8LS, England (home). *Telephone:* (1491) 671318.

ANDREW, Prudence Hastings, BA; British writer; b. 23 May 1924, London, England. *Education:* St Anne's Coll., Oxford. *Publications:* The Hooded Falcon, 1960; Ordeal by Silence, 1961; Ginger Over the Wall, 1962; A Question of Choice, 1963; Ginger and Batty Billy, 1963; The Earthworms, 1964; Ginger and No. 10, 1964; The Constant Star, 1964; A Sparkle from the Coal, 1964; Christmas Card, 1966; Mr Morgan's Marrow, 1967; Mister O'Brien, 1972; Rodge, Sylvie and Munch, 1973; Una and Grubstreet, 1973; Goodbye to the Rat, 1974; The Heroic Deeds of Jason Jones, 1975; Where Are You Going To, My Pretty Maid?, 1977; Robinson Daniel Crusoe, 1978 (in USA as Close Within My Own Circle, 1980); The Other Side of the Park, 1984.

ANDREWS, Graham, BA; Northern Irish writer; b. 3 Feb. 1948, Belfast; m. Agnes Helena Ferguson 1982. *Education:* Open University, Milton Keynes, England. *Career:* Assoc. Ed., Extro Science Fiction Magazine, 1980–81; Staff Writer, World Asscn for Orphans and Abandoned Children, 1990–91; mem. Society of Authors; RSL; BSFA. *Publications:* The Fragile Future 1990, The WAO Vocational Training Programme 1990, Darkness Audible (science fiction novel) 1991, St James Guide to Fantasy Writers (contributor) 1996, Dr Kilcasey in Space: A Bio-Bibliography of James White 2000, Gideon's Day/ Gideon of Scotland Yard 2003, The Man Who Met His Maker (play) 2004, Two Just Men: Richard S. Prather and Shell Scott; contrib. to Belfast Telegraph, Brussels Bulletin, The Guardian, F & SF, Interzone, Million, Vector, Foundation, Locus, Book and Magazine Collector. *Honours:* Aisling Gheal (Bright Vision) Award, Irish Science Fiction Asscn, 1980; First Prize in playwriting, American Theatre Co of Brussels, 2001. *Address:* Avenue du Merle 37, 1640 Rhode-Saint-Genese, Belgium.

ANDREWS, Kenneth Raymond, PhD, FBA; British academic; *Professor Emeritus of History, University of Hull;* b. 26 Aug. 1921, London; s. of Arthur Walter Andrews and Marion Gertrude Andrews; m. Ottilie Kalman 1969; two step-s. *Education:* Henry Thornton School, Clapham, London and King's Coll., London. *Career:* Southend Polytechnic 1954–56; Chiswick Polytechnic 1956–63; Lecturer, Univ. of Liverpool 1963–64; Lecturer then Sr Lecturer, Univ. of Hull 1964–79, Prof. of History 1979–88 (part time 1986–88), Prof. Emer. 1988–; conducting research in English maritime history; Vice-Pres. Hakluyt Soc. 1983–90. *Publications:* English Privateering Voyages to the West Indies 1588–95 1959, Elizabethan Privateering 1964, Drake's Voyages 1967, Last Voyage of Drake and Hawkins (ed.) 1972, The Spanish Caribbean 1978, The Westward Enterprise: English Activities in Ireland, the Atlantic and America 1480–1650 (ed.) 1979, Trade, Plunder and Settlement: Maritime Enterprise and the Genesis of the British Empire 1480–1630 1984, Ships, Money and Politics 1991, Freedom is a Constant Struggle: The Mississippi Civil Rights Movement and its Consequences 2004. *Address:* 8 Grange Drive, Cottingham, North Humberside, HU16 5RE, England.

ANDRUKHOVYCH, Yuriy; Ukrainian novelist and poet; b. 13 March 1960, Ivano-Frankivsk. *Education:* Ukrainian Institute of Polygraphy, Maxim Gorky Literary Inst., Moscow. *Career:* military service 1983–84; co-founder, literary performance group 'The Bu-Ba-Bu' (Burlesque-Bluster-Buffoonery) 1985; literary readings in American univs, including Harvard, Yale, Columbia, Pennsylvania State Univ. and La Salle Univ 1998; Fulbright Scholar in Residence Dept of Germanic and Slavic Languages, Penn State Univ.; mem. Polish experimental jazz group, Karbido. *Film screenplay:* A Military March for an Angel 1989. *Play:* Orpheus, Illegal 2006. *Recording:* album with Karbido: Samogon 2006. *Publications:* poetry: The Sky and Squares 1985, Downtown 1989, Exotic Birds and Plants 1991; fiction: Army Stories (short stories) 1989, Rekreatsii (trans. as Recreations) 1992, Moscoviada 1993, Perverzion 1996; non-fiction: Disorientation on Location (essays) 1999, 'Central-Eastern Revision' essay in anthology, My Europe 2001; contribs in trans. to Agni, Salt Hill, Exquisite Corpse. *Honours:* Blahovist 1993, Helen Shcherban-Lapika Foundation Award 1996, Novel of the Year Prize, Suchasnist 1997, Lesia & Petro Kovalev Award 1998, Leipzig Book Prize for European Understanding 2005. *Address:* c/o The National Writers' Union of Ukraine, Bankova Street 2, 01024 Kiev, Ukraine (office). *E-mail:* nspu@i.kiev.ua.

ANGEL, Albalucía Marulanda; Colombian novelist and playwright; b. 1939, Pereira, Risaralda. *Education:* Univ. de los Andes, Bogotá. *Plays:* La manzaza de piedra 1983, Siete lunas y un espejo 1991. *Publications:* Los girasoles en invierno (novel) 1970, Dos veces Alicia (novel) 1972, Estaba la pájara pinta sentada en el verde limón (novel) (Best Novel of the Year award) 1975, Oh, Gloria inmarcesible! 1979, Misiá señora (novel) 1982, Las andariegas (poetic prose) 1984. *Address:* c/o Inter-American Development Bank Cultural Center, 1300 New York Avenue NW, Washington, DC 20577, USA.

ANGEL, Leonard Jay, BA, MA, PhD; Canadian writer, dramatist and lecturer; b. 20 Sept. 1945; m. Susan Angel; one s. one d. one step-d. *Education:* McGill University, University of British Columbia. *Career:* Dept of Creative Writing, University of British Columbia 1981–82, University of Victoria 1984–86; mem. Playwrights Canada, 1976–88; Guild of Canadian Play-

wrights, chair., British Columbia region, 1978–79; Regional Representative, 1980–81; Writers' Guild of Canada, 1993. *Publications:* Antietam 1975, Isadora and G. B. 1976, The Unveiling 1981, The Silence of the Mystic 1983, Eleanor Marx 1985, How to Build a Conscious Machine 1989, Englightenment East and West 1994, The Book of Miriam 1997, contribs to The British Journal for the Philosophy of Science, Religious Studies. *Honours:* First Prize, Short Fiction, McGill Daily 1963, First Prize (joint), Playhouse Theatre Award 1971, Canada Council Artist Grants 1979, 1982. *Address:* 865 Durward Avenue, Vancouver, BC V5V 2Z1, Canada (home). *E-mail:* leonard_angel@douglas.bc .ca (home).

ANGELOU, Maya; American writer; b. (Marguerite Johnson), 4 April 1928, St Louis; d. of Bailey Johnson and Vivian Baxter; one s. *Career:* Assoc. Ed. Arab Observer 1961–62; Asst Admin., teacher, School of Music and Drama, Univ. of Ghana 1963–66; Feature Ed. African Review, Accra 1964–66; Reynold's Prof. of American Studies, Wake Forest Univ. 1981–; teacher of modern dance, Rome Opera House, Hambina Theatre, Tel-Aviv; has written several film scores; contrib. to numerous periodicals; Woman of Year in Communication 1976; numerous TV acting appearances; mem. Bd of Govs Maya Angelou Inst. for the Improvement of Child and Family Educ., Winston-Salem State Univ., NC 1998–; distinguished visiting prof. at several univs; mem. various arts orgs. *Plays:* Cabaret for Freedom 1960, The Least of These 1966, Gettin' Up Stayed On My Mind 1967, Ajax 1974, And Still I Rise 1976, Moon On a Rainbow Shawl (producer) 1988. *Theatre appearances include:* Porgy and Bess 1954–55, Calypso 19576, The Blacks 1960, Mother Courage 1964, Look Away 1973, Roots 1977, How To Make an American Quilt 1995 (feature film 1996). *Films directed include:* Down in the Delta 1998. *Publications include:* I Know Why the Caged Bird Sings 1970, Just Give Me A Cool Drink of Water 'Fore I Die 1971, Georgia, Georgia (screenplay) 1972, Gather Together In My Name 1974, All Day Long (screenplay) 1974, Oh Pray My Wings Are Gonna Fit Me Well 1975, Singin' and Swingin' and Gettin' Merry Like Christmas 1976, And Still I Rise 1976, The Heart of a Woman 1981, Shaker, Why Don't You Sing 1983, All God's Children Need Travelling Shoes 1986, Now Sheba Sings the Song 1987, I Shall Not Be Moved 1990, Gathered Together in My Name 1991, Wouldn't Take Nothing for my Journey Now 1993, Life Doesn't Frighten Me 1993, Collected Poems 1994, My Painted House, My Friendly Chicken and Me 1994, Phenomenal Woman 1995, Kofi and His Magic 1996, Even the Stars Look Lonesome 1997, Making Magic in the World 1998, A Song Flung up to Heaven 2002, Hallelujah! The Welcome Table 2005, Amazing Peace (long poem) (Quill Award for Poetry 2006) 2005. *Honours:* Hon. Amb. to UNICEF 1996–; more than 50 hon. degrees; Horatio Alger Award 1992, Grammy Award Best Spoken Word or Non-Traditional Album 1994, Lifetime Achievement Award for Literature 1999, Nat. Medal of Arts, numerous other awards. *Address:* c/o Dave La Camera, Lordly and Dame Inc., 51 Church Street, Boston, MA 02116, USA. *Telephone:* (617) 482-3593. *Fax:* (617) 426-8019.

ANGHELAKI-ROOKE, Katerina; Greek poet and translator; b. 22 Feb. 1939, Athens. *Education:* Univs of Nice, Athens and Geneva. *Career:* freelance translator 1962–; Visiting Prof. (Fulbright), Harvard Univ. 1980; Visiting Fellow, Princeton Univ. 1987. *Publications:* Wolves and Clouds 1963, Poems 63–69 1971, Magdalene the Vast Mammal 1974, The Body is the Victory and the Defeat of Dreams (in English) 1975, The Scattered Papers of Penelope 1977, The Triumph of Constant Loss 1978, Counter Love 1982, The Suitors 1984, Beings and Things on Their Own (in English) 1986, When the Body 1988, Wind Epilogue 1990, Empty Nature 1993, Tristiu 1995, The Flesh is a Beautiful Desert 1996, From Purple into Night (in English) 1997, Poems 1963–1977 1997, Poems 1978–1985 1998, Poems 1986–1996 1999, Matter Alone 2001, La Chair beau désert (in French and Greek) 2001, Translating into Love Life's End (in English) 2004; trans of works by Shakespeare, Albee, Dylan Thomas, Beckett, and from Russian of Pushkin, Mayiakorski, Lermontov. *Honours:* Greek National Poetry Prize 1985, Greek Acad. Ouranis Prize 2000. *Address:* Synesiou Kyrenes 4, 114 71 Athens, Greece (home).

ANGIER, Natalie; American journalist; b. 16 Feb. 1958, New York; d. of Keith and Adele Angier; m. Richard S. Weiss 1991; one d. *Education:* Univ. of Michigan and Barnard Coll., New York. *Career:* writer on Discover Magazine, New York 1980–83; Time Magazine, New York 1984–86; Ed. Savvy Magazine, New York 1983–84; Prof., New York Univ. Grad. Program in Science and Environmental Reporting 1987–89; joined New York Times as Reporter 1990, currently Science Corresp., Washington, DC; contribs to most, Parade, Washington Monthly, Reader's Digest, Fox TV Network, CBC and several other publs. *Publications include:* Natural Obsessions (Notable Book of the Year, New York Times and AAAS) 1988, The Beauty of the Beastly (cited as one of notable science books of the year by New York Times and Library Journal) 1995, Woman: An Intimate Geography 1999, The Best American Science and Nature Writing (ed.) 2002, The Canon: A Whirligig Tour of the Beautiful Basics of Science 2007. *Honours:* Pulitzer Prize for Reporting 1991, Journalism Award, GM Ind. Bd 1991, Lewis Thomas Award for Distinguished Writing in the Life Sciences, Marine Biology Labs 1990, Journalism Award, AAAS Award for Excellence in Journalism 1992, Distinguished Alumna Award, Barnard Coll. 1993, General Motors Int. Award, named by Forbes MediaGuide amongst seven journalists awarded its top rating of four stars. *Address:* New York Times, Washington Bureau, 1627 I Street, NW, 7th Floor, Washington, DC 20006, USA (office).

ANGLUND, Joan Walsh; American children's writer; b. 3 Jan. 1926, Hinsdale, IL. *Education:* Chicago Art Inst. *Publications:* A Friend is Someone

Who Likes You 1958, Look Out the Window 1959, The Brave Cowboy 1959, Love is a Special Way of Feeling 1960, In a Pumpkin Shell: A Mother Goose ABC 1960, Christmas Is a Time of Giving 1961, Cowboy and his Friend 1961, Nibble Nible Mousekin: A Tale of Hansel and Gretel 1962, Cowboy's Secret Life 1963, Spring is a New Beginning 1963, Childhood Is a Time of Innocence 1964, A Pocketful of Proverbs (verse) 1964, A Book of Good Tidings from the Bible 1965, What Color is Love? 1966, A Year is Round 1966, A Cup of Sun: A Book of Poems 1967, A Is for Always: An ABC Book 1968, Morning Is a Little Child (verse) 1969, A Slice of Snow: A Book of Poems 1970, Do You Love Someone? 1971, The Cowboy's Christmas 1972, A Child's Book of Old Nursery Rhymes 1973, Goodbye, Yesterday: A Book of Poems 1974, Storybook 1978, Emily and Adam 1979, Almost a Rainbow 1980, A Gift of Love (five vols) 1980, A Christmas Cookie Book 1982, Rainbow Love 1982, Christmas Candy Book 1983, A Christmas Book 1983, See the Year 1984, Coloring Book 1984, Memories of the Heart 1984, Teddy Bear Tales 1985, Baby Brother 1985, All About Me! 1986, Christmas is Here! 1986, Tubtime for Thaddeus 1986, A Mother Goose Book 1991, A Child's Year 1992, Love is a Baby 1992, The Way of Love 1992, Bedtime Book 1993, The Friend We Have Not Met 1993, Peace is a Circle of Love 1993. *Address:* JWA Inc., 3 Wherowhero Lane, Nantucket, MA, USA (office). *Website:* www.joanwalshanglund.net (office).

ANGREMY, Jean-Pierre, (Pierre-Jean Rémy); French diplomatist and writer; b. 21 March 1937, Angoulême; s. of Pierre Angremy and Alice Collebrans; m. 1st Odile Cail (divorced); one s. one d.; m. 2nd Sophie Schmit 1986 (divorced); one s. *Education:* Institut d'études politiques, Paris, Brandeis Univ., USA, Ecole nationale d' admin. *Career:* served in Hong Kong 1963–64, Beijing 1964–66, London 1966–71, 1975–79; Cultural, Scientific and Tech. Relations, Paris 1971–72; seconded to ORTF 1972–75; seconded to Ministry of Culture and Communication (Dir Theatre Dept) 1979–84; Consul, Florence 1984–87; Dir-Gen. Cultural, Scientific and Tech. Relations 1987–90; Amb. to UNESCO 1990–94; Dir Acad. de France, Rome 1994–97; Pres. Bibliothèque Nationale de France 1997–2002, Années France–Chine 2003–05, mem. Acad. française 1988. *Publications:* Désir d'Europe 1995, Le Rose et la Blanc 1997, Callas, une Vie 1997, Retour d'Hélène 1997, Aria Di Roma 1998, La Nuit de Ferrare 1999, Demi-Siècle 2000, Etat de Grâce et Dire Perdu 2001, Berlioz 2002, Chambre noire de Pekin 2004, Dictionnaire amoureux de l'Opéra 2004, and numerous other publs. *Honours:* Commdr, Légion d'honneur, des Arts et Lettres; Officier, Ordre nat. du. Mérite. *Address:* 63 Boulevard Saint-Michel, 75005 Paris, France (home). *Telephone:* 1-47-05-29-10 (home). *Fax:* 1-47-05-29-10 (home). *E-mail:* angremy@wanadoo.fr (home).

ANGUS, Ian (see Mackay, James Alexander)

ANMAR, Frank (see Nolan, William Francis)

ANNWN, David, BA, PGCE, PhD; British poet, critic and lecturer; *Assistant Lecturer, Open University*; b. 9 May 1953, Congleton, Cheshire, England; m. 1994. *Education:* Wigan Tech. Coll., Univ. Coll. of Wales, Aberystwyth, Univ. of Bath. *Career:* Postgraduate Tutor, Univ. of Aberystwyth 1975–78; Lecturer, Wakefield Coll. 1981–88, Head of English Degree Work 1988–95; Lecturer, Tutor and Examiner, Open Univ. 1995–96, currently Asst Lecturer; Lecturer in Creative Writing, Univ. of Leeds 1996; mem. Humanities and Arts Higher Educ. Network, Northern Assen of Writers in Educ., Welsh Acad. *Publications:* poetry: Foster the Ghost 1984, King Saturn's Book 1986, The Other 1988, Primavera Violin 1990, The Spirit/That Kiss 1993, Dantean Designs 1995, Danse Macabre, Death and the Printers (with Kelvin Corcoran, Alan Halsey and Gavin Selerie) 1997; prose: Inhabited Voices: Myth and History in the Poetry of Seamus Heaney, Geoffrey Hill and George Mackay Brown 1984, Catgut and Blossom: Jonathon Williams in England (ed.) 1989, A Different Can of Words (ed.) 1992, Presence, Spacing Sign: The Graphic Art of Peterjon Skelt 1993, Hear the Voice of the Bard!: The Early Bards, William Blake and Robert Duncan 1995, Poetry in the British Isles: Non-Metropolitan Perspectives 1995, Inner Celtia (with Alan Richardson) 1996, A Breton Herbal: Translations of Poems by Eugene Guillevic 1998; contrib. to anthologies and to Anglo-Welsh Review, Poetry Wales, Ambit, Iron, Scintilla, David Jones Society Journal. *Honours:* Winner Int. Collegiate Eisteddfod 1975, Ilkley Arts Festival Prize 1982, Yorkshire Arts Bursary 1985, First Prize, Cardiff Int. Poetry Competition 1996, Ferguson Centre Award 2004–07. *Address:* c/o West House Books, 40 Crescent Road, Sheffield, S7 1HN, England.

ANTHONY, Evelyn; British writer; b. 3 July 1928, d. of Henry Christian Stephens and Elizabeth Stephens (née Sharkey); m. Michael Ward-Thomas 1955; four s. two d. (and one d. deceased). *Education:* Convent of the Sacred Heart, Roehampton. *Publications include:* Imperial Highness 1953, Curse Not the King 1954, Far Fly the Eagles 1955, Anne Boleyn (US Literary Guild Award) 1956, Victoria (US Literary Guild Award) 1957, Elizabeth 1959, Charles the King 1961, The Heiress 1964, The Assassin 1970, The Tamarind Seed 1971, The Occupying Power (Yorkshire Post Fiction Prize 1973) 1973, The Persian Ransom 1975, The Silver Falcon 1977, The Grave of Truth 1979, The Defector 1980, The Avenue of the Dead 1981, Albatross 1982, The Company of Saints 1983, Voices On the Wind 1985, No Enemy But Time 1987, The House of Vandekar 1988, The Scarlet Thread 1989, The Doll's Home 1990, Exposure 1992, Bloodstones 1994, The Legacy 1997. *Honours:* Freeman City of London 1989, Liveryman of Needlemakers Co. 1989; High Sheriff of Essex 1994–95, DL (Essex) 1995. *Address:* Horham Hall, Thaxted, Essex, CM6 2NN, England.

ANTHONY, Michael; Trinidad and Tobago writer; b. 10 Feb. 1930, Mayaro; m. Yvette Francesca 1958; two s. two d. *Education:* Junior Technical Coll., San Fernando, Trinidad. *Career:* Sub-Ed., Reuters News Agency, London 1964–68; Asst Ed., Texas Star, Texaco Trinidad, Pointe-a-Pierre, Trinidad and Tobago 1972–88; Teacher of Creative Writing, Univ. of Richmond, VA, USA 1992. *Publications:* fiction: The Games Were Coming, 1963; The Year in San Fernando, 1965; Green Days by the River, 1967; Streets of Conflict, 1976; All That Glitters, 1981; Bright Road to Eldorado, 1982. Short Stories: Cricket in the Road and Other Stories, 1973; Sandra Street and Other Stories, 1973; Folk Tales and Fantasies, 1976; The Chieftain's Carnival and Other Stories, 1993. Other: Glimpses of Trinidad and Tobago, with a Glance at the West Indies, 1974; King of the Masquerade, 1974; Profile Trinidad: A Historical Survey from the Discovery to 1900, 1975; The Making of Port-of-Spain, 1757–1939, 1978; Port-of-Spain in a World War, 1939–1945, 1984; First in Trinidad, 1985; Heroes of the People of Trinidad and Tobago, 1986; A Brighter and Better Day, 1987; Towns and Villages of Trinidad and Tobago, 1988; Parade of the Carnivals of Trinidad, 1839–1989, 1989; The Golden Quest: The Four Voyages of Christopher Columbus, 1992; In the Heat of the Day, 1996; Historical Dictionary of Trinidad and Tobago, 1997; The High Tide of Intrigue, 2001; Butler, Till the Final Bell, 2002. Editor: The History of Aviation in Trinidad and Tobago, 1913–1962, 1987. Contributions: various periodicals. *Address:* c/o Ministry of Culture, ALGICO Bldg, Jerningham Avenue, Belmont, Port of Spain, Trinidad and Tobago.

ANTHONY, Patricia, BA, MA; American writer and educator; b. 29 March 1947, San Antonio, Tex.; d. of Raymond Anthony and Evelyn Anthony; m. Dennis John Hunt April 1967 (divorced 1974); one s. one d. *Education:* Univ. of Texas, Austin, Universidade Federal de Santa Catarina, Florianopolis, Brazil. *Career:* Visiting Prof. of English Literature, Univ. of Lisbon, Portugal; Assoc. Prof. of English, Universidade Federal de Santa Catarina, Florianopolis; Adjunct Prof. of Creative Writing, Southern Methodist Univ., Dallas, Tex. *Publications:* fiction: Cold Allies (Best First Novel Award, Locus 1993) 1993, Brother Termite 1993, Conscience of the Beagle 1993, Happy Policeman 1994, Cradle of Splendor 1996, God's Fires 1997, Flanders 1998; short stories: Eating Memories 1997; contribs short stories to magazines including Aboriginal SF. *Literary Agent:* c/o Meredith Bernstein Literary Agency, 2112 Broadway, Suite 503A, New York, NY 10023, USA. *Address:* 9712 Amberton Parkway, Dallas, TX 75243, USA (home). *Telephone:* (972) 231-6155 (home). *E-mail:* patanthony@mindspring.com (home); patriciaanthony@sbcglobal.net (office).

ANTHONY, Piers, BA; American writer; b. (Piers Anthony Dillingham Jacob), 6 Aug. 1934, Oxford, England; m. Carol Marble 1956; two d. *Education:* Goddard Coll., Univ. of South Florida. *Publications:* Chthon 1967, Omnivore 1968, Sos the Rope 1968, The Ring (with Robert E. Margroff) 1968, Macroscope 1969, The E.S.P. Worm (with Robert E. Margroff) 1970, Orn 1971, Prostho Plus 1971, Var the Stick 1972, Kiai! 1974, Mistress of Death 1974, Rings of Ice 1974, Triple Détente 1974, The Bamboo Bloodbath 1975, Neq the Sword 1975, Ninja's Revenge 1975, Phthor 1975, Amazon Slaughter 1976, Ox 1976, But What of Earth? (with Robert Coulson) 1976, Steppe 1976, Cluster 1977, Hasan 1977, A Spell for Chameleon 1977, Chaining the Lady 1978, Kirlian Quest 1978, The Source of Magic 1979, Castle Roogna 1979, God of Tarot 1979, The Pretender (with Frances Hall) 1979, Split Infinity 1980, Vision of Tarot 1980, Faith of Tarot 1980, Thousandstar 1980, Blue Adept 1981, Centaur Aisle 1981, Mute 1981, Juxtaposition 1982, Ogre, Ogre 1982, Viscous Circle 1982, Night Mare 1983, Dragon on a Pedestal 1983, On a Pale Horse 1983, Refugee 1983, Mercenary 1984, Bearing an Hourglass 1984, Anthonology 1985, Crewel Lye: A Caustic Yarn 1985, With a Tangled Skein 1985, Politician 1985, Executive 1985, Ghost 1986, Golem in the Gears 1986, Shade of the Tree 1986, Statesman 1986, Out of Phaze 1987, Vale of the Vole 1987, Wielding a Red Sword 1987, Being a Green Mother 1987, Dragon's Gold (with Robert E. Margroff) 1987, Bio of an Ogre 1988, For Love of Evil 1988, Heaven Cent 1988, Robot Adept 1988, Serpent's Silver (with Robert E. Margroff) 1988, Pornucopia 1988, Dead Morn 1988, Total Recall 1989, Unicorn Point 1989, And Eternity 1990, Isle of View 1990, Firefly 1990, Hard Sell 1990, Phaze Doubt 1990, Through the Ice (with Robert Kornwise) 1990, Orc's Opal (with Robert E. Margroff) 1990, Chimaera's Copper (with Robert E. Margroff) 1990, Tatham Mound 1991, Virtual Mode 1991, MerCycle 1991, Question Quest 1991, Alien Plot 1992, The Color of Her Panties 1992, Fractal Mode 1992, The Caterpillar's Question (with Jose Farmer) 1992, If I Pay Thee Not in Gold 1993, Killobyte 1993, Letters to Jenny 1993, Demons Don't Dream 1993, Chaos Mode 1993, Isle of Woman 1993, Mouvar's Magic (with Robert E. Margroff) 1993, Harpy Thyme 1994, Shame of Man 1994, Tales from the Great Turtle 1994, Geis of the Gargoyle 1995, Roc and a Hard Place 1995, Yon Ill Wind 1996, The Willing Spirit (with Alfred Tells) 1996, The Continuing Xanth Saga 1997, Hope of Earth 1997, Faun and Games 1997, Quest for the Fallen Star (with James Richey and Alan Riggs) 1998, Zombie Lover 1998, Xone of Contention 1999, Realty Check 1999, How Precious Was That While 1999, Muse of Art 1999, The Dastard 2000, Swell Foop 2001, DoOon Mode 2001, Up in a Heaval 2002, The Iron Maiden 2002, Cube Route 2003, The Magic Fart 2003, Currant Events 2004, Pet Peeve 2005, Stork Naked 2006, Relationships 2006, Air Apparent 2007, Tortoise Reform 2007. *Honours:* Science Fiction Award, Pyramid Books/Magazine of Fantasy and Science Fiction/Kent Productions 1967, British Fantasy Award 1977. *E-mail:* PiersAnthony@hipiers.com (home). *Website:* www.hipiers.com (home).

ANTIN, David, BA, MA; American academic and poet; b. 1 Feb. 1932, New York, NY; m. Eleanor Fineman 1960; one s. *Education:* City Coll., CUNY, New York Univ. *Career:* Chief Ed. and Scientific Dir, Research Information Service

1958–60; Curator, Inst. of Contemporary Art, Boston 1967; Dir Univ. Art Gallery, Univ. of California at San Diego 1968–72, Asst Prof. 1968–72, Prof. of Visual Arts 1972–. *Publications:* Definitions 1967, Autobiography 1967, Code of Flag Behavior 1968, Meditiations 1971, Talking 1972, After the War 1973, Talking at the Boundaries 1976, Who's Listening Out There? 1980, Tuning 1984, Poèmes Parlés 1984, Selected Poems 1963–73 1991, What it Means to be Avant Garde 1993, A Conversation with David Antin (with Charles Bernstein) 2002; contrib. to periodicals. *Honours:* Longview Award 1960, Univ. of California Creative Arts Award 1972, Guggenheim Fellowship 1976, Nat. Endowment for the Humanities Fellowship 1983, PEN Award for Poetry 1984, Getty Research Fellow 2002. *Address:* c/o Visual Arts Department, University of California at San Diego, 9500 Gilman Drive, La Jolla, CA 92093-0327, USA.

ANTOINE, Yves, MEd, DLitt; Canadian academic, writer and poet; b. 12 Dec. 1941, Port-au-Prince, Haiti; one d. *Education:* Univ. of Ottawa. *Career:* mem. Union of Writers, QC, Ligue des Droits et Liberté, Asscn des auteurs de l'Outaouais québécois. *Publications:* La Veillée 1964, Témoin Oculaire 1970, Au gré des heures 1972, Les sabots de la nuit 1974, Alliage 1979, Libations pour le soleil 1985, Sémiologie et personnage romanesque chez Jacques S. Alexis 1993, Polyphonie (poems and prose) 1996, La mémoire à fleur de peau 2002; contrib. to Une affligeante réalité, Le Droit, Ottawa 1987, L'indélébile, Symbiosis, Ottawa 1992, Inventeurs et savants noirs 1998, 2004. *Honours:* Guest Harambee Foundation Soc. 1988, Carter G. Woodson Award Intercultural Council of Outaouais (Québec, Canada) 1999. *Address:* 6 rue de la Sablière, Apt 2, Gatineau, QC J8Z 2V4, Canada (home).

ANTOKOLETZ, Elliott Maxim, BA, MA, PhD; American musicologist and writer; *Professor of Musicology, University of Texas, Austin;* b. 3 Aug. 1942, Jersey City, NJ; m. Juana Canabal 1972; one s. *Education:* Juilliard School of Music, Hunter Coll., Graduate School and Univ. Center, CUNY. *Career:* Lecturer and mem. of faculty string quartet, Queens Coll., CUNY 1973–76; Prof. of Musicology, Univ. of Texas, Austin 1976–, Head Musicology Div. 1992–94; Co-ed. International Journal of Musicology 1992–; mem. American Musicological Soc. *Publications:* The Music of Béla Bartók: A Study of Tonality and Progression in Twentieth-Century Music 1984, Béla Bartók: A Guide to Research 1988, Twentieth Century Music 1992, Bartók Perspectives (co-ed. with V. Fischer and B. Suchoff) 2000, Musical Symbolism in the Operas of Debussy and Bartók 2004; contrib. three chapters to The Bartók Companion, one chapter to Sibelius Studies; contrib. to scholarly books and professional journals. *Address:* c/o School of Music, University of Texas at Austin, Austin, TX 78712, USA.

ANTÓNIO, Mário; Angolan poet, writer and translator; b. (Mário António Fernandes de Oliveira), 5 April 1934, Maquela do Zombo, Angola. *Publications:* many vols of poems, essays, short stories and trans; contrib. to numerous magazines and journals.

ANTROBUS, John; British dramatist, writer and screenwriter; b. 2 July 1933, London, England; m. Margaret McCormick 1958 (divorced 1980); two s. one d. *Education:* King Edward VII Nautical Coll., Royal Military Acad., Sandhurst. *Career:* mem. Writers' Guild of America West, Writers' Guild of Great Britain. *Plays:* The Bed-Sitting Room (with Spike Milligan) 1963, Captain Oate's Left Sock 1969, Walton on Thames (revised edn as The Bed-Sitting Room 2) 1970, Crete and Sergeant Pepper 1972, Jonah 1979, Hitler in Liverpool 1980, One Orange for the Baby 1980, Up in the Hide 1980, When Did You Last See Your Trousers? (with Ray Galton) 1986. *Film screenplays:* Carry on Sergeant (with Norman Hudis) 1958, Idol on Parade 1959, The Wrong Arm of the Law (with others) 1962, The Big Job (with Talbot Rothwell) 1965, The Bed-Sitting Room (with Charles Wood) 1969. *Publications:* juvenile: The Boy with Illuminating Measles 1978, Help! I'm a Prisoner in a Toothpaste Factory 1978, Ronnie and the Haunted Rolls Royce 1982, Ronnie and the Great Knitted Robbery 1982, Ronnie and the High Rise 1992, Ronnie and the Flying Carpet 1992. *Honours:* George Devine Award 1970, Writers' Guild Award 1971, Arts Council bursaries 1973, 1976, 1980, 1982, Banff Television Festival Award for Best Comedy 1987. *Literary Agent:* Rogers, Coleridge & White Ltd, 20 Powis Mews, London, W11 1JN, England.

ANTUNES, Xana, BA; British publishing executive; *Executive Editor, CNNMoney.com;* b. 1965. *Education:* Univ. of Leeds and City Univ., London. *Career:* postgraduate diploma in journalism; began career in journalism as reporter with The Independent (newspaper) business section 1988; TV journalist on Business Daily (Channel 4); Business News Ed., Evening Standard 1992–93, est. Wall Street bureau 1993, New York Corresp. 1993–95; Deputy Business Ed. New York Post 1995–96, Business Ed. 1996–98, Deputy Ed. 1998–99, Ed. 1999–2001; host of feature writing seminars and consultant to various magazines and newspapers 2002–03; Exec. Ed. Fortune magazine 2003–05, Exec. Ed. CNNMoney.com 2005–,. *Address:* CNNMoney.com, c/o Fortune magazine, 1271 Sixth Avenue, 16th Floor, New York, NY 10020, USA (office). *Website:* money.cnn.com (office).

ANVIL, Christopher (see Crosby, Harry Clifton)

ANYANWU, Christina, BA, MSc; Nigerian journalist; b. 29 Oct. 1950, Ahiazu Mbaise Local Govt Area; m. Dr Casmir Anyanwu; one s. one d. *Education:* Owerri Girls Secondary School, Univs of Missouri and Florida, USA. *Career:* Newsweek Corresp. at Nat. Ass. 1979; with Nat. TV Authority 1979, Producer Newsline Magazine 1986; Commr of Information, Imo State 1989; Founder, Dir and Ed.-in-Chief The Sunday Magazine 1989; sentenced by special mil. tribunal in camera to life imprisonment for "spreading false news" July 1995,

sentence reduced to 15 years' imprisonment Oct. 1995, released June 1998; with Nigerian TV Authority (NTA) hosting NEWSLINE show and covering activities of OPEC as petroleum corresp.; Owner HOT 98.3 FM radio station, Abuja; elected to Senate representing Owerri dist. (People's Democratic Party) 2007–. *Honours:* Nat. Nigerian Award for Women Journalists, Ford Foundation Garnet Award, Int. Women's Media Foundation Prize for Courage 1995, Reporters Sans Frontières Award 1995, African Women's Media Center Courage in Journalism Award, Cttee to Protect Journalism Int. Press Freedom Award 1997, UNESCO/Guillermo Cano World Press Freedom Prize 1998, Mem. of the Fed. Repub. (MFR), Govt of Nigeria 2004. *Address:* Senate, National Assembly Complex, Three Arms Zone, P.M.B 141, Abuja, Nigeria. *E-mail:* senate@nassnig.org. *Website:* www.nassnig.org/senate/Senate.htm.

APPACHANA, Anjana, MFA; Indian novelist and short story writer; m.; one d. *Education:* Scindia Kanya Vidyalaya, Delhi Univ., Jawaharlal Nehru Univ., Pennsylvania State Univ. *Career:* moved to USA 1984; has taught creative writing at Pennsylvania and Arizona State Univs and YMCA Writer's Voice; Nat. Endowment for the Arts Fellowship. *Publications:* Her Mother (short story) (O. Henry Festival Prize for Fiction) 1989, Incantations and Other Stories 1992, Sharmaji (short story), Listening Now (novel) 1998; contrib. short stories to several journals, magazines and anthologies. *Address:* c/o Random House Inc., 1745 Broadway, New York, NY 10019, USA.

APPELFELD, Aharon; Israeli novelist; b. 1932, Czernowitz, Poland. *Education:* Hebrew Univ., Jerusalem. *Career:* Lecturer, Be'er Shev'a Univ. from 1984. *Publications (in Hebrew):* Smoke (stories) 1962. In the Fertile Valley (stories) 1963. Frost on the Land (stories) 1965. On the Ground Floor (stories) 1968. Pillars of the River (stories) 1971. The Skin and the Gown (novel) 1971, As an Apple of his Eye (novella) 1973, A Hundred Witnesses (stories selection) 1975, Years and Hours (novellas) 1975, The Age of Wonders (novel) 1978, First Person Essays (essays) 1979, Badenheim 1939 (novel) 1979, Searing Light (novel) 1980, The Shirt and the Stripes (novella) 1983, Tzili: The Story of a Life (novel) 1983, At One and the Same Time (novel) 1985, Tongue of Fire 1988, Katerina (novel) 1989, The Railway (novel) 1991, Laish 1994, Lost 1995, Until the Dawn's Light 1995, The Ice Mine 1997, All Whom I Have Loved 1999, The Story of a Life: A Memoir (Prix Médicis, France) 1999. *Honours:* H. H. Wingate Literary Award 1989, Nelly Sachs Prize, Dortmund, Germany 2005. *Address:* c/o Keter Publishing House, PO Box 7145, Jerusalem 91071, Israel (office).

APPELGREN, Anne Marie; Finnish writer and translator; b. 12 March 1956, Ekenaes; m.; two c. *Publications:* Novels: Salto Mortal, 1990; Skuggan av Saturnus, 1992. Non-Fiction: Astrologi i dag. Självkännedom genom symboler, 1994. Other: trans of various books into Swedish. *E-mail:* charmiene@telia.com. *Website:* www.charmiene.com.

APPIAH, Kwame Anthony, PhD; American (b. British) academic and writer; *Laurance S. Rockefeller University Professor of Philosophy and the University Center for Human Values, Princeton University;* b. 8 May 1954, London; s. of Joe Appiah and Peggy Appiah. *Education:* Kwame Nkrumah Univ. of Science and Tech., Ghana, Univ. of Cambridge, UK. *Career:* raised in Ghana; taught at Univ. of Ghana; has held position of Prof. of Philosophy and Prof. of African Studies and African-American Studies at Univ. of Cambridge, Yale Univ., Cornell Univ., Duke Univ., Harvard Univ. 1991–2002; Laurance S. Rockefeller University Prof. of Philosophy and Univ. Center for Human Values, Princeton Univ. 2002–. *Publications include:* Assertion and Conditionals 1985, For Truth in Semantics 1986, Necessary Questions: An Introduction to Philosophy 1989, Avenging Angel (novel) 1991, In My Father's House: Africa in the Philosophy of Culture (essays—Annisfield-Wolf Book Award 1993, African Studies Asscn Herskovits Award 1993) 1992, Nobody Likes Letitia (novel) 1994, Another Death in Venice (novel) 1995, Color Consciousness: The Political Morality of Race (with Amy Gutman) (North American Soc. for Social Philosophy Annual Book Award) 1996, The Dictionary of Global Culture (with Henry Louis Gates, Jr) 1996, Africana: The Encyclopedia of African and African American Experience 1999; Ed.: Early African-American Classics 1990; Co-Ed.: Critical Perspectives Past and Present (series) 1993, Identities (essays) 1995, The Ethics of Identity 2005, Cosmopolitanism: Ethics in a World of Strangers 2006. *Address:* Department of Philosophy, 208 Marx Hall, Princeton University, Princeton, NJ 08544-1006, USA (office). *Telephone:* (609) 258-4302 (office). *Fax:* (609) 258-1502 (office). *E-mail:* kappiah@princeton.edu (office); anthony_appiah@msn.com (home). *Website:* web.princeton.edu/sites/philosph (office); www.appiah.net (home).

APPLE, Max Isaac, BA, PhD; American academic and writer; b. 22 Oct. 1941, Grand Rapids, MI; one s. one d. *Education:* Michigan Univ. and Stanford Univ. *Career:* Asst Prof., Reed Coll., Portland, OR 1970–71; Asst Prof., Rice Univ. 1972–76, Assoc. Prof. 1976–80, Prof. of English 1980–2001, Prof. Emeritus 2001–; teacher of creative writing, Univ. of Pennsylvania 2001–; mem. MLA, PEN, Texas Inst. of Letters. *Publications:* Studies in English (with others) 1975, The Oranging of America and Other Stories 1976, Zip: A Novel of the Left and the Right 1978, Southwest Fiction (ed.) 1980, Three Stories 1983, Free Agents 1984, The Propheteers: A Novel 1987, Roomates: My Grandfather's Story (memoir) 1994, I Love Gootie: My Grandmother's Story 1998. *Honours:* Nat. Endowment for the Humanities Fellowship 1971, Texas Inst. of Letters Jesse Jones Award 1976, 1985, Hadassah Magazine Ribalous Award 1985.

APPLEBAUM, Anne; American writer and journalist; b. 25 July 1964, Washington, DC; m. Radek Sikorski; two c. *Education:* Univ. of Yale, LSE,

Univ. of Oxford. *Career:* Warsaw correspondent for The Economist 1988; journalist, numerous journals in Central and Eastern Europe 1988–92; Foreign Ed. and Deputy Ed. The Spectator, London; columnist, The Daily Telegraph, The Sunday Telegraph, Evening Standard; Political Ed., Evening Standard 1997; currently columnist and editiorial bd mem., The Washington Post; broadcasting work includes Newsnight (BBC2), Today (BBC Radio 4), Week in Westminster (BBC Radio 4), CNN, MSNBC, CBS, Sky News. *Publications:* non-fiction: Between East and West: Across the Borderlands of Europe 1995, Gulag: A History 2003; contrib. to Wall Street Journal, Int. Herald Tribune, Foreign Affairs, Boston Globe, Independent, Guardian, Commentaire, Suddeutsche Zeitung, Newsweek, New Criterion, Weekly Standard, New Republic, New York Review of Books, Nat. Review, New Statesman, TLS, Literary Review. *Honours:* Charles Douglas-Home Memorial Trust Award for Journalism 1992, Adolph Bentnick Prize for European non-fiction 1996. *Address:* The Washington Post, 1150 15th Street NW, Washington, DC 20071, USA. *E-mail:* applebaumanne@washpost.com. *Website:* www.washingtonpost.com; www.anneapplebaum.com.

APPLEMAN, Marjorie H., BA, MA; American dramatist and poet; b. Fort Wayne, Ind.; m. Philip Appleman. *Education:* Northwestern Univ., Indiana Univ., Univ. of Paris (Sorbonne), France. *Career:* Prof. of English and Playwriting, New York Univ., Columbia Univ.; Int. Honors Program, Indiana Univ.; mem. Authors' League of America, Circle East Theater Co., Dramatists' Guild, League of Professional Theatre Women, PEN American Center, Poets and Writers, Acad. of American Poets. *Publications:* plays: Seduction Duet 1982, The Commuter 1985, over 60 plays given in full productions or staged readings 1971–2006, Against Time (poems) 1994, Let's Not Talk About Lenny Anymore (opera libretto) 1989; contrib. to numerous anthologies and journals. *Honours:* several playwriting awards. *Address:* PO Box 5058, East Hampton, NY 11937, USA. *E-mail:* applemanmh@yahoo.com.

APPLEMAN, Philip Dean, BS, MA, PhD; American writer, poet and academic; b. 8 Feb. 1926, Kendallville, Ind.; m. Marjorie Ann Haberkorn 1950. *Education:* Northwestern Univ., Univ. of Michigan. *Career:* Fulbright Scholar, Univ. of Lyon, France 1951–52; Instructor to Prof., Indiana Univ. 1955–67, Prof. 1967–84, Distinguished Prof. of English 1984–86, Distinguished Prof. Emer. 1986–; Dir and Instructor, Int. School of America 1960–61, 1962–63; Visiting Prof., State Univ. of NY at Purchase 1973, Columbia Univ., New York 1974; Visiting Scholar, New York Univ., UCLA; John Steinbeck Visiting Writer, Long Island Univ. at Southampton 1992; mem. Acad. of American Poets, American Asscn of Univ. Profs, Authors' Guild of America, Modern Language Asscn, Nat. Council of Teachers of English, PEN American Center, Poetry Soc. of America, Poets and Writers. *Publications:* fiction: In the Twelfth Year of the War 1970, Shame the Devil 1981, Apes and Angels 1989; poetry: Kites on a Windy Day 1967, Summer Love and Surf 1968, Open Doorways 1976, Darwin's Ark 1984, Darwin's Bestiary 1986, Let There Be Light 1991, New and Selected Poems 1956–1996 1996; non-fiction: The Silent Explosion 1965; editor: 1859: Entering an Age of Crisis 1959, Darwin 1970, The Origin of Species 1975, An Essay on the Principle of Population 1976; contribs to numerous publs. *Honours:* Ferguson Memorial Award, Friends of Literature Soc. 1969, Christopher Morley Awards, Poetry Soc. of America 1970, 1975, Castanola Award, Poetry Soc. of America 1975, Nat. Endowment for the Arts Fellowship 1975, Pushcart Prize 1985, Humanist Arts Award, American Humanist Asscn 1994, Friend of Darwin Award, Nat. Center for Science Educ. 2002. *Address:* PO Box 5058, East Hampton, NY 11937, USA. *E-mail:* applemanmp@yahoo.com.

APT, Bryan Andrew, BLS, MS, MPh; American writer; b. 30 May 1965, Fort Collins, CO. *Education:* Princeton Univ., Iowa State Univ., Indiana Univ., Johns Hopkins Univ. *Publications:* Case of the Missing Detective: Mystery Down Under 1995, Search for Freedom – Distinctions between Illusory and Actual Human Freedom: Dickens and Engels 1999, Tragic Time and Comic Time in Shakespeare's Plays 1999, Under the Apple Tree: Musings and Poetry 2001, Othello: A Tragic Passage from Light to Darkness 2002, Images of Light and Darkness in Heart of Darkness: Undermining Nineteenth-Century Idealism 2003. *Honours:* Nat. Merit Scholar, US Tennis Asscn ranked player. *Address:* c/o Harper Benton Press, 1017 Burnett Avenue, Ames, IA 50010, USA (office).

ARBATOVA, Maria Ivanovna; Russian novelist, playwright and poet; b. (Maria Ivanova Gavrilina), 17 July 1957, Murom, Vladimir region; d. of Ivan Gavrilovich Gavrilin and Ludmila Ilyinichna Aisenstadt; m. 2nd Oleg Tumayevich Vitte; two s. *Education:* Moscow State Univ. and Moscow Literary Inst. (workshop of Victor Rozov). *Career:* active participant in feminist movt and other political activities 1991–; founder Psychological Club Garmonia 1991–96; Dir Women Involved with Politics Club 1996–; columnist, Obshchaya Gazeta; Cand. for State Duma 1999; Co-Chair. Partiya prav Cheloveka pressure group; commentator for Ya Sama TV talk show; mem. Union of Writers of Moscow, Union of Theatrical Artistes of Russia. *TV appearances:* I-Myself (regular appearances). *Plays:* Victoria Vassilyeva in the Eye of Strangers (USSR Competition of Young Dramatists Prize 1985), Dreams on the Bank of Dniepr (Festival of Young Dramatists Prize 1990), Detailed Interview on the Subject of Freedom (Bonn Theatre Festival Prize, Germany) 1996, Russian Mirror: Three Plays by Russian Women (Russian Theatre Archive) 1998. *Radio plays:* Late Crew, Initiation Ceremony (Europe Prize 1998). *Publications include:* I Am 40 (autobiog. novel), I Am a Woman (stories), A Will and a Way: Russian Women's Writing in the 1990s (co-author) 2002; numerous articles and essays. *Address:* EKSMO Publishers, Narognogo

Opolcheniya str. 38, 1232298 Moscow, Russia (office). *Telephone:* (095) 246-81-55 (home). *E-mail:* arbatova@cityline.ru. *Website:* www.arbatova.ru.

ARCHER, Geoffrey Wilson; British writer; b. 21 May 1944, London, England; m. Eva Janson; one s. one d. *Education:* Highgate School, London. *Career:* researcher Southern TV 1964; reporter Anglia TV, Norwich 1965–69, Tyne-Tees TV, Newcastle 1969, ITN 1969–95, Defence Correspondent 1980–95; mem. Soc. of Authors, CWA. *Publications:* fiction: Skydancer 1987, Shadow Hunter 1989, Eagle Trap 1992, Scorpion Trail 1995, Java Spider 1997, Fire Hawk 1998, The Lucifer Network 2001, The Burma Legacy 2002, Dark Angel 2004. *Address:* c/o Century/Arrow Books, 20 Vauxhall Bridge Road, London, SW1V 2SA, England. *E-mail:* ga@geoffreyarcher.info. *Website:* www.geoffreyarcher.co.uk.

ARCHER OF WESTON-SUPER-MARE, Baron (Life Peer), cr. 1992, of Mark in the County of Somerset; **Jeffrey Howard Archer;** British writer and fmr politician; b. 15 April 1940, London; s. of William Archer and Lola Archer (née Cook); m. Mary Archer 1966; two s. *Education:* Wellington School and Brasenose Coll., Oxford. *Career:* mem. GLC for Havering 1966–70; MP for Louth (Conservative) 1969–74; Deputy Chair. Conservative Party 1985–86; mem. House of Lords 1992–; sentenced to four years' imprisonment for perjury and perverting the course of justice July 2001, released July 2003. *Plays:* Beyond Reasonable Doubt 1987, Exclusive 1989, The Accused (writer and actor) 2000. *Film:* Bridget Jones's Diary (as himself) 2001. *Television:* three advertisements. *Publications:* Not a Penny More, Not a Penny Less 1975, Shall We Tell the President? 1977, Kane and Abel 1979, A Quiver Full of Arrows 1980, The First Miracle (with Craigie Aitchison) 1980, The Prodigal Daughter 1982, First Among Equals 1984, A Matter of Honour 1985, A Twist in the Tale (short stories) 1988, As the Crow Flies 1991, Honour Among Thieves 1993, Twelve Red Herrings (short stories) 1994, The Fourth Estate 1996, The Collected Short Stories 1997, The Eleventh Commandment 1998, To Cut a Long Story Short (short stories) 2000, A Prison Diary Vols I and II 2002, Sons of Fortune 2003, A Prison Diary Vol. III 2004, False Impression 2006, Cat O' Nine Tales (short stories) 2006, The Gospel According to Judas 2007. *Address:* Peninsula Heights, 93 Albert Embankment, London, SE1 7TY, England. *E-mail:* questions@jeffreyarcher.co.uk. *Website:* www.jeffreyarcher .co.uk.

ARDAI, Charles, BA; American writer and editor; b. 25 Oct. 1969, New York, NY. *Education:* Columbia Univ. *Career:* Contributing Ed., Computer Entertainment and K-Power 1985; Ed., Davis Publications 1990–91; mem. MWA. *Publications:* Great Tales of Madness and the Macabre 1990, Kingpins 1992, Futurecrime 1992, Death do us Part 2006; Contributions: Alfred Hitchcock's Mystery Magazine, Ellery Queen's Mystery Magazine, Twilight Zone, The Year's Best Horror Stories, Computer Gaming World, and others. *Honours:* Pearlman Prize for Fiction, Columbia Univ. 1991, Edgar Award for Best Short Story (for The Home Front) 2007. *Address:* 350 E 52nd St, New York, NY 10022, USA.

ARDEN, John; British playwright and novelist; b. 26 Oct. 1930, Barnsley; s. of Charles Alwyn Arden and Annie Elizabeth Layland; m. Margaretta Ruth D'Arcy (q.v.) 1957; five s. (one deceased). *Education:* Sedbergh School, King's Coll., Cambridge and Edinburgh Coll. of Art. *Career:* British Army Intelligence Corps 1949–50; architectural asst 1955–57; Fellow in Playwriting, Univ. of Bristol 1959–60; Visiting Lecturer (Politics and Drama), New York Univ. 1967; Regent's Lecturer, Univ. of California, Davis 1973; Writer in Residence, Univ. of New England, Australia 1975; mem. Corrandulla Arts and Entertainment Club 1973, Galway Theatre Workshop 1975. *Plays:* All Fall Down 1955, The Waters of Babylon 1957, Live Like Pigs 1958, Serjeant Musgrave's Dance 1959, The Happy Haven (with Margaretta D'Arcy) 1960, The Business of Good Government (with Margaretta D'Arcy) 1960, Wet Fish 1962, The Workhouse Donkey 1963, Ironhand 1963, Ars Longa Vita Brevis (with Margaretta D'Arcy) 1964, Armstrong's Last Goodnight 1964, Left Handed Liberty 1965, Friday's Hiding (with Margaretta D'Arcy) 1966, The Royal Pardon (with Margaretta D'Arcy) 1966, Muggins is a Martyr (with Margaretta D'Arcy and C.A.S.T.) 1968, The Hero Rises Up (musical with Margaretta D'Arcy) 1968, Two Autobiographical Plays 1972, The Ballygombeen Bequest (with Margaretta D'Arcy) 1972, The Island of the Mighty (with Margaretta D'Arcy) 1972, The Non-Stop Connolly Show (with Margaretta D'Arcy) 1975, Vandaleur's Folly (with Margaretta D'Arcy) 1978, The Little Gray Home in the West (with Margaretta D'Arcy) 1978, The Making of Muswell Hill (with Margaretta D'Arcy) 1979. *Radio:* The Life of Man 1956, The Bagman 1969, Keep Those People Moving (with Margaretta D'Arcy) 1972, Pearl 1977, Don Quixote (adaptation) 1980, Garland for a Hoar Head 1982, The Old Man Sleeps Alone 1982, The Manchester Enthusiasts (with Margaretta D'Arcy) 1984, Whose is the Kingdom? (with Magaretta D'Arcy) 1988, A Suburban Suicide (with Margaretta D'Arcy) 1994, Six Little Novels of Wilkie Collins (adaptation) 1997, Woe Alas, the Fatal Cashbox! 1999, Wild Ride to Dublin 2003, Poor Tom Thy Horn is Dry 2003. *Television:* Soldier Soldier 1960, Wet Fish 1962, Profile of Sean O'Casey (documentary, with Margaretta D'Arcy) 1973. *Publications:* essays: To Present the Pretence 1977, Awkward Corners (with Margaretta D'Arcy) 1988; novels: Silence Among the Weapons 1982, Books of Bale 1988, Jack Juggler and the Emperor's Whore 1995; short stories: Cogs Tyrannic 1991, The Stealing Steps 2003. *Honours:* PEN Short Story Prize 1992, V. S. Pritchett Short Story Prize 1999, Evening Standard Drama Award 1960, Arts Council Playwriting Award (with Margaretta D'Arcy) 1972. *Address:* c/o Casarotto Ramsay Ltd, National

House, 60–66 Wardour Street, London, W1V 3HP, England. *Telephone:* (20) 7287-4450. *Fax:* (20) 7287-9128.

ARGUELLES, Ivan Wallace, BA, MLS; American poet, publisher and librarian; b. 24 Jan. 1939, Rochester, MN; m. 1st Claire Birnbaum 1958 (divorced 1960); m. 2nd Marilla Calhourn Elder 1962; two s. *Education:* Univ. of Minnesota, Univ. of Chicago, New York Univ., Vanderbilt Univ. *Career:* Guest Lecturer, Rampo Coll., NJ 1978; Co-Founder Rock Steady Press, San Francisco, Calif. 1988, Pantograph Press, Berkeley, Calif. 1992. *Publications:* Instamatic Reconditioning 1978, The Invention of Spain 1978, Captive of the Vision of Paradise 1983, The Tattoed Heart of the Drunken Sailor 1983, Manicomio 1984, Nailed to the Coffin of Life 1985, What Are They Doing to My Animal? 1986, The Structure of Hell 1986, Pieces of the Bone-Text Still There 1987, Baudelaire's Brain 1988, Looking for Mary Lou: Illegal Syntax (William Carlos Williams Award, Poetry Soc. of America 1989) 1989, 'THAT' Goddess 1992, Hapax Legomenon 1993, The Tragedy of Momus 1993, Enigma and Variations: Paradise is Persian for Park 1996, Madonna Septet (two vols) 2000, Chac Prostibulario (with John M. Bennett) 2002, Triloka 2003, Inferno 2005; contribs to various anthologies and magazines. *Address:* 1740 Walnut Street, No. 4, Berkeley, CA 94709, USA. *E-mail:* iarguell@hotmail.com.

ARGUETA, Manlio; Salvadorean writer and librarian; b. 24 Nov. 1935, San Miguel. *Career:* lived in exile in Costa Rica for many years since 1973; apptd. Dir of Library, Univ. of El Salvador 1996. *Publications:* One Day of Life 1980 (trans. into English 1984), Cuscatlán (novel) 1987, Rosario de la Paz (novel) 1996, Siglo de O(g)ro 1997. *Honours:* Univ. of Cen. America Prize (for One Day of Life) 1980. *Address:* c/o Biblioteca, Universidad de El Salvador, Final 24 Avda Norte, Ciudad Universitaria, Apdo postal 2973, San Salvador, El Salvador.

ARIAS, Arturo, PhD; Guatemalan novelist and literary critic; b. 1950. *Education:* Univ. of Paris. *Career:* Pres., Latin American Studies Asscn 2001–03; currently Dir of Latin American Studies, Univ. of Redlands. *Film screenplays include:* El Norte 1984. *Publications:* novels: Despues de las bombas (trans. as After the Bombs) 1979, Itzam Na 1981, Jaguar en Llamas 1989, Los caminos de Paxil 1990, Cascabel 1998, Sopa de caracól 2003; criticism: La identidad de la palabra (trans. as The Identity of the Word) 1998, Gestos ceremoniales (trans. as Ceremonial Gestures) 1998, Miguel Angel Asturias's Mulata 2001, The Rigoberta Menchu Controversy 2001; contrib. to Rattlesnake 2003. *Honours:* Casa de las Americas Prize, Anna Seghers Scholarship (twice). *Literary Agent:* c/o Curbstone Press, 321 Jackson Street, Willimantic, CT 06226-1738, USA. *E-mail:* info@curbstone.org. *Website:* www.curbstone.org.

ARIDJIS, Homero; Mexican author, poet and diplomatist; *President Emeritus, International PEN;* b. 6 April 1940, Contepec, Michoacán; m. Betty Ferber 1965, two d. *Education:* Autonomous Univ. of Mexico 1961. *Career:* lecturer in Mexican literature at univs in USA; Cultural Attaché, Embassy in Netherlands 1972, later Amb. to Switzerland and the Netherlands; Man. Cultural Inst., Michoacán, Dir Festival Int. de Poesia 1981, 1982, 1987; f. Review Correspondencias; Chief Ed. Dialogos; Visiting Prof., Univ. of Indiana and New York Univ.; Poet-in-Residence, Columbia Univ. Translation Center, New York; co-f. Pres. Grupo de los Cien 1985 (100 internationally renowned artists and intellectuals active in environmental affairs); Nichols Chair in the Humanities and the Public Sphere, Univ. of Calif. at Irvine; Pres. International PEN 1997–2003, Pres. Emer. 2003–. *Publications include:* poetry: Los ojos desdoblados 1960, Antes del reino 1963, Ajedrez-Navegaciones 1969, Los espacios azules 1969 (Blue Spaces 1974), Quemar las naves 1975, Vivir para ver 1977, Construir la muerte 1982, Obra poética 1960–86 1987, Imágenes para el fin del milenio 1990, Nueva expulsión del paraíso 1990, El poeta en peligro de extinción 1992, Tiempo de ángeles 1994, Ojos de otro mirar 1998 (Eyes to See Otherwise: Selected Poems of Homero Aridjis 2002), El ojo de la ballena 2001; prose: La tumba de Filidor 1961, Mirándola dormir 1964, Perséfone 1967 (Persephone 1986), El poeta niño 1971, Noche de independencia 1978, Espectáculo del año dos mil 1981, Playa nudista y otros relatos 1982, 1492 vida y tiempos de Juan Cabezón de Castilla 1985, El último Adán 1986, Memorias del nuevo mundo 1988, Gran teatro del fin del mundo 1989, La leyenda de los soles 1993, El Señor de los últimos días: Visiones del año dos mil 1994, ¿En quién piensas cuando haces el amor? 1996, Apocalipsis con figuras 1997, La montaña de las mariposas 2000, El silencio de Orlando 2000, La zona del silencio 2002. *Honours:* Guggenheim Fellow 1966–67, 1979–80; Hon. DHumLitt (Indiana) 1993; Global 500 Award 1987, Novedades Novela Prize 1988, Grinzane Cavour Prize for Best Foreign Fiction 1992, Prix Roger Caillois, France 1997, Presea Generalisimo José María Morelos, City of Morelia 1998, Environmentalist of the Year Award, Latin Trade Magazine 1999, John Hay Award, Orion Soc. 2000, Forces for Nature Award, National Resources Defense Council 2001, Green Cross Millennium Award for Int. Environmental Leadership, Global Green, USA 2002. *Address:* International PEN, 9–10 Charterhouse Buildings, Goswell Road, London, EC1M 7AT, England. *Telephone:* (20) 7253-4308. *Fax:* (20) 7253-5711. *E-mail:* intpen@dircon.co.uk. *Website:* www.internatpen.org.

ARJOUNI, Jakob; German novelist and playwright; b. 8 Oct. 1964, Frankfurt am Main. *Plays:* The Garage 1988, Nobleman Daughter 1996. *Publications:* novels: Happy Birthday Turk 1987, More Beer 1987, One Man One Murder 1991, And still Drink More! 1994, Magic Hoffman 1996, One Death to Die 1997; short story collections: A Friend 1998, Kismet 2001. *Address:* c/o No Exit Press, Oldcastle Books, PO Box 394, Harpenden,

Hertfordshire AL5 1XJ, England. *E-mail:* info@noexit.co.uk. *Website:* www.noexit.co.uk.

ARKOUN, Mohammed, PhD; French/Algerian writer and academic; *Director, ARABICA journal;* b. 1 Feb. 1932, Algeria; one s. one d. *Education:* Sorbonne, Univ. of Paris. *Career:* Prof. of Islamic Studies, Sorbonne, Univ. of Paris 1961–93, Prof. Emer. 1993–; Visiting Prof., Europe, USA, Indonesia and Arab world; int. lectures; debates on TV and radio in various countries; currently Scientific Dir, ARABICA (Journal of Arabic and Islamic Studies), Brill, Leiden. *Publications:* Rethinking Islam 1995, The Unthought in Contemporary Islamic Thought 2001, Penser l'islam aujourd hui 2001, De Manhattan à Bagdad: Au delà du Bien et du Mal 2003, Le Pensée arabe 2003, L'Humanism arabe au 4e/10e Siècle 2005, Penser l'islam aujourd'hui 2005, Humanisme et Islam 2005; contrib. to books and journals. *Honours:* Commandeur, Légion d'honneur. *Address:* PO Box 12565, Ain-Diab, Casablanca, Morocco. *Website:* www.arkoum.org.

ARLEN, Leslie (see Nicole, Christopher Robin)

ARLEN, Michael John, BA; American writer; b. 9 Dec. 1930, London, England; m. Alice Albright 1972; four d. *Education:* Harvard Univ. *Career:* mem. Authors' Guild, PEN. *Publications:* Living-Room War 1969, Exiles 1970, An American Verdist 1972, Passage to Ararat (Nat. Book Award 1976) 1974, The View from Highway One 1975, Thirty Seconds 1980, The Camera Age 1982, Say Goodbye to Sam 1984; contrib. to New Yorker magazine. *Honours:* National Book Award 1975, Le Prix Bremond 1976; Hon. DLitt 1984.

ARMAH, Ayi Kwei, MFA; Ghanaian novelist and poet; b. 1939, Sekondi Takoradi. *Education:* Harvard Univ., Columbia Univ. *Career:* fmr translator, Révolution Africaine magazine; scriptwriter, Ghana TV 1964; Ed., Jeune Afrique magazine, Paris 1967–68; teacher, Coll. of Nat. Education, Chamg'omge, Tanzania, Nat. Univ. of Lesotho, various other institutes. *Publications:* novels: The Beautyful Ones are Not Yet Born 1968, Fragments 1970, Why Are We So Blest? 1972, Two Thousand Seasons 1973, The Healers 1978, Osiris Rising 1995; contrib. short stories and articles to Présense Africaine, Okyeame, Harper's, Atlantic Monthly, New African, West Africa.

ARMEL, Aliette; French writer. *Career:* critic, Magazine littéraire 1984–. *Publications:* non-fiction: Marguerita Duras et l'autobiographie 1990, Michel Leiris 1997; fiction: L'enfant abandonné (short stories) 1998, Le voyage de Bilqís (novel, trans. as Love, The Painter's Wife and The Queen of Sheba) 2002, Le Disparu de Salonique (novel) 2005; contrib. essays to Marguierite Duras: Les trois lieux de l'ecrit 1998, Les itinéraires de Michel Ragon 1999, Antigone 1999, Sylvie 2001. *Address:* 5 rue Nicolas Roret, 75013 Paris, France (home). *Telephone:* 1 55 43 99 30 (home). *Fax:* 1 55 43 99 30 (home). *E-mail:* aliette.armel@libertysurf.fr (home). *Website:* www.magazine-litteraire.com.

ARMES, Roy Philip, BA, PhD; British writer and academic; b. 16 March 1937, Norwich, England; m. Margaret Anne Johnson 1960, one s. two d. *Education:* Univ. of Bristol, Univ. of Exeter, Univ. of London. *Career:* teacher, Royal Liberty School, Romford 1960–69; Assoc. Lecturer in Film, Univ. of Surrey 1969–72; Research Fellow, Hornsey Coll. of Art 1969–72, Lecturer 1972–73; Sr Lecturer, Middlesex Polytechnic 1973–78, Reader in Film and Television 1978–; visiting lecturer at many colls and univs. *Publications:* French Cinema Since 1946 (two vols) 1966; The Cinema of Alain Resnais, 1968; French Film, 1970; Patterns of Realism, 1972; Film and Reality: An Historical Survey, 1974; The Ambiguous Image, 1976; A Critical History of British Cinema, 1978; The Films of Alain Robbe-Grillet, 1981; French Cinema, 1984; Third World Film Making and the West, 1987; Action and Image: Dramatic Structure in Cinema, 1994; contrib. to many books and periodicals.

ARMITAGE, Gary Edric, (Robert Edric), BA, PhD; British writer; b. 14 April 1956, Sheffield, England; m. Sara Jones 1978. *Education:* Hull Univ. *Publications:* Winter Garden 1985, A Season of Peace 1985, A New Ice Age 1986, Across the Autumn Grass 1986; as Robert Edric: A Lunar Eclipse 1989, In the Days of the American Museum 1990, The Broken Lands 1992, Hallowed Ground 1993, The Earth Made of Glass 1994, Elysium 1995, In Desolate Heaven 1997, The Sword Cabinet 1999, The Book of the Heathen 2000, Peacetime 2002, Cradle Song 2003, Siren Song 2004, Swan Song 2005, Gathering the Water 2006, The Kingdom of Ashes (novel) 2007; contrib. to various periodicals. *Honours:* James Tait Black Memorial Prize 1985, Trask Award 1985, Soc. of Authors Award 1994, Arts Council Bursary 1995. *Address:* Glenfinnan, Springbank Avenue, Hornsea, East Yorkshire HU18 1ED, England.

ARMITAGE, Ronda Jacqueline, DipEd; New Zealand writer, teacher and family therapist; b. 11 March 1943, Kaikoura; m. David Armitage 1966, two c. *Education:* Hamilton Teacher's Coll. *Career:* school teacher, Duvauchelle, New Zealand 1964–66, London, England 1966, Auckland, New Zealand 1968–69; adviser on children's books, Dorothy Butler Ltd, Auckland 1970–71; Asst Librarian, Lewes Priory Comprehensive School, Sussex, England 1976–77; teacher, East Sussex County Council, England 1978–; family therapist; mem. Soc. of Authors. *Publications:* Let's Talk About Drinking 1982, New Zealand 1983; children's fiction: The Lighthouse Keeper's Lunch 1977, The Trouble With Mr Harris 1978, Don't Forget, Matilda! 1978, The Bossing of Josie (aka The Birthday Spell) 1980; Ice Creams for Rosie 1981, One Moonlit Night 1983, Grandma Goes Shopping 1984, The Lighthouse Keeper's Catastrophe 1986, The Lighthouse Keeper's Rescue 1989, When Dad Did the Washing 1990, Watch the Baby, Daisy 1991, Looking After Chocolates 1992, A Quarrel of Koalas 1992, The Lighthouse Keeper's Picnic 1993, The

Lighthouse Keeper's Cat 1996, Flora and the Strawberry Red Birthday Party 1997, Queen of the Night 1999, Family Violence 1999; contrib. features in children's magazine Aquila 1998, 1999, 2000. *Honours:* New Zealand Library Asscn Esther Glen Award 1978. *Address:* Puffin Books, 80 Strand, London, WC2R 0LR (office); Old Tiles Cottage, Church Lane, Hellingly, East Sussex BN27 4HA, England (home).

ARMITAGE, Simon Robert, BA, MA; British poet and writer; b. 26 May 1963, Huddersfield, West Yorkshire, England; m. Alison Tootell 1991. *Education:* Portsmouth Polytechnic, Manchester Univ. *Career:* Probation Officer, Greater Manchester Probation Service 1988–93; Poetry Ed., Chatto and Windus 1993–95. *Publications:* Zoom! 1989, Xanadu 1992, Kid 1992, Book of Matches 1993, The Dead Sea Poems 1995, Travelling Songs 2001, Little Green Man 2001, The Universal Home Doctor 2002, The White Stuff 2004, Homer's Odyssey 2006, Tyrannosaurus Rex Versus the Corduroy Kid 2006, Sir Gawain and the Green Knight 2007; contrib. to Sunday Times, TLS, Guardian, Observer, Independent. *Honours:* Eric Gregory Award 1988, Sunday Times Young Writer of the Year 1993, Forward Poetry Prize 1993, Lannan Award 1994. *Address:* 3 Netherley, Marsden, Huddersfield HD7 6XN, England.

ARMSTRONG, David John, BA; Australian journalist; *Chief Operating Officer, Post Publishing, Bangkok*; b. 25 Nov. 1947, Sydney; s. of Allan E. Armstrong and Mary P. Armstrong; m. Deborah Bailey 1980; two d. *Education:* Marist Brothers High School Parramatta, Univ. of NSW. *Career:* Ed. The Bulletin 1985–86; Deputy Ed. The Daily Telegraph 1988–89; Ed. The Australian 1989–92, Ed.-in-Chief 1996–2002; Ed. The Canberra Times 1992–93; Ed. South China Morning Post, Hong Kong 1993–94, Ed.-in-Chief 1994–96; Ed.-in-Chief, South China Morning Post 2003–05; Chief Operating Officer, Post Publishing 2005–. *Address:* Bangkok Post Building, 136 Na Ranong Road, off Sunthorn Kosa Road, Klong Toey, Bangkok 10110, Thailand (office). *Telephone:* (2) 240-3826 (office). *Fax:* (2) 240-3679 (office). *E-mail:* david@bangkokpost.co.th (office). *Website:* www.bangkokpost.co.th (office).

ARMSTRONG, David Malet, AO, BA, BPhil, PhD, FAHA, FBA; Australian academic and writer; *Professor Emeritus of Philosophy, University of Sydney*; b. 8 July 1926, Melbourne; s. of Cdre J. M. Armstrong and Philippa Suzanne Marett; m. Jennifer Mary de Bohun Clark 1982. *Education:* Dragon School, Oxford, UK, Geelong Grammar School, Sydney Univ., Exeter Coll., Oxford, Univ. of Melbourne. *Career:* Asst Lecturer in Philosophy, Birkbeck Coll., London, UK 1954–55; Lecturer, Sr Lecturer in Philosophy, Univ. of Melbourne 1956–63; Challis Prof. of Philosophy, Univ. of Sydney 1964–91, Prof. Emer. 1992–; mem. Bd Quadrant magazine. *Publications:* Berkeley's Theory of Vision 1961, Perception and the Physical World 1961, Bodily Sensations 1962, A Materialist Theory of the Mind 1968, Belief, Truth and Knowledge 1973, Universals and Scientific Realism 1978, The Nature of the Mind and Other Essays 1983, What is a Law of Nature? 1983, Consciousness and Causality (with Norman Malcolm) 1984, A Combinatorial Theory of Possibility 1989, Universals: An Opinionated Instruction 1989, Dispositions: A Debate (with C. B. Martin and U. T. Place) 1996, A World of States of Affairs 1997, The Mind-Body Problem: An Opinionated Introduction 1999, Truth and Truthmakers 2004; contribs to scholarly books and journals. *Address:* 206 Glebe Point Road, Glebe, NSW 2037, Australia (home). *Telephone:* (2) 9660-1435 (home). *Fax:* (2) 9660-8846 (home). *E-mail:* david.armstrong@arts.usyd .edu.au.

ARMSTRONG, Jeannette Christine, DFA, BFA; Canadian (Okanagan, Penticton Indian Band) writer, poet and educator; b. 5 Feb. 1948; one s. one d. *Education:* Okanagan Coll., Univ. of Victoria, BC. *Career:* Adjunct Prof., En'owkin School of Writing, Univ. of Victoria, BC 1989–; mem. PEN Int., Writers' Union of Canada. *Publications:* Enwhisteetkwa 1982, Neekna and Chemai 1984, Slash 1985, Native Creative Process 1991, Breath Tracks 1991, Looking at the Words of Our People 1993, Whispering in Shadows 2000, Native Poetry in Canada: A Contemporary Anthology. *Honours:* Children's Book Centre Choice Award 1983. *Address:* c/o Theytus Books, Green Mountain Road, Lot 45, RR No. 2, Site 50, Comp. 8, Penticton, BC V2A 6J7, Canada.

ARMSTRONG, John Alexander, PhB, MA, PhD; American academic and writer; *Professor Emeritus, University of Wisconsin-Madison*; b. 4 May 1922, Saint Augustine, Fla; m. Annette Taylor 1952; three d. *Education:* Univ. of Chicago, Univ. of Frankfurt am Main, Germany, Columbia Univ., New York. *Career:* research analyst, War Documentation Project, Alexandria, Va 1951, 1953–54; Asst Prof., Univ. of Denver, Colo 1952; Visiting Asst Prof., Russian Inst., Columbia Univ. 1957; Asst Prof. to Philippe de Commynes Prof. of Political Science, Univ. of Wisconsin-Madison 1954–86, Prof. Emer. 1986–; mem. American Political Science Asscn, American Historical Asscn, American Asscn for Advancement of Slavic Studies (Pres. 1965–67), Council on Foreign Relations. *Publications:* Ukrainian Nationalism 1955, The Soviet Bureaucratic Elite 1959, The Politics of Totalitarianism 1961, Ideology, Politics and Government in the Soviet Union 1962, Soviet Partisans in World War II (ed.) 1964, The European Administrative Elite 1973, Nations Before Nationalism 1982; contrib. to numerous political and historical journals. *Honours:* Guggenheim Fellowships 1967, 1975, American Political Science Asscn Ralph J. Bunche Award 1983, American Asscn for Advancement of Slavic Studies Award 1997. *Address:* 40 Water Street, Saint Augustine, FL 32084, USA (home). *Telephone:* (904) 829-0171 (home).

ARMSTRONG, Karen Andersen, MA, MLitt; British writer; b. 14 Nov. 1944, Stourbridge, West Midlands; d. of John O. S. Armstrong and Eileen H. Machale. *Education:* Convent of the Holy Child Jesus, Birmingham, St Anne's Coll., Oxford. *Career:* nun 1962–69; Research Fellow, Bedford Coll., London 1973–76; Head of English, James Allen's Girls' School, London; writer and broadcaster 1982–. *Publications:* Through the Narrow Gate 1981, The Gospel According to Women 1986, Holy War 1988, Muhammaed, A Biography of the Prophet 1991, A History of God 1993, Jerusalem: One City, Three Faiths 1996, In the Beginning, A New Reading of Genesis 1996, The Battle for God – A History of Fundamentalism 2000, Islam: A Short History 2000, Buddha 2001, The Spiral Staircase: A Memoir 2004, The Great Transformation: The World in the Time of Buddha, Socrates, Confucius and Jeremiah 2006, Muhammad 2006, A Short History of Myth 2006, The Bible: A Biography 2007; regular columnist to The Guardian. *Honours:* Muslim Public Affairs Council Media Award 1999, Asscn of Muslim Social Scientists (UK) Award 2004; Open Center New York City Award 2004. *Address:* c/o Felicity Bryan, 2A North Parade, Banbury Road, Oxford, OX2 6PE, England. *Telephone:* (1865) 513816. *Fax:* (1865) 310055.

ARMSTRONG, Patrick Hamilton, BSc, DipEd, MA, PhD; Australian (b. British) academic and writer; *Honorary Research Fellow, School of Earth and Geographical Sciences, University of Western Australia*; b. 10 Oct. 1941, Leeds, Yorks.; s. of Edward Armstrong and Eunice Joan Armstrong (née Uttley); m. Moyra E. J. Irvine 1964; two s. *Education:* Univ. of Durham, UK. *Career:* Faculty, School of Earth and Geographical Sciences, Univ. of Western Australia, currently Hon. Research Fellow; Chief Examiner, Int. Baccalaureate Org.; Ed. Geographers-Biobibliographical Studies; has broadcast for Australian Broadcasting Corpn, BBC World Service. *Publications:* Discovering Ecology 1973, Discovering Geology 1974, The Changing Landscape 1975, series of children's books for Ladybird Books 1976–79, Ecology 1977, Reading and Interpretation of Australian and New Zealand Maps 1981, Living in the Environment 1982, The Earth: Home of Humanity 1984, Charles Darwin in Western Australia 1985, A Sketch Map Geography of Australia 1988, A Sketch Map Physical Geography for Australia 1989, Darwin's Desolate Islands 1992, The English Parson-Naturalist: A Companionship Between Science and Religion 2000, Darwin's Other Islands 2004; contribs to New Scientist, Geographical Magazine, East Anglian Magazine, Geography, Cambridgeshire Life, Eastern Daily Press, Work and Travel Abroad, West Australian Newspaper, Sydney Morning Herald, Weekly Telegraph; numerous articles in scholarly and scientific journals. *Address:* School of Earth and Geographical Sciences, University of Western Australia, Nedlands, WA 6009, Australia (office). *Telephone:* (8) 6488-2705 (office). *Fax:* (8) 6488-1054 (office). *E-mail:* parmstro@cyllene.uwa.edu.au (office).

ARMSTRONG OF ILMINSTER, Baron (Life Peer), cr. 1988, of Ashill in the County of Somerset; **Robert Temple Armstrong,** GCB, CVO, MA; British fmr civil servant; b. 30 March 1927, Oxford; s. of Sir Thomas Armstrong and of Lady Armstrong (née Draper); m. 1st Serena Mary Benedicta Chance 1953 (divorced 1985); two d.; m. 2nd (Mary) Patricia Carlow 1985. *Education:* Eton Coll. and Christ Church, Oxford. *Career:* Asst Prin. Treasury 1950–55, Pvt. Sec. to Econ. Sec. 1953–54; Pvt. Sec. to Chancellor of the Exchequer (Rt Hon. R. A. Butler) 1954–55; Prin. Treasury 1955–64; Asst Sec. Cabinet Office 1964–66; Asst Sec. Treasury 1966–68; Prin. Pvt. Sec. to Chancellor of the Exchequer (Rt Hon. Roy Jenkins) 1968; Under-Sec. Treasury 1968–70; Prin. Pvt. Sec. to the Prime Minister 1970–75; Deputy Under-Sec. of State, Home Office 1975–77, Perm. Under-Sec. of State 1977–79; Sec. of the Cabinet 1979–87; Perm. Sec. Man. and Personnel Office 1981–87; Head, Home Civil Service 1981–87; Chair. Biotechnology Investments Ltd 1989–2000; Chair. Forensic Investigative Assocs PLC 1997–2003; Chair. Hestercombe Gardens Trust 1995–2005, Bd of Govs Royal Northern Coll. of Music 2000–05; Sec. Radcliffe Cttee on Monetary System 1957–59; Sec. to the Dirs, Royal Opera House, Covent Garden 1968–87, Dir 1988–93; Dir Bristol and West Bldg Soc. 1988–97 (Chair. 1993–97), Bank of Ireland and other cos; Chair. Bd of Trustees, Victoria and Albert Museum 1988–98; mem. Rhodes Trust 1975–97; Fellow, Eton Coll. 1979–94; Chancellor, Univ. of Hull 1994–2006; Pres. The Literary Soc. 2004–; Trustee Leeds Castle Foundation 1987– (Chair. 2001–). *Honours:* Hon. Student, Christ Church 1985; Hon. Bencher, Inner Temple 1986; Hon. LLD. *Address:* House of Lords, Westminster, London, SW1A 0PW, England. *Telephone:* (20) 7219-4983. *Fax:* (20) 7219-1259.

ARNDT, Angelica, BA; Chilean journalist; b. 19 Aug. 1937, Santiago; d. of Eduardo Arndt and Eleonora Arndt (née Garay); m. Georges de Bourguignon 1958; two s. *Education:* Dunalastair School, Santiago, Catholic Univ. of Santiago and Colegio de Periodistas de Chile. *Career:* Ed. El Mercurio, Santiago 1974–76; int. relations columnist La Tercera 1976–77; int. relations reporter, Ercilla 1977–80, Revista Negocios 1980–81, Paula 1980–81, Chilean nat. TV 1980–81; dir, producer and ed. political and cultural programmes, Chilean nat. TV 1980–83; political interviewer, Cosas int. magazine 1982–; Research Archive Asst Hoover Inst., Stanford, CA, USA 1991, 1994; freelance political analyst, interviewer and journalist; contribs to int. journals. *Address:* Arnex, Casilia 19039, Correo 19, Lo Castillo, Santiago, Chile.

ARNOLD, Emily (see Mccully, Emily Arnold)

ARNOLD, Heinz Ludwig; German writer, critic and editor; b. 29 March 1940, Essen, Ruhr. *Education:* Univ. of Göttingen. *Career:* Ed. Text und Kritik 1963, Kritisches Lexikon zur Deutschsprachigen Gegenwartsliteratur 1978, Kritisches Lexikon zur Fremdsprachigen Gegenwartsliteratur 1983; mem.

Asscn of German Writers, PEN, Deutsche Akad. für Sprache und Dichtung, Darmstadt, OH Tulip Order. *Publications:* Brauchen wir noch die Literatur? 1972, Gespräche mit Schriftstellern 1975, Gespräch mit F. Dürrenmatt 1976, Handbuch der Deutschen Arbeiterliteratur 1977, Als Schriftsteller leben 1979, Vom Verlust der Scham und dem allmählichen Verschwinden der Demokratie 1988, Krieger Waldgänger, Anarch. Versuch über E. Jünger 1990, Querfahrt mit Dürrenmatt 1990–96, Die Drei Sprünge der Westdeutschen Gegenwartsliteratur 1993, Die Deutsche Literatur 1945–1960 (11 vols) 1995–2000, Grundzüge der Literaturwissenschaft 1996, F. Dürrenmatt, Gespräche 1996, Einigkeit und aus Ruinen 1999, Arthur Schnitzler: Ausgewählte Werke (eight vols) 1999–2002, Da schwimmen manchmal ein paar Sätze vorbei... 2001, 'Was bin ich?' Über Max Frisch 2002, Arbeiterlyrik 1842–1932 2003, Von Unvollendeten Literarische Porträts 2005; contrib. to Die Zeit, Frankfurter Rundschau, Frankfurter Allgemeine Zeitung, various radio stations. *Honours:* Hon. Prof., Univ. of Göttingen. *Address:* Tuckermannweg 10, 37085 Göttingen, Germany.

ARNOLD, Margot (see Cook, Petronelle Marguerite Mary)

ARNOTHY, Christine; French journalist and writer; b. 20 Nov. 1934, Budapest, Hungary; d. of Mr and Mrs Kovach de Szendrö; m. Claude Bellanger 1964 (died 1978); one s. one d. *Education:* Lycée français, Austria and Univ. of Paris (Sorbonne). *Career:* Literary Critic, Le Parisien Libéré, Paris 1961–, Head Literary Column 1978–; literary column in La Suisse, Geneva, Switzerland 1983–; contribs to other newspapers and magazines. *Publications:* J'ai quinze ans et je ne veux pas mourir (autobiog., Grand Prix Vérité) 1954, Dieu est en retard 1955, Il n'est pas si facile de vivre (autobiog.) 1957, Le cardinal prisonnier (Gold Cross of Merit, Hungary 1991) 1962, La saison des Américains 1964, Le jardin noir 1966, Aviva 1968, Chiche! 1970, Un type merveilleux 1972, Lettre ouverte aux rois nus 1974, Le cavalier mongol (Grand Prix de la Nouvelle, Acad. Française) 1976, J'aime la vie 1976, Le bonheur d'une manière ou d'une autre 1977, Toutes les chances plus une (Prix Interallié) 1980, Jeux de mémoire 1981, Un paradis sur mesure 1983, L'ami de la famille 1984, Les trouble-fête 1986, Vent africain (Prix des Maisons de la Presse, Prix Bernanos-Artois, Lacouture) 1989, Une affaire d'héritage 1991, Désert brûlant 1992, Voyage de noces 1994, Une question de chance 1995, La piste africaine 1997, Malins plaisirs 1999, Complot de femmes 2000, Embrasser la vie 2001; Clodomir Free ou le grand complot (cartoon text) 1975; also short stories in numerous magazines, and plays for TV and radio; works have been translated into many languages. *Honours:* Chevalier de la Légion d'Honneur; Commdr des Arts et Lettres; Chevalier de l'Ordre nat. du Mérite. *Address:* c/o Fayard, 75 rue des Saints-Pères, 75278 Paris Cedex 6, France (office); 2 rue Pedro Meylan, 1208 Genève, Switzerland (home).

ARNOULT, Erik, (Erik Orsenna), DèsScEcon, PhD; French civil servant and writer; b. 22 March 1947, Paris; s. of Claude Arnoult and Janine Arnoult (née Bodé); m. 2nd Catherine Clavier; one s. one d. *Education:* Ecole Saint-Jean de Béthune, Versailles, Institut d'Etudes Politiques, Paris, Univ. of Paris I. *Career:* lecturer Inst. d'Etudes Politiques, Paris 1975–80, Ecole Normale Supérieure 1977–81; Literary Ed. Editions Ramsay 1977–81; Sr Lecturer Université de Paris I 1978–81; Tech. Adviser to Ministry of Co-operation and Devt 1981–83, to Minister of Foreign Affairs 1990–92; Cultural Adviser to Pres. of Repub. 1983–90; Maître des Requêtes, Conseil d'Etat 1985–, Sr mem. 2000–; Pres. Centre Int. de la Mer 1991–, Ecole Nat. Supérieure du Paysage 1995–; Vice-Pres. Cytale Soc. 2000–; mem. Acad. Française. *Film screenplay:* Indochine (co-writer) (Acad. Award for Best Foreign Film). *Publications:* Espace national et déséquilibre monétaire 1977, La Vie comme à Lausanne 1997, Une comédie française 1980, L'Exposition coloniale (novel) (Prix Goncourt) 1988, Grand Amour 1993, Histoire du monde en neuf guitares 1996, Deux Etés (novel) 1996, Longtemps (novel) 1998, Portrait d'un homme heureux, André Le Nôtre 1613–1700 2000, La Grammaire est une chanson donce 2001. *Address:* Conseil d'Etat, 1 place du Palais Royal, 75001 Paris (office); 8 passage Sigaud, 75013 Paris, France (home).

ARPAIA, Bruno; Italian novelist, editor and translator; b. 1957, Ottaviano (Naples). *Education:* Univ. of Naples. *Career:* fmr journalist Il Mattino and La Repubblica; now freelance; trans. of Spanish and Latin American literature. *Publications:* novels: I forestieri (Bagutta Opera Prima Prize) 1990, Il futuro in punta di piedi 1994, Tempo perso (Premio Hammett Italia) 1997, L'angelo della storia (trans. as The Angel of History) (Campielli Prize) 2001. *Address:* c/o Canongate Books, 14 High Street, Edinburgh, EH1 1TE, Scotland.

ARRABAL, Fernando; Spanish writer; b. 11 Aug. 1932, Melilla; s. of Fernando Arrabal and Carmen Terán González; m. Luce Moreau 1958; one s. one d. *Education:* Univ. of Madrid. *Career:* political prisoner in Spain 1967; Founder "Panique" Movt with Topor, Jodorowsky, etc. *Exhibition:* Kalédescopies, Musée de Bayeux 2000. *Publications:* plays: numerous plays including Le cimetière des voitures, Guernica, Le grand cérémonial, L'architecte et l'Empereur d'Assyrie, Le jardin des délices, Et ils passèrent des menottes aux fleurs, Le ciel et la merde, Bella ciao, La Tour de Babel, L'extravagante réussite de Jésus-Christ, Karl Marx et William Shakespeare, Les délices de la chair, La traversée de l'empire, Luly, Cielito, Fando et Lis, Lettre d'amour; novels: Baal Babylone 1959, L'enterrement de la sardine 1962, Fêtes et rites de la confusion 1965, La tour prends garde, La reverdie, La vierge rouge, Bréviaire d'amour d'un haltérophile, L'extravagante croisade d'un castrat amoureux 1991, La tueuse du jardin d'hiver 1994, El Mono 1994, Le Funambule de Dieu 1998, Ceremonia por un teniente abandonado 1998, Porté disparu 2000, Levitación 2000; poetry includes: La pierre de la folie 1963, 100 sonnets 1966, Humbles paradis 1983, Liberté couleur de femme 1993, Arrabalesques 1994, Passion, Passions 1997, Le Frénétique du Spasme 1997; essays: numerous, including Le Panique, Le New York d'Arrabal, Lettre au Général Franco, Greco 1970, Lettre à Fidel Castro 1983, Goya-Dali 1992, La Dudosa Luz del Día 1994. *Films:* directed and written: Viva la Muerte, J'irai comme un cheval fou, L'arbre de Guernica, L'odyssée de la Pacific, Le cimetière des voitures, Adieu Babylone!, J.-L. Borges (Una Vida de Poesía) 1998. *Honours:* Officier, Ordre des Arts et des Lettres 1984, Chevalier, Légion d'honneur 2005; "Superdotado" Award 1942, Ford Foundation Award 1959, Grand Prix du Théâtre 1967, Grand Prix Humour Noir 1968, Obie Award 1976, Premio Nadal (Spain) 1983, World's Theater Prize 1984, Medalla de Oro de Bellas Artes (Spain) 1989, Prix du Théâtre (Acad. Française) 1993, Prix Int. Vladimir Nabokov 1994, Premio de Ensayo Espasa 1994, Grand Prix Soc. des Gens de Lettres 1996, Grand Prix de la Méditerranée 1996, Medal of Centre for French Civilization and Culture, New York 1997, Prix de la Francophonie 1998, Premio Mariano de Cavia 1998, Prix Alessandro Manzoni di Poesia 1999, Premio Nacional de las Letras, Premio Eninci Cine y Literatura 2000, Premio Nacional de Teatro 2001, Premio Ercilla Teatro 2001. *Address:* 22 rue Jouffroy d'Abbans, Paris 75017, France. *Fax:* 1-42-67-01-26. *E-mail:* arrabalf@noos.fr (home). *Website:* www.arrabal.org (home).

ARRIAGA JORDÁN, Guillermo; Mexican scriptwriter; b. 1958, Mexico City. *Career:* Prof. of Film, Instituto Tecnológico de Estudios Superiores de Monterrey. *Films:* Campeones sin límite (writer, dir) 1997, ABC discapacidad (series writer) 1999, Amores Perros (writer) 2000, Rogelio (dir) 2000, Powder Keg (writer) 2001, 21 Grams (writer, assoc. prod.) (Satellite Award for Best Original Screenplay) 2003, Los elefantes nunca olvidan (prod.) 2004, The Three Burials of Melquiades Estrada (writer, actor) 2005, Babel (writer) 2006, El Búfalo de la noche (writer, prod.) 2006. *Publications:* novels: Escuádron guillotina 1991, Un dulce olor a muerte (trans. as A Sweet Scent of Death) 1994, El Búfalo de la noche 2000. *Address:* c/o Faber and Faber Ltd, 3 Queen Square, London, WC1N 3AU, England.

ARROW, Kenneth Joseph, PhD; American economist and academic; *Professor Emeritus of Economics and Operations Research, Stanford University*; b. 23 Aug. 1921, New York; s. of Harry I. Arrow and Lillian Arrow; m. Selma Schweitzer 1947; two s. *Education:* The City College, Columbia Univ. *Career:* Capt. USAF 1942–46; Research Assoc. Cowles Comm. for Research in Econ., Univ. of Chicago 1947–49; Asst Assoc. and Prof. of Econs, Statistics and Operations Research, Stanford Univ., 1949–68; Prof. of Econs, Harvard Univ., 1968–79; Prof. of Econs and Operations Research, Stanford Univ., 1979–91, Prof. Emer. 1991–; mem. NAS, American Acad. of Arts and Sciences, American Philosophical Soc., Finnish Acad. of Sciences, British Acad., Inst. of Medicine, Pontifical Acad. of Social Sciences; Pres. Int. Soc. for Inventory Research 1983–90, Int. Econ. Asscn, Econometric Soc., American Econ. Asscn, Soc. for Social Choice and Welfare; Dir various cos. *Publications:* Social Choice and Individual Values 1951, 1963, Studies in the Mathematical Theory of Inventory and Production (with S. Karlin and H. Scarf) 1958, Studies in Linear and Nonlinear Programming (with L. Hurwicz and H. Uzawa) 1958, A Time Series Analysis of Inter-industry Demands (with M. Hoffenberg) 1959, Public Investment, The Rate of Return and Optimal Fiscal Policy (with M. Kurz) 1970, Essays in the Theory of Risk-Bearing 1971, General Competitive Analysis (with F.H. Hahn) 1971, The Limits of Organization 1973, Studies in Resource Allocation Processes (with L. Hurwicz) 1977, Collected Papers 1983–85, Social Choice and Multicriterion Decision Making (with H. Raynaud) 1985; more than 240 articles in learned journals. *Honours:* Order of the Rising Sun (Japan); Hon. LLD (City Univ., Univ. of Chicago, Washington Univ., Univ. of Pennsylvania, Ben-Gurion Univ., Harvard Univ., Univ. of Cyprus, Univ. of Buenos Aires); Hon. Dr of Social and Econ. Sciences (Vienna); Hon. ScD (Columbia Univ.) 1973; Hon. DSocSci (Yale) 1974; Hon. LLD (Hebrew Univ. Jerusalem) 1975, Hon. DPolSci (Helsinki) 1976; Hon. DLitt (Cambridge) 1985, (Harvard) 1999; Hon. DUniv (Uppsala) 1995; Hon. PhD (Univ. of Tel-Aviv) 2001; Dr hc (Univ. René Descartes) 1974, (Univ. Aix-Marseille III) 1985, (Univ. of Cyprus) 2000; Nobel Memorial Prize in Econ. Science 1972, John Bates Clark Medal, Von Neumann Prize, Medal of Univ. of Paris 1998, Nat. Medal of Science 2006. *Address:* Department of Economics, Stanford University, Stanford, CA 94305-6072 (office); 580 Constanzo Street, Stanford, CA 94305, USA (home). *Telephone:* (650) 723-9165 (office). *Fax:* (650) 725-5702 (office). *E-mail:* arrow@stanford.edu (office). *Website:* www-econ.stanford.edu/faculty/arrow.html (office).

ARROWSMITH, Pat, BA; British writer and activist; b. 2 March 1930, England. *Education:* Newham Coll., Cambridge, Univ. of Ohio, USA and Liverpool Univ. *Career:* staff mem., Amnesty International 1972–94; mem. Ver Poets, London Poetry Soc. *Publications:* poetry: Breakout 1975, On the Brink 1981, Thin Ice 1984, Nine Lives 1990, Drawing to Extinction 2000; novels: Jericho 1965, Somewhere Like This 1970, The Prisoner 1982, I Should Have Been a Hornby Train (fiction/memoir) 1995, Many are Called 1998; non-fiction: To Asia in Peace 1972, The Colour of Six Schools 1972. *Honours:* second prize Hornsey, London Competition 1977, highly commended Westminster, London Competition 1978, Ver Poets Competition prize 1993.

ARSAND, Daniel; French novelist and publisher; b. 9 July 1950, Avignon. *Career:* bookseller, publisher; established Les Editions de la Sphere 1979–. *Publications:* novels: La Province des ténèbres (trans. as The Land of Darkness) (Prix Fémina) 1998, En silence 2000. *Literary Agent:* c/o Dedalus

Ltd, Langford Lodge, St Judith's Lane, Sawtry, Cambridgeshire PE28 5XE, England. *E-mail:* info@dedalusbooks.com. *Website:* www.dedalusbooks.com.

ARTEAGA, Alfred, BA, MA, MFA, PhD; American writer, poet and university educator; *Associate Professor of Ethnic Studies, University of California, Berkeley*; b. 2 May 1950, Los Angeles, CA; m. Dec. 1972 (divorced 1995); three d. *Education:* Univ. of California, Santa Cruz, Columbia Univ. *Career:* Instructor in Mexican-American Studies, San Jose City Coll., CA 1977–87; Asst Prof. of English, Univ. of Houston 1987–90; Asst Prof. of English, Univ. of California, Berkeley 1990–98, Assoc. Prof. of Ethnic Studies 1998–. *Publications:* Cantos (poems) 1991, An Other Tongue: Nation and Ethnicity in the Linguistic Borderlands (ed.) 1994, First Words: Origins of the European Nation 1994, House with the Blue Bed (essays) 1997, Chicano Poetics: Heterotexts and Hybridities (essays) 1997, Love in the Time of Aftershocks (poems) 1998, Red (poems) 2000, Zero Act (poems) 2006, Frozen Accident (poems) 2007; Contributions: anthologies including Spivak Reader, essays and poems to journals including Stanford Humanities Review, Critical Studies, Baldus, River Styx Electronic journals. *Honours:* Rockefeller Foundation Fellow, 1993–94; Poetry Fellow, National Endowment for the Arts, 1995. *Address:* Department of Ethnic Studies, University of California, Berkeley, 506 Barrows, Berkeley, CA 94720, USA (office). *Telephone:* (510) 642-3563 (office). *Fax:* (510) 642-6456 (office). *E-mail:* arteaga@socrates.berkeley.edu (office); aa@alfredarteaga.com (home). *Website:* www.alfredarteaga.com (home).

ARTEAGA SERRANO, Rosalía, PhD; Ecuadorean politician, lawyer, journalist and writer; b. 5 Dec. 1956, Cuerca; m. Pedro Fernández de Córdova 1978; three c. *Career:* graduated in political and social sciences, holds a Master's degree in Basic Educ. and Recovery of Latin American Cultural Values; Minister of Educ. and Culture 1994–96; Vice-Pres. of Ecuador 1996–98; Interim Pres. of Ecuador 9–11 Feb. 1997; fmr Chair. Nat. Devt Council (Conade); Sec.-Gen. Amazon Cooperation Treaty Org., Brasilia 2004–07; mem. Editorial Bd Encyclopædia Britannica. *Publications:* Jerónimo, Horas, Árboles de Cuenca, La mujer y la política, La Presidenta, el secuestro de una protesta, Los Sapos y la luciernaga. *Address:* c/o Amazon Cooperation Treaty Organization, SHIS – QI 05, Conjunto 16, casa 21, Lago Sul, 71615-160 Brasília DF, Brazil (office).

ARTHUR, Elizabeth Ann; American writer; b. 15 Nov. 1953, New York, NY; m. Steven Bauer 1982. *Education:* BA, English, University of Victoria, 1978; Diploma, Education, 1979. *Career:* Visiting Instructor, Creative Writing, University of Cincinnati, 1983–84; Visiting Asst Prof., English, Miami University, 1984–85; Asst Prof., English, 1985–92, Assoc. Prof., 1992–96, Indiana University-Purdue University at Indianapolis; Visiting Assoc. Prof., English, Miami University, 1996; mem. Poets and Writers. *Publications:* Island Sojourn (memoir), 1980; Beyond the Mountain (novel), 1983; Bad Guys (novel), 1986; Binding Spell (novel), 1988; Looking for the Klondike Stone (memoir), 1993; Antarctic Navigation, (novel), 1995; Bring Deeps (novel), 2003. Contributions: New York Times; Outside; Backpacker; Ski-XC; Shenandoah. *Honours:* William Sloane Fellowship, Bread Loaf Writers' Conference, 1980; Writing Fellowship, Ossabaw Island Project, 1981; Grant in Aid, Vermont Council on the Arts, 1982; Fellowship in Prose, National Endowment for the Arts, 1982–83; Master Artist Fellowship, Indiana Arts Commission, Indianapolis, 1988; Fellowship in Fiction, National Endowment for the Arts, 1989–90; Antarctic Artists' and Writers' Grant, National Science Foundation, 1990; Critics' Choice Award for Antarctic Navigation, 1995; Notable Book, New York Times Book Review, 1995. *Literary Agent:* c/o Bloomsbury Publishing PLC, 38 Soho Square, London, W1D 3HB, England. *E-mail:* eaa@elizabetharthur.org.

ARTHUR, Rasjid Arthur James, MA; British journalist; b. 7 June 1928, Stirling, Scotland. *Education:* Edinburgh Univ. *Career:* Nat. Service, RAF 1950–52; local reporter, Stirling 1952–54; Sub-Ed. 1954–55, leader writer 1955–64, The Scotsman; Features Ed., News Ed. and writer, Central Office of Information, London 1965–78; freelance writer on environment, development and related topics 1978–; mem. Chartered Inst. of Journalists. *Publications:* many articles on environmental subjects for British and int. magazines of the water industry and for the London Press Service of the Press Asscn. *Address:* 32 Midway, Middleton Cheney, Banbury, OX17 2QW, England. *Telephone:* (1295) 712099 (office). *E-mail:* rasjid_arthur@yahoo.co.uk (office).

ASADOV, Eduard Arkadevich; Russian poet; b. 7 Sept. 1923, Merv, Turkmenistan SSR; s. of Arkady Asadov and Lidya Asadova; m. 2nd Galina Asadova 1961; one s. *Education:* Gorky Literary Inst., Moscow. *Career:* Red Army 1941, seriously wounded and lost sight 1944; started publishing 1948; mem. CPSU 1951–91. *Publications:* Again into the Line 1948, Bright Roads 1951, Snowy Evening 1956, The Soldiers Have Returned from the War 1957, Galina 1960, Lyrical Limits 1962, I Love Forever 1965, Be Happy, Dreamers 1966, Isle of Romance 1969, Goodness 1972, I Fight, I Believe, I Love 1983, The Dream of Centuries 1985, The Highest Duty 1986, Collected Works (three vols) 1987–88, Fates and Hearts 1989, Letter from the Battle Front 1993, Never Surrender, People 1997, Don't Dare To Beat a Man (novel) 1998, Don't Give up the Beloved 2000. *Address:* Astrakhansky per., 5, Apt 78, Moscow 129010, Russia. *Telephone:* (495) 280-14-58.

ASANTE, Molefi Kete, BA, MA, PhD; American academic and poet; b. 14 Aug. 1942, Vaidosta, CA; m. Kariamu Welsh 1981; two s. one d. *Education:* Oklahoma Christian Univ., Pepperdine Univ., Univ. of California at Los Angeles. *Career:* Prof., University of California at Los Angeles, 1969–73,

SUNY at Buffalo, 1973–84, Temple University, 1984–; mem. African Writers' Union, vice-pres., 1994–. *Publications:* Break of Dawn, 1964; Epic in Search of African Kings, 1979; Afrocentricity, 1980; The Afrocentric Idea, 1987; Kemet, Afrocentricity and Knowledge, 1992; Classical Africa, 1992; African American History, 1995; African Intellectual Heritage, 1996; Love Dance, 1997; African American Atlas, 1998. Contributions: journals. *Honours:* hon. degrees, citations and awards. *Literary Agent:* c/o Jay Acton, Spartan Literary Agency, 55 Fifth Avenue, New York, NY, USA. *E-mail:* jacton@timeequities.com (office). *Address:* c/o Ana Yenenga, Asante and Associates, PO Box 30004, Elkins Park, PA 19027, USA (office). *Telephone:* (215) 782-3214 (office). *E-mail:* anaroot@cs.com (office). *Website:* www.asante.net.

ASARE, Meshack; Ghanaian children's writer and illustrator; b. 1945. *Publications include:* Tawia Goes to Sea 1970, I am Kofi 1972, Mansa Helps at Home 1973, The Brassman's Secret 1981, The Canoe's Story 1982, Chipo and the Bird on the Hill 1984, Cat: In Search of a Friend 1986, Seeing the World 1989, Bury my Bones but Keep my Words: African Tales for Retelling 1991, Halima's Dilemma 1992, The Frightened Thief 1993, The Magic Goat 1997, Sosu's Call 1998, Children of the Tree 1999, Meliga's Day 2000, Nana's Son 2000, Kwajo and the Brassman's Secret: A Tale of Old Ashanti Wisdom and Gold 2002, Noma's Sand: A Tale from Lesotho 2002, L'appel de Sosu 2002. *Honours:* Noma Award for Publishing in Africa 1982, UNESCO Prize for Children and Young People's Literature in the Service of Tolerance 1999. *Address:* c/o African Books Collective, Unit 13, Kings Meadow, Ferry Hinksey Road, Oxford, OX2 0DP, England (office). *Telephone:* (1865) 726686 (office). *Fax:* (1865) 793298 (office). *E-mail:* abc@africanbookscollective.com (office). *Website:* www.africanbookscollective.com (office).

ASARO, Catherine Ann, BS, MA, PhD; American astrophysicist and writer; b. 6 Nov. 1955, Oakland, CA; m. John Kendall Cannizzo 1986, one d. *Education:* Univ. of California, Los Angeles, Harvard Univ., Univ. of Toronto, Canada. *Career:* Consultant to Lawrence Livermore Laboratory 1978–83, Biodesign 1987, Harvard-Smithsonian Center for Astrophysics 1991; Asst Prof. of Physics, Kenyon College, Gambier, Ohio 1987–90, Affiliated Scholar 1990–91; Pres., Molecudyne Research, Laurel, MD 1990–; Visiting Scientist, Max Planck Institute for Astrophysics 1991–92; Ed., Publisher, Mindsparks: The Magazine of Science and Science Fiction 1993–; Columnist, Tangent periodical; mem. SFWA; American Asscn of Physics Teachers; American Physicists Soc. *Publications:* Science Fiction: Primary Inversion 1995, Catch the Lightning 1996, The Last Hawk 1997, The Radiant Seas 1998, The Veiled Web 1999, The Quantum Rose 2000, The Phoenix Code 2000, Ascendant Sun 2000, Spherical Harmonic 2001; Contributions: anthologies including Christmas Forever, Analog, periodicals and scholarly journals including Analog, Journal of Chemical Physics, New York Review of Science Fiction, American Journal of Physics, Int. Journal of Quantitative Chemistry, SFWA Bulletin, Science Fiction Age, Pirate Writings, Physical Review Letters. *Honours:* AnLab Analog Readers Poll, Homer Award, Sapphire Award, National Readers Choice Award, Prism Award, UTC Award. *Address:* c/o Molecudyne Research, PO Box 1302, Laurel, MD 20725, USA. *E-mail:* asaro@sff.net.

ASCHERSON, (Charles) Neal, MA; British journalist, editor and writer; *Editor, Public Archaeology*; b. 5 Oct. 1932, Edinburgh, Scotland; m. 1st Corinna Adam 1958 (divorced 1984); two d.; m. 2nd Isabel Hilton 1984; one s. one d. *Education:* Eton Coll., King's Coll., Cambridge. *Career:* reporter and leader writer Manchester Guardian 1956–58; Commonwealth Correspondent The Scotsman 1959–60, Eastern Europe Correspondent 1968–75; Scottish Politics Correspondent 1975–79; reporter The Observer 1960–63, Central Europe Correspondent 1963–68, Foreign Writer 1979–85, Assoc. Ed. 1985–89, columnist 1985–90; columnist The Independent on Sunday 1990–98; Ed. Public Archaeology 1998–. *Publications:* The King Incorporated 1963, The Polish August: The Self-Limiting Revolution 1981, The Struggles for Poland 1987, Games with Shadows 1988, Black Sea 1995, Stone Voices 2002. *Honours:* Golden Insignia, Order of Merit, Poland 1992; Hon. Fellow King's Coll., Cambridge 1993; Dr hc (Strathclyde, Edinburgh, St Andrews, Open Univ., Paisley, Bradford); Reporter of the Year 1982, Journalist of the Year 1987, Granada Awards James Cameron Award 1989, David Watt Memorial Prize 1991, George Orwell Award Political Quarterly 1993, Saltire Award for Literature 1995, 50th Anniversary Award of the Political Studies Asscn 2000. *Address:* 27 Corsica Street, London, N5 1JT, England.

ASH, John, BA; British writer, poet and teacher; b. 29 June 1948, Manchester, England. *Education:* Univ. of Birmingham. *Publications:* The Golden Hordes: International Tourism and the Pleasure Periphery (with Louis Turner) 1975, Casino: A Poem in Three Parts 1978, The Bed and Other Poems 1981, The Goodbyes 1982, The Branching Stairs 1984, Disbelief 1987, The Burnt Pages 1991, A Byzantine Journey 1995, Selected Poems 1996, The Anatolikon 1999, To the City 2002. *Honours:* Ingram Merrill Foundation grant 1985, Writing Foundation Award 1986. *Address:* c/o Carcanet Press, Fourth Floor, Alliance House, Cross Street, Manchester, M2 7AP, England.

ASHBERY, John Lawrence, MA; American poet, author, critic and academic; *Charles P. Stevenson, Jr Professor of Languages and Literature, Bard College*; b. 28 July 1927, Rochester, NY; s. of Chester F. Ashbery and Helen L. Ashbery. *Education:* Deerfield Acad., Mass, Harvard, Columbia and New York Univs. *Career:* asst, Literature Dept, Brooklyn (NY) Public Library 1949; copywriter, Oxford Univ. Press, New York 1951–54; McGraw-Hill Book Co. 1954–55; went to France as a Fulbright Scholar 1955–56, 1956–57, lived there 1958–65; Art Critic, Int. edn New York Herald-Tribune, Paris 1960–65;

Co-Ed. Locus Solus, Lans-en-Vercors, France 1960–62, Art and Literature, Paris 1964–67; Art Critic, Art International, Lugano 1961–63, New York Magazine 1978–80, Newsweek 1980–85; Paris corresp. Art News, New York 1964–65, Exec. Ed. 1965–72; Prof. of English and Co-Dir MFA Program in Creative Writing, Brooklyn Coll., NY (CUNY) 1974–90, Distinguished Prof. 1980–90, Distinguished Prof. Emer. 1990–; Poetry Ed. Partisan Review, New York 1976–80; Charles Eliot Norton Prof. of Poetry, Harvard Univ. 1989–90; Charles P. Stevenson, Jr Prof. of Languages and Literature, Bard Coll., Annandale-on-Hudson, NY 1990–; Chancellor Acad. of American Poets 1988–99; Leader, Fondation d'Art de La Napoule 1989; mem. American Acad. of Arts and Letters 1980–, American Acad. of Arts and Sciences 1983–; works translated into more than 20 languages. *Plays:* The Heroes 1952, The Compromise 1956, The Philosopher 1963, Three Plays 1978. *Publications include:* poetry: Turandot and Other Poems 1953, Some Trees 1956, The Tennis Court Oath 1962, Rivers and Mountains 1966, The Double Dream of Spring 1970, Three Poems 1972, The Vermont Notebook 1975, Self-Portrait in a Convex Mirror (Pulitzer Prize 1975, Nat. Book Award 1975, Nat. Book Critics' Circle Award 1975) 1975, Houseboat Days 1979, As We Know 1979, Shadow Train 1981, A Wave 1984, Selected Poems 1985, April Galleons 1987, Flow Chart 1991, Hotel Lautréamont 1992, And the Stars Were Shining 1994, Can You Hear, Bird 1995, Wakefulness 1998, Girls on the Run 1999, Your Name Here 2000, As Umbrellas Follow Rain 2001, Chinese Whispers 2002, Where Shall I Wander 2005; novel: A Nest of Ninnies (with J. Schuyler) 1969; essays and criticism: Fairfield Porter 1983, R. B. Kitaj (with others) 1983, Reported Sightings: Art Chronicles 1957–1987 1989, Other Traditions (The Charles Eliot Norton Lectures at Harvard) 2000; numerous translations from French including works by Raymond Roussel, Max Jacob, Alfred Jarry, Antonin Artaud and Pierre Martory, including Every Question but One 1990, The Landscape is behind the Door 1994. *Honours:* Chevalier des Arts et Lettres 1993; Officier, Légion d'honneur 2002; Hon. DLitt (Southampton Coll. of Long Island Univ.) 1979, (Univ. of Rochester, NY) 1994, (Harvard Univ.) 2001; recipient of numerous awards, grants and honours, including two Guggenheim Fellowships 1967, 1973, MacArthur Fellow 1985–90, Horst Bienek Prize for Poetry (Bavarian Acad. of Fine Arts) 1991, Ruth Lilly Prize for Poetry 1992, Antonio Fraternelli Int. Prize for Poetry (Accad. Nazionale dei Lincei, Rome) 1992, Robert Frost Medal (Poetry Soc. of America) 1995, Grand Prix de Biennales Internationales de Poésie (Brussels) 1996, Gold Medal for Poetry (American Acad. of Arts and Letters) 1997, Bingham Poetry Prize 1998, Walt Whitman Citation of Merit (State of New York and New York State Writers' Inst.) 2000, Signet Soc. Medal for Achievement in the Arts 2001, Wallace Stevens Award (Acad. of American Poets) 2001. *Address:* c/o George Borchardt Inc., 136 East 57th Street, New York, NY 10022-2707; Bard College, Department of Languages and Literature, PO Box 5000, Annandale-on-Hudson, NY 12504-5000, USA (office). *Telephone:* (845) 758-7290 (office). *Website:* www.bard.edu/academics/programs/langlit (office).

ASHBY, Nora (see Africano, Lillian)

ASHCROFT, Frances Mary, PhD, ScD, FRS, FMedSci; British academic; *Royal Society Research Professor of Physiology, University of Oxford*; b. 15 Feb. 1952, d. of John Ashcroft and Kathleen Ashcroft. *Education:* Talbot Heath School, Bournemouth; Girton Coll., Cambridge. *Career:* MRC Training Fellow in Physiology, Univ. of Leicester 1978–82; Demonstrator in Physiology, Oxford Univ. 1982–85, EPA Cephalosporin Jr Research Fellow, Linacre Coll. 1983–85, Royal Soc. Univ. Research Fellow in Physiology 1985–90, Lecturer in Physiology, Christ Church 1986–87, Trinity Coll. 1988–89 (Sr Research Fellow 1992–); Tutorial Fellow in Medicine, St Hilda's Coll. 1990–91; Univ. Lecturer in Physiology 1990–96, Prof. of Physiology 1996–2001, Royal Soc. Research Prof. 2001–; G.L. Brown Prize Lecturer 1997, Peter Curran Lecturer, Yale Univ. 1999; mem. European Molecular Biology Org. *Publications:* Insulin-Molecular Biology to Pathology (jtly) 1992, Ion Channels and Disease 2000, Life at the Extremes 2000, and numerous articles in scientific journals. *Honours:* Dr hc (Open Univ.) 2003; Frank Smart Prize, Univ. of Cambridge 1974, Andrew Culworth Memorial Prize 1990, G.B. Morgagni Young Investigator Award 1991, Charter Award, Inst. of Biology 2004. *Address:* University Laboratory of Physiology, Parks Road, Oxford, OX1 3PT, England (office).

ASHE, Geoffrey Thomas, MA, FRSL; British writer and lecturer; b. 29 March 1923, London; m. 1st Dorothy Irene Train 1946 (deceased); four s. one d.; m. 2nd Maxine Lefever 1992 (divorced); m. 3rd Patricia Chandler 1998. *Education:* Univ. of British Columbia, Canada, Trinity Coll., Cambridge. *Career:* Assoc. Ed., Arthurian Encyclopedia 1986; mem. Medieval Acad. of America, Int. Arthurian Soc.; co-founder and sec., Camelot Research Cttee. *Publications:* King Arthur's Avalon 1957, From Caesar to Arthur 1960, Land to the West 1962, The Land and the Book 1965, Gandhi 1968, The Quest for Arthur's Britain 1968, Camelot and the Vision of Albion 1971, The Art of Writing Made Simple 1972, The Finger and the Moon 1973, The Virgin 1976, The Ancient Wisdom 1977, Miracles 1978, Guidebook to Arthurian Britain 1980, Kings and Queens of Early Britain 1982, Avalonian Quest 1982, The Discovery of King Arthur 1985, Landscape of King Arthur 1987, Mythology of the British Isles 1990, King Arthur: The Dream of a Golden Age 1990, Dawn Behind the Dawn 1992, Atlantis 1992, The Traveller's Guide to Arthurian Britain 1997, The Book of Prophecy 1999, The Hell-Fire Clubs 2000, Merlin 2001, Labyrinths and Mazes 2003, Merlin: The Prophet and his History 2006, The Offbeat Radicals: The British Tradition of Alternative Dissent 2007; contrib. to numerous magazines and journals. *Literary Agent:* Rogers,

Coleridge and White Ltd, 20 Powis Mews, London, W11 1JN, England. *Address:* Chalice Orchard, Well House Lane, Glastonbury, Somerset BA6 8BJ (home).

ASHER, Harry (see Freemantle, Brian Harry)

ASHER, Neal Lewis; British writer; b. 4 Feb. 1961, Billericay, Essex, England. *Education:* mechanical and production engineering ONC. *Publications:* Another England 1989, Out of the Leaflight 1991, Mason's Rats 1992, The Thrake 1993, Woodsmith 1993, Dragon in the Flower 1993, Blue Holes and Bloody Waters 1994, Mason's Rats II 1994, Stinging Things 1994, Adaptogenic 1994, The Flame 1994, Great African Vampire 1994, Stones of Straw 1994, Oceana Foods 1994, Jable Sharks 1994, Cavefish 1995, Spatterjay 1995, Jack O'Gravestones 1995, Snairls 1995, The Bacon 1996, Page Dow 1996, The Devil You Know 1996, The Berserker Captain 1996, Alternative Hospital 1996, Floundering 1996, Plastipak 1996, The Gurnard 1997, Snow in the Desert 1997, Conversations 1998, Cowl 2004, The Voyage of the Sable Keech 2006, Hilldiggers 2007. *Address:* 22 Snoreham Gardens, Latchingdon, Chelmsford, Essex CM3 6UN, England.

ASHFORD, Jeffrey (see Jeffries, Roderic Graeme)

ASHLEY, Bernard, DipEd; British writer; b. 2 April 1935, London, England. *Education:* Cambridge Inst. of Educ. *Career:* mem. Writers' Guild, BAFTA, Greenwich Theatre (bd of govs.). *Publications:* The Trouble with Donovan Croft 1974, Terry on the Fence 1975, All My Men 1977, A Kind of Wild Justice 1978, Break in the Sun 1980, Dinner Ladies Don't Count 1981, Dodgem 1982, High Pavement Blues 1983, Janey 1985, Running Scared 1986, Bad Blood 1988, The Country Boy 1989, The Secret of Theodore Brown 1989, Clipper Street 1990, Seeing off Uncle Jack 1992, Cleversticks 1993, Three Seven Eleven 1993, Johnnie's Blitz 1995, I Forgot, Said Troy 1996, A Present for Paul 1996, City Limits 1997, Tiger Without Teeth 1998, Growing Good 1999, Little Soldier 1999, Revenge House 2002, Double the Love 2002, The Bush 2003, Freedom Flight 2003, Torrent 2004, Ten Days to Zero 2005; contrib. to Books for Your Children, Junior Education, Books for Keeps, Times Educational Supplement, School Librarian. *Honours:* Hon. EdD (Greenwich) 2002, Hon. DLit (Leicester) 2004; The Other Award 1976, RTS Best Children's Entertainment Programme 1993. *Address:* 128 Heathwood Gardens, London, SE7 8ER, England (office). *Telephone:* (20) 8854-5785 (office). *Fax:* (20) 8244-0131 (office). *E-mail:* bernardashley@talktalk.net (office). *Website:* www.bashley.com.

ASHTON, Dore, BA, MA; American writer; *Professor of Art History, The Cooper Union;* b. 21 May 1928, Newark, NJ; m. 1st Adja Yunkers 1952 (died 1983); two d.; m. 2nd Matti Megged (died 2003). *Education:* Univ. of Wisconsin, Harvard Univ. *Career:* Assoc. Ed. Art Digest 1951–54, Arts, 1974–92; Art Critic, New York Times, 1955–60; Lecturer, Pratt Inst. 1962–63; Head, Dept of Humanities, School of Visual Arts 1965–68; Prof. of Art History, The Cooper Union 1969–; Adjunct Prof. of Art History, CUNY 1973, Columbia Univ. 1975, New School for Social Research 1986; Sr Lecturer, Yale Univ. 1995–; mem. Int. Asscn of Art Critics. *Publications:* Abstract Art Before Columbus 1957, Poets and the Past 1955, Philip Guston 1960, Redon, Moreau, Bresdin (co-author) 1961, The Unknown Shore 1962, Rauschenberg's Dante 1964, Richard Lindner 1969, Pol Bury 1971, Picasso on Art 1972, Cultural Guide New York 1972, The New York School: A Cultural Reckoning 1973, A Joseph Cornell Album 1974, Yes, But: A Critical Biography of Philip Guston 1976, A Fable of Modern Art 1980, Rosa Bonheur: A Life and Legend (with Denise Browne Hare) 1981, American Art Since 1945 1982, About Rothko 1983, 20th Century Artists on Art 1985, Out of the Whirlwind 1987, Fragonard in the Universe of Painting 1988, Noguchi East and West 1992, The Delicate Thread: Hiroshi Teshigahara 1997, William Tucker 2001, The Walls of the Heart: Life and Work of David Rankin 2002, The Black Rainbow: Fernando de Szyszlo 2003; Contributions: journals and magazines. *Honours:* Ford Foundation Fellow 1960, Graham Fellow 1963, Mather Award for Art Criticism, College Art Asscn 1963, Guggenheim Fellowship 1964, Nat. Endowment for the Humanities Grant 1980, Art Criticism Prize, St Louis Art Museum 1988. *Address:* The Cooper Union, Cooper Square, New York, NY 10003 (office); 21 East 11th Street, New York, NY 10003, USA (home). *Telephone:* (212) 477-6911 (home). *Fax:* (212) 353-4398 (office); (212) 477-6911 (home).

ASHTON, Robert, BA, PhD, FRHistS; British academic; *Professor Emeritus, University of East Anglia;* b. 21 July 1924, Chester; s. of Joseph Ashton and Edith Frances Ashton; m. Margaret Alice Sedgwick 1946; two d. *Education:* Magdalen Coll. School, Oxford, Univ. Coll., Southampton, London School of Econs. *Career:* Asst Lecturer, Univ. of Nottingham, later Lecturer, Sr Lecturer 1952–63; Visiting Assoc. Prof., Univ. of California, Berkeley 1962–63; Prof., Univ. of East Anglia 1963–89, Prof. Emer. 1989–; Visiting Fellow, All Souls Coll., Oxford, 1974–75, 1987; Vice-Pres. Royal Historical Soc. 1983–84. *Publications:* The Crown and the Money Market 1603–40 1960, James I by his Contemporaries 1969, The English Civil War: Conservatism and Revolution 1603–49 1978, The City and the Court 1603–1643 1979, Reformation and Revolution, 1558–1660 1984, Counter Revolution: The Second Civil War and its Origins 1646–1648 1994; contribs to Economic History Review, Bulletin of Institute of Historical Research, Past and Present, historical journals. *Address:* The Manor House, Brundall, Norwich, NR13 5JY, England (home). *Telephone:* (1603) 713368 (home).

'ĀSHŪR, Radwā, PhD; Egyptian novelist and literary critic; *Professor of English, 'Ayn Shams University, Cairo;* b. 1946, Cairo; m. Murīd Barghūthī; one s. *Education:* Univ. of Massachusetts. *Career:* resided in USA 1973–75; joined faculty 'Ayn Shams Univ., Cairo 1967–, currently Prof. of English. *Publications:* Al-Rihla (memoirs) 1983, Hajar Dāfi (novel) 1985, Khadīja wa-Sawsan (novel) 1989, Gharnāta (novel trilogy, part trans. as Granada: A Novel) (Int. Cairo Book Fair Best Novel Award 1994, Arab Women's Book Fair First Prize 1995) 1994, Taqarir sayyida ra 2001, Qatal nazif (short story, trans. as A Clean Kill) 2001. *Address:* c/o Faculty of Al-Alsun, English Department, Ain Shams University, Elkhalifa Elmaamoon Street, Abbassia, Cairo, Egypt.

ASIMOV, Janet O. Jeppson, BA, MD; American physician and writer; b. 6 Aug. 1926, Ashland, PA; m. Isaac Asimov 1973 (died 1992). *Education:* Stanford Univ., New York Univ. Coll. of Medicine, William Alanson White Inst. *Career:* mem. SFWA, William Alanson White Soc., American Acad. of Psychoanalysis, American Psychiatric Asscn. *Publications:* The Second Experiment 1974; The Last Immortal 1980, The Mysterious Cure 1985, The Package in Hyperspace 1988, Mind Transfer 1988, Murder at the Galactic Writers' Society 1995, Norby and the Terrified Taxi 1997, It's Been a Good Life by Isaac Asimov (ed.) 2002, Notes for a Memoir 2006; with Isaac Asimov: Laughing Space 1982, Norby, the Mixed-Up Robot 1983, Norby's Other Secret 1984, Norby and the Lost Princess 1985, Norby and the Invaders 1985, Norby and the Queen's Necklace 1986, Norby Finds a Villain 1987, Norby and Yobo's Great Adventure 1989, Norby and the Oldest Dragon 1990, Norby Down to Earth 1991, Norby and the Court Jester 1991, Norby and the Terrified Taxi 1993; contribs to several journals; science column in various newspapers. *Address:* 10 W 66th Street, New York, NY 10023, USA.

ASLAM, Nadeem; British writer; b. 1966, Gujranwala, Pakistan. *Education:* Manchester Univ. *Career:* wrote first short story (in Urdu) aged 13, published in Pakistani newspaper; moved to England aged 14. *Publications:* Season of the Rainbirds (Betty Trask Award, Author's Club Best First Novel Award) 1993, Maps for Lost Lovers (Kiriyama Prize 2005, Encore Award 2005) 2004. *Honours:* Royal Literary Fund grant. *Address:* c/o Faber and Faber Ltd, 3 Queen Square, London, WC1N 3AU, England.

ASMODI, Herbert; German writer; b. 30 March 1923, Heilbronn; m. 1st T. Katja; m. 2nd Mascha Freifrau von Hallberg zu Broich 2002. *Education:* Ruprecht-Karl Universität, Heidelberg. *Career:* war service 1942–45; studied 1947–52; freelance writer, Munich 1952–; wrote opera libretto Die Geschichte von dem kleinen blauen Bergsee und dem alten Adler (music by Wilfried Hiller) 1996; mem. PEN. *Plays include:* Jenseits vom Paradies 1954, Pardon wird nicht gegeben 1956, Die Menschenfresser 1959, Nachsaison 1970, Mohrenwäsche, Dichtung und Wahrheit 1969, Stirb und Werde 1965, Nasrin oder Die Kunst zu Träumen 1970, Marie von Brinvilliers 1971, Geld 1973. *Publications include:* Das Lächeln der Harpyjen 1987, Eine unwürdige Existenz 1988, Landleben 1991, Das Grosse Rendezvous 2004, Die Dame aus den Tuilerien 2004; poems: Jokers Gala 1975, Jokers Farewell 1977. *Honours:* Gerhart Hauptmann-Preis der Freien Volksbühne Berlin 1954, Tukan Prize, Munich 1971, Bayerischer Verdienstorden, Bundesverdienstkreuz. *Address:* Kufsteiner Platz 2, 81679 Munich, Germany. *Telephone:* (89) 983088. *Fax:* (89) 983088.

ASMUNDSDOTTIR, Steinunn; Icelandic journalist, writer and poet; b. 1 March 1966, Reykjavík; m.; two d. *Education:* Univ. of Iceland. *Career:* Ed. Andblaer (Breeze) magazine 1995–2000; journalist, Morgunbladid newspaper 2003–; mem. Icelandic Writers' Union. *Publications:* Frimanns Postilla (children's book) 1982, Solo on the Rainbow (poems) 1989, Words of a Goddess (poems) 1993, House on the Moor (poems) 1996; contribs to various publs. *Address:* Morgunbladid-Kaupvangur 6, 700 Egilsstadir (office); Laufas 1, 700 Egilsstadir, Iceland (home). *Telephone:* 471-1166 (office); 471-2656 (home). *E-mail:* austurland@mbl.is (office); laufas7@simmet.is (home). *Website:* www.mbl.is (office).

ASPLER, Tony, BA; British writer; b. 12 May 1939, London; one s. one d. *Education:* McGill Univ., Canada. *Career:* mem. Crime Writers of Canada (Founding Chair. 1982–84). *Publications:* Streets of Askelon 1972, One of My Marionettes 1973, Chain Reaction (with Gordon Pape) 1978, The Scorpion Sanction (with Gordon Pape) 1980, Vintage Canada 1983, The Music Wars (with Gordon Pape) 1983, Titanic (novel) 1989, Blood is Thicker than Beaujolais (novel) 1993, Cellar and Silver (with Rose Murray) 1993, Aligoté to Zinfandel 1994, The Beast of Barbaresco (novel) 1996, Death on the Douro (novel) 1997, Travels With My Corkscrew (non-fiction) 1998, The Wine Lover Cooks (with Kathleen Sloan) 1999, Canadian Wine for Dummies 2000, The Wine Atlas of Canada 2006; contribs to periodicals. *Address:* 53 Craighurst Avenue, Toronto, ON M4R 1J9, Canada. *Telephone:* (416) 488-8597. *E-mail:* tony.aspler@sympatico.ca. *Website:* www.tonyaspler.com.

ASSAD, Rifat al-, PhD; Syrian politician, newspaper publisher and fmr army officer; b. 22 Aug. 1937, Kerdaha; s. of Ali Al-Assad and Na'issa Ibad; m. Lyn Al-Khayer 1973; eight s. eight d. *Career:* officer in Syrian Army 1963–94, Founder and Commdr of Defence Regts 1965–84, mem. Regional Command of Syria 1975; Prof., Coll. of Law, Damascus Univ. 1976; Vice-Pres. of Syria 1984; Founder and Publr Al-Forsan magazine, Damascus 1966–84, Paris and London 1984–92, Al-Shah daily newspaper, Paris 1988, Shaza magazine, Paris 1986 and Memo magazine, Cyprus 1986; Founder and Pres. League of Higher Studies, Grads. and Research 1974. *Publications:* many econ. and political articles in Arabic newspapers and magazines. *Honours:* many Syrian decorations; Légion d'honneur, Hon. Decoration of Morocco. *Address:* c/o Mezzeh, Jabal, Damascus, Syria. *Telephone:* 6621623. *Fax:* 682080393.

ASSAYESH, Shahin, MPhil; Iranian publishing executive; b. 11 March 1939, Mashhad; d. of Zabihollah and Afsaneh Shamlou Assayesh; m. Nasser Meh 1959 (divorced 1987); two s. *Education:* Univ. of London, UK and Teheran and Mashhad Univs. *Career:* secondary school teacher, Tehran 1964–76; moved to UK 1976, to Canada 1983; Founder Iranian Women's Quarterly Journal 1986, then Ed. and Publisher; Pres. Iranian Women's Publications 1991–. *Address:* 278 Bloor Street, Suite 809, Toronto, Ontario, M4W 3M4, Canada. *Telephone:* (416) 920-5228. *Fax:* (416) 920-2265.

ASSOULINE, Pierre; French writer and editor; b. 1953, Casablanca, Morocco. *Career:* Ed., Lire magazine, France. *Publications:* Gaston Gallimard: Un demi-siècle d'edition française 1984, English trans. as Gaston Gallimard: A Half-Century of French Publishing 1988, Une éminence grise: Jean Jardin (1904–1976) 1986, L'homme de l'art: D. H. Kahnweiler, 1884–1979 1988, English trans. as An Artful Life: A Biography of D. H. Kahnweiler, 1884–1979 1990, Albert Londres: Vie et mort d'un grand reporter, 1884–1932 1989, Monsieur Dassault 1993, Trois hommes d'influence 1994, Hergé: Biographie 1996, Simenon: Biographie 1992, English trans. as Simenon: A Biography 1997, Germinal: l'aventure d'un film 1993, Hergé : biographie 1996, Le dernier des Camondo 1997, Le fleuve Combelle 1997, La cliente 1997, Cartier-Bresson: l'oeil du siècle 1999, Double vie 2000, Grâces lui soient rendues: Paul Durand-Ruel, le marchand des impressionnistes 2002, État limite 2003, Lutetia 2005, Rosebud: éclats de biographies 2006, Desiree Dolron: exaltation, gaze, xteriors (with Mark Haworth-Booth) 2006; Other: De nos envoyés spéciaux: les coulisses du reportage (co-author) 1977, Lourdes: Histoires d'eau 1980, Les nouveaux convertis: Enquête sur les chrétiens, des juifs et des musulmans pas comme les autres 1982, L'épuration des intellectuels 1944–1945 1985, Le fleuve combelle 1997. *Address:* c/o Lire, 17 rue de l 'Arrivée, 75733 Paris Cédex 15, France.

ASSUNÇÃO, Leilah; Brazilian playwright and novelist; b. (Maria de Lourdes Torres de Almeida Prado Teixeira), 1944, São Paulo. *Education:* São Paulo Univ. *Plays:* Vejo um Vulto na Janela, me Acudam que Sou Donzela 1963–64, Fala Baixo, senão Eu Grito (Moliere Theatre Prize) 1969, Roda côr de roda 1975, Da fala ao grito 1977, Sobrevividos 1978, A kuka de Kamaiorá 1978, Lua Nua 1986. *Publications:* Sorriso na Alvorada (novel) 1955. *Honours:* São Paulo drama critics' award for best Brazilian playwright 1969. *Address:* c/o Ministry of Culture, Esplanada dos Ministérios, Bloco B, 3 andar, 70068-900 Brasília, DF, Brazil.

ASTLEY, Neil, BA; British , writer and poetry publisher; *Editor, Bloodaxe Books;* b. England. *Education:* Univ. of Newcastle upon Tyne. *Career:* Co-Ed., Stand magazine 1976–78; founder-Ed. Bloodaxe Books 1978–. *Publications:* poetry: Darwin Survivor 1988, Biting My Tongue 1995; novels: The End of My Tether 2002, The Sheep Who Changed the World 2005; ed. anthologies: Ten North-East Poets 1980, Poetry with an Edge 1988, Tony Harrison 1991, New Blood 1999, Staying Alive: Real Poems for Unreal Times 2002, Pleased to See Me: 69 Very Sexy Poems 2002, Do Not Go Gentle: Poems for Funerals 2003, Being Alive 2004, Passiontoo: 100 Love Poems 2005, Bloodaxe Poetry Introductions 1, 2 & 3 2006–07, Soul Food: Nourishing Poems for Starved Minds (with Pamela Robertson-Pearce) 2007, Earth Shattering: Ecopoems 2007. *Honours:* Hon. DLitt (Newcastle); Eric Gregory Award. *Address:* Bloodaxe Books Ltd, Highgreen, Tarset, Northumberland, NE48 1RP, England (office). *E-mail:* editor@bloodaxebooks.com (office). *Website:* www.bloodaxebooks.com (office).

ASTOR, Gerald Morton, BA; American writer; b. 3 Aug. 1926, New Haven, CT; m. Sonia Sacoder 1949, three s. *Education:* Princeton University, Columbia University. *Career:* mem. Authors' Guild, Authors' League of America. *Publications:* The New York Cops: An Informed History, 1971; '…And a Credit to His Race': The Hard Life and Times of Joseph Louis Barrow aka Joe Louis, 1974; The Charge is Rape, 1974; A Question of Rape, 1974; Hot Paper, 1975; Photographing Sports: John Zimmerman, Mark Kauffman and Neil Leifer (with Sean Callahan), 1975; Brick Agent: Inside the Mafia for the FBI (with Anthony Villano), 1977; The Disease Detectives: Deadly Medical Mysteries and the People Who Solved Them, 1983; The 'Last' Nazi: The Life and Times of Dr. Joseph Mengele, 1985; The Baseball Hall of Fame Anniversary Book, 1988; The PGA World Golf Hall of Fame Book, 1991; Hostage: My Nightmare in Beirut (with David Jacobsen), 1991; A Blood-Dimmed Tide: The Battle of the Bulge by the Men Who Fought It, 1992; Battling Buzzards: The Odyssey of the 517th Regimental Parachute Combat Team, 1943–1945, 1993; June 6, 1944: The Voices of D-Day, 1994; Operation Iceberg: The Invasion and Conquest of Okinawa in World War II: An Oral History, 1995; Crisis in the Pacific: The Battles for the Philippines, 1996; The Mighty Eighth: The Air War in Europe by the Men Who Flew It, 1997; The Bloody Forest: Battle for the Huertgen: September 1944–January 1945, 2000. Contributions: periodicals.

ASTRUC, Alexandre, LèsL; French film director, writer and journalist; b. 13 July 1923, Paris; s. of Marcel Astruc and Huguette Haendel; m. Elyette Helies 1983. *Education:* Lycée de Saint-Germain-en-Laye, Lycée Henri IV and Faculté des Lettres, Paris. *Career:* journalist and film critic since 1945; TV reporter for Radio Luxembourg 1969–72; Film Critic, Paris Match 1970–72; contributor to Figaro-Dimanche 1977–. *Films directed include:* Le rideau cramoisi 1952, Les mauvaises rencontres 1955, Une vie 1958, La proie pour l'ombre 1960, Education sentimentale 1961, Evariste galois 1965, La longue marche 1966, Flammes sur l'Adriatique 1968, Sartre par lui-même 1976; also TV films and series. *Publications:* Les vacances 1945, La tête la première, Ciel de cendres 1975, Le serpent jaune 1976, Quand la chouette s'envole 1978, Le permissionnaire 1982, Le roman de Descartes 1989, De la caméra au stylo 1992, L'autre versant de la colline 1993, Evadiste galois 1994, Le montreur d'ombres 1996, La France au coeur 2000, Un rose en hiver 2006. *Honours:* Chevalier, Légion d'honneur; Officier, l'Ordre nat. du Mérite; Commdr des Arts et Lettres; various film prizes and other awards. *Address:* 168 rue de Grenelle, 75007 Paris, France (home). *Telephone:* 1-47-05-20-86 (home).

ASWANY, Alaa al-; Egyptian writer and dentist; b. 1957, Cairo. *Education:* Univ. of Illinois, USA. *Career:* own dental clinic. *Publications:* Umaret Yacoubian (trans. as The Yacoubian Building) 2002, Niran Sadiqa (Friendly Fire, short stories). *Address:* c/o The American University in Cairo Press, 113 Sharia Kasr el Aini Street, Cairo, Egypt (office). *E-mail:* aucpress@aucegypt .edu (office).

ASZYK, Urszula, PhD; Polish academic; *Professor, Department of Iberic Studies, University of Warsaw;* b. 26 Sept. 1944, Jedrzejów, Kielce; d. of Feliks Aszyk and Helena Aszyk (née Sutor); m. Paul Bangs 1994; two d. *Education:* Univ. of Łódź. *Career:* Lecturer in Literary and Theatrical Theory, Univ. of Łódź 1968–76; Lecturer in Polish Language and Literature Univ. Autónoma, Madrid 1976–81; Asst Prof. of Spanish Literature, Dept of Iberian Studies, Univ. of Warsaw 1981–90, Assoc. Prof. 1992–98, Prof. 2000–, Deputy Head of Dept 1982–83, Head of Section of Spanish Language and Literature 1985–1991, 1994–98; Assoc. Prof., State Univ. of New York at Stony Brook 1987–88; Visiting Prof., Univ. of San Sebastian, Spain 1989, Univ. of Mainz, Germany 1991–92, Univ. of São Paulo, Brazil 1993, Univ. of Stockholm, Sweden 1996; Sr Research Fellow, Univ. of Bristol, UK 1995–2003; Prof., Univ. of Silesia 1998–2000; mem. Int. Inst. of Theater, UNESCO 1981–, Int. Asscn of Hispanistas, Polish Asscn Polaca de Hispanistas (Pres. 2004). *Publications:* Iwo Gall's Theatre Searching (Ministry of Educ. and Science Award 1979) 1978, Spanish Contemporary Theatre (Ministry of Culture and Theatre Club Awards 1989) 1988, Iwo Gall's Works About Theatre 1993, Entre la crisis y la vanguardia. Estudios sobre el teatro español del siglo XX 1995, Federico García Lorca and the Theatre of His Time (in Polish) 1997, Federico García Lorca, Unfinished Theatre, Open Theatre (in Polish) (Ed.) 1998, The Theatre of Calderon: Tradition and Modernity (in Polish) 2002, Espacio Dramático frente al Espacio Escénico (Ed.) 2003; numerous contribs to professional journals including articles on Calderon's Theatre and Spanish Golden Age 2000. *Address:* University of Warsaw, Department of Iberic Studies, ul Obozna 8, 00 332 Warsaw, Poland (office); 2 Kenton Close, Bracknell, Berks. RG12 9AZ, England (home). *Telephone:* (1344) 429307 (home). *E-mail:* uaszyk@aol.com (home). *Website:* members.aol.com/ bangspaul2/ucv1.htm (home).

ATIYAH, Sir Michael Francis, Kt, OM, MA, PhD, ScD, FRS, PRSE; British mathematician and academic; *President, Royal Society of Edinburgh;* b. 22 April 1929, London; s. of Edward Selim Atiyah and Jean Atiyah (née Levens); m. Lily Brown 1955; three s. *Education:* Victoria Coll., Egypt, Manchester Grammar School and Trinity Coll. Cambridge. *Career:* Research Fellow, Trinity Coll., Cambridge 1954–58, Hon. Fellow 1976, Master 1990–97, Fellow 1997–; Fellow, Pembroke Coll., Cambridge 1958–61 (Hon. Fellow 1983), Univ. Lecturer 1957–61; Reader, Oxford Univ. and Fellow St Catherine's Coll., Oxford 1961–63, Hon. Fellow 1991; Savilian Prof. of Geometry, Univ. of Oxford and Fellow, New Coll., Oxford 1963–69, Hon. Fellow 1999; Prof. of Mathematics, Inst. for Advanced Study, Princeton, NJ 1969–72; Royal Soc. Research Prof., Oxford Univ. 1973–90, Fellow, St Catherine's Coll., Oxford 1973–90; Dir Isaac Newton Inst. of Math. Sciences, Cambridge 1990–96; Chancellor Univ. of Leicester 1995–2005; Pres. Royal Soc. of Edinburgh 2005–; Pres. London Math. Soc. 1974–76, Pres. Math. Asscn 1981; mem. Science and Eng Research Council 1984–89; Pres. Pugwash Confs 1997–2002; mem. Council Royal Soc. 1984–85, Pres. 1990–95; Foreign mem. American Acad. of Arts and Sciences, Swedish Acad. of Sciences, Leopoldina Acad. (Germany), NAS, Acad. des Sciences (France), Royal Irish Acad., Third World Acad. of Science, Indian Nat. Science Acad., Australian Acad. of Sciences, Chinese Acad. of Sciences, American Philosophical Soc., Ukrainian Acad. of Sciences, Russian Acad. of Sciences, Georgian Acad. of Sciences, Venezuelan Acad. of Sciences, Accad. Nazionale dei Lincei, Royal Spanish Acad. of Sciences, Norwegian Acad. of Science and Letters. *Publications:* K-Theory 1966, Commutative Algebra 1969, Geometry and Dynamics of Magnetic Monopoles 1988, Collected Works (five vols) 1988, vol. 6 2005, The Geometry and Physics of Knots 1990. *Honours:* Hon. Prof., Univ. of Edinburgh 1997–; Hon. Fellow, Darwin Coll., Cambridge 1992, Hon. FREng 1993, Hon. Faculty of Actuaries 1999, Univ. of Wales Swansea 1999; Commdr Order of the Cedars, Gold Order of Merit, Lebanon, Order of Andreas Bello (Venezuela); Hon. DSc (Bonn, Warwick, Durham, St Andrew's, Dublin, Chicago, Edinburgh, Cambridge, Essex, London, Sussex, Ghent, Reading, Helsinki, Leicester, Rutgers, Salamanca, Montreal, Waterloo, Wales, Queen's-Kingston, Keele, Birmingham, Lebanon, Open, Brown, Oxford, Prague, Chinese, Hong Kong, Heriot-Watt, York Univs, American Univ. of Beirut), Dr hc (UMIST) 1996; Fields Medal, Int. Congress of Mathematicians, Moscow 1966, Royal Medal of Royal Soc. 1968, De Morgan Medal, London Math. Soc. 1980, Copley Medal of Royal Soc. 1988, Feltrinelli Prize, Accad. Nazionale dei Lincei 1981, King Faisal Int. Prize for Science 1987, Benjamin Franklin Medal, American Philosophical Soc., Nehru Medal, Indian Nat. Science Acad., Abel Prize, Norwegian Acad. of Sciences (jtly with Isadore Singer) 2004.

Address: University of Edinburgh, Room 5619, School of Mathematics, Mayfield Road, Edinburgh, EH9 3JZ (office); Royal Society of Edinburgh, 22–26 George Street, Edinburgh, EH2 2PQ (office); 3/8 West Grange Gardens, Edinburgh, EH9 2RA, Scotland (home). *Telephone:* (131) 650-4886 (office); (131) 240-5022; (131) 667-0898 (home). *E-mail:* M.atiyah@ed.ac.uk (home). *Website:* www.maths.ed.ac.uk (office); www.royalsoced.org.uk.

ATKINSON, Kate, BA; British writer and playwright; b. 1951, York, England; m. (divorced); two d. *Education:* Univ. of Dundee. *Career:* fmrly home help, teacher and short story writer for women's magazines; writer 1988–. *Plays include:* Nice 1996, Abandonment 2000. *Publications:* Behind the Scences at the Museum (novel) (Whitbread First Novel award and Book of the Year 1996, Boeker Prize, SA, Livre Book of the Year, France) 1995, Human Croquet (novel) 1997, Emotionally Weird (novel) 2001, Not the End of the World (short stories) 2002, Case Histories (novel) 2004, One Good Turn (novel) 2006; contrib. short stories to Daily Telegraph, BBC2, BBC Radio 4, Daily Express, Daily Mail, Scotsman. *Honours:* Ian St James Award 1993. *Address:* c/o Transworld Publishers Ltd, 61–63 Uxbridge Road, London, W5 5SA, England.

ATLAN, Liliane; French writer, poet and dramatist; b. 14 Jan. 1932, Montpellier; m. 1952 (divorced 1976); one s. one d. *Education:* Sorbonne, University of Paris, CAPES. *Publications:* poetry: Lapsus 1971, Bonheur mais sur quel ton le dire 1996, Peuples d'argile, forêts d'etoiles 2000, Little Bibles for Bad Times 2003; plays: Monsieur Fugue ou le mal de terre 1967, The Messiahs 1969, The Little Car of Flames and Voices 1971, The Musicians, the Migrants 1976, Lessons in Happiness 1982, An Opera for Terezin 1997, The Red Seas 1998, My Name is No 1998, Monsieur Fugue 2000; other: videotext. *Honours:* Chevalier Ordre des Arts et des Lettres 1984; Prix Villa Medicis 1992, Radio SACD Prize 1999, Prix Mémoire de la Shoah 1999. *Address:* 70 rue du javelot, 75645 Paris cédex 13, France. *Telephone:* (1) 45-84-63-08. *Fax:* (1) 45-82-04-98. *Website:* liliane.atlan@wanadoo.fr.

ATLAS, Ronald M., BS, MS, PhD; American academic and writer; b. 1946, New York, NY. *Education:* New York State Univ., Rutgers Univ. *Career:* Nat. Research Council Research Assoc., Jet Propulsion Laboratory 1972–73; faculty mem. Univ. of Louisville 1973–, currently Prof. of Biology; Pres., American Soc. for Microbiology; Ed., CRC Critical Reviews in Microbiology. *Publications:* Handbook of Media for Environmental Microbiology 1993, Handbook of Media for Clinical Microbiology (co-author) 1995, Handbook of Microbiological Media (second edn) 1996. *Address:* American Society for Microbiology, 1752 N Street NW, Washington, DC 20036-2904; c/o University of Louisville Graduate School, Houchens Building, Room 105, Louisville, KY 40292, USA. *Telephone:* (502) 852-3957. *Fax:* (502) 852-2365. *E-mail:* r.atlas@ louisville.edu. *Website:* www.louisville.edu; www.asm.org.

ATSUMI, Ikuko; Japanese writer. *Education:* Harvard Univ., USA. *Career:* feminist poet and translator; fmr Prof. of English Literature, Aoyama Gakuin; published journal Feminist: The New Bluestocking 1977–80, issued reports on women's issues and int. feminist movts; presentations on Japanese women's movt at academic insts including Reischauer Inst. of Japanese Studies 1982. *Publications:* Mother Is (translator) 1975, The Burning Heart: Women Poets of Japan (co-author with Kenneth Rexroth) 1977, Seasons of Sacred Lust: Selected Poems of Kazuko Shiraishi (translator), Ariake (translator) 2000; papers on feminism and Japanese women's movt.

ATTALI, Jacques; French international bank official and writer; *President, Attali et Associés;* b. 1 Nov. 1943, Algiers; s. of the late Simon Attali and of Fernande Abecassis; twin brother of Bernard Attali; m. Elisabeth Allain 1981; one s. one d. *Education:* Ecole Polytechnique, Inst. d'Etudes Politiques de Paris, Ecoles des Mines de Paris, Ecole Nat. d' Admin. *Career:* started career as mining engineer, then Lecturer in Econs, Ecole Polytechnique; Auditeur, Council of State; Adviser to the Pres. 1981–91; State Councillor 1989–91; Pres. EBRD, London 1991–93; Pres. Attali et Associés (ACA) 1994–; mem. Council of State 1981–90, 1993–; Admin. KeeBoo 2000–. *Publications:* Analyse économique de la vie politique 1972, Modèles politiques 1973, Anti-économique (with Marc Guillaume) 1974, La parole et l'outil 1975, Bruits, Essai sur l'économie politique de la musique 1976, La nouvelle économie française 1977, L'ordre cannibale 1979, Les trois mondes 1981, Histoires du temps 1982, La figure de Fraser 1984, Un homme d'influence 1985, Au propre et au Figuré 1988, La vie éternelle (novel) 1989, Millennium: Winners and Losers in the Coming World Order 1991, 1492 1991, Verbatim (Tome I) 1993, Europe(s) 1994, Verbatim (Tome II) 1995, Economie de l'Apocalypse 1995, Tome III 1996, Chemins de Sagesse 1996, Au delà de nulle part 1997, Dictionnaire du XXIe siècle 1998, Les portes du ciel 1999, La femme du menteur 1999, Fraternités 1999, Blaise Pascal ou le génie français 2000, Bruits 2001, L'homme nomade 2003, Une brève histoire de l'avenir 2007. *Honours:* Dr hc (Univ. of Kent, Univ. of Haifa). *Address:* Attali et Associés 27, rue Vernet, 75008 Paris, France. *Telephone:* 1-53-57-38-38 (office). *Fax:* 1-47-23-09-91 (office). *Website:* www.aeta.net/fr (office).

ATTALLAH, Naim Ibrahim, FRSA; British publisher and financial adviser; *Chairman, Namara Group;* b. 1 May 1931, Haifa, Palestine; s. of Ibrahim Attallah and Genevieve Attallah; m. Maria Nykolyn 1957; one s. *Education:* Coll. des Frères, Haifa and Battersea Polytechnic, London. *Career:* Propr Quartet Books 1976–, Women's Press 1977–, Robin Clark 1980–, Pipeline Books 1978–2000, The Literary Review 1981–2001, The Wire 1984–2000, Acad. Club 1989–96, The Oldie 1991–2001; Group Chief Exec. Asprey PLC 1992–96, Deputy Chair. Asprey (Bond Street) 1992–98; Man. Dir Mappin and

Webb 1990–95; Exec. Dir Garrard 1990–95; Chair. Namara Group of cos 1973–, launched Parfums Namara 1985, Avant L'Amour and Après L'Amour 1985, Naïdor 1987, L'Amour de Namara 1990. *Films produced:* The Slipper and the Rose (with David Frost q.v.) 1975, Brimstone and Treacle (Exec. Producer) 1982 and several TV documentaries. *Theatre:* Happy End (Co-Presenter) 1975, The Beastly Beatitudes of Balthazar B. (Presenter and Producer) 1981, Trafford Tanzi (Co-Producer) 1982. *Publications:* Women 1987, Singular Encounters 1990, Of a Certain Age 1992, More of a Certain Age 1993, Speaking for the Oldie 1994, A Timeless Passion 1995, Tara and Claire (novel) 1996, Asking Questions 1996, A Woman a Week 1998, In Conversation with Naim Attalah 1998, Insights 1999, Dialogues 2001, The Old Ladies of Nazareth 2004, The Boy in England (memoir) 2005, In Touch with His Roots: a Second Memoir 2006. *Honours:* Hon. MA (Surrey) 1993; Retail Personality of the Year, UK Jewellery Awards 1993. *Address:* 25 Shepherd Market, London, W1J 7PP, England. *Telephone:* (20) 7499-2901. *Fax:* (20) 7499-2914. *E-mail:* nattallah@aol.com (office).

ATTAR, Samar al-, PhD; Syrian novelist and translator; *Professor of Arabic Studies, University of Sydney;* b. 1945, Damascus; m.; one d. *Education:* Damascus Univ., Dalhousie Univ. (Canada), State Univ. of NY, Binghamton (USA). *Career:* taught Arabic and English in Canada, USA, Algeria, Germany; currently Prof. of Arabic Studies, Univ. of Sydney, Australia. *Publications:* Lina: A Portrait of Damascene Girl (novel) 1982, The House on Arnus Square 1988; also scholarly studies, textbooks for teaching Arabic, trans. of Arabic poetry. *Address:* c/o Department of Arabic and Islamic Studies, University of Sydney, Sydney, NSW 2006, Australia.

ATTENBOROUGH, Sir David Frederick, Kt, OM, CH, CVO, CBE, MA, FRS; British broadcaster, naturalist and writer; b. 8 May 1926, London; s. of the late Frederick Attenborough and of Mary Attenborough; brother of Lord Attenborough; m. Jane Elizabeth Ebsworth Oriel 1950 (died 1997); one s. one d. *Education:* Wyggeston Grammar School, Leicester and Clare Coll., Cambridge. *Career:* served with RN 1947–49; editorial asst in publishing house 1949–52; with BBC Television 1952–73, Producer of zoological, archaeological, travel, political and other programmes 1952–64, Controller BBC 2 1964–68, Dir of Programmes, TV 1969–73; writer, presenter BBC series: Tribal Eye 1976, Wildlife on One, annually 1977–2004, Life on Earth 1979, The Living Planet 1984, The First Eden 1987, Lost World, Vanished Lives 1989, The Trials of Life 1990, Life in the Freezer 1993, The Private Life of Plants 1995, The Life of Birds 1998, State of the Planet 2000, The Blue Planet (narrator) 2001, The Life of Mammals 2002, Planet Earth 2006; Huw Wheldon Memorial Lecturer, RTS 1987; Pres. BAAS 1990–91, Royal Soc. for Nature Conservation 1991–96; mem. Nature Conservancy Council 1975–82; Fellow, Soc. of Film and Television Arts 1980; Int. Trustee, World Wild Life Fund 1979–86; Trustee British Museum 1980–2000, Science Museum 1984–87, Royal Botanical Gardens, Kew 1986–92. *Publications:* Zoo Quest to Guiana 1956, Zoo Quest for a Dragon 1957, Zoo Quest in Paraguay 1959, Quest in Paradise 1960, Zoo Quest to Madagascar 1961, Quest under Capricorn 1963, The Tribal Eye 1976, Life on Earth 1979, The Zoo Quest Expeditions 1982; The Living Planet 1984, The First Eden, The Mediterranean World and Man 1987, The Trials of Life 1990, The Private Life of Plants 1994, The Life of Birds (BP Natural World Book Prize) 1998, The Life of Mammals 2002, Life on Air (memoirs) 2002, Life in the Undergrowth 2005, Planet Earth 2006. *Honours:* Hon. Fellow, Clare Coll., Cambridge 1980, UMIST 1980, Inst. of Biology; Order of Merit; Hon. DLitt (Leicester, London, Birmingham, City); Hon. DSc (Liverpool, Ulster, Sussex, Bath, Durham, Keele, Heriot-Watt, Bradford, Nottingham); Hon. LLD (Bristol, Glasgow) 1977; Hon. DUniv (Open Univ.) 1980, (Essex) 1987, Antwerp 1993; Dr hc (Edin.) 1994; Special Award, Guild of TV Producers 1961, Silver Medal, Royal TV Soc. 1966, Silver Medal, Zoological Soc. of London 1966, Desmond Davis Award, Soc. of Film and TV Arts 1970, UNESCO Kalinga Prize 1982, Medallist, Acad. of Natural Sciences, Philadelphia 1982, Founders Gold Medal, Royal Geographical Soc. 1985, Int. Emmy Award 1985, Encyclopedia Britannica Award 1987, Kew Award 1996, Edin. Medal, Edin. Science Festival 1998, BP Natural World Book Prize 1998, Faraday Prize, Royal Soc. 2003, Int. Documentary Asscn Career Achievement Award 2003, Raffles Medal, Zoological Soc. of London 2004, Caird Medal, Nat. Maritime Museum 2004, British Book Awards Lifetime Achievement Award 2004. *Address:* 5 Park Road, Richmond, Surrey, TW10 6NS, England.

ATWOOD, Margaret Eleanor, CC, AM, FRSC; Canadian writer and poet; b. 18 Nov. 1939, Ottawa, ON; m. Graeme Gibson; one d. *Education:* Victoria Coll., Univ. of Toronto, Radcliffe Coll. and Harvard Univ., Cambridge, Mass. *Career:* Lecturer in English, Univ. of British Columbia, Vancouver 1964–65; Instructor in English, Sir George Williams Univ., Montreal 1967–68, Univ. of Alberta 1969–70; Asst Prof. of English, York Univ., Toronto 1971; Writer-in-Residence, Univ. of Toronto 1972–73, Maquarie Univ., Australia 1987, Trinity Univ., San Antonio, Tex. 1989; Berg Chair, New York Univ. 1986; Pres. Writers' Union of Canada 1981–82, International PEN (Canadian Centre—English Speaking) 1984–86. *Radio script:* The Trumpets of Summer (CBC Radio) 1964. *Television screenplays:* The Servant Girl (CBC) 1974, Snowbird 1981, Heaven on Earth (with Peter Pearson) 1986. *Recordings:* The Poetry and Voice of Margaret Atwood 1977, Margaret Atwood Reads From A Handmaid's Tale, Margaret Atwood Reads Unearthing Suite 1985, audio edns of her novels. *Publications:* poetry: Double Persephone 1961, The Circle Game (Gov.-Gen.'s Award 1966) 1964, Kaleidoscopes Baroque 1965, Talismans for Children 1965, Speeches for Doctor Frankenstein 1966, The Animals in That Country 1968, The Journals of Susanna Moodie 1970, Procedures for Underground 1970, Power Politics 1971, You Are Happy 1974, Selected Poems 1976, Marsh, Hawk 1977, Two-Headed Poems 1978, True Stories 1981, Notes Towards a Poem That Can Never Be Written 1981, Snake Poems 1983, Interlunar 1984, Selected Poems II: Poems Selected and New 1976–1986 1986, Selected Poems 1966–1984 1990, Margaret Atwood Poems 1965–1975 1991, Morning in the Burned House (Trillium Award for Excellence in Ontario Writing 1995) 1995; fiction: The Edible Woman 1969, Surfacing 1972, Lady Oracle 1976, Dancing Girls (short stories) 1977, Life Before Man 1979, Bodily Harm 1981, Encounters with the Element Man 1982, Murder in the Dark (short stories) 1983, Bluebeard's Egg (short stories) 1983, Unearthing Suite 1983, The Handmaid's Tale (Gov.-Gen.'s Award 1986) (adapted for the screen by Harold Pinter and directed by Volker Schlorndorf 1990) 1985, Cat's Eye (Torgi Talking Book—CNIB 1989, City of Toronto Book Award 1989, Coles Book of the Year 1989, Foundation for the Advancement of Canadian Letters/Periodical Marketers of Canada Book of the Year 1989) 1988, Wilderness Tips (short stories) (Govt of Ont. Trillium Award (with Jane Urquhart) for Excellence in Ontario Writing 1992, Periodical Marketers of Canada Book of the Year Award 1992) 1991, Good Bones (short stories) 1992, The Robber Bride (Canadian Authors' Asscn Novel of the Year 1993, Trillium Award for Excellence in Ontario Writing 1994, Commonwealth Writers' Prize for the Canadian and Caribbean Region 1994, Sunday Times Award for Literary Excellence 1994, Swedish Humour Asscn's Int. Humourous Writer Award 1995) 1993, Bones and Murder 1995, The Labrador Fiasco 1996, Alias Grace (Giller Prize 1996, Premio Mondello 1997, Salon Magazine Best Fiction of the Year 1997) 1996, The Blind Assassin (Booker Prize 2000) 2000, Oryx and Crake 2003, Telling Tales (contrib. to charity anthology) 2004, Bottle 2004, The Penelopaid 2005, The Tent (short stories) 2006, Moral Disorder (short stories) 2006; juvenile: Up in the Tree 1978, 2006, Anna's Pet 1980, For the Birds 1990, Princess Prunella and the Purple Peanut 1995, Rude Ramsay and the Roaring Radishes 2003, Bashful Bob and Doleful Dorinda 2004; non-fiction: Survival: A Thematic Guide to Canadian Literature 1972, Days of the Rebels 1815–1840 1977, Second Words: Selected Critical Prose 1982, Strange Things: The Malevolent North in Canadian Literature 1995, Negotiating with the Dead: A Writer on Writing 2002, Moving Targets: Writing With Intent 1982–2004 2004, Curious Pursuits: Occasional Writing 2005, Writing with Intent: Essays, Reviews, Personal Prose 1983–2005 2005, The Penelopiad: The Myth of Penelope and Odysseus 2005; editor: The New Oxford Book of Canadian Verse in English (ed.) 1982, The Oxford Book of Canadian Short Stories in English (with Robert Weaver) 1986, The Canlit Foodbook 1987, The Best American Short Stories (with Shannon Ravenel) 1989, The New Oxford Book of Canadian Short Stories in English (with Robert Weaver) 1995; reviews and critical articles have appeared in Canadian Literature, Maclean's, Saturday Night, This Magazine, New York Times Book Review, Globe and Mail, National Post, The Nation, Books In Canada, Washington Post, Harvard Educational Review, and many others; works have been translated into many languages, including French, German, Italian, Urdu, Estonian, Roumanian, Serbo-Croatian, Catalan, Turkish, Russian, Finnish, Dutch, Danish, Norwegian, Swedish, Portuguese, Greek, Polish, Japanese, Icelandic, Spanish, Hebrew. *Honours:* MFA Hon. Chair, Univ. of Alabama, Tuscaloosa 1985; Foreign Hon. mem. American Acad. of Arts and Sciences 1988; Order of Ont. 1990, 125th Anniversary of Canadian Confederation Commemorative Medal 1992, Chevalier, Ordre des Arts et Lettres 1994, Order of Literary Merit (Norway) 1996, Markets Initiative Order of the Forest 2006; Hon. DLitt (Trent) 1973, (Concordia) 1980, (Smith Coll., Mass) 1982, (Toronto) 1983, (Mount Holyoke) 1985, (Waterloo) 1985, (Guelph) 1985, (Oxford) 1998; Hon. LLD (Queen's Univ.) 1974; Dr hc (Victoria Coll.) 1987, (Université de Montréal) 1991, (Leeds) 1994, (McMaster) 1996, (Lakehead) 1998, (Oxford) 1998, (Cambridge) 2001, (Algoma) 2001, (Harvard) 2004, (Sorbonne Nouvelle) 2005, (Literary and Historical Soc., Univ. Coll. Dublin) 2005; E. J. Pratt Medal 1961, Pres.'s Medal, Univ. of Western Ontario 1965, First Prize, Centennial Comm. Poetry Competition 1967, Union Poetry Prize, Chicago 1969, Bess Hoskins Prize for Poetry, Chicago 1974, City of Toronto Book Award 1977, Canadian Bookseller's Asscn Award 1977, Periodical Distributors of Canada Short Fiction Award 1977, St Lawrence Award for Fiction 1978, Radcliffe Grad. Medal 1980, Molson Award 1981, Guggenheim Fellowship 1981, Welsh Arts Council Int. Writer's Prize 1982, Periodical Distributors of Canada and the Foundation for The Advancement of Canadian Letters Book of the Year Award 1983, Ida Nudel Humanitarian Award 1986, Toronto Arts Award 1986, Los Angeles Times Fiction Award 1986, Ms. Magazine Woman of the Year 1986, Arthur C. Clarke Award for Best Science Fiction 1987, Commonwealth Literary Prize (regional winner) 1987, 1994, Silver Medal for Best Article of the Year, Council for Advancement and Support of Educ. 1987, Humanist of the Year Award 1987, YWCA Women of Distinction Award 1988, First Prize, Nat. Magazine Award for Environmental Journalism 1988, Canadian Booksellers Asscn Author of the Year 1989, 1996, Harvard Univ. Centennial Medal 1990, John Hughes Prize, Welsh Devt Bd 1992, Commemorative Medal for the 125th Anniversary of Canadian Confed. 1992, Best Local Author, NOW Magazine Readers' Poll 1995, 1997, 1998, 1999, 2000, 2003, 2004, Nat. Arts Club Medal of Honor for Literature 1997, London Literature Award 1999, Int. Crime Writers' Asscn Dashiell Hammett Award 2001, Canadian Booksellers Asscn People's Choice Award 2001, Radcliffe Medal 2003, Harold Washington Literary Award 2003, Banff Centre Nat. Arts Award 2005, Edinburgh Int. Book Festival Englightenment Award 2005, Chicago Tribune Literary Prize 2005. *Literary Agent:* c/o McClelland &

Stewart, 75 Sherbourne Street, 5th Floor, Toronto, ON M5A 2P9, Canada. *Website:* www.owtoad.com. *E-mail:* atwood@owtoad.com.

AUBERT, Alvin Bernard, BA, MA; American academic and poet; b. 12 March 1930, Lutcher, LA; m. 1st Olga Alexis 1948 (divorced); one d.; m. 2nd Bernardine Tenant 1960; two d. *Education:* Southern Univ., Baton Rouge, Univ. of Michigan, Univ. of Illinois at Urbana-Champaign. *Career:* Instructor, Southern Univ. 1960–62, Asst Prof. 1962–65, Assoc. Prof. of English 1965–70; Visiting Prof. of English, Univ. of Oregon at Eugene 1970; Assoc. Prof., SUNY at Fredonia 1970–74, Prof. of English 1974–79; founder-Ed., Obsidian magazine 1975–85; Prof. of English, Wayne State Univ., Detroit 1980–92, Prof. Emeritus 1992–. *Publications:* Against the Blues, 1972; Feeling Through, 1975; South Louisiana: New and Selected Poems, 1985; If Winter Come: Collected Poems, 1994; Harlem Wrestler, 1995. *Honours:* Bread Loaf Writers Conference Scholarship 1968, NEA grants 1973, 1981, Co-ordinating Council of Literary Magazines grant 1979, Callaloo Award 1989.

AUBRY, Cécile; French author, scriptwriter and film director; b. (Anne-José Bénard), 3 Aug. 1928, Paris; d. of Lucien Bénard and Marguerite Candelier; m. Prince Brahim el Glaoui 1951 (divorced); one s. *Education:* Lycée Victor Duruy, Paris. *Career:* appeared in prin. role in Clouzot's film Manon 1948; subsequent roles in films The Black Rose 1950, Barbe Bleue 1951 and in Italian and French films 1951; author and director of numerous TV scripts and series 1961–72, including Poly, Belle et Sébastien, Sébastien Parmi les Hommes, Sébastien et la Mary Morgane, Le Jeune Fabre, etc. *Publications:* three novels 1974–85, several children's books. *Honours:* Officier, Ordre des Arts et des Lettres. *Address:* Le Moulin Bleu, 6 chemin du Moulin Bleu, 91410 St-Cyr-sous-Dourdan, France (home). *Telephone:* 1-64-59-01-06 (home). *Fax:* 1-64-59-01-06 (home).

AUCHINCLOSS, Louis Stanton, LLB, DLitt; American author and lawyer; b. 27 Sept. 1917, s. of Joseph Howland Auchincloss and Priscilla Auchincloss (née Stanton); m. Adele Lawrence 1957; three s. *Education:* Groton School, Yale Univ. and Univ. of Virginia. *Career:* admitted to New York Bar 1941, Assoc. Sullivan and Cromwell 1941–51, Hawkins, Delafield and Wood, New York 1954–58, Pnr 1958–86; Lt, USN 1941–45; Pres. American Acad. of Arts and Letters 1997–2000; Pres. Museum of the City of New York; mem. Nat. Inst. of Arts and Letters. *Publications:* The Indifferent Children 1947, The Injustice Collectors 1950, Sybil 1952, A Law for the Lion 1953, The Romantic Egoists 1954, The Great World and Timothy Colt 1956, Venus in Sparta 1958, Pursuit of the Prodigal 1959, House of Five Talents 1960, Reflections of a Jacobite 1961, Portrait in Brownstone 1962, Powers of Attorney 1963, The Rector of Justin 1964, Pioneers and Caretakers 1965, The Embezzler 1966, Tales of Manhattan 1967, A World of Profit 1969, Motiveless Malignity 1969, Edith Wharton: A Woman in Her Time 1971, I Come as a Thief 1972, Richelieu 1972, The Partners 1974, A Winter's Capital 1974, Reading Henry James 1975, The Winthrop Covenant 1976, The Dark Lady 1977, The Country Cousin 1978, Persons of Consequence 1979, Life, Law and Letters 1979, The House of the Prophet 1980, The Cat and the King 1981, Watchfires 1982, Exit Lady Masham 1983, The Book Class 1984, Honorable Men 1985, Diary of a Yuppie 1986, Skinny Island 1987, The Golden Calves 1988, Fellow Passengers 1989, The Vanderbilt Era 1989, J. P. Morgan 1990, The Lady of Situations 1991, False Gods 1992, Three Lives 1993, Tales of Yesteryear 1994, Collected Stories 1994, The Style's the Man 1994, The Education of Oscar Fairfax 1995, The Man Behind the Book 1996, La Gloire 1996, The Atonement 1997, Woodrow Wilson 2000, The Scarlet Letters 2003, East Side Story 2004; contributions to New York Review of Books, New Criterion. *Honours:* Living Landmark, New York Landmarks Conservancy 2000, Nat. Medal of Arts Award 2005. *Address:* 1111 Park Avenue, New York, NY 10028, USA (home).

AUDE, PhD; Canadian novelist; b. (Claudette Charbonneau-Tissot), 1947, Montréal. *Education:* Laval Univ. *Career:* fmr teacher in Québec. *Publications:* as Claudette Charbonneau: Contes pour hydrocéphales adultes (short stories) 1974, La contrainte (short stories) 1976; as Aude: La chaise au fond de l'oeil (novel) 1979, Les petites boîtes (juvenile, two vols short stories) 1983, L'Assembleur (novel) 1985, Banc de brume, ou les aventures de la petite fille que l'on croyait partie avec l'eau du bain (short stories) 1987, Cet imperceptible mouvement (short stories) (Prix littéraire du Gouverneur Général) 1997, L'enfant migrateur (novel) (Prix des lectrices Elle-Québec 1999) 1998, L'homme au complet (novel) 1999, Quelqu'un (novel) 2002; contrib. short stories in trans. in anthologies and journals. *Address:* c/o XYZ éditeur, 1781 rue Saint-Hubert, Montréal, QC H2L 3Z1, Canada.

AUDOUARD, Antoine; French writer; b. 6 Aug. 1956, Paris. *Education:* Pasteur de Neuilly school. *Career:* Publishing Dir Laffont-Fixot 1994–2000. *Publications:* Marie en quelques mots (novel) 1977, Le Voyage au liban (novel) 1979, Abeilles, vous avez changé de maître (novel) 1981, Passage de l'Eden, Adieu, mon unique (novel, trans. as Farewell, My Only One) 2000, Une Maison au bord du monde (non-fiction) 2001, La Peau à l'envers 2003. *Address:* c/o Canongate Books, 14 High Street, Edinburgh, EH1 1TE, Scotland.

AUEL, Jean Marie, MBA; American writer; b. 18 Feb. 1936, Chicago, Ill.; m. Ray Bernard Auel 1954; two s. three d. *Education:* Univ. of Portland. *Career:* mem. Authors' Guild, Int. Women's Forum (mem. Bd Dirs 1985–93), Mensa (Hon. Vice-Pres. 1990–), Oregon Museum of Science and Industry (mem. Bd Dirs 1993–96), Oregon Writers' Colony, PEN. *Publications:* The Clan of the Cave Bear 1980, The Valley of Horses 1982, The Mammoth Hunters 1985, The Plains of Passage 1990, The Shelters of Stone 2002. *Honours:* Hon. DLitt

(Univ. of Portland) 1984; Hon. HHD (Univ. of Maine) 1986, (Pacific Univ.) 1995; Hon. LHD (Mount Vernon Coll.) 1986; Pacific North West Booksellers Asscn Excellence in Writing Award 1980, Friends of Literature Vicki Penziner Matson Memorial Award, Chicago 1980, American Acad. of Achievement Golden Plate Award for Notable Author 1986, Smithsonian Inst. Centennial Medal 1990, Award for Contributions to Cultural Resource Management, Dept of the Interior, Sec. Manuel Lujan and the Soc. for American Archaeology 1990, Williamette Writers Distinguished Northwest Writer Award 1995, Publieksprijs voor het Nederlandse Boek for most popular foreign language book (Netherlands). *Literary Agent:* c/o Jean V. Naggar Literary Agency, 216 E 75th Street, New York, NY 10021, USA. *Website:* www .jeanmauel.co.uk.

AUERBACH, Nina Joan, BA, MA, PhD; American academic and writer; b. 24 May 1943, New York, NY. *Education:* Univ. of Wisconsin at Madison, Columbia Univ. *Career:* Adjunct Prof., Hunter College, CUNY, 1969–70; Asst Prof. of English, California State University at Los Angeles, 1970–72; Asst Prof., 1972–77, Assoc. Prof., 1977–83, Prof., 1983–, of English, University of Pennsylvania; mem. MLA of America, Victorian Soc. of America. *Publications:* Communities of Women: An Idea in Fiction, 1978; Woman and the Demon: The Life of a Victorian Myth, 1982; Romantic Imprisonment: Women and Other Glorified Outcasts, 1985; Ellen Terry: Player in Her Time, 1987; Private Theatrical: The Lives of the Victorians, 1990; Forbidden Journeys: Fairy Tales and Fantasies by Victorian Women Writers (ed. with U. C. Knoepflmacher), 1992; Our Vampires, Ourselves, 1995; Daphne Du Maurier: Haunted Heiress, 2000. Contributions: books and periodicals, incl. London Review of Books. *Honours:* Ford Foundation Fellowship, 1975–76; Radcliffe Institute Fellowship, 1975–76; Guggenheim Fellowship, 1979–80. *Address:* Department of English, University of Pennsylvania, Philadelphia, PA 19104, USA.

AUFFARTH, Susanne; German writer; b. 8 Sept. 1920, Gr Malchau. *Education:* secondary school in Uelzen. *Publications:* Olympias (drama) 1979, Lofoten (poems to Else Winter's watercolours) 1985, Der Knabe mit der Geige (fairy tales) 1989, Unvergessenes Leben (poems) 1990, Zwölf Märchen 1998, Zwischenzeit (poems) 2003, Acht Märchen, Vier Erzählungen, Dorfchronik, Der Knabe mit der Geige. *Honours:* Herta-Bläschke Gedächtnispreis, Klagenfurt 1983 and Edition L. Lyrikpreis, Bayreuth 1988. *Address:* Gr Malchau, 29597 Stoetze, Germany.

AUMBRY, Alan (see Bayley, Barrington John)

AUNG SAN SUU KYI, BA; Myanma politician; b. 19 June 1945, Rangoon; d. of the late Gen. Aung San and of Khin Kyi; m. Michael Aris 1972 (died 1999); two s. *Education:* St Francis Convent, Methodist English High School, Lady Shri Ram Coll., Delhi Univ., St Hugh's Coll., Oxford. *Career:* Asst Sec. Advisory Cttee on Admin. and Budgetary Questions UN Secr., New York 1969–71; Resident Officer, Ministry of Foreign Affairs, Bhutan 1972; Visiting Scholar Centre for SE Asian Studies, Kyoto Univ., Japan 1985–86; Fellow Indian Inst. of Advanced Studies 1987; Co-Founder, Gen. Sec. Nat. League for Democracy 1988 (expelled from party), reinstated as Gen. Sec. Oct. 1995; returned from UK 1988, under house arrest 1989–95, house arrest lifted July 1995, placed under de facto house arrest Sept. 2000, released unconditionally May 2002, placed under house arrest June 2003. *Publications:* Aung San 1984, Burma and India: Some Aspects of Colonial Life Under Colonialism 1990, Freedom from Fear 1991, Towards a True Refuge 1993, Freedom from Fear and Other Writings 1995. *Honours:* Hon. mem. Bd Council Int. Inst. for Democracy and Electoral Assistance (IDEA) 2003; numerous hon. degrees; Rafto Prize 1990, Sakharov Prize 1990, European Parl. Human Rights Prize 1991, Nobel Peace Prize 1991, Simón Bolívar Prize 1992, Liberal Int. Prize for Freedom 1995, Jawaharlal Nehru Award for Int. Understanding 1995, Freedom Award of Int. Rescue Cttee 1995, Free Spirit Prize, Freedom Forum USA 2003, ranked by Forbes magazine amongst 100 Most Powerful Women (45th) 2004, (15th) 2005, (47th) 2006. *Address:* c/o National League for Democracy, 97B West Shwegondine Road, Bahan Township, Yangon, Myanmar.

AUST, Stefan; German journalist and writer; *Editor, Der Spiegel;* b. 1 July 1946, Stade; m. Ulrike Meinhof. *Career:* Ed. Concrete magazine 1966–69; staff mem. NDR TV 1970–72; journalist Panorama (political magazine) 1972–86; Chief Ed. Der Spiegel TV 1988–94, Ed.-in-Chief Der Spiegel 1994–; Man. Dir. Der Spiegel TV GmbH 1995–; fmr. TV host with talkshow Talk in the Tower, currently Host Spiegel-TV. *Publications include:* The Baader Meinhof Complex 1985, Stammheim (film script) 1986, Mauss: A German Agent 1988, The Pirate 1990. *Honours:* Goldenen Kamera 2005. *Address:* Der Spiegel, Brandstwiete 19/Ost-West-Strasse 3, 20457 Hamburg, Germany (office). *Telephone:* (40) 30070. *Fax:* (40) 30072247. *E-mail:* spiegel@spiegel.de (office). *Website:* www.spiegel.de (office).

AUSTER, Paul, BA, MA; American writer and poet; b. 3 Feb. 1947, Newark, NJ; s. of the late Sam Auster and Queenie Auster; m. 1st Lydia Davis 1974 (divorced 1982); one s.; m. 2nd Siri Hustvedt 1982; one d. *Education:* Columbia High School, NJ, Columbia Coll., New York, Columbia Univ., New York. *Career:* worked as census taker; oil tanker utility man. on the Esso Florence; moved to Paris, France 1971, returned to USA 1974; worked as translator; Tutor in Storywriting and Trans., Princeton Univ. 1986–90; juror, Cannes Film Festival 1997; mem. PEN. *Screenplays:* Smoke 1995, Blue in the Face 1995, Lulu on the Bridge 1998. *Publications:* fiction: City of Glass 1985, Ghosts 1986, The Locked Room 1986, In the Country of Last Things 1987, Moon Palace 1989, The Music of Chance 1990, Leviathan 1992, Mr Vertigo

1994, Timbuktu 1999, True Tales of American Life 2001 (aka I Thought My Father Was God) 2001, The Book of Illusions 2002, Oracle Night 2003, The Brooklyn Follies 2005, Travels in the Scriptorium 2006; non-fiction: White Spaces 1980, The Invention of Solitude 1982, The Art of Hunger 1982, Hand to Mouth (memoir) 1989, The Red Notebook 1995, Why Write? 1996, Translations 1996, Collected Prose 2003; poetry: Unearth 1974, Wall Writing 1976, Fragments From Cold 1977, Facing the Music 1980, The Random House Book of Twentieth-Century French Poetry (ed.) 1982, Disappearances: Selected Poems 1988, Collected Poems 2003, Collected Poems 2007. *Honours:* Nat. Endowment for the Arts fellowships 1979, 1985; Prix Médicis Étranger 1993; Commandeur, Ordre des Arts et des Lettres. *Literary Agent:* Carol Mann Agency, 55 Fifth Avenue, New York, NY 10003, USA. *Website:* www.paulauster.co.uk.

AVERY, Gillian Elise; British writer and editor; b. 30 Sept. 1926, England; m. Anthony Oliver John Cockshut 1952; one d. *Career:* jr reporter, Surrey Mirror, Redhill, Surrey 1944–47; staff, Chambers's Encyclopaedia, London 1947–50; Asst Illustrations Ed., Clarendon Press, Oxford 1950–54. *Publications:* juvenile fiction: The Warden's Niece 1957, Trespassers at Charlcote 1958, James Without Thomas 1959, The Elephant War 1960, To Tame a Sister 1961, The Greatest Gresham 1962, The Peacock House 1963, The Italian Spring 1964, The Call of the Valley 1966, A Likely Lad 1971, Huck and her Time Machine 1977; adult fiction: The Lost Railway 1980, Onlookers 1983; non-fiction: Nineteenth-Century Children: Heroes and Heroines in English Children's Stories (with Angela Bull) 1965, Victorian People in Life and Literature 1970, The Echoing Green: Memories of Regency and Victorian Youth 1974, Childhood's Pattern 1975, Children and Their Books: a Celebration of the Work of Iona and Peter Opie (ed. with Julia Briggs) 1989, The Best Type of Girl: a History of Girls' Independent Schools 1991, Behold the Child: American Children and Their Books, 1621–1922 1994, Representations of Childhood Death (ed. with Kimberley Reynolds) 1999, Cheltenham Ladies: A History of the Cheltenham Ladies' College 2003; ed. of many other books. *Honours:* Guardian Award 1972. *Address:* 32 Charlbury Road, Oxford, OX2 6UU, England (office).

AVI (see Wortis, Avi)

AVICE, Claude Pierre Marie, (Pierre Barbet, David Maine, Oliver Sprigel), PhD; French writer; b. 16 May 1925, Le Mans; m. Marianne Brunswick 1952; two s. one d. *Education:* Institut Pasteur, Univ. of Paris. *Career:* pharmacist, Paris 1952–81; science fiction writer 1962–. *Publications:* Les Grognards d'Eridan (trans. as The Napoleons of Eridanus) 1970, A quoi songent les psyborgs? (trans. as Games Psyborgs Play) 1971, L'Empire du Baphomet (trans. as Baphomet's Meteor) 1972, La Planete enchantée (trans. as Enchanted Planet) 1973, Liane de Noldaz (trans. as The Joan-of-Arc Replay) 1973, L'Empereur d'Eridan (trans. as The Emperor of Eridanus) 1982; contrib. to many publications, both fiction and non-fiction. *Honours:* Int. Inst. of Science Fiction Gold Medal, Poznań, Poland. *Address:* 4 Square de l'ave du Bois, 75116 Paris, France.

AVISON, Margaret Kirkland, OC, MA; Canadian poet and writer; b. 23 April 1918, Galt, ON; d. of Rev. Dr Harold Wilson Avison and Mabel Avison (née Kirkland). *Education:* Victoria Coll., Univ. of Toronto, Indiana Univ., Univ. of Toronto School of Grad. Studies. *Career:* many different daytime jobs and occasional freelancing 1940–63; teacher, Scarborough Coll., Univ. of Toronto 1966–68; women's worker in a Toronto inner-city mission 1968–72; Writer-in-Residence, Univ. of Western Ontario 1973–74; archivist, CBC 1974–78; office man., Mustard Seed Mission 1978–86. *Publications:* poetry: Winter Sun 1960, The Dumbfounding 1966, Sunblue 1978, Winter Sun/The Dumbfounding 1982, No Time 1989, Selected Poems 1991, Not Yet But Still 1997, Concrete and Wild Carrot 2002, Always Now The Collected Poems Vol. 1 2003, Vol. 2, 2004, Vol. 3 2005, Momentary Dark 2006; other: A Kind of Perseverance (lectures) 1993. *Honours:* Hon. DLitt (Acadia Univ.) 1983, (York Univ.) 1985; Hon. Dr Sacred Letters (Emmanuel Coll., Victoria Univ.) 1988; Guggenheim Fellowship 1956; Gov.-Gen.'s Awards for Poetry 1960, 1990, Griffin Prize for Excellence in Poetry 2003. *Address:* c/o The Porcupine's Quill, 68 Main Street, Erin, ON N0B 1T0, Canada (office).

AVRIL, Nicole, LèsL; French novelist and screenwriter; b. 1939, Rambouillet; m. Jean-Pierre Elkabbach 1979. *Education:* Univ. of Lyon. *Career:* fmr actress, model, teacher of literature. *Publications:* novels: L'Été de la Saint Valentin 1972, Les Gens de Misar (Prix des Quatre Jurys au Maroc) 1972, Les Remparts d'Adrien 1975, Le Jardin des absents 1977, Monsieur de Lyon 1979, La Disgrâce (also TV adaptation 1997) 1981, Jeanne (also TV adaptation 1995) 1984, Une Personne déplacé 1996, La Première alliance 1992, Sur la peau du diable 1992, L'Impératrice 1995, Le Roman d'un inconnu (also video documentary for ARTE 2002) 1998, Il y a longtemps que je t'aime 1999, Le Roman du visage 1999, Moi, Dora Maar 2002, Le Regard de la grenouille 2003, Dernière mise en scène 2005, Dans les jardins de mon père (memoirs) 1989. *Honours:* Ordre supérieure autrichien pour l'Impératrice 1996. *Address:* c/o Mme Muriel Beyer, Editions Plon, 76 rue Bonaparte, 75006 Paris; 33 Avenue Charles Floquet, 75007 Paris, France (home). *Telephone:* 1-47-34-80-62 (home); 6-68-04-41-61 (mobile) (home).

AW, Tash, LLB; Malaysian writer; b. (Aw Ta-Shii), Taipei, Taiwan. *Education:* Univ. of Cambridge, Univ. of East Anglia, UK. *Career:* moved to England as teenager; fmrly worked at a law firm. *Publications:* The Harmony Silk Factory (Whitbread First Novel Award) 2005. *Address:* c/o Harper Perennial, 77–85 Fulham Palace Road, London, W6 8JB, England.

AWERBUCK, Diane, BA, HDipEd, MA, PhD; South African writer, lecturer and publisher; *Director of Content Development and Publisher, Electric Book Works*; b. Kimberley. *Education:* Rhodes Univ., Grahamstown, Univ. of Cape Town. *Career:* currently Lecturer, South African School of Motion Picture Medium and Live Performance (AFDA), Cape Town; Publr Electric Book Works, Cape Town. *Exhibition:* with Lisa Firer and Marlise Keith (porcelain and brushwork) 2005. *Radio:* Otherwise (with Nancy Richards) 2006. *Television:* Good Morning South Africa 2004. *Publications:* Gardening at Night (novel) 2003, The Portable Pilgrim (online column) 2003–07, Laugh It Off (anthology) 2004, 2005, 180 Degrees (anthology) 2005, Yizo Yizo (anthology) 2005, Crossing the Universe (anthology) 2007; works translated into German, Russian, Swedish and Chinese. *Honours:* Best First Book (Africa and Caribbean Region) 2004. *Address:* c/o Vintage, 20 Vauxhall Bridge Road, London, SW1V 2SA, England. *Website:* www.filmdramaschool.co.za (office).

AWOONOR, Kofi Nyidevu, PhD; Ghanaian writer, teacher, diplomatist and politician; b. 13 March 1935, Wheta; s. of Kosiwo Awoonor and Atsu Awoonor; m.; five s. one d. *Education:* Univ. of Ghana, Univ. Coll., London and State Univ. of NY, Stony Brook. *Career:* Research Fellow, Inst. of African Studies; Man. Dir Film Corpn, Accra; Longmans Fellow, Univ. of London; Asst Prof. and later Chair. Comparative Literature Program, State Univ. of NY; Visiting Prof., Univ. of Texas, Austin and New School of Social Research, New York; detained in Ghana for allegedly harbouring leader of coup 1975; on trial 1976, sentenced to one year's imprisonment Oct. 1976, pardoned Oct. 1976; fmr Chair. Dept of English and Dean of Faculty of Arts, Univ. of Cape Coast; Sec.-Gen. Action Congress Party; Amb. to Brazil 1984–90 (also accred to Cuba 1988–90); Perm. Rep. to UN 1990–94; currently Minister of State; Contributing Ed., Transition and Alcheringa; Longmans and Fairfield Fellowships. *Publications:* poetry: Rediscovery 1964, Messages 1970, Night of My Blood 1971, House by the Sea 1978, Until the Morning After (collected poems); prose: This Earth My Brother 1971, Guardians of the Sacred Word 1973, Ride Me Memory 1973, Breast of the Earth 1974 (history of African literature), Traditional African Literature (series, ed.), Alien Corn (novel) 1974, Where is the Mississippi Panorama 1974, Fire in the Valley: Folktales of the Ewes 1980, The Ghana Revolution, Ghana: A Political History 1990, Comes the Voyage at Last 1991, The Caribbean and Latin American Notebook 1992, Africa the Marginalized Continent. *Honours:* Gurrey Prize for Poetry, Nat. Book Council Award for Poetry 1979, Dillons Commonwealth Prize for Poetry (Africa Div.) 1989, Order of the Volta 1977, Agbonugla of ANLO 1997, Agbaledzigla of the Wheta Traditional Area 1998. *Address:* c/o Secretariat for Foreign Affairs, POB M212, Accra, Ghana. *Telephone:* (21) 665415 ext. 119 (office); (21) 503580 (home). *Fax:* (21) 660246 (office).

AXTON, David (see Koontz, Dean Ray)

AYCKBOURN, Sir Alan, Kt, CBE, FRSA; British playwright and theatre director; b. 12 April 1939, London; s. of Horace Ayckbourn and Irene Maud Ayckbourn (née Worley); m. 1st Christine Helen Roland 1959 (divorced 1997); two s.; m. 2nd Heather Elizabeth Stoney 1997. *Education:* Haileybury. *Career:* on leaving school went straight into the theatre as stage manager and actor with various repertory cos in England; Founder mem. Victoria Theatre Co., Stoke on Trent 1962–64; Drama Producer, BBC Radio 1964–70; Artistic Dir, Stephen Joseph Theatre, Scarborough 1971–(2008); Prof. of Contemporary Theatre, Oxford 1992. *Plays:* Mr Whatnot 1963, Relatively Speaking 1965, How the Other Half Loves 1969, Ernie's Incredible Illucinations 1969, Family Circles 1970, Time and Time Again 1971, Absurd Person Singular (Evening Standard Award for Best New Comedy 1973) 1972, The Norman Conquests (Evening Standard Award for Best New Play 1974, Plays and Players Award for Best New Play 1974) 1973, Jeeves (book and lyrics for Andrew Lloyd Webber musical) 1975 (rewritten as By Jeeves – British Regional Theatre Awards for Best Musical 1996), Absent Friends 1974, Confusions 1974, Bedroom Farce 1975, Just Between Ourselves (Evening Standard Award for Best New Play 1977) 1976, Ten Times Table 1977, Joking Apart (Co-winner Plays and Players Award for Best New Comedy 1979) 1978, Family Circles 1978, Sisterly Feelings 1979, Taking Steps 1979, Suburban Strains (musical play with music by Paul Todd) 1980, Season's Greetings 1980, Me, Myself & I (with Paul Todd) 1981, Way Upstream 1981, Intimate Exchanges 1982, It Could Be Any One Of Us 1983, A Chorus of Disapproval (London Evening Standard Award, Olivier Award and DRAMA Award for Best Comedy 1985) 1984 (film 1988), Woman in Mind 1985, A Small Family Business (London Evening Standard Award for Best New Play 1987) 1987, Henceforward... (London Evening Standard Award for Best Comedy 1989) 1987, A View from the Bridge (Plays and Players Director of the Year Award) 1987, Man of the Moment (London Evening Standard Award 1990) 1988, Mr A's Amazing Maze Plays (TMA/Martini Regional Theatre Award for Best Show for Children and Young People 1993) 1988, The Revengers' Comedies 1989, Invisible Friends 1989, Body Language 1990, This Is Where We Came In 1990, Callisto 5 1990 (rewritten as Callisto 7 1999), Wildest Dreams 1991, My Very Own Story 1991, Time of My Life 1992, Dreams From a Summer House (with music by John Pattison) 1992, Communicating Doors (Writers' Guild of GB Award for Best West End Play 1996) 1994, Haunting Julia 1994, A Word from our Sponsor (with music by John Pattison) 1995, The Champion of Paribanou 1996, Things We Do For Love (Lloyds Pvt. Banking Playwright of the Year Award 1997) 1997, Comic Potential 1998, The Boy Who Fell Into A Book 1998, House & Garden 1999, Whenever (with music by Denis King) 2000, Damsels in Distress (trilogy: GamePlan, FlatSpin, RolePlay) 2001, Snake in the Grass 2002, The Jollies 2002, Sugar Daddies 2003, Orvin – Champion of Champions (with music by Denis King) 2003, My Sister Sadie 2003, Drowning On Dry Land 2004, Private Fears in Public Places 2004, Miss Yesterday 2004, Improbable Fiction 2005, The Girl Who Lost Her Voice 2005, If I Were You 2006. *Publications:* fiction: majority of plays have been published; non-fiction: Conversations with Ayckbourn (with I. Watson) 1981, The Crafty Art of Playmaking 2002. *Honours:* Hon. Fellow (Bretton) 1982, (Cardiff) 1995; Hon. DLitt (Hull) 1981, (Keele, Leeds) 1987, (Bradford) 1994; Dr hc (York) 1992, (Wales Cardiff) 1995, (Open Univ.) 1998, (Manchester) 2003; Hon. Prof. (Hull) 2007; Variety Club of Great Britain Playwright of the Year 1974, Lifetime Achievement Award (Writers' Guild) 1993, John Ederyn Hughes Rural Wales Award for Literature 1993, Yorkshire Man of the Year 1994, Montblanc de la Culture Award for Europe 1994, Sunday Times Literary Award for Excellence 2001, Yorkshire Arts and Entertainment Personality, Yorkshire Awards 2005. *Address:* c/o Casarotto Ramsay and Associates Ltd, Waverley House, Noel Street, London, W1V 4ND, England (office). *Telephone:* (20) 7287-4450 (office). *Fax:* (20) 7287-9128 (office). *Website:* www.alanayckbourn.net.

AYRE, Richard James, BA, JP; British journalist; b. 1 Aug. 1949, Newcastle-upon-Tyne; s. of Thomas Henry Ayre and Beth Carson; pnr Guy Douglas Burch. *Education:* Univ. Coll., Durham. *Career:* Pres., Univ. of Durham Students' Union 1969–70; producer and reporter, BBC Northern Ireland 1973–76, Home News Ed., TV News 1979–84, Head of BBC Westminster 1989–92, Controller of Editorial Policy 1993–96, Deputy Chief Exec., BBC News 1996–2000; mem. Bd Food Standards Agency 2000–; Freedom of Information Adjudicator, Law Soc. 2001–; Civil Service Commr 2005–06; Bd mem. for England, Ofcom Content Bd 2006–; Benton Fellow, Univ. of Chicago 1984–85. *Address:* The Old Dairy, Burgh Hall, Burgh Parva, Melton Constable, Norfolk, NR24 2PU, England. *Telephone:* (1263) 860939. *E-mail:* richardayre@whats2hide.com (office).

AYRES, Pamela (Pam), MBE; British writer, poet and broadcaster; b. 19 March 1947, d. of Stanley William Ayres and Phyllis Evelyn Loder; m. Dudley Russell 1982; two s. *Education:* Faringdon Secondary Modern School, Berks. *Career:* served in Women's RAF 1965–69; writer and performer. *TV includes:* Opportunity Knocks 1975, The World of Pam Ayres 1977, numerous specials in UK, Hong Kong and Canada. *Radio includes:* Pam Ayres Radio Show 1995, Pam Ayres on Sunday 1996–99. *Publications include:* Some of Me Poetry 1976, Some More of Me Poetry 1976, Thoughts of a Late-Night Knitter 1978, All Pam's Poems 1978, Bertha and the Racing Pigeon 1979, The Ballad of Bill Spinks' Bedstead and Other Poems 1981, Dear Mum 1985, Guess Who? 1987, Guess What? 1987, When Dad Fills in the Garden Pond 1988, When Dad Cuts Down the Chestnut Tree 1988, Piggo and the Nosebag 1990, Piggo Has a Train Ride 1990, The Bear Who Was Left Behind 1991, Pam Ayres: The Works 1992, Guess Why? 1994, With These Hands: a Collection of Work 1997, The Nubbler 1997. *Address:* PO Box 64 Cirencester, GL7 5YD, England (office). *Telephone:* (1285) 644622 (office). *Fax:* (1285) 642291 (office). *E-mail:* acorrents@btconnect.com (office). *Website:* www.pamayres.com (office).

AYRES, Philip James, BA, PhD, FRHistS, FAHA; Australian writer and academic; *Professorial Fellow, Monash University*; b. 28 July 1944, S Australia; m. 1st Maruta Sudrabs 1965 (divorced 1981); m. 2nd Patricia San Martin 1981; one s. *Education:* Univ. of Adelaide. *Career:* Lecturer, Monash Univ. 1972–79, Sr Lecturer 1979–93, Assoc. Prof. 1993–2006, Professorial Fellow 2006–; Visiting Prof., Vassar Coll., New York 1993; Visiting Fellow, Boston Univ. 2001; mem. Australian Council, Deputy Chair. Literature Bd 2000–02. *Publications:* The Revenger's Tragedy 1977, The English Roman Life 1980, Malcolm Fraser: A Biography 1987, Classical Culture and the Idea of Rome in Eighteenth Century England 1997, Douglas Mawson 1999, Owen Dixon 2002, The Worlds of Cardinal Moran 2007; ed.: Ben Jonson: Sejanus His Fall 1990, 3rd Earl of Shaftesbury, Characteristics 1999; contribs to English Literary Renaissance, Modern Philology, Studies in Bibliography, Studies in English Literature, Studies in Philology. *Address:* 13 Harris Avenue, Glen Iris, Vic. 3146, Australia (home).

AZZOPARDI, Trezza, MA; British writer; b. 1961, Cardiff, Wales. *Education:* Univ. of East Anglia. *Career:* examiner for Norwich School of Art; Lecturer in Creative Writing, Univ. of East Anglia. *Publications:* novels: The Hiding Place (Geoffrey Faber Memorial Prize) 2000, Remember Me 2004, Winterton Blue 2007; contrib. to Neon Lit 1, Take Twenty, New Writing 9. *Address:* c/o A.P. Watt Ltd, 20 John Street, London, WC1N 2DR, England (office). *Telephone:* (20) 7405-6774 (office). *Fax:* (20) 7831-2154 (office). *E-mail:* apw@apwatt.co.uk (office). *Website:* www.apwatt.co.uk (office).

B

BAALBAKI, Layla; Lebanese writer and journalist; b. 1936, Beirut. *Career:* began writing aged 14; fmr sec. in Lebanese parl.; scholarship to Paris, France 1960. *Publications:* Anā Ahyā (novel, I Am Alive) 1958, The Disfigured Gods 1960, Safīnat Hanān ilā al-Qamar (short stories, Spaceship of Tenderness to the Moon) 1964.

BABADJHAN, Ramz; Uzbekistan poet and playwright; b. 2 Aug. 1921, s. of Nasriddin Babadjhan and Salomat Babadjhan; m. 1947; one s. two d. *Education:* Pedagogical Inst., Tashkent. *Career:* Deputy Chair. Uzbek Writers' Union; mem. CPSU 1951–91; Chair. Uzbek Republican Cttee on Relations with African and Asian Writers; Pres. Soc. on Cultural Relations with Compatriots Living Abroad 'Vatan' 1990–94; first works published 1935. *Publications include:* Dear Friends, Thank You, My Dear, The Heart Never Sleeps, Selected Poetry, A Poet Lives Twice, Living Water, Yusuf and Zuleyha, 1001 Crane, Sides, Uncle and Nephew, You Cannot Deceive a Gipsy. *Honours:* USSR State Prize 1972. *Address:* Beshchinar str. 34, 700070 Tashkent, Uzbekistan. *Telephone:* (371) 55-61-06.

BABINEAU, Jean Joseph, BEd, MA; Canadian teacher and writer; b. 10 Aug. 1952, Moncton, NB; m. Gisèle Ouellette 1993; one s. *Career:* mem. AAAPNB, CEAD. *Publications:* Bloupe 1993, Gîte 1998, Vortex 2003; contribs to Éloizes, Mœbius, Mots en Volet, Littéréalité, Satellite, Nouvelles d'Amérique, Virages, Le Front. *Honours:* Canada Council Exploration Grant 1989, New Brunswick Arts Br. Creation Grant 1998, 2002, Prix Antonine Maillet-Acadie Vie. *Address:* 12 allée Gîte, Grand-Barachois, NB, E4P 7N9, Canada.

BACHMAN, Richard (see King, Stephen Edwin)

BACKSCHEIDER, Paula, BA, MS, PhD; American academic, writer and editor; *Stevens Eminent Scholar, Auburn University;* b. 31 March 1943, Brownsville, TN; m. Nickolas Andrew Backscheider 1964; one s. one d. *Education:* Purdue Univ., Southern Connecticut State Coll. *Career:* Asst Prof., Rollins Coll., Winter Park, Fla 1973–75; Asst Prof., Univ. of Rochester 1975–78, Assoc. Prof. 1978–87, Prof. of English 1987–1990, Roswell Burrows Prof. 1991–92; Stevens Eminent Scholar, Auburn Univ. 1992–; mem. American Soc. for Eighteenth-Century Studies (Pres. 1992), Modern Language Asscn. *Publications:* An Annotated Bibliography of Twentieth-Century Studies of Women and Literature 1660–1800 (with Felicity Nussbaum and Philip Anderson) 1977, Probability, Time, and Space in Eighteenth-Century Literature (ed.) 1979, Eighteenth-Century Drama (ed.), 69 vols 1979–83, A Being More Intense: The Prose Works of Bunyan, Swift, and Defoe 1984, Daniel Defoe: Ambition and Innovation 1986, Daniel Defoe: His Life 1989, Spectacular Politics: Theatrical Power and Mass Culture in Early Modern England 1993, Popular Fiction by Women 1660–1730: An Anthology (co-ed. with John J. Richetti) 1996, The Intersections of the Public and Private Spheres in Early Modern England (co-ed. with Timothy Dykstal) 1996, Reflections on Biography 1999, Revising Women: Eighteenth-Century 'Women's Fiction' and Social Engagement (ed.) 2000, A Companion to the Eighteenth-Century Novel and Culture (co-ed. with Catherine Ingrassia) 2005, Eighteenth-Century Women Poets and Their Poetry 2005; contrib. to reference works, scholarly books and professional journals. *Honours:* American Philosophical Soc. Grants 1975, 1980, 1986, Nat. Endowment for the Humanities Fellowship 1983, American Antiquarian Soc. Fellowship 1987, British Council Prize for Best Humanities Book 1990, Guggenheim Fellowship 1991, Distinguished Alumna Award, Purdue Univ., 2001, Distinguished Teaching Award, Omicron Delta Kappa Hon. Soc. 2003, World Women's Literature Center Award (Korea) 2003, James Russell Lowell Prize 2006. *Address:* Department of English, Auburn University, Auburn, AL 36849 (office); 1930 Canary Drive, Auburn, AL 36830, USA (home). *Telephone:* (334) 844-9091 (office); (334) 821-8874 (home). *Fax:* (334) 844-9027 (office). *E-mail:* pkrb@auburn.edu (office). *Website:* www.auburn.edu/~pkrb (office).

BADAWI, (Mohamed) Mustafa, BA, PhD; British lecturer and writer; *Emeritus Fellow, St Antony's College, Oxford;* b. 10 June 1925, Alexandria, Egypt. *Education:* Alexandria Univ., Univ. of London. *Career:* Research Fellow 1947–54, Lecturer 1954–60, Asst Prof. 1960–64, Alexandria Univ., Egypt; Lecturer, Univ. of Oxford, and Brasenose Coll. 1964–92; Fellow, St Antony's Coll., Oxford 1967–; Ed., Journal of Arabic Literature, Leiden 1970; advisory bd mem., Cambridge History of Arabic Literature. *Publications:* An Anthology of Modern Arabic Verse 1970, Coleridge as Critic of Shakespeare 1973, A Critical Introduction to Modern Arabic Poetry 1975, Background to Shakespeare 1981, Modern Arabic Literature and the West 1985, Modern Arabic Drama in Egypt 1987, Early Arabic Drama 1988, Modern Arabic Literature: Cambridge History of Arabic Literature (ed.) 1992, A Short History of Modern Arabic Literature 1993; several books and vols of verse in Arabic, including Arabic trans. of Shakespeare's Macbeth 2001, King Lear 2003, Othello 2004, Hamlet 2005. *Honours:* King Faisal Int. Prize for Arabic Literature 1992, Supreme Council Award for promoting knowledge of Arabic culture, Egypt 2006. *Address:* St Antony's College, Oxford, OX2 6JF, England.

BADCOCK, Gary David; Canadian academic, writer and editor; b. 13 Jan. 1961, Bay Roberts; m. Susan Dorothy Greig 1988; two d. *Education:* BA, 1981, MA, 1984, Memorial University of Newfoundland; BD, 1987, PhD, 1991, University of Edinburgh, Scotland. *Career:* Teaching Fellow, University of Aberdeen, 1991–92; Meldrum Lecturer in Dogmatic Theology, University of Edinburgh, 1993–99; Asst Prof., Huron College, London, Ontario, 1999–2002, Assoc. Prof., 2002–. *Publications:* Disruption to Diversity: Edinburgh Divinity, 1846–1996 (ed. with D. F. Wright), 1996; Theology After the Storm, by John McIntyre (ed.), 1995; Light of Truth and Fire of Love, 1997; The Way of Life, 1998. Contributions: Co-author, books and scholarly journals. *Honours:* Leslie Tarr Award, 1998. *Address:* Faculty of Theology, Huron University College, London, ON, Canada, N6G 1H3. *E-mail:* gbadcock@uwo.ca.

BADR, Liana, BA; Palestinian writer and journalist; *Head of Cinema Department, Ministry of Culture;* b. 1950, Jerusalem; m. Yāsir 'Abd Rabbih; two s. *Education:* Beirut Arab Univ. *Career:* fmr volunteer in various Palestinian women's orgs; Culture Ed. Al Hurriyya review; after Palestinian exodus from Lebanon in 1982, lived in Damascus, Tunis and Amman, before returning in 1994; runs Cinema Dept Ministry of Culture, (founder and fmr Ed. ministry periodical Dafater Thaqafiyya). *Publications:* A Compass for the Sunflower (novel, in trans.) 1979, Stories of Love and Pursuit (short stories) 1983, A Balcony Over the Fakahani (three novellas, in trans.) 1983, I Want the Day (short stories) 1989, The Eye of the Mirror (novel, in trans.) 1991, Golden Hell (short stories) 1991, Stars of Jericho (novel) 1993, Fadwa Touqan – the shadow of narrated words (memoir of the poet) 1996; five children's books 1980–91, collection of poems 1997. *Address:* c/o Ministry of Culture, POB 147, Ramallah, Palestinian Autonomous Areas.

BAERWALD, Hans Hermann, BA, MA, PhD; American writer and academic (retd); b. 18 June 1927, Tokyo, Japan. *Education:* Univ. of California, Berkeley. *Career:* Asst Prof. of Government 1956–61, Assoc. Prof. of Government 1961–62, Miami Univ., Oxford, OH; Lecturer in Political Science, UCLA 1962–65, Assoc. Prof. of Political Science 1965–69, Prof. 1969–91. *Publications:* The Purge of Japanese Leaders Under the Occupation 1959, American Government: Structure, Problems, Policies (with Peter H. Odegard) 1962, Chinese Communism: Selected Documents (with Dan N. Jacobs) 1963, The American Republic, Its Government and Politics (with Peter H. Odegard) 1964, Japan's Parliament: An Introduction 1974, Party Politics in Japan 1986; contrib. to Asian Survey. *Honours:* Order of the Sacred Treasure with Gold and Silver Star, Japan 1989, Kun Nito Zuihosho. *Address:* 2221 Barnett Road, St Helens, CA 94574, USA (home). *Telephone:* (707) 965-0438 (home). *Fax:* (707) 965-0813 (home). *E-mail:* hanbwald@napanet.net (home).

BAGDIKIAN, Ben Haig, AB; Turkish academic and writer; b. 30 Jan. 1920, Marash; m. Marlene Griffith Bagdikian 1983; two s. *Education:* Clark Univ. *Career:* Asst Man. Ed. National News, The Washington Post; Prof., Dean, Grad. School of Journalism, Univ. of California, Berkeley. *Publications:* In the Midst of Plenty: The Poor in America 1964, The Information Machines 1973, The Effete Conspiracy and Other Crimes of the Press 1973, Caged: Eight Prisoners and Their Keepers 1976, The Media Monopoly 1983, 7th edn as The New Media Monopoly, Double Vision: Reflections on My Heritage, Life and Profession 1995; contributions: More than 200 to national magazines and journals. *Honours:* Hon. LHD (Brown Univ.) 1961, (Univ. of Rhode Island) 1992; Hon. LittD (Clark Univ.) 1963; Peabody Award 1951, Sidney Hillman Award 1955, John Simon Guggenheim Fellow 1962, Berkeley Citation 1990, James Madison Award, American Library Asscn 1998. *Address:* 25 Stonewall Road, Berkeley, CA 94705, USA.

BAHN, Paul Gerard, BA, MA, PhD; British archaeologist and writer; b. 29 July 1953, Hull, England. *Education:* Univ. of Cambridge. *Career:* Research Fellow, Univ. of Liverpool 1979–82; Sr Research Fellow, Univ. of London 1982–83; J. Paul Getty Postdoctoral Fellow 1985–86. *Publications:* Easter Island, Earth Island 1992, The Story of Archaeology 1995, Archaeology: A Very Short Introduction 1996, The Cambridge Illustrated History of Archaeology 1996, Tombs, Graves and Mummies 1996, Journey Through the Ice Age 1997, Lost Cities 1997, The Cambridge Illustrated History of Prehistoric Art 1998, Disgraceful Archaeology 1999, Wonderful Things 1999, Atlas of World Archaeology 2000, Mammoths (second edn) 2000, The Archaeology Detectives 2001, The Penguin Guide to Archaeology 2001, Archaeology: The Definitive Guide 2002, Written in Bones 2003, The Enigmas of Easter Island 2003, Archaeology: Theories, Methods and Practice (revised fourth edn) 2004, Archaeology: The Key Concepts 2004, The Bluffer's Guide to Archaeology (revised third edn) 2004, The New Penguin Dictionary of Archaeology 2004, Waking the Trance Fixed 2005, Unearthing the Past 2005, Chamanismes et Arts Prehistoriques 2006, Archaeology Essentials 2007, The Art of Creswell Crags in its European Context 2007, Ancient Obscenities 2007; contrib. to periodicals. *Literary Agent:* Watson, Little Ltd, Lymehouse Studios, 38 Georgiana Street, London, NW1 0EB, England. *E-mail:* pgbahn@anlabyrd.karoo.co.uk (home).

BAI, Fengxi; Chinese feminist and playwright; b. 1934, Wen'an, Hebei Prov.; m. Yan Zhongying; one d. *Education:* N China People's Revolutionary Univ. *Career:* became actress China Youth Theater 1954. *Publications:* The Women Trilogy: First Bathed in Moonlight 1981, An Old Friend Returning in a Stormy Night 1983, Where is Longing in Autumn? 1986. *Address:* c/o Chinese Literature Press, 24 Baiwanzhuang Road, Beijing 1000037, People's Republic of China.

BAIGELL, Matthew, BA, MA, PhD; American academic and writer; b. 27 April 1933, New York, NY; m. Renee Moses 1959, two d. *Education:* University of Vermont, Columbia University, University of Pennsylvania. *Career:* Instructor, 1961–65, Asst Prof., 1965–67, Assoc. Prof. of Art, 1967–68, Ohio State University; Assoc. Prof., 1968–72, Prof., 1972–78, Prof. II, 1978–, Rutgers, the State University of New Jersey at New Brunswick. *Publications:* A History of American Painting, 1971; A Thomas Hart Benton Miscellany (ed.), 1971; The American Scene: American Painting in the 1930s, 1974; Thomas Hart Benton, 1974; Charles Burchfield, 1976; The Western Art of Frederic Remington, 1976; Dictionary of American Art, 1979; Albert Bierstadt, 1981; Thomas Cole, 1981; A Concise History of American Painting and Sculpture, 1984; The Papers of the American Artists' Congress (1936), 1985; Artists Against War and Fascism (ed. with J. Williams), 1986; Soviet Dissident Artists: Interviews After Perestroika (with Renee Baigell), 1995; Jewish-American Artists and the Holocaust, 1997; Artist and Identity in Twentieth-Century America, 2001.

BAIGENT, Beryl, ('Snowdon'), BA, MA; British/Canadian teacher, writer and poet; *Teacher of T'ai chi and Sacred Dance*; b. 16 Dec. 1937, Llay, Wrexham, North Wales; d. of Edmund Ivor Jones and Elizabeth Bewley; m. Alan H. Baigent 1963; three d. *Education:* Univ. of Western Ontario, London, Canada. *Career:* Teacher of T'ai chi and Sacred Dance 1971–; mem. Celtic Arts Asscn, Canadian Poetry Asscn, League of Canadian Poets (Ont. Representative) 1994–96; Poetry Contests Judge, Libraries & Poetry Organ. *Publications:* The Quiet Village 1972, Pause 1974, In Counterpoint 1976, Ancestral Dreams 1981, The Sacred Beech 1985, Mystic Animals 1988, Absorbing the Dark 1990, Hiraeth: In Search of Celtic Origins 1994, Triptych: Virgins, Victims, Votives 1996, The Celtic Tree Calendar 1999, The Mary Poems 2000, And a Branch Shall Grow: The Irish Connection 2006; contribs to various anthologies and periodicals including Poetry and Spiritual Practice 2002. *Honours:* Ontario Weekly Newspaper Award 1979, Fritch Memorial, Canadian Authors Asscn 1982, Ontario Arts Council Awards 1983, 1985, 1987, Kent Writers Award 1986, Black Mountain Award 1986, Canada Council Touring Awards 1990, 1992, 1993, 1994, 1998, Forest City Poetry Award 1991, International Affairs Touring Award 1991, Welsh Arts Council Awards 1993, 1994, 1996, 1998, 1999, 2000, 2002, 2003, 2004, 2005, 2006, Muse Journal Award 1994. *Address:* PO Box 323, Thamesford, ON N0M 2M0 (office); 137 Byron Avenue, Thamesford, ON N0M 2M0, Canada (home). *Telephone:* (519) 285-2441 (home). *E-mail:* berylbaigent@yahoo.ca (home).

BAIL, Murray; Australian writer; b. 22 Sept. 1941, Adelaide, SA; m. Margaret Wordsworth 1965. *Education:* Norwood Technical High School, Adelaide. *Publications:* Contemporary Portraits and Other Stories 1975, Homesickness (Age Book of the Year Award, Nat. Book Council Award) 1980, Holden's Performance 1987, The Faber Book of Contemporary Australian Short Stories (ed.) 1988, Longhand: A Writer's Notebook 1989, Eucalyptus 1998, Camouflage (short stories) 2001, Notebooks 1970–2003 2005. *Honours:* Victorian Premier's Award 1988, Commonwealth Writers Prize 1999, Miles Franklin Award 1999. *Address:* c/o Harvill Secker, Random House, 20 Vauxhall Bridge Road, London, SW1V 2SA, England.

BAILEY, Anthony Cowper, BA, MA; British writer and journalist; b. 5 Jan. 1933, Portsmouth, England. *Education:* Merton Coll., Oxford. *Career:* staff writer, New Yorker magazine 1956–92; mem. Authors' Guild, Int. PEN, Soc. of Authors. *Publications:* Making Progress 1959, The Mother Tongue 1961, The Inside Passage 1965, Through the Great City 1967, The Thousand Dollar Yacht 1968, The Light in Holland 1970, In the Village 1971, A Concise History of the Low Countries 1972, Rembrandt's House 1978, Acts of Union: Reports on Ireland, 1973–79 1980, America, Lost and Found 1981, Along the Edge of the Forest: An Iron Curtain Journey 1983, England, First and Last 1985, Spring Jaunts: Some Walks, Excursions, and Personal Explorations of City, Country and Seashore 1986, Major André 1987, The Outer Banks 1989, A Walk Through Wales 1992, Responses to Rembrandt 1994, A Coast of Summer: Sailing New England Waters from Shelter Island to Cape Cod 1994, John Constable: A Kingdom of His Own 2006. *Honours:* Overeas Press Club Award 1974. *Address:* c/o Chatto & Windus, Random House, 20 Vauxhall Bridge Road, London, SW1V 2SA, England (office).

BAILEY, Glenda Adrianne, MA; British magazine editor; *Editor-in-Chief, Harper's Bazaar*; b. 16 Nov. 1958, Derby; d. of John Ernest Bailey and Constance Bailey (née Groome); partner Steve Sumner. *Education:* Noel Baker Grammar School, Derby and Kingston Polytechnic. *Career:* fmr consultant, Fashion Forecast, Design Direction; produced collection for Guisi Slaverio, Italy 1983; Ed. Honey 1986–88; launched Folio quarterly fashion magazine; launch Ed. Marie Claire, UK 1988–1996, Int. Editorial Consultant of all 26 editions of Marie Claire 1995, Marie Claire, USA 1996–2001; Ed.-in-Chief Harper's Bazaar, USA 2001–. *Honours:* three Magazine Editor of the Year Awards, five Magazine of the Year Awards, two Amnesty Int. Awards 1988–96, Women's Magazine Ed. of the Year, British Soc. of Magazine Eds 1990, Media Week Press Award, Periodical Publrs Award, Consumer Magazine of the Year 1991, Amnesty Int. Award 1997, Community Action Network Award 1998, 1999, named Editor of the Year by Adweek 2001. *Address:* Harper's Bazaar, 1700 Broadway, New York, NY 10019-5970, USA (office). *Telephone:* (212) 903-5000 (office). *Fax:* (212) 262-7101 (office). *E-mail:* bazaar@hearst.com (office). *Website:* www.harpersbazaar.com (office).

BAILEY, Martin, PhD; British journalist; b. 26 Oct. 1947, London, England. *Education:* LSE. *Career:* journalist, The Observer 1983–. *Publications:* Freedom Railway, 1976; Oilgate: The Sanctions Scandal, 1979; A Green Part of the World, 1984; Young Vincent: Van Gogh's Years in England, 1990; Van Gogh: Letters from Provence, 1990; Van Gogh in England: Portrait of the Artist as a Young Man, 1992. *Honours:* Journalist of the Year 1979. *Address:* c/o The Observer, 119 Farringdon Road, London, EC1R 3ER, England (office).

BAILEY, Paul, FRSL; British writer; b. (Peter Harry Bailey), 16 Feb. 1937, s. of Arthur Oswald Bailey and Helen Maud Burgess. *Education:* Sir Walter St John's School, London. *Career:* actor 1956–64, appearing in The Sport of My Mad Mother 1958 and Epitaph for George Dillon 1958; Literary Fellow at Univs. of Newcastle and Durham 1972–74; Bicentennial Fellowship 1976; Visiting Lecturer in English Literature, North Dakota State Univ. 1977–79. *Publications:* At the Jerusalem 1967, Trespasses 1970, A Distant Likeness 1973, Peter Smart's Confessions 1977, Old Soldiers 1980, An English Madam 1982, Gabriel's Lament 1986, An Immaculate Mistake (autobiog.) 1990, Hearth and Home 1990, Sugar Cane 1993, The Oxford Book of London (ed.) 1995, First Love (ed.) 1997, Kitty and Virgil 1998, The Stately Homo: A Celebration of the Life of Quentin Crisp (ed.) 2000, Three Queer Lives: Fred Barnes, Naomi Jacob and Arthur Marshall 2001, Uncle Rudolf (novel) 2002; numerous newspaper articles. *Honours:* Somerset Maugham Award 1968; E. M. Forster Award 1978; George Orwell Memorial Prize 1978. *Address:* 79 Davisville Road, London, W12 9SH, England. *Telephone:* (20) 8749-2279. *Fax:* (20) 8248-2127.

BAILEY, Sly; British publishing and media executive; *CEO, Trinity Mirror PLC*; b. (Sylvia Grice), 24 Jan. 1962, London; d. of Thomas Lewis and Sylvia Grice (née Bantick); m. Peter Bailey 1998. *Education:* St Saviours and St Olaves Grammar School for Girls. *Career:* telephone sales exec. at The Guardian 1984–87; Advertisement Sales Man., The Independent 1987–89; moved to IPC Magazines 1989, Advertising Sales Exec. 1994, mem. Bd of Dirs 1994–2003, Man. Dir TX 1997, CEO 1999–2003; mem. Bd of Dirs and CEO Trinity Mirror PLC 2003–; Dir (non-exec.) Littlewoods PLC April–Sept. 2002, EMI 2004– (Sr Ind. Dir 2007–); mem. Ind. Panel on BBC Charter Review 2004; Dir The Press Asscn; Pres. NewstrAid Benevolent Soc. *Honours:* Periodical Publrs Asscn Marcus Morris Award for Outstanding Contrib. to Publishing Industry 2002, named as one of 50 Most Powerful Woman in Britain by Management Today 2002, named as one of Britain's Most Influential Woman by Daily Mail 2003, ranked amongst top 20 of MediaGuardian's 100 Most Influential Figures in Media 2003, ranked by Fortune magazine amongst 50 Most Powerful Women in Business outside the US (23rd) 2003, (23rd) 2004, (33rd) 2005, (45th) 2006, ranked by the Financial Times amongst Top 25 Businesswomen in Europe (12th) 2005, (18th) 2006. *Address:* Trinity Mirror PLC, 1 Canada Square, Canary Wharf, London, E14 5AP, England (office). *Telephone:* (20) 7293-2203 (office). *Fax:* (20) 7293-3225 (office). *E-mail:* sly.bailey@trinitymirror.com. *Website:* www.trinitymirror.com (office).

BAILYN, Bernard, PhD; American historian and academic; *Professor Emeritus of History, Harvard University*; b. 10 Sept. 1922, Hartford, Conn.; s. of Charles Manuel Bailyn and Esther Schloss; m. Lotte Lazarsfeld 1952; two s. *Education:* Williams Coll. and Harvard Univ. *Career:* mem. Faculty, Harvard Univ. 1953–, Prof. of History 1961–66, Winthrop Prof. of History 1966–81, Adams Univ. Prof. 1981–93, Prof. Emer. 1993–, James Duncan Phillips Prof. in Early American History 1991–93, Prof. Emer. 1993–; Dir Charles Warren Center for Studies in American History 1983–94; Pitt Prof. of American Hist., Cambridge Univ. 1986–87; Dir Int. Seminar on History of Atlantic World 1995–; Ed.-in-Chief John Harvard Library 1962–70; Co-Ed. Perspectives in American History (journal) 1967–77, 1984–86; mem. American Historical Asscn (Pres. 1981), American Acad. of Arts and Sciences, Nat. Acad. of Educ., American Philosophical Soc.; Foreign mem. Russian Acad. of Sciences, Academia Europaea, Mexican Acad. of History and Geography; Sr Fellow, Soc. of Fellows; Hon. Fellow Christ's Coll., Cambridge Univ.; Corresp. Fellow, British Acad. 1989, Royal Historial Soc.; Trustee Inst. of Advanced Study, Princeton 1989–94; Trevelyan Lecturer, Cambridge Univ. 1971; Jefferson Lecturer, Nat. Endowment for the Humanities 1998. *Publications:* The New England Merchants in the 17th Century 1955, Massachusetts Shipping 1697–1714: A Statistical Study (jtly) 1959, Education in the Forming of American Society 1960, Pamphlets of the American Revolution 1750–1776, Vol. I (ed.) (Faculty Prize, Harvard Univ. Press) 1965, The Apologia of Robert Keayne (ed.) 1965, The Ideological Origins of the American Revolution (Pulitzer and Bancroft Prizes 1968) 1967, The Origins of American Politics 1968, The Intellectual Migration 1930–1960 (co-ed.) 1969, Law in American History (co-ed.) 1972, The Ordeal of Thomas Hutchinson (Nat. Book Award 1975) 1974, The Great Republic (co-author) 1977, The Press and the American Revolution (co-ed.) 1980, The Peopling of British North America 1986, Voyagers to the West (Pulitzer Prize 1986) 1986, Faces of Revolution 1990, Strangers Within the Realm (co-ed.) 1991, The Debate on the Constitution (two vols, ed.) 1993, On the Teaching and Writing of History 1994, Atlantic History 2005. *Honours:* 15 hon. degrees; Robert H. Lord Award, Emmanuel Coll. 1967, Thomas Jefferson Medal 1993, Henry Allen Moe Prize, American Philosophical Soc. 1994, Foreign Policy Asscn Medal 1998; Catton Prize, Soc. American Historians 2000. *Address:* History Department, Harvard University, Cambridge, MA 02138 (office); 170 Clifton Street, Belmont, MA 02478-2604, USA (home).

BAINBRIDGE, Dame Beryl, DBE, FRSL; British writer; b. 21 Nov. 1934, Liverpool; d. of Richard Bainbridge and Winifred Bainbridge (née Baines); m. Austin Davies 1954 (divorced); one s. two d. *Education:* Merchant Taylors' School, Liverpool, Arts Educational Schools, Tring. *Career:* columnist Evening Standard 1987–93. *Plays:* Tiptoe Through the Tulips 1976, The Warriors

Return 1977, It's a Lovely Day Tomorrow 1977, Journal of Bridget Hitler 1981, Somewhere More Central (TV) 1981, Evensong (TV) 1986. *Publications:* A Weekend with Claude 1967, Another Part of the Wood 1968, Harriet Said... 1972, The Dressmaker 1973 (film 1989), The Bottle Factory Outing (Guardian Fiction Award) 1974, Sweet William 1975 (film 1980), A Quiet Life 1976, Injury Time (Whitbread Award) 1977, Young Adolf 1978, Winter Garden 1980, English Journey (TV series) 1984, Watson's Apology 1984, Mum and Mr. Armitage 1985, Forever England 1986 (TV series 1986), Filthy Lucre 1986, An Awfully Big Adventure (staged 1992, film 1995) 1989, The Birthday Boys 1991, Something Happened Yesterday 1993, Collected Stories 1994, Northern Stories (Vol. 5.) (with David Pownall), Every Man For Himself (Whitbread Novel Prize 1996) 1996, Master Georgie 1998, According to Queeney 2001, Front Row (memoirs) 2005. *Honours:* Hon. DLitt (Liverpool Univ.) 1988; James Tait Black Fiction Prize 1996, Author of the Year 1999, James Tait Black Memorial Prize, British Book Awards 1999, David Cohen Prize, Arts Council of England 2003, Heywood Hill Literary Prize 2004. *Address:* 42 Albert Street, London, NW1 7NU, England. *Telephone:* (20) 7387-3113 (home).

BAINBRIDGE, Cyril; British writer and journalist; b. 15 Nov. 1928, Bradford, West Yorkshire, England; m. Barbara Hannah Crook 1953, one s. two d. *Education:* Negus Coll., Bradford. *Career:* reporter, Bingley Guardian 1944–45, Yorkshire Observer & Bradford Telegraph 1945–54, Press Assn 1954–63; Asst News Ed., The Times 1963–67, Deputy News Ed. 1967–69, Regional News Ed. 1969–77, Managing News Ed. 1977–82, Asst Managing Ed. 1982–88; mem. Brontë Soc., Chartered Inst. of Journalists, Soc. of Authors. *Publications:* Pavilions on the Sea, Brass Triumphant, The Brontës and Their Country, North Yorkshire and North Humberside, One Hundred Years of Journalism, The News of the World Story 1993; contrib. to newspapers, magazines and periodicals. *Address:* 6 Lea Road, Hemingford Grey, Huntingdon, Cambs PE28 9ED, England.

BAINES, John (see Salas Sommer, Dario)

BAITZ, Jon Robin; American playwright; b. 1961, Los Angeles, CA. *Publications:* plays: The Film Society, 1987; Dutch Landscape, 1989; The Substance of Fire, 1991; Three Hotels, 1993; The End of the Day, 1993. Contributions: anthologies. *Honours:* Fellow, American Acad. and Institute of Arts and Letters 1994.

BAJWA, Rupa; Indian novelist; b. 1976, Amritsar. *Publications:* The Sari Shop 2004. *Address:* c/o Penguin Books Ltd, 80 Strand, London, WC2R 0RL, England. *Website:* www.penguin.co.uk.

BAKER, Alison, BA, MLS; American writer; b. 7 Aug. 1953, Lancaster, PA. *Education:* Reed College, Indiana University. *Publications:* How I Came West, and Why I Stayed, 1993; Thousands Live!, 1996. Contributions: anthologies and periodicals. *Honours:* George Garrett Fiction Award, 1992; First Prize, O. Henry Collection, 1994.

BAKER, David Anthony, BSE, MA, PhD; American academic and poet; *Poetry Editor, The Kenyon Review;* b. 27 Dec. 1954, Bangor, Me; s. of Donald Dayle Baker and Martha Baker; m. Ann Townsend 1987; one d. *Education:* Central Missouri State Univ., Univ. of Utah. *Career:* Poetry Ed. Quarterly West 1980–81, Ed.-in-Chief 1981–83; Visiting Asst Prof., Kenyon Coll. 1983–84; Asst Ed. Kenyon Review 1983–89, Poetry Ed./Consulting Poetry Ed. 1989–94, Poetry Ed. 1994–; Asst Prof. of English, Denison Univ. 1984–90, Assoc. Prof. of English 1990–97, Thomas B. Fordham Endowed Chair in Creative Writing 1996, Prof. of English 1997–; Visiting Telluride Prof., Cornell Univ. 1985; Visiting Assoc. Prof., Univ. of Michigan 1996; Visiting Prof., Ohio State Univ. 2005; Contributing Ed. The Pushcart Prize 1992–; many poetry readings; mem. Associated Writing Programs, MLA, Nat. Book Critics Circle, Poetry Soc. of America, Poets and Writers. *Publications:* poetry: Looking Ahead 1975, Rivers in the Sea 1977, Laws of the Land 1981, Summer Sleep 1984, Haunts 1985, The Soil is Suited to the Seed: A Miscellany in Honor of Paul Bennett (ed.) 1986, Sweet Home, Saturday Night 1991, Echo for an Anniversary 1992, After the Reunion 1994, Holding Katherine 1997, The Truth About Small Towns 1998, Changeable Thunder 2001, Midwest Eclogue 2005; criticism: Meter in English: A Critical Engagement 1996, Heresy and the Ideal: On Contemporary Poetry 2000, Radiant Lyre: Essays on Lyric Poetry 2007; contrib. poems to periodicals, including The Atlantic, The Nation, The New Yorker, Poetry, The Yale Review, reviews to The Georgia Review, The Kenyon Review, Poetry. *Honours:* Bread Loaf Poetry Fellow 1989, Nat. Endowment for the Arts Fellowship 1985, Ohio Arts Council Fellowship 2000, Guggenheim Fellowship 2000; Bread Loaf Margaret Bridgman Scholar of Poetry 1982, Pushcart Press Outstanding Writer 1982, 1984, 1985, 1986, 1990, 1991, 1994, 1995, Mid-American Review James Wright Prize for Poetry 1983, Pushcart Prize 1992, 2004, 2005, Poetry Soc. of America Mary Carolyn Davies Award 1995. *Address:* The Kenyon Review, Walton House, Kenyon College, Gambier, OH 43022-9623, USA (office). *E-mail:* kenyonreview@kenyon.edu (office). *Website:* www.kenyonreview.org (office).

BAKER, Houston Alfred, Jr, BA, MA, PhD; American academic, writer, editor and poet; b. 22 March 1943, Louisville, KY; m. Charlotte Pierce-Baker 1966; one s. *Education:* Howard University, University of California at Los Angeles, University of Edinburgh. *Career:* Instructor, Howard University, 1966; Instructor, 1968–69, Asst Prof. of English, 1969–70, Yale University; Assoc. Prof. and Mem., Center for Advanced Studies, 1970–73, Prof. of English, 1973–74, University of Virginia; Prof. of English, 1974–, Dir, Afro-American Studies Program, 1974–77, Albert M. Greenfield Prof. of Human

Relations, 1982–, Dir, Center for the Study of Black Literature and Culture, 1987–, University of Pennsylvania; Fellow, Center for Advanced Study in the Behavioral Sciences, 1977–78, National Humanities Center, 1982–83; Bucknell Distinguished Scholar, University of Vermont, 1992; Berg Visiting Prof. of English, New York University, 1994; Fulbright 50th Anniversary Distinguished Fellow, Brazil, 1996; Senior Fellow, School of Criticism and Theory, Cornell University, 1996–2002; mem. College Language Asscn; English Institute, board of supervisors, 1989–91; MLA, pres., 1992. *Publications:* A Many-Colored Coat of Dreams: The Poetry of Countee Cullen, 1974; The Journey Back: Issues in Black Literature and Criticism, 1980; Blues, Ideology, and Afro-American Literature: A Vernacular Theory, 1984; Modernism and Harlem Renaissance, 1987; Afro-American Poetics: Revisions of Harlem and the Black Aesthetic, 1988; Workings of the Spirit: A Poetics of Afro-American Women's Writing, 1991; Black Studies, Rap, and the Academy, 1993. Poetry: No Matter Where You Travel, You Still Be Black, 1979; Spirit Run, 1982; Blues Journeys Home, 1985. Editor: various books. Contributions: scholarly books and journals. *Honours:* Alumni Award for Distinguished Achievement in Literature and the Humanities, Howard University, 1985; Distinguished Writer of the Year Award, Middle Atlantic Writers Asscn, 1986; Creative Scholarship Award, College Language Asscn of America, 1988; Pennsylvania Governor's Award for Excellence in the Humanities, 1990; several hon. doctorates. *Address:* c/o Center for the Study of Black Literature and Culture, University of Pennsylvania, Philadelphia, PA 19104, USA.

BAKER, Baron (Life Peer), cr. 1997, of Dorking in the County of Surrey; **Kenneth Wilfred Baker,** PC, CH; British politician and writer; b. 3 Nov. 1934, Newport, Wales; s. of the late W. M. Baker; m. Mary Elizabeth Gray-Muir 1963; one s. two d. *Education:* St Paul's School and Magdalen Coll., Oxford. *Career:* nat. service 1953–55; served Twickenham Borough Council 1960–62; as Conservative cand. contested Poplar 1964, Acton 1966; Conservative MP for Acton 1968–70, St Marylebone 1970–83, Mole Valley 1983–97; Parl. Sec. Civil Service Dept 1972–74, Parl. Pvt. Sec. to Leader of Opposition 1974–75; Minister of State and Minister for Information Tech., Dept of Trade and Industry 1981–84; Sec. of State for the Environment 1985–86, for Educ. and Science 1986–89; Chancellor of the Duchy of Lancaster and Chair. Conservative Party 1989–90; Sec. of State for the Home Dept 1990–92; mem. Public Accounts Cttee 1969–70; mem. Exec. 1922 Cttee 1978–81; Chair. Hansard Soc. 1978–81, MTT PLC 1996–97, Business Serve PLC, Northern Edge Ltd, Museum of British History, Belmont Press (London) Ltd, Monstermob, Teather & Greenwood 2003–; Pres. Royal London Soc. for the Blind; Sec. Gen. UN Conf. of Parliamentarians on World Population and Devt 1978; Chair. (non-exec.) Teather & Greenwood PLC, Monstermob, Business Serve; Dir (non-exec.) Hanson 1992–, Stanley Leisure PLC; Chair. Information Cttee, House of Lords 2002–. *Publications:* I Have No Gun But I Can Spit 1980, London Lines (ed.) 1982, The Faber Book of English History in Verse (ed.) 1988, The Faber Book of English Parodies (ed.) 1990, Unauthorized Versions (ed.) 1990, The Faber Book of Conservatism (ed.) 1993, The Turbulent Years: My Life in Politics 1993, The Prime Ministers: An Irreverent Political History in Cartoons 1995, The Kings and Queens: An Irreverent Cartoon History of the British Monarchy 1995, The Faber Book of War Poetry (ed.) 1996, Children's English History in Verse (ed.) 2000, The Faber Book of Landscape Poetry (ed.) 2000. *Honours:* Companion of Honour 1997. *Address:* House of Lords, Westminster, London, SW1A 0PW, England (office). *Telephone:* (20) 7219-3000 (office).

BAKER, Margaret Joyce; British writer; b. 21 May 1918, Reading, Berkshire, England. *Education:* King's Coll., London. *Publications:* The Fighting Cocks, 1949; Four Farthings and a Thimble, 1950; A Castle and Sixpence, 1951; The Family That Grew and Grew, 1952; Lions in the Potting Shed, 1954; The Wonderful Wellington Boots, 1955; Anna Sewell and Black Beauty, 1956; The Birds of Thimblepins, 1960; Homer in Orbit, 1961; The Cats of Honeytown, 1962; Castaway Christmas, 1963; Cut off from Crumpets, 1964; The Shoe Shop Bears, 1964; Home from the Hill, 1968; Snail's Place, 1970; The Last Straw, 1971; Boots and the Ginger Bears, 1972; The Sand Bird, 1973; Lock, Stock and Barrel, 1974; Sand in Our Shoes, 1976; The Gift Horse, 1982; Catch as Catch Can, 1983; Beware of the Gnomes, 1985; The Waiting Room Doll, 1986; Fresh Fields for Daisy, 1987. *Address:* Prickets, Old Cleeve, nr Minehead, Somerset TA24 6HW, England.

BAKER, Maureen, BA, MA, PhD; Canadian academic and writer; *Professor, University of Auckland;* b. 9 March 1948, Toronto, Ont.; m. David J. Tippin 1983. *Education:* Univ. of Toronto, Univ. of Alberta. *Career:* Asst Prof. of Sociology, Acadia Univ. 1974–76; Lecturer, Warrnambool Inst. and Kuringai Coll., Australia 1976–78; Asst Prof. of Sociology, Univ. of Toronto 1978–83; Researcher, Parl. of Canada 1983–90; Assoc. Prof. and Prof. of Sociology, McGill Univ., Montreal 1990–97; Prof. of Sociology, Univ. of Auckland, NZ 1998–, Head, Dept of Sociology 1998–2004; mem. Australian Sociology Asscn, Canadian Sociology and Anthropology Asscn, Sociological Asscn for Aotearoa/NZ. *Publications:* Families: Changing Trends in Canada 1984, (fifth edn) 2005, What will Tomorrow Bring? 1985, Aging in Canadian Society 1988, Families in Canadian Society 1989, Canada's Changing Families: Challenges to Public Policy 1994, Canadian Family Policies: Cross-National Comparisons 1995, Poverty, Social Assistance and the Employability of Mothers: Restructuring Welfare States (with D. Tippin) 1999, Families, Labour and Love 2001, Restructuring Family Policies 2006, Choices and Constraints in Family Life 2007; contribs to scholarly books and journals. *Honours:* numerous research grants. *Address:* Department of Sociology, University of Auckland, 10

Symonds Street, Auckland, New Zealand (office). *Telephone:* (9) 373-7599 (ext. 88610) (office). *Fax:* (9) 373-7439 (office). *E-mail:* ma.baker@auckland.ac.nz (office). *Website:* www.arts.auckland.ac.nz (office).

BAKER, Nicholson; American writer; b. 7 Jan. 1957, Rochester, NY; m. Margaret Brentano 1985; two c. *Education:* The School Without Walls, Rochester, Eastman Music School, Rochester, Haverford Coll., Pennsylvania. *Publications:* fiction: The Mezzanine 1990, Room Temperature 1991, Vox 1993, The Fermata 1995, The Everlasting Story of Nory 1999, A Box of Matches 2003, Checkpoint 2004; non-fiction: 'Weeds: A Talk at the Library', in Reclaiming San Francisco: history, politics, culture (anthology) 1998, U and I 1992, The Size of Thoughts 1997, Double Fold 2002; contrib. essays and short stories to periodicals, including New Yorker, Atlantic Monthly, New York Review of Books, Esquire, American Scholar, New York Times, London Review of Books, Literary Outtakes, Little Magazine, StoryQuarterly. *Address:* c/o Alfred Knopf, 1745 Broadway, New York, NY 10019, USA.

BAKER, Paul Raymond, AB, MA, PhD; American historian and academic; *Professor Emeritus of History, New York University;* b. 28 Sept. 1927, Everett, Wash.; m. Elizabeth Kemp; one c. *Education:* Stanford, Columbia and Harvard Univs. *Career:* Prof. of History, New York Univ. 1965–92, Dir of American Civilization Program 1972–92, Prof. Emer. 1999–. *Publications:* Views of Society and Manners in America, by Frances Wright D'Arusmont 1963, The Fortunate Pilgrims: Americans in Italy 1800–1860 1964, The Atomic Bomb: The Great Decision 1968, The American Experience (five vols) 1976–79, Richard Morris Hunt 1980, Stanny: The Gilded Life of Stanford White 1989; contrib. to Around the Square 1982, Master Builders 1985, The Architecture of Richard Morris Hunt 1986. *Honours:* The Turpie Award in American Studies 1994. *Address:* c/o Department of History, New York University, 53 Washington Square S, New York, NY 10012 (office); 90 Hillside Avenue, Glen Ridge NJ 07028, USA (home). *Telephone:* (212) 998-6823 (office); (973) 748-9376 (home).

BAKER, Peter Gorton; British writer; b. 28 March 1924, Eastbourne, Sussex, England. *Career:* reporter, Sussex Daily News 1944–45; chief reporter, Kinematograph Weekly 1945–53; Ed., films and filming magazine; British representative on film festival juries at Cannes, Venice, Moscow, Berlin 1953–70. *Television plays:* The Offence, Little Girl Blue, contrib. to many TV drama series. *Publications:* fiction: To Win a Prize on Sunday, Casino, Cruise, Clinic, The Bedroom Sailors, Babel Beach, Jesus. *Address:* Calle Don Juan de Málaga 6, Málaga 29015, Spain.

BAKER, Russell Wayne, DLitt; American journalist and author; b. 14 Aug. 1925, London Co., Va; s. of Benjamin R. Baker and Lucy E. Robinson; m. Miriam E. Nash 1950; two s. one d. *Education:* Johns Hopkins Univ. *Career:* served USNR 1943–45; with Baltimore Sun 1947–64; mem. Washington Bureau, New York Times 1954–62, author-columnist, editorial page 1962–; mem. American Acad., Inst. of Arts and Letters; Chair. Pulitzer Prize Bd 1992–. *Publications:* American in Washington 1961, No Cause for Panic 1964, All Things Considered 1965, Our Next President 1968, Poor Russell's Almanac 1972, The Upside Down Man 1977, Home Again, Home Again 1979, So This is Depravity 1980, Growing Up 1982, The Rescue of Miss Yaskell and Other Pipe Dreams 1983, The Good Times (memories) 1989, There's a Country in My Cellar 1990, Russell Baker's Book of American Humor 1993. *Honours:* several hon. degrees; Pulitzer Prize for distinguished commentary 1979; Pulitzer Prize for Biography 1983 and other awards. *Address:* New York Times, 229 West 43rd Street, New York, NY 10036, USA (office). *Website:* www.nytimes.com (office).

BAKER, William, BA, MPhil, PhD; American/British academic and writer; *Presidential Research Professor, Northern Illinois University;* b. 6 July 1944, Shipston, Warwicks., England; s. of the late Stanley Cohen Baker and Mabel Baker (née Woolf); m. 1969; two d. *Education:* Univs of Sussex and London, MLS, Loughborough. *Career:* Lecturer, Thurrock Tech. Coll., Essex 1969–71, Ben-Gurion Univ., Israel 1971–77, Univ. of Kent, Canterbury 1977–78, West Midlands Coll. 1978–85; Prof., Pitzer Coll., Claremont, Calif. 1981–82; Housemaster Clifton Coll. 1986–89; Prof., Northern Illinois Univ. 1989–2003, Presidential Research Prof. 2003–; Visiting Prof., Sheffield Hallam Univ.; Ed. George Eliot – George Henry Lewes Studies 1981, The Year's Work in English Studies 2000–; Co-Ed. Year's Work in English Studies, Oxford Univ. Press; Fellow, English Asscn 2003–, Humanities Inst., Univ. of Lyon III, France; mem. Bibliographical Soc. of America (Council mem.), American Library Asscn, Modern Language Asscn. *Publications:* Harold Pinter 1973, George Eliot and Judaism 1975, The Early History of the London Library 1992, Literary Theories: A Case Study in Critical Performance 1996, Nineteenth Century British Book Collectors and Bibliographers 1997, Twentieth Century British Book Collectors and Bibliographers 1999, Pre-Nineteenth Century British Book Collectors and Bibliographers 1999, The Letters of Wilkie Collins 1999, Twentieth Century Bibliography and Textual Criticism 2000, A Companion to the Victorian Novel 2002, Wilkie Collins's Library: A Reconstruction 2002, George Eliot: A Bibliographical History 2002, Nineteenth-Century Travels, Exploration and Empires – North America 2003, Middle East 2004, Redefining the Modern: Essays on Literature and Society in Honor of Joseph Wiensenfarth 2004, Harold Pinter: A Bibliographical History 2005, Shakespeare: The Critical Tradition, The Merchant of Venice 2005, History of the English Association 2007, A Wilkie Collins Chronology 2007, Jane Austen – A Critical Companion 2007; edns of letters by George Henry Lewes, George Eliot and Wilkie Collins, and four vols of George Eliot's

notebooks. *Honours:* Indiana Univ. Lilly Library Ball Brothers Foundation Fellowship 1993, Bibliographical Soc. of America Fellowship 1994–95, American Philosophical Soc. grant 1997, 'Choice' Outstanding Academic Book of the Year Awards 2000, 2006, Nat. Endowment of the Humanities Sr Fellowship 2002–03, Mellon Fellowship, Harry Ransom Humanities Research Center, Univ. of Texas 2006–07. *Address:* Department of English, Room FO 207B, Northern Illinois University, Dekalb, IL 60115, USA (office). *Telephone:* (815) 753-1857 (office). *Fax:* (815) 753-2003 (office). *E-mail:* wbaker@niu.edu (office). *Website:* www.engl.niu.edu (office).

BAKEWELL, Joan Dawson, CBE, BA; British broadcaster and writer; b. 16 April 1933, Stockport; d. of John Rowlands and Rose Bland; m. 1st Michael Bakewell 1955 (divorced 1972); one s. one d.; m. 2nd Jack Emery 1975 (divorced 2001). *Education:* Stockport High School for Girls and Newnham Coll., Cambridge. *Career:* TV critic The Times 1978–81, columnist Sunday Times 1988–90; Assoc. Newnham Coll., Cambridge 1980–91, Assoc. Fellow 1984–87; Gov. BFI 1994–99, Chair. 1999–2003. *TV includes:* Sunday Break 1962, Home at 4.30 (writer and producer) 1964, Meeting Point, The Second Sex 1964, Late Night Line Up 1965–72, The Youthful Eye 1968, Moviemakers at the National Film Theatre 1971, Film 72, Film 73, Holiday 74, 75, 76, 77, 78 (series), Reports Action (series) 1976–78, Arts UK: OK? 1980, Heart of the Matter 1988–2000, My Generation 2000, One Foot in the Past 2000, Taboo (series) 2001. *Radio includes:* Artist of the Week 1998–99, The Brains Trust 1999–, Belief 2000. *Publications:* The New Priesthood: British Television Today (jtly) 1970, A Fine and Private Place (jtly) 1977, The Complete Traveller 1977, The Heart of the Heart of the Matter 1996, The Centre of the Bed: An Autobiography 2003; contribs to journals. *Honours:* Dimbleby Award, BAFTA 1995. *Literary Agent:* Knight Ayton Management, 10 Argyll Street, London, W1V 1AB, England.

BAKHTARI, Ustad Wasef, BA, MEd; Afghan poet and academic; b. 1942, Balkh; m. Soriya Bakhtari. *Education:* Kabul Univ., Columbia Univ., USA. *Career:* fmr Prof. of Literature, Kabul Univ.; exiled from Afghanistan 1996. *Publications:* poems include: Calamity 1972.

BAKLANOV, Grigoriy Yakovlevich; Russian writer; b. 11 Sept. 1923, Voronezh; s. of Jakov Friedman and Ida Kantor; m. Elga Sergeeva 1953; one s. one d. *Education:* Gorky Inst. of Literature, Moscow. *Career:* served as soldier and officer during World War II 1941–45; mem. CPSU 1942–91; Ed.-in-Chief Znamya 1986–93. *Publications include:* In Snegiri 1954, Nine Days 1958, The Foothold 1959, The Dead Are Not Ashamed 1961, July 41 1964, Karpukhin 1965, Friends 1975, Forever Nineteen 1980, The Youngest of the Brothers 1981, Our Man 1990, Time to Gather Stones 1989, Once it was the Month of May (scenario) 1990, The Moment Between the Past and the Future 1990, Come Through the Narrow Gates 1993, Short Stories 1994, Kondratiy 1995, Short Stories 1996, And Then the Marauders Come (novel) 1996, Life Granted Twice (memoirs) 1999, My General (novel) 2000. *Honours:* USSR State Prize 1982, Russian State Prize 1997. *Address:* Lomonosovsky Prospekt 19, Apt 82, 117311 Moscow, Russia. *Telephone:* (495) 930-12-90. *Fax:* (495) 549-57-67.

BAKR, Salwā, BA; Egyptian novelist; b. June 1949, Cairo. *Education:* Ayn Shams Univ., Cairo. *Career:* film and theatre critic for Arabian language publs; concentrated on creative writing 1985–; founder, Hagar journal 1993. *Publications:* Zinat at the President's Funeral 1986, Atiyyah's Shrine 1987, About the Soul that was Spirited Away 1989, The Golden Chariot Does Not Ascend to Heaven 1991, The Wiles of Men and Other Stories (trans. by Denys Johnson Davies) 1992, Monkey Business 1992, Depicting the Nightingale 1993, Rabbits 1994, Inverse Rhythms 1996, Night and Day 1997, El-Bashmouri Vol. 1 1998, Vol. 2 2000, Dream of Years (play) 2002, Streams of Time 2003. *Address:* c/o Atelier of Writers, Karim al-Dawla Street, Talat Harb Square, Cairo, Egypt.

BA'LABAKKI, Laila (see Layla Baalbaki)

BALABAN, John, BA, AM; American academic, writer, poet and translator; b. 2 Dec. 1943, Philadelphia, PA; m. 1970, one d. *Education:* Pennsylvania State University, Harvard University. *Career:* Instructor in Linguistics, University of Can Tho, South Viet Nam, 1967–68; Instructor, 1970–73, Asst Prof., 1973–76, Assoc. Prof., 1976–82, Prof., 1982–92, of English, Pennsylvania State University; Prof. of English, Dir of Creative Writing, University of Miami, 1992–2000; Prof. of English and Poet-in-Residence, North Carolina State University, Raleigh, 2000–; mem. American Literary Trans Asscn, pres., 1994–97; National Endowment for the Arts Trans. Panel, chair, 1993–94. *Publications:* Vietnam Poems, 1970; Vietnamese Folk Poetry (ed. and trans.), 1974; After Our War (poems), 1974; Letters From Across the Sea (poems), 1978; Ca Dao Vietnam: A Bilingual Anthology of Vietnamese Folk Poetry (ed. and trans.), 1980; Blue Mountain (poems), 1982; Coming Down Again (novel), 1985; The Hawk's Tale (children's fiction), 1988; Three Poems, 1989; Vietnam: The Land We Never Knew, 1989; Words for My Daughter (poems), 1991; Remembering Heaven's Face (memoir), 1991; Vietnam: A Traveler's Literary Companion (ed. with Nguyen Qui Duc), 1996; Locusts at the Edge of Summer: New and Selected Poems and Translations, 1997; Spring Essence: The Poetry of Ho Xuan Huong (trans. and ed.), 2000. Contributions: anthologies, books, scholarly journals and periodicals. *Honours:* National Endowment for the Humanities Younger Humanist Fellow, 1971–72; Lamont Selection, Acad. of American Poets, 1974; Fulbright-Hays Senior Lectureship in Romania, 1976–77; Steaua Prize, Romanian Writers Union, 1978; National Endowment for the Arts Fellowships, 1978, 1985; Fulbright Distinguished Visiting Lectureship in Romania, 1979; Vaptsarov Medal, Union of Bulgarian Writers,

1980; National Poetry Series Book Selection, 1990; Pushcart Prize XV, 1990; William Carlos Williams Award, 1997.

BALABANOV, Alexei O.; Russian film director, producer and scriptwriter; b. 25 Feb. 1959, Sverdlovsk. *Education:* Gorky State Pedagogical Inst. *Career:* asst dir Sverdlovsk Film Studio 1983–87, freelance 1987–. *Films:* Yegor and Nastya (dir) 1989, From the History of Aerostatics in Russia (dir) 1990, Happy Days (dir and scriptwriter) 1991, The Castle (dir and scriptwriter) 1994, Secrets Shared with a Stranger (producer) 1994, The Arrival of a Train (dir and scriptwriter) 1995, Sergey Eisenstein (producer) 1995, The Brother (dir and scriptwriter) 1997, Of Freaks and Men (dir and scriptwriter) 1998, The Brother 2 (dir and scriptwriter) 2000, War (dir and scriptwriter) 2002. *Honours:* Youth Film Festival Prize, Kiev 1991, Moscow Film Festival Debut Jury Prize 1992, Kinotaur Film Festival, Sochi, Jury Prize 1994 and Best Movie Prize 1997.

BALCOMB, Mary Nelson, AA, MFA; American painter-etcher and writer; b. 29 April 1928, Ontonagon, MI; m. Robert S. Balcomb 1948, one s. one d. *Education:* American Acad. of Art, Univ. of New Mexico, Univ. of Washington. *Career:* mem. Authors' Guild Inc., New York. *Publications:* Nicolai Fechin: Russian and American Artist, 1975; Les Perhacs Sculptor, 1978; William F. Reese: American Artist, 1984; Robin-Robin: A Journal, 1995; Sergei-Bongart: Russian American Artist, 2002. Contributions: periodicals. *Honours:* Frye Art Museum Seattle Painting Award 1994, Honorarium Prix de West, Western Heritage Museum, Oklahoma City. *Address:* PO Box 1922, Silverdale, WA 98383, USA.

BALDACCI, David, BA, JD; American writer; b. 1960, Richmond, VA; m. Michelle Baldacci, two c. *Education:* Virginia Commonwealth Univ., Univ. of Virginia. *Publications:* Absolute Power 1996, Total Control 1997, The Winner 1997, The Simple Truth 1998, Saving Faith 1999, Wish You Well 2000, Last Man Standing 2001, Split Second 2003, The Camel Club 2006, The Collectors 2006, Simple Genius 2007; contrib. to periodicals. *Honours:* WHSmith Thumping Good Read Award for Fiction 1997. *Literary Agent:* c/o Aaron Priest Literary Agency, 708 Third Avenue, New York, NY 10017, USA.

BALESTRE, Jean-Marie; French editor and press executive; b. 9 April 1921, Saint-Rémy-de-Provence (Bouches-du-Rhône); s. of Joseph Balestre and Joséphine Bayol. *Education:* Lycée Charlemagne and Faculté de Droit, Paris. *Career:* sub-ed., Sport et Santé 1937, L'Auto and Droit de Vivre 1938–40; Dir Int. Gen. Presse 1947; Co-Founder and Assoc. L'Auto Journal 1950, Dir-Gen. 1952–71; Dir Semaine du Monde 1953; Asst Dir-Gen. Soc. Edn Diffusion Presse 1970–; Dir Presses Modernes de France, La Liberté de Seine-et-Marne, Centre-Presse, Oise-Matin, Editions Professionnelles de France, Brunel Editions, Editions Sport Auto, France Antilles; Dir Robert Hersant press group 1969–; Dir Agence Générale de Presse et d'Information (Hersant group) 1976–77; Treas. Office de Justification de la Diffusion de la Presse 1964–; Hon. Pres. Féd. Nat. de la Presse Hebdomadaire et Périodique; Pres. Féd. Française du Sport Automobile 1973–96, World Fed. of Automobile Clubs 1985–, Int. Fed. of Motor Sport 1978–96 (Hon. Pres. 1996–), Int. Automobile Fed. 1985–. *Honours:* Chevalier, Légion d'honneur, Officier, Ordre nat. du Mérite, Médaille de la Déportation pour Faits de Résistance; Licence d'Or, Fédération Française du Sport Automobile 1976, Personnalité de l'Année 1988. *Address:* c/o Fédération Française du Sport Automobile, 17–21 avenue du Général Mangin, 75781 Paris cedex 16, France.

BALL, Brian Neville, BA, MA; British writer; b. 19 June 1932, Cheshire, England. *Education:* University of London, University of Sheffield. *Career:* Staff Mem. to Senior Lecturer in English, Doncaster College of Education, 1965–81. *Publications:* over 50 books, including: Basic Linguistics for Secondary Schools, 3 vols, 1966–67; Lay Down Your Wife for Another, 1971; Night of the Robots (in the USA as The Regiments of Night), 1972; The Venomous Serpent (in the USA as The Night Creature), 1974; Witchfinder: The Mark of the Beast, 1976; Witchfinder: The Evil at Monteine, 1977; The Witch in Our Attic, 1979; The Baker Street Boys, 1983; Frog Island Summer, 1987; Magic on the Tide, 1995. Contributions: anthologies, newspapers, radio, and television. *Address:* c/o Hamish Hamilton Ltd, 27 Wrights Lane, London W8 5TZ, England.

BALL, Philip, BA, PhD; British science writer and editor; *Consultant Editor, Nature;* b. 30 Oct. 1962, Newport, Isle of Wight, England; s. of David Ball and Jennifer Ball; m.; one d. *Education:* Univs of Oxford and Bristol. *Career:* fmr Ed. for Physical Sciences, Nature magazine, now Consultant Ed.; lectures at various venues, including Victoria & Albert Museum, NASA,Ames Research Center, LSE; writes regularly for News@Nature; Science Writer-in-Residence, Dept of Chem., Univ. Coll., London; freelance writer. *Play:* Paracelsus the Great", London 2000. *Radio:* presenter, Small Worlds (three-part series on nano tech., BBC Radio 4). *Publications:* Designing the Molecular World: Chemistry at the Frontier (Asscn of American Publishers Award) 1994, Made to Measure: New Materials for the 21st Century 1997, The Self-Made Tapestry: Pattern Formation in Nature 1998, H_2O: A Biography of Water (Premio Acqua Scrittura, Italy 2000) 1999, Stories of the Invisible: A Guided Tour of Molecules 2001, Bright Earth: Art and the Invention of Colour (Soc. for the History of Tech. Sally Hacker Prize 2003) 2001, More Than Meets the Eye (V&A museum exhbn booklet) (Asscn of British Science Writers Award for best communication of science in a non-science context) 2001, The Ingredients: A Guided Tour of the Elements 2002, Critical Mass: How One Thing Leads to Another (Aventis Prize 2005) 2004, The Devil's Doctor: Paracelsus and the World of Renaissance Magic and Science 2006; contrib. to journals, including

Nature, Nature Materials, Journal of Materials Education, Chemistry in Britain, V&A Conservation Journal, Technology Review, Interdisciplinary Science, Physics World, Chemistry World, Angewandte Chemie Int. Edn, New Scientist, New York Times, Guardian, Financial Times, New Statesman. *Honours:* Hon. DSc (Union Coll., Schenectady, NY) 2003; numerous prizes. *Address:* Nature, 4–6 Crinan Street, London, N1 9XW, England (office). *E-mail:* p.ball@nature.com (office). *Website:* www.philipball.com.

BALLARD, James Graham (J. G.); British novelist and short story writer; b. 15 Nov. 1930, Shanghai, China; s. of the late James Ballard and Edna Ballard (née Johnstone); m. Helen Mary Mathews 1954 (died 1964); one s. two d. *Education:* Leys School, Cambridge and King's Coll., Cambridge. *Publications:* The Drowned World 1963, The Four-Dimensional Nightmare 1963, The Terminal Beach 1964, The Drought 1965, The Crystal World 1966, The Disaster Area 1967, The Atrocity Exhibition 1970, Crash 1973, Vermillion Sands 1973, Concrete Island 1974, High Rise 1975, Low-Flying Aircraft 1976, The Unlimited Dream Company 1979, Myths of the Near Future 1982, Empire of the Sun (Guardian Fiction Prize, James Tait Black Memorial Prize) 1984, The Voices of Time 1985, The Venus Hunters 1986, The Day of Forever 1986, The Day of Creation 1987, Running Wild 1988, Memories of the Space Age 1988, War Fever 1990, The Kindness of Women 1991, Rushing to Paradise 1994, A Users' Guide to the Millennium 1996, Cocaine Nights 1996, Super-Cannes 2000, The Complete Short Stories 2001, Millennium People 2003, Kingdom Come 2006. *Address:* 36 Old Charlton Road, Shepperton, Middlesex TW17 8AT, England. *Telephone:* (1932) 225692.

BALLE, Solvej; Danish writer; b. 16 Aug. 1962, S Jutland. *Education:* Univ. of Copenhagen, The Writer's School, Copenhagen. *Publications:* Lyrefugl (novel) 1984, & (short prose) 1990, Ifølge loven (short stories) 1993, Eller (prose poetry) 1998, Det umuliges kunst (essay) 2005. *Address:* Gyldendal, Klareboderne 3, 1001 Copenhagen K, Denmark. *E-mail:* gyldendal@gyldendal.dk.

BALLEM, John Bishop, BA, LLB, MA, LLM, QC; Canadian lawyer, novelist and poet; b. 2 Feb. 1925, New Glasgow, NS; m. Grace Louise Flavelle 1951; two s. one d. *Education:* Dalhousie Univ., Harvard Univ. *Career:* of counsel: Gowling Lafleur Henderson LLP; mem. Crime Writers of Canada, Int. Bar Asscn, Law Soc. of Alberta, Writers' Guild of Alberta, Writers' Union of Canada, Canadian Bar Asscn. *Publications:* Fiction: The Devil's Lighter 1973, The Dirty Scenario 1974, The Judas Conspiracy 1976, new edn as Alberta Alone 1981, The Moon Pool 1978, Sacrifice Play 1981, The Marigot Run 1983, The Oilpatch Empire 1985, Death Spiral 1989, The Barons 1991, Manchineel 2000, Murder as a Fine Art 2001, The Oilpatch Quartet 2005; poetry: Lovers and Friends 2000; other poems in various literary journals; non-fiction: The Oil and Gas Lease in Canada 1973, (4th edn) 2007; contribs: numerous short stories; legal articles in various learned journals. *Honours:* Hon. LLD (Calgary) 1993. *Address:* 700 Second Street SW, Suite 1400, Calgary, AB T2P 4V5, Canada (office).

BALMER, Josephine, BA; British poet and translator; *Chairwoman, Translators' Association;* b. 1959, Hampshire; m. Paul Dunn 1982. *Education:* Univ. Coll. London. *Career:* Reviews Ed., Modern Poetry in Translation; Chair., Translators' Asscn (UK) 2001–05; judge, Stephen Spender Prize for Poetry in Translation 2006–. *Publications:* Sappho: Poems and Fragments 1992, Classical Women Poets 1995, Catallus: Poems of Love and Hate 2004, Chasing Catullus 2004; contrib. to TLS, The New Statesman, Modern Poetry in Translation, Women's Review, The Guardian, Independent on Sunday, The Observer. *Honours:* Univ. Coll. London Platt Prize for Greek 1978, Lambda Literary Foundation Poetry Award (USA) 1988, Arts Council Write Out Hand Award 1994, Southeast Arts Writers Bursary 1997, Arthurs Foundation Award 1994, 2004, Wingate Foundation Scholarship 2004–05. *Address:* c/o Bloodaxe Books Ltd, Highgreen, Tarset, Northumberland NE48 1RP, England.

BALOGH, Mary, BA; Welsh/Canadian writer and teacher; b. 24 March 1944, Swansea, Wales; m. Robert Balogh, 1969, one s. two d. *Education:* University of Wales. *Career:* English Teacher, Kipling High School, Saskatchewan, Canada, 1967–82; Principal, English Teacher, Windthorst High School, Saskatchewan, 1982–88; mem. Saskatchewan Writers' Guild. *Publications:* Fiction: A Masked Deception, 1985; The Double Wager, 1985; Red Rose, 1985; A Chance Encounter, 1986; The Trysting Place, 1986; The First Snowdrop, 1987; The Wood Nymph, 1987; The Constant Heart, 1987; Gentle Conquest, 1987; Secrets of the Heart, 1988; The Ungrateful Governess, 1988; An Unacceptable Offer, 1988; Daring Masquerade, 1989; A Gift of Daisies, 1989; The Obedient Bride, 1989; Lady with a Black Umbrella, 1989; The Gilded Web, 1989; A Promise of Spring, 1990; Web of Love, 1990; The Incurable Matchmakers, 1990; Devil's Web, 1990; An Unlikely Duchess, 1990; A Certain Magic, 1991; Snow Angel, 1991; The Secret Pearl, 1991; The Ideal Wife, 1991; Christmas Beau, 1991; The Counterfeit Betrothal, 1992; The Notorious Rake, 1992; A Christmas Promise, 1992; Beyond the Sunrise, 1992; A Precious Jewel, 1993; Deceived, 1993; Courting Julia, 1993; Dancing with Clara, 1994; Tangled, 1994; Tempting Harriet, 1994; Dark Angel, 1994; A Christmas Belle, 1994; Longing, 1994; Lord Carew's Bride, 1995; Heartless, 1995; The Famous Heroine, 1996; Truly, 1996; The Plumed Bonnet, 1996; Indiscreet, 1997; Temporary Wife, 1997; Silent Melody, 1997; A Christmas Bride, 1997; Unforgiven, 1998; Thief of Dreams, 1998; Irresistible, 1998; The Last Waltz, 1998; One Night for Love, 1999; More than a Mistress, 2000; No Man's Mistress, 2001, A Summer to Remember 2002, Slightly Married 2003, Slightly

Wicked 2003, Slightly Scandalous 2003, Slightly Tempted 2004, Slightly Sinful 2004, Slightly Dangerous 2004, Simply Unforgettable 2005, Simply Love 2006; novellas in collections including A Regency Christmas series; short stories: Full Moon Magic, 1992; Tokens of Love, 1993; Rakes and Rogues, 1993; Moonlight Lovers, 1993. *Honours:* Best New Regency Author Award, 1985; Best Regency Author Award, 1988; Career Achievement Award, 1989, Best Regency Novel Award, 1991, Best Regency Romance Award, 1992, Career Achievement for Short Stories Award, 1993, Romantic Times; Northern Lights Best Historical Novella Award, 1996. *Literary Agent:* Maria Carvainis, 1350 Avenue of the Americas, New York, NY 10019, USA. *Address:* Box 571, Kipling, Saskatchewan, S0G 2S0 Canada (home). *Telephone:* (306) 736-2246 (home). *Fax:* (306) 736-2246 (home). *E-mail:* author@marybalogh .com (home). *Website:* www.marybalogh.com (home).

BANDELE, Biyi; Nigerian playwright and novelist; b. 13 Oct. 1967, Kafanchan. *Education:* Obafemi Awolowo Univ., Ile-Ife. *Career:* Assoc. Writer, Royal Court Theatre, London 1992–; writer-in-residence, Talawa Theatre Co. 1994–95; resident dramatist, Royal Nat. Theatre Studio 1996; mem. Soc. of Authors, Writers' Guild, PEN. *Publications:* fiction: The Man Who Came in from the Back of Beyond 1991, The Sympathetic Undertaker and Other Dreams 1991, Burma Boy (novel) 2007; plays: Rain, produced 1991, Marching for Fausa, produced 1993, Two Horsemen, produced 1994, Resurrections, produced 1994, Death Catches the Hunter, produced 1995, Things Fall Apart, produced 1997, Thieves Like Us, produced 1998; screenplays: Not Even God Is Wise Enough 1993, Bad Boy Blues 1996. *Honours:* Int. Student Playscript Competition award, Arts Council Writer's Bursary, London New Play Festival award 1994. *Literary Agent:* PFD, Drury House, 34–43 Russell Street, London, WC2B 5HA, England.

BANERJI, Sara Ann; British writer; *Lecturer in Creative Writing, Oxford University Department of Continuing Education;* b. 6 June 1932, Bucks.; d. of Sir Basil Mostyn and Anita Mostyn; m. Ranjit Banerji 1951; three d. *Education:* schools and convents in UK and Southern Rhodesia (now Zimbabwe). *Career:* fmr teacher, jockey, waitress, gardener and riding instructor. *Publications include:* Cobwebwalking 1987, The Wedding of Mayanthi Mandel 1988, The Teaplanter's Daughter 1989, Shining Agnes 1990, Absolute Hush 1991, Writing on Skin 1993, Shining Hero 2002, The Waiting Time 2005, Blood Precious 2007. *Honours:* Arts Council Award for Literature, Write Out Loud Award for radio writing. *Literary Agent:* c/o PFD, Drury House, 34–43 Russell Street, London, WC2B 5HA, England. *Telephone:* (20) 7344-1000. *Fax:* (20) 7836-9539. *E-mail:* info@pfd.co.uk. *Website:* www .pfd.co.uk; www.banerji.info; www.myspace.com/ladyacs.

BANFIELD, Stephen David, BA, DPhil, FRCO; British academic and writer; *Stanley Hugh Badock Professor of Music, University of Bristol;* b. 15 July 1951, Dulwich, London, England. *Education:* Clare Coll., Cambridge, Harvard Univ., St John's Coll., Oxford. *Career:* Lecturer, Univ. of Keele 1978–88, Sr Lecturer 1988–92; Elgar Prof. of Music, Univ. of Birmingham 1992–2003, Head, School of Performance Studies 1992–97, and Dept of Music 1996–98; Visiting Prof. of Musicology, Univ. of Minnesota, USA 1998; Stanley Hugh Badock Prof. of Music, Univ. of Bristol 2003–; mem. American Musicological Soc., Royal Musical Asscn, Soc. for American Music, Kurt Weill Foundation. *Publications:* Sensibility and English Song 1985, Sondheim's Broadway Musicals 1993, The Blackwell History of Music in Britain, Vol. VI: The Twentieth Century (ed.) 1995, Gerald Finzi 1997, Jerome Kern 2006; contrib. to scholarly books and journals. *Honours:* First Kurt Weill Prize, USA, Irving Lowens Award, USA 1995. *Address:* Department of Music, University of Bristol, Victoria Rooms, Queens Road, Bristol, BS8 1SA, England (office). *Telephone:* (117) 954-5045 (office). *E-mail:* S.D.Banfield@bristol.ac.uk (office). *Website:* www.bris.ac.uk/music (office).

BANKS, Brian Robert; British teacher, writer and poet; b. 4 Oct. 1956, Carshalton, Surrey, England; two s. two d. *Education:* Westminister Coll., Middlesex Polytechnic, Worthing Coll. *Career:* mem. Soc. de J-K Huysmans, Paris, 1890s Soc. *Publications:* The Image of J-K Huysmans 1990, Phantoms of the Belle Epoque 1993, Atmosphere and Attitudes 1993, Life and Work of Bruno Schulz 2000, Trajectory of a Comet: S. Przybyszewski, Muse & Messiah – Life and Legacy of Bruno Schulz 2006; contribs to books and journals. *Address:* 4 Meretune Court, Martin Way, Morden, Surrey, SM4 4AN, England (home). *E-mail:* love4muza@hotmail.com (home).

BANKS, Iain Menzies, BA; British writer; b. 16 Feb. 1954, Fife, Scotland. *Education:* Univ. of Stirling. *Career:* worked as technician, British Steel 1976, IBM, Greenock 1978; writes fiction as Iain Banks and science fiction as Iain M. Banks. *Publications:* as Iain Banks: The Wasp Factory 1984, Walking on Glass 1985, The Bridge 1986, Espedair Street 1987, Canal Dreams 1989, The Crow Road 1992, Complicity 1993, Whit 1995, A Song of Stone 1997, The Business 1999, Look to Windward 2000, Dead Air 2002, Raw Spirit: In Search of the Perfect Dram (non-fiction) 2003, The Steep Approach to Garbadale 2007; as Iain M. Banks: Consider Phlebas 1987, The Player of Games 1988, The State of the Art 1989, Use of Weapons 1990, Against a Dark Background 1993, Feersum Endjinn 1994, Excession 1996, Inversions 1998, The Algebraist 2004. *Honours:* Hon. DUniv (Stirling) 1997 (St Andrews) 1997; Hon. DLitt (Napier) 2003; British Science Fiction Asscn Best Novel 1997. *Address:* c/o Publicity Department, Time Warner Books UK, Brettenham House, Lancaster Place, London, WC2E 7EN, England. *Telephone:* (20) 7911-8000. *Fax:* (20) 7911-8100. *E-mail:* mail@iainbanks.net. *Website:* www .iainbanks.net.

BANKS, Lynne Reid; British writer; b. 31 July 1929, London; d. of James Reid Banks and Pat Reid Banks; m. Chaim Stephenson 1965; three s. *Education:* in Canada and Royal Acad. of Dramatic Art, London. *Career:* stage career 1949–54; freelance journalist 1954–55; news reporter (first woman in UK), Independent TV News (ITN) 1955–62; taught English in Israel 1962–71; writer, playwright and journalist 1971–. *Publications include:* The L-Shaped Room (film 1962) 1960, An End to Running 1962, Children at the Gate 1968, The Backward Shadow 1970, One More River (for children) 1973, Two Is Lonely 1974, Writing on the Wall 1975, Sarah and After: The Matriarchs 1975, The Adventures of King Midas 1976, Dark Quartet: the story of the Brontës (Yorkshire Arts Literature Award 1977) 1976, The Farthest-Away Mountain 1976, Path to the Silent Country: Charlotte Brontë's years of fame 1977, My Darling Villain 1977, I, Houdini 1978, Letters to My Israeli Sons (history) 1979, The Indian in the Cupboard (numerous children's book awards, USA, made into feature film, released 1995) 1980, Torn Country: An Oral History of the Israeli War of Independence 1980, Defy the Wilderness 1981, The Writing on the Wall 1981, Return of the Indian 1982, Maura's Angel 1984, The Warning Bell 1984, Secret of the Indian 1985, The Fairy Rebel 1985, Casualties 1986, Melusine 1988, The Magic Hare 1991, Yoshi and the Tea-Kettle (children's play) 1991, The Mystery of the Cupboard 1993, Broken Bridge 1994, Key to the Indian 1996, Harry the Poisonous Centipede 1997, Angela and Diabola 1997, Moses in Egypt 1998, Fair Exchange (for adults) 1999, Alice-by-Accident 2000, Harry the Poisonous Centipede's Big Adventure 2000, The Dungeon 2002, Stealing Stacey 2004, Tiger, Tiger 2004, Harry the Poisonous Centipede Goes to Sea 2005; works translated into other languages; plays and anthologies; contribs to newspapers including The Times, The Guardian, Observer, Times Literary and Educational Supplements, The Independent, Saga Mag. *Honours:* awards for children's literature, Australia, Italy and USA; Smarties Prize. *Literary Agent:* c/o Watson, Little Ltd, Lymehouse Studios, 38 Georgiana Street, London, NW1 0EB, England. *Telephone:* (20) 7485-5935. *Fax:* (20) 7485-6051. *Website:* www.watsonlittle .net; www.lynnereidbanks.com (office).

BANKS, Russell, BA; American writer; b. 28 March 1940, Barnstable, NH; s. of Earl Banks and Florence Banks; m. 1st Darlene Bennett (divorced 1962); one d.; m. 2nd Mary Gunst (divorced 1977); three d.; m. 3rd Kathy Walton (divorced 1988); m. 4th Chase Twichell. *Education:* Colgate Univ. and Univ. of NC at Chapel Hill. *Career:* fmr teacher of creative writing at Emerson Coll. Boston, Univ. of NH at Durham, Univ. of Ala, New England Coll.; teacher of creative writing, Princeton Univ. 1982–97; Pres. Parl. Int. des Écrivains 2001–; Guggenheim Fellowship 1976; Nat. Endowment for the Arts Fellowships 1977, 1983. *Publications include:* poetry: Waiting to Freeze 1967, 30/6 1969, Snow: Meditations of a Cautious Man in Winter 1974; novels: Family Life 1975, Hamilton Stark 1978, The Book of Jamaica 1980, The Relation of My Imprisonment 1984, Continental Drift 1985, Affliction 1989, The Sweet Hereafter 1991, Rule of the Bone 1995, Cloudsplitter 1998, The Angel on the Roof 2000, The Darling 2004; collected short stories: Searching for Survivors 1975, The New World 1978, Trailerpark 1981, Success Stories 1986; contrib. short stories to magazines and periodicals, including New York Times Book Review, Washington Post, American Review, Vanity Fair, Antaeus, Partisan Review, New England Review, Fiction International, Boston Globe Magazine. *Honours:* Best American Short Stories Awards 1971, 1985, Fels Award for Fiction 1974, O. Henry Awards 1975, St Lawrence Award for fiction 1976, John Dos Passos Award 1985, American Acad. of Arts and Letters Award 1985. *Literary Agent:* Steven Barclay Agency, 12 Western Avenue, Petaluma, CA 94952, USA. *Telephone:* (707) 773-0654. *Fax:* (707) 778-1868. *Website:* www.barclayagency.com. *Address:* 1000 Park Avenue, New York, NY 10028, USA.

BANNERMAN, Mark (see Lewing, Anthony Charles)

BANNISTER, Jo; English writer; b. 31 July 1951, Rochdale, England; d. of Alan Bannister and Marjorie Bannister. *Education:* studied in Birmingham, Nottingham, Bangor, Northern Ireland. *Career:* mem. Soc. of Authors, CWA. *Publications:* The Matrix 1981, The Winter Plain 1982, A Cactus Garden 1983, Striving With Gods (revised edn as An Unknown Death) 1984, Mosaic 1987, The Mason Codex 1988, Gilgamesh 1989, The Going Down of the Sun 1989, Shards (revised edn as Critical Angle) 1990, Death and Other Lovers 1991, A Bleeding of Innocents 1993, Sins of the Heart (aka Charisma) 1994, A Taste for Burning 1995, The Lazarus Hotel 1996, No Birds Sing 1996, The Primrose Convention 1997, Broken Lines 1999, The Hireling's Tale 1999, Changelings 2000, The Primrose Switchback 2000, Echoes of Lies 2001, True Witness 2002, Reflections 2003, The Depths of Solitude 2004, Breaking Faith 2005, The Fifth Cataract 2005, Requiem for a Dealer 2006, The Tinderbox 2006, Flawed 2007. *Honours:* British Press Award 1976, Northern Ireland Press Award 1982, Ellery Queen Readers Award 1994, Mary Higgins Clark Award 2006. *Literary Agent:* c/o Jane Gregory, Gregory & Company Authors' Agents, 3 Barb Mews, London, W6 7PA, England.

BANTOCK, Gavin Marcus August, BA, DipEd, MA; British poet and writer; b. 4 July 1939, Barnt Green, Worcestershire, England. *Education:* Univ. of Oxford. *Career:* educator in British schools 1964–69; faculty mem. Dept of English, Reitaku Univ., Chiba-ken, Japan 1969–94. *Publications:* Christ: A Poem in Twenty-Six Parts 1965, Juggernaut: Selected Poems 1968, A New Thing Breathing 1969, Anhaga 1970, Gleeman 1972, Eirenikon 1973, Isles 1974, Dragons 1979, Just Think of It 2002, Floating World 2002, SeaManShip 2003; essay collections contrib. to anthologies and numerous magazines. *Honours:* Richard Hillary Memorial Prize 1964, Alice-Hunt-Bartlett Prize

1966, Eric Gregory Award 1969, Arvon Foundation Prize 1998, Cardiff Int. Poetry Prize 1999. *Address:* c/o Peter Jay, Anvil Press Poetry, 69 King George Street, London, SE10 8PX, England. *E-mail:* gb@gol.com. *Website:* homepage .mac.com/gavinbantock.

BANVILLE, John; Irish writer; b. 8 Dec. 1945, Wexford; m. Janet Dunham; two s. *Education:* St Peter's Coll., Wexford. *Career:* fmrly night copy ed. The Irish Times, Literary Ed. 1988–99, Chief Literary Critic and Assoc. Literary Ed. 1999–2002. *Film script:* The Last September 1998. *Plays:* The Broken Jug (after Kleist) 1994, God's Gift (after Kleist's "Amphitryon") 2000. *Publications include:* novels: Nightspawn 1971, Birchwood 1973, Dr Copernicus 1976, Kepler 1983, The Newton Letter 1985, Mefisto 1987, The Book of Evidence (Guinness Peat Aviation Prize 1989) 1989, Ghosts 1993, Athena 1995, The Untouchable 1996, Eclipse 2000, Shroud 2003, The Sea (Man Booker Prize, Irish Novel of the Year) 2005; as Benjamin Black: Christine Falls 2006; nonfiction: Prague Pictures: Portraits of a City 2003; contrib. to New York Review of Books, Irish Times, Guardian, New Republic. *Honours:* Lannan Foundation Award 1998. *Literary Agent:* Ed Victor Limited, 6 Bayley Street, Bedford Square, London, WC1B 3HE, England. *Telephone:* (20) 7304-4100. *Fax:* (20) 7304-4111.

BAPTISTE, Eric; French radio executive; *Director-General, International Confederation of Societies of Authors and Composers.* *Education:* École nationale d'administration. *Career:* Gen. Man., Radio France Int. 1990–95; Vice-Pres., Radio Néo; Dir-Gen., Int. Confed. of Socs of Authors and Composers (CISAC) 1998–; chair. of govt think tank on digital convergence. *Publications:* Rapport sur les relations entre les diffuseurs télévisuels et les producteurs cinématographiques et audiovisuals 1989, L'infosphère: stratégies des medias et role de l'État 2000. *Address:* c/o CISAC, 20–26 blvd du Parc, 92200 Neuilly-sur-Seine, France. *Telephone:* 1-55-62-08-50. *Fax:* 1-55-62-08-60. *E-mail:* cisac@cisac.org. *Website:* www.cisac.org.

BAQUET, Dean Paul; American journalist and editor; *Assistant Managing Editor and Washington Bureau Chief, New York Times;* b. 21 Sept. 1956, New Orleans; s. of Edward Joseph Baquet and Myrtle (née Romano) Baquet; m. Dylan Landis 1986; one s. *Education:* Columbia Univ., New York. *Career:* investigative reporter, New Orleans 1978–84; investigative reporter, Chicago Tribune 1984–87, Chief Investigative Reporter 1987–90; investigative reporter, New York Times 1990–92, Projects Ed. 1992–95, Deputy Metropolitan Ed. 1995, Nat. Ed. 1995–2000, Asst Man. Ed. and Washington Bureau Chief 2007–; Man. Ed. Los Angeles Times 2000–05, Ed. 2005–06; mem. Bd of Dirs Cttee to Protect Journalists. *Honours:* Pulitzer Prize for Investigative Reporting 1988. *Address:* New York Times, 1627 Eye Street, NW, 7th Floor, Washington, DC 20006, USA (office). *Telephone:* (202) 862-0300 (office). *Fax:* (202) 862-0340 (office). *Website:* www.nytimes.com (office).

BARAKA, Amiri; American writer and poet; b. (Everett LeRoi Jones), 7 Oct. 1934, Newark, NJ; m. 1st Hettie Cohen 1958 (divorced 1965); m. 2nd Amina Baraka 1966; five c. *Education:* Rutgers, Howard and Columbia Univs, New School for Social Research. *Career:* served USAF 1954–57; settled in New York late 1950s; f. Totem Press 1958; active mem. Black Arts Movement; f. Black Arts Repertory Theatre/School 1964; f. Spirithouse arts and cultural org., Newark; Asst Prof. of African Studies, State Univ. of New York 1980–82, Assoc. Prof. 1983–84, Prof. 1985–2000; Poet Laureate of New Jersey 1999–2001; fmr Sec.-Gen. Nat. Black Political Ass.; fmr Chair. Congress of African People. *Plays:* The Dutchman and the Slave (Obie Award) 1964, The Baptism and the Toilet 1967, Arm Yrself or Harm Yrself 1967, Home on the Range 1968, Police 1968, The Death of Malcolm X 1969, Rockgroup 1969, Four Black Revolutionary Plays 1969, Junkies are Full of SHHH 1970, Jello 1970, BA-RA-KA 1972, Black Power Chant 1972, The Motion of History and Other Plays 1978, The Sidney Poet Heroical, in 29 Scenes 1979, General Hag's Skeezag 1992. *Publications:* poetry: Preface to a Twenty Volume Suicide Note 1961, Black Magic 1969, In Our Terribleness 1970, It's Nation Time 1970, Hard Facts 1975, Poetry for the Advanced 1979, reggae or not! 1981, Transbluesency: The Selected Poems of Amiri Baraka/LeRoi Jones 1995, Funk Lore: New Poems 1996, Somebody Blew Up America 2001, We, Why Is We Americans?; essays: Blues People: Negro Music in White America 1963, Home: Social Essays 1966, Raise Race Rays Raize: Essays Since 1965 1971, Daggers and Javelins: Essays 1974–1979 1984, The Music: Reflections on Jazz and Blues 1987, Wise, Why's Y's 1995, Jesse Jackson and Black People 1996, You Ever Hear Albert Ayler?, Black Reconstruction: DuBois and the US Struggle for Democracy and Socialism; novels: The System of Dante's Hell 1965, Tales 1967; other: The Autobiography of Leroi Jones 1984. *Honours:* PEN/Faulkner Award, Rockefeller Foundation Award for Drama, American Book Award, Langston Hughes Award, Before Columbus Foundation lifetime achievement award. *Address:* POB 3015, Newark, NJ 07103, USA. *E-mail:* wepress@con2.com. *Website:* www.amiribaraka.com.

BARAKAT, Hoda, BA; Lebanese writer and journalist; b. 1952, Beirut; m.; two c. *Education:* Lebanese Univ., Beirut. *Career:* taught for a year in village of al-Khaim, then worked as teacher and journalist during civil war; worked at Center for Lebanese Research, Beirut 1985–86; co-est. women's magazine, Shahrazad 1988; moved to Paris, France 1989. *Publications:* Za'irat (short stories, Visitors) 1985, Hajar al-Dahik (novel, The Stones of Laughter) (Al-Naqid Award) 1990, Ahl el-Hawa (novel, People of Love) 1993, Hayatt w-alaam Hammad ben Silana 1995, Bus al-awadem 1996, Harith al-Miyah (novel, The Tiller of Waters) 1998, Ya Salaam 1999; contrib. to In the House of

Silence (essays) 1998. *Address:* c/o The American University in Cairo Press, 113 Sharia Kasr el Aini Street, Cairo, Egypt.

BARAŃCZAK, Stanisław, PhD; Polish poet, translator, literary critic and academic; *Alfred Jurzykowski Professor of Polish Language and Literature, Harvard University;* b. 13 Nov. 1946, Poznań; m.; one s. one d. *Education:* Adam Mickiewicz Univ., Poznań. *Career:* on staff, Nurt magazine, Poznań 1967–71; Asst Lecturer, later Prof., Adam Mickiewicz Univ. 1969–80; Co-Founder Committee for the Defence of the Workers (and of clandestine quarterly Zapis) 1976; in the USA 1981–; Prof. of Slavic Languages and Literatures, Harvard Univ. 1981–84, Alfred Jurzykowski Prof. of Polish Language and Literature 1984–; Co-Founder and Co-Ed. Zeszyty Literackie, Paris 1983–; Assoc. Ed. The Polish Review 1986–87, Ed.-in-Chief 1987–90; mem. American Asscn for Polish-Jewish Studies, American Asscn for Advancement of Slavic Studies, PEN Polish Center, Polish Inst. of Arts and Sciences in America, Polish Writers' Asscn, Union of Polish Authors, Union of Polish Writers Abroad. *Publications:* poetry collections: Korekta twarzy (Face Correction) 1968, Jednym tchem (In One breath) 1970, Dziennik poranny (Morning Diary) 1972, Sztuczne oddychanie (Breathing Underwater) 1974, Ja wiem, że to nieształuszne (I know That It's Wrong) 1977, Atlantyda (Atlantis) 1986, Widokówka z tego świata (A Postcard from This World) 1988, The Weight of the Body 1989, Podróż zimowa (Winter Journey) 1994, Zimy i podroze (Winter and Journeys) 1997, Chirurgiczna precyzja (Surgical Precision) (Nike Prize 1999) 1998; criticism includes: Ironia i Harmonia (Irony and Harmony) 1973, Etyka i poetyka (Ethics and Poetry) 1979, Przed i po (Before and After) 1988, Tablica z Macondo (Board from Macondo) 1990, Ocalone w tłumaczeniu (Saved in Translation) 1992, Fioletowa krowa (Violet Cow) 1993, Poezja i duch h uogólnienia. Wybor esejow 1970–1995 (Poetry and the Spirit of Generalization: Selected Essays 1996; essays: Breathing Under Water and Other East European Essays 1990; numerous trans of English, American and Russian poetry and of William Shakespeare, including A Fugitive From Utopia: The Poetry of Zbigniew Herbert 1987, The Weight of the Body: Selected Poems 1989, Panorama der polnischen Literatur des 20. Jahrhunderts (in German) 1997, Polnische Lyrik aus 100 Jahren (in German) 1997; regular contrib. to Teksty Drugie. *Honours:* Chivalric Cross of the Order of Polonia Restituta 1991; Alfred Jurzykowski Foundation Literary Award 1980, Guggenheim Fellowship 1989, Terrence Des Pres Poetry Prize 1989, Special Diploma for Lifetime Achievement in Promoting Polish Culture Abroad, Polish Minister of Foreign Affairs 1993, Co-Winner PEN Best Trans. Award 1996. *Address:* Department of Slavic Languages and Literatures, Barker Center 374, 12 Quincy Street, Cambridge, MA 02138 (office); 8 Broad Dale, Newton Wille, MA 02160, USA. *Telephone:* (617) 495-4065 (office). *Fax:* (617) 496-4466 (office). *E-mail:* barancz@fas.harvard.edu (office). *Website:* www.fas.harvard.edu/~slavic/newsite/main/main.htm (office).

BARANSKAIA, Natalia Vladimirovna; Russian writer; b. 31 Dec. 1908; m. (died 1943); two d. *Education:* Moscow State Univ. *Career:* publishing and museum work, Pushkin museum –1966; contrib. to Novyi mir (New World) 1968–. *Publications include:* novels: Den' pominoveniia (trans. as Day of Remembrance) 1989, Stranstvie bezdomnykh: Zhizneopisanie 1999; short story collections: Otritsatel'naia Zhizel (trans. as A Negative Gazelle) 1977, Zhenshchina s zontikom (trans. as Woman with an Umbrella) 1981, Portret podarennyi drugu (trans. as Portrait Presented to a Friend) 1982, A Week Like Any Other (in trans.) 1989. *Address:* c/o Seal Press, 300 Queen Anne Avenue N, #375, Seattle, WA 98109, USA. *Website:* www.sealpress.com.

BARBALET, Margaret, MA; Australian writer; b. Adelaide, SA; m. Jack Barbalet 1970 (divorced 1989); three s. *Education:* Adelaide University. *Career:* Historian, Adelaide Children's Hospital, 1973–74; Research Officer, Adelaide City Council, 1973–75; Research Consultant, Commonwealth Schools Commission, 1984–88; Staff, Dept of Foreign Affairs and Trade, Australia, 1990–; mem. Australian Society of Authors. *Publications:* Far From a Low Gutter Girl: The Forgotten World of State Wards, 1983; Blood in the Rain (novel), 1986; Steel Beach (novel), 1988; The Wolf (children's book), 1991; Lady, Baby, Gypsy, Queen (novel), 1992; The Presence of Angels (novel), 2001; Reggie, Queen of the Street (children's book), 2003. *Honours:* Literature Grant, 1985; New Writers Fellowship, 1986; H. C. Coombs Creative Arts Fellow, ANU, 1998; ACT Literature Fellowship, 1999; Harold White Fellow, National Library of Australia, 2001; Writing Fellow, 2001; Literature Grant, 2002. *Address:* c/o Penguin Books, PO Box 701, Hawthorn, Vic. 3122, Australia.

BARBER, Elizabeth Jane Wayland, BA, PhD; American academic and writer; *Professor of Linguistics and Archaeology, Occidental College;* b. 2 Dec. 1940, Pasadena, CA; m. Paul Thomas Barber 1965. *Education:* Bryn Mawr Coll., Yale Univ. *Career:* Research Assoc., Princeton Univ. 1968–69; Asst Prof., Assoc. Prof., Full Prof. of Linguistics and Archaeology, Occidental Coll. 1970–. *Publications:* Archaeological Decipherment 1974, Prehistoric Textiles 1991, Women's Work: The First 20,000 Years 1994, The Mummies of Ürümchi 1998, When They Severed Earth From Sky 2005; contrib. to scholarly books and journals. *Honours:* Costume Soc. of America Davenport Book Prize, American Historical Asscn Breasted Prize in Ancient History, Guggenheim Fellowship 1979–80. *Address:* c/o Language Department, Occidental College, Los Angeles, CA 90041, USA.

BARBER, Lionel, BA; British journalist; *Editor, Financial Times;* b. 1955, London; m.; two c. *Education:* Univ. of Oxford. *Career:* journalist, The Scotsman 1978–81; Business Corresp. The Times (London) 1981–85;

Washington Corresp. and US Ed. Financial Times 1986–92, Brussels bureau chief 1992–98, News Ed. 1998–2000, Ed. Continental European Edn 2000–02, US Man. Ed. 2002–05, Ed. Financial Times 2005–; Visiting Fellow, European Univ. Inst., Florence, Italy 1996; Woodrow Wilson Foundation Fellow 1991, Eliot-Winant Fellow, British-American-Canadian Foundation 1994; Laurence Stern Fellowship, Washington Post 1985. *Publications include:* Price of Truth: Story of the Reuters Millions (with John Lawrenson) 1984, Not With Honour: Inside the Westland Scandal (co-author) 1986, Britain and the New European Agenda 1998. *Address:* Financial Times, One Southwark Bridge, London, SE1 9HL, England (office). *Telephone:* (20) 7873-3000 (office). *Fax:* (20) 7873-3924 (office). *Website:* www.ft.com (office).

BARBER, Richard William, BA, MA, PhD; British publisher and writer; b. 30 Oct. 1941, Dunmow, Essex, England; m. Helen Tolson 1970; one s. one d. *Education:* Corpus Christi Coll., Cambridge. *Career:* mem. RSL, Royal Historical Soc., Soc. of Antiquaries. *Publications:* Arthur of Albion 1961, The Knight and Chivalry 1972, Edward Prince of Wales and Aquitaine 1976, Companion Guide to South West France 1977, Tournaments 1978, The Arthurian Legends 1979, The Penguin Guide to Medieval Europe 1984, Fuller's Worthies 1987, The Worlds of John Aubrey 1988, Pilgrimages 1991, Myths and Legends of the British Isles 1998, Legends of Arthur 2000, The Holy Grail 2004; contrib. to Arthurian Literature. *Honours:* Somerset Maugham Award 1972, Times Higher Educational Supplement Book Award 1978. *Address:* Stangrove Hall, Alderton, Nr Woodbridge, Suffolk IP12 3BL, England (office).

BARBET, Pierre (see Avice, Claude Pierre Marie)

BARBOSA, Miguel; Portuguese writer, dramatist, poet and painter; b. 22 Nov. 1925, Lisbon. *Education:* Univ. of Lisbon. *Career:* mem. Accad. Internazionale Greci-Marino di Lettere, Arti e Scienze, Soc. of Portuguese Authors, Grupo de Arujos do Museu de Angueologia de Lisbon, da Umáe Brasileira de Escritos do Rio de Janeiro, Brazil; Second Sec. Institut de Sintra. *Publications:* fiction: Jrineu do Morro 1972, Mulher Mancumba 1973, A Pileca no Poleiro 1976, As Confissoes de Um Cacador de Dinossauros 1981, Esta Louca Profissao de Escritor 1983, Cartas a Um Fogo-Fatuo 1985; poetry: Dans un Cri de Couleurs 1991, Um Gesto no Rosto da Utopia 1994, Prima del Verbo 1995, Mare di Illusioni Naufragate 1995, Preludio Poético de um Vagabundo da Madrugada 1996, Mouthfuls of Red Confetti and the Hunt for God's Skull 1996, O Teu Corpo na Minha Alma 1996, A Eternidade de Un Segundo de Amor 2002, A Ninha Amante Lisboa 2003, Apologia do Silêncio 2004; Chiça! Estou farto... 2006; other: plays and short stories, contribs to various publs. *Honours:* several awards for art. *Address:* Rua Mateus Vicente de Oliveira, N° 14-2E, 2745-167, Queluz, Portugal. *Telephone:* (214) 367438.

BARBOUR, Douglas Fleming, BA, MA, PhD; Canadian academic, poet and writer; b. 21 March 1940, Winnipeg, MB; m. M. Sharon Nicoll 1966. *Education:* Acadia University, Dalhousie University, Queen's University, Kingston, ON. *Career:* Teacher, Alderwood Collegiate Institute, 1968–69; Asst Prof., 1969–77, Assoc. Prof., 1977–82, Prof. of English, 1982–, University of Alberta; mem. Asscn of Canadian University Teachers; League of Canadian Poets, co-chair., 1972–74. *Publications:* Poetry: Land Fall, 1971; A Poem as Long as the Highway, 1971; White, 1972; Song Book, 1973; He and She and, 1974; Visions of My Grandfather, 1977; Shore Lines, 1979; Vision/Sounding, 1980; The Pirates of Pen's Chance (with Stephen Scobie), 1981; The Harbingers, 1984; Visible Visions: Selected Poems, 1984; Canadian Poetry Chronicle, 1985. Other: Worlds Out of Words: The Science Fiction Novels of Samuel R. Delany, 1978; The Maple Laugh Forever: An Anthology of Canadian Comic Poetry (ed. with Stephen Scobie), 1981; Writing Right: New Poetry by Canadian Women (ed. with Marni Stanley), 1982; Tesseracts 2 (ed. with Phyllis Gollieb), 1987; B. P. Nichol and His Works, 1992; Daphne Marlatt and Her Works, 1992; John Newlove and His Works, 1992; Michael Ondaatje, 1993.

BARBOUR, Ian Graeme, BD, PhD; American physicist, theologian and academic; *Carleton Professor Emeritus, Department of Religion, Carleton College;* b. 5 Oct. 1923, Peking (now Beijing), (People's Republic of) China. *Education:* Swarthmore Coll., Duke Univ., Univ. of Chicago, Yale Univ. *Career:* Asst Prof., Assoc. Prof. of Physics, Kalamazoo Coll. 1949–53; Asst Prof. of Physics, Assoc. Prof. of Religion, Carleton Coll., Northfield, Minn. 1955–73, Prof. of Religion 1974–86, Winifred and Atherton Bean Prof. of Science, Tech. and Soc. 1981–86, Carleton Prof. Emer., Dept of Religion 1986–; Lilly Visiting Prof. of Science, Theology and Human Values Purdue Univ. 1973–74; Gifford Lecturer Univ. of Aberdeen, Scotland 1989–91; mem. American Acad. of Religion, Soc. for Values in Higher Educ. *Publications:* Christianity and the Scientist 1960, Issues in Science and Religion 1966, Science and Religion: New Perspectives on the Dialogue (ed) 1968, Science and Secularity: The Ethics of Technology 1970, Earth Might Be Fair (ed) 1971, Western Man and Environmental Ethics (ed) 1972, Myths, Models and Paradigms 1974, Finite Resources and the Human Future (ed) 1976, Technology, Environment and Human Values 1980, Energy and American Values (co-author) 1982, Religion in an Age of Science (Gifford Lectures) 1990, Ethics in an Age of Technology 1993, Religion and Science: Historical and Contemporary Issues 1997, When Science Meets Religion 2000, Nature, Human Nature and God 2002; contributions: scientific and religious journals. *Honours:* Ford Faculty Fellowship 1953–54, Harbison Award for Distinguished Teaching, Danforth Foundation 1963–64, Guggenheim Fellowship 1967–68, Fulbright Fellowship 1967–68, ACLS Fellowship 1976–77, Nat. Endowment for the Humanities

Fellowship 1976–77, Nat. Humanities Center Fellow 1980–81, American Acad. of Religion Book Award 1993, Templeton Prize for Progress in Religion 1999. *Address:* Carleton College, Northfield, MN 55057, USA. *E-mail:* ibarbour@carleton.edu.

BARER, Burl; American writer; b. 8 Aug. 1947, Walla Walla, WA; m. Britt Johnsen 1974, one s. one d. *Education:* Univ. of Washington. *Career:* mem. MWA. *Publications:* Selections from the Holy Quran, 1987; The Saint: A Complete History in Print, Radio, Film and Television, 1993; Man Overboard: The Counterfeit Resurrection of Phil Champagne, 1994; The Saint, 1997; Capture the Saint, 1998. Contributions to books and periodicals. *Honours:* Edgar Award 1994.

BARFOOT, Joan, BA; Canadian novelist and journalist; b. 17 May 1946, Owen Sound, Ont. *Education:* Univ. of Western Ont. *Career:* reporter, Religion Ed. Windsor Star 1967–69; feature and news writer, Mirror Publications, Toronto 1969–73, Toronto Sunday Sun 1973–75; with London Free Press 1976–79, 1980–94; has taught journalism and creative writing at Univ. of Western Ont.; juror, Books in Canada First Novel Award 1987, Gov.-Gen.'s Award for English Language Canadian Fiction 1995, Trillium Literary Award 1996, 1999; mem. Writers' Union of Canada, PEN Canada. *Publications:* Abra 1978, Dancing in the Dark 1982, Duet for Three 1985, Family News 1989, Plain Jane 1992, Charlotte and Claudia Keeping in Touch 1994, Some Things About Flying 1997, Getting Over Edgar 1999, Critical Injuries 2001, Luck 2005. *Honours:* Books in Canada First Novel Award 1978, Marian Engel Award 1992. *Address:* 286 Cheapside Street, London, ON N6A 2A2, Canada. *E-mail:* jbarfoot@sympatico.ca. *Website:* www3.sympatico.ca/jbarfoot.

BARGHOUTI, Mourid; Palestinian poet; b. 1944, Deir Ghassanah, Israel; m. Radwa Ashour 1970; one s. *Education:* Univ. of Cairo. *Career:* emigrated to Egypt 1963; teacher, Kuwait 1971 and Egypt; representative of the Palestinian Liberation Organization (PLO), Budapest; journalist for Palestine Radio, Cairo and Beirut; returned to Palestine 1996. *Publications:* poetry: The Palestinians, Qasa'id Al-Rasif 1980, Collected Works 1997; non-fiction: I Saw Ramallah (Naguib Mahfouz Medal) 1997, A Small Sun 2003. *Honours:* Palestine Award for Poetry 2000.

BARICCO, Alessandro; Italian writer and playwright; b. 1958, Turin. *Career:* music critic, La Repubblica; cultural correspondent, La Stampa; collaboration with French band, Air, to produce backing music for City 2003. *Plays:* Novecento 1994, Davila Roa 1996, Partita Spagnola 2003. *Publications:* novels: Castelli di rabbia (trans. as Lands of Glass) (Premio Selezione Campiello, Prix Médicis étranger) 1991, Oceano Mare (trans. as Ocean Sea) (Premio Viareggio) 1993, Seta (trans. as Silk) 1996, City 1999, Senza sangue (trans. as Without Blood) 2002, An Iliad (re-written) 2006; non-fiction: Il Genio in fuga 1988, L'anima di Hegel e le mucche del Wisconsin 1992, Barnum (collection of articles) 1995, Barnum 2 (collection of articles) 1998, Next 2002; contrib. to Il Corriere. *Honours:* several literary prizes. *Address:* c/o Canongate Books, 14 High Street, Edinburgh, EH1 1TE, Scotland.

BARICH, Bill, BA; American writer; b. 23 Aug. 1943, Winona, Minn.; partner, Imelda Healy. *Education:* Colgate Univ. *Career:* with US Peace Corps, Nigeria 1966–67; teacher, Somerset Hills School, NJ 1968–69; publicist, Alfred Knopf, New York 1971–75; staff writer, The New Yorker 1981–94; Adjunct Prof., Univ. of California, Berkeley 1988–89, 1999–; scriptwriter, NYPD Blue, 20th Century Fox 1999; mem. PEN. *Publications:* Laughing in the Hills 1980, Travelling Light 1984, Hard to Be Good 1987, Big Dreams 1994, Carson Valley 1997, Crazy for Rivers 1999, The Sporting Life 2000, A Fine Place to Daydream 2005; contribs to periodicals. *Honours:* Guggenheim Fellowship 1985, Marin Co. Arts Council Fellow 1995, San Francisco Public Library Literary Laureate 1998. *Literary Agent:* c/o Liz Darsanhoff, 236 W 26th Street, New York, NY 10001, USA. *E-mail:* barichbill@hotmail.com.

BARKER, Clive; British writer, dramatist and artist; b. 1952, Liverpool, England. *Education:* University of Liverpool. *Publications:* Fiction: The Damnation Game, 1985; The Inhuman Condition, 1985; Weaveworld, 1987; Cabal, 1988; The Great and Secret Show, 1989; Imajica, 1991; The Hellbound Heart, 1991; The Thief of Always, 1992; Emerville, 1994; Sacrament, 1996; Galilee, 1998; The Essential Clive Barker, 1999; Coldheart Canyon: A Hollywood Ghost Story, 2001; Abarat, 2002; Abarat II: Days of Magic, Nights of War 2004. Plays: Forms of Heaven: Three Plays, 1996; Incarnations: Three Plays, 1998; screenplays. *Address:* c/o HarperCollins, 10 E 53rd Street, New York, NY 10022, USA. *Website:* www.clivebarker.com.

BARKER, Dennis Malcolm; British journalist and writer; b. 21 June 1929, Lowestoft, Suffolk; m. Sarah Katherine Alwyn; one d. *Education:* Royal Grammar School, High Wycombe, Lowestoft Grammar School, Nat. Diploma in Journalism. *Career:* reporter and Sub-Ed., Suffolk Chronicle & Mercury, Ipswich 1947–48; reporter, feature writer, theatre and film critic, East Anglian Daily Times 1948–58; Ed. and Editorial Dir, East Anglian Architecture & Building Review 1956–58; Estates and Property Ed. and theatre critic, Express & Star, Wolverhampton 1958–63; Midlands correspondent, The Guardian 1963–67, reporter, feature writer, columnist 1967–91; mem. Nat. Union of Journalists, Newspaper Press Fund, Writers' Guild of GB, Broadcasting Press Guild, Soc. of Authors. *Publications:* fiction: Candidate of Promise 1969, The Scandalisers 1974, Winston Three Three Three 1987; non-fiction: Soldiering On (The People of the Forces Trilogy, Vol. I) 1981, One Man's Estate 1983, Parian Ware 1985, Ruling the Waves (The People of the

Forces Trilogy, Vol. II) 1986, Guarding the Skies (The People of the Forces Trilogy, Vol. III) 1989, Fresh Start 1990, The Craft of the Media Interview 1998, How to Deal with the Media 2000, Seize the Day (contrib.) 2001, The Guardian Book of Obituaries (contrib.) 2003, Oxford Dictionary of National Biography (contrib.) 2004, Tricks Journalists Play 2007; contrib. to BBC, Punch, The Guardian 1991–. *Address:* 67 Speldhurst Road, Chiswick, London, W4 1BY, England. *Telephone:* (20) 8994-5380.

BARKER, Elspeth; British writer; b. 16 Nov. 1940, Edinburgh; m. George Granville Barker 1989; three s. two d. *Education:* St Leonards School, Scotland; Univ. of Oxford. *Publications:* O Caledonia 1991, Anthology of Loss 1997, A Distant Cry; contrib. short stories to New Writing 2000, and to Independent on Sunday, Guardian, Harpers & Queen, TLS, Vogue, Big Issue, Sunday Times, Observer, Daily Mail. *Honours:* David Higham Award, Scottish Arts Council; Angel Literary Award; RSL Winifred Holtby Award; shortlisted for Whitbread First Novel Award 1991–92. *Address:* Bintry House, Itteringham, Aylsham, Norfolk, NR11 7AT, England.

BARKER, Howard, MA; British dramatist and poet; b. 28 June 1946, London, England. *Education:* University of Sussex. *Career:* resident dramatist, Open Space Theatre, London 1975–75. *Publications:* over 30 plays, including Collected Plays, Vol. I, 1990; poetry.

BARKER, Nicola; British writer; b. 30 March 1966, Ely, Cambridgeshire, England. *Education:* Univ. of Cambridge. *Publications:* Love Your Enemies (short stories) 1992, Reversed Forecast (novel) 1994, Small Holdings (novel) 1995, Heading Inland (short stories) 1996, Wide Open (novel) 1998, Five Miles From Outer Hope (novel) 2000, Behindlings (novel) 2002, The Three Button Trick (short stories) 2003, Clear: A Transparent Novel 2004, Darkmans (novel) 2007; contrib. to Time Out Book of London Short Stories, Food With Feeling (story adapted for BBC Radio 4). *Honours:* David Higham Prize for Fiction, jt winner, Macmillan Silver PEN Award for Fiction, Mail on Sunday/ John Llewellyn Rhys Award 1997, IMPAC Dublin Literary Award 2000, one of Granta's Best of Young British Novelists 2003. *Literary Agent:* Rogers, Coleridge & White Ltd, 20 Powis Mews, London, W11 1JN, England.

BARKER, Patricia (Pat) Margaret, CBE, BSc (Econ), FRSL; British author; b. 8 May 1943, Thornaby-on-Tees; m. David Barker 1978; one s., one d. *Education:* London School of Econs. *Career:* taught in colls of further educ. 1965–70; Patron New Writing North; mem. Soc. of Authors, PEN. *Publications:* novels: Union Street 1982, Blow Your House Down 1984, The Century's Daughter 1986 (retitled Liza's England 1996), The Man Who Wasn't There 1989; trilogy of First World War novels: Regeneration 1991, The Eye in the Door 1993, The Ghost Road (Booker Prize 1995) 1995; Another World 1998, Border Crossing 2001, Double Vision 2003, Life Class 2007. *Honours:* Hon. Fellow LSE 1998; Hon. MLitt (Teesside) 1993; Hon. DLitt (Napier) 1996, (Durham) 1998, (Hertfordshire) 1998, (London) 2002; Dr hc (Open Univ.) 1997; Fawcett Prize 1983, Guardian Prize for Fiction 1993, Northern Electric Special Arts Award 1994. *Literary Agent:* Aitken Alexander Associates Ltd, 18–21 Cavaye Place, London, SW10 9PT, England. *Telephone:* (20) 7373-8672. *Fax:* (20) 7373-6002. *E-mail:* reception@aitkenalexander.co.uk. *Website:* www .aitkenalexander.co.uk.

BARKER, Paul, MA, FRSA; British journalist, editor, writer and broadcaster; b. 24 Aug. 1935, Mytholmroyd, Yorkshire, England; m. Sally Huddleston; three s. one d. *Education:* Univ. of Oxford. *Career:* Ed. New Society 1968–86; Social Policy Ed. Sunday Telegraph 1986–88; Visiting Fellow Univ. of Bath 1986–2000; columnist London Evening Standard 1987–92, Social Policy Commentator 1992–; Assoc. Ed. The Independent Magazine 1988–90; reviewer TLS 1960–64, 1991–; essayist Prospect 1995–; columnist New Statesman 1996–99; Leverhulme Research Fellow 1993–95; Fellowship in Built Environment 2000–02; Sr Research Fellow The Young Foundation (fmrly Inst. of Community Studies). *Publications:* A Sociological Portrait 1972, One for Sorrow, Two for Joy 1972, The Social Sciences Today 1975, Arts in Society 1977, The Other Britain 1982, Founders of the Welfare State 1985, Britain in the Eighties 1989, Towards a New Landscape 1993, Young at Eighty 1995, Gulliver and Beyond 1996, Living as Equals 1996, A Critic Writes 1997, Town and Country 1998, Non-Plan 2000, From Black Economy to Moment of Truth 2004, The Rise and Rise of Meritocracy 2006. *Address:* 15 Dartmouth Park Avenue, London, NW5 1JL, England.

BARKER, Ralph Hammond; British writer; b. 21 Oct. 1917, Feltham, Middlesex, England; m. 1st Joan Muriel Harris 1948 (died 1993); one adopted d.; m. 2nd Diana Darvey 1995 (died 2000). *Education:* Hounslow Coll. *Career:* RAF 1940–46, 1949–61, retd as Flight Lieutenant. *Publications:* Down in the Drink 1955, The Ship-Busters 1957, The Last Blue Mountain 1959, Strike Hard, Strike Sure 1963, Ten Great Innings 1964, The Thousand Plan 1965, Ten Great Bowlers 1967, Great Mysteries of the Air 1967, Verdict on a Lost Flyer 1969, Aviator Extraordinary 1969, Test Cricket: England v Australia (with Irving Rosenwater) 1969, The Schneider Trophy Races 1971, One Man's Jungle 1975, The Blockade Busters 1976, The Cricketing Family Edrich 1976, The Hurricats 1978, Not Here, But in Another Place 1980, The RAF at War 1981, Innings of a Lifetime 1982, Good-Night, Sorry for Sinking You 1984, Children of the Benares 1987, Purple Patches 1987, That Eternal Summer 1990, The Royal Flying Corps in France, two vols 1994–95, combined edn 2002; Men of the Bombers 2005; contrib. to Sunday Express, The Cricketer. *Honours:* Buchpreis des Deutschen Alpenvereins 1982. *Literary Agent:* c/o Peter Knight, 20 Crescent Grove, London, SW4 7AH, England. *Telephone:* (20)

7622-1467 (office). *Address:* Old Timbers, 16 Aldercombe Lane, Caterham, Surrey CR3 6ED, England (home). *Telephone:* (1883) 343842 (home).

BARKER, Rodney, BA; American writer; b. 9 Feb. 1946, Lewisburg, Pennsylvania; m. Star York. *Education:* Knox College, San Francisco State University. *Career:* mem. International PEN. *Publications:* The Hiroshima Maidens, 1985; The Broken Circle, 1992; Dancing with the Devil, 1996; And the Waters Turned to Blood, 1997. *Literary Agent:* Janklow & Nesbit Associates, 445 Park Avenue, New York, NY 10022, USA. *E-mail:* rbarker@ cybermesa.com.

BARKLEM, Jill; British children's writer and illustrator; b. Epping; m. 1977. *Education:* studied art in London. *Publications:* Spring Story 1980, Summer Story 1980, Autumn Story 1980, Winter Story 1980, The Secret Staircase 1983, The High Hills 1986, Sea Story 1990, Poppy's Babies 1994, Wilfred's Birthday 1995, Nice for Mice 1999, Wilfred to the Rescue 2005. *Address:* Brambly Hedge, The Barn, 41 Church Hill, Epping, Essex CM16 4RA, England (office). *Telephone:* (1992) 573052. *Fax:* (1992) 575483. *E-mail:* info@ bramblyhedge.co.uk. *Website:* www.bramblyhedge.co.uk.

BARLAS, Fevziye Rahgozar, MA; Afghan journalist, short story writer and poet; b. 1955, Balkh; d. of M. Shafee Rahgozar; m. Rai Barlas. *Education:* Istanbul Univ., Turkey, Univ. of Washington, USA. *Career:* lived in Turkey early to mid 1970s; worked as writer and journalist in Ministry of Information and Culture, Kabul, and for Kabul State Radio and TV, and as trans. –1979; writings banned under Communist regime, fled to Turkey; fmr Sr Ed. and News Anchor Radio Free Europe/Radio Liberty, Munich, Germany; moved to USA 1996. *Publications:* Deyar-e Shegeftiha (poems, Wonderland) 1999, The Heavens are my Father (poems), Wondering Eyes (short stories); contrib. short stories to Persian publs in USA and Europe. *Honours:* award from then US Pres., Bill Clinton. *Address:* c/o Interdisciplinary Programs, The Graduate School, POB 352192, University of Washington, Seattle, WA 98195-2192, USA.

BARLOW, Frank, CBE, BA, BLitt, MA, DPhil FBA, FRSL; British historian and academic; b. 19 April 1911, Wolstanton, England; m. Moira Stella Brigid Garvey 1936; two s. *Education:* St John's Coll., Oxford. *Career:* Asst Lecturer, University College London 1936–40; War Service, India, Ceylon, Singapore 1941–46 (Intelligence Corps 1942–46), final rank major; Lecturer, University of Exeter 1946–49, Reader 1949–53, Prof. of History and Head of the Dept of History 1953–76, Emeritus Prof. 1976–, Deputy Vice-Chancellor 1961–63, Public Orator 1974–76,. *Publications:* The Letters of Arnulf of Lisieux 1939, Durham Annals and Documents of the Thirteenth Century 1945, Durham Jurisdictional Peculiars 1950, The Feudal Kingdom of England 1955, The Life of King Edward the Confessor (ed. and trans.) 1962, The English Church, 1000–1066 1963, William I and the Norman Conquest 1965, Edward the Confessor 1970, Winchester in the Early Middle Ages (with Martin Biddle, Olof von Feilitzen and D. J. Keene) 1976, The English Church, 1066–1154 1979, The Norman Conquest and Beyond 1983, William Rufus 1983, Thomas Beckett 1986, Introduction to Devonshire Domesday Book 1991, English Episcopal Acta, XI–XII (Exeter 1046–1257) 1995, The Carmen de Hastingae Proelio of Guy, Bishop of Amiens (ed. and trans.) 1999, The Godwins 2002; contrib. to various professional journals. *Honours:* Fereday Fellow, St John's College, Oxford 1935–38, Hon. Fellow, St John's College, Oxford 2001; Hon. DLitt (Exon) 1981. *Address:* Middle Court Hall, Kenton, Exeter, EX6 8NA, England (home). *Telephone:* (1626) 890-438 (home).

BARLTROP, Robert Arthur Horace; British journalist and writer; b. 6 Nov. 1922, Walthamstow, England; m. Mary Gleeson 1947; three s. *Education:* Forest Training Coll. *Career:* Ed., Socialist Standard 1972–78, Cockney Ancestor 1983–86; columnist and feature writer, Recorder Newspapers 1985–; mem. Inst. of Journalists. *Publications:* The Monument 1974, Jack London: The Man, the Writer, the Rebel 1977, The Bar Tree 1979, The Muvver Tongue 1980, Revolution: Stories and Essays by Jack London (ed.) 1981, My Mother's Calling Me 1984, A Funny Age 1985, Bright Summer, Dark Autumn 1986; contrib. to magazines and newspapers. *Address:* 77 Idmiston Road, London, E15 1RG, England.

BARNABY, Charles Frank, BSc, MSc, PhD; British physicist; *Consultant, Oxford Research Group;* b. 27 Sept. 1927, Andover, Hants.; s. of Charles H. Barnaby and Lilian Sainsbury; m. Wendy Elizabeth Field 1972; one s. one d. *Education:* Andover Grammar School and Univ. of London. *Career:* Physicist, UK Atomic Energy Authority 1950–57; mem. Sr Scientific Staff, MRC, Univ. Coll. Medical School 1957–68; Exec. Sec. Pugwash Confs on Science and World Affairs 1968–70; Dir Stockholm Int. Peace Research Inst. (SIPRI) 1971–81; Prof. of Peace Studies, Free Univ., Amsterdam 1981–85; Dir and Scientific Adviser, World Disarmament Campaign (UK) 1982–; Consultant, Oxford Research Group 1998–; Ed. Int. Journal of Human Rights. *Publications:* Man and the Atom 1971, Ed. Preventing the Spread of Nuclear Weapons 1971, Anti-ballistic Missile Systems (co-ed.) 1971, Disarmament and Arms Control 1973, Nuclear Energy 1975, The Nuclear Age 1976, Prospects for Peace 1980, Future Warfare (ed. and co-author) 1983, Space Weapons 1984, Star Wars Brought Down to Earth 1986, The Automated Battlefield 1986, The Invisible Bomb 1989, The Gaia Peace Atlas 1989, The Role and Control of Weapons in the 1990s 1992, How Nuclear Weapons Spread 1993, Instruments of Terror 1997, How to Build a Nuclear Bomb and Other Weapons of Mass Destruction 2003; articles in scientific journals. *Honours:* Hon. DSc (Frei Univ., Amsterdam) 1982, (Southampton) 1996. *Address:* Brandreth, Chilbolton,

Stockbridge, Hants., SO20 6HW, England. *Telephone:* (1264) 860423 (home). *Fax:* (1264) 860868. *E-mail:* frank.barnaby@btinternet.com.

BARNARD, Robert, (Bernard Bastable), BA, DrPhil; British writer; b. 23 Nov. 1936, Burnham on Crouch, Essex, England; s. of Leslie Thomas Barnard and Vera Barnard (née Nethercoat); m. Mary Louise Tabor 1963. *Education:* Balliol Coll., Oxford, Univ. of Bergen, Norway. *Career:* Lecturer in English, Univ. of New England, Armidale, NSW, 1961–66; Lecturer, then Sr Lecturer in English, Univ. of Bergen, 1966–76; Prof. of English, Univ. of Tromsø, Norway, 1976–84; mem. CWA, Brontë Soc. (chair. 1996–99, 2002–05), Soc. of Authors. *Publications:* Death of an Old Goat, 1974; A Little Local Murder, 1976; Death on the High C's, 1977; Blood Brotherhood, 1977; Unruly Son (aka Death of a Mystery Writer), 1978; Posthumous Papers (aka Death of a Literary Widow), 1979; Death in a Cold Climate, 1980; Mother's Boys (aka Death of a Perfect Mother), 1981; Sheer Torture (aka Death by Sheer Torture), 1981; Death and the Princess, 1982; The Missing Brontë (aka The Case of the Missing Brontë), 1983; Little Victims (aka School for Murder), 1983; A Corpse in a Gilded Cage, 1984; Out of the Blackout, 1985; The Disposal of the Living (aka Fête Fatale), 1985; Political Suicide, 1986; Bodies, 1986; Death in Purple Prose (aka The Cherry Blossom Corpse), 1987; The Skeleton in the Grass, 1987; At Death's Door, 1988; Death and the Chaste Apprentice, 1989; A City of Strangers, 1990; A Scandal in Belgravia, 1991; A Fatal Attachment, 1992; A Hovering of Vultures, 1993; The Masters of the House, 1994; The Bad Samaritan, 1995; The Corpse at the Haworth Tandoori, 1999; The Mistress of Alderley, 2002; The Bones in the Attic, 2002; A Cry from the Dark, 2003, The Graveyard Position 2004, Dying Flames 2005, Sins of Scarlet (short story) (CWA Award for best crime short story) 2006, A Fall from Grace 2007. As Bernard Bastable: To Die Like a Gentleman, 1993; Dead, Mr Mozart, 1995; Too Many Notes, Mr Mozart, 1995. Contributions: short stories and essays. *Honours:* CWA Cartier Diamond Dagger 2003. *Address:* Hazeldene, Houghley Lane, Leeds LS13 2DT, England. *Telephone:* (113) 263-8955.

BARNES, Christopher John, BA, MA, PhD; British academic and writer; *Professor of Slavic Languages and Literatures, University of Toronto*; b. 10 March 1942, Sheffield, Yorks.; m. Svetlana Tzapina 1994; two d. *Education:* Corpus Christi Coll., Cambridge. *Career:* Lecturer in Russian Language and Literature, Univ. of St Andrews 1967–89; Prof. and Chair. Dept of Slavic Languages and Literatures, Univ. of Toronto 1989–; mem. American Asscn for the Advancement of Slavic Studies, American Asscn of Teachers of Slavic and East European Languages, British Royal Musical Asscn, British Univs Asscn of Slavists, Canadian Asscn of Slavists, Modern Language Asscn of America. *Publications:* Studies in Twentieth-Century Russian Literature (ed.) 1976, Boris Pasternak: Collected Short Prose (ed. and trans.) 1977, Boris Pasternak: The Voice of Prose (ed. and trans., two vols) 1986, 1990, Boris Pasternak: A Literary Biography, Vol. 1, 1890–1928 1989, Vol. 2, 1928–1960 1998, Boris Pasternak and European Literature (ed.) 1990, The Moscow Piano School (ed.) 2007, Vadim Bytensky – Journey from St Petersburg (ed. and translator) 2007; contribs to scholarly journals. *Address:* Department of Slavic Languages and Literatures, University of Toronto, Toronto, ON M5S 1A1 (office); 53 Alberta Avenue, Toronto, ON M6H 2R5, Canada (home). *Telephone:* (416) 926-2074 (office); (416) 850-5102 (home). *Fax:* (416) 926-2076 (office). *E-mail:* chrjbarnes1942@yahoo.ca (home).

BARNES, Clive Alexander, CBE; British journalist and critic; *Associate Editor, Chief Drama and Dance Critic, New York Post*; b. 13 May 1927, London; s. of Arthur Lionel Barnes and Freda Marguerite Garratt; m. Patricia Winckley 1958; one s. one d. *Education:* King's Coll., London and Univ. of Oxford. *Career:* served RAF 1946–48; Admin. Officer, Town Planning Dept, London Co. Council 1952–61; also active as freelance journalist contributing articles, reviews and criticisms on music, dance, theatre, films and television to the New Statesman, The Spectator, The Daily Express, The New York Times, etc.; Chief Dance Critic, The Times, London 1961–65; Exec. Ed., Dance and Dancers, Music and Musicians, Plays and Players 1961–65; Dance Critic The New York Times 1965–78, also Drama Critic (weekdays only) 1967–77; Assoc. Ed., Chief Drama and Dance Critic, New York Post 1977–; a New York Corresp. of The Times (London) 1970–. *Publications:* Ballet in Britain Since the War, Frederick Ashton and His Ballet, Ballet Here and Now, Dance As It Happened, Dance in the Twentieth Century, Dance Scene: USA; Ed. Nureyev 1983. *Honours:* Kt Order of the Dannebrog (Denmark). *Address:* New York Post, 1211 Avenue Of The Americas, New York, NY 10036-8790, USA (office). *Telephone:* (212) 930-8000 (home). *Website:* www.nypost.com (office).

BARNES, Richard (Dick) Gordon, BA, AM, PhD; American academic, poet, writer and dramatist; b. 5 Nov. 1932, San Bernardino, CA; m. Patricia Casey 1982, five s. four d. *Education:* Pomona College, Harvard University, Claremont Graduate School. *Career:* Part-Time Instructor, 1956–58, Instructor, 1961–62, Asst Prof., 1962–67, Assoc. Prof., 1967–72, Prof., 1972–98, Prof. Emeritus, 1998–, Pomona College; numerous poetry readings. *Publications:* Poetry: A Lake on the Earth, 1982; The Real Time Jazz Band Song Book, 1990; Few and Far Between, 1994. Chapbooks: The Complete Poems of R. G. Barnes, 1972; Thirty-One Views of San Bernardino, 1975; Hungry Again the Next Day, 1978; Lyrical Ballads, 1979; All Kinds of Tremendous Things Can Happen, 1982; A Pentecostal, 1985. Plays: Nacho, 1964; A Lulu for the Lively Arts, 1965; San Antonio Noh, 1966; The Cucamonga Wrapdown, 1967; The Eighth Avatar, 1970; The Death of Buster Quinine, 1972; Purple, 1973; The Detestable Life of Alfred Furkeisar, 1975; The Bradford and Barnes Poverty Circus, 1977; Tenebrae, 1979; Come Sunday, 1982; A New Death of Buster Quinine, 1994; The Sand Mirror, 1998. Other: Trans, films and recordings. Contributions: many anthologies and magazines.

BARNES, Jim Weaver, BA, MA, PhD; American writer, poet and teacher; b. 22 Dec. 1933, Summerfield, OK; m. Carolyn 1973; two s. *Education:* Southeastern Oklahoma State University, University of Arkansas. *Career:* mem. PEN Center West; Assoc. Writing Programs. *Publications:* Fish on Poteau Mountain, 1980; American Book of the Dead, 1982; Season of Loss, 1985; La Plata Canata, 1989; Sawdust War, 1992; Paris, 1997; On Native Ground, 1997; Numbered Days, 1999; On a Wing of the Sun, 2001. Contributions: Poetry Chicago; Nation; American Scholar; Georgia Review; Poetry Northwest; Quarterly West; Prairie Schooner; Mississippi Review; Plus 400. *Honours:* National Endowment for the Arts Fellowship, 1978; Oklahoma Book Award, 1993; Camargo Foundation Fellowships, 1996, 2001; American Book Award, 1998.

BARNES, Jonathan, FBA; British academic; *Professor of Ancient Philosophy, University of Paris IV–Sorbonne*; b. 26 Dec. 1942, Much Wenlock; s. of the late A. L. Barnes and K. M. Barnes; m. Jennifer Mary Postgate 1964; two d. *Education:* City of London School and Balliol Coll., Oxford. *Career:* Lecturer in Philosophy Exeter Coll., Oxford 1967–68, Fellow Oriel Coll., Oxford 1968–78, Balliol Coll., Oxford 1978–94; Prof. of Ancient Philosophy, Univ. of Oxford 1989–94, Univ. of Geneva 1994–2002, Univ. of Paris IV–Sorbonne 2003–; visiting posts at Univ. of Chicago 1966–67, Inst. for Advanced Study, Princeton 1972, Univ. of Mass 1973, Univ. of Tex. 1981, Wissenschaftskolleg zu Berlin 1985, Univ. of Alberta 1986, Univ. of Zurich 1987, Istituto Italiano per la Storia della Filosofia 1989, 1994, 1999, Ecole Normale Supérieure, Paris 1996, Scuola Normale di Pisa 2002; mem. L' Acad. scientifique, Geneva, Aristotelian Soc., Mind Asscn. *Publications:* The Ontological Argument 1972, Aristotle's Posterior Analytics 1975, The Presocratic Philosophers 1979, Doubt and Dogmatism (with M. F. Burnyeat and M. Schofield) 1980, Aristotle 1982, Science and Speculation (with J. Brunschwig and M. F. Burnyeat) 1982, The Complete Works of Aristotle 1984, The Modes of Scepticism (with J. Annas) 1985, Early Greek Philosophy 1987, Matter and Metaphysics (with M. Mignucci 1988, Philosophia Togata (with M. Griffin) Vol. I 1989, Vol. II 1997, The Toils of Scepticism 1991, Sextus Empiricus: Outlines of Scepticism (with J. Annas) 1994, The Cambridge Companion to Aristotle 1995, Logic and the Imperial Stoa 1997, The Cambridge History of Hellenistic Philosophy (with K. Algra, J. Mansfield and M. Schofield) 1999, Porphyry: Introduction 2003. *Honours:* Hon. Fellow American Acad. of Arts and Sciences 1999; Condorcet Medal 1996, John Locke Lecturer, Univ. of Oxford 2004. *Address:* Les Charmilles, 36200 Ceaulmont (home); 12 blvd Arago, 75013 Paris, France (home). *E-mail:* jonathanbarnes@wanadoo.fr (home).

BARNES, Julian Patrick, (Dan Kavanagh, Basil Seal), BA; British writer; b. 19 Jan. 1946, Leicester, England; m. Pat Kavanagh. *Education:* City of London School, Magdalen Coll. Oxford. *Career:* lexicographer, Oxford English Dictionary Supplement 1969–72; Asst Literary Ed. New Statesman 1977–79, reviewer 1977–81, TV critic 1979–82; Contributing Ed. New Review, London 1977–78; Deputy Literary Ed. Sunday Times, London 1979–81; TV Critic The Observer 1982–86; Hon. Fellow Magdalen Coll., Oxford 1996–. *Publications:* Metroland 1980, Before She Met Me 1982, Flaubert's Parrot (Geoffrey Faber Memorial Prize, Prix Médicis 1986) 1984, Staring at the Sun 1986, A History of the World in $10\frac{1}{2}$ Chapters 1989, Talking it Over (Prix Femina Etranger 1992) 1991, The Porcupine 1992, Letters From London 1990–95 (articles) 1995, Cross Channel (short stories) 1996, England, England 1998, Love, etc. 2000, Something to Declare (essays) 2002, In the Land of Pain, by Alphonse Daudet (ed. and trans.) 2002, The Lemon Table (short stories) 2004, The Pedant in the Kitchen 2004, Arthur & George 2005; as Dan Kavanagh: Duffy 1980, Fiddle City 1981, Putting the Boot In 1985, Going to the Dogs 1987. *Honours:* Somerset Maugham Award 1981, Geoffrey Faber Memorial Prize 1985, E.M. Forster Award, US Acad. of Arts and Letters 1986, Gutenberg Prize 1987, Grinzane Cavour Prize, Italy 1988, Shakespeare Prize, Germany 1993; Officier, Ordre des Arts et des Lettres 1995. *Literary Agent:* PFD, Drury House, 34–43 Russell Street, London, WC2B 5HA, England. *Website:* www.julianbarnes.com.

BARNES, Richard John Black, FRGS, FRSA; British editor and writer; b. 13 Aug. 1950, Nyasaland, Malawi; m. Lucette Aylmer 1975; one s. one d. *Education:* Stonyhurst Coll., Royal Coll. of Agric., Polytechnic of Cen. London. *Career:* mem. Public Monuments and Sculpture Asscn. *Publications:* The Sun in the East 1983, Eye on the Hill: Horse Travels in Britain 1987, John Bell, Sculptor 1999, The Year of Public Sculpture – Norfolk 2001, The Obelisk – A Monumental Feature in Britain 2004. *Address:* c/o Frontier Publishing, Windetts Farm, Long Lane, Kirstead, Norwich, Norfolk, NR15 1EG, England. *E-mail:* frontier.pub@macunlimited.net.

BARNET, Max (see Aaron, Hugh)

BARNET, Miguel; Cuban writer; b. 28 Nov. 1950, Havana. *Career:* Pres. of Fernando Ortiz Foundation; mem. of Honor Council, Extraordinary Staff of Nuestra América of Anthrolopological Sciences Faculty, Autonomous Univ., Yucatan, Mexico. *Publications:* Cimarron 1966, Biography of a Runaway Slave 1970, Cancion de Rachel (trans. as Rachel's Song) 1979, Gallego 1981, La fuente viva 1983, Autógrafos cubanos 1989, Mapa del tiempo 1989, La vida real 1989, Oficio de ángel 1989, Con pies de gato 1993, Los orejas del conejo 1995, Reyes y sin coronas (trans. as Kings Without Crowns) 2001, Afro-Cuban Religions 2001. *Honours:* Medal of Colony City, Germany; Distinction for Nat. Culture, La Giraldillo de la Habana, Garcia Lorca Prize (Spain), Nat. Prize for

Literature 1994, Int. Book Fair Honour 2002. *Literary Agent:* c/o Curbstone Press, 321 Jackson Street, Willimantic, CT 06226-1738, USA. *E-mail:* info@curbstone.org. *Website:* www.curbstone.org.

BARNETT, Anthony Peter John, MA; British writer, poet, publisher and music historian; b. 10 Sept. 1941, London, England. *Education:* Univ. of Essex. *Career:* Editorial Dir Allardyce, Barnett, Publishers; Ed. Fable Bulletin: Violin Improvisation Studies 1993–2000, online 2000–. *Publications:* poetry: Blood Flow 1975, Fear and Misadventure 1977, The Resting Bell: Collected Poems 1987, Prose and Poetry: Carp and Rubato 1995, Anti-Beauty 1999, Miscanthus: Selected and New Poems 2005; prose: Lisa Lisa 2000; other: Desert Sands: The Recordings and Performances of Stuff Smith 1995, Black Gypsy: The Recordings of Eddie South 1999; contrib. to New Grove Dictionary of Music and Musicians, New Grove Dictionary of Jazz, anthologies, journals and periodicals. *Address:* c/o Allardyce, Barnett, Publishers, 14 Mount Street, Lewes, East Sussex BN7 1HL, England. *Website:* www.abar.net.

BARNETT, Correlli Douglas, CBE, MA; British historian; *Fellow, Churchill College, Cambridge;* b. 28 June 1927, Norbury, Surrey; s. of Douglas A. Barnett and Kathleen M. Barnett; m. Ruth Murby 1950; two d. *Education:* Trinity School, Croydon and Exeter Coll. Oxford. *Career:* Intelligence Corps 1945–48; North Thames Gas Bd 1952–57; public relations 1957–63; Keeper of Archives, Churchill Coll. Cambridge 1977–95; Defence Lecturer, Univ. of Cambridge 1980–83; Fellow, Churchill Coll., Cambridge 1977–; mem. Council, Royal United Services Inst. for Defence Studies 1973–85; mem. Cttee London Library 1977–79, 1982–84; Winston Churchill Memorial Lecturer, Switzerland 1982. *Television includes:* The Great War (BBC TV) 1964, The Lost Peace (BBC TV) 1966, The Commanders (BBC TV) 1972. *Publications:* The Hump Organisation 1957, The Channel Tunnel (with Humphrey Slater) 1958, The Desert Generals 1960, The Swordbearers 1963, Britain and Her Army 1970, The Collapse of British Power 1972, Marlborough 1974, Bonaparte 1978, The Great War 1979, The Audit of War 1986, Hitler's Generals 1989, Engage the Enemy More Closely 1991 (Yorkshire Post Book of the Year Award 1991), The Lost Victory: British Dreams, British Realities 1945–1950 1995, The Verdict of Peace: Britain Between Her Yesterday and the Future 2001. *Honours:* Hon. DSc (Cranfield Univ.) 1993; Hon. Fellow, City and Guilds of London Inst. 2003; Screenwriters' Guild Award for Best British TV Documentary (The Great War) 1964; FRSL Award for Britain and Her Army 1971; Chesney Gold Medal Royal United Services Inst. for Defence Studies 1991. *Address:* Catbridge House, East Carleton, Norwich, Norfolk, NR14 8JX, England (home). *Telephone:* (1508) 570410 (home). *Fax:* (1508) 570410 (home).

BARNETT, Paul le Page, (Dennis Brezhnev, Eve Devereux, Freddie Duff-Ware, John Grant, Armytage Ware); British writer and editor; b. 22 Nov. 1949, Aberdeen, Scotland; m. Catherine Stewart 1974; two d. *Career:* mem. West Country Writers' Asscn. *Publications:* as John Grant: Book of Time (with Colin Wilson), 1979; A Book of Numbers, 1982; The Depths of Cricket, 1986; Earthdoom (with David Langford), 1987; The Advanced Trivia Quizbook, 1987; Great Mysteries, 1988; Great Unsolved Mysteries of Science, 1989; Albion, 1991; Unexplained Mysteries of the World, 1991; The World, 1992; Monsters, 1992; The Hundredfold Problem, 1994; Encyclopedia of Fantasy Art Techniques (with Ron Tiner), 1996; Encyclopedia of Fantasy (ed. with John Clute), 1997; as Paul Barnett: Planet Earth: An Encyclopedia of Geology (ed. with A. Hallam and Peter Hutchinson); Phaidon Concise Encyclopedia of Science and Technology (contributing ed.), 1978; Strider's Galaxy, 1997; as Eve Devereux: Book of World Flags, 1992; Ultimate Card Trick Book, 1994; as Armytage Ware (joint pseudonym with Ron Tiner): Parlour Games, 1992; Conjuring Tricks, 1992; Juggling and Feats of Dexterity, 1992; Card Games, 1992; as Freddie Duff-Ware (joint pseudonym with Ron Tiner): Practical Jokes, 1993. *Address:* 17 Polsloe Road, Exeter, Devon EX1 2HL, England.

BARNHARDT, Wilton, BA, MPhil; American writer; b. 25 July 1960, Winston-Salem, NC. *Education:* Michigan State University, University of Oxford. *Publications:* Emma Who Saved My Life, 1989; Gospel, 1993; Show World, 1998. Contributions: magazines.

BARNSLEY, Victoria; British publisher; *CEO, HarperCollins UK;* b. 4 March 1954, d. of the late Thomas E. Barnsley and Margaret Gwyneth Barnsley (née Llewellin); m. Nicholas Howard 1992; one d. one step-s. *Education:* Loughborough High School, Beech Lawn Tutorial Coll., Edinburgh Univ., Univ. Coll. London, York Univ. *Career:* with Junction Books 1980–83; founder, Chair. and CEO Fourth Estate 1984–2000; CEO HarperCollins UK 2000–; Trustee Tate Gallery 1998–; Dir Tate Enterprises Ltd 1998–; council mem. Publishers Assscn 2001–. *Address:* HarperCollins, Ophelia House, 77–85 Fulham Palace Road, London, W6 8JB, England (office). *Telephone:* (20) 8741-7070 (office). *Fax:* (20) 8307-4440 (office). *E-mail:* contact@harpercollins.co.uk (office). *Website:* www.harpercollins.co.uk (office).

BARNSTONE, Willis, BA, MA, PhD; American poet, novelist and academic; b. 13 Nov. 1927, Lewiston, ME; two s. one d. *Education:* Bowdoin College, Columbia University, Yale University. *Career:* Asst Prof. of Romance Languages, Wesleyan University, 1959–62; Prof. of Comparative Literature, Spanish and Portuguese, Indiana University, 1966–; Visiting Prof., various universities, 1967–73; Senior Fulbright Prof., English Literature, Instituto Superior del Profesorado, Profesorado de Lenguas Vivas, Buenos Aires, 1975–76; Senior Fulbright Prof., English and American Literature, Peking Foreign Studies University, 1984–85; mem. PEN; Poetry Society of America. *Publications:* From This White Island, 1959; A Sky of Days, 1967; A Day in the Country, 1971; China Poems, 1976; Stickball on 88th Street, 1978; Overheard,

1979; Ten Gospels and a Nightingale, 1981; The Alphabet of Night, 1984; Five AM in Beijing, 1987; With Borges on an Ordinary Evening in Buenos Aires, 1992; ABC of Translating Poetry (illustrated), 1993; The Poetics of Translation, 1993; Funny Ways of Staying Alive: Poems and Ink Drawings, 1993; Sunday Morning in Fascist Spain: A European Memoir (1948–1953), 1995; The Secret Reader: 501 Sonnets, 1996; The Poems of Sappho: A New Translation, 1997; The Literatures of Asia, Africa and Latin America (co-ed. with Tony Barnstone), 1998; To Touch the Sky: Spiritual, Mystical and Philosophical Poems in Translation, 1999; Algebra of Night: New and Selected Poems, 1948–1998, 1998; The Apocalypse (Revelation): A New Translation with Introduction, 2000; The New Covenant: The Four Gospels and Apocalypse. Newly Translated from the Greek and Informed by Semitic Sources, 2002; Literatures of the Middle East (ed. with Tony Barnstone), 2002; Literatures of Latin America (ed.), 2002. *Honours:* Cecil Hemley Memorial Award, 1968, Lucille Medwick Memorial Awards, 1978, 1982, Gustav Davidson Memorial Awards, 1980, 1988, Emily Dickinson Award, 1985, Poetry Society of America; W. H. Auden Award, New York State Arts Council, 1986; National Poetry Competition Award, Chester H. Jones Foundation, 1988.

BARON, Carolyn, BA; American publishing executive, editor and author; *Senior President and Publisher, Dell Publishing Company;* b. 25 Jan. 1940, Detroit; d. of Gabriel Cohn and Viola Cohn; m. Richard W. Baron 1975. *Education:* Univ. of Mich. *Career:* Ed., Editorial Production Dir Holt, Rinehart & Winston, New York 1965–71; Man. Ed. E. P. Dutton Co. Inc., New York 1971–74, Exec. Ed. 1974–75; Admin. Ed. Pocket Books, Simon & Schuster, New York 1975–78, Vice-Pres., Ed.-in-Chief 1978–79; Vice-Pres., Ed.-in-Chief Crown Publs, New York 1979–81; Vice-Pres. Dell Publishing Co., New York 1981–86, Sr Pres., Publr 1986–; Sr Vice-Pres. Bantam, Doubleday, Dell 1989–. *Publications:* The History of Labor Unions in the US 1971, Re-entry Game 1974, Board Sailboats: A Buying Guide 1977; articles in magazines. *Address:* Dell Publishing Co. Inc., 1540 Broadway, New York, NY 10036, USA.

BARON, Martin, BA, MBA; American journalist; *Editor, The Boston Globe;* b. Tampa, FL. *Education:* Lehigh Univ. *Career:* state reporter, business writer The Miami Herald 1976–79; joined Los Angeles Times 1979, apptd Business Ed. 1983, Asst . Man. Ed. for 'Column One' 1991, Ed. Orange Co. Edn 1993; joined The New York Times 1996, Assoc. Man. Ed. responsible for night-time news operations 1997–99; Exec. Ed. The Miami Herald 1999–2002; Ed. The Boston Globe 2002–. *Honours:* ; Pulitzer Prize 2001, Ed. of the Year, Editor & Publisher Magazine 2002. *Address:* The Boston Globe, 135 Morrissey Boulevard, POB 2378, Boston, MA 02107-2378, USA (office). *Telephone:* (617) 929-2000 (office). *Fax:* (617) 929-3192 (office). *E-mail:* news@globe.com (office). *Website:* www.boston.com (office).

BARR, Patricia Miriam, BA, MA; British writer; b. 25 April 1934, Norwich, Norfolk, England. *Education:* Univ. of Birmingham, Univ. Coll. London. *Career:* mem. Soc. of Authors. *Publications:* The Coming of the Barbarians 1967, The Deer Cry Pavilion 1968, A Curious Life for a Lady 1970, To China with Love 1972, The Memsahibs 1976, Taming the Jungle 1978, Chinese Alice 1981, Uncut Jade 1983, Kenjiro 1985, Coromandel 1988, The Dust in the Balance 1989. *Honours:* Winston Churchill Fellowship for Historical Biography 1972. *Address:* 6 Mount Pleasant, Norwich, NR2 2DG, England.

BARRERA TYSZKA, Alberto; Venezuelan writer, journalist and screenwriter; b. 1960, Caracas. *Career:* columnist, El Nacional; writer of 'tele-novelas'. *Television series as writer:* Déjate querer 1993, Nada personal 1996, Enséñame a querer 1998, Demasiado corazón 1998, La calle de las novias 2000, Agua y aceite 2002, Un nuevo amor 2003. *Publications include:* Edición de lujo (short stories), También el corazón es un descuido (novel) 2001, La enfermedad (novel) (Premio Herralde, Spain) 2006, Hugo Chavez (biog., co-author) 2007; poetry: Amor que por demás, Edición de lujo, Coyote de ventanas, Tal vez el frío. *E-mail:* contactenos@el-nacional.com. *Website:* www .el-nacional.com.

BARRETT, Andrea, BS; American writer; b. 16 Nov. 1954, Boston, MA. *Education:* Union College, Schenectady, NY. *Publications:* Lucid Stars, 1988; Secret Harmonies, 1989; The Middle Kingdom, 1991; The Forms of Water, 1993; Ship Fever & Other Stories, 1996; The Voyage of the Narwhal, 1998; Servants of the Map, 2001. Contributions: anthologies and magazines. *Honours:* National Endowment for the Arts Fellowship in Fiction, 1992; Peden Prize, Missouri Review, 1995; Hon. Doctor of Letters, Union College, 1996; Southern Review Fiction Prize, 1996; National Book Award in Fiction, 1996; Pushcart Prize, 1997; Guggenheim Fellowship, 1997.

BARRETT, Charles Kingsley, DD, FBA; British academic (retd) and writer; b. 4 May 1917, Salford, Lancs.; s. of Rev. F. Barrett and Clara Barrett (née Seed); m. Margaret E. Heap 1944; one s. one d. *Education:* Shebbear Coll., Pembroke Coll. Cambridge and Wesley House, Cambridge. *Career:* Lecturer in Theology, Durham Univ. 1945–58, Prof. of Divinity 1958–82; Visiting Lecturer and Prof. in various European countries, USA, Canada, Australia and NZ; Pres. Studiorum Novi Testamenti Societas 1973–74; Hon. Fellow Pembroke Coll. Cambridge; mem. Royal Norwegian Soc. of Sciences and Letters 1991–. *Publications:* The Holy Spirit and the Gospel Tradition 1947, The Gospel according to St John 1955, The Epistle to the Romans 1957, From First Adam to Last 1962, Jesus and the Gospel Tradition 1967, The First Epistle to the Corinthians 1968, The Signs of an Apostle 1970, The Second Epistle to the Corinthians 1973, Essays on Paul 1982, Essays on John 1982, Freedom and Obligation 1985, Church, Ministry and Sacraments in the New

Testament 1985, Paul: An Introduction to his Thought 1994, The Acts of the Apostles, Vol. I 1994, Vol. II 1998, Jesus and the Word 1996, Jesus, Paul and John 1999, Acts: A Shorter Commentary 2002, On Paul: Aspects of his Life, Work and Influence in the Early Church 2003; several other books and many articles in learned journals and symposia. *Honours:* Dr hc (Hull, Aberdeen, Hamburg); Hon. mem. Soc. of Biblical Literature (USA); Burkitt Medal for Biblical Study 1966, Von Humboldt Forschungspreis 1988. *Address:* 22 Rosemount, Durham, DH1 5GA, England. *Telephone:* (191) 386-1340.

BARRETT, Susan Mary, MA; British writer; b. 24 June 1938, Plymouth, Cornwall, England; m. Peter Barrett 1960; one s. one d. *Education:* The Royal School, Bath, Bath Spa Univ. Coll. *Television play:* The Portrait (LWT) 1977. *Publications:* Louisa 1969, Moses 1970, The Circle Sarah Drew (with Peter Barrett) 1970, The Square Ben Drew (with Peter Barrett) 1970, Noah's Ark 1971, Private View 1972, Rubbish 1974, The Beacon 1981, Travels with a Wildlife Artist: Greek Landscape and Wildlife (with Peter Barrett) 1986, Stephen and Violet 1988, A Day in the Life of a Baby Deer: The Fawn's First Snowfall 1996, A Day in the Life of a Puppy, A Day in the Life of a Kitten (series with Peter Barrett) 1996, Making a Difference 2007. *Literary Agent:* c/o Toby Eady Associates Ltd, Third Floor, Orme Court, London, W2 4RL, England. *Telephone:* (20) 7792-0092. *Fax:* (20) 7792-0879. *E-mail:* toby@ tobyeady.demon.co.uk. *Website:* www.tobyeadyassociates.co.uk; www .susanbarrett.info.

BARRINGTON, Judith Mary, BA, MA; British poet, memoirist and critic; b. 7 July 1944, Brighton, England. *Career:* West Coast Ed., Motheroot Journal, 1985–93; Poet-in-the-Schools, Oregon, and Washington, 1986–2000; Dir, The Flight of the Mind Writing Workshops, 1984–2000; Pres., Soapstone Inc, a writing retreat; mem. National Writers Union; Poetry Society of America. *Publications:* Deviation, 1975; Why Children (co-author), 1980; Trying to Be an Honest Woman, 1985; History and Geography, 1989; An Intimate Wilderness (ed.), 1991; Writing the Memoir: From Truth to Art, 1997; Lifesaving: A Memoir, 2000; Horses and the Human Soul 2004. *Contributions:* anthologies, journals, and magazines. *Honours:* Fairlie Place Essay Prize, 1963; Jeanette Rankin Award for Feminist Journalism, 1983; Oregon Institute of Literary Arts Fellowships, 1989, 1992, 1999; Andres Berger Award in Creative Non-Fiction, 1996; Dulwich Festival Poetry Prize, 1996; Stuart H. Holbrook Award, Literary Arts Inc, 1997; Lambda Literary Award, 2001. *Address:* 622 SE 29th Avenue, Portland, OR 97214, USA. *Website:* www .judithbarrington.com.

BARROW, Jedediah (see Benson, Gerard John)

BARROW, Robin St Clair, MA, PhD, FRSC; British author and academic; *Professor of Education, Simon Fraser University;* b. 18 Nov. 1944, Oxford, England. *Education:* Univ. of Oxford, Inst. of Educ., London, Univ. of London. *Career:* Lecturer in Philosophy of Educ., Univ. of Leicester 1972–80, Personal Readership in Educ. 1980–82; Visiting Prof. of Philosophy of Educ., Univ. of Western Ontario, Canada 1977–78; Prof. of Educ., Simon Fraser Univ., Burnaby, BC 1982–, Dean of Educ. 1992–2003; mem. Philosophy of Educ. Soc. of GB (Vice-Chair. 1980–83), Northwestern Philosophy of Educ. Soc. of N America (Pres. 1984–85), Canadian Philosophy of Educ. Soc. (Pres. 1990–91). *Publications:* Athenian Democracy 1973, An Introduction to the Philosophy of Education 1974, Sparta 1975, Plato, Utilitarianism and Education 1975, Moral Philosophy for Education 1975, Greek and Roman Education 1976, Plato and Education 1976, Common Sense and the Curriculum 1976, Plato's Apology 1978, The Canadian Curriculum: A Personal View 1978, Radical Education 1978, Happiness 1979, The Philosophy of Schooling 1981, Injustice, Inequality and Ethics 1982, Language and Thought: Rethinking Language Across the Curriculum 1982, Giving Teaching Back to Teachers: A Critical Introduction to Curriculum Theory 1984, A Critical Dictionary of Educational Concepts: An Appraisal of Selected Ideas and Issues in Educational Theory and Practice 1986, Understanding Skills: Thinking, Feeling and Caring 1990, Utilitarianism: A Contemporary Statement 1991, Beyond Liberal Education (co-ed. with Patricia White) 1993, Language, Intelligence and Thought 1993, What Use is Educational Research? 2005; contribs to books and scholarly journals. *Address:* Faculty of Education, Simon Fraser University, Burnaby, BC V5A 1S6, Canada (office). *Website:* www.educ.sfu.ca (office).

BARRY, Edward William, BA; American publishing executive; b. 24 Nov. 1937, Stamford, Conn.; s. of Edward Barry and Elizabeth Cosgrove; m. Barbara H. Walker 1963; one s. one d. *Education:* Univ. of Conn. *Career:* Pres. The Free Press, New York 1972–82, Oxford Univ. Press Inc., New York 1982–2000; Sr Vice-Pres. Macmillan Publishing Co., New York 1973–82; mem. Exec. Council, Professional and Scholarly Publications 1993; mem. Advisory Bd Pace Univ. Grad. Program in Publishing 1990–; mem. Bd of Dirs Asscn of American Publrs 1995; Trustee Columbia Univ. Press 2000–. *Honours:* Hon. LittD (Univ. of Oxford) 2000. *Address:* 266 Old Poverty Road, Southbury, CT 06488-1769, USA (home). *Telephone:* (212) 251-0416 (office). *E-mail:* edwardbarry@cs.com (office).

BARRY, James P., BA; American writer and editor; b. 23 Oct. 1918, Alton, IL; m. Anne Elizabeth Jackson 1966. *Education:* Ohio State Univ. *Career:* Dir Ohioana Library Asscn 1977–88; Ed. Ohioana Quarterly 1977–88; mem. Ohioana Library Asscn. *Publications:* Georgian Bay: The Sixth Great Lake 1968), The Battle of Lake Erie 1970, Bloody Kansas 1972, The Noble Experiment 1972, The Fate of the Lakes 1972, The Louisiana Purchase 1973, Ships of the Great Lakes: 300 Years of Navigation 1973, Wrecks and Rescues of the Great Lakes 1981, Georgian Bay: An Illustrated History 1992, Old Forts

of the Great Lakes 1994, Hackercraft 2002, American Powerboats 2003. *Honours:* American Soc. of State and Local History Award 1974, Marine History Soc. of Detroit Great Lakes Historian of the Year 1995. *Address:* 353 Fairway Blvd, Columbus, OH 43213, USA.

BARRY, Sebastian, BA; Irish writer, dramatist and poet; b. 5 July 1955, Dublin. *Education:* Trinity Coll., Dublin. *Career:* writer-in-assćn and Dir of the Bd, Abbey Theatre, Dublin 1989–90; mem. Aosdána, Irish Writers' Union. *Publications:* Inherited Boundaries 1984, The Engine of Owl-Light 1987, Boss Grady's Boys (play) 1989, Fanny Hawke Goes to the Mainland Forever (verse) 1989, The Steward of Christendom 1997, Prayers of Sherkin 1997, White Woman Street 1997, The Only True History of Lizzie Finn 1997, Our Lady of Sligo 1998, The Whereabouts of Eneas McNulty 1998, The Water Colourist 1998, The Rhetorical Town: Poems 1999, Annie Dunne 2002, A Long, Long Way 2005; contrib. to periodicals. *Honours:* Arts Council Bursary 1982, Iowa Int. Writing Fellowship 1984, Hawthornden Int. Fellowships 1985, 1988, BBC/Stewart Parker Award 1989. *Literary Agent:* AP Watt Ltd, 20 John Street, London, WC1N 2DR, England.

BARSKY, Robert F., BA, MA, PhD; Canadian researcher, academic and writer; *Professor of Comparative Literature, English and French Literature, Vanderbilt University;* b. 18 May 1961, Montreal, QC; two s. *Education:* Vanier Coll., Brandeis Univ., McGill Univ., Free Univ., Brussels, Belgium. *Career:* content analysis researcher, Trans-Canada Social Policy Research Centre, Montreal 1985–91; ethnic studies and refugee studies researcher, Institut Québecois de Recherche sur la Culture, Montréal 1991–93; refugee studies researcher, Institut Nat. de la Recherche Scientifique, Montréal 1993–95; Assoc. Prof. of English, Univ. of Western Ontario, London 1995; currently Prof. of Comparative Literature, French and Italian Literature, Vanderbilt Univ., USA; Visiting Prof., IQRC/INRS 1991–96, Univ. of Western Ontario 1996, Université du Québec 2000–02; Visiting Fellow, Yale Univ. 2000, 2003, Canadian Bicentennial Prof. 2002; Founder-Ed. Ameri Quests; Founder and fmr Co-Ed. Discours social/Social Discourse: Discourse Analysis and Text Sociocriticism; Founder and fmr Ed. 415 South Street; Assoc. Ed. SubStance; mem. Scarlet Key 1992–. *Publications:* Bakhtin and Otherness 1991, Constructing a Productive Other: Discourse Theory and the Convention Refugee Hearing 1994, Introduction à la théorie littéraire 1997, Noam Chomsky: A Life of Dissent 1997, Arguing and Justifying 2000, Philosophy and the Passions (trans.) 2000, French Theory Today (co-ed. with Eric Méchoulan) 2002, Workers' Councils, by Anton Pannekoek (ed.) 2003, Marc Angenot and the Scandal of History (ed.) 2004, The Chomsky Effect 2007; contrib. to periodicals. *Honours:* Chancellor Heard Professor of the Year, Vanderbilt Univ. 2005. *Address:* Department of French and Italian, Program in Comparative Literature, Furman Hall, Vanderbilt University, PO Box 6312 Station B, Nashville, TN 37235-0001, USA (office). *Telephone:* (615) 322-2652 (office). *Fax:* (615) 343-6909 (office). *E-mail:* robert.barsky@vanderbilt.edu (office). *Website:* www.vanderbilt.edu/french_ital/barsky (office); www .ameriquests.org (home).

BARSTOW, Stanley (Stan), FRSL; British writer, playwright and script-writer; b. 28 June 1928, Horbury, Yorkshire, England; m. Constance Mary Kershaw 1951; one s. one d. *Publications:* Fiction: A Kind of Loving, 1960; Ask Me Tomorrow, 1962; Joby, 1964; The Watchers on the Shore, 1966; A Raging Calm, 1968; The Right True End, 1976; A Brother's Tale, 1980; Just You Wait and See, 1986; B-Movie, 1987; Give Us This Day, 1989; Next of Kin, 1991. Short Stories: The Desperados, 1961; A Season with Eros, 1971; The Glad Eye and Other Stories, 1984. Plays: Listen for the Trains, Love, 1970; Stringer's Last Stand (with Alfred Bradley), 1971. Non-Fiction: In My Own Time (autobiog.), 2001. Other: Television plays and scripts. *Honours:* Best British Dramatization Award, Writers Guild of Great Britain, 1974; Best Drama Series Award, British Broadcasting Press Guild, 1974; Writer's Award, RTS, 1975; Hon. MA, Open University, 1982; Hon. Fellow, Bretton College, 1985. *Literary Agent:* The Agency, 24 Pottery Lane, Holland Park, London W11 4LZ, England.

BARTH, John Simmons, MA; American novelist and academic; *Professor Emeritus in the Writing Seminars, Johns Hopkins University;* b. 27 May 1930, Cambridge, Md; s. of John J. Barth and Georgia Simmons; m. 1st Harriette Anne Strickland 1950 (divorced 1969); two s. one d.; m. 2nd Shelly Rosenberg 1970. *Education:* Johns Hopkins Univ. *Career:* Instructor Pennsylvania State Univ. 1953, Assoc. Prof. until 1965; Prof. of English, State Univ. of New York at Buffalo 1965–73, Johns Hopkins Univ. 1973–91, Prof. Emer. 1991–; Rockefeller Foundation Grant; Brandeis Univ. Citation in Literature. *Publications:* The Floating Opera 1956, The End of the Road 1958, The Sot-Weed Factor 1960, Giles Goat-Boy 1966, Lost in the Funhouse (stories) 1968, Chimera 1972, Letters 1979, Sabbatical 1982, The Friday Book (essays) 1984, The Tidewater Tales: A Novel 1987, The Last Voyage of Somebody the Sailor 1991, Once Upon a Time 1994, On With the Story (stories) 1996, Coming Soon!!! (novel) 2001, The Book of Ten Nights and a Night (stories) 2004. *Honours:* Hon. LittD (Univ. of Maryland); Hon. DHL (Pennsylvania State Univ.) 1996; Nat. Acad. of Arts and Letters Award, Nat. Book Award 1973, F. Scott Fitzgerald Award 1997, President's Medal, Johns Hopkins Univ. 1997, PEN/Malamud Award 1998, Lifetime Achievement Award, Lannan Foundation 1998, Lifetime Achievement in Letters Award, Enoch Pratt Soc. 1999. *Address:* The Writing Seminars, 135 Gilman Hall, Johns Hopkins University, 3400 North Charles Street, Baltimore, MD 21218, USA. *Telephone:* (410) 16-7563. *Website:* www.jhu.edu/writsem

BARTH, (John) Robert, AB, PhL, MA, STB, STL, PhD; American academic and writer; *James P. McIntyre Professor of English Boston College*; b. 23 Feb. 1931, Buffalo, NY. *Education:* Bellarmine Coll., Fordham Univ., Woodstock Coll., Harvard Univ. *Career:* Society of Jesus; Asst Prof. of English, Canisius Coll., Buffalo 1967–70; Asst Prof. of English, Harvard Univ. 1970–74; Assoc. Prof. of English 1974–77, Prof. of English 1977–88, Chair Dept of English 1980–83, Univ. of Missouri-Columbia; Thomas I. Gasson Prof. of English 1985–86, Dean Coll. of Arts and Sciences 1988–99, James P. McIntyre Prof. of English 1999–, Boston Coll.; mem. American Asscn of Univ. Profs, Conference on Christianity and Literature, Friends of Coleridge, Keats-Shelley Asscn, MLA, Words-worth-Coleridge Asscn (pres. 1979). *Publications:* Coleridge and Christian Doctrine 1969, Religious Perspectives in Faulkner's Fiction: Yoknapatawpha and Beyond (ed.) 1972, The Symbolic Imagination: Coleridge and the Romantic Tradition 1977, Marginalia: The Collected Works of Samuel Taylor Coleridge (ed. with George Whalley) 1984–, Coleridge and the Power of Love 1988, Coleridge, Keats and the Imagination: Romanticism and Adam's Dream-Essays in Honor of Walter Jackson Bate (ed. with John L. Mahoney) 1990, The Fountain Light: Studies in Romanticism and Religion (ed.) 2002, Romanticism and Transcendence: Wordsworth, Coleridge, and the Religious Imagination 2003; contrib. to books and journals. *Honours:* Conference on Christianity and Literature Book of the Year Award 1977, Univ. of Missouri Curators' Annual Book Award 1988. *Address:* c/o Department of English, Boston College, 24 Quincy Road, Chestnut Hill, MA 02467, USA.

BARTLETT, Christopher John, BA, PhD, FRHistS, FRSE; British writer; b. 12 Oct. 1931, Bournemouth, England; m. Shirley Maureen Briggs 1958, three s. *Education:* University College, Exeter and LSE. *Career:* Asst Lecturer, University of Edinburgh, 1957–59; Lecturer in Modern History, University of the West Indies, Jamaica, 1959–62; Queen's College, Dundee, 1962–68; Reader in International History, 1968–78, Prof. of International History, 1978–96, Head, Dept of History, 1983–88, Emeritus and Hon. Prof. of International History, 1996–2002, University of Dundee. *Publications:* Great Britain and Sea Power, 1815–53, 1963; Castlereagh, 1966; Britain Pre-eminent: Studies of British World Influence in the Nineteenth Century (ed.), 1969; The Long Retreat: A Short History of British Defence Policy, 1945–70, 1972; The Rise and Fall of the Pax Americana: American Foreign Policy in the Twentieth Century, 1974; A History of Postwar Britain, 1945–74, 1977; The Global Conflict, 1880–1990: The International Rivalry of the Great Powers, 1984; British Foreign Policy in the Twentieth Century, 1989; 'The Special Relationship': A Political History or Anglo-American Relations Since 1945, 1992; Defence and Diplomacy: Britain and the Great Powers, 1815–1914, 1993; Peace, War and the European Great Powers, 1814–1914, 1996. Contributions: UK Chapters, Annual Register, 1987–97; scholarly books and journals.

BARTLETT, Robert John, BA, MA, DPhil, FRHistS, FBA, FRSE, FSA; British academic, writer and editor; *Bishop Wardlaw Professor, University of St Andrews*; b. 27 Nov. 1950, London, England; m. Honora Elaine Hickey 1979; one s. one d. *Education:* Peterhouse, Cambridge, St John's Coll. Oxford. *Career:* Lecturer in History Univ. of Edinburgh 1980–86; mem. Inst. for Advanced Study, Princeton, NJ, and Visiting Fellow, Davis Center, Dept of History, Princeton Univ. 1983–84; Prof. of Medieval History Univ. of Chicago 1986–92; Prof. of Mediaeval History 1992–, Bishop Wardlaw Prof. 1997–, Univ. of St Andrews; Assoc. Ed. New Dictionary of National Biography 1994–; British Acad. Reader 1995–97; Sackler Scholar Mortimer and Raymond Sackler Inst. of Advanced Studies, Univ. of Tel-Aviv 2001. *Publications:* Gerald of Wales 1146–1223 1982, Trial by Fire and Water, The Medieval Judicial Ordeal 1986, Medieval Frontier Societies (ed. with Angus MacKay) 1989, The Making of Europe: Conquest, Colonization and Cultural Change 950–1350 1993, England Under the Norman and Angevin Kings 1075–1225 2000, Medieval Panorama (ed.) 2001, Life and Miracles of St Modwenna, by Geoffrey of Burton (ed. and trans.) 2002, The Miracles of St Aebbe of Coldingham and St Margaret of Scotland (ed. and trans.) 2003, The Hanged Man: A Story of Miracle, Memory and Colonialism in the Middle Ages 2004 contrib. to scholarly books and journals. *Honours:* Jr Fellow Univ. of Michigan Soc. of Fellows 1979–80, Alexander von Humboldt Fellow Univ. of Göttingen 1988–89, Wolfson Literary Prize for History 1993. *Address:* c/o Department of Mediaeval History, University of St Andrews, St Andrews, KY16 9AL, Scotland.

BARTON, Rev. John, MA, DPhil, DLitt; British academic; *Oriel and Laing Professor of the Interpretation of Holy Scripture, Oriel College, University of Oxford*; b. 17 June 1948, London; s. of Bernard A. Barton and Gwendolyn H. Barton; m. Mary Burn 1973; one d. *Education:* Latymer Upper School, London and Keble Coll. Oxford. *Career:* Jr Research Fellow, Merton Coll. Oxford 1973–74; Univ. Lecturer in Theology, Univ. of Oxford 1974–89, Reader in Biblical Studies 1989–91; Fellow, St Cross Coll. Oxford 1974–91; Oriel and Laing Prof. of the Interpretation of Holy Scripture and Fellow Oriel Coll. Oxford 1991–; Canon Theologian of Winchester Cathedral 1991–2003. *Publications:* Amos's Oracles Against the Nations 1980, Reading the Old Testament 1984, Oracles of God 1986, People of the Book? 1988, Love Unknown 1990, What is the Bible? 1991, Isaiah 1–39 1995, The Spirit and the Letter 1997, Making the Christian Bible 1997, Ethics and the Old Testament 1998, The Cambridge Companion to Biblical Interpretation 1998, Oxford Bible Commentary 2001, Joel and Obadiah 2001, The Biblical World 2003, Understanding Old Testament Ethics 2003, The Original Story (with J. Bowden) 2004, Living Belief 2005. *Honours:* Hon. DrTheol (Bonn) 1998.

Address: Oriel College, Oxford, OX1 4EW, England. *Telephone:* (1865) 276537. *E-mail:* john.barton@oriel.ox.ac.uk.

BARTOS-HÖPPNER, Barbara; German writer; b. 4 Nov. 1923, Eckersdorf, Kreis Bunzlau/Schleswig. *Career:* freelance writer of novels and children's books 1956–; Bundesverdienstkreuz. *Publications include:* Kosaken gegen Kutschum-Kahn 1959, Sturm über den Kaukasus 1963, Aljoscha und die Bärenmütze 1968, Schnüpperle (eight vols) 1969–91, Ein Ticket nach Moskau 1970, Auf dem Rücken der Pferde 1975, Tiermärchen, Wintermärchen 1977, Silvermoon (three vols) 1977, 1979, 1981, Das große Bartos-Höppner-Buch 1981, Elbsaga 1985, Das Osterbuch 1987, Norddeutsche Feste und Bräuche 1987, Kommst du mit, Kolja? 1989, Von Aachener Printen bei Zürcher Leckerli 1989, Kinderreime 1990, Muz, kleiner Muz 1990, Zaubertopf und Zauberkugel 1991, Maria 1991, Rebekka 1991, Rübezahl 1992, Die Schuld der Grete Minde 1993, Vom Himmel hoch 1999, Osterfest und Frühlingszeit 2000. *Honours:* First Prize New York Herald Tribune 1963, Hans Christian Andersen Prize 1968, European Children's Book Prize 1976, Großer Preis, Deutsche Akad. für Kinder- und Jugendliteratur 1982.

BARZUN, Jacques Martin, AB, PhD, FRSA, FRSL; American writer and academic; *Professor Emeritus, Columbia University*; b. 30 Nov. 1907, Créteil, France; s. of Henri Martin and Anna-Rose Barzun; m. 1st Mariana Lowell 1936 (died 1979); two s. one d.; m. 2nd Marguerite Lee Davenport 1980. *Education:* Lycée Janson de Sailly and Columbia Univ. *Career:* Instructor in History, Columbia Univ. 1929, Asst Prof. 1938, Assoc. Prof. 1942, Prof. 1945, Dean of Graduate Faculties 1955–58, Dean of Faculties and Provost 1958–67, Seth Low Prof. 1960–67, Univ. Prof. 1967–75; Prof. Emer. 1975–; Literary Adviser, Scribner's 1975–93; fmr Dir Council for Basic Educ., New York Soc. Library, Open Court Publications Inc., Peabody Inst.; mem. Advisory Council, Univ. Coll. at Buckingham, Editorial Bd Encyclopedia Britannica 1979–; mem. Acad. Delphinale (Grenoble), American Acad. of Arts and Letters (Pres. 1972–75, 1977–78), American Historical Asscn, Royal Soc. of Arts, American Arbitration Asscn, American Philosophical Soc., Royal Soc. of Literature, American Acad. of Arts and Sciences; Extraordinary Fellow, Churchill Coll., Cambridge 1961. *Publications:* The French Race: Theories of its Origins and their Social and Political Implications Prior to the Revolution 1932, Race: A Study in Modern Superstition 1937, Of Human Freedom 1939, Darwin, Marx, Wagner: Critique of a Heritage 1941, Romanticism and the Modern Ego (revised edn as Classic, Romantic, and Modern) 1943, Introduction to Naval History (with Paul H. Beik, George Crothers and E. O. Golob) 1944, Teacher in America 1945, Berlioz and the Romantic Century 1950, God's Country and Mine: A Declaration of Love Spiced with a Few Harsh Words 1954, Music in American Life 1956, The Energies of Art: Studies of Authors, Classic and Modern 1956, The Modern Researcher (with Henry F. Graff) 1957, Lincoln the Literary Genius 1959, The House of Intellect 1959, Science, the Glorious Entertainment 1964, The American University: How it Runs, Where it is Going 1968, On Writing, Editing and Publishing: Essays Explicative and Horatory 1971, A Catalogue of Crime (with Wendell Hertig Taylor) 1971, The Use and Abuse of Art 1974, Clio and the Doctors: Psycho-History, Quanto-History and History 1974, Simple and Direct: A Rhetoric for Writers 1975, Critical Questions 1982, A Stroll with William James 1983, A Word or Two Before You Go 1986, The Culture We Deserve 1989, Begin Here: On Teaching and Learning 1990, An Essay on French Verse for Readers of English Poetry 1991, From Dawn to Decadence: 500 Years of Western Cultural Life 2000, A Jacques Barzun Reader 2001; editor: Pleasures of Music 1950, The Selected Letters of Lord Byron 1953, New Letters of Berlioz (also trans.) 1954, The Selected Writings of John Jay Chapman 1957, Modern American Usage; translator: Diderot: Rameau's Nephew 1952, Flaubert's Dictionary of Accepted Ideas 1954, Evenings with the Orchestra 1956, Courteline: A Rule is a Rule 1960, Beaumarchais: The Marriage of Figaro 1961; contrib. of articles to various scholarly and non-scholarly periodicals and journals. *Honours:* Chevalier de la Légion d'honneur, Presidential Medal of Freedom 2004; Gold Medal for Criticism, American Acad. of Arts and Letters. *Address:* 18 Wolfeton Way, San Antonio, TX 78218, USA.

BASARA, Svetislav; Serbian writer and diplomatist; b. 1953. *Career:* currently Amb. to Cyprus. *Publications:* Bumerang, Dzon B. Malkovic, Fama o biciklistima (novel) 1988, Kinesko pismo (novel, trans. as Chinese Letters) 1984, Kratkodnevica, Looney Tunes, Mongolski bedeker, Na gralovom tragu, Najlepse price, Napuklo ogledalo, Peking by Night, Srce zemlje, Sveta mast, Ukleta zemlja. *Address:* Embassy of Serbia, 2 Vasilissis Olgas Street, Engomi, 1101 Nicosia, Cyprus. *Telephone:* 22777511. *Fax:* 22775910. *E-mail:* nicosia@scg.org.cy. *Website:* www.scg.org.cy.

BASINGER, Jeanine Deyling, BS, MS; American academic, curator and writer; *Corwin-Fuller Professor of Film Studies, Wesleyan University*; b. 3 Feb. 1936, Ravenden, AR; m. John Peter Basinger 1967, one d. *Education:* South Dakota State University. *Career:* Instructor, South Dakota State University, 1958–59; Teaching Assoc., 1971–72, Adjunct Lecturer, 1972–76, Adjunct Assoc. Prof., 1976–80, Assoc. Prof., 1980–84, Prof., 1984–88, Corwin-Fuller Prof. of Film Studies, 1988–, Wesleyan University; Founder-Curator, Wesleyan Cinema Archives, 1985–; mem. American Film Institute, trustee. *Publications:* Working with Kazan (ed. with John Frazer and Joseph W. Reed), 1973; Shirley Temple, 1975; Gene Kelly, 1976; Lana Turner, 1977; Anthony Mann: A Critical Analysis, 1979; Anatomy of a Genre: World War II Combat Films, 1986; The It's A Wonderful Life Book, 1986; A Woman's View: How Hollywood Saw Women, 1930–1960, 1993; American Cinema: 100 Years of Filmmaking, 1994; Silent Stars, 1999. Contributions: Books and periodicals. *Honours:* Distinguished Alumni Award, 1994 and Hon. PhD, 1996, South Dakota State University; Outstanding Teaching Award, Wesleyan University, 1996; William K. Everson Award, Best Film Book of the Year. *Address:* 133 Lincoln Street, Middletown, CT 06457, USA.

BASS, Cynthia, BA, MA; American writer; b. 17 Oct. 1949, Washington, DC; m. Steven Seltzer. *Education:* University of California at Berkeley. *Publications:* Sherman's March, 1994; Maiden Voyage, 1996. Contributions: periodicals.

BASS, Rick, BS; American writer; b. 7 March 1958, Fort Worth, TX. *Education:* Utah State University. *Publications:* The Deer Pasture, 1985; Wild to the Heart, 1987; Oil Notes, 1989; The Watch: Stories, 1989; Platte River, 1994; The Lost Grizzlies, 1995; In the Loyal Mountains: Stories, 1995; The Book of YAAK, 1996; Where the Sea Used to Be, 1998; Fiber, 1998; The New Wolves, 1998; Brown Dog of the YAAK, 1999; Colter, 2000; The Hermit's Story (short stories), 2002, The Diezmo: A Novel, 2005; The Lives of Rocks (short stories), 2006. Contributions: anthologies and periodicals. *Honours:* Pushcart Prize; O. Henry Award; PEN-Nelson Award, 1988. *Address:* Rt 1, Troy, MT 59935, USA.

BASS, Thomas Alden, AB, PhD; American writer; b. 9 March 1951, Chagrin Falls, OH. *Education:* Univ. of California. *Career:* mem. Authors' Guild, PEN. *Publications:* The Eudaemonic Pie (The Newtonian Casino) 1985, Camping with the Prince and Other Tales of Science in Africa 1990, Reinventing the Future: Conversations with the World's Leading Scientists 1993, Vietnamerica: The War Comes Home 1996, The Predictors 1999; contribs to Audubon, New York Times, New Yorker, Smithsonian, Wired. *Address:* 31 rue Saint Placide, Paris 75006, France. *E-mail:* tbass@hamilton.edu (office).

BASTABLE, Bernard (see Barnard, Robert)

BAT-SHAHAR, Hannah, BA; Israeli writer; b. 1944, Jerusalem. *Education:* Hebrew Univ. *Publications:* Sipurei Ha-Kos (short stories) 1987, Likroh La-Atalefim (short stories) 1990, Among the Geranium Pots (short story, in trans.) 1990, Rikud Ha-Parpar (short stories) 1993, Sham Sirot Ha-Dayig (three novellas) 1997, Yonkey Ha-Devash Ha-Metukim (short stories) 1999, Ha-Naara Mi-Agam Mishigan (novel) 2002, Nimfa Levana, Seira Meshugaat (novel) 2005. *Address:* c/o The Institute for the Translation of Hebrew Literature, POB 1005 1, Ramat Gan 52001, Israel (office). *E-mail:* hamachon@inter.net.il. *Website:* www.ithl.org.il.

BATCHELOR, John Barham, MA, PhD; British academic, writer and editor; b. 15 March 1942, Farnborough, England; m. Henrietta Jane Letts 1968; two s. one d. *Education:* Magdalene College, Cambridge, Univ. of New Brunswick. *Career:* Lecturer in English, Birmingham Univ., 1968–76; Fellow and Tutor, New College, Oxford, 1976–90; Joseph Cowen Prof. of English Literature, Univ. of Newcastle upon Tyne, 1990; Hon. Prof. (in asscn with Ruskin Programme), Univ. of Lancaster 2002–; mem. International Asscn of Profs of English; Founding Fellow, English Asscn (UK); Ed. Modern Language Review, Yearbook of English Studies. *Publications:* Mervyn Peake 1974, Breathless Hush (novel) 1974, The Edwardian Novelists 1982, H. G. Wells 1985, Virginia Woolf 1991, The Life of Joseph Conrad: A Critical Biography 1994, The Art of Literary Biography (ed.) 1995, Shakespearean Continuities (joint ed.) 1997, John Ruskin: No Wealth But Life 2000, Lady Trevelyan and the Pre-Raphaelite Brotherhood 2006; contrib. to TLS, Observer, Daily Telegraph, Economist, Articles in English, Yearbook of English Studies, Review of English Studies, Dictionary of National Biography. *Address:* c/o Department of English, University of Newcastle, Newcastle upon Tyne, NE1 7RU, England.

BATE, (Andrew) Jonathan, CBE, PhD, FBA, FRSL; British academic; *Professor of Shakespeare and Renaissance Literature, University of Warwick*; b. 26 June 1958, Sevenoaks, Kent, England; s. of Ronald Montagu Bate and Sylvia Helen Bate; m. 1st Hilary Gaskin 1984 (divorced 1995); m. 2nd Paula Jayne Byrne 1996; one s. one d. *Education:* St Catharine's Coll., Cambridge. *Career:* Harkness Fellow, Harvard Univ. 1980–81; Research Fellow, St Catherine's Coll., Cambridge 1983–85, Hon. Fellow 2000–; Fellow, Trinity Hall, Cambridge, Lecturer 1985–90; King Alfred Prof. of English Literature, Univ. of Liverpool 1991–2003; Prof. of Shakespeare and Renaissance Literature, Univ. of Warwick 2003–; Research Reader, British Acad. 1994–96; Leverhulme Personal Research Prof. 1999–2004; Gov. Bd RSC, Ed. Shakespeare Edition. *Radio:* features and reviews for BBC Radio 3 and Radio 4. *Television:* South Bank Show and other arts programmes. *Publications:* Shakespeare and the English Romantic Imagination 1986, Charles Lamb: Essays of Elia (ed.) 1987, Shakespearean Constitutions: Politics, Theatre, Criticism 1730–1830 1989, Romantic Ecology: Wordsworth and the Environmental Tradition 1991, The Romantics on Shakespeare (ed.) 1992, Shakespeare and Ovid 1993, The Arden Shakespeare: Titus Andronicus (ed.) 1995, Shakespeare: An Illustrated Stage History (ed.) 1996, The Genius of Shakespeare 1997, The Cure for Love (novel) 1998, The Song of the Earth 2000, John Clare: A Biography (Hawthornden Prize 2003, James Tait Black Memorial Prize 2004) 2003, I Am: The Selected Poetry of John Clare (ed.) 2003, Andrew Marvell: Complete Poems (ed.) 2005, William Shakespeare: Complete Works (ed.) 2007. *Honours:* Hon. Fellow, St Catherine's Coll., Cambridge; Calvin & Rose Hoffman Prize 1996, NAMI NY Book Award 2003. *Literary Agent:* Wylie Agency Ltd, 17 Bedford Square, London, WC1B 3JA. *Address:* Department of English, Room H513, University of Warwick, Coventry, CV4 7AL, England (office). *E-mail:* j.bate@warwick.ac.uk (office). *Website:* www2.warwick.ac.uk/fac/arts/english (office).

BATES, Harry (see Home, Stewart Ramsay)

BATES, Milton James, BA, MA, PhD; American academic and writer; *Professor of English, Marquette University*; b. 4 June 1945, Warrensburg, Mo.; m. 1972; one s. one d. *Education:* St Louis Univ., Univ. of California, Berkeley. *Career:* Asst Prof. of English, Williams Coll. 1975–81; Asst Prof., Marquette Univ. 1981–86, Assoc. Prof. 1986–91, Prof. of English 1991–; Fulbright Distinguished Lecturer, Beijing Foreign Studies Univ. 2000, Universidad Complutense de Madrid 2006; mem. Wallace Stevens Soc. (Sec. 1990–). *Publications:* Wallace Stevens: A Mythology of Self 1985, Sur Plusieurs Beaux Sujects: Wallace Stevens' Commonplace Book 1989, Wallace Stevens: Opus Posthumous (revised edn) 1989, The Wars We Took to Vietnam: Cultural Conflict and Storytelling 1996; contrib. articles and book reviews in journals and periodicals. *Honours:* New York Times Book Review Notable Book of the Year 1985, Wisconsin Library Asscn Outstanding Achievement in Literature 1985, Guggenheim Fellowship 1989–90, Nat. Jesuit Book Award 1999, Council for Wisconsin Writers Scholarly Book Award 1996. *Address:* Department of English, Marquette University, PO Box 1881, Milwaukee, WI 53201, USA (office).

BATTESTIN, Martin Carey, PhD; American academic and writer; *William R. Kenan, Jr Professor Emeritus of English, University of Virginia*; b. 25 March 1930, New York, NY; m. Ruthe Rootes 1963; one s. (died 1999) one d. *Education:* Princeton Univ. *Career:* instructor, Wesleyan Univ. 1956–58, Asst Prof. 1958–61; Asst Prof., Univ. of Virginia 1961–63, Assoc. Prof. 1963–67, Prof. 1967–75, William R. Kenan, Jr Prof. of English 1975–98, Chair. Dept of English 1983–86, William R. Kenan, Jr Prof. Emer. of English 1998–; Visiting Prof., Rice Univ. 1967–68; Assoc., Clare Hall, Cambridge 1972; mem. Asscn of Literary Scholars and Critics, American Soc. for 18th Century Studies, Int. Asscn of Univ. Profs of English, The Johnsonians, Modern Language Association. *Publications:* The Moral Basis of Fielding's Art: A Study of 'Joseph Andrews' 1959, The Providence of Wit: Aspects of Form in Augustan Literature and the Arts 1974, New Essays by Henry Fielding: His Contributions to 'The Craftsman' (1734–39) and Other Early Journalism 1989, Henry Fielding: A Life (with Ruthe R. Battestin) 1993, A Henry Fielding Companion 2000, Henry Fielding: 'Joseph Andrews' and 'Shamela' (ed.) 1961, Henry Fielding: The History of the Adventures of Joseph Andrews (ed.) 1967, Tom Jones: A Collection of Critical Essays (ed.) 1968, Henry Fielding: The History of Tom Jones, a Foundling (co-ed. with Fredson Bowers) (two vols) 1974, Henry Fielding: Amelia (ed.) 1983, British Novelists, 1660–1800 (ed.) 1985, The Works of Tobias Smollett (ed., mem. editorial bd, Georgia edn) 1987–, The Correspondence of Henry and Sarah Fielding (co-ed. with Clive T. Probyn) 1993, Smollett's trans. of Cervantes' Don Quixote (co-ed. with O. M. Brack) 2003; contribs to books and scholarly journals. *Honours:* American Council of Learned Socs Fellowships 1960–61, 1972, Guggenheim Fellowship 1964–65, Council of the Humanities Sr Fellow, Princeton Univ. 1971, Center for Advanced Studies, Univ. of Virginia 1974–75, Nat. Endowment for the Humanities Bicentennial Research Fellow 1975–76, Festschrift 1997, Visiting Fellow, Lincoln Coll., Oxford 1999. *Address:* 1832 Westview Road, Charlottesville, VA 22903, USA (home). *E-mail:* mcb9g@virginia.edu.

BATTIN, B. W., (S. W. Bradford, Alexander Brinton, Warner Lee, Casey McAllister), BA; American writer; b. 15 Nov. 1941, Ridgewood, NJ; m. Sandra McCraw 1976. *Education:* University of New Mexico. *Publications:* as B. W. Battin: Angel of the Night, 1983; The Boogeyman, 1984; Satan's Servant, 1984; Mary, Mary, 1985; Programmed for Terror, 1985; The Attraction, 1985; The Creep, 1987; Smithereens, 1987; Demented 1988; as Warner Lee: Into the Pit, 1989; It's Loose, 1990; Night Sounds, 1992; as S. W. Bradford: Tender Prey, 1990; Fair Game, 1992; as Alexander Brinton: Serial Blood, 1992; as Casey McAllister: Catch Me if You Can, 1993. *Address:* 711 N Mesa Road, Belen, NM 87002, USA.

BATTLES, R(oxy) E(dith) B(aker), AA, BA, MA; American writer, poet, children's author and teacher; b. 23 March 1921, Spokane, WA; m. Willis Ralph Battles 1941; one s. two d. *Education:* Bakersfield Junior Coll., California State Univ., Pepperdine Univ. *Career:* elementary teacher, Torrance Unified Schools 1959–85; instructor, Torrance Adult School 1968–88, Pepperdine Univ. 1976–79; author-in-residence, American School of Madrid, Spain 1991; instructor in creative writing, Los Angeles Harbor Coll. 1995; mem. Southwest Manuscripters. *Play:* The Lavender Castle 1996, The Sacred Submarine 1996. *Publications:* Over the Rickety Fence 1967, The Terrible Trick or Treat 1970, 501 Balloons Sail East 1971, The Terrible Terrier 1972, One to Teeter Totter 1973, Eddie Couldn't Find the Elephants 1974, What Does the Rooster Say, Yoshio? 1978, The Secret of Castle Drai 1980, The Witch in Room 6 1987, The Chemistry of Whispering Caves 1989, Barking for Rebellion (monologue) 2001; contrib. to numerous periodicals. *Honours:* National Science Award 1971, United Nations Award 1978. *Address:* 560 S Helberta Avenue, Redondo Beach, CA 90277, USA (home). *Telephone:* (310) 540-2331 (home). *E-mail:* groxy@aol.com (home).

BAUER, Caroline Feller, BA, MLS, PhD; American author and lecturer; b. 12 May 1935, Washington, DC; m. 1969, one d. *Education:* Sarah Lawrence College, Columbia University, University of Oregon. *Career:* mem. American Library Asscn; Society of Children's Book Writers. *Publications:* My Mom Travels a Lot, 1981; This Way to Books, 1983; Too Many Books, 1984; Celebrations, 1985; Rainy Day, 1986; Snowy Day, 1986; Midnight Snowman,

1987; Presenting Reader's Theater, 1987; Windy Day, 1988; Halloween, 1989; Read for the Fun of It, 1992; New Handbook for Storytellers, 1993; Putting on a Play, 1993; Valentine's Day, 1993; Thanksgiving Day, 1994; The Poetry Break, 1995; Leading Kids to Books Through Magic, 1996. *Honours:* ERSTED Award for Distinguished Teaching; Christopher Award; Dorothy McKenzie Award for Distinguished Contribution to Children's Literature.

BAUER, Douglas; American writer; b. 17 Aug. 1945, Cheyenne, WY. *Publications:* Prairie City, IA: Three Seasons at Home, 1979; Dexterity, 1989; The Very Air, 1993; The Book of Famous Iowans, 1997; The Stuff of Fiction: Advice on Craft. *Honours:* National Endowment for the Arts Fellowship; Massachusetts Artists Foundation Fellowship; Boston Public Library Literary Light.

BAUER, Steven Albert, BA, MFA; American academic, writer and poet; *Professor of English, Miami University, Oxford*; b. 10 Sept. 1948, Newark, NJ; m. Elizabeth Arthur 1982. *Education:* Trinity Coll., Hartford, CT, Univ. of Massachusetts, Amherst. *Career:* Instructor 1979–81, Asst Prof. 1981–82, Colby Coll., Waterville, ME; Asst Prof. 1982–86, Assoc. Prof. 1986–96, Prof. 1996–, of English, Dir of Creative Writing 1986–96, Internal Dir of Creative Writing 1996–2001, Miami Univ., Oxford, OH; Writing Fellowship Five Arts Work Center, Provincetown 1978–79; Allan Collins Fellowship in Prose, Bread Loaf Writers' Conf. 1981, Writing Fellowship Ossabaw Island Project 1982. *Publications:* Satyrday (novel) 1980, The River (novel) 1985, Steven Spielberg's Amazing Stories (two vols) 1986, Daylight Savings (poems) 1989, The Strange and Wonderful Tale of Robert McDoodle (The Boy Who Wanted to be a Dog) (juvenile) 1999, A Cat of a Different Color (juvenile) 2000; contrib. essays, stories and poems in many periodicals. *Honours:* Prairie Schooner Strousse Award for Poetry 1982, Indiana Arts Council Master Artist Fellowship Award 1988, Peregrine Smith Poetry Prize 1989, Parents' Choice Recommended Writer 2000. *Address:* 14100 Harmony Road, Bath, IN 47010, USA (office). *E-mail:* bauerst@muohio.edu.

BAUER, Yehuda, MA, PhD; Israeli historian and academic; *Academic Adviser, Yad Vashem*; b. 6 April 1926, Prague, Czechoslovakia; two d. *Education:* Univ. of Wales, Hebrew Univ., Jerusalem. *Career:* Served in Palmach Forces of the Haganah (Jewish Underground), 1944–45, and in Israel's War of Independence, 1948–49; Lecturer, Inst. of Contemporary Jewry, Hebrew Univ. 1961–73, Head of Div. of Holocaust Studies 1968–95, Assoc. Prof. 1973–77, Head 1973–75, 1977–79, Prof. 1977–95; Founder-Chair., Vidal Sassoon Int. Center for the Study of Antisemitism, Hebrew Univ. 1982–95; Ed., Journal of Holocaust and Genocide Studies, 1986–95; Visiting Prof., Univ. of Honolulu at Manoa, 1992, Yale Univ., 1993; Distinguished Visiting Prof., Ida E. King Chair of Holocaust Studies, Richard Stockton College, NJ, 1995–96, 2002; Dir, Int. Center for Holocaust Studies, Yad Vashem, Jerusalem, 1996–2001, Academic Adviser 2000–. *Publications:* (in English): From Diplomacy to Resistance: A History of Jewish Palestine, 1939–1945, 1970; My Brother's Keeper, 1974; Flight and Rescue, 1975; The Holocaust in Historical Perspective, 1978; The Jewish Emergence From Powerlessness, 1979; The Holocaust as Historical Experience (ed.), 1981; American Jewry and the Holocaust, 1982; History of the Holocaust, 1984; Jewish Reactions to the Holocaust, 1988; Out of the Ashes, 1989; Jews for Sale?: Nazi–Jewish Negotiations, 1939–1945, 1994; Rethinking the Holocaust, 2001. Contributions: scholarly books, yearbooks and journals. *Address:* c/o International Center for Holocaust Studies, Yad Vashem, PO Box 3477, Jerusalem 91034, Israel.

BAUMAN, Janina; British writer; b. 18 Aug. 1926, Warsaw, Poland; m. Zygmunt Bauman 1948; three d. *Education:* Acad. of Social Sciences, Univ. of Warsaw. *Career:* script ed., Polish Film 1948–68. *Publications:* Winter in the Morning 1986, A Dream of Belonging 1988; various other books and short stories published in Poland 1990–; contrib. to Jewish Quarterly, Oral History, Polin, British Journal of Holocaust Education, Thesis Eleven. *Honours:* Polityka Weekly magazine award, Poland 1991. *Address:* 1 Lawnswood Gardens, Leeds, Yorkshire LS16 6HF, England (home). *Telephone:* (113) 267-8173 (home). *E-mail:* janinabauman1@aol.com (home).

BAUMAN, Zygmunt, MA, PhD; British academic and writer; *Professor Emeritus of Sociology, University of Leeds*; b. 19 Nov. 1925, Poznań, Poland; s. of Moritz Bauman and Sophia Bauman (née Cohn); m. Janina Bauman (née Lewinson) 1948; three d. *Education:* Univ. of Warsaw. *Career:* held Chair of Gen. Sociology, Univ. of Warsaw 1964–68, Prof. Emer. 1968–; Prof. of Sociology, Univ. of Tel-Aviv 1968–71; Prof. of Sociology, Univ. of Leeds 1971–91, Prof. Emer. 1991–; mem. British Sociological Asscn, Polish Sociological Asscn. *Publications:* Culture as Praxis 1972, Hermeneutics and Social Science 1977, Memories of Class 1982, Legislators and Interpreters 1987, Modernity and the Holocaust 1989, Modernity and Ambivalence 1990, Intimations of Postmodernity 1991, Thinking Sociologically 1991, Mortality, Immortality and Other Life Strategies 1992, Postmodern Ethics 1993, Life in Fragments 1995, Postmodernity and Its Discontents 1996, Globalization: The Human Consequences 1998, Work, Consumerism and the New Poor 1998, In Search of Politics 1999, Liquid Modernity 2000, Individualized Society 2000, Community: Seeking Safety in an Uncertain World 2001, Society Under Siege 2002, Liquid Love: On the Frailty of Human Bonds 2003, Wasted Lives: Modernity and its Outcasts 2003, Europe: An Unfinished Adventure 2004, Liquid Life 2005, Liquid – Modern Fears 2006; contrib. to scholarly journals and general periodicals. *Honours:* Dr hc (Oslo) 1997, (Lapland) 1999, (Uppsala) 2000, (Prague) 2001, (Copenhagen) 2001, (Sofia) 2001, (West of

England) 2002, (London) 2003, (Leeds) 2004; Amalfi Prize for Sociology and Social Sciences 1989, Theodor W. Adorno Prize 1998. *Address:* 1 Lawnswood Gardens, Leeds, LS16 6HF, England. *Telephone:* (113) 267-8173. *Fax:* (113) 267-8173. *E-mail:* janzygbau@aol.com (home).

BAUMBACH, Jonathan; American writer and academic; b. 5 July 1933, New York; three s. one d. *Education:* AB, Brooklyn College, CUNY, 1955; MFA, Columbia University, 1956; PhD, Stanford University, 1961. *Career:* Instructor, Stanford University, 1958–60; Asst Prof., Ohio State University, 1961–64; Dir of Writing, New York University, 1964–66; Prof., English, Brooklyn College, CUNY, 1966–; Visiting professorships, Tufts University, 1970, University of Washington, 1978, 1983; mem. Teachers and Writers Collaborative, board of dirs; National Society of Film Critics, chair., 1982–84. *Publications:* The Landscape of Nightmare, 1965; A Man to Conjure With, 1965; What Comes Next, 1968; Reruns, 1974; Babble, 1976; Chez, Charlotte and Emily, 1979; Return of Service, 1979; My Father More or Less, 1984; The Life and Times of Major Fiction, 1987; Separate Hours, 1990; Seven Wives, 1994. Contributions: Movie Critic, Partisan Review, 1973–82; Articles, Fiction in Esquire; New American Review; Tri Quarterly; Iowa Review; North American Review; Fiction. *Honours:* National Endowment for the Arts Fellowship, 1978; Guggenheim Fellowship, 1980; O. Henry Prize Stories, 1980, 1984, 1988. *Address:* 320 Stratford Road, New York, NY 11218, USA.

BAUSCH, Richard Carl, BA, MFA; American author and academic; b. 18 April 1945, Fort Benning, GA; m. Karen Miller 1969, two s. one d. *Education:* George Mason University, University of Iowa. *Career:* Prof. of English, George Mason University, 1980–; mem. Associated Writing Programs. *Publications:* Real Presence, 1980; Take Me Back, 1981; The Last Good Time, 1984; Spirits and Other Stories, 1987; Mr Field's Daughter, 1989; The Fireman's Wife and Other Stories, 1990; Violence, 1992; Rebel Powers, 1993; Rare and Endangered Species: A Novella and Stories, 1994; The Selected Stories of Richard Bausch, 1996; Good Evening Mr and Mrs America, and All the Ships at Sea, 1996; In the Night Season, 1998; Someone to Watch Over Me, 1999. *Honours:* Guggenheim Fellowship, 1984.

BAUSCH, Robert Charles, BA, MA, MFA; American writer and teacher; b. 18 April 1945, Fort Benning, GA; m. 1st Geri Marrese 1970 (divorced 1982); three d.; m. 2nd Denise Natt 1982; one s. *Education:* University of Illinois, Northern Virginia College, George Mason University. *Career:* Instructor in Creative Writing, Northern Virginia Community College from 1975. *Publications:* On the Way Home, 1982; The Lives of Riley Chance, 1984; Almighty Me, 1991; The White Rooster and Other Stories, 1995; A Hole in the Earth, 2000; The Gypsy Man, 2002. Contributions: periodicals.

BAWDEN, Nina Mary, CBE, MA, JP, FRSL; English novelist; b. 19 Jan. 1925, Ilford, Essex; d. of Charles Mabey and Ellaline Ursula May Mabey; m. 1st H. W. Bawden 1947; two s. (one deceased); m. 2nd Austen S. Kark 1954 (died 2002); one d. two step-d. *Education:* Ilford Co. High School, Somerville Coll., Oxford. *Career:* Asst, Town and Country Planning Asscn 1946–47; JP, Surrey 1968; Pres. Soc. of Women Writers and Journalists 1981–; Hon. Fellow, Somerville Coll., Oxford; mem. PEN; council mem. Soc. of Authors. *Publications:* Who Calls the Tune 1953, The Odd Flamingo 1954, The Solitary Child 1956, Devil by the Sea 1958, Just Like a Lady 1960, In Honour Bound 1961, Tortoise by Candlelight 1963, A Little Love, A Little Learning 1965, A Woman of My Age 1967, The Grain of Truth 1969, The Birds on the Trees 1970, Anna Apparent 1972, George Beneath a Paper Moon 1974, Afternoon of a Good Woman 1976, Familiar Passions 1979, Walking Naked 1981, The Ice House 1983, Circles of Deceit (also adapted for TV) 1987, Family Money (also adapted for TV) 1991, In My Own Time (autobiog.) 1994, A Nice Change 1997, Dear Austen 2005; for children: The Secret Passage 1963, The Runaway Summer 1969, Carrie's War 1973 (Phoenix Award 1993) (also adapted for BBC TV 2003), The Peppermint Pig 1975 (Guardian Prize for Children's Literature 1975), The Finding 1985, Princess Alice 1985, Keeping Henry 1988, The Outside Child 1989, Humbug 1992, The Real Plato Jones 1993, Granny the Pig 1995, Off the Road 1998, Ruffian on the Stair 2001. *Honours:* Yorkshire Post Novel of the Year Award 1976, Edgar Allan Poe Award, Phoenix Award 1993, S. T. Dupont Golden Pen Award for Services to Literature 2004. *Literary Agent:* Curtis Brown Ltd, Haymarket House, 28–29 Harmarket, London, SW1Y 4SP. *Telephone:* (20) 7393-4400. *Fax:* (20) 7393-4401. *E-mail:* info@curtisbrown.co.uk. *Website:* www.curtisbrown.co.uk. *Address:* 22 Noel Road, London, N1 8HA, England; 19 Kapodistriou, Nauplion 21100, Greece. *Telephone:* (20) 7226-2839 (office). *Fax:* (20) 7359-7103.

BAXT, George; American writer; b. 11 June 1923, New York, NY. *Education:* City and Brooklyn Colls, CUNY. *Publications:* A Queer Kind of Death, 1966; A Parade of Cockeyed Creatures, 1967; I! Said the Demon, 1968; Burning Sappho, 1972; The Dorothy Parker Murder Case, 1984; The Alfred Hitchcock Murder Case: An Unauthorized Novel, 1986; The Tallulah Bankhead Murder Case, 1987; The Talking Picture Murder Case, 1990; The Mae West Murder Case, 1993; The Marlene Dietrich Murder Case, 1993; The Bette Davis Murder Case, 1994; The Clark Gable and Carole Lombard Murder Case, 1997. Contributions: Ellery Queen Mystery Magazine.

BAXTER, Charles, BA, PhD; American academic, author and poet; *Edelstein-Keller Visiting Professor of Creative Writing, University of Minnesota*; b. 13 May 1947, Minneapolis, Minn.; m. Martha Hauser, one s. *Education:* Macalester Coll., State Univ. of NY, Buffalo. *Career:* Asst Prof., Wayne State Univ. 1974–79, Assoc. Prof. 1979–85, Prof. of English 1985–89; Faculty, Warren Wilson Coll. 1986; Visiting Faculty, Univ. of Michigan 1987, Prof. of

English 1989–2003; currently Edelstein-Keller Visiting Prof. of Creative Writing, Univ. of Minnesota. *Publications:* fiction: Harmony of the World 1984, Through the Safety Net 1985, First Light 1987, A Relative Stranger 1990, Shadow Play 1993, Believers 1997, The Feast of Love 2000, Saul and Patsy 2004; non-fiction: Burning Down the House 1997; poetry: Chameleon 1970, The South Dakota Guidebook 1974, Imaginary Paintings and Other Poems 1990; contribs to numerous anthologies, journals, reviews, and newspapers. *Honours:* Nat. Endowment for the Arts Grant 1983, Guggenheim Fellowship 1985–86, Arts Foundation of Michigan Award 1991, Lila Wallace-Reader's Digest Foundation Fellowship 1992–95, Michigan Author of the Year Award 1993, Award in Literature, American Acad. of Arts and Letters 1997. *Address:* 134 Groveland Terrace, Minneapolis, MN 55403, USA.

BAXTER, Craig, BA, AM, PhD; American academic, writer and consultant; b. 16 Feb. 1929, Elizabeth, NJ; m. Barbara T. Stevens 1984 (died 2003); one s. one d. *Education:* Univ. of Pennsylvania. *Career:* US Foreign Service, Vice-Consul, Mumbai 1958–60, Political Officer, New Delhi 1961–64, Deputy Principal Officer and Political Officer, Lahore 1965–68, Analyst for India 1968–69, Sr Political Officer for Pakistan and Afghanistan 1969–71, Visiting Assoc. Prof. in Social Sciences, United State Military Acad. 1971–74, Political Counselor, Accra 1974–76, and Dhaka 1976–78, Officer-in-Charge, Int. Scientific Relations for the Near East, South Asia, and Africa 1978–80; Lecturer, Mount Vernon College, Washington, DC, 1981; Visiting Prof. of Political Science and Diplomat-in-Residence 1981–82, Prof. of Politics and History 1982–99, Chair of Dept of Political Science 1991–94, Juniata Coll., Huntingdon, Pennsylvania; consultant to various organizations; mem. American Foreign Service Asscn, Asscn for Asian Studies, American Inst. of Pakistan Studies (pres. 1993–99), American Inst. of Bangladesh Studies (pres. 1989–98). *Publications:* The Jana Sangh: A Biography of an Indian Political Party 1969, Bangladesh: A New Nation in an Old Setting 1984, Zia's Pakistan: Politics and Stability in a Frontline State (ed. and contributor) 1985, Government and Politics in South Asia (with Yogendra K. Malik, Charles H. Kennedy and Robert C. Oberst) 1987, Historical Dictionary of Bangladesh (with Syedur Rahman) 1989, Pakistan Under the Military: Eleven Years of Zia ul-Haq (with Shahid Javed Burki) 1990, Bangladesh: From a Nation to a State 1996, Pakistan 1997 (with Charles H. Kennedy) 1998, Pakistan 2000 (with Charles H. Kennedy) 2000, Pakistan on the Brink 2003; contrib. to books, encyclopedias and scholarly journals. *Honours:* Outstanding Academic Book, American Library Asscn 1996, Distinguished Asianist Mid-Atlantic Region Asscn for Asian Studies 2002. *Address:* RR No. 4, Box 103, Huntingdon, PA 16652, USA. *E-mail:* cbaxter@pennswoods.net.

BAXTER, John; Australian writer; b. 14 Dec. 1939, Sydney, NSW. *Education:* Waverly Coll., Sydney. *Career:* Dir of Publicity, Australian Commonwealth Film Unit, Sydney 1968–70; Lecturer in Film and Theatre, Hollins Coll. 1974–78; freelance TV producer and screenwriter 1978–87; Visiting Lecturer, Mitchell Coll. 1987. *Publications:* The Off Worlders, 1966, in Australia as The God Killers: Hollywood in the Thirties, 1968; The Pacific Book of Australian Science Fiction, 1970; The Australian Cinema, 1970; Science Fiction in the Cinema, 1970; The Gangster Film, 1970; The Cinema of Josef von Sternburg, 1971; The Cinema of John Ford, 1971; The Second Pacific Book of Australian Science Fiction, 1971; Hollywood in the Sixties, 1972; Sixty Years of Hollywood, 1973; An Appalling Talent: Kent Russell, 1973; Stunt: The Story of the Great Movie Stunt Men, 1974; The Hollywood Exiles, 1976; The Fire Came By (with Thomas R. Atkins), 1976; King Vidor, 1976; The Hermes Fall, 1978; The Bidders (in UK as Bidding), 1979; The Kid, 1981; The Video Handbook (with Brian Norris), 1982; The Black Yacht, 1982; Who Burned Australia? The Ash Wednesday Fires, 1984; Filmstruck, 1987; Bondi Blues, 1993; Fellini, 1993; Buñuel, 1994; Steven Spielberg: The Unauthorised Biography, 1996; Woody Allen: A Biography, 1999; Stanley Kubrick, 1999; George Lucas: Mythmaker, 2000; The Making of Dungeons and Dragons: The Movie; A Pound of Paper: Confessions of a Book Addict, 2002. Screenplays: The Time Guardian, 1988. TV Series: The Cutting Room, 1986; First Take, 1986; Filmstruck, 1986.

BAXTER, Stephen, MA, PhD; British writer; b. 1957, Liverpool, England. *Education:* Univ. of Cambridge, Univ. of Southampton. *Publications:* fiction: Raft 1991, Timelike Infinity 1992, Anti-Ice 1993, Flux 1993, Ring 1994, The Time Ships 1995, Voyage 1996, Titan 1997, Vacuum Diagrams (short stories) 1997, Gulliverzone 1997, Traces (short stories) 1998, Moonseed 1998, Webcrash 1998, Manifold 1: Time 1999, Silverhair 1999, Longtusk 2000, Manifold 2: Space 2000, The Light of Other Days (with Arthur C. Clarke) 2000, Icebones 2001, Manifold 3: Origin 2001, Evolution 2002, Phase Space (short stories) 2002, Destiny's Children 1: Coalescent 2003, Time's Eye (with Arthur C. Clarke) 2004, Exultant 2004, Sunstorm (with Arthur C. Clarke) 2005, Emperor 2006, Conqueror 2007; non-fiction: Angular Distribution Analysis in Acoustics 1986, Reengineering Information Technology (with David Lisburn) 1994, The Role of the IT/IS Manager 1996, Deep Future 2001, Omegatropic 2001, Revolutions in the Earth: James Hutton and the True Age of the Earth 2003; other: Irina (online publ.) 1996, numerous short stories, ed. of anthologies, articles and talks; contrib. to anthologies, science and computing journals, science fiction magazines, radio and television. *Honours:* John W. Campbell Award for Best Novel 1996, BSFA Award for Best Novel 1996, for Best Short Story 1998, for Best Non-Fiction 2001, Philip K. Dick Awards for Best Novel 1997, 1999. *Literary Agent:* PFD, Drury House, 34–43 Russell Street, London, WC2B 5HA, England.

BAYBARS, Taner, (Timothy Bayliss); British writer and painter; b. 18 June 1936, Cyprus; one d. *Education:* Turkish Lycée. *Career:* mem. Club de Vin d'Angoulême, Poetry Soc. of London, Arts Septemaniens of Narbonne. *Publications:* To Catch a Falling Man 1963, A Trap for the Burglar 1965, Selected Poems of Nazim Hikmet 1967, The Moscow Symphony (Hikmet) 1970, Plucked in a Far-Off Land 1970, The Day Before Tomorrow (Hikmet) 1972, Susila in the Autumn Woods 1974, Narcissus in a Dry Pool 1978, Pregnant Shadows 1981, A Sad State of Freedom 1990, Don't Go Back to Kyrenia (trans. of poems by Mehmet Yashin) 2001; contrib. to Critical Quarterly, Ambit, Orte, Détours d'Ecritures, Hudson Review, Dalhousie Review, M25, Europe, Kitap-Lik. *Literary Agent:* c/o MBA Literary Agents Ltd, 62 Grafton Way, London, W1T 5DW, England. *Address:* 2 rue de L'Evêque, 34360 Saint-Chinian, France. *E-mail:* tbaybars@wanadoo.fr.

BAYEN, Bruno; French writer, dramatist, theatre producer and translator; b. 1950, Paris. *Education:* Ecole Normale Supérieure. *Theatre includes:* Schliemann, épisodes ignorés 1982, L'éclipse du onze août 2006. *Publications:* Jean 3 Locke 1987, Restent les voyages (novel) 1990, Eloge de l'eller simple (novel) 1991, Weimarland/L'Enfant bâtard 1992, Hernando Colón, enquête sur un bâtard (novel) 1992, À trois mains 1997, Le pli de la nappe au milieu du jour (essay) 1997, La Fuite en Égypte 1999, Plaidoyer en faveur des larmes d'Héraclite, Les Excédés, La Forêt de six mois d'hiver, La Vie sentimentale 2002, Pourquoi pas tout de suite (essay) 2004. *Address:* c/o Editions Mercure de France, 26 rue de Condé, 75006 Paris; 64 avenue Jean Marlin, 75014 Paris, France (home).

BAYLEY, Barrington John, (Alan Aumbry, P. F. Woods); British writer; b. 9 April 1937, Birmingham, England; m. Joan Lucy Clarke 1969; one s. one d. *Publications:* Star Virus 1970, Annihilation Factor 1972, Empire of Two Worlds 1972, Collision with Chronos 1973, The Fall of Chronopolis 1974, The Soul of the Robot 1974, The Garments of Caean 1976, The Grand Wheel 1977, The Knights of the Limits 1978, Star Winds 1978, The Seed of Evil 1979, The Pillars of Eternity 1982, The Zen Gun 1984, The Forest of Peldain 1985, The Rod of Light 1985, Eye of Terror 1999, The Sinners of Erspia 2002, The Great Hydration 2002. *Honours:* Seiun Award for Best Foreign Science Fiction Novel Published in Japan 1984–85, BSFA Award for Best Short Fiction 1996. *Address:* 48 Turreff Avenue, Donnington, Telford, Shropshire TF2 8HE, England. *Website:* www.oivas.com/bjb.

BAYLEY, John Oliver, MA, FBA; British academic; b. 27 March 1925, s. of F. J. Bayley; m. 1st (Jean) Iris Murdoch 1956 (died 1999); m. 2nd Audhild Villers 2000. *Education:* Eton Coll. and New Coll., Oxford. *Career:* served in army 1943–47; mem. St Antony's and Magdalen Colls, Oxford 1951–55; Fellow and Tutor in English, New Coll., Oxford 1955–74; Warton Prof. of English Literature and Fellow, St Catherine's Coll., Oxford 1974–92. *Publications:* In Another Country (novel) 1954, The Romantic Survival: A Study in Poetic Evolution 1956, The Characters of Love 1961, Tolstoy and the Novel 1966, Pushkin: A Comparative Commentary 1971, The Uses of Division: Unity and Disharmony in Literature 1976, An Essay on Hardy 1978, Shakespeare and Tragedy 1981, The Order of Battle at Trafalgar 1987, The Short Story: Henry James to Elizabeth Bowen 1988, Housman's Poems 1992, Alice (novel) 1994, The Queer Captain (novel) 1995, George's Lair (novel) 1996, The Red Hat 1997, Iris and the Friends: A Year of Memories 1999, Widower's House 2001, Hand Luggage – An Anthology 2001, The Power of Delight – A Lifetime in Literature: Essays 1962–2002 2005. *Honours:* Heinemann Literary Award. *Address:* c/o St Catherine's College, Oxford, England.

BAYLEY, Peter Charles, MA; British academic and writer; *Fellow Emeritus, University College Oxford*; b. 25 Jan. 1921, Gloucester, England. *Education:* Univ. Coll., Oxford. *Career:* Fellow, Univ. Coll. Oxford 1947–72, now Fellow Emer.; Praelector in English, Univ. of Oxford 1949–72, Univ. Lecturer 1952–72; Master, Collingwood Coll., Univ. of Durham 1972–78; Berry Prof. and Head of English Dept, Univ. of St Andrews, Fife 1978–85, Berry Prof. Emer. 1985–. *Publications include:* Edmund Spenser, Prince of Poets 1971, Poems of Milton 1982, An ABC of Shakespeare 1985; Editor: The Faerie Queene, by Spenser, Book II 1965, Book 1 1966, 1970, Loves and Deaths 1972, A Casebook on Spenser's Faerie Queene 1977; contribs to Patterns of Love and Courtesy 1966, Oxford Bibliographical Guides 1971, C. S. Lewis at the Breakfast Table 1979, The Encyclopedia of Oxford 1988, University College Oxford: a Guide and Brief History, Sir William Jones 1746–94 1998. *Address:* 63 Oxford Street, Woodstock, Oxford, OX20 1TJ, England (home). *Telephone:* (1993) 812300 (home).

BAYLISS, Timothy (see Baybars, Taner)

BAYLY, Sir Christopher Alan, Kt, FBA; British historian; *Vere Harmsworth Professor of Imperial and Naval History, University of Cambridge*; b. Tunbridge Wells, Kent. *Education:* Balliol and St Antony's Colls, Oxford. *Career:* Fellow St Catharine's Coll. 1970–; Vere Harmsworth Prof. of Imperial and Naval History, Univ. of Cambridge 1991–. *Publications:* The Local Roots of Indian Politics: Allahabad 1880–1920 1975, Rulers, Townsmen and Bazaars: North Indian Society in the Age of British Expansion, 1780–1870 1983, Indian Society and the Making of the British Empire 1988, Imperial Meridian: The British Empire and the World, 1780–1830 1989, Empire and Information: Intelligence Gathering and Social Communication in India 1780–1870 1996, The Origins of Nationality in South Asia 1997, The Birth of the Modern World: Global Connections and Comparisons 1780–1914 2004, Forgotten Armies: The Fall of British Asia 1941–45 (with Tim Harper) 2004, Forgotten Wars: Freedom and Revolution in Southeast Asia (with Tim

Harper) 2006. *Honours:* Wolfson Prize for History lifetime achievement award 2005. *Literary Agent:* c/o Bruce Hunter, David Higham Associates, 5–8 Lower John Street, Golden Square, London, W1F 9HA, England. *Telephone:* (20) 7434-5900. *Fax:* (20) 7437-1072. *E-mail:* dha@davidhigham.co.uk. *Website:* www.davidhigham.co.uk. *Address:* St Catharine's College, Cambridge, CB2 1RL, England (office). *E-mail:* cab1002@cam.ac.uk (office). *Website:* www.hist .cam.ac.uk (office).

BEACH, Eric; Australian poet and writer; b. 1947, New Zealand. *Publications:* St Kilda Meets Hugo Ball, 1974; In Occupied Territory, 1977; A Photo of Some People in a Football Stadium, 1978; Weeping for Lost Babylon, 1996. Contributions: anthologies. *Address:* Minyip, Victoria 3992, Australia.

BEAGLE, Peter Soyer, BA; American writer, musician, singer and song-writer; b. 20 April 1939, New York, NY; m. 1st Enid Nordeen 1964 (divorced 1980); one s. two d.; m. 2nd Padma Hejmadi 1988. *Education:* University of Pittsburgh. *Career:* many readings, lectures, and concerts; Visiting Asst Prof., University of Washington, 1988. *Publications:* Fiction: A Fine and Private Place, 1960; The Last Unicorn, 1968; The Folk of the Air, 1986; The Innkeeper's Song, 1993; The Unicorn Sonata, 1996. Fiction Collections: The Fantasy Worlds of Peter S. Beagle, 1978; Giant Bones, 1997; The Rhinoceros Who Quoted Nietzsche, and Other Odd Acquaintances, 1997. Editor: Peter Beagle's Immortal Unicorn (with Janet Berliner), 1995. Opera Libretto: The Midnight Angel, 1993. Non-Fiction: I See By My Outfit, 1965; The California Feeling, 1969; American Denim: A New Folk Art, 1975; The Lady and Her Tiger (with Pat Derby), 1976; The Garden of Earthly Delights, 1982; In the Presence of Elephants (with Pat Derby), 1995. Contributions: anthologies, periodicals, films, and television. *Address:* 373 63rd Street, Oakland, CA 94618-1257, USA.

BEALES, Derek Edward Dawson, LittD, FBA; British historian and academic; *Professor Emeritus of Modern History, Sidney Sussex College, University of Cambridge*; b. 12 June 1931, Felixstowe; s. of the late Edward Beales and Dorothy K. Dawson; m. Sara J. Ledbury 1964; one s. one d. *Education:* Bishop's Stortford Coll. and Sidney Sussex Coll., Cambridge. *Career:* Research Fellow, Sidney Sussex Coll. Cambridge 1955–58, Fellow 1958–; Asst Lecturer in History, Univ. of Cambridge 1962–65, Lecturer 1965–80, Prof. of Modern History 1980–97, Prof. Emer. 1997–; Stenton Lecturer, Univ. of Reading 1992, Birkbeck Lecturer, Trinity Coll., Cambridge 1993; Recurring Visiting Prof., Cen. European Univ., Budapest 1995–; Ed. Historical Journal 1971–75; mem. Standing Cttee for Humanities, European Science Foundation 1994–99; Leverhulme 2000, Emer., Fellowship 2001–03. *Publications:* England and Italy 1859–60 1961, From Castlereagh to Gladstone 1969, History and Biography 1981, History, Society and the Churches (with G. Best) 1985, Joseph II, Vol. I: In the Shadow of Maria Theresa 1987, Mozart and the Habsburgs 1993, Sidney Sussex Quatercentenary Essays (with H. B. Nisbet) 1996, The Risorgimento and the Unification of Italy (2nd edn with E. Biagini) 2002, Prosperity and Plunder: European Catholic Monasteries in the Age of Revolution 2003, Enlightenment and Reform in the 18th Century 2005. *Honours:* Prince Consort Prize, Univ. of Cambridge 1960, Henry Paolucci/Walter Bagehot Prize, Intercollegiate Studies Inst., Wilmington, Del. 2004. *Address:* Sidney Sussex College, Cambridge, CB2 3HU, England (office). *Telephone:* (1223) 338833 (office). *E-mail:* derek@beales.ws.

BEAR, Carolyn Ann, (Chlöe Rayban); British writer; b. 10 April 1944, Exeter, England; m. Peter Julian Bear; two d. *Education:* Univ. of Western Australia, Univ. of Newcastle upon Tyne. *Publications:* Under Different Stars 1988, Wild Child 1991, Virtual Sexual Reality 1994, Love in Cyberia 1996, Screen Kiss 1997, Clash on the Catwalk 1997, Havana to Hollywood 1997, Street to Stardom 1997, Models Move On 1998, Terminal Chic 2000, Drama Queen 2004, My Life Starving Mum 2005, Hollywood Bliss – My Life So Far 2007. *Literary Agent:* Laura Cecil Literary Agency, 17 Alwyne Villas, London, N1 2HG, England. *E-mail:* info@lauracecil.co.uk. *Website:* www.lauracecil.co .uk; www.chloerayban.com.

BEAR, Gregory Dale, AB; American writer; b. 20 Aug. 1951, San Diego, CA, USA; m. 1st Christina Nielsen 1975 (divorced 1981); m. 2nd Astrid Anderson 1983; one s. one d. *Education:* San Diego State College. *Career:* mem. SFWA (pres. 1988–90). *Publications:* Hegira, 1979; Psychlone, 1979; Beyond Heaven's River, 1980; Strength of Stones, 1981; The Wind From a Burning Woman, 1983; Corona, 1984; The Infinity Concerto, 1984; Eon, 1985; Blood Music, 1985; The Serpent Mage, 1986; The Forge of God, 1987; Sleepside Story, 1987; Eternity, 1988; Hardfought, 1988; Early Harvest, 1988; Tangents, 1989; Queen of Angels, 1990; Heads, 1990; Anvil of Stars, 1992; Moving Mars, 1993; Legacy, 1995; Dinosaur Summer, 1998; Darwin's Radio, 1999; Vitals, 2002; Darwin's Children, 2003. *Honours:* awards from SFWA. *Address:* 506 Lakeview Road, Alderwood Manor, WA 98036, USA.

BEARD, Mary, PhD; British lecturer in classics and writer; *Professor of Classics, University of Cambridge*; b. 1 Jan. 1955, Much Wenlock, Shropshire; d. of Roy Whitbread Beard and Joyce Emily Beard; m. Robin Sinclair Cormack 1985; one d. one s. *Education:* Shrewsbury High School and Newnham Coll., Cambridge. *Career:* research in Roman history 1977–79; Lecturer in Classics, King's Coll., London 1979–83; Univ. Lecturer in Classics and Fellow, Newnham Coll., Cambridge 1984–, Reader in Classics 1999–2004, Prof. of Classics 2004–; Classics Ed. Times Literary Supplement. *Publications include:* Rome in the Late Republic (jtly) 1985, The Good Working Mother's Guide 1988, Pagan Priests (jtly) 1990, A Very Short Introduction to Classics

(jtly) 1995, The Invention of Jane Harrison 2000, Classical Art: From Greece to Rome (jtly) 2001, The Parthenon 2002, The Colosseum (with Keith Hopkins) 2005. *Address:* University of Cambridge, Newnham College, Cambridge, CB3 9DF; Faculty of Classics, Sidgwick Avenue, Cambridge, CB3 9DA, England. *Telephone:* (1223) 335162. *Fax:* (1223) 335409. *E-mail:* mb127@hermes.cam.ac .uk.

BEARDSLEY, John Douglas; Canadian writer, poet, editor, reviewer and teacher; b. 27 April 1941, Montréal, QC, Canada. *Education:* BA, University of Victoria, BC, 1976; MA, York University, Toronto, Ontario, 1978. *Career:* Chief Ed., Gregson Graham Ltd, 1980–82; Senior Instructor, Dept of English, University of Victoria, 1981–; Writer, Ed. and Graphic Designer, 1982–85, Writer, Ed. and Proofreader, 1985–, Beardsley and Assocs, Victoria. *Publications:* Going Down into History, 1976; The Only Country in the World Called Canada, 1976; Six Saanich Poems, 1977; Play on the Water: The Paul Klee Poems, 1978; Premonitions and Gifts (with Theresa Kishkan), 1979; Poems (with Charles Lillard), 1979; Pacific Sands, 1980; Kissing the Body of My Lord: The Marie Poems, 1982; Country on Ice, 1987; A Dancing Star, 1988; The Rocket, the Flower, the Hammer and Me (ed.), 1988; Free to Talk, 1992; Inside Passage, 1994; Wrestling with Angels (Selected Poems, 1960–1995), 1996; My Friends the Strangers, 1996; Our Game (ed.), 1998; No One Else is Lawrence! (with Al Purdy), 1998; The Man Who Outlived Himself (with Al Purdy), 2000. Contributions: anthologies, newspapers, magazines and periodicals. *Honours:* Canada Council Arts Award, 1978; British Columbia Millennium Book Award, 2000. *Address:* 1074 Lodge Avenue, Victoria, BC V8X 3A8, Canada.

BEATTIE, Ann, MA; American writer; *Edgar Allan Poe Professor of Literature and Creative Writing, University of Virginia*; b. 8 Sept. 1947, Washington; d. of James Beattie and Charlotte Crosby; m. Lincoln Perry. *Education:* American Univ. and Univ. of Connecticut. *Career:* Visiting Asst Prof. Univ. of Virginia, Charlottesville 1976–77, Visiting Writer 1980; Briggs Copeland Lecturer in English, Harvard Univ. 1977; Guggenheim Fellow 1977; currently Edgar Allan Poe Prof. of Literature and Creative Writing, Univ. of Virginia; mem. American Acad. and Inst. of Arts and Letters (Award in Literature 1980), PEN, Authors' Guild. *Publications:* Chilly Scenes of Winter 1976, Distortions 1976, Secrets and Surprises 1979, Falling in Place 1990, Jacklighting 1981, The Burning House 1982, Love Always 1985, Where You'll Find Me 1986, Alex Katz (art criticism) 1987, Picturing Will 1990, What Was Mine (story collection) 1991, My Life Starring Dara Falcon 1997, Park City: New and Selected Stories 1998, Perfect Recall 2001, The Doctor's House 2002, Follies 2005. *Honours:* Hon. LHD (American Univ.); PEN/Bernard Malamud Award 2000. *Address:* c/o Scribner, Simon & Schuster, 1230 Avenue of the Americas, New York, NY 10020, USA.

BEAUCHEMIN, Yves, BA, LèsL; Canadian author; b. 26 June 1941, Noranda, QC; m. Viviane St Onge 1973, two c. *Education:* Collège de Joliette, University of Montréal. *Career:* mem. Amnesty International; International PEN; Union des écrivaines et des écrivains québécois, pres., 1986–87. *Publications:* L'enfirouapé, 1974; Le matou, 1981, English trans. as The Alley Cat, 1986; Du sommet d'un arbre, 1986; Juliette Pomerleau, 1989; Finalement... les enfants, 1991; Une histoire a faire japper, 1991; Antoine et Alfred, 1992; Le second violon, 1996. Contributions: newspapers, magazines, and radio. *Honours:* Prix France-Quèbec, 1975; Prix de la communauté urbaine, Montréal, 1982; Prix des jeunes romanciers, Journal de Montréal, 1982; Prix du roman de l'ete, Cannes, France, 1982.

BEAULIEU, Victor-Lévy; Canadian author and dramatist; b. 2 Sept. 1945, Saint-Paul-de-la-Croix, QC; m. Francine Cantin, two d. *Education:* University of Rallonge. *Publications:* Jos Connaissant, 1970, English trans., 1982; Pour saluer Victor Hugo, 1971; Les Grands-Pères, 1972, English trans. as The Grandfathers: A Novel, 1975; Jack Kerouac: Essai-poulet, 1972, English trans. as Don Quixote in Nighttown, 1978; Manuel de la petite littérature de Québec, 1974; Blanche forcée, 1975; Ma Corriveau, suivi de La sorcellerie en finale sexuée, 1976; N'évoque plus que le désenchantement de ta ténèbre, mon si pauvre Abel, 1976; Sagamo Job J, 1977; Monsieur Melville, 3 vols, 1978, English trans., 1984; Una, 1980; Satan Belhumeur, 1981, English trans., 1983; Moi Pierre Leroy, prophète, martyr et un peu felé du chaudron, 1982; Entre la sainteté et le terrorisme, 1984; Docteur Ferron, 1991. Other: Television Series: Race de Monde, 1978–81; L'héritage, 1987–89; Montréal PQ, 1991–94; Bouscotte, 1997–2001. Contributions: various publications. *Honours:* Grand Prix de la Ville de Montréal, 1972; Governor-General's Award for Fiction, 1974; Beraud-Molson Prize, 1981; Prix Canada-Belgique, 1981.

BEAUMAN, Sally Vanessa, MA; British writer and journalist; b. 25 July 1944, Torquay, Devon; d. of Ronald Kinsey-Miles nd Gabrielle Kinsey-Miles (née Robinson); m. 1st Christopher Beauman 1966 (divorced 1973); m. 2nd Alan Howard; one s. *Education:* Redland High School, Bristol and Girton Coll., Cambridge. *Career:* Assoc. Ed. New York Magazine, USA 1968–72; Features Ed. Vogue 1968–69, Harper's Bazaar 1969–71; Ed. Queen 1970; Arts Ed. Telegraph Magazine 1971–79; writer (also under pseudonym, Vanessa James) 1980–; mem. Soc. of Authors. *Publications:* The Royal Shakespeare Company's Centenary Production of Henry V (ed.) 1976, The Royal Shakespeare Company: A History of Ten Decades 1982, Destiny 1987, Dark Angel 1990, Secret Lives 1994, Lovers and Liars 1994, Danger Zones 1996, Deception and Desire 1998, Sextet 1998, Rebecca's Tale 2001, The Landscape of Love 2005; contrib. to newspapers and periodicals. *Honours:* Catherine Pakenham Memorial Prize for Journalism 1970. *Literary Agent:* c/o PFD, Drury House, 34–43 Russell Street, London, WC2B 5HA, England.

BEAUMONT, Roger Alban, BS, MS, PhD; American academic and writer; b. 2 Oct. 1935, Milwaukee, WI; m. Jean Beaumont 1974; one s. two d. *Education:* Univ. of Wisconsin, Madison and Kansas State Univ. *Career:* part-time Lecturer 1965–67, 1969–73, Assoc. Dir, Center for Advanced Study in Organization Science 1970–73, Assoc. Prof. of Organization Science 1972–74, Univ. of Wisconsin, Milwaukee; Instructor, Univ. of Wisconsin, Oshkosh 1968–69; Fellow, Inter-Univ. Seminar on the Armed Forces and Society 1969–; part-time Lecturer, Marquette Univ. 1970–73; Assoc. Prof. 1974–79, Prof. of History 1979–2003, Prof. Emeritus 2003–, Texas A & M Univ.; co-founder and N American Ed., Defense Analysis 1983–90; mem. American Military Inst. (trustee 1978–81, chair. editorial advisory bd 1984–85), Dept of the Army Historical Advisory Cttee 1983–87, Int. Inst. for Strategic Studies 1974–92. *Publications:* War in the Next Decade (ed. with Martin Edmonds) 1974, Military Elites: Special Fighting Units in the Modern World 1974, Sword of the Raj: The British Army in India 1747–1947 1977, Special Operations and Elite Units 1939–1988: A Reference Guide 1988, Joint Military Operations: A Short History 1993, War, Chaos and History 1994, The Nazis' March to Chaos 2000, Right Backed by Might: The International Air Force Concept 2001; five monographs, 19 book chapters; contrib. to reference works and many scholarly journals. *Honours:* Dept of the Army Patriotic Civilian Service Award 1987, Sec. of the Navy Fellow, History Dept, US Naval Acad. 1989–90, Faculty Teaching Award, Delta Delta Delta Sorority 1994, Research Award College of Liberal Arts 1997. *Address:* 308 E Brookside Drive, Bryan, TX 77801, USA. *Telephone:* (979) 846-3282. *E-mail:* r-beaumont@tamu.edu.

BEAUSOLEIL, Claude; Canadian poet, writer, translator, editor and academic; b. 1948, Montréal, QC, Canada. *Education:* BA, Collège Sainte-Marie, University of Montréal; Bac Specialisé, MA, Université du Québec a Montréal; PhD, Sherbrooke University. *Career:* Prof. of Québec Literature, Collège Edouard-Montpetit, Longueuil, 1973–; Ed., Livrès urbaines. *Publications:* Intrusion ralentie, 1972; Journal mobile, 1974; Promenade modern style, 1975; Sens interdit, 1976; La surface du paysage, 1979; Au milieu du corps l'attraction s'insinue, 1980; Dans la matière revant comme une émeute, 1982; Le livre du voyage, 1983; Concrete City: Selected Poems 1972–82, 1983; Une certaine fin de siècle, two vols, 1983, 1991; Les livres parlent, 1984; Il y a des nuits que nous habitons tous, 1986; Extase et déchirure, 1987; Grand hotel des étrangers, 1988; Fureur de Mexico, 1992; Montréal est une vill de poèmes vous savez, 1992; L'Usage du temps, 1994. *Honours:* Prix Emile-Nelligan, 1980; Ordre des francophones d'Amérique, 1989. *Address:* c/o Union des écrivaines et des écrivains québécois, La Maison des Écrivains, 3492 Avenue Laval, Montréal H2X 3C8, Canada.

BEAVER, Paul Eli; British journalist, writer and broadcaster; b. 3 April 1953, Winchester, England; m. Ann Middleton 1978 (divorced 1993); one s. *Education:* Sheffield City Polytechnic; Henley Management College. *Career:* Ed., IPMS Magazine, 1976–80, Helicopter World, 1981–86, Defence Helicopter World, 1982–86, Jane's Videotape, 1986–87; Asst Compiler, Jane's Fighting Ships, 1987–88; Managing Ed., Jane's Defence Yearbooks, 1988–89; Publisher, Jane's Defence Weekly, 1989–93; Defence Commentator, Sky News, 1990–2001; Senior Publisher, Jane's SENTINEL, 1993–94; Group Spokesman for Jane's, 1994–; Defence and Aerospace Correspondent, CNBC Europe, 1994–97; Research Fellow, Centre for Defence and International Security Studies, Lancaster Univ., 1997–; Defence Commentator, BBC, 2001–. *Publications:* Ark Royal: A Pictorial History, 1979; U-Boats in the Atlantic, 1979; German Capital Ships, 1980; German Destroyers and Escorts, 1981; Fleet Command, 1984; Invincible Class, 1984; Encyclopaedia of Aviation, 1986; Encyclopaedia of the Fleet Air Arm Since 1945, 1987; The Gulf States Regional Security Assessment, 1993; The Balkans Regional Security Assessment, 1994; D-DAY: Private Lines, 1994; The South China Sea Regional Security Assessment, 1994; The CIS Regional Security Assessment, 1994; The North Africa Regional Security Assessment, 1994; The China and North East Asia Regional Security Assessment, 1995; Baltics and Central Europe Regional Security Assessment, 1996; The Modern Royal Navy, 1996. Contributions: many journals. *Address:* 36 Great Smith Street, London SW1P 3BU, England.

BEBB, Prudence, BA, DipEd; British writer; b. 20 March 1939, Catterick, North Yorkshire, England. *Education:* Sheffield University. *Career:* teacher, Snaith School 1961–63; History Teacher, Howden School 1963–90; mem. PEN. *Publications:* The Eleventh Emerald 1981, The Ridgeway Ruby 1983, The White Swan 1984, The Nabob's Nephew 1985, Life in Regency York 1992, Butcher, Baker, Candlestick Maker 1994, Georgian Poppleton 1994, Life in Regency Harrogate 1994, Life in Regency Scarborough 1997, Life in Regency Whitby 2000, Life in Regency Beverley 2003, Life in Regency Bridlington 2006. Contributions: Impressions, the Journal of the Northern Branch of the Jane Austen Society. *Address:* 12 Bracken Hills, Upper Poppleton, York YO26 6DH, England.

BECHMANN, Roland Philippe, LèsL, DipArch, PhD; French architect, historian and writer; b. 1 April 1919, Paris; m. Martine Cohen 1942; six d. *Education:* Univ. of the Sorbonne, Paris, Ecole Nat. Supérieure des Beaux-Arts, Paris. *Career:* architect 1945–85; Chief Ed. Aménagement et Nature 1966–2000; mem. Asscn des Journalistes de l'Environnement, Soc. des gens de Lettres, AVISTA (USA); Pres. Asscn Jean Prévost, Asscn pour les Espaces Naturels. *Works include:* Lycée Agricole Pétrarque, Avignon (inscribed on Inventory of Historical Monuments 1989) 1969, Banque Centrale, Novakchott (Mauretania) 1963. *Publications:* Les Racines des Cathedrales, L'architecture gothique, expression des conditions du milieu 1981, Des Arbres et des Hommes: La foret au Moyen Age (trans. as Trees and Man: The Forest in the Middle Ages) 1984, Carnet de Villard de Honnecourt XIII e siècle (co-author) 1986, Villard de Honnecourt Disegni (co-author) 1987, Villard de Honnecourt: La pensée technique au XIIIe siècle et sa communication 1991, L'Arbre du Ciel (novel) 1997, Villard de Honnecourt's Portfolio (CD-ROM) 2000, Le radici delle cattedrali 2006; contribs to journals. *Honours:* Croix de guerre 1944, Chevalier, Légion d'honneur 1952; Prix du premier roman, Festival de Chambéry 1997, Prix Roberval, Université de Technologie de Compiègne 2002. *Address:* 7 Villa de Buzenval, 92100 Boulogne sur Seine, France. *Telephone:* 1-46-05-53-67.

BECK, Albert (Al) William, BA, MFA; American artist, poet, writer and educator; *Artist in Residence, Culver-Stockton College*; b. 4 April 1931, Scranton, Pa; m. Carmen Federowich; two s. one d. *Education:* Northwestern Univ., US Army Admin. School, Univ. of Paris (Sorbonne), Clayton Univ., St Louis. *Career:* Dean of Students, Kansas City Art Inst., Mo. 1967–68; Assoc. Prof. of Art and Head of Art Dept, Culver-Stockton Coll. 1968–96, Artist-in-Residence 1996–; Dir Pyrapod Gallery 1996–; numerous exhbns 1956–2007; mem. Missouri Arts Council, Missouri Writers' Guild, Hannibal Arts Council, Monroe City Arts Council. *Publications:* Gnomes and Poems 1992, Sight Lines 1996, Songs from the Rainbow Worm 1997, Beaucoup Haiku 1999, God is in the Glove Compartment 2000, Survival Weapons 2001, Warm Verse, Cold Turkey 2002, Rapping Paper, Mythic Thundermugs 2002, Conversations with Lizard Bones and Wizard Stones 2003, Lifepsychles 2004, Beyond the Stars and Gripes 2005, Eclectricity 2006; contribs to professional journals. *Honours:* various painting, pottery and poetry awards. *Address:* 5987 County Road 231, Monroe City, MO 63456, USA. *E-mail:* abeck@marktwain.net.

BECK, Béatrix Marie; French/Belgian writer; b. 30 July 1914, Switzerland; d. of Christian Beck; m.; one d. *Education:* Lycée de St Germain-en-Laye and Université de Grenoble. *Career:* fmr Sec. to André Gide; journalist; mem. Jury, Prix Fémina. *Publications:* Barny 1948, Le muet 1963, Léon Morin, prêtre (Prix Goncourt) 1952, L'Enfant chat 1984, Une mort irrégulière, Des accommodements avec le ciel, Le premier mai, Abram Krol, Cou coupé court toujours, Plus loin mais où 1997, Confidences de Gorgoulle 1999, La Petite Italie 2000. *Honours:* Prix Félix Fénéon; Prix Fondation Delmas 1979; Grand Prix Nat. des Lettres 1991. *Address:* Editions Bernard Grasset, 61 rue des Saints-Pères, 75006 Paris, France (office).

BECK-COULTER, (Eva Maria) Barbara, BSc, FRSA; British (b. German) journalist; b. 14 Oct. 1941, Berlin, Germany; d. of Wilhelm Beck and Ursula Beck; m. Ian Coulter 1971; two s. one d. *Education:* Victoria-Luise Gymnasium, Hamelin, Germany, Univs of Munich and London. *Career:* mem. editorial staff, The Economist 1965–74, European Ed. 1974–80, Asst Ed. 1980–81, Surveys Ed. 1995–; Sec.-Gen. Anglo-German Foundation for the Study of Industrial Soc. 1981–91; Ed. International Management (monthly European business magazine) 1991–94; Head of Communications (Europe), Andersen Consulting 1994; broadcaster, writer and lecturer on current affairs in English and German; Chair. Reform Club 1992–93, Trustee 1995–; mem. Steering Cttee Anglo-German Koenigswinter Conf. 1982–91, Council Royal Inst. of Int. Affairs 1984–90, Academic Council Wilton Park (conf. centre) 1984–91, Int. Council Science Centre, Berlin 1990–95. *Publications:* regular articles published in The Economist and other publs over the past three decades. *Address:* The Economist, 25 St James's Street, London, SW1A 1HG (office); 9 Paget Street, London, EC1V 7PA, England (home). *Telephone:* (20) 7830-7168 (office). *E-mail:* barbarabeck@economist.com (office). *Website:* www.economist.com (office).

BECKER, Gary Stanley, PhD; American economist and academic; *University Professor of Economics, School of Business, University of Chicago*; b. 2 Dec. 1930, Pottsville, Pa; s. of Louis William and Anna Siskind Becker; m. 1st Doria Slote 1954 (deceased); m. 2nd Guity Nashat 1979; two s. two d. *Education:* Princeton Univ., Univ. of Chicago. *Career:* Asst Prof., Univ. of Chicago 1954–57; Asst and Assoc. Prof. of Econs Columbia Univ. 1957–60, Prof. of Econs 1960, Arthur Lehman Prof. of Econs 1968–69; Ford Foundation Visiting Prof. of Econs, Univ. of Chicago 1969–70, Univ. Prof., Dept of Econs, 1970–83, Depts of Econs and Sociology 1983–, Chair. Dept of Econs 1984–85; Research Assoc., Econs Research Center, NORC 1980–; Univ. Prof., Grad. School of Business, Univ. of Chicago 2002–; mem. NAS, Int. Union for the Scientific Study of Population, American Philosophical Soc. and American Econ. Asscn (Pres. 1987), Mont Pelerin Soc. (Dir 1985–, Pres. 1990–92); Fellow, American Statistical Asscn, Econometric Soc., Nat. Acad. of Educ., American Acad. of Arts and Sciences; mem. Bd of Dirs UNext.com 1999–; affil. Lexecon Corpn 1990–2002; columnist Business Week 1985–. *Publications:* The Economics of Discrimination 1957, Human Capital 1964, Human Capital and the Personal Distribution of Income: Analytical Approach 1967, Economic Theory 1971, Essays in the Economics of Crime and Punishment (ed. with William M. Landes) 1974, The Allocation of Time and Goods over the Life Cycle (with Gilbert Ghez) 1975, The Economic Approach to Human Behavior 1976, A Treatise on the Family 1991, Accounting for Tastes 1996, The Economics of Life 1996, Social Economics 2000; Family, Society and State (in German) 1996, L'Approccio Economico al Comportamento Umano 1998; numerous articles in professional journals. *Honours:* hon. degrees from Hebrew Univ. of Jerusalem 1985, Knox Coll., Galesburg, Ill. 1985, Univ. of Ill., Chicago 1988, State Univ. of New York 1990, Princeton Univ. 1991, Univs of Palermo and Buenos Aires 1993, Columbia Univ. 1993, Warsaw School of Econs 1995, Univ. of Econs, Prague 1995, Univ. of Miami 1995, Univ. of

Rochester 1995, Hofstra Univ. 1997, Univ. d'Aix-Marseille 1999, Univ. of Athens 2002; W. S. Woytinsky Award (Univ. of Mich.) 1964, John Bates Clark Medal (American Econ. Asscn) 1967, Frank E. Seidman Distinguished Award in Political Econ. 1985, Merit Award (Nat. Insts. of Health) 1986, John R. Commons Award, Nobel Prize for Economic Sciences 1992, Lord Foundation Award 1995, Irene Tauber Award 1997, Nat. Medal of Science 2000, Phoenix Prize, Univ. of Chicago 2000, American Acad. of Achievement 2001. *Address:* Department of Economics, University of Chicago, 1126 East 59th Street, Chicago, IL 60637 (office); 1308 E 58th Street, Chicago, IL 60637, USA (home). *Telephone:* (312) 702-8168 (office). *Fax:* (773) 702-8496 (office); (312) 702-8490 (office). *E-mail:* sw47@midway.uchicago.edu (office). *Website:* www.src .uchicago.edu/users/gsb1 (office).

BECKER, Heinz, PhD; German musicologist and music educator; b. 26 June 1922, Berlin. *Education:* Berlin Hochschule für Musik, Humboldt Univ., Berlin. *Career:* Asst Lecturer, Inst. of Musicology 1956–66, Habilitation 1961, Univ. of Hamburg; Prof. of Musicology, Ruhr-Univ., Bochum 1966–87; mem. Gesellschaft für Musikforschung 1951–. *Publications:* Klarinettenkonzerte des 18. Jahrhunderts 1957, Der Fall Heine-Meyerbeer 1958, Giacomo Meyerbeer: Briefwechsel und Tagebücher (ed., four vols) 1960–85, Geschichte der Instrumentation 1964, Beitrage zur Geschichte der Musikkritik 1965, Studien zur Entwicklungsgeschichte der antiken und mittelalterlichen Rohrblattinstrumente 1966, Beiträge zur Geschichte der Oper 1969, Die Couleur locale in der Oper des 19 Jahrhunderts 1976, Giacomo Meyerbeer in Selbstzeugnissen und Bilddokumenten 1980, Giacomo Meyerbeer: Ein Leben in Briefen (with G. Becker) 1983, Giacomo Meyerbeer. Weltbürger der Musik, Ausstellungskatalog zum 200 Geburtstag Meyerbeers (with Gudrun Becker) 1991, Im Auftrag de Staatsbibl. BLN, Preußischer Kulturbesitz 1991, The 19th-century Legacy, Heritage of Music 1989, Johannes Brahms 1993; contrib. articles to various music journals and other publications. *Honours:* Festschrift published in honour of 60th birthday 1982, G. Meyerbeer–Musik als Welterfahrung, Festschrift in honour of 70th birthday (ed Sieghart Döhring and Jürgen Schläder) 1992. *Address:* Wohnstift Augustinum, App 1242, Sterleyer Str 44, 23879 Mölln, Germany.

BECKER, Jürgen; German writer and editor; b. 10 July 1932, Cologne; s. of Robert Becker and Else (née Schuchardt) Becker; m. 1st Mare Becker 1954 (divorced 1965); one s.; m. 2nd Rango Bohne 1965; one step-s. one step-d. *Education:* Univ. of Cologne. *Career:* various jobs until 1959; freelance writer and contributor to W German Radio 1959–64; Reader at Rowohlt Verlag 1964–65; freelance writer; living in Cologne, Berlin, Hamburg and Rome; Dir Suhrkamp-Theaterverlag 1974; Head of Drama Dept, Deutschlandfunk Cologne; Writer in Residence, Warwick Univ. 1988; mem. Akademie der Künste Berlin, Deutsche Akademie für Sprache und Dichtung Darmstadt, PEN Club. *Publications:* Felder (short stories) 1964; Ränder (short stories) 1968, Bilder, Häuser (Radio Play) 1969, Umgebungen (short stories) 1970, Schnee (poems) 1971, Das Ende der Landschaftsmalerei (poems) 1974, Erzähl mir nichts vom Krieg (poems) 1977, In der verbleibenden Zeit (Poetry) 1979, Erzählen bis Ostende (short stories) 1981, Fenster und Stimmen (poems with Rango Bohne) 1982, Odenthals Küste (poems) 1986, Das Gedicht von der wiedervereinigten Landschaft (poem) 1988, Das Englische Fenster (poems) 1990, Frauen mit dem Rücken zum Betrachter (short stories with Rango Bohne) 1989, Foxtrott im Erfurter Stadion 1993, Korrespondenzen mit Landschaft (poems with pictures from Rango Bohne) 1996, Der fehlende Rest 1997, Aus der Geschichte der Trennungen (novel) 1999, Schnee in den Ardennen (novel) 2003; Ed. Happenings (documentary with Wolf Vostell) 1965. *Honours:* Förderpreis des Landes Niedersachsen 1964, Stipendium Deutsche Akad. Villa Massimo, Rome 1965, 1966, Group 47 Prize 1967, Literaturpreis der Stadt Cologne 1968, Literaturpreis, Bavarian Acad. of Arts 1980, Kritikerpreis 1981, Bremer Literaturpreis 1986, Peter Huchel Prize 1994, Heinrich Böll Prize 1995, Rhein Literary Prize 1998, Uwe Johnson Prize 2001. *Address:* Am Klausenberg 84, 51109 Cologne, Germany. *Telephone:* 841139.

BECKER, Lucille Ann, BA, MA, PhD; American academic and writer; *Professor Emerita of French, Drew University*; b. 4 Feb. 1929, New York City; d. of Mark Frackman and Sylvia Schwartz Frackman; m.; four s. *Education:* Univ. of Mexico, Barnard Coll., Columbia Univ., New York, Université d'Aix-Marseille, France. *Career:* part-time instructor, Columbia Univ. 1954–58, Univ. Coll., Rutgers Univ., 1958–68; Assoc. Prof. of French, Drew Univ. 1968–77, Chair. Dept of French 1976–81, Prof. of French 1977–93, Prof. Emer. of French 1993–; int. lecturer on French literature at univs in China, Hong Kong, India, Nepal, Sri Lanka, Thailand, Australia, NZ 1978–83; keynote speaker Nat. Press Club Salute to Georges Simenon, Washington, DC 1987; featured speaker, Simenon en Amérique/Simenon in America, Canadian Broadcasting System 2002; mem. American Asscn of Teachers of French, American Asscn of Univ. Profs, French Inst./Alliance Française. *Television:* featured speaker in films Simenon in America, Simenon en Amerique. *Publications:* Le Maître de Santiago, by Henry de Montherlant (co-ed.) 1965, Henry de Montherlant 1970, Louis Aragon 1971, Georges Simenon 1977, Françoise Mallet-Joris 1985, Twentieth-Century French Women Novelists 1989, Pierre Boulle 1996, Georges Simenon Revisited 1999, Cahiers Simenon 15: Sous les feux de la critique II (1945–1955) 2001, Georges Simenon – 'Maigrets' and the 'roman durs' 2006; contrib. to scholarly books and journals. *Honours:* Fulbright Scholar, France 1949–50.

BECKET, Henry S. A. (see Goulden, Joseph C.)

BECKETT, Wendy, (Sister Wendy), MA; British art writer and nun; b. 25 Feb. 1930, Johannesburg, SA. *Education:* Oxford Univ. *Career:* mem. Sacred Heart teaching order, currently living in solitude on the grounds of a Carmelite Monastery. *Television:* several series for BBC and Public Broadcasting Service (US) including Sister Wendy's Grand Tour, Sister Wendy's Story of Painting. *Publications:* A Thousand Masterpieces, The Story of Painting, Meditations, My Favourite Things, Sister Wendy's American Collection 2000, Living the Lord's Prayer (with Rowan Williams) 2007. *Literary Agent:* Toby Eady Associates Ltd, Third Floor, 9 Orme Court, London, W2 4RL, England. *Telephone:* (20) 7792-0092. *Fax:* (20) 7792-0879. *E-mail:* toby@tobyeady.demon.co.uk. *Website:* www.tobyeadyassociates.co.uk.

BECKLES WILLSON, Robina Elizabeth, BA, MA; British writer; b. 26 Sept. 1930, London, England; m. Anthony Beckles Willson, one s. one d. *Education:* University of Liverpool. *Career:* Teacher, Liverpool School of Art, 1952–56, Ballet Rambert Educational School, London, 1956–58. *Publications:* Leopards on the Loire, 1961; A Time to Dance, 1962; Musical Instruments, 1964; A Reflection of Rachel, 1967; The Leader of the Band, 1967; Roundabout Ride, 1968; Dancing Day, 1971; The Last Harper, 1972; The Shell on Your Back, 1972; What a Noise, 1974; The Voice of Music, 1975; Musical Merry-go-Round, 1977; The Beaver Book of Ballet, 1979; Eyes Wide Open, 1981; Anna Pavlova: A Legend Among Dancers, 1981; Pocket Book of Ballet, 1982; Secret Witch, 1982; Square Bear, 1983; Merry Christmas, 1983; Holiday Witch, 1983; Sophie and Nicky series, 2 vols, Hungry Witch, 1984; Music Maker, 1986; Sporty Witch, 1986; The Haunting Music, 1987; Mozart's Story, 1991; Just Imagine, 1993; Harry Stories in Animal World, 1996; Ambulance!, 1996; Very Best Friend, 1998. *Address:* 44 Popes Avenue, Twickenham, Middlesex TW2 4RE, England.

BECKWITH, Lillian; British author; b. 25 April 1916, Ellesmere Port, England; m. Edward Thornthwaite Comber 1937, one s. one d. *Education:* Ornum College, Birkenhead. *Career:* mem. Society of Authors; Mark Twain Society; Women of the Year Asscn, Consultative Committee. *Publications:* The Hebridean Stories: The Hill is Lonely, 1959; The Sea for Breakfast, 1961; The Loud Halo, 1964; Green Hand, 1967; A Rope in Case, 1968; About My Father's Business, 1971; Lightly Poached, 1973; The Spuddy, 1974; Beautiful Just, 1975; The Lillian Beckwith Hebridean Cookbook, 1976; Bruach Blend, 1978; A Shine of Rainbows, 1984; A Proper Woman, 1986; The Bay of Strangers, 1989; The Small Party, 1989; An Island Apart, 1992. *Contributions:* Countryman; Woman's Own and various other magazines for women. *Literary Agent:* Curtis Brown Ltd, Haymarket House, 28–29 Haymarket, London, SW1Y 4SP, England. *Telephone:* (20) 7393-4400. *Fax:* (20) 7393-4401. *E-mail:* info@ curtisbrown.co.uk. *Website:* www.curtisbrown.co.uk.

BEDAU, Hugo Adam, BA, MA, PhD; American academic and writer; *Professor of Philosophy Emeritus, Tufts University*; b. 23 Sept. 1926, Portland, OR; m. 1st Jan Mastin 1952 (divorced 1988); three s. one d.; m. 2nd Constance Putnam 1990. *Education:* Univ. of Redlands, Harvard Univ. *Career:* instructor, Dartmouth Coll. 1953–54; Lecturer, Princeton Univ. 1954–57, 1958–61; Assoc. Prof., Reed Coll. 1962–66; Prof. of Philosophy, Tufts Univ. 1966–99, Prof. of Philosophy Emeritus 1999–; mem. American Asscn of Univ. Profs, American Philosophical Asscn, American Soc. for Political and Legal Philosophy. *Publications:* Victimless Crimes: Two Views (with Edwin M. Schur) 1974, The Courts, the Constitution, and Capital Punishment 1977, Current Issues and Enduring Questions (with Sylvan Barnet) 1987, Death is Different: Studies in the Morality, Law, and Politics of Capital Punishment 1987, In Spite of Innocence (with Michael Radelet and Constance Putnam) 1992, Critical Thinking, Reading, and Writing (with Sylvan Barnet) 1993, Thinking and Writing About Philosophy 1996, Making Mortal Choices 1996; editor: The Death Penalty in America 1964, Civil Disobedience: Theory and Practice 1969, Justice and Equality 1971, Capital Punishment in the United States (with Chester M. Pierce) 1976, Civil Disobedience in Focus 1991; contrib. to many books, journals and magazines. *Honours:* Visiting Life Fellow Clare Hall, Cambridge 1980, 1988, Max Planck Insts, Heidelberg and Freiburg im Breisgau, 1988, Wolfson Coll., Oxford 1989, Romanell-Phi Beta Kappa Prof. of Philosophy 1995, American Soc. of Criminology August Vollmer Award 1997, Civil Liberties Union of Massachusetts Roger Baldwin Award 2002. *Address:* c/o Department of Philosophy, Tufts University, Medford, MA 02155 (office); 111 Hayward Mill Road, Concord, MA 01742, USA (home). *Telephone:* (617) 627-3230 (office). *E-mail:* habedau@aol.com.

BEDFORD, Martyn Corby, MA; British writer and critic; *Critic-in-Residence, www.youwriteon.com*; b. 10 Oct. 1959, Croydon, Surrey; m. Damaris Croxall 1994. *Education:* Univ. of East Anglia. *Career:* Lecturer in Creative Writing, Univ. of Manchester 2001–06; Critic-in-Residence, www.youwriteon.com 2006–. *Publications:* Acts of Revision (Yorkshire Post Best First Work Award) 1996, Exit, Orange & Red 1997, The Houdini Girl 1999, Black Cat 2000, The Island of Lost Souls 2006. *Literary Agent:* c/o Curtis Brown Ltd, Haymarket House, 28–29 Haymarket, London, SW1Y 4SP, England. *Telephone:* (20) 7393-4400. *Fax:* (20) 7393-4401. *E-mail:* info@ curtisbrown.co.uk. *Website:* www.curtisbrown.co.uk. www .literaryintelligence.co.uk.

BEER, Dame Gillian Patricia Kempster, DBE, LittD, FBA, FRSL; British academic, writer and college president; b. 27 Jan. 1935, Bookham, Surrey; d. of Owen Kempster Thomas and Ruth Winifred Bell, fmrly Thomas; m. John Bernard Beer 1962; three s. *Education:* St Anne's Coll., Oxford. *Career:* Asst Lecturer, Bedford Coll., London 1959–62; part-time Lecturer, Univ. of

Liverpool 1962–64; Asst Lecturer, Univ. of Cambridge 1966–71, Lecturer, then Reader in Literature and Narrative 1971–89, Prof. of English 1989–94, King Edward VII Prof. of English Literature 1994–2002, Pres. Clare Hall 1994–2001; Fellow, Girton Coll. 1965–94, Hon. Fellow 1994–; Chair. Poetry Book Soc. 1992–96, Judges, Booker Prize 1997; Pres. History of Science Section of BAAS, British Comparative Literature Asscn 2004–; Vice-Pres. British Acad. 1994–96; mem. Bd Arts Council England East 2004–; Trustee, British Museum 1992–2002. *Publications:* Meredith: a change of masks 1970, The Romance 1970, Darwin's Plots 1983, George Eliot 1986, Arguing with the Past 1989, Open Fields 1996, Virginia Woolf: The Common Ground 1996. *Honours:* Hon. Mem. American Acad. of Arts and Sciences; Hon. Fellow, Univ. of Wales (Cardiff) 1986, St Anne's Coll., Oxford 1989; Hon. DLitt (Liverpool) 1995, (Oxford); Hon. LittD (Leicester, ARU, London); Hon. DLit (Queen's Univ., Belfast); Dr hc (Sorbonne, Paris); medals from MIT and Nat. Autonomous Univ., Mexico, Rosemarie Crawshay Prize, British Acad. 1984. *Address:* Clare Hall, Herschel Road, Cambridge, CB3 9AL (office); 6 Belvoir Terrace, Cambridge, CB2 2AA, England (home). *Telephone:* (1223) 356384 (office); (1223) 356384 (home). *Fax:* (1223) 332333 (office). *E-mail:* gpb1000@cam.ac.uk (office).

BEERS, Burton Floyd, AB, MA, PhD; American academic and writer; b. 13 Sept. 1927, Chemung, New York; m. Pauline Cone Beers 1952; one s. one d. *Education:* Hobart College, Duke University. *Career:* Instructor, 1955–57, Asst Prof., 1957–61, Assoc. Prof., 1961–66, Prof., 1966–96, North Carolina State University; mem. American Historical Asscn; Asscn for Asian Studies; Asscn of Historians in North Carolina; Historical Society of North Carolina; North Carolina Literary and Historical Society; Society for Historians of American Foreign Relations; Southern Historical Asscn. *Publications:* Vain Endeavor: Robert Lansing's Attempts to End the American-Japanese Rivalry, 1962; The Far East: A History of Western Impacts and Eastern Responses, 1830–1875 (with Paul H. Clyde), sixth edn, 1975; China in Old Photographs, 1981; North Carolina's China Connection 1840–1949 (with Lawrence Kessler and Charles LaMonica), 1981; North Carolina State University: A Pictorial History (with Murray S. Downs), 1986; The Vietnam War: An Historical Case Study (with Rose Ann Mulford), 1997; Living in our World (chief exec. ed.), 1998. Contributions: Textbooks, books, scholarly journals, and periodicals. *Honours:* Alexander Quarles Holladay Medal for Excellence, North Carolina State University Board of Trustees, 1992; Medal for Excellence, Hobart and William Smith Colleges, 1994; Watauga Medal, North Carolina State University, 1998.

BEEVOR, Antony, FRSL; British historian; b. 14 Dec. 1946, London, England; m. Artemis Cooper 1986; one s. one d. *Education:* Winchester Coll., Grenoble Univ., Royal Military Acad., Sandhurst. *Career:* Exec. Council French Theatre Season 1997; Lees-Knowles Lecturer, Univ. of Cambridge 2002; Visiting Prof., Birkbeck Coll., London 2002–; cttee mem. Soc. of Authors 2001–05 (chair. 2003–05), mem. of Council 2005–; mem. steering cttee Samuel Johnson Prize 2004–; judge British Acad. Book Prize 2004, David Cohen Prize 2004; mem. Anglo Hellenic League, Friends of the British Libraries, London Library. *Publications:* The Spanish Civil War 1982, The Enchantment of Christina Von Retzen (novel) 1988, Inside the British Army 1990, Crete: The Battle and the Resistance 1991, Paris After the Liberation 1944–49 1994, Stalingrad 1998, Berlin: The Downfall 1945 2002, The Mystery of Olga Chekhova 2004, A Writer at War: Vasily Grossman with the Red Army 1941–1945 (ed. with Luba Vinogradova) 2005, The Battle for Spain – The Spanish Civil War 1936–39 2006; contrib. to TLS, Times, Telegraph, Independent, Spectator, Guardian. *Honours:* Hon. DLitt (Kent) 2004; Runciman Award 1992, Samuel Johnson Prize for Non-Fiction 1999, Wolfson Prize for History 1999, Hawthornden Prize 1999, Longman-History Today Trustees' Award 2003; Chevalier, Ordre des Arts et des Lettres 1997. *Literary Agent:* Andrew Nurnberg Associates, 45–47 Clerkenwell Green, London, EC1R 0QX, England. *Website:* www.antonybeevor.com.

BEGLEY, Louis, AB, LLB; American lawyer and writer; b. 6 Oct. 1933, Stryj, Poland; m. 1st Sally Higginson 1956 (divorced 1970); two s. one d.; m. 2nd Anka Muhlstein 1974. *Education:* Harvard Univ. *Career:* specialist in int. corporate law; writer and lecturer; mem. Bar Asscn of the City of New York, Council on Foreign Relations, American Philosophical Soc. *Publications:* fiction: Wartime Lies 1991, The Man Who Was Late 1993, As Max Saw It 1994, About Schmidt 1996, Mistler's Exit 1998, Schmidt Delivered 2000, Shipwreck 2003, Matters of Honor 2007; non-fiction: Das Gelobte Land 2002, Venedig Unter Vier Augen (with Anka Muhlstein) 2003; contrib. to periodicals. *Honours:* Irish Times-Aer Lingus Int. Fiction Prize 1991, PEN/Ernest Hemingway First Fiction Award 1992, Prix Médicis Étranger 1992, Jeanette-Schocken Preis, Bremerhaven Bürgerpreis für Literatur 1995, American Acad. of Arts and Letters Award in Literature 1995, Konrad-Adenauer Stiftung Literaturpreis 1999. *Literary Agent:* Georges Borchardt, 136 E 57th Street, New York, NY 10022, USA.

BÉGUIN, Bernard, LèsL; Swiss journalist; b. 14 Feb. 1923, Sion, Valais; s. of Bernard Béguin and Clemence Welten; m. Antoinette Waelbroeck 1948; two s. two d. *Education:* Geneva High School, Geneva Univ. and Graduate Inst. of Int. Studies. *Career:* Swiss Sec. World Student Relief 1945–46; corresp. at UN European Headquarters; Journal de Geneva 1946–70, Foreign Ed. 1947, Ed.-in-Chief 1959–70; Diplomatic Commentator, Swiss Broadcasting System 1954–59, Swiss TV 1959–70; Head of Programmes, Swiss French-speaking TV 1970–73; Deputy Dir Radio and TV 1973–86; Cen. Pres. Swiss Press Asscn 1958–60, Hon. mem. 1974–; Visiting Prof. in Professional Ethics, Univ. of

Neuchâtel 1984–88; Pres. Swiss Press Council 1985–90; Pres. Swiss Ind. Authority on Complaints concerning Broadcasting Programmes 1991–92; consultant with UNESCO (assessment of the media environment), Belarus 1994; mem. Fed. Comm. on Cartels 1964–80; mem. Bd, Swiss Telegraphic Agency 1968–71. *Journaliste, qui t'a fait roi? Les médias entre droit et liberté,* 1988. *Address:* 41 avenue de Budé, 1202 Geneva 1, Switzerland. *Telephone:* (22) 733-75-30. *Fax:* (22) 733-75-30 (home). *E-mail:* beguinb@worldcom.ch (home).

BÉGUIN, Louis-Paul, BA; French writer and poet; b. 31 March 1923, Amiens. *Education:* Sorbonne, University of Paris. *Career:* mem. PEN, Québec; Québec Writers Union. *Publications:* Miroir de Janus, 1966; Impromptu de Québec, 1974; Un homme et son langage, 1977; Problèmes de langage, 1978; Idoles et Paraboles, 1982; Yourcenar, 1982; Poèmes et pastiches, 1985; Parcours paralleles, 1988; Ange Pleureur, 1991; Poèmes depuis la tendre enfance, 1995; The Weeping Angel, 1996; Écrits des trois pignans, 1998. Contributions: newspapers and magazines. *Honours:* Poetry Award, 1967; Prix Montcalm, 1974.

BEHAR, Ruth, BA, MA, PhD; American academic, poet and writer; b. 12 Nov. 1956, Havana, Cuba; m. David Frye 1982, one s. *Education:* Wesleyan University, Princeton University. *Career:* Asst Prof., 1986–89, Assoc. Prof., 1989–94, Prof. of Anthropology, 1994–, University of Michigan at Ann Arbor. *Publications:* Santa Maria del Monte: The Presence of the Past in a Spanish Village, 1986, revised edn as The Presence of the Past in a Spanish Village: Santa Maria del Monte, 1991; Translated Woman: Crossing the Border with Esperanza's Story, 1993; Bridges to Cuba (Puentes a Cuba) (ed.), 1995; Las Visiones de una Bruja Guachichil en 1599: Hacia una Perspectiva Indígena Sobre la Conquista de San Luis Potosal, 1995; Women Writing Culture (co-ed.), 1995; The Vulnerable Observer: Anthropology That Breaks Your Heart, 1996. Contributions: anthologies, scholarly journals and literary periodicals. *Honours:* John D. and Catherine T. MacArthur Foundation Fellowship, 1988–93; Guggenheim Fellowship, 1995–96. *E-mail:* rbehar@umich.edu. *Website:* www.ruthbehar.com.

BEHBAHANI, Simin; Iranian poet; b. 1927, Tehran; d. of Abbas Khalili and Fakhr Azami Arghoon; m. 1st; m. 2nd; three c. *Publications include:* The Broken Lute 1951, Footprint 1954, Candelabrum 1955, Marble 1961, Resurrection 1971, A Line of Speed and Fire 1980, Arzhan Plain 1983, Guzinah-i Ash'ar (Selected Poems) 1988, An Mard Mard-i Hamraham (That Man, My Fellow Man) 1990, Simin Chilchiragh (Chandelier) 1991, Paper Dress 1992, A Windowful of Freedom 1995. *Honours:* Human Rights Watch-Hellman/Hammet grant 1998, Carl von Ossietzky Medal 1999. *Address:* c/o Ministry of Culture and Islamic Guidance, Baharestan Square, Tehran, Iran.

BEHRENS, Katja; German writer; b. 18 Dec. 1942, Berlin; m. Peter Behrens 1960 (divorced 1971). *Career:* trans. of contemporary American literature (including William S. Burroughs and Henry Miller) 1960–73; ed., publishing house 1973–78; writer 1978–; Guest Prof., Washington Univ., St Louis, Mo. 1986, Dartmouth Coll., Hanover, NH 1991; mem. German PEN. *Publications include:* Die Weiße Frau 1978, Die Dreizehnte Fee 1983, Im Wasser tanzen 1990, Salomo und die anderen 1992, Die Vagantin 1997, Zorro – Im Jahr des Pferdes 1999, Alles Sehen Kommt von der Seele – Die Lebensgeschichte der Helen Keller 2001, Hathaway Jones (Literaturpreis der Stadt Wiesbaden 2002, Ehrengabe der Deutschen Schillerstiftung 2003) 2003, Alles aus Liebe, sonst geht die Welt unter 2005. *Honours:* Förderpreis zum Ingeborg Bachmann Preis 1978, Förderpreis der Märkischen Kulturkonferenz 1978, Thaddäus Troll Preis 1982, Villa Massimo Stipendium in Olevano 1986, Stadtschreiberin von Mainz 1992, Künstlerhaus Schloß Wiepersdorf 1996, Premio Internazionale 'Lo Stellato' 2000, Kinder- und Jugendbuchpreis Luchs 2002. *Address:* Park Rosenhöhe 23, 64287 Darmstadt, Germany. *Telephone:* (6151) 54762. *Fax:* (6151) 54762. *E-mail:* behrenskatja@aol.com. *Website:* www.katja-behrens.de.

BEHRENS, Peter; Canadian writer and screenwriter; b. 4 Sept. 1946, Montréal. *Education:* Lower Canada Coll., Concordia Univ., McGill Univ. *Career:* Wallace Stegner Fellowship in Creative Writing, Stanford Univ.; Fellow, Fine Arts Work Center, Provincetown, MA. *Screenplays:* Night Driving (TV) 1993, Cadillac Girls 1993, Promise the Moon (TV) 1997, Kayla 1999. *Publications:* Night Driving (short stories) 1987, The Law of Dreams (novel) 2007; contrib. short stories and essays to magazines, including The Atlantic Monthly, Best Canadian Essays, Best Canadian Stories, Brick, Lost, Tin House, and to anthologies. *Honours:* Gov.-Gen's Literary Award 2006. *Literary Agent:* c/o Sarah Burnes, The Gernert Company, 136 E 57th Street, New York, NY 10022, USA. *E-mail:* himself@peterbehrens.org. *Website:* www.peterbehrens.org.

BEI DAO; Chinese poet; b. (Zhao Zhenkai), 1949, Beijing; m. Shao Fei; one d. *Career:* co-f., Jintian literary magazine, 1978–80, 1990–; worked at Foreign Languages Press, Beijing; exiled 1989–; McAndless Chair in Humanities, Eastern Michigan Univ. from 1993; Visiting Artist/Writer, Int. Inst.; Visiting Scholar, Center for Chinese Studies. *Publications:* Taiyang cheng zhaji 1978, Huida (poem) 1979, Notes from the City of the Sun (trans.) 1983, Bodong (novel, trans. as Waves) 1985, Bei Dao shi xuan (poems, trans. as The August Sleepwalker) 1986, Bai ri meng (poem) 1986, Bei Dao shi ji 1988, Old Snow (trans.) 1991, Forms of Distance (trans.) 1994, Landscape Over Zero 1996, Unlock 2000, Blue House 2000, At the Sky's Edge: Poems 1991–1996 2001; contrib. to Shi Kan, Renditions, Bulletin of Concerned Asian Scholars, Contemporary Chinese Literature (anthology) 1985, numerous other anthologies. *Honours:* hon. mem. American Acad. of Arts and Letters. *Address:* c/o Jintian magazine, PO Box 3384, Iowa City, IA 52244-3384, USA.

BEIGBEDER, Frédéric; French novelist; b. 21 Sept. 1965, Neuilly-sur-Seine. *Publications:* Mémoire d'un jeune homme dérangé 1990, Vacances dans le coma 1994, L'Amour dure trois ans 1997, Nouvelles sous ecstasy 1999, Barbie (Barbie (Universe of Fashion)) 1998, 99 francs (£9.99, aka £6.99) 2000, Dernier inventaire avant liquidation 2001, Windows on the World (Independent Foreign Fiction Prize 2005) 2004. *Address:* c/o Éditions Grasset, 61 rue des Saints-Pères, 75006 Paris, France.

BEILHARZ, Manfred; German director and producer; b. 13 July 1938, Böblingen. *Education:* Universität Tübingen, Universität München, Paris, London. *Career:* founded Studiobühne at München; Asst Dir Münchner Kammerspiele; Dir and head of literary dept, Westfälisches Landestheater 1968; Artistic Dir, Tübingen Landestheater 1970–75, City Theatre of Freiburg 1976–83, City Theatre of Kassel 1983–91, Schauspiel, Bonn 1991–92; Genralintendant, Municipal Theatre of Bonn 1997–2002; Dir Hessisches Staatstheater Wiesbaden; mem. Acad. of Performing Arts, Frankfurt, European Theatre Convention, Brussels and Paris; Vice-Pres. Hessischen Theaterakademie, Frankfurt; Pres. Int. Theatre Inst.; Chair. Dramaturgische Gesellschaft, Berlin. *Plays and opera directed:* Marat Sade, The Mother, Threepenny Opera, Mahagonny, A Romantic Woman, A Midsummer Night's Dream, Fidelio, The Hot Oven, L'enfant et les sortilèges, Love of Three Oranges, Falstaff, Spring Awakening, Schauspiel Bonn 1997, Wozzeck, Opera Bonn, Der Zerbrochne Krug. *Address:* c/o ITI, 1 rue Miollis, 75732 Paris, France. *Telephone:* 1-45-68-48-80. *Fax:* 1-45-66-48-80. *E-mail:* iti@unesco.org.

BEISSEL, Henry Eric, BA, MA; Canadian (b. German) poet, dramatist, writer, translator and editor and teacher; *Distinguished Professor Emeritus, Concordia University, Montreal;* b. 12 April 1929, Cologne, Germany; s. of Walter Beissel and Johanna Dilgen; m. 1st Ruth Heydasch; two d.; m. 2nd Arlette Francière 1981; one d. *Education:* Univs of Cologne, Germany, London, UK and Univ. of Toronto, Canada. *Career:* teacher, Univ. of Munich, Germany 1960–62, Univ. of Edmonton 1962–64, Univ. of Trinidad 1964–66; Faculty, Concordia Univ., Montréal 1966–96, Prof. of English Emer. 1997–, Distinguished Prof. Emer. 2000–; Founder-Ed. Edge Journal 1963–69; Deutscher Akademischer Austauschdienst Fellowship 1977; mem. League of Canadian Poets (Pres. 1980–81), PEN, Playwrights Canada, Writers' Union of Canada. *Plays:* The Curve (translated from Tankred Dorst, Univ. of Alberta Theatre, Edmonton) 1962, A Trumpet for Nap (translated from Tankred Dorst, Little Angel Theatre, London, UK) UK 1968–70, Mister Skinflint (Montreal, Jesu Theatre) 1969, Inook and the Sun (Stratford Shakespeare Festival, Ont.) 1973, For Crying Out Loud (Char-Lan Theatre Workshop, Williamstown, Ont.) 1975, Goya (Montreal Theatre Lab) 1976, Under Coyote's Eye (Chicago, The Other Theatre) 1978, The Emigrants (translated from Slawomir Mrozek, Saidye Bronfman Centre Theatre, Montreal) 1981, Hedda Gabler (Univ. from Henrik Ibsen, The Saidye Bronfman Centre Theatre, Montreal) 1982, The Noose (Univ. of Winnipeg Theatre) 1985, Improvisations for Mr. X (New York, Actors' Studio) 1979, The Glass Mountain (translated with Per Brask from Tor Age Bringsvaerd, Univ. of Winnipeg Theatre) 1990. *Radio:* The Double Take (translated and adapted from Luigi Pirandello, CBC) 1985, The Apple Orchard (translated and adapted from Walter Bauer, CBC) 1959, The Inseparable (translated and adapted from Walter Bauer, CBC) 1959, The Curve (translated and adapted from Tankred Dorst, CBC) 1968, All Corpses are Equal (translated and adapted with Jia-Lin Peng from Shie Min, CKUT) 1988). *Publications:* poetry: Witness the Heart 1963, New Wings for Icarus 1966, The World is a Rainbow 1968, Face on the Dark 1970, The Salt I Taste 1975, Cantos North 1980, Season of Blood 1984, Poems New and Selected 1987, Ammonite 1987, Dying I Was Born 1992, Stones to Harvest 1993, The Dragon and the Pearl 2002, Across the Sun's Warp 2003; plays: Inook and the Sun 1974, Goya 1978, Under Coyote's Eye 1980, The Noose 1989, Improvisations for Mr X 1989, Inuk 2000; other: Kanada: Romantik und Wirklichkeit 1981, Raging Like a Fire: A Celebration of Irving Layton (co-ed. with Joy Bennett) 1993; translations of poetry and plays; contrib. to journals. *Honours:* Epstein Award 1958, Davidson Award 1959, Sr Canada Council Award 1969, DAAD Fellowship, Berlin 1977, Walter-Bauer Literaturpreis, Germany 1994, First Prize (Poetry), Surrey Int. Writers' Conf. 2006. *Address:* 34 Woodview Crescent, Ottawa, ON K1B 3A9, Canada (home). *Telephone:* (613) 845-0676 (home). *E-mail:* hebe@rogers.com (home).

BEJERANO, Maya, BA, MA; Israeli librarian, poet and writer; b. 23 Feb. 1949, Haifa; m. 1983 (divorced 1988); one d. *Education:* Bar-Ilan Univ. and Hebrew Univ. of Jerusalem. *Career:* librarian, Main Public Library, Tel-Aviv. *Publications:* Bat Yaana (Ostrich) 1978, Ha-Chom Ve-Ha-Kor (The Heat and the Cold) 1981, Ibud Netunim 52 Shishah Maamarim u Maamar al Mosad Meen Makamah (Data Processing) 1982, Shirat Ha-Tsiporim (The Song of Birds) 1985, Retsef Ha-Shirim (Selected Poems) 1987, Voice 1987, Whale 1990, Anase La-Gaat Be-Tabur Bitny (Trying to Touch my Belly Button) 1997, Optical Poems: Thirteen Poems of Maya Bejerano Produced to Interactive Media Works (CD ROM) 1999; contrib. to newspapers and journals. *Honours:* Hary Harshon Prize 1976, Levi Eschol Prize 1986, Bernstein Prize for Poetry 1989, Prime Minister Award 1986, 1995–96. *Address:* c/o Ministry of Education, POB 292, 34 Shivtei Israel Street, Jerusalem 91911, Israel.

BÉJI, Hélé; Tunisian essayist and novelist; b. 1948, Tunis. *Career:* fmrly taught literature Univ. of Tunis; worked for UNESCO, Paris, France; lives in Paris. *Publications:* Le Désenchantement national: essai sur la décolonisation

1982, L'Oeil du jour (novel) 1985, Itinéraire de Paris à Tunis, Satire 1992, L'Art contre la culture, Nûba 1994, La Fièvre identitaire 1997, L'Imposture culturelle 1997, Une Force qui demeure 2006; contrib. to numerous journals, including Revue des Deux Mondes. *Address:* c/o Editions Arléa, 16 rue de l'Odéon, 75006 Paris, France (office).

BÉKÉS, Pál; Hungarian author, playwright and translator. *Career:* Iowa Int. Writing Program, USA 1997; Artistic Dir, Magyar Magic festival, UK 2003. *Publications:* 16 publications include Darvak 1979, Szerelmem útközben 1983, Lakótelepi mítoszok 1984, Törzsi viszonyok 1990, A noi partorség szeme láttara 1992. *Honours:* Fulbright Scholarship, USA 1992–93. *Address:* c/o Hungarian Cultural Centre, 10 Maiden Lane, Covent Garden, London, WC2E 7NA, England.

BEKRI, Tahar, PhD; Tunisian poet; b. 7 July 1951, Gabès; m. Annick Le Thoër 1987. *Education:* Univ. of Tunisia, Sorbonne, Univ. of Paris. *Career:* maître de conférences, Univ. of Paris X, Nanterre; mem. Soc. des Gens de Lettres de France, Maison des Ecrivains. *Publications:* Poèmes bilingues 1978, Exils 1979, Le laboureur du soleil 1983, Les lignes sont des arbres 1984, Le chant du roi errant 1985, Malek Haddad 1986, Le coeur rompu aux océans 1988, Poèmes à Selma 1989, La sève des jours 1991, Les chapelets d'attache 1993, Littératures de Tunisie et du Maghreb 1994, Les songes impatients 1997, Journal de neige et de feu 1997, Le pêcheur de lunes 1998, Inconnues saisons (translated as Unknown Seasons) 1999, De la littérature tunisienne et maghrébine 1999, Marcher sur l'oubli 2000, L'horizon incendié 2002, La brûlante rumeur de la mer 2004, Le vent sans abri 2005, Dernières nouvelles de l'été 2005, Si la musique doit mourir 2006, Le livre du souvenir 2007; contrib. to various publs. *Honours:* Officier, Mérite Culturel, Tunisia 1993; Prix Tunisie-France 2006. *Address:* 32 rue Pierre Nicole, 75005 Paris, France (home). *Telephone:* 1-43-29-33-39 (home). *Fax:* 1-43-29-33-39 (home); 1-40-97-71-51 (office). *E-mail:* taharbekri@wanadoo.fr (home); tahar.bekri@u_paris10 .fr (office). *Website:* tahar.bekri.free.fr.

BELITT, Ben, BA, MA; American academic, poet and writer; b. 2 May 1911, New York, NY. *Education:* University of Virginia. *Career:* Asst Literary Ed., The Nation, 1936–37; Faculty Mem. to Prof. of Literature and Languages, Bennington College, Vermont, 1938–; mem. Authors' Guild; PEN; Vermont Acad. of Arts and Sciences, fellow. *Publications:* Poetry: Wilderness Stair, 1955; The Enemy Joy: New and Selected Poems, 1964; Nowhere But Light: Poems, 1964–1969, 1970; The Double Witness: Poems, 1970–1976, 1977; Possessions: New and Selected Poems, 1938–1985, 1986; Graffiti, 1990. Other: School of the Soldier, 1949; Adam's Dream: A Preface to Translation, 1978; The Forged Feature: Toward a Poetics of Uncertainty, 1994; ed. and trans. of several vols; contrib. to books. *Honours:* Shelley Memorial Award in Poetry, 1936; Guggenheim Fellowship, 1947; Brandeis University Creative Arts Award, 1962; National Institute of Arts and Letters Award, 1965; National Endowment for the Arts Grant, 1967–68; Ben Belitt Lectureship Endowment, Bennington College, 1977; Russell Loines Award for Poetry, American Acad. and Institute of Arts and Letters, 1981; Rockefeller Foundation Residency, Bellagio, Italy, 1984; Williams/Derwood Award for Poetry, 1986.

BELL, Antonia (see Rae-Ellis, Vivienne)

BELL, Edward; British publisher; *Partner, Bell Lomax Literary and Sport Agency;* b. 2 Aug. 1949, s. of Eddie Bell and Jean Bell; m. Junette Bannatyne 1969; one s. two d. *Education:* Airdrie High School. *Career:* with Hodder & Stoughton 1970–85; Man. Dir Collins Gen. Div. 1985–89; launched Harper Paperbacks in USA 1989; Deputy Chief Exec., HarperCollins UK 1990–91, Chief Exec. 1991–92, Chair. 1992–2000; Chair. HarperCollins India 1994–2000; Dir (non-exec.) Haynes Publishing 2001, Be Cogent Ltd, Management Diagnostics Ltd; Chair. (non-exec.) OAG Worldwide Ltd 2001; Chair. Those Who Can Ltd 2001; Pnr, Bell Lomax Literary and Sport Agency 2002–; Gov. Kent and Surrey Inst. of Art and Design. *Address:* The Bell Lomax Agency, James House, 1 Babmaes Street, London, SW1Y 6HF, England (office). *Telephone:* (20) 7930-4447 (office). *Fax:* (20) 7925-0118 (office). *E-mail:* eddie@bell-lomax.co.uk.

BELL, Hilary; Australian playwright; b. 1966; m. Phillip Johnston. *Education:* Australia's Nat. Inst. of Drama (NIDA) Playwright Studio, Australia Film Television & Radio School (AFTRS), Juilliard School, New York, USA. *Plays:* Fortune 1995, Wolf Lullaby 1997, The Falls 2001, The Anatomy Lesson of Doctor Ruysch 2002, Shot While Dancing 2004. *Publications:* Fortune 1994, Wolf Lullaby 1996, Mirror Mirror. *Honours:* Philip Parsons Playwright Award 1994, Jill Blewett Playwright Award 1996, Eric Kocher Playwright Award 1997, Australian Writers' Guild Award 2003. *Literary Agent:* RGM Associates, PO Box 128, Surry Hills, NSW 2010, Australia. *Telephone:* 61 2 9281 3911. *Fax:* 61 2 9281 4705. *E-mail:* info@rgm .com.au. *Website:* www.rgm.com.au.

BELL, Madison Smartt, AB, MA; American writer and academic; *Director of Creative Writing Program, Goucher College;* b. 1 Aug. 1957, Nashville, TN; m. Elizabeth Spires 1985. *Education:* Princeton Univ., Hollins Coll. *Career:* Lecturer, Poetry Center of the 92nd Street YMHA, New York 1984–86; writer-in-residence, Dir of the Creative Writing Program, Goucher Coll. 1984–86, 1988–, Dir of the Kratz Center for Creative Writing 1999–, also now Prof. of English; Visiting Lecturer, Univ. of Iowa 1987–88; Visiting Assoc. Prof., Johns Hopkins Univ. 1989–95; Fellow Soc. of American Historians 2005; mem. Fellowship of Southern Writers. *Publications:* fiction: The Washington Square Ensemble 1983, Waiting for the End of the World 1985, Straight Cut 1986,

Zero db 1987, The Year of Silence 1987, Soldier's Joy 1989, Barking Man 1990, Doctor Sleep 1991, Save Me, Joe Louis 1993, All Souls' Rising (Annisfield-Wolf Award 1996) 1995, Ten Indians 1996, Master of the Crossroads 2000, Anything Goes 2002, The Stone the Builder refused 2004; non-fiction: readers' guides on various authors 1979–83, The History of the Owen Graduate School of Management 1988, Narrative Design: A Writer's Guide to Structure 1997, Narrative Design: Working with Imagination, Craft and Form 2000, Lavoisier in the Year One 2005, Toussaint Louverture: A Biography 2007; contribs fiction in many anthologies and periodicals, also essays, book reviews, etc. *Honours:* Lillian Smith Award 1989, Guggenheim Fellowship 1991, George A. and Eliza Gardner Howard Foundation Award 1991–92, Maryland State Arts Council Award 1991, NEA Fellowship 1992. *Address:* Kratz Center for Creative Writing, Goucher College, 1021 Dulaney Valley Road, Baltimore, MD 21204-2794, USA (office). *E-mail:* mbell@goucher.edu (office).

BELL, Marvin Hartley, BA, MA, MFA; American academic, poet and writer; *Flannery O'Connor Professor Emeritus of Letters, University of Iowa*; b. 3 Aug. 1937, New York, NY; m. Dorothy Murphy; two s. *Education:* Alfred Univ., Univ. of Chicago, Univ. of Iowa. *Career:* Prof., Faculty Writers' Workshop 1965–2005, Prof. Emer. 2005–; Prof. 1986–2005, Univ. of Iowa, Flannery O'Connor Prof. Emer. of Letters 2005–; Distinguished Visiting Prof., Univ. of Hawaii 1981; Visiting Lecturer, Goddard Coll. 1970; Visiting Prof., Univ. of Washington 1982; Distinguished Poet-in-Residence, Wichita State Univ. 2004; Lila Wallace-Reader's Digest Writing Fellow, Univ. of Redlands 1991–93; Woodrow Wilson Visiting Fellow, Saint Mary's Coll. of California 1994–95, Pacific Univ. 1996–97, Nebraska-Wesleyan Univ. 1996–97, Hampden-Sydney Coll. 1998–99, West Virginia Wesleyan Coll. 2000–01, Birmingham Southern Coll. 2000–01, Illinois Coll. 2002–03, Bethany Coll. 2003–04; Poetry Ed. The Iowa Review 1969–71, Guest Poetry Ed. 1980, 2005; Poetry Ed. Pushcart Prize 1991–92, 1996–97, Series Poetry Ed. 1997–2002; Prague Seminars 2002, 2004; Urban Teachers' Workshop for America Scores 2002–; Faculty, Rainier Writing Workshop, Pacific Lutheran Univ. 2004–; Faculty, Pacific Univ./Mountain Writers' Center MFA 2004–; Ed. and Publr Statements 1959–64; Poetry Ed. The North American Review 1964–69; columnist, The American Poetry Review 1975–78, 1990–92; first Poet Laureate of the State of Iowa 2000–04. *Publications:* poetry: Things We Dreamt We Died For 1966, A Probable Volume of Dreams 1969, The Escape Into You 1971, Residue of Song 1974, Stars Which See, Stars Which Do Not See 1977, These Green-Going-to-Yellow 1981, Segues: A Correspondence in Poetry (with William Stafford) 1983, Drawn by Stones, by Earth, by Things That Have Been in the Fire 1984, New and Selected Poems 1987, Iris of Creation 1990, The Book of the Dead Man 1994, Ardor: The Book of the Dead Man (vol. two) 1997, Poetry for a Midsummer's Night 1998, Wednesday: Selected Poems 1966–1997 1998, Nightworks: Poems 1962–2000 2000, Rampant 2004; other: Old Snow Just Melting: Essays and Interviews 1983, A Marvin Bell Reader: Selected Prose and Poetry 1994; contrib. to many anthologies and periodicals. *Honours:* Hon. DLitt (Alfred Univ.) 1986; Acad. of American Poets Lamont Award 1969, Guggenheim Fellowship 1977, Nat. Endowment for the Arts Fellowships 1978, 1984, Sr Fulbright Scholar 1983, 1986, American Poetry Review Prize 1982, American Acad. of Arts and Letters Award in Literature 1994, American Poetry Review Shestack Prize 2003. *Address:* 1416 E College Street, Iowa City, IA 52245, USA. *E-mail:* marvin-bell@uiowa.edu (office).

BELL, Robin, MA, MS; British writer, poet and broadcaster; b. 4 Jan. 1945, Dundee, Scotland; two d. *Education:* St Andrews Univ., Columbia Univ., New York, USA. *Radio:* Strathinver: A Portrait Album 1945–1953 (Sony Award for Best British Radio Feature 1985). *Art exhibitions:* My River, Your River (sequence for UK G8) 2005, Drawing The Tay (solo touring) 2006–. *Television:* broadcast drama and documentaries include Strathinver, The Other Thief, Melville Bay, Bittersweet Within My Heart. *Publications:* Sawing Logs 1980, Strathinver: A Portrait Album 1984, Radio Poems 1989, The Best of Scottish Poetry (ed.) 1989, Collected Poems of the Marquis of Montrose (ed.) 1990, Bittersweet Within My Heart, The Collected Poems of Mary, Queen of Scots (trans.) 1992, Scanning the Forth Bridge 1994, Le Château des Enfants 2000, Chapeau! 2002, Civil Warrior 2002, Tethering a Horse 2004, How to Tell Lies 2006. *Honours:* Best Documentary, TV and Radio Industries of Scotland Award 1984, Creative Scotland Award 2005. *Address:* The Orchard Muirton, Auchterarder, Perthshire, PH3 1ND, Scotland. *Telephone:* (1764) 662211.

BELL BURNELL, Dame S(usan) Jocelyn, DBE, PhD, FRS; British astrophysicist and fmr university administrator; *Visiting Professor, University of Oxford*; b. 15 July 1943, d. of (George) Philip Bell and (Margaret) Allison Bell (née Kennedy); m. (divorced); one s. *Career:* Lecturer, Univ. of Southampton 1968–73; part-time with Mullard Space Lab., Univ. Coll. London 1974–82; part-time with Royal Observatory, Edin. 1982–91; Chair. Physics Dept Open Univ. 1991–99; Dean of Science, Univ. of Bath 2001–04; Visiting Prof. for Distinguished Teaching, Princeton Univ. 1999–2000; Visiting Prof., Univ. of Oxford 2004–; Pres. Royal Astronomical Soc. 2002–04; Fellow Royal Soc. of Edin. 2004; discovered the first four pulsars; frequent radio and TV broadcaster on science, on being a woman in science and on science and religion. *Publications:* two books, approximately 70 scientific papers and 35 Quaker publs. *Honours:* Hon. Fellow New Hall, Cambridge 1996; 15 hon. doctorates, including Univs of Cambridge, London and Harvard; Joseph Black Medal and Cowie Book Prize, Glasgow Univ. 1962, Michelson Medal, Franklin Inst., USA 1973, J. Robert Oppenheimer Memorial Prize, Center for Theoretical Studies, Fla 1978, Beatrice M. Tinsley Prize, American Astronomical Soc. (first recipient) 1987, Herschel Medal, Royal Astronomical Soc., London 1989, Edinburgh Medal 1999, Magellanic Premium, American Philosophical Soc. 2000, Joseph Priestly Award, Dickinson Coll., Pa 2002, Robinson Medal, Armagh Observatory 2004. *Address:* University of Oxford, Astrophysics, Denys Wilkinson Building, Keble Road, Oxford, OX1 3RH, England (office). *Telephone:* (1865) 273306 (office). *Fax:* (1865) 273390 (office). *E-mail:* jocelyn@astro.ox.ac.uk (office).

BELLAMY, David James, OBE, PhD, CBiol, FIBiol; British botanist, writer, broadcaster and environmental organisation administrator; b. 18 Jan. 1933, London; s. of Thomas Bellamy and Winifred Green; m. Rosemary Froy 1959; two s. three d. *Education:* Chelsea Coll. of Science and Tech. and Bedford Coll., London Univ. *Career:* Lecturer, then Sr Lecturer, Dept of Botany, Univ. of Durham 1960–80, Hon. Prof. of Adult and Continuing Educ. 1980–82; Visiting Prof., Massey Univ., NZ 1988–89; Special Prof. of Botany, Univ. of Nottingham 1987–; TV and radio presenter and scriptwriter; Founder Dir Conservation Foundation; Pres. WATCH 1982; Pres. Youth Hostels Asscn 1983; Pres. Population Concern 1988–, Nat. Asscn of Environmental Educ. 1989–, Plantlife 1995–, Wildlife Trust's Partnership 1996–, British Inst. of Cleaning Science 1997–; Dir David Bellamy Assocs (environmental consultants) 1988–97, Bellamy & Nevard Environmental Consultants 2003–; Pres. Council Zoological Soc. of London 1991–94, BH&HPA 2000–, Camping and Caravanning Club 2002–. *Television series includes:* Life in Our Sea 1970, Bellamy on Botany 1973, Bellamy's Britain 1975, Bellamy's Europe 1977, Botanic Man 1978, Up a Gum Tree 1980, Backyard Safari 1981, The Great Seasons 1982, Bellamy's New World 1983, End of the Rainbow Show 1986, S.W.A.L.L.O.W. 1986, Turning the Tide 1986, Bellamy's Bugle 1986, 1987, 1988, Bellamy on Top of the World 1987, Bellamy's Journey to the Centre of the World 1987, Bellamy's Bird's Eye View 1989, Wheat Today What Tomorrow? 1989, Moa's Ark 1990, Bellamy Rides Again 1992, Blooming Bellamy 1993, 1994, Routes of Wisdom 1993, The Peak 1994, Bellamy's Border Raids 1996, Westwatch 1997, A Welsh Herbal 1998, Salt Solutions 1999, The Challenge 1999. *Publications include:* Peatlands 1974, Life Giving Sea 1977, Half of Paradise 1979, The Great Seasons 1981, Discovering the Countryside with David Bellamy (Vols I, II) 1982, (Vols III, IV) 1983, The Mouse Book 1983, The Queen's Hidden Garden 1984, Bellamy's Ireland 1986, Bellamy's Changing Countryside (four vols) 1988, England's Last Wilderness 1989, Wetlands 1990, Wilderness Britain 1990, Moa's Ark 1990, How Green Are You? 1991, Tomorrow's Earth 1992, World Medicine 1992, Poo, You and the Poteroo's Loo 1997, Bellamy's Changing Countryside 1998, The Glorious Trees of Great Britain 2002, Jolly Green Giant (autobiog.) 2002, The Bellamy Herbal 2003, and books connected with TV series. *Honours:* Hon. Fellow CIWEM; Hon. FLS; Dutch Order of the Golden Ark 1989; Hon. DSc; Hon. DUniv; Dr hc (CNAA) 1990; UNEP Global 500 Award 1990, Busk Medal, Royal Geographical Soc. *Address:* The Mill House, Bedburn, Bishop Auckland, Co. Durham, DL13 3NN, England. *Website:* www.wildlifebiz.com (office).

BELLAMY, Joe David, BA, MFA; American academic, writer and poet; b. 29 Dec. 1941, Cincinnati, OH; m. Connie Sue Arendsee 1964, one s. one d. *Education:* Duke University, Antioch College, University of Iowa. *Career:* Instructor, 1969–70, Asst Prof., 1970–72, Mansfield State College, Pennsylvania; Publisher and Ed., Fiction International magazine and press, 1972–84; Asst Prof., 1972–74, Assoc. Prof., 1974–80, Prof. of English, 1980–, St Lawrence University, Canton, New York; Program Consultant in American Literature, Divisions of Public Programs and Research Programs, National Endowment for the Humanities, 1976–90; Pres. and Chair, Board of Dirs, Co-ordinating Council of Literary Magazines, 1979–81, and Associated Writing Programs, 1990; Distinguished Visiting Prof., George Mason University, 1987–88; Dir, Literature Program, National Endowment for the Arts, 1990–92; Whichard Distinguished Prof. in the Humanities, East Carolina University, 1994–96; mem. National Book Critics Circle. *Publications:* Apocalypse: Dominant Contemporary Forms, 1972; The New Fiction: Interviews with Innovative Writers, 1974; Superfiction, or the American Story Transformed, 1975; Olympic Gold Medallist (poems), 1978; Moral Fiction: An Anthology, 1980; New Writers for the Eighties: An Anthology, 1981; Love Stories/Love Poems: An Anthology (with Roger Weingarten), 1982; American Poetry Observed: Poets on Their Work, 1984; The Frozen Sea (poems), 1988; Suzi Sinzinnati (novel), 1989; Atomic Love (short stories), 1993; Literary Luxuries: American Writing at the End of the Millennium, 1995. Contributions: Books, anthologies, journals and magazines. *Honours:* Bread Loaf Scholar-Bridgman Award, 1973; National Endowment for the Humanities Fellowship, 1974; Fels Award, 1976; Co-ordinating Council of Literary Magazine Award for Fiction, 1977; Kansas Quarterly-Kansas Arts Commission Fiction Prize, 1982; New York State Council on the Arts Grant in Fiction, 1984; National Endowment for the Arts Fellowship for Creative Writers, 1985; Eds' Book Award, 1989.

BELLE, Pamela Dorothy Alice, BA; British author; b. 16 June 1952, Ipswich, Suffolk; m. Steve Thomas; two s. *Education:* Univ. of Sussex, Coventry Coll. of Educ. *Career:* mem. Soc. of Authors, Historical Novel Soc. *Publications:* The Moon in the Water 1983, The Chains of Fate 1984, Alathea 1985, The Lodestar 1987, Wintercombe 1988, Herald of Joy 1989, A Falling Star 1990, Treason's Gift 1992, The Silver City 1994, The Wolf Within 1995, Blood Imperial 1996, Mermaid's Ground 1998, No Love Lost 1999; contribs to periodicals. *Address:* 61 New Road, Bromham, Chippenham, Wilts., SN15 2JB, England. *E-mail:* pam.thomas@dsl.pipex.com (office).

BELLI, Gioconda; Nicaraguan poet and writer; b. 9 Dec. 1949, Managua; m. 2nd Charles Castaldi 1987; four c. *Education:* Charles Morris Price School,

Philadelphia, INCAE (Harvard Univ. School of Business Administration in Central America), Georgetown Univ., Washington, DC. *Career:* mem., Political-Diplomatic Commission 1978–79, Int. Press Liaison 1982–83, Exec. Sec. and Spokesperson for the Electoral Campaign 1983–84, Sandinista Nat. Liberation Front; Dir of Communications and Public Relations, Ministry of Economic Planning 1979–82; Foreign Affairs Sec., Nicaragua Writer's Union 1983–88; Man. Dir, Sistema Nacional de Publicidad 1984–86. *Publications:* poetry: Sobre la grama (trans. as On the Grass) 1972, Línea de Fuego (trans. as Line of Fire) (Casa de las Américas Poetry Prize, Cuba) 1978, Truenos y arco iris 1982, Amor insurrecto (anthology) 1985, De la costilla de Eva (trans. as From Eve's Rib) 1987, El ojo de la mujer 1991, Sortilegio contra el frío 1992, Apogeo 1997; fiction: La mujer habitada (trans. as The Inhabited Woman) 1988, Sofía de los Presagios (trans. as Sophie and the Omens) 1990, El Taller de las mariposas (juvenile, trans. as The Workshop of the Butterflies) 1992, Waslala 1996, El país bajo mi piel: memorias de amor y guerra (autobiog.) 2001, El pergamino de la seducción (novel) 2005; contrib. to anthologies and periodicals. *Honours:* Nat. Univ. Poetry Prize 1972, Friedrich Ebhert Foundation Booksellers, Eds and Publishers Literary Prize, Germany 1989, Anna Seghers Literary Fellowship, Germany 1989. *E-mail:* gioconda@giocondabelli.com. *Website:* www.giocondabelli.com.

BELSHAW, Cyril Shirley, PhD, FRSC; Canadian anthropologist, writer and publisher; b. 3 Dec. 1921, Waddington, NZ; s. of Horace Belshaw and Marion L. S. Belshaw (née McHardie); m. Betty J. Sweetman 1943 (deceased); one s. one d. *Education:* Auckland Univ. Coll. and Victoria Coll., Wellington (Univ. of New Zealand), London School of Econs. *Career:* Dist Officer and Deputy Commr for Western Pacific, British Solomon Islands 1943–46; Sr Research Fellow, Australian Nat. Univ. 1950–53; Prof. Univ. of British Columbia 1953–86, Prof. Emer. 1986–; Dir Regional Training Centre for UN Fellows, Van. 1961–62; Ed. Current Anthropology 1974–84; mem. numerous UNESCO comms, working parties and consultancy groups; Pres. Int. Union of Anthropological and Ethnological Sciences 1978–83, XIth Int. Congress of Anthropological and Ethnological Sciences 1983; Exec. American Anthropological Assoc. 1969–70; Chair. Standing Cttee Social Sciences and Humanities Pacific Science Asscn 1968–76; Ed. The Anthroglobe Journal 1998–2000, 2004–; Propr Webzines of Vancouver; Man. Ed. Adam's Vancouver Dining Guide 1997–, www.anthropologising.ca 2001–. *Publications:* Island Administration in the South West Pacific 1950, Changing Melanesia 1954, In Search of Wealth 1955, The Great Village 1957, The Indians of British Columbia (with others) 1958, Under the Ivi Tree 1964, Anatomy of a University 1964, Traditional Exchange and Modern Markets 1965, The Conditions of Social Performance 1970, Towers Besieged 1974, The Sorcerer's Apprentice 1976, The Complete Good Dining Guide to Restaurants in Greater Vancouver 1984. *Honours:* Hon. Life Fellow, Royal Anthropological Inst., Pacific Science Asscn, Asscn for the Social Anthropology of Oceania; Hon. Life mem. Royal Anthropological Inst. 1978, Pacific Science Asscn 1981; World Utopian Champion 2005. *Address:* Suite 2901, 969 Richards Street, Vancouver, BC, V6B 1A8, Canada. *Telephone:* (604) 739-8130 (home). *E-mail:* editor@anthroglobe.ca (office); cyril@anthropologising.ca (home). *Website:* www.evevancouver.ca (office); www.anthroglobe.ca (office); www.anthropologising.ca (home).

BELTING, Hans, PhD; German academic and writer; b. 7 July 1935, Andernach. *Education:* Univ. of Mainz, Univ. of Rome; studied with Ernst Kitzinger, Dumbarton Oaks, Washington, DC. *Career:* Visiting Fellow, Harvard Univ.; Asst Prof. of Art History, Univ. of Hamburg 1966; Prof. of Art History, Univ. of Heidelberg 1970–80, Univ. of Munich 1980–93; Visiting Prof., Harvard Univ. 1984; Meyer Shapiro Visiting Prof., Columbia Univ. 1989, 1990; Prof. of Art History and New Media 1993–, Chair. Anthropology Programme 2000–02, School for New Media, Karlsruhe; mem. Wissenschaftkolleg, Berlin, American Acad. of Arts and Sciences, Medieval Acad. of America. *Publications:* Die Basilica de SS Martiti in Cimitile und ihr frühmittelalterlicher Freskenzyklus, 1962; Die Euphemia-Kirche am Hippodrom in Istabul und ihre Fresken (with Rudolf Naumann), 1966; Studien zur beneventanischen Malerei, 1968; Das illuminierte Buch in der spätbyzantinischen Gesellschaft, 1970; Die Oberkirche von San Francesco in Assisi: Ihre Dekoration als Aufgabe und die Genese einer neuen Wandmalerei, 1977; The Mosaics and Frescoes of St Mary Pammakaritos (with Cyril Mango and Doula Mouriki), 1978; Patronage in 13th Century Constantinople: An Atelier of Later Byzantine Book Illumination and Calligraphy (with Hugo Buchthal), 1978; Die Bibel des Niketas: Ein Werk der höfischen Buchkunst in Byanz und sein antikes Vorbild (with Guglielmo Cavallo), 1979; Das bild und sein Publikum in Mittelalter: Form und Funktion früher Bildtafeln der Passion, 1981, English trans. as The Image and Its Public in the Middle Ages, 1990; Jan van Ecyk als Erzählet (with Dagmar Eichberger), 1983; Das Ende der Kunstgeschichte?: Überlegungen zur heutigen Kunsterfahrung und historischen Kunstforschung, 1983, English trans. as The End of the History of Art?, 1987; Max Beckmann: Die Tradition als Problem in der Kunst der Moderne, 1984, English trans., 1989; Giovanni Bellini Pictà: Ikone und Bilderzählung in der venezianischen Malerei, 1985; Alex Katz: Bilder und Zeichnungen, 1989; Bild und Kult: Eine Geschichte des Bildes vor dem Zeitalter der Kunst, 1990, English trans. as Likeness and Presence: A History of the Image Before the Era of Art, 1993; Die Deutschen und ihre Kunst: Ein schwieriges Erbe, 1992, English trans. as The Germans and Their Art, 1998; Thomas Struth: Museums Photographs, 1993, English trans., 1998; Der Ort der Bilder (with Boris Groys), 1993; Die Erfindung des Gemäldes: Das erste Jahrhundert der neiderländischen Malerei (with Christiane Kruse), 1994; Das unsichtbare Meisterwerk: Die modernen Mythen der Kunst, 1998, English trans. as The Invisible Masterpiece, 2001; Identität im Zweifel: Ansichten der deutschen Kunst, 1999; Theatres: Interiors of Cinema Spaces (with Hiroshi Sugimoto), 2000; Bild-Anthropologie: Entwürfe für eine Bildwissenschaft, 2001; Hieronymous Bosch: Der Garten der Lüste, 2002, English trans. as Hieronymus Bosch: Gardens of Earthly Delights, 2002. Contributions: scholarly books and journals. *Honours:* Orden pour le mérite für Wissenschaften und Künste; Hon. Chair, University of Heidelberg; European Chair, Collège de France. *Address:* c/o Institut für Kunstwissenschaft, Staatliche Hochschule für Gestaltung, Lorenzstrasse 16, 76135 Karlsruhe, Germany. *E-mail:* hans.belting@hfg-karlsruhe.de.

BELYANIN, Andrei; Russian writer. *Career:* writer of fantasy fiction. *Publications:* Tainyi sysk carya Goroha 2000, Vek svyatogo Skiminoka 2000, Svirepyi landgraf 2000, Mech bez imeni 2000, Letuchii korabl' 2001, Dzhek Sumasshedshii Korol' 2001, Moya zhena – ved'ma 2001, Sestr nka iz Preispodnei 2001, Ryzhii rycar' 2001, Bagdadskii vor 2002, Otstrel nevest 2003, Ryzhii i Polosatyi 2003, Professional'nyi oboroten' 2003. *Address:* c/o Council for Culture and Arts, Office of the President, Kremlin, 103073 Moscow, Russia.

BEN JELLOUN, Tahar; Moroccan writer and poet; b. 1 Dec. 1944, Fès; m. Aicha Ben Jelloun 1986; two s. two d. *Education:* Lycée Regnault de Tanger, Faculté de Lettres de Rabat and Univ. of Paris. *Career:* columnist Le Monde 1973–, La Repubblica (Italy) and La Vanguardia (Spain); mem. Conseil supérieur de la langue française; UN Goodwill Amb. for Human Rights. *Publications:* fiction: Harrouda 1973, La Réclusion solitaire 1976 (trans. as Solitaire 1988), Moha le fou, Moha le sage 1978, La Prière de l'absent 1980, Muha al-ma'twah, Muha al-hakim 1982, L'Écrivain public 1983, L'Enfant de sable 1985 (trans. as The Sand Child 1987), La Nuit sacrée 1987 (trans. as The Sacred Night 1989), Jour de silence à Tanger 1990 (trans. as Silent Day in Tangier 1991), Les Yeux baissés 1991, L'Ange aveugle 1992, L'Homme rompu 1994, Corruption 1995, Le Premier amour est toujours le dernier 1995, Les Raisins de la galère 1995, La Soudure fraternelle 1995, La Nuit de l'erreur 1997, L'Auberge des pauvres 1999, Labyrinthe des Sentiments 1999, Cette aveuglante absence de lumière (trans. as This Blinding Absence of Light) (Impac Dublin Literary Award 2004) 2001, Amours sorcières 2003, Le Dernier Ami (trans. as The Last Friend) 2004, Partir 2006; poems: Hommes sous linceul de silence 1970, Cicatrice du soleil 1972, Le Discours du chameau 1974, La Mémoire future: Anthologie de la nouvelle poésie du Maroc 1976, Les Amandiers sont morts de leurs blessures 1976, A l'insu du souvenir 1980, Sahara 1987, La Remontée des cendres 1991, Poésie Complète (1966–95) 1995; plays: Chronique d'une solitude 1976, Entretien avec Monsieur Said Hammadi, ouvrier algérien 1982, La Fiancée de l'eau 1984; non-fiction: La Plus haute des solitudes: Misère sexuelle d'émigrés nord-africains 1977, Haut Atlas: L'Exil de pierres 1982, Hospitalité française: Racisme et immigration maghrebine 1984, Marseille, comme un matin d'insomnie 1986, Giacometti 1991, Le Racisme expliqué à ma fille 1998, L'islam expliqué aux enfants 2002. *Honours:* Chevalier Ordre des Arts et Lettres, Légion d'honneur; Prix de l'Amitié Franco-Arabe 1976, Médaille du Mérite Nat. (Morocco), Prix Goncourt 1987, Prix des Hemisphere 1991, UN Global Tolerance Award 1998, Prix Int. de Littérature, IMPAC, Dublin 2004. *Address:* c/o Éditions Gallimard, 5 rue Sébastien-Bottin, 75328 Paris Cedex 07, France. *E-mail:* tbjweb@gmail.com (office). *Website:* www.taharbenjelloun.org (office).

BEN-RAFAEL, Eliezer, MA, PhD; Israeli sociologist and academic; *Professor of Sociology and Weinberg Chair of Political Sociology, Tel-Aviv University*; b. 3 Oct. 1938, Brussels, Belgium; m. Miriam Neufeld 1960; two d. *Education:* Hebrew Univ., Jerusalem. *Career:* Research Fellow, Harvard Univ. 1974–75; Prof. of Sociology, Univ. of Tel-Aviv 1980–, Jima and Zalman Weinberg Chair of Political Sociology 1997–; Directeur d'Études Associé, École des Hautes Études en Sciences Sociales 1984–85; Visiting Scholar, Oxford Centre for Postgraduate Hebrew Studies 1989–90; Co-Ed., Israel Social Sciences Review 1992–; mem. Israel Soc. of Sociology, Pres. 1994–97; Vice-Pres. Int. Inst. of Sociology –2001, Pres. 2001–05; Dir Klal Yisrael Project; Leading Researcher, Int. Research About Russian-Speaking Jews (Israel-Germany and Israel). *Publications:* The Emergence of Ethnicity: Cultural Groups and Social Conflict in Israel 1982, Le kibboutz 1983, Status, Power and Conflict in the Kibbutz 1988, Ethnicity, Religion and Class in Israeli Society 1991, Language, Identity and Social Division: The Case of Israel 1994, Crisis and Transformation: The Kibbutz at Century's End 1997, Language and Communication in Israel 2000, Identités Juives, 50 sages repondent à Ben-Gourion 2001, Identity, Culture and Globalization 2001, Sociology and Ideology 2003, Contemporary Jewries: Convergence and Divergence 2003, Comparing Modernities 2005, Is Israel One? 2005, Jewry Between Tradition and Secularism 2006; contribs to professional journals. *Address:* Hadror 11, Ramat Hasharon 47203 (home); Department of Sociology, University of Tel-Aviv, Tel-Aviv 69978, Israel (office). *Telephone:* (3) 6408824 (office); (3) 5406297 (home). *Fax:* (3) 6409215 (office); (3) 5402291 (home). *E-mail:* saba@post.tau.ed.il (office).

BÉNABOU, Marcel, PhD; French writer; *Professor Emeritus of Roman History, Université de Paris VII (Denis Diderot)*; b. 1939, Meknès, Morocco; m. Isabelle Dubosc; one s. *Education:* Lycée Louis-le-Grand, Paris, Ecole Normale Supérieure and Sorbonne, Univ. of Paris. *Career:* Prof. Emer. of Roman History, Université de Paris VII (Denis Diderot); mem. Ouvroir de Littérature Potentielle (Oulipo) 1969 (secrétaire définitivement provisoire 1970–). *Publications:* Suétone, les Césars et l'histoire dans Suétone 1975, La résistance africaine à la romanisation 1976, La vie de Tacfarinas dans Les Africains IX 1978, La vie de Juba II dans Les Africains XI 1979, Un aphorisme peut en cacher un autre 1980, Locutions introuvables 1984, Alexandre au greffoir 1986, Pourquoi je n'ai écrit aucun de mes livres (trans. as Why I Have Not Written Any of my Books) (Prix de l'Humour noir Xavier Forneret) 1986, Bris de mots, Presbytères et prolétaires 1989, Jette ce livre avant qu'il soit trop tard! (trans. as Dump This Book While You Still Can!) 1992, Rendre à Cézanne 1993, Jacob, Menahem et Mimoun, une épopée familiale (trans. as Jacob, Menahem, and Mimoun: A Family Epic) 1995, L'Hannibal perdu 1997, Altitude et profondeur 1999, Un art simple et tout d'exécution (with Jacques Jouet, Harry Mathews and Jacques Roubaud) 2001, Résidence d'hiver 2001, 789 néologismes de Jacques Lacan 2002, Écrire sur Tamara (trans. as To Write on Tamara?) 2002, L'Appentis revisité 2003. *Address:* 67 rue de Rochechouart, 75009 Paris, France (home). *Website:* www.oulipo.net/oulipiens/MB.

BENACQUISTA, Tonino; French novelist and screenwriter; b. 1 Sept. 1961, Choisy-le-Roi, Paris. *Career:* fmr museum nightwatchman and train guard. *Play:* Le Contrat: un western psychanalytique en deux actes et un épilogue. *Film and television screenplays:* La Souris noire (series) 1987, Couchettes express (TV) 1994, La Débandade 1999, Les Faux-fuyants (TV) 2000, Le Coeur à l'ouvrage 2000, Le Plafond 2001, Les Morsures de l'aube 2001, Sur mes lèvres 2001, L'Outremangeur 2003, De battre mon coeur s'est arrêté 2005, La Boîte noire 2005, A Crime 2006, Les Disparus 2006. *Publications:* novels: Impossible n'est pas français (juvenile), Victor Pigeon (juvenile), Epinglé comme une pin-up dans un placard de G.I. 1985, La Maldonne des sleepings 1989, Trois carrés rouges sur fond noir 1990, La Commedia des ratés 1991, Les Morsures de l'aube 1992, Saga 1997, L'Outremangeur 2000, Quelqu'un d'autre 2001, Malavita 2004. *Honours:* Trophee 813, Grand Prix des lectrices de Elle, Prix Mystére de la Critique. *Address:* c/o Éditions Gallimard, 5 rue Sébastien-Bottin, 75328 Paris cedex 07, France (office).

BENCE-JONES, Mark, BA, MA, MRAC; British writer; b. 29 May 1930, London, England; m. Gillian Pretyman 1965; one s. two d. *Education:* Pembroke Coll., Cambridge, Royal Agricultural Coll., Cirencester. *Publications:* All a Nonsense 1957, Paradise Escaped 1958, Nothing in the City 1965, The Remarkable Irish 1966, Palaces of the Raj 1973, Clive of India 1974, The Cavaliers 1976, Burke's Guide to Irish Country Houses 1978, The British Aristocracy (co-author) 1979, The Viceroys of India 1982, Ancestral Houses 1984, Twilight of the Ascendancy 1987, A Guide to Irish Country Houses 1989, The Catholic Families 1992, Life in an Irish Country House 1996; contrib. to books and periodicals. *Address:* Glenville Park, Glenville, County Cork, Ireland.

BENEDETTI, Mario; Uruguayan writer and poet; b. 14 Sept. 1920, Paso de los Toros, Tacuarembo; s. of Brenno Benedetti and Matilde Farrugia; m. Luz López. *Education:* Colegio Alemán. *Career:* journalist on Marcha (weekly) and literary, film and theatre critic on El Diario, Tribuna Popular and La Mañana. *Publications:* fiction: Esta mañana 1949, El último viaje y otros cuentos 1951, Quién de nosotros 1953, Montevideanos 1959, La Tregua 1963, Gracias por el Fuego 1965, La muerte y otras sorpresas 1968, Con o sin nostalgia 1977, Viento del exilio 1981, El amor, las mujeres y la vida 1995; plays: Ustedes por ejemplo 1953, El Reportaje 1958, Ida y vuelta 1958; poetry: La víspera indeleble 1945, Sólo mientras tanto 1950, Poemas de la oficina 1956, Poemas del hoyporhoy 1965, Inventario 1965, Contra los puentes levadizos 1966, A ras de sueño 1967; essays: Peripecia y novela 1948, Marcel Proust y otros ensayos 1951, Literatura uruguaya siglo XX 1963, Letras del continente mestizo 1967, Sobre artes y oficios 1968. *Address:* c/o Curbstone Press, 321 Jackson Street, Willimantic, CT 06226-1738, USA.

BENEDICTUS, David Henry, BA; British writer, dramatist and reviewer; b. 16 Sept. 1938, London, England; m. Yvonne Daphne Antrobus 1971; one s. one d. *Education:* Balliol College, Oxford. *Career:* BBC News and Current Affairs, 1961, Ed., Readings, 1989–91, and Radio 3 Drama, 1992, Sr Prod., Serial Readings, 1992–95, BBC Radio; Drama Dir, 1962, Story Ed., 1965, BBC TV; Asst Dir, RSC, 1970; Writer-in-Residence, Sutton Library, Surrey, 1975, Kibbutz Gezer, Israel, 1978, Bitterne Library, Southampton, 1983–84; Antiques Correspondent, Evening Standard, 1977–80; Judith E. Wilson Visiting Fellow, Cambridge, and Fellow Commoner, Churchill College, Cambridge, 1981–82; Commissioning Ed., Drama Series, Channel 4 TV, 1984–86. *Publications:* The Fourth of June, 1962; You're a Big Boy Now, 1963; This Animal is Mischievous, 1965; Hump, or Bone by Bone Alive, 1967; The Guru and the Golf Club, 1969; A World of Windows, 1971; The Rabbi's Wife, 1976; Junk: How and Where to Buy Beautiful Things at Next to Nothing Prices, 1976; A Twentieth Century Man, 1978; The Antique Collector's Guide, 1980; Lloyd George (after Elaine Morgan's screenplay), 1981; Whose Life is it Anyway? (after Brian Clarke's screenplay), 1981; Who Killed the Prince Consort?, 1982; Local Hero (after Bill Forsyth's screenplay), 1983; The Essential London Guide, 1984; Floating Down to Camelot, 1985; The Streets of London, 1986; The Absolutely Essential London Guide, 1986; Little St Nicholas, 1990; Odyssey of a Scientist (with Hans Kalmus), 1991; Sunny Intervals and Showers, 1992; The Stamp Collector, 1994; How to Cope When the Money Runs Out, 1998. Plays: Betjemania, 1976; The Golden Key, 1982; What a Way to Run a Revolution!, 1985; You Say Potato, 1992. Contributions: newspapers and magazines.

BENEDIKT, Michael, BA, MA; American writer, poet, critic and editor; b. 26 May 1935, New York, NY. *Education:* New York Univ., Columbia Univ.

Career: Professorships in Literature and Poetry, Bennington Coll. 1968–69, Sarah Lawrence Coll. 1969–73, Hampshire Coll. 1973–75, Vassar Coll. 1976–77, Boston Univ. 1977–79; Contributing Ed., American Poetry Review 1973–; Poetry Ed., Paris Review 1974–78; mem. PEN Club of America, Poetry Soc. of America. *Publications:* The Body (verse), 1968; Sky (verse), 1970; Mole Notes (prose poems), 1971; Night Cries (prose poems), 1976; The Badminton at Great Barrington or Gustav Mahler and the Chattanooga Choo-Choo (poems), 1980. Anthologies: Modern French Theatre: The Avant-Garde, Dada and Surrealism (with George E. Wellwarth), 1964, in the UK as Modern French Plays: An Anthology from Jarry to Ionesco, 1965; Post-War German Theatre (with George E. Wellwarth), 1967; Modern Spanish Theatre (with George E. Wellwarth), 1968; Theatre Experiment, 1968; The Poetry of Surrealism, 1975; The Prose Poem: An International Anthology, 1976. Contributions: Agni Review; Ambit; Art International; Art News; London Magazine; Massachusetts Review; New York Quarterly; Paris Review; Partisan Review; Poetry. *Honours:* Guggenheim Fellowship 1968–69, Bess Hokin Prize 1969, Nat. Endowment for the Arts Prize 1970, Benedikt: A Profile (critical monograph/Festschrift) 1978, Nat. Endowment for the Arts Fellowship 1979–80, Retrospective Library of Congress (videotape) 1986. *Address:* c/o The American Poetry Review, 117 S 17th Street, Suite 910, Philadelphia, PA 19103, USA.

BENFIELD, Derek; British playwright and actor; b. Bradford, Yorkshire, England; m. Susan Elspeth Lyall Grant 1953; one s. one d. *Education:* Bingley Grammar School, RADA. *Career:* mem. Society of Authors. *Publications:* Plays: Wild Goose Chase, 1956; Running Riot, 1958; Post Horn Gallop, 1965; Murder for the Asking, 1967; Off the Hook, 1970; Bird in the Hand, 1973; Panic Stations, 1975; Caught on the Hop, 1979; Beyond a Joke, 1980; In for the Kill, 1981; Look Who's Talking, 1984; Touch & Go, 1985; Fish Out of Water, 1986; Flying Feathers, 1987; Bedside Manners, 1988; A Toe in the Water, 1991; Don't Lose the Place, 1992; Anyone for Breakfast?, 1994; Up and Running, 1995; A Fly in the Ointment, 1996; Two and Two Together, 1998; Second Time Around, 2000; In at the Deep End, 2003. *Address:* c/o Lemon Unna & Durbridge Ltd, 24 Pottery Lane, Holland Park, London W11 4LZ, England.

BENFORD, Gregory Albert, BA, MS, PhD; American physicist and science fiction writer; b. 30 Jan. 1941, Mobile, AL; m. Joan Abbe 1967; one s. one d. *Education:* Univ. of Oklahoma, Univ. of California at San Diego. *Career:* Fellow 1967–69, Research Physicist 1969–71, Lawrence Radiation Laboratory, Livermore, CA; Asst Prof. 1971–73, Assoc. Prof. 1973–79, Prof. of Physics 1979–, Univ. of California at Irvine; mem. American Physical Soc., Royal Astronomical Soc., SFWA, Social Science Exploration. *Publications:* Deeper Than the Darkness (revised edn as The Stars in the Shroud) 1970, If the Stars are Gods (with Gordon Eklund) 1977, In the Ocean of Night 1977, Find the Changeling (with Gordon Eklund) 1980, Shiva Descending (with William Rotsler) 1980, Timescape 1980, Against Infinity 1983, Across the Sea of Suns 1984, Artifact 1985, Of Space-Time and the River 1985, In Alien Flesh 1986, Heart of the Comet (with David Brin) 1986, Great Sky River 1987, Under the Wheel (with others) 1987, Hitler Victorious: Eleven Stories of the German Victory in World War II (ed. with Martin H. Greenberg) 1987, We Could Do Worse 1988, Tides of Light 1989, Beyond the Fall of Night (with Arthur C. Clarke) 1990, Centigrade 233 1990, Matter's End (ed.) 1991, Chiller 1993, Furious Gulf 1994, Far Futures 1995, Sailing Bright Eternity 1995, Foundation's Fear 1997, Immersion and Other Short Novels 2002, Beyond Infinity 2004, The Sunborn 2005. *Honours:* Woodrow Wilson Fellowship 1963–64, SFWA Nebula Awards 1975, 1981, BSFA Award 1981, World Science Fiction Convention John W. Campbell Award 1981, Ditmar Award, Australia 1981, various grants. *Address:* c/o Orbit, Brettenham House, Lancaster Place, London, WC2E 7EN, England.

BENÍTEZ, Sandra, BS, MA; American writer; b. 26 March 1941, Washington, DC; m. James F. Kondrick 1980, two s. *Education:* Northeast Missouri State University. *Career:* Distinguished Edelstein-Keller Writer-in-Residence, University of Minnesota, 1997; mem. Authors' Guild; Poets and Writers. *Publications:* A Place Where the Sea Remembers, 1993; Bitter Grounds, 1997; The Weight of All Things, 2000. *Honours:* Minnesota Book Award for Fiction, 1993; Barnes and Noble Fiction Award, 1994.

BENJAMIN, David (see Slavitt, David Rytman)

BENN, Rt Hon. Anthony (Tony) Neil Wedgwood, PC, MA; British politician, writer and broadcaster; b. 3 April 1925, London; s. of William Wedgwood Benn (1st Viscount Stansgate), PC and Margaret Eadie (née Holmes); m. Caroline de Camp 1949 (died 2000); three s. one d. *Education:* Westminster School and New Coll., Oxford. *Career:* RAF pilot 1943–45; Univ. of Oxford 1946–49; Producer, BBC 1949–50; Labour MP for Bristol SE 1950–60, compelled to leave House of Commons on inheriting peerage 1960, re-elected and unseated 1961, renounced peerage and re-elected 1963, contested and lost Bristol E seat in 1983, re-elected as mem. for Chesterfield 1984–2001; Nat. Exec. Labour Party 1959–94; Chair. Fabian Soc. 1964; Postmaster-Gen. 1964–66; Minister of Tech. 1966–70, of Power 1969–70; Shadow Minister of Trade and Industry 1970–74; Sec. of State for Industry and Minister of Posts and Telecommunications 1974–75; Sec. of State for Energy 1975–79; Vice-Chair. Labour Party 1970, Chair. 1971–72; Chair. Labour Party Home Policy Cttee 1974–82; cand. for Leadership of Labour Party 1976, 1988, for Deputy Leadership 1971, 1981; Pres. EEC Energy Council 1977, Labour Action for Peace 1997–; currently Pres. Steering Cttee Stop the War Coalition; Visiting Prof. of Politics, LSE 2001–02; Pres. Socialist

Campaign Group of Labour MPs; fmr mem. Bureau Confed. of Socialist Parties of the European Community; numerous TV and radio broadcasts. *Television:* Speaking Up in Parliament 1993, Westminster Behind Closed Doors 1995, New Labour in Focus 1998, Tony Benn Speaks 2001. *Recordings:* The BBC Benn Tapes 1994, 1995, Writings on the Wall (with Roy Bailey) 1996, Tony Benn's Greatest Hits 2003, An Audience with Tony Benn 2003. *Publications:* The Privy Council as a Second Chamber 1957, The Regeneration of Britain 1964, The New Politics 1970, Speeches by Tony Benn 1974, Arguments for Socialism 1979, Arguments for Democracy 1981, Parliament, People and Power 1982, The Sizewell Syndrome 1984, Writings on the Wall: A Radical and Socialist Anthology 1215–1984 (ed.) 1984, Out of the Wilderness: Diaries 1963–67 1987, Office Without Power: Diaries 1968–72 1988, Fighting Back: Speaking Out for Socialism in the Eighties 1988, Against the Tide: Diaries 1973–76 1989, Conflicts of Interest: Diaries 1977–80 1990, A Future for Socialism 1991, End of an Era: Diaries 1980–90 1992, Common Sense: A New Constitution for Britain (with Andrew Hood) 1993, Years of Hope: Diaries 1940–1962 1994, The Benn Diaries 1940–1990 1995, Free at Last: Diaries 1991–2001 2002, Free Radical: New Century Essays 2003, Dare to be a Daniel (memoir) 2004. *Honours:* Freeman of the City of Bristol 2003; Hon. Fellow, New Coll. Oxford 2005; Hon. LLD (Strathclyde, Williams Coll., USA, Brunel, Bristol, Univ. of West of England, Univ. of N London); Hon. DTech (Bradford); Hon. DSc (Aston); Dr hc (Paisley). *Address:* 12 Holland Park Avenue, London, W11 3QU, England (office). *Telephone:* (20) 7229-0779 (office). *Fax:* (20) 7229-9693 (office). *E-mail:* tony@tbenn.fsnet.co.uk (office).

BENNACK, Frank Anthony, Jr; American publishing executive; *Vice-Chairman of the Board and Chairman, Executive Committee, Hearst Corporation;* b. 12 Feb. 1933, San Antonio; s. of Frank Bennack and Lula Connally; m. Luella Smith 1951; five d. *Education:* Univ. of Maryland and St Mary's Univ. *Career:* advertising account exec. San Antonio Light 1950–53, 1956–58, Advertising Man. 1961–65, Asst Publr 1965–67, Publr 1967–74; Gen. Man. (newspapers), Hearst Corpn New York 1974–76, Exec. Vice-Pres. and COO 1975–78, Pres. and CEO 1978–2002, Vice-Chair. Bd, Chair. Exec. Cttee 2002–; Chair. Museum of TV and Radio, NY City 1991–; Pres. Tex. Daily Newspaper Asscn 1973–; mem. Bd of Dirs J.P. Morgan Chase & Co., Wyeth, Polo Ralph Lauren Corpn, Metropolitan Opera of New York; Dir, Vice-Chair. Lincoln Center for the Performing Arts; Dir Newspaper Asscn of American (fmrly American Newspaper Publrs Asscn), Chair. 1992–93; Gov., Vice-Chair. New York Presbyterian Hosp.; mem. Bd of Dirs Mfrs Hanover Trust Co., New York. *Address:* Hearst Corporation, 959 8th Avenue, New York, NY 10019, USA (office). *Telephone:* (212) 649-2000 (office). *Fax:* (212) 649-2108 (office). *Website:* www.hearstcorp.com (office).

BENNASSAR, Bartolomé; French academic, historian and novelist; b. 8 April 1929, Nîmes; m. 1954, one s. two d. *Education:* University of Montpellier, University of Toulouse. *Career:* Prof. of History, High Schools of Rodez, Agen and Marseille; Asst Prof., Prof., then Pres., University of Toulouse Le Mirail. *Publications:* Valladolid au siècle d'or 1967, Recherches sur les grandes épidémies dans le Nord de l'Espagne 1969, L'Homme espagnol (trans. as The Spanish Character) 1975, L'Inquisition espagnole XV–XIX 1979, Un siècle d'or espagnol 1982, Histoire d'Espagnols 1985, Les Chrétiens d'Allah 1989, 1492: Un monde nouveau? 1991, Histoire de la tauromachie 1993, Franco 1995, Le Voyage en Espagne 1998; fiction: Le Baptême du Mort 1962, Picture: le dernier saut 1970, Les Tribulations de Mustafa des Six-Fours 1995; contrib. to Annales ESC, L'Histoire, Historia. *Honours:* Bronze Medal, Centre National de la Recherche Scientifique; Dr hc (University of Valladolid, Spain).

BENNETT, Alan, BA; British playwright and actor; b. 9 May 1934, Leeds; s. of Walter Bennett and Lilian Mary Peel. *Education:* Leeds Modern School, Exeter Coll., Oxford. *Career:* Jr Lecturer, Modern History, Magdalen Coll., Oxford 1960–62; co-author and actor Beyond the Fringe, Edin. 1960, London 1961, New York 1962; Trustee Nat. Gallery 1993–98. *Plays:* On the Margin (TV series, author and actor) 1966, Forty Years On (author and actor) 1968, Getting On 1971, Habeas Corpus 1973, The Old Country 1977, Enjoy 1980, Kafka's Dick 1986, Single Spies 1988, The Wind in the Willows (adapted for Nat. Theatre) 1990, The Madness of George III 1991 (film 1995), The Lady in the Van 1999, The History Boys (Royal Nat. Theatre, London) (Evening Standard Award for Best Play 2004, Critics Circle Theatre Award for Best New Play 2005, Olivier Award for Best New Play 2005, New York Drama Critics' Circle Play of the Year 2006, Drama Desk Award for Best Play 2006, Tony Award for Best Play 2006) 2004. *Radio:* The Last of the Sun 2004. *Television scripts:* A Day Out (film) 1972, Sunset Across the Bay (TV film) 1975, A Little Outing, A Visit from Miss Prothero (plays) 1977, Doris and Doreen, The Old Crowd, Me! I'm Afraid of Virginia Woolf, All Day on the Sands, Afternoon Off, One Fine Day 1978–79, Intensive Care, Our Winnie, A Woman of No Importance, Rolling Home, Marks, Say Something Happened, An Englishman Abroad 1982, The Insurance Man 1986, Talking Heads (Olivier Award) 1992, 102 Boulevard Haussmann 1991, A Question of Attribution 1991, Talking Heads 2 1998. *Films:* A Private Function 1984, Prick Up Your Ears 1987, The Madness of King George 1994, The History Boys 2006. *Television documentaries:* Dinner at Noon 1988, Poetry in Motion 1990, Portrait or Bust 1994, The Abbey 1995, Telling Tales 1999. *Publications:* Beyond the Fringe (with Peter Cook, Jonathan Miller and Dudley Moore) 1962, Forty Years On 1969, Getting On 1972, Habeas Corpus 1973, The Old Country 1978, Enjoy 1980, Office Suite 1981, Objects of Affection 1982, The Writer in Disguise 1985, Two Kafka Plays 1987, Talking Heads 1988, Single

Spies 1989, Poetry in Motion 1990, The Lady in the Van 1991, The Wind in the Willows (adaptation) 1991, The Madness of George III 1992, Writing Home (autobiog.) 1994, Diaries 1997, The Clothes They Stood Up In 1998, Talking Heads 2 1998, The Complete Talking Heads 1998, A Box of Alan Bennett 2000, Father, Father! Burning Bright 2000, The Laying on of Hands 2001, The History Boys 2004, Untold Stories 2005; regular contrib. to London Review of Books. *Honours:* Hon. Fellow Royal Acad. 2000; Hon. Fellow Exeter Coll., Oxford; Hon. DLitt (Leeds); Evening Standard Award 1961, 1969, Hawthornden Prize 1988, two Olivier Awards 1993, Evening Standard Film Award 1996, Lifetime Achievement Award, British Book Awards 2003, Evening Standard Best Play Award 2004, Olivier Award for outstanding contribution to British theatre 2005, British Book Awards Reader's Digest Author of the Year 2006. *Literary Agent:* PFD, Drury House, 34–43 Russell Street, London, WC2B 5HA, England. *Telephone:* (20) 7376-7676.

BENNETT, Amanda; American newspaper editor; *Editor and Executive Vice-President, The Philadelphia Enquirer. Education:* Harvard Univ. *Career:* 23 years with The Wall Street Journal, fmr positions include Auto Industry Reporter, Detroit 1970s–1980s, Pentagon and State Dept Reporter, Beijing Corresp., Man. Ed./Reporter, Nat. Econs Corresp., Atlanta Bureau Chief 1994–98; fmr Man. Ed./Projects The Oregonian, Portland, co-leader of Pulitzer Prize-winning reporting team 2001; Ed. The Lexington Herald-Leader, Ky 2001–03; Ed. and Exec. Vice-Pres. The Philadelphia Enquirer 2003–; fmr Pulitzer Prize juror, mem. Pulitzer Prize Bd 2002–; fmr Nat. Headliners' Judge. *Publications include:* Death of the Organization Man 1991, The Man Who Stayed Behind (co-author) 1993, In Memoriam (co-author) 1998, Your Child's Symptoms. *Honours:* Pulitzer Prize in Nat. Reporting (co-recipient) 1997, Pulitzer Prize in Public Service (co-recipient) 2000. *Address:* The Philadelphia Inquirer, PO Box 8263, Philadelphia, PA 19101, USA (office). *Telephone:* (215) 854-2529 (office). *Website:* www.philly.com/mld/inquirer (office).

BENNETT, Bruce Harry, AO, BA, DipEd, MA, DLitt; Australian academic, editor and writer; b. 23 March 1941, Perth, WA; m. Patricia Ann Bennett 1967; one s. one d. *Education:* Univ. of Western Australia, Univ. of Oxford, Univ. of London, Univ. of NSW. *Career:* Lecturer, Univ. of Western Australia 1968–75, Sr Lecturer 1975–85, Assoc. Prof. 1985–90; Co-Ed. Westerly: A Quarterly Review 1975–92; Prof. of English, School of Humanities and Social Sciences, Univ. of New South Wales, Australian Defence Force Acad.; Overseas Fellow, Churchill Coll. Cambridge, UK 2005; Visiting Prof. of Australian Studies, Georgetown Univ., Washington, DC, USA 2005–06; mem. Asscn for the Study of Australian Literature (Pres. 1983–85), Australian Soc. of Authors, Asscn of Commonwealth Literature and Language Studies (also Vice-Chair.), MLA of America, PEN International, Australia-India Council 2002–; Fellow, Australian Acad. of the Humanities 1995. *Publications:* Place, Region and Community 1985, An Australian Compass: Essays on Place and Direction in Australian Literature 1991, Spirit in Exile: Peter Porter and his Poetry 1991, Oxford Literary History of Australia (co-ed.) 1998, Australian Short Fiction: A History 2002; other: ed. or co-ed. of various vols, including: Resistance and Reconciliation: Writing in the Commonwealth 2003; contribs to many books and journals. *Honours:* Rhodes Scholar, Pembroke Coll. Oxford 1964–67, Western Australia Premier's Award, Historical and Critical Studies 1992. *Address:* c/o School of Humanities and Social Sciences, University of New South Wales, Australian Defence Force Academy, Canberra, ACT 2600, Australia.

BENNETT, John J.; American writer; b. 8 Aug. 1938, New York, NY. *Education:* George Washington University; University of Munich. *Publications:* Tripping in America, 1984; Crime of the Century, 1986; The New World Order, 1991; Bodo (novel), 1995; Karmic Four-Star Buckaroo, 1997. *Contributions:* Chicago Review; Exquisite Corpse; Northwest Review; Transatlantic Review; New York Quarterly; Seattle Weekly. *Honours:* First Prize for Fiction, Iron Country, 1978; William Wantling Award, 1987; Darrell Bob Houston Award, 1988.

BENNETT, Paul Lewis, BA, AM; American academic, poet and writer; b. 10 Jan. 1921, Gnadenhutten, OH; m. Martha Jeanne Leonhart 1941 (died 1995); two s. *Education:* Ohio University, Harvard University. *Career:* Instructor, Samuel Adams School of Social Studies, Boston, 1945–46; Teaching Asst, Harvard University, 1945–46; Instructor in English, University of Maine, Orono, 1946–47; Instructor to Prof. of English, 1947–86, Poet-in-Residence, 1986–, Denison University; Gardener and Orchardist, 1948–; Consultant, Aerospace Laboratories, Owens-Corning Fiberglass Corp, 1964–67, Ohio Arts Council, 1978–81, Ohio Board of Regents, 1985–86. *Publications:* Poetry: A Strange Affinity, 1975; The Eye of Reason, 1976; Building a House, 1986; The Sun and What It Says Endlessly, 1995; Appalachian Mettle, 1997. Fiction: Robbery on the Highway, 1961; The Living Things, 1975; Follow the River, 1987; Fact Book: Max: The Tail of a Waggish Dog, 1999. Contributions: many periodicals. *Honours:* National Endowment for the Arts Fellowship, 1973–74; Significant Achievement Award, Ohio University, 1992.

BENNETT, Ronan, BA, PhD; Northern Irish writer; b. 1956, Belfast; m. Georgina Henry. *Education:* King's Coll., London. *Television screenplays:* Love Lies Bleeding 1993, A Man You Don't Meet Every Day 1994, Rebel Heart 2001, Fields of Gold 2002. *Film screenplays:* A Further Gesture (aka The Break) 1997, Lucky Break 2001, Face 1997, Do Armed Robbers Have Love Affairs? (short) 2002, The Hamburg Cell 2004. *Publications:* novels: The Second Prison 1991, Overthrown by Strangers 1992, The Catastrophist 1998,

Havoc, in its Third Year (Hughes & Hughes/Sunday Independent Irish Novel of the Year) 2004, Zugzwang 2006; non-fiction: Stolen Years: Before and After Guildford (with Paul Hill) 1990, Fire and Rain 1994. *Literary Agent:* David Godwin Associates, 55 Monmouth Street, London, WC2H 9DG, England. *Telephone:* (20) 7240-9992. *Fax:* (20) 7240-3007. *E-mail:* sophie@davidgodwinassociates.co.uk. *Website:* www.davidgodwinassociates.co.uk.

BENNETT, William John, BA, PhD, JD; American academic, lawyer, broadcaster and fmr government official; b. 31 July 1943, Brooklyn, New York; m. Elyane Glover 1982; two s. *Education:* Williams Coll., Univ. of Texas, Harvard Univ. Law School. *Career:* Asst Prof., Univ. of Southern Mississippi 1967–68, Univ. of Texas 1970, Univ. of Wisconsin 1973; Resident Adviser and Tutor, Harvard Univ. 1969–71; Asst Prof. and Asst to the Pres., Boston Univ. 1971–76; Exec. Dir Nat. Humanities Center, NC 1976–79, Pres. and Dir 1979–81; Adjunct Assoc. Prof. NC State Univ., Raleigh 1979–81, Univ. of NC 1979–81; Pres. Nat. Endowment for the Humanities, Washington, DC 1981–85; Sec. for Educ. 1985–88; Pnr Dunnells, Duvall, Bennett and Porter, Washington, DC 1988; Dir Nat. Drug Policy 1989–90; Co-Dir Empower America 1993; host Bill Bennett's Morning in America (radio talk show) 2004–; mem. American Soc. for Political and Legal Philosophy, Nat. Acad. of Education, Nat. Humanities Faculty, Soc. for Values in Higher Education, Southern Education Communications Asscn; Chair. Americans for Victory Over Terrorism; co-Chair. Partnership for a Drug-Free America; Washington Fellow, Claremont Inst.; Contrib. CNN; fmr Democrat, joined Republican Party 1986. *Publications include:* Counting by Race: Equality from the Founding Fathers to Bakke and Weber (with Terry Eastland) 1979, Our Children and Our Country: Improving America's Schools and Affirming the Common Culture 1988, The De-Valuing of America: The Fight for Our Culture and Our Children 1992, The Book of Virtues: A Treasury of Great Moral Stories 1993, The Index of Leading Cultural Indicators: Facts and Figures of the State of American Society 1994, The Moral Compass: Stories for a Life's Journey 1995, Our Sacred Honor 1997, Children's Book of Heroes 1997, Book of Virtures for Young People 1997, Children's Book of America 1998, Death of Outrage: Bill Clinton and the Assault on American Ideals 1998, Children's Book of Faith 2000, Broken Hearth: Reversing the Moral Collapse of the American Family 2001, Children's Book of Home and Family 2002, Why We Fight: Moral Clarity and the War on Terrorism 2003, America: The Last Best Hope Volume I 2006. *Address:* c/o Claremont Institute, 937 West Foothill Boulevard, Suite E, Claremont, CA 91711; 862 Venable Place NW, Washington, DC 20012, USA. *Website:* bennettmornings.com.

BENNOUNA, Khnata; Moroccan writer. *Career:* currently high school Principal, Casablanca. *Publications:* fiction: Liyasqet Assamt (trans. as Down with Silence!) 1967, Annar wa Al-'ikhtiyar (trans. as Fire and Choice) (Morocco Literary Prize 1971) 1969, Assawt wa Assurah (trans. as Sound and Image) 1975, Al-A'asifah (trans. as The Tempest) 1979, Al-Ghad wa Al-Ghadab (novel, trans. as Tomorrow and Wrath) 1981, Assamt Annatiq (trans. as Talking Silence) 1987. *Address:* c/o Union des Ecrivains du Maroc, 5 rue Ab Bakr Seddik, Rabat, Morocco.

BENSLEY, Connie; British poet and writer; b. 28 July 1929, London, England; m. J. A. Bensley 1952 (divorced 1976); two s. *Career:* Poetry Ed., PEN Magazine 1984–85; mem. Poetry Soc.; judge on panel for Forward Prizes for poetry 2003. *Publications:* Progress Report 1981, Moving In 1984, Central Reservations 1990, Choosing to be a Swan 1994, The Back and the Front of It 2000, Private Pleasures 2007; contrib. to Observer, Poetry Review, Spectator, TLS. *Honours:* first place TLS Poetry Competition 1986, second place Leek Poetry Competition 1988, prizewinner Arvon/Observer Poetry Competition 1994, second place Tate Gallery Poetry Competition 1995. *Address:* 49 Westfields Avenue, Barnes, London, SW13 0AT, England (home). *Telephone:* (20) 8878-6260 (home).

BENSON, Eugene, BA, MA, PhD; Canadian/ Northern Irish academic and writer; b. 6 July 1928, Larne, Northern Ireland; m. Renate Niklaus 1968; two s. *Education:* Nat. Univ. of Ireland, Univ. of Western Ontario, Univ. of Toronto. *Career:* Lecturer, Royal Military Coll., Kingston, ON 1960–61; Asst Prof. of English, Laurentian Univ. 1961–64; Asst Prof., Univ. of Guelph 1965–67, Assoc. Prof. 1967–71, Prof. of English 1971–93, Univ. Prof. Emeritus 1994–; mem. Asscn of Canadian Theatre Historians, Canadian Asscn of Irish Studies, Writers' Union of Canada (chair. 1983–84, elected life mem. 2001), PEN Canada (co-pres. 1984–85). *Publications:* Encounter: Canadian Drama in Four Media (anthology, ed.) 1973, The Bulls of Ronda (novel) 1976, Power Game, or the Making of a Prime Minister (novel) 1980, J. M. Synge 1982, English-Canadian Theatre (co-author) 1987, Oxford Companion to Canadian Theatre (co-ed.) 1989, Encyclopedia of Post-Colonial Literatures in English (co-ed.) 1994, The Oxford Companion to Canadian Literature (co-ed.) 1997. *Address:* 55 Palmer Street, Guelph, ON N1E 2P9, Canada.

BENSON, Gerard John, (Jedediah Barrow); British poet, writer, editor and actor; *Editor/Administrator, Poems on the Underground*; b. 9 April 1931, London, England; m. 2nd; one s. one d. *Education:* Rendcomb Coll., Univ. of Exeter, Cen. School of Speech and Drama, Univ. of London, IPA. *Career:* Resident Tutor, Arvon Foundation and Taliesen Trust; Sr Lecturer, Cen. School of Speech and Drama; Co-originator and Admin. of Poems on the Underground 1986–; Arts Council Poet-in-Residence, Dove Cottage, Wordsworth Trust 1994–; British Council Poet-in-Residence, Cairo and Alexandria 1997; British Council Writer-in-Residence, Stavanger and Kristiansand 1998; Poetry in Practice, Poet-in-Residence, Ashwell Medical Centre, Bradford 2000–01; poet and lecturer, Aldebugh Poetry Festival 2002, 2003, 2005; mem. Barrow Poets, Quaker Arts Network, Poems on the Underground, Poetry Soc. Educ. Advisory Panel, Nat. Asscn of Writers in Educ. (Chair. 1992), Soc. of Authors. *Publications:* Name Game 1971, Gorgon 1983, This Poem Doesn't Rhyme (ed.) 1990, Tower Block Poet: Sequence of 15 poems commissioned by BBC Radio 1990, Poems on the Underground anthologies (co-ed.) 1991–2006, The Magnificent Callisto 1993, Does W Trouble You? (ed.) 1994, Evidence of Elephants 1995, In Wordsworth's Chair 1995, Love Poems on the Underground 1996, Bradford and Beyond 1997, Nemo's Almanac (ed. and author) 1997–2006, Hlep! (15 poems with woodcuts by Ros Cuthbert) 2001, The Poetry Business 2002, To Catch an Elephant (poems for children) 2002, The Carnival of the Animals – poems and music for children (co-ed.) 2005, Omba Bolomba (poems for children) 2005; contrib. to newspapers, journals, reviews and the internet. *Honours:* Signal Award for Poetry 1991. *Address:* 46 Ashwell Road, Manningham, Bradford, West Yorks., BD8 9DU, England (home). *Telephone:* (1274) 541316 (office). *Fax:* (1274) 541316 (office). *E-mail:* gerardjbenson@hotmail.com (home).

BENTLEY, Eric, BA, BLitt, PhD; American (b. British) dramatist, critic and scholar; b. 14 Sept. 1916, Bolton, Lancs., England; m. 1st Maja Tschernjakow (divorced); m. 2nd Joanne Davis 1953; two s. *Education:* Univ. of Oxford, Yale Univ. *Career:* drama critic, New Republic 1952–56; Brander Matthews Prof. of Dramatic Literature, Columbia Univ., New York 1953–69; Charles Eliot Norton Prof. of Poetry, Harvard Univ. 1960–61; Katharine Cornell Prof. of Theatre, State Univ. of New York at Buffalo 1975–82; Fulbright Prof., Belgrade 1980; Prof. of Comparative Literature, Univ. of Maryland, College Park 1982–89; mem. American Acad. of Arts and Sciences, American Acad. of Arts and Letters. *Publications:* The Playwright as Thinker 1946, Bernard Shaw 1947, In Search of Theatre 1953, The Theatre of Commitment 1967, Theatre of War 1972, Rallying Cries (three plays) 1977, The Kleist Variations (three plays) 1982, Monstrous Martyrdoms (three plays) 1985, The Pirandello Commentaries 1985, The Brecht Memoir 1986, Thinking About the Playwright 1987, Bentley on Brecht 1999. *Honours:* Hon. DFA (Wisconsin) 1975; Hon. LittD (East Anglia) 1979; Dr hc (New School for Social Research) 1992; Festschrift: The Play and its Critic 1986, Florida Theatre Festival named in his honour 1992, Robert Lewis Award for Life Achievement in the Theatre 1992, inducted into Theatre Hall of Fame 1997. *Literary Agent:* c/o Jack Tantleff, William Morris Agency, 1325 Avenue of the Americas, New York, NY 10019, USA. *Telephone:* (212) 586-5100. *Fax:* (212) 246-3583. *Website:* www.wma.com. *Address:* 194 Riverside Drive, New York, NY 10025, USA (home). *E-mail:* ericbentley@verizon.net (home).

BERENBAUM, Michael, AB, PhD; American academic, museum and foundation executive and writer; b. 31 July 1945, Newark, NJ; m. Melissa Patack, 25 June 1995, one s. one d. *Education:* Queens College, CUNY, Jewish Theological Seminary, Hebrew University, Boston University, Florida State University. *Career:* Hymen Goldman Prof. of Theology, Georgetown University, 1983–97; Senior Scholar, Religious Action Center, 1986–89; Adjunct Prof. of Judaic Studies, American University, 1987; Project Dir, United States Holocaust Memorial Museum, 1988–93; Dir, United States Holocaust Research Institute, 1993–97; Pres. and CEO, Survivors of Shoah Visual History Foundation, 1997–; Prof. of Theology, University of Judaism, 1998–. *Publications:* The World Must Know: A History of the Holocaust, 1993; Anatomy of the Auschwitz Death Camp (ed. with Israel Gutman), 1994; What Kind of God? (ed. with Betty Rogers Rubenstein), 1995; Witness to the Holocaust: An Illustrated Documentary History of the Holocaust in the Words of Its Victims, Perpetrators and Bystanders, 1997; The Holocaust and History: The Known, the Unknown, the Disputed and the Reexamined, 1998. *Honours:* Silver Angel Award, 1981; Simon Rockower Memorial Award, 1986, 1987.

BERENDT, John Lawrence, BA; American writer and journalist; b. 5 Dec. 1939, Syracuse, NY; s. of Ralph Berendt and Carol Berendt (née Deschere). *Education:* Nottingham High School, Syracuse, Harvard Univ. *Career:* Assoc. Ed. Esquire 1961–69, columnist 1982–94; Ed. New York magazine 1977–82; freelance writer 1982–; mem. PEN, The Century Asscn. *Publications:* Midnight in the Garden of Good and Evil 1994, The City of Falling Angels 2005. *Literary Agent:* c/o The Penguin Press, 375 Hudson Street, New York, NY 10014, USA. *Address:* c/o Hodder & Stoughton, 338 Euston Road, London, NW1 3BH, England.

BERESFORD, Elisabeth, MBE; British writer; b. Paris, France; one s. one d. *Career:* Founder Alderney Youth Trust. *Publications:* children's fiction: The Television Mystery 1957, Trouble at Tullington Castle 1958, Gappy Goes West 1959, Two Gold Dolphins 1961, Game, Set and Match 1965, The Hidden Mill 1965, The Black Mountain Mystery 1967, Sea-Green Magic 1968, Stephen and the Shaggy Dog 1970, The Wandering Wombles 1970, Dangerous Magic 1972, The Secret Railway 1973, The Wombles at Work 1973, The Wombles Annual 1975–78, Snuffle to the Rescue 1975, Orinoco Runs Away 1975, Bungo Knows Best 1976, Tobermory's Big Surprise 1976, Wombling Free 1978, The Happy Ghost 1979, Curious Magic 1980, The Four of Us 1982, The Animals Nobody Wanted 1982, The Tovers 1982, The Adventures of Poon 1984, One of the Family 1985, The Ghosts of Lupus Street School 1986, The Secret Room 1987, Emily and the Haunted Castle 1987, The Oscar Puffin Book 1987, Once Upon a Time Stories 1988, The Island Railway Armada Adventure 1989, Rose 1992, Charlie's Ark 1992, The Wooden Gun 1992, Tim the Trumpet 1992, Jamie and the Rola Polar Bear 1993, Lizzy's War 1993, Rola Polar Bear and the Heatwave 1995, Lizzy's War, Part II 1996, The Smallest Whale 1996, Chris the Climber 1997, Island Treasure 1998, Shansi's Surprise 1998, Ghost of

Wimbledon Common 1998, Orinoco the Magnificent 1998, Tomsk to the Rescue 1998, Beautiful Boating Weather 1998, Camping and Cloudberries 1998, Six Womble Picture Books 1998, Seven Womble Picture Books 1999, Bigfoot Womble (audiobook) 1999, Pirate Gold 2000, Tommy in Trouble 2000, Tessa on TV 2000, The Sleep Wombler 2001, Lizzy Fights On (also audiobook) 2001; adult fiction: Paradise Island 1963, Escape to Happiness 1964, Roses Round the Door 1965, Island of Shadows 1966, Veronica 1967, A Tropical Affair 1968, Saturday's Child 1969, Love Remembered 1970, Love and the SS Beatrice 1972, Pandora 1974, The Steadfast Lover 1980, The Silver Chain 1980. *Literary Agent:* The Agency, 24 Pottery Lane, Holland Park, London, W11 4LZ, England. *Address:* Little Street, Alderney, GY9 3TT, Channel Islands (home).

BERESFORD-HOWE, Constance, BA, MA, PhD; Canadian academic and novelist; b. 10 Nov. 1922, Montréal, QC; m. 1960, one s. *Education:* McGill University, Brown University. *Career:* mem. International PEN; International PEN, Writers in Prison Committee. *Publications:* The Book of Eve, 1973; A Population of One, 1976; The Marriage Bed, 1980; Night Studies, 1984; Prospero's Daughter, 1989; A Serious Widow, 1990. *Honours:* Dodd Mead Intercollegiate Literary Fellowship, 1948; Canadian Booksellers Award, 1974.

BERG, Elizabeth; American writer; b. 2 Dec. 1948; m. Howard Berg 1974 (divorced); two d. *Education:* University of Minnesota, St Mary's College. *Publications:* Family Traditions: Celebrations for Holidays and Everyday, 1992; Durable Goods, 1993; Talk Before Sleep, 1994; Range of Motion, 1995; The Pull of the Moon, 1996; Joy School, 1997; What We Keep, 1998; Until the Real Thing Comes Along, 1999; Escaping Into the Open: The Art of Writing True, 1999; Open House, 2000; Never Change, 2001; Ordinary Life, 2002. Contributions: periodicals. *Honours:* New England Book Award for Fiction 1997.

BERG, Stephen Walter, BA; American poet and writer; *Joint Editor, American Poetry Review;* b. 2 Aug. 1934, Philadelphia, PA; m. Millie Lane 1959; two d. *Education:* Univ. of Pennsylvania, Boston Univ., Univ. of Iowa, Indiana Univ. *Career:* teacher, Temple Univ., Philadelphia, Princeton Univ., Haverford Coll., Pennsylvania; Prof., Philadelphia Coll. of Art; Poetry Ed., Saturday Evening Post 1961–62; Founding Ed. (with Stephen Parker and Rhoda Schwartz), American Poetry Review 1972–. *Publications:* poetry: Berg Goodman Mezey 1957, Bearing Weapons 1963, The Queen's Triangle: A Romance 1970, The Daughters 1971, Nothing in the Word: Versions of Aztec Poetry 1972, Grief: Poems and Versions of Poems 1975, With Akmatova at the Black Gates: Variations 1981, In It 1986, First Song, Bankei, 1653 1989, Homage to the Afterlife 1991, New and Selected Poems 1992, Oblivion: Poems 1995; editor: Naked Poetry: Recent American Poetry in Open Forms (with Robert Mezey) 1969, Between People (with S. J. Marks) 1972, About Women (with S. J. Marks) 1973, The New Naked Poetry (with Robert Mezey) 1976, In Praise of What Persists 1983, Singular Voices: American Poetry Today 1985, The Body Electric: America's Best Poetry from The American Poetry Review (co-ed.) 2001; other: Sea Ice: Versions of Eskimo Songs 1988; contrib. to periodicals. *Honours:* Rockefeller-Centro Mexicano de Escritores Grant, 1959–61; National Trans. Center Grant, 1969; Frank O'Hara Prize, Poetry magazine, 1970; Guggenheim Fellowship, 1974; National Endowment for the Arts Grant, 1976; Columbia University Trans. Center Award, 1976. *Address:* 2005 Mount Vernon Street, Philadelphia, PA 19130, USA. *Address:* The American Poetry Review, 117 S 17th Street, Suite 910, Philadelphia, PA 19103, USA (office). *Telephone:* (215) 496-0439. *Fax:* (215) 569-0808. *E-mail:* sberg@aprweb.org. *Website:* www.aprweb.org.

BERGÉ, Carol; American writer, poet, editor, publisher and antiques dealer; b. 4 Oct. 1928, New York, NY; m. Jack Henry Bergé 1955; one s. *Education:* New York Univ., New School for Social Research, New York. *Career:* Ed. 1970–84, Publisher 1991–93, CENTER Magazine and Press; Distinguished Prof. of Literature, Thomas Jefferson Coll., Allendale, MI 1975–76; Instructor, Goddard Coll. 1976; Teacher, Univ. of California Extension Program, Berkeley 1976–77; Assoc. Prof., Univ. of Southern Mississippi 1977–78; Ed., Mississippi Review 1977–78; Visiting Prof., Univ. of New Mexico 1978–79, 1987; Visiting Lecturer, Wright State Univ., Dayton, OH 1979, SUNY at Albany 1980–81; proprietor, Blue Gate Gallery of Art and Antiques 1988–; mem. Authors' League, MacDowell Fellows' Asscn, Nat. Press Women, Poets & Writers. *Publications:* fiction: The Unfolding 1969, A Couple Called Moebius 1972, Acts of Love: An American Novel 1973, Timepieces 1977, The Doppler Effect 1979, Fierce Metronome 1981, Secrets, Gossip and Slander 1984, Zebras, or, Contour Lines 1991; poetry: The Vulnerable Island 1964, Lumina 1965, Poems Made of Skin 1968, The Chambers 1969, Circles, as in the Eye 1969, An American Romance 1969, From a Soft Angle: Poems About Women 1972, The Unexpected 1976, Rituals and Gargoyles 1976, A Song, A Chant 1978, Alba Genesis 1979, Alba Nemesis 1979; editor: Light Years: The New York City Coffeehouse Poets of the 1960s 2004; reportage: The Vancouver Report 1965; contrib. to anthologies and periodicals. *Honours:* New York State Council on the Arts CAPS Award 1974, NEA Fellowship 1979–80. *Address:* 2070 Calle Contento, Santa Fe, NM 87505, USA. *Telephone:* (505) 438-3979. *E-mail:* carolberge@earthlink.net.

BERGEL, Hans; German writer; b. 26 July 1925, Kronstadt, Romania. *Education:* University of Cluj-Napoca. *Career:* mem. Die Künstlergilde, Esslingen; PEN International; Institut für deutsche Kultur und Geschichte Südosteuropas, Munich. *Publications:* Rumänien, Portrait einer Nation, 1969;

Ten Southern European Short Stories, 1972; Die Sachsen in Siebenburgen nach dreissig Jahren Kommunismus, 1976; Der Tanz in Ketten, 1977; Siebenburgen, 1980; Gestalten und Gewalten, 1982; Hermann Oberth oder Der mythische Traum vom Fliegen, 1984; Der Tod des Hirten, 1985; Literaturgeschichte der Deutschen in Siebenburgen, 1987; Das Venusherz (short novel), 1987; Weihnacht ist uberall (eleven short stories), 1988. Contributions: periodicals. *Honours:* Short Story Prize, Bucharest, 1957, Bonn, 1972; Georg Dehio Prize, Esslingen, 1972; Goethe Foundation Prize, Basel, 1972; Medien Prizes, Bavarian Broadcasting Company, 1983, 1989; Bundesverdienstkreuz, 1987; Saxon of Transylvania Culture Prize, 1988; Geyphius-Prize, 1990.

BERGEN, David, BEd; Canadian novelist; b. 1957, Port Edward, BC. *Career:* worked as a carpenter, bricklayer and orderly; teacher English in high school. *Publications:* Sitting Opposite My Brother (short stories) 1993, A Year of Lesser (novel) (New York Times Notable Book, McNally Robinson Book of the Year Award) 1996, See the Child (novel) 1999, The Case of Lena S. (novel) (Carol Shields Winnipeg Book Award) 2002, The Time in Between (novel) (Scotiabank Giller Prize 2006) 2005. *Address:* c/o Random House, 1745 Broadway, New York, NY 10019, USA (office).

BERGENHEIM, Richard C., BA, MA; American teacher; *Editor, Christian Science Monitor;* s. of Robert Bergenheim. *Education:* Principia Coll., Elsah, IL and Shakespeare Inst., Univ. of Birmingham, England. *Career:* teacher of Christian Science 1982–; mem. bd of dirs and Ed.-in-Chief The Christian Science Publishing Soc. 1988–94, Ed. Christian Science Monitor 2005–. *Address:* The Christian Science Monitor, One Norway Street, Boston, MA 02115, USA (office). *Telephone:* (617) 450-2000 (office). *E-mail:* richard@bergenheim.com. *Website:* bergenheim.com; www.csmonitor.com.

BERGER, François, LenD; Swiss barrister, poet and writer; b. 16 May 1950, Neuchâtel. *Education:* Neuchâtel Univ., Vienna Univ. *Career:* Barrister, Neuchâtel; mem. Asscn des écrivains de langue française, Asscn des écrivains neuchâtelois et jurassiens; Pres., Canton of Neuchâtel Literature Cttee; Pres. Autrices et auteurs de Suisse; mem. Soc. Européenne de Culture. *Publications:* poetry: Mémoire d'anges, 1981; Gestes du veilleur, 1984; Le Pré, 1986; Les Indiennes, 1988; Le Repos d'Ariane, 1990; fiction: Le jour avant, 1995; Le Voyage de l'Ange, 1999; L'Anneau de sable 2001; L'Amour à Trieste 2004; contribs to several anthologies and to L'Express/Feuille d'Avis de Neuchâtel (newspaper). *Honours:* Louise Labé Prize, Paris, 1982; Citation of Distinction, Schiller Foundation, Zürich, 1984; Auguste Bachelin Prize, Neuchâtel, 1988, Prix du roman poétique, Soc. de poètes et d'écrivains d'expression française, Geneva, 2002. *Address:* 28 Rebatte, 2068 Hauterive, Neuchâtel, Switzerland (home). *Telephone:* (32) 724-03-71 (office). *Fax:* (32) 724-03-72. *E-mail:* etudeberger@vtx.ch (office).

BERGER, John; British author and art critic; b. 5 Nov. 1926, London; s. of the late S. J. D. Berger and Miriam Berger (née Branson). *Education:* Cen. School of Art and Chelsea School of Art, London. *Career:* began career as painter and teacher of drawing; exhbns at Wildenstein, Redfern and Leicester Galleries, London; Art Critic Tribune, New Statesman; Visiting Fellow BFI 1990–; numerous TV appearances including Monitor, two series for Granada; Scenario: La Salamandre (with Alain Tanner), Le Milieu du Monde, Jonas (New York Critics Prize for Best Scenario of Year 1976). *Plays:* The Three Lives of Lucy Cabrol (with Simon McBurney) 1994, Isabelle (with Nella Bielski) 1998. *Radio:* Will It Be A Likeness? 1996. *Publications:* fiction: A Painter of Our Time 1958, The Foot of Clive 1962, Corker's Freedom 1964, G (Booker Prize, James Tait Black Memorial Prize) 1972, Pig Earth 1979, Once in Europa 1989, Lilac and Flag 1991, To The Wedding 1995, Photocopies 1996, King: A Street Story 1999, Here is Where we Meet 2005; theatre: Question of Geography (with Nella Bielski) 1984 (staged in Marseille, Paris and by RSC, Stratford), Francisco Goya's Last Portrait (with Nella Bielski) 1989, I Send You This Cadmium Red (with John Christie) 2000; non-fiction: Marcel Frishman 1958, Permanent Red 1960, The Success and Failure of Picasso 1965, A Fortunate Man: The Story of a Country Doctor (with J. Mohr) 1967, Art and Revolution, Moments of Cubism and Other Essays 1969, The Look of Things, Ways of Seeing 1972, The Seventh Man 1975 (Prize for Best Reportage, Union of Journalists and Writers, Paris 1977), About Looking 1980, Another Way of Telling (with J. Mohr) 1982, And Our Faces, My Heart, Brief as Photos 1984, The White Bird 1985 (USA as The Sense of Sight 1985), Keeping a Rendezvous (essays and poems) 1992, Titian: Nymph and Shepherd (with Katya Berger) 1996, Steps Towards a Small Theory of the Visible 1996, The Shape of a Pocket 2001, John Berger Selected Essays (ed. by Geoff Dyer) 2001; poetry: Pages of the Wound: Poems, Drawings, Photographs 1956–96 1996; translations: (with A. Bostock): Poems on the Theatre by B. Brecht 1960, Return to My Native Land by Aimé Césaire 1969; Oranges for the Son of Alexander Levy by Nella Bielski (with Lisa Appignanesi) 1982. *Honours:* George Orwell Memorial Prize 1977. *Address:* Quincy, Mieussy, 74440 Taninges, France.

BERGER, Thomas Louis, BA; American writer; b. 20 July 1924, Cincinnati, OH; s. of Thomas C. Berger and Mildred Berger; m. Jeanne Redpath 1950. *Education:* Univ. of Cincinnati and Columbia Univ. Grad. School. *Career:* mil. service 1943–46; Assoc. Ed., Popular Science Monthly 1952–53; Distinguished Visiting Prof. Southampton Univ. 1975–76; Visiting Lecturer, Yale Univ. 1981, 1982; Regents Lecturer, Univ. of Calif. at Davis 1982; Dial Fellow 1962. *Play:* Other People 1970. *Publications:* Crazy in Berlin 1958, Reinhart in Love 1962, Little Big Man 1964, Killing Time 1967, Vital Parts 1970, Regiment of

Women 1973, Sneaky People 1975, Who is Teddy Villanova? 1977, Arthur Rex 1978, Neighbors 1980, Reinhart's Women 1981, The Feud 1983, Nowhere 1985, Being Invisible 1987, The Houseguest 1988, Changing the Past 1989, Orrie's Story 1990, Meeting Evil 1992, Robert Crews 1994, Suspects 1996, The Return of Little Big Man 1999, Best Friends 2003, Adventures of the Artificial Woman 2004. *Honours:* Hon. LittD (Long Island) 1986; Rosenthal Award, Nat. Inst. of Arts and Letters 1965, Western Heritage Award 1965, Ohiona Book Award 1982. *Literary Agent:* Don Congdon Associates, 156 Fifth Avenue, Suite 625, New York, NY 10010-7002. *Telephone:* (212) 645-1229 (office). *Fax:* (212) 727-2688 (office). *E-mail:* doncongdon@aol.com (office). *Address:* PO Box 11, Palisades, NY 10964, USA.

BERGMAN, Ingmar; Swedish film director, theatre producer and screenwriter; b. 14 July 1918, Uppsala; m. 1st Else Fisher 1943 (divorced); m. 2nd Ellen Lundström 1945 (divorced); m. 3rd Gun Grut 1951 (divorced); m. 4th Käbi Laretei 1959 (divorced); m. 5th Ingrid Karlebovon Rosen 1971 (died 1995); one d.; eight c. by previous marriages. *Education:* Stockholm Univ. *Career:* producer Royal Theatre, Stockholm 1940–42; scriptwriter and producer Svensk Filmindustri 1940–44; theatre-Dir Helsingborg 1944–46, Gothenburg 1946–49, Malmo 1954–63; leading Dir Royal Dramatic Theatre, Stockholm 1963; Dir Mme de Sade Theatre 1989; Chair. European Cinema Soc. 1989–; has written the scripts of most of his films; mem. Swedish Acad. of Letters. *Films include:* Crisis 1945, It Rains on Our Love 1946, A Ship Bound for India 1947, Music in Darkness 1947, Port of Call 1948, Prison 1948, Thirst 1949, To Joy 1949, Summer Interlude 1950, This Can't Happen Here 1950, Waiting Women 1952, Summer with Monika 1952, Sawdust and Tinsel 1953, A Lesson in Love 1954, Journey into Autumn 1955, Smiles of a Summer Night 1955, The Seventh Seal 1956, Wild Strawberries 1957, So Close to Life 1957, The Face 1958, The Virgin Spring 1959, The Devil's Eye 1960, Through a Glass Darkly 1961, Winter Light 1962, The Silence 1962, Now About these Women 1963, Episode in Stimulantia 1965, Persona 1966, The Hour of the Wolf 1967, Shame 1968, The Rite 1970, A Passion 1970, The Touch 1971, Cries and Whispers 1972, Scenes from a Marriage 1974, The Magic Flute 1975, Face to Face 1975, The Serpent's Egg 1977, Sonate d'automne 1978, Aus dem Leben der Marionetten 1980, Fårö Document 1980, Fanny and Alexander 1981, After the Rehearsal 1984, Private Confessions 1998; scriptwriter, The Best Intentions 1991, Faithless 2000, Persona (video) 2002. *Plays include:* A Painting on Wood, The City, The Rite (TV play), The Lie (TV play), Scenes from a Marriage (TV play); Dir To Damascus 1974, The Merry Widow, Twelfth Night 1975, 1980, Tartuffe 1980, King Lear 1985, John Gabriel Borkman 1985, Miss Julie 1986, Hamlet 1986, Maria Stuart 2000. *Television includes:* Scenes from a Marriage 1974, The Magic Flute 1975, Face to Face 1975, The Making Noise and Acting Up 1996, Saraband 2003, Bergmanova Sonata (play) (writer) 2005. *Publications:* Four Stories 1977, The Magic Lantern (autobiog.) 1988, Fanny and Alexander 1989, Images: My Life in Film 1993, Sunday's Child 1994, Private Confessions 1997. *Honours:* Commdr, Légion d'honneur 1985; Dr hc (Rome) 1988; Erasmus Prize 1965, Award for Best Dir Nat. Soc. of Film Critics 1970, Order of the Yugoslav Flag 1971, Luigi Pirandello Int. Theatre Prize 1971, Goethe Award (Frankfurt) 1976, Gold Medal of Swedish Acad. 1977, European Film Award 1988, Le Prix Sonning 1989, Praemium Imperiale Prize (Japan) 1991, Dorothy and Lilian Gish Prize 1995.

BERGON, Frank, BA, PhD; American novelist and academic; b. 24 Feb. 1943, Ely, Nevada, USA; m. Holly St John Bergon 1979. *Education:* Boston College, Stanford University, Harvard University. *Career:* Teaching Fellow, Harvard University, 1968–70; Lecturer, Newton College, 1971–72; Prof. of English, 1972–, Dir, American Culture Program, 1982–85, Vassar College; Visiting Assoc. Prof., University of Washington, 1980–81; mem. MLA; Western Literature Asscn; Asscn of the Study of Literature and the Environment. *Publications:* Stephen Crane's Artistry, 1975; Looking Far West: The Search for the American West in History, Myth and Literature (co-ed.), 1978; The Western Writings of Stephen Crane (ed.), 1979; The Wilderness Reader (ed.), 1980; Shoshone Mike (novel), 1987; A Sharp Lookout: Selected Nature Essays of John Burroughs (ed.), 1987; The Journals of Lewis & Clark (ed.), 1989; The Temptations of St Ed & Brother S (novel), 1993; Wild Game (novel), 1995. Contributions: American Literary History; Terra Nova; Journal of Nature and Culture. *Honours:* Wallace Stegner Fellowship 1965–66. *Address:* 136 Chapel Hill Road, Highland, NY 12528, USA. *E-mail:* bergon@vassar.edu.

BERGONZI, Bernard; British writer, poet and academic; b. 13 April 1929, London, England. *Education:* BLitt, 1961, MA, 1962, Wadham College, Oxford. *Career:* Senior Lecturer, 1966–71, Prof. of English, 1971–92, Prof. Emeritus, 1992–, University of Warwick, Coventry. *Publications:* The Early H. G. Wells, 1961; Heroes' Twilight, 1965; Innovations: Essays on Art and Ideas, 1968; T. S. Eliot: Four Quartets: A Casebook, 1969; The Situation of the Novel, 1970; T. S. Eliot, 1972; The Turn of a Century, 1973; H. G. Wells: A Collection of Critical Essays, 1975; Gerard Manley Hopkins, 1977; Reading the Thirties, 1978; Years: Sixteen Poems, 1979; Poetry 1870–1914, 1980; The Roman Persuasion (novel), 1981; The Myth of Modernism and Twentieth Century Literature, 1986; Exploding English, 1990; Wartime and Aftermath, 1993; David Lodge, 1995; War Poets and Other Subjects, 1999; A Victorian Wanderer, 2003, A Study in Greene 2006. *Address:* 19 St Mary's Crescent, Leamington Spa, CV31 1JL, England.

BERGOUNIOUX, Pierre; French writer, literary critic, teacher and sculptor; b. 25 May 1949, Brive-la-Gaillarde, Corrèze. *Education:* Ecole Normale Supérieure de Saint-Cloud. *Career:* teacher of French in Paris schools. *Publications:* novels: Catherine 1984, Ce pas et le suivant 1985, La Bête faramineuse 1986, La Maison rose 1987, L'Arbre sur la rivière 1988, C'était nous 19889, La Mue 1991, L'Orphelin 1992, Le Matin des origines 1992, Le Grand Sylvain 1993, La Toussaint 1994, Miette 1996, La Mort de Brune 1996, La Ligne 1997, Les Forges de Syam 2001, L'Eau, le Feu 2001, Un Peu de bleu dans le paysage 2001, Le Premier mot 2001; non-fiction: B-17 G 2001, Jusqu'à Faulkner (literary criticism) 2002, École: mission accomplie 2006, Carnet de notes (journal) 1980–1990 2006. *Honours:* Prix Alain Fournier, Grand Prix de littérature de la SGDL for lifetime achievement 2002, Prix Virgile 2002. *Address:* c/o Editions Gallimard, 5 rue Sebastien-Bottin, 75007 Paris, France (office).

BERGSON, Leo (see Stebel, Sidney Leo)

BERKELEY, Humphry John, BA, MA; British writer and fmr politician; b. 1 Feb. 1926, Marlow, England. *Education:* Pembroke College, Cambridge. *Career:* MP, Conservative Party, Lancaster, 1959–66, joined Labour Party, 1970; Chair., United Nations Asscn of Great Britain and Northern Ireland, 1966–70; mem. Savile Club. *Publications:* The Power of the Prime Minister, 1968; Crossing the Floor, 1972; The Life and Death of Rochester Sneath, 1974; The Odyssey of Enoch: A Political Memoir, 1977; The Myth That Will Not Die: The Formation of the National Government, 1978; Faces of the Eighties (with Jeffrey Archer), 1987. Contributions: Times; Sunday Times; Daily Telegraph; Financial Times; Spectator; New Statesman. *Address:* 3 Pages Yard, Church Street, Chiswick, London W4 2PA, England.

BERKOFF, Steven; British actor, writer and director; b. 3 Aug. 1937, Stepney, London; s. of Alfred Berkoff and Pauline Berkoff; m. 1st Alison Minto 1970; m. 2nd Shelley Lee 1976 (divorced). *Education:* Hackney Downs Grammar School, Webber-Douglas School of Drama. *Films include:* Octopussy, First Blood 2, Beverly Hills Cop, Absolute Beginners, War and Remembrance (TV) 1988, The Krays 1990, Decadence 1994, Rancid Aluminium 2000, Head in the Clouds 2004, Brides 2004, Forest of the Gods 2005. *Plays/Productions include:* Agamemnon (London) 1973, The House of Usher 1974, The Trial 1976, East 1978, Hamlet 1980, 2001, Greek 1980, Decadence 1981, Agamemnon (USA) 1984, Harry's Xmas 1985, Kvetch 1986, 1991, Sink the Belgrano 1987, Coriolanus 1988, Metamorphosis 1988, Salome 1989, The Trial 1991, Brighton Beach Scumbags 1994; Dir West (London) 1983, Acapulco (LA) 1990, One Man (London) 1993, Coriolanus 1996, Mermaid 1996, Massage (LA and Edinburgh) 1997, Shakespeare's Villains 1998, Messiah 2000 (London 2003), Dir Sip and Shiver (Los Angeles) 2004, Dir Richard II (Ludlow Festival) 2005. *Publications:* America 1988, I am Hamlet 1989, A Prisoner in Rio 1989, The Theatre of Steven Berkoff (photographic) 1992, Coriolanus in Deutschland 1992, Overview (collected essays) 1994, Free Association (autobiog.) 1996, Graft: Tales of an Actor 1998, Shopping in the Santa Monica Mall, Ritual in Blood, Messiah, Oedipus 2000, The Secret Love Life of Ophelia 2001, Tough Acts 2003. *Honours:* Evening Standard Award for Comedy of the Year 1991. *Website:* www.stevenberkoff.com.

BERKOVÁ, Alexandra, PhD; Czech writer; b. 2 July 1949, Trencin, Slovakia; m. Vladimir Novák; one s. one d. *Education:* Charles Univ., Prague. *Career:* ed. 1973–81; television screenwriter 1983–91; freelance writer 1985–; founder New Humanity feminist org. 1992–; teacher of creative writing in high schools 1995–; mem. PEN Club 1989–. *Publications include:* Knížka s červeným obalem (short stories, trans. as Book with a Red Cover) 1986, Magorie (novel, trans. as Land of Fools) (Egon Hostorský Prize) 1991, The Sorrows of a Devoted Scoundrel (novel, title in trans.) 1993. *Address:* c/o Ministry of Culture, Maltéské nám. 471/1, 118 11 Prague 1, Czech Republic.

BERKSON, William (Bill) Craig; American poet, critic, editor and academic; *Professor and Co-ordinator of Public Lectures Programme, San Francisco Art Institute*; b. 30 Aug. 1939, New York, NY; m. 1st Lynn O'Hare 1975 (divorced); one s. one d.; m. 2nd Constance Lewallen 1998. *Education:* Brown Univ., Columbia Univ., New School for Social Research, New York, New York Univ. Inst. of Fine Arts. *Career:* Instructor, New School for Social Research, 1964–69; Visiting Fellow, Yale Univ. 1969–70; Ed. and Publr Big Sky magazine and books 1971–78; Adjunct Prof., Southampton Coll., Long Island Univ. 1980, Marin Community Coll. 1983–84; Assoc. Prof., California Coll. of Arts and Crafts 1983–84; Prof. and Co-ordinator of Public Lectures Programme, San Francisco Art Inst. 1984–, Dir Letters and Science 1994–99; Visiting Artist/Scholar, American Acad. in Rome 1991. *Publications:* Saturday Night: Poems, 1960–1961 1961, Shining Leaves 1969, Two Serious Poems and One Other (with Larry Fagin) 1972, Recent Visitors 1973, Hymns of St Bridget (with Frank O'Hara) 1975, Enigma Variations 1975, Ants 1975, 100 Women 1975, Blue is the Hero: Poems, 1960–1975 1976, Red Devil 1983, Lush Life 1983, Start Over 1984, Serenade 2000, Fugue State 2001, Hymns of St Bridget and Other Writings (with Frank O'Hara) 2002, 25 Grand View 2002, The Sweet Singer of Modernism and Other Art Writings 2003, Gloria 2005, What's Your Idea of a Good Time? (with Bernadette Mayer) 2006; other: ed. or co-ed. of several books; contribs to anthologies, periodicals, quarterlies and journals. *Honours:* Dylan Thomas Memorial Award 1959, Poets Foundation Grant 1968, Yaddo Fellowship 1968, National Endowment for the Arts Fellowship 1980, Briarcombe Fellowship 1983, Artspace Award 1990, Fund for Poetry Awards 1995, 2001. *Address:* 25 Grand View Avenue, San Francisco, CA 94114, USA (home). *Telephone:* (415) 826-2947 (home). *E-mail:* berkson@pacbell.net.

BERMAN, David, BA, MA, PhD; American academic and writer; *Associate Professor of Philosophy, Trinity College, Dublin*; b. 20 Nov. 1942, New York, NY; s. of Seymour Berman and Marion Berman; m. 1st Aileen Jill Mitchell

1970 (divorced 2001); two s. two d.; m. 2nd Patricia O'Riordan 2002. *Education:* New School for Social Research, New York, Univ. of Denver, Trinity Coll., Dublin, St Vincent's Hospital, Dublin. *Career:* Sr Lecturer in Philosophy, Trinity Coll., Dublin 1981–94, Fellow 1984, Assoc. Prof. of Philosophy 1994–, Head of Philosophy Dept 1997–2002. *Publications:* A History of Atheism in Britain: From Hobbes to Russell 1988, George Berkeley's Alciphron or the Minute Philosopher in Focus (ed.) 1993, George Berkeley: Idealism and the Man 1994, Arthur Schopenhauer's World as Will and Idea (ed.) 1995, Berkeley: Experimental Philosophy 1997, The Irish Enlightenment and Counter-Enlightenment (co-ed. with P. O'Riordan, six vols) 2002, Berkeley and Irish Philosophy 2005; contrib. to reference works, books, scholarly journals. *Address:* Department of Philosophy, Trinity College, University of Dublin, Dublin 2, Ireland (office). *E-mail:* dberman@tcd.ie (office).

BERMAN, Sabina; Mexican playwright, poet and theatre director; b. 21 Aug. 1956, Mexico City, DF. *Education:* Universidad Nacional Autónoma de México. *Film screenplay:* Tía Alejandra (Premio de la Academia de Artes y Ciencias Cinematográficas) 1974. *Plays:* Mariposa (Premio de Poesía Pluridimensional Juguete) 1974, El jardín de las delicias (aka El suplicio del placer) 1976, Yankee (aka Bill) (Premio de Teatro Instituto Nacional de Bellas Artes) 1979, Rompecabezas (aka Un buen trabajador de piolet) (Premio de Teatro Instituto Nacional de Bellas Artes) 1981, La maravillosa historia del niño pingüica, de cómo supo de su gran destino y de cómo comprobó su grandeza (Premio de Teatro Instituto Nacional de Bellas Artes) 1982, Herejía (aka Anatema) (Premio de Teatro Instituto Nacional de Bellas Artes) 1983, Aguila o sol 1985, Muerte súbita 1987, Volar la tecnología maharishi del campo unificado 1987, Caracol y colibrí 1990, La grieta 1990, La guerra culta 1991, Los ladrones del tiempo 1991, Entre Villa y una mujer desnuda 1993, El árbol de humo 1993, Krisis 1996, Los carvajales, En el nombre de Dios. *Publications:* poetry: Año internacional de la mujer (poems) (Premio de Poesía Pluridimensional Máscaraz, Premio de Cuento Latinoamericano) 1975, Poemas de agua 1986, Shanik 1986, Lunas 1988, Katún 1988; prose: La bobe (novel) 1990, Mujeres y poder (collection of interviews) (Nat. Journalism Award) 2000. *Honours:* Fondo Nacional grants 1993, 1994. *Address:* c/o International PEN (Mexican Centre), Heriberto Frias 1452-407, Col. de Valle, México, DF 03100, Mexico.

BERNARD, David Kane, BA, JD; American pastor, author and editor; b. 20 Nov. 1956, Baton Rouge; m. Connie Sharpe Bernard 1981, two s. one d. *Education:* Rice University, Wesley Biblical Seminary, University of Texas. *Career:* Instructor, Administrator, Jackson College of Ministries, 1981–86; Assoc. Ed., United Pentecostal Church International, 1986–; Pastor, New Life United Pentecostal Church, Austin, Texas, 1992–; mem. Society for Pentecostal Studies. *Publications:* In Search of Holiness, 1981; The Oneness of God, 1983; The New Birth, 1984; Practical Holiness, 1985; A History of Christian Doctrine, 3 vols, 1995–99; Spiritual Gifts, 1997. Contributions: Pentecostal Herald; Forward. *Honours:* Word Aflame Press Writer of the Year, 1987.

BERNARD, Oliver Owen, BA, ACSD; British poet and translator; b. 6 Dec. 1925, Chalfont St Peter, Buckinghamshire, England; two s. two d. *Education:* Westminster School, Goldsmiths Coll., Central School of Speech and Drama. *Career:* RAFVR 1943–47; teacher of English, Paris and Corsica 1947–56; copywriter, London 1957–64; teacher of English, Suffolk and Norfolk 1964–74; advisory teacher of drama, Norfolk Education Cttee 1974–81; mem. British Actors' Equity Asscn, Speak-a-Poem (cttee mem.), William Morris Soc., Dominicans for Peace and Justice. *Film:* Rimbaud: A Season in Hell (video performance filmed by Martin Jones). *Publications:* Country Matters 1960, Rimbaud: Collected Poems (translating ed.) 1961, Apollinaire: Selected Poems (trans.) 1965, Moons and Tides 1978, Poems 1983, Five Peace Poems 1985, The Finger Points at the Moon (trans.) 1989, Salvador Espriu: Forms and Words 1990, Getting Over It (autobiog.) 1992, Quia Amore Langueo (trans.) 1995, Verse Etc 2001; contrib. to various publications. *Honours:* Poetry Soc. Gold Medal for Verse Speaking 1982. *Address:* 1 East Church Street, Kenninghall, Norwich NR16 2EP, England. *Telephone:* (1953) 887768.

BERNAYS, Anne Fleischman, BA; American writer and teacher; b. 14 Sept. 1930, New York, NY; m. Justin Kaplan 1954; three d. *Education:* Barnard Coll. *Career:* Writing Instructor, Nieman Foundation, Harvard Univ. 1993–; mem. PEN New England. *Publications:* Growing Up Rich (novel), Professor Romeo (novel), What If? (non-fiction, with Pamela Painter), Back Then (non-fiction, with Justin Kaplan), Trophy House (novel) 2005, The Language of Names (with Justin Kaplan); contribs to New York Times Book Review, Nation, Sports Illustrated, Travel and Leisure, Sophisticated Traveller. *Honours:* Edward Lewis Wallant Award, Bellagio Study and Conf. Centre Residency. *Literary Agent:* Sterling Lord Literistic Inc., 65 Bleecker Street, New York, NY 10012, USA. *Address:* 16 Francis Avenue, Cambridge, MA 02138, USA. *Telephone:* (617) 354-2577 (home). *Fax:* (617) 868-3209 (home). *E-mail:* AFBernays@aol.com (home).

BERNE, Stanley, BS, MA, PhD; American academic and writer; *Research Professor Emeritus, Eastern New Mexico University at Portales;* b. 8 June 1923, Port Richmond, Staten Island, NY; s. of William Berne and Irene Berne (née Daniels); m. Arlene Zekowski 1952. *Education:* Rutgers Univ., New York Univ., Louisiana State Univ., Baton Rouge, Marlborough Univ. *Career:* mem. Army of Occupation Japan 1942–46; Assoc. Prof. of English, Eastern New Mexico Univ. at Portales 1960–80, Research Prof. of English 1980–; Chair.

American-Canadian Publrs Inc. 1980–97; mem. Bd Dirs New Arts Foundation Inc., Santa Fe 1990–; mem. PEN, New England Small Press Asscn, Rio Grande Writers' Asscn, Santa Fe Writers. *Television:* host, co-prod. Future Writing Today (series on KENW-TV, PBS) 1984–85. *Publications:* A First Book of the Neo-Narrative 1954, Cardinals and Saints: On the aims and purposes of the arts in our time 1958, The Dialogues 1962, The Multiple Modern Gods and Other Stories 1964, The Unconscious Victorious and Other Stories 1969, The New Rubaiyat of Stanley Berne (poems) 1973, Future Language 1976, The Great American Empire 1981, Every Person's Little Book of P-L-U-T-O-N-I-U-M (with Arlene Zekowski) 1992, Alphabet Soup: A Dictionary of Ideas 1993, To Hell with Optimism! 1996, Gravity Drag 1998, Swimming to Significance 1999, At One with Birds 2000, Extremely Urgent Messages 2000, Empire Sweets, or How I Learned to Live and Love in the Greatest Empire on Earth 2003, Legal Tender, or It's All About Money! 2003, You and Me, or How to Survive in the Greatest Empire on Earth! 2003; contrib. to anthologies and other publications. *Honours:* Medal of Philippine Liberation 1946; Eastern New Mexico Univ. literary research awards 1966–76, St-John Perse Award for Int. Prose 1998. *Address:* c/o Pamela Tree, Rising Tide Press, PO Box 6136, Santa Fe, NM 87502-6136, USA.

BERNSTEIN, Carl, LLD; American journalist and author; b. 14 Feb. 1944, Washington; s. of Alfred Bernstein and Sylvia Walker; m. Nora Ephron 1976 (divorced); two s. *Education:* Univ. of Maryland and Boston Univ. *Career:* copyboy, reporter, Washington Star 1960–65; reporter Elizabeth (NJ) Journal 1965–66; Washington Post 1966–77; Washington bureau chief, ABC 1979–81; corresp. ABC News, New York 1981–84; Corresp., contrib. Time Magazine 1990–91; Visiting Prof. New York Univ. 1992–93; Exec. Vice-Pres. and Exec. Dir Voter.com –2001; contributing ed. Vanity Fair 1997–; frequent political commentator on network TV; fmr rock and music critic for the Washington Post. *Publications:* All the President's Men (with Bob Woodward) (Pulitzer Prize 1977) 1974, The Final Days (with Bob Woodward) 1976, Loyalties: A Son's Memoir 1989, His Holiness: John Paul II and the Hidden History of Our Time (with Marco Politi) 1996, A Woman in Charge: the Life of Hillary Rodham Clinton 2007; numerous articles in The New Republic, Rolling Stone, The New York Times, Newsweek and Der Spiegel. *Honours:* Drew Pearson Prize for investigative reporting of Watergate 1972, George Polk Memorial Award and other awards for journalism. *Address:* c/o Knopf Publishing/Author Mail, 1745 Broadway, New York, NY 10019, USA (office). *Website:* www.randomhouse.com/knopf (office).

BERNSTEIN, Charles, AB; American academic, poet, writer and editor; *Professor of English, University of Pennsylvania;* b. 4 April 1950, New York, NY; s. of Herman Joseph Bernstein and Sherry Bernstein (née Kegel); m. Susan Bee Laufer 1977; one s. one d. *Education:* Harvard Coll. *Career:* freelance writer in the medical field 1976–89; Visiting Lecturer in Literature, Univ. of California, San Diego 1987; Lecturer in Creative Writing, Princeton Univ. 1989, 1990; David Gray Prof. of Poetry and Letters, State Univ. of NY, Buffalo 1990–2003; Prof. of English, Univ. of Pennsylvania 2003–; Curator Poetry Plastique exhbn; Fellow, American Acad. of Arts and Sciences. *Music:* libretto for Shadowtime (opera with music by Brian Ferneyhough), premiered Munich Biennalle 2004. *Radio:* Host and Producer of LINEbreak, Close Listening. *Publications:* poetry: Asylums 1975, Parsing 1976, Shade 1978, Poetic Justice 1979, Senses of Responsibility 1979, Legend (with others) 1980, Controlling Interests 1980, Disfrutes 1981, The Occurrence of Tune 1981, Stigma 1981, Islets/Irritations 1983, Resistance 1983, Veil 1987, The Sophist 1987, Four Poems 1988, The Nude Formalism 1989, The Absent Father in Dumbo 1990, Fool's Gold (with Susan Bee) 1991, Rough Trades 1991, Dark City 1994, The Subject 1995, Republics of Reality: Poems 1975–1995 2000, With Strings 2001; essays: Content's Dream: Essays 1975–1984 1986, A Poetics 1992, My Way: Speeches and Poems 1999, With Strings 2001, Girly Man 2006; editor: L=A=N=G=U=A=G=E Book (with Bruce Andrews, four vols) 1978–84, The Politics of Poetic Form: Poetry and Public Policy 1990, Close Listening: Poetry and the Performed Word 1998; contrib. to numerous anthologies, collections and periodicals. *Honours:* William Lyon Mackenzie King Fellow, Simon Fraser Univ. 1973, Nat. Endowment for the Arts Fellowship 1980, Guggenheim Fellowship 1985, Foundation Fellowship, Univ. of Auckland, NZ 1986, New York Foundation for the Arts Fellowships 1990, 1995, Roy Harvey Pearce/Archive for New Poetry Prize 2000. *Address:* 119 Bennet Hall, University of Pennsylvania, Philadelphia, PA 19104-6273, USA. *E-mail:* charles.bernstein@english.upenn.edu (office). *Website:* epc.buffalo.edu/authors/bernstein.html (office).

BERNSTEIN, Marcelle; British writer and journalist; b. 14 June 1945, Manchester; m. Eric Clark 1972; one s. two d. *Career:* staff, The Guardian, Daily Mirror, The Observer; mem. Soc. of Authors. *Publications:* Nuns 1976, Sadie 1983, Salka 1986, Lili 1988, Body and Soul (dramatised as a prizewinning six-part TV series) 1991, Sacred and Profane 1995 (filmed as Le Pacte du Silence 2003), Saints and Sinners 1998; contribs: Sunday Times, Daily Mail, Daily Telegraph, New Statesman, Washington Post, Melbourne Age, Woman's Journal (US). *Honours:* Arts Council Award 1986, Helene Heroys Award 1988. *Literary Agent:* Carole Blake, Blake Friedmann Agency, 122 Arlington Road, London NW1 7HP, England.

BERNSTEIN, Robert Louis; American publisher; b. 5 Jan. 1923, New York, NY; s. of Alfred and Sylvia Bernstein; m. Helen Walter 1950; three s. *Education:* Harvard Univ. *Career:* US Army Air Force 1943–46; with Simon & Schuster (book publrs) 1946–57, Gen. Sales Man. 1950–57; Random House Inc. 1958–61, Vice-Pres. (Sales) 1961–63, First Vice-Pres. 1963–65, Pres. and

CEO 1966–89, Chair. 1975–89; Publr at Large, Adviser John Wiley & Sons Inc. 1991–98; Vice-Chair. Asscn of American Publrs 1970–72, Chair. 1972–73; Chair. Asscn of American Publrs Cttee on Soviet-American Publishing Relations 1973–74, on Int. Freedom to Publish 1975; Chair. US Helsinki Watch Cttee New York, 1971–92, Founding Chair. 1992; Chair. Fund for Free Expression 1975–90, Founding Chair. 1990; Founding Chair. Human Rights Watch 1975–, now Emer. Bd Mem.; Co-Chair. Human Rights in China 1999–; fmr mem. Council on Foreign Relations, Nat. Advisory Cttee Amnesty Int.; mem. Americas Watch, Asia Watch, Middle East Watch, Africa Watch, Advisory Cttee Carter-Menil Human Rights Foundation, Advisory Bd Robert F. Kennedy Foundation Human Rights Award, Int. Liberal Education Bd Bard Coll.; Vice-Pres. Bd of Dirs Aaron Diamond Foundation, The Century Asscn. *Honours:* Hon. LLD (New School for Social Research) 1991, (Hofstra) 1998; Human Rights Award (Lawyers' Cttee for Human Rights) 1987, Spirit of Liberty Award for the American Way 1989, Barnard Medal of Distinction, Barnard Coll. 1990, Liberty Award, Brandeis Univ. 1994, Eleanor Roosevelt Human Rights Award 1998 and other awards. *Address:* 277 Park Avenue, 49th Floor, New York, NY 10172-0003, USA (office). *E-mail:* r.l.bernstein@att .net.

BERRADA, Mohamed; Moroccan literary critic, translator and writer; *Professor of Arab Literature, University Mohammed V Souissi;* b. 1938. *Education:* schools in Morocco, Egypt and France. *Career:* trans. of literary criticism of Roland Barthes, Bakhtin and Moroccan philosophers, and cultural critics Mohammed Aziz Lehbabi and Abdelkebir Khatibi; Prof. of Arab Literature Univ. Mohammed V Souissi, Rabat; teacher Nat. Inst. of Dramatic Arts. *Publications:* Frantz Fanon 'aw Maa'rakatu Ashshua'ub Al-Mutakhallifah (co-author, trans. as Frantz Fanon and the Struggle of Developing Countries) 1963, Salkh Al-Jild (fiction, trans. as Skinning) 1979, Mohammed Mandur wa Tanthir Annaqd Al-A'rabi (trans. as Mohammed Mandur and the Theorization of Arab Criticism) 1986, Lua'bat Annisyan (fiction, trans. as The Game of Forgetting) 1987, Le Jeu de l'Oubli (novel) 1990, Lumière Fuyante (novel) 1998, Maroc Musique de l'Ombre 2001, Comme un été qui ne reviendra pas: Le Caire 1955–1996 (novel) 2001; trans. of Mohammed Aziz Lehbabi's Mina Lmunghalaq 'ila Lmunfatah' (From the Closed to the Open), Tahar Ben Jelloun's H'adith Al-Jamal (Talk of the Camel) 1971, Abdellatif Laâbi's Aas'a-'id tah't Al-Kimamah (Muzzled Poems) 1982, Abdelkebir Khatibi's Fi Lkitaba wa Ttajriba (On Writing and Experience) 1990. *Address:* c/o Université Mohammed V Souissi, BP 8007, N.U. Agdal, Rabat, Morocco.

BERRIDGE, Elizabeth, FRSL; British author and critic; b. 3 Dec. 1919, London, England; m. Reginald Moore 1940; one s. one d. *Education:* studied in London and Geneva, Switzerland. *Career:* critic, BBC, Spectator, Books and Bookmen, Tribune, Country Life 1952–74; Fiction Reviewer, Daily Telegraph 1967–88, Evening Standard; Judge, David Higham First Novel Award 1989–97; mem. and Trustee Chase Charity; Fellow, PEN. *Publications:* House of Defence 1945, Story of Stanley Brent 1945, Be Clean, Be Tidy 1949, Upon Several Occasions 1953, Across the Common 1964, Rose Under Glass 1967, Sing Me Who You Are 1972, That Surprising Summer 1973, The Barretts at Hope End (ed.) 1974, Run for Home 1981, Family Matters 1981, People at Play 1982, Touch and Go (radio play) 1995, Tell It to a Stranger (short stories) 2000; contribs to periodicals. *Honours:* Yorkshire Post Book of the Year Award 1964. *Literary Agent:* David Higham Associates, 5–8 Lower John Street, Golden Square, London, W1F 9HA, England.

BERRY, Adrian Michael (see Camrose, 4th Viscount)

BERRY, James, OBE; British poet, writer and editor; b. 1925, Fair Prospect, Jamaica. *Career:* emigrated to UK 1948. *Publications:* Bluefoot Traveller: An Anthology of West Indian Poets in Britain (ed.) 1976, Fractured Circles 1979, News for Babylon: The Chatto Book of West Indian-British Poetry (ed.) 1984, Chain of Days 1985, The Girls and Yanga Marshall (short stories) 1987, A Thief in the Village and Other Stories (Smarties Prize Grand Prix 1987) 1988, Don't Leave an Elephant to Go and Chase a Bird 1990, When I Dance (poems) (Signal Poetry Award 1988) 1991, Ajeema and his Son 1992, Hot Earth, Cold Earth 1995. *Honours:* C. Day-Lewis Fellowship, Greater London Arts Asscn Fellowship 1977, Nat. Poetry Competition Award 1981, Poetry Soc. Prize 1981, Soc. of Authors Cholmondeley Award for Poetry 1991, Boston Globe/Horn Book Award 1993. *Address:* c/o Penguin Books Ltd, 80 Strand, London, WC2R 0RL, England.

BERRY, Wendell, MA; American writer; b. 5 Aug. 1934, Henry County, Ky; m. Tanya Amyx 1957; one s. one d. *Education:* Univ. of Kentucky. *Career:* mem. Faculty, Univ. of Kentucky 1964–77, 1987, Distinguished Prof. of English 1971–72. *Publications:* novels: Nathan Coulter 1962, A Place on Earth 1967, The Memory of Old Jack 1974, Remembering 1988, The Discovery of Kentucky 1991, Fidelity 1992, A Consent 1993, Watch With Me 1994, A World Lost 1996, Jayber Crow 2001; short stories: The Wild Birds 1986; poetry: The Broken Ground 1964, Openings 1968, Findings 1969, Farming: A Handbook 1970, The Country of Marriage 1973, Clearing 1977, A Part 1980, The Wheel 1982, Collected Poems 1985, Sabbaths 1987, Sayings and Doings and an Eastward Look 1990, Entries 1994, The Farm 1995, A Timbered Choir: The Sabbath Poems 1979–1997 1999; essays: The Long-Legged House 1969, The Hidden Wound 1970, The Unforeseen Wilderness 1971, A Continuous Harmony 1972, The Unsettling of America 1977, Recollected Essays 1965–80 1981, The Gift of Good Land 1981, Standing by Words 1985, Life is a Miracle: An Essay Against Modern Superstition 2000; co-ed. Meeting the

Expectations of the Land 1985, Home Economics 1987, What Are People For? 1990, Harland Hubbard: Life and Work 1990, Standing on Earth 1991, Another Turn of the Crank. *Address:* Lanes Landing Farm, Port Royal, KY 40058, USA.

BERTI, Eduardo; Argentine writer and journalist; b. 1964, Buenos Aires. *Career:* lives in Paris, France; writes for TV documentaries, including La cueva, Rocanrol. *Publications:* Los pájaros (short stories) 1979, Spinetta (essays) 1988, Rockología (essays) 1990, Agua (novel) 1997, La mujer de Wakefield (novel) 1999, La vida imposible (short stories) 2002; contrib. short stories to numerous publications. *Address:* c/o Pushkin Press, 123 Biddulph Mansions, Elgin Avenue, London, W9 1HU, England.

BERTOLINO, James, BS, MFA; American poet, writer and teacher; b. 4 Oct. 1942, Hurley, WI; m. Lois Behling 1966. *Education:* University of Wisconsin, Cornell University. *Career:* Teacher, Washington State University, 1970–71, Cornell University, 1971–74, University of Cincinnati, 1974–84, Washington Community Colleges, 1984–91, Chapman University, 1989–96, Western Washington University, 1991–96. *Publications:* Poetry: Employed, 1972; Soft Rock, 1973; The Gestures, 1975; Making Space for Our Living, 1975; The Alleged Conception, 1976; New & Selected Poems, 1978; Precint Kali, 1982; First Credo, 1986; Snail River, 1995. Chapbooks: Drool, 1968; Day of Change, 1968; Stone Marrow, 1969; Becoming Human, 1970; Edging Through, 1972; Terminal Placebos, 1975; Are You Tough Enough for the Eighties?, 1979; Like a Planet, 1993. Contributions: Poetry in 27 anthologies; Prose in 3 anthologies; Poetry, stories, essays, and reviews in periodicals. *Honours:* Hart Crane Poetry Award, 1969; Discovery Award, 1972; National Endowment for the Arts Fellowship, 1974; Quarterly Review of Literature International Book Awards, 1986, 1995; Djerassi Foundation Residency, 1987; Bumbershoot Big Book Award, 1994.

BESS, Clayton (see Locke, Robert Howard)

BESSON, Philippe; French writer and lawyer; b. 29 Jan. 1967, Barbezieux, Charente. *Education:* Lycée Montaigne de Bordeaux, École Supérieure de Commerce de Rouen. *Career:* lawyer and teacher of social law, Paris 1989. *Publications:* En l'absence des hommes (trans. as In the Absence of Men) (Prix Emmanuel-Roblès) 2001, Son frère 2001, L'arrière-saison (Grand Prix TRL-Lire 2003) 2002, Un garcon d'Italie 2003. *E-mail:* phillipebesson@free.fr. *Website:* www.phillipebesson.free.fr.

BETHEL, Marion, BL; Bahamian poet, writer and lawyer; b. 1953, Nassau. *Education:* Univ. of Cambridge. *Career:* has private law practice; teacher and consultant on education; Alice Naumburg Proskauer Fellow, Bunting Inst. of Radcliffe Coll. 1997–08; fmr nat. chair. Caribbean Asscn for Feminist Research and Action (CAFRA), Bahamas; Guest Poet, Int. Writers Workshop, Hong Kong Baptist Univ. 2006, 16th Medellin Poetry Festival 2006. *Publications include:* Guanahaní, mi amor (poems) (Casa de las Américas Prize) 1994; several essays; contrib. to journals, including Callaloo, Caribbean Writer, Lignum Vitae, Massachusetts Review, Moving Beyond Boundaries, River City, WomanSpeak, and to anthologies. *Honours:* Univ. of Miami Writer's Summer Inst. James Michener Fellowship 1991, Bahamas Nat. Poetry Award 1996. *Address:* POB N3645, Nassau, NP, Bahamas (office). *Telephone:* (242) 326-3481 (office). *Fax:* (242) 326-3483 (office). *E-mail:* missma@batelnet.bs (home); mbethel@searschambers.com (office).

BETTARINI, Mariella, DipEd; Italian writer, poet and teacher; b. 31 Jan. 1942, Florence. *Career:* elementary school teacher; co-founder, Ed. and Publisher, Salvo Imprevisti 1973. *Publications:* Il pudore e l'effondersi, 1966; Il leccio, 1968; La rivoluzione copernicana, 1970; Terra di tutti e altre poesie, 1972; Dal vero, 1974; In bocca alla balena, 1977; Storie d'Ortensia: Romanza, 1978; Felice di essere: Scritti sulla condizione della donna e sulla sessualità, 1978; Diario fiorentino, 1979; Chi è il poeta? (co-ed.), 1980; Ossessi oggetti-Spiritate materie, 1981; Il viaggio-Il corpo, 1982; La nostra gioventù: 18 gennaio 1976, 1982; Poesie vegetali, 1982; Psicografia, 1982; Vegetali figure: 1978–82, 1983; I Guerrieri di Riace di Mario Grasso, 1984; Tre lustri ed oltre: Antologia poetica 1963–1981, 1986; Amorosa persona, 1989.

BETTS, Raymond Frederick, BA, MA, PhD; American academic and writer; b. 23 Dec. 1925, Bloomfield, NJ, USA; m. Irene Donahue 1956; two s. one d. *Education:* Rutgers University, Columbia University; Doctorat d'Université, University of Grenoble; Certificat d'Études africaines, Institut d'Études Politiques, University of Paris. *Career:* Instructor to Asst Prof., Bryn Mawr College, 1956–61; Asst Prof. to Prof., Grinnell College, 1961–71; Prof. of History, 1971–98, Dir, Gaines Center for the Humanities, 1983–98, University of Kentucky; Contributing Ed., Britannia Com, 1999–; mem. African Studies Asscn; American Historical Asscn; French Colonial Historical Society; Society for French Historical Studies. *Publications:* Assimilation and Asscn in French Colonial Theory, 1890–1914, 1961; The Scramble for Africa (ed.), 1966; Europe Overseas: Phases of Imperialism, 1968; The Ideology of Blackness (ed.), 1971; The False Dawn: European Imperialism in the Nineteenth Century, 1975; Tricouleur: A Brief History of Modern French Colonial Empire, 1978; Europe in Retrospect: A Brief History of the Last Two Hundred Years, 1979; Uncertain Dimensions: Western Overseas Empires in the Twentieth Century, 1985; France and Decolonisation, 1991; Decolonization, 1998. Contributions: Books and scholarly journals. *Honours:* Hallam Book Awards, University of Kentucky, 1976, 1986; Great Teacher Award, University of Kentucky, 1979, 1998; Outstanding Kentucky Humanist Award, Kentucky Humanities Council, 1989. *Address:* 311 Mariemont Drive, Lexington, KY 40505, USA.

BEUTLER, Maja; Swiss writer; b. 8 Dec. 1936, Berne; m. Urs Bentler 1961; two s. one d. *Education:* Dolmetscher Schüle, Zürich, France, UK and Italy. *Career:* trans. for UNESCO, Rome; radio presenter (Italian and German) for Swiss Int. radio 1962–70; currently radio presenter and writer. *Publications:* novels: Fuss fassen 1980, Die Wortfalle (2nd edn) 1990, Die Stunde, da wir fliegen Lerhen 1994; short stories: Flissingen fehlt auf der Karte 1976, Das Bildnis der Doña Quichotte 1989; plays: Das Blaue Gesetz 1979, Das Marmelspiel 1985, Lady Macbeth Wäscht Sich Die Hände Nicht Mehr 1994; collected radio contribs: Wärchtig 1986, Beiderlei 1991, Tagwärts 1996. *Honours:* Schillerstiftung Prize for works 1983, Weltpreis für Drama 1985, Literaturpreis, Stadt Berne 1989. *Address:* Schosshaldenstr. 22A, 3006 Berne, Switzerland. *Telephone:* (31) 3523538. *Fax:* (31) 3523538. *E-mail:* maja .beutler@swissonline.ch.

BEVERLEY, Jo; British writer; b. 22 Sept. 1947, Morecambe, Lancashire, England; m. Kenneth Beverley 1971, two s. *Education:* University of Keele. *Career:* mem. Canadian Romance Authors Network; Romance Writers of America; SF Canada; Writers' Union of Canada. *Publications:* Lord Wray-bourne's Betrothed, 1988; The Stanforth Secrets, 1989; The Stolen Bride, 1990; If Fancy Be the Food of Love, 1991; Emily and the Dark Angel, 1991; The Fortune Hunter, 1991; An Arranged Marriage, 1991; The Christmas Angel, 1992; An Unwilling Bride, 1992; Lord of My Heart, 1992; Dark Champion, 1993; My Lady Notorious, 1993; Forbidden, 1994; Dangerous Joy, 1995; Tempting Fortune, 1995; The Shattered Rose, 1996; Something Wicked, 1997; Forbidden Magic, 1998; Lord of Midnight, 1998. Contributions: anthologies. *Honours:* Career Achievement for Regency Romance, 1992, and for Regency Historical, 1997, Romantic Times; Inducted, Romance Writers of America Hall of Fame, 1993. *Address:* c/o The Rotrosen Agency, 318 East 51st Street, New York, NY 10022, USA. *E-mail:* jo@jobev.com. *Website:* members.shaw.ca/ jobev.

BEWES, Richard Thomas, OBE, MA; British ecclesiastic and writer; b. 1 Dec. 1934, Nairobi, Kenya; m. Elisabeth Ingrid Jaques 1964 (died 2006); two s. one d. *Education:* Marlborough School, Emmanuel Coll., Cambridge, Ridley Hall Theological Coll., Cambridge. *Career:* Rector of All Souls Church, Langham Place, London 1983–2004; Prebendary St Paul's Cathedral, London 1986–; mem. Guild of British Songwriters. *Publications:* Talking About Prayer 1979, The Pocket Handbook of Christian Truth 1981, The Church Reaches Out 1981, John Wesley's England 1981, The Church Overcomes 1983, On the Way 1984, Quest for Life 1985, The Church Marches On 1986, When God Surprises 1986, A New Beginning 1989, The Resurrection 1989, Does God Reign? 1995, Speaking in Public – Effectively 1998, Open Home Open Bible 2000, The Lamb Wins 2000, The Stone That Became a Mountain 2001, Ten Steps in Prayer 2001, Words That Circled the World 2001, The Top 100 Questions 2002, Wesley Country 2003, Beginning the Christian Life 2004, 150 Pocket Thoughts 2004. *Honours:* Freeman of the City of Charlotte, NC 1985. *Address:* Christian Focus, Geanies House, Fearn, Tain, Ross-shire IV20 1TW, Scotland (office). *Telephone:* (1862) 871011 (office). *Fax:* (1862) 871699 (office). *E-mail:* info@christianfocus.com (office). *Website:* www.christianfocus.com (office).

BEYALA, Calixthe, BA; Cameroonian novelist; b. 1961, Douala; m. (divorced); two c. *Career:* lives in Paris, France. *Publications:* novels: C'est le soleil qui m'a brûlée 1987, Tu t'appelleras Tanga 1988, Seul le Diable le savait (aka La Négresse rousse) 1990, Le Petit prince de Belleville 1992, Maman a un amant (Grand Prix Littéraire de l'Afrique Noire) 1993, Asséze l'africaine (Prix François Mauriac de l'Académie française, Prix tropique) 1994, Les Honneurs perdus (Grand prix du roman de l'Académie française) 1996, La Petite fille du réverbère (Grand Prix de l'Unicef) 1997, Amours sauvages 1999, Comment cuisiner son mari à l'africaine 1999, Les Arbres en parlent encore 2002, Femme nue, femme noire 2003, La Plantation 2005; essays: Lettre d'une africaine à ses sœurs occidentales 1995, Lettre d'une afro-française à ses compatriotes 2000. *Honours:* Chevalier, Ordre des Arts et des Lettres; Prix de l'Action Communautaire 2000, Prix Genova 2002. *Address:* c/o Collectif Egalité, 9 rue roger Gobaut, 93500 Pantin, France. *E-mail:* calixthe.beyala@ online.fr. *Website:* calixthe.beyala.free.fr.

BEZMOZGIS, David, BA; Canadian (b. Latvian) writer; b. 1973, Riga, Latvia. *Education:* McGill Univ., Montréal, Univ. of Calif. Film School. *Career:* emigrated with parents to Toronto, Canada 1980. *Films directed:* L. A. Mohel (documentary) 1999, The Diamond Nose 2000. *Play:* The Last Waltz: An Inheritance. *Publications:* Natasha and Other Stories (Reform Judaism Prize for Jewish Fiction 2004, The Jewish Quarterly Wingate Literary Prize for fiction 2005) 2004, The Second Strongest Man (short story), Roman Berman, Massage Therapist (short story), Tapka (short story); contrib. short stories to Harper's, The New Yorker, Zoetrope: All Story. *Literary Agent:* c/o Ira Silverberg, Donadio & Olson, 121 W 27th Street, Suite 704, New York, 10001, USA. *Address:* c/o Random House UK Ltd, Random House, 20 Vauxhall Bridge Road, London SW1V 2SA, England (office).

BHARTIA, Shobhana; Indian newspaper executive; b. 4 Jan. 1957, Calcutta (now Kolkata); d. of Birla and Manorama Devi; m. Shyam Sunder Bhartia 1974; two s. *Education:* Loreto House, Calcutta. *Career:* Exec. Dir The Hindustani Times Ltd 1986–, Vice-Chair. and Editorial Dir; Dir Press Trust of India Ltd 1987, Indian Airlines, New Delhi 1988–90, Air Travel Bureau Pvt. Ltd 1989; Chair. and Treas. Bd of Govs, Delhi Coll. of Arts and Commerce 1988–90; Chair. HT Vision Ltd 1990–; Chair. Bd of Govs Shyama Prasad Mukherjee Coll. (for Women) 1992; mem. Sri Mata Vaishnu Devi Shrine Bd, Katra 1991; Pres. FICCI (women's org.), Leader dels to Australia, NZ, the Philippines and to World Congress of Women Conf. (Moscow, fmr USSR) 1987–88. *Honours:* Int. Cultural Devt Org. Award 1989, Mahila Shiromani Award 1990, Lok Shri Award, Inst. of Econ. Studies 1990, Vijaya Shri Award, Int. Friendship Soc. of India 1991, Delhi Chamber of Commerce Outstanding Businesswoman Award 2001, Padma Shri 2005. *Address:* Hindustani Times House, 18–20 Kasturba Gandhi Marg, New Delhi, 110 065, India. *Telephone:* (11) 3317955 (office); (11) 6830260 (home). *Fax:* (11) 3319021 (office).

BHATTACHARYA, Nalinaksha, BSc; Indian civil servant and writer; b. 2 April 1949, Kolkata; m. Manju Bhattacharya 1982. *Education:* University of Calcutta, London School of Journalism. *Publications:* Hem and Football, novel, 1992; Hem and Maxine, novel, 1995; A Fistful of Desire, novel, 1997; Short stories. Contributions: BBC World Service; London Magazine; New Writing 5. *Honours:* First Prize in Short Story Writing, American University Centre, Kolkata, 1977. *Address:* Sector 8/121, R. K. Puram, New Delhi 110022, India.

BHATTACHARYYA, Birendra Kumar, BSc, MA, PhD; Indian journalist and writer; b. 16 March 1924, Suffry Sibsagar, Assam; s. of Sashidhar and Aideo Bhattacharyya; m. Binita Bhattacharyya 1958; two s. one d. *Education:* Jorhat Govt High School, Cotton Coll., Gauhati, Calcutta Univ. and Gauhati Univ. *Career:* fmr science teacher, Ukrul High School, Manipur; Ed. Ramdhenu 1951–61, Sadiniya Navayung 1963–67; Lecturer in Journalism, Gauhati Univ. 1974–; Exec. mem. Janata Party, Assam; Sec. Archaeological Soc. of Assam. *Publications:* novels: Iyaruingam (won Akademi Award), Rajpathe Ringiai (Call of the Main Street), Mother, Sataghai (Killer), Mrityunjay, Pratipad, Nastachandra, Ballart, Kabar Aru Phul, Ranga Megh, Daint; collections of short stories: Kolongajioboi (Still Flows the Kolong), Satsari (Necklace); Aurobindo (biog.), A Survey of Assamese Modern Culture (in Assamese), Munichunir Pohar, Kalar Humuniyah, Naga Kakar Sadhu, Chaturanga, Phul Konwarar Pathighora, Sandhya Swar. *Honours:* Sahitya Akademi Award for Assamese Literature 1961, Jnanpitho Award 1979. *Address:* Kharghuli Development Area, Guwahati 781004, India. *Telephone:* 25019.

BIANCONI, Lorenzo Gennaro, PhD; Swiss/Italian musicologist; *Professor of Musical Dramaturgy, University of Bologna;* b. 14 Jan. 1946, Muralto, Switzerland; m. Giuseppina La Face 1979; two s. *Education:* Univ. of Heidelberg, Germany, studied music theory with Luciano Sgrizzi in Lugano, Switzerland. *Career:* collaborator, Répertoire International des Sources Musicales, Italy 1969–70; mem., German Inst., Venice 1974–76; guest asst, German Historical Inst., Rome 1976; guest Prof., Princeton Univ., USA 1977; Prof. of Musical Dramaturgy, Univ. of Bologna, Italy 1977–; Prof. of the History of Music, Siena Univ., Arezzo, Italy 1980–83; Co-Ed., Rivista Italiana di Musicologia 1973–79; Ed., Acta Musicologica 1987–91; Head of Programme Cttee, 14th Int. Musicological Congress, Bologna 1987; Co-Ed., Musica e Storia 1993–; Co-Ed., Il Saggiatore Musicale 1994–; Ed., Historiae Musicae Cultores 1999–; Head of Music Dept, Bologna Univ., Italy 1998–2001; hon. mem. Accademia Filarmonica, Bologna; corresponding mem., American Musicological Soc. *Publications:* B. Marcello, Sonates pour clavecin (ed. with Luciano Sgrizzi) 1971, P. M. Marsolo, Madrigali a 4 voci (1614) 1973, A Il Verso, Madrigali a 3 e a 5 voci (1605–19) 1978, Il Seicento 1982, La Drammaturgia Musicale 1986, Storia dell'Opera Italiana 1987, I Libretti Italiani di G. F. Händel (with G. La Face) 1992, Il Teatro d'Opera in Italia 1993, G. Frescobaldi, Madrigali a 5 voci (with M. Privitera) 1996, Guida al percorso museale (Museo della Musica, Bologna) 2004. *Honours:* Dent Medal of the Royal Musical Asscn 1983, Premio Imola per la Critica 1994. *Address:* Dipartimento di Musica e Spettacolo, Università di Bologna, via Barberia 4, 40123, Bologna (office); via A. Frank 17, 40068 San Lazzaro di Savena, Bologna, Italy (home). *Telephone:* 051 2092156 (office). *Fax:* 051 2001 (office). *E-mail:* lorenzo.bianconi@unibo.it (office).

BIBBY, Peter Leonard, BA, DipEd; British poet, writer, dramatist and screenwriter; b. 21 Dec. 1940, London, England; m. 1967; two s. two d. *Education:* University of Western Australia, Murdoch University. *Career:* fmr Ed., Fellowship of Australian Writers, Bagabala Books; mem. Australian Film Institute, Australian Writers' Guild, Computer Graphics Asscn, Fellowship of Australian Writers. *Publications:* Island Weekend 1960; contrib. to various anthologies and journals. *Honours:* Tom Collins Literary Awards, 1978, 1982; Lyndall Hadow National Short Story Award, 1983; Donald Stuart National Short Story Award, 1985.

BIBERGER, Erich Ludwig; German poet, writer and editor; b. 20 July 1927, Passau. *Education:* studied in Passau. *Career:* founder-Dir, Internationale Regensbürger Literaturtage, 1967–94, Internationale Jungautoren-Wettbewerbe, 1972–94; Founder-Ed., RSG Studio International, 1973–, RSG Forum 15/25, 1977–; mem. Regensburg Asscn of Authors, chair., 1960–, hon. pres., 1999–; Humboldt-Gesellschaft für Wissenschaft und Kunst, 1993–; Bayerischer Kulturrat, 1998–; established the Erich-und-Maria-Biberger Preises für Verdienste um die Literatur 1995. *Publications:* Dreiklang der Stille (poems), 1955; Rundgang über dem Nordlicht (prose), 1958; Die Traumwelle (novel), 1962; Denn im Allsein der Welt (poems), 1966; Gar mancher (satirical verses), 1967; Anthology Quer, 1974; Anthology 3, 1979; Andere Wege bis Zitterluft (poems), 1982; Nichts als das Meer (poems), 1984; Zwei Pfund Morgenduft (feuilletons), 1987; Drei Millimeter Erd-Kugel, Trei Milimetristerapamanteasca (poems), 1997; Fantasieschutzgebiet, Imagainationis hortulus (haiku), 1998.

BICHSEL, Peter; Swiss writer; b. 24 March 1935, Lucerne; m. Therese Spörri 1956; one s. one d. *Education:* Teacher's Coll., Solothurn. *Career:* writer-in-residence, Oberlin Coll., Ohio 1971–72; Visiting Lecturer, Univ. of Essen 1980, Univ. of Frankfurt am Main 1982, Dartmouth Coll., Hanover, NH 1987, Middlebury Coll., Vermont 1989, CUNY 1992; mem. Akademie der Künste; corresponding mem. Deutsche Akademie für Sprache und Dichtung, Darmstadt. *Publications:* Eigentlich möchte Frau Blum den Milchmann kennenlernen 1964, Das Gästehaus 1965, Die Jahreszeiten 1967, Kindergeschichten 1969, Des Schweizers Schweiz 1969, Geschichten zur falschen Zeit 1979, Der Leser: Das Erzählen 1982, Der Busant: Von Trinkern, Polizisten und der schönen Magelone 1985, Schulmeistereien 1985, Irgendwo anderswo 1986, Im Gegenteil 1990, Zur Stadt Paris 1993, Die Totaldemokraten 1998, Cherubin Hammer und Cherubin Hammer 1999, Alles von mir gelernt 2000, Eisenbahnfatzen 2002, Columnen Kolumnen 2005. *Honours:* hon. mem. American Asscn of Teachers of German; DTheol hc (Basel) 2004; Gruppe 47 Prize 1965, Lessing Prize, Hamburg 1965, Arts Prize, Solothurn 1979, Literature Prize, Bern 1979, Johann Peter Hebel Prize 1986, Culture Prize, Lucerne 1989, Gottfried Keller Prize, Zurich 1999, Veillon Prize, Lausanne 2000. *Address:* Nelkenweg 24, 4512 Bellach, Switzerland.

BIDART, Frank; American poet and academic; b. 1939, Bakersfield, CA. *Education:* Univ. of Calif., Harvard Univ. *Career:* teacher, Wellesley Coll.; elected Chancellor, Acad. of American Poets 2003. *Publications:* poetry: Golden State 1973, The Sacrifice 1983, In the Western Night: Collected Poems 1965–90 1990, Desire 1997, Music Like Dirt 2002, Robert Lowell: Collected Poems (co-ed.) 2003, Star Dust 2005. *Honours:* Lila Wallace–Reader's Digest Foundation Writer's Award, American Acad. of Arts and Letters Morton Dauwen Zaubel Award, Poetry Soc. of America Shelley Award. *Address:* c/o English Department, Wellesley College, 106 Central Street, Wellesley, MA 02481, USA (office). *Website:* www.wellesley.edu.

BIDDISS, Michael Denis, MA, PhD, FRHistS; British academic and writer; *Professor Emeritus of History, University of Reading*; b. 15 April 1942, Farnborough, Kent; s. of Daniel Biddiss and Eileen Biddiss (née Jones); m. Ruth Margaret Cartwright 1967; four d. *Education:* Queens' Coll., Cambridge, Centre des Hautes Etudes Européennes, Univ. of Strasbourg, France. *Career:* Fellow in History, Downing Coll., Cambridge and Dir of Studies in History, Social and Political Sciences 1966–73; lecturer, then Reader in History, Univ. of Leicester 1973–79; Prof. of History, Univ. of Reading 1979–2004, Prof. Emer. 2004–, Dean Faculty of Letters and Social Sciences 1982–85; Visiting Prof., Univ. of Victoria, Canada 1973, Univ. of Cape Town 1976, 1978, Univ. of Cairo 1985, Monash Univ., Australia 1989, Univ. of Nanjing, China 1997; Chair. History at the Univs Defence Group 1984–87; mem. Council, The Historical Asscn 1985– (Pres. 1991–94), Vice-Pres. Royal Historical Soc. 1995–99 (mem. Council 1988–92); Lister Lecturer, BAAS 1975. *Publications:* Father of Racist Ideology 1970, Gobineau: Selected Political Writings (ed.) 1970, Disease and History (co-author) 1972, The Age of the Masses 1977, Images of Race (ed.) 1979, Thatcherism (co-ed.) 1987, The Nuremberg Trial and the Third Reich (co-author) 1992, The Uses and Abuses of Antiquity (co-ed.) 1999, The Humanities in the New Millennium (co-ed) 2000. *Honours:* Hon. Fellow, Faculty of the History of Medicine (Pres. 1994–98), Soc. of Apothecaries 1986–; Osler Medallist, Soc. of Apothecaries of London 1989, Locke Medallist, Soc. of Apothecaries of London 1996, Sydenham Medallist, Soc. of Apothecaries of London 2000. *Address:* c/o School of History, University of Reading, Whiteknights, Reading, RG6 6AA, England (office).

BIDGOOD, Ruth, MA; Welsh poet and local historian; b. 20 July 1922, Seven Sisters, Glamorgan; m. David Edgar Bidgood 1946; two s. one d. *Education:* Univ. of Oxford. *Career:* coder, WRNS; Sub-Ed., Chambers Encyclopaedia; Fellow Academi Gymreig, English Speaking Section. *Publications:* The Given Time 1972, Not Without Homage 1975, The Print of Miracle 1978, Lighting Candles 1982, Kindred 1986, Selected Poems 1992, The Fluent Moment 1996, Singing to Wolves 2000, Parishes of the Buzzard (non-fiction) 2000, New and Selected Poems 2004, Symbols of Plenty 2006; contrib. to literary and historical reviews, magazines and journals. *Honours:* Welsh Arts Council Awards 1976, 1993, 1997. *Address:* 2 Wylfa, Beulah, Llanwrtyd Wells, Powys, Wales (home).

BIEBER, Konrad, LèsL, PhD; American writer and translator; *Professor of French and Comparative Literature Emeritus, State University of New York*; b. 24 March 1916, Berlin, Germany; m. Tamara Siew 1939 (died 1995); one s. *Education:* Sorbonne, Univ. of Paris, Yale Univ. *Career:* instructor in French, Yale Univ. 1948–53; instructor, Middlebury French Summer School 1949–51, 1956; Visiting Lecturer in French and Comparative Literature, Univ. of Colorado at Boulder 1952; Asst Prof. 1953–57, Assoc. Prof. 1957–60, Prof. of French and Chair Dept of French 1959–68, Connecticut Coll., New London; Prof. of French and Comparative Literature 1968–86, Prof. Emeritus 1986–, SUNY. *Publications:* L'Allemagne vue par les Écrivains de la Résistance Française 1954, Simone de Beauvoir 1979, Outwitting the Gestapo (trans. of Lucie Aubrac's Ils partiront dans l'Ivresse) 1993; contrib. to encyclopedias, dictionaries, books and journals. *Honours:* Guggenheim Fellowship 1957–58, Chevalier, Ordre des Palmes Académiques 1970, Book of the Month and History Club selections 1993. *Address:* 1211 Foulkeways, Gwynedd, PA 19436, USA.

BIELSKI, Alison Joy Prosser; Welsh poet, writer and fmr lecturer; b. 24 Nov. 1925, Newport, Gwent; m. 1st Dennis Ford Treverton Jones 1948; m. 2nd Anthony Edward Bielski 1955; one s. one d. *Career:* Lecturer Writers on Tour, Welsh Arts Council; mem. Gwent Poetry Soc., Soc. of Women Writers and Journalists, Welsh Acad., Welsh Union of Writers. *Publications:* The Story of the Welsh Dragon 1969, Across the Burning Sand 1970, Eve 1973, Flower Legends of the Wye Valley 1974, Shapes and Colours 1974, The Lovetree 1974, Mermaid Poems 1974, Seth 1980, Night Sequence 1981, Eagles 1983, The Story of St Mellons 1985, That Crimson Flame 1996, The Green-Eyed Pool 1997, Sacramental Sonnets 2003; contrib. to anthologies and journals. *Honours:* premium prize Poetry Soc. 1964, Anglo-Welsh Review Poetry Prize 1970, Arnold Vincent Bowen Poetry Prize 1971, Orbis Poetry Prize 1984, second prize Soc. of Women Writers and Journalists Julia Cairns Trophy 1984, 1992.

BIELSKI, Nella; French (b. Russian) playwright and novelist; m. 1962. *Education:* Moscow Univ. *Career:* lives in Paris, writes in French. *Publications include:* Voronej, Oranges for the Son of Alexander Levy (novel), After Arkadia (novel), Isabella (screenplay), A Question of Geography (play), The Year Is '42 (novel), Last Portrait of Francisco Goya (theatre plays co-written with John Berger), Pulpe de l'étreinte (essay on poet Rainer Maria Rilke); contrib. to Granta magazine. *Address:* c/o Bloomsbury Publishing plc, 38 Soho Square, London, W1D 3HB, England.

BIERMANN, Wolf; German poet, songwriter and musician; b. 15 Nov. 1936, Hamburg; m. Pamela Rüsche; seven s. three d. *Education:* Humboldt Univ., Berlin. *Career:* Asst Dir Berliner Ensemble, 1957–59; song and guitar performances throughout Germany. *Recordings:* albums: Wolf Biermann (Ost) zu Gast bei Wolfgang Neuß (West) 1965, Vier neue Lieder 1968, Chausseestraße 131 1969, Warte nicht auf bessre Zeiten 1973, ah-jaa! 1974, Liebeslieder 1975, Es gibt ein Leben vor dem Tod 1976, Das geht sein' Sozialistischen Gang 1977, Der Friedensclown (Kinderlieder) 1977, Trotzalledem 1978, Halfte des Lebens 1979, Eins in die Fresse, mein Herzblatt 1980, Wir miissen vor Hoffnung verrückt sein 1982, Im Hamburger Federbett 1983, Die Welt ist schon 1985, Seelengeld 1986, VEB-volkseigener Biermann 1988, Gut Kirschenessen 1990, Nur wer sich andert, bleibt sich treu 1991, Süßes Leben – saures Leben 1996, Brecht, deine Nachgeborenen 1999, Paradies uff Erden – ein Berliner Bilderbogen 1999, Ermutigung im Steinbruch der Zeit 2001, Großer Gesang des Jizchak Katzenelson vom Ausgerotteten Jtidischen Volk 2004. *Publications:* Die Drahtharfe: Balladen, Gedichte, Lieder 1965, Mit Marx-und Engelszungen 1968, Der Dra-Dra (play) 1970, Für meine Genossen 1972, Deutschland: Ein Wintermärchen 1972, Nachlass I 1977, Wolf Biermann, Poems and Ballads 1977, Preussicher Ikarus 1978, Verdrehte welt das seh'ich gerne 1982, Und als ich von Deutschland nach Deutschland: Three Contemporary German Poets 1985, Affenels und Barrikade 1986, Alle Lieder 1991, Der Sturz des Dadalus 1992, Großer Gesang des Jizchak Katzenelson vom ausgerotteten jiidischen Volk 1994, Alle Gedichte 1995, Wie man Verse macht und Lieder – eine Poetik in acht Gangen 1997, Paradies uff Erden – ein Berliner Bilderbogen 1999, Wolf Biermann und andere Autoren: Die Ausbürgerung. Anfang vom Ende der DDR. Herausgegeben von Fritz Pleitgen 2001, Uber Deutschland Unter Deutschen. Essays, Kiepenheuer & Witsch 2002, Wolf Biermanns Nachdichtung ins Deutsche der 'Elf Entwiirfe für meinen Grabspruch' von Bob Dylan 3003, Das ist die feinste Liebeskunst – Die Sonette des William Shakespeares als Gedichte und Lieder von Wolf Biermann 2004. *Honours:* Büchner Prize 1991, Möricke Prize 1991, Heine Prize 1993. *Address:* c/o Verlag Kiepenheuer und Witsch, Rondorferstrasse 5, 5000 Cologne-Marienurg, Germany.

BIGSBY, Christopher William Edgar, BA, MA, PhD, FRSL; British academic, broadcaster and novelist; b. 27 June 1941, Dundee, Scotland. *Education:* Sheffield Univ., Nottingham Univ. *Career:* Lecturer in American Literature, Univ. Coll. of Wales 1966–69; Lecturer 1969–73, Sr Lecturer 1973–85, Prof. of American Literature 1985–, Univ. of East Anglia. *Publications:* Confrontation and Commitment: A Study of Contemporary American Drama, 1967; Edward Albee, 1969; The Black American Writer (ed.), 1969; Three Negro Plays, 1969; Dada and Surrealism, 1972; Approaches to Popular Culture, 1975; Tom Stoppard, 1976; Superculture, 1976; Edward Albee, 1976; The Second Black Renaissance, 1980; Contemporary English Drama, 1981; Joe Orton, 1982; A Critical Introduction to 20th Century American Drama, 3 vols, 1982, 1984, 1985; The Radical Imagination and the Liberal Tradition, 1982; David Mamet, 1985; Cultural Change in the United States since World War II, 1986; Plays by Susan Glaspell, 1987; File on Miller, 1988; Modern American Drama: 1945–1990, 1992, revised edn as Modern American Drama: 1945–2000, 2000; Hester (novel), 1994; Pearl (novel), 1995; 19th Century American Short Stories (ed.), 1995; Portable Arthur Miller (ed.), 1995; Still Lives (novel), 1996; Cambridge Companion to Arthur Miller (ed.), 1998; Cambridge History of American Theatre (joint ed.), three vols, 1998, 1999, 2000; Contemporary American Playwrights, 1999; Writers in Conversation (ed.), 2000. Contributions: Radio; Television; TLS; Times Higher Education Supplement; Sunday Independent; American Quarterly; Modern Drama; Theatre Quarterly; Guardian; Sunday Telegraph. *Address:* 3 Church Farm, Colney, Norwich, England.

BILGRAMI, Akeel, BA, PhD; Indian academic; *Johnsonian Professor of Philosophy, Columbia University*; b. 28 Feb. 1950, Hyderabad; m. Carol Rovane 1990; one d. *Education:* Univ. of Bombay, Univ. of Oxford, UK, Univ. of Chicago, USA. *Career:* Prof. of Philosophy, Columbia Univ. 1985–, Chair of Philosophy Dept and Johnsonian Prof. of Philosophy, Columbia Univ.; mem. American Philosophical Soc. *Publications:* Belief and Meaning 1992, Self-Knowledge and Intentionality 1996, Internal Dialectics: The Moral Psychology of Identity; contrib. to Journal of Philosophy, Philosophical Quarterly,

Philosophical Topics. *Honours:* Rhodes Scholarship 1971, Whitney Humanities Fellow 1992. *Address:* Department of Philosophy, Columbia University, 1150 Amsterdam Avenue, 708 Philosophy Hall, MC 4971, New York, NY 10027, USA (office). *Telephone:* (212) 854-3196 (office). *Fax:* (212) 854-4986 (office). *E-mail:* ab41@columbia.edu (office). *Website:* www.columbia.edu/cu/philosophy/Faculty/_facultypages/akeelbilgrami (office).

BILLETDOUX, Raphaële; French novelist and film director; b. 1951, Neuilly. *Film:* La Femme enfant (screenplay writer and director) 1980. *Publications:* Jeune fille en silence 1971, L'Ouverture des bras de l'homme 1973, Prends garde à la douceur des choses 1976, La Lettre d'excuse 1980, Mes nuits sont plus belles que vos jours (Night Without Day) (Prix Renaudot) 1985, Chère Madame ma fille cadette 1987, Entrez et fermez la porte 1991, Mélanie dans un vent terrible 1994, De l'air 2001. *Address:* c/o Editions du Seuil, 27 rue Jacob, 75006 Paris, France (office).

BILLING, Graham John; New Zealand author, dramatist and poet; b. 12 Jan. 1936, Dunedin; m. Rowan Innes Cunningham 1978; one s. one d. (by previous m.). *Education:* Otago University. *Career:* staff, Dunedin Evening Star, 1958–62; Antarctic Division, DSIR, 1962–64; New Zealand Broadcasting Corporation News Service and TV Service, 1964–67; Staff, Dominion Sunday Times, 1967–69; Lecturer, writing, Mitchell College Advanced Education, Bathurst, Australia, 1974–75. *Publications:* Forbush and the Penguins, 1965; The Alpha Trip, 1969; Statues, 1971; The Slipway, 1973; The Primal Therapy of Tom Purslane, 1980; Changing Countries (poems), 1980. Non-Fiction: South: Man and Nature in Antarctica, 1965; New Zealand, the Sunlit Land, 1966; The New Zealanders, 1974. Radio Plays: Forbush and the Penguins, 1965; Mervyn Gridfern versus the Babsons, 1965; The Slipway, 1976; The Prince of Therapy of Tom Purslane, 1980.

BILLINGTON, James Hadley, PhD; American historian, academic and librarian; *Librarian of Congress;* b. 1 June 1929, Bryn Mawr, Pa; s. of Nelson Billington and Jane Coolbaugh; m. Marjorie A. Brennan 1957; two s. two d. *Education:* Princeton Univ. and Univ. of Oxford. *Career:* army service 1953–56; Instructor in History, Harvard Univ. 1957–58, Fellow Russian Research Center 1958–59, Asst Prof. of History 1958–61; Assoc. Prof. of History, Princeton Univ. 1962–64, Prof. 1964–73; Dir Woodrow Wilson Int. Center for Scholars, Washington, DC 1973–87; Librarian of Congress, Library of Congress, Washington, DC 1987–; Visiting Research Prof. Inst. of History of USSR Acad. of Sciences 1966–67, Univ. of Helsinki 1960–61, Ecole des Hautes Etudes en Sciences Sociales, Paris 1985, 1988; visiting lecturer to various univs in Europe and Asia, etc.; Guggenheim Fellow 1960–61; mem. American Acad. of Arts and Sciences, American Philosophical Soc.; Chair. Bd of Foreign Scholarships (Fulbright Program) 1971–73; writer/host The Face of Russia (TV series) 1998. *Publications:* Mikhailovsky and Russian Populism 1958, The Icon and the Axe: An Interpretive History of Russian Culture 1966, Fire in the Minds of Men: Origins of the Revolutionary Faith 1980, Russia Transformed: Breakthrough to Hope 1992, The Face of Russia 1998, Russia in Search of Itself 2004; contribs to books and journals. *Honours:* Chevalier Ordre des Arts et des Lettres; Kt Commdr's Cross of the Order of Merit (Germany) 1996; 22 hon. degrees; Gwangha Medal (Repub. of Korea), Woodrow Wilson Award 1992, Pushkin Medal 1999, Univ. of Calif. at LA Medal 2000. *Address:* Library of Congress, 101 Independence Avenue, Washington, DC 20540-0002, USA. *Telephone:* (202) 707-5205. *Fax:* (202) 707-1714. *Website:* www.loc.gov.

BILLINGTON, Michael Keith, BA; British drama critic and author; b. 16 Nov. 1939, Leamington Spa; s. of Alfred R. Billington and Patricia Bradshaw; m. Jeanine Bradlaugh 1977; one d. *Education:* Warwick School and St Catherine's Coll., Oxford. *Career:* Public Liaison Officer, Theatre Royal, Lincoln 1962–64; writer on theatre, film and cinema, The Times 1965–71; Drama Critic, The Guardian 1971–, Country Life 1988–; presenter of various BBC Radio arts programmes including Options, Kaleidoscope, Meridian, etc. 1971–91; writer on London arts scene for The New York Times 1984–94; writer and presenter of TV profiles of Peter Hall, Alan Ayckbourn, Peggy Ashcroft 1988–90. *Publications:* The Modern Actor 1973, Alan Ayckbourn 1983, Tom Stoppard 1987, Peggy Ashcroft 1988, One Night Stands 1993, The Life and Work of Harold Pinter 1996, Stage and Screen Lives (Ed.) 2001. *Honours:* IPC Critic of the Year 1974, Theatre Critic of the Year 1993, 1995, 1997. *Address:* 15 Hearne Road, London, W4 3NJ, England. *Telephone:* (20) 8995-0455. *Fax:* (20) 8742-3496 (home). *E-mail:* michael.billington@guardian.co.uk (office).

BILLINGTON, Rachel Mary, BA; British writer; b. 11 May 1942, Oxford, England; m. 1967; two s. two d. *Education:* Univ. of London. *Career:* Vice-Pres. PEN; Co-Ed. Inside Time (newspaper for prisoners); mem. Soc. of Authors. *Publications include:* Loving Attitudes 1988, Theo and Matilda 1990, The First Miracles 1990, Bodily Harm 1992, The Family Year 1992, The Great Umbilical 1994, Magic and Fate 1996, The Life of Jesus (juvenile) 1996, Perfect Happiness 1996, Tiger Sky 1998, The Life of St Francis (juvenile) 1999, A Woman's Life, Far Out! (juvenile) 2002, The Space Between 2004, One Summer 2006, There's More to Life (juvenile) 2006; contrib. to various publications, radio and television. *Address:* The Court House, Poyntington, nr Sherborne, Dorset DT9 4LF, England.

BINCHY, Maeve, BA; Irish writer; b. 28 May 1940, Dalkey, Co Dublin; d. of William Binchy and Maureen Blackmore; m. Gordon Thomas Snell 1977. *Education:* Univ. Coll. Dublin. *Career:* teacher of history and French, Pembroke School, Dublin 1961–68; columnist, Irish Times 1968–2000. *Publications:* short story collections: Central Line 1978, Victoria Line 1980,

Dublin Four 1982, Victoria Line/Central Line (revised edn of two earlier titles, aka London Transports) 1983, This Year it Will be Different 1996, Return Journey 1998; novels: Silver Wedding 1979, Light a Penny Candle 1982, The Lilac Bus 1984, Echoes 1985, Firefly Summer 1987, Circle of Friends 1990, The Copper Beech 1992, The Glass Lake 1994, Evening Class 1996, Tara Road 1999, Scarlet Feather 2000, Quentins 2002, Nights of Rain and Stars 2004, Whitethorn Woods 2006; non-fiction: Aches and Pains 2000; other: several plays. *Honours:* Hon. DLit (Nat. Univ. of Ireland) 1990, (Queen's Belfast) 1998; Int. Television Festival Golden Prague Award, Czech TV 1979, Jacobs Award 1979, WHSmith Fiction Award 2001, Irish PEN/A T Cross Award for Literature 2007. *Literary Agent:* Christine Green, 6 Whitehorse Mews, Westminster Bridge Road, London, SE1 7QD, England. *E-mail:* info@christinegreen.co.uk. *Website:* www.christinegreen.co.uk. *Address:* PO Box 6737, Dun Laoghaire, Co Dublin, Ireland. *Website:* www.maevebinchy.com.

BINDING, Tim; British writer and scriptwriter; b. 1947, Germany. *Career:* fmrly Editorial Dir Picador, Penguin Books; Commissioning Ed., Simon & Schuster. *Television:* The Last Salute (with Simon Nye). *Publications:* fiction: In the Kingdom of Air 1993, A Perfect Execution 1996, Island Madness (aka Lying with the Enemy) 1998, Anthem 2003, Man Overboard 2005; non-fiction: Firebird: Writing Today (ed.) 1983, On Ilkley Moor: The Story of an English Town 2001; contrib. to Granta 56. *Honours:* Soc. of Authors Travelling Scholarship 2004. *Address:* c/o Picador, 20 New Wharf Road, London, N1 9RR, England.

BINEBINE, Mahi; Moroccan novelist and artist; b. 13 Feb. 1959, Marrakesh; m.; three d. *Career:* teacher of mathematics, painter; painting exhibited in Guggenheim Museum, New York. *Publications:* novels: Le Sommeil de l'esclave 1992 (Prix Méditerranée Maghreb 1993), Les Funérailles du lait 1994, L'Ombre du Poète 1997, Cannibales (translated as Welcome to Paradise) 1999, Pollens 2001 (Prix de l'Amitié Franco-Arabe 2001), Terre d'ombre brulée 2005; illustrator: L'Ecriture au tournant by Abdellatif Laâbi 2000, Le griot de Marrakech 2006. *Literary Agent:* 90 rue Yougoslavie, Gueliz, Marrakesh, Morocco; c/o Granta Books, 2–3 Hanover Yard, Noel Road, London, N1 8BE, England. *Telephone:* (620) 967837 (Spain). *Fax:* 24-49-31-24 (Marrakesh). *Website:* www.granta.co.uk. *Telephone:* 61-35-19-59 (office). *Fax:* 24-49-31-24 (office). *E-mail:* binebine@gmail.com (office); mahibinebine@hotmail.com (home). *Website:* www.mahibinebine.com.

BINGHAM, Hon. Charlotte Marie-Thérèse; British writer; b. 29 June 1942, d. of Baron Clanmorris (John) and Madeleine Mary (née Ebel) Bingham; m. Terence Brady 1964; one s. one d. *Education:* The Priory (Haywards Heath) and Univ. of Paris (Sorbonne). *Career:* writer of screenplays with Terence Brady. *Stage plays include:* I Wish, I Wish 1989. *TV includes:* Series: Boy Meets Girl, Take Three Girls, Upstairs Downstairs, Away From it All, No—Honestly, Yes—Honestly, Pig in the Middle, Thomas and Sarah, Father Matthew's Daughter, Oh Madeleine!, Forever Green, The Upper Hand; Films: Love With a Perfect Stranger 1986, Losing Control 1987, The Seventh Raven 1987, The Magic Moment 1988. *Publications include:* Coronet Among the Weeds 1963, Lucinda 1965, Coronet Among the Grass 1972, Victoria (jtly) 1972, Rose's Story (jtly) 1973, Victoria and Company (jtly) 1974, Belgravia 1983, Country Life 1986, At Home 1987, To Hear a Nightingale 1988, The Business 1989, In Sunshine or in Shadow 1991, Stardust 1992, By Invitation 1993, Nanny 1993, Change of Heart 1994, Debutantes 1995, The Nightingale Sings 1996, Grand Affair 1997, Love Song 1998, The Kissing Garden 1999, The Love Knot 2000, The Blue Note 2000, The Season 2001, Summertime 2001, Distant Music 2002, The Chestnut Tree 2002, Out of the Blue 2006, In Distant Fields 2006, The White Marriage 2007. *Address:* c/o United Authors, Garden Studios, 11–15 Betterton Street, London, WC2H 9BP, England.

BINGHAM, Kate; British poet, novelist and screenwriter; b. 1971, London. *Education:* Univ. of Oxford. *Publications:* novels: Mummy's Legs 1998, Slipstream 2000; poetry: Cohabitation 1998, Eighteenth 2003, Quicksand Beach 2006. *Honours:* Soc. of Authors Eric Gregory Award 1996, Prizewinner, Nat. Poetry Competition 2003. *Literary Agent:* c/o Seren Books, 1st and 2nd Floors, 38–40 Nolton Street, Bridgend, Glamorgan, CF31 3BN, Wales.

BIRCH, Carol; British novelist; b. 3 Jan. 1951, Manchester, England; m. Martin Lucas Butler 1990; two s. *Education:* Univ. of Keele. *Career:* mem. Soc. of Authors. *Publications:* Life in the Palace 1988, The Fog Line 1989, The Unmaking 1992, Songs of the West 1994, Little Sister 1998, Come Back Paddy Riley 2000, Turn Again Home 2003, In a Certain Light 2004, The Naming of Eliza Quinn 2005; contrib. to TLS, Independent, New Statesman. *Honours:* David Higham Prize, Geoffrey Faber Memorial Award. *Literary Agent:* Mic Cheetham Agency, 11–12 Dover Street, London, W1X 3PH, England.

BIRD, Charles (see Wittich, John Charles Bird)

BIRD, Kai, BA, MSc; American writer; b. 2 Sept. 1951, Eugene, OR; m. Susan Gloria Goldmark 1975; one s. *Education:* Carleton Coll., Northwestern Univ. *Publications:* The Chairman: John J. McCloy, The Making of the American Establishment 1992, Hiroshima's Shadow: Writings on the Denial of History and the Smithsonian Controversy (ed. with Lawrence Lifshultz) 1998, The Color of Truth: McGeorge Bundy and William Bundy, Brothers in Arms: A Biography 1998, American Prometheus: The Triumph and Tragedy of J. Robert Oppenheimer (with Martin J. Sherwin) (Pulitzer Prize in Biography 2006) 2005; contrib. to periodicals and journals. *Honours:* John D. and Catherine T. MacArthur Foundation Writing Fellowship, German Marshall Fund Fellow, Alicia Patterson Journalism Fellowship, Guggenheim Fellowship, Fellow Woodrow Wilson Center for Int. Scholarship 2001–02. *Address:* 1914 Biltmore Street NW, Washington, DC 20009, USA.

BIRDSELL, Sandra Louise; Canadian writer; b. 22 April 1942, Hamiota, Manitoba; m. Stanley Vivian Birdsell 1959 (divorced 1984); one s. two d. *Career:* several writer-in-residencies; instructor in English, Capilano Coll., N Vancouver; mem. Manitoba Writers' Guild, PEN Int., Writers' Guild of Canada, Writers' Union of Canada. *Publications:* Night Travellers (short stories) 1982, Ladies of the House (short stories) 1984, The Missing Child (novel) 1989, The Chrome Suite (novel) 1992, The Two-Headed Calf (short stories) 1997, The Town That Floated Away (juvenile) 1997, The Russländer (novel) 2001, Katya (novel) 2004; contrib. to various publications. *Honours:* Gerald Lampert Memorial Award 1982, WHSmith/Books in Canada First Novel Award 1989, McNally Robinson Award for Manitoba Book of the Year 1992. *Address:* c/o Random House of Canada Ltd, One Toronto Street, Unit 300, Toronto, ON M5C 2V6, Canada. *Website:* www.sandrabirdsell.com.

BIRLEY, Julia Davies, BA; British writer; b. 13 May 1928, London, England; m. 1954; one s. three d. *Education:* Univ. of Oxford. *Career:* mem. PEN, Charlotte Yonge Soc. *Publications:* fiction: The Children on the Shore, The Time of the Cuckoo, When You Were There, A Serpent's Egg, Dr Spicer; also short stories and plays; contrib. to The Guardian. *Address:* Upper Bryn, Longtown, Hereford HR2 0NA, England.

BIRMINGHAM, Stephen, BA; American writer; b. 28 May 1931, Hartford, CT; m. Janet Tillson 1951 (divorced); one s. two d. *Education:* Williams College, University of Oxford. *Career:* Advertising Copywriter, Needham, Harper & Steers Inc, 1953–67; mem. New England Society of the City of New York. *Publications:* Young Mr Keefe, 1958; Baraba Greer, 1959; The Towers of Love, 1961; Those Harper Women, 1963; Fast Start, Fast Finish, 1966; Our Crowd: The Great Jewish Families of New York, 1967; The Right People, 1968; Heart Troubles, 1968; The Grandees, 1971; The Late John Marquand, 1972; The Right Places, 1973; Real Lace, 1973; Certain People: America's Black Elite, 1977; The Golden Dream: Suburbia in the 1970s, 1978; Jacqueline Bouvier Kennedy Onassis, 1978; Life at the Dakota, 1979; California Rich, 1980; Duchess, 1981; The Grandes Dames, 1982; The Auerbach Will, 1983; The Rest of Us, 1984; The LeBaron Secret, 1986; America's Secret Aristocracy, 1987; Shades of Fortune, 1989; The Rothman Scandal, 1991; Carriage Trade, 1993. Contributions: periodicals.

BISCHOFF, David Frederick; American writer; b. 15 Dec. 1951, Washington, DC. *Career:* staff mem., NBC-TV, Washington, DC, 1974–; Assoc. Ed., Amazing Magazine; mem. faculty Masters Program for Popular Fiction, Seton Hill Univ. *Publications:* The Seeker (with Christopher Lampton), 1976; Quest (children's), 1977; Strange Encounters (children's), 1977; The Phantom of the Opera (children's), 1977; The Woodman (with Dennis R. Bailey), 1979; Nightworld, 1979; Star Fall, 1980; The Vampires of the Nightworld, 1981; Tin Woodman (with Dennis Bailey), 1982; Star Spring, 1982; War Games, 1983; Mandala, 1983; Day of the Dragonstar (with Thomas F. Monteleone), 1983; The Crunch Bunch, 1985; Destiny Dice, 1985; Galactic Warriors, 1985; The Infinite Battle, 1985; The Macrocosmic Conflict, 1986; Manhattan Project, 1986; The Unicorn Gambit, 1986; Abduction: The UFO Conspiracy, 1990; Revelation: The UFO Conspiracy, 1991; Deception: The UFO Conspiracy, 1991; Aliens Versus Predator: Hunter's Planet, 1994. *E-mail:* david.bischoff@gmail.com.

BISHER, Badrya al-; Saudi Arabian writer; b. 1967, Riyadh; m. *Education:* Univ. of Riyadh. *Career:* writer for weekly literary magazine, Al-Yamama. *Publications:* short story collections: Nihayat al-lu'ba (The End of the Game) 1992, Masa' al-arbia' (The Evening of the Weekend) 1994; contrib. to Voices of Change: Short Stories by Saudi Arabian Women Writers 1997. *Address:* c/o Dar al-Adab, PO Box 11-4123, Beirut, Lebanon. *E-mail:* d_aladab@cyberia.net.lb.

BISHOP, James Drew, BA; British journalist; b. 18 June 1929, London; s. of the late Sir Patrick Bishop and Vera Drew; m. Brenda Pearson 1959; two s. *Education:* Haileybury Coll., Hertford and Corpus Christi Coll., Cambridge. *Career:* reporter, Northampton Chronicle 1953; editorial staff of The Times (London) 1954–70, Foreign Corresp. 1957–64, Foreign News Ed. 1964–66, Features Ed. 1966–70; Ed. The Illustrated London News 1971–87, Newsweek Int. Diary 1977–88; Dir Int. Thomson Publishing Co. 1980–85; Editorial Dir Orient Express, Connections and Natural World Magazines 1981–94; Ed.-in-Chief Illustrated London News Publs 1987–94; contrib. to The Annual Register 1960–88, mem. Advisory Bd 1970–; Chair. Editorial Bd Natural World 1981–97, Asscn of British Eds 1987–95; Chair. Nat. Heritage 1998– (Trustee 1994–). *Publications:* A Social History of Edwardian Britain 1977, Social History of the First World War 1982, The Story of The Times (with O. Woods) 1983, Illustrated Counties of England (ed.) 1985, The Sedgwick Story 1998. *Address:* Black Fen, Stoke by Nayland, Suffolk, CO6 4QD, England (home). *Telephone:* (1206) 262315 (office). *Fax:* (1206) 262876 (office). *E-mail:* jamesbishop3@compuserve.com (home).

BISHOP, Jan (see McConchie, Lyn)

BISHOP, Michael Lawson, (Philip Lawson (with Paul Di Filippo), BA, MA; American writer, poet and teacher; b. 12 Nov. 1945, Lincoln, NE; s. of Lee O. Bishop and Maxine Elaine Matison; m. Jeri Whitaker 1969; one s. one d. *Education:* Univ. of Georgia. *Career:* Writer-in-Residence, LaGrange Coll. 1997–; mem. Science Fiction and Fantasy Writers of America Inc. (SFWA), Science Fiction Poetry Asscn, Georgia Writers Inc. *Publications:* fiction: A Funeral for the Eyes of Fire (aka Eyes of Fire) 1975, And Strange at Ecbatan the Trees 1976, Stolen Faces 1977, A Little Knowledge 1977, Transfigurations 1979, Under Heaven's Bridge (with Ian Watson) 1981, No Enemy but Time 1982, Who Made Steve Cry? 1984, Ancient of Days 1985, The Secret Ascension, or, Philip K. Dick Is Dead, Alas 1987, Unicorn Mountain 1988, Apartheid, Superstrings and Mordecai Thubana 1989, Count Geiger's Blues 1992, Brittle Innings 1994; as Philip Lawson (jt pseudonym with Paul di Filippo): Would It Kill You to Smile? 1998, Muskrat Courage 2000; short stories: Catacomb Years 1979, Blooded on Arachne 1982, One Winter in Eden 1984, Close Encounters with the Deity 1986, Emphatically Not SF, Almost 1990, At the City Limits of Fate 1996, Brighten to Incandescence 2003; non-fiction: A Reverie for Mister Ray: Reflections on Life, Death and Speculative Fiction 2005; poetry: Windows and Mirrors 1977, Time Pieces 1999, Novella Collection: Blue Kansas Sky 2000; editor: Changes (anthology with Ian Watson) 1982, Light Years and Dark (anthology) 1984, Nebula Awards: SFWA's Choices for the Best Science Fiction and Fantasy (Vols 23–25) 1989–91, A Cross of Centuries: 25 Imaginative Tales about the Christ 2007; contrib. to anthologies and periodicals. *Honours:* Hon. LHD (LaGrange Coll.) 2001; Phoenix Award 1977, Clark Ashton Smith Award 1978, Science Fiction Poetry Asscn Rhysling Award 1979, SFWA Nebula Awards 1981, 1982, Mythopoetic Fantasy Award 1988, Locus Award for Best Fantasy Novel 1994, Southeastern Science Fiction Asscn Award for Best Short Fiction 2004, 2006. *Address:* PO Box 646, Pine Mountain, GA 31822, USA (home). *Telephone:* (706) 663-4461 (home). *E-mail:* mlbishop@juno.com (home). *Website:* www.michaelbishop-writer.com.

BISHOP, Pike (see Obstfeld, Raymond)

BISKIND, Peter; American film critic and writer. *Career:* fmr documentarist; Exec. Ed., Premiere magazine for nine years; Ed.-in-Chief, American Film magazine for five years; fmr Contributing Ed., Vanity Fair. *Publications:* Seeing is Believing: How Hollywood Taught Us to Stop Worrying and Love the Fifties 1983, The Godfather Companion 1991, Easy Riders, Raging Bulls: How the Sex, Drugs and Rock 'n' Roll Generation Saved Hollywood 1998, Down and Dirty Pictures: Miramax, Sundance and the Rise of Independent Film 2004, Gods and Monsters: Movers, Shakers, and Other Casualties of the Hollywood Machine 2004; contrib. to New York Times, Washington Post, Rolling Stone. *Address:* c/o Bloomsbury Publishing Plc, 38 Soho Square, London, W1D 3HB, England.

BISSETT, Bill; Canadian poet and artist; b. 23 Nov. 1939, Halifax, NS. *Education:* Dalhousie Univ., Univ. of British Columbia. *Career:* Ed. Printer Blewointmentpress, Vancouver 1962–83. *Exhibitions:* art shows at Van Art Gallery, BC, Modern Art, Ont., Harbour Front, Ont. *Publications:* The Jinx Ship and other Trips: Poems-drawings-collage 1966, We Sleep Inside Each Other All 1966, Fires in the Temple 1967, Where Is Miss Florence Riddle 1967, What Poetiks 1967, Gossamer Bed Pan 1967, Lebanon Voices 1967, Of the Land/Divine Service Poems 1968, Awake in the Red Desert 1968, Killer Whale 1969, Sunday Work? 1969, Liberating Skies 1969, The Lost Angel Mining Company 1969, The Outlaw 1970, Blew Trewz 1970, Nobody Owns the Earth 1971, Air 6 1971, Dragon Fly 1971, Four Parts Sand: Concrete Poems 1972, The Ice Bag 1972, Poems for Yoshi 1972, Drifting into War 1972, Air 10-11-12 1973, Pass the Food, Release the Spirit Book 1973, The First Sufi Line 1973, Vancouver Mainland Ice and Cold Storage 1973, Living with the Vishyan 1974, What 1974, Drawings 1974, Medicine My Mouths on Fire 1974, Space Travel 1974, You Can Eat it at the Opening 1974, The Fifth Sun 1975, The Wind up Tongue 1975, Stardust 1975, An Allusyun to Macbeth 1976, Plutonium Missing 1976, Sailor 1978, Beyond Even Faithful Legends 1979, Soul Arrow 1980, Northern Birds in Color 1981, Parlant 1982, Seagull on Yonge Street 1983, Canada Geese Mate for Life 1985, Animal Uproar 1987, What we Have 1989, Hard 2 Beleev 1990, Incorrect Thoughts 1992, Vocalist with the Luddites, Dreaming of the Night 1992, The Last Photo of the Human Soul 1993, Th Influenza uv Logik 1995, loving without being vulnrabul 1997, Offthroad (cassette) 1998, Skars on the Seehors 1999, B leev abul char ak trs 2000, Offthroad (with CD) 2000, rainbow mewsick (ed.) 2002, peter among th towring boxes 2002, unmatching phenomena I (with CD) 2002, rumours uv hurricane (CD) 2003, narrativ enigma 2004, northern wild roses 2005, deth interrupts th dansing (CD) 2006. *Honours:* People's Poets 1992, Dorothy Livesay Poetry Award 1993, 2003. *Address:* PO Box 272, Str F, Toronto, ON M4Y 2L7, Canada. *Telephone:* (416) 924-4201 (office). *E-mail:* centralianwings@sympatico.ca (office).

BISSON, Thomas Noel, PhD; American historian and academic; *Henry Charles Lea Professor of Medieval History, Harvard University;* b. 30 March 1931, New York; s. of Thomas A. Bisson and Faith W Bisson; m. Margaretta C. Webb 1962; two d. *Education:* Port Washington High School, New York, Haverford Coll., Univ. of Calif., Berkeley and Princeton Univ. *Career:* Instructor in History, Amherst Coll. 1957–60; Asst Prof. Brown Univ. 1960–65; Assoc. Prof. Swarthmore Coll. 1965–67; Assoc. Prof. Univ. of Calif. (Berkeley) 1967–69, Prof. 1969–87; Prof. Harvard Univ. 1986–, Henry Charles Lea Prof. of Medieval History 1988–, Chair. Dept of History 1991–95; mem. American Philosophical Soc.; Fellow, Medieval Acad. of America (Pres. 1994–95), Royal Historical Soc., British Acad. etc.; Guggenheim Fellow 1964–65. *Publications:* Assemblies and Representation in Languedoc in the Thirteenth Century 1964, Medieval Representative Institutions: Their Origins and Nature 1973, Conservation of Coinage: Monetary Exploitation and its Restraint in France, Catalonia and Aragon (c. AD 1000–c. AD 1225) 1979, Fiscal Accounts of Catalonia under the Early Count-Kings 1151–1213 (2 vols) 1985, The Medieval Crown of Aragon: a Short History 1986, Medieval France and her Pyrenean Neighbors 1989, Tormented Voices: Power, Crisis and Humanity in Rural Catalonia 1140–1200 1998; articles in journals. *Honours:* Creu de Sant Jordi (Generalitat of Catalonia) 2001; Dr hc (Barcelona) 1991. *Address:* Department of History, Robinson Hall, Harvard University, Cambridge, MA 02138 (office); 21 Hammond Street, Cambridge, MA 02138, USA (home). *Telephone:* (617) 495-5221 (office). *E-mail:* tnbisson@fas.harvard.edu (office). *Website:* www.fas.harvard.edu/~history (office).

BISSOONDATH, Neil Devindra, BA; Canadian author; b. 19 April 1955, Arima, Trinidad. *Education:* York University, Toronto, Canada. *Publications:* Digging Up the Mountains (short stories), 1985; A Casual Brutality (novel), 1988; On the Eve of Uncertain Tomorrows (short stories), 1990; The Innocence of Age (novel), 1992; In Selling Illusions: The Cult of Multiculturalism in Canada, 1994; Doing the Heart Good, 2001. Contributions: periodicals. *Honours:* Canadian Authors' Asscn Literary Award 1993.

BISWAS, Brian, BA, MS; American writer; b. 7 March 1957, Columbus, OH; m. Elizabeth Phelan 1977; one s. one d. *Education:* Antioch Coll., Univ. of Illinois. *Publications:* short stories: The Bridge 1991, Solitary Confinement 1992, The Museum of North African Treasures 1992, A Sea Voyage 1992, The Nature of Love 1993, Fare-Thee-Well 1993, Others 1993, The Vulture 1997, A Betrayal 1999, Apologia Du Amore 2000, The Crystal 2000, A Soldier's Lament 2003, The Town That Went to Sleep 2004, Death in the Afternoon 2004, The Room at the End of the World 2005, The Moons of Jupiter 2005, Hoag's Object 2006; contrib. to various literary journals. *Address:* 412 Holly Lane, Chapel Hill, NC 27517, USA. *E-mail:* bbiswas@email.unc.edu.

BJØRNSTAD, Ketil; Norwegian musician (piano), composer and writer; b. 25 April 1952, Oslo. *Education:* studied piano with Amalie Christie and Robert Riefling, Oslo, further studies in London and Paris. *Career:* professional debut with Oslo Philharmonic 1969; performed with experimental Svein Finnerud Trio 1971; first recording of own music Åpning 1973; collaborations with numerous Norwegian and int. musicians from fields of jazz, folk, rock, avant-garde and classical music, including Ole Paus, Jon Christensen, Terje Rypdal, David Darling, Cornelis Vreeswijk, Randi Stene, Lars Anders Tomter, Anneli Drecker, Nora Taksdal, Lill Lindfors; has toured in Europe, Asia and USA and performed at jazz festivals in Frankfurt, Neuwied, Ingolstadt, Hamburg, Stans, Vienna, Voss, Molde, Modena, Ravenna, Nancy, Porto, Montreal, Shanghai, Warsaw and London; UK tour with Contemporary Music Network 2006; has published over 20 novels, also poetry, essays, literary and music criticism. *Recordings include:* Åpning 1973, Berget det blå 1974, Tredje dag 1975, Lise Madsen, Moses & de Andre (with Ole Paus) 1975, Finnes du noensteds ikveld 1976, Selena 1977, Musikk for en lang natt 1977, Leve Patagonia 1978, Svart Piano 1979, Tidevann 1980, Och människor ser igen (with Lill Lindfors) 1980, 30-års-krigen (with Stavangerenseblet) 1981, Engler i sneen 1982, Bjørnstad/Paus/Hamsun 1982, Aniara (with Lindfors/Fristorp) (1983) 1983, Mine dager i Paris 1983, Preludes Vol. 1 1984, Människors makt (with Lill Lindfors) 1985, Natten (with Sissel I. Andersen) 1985, Preludes Vol. 2 1986, Three Ballets 1987, Karen Mowat-suite 1988, The Shadow (with Randi Stene) 1990, Odyssey 1991, Rift 1991, Messe for en såret jord (with Randi Stene and Lars Anders Tomter) 1992, Løsrivelse (with Kari Bremnes) 1993, Water Stories 1993, For den som elsker 1994, Sanger fra en klode 1995, Salomos Høysang 1995, The Sea 1995, Haugtussa 1996, The River (with David Darling) 1997, Reisetid 1997, The Sea II 1997, Ett Liv (with Lill Lindfors) 1998, The Rosenborg Tapes Vol. 1 1998, The Rosenborg Tapes Vol. 2 1999, Himmelrand – Tusenårsoratoriet 1999, Epigraphs (with David Darling) 2000, Grace 2001, Old 2001, The Nest 2003, Seafarer's Song 2004, Floating 2005. *Compositions:* Minotauros (ballet) 1997, IZZAT (youth opera) 2006. *Film soundtracks:* Forever Mozart 1996, Museum of Modern Art 1999, Histoire du Cinéma 1999, Eloge d'Amour 2001, Engler i sneen 1983, Nous sommes touts encore ici 1997, Emporte moi 1999, Trofast 2004, Ae Fond Kiss 2005, Loneliness in the Net 2006. *Plays:* Ildlandet (musical) 1984, Spill 1995, Forestillinger 1997. *Publications:* fiction: Nattsvermere 1974, Kråker og Krigere 1975, Pavane 1976, Vinterbyen 1977, Landet på andre siden 1979, Bingo 1981, Oda! 1983, Det personlige motiv 1985, G-moll-balladen 1986, Oppstigning fra det usynlig 1988, Stormen 1989, Skumringsmulighetene 1990, Villa Europa 1992, Historien om Edvard Munch 1993, Barnevakt 1994, Drift 1996, Drømmen om havet 1996, Veien til Dhaka 1997, Nåde, Fall 1999, Ludvig Hassels tusenårsskifte 2000, Jæger 2001, Mannen som gikk på jorden (jtly) 2002, Tesman 2003, Til Musikken 2004; poetry: Alene ut 1972, Nærmere 1973; non-fiction: Reisen til Gallia (essays, with Ole Paus) 1998, Flammeslukeren (biography) 2005, Liv Ullmann: Livslinjer (biography) 2005. *Literary Agent:* Kjell Kalleklev Management, Georgernes Verft 3, 5011 Bergen, Norway. *Telephone:* 55-55-76-30. *Fax:* 55-55-76-31. *E-mail:* kjell@kalleklev.no. *Website:* www.kalleklev.no; www.ketilbjornstad.com.

BLACK OF CROSSHARBOUR, Baron (Life Peer), cr. 2001, of Crossharbour in the London Borough of Tower Hamlets; **Conrad M. Black,** Kt, PC, OC, LittD, LLD; British (b. Canadian) publisher and business executive; b. 25 Aug. 1944, Montreal, Québec; s. of George Montegu and Jean Elizabeth Black (née Riley); m. 1st Joanna Catherine Louise Black 1978 (divorced 1991); two s. one d.; m. 2nd Barbara Amiel 1992. *Education:* Carleton, Laval, McGill Univs. *Career:* Chair. and CEO Ravelston Corpn Ltd; Chair. Hollinger Int. 1985–2004, acquired Daily Telegraph newspaper group 1985, Chair. Telegraph Group – 2004; CEO Chair. Argus Corpn 1978–2005; Chair. Conrad Black Capital Corpn; Patron The Malcolm Muggeridge Foundation; mem. Advisory Bd, The Nat. Interest, Washington, DC; convicted of three counts of fraud July 2007. *Publications:* Duplessis 1977, A Life in Progress (autobiog.) 1994, Franklin D. Roosevelt: Champion of Freedom 2003, Richard Milhous Nixon: The Invincible Quest 2007. *Honours:* Hon. LLD (St Francis Xavier) 1979, (McMaster) 1979. *Address:* 3044 Bloor Street West, Suite 296, Toronto, ON M8X 2Y8, Canada; c/o 9 Montague Gardens, London, W3 9PT, England.

BLACK, David, BA, MFA; American writer; b. 21 April 1945, Boston, MA; m. Deborah Hughes Keehn 1968, one s. one d. *Education:* Amherst College, Columbia University. *Career:* Writer-in-Residence, Mt Holyoke College, 1982–86; Contributing Ed., Rolling Stone, 1986–89; mem. International Asscn of Crime Writers; MWA; PEN; Writers' Guild-East. *Publications:* Mirrors, 1968; Ekstasy, 1975; Like Father, 1978; The King of Fifth Avenue, 1981; Minds, 1982; Murder at the Met, 1984; Medicine Man, 1985; Peep Show, 1986; The Plague Years, 1986. Other: various television scripts. Contributions: numerous national and international magazines. *Honours:* Gold Medal for Excellence in Writing, Writers' Foundation of America, 1992.

BLACK, Jim (see Haining, Peter Alexander)

BLACK, Robert (see Holdstock, Robert)

BLACKBOURN, David Gordon, PhD, FRHistS; British historian and academic; *Coolidge Professor of History and Director of Minda de Gunzburg Center for European Studies, Harvard University*; b. 1 Nov. 1949, Spilsby, Lincs.; s. of Harry Blackbourn and Pamela Jean Blackbourn (née Youngman); m. Deborah Frances Langton 1985; one s. one d. *Education:* Leeds Modern Grammar School, Christ's Coll., Cambridge. *Career:* Research Fellow, Jesus Coll., Cambridge 1973–76; Lecturer in History, Queen Mary Coll., Univ. of London 1976–79, Birkbeck Coll. 1979–85, Reader in Modern History 1985–89, Prof. of Modern European History 1989–92; Coolidge Prof. of History Harvard Univ. 1992–, Dir, Minda de Gunzburg Center for European Studies 2007–; lectures and contribs to confs in UK, Ireland, Germany, France, Italy, Yugoslavia, USA and Canada 1973–; Fellow Inst. for European History, Mainz, FRG 1974–75; Research Fellow, Alexander von Humboldt Foundation, Bonn-Bad Godesberg, FRG 1984–85, 1994–95; Visiting Kratter Prof. of German History, Stanford Univ., Calif., USA 1989–90; Fellow Guggenheim Foundation, New York 1994–95; Sec. German History Soc. 1978–81, mem. Cttee 1981–86; mem. Acad. Man. Cttee, German Historical Inst., London 1983–92; mem. Editorial Bd Past and Present 1988–; mem. European Sub-Cttee of Labour Party Nat. Exec. Cttee 1978–80, Academic Man. Cttee, Inst. for European History, Mainz, Germany 1995–2005, Cttee on Hon. Foreign mems, American Historical Asscn 2000–02; Pres. Conf. Group on Cen. European History, American Historical Asscn 2003–04; mem. Advisory Bd, Edmund Spevack Memorial Foundation, 2003–, mem. Academic Bd, Friends of the German Historical Institute, Washington, 2004–; Ed. Penguin Custom Editions: The Western World Database 2000–; consultant to SMASH/The History Channel, USA; gave Annual Lecture of German Historical Inst., London 1998, Malcolm Wynn Lecture, Stetson Univ., Florida 2002, George C. Windell Memorial Lecture, Univ. of New Orleans 2006, Crayenborgh Lecture, Leiden Univ., Netherlands 2007. *Publications:* Class, Religion and Local Politics in Wilhelmine Germany 1980, The Peculiarities of German History (with Geoff Eley) 1984, Populists and Patricians: Essays in Modern German History 1987, Volksfrömmigkeit und Fortschrittsglaube im Kulturkampf 1988, The German Bourgeoisie (ed. with Richard J. Evans) 1991, Marpingen: Apparitions of the Virgin Mary in Bismarckian Germany 1993, The Fontana History of Germany: the Long Nineteenth Century, 1780–1918 1997, The Conquest of Nature: Water, Landscape and the Making of Modern Germany 2006; scholarly articles in English, German, French, Serbo-Croat, Japanese and Italian; contribs to several magazines and the BBC. *Honours:* American Historical Asscn Book Prize 1996, Walter Channing Cabot Fellow, Harvard Univ. 2003–04. *Address:* Minda de Gunzburg Center for European Studies, Harvard University, 27 Kirkland Street, Cambridge, MA 02138, USA (office). *Telephone:* (617) 495-4303, ext. 228 (office). *Fax:* (617) 495-8509 (office). *E-mail:* dgblackb@fas.harvard.edu (office). *Website:* www.fas.harvard.edu/~history (office).

BLACKBURN, Alexander Lambert, MA, PhD; American academic, writer and editor; *Professor Emeritus of English, University of Colorado at Colorado Springs*; b. 6 Sept. 1929, Durham, NC; m. Inés Dölz 1975; two s. one d. *Education:* Yale Univ., Univ. of N Carolina, Univ. of Cambridge, UK. *Career:* instructor, Hampden-Sydney Coll. 1960–61, Univ. of Pennsylvania 1963–65; Lecturer, Univ. of Maryland European Div. 1967–72; Prof. of English, Univ. of Colorado at Colorado Springs 1973–95, Prof. Emer. of English 1996–; Founder and Ed.-in-Chief Writers' Forum 1974–95; mem. Authors' Guild, PEN West, Colorado Authors' League, Western American Literature Asscn. *Publications:* The Myth of the Picaro 1979, The Cold War of Kitty Pentecost (novel) 1979, The Interior Country: Stories of the Modern West (ed.) 1987, A Sunrise Brighter Still: The Visionary Novels of Frank Waters 1991, Higher Elevations: Stories from the West (ed.) 1993, Suddenly a Mortal Splendor (novel) 1995, Creative Spirit: Towards a Better World 2001, Meeting the Professor: Growing Up in the William Blackburn Family 2004. *Honours:* Faculty Book Award Colorado Univ. 1993, Int. Peace Writing Award 2003, Frank Waters Award for Excellence in Literature 2005. *Address:* 6030 Twin Rock Court, Colorado Springs, CO 80918, USA (home). *Telephone:* (719) 599-4023 (home). *E-mail:* idb99@yahoo.com (home).

BLACKBURN, Julia, BA, FRSL; British writer; b. 12 Aug. 1948, London; d. of Thomas Blackburn and Rosalie de Meric; m. 1st Hein Bonger 1978 (divorced); one d. one s.; m. 2nd Herman Makkink 1999. *Education:* Univ. of York.

Publications include: The White Men 1979, Charles Waterton 1989, The Book of Colour 1991, Daisy Bates in the Desert 1994, The Emperor's Last Island 1997, The Leper's Companions 1999, For A Child: Selected Poems by Thomas Blackburn (ed and introduction) 2000, Old Man Goya 2002, With Billie (biog.) 2005. *Literary Agent:* Toby Eady, 9 Orme Court, London W2 4RL, England. *Address:* Sandpit, Thorington Road, Bramfield, Suffolk, IP19 9H2, England (home). *Telephone:* (1986) 784215 (home). *Fax:* (1986) 784665 (home). *E-mail:* julia@makkandblack.freeserve.co.uk (home).

BLACKBURN, Simon W., PhD, DPhil, FBA; British academic; *Professor of Philosophy, University of Cambridge;* b. 12 July 1944, Bristol; s. of Cuthbert Blackburn and Edna Blackburn; m. Angela Bowles 1968; one s. one d. *Education:* Clifton Coll. Bristol and Trinity Coll., Cambridge. *Career:* Research Fellow, Churchill Coll. Cambridge 1967–69; Fellow and Tutor in Philosophy, Pembroke Coll. Oxford 1969–90; Ed. Mind 1984–90; Edna J. Koury Distinguished Prof. of Philosophy, Univ. of NC 1990–2000; Adjunct Prof., ANU 1993–; Prof. of Philosophy, Univ. of Cambridge 2001–. *Publications:* Reason and Prediction 1970, Spreading the Word 1984, Essays in Quasi-Realism 1993, Oxford Dictionary of Philosophy 1994, Ruling Passions 1998, Think 1999, Being Good 2001, Lust 2004, Truth: A Guide for the Perplexed 2005, Plato's Republic: A Biography 2006. *Honours:* Hon. LLD (Sunderland). *Address:* Faculty of Philosophy, University of Cambridge, Sidgwick Avenue, Cambridge, CB3 9DA (office); 141 Thornton Road, Cambridge, CB3 0NE, England (home). *Telephone:* (1223) 528278 (office). *E-mail:* swb24@cam.ac.uk (office). *Website:* www.phil.cam.ac.uk/~swb24/ (office).

BLACKMAN, Malorie; British writer; b. 1962, London; one d. *Education:* Honor Oak Grammar School, Thames Polytechnic. *Career:* database man. for Reuters; full-time writer 1990–. *Publications include:* juvenile: Not So Stupid! 1990, Elaine You're a Brat 1991, Girl Wonder and the Terrific Twins 1991, That New Dress 1991, A New Dress for Maya 1992, Hacker 1992, Girl Wonder's Winter Adventures 1992, Trust Me 1992, Betsey Biggalow the Detective 1992, Betsey Biggalow is Here! 1993, Operation Gadgetman! 1993, Hurricane Betsey 1993, Crazy Crocs 1994, Rachel and the Difference Thief 1994, Magic Betsey 1994, My Friend's a Gris-Quok! 1994, All Aboard 1995, Deadly Dare 1995, Truth! 1995, Jack Sweettooth the 73rd 1995, Whizziwig 1995, Mrs Spoon's Family 1995, A.N.T.I.D.O.T.E. 1996, Betsey's Birthday Surprise 1996, Grandma's Haunted Handbag 1996, Peril on Planet Pelia 1997, The Mellion Moon Mystery 1997, The Computer Ghost 1997, The Secret of the Terrible Hand 1997, Space Race 1997, Pig Heart Boy 1997, Quasar Quartz Quest 1998, Lie Detectives 1998, Aesop's Fables 1998, Words Last Forever 1998, Fangs 1998, Tell Me No Lies 1999, Dangerous Reality 1999, Forbidden Game 1999, Dizzy's Walk 1999, Whizziwig Returns 1999, Hostage 1999, Marty Monster 1999, Noughts and Crosses 2001, Snow Dog 2001, The Monster Crisp-Guzzler 2002, Dead Gorgeous 2002, I Want A Cuddle 2002, Jessica Strange 2002, The Amazing Adventures of Girl Wonder 2003, An Eye for an Eye 2003, Sinclair the Wonder Bear 2003, Cloud Busting 2004, Knife Edge 2004, Ellie and the Cat 2004, Unheard Voices (ed., stories and poems about slavery); contrib. to A Christmas Tree of Stories 1999, Animal Avengers 1999. *Honours:* Young Telegraph's Fully Booked Award, WHSmith Mind Boggling Book Award 1994, Children's Book Award 2001, Children's Book Circle Eleanor Farjeon Award 2005. *Address:* c/o Random House UK Ltd, 20 Vauxhall Bridge Road, London, SW1V 2SA, England.

BLACKWELL, Julian Toby; British bookseller; b. 10 Jan. 1929, s. of the late Sir Basil Henry Blackwell and Marion Christine Soans; m. Jennifer Jocelyn Darley Wykeham 1953; two s. one d. *Education:* Winchester Coll. and Trinity Coll., Oxford. *Career:* served 5th Royal Tank Regt 1947–49; 21st SAS (TA) 1950–59; Dir and Chair. various Blackwell cos 1956–; Chair. The Blackwell Group Ltd 1980–94; Pres. Blackwell Ltd 1995–, Chair. 1996–99; Chair. Council, ASLIB 1966–68; Pres. Booksellers' Asscn 1980–82; Chair. Thames Business Advice Centre 1986–97, Heart of England TEC 1989–94, Fox FM 1989–98, Cottontail Ltd 1990–; Chair. Son White Memorial Trust 1991–; DL (Oxfordshire) 1988. *Honours:* Hon. DLitt (Robert Gordon) 1997, DUniv (Sheffield Hallam) 1998. *Address:* c/o Blackwell, 50 Broad Street, Oxford, OX1 3BQ, England. *Telephone:* (1865) 792111. *Website:* www.blackwell.com.

BLADES, Ann; Canadian writer and illustrator; b. 16 Nov. 1947, Vancouver, BC; d. of Arthur Sager and Dorothy Sager; m. David Morrison 1984; two s. *Education:* Croft House School, Vancouver and Univ. of British Columbia. *Career:* elementary school teacher, nr Mile 18, BC 1967–71; Registered Nurse 1974–80; illustrator 1968–; artist 1982–; exhbns include Vancouver Art Gallery 1971, Biennale of Illustrations, Bratislava, Czechoslovakia 1977, Art Gallery of Ontario 1977, Master Eagle Gallery, New York 1980, Dunlop Art Gallery 1982, Bau Xi Galleries, Toronto and Vancouver 1982–91, Canada at Bologna 1990. *Publications include:* writer and illustrator: Mary of Mile 18 (Book of the Year Award, CACL—Canadian Asscn of Children's Librarians, Hon. List German and Austrian Kinderbuchpreis 1976) 1971, A Boy of Taché (A Child Study Assn Best Children's Book 1977) 1973, A Cottage at Crescent Beach 1977, By the Sea: An Alphabet Book (Elizabeth Mrazik-Cleaver Canadian Picture Book Award 1986) 1985, Seasons Board Books 1989, Back to the Cabin 1996, Wolf and the Seven Little Kids: Based on a Tale from the Brothers Grimm; illustrations: Jacques the Woodcutter 1977, A Salmon for Simon (Children's Literature Award for Illustration, Canada Council 1979, Amelia Frances Howard-Gibbon Award, CACL) 1978, Six Darn Cows 1979, Pettranella 1980, A Candle for Christmas 1986, Ida and the Wool Smugglers 1987, A Guide to Authors and Illustrators 1988, Anna's Pet 1989, Spring 1989, Summer 1989, Fall 1989, Winter 1989, The Singing Basket 1990, A Dog Came,

Too 1992, A Ride for Martha 1993, Pond Seasons 1997. *Telephone:* (604) 538-5852.

BLAINEY, Geoffrey Norman, AC; Australian historian and author; b. 11 March 1930, Melbourne; s. of Rev. Samuel C. Blainey and Hilda Blainey; m. Ann Heriot 1957; one d. *Education:* Ballarat High School, Wesley Coll., Univ. of Melbourne. *Career:* freelance historian 1951–61; Reader in Econ. History, Univ. of Melbourne 1963–68, Prof. 1968–76, Ernest Scott Prof. of History 1977–88, Dean of Faculty of Arts 1982–87; Prof. of Australian Studies, Harvard Univ. 1982–83; columnist in daily newspapers 1974–; Commr Australian Heritage Comm. 1976–77, Chair. Australia Council 1977–81, Chair., Fed. Govt's Australia-China Council 1979–84, Chair. Commonwealth Literary Fund 1971–73; Pres. Council, Queen's Coll., Univ. of Melbourne 1971–89; Chair. Australian Selection Cttee Commonwealth Fund (Harkness) Fellowships 1983–90; Chancellor Univ. of Ballarat 1994–98; Dir Royal Humane Soc. 1996–2004; Gov. Ian Potter Foundation 1991–; Councillor Australian War Memorial 1997–2004; Del. to Australian Constitutional Convention 1998; Councillor Nat. Council for the Centenary of Fed. 1997–2002 (Chair. 2001–02). *Publications include:* The Peaks of Lyell 1954, Centenary History of the University of Melbourne 1957, Gold and Paper: a History of the National Bank 1958, Mines in the Spinifex 1960, The Rush That Never Ended 1963, A History of Camberwell 1965, If I Remember Rightly: The Memoirs of W. S. Robinson 1966, The Tyranny of Distance 1966, Wesley College: The First Hundred Years (co-author and ed.) 1967, Across a Red World 1968, The Rise of Broken Hill 1968, The Steel Master 1971, The Causes of War 1973, Triumph of the Nomads: A History of Ancient Australia 1975, A Land Half Won 1980, Our Side of the Country 1984, All for Australia 1984, The Great Seesaw 1988, A Game of Our Own 1990, Eye on Australia 1991, Odd Fellows 1992, The Golden Mile 1993, Jumping over the Wheel 1993, A Shorter History of Australia 1994, White Gold 1997, A History of AMP 1999, In Our Time 1999, A Short History of the World 2000, This Land is all Horizons 2001, Black Kettle and Full Moon: Daily Life in a Vanished Australia 2003, A Very Short History of the World 2004, A Short History of the Twentieth Century 2005, A History of Victoria 2006. *Honours:* Gold Medal, Australian Literature Soc. 1963, Capt. Cook Bicentenary Literary Award 1970, Britannica Award for dissemination of learning, NY 1988, Dublin Prize 1986, Australian Author's Society Book of the Year 2000. *Address:* PO Box 257, East Melbourne, Vic. 3002, Australia. *Telephone:* (3) 9417-7782. *Fax:* (3) 9417-7920 (home). *E-mail:* ablainey@netlink.com.au.

BLAIR, Claude, CVO, OBE, BA, MA, LittD, FSA; British antiquary and art historian; b. 30 Nov. 1922, Manchester, England. *Education:* Univ. of Manchester. *Career:* Asst, Tower of London Armouries 1951–56; Hon. Ed., Journal of Arms and Armour Soc. 1953–77; Asst Keeper Metalwork 1956–72, Deputy Keeper Metalwork 1966–72, Keeper Metalwork 1972–82, Victoria & Albert Museum, London; consultant, Christie's, London 1982–2000. *Publications:* European Armour 1958, European and American Arms 1962, Pistols of the World 1968, Three Presentation Swords in the Victoria and Albert Museum 1972, The James A. de Rothschild Collection at Waddesdon Manor: Arms, Armour and Base-Metalwork 1974, Pollard's History of Firearms 1983, A History of Silver 1987, The Crown Jewels (gen. ed. and contrib.) 1998. *Honours:* Soc. of Antiquaries Gold Medal 1998. *Literary Agent:* MBA Literary Agents Ltd, 62 Grafton Way, London, W1T 5DW, England. *Address:* 90 Links Road, Ashtead, Surrey KT21 2HW, England.

BLAIR, David Chalmers Leslie, Jr, BA; American/British writer, composer and artist; b. 8 April 1951, Long Beach, Calif.; descendant of 13th Earl of Rothes, Scotland. *Education:* California State Univ. at Long Beach, Univ. of Aix-en-Provence; teaching certificate, English as a Second Language. *Career:* music has been performed in California and New York and worldwide in Denmark, Sweden, Ukraine and elsewhere. *Recordings:* 109 albums, including Sir Blair of Rothes, Her Garden of Earthly Delights, St Luke Passion, Europe. *Publications:* Death of an Artist 1982, Vive la France 1993, Death of America 1994, Mother 1998, Evening in Wisconsin 2001, The Girls (& Women) I Have Known 2001, A Small Snack Shop in Stockholm-Sweden 2002. *Address:* 19331 105th Avenue, Cadott, WI 54727, USA. *Telephone:* (715) 382-4925.

BLAIR, Emma (see Blair, Iain John)

BLAIR, Iain John, (Emma Blair); Scottish novelist; b. 12 Aug. 1942, Glasgow; m. 1st 1975 (divorced); two s.; m. 2nd Jane Blanchard 2004. *Education:* Royal Scottish Acad. of Music and Dramatic Art. *Career:* mem. Romantic Novelists Asscn, British Actors Equity. *Publications:* Where No Man Cries 1982, Nellie Wildchild 1983, Hester Dark 1984, This Side of Heaven 1985, Jessie Gray 1985, The Princess of Poor Street 1986, Street Song 1986, When Dreams Come True 1987, A Most Determined Woman 1988, The Blackbird's Tale 1989, Maggie Jordan 1990, Scarlet Ribbons 1991, The Water Meadows 1992, The Sweetest Thing 1993, The Daffodil Sea 1994, Passionate Times 1995, Half Hidden 1996, Flower of Scotland 1997, An Apple from Eden 1998, Goodnight, Sweet Prince 1999, Wild Strawberries 2000, Forget-Me-Not 2001, Moonlit Eyes 2002, Finding Happiness 2003, Twilight Time 2004, Little White Lies 2005, Three Bites of the Cherry 2006. *Literary Agent:* Rogers, Coleridge & White Ltd, 20 Powis Mews, London, W11 1JN, England. *Website:* www.emmablair.com.

BLAIR, Jessica (see Spence, William John Duncan)

BLAIS, Marie-Claire, CC; Canadian writer; b. 5 Oct. 1939, Québec City; d. of Fernando Blais and Veronique Nolin. *Education:* studied in Québec, Paris, France and USA. *Career:* Guggenheim Foundation Fellowship, New York 1963, 1964; Hon. Prof. Calgary Univ. 1978; mem. Royal Soc. of Canada, Acad. Royale de Belgique, Acad. des Lettres françaises. *Publications:* La belle bête 1959, Tête blanche 1960, Le jour est noir 1962, Existences (poems), Une saison dans la vie d'Emmanuel 1965, L'insoumise 1966, David Sterne 1967, Manuscrits de Pauline Archange 1968, Vivre, vivre 1969, Les voyageurs sacrés 1966, Les apparences 1970, Le loup 1972, Un Joualonais sa Joualonie 1973, Theatre radiophonique 1974, Une liaison parisienne 1976, Les nuits de l'underground 1978, Le sourd dans la ville 1980, Visions d'Anna 1982, Pierre 1984, Dans la foudre et la lumière 2002 (novels); Pays voilés (poems) 1964; L'océan 1967, L'exécution 1968, Fièvre 1974, La nef des sorcières 1976, Sommeil d'hiver 1985, Fière 1985, L'île 1988 (plays), L'ange de la solitude (novel) 1989, Un jardin dans la tempête (play) 1990, Parcours d'un Ecrivain: Notes Americaines (essay) 1993, L'Exile (short stories) 1993, Soifs (novel) 1995, Dans la foudre et la lumière (novel), Théatre (Ed.), Des Rencontres Humaines 2002, Noces à midi au-dessus de l'abîme (play) 2004, Augustino et le choeur de la destruction (play) 2007. *Honours:* Hon. mem. Boivin Center of French Language and Culture, Univ. of Massachusetts, USA; Chevalier de la Légion d'honneur; Dr hc (York Univ., Toronto) 1975, (Lyon) 2003, (Ottawa) 2004, (Lyon) 2005; Prix de la langue française 1961, Prix France-Québec 1964, Prix Médicis 1966, Prix de l'Acad. Française 1983, Prix Athanase-David (Québec) 1983, Prix Nessim Habif (Acad. Royale de Belgique) 1991, Prix de la Fondation Prince Pierre de Monaco, Prix du Gouverneur Général (Canada) (three times), Prix Gilles Corbeil 2006 and others. *Literary Agent:* Agence Goodwin, 839 Sherbrooke Estate, Suite 2, Montréal, H26 1K6, Canada. *Telephone:* (514) 598-5252. *Fax:* (514) 598-1878. *Address:* 427 Grosvenor Avenue, Westmount, Québec H3Y 255, Canada. *Telephone:* (514) 937-0212.

BLAISE, Clark Lee, AB, MFA; American/Canadian writer and teacher; *Professor Emeritus, University of Iowa;* b. 10 April 1940, Fargo, ND; m. Bharati Mukherjee 1963; two s. *Education:* Denison Univ., Univ. of Iowa. *Career:* Prof., Concordia Univ. 1966–78, York Univ. 1978–80, Skidmore Coll. 1980–81, 1982–83; Visiting Prof., Univ. of Iowa 1981–82, Prof. Emer. 1998–, Dir Int. Writing Program 1990–; Writer-in-Residence, David Thompson Univ. Center 1983, Emory Univ. 1985; Adjunct Prof., Columbia Univ., New York 1986; Visiting Prof., Univ. of California, Berkeley 1998–2000; Distinguished Writer, Long Island Univ. –2005, Southhampton Coll. 2005; mem. PEN. *Publications:* A North American Education 1973, Tribal Justice 1974, Days and Nights in Calcutta (with B. Mukherjee) 1977, Here and Now (co-ed.) 1977, Lunar Attractions 1978, Lusts 1983, Resident Alien 1986, The Sorrow and the Terror: The Haunting Legacy of the Air India Tragedy 1987, Man and His World 1992, I Had a Father: A Post-Modern Autobiography 1993, If I Were Me (novel) 1997, New and Selected Stories (four vols) 2000–06, Time Lord: Sir Sandford Fleming and the Creation of Standard Time 2000; contribs to various publs. *Honours:* Hon. PhD (Denison Univ.) 1979, (McGill Univ.) 2005; Nat Endowment for the Arts grant 1982, Guggenheim Fellowship, Canada Council grants, Lifetime Achievement Award, American Acad. of Arts and Letters 2003. *Literary Agent:* Janklow & Nesbit Associates, 445 Park Avenue, New York, NY 10022, USA. *Address:* 130 Rivoli Street, San Franciso, CA 94117, USA (home). *Telephone:* (631) 804-7264 (home). *Fax:* (415) 759-9810 (home). *E-mail:* clarquito@aol.com (home).

BLAKE, James Carlos; American/Mexican writer; b. May 1948, Tampico, Mexico. *Career:* mem. Texas Institute of Letters. *Publications:* The Pistoleer, 1995; The Friends of Pancho Villa, 1996; In the Rogue Blood, 1997; Red Grass River: A Legend, 1998; Borderlands: Short Fiction, 1999; Wildwood Boys: A Novel, 2000. *Honours:* First Prize, Quarterly West Novella Competition, 1991; Los Angeles Times Book Prize, 1997; Chautauqua South Fiction Award, Library Foundation, Martin County, FL, 1999; Southwest Book Award, Border Regional Library Asscn, 1999. *Address:* c/o HarperCollins Publishers, 10 East 53rd Street, New York, NY 10022, USA. *Website:* www.harpercollins.com/authors/15763/James_Carlos_Blake/index.aspx.

BLAKE, Jennifer (see Maxwell, Patricia Anne)

BLAKE, Ken (see Holdstock, Robert)

BLAKE, Norman Francis, BA, BLitt, MA; British academic, writer, editor and translator; *Professor Emeritus of English Language and Linguistics, University of Sheffield;* b. 19 April 1934, Ceara, Brazil. *Education:* Univ. of Oxford. *Career:* Lecturer in English Language and Linguistics, Univ. of Sheffield 1959–68, Sr Lecturer 1968–73, Prof. 1973–2004, Prof. Emer. 2004–. *Publications:* The Saga of the Jomsvikings 1962, The Phoenix 1964, Caxton and His World 1969, William Caxton's Reynard the Fox 1970, Middle English Religious Prose 1972, Selections from William Caxton 1973, Caxton's Quattuor Sermiones 1973, Caxton's Own Prose 1975, Caxton: England's First Publisher 1976, The English Language in Medieval Literature 1977, Non-Standard Language in English Literature 1981, Shakespeare's Language 1983, Textual Tradition of the Canterbury Tales 1985, William Caxton: A Bibliographical Guide 1985, Traditional English Grammar and Beyond 1988, The Language of Shakespeare (with R.E. Lewis and A.S.G. Edwards) 1989, An Introduction to the Languages of Literature 1990, William Caxton and English Literary Culture 1991, The Cambridge History of the English Language, Vol. II: 1066–1476 1992, Introduction to English Language (with J. Moorhead) 1993, William Caxton 1996, Essays in Shakespeare's Language 1996, History of the English Language 1996, Shakespeare's Non-Standard English – A Dictionary of his Informal Langauge 2004. *Address:* c/o Department of English Language and Linguistics, University of Sheffield, Sheffield, S10 2TN, England (office).

BLAKE, Quentin Saxby, OBE, CBE, RDI, MA, FCSD; British artist, writer, illustrator and teacher; b. 16 Dec. 1932, Sidcup, Kent; s. of William Blake and Evelyn Blake. *Education:* Downing Coll., Cambridge, London Inst. of Educ., Chelsea School of Art. *Career:* freelance illustrator 1957–; Tutor, Royal Coll. of Art 1965–86, Head of Illustration Dept 1978–86, Visiting Prof. 1989–; first British Children's Laureate 1999–2001; Sr Fellow RCA 1988. *Exhibitions:* Quentin Blake – 50 Years of Illustration, The Gilbert Collection, Somerset House, London 2003–04; Quentin Blake at Christmas, Dulwich Picture Gallery, London 2004–05. *Publications include:* Patrick 1968, Angelo 1970, Mister Magnolia 1980, Quentin Blake's Nursery Rhyme Book 1983, The Story of the Dancing Frog 1984, Mrs Armitage on Wheels 1987, Mrs Armitage Queen of the Road, Quentin Blake's ABC 1989, All Join In 1992, Cockatoos 1992, Simpkin 1993, La Vie de la Page 1995, The Puffin Book of Nonsense Verse 1996, Mrs Armitage and the Big Wave 1997, The Green Ship 1998, Clown 1998, Drawing for the Artistically Undiscovered (with John Cassidy) 1999, Fantastic Daisy Artichoke 1999, Words and Pictures 2000, The Laureate's Party 2000, Zagazoo 2000, Tell Me a Picture 2001, Loveykins 2002, A Sailing Boat in the Sky 2002, Laureate's Progress 2002, Angel Pavement 2004, The Life of Birds 2005; illustrations for over 250 works for children and adults, including collaborations with Roald Dahl, Russell Hoban, Joan Aiken, Michael Rosen, John Yeoman, Michael Morpurgo. *Honours:* Hon. Fellow, Brighton Univ. 1996, Downing Coll. Cambridge 2000, Cardiff Univ. 2006, Hon. RA; Chevalier, Ordre des Arts et des Lettres 2002; Dr hc (London Inst.) 2000, (Northumbria) 2001, (RCA) 2001, (Open Univ.) 2006, (Loughborough) 2007; Hon. DLitt (Cambridge Univ.) 2004. *Address:* Flat 8, 30 Bramham Gardens, London, SW5 0HF, England. *Telephone:* (20) 7373-7464 (office). *Fax:* (20) 7370-1023 (office). *E-mail:* zagazoo2002@yahoo.com (office). *Website:* www.quentinblake.com.

BLAKE-HANNAH, Barbara Makeda; Jamaican/British author, cultural historian and filmmaker; *Managing Director, Jamaica Media Productions Ltd;* b. 5 June 1941, d. of Evon Blake and Veronica Stewart; m. Deeb Roy Hanna 1984; one s. *Education:* Hampton High School, Wolmers Girls' School and Inst. of Public Relations, London. *Career:* TV reporter and interviewer in UK 1968–72, Cuban Film Week 1975; Organizer Annual Festival of Black and Third World Films 1974–85; Special Asst to Minister of Information and Culture 1976–77; Dir of Public Relations Kingston 1978, Montego Bay 1980; mem. Senate 1984–87; Founder and Man. Dir Jamaica Media Productions Ltd 1982–; columnist and feature writer for numerous magazines and newspapers; reporter and interviewer, Jamaica Broadcasting Corpn, RJR-Radio Jamaica, KLAS-FM, IRIE-FM 1972–96; has been a Rastafarian for 30 years, considered an Elder Empress of the Jamaican faith; lecturer at Univ. of West Indies, Vienna, New York, Florida (FIU), USVI. *Film and TV includes:* documentaries and features: Kids Paradise – The Movie, Hotel Kids Paradise – the Great Lost Treasure Hunt, Race, Rhetoric, Rastafari, The Peaceful Gun, By The Land We Live, The Road through the Blue Mountains 2002. *Publications:* Rastafari – The New Creation 1981, Joseph – A Rasta Reggae Fable 1992. *Honours:* UN Peace Medal 1974, Gold Adowa Centenary Medal Ethiopian Crown Council 1997. *Address:* PO Box 727, Kingston 6, Jamaica (office). *Telephone:* (876) 384-2923 (office). *E-mail:* jamediapro@hotmail.com (office); i_makeda@yahoo.com (home). *Website:* www.geocities.com/jamaicamediaproductions (office).

BLAMIRES, Harry, BA, MA; British academic and writer; b. 6 Nov. 1916, Bradford, Yorks.; m. Nancy Bowles 1940; five s. *Education:* Univ. Coll., Oxford. *Career:* Head, English Dept, King Alfred's Coll., Winchester 1948–72, Dean Arts and Sciences 1972–76; Clyde Kilby Visiting Prof. of English, Wheaton Coll., Wheaton, Ill. 1987; mem. Soc. of Authors. *Publications:* Repair the Ruins 1950, The Devil's Hunting Grounds 1954, Cold War in Hell 1955, Blessing Unbounded 1955, The Faith and Modern Error 1956, The Will and the Way 1957, The Kirkbride Conversations 1958, The Offering of Man 1959, The Christian Mind 1963, A Defence of Dogmatism 1965, The Bloomsday Book: Guide to Joyce's Ulysses 1966, Word Unheard: Guide Through Eliot's Four Quartets 1969, Milton's Creation 1971, A Short History of English Literature 1974, Where Do We Stand? 1980, Twentieth-Century English Literature 1982, Guide to 20th Century Literature in English 1983, On Christian Truth 1983, Words Made Flesh (aka The Marks of the Maker) 1985, The Victorian Age of Literature 1988, Meat Not Milk 1988, The Age of Romantic Literature 1989, A History of Literary Criticism 1991, The Queen's English 1994, The Cassell Guide to Common Errors in English 1997, The Penguin Guide to Plain English 2000, The Post-Christian Mind 2001, Compose Yourself – and Write Good English 2003, New Town, a fable 2005. *Honours:* Hon. DLitt (Southampton) 1993. *Address:* Pinfold, 3 Glebe Close, Keswick, Cumbria CA12 5QQ, England. *Telephone:* (1768) 775232.

BLANCHARD, Stephen Thomas; British writer; b. 8 Dec. 1950, Hull, Yorkshire, England; m. Sarah Rookledge, two s. one d. *Education:* University of Liverpool. *Career:* carpenter, antique dealer, postman; mem. Society of Authors. *Publications:* Fiction: Gagarin and I 1995, Wilson's Island 1997, The Paraffin Child 1999. Contributions: stories and articles in magazines. *Honours:* McKitterick Prize, Society of Authors 1996; First Novel Award, Yorkshire Post 1996. *Literary Agent:* Rachel Calder, The Sayle Literary Agency, Bickerton House, 25–27 Bickerton Road, London N19 5JT, England.

Address: 74 Rectory Grove, London, SW4 0ED, England (home). *E-mail:* stephenblanchard@ukgateway.net.

BLAND, Peter; British poet, reviewer, actor and dramatist; b. 12 May 1934, Scarborough, Yorks.; m. Beryl Matilda Connolly 1956; one s. two d. *Education:* Victoria Univ. of Wellington, NZ. *Career:* journalist and talks producer, NZ Broadcasting Corpn 1960–64; co-founder, dir, actor and dramatist, Downstage Theatre, Wellington 1964–68; actor, West End plays and numerous television productions, London; leading role, Came a Hot Friday (New Zealand film), 1985. *Publications:* Poetry: My Side of the Story, 1964; The Man with the Carpet Bag, 1972; Mr Maui, 1976; Stone Tents, 1981; The Crusoe Factor, 1985; Selected Poems, 1987; Paper Boats, 1991; Selected Poems, 1998; Ports of Call, 2003. Plays: Father's Day, 1967; George the Mad Ad Man, 1967; Memoir: Sorry, I'm a Stranger Here Myself 2004. Contributions: anthologies and periodicals. *Honours:* Macmillan-Brown Prize for Creative Writing, Victoria Univ. of Wellington, 1958; Melbourne Arts Festival Literary Award, 1960; Queen Elizabeth II Arts Council Drama Fellowship, 1968; Cholmondeley Award for Poetry, 1977; Best Film Actor Award, Guild of Film and TV Arts, NZ, 1985; Poetry Book Soc. Recommendation, 1987; Observer/Arvon Foundation Int. Poetry Prize, 1990. *Address:* 17 Tower Road, Worthing, West Sussex, BN11 1DP (home); c/o Carcanet Press, Fourth Floor, Alliance House, Cross Street, Manchester M2 7AP, England (office). *Telephone:* (1903) 820401 (home).

BLANDIANA, Ana, BA; Romanian writer and poet; b. 25 March 1942, Timişoara; m. Romulus Rusan 1960. *Education:* Univ. of Cluj. *Career:* columnist Romania literary magazine 1974–88; has given numerous lectures on cultural and civic issues in the UK, France, Netherlands, Norway, Austria and Germany; has participated in int. seminars on human rights and multiculturalism in Canada, France, Greece, Germany, USA, Norway and Russian Fed., confs at Univ. of Rome 1991, The German Rectors' Conf., Bonn 1992, Free Univ. of Berlin 1992, Univ. of Paris, Sorbonne 1993, Univ. of Vienna 1994, Univ. of Prague 1994, Univ. of Heidelberg, Austria 1995, INALCO, Paris 1996, and poetry festivals in Finland, Paris, Romania, USA, Italy, UK, France, Austria and Norway; Pres. Academia Civica Foundation, Romanian PEN Centre (has participated in several int. confs). *Publications include:* poetry: First Person in the Plural 1964, The Vulnerable Heel 1966, The Third Sacrament 1960, 50 Poems 1970, October, November, December 1982, Poems 1974, The Sleep in the Sleep 1977, Events in my Garden 1980, The Eye of the Cricket 1981, The Sand Hour 1984, The Prey Star 1986, Other Events in my Garden 1987, Events on my Street 1988, Poems 1988, The Architecture of the Waves 1990, 100 Poems 1991; essays: The Witness Quality 1970, I Write, You Write, He/She Writes 1975, The Most Beautiful of the Possible Worlds 1978, Passage of Mirrors 1983, Self-portrait with Palimpsest 1985, City of Syllables 1987; short stories: Four Seasons 1977, Projects of the Past 1982, Imitation of a Nightmare 1995; novel: The Drawer with Applause 1992, The Sun After the Death 2002. *Honours:* Romanian Writers' Union Poetry Prize 1969, 2000, Romanian Acad. Poetry Prize 1970, Asscn of Writers in Bucharest Poetry Prize 1980, Int. Herder Prize, Austria 1982, Opera Omnia Prize 2002, Int. Vilenica Prize, Slovenia 2002. *Address:* Academia Civica, Piata Amzei 13 et 2, CP 22-216, Bucharest (office); Str. Transilvaniei 56, 70778 Bucharest, Romania (home). *Telephone:* (21) 3129852 (office). *Fax:* (21) 3125854 (office); (21) 3111112 (home). *E-mail:* acivica@fx.ro (office). *Website:* www.memorialsighet.ro (office).

BLANNING, Timothy Charles William, LittD, FBA; British academic; *Professor of Modern European History, University of Cambridge*; b. 21 April 1942, Wells, Somerset; s. of Thomas Walter Blanning and Gwendolen Marchant-Jones; m. Nicky Susan Jones 1988; one s. one d. *Education:* King's School, Bruton, Somerset, Sidney Sussex Coll., Cambridge. *Career:* Research Fellow, Sidney Sussex Coll. 1965–68, Fellow 1968–, Asst Lecturer in History, Cambridge Univ. 1972–76, lecturer 1976–87, Reader in Modern European History 1987–92, Prof. of Modern European History 1992–. *Publications:* Joseph II and Enlightened Despotism 1970, Reform and Revolution in Mainz 1743–1803 1974, The French Revolution in Germany 1983, The Origins of the French Revolutionary Wars 1986, The French Revolution: Aristocrats versus Bourgeois? 1987, Joseph II 1994, The French Revolutionary Wars 1787–1802 1996, The French Revolution: Class War or Culture Clash? 1998, The Culture of Power and the Power of Culture 2002; Ed.: The Oxford Illustrated History of Modern Europe 1996, The Rise and Fall of the French Revolution 1996, History and Biography: Essays in Honour of Derek Beales (with Peter Wende), Reform in Great Britain and Germany 1750–1850 1999, The Short Oxford History of Europe: The Eighteenth Century 2000, The Short Oxford History of Europe: The Nineteenth Century 2000. *Address:* Sidney Sussex College, Cambridge, CB2 3HU, England. *Telephone:* (1223) 335308. *Fax:* (1223) 335968 (office). *E-mail:* tcb1000@cam.ac.uk (office).

BLASER, Robin Francis, MA; American academic and poet; b. 18 May 1925, Denver, CO. *Education:* University of California at Berkeley. *Career:* Prof. of English, Centre for the Arts, Simon Fraser University, Burnaby, BC, Canada 1972–86. *Publications:* The Moth Poem 1964, Les Chimères 1965, Cups 1968, The Holy Forest Section 1970, Image-nations 1-12 and The Stadium of the Mirror 1974, Image-nations 13–14 1975, Suddenly 1976, Syntax 1983, The Faerie Queene and the Park 1987, Pell Mell 1988, The Holy Forest 1993, Libretto for Sir Harrison Birtwistle's The Last Supper 2000, Wanderer (with M. Quartermain) 2002, The Irreparable 2003. *Honours:* Poetry Society Award 1965, Canada Council Grant 1989–90, Fund for Poetry Award, New York 1995. *Address:* 1636 Trafalgar Street, Vancouver, BC V6K 3R7, Canada.

BLASHFORD-SNELL, Col John Nicholas, OBE, FRGS, FRSGS; British explorer, writer and broadcaster; *Chairman, Scientific Exploration Society*; b. 22 Oct. 1936, Hereford; s. of the late Rev. Prebendary Leland John Blashford-Snell and Gwendolen Ives Blatshford-Snell (née Sadler); m. Judith Frances Sherman 1960; two d. *Education:* Victoria Coll., Jersey, RMA, Sandhurst. *Career:* commissioned, Royal Engineers 1957; Commdr Operation Aphrodite (Expedition), Cyprus 1959–61; Instructor, Jr Leaders Regt Royal Engineers 1962–63; Instructor, RMA, Sandhurst 1963–66; Adjt, 3rd Div. Engineers 1966–67; Commdr The Great Abbai Expedition (Blue Nile) 1968; attended Staff Coll., Camberley 1969; Chair. Scientific Exploration Soc. 1969–; Commdr Dahlak Quest Expedition 1969–70, British Trans-Americas Expedition (Darien Gap) 1971–72; Officer Commdg 48th Field Squadron, Royal Engineers 1972–74; Commdr, Zaire River Expedition 1974–75; CO, Jr Leaders Regt, Royal Engineers 1976–78; Dir of Operations, Operation Drake 1978–81; Staff Officer, Ministry of Defence 1978–91, Consultant 1992–; Commdr, Fort George Volunteers 1982; Operations Dir, Operation Raleigh 1982–88, Dir-Gen. 1989–91; Dir SES Tibet Expedition 1987; Leader, Kalahari Quest Expedition 1990, Karnali Quest Expedition 1991, Karnali Gorges Expedition 1992, numerous exploration projects thereafter; Trustee, Operation New World 1995–; Chair. Just a Drop Charity 2001–04, Pres. 2004–, The Liverpool Construction-Crafts Guild 2003–05, Pres. 2005–; Pres. The British Travel Health Asscn 2006–. *Publications:* Weapons and Tactics (with T. Wintringham) 1970, The Expedition Organiser's Guide (with Richard Snailham) 1970, Where the Trails Run Out 1974, In the Steps of Stanley 1975, Expeditions the Experts' Way (with A. Ballantine) 1977, A Taste for Adventure 1978, Operation Drake (with M. Cable) 1981, In the Wake of Drake (with M. Cable) 1982, Mysteries: Encounters with the Unexplained 1983, Operation Raleigh, The Start of an Adventure 1987, Operation Raleigh, Adventure Challenge (with Ann Tweedy) 1988, Operation Raleigh, Adventure Unlimited (with Ann Tweedy) 1990, Something Lost Behind the Ranges 1994, Mammoth Hunt (with Rula Lenska) 1996, Kota Mama: Retracing the Lost Trade Routes of Ancient South American Peoples (with Richard Snailham) 2000, East to the Amazon (with Richard Snailham) 2002. *Honours:* Freeman of the City of Hereford, Hon. Pres. The Vole Club 1996–; Hon. Life Pres. The Centre for Fortean Zoology 2003–; Hon. DSc (Durham); Hon. DEng (Bournemouth) 1997; The Livingstone Medal, The Darien Medal (Colombia) 1972, The Segrave Trophy, Paul Harris Fellow (Rotary Int.), Royal Geographical Soc. Patrons' Medal 1993, Gold Medal (Inst. of Royal Engineers) 1994, La Paz Medal (Bolivia) 2000. *Address:* c/o Scientific Exploration Society, Expedition Base, Motcombe, nr Shaftesbury, Dorset SP7 9PB, England. *Telephone:* (1747) 854456 (office). *Fax:* (1747) 851351 (office). *E-mail:* jbs@ses-explore.org (office). *Website:* www.ses-explore.org (office).

BLATTY, William Peter, MA, DHumLitt; American writer and screenwriter; b. 7 Jan. 1928, New York, NY; s. of Peter Blatty and Mary (née Mouakad) Blatty; m. Julie Alicia Witbrodt 1983; three s. three d. *Education:* Georgetown Univ., George Washington Univ. and Seattle Univ. *Career:* served in USAF 1951–54; ed. with US Information Agency 1955–57; Publicity Dir Univ. Southern Calif. 1957–58; Public Relations Dir Loyola Univ., Los Angeles 1959–60. *Screenplays:* The Man from the Diner's Club 1961, Promise Her Anything 1962, John Goldfarb, Please Come Home 1963, A Shot in the Dark 1964, The Great Bank Robbery 1967, What Did You Do in the War, Daddy? 1965, Gunn 1967, Darling Lili 1968, Twinkle, Twinkle, 'Killer' Kane (Golden Globe for Best Movie Screenplay) 1973, Mastermind 1976, The Ninth Configuration (also dir) 1978, The Exorcist (Golden Globe for Best Movie Screenplay 1980) 1973, The Exorcist III 1990, Exorcist: The Beginning 2004. *Writing for television:* Watts Made Out of Thread (series episode) (American Film Festival Blue Ribbon and Gabriel Award). *Publications:* Which Way to Mecca, Jack? 1959, John Goldfarb, Please Come Home 1963, I, Billy Shakespeare 1965, Twinkle, Twinkle, 'Killer' Kane 1966, The Exorcist 1970, I'll Tell Them I Remember You (autobiog.) 1973, The Exorcist: From Novel to Film 1974, The Ninth Configuration 1978, Legion 1983, Demons Five, Exorcists Nothing 1996, Elsewhere 1999. *Honours:* Acad. Award of Acad. Motion Picture, Arts and Sciences 1973, Acad. of Fantasy, Science Fiction and Horror award 1980, Stoker Award for Lifetime Achievement 1998.

BLAYNE, Diana (see Kyle, Susan Eloise Spaeth)

BLAŽKOVÁ, Jaroslava; Slovak novelist and editor; b. 1933, Valasské Mezirící, Moravia. *Education:* Comenius Univ., Bratislava. *Career:* moved between Slovakia and Czech lands in her youth; worked at Slovak Radio and later in culture section of Smena newspaper; started publishing short stories in various periodicals from 1956; settled in Canada after Soviet invasion of Czechoslovakia; worked for Canadian Broadcasting Corpn and later for 68 Publishers. *Publications:* Nylon Moon (novel) 1960, Fireworks for Grandad (juvenile novel) (UNESCO Prize) 1963, Poviedka plná snehu (short story, A Tale Full of Snow) 1964, Little Lamb and the Big Shots (juvenile short stories) 1964.

BLEAKLEY, David Wylie, OBE, BA, MA; Northern Irish educator and writer; b. 11 Jan. 1925, Belfast; m. Winifred Wason 1949, three s. *Education:* Ruskin Coll., Oxford, Queen's Univ., Belfast. *Career:* Principal, Belfast Further Education Centre 1955–58; MP, Labour Party, Victoria, Parliament of Northern Ireland, Belfast 1958–65; Lecturer in Industrial Relations, Kivukoni Coll., Dar-es-Salaam 1967–69; Head of Dept of Economics and Political Studies, Methodist Coll., Belfast 1969–79; Minister of Community Relations, Govt of Northern Ireland 1971; Mem. Northern Ireland Labour Party, East Belfast, Northern Ireland Assembly 1973–75; Visiting Sr Lecturer in Peace Studies, Univ. of Bradford 1974–; Chief Exec., Irish Council of Churches 1980–92; apptd Privy Councillor 1971; mem. Church Mission Soc. (pres. 1983–97). *Publications:* Ulster Since 1800: Regional History Symposium, 1958; Young Ulster and Religion in the Sixties, 1964; Peace in Ulster, 1972; Faulkner: A Biography, 1974; Saidie Patterson: Irish Peacemaker, 1980; In Place of Work, 1981; The Shadow and Substance, 1983; Beyond Work: Free to Be, 1985; Will the Future Work?, 1986; Europe: A Christian Vision, 1992; Ageing and Ageism in a Technological Society, 1994; Peace in Ireland: Two States, One People, 1995; C. S. Lewis: At Home in Ireland, 1998; contrib. to BBC and periodicals. *Honours:* Hon. MA (Open Univ) 1975.

BLEASDALE, Alan; British playwright and novelist; b. 23 March 1946, s. of George Bleasdale and Margaret Bleasdale; m. Julia Moses 1970; two s. one d. *Education:* Wade Deacon Grammar School, Widnes, Padgate Teachers Training Coll. *Career:* schoolteacher 1967–75. *Publications:* Scully 1975, Who's Been Sleeping in My Bed? 1977, No More Sitting on the Old School Bench 1979, Boys from the Blackstuff 1982, Are You Lonesome Tonight? (Best Musical, Evening Standard Drama Awards 1985) 1985, No Surrender (film script) 1986, Having a Ball 1986, It's a Madhouse 1986, The Monocled Mutineer (televised 1986) 1986, GBH (TV series) 1991, On the Ledge 1993, Jake's Progress (TV) 1995, Oliver Twist 1999 (Best Drama Series, TV and Radio Industries Club 2000). *Honours:* Hon. DLitt (Liverpool Polytechnic) 1991; BAFTA Writers Award 1982, Royal TV Soc. Writer of the Year 1982; Best Writer Monte Carlo Int. TV Festival 1996 (for Jake's Progress). *Address:* c/o The Agency, 24 Pottery Lane, Holland Park, London, W11 4LZ, England. *Telephone:* (20) 7727-1346. *E-mail:* info@theagency.co.uk.

BLEDSOE, Lucy Jane, BA; American sriter and editor; b. 1 Feb. 1957, Portland, OR; pnr Patricia E. Mullan. *Education:* Williams College, University of California at Berkeley. *Career:* Instructor, University of California Graduate Program of Creative Writing; Instructor, Creative Writing workshops in adult literacy programmes; mem. Media Alliance; National Writers Union; PEN. *Publications:* Sweat: Stories and a Novella, 1995; The Big Bike Race, 1995; Working Parts, 1997; Tracks in the Snow, 1997. Editor: Gay Travels, 1998; Lesbian Travels, 1998. Contributions: books and magazines. *Honours:* PEN Syndicated Fiction Award, 1985; Creative Writing Fellowship, Money for Women/Barbara Deming Memorial Fund, 1989; Gay/Lesbian/Bisexual Award for Literature, 1998.

BLEGVAD, Peter; American singer, songwriter and cartoonist; b. 14 Aug. 1951, New York. *Career:* founder mem., Slapp Happy 1971–; collaborations with Henry Cow, Faust, Golden Palominos, John Greaves, Chris Cutler, Lisa Herman; creator of Leviathan cartoon strip, Independent on Sunday 1992–99. *Recordings include:* albums: with Slapp Happy: Sort Of 1973, Slapp Happy 1974, Ça Va 1998; with Slapp Happy and Henry Cow: Desperate Straights, In Praise Of Learning; solo: Kew Rhône (with John Greaves and Lisa Herman) 1977, Smell of a Friend by The Lodge (with John Greaves), Dr Huelsenbeck's Mentale Heilmethode (with John Greaves) 1992, The Naked Shakespeare 1983, Knights Like This 1985, Downtime 1989, King Strut & Other Stories 1990, Unearthed (with John Greaves) 1995, Just Woke Up (with John Greaves and Chris Cutler) 1995, Hangman's Hill 1998, Choices Under Pressure 2001, Orpheus the Lowdown (with Andy Partridge) 2004. *Publication:* The Book of Leviathan 2001. *Address:* c/o Voiceprint UK, POB 50, Houghton-le-Spring, Tyne & Wear DH4 5YP, England. *E-mail:* info@voiceprint.co.uk. *Website:* www.voiceprint.co.uk.

BLICKER, Seymour, BA; Canadian writer; b. 12 Feb. 1940, Montréal, QC; m. Susan Wanda Colman 1963; three s. one d. *Education:* Loyola Coll. 1962. *Career:* Special Lecturer, Creative Writing, Concordia Univ. 1978–90; mem. Writers Guild of Canada, Playwrights Union of Canada, Acad. of Canadian Cinema and Television Writers' Guild of America West. *Film and television:* various works including episodes of Emmy Award-winning The Barney Miller Show, Side Street series (CBC), Urban Angel series and the film The Kid starring Rod Steiger. *Publications:* fiction: Blues Chased a Rabbit 1969, Shmucks 1972, The Last Collection 1976. Stage Plays: Up Your Alley 1987, Never Judge a Book By Its Cover 1987, Pals 1995, Home Free 1998, Pipe Dreams 1999, Found Money 2003. *Honours:* Canada Council Sr Arts Fellowship 1974, British Council Int. New Playwriting Award for the Americas Region 1997. *Address:* 7460 Kingsley Road, No. 804, Montréal, QC H4W 1P3, Canada. *Telephone:* (514) 485-8263; (819) 322-6232. *Fax:* (514) 485-8263; (819) 322-6232. *E-mail:* seymour.blicker@sympatico.ca.

BLOCH, Chana, MA, PhD; American academic, poet, translator, critic and essayist; *Professor Emerita of English, Mills College, Oakland*; b. 15 March 1940, New York, NY; m. 1st Ariel Bloch 1969 (divorced); two s.; m. 2nd David Sutter 2003. *Education:* Cornell Univ., Brandeis Univ., Univ. of California at Berkeley. *Career:* Instructor of English, Hebrew Univ., Jerusalem 1964–67; Assoc. in Near Eastern Studies, Univ. of California at Berkeley 1967–69; Instructor, Mills College, Oakland, CA 1973–75, Asst Prof. 1975–81, Assoc. Prof. 1981–87, Chair., Dept of English 1986–89, Prof. of English 1987–2003, Dir, Creative Writing Program 1993–2001, Prof. Emerita 2002–; mem. PEN, Poetry Soc. of America, MLA. *Publications:* poetry: The Secrets of the Tribe 1981, The Past Keeps Changing 1992, Mrs Dumpty 1998; literary criticism: Spelling the Word: George Herbert and the Bible 1985; trans.: Dahlia Ravikovitch: A Dress of Fire 1978, Yehuda Amichai: The Selected Poetry (with Stephen Mitchell) 1986, Dahlia Ravikovitch: The Window: New and Selected Poems (with Ariel Bloch) 1989, The Song of Songs: A New Translation, Introduction and Commentary (with Ariel Bloch) 1995, Open Closed Open, by Yehuda Amichai (with Chana Kronfeld) 2000, The Poetry of Dahlia Ravikovitch (with Chana Kronfeld) 2007; contribs to poetry, trans, criticism and essays in various anthologies and periodicals. *Honours:* Discovery Award, Poetry Centre, New York 1974, Trans. Award, Columbia Univ. 1978, Nat. Endowment for the Humanities Fellowship 1980, Book of the Year Award, Conf. on Christianity and Literature 1986, Writers Exchange Award, Poets and Writers 1988, Rockefeller Foundation Residency, Bellagio Study Center 2004, Yaddo Residencies 1988, 1990, 1993, 1994, 1995, 1996, 1997, 1999, 2001, MacDowell Colony Residencies 1988, 1992, 1993, 2000, Djerassi Foundation Residencies 1989, 1991, Nat. Endowment for the Arts Fellowships 1989–90, 1999, Felix Pollak Prize 1998, California Book Award Silver Medal in Poetry 1999, PEN Award for Poetry in Trans. 2001, Alice Fay di Castagnola Award, Poetry Soc. of America 2004. *Address:* 12 Menlo Place, Berkeley, CA 94707, USA (home). *Fax:* (510) 524-8459 (home). *Website:* www.mindspring.com/~chanab.

BLOCK, Lawrence; American novelist; m. Lynne. *Career:* mem. MWA (past pres.), Private Eye Writers of America (past pres.). *Publications:* You Could Call it Murder 1961, Mona 1961, Cinderella Sims 1961, Coward's Kiss 1961, The Girl With the Long Green Heart 1965, Deadly Honeymoon 1967, After the First Death 1969, The Specialists 1969, Such Men are Dangerous 1969, The Triumph of Evil 1971, Ronald Rabbit is a Dirty Old Man 1971, Not Comin' Home to You 1974, Ariel 1980, Random Walk 1988, Small Town 2003; Evan Tanner series: The Thief who Couldn't Sleep 1966, The Canceled Czech 1966, Tanner's Twelve Swingers 1967, Two for Tanner (aka The Scoreless Thai) 1968, Tanner's Tiger 1968, Here Comes a Hero 1968, Me Tanner, You Jane 1970, Tanner on Ice 1998; Matthew Scudder series: The Sins of the Fathers 1976, In the Midst of Death 1976, Time to Murder and Create 1977, A Stab in the Dark 1981, Eight Million Ways to Die 1982, When the Sacred Ginmill Closes 1986, Out on the Cutting Edge 1989, A Ticket to the Boneyard 1990, A Dance at the Slaughterhouse 1991, A Walk Among the Tombstones 1992, The Devil Knows You're Dead 1993, A Long Line of Dead Men 1994, Even the Wicked 1996, Everybody Dies 1998, Hope to Die 2001; Bernie Rhodenbarr series: Burglars Can't be Choosers 1977, The Burglar in the Closet 1978, The Burglar Who Liked to Quote Kipling 1979, The Burglar Who Studied Spinoza 1980, The Burglar Who Painted Like Mondrian 1983, The Burglar Who Traded Ted Williams 1994, The Burglar Who Thought he was Bogart 1995, The Burglar in the Library 1997, The Burglar in the Rye 1999, The Burglar on the Prowl 2004; Chip Harrison series: No Score 1970, Chip Harrison Scores Again 1971, Make Out With Murder (aka The Five Little Rich Girls) 1974, The Topless Tulip Caper 1975; Keller series: Hit Man 1998, Hit List 2000, Hit Parade 2006; contrib. anthologies; articles and short stories in American Heritage, Redbook, Playboy, Cosmopolitan, GQ, New York Times. *Honours:* Nero Wolfe Award 1979, four Shamus Awards, Japanese Maltese Falcon awards 1986, 1989, four Edgar Awards, Philip Marlowe Award, Life Achievement award, Private Eye Writers of America, MWA Grand Master, two Société 813 trophies, presented with the key to the city of Muncie, IN. *Address:* 299 W 12th Street, Suite 12-D, New York, NY 10014, USA. *E-mail:* LawBloc@aol.com. *Website:* www.lawrenceblock.com.

BLOEM, Marion; Dutch novelist, film-maker and artist; b. 24 Aug. 1952. *Education:* State Univ. of Utrecht. *Films:* shorts: Feest (scriptwriter, dir, prod.) 1978, Buitenspel (scriptwriter, dir, prod.) 1979, Aanraken (script with Ivan Wolffers, dir, prod.) 1980, Nieuwsgierig (script with Ivan Wolffers, dir, prod.) 1980, Borsten (script with Ivan Wolffers, dir, prod.) 1981, De Tovenaarsleerling (scriptwriter, dir) (VPRO Kid Screen Award 1987) 1986; documentaries: Het land van mijn ouders (scriptwriter, dir) 1983, Wij komen als vrienden (scriptwriter, dir, prod.) 1984. *Video and television:* Vrijheid (dir, prod.), Lot (script, dir) 1984, Screentest (script, dir) 1985, Cursus voor beginners in de liefde (script with Ivan Wolffers, dir) 1988, Walden Place (script, dir, prod.) 1993, De kunst van het vertellen (dir, prod.) 1999, Liefde is soms lastig, liefste 2002. *Radio:* De stem van mijn vader (scriptwriter) 1996. *Publications:* Geen gewoon Indisch meisje (novel, trans. as Not an Ordinary Indonesian Girl) 1983, Kermis achter kerk (juvenile) 1984, Brieven van Souad (juvenile) 1986, Waar schuil je als het regent? (juvenile) 1987, Lange reizen korte liefdes (novel) 1987, Rio (novel) 1987, Meisjes vechten niet (novel) 1988, Vaders van betekenis (novel) 1989, Gezichten van Zon (poems) 1990, Matabia (juvenile) (Jenny Smelik IBBY Prize 1992) 1990, Vliegers onder het matras (short stories) 1990, Zwartwit in en achter kleuren (poems) 1992, Schilderijen en gedichten (poems) 1992, De honden van Slip (novel, trans. as Slipi's Dogs) 1992, Blauwen noemden ze ons (poems) 1993, De leugen van de kaketoe (novel, trans. as The Cockatoo's Lie) 1993, Op de brug naar de tempel (poems) 1994, Hoop op nieuwe woorden (poems and silk prints) 1995, De geheime plek (juvenile) 1995, Muggen mensen olifanten (short stories) 1995, De smaak van het onbekende (novel) 1995, De droom van de magere tijger (juvenile) 1996, Mooie meisjesmond (novel) 1997, Ver van familie (novel) 1999, Voor altijd moeder (short stories and poems) 2001, Games4Girls (novel) 2001, Amsterdam, A Traveller's Literary Companion 2001, Liefde is soms lastig liefste (poems) 2002, Thuis (art book) 2003, De V van Venus (novel) 2004, Zo groot als Hugo (illustrated biog.) 2004, De kleine krijger (juvenile) 2005. *Honours:* Du Perron Prize 1993. *Address:* c/o Arbeiderspers, Herengracht 376, 1016 CH Amsterdam, The Netherlands. *Website:* www.marionbloem.com.

BLOND, Anthony, MA; British author; b. 20 March 1928, Sale, England; m. Laura Hesketh 1981, one s. *Education:* New Coll., Oxford. *Career:* active with Anthony Blond Ltd 1957–71; Dir, Blond and Brigg Ltd publishers, London 1971–90; with Muller Blond & White. *Publications:* The Publishing Game

1971, Family Business 1978, The Lord My Light 1982, A Book on Books 1983, Blond's Roman Emperors 1994, Carnets d'un Promeneur Anglais en France 1997; contrib. to Literary Review, Spectator. *Address:* 9 rue Thiers, 87300 Bellac, France (home); Muller Blond & White, 55/57 Great Ormond Street, London, WC1N 3HZ, England (office).

BLONDEL, Jean Fernand Pierre, BLitt; French political scientist and writer; *Professorial Fellow, European University Institute;* b. 26 Oct. 1929, Toulon; m. 1st Michele Hadet 1954 (divorced); m. 2nd Teresa Ashton 1982; two d. *Education:* Institut d'etudes politiques, Paris, Univ. of Paris, St Antony's Coll., Oxford, England, Univ. of Manchester, UK. *Career:* Lecturer in Political Institutions, Univ. of Keele, UK 1958–63; Fellow, American Council of Learned Socs 1963–64; Founding Prof. Dept of Govt, Univ. of Essex 1964–83; Co-founder and Dir European Consortium of Political Research 1970–78; Scholar, Russell Sage Foundation 1984–85; Prof. of Political Science, European Univ. Inst., Florence, Italy 1985–94, Professorial Fellow 1994–; Visiting Prof., Univ. of Siena 1995–; mem. American Political Science Asscn, Asscn Française de Science Politique, British Political Studies Asscn. *Publications:* Voters, Parties and Leaders 1963, An Introduction to Conservative Government 1969, Comparative Legislatures 1973, Political Parties 1978, World Leaders 1980, The Discipline of Politics 1982, The Organisation of Governments 1982, Government Ministers in the Contemporary World 1985, Political Leadership 1993, Governing Together (ed. with F. Muller-Rommel) 1993, Comparative Government (second edn) 1995, Party and Government (ed. with M. Cotta) 1996, People and Parliament in the European Union (with R. Sinnott and P. Svensson) 1998, Democracy, Governance and Economic Performance (ed. with I. Marsh and T. Inoguchi) 1999, The Nature of Party Government (ed. with M. Cotta) 2000, Cabinets in Eastern Europe (with F. Muller-Rommel) 2001; contrib. to professional journals. *Honours:* Dr hc (Univ. of Salford) 1990, (Univ. of Essex) 1992, (Catholic Univ. of Louvain) 1992, (Univ. of Turku) 1995; Hon. mem. American Science Acad. 2004–, Swedish Royal Acad. of Sciences; Johan Skytte Prize 2004. *Address:* c/o European University Institute, Via dei Roccettini 9, 50016 San Domenico di Fiesole, Italy (office); 15 Marloes Road, London, W8 6LQ, England (home). *Telephone:* (055) 21-00-38 (office); (20) 7370-6008 (home). *E-mail:* jean.blondel@iue.it.

BLOOM, Harold, PhD; American academic and writer; *Sterling Professor of Humanities and English, Yale University;* b. 11 July 1930, New York; s. of William Bloom and Paula Lev; m. Jeanne Gould 1958; two s. *Education:* Cornell and Yale Univs, Pembroke Coll., Univ. of Cambridge, UK. *Career:* mem. Faculty, Yale Univ. 1955–, Prof. of English 1965–77, DeVane Prof. of Humanities 1974–77, Prof. of Humanities 1977–, Sterling Prof. of Humanities and English 1983–; Visiting Prof., Hebrew Univ. Jerusalem 1959, Breadloaf Summer School 1965–66, Soc. for Humanities, Cornell Univ. 1968–69; Visiting Univ. Prof., New School of Social Research, New York 1982–84; Charles Eliot Norton Prof. of Poetry, Harvard Univ. 1987–88; Berg Visiting Prof. of English, New York Univ. 1988–2004; mem. American Acad. and Inst. of Arts and Letters, American Philosophical Soc.; Fulbright Fellow 1955, Guggenheim Fellow 1962. *Publications:* Shelley's Mythmaking 1959, The Visionary Company 1961, Blake's Apocalypse 1963, Commentary to Blake 1965, Yeats 1970, The Ringers in the Tower 1971, The Anxiety of Influence 1973, Wallace Stevens: The Poems of Our Climate 1977, A Map of Misreading 1975, Kabbalah and Criticism 1975, Poetry and Repression 1976, Figures of Capable Imagination 1976, The Flight to Lucifer: A Gnostic Fantasy 1979, Agon: Towards a Theory of Revisionism 1981, The Breaking of the Vessels 1981, The Strong Light of the Canonical 1987, Freud: Transference and Authority 1988, Poetics of Influence: New and Selected Criticism 1988, Ruin the Sacred Truths 1989, The Book of J 1990, The American Religion 1991, The Western Canon 1994, Omens of Millennium 1996, Shakespeare: The Invention of the Human 1998, How to Read and Why 2000, Stories and Poems for Extremely Intelligent Children of All Ages 2000, Genius: A Mosaic of One Hundred Exemplary Creative Minds 2002, Hamlet: Poem Unlimited 2003, Best Poems of the English Language: Chaucer to Hart Crane 2003, Where Shall Wisdom be Found? 2004, The Names Divine: Jesus and Yahweh 2005, Yetziat: Fallen Angels, Demons and Devils 2006. *Honours:* Dr hc (St Michael's Coll.), (Univ. of Rome), (Univ. of Bologna), (Univ. of Coimbra), (Boston Coll.), (Yeshiva Univ.), (Univ. of Mass. at Dartmouth), (Univ. of Buenos Aires); Newton Arvin Award 1967; Melville Cane Award, Poetry Soc. of America 1970; Zabel Prize, American Inst. of Arts and Letters 1982; MacArthur Foundation Fellowship 1985; Christian Gauss Prize 1989, Gold Medal for Criticism, American Acad. of Arts and Letters 1999, Int. Prize of Catalonia 2002, Alfonso Reyes Prize (Mexico) 2003, Hans Christian Anderson Bicentennial Prize (Denmark) 2005. *Address:* Department of English, WHC 202, Yale University, 63 High Street, POB 208302, New Haven, CT 06520-8302, USA (office). *Telephone:* (203) 432-0029 (office). *E-mail:* harold.bloom@yale.edu (office). *Website:* www.yale.edu/english (office).

BLOOM, Valerie, DipEd, BA, MA; British/Jamaican poet and novelist; b. 15 Sept. 1956, Clarendon, Jamaica; d. of John Wright and Edna Wright; m. Douglas Bloom; one s. two d. *Education:* Univ. of Kent, Canterbury. *Career:* emigrated to England 1979; librarian, steel band instructor, arts officer, teacher, the Arvon Foundation, resident poet for numerous orgs internationally; mem. Bd Poetry Book Soc. *Radio:* producer and contributor to various poetry and literature programmes. *Television:* various schools and entertainment programmes. *Publications:* poems: Touch Mi! Tell Mi! 1983, Duppy Jamboree and Other Jamaican Poems 1992, Fruits (Smarties Bronze Award) 1997, Ackee, Breadfruit, Callaloo: An Edible Alphabet 1999, Let me Touch the

Sky 2000, New Baby 2000, The World is Sweet 2000, Hot Like Fire 2002, Whoop an' Shout 2003, A Twist in the Tale 2004; novel: Surprising Joy 2003; editor: On a Camel to the Moon and other poems about journeys 2001, One River, Many Creeks: Poems from Around the World 2003; contribs to numerous anthologies. *Honours:* Hon. MA (Univ. of Kent); Community Award for Literature, Voice newspaper. *Literary Agent:* c/o Clare Pearson, West Hill House, 6 Swains Lane, London, N6 6QU, England. *Telephone:* (20) 7700-7763. *Fax:* (20) 7700-7866. *E-mail:* clare@eddisonpearson.com. *Website:* www.eddisonpearson.com. *Address:* c/o Pan Macmillan Ltd, 20 New Wharf Road, London, N1 9RR, England. *Telephone:* (20) 7014-6000. *Fax:* (20) 7014-6001. *E-mail:* vblo@aol.com (home). *Website:* www.valbloom.co.uk.

BLOUNT, Roy Alton, Jr, (Noah Sanders, C. R. Ways), BA, MA; American writer, poet and screenwriter; b. 4 Oct. 1941, Indianapolis, IN; m. 1st Ellen Pearson 1964 (divorced 1973); one s. one d.; m. 2nd Joan Ackermann 1976 (divorced 1990). *Education:* Vanderbilt Univ., Harvard Univ. *Career:* staff, Decatur-DeKalb News, GA 1958–59, Morning Telegraph, New York 1961, New Orleans Times-Picayune 1963; reporter, editorial writer and columnist, Atlanta Journal 1966–68; staff writer, Sports Illustrated 1968–74, Assoc. Ed. 1974–75; Contributing Ed., Atlantic Monthly 1983–. *Publications:* About Three Bricks Shy of a Load (revised edn as About Three Bricks Shy–and the Load Filled Up: The Story of the Greatest Football Team Ever) 1974, Crackers: This Whole Many-Sided Thing of Jimmy, More Carters, Ominous Little Animals, Sad-Singing Women, My Daddy and Me 1980, One Fell Soup, or, I'm Just a Bug on the Windshield of Life 1982, What Men Don't Tell Women 1984, Not Exactly What I Had in Mind 1985, It Grows on You: A Hair-Raising Survey of Human Plumage 1986, Soupsongs/Webster's Ark 1987, Now, Where Were We? 1989, First Hubby 1990, Camels Are Easy, Comedy's Hard 1991, Roy Blount's Book of Southern Humor 1994, Be Sweet: A Conditional Love Story 1998, If Only You Knew How Much I Smell You 1998, I Am Puppy, Hear Me Yap 2000, Am I Pig Enough For You Yet? 2001, Robert E. Lee 2003, I Am the Cat, Don't Forget That 2004, Long Time Leaving: Dispatches From Up South 2007; contrib. to many anthologies and periodicals. *Literary Agent:* ICM, 40 W 57th Street, New York, NY 10019, USA.

BLUME, Judy, BS; American writer; b. 12 Feb. 1938, Elizabeth, NJ; d. of Rudolph and Esther (née Rosenfeld) Sussman; m. 1st John M. Blume 1959 (divorced 1975); one s. one d.; m. 2nd George Cooper 1987; one step-d. *Education:* New York Univ. *Career:* founder and Trustee The Kids Fund 1981; mem. PEN Club, Authors' Guild, Nat. Coalition Against Censorship, Soc. of Children's Book Writers. *Publications:* juvenile fiction: The One in the Middle Is the Green Kangaroo 1969, Iggie's House 1970, Are You There God? It's Me, Margaret (Outstanding Children's Book) 1970, Then Again, Maybe I Won't 1971, Freckle Juice 1971, It's Not the End of the World 1972, Tales of a Fourth Grade Nothing 1972, Otherwise Known as Sheila the Great 1972, Deenie 1973, Blubber 1974, Forever 1975, Starring Sally J. Freedman as Herself 1977, Superfudge 1980, Tiger Eyes 1981, The Pain and the Great One 1984, Just As Long As We're Together 1987, Fudge-a-mania 1990, Here's to You, Rachel Robinson 1993, Summer Sisters 1998, Places I Never Meant To Be (ed.) 1999, Double Fudge 2002; adult fiction: Wifey 1978, Smart Women 1983; nonfiction: Letters to Judy: What Kids Wish They Could Tell You 1986, The Judy Blume Memory Book 1988. *Honours:* Hon. LHD (Kean Coll.) 1987; Chicago Public Library Carl Sandburg Freedom to Read Award 1984, American Civil Liberties Union Award 1986, American Library Asscn Margaret A. Edwards Award for Lifetime Achievement 1996; Nat. Book Foundation Medal for Distinguished Contribution to American Letters 2004. *Literary Agent:* Harold Ober Associates, 425 Madison Avenue, New York, NY 10017-1110, USA. *Website:* www.judyblume.com.

BLUMENTHAL, Michael Charles, BA, JD; American writer, poet and academic; b. 8 March 1949, Vineland, NJ; one s. *Education:* SUNY at Binghamton, Cornell University. *Career:* Bingham Distinguished Poet-in-Residence, University of Louisville, 1982; Briggs-Copeland Lecturer, Asst Prof. of Poetry, 1983–88, Assoc. Prof. of English, Dir of Creative Writing, 1988–93, Harvard University; Senior Fulbright Lecturer in American Literature, Eötvös Lorand University, Budapest, 1992–95; Distinguished Visiting Writer-in-Residence, Boise State University, 1996; Assoc. Prof. of English, University of Haifa, 1996; Visiting Writer, Southwest Texas State University, 1997–98; Distinguished Visiting Poet-in-Residence, Wichita State University, 1999; Distinguished Writer-in-Residence, Santa Clara University, CA, 2001; Lecturer in Creative Non-Fiction, American University of Paris, 2001–02; Distinguished Visiting Prof. of American Literature, Université Jean Monnet, Saint-Etienne, France, 2001–; mem. Associated Writing Programs; PEN American Center; Poetry Society of America; Poets and Writers. *Publications:* Sympathetic Magic, 1980; Days We Would Rather Know, 1984; Laps, 1984; Against Romance, 1987; The Wages of Goodness, 1992; To Wed & To Woo: Poets on Marriage (ed.), 1992; Weinstock Among the Dying, 1993; When History Enters the House: Central European Essays, 1998; Dusty Angel, 1999; All My Mothers and Fathers, 2002. Contributions: Reviews, quarterlies and journals. *Honours:* First Book Prize, Water Mark Poets of North America, 1980; Juniper Prize, University of Massachusetts, 1984; Lavan Younger Poets Prize, Acad. of American Poets, 1986; Guggenheim Fellowship, 1989; Harold U. Ribelow Prize for Jewish Fiction, Hadassah magazine, 1994. *E-mail:* mcblume@attglobal.net.

BLUNDELL, Sue, BA, DipContEd, PhD; British lecturer and writer; b. 4 Aug. 1947, Manchester, England. *Education:* Westfield Coll., London, Goldsmiths Coll., London. *Career:* part-time Lecturer, Birkbeck Coll., London 1979–2004;

Asst Lecturer of Classical Civilization, Open Univ. 1986–; academic tutor, Architectural Asscn, London 1994–. *Publications:* The Origins of Civilisation in Greek and Roman Thought 1986, Women in Ancient Greece 1995, The Sacred and the Feminine in Ancient Greece (ed. with Margaret Williamson) 1998, Women in Classical Athens 1998, Epicurus on Happiness (dramatic monologue, performed at British Museum) 2001; contrib. to Women's Dress in the Ancient Greek World 2002, Greek Art in View: Studies in Honour of Brian Sparkes 2004. *Address:* 59b Goodge Street, London, W1T 1TJ, England. *Telephone:* (20) 7580-4917. *E-mail:* sblundell@aaschool.ac.uk.

BLY, Robert Elwood, MA; American writer and poet; b. 23 Dec. 1926, Madison, Minn.; s. of Jacob Thomas Bly and Alice Bly (née Aws); m. 1st Carolyn McLean 1955 (divorced 1979); m. 2nd Ruth Counsell 1980; five c. *Education:* Harvard Univ. and Univ. of Iowa. *Career:* served USN 1944–46; founder and Ed. The Fifties 1958–, later The Sixties and Seventies Press; f. American Writers Against the Vietnam War 1966. *Publications include:* poems: Silence in the Snowy Fields 1962, The Light Around the Body 1967, Chrysanthemums 1967, Ducks 1968, The Morning Glory: Another Thing That Will Never Be My Friend 1969, The Teeth Mother Naked at Last 1971, Poems for Tennessee (with William Stafford and William Matthews) 1971, Christmas Eve Service at Midnight at St Michael's 1972, Water Under the Earth 1972, The Dead Seal Near McClure's Beach 1973, Sleepers Joining Hands 1973, Jumping out of Bed 1973, The Hockey Poem 1974, Point Reyes Poems 1974, Old Man Rubbing his Eyes 1975, The Loon 1977, Visiting Emily Dickinson's Grave and Other Poems 1979, This Tree Will Be Here for a Thousand Years 1979, Finding An Old Ant Mansion 1981, The Man in the Black Coat Turns 1982, Four Ramages 1983, The Whole Moisty Night 1983, Out of the Rollling Ocean 1984, Mirabai Versions 1984, In the Month of May 1985, A Love of Minute Particulars 1985, Loving a Woman in Two Worlds 1985, Selected Poems (ed.) 1986, The Moon on the Fencepost 1988, The Apple Found in the Plowing 1989, What Have I Ever Lost By Dying?: Collected Prose Poems 1993, Gratitude to Old Teachers 1993, Meditations on the Insatiable Soul 1994, Morning Poems 1997, Eating the Honey of Words: New and Selected Poems 1999, The Best American Poetry (ed.) 1999, The Night Abraham Called to the Stars 2001; prose poems: The Morning Glory 1973, This Body is Made of Eating the Honey of Words: New and Selected Poems 1999, The Best American Poetry (ed.) 1999, This Body is Made of Camphor and Gopherwood 1977; prose: Iron John 1990; criticism: Leaping Poetry 1975, Forty Poems Touching on Recent American History (ed.) 1967, A Poetry Reading Against the Vietnam War 1966, The Sea and the Honeycomb 1966, The Soul is Here for its Own Joy 1995; trans. of vols of poetry from Swedish, Norwegian, German, Spanish and Hindi. *Honours:* Fulbright Award 1956–57, Amy Lowell Fellow 1964–65, Guggenheim Fellow 1965–66, Rockefeller Foundation Fellow 1967, Nat. Book Award in Poetry 1968. *Address:* 1904 Girard Avenue South, Minneapolis, MN 55403, USA.

BLYTH, Alan, MA; British music critic and editor; b. 27 July 1929, London, England; m. Ursula Zumloh. *Education:* Univ. of Oxford. *Career:* critic, The Times 1963–76; Assoc. Ed., Opera 1967–84; Music Ed., Encyclopaedia Britannica 1971–76; critic, Daily Telegraph 1976–89; mem. Critics' Circle, Garrick Club. *Publications:* The Enjoyment of Opera 1969, Colin Davis: A Short Biography 1972, Opera on Record (ed.) 1979, Remembering Britten 1980, Wagner's Ring: An Introduction 1980, Opera on Record 2 (ed.) 1983, Opera on Record 3 (ed.) 1984, Song on Record (ed.) Vol. 1 1986, Vol. 2 1988, Choral Music on Record 1990, Opera on CD 1992, Opera on Video 1995, Heddle Nash: The Recorded Legacy 2007; contrib. entries on singers to New Grove Dictionary 1980, 2000; contrib. to Gramophone, BBC. *Address:* c/o Paul Campion, 20 City Harbour, 8 Selsdon Way, London, E14 9GR, England (office).

BLYTH, Myrna, BA; American magazine editor; *Commissioner, President's Commission on White House Fellows;* b. 22 March 1939, New York; d. of Benjamin Greenstein and Betty Greenstein (née Austin); m. Jeffrey Blyth 1962; two s. *Education:* Bennington Coll. *Career:* Sr Ed. Datebook 1960–62, Ingenue 1963–68; Book Ed. Family Health 1968–71; Book and Fiction Ed., then Assoc. Ed. Family Circle 1972–78, Exec. Ed. 1978–81; Ed.-in-Chief Ladies' Home Journal 1981–2002, Sr Vice-Pres. and Publishing Dir 1987–2002, Ed. Dir Meredith Corpn New York magazines 2002–03, Editorial Dir New Product Devt, Meredith Publishing Group 2002–03; Founding Ed.-in-Chief and Publishing Dir More magazine 1998; currently Commr on Pres.'s Comm. on White House Fellows; mem. Advisory Cttee for the Office of Research in Women's Health, NIH; mem. Exec. Bd American Soc. of Magazine Eds; mem. Bd Govs Overseas Press Club, Child Care Action Campaign, Advisory Bd ThirdAge Media and Research America; mem. Authors' Guild, Women's Media Group; fmr mem. Advisory Bd; fmr Pres. New York Women in Communications Inc.; mem. Del. to UN Fourth World Conf. on Women, Beijing. *Publications include:* For Better and For Worse, Cousin Suzanne, Spin Sisters – How the Women of the Media Sell Unhappiness and Liberalism to the Women of America 2004, How to Raise an American 2007; contrib. of short stories and non-fiction articles to New Yorker, New York, McCall's, Redbook, The Reader's Digest. *Honours:* Matrix Award, New York Women in Communications Inc. 1988, Magazine of the Year Award, Clarion Award 1984, 1989, MagazineWeek Publishing Excellence Award 1991, Henry Johnson Fisher Award, Magazine Publr Asscn 1999, Women of Achievement Award, New York City Comm. on Status of Women 2000, Matrix Award, New York Women in Communications, Headliner Award, Women in Communications, Inc., Publishing Exec. of the Year Award, Advertising Age magazine 2001,

Innovator Award, Isis Fund, Soc. for Women's Health Research, Athena Award, Partnership for Women's Health, Columbia Univ. *Address:* c/o Meredith Corporation, 125 Park Avenue, New York, NY 10017-5529, USA. *Website:* www.howtoraiseanamerican.com.

BLYTHE, Ronald George, FRSL, DLitt; British writer; b. 6 Nov. 1922, Acton, Suffolk, England; s. of George and Matilda Blythe. *Education:* St Peter's and St Gregory's School, Sudbury, St Edmundsbury. *Career:* Lay Canon, St Edmundsbury Cathedral 2003; mem. Soc. of Authors, John Clare Soc. (pres.), Fabian Soc., Kilvert Soc., Robert Bloomfield Soc., The Woodland Trust (patron). *Films:* Akenfield 1974; art films for BBC. *Publications:* A Treasonable Growth 1960, Immediate Possession 1961, The Age of Illusion 1963, Akenfield 1969, William Hazlett: Selected Writings (ed.) 1970, The View in Winter 1979, From the Headlands 1982, The Stories of Ronald Blythe 1985, Divine Landscapes 1986, Each Returning Day 1989, Word from Wormingford 1997, First Friends 1998, Going to Meet George 1998, Talking About John Clare 1999, Out of the Valley 2000, The Circling Year 2001, Talking to the Neighbours 2002, The Assassin 2004, Borderland 2004, A Writer's Day Book 2006; other: critical studies of Jane Austen, Thomas Hardy, Leo Tolstoy, Henry James, Literature of the Second World War; ed. of various authors' works; contrib. to Observer, Sunday Times, New York Times, Listener, Atlantic Monthly, London Magazine, Tablet, New Statesman, Bottegue Oscure, Guardian. *Honours:* Hon. MA (East Anglia) 1991, Hon. MLitt (Lambeth) 2001, Hon. DLitt (Anglia Ruskin Univ.) 2001, (Essex) 2002; Heinemann Award 1969, Soc. of Authors Travel Scholarship 1970, Angel Prize for Literature 1986, Benson Medal for Literature 2006. *Address:* Bottengoms Farm, Wormingford, Colchester, Essex, England. *Telephone:* (1206) 271308.

BOADEN, Helen, BA; British broadcasting executive; *Director, BBC News;* b. 1 March 1956, Essex; d. of William John Boaden and Barbara Mary Boaden; m. Stephen Burley 1994. *Education:* Univ. of Sussex. *Career:* Care Asst, Hackney Social Services, London 1978; Reporter, Radio WBAI, NY, USA 1979, Radio Tees and Radio Aire 1980–83; Producer, BBC Radio Leeds 1983–85; Reporter, File on 4, Radio 4 1985–91, Brass Tacks, BBC 2 1985–91; Presenter, Woman's Hour, Radio 4 1985–91, Verdict, Channel 4 1991–; Ed., File on 4, Radio 4 1991–94; Head of Network Current Affairs, BBC Manchester (first woman in position) 1994–97; Head of Business Programmes, BBC News 1997, Head of Current Affairs and Business Programmes 1998–2000; Controller, BBC Radio 4 2000–04, BBC 7 2002–04; Dir BBC News 2004–; Chair. Radio Acad. 2003–. *Honours:* Hon. doctorates (E Anglia, Sussex, York); Sony Gold Award (File on 4 investigation into AIDS in Africa in 1987, Sony Gold Award for File on 4 investigation into bullying in Feltham Young Offenders Inst. 1993, Radio Station of the Year 2003, 2004. *Address:* BBC, Television Centre, Wood Lane, London, W12 7RJ, England (office). *Telephone:* (20) 8743-8000 (office). *Website:* www.bbc.co.uk (office).

BOARDMAN, Sir John, Kt, MA, FSA, FBA; British archaeologist; *Professor Emeritus of Classical Archaeology and Art, University of Oxford;* b. 20 Aug. 1927, s. of the late Frederick Boardman and Clare Wells; m. Sheila Stanford 1952; one s. one d. *Education:* Chigwell School and Magdalene Coll., Cambridge. *Career:* Asst Dir British School, Athens 1952–55; Asst Keeper, Ashmolean Museum, Oxford 1955–59; Reader in Classical Archaeology, Univ. of Oxford 1959–78, Lincoln Prof. of Classical Archaeology and Art 1978–94, Hon. Fellow 1995, now Prof. Emer.; Fellow, Merton Coll. Oxford 1973–78, Hon. Fellow 1978–, Sub-Warden 1975–78; Prof. of Ancient History, Royal Acad. of Arts 1989–; conducted excavations on Chios 1953–55, Crete 1964–65, in Tocra, Libya 1964–65; Visiting Prof., Columbia Univ. 1965; Geddes-Harrower Prof., Univ. of Aberdeen 1974; Fellow, Inst. of Etruscan Studies, Florence 1983, Austrian and German Archaeological Insts; Foreign mem. Royal Danish Acad.; Assoc. mem. Acad. des Inscriptions et des Belles Lettres, Institut de France; Corresp. mem. Bavarian Acad. of Sciences; Foreign mem. American Philosophical Soc., Accad. dei Lincei, Rome, Russian Acad. of Sciences. *Publications include:* Cretan Collection in Oxford 1961, Island Gems 1963, Archaic Greek Gems 1968, Athenian Black Figure Vases 1974, Escarabeos de Piedra de Ibiza 1984, The Oxford History of the Classical World (with others) 1986, Athenian Red Figure Vases: Classical period 1989, Oxford History of Classical Art 1993, The Diffusion of Classical Art in Antiquity 1994, Greek Sculpture, Later Classical 1995, Runciman Prixoe 1995, Early Greek Vase Painting 1997, Persia and the West 2000, The History of Greek Vases 2001, Greek Gems and Finger Rings 2001, The Archaeology of Nostalgia 2002, Classical Phoenician Scarabs 2003, The World of Ancient Art 2006; articles in learned journals. *Honours:* Hon. RA; Hon. MRIA; Dr hc (Athens) 1991, (Sorbonne) 1994; Kenyon Medal (British Acad.) 1995. *Address:* 11 Park Street, Woodstock, Oxford, OX20 1SJ, England (home). *Telephone:* (1993) 811259 (home). *Fax:* (1865) 278082 (office). *E-mail:* john.boardman@ashmus.ox.ac.uk (office).

BOAST, Philip James; British writer; b. 30 April 1952, London, England; m. Rosalind Thorpe 1981, two s. one d. *Education:* Mill Hill School. *Publications:* The Assassinators, 1976; London's Child, 1987; The Millionaire, 1989; Watersmeet, 1990; Pride, 1991; The Londons of London, 1992; Gloria, 1993; London's Daughter, 1994; City, 1994; The Foundling, 1995; Resurrection, 1996; Deus, 1997; Sion, 1998; Era, 2000. Contributions: Science Fiction Monthly. *Address:* Upper Thornehill, 27 Church Road, St Marychurch, Torquay, Devon TQ1 4QY, England. *E-mail:* philipboast@beeb.net.

BOBIS, Merlinda Carullo, PhD; Philippine/Australian poet, novelist and dramatist; *Senior Lecturer, Faculty of Creative Arts, University of Wollon-*

gong; b. 25 Nov. 1959, Albay; d. of Nicolas Bobis and Amprao Carullo Bobis; m. *Education:* Bicol Univ. High School, Aquinias Univ., Legaspi City, Univ. of Sto Tomas, Univ. of Wollongong, Australia. *Career:* Lecturer in Creative Writing in Australia and the Philippines for over 17 years; currently Sr Lecturer Faculty of Creative Arts, Univ. of Wollongong; regularly performs plays and poetry on radio and at festivals. *Plays include:* Rita's Lullaby (Ian Reed Radio Drama Prize) 1995. *Publications:* Cantata of the Warrior Woman Daragang Magayon (epic poem) 1993, Rituals (poems) 1990, Flight is Song on Four Winds (poems) 1990, Summer Was A Fast Train Without Terminals (poems) 1998, Rita's Lullaby (poetic drama) (Prix Italia, Australian Writers' Guild Award) 1998, White Turtle (short stories) (Philippine Nat. Book Award for Fiction 2000) 1999, Fish-Hair Woman (novel), Banana Heart Summer (novel) 2005. *Honours:* Steele Rudd Award for Best Collection of Australian Short Stories 2000, Ministry for the Arts Writers' Fellowship 2000. *Address:* Faculty of Creative Arts, University of Wollongong, Wollongong, NSW 2522, Australia. *E-mail:* merlinda_bobis@uow.edu.au.

BOCEK, Alois (see Vanicek, Zdenek)

BOCHEŃSKI, Jacek; Polish writer, journalist and translator; b. 29 July 1926, Lvov; m.; one d. *Education:* State Coll. of Theatrical Arts, Warsaw. *Career:* Co-Founder and Ed. Zapis 1977–81; Pres. Polish PEN Club 1996–99. *Radio:* Caprices of an Old Gentleman (weekly five-minute slot) 2001–02. *Television and stage plays:* Taboo, After the Collapse. *Publications include:* novels: Farewell to Miss Syngilu 1960, Divine Julius – Notes of an Antiquary (also translated into German) 1961, Taboo 1965, Naso Poet 1969, After the Collapse (Solidarity Prize 1987) 1987, Caprices of an Old Gentleman 2004; stories: Violets Are Unlucky 1949, Bloody Italian Rarities 1982, Retro 1990; travel book: Farewell to Miss Syngilu or the Elephant and the Polish Question; trans: Tabu 1960, Der Täter heißt Ovid 1975, État de Pesanteur 1995; several essays and contribs to magazines on media ethics and the civic responsibilities of cultural figures. *Address:* ul. Sonaty 6 m. 801, 02-744 Warsaw, Poland (home). *Telephone:* (22) 8435853 (home). *E-mail:* jacek .bochenski@poczta.gazeta.pl (home).

BÖCK, Emmi; German writer and folklorist; b. 17 June 1932, Zweibrücken; d. of Robert Böck and Klara Heist. *Education:* Gnadenthal Coll., Ingolstadt and Univ. of Munich. *Career:* freelance book reviewer and writer 1961–; Researcher for Bavarian State Foundation (Bayer Landesstiftung) on collection of folklore from Oberpfalz 1980, from Middle-Franconia 1989; research on regional collection of folklore, Neuburg/Donau 1988. *Publications include:* Ingolstadt. Bildband 1966, Sagen und Legenden aus Ingolstadt und Umgebung 1973, Die Hallertau. Bildband 1973, Sagen aus der Hallertau 1975, Sagen aus Niederbayern 1977, Sagen aus Eichstätt und Umgebung 1977, Regensburger Stadtsagen 1982, Bayerische Legenden 1984, Sagen aus der Oberpfalz, Aus der Literatur 1986, Sitzweil, Oberpfälzer Sagen aus dem Volksmund 1987, Sagen aus dem Neuburg-Schrobenhauser Land 1989, Bayerische Schwänke 1991, Köschinger Sagenbiachl 1993, Sagen aus Mittelfranken. Aus der Literatur 1995, Kleine Regensburger Volkskunde 1996, Legenden und Mirakel aus Ingolstadt und Umgebung 1998, Baustellen des Himmels (co-author) 2001, Nürnberger Stadtsagen 2002. *Honours:* Bundesverdienstkreuz 1981, Bayerischer Verdienstorden 1987; Kulturpreis der Stadt Ingolstadt 2000.

BOCOCK, Robert James, PhD; British sociologist, writer and lecturer; b. 29 Sept. 1940, Lincoln, Lincolnshire, England. *Education:* University of London, Brunel University. *Career:* Lecturer in Sociology, Brunel University, 1966–79, Open University, Buckinghamshire, 1979–; mem. Asscn of University Teachers; British Sociological Asscn. *Publications:* Ritual in Industrial Society, 1974; Freud and Modern Society, 1976; An Introduction to Sociology, 1980; Sigmund Freud, 1983; Religion and Ideology (ed.), 1985; Hegemony, 1986; Consumption, 1993. Contributions: journals.

BODANIS, David; American academic and writer; b. Chicago; m.; two c. *Education:* studied mathematics, physics and economics Univ. of Chicago. *Career:* copy boy, Int. Herald Tribune, Paris 1977; sr assoc. mem., St Antony's Coll., Oxford 1988, Lecturer in Social Science, Univ. of Oxford 1991–97; business consultant mid-1990s–, working with companies, including Accenture, BMW, General Motors, Microsoft, Pfizer and Shell, and with governments; gives lectures and workshops. *Television:* The Secret Family (documentary, Discovery Channel and CBC). *Publications:* Being Human: A Day in the Life of the Human Body 1984, The Body Book: A Fantastic Voyage to the World Within 1984, The Secret House 1986, Web of Words: The Ideas Behind Politics 1988, The Secret Garden 1993, The Secret Family: 24 Hours Inside the Mysterious World of Our Minds and Bodies 1997, E=mc2: A Biography of the World's Most Famous Equation 2000, Electric Universe: How Electricity Switched on the Modern World (Royal Soc. Aventis Prize 2006) 2005, Passionate Minds: The Great Enlightenment Love Affair 2006; contrib. to journals, including Popular Science. *E-mail:* contact.david@virgin.net. *Website:* www.davidbodanis.com.

BODEN, Group Captain Anthony Norman, BA; British writer; b. 21 April 1938, Altrincham, Cheshire, England; m. Elizabeth Anne Miles; one s. one d. *Education:* Open Univ. *Career:* RAF, retiring in the rank of Group Capt. 1957–89; Festival Admin. Three Choirs Festival, Gloucester 1989–99; mem. Ivor Gurney Soc. (Chair. 1995–2002), Ivor Gurney Estate (Trustee), Edward Thomas Fellowship, Friends of the Dymock Poets. *Publications:* Stars in a Dark Night: The Letters of Ivor Gurney to the Chapman Family 1986, F. W. Harvey: Soldier Poet 1988, Three Choirs: A History of the Festival 1992, The

Parrys of the Golden Vale 1998, Thomas Tomkins: The Last Elizabethan 2005. *Honours:* Officer (Brother) of the Order of St John 1987. *Address:* Chosen Hay, The Green, Churchdown, Gloucester, GL3 2LF, England. *Website:* www .anthonyboden.co.uk.

BODEN, Margaret Ann, OBE, ScD, PhD, FBA; British cognitive scientist and academic; *Research Professor of Cognitive Science, University of Sussex*; b. 26 Nov. 1936, London; d. of Leonard F. Boden and Violet Dorothy Boden (née Dawson); m. John R. Spiers 1967 (divorced 1981); one s. one d. *Education:* Newnham Coll., Cambridge (Major Scholar) and Harvard Grad. School (Harkness Fellow). *Career:* Lecturer in Philosophy, Univ. of Birmingham 1959–65; Lecturer, then Reader in Philosophy and Psychology, Univ. of Sussex 1965–80, Prof. 1980–, Founding Dean School of Cognitive and Computing Sciences 1987, Research Prof. of Cognitive Science 2002–; Curator Univ. of London Inst. for Advanced Study 1995–; co-founder, Harvester Press Ltd 1970–, Dir 1970–85; Vice-Pres. British Acad. 1989–91, Royal Inst. of GB 1993–95, Chair. of Council 1993–95, mem. of Council 1992–95; mem. Advisory Bd for the Research Councils 1989–90, Academia Europaea 1993–, Animal Procedures Cttee 1995–99; Fellow, American Asscn for Artificial Intelligence 1993–, European Coordinating Cttee for Artificial Intelligence 1999–. *Publications:* Purposive Explanation in Psychology 1972, Artificial Intelligence and Natural Man 1977, Piaget 1979, Minds and Mechanisms 1981, Computer Models of Mind 1988, Artificial Intelligence in Psychology 1989, The Philosophy of Artificial Intelligence (ed.) 1990, Dimensions of Creativity (ed.) 1994, Artificial Intelligence and the Mind (co-ed.) 1994, The Philosophy of Artificial Life (ed.) 1996, Artificial Intelligence (ed.) 1996, The Creative Mind (2nd edn) 2004, Mind as Machine 2006. *Honours:* Hon. DSc (Sussex) 2001, (Bristol) 2002, Hon. DUniv (Open) 2004. *Address:* c/o Centre for Research in Cognitive Science, University of Sussex, Falmer, Brighton, BN1 9QJ, England (office). *Telephone:* (1273) 678386 (office). *Fax:* (1273) 671320 (office). *E-mail:* maggieb@cogs.susx.ac.uk (office). *Website:* www.cogs.susx.ac.uk (office).

BØDKER, Cecil; Danish novelist, poet and playwright; b. 1927, Fredericia. *Career:* apprenticed and qualified as a silversmith 1948; worked for four years for Georg Jensen, Copenhagen and Markstroem's, Uppsala, Sweden; turned to writing full time in mid-1950s. *Publications:* poetry: Luseblomster (Edith Rhodes grant 1956) 1955; juvenile: Silas og den sorte hoppe 1967, Silas og Ben-Godik 1969, Timmerlis 1969, Leoparden 1970, Dimma Gole 1971, Silas fanger et firspand 1972, Silas stifter familie 1976, Silas på Sebastiansbjerget 1977, Silas og Hestekragen mødes igen 1978, Silas møder Matti 1979, Syv år for Rakel 1982, Silas – livet i bjergbyen 1984, Silas – de blå heste 1985, Silas – Sebastians arv 1986, Ægget der voksede 1987, Silas – ulverejsen 1988, Silas – testamentet 1992, Silas og flodrøverne 1998, Silas – fortrøstningens tid 2001; fiction: Salthandlerskens hus 1972, Marias barn. Drengen 1983, Marias barn. Manden 1984, Maria fra Nazaret 1988, Hungerbarnet 1990, Men i hvert fald i live 1995, Siffrine 2003; also short stories, radio and theatre plays. *Honours:* The Critics' Award 1961, Ministry of Culture Children's Book Prize 1968, Hans Christian Andersen Award 1976, The Golden Laurels 1985, Danish Acad. Grand Prize 1998. *Address:* c/o Gyldendal, Klareboderne 3, 1001 Copenhagen K, Denmark. *E-mail:* gyldendal@gyldendal.dk. *Website:* www .gyldendal.dk.

BOENISCH, Peter H.; German journalist; b. 4 May 1927, Berlin; s. of Konstantin Boenisch and Eva Boenisch (née Premysler); m. 1st Victoria von Schack 1959 (divorced); m. 2nd Susanne Fischer (divorced); m. 3rd Julia Schramm 1998; one d. *Education:* Dr Hugo Eckner Coll., Berlin Univ. *Career:* Political Ed. Die Neue Zeitung 1945–49; Ed. Tagespost 1949–52; Special Asst to Pres. Nordwest-Deutsche-Rundfunk 1952–55; Ed. Kindler Publishing Co. 1955–59, Springer Publishing Corpn (Berliner Illustrierte, Bild-Zeitung, Bild am Sonntag) 1959–81; Chair. Ed. Bd Die Welt 1978–81; fmr Vice-Chair. Axel Springer Group, responsible for planning and Devt; Chief Govt Spokesman and Leader, Fed. Press and Information Office 1983–85; Man. Dir of Burda Magazines 1986–92; mem. Bd of Dirs Axel Springer Verlag 1999. *Honours:* Bundesverdienstkreuz, Bayerischer Verdienstorden 1976, Order of Leopold II (Belgium) 1985. *Address:* Kaltenbrunnerstr. 14, 83703 Gmund, Germany.

BOESCHE-ZACHAROW, Tilly; German writer and publisher; b. 31 Jan. 1928, Elbing; d. of Ernst Großkopf and Maria Großkopf; m. Hans Boesche 1950 (divorced 1963); two s. two d. *Education:* in Berlin. *Career:* fmr clerk and bookseller; writer 1950–; ed. and publr 1980–, ed. of four children's books, fairy tales, books on religious philosophy, feminism, etc.; has written 300 romantic thrillers (under various pseudonyms including Eva Trojan, Ilka Korff, Eve Jean, etc.). *Publications include:* Dream of Jalna 2001, The Small Line Between Sky and Water 2001, The Rabbi 2001, Pintus of Seehausen 2001, O Israel, They Want to Kill You 2001. *Honours:* Hon. DLitt (World Univ., AZ) 1987; Dr hc 1981; Dip. di merito, Dip. d'Honore, European Banner of Arts 1984; Studiosis Humanitas 1985. *Address:* Laurinsteig 14A, 13465 Berlin, Germany. *Telephone:* (30) 4019009.

BOFF, Leonardo Genezio Darci, DPhil, DTheol; Brazilian academic, writer and editor; b. 14 Dec. 1938, Concórdia, SC; s. of Mansueto Boff and Regina Fontana Boff. *Education:* Inst. Teológico Franciscano, Petrópolis and Nat. Univ. of Rio de Janeiro. *Career:* Prof. of Systematic Theology and of Franciscan Spirituality, Inst. Teológico Franciscano, Petrópolis, Rio de Janeiro 1971–92, also Prof. of Theology of Liberation; Adviser to Latin American Conf. of Religions (CLAR) 1971–80, to Nat. Conf. of Brazilian Bishops (CNBB) 1971–80; mem. Editorial Bd of Revista Eclesiástica Brasileira 1971–92; mem. Bd of Dirs Vozes publishing house 1971–92; Pres.

Bd of Eds, Theology and Liberation collection 1985–; mem. Editorial Bd Concilium; ordered by Roman Curia to begin unspecified period of 'obedient silence' 1985. *Publications:* Jesus Christ Liberator 1971, Die Kirche als Sakrament im Horizont der Welterfahrung 1972, Theology of Captivity and Liberation 1972, Ecclesiogenesis 1977, The Maternal Face of God 1979, Church: Charisma and Power 1980, Theology Listening to People 1981, St Francis: A Model for Human Liberation 1984, Trinity and Society 1988, The Gospel of the Cosmic Christ 1989, The New Evangelization: The Perspective of the Oppressed 1990, Ecology and Spirituality 1991, Mística e Espiritualidade 1994, Nova Era: a Consciência Planetária 1994. *Honours:* Dr hc (Turin, Lund); Paz y Justicia Award, Barcelona, Menschenrechte in der Kirche Award, Herbert Haag Foundation, FRG and Switzerland, Right Livelihood Award, Stockholm 2001. *Address:* Pr. Martins Leão 12/204, Alto Vale Encantado, 20531-350 Rio de Janeiro, Brazil. *Telephone:* (21) 326-5293. *Fax:* (21) 326-5293.

BOGAARDS, Carla; Dutch novelist and poet; b. 12 July 1947, Voorburg. *Publications:* Ik kom op niets 1982, Lena en de mannen 1985, De reigers van Amsterdam 1987, De bruinvisvrouw 1989, Lillian sugar baby 1990, Meisjesgenade 1992, Eigen vlees en bloed 1995, God bewogen 1997, Het gezichtsbedrog 2000. *Literary Agent:* c/o J.M. Meulenhoff BV, PO Box 100, 1000 Amsterdam AC, Netherlands.

BOGDANOR, Vernon, CBE, MA, FRSA, FBA; British academic; *Professor of Government, University of Oxford*; b. 16 July 1943, London; s. of Harry Bogdanor and Rosa Weinger; m. Judith Beckett 1972 (divorced 2000); two s. *Education:* Queen's Coll. and Nuffield Coll. Oxford. *Career:* Fellow, Brasenose Coll. Oxford 1966–, Sr Tutor 1979–85, 1996–97; mem. Council of Hansard Soc. for Parl. Govt 1981–97; Special Adviser, House of Lords Select Cttee on European Communities 1982–83; adviser to Govts of Czech Repub., Slovakia, Hungary and Israel on constitutional and electoral matters 1988–; Reader in Govt Univ. of Oxford 1989–96, Prof. of Govt 1996–; Special Adviser, House of Commons Public Service Cttee 1996; Gresham Prof. of Law, Gresham Coll., London 2004–07; mem. UK del. to CSCE Conf. Oslo 1991; Mishcon Lecturer 1994; Magna Carta Lecturer 2006. *Publications:* Devolution 1979, The People and the Party System 1981, Multi-party Politics and the Constitution 1983, What is Proportional Representation? 1984, The Blackwell Encyclopaedia of Political Institutions (ed.) 1987, Comparing Constitutions (co-author) 1995, The Monarchy and the Constitution 1995, Politics and the Constitution 1996, Power and the People 1997, Devolution in the United Kingdom 1999, The British Constitution in the Twentieth Century (ed.) 2003, Joined-Up Government (ed.) 2005. *Honours:* Hon. Fellow Soc. for Advanced Legal Studies 1997. *Address:* Brasenose College, Oxford, OX1 4AJ, England. *Telephone:* (1865) 277830. *Fax:* (1865) 277822.

BOGDANOV, Vsevolod Leonidovich; Russian journalist; *President, International Confederation of Journalists' Unions*; b. 6 Feb. 1944, Arkhangelsk Region; m.; two d. *Education:* Leningrad State Univ. *Career:* corresp., ed. in newspapers, radio and TV Magadan 1961–76; Head Chief Dept of Periodicals State Cttee of Publs 1976–89; Dir-Gen. TV programmes State Radio and TV Cttee 1989–92; Chair. Russian Union of Journalists 1992–; Pres. Nat. Journalist Trade Union 1999–; Pres. Int. Confed. of Journalists' Unions 1999–. *Address:* Union of Journalists, Zubovsky blvd 4, 119021 Moscow, Russia (office). *Telephone:* (495) 201-51-01 (office).

BOGDANOVICH, Peter; American film director, writer, producer and actor; b. 30 July 1939, Kingston, NY; s. of Borislav Bogdanovich and Herma (Robinson) Bogdanovich; m. 1st Polly Platt 1962 (divorced 1970); two d.; m. 2nd L. B. Straten 1988. *Career:* Actor, American Shakespeare Festival, Stratford, Conn. 1956, NY Shakespeare Festival 1958; Dir, Producer off-Broadway plays The Big Knife 1959, Camino Real, Ten Little Indians, Rocket to the Moon 1961, Once in a Lifetime 1964; film feature-writer for Esquire, New York Times, Village Voice, Cahiers du Cinéma, Los Angeles Times, New York Magazine, Vogue, Variety etc. 1961–; owner The Holly Moon Co. Inc. 1992–; mem. Dirs Guild of America, Writers' Guild of America, Acad. of Motion Picture Arts and Sciences. *Films include:* The Wild Angels (2nd unit dir, co-writer, actor) 1966, Targets (dir, co-writer, producer, actor) 1968, The Last Picture Show (dir, co-writer) 1971, Directed by John Ford (dir, writer) 1971, What's Up Doc? (dir, co-writer, producer) 1972, Paper Moon (dir, producer) 1973, Daisy Miller (dir, producer) 1974, At Long Last Love (dir, writer, producer) 1975, Nickelodeon (dir, co-writer) 1976, Saint Jack (dir, co-writer, actor) 1979, They All Laughed (dir, writer) 1981, Mask (dir) 1985, Illegally Yours (dir, producer) 1988, Texasville (dir, producer, writer) 1990, Noises Off (dir, exec. producer) 1992, The Thing Called Love (dir) 1993, Who The Devil Made It (dir) 1997, Mr Jealousy (actor) 1997, Highball (actor) 1997, Coming Soon (actor) 1999, Rated X (actor) 2000, The Independent (actor) 2000, The Cat's Meow (dir) 2003, Scene Stealers (actor) 2003. *Television:* The Great Professional: Howard Hawks (co-dir, wrote), BBC 1967; dir: Saintly Switch 1999, The Sopranos 1999, Hustle 2004, The Mystery of Natalie Wood 2004; regular commentator for CBS This Morning 1987–89; actor: Northern Exposure, CBS 1993, Fallen Angels 1995, Painted Word 1995, To Sir With Love II 1996, Naked City: A Killer Christmas 1998. *Publications:* The Cinema of Orson Welles 1961, The Cinema of Howard Hawks 1962, The Cinema of Alfred Hitchcock 1963, John Ford 1968, Fritz Lang in America 1969, Allan Dwan, the Last Pioneer 1971, Pieces of Time, Peter Bogdanovich on the Movies 1961–85, The Killing of the Unicorn: Dorothy Stratten (1960–80) 1984, A Year and a Day Calendar (ed.) 1991, This is Orson Welles (with Orson Welles) 1992, Who the Devil Made It 1997, Who the Hell's In It? 2004. *Honours:* NY Film Critics' Award (1971) and BAFTA Award for Best Screenplay (The Last Picture Show) 1971, Writers' Guild of America Award for Best Screenplay (What's Up, Doc?) 1972, Pasinetti Award, Critics' Prize, Venice Festival (Saint Jack) 1979 and other awards and prizes. *Address:* c/o William Pfeiffer, 30 Lane of Acres, Haddonfield, NJ 08033; c/o CAA, 9830 Wilshire Boulevard, Beverly Hills, CA 90212-1804, USA (office).

BOGUSLAVSKAYA, Zoya Borisovna; Russian writer, playwright and critic; b. 16 April 1929, Moscow; d. of Boris Lvovich Boguslavsky and Emma Iosifovna Boguslavskaya; m. Andrei Andreyevich Voznesensky; one s. *Education:* Moscow State Inst. of Arts and Inst. of History of Art, USSR Acad. of Sciences. *Career:* Ed., Sovetsky Pisatel publishing house; Lecturer, Moscow Higher School of Theatre Art; Head Div. of Literature, USSR State Cttee on Lenin's and State Prizes; critic in various newspapers and magazines; Founder Festival of Arts Christmas Carousel (Moscow-Paris); Guest Writer, Columbia Univ., New York, USA, Catholic Acad., Stuttgart, Germany; mem. Editorial Bd several literary magazines and journals, including Elite, Rabotnitsa, Marina (American-Russian magazine published in USA); mem. Asscn of Women-Writers of Russia, Russian Writers' Union 1960, Int. Asscn of Women-Writers in Paris; mem. Bd Dirs Russian PEN-Centre; est. Russian Ind. Triumph and Foundation Prizes; juror, Neustadt Prize 1994. *Publications include:* novels and short stories: And Tomorrow 1959, Seven Hundred in New Banknotes, The Defence, Obsession, Kinship, Change, Ghost, Mediators, By Transit, Races 1981, Leonid Leonov, Vera Panova, American Women (winner, Bravo! TV-show Prize, Yunost journal Prize), Ludmila Gutsko's Disappearance, or Change of Landmarks; plays: Windows Overlooking the South, Contact, Promise (banned for political reasons); essays: Unthought-Up Stories, Time of Lubimov and Vysotsky, Lisa and Baryshnikov, One Way Ticket. *Address:* Kotelnicheskaya nab 1/15, korpus B, apt 62, 109240 Moscow, Russia. *Telephone:* (495) 227-49-90.

BOHJALIAN, Chris; American novelist and journalist; b. 12 Aug. 1960, White Plains, NY; m. Victoria Blewer 1984. *Career:* mem. PEN. *Publications:* A Killing in the Real World, 1988; Hangman, 1990; Past the Bleachers, 1992; Water Witches, 1995; Midwives, 1997; The Law of Similars, 1999; Trans-Sister Radio, 2000; The Buffalo Soldier, 2002; Idyll Banter, 2003. *Honours:* New England Booksellers' Asscn Discovery Prize, New England Book Award 2002.

BOISVERT, France, MLitt, PhD; Canadian teacher, writer and poet; b. 10 June 1959, Sherbrooke, QC; one s. *Career:* teacher of French and French Canadian literature; mem. Union des écrivaines et des écrivains québécois, Asscn internationale des Études québécoises, Élue au Conseil d' admin de l'UNEQ (1992–93, 1995). *Publications:* Les Samouraïlles (fiction) 1987, Li Tsing-tao ou Le grand avoir (fiction) 1989, Massawippi (poem) 1992, Comme un vol de gerfauts (poem) 1993, Les Vents de l'Aube (prose) 1997, Le Voyageur aux yeux d'onyx (prose) 2002, Communistoland (fiction) 2007; contribs to Liberté, La Presse, Le Devoir. *Honours:* Minister of Culture, Québec bursaries 1989, 1990, 1991. *Address:* A/S Collège Lionel-Groulx, 100 rue Duquet, Sainte-Thérèse, QC J7E 3G6, Canada (office). *Telephone:* (450) 430-3120 (office). *Fax:* (450) 971-7883 (office). *E-mail:* france59boisvert@yahoo.ca (home). *Website:* www.clq.qc.ca (office); www.litterature.org/detailauteur.asp?numero=80 (office); felix.cyberscol.qc.ca/lq/auteurB/boisve_f/boisvert.html (office).

BOK, Derek, MA, JD; American legal scholar, university administrator and academic; *300th Anniversary University President Emeritus, Professor Emeritus and Faculty Chair, Hauser Center for Non-Profit Organizations, Harvard University*; b. 22 March 1930, Bryn Mawr, Pa; s. of late Curtis Bok and Margaret Plummer (now Mrs. W. S. Kiskadden); m. Sissela Ann Myrdal (d. of Karl Gunnar and Alva Myrdal) 1955; one s. two d. *Education:* Univs of Stanford, Harvard, George Washington and Inst. of Political Science, Paris Univ. *Career:* served US Army 1956–58; Asst Prof. of Law, Harvard Univ. 1958–61, Prof. 1961–, Dean 1968–71, 300th Anniversary Univ. Prof. 1991–, now Emer.; Pres. Harvard Univ. 1971–91, now Pres. Emer., Interim Pres. 2006–; Dir, Nat. Chair. Common Cause 1999–; Chair. Spencer Foundation 2002–; Faculty Chair. Hauser Center for Non-Profit Orgs 2002–. *Publications include:* The First Three Years of the Schuman Plan, Cases and Materials on Labor Law (with Archibald Cox), Labor and the American Community (with John Dunlop), The Federal Government and the University, Beyond the Ivory Tower: Social Responsibilities of the Modern University 1982, Higher Learning 1986, Universities and the Future of America 1990, The Cost of Talent 1993, The State of the Nation 1997, The Shape of the River (jtly) 1998, The Trouble with Government 2001, Universities in the Marketplace: the commercialization of higher education 2004. *Address:* Hauser Center for Nonprofit Organizations, 5 Bennett Street, Cambridge, MA 02138 (office); John F. Kennedy School of Government, Harvard University, 79 John F. Kennedy Street, Cambridge, MA 02138, USA (office). *Telephone:* (617) 495-1199 (office). *Fax:* (617) 496-6886 (office). *E-mail:* derek_bok@harvard.edu (office). *Website:* www.ksg.harvard.edu/hauser (office).

BOK, Sissela, BA, MA, PhD; American (b. Swedish) philosopher and writer; *Distinguished Fellow, Harvard Center for Population and Development Studies*; b. 2 Dec. 1934, Stockholm, Sweden; d. of Gunnar Myrdal and Alva Myrdal; m. Derek Bok 1955; one s. two d. *Education:* George Washington Univ., Harvard Univ. *Career:* Lecturer, Simmons Coll., Boston 1971–72, Harvard-MIT Div. of Health Sciences and Tech., Cambridge 1975–82, Harvard Univ. 1982–84; Assoc. Prof. 1985–89, Prof. of Philosophy 1989–92, Brandeis Univ.; Fellow, Center for Advanced Study, Stanford, Calif. 1991–92;

Distinguished Fellow, Harvard Center for Population and Devt Studies 1993–; mem. Pulitzer Prize Bd 1988–97, Chair. 1996–97; Fellow, Hasting Center 1972–2002, Dir 1976–84, 1994–97; mem. American Philosophical Asscn. *Publications:* Lying: Moral Choice in Public and Private Life 1978, Secrets: On the Ethics of Concealment and Revelation 1982, Alva: Ett kvinnoliv 1987, A Strategy for Peace 1989, Alva Myrdal: A Daughter's Memoir 1991, Common Values 1996, Mayhem: Violence as Public Entertainment 1998, Euthanasia and Physician-Assisted Suicide (with Gerald Dworkin and Ray Frey) 1998; contrib. to scholarly publications. *Honours:* Dr hc (Mount Holyoke Coll.) 1985, (George Washington Univ.) 1986, (Clark Univ.) 1988, (Univ. of Massachusetts) 1991, (Georgetown Univ.) 1992; George Orwell Award 1978, Melcher Awards 1978, 1991, Abram L. Sacher Silver Medallion, Brandeis Univ. 1985, St Botolph Foundation Award 2002, Radcliffe Coll. Grad. Soc. Medal 1993, Barnard Coll. Medal of Distinction 1995, Centennial Medal, Grad. School of Arts and Sciences, Harvard Univ. 1998, Commonwealth Humanities Lecturer 2006. *Address:* Harvard Center for Population and Development Studies, 9 Bow Street, Cambridge, MA 02138, USA (office). *E-mail:* sbok@hsph.harvard.edu (office).

BOKHARI, Salim; Pakistani journalist; *Editor, The News, Lahore. Career:* correspondent for numerous publications and TV and radio broadcasts, including The International News and CNN; Ed., The News, Lahore. *Honours:* President's Award for Pride of Performance. *Address:* c/o The News, al-Rahman Bldg, Murree Road, Rawalpindi, Pakistan (office).

BOLAM, Robyn, (Marion Lomax), BA, DPhil; British academic, poet and editor; *Professor of Literature, St Mary's College, University of Surrey;* b. (Marion Bolam), 20 Oct. 1953, Newcastle upon Tyne; m. Michael Lomax 1974, divorced 1999. *Education:* Univ. of Kent; Univ. of York. *Career:* Part-time Lecturer, King Alfred's Coll. 1983–86; Creative Writing Fellow, Univ. of Reading 1987–88; Lecturer, later Sr Lecturer in English, St Mary's Coll., Univ. of Surrey 1988–95, Prof. of Literature 1995–; Writer-in-Residence, University of Stockholm, March–May 1998; published as Marion Lomax – 2000, as Robyn Bolam 2000–; mem. Nat. Asscn for Writers in Educ., Poetry Soc., Soc. of Authors, Higher Educ. Acad., English Asscn. *Opera:* libretto for Beyond Men and Dreams (composer Bennett Hogg), Royal Opera House Garden Venture 1991. *Publications:* poetry: The Peepshow Girl 1989, Raiding the Borders 1996, New Wings 2007; non-fiction: Stage Images and Traditions: Shakespeare to Ford 1987, Eliza's Babes: Four Centuries of Women's Poetry in English, c. 1500–1900 2005; editor: Time Present and Time Past: Poets at the University of Kent 1965–1985 1985, Four Plays by John Ford 1995, The Rover, by Alpha Behn 1995, Out of the Blue (with Steven Harman) 1998; contribs to collections of essays, anthologies and periodicals. *Honours:* E.C. Gregory Award, Soc. of Authors 1981, First Prize, Cheltenham Festival Poetry Competition 1981, Hawthornden Fellowship 1993. *Address:* c/o Bloodaxe Books Ltd, Highgreen, Tarset, Northumberland NE48 1RP, England.

BOLAND, Eavan Aisling, BA; Irish poet and academic; *Melvin and Bill Lane Professor for the Director of the Creative Writing Program, Stanford University;* b. 24 Sept. 1944, Dublin; d. of Frederick Boland and Frances Kelly; two d. *Education:* schools in London, New York, USA and Dublin, and Trinity Coll., Dublin. *Career:* Lecturer Trinity Coll., Dublin 1967–68 and School of Irish Studies, Dublin; fmr writer-in-residence Trinity Coll. and Univ. Coll. Dublin; fmr poet-in-residence Nat. Maternity Hosp. in its centenary year 1994; fmr Hurst Prof. Washington Univ., Advisory Bd Int. Writers' Center; fmr Regent's Lecturer Univ. of California at Santa Barbara; Chair. judging panel Irish Times-Aer Lingus Irish Literature Prizes; Melvin and Bill Lane Prof. for the Dir of the Creative Writing Program 1995–2000, 2002–, Bella Mabury and Eloise Mabury Knapp Prof. in Humanities, Stanford Univ., Calif. 1995–; reviewer Irish Times; mem. bd Irish Arts Council; mem. Irish Acad. of Letters; Macaulay Fellowship 1967. *Publications:* poetry: 23 Poems 1962, New Territory 1967, The War Horse 1976, In her Own Image 1980, Night Feed 1982, The Journey and Other Poems 1987, Selected Poems 1989, A Kind of Scar – The Woman Poet in a National Tradition 1989, Outside History – Selected Poems 1980–1990 1990, In a Time of Violence 1994, A Dozen Lips 1994, Collected Poems 1995, An Origin Like Water – Collected Poems 1967–1987 1996, The Lost Land 1998, Against Love Poetry 2001, Code 2001; prose: W. B. Yeats and his World (with Michael MacLiammoir) 1971, Object Lessons: The Life of the Woman and the Poet in Our Time 1995; other: The Making of a Poem: A Norton Anthology of Poetic Forms (ed., with Mark Strand) 2000. *Honours:* Dr hc (Nat. Univ. of Ireland), (Univ. of Strathclyde, UK), (Holy Cross Coll., Boston, USA), (Colby Coll., Maine, USA); Irish-American Foundation Award 1983, Ireland–American Fund 1994, Lannan Award for Poetry 1994. *Address:* English Department, Stanford University, Mail Code 2087, Building 460, Room 219A, Stanford, CA 94305-2087, USA (office). *Telephone:* (650) 725-1207 (office). *Fax:* (650) 723-3679 (office). *E-mail:* boland@stanford.edu (office). *Website:* www.stanford.edu (office).

BOLGER, Dermot; Irish writer, dramatist and poet; b. 6 Feb. 1959, Finglas, Dublin; s. of Roger Bolger and the late Bridie Flanagan; m. Bernadette Clifton 1988; two s. *Education:* St Canice's BNS, Finglas and Benevin Coll. Finglas. *Career:* worked as factory hand, library asst and professional author; founder and Ed. Raven Arts Press 1979–92; founder and Exec. Ed. New Island Books, Dublin 1992–; mem. Arts Council of Ireland 1989–93; elected mem. Aosdána 1991–; Playwright in Association, The Abbey (Nat.) Theatre 1997; Writer Fellow, Trinity Coll., Dublin 2003. *Plays:* The Lament for Arthur Cleary 1989, Blinded by the Light 1990, In High Germany 1990, The Holy Ground 1990, One Last White Horse 1991, A Dublin Bloom 1994, April Bright 1995, The Passion of Jerome 1999, Consenting Adults 2000, From These Green Heights 2004. *Television screenplay:* Edward No Hands 1996. *Publications:* novels: Night Shift 1985, The Woman's Daughter 1987, The Journey Home 1990, Emily's Shoes 1992, A Second Life 1994, Father's Music 1997, Finbar's Hotel (co-author) 1997, Ladies Night at Finbar's Hotel (co-author) 1999, Temptation 2000, The Valparaiso Voyage 2001, The Family on Paradise Pier 2005; poetry: The Habit of Flesh 1979, Finglas Lilies 1980, No Waiting America 1981, Internal Exile 1986, Leinster Street Ghosts 1989, Taking My Letters Back, New and Selected Poems 1998, The Chosen Moment 2004; editor: The Dolmen Book of Irish Christmas Stories 1986, The Bright Wave: Poetry in Irish Now 1986, 16 on 16: Irish Writers on the Easter Rising 1988, Invisible Cities: The New Dubliners: A Journey through Unofficial Dublin 1988, Invisible Dublin: A Journey through its Writers 1992, The Picador Book of Contemporary Irish Fiction 1993, 12 Bar Blues (with Aidan Murphy) 1993, The New Picador Book of Contemporary Irish Fiction 2000, Druids, Dudes and Beauty Queens: The Changing Face of Irish Theatre 2001. *Honours:* A. E. Memorial Prize 1986, Macauley Fellowship 1987, A. Z. Whitehead Prize 1987, Samuel Beckett Award 1991, Edinburgh Fringe First Awards 1991, 1995, Stewart Parker BBC Award 1991, The Hennessy Irish Literature Hall of Fame Award 2003. *Literary Agent:* A. P. Watt Ltd, 20 John Street, London, WC1N 2DR, England. *Telephone:* (20) 7405-6774. *Fax:* (20) 7831-2154.

BON, François; French writer; b. 22 May 1953, Luçon, Vendée. *Education:* École Nat. Supérieure d'Arts et Métiers. *Career:* founder, literary collective website remue.net 2001; writer-in-residence Acad. de France, Rome 1984–85, Deutscher Akademischer Austauschdienst, Berlin 1987–88, Robert Bosch Stiftung, Stuttgart, 1991–92, Centre Dramatique Nat. de Nancy 1998–99, Théâtre Ouvert, Paris 1999–2000. *Plays:* Scène (Centre Dramatique Régional de Tours) 1998, Au buffet de la gare d'Angoulême (Centre Dramatique Régional de Tours) 1998, Vie de Myriam C. (Centre Dramatique Nat. de Nancy) 1998, Fariboles (Centre Dramatique Nat. de Nancy) 1999, Qui se déchire (France-Culture) 2000, Bruit (Théâtre Ouvert, Paris) 2000, Quatre avec le mort (Théâtre de la Comédie Française) 2002, Daewoo (Festival d'Avignon) 2004. *Publications:* Sortie d'usine 1982, Limite 1985, Le Crime de Buzon 1986, Décor ciment 1988, Calvaire des chiens 1990, La Folie Rabelais (essay) 1990, L'Enterrement 1990, Temps Machine 1992, Un Fait divers 1993, Dans la ville invisible (juvenile) 1995, C'était toute une vie 1995, Parking 1996, Voleurs de feu, vies singulières des poètes (juvenile) 1996, 30, rue de la Poste (juvenile) 1996, Le Solitaire (non-fiction) 1996, Impatience 1998, Prison 1998, Dehors est la ville (non-fiction) 1998, Autoroute (juvenile) 1999, Pour Koltès (essay) 2000, Tous les mots sont adultes 2000, Paysage fer (Prix France Culture La Ville à Lire) 2000, Mécanique 2001, Quoi faire de son chien mort? et autres textes courts pour la scène 2002, Rolling Stones, une biographie (Soc. des Gens de Lettres Prix d'automne) 2002, Billancourt (non-fiction) 2003, Daewoo (novel) 2004, Monument 70 2006. *Honours:* Chevalier, Ordre des Arts et des Lettres 1998. *Address:* c/o Editions Fayard, 75 rue des Saints-Pères, 75278 Paris, Cédex 06, France. *E-mail:* fb@tierslivre.net. *Website:* www.tierslivre.net.

BONA, Dominique Henriette Marie; French journalist and writer; b. 29 July 1953, Perpignan; d. of Arthur Conte and Colette Conte; m. Philippe Bona 1973; one s. one d. *Education:* Cours Dupanloup, Boulogne, Lycée Victor Duruy and Univ. of Paris IV (Paris-Sorbonne). *Career:* journalist on Quotidien de Paris 1980–85, on Figaro 1985–; writer of novels and biographies; mem. Jury Prix Renaudot 1999–. *Publications:* novels: Les heures volées 1981, Argentina 1984, Malika (Prix Interallié) 1992, Le manuscit de Port-Ebène (Prix Renaudot) 1998; biographies: Romain Gary (Grand Prix de la Biographie, Acad. Française) 1987, Les yeux noirs ou les vies extraordinaires des sœurs Hérédia (Grand Prix de la Femme, Prix Lutèce, Prix de l'Enclave des Papes 1990) 1989, Gala 1994, Stefan Zweig, l'ami blessé 1996, Berthe Morisot, Le Secret de la femme en noir (Prix Goncourt de la Biographie) 2000, Il n'y a qu'un amour 2003. *Honours:* Chevalier des Arts et Lettres, l'Ordre nat. du Mérite. *Address:* c/o Editions Grasset, 61 rue des Saints-Pères, 75006 Paris, France. *Telephone:* 1-44-39-22-13. *Fax:* 1-44-39-22-41. *E-mail:* hwarneke@grasset.fr. *Website:* www.grasset.fr.

BONANNO, David; American; *Joint Editor, American Poetry Review. Career:* joint Ed., American Poetry Review 1973–; teaches workshops on poetry and literary publishing; co-ordinator, poetry-in-the-high-schools programme in Philadelphia; mem. Literary Advisory panel, Pennsylvania Council on the Arts. *Publications:* The Body Electric: America's Best Poetry from The American Poetry Review (co-ed.) 2001. *Address:* The American Poetry Review, 117 S 17th Street, Suite 910, Philadelphia, PA 19103, USA (office). *Telephone:* (215) 496-0439. *Fax:* (215) 569-0808. *E-mail:* dbonanno@aprweb.org. *Website:* www.aprweb.org.

BOND, Edward; British playwright, director and poet; b. 18 July 1934, London; m. Elisabeth Pablé 1971. *Career:* Northern Arts Literary Fellowship 1977–79; resident theatre writer, Univ. of Essex 1982–83. *Publications:* plays: The Pope's Wedding 1962, Saved 1965, Narrow Road to the Deep North 1968, Early Morning 1968, Passion 1971, Black Mass 1971, Lear 1972, The Sea 1973, Bingo 1974, The Fool 1976, A-A-America! (Grandma Faust and The Swing) 1976, Stone 1976, The Bundle 1978, The Woman 1979, The Worlds 1980, The Activist Papers 1980, Restoration 1981, Summer: A Play for Europe 1982, Derek 1983, Human Cannon 1985, The War Plays (Red Black and Ignorant, The Tin Can People, Great Peace) 1985, Jackets 1989, In the Company of Men 1990, September 1990, Olly's Prison 1993, Tuesday 1993, Coffee: A Tragedy 1994, At the Inland Sea (A Play for Young People) 1996,

Eleven Vests (A Play for Young People) 1997, The Crime of the Twenty-first Century 1999, The Children (A Play for Two Adults and Sixteen Children) 2000, Chair 2000, Have I None 2000, Existence 2002, Born 2004, The Balancing Act 2004, The Short Electra 2004, My Day (Song Cycle for Children) 2005, The Under Room 2006, Arcade 2006, June 2007, People 2007, Collected Plays (eight vols) 1977–2007 2007; short stories: Fables 1982; opera librettos of music by Hans Werner Henze: We Come to the River 1977, The English Cat 1983; ballet libretto of music by Henze: Orpheus 1982; translations: Chekhov's The Three Sisters 1967, Wedekind's Spring Awakening 1974, Wedekind's Lulu: A Monster Tragedy (with Elisabeth Bond-Pablé) 1992; other: Theatre Poems and Songs 1978, Collected Poems 1978–1985 1987, Notes on Post-Modernism 1990, Letters (five vols) 1994–2001, Notes on Imagination 1995, Selected Notebooks Vol. 1 2000, Vol. 2 2001, The Hidden Plot: Notes on Theatre and the State 2000. *Honours:* City of Lyon Medal 2007; Hon. DLitt (Yale) 1977; George Devine Award 1968, John Whiting Award 1968, Obie Award 1976. *Address:* c/o Casarotto Ramsay, Waverley House, 7–12 Noel Street, London, W1F 8GQ, England (office). *Telephone:* (20) 7287-4450 (office). *Fax:* (20) 7287-9128 (office). *E-mail:* agents@casarotto.uk.com (office). *Website:* www.casarotto.uk.com (office).

BOND, (Thomas) Michael, OBE; British author; b. 13 Jan. 1926, Newbury, Berkshire, England; m. 1st Brenda Mary Johnson 1950 (divorced 1981); one d. one s.; m. 2nd Susan Marfrey Rogers 1981. *Education:* Presentation Coll. *Publications:* for children: A Bear Called Paddington 1958, More About Paddington 1959, Paddington Helps Out 1960, Paddington Abroad 1961, Paddington at Large 1962, Paddington Marches On 1964, Paddington at Work 1966, Here Comes Thursday 1966, Thursday Rides Again 1968, Paddington Goes to Town 1968, Thursday Ahoy 1969, Parsley's Tail 1969, Parsley's Good Deed 1969, Parsley's Problem Present 1970, Parsley's Last Stand 1970, Paddington Takes the Air 1970, Thursday in Paris 1971, Michael Bond's Book of Bears 1971, Michael Bond's Book of Mice 1971, The Day the Animals Went on Strike 1972, Paddington Bear 1972, Paddington's Garden 1972, Parsley Parade 1972, The Tales of Olga de Polga 1971, Olga Meets her Match 1973, Paddington's Blue Peter Story Book 1973, Paddington at the Circus 1973, Paddington Goes Shopping 1973, Paddington at the Seaside 1974, Paddington at the Tower 1974, Paddington on Top 1974, Windmill 1975, How to Make Flying Things 1975, Eight Olga Readers 1975, Olga Carries On 1976, Paddington Takes the Test 1979, Paddington's Cartoon Book 1979, J. D. Polson and the Liberty Head Dime 1980, J. D. Polson and the Dillogate Affair 1981, Paddington on Screen 1981, Olga Takes Charge 1982, The Caravan Puppets 1983, Paddington at the Zoo 1984, Paddington's Painting Exhibition 1985, Oliver the Greedy Elephant 1985, Paddington Minds the House 1986, Paddington at the Palace 1986, Paddington's Busy Day 1987, Paddington and the Magical Maze 1987, Paddington: A Classic Collection 1997, Paddington and the Christmas Surprise 1997, Paddington at the Carnival 1998, Paddington and the Tutti Frutti Rainbow 1998, Paddington – My Scrapbook 1999, Paddington's Party Tricks 2000, Paddington in Hot Water 2000, Paddington Goes to Hospital 2001, Paddington Treasury 2001, Olga Moves House 2001, Olga Follows her Nose 2002, Paddington and the Grand Tour 2003; for adults: Monsieur Pamplemousse 1983, Monsieur Pamplemousse and the Secret Mission 1984, Monsieur Pamplemousse on the Spot 1986, Monsieur Pamplemousse Takes the Cure 1987, The Pleasures of Paris, Guide Book 1987, Monsieur Pamplemousse Aloft 1989, Monsieur Pamplemousse Investigates 1990, Monsieur Pamplemousse Rests his Case 1991, Monsieur Pamplemousse Stands Firm 1992, Monsieur Pamplemousse on Location 1992, Monsieur Pamplemousse Takes the Train 1993, Bears and Forebears (autobiog.) 1996, Monsieur Pamplemousse Afloat 1998, Monsieur Pamplemousse on Probation 2000, Monsieur Pamplemousse on Vacation 2002, Monsieur Pamplemousse Hits the Headlines 2003, Monsieur Pamplemousse and the Militant Midwives 2006. *Literary Agent:* The Agency, 24 Pottery Lane, Holland Park, London, W11 4LZ, England.

BOND, Nancy Barbara, BA, DipLib; American librarian and writer; b. 8 Jan. 1945, Bethesda, MD. *Education:* Mount Holyoke Coll., Coll. of Librarianship, Wales. *Career:* part-time instructor, Simmons Coll., Centre for the Study of Children's Literature 1979–2001. *Publications:* A String in the Harp 1976, The Best of Enemies 1978, Country of Broken Stone 1980, The Voyage Begun 1981, A Place to Come Back To 1984, Another Shore 1988, Truth to Tell 1994, The Love of Friends 1997. *Honours:* Int. Reading Assn Award 1976, Newbery Honour 1976, Welsh Arts Council Tir na n'Og Award 1976. *Address:* 109 The Valley Road, Concord, MA 01742, USA.

BONDER, Nilton, BS, MA; Brazilian writer and rabbi; *Rabbi of the Jewish Congregation of Brazil*; b. 27 Dec. 1957, Porte Alegre; m. Esther Bonder 1991; one s. one d. *Education:* Catholic Univ. of Rio de Janeiro, Jewish Theological Seminary, New York City. *Publications:* A Tractade on Impunity 1993, The Art of Saving Yourself 1994, The Jewish Way of Problem Solving 1995, Secret Portals 1996, The Kabbalah of Money 1996, The Kabbalah of Envy 1997, The Kabbalah of Food 1998, The Immoral Soul 2001, Boundaries of Intelligence 2002, The Kabbalah of Time 2003, Heaven's Criminal Code 2004. *Literary Agent:* c/o Karen Schindler, PO Box 19051, 04599-970 São Paulo, SP, Brazil. *Telephone:* 22610-380 (Brazil) (office). *Fax:* 24935-735 (Brazil) (office). *E-mail:* nbonder@globo.com (office). *Website:* www.niltonbonder.org.

BONNEFOY, Yves Jean, LèsL; French writer; b. 24 June 1923, Tours; s. of Elie Bonnefoy and Hélène Maury; m. Lucille Vines 1968; one d. *Education:* Lycée Descartes, Tours, Faculté des Sciences, Poitiers and Faculté des Lettres, Paris. *Career:* Prof. Collège de France 1981; contrib. to Mercure de France, Critique, Encounter, L'Ephémère, La Nouvelle Revue Française etc.; has travelled in Europe, Asia and N America; lectures or seminars at Brandeis, Johns Hopkins, Princeton, Williams Coll., Calif., Geneva, Nice, Yale, CUNY, NY and other univs. *Publications:* poems: Du mouvement et de l'immobilité de Douve 1953 (English 1968), Hier régnant désert 1958, Pierre écrite 1964 (English 1976), Selected Poems 1968, Dans le leurre du seuil 1975, Poèmes (1947–1975) 1978, Ce qui fut sans lumière 1987, Entretiens sur la Poesie 1990, Début et fin de la neige 1991, Les planches courbes 2001; essays: L'Improbable 1959, Arthur Rimbaud 1961 (English trans. 1973), Un rêve fait à Mantoue 1967, Le nuage rouge 1977, Rue traversière 1977; on art: Peintures murales de la France Gothique 1954, Miró 1963, Rome 1630 1969, L'Arrière-Pays 1972, Entretiens sur la poésie 1981, La Présence et l'Image 1983, Récits en rêve 1987, La Vérité de Parole 1988, Alberto Giacometti 1991, La vie errante 1993, Remarques sur le dessin 1993, Dessin, couleur et lumière 1995, Théâtre et poésie: Shakespeare et Yeats, l'Encore aveugle 1998, Zao-Wou-ki (jtly) 1998, Lieux et destins de l'image 1999, La Communauté des traducteurs 2000, Baudelaire: Le Tentation de l'oubli 2000, Keats et Léopardi 2000, Sous l'Horizon du Langage 2001, Remarques sur le regard 2001, Breton à l'avant de soi 2001, Poésie et architecture 2001, L'Enseignement de Léopardi 2001, Le poète et le flot mouvant des multitudes 2003, Le sommeil de personne 2004, La stratégie de l'énigme 2006, L'imaginaire métaphysique 2006, Goya: les peintures noires 2006, Dans un débris de miroir 2006; co-ed. L'Ephémère, trans. of Shakespeare, W. B. Yeats, Keats, Léopardi. *Honours:* Commdr des Arts et des Lettres; Hon. DHumLitt (American Coll., Paris, Univ. of Chicago, Univ. of Neuchâtel, Trinity Coll., Dublin, Rome, Edin., Siena); Prix Montaigne 1980, Grand Prix de poésie (Acad. Française) 1981, Prix Florence Gould 1987, Grand Prix national 1993, Prix de la Fondation Cino-del-Duca 1995, Prix Balzan 1995, Prix Prince Louis de Polignac 1998, American Acad. of Arts and Letters Award, and numerous other prizes. *Address:* Collège de France, 11 place Marcelin Berthelot, 75005 Paris, France. *E-mail:* yves.bonnefoy@college-de-france.fr (office).

BONNER, Elena Georgievna; Russian human rights activist and writer; b. 25 Feb. 1923, Turkmenistan; m. 2nd Andrei Sakharov 1972 (died 1989); one s. one d. *Education:* First Leningrad Medical Inst. *Career:* active as nurse 1941–45; partially blinded; Lt 1945; doctor 1953–83; founder of Moscow group to monitor observation of 1975 Helsinki accords; regular visitor to Sakharov during latter's exile in Gorky 1980–84; sentenced to five years' exile 1984, released 1986; political activist after husband's death; Chair. Comm. for perpetuation of Andrei Sakharov's memory. *Publications:* Alone Together (memoirs) 1986, Mothers and Daughters (memoir) 1991. *Address:* A. D. Sakharova Museum, Zemlyanoy val 57, Bldg 6, 107120 Moscow, Russia.

BONNER, Gerald, MA, FSA; British academic (retd); *Reader Emeritus, University of Durham*; b. 18 June 1926, London; s. of Frederick J. Bonner and Constance E. Hatch; m. Priscilla J. Hodgson 1967; one s. one d. *Education:* The Stationers' Co.'s School, London and Wadham Coll. Oxford. *Career:* mil. service 1944–48; Asst Keeper, Dept of Manuscripts, British Museum 1953–64; Lecturer in Theology, Univ. of Durham 1964, promoted to personal Readership 1969, Reader Emer. 1989–; Convener and Sec. Bedan Conf. Durham 1973; Distinguished Prof. of Early Christian Studies, Catholic Univ. of America 1991–94; delivered Cathedral Lecture, Durham 1970, Augustine Lecture, Villanova Univ. Pa, 1970, Otts Lectures, Davidson Coll. NC 1992; Visiting Prof. in Augustinian Studies, Villanova Univ. Pa 1999. *Publications:* The Warfare of Christ 1962, St Augustine of Hippo: Life and Controversies 1963, Famulus Christi: Essays in Commemoration of the Thirteenth Centenary of the Venerable Bede (ed.) 1976, God's Decree and Man's Destiny 1987, St Cuthbert, His Cult and His Community (ed. with D. Rollason and C. Stancliffe), Church and Faith in the Patristic Tradition: Augustine, Pelagianism and Early Christian Northumbria 1996, Augustine of Hippo: The Monastic Rules 2004, Freedom and Necessity: St Augustine's Teaching on Divine Power and Human Freedom 2007; articles in the Augustinus-Lexikon (Basle) and other learned journals. *Honours:* Johannes Quasten Medal 1994. *Address:* 7 Victoria Terrace, Durham, DH1 4RW, England (home). *Telephone:* (191) 386-3407.

BONNER, Terry Nelson (see Krauzer, Steven Mark)

BONTLY, Thomas John, BA, PhD; American academic and writer; b. 25 Aug. 1939, Madison, Wisconsin; m. Marilyn R. Mackie 1962; one s. *Education:* University of Wisconsin at Madison, Corpus Christi College, Cambridge, Stanford University. *Career:* Asst Prof., 1966–71, Assoc. Prof., 1971–76, Co-ordinator of Creative Writing, 1975–77, 1987–90, 1995–97, and Chair., 1979–82, Dept of English, Prof., 1976–, University of Wisconsin-Milwaukee; Fulbright Senior Lectureship, West Germany, 1984; mem. Council for Wisconsin Writers, board of dirs, 1991–. *Publications:* Fiction: The Competitor, 1966; The Adventures of a Young Outlaw, 1974; Celestial Chess, 1979; The Giant's Shadow, 1989. Other: Short stories in anthologies and many periodicals; Essays and reviews. *Honours:* Wallace Stegner Creative Writing Fellowship, 1965–66; Maxwell Perkins Commemorative Award, 1966; First Prizes for Short Fiction, Council for Wisconsin Writers, 1975, 1989, 1997; Wisconsin Arts Board New Work Award, 1990. *Literary Agent:* Curtis Brown Ltd, 10 Astor Place, New York, NY 10003, USA. *Address:* Department of English, University of Wisconsin-Milwaukee, Milwaukee, WI 53201, USA.

BOOKER, Christopher John Penrice; British journalist and writer; b. 7 Oct. 1937, Eastbourne, Sussex, England; m. Valerie Patrick 1979; two s. *Education:* Corpus Christi Coll., Cambridge. *Career:* contributor 1959–97,

Way of the World column 1987–90, Daily Telegraph; Liberal News 1960; jazz critic 1961, columnist 1990–, Sunday Telegraph; Ed. 1961–63, regular contributor 1965–, Private Eye; resident scriptwriter, That Was the Week That Was 1962–63; contributor, Spectator 1962–. *Publications:* The Neophiliacs: A Study of the Revolution in English Life in the 50s and 60s 1969, Goodbye London (with Candida Lycett-Green) 1973, The Booker Quiz 1976, The Seventies 1980, The Games War: A Moscow Journal 1981, The Repatriations from Austria in 1945 1990, The Mad Officials: How the Bureaucrats are Strangling Britain (with Richard North) 1994, The Castle of Lies: Why Britain Must Get Out of Europe (with Richard North) 1996, A Looking Glass Tragedy: The Controversy Over the Repatriations from Austria in 1945 1997, The Great Deception: The Secret History of the European Union (with Richard North) 2003, The Seven Basic Plots: Why We Tell Stories 2004. *Honours:* co-winner Campaigning Journalist of the Year 1973, Aims of Industry Free Enterprise Award 1992. *Address:* The Old Rectory, Litton, Bath BA3 4PW, England (office). *Telephone:* (1761) 241263 (office). *Fax:* (1761) 241260 (office). *E-mail:* cblitton@aol.com.

BOOS, Jürgen, BEcons; German publisher; *Director, Frankfurt Book Fair.* *Education:* Universität Mannheim. *Career:* Sales Man. at publisher, Droemer 1991, then at Carl Hanser 1992; Man., Lange & Springer scientific book shop, Berlin 1993; Head of Int. Sales at publisher, Julius Springer 1996; mem. of exec. bd, responsible for marketing, sales and distribution at publisher, Wiley-VCH 1997–2005; Dir, Frankfurt Book Fair 2005–. *Address:* Ausstellungs- und Messe GmbH, Frankfurt Book Fair, Reineckstr. 3, 60313 Frankfurt am Main, Germany. *E-mail:* info@book-fair.com. *Website:* www.frankfurt-book-fair.com.

BOOTH, Geoffrey Thornton, (Edward Booth O. P.), BA, MA, PhD; British writer, teacher and priest; b. 16 Aug. 1928, Evesham, Worcestershire, England. *Education:* Univ. of Cambridge. *Career:* entered English province, Order of Dominicans, 1952; Ordained, Roman Catholic Priest, 1958; Lecturer, Pontifical Beda College, 1978–80, Pontifical University of St Thomas, 1980–88, Rome. *Publications:* Aristotelian Aporetic Ontology in Islamic and Christian Thinkers, 1983; Saint Augustine and the Western Tradition of Self Knowing: The Saint Augustine Lecture 1986, 1989. Contributions: The New Grove Dictionary of Music and Musicians, 1980; La Production du livre universitaire au moyen age: Exemplar et Pecia, 1988; Kategorie und Kategorialität, Historisch-Systematische Untersuchungen zum Begriff der Kategorie im philosophischen Denken, Festschrift für Klaus Hartmann, 1990; Gott und sein Bild–Augustins De Trinitate im Spiegel der neueren Forschung, 2000; Also many articles and book reviews in journals.

BOOTH, Rosemary, (Frances Murray), DipEd, MA; British teacher and author; b. 10 Feb. 1928, Glasgow, Scotland; m. Robert Edward Booth 1950, three d. *Education:* University of Glasgow, University of St Andrews, Dundee College of Education. *Career:* history teacher. *Publications:* Ponies on the Heather, 1966; The Dear Colleague, 1972; The Burning Lamp, 1973; The Heroine's Sister, 1975; Ponies and Parachutes, 1975; Red Rowan Berry, 1976; Castaway, 1978; White Hope, 1978; Payment for the Piper, 1983, US edn as Brave Kingdom; The Belchamber Scandal, 1985; Shadow Over the Islands, 1986.

BOOTH, Stephen, BA; British journalist and novelist; b. 1952, Burnley, Lancs., England; m. *Education:* Birmingham Polytechnic. *Career:* fmrly sports reporter and journalist on local newspapers, night shift sub-ed. on Scottish Daily Express, production ed. on Farming Guardian. *Publications:* novels: Black Dog 2000, Dancing with the Virgins 2001, Blood on the Tongue 2002, Blind to the Bones 2003, One Last Breath 2004, The Dead Place 2005, Scared to Live 2006. *Honours:* Lichfield Prize, Lichfield Int. Arts Festival 1999, Barry Award for Best British Crime Novel 2000, 2001, CWA Dagger in the Library 2003. *Address:* c/o HarperCollins Publishers Ltd, 77–85 Fulham Palace Road, London, W6 8JB, England. *Telephone:* (20) 8741-7070. *Website:* www.stephen-booth.com.

BORCHERS-CARLÉ, Elisabeth; German writer; b. 27 Feb. 1926, Homberg; d. of Rudolf Sarbin and Claire Sarbin (née Beck); m. (widowed and remarried); two s. *Career:* Ed. Luchterhand 1960–71, Suhrkamp Verlag and Insel Verlag 1971–98; mem. PEN, Acad. of Sciences and Literature, Mainz, Acad. of Language and Poetry, Darmstadt. *Publications:* poetry, prose, translations, children's books. *Honours:* Erzahlerpreis Suddeutscher Rundfunk, German Industry Culture Prize, Roswitha-Gedenk-Medaille 1976, Friedrich-Hölderlin-Preis 1986. *Address:* Arndtstrasse 17, 60325 Frankfurt, Germany (home). *Telephone:* (69) 746391 (home). *Fax:* (69) 74093909 (home).

BORDEN, Anthony, BA; American journalist; *Executive Director, Institute for War and Peace Reporting.* *Education:* Yale Univ. *Career:* freelance and staff reporter, New York 1983–88; Staff Reporter, American Lawyer (magazine), New York 1988–90; Launch Ed. Transitions, Inst. for Journalism, London/Prague 1998; Ed. War Report, London 1992–98; Consultant, Dept for Int. Devt, UK Govt 1999–2002; Founder and Exec. Dir Inst. for War and Peace Reporting 1991–; Assoc. Gov. New End Primary School, London; mem. Exec. Cttee New End Second Century Campaign. *Publications:* Breakdown: War and Reconstruction in Yugoslavia (co-ed.) 1992, An Elections Handbook for Bosnian Journalists (co-ed.) 1996, Reporting Macedonia: The New Accommodation (co-ed.) 1998, Out of Time: Draskovic, Djindjic and Serbian Opposition Against Milosevic (co-ed.) 2000; numerous contribs to newpapers and journals. *Honours:* One World Media Awards, New Media Award 2004. *Address:* Institute for War and Peace Reporting, Lancaster House, 33 Islington High Street, London, N1 9LH, England (office). *Telephone:* (20) 7713-7130 (office). *Fax:* (20) 7713-7140 (office). *E-mail:* tony@iwpr.net (office). *Website:* www.iwpr.net (office).

BORDEN, Louise Walker, BA; American writer; b. 30 Oct. 1949, Cincinnati, OH; m. Peter A. Borden 1971; one s. two d. *Education:* Denison Univ. *Career:* mem. Soc. of Children's Book Writers, Authors' Guild. *Publications:* Caps, Hats, Socks and Mittens 1989, The Neighborhood Trucker 1990, The Watching Game 1991, Albie the Lifeguard 1993, Just in Time for Christmas 1994, Paperboy 1996, The Little Ships 1997, Thanksgiving Is... 1997, Goodbye, Charles Lindbergh 1998, Good Luck, Mrs K! 1999, A. Lincoln and Me 1999, Sleds on Boston Common 2000, Fly High 2001, America Is... 2002, Touching the Sky – Flying Adventures of Wilbur and Orville Wright 2003, Sea Clocks – The Story of Longitude 2004, The A+ Custodian 2004, The Greatest Skating Race – A WW2 Story from the Netherlands 2004, The Journey That Saved Curious George – The True Wartime Escape of Margret and H. A. Rey 2005, The Last Day of School 2006, Across the Blue Pacific – A WW2 Story 2006. *Honours:* Parents' Choice Award 1997, Silver Gertie Award 1998, Christopher Award 1999, Goodall Award 2000, Ohioana Children's Literature Award 2002, Denison Univ. Alumni Citation Award 2002. *Address:* 628 Myrtle Avenue, Terrace Park, OH 45174, USA. *Fax:* (513) 831-9032. *Website:* www.louiseborden.com.

BORDEN, William Vickers, AB, MA; American writer, poet, dramatist and editor; *Professor Emeritus, University of North Dakota;* b. 27 Jan. 1938, Indianapolis, IN; m. Nancy Lee Johnson 1960; one s. two d. *Education:* Columbia Univ., Univ. of California at Berkeley. *Career:* instructor 1962–64, Asst Prof. 1966–70, Assoc. Prof. 1970–82, Prof. of English 1982–90, Chester Fritz Distinguished Prof. of English 1990–97, Prof. Emeritus 1998–, Univ. of North Dakota; Fiction Ed., North Dakota Quarterly 1986–2002; mem. American Soc. of Composers, Authors and Publishers, Authors' League of America, Dramatists' Guild, PEN, Authors' Guild, The Playwrights' Center. *Plays include:* The Last Prostitute 1980, Tap Dancing Across the Universe 1981, Loon Dance 1982, The Only Woman Awake is the Woman Who Has Heard the Flute 1983, Makin' It 1984, The Consolation of Philosophy 1986, Sakakawea (musical drama) 1987, When the Meadowlark Sings 1988, Meet Again 1990, Turtle Island Blues 1991, Don't Dance Me Outside 1993, Gourmet Love 1996, Dirty Laundry 1999, Bluest Reason 2001, Wonderful World 2004, Falling 2004, Many Worlds 2005. *Publications:* fiction: Superstore (novel) 1967, many short stories; poetry: Slow Step and Dance (chapbook) 1991, Eurydice's Song 1999; numerous screenplays, radio plays and video scripts; contrib. to many anthologies and periodicals. *Honours:* North Dakota Centennial Drama Prize 1989, American Soc. of Composers, Authors and Publishers Awards 1990, 1991, 1992, Burlington Northern Award, Univ. of North Dakota 1990, Minnesota Distinguished Artist Award 1992, Minnesota State Arts Board Career Opportunity Grant 1996. *Address:* 7996 S FM 548, Royse City, TX 75189, USA (office). *Telephone:* (214) 828-1202 (office); (214) 828-1202 (home). *E-mail:* borden@ev1.net. *Website:* www.intraart.com/williamborden.

BORDIER, Roger; French writer; b. 5 March 1923, Blois; s. of Robert Bordier and Valentine Jeufraux; m. Jacqueline Bouchaud. *Education:* secondary school. *Career:* journalist in the provinces, later in Paris; contrib. to Nouvelles Littéraires and Aujourd'hui; radio and TV writer. *Publications:* poems: Les épicentres 1951; novels: La cinquième saison 1959, Les blés 1961, Le mime 1963, L'entracte 1965, Un âge d'or 1967, Le tour de ville 1969, Les éventails 1971, L'océan 1974, Meeting 1976, Demain l'été 1977; plays: Les somnambules 1963, Les visiteurs 1972; essays: L'objet contre l'art 1972, Le progrès: Pour qui? 1973, L'art moderne et l'objet 1978; novels: La grande vie 1981, Les temps heureux 1983, La longue file 1984, 36 La fête 1985, La belle de mai 1986, Les saltimbanques de la Révolution 1989, Vel d'hib 1989, Les fusils du 1er Mai 1991, Chroniques de la Cité Joyeuse 1995, L'interrogatoire, dialogue 1998, Le Zouave du Pont de l'Alma 2001, A la recherche de Paris (essay) 2004. *Honours:* Officier, Ordre des Artes et Lettres; Prix Renaudot 1961. *Address:* Editions Albin Michel, 22 rue Huyghens, 75014 Paris, (office); 8 rue Geoffroy St Hilaire, 75005 Paris, France.

BORDO, Susan Rebecca, BA, PhD; American academic and writer; b. 24 Jan. 1947, Newark, NJ; m. 1968 (divorced 1971). *Education:* Carleton University, SUNY at Stony Brook. *Career:* Assoc. Prof. of Philosophy, 1987–93, Joseph C. Georg Prof., 1991–94, Le Moyne College, Syracuse, New York; Visiting Assoc. Prof., Duke University, 1989; Prof. of Philosophy, Otis A Singletary Chair in the Humanities, University of Kentucky, Lexington, 1994–; mem. American Philosophical Asscn; Society for Phenomenology and Existential Philosophy; Society for Women in Philosophy; American Studies Asscn. *Publications:* The Flight to Objectivity: Essays on Cartesianism and Culture, 1987; Gender-Body-Knowledge: Feminist Reconstructions of Being and Knowing (co-ed.), 1989; Unbearable Weight: Feminism, Western Culture, and the Body, 1993; Twilight Zones: The Hidden Life of Cultural Images from Plato to O. J., 1997; Feminist Interpretation of Descartes (ed.), 1999; The Male Body: A New Look at Men in Public and in Private, 1999. *Honours:* Visiting Scholar in Women's Studies, Douglass College, Rutgers University, 1985; ACLS-Ford Foundation Fellowship, 1988; Rockefeller Humanist-in-Residence, Duke University and University of North Carolina Center for Research on Women, 1987–88; Scholar of the Year Award, Le Moyne College, 1990; Notable Book of the Year, New York Times, 1993; Distinguished Publication Award, Asscn for Women in Psychology, 1994. *Address:* Department of English, University of Kentucky, 1215 Paterson Office Tower, Lexington, KY 40506, USA.

BORGE MARTÍNEZ, Tomás; Nicaraguan politician, writer, poet and journalist; b. 13 Aug. 1930, Matagalpa; s. of Tomás Borge Delgado and Ana Martínez Rivera; m. 1st Yelba Mayorga (assassinated by Nat. Guard 1979); m. 2nd Josefina Cerda; eight d. *Education:* Nat. Univ. León and Granada. *Career:* first took part in activities against Somoza 1943, sentenced to eight years in prison 1956, escaped 1958, founder Frente Sandinista de Liberación Nacional (FSLN) 1961, guerrilla leader in Río Coco-Bocay, Pancasán and in clandestine struggle in the cities, captured by Somoza's agents 1976 and sentenced to 180 years of imprisonment, suffered torture and thirty months isolation, liberated in 1978 after attack on Nat. Palace; mem. Nat. Directorate FSLN 1978–; Minister of the Interior 1979–90, Adjoint Commdr Armed Forces, First Vice-Pres. Perm. Conference of Political Parties in Latin America (COPPPAL); founder Espartaco (magazine) 1946 and El Universitario (newspaper) 1950; jury mem. Festival of New Latin American Film 1990, House of Americas Award 1991. *Publications:* Carlos, el Amanecer ya no es una Tentación 1979, Los Primeros Pasos 1981, Estamos Creando una Nueva Sociedad 1981, La Mujer en la Revolución 1983, La Revolución Combate Contra la Teología de la Muerte 1983, El Axioma de la Esperanza 1984, Nicaragua: Justicia y Revolución 1986, Cristianismo y Revolución 1987, Una Relación Mágica 1989, La Paciente Impaciencia (House of America Award) 1989, La Ceremonia Esperada 1990. *Honours:* Dr hc Autonomous Univ. of Puebla, Mexico 1981. *Address:* Apartado 1229, Managua, Nicaragua. *Telephone:* 43853-52.

BORIS, Martin, BA, MA; American writer; b. 7 Aug. 1930, New York, NY; m. Gloria Shanf 1952, one s. two d. *Education:* New York University, University Heights, New York University, Washington Square, Long Island University, Brooklyn College of Pharmacy. *Publications:* Two and Two, 1979; Woodridge 1946, 1980; Brief Candle, 1990.

BORN, Anne, MA, MLitt; British poet, reviewer and translator; b. 9 July 1930, Cooden Beach, Sussex, England; m. Povl Born 1950; three s. one d. *Education:* Univ. of Copenhagen, Univ. of Oxford. *Career:* writer-in-residence, Barnstaple 1983–85, Kingsbridge 1985–87, Buckinghamshire 1996; Fellow of Hawthornden Castle; Sr Mem. St Hugh's Coll., Oxford; mem. Soc. of Authors, Trans' Asscn (chair. 1987, 1993–95), Univ. Women's Club, Devonshire Asscn (vice-chair. 2003–), FANY Corps. *Publications:* 13 poetry collections, four history books, 40 translated books (including Jens Christian Grøndahl's Silence in October, Lucca and Virginia, and Per Petterson's In the Wake); contribs to TLS, Ambit, Rialto, Green Book, Scratch, Cimarron Review, Tears in the Fence, The Frogmore Papers, Other Poetry, Salzburg Poetry Review, Troubleshare, Oasis, Links, Seam, Odyssey South. *Honours:* some 20 prizes and commendations; Freeman of the City of London. *Address:* Oversteps, Froude Road, Salcombe, South Devon TQ8 8LH, England. *Telephone:* (1548) 843713 (office). *Fax:* (1548) 844384 (office). *E-mail:* anne@oversteps.fsnet.co.uk.

BORNHOLDT, Jenny, BA; New Zealand poet; *Te Mata Estate New Zealand Poet Laureate*; b. 1960, Lower Hutt; m. Gregory O'Brien. *Education:* Victoria Univ. *Career:* Te Mata Estate New Zealand Poet Laureate 2005–. *Publications:* This Big Face 1988, Moving House 1989, Waiting Shelter 1991, How We Met 1995, My Heart Goes Swimming (ed. with Gregory O'Brien) 1996, Miss New Zealand: Selected Poems 1997, An Anthology of New Zealand Poetry in English (ed. with Gregory O'Brien and Mark Williams) (Montana New Zealand Book Award for Poetry 1997) 1997, These Days VUP 2000, Summer 2003. *Honours:* Meridian Energy Katherine Mansfield Fellow, Menton France 2002. *Address:* c/o Victoria University Press, PO Box 600, Wellington, New Zealand (office). *E-mail:* victoria-press@vuw.ac.nz.

BORSON, Ruth (Roo) Elizabeth, BA, MFA; Canadian/American poet and essayist; b. 1952, Berkeley, CA, USA. *Education:* Univ. of California at Santa Barbara, Goddard Coll., Univ. of British Columbia. *Career:* writer-in-residence, Univ. of Western Ontario 1987–88, Concordia Univ. 1993, Massey Coll., Univ. of Toronto 1998, Green Coll., Univ. of British Columbia 2000; writer-in-residence Univ. of Guelph 2005; mem. Int. PEN, Pain Not Bread, Writers' Union of Canada. *Publications:* Landfall 1977, Rain 1980, In the Smoky Light of the Fields 1980, A Sad Device 1982, The Whole Night, Coming Home 1984, The Transparence of November/Snow (with Kim Maltman) 1985, Intent, or the Weight of the World 1989, Night Walk: Selected Poems 1994, Water Memory 1996, Introduction to Wang Wei (with Kim Maltman and Andy Patton) 2000, Short Journey Upriver Toward Oishida (Governor General's Literary Award 2004, Griffin Canadian Poetry Prize 2005, Pat Lowther Award 2005) 2004; contrib. to many anthologies and periodicals. *Honours:* Univ. of British Columbia MacMillan Prize for Poetry 1977, CBC first prize for poetry 1982, CBC third prize for poetry 1989, CBC third prize for personal essay 1990, Malahat Long Poem Prize 1993, Gov. Gen.'s Award 2004, Griffin Poetry Prize 2005. *Address:* c/o McClelland and Stewart Ltd, The Canadian Publishers, 75 Sherbourne Street, Fifth Floor, Toronto, ON M5A 2P9, Canada.

BORTNIK, Aida; Argentine scriptwriter; b. 16 July 1941, Buenos Aires. *Career:* scriptwriter in Spain and Argentina. *Screenplays include:* Sebastián y su amigo el artista (TV) 1971, La Tregua (The Truce) 1974, Una mujer (A Woman) 1975, Crecer de golpe (Growing Up Suddenly) 1977, La isla (The Island) 1979, Hombres en pugna (TV mini-series) 1980, Un tiro al aire 1980, Volver (To Return) 1982, Ruggero (TV series) 1983, La historia oficial (The Official Story) (Acad. Award for Best Foreign Language Film (jtly) 1985) 1985, Pobre mariposa (Poor Butterfly) 1986, Old Gringo 1989, Tango feroz: la leyenda de Tanguito (aka Tanguito) 1993, Caballos salvajes (Wild Horses)

1995, Cenizas del paraíso (Ashes from Paradise) 1997, La soledad era ésto (This Was Solitude) 2002.

BOSHER, John Francis, PhD, FRSC, FRHistS; Canadian historian and academic; b. 28 May 1929, Sidney, BC; s. of John Ernest Bosher and Grace Simister; m. Kathryn Cecil Berry 1968; one s. three d. *Education:* Univ. of British Columbia, Univ. of Paris and Univ. of London. *Career:* Jr Admin. Asst and Personnel Selection Officer Civil Service Comm., Ottawa 1951–53; Asst Lecturer King's Coll., London 1956–59; Asst Prof. Univ. of British Columbia 1959–67; Prof. of History Cornell Univ. 1967–69, York Univ., Toronto 1969–96; Visiting Fellow All Souls Coll., Oxford 1991–92. *Publications:* The Single Duty Project: A Study of the Movement for a French Customs Union in the 18th Century 1964, French Finances 1775–1795: From Business to Bureaucracy 1970, French Society and Government: Essays in Honour of Alfred Cobban (Ed.) 1973, The Canada Merchants 1713–1763, 1987, The French Revolution 1988, Men and Ships in the Canada Trade 1660–1760: a Biographical Dictionary 1992, Business and Religion in the Age of New France 1600–1760 1994, The Gaullist Attack on Canada 1998; numerous articles on France. *Address:* 280 Chapel Street, Ottawa, ON K1N 7Y9, Canada. *Telephone:* (613) 565-6724. *E-mail:* jfbosher@attcanada.ca (home).

BOSLEY, Keith Anthony, BA; British poet and translator; b. 16 Sept. 1937, Bourne End, Buckinghamshire; m. Satu Salo 1982; three s. *Education:* Univs of Reading, Paris and Caen. *Career:* staff, BBC 1961–93; Visiting Lecturer, BBC and British Council, Middle East, 1981; corresponding mem. Finnish Literature Soc., Helsinki. *Publications:* The Possibility of Angels, 1969; And I Dance, 1972; Dark Summer, 1976; Mallarmé: The Poems (trans.), 1977; Eino Leino: Whitsongs (trans.), 1978; Stations, 1979; The Elek Book of Oriental Verse, 1979; From the Theorems of Master Jean de La Ceppède (trans.), 1983; A Chiltern Hundred, 1987; The Kalevala (trans.), 1989; I Will Sing of What I Know (trans.), 1990; Luis de Camões: Epic and Lyric (trans.), 1990; The Kanteletar (trans.), 1992; The Great Bear (trans.), 1993; Aleksis Kivi: Odes (trans.), 1994; André Frénaud: Rome the Sorceress (trans.), 1996; Eve Blossom has Wheels: German Love Poetry, 1997; Skating on the Sea: Poetry from Finland, 1997; An Upton Hymnal, 1999. Contributions: many newspapers, reviews, magazines and journals. *Honours:* Finnish State Prize for Translation 1978; First Prize, British Comparative Literature Asscn Translation Competition, 1980; First Prize, Goethe Soc. Translation Competition, 1982; Knight, First Class, Order of the White Rose of Finland, 1991; Pension, Royal Literary Fund, 2001. *Address:* 108 Upton Road, Upton-cum-Chalvey, Slough SL1 2AW, England (home). *Telephone:* (1753) 525249 (home). *Fax:* (1753) 525249 (home). *E-mail:* bosleykssg@msm.com (home).

BOTELHO, (Maria) Fernanda; Portuguese novelist and poet; b. 1926, Oporto. *Education:* Univs of Coimbra and Lisbon. *Career:* co-f. magazine, Távola Redonda 1950s; regular contrib. to experimental magazines of 1950s. *Publications:* As Coordenadas Líricas (poems) 1951, O Enigma das Sete Alíneas (fiction) 1956, O Ângulo Raso (fiction) 1957, Calendário Privado (fiction) 1958, A Gata e a Fábula (fiction) 1960, Xerazade e os Outros (fiction) 1964, Terra sem Música (fiction) 1969, Lourenço é nome de Jogral (fiction) 1971, Esta Noite Sonhei com Brueghel (fiction) 1987, Festa em Casa de Flores (fiction) 1990, Dramaticamente Vestida de Negro (fiction) 1994, As Contadoras de Histórias (Portuguese Writers' Asscn Prize) 1998. *Honours:* Grand Official of the Order of Merit (Portugal), Order of Leopold I (Belgium); Prémio Camilo Castelo Branco, Prémio da Crítica, Prémio Eça de Queirós. *Address:* c/o Editora Presença, Estrada das Palmeiras 59, Queluz de Baixo, 2730-132 Barcarena, Portugal. *Website:* www.presenca.pt.

BOTSFORD, Keith, (I. I. Magdalen); Italian/American journalist and novelist; b. 29 March 1928, Brussels, Belgium. *Career:* Prof. of Journalism, History and Int. Relations, Boston, USA; journalist, sports writer, food writer and US correspondent for journals, incl. The Sunday Times, The Independent, La Stampa. *Publications:* as Keith Botsford: fiction: Master Race 1955, The Eighth Best-Dressed Man in the World 1958, Benvenuto 1961, The Marchman 1965, Dominguin 1972, The Mothers 2001; non-fiction: Driving Ambition (with Alan Jones) 1981, Keke (with Keke Rosberg) 1985, The Champion of Formula 1 1988, The Republic of Letters (with Saul Bellow) 1999, Editors (with Saul Bellow) 2001; as I. I. Magdalen: fiction: The Search for Anderson 1982, Ana P. 1983, Lennie and Vance and Benji 2002, Emma H. 2003. *Address:* c/o The Toby Press, PO Box 8531, New Milford, CT 06776-8531, USA. *Website:* www.tobypress.com.

BOTTING, Douglas Scott, MA, FRGS; British writer; b. 22 Feb. 1934, London, England; m. 1964; two d. *Education:* St Edmund Hall, Oxford. *Career:* mem. King's African Rifles, East Africa; exploration film-maker, BBC TV; Special Corresp., BBC, Geographical Magazine, Time-Life and other periodicals; mem. Royal Inst. of Int. Affairs, Soc. of Authors, Biographers' Club, NCICA, Friends of Soqotra. *Publications:* Island of the Dragon's Blood 1958, The Knights of Bornu 1961, One Chilly Siberian Morning 1965, Humboldt and the Cosmos 1973, Wilderness Europe 1976, Rio de Janeiro 1977, The Pirates 1978, The Second Front 1978, The U-Boats 1979, The Giant Airships 1980, The Aftermath in Europe 1945, Nazi Gold 1984, The Story of the Worlds's Greatest Robbery 1984, In the Ruins of the Reich 1985, Wild Britain 1988, Hitler's Last General: The Case Against Wilhelm Mohnke 1989, America's Secret Army 1989, Gavin Maxwell: A Life 1993, Sex Appeal: The Art and Science of Sexual Attraction (with Kate Botting) 1995, Gerald Durrell: The Authorised Biography 1999, The Saga of Ring of Bright Water 2000, Dr Eckener's Dream Machine: The Historic Saga of the Round-the-World

Zeppelin 2001, Hitler and Women – the Love Life of Adolf Hitler 2004, My Darling Enemy 2007; contrib. to Oxford Dictionary of National Biography, BBC TV and radio, various periodicals. *Address:* 2 The Old School House, 1 Dinton Road, Kingston upon Thames, Surrey KT2 5JT (home); c/o Johnson & Alcock Ltd, Clerkenwell House, 45–47 Clerkenwell Green, London, EC1R 0HT, England (office). *E-mail:* douglasbotting@compuserve.com (home).

BOUBLIL, Alain Albert; French writer and dramatist; b. 5 March 1941, Tunis; four s. *Career:* wrote libretto and lyrics for: La Révolution Française 1973, Les Misérables 1980, Abbacadabra 1984, Miss Saigon 1989, Martin Guerre 1996; Le Journal d'Adam et Eve (play) 1994. *Honours:* two Tony Awards, Two Grammy Awards, two Victoire de la Musique Awards, Molière Award (all for Les Misérables), Evening Standard Drama Award (for Miss Saigon), Laurence Olivier Award (for Martin Guerre).

BOUCHARDEAU, Huguette; French politician, writer and editor; b. 1 June 1935, St-Etienne; d. of Marius Briaut and Rose Briaut (née Noël); m. Marc Bouchardeau 1955; one s. two d. *Career:* teacher of philosophy, Lycée Honoré d'Urfé 1961–70; Lecturer in Educ. Sciences, Univ. of Lyon 1970; Sec.-Gen. Parti Socialiste unifié 1979–83; unsuccessful presidential cand. 1981; Sec. of State for Environment and Quality of Life 1983–84; Minister for the Environment 1984–86; Founder, Ed. H.B. Editions 1995–; Mayor Aigues-Vives 1995–. *Publications:* Pas d'histoire, les femmes 1977, Hélène Brion: La voie feministe 1978, Un coin dans leur monde 1980, Le ministère du possible 1986, Choses dites de profil 1988, George Sand, La lune et les sabots 1990, Rose Noël 1990, La grande verrière 1991, Carnets de Prague 1992, Le Déjeuner 1993, La Famille Renoir 1994, Simone Weil 1995, Les Roches rouges 1996, Faute de regard 1997, Agatha Christie 1999, Voyage autour de ma bibliothèque 2000, Elsa Triolet 2001, Mes Nuits avec Descartes 2002, Nathalie Sarraute 2003, Differents receuils de textes choisis de G. Saud 2003–04. *Honours:* Chevalier Légion d'honneur. *Address:* H.B. Editions, 8 rue Ménard, 30000 Nîmes, France (office). *E-mail:* bouchardeau-hb-editions@wanadoo.fr (office).

BOUCHÈNE, Abderrahmane; Algerian publisher; b. 1941, Algiers; m.; four c. *Education:* Algeria and Lausanne Univs. *Career:* worked in family clothing shop; admin. posts at Société nat. d'édition et de diffusion, Entreprise nat. du livre and Ministry of Culture; f. Editions Bouchène publishing house, Kouba, in late 1980s; by 1990 owner of two bookshops in Algiers, one in Riad-El-Feth; forced to flee Algeria and close business 1994; exile in Tunisia 1994–96; moved to Paris and set up new co. specializing in Algerian historical texts and historical anthropology of Maghreb socs. *Address:* Editions Bouchène, 113–115 rue Danielle-Casanova, 93200 Saint-Denis, Paris, France (office). *Telephone:* 1-48-20-93-75 (office). *E-mail:* edbouchene@aol.com (office).

BOUCHER, David Ewart George, BA, MSc, PhD, FRHistS; British academic, writer and editor; b. 15 Oct. 1951, Ebbw Vale, Monmouthshire, Wales; m. Clare Mary French Mullen 1979, two d. *Education:* Univ. Coll., Swansea, LSE and Univ. of Liverpool. *Career:* Tutorial Fellow, 1980–83; Temporary Lecturer in Politics, 1983–84, University College, Cardiff; Lecturer, 1985–88, Senior Lecturer in Politics, 1988–89, La Trobe University, Melbourne, Australia; Research Fellow, 1989–90, Lecturer, 1990, Senior Lecturer in Politics, 1991, Australian National University, Canberra; Reader, 1995–98, Prof. of Political Theory and Government, 1998–2000, University of Wales, Swansea; Professorial Fellow, Cardiff University, 2000–; mem. Political Studies Asscn. *Publications:* Texts in Context: Revisionist Methods for Studying the History of Ideas, 1985; The Social and Political Thought of R. G. Collingwood, 1989; A Radical Hegelian: The Political Thought of Henry Jones (with Andrew Vincent), 1994; Political Theories of International Relations: From Thucydides to the Present, 1998; Steel Skill and Survival, 2000; British Idealism and Political Theory (with Andrew Vincent), 2000; Politics, Poetry and Protest: Bob Dylan and Leonard Cohen, 2003. Editor: Essays in Political Philosophy, by R. G. Collingwood, 1989; The New Leviathan, revised edn, by R. G. Collingwood, 1992; The Social Contract from Hobbes to Rawls (with Paul Kelly), 1994; Philosophy, Politics and Civilization (with T. Modood and J. Connelly), 1995; The British Idealists, 1997; Social Justice: From Hume to Walzer (with Paul Kelly), 1998; Political Thinkers (with Paul Kelly), 2003. Contributions: scholarly journals. *Address:* School of European Studies, University of Wales, Cardiff, Cardiff CF10, Wales. *E-mail:* boucherde@cardiff.ac.uk.

BOUČKOVÁ, Tereza; Czech writer; b. 24 May 1957, Prague; d. of Pavel Kohout and Anna Cornová; m. Jiří Bouček; one s. two adopted s. *Career:* mem. Int. PEN. *Publications:* Indiánský běh 1991, Daleko od stromu 1991, Křepelice 1993, Když milujete muže 1995, Zlodějina 1995, Krákorám 1998, Rok perel 2000, Jen si tak trochu schnít 2004. *Address:* c/o Czech PEN Centre, Vodièkova str. 32, 110 00 Prague 1, Czech Republic (office).

BOUDJEDRA, Rachid, BPhil; Algerian poet, writer and playwright; b. 5 Sept. 1941, Aïn Beïda, Constantinois; m. *Education:* Univ. of the Sorbonne. *Career:* lived in France 1969–72, Morocco 1972–75; worked in Ministry of Information and Culture 1977; columnist weekly magazine Révolution africaine; Reader SNED, lecturer IEP Alger 1981; mem. Ligue des droits de l'homme. *Publications:* La Répudiation (novel) 1969, L'Insolation 1972, L'Escargot entêté 1977, Topographie idéale pour une agression caractérisée 1975, Les 1001 Années de la nostalgie 1979, Le Vainqueur de coupe 1981, Le Démantèlement 1982, Greffe 1984, La Macération 1985, La Pluie 1987, La Prise de Gibraltar 1987, Le Désordre des choses 1991, FIS de la haine (non-fiction) 1994, Philippe Djian 1992, Barbès-Palace 1993, Timimoun 1994, Mines de rien 1995, Lettres algériennes 1995, La Vie à l'endroit 1997, Fascination 2000, Le Directeur des promenades 2002, Cinq Fragments du désert 2001, Les Funérailles 2003, Peindre l'Orient 2003. *Address:* c/o Ministry of Communications and Culture, Les Annassers, BP 100, Kouba, Algiers, Algeria.

BOULANGER, Daniel; French writer; b. 24 Jan. 1922, Compiègne, Oise; s. of Michel Boulanger and Hélène Bayart; m. 2nd Clémence Dufour; four s. three d. *Education:* Petit Séminaire Saint-Charles, Chauny. *Career:* sub-ed., Affaires économiques 1946–48; writer 1948–; wrote scripts or screenplays for over 100 films, including Cartouche 1962, L'Homme de Rio 1963, Les Tribulations d'un Chinois en Chine 1965, La Vie de Château 1966, Le Voleur 1967, Le Diable par la Queue 1968, Le Roi de Coeur (Prix Louis-Delluc) 1969, Les Maries de l'An II 1971, L'Affaire Dominici 1973, Police Python 1975, Une femme fidèle 1976, La Menace 1976, Cheval d'Orgueil 1980, Chouans 1988, La Révolution Française 1989; numerous plays; mem. Acad. Goncourt 1983. *Publications include:* (novels, novellas and short stories) Les Noces du Merle 1963 (Prix de la Nouvelle 1963), Retouches 1969 (Prix Max Jacob 1970), Vessies et Lanternes 1971 (Prix de l'Académie française 1971), Fouette Cocher 1974 (Prix Goncourt de la Nouvelle 1974), Jules Bouc 1987, La Confession d'Omer 1991, Un Eté à la diable 1992, Ursacq 1993, A la courte paille 1993, Le Retable Wasserfall et Etiquettes 1994, Caporal Supérieur 1994, Le Miroitier 1995, Taciturnes 1995, Tombeau d'Héraldine 1997, Talbard 1998, Le Ciel de Bargetal 1999, Clémence et Auguste 2000, Les Mouches et l'âne 2001, Cache-Cache 2002, Du temps qu'on plaisantait 2003, La Poste de Nuit 2004; several collections of poetry including L'été des femmes 1964, Le chemin des caracoles, Fête Ste. Beuve 1966, Memoire de la Ville 1970. *Honours:* Officier Légion d'honneur, Officier Ordre nat. du Mérite, Commdr des Arts et Lettres; Prix Pierre de Monaco for complete body of work 1979, Prix Kléber Haedens 1983. *Address:* 22 rue du Heaume, 60300 Senlis, France.

BOULARÈS, Mohamed Habib; Tunisian politician, writer and journalist; b. 29 July 1933, Tunis; s. of Sadok Ben Mohamed and Zoubeida Bent Abdelkader Aziz; m. Line Poinsignon 1966; one d. *Education:* Collège Sadiki, Tunis. *Career:* mem. staff exec. office, Parti Destourien 1955; Deputy Ed. daily Essabah 1956; in charge of publications, Ministry of Information 1957; Ed. Nat. Radio news service 1958; Ed. Al Amal (Parti Destourien daily newspaper) 1960; first Man. Dir Tunis Afrique Presse news agency 1961; Dir Radio Télévision Tunisienne, Dir of Information, Ministry of Cultural Affairs and Information 1962; mem. Econ. and Social Council 1964–70; Minister of Cultural Affairs and Information 1970; Dir Ecole Internationale de Bordeaux, France 1972–73; teacher, Institut de Langues Orientales, Paris for four years; mem. Parl. 1981–86, 1989–94, 1994–; Amb. to Egypt 1988; Minister of Culture 1988–89, of Culture and Information 1989–90, of Foreign Affairs 1990–91, of Nat. Defence Feb.–Oct. 1991; Special Adviser to Pres. of Repub. March 1990; Pres. Nat. Ass. 1991–94; (Mediterranean Africa prize of Asscn des Ecrivains en langue française ADELF) 1984. *Publications:* L'Islam, la peur et l'espérance (trans. in English); several other non-fiction works and plays. *Honours:* Grand Officier Ordre de l'Indépendence, Grand Cordon Ordre de la République, Commdr Ordre du 7 Novembre, numerous foreign decorations. *Address:* c/o Assemblée Nationale, 2000 Le Bardo, Tunis, Tunisia. *Telephone:* (1) 510-200. *Fax:* (1) 514-608.

BOULLOSA, Carmen; Mexican novelist, poet and playwright; *Disinguished Lecturer, City College, City University of New York*; b. 1954, Mexico City; m. Alejandro Aura; two c. *Education:* Univ. Iberoamericana, Univ. Nacional Autónoma de México. *Career:* Disinguished Lecturer City Coll., CUNY; Visiting Prof. and Andrés Bello Chair NY Univ. 2002–03; Visiting Prof. Columbia Univ. 2003–04; has held visiting appts at San Diego State Univ., Georgetown Univ., La Sorbonne (France); lectured at Brown, Princeton, Irvine, UCLA and insts in England, Germany, Austria, France, Spain, Argentina, Ecuador, Venezuela, Colombia; co-f. (with Salman Rushdie) Mexico City House for Persecuted Writers; Fellow NY Public Library's Center for Scholars and Writers 2001. *Plays:* Cocinar hombres 1985, Teatro Herético: Propusieron a Maria 1987, Pesca de piratas 1993, Mi versión de los hechos 1997, Los Totoles (Mexico City Critics Play of the Year) 2000. *Publications:* novels: Mejor desaparece 1987, Antes 1989, Son vacas, somos puercos 1991, El médico de los piratas 1992, Llanto 1992, La milagrosa 1993, Duerme 1994, Quiza 1995, Cielos de la tierra 1997, Treinta años 1999, De un salto descabalga la reina 2002, La otra mano de Lepanto 2005; juvenile: La midas 1986, Sólo para muchachos 1997; essays: Papeles irresponsables 1989; poems: La memoria vacía 1978, El hilo olvida 1979, Ingobernable 1979, Lealtad 1981, Abierta 1983, La salvaja 1988, Soledumbre 1992, Envenenada: antología personal 1993, Niebla 1997, Jardín Elíseo 1999, La delirios 1998, La bebida 2002, Salto de mantarraya (y otros dos) 2002; art books, ed. of other books; contrib. to anthologies and publications. *Honours:* Premio Xavier Villarutia. *E-mail:* labebida@hotmail.com. *Website:* www.carmenboullosa.net.

BOULTON, Adam, BA, MA; British journalist; *Political Editor, Sky News*; b. 15 Feb., Reading; three d.; m. Angela Hunter 2006. *Education:* Westminster School, Christ Church, Oxford and School of Advanced Int. Studies, Washington, DC. *Career:* jr staff mem., BBC External Services 1982; Political Ed., TV-am from launch in 1983; f. mem. and Political Ed., Sky News, establishing the Sky News political team 1989–; contrib. articles to numerous publications, including The Times, The Independent, The Business, Scotland on Sunday. *Television programmes:* presenter Sunday with Adam Boulton (Plain English Campaign Nat. Programme Award 2001) 1994–, Tonight 1995–98, Forum (roadshow), Answer the Question, The Boulton Factor.

Address: c/o BSkyB PLC, Victoria House, 98 Victoria Street, London, SW1E, England. *Website:* www.sky.com/skynews.

BOULTON, James Thompson, BA, BLitt, PhD, FRSL, FBA; British academic emeritus and writer; b. 17 Feb. 1924, Pickering, Yorkshire; m. Margaret Helen Leary 1949; one s. one d. *Education:* Univ. Coll., Univ. of Durham, Lincoln Coll., Univ. of Oxford, Univ. of Nottingham. *Career:* Pilot, RAF 1943–46; Lecturer, Univ. of Nottingham, becoming Sr Lecturer, Reader in English Literature 1951–63, Prof. 1964–75, Dean, Faculty of Arts 1970–73; Prof. of English Studies and Head of Dept, Univ. of Birmingham 1975–88, Prof. Emer. 1989–, Dean, Faculty of Arts 1981–84, Public Orator 1984–88, Dir, Inst. for Advanced Research in Arts and Social Sciences 1987–99, Deputy Dir 1999–. *Publications:* Edmund Burke – Sublime and Beautiful (ed.) 1958, The Language of Politics in the Age of Wilkes and Burke 1963, Samuel Johnson – The Critical Heritage 1971, Defoe – Memoirs of a Cavalier (ed.) 1972, The Letters of D. H. Lawrence (ed.) (eight vols) 1979–2000, Selected Letters of D. H. Lawrence (ed.) 1997, The Writings and Speeches of Edmund Burke, Vol. One (co-ed.) 1997, D. H. Lawrence – Late Essays and Articles (ed.) 2004, James Boswell – An Account of Corsica (co-ed.) 2006. *Honours:* Hon. DLitt (Durham) 1991, (Nottingham) 1993. *Address:* Tyn y Ffynnon, Nant Peris, Caernarfon, LL55 4UH, England (office). *Telephone:* (1286) 872281.

BOURAOUI, Hédi, LèsL, MA, PhD; Canadian poet, writer and academic; *Writer-in-Residence, Strong College, York University*; b. 16 July 1932, Sfax, Tunisia. *Education:* Université de Toulouse, France, Indiana Univ., USA, Cornell Univ., Ithaca, USA. *Career:* Master, Strong Coll., York Univ. 1978–88, now Univ. Prof. Emeritus, Writer-in-Residence 2005–; Jt Ed.-in-Chief poetry review, Envol; Jt Ed.-in-Chief, LittéRéalité; Deputy Gov. to the Bd of Govs, American Biographical Inst. Research Asscn 1995; mem. Royal Soc. of Canada (Acad. des Lettres et Sciences Humaines). *Publications:* poetry: Musocktail 1966, Tremblé 1969, Eclate-Module 1972, Vésuviade 1976, Haïtuvois, suivi de Antillades 1980, Vers et l'Envers 1982, Ignescent 1982, Echosmos 1986, Arc-en-Terre 1991, Emigressence 1992, Nomadaime 1995, Illuminations Autistes (Pensées-Eclairs) 2003, Struga, suivi de Margelle d'un Festival 2003, Sfaxitude 2005, Livr'Errance 2005; novels: L'Icônaison 1985, Bangkok Blues 1994, Retour à Thyna 1996, La Pharaone 1998, Ainsi parle la Tour CN 1999, La Composée 2001, La Femme d'entre les lignes 2002, Sept Portes pour une Brûlance 2005; numerous essays and works of criticism. *Honours:* Grand Prix du Salon du livre de Toronto 1998, Prix du Nouvel Ontario 1999, Salon du livre de Toronto Prix Christine Dumitriu van Saanen 2000, Prix Int. de Poésie Emmanuel Roblès 2004, APFUCC Prix du Meilleur Ouvrage d'Érudition 2006; Officier, Ordre des Palmes académiques 2004. *Address:* 332 Strong College, York University, 4700 Keele Street, Toronto, ON M3J 1P3, Canada (office). *Telephone:* (416) 736-2100 ext. 77323 (office). *E-mail:* bouraoui@yorku.ca (office). *Website:* www.hedibouraoui.com; www.arts.yorku.ca/french/cmc.

BOURAOUI, Nina; French writer; b. 31 July 1967, Rennes; d. of Rachid Bouraoui and Maryvonne Henry-Bouraoui. *Education:* Lycée Français, Algiers, Algeria and Zurich, Switzerland, Inst. Catholique, Paris and Univ. of Paris II (Panthéon-Assas). *Career:* moved to Algiers with her family 1967, stayed there until aged 15, family then lived in Switzerland and UAE, moved to Paris to pursue her univ. studies. *Publications include:* La voyeuse interdite (Prix du Livre Inter) 1991, Poing mort 1992, Le bal des murènes 1996, L'âge blessé 1998, Garçon manqué 2000, Le jour du séisme 2001, La vie heureuse 2002, Poupée Bella 2004. *Address:* 47 rue Claude Bernard, 75005 Paris, France. *Telephone:* (1) 43-37-54-31.

BOURJAILY, Vance, BA, DLit; American novelist and academic; b. 17 Sept. 1922, Cleveland; s. of Monte Ferris Bourjaily and Barbara Webb Bourjaily; m. 1st Bettina Yensen 1946; one s. two d.; m. 2nd Yasmin Mogul 1985; one s. *Education:* Handley High School, Va and Bowdoin Coll., Maine. *Career:* American Field Service 1942–44; US Army 1944–46; Publisher, Record, New Castle, Va 1947–48; Staff Writer, San Francisco Chronicle 1949–50; Ed. Discovery 1951–53; Instructor, Mexico City Coll. 1953; Dramatic Critic, The Village Voice 1955–56; freelance TV writer 1956–57; Visiting Lecturer, Univ. of Iowa 1957–59, Prof. 1961; Specialist, US State Dept 1960; Boyd Prof. of English, La. State Univ. 1989, now Prof. Emer. *Publications:* novels: The End of My Life 1947, The Hound of Earth 1953, The Violated 1957, Confessions of a Spent Youth 1960, The Man Who Knew Kennedy 1967, Brill Among the Ruins 1970, Now Playing at Canterbury 1976, The Great Fake Book 1986, Old Soldier 1990, Fishing by Mail: The Outdoor Life of a Father and Son 1993; non-fiction: The Unnatural Enemy 1963, Country Matters 1973; plays: Time is a Dancer 1950, The Quick Years 1956, Confessions 1971. *Honours:* Acad. Award in Literature, American Acad. of Arts and Letters 1993. *Address:* c/o Department of English, 260 Allen Hall, Louisiana State University, Baton Rouge 70803, USA.

BOURKE, Joanna, MA; New Zealand historian and writer; *Professor of History, Birkbeck College, London*; b. 1963. *Education:* Auckland Univ. *Career:* brought up by missionary parents in Zambia, Solomon Islands and Haiti; has held academic posts in Australia, New Zealand and Cambridge, England; currently Prof. of History, Birkbeck Coll., London. *Publications:* Husbandry to Housewifery: Women, Economic Change and Housework in Ireland, 1890–1914 1993, Working-Class Cultures in Britain 1890–1960 1996, Dismembering the Male: Men's Bodies, Britain and the Great War 1999, An Intimate History of Killing (Fraenkel Prize in Contemporary History 1998, Wolfson Prize for Historical Writing 2000) 1999, The Second World War: A People's History 2001, The Misfit Soldier: Edward Casey's War Story, 1914–32

(ed.) 2001, Fear: A Cultural History of the Twentieth Century 2004; contrib. numerous chapters and articles to scholarly books and journals, on Irish history, British social history and the history of warfare. *Address:* c/o School of History, Classics and Archaeology, Birkbeck College, Malet Street, London, WC1E 7HX, England (office). *E-mail:* j.bourke@bbk.ac.uk (office). *Website:* www.bbk.ac.uk/hca/staff/bourke (office).

BOURNE, Stephen Robert Richard, MA, FCA, FRSA; British publisher; *CEO, Cambridge University Press*; b. 20 March 1952, Kampala, Uganda; s. of Colyn M. Bourne and Kathleen Bourne; m. Stephanie Ann Bickford 1978; one s. one d. *Education:* Berkhamsted School, Univ. of Edinburgh. *Career:* with Deloitte Haskins and Sells, London and Hong Kong 1974–80; with Exxon Chemical Asia-Pacific, Hong Kong 1980–86; Financial Dir Asia, Dow Jones Telerate, London and Hong Kong 1986–89, Gen. Man. Northern Europe 1989–94; Man. Dir, Financial Printing Div., St Ives PLC, London 1994–96; Devt Dir, Cambridge Univ. Press 1997–2000, Chair. of Printing Div. 2000–02, CEO 2002–; Bd mem., Britten Sinfonia, The Wine Soc.; mem. Publishing Studies Advisory Bd, Univ. Coll. London, City Univ., London Coll. of Communication; Fellow, Clare Hall, Cambridge, Inst. of Printing; Liveryman and Chair. Trade and Industry Forum, The Stationers' Co. *Address:* Cambridge University Press, The Edinburgh Building, Shaftesbury Road, Cambridge, CB2 2RU (office); Falmouth Lodge, Snailwell Road, Newmarket, CB8 7DN, England (home). *Telephone:* (1223) 325184 (office). *Fax:* (1223) 325701 (office). *E-mail:* sbourne@cambridge.org (office). *Website:* www.cambridge.org (office).

BOUZFOUR, Ahmed; Moroccan author. *Publications:* Nanna (short story), Qounqous (short story collection) 2003; contrib. to Aljamía, Banipal. *Address:* c/o Union des écrivains du Maroc, Rabat, Morocco.

BOVA, Benjamin (Ben) William, BA, MA; American writer, editor and lecturer; b. 8 Nov. 1932, Philadelphia, PA. *Education:* Temple Univ., SUNY at Albany. *Career:* Editorial Dir, Omni Magazine; Ed., Analog Magazine; Lecturer; Fellow British Interplanetary Soc.; mem. Nat. Space Soc. (pres. emeritus), PEN, SFWA. *Publications:* fiction: The Star Conquerors 1959, Star Watchman 1964, The Weathermakers 1967, Out of the Sun 1968, The Dueling Machine 1969, Escape! 1969, Exiled from Earth 1971, THX1138 (with George Lucas) 1971, Flight of Exiles 1972, As on a Darkling Plain 1972, When the Sky Burned 1972, Forward in Time 1973, Gremlins, Go Home! 1974, End of Exile 1975, The Starcrossed 1975, City of Darkness 1976, Millennium 1976, The Multiple Man 1976, Colony 1978, Maxwell's Demons 1978, Kinsman 1979, Voyagers 1981, Test of Fire 1982, The Winds of Altair 1983, Orion 1984, The Astral Mirror 1985, Privateers 1985, Prometheans 1986, Voyagers II: The Alien Within 1986, Battle Station 1987, The Kinsman Saga 1987, Vengeance of Orion 1988, Peacekeepers 1988, Cyberbooks 1989, Voyagers III: Star Brothers 1990, Future Crime 1990, Orion in the Dying Time 1990, The Trikon Deception 1992, Mars 1992, To Save the Sun 1992, Triumph 1993, Challenges 1993, Empire Builders 1993, Sam Gunn Unlimited 1993, Orion and the Conqueror 1994, To Fear the Light 1994, Death Dream 1994, Orion Among the Stars 1995, Brothers 1996, Moonrise 1996, Twice Seven 1998, Sam Gunn Forever 1998, Moonwar 1998, Return to Mars 1999, Venus 2000, Jupiter 2001, The Precipice 2001, The Rock Rats 2002, Saturn 2003, Tales of the Grand Tour 2004, The Silent War 2004, Powersat 2005, Mercury 2005, Titan 2006; non-fiction: The Milky Way Galaxy 1961, Giants of the Animal World 1962, Reptiles Since the World Began 1964, The Uses of Space 1965, In Quest of Quasars 1970, Planets, Life & LGM 1970, The Fourth State of Matter 1971, The Amazing Laser 1972, The New Astronomies 1972, Starflight and Other Improbabilities 1973, Man Changes the Weather 1973, Survival Guide for the Suddenly Single (with Barbara Berson) 1974, The Weather Changes Man 1974, Workshops in Space 1974, Through Eyes of Wonder 1975, Science: Who Needs it? 1975, Notes to a Science Fiction Writer 1975, Closeup: New Worlds (with Trudy E. Bell) 1977, Viewpoint 1977, The Seeds of Tomorrow 1977, The High Road 1981, Vision of the Future: The Art of Robert McCall 1982, Assured Survival 1984, Star Peace 1986, Welcome to Moonbase! 1987, Interactions (with Sheldon Glashow) 1988, The Beauty of Light 1988, First Contact (ed. and contrib.) 1990, The Craft of Writing Science Fiction that Sells 1994, Space Travel 1997, Immortality 1998, The Story of Light 2001, Faint Echoes, Distant Stars 2004. *Honours:* Distinguished Alumnus Temple Univ. 1981, Alumni Fellow 1982. *Address:* c/o Hodder, 338 Euston Road, London, NW1 3BH, England. *Website:* www.benbova.com.

BOWDEN, Jim (see Spence, William John Duncan)

BOWDEN, Roland Heywood; British poet and dramatist; b. 19 Dec. 1916, Lincoln, England; m. 1946, one s. one d. *Education:* School of Architecture, Liverpool University 1934–39. *Career:* mem. National Poetry Secretariat. *Publications:* Poems From Italy, 1970; Every Season is Another, 1986. Plays: Death of Paolini, 1980; After Neruda, 1984; The Fence, 1985. Contributions: Arts Review: London Magazine; Panurge; Words International. *Honours:* Arts Council Drama Bursary, 1978; Cheltenham Festival Poetry Prize, 1982; First Prize, All-Sussex Poets, 1983.

BOWEN, Kevin; American poet and translator; m.; two c. *Career:* served with the US Army in Viet Nam 1968–69; currently Dir William Joiner Centre for the Study of War and its Social Consequences, Univ. of Massachusetts in Boston. *Publications:* poetry: Playing Basketball with the Viet-Cong 1994; editor: Mountain Poetry: Vietnamese Poetry from the Wars 1948–93 1998, 6 Vietnamese Poets 2002; contrib. to Distant Road 1999. *Address:* c/o Curbstone

Press, 321 Jackson Street, Willimantic, CT 06226-1738, USA. *E-mail:* info@curbstone.org. *Website:* www.curbstone.org.

BOWEN, Lynne, BSc, MA; Canadian writer; *Co-Chair of Creative Non-Fiction Writing, Rogers Communications*; b. 22 Aug. 1940, Indian Head,SK; d. of Desmond and Isobel Crossley; m. Richard Allen Bowen; two s. one d. *Education:* Univ. of Alberta, Univ. of Victoria. *Career:* Co-Chair. of Creative Non-Fiction Writing, Rogers Communications 1992–; Co-Chair., Creative Writing Program, Univ. of BC 2000–02; mem. Writers' Union of Canada, PEN Int. *Publications:* Boss Whistle: The Coal Miners of Vancouver Island Remember 1982, Three Dollar Dreams 1987, Muddling Through: The Remarkable Story of the Barr Colonists 1992, Those Lake People: Stories of Cowichan Lake 1995, Robert Dunsmuir, Laird of the Mines 1999. *Honours:* Canadian Historical Asscn Regional Certificates of Merit 1984, 1993, Lieutenant Gov.'s Medal 1987, Hubert Evans Non-Fiction Prize 1993, City of Nanaimo Excellence in Culture Award 1999, Concordia Univ. Coll. of Alberta Distinguished Alumni Award 2000. *Address:* 4982 Fillinger Crescent, Nanaimo, BC V9V 1J1, Canada (office). *E-mail:* lynne@island.net.

BOWEN, William Gordon, PhD; American academic; *Trustee, Andrew W. Mellon Foundation*; b. 6 Oct. 1933, Cincinnati, Ohio; s. of Albert A. Bowen and Bernice Pomert; m. Mary Ellen Maxwell 1956; one s. one d. *Education:* Denison and Princeton Univs. *Career:* Asst Prof. of Econs, Princeton Univ. 1958–61, Assoc. Prof. 1961–65, Prof. 1965–87; Dir of Graduate Studies, Woodrow Wilson School of Public and Int. Affairs, Princeton Univ. 1964–66; Provost, Princeton Univ. 1967–72, Pres. 1972–88; lecturer Oxford Univ. 2000; Pres. Andrew W. Mellon Foundation, New York 1988, now Trustee; Dir NCR Corpn 1975–91; Regent Smithsonian Inst. 1980, now Regent Emer.; Trustee, Denison Univ. 1966–75, 1992–2000, Center for Advanced Study in the Behavioral Sciences 1973–84, 1986–92, Reader's Digest 1985–97, American Express 1988–, ISTOR 1995–, Merck and Co. 1986–, Ithaka Harbors, Inc., Univ. Corpn for Advanced Internet Devt 1998–; mem. Bd of Overseers Teachers Insurance and Annuity Asscn and Coll. Retirement Equities Fund 1995–; Dr hc. (Oxford) 2001. *Publications:* The Wage-Price Issue: A Theoretical Analysis 1960, Performing Arts: The Economic Dilemma (with W. J. Baumol) 1966, The Economics of Labor Force Participation (with T. A. Finegan) 1969, Ever the Teacher 1987, Prospects for Faculty in the Arts and Sciences 1989 (with J. A. Sosa), In Pursuit of the PhD 1992 (with Neil L. Rudenstine), Inside the Boardroom: Governance by Directors and Trustees 1994, (with T. Nygren, S. Turner and E. Duffy) The Charitable Nonprofts 1994, Universities and Their Leaderships (ed. Harold Shapiro) 1998, The Shape of the River: Long-Term Consequences of Considering Race in College and University Admissions (with Derek Bok) 1998, The Game of Life: College Sports and Educational Values 2001, At a Slight Angle to the Universe (also Romanes Lecture, Univ. of Oxford) 2001, Reclaiming the Game: College Sports and Educational Values (with Sarah A. Levin) 2003. *Honours:* Joseph Henry Medal, Smithsonian Inst. 1996, Grawemeyer Award in Educ., Univ. of Louisville 2001. *Address:* Andrew W. Mellon Foundation, 140 East 62nd Street, New York, NY 10021, USA (office). *Telephone:* (212) 838-8400 (office). *Fax:* (212) 223-2778 (office). *Website:* www.mellon.org (office).

BOWERING, George Henry, OC, MA; Canadian writer, poet and lecturer; b. 1 Dec. 1936, Penticton, BC; s. of Ewart Bowering and Pearl Bowering (née Brinson); m. Angela Luoma 1962 (died 1999); one d. *Education:* Victoria Coll., Univ. of British Columbia, Univ. of Western Ontario. *Career:* served as Royal Canadian Air Force photographer 1954–57; lecturer Univ. of Calgary 1963–66; writer-in-residence Sir George Williams Univ., Montreal 1967–68, lecturer 1968–71; lecturer Simon Fraser Univ., Burnaby, BC 1972–2001; Parl. Poet Laureate 2002–04. *Play:* The Home for Heroes 1962. *Radio plays:* George Vancouver CBC) 1972, Sitting in Mexico (CBC) 1973, Music in the Park (CBC) 1986, The Great Grandchildren of Bill Bissett's Mice (CBC) 1989. *Television play:* What Does Eddie Williams Want? (CBC) 1966. *Publications:* poetry collections: Sticks & Stones 1963, Points on the Grid 1964, The Man in Yellow Boots/El hombre de las botas amarillas 1965, The Silver Wire 1966, Rocky Mountain Foot 1969, The Gangs of Kosmos 1969, Touch: Selected Poems 1960–1969 1971, In the Flesh 1974, The Catch 1976, Poem & Other Baseballs 1976, The Concrete Island 1977, Another Mouth 1979, Particular Accidents: Selected Poems 1981, West Window: Selected Poetry 1982, Smoking Poetry 1982, Smoking Mirrow 1982, Seventy-One Poems for People 1985, Delayed Mercy & Other Poems 1986, Urban Snow 1992, George Bowering Selected: Poems 1961–1992 1993; chapbooks: How I Hear Howl 1967, Two Police Poems 1969, The Sensible 1972, Layers 1–13 1973, In Answer 1977, Uncle Louis 1980, Spencer & Groulx 1985, Quarters 1991, Do Sink 1992, Sweetly 1992, Blondes on Bikes 1997, A, You're Adorable 1998, 6 Little Poems in Alphabetical Order 2000, Some Writers 2001, Joining the Lost Generation 2002; long poems: Sitting in Mexico 1965, George,Vancouver 1970, Geneve 1971, Autobiology 1972, Curious 1973, At War With the U.S. 1974, Allophanes 1976, Ear Reach 1982, Kerrisdale Elegies 1984, His Life: A Poem 2000, Baseball: A poem in the magic number 9 2003; novels: Mirror on the Floor 1967, A Short Sad Book 1977, Burning Water 1980, En eaux troubles 1982, Caprice 1987, Harry's Fragments 1990, Shoot! 1994, Parents from Space 1994, Piccolo Mondo 1998, Diamondback Dog 1998; short story collections: Flycatcher & Other Stories 1974, Concentric Circles 1977, Protective Footwear 1978, A Place to Die 1983, The Rain Barrel 1994, Standing on Richards 2004; non-fiction: Al Purdy 1970, Three Vancouver Writers 1979, A Way with Words 1982, The Mask in Place 1983, Craft Slices 1985, Errata 1988, Imaginary Hand 1988, The Moustache: Memories of Greg Curnoe (memoir) 1993, Bowering's B.C. 1996, Egotists and Autocrats – the Prime Ministers of Canada 1999, A Magpie Life (memoir) 2001, Cars (memoir) 2002, Stone Country 2003. *Honours:* Hon. DLit (British Columbia) 1997, (Western Ontario) 2003; Gov.-Gen.'s Award for poetry 1967, for fiction 1980, bp Nichol Chapbook Awards for Poetry 1991, 1992, Canadian Authors' Asscn Award for Poetry 1993. *Address:* 303 Fielden Avenue, Port Colborne, ON L3K 4T5, Canada (home). *Telephone:* (905) 834-0642 (home). *E-mail:* bowering@sfu.ca (home).

BOWERING, Marilyn Ruthe, MA; Canadian writer and poet; *University-College Professor, Malaspina University College*; b. 13 April 1949, Winnipeg, Man.; d. of Herbert James Bowering and Elnora May Bowering; m. Michael S. Elcock 1982; one d. *Education:* Univs of Victoria, British Columbia and New Brunswick. *Career:* instructor in continuing educ., Univ. of British Columbia 1977; ed., writer, Gregson/Graham Marketing and Communications 1978–80; ed., Noel Collins and Blackwells, Edinburgh, UK 1980–82; Visiting Lecturer, Dept of Creative Writing, Univ. of Victoria 1978–80, Lecturer 1982–86, 1989, Visiting Assoc. Prof. 1993–98; Writer-in-Residence, Memorial Univ. of Newfoundland 1995; Univ.-Coll. Prof., Malaspina Univ. Coll. 1998–; mem. Writers' Union of Canada, PEN. *Radio programmes include:* Grandfather Was a Soldier 1983, Anyone Can See I Love You 1986, Laika and Folchakov – A Journey in Time and Space 1987, A Cold Departure 1989. *Plays:* Hajimari-No-Hajimari – Four Myths of the Pacific Rim 1986, Anyone Can See I Love You 1988, Temple of the Stars 1996. *Film script:* Divine Fate (Heart of the Festival Award, Earth Peace Int. Film Festival 1994, UNICEF Award for Animation, Int. Animation Festival 1994) 1993. *Publications:* poetry: The Liberation of Newfoundland 1973, One Who Became Lost 1976, Many Voices: An Anthology of Contemporary Canadian Indian Poetry (co-ed. with David A. Day) 1977, The Killing Room 1977, Third/Child Zian 1978, The Book of Glass 1978, Sleeping with Lambs 1980, Giving Back Diamonds 1982, The Sunday Before Winter – New and Selected Poetry 1984, Anyone Can See I Love You 1987, Grandfather was a Soldier 1987, Calling All the World – Laika and Folchakov 1989, Love As It Is 1993, Interior Castle 1994, Autobiography 1996, Human Bodies: New and Collected Poems, 1987–1999 1999, The Alchemy of Happiness 2003; fiction: The Visitors Have All Returned 1979, To All Appearances a Lady (New York Times Notable Book 1990) 1990, Visible Worlds (Ethel Wilson Fiction Prize) 1997, Cat's Pilgrimage 2004, What It Takes To Be Human 2006; non-fiction: Guide to the Labor Code of British Columbia (ed.) 1980; contribs to anthologies and journals. *Honours:* Gov.-Gen.'s Award for Poetry, CBC Literary Prize, Commonwealth Poetry and Photography Prizes, Canada Council Project Awards 1972, 1986, Canada Council Arts Awards 1973, 1977, 1980, 1981, 1984, Du Maurier Award for Poetry (Gold) 1977, Nat. Magazine Awards for Poetry 1978, 1988, Malahat Review Long Poem Prize 1994, Pat Lowther Award for Autobiography 1997. *Literary Agent:* c/o Jackie Kaiser, Westwood Creative Artists Ltd, 94 Harbord Street, Toronto, ON M5S 1G6, Canada. *Telephone:* (416) 964-3302. *Fax:* (416) 975-9209. *E-mail:* jackie@wcaltd.com. *Address:* Department of Creative Writing, Malaspina University College, 900 Fifth Street, Nanaimo, BC V9R 5S5, Canada (office). *E-mail:* info@marilynbowering.com. *Website:* www.marilynbowering.com.

BOWKER, Gordon, MA, PhD; British writer and journalist; b. 19 March 1934, Birmingham. *Education:* Univ. of Nottingham, Univ. . of London. *Career:* teacher, Goldsmiths Coll., London 1966–91; mem. PEN, Soc. of Authors, Writers' Guild. *Publications:* Under Twenty (ed.) 1966, Freedom: Reason or Revolution (ed.) 1970, Malcolm Lowry Remembered (ed.) 1985, Malcolm Lowry: Under the Volcano (ed.) 1988, Apparently Incongruous Parts: The Worlds of Malcolm Lowry (co-ed.) 1990, Pursued by Furies: A Life of Malcolm Lowry 1993, Through the Dark Labyrinth 1996, George Orwell (aka Inside George Orwell) 2003. *Literary Agent:* David Higham Associates, 5–8 Lower John Street, Golden Square, London, W1F 9HA, England.

BOWKER, John Westerdale, BA; British academic and writer; b. 30 July 1935, London, England. *Education:* Univ. of Oxford. *Career:* Fellow, Corpus Christi Coll., Cambridge 1962–74; Lecturer, Univ. of Cambridge 1965–74; Prof. of Religious Studies, Univ. of Lancaster 1974–85; Fellow, Dean, Trinity Coll., Cambridge 1984–93; Hon. Cannon, Canterbury Cathedral 1985–; Gresham Prof. 1992–97, Fellow 1997–, Gresham Coll., London. *Publications:* The Targums and Rabbinic Literature 1969, Problems of Suffering in Religions of the World 1970, Jesus and the Pharisees 1973, The Sense of God: Sociological, Anthropological and Psychological Approaches to the Origin of the Sense of God 1973, Uncle Bolpenny Tries Things Out 1973, The Religious Imagination and the Sense of God 1978, Worlds of Faith 1983, Violence and Aggression (ed.) 1984, Licensed Insanities 1987, The Meanings of Death 1991, A Year to Live 1991, Hallowed Ground 1993, Is God a Virus? Genes, Culture and Religion 1995, The Oxford Dictionary of World Religions 1997, World Religions 1997, The Complete Bible Handbook 1998, What Muslims Believe 1998, God: A Brief History 2002, The Sacred Neuron: Extraordinary New Discoveries Linking Science and Religion 2005. *Honours:* Harper Collins Biennial Prize 1993, Benjamin Franklin Award 1999. *Address:* c/o Gresham College, Barnard's Inn Hall, Holborn, London, EC1N 2HH; 14 Bowers Croft, Cambridge, CB1 8RP, England.

BOWLER, Peter John, BA, MSc, PhD, FBA; British academic and writer; *Professor of History of Science, Queen's University*; b. 8 Oct. 1944, Leicester; m. Sheila Mary Holt 1966; one s. one d. *Education:* Univ. of Cambridge, Univ. of Sussex, Univ. of Toronto. *Career:* Asst Prof., Univ. of Toronto 1971–72; Lecturer, Science Univ. of Malaysia, Penang 1972–75; Asst Prof., Univ. of

Winnipeg 1975–79; Lecturer, Queen's Univ., Belfast 1979–87, Reader 1987–92, Prof. of History of Science 1992–; mem. Royal Irish Acad., British Soc. for the History of Science, History of Science Soc. *Publications:* Fossils and Progress: Paleontology and the Idea of Progressive Evolution in the Nineteenth Century 1976, The Eclipse of Darwinism: Anti-Darwinian Evolution Theories in the Decades Around 1900 1983, Evolution: The History of an Idea 1984, Theories of Human Evolution: A Century of Debate 1844–1944 1986, The Non-Darwinian Revolution: Reinterpreting a Historical Myth 1988, The Mendelian Revolution: The Emergence of Hereditarian Concepts in Modern Science and Society 1989, The Invention of Progress: The Victorians and the Past 1990, Darwin: L'origine delle specie 1990, Charles Darwin: The Man and his Influence 1990, The Fontana History of the Environmental Sciences 1992, US edn as The Norton History of the Environmental Sciences 1993, Biology and Social Thought 1850–1914, 5 lectures 1993, Darwinism 1993, E. Ray Lankester and the Making of Modern British Biology (ed. and co-author with J. Lester) 1995, Life's Splendid Drama: Evolutionary Biology and the Reconstruction of Life's Ancestry 1860–1940 1996, Reconciling Science and Religion: The Debate in Early Twentieth-Century Britain 2001; contrib. to journals. *Address:* c/o School of History and Anthropology, Queen's University of Belfast, Belfast BT7 1NN, Northern Ireland.

BOWLT, John Ellis, BA, MA, PhD; American academic and writer; *Professor, Department of Slavic Languages and Literatures, UCLA*; b. 6 Dec. 1943, London, England; m. Nicoletta Misler 1981. *Education:* Univ. Univ. of Birmingham, Univ. Univ. of St Andrews. *Career:* Lecturer, Univ. of St Andrews 1968–79, Univ. of Birmingham 1970; Asst Prof., Univ. of Kan., USA 1970–71; Asst to Assoc. Prof. 1971–81, Assoc. Prof. to Prof. 1981–88, Univ. of Tex.; Visiting Prof., Univ. of Otago, New Zealand 1982, Hebrew Univ., Jerusalem 1985; Prof., Univ. of Southern Calif., LA 1988–; mem. American Asscn for the Advancement of Slavic Studies, Coll. Art Asscn, New York; British Council Scholarship 1966–68; Woodrow Wilson Nat. Fellowship 1971; Yale Univ. Nat. Humanities Inst. Fellow 1977–78; Sr Fellow, Wolfsonian Foundation, Miami 1995; Casden Inst. for Jewish Studies Faculty Research Grant 2003; Int. Research and Exchanges Bd IARO grantee 2004. *Publications:* Russian Formalism (ed. with Stephen Bann) 1973, The Russian Avant-Garde: Theory and Criticism 1902–1934 1976, The Silver Age: Russian Art of the Early Twentieth Century 1979, The Life of Vasilii Kandinsky in Russian Art (with Rose Carol Washton-Long) 1980, Pavel Filonov: A Hero and his Fate (with Nicoletta Misler) 1984, Mikalojus Konstantinas Ciurlionis: Music of the Spheres (with Alfred Senn and Danute Staskevicius) 1986, Russian Samizdat Art (co-author) 1986, Gustav Kluzis 1988, Aus Vollem Halse: Russische Buchillustration und Typographie 1900–1930 (with B. Hernad) 1993, Russian and East European Paintings in the Thyssen-Bornemisza Collection (with Nicoletta Misler) 1993, The Salon Album of Vera Sudeikin-Stravinsky 1995, Painting Revolution 1999, Spheres of Light, Stations of Darkness: The Art of Solomon Nikritin 2004; contrib. to books, scholarly journals, periodicals and exhibition catalogues. *Honours:* Fulbright-Hays Award, Paris 1981, ACLS Award, Italy 1984, 2007–08. *Address:* c/o Department of Slavic Languages and Literatures, University of Southern California, Box 4353, Los Angeles, CA 90095-4353, USA (office). *Telephone:* (213) 740-2735 (office). *Fax:* (213) 740-8550 (office). *Website:* www.usc.edu/schools/college/sll.

BOYCOTT, Rosie; British journalist and author; b. 13 May 1951, d. of Charles Boycott and Betty Boycott; m. 1st David Leitch (divorced); one d.; m. 2nd Charles Howard 1999. *Education:* Cheltenham Ladies Coll., Kent Univ. *Career:* f. Spare Rib 1972; est. Virago Books 1973; worked on Village Voice (magazine), New York; subsequently edited Arabic women's magazine in Kuwait; Features Ed. Honey; Deputy Ed. Daily Mail's Male and Femail pages; Ed. Discount Traveller; Commissioning Ed. The Sunday Telegraph; Deputy Ed. Harpers & Queen 1989; Deputy Ed. and Features Ed. (British) Esquire 1991, Ed. 1992–96, of Ind. on Sunday 1996–98, of the Ind. 1998, of the Express 1998–2001, of the Express on Sunday 1998–2001; Chair., Panel of Judges, Orange Prize for Fiction 2001; mem. Exec. Cttee English PEN. *Publications:* A Nice Girl Like Me (autobiog.) 1983, All For Love 1985, Our Farm: A Year in the Life of a Smallholding 2007. *Address:* c/o Bloomsbury Publishing Plc, 36 Soho Square, London, W1D 3QY, England (office).

BOYD, William Andrew Murray, CBE, MA, FRSL; British writer; b. 7 March 1952, Ghana; s. of Dr Alexander Murray Boyd and Evelyn Boyd; m. Susan Anne (née Wilson) Boyd 1975. *Education:* Gordonstoun School, Glasgow Univ., Jesus Coll., Oxford. *Career:* lecturer in English, St Hilda's Coll., Oxford 1980–83; TV critic, New Statesman 1981–83. *Film appearance:* Rabbit Fever 2006. *Publications include:* A Good Man in Africa (Whitbread Prize 1981, Somerset Maugham Award 1982) 1981 (screenplay 1994), On the Yankee Station 1981, An Ice-Cream War (John Llewellyn Rhys Prize) 1982, Stars and Bars 1984 (screenplay 1988), School Ties 1985, The New Confessions 1987, Scoop (screenplay) 1987, Brazzaville Beach (McVities Prize and James Tait Black Memorial Prize) 1990, Aunt Julia and the Scriptwriter (screenplay) 1990, Mr Johnson (screenplay) 1990, Chaplin (screenplay) 1992, The Blue Afternoon (novel) 1993, A Good Man in Africa (screenplay) 1994, The Destiny of Nathalie 'X' 1995, Armadillo 1998 (screenplay 2001), Nat Tate: An American Artist 1998, The Trench (screenplay, also dir) 1999, Sword of Honour (screenplay) 2001, Any Human Heart 2002, Fascination 2004, Bamboo 2005, A Waste of Shame (screenplay) 2005, Restless (novel) (Costa Book Award for Novel of the Year 2007) 2006. *Honours:* Hon. DLitt (St Andrews), (Glasgow), (Stirling); Officier, Ordre des Arts et des Lettres. *Literary Agent:* The Agency, 24 Pottery Lane, Holland Park, London, W11 4LZ, England.

BOYLE, Thomas Coraghessan (T. C.), BA, MFA, PhD; American academic and writer; *Professor, Department of English, University of Southern California*; b. 2 Dec. 1948, Peekskill, NY; m. Karen Kvashay 1974; two s. one d. *Education:* SUNY at Potsdam, Univ. of Iowa. *Career:* Founder-Dir, Creative Writing Program 1978–86, Asst Prof. of English 1978–82, Assoc. Prof. of English 1982–86, Prof. of English 1986–, Univ. of Southern California; mem. Nat. Endowment of the Arts literature panel 1986–87; Nat. Endowment for the Arts grants 1977, 1983; Guggenheim Fellowship 1988. *Publications:* Descent of Man 1979, Water Music 1982, Budding Prospects 1984, Greasy Lake 1985, World's End 1987, If the River was Whiskey 1989, East is East 1990, The Road to Wellville 1993, Without a Hero 1994, The Tortilla Curtain 1995, Riven Rock 1998, T.C. Boyle Stories 1998, A Friend of the Earth 2000, After the Plague 2001, Drop City 2003, The Inner Circle 2004, Tooth and Claw 2006, Talk Talk 2006; contrib. to numerous anthologies and periodicals. *Honours:* Hon. DHumLitt (SUNY) 1991; PEN/Faulkner Award 1988, Commonwealth Club of California Gold Medal for Literature 1988, O. Henry Short Story Awards 1988, 1989, Prix Passion Publishers' Prize, France 1989, Eds' Choice, New York Times Book Review 1989, Harold D. Vursell Memorial Award, American Acad. of Arts and Letters 1993, Prix Médicis Étranger 1997. *Address:* Department of English, University of Southern California, Los Angeles, CA 90089, USA (office). *Telephone:* (213) 740-3734 (office). *E-mail:* tcb@tcboyle.com (office). *Website:* www.tcboyle.com.

BOYNE, John, BA, MA; Irish novelist; b. 1971, Dublin. *Education:* Trinity Coll., Dublin and Univ. of East Anglia. *Career:* fmr creative writing teacher, Irish Writers' Centre; Univ. of East Anglia Writing Fellowship 2005. *Publications:* novels: The Thief of Time 2000, The Congress of Rough Riders 2001, Crippen 2004, The Boy in the Striped Pyjamas (juvenile) 2006, Next of Kin 2006. *Honours:* Curtis Brown Prize. *Literary Agent:* c/o Simon Trewin, PFD, Drury House, 34–43 Russell Street, London, WC2B 5HA, England. *Telephone:* (20) 7344-1000. *E-mail:* strewin@pfd.co.uk. *Website:* www.pfd.co.uk. *E-mail:* info@johnboyne.com. *Website:* www.johnboyne.com.

BRABCOVÁ, Zuzana; Czech novelist; b. 23 March 1959, Prague; d. of Jiří Brabec and Zina Trochová; m.; one d. *Career:* fmr librarian and cleaner; Ed. at publisher, Český spisovatel (Czech Writer) 1995–. *Publications:* Daleko od stromu (Far from the Tree) 1984, Zlodějina (Thievery) 1995, Rok perel 2000. *Honours:* Jiří Orten Prize. *Address:* c/o Czech PEN Centre, Vodièkova str. 32, 110 00 Prague 1, Czech Republic (office).

BRACKENBURY, Alison, BA; British poet and writer; b. 20 May 1953, Gainsborough, Lincolnshire, England. *Education:* St Hugh's Coll., Oxford. *Radio play:* The Country of Afternoon 1985. *Publications:* Journey to a Cornish Wedding 1977, Two Poems 1979, Dreams of Power and Other Poems 1981, Breaking Ground and Other Poems 1984, Christmas Roses and Other Poems 1988, Selected Poems 1991, 1829 1994, After Beethoven 1999, The Story of Sigurd 2002, Bricks and Ballads 2004; contrib. to journals, including PN Review. *Honours:* Eric Gregory Award 1982, Cholmondeley Award 1997. *Address:* c/o Carcanet Press, Fourth Floor, Alliance House, Cross Street, Manchester, M2 7AP, England. *Website:* www.alisonbrackenbury.co.uk.

BRADBURY, Edward P. (see Moorcock, Michael John)

BRADBURY, Ray Douglas; American writer, poet and dramatist; b. 22 Aug. 1920, Waukegan, Ill.; s. of Leonard Bradbury and Esther Bradbury; m. Marguerite Susan McClure 1947; four d. *Education:* public schools. *Career:* mem. SFWA (pres. 1951–53), Screen Writers' Guild of America (bd of dirs 1957–61). *Plays:* The Meadow 1948, Way in the Middle of the Air 1962, The Anthem Sprinters and Other Antics 1963, The World of Ray Bradbury 1964, The Wonderful Ice-Cream Suit 1965, Leviathan 99 1966, The Day it Rained Forever (play of novel A Medicine for Melancholy) 1966, The Pedestrian 1966, Christus Apollo 1969, Madrigals for the Space Age 1972, Pillars of Fire and Other Plays for Today, Tomorrow, and Beyond Tomorrow 1975, That Ghost, That Bride of Time: Excerpts from a Play-in-Progress 1976, The Martian Chronicles 1977, A Device Out of Time 1986, Falling Upward 1988. *Screenplays:* It Came from Outer Space 1952, Moby Dick 1954, Icarus Montgolfier Wright 1961, The Picasso Summer 1968; TV scripts include Alfred Hitchcock Show, Twilight Zone. *Publications:* fiction: The Martian Chronicles 1950, Fahrenheit 451 1953, Switch on the Night 1955, Dandelion Wine 1957, Something Wicked This Way Comes 1962, R is for Rocket 1962, S is for Space 1966, The Halloween Tree 1972, Death is a Lonely Business 1985, A Graveyard for Lunatics 1990, Green Shadows, White Whale 1992; short story collections: Dark Carnival 1947, The Illustrated Man 1951, The Golden Apples of the Sun 1953, The October Country 1955, A Medicine for Melancholy 1959, The Ghoul Keepers 1961, The Small Assassin 1962, The Machineries of Joy 1964, The Vintage Bradbury 1965, The Autumn People 1965, Tomorrow Midnight 1966, Twice Twenty-Two 1966, I Sing the Body Electric! 1969, Bloch and Bradbury: Ten Masterpieces of Science Fiction (with Robert Bloch) 1969, Whispers From Beyond (with Robert Bloch) 1972, Harrap 1975, Long After Midnight 1976, To Sing Strange Songs 1979, The Stories of Ray Bradbury 1980, The Dinosaur Tales 1983, A Memory of Murder 1984, The Toynbee Convector 1988, Kaleidoscope 1994, Quicker Than the Eye 1996, Driving Blind 1997; non-fiction: Teacher's Guide: Science Fiction 1968, Zen and the Art of Writing 1973, Mars and the Mind of Man 1973, The Mummies of Guanajuato 1978, Beyond 1984: Remembrance of Things Future 1979, Los Angeles 1984, Orange County 1985, Yestermorrow: Obvious Answers to

Impossible Futures 1991, Ray Bradbury on Stage: A Chrestomathy of his Plays 1991, Journey to Far Metaphor: Further Essays on Creativity, Writing, Literature and the Arts 1994, The First Book of Dichotomy, The Second Book of Symbiosis 1995, Bradbury Speaks: Too Soon from the Cave, Too Far from the Stars 2005; poetry: Old Ahab's Friend, and Friend to Noah, Speaks his Piece: A Celebration 1971, When Elephants Last in the Dooryard Bloomed 1972, That Son of Richard III: A Birth Announcement 1974, Where Robot Mice and Robot Men Run Round in Robot Towns 1977, Twin Hieroglyphs That Swim the River Dust 1978, The Bike Repairman 1978, The Author Considers his Resources 1979, The Aqueduct 1979, The Attic Where the Meadow Greens 1979, The Last Circus 1980, The Ghosts of Forever 1980, The Haunted Computer and the Android Pope 1981, The Complete Poems of Ray Bradbury 1982, The Love Affair 1983, Forever and the Earth 1984, Death Has Lost its Charm for Me 1987. *Honours:* O. Henry Prizes 1947, 1948, Nat. Inst. of Arts and Letters Award 1954, Writers' Club Award 1974, Balrog Award for Best Poet 1979, PEN Body of Work Award 1985, Nat. Book Foundation Hon. Medal 2000, Pulitzer Prize Special Citation 2007. *Address:* c/o Bantam Doubleday Dell, 1540 Broadway, New York, NY 10036 (office); c/o Avon Books, 1350 Avenue of the Americas, New York, NY 10019 (office); 10265 Cheviot Drive, Los Angeles, CA 90064, USA.

BRADBY, Tom, MA; British journalist and writer; *Political Editor, ITV News;* b. 1967, Malta; m.; three c. *Education:* Sherborne School, Univ. of Edinburgh. *Career:* editorial trainee ITN 1990, Producer, for political Ed. ITV News 1992–93, NI Correspondent 1993–96, Political Correspondent 1996–98, Asia Correspondent, based in Hong Kong 1998–2001, Royal Correspondent, then UK Ed. 2001–05, Political Ed. 2005–. *Publications:* novels: Shadow Dancer 1998, The Sleep of the Dead 2001, The Master of Rain 2002, The White Russian 2003, The God of Chaos 2004. *Address:* ITN, 200 Gray's Inn Road, London, WC1X 8XZ, England. *E-mail:* tom.bradby@itn.co.uk. *Website:* www.itn.co.uk.

BRADFORD, Barbara Taylor, OBE; British writer and journalist; b. Leeds, England; d. of Winston Taylor and Freda Walker; m. Robert Bradford 1963. *Career:* reporter, Yorkshire Evening Post 1949–51, Women's Ed. 1951–53; Fashion Ed. Woman's Own 1953–54; columnist, London Evening News 1955–57; Exec. Ed. London American 1959–62; Ed. Nat. Design Center Magazine 1965–69; syndicated columnist, Newsday Specials, Long Island 1968–70; nat. syndicated columnist, Chicago Tribune-New York (News Syndicate), New York 1970–75, Los Angeles Times Syndicate 1975–81; Dir Library of Congress, DL; mem. Bd American Heritage Dictionary, Police Athletic League, Author's Guild Foundation 1989–; Girls Inc. *Television:* ten novels adapted into TV mini-series. *Publications:* Complete Encyclopaedia of Homemaking Ideas 1968, A Garland of Children's Verse 1968, How to be the Perfect Wife 1969, Easy Steps to Successful Decorating 1971, How to Solve your Decorating Problems 1976, Decorating Ideas for Casual Living 1977, Making Space Grow 1979, A Woman of Substance (novel) 1979, Luxury Designs for Apartment Living 1981, Voice of the Heart 1983, Hold the Dream 1985, Act of Will (novel) 1986, To Be The Best 1988, The Women in his Life (novel) 1990, Remember (novel) 1991, Angel (novel) 1993, Everything to Gain (novel) 1994, Dangerous to Know (novel) 1995, Love in Another Town (novel) 1995, Her Own Rules 1996, A Secret Affair 1996, Power of a Woman 1997, A Sudden Change of Heart 1998, Where You Belong 2000, The Triumph of Katie Byrne 2001, Three Weeks in Paris 2002, Emma's Secret 2003, Just Rewards 2006, The Ravenscar Dynasty 2007. *Honours:* Hon. DLitt (Leeds) 1990, (Bradford) 1995; Hon. DHumLit (Teikyo Post Univ.) 1996; numerous awards and prizes. *Address:* Bradford Enterprises, 450 Park Avenue, New York, NY 10022, USA. *Telephone:* (212) 308-7390. *Fax:* (212) 935-1636. *Website:* www.barbarataylorbradford.com.

BRADFORD, Karleen, BA; Canadian writer; b. 16 Dec. 1936, Toronto, ON; m. James Creighton Bradford 1959, two s. one d. *Education:* University of Toronto. *Career:* Chair., Public Lending Right Commission of Canada 1998–2000; mem. PEN, IBBY, Writers' Union of Canada. *Publications:* A Year for Growing 1977, The Other Elizabeth 1982, Wrong Again, Robbie 1983, I Wish There Were Unicorns 1983, The Stone in the Meadow 1984, The Haunting at Cliff House 1985, The Nine Days Queen 1986, Write Now! 1988, Windward Island 1989, There Will be Wolves 1992, Thirteenth Child 1994, Animal Heroes 1995, Shadows on a Sword 1996, More Animal Heroes 1996, Dragonfire 1997, A Different Kind of Champion 1998, Lionhearts Scribe 1999, Whisperings of Magic 2001, With Nothing But Our Courage 2002, You Can't Rush a Cat 2003, Angeline 2004. *Honours:* Canadian Library Asscn Young Adult Novel Award 1993. *Address:* RR No. 2, Owen Sound, ON N4K 5N4, Canada.

BRADFORD, S. W. (see Battin, B. W.)

BRADFORD, Sarah Mary Malet, (Viscountess Bangor); British biographer and historian; b. 3 Sept. 1938, Bournemouth; d. of the late Brig. Hilary Anthony Hayes and Mary Beatrice de Carteret Malet; m. 1st Anthony John Bradford 1959; one s. one d.; m. 2nd Viscount Bangor 1976. *Education:* St Mary's Convent, Shaftesbury and Lady Margaret Hall, Oxford. *Career:* manuscript expert at Christie's 1975–78. *Publications:* Portugal and Madeira 1969, Portugal 1973, Cesare Borgia 1976, The Englishman's Wine 1969, re-published as The Story of Port 1978, Disraeli 1982, Princess Grace 1984, King George VI 1989, Sacheverell Sitwell 1993, Elizabeth – A Biography of Her Majesty The Queen 1996, America's Queen – The Life of Jacqueline Kennedy Onassis 2000, Lucrezia Borgia – Life, Love and Death in Renaissance Italy

2004, Diana 2006; contribs to periodicals. *Literary Agent:* Aitken Alexander Associates Ltd, 18–21 Cavaye Place, London, SW10 9PT, England. *Telephone:* (20) 7373-8672. *Fax:* (20) 7373-6002. *E-mail:* reception@aitkenalexander.co.uk. *Website:* www.aitkenalexander.co.uk.

BRADHURST, Jane, BA, MSc, DipEd; Australian artist, writer, dramatist and poet; b. 28 Oct. 1926, Sydney, NSW; d. of Frank Bradhurst and Winifred Bradhurst; m. Colin Russell-Jones (deceased); two s. one d. *Education:* Univ. of Sydney, Univ. of Canberra, Goulburn CAE. *Career:* eight solo exhbns; works in main lobby of Australian Embassy, Washington, DC, USA to celebrate opening of Nat. Museum of Australia; 16 works acquired by Nat. Gallery of Australia 2005; mem. ACT Writers' Centre, Australian Writers' Guild. *Publications:* five novels and two vols of plays, including The Flowers of the Snowy Mountains 1977, Document of Our Day: Women of the Pre-Pill Generation 1986, Three One Act Plays 1987, Duet String Trio Quartet 1987, Animalia in Australia 1992, 100 Poems 1993, The BD II 1995, Love in a Hot Climate 1996, Three Festival Plays 1998, Summertime (musical) 1998, There is no Mystery (anthology) 1999, Mystery in Manhattan 2000, Always on Call: Tales of an Outback Doctor 2002, Outback Lives and Border Fence Brides – more tales of an outback doctor 2004. *Honours:* Jt Winner, Best Play, Int. Women's Year 1975, Best Play, Fed. of Australian Drama 1975, Jt Winner, Everyman 1979. *Address:* PO Box 9009, Deakin, ACT 2600 (office); 50 Beauchamp Street, Deakin, ACT 2600, Australia (home). *Telephone:* (2) 62814633 (home).

BRADLEE, Benjamin Crowninshield, AB; American newspaper editor; *Vice-President at Large, Washington Post;* b. 26 Aug. 1921, Boston; s. of Frederick Bradlee and Josephine de Gersdorff; m. 1st Jean Saltonstall 1942; one s.; m. 2nd Antoinette Pinchot 1956; one s. one d.; m. 3rd Sally Quinn 1978, one s. *Education:* Harvard Univ. *Career:* reporter, NH Sunday News, Manchester 1946–48, Washington Post 1948–51; Press Attaché, US Embassy, Paris 1951–53; European corresp. Newsweek, Paris 1953–57; reporter, Washington Bureau, Newsweek 1957–61, Sr Ed. and Chief of Bureau 1961–65; Man. Ed. Washington Post 1965–68, Vice-Pres. and Exec. Ed. 1968–91, Vice-Pres. at Large 1991–; Chair. History of St Mary's City Comm. 1992–. *Publications:* That Special Grace 1964, Conversations with Kennedy 1975, A Good Life: Newspapering and Other Adventures (autobiog.) 1995. *Honours:* Burton Benjamin Award 1995. *Address:* c/o Washington Post, 1150 15th Street, NW, Washington, DC 20071-0001 (office); 3014 N Street, NW, Washington, DC 20007-3404, USA (home).

BRADLEY, Clive, CBE, MA; British publishing and media executive and barrister; *Convenor, Confederation of Information Communication Industries;* b. 25 July 1934, London; s. of the late Alfred Bradley and Annie Kathleen Bradley. *Education:* Felsted School, Essex, Clare Coll., Cambridge and Yale Univ., USA. *Career:* barrister (Middle Temple); with BBC 1961–63; Broadcasting Officer, Labour Party 1963–65; Political Ed., The Statist 1965–67; Group Labour Adviser, Int. Publishing Corpn and Deputy Gen. Man. Mirror Group Newspapers 1967–73; Dir The Observer 1973–75; Chief Exec. The Publishers Asscn 1976–97; Convenor Confed. of Information Communication Industries 1984–; Chair. Central London Valuation Tribunal, Richmond upon Thames Arts Council 2003–; Deputy Chair. Age Concern, Richmond 2001–03; Gov. Felsted School. *Publications:* many articles and broadcasts on politics, econs, industrial relations, industry media and current affairs. *Address:* 8 Northumberland Place, Richmond-upon-Thames, Surrey TW10 6TS, England (home). *Telephone:* (20) 8940-7172 (home). *Fax:* (20) 8940-7603 (home). *E-mail:* bradley_clive@btopenworld.com (home).

BRADLEY, George, BA; American writer and poet; b. 22 Jan. 1953, Roslyn, New York; m. Spencer Boyd 1984; one d. *Education:* Yale Univ., Univ. of Virginia. *Publications:* Terms to Be Met 1986, Of the Knowledge of Good and Evil 1991, The Fire Fetched Down 1996, The Yale Younger Poets Anthology (ed.) 1998, Some Assembly Required 2001; contribs to periodicals. *Honours:* Acad. of American Poets Prize 1978, Yale Younger Poets Prize 1985, Lavan Younger Poets Award 1990, Witter Bynner Prize 1992. *Address:* 82 W Main Street, Chester, CT 06412, USA.

BRADLEY, John, BA, MA, MFA; American teacher, writer and poet; b. 26 Sept. 1950, New York, NY; m. Jana Brubaker 1988, one s. *Education:* University of Minnesota, Colorado State University, Bowling Green State University. *Career:* Instructor in English, Bowling Green State University, 1989–91, Northern Illinois University, 1992–. *Publications:* Love in Idleness: The Poetry of Roberto Zingarello, 1989; Atomic Ghost: Poets Respond to the Nuclear Age, 1995; Learning to Glow: A Nuclear Reader, 2000. Contributions: Ironwood; Rolling Stone; Poetry East. *Honours:* NEA Fellowship.

BRADLEY, John Edmund, Jr, BA; American writer; b. 12 Aug. 1958, Opelousas, LA. *Education:* Louisiana State University. *Publications:* Tupelo Nights, 1988; The Best There Ever Was, 1990; Love & Obits, 1992; Smoke, 1994; My Juliet, 2000. Contributions: Esquire, Sports Illustrated and other periodicals.

BRADWELL, James (see Kent, Arthur William Charles)

BRADY, Conor, BA, MA; Irish journalist and academic; *Commissioner, Garda Síochána Ombudsman Commission;* b. 24 April 1949, Dublin; s. of Conor Brady and Amy MacCarthy; m. Ann Byron 1971; two s. *Education:* Mount St Joseph Cistercian Abbey, Univ. Coll. Dublin. *Career:* reporter Irish Times 1969–73, Asst Ed. 1977–81, Dir and Deputy Ed. 1984–86, Ed. and Group Editorial Dir 1986–2002, Ed. Emer. 2002–; Ed. Garda Review 1973–74; Tutor,

Dept of Politics, Univ. Coll. Dublin 1973–74 Presenter/Reporter RTE News At One and This Week 1974–75; Ed. The Sunday Tribune 1981–82; Chair. Bd of Counsellors, European Journalism Centre, Maastricht 1993–98; Pres. World Eds' Forum, Paris 1995–2000; mem. Bd of Dirs World Press Freedom Cttee, Federation International des Editeurs de Journeaux 1995–2000; Commr, Garda Síochána Ombudsman Comm. 2006–; Visiting Prof., John Jay Coll., CUNY; Sr Teaching Fellow, Michael Smurfit Grad. School of Business, Univ. Coll. Dublin; Chair. British-Irish Asscn; Cttee Mem. UNESCO Int. Press Freedom. *Publication:* Guardian of the Peace 1974. *Honours:* Award for Outstanding Work in Irish Journalism 1979. *Address:* Garda Síochána Ombudsman Commission, 31-35 Bow Street, Smithfield, Dublin 7, Ireland (office). *Telephone:* (1) 8280370 (office). *Fax:* (1) 8280371 (office). *E-mail:* info@ gsoc.ie (office). *Website:* www.gardaombudsman.ie (office).

BRADY, James Winston, AB; American writer and broadcaster; b. 15 Nov. 1928, New York, NY; m. Florence Kelly 1958, two d. *Education:* Manhattan College, New York University. *Publications:* fiction: Paris One, 1977; Nielsen's Children, 1979; Press Lord, 1981; Holy Wars, 1983; Designs, 1986. Non-Fiction: The Coldest War, 1990; Fashion Show, 1992. Contributions: Parade; Esquire; Advertising Age; TV Guide; People; Harper's Bazaar. *Honours:* Emmy Award 1973–74.

BRADY, Joan, BS; American/British writer; b. 4 Dec. 1939, San Francisco, CA; m. Dexter Masters 1963; one s. *Education:* Columbia Univ., Open Univ. *Publications:* The Imposter (novel) 1979, The Unmaking of a Dancer (autobiog.) 1982, Theory of War (novel) (Whitbread Novel of the Year and Book of the Year 1993, Prix du Meilleur Livre Étranger 1995) 1992, Prologue (autobiog.) 1994, Death Comes for Peter Pan (novel) 1996, The Emigré (novel) 1999, Bleedout (novel) 2005; contrib. to Harpers, London Times, Sunday Times, Telegraph, Independent. *Honours:* NEA grant 1986. *Literary Agent:* The Saddler Literary Agency, 9 Curzon Road, London, W5 1NE, England. *Telephone:* (20) 8991-8082. *Fax:* (20) 8997-5610. *E-mail:* js-kg@tiscali.co.uk; jbrady@btinternet.com.

BRADY, Nicholas (see Levinson, Leonard)

BRADY, Terence Joseph, BA; British dramatist, writer and actor; b. 13 March 1939, London, England; m. Charlotte Mary Therese Bingham, one s. one d. *Education:* Trinity College, Dublin. *Career:* actor in films, radio and television; mem. Point-to-Point Owners Asscn; Society of Authors. *Publications:* Rehearsal, 1972; Victoria (with Charlotte Bingham), 1972; Rose's Story (with Charlotte Bingham), 1973; Victoria and Company (with Charlotte Bingham), 1974; The Fight Against Slavery, 1976; Yes–Honestly, 1977; Point-to-Point (with Michael Felton), 1990. Other: Television Films: Losing Control, 1987; The Seventh Raven, 1987; This Magic Moment, 1988; Riders, 1990; Polo, 1993. Contributions: Stage, radio, television series and periodicals. *Honours:* BBC Radio Writers' Guild Award, 1972.

BRAGG, Baron (Life Peer), cr. 1998, of Wigton in the County of Cumbria; **Melvyn Bragg,** MA, FRSL, FRTS; British author and television presenter; *Controller of Arts and Features, London Weekend TV;* b. 6 Oct. 1939, Carlisle; s. of Stanley Bragg and Mary E. Park; m. 1st Marie-Elisabeth Roche 1961 (deceased); one d.; m. 2nd Catherine M. Haste 1973; one s. one d. *Education:* Nelson-Thomlinson Grammar School, Wigton and Wadham Coll., Oxford. *Career:* BBC Radio and TV Producer 1961–67; TV Presenter and Ed. the South Bank Show for ITV 1978–; Head of Arts, London Weekend TV 1982–90, Controller of Arts and Features 1990–; Deputy Chair. Border TV 1985–90, Chair. 1990–96; novelist 1965–; writer and broadcaster 1967–, writer and presenter of BBC Radio Four's Start the Week 1988–98, In Our Time 1998–, Routes of English 1999–, The Adventure of English 2001; mem. Arts Council and Chair. Literature Panel of Arts Council 1977–80; Pres. Cumbrians for Peace 1982–, Northern Arts 1983–87, Nat. Campaign for the Arts 1986–; Gov. LSE 1997–; Chancellor Leeds Univ. 1999–; mem. Bd Really Useful Co. 1989–90; Pres. Nat. Acad. of Writing; Pres. MIND; Appeal Chair. Royal Nat. Inst. for the Blind Talking Books Appeal 1998–2005. *Plays:* Mardi Gras 1976, Orion 1977, The Hired Man 1985, King Lear in New York 1992. *Screenplays:* Isadora, The Music Lovers, Jesus Christ Superstar, A Time to Dance. *Publications:* novels: For Want of a Nail 1965, The Second Inheritance 1966, Without a City Wall 1968, The Hired Man 1969, A Place in England 1970, The Nerve 1971, The Hunt 1972, Josh Lawton 1972, The Silken Net 1974, A Christmas Child 1976, Autumn Manoeuvres 1978, Kingdom Come 1980, Love and Glory 1983, The Cumbrian Trilogy 1984, The Maid of Buttermere 1987, A Time to Dance (televised 1992) 1990, Crystal Rooms 1992, Credo 1996, The Sword and the Miracle 1997, The Soldier's Return 1999, A Son of War 2001; non-fiction: Speak for England 1976, Land of the Lakes 1983, Laurence Olivier 1984, Rich, The Life of Richard Burton 1988, The Seventh Seal: A Study on Ingmar Bergman 1993, On Giants' Shoulders 1998, The Adventure of English 2003, Crossing the Lines 2004, Twelve British Books That Changed the World 2006. *Honours:* Hon. Fellow, Lancashire Polytechnic 1987, The Library Asscn 1994, Wadham Coll. Oxford 1995, Univ. of Wales, Cardiff 1996; Domus Fellow, St Catherine's Coll., Oxford 1990; Hon. DLitt (Liverpool) 1986, (CNAA) 1990, (Lancaster) 1990, (South Bank) 1997, (Leeds) 2000, (Bradford) 2000; Hon. DUniv (Open Univ.) 1988; Hon. DCL (Northumbria) 1994; Hon. DSc (UMIST) 1998, (Brunel) 2000; Dr hc (St. Andrews) 1993, (Sunderland) 2001; John Llewellyn-Rhys Memorial Award 1968, PEN Award for Fiction 1970, Richard Dimbleby Award for Outstanding Contribution to Television 1987, Ivor Novello Award for Best Musical 1985, VLV Award 2000, WHSmith Literary Award 2000, four Prix Italia awards, various BAFTA Awards. *Address:* 12

Hampstead Hill Gardens, London, NW3 2PL, England (office). *Telephone:* (20) 7261-3128 (office). *Fax:* (20) 7261-3299 (office). *E-mail:* melvyn.bragg@ granadamedia.com (office).

BRAINARD, Cecilia Manguerra; American (b. Philippine) writer; b. 1948, Cebu, Philippines; m. Lauren R. Brainard; three s. *Education:* St Theresa's Coll., Cebu and Maryknoll Coll., Quezon City. *Career:* worked in communications and as documentary scriptwriter and asst dir of development 1969–81; freelancer writer 1981–; teacher in Animation Dept, Univ. of Southern California; creative writing teacher, UCLA-Extension Writers' Programme; gives lectures worldwide. *Publications include:* Woman with Horns and Other Stories 1988, When the Rainbow Goddess Wept (novel, aka Song of Yvonne) 1991, Philippine Woman in America (essays) 1991, Seven Stories from Seven Sisters (ed.) 1992, Fiction by Filipinos in America (ed.) 1993, The Beginning and Other Asian Folktales (ed.) 1995, Acapulco at Sunset and Other Stories 1995, Journey of 100 Years: Reflections on the Centennial of Philippine Independence (ed.), Growing Up Filipino: Stories for Young Adults (ed.), Contemporary Fiction by Filipinos in America (ed.) 1998, Magdalena (novel) 2002, Cecilia's Diary 1962–1968 2003, Behind the Walls: Life of Convent Girls (co-ed.) 2005. *Honours:* Fortner Prize (for short story, The Balete Tree) 1985, California Arts Council Fellowship in Fiction 1989–90, City of Los Angeles cultural grant 1990–91, Brody Arts Fund Fellowship 1991, Los Angeles Board of Education Special Recognition Award 1991, Filipino Women's Network Literature Award 1992, Makati Rotarian Award 1994, Outstanding Individual Award from the City of Cebu, Philippines 1998, Filipinas Magazine Achievement Award for Arts and Culture 2001. *Address:* PO Box 5099, Santa Monica, CA 90409, USA (home). *E-mail:* CBrainard@aol.com (home). *Website:* www.ceciliabrainard.com.

BRAINE, David, BA, BPhil; British academic and writer; *Honorary Research Fellow, University of Aberdeen;* b. 2 Sept. 1940, Devonshire, England. *Education:* Magdalen Coll., Oxford. *Career:* Lecturer, Univ. of Aberdeen 1965–89, Hon. Lecturer 1989–2002, Hon. Research Fellow 2002–; mem. American Catholic Philosophical Asscn, Aristotelian Soc. *Publications:* Medical Ethics and Human Life 1982, The Reality of Time and the Existence of God 1988, Ethics, Technology and Medicine (ed. and contributor, with Harry Lesser) 1988, The Human Person: Animal and Spirit 1992; contrib. to scholarly books and professional journals. *Honours:* Demyship, Magdalen Coll., Oxford, Gifford Fellow Univ. of Aberdeen 1981–87. *Address:* 104–106 High Street, Old Aberdeen, AB2 3HE, Scotland.

BRAITHWAITE, Eustace, MSc; Guyanese writer and diplomatist; b. 27 June 1922. *Education:* New York Univ. and Cambridge Univ. *Career:* RAF, Second World War; schoolteacher, London 1950–57; Welfare Officer, London Co. Council 1958–60; Human Rights Officer, World Veterans Foundation, Paris 1960–63; Lecturer and Educ. Consultant, UNESCO, Paris 1963–66; Perm. Rep. of Guyana to UN 1967–68; Amb. to Venezuela 1968–69. *Publications:* To Sir, With Love 1959, A Kind of Homecoming 1961, Paid Servant 1962, A Choice of Straws 1965, Reluctant Neighbours 1972, Honorary White 1976. *Honours:* Franklin Prize, Ainsfield Wolff Literary Award for To Sir, With Love.

BRAITHWAITE, Sir Rodric Quentin, GCMG; British fmr diplomatist; *Senior Consultant in Global Investment Banking, Deutsche Bank;* b. 17 May 1932, London; s. of Henry Warwick Braithwaite and Lorna Constance Davies; m. Gillian Mary Robinson 1961; four s. (one deceased) one d. *Education:* Bedales School, Christ's Coll., Cambridge. *Career:* mil. service 1950–52; joined Foreign Service 1955; Third Sec., Jakarta 1957–58; Second Sec., Warsaw 1959–61; Foreign Office 1961–63; First Sec. (Commercial), Moscow 1963–66; First Sec., Rome 1966–69; FCO 1969–72, Head of European Integration Dept (External) 1973–75, Head of Planning Staff 1979–80, Asst Under-Sec. of State 1981, Deputy Under-Sec. of State 1984–88; Head of Chancery, Office of Perm. Rep. to EEC, Brussels 1975–78; Minister, Commercial, Washington 1982–84; Amb. to Soviet Union 1988–92; Foreign Policy Adviser to Prime Minister 1992–93; Chair. Jt Intelligence Cttee 1992–93; currently Sr Consultant in Global Investment Banking, Deutsche Bank AG, London; Chair. Britain Russia Centre 1994–2000, Moscow School of Political Studies 1998–; mem. European Strategy Bd ICL 1994–2000, Supervisory Bd Deutsche Bank Moscow 1998–99, Bd Ural Mash Zavody (Moscow and Ekaterinburg) 1998–99; mem. Advisory Bd Sirocco Aerospace 2000–; mem. RAM 1993–2002 (Chair. of Govs 1998–2002); Visiting Fellow All Souls Coll. Oxford 1972–73. *Publications:* Engaging Russia (with Blackwill and Tanaka) 1995, Russia in Europe 1999, NATO at Fifty: Perspectives of the Future of the Atlantic Alliance (jtly) 1999, Across the Moscow River 2002, Moscow 1941 2006. *Honours:* Hon. Fellow Christ's Coll. Cambridge; Hon. FRAM; Hon. Prof. (Birmingham) 2000; Dr hc (Birmingham) 1998. *Address:* Deutsche Bank AG, 6th Floor, Winchester House, Great Winchester Street, London, EC2N 2DB, England (office). *Telephone:* (20) 7545-8000 (office). *Fax:* (20) 7545-4577 (office).

BRAMPTON, Sally; British editor and novelist; one d. *Career:* fmr Ed., British Elle magazine, Red magazine; Prof., Central Saint Martins College of Art and Design. *Publications:* Good Grief 1992, Lovesick 1995, Concerning Lily 1998, Love, Always 2000. *Address:* c/o Arrow, Random House, 20 Vauxhall Bridge Road, London, SW1V 2SA, England. *E-mail:* sallybrampton@ hotmail.com.

BRANCH, Edgar Marquess, MA, PhD; American academic, editor and writer; *Research Professor Emeritus and Associate in American Literature, Miami University;* b. 21 March 1913, Chicago, IL; s. of Raymond Sydney

Branch and Marian Marquess Branch; m. Mary Josephine Emerson 1939; one s. two d. *Education:* Univ. Coll., London, England, Beloit Coll., Brown Univ., Univ. of Chicago, Univ. of Iowa. *Career:* Instructor, Miami Univ., Oxford, OH 1941–43, Asst Prof. 1943–49, Assoc. Prof. 1949–57, Prof. 1957–64, Chair. Dept of English 1959–64, Research Prof. 1964–78, Emer. and Assoc. in American Literature 1978–; mem. Modern Language Asscn (MLA) of America, Nat. Council of Teachers of English, James T. Farrell Soc., Mark Twain Circle of America. *Publications:* The Literary Apprenticeship of Mark Twain 1950, James T. Farrell 1963, Clemens of the Call 1969, James T. Farrell 1971, Men Call Me Lucky 1985, Mark Twain and the Starchy Boys 1992, Studs Lonigan's Neighborhood and the Making of James T. Farrell 1996, A Paris Year: Dorothy and James T. Farrell in Paris 1931–32 1998; contrib. to anthologies, magazines and journals. *Honours:* Nat. Endowment for the Humanities Fellowships 1971–72, 1976–77, Miami Univ. Benjamin Harrison Medallion 1978, Guggenheim Fellowship 1978–79, Beloit Coll. Distinguished Service Citation 1979, Mark Twain Circle of America Lifetime Achievement Award 1992, Soc. for the Study of Midwestern Literature Mid-American Award for Distinguished Contributions to the Study of Midwestern Literature 1994, first MLA Prize for Distinguished Scholarly Edition 1995, Ohioana Library Asscn Pegasus Award 1996. *Address:* 4810 Bonham Road, Oxford, OH 45056, USA (home). *Telephone:* (513) 523-4854 (home). *E-mail:* ebranch@lib.muohio.edu (home).

BRANCH, Taylor, AB; American writer; b. 14 Jan. 1947, Atlanta, GA; m. Christina Macy; one s. one d. *Education:* Univ. of North Carolina at Chapel Hill, Princeton Univ. *Career:* staff, The Washington Monthly magazine, Washington, DC 1971–73, Harper's magazine, New York 1973–75, Esquire magazine, New York 1975–76. *Publications:* Blowing the Whistle: Dissent in the Public Interest (with Charles Peters) 1972, Second Wind: The Memoirs of an Opinionated Man (with Bill Russell) 1979, The Empire Blues 1981, Labyrinth (with Eugene M. Propper) 1982, Parting the Waters: America in the King Years 1954–63 (Nat. Book Critics Circle Award for General Non-fiction 1988, Pulitzer Prize in History 1989) 1988, Pillar of Fire: America in the King Years 1963–65 1998, At Canaan's Edge 2006; contrib. articles to magazines and journals, including The Washington Monthly. *Honours:* Christopher Award 1988; Nat. Humanities Medal 1999. *Address:* 1806 South Road, Baltimore, MD 21209, USA (office). *E-mail:* info@taylorbranch.com. *Website:* www.taylorbranch.com.

BRAND, Alice Glarden, BA, MEd, DEd; American poet, writer and academic; b. 8 Sept. 1938, New York, NY; m. Ira Brand 1960, three c. *Education:* University of Rochester, City College, CUNY, Rutgers University. *Career:* Asst Prof., 1980–86, Assoc. Prof. of English, 1987, University of Missouri at St Louis; Visiting Scholar, University of California at Berkeley, 1982–83; Assoc. Prof. of English and Dir of Writing, Clarion University of Pennsylvania, 1987–89; Assoc. Prof., 1989–91, Dir of Composition, 1989–93, Prof. of English, 1992–99, SUNY at Brockport; many workshops, lectures and readings; mem. Acad. of American Poets; MLA; National Council of Teachers of English; Poetry Society of America; Poets and Writers. *Publications:* Poetry: As it Happens, 1983; Studies on Zone, 1989. Other: Therapy in Writing: A Psycho-Educational Enterprise, 1980; The Psychology of Writing: The Affective Experience, 1989; Presence of Mind: Writing and the Domain Beyond the Cognitive (ed. with Richard L. Graves), 1994; Court of Common Pleas, 1996; Writing in the Majors: A Guide to Disciplinary Faculty, 1998. Contributions: numerous anthologies and periodicals. *Honours:* New Jersey State Council on the Arts Fellowship in Poetry, 1981; Residencies, Yaddo Artist's Colony, 1986, 1987, 1991; Wildwood Poetry Prize, 1988; Hon. Mention, National Writers' Union National Poetry Competition, 1993.

BRAND, Dionne, BA, MA; Canadian poet, novelist, essayist and film-maker; b. 1953, Guayguayare, Trinidad. *Education:* Univ. of Toronto, Ontario Inst. for Studies in Education. *Career:* f. mem., ed., Our Lives newspaper; extensive community work; f. mem., fmr Chair., Women's Issues Committee of the Ontario Coalition of Black Trade Unionists; fmr writer-in-residence, Halifax City Regional Library; fmr teacher of poetry, West Coast Women and Words Society Summer School and Retreat; Writer-in-residence, Univ. of Toronto, 1990–91; Teacher, creative writing, Univ. of Guelph, 1991–92; Documentary films: Older, Stronger, Wiser (assoc. dir), 1989, Sisters in the Struggle (co-dir), 1991, Long Time Comin' (co-dir), 1993. *Publications:* Poetry: 'Fore Day Morning: Poems, 1978; Earth Magic: Poetry for Young People, 1978; Primitive Offensive, 1982; Winter Epigrams and Epigrams to Ernesto Cardenal in Defense of Claudia, 1983; Chronicles of the Hostile Sun, 1984; No Language is Neutral, 1990; Land to Light On, 1997; At the Full and Change of the Moon, 1999; Thirsty, 2001. Other: Rivers Have Sources, Trees Have Roots: Speaking of Racism (with Krisantha Sri Bhaggiydatta), 1986; Sight Specific: Lesbians and Representation, 1988; Sans Souci (short stories), 1988; No Burden to Carry: Narratives of Black Working Women in Ontario 1920s to 1950s (with Lois de Shield), 1991; Bread out of Stone (essays), 1994; In Another Place, Not Here (novel), 1996. Contributions: journals incl.: Spear, Fuse Magazine, Network, the Harriet Tubman Review, Fireweed, Poetry Canada Review, Canadian Women Studies, Resources for Feminist Research, Canadian Women Poets; Anthologies: Grammar of Dissent: Poetry and Prose by Claire Harris, M. Nourbese Philip and Dionne Brand, 1994; Other Voices; The Penguin Book of Caribbean Verse; Poetry by Canadian Women; Stories by Canadian Women; Her True-True Name: An Anthology of Women's Writing from the Caribbean; Other Solitudes: Canadian Multicultural Fictions;

Eyeing the North Star: Directions in African-Canadian Literature. *Honours:* Gov.-Gen.'s Literary Award, 1997.

BRAND, Stewart, BS; American editor, writer and publisher; *President, The Long Now Foundation;* b. 14 Dec. 1938, Rockford, Ill.; m. 1st Lois Jennings 1966 (divorced 1972); m. 2nd Ryan Phelan 1983; one s. from a previous relationship. *Education:* Phillips Exeter Acad., Stanford Univ. *Career:* served US Army 1960–62; fmrly with Merry Pranksters; consultant to Gov. of Calif. 1976–78; research scientist Media Lab., MIT 1986; Visiting Scholar Royal Dutch/Shell 1986; f. America Needs Indians, The Well (Internet bulletin Bd) 1984–; co-f. Global Business Network consultancy 1988–, The Long Now Foundation 1996– (also Pres.), All Species project 2000–; Trustee Santa Fe Inst. 1989–. *Television:* How Buildings Learn (writer and presenter) 1997. *Publications:* Two Cybernetic Frontiers 1974, The Media Lab 1987, How Buildings Learn 1994, The Clock of the Long Now 1999; editor, publr: The Last Whole Earth Catalog 1968–71 (Nat. Book Award), Whole Earth Epilog 1974, The Co-Evolution Quarterly 1974–85, The Next Whole Earth Catalog 1980–81, Whole Earth Software Catalog (ed.-in-chief) 1983–85. *Address:* The Long Now Foundation, POB 29462, Presidio of San Francisco, CA 94129-0462, USA (office). *Telephone:* (415) 561-6582 (office). *Fax:* (415) 561-6297 (office). *E-mail:* services@longnow.org (home). *Website:* www.longnow.org (office).

BRANDON, Sheila (see Rayner, Claire Berenice)

BRANDT, Diana (Di) Ruth, BTh, BA, MA, PhD; Canadian poet and writer; b. 31 Jan. 1952, Winkler, Manitoba, Canada; m. Les Brandt 1971 (divorced 1990); two d. *Education:* Canadian Mennonite Bible College, University of Manitoba, University of Toronto. *Career:* Faculty, University of Winnipeg, 1986–95; Writer-in-Residence, University of Alberta, 1995–96; Research Fellow, University of Alberta, 1996–97; Assoc. Prof. of English and Creative Writing, University of Windsor, 1997–; mem. Canadian PEN; League of Canadian Poets; Manitoba Writers' Guild; Writers' Union of Canada. *Publications:* Poetry: questions i asked my mother, 1987; Agnes in the sky, 1990; mother, not mother, 1992; Jerusalem, beloved, 1995. Other: Wild Mother Dancing: Maternal Narrative in Canadian Literature, 1993; Dancing Naked: Narrative Strategies for Writing Across Centuries, 1996. Contributions: various publications. *Honours:* Gerald Lampert Award for Best First Book of Poetry in Canada, 1987; McNally Robinson Award for Manitoba Book of the Year, 1990; Silver National Magazine Award, 1995; Canadian Authors' Asscn National Poetry Award, 1996.

BRANDT, Jorgen Gustava; Danish poet, novelist and essayist; b. 1929. *Career:* worked for the Cultural Dept, Danish Radio. *Publications:* Her omkring 1974, Jatháram 1976, Ophold 1977, Lyset i stenene 1977, Almanak 1977, Köbenhavnerluft 1977, Idiotes: Med blade af livet i klostret 20 1980, Hop: Nye digte 1982, By: Byen i digte 1983, Selected Longer Poems 1983, Harlekinade 1985, Scala suite 1986. *Address:* c/o Curbstone Press, 321 Jackson Street, Willimantic, CT 06226-1738, USA. *E-mail:* info@curbstone.org. *Website:* www.curbstone.org.

BRANFIELD, John Charles, MA, MEd; British writer and teacher; b. 19 Jan. 1931, Burrow Bridge, Somerset; m. Kathleen Elizabeth Peplow; two s. two d. *Education:* Queens' Coll., Cambridge, Univ. of Exeter. *Publications:* A Flag in the Map 1960, Look the Other Way 1963, In the Country 1966, Nancekuke 1972, Sugar Mouse 1973, The Fox in Winter 1980, Thin Ice 1983, The Falklands Summer 1987, The Day I Shot My Dad 1989, Lanhydrock Days 1991, A Breath of Fresh Air 2001, Ella and Charles Naper Art and Life at Lamorna 2003, Charles Simpson, Painter of Animals and Birds, Coastline and Moorland 2005. *Address:* Mingoose Villa, Mingoose, Mount Hawke, Truro, Cornwall, TR4 8BX, England.

BRANIGAN, Keith, BA, PhD; British academic and writer; *Professor of Prehistory and Archaeology, University of Sheffield;* b. 15 April 1940, Bucks.; m. Kuabrat Sivadith 1965; one s. two d. *Education:* Univ. of Birmingham. *Career:* Research Fellow, Univ. of Birmingham 1965–66; Lecturer, Univ. of Bristol 1966–67; Prof. of Prehistory and Archaeology, Univ. of Sheffield 1976–; mem. Prehistory Soc. (vice-pres. 1984–86); Dir Sheffield Centre for Aegean Archaeology 1997–2003; Fellow, Soc. of Antiquaries 1970–. *Publications:* Copper and Bronzeworking in Early Bronze Age Crete 1968, The Foundations of Palatial Crete: A Survey of Crete in the Early Bronze Age 1970, The Tombs of Mesara: A Study of Funerary Architecture and Ritual in Southern Crete, 2800–1700 B.C. 1970, Latimer: Belgic, Roman, Dark Age, and Early Modern Farm 1971, Town and Country: The Archaeology of Verulamium and the Roman Chilterns 1973, Reconstructing the Past: A Basic Introduction to Archaeology 1974, Aegean Metalwork of the Early and Middle Bronze Ages 1974, Atlas of Ancient Civilizations 1976, Prehistoric Britain: An Illustrated Survey 1976, The Roman West Country: Classical Culture and Celtic Society (ed. with P. J. Fowler) 1976, The Roman Villa in South-West England 1977, Gatcombe: The Excavation and Study of a Romano-British Villa Estate, 1967–1976 1978, Rome and the Brigantes: The Impact of Rome on Northern England (ed.) 1980, Roman Britain: Life in an Imperial Province 1980, Hellas: The Civilizations of Ancient Greece (with Michael Vickers) 1980, Atlas of Archaeology 1982, Prehistory 1984, The Catuvellauni 1986, Archaeology Explained 1988, Romano-British Cavemen (with M. J. Dearne) 1992, Dancing with Death: Life and Death in Southern Crete c.3000–2000 B.C. 1993, Lexicon of the Greek and Roman Cities and Place Names in Antiquity, c.1500 B.C.– A.D. 500 (ed. with others) 1993, The Archaeology of the Chilterns (ed.) 1994, Barra: Archaeological Research on Ben Tangaval (with P. Foster) 1995, Cemetery and Society in the Aegean Bronze Age (ed.) 1998, From Barra to

Berneray (with P. Foster) 2000, Barra and the Bishop's Isles (with P. Foster) 2002, Urbanism in the Aegean Bronze Age (ed.) 2002, The Roman Chilterns (with R. Niblett) 2004, From Clan to Clearance 2005; contribs to professional journals. *Address:* Department of Prehistory and Archaeology, University of Sheffield, Sheffield, S10 2TN, England (office). *Telephone:* (114) 222-2900 (office); (114) 258-1523 (home). *E-mail:* archaeology@sheffield.ac.uk (office).

BRANSCOMBE, Peter John, MA, PhD; British academic (retd) and musicologist; *Emeritus Professor, University of St Andrews;* b. 7 Dec. 1929, Sittingbourne, Kent; m. Marina Elizabeth Riley 1967; two s. one d. *Education:* Dulwich Coll., London, Worcester Coll., Oxford, Bedford Coll., London. *Career:* appearances on BBC radio and TV, Austrian radio, Scottish TV; Lecturer in German, Univ. of St Andrews 1959–69, Sr Lecturer 1970–79, Prof. of Austrian Studies 1979–, Emer. Prof. 1996–; Gov., Royal Scottish Acad. of Music 1967–73; mem. Scottish Early Music Consort (advisory cttee 1981–89), Royal Musical Asscn, MHRA, Int. Nestroy Soc., Internationales Franz Schubert Institut, Schubert Inst. (UK), Haydn Soc. of Great Britain, W. H. Auden Soc., Scottish Arts Council (music cttee 1974–81, council 1976–79), Conf. of Univ. Teachers of German in Scotland (Chair. 1983–85). *Publications:* Mozart and his World in Contemporary Pictures (trans.) 1961, Mozart: A Documentary Biography (co-trans.) 1965, Schubert Studies: Problems of Style and Chronology (co-ed.) 1982, Mozart: Die Zauberflöte 1991, Johann Nestroy Sämtliche Werke (ed.) Vols 35 1998, 36 2000, 37 2001, 38 1996; contrib. some 120 articles to New Grove Dictionary of Music and Musicians 1980, 2001, some 120 articles to New Grove Dictionary of Opera 1992, contrib. to various professional journals. *Address:* 32 North Street, St Andrews, Fife KY16 9AQ, Scotland.

BRANTENBERG, Gerd, cand. philol.; Norwegian novelist; b. 27 Oct. 1941, Oslo. *Education:* Fredrikstad Grammar School, Royal High Commercial Inst., Edinburgh, Scotland, Univ. of Oslo. *Career:* high school teacher 1971–82; full-time writer 1982–; reading tours in Scandinavia, England, Germany, USA, Canada; monthly columnist Fredriksstad Blad and Blikk; feminist activist; initiated Refugee Centre for battered wives and rape victims, Oslo; f. Women's High School, Denmark, Lesbian Movements, Copenhagen and Oslo; co-organizer Int. Feminist Book Fairs, London 1984, Oslo 1986, Barcelona 1990, Amsterdam 1992; co-f. Literary Women's Forum 1978; bd mem. Union of 1948, Denmark and Norway; mem. Norwegian Writers' Union (bd mem. 1981–83). *Publications:* Opp alle jordens homofile (novel, trans. as What Comes Naturally 1986) 1973, Egalias døtre (novel, trans. as The Daughters of Egalia 1985) 1977, Ja, vi slutter (novel) 1978, Sangen om St. Croix (novel) 1979, Favntak (novel) 1983, Ved fergestedet (novel) 1985, På sporet av den tapte lyst (co-author, literary criticism) 1986, For alle vinder (novel, trans. as The Four Winds 1996) 1989, Eremitt og entertainer (essays) 1991, Ompadorastedet (juvenile) 1992; contrib. numerous short stories and articles. *Address:* c/o Seal Press, Avalon Publishing Group, 1400 65th Street, Suite 250, Emeryville, CA 94608, USA.

BRANTLINGER, Patrick Morgan, BA, MA, PhD; American academic and writer; *Professor of English, Indiana University;* b. 20 March 1941, Indianapolis, IN; m. Ellen Anderson 1963, two s. one d. *Education:* Antioch Coll., Harvard Univ. *Career:* Asst Prof. of English, Indiana Univ. 1968–74, Assoc. Prof. of English 1974–79, Prof. of English 1979–, Chair Dept of English 1990–94; Ed., Victorian Studies 1980–90; mem. Midwest Victorian Studies Asscn, MLA. *Publications:* The Spirit of Reform: British Literature and Politics, 1832–1867 1977, Bread and Circuses: Theories of Mass Culture and Social Decay 1983, Rule of Darkness: British Literature of Imperialism, 1830–1914 1986, Crusoe's Footprints: Cultural Studies in Britain and America 1990, Fictions of State: Culture and Credit in Britain, 1694–1994 1996, The Reading Lesson: Mass Literacy as Threat in Nineteenth Century British Fiction 1998, Who Killed Shakespeare? What's Happened to English Since the Radical Sixties 2001, Dark Vanishings: Discourse on the Extinction of Primitive Races, 1800–1930 2003; contrib. to scholarly books and journals. *Honours:* Guggenheim Fellowship 1978, Nat. Endowment for the Humanities Fellowship 1983. *Address:* c/o Department of English, Indiana University, Bloomington, IN 47405, USA (office).

BRATA, Sasthi; Indian writer and poet; b. (Sasthibrata Chakravarti), 16 July 1939, Kolkata; m. Pamela Joyce Radcliffe (divorced). *Education:* Univ. of Calcutta. *Career:* London columnist, Statesman 1977–80. *Publications:* Eleven Poems 1960, Confessions of an Indian Woman Eater 1971, She and He 1973, Encounter (short stories) 1978, The Sensorous Guru: The Making of a Mystic President 1980, Traitor to India, Search for Home, My God Died Young, India: The Perpetual Paradox, India: Labyrinths in the Lotus Land. *E-mail:* sasthi.brata@ntlworld.com. *Website:* www.sasthi-brata.com.

BRATHWAITE, Edward Kamau, BA, CertEd, DPhil; Barbadian academic, poet, writer and editor; b. 11 May 1930, Bridgetown; m. Doris Monica Welcome 1960; one s. *Education:* Harrison Coll., Barbados, Pembroke Coll., Cambridge and Univ. of Sussex. *Career:* education officer Ministry of Education, Ghana 1955–62; tutor Extramural Dept, Univ. of the West Indies, St Lucia 1962–63; Lecturer 1963–76, Reader 1976–82, Prof. of Social and Cultural History from 1982, Univ. of the West Indies, Kingston; founding Sec. Caribbean Artists Movement 1966; Ed. Savacou magazine 1970–; Visiting Fellow Harvard Univ. 1987; several visiting professorships. *Publications:* poetry: Rights of Passage 1967, Masks 1968, Islands 1969, Penguin Modern Poets 15 (with Alan Bold and Edwin Morgan) 1969, Panda No. 349 1969, The Arrivants: A New World Trilogy 1973, Days and Nights 1975, Other Exiles

1975, Poetry '75 International 1975, Black + Blues 1976, Mother Poem 1977, Soweto 1979, Word Making Man: A Poem for Nicolas Guillen 1979, Sun Poem 1982, Third World Poems 1983, X-Self 1987, Sappho Sakyi's Meditations 1989, Shar 1990; other: Folk Culture of the Slaves in Jamaica 1970, The Development of Creole Society in Jamaica, 1770–1820 1971, Caribbean Man in Space and Time 1974, Contradictory Omens: Cultural Diversity and Integration in the Caribbean 1974, Our Ancestral Heritage: A Bibliography of the Roots of Culture in the English-Speaking Caribbean 1976, Wars of Respect: Nanny, Sam Sharpe, and the Struggle for People's Liberation 1977, Jamaica Poetry: A Checklist 1686–1978 1979, Barbados Poetry: A Checklist, Slavery to the Present 1979, Kumina 1982, Gods of the Middle East 1982, National Language Poetry 1982, The Colonial Encounter: Language 1984, History of the Voice: The Development of a National Language in Anglophone Caribbean Poetry 1984, Jah Music 1986, Roots 1986; editor: Iouanaloa: Recent Writing from St Lucia 1963, New Poets from Jamaica 1979, Dream Rock 1987. *Honours:* Arts Council of Great Britain Bursary 1967, Camden Arts Festival Prize 1967, Cholmondeley Award 1970, Guggenheim Fellowship 1972, Bussa Award 1973, Casa de las Américas Prize, Cuba 1976, Fulbright Fellowships 1982–83, 1987–88, Inst. of Jamaica Musgrave Medal 1983. *Address:* c/o University of the West Indies, Mona, Kingston 7, Jamaica.

BRAULT, Jacques, MA; Canadian poet, writer, critic and teacher; b. 29 March 1933, Montréal, QC. *Education:* Univ. of Montréal, Univ. of Paris, Univ. of Poitiers. *Career:* teacher, Institut des Sciences Médiévales; Faculty of Letters, Univ. of Montréal. *Publications:* poetry: La poésie et nous (with others) 1958, Mémoire 1965, La poésie ce matin 1971, L'en dessous, l'admirable (trans. as Within the Mystery) 1972, Poèmes des quatre côtés 1975, Trois fois passera 1981, Moments fragiles 1981, Poèmes 1986, Il n'y a plus de chemin (trans. as On the Road No More) 1990, Au petit matin (with Robert Melancon) 1993, Au bras de ombres 1997; prose: Nouvelles (short stories) 1963, Alain Grandbois 1968, Miron le magnifique 1969, Trois partitions (plays) 1972, Chemin faisant 1975, Agonie (novel, trans. as Death-watch) 1984, La poussière de chemin 1989, Ô saison, ô châteaux 1991, Que la vie est quotidienne 1993, Au fonds du jardin 1996. *Honours:* Prix France-Canada 1968, Gov.-Gen.'s Literary Award 1971, Prix Duvernay 1979, Prix du Athanse-David 1986. *Address:* c/o Faculty of Letters, Université de Montréal, CP 6128, Succursale Centre-ville, Montréal, QC H3C 3J7, Canada.

BRAUN, Volker; German poet and playwright; b. 7 May 1939, Dresden. *Education:* Univ. of Leipzig. *Career:* Asst Dir Deutsches Theater, Berlin 1972–77, Berlin Ensemble 1979–90; mem. Akad. der Künste, Berlin. *Plays:* Grosser Frieden 1979, Dmitri 1982, Die Ubergangsgesellschaft 1987, Lenins Tod 1988, Transit Europa: Der Ausflug der Toten 1988, Böhmen am Meer 1992. *Publications:* poetry: Gegen die symmetrische Welt 1974, Training des aufrechten Gangs 1979, Langsamer knirschender Morgen 1987, Der Stoff zum Leben 1990, Lustgarten Preussen 1996; prose: Unvollendete Geschichte 1977, Hinze-Kunze-Roman 1985, Bodenloser Satz 1990, Der Wendehals: Eine Enterhaltung 1995, Das Wirklichgewollte 2000; essays: Verheerende Folgen magnelnden Anscheins innerbetrieblicher Demokratie 1988. *Honours:* Heinrich Mann Prize 1980, Bremen Literature Prize 1986, Nat. Prize, First Class 1988, Berlin Prize 1989, Schiller Commemorative Prize 1992, Büchner Prize 2000. *Address:* Wolfshagenerstrasse 68, 13187 Berlin, Germany (home).

BRAVERMAN, Melanie; American writer; b. 9 Oct. 1960, Iowa City, IA; Companion of Sally Randolph. *Education:* Evergreen State College. *Publications:* East Justice (novel) 1996. *Honours:* Fellow in Poetry and Fiction, Massachusetts Cultural Council, 1996. *Literary Agent:* Edite Kroll Literary Agency, 12 Grayhurst Park, Portland, ME 04102, USA. *E-mail:* mrb@well .com.

BRAX, Najwa Salam, BA, MA; Lebanese poet, writer and academic; b. 3 Sept. 1948, Aley; m. Ghazi Brax 1981. *Education:* Lebanese Univ., Queens Coll., CUNY. *Career:* teacher of Arabic literature 1972–86; Prof. of Arabic Language, Columbia Univ., New York 2003, New School Univ. 2005–. *Publications:* in English: Dr Dahesh: A Great Writer and his Literary Works 1981, Halim Dammous and Spirituality in his Writings 1984, Dahesh as I Knew Him, Wings 1993, Zephyrus Wings 1994, Daring Wings 1996, Growing Wings 1998, Ethereal Wings 1999; contribs to more than 150 US, Canadian, Italian, Indian and British publs. *Honours:* more than 160 poetry awards 1990–. *Address:* 150-16 60th Avenue, Flushing, NY 11355, USA (home).

BRAY, John Jefferson, LLB, LLD; Australian barrister, retd chief justice and poet; b. 16 Sept. 1912, Adelaide, SA. *Education:* University of Adelaide. *Career:* admitted to South Australian Bar, 1933; Chief Justice of South Australia, 1967–78; Chancellor, University of Adelaide, 1968–83; mem. Australian Society of Authors; Friendly Street Poets, Adelaide. *Publications:* Poems, 1962; Poems 1961–71, 1972; Poems 1972–79, 1979; The Bay of Salamis and Other Poems, 1986; Satura: Selected Poetry and Prose, 1988; The Emperor's Doorkeeper (occasional addresses), 1988; Seventy Seven (poems), 1990. *Contributions:* periodicals. *Honours:* South Australian Non-Fiction Award, Adelaide Festival of the Arts, 1990. *Address:* 39 Hurtle Square, Adelaide, SA 5000, Australia.

BRAYBROOKE, Neville Patrick Bellairs; British writer, poet and dramatist; b. 30 May 1923, London, England. *Publications:* London Green: The Story of Kensington Gardens, Hyde Park, Green Park and St James' Park 1959, The Idler (novel) 1960, The Delicate Investigation (play) 1969, Four Poems for Christmas 1986, Dialogue With Judas (poem) 1989, Two Birthdays (poem) 1996, Life of Olivia Manning (with Isobel English) 2001, Olivia

Manning: A Life (with June Braybrooke) 2004; contrib. to periodicals. *Address:* 29 Castle Road, Cowes PO31 7QZ, Isle of Wight.

BRAYFIELD, Celia Frances; British author and journalist; *Senior Lecturer in Creative Writing, Brunel University, London;* b. 21 Aug. 1945, Wembley Park; d. of the late Felix Brayfield and Ada Ellen Brayfield (née Jakeman); one d. *Education:* St. Paul's Girls' School, Universitaire de Grenoble. *Career:* feature writer, Daily Mail 1969–71, TV critic, Evening Standard 1974–82, The Times 1983–88; columnist, Sunday Telegraph 1989–90, The Times 1998–; contrib. to numerous other media; Dir Nat. Acad. of Writing 1999–2003; Sr Lecturer in Creative Writing, Brunel Univ., London 2005–; Trustee One Parent Families 1988–; mem. Soc. of Authors. *Publications:* The Body Show Book 1981, Glitter: The Truth About Fame 1985, Pearls 1987, The Prince 1990, White Ice 1993, Harvest 1995, Bestseller 1996, Getting Home 1998, Sunset 1999, Heartswap 2000, Mr Fabulous and Friends 2003, Wild Weekend 2004, Deep France 2004; contrib. various journals, magazines and newspapers. *Literary Agent:* Curtis Brown Ltd, Haymarket House, 28–29 Haymarket, London, SW1Y 4SP, England. *Telephone:* (20) 7393-4400. *Fax:* (20) 7393-4401. *E-mail:* info@curtisbrown.co.uk. *Website:* www.curtisbrown.co.uk; www.celiabrayfield.com.

BRECHER, Michael, PhD, FRSC; Canadian academic; *R. B. Angus Professor of Political Science, McGill University;* b. 14 March 1925, Montreal; s. of Nathan Brecher and Gisela Hopmeyer; m. Eva Danon 1950; three d. *Education:* McGill and Yale Univs. *Career:* mem. Faculty, McGill Univ. 1952–, R. B. Angus Prof. of Political Science 1993–; Pres. Int. Studies Asscn 1999–2000; Visiting Prof. Univ. of Chicago 1963, Hebrew Univ. Jerusalem 1970–75, Univ. of Calif. Berkeley 1979, Stanford Univ. 1980; Nuffield Fellow 1955–56; Rockefeller Fellow 1964–65; Guggenheim Fellow 1965–66; f. Shashtri Indo-Canadian Inst. 1968. *Publications:* The Struggle for Kashmir 1953, Nehru: A Political Biography 1959, The New States of Asia 1963, Succession in India 1966, India and World Politics 1968, Political Leadership in India 1969, The Foreign Policy System of Israel 1972, Israel, the Korean War and China 1974, Decisions in Israel's Foreign Policy 1975, Studies in Crisis Behavior 1979, Decisions in Crisis 1980, Crisis and Change in World Politics 1986, Crises in the 20th Century (Vols I, II) 1988, Crisis, Conflict and Instability 1989, Crises in World Politics 1993, A Study of Crisis 1997, 2000, Millennial Reflections on International Studies (Vols 1–5) 2002; over 85 articles in journals. *Honours:* Watumull Prize (American Hist. Asscn) 1960, Killam Awards (Canada Council) 1970–74, 1976–79, Woodrow Wilson Award (American Political Science Asscn) 1973, Fieldhouse Award for Distinguished Teaching (McGill Univ.) 1986, Distinguished Scholar Award (Int. Studies Asscn) 1995, Léon-Gérin Quebec Prize 2000, Award for High Distinction in Research, McGill Univ. 2000. *Address:* Department of Political Science, McGill University, 855 Sherbrooke Street West, Montreal, PQ H3A 2T7, Canada (office); 5 Dubnov Street, PO Box 4438, Jerusalem 91043, Israel (home). *Telephone:* (514) 398-4816 (McGill) (office). *Fax:* (514) 398-1770 (McGill) (office). *E-mail:* michael.brecher@mcgill.ca (office). *Website:* www .mcgill.ca/politicalscience (office).

BREE, Marlin, BA; American author and publisher; b. 16 May 1933, Norfolk, Neb.; m. Loris Gutzmer 1963; one s. *Education:* Univ. of Nebraska, Lincoln. *Career:* Ed.'s Reporter, Stars and Stripes Newspaper, 1956; Ed., Sunday Magazine, Minneapolis Star-Tribune, 1968–72; Columnist, Corporate Report Magazine, 1973–77; Editorial Dir, Marlor Press, 1983–; mem. Minnesota Press Club, Pres. 1963; Chair. Midwest Book Awards 1992; Judge, Boating Writers Int. Writing Contest 2007. *Publications:* Alone Against the Atlantic (co-author) 1981, In the Teeth of the Northeaster 1988, Call of the North Wind 1996, Kid's Travel Fun Book (co-author and illustrator) 2000, Wake of the Green Storm: A Survivor's Tale 2001, Broken Seas: True Tales of Extraordinary Seafaring Adventures 2005. *Honours:* Golden Web Award 2004, West Marine Writer's Award 2205. *Address:* 4304 Brigadoon Drive, St Paul, MN 55126, USA. *E-mail:* marlin.marlor@minn.net. *Website:* www .marlinbree.com.

BREEZE, Jean 'Binta'; Jamaican dub poet, writer and film director; b. 1956; m. 1st (divorced 1978); three c. *Education:* Jamaica School of Drama, Kingston. *Career:* jt Ed., Critical Quarterly. *Film screenplays include:* Hallelujah Anyhow 1990. *Recordings include:* Tracks 1991, Hearsay 1994, Riding on de Riddym 1996. *Publications:* poetry: Riddym Ravings and other poems 1988, Spring Cleaning 1992, On the Edge of an Island 1997, Song Lines 1997, The Arrival of Brighteye and other poems 2000. *Address:* c/o Bloodaxe Books Ltd, Highgreen, Tarset, Northumberland NE48 1RP, England. *Website:* www.bloodaxebooks.com.

BRÉGOU, Christian Robert; French publisher; b. 19 Nov. 1941, Neuilly-sur-Seine, Hauts-de-Seine. *Education:* École Supérieure des Sciences Économiques et Commerciales. *Career:* apptd Financial Dir Havas Group 1971; Dir-Gen. CEP Communication 1975, Pres. 1979–97; Pres. Dir-Gen. Groupe de la Cité 1988, Groupe Expansion 1994, l'Express 1995–97; adviser Socpresse SA 1997; Pres. media group DI (Desfossés International—part of LVMH Group) 2001–. *Address:* D.I Group, 48 rue Notre-Dame-des-Victoires, 75081 Paris Cedex 02, France.

BREILLAT, Catherine; French film director, screenwriter and novelist; *Professor of Auteur Cinema, European Graduate School;* b. 1948, Bressuire. *Career:* Prof. of Auteur Cinema, European Grad. School, Switzerland. *Film roles include:* Last Tango in Paris 1972, Dracula Père et Fils 1977. *Films directed include:* Une vraie jeune fille (A Real Young Girl) 1975 (released 2000), Tapage nocturne (Nocturnal Uproar) 1979, 36 Fillette (Virgin) 1988, Sale comme un ange (Dirty Like an Angel) 1990, Parfait Amour (Perfect Love, jtly) 1996, Romance 1999, À ma soeur! (Fat Girl) 2001, Brève traversée (Brief Crossing) 2001, Scènes intimes 2002, Sex is Comedy 2002, Anatomie de l'enfer 2004, Une Vieille Maîtresse (An Elderly Mistress) 2007. *Publications include:* L'homme facile (novel), Tapage nocturne 1979, Romance 1999, Le livre du plaisir 1999, Une vraie jeune fille 2000, À ma soeur! 2001, Pornocratie 2001, Ein Mädchen 2001. *Screenplays include:* Catherine et Cie (Catherine & Co., jtly) 1975, Bilitis 1977, La peau (The Skin) 1981, Et la nave va (And the Ship Sails On) 1983, L'araignée de satin (The Satin Spider) 1984, Police 1985, Milan noir (Black Milan, jtly) 1987, Zanzibar (jtly) 1988, La nuit de l'océan (The Night of the Ocean, jtly) 1988, Aventure de Catherine C. (The Adventure of Catherine C., jtly) 1990, Le diable au corps 1990, La Thune (Money, jtly) 1991, Couples et amants (Couples and Lovers, jtly) 1994, Viens jouer dans la cour des grands (TV) 1997, Selon Matthieu 2000. *Address:* c/o European Graduate School, Ringacker, 3953 Leuk-Stadt, Switzerland (office). *Telephone:* (27) 474 9917 (office). *Fax:* (27) 474 9969 (office).

BRENDEL, Alfred; Austrian pianist and writer; b. 5 Jan. 1931, Wiesenberg; s. of Ing. Albert and Ida Brendel (née Wieltschnig); m. 1st Iris Heymann-Gonzala 1960 (divorced 1972); one d.; m. 2nd Irene Semler 1975; one s. two d. *Career:* studied piano under Sofija Deželić (Zagreb), Ludovika v. Kaan (Graz), Edwin Fischer (Lucerne), Paul Baumgartner (Basel), Edward Steuermann (Salzburg); studied composition under A. Michl (Graz) and harmony under Franjo Dugan (Zagreb); first piano recital Musikverein Graz 1948; concert tours through Europe, Latin America, North America 1963–, Australia 1963, 1966, 1969, 1976; has appeared at many music festivals, including Salzburg 1960–, Vienna, Edinburgh, Aldeburgh, Athens, Granada, Puerto Rico, London Proms and has performed with most of the major orchestras of Europe and USA, etc.; mem. American Acad. of Arts and Sciences. *Recordings:* extensive repertoire; Beethoven's Complete Piano Works, Beethoven Sonatas, Beethoven Concertos (with Vienna Philharmonic Orchestra and Simon Rattle) 1998. *Publications:* essays on music and musicians in Phono, Fono Forum, Österreichische Musikzeitschrift, Music and Musicians, Hi-Fi Stereophonie, New York Review of Books, Die Zeit, Frankfurter Allgemeine Zeitung, Musical Thoughts and Afterthoughts 1976, Nachdenken über Musik 1977, Music Sounded Out (essays) 1990, Musik beim Wort genommen 1992, Fingerzeig 1996, Störendes Lachen während des Jaworts 1997, One Finger Too Many 1998, Kleine Teufel 1999, Collected Essays on Music 2000, Alfred Brendel on Music 2001, Augerechnet Ich (aka The Veil of Order: In Conversation with Martin Meyer) 2001, Spiegelbild und Schwarzer Spuk (poems) 2003, Cursing Bagels (poems) 2004. *Honours:* Hon. RAM; Hon. RCM; Hon. Fellow, Exeter Coll. Oxford 1987; Commdr, Ordre des Arts et des Lettres 1985, Hon. KBE 1989, Ordre pour le Mérite (Germany) 1991; Hon. DMus (London) 1978, (Oxford) 1983, (Warwick) 1991, (Yale) 1992, (Exeter) 1998, (Southampton) 2002, Hon. DLitt (Sussex) 1981, Dr hc (Cologne) 1995; Premio Città de Bolzano, Concorso Busoni 1949, Grand Prix du Disque 1965, Edison Prize (five times 1973–87), Grand Prix des Disquaires de France 1975, Deutscher Schallplattenpreis (four times 1976–84, 1992), Wiener Flötenuhr (six times 1976–87), Gramophone Award (six times 1977–83), Japanese Record Acad. Award (five times 1977–84, with Scottish Symphony Orchestra/ Sir Charles Mackerras 2002), Japanese Grand Prix 1978, Franz Liszt Prize (four times 1979–83), Frankfurt Music Prize 1984, Diapason D'Or Award 1992, Heidsieck Award for Writing on Music 1990, Hans von Bülow-Medaille, Kameradschaft der Berliner Philharmoniker eV, 1992, Cannes Classical Award 1998, Ehrenmitgliedschaft der Wiener Philharmoniker 1998, Léonie Sonnings Musikpris, Denmark 2002, Ernst von Siemens Musikpreis 2004. *Address:* c/o Ingpen & Williams, 7 St George's Court, 131 Putney Bridge Road, London, SW15 2PA, England (office). *Telephone:* (20) 8874-3222 (office). *Fax:* (20) 8877-3113 (office). *E-mail:* info@ingpen.co.uk (office).

BRENDON, Piers George Rundle, MA, PhD; British writer and broadcaster; b. 21 Dec. 1940, Stratton, Cornwall; m. Vyvyen Davis 1968; two s. *Education:* Magdalene Coll., Cambridge. *Career:* Lecturer in History, Cambridgeshire Coll. of Arts and Tech. 1966–79, Head, Dept of History 1977–79; Keeper of the Archives Centre and Fellow, Churchill Coll., Cambridge 1995–2001. *Publications:* Reading They've Liked (co-ed. with William Shaw) 1967, Reading Matters (co-ed. with William Shaw) 1969, By What Authority? (co-ed. with William Shaw) 1972, Hurrell Froude and the Oxford Movement 1974, Hawker of Morwenstow: Portrait of a Victorian Eccentric 1975, Eminent Edwardians 1979, The Life and Death of the Press Barons 1982, Winston Churchill: A Brief Life 1984, Ike: The Life and Times of Dwight D. Eisenhower 1986, Our Own Dear Queen 1986, Thomas Cook: 150 Years of Popular Tourism 1991, The Windsors: A Dynasty Revealed 1995, The Motoring Century: The Story of the Royal Automobile Club 1997, The Dark Valley: A Panorama of the 1930s 2000; contrib. to periodicals, including The Guardian, The Independent, The Oldie. *Address:* 4B Millington Road, Cambridge, CB3 9HP, England. *Telephone:* (1223) 351886 (home). *Fax:* (1223) 329729 (home). *E-mail:* pb204@cam.ac.uk (home).

BRENT, Madeleine (see O'Donnell, Peter)

BRENTON, Howard, BA; British playwright; b. 13 Dec. 1942, Portsmouth; s. of Donald Henry Brenton and Rose Lilian Brenton (née Lewis); m. Jane Fry 1970; two s. *Education:* Chichester High School for Boys and St Catharine's Coll., Cambridge. *Career:* resident writer, Royal Court Theatre, London 1972–73; writer-in-residence, Warwick Univ. 1978–79; Granada Artist in Residence, Univ. of Calif. at Davis 1997; Arts and Humanities Research Bd

Fellowship, Birmingham Univ. 2000. *Publications:* Notes from a Psychotic Journal and Other Poems 1969, Revenge 1969, Christie in Love (plays) 1969, Scott of the Antarctic (or what God didn't see) 1970, Lay By (co-author) 1972, Plays for Public Places 1972, Hitler Dances 1972, Magnificence 1973, Brassneck (with David Hare) 1973, The Churchill Play 1974, Government Property 1975, The Saliva Milkshake 1975, Weapons of Happiness 1976, The Paradise Run (TV play) 1976, Sore Throats 1979, Plays for the Poor Theatre 1980, The Romans in Britain 1980, Thirteenth Night 1981, The Genius 1983, Desert of Lies (TV play) 1983, Sleeping Policemen (with Tunde Ikoli) 1983, Bloody Poetry 1984, Pravda (with David Hare) 1985, Dead Head 1986, Greenland 1988, Diving for Pearls (novel) 1989, Iranian Nights (with Tariq Ali) 1989, Hess is Dead 1990, Moscow Gold (with Tariq Ali) 1990, Berlin Bertie 1992, Hot Irons (Essays and Diaries) 1995, Playing Away (opera) 1994, Goethe's Faust, Parts I and II (adaptation) 1995, Plays I 1996, Plays II 1996, in Extremis 1997, Ugly Rumours (with Tariq Ali) 1998, Collateral Damage (with Tariq Ali and Andy de la Tour), Nasser's Eden (play for radio) 1999, Snogging Ken (with Tariq Ali and Andy de la Tour) 2000, Kit's Play 2000, Spooks (TV series) 2002–05, Paul (play) 2005, In Extremis (play) 2006. *Honours:* Hon. Dr of Arts (Univ. of N London) 1996; John Whiting Award 1970, Standard Best Play of the Year Award 1976, Standard Best Play of the Year (jtly with David Hare) 1985. *Address:* c/o Cassarotto Ramsay Ltd, 60/66 National House, Wardour Street, London, W1V 4ND, England. *Telephone:* (20) 7287-4450. *Fax:* (20) 7287-9128.

BRETT, Simon Anthony Lee, BA; British writer; b. 28 Oct. 1945, Surrey, England; m. Lucy Victoria McLaren 1971, two s. one d. *Education:* Wadham Coll., Oxford. *Career:* mem. CWA (chair. 1986–87), Detection Club, PEN, Soc. of Authors (chair. 1995–97). *Publications:* 17 Charles Paris crime novels 1975–97; A Shock to the System 1984; Dead Romantic 1985; six Mrs Pargeter crime novels 1986–99; The Booker Book 1989; How to be a Little Sod 1992; Singled Out 1995; The Body on the Beach 2000; The Hanging in the Hotel 2003, The Stabbing in the Stables 2006, Death Under the Dryer 2007; editor: The Detection Collection (short stories) 2005 and several Faber books; other: After Henry (radio and television series), 1985–92, On Second Thoughts 2006. *Honours:* Writers' Guild Best Radio Feature 1973, Broadcasting Press Guild Outstanding Radio Programme 1987. *Address:* Frith House, Burpham, Arundel, West Sussex BN18 9RR, England.

BRETTON, Barbara; American writer; b. 25 June 1950, New York, NY; m. Roy Bretton 1968. *Education:* Queens College, CUNY. *Career:* mem. Romance Writers of America. *Publications:* Love Changes, 1983; The Sweetest of Debts, 1984; No Safe Place, 1985; Starfire, 1985; The Edge of Forever, 1986; Promises in the Night, 1986; Shooting Star, 1986; Somewhere in Time, 1992; One and Only, 1994; The Invisible Groom, 1994; Tomorrow and Always, 1994; Destiny's Child, 1995; Maybe This Time, 1996; Guilty Pleasure, 1996; Operation: Baby, 1997; Sleeping Alone, 1997; The Perfect Wife, 1997; Always, 1998; Operation: Family, 1998. Contributions: anthologies and periodicals.

BREW, (Osborne Henry) Kwesi, BA; Ghanaian fmr ambassador and poet; b. 27 May 1928, Cape Coast. *Education:* University College of the Gold Coast, Legon. *Career:* fmr Ghanian Ambassador to Britain, India, France, USSR, Germany and Mexico. *Publications:* The Shadows of Laughter, 1968; African Panorama and Other Poems, 1981. Contributions: anthologies and periodicals. *Honours:* British Council Prize. *Address:* c/o Greenfield Review Press, PO Box 80, Greenfield Center, NY 12833, USA.

BREWER, Derek Stanley, LittD, PhD; British academic; *Professor Emeritus of English, University of Cambridge*; b. 13 July 1923, Cardiff; s. of Stanley Leonard Brewer and Winifred Helen Forbes; m. Lucie Elisabeth Hoole 1951; three s. two d. *Education:* Crypt Grammar School, Gloucester, Magdalen Coll., Oxford. *Career:* war service in infantry 1942–45; Asst Lecturer then Lecturer, Univ. of Birmingham 1949–56, Sr Lecturer 1958–64; Prof., Int. Christian Univ., Tokyo 1956–58; Lecturer, Univ. of Cambridge 1965–76, Reader 1976–83, Prof. 1983–90, Prof. Emer. 1990–; f. D. S. Brewer Ltd (now part of Boydell and Brewer), publrs of academic books; Fellow, Emmanuel Coll., Cambridge 1965–77, Master 1977–90, Life Fellow 1990–; Corresp. Fellow Medieval Soc. of America 1987; Franqui Prof. des Sciences Humaines (Belgium) 1998. *Publications include:* Chaucer 1953, Proteus 1958, Chaucer's Parlement of Foulys (ed.) 1960, Malory's Morte d'Arthur Parts 7 and 8 (ed.) 1968, Chaucer and his World 1978, Symbolic Stories 1980, English Gothic Literature 1983, Introduction to Chaucer 1984, Medieval Comic Tales (ed.) 1996, A Critical Companion to the Gawain-poet (ed.) 1996, A New Introduction to Chaucer 1998, Seatonian Exercises and other verses 2000, The World of Chaucer 2000. *Honours:* Hon. Fellow English Assen 2001; Hon. mem. Japan Acad. 1981; hon. degrees from Univs of Keio (Tokyo), Harvard, York, Birmingham, Paris IV (Sorbonne), Liège, Williams Coll., USA; Seatonian Prize for Poetry (ten times); Medal, Japan Acad. 1997; Medal des Sciences Humaines (Belgium) 1998. *Address:* Emmanuel College, Cambridge, CB2 3AP (office); 240 Hills Road, Cambridge, CB2 2QE, England. *Telephone:* (1223) 210782 (home); (1223) 334200. *Fax:* (1223) 241104. *E-mail:* dsb27@cam.ac.uk (office).

BREWSTER, Elizabeth Winifred, BLS, MA, PhD; Canadian academic and writer; *Professor Emerita of English, University of Saskatchewan*; b. 26 Aug. 1922, Chipman, NB; d. of Frederick Brewster and Ethel Brewster (née Day). *Education:* Univ. of New Brunswick, Radcliffe Coll., King's Coll., London, Univs of Toronto and Indiana, USA. *Career:* Faculty mem. Univ. of Saskatchewan 1972–, Prof. of English 1980–90, Prof. Emer. 1990–; staff

mem. numerous libraries; mem. League of Canadian Poets, Writers' Union of Canada, Assen of Canadian Univ. Teachers of English, Canadian Assen of Commonwealth Literature and Language Studies, PEN Club Int. *Publications include:* poetry: East Coast 1951, Lillooet 1954, Roads 1957, Passage of Summer 1969, Sunrise North 1972, In Search of Eros 1974, It's Easy to Fall 1977, Sometimes I Think of Moving 1977, It's Easy to Fall on the Ice 1977, The Way Home 1982, Digging In 1982, Selected Poems of Elizabeth Brewster 1944–84 1985, Entertaining Angels 1988, Spring Again 1990, The Invention of Truth 1991, Wheel of Change 1993, Footnotes to the Book of Job 1995, Away From Home (autobiog.) 1995, Garden of Sculpture 1998, Burning Bush 2000, Jacob's Dream 2002, Collected Poems Vol. 1 2003, Bright Centre 2005; novels: The Sisters 1974, Junction 1982; short stories: A House Full of Women 1983, Visitations 1987. *Honours:* mem. Order of Canada 2001; Hon. DLitt (New Brunswick) 1982; Canada Council Sr Artists Awards for Poetry 1971–72, 1976, 1978–79, 1985–86, Pres.'s Medal for Poetry, Univ. of Western Ontario 1980, Literary Award, Canadian Broadcasting Corp. 1991, Saskatoon Arts Bd Award for Lifetime Excellence in the Arts 1995, Saskatchewan Book Award for Poetry 2003. *Address:* Department of English, 320 Arts Tower, 9 Campus Drive, University of Saskatchewan, Saskatoon, SK S7N 5A5 (office); 206 Colony Square, 910 9th Street E, Saskatoon, SK S7H 0N1, Canada (home). *Telephone:* (306) 966-5486 (office); (306) 343-7695 (home). *Fax:* (306) 966-5951 (office). *Website:* www.usask.ca/english (office).

BREYTENBACH, Breyten; South African poet and writer; b. 16 Sept. 1939, Bonnievale. *Education:* Univ. of Cape Town. *Publications:* Sinking Ship Blues 1977, And Death White as Words: Anthology 1978, In Africa Even the Flies Are Happy: Selected Poems 1964–77 1978, Mouroir: Mirrornotes of a Novel 1984, End Papers 1986, Judas Eye 1988, All One Horse 1990, The Memory of Birds in Times of Revolution (essays) 1996. *Honours:* Rapport Prize 1986. *Address:* c/o Faber and Faber Ltd, 3 Queen Square, London, WC1N 3AU, England.

BREZHNEV, Dennis (see Barnett, Paul Le Page)

BRIANÇON, Pierre, LLM; French journalist; b. 3 Aug. 1954, Tunis, Tunisia; s. of Claude Briançon and Geneviève Pochard; three c. *Education:* Université Paris II, Institut d'Etudes Politiques, Paris. *Career:* journalist, Forum International 1979; Econs and Business Ed. Libération 1981–88, Moscow Corresp. 1988–91, USA Bureau Chief, Washington 1992–95, Ed.-in-Chief 1996–98; contrib. France Inter radio 1982–86; Asst Editorial Dir L'expansion 1998–2000; Dir. Startup Avenue (econ. information site) 2000–; Pres., Dir-Gen. B to B Avenue.com. *Publications:* A Droite en sortant de la gauche? 1986, Héritiers du désastre 1992. *Address:* B to B Avenue, 12 rue Charlot, 75003 Paris, France (office).

BRIDGEMAN, Viscountess Victoria Harriet Lucy, MA, FRSA; British fine arts specialist, library executive and editor; *Managing Director, The Bridgeman Art Library*; b. 30 March 1942, Co. Durham; d. of Ralph Meredyth Turton and Mary Blanche Turton (née Chetwynd Stapylton); m. Viscount Bridgeman 1966; four s. (one deceased). *Education:* St Mary's School, Wantage, Trinity Coll., Dublin. *Career:* Exec. Ed. The Masters 1965–69; Ed. Discovering Antiques 1970–72; est. own co. producing books and articles on fine and decorative arts; founder and Man. Dir The Bridgeman Art Library 1971–; Cttee mem. British Assen of Picture Libraries and Agencies; founder Artists' Collecting Soc. 2006. *Publications:* Encyclopaedia of Victoriana, Needlework: An Illustrated History, The British Eccentric 1975, Society Scandals 1977, Beside the Seaside 1977, Guide to the Gardens of Europe 1980, The Last Word 1982 (all jtly with Elizabeth Drury), eight titles in Connoisseur's Library series. *Honours:* European Woman of the Year (Arts Section) Award 1997, Int. Business Woman of the Year 2005. *Address:* The Bridgeman Art Library, 17–19 Garway Road, London, W2 4PH, England (office); The Bridgeman Art Library International, 65 East 93rd Street, New York, NY 10128, USA (office); The Bridgeman Art Library, 36 rue des Bourdonnais, 75001 Paris, France (office); 19 Chepstow Road, London, W2 5BP (home); Watley House, Sparsholt, Nr Winchester, Hants., SO21 2LU, England (home). *Telephone:* (20) 7727-4065 (office); (20) 7727-5400 (London) (home); (1962) 776297 (Hants.) (home). *Fax:* (20) 7792-8509 (office); (20) 7792-9178 (home); (1962) 776297 (Hants.). *E-mail:* harriet.bridgeman@bridgeman.co.uk (office). *Website:* www .bridgeman.co.uk (office).

BRIEN, Alan, BA; British novelist and journalist; b. 12 March 1925, Sunderland, England; m. 1st Pamela Mary Jones 1947, three d.; m. 2nd Nancy Newbold Ryan 1961, one s. one d.; m. 3rd Jill Sheila Tweedie 1973. *Education:* Jesus College, Oxford. *Career:* Assoc. Ed., Mini-Cinema, 1950–52, Courier, 1952–53; Film Critic, Columnist, Truth, 1953–54; TV Critic, Observer, 1954–55; Film Critic, 1954–56, New York Correspondent, 1956–58, Evening Standard; Drama Critic, Features Ed., 1958–61, Columnist, 1963–65, Spectator; Columnist, Sunday Daily Mail, 1958–62, Sunday Dispatch, 1962–63; Political Columnist, Sunday Pictorial, 1963–64; Drama Critic, Sunday Telegraph, 1964–67; Columnist New Statesman, 1966–72, Punch, 1972–84; Diarist, 1967–75, Film Critic, 1976–84, Sunday Times. *Publications:* Domes of Fortune, 1979; Lenin: The Novel, 1986; Heaven's Will (novel), 1989; And When Rome Falls (novel), 1991. Contributions: various professional journals.

BRIERLEY, David, BA; British author; b. 30 July 1936, Durban, South Africa; m. (separated); one d. *Education:* Univ. of Oxford. *Publications:* Cold War, 1979; Blood Group O, 1980; Big Bear, Little Bear, 1981; Shooting Star, 1983; Czechmate, 1984; Skorpion's Death, 1985; Snowline, 1986; One Lives,

One Dies, 1987; On Leaving a Prague Window, 1995; The Horizontal Woman, 1996; The Cloak-and-Dagger Girl, 1998; Death & Co, 1999.

BRIGGS, Baron (Life Peer), cr. 1976, of Lewes in the County of Sussex; **Asa Briggs,** BSc, MA, FBA; British historian; b. 7 May 1921, Keighley, Yorks.; s. of William Walker Briggs and Jane Briggs; m. Susan Anne Banwell 1955; two s. two d. *Education:* Keighley Grammar School and Sidney Sussex Coll., Cambridge. *Career:* Fellow, Worcester Coll., Oxford 1945–55, Reader in Recent Social and Econ. History, Univ. of Oxford 1950–55; Prof. of Modern History, Leeds Univ. 1955–61; Prof. of History, Univ. of Sussex 1961–76, Dean of Social Studies 1961–65, Pro-Vice-Chancellor 1961–67, Vice-Chancellor 1967–76; Provost Worcester Coll., Oxford 1976–91; Chancellor, Open Univ. 1979–94; Pres. Workers Educational Asscn 1958–67; Chair. Appts Comm. Press Council 1972–88; mem. Univ. Grants Cttee 1959–67; Trustee, Int. Broadcast Inst. 1968–86, Hon. Trustee 1990–; Gov. British Film Inst. 1970–76, Chair. European Inst. of Educ. 1974–84; mem. Council of UN Univ. 1974–80; Chair. Cttee on Nursing 1970–72, Heritage Educ. Group 1976–86, Commonwealth of Learning 1988–93; Pres. Social History Soc. 1976–, Ephemera Soc. 1984–, Victorian Soc. 1983–; Vice-Pres. Historical Asscn 1986–; Vice-Chair. of Council, UN Univ. 1974–80. *Publications:* Patterns of Peacemaking (with D. Thomson and E. Meyer) 1945, History of Birmingham, 1865–1938 1952, Victorian People 1954, Friends of the People 1956, The Age of Improvement 1959 (revised Edn 2000), Ed. Chartist Studies 1959, History of Broadcasting, Vol. I 1961, Vol. II 1965, Vol. III 1970, Vol. IV 1979, Vol. V 1995, Victorian Cities 1963, The Nineteenth Century (ed.) 1970, Cap and Bell (with Susan Briggs) 1972, Essays in the History of Publishing (ed.) 1974, Essays in Labour History 1918–1939 1977, Governing the BBC 1979, From Coalbrookdale to the Crystal Palace 1980, The Power of Steam 1982, Marx in London 1982, A Social History of England 1983 (Haut-Brion: An Illustrious Lineage 1994), The BBC—The First Fifty Years 1985, The Collected Essays of Asa Briggs, (Vol. 1, 2, 3), The Franchise Affair (with Joanna Spicer) 1986, Victorian Things 1988, The Longman Encyclopedia (ed.) 1989, The Channel Islands: Occupation and Liberation 1940–45 1995, Fins de Siècle (co-ed.) 1996; co-author Modern Europe 1789–1989 1996, The History of Bethlem 1997, Chartism 1998, Go to It! War: Working for Victory on the Home Front, 1939–45, Michael Young: Social Entrepreneur 2000, A Social History of the Media (with Peter Burke) 2002. *Honours:* Hon. mem. American Acad. of Arts and Sciences 1970–; Hon. LLD, Hon. DLitt, Hon. DSc; Marconi Medal for Services to Study of Broadcasting 1975, Medal of French Acad. for Architecture 1982, Wolfson History Prize 2001. *Address:* 26 Oakmede Way, Ringmer, East Sussex, BN8 5JL (office); The Caprons, Keere Street, Lewes, Sussex, England (home). *Telephone:* (1273) 814472 (office); (1273) 474704 (home). *Fax:* (1273) 814462 (office); (1273) 474704 (home). *E-mail:* veronica .humphrey@btinternet.com.

BRIGGS, Raymond Redvers, NDD, DFA, FSCD, FRSL; British writer, illustrator and cartoonist; b. 18 Jan. 1934, Wimbledon, London; s. of Ernest R. Briggs and Ethel Bowyer; m. Jean Taprell Clark 1963 (died 1973). *Education:* Rutlish School, Merton, Wimbledon School of Art and Slade School of Fine Art, London. *Career:* freelance illustrator 1957–; part-time lecturer in illustration Brighton School of Art 1961–87; children's author 1961–; mem. RSL, Soc. of Authors. *Publications:* The Strange House 1961, Midnight Adventure 1961, Ring-a-Ring o' Roses 1962, Sledges to the Rescue 1963, The White Land 1963, Fee Fi Fo Fum 1964, The Mother Goose Treasury 1966, Jim and the Beanstalk 1970, The Fairy Tale Treasury 1972, Father Christmas 1973 (also film version), Father Christmas Goes on Holiday 1975, Fungus the Bogeyman 1977, The Snowman 1978 (also film version), Gentleman Jim 1980 (also stage version), When the Wind Blows 1982 (stage and radio versions 1983, animated film version 1987), The Tinpot Foreign General and the Old Iron Woman 1984, The Snowman Pop-Up 1986, Unlucky Wally 1987, Unlucky Wally Twenty Years On 1989, The Man 1992, The Bear 1994 (also film version), Ethel and Ernest 1998, UG 2001, Blooming Books (with Nicolette Jones) 2003, The Puddleman 2004. *Honours:* awards include Kate Greenaway Medal 1966, 1973, BAFTA Award, Francis Williams Illustration Award (Victoria & Albert Museum) 1982, Broadcasting Press Guild Radio Award 1983, Children's Author of the Year 1992, Kurt Maschler Award 1992, Illustrated Book of the Year Award 1998, Smarties Silver Award 2001. *Address:* Weston, Underhill Lane, Westmeston, nr Hassocks, Sussex, BN6 8XG, England.

BRIJS, Stefan; Belgian writer; b. 29 Dec. 1969, Genk. *Publications:* De verwording (novel) 1997, Kruistochten (essays) 1998, Arend (novel) 2000, Twee levens (short story) 2001, Villa Keetje Tippel (biog.) 2001, De engelenmaker (novel) (Gouden Uil Prijs van de Lezer, De Vijfjaarlijkse Prijs voor Proza van de Koninklijke Academie voor Nederlandse Taal- en Letterkunde 2006) 2005, Korrels in Gods grote zandbak (essays) 2006. *Address:* c/o Uitgeverij Atlas, Herengracht 481, 1017 BT Amsterdam, The Netherlands (office). *Telephone:* (20) 524 98 00 (office). *Fax:* (20) 627 68 51 (office). *E-mail:* mail@stefanbrijs.be; atlas@uitgeverijatlas.nl (office). *Website:* www .stefanbrijs.be; www.uitgeverijatlas.nl (office).

BRINDLEY, Lynne Janie, MA, FLA, FRSA, CCMI; British librarian; *Chief Executive, The British Library*; b. 2 July 1950, London; d. of Ivan Blowers and Janie Blowers (née Williams); adopted d. of Ronald Williams and Elaine Williams (née Chapman); m. Timothy Stuart Brindley 1972. *Education:* Truro High School, Univ. of Reading, Univ. Coll. London. *Career:* Head of Marketing and of Chief Exec.'s Office, British Library 1979–85, Chief Exec. British Library 2000–; Dir of Library and Information Services, also Pro-Vice Chancellor, Aston Univ. 1985–90; Prin. Consultant, KPMG 1990–92; Librarian and Dir of Information Services, LSE 1992–97; Librarian and Pro-Vice Chancellor, Univ. of Leeds 1997–2000, Visiting Prof. of Knowledge Man., 2000–; Visiting Prof. of Information Man., Leeds Metropolitan Univ. 2000–03; mem. Int. Cttee on Social Science Information, UNESCO 1992–97, Lord Chancellor's Advisory Cttee on Public Records 1992–98, Stanford Univ. Advisory Council for Libraries and Information Resources 1999–, Resource Bd 2002–, EPSRC User Panel 2002–04, Ithaka Bd; Trustee Thackray Medical Museum, Leeds 1999–2001; Fellow Univ. Coll. London 2002. *Publications:* numerous articles on electronic libraries and information man. *Honours:* Freeman, City of London 1989; Liveryman, Goldsmiths' Co. 1993; Hon. DLitt (Nottingham Trent) 2001, (Oxford) 2002, (Leicester) 2002, (Sheffield) 2004, (Reading) 2004; Hon. DPhil (London Guildhall) 2002; Hon. DSc (City) 2005. *Address:* The British Library, 96 Euston Road, London, NW1 2DB, England (office). *Telephone:* (20) 7412-7273 (office). *Fax:* (20) 7412-7268 (office). *E-mail:* chief-executive@bl.uk (office). *Website:* www.bl.uk (office).

BRINGHURST, Robert, BA, MFA; Canadian poet and writer; *Adjunct Professor, Frost Centre for Native Studies and Canadian Studies, Trent University*; b. 16 Oct. 1946, Los Angeles, CA, USA; one d. *Education:* MIT, Univ. of Utah, Defense Language Inst., Indiana Univ., Univ. of British Columbia. *Career:* Gen. Ed. Kanchenjunga Poetry Series 1973–79; Reviews Ed. Canadian Fiction Magazine 1974–75; Visiting Lecturer, Univ. of British Columbia 1975–77, Lecturer 1979–80; poet-in-residence Banff School of Fine Arts 1983, Ojibway and Cree Cultural Centre Writers' Workshops 1985–86, Univ. of Western Ontario 1998–99; Adjunct Prof., Frost Centre for Native Studies and Canadian Studies, Trent Univ. 1998–, and Centre for Studies in Publishing 2000–, Simon Fraser Univ.; Ashley Fellow, Trent Univ. 1994; Contributing Ed. Fine Print: A Review for the Arts of the Book 1985–90; writer-in-residence Univ. of Edinburgh 1989–90; Philips Fund Research Fellow, American Philosophical Soc. 2000. *Publications:* The Shipwright's Log 1972, Cadastre 1973, Eight Objects 1975, Bergschrund 1975, Jacob Singing 1977, The Stonecutter's Horses 1979, Tzuhalem's Mountain 1982, The Beauty of the Weapons: Selected Poems 1972–82 1982, Visions: Contemporary Art in Canada 1983, The Raven Steals the Light 1984, Ocean, Paper, Stone 1984, Tending the Fire 1985, The Blue Roofs of Japan 1986, Pieces of Map, Pieces of Music 1986, Conversations with Toad 1987, The Black Canoe 1991, The Elements of Typographic Style 1992, The Calling: Selected Poems 1970–95 1995, Elements 1995, Boats is Saintlier than Captains 1997, Native American Oral Literatures and the Unity of the Humanities 1998, A Story as Sharp as a Knife: The Classical Haida Mythtellers and Their World 1999, A Short History of the Printed Word 1999, The Book of Silences 2001, Ursa Major 2003, Prosodies of Meaning 2003, Carving the Elements: A Companion to the Fragments of Parmenides 2004, The Solid Form of Language 2004, New World Suite No. 3 2005, The Old in Their Knowing 2005, The Silence That Is Not Poetry — And The Silence That Is 2006; translations: Nine Visits to the Mythworld (by Ghandl of the Qayahl Llaanas) 2000, Being in Being: The Collected Works of Skaay of the Qquuna Qiighawaay 2001, The Fragments of Parmenides 2003; contrib.: many anthologies. *Honours:* Macmillan Prize 1975, Alcuin Soc. Design Awards 1984, 1985, Canadian Broadcasting Corporation Poetry Prize 1985, Guggenheim Fellowship 1987–88; Edward Sapir Prize 2004, Lt-Gov.'s Award for Literary Excellence 2005. *Address:* POB 51, Heriot Bay, BC V0P 1H0, Canada. *Fax:* (250) 285-2670.

BRINK, André Philippus, MA; South African writer and academic; *Honorary Professor, Department of English Language and Literature, University of Cape Town*; b. 29 May 1935, Vrede; s. of Daniel and Aletta (née Wolmarans) Brink; three s. one d. *Education:* Lydenburg High School, Potchefstroom Univ., Sorbonne, Paris. *Career:* began writing at an early age; first novel (Afrikaans) published 1958; on return from Paris became mem. and spokesman of young Afrikaans writers' group Sestigers; returned to Paris 1968; went back to South Africa to resist apartheid through writing; novel Kennis van die Aand banned 1973 (first Afrikaans novel to be banned); began to write in English as well; Dir several plays, but abandoned theatre owing to censorship; resumed playwriting 1996; Founder-mem. Afrikaans Writers' Guild; Prof. of Afrikaans and Dutch Literature, Rhodes Univ. (previously lecturer) 1980–89; Prof. of English, Univ. of Cape Town 1991–2000, now Hon. Prof. *Publications include:* File on a Diplomat 1966, Looking on Darkness (novel) 1974, An Instant in the Wind (novel) 1976, Rumours of Rain (novel) 1978, A Dry White Season (novel) 1979, A Chain of Voices (novel) 1982, Mapmakers (essays) 1983, The Wall of the Plague (novel) 1984, The Ambassador (novel) 1985, A Land Apart (co-ed with J M Coetzee) 1986, States of Emergency (novel) 1988, An Act of Terror (novel) 1991, The First Life of Adamastor (novel) 1993, On the Contrary (novel) 1993, Imaginings of Sand (novel) 1996, Reinventing a Continent (essays) 1996, Devil's Valley (novel) 1998, The Rights of Desire (novel) 2000, The Other Side of Silence (novel) 2002, Before I Forget (novel) 2004, Praying Mantis 2004; several plays 1965–75, The Jogger 1997. *Honours:* Chevalier Légion d'honneur 1983; Commdr Ordre des Arts et des Lettres 1992; Hon. DLitt (Witwatersrand) 1985, (Univ. of Free State) 1997, (Montpellier) 1998, (Rhodes) 2001, (Pretoria) 2003; Reina Prinsen Geerlings Prize 1964, CNA Award for Literature, South Africa 1965, 1978 and 1982, Martin Luther King Memorial Prize 1979, Prix Médicis Etranger, France 1979, Biannual Freedom of Speech Prize by Monismanien Foundation, Univ. of Uppsala 1991, Premio Mondello (Italy) 1997, Commonwealth Prize for Literature (Africa) 2003, Sunday Times Fiction Award 2004. *Address:* Department of English Language and

Literature, University of Cape Town, Rondebosch 7701, South Africa (office). *Fax:* (21) 685-3945 (home). *Website:* web.uct.ac.za/depts/english.

BRINKLEY, Alan, BA, PhD; American historian and academic; *Provost and Allan Nevins Professor of History, Columbia University*; b. 2 June 1949, Washington, DC; s. of the late David Brinkley; m. Evangeline Morphos 1989; one d. *Education:* Princeton and Harvard Univs. *Career:* Asst Prof. of History, MIT 1978–82; visiting position, Harvard Univ. 1980, Dunwalke Assoc. Prof. of American History 1982–88; Prof. of History, Grad. School and Univ. Center, CUNY 1988–91; visiting positions, Princeton Univ. 1991, Univ. of Turin 1992, New York Univ. 1993, École des Hautes Études en Sciences Sociales, Paris 1996; Prof. of History, Columbia Univ. 1991–98, Allan Nevins Prof. of History 1998–, Provost 2003–; Harmsworth Prof. of American History, Univ. of Oxford 1998–99; Fellow, Soc. of American Historians 1984– (Exec. Bd mem. 1989–); mem. American Historical Asscn, Org. of American Historians (Exec. Bd mem. 1990–93), Century Foundation (Trustee 1995–, Chair. 1999–), Nat. Humanities Center (Trustee 2004–), American Acad. of Arts and Sciences. *Publications:* Voices of Protest: Huey Long, Father Coughlin, and the Great Depression 1982, American History: A Survey 1983, The Unfinished Nation: A Concise History of the American People 1993, The End of Reform: New Deal Liberalism in Recession and War 1995, Eyes of the Nation: A Visual History of the United States (with others) 1997, New Federalist Papers (with Kathleen Sullivan and Nelson Polsby) 1997, Liberalism and Its Discontents 1998, The Chicago Handbook for Teachers (co-ed.) 1999, The Reader's Companion to the American Presidency (co-ed.) 2000; contribs to scholarly books and journals. *Honours:* Nat. Endowment for the Humanities Fellowship 1972–73, American Council of Learned Socs Fellowship 1981, Robert L. Brown Prize, Louisiana Historical Asscn 1982, Nat. Book Award for History 1983, Guggenheim Fellowship 1984–85, Woodrow Wilson Center for Int. Scholars Fellowship 1985, Joseph R. Levenson Memorial Teaching Prize, Harvard Univ. 1987, Nat. Humanities Center Fellowship 1988–89, Media Studies Center Fellowship 1993–94, Russell Sage Foundation Fellowship 1996–97, Great Teacher Award, Columbia Univ. 2003. *Address:* Office of the Provost, 205 Low Library, Columbia University, New York, NY 10027, USA (office). *Telephone:* (212) 854-2403 (office). *E-mail:* ab65@columbia.edu (office). *Website:* www.columbia .edu/cu/history (office).

BRINKLEY, Douglas Gregg, BA, MA, PhD; American academic and writer; b. 14 Dec. 1960, Atlanta, GA; m.; two c. *Education:* Ohio State Univ. and Georgetown Univ. *Career:* Instructor, US Naval Acad. 1987; Visiting Research Fellow, Woodrow Wilson School of Public Policy and Int. Affairs 1987–88; Lecturer, Princeton Univ. 1988; Asst Prof. of History, Hofstra Univ. 1989–93; Visiting Assoc. Dir 1993–94, Dir from 1994, Eisenhower Center for American Studies, Assoc. Prof. of History 1993–96; Ambrose Prof. of American History, Univ. of New Orleans 1997–; Prof. of History, Tulane Univ.; Contributing Ed., LA Times, American History; mem. Council on Foreign Relations, Theodore Roosevelt Asscn, Franklin and Eleanor Roosevelt Inst., Century Asscn, National D-Day Museum. *Publications:* Jean Monnet: The Path of European Unity (ed. with Clifford Hackett) 1991, The Atlantic Charter (ed. with D. Facey-Crowther) 1992, Dean Acheson: The Cold War Years, 1953–1971 1992, Driven Patriot: The Life and Times of James Forrestal (with Townsend Hoopes) 1992, Dean Acheson and the Making of US Foreign Policy (ed.) 1993, Theodore Roosevelt: The Many-Sided American (ed. with Gable and Naylor) 1993, The Majic Bus: An American Odyssey 1993, Franklin Roosevelt and the Creation of the United Nations (with Townsend Hoopes) 1997, John F. Kennedy and Europe (ed.) 1997, Hunter S. Thompson: The Proud Highway Saga of a Desperate Southern Gentleman 1955–1967 (ed.) 1997, American Heritage: History of the United States 1998, The Unfinished Presidency: Jimmy Carter's Journey Beyond The White House 1998, Rosa Parks: A Biography 2000, Hunter S. Thompson: Fear and Loathing in America (ed.) 2001, Wheels for the World: Henry Ford, his Company and a Century of Progress 2004, Tour of Duty: John Kerry and the Vietnam War 2004, The Boys of Pointe Du Hoc: Ronald Reagan, D-Day and the US Army 2nd Ranger Battalion 2005, Parish Priest (with Julie M. Fenster) 2006, The Great Deluge 2006; contrib. to books, popular magazines and scholarly journals. *Honours:* Hon. DH (Trinity Coll., CT) 1997; New York Times Notable Book of the Year Citations 1993, 1998, Hofstra Univ. Stessin Award for Distinguished Scholarship 1993, Theodore and Franklin Roosevelt Naval History Prize 1993, Bernath Lecture Prize 1996. *Address:* c/o Department of History, 125A Hebert Hall Annex, Tulane University, New Orleans, LA 70118, USA (office). *E-mail:* dbrinkl@tulane.edu (office).

BRINTON, Alexander (see Battin, B. W.)

BRISCO, Patty A. (see Matthews, Patricia Anne)

BRISTOW, Robert O'Neil, BA, MA; American author; b. 17 Nov. 1926, St Louis, Mo.; m. 1st Gaylon Walker 1950 (divorced); two s. two d; m. 2nd Gail Hamiter Rosen 2003. *Education:* Univ. of Oklahoma. *Career:* Writer-in-Residence, Winthrop Coll., SC 1961–87. *Publications:* Time for Glory 1968, Night Season 1970, A Faraway Drummer 1973, Laughter in Darkness 1974; more than 200 short stories published in magazines and journals. *Honours:* Award for Literary Excellence 1969, Friends of American Writer's Award 1974. *Address:* 613 1/2 Charlotte Avenue, Rock Hill, SC 29730, USA. *E-mail:* bobbristow@comporium.net.

BRISVILLE, Jean-Claude Gabriel; French writer; b. 28 May 1922, Bois-Colombes/Hauts-de-Seine; s. of Maurice Brisville and Geneviève Gineste; m. 2nd Irène Kalaschnikowa 1963; one s. one d. by first m. *Education:* Lycée Jacques Decour, Paris. *Career:* literary journalist 1946–; Reader, Hachette 1951–58; Sec. to Albert Camus 1957–59; Deputy Literary Dir Juilliard 1959–64, Literary Dir 1964–70; Head of Drama Video Section, ORTF 1971–75; Literary Dir Livre de poche 1976–81. *Publications:* narrative works: Prologue 1948, D'un amour (Prix Sainte-Beuve) 1954, La Fuite au Danemark 1962, La Zone d'ombre 1976; plays: Le Fauteuil à bascule (Prix Ibsen, Prix de la meilleure création dramatique) 1982, Le Bonheur à Romorantin, L'entretien de M. Descartes avec M. Pascal le jeune, La Villa bleue, Les Liaisons dangereuses (adaptation), Le Souper (Prix du Théâtre, Acad. Française) 1990, L'Officier de la Garde 1990, L'Antichambre 1991, Contre-jour 1993, Dernière Salve 1995; essays; stories for children. *Honours:* Chevalier, Légion d'honneur, Chevalier, Ordre des Arts et des Lettres; Prix du Théâtre de la Société des Auteurs et Compositeurs Dramatiques (SACD). *Address:* SACD, 12 rue Ballu, 75009 Paris, France.

BRITTAN, Sir Samuel, Kt, MA; British writer and journalist; *Columnist, Financial Times*; b. 29 Dec. 1933, London; brother of Lord Brittan of Spennithorne. *Education:* Kilburn Grammar School, Jesus Coll., Cambridge. *Career:* journalist on The Financial Times 1955–61, prin. economic commentator 1966–, Asst Ed. 1978–95; Econs Ed. The Observer 1961–64; Adviser, Dept of Econ. Affairs 1965; Research Fellow, Nuffield Coll., Oxford 1973–74, Visiting Fellow 1974–82; Visiting Prof., Chicago Law School, USA 1978; mem. Peacock Cttee on Finance of the BBC 1985–86. *Publications:* Steering the Economy (3rd edn 1970), Left or Right: The Bogus Dilemma 1968, The Price of Economic Freedom: A Guide to Flexible Rates 1970, Is There an Economic Consensus? 1973, Capitalism and the Permissive Society 1973 (new edn A Restatement of Economic Liberalism 1988), The Delusion of Incomes Policy (with Peter Lilley) 1977, The Economic Consequences of Democracy 1977, How to End the 'Monetarist' Controversy 1981, Role and Limits of Government: Essays in Political Economy 1983, There Is No Such Thing As Society 1993, Capitalism with a Human Face 1995, Essays, Moral, Political and Economic 1998, Against the Flow 2005. *Honours:* Hon. Prof. of Politics Univ. of Warwick 1987–92; Hon. Fellow Jesus Coll., Cambridge 1988; Chevalier, Légion d'honneur 1993; Hon. DLitt (Heriot-Watt) 1985; Hon. DUniv (Essex) 1995; first winner Sr Harold Wincott Award for financial journalists 1971, George Orwell Prize for political journalism 1980, Ludwig Erhard Prize 1987. *Address:* The Financial Times, Number 1 Southwark Bridge, London, SE1 9HL, England (office). *Telephone:* (20) 7873-3000 (office). *Fax:* (20) 7873-4343 (office). *Website:* www.samuelbrittan.co.uk.

BROBST, Richard Alan, BA; American teacher, poet, writer and editor; b. 13 May 1958, Sarasota, FL; m. Pamela Millace 1986, two s. one d. *Education:* University of Florida. *Career:* Co-founder and Ed., Albatross Poetry Journal, 1986–99; Resident Poet, Charlotte County Schools, 1989–. *Publications:* Inherited Roles, 1997; Dancing With Archetypes, 1998; Songs From the Lost Oaks, 1999; The Cody Star, 2000. Contributions: anthologies and periodicals. *Honours:* winner Duanne Locke Chapbook Series 1997. *Address:* 17145 Urban Avenue, Port Charlotte, FL 33954, USA. *E-mail:* aliasd13@aol.com.

BROCK, William Ranulf, MA, PhD, FBA, FRHistS; British historian; *Professor Emeritus of Modern History, University of Glasgow*; b. 16 May 1916, Farnham, Surrey; s. of Stewart E. Brock and Katherine Temple Roberts; m. Constance H. Brown 1950 (died 2000); one s. one d. *Education:* Christ's Hosp., Horsham and Trinity Coll., Cambridge. *Career:* Fellow, Selwyn Coll., Cambridge 1947–, Life Fellow 1967; Prof. of Modern History, Univ. of Glasgow 1967–81, Prof. Emer. 1981–. *Publications:* Lord Liverpool and Liberal Toryism 1941, Character of American History 1960, An American Crisis 1865–67 1963, Conflict and Transformations, USA 1844–77 1973, Parties and Political Conscience 1979, Scotus Americanus 1981, Investigation and Responsibility 1984, Welfare, Democracy and the New Deal 1988, Selwyn College: a history (with P. H. M. Cooper) 1994. *Honours:* Hon. LittD (Keele) 1998. *Address:* 49 Barton Road, Cambridge, CB3 9LG, England. *Telephone:* (1223) 529655. *E-mail:* wrb20@cam.ac.uk (home).

BROCKMAN, John, MBA; American editor, publisher and literary agent; *Chief Executive Officer, Brockman Inc.*; b. 16 Feb. 1941, Boston, MA; m. Katinka Matson; one s. *Education:* Babson Inst. of Business Admin, Columbia Univ., NY. *Career:* multimedia artist 1965–69; f. and CEO Brockman Inc. literary and software agency 1973–; f. and Pres. Edge Foundation, Ed. and Publisher Edge website 1988–; co-f. and Chair. Content.com Inc. (web-based digital publishing co.); agent and co-f. The Reality Club; co-f. rightscenter.com. *Publications:* By the Late John Brockman 1969, Doing Science: The Reality Club (ed.) 1988, The Third Culture: Beyond the Scientific Revolution 1995, Digerarti: Encounters with the Cyber Elite 1996, The Greatest Inventions in the Past Two Thousand Years (ed.) 2000, The Next Fifty Years: Science in the First Half of the Twenty-First Century (ed.) 2003, The New Humanists: Science at the Edge (ed.) 2004, What is Your Dangerous Idea? 2006. *Address:* Brockman Inc., 5 E 59th Street, New York, NY 10022, USA. *E-mail:* editor@ edge.org. *Website:* www.brockman.com; www.edge.org.

BRODBER, Erna, MSc, PhD; Jamaican novelist and sociologist; b. 21 April 1940, Woodside, St Mary. *Education:* Univ. Coll. of the W Indies (now UWI), Kingston. *Career:* fmr civil servant, teacher, sociology lecturer; fmr Fellow/ staff mem. Inst. for Social and Econ. Research (ISER), Mona; fmr Lecturer Univ. of the W Indies, Mona; Whichard Distinguished Prof. in Women's Studies E Carolina Univ. Thomas Harriot Coll. of Arts and Sciences 2003. *Publications:* fiction: Jane and Louisa Will Soon Come Home 1980, Myal (Commonwealth Regional Prize for Literature) 1988, Louisiana 1997, Rainmaker's Mistake 2007; non-fiction: People of my Jamaican village 1999, Standing Tall etc. 2003, The Continent of Black Consciousness 2003, The Second Generation of Freemen in Jamaica, Woodside Pear Tree Grove; contribs to ISER and UNESCO. *Honours:* Order of Distinction, Jamaica; Musgrave Gold Award for Literature and Orature, Prince Claus Laureate. *Address:* Woodside, Pear Tree Grove, St. Mary/ St Catherine, Jamaica (home). *Telephone:* 819-7721 (home); 410-8737 (home). *E-mail:* ernabrodber_1@yahoo .com (home).

BRODER, David Salzer; American journalist, editor and writer; b. 11 Sept. 1929, Chicago Heights, IL; m. Ann Creighton Collar 1951; four s. *Education:* BA, 1947, MA, 1951, University of Chicago. *Career:* Reporter, Pantagraph, Bloomington, IL, 1953–55, Congressional Quarterly, Washington, DC, 1955–60, Washington Star, 1960–65, New York Times, 1965–66; Reporter, 1966–75, Assoc. Ed., 1975–, Washington Post; Syndicated Columnist; mem. American Acad. of Arts and Sciences, fellow; American Political Science Asscn; American Society of Public Administration; Gridiron Club; National Press Club. *Publications:* The Republican Establishment (with Stephen Hess), 1967; The Party's Over: The Failure of Politics in America, 1972; Changing of the Guard: Power and Leadership in America, 1980; Behind the Front Page: A Candid Look at How the News is Made, 1987; The Man Who Would be President: Dan Quayle (with Bob Woodward), 1992; Democracy Derailed: Initiative Campaigns and the Power of Money, 2000. *Contributions:* Books, newspapers and magazines. *Honours:* Fellow, John F. Kennedy School of Government, Harvard University, 1969–70; Pulitzer Prize in Journalism, 1973; Poynter Fellow, Yale University and Indiana University, 1973; Carey McWilliams Award, 1983; Fourth Estate Award, National Press Club, 1988; Elijah Parrish Lovejoy Award, 1990. *Address:* c/o Washington Post, 1150 15th Street NW, Washington, DC 20071, USA.

BRODERICK, Damien Francis; Australian writer; b. 22 April 1944, Melbourne, Vic. *Education:* BA, Monash University, 1966; PhD, Deakin University, 1990. *Career:* Writer-in-Residence, Deakin University, 1986; Senior Fellow, University of Melbourne. *Publications:* A Man Returned (short stories), 1965; The Zeitgeist Machine (ed.), 1977; The Dreaming Dragons, 1980; The Judas Mandala, 1982; Valencies (with Rory Barnes), 1983; Transmitters, 1984; Strange Attractors (ed.), 1985; The Black Grail, 1986; Striped Holes, 1988; Matilda at the Speed of Light (ed.), 1988; The Dark Between the Stars (short stories), 1991; The Lotto Effect, 1992; The Sea's Furthest End, 1993; The Architecture of Babel: Discourses of Literature and Science, 1994; Reading by Starlight: Postmodern Science Fiction, 1995; The White Abacus, 1997; Zones (with Rory Barnes), 1997; Theory and its Discontents, 1997; The Spike, 1997; Not the Only Planet (ed.), 1998; Centaurus (co-ed. with David G. Hartwell), 1999; The Last Mortal Generation, 1999; Stuck in Fast Forward (with Rory Barnes), 1999; The Book of Revelation (with Rory Barnes), 1999; Transrealist Fiction, 2000; The Game of Stars and Souls, 2000; Earth is But a Star (ed.), 2001; Transcension, 2002; Jack and the Aliens, 2002. *Contributions:* periodicals. *Honours:* Australian Science Fiction Achievement Awards, 1981, 1985, 1989; Aurealis Award, 1998; Ditmar Award, 1998. *Literary Agent:* Richard Curtis Associates Inc., 171 E 74th Street, Second Floor, New York, NY 10021, USA. *Website:* www.curtisagency .com; www.thespike.us.

BRODEUR, Hélène, BA; Canadian writer; b. 13 July 1923, Val Racine, QC; m. Robert L. Nantais 1947; three s. two d. *Education:* Teacher's Certificate, Ottawa University Normal School; Ottawa University, Canadian Government College. *Career:* Writer-in-Residence, Visiting Prof., French Creative Writing, Ottawa University; mem. Ontario Authors Asscn; Union des écrivains; PEN International; Press Club. *Publications:* Chroniques du Nouvel-Ontario, Vol. 1, La quête d'Alexandre, 1981, Vol. 2, Entre l'aube et le jour, 1983, Vol. 3, Les routes incertaines, 1986, Vol. 4 L'Ermitage, 1996; Alexander, 1983; Rose-Delima, 1987; The Honourable Donald, 1990. Miniseries for Television: Les Ontariens, 1983. *Contributions:* Extension Magazine, 1968; A serial, Murder in the Monastery. *Honours:* Champlain Award, 1981; Le Droit Award, 1983; Prix du Nouvel-Ontario, 1984.

BRODEUR, Paul Adrian, Jr, BA; American writer; b. 16 May 1931, Boston, MA; m. (divorced); one s. one d. *Education:* Harvard Coll. *Career:* staff writer, The New Yorker magazine 1958–96; Lecturer, Columbia Univ. Graduate School of Journalism 1969–80, Boston Univ. School of Public Communications 1978–79, Univ. of California at San Diego 1989. *Publications:* The Sick Fox 1963, The Stunt Man 1970, Downstream 1972, Expendable Americans 1974, The Zapping of America 1977, Outrageous Misconduct 1985, Restitution 1985, Currents of Death 1989, The Great Power-Line Coverup 1993, Secrets 1997; contrib. to The New Yorker. *Honours:* Sidney Hillman Prize 1973, Columbia Univ. Nat. Magazine Award 1973, American Asscn for the Advancement of Science Award 1976, Guggenheim Fellowship 1976–77, Alicia Patterson Foundation Fellowship 1978, American Bar Asscn Certificate of Merit 1983, UNEP Global 500 Honor Roll 1989, American Soc. of Professional Journalists Public Service Award 1990. *Address:* PO Box 793, North Truro, MA 02652, USA (office).

BRODY, Jane Ellen, MS; American journalist; b. 19 May 1941, Brooklyn; d. of Sidney Brody and Lillian Kellner; m. Richard Engquist 1966; twin s. *Education:* New York State Coll. of Agric., Cornell Univ. and Univ. of Wis. *Career:* reporter, Minn. Tribune 1963–65; science writer, personal health columnist, New York Times 1965–; mem. Advisory Council, New York State Coll. of Agric. 1971–77. *Publications:* Secrets of Good Health (with R.

Engquist) 1970, You Can Fight Cancer and Win (with A. Holleb) 1977, Jane Brody's Nutrition Book 1981, Jane Brody's New York Times Guide to Personal Health 1982, Jane Brody's Good Food Book 1985, Jane Brody's Good Food Gourmet 1990, Jane Brody's Good Seafood Book (with Richard Flaste) 1994, Jane Brody's Cold and Flu Fighter 1995, Jane Brody's Allergy Fighter 1997, The New York Times Book of Health 1997, The New York Times Book of Women's Health 2000, The New York Times Book of Alternative Medicine 2001. *Honours:* numerous awards including Howard Blakeslee Award, American Heart Asscn 1971, Science Writers' Award, ADA 1978, J.C. Penney–Univ. of Mo. Journalism Award 1978, Lifeline Award, American Health Foundation 1978. *Address:* c/o New York Times, 229 W 43rd Street, New York, NY 10036-3913, USA.

BRØGGER, Suzanne; Danish writer, poet and dramatist; b. 18 Nov. 1944, Copenhagen; m. Keld Zeruneith 1991. *Education:* Univ. of Copenhagen. *Career:* mem. Danish Acad. *Publications include:* Fri os fra kærlighed (Deliver Us From Love) 1973, Kærlighedens veje og vildveje (Love's Paths and Pitfalls) 1975, Creme Fraiche (Crème Fraîche) 1978, Ja (Yes) 1984, Efter Orgiet (play, After the Orgy) 1991, Transparence (Transparency) 1993, Mørk (play, Dark) 1994, En gris der har været oppe at slås kan man ikke stege (A Fighting Pig is Too Tough to Eat) 1979, Tone (epic poem) 1981, Vølvens spådom (Völuspā, adaptation) 1994, The Jade Cat (novel, in trans.) 1997. *Honours:* Gabor Prize 1987. *Address:* Knudstrup Gl Skole, 4270 Hong, Denmark; c/o Gyldendal, Klareboderne 3, 1001 Copenhagen K, Denmark. *Website:* www.gyldendal.dk.

BROKAW, Thomas (Tom) John, BA; American broadcast journalist and writer; b. 6 Feb. 1940, Webster, S Dakota; s. of Anthony O. Brokaw and Eugenia Conley; m. Meredith Lynn Auld 1962; three d. *Education:* Univ. of South Dakota. *Career:* morning news KMTV, Omaha 1962–65; news ed., anchorman, WSB-TV, Atlanta 1965–66; reporter, corresp., anchorman KNBC-TV, Los Angeles 1966–73; White House corresp. NBC, Washington, DC 1973–76; anchorman, Saturday Night News, New York 1973–76; host, Today Show, New York 1976–82; anchorman, NBC Nightly News 1982–2004 (retd), Corresp. Exposé NBC 1991–2004; mem. Bd of Dirs Council on Foreign Relations, Cttee to Protect Journalists, Int. Rescue Cttee; mem. advisory cttee Reporters Cttee for Freedom of Press, Gannett Journalism Center, Columbia Univ.; Trustee, Norton Simon Museum of Art, Pasadena, Calif.; mem. American Acad. of Arts and Sciences. *Publication:* The Greatest Generation 1998, The Greatest Generation Speaks 1999, An Album of Memories 2001, A Long Way from Home 2002. *Honours:* Dr hc (Univ. of South Dakota), (Washington Univ.), St. Louis), (Syracuse Univ.), (Hofstra Univ.), (Boston Coll.), (Emerson Coll.), (Simpson Coll.), (Duke Univ.) 1991, (Notre Dame Univ.) 1993; Hon. DHL (Dartmouth Coll.) 2005; two Dupont Awards, Peabody Award, Alfred I. duPont-Columbia Univ. Award for Excellence in Broadcast Journalism 1997, seven Emmy Awards including Emmy for Outstanding Interview 2003, Records of Achievement Award, Foundation for the Nat. Archives 2005, George Catlett Marshall Medal, Asscn of the US Army 2005, Edward R. Murrow Award for Lifetime Achievement in Broadcasting, Wash. State Univ. 2006, Sylvanus Thayer Award, US Military Acad. at West Point 2006, Walter Cronkite Award for Journalism Excellence, Ariz. State Univ. 2006; elected to TV Hall of Fame 1997. *Address:* c/o Board of Directors, Council on Foreign Relations, The Harold Pratt House, 58 East 68th Street, New York, NY 10021, USA.

BROKS, Paul, DPhil; British neuropsychologist. *Education:* Univs of Sheffield and Oxford. *Career:* practising neuropsychologist, Leeds and Sheffield; academic posts at Birmingham and Sheffield; Sr Clinical Lecturer, Univ. of Plymouth 2000; columnist Prospect Magazine. *Publications:* Into the Silent Land: Travels in Neuropsychology 2003; contrib. to Schitzotypy: Implications for Illness and Health 1997, numerous journals. *Address:* Department of Psychology, University of Plymouth, Portland Square, Plymouth, England. *Telephone:* (1752) 233826. *E-mail:* p.broks@plymouth.ac.uk.

BROMBERT, Victor Henri, BA, MA, PhD; American writer and academic; *Professor Emeritus of Romance and Comparative Literatures, Princeton University;* b. 11 Nov. 1923, Germany; m. Beth Anne Archer 1950; one s. one d. *Education:* Yale Univ., Univ. of Rome, Italy. *Career:* Faculty, Yale Univ. 1951–58, Assoc. Prof. 1958–61, Prof. 1961–75, Benjamin F. Barge Prof. of Romance Literatures 1969–75; Henry Putnam Univ. Prof. of Romance and Comparative Literatures, Princeton Univ. 1975–99, Prof. Emer. of Romance and Comparative Literatures 1999–; many visiting lectureships and professorships; mem. American Comparative Literature Asscn, American Asscn of Teachers of French, American Philosophical Soc., Modern Language Asscn (Pres. 1989), Soc. des Études Françaises, Soc. des Études Romantiques; Fellow, American Acad. of Arts and Sciences. *Publications:* The Criticism of T. S. Eliot 1949, Stendhal et la Voie Oblique 1954, The Intellectual Hero 1961, Stendhal: A Collection of Critical Essays (ed.) 1962, The Novels of Flaubert 1966, Stendhal: Fiction and the Themes of Freedom 1968, Flaubert par lui-même 1971, La Prison romantique 1976, The Romantic Prison: The French Tradition 1978, Victor Hugo and the Visionary Novel 1984, The Hidden Reader 1988, In Praise of Antiheroes 1999, Trains of Thought 2002, Les trains du souvenir 2005; contribs to many books, journals and periodicals. *Honours:* Commdr, Ordre des Palmes académiques; Hon. LHD (Chicago) 1981; Hon. HLD (Toronto) 1997; Fulbright Fellowship 1950–51, Guggenheim Fellowships 1954–55, 1970, Nat. Endowment for the Humanities Sr Fellow 1973–74, Rockefeller Foundation Resident Fellow, Bellagio, Italy 1975, 1990, Médaille Vermeil de la Ville de Paris 1985. *Address:* 49 Constitution Hill W, Princeton, NJ 08540, USA (home).

BROMIGE, David Mansfield, BA, ABD, MA; Canadian poet, writer and academic; *Lecturer, University of San Francisco*; b. 22 Oct. 1933, London, England; m., one s. one d. *Education:* Univ. of British Columbia, Univ. of California at Berkeley. *Career:* Poetry Ed., Northwest Review 1962–64; instructor, Univ. of California at Berkeley 1965–69; Lecturer, California Coll. of Arts and Crafts 1969, Univ. of San Francisco 2000–; Prof. of English, Sonoma State Univ., CA 1970–93; contributing ed., Avec, Penngrove 1986–, Kaimana, Honolulu 1989–. *Publications:* The Gathering 1965, Please, Like Me 1968, The Ends of the Earth 1968, The Quivering Roadway 1969, Threads 1970, Ten Years in the Making 1973, Three Stories 1973, Birds of the West 1974, Out of My Hands 1974, Spells and Blessings 1974, Tight Corners and What's Around Them 1974, Credences of Winter 1976, Living in Advance 1976, My Poetry 1980, P-E-A-C-E 1981, In the Uneven Steps of Hung Chow 1982, It's the Same Only Different 1984, The Melancholy Owed Categories 1984, You See 1985, Red Hats 1986, Desire 1988, Men, Women and Vehicles 1990, Tiny Courts in a World Without Scales 1991, They Ate 1992, The Harbormaster of Hong Kong 1993, A Cast of Tens 1994, Romantic Traceries 1994, From the First Century 1995, Piccolomondo 1998, Establishing 1999, Authenticizing 2000; contrib. to anthologies and periodicals. *Honours:* Macmillan Poetry Prize 1957–59, Poet Laureate Univ. of California (all campuses) 1965, NEA Discovery Award 1969, Canada Council Grant in Poetry 1976–77, NEA Poetry Fellowship 1980, Pushcart Prize in Poetry 1980, Western States Arts Federation Prize in Poetry 1988, Gertrude Stein Award in Innovative Writing 1994, Living Treasure Award, Sonoma County 1994, Fund for Poetry Award 1998. *Address:* c/o Chax Press, 101 Sixth Street, No. 6, Tucson, AZ 85701-1000, USA.

BRONNER, Leila Leah, BA, MA, LittD; American academic and writer; b. 22 April 1930, Czechoslovakia; m. Joseph Bronner 1950; three c. *Education:* Beth Jacob Teachers Seminary of America, Hebrew University, Jerusalem, University of the Witwatersrand, University of Pretoria. *Career:* Assoc. Prof., University of the Witwatersrand, 1960–84; Senior Lecturer, Hebrew Teachers College, 1966–78; Visiting Fellow, Harvard University, 1984; Visiting Prof., Yeshiva University, 1985–87; Visiting Scholar, University of Southern California at Los Angeles, 1986–87; Adjunct Assoc. Prof., University of Judaism, 1987–90; Prof., Institute of Bible and Jewish Studies, 1991–; mem. American Society for Religion; Asscn of Jewish Studies; National Asscn of Profs of Hebrew; Ou Testamentiese Werkgemeenskap in Suid Africa; Society for Biblical Literature; World Union of Jewish Studies, Jerusalem. *Publications:* Sects and Separatism During the Second Jewish Commonwealth, 1967; The Stories of Elijah and Elisha, 1968; Biblical Personalities and Archaeology, 1974; From Eve to Esther: The Rabbinic Reconstruction of Biblical Woman, 1994; Stories of Biblical Mothers: Maternal Power in the Hebrew Bible. Contributions: numerous books and journals. *Honours:* Leila Bronner School, Johannesburg, named after her. *Address:* 180 N Las Palmas Avenue, Los Angeles, CA 90004, USA.

BRØNNUM, Jakob, MA; Danish writer and poet; b. 16 April 1959, Copenhagen; m. Anette Brønnum 1995. *Career:* Ed., Præsteforeningens Blad 1997–; Chair., Baltic Writers' Council 1999–2002; mem. Danish Writers' Asscn. *Publications:* Skyggedage (prose) 1989, Europadigte (poems) 1991, Den Lange Sondag (novel) 1994, Morke (novel) 1996, Sjaelen og Landskaberne (poems) 1997, Kulturhistoriske Årstal (reference) 2001, Kun sig selv (novel) 2004, Vejen ud og vejen hjem (poems) 2004; contrib. to Literaturnaja Gazetta, Parnasso (Finland).

BROOKE, Christopher Nugent Lawrence, CBE, MA, LittD, FBA, FRHistS, FSA; British historian and academic; *Professor Emeritus, University of Cambridge*; b. 23 June 1927, Cambridge; s. of Zachary Nugent Brooke and Rosa Grace Brooke (née Stanton); m. Rosalind Beckford Clark 1951; three s. (one deceased). *Education:* Winchester Coll., Gonville and Caius Coll., Cambridge. *Career:* Asst Lecturer, Univ. of Cambridge 1953–54, Lecturer 1954–56; Prof. of Medieval History, Univ. of Liverpool 1956–67; Prof. of History, Westfield Coll., London 1967–77; Dixie Prof. of Ecclesiastical History, Univ. of Cambridge 1977–94, Prof. Emer. 1994–; Pres. Soc. of Antiquaries 1981–84; Fellow Gonville and Caius Coll. Cambridge 1949–56, 1977–; Corresp. Fellow Medieval Acad. of America; corresp. mem., Monumenta Germaniae Historica, Bavarian Acad. of Sciences; Fellow Società Internazionale di Studi Francescani; mem. Royal Comm. on Historical Monuments 1977–83, Reviewing Comm. on Export of Works of Art 1979–82. *Publications:* The Letters of John of Salisbury vol. I (ed.) 1955, The Dullness of the Past 1957, Carte Nativorum (ed.) 1960, From Alfred to Henry III 1961, The Saxon and Norman Kings 1963, Europe in the Central Middle Ages 1964, Gilbert Foliot and his Letters (with A. Morey) 1965, The Letters and Charters of Gilbert Foliot (ed. with A. Morey) 1967, Time the Archsatirist 1968, The Twelfth Century Renaissance 1969, Structure of Medieval Society 1971, Medieval Church and Society (selected papers) 1971, Heads of Religious Houses, England and Wales 940–1216 (ed. with D. Knowles and V. London) 1972, The Monastic World (with Wim Swaan) 1974, London 800–1216 (with G. Keir) 1975, Marriage in Christian History 1977, The Letters of John of Salisbury vol. II (ed.) 1979, Oxford (fmrly Nelson's) Medieval Texts (gen. ed.) 1979–87, Nelson's History of England (gen. ed.), Councils and Synods Vol. I (ed. with D. Whitelock and M. Brett) 1981, Popular Religion in the Middle Ages, 1000–1300 (with Rosalind Brooke) 1984, A History of Gonville and Caius College 1985, The Church and the Welsh Border in the Central Middle Ages 1986, Oxford and Cambridge (with Roger Highfield and Wim Swaan) 1988, A History of the University of Cambridge (four vols) 1988–2004, The Medieval

Idea of Marriage 1989, David Knowles Remembered (with R. Lovatt, D. Luscombe and A. Sillem) 1991, Churches and Churchmen in Medieval Europe (with R. B. Brooke) 1999, Jane Austen: Illusion and Reality 1999, A History of Emmanuel College, Cambridge (with S. Bendall and P. Collinson) 1999, The Age of the Cloister 2001; contrib. articles and reviews to professional journals. *Honours:* Hon. DUniv (York) 1984; Lord Mayor's Midsummer Prize City of London 1981. *Address:* Gonville and Caius College, Cambridge, CB2 1TA, England.

BROOKE, Robert Taliaferro (Tal), BA, MDiv; American author and lecturer; b. 21 Jan. 1945, Washington, DC. *Education:* Univ. of Virginia, Princeton Univ. *Career:* Vice-Pres. of Public Relations, Telecom Inc 1982–83; Pres. and Chair., Spiritual Counterfeits Project Inc, Conservative think-tank, Berkeley, CA 1989–; founder End Run Publ. 1999–; lecturer on Eastern thought and the occult at colls, univs, conventions and seminars in the USA and abroad; many radio and television appearances; mem. Int. Platform Asscn, Authors' Guild, Soc. of the Cincinnati. *Publications:* Lord of the Air 1976, 1990, The Other Side of Death 1979, Riders of the Cosmic Circuit 1986, Millennium Edition 2002, Avatar of Night 1987, Harvest (with Chuck Smith) 1988, When the World Will Be As One 1989, Virtual Gods 1997, Conspiracy to Silence the Son 1998, One World 2000, The Mystery of Death 2001. *Honours:* Spring Arbor National Bestseller 1989, first place Critical Review Category, National EPA Awards 1991. *Address:* SCP Inc, PO Box 4308, Berkeley, CA 94704, USA. *Website:* www.endrunpublishing.com.

BROOKE-ROSE, Christine, PhD; British academic (retd), writer and critic; b. 1923, Geneva, Switzerland. *Education:* Univs of London and Oxford. *Career:* researcher and critic 1955–; reviewer Times Literary Supplement, The Times, Observer, The Sunday Times, The Listener, The Spectator, The London Magazine 1956–68; Lecturer, Univ. of Paris 1969–75, Prof. of English Language and Literature 1975–88. *Publications:* 15 novels: The Languages of Love 1957, The Sycamore Tree 1958, The Dear Deceit 1960, The Middlemen 1961, Out (Soc. of Authors Travelling Prize 1965) 1964, Such (James Tait Black Memorial Prize 1966) 1965, Between 1968, Thru 1975, Amalgamemnon 1984, Xorandor 1986, Verbivore 1990, Textermination 1991, Remake 1996, Next 1998, Subscript 1999; criticism: A Grammar of Metaphor 1958, A ZBC of Ezra Pound 1971, A Rhetoric of the Unreal 1981, Stories, Theories and Things 1991, Invisible Author 2002; short stories: Go When You See the Green Man Walking 1969; five critical books. *Honours:* Hon. Fellow Somerville Coll. Oxford 1996; Hon. DLitt (East Anglia) 1988; Arts Council Translation Prize 1969. *Address:* c/o Cambridge University Press, POB 110, Cambridge, CB2 3RL, England.

BROOKENS, Diane, BEd, MA; British/American teacher, poet and writer; *Founder and Director, Naturama School of Drama*; b. 29 May 1952, Raleigh, NC, USA; d. of the late Floyd Brigham Brookens and Marjorie Brookens (née Snape). *Education:* Univ. of London, Hertfordshire Univ. *Career:* Founder-Dir, Naturama School of Drama 1985– (devised own form of drama, Naturama, exploring nature and human nature through drama); appearances on radio and TV, including poetry readings on BBC Radio Lancashire 1997–2004; poetry performances at 125th Anniversary of The Winter Gardens, Blackpool 2003; mem. Asscn of Lamda Teachers, Writers' Guild of GB, Actors' Equity. *Publications:* The Artistic Value of the American Musical 1977, Timothy Earle and Other Poems for Children 1986, Poems from a Chrysalis 1997, A Linguistic Analysis of Past Life Regression 1998, Across the Atlantic: Memories of America 2000, Back to Blackpool: The Lancashire Poems 2001; contrib. to poetry magazines and reviews. *Honours:* first prize for self-publishing poetry, David Thomas Charitable Trust, Writers News and Writing Magazine 1998. *E-mail:* dbrookens1@talktalk.net. *Website:* www.dianebrookens.com; www.naturama.info.

BROOKNER, Anita, CBE, BA, PhD, FRSL; British academic, writer and art historian; b. 16 July 1928, London; d. of Newson Brookner and Maude Brookner. *Education:* James Allen's Girls' School, King's Coll., London, Courtauld Inst. and Paris. *Career:* Visiting Lecturer in Art History, Univ. of Reading 1959–64; Lecturer, Courtauld Inst. of Art 1964–77, Reader in Art History 1977–87; Slade Prof., Univ. of Cambridge 1967–68; Fellow, New Hall Cambridge, King's Coll. London. *Publications:* fiction: A Start in Life 1981, Providence 1982, Look at Me 1983, Hôtel du Lac (Booker Prize) 1984, Family and Friends 1985, A Misalliance 1986, A Friend from England 1987, Latecomers 1988, Lewis Percy 1989, Brief Lives 1990, A Closed Eye 1991, Fraud 1992, A Family Romance 1993, A Private View 1994, Incidents in the rue Laugier 1995, Altered States 1996, Soundings 1997, Visitors 1997, Falling Slowly 1998, Undue Influence 1999, The Bay of Angels 2000, The Next Big Thing 2002, The Rules of Engagement 2003, Leaving Home 2005; non-fiction: An Iconography of Cecil Rhodes 1956, J. A. Dominique Ingres 1965, Watteau 1968, The Genius of the Future: Studies in French Art Criticism 1971, Greuze: The Rise and Fall of an Eighteenth-Century Phenomenon 1972, Jacques-Louis David, a Personal Interpretation: Lecture on Aspects of Art 1974, Jacques-Louis David 1980; editor: The Stories of Edith Wharton (two vols) 1988, 1988; contrib. to books and periodicals, including Burlington Magazine. *Honours:* Hon. DLitt (Loughborough Univ. of Tech.) 1990; Dr hc (Smith Coll., USA); Commdr, Ordre des Arts et Lettres 2002. *Address:* 68 Elm Park Gardens, London, SW10 9PB, England. *Telephone:* (20) 7352-6894.

BROOKS, George Edward, MA, PhD; American academic, historian and writer; *Professor, Indiana University*; b. 20 April 1933, Lynn, MA; m. 1st Mary C. Crowley 1957; two s.; m. 2nd Elaine Claire Rivron 1985; two d. *Education:*

Dartmouth Coll., Boston Univ. *Career:* instructor, Boston Univ. 1960, 1962; Asst Prof., Indiana Univ. 1962–68, Assoc. Prof. 1968–75, Prof. 1975–; Visiting Assoc. Prof., Tufts Univ. 1969; Visiting Fulbright Prof., Univ. of Zimbabwe 1984; Visiting Prof., Shandong Univ., People's Repub. of China 1985; mem. Liberian Studies Asscn, MANSA/Mande Studies Asscn, World History Asscn (mem. Exec. Council 1990–93); Fellow, African Studies Asscn. *Publications:* New England Merchants in Africa: A History Through Documents 1802–1865 (co-ed. with Norman R. Bennett) 1965, Yankee Traders, Old Coasters and African Middlemen: A History of American Legitimate Trade with West Africa in the Nineteenth Century 1970, The Kru Mariner in the Nineteenth Century: An Historical Compendium 1972, Themes in African and World History 1973, Perspectives on Luso-African Commerce and Settlement in The Gambia and Guinea-Bissau Region, 16th–19th Centuries 1980, Kola Trade and State-Building: Upper Guinea Coast and Senegambia, 15th–17th Centuries 1980, Western Africa to c. 1860 A.D.: A Provisional Historical Schema Based on Climate Periods 1985, Landlords and Strangers: Ecology, Society, and Trade in Western Africa, 1000–1630 1993, The Aspen World History Handbook: An Organizational Framework, Lessons, and Book Reviews for Non-Centric World History (co-ed. with Dik A. Daso, Marilynn Hitchens, and Heidi Roupp) 1994, Getting Along Together: World History Perspectives for the 21st Century 1999, Eurafricans in Western Africa: Commerce, Social Status, Gender and Religious Observance from the Sixteenth to the Eighteenth Century 2003; contrib. to many scholarly books and journals. *Honours:* Ford Foundation Training Fellowship 1960–62, Social Science Research Council grant 1971–72, Nat. Endowment for the Humanities grant 1976–77, Indiana Univ. Pres.'s Council on Int. Programs Award 1978, American Council of Learned Socs grant 1990, Visiting Fellowship, Africa: Precolonial Achievement Conf., Humanities Research Centre, ANU 1995. *Address:* 1615 E University Street, Bloomington, IN 47401-5201, USA (office). *Website:* www.indiana.edu (office).

BROOKS, Melvin (Mel) Kaminsky; American actor, writer, producer and director; b. 28 June 1926, Brooklyn, New York, NY; m. 1st Florence Baum; two s. one d.; m. 2nd Anne Bancroft 1964 (died 2005); one s. *Career:* script writer for TV series Your Show of Shows 1950–54, Caesar's Hour 1954–57, Get Smart 1965; set up feature film production co. Brooksfilms. *Television:* Get Smart (writer) 1965–70, The Nutt House (writer) 1989, Mad About You (Emmy Award for Outstanding Guest Actor in a Comedy Series 1997, 1998, 1999),. *Films include:* The Critic (writer, cartoon) (Academy Award 1964) 1963, The Producers (writer, dir) (Acad. Award for Best Screenplay) 1968, The Twelve Chairs (writer, dir, actor) 1970, Shinbone Alley (writer) 1971, Blazing Saddles (writer, dir, actor) 1974, Young Frankenstein (writer, dir) 1974, Silent Movie (writer, dir, actor) 1976, High Anxiety (writer, dir, actor, producer) 1977, The Muppet Movie (actor) 1979, The Elephant Man (exec. producer) 1980, History of the World Part I (writer, dir, actor, producer) 1981, My Favourite Year 1982, To Be or Not to Be (actor, producer) 1983, The Doctor and the Devils (exec. producer) 1985, Solarbabies (exec. producer) 1986, Fly I 1986, Spaceballs (writer, dir, actor, producer) 1987, 84 Charing Cross Road (exec. producer) 1987, Fly II 1989, Life Stinks (writer, dir, actor, producer) 1991, The Vagrant (exec. producer) 1992, Robin Hood: Men in Tights (writer, dir, actor, producer) 1993, The Little Rascals (actor) 1994, Dracula: Dead and Loving It (writer, dir, actor, producer) 1995, Svitati (actor) 1999, The Producers: The Movie Musical 2005. *Musical:* The Producers: The New Mel Brooks Musical (producer, co-writer, composer) (Tony Awards for Best Book, Best Score, Best Musical 2001, Evening Standard Award for Best Musical 2004, Critics Circle Theatre Award for Best Musical 2005) 2001. *Address:* c/o The Culver Studios, 9336 W Washington Boulevard, Culver City, CA 90232, USA.

BROSMAN, Catharine Savage, BA, MA, PhD; American academic, poet and writer; *Professor Emerita of French, Tulane University*; b. 7 June 1934, Denver, Colo; d. of Paul Victor Hill and Della Hill (née Stanforth); m. Paul W. Brosman, Jr 1970 (divorced 1993); one d. *Education:* Rice Univ. *Career:* Instructor, Rice Univ. 1960–62; Asst Prof. of French, Sweet Briar Coll. 1962–63, Univ. of Florida 1963–66; Assoc. Prof. of French, Mary Baldwin Coll. 1966–68; Assoc. Prof. of French, Tulane Univ. 1968–72, Prof. of French 1972–92, Andrew W. Mellon Prof. of Humanities 1990, Kathryn B. Gore Prof. of French 1992–96, Prof. Emerita 1997–; De Velling and Willis Visiting Prof., Univ. of Sheffield, UK 1996. *Publications:* poetry (with prose): Watering 1972, Abiding Winter 1983, Journeying from Canyon de Chelly 1990, The Shimmering Maya and Other Essays 1994, Passages 1996, The Swimmer and Other Poems 2000, Places in Mind 2000, Finding Higher Ground: A Life of Travels 2003, Petroglyphs: Poems and Prose 2003, The Muscled Truce 2003, Range of Light 2007; non-fiction: André Gide: l'évolution de sa pensée religieuse 1962, Malraux, Sartre, and Aragon as Political Novelists 1964, Roger Martin du Gard 1968, Jean-Paul Sartre 1983, Jules Roy 1988, Art as Testimony: The Work of Jules Roy 1989, An Annotated Bibliography of Criticism on André Gide, 1973–1988 1990, Simone de Beauvoir Revisited 1991, Visions of War in France: Fiction, Art, Ideology 1999, Existential Fiction 2000, Albert Camus 2000; editor: French Novelists, 1900–1930 1988, French Novelists, 1930–1960 1988, French Novelists since 1960 1989, Nineteenth-Century French Fiction Writers, 1800–1860: Romantics and Realists 1992, Nineteenth-Century French Fiction Writers, 1860–1900: Naturalists and Beyond 1992, Twentieth-Century French Culture, 1900–1975 1995, Retour aux 'Nourritures terrestres': Le Centenaire d'un bréviaire (with David H. Walker) 1997; contrib. to Southern Review, Sewanee Review, Southwest Review, New England Review, Georgia Review, Shenandoah, Critical Quarterly, Interim, American Scholar, South Carolina Review, Europe (Paris), Nouvelle Revue Française. *Honours:* Third Place Award, Best Poems of 1973, Distinguished Alumna Award, Rice Univ. 2000. *Address:* 1550 Second Street, Suite 7-I, New Orleans, LA 70130 (home); 417 East Kiowa Street, Suite 406, Colorado Springs, CO 80903, USA (summer) (home). *Telephone:* (504) 899-6016 (home); (719) 227-1368 (summer) (home). *E-mail:* cbrosman@tulane.edu (home).

BROSSARD, Nicole, LèsL; French-Canadian poet and novelist; b. 1943, Montréal, QC. *Education:* Université de Montréal, Université du Québec, Montréal. *Career:* mem. Académie des Lettres du Québec 1993–. *Publications:* poetry: Mécanique jongleuse (trans. as Daydream Mechanics) 1973, Le centre blanc 1978, The Story So Far 6 (ed.) 1978, Amantes (trans. as Lovhers) 1980, Double Impression 1984, Mauve 1984, Journal intime (trans. as Intimate Journal) 1984, Character/Jeu de lettres 1986, Sous la langue/Under Tongue (bilingual edn) 1987, A tout regard 1989, Installations (trans. as Installations) 1989, Langues obscures 1991, Anthologie de la poésie des femmes au Québec (ed.) 1991, La Nuit verte du parc labyrinthe (trilingual edn) 1992, Vertige de l'avant-scène 1997, Musée de l'os et de l'eau (trans. as Museum of Bone and Water) 1999, Au présent des veines 1999, Poèmes à dire la francophonie 2002, Cahier de roses et de civilisation 2003, Je m'en vais à Trieste 2003; fiction: Un livre (trans. as A Book) 1970, Sold-Out (trans. as Turn of a Pang) 1973, French Kiss (trans.) 1974, L'amèr (trans. as These Our Mothers, or, The Disintegrating Chapter) 1977, Le Sens apparent (trans. as Surfaces of Sense) 1980, Picture Theory (trans.) 1982, Le Désert mauve (trans. as Mauve Desert) 1987, Baroque d'aube (trans. as Baroque at Dawn) 1995, Hier (trans. as Yesterday, at the Hotel Clarendon) 2001, The Blue Books 2003; essays: La Lettre aérienne (trans. as The Aerial Letter) 1985; contrib. to numerous anthologies. *Honours:* Dr hc (Western Ontario) 1991, (Sherbrooke) 1997; Gov.-Gen. Prizes 1974, 1984, Therafields Foundation Chapbook Award 1986, Foundation Les Forges Grand Prix de Poésie 1989, 1999, Prix Athanase-David 1991, Prix W. O. Mitchell 2003. *Address:* 34 avenue Robert, Outrement, QC H3S 2P2, Canada. *E-mail:* nicolebrossard60@hotmail.com.

BROTTON, Jerry, BA, MA, PhD; British historian, academic and writer; *Senior Lecturer in Renaissance Studies, Queen Mary, University of London*. *Education:* Univs of Sussex, Essex and London. *Career:* Sr Lecturer in Renaissance Studies, School of English and Drama, Queen Mary, Univ. of London; Sr Visiting Fellow, Centre for Editing Lives and Letters; Visiting Research Fellow, The Globe theatre, London; Trustee, J. B. Harley Trust. *Television:* Leonardo (contrib., BBC 1), Medici (series consultant and contrib., Channel 4), Newsnight Review (BBC 2). *Publications:* Trading Territories: Mapping the Early Modern World 1997, Global Interests: Renaissance Art between East and West (with Lisa Jardine) 2000, The Renaissance Bazaar: From the Silk Road to Michelangelo 2002, The Renaissance: A Very Short Introduction 2006, The Sale of the Late King's Goods: Charles I and his Art Collection 2006; contrib. of articles and reviews to Literary Review, BBC History Magazine, The New Statesman. *Honours:* Leverhulme Research Fellow 2002, Arts and Humanities Research Council Research Leave Scheme 2006–07. *Address:* School of English and Drama, Queen Mary, University of London, Mile End Road, London, E1 4NS, England (office).

BROUMAS, Olga, BA, MFA; Greek poet and translator; b. 6 May 1949, Hermoupolis; m. Stephen Edward Bangs 1973 (divorced 1979). *Education:* Univ. of Pennsylvania, Univ. of Oregon at Eugene. *Career:* Instructor, Univ. of Oregon 1972–76; Visiting Assoc. Prof., Univ. of Idaho 1978; Poet-in-Residence, Goddard Coll., Plainfield, Vt 1979–81, Women Writers' Center, Cazenovia, New York 1981–82; Founder-Assoc. Faculty, Freehand Women Writers' and Photographers' Community, Provincetown, Mass 1982–87; Visiting Assoc. Prof., Boston Univ. 1988–90; Fanny Hurst Poet-in-Residence 1990, Dir Creative Writing 1995–, Brandeis Univ. *Publications:* Restlessness 1967, Caritas 1976, Beginning with O 1977, Soie Sauvage 1980, Pastoral Jazz 1983, Black Holes Black Stockings 1985, Perpetua 1989, Sappho's Gymnasium 1994, Rave: Poems 1975–1999 1999; translations of poems and essays of Greek Nobel Laureate, Odysseas Elytis: What I Love 1986, The Little Mariner 1988, Open Papers, Selected Essays 1995, Eros, Eros, Eros: Poems, Selected and Last 1998. *Honours:* Yale Younger Poets Award 1977, Nat. Endowment for the Arts Grant 1978, Guggenheim Fellowship 1981–82. *Address:* 162 Mill Pond Drive, Brewster, MA 02631, USA.

BROVINA, Flora, PhD; Albanian poet, pediatrician and activist; b. 30 Sept. 1949, Skënderaj, Kosova; m.; two s. *Education:* Medical School of Prishtina Univ., Medical School of Univ. of Zagreb. *Career:* newspaper journalist, Rilindja, Prishtina 1973–81; pediatrician –1989; founder, League of Albanian Women of Kosova 1992; est. Center for the Rehabilitation of Women and Children 1998, imprisoned by Serbian Paramilitary 1999, released 2000; subsequently est. centre for war orphans; fmr editorial bd mem. Kosovarja and Teuta magazines. *Publications:* Verma emrin tim (Call Me by My Name) 1973, Bimë e zë (Plant and Voice) 1979, Snowball Flower 1988, Mat e çmat (With the Tape it Measures) 1995. *Honours:* Swedish PEN Club Tucholsky Award 1999, honoured by AAAS 2001, UNIFEM and Int. Alert UN Millennium Peace Prize for Women 2001, American PEN Center Barbara Goldsmith Freedom to Write Award 2000, Dutch PEN Award 2000, Foundation of Child and Family/UNESCO Woman of the Balkans Award 2000, Jonathan Mann Award for Health and Human Rights 2000, (jtly) 2004, La Ferthe Award 2000, Heinrich Böll Foundation Human Rights Award, Berlin 2000.

BROWN, Andrew; British writer. *Career:* Scandinavian correspondent and reporter, The Spectator 1980s; Religious Affairs correspondent, writer, Independent 1986–96; currently writes for the Guardian, writes and presents analysis programmes for BBC Radio 4. *Publications:* Watching the Detectives 1988, The Darwin Wars: The Scientific Battle for the Soul of Man 2002, In the Beginning was the Worm: Finding the Secrets of Life in a Tiny Hermaphrodite 2003; contrib. to News of the World, Vogue, New York Review of Books, Guardian, Times, Sunday Telegraph, Daily Mail, Daily Express, Church Times, New Statesman, Salon, Waterlog. *Honours:* Templeton Prize 1995. *Address:* c/o Simon & Schuster, HarperCollins Publishers Ltd, Customer Services, Westerhill Road, Bishopbriggs, Glasgow G64 2QT, Scotland. *E-mail:* readers_editor@darwinwars.com. *Website:* www.darwinwars.com; www.thewormbook.com.

BROWN, Archibald Haworth, CMG, BSc, MA, FBA; British academic and writer; *Emeritus Professor of Politics, University of Oxford*; b. 10 May 1938, Annan, Scotland; m. Patricia Susan Cornwell 1963; one s. one d. *Education:* LSE, Univ. of Oxford. *Career:* Lecturer in Politics, Glasgow Univ. 1964–71; British Council Exchange Scholar, Moscow Univ. 1967–68; Lecturer in Soviet Institutions, Univ. of Oxford 1971–89, Prof. of Politics 1989–2005, Emer. Prof. 2005–; Visiting Prof. and Henry L. Stimson Lecturer, Yale Univ. 1980; Visiting Prof., Univ. of Connecticut 1980, Columbia Univ. 1985, Univ. of Texas at Austin 1990–91; Distinguished Visiting Fellow, Kellogg Inst. for Int. Studies, Univ. of Notre Dame 1998; mem. American Assen for the Advancement of Slavic Studies, American Political Science Assen, British Nat. Assen for Slavonic and East European Studies, Political Studies Assen of the UK, Acad. of Learned Socs for the Social Sciences. *Publications:* Soviet Politics and Political Science 1974, The Soviet Union Since the Fall of Khrushchev (ed. with Michael Kaser) 1975, Political Culture and Political Change in Communist States (ed. with Jack Gray) 1977, Authority, Power, and Policy in the USSR: Essays Dedicated to Leonard Schapiro (ed. with T. H. Rigby and Peter Reddaway) 1980, The Cambridge Encyclopedia of Russia and the Soviet Union (ed. with John Fennell, Michael Kaser, and Harry T. Willetts) 1982, Soviet Policy for the 1980s (ed.) 1982, Political Culture and Communist Studies (ed.) 1984, Political Leadership in the Soviet Union (ed.) 1989, The Soviet Union: A Biographical Dictionary (ed.) 1990, New Thinking in Soviet Politics (ed.) 1992, The Cambridge Encyclopedia of Russia and the Former Soviet Union (ed. with Michael Kaser and Gerald S. Smith) 1994, The Gorbachev Factor 1996, The British Study of Politics in the Twentieth Century (ed. with Jack Hayward and Brian Barry) 1999, Contemporary Russian Politics: A Reader 2001, Gorbachev, Yeltsin and Putin: Political Leadership in Russia's Transition (ed. with Lilia Shevtsova) 2001, The Demise of Marxism-Leninism in Russia (ed.) 2004, Seven Years that Changed the World: Perestroika in Perspective 2006; contrib. to scholarly journals and symposia. *Honours:* foreign hon. mem., American Acad. of Arts and Sciences. *Address:* St Antony's College, University of Oxford, Oxford, OX2 6JF, England.

BROWN, Craig Edward Moncrieff; British journalist and writer; b. 23 May 1967, England; m. Frances Welch 1987; one s. one d. *Education:* Eton, Univ. of Bristol. *Career:* columnist (as Wallace Arnold), The Spectator 1987–, The Times 1988, Private Eye 1989–, Independent on Sunday 1991, The Evening Standard 1993–, The Guardian (as Bel Littlejohn) 1995–; restaurant columnist, Sunday Times 1988–93. *Radio:* This is Craig Brown (BBC Radio 4) 2003. *Publications:* The Marsh Marlowe Letters 1983, A Year Inside 1988, The Agreeable World of Wallace Arnold 1990, Rear Columns 1992, Welcome to My Worlds 1993, Craig Brown's Greatest Hits 1993, The Hounding of John Thenos 1994, The Private Eye Book of Craig Brown Parodies 1995, This is Craig Brown 2003, 1966 and All That 2005. *Address:* c/o The Spectator, 56 Doughty Street, London, WC1N 2LL, England.

BROWN, Dan; American writer; b. 1965, Exeter, NH; m. Blythe Newlon 1997. *Education:* Phillips Exeter Acad., Amherst Coll. *Career:* English teacher 1986–1996. *Publications:* 187 Men to Avoid (as Danielle Brown) 1995, Digital Fortress 1998, Angels and Demons 2001, Deception Point 2002, The Da Vinci Code (British Book Award for Book of the Year 2005) 2003. *Literary Agent:* Heide Lange, Sandford J. Greenburger Associates Inc., 55 Fifth Avenue, New York, NY 10003, USA. *Telephone:* (212) 206-5600. *Fax:* (212) 463-8718. *Website:* www.danbrown.com.

BROWN, Diana, AA, BA, MLS, MA; American research librarian and author; b. 8 Aug. 1928, Twickenham, England; m. Ralph Herman Brown 1964 (deceased); two d. *Education:* San Jose City Coll., San Jose State Univ. *Career:* Librarian, Signetics Corp, Sunnyvale, CA 1978–79, NASA/Ames Research Center, Moffett Field 1979–80; Academic Information Specialist, University of Phoenix, San Jose Division 1984–86; Research Librarian, San Jose Public Library from 1988; mem. Authors' Guild, Jane Austen Society, Special Libraries Assen. *Publications:* The Emerald Necklace, 1980; Come Be My Love, 1981; A Debt of Honour, 1981; St Martin's Summer, 1981; The Sandalwood Fan, 1983; The Hand of a Woman, 1984; The Blue Dragon, 1988. *Honours:* American Library Assen Booklist for Outstanding Adult Novel 1984.

BROWN, Eleanor; British poet and writer; b. 1969; m.; one s. one d. *Education:* Univ. of York. *Career:* Writing Fellow, Univ. of Strathclyde, Univ. of Glasgow. *Plays:* Philoctetes by Sophocles (adaptation) 1997, Franziska by Frank Wedekind (adaptation) 1998. *Publications:* poetry: Maiden Speech 1996. *Address:* c/o Bloodaxe Books Ltd, Highgreen, Tarset, Northumberland

NE48 1RP, England. *Telephone:* (1434) 240500. *Fax:* (1434) 240505. *Website:* www.bloodaxebooks.com.

BROWN, Ian James Morris, MA, DipEd, MLitt, PhD, FRSA; British academic and playwright; b. 28 Feb. 1945, Barnet, England; m. 1st Judith Sidaway 1969 (divorced 1997); m. 2nd Nicola Axford 1997; one s. one d. *Education:* University of Edinburgh, Crewe and Alsager College. *Career:* Lecturer in Drama, Dunfermline College, Edinburgh, 1971–76; Senior Principal Lecturer, Crewe and Alsager College, 1978–86; Drama Dir, Arts Council of Great Britain, 1986–94; Reader in Drama, 1994–95, Head of Drama, 1995–99, Prof. of Drama, 1999–2002, Dean of Arts, 1999–2002, Queen Margaret University College, Edinburgh; Dir, Scottish Centre for Cultural Management and Policy, 1996–2002; mem. Scottish Society of Playwrights, chair., 1973–75, 1984–87, 1997–99; BTI, chair., 1985–87. *Publications:* Plays: Mother Earth, 1970; The Bacchae, 1972; Carnegie, 1973; The Knife, 1973; Rabelais, 1973; The Fork, 1976; New Reekie, 1977; Mary, 1977; Runners, 1978; Mary Queen and the Lock Tower, 1979; Pottersville, 1982; Joker in the Pack, 1983; Beatrice, 1989; First Strike, 1990; The Scotch Play, 1991; Wasting Reality, 1992; Margaret, 2000; A Great Reckoning, 2000. Poetry: Poems for Joan, 2001.

BROWN, John Russell, BA, BLitt, PhD; British academic, theatre director and writer; *Visiting Professor of Theatre, Middlesex University*; b. 15 Sept. 1923, Bristol, England; m. Hilary Sue Baker 1961; one s. two d. *Education:* Univ. of Oxford, Univ. of Birmingham. *Career:* Fellow Shakespeare Inst., Stratford-upon-Avon 1951–53; Faculty 1955–63, Head Dept of Drama and Theatre Arts 1964–71, Univ. of Birmingham; Prof. of English Sussex Univ. 1971–82; Assoc. Dir and Head of Script Dept, Nat. Theatre, London 1973–88; Prof. of Theatre Arts, SUNY at Stony Brook 1982–85; Artistic Dir Project Theatre 1985–89; Prof. of Theatre 1985–97, Univ. of Michigan; Consultant 1994–2000, Hon. Visiting Prof. 2000–, Middlesex Univ.; dir of various theatre productions in Europe and N America; Visiting Lecturer or Prof. in Europe, N America and New Zealand; mem. Theatre Museum (advisory council 1974–83, chair. 1979–83), Arts Council of Great Britain (drama panel chair. 1980–83). *Publications:* Shakespeare and his Comedies 1957, Shakespeare: The Tragedy of Macbeth 1963, Shakespeare's Plays in Performance 1966, Effective Theatre 1969, Shakespeare's The Tempest 1969, Shakespeare's Dramatic Style 1970, Theatre Language 1972, Free Shakespeare 1974, Discovering Shakespeare 1981, Shakespeare and His Theatre 1982, A Short Guide to Modern British Drama 1983, Shakescenes 1993, William Shakespeare: Writing for Performance 1996, What is Theatre?: An Introduction and Exploration 1997, New Sites for Shakespeare 1999, William Shakespeare: The Tragedies 2001, Shakespeare and the Theatrical Event 2002, Shakespeare Dancing 2005; General Ed. Stratford-upon-Avon Studies 1960–67, Stratford-upon-Avon Library 1964–69, Theatre Production Studies 1981–2002, Theatre Concepts 1992–2001, Theatres of the World 2001, Oxford Illustrated History of Theatre 1995; editor: various plays of Shakespeare; contrib. to scholarly journals. *E-mail:* jrbathooe@freezone.co.uk. *Address:* 318 The Circle, Queen Elizabeth Street, London SE1 (office); Court Lodge, Hooe, Battle, East Sussex TN33 9HJ, England (home).

BROWN, Malcolm Carey, BA, MA; British historian; b. 7 May 1930, Bradford, West Yorkshire, England; m. Beatrice Elsie Rose Light 1953, two s. one d. *Education:* St John's College, Oxford. *Career:* general trainee, BBC, 1955; Production Asst, BBC TV, 1958–60; Television Documentary Producer, BBC, 1960–86; Freelance Historian, Imperial War Museum, 1989–; Hon. Research Fellow, Centre for First World War Studies, University of Birmingham, 2002. *Publications:* Scapa Flow (co-author), 1968; Tommy Goes to War, 1978; Christmas Truce (co-author), 1984; A Touch of Genius (co-author), 1988; The Letters of T. E. Lawrence (ed.), 1988; The Imperial War Museum Book of the First World War, 1991; The Imperial War Museum Book of the Western Front, 1993; The Imperial War Museum Book of the Somme, 1996; The Imperial War Museum Book of 1918: Year of Victory, 1998; Verdun 1916, 1999; Spitfire Summer, 2000.

BROWN, Marc, BFA; American children's writer, illustrator and television producer; b. 25 Nov. 1946, Erie, PA; m. Laurie Krasny Brown; three c. *Education:* Cleveland Art Inst. *Career:* worked on fmr First Lady, Barbara Bush's literacy initiative 1992, 2003, 2004, 2005; featured author and speaker at Library of Congress Nat. Book Festival 2001, 2004; represented USA at Children's Book Festival, Moscow, Russia 2003; Hon. Co-Chair. Nat. Braille Press 'Readbooks! Because Braille Matters' programme 2003; speaker at 'Celebration of Reading' 2003; mem. bd of dirs Cleveland Inst. of Art 2000–; mem. bd of overseers Boston Museum of Fine Arts 2003–; mem. advisory council Harvard Center for Soc. and Health, Harvard School of Public Health 2003–. *Publications include:* juvenile: Arthur Accused, Arthur Babysits, Arthur Chapter Books 1–6, Arthur Goes to Camp, Arthur Helps Out, Arthur Loses his Marbles, Arthur Lost and Found, Arthur Makes the Team, Arthur Meets the President, Arthur Plays the Blues, Arthur Rocks with Binky, Arthur Tells a Story, Arthur Writes a Story, Arthur and the 1,001 Dads, Arthur and the Bad-Luck Brain, Arthur and the Best Coach Ever, Arthur and the Big Blow-Up, Arthur and the Comet Crisis, Arthur and the Cootie-Catcher, Arthur and the Crunch Cereal Contest, Arthur and the Dog Show, Arthur and the Double Dare, Arthur and the Goalie Ghost, Arthur and the Lost Diary, Arthur and the Nerves of Steal, Arthur and the No-Brainer, Arthur and the Pen Pal Playoff, Arthur and the Perfect Brother, Arthur and the Poetry Contest, Arthur and the Popularity Test, Arthur and the Race to Read, Arthur and the Recess Rookie, Arthur and the Scare-Your-Pants-Off-Club, Arthur and the Seventh-Inning Stretcher, Arthur and the True

Francine, Arthur and the World Record, Arthur's April Fool, Arthur's Baby, Arthur's Birthday, Arthur's Chicken Pox, Arthur's Christmas, Arthur's Computer Disaster, Arthur's Eyes, Arthur's Family Vacation, Arthur's First Sleepover, Arthur's Halloween, Arthur's Heart Mix-Up, Arthur's Homework, Arthur's Jelly Beans, Arthur's Mystery Babysitter, Arthur's Mystery Envelope, Arthur's New Puppy, Arthur's Nose, Arthur's Off to School, Arthur's Perfect Christmas, Arthur's Pet Business, Arthur's TV Trouble, Arthur's Teacher Moves In, Arthur's Teacher Trouble, Arthur's Thanksgiving, Arthur's Tooth, Arthur's Underwear, Arthur's Valentine, Arthur, It's Only Rock 'N' Roll, BINKY Rules, Buster Baxter, Cat Saver, Buster Makes the Grade, Buster's Dino Dilemma, Buster's New Friend, D.W. Go To Your Room!, D.W. Thinks Big, D.W.'s Guide to Preschool, D.W.'s Library Card, D.W.'s Lost Blankie, D.W. All Wet, D.W. Flips, D.W. Rides Again, D.W. The Big Boss, D.W. the Picky Eater, D.W.'s Perfect Present, Francine the Superstar, Francine, Believe It or Not, Good Night, D.W., King Arthur, Locked in the Library!, Muffy's Secret Admirer, Scared Silly, The Mystery of the Stolen Bike, What's the Big Secret?, When Dinosaurs Die, Who's in Love with Arthur?; Postcards from Buster series: Buster Changes his Luck, Buster Hits the Trail, Buster on the Farm, Buster on the Town, Buster Plays Along, Buster and the Dance Contest, Buster and the Giant Pumpkin, Buster's Sugartime, Buster Catches a Wave, Buster Climbs the Walls, Buster Hunts for Dinosaurs, Buster and the Great Swamp; Dino Life Guides for Families series: Dinosaurs Beware (American Library Asscn Notable Book 1982), Dinosaurs to the Rescue!: A Guide to Protecting Our Planet, Dinosaurs Travel: A Guide for Families on the Go, Dinosaurs Alive and Well!: A Guide to Good Health, Dinosaurs Divorce: A Guide for Changing Families, How To Be A Friend. *Honours:* New York Festival Bronze Medal for Best Writing 1997, Silver Medal for Best Writing 1998, Gold Medal for Best Animation 1998, Silver Medal for Children's Programs (age 2–6) 1999, Gold Medal for Children's Programs (age 2–6) 2000, 2003, Grand Award for Best Children's Youth Program 2003; Weekly Reader Children's Book Club Award (for Arthur's Nose) 1992, Atlantic Film Festival Award 1997, Alliance for Children and Television Awards of Excellence for Best Animated Program 1997, 1998, US Int. Film and Video Festival Awards 1997, 1998, 1999, 2000, 2001, 2002, Parents' Choice Award 1997, 2001, 2002, Worldfest Houston Award for TV Series for Family/Children 1997, 1998, 1999, 2000, 2001, 2002, Worldfest Flagstaff Award for TV Series for Family/Children 1999, Daytime Emmy Award for Outstanding Children's Animated Program 1997, 1998, 1999, 2001, Parenting Magazine Video Magic Award 1998, Prix Jeunesse Int. 1998, Parent's Guide to Children's Media Inc. Award for Outstanding Achievement in Classic Television Programs 1999, 2000, 2001, 2002, Unda-USA Gabriel Award for Outstanding Achievement in Children's Programs 1999, 2002, Clarion Award for Children's Educational Television Program 1999, 2000, 2001, Director's Choice Award 2000, Print Magazine Award of Design Excellence 2000, George Foster Peabody Award for Excellence in Broadcasting and Cable Television 2001, Environmental Protection Agency Nat. Environmental Asthma Educator Award (for Buster's Breathless) 2002, American Council for the Blind Vernon Henley Award 2002, Humanitas Award 2002, 2004, 2005; Hon. DArts (Cleveland Inst. of Art) 2000. *Address:* PO Box 873, West Tilbury, MA 02575 (home); c/o Author Mail, Little, Brown and Company, 237 Park Avenue, New York, NY 10017, USA (office). *Telephone:* (508) 696-5888 (office). *Fax:* (508) 693-6540 (office). *E-mail:* j.hartnett@arthurworldwide.com. *Website:* www.marcbrownstudios.com.

BROWN, Patricia Ann Fortini, MA, PhD; American academic and art historian; *Professor, Princeton University*; b. 16 Nov. 1936, Oakland, CA; m. 1st Peter Claus Meyer 1957 (divorced 1978); two s.; m. 2nd Peter Robert Lamont Brown 1980 (divorced 1989). *Education:* Univ. of California at Berkeley. *Career:* Asst Prof., Princeton Univ. 1983–89, Assoc. Prof. 1989–91, Andrew W. Mellon Prof. 1991–95, Prof. 1997–, Chair. Dept of Art and Archaeology 1999–; Slade Prof. of Fine Arts, Univ. of Cambridge 2001; mem. Renaissance Soc. of America, American Acad. in Rome, Coll. Art Asscn. *Publications:* Venetian Narrative Painting in the Age of Carpaccio 1988, Venice and Antiquity: The Venetian Sense of the Past 1996, The Renaissance in Venice: A World Apart 1997, Private Lives in Renaissance Venice 2004, Art Architecture and the Family 2004; contrib. to Art History, Christian Science Monitor, Monitor Book Review, Burlington Magazine, Renaissance Quarterly, Biography, Journal of the Society of Architectural Historians. *Honours:* Premio Salotto Veneto (Italy), Phyllis Goodhart Gordan Book Prize 1998. *Address:* Department of Art and Archaeology, Princeton University, Princeton, NJ 08544, USA (office).

BROWN, Paul, BSc, MScSoc, PhD; Australian playwright and lecturer. *Education:* Univ. of New South Wales. *Career:* fmrly documentary maker for television, Campaign Man. for Greenpeace Australia; founder, Death Defying Theatre (now Urban Theatre Projects) 1981; Lecturer in History and Philosophy of Science. *Plays:* Aftershcoks 1993, Room 207 Nikola Tesla 2003. *Literary Agent:* RGM Associates, PO Box 128, Surry Hills, NSW 2010, Australia. *Telephone:* (2) 9281-3911. *Fax:* (2) 9281-4705. *E-mail:* info@rgm.com.au. *Website:* www.rgm.com.au.

BROWN, Peter Robert Lamont, MA; British academic and writer; b. 26 July 1935, Dublin, Ireland; m. 1st Friedl Esther 1959, two d.; m. 2nd Patricia Ann Fortini 1980; m. 3rd Elizabeth Gilliam 1989. *Education:* New College, Oxford. *Career:* Harmsworth Senior Scholar, 1956, Lecturer in Medieval History, 1970–75, Merton College, Oxford; Fellow, All Souls College, Oxford, 1956–75; Special Lecturer in Late Roman and Early Byzantine History,

1970–73, Reader, 1973–75, University of Oxford; Prof. of History, Royal Holloway College, London, 1975–78; Prof. of History and Classics, University of California at Berkeley, 1978–86; Visiting Prof., 1983–86, Rollins Prof. of History, 1986–, Princeton University. *Publications:* Augustine of Hippo: A Biography, 1967; The World of Late Antiquity, 1971; Religion and Society in the Age of St Augustine, 1971; The Making of Late Antiquity, 1978; The Cult of the Saints: Its Rise and Function in Latin Christianity, 1980; Society and the Holy in Late Antiquity, 1982; The Body and Society: Men, Women and Sexual Renunciation in Early Christianity, 1989; Power and Persuasion in Late Antiquity: Towards a Christian Empire, 1992; Authority and the Sacred: Aspects of the Christianization of the Roman World, 1995; The Rise of Western Christendom: Triumph and Diversity, AD 200–1000, 1996. Contributions: scholarly journals. *Honours:* Fellow, American Acad. of Arts and Sciences, 1978; several hon. doctorates.

BROWN, Rebecca; American writer, journalist and teacher; b. 1956. *Publications:* Evolution of Darkness and Other Stories 1984, The Haunted House 1986, The Children's Crusade 1989, The Terrible Girls 1990, Annie Oakley's Girl 1993, The Gifts of the Body 1994, What Keeps Me Here: A Book of Stories 1996, Dogs: A Modern Bestiary 1997, The End of Youth 2003, Excerpts from a Family Medical Dictionary 2003. *Honours:* Lambda Literary Award, Boston Book Review Award, Washington State Governor's Award, Pacific Northwest Bookseller's Award. *Address:* c/o Granta, 1755 Broadway, New York, NY 10019, USA. *Telephone:* (212) 246-1313. *Fax:* (212) 586-8003. *Website:* www.granta.com.

BROWN, Rita Mae, PhD; American writer and scriptwriter; b. 28 Nov. 1944, Hanover, PA; d. of Ralph and Julia Brown. *Education:* Broward Jr Coll., Univ. of New York, School of Visual Arts and Inst. of Policy Studies. *Career:* Lecturer, Fed. City Coll. 1970–71; mem. Faculty Goddard Coll. 1973–; Pres. American Artists Inc., VA 1980–; mem. Bd of Dirs Human Rights Campaign Fund, New York 1986. *TV includes:* I Love Liberty 1982, The Long Hot Summer 1985, My Two Loves 1986, The Mists of Avalon 1986, The Girls of Summer 1989, Rich Men, Single Women 1989, Southern Exposure 1990, The Thirty Nine Year Itch 1990, The Woman Who Loved Elvis 1992, A Family Again 1994, Cat on the Scent 1999, Loose Lips 1999, Out Foxed 2000, Pawing Through the Past 2000. *Publications include:* The Hand that Rocks the Cradle 1971, Rubyfruit Jungle 1973, A Plain Brown Rapper 1976, Six of One 1978, Southern Discomfort 1982, Sudden Death 1983, High Hearts 1986, Starting From Scratch: A Different Kind of Writer's Manual 1988, Bingo 1988, Wish You Were Here 1990, Rest in Pieces 1991, Dolley 1992, Murder at Monticello 1992, Venus Envy 1994, Pay Dirt 1995, Riding Shotgun 1996, Murder, She Meowed 1996, Outfoxed 2000, Hotspur 2002. *Honours:* Award for Best Variety Show, TV Writers' Guild of America 1982. *Address:* Teatime Farm, 1295 Greenfield Road, Afton, VA 22920, USA. *Website:* www.ritamaebrown.com.

BROWN, Rosellen, BA, MA; American writer, poet and academic; b. 12 May 1939, Philadelphia, PA; m. Marvin Hoffman 1963, two d. *Education:* Barnard College, Brandeis University. *Career:* Instructor, Tougaloo College, Mississippi, 1965–67; Staff, Bread Loaf Writer's Conference, Middlebury, Vermont, 1974, 1991, 1992; Instructor, Goddard College, Plainfield, Vermont, 1976; Visiting Prof. of Creative Writing, Boston University, 1977–78; Assoc. Prof. in Creative Writing, University of Houston, 1982–85, 1989–. *Publications:* Some Deaths in the Delta and Other Poems, 1970; The Whole World Catalog: Creative Writing Ideas for Elementary and Secondary Schools (with others), 1972; Street Games: A Neighborhood (short stories), 1974; The Autobiography of My Mother (novel), 1976; Cora Fry (poems), 1977; Banquet: Five Short Stories, 1978; Tender Mercies (novel), 1978; Civil Wars: A Novel, 1984; A Rosellen Brown Reader: Selected Poetry and Prose, 1992; Before and After (novel), 1992; Cora Fry's Pillow Book (poems), 1994; Half a Heart, 2000. Contributions: books, anthologies and periodicals. *Honours:* Woodrow Wilson Fellow, 1960; Howard Foundation Grant, 1971–72; National Endowment for the Humanities Grants, 1973–74, 1981–82; Radcliffe Institute Fellow, 1973–75; Great Lakes Colleges New Writers Award, 1976; Guggenheim Fellowship, 1976–77; American Acad. and Institute of Arts and Letters Award, 1988; Ingram Merrill Grant, 1989–90.

BROWN, Sandra; American writer; b. 1948, Waco, Tex.; m. Michael Brown 1968; one s. one d. *Education:* Texas Christian Univ. *Career:* fmr model, Dallas Apparel Mart, and in TV, including weathercasting for WFAA-TV in Dallas; feature reporter, PM Magazine; has written 65 novels since 1981; has had 20 books on New York Times bestseller list since 1990; attended numerous Roman Writers of America confs; mem. Authors' Guild, Mystery Writers of America, Int. Asscn of Crime Writers, Novelists, Inc., Literacy Partners. *Publications include:* Love's Encore (as Rachel Ryan), Love Beyond Reason, Slow Heat in Heaven 1988, Best Kept Secrets 1989, Mirror Image 1990, Breath of Scandal 1991, French Silk 1992 (also ABC-TV film), Where There's Smoke 1993, Charade 1994, The Witness, Exclusive 1996, Long Time Coming 1997, Fat Tuesday 1997, Unspeakable 1998, The Alibi 1999, The Switch 2000, Words of Silk 2001, Seduction by Design 2001, Envy 2001, The Crush 2002, A Kiss Remembered 2002, Standoff 2003, Hello, Darkness 2003, White Hot 2004, Led Astray 2005, Chill Factor 2005, Ricochet 2006. *Honours:* Distinguished Circle of Success, American Business Women's Asscn, B'nai B'rith Distinguished Literary Achievement Award, A.C. Greene Award, Lifetime Achievement Award, Romance Writers of America. *Address:* c/o Simon & Schuster, Inc., 1230 Avenue of the Americas, New York, NY 10020, USA. *E-mail:* sandrab@sandrabrown.net. *Website:* www.sandrabrown.net.

BROWN, Stewart, MA, PhD; British academic, writer, poet and editor; *Director, Centre of West African Studies, University of Birmingham*; b. 14 March 1951, Lymington, Hants.; m. Priscilla Margaret Brant 1976; one s. one d. *Education:* Falmouth School of Art, Univ. of Sussex, Univ. of Wales. *Career:* Lecturer in English, Bayero Univ., Kano, Nigeria 1980–83; Reader in African and Caribbean Literature, Univ. of Birmingham 1988–, Dir Centre of West African Studies 2004–; mem. Welsh Acad. *Publications:* Mekin Foolishness (poems) 1981, Caribbean Poetry Now 1984, Zinder (poems) 1986, Lugard's Bridge (poems) 1989, Voiceprint: An Anthology of Oral and Related Poetry from the Caribbean (co-ed. with Mervyn Morris and Gordon Rohler) 1989, Writers from Africa: A Readers' Guide 1989, New Wave: The Contemporary Caribbean Short Story 1990, The Art of Derek Walcott: A Collection of Critical Essays 1991, The Heinemann Book of Caribbean Poetry (with Ian McDonald) 1992, The Art of Kamau Brathwaite: A Collection of Critical Essays 1995, The Pressures of the Text: Orality, Texts and the Telling of Tales 1995, Caribbean New Voices I 1996, The Oxford Book of Caribbean Short Stories (with John Wickham) 1998, African New Voices 1999, Elsewhere: New and Selected Poems 1999, All are Involved: The Art of Martin Carter 2000, Kiss and Quarrel: Youba/English, Strategies of Mediation 2000, The Oxford Book of Caribbean Verse (with Mark McWatt) 2005. Contributions: anthologies and periodicals. *Honours:* Hon. Fellow, Centre for Caribbean Studies, Univ. of Warwick 1990; Eric Gregory Award 1976, Southwest Arts Literature Award 1978. *Address:* Centre of West African Studies, University of Birmingham, Edgbaston, Birmingham B15 2TT, England (office). *Telephone:* (121) 414-5128 (office). *E-mail:* s.brown@bham.ac.uk (office).

BROWN, Terence, MA, PhD; Irish academic, writer and editor; *Professor of Anglo-Irish Literature, Trinity College, Dublin*; b. 17 Jan. 1944, Loping, China; m. Suzanne Marie Krochalis 1969; one s. one d. *Education:* Trinity Coll., Dublin. *Career:* Lecturer, Trinity Coll., Dublin 1968–82, Dir of Modern English 1976–83, Fellow 1976–86, Registrar 1980–81, Assoc. Prof. of English 1982–93, Prof. of Anglo-Irish Literature 1993–; mem. Int. Asscn for the Study of Irish Literatures, Royal Irish Acad., Academia Europaea, Int. Asscn of Prof. of English. *Publications:* Time Was Away: The World of Louis MacNeice (co-ed. with Alec Reid) 1974, Louis MacNeice: Sceptical Vision 1975, Northern Voices: Poets from Northern Ulster 1975, The Irish Short Story (co-ed. with Patrick Rafroidi) 1979, Ireland: A Social and Cultural History, 1922–1979 1981, revised edn as Ireland: A Social and Cultural History, 1922 to the Present 1985, The Whole Protestant Community: The Making of a Historical Myth 1985, Hermathena (co-ed. with N. Grene) 1986, Samuel Ferguson: A Centenary Tribute (co-ed. with B. Hayley) 1987, Ireland's Literature: Selected Essays 1988, Traditions and Influence in Anglo-Irish Literature (co-ed. with N. Grene) 1989, The Field Day Anthology of Irish Writing (contributing ed.) 1991, James Joyce: Dubliners (ed.) 1992, Celticism (ed.) 1996, Journalism: Derek Mahon, Selected Prose (ed.) 1996, The Life of W. B. Yeats: A Critical Biography 1999, 2001; contributing ed., The Encyclopaedia of Ireland 2003. *Honours:* Hon. Companion of St Michael and St George, 2002. *Address:* Department of English, Trinity College, Dublin 2, Ireland (office). *E-mail:* tbrown@tcd.ie (office).

BROWN, Christina Hambley (Tina), MA, CBE; British writer and magazine editor; b. 21 Nov. 1953, Maidenhead; d. of the late George Hambley Brown and Bettina Iris Mary Brown (née Kohr); m. Harold Matthew Evans 1981; one s. one d. *Education:* Univ. of Oxford. *Career:* columnist, Punch magazine 1978; Ed.-in-Chief Tatler Magazine 1979–83, of Vanity Fair Magazine, New York 1984–92, London 1991–92; Ed. The New Yorker 1992–98, Talk magazine 1999–2002; Partner and Chair. Talk Media 1998–, Talk Miramax Books 1998–; columnist, Washington Post 2003–. *Publications:* Under the Bamboo Tree (play) (Sunday Times Drama Award) 1973, Happy Yellow (play) 1977, Loose Talk 1979, Life as a Party 1983, The Icarus Complex 2005, The Diana Chronicles 2007. *Honours:* Most Promising Female Journalist, Katherine Pakenham Prize Sunday Times 1973, Young Journalist of the Year 1978, Univ. of Southern Calif. Distinguished Achievement in Journalism Award 1994. *Literary Agent:* Ed Victor Ltd, 6 Bayley Street, Bedford Square, London, WC1B 3HE, England. *Address:* c/o Miramax, 375 Greenwich Street, New York, NY 10013, USA (office). *Fax:* (212) 830-5838 (office).

BROWN, Wayne; Trinidadian poet and writer; b. 1944, Woodbrook. *Career:* teacher, Univ. of the West Indies; columnist, Trinidad Express. *Publications:* poetry: On the Coast (Commonwealth Prize for Poetry) 1972, Derek Walcott: Selected Poetry (ed.) 1981, Voyages 1989, Jullia Rypinski: The Light and the Dark – Selected Poems (ed.) 2003, M. G. Smith: In the Kingdom of Light – Collected Poems (ed.) 2003; non-fiction: Edna Manley: The Private Years 1900–38 1976. *Address:* c/o University of the West Indies, St Augustine Campus, St Augustine, Trinidad.

BROWNE, Michael Dennis; American academic, writer and poet; b. 28 May 1940, Walton-on-Thames, England; m. Lisa Furlong McLean 1981; one s. two d. *Education:* BA, Hull University, 1962; University of Oxford, 1962–63; Ministry of Education Teacher's Certificate, 1963; MA, University of Iowa, 1967. *Career:* Visiting Lecturer, University of Iowa, 1967–68; Instructor, 1967, 1968, Visiting Adjunct Asst Prof., 1968, Columbia University; Faculty, Bennington College, Vermont, 1969–71; Visiting Asst Prof., 1971–72, Asst Prof., 1972–75, Assoc. Prof., 1975–83, Prof., 1983–, University of Minnesota; mem. The Loft; Poetry Society of America. *Publications:* The Wife of Winter, 1970; Sun Exercises, 1976; The Sun Fetcher, 1978; Smoke From the Fires, 1985; You Won't Remember This, 1992; Selected Poems 1965–1995, 1997. Contributions: numerous anthologies and journals. Other: Texts for various

musical compositions. *Honours:* Fulbright Scholarship, 1965–67; Borestone Poetry Prize, 1974; National Endowment for the Arts Fellowships, 1977, 1978; Bush Fellowship, 1981; Loft-McKnight Writers' Award, 1986; Minnesota Book Award for Poetry, 1993, 1998. *Address:* 2111 E 22nd Street, Minneapolis, MN 55404, USA.

BROWNJOHN, Alan Charles, MA, FRSL; British poet, novelist and critic; b. 28 July 1931, London. *Education:* Merton Coll., Oxford. *Career:* Lecturer, Battersea Coll. of Educ. 1965–76, Polytechnic of the South Bank 1976–79; Visiting Lecturer, London Metropolitan Univ. 2001–03; poetry critic, New Statesman 1968–76, Encounter 1978–82, Sunday Times 1990–; mem. Arts Council of Great Britain (literature panel 1968–72), Poetry Soc. (chair. 1982–88), Writers' Guild of Great Britain, Soc. of Authors. *Publications:* poetry: Travellers Alone 1954, The Railings 1961, The Lions' Mouths 1967, Sandgrains on a Tray 1969, Penguin Modern Poets 14 1969, First I Say This: A Selection of Poems for Reading Aloud 1969, Brownjohn's Beasts 1970, Warrior's Career 1972, A Song of Good Life 1975, A Night in the Gazebo 1980, Collected Poems 1982, The Old Flea-Pit 1987, The Observation Car 1990, In the Cruel Arcade 1994, The Cat Without E-Mail 2001, The Men Around her Bed 2004, Collected Poems 2006; fiction: To Clear the River 1964, The Way You Tell Them 1990, The Long Shadows 1997, A Funny Old Year 2001; non-fiction: Philip Larkin 1975, Meet and Write 1985–87, The Gregory Anthology 1990; translations: Torquato Tasso (play, Goethe) 1985, Horace (play), Corneille (play) 1996. *Address:* 2 Belsize Park, London, NW3, England (home). *Telephone:* (20) 7794-2479 (home).

BROWNLOW, Kevin; British film historian and television director; b. 2 June 1938, Crowborough, Sussex; s. of Robert Thomas Brownlow and Niña Fortnum; m. Virginia Keane 1969; one d. *Education:* Univ. Coll. School, Hampstead. *Career:* joined World Wide Pictures 1955; became film ed., then co-dir 1964; with Thames TV 1975–90. *Films include:* It Happened Here 1964, Winstanley 1975 (both with Andrew Mollo). *Television includes:* 13-part series Hollywood 1980, three-part Unknown Chaplin 1983, three-part British Cinema 1986, three-part Buster Keaton: A Hard Act to Follow 1987, two-part Harold Lloyd 1988, three-part D. W. Griffith 1993, six-part Cinema Europe: The Other Hollywood 1995 (all with David Gill), Universal Horror 1998, Lon Chaney: A Thousand Faces 2000, The Tramp and the Dictator (with Michael Kloft) 2002, Cecil B. De Mille: American Epic 2003; with Christopher Bird: Buster Keaton: So Funny It Hurt 2004, Garbo 2005, I'm King Kong: The Exploits of Merion C. Cooper 2005. *Publications:* Parade's Gone By 1968, The War, the West and the Wilderness 1978, Napoleon (Abel Gance's Classic Film) 1983, Behind the Mask of Innocence 1990, David Lean: A Biography 1996, Mary Pickford Rediscovered 1999. *Address:* c/o Photoplay Productions, 21 Princess Road, London, NW1 8JR, England (office). *Telephone:* (20) 7722-2500.

BROXHOLME, John Franklin, (Duncan Kyle, James Meldrum); British writer; b. 11 June 1930, Bradford, England; m. Alison Millar Hair 1956, three c. *Education:* Bradford, England. *Publications:* as Duncan Kyle: A Cage of Ice, 1970; Flight into Fear, 1972; A Raft of Swords, 1973; The Suvarov Adventure, 1974; Terror's Cradle, 1975; White-Out, 1976; In Deep, 1976; Black Camelot, 1978; Green River High, 1979; Stalking Point, 1981; The King's Commissar, 1984; The Dancing Men, 1985; The Honey Ant, 1988; as James Meldrum: The Semonov Impulse, 1975.

BROYLES, William Dodson, Jr, MA; American journalist; b. 8 Oct. 1944, Houston; s. of William Dodson and Elizabeth (née Bills) Broyles; m. Sybil Ann Newman 1973; one s. one d. *Education:* Rice Univ., Houston, Oxford Univ. *Career:* US Marine Corps Reserve 1969–71; teacher Philosophy US Naval Acad. 1970–71; Asst Supt Houston Public Schools 1971–72; Ed.-in-Chief Texas Monthly 1972–82; Ed.-in-Chief California Magazine 1980–82; Ed.-in-Chief Newsweek Magazine 1982–84; Columnist, US News and World Report 1986; Co-producer, exec. consultant China Beach (TV programme) 1988–; screenwriter Apollo 13 1995. *Honours:* Bronze Star.

BRUCE, (William) Harry; Canadian journalist, editor and writer; b. 8 July 1934, Toronto, ON; m. Penny Meadows 1955; two s. one d. *Education:* BA, Mount Allison University, 1955; LSE, 1956–57; Massey College, University of Toronto, 1969–70. *Career:* Reporter, Ottawa Journal, 1955–59, Globe and Mail, 1959–61; Asst Ed., 1961–64, Columnist, 1970–71, Maclean's; Managing Ed., Saturday Night, 1964–65, Canadian Magazine, 1965–66; Assoc. Ed. and Columnist, Star Weekly, 1967–68; Columnist, Toronto Daily Star, 1968–69; Talk-show Host, CBC-TV, Halifax, NS, 1972; Ed., 1979–80, Exec. Ed., 1981, Atlantic Insight; Ed., Atlantic Salmon Journal, 1991–. *Publications:* The Short Happy Walks of Max MacPherson, 1968; Nova Scotia, 1975; Lifeline, 1977; R.A.: The Story of R. A. Jodrey, Entrepreneur, 1979; A Basket of Apples: Recollections of Historic Nova Scotia, 1982; The Gulf of St Lawrence, 1984; Each Moment as it Flies, 1984; Movin' East: The Further Writings of Harry Bruce, 1985; The Man and the Empire: Frank Sobey, 1985; Down Home: Notes of a Maritime Son, 1988; Maud: The Life of L. M. Montgomery, 1992; Corporate Navigator, 1995. Contributions: various anthologies and periodicals. *Honours:* Evelyn Richardson Memorial Literary Award, 1978; Brascan Award for Culture, National Magazine Awards, 1981; Top Prize for Magazine Writing, Atlantic Journalism Awards, 1983, 1984, 1986, 1993; City of Dartmouth Book Award, 1989; Booksellers' Choice Award, Atlantic Provinces Booksellers' Asscn, 1989.

BRUCE, Robert Vance, BS, AM, PhD; American historian and academic; *Professor Emeritus, Boston University*; b. 19 Dec. 1923, Malden, Mass.

Education: Massachusetts Inst. of Tech., Univ. of New Hampshire, Boston Univ. *Career:* Instructor, Univ. of Bridgeport 1947–48; History Master, Lawrence Acad., Groton, Mass 1948–51; Research Asst to Benjamin P. Thomas 1953–54; Instructor to Prof. of History, Boston Univ. 1955–84, Prof. Emer. 1984–; Visiting Prof., Univ. of Wisconsin at Madison 1962–63; Fellow, American Asscn for the Advancement of Science, Soc. of American Historians. *Publications:* Lincoln and the Tools of War 1956, 1877: Year of Violence 1959, Bell: Alexander Graham Bell and the Conquest of Solitude 1973, The Launching of Modern American Science, 1846–1876 1987; contribs to various publs. *Honours:* Guggenheim Fellowship 1957–58, Huntington Library Fellow 1966, Pulitzer Prize in History 1988, Distinguished Alumni Award, Boston Univ. 1991. *Address:* 3923 Westpark Court NW, Olympia, WA 98502, USA (home). *E-mail:* yov1877@webtv.com (home).

BRUCE-LOCKHART, Robin, MSI; British writer; b. 13 April 1920, London; s. of Robert Bruce-LockhartKCMG; m. 1st Margaret Crookdake 1941 (divorced 1953); one d.; m. 2nd Eila McLean 1987. *Education:* Royal Naval Coll., Dartmouth, Univ. of Cambridge. *Career:* Foreign Man., Financial Times 1946–53; General Man., Beaverbrook Newspapers, Daily Express, Sunday Express, Evening Standard 1953–60; mem. London Stock Exchange 1960; mem. Sussex Author Asscn (chair. 1970–78). *Publications:* Half Way to Heaven: The Secret Life of the Carthusians 1965, Reilly: Ace of Spies 1967, Reilly: The First Man 1987, Listening to Silence 1997, O Bonitas 2000. *Address:* 11–12 Dover Street, London, W1S, England (office).

BRUCHAC, Joseph, AB, MA, PhD; American author, poet, publisher and editor; b. 16 Oct. 1942, Saratoga Springs, NY; m. Carol Worthen 1964, two s. *Education:* Cornell University, Syracuse University, SUNY at Albany, Union Institute, OH. *Career:* co-founder, Dir, Greenfield Review Press, 1969–; Ed., Greenfield Review literary magazine, 1971–90; Visiting Scholar and Writer-in-Residence at various institutions; Mem., Dawnland Singers, 1993–; mem. National Asscn for the Preservation and Perpetuation of Storytelling; PEN; Poetry Society of America. *Publications:* fiction and poetry: Indian Mountain and Other Poems, 1971; Turkey Brother and Other Iroquois Folk Tales, 1976; The Dreams of Jesse Brown (novel), 1977; Stone Giants and Flying Heads: More Iroquois Folk Tales, 1978; The Wind Eagle and Other Abenaki Stories, 1984; Iroquois Stories, 1985; Walking With My Sons and Other Poems, 1986; Near the Mountains: New and Selected Poems, 1987; Keepers of the Earth (short stories), 1988; The Faithful Hunter: Abenaki Stories, 1988; Long Memory and Other Poems, 1989; Return of the Sun: Native American Tales from the Northeast Woodlands, 1989; Hoop Snakes, Hide-Behinds and Side-Hill Winders: Tall Tales from the Adirondacks, 1991; Keepers of the Animals (with Michael Caduto) (short stories), 1991; Thirteen Moons on Turtle's Back (with Jonathan London) (poems and stories), 1992; Dawn Land (novel), 1993; The First Strawberries, 1993; Flying With the Eagle, Racing the Great Bear (short stories), 1993; The Girl Who Married the Moon (with Gayle Ross) (short stories), 1994; A Boy Called Slow, 1995; The Boy Who Lived With Bears (short stories), 1995; Dog People (short stories), 1995; Long River (novel), 1995; The Story of the Milky Way (with Gayle Ross), 1995; Beneath Earth and Sky, 1996; Children of the Long House (novel), 1996; Four Ancestors: Stories, Songs and Poems from Native North America, 1996. Other: Survival This Way: Interviews with Native American Poets, 1987; The Native American Sweat Lodge: History and Legends, 1993; Roots of Survival: Native American Storytelling and the Sacred, 1996. Editor: Over 15 books. Contributions: many anthologies, books and periodicals. *Honours:* National Endowment for the Arts Fellowship, 1974; Rockefeller Foundation Humanities Fellowship, 1982–83; American Book Award, 1985; Notable Children's Book in the Language Arts Award, 1993; Scientific American Young Readers Book Award, 1995; Parents Choice Award, 1995; American Library Asscn Notable Book Award, 1996; Knickerbocker Award for Juvenile Literature, New York Library Asscn, 1996.

BRUCKNER, Pascal, DèsSc, PhD; French writer and lecturer; b. 15 Dec. 1948, Paris; s. of René Bruckner and Monique Bruckner; m. Violaine Barret 1970 (divorced 1973); one s.; also one d. by Caroline Thompson. *Education:* Lycée Henri IV, Univs de Paris I (Sorbonne), Paris VII (Jussieu). *Career:* annual travels in Asia 1977–90; lecturer Inst. d'Etudes Politiques, Paris 1990–; Visiting Prof. Univs of San Diego and New York 1986–95. *Theatre:* many of his books have been played on stage throughout Europe and in India. *Publications:* Le Nouveau Désordre Amoureux 1977, Lune de Fiel 1982 (adapted for screen by Roman Polanski under the title Bitter Moon 1992), Le sanglot de l'homme blanc 1983, Le Divin Enfant 1992, La Tentation de l'Innocence 1995, Les Voleurs de Beauté 1997, Les ogres anonymes 1998, L' Euphorie perpétuelle, essai sur Le devóir de bonheur 2000, Misère de la prospérité. La religion marchande et ses ennemis (Sénat Prix du Livre d'économie) 2002; translations in 25 countries. *Honours:* Chevalier des Arts et des Lettres, Légion d'honneur 2002; Prix Médicis de l'Essai 1995, Prix Renaudot 1997. *Address:* 8 rue Marie Stuart, 75002 Paris, France. *Telephone:* 1-40-26-68-79. *Fax:* 1-40-56-34-37. *E-mail:* bruckner@wanadoo.fr (home).

BRULOTTE, Gaëtan, BA, MA, PhD; Canadian academic and writer; *Professor of French Literature, University of South Florida, Tampa*; b. April 1945, Lévis, QC. *Education:* Laval Univ., École des Hautes Études en Sciences Sociales, Paris. *Career:* instructor, Laval Univ. 1969; Prof. of French, Trois-Rivières Coll. 1970–83; Visiting Prof., Université du Québec à Trois-Rivières 1973, 1980, 1981, 1989, 1990, Univ. of New Mexico 1981, 1982, 1983, 1984, 1993–94, Univ. of California, Santa Barbara 1982, Brevard Community Coll. 1983–84, Université Stendhal 1993, Sorbonne, Paris 1994; Distinguished Visiting Prof., New Mexico State Univ. 1988; Visiting Prof., Univ. of South Florida, Tampa 1984–88, Prof. of French Literature 1988–, Distinguished Univ. Prof. 2005; mem. Int. Comparative Literature Asscn, Int. Council on Francophone Studies, MLA. *Play:* Le Client (stage production by La Patience, France; Dir Charles Tordjman, cr. in residence at Théâtre de La Mure, France) 2001. *Radio:* Seuils (The Threshold of the Imagination; director and producer of 15 half-hour radio programmes, CFCQ FM, Trois-Rivières) 1979, Le Surveillant (Radio-Canada FM) 1979, Le Balayeur (Radio-Canada FM) 1979, Les Ecrivains (director and producer of 31 half-hour radio programmes on the craft of writing, CFCQ FM, Trois-Rivières) 1980–81, L'Indication (Radio-Canada FM) 1980, Histoire d'Albert (Radio-Canada FM) 1980, En voitur (Radio-Canada FM) 1981, Les Cadenas (Radio-Canada FM) 1981, Le Client (radio drama; First Prize, XIth Concours d'oeuvres dramatiques radio-phoniques de Radio-Canada) 1983, La Contravention, Monsieur Desfossés (Radio-Canada FM) 1986, Le Bail, L'Exclusion de Hoper (Radio-Canada FM) 1987, La fulgurante ascension de Bou (Radio-Canada FM) 1994. *Television:* L'Emprise (TV script with Jean Sarrazin), Les Beaux Dimanches (part of series Les Chemins de l'imaginaire, CBC) 1980. *Publications:* L'Imaginaire et l'écriture: Ghelderode 1972, Aspects du texte érotique (revised edn as Oeuvres de chair: Figures du discours érotique) 1977, L'Emprise (novel, translated as Double Exposure) 1979, Écrivains de la Mauricie (ed.) 1981, Le Surveillant (short stories, trans. as The Secret Voice) 1982, Ce qui nous tient 1988, L'Univers du peintre Jean Paul Lemieux (critical essay) 1996, Les cahiers de Limentinus: Lectures fin de Siècle (essays) 1998, Epreuves (short stories) 1999, Le Client (play) 2001, La Vie de Biais (short stories) 2002, La chambre des lucidités (essay) 2003, Encyclopedia of Erotic Literature (2 vols) 2006; contrib. to books, anthologies, textbooks, scholarly journals and periodicals. *Honours:* Adrienne-Choquette Award 1981, France-Québec Award 1983, First Prize, XI CBC Radio Drama Contest 1983, Trois-Rivières Literary Grand Prize 1989, John-Glassco Trans. Award 1990, Artist/Scholar of the Year (Phi Kappa Phi), 1998, Theodore and Venette Ashkounes-Ashford Distinguished Scholar Award 1999, Odyssee Award, Quebec 2002, Presidential Award for Faculty Excellence 2003, Outstanding Research Achievement 2004. *Address:* World Languages, University of South Florida, 4202 E. Fowler Avenue, CPR 424, Tampa, FL 33620, USA (office). *Telephone:* (813) 974-2782 (office); (813) 264-2963 (home). *Fax:* (813) 974-1718 (office). *E-mail:* brulotte@chumal.cas .usf.edu (office). *Website:* www.gbrulotte.com.

BRUMMER, Alexander, BSc, MBA; British journalist; b. 25 May 1949, Hove, England; m. Tricia Brummer; two s. *Education:* University of Southampton, University of Bradford Management Center. *Career:* fmr Financial Ed., The Guardian. *Publications:* American Destiny 1986, Hanson: A Biography 1994, Weinstock: A Biography 1998.

BRUNA, Hendrik (Dick); Dutch children's writer and illustrator; b. 1927, Utrecht; m. Irene de Jongh 1953; two s. one d. *Career:* creator, numerous illustrated children's book characters, including Miffy 1955–. *Publications (in translation):* Miffy series: Miffy, Miffy at the Zoo, Miffy in the Snow, Miffy at the Seaside, Miffy Goes Flying, Miffy's Birthday, Miffy at the Playground, Miffy in Hospital, Miffy's Dream, Miffy's Bicycle, Miffy at School, Miffy Goes to Stay, Grandpa and Grandma Bunny, Miffy is Crying, Miffy's House, Auntie Alice's Party, Miffy in the Tent (De Zilveren Penseel 1996), Dear Grandma Bunny (De Zilveren Griffel 1997), Miffy at the Gallery, Miffy and Melanie, Miffy the Ghost, Miffy the Fairy, Miffy Dances, Miffy's Letter, The New Baby, Miffy's Garden; Poppy Pig series: Poppy Pig, Poppy Pig's Garden, Poppy Pig's Birthday, Poppy Pig is Sick, Poppy Pig Goes on Holiday, Poppy Pig's Shop, A Song for Poppy Pig; Snuffy series: Snuffy, Snuffy and the Fire, Snuffy's Puppies; Boris and Barbara series: Boris Bear (De Gouden Penseel 1990), Boris and Barbara, Boris on the Mountain, Boris in the Snow, Boris, Barbara and Benny, Boris Bear's Boat, Boris and the Umbrella, Boris the Pilot, Barbara's Clothes Chest, Boris the Champion; other titles: The Apple, The Bird, Kitty Nell, Tilly and Tessa, The Egg, The King, Circus, The Fish, The Sailor, B is for Bear, A Book Without Words, My Vest is White, Animal Book, Flower Book, I Can Read, I Can Read More, I Can Read Much More, I Can Read Difficult Words, I Can Do Sums, Christmas, Farmer John, The Rescue, The Orchestra, Spring, Summer, Autumn and Winter, Stop at the Kerb!. *Honours:* many prizes for illustration on posters; Companion of the Order of Oranje-Nassau 1993. *Address:* c/o Egmont Books Ltd, 239 Kensington High Street, London, W8 6SA, England. *Website:* www.miffy.com.

BRUNNER, Eva; Swiss writer, playwright and translator; b. 26 Nov. 1952, Lucerne. *Education:* American Coll. of Rome, Univ. of Charleston, West Virginia. *Career:* mem. Swiss Writers' Asscn. *Plays:* Kalt 1984, Granit 1985, Von Wegen Abwege 1988, Alles Wird Gut 1994, Die Strick-Trilogie 1997, Sutters Salut 1998, Intimi.Date 2003. *Radio plays:* Geist trug die Steine, Ich trag' sie alleine 1988, Herrscher und Herrscherin 1989, Der Schweiz den Rückenkehren? 1991, Frieda Flachmann 1997, Im Paradies der Plauderer 1999, Blauensee 2006. *Honours:* various scholarships. *Address:* Kuglerstrasse 22, 10439 Berlin, Germany. *E-mail:* evabrunner@aol.com. *Website:* www .barkinarts.com (office).

BRUNSKILL, Ronald William, MA, PhD, OBE; British architect (retd), lecturer and writer; b. 3 Jan. 1929, Lowton, England; m. Miriam Allsopp 1960, two d. *Education:* Univ. of Manchester. *Career:* Commonwealth Fund Fellow in Architecture and Town Planning, MIT 1956–57; Architect, Williams Deacon's Bank 1957–60; Lecturer 1960–73, Senior Lecturer 1973–84, Reader in Architecture 1984–89, Hon. Fellow, School of Architecture 1989–95, University of Manchester; Partner 1966–69, Consultant 1969–73, Carter,

Brunskill & Assocs, architects; Visiting Prof., University of Florida at Gainesville 1969–70; Pres., Vernacular Architect Group 1974–77; Hon. Visiting Prof. 1994–95, Prof., School of the Built Environment 1995–2001, De Montfort University; mem. Cumberland and Westmorland Antiquarian and Archaeological Society, vice-pres. 1975–90, pres. 1990–93; Historic Buildings Council for England 1978–84; Cathedrals Advisory Committee for England 1981–91; Cathedrals Fabric Commission 1991–96; Ancient Monuments Society, hon. architect 1983–88, vice-chair. 1988–90, chair. 1990–2000, pres. 2004–; Royal Commission on the Ancient and Historical Monuments for Wales 1983–97, vice-chair. 1993–97; British Historic Buildings Trust, trustee 1985–92; Historic Buildings and Monuments Commission 1989–95; Friends of Friendless Churches, chair. 1990–98, pres. 1999–. *Publications:* Illustrated Handbook of Vernacular Architecture 1971, Vernacular Architecture of the Lake Counties 1974, English Brickwork (with Alec Clifton-Taylor) 1977, Traditional Buildings of Britain 1981, Traditional Farm Buildings of Britain 1982, Timber Building in Britain 1985, Brick Building in Britain 1990, Houses and Cottages of Britain 1997, Traditional Farm Buildings of Britain and Their Conservation 1999, Vernacular Architecture: An Illustrated Handbook 2000, Traditional Buildings of Cumbria 2002; contribs to scholarly journals. *Honours:* Fellow, Society of Antiquaries 1975–; Pres.'s Award, Manchester Society of Architects 1977; Hon. Doctor of Art, De Montfort University. *Address:* 8 Overhill Road, Wilmslow, SK9 2BE, England. *Telephone:* (1625) 522099.

BRUSSIG, Thomas; German writer, poet and playwright; b. 1965, Berlin. *Publications:* Wasserfarben (poems) 1991, Helden wie wir (trans. as Heroes Like Us) 1995, Am kürzeren Ende der Sonnenallee (Drehbuchpreis der Bundesregierung, with Leander Haußmann) 1999, Heimsuchung (play) 2000, Leben bis Männer 2001, Wie es leuchtet 2004; contrib. to Die Welt, Die Welt am Sonntag, FAZ, Tageszeitung, Süddeutsche Zeitung, Max, Wir sind nostalgisch, weil wir Menschen sind (essay in Sehnsucht nach dem Kommunismus) 2001. *Honours:* Hans-Fallada-Preis der Stadt Neumünster 2000. *Website:* www.thomasbrussig.de.

BRUTON, Eric, (Eric Moore); British author and businessman; b. 1915, London, England. *Career:* Managing Dir, NAG Press Ltd, Colchester, 1963–93, Diamond Boutique Ltd, 1965–80; Chair., Things & Ideas Ltd, 1970–78; mem. British Horological Institute, 1955–62; CWA, 1959–62; Gemmological Asscn of Great Britain, council mem., 1972–91, pres., 1994–95; National Asscn of Goldsmiths, pres., 1983–85. *Publications:* True Book about Clocks, 1957; Death in Ten Point Bold, 1957; Die Darling Die, 1959; Violent Brothers, 1960; True Book about Diamonds, 1961; The Hold Out, 1961; King Diamond, 1961; The Devil's Pawn, 1962; Automation, 1962; Dictionary of Clocks and Watches, 1962; The Laughing Policeman, 1963; The Longcase Clock, 1964; The Finsbury Mob, 1964; The Smithfield Slayer, 1964; The Wicked Saint, 1965; The Fire Bug, 1967; Clocks and Watches 1400–1900, 1967; Clocks and Watches, 1968; Diamonds, 1970; Antique Clocks and Clock Collecting, 1974; The History of Clocks, 1978; The Wetherby Collection of Clocks, 1980; Legendary Gems, 1984; Collector's Dictionary of Clocks and Watches, 1999.

BRUTUS, Dennis, BA; South African academic and poet; *Professor Emeritus of Africana Studies, University of Pittsburgh;* b. 28 Nov. 1924, Salisbury, S Rhodesia (now Harare, Zimbabwe); s. of Francis Henry Brutus and Margaret Winifred Brutus (née Bloemetjie); m. May Jaggers 1950; four s. four d. *Education:* Paterson High School, Port Elizabeth, Fort Hare and Witwatersrand Univs. *Career:* language teacher, Paterson High School, Cen. Indian High School; office boy and law student, Witwatersrand Univ.; imprisoned for opposition to apartheid 1964–65, exiled 1966, political asylum in USA 1983; Dir World Campaign for Release of S African Political Prisoners; worked for Int. Defence and Aid Fund, fmrly UN Rep.; Visiting Prof. Denver Univ.; Prof. of English, Northwestern Univ., Evanston, Ill.; Visiting Prof., English Dept, African and Afro-American Studies and Research Center, Univ. Tex. 1974–75; Visiting Prof., Dept of English, Amherst Coll., Mass. 1982–83, Dartmouth Coll., NH 1983; Adjunct Prof., Northeastern Univ., Boston, Mass. 1984; Prof., Dept of Africana Studies, Univ. of Pittsburgh, now Prof. Emer.; Pres. S African Non-Racial Olympic Cttee (SAN-ROC); Chair. Int. Campaign Against Racism in Sport (ICARIS), Africa Network from 1984; Dir Program on African and African-American Writing in Africa and the Diaspora from 1989; Interport lecturer Univ. of Pittsburgh; Founding Chair., Exec. mem. African Literature Asscn, fmr Chair. ARENA (Inst. for Study of Sport and Social Issues); mem. of Bd, Black Arts Celebration, Vice-Pres. Union of Writers of the African People; mem. Bd of Dirs UN Asscn of Chicago and Ill., Editorial Bd Africa Today; Dir Troubadour Press; Fellow, Int. Poetry Soc.; mem. Modern Language Asscn 1972, Int. Platform Asscn 1979–. *Publications:* Sirens, Knuckles, Boots 1963, Letters to Martha and Other Poems from a South African Prison 1968, Poems from Algiers 1970, Thoughts Abroad (as John Bruin) 1971, A Simple Lust 1973, China Poems 1975, Strains 1975, Stubborn Hope 1978, 1979, 1983, Salutes and Censures 1980, Airs and Tributes 1988, Still the Sirens 1993. *Honours:* Dr hc (Univ. of Mass., Amherst), (Northeastern Univ., Boston), (Univ. of the District of Columbia); Hon. HLD (Worcester State Coll.) 1982; Mbari Prize for Poetry in Africa, Chancellor's Prize for Bilingualism (Univ. of S Africa), Freedom Writers' Award, Kenneth David Kaunda Humanism Award, Int. Jury Books Abroad Award 1976, Nat. Council for Black Studies Academic Excellence Award 1982, UN Human Rights Day Award 1983, Paul Robeson Award, Langston Hughes Award. *Address:* c/o Department of Africana Studies, 4140 Wesley W. Posvar Hall, University of Pittsburgh, 230 South Bouquet Street, Pittsburgh, PA 15260, USA (office).

BRYANT, Dorothy Mae, BA, MA; American writer, dramatist, teacher and publisher; b. 8 Feb. 1930, San Francisco, CA; m. 1st 1949 (divorced 1964); one s. one d.; m. 2nd Robert Bryant 1968; one step-s. one step-d. *Education:* San Francisco State Univ. *Career:* teacher high school 1953–64, San Francisco State Univ., San Francisco Mission Adult School, Golden Gate Coll. 1961–64, Contra Costa Coll. 1964–76; Publisher, Ata Books 1978–. *Plays:* Dear Master 1991, Tea with Mrs Hardy 1992, The Panel 1996, The Trial of Cornelia Connelly 1996, Posing for Gauguin 1998. *Publications:* fiction: Ella Price's Journal 1972, The Kin of Ata Are Waiting for You 1976, Miss Giardino 1978, The Garden of Eros 1979, Prisoners 1980, Killing Wonder 1981, A Day in San Francisco 1983, Confessions of Madame Psyche 1986, The Test 1991, Anita, Anita 1993, The Berkeley Pit 2005; non-fiction: Writing a Novel 1979, Myths to Lie By: Essays and Stories 1984, Literary Lynching 2002. *Honours:* American Book Award 1987, Bay Area Theatre Critics Circle Award for Best Script 1991. *E-mail:* dorbob@CWnet.com.

BRYANT, John; British journalist; *Editor-in-Chief, Telegraph Newspapers.* *Career:* trainee journalist The Scotsman; fmr Exec. Ed. The Daily Mail; fmr Managing Ed. The Times 1986, then Deputy Ed.; fmr Ed. The Sunday Correspondent 1990, The European; Consulting Ed. The Daily Mail –2005; Ed.-in-Chief Telegraph Newspapers 2005–, acting Ed. The Daily Telegraph 2005–. *Publications:* non-fiction: 3:59.4 2005, The London Marathon 2006. *Address:* Telegraph Group Ltd, 1 Canada Square, Canary Wharf, London, E14 5DT, England (office). *E-mail:* john.bryant@telegraph.co.uk (office). *Website:* www.telegraph.co.uk (office).

BRYANT, Joseph Allen, Jr; American academic and writer; b. 26 Nov. 1919, Glasgow, KY; m. 1st Mary Virginia Woodruff 1946; two s.; m. 2nd Sara C. Bryant 1993. *Education:* AB, Western Kentucky University, 1940; MA, Vanderbilt University, 1941; PhD, Yale University, 1948. *Career:* Instructor to Assoc. Prof., Vanderbilt University, 1945–56; Assoc. Prof., University of the South at Sewanee, 1956–59, Duke University, 1959–61; Prof., University of North Carolina, Greensboro, 1961–68, Syracuse University, 1968–71, University of Kentucky, 1973–90; mem. MLA. *Publications:* Hippolyta's View: Some Christian Aspects of Shakespeare's Plays, 1961; The Compassionate Satirist: Ben Jonson and His Imperfect World, 1972; Understanding Randall Jarrell, 1986; Shakespeare and the Uses of Comedy, 1986; Twentieth Century Southern Literature, 1997. *Honours:* Hon. DLitt, University of the South, 1993.

BRYCE ECHENIQUE, Alfredo; Peruvian writer; b. 19 Feb. 1939, Lima. *Publications:* Huerto cerrado (short stories) 1968, Un mundo para Julius (novel) 1970, La felicidad ja ja (short stories) 1974, Tantas veces Pedro (novel) 1977, A vuelo de buen cubero y otras crónicas (non-fiction) 1977, La vida exagerada de Martín Romaña (novel) 1981, El hombre que hablaba de Octavia de Cádiz 1984, Magdalena peruana y otros cuentos (short stories) 1986, Crónicas personales 1986, La última mudanza de Felipe Carrillo (novel) 1988, Dos señoras conversan (novella) 1990, Permiso para vivir (Antimemorias) (memoir) 1993, No me esperen en abril (novel) 1995, A trancas y barrancas (articles) 1997, Reo de nocturnidad (novel) 1997, Guía triste de París (short stories) 1999, La amigdalitis de Tarzán (novel) 1999, El huerto de mi amada 2002. *Honours:* Premio Nacional de Literatura de Perú 1972, Premio Passion, France 1983, Encomienda de Isabel la Católica, Spain 1993, Premio Nacional de Narrativa, Spain 1998, Encomienda de Alfonso X El Sabio, Spain 2000, Premio Grinzane Cavour, Piemonte, Italy 2002, Premio Planeta, Spain 2002; Commdr, Ordre des Arts et des Lettres 2000. *Address:* c/o Alfaguara, Avenida San Felipe 731, Jesús María, Lima, Peru.

BRYSON, Bill; American writer; b. 1951, Des Moines, IA; m.; four c. *Education:* Drake Univ. *Career:* travelled to England and worked as orderly in mental hosp. 1973; worked as journalist for The Times and the Independent; returned with his family to USA 1993; apptd to selection panel, Book of the Month Club 2001; Commissioner for English Heritage; Chancellor Univ. of Durham 2005–; Pres. Campaign to Protect Rural England 2007–. *Publications:* Penguin Dictionary of Troublesome Words (re-printed as Bryson's Dictionary of Troublesome Words) 1985, The Lost Continent 1987, The Mother Tongue: English and How It Got That Way, Made in America 1994, Neither Here Nor There: Travels in Europe 1995, Notes From a Small Island 1995, A Walk in the Woods 1998, I'm a Stranger Here Myself (essays, aka Notes From a Big Country) 1999, In a Sunburned Country (aka Down Under) 2000, The Best American Travel Writing (ed.), African Diary 2002, A Short History of Nearly Everything (Aventis Prize 2004, Descartes Science Communication Prize 2005) 2003, The Life and Times of the Thunderbolt Kid (memoirs) 2006, Shakespeare: A Short Life (biog.) 2007. *Honours:* Hon. DCL (Durham) 2004, Hon. OBE 2006. *Literary Agent:* The Marsh Agency, 11 Dover Street, London, W1S 4LJ, England. *Telephone:* (20) 7399-2800. *Fax:* (20) 7399-2801. *Website:* www.marsh-agency.co.uk. *Address:* c/o Publicity Department, Transworld Publishers, 61–63 Uxbridge Road, London, W5 5SA, England. *Website:* www.cpre.org.uk.

BRZEZINSKI, Zbigniew Kazimierz, PhD; American academic and fmr government official; *Counsellor, Center for Strategic and International Studies;* b. 28 March 1928, Warsaw, Poland; s. of Tadeusz Brzezinski and Leonia Roman; m. Emilie Anna (Muska) Benes 1955; two s. one d. *Education:* McGill and Harvard Univs. *Career:* settled in N America 1938; Instructor in Govt and Research Fellow, Russian Research Center, Harvard Univ. 1953–56;

Asst Prof. of Govt, Research Assoc. of Russian Research Center and of Center for Int. Affairs, Harvard Univ. 1956–60; Assoc. Prof. of Public Law and Govt, Columbia Univ. 1960–62, Prof. 1962–89 (on leave 1966–68, 1977–81) and Dir Research Inst. on Communist Affairs 1961–77 (on leave 1966–68); mem. Policy Planning Council, Dept of State 1966–68; mem. Hon. Steering Cttee, Young Citizens for Johnson 1964; Dir Foreign Policy Task Force for Vice-Pres. Humphrey 1968; Asst to the Pres. for Nat. Security Affairs 1977–81; mem. Nat. Security Council 1977–81; Counsellor, Center for Strategic and Int. Studies, Washington, DC 1981–; Robert E. Osgood Prof. of American Foreign Policy, Paul Nitze School of Advanced Int. Studies, Johns Hopkins Univ. 1989–; Fellow, American Acad. of Arts and Sciences 1969–; mem. Council on Foreign Relations, New York, Bd of Trustees, Freedom House; Guggenheim Fellowship 1960, Ford Fellowship 1970. *Publications include:* Political Controls in the Soviet Army 1954, The Permanent Purge–Politics in Soviet Totalitarianism 1956, Totalitarian Dictatorship and Autocracy (with Carl Joachim Friedrich) 1957, The Soviet Bloc–Unity and Conflict 1960, Ideology and Power in Soviet Politics 1962, Africa and the Communist World (ed. and contrib.) 1963, Political Power: USA/USSR (with Samuel P. Huntington) 1964, Alternative to Partition: For a Broader Conception of America's Role in Europe 1965, Dilemmas of Change in Soviet Politics (ed. and contrib.) 1969, Between Two Ages: America's Role in the Technetronic Era 1970, The Fragile Blossom: Crisis and Change in Japan 1972, The Relevance of Liberalism 1977, Power and Principle: Memoirs of the National Security Adviser 1977–1981 1983, Game Plan: A Geostrategic Framework for the Conduct of the US-Soviet Contest 1986, In Quest of National Security 1988, The Grand Failure: The Birth and Death of Communism in the 20th Century 1989, Out of Control: Global Turmoil on the Eve of the Twenty-First Century 1993, The Grand Chessboard: American Primacy and its Geostrategic Imperatives 1996; contrib. to many publications, journals and periodicals. *Honours:* Dr hc (Alliance Coll.) 1966, (Coll. of the Holy Cross) 1971, (Fordham Univ.) 1979, (Williams Coll.) 1986, (Georgetown Univ.) 1987, (Catholic Univ. of Lublin) 1990, (Warsaw Univ.) 1991; Presidential Medal of Freedom 1981, Order of White Eagle (Poland) 1995, Order of Merit (Ukraine) 1996, Masaryk Order 1998, Gedymim Order 1998. *Address:* Center for Strategic and International Studies, 1800 K Street NW, Washington, DC 20006, USA (office). *Telephone:* (202) 833-2408 (office). *Fax:* (202) 833-2409 (office). *E-mail:* zb@csis.org (office). *Website:* www.csis.org (office).

BUARQUE, Chico; Brazilian singer, songwriter, musician (guitar), writer and poet; b. (Francisco Buarque de Holllanda), 19 June 1944, Rio de Janeiro; s. of Sérgio Buarque de Hollanda and Maria Amélia Cesário de Hollanda; brother of vocalist Miucha, uncle of Bebel Gilberto. *Career:* left Univ. of São Paulo to absorb local Bossa Nova scene and began writing songs; came to prominence when compositions recorded by singer Nara Leao. *Recordings include:* albums: Pedro Pedriero 1965, Chico Buarque de Hollanda 1966, Morte e Vida Severina 1966, Umas e outras 1969, Chico Buarque na Itália 1969, Apesar de você 1970, Per un pugno di samba 1970, Construção 1971, Quando o carnaval chegar 1972, Caetano e Chico juntos e ao vivo 1972, Chico canta 1973, Sinal fechado 1974, Chico Buarque & Maria Bethânia ao vivo 1975, Meus caros amigos 1976, Cio da Terra 1977, Os saltimbancos 1977, Gota d'água 1977, Chico Buarque 1978, Ópera do malandro 1979, Vida 1980, Show 1° de Maio 1980, Almanaque 1981, Saltimbancos trapalhões 1981, Chico Buarque en espanhol 1982, Para viver um grande amor 1983, O grande circo místico 1983, Chico Buarque 1984, O Corsário do rei 1985, Ópera do malandro 1985, Malandro 1985, Melhores momentos de Chico & Caetano 1986, Francisco 1987, Dança da meia-lua 1988, Chico Buarque ao vivo Paris Le Zenith 1990, Paratodos 1993, Uma palavra 1995, Terra 1997, As Cidades 1998, Chico ao Vivo 1999, Cambaio 2001, Chico Buarque Duetos 2002, Carioca 2006. *Film music:* Anjo assassino 1966, Garota de Ipanema 1967, Roda Vida (play, also score) 1968, Quando o carnaval chegar 1972, Os saltimbancos trapalhões 1981, Ópera do malandro 1986, Ed Mort 1996, O mandarim 1995. *Publications:* A Banda (songbook) 1966, Fazenda modelo (novel) 1974, Chapeuzinho Amarelo (poems) 1979, A bordo do Rui Barbosa 1981, Estorvo (novel) 1991, Benjamim (novel) 1995, Budapeste 2003. *Address:* c/o Discmedi SA, Ronda Guinardó, 59 Bis, Baixos, 08024 Barcelona, Spain. *Website:* www .chicobuarque.com.br.

BUCHANAN, Mark; American writer. *Publications:* Ubiquity: The Science of History, or Why the World is Simpler Than We Think, 2000; Nexus: Small Worlds and the Groundbreaking Science of Networks, 2002; Small World: Uncovering Nature's Hidden Networks, 2002.

BUCHANAN, Patrick (Pat) Joseph, MS; American journalist and fmr government official; b. 2 Nov. 1938, Washington; s. of William Buchanan and Catherine Crum; m. Shelley A. Scarney 1971. *Education:* Georgetown and Columbia Univs. *Career:* editorial writer, St Louis Globe Democrat 1962–64, asst editorial writer 1964–66; Exec. Asst to Richard Nixon 1966–69; Special Asst to Pres. Nixon 1969–73; consultant to Pres. Nixon and Pres. Ford 1973–74; Asst to Pres., Dir of Communications, White House, Washington, DC 1985–87; syndicated columnist, political commentator, New York Times special features 1975–78; Chicago Tribune-New York News Syndicate 1978–85, Tribune Media Services 1987–91, 1993–95; commentator, NBC Radio Network 1978–82; co-host Crossfire (TV Show) Cable News Network 1982–85, 1987–91, 1993–95, 1997–; appeared as host and panellist in TV shows 1978–; Ed.-in-Chief PJB—From the Right (newsletter) 1990–91; moderator Capital Gang TV show CNN 1988–92; Chair. The American Cause 1993–95, 1997–, Pat Buchanan & Co., Mutual Broadcasting System 1993–95;

Cand. for Republican Presidential nomination 1992, 1996; Republican. *Publications:* The New Majority 1973, Conservative Votes, Liberal Victories 1975, Right from the Beginning 1988; Barry Goldwater, The Conscience of A Conservative 1990, The Great Betrayal 1998, A Republic, not an Empire 2000, State of Emergency 2006. *Address:* The American Cause, 501 Church Street, Suite 217, Vienna, VA 22180 (office); 1017 Savile Lane, McLean, VA 22101, USA. *Telephone:* (703) 255-2632 (office). *Fax:* (703) 255-2219 (office). *E-mail:* webmaster@theamericancause.org (office). *Website:* www.theamericancause .org (office).

BUCHER, Werner; Swiss poet, writer, journalist and editor; b. 19 Aug. 1938, Zürich; m. Josiane Fidanza 1968. *Career:* mem. Swiss Writers' Union. *Publications:* Nicht Solche Aengste, du... (poems), 1974; Zeitzünder 3: Dank an den Engel, 1987; Was ist mit Lazarus?, 1989; Einst & Jetzt & Morgen (poems), 1989; Ein anderes Leben: Versuch, sich einem Unbekannten anzunahern; De Wand: Roman; Eigentlich wunderbar, das Leben...: Tagtag-Gedichte und Nachtnacht-Nachrichten; Das bessere Ende: Gedichte; Mouchette (poem), 1995; Wegschleudern die Brillen, die Lügen (poems), 1995; Unruhen, 1997; Wenn der zechpreller gewinnt (poems), 1997; Urwaldhus, Tierhag, Ochsenhutte & Co, Die Schonsten Ostschweizer Beizen, 1997; Im Schatten des Campanile, 2000; Weitere Stürme sind angesagt (poems), 2002. Contributions: Entwürfe; Tobel und Hoger; Listerarisches aus dem Appenzellerland, 2001. *Address:* Wirtschaft Rütegg, 9413 Oberegg, Switzerland (office). *Telephone:* (71) 888 15 56 (office). *E-mail:* info@wernerbucher.ch (office). *Website:* www.wernerbucher.ch.

BUCHOLZ, Arden, MA, PhD; American historian; *Distinguished Teaching Professor of History, State University of New York at Brockport;* b. 14 May 1936, Chicago, IL; m. Sue Tally 1962; two c. *Education:* Dartmouth Coll., Univ. of Vienna, Univ. of Chicago. *Career:* teacher of English, Amerikan Orta Okulu, Talas-Kayseri, Turkey 1958–60; served to Lt, US Army, including Counterintelligence in Germany 1961–64; teacher of History, Latin School of Chicago 1965–70; Distinguished Teaching Prof. of History, State Univ. of New York at Brockport 1970–; Programme Co-Dir, Brunel Univ., Uxbridge, UK 1987–88. *Publications:* Hans Delbruck and the German Military Establishment 1985, Moltke, Schlieffen, and Prussian War Planning 1991, Delbruck's Modern Military History 1997, Moltke and The German Wars, 1864–1871 2001. *Honours:* Outstanding Book in Mil. History Citation, Int. Comm. on Mil. History 1991. *Address:* 306 Main Street, Brockport, NY 14420, USA (home). *Telephone:* (585) 637-3099 (home). *E-mail:* abucholz@brockport.edu.

BUCHT, Gunnar, PhD; Swedish composer and writer; b. 5 Aug. 1927, Stocksund; m. Bergljot Krohn 1958. *Education:* studied composition with Karl Birger-Blomdahl, Carl Orff, Goffredo Petrassi, Max Deutsch, piano with Yngve Flyckt. *Career:* debut as composer and pianist 1949; Chair., Soc. of Swedish Composers 1963–69; teacher, Stockholm Univ. 1965–69; Vice-Pres., Int. Soc. for Contemporary Music 1969–72; cultural attaché to the Swedish Embassy at Bonn 1970–73; Prof. of Composition, Royal Coll. of Music 1975–85, Dir 1987–93; mem. Royal Acad. of Music. *Compositions include:* 12 symphonies 1952–97, two cello concertos 1955–90, three string quartets 1951, 1959, 1997, String Quintet 1950, Sonata for piano and percussion 1955, La fine della diaspora for tenor, chorus and orchestra (Quasimodo) 1957, The Pretenders (opera, after Ibsen) 1966, Symphonie pour la musique libérée for tape 1969, Lutheran Mass 1973, Journées oubliées 1975, Au delá 1977, Violin Concerto 1978, The Big Bang – and After 1979, Georgica 1980, En Clairobscur for chamber orchestra 1981, One Day I Went Out Into The World novel for orchestra 1983–84, Blad från mitt gulsippeänge for clarinet and piano 1985, Fresques mobiles 1986, Unter Vollem Einsatz for organ and five percussionists 1987, Tönend bewegte Formen for orchestra 1987, Piano Concerto 1994, Coup sur Coup for percussion 1995, Concerto de Marle for viola and orchestra 1996, Movements in Space for orchestra 1996, Panta Rei for soli, chorus and orchestra 1998–99, Alienus' Dream for orchestra 1999, Partita for two violins 2001, Den starkare (Strindberg) monodram for mezzo-soprano and orchestra 2001, Superstrings for orchestra 2002, Tre per due for two violins 2002. *Recordings:* Symphony 7, Violin Concerto, Piano Concerto, Georgica, Cantata, Quatre pièces pour le pianiste, Coup sur Coup, Sections of One Day I Went Out Into the World, Odysseia (Kazantzakis) half-scenic oratorio for soli, chorus and orchestra, part one 2000–03, The Infinite Melody for orchestra 2004. *Publications:* Electronic Music in Sweden 1977, Europe in Music 1996, Född på Krigsstigen (autobiog.) 1997, Rum, rörelse, tid 1999, Pythagoras' String 2005; contrib. to Swedish Journal of Musicology, Nordic Journal of Aesthetics. *Honours:* Royal Medal Litteris et artibus, Royal Acad. of Music För tonkonstensfrämjande. *Address:* Burge Hablingbo, 62011 Havdhem (home); Rådmansgatan 74, 11360 Stockholm, Sweden. *Telephone:* (08) 736 60 31 (home). *E-mail:* gb.bucht@telia.com (home). *Website:* www.gunnarbucht.com.

BUCHWALD, Christoph; German publishing executive. *Career:* fmrly Ed. Hanser, Munich; fmrly Publr Luchterhand Literaturverlag; now with Suhrkamp Verlag KG, Frankfurt 1998–. *Address:* Suhrkamp Verlag KG, Frankfurt a.M., Postfach 101945, Germany (office). *Telephone:* (69) 756010 (office). *Fax:* (69) 75601522 (office). *Website:* www.suhrkamp.de (office).

BUCK, Joan Juliet; American writer and magazine editor; b. Los Angeles; m. John Heilpern (divorced). *Career:* raised in Paris and London; fmr journalist with numerous magazines including Interview, WWD (as London and Italian Corresp.), The Observer Magazine, Condé Nast, Vogue USA, The New Yorker; Ed.-in-Chief French Vogue 1994–2000, now TV critic Vogue Magazine, New York; mem. PEN Newsletter Cttee. *Film appearance:*

Greyfriars Bobby: The True Story of a Dog 1961. *Television appearance:* as herself in Fashion Victim: The Killing of Gianni Versace (TV) 2001. *Publications include:* The Only Place To Be 1982, Daughter of the Swan 1989; contrib. to numerous magazines. *Address:* c/o Vogue Magazine, 350 Madison Avenue, New York, NY 10017, USA. *Telephone:* (212) 286-2860.

BUCKLEY, William Frank, Jr; American editor and author; b. 24 Nov. 1925, New York; s. of William Frank Buckley and Aloise (Steiner) Buckley; m. Patricia Taylor 1950; one s. *Education:* Univ. of Mexico and Yale Univ. *Career:* on staff American Mercury 1952; Ed. National Review 1955–88, Ed.-in-Chief 1988–90, Ed.-at-Large 1991–2004; syndicated columnist 1962–; host of weekly TV series Firing Line 1966–99; lecturer New School for Social Research 1967; mem. USIA Advisory Comm. 1969–72; mem. US del. to UN 1973; contrib. to Harper's, Esquire, Foreign Affairs, Atlantic, etc. *Publications:* God and Man at Yale 1951, Up from Liberalism 1959, Rumbles Left and Right 1963, The Unmaking of a Mayor 1966, The Jeweler's Eye 1968, The Governor Listeth 1970, Cruising Speed 1971, Inveighing We Will Go 1972, Four Reforms 1973, United Nations Journal 1974, Execution Eve 1975, Saving the Queen 1976, Airborne 1976, Stained Glass 1978, A Hymnal 1978, Who's on First 1980, Marco Polo, If You Can 1982, Atlantic High 1982, Overdrive 1983, The Story of Henri Tod 1984, See You Later, Alligator 1985, Right Reason (articles and essays) 1985, The Temptation of Wilfred Malachey 1985, High Jinx 1986, Racing through Paradise 1987, Mongoose RIP 1988, On the Firing Line 1989, Gratitude 1990, Tucker's Last Stand 1991, Windfall: The End of the Affair 1992, Happy Days Were Here Again 1993, A Very Private Plot 1994, Buckley! The Right Word 1996, Nearer My God–An Autobiography of Faith 1997, The Lexicon 1998, The Redhunter: A Novel Based on the Life of Senator Joe McCarthy 1999, Spytime 2000, Elvis in the Morning 2001, Nuremberg: The Reckoning 2002, Getting it Right 2003, The Fall of the Berlin Wall 2004; co-author McCarthy and His Enemies 1954; Ed. The Committee and Its Critics 1962, Odyssey of a Friend 1970, Did You Ever See a Dream Walking 1970. *Honours:* numerous hon. degrees; numerous awards including Presidential Medal of Freedom 1991. *Address:* National Review, 215 Lexington Avenue, New York, NY 10016-6023, USA. *Telephone:* (212) 679-7330. *Website:* www.nationalreview.com.

BUCKLEY, William K., BA, MA, PhD; American academic, writer and poet; *Professor, Indiana University Northwest;* b. 14 Nov. 1946, San Diego, Calif.; m. Mary Patricia 1969; one s. *Education:* Univ. of San Diego, California State Univ. at San Diego, Miami Univ., Oxford, OH. *Career:* instructor, San Diego Community Colls 1972–74; Co-founder and Co-Ed. Recovering Literature 1972–85; Dir Learning Skills Center, California State Univ. at San Diego 1974–75; Teaching Fellow, Miami Univ., Oxford, OH 1975–79; Visiting Asst Prof., Hanover Coll. 1979–82; Visiting Asst Prof., Indiana Univ. Northwest, Gary, Ind. 1982–84; Prof. 1985–; mem. Acad. of American Poets. *Publications:* A Half-Century of Céline (co-author) 1983, Critical Essays on Louis-Ferdinand Céline (ed.) 1989, Senses' Tender: Recovering the Novel for the Reader 1989, New Perspectives on the Closing of the American Mind (co-ed.) 1992, Lady Chatterley's Lover: Loss and Hope 1993; poetry: By the Horses Before the Rains (Modern Poetry journal Best Chapbook of the Year 1997) 1996, Heart Maps 1997, 81 Mygrations 1998, Athena in Steeltown 1999, Sylvia's Bells 2002, Lost Heartlands Found 2004, On Heartland Soils 2005. *Address:* Department of English, Indiana University Northwest, 3400 Broadway, Gary, IN 46408, USA (office). *Telephone:* (219) 980-6570 (office). *E-mail:* wbuckley@iun.edu (office).

BUDBILL, David, BA, MDiv; American writer, poet and dramatist; b. 13 June 1940, Cleveland, OH. *Education:* Muskingum College, New Concord, OH, Columbia University, Union Theological Seminary, New York. *Career:* Poet-in-Residence, Niagara Erie Writers, Buffalo, NY, 1984, Jamestown Community College, Jamestown, New York, 1986, 1987; mem. PEN; Dramatists' Guild. *Publications:* Barking Dog, 1968; The Chain Saw Dance, 1977; Pulp Cutters' Nativity, 1981; From Down to the Village, 1981; Why I Came to Judevine, 1987; Judevine: The Complete Poems, 1991; Danvis Tales: Selected Stories by Rowland Robinson (ed.), 1995; Little Acts of Kindness, 1995; Moment to Moment, 1999. Play: Two for Christmas, 1996. Contributions: many anthologies and periodicals. *Honours:* Williamstown Repertory Theatre Playwright's Fellowship, 1965; Publication Grant, American Studies Institute, 1967; Poetry Fellowships, Vermont Council on the Arts, 1973, 1977, 1979; Kirkus Reviews Best Books, 1974, 1976; Guggenheim Fellowship, 1982–83; Playwriting Fellowship, National Endowment for the Arts, 1991; San Francisco Bay Area Critics' Circle Award, 1991.

BUDD, Holly (see Judd, Alan)

BUDRYS, Algirdas Jonas; Lithuanian/American writer, editor and publisher; b. 9 Jan. 1931, Königsberg, Germany; m. Edna F. Duna 1954; four s. *Education:* University of Miami, Columbia University. *Career:* Ed.-in-Chief, Regency Books, 1962–63; Playboy Press, 1963–65; Operations Man., Woodall Publishing Co, 1974–75; Pres., Unifont Co 1975–; Ed. and Publisher, Tomorrow Speculative Fiction magazine, 1992–; mem. Science Fiction Hall of Fame. *Publications:* Fiction: False Night, 1954, revised edn as Some Will Not Die, 1962; Man of Earth, 1955; Who?, 1958; The Falling Torch, 1959; Rogue Moon, 1960; The Iron Thorn, 1967; Michaelmas, 1977; Hard Landing, 1993. Collections: The Unexpected Dimension, 1960; The Furious Future, 1963; Blood and Burning, 1979. Non-Fiction: Truman and the Pendergasts, 1963; Bicycles: How They Work and How to Fix Them, 1976; Writing to the

Point, 1994. Contributions: numerous magazines. *Address:* 824 Seward Street, Evanston, IL 60202, USA.

BUECHNER, (Carl) Frederick; American writer and minister; b. 11 July 1926, New York, NY; m. Judith Friedrike Merck 1956; three c. *Education:* AB, Princeton University, 1947; BD, Union Theological Seminary, 1958. *Career:* Teacher of Creative Writing, New York University, summers, 1954, 1955; Ordained Minister, United Presbyterian Church, 1958; Chair., Dept of Religion, 1958–67, Minister, 1960–67, Phillips Exeter Acad.; William Belden Noble Lecturer, Harvard University, 1969; Russell Lecturer, Tufts University, 1971; Lyman Beecher Lecturer, Yale University, 1977; Harris Lector, Bangor Seminary, 1979; Smyth Lecturer, Columbia Seminary, 1981; Lecturer, Trinity Institute, 1990; mem. Council on Religion in Independent Schools, regional chair., 1958–63; National Council of Churches, committee on literature, 1954–57; Presbytery of Northern New England. *Publications:* A Long Day's Dying, 1950; The Season's Difference, 1952; The Return of Ansel Gibbs, 1958; The Final Beast, 1965; The Magnificent Defeat, 1966; The Hungering Dark, 1969; The Alphabet of Grace, 1970; The Entrance to Porlock, 1970; Lion Country, 1971; Open Heart, 1972; Wishful Thinking, 1973; The Faces of Jesus, 1974; Love Feast, 1974; Telling the Truth, 1977; Treasure Hunt, 1977; The Book of Bebb, 1979; Peculiar Treasures, 1979; Godric, 1980; The Sacred Journey, 1982; Now and Then, 1983; A Room Called Remember, 1984; Brendan, 1987; Whistling in the Dark, 1988; The Wizard's Tide, 1990; Telling Secrets, 1991; The Clown in the Belfry, 1992; Listening to Your Life, 1992; The Son of Laughter, 1993; The Longing for Home, 1996; On the Road with the Archangel, 1997; The Storm, 1998; The Eyes of the Heart, 1999; Speak What We Feel, 2001. *Honours:* O'Henry Prize, 1955; Richard and Hinda Rosenthal Award, 1958. *Address:* RR1, Box 1145, Pawlet, VT 05761, USA.

BUICAN, Denis, DèsScNat, DèsL et ScHum; Romanian/French academic, biologist and philosopher of biology; *Honorary Professor, Université de Paris X Nanterre;* b. 21 Dec. 1934, Bucharest; s. of Dumitru Peligrad and Elena Buican. *Education:* Bucharest Univ., Faculté des Sciences de Paris, Univ. de Paris I-Sorbonne. *Career:* teaching asst, Bucharest Univ. 1956–57, Prin. Scientific Researcher 1957–60, Course Leader Gen. Biology and Genetics with History of Science course 1960–69, Invited Prof. 1990–; Invited Prof. First Class, History of Sciences, Faculté des Sciences, Univ. de Paris 1969–70, Univ. de Paris-Sorbonne 1970–74, Assoc. Prof., History and Philosophy of Science 1970–74; Assoc. Prof., History and Philosophy of Science, Univ. of Dijon 1974–80; Assoc. Prof., History of Sciences, Univ. de Paris I Panthéon-Sorbonne 1980–83; Assoc. Prof. First Class, History of Sciences, Univ. de Paris X 1983–86; Invited Prof. Collège de France 1984, 1993; Prof. First Class, Univ. de Paris X Nanterre 1986–2003, Hon. Prof. 2003–. *Publications include:* Histoire de la génétique et de l'évolutionnisme en France 1984, La Génétique et l'évolution 1986, Génétique et pensée évolutionniste 1987, Darwin et le darwinisme 1987, Lyssenko et le lyssenkisme 1988, L'Evolution et les évolutionnismes 1989, La Révolution de l'évolution 1989, L'Explosion biologique, du néant au Sur-être 1991, Dracula et ses avatars de Vlad l'Empaleur à Staline et Ceaucescu 1991, Charles Darwin 1992, Mendel et la génétique d'hier et d'aujourd'hui 1993, Les Métamorphoses de Dracula 1993, Biognoséologie: Evolution et révolution de la connaissance 1993, Jean Rostand 1994, Histoire de la Biologie 1994, Evolution de la pensée biologique 1995, L'Evolution aujourd'hui 1995, L'Evolution: la grande aventure de la vie 1995, Ethologie comparée 1996, Dictionnaire de la Biologie 1997, L'Evolution et les théories évolutionnistes 1997, L'Epopée du vivant, L'Evolution de la biosphère et les avatars de l'Homme 2003, Le Darwinisme et les évolutionnismes 2005; poetry books: Arbre seul 1974, Lumière aveugle 1976, Mamura 1993, Spice (poèmes anciens et nombreaux) 2006. *Honours:* Hon. Citizen of Saliste (Romania) 2003; Grand Prix, Acad. Française 1989. *Address:* 15 rue Poliveau, 75005 Paris, France (home). *Telephone:* 1-43-36-33-97 (home).

BUIDA, Yuri; Russian author; b. 1954, USSR. *Publications:* Don Domino (novel), Yermo (novel), Boris and Gleb (novel), The Prussian Bride (short stories) 1998, Zero Train (novel) 2001; contrib. to Glas, Novy Mir, Znamya, Oktyabr, Volga. *Address:* c/o Dedalus Ltd, Langford Lodge, St Judith's Lane, Sawtry, Cambridgeshire PE28 5XE, England. *E-mail:* info@dedalusbooks.com. *Website:* www.dedalusbooks.com.

BUISSERET, David Joseph, PhD, FRHistS; British/American writer, historian and academic; b. 18 Dec. 1934, Totland Bay, Isle of Wight, England; m. Patricia Connolly 1961; three s. two d. *Education:* Corpus Christi Coll., Cambridge. *Career:* Research Fellow, Corpus Christi Coll. 1961–64; Lecturer to Sr Lecturer, Univ. of the West Indies 1964–72, Reader 1972–75, Prof. of History 1975–80; Ed. The Jamaican Historical Review 1968–80, Terrae Incognitae 1982–; Dir Hermon Dunlap Smith Center for the History of Cartography, Newberry Library, Chicago 1980–95; Jenkins and Virginia Garrett Prof. in Southwestern Studies and the History of Cartography, Univ. of Texas, Arlington 1995–2006. *Publications:* Sully and the Growth of Centralized Government in France, 1598–1610 1969, The Wars of Religion (Vol. 10 of the Hamlyn History of the World) 1969, Historic Jamaica from the Air (with J. S. Tyndale-Biscoe) 1969, Les Oeconomies Royales de Sully (co-ed. with Bernard Barbiche) Vol. I 1970, Vol. II 1988, The Fortifications of Kingston, 1660–1900 1971, Huguenots and Papists 1972, A Popular History of the Port of Kingston 1973, Port Royal, Jamaica (with Michael Pawson) 1975, Historic Architecture of the Caribbean 1980, Henry IV 1984, Histoire de l'Architecture dans la Caraibe 1984, Skokie: A Community History using Old Maps (with Gerald Danzer) 1985, From Sea Charts to Satellite Images: Interpreting North American History through Maps (ed.) 1990, Historic

Illinois from the Air 1990, A Guidebook to Resources for Teachers of the Columbian Encounter (co-ed. with Tina Reithmaier) 1992, Monarchs, Ministers and Maps: The Emergence of Cartography as a Tool of Government in Early Modern Europe (ed.) 1992, Elk Grove: A Community History in Maps (with James Issel) 1996, Rural Images: The Estate Map in the Old and New Worlds (ed.) 1996, Envisioning the City 1998, France in America (ed.) 1998, Creolization in the Americas (with Steven Reinhardt) 2000, Ingénieurs et Fortifications avant Vauban: l'Organisation d'un service royal aux XVIe-XVIIe Siècles 2001, The Mapmaker's Quest: Depicting New Worlds in Renaissance Europe 2003, A Cartographic History of Arlington and the Dallas-Fort Worth Area 2006; contrib. to scholarly books and journals. *Honours:* Chevalier, Ordre des Palmes académiques 1993; Inst. of Jamaica Centennial Medal 1979, various grants. *Address:* 5126 Lunt Avenue, Skokie, IL 60077, USA (home). *Telephone:* (847) 679-2885 (home). *E-mail:* buisser@uta.edu (office).

BUKHT, Baidar, MA; Pakistani journalist; *Chief News Editor, Daily Jang, Lahore. Career:* Sub-Ed., Daily Jang 1982, currently Chief News Ed.; involved in setting up Daily Pakistan and Daily Khabrain newspapers. *Honours:* President's Award for Pride of Performance (Journalism) 2005. *Address:* Daily Jang, 13 Davis Road, Lahore, Pakistan (office). *Website:* www.jang.com.pk.

BULARD, Martine, LèsL; French newspaper editor; b. 12 June 1952. *Career:* apptd Chief Econ. Columnist on L'Humanité newspaper (organ of the French Communist Party) 1980, fmr Ed.-in-Chief L'Humanité Dimanche; currently columnist for Le Monde diplomatique. *Address:* Le Monde diplomatique, 1 avenue Stephen-Pichon, 75013 Paris, France (office). *Telephone:* 1-53-94-96-26 (office). *Fax:* 1-53-94-96-01 (office). *Website:* mondediplo.com (office).

BULLOCK, Michael; British/Canadian dramatist, writer and poet; *Professor Emeritus, University of British Columbia;* b. 19 April 1918, London, England; m. Charlotte Schneller; one s. one d. *Education:* Hornsey Coll. of Art, London. *Career:* Commonwealth Fellow 1968, Prof. of Creative Writing 1969–83, Prof. Emeritus 1983–, Univ. of British Columbia, Vancouver, Canada; McGuffey Visiting Prof. of English, Ohio Univ., Athens, OH, USA 1969; New Asia Ming Yu Visiting Scholar 1989, writer-in-residence 1996, New Asia Coll., Chinese Univ. of Hong Kong; Adviser, New Poetry Soc. of China 1995–. *Publications:* poetry: Transmutations 1938, Sunday is a Day of Incest 1961, World Without Beginning Amen 1963, Two Voices in My Mouth/Zwei Stimmen in meinem Mund 1967, A Savage Darkness 1969, Black Wings White Dead 1978, Lines in the Dark Wood 1981, Quadriga for Judy 1982, Prisoner of the Rain 1983, Brambled Heart 1985, Dark Water 1987, Poems on Green Paper 1988, The Secret Garden 1990, Avatars of the Moon 1990, Labyrinths 1992, The Walled Garden 1992, The Sorcerer with Deadly Nightshade Eyes 1993, The Inflowing River 1993, Moons and Mirrors 1994, Dark Roses 1994, Stone and Shadow 1996, Der Grüne Mond 1997, Sonnet in Black and Other Poems 1998, Erupting in Flowers 1999, Nocturnes: Poems of Night 2000, Wings of the Black Swan: Poems of Love and Loss 2001, Colours 2003; fiction: Sixteen Stories as They Happened 1969, Green Beginning Black Ending 1971, Randolph Cranstone and the Pursuing River 1975, Randolph Cranstone and the Glass Thimble 1977, The Man with Flowers Through his Hands 1985, The Double Ego 1985, Randolph Cranstone and the Veil of Maya 1986, The Story of Noire 1987, Randolph Cranstone Takes the Inward Path 1988, The Burning Chapel 1991, The Invulnerable Ovoid Aura, Stories and Poems 1995; plays: Not to Hong Kong 1971, Sokotra 1997; other: Selected Works, 1936–1996 (co-eds Peter Loeffler and Jack Stewart) 1998; contrib. to many anthologies. *Honours:* Schlegel-Tieck German Trans. Prize 1966, British New Fiction Soc. Book of the Month 1977, Canada Council French Trans. Award 1979, San Francisco Review of Books Best Book List 1982, San Jose Mercury News Best Book List 1984, Okanagan Short Fiction Award 1986. *Address:* Suite 103, 3626 W 28th Avenue, Vancouver, BC V6S 1S4, Canada (office). *Telephone:* (604) 224-4756 (office). *Fax:* (604) 224-4740 (office). *E-mail:* michaelhbullock@hotmail.com (office). *Website:* www.m_bullock.tripod.com (office).

BUNCH, Richard Alan, AA, BA, MA, MDiv, DD, JD; American teacher, poet and writer; b. 1 June 1945, Honolulu, HI; s. of Thornton Carlisle Bunch and DeLores Virginia Veal Bunch; m. Rita Anne Glazar 1990; one s. one d. *Education:* Napa Valley Coll., Stanford Univ., Univ. of Arizona, Vanderbilt Univ., Temple Univ., Univ. of Memphis, Sonoma State Univ. *Career:* staff mem., Nashville Human Rights Forum, Vanderbilt Univ. 1974–75; law clerk, Circuit Court, Memphis 1979–81; Attorney, Horne and Peppel, Memphis 1981–83; law clerk, Tennessee Court of Appeals, Memphis 1983; Assoc. News Ed. and features writer, Napa Valley Times 1985–86; teaching asst in philosophy, Vanderbilt Univ. 1973–74; instructor in philosophy, Belmont Univ. 1973–74, Chapman Univ. 1986–87; instructor in law, Univ. of Memphis 1982–83; instructor in history and humanities, Napa Valley Coll. 1985–, Diablo Valley Coll. 1991–94, 1997, Solano Coll. 1988–; instructor in law 1986–87, in Philosophy 1990–91, Sonoma State Univ.; Lecturer, Univ. of California, Berkeley 1995; judge Davis Poetry Contest for Teens 2002, 2004; mem. Ina Coolbrith Poetry Circle. *Publications:* poetry: Summer Hawk 1991, Wading the Russian River 1993, A Foggy Morning 1996, Santa Rosa Plums 1996, South by Southwest 1997, Rivers of the Sea 1998, Sacred Space 1998, Greatest Hits: 1970–2000 2001, Running for Daybreak 2004; play: The Russian River Returns 1999; prose: Night Blooms 1992, Hawking Moves: Plays, Poems and Stories 2007; contrib. poems to Oregon Review, Orbis, Hawaii Review, California Quarterly, short stories to The Plaza 2000, Goose River Anthologies 2003, 2004, 2005, Poetry Nottingham, Poetry New Zealand.

Honours: grand prize Ina Coolbirth Nat. Poetry Day Contest 1989, Jessamyn West Prize 1990. *Address:* 248 Sandpiper Drive, Davis, CA 965616, USA.

BURCH, Claire, BA; American writer, poet and filmmaker; b. 19 Feb. 1925, New York, NY; m. Bradley Bunch 1944 (deceased); one s. (deceased) two d. *Education:* Washington Square Coll. *Career:* mem. Writers' Guild. *Publications:* Stranger in the Family 1972, Notes of a Survivor 1972, Shredded Millions 1980, Goodbye My Coney Island Baby 1989, Homeless in the Eighties 1989, Solid Gold Illusion 1991, You Be the Mother Follies 1994, Homeless in the Nineties 1994, Stranger on the Planet: The Small Book of Laurie 1996; contrib. to periodicals. *Honours:* Carnegie Awards 1978, 1979, California Arts Council grants 1991, 1992, 1993, 1994, Seva Foundation Award 1996. *Address:* c/o Regent Press, 6020A Adeline, Oakland, CA 94808, USA.

BURCHILL, Julie; British journalist and writer; b. 3 July 1959, Bristol; m. 1st Tony Parsons (divorced); m. 2nd Cosmo Landesman (divorced); m. 3rd Daniel Raven. *Career:* journalist NME (New Music Express) 1976–79, The Face, 1979–84, Mail on Sunday, 1984–93, Sunday Times, 1993–94, Guardian, 1998–2003, The Times 2003–06; freelance journalist Sunday Express; co-founder Modern Review. *TV includes:* Prince (film), several plays. *Publications:* The Boy Looked at Johnny 1979, Love It or Shove It 1983, Girls on Film 1986, Damaged Goods 1987, Ambition 1989, Sex and Sensibility 1992, No Exit 1993, I Knew I Was Right (autobiog.) 1998, Diana 1998, Married Alive 1998, On Beckham 2002, Sugar Rush 2004, Made in Brighton (with Daniel Raven) 2007, Sweet 2007. *Literary Agent:* Simpson Fox, 52 Shaftesbury Avenue, London, W1V 7OE, England.

BURDA, Hubert, DPhil; German publisher and author; b. 9 Feb. 1940, Heidelberg; s. of Dr Franz Burda and Aenne Lemminger. *Education:* Univ. of Munich. *Career:* Man. Bild & Funk 1966–74; partner, Burda GmbH 1974, now Chair. Burda Group; Co-Publr Elle-Verlag GmbH, Munich; co-f. Europe Online SA, Luxembourg; Publr Anna, Bunte, Burda Moden, Das Haus, Elle, Elle Bistro, Elle Deco, Elle TopModel, Focus, Focus Online, Focus TV, Freundin, Freizeit Revue, Futurekids, Glücks Revue, Haus + Garten, Lisa, Lisa Kochen & Backen, Lisa Wohnen & Dekorieren, Mein schöner Garten, Meine Familie & ich, Norddeutsche Neueste Nachrichten, Schweriner Volkszeitung, Starwatch Navigation, Super Illu, Super TV, TraXXX, Verena; mem. Bd German School of Journalism, Munich; f. Petrarca Prize (for poetry), Bambi (Media-Prize), Corp. Art Prize 1997. *Address:* Arabellastrasse 23, 81925 Munich, Germany.

BUREAU, Jérôme, DHist; French journalist; b. 19 April 1956, Paris; m. Fabienne Pauly 1999; two c. (and two from a previous marriage). *Career:* journalist with Libération 1978–81; Sr Reporter L'Équipe Magazine 1981–87, Ed.-in-Chief 1989–93; Ed.-in-Chief Le Sport 1987–88; Editorial Dir L'Équipe, L'Équipe-TV 1997–, L'Équipe Magazine, Vélo, XL, Tennis de France 1993–, lequipe.fr 1999–2003; TV and Radio Producer, Sport FM 2004–. *Publications:* L'Amour-Foot 1986, Les Géants du football 1996. *Address:* 34 bis avenue Bernard Palissy 92, 92210 Saint-Cloud; 102 avenue Denfert-Rochereau, 75014 Paris, France (home). *E-mail:* jereome.bureau6@wanadoo.fr (office).

BURENGA, Kenneth L.; American publishing executive; b. 30 May 1944, Somerville, NJ; s. of Nicholas Burenga and Louanna Chamberlin; m. Jean Case 1964; one s. one d. *Education:* Rider Coll. *Career:* budget accountant, Dow Jones & Co., S Brunswick, NJ 1966–67, Asst Man. data processing control 1968–69, staff asst for systems devt 1970–71, Man. systems devt and control 1972–76, circulation marketing Man. 1977–78, circulation sales dir 1979–80, Vice-Pres. circulation and circulation dir 1980–86; Chief Financial Officer and Admin. Officer, Dow Jones & Co., New York 1986–88, Exec. Vice-Pres., Gen. Man. 1989–91, Pres. COO 1991, Pres. and CEO –1998 (retd); fmr Gen. Man. Wall Street Journal 1989; mem. Bd of Dirs Dow Jones Courier.

BURGIN, Richard Weston, MA, MPhil; American academic, writer and editor; *Professor of Communication and English, St Louis University;* b. 30 June 1947, Boston, MA; m. Linda K. Harris 1991; one s. one step-d. *Education:* Brandeis Univ., Columbia Univ. *Career:* instructor, Tufts Univ., Mass 1970–74; Critic-at-Large, Boston Globe Magazine 1973–74; Founding Ed. and Dir New York Arts Journal 1976–83; Visiting Lecturer, Univ. of California at Santa Barbara 1981–84; Assoc. Prof. of Humanities, Drexel Univ., Phila 1984–96; Founder-Ed. Boulevard literary journal 1985–; Prof. of Communication and English, St Louis Univ., Mo. 1996–; mem. Nat. Book Critics Circle 1988–. *Recordings of compositions:* In All Of The World 2000, House Of Sun 2001, Doll Of Dreams 2002, Don't Go There 2005, Cold Ocean 2005. *Publications:* Conversations with Jorge Luis Borges 1969, The Man with Missing Parts (novella) 1974, Conversations with Isaac Bashevis Singer 1985, Man Without Memory (short stories) 1989, Private Fame (short stories) 1991, Fear of Blue Skies (short stories) 1998, Jorge Luis Borges: Conversations (ed.) 1998, Ghost Quartet (novel) 1999, The Spirit Returns (short stories) 2001, Stories and Dreamboxes (short stories, with illustrations by Gloria Vanderbilt) 2002, The Identity Club: New and Selected Stories (accompanied by CD, Don't Go There) 2005, Don't Go There 2005, Cold Ocean 2005, The Conference on Beautiful Moments (short stories) 2006; contribs to numerous anthologies, reviews, journals and newspapers. *Honours:* Pushcart Prizes 1983, 1986, 1999, 2002, Best American Mystery Stories 2005, various hon. mentions and listings. *Address:* 7545 Cromwell Drive, Apt 2N, St Louis, MO 63105, USA (office). *Telephone:* (314) 862-2643 (office). *Fax:* (314) 862-2982 (office). *E-mail:* kingd@slu.edu (office). *Website:* www.richardburgin.net.

BURGIN, Victor, ARCA, MFA; British artist, writer and academic; *Millard Professor of Fine Art, Goldsmiths College, London*; b. 24 July 1941, Sheffield; s. of Samuel Burgin and Gwendolyne A. Crowder; m. 1st Hazel P. Rowbotham 1964 (divorced 1975); m. 2nd Francette Pacteau 1988; two s. *Education:* Firth Park Grammar School, Sheffield, Sheffield Coll. of Art, Royal Coll. of Art, London and Yale Univ., USA. *Career:* Sr Lecturer, Trent Polytechnic, Nottingham 1967–73; Prof. of History and Theory of Visual Arts, Faculty of Communication, Polytechnic of Cen. London 1973–; Prof. of Art History, Univ. of Calif., Santa Cruz 1988–95, Prof. of History of Consciousness 1995–2001, Prof. Emer. of History of Consciousness 2001–; Millard Prof. of Fine Art Goldsmiths Coll., Univ. of London 2001–; Deutscher Akademischer Austauschdienst Fellowship 1978–79; Picker Professorship, Colgate Univ., Hamilton, New York 1980; mem. arts advisory panel, Arts Council of Great Britain 1971–76, 1980–81; numerous mixed and solo exhbns at galleries around the world from 1965. *Publications:* Work and Commentary 1973, Thinking Photography 1982, The End of Art Theory 1986, Between 1986, Passages 1991, In/Different Spaces 1996, Some Cities 1996, Venice 1997, Shadowed 2000, The Remembered Film 2005; contrib. to exhbn catalogues. *Honours:* Hon. DUniv (Sheffield Hallam). *Address:* c/o Goldsmiths College, New Cross, London, SE14 6NW, England (office). *Telephone:* (20) 7919-7671 (office). *Fax:* (20) 7919-7673 (office). *E-mail:* v.burgin@gold.ac.uk. *Website:* www.goldsmiths.ac.uk/departments/visual-arts (office).

BURKE, Gregory; British playwright; b. 1969, Dunfermline, Scotland. *Career:* writer-in-residence at the Nat. Theatre Studio. *Plays:* Gagarin Way 2001, The Straits 2003, Black Watch 2006. *Honours:* Pearson Television Bursary 2002. *Address:* c/o Faber & Faber Ltd, 3 Queen Square, London, WC1N 3AU, England. *Telephone:* (20) 7465-0045. *Fax:* (20) 7465-0034. *Website:* www.faber.co.uk.

BURKE, James Lee, BA, MA; American writer; b. 5 Dec. 1936, Houston, TX; m. Pearl Pai 1960; one s. three d. *Education:* Univ. of Southwest Louisiana, Univ. of Missouri. *Career:* mem. Amnesty Int. *Publications:* Half of Paradise 1965, To the Bright and Shining Sun 1970, Lay Down My Sword and Shield 1971, Two for Texas 1983, The Convict and Other Stories 1985, The Lost Get-Back Boogie 1986, The Neon Rain 1987, Heaven's Prisoners 1988, Black Cherry Blues 1989, A Morning for Flamingos 1990, A Stained White Radiance 1992, Texas City, Nineteen Forty-Seven 1992, In the Electric Mist with Confederate Dead 1993, Dixie City Jam 1994, Burning Angel 1995, Heartwood 1999, Purple Cane Road 2000, Bitterroot 2001, Jolie Blon's Bounce 2002, White Doves at Morning 2002, Last Car to Elysian Fields 2003, In the Moon of Red Ponies 2004, Crusader's Cross 2005, Pegasus Descending 2006, The Tin Roof Blowdown 2007; contrib. to periodicals. *Honours:* Bread Loaf Fellow 1970, Southern Federation of State Arts Agencies grant 1977, Guggenheim Fellowship 1989, MWA Edgar Allan Poe Awards 1989, 1998. *Address:* c/o Orion Publishing Group Ltd, Orion House, 5 Upper St Martin's Lane, London, WC2H 9EA, England.

BURKE, John Frederick, (Owen Burke, Harriet Esmond, Jonathan George, Joanna Jones, Robert Miall, Sara Morris, Martin Sands); British author; b. 8 March 1922, Rye, Sussex; m. 1st Joan Morris 1940; five d.; m. 2nd Jean Williams 1963; two s. *Education:* Holt High School, Liverpool. *Career:* Production Man., Museum Press; Editorial Man., Paul Hamlyn Books for Pleasure Group: European Story Ed., 20th Century Fox Productions; mem. Society of Authors, Danish Club. *Publications:* Swift Summer 1949, An Illustrated History of England 1974, Dr Caspian Trilogy 1976–78, Musical Landscapes 1983, Illustrated Dictionary of Music 1988, A Traveller's History of Scotland 1990, Bareback 1998, Death by Marzipan 1999, We've Been Waiting for You 2000, Stalking Widow 2000, The Second Strain 2002, Wrong Turnings 2004, Hang Time 2007; other: film and TV novelizations. Contributions: The Bookseller, Country Life, Denmark. *Honours:* Atlantic Award in Literature 1948–49. *Literary Agent:* David Higham Associates, 5–8 Lower John Street, Golden Square, London, W1F 9HA, England. *Address:* 5 Castle Gardens, Kirkcudbright, Dumfries & Galloway, DG6 4JE, Scotland (home). *Telephone:* (1557) 331837 (home).

BURKE, (Ulick) Peter, MA, FRHistS, FBA; British historian and academic; *Professor Emeritus of Cultural History, University of Cambridge*; b. 16 Aug. 1937, Stanmore; s. of John Burke and Jenny Burke (née Colin); m. 1st Susan Patricia Dell 1972 (divorced 1983); m. 2nd Maria Lucía García Pallares 1989. *Education:* St Ignatius' Coll., Stamford Hill, St John's Coll., Oxford, St Antony's Coll., Oxford. *Career:* Asst Lecturer, then Lecturer, then Reader in History (later Intellectual History), School of European Studies, Univ. of Sussex 1962–78; Lecturer in History, Univ. of Cambridge 1979–88, Reader in Cultural History 1988–96, Prof. of Cultural History 1996–2004, Prof. Emer. 2004–; Fellow, Emmanuel Coll. Cambridge 1979–; Visiting Prof., Univ. of São Paulo, Brazil 1986, 1987, Nijmegen Univ. 1992–93, Groningen Univ. 1998–99, Heidelberg Univ. 2002; Fellow, Wissenschaftskolleg, Berlin 1989–90, Netherlands Inst. for Advanced Study 2005–. *Publications:* The Renaissance Sense of the Past 1969, Culture and Society in Renaissance Italy 1972, Venice and Amsterdam 1974, Popular Culture in Early Modern Europe 1978, Sociology and History 1980, Montaigne 1981, Vico 1985, Historical Anthropology of Early Modern Italy 1987, The Renaissance 1987, The French Historical Revolution: The Annales School 1929–1989 1990, The Fabrication of Louis XIV 1992, History and Social Theory 1992, Antwerp: A Metropolis in Europe 1993, The Art of Conversation 1993, The Fortunes of the Courtier 1995, Varieties of Cultural History 1997, The European Renaissance 1998, A Social History of Knowledge 2000, Eyewitnessing 2001, (jtly) A Social History of the Media 2002, Languages and Communities in Early Modern Europe 2004. *Honours:* Erasmus Prize, Academia Europaea 1999. *Address:* Emmanuel College, Cambridge, CB2 3AP (office); 14 Warkworth Street, Cambridge, CB1 1EG, England (home). *Telephone:* (1223) 334272. *Fax:* (1223) 334426 (office). *E-mail:* upb1000@cam.ac.uk (home). *Website:* www.hist.cam.ac.uk (office).

BURKHOLZ, Herbert Laurence, BA; American author; b. 9 Dec. 1932, New York, NY; m. Susan Blaine 1961, two s. *Education:* New York University. *Career:* Writer-in-Residence, College of William and Mary, 1975. *Publications:* Sister Bear, 1969; Spy, 1969; The Spanish Soldier, 1973; Mulligan's Seed, 1975; The Death Freak, 1978; The Sleeping Spy, 1983; The Snow Gods, 1985; The Sensitives, 1987; Strange Bedfellows, 1988; Brain Damage, 1992; Writer-in-Residence, 1992; The FDA Follies, 1994. Contributions: New York Times; Town & Country; Playboy; Penthouse; Longevity. *Honours:* Distinguished Scholar 1976.

BURLATSKY, Fedor Mikhailovich, DPhil; Russian journalist, writer and politician; b. 4 Jan. 1927, Kiev; s. of Mikhail Burlatsky and Sofia Burlatsky; m. 1st Seraphyma Burlatsky 1952 (divorced 1974); two s.; m. 2nd Kyra Burlatsky 1974; one d. *Education:* Tashkent Law Inst. *Career:* journalist Tashkent 1948–50; post grad. at Inst. of State Law, USSR Acad. of Sciences 1950–53; journalist with Kommunist 1953–59; head of section in Cen. Cttee Dept for Liaison with Communist and Workers' Parties of Socialist Countries 1959–65; political observer with Pravda 1965–67; Deputy Dir of USSR Inst. of Sociological studies 1968–72; head of section, USSR Inst. of State and Law (later Chief Scientific Researcher 1990–) and Head of Philosophy Dept, Inst. of Social Science, Cen. Cttee of CPSU 1975–88; Vice-Pres. Soviet Assoc. of Political Science 1976, currently Pres.; USSR People's Deputy 1989–91; Chair. Sub cttee on Humanitarian, Scientific and Cultural Co-operation, Cttee on Foreign Affairs 1989–91; political observer Literaturnaya Gazeta 1983–90, Ed.-in-Chief 1990–91; Chair. of Public Comm. for Int. Co-operation on Humanitarian Problems and Human Rights 1987–90; Dir Public Consultative Council to Chair. of State Duma 1993–96; Chief Scientific Researcher Inst. of State and Law 1992–; Visiting Prof. Heidelberg Univ. 1988, Harvard Univ. 1992, Oxford Univ. 1993; Pres. Euro-Asian Fund for Humanitarian Co-operation 1996–, Int. League for Defence of Culture; Chair., Scientific Council on Politology, Pres. Russian Acad. of Sciences 1995–; mem. Acad. of National Sciences 1993, Acad. of Socio-Political Sciences 1996. *Publications include:* Mao Zedong (biography) 1976, The Modern State and Politics 1978, The Legend of Machiavelli 1987, New Thinking 1988, Leaders and Advisers 1990, Khrushchev and the First Russian Spring 1992, The End of the Red Empire 1993, Russian Sovereigns–Age of the Reformation 1996. *Honours:* Italian Senate Prize 1988. *Address:* Institute of State and Law, Znamenka str. 10, 119841 Moscow, Russia (office); Novovagankovsky per. 22, Apt 90, 123022 Moscow, Russia (home). *Telephone:* (495) 291-88-16 (office); (495) 291-85-06 (home). *Fax:* (495) 291-87-56 (office). *E-mail:* isl-ran@rinet.ru (office).

BURLEIGH, Michael Christopher Bennet, BA, PhD, FRHistS; British historian and journalist; b. 3 April 1955, London, England; m. Linden Mary Brownbridge 1990. *Education:* Univ. Coll. London, Bedford Coll., London. *Career:* Weston Jr Research Fellow, New Coll., Oxford 1984–87; British Acad. Postdoctoral Fellow, Queen Mary Coll. 1987–88; Lecturer, LSE 1988–93, Reader in Int. History 1993–95; Distinguished Research Prof. in Modern European History, Univ. of Cardiff 1995–2000; Raoul Wallenburg Visiting Prof. of Human Rights, Rutgers Univ. 1999–2000; William R. Kenan Prof. of History, Washington and Lee Univ. 2000. *Television:* writer and presenter, Dark Enlightenment (More 4). *Publications:* Prussian Society and the German Order 1984, Germany Turns Eastwards: A Study of 'Ostforschung' in the Third Reich 1988, The Racial State: Germany 1933–1945 1991, Death and Deliverance: 'Euthanasia' in Germany 1994, Confronting the Nazi Past: New Debates on Modern German History (ed.) 1996, Ethics and Extermination: Reflections on Nazi Genocide 1997, The Third Reich: A New History 2000, Earthly Powers: The Conflict Between Religion and Politics from the French Revolution to the Great War 2005, Sacred Causes: Politics and Religion from the European Dictators to Al-Qaeda 2006. *Honours:* BFI Award for Archival Achievement 1992, New York Film and TV Festival Bronze Medal 1993, Samuel Johnson Prize for non-fictions 2001. *Address:* c/o HarperCollins Publishers, 77–85 Fulham Palace Road, Hammersmith, London, W6 8JB, England.

BURLEY, William John; British writer; b. 1 Aug. 1914, Falmouth, Cornwall, England; m. Muriel Wolsey 1938, two s. *Education:* Balliol College, Oxford. *Career:* mem. Authors Copyright and Lending Society; CWA; South West Writers. *Publications:* A Taste of Power, 1966; Three Toed Pussey, 1968; Death in Willow Pattem, 1969; Guilt Edged, 1971; Death in a Salubrious Place, 1973; Wycliffe and the Schoolgirls, 1976; The Schoolmaster, 1977; Charles and Elizabeth, 1979; Wycliffe and the Beales, 1983; Wycliffe and the Four Jacks, 1985; Wycliffe and the Quiet Virgin, 1986; Wycliffe and the Windsor Blue, 1987; Wycliffe and the Tangled Web, 1988; Wycliffe and the Cycle of Death, 1989; Wycliffe and a Dead Flautist, 1991; Wycliffe and the Last Rites, 1992; Wycliffe and the Dunes Mystery, 1993; Wycliffe and the House of Fear, 1995; Wycliffe and the Redhead, 1997; Wycliffe and the Guild of Nine, 2000. Novels successfully adapted for television, fourth series.

BURN, Gordon, BA; British writer; b. 16 Jan. 1948, Newcastle upon Tyne. *Education:* Univ. of London. *Publications:* Somebody's Husband, Somebody's Son: The Story of Peter Sutcliffe 1984, Pocket Money 1986, Alma Cogan: A Novel 1991, Fullalove (novel) 1995, Happy Like Murderers 1998, On the Way to Work (with Damien Hirst) 2001, The North of England Home Service 2003, Best and Edwards (biog.); Contributions: The Guardian, The Observer. *Honours:* Hon. DLitt (Univ. of Plymouth) 1992; Whitbread First Novel Award 1991. *Literary Agent:* Aitken Alexander Associates Ltd, 18–21 Cavaye Place, London, SW10 9PT, England. *Telephone:* (20) 7373-8672. *Fax:* (20) 7373-6002. *E-mail:* reception@aitkenalexander.co.uk. *Website:* www.aitkenalexander.co.uk.

BURN, Michael Clive; British writer and poet; b. 11 Dec. 1912, London, England; m. Mary Walter 1947. *Education:* Winchester and New Coll., Oxford. *Career:* POW, Colditz 1944; staff The Times 1938–39; correspondent, Vienna, Budapest, Belgrade 1947–49; mem. Soc. of Authors. *Publications:* Yes Farewell 1946, The Modern Everyman 1948, Childhood at Oriol 1951, The Midnight Diary 1952, Poems to Mary 1953, The Flying Castle 1954, Mr Lyward's Answer 1956, The Trouble with Jake 1967, The Debatable Land 1970, Out on a Limb 1973, Open Day and Night 1978, Mary and Richard 1988, Turned Towards the Sun: An Autobiography 2003; contrib. articles and poems to Encounter, Guardian, TLS. *Honours:* Keats Poetry First Prize 1973. *Address:* Beudy Gwyn, Minffordd, Gwynedd, Wales. *Telephone:* (1766) 770395.

BURNET, Sir James William Alexander (Alastair), Kt; British journalist; b. 12 July 1928, Sheffield, Yorks.; s. of the late Alexander Burnet and Schonaid Burnet; m. Maureen Campbell Sinclair 1958. *Education:* The Leys School, Cambridge and Worcester Coll., Oxford. *Career:* Sub-Ed. and Leader Writer, Glasgow Herald 1951–58, Leader Writer, The Economist 1958–62; Political Ed., Independent Television News (ITN) 1963–64, with ITN 1976–91, Dir 1982–90, Assoc. Ed. ITN 1981–91; Ed. The Economist 1965–74; Ed. Daily Express 1974–76; Contributor to TV current affairs programmes, This Week, Panorama, News at Ten, etc.; Ind. Dir Times Newspapers Holdings Ltd 1982–2002; mem. Council of the Banking Ombudsman 1985–96; Dir United Racecourses Ltd 1985–94. *Honours:* Hon. Vice-Pres. Inst. of Journalists 1990 Richard Dimbleby Award, BAFTA 1966, 1970, 1979, Royal Television Society Judges' Award 1981, Hall of Fame 1999. *Address:* 43 Hornton Court, Campden Hill Road, London, W8 7RU, England. *Telephone:* (20) 7937-7563.

BURNHAM, Sophy, BA; American writer and dramatist; b. 12 Dec. 1936, Baltimore, MD; m. David Bright Burnham 1960 (divorced 1984); two d. *Education:* Smith Coll. *Career:* Acquisitions Ed., David McKay Inc, 1971–73; Contributing Ed., Town & Country, 1975–80, New Art Examiner, 1985–86; Independent Consultant to various organizations, 1975–88; Adjunct Lecturer, George Mason University, 1982–83; Staff Writer, New Woman magazine, 1984–92; Staff Writer and Columnist, Museum & Arts/Washington, 1987–96; Exec. Dir, Fund for New American Plays, John F. Kennedy Center for the Performing Arts, Washington, DC, 1992–96; mem. Authors' Guild; Authors League of America; Cosmos Club. *Publications:* The Exhibits Speak, 1964; The Art Crowd, 1973; The Threat to Licensed Nuclear Facilities (ed.), 1975; Buccaneer (novel), 1977; The Landed Gentry, 1978; The Dogwalker (novel), 1979; A Book of Angels, 1990; Angel Letters, 1991; Revelations (novel), 1992; The President's Angel (novel), 1993; For Writers Only, 1994; The Ecstatic Journey: Walking the Mystical Path in Everyday Life, 1997; The Treasure of Montségur (novel), 2002; The Path of Prayer, 2002. Plays: Penelope, 1976; The Witch's Tale, 1978; The Study, 1979, revised edn as Snowstorms, 1993; Beauty and the Beast, 1979; The Nightingale, 1980; The Meaning of Life, 2001; Prometheus, 2002. Contributions: essays and articles in many periodicals; seminars, talks, workshops. *Honours:* Daughter of Mark Twain, Mark Twain Society, 1974; First Prize, Women's Theatre Award, Seattle, 1981; Helene Wurlitzer Foundation Grants, 1981, 1983, 1991; Virginia Duvall Mann Award, 1993. *E-mail:* sophyb@sophyburnham.com. *Website:* www.sophyburnham.com.

BURNS, Alan; British writer, dramatist and academic; b. 29 Dec. 1929, London, England; m. 1st Carol Lynn 1954; m. 2nd Jean Illien 1980; one s. two d. *Education:* Merchant Taylors' School, London. *Career:* C. Day-Lewis Writing Fellow, Woodberry Down School, 1973; Prof. of English, University of Minnesota, 1977–90; Writer-in-Residence, Associated Colleges of the Twin Cities, Minneapolis-St Paul, 1980; Writing Fellow, Bush Foundation of Minnesota, 1984–85; Lecturer, Lancaster University, 1993–96. *Publications:* Buster, 1961; Europe After the Rain, 1965; Celebrations, 1967; Babel, 1969; Dreamerika, 1972; The Angry Brigade, 1973; The Day Daddy Died, 1981; Revolutions of the Night, 1986; Art by Accident, 1997. Plays: Palach, 1970; To Deprave and Corrupt, 1972; The Imagination on Trial, 1981. Contributions: journals and periodicals. *Honours:* Arts Council Maintenance Grant, 1967, and Bursaries, 1969, 1973. *Address:* Creative Writing Dept, Lancaster University, Lancaster LA1 4YN, England.

BURNS, James MacGregor; American political scientist, historian, academic and writer; b. 3 Aug. 1918, Melrose, Massachusetts; m. 1st Janet Rose Dismorr Thompson 1942 (divorced 1968); two s. two d.; m. 2nd Joan Simpson Meyers 1969 (divorced 1991). *Education:* BA, Williams College, 1939; Postgraduate Studies, National Institute of Public Affairs, 1939–40; MA, 1947, PhD, 1947, Harvard University; Postdoctoral Studies, LSE, 1949. *Career:* Faculty, 1941–47, Asst Prof., 1947–50, Assoc. Prof., 1950–53, Prof. of Political Science, 1953–88, Prof. Emeritus, 1988–, Williams College; Senior Scholar, Jepson School of Leadership, University of Richmond, 1990–93; Scholar-in-Residence, Center for Political Leadership and Participation, University of Maryland at College Park, 1993–; mem. American Civil Liberties Union; American Historical Asscn; American Legion; American

Philosophical Asscn; American Political Science Asscn, pres., 1975–76; International Society of Political Psychology, pres., 1982–83; New England Political Science Asscn, pres., 1960–61. *Publications:* Okinawa: The Last Battle (co-author), 1947; Congress on Trial: The Legislative Process and the Administrative State, 1949; Government by the People: The Dynamics of American National Government and Local Government (with Jack Walter Peltason and Thomas E. Cronin), 1952; Roosevelt: The Lion and the Fox, 1956; Functions and Policies of American Government (with Jack Walter Peltason), 1958; John Kennedy: A Political Profile, 1960; The Deadlock of Democracy: Four-Party Politics in America, 1963; Presidential Government: The Crucible of Leadership, 1966; Roosevelt: The Soldier of Freedom, 1970; Uncommon Sense, 1972; Edward Kennedy and the Camelot Legacy, 1976; State and Local Politics: Government by the People, 1976; Leadership, 1978; The American Experiment: Vol. I, The Vineyard of Liberty, 1982, Vol. II, The Workshop of Democracy, 1985, Vol. III, The Crosswinds of Freedom, 1989; The Power to Lead: The Crisis of the American Presidency, 1984; Cobblestone Leadership: Majority Rule, Minority Power (with L. Marvin Overby), 1990; A People's Charter: The Pursuit of Rights in America (with Stewart Burns), 1991; Dead Centre: Clinton-Gore Leadership and the Perils of Moderation (with Georgia Sorenson), 2000; The 3 Roosevelt's: Patrician Leaders Who Transformed America, 2001; Running Alone: Presidential Leadership JFK to Bush II (with Susan Dunn) 2006. *Honours:* Tamiment Institute Award for Best Biography, 1956; Woodrow Wilson Prize, 1957; Pulitzer Prize in History, 1971; National Book Award, 1971; Francis Parkman Prize, Society of American Historians, 1971; Sarah Josepha Hale Award, 1979; Christopher Awards, 1983, 1990; Harold D. Lassell Award, 1984; Robert F. Kennedy Book Award, 1990; Rollo May Award in Humanistic Services, 1994. *Address:* Highgate Barn, High Mowing, Bee Hill Road, Williamstown, MA 01267, USA. *Telephone:* (413) 458-8607.

BURNS, Jim, BA; British writer and poet; b. 19 Feb. 1936, Preston, Lancashire. *Education:* Bolton Inst. of Tech. *Career:* Ed., Move 1964–68, Palantir 1976–83; Jazz Ed., Beat Scene 1990–. *Publications:* A Single Flower 1972, The Goldfish Speaks from Beyond the Grave 1976, Fred Engels in Woolworth's 1977, Internal Memorandum 1982, Out of the Past: Selected Poems 1961–1986 1987, Confessions of an Old Believer 1996, The Five Senses 1999, As Good a Reason as Any 1999, Beats, Bohemians and Intellectuals 2000, Take it Easy 2003, Short Statements 2006, Laying Something Down 2007; contrib. to London Magazine, Stand, Ambit, Jazz Journal, Critical Survey, The Guardian, New Statesman, Tribune, New Society, Penniless Press, Prop, Verse. *Address:* 11 Gatley Green, Gatley, Cheadle, Cheshire SK8 4NF, England. *Telephone:* (161) 428-7996 (home).

BURNS, John Fisher; British journalist; *Chief of Bureau for Pakistan and Afghanistan, Washington Post;* b. 4 Oct. 1944, Nottingham, England; s. of Air Cdre R. J. B. Burns and Dorothy Burns (née Fisher); m. 1st Jane Pequegnat 1972 (divorced); m. 2nd Jane Scott-Long 1991; two s. one d. *Education:* Stowe School, McGill Univ., Canada and Harvard Univ., USA. *Career:* Foreign Corresp. New York Times 1975–80, Soviet Union 1981–84, China 1984–86, Canada 1987–88, Afghanistan 1989–90, Persian Gulf 1990, Balkans 1991–94, India 1994–98, Special Corresp. for Islamic Affairs 1999–2002; Chief of Bureau for Pakistan and Afghanistan, Washington Post 2002–. *Honours:* Pulitzer Prize for Int. Reporting 1993 (co-winner for reporting from Bosnia), 1997 (for coverage of the Taliban regime in Afghanistan); George Polk Prize for Foreign Correspondence 1978, 1997. *Address:* The Washington Post, 1150 15th Street, NW, Washington, DC 20071, USA (office). *Telephone:* (202) 334-6000 (office). *Website:* www.washingtonpost.com (office).

BURNS, Ralph, MFA; American poet, editor and academic; b. 8 June 1949, Norman, OK; m. Candace Wilson Calhoun 1974; one s. *Education:* University of Montana. *Career:* Prof., University of Arkansas at Little Rock, 1985–; Ed., Crazyhorse magazine. *Publications:* Us, 1983; Any Given Day, 1985; Mozart's Starling, 1991; Swamp Candles, 1996. *Honours:* Two National Endowment for the Arts Fellowships; Iowa Poetry Prize, 1996. *Address:* 315 Linwood Court, Little Rock, AR 72205, USA.

BURNS, Rex Sehler, AB, MA, PhD; American academic and writer; *Emeritus Professor of English, University of Colorado at Denver;* b. 13 June 1935, San Diego, CA; m. Terry Fostvedt 1987 (divorced 1996); three s. one d. *Education:* Stanford Univ., Univ. of Minnesota. *Career:* Asst Prof., Central Missouri State Coll. 1965–68; Assoc. Prof. 1968–75, Prof. of English 1975–2000, Chair Dept of English 1996–99, Emeritus Prof. of English 2000–, Univ. of Colorado at Denver; Fulbright Lecturer, Aristotle Univ., Thessaloniki 1969–70, Universidad Católica, Buenos Aires 1974; book reviewer, Rocky Mountain News 1982–92; Sr Lecturer, Univ. of Kent, Canterbury 1992–93; mem. Int. Asscn of Crime Writers, MWA. *Publications:* fiction: The Alvarez Journal 1975, The Farnsworth Score 1977, Speak for the Dead 1978, Angle of Attack 1979, The Avenging Angel 1983, Strip Search 1984, Ground Money 1986, Suicide Season 1987, The Killing Zone 1988, Parts Unknown 1990, When Reason Sleeps 1991, Body Guard 1991, Endangered Species 1993, Blood Line 1995, The Leaning Land 1997; non-fiction: Success in America: The Yeoman Dream and the Industrial Revolution 1976, Crime Classics: The Mystery Story from Poe to the Present (ed., with Mary Rose Sullivan) 1990; contrib. to periodicals and anthologies, Starz Encore Mystery Channel. *Honours:* MWA Edgar Allan Poe Award 1976, Colorado Authors League Awards 1978, 1979, 1980, Univ. of Colorado System Pres.'s Teaching Scholar (lifetime title) 1990, Univ. Service Award.

BURNSIDE, John; Scottish poet and novelist; b. 19 March 1955, Dunfermline, Fife. *Publications:* Physical Diagnosis 1981, The Hoop 1988, Common Knowledge 1991, Feast Days 1992, The Myth of the Twin 1994, Swimming in the Flood 1995, The Dumb House 1997, A Normal Skin 1997, Sense Data 1998, The Mercy Boys 1999, Love for Love 2000, Burning Elvis 2000, The Asylum Dance 2000, The Locust Room 2001, The Light Trap 2002, The Forest of Beguilement 2003, The Shifting Stars 2003, Antimony 2003, The Good Neighbour 2005, A Lie About My Father 2006, Selected Poems 2006, The Devil's Footprints (novel) 2007, Gift Songs 2007; contrib. to newspapers, journals and periodicals. *Honours:* Scottish Arts Council Book Awards 1988, 1991, Geoffrey Faber Memorial Prize 1994, Whitbread Prize for Poetry 2000. *Address:* c/o Jonathon Cape, 20 Vauxhall Bridge Road, London, SW1V 2SA, England (office).

BURRINGTON, Ernest; British newspaper executive; b. 13 Dec. 1926, s. of the late Harold Burrington and of Laura Burrington; m. Nancy Crossley 1950; one s. one d. *Career:* reporter, Oldham Chronicle 1941–44, reporter and sub-ed. 1947–49; mil. service 1945–47; sub-ed. Bristol Evening World 1950; sub-ed. Daily Herald, Manchester 1950, night ed. 1955, London night 1957; night ed. IPC Sun 1964, Asst ed. 1965; Asst ed. and night News Int. Sun 1969; deputy night ed. Daily Mirror 1970; Deputy Ed. Sunday People 1971, Assoc. Ed. 1972; Ed. The People 1985–88, 1989–90; Dir Mirror Group Newspapers 1985–92, Deputy Chair. and Asst Publr 1988–91, Man. Dir 1989–91, Chair. 1991–92; Chair. Syndication Int. 1989–92; Deputy Chair. Mirror Publishing Co. 1989–91; Dir Mirror Group Magazine and Newsday Ltd 1989–92, Legionstyle Ltd 1991–92, Mirror Colour Print Ltd 1991–92; Dir (non-exec.) Sunday Correspondent 1990, The European 1990–91, IQ Newsgraphics 1990–92, Sygma Picture Agency, Paris 1990–91; Deputy Publr Globe Communications, Montreal, Canada 1993–95, Exec. Vice-Pres. and Assoc. Publr 1995–96; Pres. Atlantic Media 1996–98; Consultant Head of Marketing Harveys PLC, UK 1998–2000; mem. Council Nat. Press Asscn 1988–92, Int. Press Inst. British Exec. 1988–92; Trustee Int. Centre for Child Studies 1986–90; Life mem. NUJ 1960–. *Honours:* Hon. Life mem. NUJ 1996; Hon. Red Devil (Manchester United Football Club) 1985. *Address:* 17499 Tiffany Trace Drive, Boca Raton, FL 33487, USA; South Hall, Dene Park, Shipbourne Road, Tonbridge, TN11 9NS, England. *Telephone:* (561) 995-9897 (USA); (1732) 368517 (England). *Fax:* (561) 995-9897 (USA); (1732) 368517 (England). *E-mail:* burringtone@aol.com (home).

BURROW, John Anthony, MA, FBA; British academic and writer; b. 1932, Loughton. *Education:* Christ Church, Oxford. *Career:* Fellow, Jesus Coll., Oxford 1961–75; Winterstoke Prof., Univ. of Bristol 1976–98. *Publications:* A Reading of Sir Gawain and the Green Knight, 1965; Geoffrey Chaucer: A Critical Anthology, 1969; Ricardian Poetry: Chaucer, Gower Langland and the Gawain Poet, 1971; Sir Gawain and the Green Knight, 1972; English Verse 1300–1500, 1977; Medieval Writers and Their Work, 1982; Essays on Medieval Literature, 1984; The Ages of Man, 1986; A Book of Middle English, 1992; Langlands Fictions, 1993; Thomas Hoccleve, 1994; Thomas Hoccleve's Complaint and Dialogue, 1999; The Gawain-Poet, 2001; Gestures and Looks in Medieval Narrative, 2002. *Address:* 9 The Polygon, Clifton, Bristol, BS8 4PW England.

BURROW, John Wyon, MA, PhD, FBA, FRHistS; British historian and academic; *Emeritus Fellow, Balliol College, University of Oxford*; b. 4 June 1935, Southsea; s. of Charles Burrow and Alice Burrow (née Vosper); m. Diane Dunnington 1958; one s. one d. *Education:* Exeter School and Christ's Coll., Cambridge. *Career:* Research Fellow, Christ's Coll. Cambridge 1959–62; Fellow and Dir of Studies in History, Downing Coll. Cambridge 1962–65; Reader, School of European Studies, Univ. of E Anglia 1965–69; Reader in History, Univ. of Sussex 1969–82, Prof. of Intellectual History 1982–95; Visiting Fellow All Souls Coll. Oxford Univ. 1994–95, Prof. of European Thought and Fellow of Balliol Coll. 1995–2000, Emer. Fellow 2001–; Research Prof. of History, Univ. of Sussex 2000–; Visiting Prof. Univ. of Calif. Berkeley 1981; Visiting Fellow, History of Ideas Unit, ANU 1983; Carlyle Lecturer, Univ. of Oxford 1985; Ed. History of European Ideas 1996–2006; Distinguished Visiting Prof., Ben Gurion Univ. of the Negev 1998; delivered Gauss Seminars, Princeton Univ. 1988. *Publications:* Evolution and Society 1966, A Liberal Descent 1981, That Noble Science of Politics (with S. Collini and D. Winch) 1983, Gibbon 1985, Whigs and Liberals 1988, The Crisis of Reason 2000. *Honours:* Hon. Dr Political Sciences (Bologna) 1988; Wolfson Prize for History 1981. *Address:* Balliol College, Oxford, OX1 3BJ; 22 Bridge Street, Witney, Oxon. OX18 2HY, England (home). *Telephone:* (1993) 201396.

BURROWAY, Janet Gay, BA, MA; American academic, writer and poet; *Robert O. Lawson Distinguished Professor Emerita, Florida State University*; b. 21 Sept. 1936, Tucson, AZ; d. of Paul M. Burroway and Alma May Burroway (née Milner); m. 1st Walter Eysselinck 1961 (divorced 1973); two s.; m. 2nd William Dean Humphries 1978 (divorced 1981); m. 3rd Peter Ruppert 1993; one step-d. *Education:* Univ. of Arizona, Barnard Coll., Univ. of Cambridge, UK, Yale School of Drama. *Career:* Instructor, Harpur Coll., Binghamton, New York, 1961–62; Lecturer, Univ. of Sussex, UK 1965–70; Assoc. Prof., Florida State Univ. 1972–77, Prof. 1977–, MacKenzie Prof. of English 1989–95, Robert O. Lawson Distinguished Prof. 1995–2002, Robert O. Lawson Distinguished Prof. Emer. 2002–; fiction reviewer, Philadelphia Enquirer 1986–90; reviewer, New York Times Book Review 1991–; essay-columnist, New Letters: A Magazine of Writing and Art 1994–; mem. Associated Writing Programs, Authors' Guild. *Dance:* texts for dance: Dadadata, Text/tiles, The Empty Dress, Quiltings (all Florida State Univ.) 1995–2000. *Plays:* Medea With Child 1997, Sweepstakes 1999, Parts of Speech 2004. *Radio:* adaptation of Opening Nights for NPR 1996. *Television:* The Beauty Operators (Thames Television) 1970, Hoddinott Veiling (ATV Network TV; UK entry in the 1970 Monte Carlo Festival) 1970. *Publications:* fiction: Descend Again 1960, The Dancer From the Dance 1965, Eyes 1966, The Buzzards 1969, The Truck on the Track 1970, The Giant Jam Sandwich 1972, Raw Silk 1977, Opening Nights 1985, Cutting Stone 1992; poetry: But to the Season 1961, Material Goods 1980; other: Writing Fiction: A Guide to Narrative Craft 1982, Embalming Mom (essays) 2002, Imaginative Writing: The Elements of Craft 2002, From Where You Dream: The Process of Writing Fiction (ed.); contribs to numerous journals and periodicals. *Honours:* Nat. Endowment for the Arts Fellowship 1976, Yaddo Residency Fellowships 1985, 1987, Lila Wallace-Reader's Digest Fellow 1993–94, Carolyn Benton Cockefaire Distinguished Writer-in-Residence, Univ. of Missouri 1995, Woodrow Wilson Visiting Fellow, Furman Univ., Greenville, S Carolina 1995, Visiting Writer, Erskine Coll., Due West, S Carolina 1997, Drury Coll., Springfield, Ill. 1999. *Address:* 240 De Soto Street, Tallahassee, FL 32303, USA; 59 Carlton Mansions, Randolph Avenue, London, W9 1NR, England. *Telephone:* (850) 222-8272 (Florida). *Fax:* (850) 222-8272 (Florida). *E-mail:* jburroway@english.fsu.edu (office). *Website:* www.janetburroway.com.

BURTON, Anthony George Graham; British writer and broadcaster; b. 24 Dec. 1934, Thornaby, England; m. 28 March 1959; two s. one d. *Career:* mem. Outdoor Writers' Guild. *Publications:* A Programmed Guide to Office Warfare 1969, The Jones Report 1970, The Canal Builders 1972, The Reluctant Musketeer 1973, Canals in Colour 1974, Remains of a Revolution 1975, The Master Idol 1975, The Miners 1976, The Navigators 1976, Josiah Wedgwood 1976, Canal 1976, Back Door Britain 1977, A Place to Stand 1977, Industrial Archaeological Sites of Britain 1977, The Green Bag Travellers 1978, The Past At Work 1980, The Rainhill Story 1980, The Past Afloat 1982, The Changing River 1982, The Shell Book of Curious Britain 1982, The National Trust Guide to Our Industrial Past 1983, The Waterways of Britain 1983, The Rise and Fall of King Cotton 1984, Walking the Line 1985, Wilderness Britain 1985, Britain's Light Railways 1985, The Shell Book of Undiscovered Britain and Ireland 1986, Britain Revisited 1986, Landscape Detective 1986, Opening Time 1987, Steaming Through Britain 1987, Walk the South Downs 1988, Walking Through History 1988, The Great Days of the Canals 1989, Cityscapes 1990, Astonishing Britain 1990, Slow Roads 1991, The Railway Builders 1992, Canal Mania 1993, The Grand Union Canal Walk 1993, The Railway Empire 1994, The Rise and Fall of British Shipbuilding 1994, The Cotswold Way 1995, The Dales Way 1995, The West Highland Way 1996, The Southern Upland Way 1997, William Cobbett: Englishman 1997, The Wye Valley Walk 1998, The Caledonian Canal 1998, Best Foot Forward 1998, The Cumbria Way 1999, The Wessex Ridgeway 1999, Thomas Telford 1999, Weekend Walks: Dartmoor and Exmoor 2000, Weekend Walks: The Yorkshire Dales 2000, Traction Engines 2000, Richard Trevithick 2000, The Orient Express 2001, Weekend Walks: The Peak District 2001, The Anatomy of Canals: The Early Years 2001, The Daily Telegraph Guide to Britain's Working Past 2002, The Anatomy of Canals: The Mania Years 2002, Daily Telegraph Guide to Britain's Maritime Past 2003, Hadrian's Wall Path 2003, The Anatomy of Canals: Decline & Renewal 2003, On the Rails 2004, The Ridgeway 2005. *Literary Agent:* Sara Menguc, 4 Hatch Place, Kingston upon Thames, KT2 5NB, England. *Address:* 31 Lansdown, Stroud, Gloucestershire, GL5 1BG, England (home). *Fax:* (1453) 751541 (office). *E-mail:* tony.pip@btinternet.com (office).

BURTON, Gabrielle, BA, MFA; American writer; b. 21 Feb. 1939, Lansing, MI; m. Roger V. Burton 1962; five d. *Education:* Marygrove Coll., Michigan, American Film Inst., Los Angeles. *Career:* teacher, Fiction in the Schools, Writers in Educ. Project, New York 1985; various prose readings and workshops; Equinoxe Fellow, Bordeaux, France 2000. *Publications:* I'm Running Away From Home But I'm Not Allowed to Cross the Street 1972, Heartbreak Hotel 1986, Manna From Heaven (screenplay, filmed, DVD 2005) 2000; contribs to numerous publs. *Honours:* MacDowell Colony Fellowships 1982, 1987, 1989, Yaddo Fellowship 1983, Maxwell Perkins Prize 1986, Great Lakes Colleges Asscn Award 1987, Bernard De Voto Fellow in Non-Fiction, Bread Loaf Writers' Conf. 1994, Mary Pickford Foundation Award for First Year Screenwriter 1996, First Prize, Austin Film Festival Screenwriting Contest 2000, Nicholl Fellow 2000. *Address:* 29 Paloma Avenue, Venice, CA 90291, USA. *Telephone:* (310) 714-1739.

BURTON, Tim; American film director and screenwriter; b. 25 Aug. 1958, Burbank, Calif.; pnr Helena Bonham Carter; one s. *Education:* Calif. Arts Inst. *Career:* began career as animator, Walt Disney Studios (projects included The Fox and the Hound and The Black Cauldron). *Films as director:* Vincent (also animator) 1982, Luau 1982, Hansel and Gretel (TV) 1982, Frankenweenie (short, for Disney) 1984, Pee-Wee's Big Adventure 1985, Alfred Hitchcock Presents (TV episode, The Jar) 1985, Beetlejuice 1988, Batman 1989, Edward Scissorhands (also prod.) 1991, Batman Returns (also prod.) 1992, Ed Wood (also prod.) 1994, Mars Attacks! (also prod.) 1996, Sleepy Hollow 1999, Planet of the Apes 2001, Big Fish 2003, Charlie and the Chocolate Factory 2005, Corpse Bride (also prod.) 2005. *Films as producer:* Beetlejuice (TV series) 1993, Family Dog (TV series) 1993, The Nightmare Before Christmas 1993, Cabin Boy 1994, Batman Forever 1996, James and the Giant Peach 1996, Lost in Oz (TV series) 2000. *Film screenplays:* The Island of Doctor Agor 1971, Stalk of the Celery 1979, Vincent 1982, Luau 1982, Beetlejuice (story) 1988, (TV series creator) 1989, Edward Scissorhands (story) 1990, The Nightmare

Before Christmas (story) 1993, Lost in Oz (TV pilot episode story) 2000, Point Blank (TV series) 2002. *Publications:* My Art and Films 1993, The Melancholy Death of Oyster Boy and Other Stories 1997, Burton on Burton 2000; various film tie-in books. *Honours:* short-length film awards include two from Chicago Film Festival. *Literary Agent:* Chapman, Bird & Grey, 1990 South Bundy Drive, Suite 200, Los Angeles, CA 90025, USA. *Website:* www.timburton.com.

BUSBY, F. M., BSc, BScEE; American writer; b. 11 March 1921, Indianapolis, IN; m. Elinor Doub 1954; one d. *Education:* Washington State Univ. *Career:* mem. SFWA (vice-pres. 1974–76), Spectator Amateur Press Soc. *Publications:* Cage a Man 1973, The Proud Enemy 1975, Rissa Kerguelen 1976, The Long View 1976, All These Earths 1978, The Demu Trilogy 1980, Zelde M'tana 1980, Star Rebel 1984, The Alien Debt 1984, Rebel's Quest 1985, Rebels' Seed 1986, Getting Home (short stories) 1987, The Breeds of Man 1988, Slow Freight 1991, The Singularity Project 1993, Islands of Tomorrow 1994, Arrow from Earth 1995, The Triad Worlds 1996; contrib. approximately 45 shorter works in anthologies and magazines. *Address:* 2852 14th Avenue W, Seattle, WA 98119, USA (home). *E-mail:* fmbusby001@aol.com (home).

BUSBY, Roger Charles; British writer and public relations officer; b. 24 July 1941, Leicester, England. *Education:* Certificate in Journalism, University of Aston, Birmingham. *Career:* Journalist, Caters News Agency, Birmingham, 1959–66; Journalist, Birmingham Evening Mail, 1966–73; Head of Public Relations, Devon & Cornwall Police, 1973–; mem. CWA; Institute of Public Relations; National Union of Journalists. *Publications:* Main Line Kill, 1968; Robbery Blue, 1969; The Frighteners, 1970; Deadlock, 1971; A Reasonable Man, 1972; Pattern of Violence, 1973; New Face in Hell, 1976; Garvey's Code, 1978; Fading Blue, 1984; The Hunter, 1986; Snow Man, 1987; Crackhot, 1990; High Jump, 1992. *Address:* Sunnymoor, Bridford, Nr Exeter, Devon, England.

BUSH, Duncan Eric, BA, DPhil; British poet, writer and teacher; *Editor, The Amsterdam Review;* b. 6 April 1946, Cardiff, Wales; m. Annette Jane Weaver 1981; two s. *Education:* Univ. of Warwick, Duke Univ., USA, Wadham Coll., Oxford. *Career:* European Ed. The Kansas Quarterly and Arkansas Review; writing tutor with various insts; Co-founder and Ed. The Amsterdam Review 2004–; mem. Welsh Acad., Soc. of Authors. *Publications:* Aquarium 1983, Salt 1985, On Censorship (ed.) 1985, Black Faces, Red Mouths 1986, The Genre of Silence 1987, Glass Shot 1991, Masks 1994, The Hook 1997, Midway 1998; contrib. to BBC and periodicals. *Honours:* Eric Gregory Award for Poetry 1978, Barbara Campion Memorial Award for Poetry 1982, Welsh Arts Council Prizes for Poetry, Arts Council of Wales Book of the Year 1995. *Address:* Godre Waun Oleu, Brecon Road, Ynyswen, Penycae, Powys, SA9 1YY, Wales (office). *Telephone:* (1639) 730652 (office). *E-mail:* dcolophon@excite.com (office).

BUSH, Ronald, BA, PhD; American academic and writer; *Drue Heinz Professor of American Literature, Oxford University;* b. 16 June 1946, Philadelphia, Pa; m. Marilyn Wolin 1969; one s. *Education:* Univ. of Pennsylvania, Univ. of Cambridge, UK, Princeton Univ. *Career:* Asst to Assoc. Prof., Harvard Univ. 1974–82; Assoc. Prof. 1982–85, Prof. 1985–97, Calif. Inst. of Tech.; Visiting Fellow, Exeter Coll., Oxford 1994–95; Drue Heinz Prof. of American Literature, Univ. of Oxford, 1997–; Visiting Fellow, Program in American Civilization, Harvard Univ. 2004. *Publications:* The Genesis of Ezra Pound's Cantos 1976, T. S. Eliot: A Study in Character and Style 1983, T. S. Eliot: The Modernist in History (ed.) 1991, Prehistories of the Future: The Primitivist Project and the Culture of Modernism (co-ed. with Elazar Barkan) 1995, Claiming the Stones/Naming the Bones: Cultural Property and the Negotiation of National and Ethnic Identity (co-ed. with Elazar Barken) 2003; contribs to scholarly books and journals. *Honours:* Nat. Endowment for the Humanities Fellowships 1977–78, 1992–93, AHRB Research Award 2003–04. *Address:* St John's College, Oxford, OX1 3JP, England (office). *Telephone:* (1865) 277300. *E-mail:* ron.bush@ell.ox.ac.uk (office).

BUSHNELL, Candace; American writer; b. 1959, Glastonbury, CT; m. Charles Askegard 2002. *Education:* Rice Univ., TX and New York Univ. *Career:* wrote 'Sex and the City' column, New York Observer 1994–96 (made into TV series); host, TV programme Sex, Lives and Video Clips (VH-1) 1997. *Publications:* novels: Sex and the City 1997, Four Blondes 2000, Trading Up 2003, Lipstick Jungle 2005. *Address:* c/o Hyperion Editorial Department, 77 W 66th Street, 11th Floor, New York, NY 10023, USA. *E-mail:* beth.dickey@abc.com. *Website:* www.candacebushnell.com.

BUTALA, Sharon Annette, OC, BA, BEd; Canadian writer; b. 24 Aug. 1940, Nipawin, Sask.; d. of Achille Antoine Le Blanc and Margaret Amy Graham; m. Peter Butala 1976; one s. *Education:* Univ. of Saskatchewan. *Career:* mem. PEN Canada, Saskatchewan Writers' Guild, Writers' Union of Canada. *Publications:* fiction: Country of the Heart (novel) 1984, Queen of the Headaches (short stories) 1985, The Gates of the Sun (novel) 1986, Luna (novel) 1988, Fever (short stories) 1990, Upstream: Le Pays d'en Haut (autobiographical novel) 1991, The Fourth Archangel (novel) 1992, The Garden of Eden 1998, Real Life 2002; non-fiction: Harvest 1992, The Perfection of the Morning (autobiog.) 1994, Coyote's Morning Cry 1995, Wild Stone Heart 2000, Old Man on his Back 2002, Lilac Moon: Dreaming of the Real West 2005; contrib. to periodicals. *Honours:* Hon. LLD (Univ. of Regina) 2000; Hon. DLitt (Univ. of Saskatchewan) 2004; Canada 125 Commemorative Medal 1993, Saskatchewan Book Award for Non-Fiction 1994, 2005, Marian Engel Award 1998, Queen's Golden Jubliee Medal 2002, Saskatchewan Centennial Medal 2005. *Address:* c/o The Writers' Union of

Canada, 90 Richmond Street E, Suite 200, Toronto, ON M5C 1P1, Canada. *Telephone:* (306) 295-3810.

BUTLER, Gwendoline Williams, (Jennie Melville), MA; British author; b. 19 Aug. 1922, London, England; m. Lionel Butler 1949 (deceased), one d. *Education:* Lady Margaret Hall, Oxford. *Career:* historical crime critic, Crime Time Magazine 1999–2002; mem. CWA panel, Reform Club, Detection Club (hon. sec. 1992–95), MWA. *Publications:* Receipt for Murder, 1956; Dead in a Row, 1957; The Dull Dead, 1958; The Murdering Kind, 1958; The Interloper, 1959; Death Lives Next Door, US edn as Dine and Be Dead, 1960; Make Me a Murderer, 1961; Coffin on the Water, 1962; Coffin in Oxford, 1962; Coffin for Baby, 1963; Coffin Waiting, 1963; Coffin in Malta, 1964; A Nameless Coffin, 1966; Coffin Following, 1968; Coffin's Dark Number, 1969; A Coffin form the Past, 1970; A Coffin for Pandora, 1973, US edn as Olivia, 1974; A Coffin for the Canary, US edn as Sarsen Place, 1974; The Vesey Inheritance, 1975; Brides of Friedberg, US edn as Meadowsweet, 1977; The Red Staircase, 1979; Albion Walk, 1982; Coffin on the Water, 1986; Coffin in Fashion, 1987; Coffin Underground, 1988; Coffin in the Black Museum, 1989; Coffin and the Paper Man, 1990; Coffin the Museum of Crime, 1990; Coffin on Murder Street, 1992; Cracking Open a Coffin, 1992; A Coffin for Charley, 1993; The Coffin Tree, 1994; A Dark Coffin, 1995; A Double Coffin, 1996; Butterfly, 1996; Let There Be Love, 1997; Coffin's Game, 1997; A Grave Coffin, 1998; Coffin's Ghost, 1999; The King Cried Murder, 2000; A Cold Coffin, 2000; Coffin Knows the Answer. As Jennie Melville: Come Home and Be Killed, 1962; Burning Is a Substitute for Loving, 1963; Murderers' Houses, 1964; There Lies Your Love, 1965; Nell Alone, 1966; A Different Kind of Summer, 1967; The Hunter in the Shadows, 1969; A New Kind of Killer, An Old Kind of Death, 1970, US edn as A New Kind of Killer, 1971; Ironwood, 1972; Nun's Castle, 1973; Raven's Forge, 1975; Dragon's Eye, 1976; Axwater, US edn as Tarot's Tower, 1978; Murder Has a Pretty Face, 1981; The Painted Castle, 1982; The Hand of Glass, 1983; Listen to the Children, 1986; Death in the Garden, 1987; Windsor Red, 1988; A Cure for Dying, 1989; Witching Murder, 1990; Footsteps in the Blood, 1990; Dead Set, 1992; Whoever Has the Heart, 1993; Baby Drop, 1994; The Morbid Kitchen, 1995; The Woman Who Was Not There, 1996; Revengeful Death, 1997; Stone Dead, 1998; Dead Again, 1999. *Honours:* Silver Dagger, CWA, 1973; Silver Rose Bowl, Romantic Novelists Asscn, 1981; Ellery Queen Short Story Award; Judge Ellis Peters Memorial Historical Crime Fiction Contest, 2000; FRSA.

BUTLER, Leo; British playwright; b. 1975, S Yorkshire, England. *Plays:* Made of Stone 2000, Redundant 2001, Devotion 2002, Lucky Dog 2004, The Early Bird 2006. *Honours:* George Devine Award 2001. *Literary Agent:* c/o A & C Black Publishers Ltd., 38 Soho Square, London, W1D 3HB, England. *Telephone:* (20) 7758-0200. *Fax:* (20) 7758-0222. *Website:* www.acblack.com.

BUTLER, Marilyn Speers, DPhil, FRSL, FRSA; British academic; b. (Marilyn S. Evans), 11 Feb. 1937, Kingston-upon-Thames, Surrey; d. of Trevor Evans and Margaret Evans (née Gribbin); m. David Edgeworth Butler 1962; three s. *Education:* Wimbledon High School, St Hilda's Coll. Oxford. *Career:* BBC trainee and producer 1960–62; Jr Research Fellow, St Hilda's Coll. Oxford 1970–73; Fellow and Tutor, St Hugh's Coll. Oxford 1973–86; King Edward VII Prof. of English Literature, Cambridge Univ. 1986–93; Fellow King's Coll. Cambridge 1987–93; Rector Exeter Coll., Oxford 1993–; Titular Prof. of English Language and Literature, Univ. of Oxford 1998–; British Acad. Reader 1982–85; Foreign mem. US Acad. of Arts and Sciences 1999; Hon. Fellow St Hilda's Coll. Oxford, St Hugh's Coll. Oxford, King's Coll. Cambridge. *Publications:* Maria Edgeworth: A Literary Biography 1972, Jane Austen and the War of Ideas 1975, Peacock Displayed 1979, Romantics, Rebels and Reactionaries 1981, Burke, Paine, Godwin and the Revolution Controversy (ed.) 1984, Collected Works of Wollstonecraft (Ed. with J. Todd) 1989, Edgeworth's Castle Rackrent and Ennui (ed.) 1992, Mary Shelley's Frankenstein (ed.) 1993, Jane Austen's Northanger Abbey (ed.) 1995, Collected Works of Edgeworth (ed. with M. Myers), 12 Vols, 1999. *Honours:* Hon. LittD (Leicester) 1992, (Birmingham) 1993, (Oxford Brookes) 1994, (Williams Coll., Mass) 1995, (Lancaster, Warwick, Surrey) 1997, (Kingston) 1998, (Open) 2000, (Roehampton) 2000. *Address:* 151 Woodstock Road, Oxford, OX2 7NA, England (home). *Telephone:* (1865) 558323 (home). *E-mail:* marilyn.butler@exeter.ox.ac.uk (home).

BUTLER, Robert Olen, BS, MA; American writer, screenwriter and academic; b. 20 Jan. 1945, Granite City, IL; m. 1st Carol Supplee 1968 (divorced 1972); m. 2nd Marylin Geller 1972 (divorced 1987); two s.; m. 3rd Maureen Donlan 1987 (divorced 1995); m. 4th Elizabeth Dewberry 1995. *Education:* Northwestern University, University of Iowa, New School for Social Research, New York. *Career:* Ed.-in-Chief, Energy User News, 1975–85; Prof., Master of Fine Arts in Creative Writing Program, McNeese State University, 1985–; Faculty, various summer writing conferences; mem. Writers Guild of America West. *Publications:* The Alleys of Eden, 1981; Sun Dogs, 1982; Countrymen of Bones, 1983; On Distant Ground, 1985; Wabash, 1987; The Deuce, 1989; A Good Scent from a Strange Mountain, 1992; They Whisper, 1994; Coffee, Cigarettes, and a Run in the Park, 1996; Tabloid Dreams, 1996; The Deep Green Sea, 1998. Other: several screenplays. Contributions: anthologies, newspapers, and journals. *Honours:* Charter Recipient, Tu Do Chinh Kien Award, Vietnam Veterans of America, 1987; Emily Clark Balch Award, Virginia Quarterly Review, 1991; Southern Review/Louisiana State University Prize for Short Fiction, 1992; Hon. Doctor of Humane Letters, McNeese State University, 1993; Notable Book Citation, American Library Asscn, 1993; Richard and Hinda Rosenthal Foundation

Award, American Acad. of Arts and Letters, 1993; Guggenheim Fellowship, 1993; Pulitzer Prize for Fiction, 1993; National Endowment for the Arts Fellowship, 1994; Lotos Club Award of Merit, 1996; William Peden Prize, Missouri Review, 1997; Author of the Year Award, Illinois Asscn of Teachers of English, 1997. *E-mail:* dewbutler@sprynet.com.

BUTLIN, Martin Richard Fletcher, CBE, MA, DLit, FBA; British museum curator and art historian; b. 7 June 1929, Birmingham; s. of K. R. Butlin and Helen M. Butlin (née Fletcher); m. Frances C. Chodzko 1969. *Education:* Trinity Coll., Cambridge and Courtauld Inst. of Art., Univ. of London. *Career:* Asst Keeper, Tate Gallery, London 1955–67, Keeper of the Historic British Collection 1967–89; consultant to Christie's 1989–. *Publications:* A Catalogue of the Works of William Blake in the Tate Gallery 1957, 1971, 1990, Samuel Palmer's Sketchbook of 1824 1962, Turner Watercolours 1962, Turner (with Sir John Rothenstein) 1964, Tate Gallery Catalogues: The Modern British Paintings, Drawings and Sculpture (with Mary Chamot and Dennis Farr) 1964, The Later Works of J. M. W. Turner 1965, William Blake 1966, The Blake-Varley Sketchbook of 1819 1969, The Paintings of J. M. W. Turner (with E. Joll) 1977, 1984, The Paintings and Drawings of William Blake 1981, Aspects of British Painting 1550–1800 1988, Turner at Petworth (with Mollie Luther and Ian Warrell) 1989, The Oxford Companion to J. M. W. Turner ed. (with Evelyn Joll and Luke Herrmann) 2001; catalogues, articles, reviews etc. *Honours:* Mitchell Prize (jtly) 1978. *Address:* 74C Eccleston Square, London, SW1V 1PJ, England (home).

BUTLIN, Ron, MA, DipCDAE; British poet and writer; b. 17 Nov. 1949, Edinburgh, Scotland; m. Regula Staub 1993. *Education:* Univ. of Edinburgh. *Career:* Writer-in-Residence, Univ. of Edinburgh 1983, 1985, Midlothian Region 1990–91, Craigmillar Literary Trust 1997–98, Univ. of St Andrews 1998–, Univ. of Stirling 1993 (Examiner in Creative Writing 1997–); mem. Scottish Arts Council (mem. Literature Cttee 1995–96). *Libretti:* Faraway Pictures (children's opera) 2000, The Voice Inside (concerto, BBC Radio 3 commission) 2001, Good Angel, Bad Angel (opera, with Lyell Cresswell), Edward Harper's Voice of a City (SCO commission) 2006, Edward Harper's 2nd Symphony (SCO commission) 2006. *Publications:* Creature Tamed by Cruelty 1979, The Exquisite Instrument 1982, The Tilting Room 1984, Ragtime in Unfamiliar Bars 1985, The Sound of My Voice 1987, Faber Book of Twentieth Century Scottish Poetry 1992, Histories of Desire 1995, Night Visits 1997, When We Jump We Jump High! (ed.) 1998, Our Piece of Good Fortune 2002, Panther Book of Scottish Short Stories 2002, Vivaldi and the Number 3 2003, Without a Backward Glance: Selected Poems 2005, Belonging (novel) 2006, No More Angels (stories) 2007; contrib. to reviews, periodicals and journals. *Honours:* Writing Bursaries 1977, 1987, 1990, 1994, 2002, Scottish Arts Council Book Awards 1982, 1984, 1985, Scottish-Canadian Writing Fellow 1984, Poetry Book Soc. Recommendation 1985, Prix Mille Pages for Best Foreign Novel 2004, Prix Lucioles for Best Foreign Novel 2005. *Address:* 7W Newington Place, Edinburgh, EH9 1QT, Scotland (home). *Telephone:* (131) 667-0394 (home). *E-mail:* ronbutlin@blueyonder.co.uk (home).

BUTOR, Michel; French writer and lecturer; b. 14 Sept. 1926, Mons-en-Baroeul, Nord; s. of Emile Butor and Anne Brajeux; m. Marie-Josephe Mas 1958; four d. *Education:* Univ. of Paris. *Career:* teacher at Sens, France 1950, Minieh, Egypt 1950–51, Manchester, England 1951–53, Salonica, Greece 1954–55, Geneva, Switzerland 1956–57; Visiting Prof. Bryn Mawr and Middlebury, USA 1960, Buffalo, USA 1962, Evanston, USA 1965, Albuquerque, USA 1969–70, 1973–74, Nice and Geneva 1974–75; Assoc. Prof. Vincennes 1969, Nice 1970–73; Prof. of Modern French Literature, Geneva 1975–91; Reader Éditions Gallimard 1958–. *Publications:* novels: Passage de Milan 1954, L'emploi du temps 1956, La modification 1957, Degrés 1960, Intervalle 1973; essays: Le Génie du lieu 1958, Répertoire 1960, Histoire extraordinaire 1961, Mobile 1962, Réseau aérien 1963, Description de San Marco 1963, Les oeuvres d'art imaginaires chez Proust 1964, Répertoire II 1964, Portrait de l'artiste en jeune singe 1967, Répertoire III 1968, Essais sur les essais 1968, Les mots dans la peinture 1969, La rose des vents 1970, Le génie du lieu II 1971, Dialogue avec 33 variations de L. van Beethoven 1971, Répertoire IV 1974, Matière de rêves 1975, Second sous-sol 1976, Troisième dessous 1977, Boomerang 1978, Quadruple Fond 1981, Répertoire V 1982; poetry: Illustrations 1964, 6,801.000 litres d'eau par second 1965, Illustrations II 1969, Travaux d'approche 1972, Illustrations III 1973, Illustrations IV 1976, Envois 1980, Brassée d'Avril 1982, Exprès 1983, Herbier Lunaire 1984, Mille et un plis 1985, Le Retour du Boomerang 1988, Improvisations sur Flaubert 1991, Patience, Collation 1991, Transit A, Transit B 1993, Improvisations sur Michael Butor 1994, L'Utilité Poétique 1995, Le Japon depuis la France, un rêve à l'ancre 1995, Curriculum Vitae 1996 (jtly), Gyroscope 1996, Ici et là 1997, Improvisations sur Balzac 1998, Entretiens 1999, M. Butor par M. Butor 2003, Anthologie nomade 2004, L'Horticulteur itinérant 2004, Octogénaire 2006, Seize Lustres 2006, Oeuvres complètes I–IV 2006, V–VI 2007. *Honours:* Chevalier, Ordre nat. du Mérite, Ordre des Arts et des Lettres; Hon. PhD (Univ. of Mainz) 1995, (Univ. of Massachusetts) 1999, (Univ. of Thessaloniki) 2001; Prix Felix Féneon 1957, Prix Renaudot 1957, Grand prix de la critique littéraire 1960. *Address:* à l'Ecart, 216 Place de l'Eglise, 74380 Lucinges, France.

BUTTERWORTH, Jeremy (Jez); British writer, playwright and film director; b. 4 March 1969, London; m. Gilly Richardson. *Education:* Verulam School, St Albans, Univ. of Cambridge. *Films as director:* Mojo 1997, Birthday Girl 2001. *Plays:* Mojo 1995, Birthday Girl (with Tom Butterworth) 2001, The Night Heron 2002. *Honours:* George Dence Award for Most Promising Playwright 1995, Writers' Guild New Writer of the Year Award 1995, Evening Standard Award for Most Promising Playwright 1995, Olivier Award for Britain's Best Comedy 1995. *Literary Agent:* Curtis Brown Ltd, Haymarket House, 28–29 Haymarket, London, SW1Y 4SP, England. *Telephone:* (20) 7393-4400. *Fax:* (20) 7393-4401. *E-mail:* info@curtisbrown.co.uk. *Website:* www.curtisbrown.co.uk.

BUTTERWORTH, (David) Neil, BA, MA; British fmr composer, conductor, writer and broadcaster; b. 4 Sept. 1934, London; m. Anne Mary Barnes 1960; three d. *Education:* Univ. of London, Guildhall School of Music, London, Univ. of Nottingham. *Career:* Lecturer, Kingston Coll. of Tech. 1960–68; Head of Music Dept, Napier Coll., Edinburgh 1968–87; conductor Edinburgh Schools Choir 1968–72, Glasgow Orchestral Soc. 1975–83, 1989–2002, Edinburgh Chamber Orchestra 1983–85; music critic, Times Educational Supplement 1993–97; Winston Churchill Travelling Fellowship 1975; mem. Inc. Soc. of Musicians, Performing Right Soc., Scottish Soc. of Composers. *Compositions include:* two horn concertos, Overture Budapest, A Scott Cantata, Dunblane, In Memory of Auschwitz, Partita, Dances for Dalkeith, Count Dracula (opera), many songs and instrumental works. *Publications:* Haydn 1970, 400 Aural Training Exercises 1970, A Musical Quiz Book 1974, Dvořák 1978, A Dictionary of American Composers 1983, revised edn 2005, Aaron Copland 1984, 20th Century Sight-singing Exercises 1984, Sight-singing Exercises from the Masters 1984, Vaughan Williams 1989, Neglected Music 1991, The American Symphony 1998; contrib. to periodicals, including Classic CD, Classical Music, Musical Opinion, The Scotsman, The Herald. *Honours:* Hon. FLCM; Guildhall School of Music and Drama Conducting Prize 1961. *Address:* The Lodge, 42 E High Street, Greenlaw, Berwickshire, TD10 6UF, Scotland. *Telephone:* (1361) 810408 (home).

BUTTERWORTH, Nick; British children's writer and illustrator; b. 1946, Kingsbury, London; m.; two c. *Career:* worked as a typographic designer, printing dept, Nat. Children's Home; fmr graphic designer with agencies in London, later freelance; fmr TV presenter Rub-a-Dub-Tub (TV-AM); produced Upney Junction illustrated serial, Sunday Express magazine; created successful 'Percy the Park Keeper' series of children's books; numerous collaborations with illustrator, Mick Inkpen. *Publications include:* Windy Day at Upney Junction 1983, Monster at Upney Junction 1983, Invasion at Upney Junction 1983, Treasure Trove at Upney Junction 1983, The Gravedigger File 1983, The Nativity Play 1985, The House on the Rock 1986, The Lost Sheep 1986, The Precious Pearl 1986, The Two Sons 1986, Who Made... (series with Mick Inkpen) 1987–, Nice or Nasty: A Book of Opposites 1987, I Wonder... (series with Mick Inkpen) 1987–, Sports Day! 1988, The Fox's Story: Jesus is Born 1988, The Mouse's Story: Jesus and the Storm 1988, The Magpie's Story: Jesus and Zacchaeus 1988, The Cat's Story: Jesus at the Wedding 1988, Just Like Jasper 1989, The Ten Silver Coins 1989, The Good Stranger 1989, The Little Gate 1989, The Rich Farmer 1989, One Snowy Night 1989, The School Trip 1990, Wonderful Earth 1990, Amanda's Butterfly 1991, Field Day 1991, Jasper's Beanstalk 1992, My Dad is Awesome 1992, My Grandma is Wonderful 1992, Rescue Party 1993, The Secret Path 1994, My Mom is Excellent 1994, The Cross Rabbit 1995, The Fox's Hiccups 1995, A Year in Percy's Park 1995, The Badger's Bath 1996, The Hedgehog's Balloon 1996, Jill the Farmer and her Friends 1996, Jack the Carpenter and his Friends 1996, Thud! 1997, The Owl's Lesson 1997, One Warm Fox 1997, Jake in Trouble 1998, Learn with Percy: A-B-C 1998, Learn with Percy: 1-2-3 1998, Jingle Bells 1998, Percy's Bumpy Ride 1999, The Lost Acorns 2000, Q Pootle 5 2000, Owl Takes Charge 2000, Percy the Park Keeper and his Friends (series) 2001–, My Family 2002, Make a Wish 2002, Albert Le Blanc 2002, Q Pootle 5 in Space 2004, Whisperer 2004, Tiger 2006, Tiger in the Snow 2006, Animal Tales 2006. *Address:* c/o HarperCollins Childrens Books, 77–85 Fulham Palace Road, Hammersmith, London, W6 8JB, England.

BUTTROSE, Ita Clare, AO, OBE; Australian editor, broadcaster, writer and publishing executive; b. 17 Jan. 1942, Sydney; d. of Charles Oswald Buttrose and Mary Clare Buttrose (née Rodgers); m. 1st Alasdair MacDonald 1963 (divorced); m. 2nd Peter Sawyer 1979 (divorced); one s. one d. *Education:* Sacred Heart Convent, Rose Bay, Sydney and Dover Heights High School, Sydney. *Career:* joined Australian Consolidated Press Pty Ltd 1958, Dir 1974–81, Publr Women's Div. 1977–80; Founding Ed. Cleo 1972–75; Ed. Australian Women's Weekly 1975–76, Ed.-in-Chief 1976–77, columnist and feature writer 1998–; Sub-Ed. Woman's Own, UK 1967–69; Ed.-in-Chief The Daily Telegraph and The Sunday Telegraph, Sydney 1981–84; Dir News Ltd Australia 1981–84; Ed.-in-Chief The Sun-Herald 1988; Publishing Consultant, Woman's Day and Portfolio magazines 1983–88; Ed. Ita Magazine 1989–94; CEO Capricorn Publishing Pty Ltd 1988–94; Broadcaster Radio 2KY, 2UE, Sydney 1984–87, Radio 3UZ, Melbourne 1988–90; TV personality Beauty & the Beast Foxtel and Network TEN 1996–; Dir TV and Telecasters Pty Ltd 1991–93, Prudential Corpn Australia Ltd 1990–96; Dir Hope Town Special School Wyong Ltd 1990–; Chair. Nat. Advisory Cttee on AIDS (NACAIDS) 1984–88, Chair. AIDS Trust of Australia 1990–94; Convenor First Nat. Family Summit, Canberra; Communications Strategist, World Vision Australia 1995–97; Chair. Australian Services Nurses Nat. Memorial Fund Cttee 1997–99; Nat. Spokesperson Arthritis Foundation of Australia 1997–99, 2001–, Pres. 2003–; Dir Sydney Symphony Council 1996–, The Smith Family 1997, Prostate Cancer Foundation 2002–; Fellow, Australian Inst. of Co. Dirs, Autralian Inst. of Man.; Assoc. Fellow Professional Marketing Asscn; mem. Council Australian Nat. Art Gallery 1989–, Australian Soc. of Authors, Chief

Exec. Women; mem. Program Reference Group 2001, Australian Govt's Women Speak Conf.; Amb. Melbourne Museum 2001–; Patron Active Ageing Week 2004. *Publications include:* A Guide to Modern Etiquette 1985, Early Edition: My First Forty Years 1985, A Passionate Life 1998, A Word to the Wise 1999, What is Love? 2000, Motherguilt (co-author). *Honours:* honoured by UN for convening Australia's first Nat. Family Summit 1992, RSA Hartnett Medal (first woman recipient) 1992, Centenary Medal for service to Australian society in business leadership 2003, twice voted Australia's Most Admired Woman. *Address:* POB 648, Double Bay, NSW 1360, Australia. *Telephone:* (2) 9361-6636. *Fax:* (2) 9361-5757.

BUTTS, Anthony, BA, MA, MFA; American writer and poet; b. 28 July 1969, Detroit, MI. *Education:* Wayne State University, Western Michigan University, University of Missouri at Columbia. *Career:* co-host, Different Voices interview show (KOPN-FM Radio); mem. Conference on Christianity and Literature; assoc. mem. Acad. of American Poets. *Publications:* Fifth Season 1997, Evolution 1998.

BUZAN, Barry, BA, PhD, FBA, ACSS; British/Canadian academic, writer and editor; *Professor of International Relations, London School of Economics*; b. 28 April 1946, London; m. Deborah Skinner 1973. *Education:* Univ. of British Columbia, London School of Econs. *Career:* Research Fellow, Inst. of Int. Relations, Univ. of British Columbia 1973–75; Lecturer, Univ. of Warwick 1976–83, Sr Lecturer 1983–88, Reader, Dept of Int. Studies 1988–89, Prof., Dept of Politics and Int. Studies 1990–95; Dir Project on European Security, Copenhagen Peace Research Inst. 1988–2003; Ed. European Journal of International Relations 2004–; Research Prof. of Int. Studies, Univ. of Westminster 1995–2002; Olof Palme Visiting Prof., Sweden 1997–98; Prof. of Int. Relations, LSE 2002–; Hon. Prof., Univ. of Copenhagen 2005–. *Publications:* Seabed Politics 1976, Change and the Study of International Relations: The Evaded Dimension (ed. with R. J. Barry Jones) 1981, People, States, and Fear: The National Security Problem in International Relations 1983, second edn as An Agenda for International Security Studies in the Post-Cold War Era 1991, South Asian Insecurity and the Great Powers (co-author) 1986, An Introduction to Strategic Studies: Military Technology and International Relations 1987, The International Politics of Deterrence (ed.) 1987, The European Security Order Recast: Scenarios for the Post-Cold War Era (co-author) 1990, The Logic of Anarchy: Neorealism to Structural Realism (co-author) 1993, Identity, Migration and the New Security Agenda in Europe (co-author) 1993, The Mind Map Book (with T. Buzan) 1993, Security: A New Framework for Analysis (co-author) 1998, Anticipating the Future: Twenty Millennia of Human Progress (with G. Segal) 1998, The Arms Dynamic in World Politics (with E. Herring) 1998, International Systems in World History: Remaking the Study of International Relations (with R. Little) 2000, Regions and Powers: The Structure of International Security (with O. Waever) 2003, From International to World Society 2004, The United States and the Great Powers 2004; contrib. to many scholarly publications. *Honours:* Francis Deak Prize, American Journal of International Law 1982. *Address:* Department of International Relations, London School of Economics, Houghton Street, London, WC2A 2AE (office); Garden Flat, 17 Lambolle Road, London, NW3 4HS, England (home). *E-mail:* b.g.buzan@lse.ac.uk (office).

BYAM SHAW, Nicholas Glencairn; British publisher; b. 28 March 1934, London; s. of the late Lt-Commdr David Byam Shaw and Clarita Pamela Clarke; m. 1st Joan Elliott 1956 (divorced 1973); two s. one d.; m. 2nd Suzanne Filer (née Rastello) 1974; m. 3rd Constance Mary Wilson (née Clarke) 1987. *Education:* Royal Naval Coll., Dartmouth. *Career:* served RN, retiring with rank of Lt 1951–56; on staff of Collins (printers and publrs), Sales Man. 1956–64; joined Macmillan Publrs Ltd as Sales Man. 1964, Deputy Man. Dir 1968, Man. Dir 1970–90, Chair. 1990–97, Deputy Chair. 1998–99; Dir St Martin's Press 1980–99 (Deputy Chair. 1997–99), Pan Books Ltd 1983–99 (Chair. 1986–99), Gruppe Georg von Hotzbrinck, Stuttgart, Germany 1996–99; mem. British Council Publrs' Advisory Cttee, Byam Shaw School Council. *Address:* 9 Kensington Park Gardens, London, W11 3HB, England. *Telephone:* (20) 7221-4547.

BYATT, Dame Antonia Susan (A.S.), (Dame Antonia Duffy), DBE, BA, FRSL; British writer; b. 24 Aug. 1936, Sheffield, Yorkshire; d. of His Honour John F. Drabble, QC and the late Kathleen M. Bloor; sister of Margaret Drabble; m. 1st Ian Charles Rayner Byatt 1959 (divorced 1969); one s. (deceased) one d.; m. 2nd Peter John Duffy 1969; two d. *Education:* Sheffield High School, The Mount School, York, Newnham Coll., Cambridge, Bryn Mawr Coll., PA, USA and Somerville Coll., Oxford. *Career:* Extra-Mural Lecturer, Univ. of London 1962–71; Lecturer in Literature, Cen. School of Art and Design 1965–69;

Lecturer in English, Univ. Coll., London 1972–81, Sr Lecturer 1981–83; Assoc. Newnham Coll., Cambridge 1977–82; mem. BBC Social Effects of TV Advisory Group 1974–77; mem. Bd of Creative and Performing Arts 1985–87, Bd of British Council 1993–98; Kingman Cttee on English Language 1987–88; Man. Cttee Soc. of Authors 1984–88 (Chair. 1986–88); mem. Literature Advisory Panel of the British Council 1990–98; broadcaster, reviewer and judge of literary prizes; Fellow English Asscn. *Radio:* dramatisation of quartet of novels (BBC Radio) 2002. *Television:* profile on Scribbling (series, BBC 2) 2002. *Films:* Angels and Insects 1996, Possession 2002. *Publications:* fiction: The Shadow of the Sun 1964, The Game 1967, The Virgin in the Garden 1978, Still Life (PEN/Macmillan Silver Pen for Fiction 1986) 1985, Sugar and Other Stories 1987, Possession: A Romance (Booker Prize 1990, Irish Times–Aer Lingus Int. Fiction Prize 1990, Eurasian Regional Award of the Commonwealth Writers' Prize 1991) 1990 filmed 2002, Angels and Insects (novellas) 1992 filmed 1996, The Matisse Stories 1993, The Djinn in the Nightingale's Eye (Mythopoeic Fantasy Award 1998) 1994, Babel Tower 1996, Elementals, Stories of Fire and Ice 1998, The Biographer's Tale 2000, A Whistling Woman 2002, Little Black Book of Stories 2003; non-fiction: Degrees of Freedom: The Novels of Iris Murdoch (revised edn as Degrees of Freedom: The Early Novels of Iris Murdoch) 1965, Wordsworth and Coleridge in Their Time (revised edn as Unruly Times: Wordsworth and Coleridge in Their Time) 1970, Iris Murdoch 1976, Passions of the Mind (selected essays) 1991, Imagining Characters: Conversations About Women Writers (with Ignês Sodré) 1995, New Writing 4 (ed. with Alan Hollinghurst) 1995, New Writing 6 (co-ed.) 1997, The Oxford Book of English Short Stories (ed.) 1998, On Histories and Stories (essays) 2000, Portraits in Fiction 2001, Bird Hand Book (with V. Schrager) 2001; ed. and introduction to numerous works by other writers. *Honours:* Hon. Fellow, Newnham Coll. Cambridge 1999, London Inst. 2000, Univ. Coll. London 2004, Somerville Coll. Oxford 2005; Chevalier, Ordre des Arts et Lettres 2003; Hon. DLitt (Bradford) 1987, (Durham, York) 1991, (Nottingham) 1992, (Liverpool) 1993, (Portsmouth) 1994, (London) 1995, (Cambridge) 1999, (Sheffield) 2000, (Kent at Canterbury) 2004; Premio Malaparte Award, Capri 1995, Toepfer Foundation Shakespeare Prize, Hamburg 2002. *Literary Agent:* c/o Rogers Coleridge and White, 20 Powis Mews, London, W11 1JN, England. *Telephone:* (20) 7221-3717 (office). *Fax:* (20) 7229-9084 (office). *Website:* www.asbyatt.com.

BYNG, Jamie, BA; British publishing director; *Director, Canongate Books*; b. 1969, Winchester; s. of the Earl of Strafford; m. (separated); two s. *Education:* Edinburgh Univ. *Career:* joined Canongate Books as unpaid worker 1994, bought the co. 1994, Dir 1994–. *Address:* Canongate Books, 14 High Street, Edinburgh EH1 1TE, Scotland (office). *Telephone:* (131) 557-5111 (office). *Fax:* (131) 557-5211 (office). *E-mail:* info@canongate.co.uk (office). *Website:* www .canongate.co.uk (office).

BYRD, Harry Flood, Jr, American newspaper executive and politician; b. 20 Dec. 1914, s. of Harry Flood Byrd, Sr; m. Gretchen B. Thomson 1941 (died 1989); two s. one d. *Education:* John Marshall High School, Richmond, Va Mil. Inst. and Univ. of Va. *Career:* Ed. and writer, Winchester Evening Star 1935, Ed. and Publr 1935–81, Ed. and Publr Harrisonburg Daily News-Record 1937–2000; also active in firm of H. F. Byrd, Inc., apple growers; mem. Va State Senate 1947–65; mem. Democratic State Cen. Cttee 1940–70; served in USNR 1941–46; Dir Associated Press 1950–66; US Senator from Va (succeeding his father) 1965–83; Ind. *Address:* Rockingham Publishing Co. Inc., 2 North Kent Street, Winchester, VA 22601 (office); 411 Tennyson Avenue, Winchester, VA 22601, USA (home). *Telephone:* (540) 662-7745 (office). *Fax:* (540) 667-6729 (office).

BYRD, Robert C., JP; American politician; *Senator from West Virginia*; b. 20 Nov. 1917, North Wilkesboro, NC; s. of Cornelius Sale and Ada Byrd; m. Erma O James 1936; two d. *Education:* George Washington Univ. Law School and Washington Coll. of Law (American Univ.). *Career:* mem. W Va House of Delegates 1946–50, W Va Senate 1950–52; mem. US House of Reps rep. 6th Dist of W Va 1952–58; Senator from West Virginia 1959–; Asst Democratic Leader in Senate 1971–77, Majority Leader 1977–81, Minority Leader 1981–87, Majority Leader 1987–88; Chair. Appropriations Cttee 2001–; mem. Senate Appropriations, Armed Services and Rules and Admin. Cttees; Democrat. *Publications:* The Senate 1789–1989 (four vols) 1989–94, The Senate of the Roman Republic: Addresses on the History of Roman Constitutionalism 1995, Losing America 2004. *Address:* 311 Hart Senate Office Building, Washington, DC 20510-0001, USA. *Telephone:* (202) 224-3954 (office). *Website:* byrd.senate.gov (office).

C

CABOT, Meggin (Meg) Patricia, (Patricia Cabot, Jenny Carroll), BFA; American writer; b. Bloomington, IN; m. *Education:* Indiana Univ. *Career:* frmly illustrator, asst man. of undergraduate dormitory, New York Univ. *Publications:* as Patricia Cabot, adult fiction: Where Roses Grow Wild 1998, Portrait of my Heart 1999, An Improper Proposal 1999, A Little Scandal 2000, Lady of Skye 2001, Educating Caroline 2001, Kiss the Bride 2002, contrib. novella to anthology A Season in the Highlands 2000; as Meg Cabot, juvenile fiction: The Princess Diaries 2000, The Princess Diaries, Vol. II: Princess in the Spotlight 2001, The Princess Diaries, Vol. III: Princess in Love 2002, Nicola and the Viscount 2002, All-American Girl 2002, The Boy Next Door 2002, She Went All the Way 2002, Victoria and the Rogue 2003, The Princess Diaries, Vol. IV: Princess in Waiting 2003, Princess Lessons: A Princess Diaries Book 2003, The Princess Diaries, Vol. IV and a Half: Project Princess 2003, Boy Meets Girl 2004, The Princess Diaries, Vol. V: Princess in Pink 2004, Perfect Princess: A Princess Diaries Book 2004, Teen Idol 2004, The Princess Diaries: Sixsational 2005, All American Girl: Ready or Not 2005, Avalon High 2005, The Princess Diaries: Seventh Heaven 2006; as Jenny Carroll, juvenile fiction: The Mediator: Shadowland 2000, 1-800-WHERE-R-YOU: When Lightning Strikes 2001, The Mediator: Ninth Key 2001, The Mediator: Reunion 2001, 1-800-WHERE-R-YOU: Code Name Cassandra 2001, The Mediator: Darkest Hour 2001, 1-800-WHERE-R-YOU: Safe House 2002, 1-800-WHERE-R-YOU: Sanctuary 2002, Haunted: A Tale of the Mediator 2003. *Literary Agent:* The Marsh Agency, 11 Dover Street, London, W1S 4LJ, England. *Telephone:* (20) 7399-2800. *Fax:* (20) 7399-2801. *Website:* www.marsh-agency.co.uk; www.megcabot.com.

CADE, Robin (see Nicole, Christopher Robin)

CAFFREY, Idris; British writer; b. 16 Nov. 1949, Rhayader, Powys, Wales. *Education:* Swansea Coll. of Education. *Publications:* Pacing Backwards 1996, Pathways 1997, Other Places 1998, Warm Rain 2000, Touch the Earth 2001, Departures and Returns 2002, Relatively Unscathed 2007. *Address:* 5 Lyndale, Wilnecote, Tamworth B77 5DX, England.

CAHILL, Mike (see Nolan, William Francis)

CAIPÍN, Áine an (see Wilton-Jones, Anni)

CAIRNCROSS, Frances Anne, BA, MA; British journalist and academic; *Rector, Exeter College, Oxford;* b. 30 Aug. 1944, Otley, Yorks.; d. of Alexander Kirkland Cairncross and Mary Frances Cairncross; m. Hamish McRae 1971, two d. *Education:* St Anne's Coll., Oxford and Brown Univ., Providence, RI, USA. *Career:* staff mem. The Times 1967–69, The Banker 1969, The Observer 1969–71; Econs Corresp., The Guardian 1973–81, Women's Ed. 1981–84; Britain Ed., The Economist 1984–89, Public Policy Ed. 1997–2000, Man. Ed. 2000–04; Chair., Econ. and Social Research Council 2001–07; High Sheriff of London 2004–05; elected to Rectorship of Exeter Coll., Oxford 2004–; Pres., BAAS 2005–06; Sr Fellow at School of Public Policy, UCLA. *Publications:* Capital City (with Hamish McRae) 1971, The Second Great Crash 1973, The Guardian Guide to the Economy 1981, Changing Perceptions of Economic Policy 1981, Second Guardian Guide to the Economy 1983, Guide to the Economy 1987, Costing the Earth 1991, Green, Inc. 1995, The Death of Distance 1997, The Company of the Future 2002. *Honours:* Hon. Fellowship St Anne's Coll., Oxford, St Peter's Coll., Oxford; Visiting Fellowship Nuffield Coll.; Dr hc (Univs of Glasgow, Birmingham, City, Loughborough, Trinity Coll. Dublin, East Anglia). *Address:* Exeter College, Oxford, OX1 3DP, England (office). *Telephone:* (1865) 279647 (office). *Website:* www.exeter.ox.ac.uk (office).

CAIRNS, David Adam, CBE, MA; British journalist and musicologist; b. 8 June 1926, Loughton, Essex; s. of Sir Hugh William Bell Cairns and Barbara Cairns (née Smith); m. Rosemary Goodwin 1959; three s. *Education:* Winchester Coll., Oxford, Princeton Univ. Graduate Coll., USA. *Career:* Library Clerk, House of Commons 1951–53; critic, Record News 1954–56; mem. editorial staff, Times Educational Supplement 1955–58; music critic, Spectator 1958–63, Evening Standard 1958–63; asst music critic, Financial Times 1963–67; music critic, New Statesman 1967–70; mem. staff, Philips Records, London 1968–70, Classic Programme Co-ordinator 1970–73; asst music critic, Sunday Times 1975–84, music critic 1985–92; Leverhulme Research Fellow 1972–74; Distinguished Visiting Prof., Univ. of California, Davis 1985; Distinguished Visiting Scholar, Getty Center for the History of Art and Humanities 1992; Visiting Resident Fellow, Merton Coll., Oxford 1993. *Publications:* The Memoirs of Hector Berlioz (ed. and trans.) 1969, Responses: Musical Essays and Reviews (co-author) 1973, The Magic Flute (ENO Opera Guide) 1980, Falstaff (ENO Opera Guide) 1982, Berlioz: The Making of an Artist 1803–1832 1989, Berlioz: Servitude and Greatness 1832–1869 (Whitbread Biog. of the Year 2000, Samuel Johnson Non-Fiction Prize 2000) 1999, Mozart and his Operas 2006; contrib. to articles on Beethoven and Berlioz, in Viking Opera Guide 1993. *Honours:* Officier, Ordre des Arts et des Lettres 1991; Hon. DLitt (Southampton) 2001; British Acad. Derek Allen Memorial Prize 1990, Royal Philharmonic Soc. Award 1990, 1999, Yorkshire Post Prize 1990. *Address:* 49 Amerland Road, London, SW18 1QA, England. *Telephone:* (20) 8870-4931.

CALCAGNO, Anne; American academic, writer and poet; b. 14 Nov. 1957, San Diego, CA; m. Leo 1986, one s. one d. *Education:* BA, English, Williams College, 1979; MFA, Fiction and Poetry, University of Montana, 1984. *Career:* Part-time Lecturer, North Park College and American Conservatory of Music, Chicago, 1989–91; Teacher, School of the Art Institute of Chicago, 1990–93; Artist-in-Education, Illinois Arts Council, 1992–93; Lecturer, 1992–93, Assoc. Prof. of English, 1993–, DePaul University; mem. Associated Writing Programs; Authors' Guild; Poets and Writers. *Publications:* Pray for Yourself (short stories), 1993; Travelers Tales, Italy (ed.), 1998. Contributions: anthologies and periodicals. *Honours:* National Endowment for the Arts Creative Writing Fellowship, 1989; Illinois Arts Council Artists Fellowship, 1993; James D. Phelan Literary Award, San Francisco Foundation, 1993; Silver Medal, ForeWord Travel Book of the Year, 1999; Ed.'s Choice Award, Journey Woman, 1999; Illinois Arts Council Literary Award, 2003. *Address:* c/o Department of English, DePaul University, 802 W Belden Ave, Chicago, IL 60614-3214, USA.

CALDECOTT, Moyra, BA, MA; British author; b. 1 June 1927, Pretoria, South Africa; m. Oliver Zerffi Stratford Caldecott 1951; two s. one d. *Education:* University of Natal. *Publications:* The Weapons of the Wolfhound 1976, The Sacred Stones, Vol. I, The Tall Stones 1977, Vol. II, The Temple of the Sun 1977, Vol. III, Shadow on the Stones 1978, Adventures by Leaf Light 1978, The Lily and the Bull 1979, Child of the Dark Star 1980, The King of Shadows: A Glastonbury Story 1981, The Twins of the Tylwyth Teg 1983, Taliesin and Avagddu 1983, Bran, Son of Llyr 1985, The Tower and the Emerald 1985, Guardians of the Tall Stones 1986, The Son of the Sun 1986, The Silver Vortex 1987, Etheldreda 1987, Women in Celtic Myth 1988, Daughter of Amun 1989, The Green Lady and the King of Shadows 1989, The Daughter of Ra 1990, The Crystal Legends 1990, Myths of the Sacred Tree 1993, The Winged Man 1994, Mythical Journeys: Legendary Quests 1996, The Waters of Sul 1998; contrib. to anthologies and periodicals. *Electronic publications:* Hatshepsut: Daughter of Amun 2000, Akhenaten: Son of the Sun 2000, Tutankhamun and the Daughter of Ra 2000, The Ghost of Akhenaten, The Eye of Callanish, Weapons of the Wolfhound, Etheldreda, The Green Lady and the King of Shadows, Three Celtic Tales, Crystal Legends, The Tall Stones, The Temple of the Sun, Shadow on the Stones, The Silver Vortex, The Lily and the Bull, The Tower and the Emerald, Child of the Dark Star.

CALDER, Angus Lindsay Ritchie, MA, DPhil; Scottish writer and poet; b. 5 Feb. 1942, Sutton, Surrey, England; m. 1st Jenni Daiches; m. 2nd Kate Kyle; two s. two d. *Education:* King's College, Cambridge, University of Sussex. *Career:* Lecturer in Literature, University of Nairobi 1968–71; Staff Tutor in Arts, Open University in Scotland 1979–93; Visiting Prof. of English, University of Zimbabwe 1992; Ed., Journal of Commonwealth Literature; freelance writer 1994–; mem. Scottish PEN. *Publications:* The People's War: Britain 1939–1945 1969, Russia Discovered: Nineteenth Century Fiction 1976, Revolutionary Empire: The Rise of the English-Speaking Empires 1981, The Myth of the Blitz 1991, Revolving Culture: Notes From the Scottish Republic 1994, Waking in Waikato (poems) 1997, Horace in Tollcross (poems) 2000, Scotlands of the Mind (poems) 2002, Colours of Grief (poems) 2002, Gods, Mongrels and Demons: 101 Brief but Essential Lives 2003, Disasters and Heroes: War, Memory and Representation 2004, Dipa's Bowl (poems) 2004, Sun Behind the Castle: Edinburgh Poems 2004; contribs to Cencrastus, Chapman, Herald, London Review of Books, New Statesman, Scotland on Sunday, TLS, The Drouth. *Honours:* Eric Gregory Award 1967, John Llewellyn Rhys Memorial Prize 1970, Scottish Arts Council Book Awards 1981, 1994, Scottish Arts Council Writer's Bursary 2002. *Address:* c/o Jenny Brown, 42 The Causeway, Edinburgh, EH15 3PZ, Scotland (office). *Telephone:* (131) 620-1556 (office). *E-mail:* jenny-brown@blueyonder.co.uk (office).

CALDER, Elisabeth (Liz) Nicole, BA; British publisher; *Publishing Director, Book Division, Bloomsbury Publishing plc;* b. 20 Jan. 1938, New Zealand; d. of Ivor George Baber and Florence Mary Baber; m. 1st Richard Henry Calder (divorced 1972); one s. one d.; m. 2nd Louis Baum 2000. *Education:* Palmerston North Girls' High School, NZ and Univ. of Canterbury, NZ. *Career:* catwalk model in Brazil 1965–68; reader Metro-Goldwyn-Mayer Story Dept 1969–70; Publicity Man. Victor Gollancz 1971–74, Editorial Dir 1975–78; Editorial Dir (fiction), Jonathan Cape 1979–86; Founding Publishing Dir Book Div., Bloomsbury Publishing 1986–; co-f. Women in Publishing 1979; co-f. Groucho Club, London 1984; f. Parati Int. Literary Festival, Brazil 2003–; Chair. Royal Court Theatre 2001–05, Vice-Chair. 2005–. *Honours:* Order of Merit for services to culture, Brazil 2004. *Address:* Bloomsbury Publishing plc, 38 Soho Square, London, W1V 5DF, England. *Telephone:* (20) 7494-2111. *Website:* www.bloomsbury.com.

CALDER, John Mackenzie; British publisher, critic, playwright and theatre administrator; *Managing Director, Calder Publishers Ltd;* b. 25 Jan. 1927; m. 1st Mary A. Simmonds 1949; one d.; m. 2nd Bettina Jonic 1960 (divorced 1975); one d. *Education:* Gilling Castle, Yorks., Bishops Coll. School, Canada, McGill Univ., Montreal, Sir George Williams Coll. and Univ. of Zürich, Switzerland. *Career:* Founder and Man. Dir John Calder (Publishers) Ltd 1950–91, Calder Publrs Ltd 1991–, Calder and Boyars Ltd 1964–75, f. Calder Bookshop; expanded to Edin. 1971; organized literature confs, Edin.

Festival 1962, 1963, Harrogate Festival 1969; f. Ledlanet Nights (music and opera festival) Kinross-shire 1963–74; Pres. Riverrun Press Inc., New York 1978–; Prof. of Literature and Philosophy, Ecole Active Bilingue, Paris 1994–96; Lecturer in History, Univ. of Paris-Nanterre 1995; acquired bookselling business of Better Books, London 1969; Chair. North American Book Clubs 1982–89, Fed. of Scottish Theatres 1972–74; Co-founder Defence of Literature and the Arts Soc.; Dir of other cos associated with opera, publishing etc.; f. Samuel Beckett Theatre, Waterloo, London; Theatre Admin. Godot Co. *Plays include:* Lorca, The Voice, The Trust. *Publications:* A Samuel Beckett Reader, The Burroughs Reader 1981, New Beckett Reader 1983, Henry Miller Reader 1985, Nouveau Roman Reader 1986, The Defence of Literature 1991, The Garden of Eros 1992, The Philosophy of Samuel Beckett 1998, What's Wrong, What's Right (poetry) 1999, Pursuit (autobiography) 2001. *Honours:* Chevalier des Arts et des Lettres; Officier, Ordre nat. du Mérite; Dr hc (Edinburgh, Zurich). *Address:* Calder Publications Ltd, 51 The Cut, London, SE1 8LF, England (office); Riverrun Press Inc., 100 Newfield Avenue, Edison, NJ 08837, USA (office); 9 rue de Ramainville, 93100 Montreuil, France. *Telephone:* (20) 7633-0599 (UK) (home); 1-49-88-75-12 (France). *Fax:* 1-48-59-66-68 (France). *E-mail:* info@calderpublications.com (office). *Website:* www.calderpublications.com (office).

CALDER, Nigel David Ritchie, MA; British writer; b. 2 Dec. 1931, London, England; m. Elisabeth Palmer 1954; two s. three d. *Education:* Sidney Sussex Coll., Cambridge. *Career:* research physicist, Mullard Research Laboratories, Redhill, Surrey 1954–56; staff writer 1956–60, Science Ed. 1960–62, Ed. 1962–66, New Scientist; Science Correspondent, New Statesman 1959–62, 1966–71; mem. Asscn of British Science Writers, Royal Astronomical Soc. *Publications:* The Environment Game (aka Eden Was No Garden: an Inquiry into the Environment of Man) 1967, Technopolis: Social Control of the Uses of Science 1969, Violent Universe: An Eyewitness Account of the New Astronomy 1970, The Mind of Man: An Investigation into Current Research on the Brain and Human Nature 1970, Restless Earth: A Report on the New Geology 1972, The Life Game: Evolution and the New Biology 1974, The Weather Machine: How Our Weather Works and Why it is Changing 1975, The Human Conspiracy 1976, The Key to the Universe: A Report on the New Physics 1977, Spaceships of the Mind 1978, Einstein's Universe 1979, Nuclear Nightmares: An Investigation into Possible Wars 1980, The Comet is Coming!: The Feverish Legacy of Mr Halley 1981, Timescale: An Atlas of the Fourth Dimension 1984, 1984 and Beyond: Nigel Calder Talks to his Computer About the Future 1984, The English Channel 1986, The Green Machines 1986, Future Earth: Exploring the Frontiers of Science (ed. with John Newell) 1989, Scientific Europe 1990, Spaceship Earth 1991, Giotto to the Comets 1992, Beyond This World 1995, The Manic Sun 1997, Magic Universe: The Oxford Guide to Modern Science 2003, Albert Einstein: Relativity (intro.) 2006; contrib. to TV documentaries, numerous periodicals. *Honours:* hon. fellow American Asscn for the Advancement of Science 1986; UNESCO Kalinga Prize 1972. *Address:* 26 Boundary Road, Northgate, Crawley, West Sussex RH10 8BT, England. *Telephone:* (1293) 549969 (office). *Fax:* (1293) 547083 (office). *E-mail:* nc@windstream.demon.co.uk.

CALDERWOOD, James Lee; American academic and writer; b. 7 April 1930, Corvallis, OR, USA; m. Cleo Xeniades Calderwood 1955; two s. *Education:* BA, University of Oregon, 1953; PhD, University of Washington, 1963. *Career:* Instructor, Michigan State University, 1961–63; Asst Prof., University of California at Irvine, 1963–66; Asst Prof., 1966–68, Assoc. Prof., 1968–71, Prof., 1971–94, Assoc. Dean of Humanities, 1974–94, Prof. Emeritus, 1994–, University of California at Irvine. *Publications:* Shakespearean Metadrama, 1971; Metadrama in Shakespeare's Henriad, 1979; To Be and Not to Be: Negation and Metadrama in Hamlet, 1983; If It Were Done: Tragic Action in Macbeth, 1986; Shakespeare and the Denial of Death, 1987; The Properties of Othello, 1989; A Midsummer Night's Dream, 1992. Editor: Forms of Poetry (with H. E. Toliver), 1968; Perspectives on Drama (with H. E. Toliver), 1968; Perspectives on Poetry (with H. E. Toliver), 1968; Perspectives on Fiction (with H. E. Toliver), 1968; Forms of Drama (with H. E. Toliver), 1969; Essays in Shakespearean Criticism (with H. E. Toliver), 1969; Shakespeare's Love's Labour's Lost, 1970; Forms of Prose Fiction (with H. E. Toliver), 1972; Forms of Tragedy (with H. E. Toliver), 1972. Contributions: scholarly journals. *Honours:* Alumni Achievement Award, University of Oregon, 1991. *Address:* 1323 Terrace Way, Laguna Beach, CA 92651, USA.

CALDWELL, Grant; Australain writer, poet and teacher; b. 6 March 1947, Melbourne, Vic. *Career:* Ed.-Publisher, MEUSE art and literature magazine, 1980–82; Teacher, Victoria College of the Arts, University of Melbourne, 1995–2000. *Publications:* Poetry: The Screaming Frog That Ralph Ate, 1979; The Bells of Mr Whippy, 1982; The Nun Wore Sunglasses, 1984; The Life of a Pet Dog, 1993; You Know What I Mean, 1996. Other: The Revolt of the Coats (short stories), 1988; Malabata (autobiog.), 1991. Contributions: anthologies, newspapers and magazines. *Address:* c/o Hale and Iremonger, 19 Eve Street, Erskineville, NSW 22043, Australia.

CALDWELL-MOORE, Sir Patrick Alfred, (R. T. Fishall), Kt, CBE, FRS; English astronomer and writer; b. 4 March 1923, Pinner, Middx; s. of the late Capt. Caldwell-Moore, MC and Gertrude Lilian Moore (née White). *Education:* privately. *Career:* Officer, Bomber Command, RAF 1940–45; Ed. Year Book of Astronomy 1962–; Dir Armagh Planetarium 1965–68; freelance 1968–; Pres. British Astronomical Asscn 1982–84, then Life Hon. Vice-Pres.; mem. Royal Astronomical Soc. of Canada, Royal Astronomical Soc. of NZ. *Play:* Quintet (Chichester) 2002. *Television includes:* The Sky at Night (BBC) 1957–. *Radio:*

frequent broadcaster on radio. *Compositions:* Perseus (opera) 1975, Theseus 1982, Galileo 2003. *Publications include:* The Amateur Astronomer 1970, Atlas of the Universe 1970, Guide to the Planets 1976, Guide to the Moon 1976, Guide to the Stars 1977, Guide to Mars 1977, Out of the Darkness: The Planet Pluto (jtly) 1980, The Unfolding Universe 1982, Travellers in Space and Time 1983, History of Astronomy 1983, The Return of Halley's Comet (with Heather Couper) 1984, The Story of the Earth (with Peter Cattermole) 1985, Patrick Moore's Armchair Astronomy 1985, Stargazing 1985, Exploring the Night Sky with Binoculars 1986, The A–Z of Astronomy 1986, TV Astronomer 1987, Astronomy for the Under Tens 1987, Astronomers' Stars 1987, The Planet Uranus (jtly) 1988, Space Travel for the Under Tens 1988, The Planet Neptune 1989, Mission to the Planets 1990, The Universe for the Under Tens 1990, A Passion for Astronomy 1991, Fireside Astronomy 1992, The Starry Sky 1994, The Great Astronomical Revolution 1994, Stars of the Southern Skies 1994, Guinness Book of Astronomy 1995, Passion for Astronomy 1995, Teach Yourself Astronomy 1995, Eyes on the Universe 1997, Brilliant Stars 1998, Patrick Moore on Mars 1999, Yearbook of Astronomy AD 1000 (with Allan Chapman) 1999, Astronomy Data Book 2000, Eighty Not Out 2003, Stars of Destiny 2004, Venus 2004, Patrick Moore The Autobiography 2004, Patrick Moore on the Moon 2005, Bang! The Complete History of the Universe (with Brian May and Chris Lintott) 2006, Moore on Mercury 2007. *Honours:* Hon. DSc (Lancaster) 1974, (Hatfield Polytechnic) 1989, (Birmingham) 1990, (Portsmouth) 1997, (Leicester) 1996; Dr hc (Keele) 1994; Lorimer Gold Medal 1962, Goodacre Medal (British Astronomical Asscn) 1968, Jackson Gwilt Gold Medal (Royal Astronomical Soc.) 1977, Roberts-Klumpke Medal (Astronomical Soc. of the Pacific) 1979, Royal Astronomical Soc. Millennium Award 2000, BAFTA Special Award 2002, Minor Planet No. 2602 is named in his honour. *Address:* Farthings, 39 West Street, Selsey, Sussex, PO20 9AD, England. *Telephone:* (1243) 603668. *Fax:* (1243) 607237 (office); (1243) 607237 (home).

CALHOUN, Craig Jackson, BA, MA, PhD; American academic, writer and editor; *Professor of Sociology, New York University;* b. 16 June 1952, Watseka, Ill.; m. Pamela F. DeLargy; two c. *Education:* Univ. of Southern California, Columbia Univ., New York, Univ. of Manchester and St Antony's Coll., Oxford, UK. *Career:* Instructor, Univ. of N Carolina, Chapel Hill 1977–80, Asst Prof. 1980–85, Assoc. Prof. 1985–89, Prof. of Sociology and History 1989–96, Dir Univ. Center for Int. Studies 1993–96; Ed. Comparative Social Research 1988–93, Sociological Theory 1994–99; Visiting Lecturer, Univ. of Oslo 1991, Prof. (part-time) 1993–; Prof. of Sociology and Chair. Dept of Sociology, New York Univ. 1996–; Pres. Social Science Research Council 1999–; Consulting Ed. McGraw-Hill Publrs 1990–2000; mem. Editorial Bds Thesis Eleven, European Journal of Social Theory, Ethnicities, British Journal of Sociology, Irish Journal of Sociology, Journal of Civil Society; mem. American Anthropological Asscn, American Historical Asscn, American Sociological Asscn, Int. Sociological Asscn, Int. Studies Asscn, Royal Anthropological Inst., Social Science History Asscn, Soc. for the Study of Social Problems, Sociological Research Asscn. *Publications:* The Question of Class Struggle: Social Foundations of Popular Radicalism During the Industrial Revolution 1982, Sociology (with Donald Light and Suzanne Keller) 1989, Neither Gods Nor Emperors: Students and the Struggle for Democracy in China 1995, Critical Social Theory: Culture, History and the Challenge of Difference 1995, Nationalism 1997; editor: The Anthropological Study of Education (with F. A. J. Ianni) 1976, Structures of Power and Constraint: Essays in Honor of Peter M. Blau (with W. R. Scott and M. Meyer) 1990, Habermas and the Public Sphere 1992, Contradictions: Perspectives in Theory and Culture (series ed., 17 vols) 1992–, Bourdieu: Critical Perspectives (with E. LiPuma and M. Postone) 1993, Social Theory and the Politics of Identity 1994, Hannah Arendt and the Meaning of Politics (co-ed.) 1997, Dictionary of the Social Sciences 2002, The Classical Social Theory Reader (with J. Gerteis, J. Moody et al) 2002, Understanding September 11: Perspectives from the Social Sciences (with P. Price and A. Timmer) 2002, Lessons of Empire: Imperial Histories and American Power (with Frederick Cooper and Kevin W. Moore) 2005, Sociology in America: The ASA Centennial History 2007; contrib. of articles and chapters in books and scholarly journals, reviews, translations. *Honours:* W. K. Kellogg Nat. Fellowship 1982–85, American Sociological Asscn Distinguished Contrib. to Scholarship Award (Section on Political Sociology) 1995. *Address:* Department of Sociology, New York University, 269 Mercer Street, New York, NY 10003 (office); Social Science Research Council, 810 Seventh Avenue, 31st Floor, New York, NY 10019, USA (office). *Telephone:* (212) 998-8348 (office); (212) 377-2700 (office). *Fax:* (212) 995-4140 (office); (212) 377-2727 (office). *E-mail:* craig.calhoun@nyu.edu (office); calhoun@ssrc.org (office). *Website:* www.ssrc.org/calhoun.

CALINESCU, Matei, BA; Romanian literary critic and academic; *Professor Emeritus of Comparative Literature, Indiana University, Bloomington;* b. 1934; m. *Education:* I. L. Caragiale Lycee. *Career:* first published in Romania; emigrated to USA 1973; Prof., now Emer., of Comparative Literature Indiana Univ., Bloomington 1973–; Prof. Emer. of W European Studies; has published several books in Romania since collapse of Ceauşescu regime; Guggenheim Fellowship 1976–77, Woodrow Wilson Center Fellowship, Washington, DC 1995–96. *Publications include:* Five Faces of Modernity: Modernism, Avant-Garde, Decadence, Kitsch, Postmodernism 1987, Exploring Postmodernism (ed., with D. W. Fokkema) 1987, Rereading 1993, Amtintiri in dialog (with Ion Vianu) 1994, Despre Ioan P. Culianu oi Mircea Eliade 2002, Portretul lui M 2003; two books of poetry, a novel, several vols of literary criticism; contrib. articles and essays to books, anthologies and journals including Daedalus, The

Yale Journal of Criticism, Poetics Today, East European Politics and Societies, Salmagundi, The Comparatist. *Address:* c/o Indiana University, 107 S Indiana Avenue, Bloomington, IN 47405-7000, USA. *Telephone:* (812) 856-3342. *E-mail:* calinesc@indiana.edu.

CALISHER, Hortense, (Jack Fenno), AB; American author; b. 20 Dec. 1911, New York; d. of Joseph H. Calisher and Hedwig Calisher (née Lichtstern); m. 1st Heaton Bennet Heffelfiner 1935; one s. one d.; m. 2nd Curtis Harnack 1959. *Education:* Barnard Coll., New York. *Career:* Adjunct Prof. of English, Barnard Coll. 1956–57; Visiting Lecturer, State Univ. of Iowa 1957, 1959–60, Stanford Univ. 1958, Sarah Lawrence Coll. Bronxville, New York 1962, 1967; Adjunct Prof. Columbia Univ., New York 1968–70, City Coll. of New York 1969; Visiting Prof. of Literature, Brandeis Univ. 1963–64, Univ. of Pennsylvania 1965, State Univ. of New York, Purchase 1971–72; Regent's Prof. Univ. of Calif. 1976; Visiting Prof., Bennington Coll. 1978, Washington Univ., St Louis 1979, Brown Univ. 1986; Guggenheim Fellow 1952, 1955; mem. American Acad. and Inst. Arts and Letters (Pres. 1987–90); American PEN (Pres. 1986–87). *Publications include:* novels: False Entry 1961, Textures of Life 1963, Journal from Ellipsia 1965, The Railway Police and The Last Trolley Ride (two novellas) 1966, The New Yorkers 1966, Queenie 1971, Standard Dreaming 1972, Eagle Eye 1973, On Keeping Women 1977, Mysteries of Motion 1983, The Bobby Soxer (Kafka Prize) 1986, Age 1987, The Small Bang (as Jack Fenno) 1992, In the Palace of the Movie King 1993, In the Slammer with Carol Smith 1996, Sunday Jews 2002; novellas: (collected) Modern Library 1997; short stories: In the Absence of Angels 1951, Tale for the Mirror 1962, Extreme Magic 1964, Saratoga, Hot 1985; Herself (autobiog.) 1972, Kissing Cousins 1988 (memoir), Tattoo for a Slave (memoir) 2004. *Honours:* Hon. LittD (Skidmore Coll.) 1980; Hon. LLD (Grinnell) 1986; Acad. of Arts and Letters Award 1967, Nat. Council Arts Award 1967, Nat. Endowment for the Arts Award For Lifetime Achievement 1989. *Address:* c/o Calisher-Harnack, 205 West 57th Street, New York, NY 10001, USA. *E-mail:* hcalisher@aol.com (office).

CALLAGHAN, Barry, BA, MA; Canadian writer, poet, editor, publisher and translator and academic; *Distinguished Scholar and Professor Emeritus, York University*; b. 5 July 1937, Toronto, Ont.; one s. *Education:* St Michael's College, University of Toronto. *Career:* Teacher, Atkinson College, York University, Toronto, 1965–2003, Distinguished Scholar and Prof. Emer. 2003–; Literary Ed., Telegram, Toronto, 1966–71; Host and Documentary Producer, Weekend, CBC-TV, 1969–72; Founder-Publisher, Exile, 1972–, Exile Editions, 1976–; Writer-in-Residence, University of Rome, 1987, Nat. Univ. of Mexico, Mexico City 2004. *Publications:* Poetry: The Hogg Poems and Drawings 1978, As Close As We Came 1982, Stone Blind Love 1987, Hogg: The Poems and Drawings 1997, Hogg, Seven Last Words 2001; fiction: The Black Queen Stories 1982, The Way the Angel Spreads Her Wings 1989, When Things Get Worst 1993, A Kiss is Still a Kiss 1995; non-fiction: Barrelhouse Kings 1998, Raise You Five 1964–2004 Vol. I (essays) 2005, Raise You Ten 1964–2004 Vol. II (essays) 2006; editor: various anthologies and books. *Honours:* many National Magazine Awards; Gold Medal for Journalism, University of Western Ontario 1979, 1985; Co-Winner, International Authors Festival Award, Toronto 1986; Pushcart Prize for Prose, USA 1990, Toronto Arts Award 1993, inaugural winner W.D. Mitchell Prize for Fiction and Editorial Mentoring 1998; Hon. Doctor of Letters (SUNY) 1999, Hon. Doctor of Laws (Guelph Univ., Ontario) 2001. *Address:* 20 Dale Avenue, Toronto, ON M4W 1K4, Canada. *Telephone:* (416) 922-8221 (home). *Fax:* (416) 969-9556 (home). *E-mail:* exile@eol.ca (home).

CALLICOTT, John Baird; American academic and writer; b. 9 May 1941, Memphis, TN; m. 1st Ann Nelson Archer 1963 (divorced 1985); one s.; m. 2nd Frances Moore Lappe 1985 (divorced 1990). *Education:* BA, Rhodes College, 1963; MA, 1966, PhD, 1972, Syracuse University. *Career:* Lecturer, Syracuse University, 1965–66; Instructor, University of Memphis, 1966–69; Asst Prof., 1969–74, Assoc. Prof., 1974–82, Prof. of Philosophy, 1982–95, Prof. of Natural Resources, 1984–95, University of Wisconsin at Stevens Point; Prof. of Philosophy, University of North Texas, 1995–; mem. American Philosophical Asscn; American Society for Environmental History; International Society for Ecosystem Health; International Society for Environmental Ethics, pres., 1997–2000; Society for Asian and Comparative Philosophy; Society for Conservation Biology. *Publications:* Plato's Aesthetics: An Introduction to the Theory of Forms, 1972; Clothed-in-Fur and Other Tales: An Introduction to An Ojibwa World View, 1982; In Defense of the Land Ethic: Essays in Environmental Philosophy, 1989; Earth's Insights: A Survey of Ecological Ethics from the Mediterranean Basin to the Australian Outback, 1994; Beyond the Land Ethic: More Essays in Environmental Philosophy, 1999. Editor: several books. Contributions: many books and numerous journals. *Honours:* Woodrow Wilson Fellow, 1963–64; University Scholar Award, University of Wisconsin at Stevens Point, 1995. *Address:* c/o Department of Philosophy and Religion, University of North Texas, PO Box 310920, Denton, TX 76203-0920, USA.

CALLIL, Carmen Thérèse, BA, FRSA; Australian/British publisher and writer; b. 15 July 1938, Melbourne; d. of Lorraine Claire Allen and Frederick Alfred Louis Callil. *Education:* Star of the Sea Convent, Loreto Convent, Melbourne and Melbourne Univ. *Career:* settled in England 1963; Buyer's Asst, Marks and Spencer 1963–65; Editorial Asst, Hutchinson Publishing Co. 1965–66, B. T. Batsford 1966–67, Publicity Man., Granada Publishing 1967–70, André Deutsch 1971–72; f. Carmen Callil Ltd, Book Publicity Co. and Virago Press 1972; Chair. and Man. Dir Virago Press 1972–82, Chair. 1982–95, Man. Dir Chatto and Windus, The Hogarth Press 1983–93; Publr-at-Large Random House, UK 1993–94; Ed.-at-Large Knopf, New York 1993–94; mem. Bd Channel 4 1985–91, Random Century Bd 1989–94; Gov. Museum of London 1992–; Chair. Booker Prize for Fiction 1996. *Publications:* The Modern Library: The 200 Best Novels in England Since 1950 (jtly) 1999, Bad Faith: A Forgotten History of Family and Fatherland 2006. *Honours:* Hon. DLitt (Sheffield) 1994, (Oxford Brookes Univ.) 1995; Hon. DUniv (York) 1995, (Open) 1997; Int. Women's Writing Guild Distinguished Service Award. *Literary Agent:* c/o Rogers, Coleridge & White Literary Agency, 20 Powis Mews, London, W11 1JN, England. *Telephone:* (20) 7221-3717. *Fax:* (20) 7229-9084. *E-mail:* info@rcwlitagency.co.uk. *Website:* www.rcwlitagency.co.uk.

CALLISON, Brian Richard; British writer; b. 13 July 1934, Manchester, England; m. Phyllis Joyce Jobson 1958, two s. *Education:* Dundee College of Art. *Career:* mem. Royal Institute of Nagivation; Society of Authors. *Publications:* A Flock of Ships, 1970; A Plague of Sailors, 1971; Dawn Attack, 1972; A Web of Salvage, 1973; Trapp's War, 1974; A Ship is Dying, 1976; A Frenzy of Merchantmen, 1977; The Judas Ship, 1978; Trapp's Peace, 1979; The Auriga Madness, 1980; The Sextant, 1981; Spearfish, 1982; Bone Collectors, 1984; Thunder of Crude, 1986; Trapp and World War Three, 1988; The Trojan Hearse, 1990; Crocodile Trapp, 1993; Ferry Down, 1998; The Stollenberg Legacy, 2000.

CALLOW, Philip Kenneth; British writer and poet; b. 26 Oct. 1924, Birmingham, England. *Education:* St Luke's College, Exeter 1968–70. *Career:* Open Univ. *Publications:* The Hosanna Man, 1956; Common People, 1958; Native Ground, 1959; Pledge for the Earth, 1960; The Honeymooners, 1960; Turning Point, 1961; Clipped Wings, 1963; The Real Life, 1964; In My Own Land, 1965; Going to the Moon, 1968; The Bliss Body, 1969; Flesh of Morning, 1971; The Lamb, 1971; Bare Wires, 1972; Yours, 1972; Son and Lover: The Young D. H. Lawrence, 1975; The Story of My Desire, 1976; Janine, 1977; The Subway to New York, 1979; Cave Light, 1981; Woman with a Poet, 1983; New York Insomnia, 1984; Poetry: Icons, 1987; Soliloquires of an Eye, 1990; Some Love, 1991. *Address:* Little Thatch, Haselbury, Nr Crewkerne, Somerset, England.

CALLOW, Simon Philip Hugh, CBE; British actor, director and writer; b. 15 June 1949, s. of Neil Callow and Yvonne Mary Callow. *Education:* London Oratory Grammar School, Queen's Univ., Belfast, Drama Centre. *Career:* debut Edinburgh Festival 1973; repertory seasons, Lincoln and Traverse Theatre, Edin.; work at the fringe theatre, the Bush, London; joined Joint Stock Theatre Group 1977, Nat. Theatre 1979; regular book reviewer The Guardian. *Stage appearances include:* Passing By 1975, Plumbers Progress 1975, Arturo Ui 1978, Titus Andronicus 1978, Mary Barnes 1978, As You Like It 1979, Amadeus 1979, Sisterly Feeling 1979, Total Eclipse 1982, Restoration 1982, The Beastly Beatitudes of Balthazar B 1982, The Relapse 1983, On The Spot 1984, Melancholy Jacques 1984, Kiss of the Spider Woman 1985, Faust 1988, Single Spies 1988, 1989, The Destiny of Me 1993, The Alchemist 1996, The Importance of Being Oscar 1997, Chimes at Midnight 1997, The Mystery of Charles Dickens 2000–02, Through the Leaves 2003, The Holy Terror 2004, The Woman in White (Palace Theatre, London) 2005, Aladdin (Richmond Theatre, London) 2005, Present Laughter (tour) 2006. *Films include:* Amadeus 1983, A Room With A View 1984, The Good Father 1985, Maurice 1986, Manifesto 1987, Mr and Mrs Bridge 1991, Postcards from the Edge 1991, Soft Top Hard Shoulder 1992, Four Weddings and A Funeral 1994, Jefferson in Paris 1994, Victory 1994, Le Passager Clandestin 1995, England, My England 1995, Ace Ventura: When Nature Calls 1995, James and the Giant Peach (voice) 1996, The Scarlet Tunic 1996, Woman In White 1997, Bedrooms and Hallways 1997, Shakespeare in Love 1997, No Man's Land 2000, Thunderpants 2001, A Christmas Carol 2001, George and the Dragon 2002, Phantom of the Opera 2004, Rag Tale 2005, Bob The Butler 2005. *TV appearances:* Wings of Song 1977, Instant Enlightenment inc. VAT 1979, La Ronde 1980, Man of Destiny 1982, Chance in a Million 1982–84, Deadhead 1984, Handel 1985, David Copperfield 1986, Cariani and the Courtesan 1987, Old Flames 1989, Patriot Witness 1989, Trial of Oz 1991, Bye Bye Columbus 1992, Femme Fatale 1993, Little Napoleons 1994, An Audience with Charles Dickens 1996, A Christmas Dickens 1997, The Woman in White 1998, Trial-Retribution 1999, 2000, Galileo's Daughter, The Mystery of Charles Dickens 2002, Angels in America 2003, Miss Marple 2004, Midsomer Murders 2006. *Directed:* Loving Reno 1983, Passport 1985, Nicolson Fights Croydon 1986, Amadeus 1986, The Infernal Machine 1986, Così Fan Tutte 1987, Jacques and His Master 1987, Shirley Valentine (theatre production) 1988/89, Die Fledermaus 1989/90, Facades 1988, Single Spies 1988/89, Stevie Wants to Play the Blues 1990, The Ballad of the Sad Café (film) 1991, Carmen Jones (Evening Standard Olivier Award) 1991, My Fair Lady 1992, Shades 1992, The Destiny of Me 1993, Carmen Jones 1994, Il Trittico 1995, Les Enfants du Paradis (RSC) 1996, Stephen Oliver Trilogy 1996, La Calisto 1996, Il Turco in Italia 1997, HRH 1997, The Pajama Game 1999, The Consul 1999, Tomorrow Week (play for radio) 1999, Le Roi Malgré Lui 2003, Everyman 2003, Jus' Like That 2004. *Publications:* Being An Actor 1984 (expanded edn 2004), A Difficult Actor: Charles Laughton 1987, Shooting the Actor, or the Choreography of Confusion (with Dusan Makevejev) 1990 (expanded edn 2004), Acting in Restoration Comedy 1991, Orson Welles: The Road to Xanadu 1995, Les Enfants du Paradis 1996, Snowdon – On Stage 1996, The National 1997, Love is Where it Falls 1999, Shakespeare on Love 2000, Charles Laughton's the Night of the Hunter 2000, Oscar Wilde and His Circle 2000, The Nights of the Hunter 2001, Henry IV Part 1 2002, Henry IV Part 2 2003, Dicken's

Christmas 2003, Orson Welles: Hello Americans 2006; translations of works of Cocteau, Kundera, Prévert, Chabrier; weekly column in Sunday Express, Independent, Country Life; contrib. to The Times, The Sunday Times, The Guardian, The Observer, Evening Standard, etc. *Honours:* Hon. DLitt (Queen's Univ., Belfast) 1999, (Birmingham) 2000; Evening Standard Patricia Rothermere Award 1999. *Address:* c/o BAT, 180 Wardour Street, London, W1V 3AA, England. *Telephone:* (20) 7413-0869 (office). *Fax:* (20) 7413-0870 (office). *E-mail:* karen@ichkin.freeserve.co.uk (office).

CALLWOOD, June, CC; Canadian journalist; b. 2 June 1924, Chatham; d. of Harold Callwood and Gladys Lavoie; m. Trent Frayne 1944; two s. (one deceased) two d. *Career:* Columnist Toronto Globe and Mail 1983–89; Guest Lecturer on Human Rights, Univ. of Ottawa 1984; Margaret Laurence Lecture 1993; Writer-in-Residence, North York Public Library 1995–96; Founding mem. and Vice-Pres. Canadian Civil Liberties Asscn 1965–88 (Hon. Dir for Life 1988); Pres. and Founder Nellie's Hostel for Women 1974-78, Dir 1985–89, 1990–92; Pres. and Founder Jessie's Centre for Teenagers 1982–83, 1987–89; Pres. and Founding mem. Learnx Foundation 1977–79, Justice for Children 1979–80; Pres. and Founder Casey House Hospice (for AIDS) 1988–89, Hon. Dir 1989–; Pres. Casey House Foundation 1992–93 (Hon. Dir 1993–), Maggie's Prostitute Community Service Org. 1990–94; Chair. The Writers' Union of Canada 1979–80 (Life mem. 1994–); mem. Council, Amnesty International (Canada) 1978–85; Dir Canadian Inst. for Admin. of Justice 1983–84, The Electronic Rights Licensing Agency 1997–99; Vice-Pres. PEN (Canada) 1987–88, Dir 1988–89, Pres. 1989–90; Vice-Pres. Ward's Retreat 1990–91, Book and Periodical Council 1994–95 (Chair. 1995–96), Bd of Govs Etobicoko Gen. Hosp. 1994–98; Dir Frosst Health Care Foundation 1999–2002; Judge, Gov.-Gen.'s Literary Awards 1983–86, 2003; involved in many other public and humanitarian activities; Bencher Law Soc. of Upper Canada 1987–91, Duthie Lecture, Simon Fraser Univ. 1990, Sechelt, B.C. Margaret Laurence Lecture 1993; Harmony Movement Patron 1994–; Co-Chair. Campaign Against Child Poverty 1997–; Bruce Hutchison Lecture 1998, Carmelita Lawlor Lecture, Univ. of Toronto 2000; mem. Advisory Cttee Law Comm. of Canada 2000–; First Lecturer Dalton Camp Lectures, St Thomas 2002. *Radio includes:* Court of Opinions 1959–67, Human Sexuality 1966. *Television includes:* Generations (host) 1966, In Touch 1975–78, Callwood's National Treasures 1991–98, Caregivers 1998. *Publications:* Love, Hate, Fear and Anger 1964, The Law is Not for Women 1973, Portrait of Canada 1981, Emma 1984, Emotions 1986, Twelve Weeks in Spring 1986, Jim: A Life with AIDS 1988, The Sleepwalker 1990, June Callwood's National Treasurers 1994, Trial Without End 1995, The Man Who Lost Himself 2000, and 16 other books. *Honours:* Order of Ontario 1988; Hon. DUniv (Ottawa) 1987; Hon. Dr of Sacred Letters (Trinity Coll.) 1988; Hon. LLD (Memorial Univ., Newfoundland, Univ. of Toronto, York Univ.) 1988, (Univ. of Western Ont.) 1993, (McMaster) 1994, (Law Soc. of Upper Canada, Univ. of Calgary) 1997; Hon. LittD (Carleton Univ., Univ. of Alberta) 1988, (Guelph Univ.) 1989, (Univ. of New Brunswick) 1990; Hon. DCL (Acadia Univ.) 1993; Hon. DHumLitt (Mount St Vincent Univ.) 1993; City of Toronto Award of Merit 1974, Canadian Newspaper Hall of Fame 1984, Toronto Arts Foundation Lifetime Achievement Award 1990, Canadian Journalism Foundation Lifetime Achievement Award 2004, and other awards. *Address:* 21 Hillcroft Drive, Toronto, Ont., M9B 4X4, Canada. *Telephone:* (416) 231-1923. *Fax:* (416) 231-1923. *E-mail:* jcall@sympatico.ca (home).

CALVERT, Peter Anthony Richard, MA, PhD, FRHistS; British academic and writer; *Professor Emeritus of Comparative and International Politics, University of Southampton;* b. 19 Nov. 1936, Islandmagee, Co. Antrim, NI; s. of the late Raymond Calvert and Irene Calvert; m. Susan Ann Milbank 1987. *Education:* Campbell Coll., Belfast, Queens' Coll., Cambridge, Univ. of Michigan, Ann Arbor, USA. *Career:* Lecturer, Univ. of Southampton 1964–71, Sr Lecturer 1971–74, Reader 1974–83, Prof. of Comparative and Int. Politics 1984–2002, Prof. Emer. 2002–; mem. Royal Historical Soc., Royal Inst. of Int. Affairs. *Publications:* The Mexican Revolution 1910–1914 1968, A Study of Revolution 1970, The Falklands Crisis 1982, Guatemala 1985, The Foreign Policy of New States 1986, Argentina: Political Culture and Instability (with Susan Calvert) 1989, Revolution and Counter Revolution 1990, Latin America in the 20th Century (with Susan Calvert) 1990, 1993, An Introduction to Comparative Politics 1993, International Politics of Latin America 1994, Politics and Society in the Third World (with Susan Calvert) 1995, 2001, Revolution and International Politics 1996, The South, the North and the Environment (with Susan Calvert) 1999, Comparative Politics: An Introduction 2002, A Political and Economic Dictionary of Latin America 2004, Politics and Society in the Developing World (with Susan Calvert) 2007; editor: The Process of Political Succession 1987, The Central American Security System 1988, Political and Economic Encyclopedia of South America and the Caribbean 1991, The Resilience of Democracy (with Peter Burnell) 1999, Civil Society in Democratization (with Peter Burnell) 2004, Border and Territorial Disputes of the World (fourth edn) 2004. *Address:* School of Social Sciences, University of Southampton, Southampton, SO17 1BJ, England (office). *E-mail:* pcpol@socsci.soton.ac.uk (office). *Website:* www.soton.ac.uk (office).

CALVOCORESSI, Peter John Ambrose; British writer, book publisher and university lecturer; b. 17 Nov. 1912, Karachi, Pakistan; s. of Pandia J. Calvocoressi and Irene Calvocoressi (née Ralli); m. 1st Barbara Dorothy Eden 1938 (died 2004); two s.; m. 2nd Rachel Scott 2006. *Education:* Eton Coll. and Balliol Coll., Oxford. *Career:* called to Bar 1935; RAF Intelligence 1940–45;

assisted Trial of Major War Criminals, Nuremberg 1945–46; on staff, Royal Inst. of Int. Affairs 1949–54; partner Chatto & Windus, publishers 1955–65; Reader in Int. Relations, Sussex Univ. 1965–71; Ed. Dir Penguin Books 1972, Publr and Chief Exec. 1973–76; Chair. Open Univ. Educational Enterprises Ltd 1979–88; mem. UN sub-comm. on the Prevention of Discrimination 1961–71; Chair. The London Library 1970–73. *Publications:* Nuremberg: The Facts, the Law and the Consequences 1947, Survey of International Affairs: Vols for 1947–48, 1949–50, 1951, 1952 and 1953, Middle East Crisis (with Guy Wint) 1957, South Africa and World Opinion 1961, World Order and New States 1962, Total War (with Guy Wint) 1972, The British Experience: 1945–75, Top Secret Ultra 1980, A Time for Peace 1987, Who's Who in the Bible 1987, Resilient Europe 1991, Threading My Way 1994, Fall Out: World War II and the Shaping of Postwar Europe 1997, World Politics 1945–2000 2001. *Honours:* Hon. DUniv (Open Univ.) 1989. *Address:* Old Mill Lane Farmhouse, Marnhull, Dorset, DT10 1JX, England. *Telephone:* (1258) 820562 (home).

CAMDESSUS, Michel Jean; French international civil servant; *Honorary Governor, Banque de France;* b. 1 May 1933, Bayonne; s. of Alfred Camdessus and Madeleine Cassembon; m. Brigitte d'Arcy 1957; two s. four d. *Education:* Notre Dame Coll., Betharram, Inst. of Political Studies, Paris, Nat. School of Admin. *Career:* civil servant, Treasury, Ministry of Finance 1960–66; Chief, Bureau of Industrial Affairs, Treasury, Ministry of Econ. and Finance 1969–70; Chair. 'Investissements' Sub-Cttee of Treasury 1971; Deputy Dir of Treasury 1974–82, Dir 1982–84; Financial Attaché, Perm. Representation, EEC, Brussels 1966–69; mem. Monetary Cttee, EEC 1978, Pres. 1982; Sec. Conseil de Direction du Fonds de Développement Economique et Social 1971; Asst Dir 'Épargne et Crédit' Sub-Cttee 1972; Deputy Gov. Banque de France 1984, Gov. 1984–87, Hon. Gov. 1987–; Man. Dir IMF 1987–2000; Pres. Club de Paris 1978–84; Chair. Centre d'études prospectives et d'informations inter-nationales (CEPII) 2000–04, Semaines Sociales de France 2001–; UN Sec.-Gen. Special Envoy to the Monterrey Conf. 2002; Dir Banque Européenne d'Investissements, Banque Cen. des États de l'Afrique de l'Ouest, Air France, Soc. Nat. des Chemins de fer Français, Crédit Lyonnais (all 1978); Personal Rep. to Africa for French Govt and G8 Heads of State 2002. *Publications:* Notre foi dans ce siècle (with M. Albert, J. Boissonnat), Eau (with Bertrand Badré, Ivan Chéret, Pierre-Frédéric Tenière-Buchot) 2004, Le Sursaut: Vers une nouvelle croissance pour la France 2004. *Honours:* Commdr, Légion d'honneur; Chevalier, Ordre nat. du Mérite; Croix de la Valeur militaire. *Address:* Banque de France, 09–1060, 75049 Paris Cedex 01 (office); 27 rue de Valois, 75001 Paris, France (home). *Telephone:* 1-42-97-73-38 (office). *Fax:* 1-42-97-76-42 (office). *E-mail:* cyliane.huot@banque-france.fr (office).

CAMERON, Dame Averil Millicent, DBE, MA, PhD, FBA, FSA; British historian of late antiquity and Byzantine studies and writer; *Warden, Keble College, University of Oxford;* b. 8 Feb. 1940, Leek, Staffs.; d. of Tom Roy Sutton and Millicent Drew; m. Alan Douglas Edward Cameron 1962 (divorced 1980); one s. one d. *Education:* Somerville Coll., Oxford, Univ. Coll., London. *Career:* Asst Lecturer Classics, King's Coll., London 1965, Lecturer 1968, Reader in Ancient History 1970, Prof. 1978–88, Prof. Late Antique and Byzantine Studies 1988–94, Dir Centre for Hellenic Studies 1989–94, Fellow 1987–; Warden of Keble Coll., Oxford 1994–; Prof. of Late Antique and Byzantine History, Oxford Univ. 1997–; Pro-Vice-Chancellor Univ. of Oxford 2001–; Visiting Prof., Columbia Univ., New York 1967–68; Visiting Mem., Inst. for Advanced Study, Princeton 1977–78, Distinguished Visitor 1992; Summer Fellow, Dumbarton Oaks 1980; Sather Prof. of Classical Literature, Univ. of Calif. 1985–86; Visiting Prof. Coll. de France 1987, Lansdowne Lecturer, Victoria, BC 1992; Hon. Fellow Somerville Coll., Oxford; Ed. Journal of Roman Studies 1985–90; Pres. Soc. for the Promotion of Roman Studies 1995–98, Ecclesiastical History Soc. 2005–06, Council for British Research in the Levant 2005–; Chair. Cathedrals Fabric Comm. for England 1999–2005, Review Group on the Royal Peculiars 1999–2000. *Publications:* Procopius 1967, Agathias 1970, Corippus, In laudem Iustini minoris 1976, Images of Women in Antiquity (ed.) 1983, Continuity and Change in Sixth-Century Byzantium 1981, Constantinople in the Eighth Century (ed.) 1984, Procopius and the Sixth Century 1985, 1996, History as Text (ed.) 1989, The Greek Renaissance in the Roman Empire (ed.) 1990, Christianity and the Rhetoric of Empire 1991, The Byzantine and Early Islamic Near East I (ed.) 1992, II (ed.) 1994, III (ed.) 1995, The Later Roman Empire 1993, The Mediterranean World in Late Antiquity A.D. 395–600 1993, Changing Cultures in Early Byzantium (ed.) 1996, Cambridge Ancient History Vol. XIII. The Late Empire (ed.) 1998, Eusebius, Life of Constantine (ed. and trans.) 1999, Cambridge Ancient History Vol. XIV. Late Antiquity: Empire and Successors (ed.) 2000, Fifty Years of Prosopography (ed.) 2003, Cambridge Ancient History Vol. XII. The Crisis of Empire (ed.) 2005. *Honours:* Hon. DLitt (Warwick, St Andrews, Queen's, Belfast, Aberdeen, London); Hon. DTheol (Lund). *Address:* Keble College, Oxford, OX1 3PG, England. *Telephone:* (1865) 272700 (office). *Fax:* (1865) 272785 (office). *E-mail:* averil.cameron@keb.ox.ac.uk (office). *Website:* www.keble.ox.ac.uk (office).

CAMERON, Charla (see Skinner, Gloria Dale)

CAMERON, Donald Allan, (Silver Donald Cameron), MA, PhD; Canadian author; b. 21 June 1937, Toronto, Ont.; s. of Dr Maxwell A Cameron and Hazel Robertson Cameron; m. 1st Catherine Ann Cahoon 1959; three s. one d.; m. 2nd Lulu Terrio 1980 (died 1996); one s.; m. 3rd Marjorie L. Simmins 1998. *Education:* Univ. of British Columbia, Univ. of California, USA, Univ. of London, UK. *Career:* Assoc. Prof. of English, Univ. of New Brunswick

1968–71; Writer-in-Residence, Univ. Coll. of Cape Breton, NS 1978–80, Dean, School of Community Studies 1994–96, Special Asst to the Pres. 1997–99; Writer-in-Residence, Univ. of Prince Edward Island 1985–86, Nova Scotia Coll. of Art and Design 1987–88; columnist, Halifaz (NS) Herald 1998–; mem. Writers Fed., NS. *Publications:* Faces of Leacock 1967, Conversations with Canadian Novelists 1973, The Education of Everett Richardson 1977, Seasons in the Rain (essays) 1978, Dragon Lady 1980, The Baitchopper (children's novel) 1982, Schooner: Bluenose and Bluenose II 1984, Outhouses of the West 1988, Wind, Whales and Whisky: A Cape Breton Voyage 1991, Lifetime: A Treasury of Uncommon Wisdoms (co-author) 1992, Once Upon a Schooner: An Offshore Voyage In Bluenose II 1992, Iceboats to Superferries: An Illustrated History of Marine Atlantic (co-author), Sniffing the Coast: An Acadian Voyage 1993, Sterling Silver: Rants, Raves and Revelations 1994, The Living Beach 1998, Sailing Away from Winter 2007; other: numerous articles, radio dramas, short stories, TV scripts and stage plays. *Honours:* Hon. DCL (King's Coll., London) 2004; four Nat. Magazine Awards, Best Short Film, Canadian Film Celebration, City of Dartmouth Book Award 1992, Atlantic Provinces Booksellers Choice Award 1992. *Address:* 24 Armshore Drive, Halifax, NS B3N 1M5, Canada. *Telephone:* (902) 446-5577. *E-mail:* sdc@silverdonaldcameron.ca (home). *Website:* www.silverdonaldcameron.ca; www.sailingawayfromwinter.blogspot.com.

CAMERON, Matt; Australian playwright and screenwriter. *Plays:* Mr Melancholy 1995, Footprints on Water 1997, Tear From a Glass Eye 1998, The Eskimo Calling 2000, Whispering Death 2000, Man the Balloon 2001, Ruby Moon 2003. *Television writing:* SeaChange 1998, Small Tales and True 1998, Introducing Gary Petty (also co-creator and writer) 2000. *Honours:* ANPC New Dramatists' Award, Wal Cherry Play of the Year Award, British Council Int. New Playwriting Award, Centenary Medal for Service to Australian Soc. and Literature, AWGIE Award for Best Television Comedy. *Literary Agent:* RGM Associates, PO Box 128, Surry Hills, NSW 2010, Australia. *Telephone:* (2) 9281-3911. *Fax:* (2) 9281-4705. *E-mail:* info@rgm.com.au. *Website:* www.rgm.com.au.

CAMERON WATT, Donald, MA, DLitt, FBA, FRHistS; British historian and academic; *Professor Emeritus of International History, London School of Economics;* b. 17 May 1928, Rugby; s. of Robert Cameron Watt and Barbara Bidwell; m. 1st Marianne R. Grau 1951 (died 1962); m. 2nd Felicia Cobb Stanley 1962 (died 1997); one s., one step-d. *Education:* Rugby School and Oriel Coll., Oxford. *Career:* Asst Ed. (Foreign Office Research Dept), Documents on German Foreign Policy 1918–1945, 1951–54, 1951–59; Asst Lecturer in Political History, LSE 1954–56, Lecturer in Int. History 1957–63, Sr Lecturer 1964–65; Reader in Int. History, Univ. of London 1966–72, Prof. in Int. History 1972–82, Stevenson Prof. of Int. History 1982–93, Prof. Emer. 1993–; Ed. Survey of Int. Affairs, Royal Inst. of Int. Affairs 1962–71; Historian, Cabinet Office Historical Section 1977–94; Rockefeller Fellow in Social Sciences 1960–61; Fellow Polish Acad. of Arts and Sciences, Kraków; fmr FRSA; Sec. Comm. for History of Int. Relations 1982–95, Vice Pres. 1995–. *Publications:* Oxford Poetry 1950 (ed.) 1951, Britain and the Suez Canal 1956, Documents on the Suez Crisis 1957, Britain Looks to Germany 1965, Personalities and Policies 1965, A History of the World in the 20th Century 1967, Contemporary History in Europe 1969, Hitler's Mein Kampf (ed.) 1969, 1992, Current British Foreign Policy 1970–72, Too Serious a Business 1975, 1992, Succeeding John Bull, America in Britain's Place 1900–1975 1983, Documents on British Foreign Affairs 1867–1939 1985–97, How War Came 1989, Argentina Between the Great Powers 1990. *Honours:* Hon. Fellow Oriel Coll., Oxford 1998; Wolfson Prize for History 1990. *Address:* c/o Department of International History, London School of Economics, Aldwych, London, WC2A 2AE, England. *Website:* www.lse.ac.uk/collections/internationalHistory.

CAMILLERI, Andrea; Italian novelist; b. Porto Empedocle, nr Agrigento; m.; three c. *Career:* dir and scriptwriter since World War II; especially known for crime TV productions featuring Lt Sheridan and Insp. Maigret; as novelist created Insp. Montalbano. *Publications:* La forma dell'acqua (trans. as The Shape of Water) 1994, Il cane di terracotta (trans. as The Terracotta Dog) 1996, Il ladro di merendine (trans. as The Snack Thief) 1996, La voce del violino (trans. as The Voice of the Violin) 1997, Un mese con Montalbano 1998, Gli arancini di Montalbano 1999, La gita a Tindari (trans. as Excursion to Tindari) 2000, L'odore della notte (trans. as The Scent of the Night) 2001, La paura di Montalbano 2002. *Honours:* numerous literary awards. *Address:* c/o Picador, 20 New Wharf Road, London, N1 9RR, England. *Website:* www.andreacamilleri.net.

CAMPBELL, Alistair Te Ariki, BA, DipEd; New Zealand poet, dramatist and novelist; b. 25 June 1925, Rarotonga, Cook Islands; m. 1st Fleur Adcock 1952; m. 2nd Meg Andersen 1958; three s. two d. *Education:* Victoria Univ. of Wellington, Wellington Teachers' Coll. *Career:* teacher 1954–; Ed., Dept of Educ. 1955–72, Sr Ed. NZ Council for Educational Research 1972–87; Writer's Fellow, Victoria Univ. of Wellington 1992; mem. PEN International, New Zealand Centre. *Publications:* poetry: Mine Eyes Dazzle 1950, Sanctuary of Spirits 1963, Wild Honey 1964, Blue Rain 1967, Kapiti: Selected Poems 1972, Dreams, Yellow Lions 1975, The Dark Lord of Savaiki 1980, Collected Poems 1981, Soul Traps 1985, Stone Rain: The Polynesian Strain 1992, Death and the Tagua 1995, Pocket Collected Poems 1996, Gallipoli and Other Poems 1999, Maori Battalion 2001, Poets in Our Youth: Four Letters in Verse 2002; fiction: The Frigate Bird 1989, Sidewinder 1991, Tia 1993, Fantasy with Witches 1998, The Dark Lord of Saviki: Collected Poems 2005; autobiography: Island to Island 1984; plays: The Suicide 1965, When the Bough Breaks 1970;

children's story: The Happy Summer 1961; contrib. to Landfall, New Zealand Listener, Poetry New Zealand, New Zealand Poetry Yearbook, Comment, Poetry Australia, Poetry New Zealand. *Honours:* Hon. DLitt (Victoria Univ. of Wellington) 1999; Officer of the NZ Order of Merit; La Spezia Int. Film Festival Gold Medal for TV documentary 1974, NZ Book Award for Poetry 1982, Pacific Islands Artists Award 1998, Prime Minister's Award for Literary Achievement 2005. *Address:* 4B Rawhiti Road, Pukerua Bay, Wellington, New Zealand. *Telephone:* (4) 2399580 (home). *E-mail:* meg.campbell@actrix.gen.nz (home).

CAMPBELL, Donald; British poet and dramatist; b. 25 Feb. 1940, Caithness, Scotland; m. Jean Fairgrieve 1966; one s. *Career:* writer-in-residence, Edinburgh Education Dept 1974–77, Royal Lyceum Theatre 1981–82; Fellow in Creative Writing, Univ. of Dundee 1987–89; William Soutar Fellow, Perth Libraries 1991–93; Royal Literary Fund Fellow, Napier Univ. 2000–02. *Publications:* poetry: Poems 1971, Rhymes 'n' Reasons 1972, Murals: Poems in Scots 1975, Blether: A Collection of Poems 1979, A Brighter Sunshine 1983, Selected Poems 1870–90 1990, Playing for Scotland 1996, Edinburgh: A cultural and literary history 2003; plays for stage, radio and television. *Address:* 85 Spottiswoode Street, Edinburgh, EH9 1BZ, Scotland.

CAMPBELL, Ewing, BBA, MA, PhD; American writer and academic; b. 26 Dec. 1940, Alice, TX. *Education:* North Texas State University, University of Southern Mississippi, Oklahoma State University. *Career:* Lecturer, University of Texas at Austin, 1981–82, Oklahoma State University, 1982–83, Wharton Community College, 1983–84; Asst Prof., 1984–90, Assoc. Prof., 1990–, Full Prof., 1999–, Texas A & M University; mem. Texas Institute of Letters. *Publications:* Fiction: Weave It Like Nightfall, 1977; The Way of Sequestered Places, 1982; The Rincón Triptych, 1984; The Tex-Mex Express, 1993; Madonna, Maleva, 1995. Short Fiction: Piranesi's Dream, 1986. Criticism: Raymond Carver: A Study of the Short Fiction, 1992. Contributions: Stories and articles to many periodicals. *Honours:* Fulbright Scholar, Argentina, 1989, Spain, 1997; National Endowments for the Arts Fellowship, 1990; Dobie-Paisano Ralph A. Johnston Award, 1992; Chris O'Malley Fiction Prize, 1998; American Literary Fiction Prize, 2002. *Address:* c/o Rager Media, 1016 West Abbey, Medina, OH 44256, USA.

CAMPBELL, Ian, MA, PhD; British academic and writer; *Professor of Scottish and Victorian Literature, University of Edinburgh;* b. 25 Aug. 1942, Lausanne, Switzerland. *Education:* Univ. of Aberdeen, Univ. of Edinburgh. *Career:* Reader in English 1967–92, Prof. of Scottish and Victorian Literature 1992–, Univ. of Edinburgh; British Council appointments in France, Germany; mem. Carlyle Soc. (pres.), Scottish Asscn for the Speaking of Verse, Asscn for Scottish Literary Studies (council mem.). *Publications:* Thomas Carlyle Letters (33 vols) 1970–2005, Carlyle 1974, Nineteenth Century Scottish Fiction: Critical Essays 1978, Thomas and Jane 1980, Kailyard 1981, Lewis Grassic Gibbon 1986, Spartacus 1987, Gibbon's Complete Works (ed.); contrib. to numerous papers to learned journals. *Honours:* British Acad. Research Fellowship 1980. *Address:* Department of English Literature, University of Edinburgh, David Hume Tower, George Square, Edinburgh, EH8 9JX, Scotland. *E-mail:* Ian.Campbell@ed.ac.uk.

CAMPBELL, John Malcolm, MA, PhD; British writer; b. 2 Sept. 1947, London, England; m. Alison McCracken 1972; one s. one d. *Education:* Charterhouse, Univ. of Edinburgh. *Career:* mem. Soc. of Authors. *Publications:* Lloyd George: The Goat in the Wilderness 1977, F. E. Smith, First Earl of Birkenhead 1983, Roy Jenkins: A Biography 1983, Nye Bevan and the Mirage of British Socialism 1987, The Experience of World War II (ed.) 1989, Makers of the Twentieth Century (ed.) 1990–92, Edward Heath 1993, Margaret Thatcher: Vol. I: The Grocer's Daughter 2000, Vol. II: The Iron Lady 2003, If Love Were All... the Story of Frances Stevenson and David Lloyd George 2006; contrib. book reviews to The Times, TLS, The Independent, Sunday Telegraph, etc. *Honours:* Yorkshire Post Best First Book Award 1977, NCR Book Award for Non-Fiction 1994. *Address:* 2 Lansdowne Crescent, London, W11 2NH, England.

CAMPBELL, Judith (see Pares, Marion)

CAMPBELL, Philip Henry Montgomery, PhD, FInstP, FRAS; British journalist and academic; *Editor-in-Chief, Nature;* b. 19 April 1951, s. of Hugh Campbell and Mary Montgomery Campbell; m. Judie Yelton 1980 (died 1992); two s. *Education:* Shrewsbury School, Univ. of Bristol, Queen Mary Coll., London, Univ. of Leicester. *Career:* postdoctoral research asst, Dept of Physics, Univ. of Leicester 1977–79; Asst Ed. Nature journal 1979–82, Physical Sciences Ed. 1982–88, Ed., Nature journal and Ed.-in-Chief Nature journal and Nature publications 1995–, Dir Nature Publishing Group 1997–; founding Ed. Physics World magazine 1988–95; Trustee Cancer Research UK. *Radio:* broadcasts on BBC World Service. *Publications:* numerous papers and articles in journals, magazines and newspapers. *Honours:* Hon. DSc (Leicester) 1999. *Address:* c/o Nature Publishing Group, The Macmillan Building, 4 Crinan Street, London, N1 9XW, England. *Telephone:* (20) 7833-4000. *Fax:* (20) 7843-4596. *E-mail:* exec@nature.com. *Website:* www.nature.com.

CAMPBELL, Ramsey; British writer and film critic; b. 4 Jan. 1946, Liverpool, England; m. Jenny Chandler 1971, one s. one d. *Career:* film reviewer, BBC Radio Merseyside 1969–; full-time writer 1973–; mem. British Fantasy Society (fmr pres.), Soc. of Fantastic Films. *Publications:* Fiction: The Doll Who Ate His Mother, 1976; The Face That Must Die, 1979; The Parasite,

1980; The Nameless, 1981; Incarnate, 1983; The Claw, 1983, US edn as Night of the Claw; Obsession, 1985; The Hungry Moon, 1986; The Influence, 1988; Ancient Images, 1989; Midnight Sun, 1990; The Count of Eleven, 1991; The Long Lost, 1993; The One Safe Place, 1995; The House on Nazareth Hill, 1996; The Last Voice They Hear, 1998; Silent Children, 2000; The Darkest Part of the Woods, 2002; The Overnight, 2003. Short Stories: The Inhabitant of the Lake and Less Welcome Tenants, 1964; Demons by Daylight, 1973; The Height of the Scream, 1976; Dark Companions, 1982; Cold Print, 1985; Black Wine (with Charles L. Grant), 1986; Night Visions 3 (with Clive Barker and Lisa Tuttle), 1986; Scared Stiff, 1987; Dark Feasts: The World of Ramsey Campbell, 1987; Waking Nightmares, 1991; Alone With the Horrors, 1993; Strange Things and Stranger Places, 1993; Ghosts and Grisly Things, 1998; Told by the Dead, 2003. Novella: Needing Ghosts, 1990. Other: Ramsey Campbell, Probably (collected non-fiction), 2002. *Honours:* Liverpool Daily Post and Echo Award for Literature, 1993; World Fantasy Award, Bram Stoker Award, Best Collection, 1994; Best Novel, International Horror Guild, 1998; Grand Master, World Horror Convention, 1999; Lifetime Achievement Award, Horror Writers' Asscn, 1999. *Address:* 31 Penkett Road, Wallasey CH45 7QF, Merseyside, England. *Website:* www.ramseycampbell.com.

CAMPION, Daniel Ray, AB, MA, PhD; American editor, poet and literary critic; *Manager of Editorial Services, ACT, Inc.*; b. 23 Aug. 1949, Oak Park, Ill.; s. of Raymond E. Campion and Wilma F. Campion; m. JoAnn E. Castagna. *Education:* Univ. of Chicago, Univ. of Illinois, Chicago, Univ. of Iowa. *Career:* Production Ed. Encyclopaedia Britannica Inc., Chicago, Ill. 1972–74; Children's Book Ed., Follett Publishing Co., Chicago 1977–78; Teaching and Research Asst, Univ. of Iowa 1978–84; Test Specialist Sr Ed. and Man. Editorial Services, ACT Inc. 1984–; mem. Authors' Guild, MLA, Midwest MLA, Nat. Council of Teachers of English, Soc. for the Study of Midwestern Literature. *Publications:* Walt Whitman: The Measure of his Song (co-ed.) 1981, Calypso (poems) 1981, Peter De Vries and Surrealism 1995; contrib. of poetry and articles to periodicals, including College English, Literary Magazine Review, The Writer's Chronicle, Hispanic Journal, Rolling Stone, Chicago Tribune, Chicago Reader, Ascent, Poet Lore, English Journal, Poetry, The North American Review. *Honours:* Univ. of Chicago Festival of the Arts Poetry Award 1967, Triton Coll. All-Nations Poetry Contest Award, River Grove, Ill. 1975, Illinois Arts Council Poetry Award 1979. *Address:* 1700 Rochester Avenue, Iowa City, IA 52245-6035, USA. *E-mail:* dan.campion@act.org (office).

CAMPTON, David; British playwright and children's writer; b. 5 June 1924, Leicester. *Education:* Wyggeston Boys' School. *Career:* mem. Writers Guild of Great Britain. *Publications:* On Stage: Containing 17 Sketches and 1 Monologue, 1964; Resting Place, 1964; The Manipulator, 1964; Split Down the Middle, 1965; Little Brother, Little Sister and Out of the Flying Pan, 1966; Two Leaves and a Stalk, 1967; Angel Unwilling, 1967; Ladies Night: 4 Plays for Women, 1967; More Sketches, 1967; Laughter and Fear, 9 One-Act Plays, 1969; The Right Place, 1969; On Stage Again: Containing 14 Sketches and 2 Monologues, 1969; Now and Then, 1970; The Life and Death of Almost Everybody, 1970; Timesneeze, 1970; Gulliver in Lilliput (reader), 1970; Gulliver in The Land of Giants (reader), 1970; The Wooden Horse of Troy (reader), 1970; Jonah, 1971; The Cagebirds, 1971; Us and Them, 1972; Carmilla, 1972; In Committee, 1972; Come Back Tomorrow, 1972; Three Gothic Plays, 1973; Modern Aesop (reader), 1976; One Possessed, 1977; What Are You Doing Here?, 1978; The Do-It-Yourself Frankenstein Outfit, 1978; Zodiac, 1978; After Midnight: Before Dawn, 1978; Pieces of Campton, 1979; Parcel, 1979; Everybody's Friend, 1979; Who Calls?, 1980; Attitudes, 1980; Freedom Log, 1980; Dark Wings, 1981; Look-Sea, 1981; Great Whales, 1981; Who's a Hero, Then?, 1981; Dead and Alive, 1983; But Not Here, 1984; Singing in the Wilderness, 1986; Mrs Meadowsweet, 1986; The Vampyre (children's book), 1986; Our Branch in Brussels, 1986; Cards, Cups and Crystal Ball, 1986; Can You Hear the Music?, 1988; The Winter of 1917, 1989; Smile, 1990; Becoming a Playwright, 1992; The Evergreens, 1994; Permission to Cry, 1996. Contributions: Amateur Stage; Writers News; Drama; Whispers. *Honours:* Hon. DLit (Univ. of Leicester) 2006. *Address:* 35 Liberty Road, Glenfield, Leicester, LE3 8JF, England. *Telephone:* (116) 2873951 (office). *E-mail:* davidcampton@aol.com (office).

CAMROSE, 4th Viscount (cr. 2001), of Hackwood Park, Southampton; **Adrian Michael Berry,** FRGS, FRAS; British writer and journalist; b. 15 June 1937, London, England; m. Marina Beatrice 1967; one s. one d. *Education:* Eton, Christ Church, Oxford. *Career:* correspondent, Time Magazine, New York 1965–67; science correspondent, Daily Telegraph, London 1977–96, Consulting Ed. (science) 1996–; Fellow British Interplanetary Soc. 1986–. *Publications:* The Next Ten Thousand Years: A Vision of Man's Future in the Universe 1974, The Iron Sun: Crossing the Universe Through Black Holes 1977, From Apes to Astronauts 1981, The Super Intelligent Machine 1983, High Skies and Yellow Rain 1983, Koyama's Diamond (fiction) 1984, Labyrinth of Lies (fiction) 1985, Ice With Your Evolution 1986, Computer Software: The Kings and Queens of England 1985, Harrap's Book of Scientific Anecdotes 1989, The Next 500 Years 1995, Galileo and the Dolphins 1996, The Giant Leap 1999. *Address:* 11 Cottesmore Gardens, Kensington, London, W8 5PR, England.

CANIN, Ethan, BA, MFA, MD; American writer; b. 19 July 1960, Ann Arbor, MI. *Education:* Stanford University, University of Iowa, Harvard University. *Publications:* Emperor of the Air, 1988; Blue River, 1991; The Palace Thief, 1994; For Kings and Planets, 1998; Carry Me Across the Water, 2001. Contributions: anthologies and periodicals.

CANNADINE, David Nicholas, DPhil, LittD, FRHistS, FBA, FRSA, FRSL; British historian and academic; *Queen Elizabeth the Queen Mother Professor of British History, Institute of Historical Research, University of London*; b. 7 Sept. 1950, s. of Sydney Douglas Cannadine and Dorothy Mary Hughes; m. Linda Jane Colley (q.v.) 1982; one d. (deceased). *Education:* King Edward's Five Ways School, Birmingham, Clare Coll., Cambridge, St John's Coll., Oxford, Princeton Univ., USA. *Career:* Resident Fellow, St John's Coll. Cambridge 1975–77, Asst Lecturer in History 1976–80, Lecturer 1980–88; Fellow, Christ's Coll. Cambridge 1977–88, Dir of Studies in History 1977–83, Tutor 1979–81; Prof. of History, Columbia Univ., New York 1988–92, Moore Collegiate Prof. 1992–98; Dir Inst. of Historical Research Univ. of London 1998–2003, Prof. 1998–2003, Queen Elizabeth the Queen Mother Prof. of British History 2003–, Hon. Fellow 2005–; Visiting mem. Inst. for Advanced Study 1980–81, Princeton, NJ, Visiting Fellow Council of the Humanities 2003–05; Visiting Prof., Birkbeck Coll., Univ. of London 1995–97; Visiting Fellow, Whitney Humanities Center, Yale Univ. 1995–96; Visiting Scholar, Pembroke Coll., Cambridge 1997; Pres. Worcs. Historical Soc. 1999–; Vice-Pres. British Records Soc. 1998–, Royal Historical Soc. 1998–2002; Chair. IHR Trust 1999–2003; mem. Advisory Bd Centre for Study of Soc. and Politics, Kingston Univ. 1998–2003, ICBH 1998–2003, Advisory Council Warburg Inst. 1998–2003, Inst. of US Studies 1999–2004, Public Record Office 1999–2004, Inst. of English Studies 2000–03, Inst. of Latin American Studies 2000–04, Kennedy Memorial Trust 2000–, Nat. Trust Eastern Regional Cttee 2000–, Royal Mint Advisory Cttee 2004–, Editorial Bd History of Parliament 2004–, Advisory Council Inst. for the Study of the Americas 2004–; Gov. Ipswich School 1982–88; Fellow, Berkeley Coll., Yale Univ. 1985, J. P. Morgan Library, New York 1992–98; American Council of Learned Socs Fellowship 1990–91; regular radio and TV broadcaster; Ed.-in-Chief Journal of Maritime History 1999–; Gen. Ed. Studies in Modern History 1979–2002, Penguin History of Britain 1989–, Penguin History of Europe 1991–, Historical Research 1998–2003; Trustee Kennedy Memorial Scholarship Fund 1999–, Nat. Portrait Gallery 2000– (Chair. of Trustees 2005–), British Empire and Commonwealth Museum 2003–, Commr English Heritage 2001–; Visiting Fellow, Australian Nat. Univ. 2005, Nat. Humanities Center, North Carolina 2006. *Radio:* A Point of View (BBC Radio 4) 2005–06. *Publications:* Lords and Landlords: The Aristocracy And The Towns 1774–1967 1980, (ed. and contrib.) Patricians, Power and Politics in Nineteenth-Century Towns 1982, (jt and contrib.) H. J. Dyos, Exploring the Urban Past 1982, (jt and contrib.) Rituals of Royalty: Power and Ceremonial in Traditional Societies 1987, The Pleasures of the Past 1989, (ed. and contrib.) Winston Churchill's Famous Speeches 1989, (jt and contrib.) The First Modern Society: Essays in English History in Honour of Lawrence Stone 1989, The Decline and Fall of the British Aristocracy (Lionel Trilling Prize) 1990, G. M. Trevelyan: A Life in History 1992, Aspects of Aristocracy: Grandeur and Decline in Modern Britain 1994, (jt and contrib.) History and Biography: Essays in Honour of Derek Beales 1996, Class in Britain 1998, History in Our Time 1998, Making History Now 1999, Ornamentalism: How the British Saw Their Empire 2001, In Churchill's Shadow: Confronting the Past in Modern Britain 2002, What is History Now? (ed.) 2002, History and the Media (ed.) 2004, Winston Churchill in the 21st Century (co-ed. and contrib.) 2004, Admiral Lord Nelson, his context and legacy (ed.) 2005, Mellon 2006; numerous contribs to other books and learned journals. *Honours:* Hon. Fellow, Christ's Coll. Cambridge 2005 Hon. DLitt (East Anglia) 2001, (South Bank) 2001, (Birmingham) 2002; T. S. Ashton Prize (Econ. History Soc.) 1977, Silver Jubilee Prize (Agric. History Soc.) 1977, Lionel Trilling Prize 1991, Governors' Award 1991, Dean's Distinguished Award in the Humanities, Columbia Univ. 1996. *Address:* Institute of Historical Research, Senate House, Malet Street, London, WC1E 7HU, England (office). *Telephone:* (20) 7664-4893 (office). *Fax:* (20) 7664-4894 (office). *Website:* www.history.ac.uk (office).

CANNON, Frank (see Mayhar, Ardath)

CANNON, Steve, BA; American writer, dramatist, educator and publisher; b. 10 April 1935, New Orleans, LA; one s. (deceased). *Education:* University of Nebraska. *Career:* Prof. of Humanities, Medgar Evers College, CUNY, 1971–92; mem. PEN, New York Chapter. *Publications:* Groove, Bang and Jive Around, 1969; Introduction to Rouzing the Rubble, 1991; Reminicin' in C, 1995. Plays: The Set Up, 1991; Chump Change, 1992; Nothing to Lose, 1993; Now What, What Now?, 1994; En Vogue, 1994; Top of the World, 1995; Marvellous, 1996.

CANTALUPO, Charles, BA, MA, PhD; American academic, poet and writer; b. 17 Oct. 1951, Orange, NJ; m. 1st Catherine Musello 1976 (died 1983); one s. (deceased); m. 2nd Barbara Dorosh 1988; one s. three d. *Education:* Univ. of Kent at Canterbury, Washington Univ., St Louis, Rutgers Univ. *Career:* Teaching Asst, 1973–76, Instructor, 1977–79, Rutgers Univ.; Instructor, 1980–81, Asst Prof., 1981–89, Assoc. Prof., 1989–96, Prof. of English, 1996–99, Prof. of English and Comparative Literature, 1999–2001, Prof. of English, Comparative Literature and African Studies, 2002–, Pennsylvania State Univ., Schuylkill Haven. *Publications:* The Art of Hope (poems), 1983; A Literary Leviathan: Thomas Hobbe's Masterpiece of Language, 1991; The World of Ngugi wa Thiong'o (ed.), 1995; Poetry, Mysticism, and Feminism: From th' Nave to the Chops, 1995; Ngugi wa Thiong'o: Text and Contexts (ed.), 1995; Anima/l Wo/man and Other Spirits (poems), 1996; We Have Our Voice: Selected Poems of Reesom Haile (trans.), 2000; We Invented the Wheel: Poems by Reesom Haile (trans.), 2002; Light the Lights (poems), 2004. Contributions: books, anthologies, scholarly journals, periodicals, newspapers and websites. *Honours:* American Acad. of Poets Prize, 1976.

CANTSIN, Monty (see Home, Stewart Ramsay)

CANTWELL, Aston (see Platt, Charles Michael)

CAPIE, Forrest Hunter, BA, MSc, PhD, FRSA; British academic; *Official Historian, Bank of England, London*; b. 1 Dec. 1940, Glasgow, Scotland; m. Dianna Dix 1967. *Education:* Univ. of Auckland, New Zealand, Univ. of London. *Career:* Lecturer, Univ. of Warwick 1972–74, Univ. of Leeds 1974–79; Visiting Lecturer 1978–79, Lecturer 1979–82, Sr Lecturer 1982–83, Reader 1983–86, Prof. of Economic History 1986–, City Univ., London; various guest lectureships; Ed., Economic History Review 1993–; Official Historian Bank of England 2004–; mem. Asscn of Business Historians, Cliometrics Soc., Economic History Asscn, Economic History Soc., Royal Economic Soc., Western Economics Asscn. *Publications:* The British Economy Between the Wars (with M. Collins) 1983, Depression and Protectionism: Britain Between the Wars 1983, A Monetary History of the United Kingdom, 1870–1982: Data Sources and Methods (with A. Webber) 1985, Financial Crises and the World Banking System (ed. with G. E. Wood) 1986, Monetary Economics in the 1980s: Some Themes from Henry Thornton (ed. with G. E. Wood) 1989, A Directory of Economic Institutions (ed.) 1990, Unregulated Banking: Chaos or Order? (ed. with G. E. Wood) 1991, Major Inflations in History (ed.) 1991, Protectionism in the World Economy (ed.) 1992, Did the Banks Fail British Industry? (with M. Collins) 1992, Monetary Regimes in Transition (ed. with M. Bordo) 1993, A History of Banking (ed., 10 vols) 1993, Tariffs and Growth 1994, The Future of Central Banking (with Charles Goodhart, Stanley Fischer and Norbert Schnadt) 1994, Monetary Economics in the 1990s (ed. with G. E. Wood) 1996, Asset Prices and the Real Economy (ed. with G. E. Wood) 1997, Policy Makers on Policy (ed. with G. E. Wood) 2001, World Economic Liberalization in Historical Perspective 2001, Capital Controls: A Cure Worse Than the Disease 2002; contrib. to scholarly books and journals. *Honours:* several grants and fellowships. *Address:* Bank of England, Threadneedle Street, London, EC2R 8AH, England (office). *Telephone:* (20) 7601-3680 (office). *E-mail:* forrest.capie@bankofengland.co.uk (office).

CAPUTO, Philip Joseph, BA; American writer and screenwriter; b. 10 June 1941, Chicago, IL; m. 1st Jill Esther Ongemach 1969 (divorced 1982); two s.; m. 2nd Marcelle Lynn Besse 1982 (divorced 1985); m. 3rd Leslie Blanchard Ware 1988. *Education:* Purdue Univ., Loyola Univ. *Career:* staff 1969–72, Foreign Correspondent 1972–77, Chicago Tribune; freelance writer 1977–; screenwriter, Mercury-Douglas Productions, Paramount Pictures 1987–; mem. Authors' Guild. *Publications:* A Rumor of War (memoir) 1977, Horn of Africa (novel) 1980, Del Corso's Gallery (novel) 1983, Indian Country: A Novel 1987, Means of Escape (memoir) 1991, Equation for Evil (novel) 1996, Exiles (three novellas) 1997, The Voyage (novel) 1999, Acts of Faith 2005; contrib. to various periodicals. *Honours:* Pulitzer Prize for Reporting (with George Bliss) 1973, George Polk Award 1973, Overseas Press Club Award, Sidney Hillman Award. *Literary Agent:* Aaron M. Priest Literary Agency, 708 Third Avenue, 23rd Floor, New York, NY 10017, USA.

CARD, Orson Scott, (Brian Green, Byron Walley), BA, MA; American writer; b. 24 Aug. 1951, Richland, WA; m. Kristine Allen 1977, two s. three d. *Education:* Brigham Young University, University of Utah. *Career:* mem. Authors' Guild; SFWA. *Publications:* Capitol, 1978; Hot Sleep: The Worthing Chronicle, 1978; A Planet Called Treason, 1979, revised edn as Treason, 1988; Songmaster, 1980; Unaccompanied Sonata and Other Stories, 1980; Saintspeak: The Mormon Dictionary, 1981; Ainge, 1982; Hart's Hope, 1983; A Woman of Destiny, 1983, revised edn as Saints, 1988; The Worthing Chronicle, 1983; Ender's Game, 1985; Speaker for the Dead, 1986; Cardography, 1987; Free Lancers (with others), 1987; Seventh Son, 1987; Wyrms, 1987; Characters and Viewpoint, 1988; Red Prophet, 1988; Folk of the Fringe, 1989; The Abyss, 1989; Prentice Alvin, 1989; How to Write Science Fiction and Fantasy, 1990; Eye for Eye–The Tunesmith (with Lloyd Biggle), 1990; Maps in a Mirror: The Short Fiction of Orson Scott Card, 1990; Worthing Saga, 1990; Xenocide, 1991; The Changed Man, 1992; Cruel Miracles, 1992; Flux, 1992; The Memory of Earth, 1992; Lost Boys, 1992; The Call of the Earth, 1993; Monkey Sonatas, 1993; The Ships of Earth, 1993; Lovelock (with Kathryn H. Kidd), 1994; Earthfall, 1994; Turning Hearts: Short Stories on Family Life (ed. with David C. Dollahite), 1994; Alvin Journeyman, 1995; Earthborn, 1995; Children of the Mind, 1996; Pastwatch: The Redemption of Christopher Columbus, 1996; Treasure Box, 1996; Stone Tables, 1997; Heartfire, 1998; Homebody, 1998; Enchantment, 1999; Ender's Shadow, 1999; Magic Mirror 1999, Sarah 2000, Shadow of the Hegemon 2001, Rebekah, 2001, Shadow of the Hegemon, 2001, Shadow Puppets 2002, The Crystal City 2003. Contributions: periodicals. *Honours:* John W. Campbell Award, World Science Fiction Convention, 1978; Utah State Institute of Fine Arts Prize, 1980; Hamilton-Brackett Awards, 1981, 1986; Nebula Awards, 1985, 1986; Hugo Awards, 1986, 1987; Locus Awards, 1987, 1988, 1989; Mythopoeic Fantasy Award, Mythopoeic Society, 1988. *Address:* c/o Barbara Bova, 3951 Gulf Shore Blvd, PH1B, Naples, FL 34103, USA.

CARDENAL, Ernesto; Nicaraguan poet and priest; b. 20 Jan. 1925, Granada. *Education:* Univ. of Mexico, Columbia Univ., New York. *Career:* Roman Catholic priest 1965–; Minister of Culture 1979–90. *Publications:* Proclama del conquistador 1947, Gethsemani Ky 1960, Hora 0 1960, Epigramas 1961, Poemas 1961, Salmos 1964, Oración por Marilyn Monroe y otros poemas 1965, La voz de un monje en la era nuclear 1965, El estrecho dudoso 1966, Homenaje a los Indios Americanos 1969, Mayapán 1970, Vida en el amor 1971, La hora cero y otros poemas 1971, Canto nacional al F.S.L.N. 1972, Oráculo sobre Managua 1973, El evangelio en solentiname 1975, La santidad de la revolución 1976, Cátulo marcial 1978, Nueva antología poética 1978, Viaje a New York 1980, Nostalgia del futuro 1982, Crónica de un reencuentro 1982, Waslala 1983, Vuelos de victoria 1984, With Walker in Nicaragua and other early poems 1949–54 1984, Quetzalcoatl 1985, Nuevo cielo y tierra nueva 1985, From Nicaragua with Love: Poems 1976–1986 1986, Cántico cósmico 1989, La noche iluminada de palabras 1991, Los ovnis de oro 1991, El telescopio en la noche oscura 1993, Del monasterio al mundo: correspondencia entre Ernesto Cardenal y Thomas Merton 1998, Vida perdida 1999, Los años de Granada 2002, Las ínsulas extrañas 2002, La revolución perdida 2003. *Honours:* Premio de la Paz 1980. *E-mail:* escritor@ibw.com.ni. *Website:* www.ernestocardenal.org/sitiooficialernestocardenal/.

CARDOSO PIRES, José Augusto Neves; Portuguese novelist and dramatist; b. 2 Oct. 1925, Peso, Castelo, Branco. *Education:* University of Lisbon. *Career:* literary dir of various publishing houses in Lisbon. *Publications:* Historuas de amor, 1952; Estrada 43, 1955; A ancorado, 1958; Jogos de azar, 1963; O hospede de Job, 1963; O delfin, 1968; Dinossauro excelentissimo, 1972; O burro-em-pe, 1978; Ballad of Dogs' Beach: Dossier of a Crime, 1982; Alexandra Alpha, 1987; A Republica dos Corvos, 1988. Plays: O render dos herois, 1960; Corpo-delito na sala de espelhos, 1980. *Honours:* Grande Premio do Romance e da Novela 1983.

CAREW, Jan Rynveld; Guyanese academic, writer and poet; b. 24 Sept. 1925, Agricola. *Career:* Lecturer in Race Relations, University of London Extra-Mural Dept, 1953–57; Writer and Ed., BBC Overseas Service, London, 1954–65; Ed., African Review, Ghana, 1965–66; CBC Broadcaster, Toronto, 1966–69; Senior Fellow, Council of Humanities and Lecturer, Dept of Afro-American Studies, Princeton University, 1969–72; Prof., Dept of African-American Studies, Northwestern University, 1972–87; Visiting Clarence J. Robinson Prof. of Caribbean Literature and History, George Mason University, 1989–91; Visiting Prof. of International Studies, Illinois Wesleyan University, 1992–93. *Publications:* Streets of Eternity, 1952; Black Midas, 1958, US edn as A Touch of Midas; 1958; The Last Barbarian, 1961; Green Winter, 1964; University of Hunger, 1966; The Third Gift, 1975; The Origins of Racism and Resistance in the Americas, 1976; Rape of the Sun-people, 1976; Children of the Sun, 1980; Sea Drums in My Blood, 1981; Grenada: The Hour Will Strike Again, 1985; Fulcrums of Change, 1987. *Address:* Dept of African-American Studies, Northwestern University, Evanston, IL 60208, USA.

CAREY, John, MA, DPhil, FRSL, FBA; British literary critic and academic; *Merton Professor Emeritus of English Literature, University of Oxford*; b. 5 April 1934, s. of Charles William and Winifred Ethel Carey (née Cook); m. Gillian Mary Florence Booth 1960; two s. *Education:* Richmond and E Sheen County Grammar School, St John's Coll., Oxford. *Career:* served in E Surrey Regt 1953–54; Harmsworth Sr Scholar, Merton Coll., Oxford 1957–58; Lecturer, Christ Church, Oxford 1958–59; Andrew Bradley Jr Research Fellow, Balliol Coll., Oxford 1959–60; Tutorial Fellow, Keble Coll., Oxford 1960–64, St John's Coll. 1964–75; Merton Prof. of English Literature, Univ. of Oxford 1976–2001, Prof. Emer. 2001–; Chief Book Reviewer, Sunday Times (London) 1976–; T. S. Eliot Memorial Lecturer, Univ. of Kent 1989; Northcliffe Lecturer, Univ. Coll., London 2004; Chair. Booker Prize Judges 1982, 2003, Int. Booker Prize Judges 2005; Judge, WH Smith Prize 1989–95. *Publications:* The Poems of John Milton (co-ed. with Alastair Fowler) 1968, Milton 1969, The Violent Effigy: A Study of Dickens' Imagination 1973, Thackeray: Prodigal Genius 1977, John Donne: Life, Mind and Art 1981, The Private Memoirs and Confessions of a Justified Sinner, by James Hogg (ed.), William Golding: The Man and His Books (ed.) 1986, Original Copy: Selected Reviews and Journalism 1987, The Faber Book of Reportage (ed.) 1987, John Donne (Oxford Authors) (ed.) 1990, The Intellectuals and the Masses 1992, The Faber Book of Science (ed.) 1995, The Faber Book of Utopias (ed.) 1999, Pure Pleasure 2000, What Good are the Arts? 2005; articles in Review of English Studies, Modern Language Review, etc. *Honours:* Hon. Fellow, St John's Coll. Oxford 1991, Balliol Coll. Oxford 1992; Hon. Prof. Univ. of Liverpool 2004–. *Address:* Brasenose Cottage, Lyneham, Oxon., OX7 6QL; 57 Stapleton Road, Headington, Oxford, England. *Telephone:* (1865) 764304. *E-mail:* john .carey53@ntlworld.com (home).

CAREY, Peter Philip, FRSL; Australian writer and academic; *Director, Creative Writing Program, Hunter College, CUNY*; b. 7 May 1943, Bacchus Marsh, Vic.; m. 2nd Alison Summers 1985 (divorced); two s. *Education:* Geelong Grammar School and Monash Univ. *Career:* fmr Pnr, McSpedden Carey Advertising Consultants, Sydney; writer-in-residence, New York Univ. 1990; fmr teacher Columbia Univ. and Princeton Univ.; currently Dir, Creative Writing Program, Hunter Coll., CUNY. *Screenplay:* Bliss (jtly), Until the End of the World (jtly). *Publications:* The Fat Man in History (short stories, aka Exotic Pleasures 1981) 1974, War Crimes (short stories) (NSW Premier's Award) 1979, Bliss (novel) (Miles Franklin Award, Nat. Book Council Award, NSW Premier's Award) 1981, Illywhacker (novel) (Age Book of the Year Award, Nat. Book Council Award, Victorian Premier's Award) 1985, Oscar and Lucinda (Booker Prize for Fiction 1988, Miles Franklin Award, Nat. Book Council Award, Adelaide Festival Award, Foundation for Australian Literary Studies Award) 1988, Until the End of the World 1990, The Tax Inspector (novel) 1991, The Unusual Life of Tristan Smith (novel) (Age Book of the Year Award) 1994, Collected Stories 1995, The Big Bazoohley (children's novel) 1995, Jack Maggs 1997, The True History of the Kelly Gang (Booker Prize 2001) 2000, 30 Days in Sydney: A Wildly Distorted Account 2001, My Life as a Fake 2003, Wrong About Japan 2005, Theft: A Love Story 2006. *Honours:* Hon. LittD (Queensland). *Literary Agent:* Department of English, Hunter College, The City University of New York, 695 Park Avenue, New York, NY 10021; c/o Amanda Urban, ICM, 40 West 57th Street, New York, NY 10019, USA (office). *Telephone:* (212) 772-5164 (office). *Fax:* (212) 772-5411 (office). *Website:* sapientia.hunter.cuny.edu/~creativewriting (office).

CARFAX, Catherine (see Fairburn, Eleanor M.)

ČARIJA, Jelena; Croatian novelist; b. 1980, Split. *Education:* Zagreb Drama and Film Acad. *Career:* won award in 2002 for then unpublished novel Klonirana, orig. written as filmscript; currently studying production. *Publications:* Klonirana (novel) 2003. *Address:* c/o Rende, Hadži Đerina 7, II sprat, stan br. 8, 11000 Belgrade, Serbia. *E-mail:* info@rende.co.yu. *Website:* www.rende.co.yu.

CARKEET, David Corydon, AB, MA, PhD; American academic and writer; b. 15 Nov. 1946, Sonora, CA; m. Barbara Lubin 1975; three d. *Education:* University of California at Davis, University of Wisconsin, Indiana University. *Career:* Asst Prof., 1973–79, Assoc. Prof., 1979–87, Prof., 1987–, University of Missouri. *Publications:* Fiction: Double Negative, 1980; The Greatest Slump of All Time, 1984; I Been There Before, 1985; The Full Catastrophe, 1990; The Error of Our Ways, 1997. Young Adult Fiction: The Silent Treatment, 1988; Quiver River, 1991. Contributions: scholarly journals; Short stories and popular essays in periodicals. *Honours:* James D. Phelan Award in Literature, San Francisco Foundation, 1976; Notable Books of the Year, New York Times Book Review, 1981, 1990, 1997; O. Henry Award, 1982; National Endowment for the Arts Fellowship, 1983.

CARLE, Eric; American children's writer and illustrator; b. 1929, Syracuse, NY; m. Barbara; one s. one d. *Education:* Akademie der bildenden Künste, Stuttgart. *Career:* fmrly graphic designer promotion dept, New York Times, art dir of an advertising agency; co-f. Eric Carle Museum of Picture Book Art, Amherst, MA 2002. *Publications:* 1, 2, 3 to the Zoo 1968, The Very Hungry Caterpillar 1969, Pancakes, Pancakes! 1970, The Tiny Seed 1970, Do You Want to Be My Friend? 1971, Rooster's Off to See the World 1972, The Very Long Tail 1972, The Very Long Train 1972, The Secret Birthday Message 1972, Walter the Baker 1972, Have You Seen My Cat? 1973, I See a Song 1973, My Very First Book of Numbers 1974, My Very First Book of Colors 1974, My Very First Book of Shapes 1974, My Very First Book of Words 1974, All About Arthur 1974, The Mixed-Up Chameleon 1976, Eric Carle's Storybook, Seven Tales by the Brothers Grimm 1976, The Grouchy Ladybug 1977, Watch Out! A Giant! 1978, Seven Stories by Hans Christian Andersen 1978, Twelve Tales from Aesop 1980, The Honeybee and the Robber 1981, Catch the Ball! 1982, Let's Paint A Rainbow 1982, What's For Lunch? 1982, The Very Busy Spider 1984, All Around Us 1986, Papa, Please Get the Moon for Me 1986, My Very First Book of Sounds 1986, My Very First Book of Food 1986, My Very First Book of Tools 1986, My Very First Book of Touch 1986, My Very First Book of Motion 1986, My Very First Book of Growth 1986, My Very First Book of Homes 1986, My Very First Book of Heads 1986, All in a Day (with others) 1986, A House for Hermit Crab 1987, Eric Carle's Treasury of Classic Stories for Children 1988, The Very Quiet Cricket 1990, Draw Me a Star 1992, Today is Monday 1993, My Apron 1994, The Very Lonely Firefly 1995, Little Cloud 1996, The Art of Eric Carle 1996, From Head to Toe 1997, Flora and Tiger: 19 very short stories from my life 1997, Hello, Red Fox 1998, You Can Make a Collage: A Very Simple How-to Book 1998, The Very Clumsy Click Beetle 1999, Does A Kangaroo Have A Mother, Too? 2000, Dream Snow 2000, "Slowly, Slowly, Slowly," said the Sloth 2002, Where Are You Going? To See My Friend! (with Kazuo Iwamura) 2003, Mister Seahorse 2004, 10 Little Rubber Ducks 2005; many books illustrated for other authors. *Honours:* PhD hc (Coll. of Our Lady the Elms, Chicopee, MA) 2001, (Niagara Univ., Niagara, NY) 2002; Silver Medal, Milan, Italy 1989, David McCord Children's Literature Citation, Framingham State Coll. and Nobscot Reading Council of the Int. Reading Asscn 1995, Univ. of Southern Mississippi Medallion from DeGrumond Collection 1997, Catholic Library Asscn Regina Medal 1999, Pittsburgh Children's Museum Outstanding Friend of Children 1999, Mainichi Newspaper Japan Picture Book Award for Lifetime Achievement 2000, Officer's Cross of the Order of Merit of the Federal Republic of Germany 2001, American Library Asscn Laura Ingalls Wilder Award 2003. *Address:* PO Box 485, Northampton, MA 01060, USA. *Website:* www.eric-carle.com; www .picturebookart.org.

CARLILE, Henry David, AA, BA, MA; American academic, poet and writer; b. 6 May 1934, San Francisco, CA; one d. *Education:* Grays Harbor College, University of Washington. *Career:* Instructor, 1967–69, Asst Prof., 1969–72, Assoc. Prof., 1972–78, Prof. of English, 1980–, Portland State University; Visiting Lecturer, Writers Workshop, University of Iowa, 1978–80. *Publications:* The Rough-Hewn Table, 1971; Running Lights, 1981; Rain, 1994. Contributions: many anthologies, reviews, and journals. *Honours:* National Endowment for the Arts Discovery Grant, 1970, and Fellowship in Poetry, 1976; Devins Award, 1971; PEN Syndicated Fiction Awards, 1983, 1986; Ingram Merrill Poetry Fellowship, 1985; Helen Foundation Award, 1986; Pushcart Prizes, 1986, 1992; Poetry Award, Crazyhorse, 1988; Oregon Arts Commission Literary Fellowship, 1994.

CARLSEN, Chris (see Holdstock, Robert)

CARMICHAEL, Jack Blake, BA, PhD; American writer, poet and editor; *President, Dynamics Press;* b. 31 Jan. 1938, Ravenswood, West Virginia; m. Julie Ann Carmichael 1981; four d. *Education:* Ohio Wesleyan University, Michigan State University, University of Oregon. *Career:* Ed., Pres. and Publisher, Dynamics Press 1990–; mem. Acad. of American Poets. *Publications:* Fiction: A New Slain Knight, 1991; Black Knight, 1991; Tales of the Cousin, 1992; Memoirs of the Great Gorgeous, 1992; The Humpty Boys in Michigan, 1996; Here Me America, with other poems and short stories, 1999. Contributions: poems in anthologies and journals. *Honours:* Hon. Co-Chair. Business Advisory Council; Outstanding Achievement Award, American Poetry Asscn 1990, Poet of the Year, Materials Dynamics 2003, Nat. Republican Congressional Cttee Leadership Award 2004. *Address:* c/o Dynamics Press, 519 S Rogers Street, Mason, MI 48854, USA. *Telephone:* (517) 676-5211 (office). *Fax:* (517) 676-3395 (office). *E-mail:* jackbcarmi@ prodigy.net (office).

CARMICHAEL, Joel, BA, MA; American author, editor and translator; b. 31 Dec. 1915, New York, NY. *Education:* University of Oxford, Sorbonne, University of Paris, École Nationale des Langues Orientales Vivantes. *Career:* European Correspondent, The Nation magazine, 1946–47; Ed., Midstream magazine, 1975–87, 1990–2000. *Publications:* An Illustrated History of Russia, 1960; The Death of Jesus, 1962; A Short History of the Russian Revolution, 1964; The Shaping of the Arabs: A Study in Ethnic Identity, 1967; Karl Marx: The Passionate Logician, 1967; An Open Letter to Moses and Muhammed, 1968; A Cultural History of Russia, 1968; Arabs and Jews, 1969; Trotsky: An Appreciation of His Life, 1976; Stalin's Masterpiece, 1977; Arabs Today, 1977; St Paul and the Jews, 1980; The Birth of Christianity: Reality and Myth, 1989; The Satanizing of the Jews: Origin and Development of Mystical Anti-Semitism, 1992; The Unriddling of Christian Origins: A Secular Account, 1995. Translations: (from Russian) The Russian Revolution 1917, N. N. Sukhanov, 1955; Anna Karenina, Leo Tolstoy, 1975. Contributions: journals and periodicals. *Honours:* Fulbright Fellowship 1949–51.

CARNERO, Guillermo, BEcons, PhD; Spanish poet and writer; b. 1947, Valencia. *Education:* Universidad de Alicante. *Career:* Visiting Prof., Univs of Virginia, Berkeley and Harvard in USA, and Universidad Menéndez Pelayo; fmr Co-Dir of Clásicos Taurus collection; Ed., (vols 6–8) Historia de la Literatura Española; mem. editorial bd of the literary magazines Castilla, Dieciocho, Hispanic Review, Ínsula, La Nueva Literatura Hispánica, Studi Ispanici, Voz y Letra, and Dir of literary journal, Anales de Literatura Española; bd mem., March Foundation, Sociedad Estatal de Conmemoraciones Culturales for centenary of Rafael Alberti, 'Tres mitos españoles: Don Quijote, Don Juan Tenorio y La Celestina' (exhibition at Museo del Prado and Centro Cultural Conde Duque). *Publications:* poetry: Dibujo de la muerte 1967, El sueño de Escipión 1971, Variaciones y figuras sobre un tema de La Bruyére 1974, El azar objetivo 1975, Ensayo de una teoría de la visión (Poesía 1966–1977) 1979, Música para fuegos de artificio 1989, Divisibilidad indefinida 1990, Dibujo de la muerte. Obra poética completa 1998, Verano inglés (Premio Nacional de Literatura 2000, Premio Nacional de la Crítica 2000, Premio Fastenrath de la Real Academia Española 2002) 1999, Ut pictura poesis (anthology) 2001, Sepulcros y jardines 2001, Espejo de gran niebla 2002, Poemas arqueológicos 2003; prose: El grupo 'Cántico' de Córdoba. Un episodio clave en la historia de la poesía española de posguerra 1976, Los orígenes del Romanticismo reaccionario español. El matrimonio Böhl de Faber 1978, La cara oscura del Siglo de las luces 1983, Las armas abisinias. Ensayos sobre literatura y arte del siglo XX 1989, Estudios sobre el teatro español del Siglo XVIII 1997, Espronceda 1999. *Honours:* Premio Nacional de la Crítica Valenciana 2000, 2003. *Address:* c/o Anales de Literatura Española, Universidad de Alicante, Dpto de Filología Española, Lingüística General y Teoría de la Literatura, Carretera San Vicente del Raspeig s/n, 03690 San Vicente del Raspeig, Alicante, Spain (office). *E-mail:* dfelg@ua.es.

CAROFIGLIO, Gianrico; Italian novelist; b. 1961. *Career:* judge in town of Bari, southern Italy. *Publications:* Testimone inconsapevole (trans. as Involuntary Witness) (Marisa Rusconi Prize, Rhegium Julii Award, Fortunato Seminara Award) 2002, Ad occhi chiusi (trans. as A Walk in the Dark) 2003. *Address:* c/o Bitter Lemon Press, 37 Arundel Gardens, London, W11 2LW, England. *E-mail:* books@bitterlemonpress.com.

CARON, Louis; Canadian author, poet and dramatist; b. 1942, Sorel, QC. *Career:* mem. Académie des lettres de Québec 1995–. *Publications:* L'illusionnisie suivi de Le guetteur, 1973; L'emmitouflé, 1977, English trans. as The Draft-Dodger, 1980; Bonhomme sept-heures, 1978; Le canard de bois, 1981; La corne de brume, 1982; Le coup de poing, 1990; La tuque et le béret, 1992; Le bouleau et l'epinette, 1993. Other: many radio and television plays. *Honours:* Prix Hermes, France, 1977; Prix France-Canada, 1977; Prix Ludger-Duvernay, Société Saint-Jean-Baptiste, Montréal, 1984.

CARPELAN, Bo, MA; Finnish poet, writer and translator; b. 1926, Helsinki; s. of Bertel Gustaf Carpelan and Ebba Adele Lindahl; m. Barbro Eriksson; two c. *Education:* Univ. of Helsinki. *Career:* librarian, Helsinki City Library 1946–80; critic, Hufvudstadsbladet newspaper 1949–64; writes in Swedish. *Publications include:* poetry: Som en dunkel värme 1946, Minus sju 1952, Den svala dagen 1961, Anders i stan 1962, En gammal mans dag 1966, En och/ja Erkki 1966, 73 dikter 1966, Bonny och Clyde på Åland 1969, Gården 1969, Paavo 1969, Källan 1973, I de mörka rummen, i de ljusa (Nordic Council Literature Prize 1977) 1976, Slaktmånad 1978, Kesäkuu 1981, År som löv 1989, I det sedda 1995, Namnet på tavlan Klee målade 1999, Ögonblickets tusen årstider: dikter, fragment, marginalia 2001; fiction: Bågen 1968, Rösterna i den sena timmen 1971, Din gestalt bakom dörren 1975, Vandrande skugga 1977, Axel 1986, Urwind (Finlandia Prize) 1993, Benjamins bok 1997, Berg (Finlandia Prize) 2005; juvenile: Anders på ön 1959, Anders i stan 1962; translator: Greek classics and works by Sándor Csoóri, Osip Mandelstam, Marina Tsvetayeva, Paavo Haavikko, Lassi Nummi, Edith Södergran, Sirkka Turkka; opera libretto: Erik Bergman's Det sjungande trädet. *Honours:* Professor Artium 1980; Finnish State Literature Prize, Acad. of Sweden Nordic Prize 1997, Prix Européen de Littérature 2006. *Address:* c/o Carcanet Press, Fouth Floor, Alliance House, Cross Street, Manchester, M2 7AP, England. *E-mail:* info@carcanet.co.uk.

CARPENTER, Bogdana Maria Magdalena, MA, PhD; American (b. Polish) academic, writer and translator; *Professor of Slavic Languages and Literatures, University of Michigan at Ann Arbor;* b. 2 June 1941, Czestochowa, Poland; d. of Jozef Chetkowski and Maria Gordon-Chetkowska; m. John Randell Carpenter 1963; one s. one d. *Education:* Univ. of Warsaw, Univ. of California, Berkeley. *Career:* Acting Asst Prof. 1971–73, Lecturer 1973–74, Univ. of California, Berkeley; Asst Prof., Univ. of Washington, Seattle 1974–83; staff reviewer, World Literature Today 1977–; Asst Prof., Univ. of Michigan, Ann Arbor 1983–85, Assoc. Prof. 1985–91, Prof. of Slavic Languages and Literatures 1991–, Chair. Dept of Slavic Languages and Literatures 1991–95; mem. The Polish Review (Advisory Bd 1993–). *Publications:* The Poetic Avant-Garde in Poland, 1918–1939 1983, Cross Currents: A Yearbook of Central European Culture (assoc. ed.) 1987–93, Monumenta Polonica: The First Four Centuries of Polish Poetry 1989, Czeslaw Milosz' To Begin Where I Am (essays, ed. with Madeleine Levine) 2001; translator: Works by Zbigniew Herbert (with John Carpenter): Selected Poems of Zbigniew Herbert 1977, Report from the Besieged City and Other Poems 1987, Still Life with a Bridle 1991, Mr Cogito 1993, Elegy for Departure and Other Poems 1999, The King of Ants 1999; contrib. to books, scholarly journals and general periodicals. *Honours:* Golden Cross of Merit (Poland) 1999; Poetry Soc. of America Witter Bynner Poetry Trans. Prize 1979, Nat. Endowment for the Humanities Trans. grant 1987–88, ACLS Fellowship 1990–91, First Prize, American Council for Polish Culture Clubs 1991, Columbia Univ. Trans. Center Merit Award 1992, Nat. Endowment for the Arts Trans. grant 2006-07. *Address:* Department of Slavic Languages and Literatures, 3040 Modern Languages Building, University of Michigan, Ann Arbor, MI 48109-1275 (office); 1606 Granger, Ann Arbor, MI 48104, USA (home). *Telephone:* (764) 763-5715 (office). *E-mail:* bogdana@umich.edu (office). *Website:* www.lsa.umich.edu/slavic (office).

CARPENTER, Lucas, BS, MA, PhD; American academic, writer, poet and editor; *Charles Howard Candler Professor of English, Oxford College of Emory University;* b. 23 April 1947, Elberton, GA; m. Judith Leidner 1972; one d. *Education:* Coll. of Charleston, Univ. of North Carolina at Chapel Hill, State Univ. of NY (SUNY), Stony Brook. *Career:* Instructor, SUNY, Stony Brook 1973–78; Instructor, Suffolk Community Coll. 1978–80, Assoc. Prof. of English 1980–85; Assoc. Prof. of English, Oxford Coll. of Emory Univ. 1985–94, Prof. of English 1994–, Charles Howard Candler Prof. of English 2000–; Editorial Consultant, Prentice-Hall Inc. 1981–; Resident Fellow in Poetry and Fiction Writing, Hambidge Center for the Creative Arts 1991; mem. Nat. Council of Teachers of English, Poetry Atlanta, Poetry Soc. of America, Southeast MLA, Poets and Writers. *Publications:* A Year for the Spider (poems) 1972, The Selected Poems of John Gould Fletcher (co-ed. with E. Leighton Rudolph) 1988, The Selected Essays of John Gould Fletcher (ed.) 1989, John Gould Fletcher and Southern Modernism 1990, The Selected Correspondence of John Gould Fletcher (co-ed. with E. Leighton Rudolph) 1996, Perils of the Affect (poems) 2002; contrib. to anthologies, scholarly journals and periodicals. *Honours:* Oxford Coll. Prof. of the Year Awards 1994, 1996, 2003, Fulbright Distinguished Scholar, Belgium 1999. *Address:* Department of English, Oxford College of Emory University, Oxford, GA 30054, USA (office).

CARR, Caleb, BA; American writer and historian; b. 2 Aug. 1955, New York, NY. *Education:* Kenyon Coll., New York Univ. *Publications:* Casing the Promised Land 1980, America Invulnerable: The Quest for Absolute Security, from 1812 to Star Wars (with James Chace) 1988, The Devil Soldier: The Story of Frederick Townsend Ward 1991, The Alienist 1994, The Angel of Darkness 1997, Killing Time 2000, The Mysterious Island 2001, The Lessons of Terror 2002, The Italian Secretary 2005; contrib. to professional journals, newspapers and periodicals. *Address:* c/o Random House Inc. Author Mail, 1745 Broadway, New York, NY 10019, USA.

CARR, Glyn (see Styles, (Frank) Showell)

CARR, Margaret, (Martin Carroll, Carole Kerr, Belle Jackson); English writer; b. 25 Nov. 1935, Salford. *Publications:* Begotten Murder 1967, Spring into Love 1967, Blood Vengeance 1968, Goodbye is Forever 1968, Too Beautiful to Die 1969, Hear No Evil 1971, Tread Warily at Midnight 1971, Sitting Duck 1972, Who's the Target? 1974, Not for Sale 1975, Shadow of the Hunter 1975, A Time to Surrender 1975, Out of the Past 1976, Twin Tragedy 1977, Lamb to the Slaughter 1978, The Witch of Wykham 1978, Daggers Drawn 1980, Stolen Heart 1981, In the Dark of the Day 1988, Valdez's Lady 1989, Deadly Pursuit 1991, Dark Intruder 1991. *Address:* Waverly, Wavering Lane, Gillingham, Dorset SP8 4NR, England.

CARR, Pat Moore, BA, MA, PhD; American writer and university teacher; b. 13 March 1932, Grass Creek, WY; m. 1st Jack Esslinger 1955 (divorced 1970); m. 2nd Duane Carr 1971; one s. three d. *Education:* Rice Univ., Tulane Univ. *Career:* teacher, Texas Southern Univ. 1956–58, Univ. of New Orleans 1961, 1965–69, 1987–88, Univ. of Texas at El Paso 1969–79, Univ. of Arkansas at Little Rock 1983, 1986–87, Western Kentucky Univ. 1988–96; mem. Int. Women's Writing Guild (bd mem. 1996–), Texas Inst. of Letters, PEN. *Publications:* fiction: The Grass Creek Chronicle 1976, Bluebirds 1993, Beneath the Hill 1999, If We Must Die 2002, Border Ransom 2006; short story collections: The Women in the Mirror 1977, Night of the Luminarias 1986, Sonahchi 1988, Our Brothers' War 1993; criticism: Bernard Shaw 1976, Mimbres Mythology 1979, In Fine Spirits 1986; contrib. articles and short stories in numerous publications, including The Southern Review, Best American Short Stories. *Honours:* South and West Fiction Award 1969, Library of Congress Marc IV Award for Short Fiction 1970, Nat. Endowment for the Humanities Award 1973, Iowa Fiction Award 1977, Texas Inst. of Letters Short Story Award 1978, Arkansas Endowment for the Humanities Award 1985, Green Mountain Short Fiction Award 1986, First Stage Drama Award 1990, Al Smith Fellowship in Fiction 1995, Chateau de Lavigny Writing Fellowship 1999, Texas Council of the Arts Literary Award 2000. *Address:* 10695 Venice Road, Elkins, AR 72727, USA. *Telephone:* (479) 643-3647 (home). *E-mail:* patcarr313@aol.com (home).

CARR, Sir (Albert) Raymond Maillard, Kt, MA, DLitt, FRSL, FRHistS, FBA; British historian; b. 11 April 1919, Bath; s. of Reginald Henry Maillard Carr and Ethel Gertrude Marion Carr; m. Sara Ann Mary Strickland 1950; three s. one d. *Education:* Brockenhurst School and Christ Church, Oxford. *Career:* Gladstone Research Exhibitioner, Christ Church 1941; Fellow, All Souls Coll., Oxford 1946–53, New Coll. 1953–64, St Antony's Coll. 1964–; Dir Latin American Centre 1964–68, Chair. Soc. for Latin American Studies 1966–68; Prof. of History of Latin America, Univ. of Oxford 1967–68, Warden St Antony's Coll. 1968–87; mem. Nat. Theatre Bd 1980; Corresp. mem. Royal Acad. of History, Madrid 1968. *Publications:* Spain 1808–1939 1966, Latin American Affairs (ed.) 1969, The Republic and the Civil War in Spain (ed.) 1971, English Fox Hunting 1976, The Spanish Tragedy: The Civil War in Perspective 1977, Spain: Dictatorship to Democracy (co-author) 1979, Modern Spain 1980, Fox-Hunting (with Sara Carr) 1982, Puerto Rico: A Colonial Experiment 1984, The Spanish Civil War (ed.) 1986, The Chances of Death: A Diary of the Spanish Civil War (ed.) 1995, Visiones de fin de siglo 1999, Spain: A History (ed.) 2001; contrib. to scholarly books and journals. *Honours:* Hon. Fellow, Christ Church Coll., St Antony's Coll., Oxford, Univ. of Exeter; Grand Cross of the Order of Alfonso El Sabio (for services to Spanish history) 1983; Hon. DLitt (Madrid); Prince of Asturias Award in Social Sciences 1999. *Address:* 58 Fitzgeorge Avenue, London, W14 0SW, England (home). *Telephone:* (20) 7603-6975 (home).

CARR, Roberta (see Roberts, Irene)

CARR, Terry Gene, (Norman Edwards), AA; American writer, editor and lecturer; b. 19 Feb. 1937, Grants Pass, OR. *Education:* City College of San Francisco, University of California at Berkeley. *Career:* Ed., Ace Books 1964–71, SFWA Bulletin 1967–68; founder, SFWA Forum 1967–68. *Publications:* Warlord of Kor (with Ted White), 1963; World's Best Science Fiction (ed.), 7 vols, 1965–71; Universe (ed.), 13 vols, 1971–83; The Best Science Fiction of the Year (ed.), 13 vols, 1972–84; The Light at the End of the Universe (short stories), 1976; Cirque, 1977; Classic Science Fiction: The First Golden Age (ed.), 1978; The Year's Finest Fantasy (ed.), 1978–84; Between Two Worlds, 1986; Spill! The Story of the Exxon Valdez, 1991.

CARRÈRE, Emmanuel; French writer, screenwriter and director; b. 9 Dec. 1957, Paris; s. of Hélène Carrère d'Encausse; m.; two c. *Television:* Léon Morin prêtre (adaptation) 1991, Monsieur Ripois (adaptation) 1993, Le Blanc à lunettes (adaptation) 1995, Pêcheur d'Islande (adaptation) 1996, Les Clients d'Avrenos (adaptation) 1996, Denis (with others) 1998, Désiré Landru (story) 2005. *Films:* La Classe de neige (screenplay, with Claude Miller) (Prix spécial du jury, Cannes Film Festival) 1998, Retour à Kotelnitch (screenplay, also dir) 2003, La Moustache (screenplay, also dir) 2005. *Publications:* Werner Herzog (essay) 1982, L'Amie du jaguar 1983, Bravoure 1984, La Moustache 1986, Le Détroit de Behring 1986, Hors d'atteinte 1988, Je suis vivant et vous êtes morts (biog.) 1993, La Class de neige (Prix Fémina) 1995, L'Adversaire 2000. *Address:* c/o Editions P.O.L., 33 rue Saint-André-des-Arts, 75006 Paris, France.

CARRÈRE D'ENCAUSSE, Hélène, DèsSc; French political scientist; *Secretary for Life, Académie Française;* b. 6 July 1929, Paris; d. of Georges Zourabichvili and Nathalie von Pelken; m. Louis Carrère 1952; one s. two d. *Education:* Sorbonne, Paris. *Career:* fmr Prof. Univ. of Paris (Sorbonne); now Prof. Inst. of Etudes Politiques, Paris and Dir of Research, Fondation Nationale des Sciences Politiques; fmr mem. Bd of Dirs East-West Inst. for Security Studies; Visiting Prof. at numerous univs in USA; mem. Acad. Française, Sec. for Life 2000–; foreign mem. Russian Acad. of Science 2003–; Assoc. mem. Acad. Royale de Belgique; mem. European Parl. 1994–99; Foreign mem. Russian Acad. of Sciences. *Publications include:* Le marxisme et l'Asie 1965, Réforme et révolution chez les musulmans de l'Empire russe 1966, L'URSS et la Chine devant les révolutions dans les sociétés pré-industrielles 1970, L'Empire éclaté 1978, Lénine: la révolution et le pouvoir 1979, Staline: l'ordre par la terreur 1979, Le pouvoir confisqué 1982, Le Grand Frère 1983, La déstalinisation commence 1984, Ni paix ni guerre 1986, Le Grand Défi: bolcheviks et nations 1917–30 1987, Le Malheur russe 1988, La Gloire des nations ou la fin de l'Empire soviétique 1991, Victorieuse Russie 1992, Nicholas II: la transition interrompue 1996, Lénine 1998, La Russie inachevée 2000, Catherine II 2002, L'Impératrice et l'abbé un duel littéraire ivédit 2003. *Honours:* Hon. mem. Acad. of Georgia; Officier, Légion d'honneur, Commdr Légion d'honneur 2005; Dr hc (Montréal); Prix Aujourd'hui 1978, Prix de la Fondation Louis-Weiss 1986. *Address:* Académie Française, 23 quai Conti, 75006 Paris, France (office). *Telephone:* 1-44-41-43-00 (office). *Fax:* 1-43-29-47-45 (office). *Website:* www.academie-francaise.fr (office).

CARRIER, Roch, BA, MA; Canadian author, dramatist and poet; b. 13 May 1937, Sainte-Justine-de-Dorchester, QC; m. Diane Gosselin 1959, two d. *Education:* Collège Saint-Louis, University of Montréal, Sorbonne, University of Paris. *Career:* Sec.-Gen., Théatre du Nouveau Monde, Montréal; teacher, Collège Militaire, St-Jean; Dir, Canada Council –1997. *Publications:* Fiction: Jolis deuils, 1964; La guerre, yes sir!, 1968, English trans., 1970; Floralie, ou es-tu?, 1969, English trans. as Floralie, Where Are You?, 1971; Il est par la le soleil, 1970, English trans. as Is it the Sun, Philibert?, 1972; Le deux-millième é'tage, 1973, English trans. as They Won't Demolish Me!, 1974; Le jardin des délices, 1975, English trans. as The Garden of Delights, 1978; Les enfants du bonhomme dans la lune, 1979, English trans. as The Hockey Sweater and Other Stories, 1979; Il n'y a pas de pays sans grand-père, 1979, English trans. as No Country Without Grandfathers, 1981; Les fleurs vivent-elles ailleurs que sur la terre, 1980; La dame qui avait des chaines aux cheville, 1981; De l'amour dans la feraille, 1984, English trans. as Heartbreaks Along the Road, 1987; La fleur et autres personnages, 1985; Prières d'un enfant très très sage, 1988; L'homme dans le placard, 1991; Fin, 1992; The Longest Home Run, 1993; Petit homme tornade, 1996. Plays: La celeste bicyclette, 1980, English trans. as The Celestial Bycycle, 1982; Le cirque noir, 1982; L'ours et le kangourou, 1986. Other: various poems. *Honours:* Prix Littéraire de la Province de Québec, 1965; Grand Prix Littéraire de la Ville de Montréal, 1980; Québec Writer of the Year, 1981.

CARRIER, Warren Pendleton, AB, MA, PhD; American academic, writer and poet; b. 3 July 1918, Cheviot, OH; m. 1st Marjorie Jane Regan 1947 (deceased); one s.; m. 2nd Judy Lynn Hall 1973; one s. *Education:* Wabash Coll., Miami Univ., Oxford, OH, Harvard Univ., Occidental Coll. *Career:* Founder-Ed., Quarterly Review of Literature 1943–44; Assoc. Ed., Western Review 1949–51; Asst Prof., Univ. of Iowa 1949–52; Assoc. Prof., Bard Coll. 1953–57; Faculty, Bennington Coll. 1955–58; Visiting Prof., Sweet Briar Coll. 1958–60; Prof., Deep Springs Coll., CA 1960–62, Portland State Univ., Oregon 1962–64; Prof., Chair Dept of English, Univ. of Montana 1964–68; Assoc. Dean, Prof. of English and Comparative Literature, Chair Dept of Comparative Literature, Livingston Coll., Rutgers Univ. 1968–69; Dean Coll. of Arts and Letters, San Diego State Univ. 1969–72; Vice-Pres. Academic Affairs, Univ. of Bridgeport, CT 1972–75; Chancellor, Univ. of Wisconsin at Platteville 1975–82. *Publications:* City Stopped in Time 1949, The Hunt 1952, The Cost of Love 1953, Reading Modern Poetry (co-ed.) 1955, Bay of the Damned 1957, Toward Montebello 1966, Leave Your Sugar for the Cold Morning 1977, Guide to World Literature (ed.) 1980, Literature from the World (co-ed.) 1981, The Diver 1986, Death of a Chancellor 1986, An Honorable Spy 1992, Murder at the Strawberry Festival 1993, An Ordinary Man 1997, Death of a Poet 1999, Risking the Wind 2000, Justice at Christmas 2000, Coming to Terms 2004; contrib. to periodicals. *Honours:* Nat. Foundation for the Arts Award for Poetry 1971, Collady Prize for Poetry 1986. *Address:* 69 Colony Park Circle, Galveston, TX 77551, USA.

CARRIÈRE, Jean-Claude; French writer and screenwriter; b. 19 Sept. 1931, Colombières-sur-Orb, Hérault, Languedoc-Roussillon. *Film screenplays:* Rupture 1961, Le Soupirant 1962, Le Journal d'une femme de chambre 1964, Le Bestiaire d'amour 1965, Yoyo 1965, Viva María! 1965, Miss Muerte 1966, Tant qu'on a la santé 1966, Cartes sur table 1966, Hotel Paradiso 1966, Le Voleur 1967, Belle de jour 1967, Pour un amour lointain 1968, La Pince à ongles 1969, La Voie lactée 1969, Le Grand amour 1969, Borsalino 1970, L'Alliance 1971, Taking Off 1971, Le Droit d'aimer 1972, Le Charme discret de la bourgeoisie 1972, Un homme est mort 1972, Le Moine 1973, Dorotheas Rache 1974, France société anonyme 1974, Le Fantôme de la liberté 1974, La Femme aux bottes rouges 1974, Sérieux comme le plaisir 1975, La Chair de l'orchidée 1975, Der Dritte Grad 1975, Leonor 1975, Les Oeufs brouillés 1976, Le Diable dans la boîte 1977, Le Gang 1977, Julie pot de colle 1977, Cet obscur objet du désir 1977, Le Franc-tireur 1978, Un papillon sur l'épaule 1978, Photo-souvenir 1978, Chaussette surprise 1978, Slachtvee 1979, L'Homme en colère 1979, Retour à la bien-aimée 1979, Die Blechtrommel 1979, L'Associé 1979, Sauve qui peut (la vie) 1980, Lundi 1980, Le Bouffon 1981, Black Mirror 1981, Die Fälschung 1981, La Double vie de Théophraste Longuet 1981, Je tue il 1982, L'Accompagnateur 1982, Le Retour de Martin Guerre 1982, L'Indiscrétion 1982, Antonieta 1982, Credo 1983, Danton 1983, Itinéraire bis 1983, Le Jardinier récalcitrant 1983, Il Generale dell'armata morte 1983, La Joven y la tentación 1984, L'Aide-mémoire 1984, Un amour de Swann 1984, Les Étonnements d'un couple moderne 1985, Auto défense 1985, Les Exploits d'un jeune Don Juan 1987, La Nuit Bengali 1988, The Unbearable Lightness of Being 1988, Une femme tranquille 1989, J'écris dans l'espace 1989, Bouvard et Pecuchet 1989, Valmont 1989, Milou en mai 1990, Es ist nicht leicht ein Gott zu sein 1990, Cyrano de Bergerac 1990, At Play in the Fields of the Lord 1991, La Controverse de Valladolid 1992, Le Retour de Casanova 1992, The Night and the Moment 1995, Le Hussard sur le toit 1995, Une femme explosive 1996, Golden Boy 1996, Der Unhold 1996, L'Associé 1996, Les Paradoxes de Buñuel 1997, Chinese Box 1997, Clarissa 1998, La Guerre dans le Haut Pays 1999, Salsa 2000, Rien, voilà l'ordre 2003, Birth 2004, Galilée ou L'amour de Dieu 2005, Marie-Antoinette 2006, Goya's Ghosts 2006. *Television writing:* Robinson Crusoé (series) 1964, The Mahabharata (mini series) 1989, Associations de bienfaiteurs (mini series) 1995, Ruy Blas (TV play) 2002, Les Thibault (mini series) 2003. *Television and film appearances:* Le Journal d'une femme de chambre 1964, La Voie lactée 1969, L'Alliance 1971, Un peu de soleil dans l'eau froide 1971, Le Jardin des supplices 1976, Le Jeu du solitaire 1976, Julie pot de colle 1977, Photo-souvenir 1978, Chaussette surprise 1978, Ils sont grands, ces petits 1979, L'Amour nu 1981, La Double vie de Théophraste Longuet 1981, L'Écarteur 1982, L'Homme de la nuit (TV series) 1983, Vive les femmes! 1984, Sueurs froides (episode of À la mémoire d'un ange) 1988, Bouvard et Pecuchet (voice) 1989, Eugénie Grandet (voice) 1994, The Night and the Moment 1995, Le Parfum de Jeannette (voice) 1996, Jaya Ganga 1998, Buñuel y la mesa del rey Salomón 2001, Madame de... 2001, Les Thibault (TV series) 2003, Avida 2006. *Films:* Heureux anniversaire (prod.) 1962, La Pince à ongles (dir) 1969, L'Unique (dir) 1986. *Publications:* novels: Monsieur Hulot's Holiday 1959, L'Alliance 1971, Mon Oncle 1974, Please Mr Einstein 2006; plays: The Mahabharata 1989, Milou in May 1990, Chinese Box and a Film-maker's Diary 1998, The Little Black Book 2003, The Controversy of Valladolid 2005; non-fiction: The Secret Language of Film 1994, Violence and Compassion (with The Dalai Lama) 2001. *Address:* c/o Harvill Secker, 20 Vauxhall Bridge Road, London, SW1V 2SA, England. *E-mail:* harvillseckereditorial@randomhouse.co.uk.

CARRIÈRE, Jean Paul Jacques; French author; b. 6 Aug. 1928, Nîmes; s. of Edmond Carrière and Andrée Paoli; m. 1st Michèle Bollé; two s.; m. 2nd Françoise Battistini 1978; one s. *Education:* Coll. Saint Stanislas, Coll. de l'Assomption and Lycée Alphonse Daudet, Nîmes. *Career:* disc-jockey, Manosque 1958–63; producer, Radio Languedoc-Roussillon 1965–74; television producer, ORTF 1969–; mem. PEN Club. *Publications:* Les forêts du nouveau monde 1956, Lettre à un père sur une vocation incertaine 1956, Retour à Uzes 1968, L'Epervier de Maheux 1972, Jean Giono 1973, L'univers de Jean Carrière 1975, Noémie, Céléstin, Joseph et autres paysans d'Ardèche 1976, La Caverne des Pestiférés (two vols) 1978, 1979, Le nez dans l'herbe 1980, Les années sauvages (novel) 1986, Julien Gracq 1986, Le Prix du Goncourt (novel) 1986, Le Dernier Été d'Occident 1987, Voyage d'hiver en Provence 1987, Cévennes 1988, Jean Fusaro, ou La chorégraphie de l'instant 1988, Un grain de beauté sur la lune (novel) 1990, Sigourney Weaver ou Portrait et itinéraire d'une femme accomplie 1989, Droits, Devoirs et Crocodile: essai politique (co-author) 1992, L'Indifférence des Etoiles (novel) 1994, Achigan (novel) 1995, L'Etoffe des rêves (novel) 1996, L'Empire des songes (novel) 1996, Un jardin pour l'éternel (novel) 1997, Le fer dans la plaie (novel) 1999, L'outsider 2002. *Honours:* Prix de l'Acad. Française 1968, Prix Goncourt 1972, Prix des Journalistes de la Presse Parisienne 1999, Prix du Roman de l'Été 1999, Screen Laurel Award, Writer's Guild of America 2000, Prix du Sud 2000. *Address:* Les Broussanes, Domessargues, 30350 Ledignan; Le Devois, Super Camprieu, 30750 Trèves, France. *Telephone:* 66-83-30-76; 67-82-61-12. *Fax:* 66-83-33-84.

CARRINGTON, Ruth (see James, Michael Leonard)

CARROLL, Jenny (see Cabot, Meggin (Meg) Patricia)

CARROLL, Martin (see Carr, Margaret)

CARROLL, Paul Donnelly Michael, MA; American academic, poet and writer; b. 15 July 1927, Chicago, IL; m. Maryrose Carroll 1979, one s. *Education:* University of Chicago. *Career:* Poetry Ed., Chicago Review, 1957–59; Ed., Big Table Magazine, 1959–61, Big Table Books, Follett Publishing Company, 1966–71; Visiting Poet and Prof., University of Iowa, 1966–67; Prof. of English, University of Illinois, 1968–. *Publications:* Edward Dahlberg Reader (ed.), 1966; The Young American Poets, 1968; The Luke Poets, 1971; New and Selected Poems, 1978; The Garden of Earthly Delights, 1986; Poems, 1950–1990, 1990. Contributions: periodicals.

CARRUTH, Hayden, AB, MA; American poet, writer and academic; *Professor Emeritus, Syracuse University*; b. 3 Aug. 1921, Waterbury, CT; m. 1st Sara Anderson 1943; one d.; m. 2nd Eleanor Ray 1952; m. 3rd Rose Marie Dorn 1961; one s.; m. 4th Joe-Anne McLaughlin 1989. *Education:* Univ. of North Carolina, Univ. of Chicago. *Career:* Ed.-in-Chief, Poetry magazine 1949–50; Assoc. Ed., Univ. of Chicago Press 1950–51; Project Administrator, Intercultural Publications Inc., New York 1952–53; poet-in-residence, Johnson State Coll., Vermont 1972–74; Adjunct Prof., Univ. of Vermont 1975–78; Poetry Ed., Harper's magazine 1977–83; Prof. 1979–85, 1986–91, Syracuse Univ., Prof. Emeritus 1991–; Prof., Bucknell Univ. 1985–86. *Publications:* poetry: The Crow and the Heart, 1946–1959 1959, In Memoriam: G.V.C. 1960, Journey to a Known Place 1961, The Norfolk Poems: 1 June to 1 September 1961 1962, North Winter 1964, Nothing for Tigers: Poems, 1959–1964 1965, Contra Mortem 1967, For You 1970, The Clay Hill Anthology 1970, The Bird/Poem Book: Poems on the Wild Birds of North America (ed.) 1970, From Snow and Rock, From Chaos: Poems, 1965–1972 1973, Dark World 1974, The Bloomingdale Papers 1975, Loneliness: An Outburst of Hexasyllables 1976, Aura 1977, Brothers, I Loved You All 1978, Almanach du Printemps Vivarois 1979, The Mythology of Dark and Light 1982, The Sleeping Beauty 1983, If You Call This Cry a Song 1983, Asphalt Georgics 1985, Lighter Than Air Craft 1985, The Oldest Killed Lake in North America 1985, Mother 1985, The Selected Poetry of Hayden Carruth 1986, Sonnets 1989, Tell Me Again How the White Heron Rises and Flies Across the Nacreous River at Twilight Toward the Distant Islands 1989, Collected Shorter Poems, 1946–1991 1992, Collected Longer Poems 1994, Scrambled Eggs and Whiskey: Poems,

1991–1995 1995, Doctor Jazz 2003; prose: Appendix A (novel) 1963, After 'The Stranger': Imaginary Dialogues with Camus 1964, A New Directions Reader (ed. with James Laughlin) 1964, The Voice That is Great Within Us: American Poetry of the Twentieth Century (ed.) 1970, Working Papers: Selected Essays and Reviews 1981, Effluences from the Sacred Caves: More Selected Essays and Reviews 1984, Sitting In: Selected Writings on Jazz, Blues, and Related Topics 1986, Beside the Shadblow Tree (memoir) 2000, Letters to Jane 2004; contrib. to various periodicals. Honours: Bess Hokin Prize 1954, Vachel Lindsay Prize 1956, Levinson Prize 1958, Harriet Monroe Poetry Prize 1960, Bollingen Foundation Fellowship 1962, Helen Bullis Award 1962, Carl Sandburg Award 1963, Emily Clark Balch Prize 1964, Eunice Tietjens Memorial Prize 1964, Guggenheim Fellowships 1965, 1979, Morton Dauwen Zabel Prize 1967, Nat. Endowment for the Humanities Fellowship 1967, Governor's Medal, Vermont 1974, Sheele Memorial Award 1978, Lenore Marshall Poetry Prize 1978, Whiting Writers Award 1986, Nat. Endowment for the Arts Sr Fellowship 1988, Ruth Lilly Poetry Prize 1990, Nat. Book Critics Circle Award in Poetry 1993, Nat. Book Award for Poetry 1996. Address: 4788 Bear Path Road, Munnsville, NY 13409, USA (home). Telephone: (315) 495-6665.

CARRUTHERS, Peter Michael; British philosopher, academic and writer; b. 16 June 1952, Manila, Philippines; m. Susan Levi 1978; two s. Education: Univ. of Leeds, Balliol Coll., Oxford. Career: Lecturer, University of St Andrews, 1979–81, Queens University of Belfast, 1981–83, University of Essex, 1985–91; Visiting Prof., University of Michigan, 1989–90; Senior Lecturer, 1991–92, Prof., 1992–, University of Sheffield; mem. Aristotelian Society. Publications: The Metaphysics of the Tractatus, 1990; Introducing Persons: Theories and Arguments in the Philosophy of Mind, 1991; Human Knowledge and Human Nature: A New Introduction to the Ancient Debate, 1992; The Animals Issue: Moral Theory in Practice, 1992. Contributions: journals. Address: Department of Philosophy, University of Maryland, College Park, MD 20742, USA. Telephone: (301) 405-5689. E-mail: pcarruth@umd .edu.

CARSON, Anne, MA, PhD; Canadian academic, poet and writer; John MacNaughton Professor of Classics, McGill University; b. 21 June 1950, Toronto, ON. Education: Univ. of Toronto. Career: Prof. of Classics, Univ. of Calgary 1979–80, Princeton Univ. 1980–87, Emory Univ. 1987–88; John MacNaughton Prof. of Classics, McGill Univ. 1988–, Dir of Grad. Studies, Classics; Guggenheim Fellowship 1999; John D. and Catherine T. MacArthur Foundation Fellowship 2001. Publications: Eros the Bittersweet: An Essay 1986, Short Talks 1992, Plainwater 1995, Glass, Irony and God 1995, Autobiography of Red 1998, Economy of the Unlost 1999, Men in the Off Hours (Griffin Poetry Prize 2001) 2000, The Beauty of the Husband (Poetry Book Soc. T. S. Eliot Prize) 2001, Sophocles' Electra 2001, If Not, Winter: Fragments of Sappho (trans.) 2002, Decreation 2006; contribs to anthologies and journals. Honours: Lannan Literary Award 1996, Pushcart Prize for Poetry 1997. Address: Department of Classics, Room 823, Stephen Leacock Building, 855 Sherbrooke Street West, Montréal, PQ H3A 2T7 (office); 5900 Esplanade Avenue, Montréal, PQ H2T 3A3, Canada (home). E-mail: decreation@hotmail.com (office). Website: www.arts.mcgill.ca/programs/ classic.

CARSON, Ciaran, BA; Northern Irish poet; Professor of Poetry, Queen's University Belfast; b. 9 Oct. 1948, Belfast; m. Deidre Shannon 1982; two s. one d. Education: Queen's Univ., Belfast. Career: Traditional Arts Officer, Arts Council of Northern Ireland 1975–98; Prof. of Poetry, Dir, Seamus Heaney Centre for Poetry, Queen's Univ. Belfast. Publications: poetry: The New Estate 1976, The Lost Explorer 1978, Irish Traditional Music 1986, The Irish For No (Alice Hunt Bartlett Award) 1987, Belfast Confetti (Irish Times Irish Literature Prize for Poetry) 1990, First Language: Poems (T. S. Eliot Prize) 1993, Belfast Frescoes (with John Kindness) 1995, Letters from the Alphabet 1995, Opera Et Cetera 1996, The Alexandrine Plan (adaptations of other poets' sonnets) 1998, The Ballad of HMS Belfast: A Compendium of Belfast Poems 1999, The Twelfth of Never 1999, Breaking News (Forward Poetry Prize for best poetry collection) 2003, The Midnight Court: A New Translation of Cúirt An Mhéan Oíche by Brian Merriman 2005; prose: Last Night's Fun: About Time, Food and Music 1996, The Star Factory (Yorkshire Post Book Award for Book of the Year) 1997, Fishing for Amber 1999, Shamrock Tea (novel) 2001, The Inferno of Dante Alighieri (trans.) 2002; contrib. to TLS, New Yorker, Irish Review, Honest Ulsterman, London Review of Books. Honours: Eric Gregory Award 1978. Address: Seamus Heaney Centre for Poetry, Queen's University, Belfast, BT7 1NN, Ireland. E-mail: c.carson@qub .ac.uk. Website: www.qub.ac.uk/en/staff/carson/index.htm.

CARSON, Paul, BA, MB, BChir, BAO, DFPA; Northern Irish doctor and novelist; Medical Director, Slievemore Clinic; b. 1949, Belfast, Co. Down. Education: Garron Tower school, Trinity Coll., Dublin. Career: Medical Dir, Slievemore Clinic, Dublin 1984–. Publications: novels: Scalpel 1997, Cold Steel 1999, Final Duty 2000, Ambush 2004, Betrayal 2005; also five health books, two children's books, and numerous medical publications. Address: c/o William Heinemann, Random House UK Ltd, 20 Vauxhall Bridge Road, London, SW1V 2SA, England. Website: www.randomhouse.co.uk.

CARTANO, Tony, LèsL, DipES; French author and editor; b. 27 July 1944, Bayonne; m. Françoise Perrin 1966, one s. one d. Education: University of Paris. Career: Dir Foreign Dept, Editions Albin Michel, Paris. Publications: Le Single Hurteur, 1978; Malcolm Lowry (essay), 1979; Blackbird, 1980; La

Sourde Oreille, 1982; Schmutz, 1987; Le Bel Arturo, 1989; Le soufflé de Satan, 1991; American Boulevard (travel book), 1992. Honours: Chevalier, Ordre des Arts et des Lettres.

CĂRTĂRESCU, Mircea, PhD; Romanian poet and novelist; b. 1 June 1956, Bucharest. Education: Univ. of Bucharest. Career: teacher of Romanian language and literature, Bucharest 1980–89; fmr Ed. Contrapunct literary journal; Assoc. Prof. of Romanian Literature, Univ. of Bucharest 1991–; Visiting Prof., Univ. of Amsterdam 1994–95; mem. Romanian Writers' Union, PEN Romania, ASPRO. Publications: poetry: Faruri, vitrine, fotografii (Romanian Writers' Union Literary Debut Prize) 1980, Aer cu diamante 1982, Poeme de amor 1983, Totul 1985, Levantul (Romanian Writers' Union Prize) 1990, Dragostea 1994; fiction: Desant '83 1983, Visul (Romanian Acad. Prize) 1989, Travesti (Romanian Writers' Union Prize) 1994, Orbitor (ASPRO Prize) 1996. Address: c/o Department of Romanian Literature, Faculty of Letters, University of Bucharest, Str Edgar Quinet nr 5–7, Sector 1, Bucharest, Romania (office). E-mail: info@unibuc.ro (office).

CARTER, (Edward) Graydon; Canadian magazine editor; Editor-in-Chief, Vanity Fair; b. 14 July 1949, s. of E. P. Carter and Margaret Ellen Carter; m. Anna Scott 2005; three s. one d. Education: Carleton Univ., Univ. of Ottawa. Career: Ed. The Canadian Review 1973–77; writer, Time 1978–83, Life 1983–86; Founder, Ed. Spy 1986–91; Ed. New York Observer 1991–92; Ed.-in-Chief, Vanity Fair 1992–. Television as executive producer: 9/11 (CBS) 2002. Film as producer: The Kid Stays in the Picture 2002. Publications: Vanity Fair's Hollywood 2000, What We've Lost 2004, Oscar Night: 75 Years of Hollywood Parties 2004. Honours: Hon. Ed. Harvard Lampoon 1989; Advertising Age Editor of the Year 1996, Nat. Magazine Award for Gen. Excellence 1997, 1999, Nat. Magazine Award for Photography 2000, 2002, Nat. Magazine Award for Reviews and Criticism 2003. Address: Vanity Fair, Condé Nast Building, 4 Times Square, New York, NY 10036-6522, USA (office). Website: www.vanityfair.com (office).

CARTER, James (Jimmy) Earl, Jr, BSc; American politician, international political consultant and farmer; Chairman, Carter Center; b. 1 Oct. 1924, Plains, GA; s. of the late James Earl Carter, Sr and Lillian Gordy; m. Eleanor Rosalynn Smith 1946; three s. one d. Education: Plains High School, Georgia Southwestern Coll., Georgia Inst. of Tech., US Naval Acad., Annapolis, Md, Union Coll., New York State. Career: served in USN 1946–53, attained rank of Lt (submarine service); peanut farmer, warehouseman 1953–77, businesses Carter Farms, Carter Warehouses, Ga; State Senator, Ga 1962–66; Gov. of Georgia 1971–74; Pres. of USA 1977–81; Distinguished Prof., Emory Univ., Atlanta 1982–; leader int. observer teams Panama 1989, Nicaragua 1990, Dominican Repub. 1990, Haiti 1990; host peace negotiations Ethiopia 1989; visit to Democratic People's Repub. of Korea (in pvt. capacity) June 1994; negotiator in Haitian crisis Sept. 1994; visit to Bosnia Dec. 1994; f. Carter Presidential Center 1982; Chair. Bd of Trustees, Carter Center Inc. 1986–, Carter-Menil Human Rights Foundation 1986–, Global 2000 Inc. 1986–, Council of Freely Elected Heads of Govt 1986–, Council of Int. Negotiation Network 1991–; mem. Sumter County, Ga, School Bd 1955–62 (Chair. 1960–62), Americus and Sumter County Hospital Authority 1956–70, Sumter County Library Bd 1961; Pres. Plains Devt Corpn 1963; Georgia Planning Asscn 1968; Dir Ga Crop Improvement Asscn 1957–63 (Pres. 1961); Chair. West Cen. Ga Area Planning and Devt Comm. 1964; State Chair. March of Dimes 1968–70; District Gov. Lions Club 1968–69; Chair. Congressional Campaign Cttee, Democratic Nat. Cttee 1974; Democrat. Publications: Why Not the Best? 1975, A Government as Good as Its People 1977, Keeping Faith: Memoirs of a President 1982, The Blood of Abraham: Insights into the Middle East 1985, Everything to Gain: Making the Most of the Rest of Your Life 1987, An Outdoor Journal 1988, Turning Point: A Candidate, a State and a Nation Come of Age 1992, Always a Reckoning (poems) 1995, Sources of Strength 1997, The Virtues of Ageing 1998, An Hour Before Daylight 2001, The Hornet's Nest (novel) 2003, Our Endangered Values 2005, Palestine: Peace Not Apartheid 2006. Honours: several hon. degrees; Ansel Adams Conservation Award, Wilderness Society 1982, World Methodist Peace Award 1984, Albert Schweitzer Prize for Humanitarianism 1987, Onassis Foundation Award 1991, Notre Dame Univ. Award 1992, Matsunaga Medal of Peace 1993, J. William Fulbright Prize for Int. Understanding 1994, shared Houphouët Boigny Peace Prize, UNESCO 1995, UNICEF Int. Child Survival Award (jtly with Rosalynn Carter) 1999, Presidential Medal of Freedom 1999, Eisenhower Medallion 2000, Nobel Peace Prize 2002. Address: The Carter Center, 453 Freedom Parkway, 1 Copenhill Avenue NE, Atlanta, GA 30307, USA (office). Telephone: (404) 420-5100 (office). Fax: (404) 420-5196 (office). E-mail: carterweb@emory.edu (office). Website: www.cartercenter.org (office).

CARTER, Robert Ayres, AB; American writer and lecturer; b. 16 Sept. 1923, Omaha, NE; m. 1983; two s. Education: New School for Social Research, New York. Career: mem. Poets and Writers, MWA, Int. Asscn of Crime Writers; life mem. The Players. Publications: Manhattan Primitive 1972, Written in Blood (aka Casual Slaughters) 1992, Final Edit 1994, The Language of Stones 2004, The Giants' Dance 2005, Whitemantle 2006; three textbooks; contrib. to Publishers Weekly; International Journal of Book Publishing. Honours: Fulbright Scholar 1949. Address: 510 N Meadow Street, Richmond, VA 23220, USA.

CARTER, Stephen Lisle, BA, JD; American academic and lawyer; William Nelson Cromwell Professor of Law, Yale University; b. 1954, Washington, DC; m.; c. Education: Stanford and Yale Univs. Career: fmr Note Ed. Yale Law

Journal; admitted to Bar, Washington, DC 1981; law clerk, Judge Spottswood W. Robinson III, US Court of Appeal, Washington, DC 1979–80; law clerk, Justice Thurgood Marshall, US Supreme Court 1980–81; Assoc. Shea & Gardner, Washington, DC 1981–82; Asst Prof. of Law, Yale Univ. 1982–84, Assoc. Prof. 1984–85, Prof. 1986–91, William Nelson Cromwell Prof. of Law 1991–; Official Adviser to US Pres. Bill Clinton 1993. *Publications include:* Reflections of an Affirmative Action Baby 1991, The Culture of Disbelief 1993, The Confirmation Mess 1994, Integrity 1996, The Dissent of the Governed 1998, Civility 1998, God's Name in Vain 2000, The Emperor of Ocean Park 2002, New England White 2007. *Honours:* Hon. LLD (Univ. of Notre Dame) 1996. *Address:* Yale Law School, POB 208215, New Haven, CT 06520 (office); c/o Knopf Publishing (Author Mail), 1745 Broadway, New York, NY 10019, USA (office). *E-mail:* stephen.carter@yale.edu (office). *Website:* www.law.yale .edu/outside/html/home/index.htm (office).

CARTWRIGHT, Justin, (Suzy Crispin, Penny Sutton); British writer; b. 1933, South Africa. *Education:* Univ. of Oxford. *Career:* fmr copywriter and film-maker. *Publications:* Fighting Men 1977, The Revenge 1978, The Horse of Darius 1980, Freedom for the Wolves 1983, Interior 1988, Look at it This Way 1990, Masai Dreaming 1993, In Every Face I Meet 1995, Not Yet Home 1996, Leading the Cheers (Whitbread Novel of the Year) 1998, Half in Love 2002, White Lightning 2002, The Promise of Happiness (Hawthornden Prize 2005, Sunday Times Fiction Award, South Africa 2005) 2004, The Song Before It Is Sung 2007. *Literary Agent:* PFD, Drury House, 34–43 Russell Street, London, WC2B 5HA, England.

CARWARDINE, Richard John, BA, MA, DPhil, FBA; British academic and writer; *Rhodes Professor of American History, University of Oxford;* b. 12 Jan. 1947, Cardiff, Wales; m. Linda Margaret Kirk 1975. *Education:* Univ. of Oxford. *Career:* Lecturer, Univ. of Sheffield, later Sr Lecturer, Reader, Prof. 1971–2002; Visiting Prof., Syracuse Univ., New York 1974–75; Visiting Fellow, Univ. of North Carolina, Chapel Hill 1989; Rhodes Prof. of American History, Univ. of Oxford 2002–; Fellow, St Catherine's Coll. *Publications:* Transatlantic Revivalism: Popular Evangelicalism in Britain and America 1790–1865 1978, Evangelicals and Politics in Antebellum America 1993, Lincoln 2003, Lincoln: A Life of Purpose and Power 2006. *Honours:* Lincoln Prize Laureate 2004. *Address:* St Catherine's College, Oxford, OX1 3UJ, England (office).

CARY, Jud (see Tubb, Edwin Charles)

CARY, Lorene Emily, BA, MA; American writer; b. 29 Nov. 1956, Philadelphia, PA; m. R. C. Smith 1983; two d. one step-s. *Education:* University of Pennsylvania, University of Sussex. *Career:* Assoc. Ed., TV Guide, 1980–82; Contributing Ed., Newsweek Magazine, 1991; Lecturer, University of Pennsylvania, 1995–; mem. PEN, Authors' Guild. *Publications:* Black Ice, 1991; The Price of a Child, 1995; Pride, 1998. *Honours:* Hon. DLitt.

CASEY, John Dudley, BA, LLB, MFA; American writer and academic; b. 18 Jan. 1939, Worcester, Mass; m. Rosamond Pinchot Pittman 1982; four d. *Education:* Harvard Coll., Harvard Law School, Univ. of Iowa. *Career:* Prof., Univ. of Virginia, later Henry Hoynes Prof. of English 1972–92, 1999–; Guggenheim Foundation Fellowship 1979–80, Nat. Endowment for the Arts Fellowship 1983, Ingram Merril Foundation Fellowship 1990; residency, American Acad. in Rome 1990–91; mem. PEN. *Publications:* An American Romance (novel) 1977, Testimony and Demeanor (short stories) 1979, Spartina (novel) (Nat. Book Award) 1989, Avid (short story) (O. Henry Award) 1989, Supper at the Black Pearl 1996, The Half-Life of Happiness (novel) 1998; contrib. stories, articles and reviews in newspapers and magazines, including The New Yorker, The New York Times Magazine, Esquire, Harper's. *Honours:* Friends of American Writers Award 1980, American Acad. of Arts and Letters Strauss Living Award 1991–97, Nat. Book Award 1989. *Address:* Department of English, University of Virginia, 219 Bryan Hall, PO Box 400121, Charlottesville, VA 22904-4121, USA (office). *E-mail:* jdc@virginia.edu (office).

CASS, Sir Geoffrey Arthur, Kt, MA, CCMI; British publishing executive and arts and lawn tennis administrator; b. 11 Aug. 1932, Bishop Auckland; s. of the late Arthur Cass and Jessie Cass (née Simpson); m. Olwen Mary Richards, JP, DL 1957; four d. *Education:* Queen Elizabeth Grammar School, Darlington and Jesus Coll., Oxford. *Career:* Nuffield Coll., Oxford 1957–58; RAF 1958–60; ed. Automation 1960–61; Consultant, PA Man. Consultants Ltd 1960–65; Pvt. Man. Consultant, British Communications Corpn and Controls and Communications Ltd 1965; Dir Controls and Communications Ltd 1966–69; Dir George Allen & Unwin 1965–67, Man. Dir 1967–71; Dir Weidenfeld Publrs. 1972–74, Univ. of Chicago Press, UK 1971–86; Chief Exec. Cambridge Univ. Press 1972–92, Consultant 1992–; Sec. Press Syndicate, Univ. of Cambridge 1974–92; Univ. Printer 1982–83, 1991–92; Fellow, Clare Hall, Cambridge 1979–; Trustee Shakespeare Birthplace Trust 1982–94 (Life Trustee 1994–); Chair. Royal Shakespeare Co. 1985–2000 (Deputy Pres. 2000–), Royal Shakespeare Theatre Trust 1983–; British Int. Tennis and Nat. Training 1985–90, Nat. Ranking Cttee; mem. Bd of Man., Lawn Tennis Asscn of GB 1985–90, 1993–2000, Deputy Pres. 1994–96, Pres. 1997–99, Chair. British Tennis Foundation 2003–; mem. Cttee of Man., Wimbledon Championships 1990–2002; Pres., Chair. or mem. numerous other trusts, bds, cttees, charitable appeals and advisory bodies particularly in connection with theatre, sport and medicine; Oxford tennis Blue and badminton; played in Wimbledon Tennis Championships 1954, 1955, 1956, 1959; British Veterans Singles Champion, Wimbledon 1978. *Publications:* articles in professional journals. *Honours:* Hon. Fellow, Jesus Coll., Oxford 1998; Chevalier, Ordre des Arts et Lettres. *Address:* Middlefield, Huntingdon Road, Cambridge, CB3 0LH, England.

CASS, Zoe (see Low, Lois Dorothea)

CASSELLS, Cyrus Curtis, BA; American poet, teacher and translator; b. 16 May 1957, Dover, DE. *Education:* Stanford University. *Career:* mem. PEN; Poetry Society of America. *Publications:* The Mud Actor, 1982; Soul Make a Path Through Shouting, 1994; Beautiful Signor, 1997. *Contributions:* Southern Review; Callaloo; Translation; Seneca Review; Quilt; Sequoia. *Honours:* Acad. of American Poets Prize, 1979; National Poetry Series Winner, 1982; Callaloo Creative Writing Award, 1983; Massachusetts Artists Foundation Fellowship, 1985; National Endowment for the Arts Fellowship, 1986; Lavan Younger Poets Award, 1992; Lannan Award, 1993; William Carlos Williams Award, 1994.

CASSIDY, Anne; British children's writer; b. 1952; m.; one s. *Publications:* A Big Bunch of Balloons, A Family Affair, Accidental Death, Big Girl's Shoes, Blood Money, Brotherly Love, Cleo and Leo, Death by Drowning, Driven to Death, Good Days, Bad Days, Jasper and Jess, Love Letters, Missing Judy, Naughty Nancy, Optical Illusions, Patsy Kelly Investigates, Snow White, Spider Pie, Temples, The End of the Line, The Hidden Child, The Queen's Dragon, The Sassy Monkey, Toby's Trousers, Tough Love, Looking for JJ (Booktrust Teenage Book of the Year, Staffordshire YTF Book Award 2005) 2004, The Story of my Life 2006. *Address:* c/o Scholastic UK, 24 Eversholt Street, London, NW1 1DB, England. *Website:* www.annecassidy.com.

CASTEL, Albert Edward, BA, MA, PhD; American historian and academic; b. 11 Nov. 1928, Wichita, KS; m. GeorgeAnn Bennett 1959; one s. one d. *Education:* Wichita State Univ., Univ. of Chicago. *Career:* Instructor, Univ. of California at Los Angeles 1957–58; Asst Prof., Waynesburg Coll., PA 1958–60; Asst Prof. 1960–63, Assoc. Prof. 1963–67, Prof. 1967–91, Western Michigan Univ. *Publications:* A Frontier State at War 1958, William Clarke Quantrill 1962, Sterling Price and the Civil War in the West 1968, The Guerrilla War 1974, The Yeas and Nays: Key Congressional Votes (co-author) 1975, Fort Sumter: 1861 1976, The Presidency of Andrew Johnson 1979, Decision in the West: The Atlanta Campaign of 1864 1992, Winning and Losing in the Civil War: Essays and Stories 1996, Bloody Bill Anderson (co-author) 1998, Tom Taylor's Civil War 2000, Articles of War 2001; contrib. to many scholarly journals. *Honours:* American Historical Asscn Albert J. Beveridge Award 1957, Civil War Times Illustrated Best Author Award 1979, Eastern Nat. Park and Monument Asscn Peterson Award 1989, Atlanta Civil War Round Table Harwell Award 1993, Gettysburg Coll. Lincoln Prize 1993, Civil War Round Table of Kansas City Truman Award 1994. *Address:* 166 Westwood Drive, Hillsdale, MI 49242, USA.

CASTEL-BLOOM, Orly; Israeli novelist; b. 1960, Tel-Aviv. *Education:* Tel-Aviv Univ. *Publications:* novels: Heichan Ani Nimtzet (trans. as Where Am I?) 1990, Dolly City 1992, Ha-Mina Lisa (trans. as The Mina Lisa) 1995, Taking the Trend 1998, Human Parts (Wizo Prize 2005) 2002; short story collections: Not Far from the Centre of Town 1987, Hostile Surroundings 1989, Unbidden Stories 1993, Free Radicals 2000, Selected Stories 1987–2004 2004; juvenile: Let's Behave Ourselves 1997. *Honours:* Tel-Aviv Prize for Literature 1990, Newman Prize 2003. *Address:* c/o Jewish Book Council, PO Box 38247, London, NW3 5YQ, England.

CASTELL, Megan (see Williams, Jeanne)

CASTER, Sylvie; French journalist and writer; b. 1952. *Education:* studied in Bordeaux. *Publications:* Les Chênes verts 1980, La France fout la camp 1982, Nel est mort 1985, Bel-Air 1991, H. B., la bombe humaine 1994, La petite Sibérie 1995, Dormir (Prix Jean Freustié 2003, Prix Charles Exbrayat 2003) 2002. *Address:* c/o Editions Fayard, 75 rue des Saints-Pères, 75278 Paris, Cédex 06, France.

CASTILLO, Michel Xavier Janicot del, LèsL, LenP; French writer; b. 2 Aug. 1933, Madrid, Spain; s. of Michel Janicot and Isabelle del Castillo. *Education:* Coll. des jésuites d'Ubeba, Spain, Lycée Janson-de-Sailly, Paris. *Career:* mem. Soc. des gens de lettres, PEN. *Publications:* Tanguy 1957, La Guitare 1958, Le Colleur d'affiches 1959, Le Manège espagnol 1960, Tara 1962, Gerardo Laïn 1969, Le Vent de la nuit 1973, Le Silence des pierres 1975, Le Sortilège espagnol 1977, Les Cyprès meurent en Italie 1979, Les Louves de l'Escurial 1980, La nuit du décret 1981, La Gloire de Dina 1984, Nos Andalousies 1985, Le Démon de l'oubli 1987, Mort d'un poète 1989, Une Femme en Soi 1991, Le Crime des Pères 1993, Rue des Archives 1994, Mon frère l'idiot 1995, La Tunique d'infamie 1997, De père français 1998, Colette, une certaine France (Prix Femina 1999), L'Adieu au siècle 2000, Droit d'auteur 2000. *Honours:* Chevalier Légion d'honneur; Commdr des Jess. et Lettres; Prix des Neufs 1957, Prix des Magots 1973, Grand Prix des libraires 1973, Prix Chateaubriand 1975, Prix Renaudot 1981, Prix Maurice Genevoix 1994. *Address:* Editions Stock, 27 rue Cassette, 75006 Paris (office); Le Colombier, 7 avenue Camille Martin, 30190 La Calmette, France (home).

CASTLEDEN, Rodney, DipEd, MA, MSc; British geomorphologist, writer, archaeologist and composer; b. 23 March 1945, Worthing, Sussex; s. of Dennis Castleden and Gwendoline Dennett; m. Sarah Dee 1987. *Education:* Hertford Coll., Univ. of Oxford. *Career:* freelance writer, researcher; mem. Soc. of Authors, Sussex Archaeological Soc. *Composition:* Winfrith (chamber opera) 2000, revised 2003. *Publications:* Classic Landforms of the Sussex Coast 1982,

The Wilmington Giant: The Quest for a Lost Myth 1983, Classic Landforms Series (ed.) 1983–99, The Stonehenge People: An Exploration of Life in Neolithic Britain 1987, The Knossos Labyrinth 1989, Minoans: Life in Bronze Age Crete 1990, Book of British Dates 1991, Neolithic Britain 1992, The Making of Stonehenge 1993, World History: A Chronological Dictionary of Dates 1994, British History: A Chronological Dictionary of Dates 1994, The Cerne Giant 1996, Knossos, Temple of the Goddess 1996, Atlantis Destroyed 1998, Out in the Cold 1998, The English Lake District 1998, The Search for King Arthur 1999, Ancient British Hill Figures 2000, History of World Events 2003, Britain 3000 BC 2003, Infamous Murderers 2004, Serial Killers 2004, The World's Most Evil People 2005, Mycenaeans 2005, People Who Changed the World 2005, Events that Changed the World 2005, The Attack on Troy 2006, English Castles 2006, Castles of the Celtic Lands 2006, The Book of Saints 2006, Assassinations and Conspiracies 2006, Natural Disasters That Changed the World 2007; contrib. 100 articles published in various journals and magazines. *Address:* Rookery Cottage, Blatchington Hill, Seaford, East Sussex, BN25 2AJ, England (home). *Telephone:* (1323) 873985 (office). *E-mail:* rodney@castleden.fsnet.co.uk (home).

CASTRO, Brian Albert, MA; Australian writer and teacher; b. 16 Jan. 1950, Kowloon, Hong Kong; m. Josephine Mary Gardiner 1976. *Education:* University of Sydney. *Career:* journalist, Asiaweek, Hong Kong 1983–87, All-Asia Review of Books, Hong Kong 1989–; writer-in-residence, Mitchell College, NSW 1985; Visiting Fellow, Nepean College, Kingswood, NSW 1988; Tutor in Literary Studies, University of Western Australia 1989–. *Publications:* Birds of Passage 1982, Pomeroy 1991, Double-Wolf 1991, After China 1992, Drift 1994, Stepper 1998, Shanghai Dancing 2003, The Garden Book 2005; Contributions: anthologies and periodicals. *Honours:* Book of the Year Award 1992.

CAULDWELL, Frank (see King, Francis Henry)

CAULO, Ralph Daniel, MA; American publishing executive; *Vice-Chairman, WRC Media Inc.*; b. 7 Jan. 1935; two s. one d. *Education:* Univ. of Redlands. *Career:* SW Regional Man. Schools Dept Harcourt Brace Jovanovich Inc. 1974–75, Man. Gen. Sales 1975–78, Deputy Dir 1978–79, Vice-Pres. 1979–81, Sr Vice-Pres. 1981–83, Exec. Vice-Pres. 1983–88, Pres. and COO 1988–89, Pres. and CEO 1989–91; Exec. Vice-Pres., later Pres. Simon & Schuster 1991–98; consultant to Ripplewood Holdings LLC from 1998; Dir and Vice-Chair. Bd of Dirs WRC Media Inc. 1999–, (interim CEO 2005). *Address:* WRC Media Inc., 512 Seventh Avenue, New York, NY 10018, USA (office).

CAUTE, (John) David, MA, DPhil, JP, FRSL; British writer; b. 16 Dec. 1936; m. 1st Catherine Shuckburgh 1961 (divorced 1970); two s.; m. 2nd Martha Bates 1973; two d. *Education:* Edinburgh Acad., Wellington, Wadham Coll., Oxford. *Career:* St Antony's Coll. 1959; army service Gold Coast 1955–56; Henry Fellow, Harvard Univ. 1960–61; Fellow, All Souls Coll., Oxford 1959–65; Visiting Prof. New York Univ. and Columbia Univ.; 1966–67; Reader in Social and Political Theory, Brunel Univ. 1967–70; Regents' Lecturer, Univ. of California 1974, Visiting Prof. Univ. of Bristol 1985; Literary Ed. New Statesman 1979–80; Co-Chair. Writers' Guild 1982. *Plays:* Songs for an Autumn Rifle 1961, The Demonstration 1969, The Fourth World 1973, Brecht and Company (BBC TV) 1979. *Radio plays:* The Demonstration 1971, Fallout 1972, The Zimbabwe Tapes (BBC Radio) 1983, Henry and the Dogs (BBC Radio) 1986, Sanctions (BBC Radio) 1988, Animal Fun Park (BBC Radio) 1995. *Publications:* At Fever Pitch (novel) (Authors' Club Award 1960, John Llewelyn Rhys Award 1960) 1959, Comrade Jacob (novel) 1961, Communism and the French Intellectuals 1914–1960 1964, The Left in Europe Since 1789 1966, The Decline of the West (novel) 1966, Essential Writings of Karl Marx (ed.) 1967, Fanon 1970, The Confrontation: a trilogy, The Demonstration (play), The Occupation (novel), The Illusion 1971, The Fellow-Travellers 1973, Collisions: Essays and Reviews 1974, Cuba, Yes? 1974, The Great Fear: The Anti-Communist Purge Under Truman and Eisenhower 1978, Under the Skin: the Death of White Rhodesia 1983, The Baby-Sitters (novel, as John Salisbury) 1978, Moscow Gold (novel, as John Salisbury) 1980, The K-Factor (novel) 1983, The Espionage of the Saints 1986, News from Nowhere (novel) 1986, Sixty Eight: the Year of the Barricades 1988, Veronica of the Two Nations (novel) 1989, The Women's Hour (novel) 1991, Joseph Losey: A Revenge on Life 1994, Dr Orwell and Mr Blair (novel) 1994, Fatima's Scarf (novel) 1998, The Dancer Defects: The Struggle for Cultural Supremacy During the Cold War 2003. *Address:* 41 Westcroft Square, London, W6 0TA, England.

CEBRIÁN ECHARRI, Juan Luis; Spanish writer and journalist; b. 30 Oct. 1944, Madrid; s. of Vicente Cebrián and Carmen Echarri; m. 1st María Gema Torallas 1966 (divorced); two s. two d.; m. 2nd Teresa Aranda 1988; one s. one d. *Education:* Univ. of Madrid. *Career:* Founder-mem. of magazine Cuadernos para el Diálogo, Madrid 1963; Sr Ed. newspapers Pueblo, Madrid 1962–67, Informaciones, Madrid 1967–69; Deputy Ed.-in-Chief, Informaciones 1969–74, 1974–76; Dir News Programming, Spanish TV 1974; Ed.-in-Chief newspaper El País, Madrid 1976–88; CEO PRISA 1988–, Canal Plus 1989–, Estructura 1989–; Publr, CEO El País 1988–; Vice-Pres. SER 1990–; mem. Int. Press Inst. (Vice-Pres. 1982–86, Chair. 1986–88). *Publications:* La Prensa y la Calle 1980, La España que bosteza 1980, ¿Qué pasa en el mundo? 1981, Crónicas de mi país 1985, El Tamaño del elefante 1987, Red Doll 1987, La isla del viento 1990, El siglo de las sombras 1994. *Honours:* Dr hc (Iberoamericana Univ., Santo Domingo) 1988; Control Prize for Outstanding Newspaper Ed. 1976, 1977, 1978, 1979; Víctor de la Serna Prize for Journalism, Press Asscn

Fed. 1977; Outstanding Ed. of the Year (World Press Review, New York) 1980, Spanish Nat. Journalism Prize 1983; Freedom of Expression Medal, F. D. Roosevelt Four Freedoms Foundation 1986; Medal of Honor, Univ. of Miss. 1986; Trento Int. Prize for Journalism and Communication 1987; Gold Medal, Spanish Inst. New York 1988. *Address:* Gran Vía 32-6a, 28013 Madrid, Spain.

CEDERING, Siv; American (b. Swedish) writer, poet and artist; b. 5 Feb. 1939, Sweden; m. Hans Van de Bovenkamp; one s. two d. *Career:* mem. Co-ordinating Council of Literary Magazines; PEN; Poetry Society of America; Poets and Writers. *Publications:* for children: The Blue Horse 1979, Grisen Som Ville Bli Ren (The Pig Who Wanted to be Clean) 1983, Polis, Polis, Potatis Gris (The Pig and the Stolen Cakes) 1985, Grisen Som Ville Bli Julskinka (The Pig and the Christmas Ham) 1986, Grisen Far Till Paris (The Pig Goes to Paris) 1987, Mannen I Ödebyn (The Man in the Deserted Village) 1988; novels: Leken i Grishuset (The Pighouse Game) 1980, Oxen (The Ox) 1981; poetry: Cup of Cold Water 1973, Letters from the Island 1973, From Helge 1974, Moher Is 1975, How to Eat a Fortune Cookie 1976, The Juggler 1977, Twelve Pages from the Floating World 1983, Letters from the Floating World 1984, Letters from an Observatory: New and Selected Poems 1973–98 1998. *Honours:* New York Foundation Fellowships 1985, 1992. *Address:* PO Box 89, Sagaponack, NY 11962, USA. *E-mail:* cedering@cedering.com. *Website:* www .cedering.com.

CELATI, Gianni; Italian novelist; b. 1937, Sondrio, Ferrara, Italy. *Career:* Lecturer in Anglo-American Literature, University of Bologna. *Publications:* Comiche, 1971; Le avventure di Guizzardi, 1971; Il chiodo in testa, 1975; Finzioni occidentali, 1975; La banda dei sospiri, 1976; La bottega dei mimi, 1977; Lunario del paradiso, 1978; Narratori delle pianure, 1985; Quattro novelle sulle apparenze, 1987; Verso la foce, 1989; Parlamenti buffi, 1989; Profili delle nuvole, 1989; ed. and translator. *Honours:* Mondello Prize 1990.

CERCAS, Javier; Spanish novelist; b. 6 April 1962, s. of José and Blanca Cercas; m. Mercè Mas; one s. *Education:* Univ. Autónoma, Barcelona. *Career:* teacher, Univ. of Illinois –1989; Lecturer in Spanish Literature, Univ. of Gerona 1989–. *Publications:* El móvil (trans. as The Motive) 1987, El inquilino (trans. as The Tenant) 1989, La obra literaria de Gonzalo Suárez 1993, El vientre de la balleria (trans. as The Belly of the Whale) 1997, Una buena temporada 1999, Relatos reales (trans. as True Tales) 2000, Soldados de Salamina (trans. as Soldiers of Salamis) (Independent Foreign Fiction Prize 2004) 2001, La velocidad de la luz (trans. as The Speed of Light) 2005; contrib. to El País. *Honours:* Premi Libreter 2001, Premi Ciutat de Barcelona 2002, Premio de la Crítica de Chile 2002, Premio Salambó 2002, Premio Qué Leer 2002, Premio Extremadura 2002, Premio Cálamo 2002, Premio Grinzane-Cavour 2003. *Address:* c/o Bloomsbury Publishing PLC, 38 Soho Square, London, W1V 5DF, England. *Website:* www.bloomsbury.com.

CERONETTI, Guido; Italian writer, philosopher, poet and translator; b. 1927, Turin. *Publications:* La carta è stanca 1976, La musa ulcerosa: Scritti vari e inediti 1978, Un viaggio in Italia 1981-83 1983, Albergo Italia 1985, Briciole di colonna 1987, Aquilegia: Favola sommersa 1988, Amor di busta 1991, Silence of the Body: Materials for the Study of Medicine (co-author) 1993, N.U.E.D.D. (Nuovi ultimi esasperati deliri disarmati) 2001. *Address:* c/o Einaudi Editore, Via Biancamo 2, 10121 Turin, Italy.

CERVANTES, Lorna Dee; American poet and academic; *Associate Professor of English, University of Colorado at Boulder;* b. 1954, San Jose, CA. *Career:* Assoc. Prof. of English and Dir Creative Writing Program, Univ. of Colorado at Boulder; founding Ed. and Publr Mango (literary magazine), Red Dirt (poetry journal); Visiting Scholar Mexican American Studies Program, Univ. of Houston 1994–95. *Publications:* Emplumada (American Book Award 1982) 1981, From the Cables of Genocide: Poems on Love and Hunger (Paterson Prize for Best Book of Poetry 1991, Latino Literature Award) 1991. *Honours:* NEA fellowships 1978, 1993, Nat. Asscn of Chicano Scholars Outstanding Chicana Scholar 1993, Pushcart Prize 1980, Lila-Wallace Reader's Digest Fund Writers' Award 1995. *Address:* Hellems 103, Department of English, University of Colorado, UCB 226, Boulder, CO 80309-0226, USA. *E-mail:* Lorna.Cervantes@colorado.edu.

CÉSAIRE, Aimé Fernand, LèsL; French politician, poet and dramatist; b. 25 June 1913, Basse-Pointe, Martinique; s. of Fernand Césaire and Marie Césaire (née Hermine); m. Suzanne Roussi 1937; four s. two d. *Education:* Fort-de-France, Martinique, Lycée Louis-le-Grand, Ecole Normale Supérieure and the Sorbonne, Paris. *Career:* teaching career 1940–45; mem. Constituent Assemblies 1945 and 1946; Deputy for Martinique 1946–93; Pres. Parti Progressiste Martiniquais; Mayor of Fort-de-France 1945–2001; Pres. Conseil régional, Martinique 1983–86; Pres. Soc. of African Culture, Paris. *Publications:* verse: Les armes miraculeuses 1946, Cahier d'un retour au pays natal 1947, Soleil cou coupé 1948, Corps perdu 1960, Ferrements 1960, Cadastre 1961, L'Etat de l'union 1966, Moi, laminaire 1982; poetry: Aimé Césaire: The Collected Poetry 1983, Oeuvres complètes et inédites 1994; essays: Discours sur le colonialisme; plays: Et les chiens se taisaient 1956, La tragédie du roi Christophe 1964, Une saison au Congo 1966, Une tempête (adaptation of Shakespeare) 1969; other: Toussaint L'ouverture: La révolution française et le problème colonial 1960. *Honours:* Grand Prize for Verse 1982. *Address:* c/o La Mairie, boulevard de général de Gaulle, 97200 Fort-de-France, Martinique, West Indies.

CHABON, Michael, MFA; American writer; b. 1964, Columbia, MD; m.; one s. one d. *Education:* Univ. of Pittsburgh, Univ. of Calif., Irvine. *Publications:* The

Mysteries of Pittsburgh 1988, A Model World (short stories) 1991, The Wonder Boys 1995, Werewolves in Their Youth (short stories) 1995, The Amazing Adventures of Kavalier & Clay (Pulitzer Prize for fiction 2001) 2000, The Final Solution 2005, The Yiddish Policemen's Union (novel) 2007; contrib. short stories to several magazines. *Honours:* Publishers Weekly Best Book 1995, New York Times Notable Book 1995, O. Henry Award 1999. *Literary Agent:* Steven Barclay Agency, 12 Western Avenue, Petaluma, CA 94952, USA. *Telephone:* (707) 773-0654. *Fax:* (707) 778-1868. *Website:* www.barclayagency .com.

CHADWICK, Cydney; American writer and editor; b. 12 July 1959, Oakland, Calif. *Education:* Sonoma State Univ., Kootenay School of Writing. *Career:* Regional Sales Man., Chadwick Marketing, Penngrove, Calif. 1984–92; Exec. Dir Syntax Projects for the Arts; freelance typesetter, designer, ed. and manuscript consultant; Fellow, California Arts Council 1997; mem. PEN West. *Publications:* Enemy Clothing (stories) 1993, Dracontic Nodes (chapbook) 1993, Persistent Disturbances (stories, chapbook) 1994, Oeuvres (story, chapbook) 1994, The Gift Horse's Mouth (story, chapbook) 1995, Interims (stories, chapbook) 1997, Inside the Hours (fiction) 1998, Benched (novella) 2000, Flesh and Bone 2001, Under the Sun 2003, Cut and Run 2005. *Honours:* Gertrude Stein Award in Innovative Writing 1995, New American Writing Award in Fiction 1998, Nat. Endowment for the Arts Creative Writing Fellowship 2001, ind. Book Publrs' Award 2002. *Address:* PO Box 1059, Penngrove, CA 94951, USA (home). *Telephone:* (707) 793-2114 (office). *Fax:* (707) 769-0880 (office). *E-mail:* aveclivres@yahoo.com (home). *Website:* www.avecbooks.org.

CHADWICK, Geoffrey (see Wall, Geoffrey)

CHADWICK, Sir Henry, KBE, MusB, DD, FBA; British academic; *Professor Emeritus, University of Cambridge;* b. 23 June 1920, Bromley, Kent; s. of John Chadwick and Edith M. Chadwick; m. Margaret E. Brownrigg 1945; three d. *Education:* Eton Coll. and Magdalene Coll., Cambridge. *Career:* Fellow, Queens' Coll. Cambridge 1946–58, Hon. Fellow 1958–; Regius Prof. of Divinity, Univ. of Oxford 1959–69; Dean of Christ Church 1969–79; Regius Prof. of Divinity, Univ. of Cambridge 1979–83, Prof. Emer. 1983–, Fellow, Magdalene Coll. 1979–86; Master, Peterhouse, Cambridge 1987–93, Hon. Fellow 1993; Del. Oxford Univ. Press 1960–79. *Publications:* Origen Contra Celsum 1953, Sentences of Sextus 1959, Early Christian Thought and the Classical Tradition 1966, The Early Church 1967, Priscillian of Avila 1976, Boethius 1981, History and Thought of the Early Church 1982, Augustine 1986, Heresy and Orthodoxy in the Early Church 1991, Augustine's Confessions 1991, Tradition and Exploration 1994, The Church in Ancient Society from Galilee to Gregory the Great 2001, East and West: The Making of a Rift in the Church 2003. *Honours:* German Order pour le mérite 1993; Dr hc (Glasgow, Leeds, Manchester, Surrey, Uppsala, Yale, Harvard, Jena and Chicago); Humboldt Prize 1983, Lucas Prize (Tübingen) 1991. *Address:* 46 St John Street, Oxford, OX1 2LH, England. *Telephone:* (1865) 512814.

CHADWICK, (William) Owen, OM, KBE, FBA, FRSE; British historian (retd); b. 20 May 1916, Bromley, Kent; s. of John Chadwick and Edith Chadwick (née Horrocks); m. Ruth Hallward 1949; two s. two d. *Education:* St John's Coll., Cambridge. *Career:* Fellow, Trinity Hall, Cambridge 1947–56; Master of Selwyn Coll., Cambridge 1956–83, Fellow 1983–; Dixie Prof. of Ecclesiastical History, Univ. of Cambridge 1958–68, Regius Prof. of Modern History 1968–83; Vice-Chancellor Univ. of Cambridge 1969–71; Pres. British Acad. 1981–85; Chancellor Univ. of East Anglia 1985–94; Chair. of Trustees Nat. Portrait Gallery 1988–94. *Publications:* From Bossuet to Newman 1957, The Victorian Church (two vols) 1966–70, John Cassian (2nd edn) 1968, The Reformation (20th edn) 1986, The Secularization of the European Mind 1976, The Popes and European Revolution 1981, Britain and the Vatican during the Second World War 1987, Michael Ramsey: A Life 1990, The Christian Church in the Cold War 1992, A History of Christianity 1995, A History of the Popes 1830–1914 1998, The Early Reformation on the Continent 2001; numerous articles and reviews in learned journals. *Honours:* Hon. mem. American Acad. of Arts and Sciences; Hon. DD (St Andrews) 1960, (Oxford) 1973, (Wales) 1993: Hon. DLitt (Kent) 1970, (Columbia Univ.) 1977, (East Anglia) 1977, (Bristol) 1977, (London) 1983, (Leeds) 1986, (Cambridge) 1987; Hon. LLD (Aberdeen) 1986; Wolfson Literary Award 1981. *Address:* 67 Grantchester Street, Cambridge, CB3 9HZ, England. *Telephone:* (1223) 314000 (home).

CHADWICK, Whitney, BA, MA, PhD; American art historian and academic; *Professor of Art and Art History, San Francisco State University;* b. 28 July 1943, New York; d. of Cecil Chadwick and Helen Reichert; m. Robert A. Bechtle 1982. *Education:* Middlebury Coll. and Pennsylvania State Univ. *Career:* teacher at MIT 1972–78, Univ. of California, Berkeley 1977, Stanford Univ. 1990; Prof. of Art and Art History, San Francisco State Univ. 1978–; mem. Bd of Dirs Coll. of Art Asscn 1989–92; Nat. Endowment for the Humanities Fellow 1981; Sr Fellow, American Council of Learned Socs 1988. *Publications:* Myth in Surrealist Painting 1929–1939: Dali, Ernst, Masson 1980, Women Artists and the Surrealist Movement 1985, Women, Art and Society 1990, Significant Others: Creativity and Intimate Partnership (co-ed) 1993, Leonora Carrington: La Realidad de la Imaginación 1994, American Dreamer: The Art of Philip C. Curtis 1999 (co-author), Amazons in the Drawing Room: The Art of Romaine Brooks (co-author) 2000. *Address:* Art Department, San Francisco State University, FA 268, 1600 Holloway Avenue, San Francisco, CA 94132 (office); 871 DeHaro Street, San Francisco, CA

94107, USA. *Telephone:* (415) 338-6524 (office). *Fax:* (415) 338-6537 (office). *E-mail:* wchad@sfsu.edu (office). *Website:* www.sfsu.edu/~artdept (office).

CHAGALL, David, BA; American writer and journalist; b. 22 Nov. 1930, Philadelphia, Pa; m. Juneau Joan Alsin 1957. *Education:* Swarthmore Coll., Pennsylvania State Univ., Univ. of Paris (Sorbonne), France. *Career:* Assoc. Ed., IEE 1960–61; Investigative Reporter, Nation Magazine, 1975–; Ed., Publr, Inside Campaigning 1984; Contributing Ed., Los Angeles Magazine 1986–89; Host, TV series, The Last Hour 1994–; Chair. Selective Service Bd 1999; mem. Authors' Guild, American Acad. of Political Science. *Publications:* The Century God Slept 1963, Diary of a Deaf Mute 1971, The Spieler for the Holy Spirit 1972, The New Kingmakers 1981, Television Today 1981, The Sunshine Road 1988, The World's Greatest Comebacks 1989, Surviving the Media Jungle 1996, Media and Morality 1999, Target: Special Victims of the Holocaust 2000; contribs to periodicals. *Honours:* Carnegie Award 1964, Nat. Book Award 1972, Health Journalism Award 1980, Presidential Achievement Award 1982. *Address:* PO Box 85, Agoura Hills, CA 91376, USA. *E-mail:* dchagall@aol.com.

CHAKRABORTI, Rajorshi, PhD; Indian writer; b. 1978, Calcutta. *Education:* Hull Univ. and Univ. of Edinburgh, UK. *Career:* teacher of literature and creative writing, Univ. of Edinburgh; regular tutor in creative writing at Scottish univ. int. summer school. *Publication:* Or the Day Seizes You 2006. *Honours:* Philip Larkin Prize. *Address:* c/o Marketing and Promotions Department, Penguin Books India Pvt Ltd, 11 Community Centre, Panchsheel Park, 110017 New Delhi, India (office).

CHALFONT, Baron (Life Peer), cr. 1964, of Llantarnam in the County of Monmouthshire; **(Arthur) Alun Gwynne Jones,** PC, OBE, MC, FRSA; British politician and writer; b. 5 Dec. 1919, Llantarnam, Wales; s. of Arthur Gwynne Jones and Eliza Alice Hardman; m. Dr Mona Mitchell 1948; one d. (deceased). *Education:* West Monmouth School. *Career:* commissioned into S. Wales Borderers (24th Foot) 1940; served in Burma 1941–44, Malaya 1955–57, Cyprus 1958–59; resgnd comm. 1961; Defence Corresp. The Times, London 1961–64; consultant on foreign affairs to BBC TV, London 1961–64; Minister of State for Foreign Affairs 1964–70, Minister for Disarmament 1964–67, 1969–70, in charge of day-to-day negotiations for Britain's entry into Common Market 1967–69; Perm. Rep. to WEU 1969–70; Foreign Ed. New Statesman 1970–71; Chair. All-Party Defence Group House of Lords 1980–96, Pres. 1996–; Chair. Industrial Cleaning Papers 1979–86, Peter Hamilton Security Consultants Ltd 1984–86, UK Cttee for Free World 1981–89, European Atlantic Group 1983–, VSEL Consortium PLC 1987–93, Marlborough Stirling Group 1994–99; Deputy Chair. IBA 1989–90; Chair. Radio Authority 1991–94; Pres. Hispanic and Luso Brazilian Council 1975–80, Royal Nat. Inst. for Deaf 1980–87, Llangollen Int. Music Festival 1979–90; Chair. Abington Corpn (Consultants) Ltd 1981–, Nottingham Building Soc. 1983–90, Southern Mining Corpn 1997–99; Dir W. S. Atkins Int. 1979–83, IBM UK Ltd 1973–90 (mem. IBM Europe Advisory Council 1973–90), Lazard Brothers and Co. Ltd 1983–90, Shandwick PLC 1985–95, Triangle Holdings 1986–90, TV Corpn PLC 1996–2001; Pres. Freedom in Sport Int.; mem. IISS, Royal Inst.; Hon. Fellow, Univ. Coll. Wales, Aberystwyth 1974. *Publications:* The Sword and the Spirit 1963, The Great Commanders (ed.) 1973, Montgomery of Alamein 1976, Waterloo: Battle of Three Armies (ed.) 1979, Star Wars: Suicide or Survival 1985, Defence of the Realm 1987, By God's Will: A Portrait of the Sultan of Brunei 1989, The Shadow of My Hand (autobiog.) 2000; contrib. to The Times and nat. and professional journals. *Address:* House of Lords, London, SW1A 0PW, England.

CHALIDZE, Valeriy Nikolayevich; Russian writer, physicist and publisher; b. 1938, Moscow; m. *Education:* Moscow Univ., then Faculty of Physics, Tbilisi Univ. 1965. *Career:* head of research unit in Plastics Research Inst., Moscow 1965–70; removed from post 1970; mem. of USSR Human Rights Cttee; dissident activity 1969–, when started samizdat journal Obshchestvennyye problemy (Problems of Society), trip to USA to lecture on human rights in USSR, subsequently deprived of Soviet citizenship 1972; currently living in New York. *Publications include:* numerous samizdat articles and books and Ugolovnaya Rossiya (Capital Punishment in Russia) 1977, USSR – The Workers' Movement 1978. A Foreigner in the Soviet Union. A Juridical Memoir 1980, Communism Vanquished (Stalin) 1981, The Responsibility of a Generation 1982, National Problems and Perestroika 1988, The Dawn of the Legal Reform 1990, Responsibility of the Generation 1991, A Hierarchical Man 1991.

CHAMBERLAIN, Lesley, BA, MLitt; British writer; b. 26 Sept. 1951, Rochford, Essex; one d.; m. Pavel Seifter 1999. *Education:* Univ. of Exeter and Wolfson Coll., Oxford. *Career:* Lecturer, Portsmouth Polytechnic 1977–86; corresp. and Sr Sub-Ed. Reuters, Moscow 1978–79; freelance writer and teacher 1986–, regular contrib. to The TLS, Los Angeles Times Book Review, The Independent and other nat. publs. *Publications include:* The Food and Cooking of Russia 1982, The Food and Cooking of Eastern Europe 1989, In the Communist Mirror 1990, Volga, Volga A Journey Down the Great River 1994, Nietzsche in Turin 1996, In a Place Like That 1998, The Secret Artist – A Close Reading of Sigmund Freud 2000, Girl in a Garden (novel) 2003, Motherland: A Philosophical History of Russia 2004, The Philosophy Steamer: Lenin and the Exile of the Intelligentsia 2006. *Address:* c/o Atlantic Books, Ormond House, 26–27 Boswell Street, London, WC1N 3JZ, England (office). *Website:* www.lesleychamberlain.co.uk.

CHAMBERLAND, Paul, BPhil; Canadian poet and essayist; *Associate Professor, Université du Québec à Montréal*; b. 16 May 1939, Longueuil, QC. *Education:* Collège Saint-Laurent, Univ. of Québec, Montréal and Sorbonne, Univ. of Paris. *Career:* co-founder literary journal, Parti pris 1963; Assoc. Prof. in Département d'Études Littéraires, Université du Québec à Montréal 1985–; mem. Union des écrivaines et des écrivains québécois. *Publications include:* poetry: Genèses 1962, Le Pays 1963, Terre Québec 1964, L'Afficheur hurle 1964, L'Inavouable 1967, Éclats de la pierre noire d'où rejaillit ma vie: poèmes suivis d'une révélation 1966–1969 1972, Demain les dieux naîtront 1974, Le Prince de sexamour 1976, Extrême survivance, extrême poésie 1978, Terre souveraine 1979, L'Enfant doré: 1974–1977 1980, Émergence de l'adultenfant (poems and essays) 1981, Fidèles d'amour 1981, Le Courage de la poésie: fragments d'art total 1981, Du côté hiéroglyphe de ce qu'on appelle le réel: suivi de Devant le temple de Louxor le 31 juillet 1980 1982, Aléatoire instantané 1983, Le recommencement du monde: méditations sur le processus apocalyptique 1983, Compagnons chercheurs 1984, Phoenix intégral: poèmes 1975–1987 1988, Intarsia 1990, Le Multiple événement terrestre: géogrammes 1 1979–1985 1991, L'Assaut contre les vivants: géogrammes 2 1986–1991 1994, Témoin nomade: carnets I 1975–1981 1995, Dans la proximité des choses 1996, Le Froid coupant du dehors: géogrammes 3 1992–1996 1997, Intime faiblesse des mortels (Estuaire Prix de Poésie Terrasses Saint-Sulpice) 1999, Au seuil d'une autre Terre 2003; non-fiction: En nouvelle barbarie (essay) (Spirale Prix de l'essai 2000), Une politique de la douleur (essay) 2004; contrib. to Estuaire, Forces, Hobo-Québec, La Barre du jour, Liberté, Mainmise, Possibles. *Honours:* Prix de la Province de Québec 1964, Prix Édouard J. Maunick 1991. *Address:* Département d'Études Littéraires, Université du Québec à Montréal, CP 8888, succ. Centre-ville, Montréal, QC H3C 3P8, Canada (office). *E-mail:* etudes.litteraires@uqam.ca.

CHAMBERLIN, Ann; American writer and dramatist; b. 28 March 1954, Salt Lake City, UT; m. Curt F. Setzer 1978, two s. *Education:* Brigham Young University, University of Utah, University of Tel-Aviv, Israel. *Publications:* The Virgin and the Tower, 1979; Tamar, 1994; Sofia, 1996; The Sultan's Daughter, 1997; The Reign of the Favored Women, 1999; Leaving Eden, The Merlin of St Gilles' Well, 1999; The Merlin of the Oak Wood, 2001. *Honours:* several book and drama awards. *Address:* PO Box 71114, Salt Lake City, UT 84171, USA. *E-mail:* setzers@msn.com. *Website:* www.annchamberlin.com.

CHAMBERS, Aidan; British writer and publisher; b. 27 Dec. 1934, Chester-le-Street, County Durham; m. Nancy Harris Lockwood 1968. *Education:* Borough Road Coll., Isleworth, Univ. of London. *Career:* mem. Soc. of Authors, School Library Asscn (Pres. 2003–06). *Publications:* The Reluctant Reader 1969, Introducing Books to Children 1973, Breaktime 1978, Seal Secret 1980, The Dream Cage 1981, Dance on My Grave 1982, The Present Takers 1983, Booktalk 1985, Now I Know 1987, The Reading Environment 1991, The Toll Bridge 1992, Tell Me: Children, Reading and Talk 1993, Only Once 1998, Postcards From No Man's Land 1999, Reading Talk 2001, This is All: ThePillow Book of Cordelia Kenn 2005; contrib. to numerous magazines and journals. *Honours:* Dr hc (Umeå Univ., Sweden) 2003; Children's Literature Award for Outstanding Criticism 1978, Eleanor Farjeon Award 1982, Silver Pencil Awards 1985, 1986, 1994, Carnegie Medal 1999, Stockport School Book Award KS4 2000, Hans Christian Andersen Award 2002, Michael L. Printz Award 2003, J. Hunt Award 2003. *Address:* Lockwood, Station Road, Woodchester, Stroud, Glos. GL5 5EQ, England. *Telephone:* (1453) 872208. *E-mail:* aidanchambers@onetel.com. *Website:* www.aidanchambers.co.uk.

CHAMLING, Pawan Kumar; Indian politician, poet and writer; *Chief Minister of Sikkim*; b. 22 Sept. 1950, Yangang Busty, South Sikkim; s. of Shri Ash Bahadur Chamling and Smt. Asharani Chamling; m. Tika Maya Chamling; four s. four d. *Career:* began career as ind. farmer; entered politics in 1973; Vice-Pres. Dist Youth Congress 1975; Pres. Sikkim Handicapped Persons Welfare Mission 1976–77; Ed. Nava Jyoti 1976–77, Founder Nirman Prakashan 1977, Ed. Nirman (quarterly literary magazine) 1977; Gen. Sec. and Vice-Pres. Sikkim Prajatantra Congress 1978–84; Pres. of Yangang Gram Panchayat 1982; mem. Sikkim Legis. Ass. 1985–; Minister for Industries, Printing and Information and Public Relations 1989–92; formed Sikkim Democratic Front Party 1993, Leader 1993–; Chief Minister of Sikkim 1994–; Chair. Sikkim Distilleries Ltd 1985–. *Publications include:* Veer koh Parichaya (poem) 1967, Antahin Sapana Meroh Bipana 1985, Perennial Dreams and My Reality, Prarambhek Kabitaharu 1991, Pratiwad 1992, Damthang Heejah ra Aajah 1992, Ma koh Hun 1992, Sikkim ra Narikon Maryadha 1994, Crucified Prashna Aur Anya Kabitaye 1996, Sikkim ra Prajatantra 1996, Democracy Redeemed 1997, Prajatantra koh Mirmireymah 1997, Meroh Sapana Ko Sikkim 2002, Perspectives and Vision 2002. *Honours:* Hon. PhD (Manipal Univ.) 2003; numerous awards including Chinton Puraskar 1987, Bharat Shiromani 1996, Man of the Year 1998, The Greenest Chief Minister of India 1998, Man of Dedication 1999, Secular India Harmony Award 1998, Manav Sewa Puraskar 1999, Pride of India Gold Award 1999, Best Citizen of India 1999, Poets' Foundation Award 2001, Nat. Citizens of India Award 2002. *Address:* CM Secretariat, Tashiling, Gangtok, Sikkim 737 101 (office); Ghurpisay, Namchi, South Sikkim 737 126, India (home). *Telephone:* (3592) 222263 (office); (3592) 228200 (office); (3592) 222536 (home); (3595) 263748 (home). *Fax:* (3592) 222245 (office); (3592) 224710 (home). *E-mail:* cm-skm@nic.in (office). *Website:* sikkim.nic.in (office).

CHAMOISEAU, Patrick, LèsDP; French writer; b. 12 March 1953, Fort de France, Martinique; m. Ghislaine Chamoiseau 1975, one c. *Education:* Univ. of Sceaux, France. *Publications:* Manman Dlo contre la fée Carabosse, Chronique des sept misères 1986, Solibo Magnifique (trans. as Solibo Magnificent) 1988, Martinique 1988, Eloge de la créolité (co-author) 1989, Lettres créoles: Traces antillaises et continentales de la littérature (co-author) 1991, Texaco 1992, Antan d'enfance 1993, Au temps de l'antan (trans. as Creole Folktales) 1994, Guyane: Traces-mémoires du bagne 1994, Chemin-d'école (trans. as School Days) 1994, Biblique des derniers gestes 2001. *Honours:* Prix Goncourt 1992, Prix Garbet de la Caraibe 1993. *Address:* 31 Favorite, 97232 Larentin, Martinique. *E-mail:* chamoiseau@cgit.com.

CHAMORRO BARRIOS, Cristiana; Nicaraguan foundation director and editor; *Director, Fundación Violeta Barrios de Chamorro*; d. of Pedro Joaquin Chamorro Cardenal and Violeta Barrios de Chamorro. *Career:* Dir Diario La Prensa 1986–91, Chair. Bd Dirs 1991–93, currently Ed. and Dir; Vice-Pres. Comm. for the Freedom of Expression 1987–93; Adviser to Pres. of Nicaragua Violeta Barrios de Chamorro 1991–96; Ed. Servicio Especial de Mujeres (SEM), Costa Rica; Founder and Dir Fundación Violeta Barrios de Chamorro (non-profit org. for peace, democracy and freedom of expression). *Address:* Fundación Violeta Barrios de Chamorro, Malaga Building Spain Seat, B-9 Module, Managua, Nicaragua (office). *Telephone:* (505) 268-6500 (office). *Fax:* (505) 268-6502 (office). *E-mail:* cristiana.chamorro@ibw.com.ni (office).

CHAMPION, Larry Stephen, MA, PhD; American academic and writer; b. 27 April 1932, Shelby, NC; m. Nancy Ann Blanchard 1956; one s. two d. *Education:* Davidson Coll., Univ. of Virginia, Univ. of North Carolina. *Career:* instructor, Davidson Coll. 1955–56, Univ. of North Carolina, Chapel Hill 1959–60; instructor, North Carolina State Univ. 1960–61, Asst Prof. 1961–65, Assoc. Prof. 1965–68, Prof. of English 1968–94; mem. Cttee of Correspondents World Shakespeare Bibliography, MLA, Nat. Council of Teachers of English, Renaissance English Text Soc., Renaissance Soc. of America, Int. Shakespeare Soc., Shakespeare Asscn of America. *Publications:* Ben Jonson's 'Dotages': A Reconsideration of the Late Plays 1967, The Evolution of Shakespeare's Comedy: A Study in Dramatic Perspective 1970, Quick Springs of Sense: Studies in the Eighteenth Century (ed.) 1974, Shakespeare's Tragic Perspective: The Development of his Dramatic Technique 1976, Tragic Patterns in Jacobean and Caroline Drama: A Study in Perspective 1977, Perspective in Shakespeare's English Histories 1980, King Lear: An Annotated Bibliography Since 1940 (two vols) 1981, Thomas Dekker and the Traditions of English Drama 1985, The Essential Shakespeare: An Annotated Bibliography of Major Modern Studies 1986, The Noise of Threatening Drum: Dramatic Strategy and Political Ideology in Shakespeare and the English Chronicle Plays 1990; contrib. to books and scholarly journals. *Honours:* Acad. of Outstanding Teachers Award 1966, Alumni Distinguished Prof. 1987. *Address:* 5320 Sendero Drive, Raleigh, NC 27612, USA. *Telephone:* (919) 787-3072 (home); (919) 523-1749 (home). *E-mail:* lac32@bellsouth.net (home).

CHAMPION DE CRESPIGNY, (Richard) Rafe, (Rafe de Crespigny), BA, MA, PhD, FAHA; Australian historian and writer; *Adjunct Professor of Asian Studies, Australian National University*; b. 16 March 1936, Adelaide, S Australia; s. of (Richard) Geoffrey Champion de Crespigny and Kathleen Champion de Crespigny (née Cudomore); m. Christa Charlotte Boltz; one s. one d. *Education:* Univ. of Cambridge, UK, Univ. of Melbourne, Australian Nat. Univ. *Career:* Lecturer, ANU, Canberra 1964–70, Sr Lecturer 1970–73, Reader in Chinese 1973–, Master Univ. House 1991–2001, Adjunct Prof. of Asian Studies 1999–; mem. Chinese Studies Asscn of Australia (Pres. 1999–2001). *Publications:* The Biography of Sun Chien 1966, Official Titles of the Former Han Dynasty (with H. H. Dubs) 1967, The Last of the Han 1969, The Records of the Three Kingdoms 1970, China: The Land and its People 1971, China This Century: A History of Modern China 1975, Portents of Protest 1976, Northern Frontier 1984, Emperor Huan and Emperor Ling 1989, Generals of the South 1990, To Establish Peace 1996, A Biographical Dictionary of Later Han to the Three Kingdoms 2006. *Honours:* Australian Centerary Medal 2003. *Address:* Faculty of Asian Studies, Australian National University, Canberra, ACT 0200, Australia (office). *E-mail:* rafe.decrespigny@anu.edu.au (office). *Website:* www.anu.edu.au/asianstudies (office).

CHAN, Stephen; New Zealand/British academic, writer and poet; b. 11 May 1949, Auckland, New Zealand. *Education:* BA, 1972, MA, 1975, University of Auckland; MA, King's College, London, 1977; PhD, University of Kent, Canterbury, 1992. *Career:* International Civil Servant, Commonwealth Secretariat, 1977–83; Lecturer in International Relations, University of Zambia, 1983–85; Faculty, University of Kent, 1987–96; Prof. in International Relations and Ethics, Head of International Studies, Dean of Humanities, Nottingham Trent University, 1996–. *Publications:* The Commonwealth Observer Group in Zimbabwe: A Personal Memoir, 1985; Issues in International Relations: A View from Africa, 1987; The Commonwealth in World Politics: A Study of International Action, 1965–85, 1988; Exporting Apartheid: Foreign Policies in Southern Africa, 1978–1988, 1990; Social Development in Africa Today: Some Radical Proposals, 1991; Kaunda and Southern Africa: Image and Reality in Foreign Policy, 1991; Twelve Years of Commonwealth Diplomatic History: Commonwealth Summit Meetings, 1979–1991, 1992; Mediation in South Africa (ed. with Vivienne Jabri), 1993; Renegade States: The Foreign Policies of Revolutionary States (ed. with Andrew Williams), 1994; Towards a Multicultural Roshamon Paradigm in International Relations, 1996; Portuguese Foreign Policy in Southern Africa (with M. Venancio), 1996; Theorists and Theorising in International Relations (ed. with Jarrold Wiener), 1997; War and Peace in Mozambique (with M. Vanancio), 1998; Giving Thought: Currents in International Relations (ed. with Jarrold

Wiener), 1998; Twentieth Century International History (ed. with Jarrold Wiener), 1998; Zambia and the Decline of Kaunda 1984–1998, 2000; Security and Development in Southern Africa, 2001. Poetry: Postcards from Paradise (with Rupert Glover and Merlene Young), 1971; Arden's Summer, 1975; Songs of the Maori King, 1986; Crimson Rain, 1991. *Honours:* Visiting fellowships; Hon. LittD, WAAC, Istanbul; Hon. Prof., University of Zambia, 1993–95. *Address:* School of Oriental and African Studies, University of London, Thornhaugh Street, Russell Square, London, WC1H 0XG, England. *E-mail:* sc5@soas.ac.uk. *Website:* www.stephen-chan.com.

CHANCE, Jane, BA, AM, PhD; American academic, writer, poet and editor; *Professor of English, Rice University;* b. 26 Oct. 1945, Neosho, MO; m. 1st Dennis Carl Nitzsche 1966 (divorced 1967); one d.; m. 2nd Paolo Passaro 1981 (divorced 2002); two s. *Education:* Purdue Univ., Univ. of Illinois. *Career:* Lecturer, Univ. of Saskatchewan 1971–72, Asst Prof. of English 1972–73; Asst Prof., Rice Univ. 1973–77, Assoc. Prof. 1977–80, Prof. of English 1980–, founder and first Pres. Medieval Studies Program 1987–92; Dir NEA Summer Seminar for Coll. Teachers on Chaucer and Mythography 1985, on the Literary Traditions of Medieval Women 1997; mem., Inst. for Advanced Study, Princeton, NJ 1988–89; Gen. Ed., Library of Medieval Women 1988–; mem. Exec. Cttee and Vice-Pres. Texas Faculty Asscn 1995–2000; Visiting Research Fellow Inst. for Advanced Studies in the Humanities, Univ. of Edinburgh 1994; Eccles Research Fellow Univ. of Utah, Humanities Centre 1994–95; various guest and plenary lectures; Series Ed. Greenwood Guides to Historic Events in the Medieval World 2001–, Praeger Series on the Middle Ages 2003–; mem. American Asscn of Univ. Profs, Authors' Guild, Christine de Pizan Soc., Int. Asscn of Neo-Latin Studies, Int. Soc. in Classical Studies, Medieval Acad. of America, MLA, South Central MLA Scientia (sec. 1982–83, acting dir 1983–84). *Publications:* The Genius Figure in Antiquity and the Middle Ages 1975, Tolkien's Art: A 'Mythology for England' 1979, Woman as Hero in Old English Literature 1986, Tolkien's Lord of the Rings: The Mythology of Power 1992, Medieval Mythography (two vols) 1994, 2000, The Mythographic Chaucer: The Fabulation of Sexual Politics 1995; editor: Christine de Pizan, Letter of Othea to Hector 1990, Gender and Text in the Later Middle Ages 1996, The Assembly of Gods 1999, Tolkien the Medievalist 2003, Tolkien and the Invertion of Myth 2004, Tolkien's Modern Middle Ages 2005, Women Medievalists and the Academy 2005; contrib. to scholarly books and journals. *Honours:* Hon. Research Fellow Univ. Coll. London 1977–78; Nat. Endowment for the Humanities Fellowship 1977–78, Guggenheim Fellowship 1980–81, Rockefeller Foundation residency, Bellagio, Italy 1988, South Central MLA Best Book Award 1994, Soc. for Medieval Feminist Scholarship Best Essay Prize 2005. *Address:* Department of English MS-30, Rice University, PO Box 1892, Houston TX 77251-1892 (office); 2306 Wroxton Road, Houston, TX 77005, USA (home). *Telephone:* (713) 348-2625 (office); (713) 524-3282 (home). *Fax:* (713) 348-5991 (office); (713) 524-3282 (home). *E-mail:* jchance@rice.edu. *Website:* www.ruf.rice.edu/~jchance.

CHANCE, Megan, BA; American writer; b. 31 Dec. 1959, Columbus, OH; m. Kany Levine 1995; two d. *Education:* Western Washington University. *Career:* mem. Romance Writers of America. *Publications:* A Candle in the Dark, 1993; After the Frost, 1994; The Portrait, 1995; A Heart Divided, 1996; Fall from Grace, 1977; The Way Home, 1997; The Gentleman Caller, 1998; A Season in Eden, 1999; Susannah Morrow, 2002. *Honours:* Reviewer's Choice Award for Best First Historical Novel, Romantic Times, 1993; RITA Award for Excellence in Romantic Fiction, 1994; Emerald City Keeper Award for Best Historical Romance, 1997.

CHANCELLOR, Alexander Surtees, BA; British journalist; b. 4 Jan. 1940, Ware, Herts.; s. of Sir Christopher Chancellor, CMG and Sylvia Mary Chancellor (née Paget); m. Susanna Elizabeth Debenham 1964; two d. *Education:* Eton Coll., Trinity Hall, Cambridge. *Career:* Reuters News Agency 1964–74, Chief Corresp., Italy 1968–73; ITV News 1974–75; Ed. The Spectator 1975–84; Ed. Time and Tide 1984–86; Deputy Ed. Sunday Telegraph 1986; Washington Ed. The Independent 1986–88; Ed. The Independent Magazine 1988–92; The New Yorker (Ed. The Talk of the Town) 1992–93; Columnist The Times 1992–93, The Guardian 1996–, Slate 1997, The Daily Telegraph 1998–2004, Saga Magazine 2002–. *Publication:* Some Times in America 1999. *Address:* The Court House, Stoke Park, Stoke Bruerne, Towcester, NN12 7RZ, England. *Telephone:* (1604) 862329 (home). *E-mail:* chancellor@dial.pipex.com.

CHANDLER, Frank (see Harknett, Terry)

CHANDLER, Kenneth A.; British journalist; b. 2 Aug. 1947, Westcliff-on-Sea, Essex; s. of Leonard Gordon Chandler and Beatrix Marie Chandler (née McKenzie); m. Erika Schwartz; five c. *Career:* Man. Ed. The New York Post 1978–86, 1993–99, Ed.-in-Chief, then Publr 1999–2002; Ed. Boston Herald 1986–93, Editorial Dir 2004–06; f. ChandlerMedia (media consulting firm) 2006; Exec. Producer Fox TV's A Current Affair 1993; CEO Natural Energy Solutions Corpn 2002–03. *E-mail:* kchandler@chandlermedia.com. *Website:* chandlermedia.com (office).

CHANDRA, Ramesh, BSc; Indian newspaper executive; b. 15 Aug. 1925, Najibabad, Uttar Pradesh; s. of Raibahadur Sahu Jagmandar Das and Asharfi Devi; m. Chandrakanta Jain 1948; two s. *Education:* Banaras Hindu Univ. *Career:* fmr Sr Vice-Chair. Municipal Bd Najibabad; joined Times of India 1959; Exec. Dir Bennett, Coleman & Co. Ltd (The Times of India Group of Publs); fmr Chair. Press Trust of India; fmr Pres. Indian Newspaper Soc.; Pres. Chrysanthemum Soc. of India, All India Digambar Jain Parishad; Man.

Trustee, Bharatiya Jnanpith; Thomson Foundation Fellow, UK 1968. *Publications:* articles on newspaper management in various journals. *Address:* Bharatiya Jananpith, 18 Institutional Area, Lodi Road, New Delhi 110003 (office); C-48 Gulmohar Park, New Delhi 110049, India (home). *Telephone:* (11) 331-8191 (office); (11) 685-2909 (home). *Fax:* (11) 465-4197 (office); (11) 696-9523 (home). *E-mail:* jnanpith@satyam.net.in (office).

CHANDRA, Vikram, BA, MA, MFA; Indian writer and academic; *Senior Lecturer, University of California, Berkeley;* b. 23 July 1961, New Delhi. *Education:* St Xavier's Coll., Mumbai, Pomona Coll., Johns Hopkins Univ. and Univ. of Houston, USA. *Career:* Adjunct Prof., Univ. of Houston 1987–93; Visiting Writer, George Washington Univ. 1994–95, Assoc. Prof. 1995–2005; Sr Lecturer, Univ. of California, Berkeley 2005–. *Publications:* Red Earth and Pouring Rain 1995, Love and Longing in Bombay 1997, Sacred Games 2006; contribs to several periodicals. *Honours:* Discovery Prize, Paris Review 1994, David Higham Prize, Book Trust, London 1995, Commonwealth Writers Prize for Best First Published Book 1996, and for Best Book, Eurasia region 1998. *Literary Agent:* c/o Janklow & Nesbit Associates, 445 Park Avenue, New York, NY 10022-2606, USA. *E-mail:* vikram@vikramchandra.com (office). *Website:* www.vikramchandra.com (office).

CHANEY, Edward Paul de Gruyter, BA, MPhil, PhD, FSA, FRSA; British academic and writer; *Professor of Fine and Decorative Arts, Southampton Solent University;* b. 11 April 1951, Hayes, Middlesex; m. Lisa Maria Jacka 1973 (divorced); two d. *Education:* Univ. of Reading, Warburg Inst., London, European Univ. Inst., Florence. *Career:* Lecturer, Univ. of Pisa 1979–85; Adjunct Asst Prof., Charles A. Strong Center, Georgetown Univ. Florence Program, Villa Le Balze, Florence 1982, 1983; Assoc., Harvard Univ. Center for Italian Renaissance Studies, Villa I Tatti, Florence 1984–85; Shuffrey Research Fellow in Architectural History, Lincoln Coll., Oxford 1985–90; part-time History of Art Lecturer, Oxford Polytechnic 1991, Oxford Brookes Univ. 1993–; historian, London Division, English Heritage 1991–93; currently Prof. of Fine and Decorative Arts and Chair of History of Collecting Research Centre, Southampton Solent Univ.; mem. of Exec. Cttee or editorial Bd, Wyndham Lewis Soc., Walpole Soc., Catholic Record Soc., British Art Journal, British-Italian Soc. *Publications:* Oxford, China and Italy: Writings in Honour of Sir Harold Acton on his Eightieth Birthday (ed. with N. Ritchie) 1984, The Grand Tour and the Great Rebellion: Richard Lassels and 'The Voyage of Italy' in the Seventeenth Century 1985, Florence: A Travellers' Companion (with Harold Acton) 1986, England and the Continental Renaissance: Essays in Honour of J. B. Trapp (ed. with Peter Mack) 1990, English Architecture: Public and Private: Essays for Kerry Downes (ed. with John Bold) 1993, The Evolution of the Grand Tour: Anglo-Italian cultural relations since the Renaissance 1998, The Stuart Portrait: Status and Legacy (with G. Worsdale) 2001, Richard Eurich (1903–1992): Visionary Artist (with C. Clearkin) 2003, The Evolution of English Collecting: Receptions of Italian Art in the Tudor and Stuart Periods 2003, Inigo Jones's Roman Sketchbook 2005; contrib. to reference works, books, scholarly journals, periodicals, newspapers, TV and radio etc. *Honours:* Hon. Dottore di Laurea in Lingue e Letterature Straniere (Univ. of Pisa) 1983; hon. life mem., British Inst. of Florence 1984; hon. assoc., Soc. of Fine Art Auctioneers; Commendatore of the Italian Repub. 2003. *Address:* Southampton Solent University, E Park Terrace, Southampton, SO14 0RF, England (office). *Telephone:* (2380) 319478 (office). *E-mail:* edward.chaney@solent.ac.uk (office).

CHANG, Jung, PhD; British writer; b. 25 March 1952, Yibin, Sichuan Province, China; d. of Chang Shou-Yu and Xia De-Hong; m. Jon Halliday 1991. *Education:* Sichuan Univ., Univ. of York. *Career:* fmrly worked as a peasant, a 'barefoot doctor', a steelworker and an electrician; Asst Lecturer Sichuan Univ.; moved to UK to study linguistics 1978; now full-time writer. *Publications:* Madame Sun Yet-sen (with Jon Halliday) 1986, Wild Swans: Three Daughters of China (NCR Book Award 1992, UK Writers' Guild Best Non-Fiction Book 1992, Fawcett Soc. Book Award 1992, Book of the Year 1993, Golden Bookmark Award, Belgium 1993, 1994, Best Book Award, Humo, Belgium 1993) 1991, Mao: the Unknown Story (with Jon Halliday) 2005. *Honours:* Dr hc (Buckingham) 1996, (Warwick, York) 1997, (Open Univ.) 1998; Bjørnsonordenen, Den Norske Orden for Literature, Norway 1995. *Literary Agent:* Aitken Alexander Associates Ltd, 18–21 Cavaye Place, London, SW10 9PT, England. *Telephone:* (20) 7373-8672. *Fax:* (20) 7373-6002. *E-mail:* reception@aitkenalexander.co.uk. *Website:* www.aitkenalexander.co.uk.

CHANG, Lan Samantha, MFA, MPA, BA; Chinese-American writer; b. 1956, Appleton, WI; m. *Education:* Yale Univ., Harvard Univ., Stanford Univ. and Iowa Univ. *Career:* Wallace Stegner and Truman Capote fellowships, Stanford Univ.; Briggs-Copeland Lecturer in Creative Writing, Harvard Univ.; Dir Iowa Writers' Workshop 2005. *Publications:* Hunger: A Novella and Stories 1998, Inheritance 2004; contribs to Atlantic Monthly, Ploughshares, Best American Short Stories. *Honours:* Henfield/Transatlantic Review Award. *Address:* c/o W. W. Norton & Co. Inc., 500 Fifth Avenue, New York, NY 10110, USA.

CHANNER, Colin; Jamaican novelist; b. 1963, Kingston. *Career:* teacher of fiction writing in London and New York; bass player for reggae band Pipecock Jaxxon; founder and artistic dir of Calabash Int. Literary Festival. *Publications:* novels: Waiting in Vain 1998, I'm Still Waiting (novella, featured in anthology Got to be Real) 2001, Satisfy My Soul 2002, Passing Through 2004. *Address:* c/o Ballentine/One World, 1745 Broadway, New York, NY 10019,

USA. *Telephone:* (212) 782-9000. *Website:* www.randomhouse.com. *E-mail:* colin@colinchanner.com. *Website:* www.colinchanner.com.

CHAO, Patricia, BA, MA; American novelist and poet. *Education:* Brown Univ., New York Univ. *Career:* Creative Writing Teacher, Sarah Lawrence Coll., Bronxville, NY; Ed. Global City Review special issue 1996. *Publications:* novels: Monkey King 1997, Mambo Peligroso 2005; contribs to periodicals and books. *Honours:* Rose Low Memorial Poetry Prize, Brown Univ. 1978, Fellowship, New York Univ. Master's Programme in Creative Writing 1990–92, Dean's Fiction Prize, New York Univ. 1992, New Voice Award for Poetry, The Writer's Voice 1996, New York Foundation of the Arts Fellowship 2002.

CHAPLIN, Jenny Telfer, (Tracie Telfer, Wendy Wentworth), DCE, FSA; British editor, publisher, novelist, poet and public speaker; b. 22 Dec. 1928, Glasgow, Scotland; m. J. McDonald Chaplin 1951; one d. *Education:* Jordanhill Coll. of Educ., Glasgow. *Career:* Founder, Ed. and Publr International: The Writers Rostrum 1984–93; public speaker 2004–; Fellow, Soc. of Antiquaries, Scotland 2000. *Publications:* Tales of a Glasgow Childhood 1994, Alone in a Garden 1994, Happy Days in Rothesay 1995, From Scotland's Past 1996, Childhood Days in Glasgow 1996, Thoughts on Writing (with Fay Goldie and V. Cuthbert) 1996, An Emigrant's Farewell, in A Scottish Childhood Vol. II, anthology of memoirs from famous Scottish people 1998, We Belonged to Glasgow 2001; novels as Jenny Telfer Chaplin: The Kinnon Trilogy: The Kinnons of Candleriggs 2004, The Widow of Candleriggs 2005, The Ashes of Candleriggs 2006; contrib. to The Scots Magazine, The Highlander Magazine, Scottish Memories, The Scottish Banner, anthologies. *Honours:* Proclaimed Champion Poet of Largs, Ayrshire 2000. *Address:* Tigh na Mara Cottage, 14 Ardbeg Road, Rothesay, Bute, PA20 0NJ, Scotland (home). *Telephone:* (1700) 502737 (home).

CHAPLINA, Natalya; Russian newspaper editor; b. 15 Feb. 1957, Leningrad (now St Petersburg); m 2nd Viktor Cherkesov 1996; two d. *Education:* St Petersburg State Univ. *Career:* journalist 1975–; Founder and Ed.-in-Chief Chas Pik (first ind. newspaper in Russian Fed.) 1990–2003, fmr Chair. Bd Dirs; Project Dir RosBalt (news agency) 2003–. *Publications:* has written five books. *Honours:* USSR Journalists' Union award 1991, Russian Journalists' Union award 1994. *Address:* Rosbalt News Agency, 7 Konnogvardeisky Boulevard, 190000 St Petersburg, Russia (office). *Telephone:* (812) 320-50-30 (office); (812) 320-50-48 (office). *Fax:* (812) 320-50-31 (office). *E-mail:* rosbalt@rosbalt.ru (office). *Website:* www.rosbaltnews.com (office).

CHAPMAN, (F.) Ian, CBE, CBIM, FRSA, FFCS; British publisher; *Vice-President, National Academy of Writing;* b. 26 Oct. 1925, St Fergus, Aberdeenshire, Scotland; s. of the late Rev. Peter Chapman and Frances Burdett; m. Marjory Stewart Swinton, MA 1953; one s. one d. *Education:* Shawlands Acad., Ommer School of Music, Glasgow. *Career:* served in RAF 1943–44; miner (nat. service) 1945–47; with William Collins Sons & Co. Ltd (fmrly W.M. Collins Holdings PLC, now Harper Collins) 1947, Man. Trainee New York br. 1950–51, Sales Man. London br. 1955; mem. main operating Bd, Group Sales Dir 1959, Jt Man. Dir 1967–76, Deputy Chair. 1976–81, Chair. CEO 1981–89; Deputy Chair. Orion Publishing Group 1993–94, Dir William Collins overseas cos 1968–89: Canada 1968–89, USA 1974–89, S. Africa 1978–89, NZ 1978–89, William Collins Int. Ltd 1975–89; Chair. Scottish Radio Holdings PLC (fmrly Radio Clyde) 1972–96 (Hon. Pres. 1996–2000), Harvill Press 1978–89, Hatchards Ltd 1976–89, William Collins Publrs Ltd 1979–81, The Listener Publs PLC 1988–93, RadioTrust PLC 1997–2001, Guinness Publrs Ltd 1991–98; Dir Pan Books Ltd 1962–84 (Chair. 1973–76), Book Tokens Ltd 1981–94, Ind. Radio News 1984–85, Stanley Botes Ltd 1986–89, Guinness PLC (non-exec.) 1986–91; Pres.-Dir Gen. Guinness Media SAS, Paris 1996–99; f. Chapmans Publrs. Chair. and Man. Dir 1989–94; Trustee Book Trade Benevolent Soc. 1982–2003; Trustee The Publrs Asscn 1989–97; mem. Gov. Council SCOTBIC; mem. Council Publishers Asscn 1962–77, Vice-Pres. 1978, Pres. 1979–81; Chair. Nat. Acad. of Writing 2000–03, Vice-Pres. 2003–; mem. Bd Book Devt Council 1967, Ancient House Bookshop 1972–89, Scottish Opera, Theatre Royal Ltd 1974–79, IRN Ltd 1983–85; Chair. Advisory Bd Strathclyde Univ. Business School 1985–88. *Honours:* Hon. DLitt (Strathclyde Univ.) 1990; Scottish Free Enterprise Award 1985. *Address:* Kenmore, 46 The Avenue, Cheam, Surrey, SM2 7QE, England (home). *Telephone:* (20) 8642-1820 (home). *Fax:* (20) 8642-7439 (home). *E-mail:* fic@onetel.net.uk (home).

CHAPMAN, Jean, BA; British writer; b. 30 Oct. 1939, England; m. Lionel Alan Chapman 1951, one s. two d. *Education:* Open Univ. *Career:* creative writing tutor, East Midlands arts and community colls; mem. Society of Authors; Chair., Romantic Novelists Asscn. *Publications:* The Unreasoning Earth, 1981; Tangled Dynasty, 1984; Forbidden Path, 1986; Savage Legacy, 1987; The Bellmakers, 1990; Fortune's Woman, 1992; A World Apart, 1993; The Red Pavilion, 1995; The Soldier's Girl, 1997; This Time Last Year, 1999; A New Beginning, 2001; And a Golden Pear, 2002. Other: many short stories. *Address:* 3 Arnesby Lane, Peatling Magna, Leicester LE8 5UN, England.

CHAPMAN, Stanley David, BSc, MA, PhD; British fmr academic and writer; b. 31 Jan. 1935, Nottingham; m.; two s. *Education:* LSE, Univ. of Nottingham, Univ. of London. *Career:* Lecturer 1968–73, Pasold Reader in Business History 1973–, Prof. 1993–97, Emer. Prof. 1998–, Univ. of Nottingham; Ed., Textile History Bi Annual 1984–2002. *Publications:* The Early Factory Masters 1967, The Beginnings of Industrial Britain 1970, The History of Working Class Housing 1971, The Cotton Industry in the Industrial

Revolution 1972, Jesse Boot of Boots the Chemists 1974, The Devon Cloth Industry in the 18th Century 1978, European Textile Printers in the 18th Century (with S. Chassagne) 1981, Stanton and Staveley 1981, The Rise of Merchant Banking 1984, Merchant Enterprise in Britain from the Industrial Revolution to World War I 1992, Hosiery and Knitwear: Four Centuries of Small-Scale Industry in Britain 1589–2000 2002, Southwell Town and People (with D. Walker, Ed.) 2006. *Address:* Rochester House, Halam Road, Southwell, Nottinghamshire NG25 0AD, England.

CHAPPELL, Fred Davis, BA, MA; American poet, writer and fmr teacher; b. 28 May 1936, Canton, NC; m. Susan Nicholls 1959; one s. *Education:* Duke Univ. *Career:* teacher, Univ. of North Carolina at Greensboro 1964–2004; Poet Laureate, North Carolina 1997–2003. *Publications:* poetry: The World Between the Eyes 1971, River 1975, The Man Twiced Married to Fire 1977, Bloodfire 1978, Awakening to Music 1979, Wind Mountain 1979, Earthsleep 1980, Driftlake: A Lieder Cycle 1981, Midquest 1981, Castle Tzingal 1984, Source 1985, First and Last Words 1989, C: 100 Poems 1993, Spring Garden: New and Selected Poems 1995, Poetry Collection: Family Gathering 2000, Backsass 2004; fiction: It is Time, Lord 1963, The Inkling 1965, Dagon 1968, The Gaudy Place 1972, Moments of Light (short story) 1980, I Am One of You Forever 1985, Brighten the Corner Where You Are 1989, More Shapes Than One (short story) 1991, Farewell, I'm Bound to Leave You 1996, Look Back All the Green Valley 1999; other: Plow Naked: Selected Writings on Poetry 1993, A Way of Happening: Observations of Contemporary Poetry 1998. *Honours:* Rockefeller Grant 1967–68, Nat. Inst. of Arts and Letters Award 1968, Académie Française Prix de Meilleur des Livres Étrangers 1972, Sir Walter Raleigh Prize 1972, Roanoke-Chowan Poetry Prizes 1972, 1975, 1979, 1980, 1985, 1989, North Carolina Award in Literature 1980, Bollingen Prize in Poetry 1985, World Fantasy Awards 1992, 1994, Ingersoll Foundation T. S. Eliot Prize 1993, Aiken Taylor Award in Poetry 1996, Thomas Wolfe Prize 2006, Caroliniana Award 2007. *Address:* 305 Kensington Road, Greensboro, NC 27403, USA. *Telephone:* (336) 275-8851.

CHAPPLE, John Alfred Victor, MA; British academic and writer; *Professor Emeritus, Hull University;* b. 25 April 1928, Barnstaple, Devon. *Education:* Univ. Coll., London. *Career:* Asst, Univ. Coll. 1953–55; Research Asst Yale Univ. 1955–58; Asst Lecturer, Aberdeen Univ. 1958–59; Asst Lecturer, Univ. of Manchester 1959–61, Lecturer 1961–67, Sr Lecturer 1967–71; Prof., Univ. of Hull 1971–92, Prof. Emer. 1992–; Visiting Fellow, Corpus Christi Coll. Cambridge 1991–92; mem. Gaskell Soc. (Pres. 1992–), Int. Asscn of Univ. Profs of English, Larkin Soc., Johnson Soc., Friends of Erasmus, Darwin House. *Publications:* The Letters of Mrs Gaskell 1966, Documentary and Imaginative Literature 1880–1920 1970, Elizabeth Gaskell: A Portrait in Letters 1980, Science and Literature in the 19th Century 1986, Private Voices: The Diaries of Elizabeth Gaskell and Sophia Holland 1996, Elizabeth Gaskell: The Early Years 1997, Further Letters of Mrs Gaskell 2000, 2003. *Address:* 8 Lomax Close, Lichfield, WS13 7EY, England.

CHARBONNEAU, Eileen, BA; American writer; b. 11 April 1951, Long Island, NY; m. Edward Gully 1972; two d. one s. *Education:* State Univ. of NY, Fredonia, River Arts Film School, Woodstock, NY, New School for Social Research. *Publications:* The Ghosts of Stony Clove 1988, In the Time of the Wolves 1994, The Mound Builders' Secret 1994, Disappearance at Harmony Festival 1994, Honor to the Hills 1995, Waltzing in Ragtime 1996, The Randolph Legacy 1997, Rachel LeMoyne 1998, The Connor Emerald 2000; contrib. to periodicals. *Honours:* Romance Writers of America Golden Medallion Award 1989, American Library Asscn Best Books Citations 1994, Council of Books for Children Best Books Citation 1996, Washington Post Book World 1998, Christopher Columbus Screenwriting Award 1999, Washington Romance Writers of America Lifetime Achievement Award 2004. *Address:* PO Box 20, Cold Spring, NY 10516, USA. *E-mail:* eileencharbonneau@hotmail.com.

CHARBONNEAU-TISSOT, Claudette (see Aude)

CHARKIN, Richard Denis Paul, MA; British publishing executive; *CEO, Macmillan Ltd;* b. 17 June 1949, London; s. of Frank Charkin and Mabel Doreen Charkin (née Rosen); m. Susan Mary Poole 1972; one s. two d. *Education:* Haileybury, Imperial Service Coll., Univ. of Cambridge and Harvard Business School. *Career:* Science Ed. Harrap & Co. 1972; Sr Publishing Man. Pergamon Press 1973; Medical Ed. Oxford Univ. Press 1974, Head of Science and Medicine 1976, Head of Reference 1980; Man. Dir Academic and Gen. 1984; joined Octopus Publishing Group (Reed Int. Books) 1988; Chief Exec. Reed Consumer Books 1989–94, Exec. Dir Reed Books Int. 1988–96, Chief Exec. 1994–96; CEO Current Science Group 1996–97; CEO Macmillan Ltd 1998–; Visiting Fellow Green Coll. Oxford 1987; Chair. Common Purpose 1998–; mem. man. cttee John Wisden; mem. Publishers Asscn (vice-pres. 2004–05, pres. 2005–06). *Address:* Macmillan Ltd, The Macmillan Building, 4 Crinan Street, London, N1 9XW (office); 3 Redcliffe Place, London, SW10 9DB, England (home). *Telephone:* (20) 7843-3600 (office). *Fax:* (20) 7843-3648 (office). *E-mail:* richard@macmillan.com (office). *Website:* www.macmillan.co.uk.

CHARLES, Nicholas J. (see Kuskin, Karla Seidman)

CHARLES-ROUX, Edmonde; French writer; *President, Académie Goncourt;* b. 17 April 1920, Neuilly-sur-Seine; d. of François Charles-Roux and Sabine Gounelle; m. Gaston Defferre 1973 (deceased). *Education:* Italy. *Career:* served as nurse, then in Resistance Movt, during Second World War, in which she was twice wounded; reporter, magazine Elle 1947–49; Features Ed., French edn of Vogue 1949–54, Ed.-in-Chief 1954–66; mem. Académie Goncourt 1983–, Pres. 2002–. *Publications:* Oublier Palerme 1966, Elle Adrienne 1971, L'irrégulière ou mon itinéraire Chanel 1974, Le temps Chanel 1979, Stèle pour un bâtard, Don Juan d'Autriche: 1980, Une enfance sicilienne 1981, Un désir d'Orient: La jeunesse d'Isabelle Eberhardt 1988, Nomade j'étais: Les années africaines d'Isabelle Eberhardt 1995, L'homme de Marseille 2001. *Honours:* Croix de guerre 1940–45, Officier, Légion d'honneur 2003; Prix Goncourt 1966, Grand Prix Littéraire de Provence 1977. *Address:* Editions Grasset, 61 rue des Saints-Pères, Paris 75006, France (office).

CHARNAS, Suzy McKee, BA, MA; American writer; b. 22 Oct. 1939, New York, NY; m. Stephen Charnas 1968; one step-s. one step-d. *Education:* Barnard College, New York University. *Career:* mem. Authors' Guild; SFWA; Dramatists Guild. *Publications:* Walk to the End of the World, 1974; Motherlines, 1979; The Vampire Tapestry, 1980; The Bronze King, 1985; Dorothea Dreams, 1986; The Silver Glove, 1988; The Golden Thread, 1989; The Kingdom of Kevin Malone, 1993; Vampire Dreams (play), 1990; The Furies, 1994; The Ruby Tear, 1997; The Conqueror's Child, 1999, Stagestruck Vampires 2004, My Father's Ghost 2002. Contributions: Womens Review of Books. *Honours:* Nebula Award, 1980; Hugo Award, 1989; Tiptree Award, 1999. *Address:* 212 High Street NE, Albuquerque, NM 87102, USA. *E-mail:* pagemail@swcp.com. *Website:* www.suzymckeecharnas.com.

CHARRY, Brinda S.; Indian writer; b. Bangalore. *Education:* Syracuse Univ., USA. *Career:* teaches at Syracuse Univ., NY. *Publications:* The Hottest Day of the Year (novel) 2001, Shadow (short story) 2003; contrib. to Indian periodicals. *Honours:* Katha Awards 1998, 2003, winner Asian Age Short Story Competition, winner Hindu-Picador Short Story Competition. *Address:* c/o Penguin Books India Pvt Ltd, #11 Community Centre, Panchsheel Park, New Delhi, India.

CHARTERIS, Richard, BA, MA, PhD, FAHA, FRHistS; New Zealand musicologist, writer and editor; *Professor in Historical Musicology, University of Sydney;* b. 24 June 1948, Chatham Islands. *Education:* Victoria Univ., Wellington, Univ. of Canterbury, NZ, Univ. of London, UK. *Career:* Research Fellow in Music Dept, Univ. of Sydney 1976–90; Sr Research Fellow (Reader) 1991–94, Prof. in Historical Musicology, Music Dept, Univ. of Sydney 1995–. *Publications include:* more than 160 books and editions devoted to the music of Johann Christian Bach, Giovanni Bassano, John Coprario, Alfonso Ferrabosco the Elder, Domenico Maria Ferrabosco, Andrea and Giovanni Gabrieli, Adam Gumpelzhaimer, Hans Leo Hassler, John Hingeston, Thomas Lupo, Claudio Monteverdi, Johann Georg von Werdenstein and others, and mostly in the series Corpus Mensurabilis Musicae, Musica Britannica, Recent Researches in the Music of the Baroque Era, Boethius Editions, Fretwork Editions, King's Music Editions, Baroque and Classical Music Series; and books on composers, music and early sources in the series Boethius Editions, Thematic Catalogues Series, Annotated Reference Tools in Music, Detroit Studies in Music Bibliography, Musicological Studies and Documents and Altro Polo. *Honours:* Sr Scholar 1970–71, Mary Duncan Scholar 1975, Louise Dyer Award Royal Musical Asscn 1975, Australian Acad. of Humanities Travelling Fellow 1979–80, Top Award Australian Hi Fi FM Classical Music Section 1988, Australian Centenary Medal 2003. *Address:* Music Department J09, University of Sydney, Sydney, NSW 2006, Australia (office). *Website:* www-personal.arts.usyd.edu.au/charteris (office).

CHARYN, Jerome, BA; American writer and educator; b. 13 May 1937, New York, NY. *Education:* Columbia College. *Career:* English Teacher, High School of Music and Art, School of Performing Arts, New York City, 1962–64; Asst Prof., Stanford University, 1965–68; Prof., Lehman College, CUNY, 1968–80; Founding Ed., The Dutton Review, 1970; Lecturer, Princeton University, 1980–86; Prof. of Film Studies, American University of Paris, 1995–; mem. PEN; Authors' Guild; Writers Guild of America; International Asscn of Crime Writers. *Publications:* Once Upon a Droshky, 1964; On the Darkening Green, 1965; Going to Jerusalem, 1967; American Scrapbook, 1969; The Single Voice: An Anthology of Contemporary Fiction, 1969; The Troubled Vision, 1970; The Tar Baby, 1973; Blue Eyes, 1975; Marilyn the Wild, 1976; The Franklin Scare, 1977; Secret Isaac, 1978; The Seventh Babe, 1979; Darlin' Bill, 1980; Panna Maria, 1982; Pinocchio's Nose, 1983; The Isaac Quartet, 1984; Metropolis, 1986; Paradise Man, 1987; Movieland, 1989; The Good Policeman, 1990; Maria's Girls, 1992; Montezuma's Man, 1993; Little Angel Street, 1994; El Bronx, 1997; The Dark Lady from Belorusse, 1997; Death of a Tango King, 1998; Citizen Sidel, 1999; Captain Kidd, 1999; The Black Swan, 2000; Hurricane Lady, 2001; Sizzling Chops and Devilish Spins, 2001; The Isaac Quartet, 2002; Bronx Boy, 2002; Gangsters and Gold Diggers, 2003. *Honours:* Commdr, Ordre des Arts et des Lettres, 2002. *Address:* 302 W 12th Street, Apt 10c, New York, NY 10014, USA. *E-mail:* jeromecharyn@aol .com. *Website:* www.jeromecharyn.com.

CHASE, Elaine Raco, AA; American writer; b. 31 Aug. 1949, Schenectady, NY; m. Gary Dale Chase 1969; one s. one d. *Education:* Albany Business College, Union College, SUNY. *Career:* mem. Romance Writers of America; Sisters in Crime, national pres., 1995–96. *Publications:* Rules of the Game, 1980; Tender Yearnings, 1981; A Dream Come True, 1982; Double Occupancy, 1982; Designing Woman, 1982; No Easy Way Out, 1983; Video Vixen, 1983; Best Laid Plans, 1983; Special Delivery, 1984; Lady Be Bad, 1984; Dare the Devil, 1987; Dark Corners, 1988; Partners in Crime, 1994; Amateur Detective

(non-fiction), 1996. Contributions: several publications. *Honours:* Walden Book Award, 1985; Top Romantic Supsense Series Award, 1987–88.

CHASE BRENES, Alfonso; Costa Rican writer, poet and academic; b. 19 Oct. 1944, Cartago. *Career:* fmr Dir of Publications, Ministry of Culture; faculty mem., Universidad Nacional, Heredia 1974–, currently Prof. of Literature; fmr Scholar-in-Residence, Arkansas Univ., USA; founder, Asociación de Escritores de América Central 1993, Costa Rica PEN 1955; mem. Costa Rican chapter of the Int. Bd on Books for Young People (IBBY). *Publications include:* poetry: Los reinos de mi mundo 1966, El árbol del tiempo 1967, Para escribir sobre el agua 1970, Cuerpos 1972, El libro de la patria 1975, Los pies sobre la tierra 1978, Obra en marcha 1982, El tigre luminoso 1982, Entre el ojo y la noche 1990, Jardines de asfalto (Premio Nacional Aquileo J. Echeverría) 1995; prose: Las puertas de la noche 1974, Mirar con inocencia 1975, Días y territorios 1980; also essays, children's books. *Address:* c/o Escuela de Estudios Generales, Universidad Nacional, Apdo 86-3000, Heredia, Costa Rica. *E-mail:* jmora@una.ac.cr.

CHASE-RIBOUD, Barbara Dewayne, MFA, PhD; American/French sculptor and writer; b. 26 June 1939, Philadelphia, PA; d. of Charles Edward Chase and Vivian May Braithwaite West Chase; m. 1st Marc Eugene Riboud 1961 (divorced 1981); m. 2nd S. G. Tosi 1981; two s. *Education:* Yale Univ. *Career:* rep. in perm. collections in USA and France; Fellow John Hay Whitney Foundation 1958, Nat. Endowment for Arts 1973. *Exhibitions include:* solo: Berkeley Museum, CA 1973, MIT 1973, Museum of Modern Art, Paris 1974, Kunstmuseum, Düsseldorf, Germany 1974, Bronx Museum, New York 1979, Pasadena Coll., CA 1990, Metropolitan Museum of Art, New York 1999, Walters Museum Washington, DC 2000; numerous group exhbns in Italy, France, USA, Germany, Australia, UK, China, Philadelphia Art Museum 2005–06, Shanghai Museum of Contemporary Art 2005–06. *Publications include:* From Memphis and Peking, Poems 1974, Sally Hemings, A Novel 1979, Study of a Nude Woman as Cleopatra 1987, Valide 1986, Echo of Lions 1989, The President's Daughter 1995, Roman Egyptian 1995, The Sculpture of Barbara Chase-Riboud, Selz, Jansen A., Abrams 2001, Hottentot Venus 2003, Ragtime Girl 2005, Untitled Poems 2005. *Honours:* Kt of French Repub. 1996, Chevalier, Ordre des Arts et des Lettres; Hon. PhD (Temple Univ.), (Univ. of Connecticut), (Mullenberg Coll.), (Dillard Univ.) 2005; Kafka Prize 1979, Acad. of Italy Gold Medal 1979, Carl Sandburg Poetry Prize 1988, US Gen. Services Design Award for Best Public Sculpture 1998, American Library Asscn Black Caucus Prize for Best Fiction 2004. *Literary Agent:* Sandra Dijkstra Agency, PMB515, 1155 Camino de Mar, Del Mar, CA 92014, USA. *Telephone:* (858) 755-3115. *Fax:* (858) 794-2822. *E-mail:* sdla@dijkstraagency .com. *Website:* www.dijkstraagency.com. *Address:* 3 rue Auguste Comte, 75006 Paris, France; Palazzo Ricci, 146 via Guilia, 00186 Rome, Italy. *Telephone:* (1) 43-29-69-63. *Fax:* (1) 43-29-47-53. . *Website:* www.chase-riboud .com.

CHÂTELET, Noëlle, DèsL; French writer and actress; *Professor, University of Paris V—René Descartes;* b. 16 Oct. 1944, Meudon, Seine; d. of Robert Jospin and Mireille Jospin (née Dandieu); m. François Chatelet (deceased); one s. *Education:* Lycée mixte de Meaux, Lycée Hélène Boucher, Paris, Univs of Sorbonne and Paris VIII—Vincennes Saint-Denis. *Career:* Asst, Asst Lecturer then Lecturer of Communication Studies, Univ. of Paris XI—Sud Orsay 1970–89; Dir French Inst. of Florence, Italy 1989–91; Head Dept of Culture, Univ. of Versailles—Saint-Quentin 1991–93; apptd Lecturer, Univ. of Paris V—René Descartes 1993, now Prof.; Co-Chair. Maison des écrivains 1995–; mem. Cttee Soc. des gens de lettres 1996–; jury mem. for various literary awards in France; mem. support cttee for Lionel Jospin, her brother, during French presidential election 2002. *Films include:* Les Autres 1972, Vera Baxter 1977, La Banquiére 1980. *Television includes:* Les Buddenbrooks 1978–79, La Vie de Berlioz 1982. *Publications include:* Le corps à corps culinaire (essay) 1972, Histoires de bouches (Prix Goncourt de la nouvelle) 1987, A contre-sens 1989, La Courte échelle (Rene Fallet Prize, Francophone Schools and Univs Prize) 1991, A Table 1992, Trompe l'oeil (essay) 1993, La dame en bleu (Anna de Noailles Prize, Acad. française) 1996, La femme coquelicot 1997, Devenu Corps sur mesure (essay) 1998, La petite aux tournesois 1999, La tête en bas 2002, La dernière leçon 2004. *Address:* Université Paris V—René Descartes, Département linguistique, 12 rue Cujas, 75005 Paris, France (office).

CHATTERJEE, Debjani; Indian writer, poet, editor, storyteller and translator; b. 21 Nov. 1952, Delhi, India; m. Brian D'Arcy 1983. *Education:* BA, American University in Cairo, 1972; MA, University of Kent, Canterbury, 1973; PhD, University of Lancaster, 1977; PGCE, Sheffield City Polytechnic, 1981. *Career:* Chair. National Asscn of Writers in Education; Vice-Chair. Bengali Women's Support Group and Book Project 1985–; mem. Poetry Society, India, UK, Arts Council of England, Literature Advisory Group 1996–99, Mini Mushaira 1996–. *Publications:* Peaces; Poems for Peace, 1987; Whistling Still: Bloody Lyres, 1989; I Was That Woman, 1989; Northern Poetry, Vol. II, 1991; The Sun Rises in the North, 1993; A Little Bridge, 1997; Albino Gecko, 1998; Songs in Exile (trans.), 1999; Cette-Femme La..., 2000; The Redbeck Anthology of British South Asian Poetry, 2000; Animal Antics, 2000; My Birth Was Not in Vain: Selected Poems by Seven Bengali Women, 2001, Jade Horse Torso: Poems and Translations 2003, Rainbow World: Poems from Many Cultures 2003, Generations of Ghazals: Ghazals by Nasir Kazmi & Basir Sultan Kazmi 2003, Daughters of a Riverine Land 2003. Other: The Role of Religion in A Passage to India, 1984; The Elephant-Headed God and Other Hindu Tales, 1989; Barbed Lines, 1990; Sweet and Sour, 1993; The Parrot's

Training (trans.), 1993; The Monkey God and Other Hindu Tales, 1993; Sufi Stories from Around the World, 1994; Nyamia and the Bag of Gold, 1994; Home to Home, 1995; The Most Beautiful Child, 1996; Album (trans.), 1997; The Message of Thunder and Other Plays, 1999; The Snake Prize and Other Folk Tales from Bengal, 1999, Who Cares? Reminiscences of Yemeni Carers in Sheffield 2001. *Honours:* Shankars International Children's Competition Poetry Prize; Lancaster LitFest Poems Competition Winner; Peterloo Poets Open Poetry Competition Afro-Caribbean/Asian Prize; Southport Writers' Circle Poetry Competition, second prize; Artrage Annual Literature Award; Raymond Williams Community Publishing Prize, 1990; Yorkshire and Humberside Arts Writer's Award, 1995. *Address:* 11 Donnington Road, Sheffield S2 2RF, England. *Website:* mysite.freeserve.com/DebjaniChatterjee.

CHATTERJEE, Margaret, PhD; Indian philosopher and writer; b. 13 Sept. 1925, London; d. of Norman Herbert and Edith Gantzer; m Nripendranath Chatterjee 1946; two d. one s. *Education:* Parkstone Grammar School, Somerville Coll., Oxford, UK and Univ. of Delhi. *Career:* moved to India 1946; teacher of Philosophy Univ. of Delhi 1956–90, Prof. of Comparative Religion 1976–77; Visiting Prof., Drew Univ., NJ, USA 1983, Westminster Coll., Oxford 1992–; Dir Indian Inst. of Advanced Study, Simla 1986–89, Visiting Scholar 2005; Visiting Fellow, Woodbrooke, Birmingham, UK 1990; Spalding Visiting Fellow in Indian Philosophy, Wolfson Coll., Oxford 1991; Commonwealth Visiting Fellow, Univ. of Calgary, Canada 1991; Pres. Int. Soc. for Metaphysics 1985–90. *Publications include:* Our Knowledge of Other Selves 1963, Philosophical Enquiries 1968, The Existentialist Outlook 1974, The Language of Philosophy 1981, Gandhi's Religious Thought 1983, The Religious Spectrum 1984, The Concept of Spirituality 1988, The Philosophy of Nikunja Vihari Banerjee 1990, Gandhi and his Jewish Friends 1992, Rabbi Abraham Isaac Kook and Sri Aurobindo – Towards a Comparison, Gandhi and the Challenge of Religious Diversity – Religious Pluralism Revisited 2005; poetry: The Spring and the Spectacle 1967, Towards the Sun 1970, The Sandalwood Tree 1972, The Sound of Wings 1978, The Rimless World 1987; short stories: At the Homeopath's 1975. *Address:* 49 Kala Kunj, A/0 Shalimar Bagh, Delhi 110052, India (home).

CHATTERTON-NEWMAN, Roger; British author; b. 17 March 1949, Haslemere, Surrey, England. *Career:* Editorial Staff, Haymarket Publishing, 1970–89; Deputy Ed., PQ International. *Publications:* A Hampshire Parish, 1976; Brian Boru, King of Ireland, 1983; Murtagh and the Vikings, 1986; Betwixt Petersfield and Midhurst, 1991; Edward Bruce: A Medieval Tragedy, 1992; Polo at Cowdray, 1992; Murtagh the Warrior, 1996. Contributions: Hampshire Magazine; Horse and Hound; Polo Quarterly International; West Sussex History; Downs Country; International Polo Review; The Ring Fort Annual.

CHAUDHURI, Amit, BA, DPhil; Indian writer; b. 15 May 1962, Kolkata, India; m. Rinka Khastgir 1991. *Education:* Univ. of London, Balliol Coll., Oxford. *Career:* Creative Arts Fellow, Wolfson Coll., Oxford 1992–95; Leverhulme Fellow in English, Univ. of Cambridge 1997–99. *Publications:* A Strange and Sublime Address 1991, Afternoon Raag 1993, Freedom Song 1998, A New World 2000, Real Time: Stories and a Reminiscence 2002, D. H. Lawrence and 'Difference': Postcoloniality and the Poetry of the Present 2003; contrib. to anthologies and periodicals, including London Review of Books. *Honours:* Betty Trask Award 1991, Commonwealth Writers' Prize for Best First Book 1992, K. Blundell Trust Award 1993, Southern Arts Literature Prize 1993, Arts Council of Great Britain Writers' Award 1993–94, Soc. of Authors Encore Prize 1994, Los Angeles Times Book Award for Fiction 2000. *Literary Agent:* AP Watt Ltd, 20 John Street, London, WC1N 2DR, England. *Address:* 6 Sunny Park, Flat 10, Eighth Floor, Kolkata 700019, India.

CHÉDID, Andrée, BA; French writer; b. 20 March 1920, Cairo; d. of Selim Saab and Alice K. Haddad; m. Louis A. Chedid 1942; one s. one d. *Education:* French schools, Cairo and Paris, American Univ. in Cairo. *Career:* has lived in Paris since 1946. *Publications include:* poetry: Fraternité de la parole 1975, Epreuves du vivant 1983, Textes pour un poème 1949–1970, 1987, Poèmes pour un texte 1970–91, Par delà les mots 1995, Fugitive Suns: Selected Poetry 1999; novels: Le Sommeil délivré 1952, Le Sixième Jour 1960, L'Autre 1969, Nefertiti et le rêve d'Akhnaton 1974, La Maison sans racines 1985, L'Enfant multiple 1989, Lucy: La Femme Verticle 1998, Le Message 2000; plays: Bérénice d'Egypte, Les Nombres, Le Montreur 1981, Echec à la Reine 1984, les saisons de passage 1996; short stories: Les Corps et le temps 1979, Mondes Miroirs Magies 1988, A la Mort, A la Vie 1992, La Femme de Job 1993, Les Saisons de passage 1996, Le Jardin perdu 1997, Territoires du Souffle 1999, Le Cœur demeure 1999; essays, children's books. *Honours:* Prix Louise Labé 1966, L'aigle d'or de la poésie 1972, Grand Prix des Lettres Françaises de l'Acad. Royale de Belgique 1975, Prix de l'Afrique Méditerranéenne 1975, Prix de l'Acad. Mallarmé 1976, Prix Goncourt for short story 1979, Prix de Poésie (Soc. des Gens de Lettres) 1991, Prix PEN Club Int. 1992, Prix Paul Morand, Acad. Française 1994, Prix Albert Camus 1996, Prix Poésie de la SALEH 1999; Officier, Légion d'honneur, Commdr des Arts et des Lettres. *Address:* c/o Flammarion, 26 rue Racine, 75006 Paris, France. *Telephone:* 1-40-51-31-00.

CHEETHAM, Anthony John Valerian, BA; British publisher; *Executive Chairman, Quercus Publishing plc;* b. 12 April 1943, s. of Sir Nicolas John Alexander Cheetham; m. 1st Julia Rollason 1969 (divorced); two s. one d.; m. 2nd Rosemary de Courcy 1979 (divorced); two d.; m. 3rd Georgina Capel 1997. *Education:* Eton Coll., Balliol Coll., Oxford. *Career:* Editorial Dir Sphere Books 1968; Man. Dir Futura Publs 1973, Macdonald Futura 1979; Chair.

Century Publishing 1982–85; Man. Dir Century Hutchinson 1985; Chair. and CEO Random Century Group 1989–91; Founder and CEO Orion Publishing Group (fmrly Orion Books) 1991–2006; Exec. Chair. Quercus Publishing plc 2006–. *Publication:* Richard III 1972. *Address:* Quercus Publishing plc, 21 Bloomsbury Square, London, WC1A 2QA, England (office). *Telephone:* (20) 7291-7200 (office). *Fax:* (0870) 7301482 (office). *E-mail:* mail@quercusbooks.co.uk (office). *Website:* www.quercusbooks.co.uk (office).

CHELES, Luciano, BA, MPhil, PhD; Italian academic; *Professor of Italian Studies, University of Poitiers;* b. 7 Sept. 1948, Cairo, Egypt. *Education:* Univs of Reading, Essex and Lancaster. *Career:* Sr Lecturer in Italian Studies, Univ. of Lancaster 1994–2000; Visiting Lecturer, Univ. of Lyons II, France 1994–95, 1996; Prof. of Italian Studies, Univ. of Poitiers, France 2000–; mem. Asscn for the Study of Modern Italy, Istituto di Studi Rinascimentali, Soc. for Renaissance Studies, Groupe d'Etudes et de Recherches sur la Culture Italienne. *Publications:* The Studiolo di Urbino: An Iconographic Investigation (revised Italian edn as Lo Studiolo di Urbino: Iconografia di un microcosmo principesco) 1986, Neo-Fascism in Europe (ed. with R. G. Ferguson and M. Vaughan, revised edn as The Far Right in Western and Eastern Europe) 1991, Grafica Utile: L'affiche d'utilité publique en Italie, 1975–1995 1995, The Art of Persuasion: Political Communication in Italy, from 1945 to the 1990s (co-ed. with L. Sponza) 2001; contrib. to scholarly books and journals. *Honours:* Frontino-Montefeltro Prize 1992. *Address:* Département d'Études Italiennes, Université de Poitiers, 86000 Poitiers, France. *E-mail:* luciano.cheles@laposte.net (office).

CHEN, Jiangong; Chinese writer; b. Nov. 1949, Beihai, Guangxi Prov. *Education:* Peking Univ. *Career:* joined Beijing Writers' Asscn 1981; Sec. of Secr., Chinese Writers' Asscn 1995–2001, 2003–, Vice-Chair. 2001–. *Publications:* A Girl with the Eyes of a Red Phoenix, Selected Novels by Chen Jiangong, No. 9 Huluba Alley, Letting Go, Curly Hair, Previous Offence. *Address:* c/o Beijing Writers' Association, Beijing, People's Republic of China.

CHEN, Jo-Hsi, BA, MA; Taiwanese novelist; b. 15 Nov. 1938, Taiwan. *Education:* Taiwan National University, Johns Hopkins University. *Career:* has lived and worked in Taiwan, USA, China, Hong Kong, Canada; Lecturer, University of California at Berkeley 1983. *Publications:* Fiction: Mayor Yin, 1976; Selected Works by Jo-Hsi Chen, 1976; The Old Man, 1978; Repatriation, 1978; The Execution of Mayor Yin, and Other Stories from the Great Proletarian Cultural Revolution, 1978; Inside and Outside the Wall, 1981; Tu Wei, 1983; Selected Short Stories by Jo-Hsi Chen, 1983; Foresight, 1984; The Two Hus, 1985; Paper Marriage, 1986; The Old Man and Other Stories, 1986; Woman from Guizhou, 1989; Wangzhou's Sorrows, 1995; Home of Daughters, 1998; Create a Paradise, 1998. Other: Reminiscences of the Cultural Revolution, 1979; Random Notes, 1981; Democracy Wall and the Unofficial Journals, 1982; Read to Kill Time, 1983; Flower Grown Naturally, 1987; Trip to Tibet, 1988; Trip to Inner Mongolia, 1988. *Honours:* Wu Zhuoliu Prize 1978.

CHEN, Li; Taiwanese poet, essayist and translator; b. 1954, Hualien; m. Chang Fen-ling. *Education:* Nat. Taiwan Normal Univ. *Career:* started writing poetry early 1970s; secondary school teacher 1975–; guest lecturer Nat. Dong Hwa Univ.; also trans. poetry of Szymborska, Plath, Heaney, Neruda, Paz into Chinese. *Publications:* Intimate Letters: Selected Poems of Chen Li (with English trans. by Chang Fen-ling) 1997. *Address:* c/o Council for Cultural Affairs, 102 Ai Kuo East Road, Taipei, Taiwan.

CHEN, Zhongshi; Chinese novelist; *Chairman, Shaanxi Provincial Writers' Association;* b. 1942, Xian, Shanxi Prov. *Career:* Chair. Shaanxi Prov. Writers' Asscn 1993–; Vice-Chair. Chinese Writers' Asscn 2001. *Publications:* White Deer Height (Mao Dun Prize for Literature 1997), Early Summer, Mr. Blue Gown, The Cellar 1994. *Address:* Shanxi Provincial Writers' Association, Xian, People's Republic of China.

CHENEY-COKER, Syl; Sierra Leonean academic and poet; b. 28 June 1945, Freetown; m. *Education:* Univs of Oregon, California and Wisconsin. *Career:* Prof. of English, Univ. of the Philippines, Quezon City 1975–77; Sr Lecturer, Univ. of Maiduguri, Nigeria 1977–88; writer-in-residence, Univ. of Iowa 1988; Ed. of newspaper, Vanguard, Freetown –1997; writer in the City of Asylum programme, Las Vegas, USA; returned to Sierra Leone 2003. *Publications:* poetry: The Road to Jamaica 1969, Concerto for an Exile 1973, The Graveyard Also Has Teeth 1980, The Blood in the Desert's Eyes 1990; novel: The Last Harmattan of Alusine Dunbar (Commonwealth Writers Prize) 1990. *Address:* c/o Ministry of Tourism and Culture, Ministerial Bldg, George Street, Freetown, Sierra Leone.

CHENG, Naishan; Chinese writer; b. 14 June 1946, Shanghai; d. of Cheng Xueqiao and Pan Zuojun; m. Yan Erchun 1969; one d. *Education:* Shanghai Educational Inst. *Career:* family left China 1949, returned 1956; teacher 1965–85; writer 1985–; invited to speak in Germany, USA and Philippines 1986–; moved to Hong Kong 1990s. *Publications:* The Blue House 1983, The Clove Villa 1984, The Poor Street 1984, Daughters' Tribulations 1985, The Bankers 1989, The Piano Tuner 1989. *Address:* Lane 48, No. 36, Yu Yuan Road, 200040 Shanghai, People's Republic of China. *Telephone:* (21) 2531652.

CHERKOVSKI, Neeli, (Neeli Cherry), BA; American writer, poet and editor; b. 1945, Los Angeles, CA, USA; pnr Jesse Guinto Cabrera 1983. *Education:* San Bernardino Community Coll., California State Univ., Hebrew Union Coll. Jewish Inst. of Religion. *Publications:* poetry: Anthology of Los Angeles Poets (co-ed.), 1972; Don't Make a Move, 1973; Public Notice, 1975; The Waters Reborn, 1975; Love Proof, 1981; Clear Wind, 1983; Ways in the Wood, 1993;

Animal, 1996; Elegy for Bob Kaufman, 1996; prose: Ferlinghetti: A Life, 1979; Whitman's Wild Children, 1988; Hank: The Life of Charles Bukowski, 1991. *Address:* c/o Synaesthesia Press, PO Box 1763, Tempe, AZ 85280, USA.

CHERNOW, Ron, BA, MA; American writer; b. 3 March 1949, New York, NY; m. Valerie Stearn 1979 (died 2006). *Education:* Yale Coll., Pembroke Coll., Cambridge. *Career:* fmr freelance journalist; Dir of Financial Policy Studies for think tank, Twentieth Century Fund 1982; book reviewer, essayist, TV and radio commentator; mem. PEN American Center (fmr sec., pres. 2006–), Authors' Guild. *Publications:* The House of Morgan: An American Banking Dynasty and the Rise of Modern Finance (Nat. Book Award for Nonfiction 1990) 1990, The Warburgs: The Twentieth-Century Odyssey of a Remarkable Jewish Family (George S. Eccles Prize for the best business book 1993) 1993, The Death of the Banker: The Decline and Fall of the Great Financial Dynasties and the Triumph of the Small Investor (essays) 1997, Titan: The Life of John D. Rockefeller Sr 1998, Alexander Hamilton 2004; contrib. to New York Times, Wall Street Journal. *Honours:* United Steelworkers of America Jack London Award 1980, English-Speaking Union of the United States Ambassador Book Award 1990. *Address:* c/o PEN American Center, 588 Broadway, Suite 303, New York, NY 10012, USA (office). *E-mail:* pen@pen.org (office).

CHERRY, Carolyn Janice, (C. J. Cherryh), BA, MA; American writer; b. 1 Sept. 1942, St Louis, MO. *Education:* University of Oklahoma, Johns Hopkins University. *Career:* mem. National Space Society, SFWA. *Publications:* The Faded Sun, 1978; Downbelow Station, 1981; The Pride of Chanur, 1982; Chanur's Venture, 1984; Forty Thousand in Gehenna, 1984; Cuckoo's Egg, 1985; Chanur's Homecoming, 1986; Visible Light, 1986; Angel with the Sword, 1987; The Paladin, 1988; Rusalka, 1989; Rimrunners, 1990; Chernevog, 1991; Heavy Time, 1991; Chanur's Legacy, 1992; The Goblin Mirror, 1993; Hellburner, 1993; Faery in Shadow, 1994; Tripoint, 1994; Fortress in the Eye of Time, 1995; Invader, 1995; Rider at the Gate, 1995; Cloud's Rider, 1996; Lois and Clark, 1996; Inheritor, 1996; Fortress of Owls, 1998. *Honours:* John Campbell Award, 1977; Hugo Awards, 1979, 1982, 1989.

CHERRY, Neeli (see Cherkovski, Neeli)

CHERRYH, C. J. (see Cherry, Carolyn Janice)

CHESSEX, Jacques; Swiss novelist and poet; b. 1 March 1934, Payerne. *Education:* Univ. of Lausanne. *Publications:* La Tête ouverte 1962, La Confession du pasteur Burg 1967, A Father's Love 1973, L'Ardent Royaume 1975, Le Séjour des morts 1977, Les Yeux jaunes 1979, Où vont mourir les oiseaux 1980, Judas le transparent 1983, Jonas 1987, Morgane Madrigal 1990, Sosie d'un saint 2000, Monsieur 2001; poetry: Le Jour proche 1954, Chant de printemps 1955, Une Voix la nuit 1957, Batailles dans l'air 1959, Le Jeûne de huit nuits 1966, L'Ouvert obscur 1967, Elégie, soleil du regret 1976, Le Calviniste 1983, Feux d'orée 1984, Comme l'os 1988; non-fiction: Maupassant et les autres 1981, Mort d'un cimetière 1989, Flaubert, ou le désert en abîme 1991, Notes sur Saura 2001. *Honours:* Prix Goncourt 1973; Commdr, Ordre des Arts et des Lettres 1984, Chevalier, Légion d'honneur 2002. *Address:* c/o Editions Grasset, 61 rue des Sts-Pères, 75006 Paris, France.

CHEUNG, Angelica, BA, MBA; Chinese journalist; *Editorial Director, Vogue China*; m.; one d. *Education:* studied law and languages, Peking Univ., Univ. of Southern Australia. *Career:* fmrly journalist for newspapers and magazines in Hong Kong, then Ed.-in-Chief Marie Claire (Hong Kong), then Editorial Dir, Elle China; Editorial Dir, Vogue China (launched Sept. 2005 by Condé Nast Int. Ltd and China Pictorial Publishing House) 2005–. *Address:* Vogue China, Rm 505, Tower C1, Beijing Oriental Plaza, 1 East Changan Avenue, Beijing 100738, China (office). *Telephone:* (10) 85187700 (office). *Fax:* (10) 85189686 (office). *E-mail:* voguechina@condenast.com.cn (office). *Website:* www.vogue.com.cn.

CHEUSE, Alan, BA, PhD; American author, critic and teacher; b. 23 Jan. 1940, Perth Amboy, NJ; m. 1st Mary Agan 1964 (divorced 1974), one s.; m. 2nd Marjorie Pryse 1974, two d.; m. 3rd Kristin M. O'Shee 1991. *Education:* Lafayette Coll., Rutgers Univ. *Career:* faculty mem., Bennington Coll. 1970–78, George Mason Univ. 1987–; Co-Dir, Bennington Summer Writing Workshops 1978–85, Acting Dir 1986–87; Visiting Lecturer, Univ. of Tennessee 1980–83, Univ. of Virginia 1987; Visiting Fellow, Univ. of the South 1984; Writing Program, Univ. of Michigan 1984–86; Visiting Writer, Univ. of Houston 1991–92; mem. Nat. Book Critics Circle, PEN. *Radio:* book commentator All Things Considered (Nat. Public Radio) 1983–, producer and host The Sound of Writing (Center for the Book/Nat. Public Radio) 1988–99. *Publications:* fiction: Candace & Other Stories 1980, The Bohemians 1982, The Grandmothers' Club 1986, The Tennessee Waltz and Other Stories 1990, The Light Possessed 1990, Lost and Old Rivers 1999; other: Fall Out of Heaven 1987, The Sound of Writing: Stories from the Radio (ed. with Caroline Marshall) 1991, Listening to Ourselves: More Stories from the Sound of Writing (ed. with Caroline Marshall) 1994, Talking Horse: Bernard Malamud on Life and Work (ed. with Nicholas Delbanco) 1996, Listening to the Page: Adventures in Reading and Writing 2001, Writer's Workshop in a Book (ed. with Lisa Alvarez) 2007, Seeing Ourselves: Great American Short Fiction (ed.) 2007, The Fires 2007; contrib. to anthologies, reference books, reviews, journals and newspapers. *Honours:* NEA Creative Writing Fellowship 1979–80, New York Times Notable Book of the Year citation 1982, Antioch Review Prize for Distinguished Non-Fiction 2001. *Address:* 3611 35th Street NW, Washington, DC 20016, USA.

CHEVALIER, Tracy, MA; American writer; b. Oct. 1962, Washington, DC; m.; one s. *Education:* Oberlin Coll., Univ. of East Anglia, England. *Career:* moved to London, England 1984; fmr reference book ed. –1993. *Publications:* novels: The Virgin Blue 1997, Girl with a Pearl Earring 1999, Falling Angels 2001, The Lady and the Unicorn 2003, Burning Bright 2007. *Literary Agent:* c/o Jonny Geller, Curtis Brown, Haymarket House, 28–29 Haymarket, London, SW1Y 4SP, England. *Telephone:* (20) 7393-4400. *E-mail:* hello@tchevalier.com. *Website:* www.tchevalier.com.

CHIASSON, Dan, PhD; American poet, literary critic and academic; b. Burlington, VT. *Education:* Amherst Coll., Harvard Univ. *Career:* teacher Wellesley Coll.; Asst Prof. Dept of English, State Univ. of New York at Stony Brook, also Dir Poetry Center. *Publications:* poetry: The Afterlife of Objects 2002, Natural History 2005; criticism: One Kind of Everything: Poem and Person in Contemporary America; contrib. articles to New York Times, The Threepenny Review, Poetry, Slate. *Honours:* Pushcart Prize, Whiting Writers' Award 2004. *Address:* c/o English Department, Wellesley College, 106 Central Street, Wellesley, MA 02481, USA. *Website:* www.wellesley.edu.

CHICHETTO, James William, BA, MA,; American writer, ecclesiastic, poet, academic and editor; *Professor of Writing and Communications, Stonehill College*; b. 5 June 1941, Boston, Mass; s. of Frank A. Chichetto and Christina Chichetto (née McInnis). *Education:* Stonehill Coll., Holy Cross Coll., Wesleyan Univ., Chicago Univ., Catholic Univ. *Career:* ordained priest, Congregation of Holy Cross 1968; educator and missionary, Peru 1968–72; Assoc. Ed. Gargoyle Magazine 1974–80; Ed. 1982–87, Artist 1990–, The Connecticut Poetry Review; Prof. of Writing and Communications, Stonehill Coll., North Easton, Mass 1982–; art work for The Connecticut Poetry Review 1995–2005 (in archives at John Hay Library, Brown Univ., Providence, RI); mem. Connecticut Literary Forum, Nat. Asscn of Scholars, Directory of American Scholars, Massachusetts Foundation for Humanities Scholars, Asscn of Literary Scholars and Critics; Fellow, World Literary Acad. *Publications:* Poems 1975, Dialogue: Emily Dickinson and Christopher Cauldwell 1978, Stones: A Litany 1980, Gilgamesh and Other Poems 1983, Victims 1987, Homage to Father Edward Sorin 1992, Dream of Norumbega 2000, Reckoning Genocide 2002, Dream of Norumbega Book II (An Epic Poem on the United States of America) 2005; play: The Bakers' Wind; contrib. to Boston Phoenix, Colorado Review, Boston Globe, The Manhattan Review, The Patterson Review, The Connecticut Poetry Review, America, Harpers, East West Literary Journal, National Catholic Reporter, etc.; to anthologies, books: Perversions of Justice, Indigenous Peoples of Angloamerican Law 2003, Blood To Remember: American Poets on the Holocaust 1991, And What the Rough Beast 2000, Mr. Cogito (translations), Hitler's Priests, Catholic Clergy in National Socialism (translations) 2007 and others. *Honours:* book grants, Nat. Endowment for the Arts 1980, 1983, Nat. Endowment for the Humanities 1992, 1993, 1994, Sri Chinmoy Poetry Award 1984, Stonehill Alumni Service Award 1997, Connecticut Literary Forum Award 2003, CPR Talent Award 2005, Stonehill Devt Grant 2007. *Address:* Stonehill College, North Easton, MA 02357, USA (office). *Telephone:* (508) 565-1271 (office). *E-mail:* jchichetto@stonehill.edu (office).

CHILDISH, Billy; British singer, songwriter, musician (guitar), writer and poet and painter; b. (Stephen Hamper), 1 Dec. 1959, Chatham, Kent; m. Julie Childish; one c. *Career:* mem. various bands, including Pop Rivets, the Milkshakes, Thee Mighty Caesars, the Delmonas, Thee Headcoats, the Natural Born Lovers, The Buff Medways. *Recordings include:* albums: I Remember, I've Got Everything Indeed, Laughing Gravy, Plump Prizes and Little Gems, The 1982 Cassettes, Which Dead Donkey Daddy?, Talkin' Bout Milkshakes, Acropolis Now, In Tweed We Trust, Ypres 1917 Overture 1987, Play: Capt'n Calypso's Hoodoo Party 1988, Poems of Laughter and Violence 1988, Long Legged Baby 1989, I Am the Billy Childish 1991, The Original Chatham Jack 1992, At the Bridge 1993, Live in the Netherlands 1993, Hunger at the Moon 1994, Live 1994, Devil in the Flesh 1998, The Cheeky Cheese 1999, In Blood 1999, I Am the Object of Your Desire 2000, Steady the Buffs 2002, Here Come the Fleece 2002, Medways 2003, Medway Wheelers 2005, Heavens Journey (with The Chatham Singers) 2005, Punk Rock at the British Legion Hall 2007. *Publications:* Poems from the Barrier Block 1984, Monks Without God 1986, Companions in a Death Boat 1987, To the Quick 1988, Girl in the Tree 1988, Maverick Verse 1988, Admissions to Strangers 1989, Death of a Wood 1989, The Silence of Words (short stories) 1989, The Deathly Flight of Angels 1990, Like a God I Love All Things 1990, Child's Death Letter 1990, The Hart Rises 1991, Poems of Laughter and Violence: Selected Poetry 1981–86 1992, Poems to Break the Harts of Impossible Princesses 1994, Days With a Hart Like a Dog 1994, Big Hart and Balls 1995, Messerschmitt Pilot's Severed Hand 1996, My Fault (novel) 1996, Billy Childish and his Famous Headcoat 1997, Notebooks of a Naked Youth (novel) 1997, I'd Rather You Lied: Selected Poems 1980–1998 1999, Chatham Town Welcomes Desperate Men (poems) 2001, Chathams Burning 2004, Knite of the Sad Face 2004, Sex Crimes of the Futcher 2005. *Address:* c/o Hangman Books, 11 Boundary Road, Chatham, Kent ME4 6TS, England. *Website:* www.billychildish.com.

CHILTON, Bruce, AB, MDiv, PhD; American academic and writer; b. 27 Sept. 1949, Roslyn, NY; m. Odile Sevault 1982, two s. *Education:* Bard Coll., St John's Coll., Cambridge. *Career:* Lecturer in Biblical Studies, Sheffield Univ., England 1976–85; Lillian Claus Prof. of the New Testament, Yale Univ. 1985–87; Bernard Iddings Prof. of Religion, Bard Coll., Annandale, NY 1987–; Rector, Church of St John the Evangelist 1987–; Bishop Henry Martin

Memorial Lecturer, Univ. Coll. of Emmanuel and St Chad; mem. Studiorum Novi Testamenti Societas, Soc. of Biblical Literature. *Publications:* The Glory of Israel: The Theology and Provinence of the Isaiah Targum 1983, The Kingdom of God in the Teaching of Jesus (ed.) 1984, A Galilean Rabbi and his Bible: Jesus' Own Interpretation of Isaiah 1984, Targumic Approaches to the Gospels: Essays in the Mutual Definition of Judaism and Christianity 1986, The Isaiah Targum (trans.) 1987, Beginning New Testament Study 1986, Jesus and the Ethics of the Kingdom (co-author) 1988, Profiles of a Rabbi: Synoptic Opportunities in Reading about Jesus 1989, The Temple of Jesus: His Sacrificial Program within a Cultural History of Sacrifice 1992, A Feast of Meanings: Eucharistic Theologies from Jesus through Johannine Circles 1994, Studying the Historical Jesus: Evaluations of the State of Current Research (co-ed.) 1994, Judaic Approaches to the Gospel 1994, Judaism in the New Testament: Practices and Beliefs (co-author) 1995, Revelation: The Torah and the Bible (co-author) 1995, Pure Kingdom: Jesus' Vision of God 1996, The Body of Faith: Israel and the Church (co-author) 1996, Trading Places: The Intersecting Histories of Judaism and Christianity (co-author) 1996, The Intellectual Foundations of Christian and Jewish Discourse: The Philosophy of Religious Argument (co-author) 1997, Jesus' Prayer and Jesus' Eucharist: His Personal Practice of Spirituality 1997, Trading Places Sourcebook: Readings in the Intersecting Histories of Judaism and Christianity 1997, Rabbi Jesus: An Intimate Biography 2000, Rabbi Paul: An Intellectual Biography 2004, Mary Magdalene: A Biography 2005, The Cambridge Companion to the Bible 2007. *Honours:* Heinrich Hertz Scholar, Germany, Asher Edelman Fellow Bard Coll., Evangelical Fellow, Pew Charitable Trust. *Address:* Faculty of Religion, Bard College, Annandale, NY 12504, USA (office). *Telephone:* (845) 758-7335 (office). *E-mail:* chilton@bard.edu (office). *Website:* www.bard.edu (office).

CHIMOMBO, Steve, PhD; Malawi poet, playwright and literary critic; *Professor of English, University of Malawi;* b. 1945, Zomba. *Education:* Univ. of Malawi, Wales and Univ. of Columbia, USA. *Career:* Prof. of English, Univ. of Malawi; Ed. Wasi Writer journal. *Plays:* The Rainmaker 1978, Wachiona Ndani? 1983, Sister! Sister! 1995. *Publications:* poetry: Vipya 1966, Napolo Poems 1987, Python!, Python! 1992, Referendum of the Forest Creatures 1993; novel: The Basket Girl 1990; criticism: Oral Literature in Malawi 1860–1986 1987, Malawian Oral Literature: The Aesthetics of Indigenous Arts 1988. *Address:* c/o University Office, University of Malawi, POB 278, Zomba, Malawi (office).

CHINODYA, Shimmer, (B. Chirasha), MA; Zimbabwean novelist; b. 1957, Gweru; m. *Education:* Univ. of Zimbabwe, Univ. of Iowa, USA. *Career:* curriculum developer, materials designer, ed. and screenwriter; Distinguished Visiting Prof. in Creative Writing, St Lawrence Univ., New York 1995–97. *Film script:* Everyone's Child 1994. *Publications:* Dew in the Morning 1982, Farai's Girls 1984, Child of War (as B. Chirasha) 1985, Harvest of Thorns 1990, Can We Talk and Other Stories 1998, Tale of Tamari 2004, Chairman of Fools 2005; several children's books as B. Chirasha. *Honours:* Commonwealth Writers Prize for African Literature 1990; numerous fellowships and prizes. *Address:* 39 Lorraine Drive, Bluff Hill, PO Westgate, Harare, Zimbabwe. *E-mail:* shimmerchi2000@yahoo.com.

CHIPASULA, Frank Mkalawile, BA, MA, PhD; Malawi poet; b. 1949, Likoma Island, Lake Malawi. *Education:* Chancellor Coll., Univ. of Malawi, Univ. of Zambia, and Brown and Yale Univs, USA. *Career:* fmr teacher, Brown and Yale Univs, St Olaf Coll., Northfield, MN; fmr Assoc. Prof. of Black Studies, Univ. of Nebraska at Omaha, USA. *Publications:* poetry: Visions and Reflections 1972, O Earth, Wait for Me 1984, When My Brothers Come Home: Poems from Central and Southern Africa (ed.) 1985, Nightwatcher, Nightsong 1986, Whispers in the Wings 1991, In a Dark Season (novel), The Heinemann Book of African Women's Poetry (co-ed.) 1995. *Honours:* hon. mention Noma Award for Publishing in Africa 1985, BBC Poetry Prize 1989. *Address:* c/o Heinemann Publishers Ltd, Halley Court, Jordan Hill, Oxford, OX2 8EJ, England.

CHIRASHA, B. (see Chinodya, Shimmer)

CHISHOLM, Anne, FRSL; British biographer and reviewer; m. Michael Davie. *Career:* mem. RSL (mem. of council). *Publications:* non-fiction: Philosophers of the Earth 1972, Nancy Cunard: A Biography 1979, Faces of Hiroshima: A Report 1985, Beaverbrook: A Life (with Michael Davie) 1992, Rumer Godden: A Storyteller's Life 1998. *Honours:* Silver PEN Award 1979. *Address:* c/o Pan Macmillan Ltd, 20 New Wharf Road, London, N1 9RR, England. *Website:* www.macmillan.co.uk.

CHITHAM, Edward Harry Gordon, , PGCE, MA, PhD, FRSA; British education consultant and writer; b. 16 May 1932, Harborne, Birmingham; m. Mary Patricia Tilley 1962; one s. two d. *Education:* Jesus Coll., Cambridge, Univ. of Birmingham, Univ. of Warwick, Univ. of Sheffield. *Career:* mem. Asscn of Classics Teachers, Gaskell Soc., Brontë Soc. *Publications:* The Black Country 1972, Ghost in the Water 1973, The Poems of Anne Brontë 1979, Brontë Facts and Brontë Problems (with T. J. Winnifrith) 1983, Selected Brontë Poems (with T. J. Winnifrith) 1985, The Brontës' Irish Background 1986, A Life of Emily Brontë 1987, Charlotte and Emily Brontë (with T. J. Winnifrith) 1989, A Life of Anne Brontë 1991, A Bright Start 1995, The Poems of Emily Brontë (with Derek Roper) 1996, The Birth of Wuthering Heights: Emily Brontë at Work 1998, A Brontë Family Chronology 2003, Harborne: A History 2004, Rowley Regis: A History 2006; contrib. to Byron Journal,

Gaskell Society Journal, ISIS Magazine, Brontë Society Transactions. *Address:* 25 Fugelmere Close, Harborne, Birmingham, B17 8SE, England.

CHITTICK, William C., BA, PhD; American writer and academic; *Professor of Religious Studies, State University of New York, Stony Brook;* b. 29 June 1943, Milford, Conn.; s. of Oliver B. Chittick and Margaret Clark Chittick; m. Sachiko Murata. *Education:* Coll. of Wooster, OH, Univ. of Tehran, Iran. *Career:* Asst Prof., Center for the Humanities, Aryamehr Tech. Univ., Tehran 1974–78; Asst Prof., Imperial Iranian Acad. of Philosophy, Tehran 1978–79; Asst Ed., Encyclopaedia Iranica, Columbia Univ. 1981–84; Asst Prof. of Religious Studies, Dept of Asian and Asian American Studies, State Univ. of New York, Stony Brook 1983–91, Prof. of Religious Studies 1991–; Visiting Prof. of Arabic Literature, Harvard Univ. 1996; Directeur d'études, L'École des Hautes Études en Sciences Social, Paris 2004. *Publications include:* A Shi'ite Anthology 1981, The Sufi Path of Love 1983, The Psalms of Islam 1988, The Sufi Path of Knowledge 1989, Faith and Practice of Islam 1992, Imaginal Worlds 1994, The Vision of Islam (co-author) 1996, The Self-Disclosure of God 1998, Sufism: A Short Introduction 2000, The Heart of Islamic Philosophy 2001, Me & Rumi: The Autobiography of Shams-i Tabrizi 2004, The Elixir of the Gnostics 2005, The Sufi Doctrine of Rumi: Illustrated Edition 2005, Science of the Cosmos, Science of the Soul 2007, The Inner Journey: Views from the Islamic Tradition 2007. *Honours:* Fellowship for ind. Study and Research, Nat. Endowment for the Humanities 1986–87, Fellowship for Univ. Profs, Nat. Endowment for the Humanities 1993–94, World Prize for the Book of the Year in Iranian Studies within the American Countries (Iran) 2005, Mevlâna Arastirmalari Özel Ödülü, Kombassan Foundation (Konya Turkey) 2000. *Address:* Department of Asian and Asian American Studies, State University of New York, Stony Brook, NY 11794-8081, USA (office). *Telephone:* (631) 632-7316 (office). *E-mail:* wchittick@notes.cc.sunysb.edu (office).

CHITTY, Susan Elspeth, Lady Chitty; British writer, journalist and lecturer; b. 18 Aug. 1929, London, England; m. Sir Thomas Willes Chitty 1951, one s. three d. *Education:* Somerville Coll., Oxford. *Publications:* fiction: The Diary of a Fashion Model 1958, White Huntress 1963, My Life and Horses 1966; non-fiction: The Woman Who Wrote Black Beauty 1972, The Beast and the Monk 1975, Charles Kingsley and North Devon 1976, On Next to Nothing (with Thomas Willes Chitty) 1976, The Great Donkey Walk (with Thomas Willes Chitty) 1977, The Young Rider 1979, Gwen John 1876–1939 1981, Now to My Mother 1985, That Singular Person Called Lear 1988; editor: The Intelligent Woman's Guide to Good Taste 1958, The Puffin Book of Horses 1975, Antonia White: Diaries 1926–1957 two vols 1991–92, Playing the Game: Biography of Henry Newbolt 1997. *Address:* Bow Cottage, West Hoathly, Sussex RH19 4QF, England (home).

CHITTY, Sir Thomas Willes, (Thomas Hinde), Bt; British writer; b. 2 March 1926, Felixstowe; s. of Sir (Thomas) Henry Willes Chitty and the late Ethel Constance; m. Susan Elspeth Chitty (née Hopkinson) 1951; one s. three d. *Education:* Winchester Coll. and Univ. Coll., Oxford. *Career:* served in RN 1944–47; with Shell Group 1953–60; Granada Arts Fellow, Univ. of York 1964–65; Visiting Lecturer, Univ. of Ill., USA 1965–67; Visiting Prof., Boston Univ. 1969–70; now freelance writer. *Achievements:* expedition on foot and donkey with wife and two young daughters, Santiago to Salonika 1975–76. *Publications include:* fiction: Mr Nicholas 1952, Happy As Larry 1957, For the Good of the Company 1961, A Place Like Home 1962, The Cage 1962, Ninety Double Martinis 1963, The Day the Call Came 1964, Games of Chance 1965, The Village 1966, High 1968, Bird 1970, Generally a Virgin 1972, Agent 1974, Our Father 1975, Daymare 1980; non-fiction: Spain 1963, On Next to Nothing (with Susan Elspeth Chitty) 1976, The Great Donkey Walk (with Susan Elspeth Chitty) 1977, The Cottage Book 1979, Sir Henry and Sons (autobiog.) 1980, Stately Gardens of Britain 1983, A Field Guide to the English Country Parson 1983, Forests of Britain 1984, The Domesday Book: England's Heritage, Then and Now 1986, Courtiers: 900 Years of Court Life 1986, Tales from the Pump Room: An Informal History of Bath 1988, Capability Brown 1986, Imps of Promise: A History of the King's School Canterbury 1990, Looking-Glass Letters (ed.) (letters of Lewis Carroll) 1991, Paths of Progress, A History of Marlborough College 1992, A History of Highgate School 1993, A History of King's College School 1994, Carpenter's Children: A History of the City of London School 1995, An Illustrated History of the University of Greenwich 1996, The Martlet and the Griffen: A History of Abingdon School 1997. *Address:* c/o Andrew Hewson, John Johnson, 45–47 Clerkenwell Green, London, EC1R 0HT (office); Bow Cottage, West Hoathly, Sussex, RH19 4QF, England. *Telephone:* (20) 7251-0125 (office); (1342) 810269. *E-mail:* thomas .chitty@ukgateway.net (home).

CHO, Ramaswamy, BSc, BL; Indian journalist, playwright, actor, lawyer and politician; b. 5 Oct. 1934, Madras (now Chennai); s. of R. Srinivasan and Rajammal Srinivasan; m. 1966; one s. one d. *Education:* P.S. High School, Loyola Coll., Vivekananda Coll., Madras and Madras Law Coll., Madras Univ. *Career:* started practice as lawyer, Madras High Court 1957; Legal Adviser to T.T.K. Group of Cos. 1961–; film scriptwriter and actor 1966–; theatre dir, actor and playwright 1958–; Ed. Tamil political fortnightly Thuglak 1970–; Pres. People's Union of Civil Liberties, Tamilnadu 1980–82; nominated mem. of Rajya Sabha (Parl.); has acted in 180 films, written 14 film scripts, directed four films; written, directed and acted in four TV series and 23 plays in Tamil. *Publications:* 23 plays and 10 novels in Tamil; numerous articles on politics, in English and Tamil. *Honours:* Haldi Gati Award, Maharana of Mewar, for nat. service through journalism 1985, Veerakesari Award for investigative journalism 1986, B. D. Goenka Award for Excellence in Journalism, Panchajanya Award for promotion of nationalism 1998. *Address:* 46 Greenways Road, Chennai, 600028; 35 Meena Bagh, New Delhi, 110011, India. *Telephone:* (44) 4936913 (Chennai); (11) 3792520 (New Delhi). *Fax:* (44) 24936915 (office).

CHOMSKY, (Avram) Noam, MA, PhD; American theoretical linguist and writer; *Professor Emeritus, Department of Linguistics, Massachusetts Institute of Technology*; b. 7 Dec. 1928, Philadelphia, PA; s. of William Chomsky and Elsie Simonofsky; m. Carol Schatz 1949; one s. two d. *Education:* Univ. of Pennsylvania. *Career:* Asst Prof., MIT 1955–58, Assoc. Prof. 1958–61, Prof. of Modern Languages 1961–66, Ferrari P. Ward Prof. of Modern Languages and Linguistics 1966–76, Institute Prof. 1976–; Visiting Prof., Columbia Univ. 1957–58; NSF Fellow, Princeton Inst. for Advanced Study 1958–59; American Council of Learned Socs Fellow, Center for Cognitive Studies, Harvard Univ. 1964–65; Linguistics Soc. of America Prof., Univ. of California at Los Angeles 1966; Beckman Prof., Univ. of California at Berkeley 1966–67; John Locke Lecturer, Univ. of Oxford 1969; Shearman Lecturer, Univ. Coll. London 1969; Bertrand Russell Memorial Lecturer, Univ. of Cambridge 1971; Nehru Memorial Lecturer, Univ. of New Delhi 1972; Whidden Lecturer, McMaster Univ. 1975; Huizinga Memorial Lecturer, Univ. of Leiden 1977; Woodbridge Lecturer, Columbia Univ. 1978; Kant Lecturer, Stanford Univ. 1979; Jeanette K. Watson Distinguished Visiting Prof., Syracuse Univ. 1982; Pauling Memorial Lecturer, Oregon State Univ. 1995; mem. American Acad. of Arts and Sciences, Linguistic Soc. of America, American Philosophical Asscn, American Acad. of Political and Social Science, NAS, Bertrand Russell Peace Foundation, Deutsche Akademie der Naturforscher Leopoldina, Nat. Acad. of Sciences, Royal Anthropological Inst., Utrecht Soc. of Arts and Sciences; Fellow, American Asscn for the Advancement of Science; Corresp. Fellow, British Acad. *Publications include:* Syntactic Structures 1957, Current Issues in Linguistic Theory 1964, Aspects of the Theory of Syntax 1965, Cartesian Linguistics 1966, Topics in the Theory of Generative Grammar 1966, Language and Mind 1968, The Sound Pattern of English (with Morris Halle) 1968, American Power and the New Mandarins 1969, At War with Asia 1970, Problems of Knowledge and Freedom 1971, Studies on Semantics in Generative Grammar 1972, For Reasons of State 1973, The Backroom Boys 1973, Counter-revolutionary Violence (with Edward Herman) 1973, Peace in the Middle East? 1974, Reflections on Language 1975, The Logical Structure of Linguistic Theory 1975, Essays on Form and Interpretation 1977, Human Rights and American Foreign Policy 1978, Language and Responsibility 1979, The Political Economy of Human Rights (two vols, with Edward Herman) 1979, Rules and Representations 1980, Lectures on Government and Binding 1981, Radical Priorities 1981, Towards a New Cold War 1982, Concepts and Consequences of the Theory of Government and Binding 1982, Fateful Triangle: The United States, Israel and the Palestinians 1983, Modular Approaches to the Study of the Mind 1984, Turning the Tide 1985, Knowledge of Language: Its Nature, Origins and Use 1986, Barriers 1986, Pirates and Emperors 1986, Generative Grammar: Its Basis, Development and Prospects 1987, On Power and Ideology 1987, Language and Problems of Knowledge 1987, Language in a Psychological Setting 1987, The Chomsky Reader 1987, The Culture of Terrorism 1988, Manufacturing Consent (with Edward Herman) 1988, Language and Politics 1988, Necessary Illusions 1989, Deterring Democracy 1991, What Uncle Sam Really Wants 1992, Chronicles of Dissent 1992, Year 501: The Conquest Continues 1993, Rethinking Camelot: JFK, the Vietnam War and US Political Culture 1993, Letters from Lexington: Reflections on Propaganda 1993, The Prosperous Few and the Restless Many 1993, Language and Thought 1994, World Orders, Old and New 1994, The Minimalist Program 1995, Powers and Prospects 1996, Class Warfare 1996, The Common Good 1998, Profit over People 1998, The New Military Humanism 1999, New Horizons in the Study of Language and Mind 2000, Rogue States: The Rule of Force in World Affairs 2000, A New Generation Draws the Line 2000, Architecture of Language 2000, Propaganda and the Public Mind 2001, 9-11 2001, Understanding Power 2002, On Nature and Language 2002, Middle East Illusions 2003, Hegemony or Survival: America's Quest for Global Dominance 2003, Failed States: America 2006; numerous lectures, contribs. to scholarly journals. *Honours:* Hon. Fellow, British Psychological Soc. 1985, Royal Anthropological Inst.; Hon. DHL (Chicago) 1967, (Loyola Univ., Swarthmore Coll.) 1970, (Bard Coll.) 1971, (Mass.) 1973, (Maine, Gettysburg Coll.) 1992, (Amherst Coll.) 1995, (Buenos Aires) 1996; Hon. DLitt (London) 1967, (Delhi) 1972, Visva-Bharati (West Bengal) 1980, (Pa) 1984, (Cambridge) 1995; hon. degrees (Tarragona) 1998, (Guelph) 1999, (Columbia) 1999, (Connecticut) 1999, (Pisa) 1999, (Harvard) 2000, (Toronto) 2000, (Western Ontario) 2000, Kolkata (2001); George Orwell Award, Nat. Council of Teachers of English 1987, Kyoto Prize in Basic Sciences 1988, James Killian Award, MIT 1992, Helmholtz Medal, Berlin Brandenburgische Akad. Wissenschaften 1996, Benjamin Franklin Medal, Franklin Inst., Philadelphia 1999, Rabindranath Tagore Centenary Award, Asiatic Soc. 2000, Peace Award, Turkish Publrs Asscn 2002. *Address:* Department of Linguistics and Philosophy, Massachusetts Institute of Technology, 77 Massachusetts Avenue, Bldg. 32-D808, Cambridge, MA 02139 (office); 15 Suzanne Road, Lexington, MA 02420, USA (home). *Telephone:* (617) 253-7819 (office); (781) 862-6160 (home). *Fax:* (617) 253-9425 (office). *E-mail:* chomsky@mit.edu (office). *Website:* web.mit.edu/linguistics/www (office).

CHORLTON, David; British writer, poet and artist; b. 15 Feb. 1948, Spittal-an-der-Drau, Austria; m. Roberta Elliott 1976. *Education:* Stockport Coll. *Publications:* Without Shoes 1987, The Village Painters 1990, Measuring Time 1990, Forget the Country You Came From 1992, Outposts 1994, Assimilation 2000, Common Sightings 2001, A Normal Day Amazes Us 2003, Return to Waking Life 2004, Waiting for the Quetzal 2006; contrib. to many reviews and journals. *Address:* 118 W Palm Lane, Phoenix, AZ 85003, USA. *Telephone:* (602) 253-5055.

CHOUAKI, Aziz, DipLit; French (b. Algerian) writer, playwright, poet and musician; b. 1951, Algiers. *Education:* Univ. of Algiers. *Career:* guitarist in rock groups 1975; writer 1982–; artistic dir Triangle jazz club, Algiers; moved to France 1991. *Plays:* Poussières d'Ange (play, Théâtre Jean Vilar, Vitry sur Seine), Fruits de Mer (24 radio plays, for Radio Suisse Romande) 1993, Brisants de mémoire (five short dramas) 1995, Les Oranges (play, TILF, La Villette) 1997, Boudin-purée (play, Gare au Théâtre, Vitry sur Seine) 1998, Bazar (play, La Laiterie, Strasbourg) 1999, Le Père indigne (play, Gare au Théâtre, Vitry) 1999, El Maestro (play, ARC, Creusot) 2000, Le Trésor (play, Théâtre SaulCy, Metz) 2000, Le Portefeuille (play, La Laiterie, Strasbourg) 2001, L'Arrêt de bus (play) 2003, Le tampon vert (lectures, Théâtre des Amandiers, Nanterre) 2004, Une Virée (play, Théâtre des Amandiers, Nanterre) 2004. *Publications:* Argo (poems and novellas) 1982, Baya (novel) 1989, L'Etoile d'Alger (novel, trans. as The Star of Algiers) 1998, Aigle (novel) 2000, Une enfance outremer 2001, Avoir 20 ans à Alger (fiction) 2001, Arobase (novel) 2004.

CHOYCE, Lesley, BA, MA,; Canadian academic, writer, poet and editor; b. 21 March 1951, Riverside, NJ, USA; m. Terry Paul 1974; two d. *Education:* Rutgers University, Montclair State College, CUNY. *Career:* Ed., Pottersfield Press, 1979–; Prof., Dalhousie University, 1986–. *Recordings:* Long Lost Planet 1996, Sea Level 1998. *Publications:* Adult Fiction: Eastern Sure, 1981; Billy Botzweiler's Last Dance, 1984; Downwind, 1984; Conventional Emotions, 1985; The Dream Auditor, 1986; Coming Up for Air, 1988; The Second Season of Jonas MacPherson, 1989; Magnificent Obsessions, 1991; Ecstasy Conspiracy, 1992; Margin of Error, 1992; The Republic of Nothing, 1994; The Trap Door to Heaven, 1996; Beautiful Sadness, 1997; Dance the Rocks Ashore, 1997; World Enough, 1998, The Summer of Apartment X 1999, Cold Clear Morning 2001. Young Adult Fiction: Skateboard Shakedown, 1989; Hungry Lizards, 1990; Wavewatch, 1990; Some Kind of Hero, 1991; Wrong Time, Wrong Place, 1991; Clearcut Danger, 1992; Full Tilt, 1993; Good Idea Gone Bad, 1993; Dark End of Dream Street, 1994; Big Burn, 1995; Falling Through the Cracks, 1996, Couleurs Troubles 1997, Roid Rage 1999, Refuge Cove 2002, Shoulder the Sky 2002. Poetry: Re-Inventing the Wheel, 1980; Fast Living, 1982; The End of Ice, 1985; The Top of the Heart, 1986; The Man Who Borrowed the Bay of Fundy, 1988; The Coastline of Forgetting, 1995; Beautiful Sadness, 1998, Caution to the Wind 2000. Non-Fiction: An Avalanche of Ocean, 1987; December Six: The Halifax Solution, 1988; Transcendental Anarchy (autobiog.), 1993; Nova Scotia: Shaped by the Sea, 1996. Editor: Chezzetcook, 1977; The Pottersfield Portfolio, 7 vols, 1979–85; Visions from the Edge (with John Bell), 1981; The Cape Breton Collection, 1984; Ark of Ice: Canadian Futurefiction, 1992. *Honours:* Event Magazine's Creative Nonfiction Competition Winner, 1990; Dartmouth Book Awards, 1990, 1995; Ann Connor Brimer Award for Children's Literature, 1994; Authors Award, Foundation for the Advancement of Canadian Letters 1995, Landmar East Literacy Award 2000, Poet Laureate Peter Gzowski Invitational Golf Tournament 2000. *Address:* 83 Leslie Road, East Lawrencetown, NS B2Z 1P8, Canada.

CHRISTENSEN, Inger; Danish poet, playwright and essayist; b. 16 Jan. 1935. *Plays:* Intriganterne 1972, En vinteraften i Ufa og andre spil 1987. *Publications include:* poetry: Lys 1962, Graes 1963, Det 1969, Brev i april 1970, Alfabet 1981, Sommerfugledalen - et requiem 1991, Samlede digte 1998; novels: Evighedsmaskinen 1964, Det malede vaerelse 1976; juvenile fiction: Den store ukendte rejse 1982; essays: Del af labyrinten 1982, Hemmelighedstilstanden 2000. *Address:* c/o Bloodaxe Books Ltd, Highgreen, Tarset, Northumberland NE48 1RP, England.

CHRISTENSEN, Lars Saabye; Norwegian poet, writer and playwright; b. 21 Sept. 1953, Oslo. *Career:* Ed., Signaler 1986–90. *Plays:* Columbus' ankomst (Hørespillprisen 1981–82) 1981, Mekka 1994. *Publications:* poetry: Historien om Gly (Tarjei Vesaas' Debutantpris) 1976, Ordbok 1977, Kamelen i mitt hertje 1978, Jaktmarker 1979, Paraply 1982, Åsteder 1986, Stempler 1989, Versterålen: Lyset, livet, landskapet 1989, Hvor er det blitt av alle gutta 1991, Den akustiske skyggen 1993, Nordmarka 1993, Den andre siden av blått 1996, Falleferdig himmel 1998, Pasninger 1998, Under en sort paraply (with Niels Fredriok Dahl) 1998, Pinnsvinsol 2000, Mann for sin katt 2000, Sanger & steiner 2003; novels: Amatøren 1977, Billettene 1980, Jokeren 1981, Beatles 1984, Blodets bånd 1985, Sneglene 1987, Herman (trans. as Herman) 1988, Bly (Bokhandlerprisen) 1990, Gutten som ville være en av gutta 1992, Jubel 1995, Halvbroren (trans. as The Half Brother) (Bokhandlerprisen) 2001, Maskeblomstfamilien 2003, Circus 2007; other fiction: Ingens 1992, Den Misunnnelige frisøren 1997, Noen som elsker hverandre 1999, Kongen som ville ha mer enn en krone (with Randall Meyers and Anita Killi) 1999; contrib. to Alexandrias aske 1993. *Honours:* Commdr, Order of St Olaf 2006 Cappelenprisen 1984, Rivertonprisen 1987, Kritikerpris 1988, Amandaprisen 1991, Doblougprisen 1993, Riksmålprisen 1997, Sargsborgrisen 1999, Aamoudt-statuetten 2001, Brageprisen 2001, Den norske leserprisen 2001, Natt & Dags bokpris 2001, Nordisk Råds Litteratuur Pris 2002. *Literary Agent:* J. W. Cappelens Forslag AS, PB 350, 0101, Oslo, Norway. *Telephone:* 22365000. *Fax:* 22365040. *Website:* www.cappelen.no.

CHRISTIAN, Beatrix; Australian playwright and screenwriter. *Education:* Nat. Inst. of Drama. *Career:* affiliate writer and writer-in-residence, Sydney Theatre Co 1993–94; writer-in-residence, Sydney Theatre Co 2002. *Plays:* Inside Dry Water 1993, Blue Murder 1994, The Governor's Family 1997, Faust's House, Fred, Old Masters, The Promised Land, Spumante Romantica, Ten Things Not to Do on a First Date, Then the Mountain Comes; adaptations: A Doll's House (Ibsen), Life is a Dream (Calderón de la Barca); adaptations with Benedict Andrews: Three Sisters (Chekhov). *Television writing:* White Colour Blue. *Film screenplay:* Jindabyne 2005. *Honours:* Sydney Critics' Circle Award for Best Australian Play, New York New Dramatists' Award 1997, Queensland Premier's Literary Award. *Literary Agent:* RGM Associates, PO Box 128, Surry Hills, NSW 2010, Australia. *Telephone:* (2) 9281-3911. *Fax:* (2) 9281-4705. *E-mail:* info@rgm.com.au. *Website:* www.rgm.com.au.

CHRISTIAN, John (see Dixon, Roger)

CHRISTOPHER, Nicholas, AB; American poet and writer; b. 28 Feb. 1951, New York, NY; m. Constance Barbara Davidson 1980. *Education:* Harvard College. *Career:* Adjunct Prof. of English, New York Univ.; Lecturer, currently Prof. The Writing Div., School of the Arts, Columbia Univ. *Publications:* On Tour with Rita (poems) 1982, A Short History of the Island of Butterflies (poems) 1986, The Soloist (novel) 1986, Desperate Characters (poems) 1988, Under 35: The New Generation of American Poets (ed.) 1989, In the Year of the Comet (poems) 1992, 5 Degrees and Other Poems 1994, Walk and Other Poems 1995, Veronica (novel) 1996, Somewhere in the Night: Film Noir and the American City 1997, The Creation of the Night Sky (poems) 1998, Atomic Field: Two Poems 2000, A Trip to the Stars (novel) 2000, Franklin Flyer (novel) 2002, Crossing the Equator: New & Selected Poems 1972–2004 2004; contribs to anthologies and periodicals. *Honours:* New York Foundation for the Arts Fellowship 1986, National Endowment for the Arts Fellowship 1987, Peter I. B. Lavan Award, Acad. of American Poets 1991, Guggenheim Fellowship 1993, Melville Cane Award 1994. *Literary Agent:* Janklow & Nesbit Associates, 445 Park Avenue, New York, NY 10022, USA.

CHROBÁKOVÁ-REPAR, Stanislava; Slovak poet and writer; b. 1960, Bratislava. *Career:* fmr Ed. Romboid literary journal of the Slovak Writers' Union. *Publications:* Zo spoločnej zimy 1994, Na hranici jazyka 1997. *Address:* c/o Literarne Informacne Centrum, Nam. SNP 12, 81224 Bratislava, Slovakia. *Telephone:* (7) 5296-4475. *Fax:* (7) 5296-4563. *E-mail:* lic@litcentrum.sk.

CHUDAKOV, Aleksandr, PhD; Russian writer and academic; *Teacher of Russian Literature, Moscow State University;* b. 1938, Shchuchensk, N Kazakhstan; m. Marietta Omarovna Chudakova. *Education:* Moscow State Univ. *Career:* mem. faculty Russian Acad. of Sciences Inst. of World Literature 1964–; teacher of Russian literature Moscow State Univ. 1969–; Visiting Prof. Univs of Hamburg, Michigan, Los Angeles, Seoul, Cologne 1988–. *Publications:* Poetika Chekhova (trans. as Chekhov's Poetics) 1971, Mir Chekhova: Vozniknovenie i utverzhdenie (trans. as Chekhov's World: Origins and Affirmation) 1986, Anton Pavlovich Chekhov: Biografiia pisatelia (trans. as Anton Pavlovich Chekhov: A Writer's Life) 1987, Chekhov v Taganroge (trans. as Chekhov in Taganrog) 1987, Slovo – Veshch' – Mir: Ot Pushkina do Tolstogo (trans. as The Word – The Thing – The World: From Pushkin to Tolstoy) 1992, Lozhitsia mgla na starye stupeni (autobiog. novel, trans. as A Gloom is Cast Upon the Ancient Steps) (Znamya Magazine Prize for a Work of Literature Affirming Liberal Values) 2000; memoirs of Viktor Shklovsky, Viktor Vinogradov, Lidia Ginzburg; contrib. hundreds of articles in journals and magazines, including Novy mir. *Address:* c/o Moscow M. V. Lomonosov State University, Vorob'ovy Hills, 119992 Moscow, Russia. *Website:* www.msu.ru.

CHUNN, Louise; New Zealand magazine editor; *Editor, Good Housekeeping;* m. 2nd Andrew Anthony 2001; one s. two d. *Education:* Auckland Univ. *Career:* Ed. trade magazines, Auckland; writer Auckland Star evening newspaper; moved to USA, asst ed. Cornell Univ. alumni magazine; moved to London, news reporter Fashion Weekly 1982–83; Features Ed., then Deputy Ed. Just 17 magazine 1983–85, Ed. 1985–1986; Deputy Ed. Elle 1986–89; women, parents and style pages ed. Guardian newspaper 1989–95; Features Ed., Features Dir, then Deputy Ed., Vogue 1995–98; Ed. ES magazine 1998–2000; Deputy Ed. In Style 2000–02, Ed. 2002–06; Ed. Good Housekeeping 2006–. *Honours:* PPA Consumer Magazine of the Year 2004, EMAP Writer of the Year 1984.

CHURCH, Robert; British author; b. 20 July 1932, London; m. Dorothy June Bourton 1953; two d. *Education:* Beaufoy Coll., London. *Career:* Army 1950–52; Metropolitan Police 1952–78; Probation Service 1978–88. *Publications:* Murder in East Anglia 1987, Accidents of Murder 1989, More Murder in East Anglia 1990, Anglian Blood (co-ed.) 1995, Well Done Boys 1996; contrib. to miscellaneous journals. *Honours:* Salaman Prize for Non-Fiction 1997. *Address:* Woodside, 7 Crome Walk, Gunton Park, Lowestoft, Suffolk NR32 4NF, England (home). *Telephone:* (1502) 518072 (home).

CHURCHILL, Caryl, BA; British playwright; b. 3 Sept. 1938, London; d. of Robert Churchill and Jan Churchill (née Brown); m. David Harter 1961; three s. *Education:* Trafalgar School, Montreal, Canada, Lady Margaret Hall, Oxford. *Career:* first play, Downstairs, performed at Nat. Union of Students Drama Festival 1958; numerous radio plays and several TV plays. *Stage plays include:* Having a Wonderful Time (Oxford Players, 1960), Owners (Royal Court, London) 1972, Objections to Sex and Violence (Royal Court) 1975, Vinegar Tom (Monstrous Regiment toured 1976), Light Shining in Buckinghamshire (performed by Joint Stock Co., Edinburgh Festival 1976, then

Royal Court), Traps (Royal Court) 1977, Cloud Nine (Joint Stock Co., Royal Court) 1979, 1980, Lucille Lortel Theater, New York 1981–83, Top Girls (Royal Court) 1982, 1983, Public Theater, New York 1983, Fen (Joint Stock Co., Almeida Theatre, London 1983, Royal Court 1983, Public Theater, New York 1983), Softcops (RSC 1984), A Mouthful of Birds (Joint Stock, Royal Court and tour 1986), Serious Money (Royal Court 1987, Wyndham Theatre 1987, Public Theater New York 1988), Icecream (Royal Court 1989, Public Theater New York 1990), Mad Forest (Cen. School of Drama, Nat. Theatre Bucharest, Royal Court 1990), Lives of the Great Poisoners (Second Stride Co. Riverside Studios, London and tour 1991), The Skriker (Nat. Theatre 1994), Thyestes (by Seneca, translation; Royal Court Theatre Upstairs 1994); Hotel (Second Stride Co., The Place) 1997, This Is A Chair (Royal Court) 1997, Blue Heart (Out of Joint, Royal Court) 1997, Far Away (Royal Court) 2000, (Albery) 2001, A Number (Royal Court) 2002. *Radio:* The Ants, Not . . Not . . not . . not enough Oxygen, Abortive, Schreiber's Nervous Illness, Identical Twins, Perfect Happiness, Henry's Past. *Television:* The Judge's Wife, The After Dinner Joke, The Legion Hall Bombing, Fugue (jtly). *Publications:* Owners 1973, Light Shining 1976, Traps 1977, Vinegar Tom 1978, Cloud Nine 1979, Top Girls 1982, Fen 1983, Fen and Softcops 1984, A Mouthful of Birds 1986, Serious Money 1987, Plays I 1985, Plays II 1988, Objections to Sex and Violence in Plays by Women Vol. 4 1985, Ice Cream 1989, Mad Forest 1990, Lives of the Great Poisoners 1992, The Striker 1994, Thyestes 1994, Blue Heart 1997, This is a Chair 1999, Far Away 2000, A Number 2002; anthologies. *Address:* c/o Casarotto Ramsay Ltd, National House, 60–66 Wardour Street, London, W1V 3HP, England. *Telephone:* (20) 7287-4450. *Fax:* (20) 7734-9293.

CHUTE, Robert Maurice, ScD; American poet, biologist and academic (retd); *Professor Emeritus of Biology, Bates College;* b. 13 Feb. 1926, Bridgton, Me; s. of James Cleveland and Elizabeth Davis Chute; m. Virginia Hinds 1946; one s. one d. *Education:* Fryeburg Acad., Univ. of Maine, Johns Hopkins Univ. School of Hygiene and Public Health. *Career:* Instructor and Asst Prof., Middlebury Coll. 1953–59; Asst Prof. Northridge State Coll. 1959–61; Assoc. Prof. and Chair. of Biology, Lincoln Univ. 1961; Prof. and Chair. of Biology, then Dana Prof. of Biology, Bates Coll. 1962–93, Prof. Emer. 1993–; Fellow, AAAS. *Publications:* Environmental Insight 1971, Introduction to Biology 1976, Sweeping the Sky: Soviet Women Flyers in Combat 1999; poetry: Quiet Thunder 1975, Uncle George (poems) 1977, Voices Great and Small 1977, Thirteen Moons/Treize Lunes 1982, Samuel Sewell Sails for Home 1986, When Grandmother Decides to Die 1989, Woodshed on the Moon: Thoreau Poems, Barely Time to Study Jesus 1996, Androscoggin Too 1997, Sweeping the Sky 1999, Bent Offerings 2003; trans.: Thirteen Moons into Micmac Maliseet (native American) 2002; contribs to Kansas Quarterly, Beloit Poetry Review, Bitterroot, South Florida Poetry Review, North Dakota Review, Cape Rock, Fiddlehead, Greenfield Review, Literary Review. *Honours:* Me Arts and Humanities Award 1978, Chad Walsh Award (Beloit Poetry Journal) 1997, Maine Writers and Publrs Alliance Poetry Competition 2001. *Address:* 85 Echo Cove Lane, Poland Spring, ME 04274, USA. *Telephone:* (207) 998-4338.

ÇIÇEKOĞLU, Feride, PhD; Turkish writer; b. 27 Jan. 1951, Ankara; d. of Hasan and Nihal Çiçekoğlu; m. Zafer Aldemir 1986; one d. *Education:* Middle East Tech. Univ. and Univ. of Pennsylvania (USA). *Career:* teacher 1977–80; political prisoner 1980–84; Ed., writer and Film Consultant 1984–92; apptd Sec-Gen. Cultural Foundation for Audiovisual and Cinema, Istanbul 1991. *Film:* Journey of Hope (Acad. Award) 1991. *Publications include:* Don't let Them Shoot the Kite (book) 1986, (screenplay, Golden Orange Award) 1989, The Other Side of the Water (book) 1990, (screenplay) 1991, Did Your Father Ever Die 1990, Melekler Evi (screenplay) 2001. *Address:* TÜRSAK, Fahri Gizden Sok 16/2, Gayrettepe, Istanbul, Turkey. *Telephone:* (1) 2721102. *Fax:* (1) 2728602.

CIFERRI, Elvio, DLitt; Italian writer, historian and academic; *Professor of Italian Literature, Leopoldo and Alice Franchetti Institute;* b. 1 April 1965, Città di Castello; s. of Luigi Ciferri and Elena Massimina Radicchi del Citerna. *Education:* Perugia Univ. *Career:* Prof. of History and Italian Literature, Perugia 1992; Prof., Leopoldo and Alice Franchetti Inst., Città di Castello 1999–. *Publications:* non-fiction: Editti e notificazioni di mons. Giovanni Muzi vescovo di Città di Castello 1989, Luigi Piccardini e il suo tempo 1993, Tifernati illustri (three vols) 2000–03; contrib. to numerous journals, Bibliotheca Sanctorum, Encyclopedia of the Romantic Era 2004, Encyclopedia of World Geography 2005, Encyclopedia of the French Revolutionary and Napoleonic Wars 2006. *Honours:* Gold Medal Atheste Prize for historical research 2002. *Address:* Via Toscana 51, 06010 Lerchi, Italy (home). *Telephone:* (75) 8554902 (home). *E-mail:* elcif@tiscali.it (home). *Website:* www.elviociferri.it.

CIRESI, Rita; American writer and academic; b. 29 Sept. 1960, New Haven, CT. *Education:* BA, New College, 1981; MA, University of Iowa, 1983; MFA, Pennsylvania State University, 1988. *Career:* Asst Prof. of English, Hollins College, 1992–95; Asst Prof., 1995, Assoc. Prof., 1995–, University of South Florida; mem. American Italian Historical Asscn; Associated Writing Programs; Italian American Writers' Asscn. *Publications:* Mother Rocket, 1993; Blue Italian, 1996; Pink Slip, 1999; Sometimes I Dream in Italian, 2000. Contributions: anthologies, reviews and quarterlies. *Honours:* Master Fellowship, Pennsylvania Council on the Arts, 1989; Flannery O'Connor Award, 1991; Teaching Fellow, Wesleyan Writers Conference, 1995; William Faulkner Prize, 1997. *Address:* c/o Department of English, University of South Florida, Tampa, FL 33634, USA.

CISNEROS, Sandra, BA; American writer and poet; b. 20 Dec. 1954, Chicago, IL. *Education:* Loyola Univ. *Publications:* Bad Boys 1980, The House on Mango Street 1983, The Rodrigo Poems 1985, My Wicked, Wicked Ways 1987, Woman Hollering Creek and Other Stories 1991, Hairs-Pelitos 1994, Loose Women 1994, Caramelo 2002; contrib. to periodicals. *Honours:* National Endowment for the Arts Fellowships 1982, 1987, American Book Award 1985, Lannan Foundation Award 1991, John D. and Catherine T. MacArthur Foundation Fellowship 1995. *Literary Agent:* Susan Bergholz Literary Services, 17 W 10th Street, Suite 5, New York, NY 10011, USA.

CIXOUS, Hélène, DèsSc; French academic and author; b. 5 June 1937, Oran, Algeria; d. of Georges Cixous and Eve Klein; one s. one d. *Education:* Lycée d'Alger, Lycée de Sceaux, Sorbonne. *Career:* mem. staff. Univ. of Bordeaux 1962–65; Asst Lecturer, Sorbonne 1965–67; Lecturer, Univ. of Paris X (Nanterre) 1967–68; helped found Univ. of Paris VIII (Vincennes) 1968, Chair. and Prof. of Literature 1968–, Founder and Dir Centre d'Etudes Féminines 1974–; Co-Founder of journal Poétique 1969. *Theatre:* Portrait de Dora 1976, Le nom d'Oedipe 1978, La prise de l'école de Madhubaï 1984, L'Histoire terrible mais inachevée de Norodom Sihanouk, roi du Cambodge 1985, L'Indiade ou l'Inde de leurs rêves 1987, On ne part pas on ne revient pas 1991, Voile noire voile blanche 1994, L'Histoire qu'on ne connaîtra jamais 1994, La Ville Parjure ou le Réveil des Erinyes 1994, Tambours sur la digue 1999 (Molière Award 2000), Rouen la trentième nuit de mai 31 2001. *Publications* include: Le Prénom de Dieu 1967, Dedans 1969, Le Troisième corps, Les Commencements 1970, Un vrai jardin 1971, Neutre 1972, Tombe, Portrait du Soleil 1973, Révolutions pour plus d'un Faust 1975, Souffles 1975, La 1976, Partie 1976, Angst 1977, Préparatifs de noces au-delà de l'abîme 1978, Vivre l'orange 1979, Ananké 1979, Illa 1980, With ou l'art de l'innocence 1981, Limonade tout était si infini 1982, Le Livre de Promethea 1983, Manne 1988, Jours de l'An 1990, L'Ange au secret 1991, Déluge 1992, Beethoven à jamais 1993, La fiancée juive 1995, Messie 1996, Or, les lettres de mon père 1997, Osnabrück 1999, Les Rêveries de la femme sauvage 2000, Le Jour où je n'étais pas là 2000, Portrait de Jacques Derrida en jeune saint juif 2001, Benjamin à Montaigne, il ne faut pas le dire 2001, Manhattan. Lettres de la Préhistoire 2002; Essays: L'exil de James Joyce 1969, Prénoms de personne 1974, La Jeune née 1975, La venue à l'écriture 1977, Entre l'écriture 1986, L'heure de Clarice Lispector 1989, Reading with Clarice Lispector 1990, Readings, the Poetics of Blanchot, Joyce, Kafka, Lispector, Tsvetaeva 1992, Three Steps on the Ladder of Writing 1993, Photos de racines 1994, Stigmata 1998, Escaping Texts 1998. *Honours:* Southern Cross of Brazil 1989; Chevalier de la Légion d'honneur 1994; Officier Ordre nat. du Mérite 1998; Dr hc (Queen's Univ., Kingston, Canada) 1991, (Edmonton, Canada) 1992, (York, UK) 1993, (Georgetown, Washington, DC, USA) 1995, (Northwestern, Chicago, USA) 1996; Prix Médicis 1969, Prix des critiques for best theatrical work of the year 1994, 2000, Amb. of Star Awards, Pakistan 1997. *Address:* Éditions Galilée, 9 rue Linné, 75005 Paris (office); Centre d'études féminines, Université Paris VIII, 2 rue de la Liberté, 93526 Saint-Denis cedex 2, France.

CLANCY, Joseph Patrick Thomas, BA, MA, PhD; American teacher, writer and poet; b. 8 March 1928, New York, NY; m. Gertrude Wiegand 1948; four s. four d. *Education:* Fordham University. *Career:* Faculty, 1948, Prof., 1962, Marymount Manhattan College; mem. American Literary Trans' Asscn; Dramatists' Guild; Yr Academi Gymreig; Eastern States Celtic Asscn; St Davids Society of New York. *Publications:* The Odes and Epodes of Horace, 1960; Medieval Welsh Lyrics, 1965; The Earliest Welsh Poems, 1970; 20th Century Welsh Poems, 1982; Gwyn Thomas: Living a Life, 1982; The Significance of Flesh: Poems, 1950–83, 1984; Bobi Jones: Selected Poems, 1987. Contributions: Poetry Wales; Planet; Anglo Welsh Review; Book News from Wales; Epoch; College English; America. *Honours:* American Philosophical Society Fellowships, 1963, 1968; National Trans. Centre Fellowship, 1968; Welsh Arts Council, Literature Award, 1971, Major Bursary, 1972; National Endowment for the Arts Trans. Fellowship, 1983; St Davids Society of New York Annual Award, 1986.

CLANCY, Laurence James; Australian academic and writer; b. 2 Dec. 1942, Melbourne, Vic.; m. (divorced); two s. *Education:* BA, Melbourne University, 1964; MA, La Trobe University, 1973. *Career:* mem. PEN International. *Publications:* A Collapsible Man, 1975; The Wife Specialist, 1978; Xavier Herber, 1981; Perfect Love, 1983; The Novels of Vladimir Nabokov, 1984; City to City, 1989; A Reader's Guide to Australian Fiction, 1992; The Wild Life Reserve, 1994. Contributions: newspapers and journals. *Honours:* Co-Winner, National Book Council Award, 1975; Australian Natives Asscn Award, 1983. *Address:* 227 Westgarth Street, Northcote, Vic. 3070, Australia.

CLANCY, Thomas (Tom) L., Jr, BA; American writer; b. 12 March 1947, Baltimore, Md; m. 1st Wanda Thomas 1969 (divorced 1998); one s. three d.; m. 2nd Alexandra Marie Llewellyn 1999. *Education:* Loyola Coll. *Career:* co-founder of computer game developer, Red Storm Entertainment 1996 (company later sold, but continues to use his name). *Publications:* The Hunt for Red October 1984, Red Storm Rising 1986, Patriot Games 1987, Cardinal of the Kremlin 1988, Clear and Present Danger 1989, The Sum of all Fears 1991, Without Remorse 1992, Submarine 1993, Debt of Honour 1994, Tom Clancy's Op Centre (with Steve Pieczenik) 1994, Reality Check 1995, Games of State: Op Centre 03 (with Steve Pieczenik) 1996, Tom Clancy's Op Centre II (with Steve Pieczenik) 1996, Executive Orders 1996, Into the Storm (with Fred Franks Jr) 1997, Rainbow Six 1998, Carrier 1999, The Bear and the Dragon 2000, Red Rabbit 2002, The Teeth of the Tiger 2003, Battle Ready (with Tony Zinni and Tony Koltz) 2004. *Address:* c/o Michael Joseph Ltd, 80 Strand, London, WC2R 0RL, England.

CLARE, Ellen (see Sinclair, Olga Ellen)

CLARK, Anne (see Amor, Anne Clark)

CLARK, Brian Robert, BA, FRSL; British dramatist; b. 3 June 1932, Bournemouth, England; m. 1st Margaret Paling 1961; two s.; m. 2nd Anita Modak 1983; one step-s. one step-d.; m. 3rd Cherry Potter 1990. *Education:* Redland College of Education, Bristol, Central School of Speech and Drama, London, Nottingham University. *Career:* Staff Tutor in Drama, University of Hull, 1966–70; Founder, Amber Lane Press, 1978. *Publications:* Group Theatre, 1971; Whose Life is it Anyway?, 1978; Can You Hear Me at the Back?, 1979; Post Mortem, 1979; The Petition, 1986; In Pursuit of Eve–A dramatic sonnet sequence, 2001. Other: Over 30 television plays, 1971–; several stage plays. *Honours:* Society of West Theatre Award for Best Play 1977.

CLARK, Candida; British writer; *Lecturer in Creative Writing, Birkbeck University of London;* b. 1970. *Education:* Univ. of Cambridge. *Career:* worked as film scriptwriter, TV arts presenter; West Midlands Arts Fellow Warwick Writing Programme 2001; currently Lecturer in Creative Writing, Birkbeck Univ. of London; Arts and Cultures Ed. online current affairs magazine, openDemocracy.net; Mentor Arvon Foundation's post-MA masterclass series. *Publications:* novels: The Last Look 1998, The Constant Eye 2000, The Mariner's Star 2002, Ghost Music 2003, A House of Light 2005, The Chase 2006; contrib. reviews to The Observer, The Daily Telegraph, poetry and short fiction in various anthologies, newspapers and magazines. *Address:* School of English & Humanities, Birkbeck, University of London, Malet Street, London, WC1E 7HX, England (office). *Telephone:* (20) 7679-1030.

CLARK, Curt (see Westlake, Donald Edwin)

CLARK, David Ridgley, BA, MA, PhD; American academic and writer; b. 17 Sept. 1920, Seymour, CT; m. Mary Adele Matthieu 1948; two s. two d. *Education:* Wesleyan Univ., Yale Univ. *Career:* instructor 1951–57, Asst Prof. 1957–58, Assoc. Prof. 1958–65, Prof. 1965–85, Univ. of Massachusetts; Visiting Prof. St Mary's Coll., Notre Dame, IN 1985–87, Williams Coll., Williamstown, MA 1989–91; mem. American Conference for Irish Studies, Int. Asscn for the Support of Anglo-Irish Literature, MLA of America. *Publications:* A Curious Quire 1962, W. B. Yeats and the Theatre of Desolate Reality 1965, Irish Renaissance 1965, Dry Tree 1966, Reading Poetry (with Fred B. Millett and Arthur Hoffman 1970, Riders to the Sea 1970, A Tower of Polished Black Stones: Early Versions of the Shadowy Waters 1971, Twentieth Century Interpretations of Murder in the Cathedral 1971, Druid Craft 1971, Lyric Resonance 1972, That Black Day: The Manuscripts of Crazy Jane on the Day of Judgement 1980, Yeats at Songs and Choruses 1983, W. B. Yeats: The Writing of Sophocles' King Oedipus (with James McGuire) 1989, W. B. Yeats: The Winding Stair (1929): Manuscript Materials 1995, W. B. Yeats: Words for Music Perhaps and Other Poems (1932): Manuscript Materials 1999, The Collected Works of W. B. Yeats, Vol. II, The Plays 2001, Parnell's Funeral and Other Poems, from A Full Moon in March: Manuscript Materials 2003. *Honours:* W.B. Yeats Soc. of New York M. L. Rosenthal Award 2004. *Address:* 481 Holgerson Road, Sequim, WA 98382, USA.

CLARK, Eric; British author and journalist; b. 29 July 1937, Birmingham; s. of Horace Clark and Hilda Milchley; m. Frances Robina Grant 1958 (divorced 1971); m. 2nd Marcelle Bernstein 1972; one s. two d. *Education:* Handsworth Grammar School, Birmingham. *Career:* staff of various newspapers including Daily Mail, The Guardian, The Observer until 1972; Full-time Author, 1972–; mem. Society of Authors, Authors' Guild, PEN International UK Centre (Fellow), Nat. Union of Journalists, Int. Fed. of Journalists, Mystery Writers of America. *Publications:* Len Deighton's London Dossier (co-author), 1967; Everybody's Guide to Survival, 1969; Corps Diplomatique, 1973, US edn as Diplomat, 1973; Black Gambit, 1978; The Sleeper, 1979; Send in the Lions, 1981; Chinese Burn, 1984, US edn as China Run, 1984; The Want Makers (Inside the Hidden World of Advertising), 1988; Hide and Seek, 1994; The Real Toy Story, 2006. Contributions: Observer; Sunday Times; Daily Mail; Daily Telegraph; Washington Post; Los Angeles Times; Melbourne Age. *Address:* c/o Bill Hamilton, A. M. Heath Agency, 6 Warwick Court, London WC1R 5DJ, England.

CLARK, Johnson (John) Pepper, BA; Nigerian poet, dramatist and academic; b. 3 April 1935, Kiagbodo; s. of Fuludu Bekederemo Clark; m. Ebunoluwa Bolajoko Odutola; one s. three d. *Education:* Govt Coll. Ughelli, Univ. Coll. Ibadan, Princeton Univ. *Career:* Ed. The Horn (Ibadan) 1958; head of features, editorial writer Express Group of Newspapers, Lagos 1961–62; Research Fellow Inst. of African Studies, Univ. of Lagos 1963–64, Lecturer, Dept of English 1965–69, Sr Lecturer 1969–72, Prof. of English 1972–80; consultant UNESCO 1965–67; Ed. Black Orpheus (journal) 1965–78; Visiting Distinguished Fellow, Center for Humanities, Wesleyan Univ., Conn. 1975–76; Visiting Research Prof., Inst. of African Studies, Univ. of Ibadan 1979–80; Distinguished Visiting Prof. of English, Writer in Residence, Lincoln Univ., Pa 1989; Visiting Prof. of English, Yale Univ., Conn. 1990; Trustee, mem. Petroleum (Special) Trust Fund and Man. Bd, Abuja 1995–; mem. Nat. Council of Laureates (Nigeria) 1992. *Drama includes:* Song of a Goat 1961, Three Plays 1964, Ozidi 1968, The Bikoroa Plays 1985, The Wives' Revolt. *Poetry published includes:* Poems 1962, A Reed in the Tide 1965, Casualties

1970, A Decade of Tongues 1981, State of the Union 1985, Mandela and Other Poems 1988, A Lot From Paradise 1997. *Other publications:* America, Their America 1964, The Example of Shakespeare 1970, Transcription and Translation from the Oral Tradition of the Izon of the Niger Delta; The Ozidi Saga (trans.) 1977, The Hero as a Villain 1978. *Honours:* Nigerian Nat. Merit Award, Nigerian Nat. Order of Merit; Foundation Fellow Nigerian Acad. of Letters 1996. *Address:* 23 Oduduwa Crescent, GRA, Ikeja, Lagos; Okemeji Place, Funama, Kiagbodo, Burutu Local Government Area, Delta State, Nigeria. *Telephone:* (1) 497-8436 (Lagos). *Fax:* (1) 497-8463 (Lagos).

CLARK, Jonathan Charles Douglas, PhD, FRHistS; British historian and academic; *Joyce and Elizabeth Hall Distinguished Professor of British History, University of Kansas*; b. 28 Feb. 1951, London; s. of Ronald James Clark and Dorothy Margaret Clark; m. Katherine Redwood Penovich 1996. *Education:* Univ. of Cambridge. *Career:* Research Fellow, Peterhouse, Cambridge 1977–81; Research Fellow, The Leverhulme Trust; Fellow, All Souls Coll., Oxford 1986–95, Sr Research Fellow 1995; Joyce and Elizabeth Hall Distinguished Prof. of British History, Univ. of Kan., USA 1995–; Visiting Prof., Cttee on Social Thought, Univ. of Chicago 1993; Visiting Prof., Forschungszentrum Europäische Aufklärung, Potsdam 2000, Univ. of Northumbria 2001–03; Visiting Distinguished Lecturer, Univ. of Manitoba 1999; mem. Ecclesiastical History Soc., Church of England Record Soc., N American Conf. on British Studies, British Soc. for Eighteenth Century Studies. *Publications:* The Dynamics of Change 1982, English Society 1688–1832 1985, Revolution and Rebellion 1986; The Memoirs and Speeches of James, 2nd Earl Waldegrave (ed.) 1988, Ideas and Politics in Modern Britain (ed.) 1990, The Language of Liberty 1660–1832 1993, Samuel Johnson 1994, Edmund Burke's Reflections on the Revolution in France (ed.) 2001, English Society 1660–1832 (revised edn) 2000, Samuel Johnson in Historical Context (jt ed.) 2002, Our Shadowed Present 2003; articles on British and American history. *Address:* Department of History, University of Kansas, 1445 Jayhawk Boulevard, Lawrence, KS 66045-7590, USA (office). *Telephone:* (785) 864-3569 (office). *Fax:* (785) 864-5046 (office). *E-mail:* jcdclark@ku.edu (office). *Website:* www.history.ku.edu (office).

CLARK, LaVerne Harrell, BA, MA, MFA; American writer, photographer and lecturer; b. 6 June 1929, Smithville, Tex.; s. of (James) Boyce Harrell and (Isabella) Belle Harrell (née Bunte); m. L. D. Clark 1951. *Education:* Texas Woman's Univ., Columbia Univ., Univ. of Arizona. *Career:* reporter and librarian, Fort Worth Press 1950–51; Sales and Advertising Dept, Columbia Univ. Press 1951–53; Asst Promotion News Dept, Episcopal Diocese, New York 1958–59; Founding Dir, Poetry Centre, Univ. of Arizona 1962–66, photographer 1966–99; mem. Texas Inst. of Letters, PEN, Nat. League of American Pen Women, Western Writers of America, Soc. of Southwestern Authors, Mari Sandoz Heritage Soc. (Hon. Bd mem.), Westerners International, Women in Communications, Women Writing the West, Golden Key Honor Soc. *Photographic work:* many published photographs, including book illustrations and informal portraits of over 500 well-known American poets and writers. *Exhibition:* Photographic Portraits, 20th Century Poets, Texas Woman's Univ. Main Library Gallery, Denton, Tex. *Television:* 1970s documentary on her book, They Sang for Horses (KUAT-TV, Univ. of Arizona, Tucson), documentary, The Writing Life, with husband, writer, L. D. Clark (BCAT-TV, Bastrop, Tex.) 2001. *Publications:* They Sang for Horses 1966, (revised edn) 2001, The Face of Poetry 1976, Focus 101 1979, Revisiting the Plains Indians Country of Mari Sandoz 1979, The Deadly Swarm and Other Stories 1985, Keepers of the Earth 1997, Mari Sandoz's Native Nebraska 2000; contribs to Let's Hear It: Stories by 21 Texas Women Writers 2003 and to periodicals and anthologies. *Honours:* American Philosophical Soc. grant 1967–69, Univ. of Chicago Folklore Prize 1967, Biennial Letters Contest Non-Fiction Award 1968, Distinguished Alumna Award 1973, Julian Ocean Literary Prize 1984, Westerners International Philip A. Danielson Award 1992, Western Writers of America Award for Best First Novel 1998, 19 awards from Nat. League of American Pen Women 1967–94. *Address:* 604 Main Street, Smithville, TX 78957, USA (home). *E-mail:* lhldclark@aol.com (home). *Website:* www.writersregister.com/artists/TX7; www.artisticnetwork.net/artist/349.

CLARK, Mary Higgins, BA; American writer and business executive; b. 24 Dec. 1931, New York; d. of Luke Higgins and Nora Durkin; m. Warren Clark 1949 (died 1964); two s. three d. *Education:* Fordham Univ. *Career:* advertising asst Remington Rand 1946; stewardess, Pan Am 1949–50; radio scriptwriter, producer Robert G. Jennings 1965–70; Vice-Pres., Pnr, Creative Dir, Producer Radio Programming, Aerial Communications, New York 1970–80; Chair. and Creative Dir D.J. Clark Enterprises, New York 1980–; mem. American Acad. of Arts and Sciences, Mystery Writers of America, Authors League. *Publications:* Aspire to the Heavens, A Biography of George Washington 1969, Where Are the Children? 1976, A Stranger is Watching 1978, The Cradle Will Fall 1980, A Cry in the Night 1982, Stillwatch 1984, Weep No More, My Lady 1987, While My Pretty One Sleeps 1989, The Anastasia Syndrome 1989, Loves Music, Loves to Dance 1991, All Around the Town 1992, I'll Be Seeing You 1993, Remember Me 1994, The Lottery Winner 1994, Bad Behavior 1995, Let Me Call You Sweetheart 1995, Silent Night 1996, Moonlight Becomes You 1996, My Gal Sunday 1996, Pretend You Don't See Her 1997, The Plot Thickens 1997, You Belong to Me 1998, All Through the Night 1998, We'll Meet Again 1999, Before I Say Good-Bye 2000, Deck the Halls (with Carol Higgins Clark) 2000, Daddy's Little Girl 2002, On the Street Where You Live 2002, Mount Vernon Love Story: A Novel of George and Martha Washington 2002, The Second Time Around 2003, Nighttime is My Time 2004, Two Little Girls in Blue 2006. *Honours:* several hon. degrees; Grand Prix de Littérature Policière, France 1980. *Address:* 210 Central Park South, New York, NY 10019, USA.

CLARK, Patricia Denise, (Claire Lorrimer, Patricia Robins, Susan Patrick); British writer and poet; b. 1 Feb. 1921, Hove, Sussex. *Career:* mem. Soc. of Authors, Romantic Novelists' Asscn. *Publications:* as Claire Lorrimer: A Voice in the Dark 1967; The Shadow Falls 1974, Relentless Storm 1975, The Secret of Quarry House 1976, Mavreen 1976, Tamarisk 1978, Chantal 1980, The Garden (a cameo) 1980, The Chatelaine 1981, The Wilderling 1982, Last Year's Nightingale 1984, Frost in the Sun 1986, House of Tomorrow (biog.) 1987, Ortolans 1990, The Spinning Wheel 1991, Variations (short stories) 1991, The Silver Link 1993, Fool's Curtain 1994, Beneath the Sun 1996, Connie's Daughter 1997, The Reunion 1997, The Woven Thread 1998, The Reckoning 1998, Second Chance 1998, An Open Door 1999, Never Say Goodbye 2000, Search for Love 2000, For Always 2001, The Faithful Heart 2002 Deception 2003, Over My Dead Body 2003, Troubled Waters 2004, Dead Centre 2005, Infatuation 2007, You Never Know (autobiography) 2007; as Patricia Robins: To the Stars 1944, See No Evil 1945, Three Loves 1949, Awake My Heart 1950, Beneath the Moon 1951, Leave My Heart Alone 1951, The Fair Deal 1952, Heart's Desire 1953, So This is Love 1953, Heaven in Our Hearts 1954, One Who Cares 1954, Love Cannot Die 1955, The Foolish Heart 1956, Give All to Love 1956, Where Duty Lies 1957, He Is Mine 1957, Love Must Wait 1958, Lonely Quest 1959, Lady Chatterley's Daughter 1961, The Last Chance 1961, The Long Wait 1962, The Runaways 1962, Seven Loves 1962, With All My Love 1963, The Constant Heart 1964, Second Love 1964, The Night is Thine 1964, There Is But One 1965, No More Loving 1965, Topaz Island 1965, Love Me Tomorrow 1966, The Uncertain Joy 1966, The Man Behind the Mask 1967, Forbidden 1967, Sapphire in the Sand 1968, Return to Love 1968, Laugh on Friday 1969, No Stone Unturned 1969, Cinnabar House 1970, Under the Sky 1970, The Crimson Tapestry 1972, Play Fair with Love 1972, None But He 1973, Fulfilment 1993, Forsaken 1993, Forever 1993, The Legend 1997. *Address:* Chiswell Barn, Marsh Green, Edenbridge, Kent, TN8 5PR, England. *Website:* www.clairelorrimer.com.

CLARKE, Sir Arthur Charles, Kt, CBE, BSc; British writer and underwater explorer; b. 16 Dec. 1917, Minehead, Somerset; s. of Charles Wright Clarke and Nora Mary Willis; m. Marilyn Mayfield 1953 (divorced 1964). *Education:* Huish's Grammar School, Taunton and King's Coll., London. *Career:* auditor HM Exchequer and Audit Dept 1936–41; RAF 1941–46; Inst. of Electrical Engineers 1949–50; Technical Officer on first G.C.A. radar 1943; originated communications satellites 1945; Chair. British Interplanetary Soc. 1947–50, 1953; Asst Ed. Physics Abstracts 1949–50; engaged on underwater exploration on Great Barrier Reef of Australia and coast of Ceylon (Sri Lanka) 1954–; has lived in Sri Lanka since 1956; Chancellor, Univ. of Moratuwa, Sri Lanka, 1979–2002, Int. Space Univ. 1989–2002; Vikram Sarabhai Prof., Physical Research Lab., Ahmedabad 1980; extensive lecturing, radio and TV, UK and USA; Dir Rocket Publishing Co. (UK), Underwater Safaris Sri Lanka; Trustee, Spaceguard Foundation, Inst. of Integral Educ. Sri Lanka; mem. Royal Asiatic Soc., British Astronomical Asscn, Science Fiction Writers of America, Astronomical Soc. of the Pacific; Fellow, King's Coll. London, Royal Astronomical Soc., Int. Space Hall of Fame 1989, Int. Aerospace Hall of Fame 1989; Patron, British Sub-Aqua Club, Sri Lanka Asscn for Advancement of Science, Sri Lanka Animal Welfare Asscn, Science Fiction Foundation, Arthur C. Clarke Inst. for Modern Techs Sri Lanka, Dian Fossey Gorilla Fund, Sri Lanka Astronomical Asscn, Earthkind, Rehabilitation Hospital Soc. Ltd Sri Lanka; Vice-Patron, British Polio Fellowship; bd mem., Nat. Space Soc. (USA), IAU (SETI) Comm. 51, Lindbergh Award Nominations Cttee (USA), Space Generation Foundation (USA), Planetary Soc. (USA), Buckminster Fuller Inst. *Film screenplay:* 2001: A Space Odyssey (with Stanley Kubrick) 1964–68. *Television work:* Arthur C. Clarke's Mysterious World 1980, World of Strange Powers 1984, Arthur C. Clarke's Mysterious Universe 1994 (all as writer and host). *Publications:* non-fiction: Voices from the Sky 1945, Interplanetary Flight 1950, The Making of a Moon 1951, The Exploration of Space 1951, The Young Traveller in Space (aka Going into Space) 1954, The Exploration of the Moon (with R. A. Smith) 1954, The Coast of Coral 1956, The Reefs of Taprobane 1957, Voice across the Sea 1958, Boy Beneath the Sea (with Mike Wilson) 1958, The Challenge of the Spaceship 1960, The Challenge of the Sea 1960, The First Five Fathoms (with Mike Wilson) 1960, Indian Ocean Adventure (with Mike Wilson) 1961, Profiles of the Future 1962, Man and Space (with the eds of Life) 1964, The Treasure of the Great Reef (with Mike Wilson) 1964, Indian Ocean Treasure (with Mike Wilson) 1964, Voices from the Sky 1965, The Promise of Space 1968, First on the Moon (with the Apollo XI Astronauts) 1970, Into Space (with Robert Silverberg) 1971, Beyond Jupiter (with Chesley Bonestell) 1972, Report on Planet Three (with the Apollo XI Astronauts) 1972, The View from Serendip 1977, Arthur C. Clarke's Mysterious World (with Simon Welfare and John Fairley, also TV series) 1980, 1984: Spring 1984, Ascent to Orbit: A Scientific Autobiography 1984, Arthur C. Clarke's World of Strange Powers (with Simon Welfare and John Fairley) 1984, The Odyssey File (with Peter Hyams) 1984, Arthur C. Clarke's Chronicles of the Strange and Mysterious (with Simon Welfare and John Fairley) 1987, Astounding Days: A Science Fictional Autobiography 1989, How the World Was One 1992, Arthur C. Clarke's A–Z of Mysteries (with Simon Welfare and John Fairley) 1993, By Space Possessed 1993, The Snows of Olympus 1994, 'Greetings, Carbon-Based Bipeds!' (with Peter Hyams) 1999; fiction: Prelude to Space 1951, The Sands of Mars 1951, Islands in the Sky

1952, Against the Fall of Night 1953, Childhood's End 1953, Expedition to Earth 1953, Earthlight 1955, Reach for Tomorrow 1956, The City and the Stars 1956, Tales from the White Hart (short stories) 1957, The Deep Range 1957, The Other Side of the Sky 1958, Across the Sea of Stars 1959, A Fall of Moondust 1961, From the Oceans, From the Stars 1962, Tales of Ten Worlds (short stories) 1962, Dolphin Island 1963, Glide Path 1963, Prelude to Mars 1965, The Nine Billion Names of God (short stories) 1967, The Lion of Comarre 1968, 2001: A Space Odyssey 1968, The Lost Worlds of 2001 1972, Of Time and Stars 1972, The Wind from the Sun 1972, Rendezvous with Rama 1973, The Best of Arthur C. Clarke 1973, Imperial Earth 1975, The Fountains of Paradise 1979, 2010: Odyssey Two 1982, The Sentinel (short stories) 1984, The Songs of Distant Earth 1986, 2061: Odyssey Three 1988, Cradle (with Gentry Lee) 1988, Rama II (with Gentry Lee) 1989, A Meeting with Medusa (short stories) 1989, Tales from Planet Earth (short stories) 1990, The Ghost from the Grand Banks 1990, More than One Universe (short stories) 1991, The Garden of Rama (with Gentry Lee) 1991, The Hammer of God 1993, Rama Revealed (with Gentry Lee) 1993, Richter 10 (with Mike McQuay) 1996, 3001: The Final Odyssey 1997, Trigger (with Mike Kube-McDowell) 1998, The Light of Other Days (with Stephen Baxter) 2000, Greetings, Carbon-Based Bipeds! 2000, Collected Short Stories 2001, The Other Side of the Sky (short stories) 2003, Time's Eye (with Stephen Baxter) 2004, Sunstorm (with Stephen Baxter) 2005; ed. of various books; contrib. to journals and periodicals. *Honours:* Assoc. Fellow, Third World Acad. of Sciences 1987, Freedom of Minehead, Somerset 1992, Paul Harris Fellow and Hon. Rotary Mem. 2001, Hon. Fellow, British Interplanetary Soc., American Astronautical Asscn, Int. Acad. of Astronautics 1960, AIAA 1976, Inst. of Engineers, Sri Lanka 1983, Ceylon Coll. of Physicians 1991; Hon. DSc (Beaver Coll.) 1971, (Moratuwa) 1979, (Int. Space Univ., France) 2005; Hon. DLitt (Bath) 1988, (Liverpool) 1995, (Baptist Univ. of Hong Kong) 1996; UNESCO Kalinga Prize 1961, Stuart Ballantine Gold Medal, Franklin Inst. 1963, Aviation Space Writers' Asscn Robert Ball Award 1965, AAAS-Westinghouse Science Writing Prize 1969, AIAA Aerospace Communications Award 1974, SFWA Nebula Awards 1973, 1974, 1979, John W. Campbell Award 1974, Hugo Award 1956, 1974, 1980, Galaxy Award 1979, IEEE Centennial Medal 1984, Marconi Int. Fellowship 1982, E. M. Emme Astronautical Literature Award 1984, Vidya Jyothi Medal 1986, SFWA 'Grand Master' 1986, Charles A. Lindbergh Award 1987, Space Explorers' Asscn, Riyadh Special Achievement Award 1989, Int. Science Policy Foundation Medal 1992, Lord Perry Award for Distance Educ. 1992, NASA Distinguished Public Service Medal 1995, BIS Space Achievement Medal and Trophy 1995, Mohamed Sahabdeen Award for Science 1996, Int. Acad. of Astronautics Von Karman Award 1996, Univ. of Illinois Presidential Award 1997, Explorers Club Communications Award 2001, Aerospace Historical Soc. Von Karman Wings Award 2001, Isaac Asimov Memorial Award 2001, Robert A. Heinlein Award 2004, Nat. Arts Council, Sri Lanka Sahithyaratna Lifetime Achievement Award 2005, Sri Lanka-bhimanya Award 2005. *Literary Agent:* David Higham Associates, 5 Lower John Street, Golden Square, London, W1R 3PE, England. *Address:* 25 Barnes Place, Colombo 7, Sri Lanka. *Telephone:* (11) 2699757; (11) 2694255. *Fax:* (11) 2698730.

CLARKE, Austin; Canadian writer; b. 1934, Barbados. *Education:* Univ. of Toronto. *Career:* fmrly journalist and broadcaster, teacher of creative writing and cultural attaché in the USA. *Publications:* novels: Survivors of the Crossing 1964, The Meeting Place 1967, Storm of Fortune 1971, The Bigger Light 1975, The Prime Minister 1977, Proud Empires 1988, The Origin of Waves 1997, The Question 1999, The Polished Hoe 2004; short story collections: Among Thistles and Thorns 1965, When He Was Free and Young and He Used to Wear Silks 1971, When Women Rule 1985, Nine Men Who Laughed 1986, In This City 1992, There are No Elders 1993; memoir: Growing Up Stupid Under the Union Jack 1980. *Honours:* Commonwealth Writers' Prize (UK), W. O. Mitchell Prize (Canada), Giller Prize (Canada). *Literary Agent:* The Bukowski Agency, 14 Prince Arthur Avenue, Suite 202, Toronto, ON M5R 1A9, Canada. *Website:* www .thebukowskiagency.com.

CLARKE, Brenda Margaret Lilian, (Brenda Honeyman, Kate Sedley); British writer; b. 30 July 1926, Bristol, England; m. Ronald John Clarke 1955; one s. one d. *Publications:* The Glass Island 1978, The Lofty Banners 1980, The Far Morning 1982, All Through the Day 1983, A Rose in May 1984, Three Women 1985, Winter Landscape 1986, Under Heaven 1988, An Equal Chance (aka Riches of the Heart) 1989, Sisters and Lovers 1990, Beyond the World 1991, A Durable Fire 1993, Sweet Auburn 1995; as Brenda Honeyman: Richard by Grace of God 1968, The Kingmaker 1969, Richmond and Elizabeth 1970, Harry the King 1971, Brother Bedford 1972, Good Duke Humphrey 1973, The King's Minions 1974, The Queen and Mortimer 1974, Edward the Warrior 1975, All the King's Sons 1976, The Golden Griffin 1976, At the King's Court 1977, A King's Tale 1977, Macbeth, King of Scots 1977, Emma, the Queen 1978, Harold of the English 1979; as Kate Sedley: Death and the Chapman 1991, The Plymouth Cloak 1992, The Hanged Man 1993, The Holy Innocents 1994, The Eve of St Hyacinth 1995, The Wicked Winter 1996, The Brothers of Glastonbury 1997, The Weaver's Inheritance 1998, The Saint John's Fern 1999, The Goldsmith's Daughter 2001, The Lammas Feast 2002, Nine Men Dancing 2003, The Midsummer Rose 2004, The Burgundian's Tale 2005, The Prodigal Son 2006, The Three Kings of Cologne 2007. *Address:* 25 Torridge Road, Keynsham, Bristol, BS31 1QQ (home); David Grossman Literary Agency Ltd, 118b Holland Park Avenue, London, W11 4UA, England (office).

CLARKE, George Elliott, BA, MA, PhD; Canadian poet and playwright; *E. J. Pratt Professor of Canadian Literature, University of Toronto;* b. 1960, Windsor, NS. *Education:* Univ. of Waterloo, Dalhousie Univ., Queen's Univ. *Career:* parliamentary researcher, Toronto 1982–83, parliamentary aide, Ottawa 1987–91; fmr newspaper ed. in Halifax and Waterloo, social worker in Halifax; columnist, Halifax Herald; Lecturer in English and Canadian Studies, Duke Univ. 1994–99; Visiting Seagrams Chair in Canadian Studies, McGill Univ. 1998–99; Prof. of English, Univ. of Toronto 1999–2003, E. J. Pratt Prof. of Canadian Literature 2003–. *Play:* Whylah Falls: The Play 1999. *Publications:* poetry: Saltwater Spirituals and Deeper Blues 1983, Whylah Falls 1990, Provençal Songs 1993, Lush Dreams, Blue Exile: Fugitive Poems 1978–93 1993, Provençal Songs II 1997, Gold Indigoes 2000, Execution Poems 2001, Blue Vancouver 2001, Illuminated Verses 2005; libretti: Beatrice Chancy 1996, Québécité: A Jazz Fantasia in Three Cantos 2003; novel: George and Rue 2005; essays: Sins and Innocence 2002; editor: Other Voices: Writings by Blacks in Canada 1985, Eyeing the North Star: Directions in African–Canadian Literature 1997. *Honours:* Hon. LLD (Dalhousie) 1999, Dr hc (New Brunswick) 2000, (Alberta) 2005; Nova Scotia Arts Council Portia White Prize for Artistic Achievement 1998, Bellagio Center Fellowship 1998, Outstanding Writer in Film and Television 2000, Martin Luther King Jr Award 2004, Pierre Elliott Trudeau Fellows' Prize, Montréal 2005, Univ. of Toronto Distinguished Teaching Award 2005, Univ. of Toronto Black Alumni Asscn Faculty Achievement Award 2005, Univ. of Toronto Undergraduate Teaching Award 2005, Planet Africa TV Renaissance Award 2005. *Literary Agent:* The Bukowski Agency, 14 Prince Arthur Avenue, Suite 202, Toronto, ON M5R 1A9, Canada. *E-mail:* assistant@thebukowskiagency.com. *Website:* www.thebukowskiagency.com.

CLARKE, Gillian, BA; British poet, writer, editor, translator and academic; *Tutor of Writing, University of Glamorgan;* b. 8 June 1937, Cardiff, Glamorgan, Wales; d. of Penri Williams and Ceinwen Evans; m. 2nd David Thomas; one d. two s. (from previous m.) *Education:* Univ. Coll., Cardiff. *Career:* Lecturer, Gwent Coll. of Art and Design, Newport 1975–82; Ed., Anglo-Welsh Review 1976–84; Pres., Ty Newydd (Welsh creative writers' house), Gwynedd 1993–; Tutor in Writing, Univ. of Glamorgan 1993–; appointed 'Capital Poet' of Cardiff, funded by Cardiff City and County Council 2005–, to commemorate Cardiff's 2005 celebrations; Fellow Univ. of Wales, Cardiff 1984; mem. Welsh Acad. (chair. 1988–93). *Publications:* poetry: Snow on the Mountain 1971, The Sundial 1978, Letter From a Far Country 1982, Selected Poems 1985, Letting in the Rumour 1989, The King of Britain's Daughter 1993, Collected Poems 1997, Five Fields 1998, The Animal Wall 1999, Nine Green Gardens 2000, Making the Beds for the Dead 2004; editor: The Poetry Book Society Anthology 1987–88 1987, The Whispering Room 1996, I Can Move the Sea (anthology) 1996; also translations. *Honours:* Hon. Fellow Univ. of Wales, Aberystwyth 1995, Swansea 1996, Lampeter 2002, Hon. MA (Univ. of Wales) 2002; Cholmondeley Award for Poetry 1997, Owain Glyndwr Award for Outstanding Contribution to Arts in Wales 1999. *Address:* Blaen Cwrt, Talgarreg, Llandysul, Ceredigion, SA44 4EU, Wales. *Website:* www.gillianclarke.co.uk.

CLARKE, (Victor) Lindsay, BA; British writer; b. 14 Aug. 1939, Halifax, West Yorkshire, England; m. Phoebe Clare Mackmin 1980; one d. *Education:* King's Coll., Cambridge. *Career:* Co-ordinator of Liberal Studies, Norwich City Coll.; Co-Dir, European Centre, Friends World Coll.; writer-in-residence and Assoc. Lecturer in Creative Writing, Univ. of Wales, Cardiff. *Publications:* Sunday Whiteman 1987, The Chymical Wedding 1989, Alice's Masque 1994, Essential Celtic Mythology 1997, Parzival and the Stone from Heaven 2001, The War at Troy 2004. *Honours:* Whitbread Award for the Novel 1989. *Literary Agent:* PFD, Drury House, 34–43 Russell Street, London, WC2B 5HA, England.

CLARKE, Mary; British editor and writer; b. 23 Aug. 1923, London, England. *Career:* London Correspondent, Dance Magazine, New York 1943–55; Asst Ed. and Contributor, Ballet Annual 1952–63; Asst Ed. 1954–63, Ed. 1963–, Dancing Times; London Ed., Dance News, New York 1955–70; Dance Critic, The Guardian 1977–94 (retd). *Publications:* The Sadler's Wells Ballet: A History and Appreciation 1955, Six Great Dancers 1957, Dancers of Mercury: The Story of Ballet Rambert 1962, Ballet: An Illustrated History (with Clement Crisp) 1973, Making a Ballet (with Clement Crisp) 1974, Introducing Ballet (with Clement Crisp) 1976, Encyclopedia of Dance and Ballet (ed. with David Vaughan) 1977, Design for Ballet (with Clement Crisp) 1978, Ballet in Art (with Clement Crisp) 1978, The History of Dance (with Clement Crisp) 1981, Dancer: Men in Dance (with Clement Crisp) 1984, Ballerina (with Clement Crisp) 1987; contrib. to Encyclopaedia Britannica, New Dictionary of National Biography, newspapers, magazines. *Honours:* Knight, Order of Dannebrog, Denmark 1992; second prize Cafe Royal Literary Prize for Best Book on the Theatre 1955, Royal Acad. of Dancing Queen Elizabeth II Coronation Award 1990, Polish Ministry of Culture Nijinsky Medal 1995. *Address:* 54 Ripplevale Grove, London, N1 1HT, England.

CLARKE, Robert (see Platt, Charles Michael)

CLARKE, Susanna; British writer; b. 1959, Nottingham; pnr Colin Greenland. *Education:* St Hilda's Coll., Oxford. *Career:* fmrly worked in non-fiction publishing and as teacher of English; Ed., Simon and Schuster 1993–2003. *Publications:* short stories: The Ladies of Grace Adieu, in Starlight 1 1996, Stopp't-Clock Yard, in Sandman: Book of Dreams 1996, On Lickerish Hill, in

Black Swan, White Raven 1997, Mrs Mabb, in Starlight 2 1998, The Duke of Wellington Misplaces his Horse, in A Fall of Stardust 1999, Mr Simonelli, or the Fairy Widower, in Black Heart, Ivory Bones 2000, Tom Brightwind, or How the Fairy Bridge was Built at Thoresby, in Starlight 3 2001, Antickes and Frets (New York Times) 31 Oct. 2004, The Ladies of Grace Adieu and Other Stories 2006; novel: Jonathan Strange & Mr Norrell (British Book Award for Newcomer of the Year Award 2005, World Science Fiction Soc. Hugo Award 2005) 2004. *Address:* c/o Bloomsbury Publishing PLC, 38 Soho Square, London, W1D 3HB, England. *Website:* www.jonathanstrange.com.

CLARKSON, Ewan, MA; British writer; b. 23 Jan. 1929, England. *Education:* University of Exeter. *Publications:* Break for Freedom, 1967; Halic: The Story of a Grey Seal, 1970; The Running of the Deer, 1972; In the Shadow of the Falcon, 1973; Wolf Country: A Wilderness Pilgrimage, 1975; The Badger of Summercombe, 1977; The Many Forked Branch, 1980; Wolves, 1980; Reindeer, 1981; Eagles, 1981; Beavers, 1981; In the Wake of the Storm, 1984; Ice Trek, 1986; King of the Wild, 1990; The Flight of the Osprey, 1995. *Address:* Moss Rose Cottage, Preston, Newton Abbot, Devon TQ12 3PP, England.

CLARKSON, J. F. (see Tubb, Edwin Charles)

CLARKSON, Stephen, BA, FRSC; Canadian academic and writer; *Professor of Political Economy, University of Toronto*; b. 21 Oct. 1937, London, England; m. Christina McCall 1978 (divorced); three d. *Education:* Upper Canada Coll., Sorbonne, Univ. of Paris. *Career:* Lecturer, Univ. of Toronto 1964–65, Asst Prof. 1965–67, Assoc. Prof. 1967–80, Prof. of Political Economy 1980–; Sr Fellow, Columbia Univ. 1967–68; Policy Chair., Liberal Party, Ontario 1969–73; Dir, Maison Française de Toronto 1972; Jean Monnet Fellow, European Univ. Inst. 1995–96; Killam Research Fellow 1999–2001; Woodrow Wilson Fellow 2000–01; Sr Fellow, Centre for Int. Governance Innovation 2006; mem. Canadian Inst. of Int. Affairs, Canadian Political Science Asscn, Int. Political Science Asscn, Univ. League for Social Reform (pres.). *Publications:* An Independent Foreign Policy for Canada? (ed.) 1968, L'Analyse Soviétique des problèmes indiens de sous-développement 1970, Visions 2020: Fifty Canadians in Search of a Future (ed.) 1970, City Lib: Parties and Reform in Toronto 1972, The Soviet Theory of Development: India and the Third World in Marxist-Leninist Scholarship 1978, Canada and the Reagan Challenge: Crisis in the Canadian-American Relationship 1982, Trudeau and Our Times, Vol. 1: The Magnificent Obsession (co-author) 1990, Vol. 2: The Heroic Delusion (co-author) 1994, Uncle Sam and Us: Globalization, Neoconservatism and the Canadian State 2002, The Big Red Machine: How the Liberal Party Dominates Canadian Politics 2005; contrib. to scholarly books and professional journals. *Honours:* Rhodes Scholar 1959, Woodrow Wilson Fellow 1961, John Porter Prize 1984, Governor-General's Award for Non-Fiction 1990. *Address:* c/o University College, 15 King's College Circle, Toronto, ON M5S 3G3, Canada. *Telephone:* (416) 978-2682 (office). *Fax:* (416) 978-5566 (office). *E-mail:* stephen.clarkson@utoronto.ca (office).

CLAUDEL, Philippe; French writer and screenwriter; b. 1962, Dombasle-sur-Meurthe; m. Dominique Kucharzewski; one d . *Films:* Sur le bout des doigts (screenplay) 2002, Les Âmes grises (screenplay) 2005. *Publications:* novels: J'abandonne (Prix France Télévision) 2000, Meuse l'oubli (Premier Roman) 2000, Quelques-uns des cent regrets (Prix Marcel Pagnol) 2000, Au revoir Monsieur Friant 2001, Le Bruit des trousseaux 2002, Mirhaela 2002, Barrio Flores 2002, Le Café de l'Excelsior 2002, Les Petites mécaniques (Prix Goncourt de la Nouvelle) 2003, Les Âmes grises (Prix Renaudot 2003, Prix des lectrices de Elle Roman 2004) 2003, Trois petites histoires de jouets 2004, La Petite fille de Monsieur Linh 2005; other: La Mort dans le paysage (with Nicolas Matula) 2002. *Address:* c/o Editions Stock, 31 rue de Fleurus, 75006 Paris, France. *E-mail:* phclaudel@aol.com. *Website:* www.editions-stock.fr.

CLAUS, Hugo; Belgian writer, poet, screenwriter, translator and stage and film director; b. 5 April 1929, Bruges; m. 1st Elly Overzier 1955 (divorced); m. 2nd Sylvia Kristel (divorced); m. 3rd Veerle Claus-De Wit. *Films include:* De Vijanden (dir) 1967, Vrijdag (dir) 1980, Het Sacrament (dir) 1989. *Publications:* Kleine reeks, 1947; Registreren (poems), 1948; De blijde en onvoorziene week (with Karel Appel), 1950; De metsiers (novel, The Duck Hunt), 1950; Zonder vorm van proces, 1950; Tancredo Infrasonic, 1950; Over het werk van Corneille, 1951; De hondsdagen, 1952; Een huis dat tussen nacht en morgen staat, 1953; Natuurgetrouw, 1954; De Oostakkerse gedichten (poems), 1955; Paal en Perk (with Corneille), 1955; Een bruid in de morgen (A Bride in the Morning), 1955; De Koele Minnaar, 1956; Het lied van de moordenaar, 1957; Suiker (play), 1958; De zwarte keizer, 1958; Mama, kijk, zonder handen!, 1959; Een geverfde ruiter, 1961; De dans van de reiger, 1962; Omtrent Deedee, 1963; Love Song (with Karel Appel), 1963; De verwondering (novel), 1963; Karel Appel, schilder (Karel Appel, painter), 1963; De man van Tollund, 1963; Het teken van de Hamster, 1964; Louis Paul Boon, 1964; Oog om oog (with van Sanne Sannes), 1964; Gedichten 1948–1963, 1965; Het landschap, 1965; Die schilderijen van Roger Raveel, 1965; Acht toneelstukken, 1966; Relikwie, 1967; De vijanden, 1967; De avonturen van Belgman, 1967; Morituri, 1968; Masscheroen, 1968; Reconstructie (libretto, with others), 1969; Motet, 1969; Genesis (with Roger Raveel), 1969; Natuurgetrouwer, 1969; Vrijdag (play, Friday), 1969; Tand om tand, 1970; Het leven en de werken van Leopold II (play, The Life and Works of Leopold II), 1970; Heer Everzwijn, 1970; Van horen zeggen, 1970; Dag, jij, 1971; Schola Nostra, 1971; Schola Nostra door Dorothea van Male, 1971; Interieur, 1971; Gebed om geweld, 1972; Het Jaar van de kreeft (novel), 1972; De vossejacht, toonelstuk naar Ben Jonson, 1972; Schaamte (novel), 1972; Figuratief, 1973; In het Wilde Westen, De groene ridder, deel 1, 1973; De paladijnen, De groene ridder, deel 2, 1973; Aan de evenaar, De groene ridder, deel 7, 1973; Pas de deux, 1973; Gekke Gerrit, 1973; Wangebeden, 1973; De groene ridder, 1973; Thuis (Back Home), 1975; Het graf van Pernath, 1976; Het Jansenisme, 1977; Jessica!, 1977; De vluchtende Atalanta, 1977; Het huis van Labdakos (play), 1977; De Wangebeden, 1978; Zwart, 1978; Het verlangen (novel, Desire), 1978; Claustrum, 1979; Fuga, 1979; Gedichten 1969–1978, 1979; Het Teken van de Hamster, 1979; Dertien manieren om een fragment van Alechinsky te zien, 1980; De verzoeking, 1980; Ontmoetingen met Corneille en Karel Appel, 1980; Phaedra, 1980; Een Hooglied, 1981; Jan de Lichte, 1981; Almanak, 1982; Mexico vandaag (with Freddy de Vree), 1982; Het haar van de hond (The Hair of the Dog), 1982; Het verdriet van België (novel, The Sorrow of Belgium), 1983; Serenade, 1984; Blindeman, 1985; Georg Faust (libretto), 1985; Alibi, 1985; De mensen Hiernaast, 1985; Een weerzinwekkend bezoek, 1985; Gevulde contouren, 1985; Wyckaert (with Freddy de Vree), 1986; Bewegen, 1986; Evergreens, 1986; Gedichten van Hugo Claus, 1986; Het verschijnsel, 1986; Sonnetten, 1986; Hugo Claus: Selected Poems, 1986; Bewegen (with van Willy Legendre), 1986; In Kolonos, 1986; Sporen, 1987; Hymen, 1987; Voor Pierre, 1987; Sonnetten, 1987; Mej honderd gedichten, 1987; Chateau Migraine, 1987; Beelden, 1987; Een zachte vernieling, 1988; Het schommelpaard, 1988; Toneel I, 1988; Gilles en de nacht, 1989; Toneel II, 1989; De zwaardvis (novella, The Swordfish), 1989; Kort dagboek, 1989; Perte Totale, 1989; Four Works for the Theatre, 1990; Toneel III, 1991; De Sporen, 1993; Onder de torens, 1993; Toneel IV, 1993; Belladonna (novel), 1994; Gedichten 1948–1993, 1994; De eieren van de kaaiman, 1995; De verlossing, 1996; Visite: Winteravond, 1996; De Geruchten (novel), 1996; Onvoltooid verleden, 1997; Zoek de zeven, 1997; De Komedianten (Pas de deux II), 1997; Oktober '43, 1998; Voor de reiziger, 1998; De aap in Efese, 1998; Het laatste bed, 1998, Verhalen, 1999; Het huis van de liefde, 1999; Wreed geluk, 1999. *Honours:* State Prize for Dutch Letters, Herman Gorter Prize.

CLAVEL, Bernard; French writer; b. 29 May 1923, Lons-le-Saunier; s. of Henri Clavel and Héloïse Dubois; m. 2nd Josette Pratte 1982; three s. (from first marriage). *Education:* primary school. *Career:* left school aged 14 and apprenticed as pâtissier 1937; subsequently held various jobs on the land and in offices; painter and writer since age 15; has written numerous plays for radio and television and contributed to reviews on the arts and pacifist journals. *Publications include:* L'Ouvrier de la nuit 1956, Qui m'emporte 1958, L'espagnol 1959, Malataverne 1960, La maison des autres 1962, Celui qui voulait voir la mer 1963, Le coeur des vivants 1964, Le voyage du père 1965, L'Hercule sur la place 1966, Les fruits de l'hiver 1968, Victoire au Mans 1968, L'espion aux yeux verts 1969, Le tambour du bief 1970, Le massacre des innocents 1970, Le seigneur du fleuve 1972, Le silence des armes 1974, Lettre à un képi blanc 1975, La boule de neige 1975, La saison des loups 1976, La lumière du lac 1977, Ecrit sur la neige 1977, La fleur de sel 1977, La femme de guerre 1978, Le Rhône ou la métamorphose d'un dieu 1979, Le chien des Laurentides 1979, L'Iroquoise 1979, Marie Bon Pain 1980, La bourrelle 1980, Felicien le fantôme (with Josette Pratte) 1980, Terres de Mémoire 1980, Compagnons du Nouveau-Monde 1981, Arbres 1981, Odile et le vent du large 1981, Le Hibou qui avait avalé la lune 1981, L'Homme du Labrador 1982, Harricana 1983, L'Or de la terre 1984, Le mouton noir et le loup blanc 1984, Le roi des poissons 1984, L'oie qui avait perdu le nord 1985, Miserere 1985, Bernard Clavel qui êtes-vous? 1985, Amarok 1986, Au cochon qui danse 1986, L'Angélus du soir 1988, Le grand voyage de Quick Beaver 1988, Quand j'étais capitaine 1990, Retour au pays 1990, Meurtre sur le Grandvaux 1991, La révolte à deux sous 1992, Cargo pour l'enfer 1993, Les roses de Verdun 1994, Le Carcajou 1995, Jésus le fils du charpentier 1996, Contes et légendes du Bordelais 1997, La Guinguette 1997, Le Soleil des morts 1998, Achille le singe 1998, Les Petits bonheurs 1999, Le Commencement du monde 1999, La Louve du Noirmont 2000, Le Cavalier du Baïkal 2000, Histoires de chiens 2000, Brutus 2001, La Retraîte aux flambeaux 2002, La Table du roi 2003, Les Grands malheurs 2004, numerous essays, short stories and children's books. *Honours:* Prix Eugène Leroy, Prix populiste, Prix Jean Macé, Prix Goncourt (for Les fruits de l'hiver) 1968, Grand Prix littéraire de la Ville de Paris 1968, Prix Ardua de l'Université 1997, Prix des maisons de la presse 1998. *Address:* 8 rue Crébillon, 75006 Paris, France (office). *E-mail:* iroquoise.jp@wanadoo.fr (office). *Website:* www.bernard-clavel.com.

CLAYTON, John J., AB, MA, PhD; American fmr academic and writer; *Professor Emeritus of English, University of Massachusetts at Amherst*; b. 5 Jan. 1935, New York, NY; m. 1st Marilyn Hirsch 1956 (divorced 1974); one s. one d.; m. 2nd Marlynn Krebs (divorced 1983); one s.; m. 3rd Sharon Dunn 1984; one s. *Education:* Columbia Univ., New York Univ., Indiana Univ. *Career:* instructor, Univ. of Victoria, BC 1962–63; Lecturer Overseas Division, Univ. of Maryland 1963–64; Asst Prof. of Humanities, Boston Univ. 1964–69; Assoc. Prof. 1969–75, Prof. (now Emer.) of English 1975–, Univ. of Massachusetts at Amherst. *Publications:* Saul Bellow: In Defense of Man 1968, What Are Friends For? (novel) 1979, Bodies of the Rich (short stories) 1984, Gestures of Healing: Anxiety and the Modern Novel 1991, Radiance (collection of stories) 1998, The Man I Never Wanted To Be (novel) 1998, Kuperman's Fire (novel) 2007, Wrestling with Angels (stories) 2007; editor: The D. C. Heath Introduction to Fiction; contrib. to anthologies and periodicals. *Honours:* second prize O. Henry Prize Stories 1995, Ohio State Univ. Award in short fiction 1998, Pushcart Prize 1998, 2006. *Address:* 12

Lawton Road, Leverett, MA 01054, USA. *Telephone:* (413) 548-9645. *E-mail:* jclayton@english.umass.edu. *Website:* www.johnj.clayton.

CLAYTON, Martin David, BA, MA; British art historian and writer; b. 30 Dec. 1967, Harrogate, England. *Education:* Christ's Coll., Cambridge. *Career:* Asst Curator, Royal Library, Windsor Castle. *Publications:* Leonardo da Vinci: The Anatomy of Man 1992, Poussin: Works on Paper 1995, Leonardo da Vinci: A Curious Vision 1996, Canaletto in Venice 2005. *Address:* c/o Royal Library, Windsor Castle, Berkshire, England.

CLEARY, Jon Stephen; Australian author; b. 22 Nov. 1917, Sydney, NSW; s. of Mathew Cleary and Ida F. Brown; m. Constantine E. Lucas 1946 (deceased); two d. (one deceased). *Education:* Marist Brothers School, NSW. *Career:* various jobs, including bush-working and commercial art 1932–40; served in Australian Imperial Forces, Middle East, New Britain, New Guinea 1940–45; full-time writer since 1945, except for three years as journalist, Australian News and Information Bureau, London and New York 1948–51. *Cinema:* The Siege of Pinchgut 1958, The Sundowners 1960, The Green Helmet 1960. *Television includes:* No Friend like an Old Friend (CBS) 1951, Just Let Me Be (ATV) 1958, Bus Stop (Fox) 1967. *Publications include:* two books of short stories 1983; novels: These Small Glories 1945, You Can't See Round Corners 1948, The Long Shadow 1949, Just Let Me Be 1950, The Sundowners 1952, The Climate of Courage 1954, Justin Bayard 1955, The Green Helmet 1957, Back of Sunset 1959, The Siege of Pinchgut 1959, North from Thursday 1960, The Country of Marriage 1961, Forests of the Night 1962, Pillar of Salt 1963, A Flight of Chariots 1964, The Fall of An Eagle 1965, The Pulse of Danger 1966, The High Commissioner 1966, The Long Pursuit 1968, Season of Doubt 1969, Remember Jack Hoxie 1970, Helga's Webb 1971, The Liberators 1971, The Ninth Marquess 1972, Ransom 1973, Peter's Pence 1974, The Safe House 1975, A Sound of Lightning 1976, High Road to China 1977, Vortex 1977, The Beaufort Sisters 1979, A Very Private War 1980, The Golden Sabre 1981, The Faraway Drums 1981, Spearfield's Daughter 1982, The Phoenix Tree 1984, The City of Fading Light 1985, Dragons at the Party 1987, Now and Then, Amen 1988, Babylon South 1989, Murder Song 1990, Pride's Harvest 1991, Dark Summer 1992, Bleak Spring 1993, Autumn Maze 1994, Winter Chill 1995, Endpeace 1996, A Different Turf 1997, Five-Ring Circus 1998, Dilemma 1999, Bear Pit 2000, Yesterday's Shadow 2001, The Easy Sin 2002, Degrees of Connection 2003, Miss Ambar Regrets 2004, Morning's Gone 2006, Four-Cornered Circle 2007. *Honours:* winner, ABC Nat. Play Competition 1945, Crouch Literary Prize 1951, Edgar Award for Best Crime Novel 1974, First Lifetime Award, Australian Crime Writers Soc. 1998, Ned Kelly Award for Best Crime Novel 2003. *Address:* c/o HarperCollins, 23 Ryde Road, Pymble, NSW 2073, Australia.

CLEMENS, Kate (see Mackey, Mary)

CLÉMENT, Paul (see Amette, Jacques-Pierre)

CLIFTON, (Thelma) Lucille; American poet, writer and academic; b. 27 June 1936, Depew, NY; m. Fred James Clifton 1958 (died 1984); two s. four d. *Education:* Howard Univ., Fredonia State Teachers Coll. *Career:* poet-in-residence Coppin State Coll. 1974–79; Poet Laureate of Maryland 1974–85; Prof. of Literature and Creative Writing Univ. of Calif. at Santa Cruz 1985–89; Distinguished Prof. of Literature St Mary's Coll. of Maryland 1989–91, Distinguished Prof. of Humanities 1991–, Hilda C. Landers Endowed Chair in the Liberal Arts 2000–; Blackburn Prof. of Creative Writing Duke Univ. 1998–; mem. Acad. of American Poets (chancellor 1999–), Authors' Guild, Authors' League of America, Int. PEN, Poetry Soc. of America. *Publications:* poetry: Good Times 1969, Good News about the Earth: New Poems 1972, An Ordinary Woman 1974, Two-Headed Woman 1980, Good Woman: Poems and a Memoir 1969–1980, 1987, Next: New Poems 1987, Ten Oxherding Pictures 1988, Quilting: Poems 1987–1990, 1991, The Book of Light 1993, The Terrible Stories 1998, Blessing the Boats: New and Selected Poems 1988–2000 2000; prose: Generations of Americans: A Memoir 1976, over 20 books for children 1970–2001; contribs to anthologies and periodicals. *Honours:* NEA Awards 1969, 1970, 1972, Univ. of Massachusetts Juniper Prize 1980, American Library Asscn Coretta Scott King Award 1984, Loyola Coll. in Maryland Andrew White Medal 1993, named Maryland Living Treasure 1993, Lannan Literary Award for Poetry 1997, Lenore Marshall Poetry Prize 1998, Los Angeles Times Poetry Prize 1998, Lila Wallace/Reader's Digest Award 1999, Nat. Book Award for Poetry 2001, Pushcart Prize 2001, Emmy Award. *Address:* c/o Faculty of Humanities, St Mary's College of Maryland, St Mary's City, MD 20686, USA.

CLOSETS, François de; French writer, journalist and producer; b. 25 Dec. 1933, Enghien-les-Bains; s. of Louis-Xavier de Closets and Marie-Antoinette Masson; m. 1st Danièle Lebrun; one s.; m. 2nd Janick Jossin 1970; one s. one d. *Education:* Lycée d'Enghien, Faculté de Droit de Paris and Inst. d'Etudes Politiques, Paris. *Career:* Ed. then special envoy of Agence France-Presse in Algeria 1961–65; scientific journalist, Sciences et Avenir 1964–, Acualités Télévisées 1965–68; contrib. L'Express 1968–69; Head of Scientific Service, TV Channel 1 1969–72; Head of Scientific and Tech. Service of TV Channel 2 1972; contrib. to Channel 1 1974; Asst Ed.-in-Chief TF1; Co-producer l'Enjeu (econ. magazine) 1978–88; Dir of Econ. Affairs, TFI 1987; Co-producer, Médiations magazine 1987–93; Producer, illustrator "Savoir Plus" for France 2 1992–2000, "Les Grandes Enigmes de la Science" for France 2 1992–2003. *Publications:* L'Espace, terre des hommes, La lune est à vendre 1969, En danger de progrès 1970, Le Bonheur en plus 1974, La France et ses mensonges 1977, Scénarios du futur (Vol. I) 1978, Le monde de l'an 2000 (Vol. II) 1979, Le

Système EPM 1980, Toujours plus 1982, Tous ensemble pour en finir avec la syndicatrie 1985, La Grande Manip 1990, Tant et Plus 1992, Le Bonheur d'apprendre, et comment on l'assassine 1996, Le compte à Rebours 1998, L'Imposture informatique 2000, La dernière liberté 2001, Ne dites pas à Dieu ce qu'il doit faire 2004. *Honours:* Grand Prix du reportage du Syndicat des journalistes et écrivains 1966, Prix Cazes 1974, 7 d'or du meilleur journaliste 1985, Prix Aujourd'hui 1985, Roland Dorgelès Prize 1997. *Address:* France 2, 7 esplanade Henri de France, 75907 Paris Cedex 15 (office); VM Group, 99 rue leblanc, Paris 75015 (office); 1 Villa George Sand, Paris 75016, France (home). *Telephone:* 1-53-90-16-71, ext. 75 (office). *Fax:* 1-45-45-45-33 (office). *E-mail:* f.declosets@france2.fr (office).

CLOUDSLEY, Timothy, MA; British university lecturer, poet and writer; b. 18 Sept. 1948, Cambridge; two s. *Education:* Cambridge Univ., Durham Univ. *Career:* Lecturer in Sociology, Newcastle Univ. 1972–74, Napier Univ., Edinburgh 1974–76, Heriot-Watt Univ., Edinburgh 1976–77, Glasgow Caledonian Univ. 1977–97; mem. of arts and literature org., Open Circle, Glasgow (literary sec. 1990–96). *Publications:* Poems to Light (Through Love and Blood) 1980, Mair Licht (anthology) 1988, The Construction of Nature (social philosophy) 1994, Coincidence (anthology) 1995, Incantations from Streams of Fire 1997, Poems 1998; contrib. to Northlight Poetry Review, Understanding Magazine, Interactions, Romantic Heir, The People's Poetry, Cadmium Blue Literary Journal, Le Journal des Poètes, Dandelion Magazine, Consciousness, Literature and the Arts, The European Legacy, Shadow, Indigenous Affairs; to electronic literary journals www.raunchland.co.uk, www.aber.ac.uk/tfts/journal. *Address:* 10 Battishill Street, Islington, London, N1 1TE, England (home).

CLOUGH, Brenda Wang, BA; American writer; b. 13 Nov. 1955, Washington, DC; m. Lawrence A. Clough 1977; one d. *Education:* Carnegie Mellon University. *Publications:* The Crystal Crown, 1984; The Dragon of Mishbil, 1985; The Realm Beneath, 1986; The Name of the Sun, 1988; An Impossible Summer, 1992; How Like a God, 1997; Doors of Death and Life, 2000. Contributions: Short stories in anthologies and periodicals. *Address:* 1941 Barton Hill Road, Reston, VA 20191, USA. *Website:* www.sff.net/people/Brenda.

CLOUTIER, Cécile, BA, LèsL, MA, PhD; Canadian poet, writer and academic; b. 13 June 1930, Québec, QC; m. Jerzy Wojciechowski 1966; two d. *Education:* Collège de Sillery, Université Laval, Université de Paris, McMaster Univ., Univ. of Toronto, Université de Tours. *Career:* Prof. of French and Québec Literature, Univ. of Ottawa 1958–64; Prof. of Aesthetics and French and Québec Literature, Univ. of Toronto 1964–95, Prof. Emerita 1995–; mem. Asscn des Écrivains de Langue française, PEN Club de France, Société des Écrivains, Société des Gens de Lettres de Paris, Union des écrivaines et des écrivains québécois. *Publications:* Mains de sable 1960, Cuivre et soies 1964, Cannelles et craies 1969, Paupières 1970, Câblogrammes 1972, Chaleuils 1979, Springtime of Spoken Words 1979, Près 1983, Opuscula Aesthetica Nostra: Essais sur l'Esthétique 1984, La Girafe 1984, L'Échangeur 1985, L'Écouté 1986, Solitude Rompue 1986, Lampées 1990, Périhélie 1990, La Poésie de l'Hexagone 1990, Ancres d'Encre 1993, Ostraka; contrib. to various publications. *Honours:* Société des Écrivains de France medal 1960, Centennial Medal, Canada 1967, Gov.-Gen.'s Award for Poetry 1986, Société des Poètes français medal 1994. *Address:* La Chacunière, 44 Farm Greenway, Don Mills, ON M2A 3M2 (home); Department of French Studies, University of Toronto, 50 rue Saint-Joseph, Toronto, M5S 1J4, Canada (office). *Telephone:* (416) 445-6287 (home); (416) 978-7165 (office).

CLUYSENAAR, Anne, (Alice Andrée), BA; Irish academic, poet, songwriter, librettist and painter; b. 15 March 1936, Brussels, Belgium; d. of John Cluysenaar and Sybil Fitzgerald Hewat; m. Walter Freeman Jackson 1976; three step-c. *Education:* Trinity Coll., Dublin, Univ. of Edinburgh. *Career:* Asst Lecturer, Univ. of Manchester 1957–58; reader to (blind) critic and novelist, Percy Lubbock 1959; Librarian, Chester Beatty Library of Oriental Manuscripts, Dublin; Lecturer, King's Coll., Aberdeen 1963–65, Univ. of Lancaster 1965–71, Huddersfield Polytechnic 1972, Univ. of Birmingham 1973–76, Sheffield City Polytechnic 1976–89; part-time Lecturer, Univ. of Wales, Cardiff 1990–2002; founder, Ed. Sheaf 1979; founder Dir Verbal Arts Asscn 1983–86; co-founder and sec. Usk Valley Vaughan Asscn 1995–; founding Gen. Ed., now Poetry Ed., U.V.V.A. journal Scintilla 1997–; Fellow Welsh Acad. 2001. *Publications:* A Fan of Shadows 1967, Nodes 1971, Introduction to Literary Stylistics 1976, Selected Poems of James Burns Singers (ed.) 1977, Double Helix 1982, Timeslips: New and Selected Poems 1997, Henry Vaughan Selected Poems (ed.) 2004, The Hare That Hides Within (co-ed.) 2004; contrib. poems to New Poets of Ireland 1963, Poetry Introduction 4 1978, Virago Book of Love Poetry 1990, Hepworth 1992, Private People 1999, Poetry in the Parks 2000, The White Page 2000, Parents 2000, Blodeuedd 2001, Birdsong 2002, Making Worlds 2003, Agenda 2004; essays in British Poetry Since 1960 1972, The Life of Metrical and Free Verse in Twentieth-Century Poetry 1997, Poets on Poets 1997; contribs to Stand, Planet, New Welsh Review, Poetry Wales and others. *Honours:* Trinity Coll., Dublin Vice-Chancellor's Prize for Poetry. *Address:* Little Wentwood Farm, Llantrisant, Usk, Gwent NP15 1ND, Wales (home). *Telephone:* (1291) 673797 (home). *E-mail:* anne.cluysenaar@virgin.net (home).

COASE, Ronald Harry, BCom, DScEcon; British economist and academic; *Clifton R. Musser Professor Emeritus of Economics, The Law School, University of Chicago;* b. 29 Dec. 1910, London; s. of Henry Coase and Rosalie

Coase; m. Marian Hartung 1937. *Education:* LSE. *Career:* Asst Lecturer, Dundee School of Econs 1932–34; Asst Lecturer, Univ. of Liverpool 1934–35; Asst Lecturer to Reader, LSE, 1935–40, 1946–51; Head, Statistical Division, Forestry Comm. 1940–41; Statistician, later Chief Statistician, Central Statistical Office, Offices of War Cabinet, 1941–46; Prof., Univ. of Buffalo 1951–58; Prof., Univ. of Virginia 1958–64; Ed., Journal of Law and Economics 1964–92; Clifford R. Musser Prof. of Econs, Univ. of Chicago 1964–82, Prof. Emer. and Senior Fellow in Law and Econs 1982–; Fellow, American Acad. of Arts and Sciences; Distinguished Fellow, American Econ Asscn; Corresponding Fellow, British Acad.; European Acad.; Hon. Fellow, LSE, Royal Economic Society. *Publications:* British Broadcasting: a study in Monopoly 1950, The Firm, the Market and the Law 1988, Essays on Economics and Economists 1994. *Honours:* numerous hon. degrees; Rockefeller Fellow, 1948; Senior Research Fellow, Hoover Institution, Stanford Univ. 1977; Nobel Prize for Economic Science 1991. *Address:* University of Chicago Law School, 1111 East 60th Street, Chicago, IL 60637 (office); The Hallmark, Apt 1100, 2960 N Lake Shore Drive, Chicago, IL 60657, USA (home). *Telephone:* (773) 702-7342 (office). *Website:* www.law.uchicago.edu (office).

COATES, Kenneth Sidney, BA; British academic and writer; b. 16 Sept. 1930, Leek, Staffs., England; m. Tamara Tura 1969; three s. three d. (one deceased). *Education:* Univ. of Nottingham. *Career:* Asst Tutor to Sr Tutor, Univ. of Nottingham 1960–80, Reader 1980–89, Special Prof. in Adult Educ. 1990–2004; MEP (Labour Party, then Ind. Labour) 1989–99; Ed. The Spokesman; mem. Bertrand Russell Peace Foundation. *Publications:* Industrial Democracy in Great Britain (with A. J. Topham) 1967, Readings and Witnesses for Workers' Control (co-ed.) 1968, Poverty: The Forgotten Englishman (with R. L. Silburn) 1970, The New Unionism (with A. J. Topham) 1972, Trade Unions in Britain (with A. J. Topham) 1980, Heresies: The Most Dangerous Decade 1984, Trade Unions and Politics (with A. J. Topham) 1986, Think Globally, Act Locally 1988, The Making of the Transport and General Workers' Union (with A. J. Topham) 1991, A European Recovery Programme 1993, Full Employment for Europe (with Stuart Holland) 1995, Common Ownership: Clause Four and the Labour Party 1995, The Right to Work: The Loss of Our First Freedom 1995, Dear Commissioner (ed.) 1996, The Blair Revelation (co-author) 1996, Community Under Attack: The Struggle for Survival in the Coalfield Communities of Britain (co-author) 1997, Straw Wars 2001, Third Way... Where To? (with Michael Barratt Brown) 2001, Tony Blair – The Old New Goes to War 2003, Workers' Control – Another World is Possible 2003, Dealing with the Hydra? 2003, Empire No More! 2004, The Social Europe We Need (with Beatty, Blackburn, Brie and Fothergill) 2004. *Address:* Russell House, Bulwell Lane, Nottingham, NG6 0BT, England (office). *Telephone:* (1159) 784504 (office). *Fax:* (1159) 420433 (office). *E-mail:* elfeuro@compuserve.com (office). *Website:* www .spokesmanbooks.com.

COBEN, Harlan, BA; American writer; b. 4 Jan. 1962, Newark, NJ; m. Anne Armstrong 1988; two s. two d. *Education:* Amherst Coll. *Career:* mem. MWA, Sisters in Crime. *Publications:* novels: Play Dead 1990, Miracle Cure 1991, Deal Breaker (World Mystery Conference Anthony Award for Best Paperback Original Novel 1996) 1995, Drop Shot 1996, Fade Away (MWA Edgar Award for Best Paperback Original Mystery Novel, Shamus Award for Best Paperback Original Novel, Private Eye Writers of America 1997) 1996, Back Spin 1997, One False Move (WH Smith Fresh Talent Award) 1997, The Final Detail 1999, Darkest Fear 2000, Tell No One 2001, Gone For Good (WH Smith Thumping Good Read Award) 2002, No Second Chance 2003, Just One Look 2004, The Innocent 2005, Promise Me 2006, The Woods 2007; short stories: A Simple Philosophy 1999, The Key to My Father 2003. *Literary Agent:* Aaron Priest Literary Agency, 708 Third Avenue, New York, NY 10017, USA. *E-mail:* me@harlancoben.com. *Website:* www.harlancoben.com.

COBURN, Andrew; American writer; b. 1 May 1932, Exeter, NH. *Education:* Suffolk University, Boston. *Publications:* Fiction: The Trespassers, 1974; The Babysitter, 1979; Off Duty, 1980; Company Secrets, 1982; Widow's Walk, 1984; Sweetheart, 1985; Love Nest, 1987; Goldilocks, 1989; No Way Home, 1992; Voices in the Dark, 1994; Birthright, 1997. Contributions: Transatlantic Magazine. *Honours:* Hon. DLitt, Merrimack College, USA, 1986. *Address:* 303 Walnut Street, Westfield, NJ 07090, USA.

COBURN, Donald Lee; American dramatist; b. 4 Aug. 1938, Baltimore, MD; m. 1st Nazlee Joyce French 1964 (divorced 1971); one s. one d.; m. 2nd Marsha Woodruff Maher 1975. *Education:* public schools in Baltimore. *Career:* mem. Authors League of America; Dramatists Guild of America; Société des Auteurs et Compositeurs; Texas Institute of Letters; Writers Guild of America. *Plays:* The Gin Game, 1977; Bluewater Cottage, 1979; The Corporation Man, 1981; Currents Turned Awry, 1982; Guy, 1983; Noble Adjustment, 1986; Anna-Weston, 1988; Return to Blue Fin, 1991. *Screenplays:* Flights of Angels, 1987; A Virgin Year, 1992. *Honours:* Pulitzer Prize in Drama, 1978; Golden Apple, 1978. *Address:* c/o Writers' Guild of America, 555 W 57th Street, New York, NY 10019, USA.

COCKE, Ulla, BA; Swedish magazine editor; b. 14 April 1947, d. of Gert and Lisa Ljungstrom; m. Thomas Cocke 1974; one d. *Education:* Stockholm Univ. *Career:* journalist 1980–; Ed-in-Chief Min Värld 1984, Hemmets Veckotidning weekly magazine 1985. *Address:* Hemmets Veckotidning, Allers Förlag AB, Box 277 10, 115 91 Stockholm, Sweden. *Telephone:* (40) 385 900. *Website:* www .annons.allersforlag.se.

CODINA, Pedro Jeta Ramirez; Spanish journalist and newspaper executive; *Director, El Mundo;* b. 26 March 1952, Logroño; m. 1st Rocío Fernández Iglesias; m. 2nd Agatha Ruíz de la Prada; one s. one d. *Education:* Univ. of Navarre. *Career:* Prof. of Contemporary Spanish Literature, Lebanon Valley Coll., PA, U.S.A. 1973–74; with La Actualidad Económica 1974–76; wrote a weekly column for ABC; corresp. for El Noticiero Universal, Madrid; Dir. of Diario 16 1980; currently Dir. El Mundo. *Address:* El Mundo, Pradillo 42, 28002 Madrid, Spain (office). *Telephone:* (91) 5864800 (office). *Fax:* (91) 5864848 (office). *Website:* www.elmundo.es (office).

CODRESCU, Andrei, BA; American academic, writer, poet, editor and radio and television commentator; *MacCurdy Distinguished Professor of English, Louisiana State University;* b. 20 Dec. 1946, Sibiu, Romania; m. Alice Henderson 1969 (divorced 1998); two s.; m. Laura Cole 2000. *Education:* Univ. of Bucharest. *Career:* MacCurdy Distinguished Prof. of English, Louisiana State Univ. 1966–; commentator, All Things Considered, Nat. Public Radio; Ed., Exquisite Corpse, literary journal. *Film:* Road Scholar (for PBS) 1994. *Publications:* fiction: The Repentence of Lorraine 1994, The Blood Countess 1995, Messiah 1999, Casanova in Bohemia 2002, Wakefield 2004; poetry: Comrade Past and Mister Present 1991, Belligerence 1993, Alien Candor: Selected Poems, 1970–1995 1996, It Was Today 2004; essays: Raised by Puppets Only to be Killed by Research 1987, Craving for Swan 1988, The Disappearance of the Outside: A Manifesto for Escape 1990, The Hole in the Flag: A Romanian Exile's Story of Return and Revolution 1991, Road Scholar: Coast to Coast Late in the Century 1993, The Muse is Always Half-Dressed in New Orleans 1995, Zombification: Essays from NPR 1995, The Dog With the Chip in his Neck: Essays from NPR & Elsewhere 1996, Ay, Cuba! A Socio-Erotic Journey 1999, New Orleans, Mon Amour 2006; editor: American Poetry Since 1970: Up Late 1988, The Stiffest of the Corpse: An Exquisite Corpse Reader, 1983–1990 1990, American Poets Say Goodbye to the 20th Century 1996; numerous syndicated radio and newspaper contributions. *Honours:* George Foster Peabody Award 1995, American Civil Liberties Union Freedom of Speech Award 1995, Romanian Cultural Foundation Literature Prize 1996. *Address:* Department of English, 26 Allen Hall, Louisiana State University, Baton Rouge, LA 70803, USA (office). *Telephone:* (225) 578-2823 (office). *E-mail:* acodrescu@aol.com (office). *Website:* www.codrescu.com.

CODY, James (see Rohrbach, Peter Thomas)

COE, Jonathan, BA, MA, PhD; British writer; b. 19 Aug. 1961, Birmingham, England; m. Janine McKeown 1989. *Education:* Trinity Coll., Cambridge, Warwick Univ. *Career:* fmr legal proofreader. *Publications:* The Accidental Woman 1987, A Touch of Love 1989, The Dwarves of Death 1990, Humphrey Bogart: Take It and Like It 1991, James Stewart: Leading Man 1994, What A Carve Up! 1994, The House of Sleep 1997, The Rotters' Club 2001, The Closed Circle 2004, Like a Fiery Elephant: the Story of B. S. Johnson (BBC Four Samuel Johnson Prize for non-fiction 2005) 2004, The Rain Before It Falls 2007; contrib. to periodicals. *Honours:* John Llewellyn Rhys Prize 1995, Prix du Meilleur Livre Étranger 1996, Writers' Guild Award 1997, Prix Médicis Étranger 1998, Bollinger Everyman Wodehouse Prize 2001. *Literary Agent:* Peake Associates, 14 Grafton Crescent, London, NW1 8SL, England.

COE, Tucker (see Westlake, Donald Edwin)

COELHO, Paulo; Brazilian writer; b. Aug. 1947, Rio de Janeiro. *Education:* law school. *Career:* fmr playwright, theatre director and popular songwriter; imprisoned for alleged subversive activities against Brazilian Govt 1974; regular columnist for O Globo (newspaper) 2007–; elected mem. Brazilian Acad. of Arts 2002–. *Publications:* Arquivos do inferno 1982, O Diário de um mago (trans. as The Pilgrimage, aka The Diary of a Magus: The Road to Santiago) 1987, O Alquimista (trans. as The Alchemist) 1988, Brida 1990, O Dom Supremo (trans. as The Gift) 1991, As Valkírias (trans. as The Valkyries) 1992, Maktub 1994, Na margem do rio Piedra eu sentei e chorei (trans. as By the River Piedra I Sat Down and Wept) 1994, Frases 1995, O Monte Cinco (trans. as The Fifth Mountain) 1996, Cartas de Amor do Profeta (trans. as Love Letters from a Prophet) 1997, Manual do guerreiro da luz (trans. as Manual of the Warrior of Light) 1997, Veronika decide morrer (trans. as Veronika Decides to Die) 1998, Palavras essenciais (trans. as The Confessions of a Pilgrim) 1999, O demônio e a Srta Prym (trans. as The Devil and Miss Prym) 2000, Histórias para pais, filhos e netos (trans. as Fathers, Sons and Grandsons) 2001, Onze minutos (trans. as Eleven Minutes) 2003, O Gênio e as Rosas (trans. as The Genie and the Roses, juvenile) 2004, O Zahir (trans. as The Zahir) 2005, Like the Flowing River (thoughts and short stories) 2006, A Bruxa do Portobello (The Witch of Portobello) 2007. *Honours:* Chevalier, Ordre des Arts et des Lettres 1996, Comendador de Ordem do Rio Branco, Brazil 1998, Chevalier, Légion d'honneur 2000, Order of St Sophia, Ukraine 2004, Cruz do Mérito do Empreendedor Juscelino Kubitschek 2006; Prix Lectrices d'Elle, France 1995, Golden Book Awards, Yugoslavia 1995, 1996, 1997, 1998, 1999, 2000, Flaiano Int. Award, Italy 1996, Super Grinzane Cavour Book Award, Italy 1996, Golden Medal of Galicia, Spain 1999, Crystal Mirror Award, Poland 2000, XXIII Premio Internazionale Fregene, Italy 2001, Bambi Award, Germany 2001; Budapest Prize, Hungary 2005. *Literary Agent:* Sant Jordi Asociados Agencia Literaria SL, Arquitecte Sert no. 31, 5° 1a, 08005 Barcelona, Spain. *Address:* c/o HarperCollins, 77–85 Fulham Palace Road, Hammersmith, London, W6 8JB, England. *E-mail:* autor@paulocoelho .com. *Website:* www.paulocoelho.com.

COETZEE, John Maxwell (J. M.), MA, PhD; South African writer and academic; b. 9 Feb. 1940, Cape Town; one s. one d. *Education:* Univ. of Cape

Town, Univ. of Texas. *Career:* Asst Prof. of English, State Univ. of NY Buffalo 1968–71; Lecturer, Univ. of Cape Town 1972–76, Sr Lecturer 1977–80, Assoc. Prof. 1981–83, Prof. of Gen. Literature 1984–2001, attached to Univ. of Adelaide, Australia 2002–; Prof. of Social Thought, Univ. of Chicago, USA 2001–, Distinguished Service Prof. *Publications:* Dusklands 1974, In the Heart of the Country 1977, Waiting for the Barbarians 1980, Life and Times of Michael K (Booker-McConnell Prize 1983, Prix Femina Etranger 1985) 1983, Foe 1986, White Writing 1988, Age of Iron (Sunday Express Book of the Year Prize 1990) 1990, Doubling the Point: Essays and Interviews (ed. by David Atwell) 1992, The Master of Petersburg (Premio Mondello 1994, Irish Times Int. Fiction Prize 1995) 1994, Giving Offence: Essays on Censorship 1996, Boyhood 1997, The Lives of Animals (lecture) 1999, Disgrace (Booker Prize 1999, Commonwealth Writers Prize 2000) 1999, The Humanities in Africa 2001, Stranger Shores: Essays 1986–1999 2001, Youth 2002, Elizabeth Costello: Eight Lessons 2003, Slow Man (novel) 2005, Inner Workings (essays) 2007, Diary of a Bad Year (novel) 2007. *Honours:* Dr hc (Strathclyde) 1985, (State Univ. of New York) 1989, (Cape Town) 1995, (Oxford) 2002; CNA Literary Award 1977, 1980, 1983, Geoffrey Faber Prize 1980, James Tait Black Memorial Prize 1980, Jerusalem Prize 1987, Prix Meilleur Livre 2002, Premio Grinzane 2003, Nobel Prize for Literature 2003. *Address:* POB 3045, Newton, SA 5074, Australia. *E-mail:* john.coetzee@adelaide.edu.au (home).

COFFEY, Brian (see Koontz, Dean Ray)

COFFEY, Marilyn June; American writer, poet and academic; b. 22 July 1937, Alma, NE; m. 1961 (divorced); one s. *Education:* BA, University of Nebraska, 1959; MFA, Brooklyn College, CUNY, 1981. *Career:* Faculty, Pratt Institute, New York, 1966–69, 1973–90; Adjunct Communication Instructor, St Mary's College, Lincoln, NE, 1990–92; Assoc. Prof. of Creative Writing, Ft Hays State University, 1992–; mem. E. A. Burnett Society, charter mem.; Poets and Writers. *Publications:* Marcella (novel), 1973; Great Plains Patchwork (non-fiction), 1989; A Cretan Cycle: Fragments Unearthed From Knossos (poems), 1991; Creating the Classic Short Story: A Workbook, 1995; Delicate Footsteps: Poems About Real Women, 1995. Contributions: anthologies, journals, reviews, and newspapers. *Honours:* Pushcart Prize, 1976; Master Alumnus, University of Nebraska, 1977; Winner, Newark Public Library Competitions, NJ, 1985, 1987–88; several grants. *Address:* c/o Department of English, Fort Hays State University, Hays, KS 67601, USA.

COFFEY, Shelby, III; American journalist; m. Mary Lee Coffey. *Education:* Univ. of Virginia. *Career:* with Washington Post 1968–85, latterly Asst Man. Ed. for nat. news and Deputy Man. Ed. for features; Ed. US News and World Report 1985–86; Ed. Dallas Times Herald 1986; Deputy Assoc. Ed. Los Angeles Times, subsequently Exec. Ed. 1986–89, Ed. and Exec. Vice-Pres. 1989. *Honours:* Nat. Press Foundation Ed. of the Year 1994. *Address:* c/o Los Angeles Times, Times Mirror Co., Times Mirror Square, Los Angeles, CA 90053, USA.

COFFMAN, Virginia Edith, (Victor Cross, Virginia Du Vaul, Jeanne Duval, Anne Stanfield), AB; American author; b. 30 July 1914, San Francisco, CA. *Education:* University of California at Berkeley. *Publications:* Survivor of Darkness, 1973; The Ice Forest, 1976; Looking Glass, 1979; The Lombard Cavalcade, 1982; Dark Winds, 1985; The Royles (three vols) 1991–94.

COGSWELL, Frederick William; Canadian academic, author, poet, editor and translator; b. 8 Nov. 1917, East Centreville, NB, Canada; m. 1st Margaret Hynes 3 July 1944 (died 2 May 1985); two d.; m. 2nd Gail Fox 8 Nov. 1985. *Education:* BA, 1949, MA, 1950, University of New Brunswick; PhD, University of Edinburgh, 1952. *Career:* Asst Prof., 1952–57, Assoc. Prof., 1957–61, Prof., 1961–83, Prof. Emeritus 1983–, University of New Brunswick; Ed., Fiddlehead Magazine, 1952–66, Humanities Asscn Bulletin, 1967–72; mem. League of Canadian Poets; PEN; Writers Federation of New Brunswick. *Publications:* The Stunted Strong, 1955; The Haloed Tree, 1956; Testament of Cresseid, 1957; Descent from Eden, 1959; Lost Dimensions, 1960; A Canadian Anthology, 1960; Five New Brunswick Poets, 1962; The Arts in New Brunswick, 1966; Star People, 1968; Immortal Plowman, 1969; In Praise of Chastity, 1970; One Hundred Poems of Modern Québec, 1971; The Chains of Liliput, 1971; The House Without a Door, 1973; Against Perspective, 1979; A Long Apprenticeship: Collected Poems, 1980; Pearls, 1983; The Edge to Life, 1987; The Best Notes Merge, 1988; Black and White Tapestry, 1989; Unfinished Dreams: Contemporary Poetry of Acadie, 1990; Watching an Eagle, 1991; When the Right Light Shines, 1992; In Praise of Old Music, 1992; In My Own Growing, 1993; As I See It, 1994; In Trouble With Light, 1996. *Honours:* Order of Canada.

COHAN, Tony, (Anthony Robert Cohan), BA; American writer; b. 28 Dec. 1939, New York, NY; m. 1974; one d. *Education:* Univ. of California. *Career:* mem. Authors' Guild, PEN. *Publications:* Nine Ships 1975, Canary 1981, The Flame 1983, Opium 1984, Agents of Desire 1997, Mexicolor 1997, On Mexican Time 2000, Native State 2003, Mexican Days 2006. *Honours:* Notable Book of the Year 1981. *Address:* PO Box 1170, Venice, CA 90294, USA. *E-mail:* tobo101@cs.com (home).

COHEN, Leonard, BA, CC; Canadian singer and songwriter; b. 21 Sept. 1934, Montreal; s. of Nathan B. Cohen and Masha Klinitsky; two c. *Education:* McGill Univ. *Career:* f. country-and-western band, The Buckskin Boys 1951; initially wrote poetry, winning McGill Literary Award for first collection; moved to New York in early 1960s. *Recordings include:* albums: The Songs of Leonard Cohen 1968, Songs From A Room 1969, Songs of Love and Hate 1971,

Live Songs 1973, New Skin For the Old Ceremony 1974, Greatest Hits 1975, The Best of Leonard Cohen 1976, Death of a Ladies' Man 1977, Recent Songs 1979, Various Positions 1985, I'm Your Man 1988, The Future 1992, Cohen Live 1994, More Best Of 1997, Live Songs 1998, Ten New Songs 2001, Field Commander Cohen 2001, The Essential Leonard Cohen 2002, Dear Heather 2004. *Film:* Leonard Cohen I'm Your Man 2006. *Publications:* Let Us Compare Mythologies (McGill Literary Award) 1956, The Spice-Box of Earth 1961, The Favourite Game (Quebec Literary Prize) 1963, Flowers for Hitler 1964, Beautiful Losers 1966, Parasites of Heaven 1966, Selected Poems 1956–1968 1968, The Energy of Slaves 1972, Death of a Ladies' Man 1978, Book of Mercy (Canadian Authors' Asscn Literary Award) 1984, Stranger Music: Selected Poems and Songs 1993, Book of Longing (poems) 2006. *Honours:* hon. degree (Dalhousie Univ.) 1970, (McGill Univ.) 1992; numerous awards including William Harold Moon Award (Recording Rights Org. of Canada) 1984, Juno Hall of Fame 1991, Gov. Gen.'s Performing Arts Award 1993. *Literary Agent:* 5042 Wilshire Boulevard, Suite 845, Los Angeles, CA 90036, USA.

COHEN, Marcel; French writer; b. 9 Oct. 1937, Asnières. *Education:* École Supérieure de Journalisme and École du Louvre, Paris. *Publications:* Galpa 1969, Malestroit: Chroniques du Silence 1973, Voyage à Waizata 1976, Murs 1979, Du désert au livre: Entretiens avec Edmond Jabès (trans. as From the Desert to the Book) 1981, Miroirs (trans. as Mirrors) 1981, Je ne sais pas le nom 1986, Le grand paon-de-nuit (trans. as The Peacock Emperor Moth) 1990, Lettre à Antonio Saura (translated as In Search of a Lost Ladino: Letter to Antonio Saura) 1997, Assassinat d'un garde 1998, Faits 2002, Faits II 2007; contrib. to anthologies, journals and magazines. *Address:* 197 rue de Grenelle, 75007 Paris, France.

COHEN, Michael Joseph, BA, PhD; British academic and writer; *Lazarus Philips Chair in History, Bar-Ilan University;* b. 29 April 1940, London, England. *Education:* University of London, LSE. *Career:* Lecturer 1972–77, Senior Lecturer 1977–81, Assoc. Prof. 1981–86, Prof. 1986–, Lazarus Philips Chair of History 1990–, Bar Ilan University; Visiting Prof., Stanford University 1977, 1981, Hebrew University, Jerusalem 1978–80, 1981–83, Duke University and University of North Carolina, Chapel Hill 1980–81, University of British Columbia 1985–86; Bernard and Audre Rapaport Fellow, American Jewish Archives, Cincinnati 1988–89; Meyerhoff Visiting Prof. of Israel Studies, University of Maryland, College Park 1992–98; Mem., Institute of Advanced Studies, Princeton 1998; Visiting Prof., San Diego State University 1999, Centre for International Studies, LSE 2002–03. *Publications:* Palestine: Retreat From the Mandate, 1936–45 1978, Palestine and the Great Powers 1945–48 1982, Churchill and the Jews 1985, The Origins of the Arab-Zionist Conflict, 1914–1948 1987, Palestine to Israel: From Mandate to Independence 1988, Truman and Israel 1990, Fighting World War Three from the Middle East: Allied Contingency Plans, 1945–1954 1997, Strategy and Politics in the Middle East 1954–1960: Defending the Northern Tier 2004. Editor: The Weizmann Letters, Vols XX, XXI, 1936–1945 1979, The History of the Founding of Israel, Part III, The Struggle for the State of Israel, 1939–1948, 10 vols 1988, Bar-Ilan Studies in Modern History 1991, British Security Problems in the Middle East During the 1930s: The Conquest of Abyssinia to World War Two (with Martin Kolinsky) 1992, The Demise of Empire: Britain's Responses to Nationalist Movements in the Middle East, 1943–1955 (with Martin Kolinsky) 1998. Contributions: scholarly journals. *Address:* c/o General History Department, Bar-Ilan University, 52900 Ramat-Gan, Israel.

COHEN, Morton Norton, (John Moreton), AB, MA, PhD, FRSL; Canadian academic and writer; b. 27 Feb. 1921, Calgary, AB. *Education:* Tufts Univ., Columbia Univ. *Career:* Tutor to Prof., City Coll., CUNY 1952–81, mem. doctoral faculty, CUNY 1964–81, Deputy Exec. Officer PhD Programme in English 1976–78, 1979–80, Prof. Emeritus 1981–; mem. Lewis Carroll Soc., Lewis Carroll Soc. of North America, Lewis Carroll Soc. of Japan, Century Asscn, New York. *Publications:* Rider Haggard: His Life and Works 1960, A Brief Guide to Better Writing (co-author) 1960, Rudyard Kipling to Rider Haggard: The Record of a Friendship 1965, Lewis Carroll's Photographs of Nude Children (aka Lewis Carroll, Photographer of Children: Four Nude Studies) 1978, The Russian Journal II 1979, The Letters of Lewis Carroll (ed., two vols) 1979, Lewis Carroll and the Kitchins 1980, Lewis Carroll and Alice 1832–1882 1982, The Selected Letters of Lewis Carroll 1982, Lewis Carroll and the House of Macmillan (co-ed.) 1987, Lewis Carroll: A Biography 1995, Reflections in a Looking Glass (A Celebration of Lewis Carroll's Photographs) 1998, Lewis Carroll and his Illustrators 2003; contrib. to many magazines, journals, papers and books. *Honours:* Fulbright Fellow 1954–55, 1974–75, Guggenheim Fellowship 1966–67, Nat. Endowment for the Humanities research grant 1974–75, Guggenheim Foundation publication grant 1979. *Address:* 55 E Ninth Street, Apt 10-D, New York, NY 10003, USA (home); AP Watt Ltd, 20 John Street, London, WC1N 2DR, England (office).

COHEN, Stephen Frand, BA, MA, PhD; American academic and writer; *Professor of Russian Studies and History, New York University;* b. 25 Nov. 1938, Indianapolis, IN; m. 1st Lynn Blair 1962 (divorced); one s. one d.; m. 2nd Katrina vanden Heuvel 1988; one d. *Education:* Indiana Univ., Columbia Univ. *Career:* Instructor, Columbia Coll. 1965–68; Jr Fellow 1965–68, Sr Fellow 1971–73, 1976–77, 1985, Assoc. 1972–85, Visiting Prof. 1973–84, Visiting Scholar 1980–81, Columbia Univ.; Asst Prof. 1968–73, Assoc. Prof. 1973–80, Prof. 1980–98, Prof. Emeritus 1998–, Princeton Univ.; Prof. of Russian Studies and History, New York Univ. 1998–; Contributing Ed., The Nation; mem. American Asscn for the Advancement of Slavic Studies,

American Historical Asscn, American Political Science Asscn, Council on Foreign Relations. *Documentary films:* (with Rosemarie Reed): Conversations with Gorbachev 1994, Russia Betrayed? 1995, Widow of the Revolution 2000. *Publications:* The Great Purge Trial (co-ed.) 1965, Bukharin and the Bolshevik Revolution: A Political Biography, 1888–1938 1973, The Soviet Union Since Stalin (co-ed.) 1980, An End to Silence: Uncensored Opinion in the Soviet Union (ed.) 1982, Rethinking the Soviet Experience: Politics and History Since 1917 1985, Sovieticus: American Perceptions and the Soviet Realities 1985, Voices of Glasnost: Interviews with Gorbachev's Reformers (co-author and co-ed.) 1989, Failed Crusade: America and the Tragedy of Post-Communist Russia 2000, (revised and expanded edn) 2001, The Question of Questions: Why Did the Soviet Union? (in Russian) 2007; contrib. to books, scholarly journals and periodicals. *Honours:* Guggenheim Fellowships 1976–77, 1989, Rockefeller Foundation Humanities Fellowship 1980–81, Nat. Endowment for the Humanities Fellowship 1984–85, Page One Award for Column Writing 1985, Fulbright-Hays Faculty Research Abroad Fellowship 1988–89, Indiana Univ. Distinguished Alumni Award 1998, New York Univ. Award for Excellence in Teaching 2001, Columbia Univ. Harriman (Russian) Inst. Alumnus of the Year 2002. *Address:* Department of Russian Studies, New York University, 19 University Place, New York, NY 10003-4556, USA (office). *Telephone:* (212) 998-8289 (office). *Fax:* (212) 995-4604 (office).

COHN, Samuel Kline, Jr, BA, MA, PhD; American academic and writer; b. 13 April 1949, Birmingham, AL; m. Genevieve A. Warwick 1994, two s. *Education:* Union College, University of Wisconsin at Madison, Università degli Studi di Firenze, Harvard University. *Career:* Asst Prof., Wesleyan University, 1978–79; Asst Prof., 1979–85, Assoc. Prof., 1986–89, Prof. of History, 1989–95, Brandeis University; Visiting Prof., Brown University, 1990–91; Prof. of Medieval History, University of Glasgow, 1995–; mem. American Historical Asscn, Society for Italian Historical Studies. *Publications:* The Laboring Classes in Renaissance Florence, 1980; Death and Property in Siena 1205–1800: Strategies for the Afterlife, 1988; The Cult of Remembrance and the Black Death: Six Renaissance Cities in Central Italy, 1992; Portraits of Medieval and Renaissance Living: Essays in Memory of David Herlihy (ed.), 1996; Women in the Streets: Essays on Sex and Power in the Italian Renaissance, 1996; The Black Death and the Transformation of the West (with David Herlihy), 1996; Creating the Florentine State: Peasants and Rebellion 1348–1434, 1999. Contributions: scholarly books and journals. *Honours:* Hon. FRHistS; Hon. Krupp Foundation Fellowship, 1976; Fulbright-Hays Fellowship, Italy, 1977; Fellow, Center for European Studies, Harvard University, 1977–; National Endowment for the Humanities Research Fellowship, 1982–83; Guest Fellow, Villa I Tatti, Settignano, Italy, 1988–89; Howard R. Marraro Prize, American Catholic Historical Asscn, 1989; Outstanding Academic Book Selection, Choice magazine, 1993; Villa I Tatti Fellowship, 1993–94; Guggenheim Fellowship, 1994–95. *Address:* Department of History (Medieval), 10 University Gardens, Glasgow G12 8QQ, USA. *E-mail:* s.cohn@history.arts.gla.ac.uk.

COKER, Christopher; British academic and writer; *Professor of International Relations, London School of Economics. Career:* NATO Fellow 1981–; currently Prof. of Int. Relations, LSE; adviser to several UK Conservative Party think tanks including Inst. for European Defence and Strategic Studies and Centre for Policy Studies; visiting lecturer, Jt Staff Coll., Royal Coll. of Defence Studies, London, NATO Coll., Rome, Centre for Int. Security, Geneva, Nat. Inst. for Defence Studies, Tokyo; mem. Washington Strategy Seminar, Inst. for Foreign Policy Analysis, Cambridge, MA, Black Sea Univ. Foundation, Moscow School of Politics; fmr Ed. Atlantic Quarterly; fmr mem. Council of Royal United Services Inst. *Publications:* A Nation in Retreat 1991, Britain's Defence Policy in the 1990s: An Intelligent Person's Guide to the Defence Debate 1992, War and the Twentieth Century 1994, Twilight of the West 1997, War and the Illiberal Conscience 1998, Humane Warfare 2001, Waging War without Warriors 2002, The Future of War: the Re-enchantment of War in the Early 21st Century 2004; numerous contribs to books, newspapers and journals, including Wall Street Journal, The Times, Independent, The Spectator, The Times Literary Supplement. *Address:* Department of International Relations, London School of Economics, Houghton Street, London, WC2A 2AE, England (office). *Telephone:* (20) 7955-7387 (office). *E-mail:* c.coker@lse.ac.uk (office). *Website:* www.lse.ac.uk (office).

COLE, Babette, BA; British writer; b. 10 Sept. 1949, Jersey; d. of Frederick Cole and Iris Cole (née Horseford). *Education:* Convent FCJ, St Helier and Canterbury Coll. of Art. *Career:* mem. staff BBC, Children's TV; lived in Okavango Swamps, Botswana 1976; writer of children's books; owns stud farm in UK and breeds and rides show hunters; Fellow Kent Inst. of Art and Design, British Book Awards Acad. *Publications include:* Promise Solves the Problem 1976, Nungu and the Hippo 1978, Nungu and the Elephant 1980, Promise and the Monster 1981, Don't Go Out Tonight 1981, Beware of the Vet 1982, Nungu and the Crocodile 1983, The Trouble with Mum 1983, The Hairy Book 1984, The Trouble with Dad 1985, The Slimey Book 1985, Princess Smartypants 1986, Prince Cinders 1987, The Smelly Book 1987, The Trouble with Gran 1987, The Trouble with Grandad 1988, King Changealot 1988, The Silly Book 1989, Cupid 1989, Three Cheers for Errol 1989, Hurrah for Ethelyn 1991, Beastly Birthday Book 1991, The Trouble with Uncle 1992, Tarzanna 1992, Supermoo! 1992, Bible Beasties 1992, Mummy Laid an Egg (sold one million copies) (Best Illustrated Children's Book of the Year) 1993, Dr Dog 1994, Winni Allfours 1995, Drop Dead 1996, four mini-novelties: My Dog, My Cat, My Fish, My Horse 1997, The Bad Good Manners Book 1997, Two of Everything 1997, four more mini-novelties: My Aunt etc. 1997, Hair in Funny Places 1999, Lady Lupin's Book of Etiquette 2001, True Love 2001, Animals Scare Me Stiff 2002, Mummy Never Told Me 2003, The Wind in the Willows Pop-Up Book, The Hairy Book 2003, That's Why 2006. *Honours:* 2nd Place, Kate Greenaway Prize 1986, 1987, Smarties Prize 1987, Intermediate Side Saddle Rider of the Year 1998. *Literary Agent:* c/o Rosemary Sandberg Ltd, 6 Bayley Street, London, WC1B 3HB, England. *Telephone:* (20) 7304-4110. *E-mail:* babette@babette-cole.com. *Website:* www.babette-cole.com.

COLE, Barry; British writer and poet; b. 13 Nov. 1936, Woking, Surrey; m. Rita Linihan 1959; three d. *Career:* Northern Arts Fellow in Literature, Univs. s of Durham and Newcastle upon Tyne, 1970–72. *Publications:* Blood Ties, 1967; Ulysses in the Town of Coloured Glass, 1968; A Run Across the Island, 1968; Moonsearch, 1968; Joseph Winter's Patronage, 1969; The Search for Rita, 1970; The Visitors, 1970; The Giver, 1971; Vanessa in the City, 1971; Pathetic Fallacies, 1973; Dedications, 1977; The Edge of the Common, 1989; Inside Outside: New and Selected Poems, 1997; Lola and the Train, 1999; Ghosts Are People Too, 2003. Contributions: The Oxford Book of Twentieth Century Verse, British Poetry Since 1945 (anthology). *Address:* 68 Myddelton Square, London EC1rR 1XP, England. *Telephone:* (20) 278-2837 (home). *E-mail:* barryh.cole@virgin.net (home).

COLE, John Morrison; Northern Irish journalist, broadcaster and writer; b. 23 Nov. 1927, Belfast, Northern Ireland; m. Margaret Isobel Williamson 1956; four s. *Education:* University of London. *Career:* mem. Athenaeum Club. *Publications:* The Poor of the Earth, 1976; The Thatcher Years, 1987; As It Seemed to Me: Political Memoirs, 1995. Contributions: Guardian; New Statesman. *Honours:* Granada Television Newspaper Award, 1960; RTS Broadcast Journalist of the Year Award, 1990; BAFTA Richard Dimbleby Award, 1992; Hon. Doctorates, Open University, 1992, Queen's University, Belfast, 1992, University of Ulster, 1992, University of St Andrews, 1993.

COLE, Martina; British novelist; b. Essex, England. *Publications:* Dangerous Lady 1992, The Ladykiller 1993, Goodnight Lady 1994, The Jump 1995, The Runaway 1997, Two Women 1999, Broken 2000, Faceless 2001, Maura's Game 2002, The Know 2003, The Graft 2004, The Take (British Book Awards Worldbooks Crime Thriller of the Year 2006) 2005, Close 2006. *Address:* c/o Hodder Headline, 338 Euston Road, London, NW1 3BH, England. *Website:* www.martinacole.co.uk.

COLE, Peter; American poet and translator; b. 1957, Paterson, NJ. *Career:* Visiting Prof., Wesleyan Univ., Middlebury Coll.; editorial bd mem., Ibis Editions. *Publications:* poetry: Rift 1990, Hymns and Qualms 1998; nine books of translations from Hebrew and Arabic poetry and prose. *Honours:* National Endowment for the Humanities Fellowship, National Endowment for the Arts Fellowship, John Simon Guggenheim Foundation Fellowship; MLA Scaglione Translation Prize, TLS Porjes Hebrew Translation Prize. *Address:* c/o Ibis Editions, PO Box 8074, German Colony, Jerusalem, Israel. *E-mail:* ibis@netvision.net.il. *Website:* www.ibiseditions.com.

COLEGATE, Isabel, FRSL; British writer; b. 10 Sept. 1931, London; d. of Arthur Colegate and Winifred Colegate; m. Michael Briggs 1953; two s. one d. *Education:* Runton Hill School, Norfolk. *Career:* literary agent, Anthony Blond Ltd, London 1952–57. *Publications include:* The Blackmailer 1958, A Man of Power 1960, The Great Occasion 1962, Statues in a Garden 1964, The Orlando Trilogy 1968–72, News From the City of the Sun 1979, The Shooting Party 1980 (WH Smith Literary Award; filmed 1985), A Glimpse of Sion's Glory 1985, Deceits of Time 1988, The Summer of the Royal Visit 1991, Winter Journey 1995, A Pelican in the Wilderness – Hermits Solitaries and Recluses 2002. *Honours:* Dr hc (Bath) 1988. *Address:* c/o PFD, Drury House, 34–43 Russell Street, London, WC2B 5HA, England. *Telephone:* (20) 7344-1000. *Fax:* (20) 7836-9539.

COLEMAN, Jane Candia, BA; American writer and poet; *fiction mentor MFA Program, Carlow University, Pittsburgh;* b. 1 Jan. 1939, Pittsburgh, PA; m. Bernard Coleman 1965 (divorced 1989); two s. *Education:* University of Pittsburgh. *Career:* fiction mentor MFA Program, Carlow University, Pittsburgh; mem. Authors' Guild, Women Writing the West. *Publications:* No Roof But Sky (poems), 1990; Stories From Mesa Country, 1991; Discovering Eve (short stories), 1993; Shadows in My Hands (memoir), 1993; The Red Drum (poems), 1994; Doc Holliday's Woman (novel), 1995; Moving On (short stories), 1997; I, Pearl Hart (novel), 1998; The O'Keefe Empire (novel), 1999; Doc Holliday's Gone (novel), 1999; Borderlands (short stories), 2000; Desperate Acts (novel), 2001; The Italian Quartet (novel), 2001; Mountain Time (memoir), 2001; Country Music (short stories), 2002; Wives and Lovers (short stories), 2002, Matchless (novel) 2003, Tombstone Travesty (novel) (Willa Award) 2004. Contributions: periodicals. *Honours:* Western Heritage Awards, 1991, 1992, 1994, Spur Awards for short fiction Western Writers of America 1993, 1995, Arizona Comm. on the Arts Poetry Grant 1993. *Address:* 1702 E Lind Road, Tucson, AZ 85719, USA. *Telephone:* (520) 785-5588.

COLEMAN, Terence (Terry) Francis Frank, LLB, FRSA; British journalist and writer; b. 13 Feb. 1931, s. of Jack Coleman and D. I. B. Coleman; m. 1st Lesley Fox-Strangeways Vane 1954 (divorced); two d.; m. 2nd Vivien Rosemary Lumsdaine Wallace 1981; one s. one d. *Education:* 14 schools and Univ. of London. *Career:* fmr reporter, Poole Herald; fmr Ed. Savoir Faire; fmr Sub-Ed. Sunday Mercury, Birmingham Post; Reporter then Arts Corresp. The

Guardian 1961–70, Chief Feature Writer 1970–74, 1976–79, New York Corresp. 1981, Special Corresp. 1982–89; Special Writer with Daily Mail 1974–76; Assoc. Ed. The Independent 1989–91; columnist, The Guardian 1992–. *Publications:* The Railway Navvies 1965 (Yorkshire Post Prize for Best First Book of the Year), A Girl for the Afternoons 1965, Providence and Mr Hardy (with Lois Deacon) 1966, The Only True History: collected journalism 1969, Passage to America 1972, An Indiscretion in the Life of an Heiress (Hardy's first novel) (ed.) 1976, The Liners 1976, The Scented Brawl: Collected Journalism 1978, Southern Cross 1979, Thanksgiving 1981, Movers and Shakers: Collected Interviews 1987, Thatcher's Britain 1987, Empire 1994, W. G. Grace: A Biography 1997, Nelson: The Man and the Legend (biog.) 2001, Olivier: The Authorised Biography 2005. *Honours:* Feature Writer of the Year, British Press Awards 1982, Journalist of the Year (What the Papers Say Award) 1988. *Literary Agent:* PFD, 34–43 Russell Street, London, WC2B 5HA, England. *Telephone:* (20) 7720-2651 (home).

COLEMAN, Wanda; American poet and writer; b. 13 Nov. 1946, Los Angeles, CA. *Publications:* Mad Dog Black Lady, 1979; Imagoes, 1983; Heavy Daughter Blues: Poems and Stories, 1968–1986, 1987; A War of Eyes and Other Stories, 1988; Women for All Seasons: Poetry and Prose About the Transitions in Women's Lives (ed. with Joanne Leedom-Ackerman), 1988; Dicksboro Hotel and Other Travels, 1989; African Sleeping Sickness: Stories and Poems, 1990; Hand Dance, 1993; Native in a Strange Land: Trials & Tremors, 1996; Bathwater Wine, 1998; Mambo Hips & Make Believe: A Novel, 1999. Contributions: anthologies and periodicals. *Honours:* Fellowships, Acad. of American Poets Lenore Marshall Poetry Prize 1999.

COLERIDGE, Geraldine Margaret (Gill); British literary agent; b. 26 May 1948, d. of Antony Duke Coleridge and June Marian Caswell; m. David Roger Leeming 1974; two s. *Education:* Queen Anne's School, Caversham and Marlborough Secretarial Coll., Oxford. *Career:* mem. staff, BPC Partworks, Sidgwick & Jackson, Bedford Square Book Bang –1971; Publicity Man. Chatto & Windus 1971–72; Dir and Literary Agent, Anthony Sheil Assocs 1973–88; Partner, Rogers, Coleridge & White, Literary Agents 1988–; Pres. Assoc. of Authors' Agents 1988–91; mem. British Library Publishing Bd 1993–2003; mem. Public Lending Right Bd 2000–. *Address:* Rogers, Coleridge & White, 20 Powis Mews, London, W11 1JN, England (office). *Telephone:* (20) 7221-3717 (office). *Fax:* (20) 7229-9084 (office).

COLERIDGE, Nicholas David; British publisher, journalist and author; *Vice-President, Condé Nast International;* b. 4 March 1957, s. of David Ean Coleridge and Susan Coleridge (née Senior); m. Georgia Metcalfe 1989; three s. one d. *Education:* Eton, Trinity Coll., Cambridge. *Career:* Assoc. Ed. Tatler 1979–81; columnist Evening Standard 1981–84; Features Ed. Harpers and Queen 1985–86, Ed. 1986–89; Editorial Dir Condé Nast Publs 1989–91, Man. Dir Condé Nast UK 1992–, Vice-Pres. Condé Nast Int. 1999–; Chair. British Fashion Council 2000–03, Fashion Rocks for The Prince's Trust 2003, Periodical Publrs Assen 2004–; mem. Council RCA 1995–2000. *Publications:* Tunnel Vision 1982, Around the World in 78 Days 1984, Shooting Stars 1984, The Fashion Conspiracy 1988, How I Met My Wife and Other Stories 1991, Paper Tigers 1993, With Friends Like These 1997, Streetsmart 1999, Godchildren 2002, A Much Married Man 2006. *Honours:* Young Journalist of the Year, British Press Awards 1983, Mark Boxer Award for Editorial Excellence 2001. *Address:* Condé Nast, Vogue House, Hanover Square, London, W1S 1JU (office); 38 Princedale Road, London, W11 4NL; Rignell Farm, Barford St Michael, Oxon., OX15 0PN, England. *Telephone:* (20) 7221-4293. *Website:* www.condenast.co.uk (office).

COLES, Donald Langdon, BA, MA; Canadian academic and poet; b. 12 April 1928, Woodstock, ON; m. 1958; one s. one d. *Education:* Victoria Coll., Univ. of Toronto. *Career:* Fiction Ed., The Canadian Forum, 1975–76; Dir, Creative Writing Programme, York University, 1979–85; Poetry Ed., May Studio, Banff Centre for the Fine Arts, 1984–93; mem. PEN International. *Publications:* Sometimes All Over, 1975; Anniversaries, 1979; The Prinzhorn Collection, 1982; Landslides, 1986; K in Love, 1987; Little Bird, 1991; Forests of the Medieval World, 1993; Someone Has Stayed in Stockholm: Selected and New Poems, 1994; Kurgan, 2000. Contributions: Saturday Night; Canadian Forum; London Review of Books; Poetry (Chicago); Globe and Mail; Arc; Ariel. *Honours:* CBC Literary Competition, 1980; Gold Medal for Poetry, National Magazine Awards, 1986; Gov.-Gen.'s Award for Poetry, Canada, 1993; Trillium Prize, Ontario, 2000. *Address:* 122 Glenview Ave, Toronto, Ontario M4R 1P8, Canada.

COLES, Robert Martin, AB, MD; American child psychiatrist; b. 12 Oct. 1929, Boston, Mass.; s. of Philip W. Coles and Sandra Coles (née Young); m. Jane Hallowell 1960; three s. *Education:* Harvard Coll. and Columbia Univ. *Career:* Intern, Univ. of Chicago clinics 1954–55; Resident in Psychiatry, Mass. Gen. Hosp., Boston 1955–56, McLean Hosp., Belmont 1956–57; Resident in Child Psychiatry, Judge Baker Guidance Center, Children's Hosp., Roxbury, Mass. 1957–58, Fellow 1960–61; mem. psychiatric staff, Mass. Gen. Hosp. 1960–62; Clinical Asst in Psychiatry, Harvard Univ. Medical School 1960–62; Research Psychiatrist in Health Services, Harvard Univ. 1963–, lecturer in Gen. Educ. 1966–, Prof. of Psychiatry and Medical Humanities, Harvard Univ. Medical School 1977–; numerous other professional appts; mem. American Psychiatric Assen; Fellow, American Acad. of Arts and Sciences etc. *Publications:* Harvard Diary 1988, Times of Surrender: Selected Essays 1989, The Spiritual Life of Children; numerous books and articles in professional journals. *Honours:* awards include Pulitzer Prize for

vols II and III of Children of Crisis 1973, Sara Josepha Hale Award 1986. *Address:* Harvard Health Services, Harvard University, 75 Mt. Auburn Street, Cambridge, MA 02138 (office); 81 Carr Road, Concord, MA 01742, USA (home). *Telephone:* (617) 495-3736 (office); (617) 369-6498 (home).

COLFER, Eoin; Irish children's writer; b. 14 May 1965, Wexford; m. Jackie; two s. *Career:* fmr teacher. *Publications:* juvenile: Benny and Omar 1998, Benny and Babe 1999, The Wish List 2000, Artemis Fowl 2001, Artemis Fowl: The Arctic Incident 2002, Artemis Fowl: The Eternity Code 2003, The Seventh Dwarf (novella) 2004, The Legend of Spud Murphy 2004, The Supernaturalist 2004, The Artemis Fowl Files 2004, Artemis Fowl: The Opal Deception 2005, Artemis Fowl and the Lost Colony 2006, Half Moon Investigations 2006; for younger children: Going Potty 1999, Ed's Funny Feet 2000, Ed's Bed 2001; has also written plays. *Honours:* British Book Awards WH Smith Children's Book of the Year 2001, WH Smith Book Award 2002, German Children's Book Award 2004. *Address:* 1 Priory Hall, Spawell Road, Wexford, Ireland (office); Brookes Batchellor LLP, 102–108 Clerkenwell Road, London, EC1M 5SA, England. *Website:* www.eoincolfer.com.

COLL, Steve; American editor and journalist; *President, New America Foundation.* *Career:* joined The Washington Post 1985, Financial Corresp., Investigative Corresp., South Asia Corresp. 1989–92, Managing Ed. 1998–2004, Assoc. Ed. 2004–05; Staff Writer, The New Yorker 2005–; Pres. New America Foundation 2007–. *Publications:* The Taking of Getty Oil: The Full Story of the Most Spectacular – and Catastrophic – Takeover of All Time, The Deal of the Century: The Break Up of AT&T 1986, Eagle on the Street (with David A. Vise) 1991, On the Grand Trunk Road: A Journey into South Asia 1993, Ghost Wars: The Secret History of the CIA, Afghanistan and bin Laden, from the Soviet Invasion to September 10, 2001 (Pulitzer Prize 2005) 2004. *Honours:* Pulitzer Prize 1990, SAJA Journalism Leader Award 2002. *Address:* New America Foundation, 1630 Connecticut Avenue, N.W., 7th Floor, Washington, DC 20009, USA England (office). *Telephone:* (202) 986-2700 (office). *Fax:* (202) 986-3696 (office). *E-mail:* president@newamerica.net (office). *Website:* www.newamerica.net (office).

COLLEY, Linda Jane, PhD, FRSL, FBA; British academic and writer; *Shelby M.C. Davis 1958 Professor of History, Princeton University;* b. 13 Sept. 1949, d. of Roy Colley and the late Marjorie Colley (née Hughes); m. David Nicholas Cannadine (q.v.) 1982; one d. (deceased). *Education:* Univs of Bristol and Cambridge. *Career:* Eugenie Strong Research Fellow, Girton Coll., Cambridge 1975–78; Fellow, Newnham Coll., Cambridge 1978–79, Christ's Coll., Cambridge 1979–81; Asst Prof. of History, Yale Univ. 1982–85, Assoc. Prof. 1985–90, Prof. of History 1990–92, Richard M. Colgate Prof. of History 1992–98, Dir Lewis Walpole Library 1982–96; Prof. School of History, LSE 1998–2003, Leverhulme Personal Research Prof., European Inst. 1998–2003; Shelby M.C. Davis 1958 Prof. of History, Princeton Univ. 2003–; mem. Bd British Library 1999–2003; mem. Advisory Bd Tate Britain 1999–2003, Paul Mellon Centre for British Art 1999–2003; Visiting Fellowship, Humanities Research Centre, ANU, Canberra 2005; Glaxo-Smith-Kline Sr Fellowship Nat. Humanities Center, NC 2006. *Publications:* In Defiance of Oligarchy: The Tory Party 1714–60 1982, Namier 1989, Crown Pictorial: Art and the British Monarchy 1990, Britons: Forging the Nation 1707–1837 (Wolfson Prize 1993) 1992, Captives: Britain, Empire and the World 1600–1850 2002, The Ordeal of Elizabeth Marsh: A Woman in World History 2007; numerous articles and reviews in UK and American learned journals. *Honours:* Hon. Fellow, Christ's Coll., Cambridge 2005; Dr hc (South Bank, London) 1999, (Essex) 2004, (East Anglia) 2005, (Bristol) 2006; Wolfson Prize 1993, Anstey Lecturer Univ. of Kent 1994; William Church Memorial Lecturer, Brown Univ. 1994, Distinguished Lecturer in British History, Univ. of Texas 1995, Trevelyan Lecturer, Univ. of Cambridge 1997, Wiles Lecturer, Queen's Univ. Belfast 1997, Prime Minister's Millennium Lecture 2000, Raleigh Lecturer, British Acad. 2002, Nehru Lecturer 2002, Bateson Lecturer, Oxford 2003, Chancellor Dunning Trust Lecturer, Queen's Univ., Ont. 2004, Byrn Lecturer, Vanderbilt Univ. 2005, Annual Lecture in Int. History, LSE 2006. *Literary Agent:* c/o Gill Coleridge, RCW Ltd, 20 Powis Mews, London, W11 1JN, England. *Address:* Department of History, Princeton University, 129 Dickinson Hall, Princeton, NJ 08544-1017, USA (office). *Telephone:* (609) 258-8076 (office). *E-mail:* lcolley@princeton.edu (office). *Website:* his.princeton.edu (office).

COLLIER, Catrin (see Watkins, Karen Christna)

COLLIER, Michael Robert, BA, MFA; American academic, poet, writer and editor; b. 25 May 1953, Phoenix, AZ; m. Katherine A. Branch 1981, two s. *Education:* Connecticut College, University of Arizona. *Career:* Lecturer in English, George Mason University, 1982, Trinity College, Washington, DC, 1982–83; Writing Staff, The Writer's Center, Bethesda, MD, 1982–85; Visiting Lecturer, 1984–85, Adjunct Instructor, 1985–86, Asst Prof. of English, 1986–90, Prof. of English, 1995–, University of Maryland at College Park; Visiting Lecturer, Johns Hopkins University, 1986–89, Yale University, 1990, 1992; Teacher, Warren Wilson College, 1991–93, 1996; Assoc. Staff, 1992–94, Dir, 1994–, Bread Loaf Writers' Conference, Middlebury College; mem. Acad. of American Poets; Poetry Society of America. *Publications:* Poetry: The Clasp and Other Poems, 1986; The Folded Heart, 1989; The Neighbor, 1995; The Ledge, 2000. Editor: The Wesleyan Tradition: Four Decades of American Poetry, 1993; The New Bread Loaf Anthology of Contemporary American Poetry (with Stanley Plumly), 1999; The New American Poets: A Bread Load Anthology, 2000. Contributions: anthologies, journals and magazines. *Honours:* Writing Fellow, Fine Arts Work Center, Provincetown, 1979–80;

'Discovery' The Nation Award, 1981; Margaret Bridgeman Scholar in Poetry, 1981, Theodore Morrison Fellow in Poetry, 1986, Bread Loaf Writers' Conference; National Endowment for the Arts Creative Writing Fellowships, 1984, 1994; Alice Faye di Castagnola Award, Poetry Society of America, 1988; Fellow, Timothy Dwight College, Yale University, 1992–96; Guggenheim Fellowship, 1995–96; Maryland Arts Council Grant, 2000; Poet Laureate of Maryland, 2001.

COLLINS, Billy, PhD; American poet and academic; *Distinguished Professor, Lehman College, City University of New York*; b. 22 March 1941, New York; m. Diane Collins 1979. *Education:* Holy Cross Coll., Univ. of California at Riverside. *Career:* Prof. of English Lehman Coll., City Univ. of New York 1969–2001, Distinguished Prof. 2001–; Visiting Writer Poets House, N Ireland 1993–96, Lenoir-Rhyne Coll. 1994, Ohio State Univ. 1998; Resident Poet Burren Coll. of Art, Ireland 1996, Sarah Lawrence Coll. 1998–2000; Adjunct Prof. Columbia Univ. 2000–01; conducts summer poetry workshops at Univ. Coll. Galway, Ireland; Library of Congress's Poet Laureate Consultant in Poetry 2001, US Poet Laureate 2001–03; Fellow, New York Foundation for the Arts, Nat. Endowment for the Arts, Guggenheim Foundation; NEA Fellowship 1993; Guggenheim Fellowship 1995. *Publications include:* Pokerface 1977, Video Poems 1980, The Apple that Astonished Paris 1988, Questions About Angels 1991, The Art of Drowning 1995, Picnic, Lightning 1998, Taking Off Emily Dickinson's Clothes 2000, Sailing Alone Around the Room: New and Selected Poems 2001, Nine Horses 2002, The Trouble with Poetry 2005, The Apple That Astonished Paris 2006; editor: Poetry 180: A Turning Back to Poetry, 180 More: Extraordinary Poems for Everyday Life; poems in many anthologies, including The Best American Poetry 1992, 1993, 1997 and periodicals, including Poetry, American Poetry, Review, American Scholar, Harper's, Paris Review and The New Yorker. *Honours:* New York Foundation for the Arts Poetry Fellowship 1986, Nat. Endowment for the Arts Creative Writing Fellowship 1988, Nat. Poetry Series Competition Winner 1990, Bess Hokin Prize 1991, Literary Lion, New York Public Library 1992, Frederick Bock Prize 1992, Guggenheim Fellowship 1993, Levinson Prize 1995, Paterson Poetry Prize 1999, J. Howard and Barbara M. J. Wood Prize 1999, Pushcart Prize 2002, New York State Poet Laureate 2004(–06). *Address:* c/o Lehman College, 250 Bedford Park Boulevard West, Business Office, Shuster Hall Building, Bronx, New York, NY 10468, USA (office); 185 Route 202, Somers, NY 10589 (home). *Website:* www.lehman.cuny.edu (office); www.bigsnap.com (home). *Literary Agent:* Steven Barclay Agency, 12 Western Avenue, Petaluma, CA 94952, USA. *Telephone:* (707) 773-0654. *Fax:* (707) 778-1868. . *Website:* www.barclayagency.com.

COLLINS, Gail, BA, MA; American writer, editor and columnist; b. 25 Nov. 1945, Cincinnati, OH; m. Dan Collins. *Education:* Marquette Univ., Univ. of Mass., Columbia Univ. *Career:* early career writing for newspapers in Milwaukee and Conn.; f. Conn. State News Bureau 1970s; columnist, United Press Int., New York Daily News 1985–91, New York Newsday 1991–95; mem. Editorial Bd, New York Times 1995–, later Op-Ed columnist, Editorial Page Ed. (first woman) 2001–07. *Publications include:* The Millennium Book (with Dan Collins), Scorpion Tongues: The Irresistible History of Gossip in American Politics 1998, America's Women: Four Hundred Years of Dolls, Drudges, Helpmates and Heroines 2003. *Address:* c/o New York Times, 500 Seventh Avenue, Eighth Floor, New York, NY 10018, USA.

COLLINS, Jackie; British novelist; sister of Joan Collins (q.v.); *Mini-series:* Hollywood Wives (ABC TV), Lucky Chances (NBC TV), Lady Boss (NBC TV). *Screenplays:* Yesterday's Hero, The World is Full of Married Men, The Stud. *Publications:* The World is Full of Married Men 1968, The Stud 1969, Sunday Simmons and Charlie Brick 1971, Lovehead 1974, The World is Full of Divorced Women 1975, Lovers and Gamblers 1977, The Bitch 1979, Chances 1981, Hollywood Wives 1983, Lucky 1985, Hollywood Husbands 1986, Rock Star 1988, Lady Boss 1990, American Star 1993, Hollywood Kids 1994, Vendetta – Lucky's Revenge 1996, Thrill 1998, LA Connections (four-part serial novel) 1998, Dangerous Kiss 1999, Hollywood Wives: The New Generation 2001, Lethal Seduction 2001, Deadly Embrace 2002, Hollywood Divorces 2003. *Address:* c/o Simon and Schuster, 1230 Avenue of the Americas, New York, NY 10020, USA. *Fax:* (310) 278-6517.

COLLINS, James (Jim) Lee; American author and editor; b. 30 Dec. 1945, Beloit, WI; m. Joan Hertel 1974, two s. *Career:* mem. Colorado Authors League; National Writers Club; Western Writers of America. *Publications:* Comanche Trail, 1984; Gone to Texas, 1984; War Clouds, 1984; Campaigning, 1985; Orphans Preferred, 1985; Riding Shotgun, 1985; Mister Henry, 1986; The Brass Boy, 1987; Spencer's Revenge, 1987; Western Writers Handbook, 1987; Settling the American West, 1993. Contributions: The Blue and the Gray; Writers Digest Magazine.

COLLINS, Joan Henrietta, OBE; British actress and author; b. 23 May 1933, London; d. of Joseph William and Elsa (née Bessant) Collins; sister of Jackie Collins (q.v.); m. 1st Maxwell Reed 1954 (divorced 1957); m. 2nd George Anthony Newley 1963 (divorced 1970); one s. one d.; m. 3rd Ronald S. Kass 1972 (divorced 1983); one d.; m. 4th Peter Holm 1985 (divorced 1987); m. 5th Percy Gibson 2002. *Education:* RADA. *Career:* actress in numerous stage, film, and TV productions, producer and author. *Plays include:* The Last of Mrs Cheyne, London 1979–80, Private Lives London 1990, Broadway 1991, Love Letters, USA tour 2000, Over the Moon, London 2001, Full Circle (UK tour) 2004. *Films include:* I Believe in You 1952, Our Girl Friday 1953, The Good Die Young 1954, Land of the Pharaohs 1955, The Virgin Queen 1955, The Girl in the Red Velvet Swing 1955, The Opposite Sex 1956, Island in the Sun 1957, Sea Wife 1957, The Bravados 1958, Seven Thieves 1960, Road to Hong Kong 1962, Warning Shot 1966, The Executioner 1969, Quest for Love 1971, Revenge 1971, Alfie Darling 1974, The Stud 1979, The Bitch 1980, The Big Sleep, Tales of the Unexpected, Neck 1983, Georgy Porgy 1983, Nutcracker 1984, Decadence 1994, In the Bleak Midwinter 1995, Hart to Hart 1995, Annie: A Royal Adventure 1995, The Clandestine Marriage 1998, Joseph and the Amazing Technicolor Dreamcoat 1999, The Flintstones – Viva Rock Vegas 2000, These Old Broads 2000, Clandestine Marriage 2001, Ozzie 2001. *Television appearances include:* Dynasty (series) 1981–89, Cartier Affair 1985, Sins 1986, Monte Carlo 1986, Tonight at 8.30 1991, Pacific Palisades (series) 1997, Will and Grace 2000, Guiding Light 2002, Hotel Babylon 2006, Footballers Wives 2006. *Publications include:* Past Imperfect 1978, The Joan Collins Beauty Book 1980, Katy, A Fight for Life 1982, Prime Time 1988, Love and Desire and Hate 1990, My Secrets 1994, Too Damn Famous 1995, Second Act 1996, My Friends' Secrets 1999, Star Quality 2002, Joan's Way 2002, Misfortune's Daughters 2004. *Honours:* Best TV Actress, Golden Globe, 1982; Favourite TV Performer, People's Choice 1985. *Address:* c/o Paul Keylock, 16 Bulbecks Walk, South Woodham Ferrers, Essex, CM3 5ZN, England (office). *Telephone:* (1245) 328367 (office). *Fax:* (1245) 328625 (office). *E-mail:* pkeylock@aol.com (office). *Website:* www.joancollins.net (office).

COLLINS, Merle, BA, MA, PhD; Grenadian poet and novelist; *Professor of Comparative Literature, University of Maryland*; b. 29 Sept. 1950, d. of John Collins and Helena Collins. *Education:* Univ. of the West Indies, Georgetown Univ., USA and LSE, UK. *Career:* fmr high school teacher in Grenada and St Lucia; research co-ordinator for govt 1981; writer-in-residence, London Borough of Waltham Forest, England 1987; Lecturer in Caribbean Studies, Univ. of North London 1990–95; Prof. of Creative Writing and Caribbean Literature, Univ. of Maryland, USA 1995, Faculty Dir Maryland in Mexico Programme 1997, currently Prof. of Comparative Literature; mem. African Dawn music and poetry group 1985–; numerous appearances on TV and radio programmes; reviewer for Ariel, Journal of the Asscn of Caribbean Women Writers. *Publications:* Because the Dawn Breaks (poems) 1985, Angel (novel) 1987, Rain Darling (short stories) 1990, Rotten Pomerack (poems) 1992, The Colour of Forgetting (novel) 1995; contribs to Callaloo: A Grenada Anthology 1984, Watchers and Seekers: Creative Writing by Black Women in Britain 1987, Facing the Sea: An Anthology of Writing from the Caribbean 1990, Penguin Modern Poets Vol. 8 1996, The Oxford Book of Caribbean Short Stories 1999. *Address:* c/o Department of English, University of Maryland, 3101 Susquehanna Hall, College Park, MD 20742, USA (office). *E-mail:* collinsm@umd.edu (office). *Website:* www.english.umd.edu (office).

COLLINS, Michael, PhD; Irish writer and athlete; b. 1964, Limerick. *Education:* Univ. of Notre Dame, USA. *Career:* taught at various colls, including Art Inst. of Chicago, Western Washington Univ., Univ. of Notre Dame; worked for Microsoft, USA; as an 'extreme' athlete, has won The Last Marathon, Antarctica (co-winner) 1997, Redwoods Marathon 1997, The Himalayan 100 Mile Stage Race 1999, The Everest Challenge Marathon 1999, The North Pole Marathon 2006; also completed The Sahara Half Marathon 2005. *Publications:* novels: The Meat Eaters 1993, The Life and Times of a Teaboy 1995, Emerald Underground 1999, The Keepers of Truth (Kerry Ingredients Irish Novel of the Year) 2000, The Resurrectionists (PNBA Novel of the Year 2003) 2002, Exodus 2004, Lost Souls (USA Today Editor's Choice) 2005, The Secret Life of E. Robert Pendleton 2006; short stories: The Man Who Dreamt of Lobsters 1993, The Feminists Go Swimming 2003. *Honours:* Hennessy/Sunday Tribune Award, Ireland, Pushcart Prize for short stories. *Address:* c/o Weidenfeld & Nicolson, Orion House, 5 Upper St Martin's Lane, London, WC2H 9EA, England (office). *E-mail:* michaelcollinsauthor@michaelcollinsauthor.net. *Website:* www.michaelcollinsauthor.net.

COLLINSON, Patrick, CBE, PhD, FBA, FRHistS, FAHA; British historian and academic; *Professor Emeritus of Modern History, University of Cambridge*; b. 10 Aug. 1929, Ipswich; s. of William Cecil Collinson and Belle Hay Collinson (née Patrick); m. Elizabeth Albinia Susan Selwyn 1960; two s. two d. *Education:* King's School, Ely, Pembroke Coll., Cambridge and Univ. of London. *Career:* Research Asst, Univ. Coll. London 1955–56; Lecturer in History, Univ. of Khartoum, Sudan 1956–61; Lecturer in Ecclesiastical History, King's Coll. London 1961–69; Prof. of History, Univ. of Sydney, Australia 1969–75; Prof. of History, Univ. of Kent at Canterbury 1976–84; Prof. of Modern History, Univ. of Sheffield 1984–88; Regius Prof. of Modern History, Univ. of Cambridge 1988–96, now Emer.; Ford's Lecturer in English History, Univ. of Oxford 1979; Visiting Prof. Univ. of Richmond, VA 1999; Assoc. Visiting Prof., Univ. of Warwick 2000–03; Fellow Trinity Coll., Cambridge 1988–; Chair. Advisory Ed. Bd Journal of Ecclesiastical History 1982–93; Pres. Ecclesiastical History Soc. 1985–86, Church of England Record Soc. 1991–92; mem. Council British Acad. 1986–89. *Publications:* The Elizabethan Puritan Movement 1967, Archbishop Grindal 1519–1583: The Struggle for a Reformed Church 1979, The Religion of Protestants: the Church in English Society 1559–1625 (The Ford Lectures 1979) 1982, Godly People: Essays on English Protestantism and Puritanism 1984, English Puritanism 1984, The Birthpangs of Protestant England: Religious and Cultural Change in the 16th and 17th Centuries 1988, Elizabethan Essays 1993, A History of Canterbury Cathedral (jtly) 1995, The Reformation in English Towns (jtly) 1998, A History of Emmanuel College, Cambridge (jtly) 1999, Short Oxford History of the British Isles: The Sixteenth Century (ed) 2002, Reformation 2003, Elizabethans 2003, Conferences and Combination Lectures in the

Elizabethan Church (jtly) 2003, Oxford Dictionary of National Biography 2004, From Cranmer to Sancroft 2006. *Honours:* Hon. DUniv (York) 1988; Hon. DLitt (Kent) 1989, (Trinity Coll. Dublin) 1992, (Sheffield) 1994, (Oxford) 1997, (Essex) 2000, (Warwick) 2003; Medlicott Medal, Historical Asscn 1998. *Address:* Trinity College, Cambridge, CB2 1TQ (office); New House, Crown Square, Shaldon, Devon TQ14 0DS, England (home). *Telephone:* (1223) 338400 (office); (1626) 871245 (home). *Fax:* (1433) 650918; (1626) 871245 (home). *E-mail:* patrickcollinson@btinternet.com (home).

COLLIS, Louise Edith, BA; British writer; b. 29 Jan. 1925, Arakan, Burma; d. of the late Maurice Collis and Eleanor Collis. *Education:* Reading Univ. *Career:* mem. Soc. of Authors, Int. Asscn of Art Critics. *Publications:* Without a Voice 1951, A Year Passed 1952, After the Holiday 1954, The Angel's Name 1955, Seven in the Tower 1958, The Apprentice Saint 1964, Solider in Paradise 1965, The Great Flood 1966, A Private View of Stanley Spencer 1972, Maurice Collis Diaries (ed.) 1976, Impetuous Heart: The Story of Ethel Smyth 1984; contrib. to Books and Bookmen, Connoisseur, Art and Artists, Arts Review, Collectors Guide, Art and Antiques. *Address:* 65 Cornwall Gardens, London, SW7 4BD, England. *Telephone:* (20) 7937-1950.

COLOMBANI, Jean-Marie; French journalist; b. 7 July 1948, Dakar, Senegal; m. Catherine Sénès 1976; five c. *Education:* Lycée Hoche, Versailles, Lycée La Pérouse, Nouméa, New Caledonia, Univ. of Paris II-Assas, Univ. of Paris I Panthéon-Sorbonne, Inst. d'Etudes Politiques, Paris and Inst. d'Etudes Supérieures de Droit Public. *Career:* journalist, ORTF, later Office of FR3, Nouméa 1973; Ed. Political Service, Le Monde 1977, Head of Political Service 1983, Ed.-in-Chief 1990, Deputy Editorial Dir 1991; Man. Dir S.A.–Le Monde March–Dec. 1994, Chair. of Bd and Dir of Publs 1994–2007, mem. Bd Dirs 2007–; Chair. Advisory Council, Midi-Libre Group 2000–. *Publications:* Contradictions: entretiens avec Anicet Le Poro 1984, L'utopie calédonienne 1985, Portrait du président ou le monarque imaginaire 1985, Le mariage blanc (co-author) 1986, Questions de confiance: entretiens avec Raymond Barre 1987, Les héritiers (co-author), La France sans Mitterrand 1992, La gauche survivra-t-elle aux socialistes? 1994, Le Double Septennat de François Mitterrand, Dernier Inventaire (jtly) 1995, De la France en général et de ses dirigeants en particulier 1996, Le Résident de la République 1998, La Cinquième ou la République des phratries (co-author) 1999, Les infortunes de la Republique 2000, Tous Américains? 2002. *Address:* c/o Le Monde, 21 bis rue Claude Bernard, 75242 Paris cedex 05 (office); 5 rue Joseph Bara, 75006 Paris, France (home).

COLOMBO, John Robert, CM, OC, BA, DLitt; Canadian editor, author and consultant; b. 24 March 1936, Kitchener, Ont.; m. Ruth F. Brown 1959; two s. one d. *Education:* Kitchener-Waterloo Collegiate Inst., Waterloo Coll. and Univ. Coll., Univ. of Toronto. *Career:* editorial asst, Univ. of Toronto Press 1957–59; Asst Ed. The Ryerson Press 1960–63; Consulting Ed. McClelland & Stewart 1963–70, Ed.-at-Large 1963–; Gen. Ed. The Canadian Global Almanac 1992–2000; TV Presenter Unexplained Canada Series, Space Network 2006; Consultant, American Man. Asscn/Canadian Man. Centre. *Publications include:* over 180 books of poetry, prose, reference, science fiction anthologies and translations including Colombo's Canadian Quotations 1974, Colombo's Canadian References 1976, Colombo's Book of Canada 1978, Canadian Literary Landmarks 1984, 1,001 Questions about Canada 1986, Colombo's New Canadian Quotations 1987, Mysterious Canada 1988, Songs of the Great Land 1989, Mysterious Encounters 1990, The Dictionary of Canadian Quotations 1991, UFOs over Canada 1991, Dark Visions 1992, Worlds in Small 1992, The Mystery of the Shaking Tent 1993, Walt Whitman's Canada 1993, Voices of Rama 1994, 1995, Close Encounters of the Canadian Kind 1995, Ghost Stories of Ontario 1995, Haunted Toronto 1996, Iron Curtains 1996, The New Consciousness 1997, Weird Stories 1999, Ghosts in our Past 2000, The UFO Quote Book 2000, 1000 Questions about Canada 2001, Famous Lasting Words 2001, The Penguin Book of Canadian Jokes 2002, The Penguin Treasury of Popular Canadian Poems and Songs 2002, The Penguin Book of More Canadian Jokes 2003, O Rare Denis Saurat 2003, True Canadian Ghost Stories 2003, The Midnight Hour 2004, The Denis Saurat Reader 2004, The Monster Book of Canadian Monsters 2004, The Native Series 2005, Early Earth 2006, All the Poems 2006, All the Aphorisms 2006, Autumn in August 2006, Miniatures 2006, The Penguin Dictionary of Popular Canadian Quotations 2006. *Honours:* Order of Cyril and Methodius 1979; Esteemed Kt of Mark Twain 1979; Hon. DLitt (York Univ., Toronto) 1998; Centennial Medal 1967, Harbour Front Literary Prize 1985. *Address:* 42 Dell Park Avenue, Toronto, ON M6B 2T6, Canada. *Telephone:* (416) 782-6853. *Fax:* (416) 782-0285. *E-mail:* jrc@ca.inter.net (office). *Website:* www.colombo.ca (home).

COLQUHOUN, Keith; British journalist and novelist; b. 5 Aug. 1937, London, England; three s. three d. *Career:* Chief Sub-Ed., London Daily Herald, Sun, 1959–70; Managing Ed., Observer, 1970–77; News Ed., Far Eastern Economic Review, Hong Kong, 1977–80; Asian Affairs Writer, The Economist 1980–2005; consultant ICC, Paris 2005–. *Publications:* The Money Tree, 1958; Point of Stress, 1960; The Sugar Coating, 1973; St Petersburg Rainbow, 1975; Goebbels and Gladys, 1981; Filthy Rich, 1982; Kiss of Life, 1983; Foreign Wars, 1985; Mad Dog, 1992; Killing Stalin, 2002. *Address:* 52 West Stockwell Street, Colchester, Essex, England. *Telephone:* (1206) 533938.

COLVIN, Sir Howard Montagu, Kt, CVO, CBE, MA, FBA, FRHistS, FSA; British architectural historian; b. 15 Oct. 1919, s. of late Montagu Colvin; m. Christina E. Butler 1943 (died 2003); two s. *Education:* Trent Coll., Univ. Coll., London. *Career:* served in RAF 1941–46; Asst Lecturer, Univ. Coll. London 1946–48, Fellow 1974; Fellow, St John's Coll. Oxford 1948–87, Tutor in History 1948–78, Librarian 1950–84, Emer. Fellow 1987–; Reader in Architectural History, Univ. of Oxford 1965–87; mem. Historic Buildings Council for England 1970–84, Historic Buildings and Monuments Comm. 1984–85, Historic Buildings Advisory Cttee 1984–2001, Royal Comm. on Ancient and Historical Monuments of Scotland 1977–89, Royal Comm. on Historical Manuscripts 1981–88, Royal Fine Art Comm. 1962–72, Royal Comm. on Historical Monuments, England 1963–76, etc. *Publications include:* The White Canons in England 1951, A Biographical Dictionary of English Architects 1660–1840 1954, The History of the King's Works (gen. and part author) 1963–82, A History of Deddington 1963, Building Accounts of King Henry III 1971, Unbuilt Oxford 1983, Calke Abbey, Derbyshire 1985, The Canterbury Quadrangle, St John's College, Oxford 1988, All Souls: An Oxford College and Its Buildings (with J. S. G. Simmons) 1989, Architecture and the After-Life 1991, A Biographical Dictionary of British Architects 1600–1840 1978, Essays in English Architectural History 1999; catalogues; articles in learned journals. *Honours:* Hon. FRIBA; Hon. FSA (Scotland); Hon. DUniv (York) 1978; Wolfson Literary Award 1978. *Address:* 50 Plantation Road, Oxford, OX2 6JE, England (home). *Telephone:* (1865) 557460 (home). *Fax:* (1865) 277435 (office).

COLVIN, Marie Catherine, BA; American journalist; *Foreign Affairs Correspondent, The Sunday Times (UK)*; b. 12 Jan. 1956, New York; d. of William Joseph Colvin and Rosemarie Marron; m. Patrick Bishop 1989 (divorced). *Education:* Yale Univ. *Career:* with United Press Int. (UPI), New York and Washington, DC 1982–84, Paris Bureau Chief 1984–86; Middle East Corresp., The Sunday Times, London 1986–96, Foreign Affairs Corresp. 1996–. *Television:* Behind the Myth: Yasser Arafat (BBC documentary), Martha Gelhorn (BBC documentary). *Honours:* Woman of the Year (for work in Timor-Leste), Women of the Year Foundation, London 2000, Courage in Journalism Award, Int. Women's Media Foundation, USA 2000, Journalist of the Year, USA Foreign Corresps' Asscn 2001, Foreign Reporter of the Year, UK Press Awards 2001. *Address:* c/o Sunday Times Foreign Desk, 1 Pennington Street, London, E1 9XW, England (office). *Telephone:* (20) 7782-5701 (office). *Fax:* (20) 7782-5050 (office). *E-mail:* mariecolvin@hotmail.com (home).

COMAROFF, John Lionel; American writer; *Harold H. Swift Distinguished Service Professor of Anthropology and Social Sciences, University of Chicago*; b. 1 Jan. 1945, Cape Town, South Africa; m. Jean Rakoff 1967; one s. one d. *Education:* BA, University of Cape Town, 1966; PhD, University of London, 1973. *Career:* Lecturer in Social Anthropology, University College of Swansea, 1971–72, University of Manchester, 1972–78; Visiting Asst Prof. of Anthropology, 1978, Assoc. Prof. of Anthropology and Sociology, 1981–87, Prof. of Anthropology and Social Sciences, 1987–96, Harold H. Swift Distinguished Service Prof. of Anthropology and Social Sciences, 1996–, University of Chicago; Directeur d'Études, 1988, Directeur d'Études Associé, 1995, École des Hautes Études en Sciences Sociales, Paris; mem. Royal Anthropological Institute, fellow; African Studies Asscn; International African Institute, fellow; Asscn of Social Anthroplogists; American Anthropological Asscn, fellow; Asscn of Political and Legal Anthropology, pres., 1995–96. *Publications:* The Structure of Agricultural Transformation in Barolong, 1977; Rules and Processes: The Cultural Logic of Dispute in an African Context (with S. A. Roberts), 1981; Of Revelation and Revolution: Christianity and Colonialism in South Africa (with Jean Comaroff), 1991; Ethnography and the Historical Imagination (with Jean Comaroff), 1992; Modernity and its Malcontents: Ritual and Power in Africa (ed. with Jean Comaroff), 1993; Perspectives on Nationalism and War (ed. with Paul C. Stern), 1993. Contributions: scholarly books and journals. *Honours:* National Endowment for the Humanities Grants, 1984–85, 1986–87; National Science Foundation Grants, 1986–87, 1993; Spencer Foundation Grant, 1991; Laing Prize, University of Chicago, 1993; American Acad. of Arts and Sciences, 1995; Spencer Foundation Mentor Award, 1996. *Address:* c/o Dept of Anthropology, University of Chicago, 1126 E 59th Street, Chicago, IL 60637, USA.

COMINI, Alessandra, MA, PhD; American art historian, academic and author; *University Distinguished Professor Emerita of Art History, Southern Methodist University*; b. 24 Nov. 1934, Winona, Minnesota, USA; d. of Raiberto Comini and Megan Laird. *Education:* Barnard College, Univ. of California, Berkeley, Columbia Univ. *Career:* Instructor, Columbia Univ. 1968–69; Asst Prof., Southern Methodist Univ. 1969–74, Visiting Asst Prof. 1970, 1973, Assoc. Prof. 1974–75, Prof. 1976–, Univ. Distinguished Prof. of Art History 1983–, now Emer.; Alfred Hodder Fellow, Princeton Univ. 1972–73; Visiting Asst Prof., Yale Univ. 1973; Assoc. Ed. Arts Magazine 1977–88; Lansdown Prof., Univ. of Victoria, BC 1981; Visiting Distinguished Prof., California State Univ., Chico 1990; Distinguished Visiting Fellow, European Humanities Research Centre, Univ. of Oxford 1996; mem. Coll. Art Asscn of America, Texas Inst. of Letters, Women's Caucus for Art. *Publications:* Schiele in Prison 1973, Egon Schiele's Portraits 1974, Gustav Klimt 1975, Egon Schiele 1976, The Fantastic Art of Vienna 1978, The Changing Image of Beethoven: A Study in Mythmaking 1987, Egon Schiele's Nudes 1994, In Passionate Pursuit: A Memoir 2004; contribs to books, journals, magazines and exhbn catalogues. *Honours:* Charles Rufus Morey Book Award, Coll. Art Asscn of America 1976, Grand Decoration of Honour for Services to the Austrian Repub. 1990, Lifetime Achievement Award, Women's Caucus for Art 1995. *Address:* 2900 McFarlin, Dallas, TX 75205, USA (home). *Telephone:* (214) 369-8523 (home). *Fax:* (214) 369-8523 (home). *E-mail:* acomini@smu.edu.

COMPAGNON, Antoine Marcel Thomas; French (b. Belgian) academic and writer; *Blanche W. Knopf Professor of French and Comparative Literature, Columbia University*; b. 20 July 1950, Brussels, Belgium; s. of Gen. Jean Compagnon and Jacqueline Terlinden. *Education:* Lycée Condorcet, The Maret School, Washington, DC, USA, Prytanée Militaire, La Flèche, Ecole Polytechnique, Paris, Ecole Nat. des Ponts et Chaussées, Paris, Univ. of Paris VII. *Career:* with Fondation Thiers and Research Attaché, CNRS 1975–78; Asst Lecturer, Univ. of Paris VII 1975–80; Asst Lecturer, Ecole des Hautes Etudes en Sciences Sociales, Paris 1977–79; Lecturer, Ecole Polytechnique, Paris 1978–85; teacher at French Inst., London 1980–81; Lecturer, Univ. of Rouen 1981–85; Prof. of French, Columbia Univ., New York 1985–91; Visiting Prof., Univ. of Pennsylvania 1986, 1990; Prof., Univ. of Le Mans 1989–90; Blanche W. Knopf Prof. of French and Comparative Literature, Columbia Univ., New York 1991–; Prof., Univ. of Paris IV-Sorbonne 1994–2006, Collège de France 2006–; Sec. Gen. Int. Asscn of French Studies 1998–; Guggenheim Fellow 1988; Visiting Fellow, All Souls Coll., Oxford 1994; Fellow, American Acad. of Arts and Sciences 1997, Academia Europaea 2006. *Publications:* La Seconde Main ou le travail de la citation 1979, Le Deuil antérieur 1979, Nous, Michel de Montaigne 1980, La Troisième République des lettres, de Flaubert à Proust 1983, Ferragosto 1985, critical edn of Marcel Proust, Sodome et Gomorrhe 1988, Proust entre deux siècles 1989, Les Cinq Paradoxes de la modernité 1990, Chat en poche: Montaigne et l'allégorie 1993, Connaissez-vous Brunetière? 1997, Le Démon de la théorie 1998, Baudelaire devant l'innombrable 2003, Les Antimodernes 2005; numerous articles on French literature and culture. *Honours:* Officier des Palmes académiques; Chevalier de la Légion d'honneur. *Address:* Columbia University, Department of French and Romance Philology, 513 Philosophy Hall, 1150 Amsterdam Avenue, New York, NY 10027 (office); 29 Claremont Avenue, New York, NY 10027, USA (home); 36 rue de Moscou, 75008 Paris, France (home). *Telephone:* (212) 854-2500 (office); (212) 222-2550 (New York) (home); 1-43-87-71-48 (Paris) (home). *Fax:* (212) 854-5863 (office). *E-mail:* amc6@columbia.edu (office); antoine.compagnon@wanadoo.fr (home). *Website:* www.columbia.edu/cu/french (office).

COMPTON, David Guy, (Guy Compton, Frances Lynch); British writer; b. 19 Aug. 1930, London, England. *Education:* Cheltenham College, Gloucester. *Career:* Ed., Reader's Digest Condensed Books, London, 1969–81. *Publications:* Too Many Murderers, 1962; Medium for Murder, 1963; Dead on Cue, 1964; Disguise for a Dead Gentleman, 1964; High Tide for Hanging, 1965; The Quality of Mercy, 1965; Farewell Earth's Bliss, 1966; The Silent Multitude, 1966; And Murder Came Too, 1966; Synthajoy, 1968; The Palace, 1969; The Electric Crocodile, 1970; Hot Wireless Sets, Aspirin Tablets, the Sandpaper Sides of Used Matchboxes and Something that Might Have Been Castor Oil, 1971; The Missionaries, 1972; The Continuous Katherine Mortenhoe, 1974; Twice Ten Thousand Miles, 1974; The Fine and Handsome Captain, 1975; Stranger at the Wedding, 1977; A Dangerous Magic, 1978; A Usual Lunacy, 1978; Windows, 1979; In the House of Dark Music, 1979; Ascendancies, 1980; Scudder's Game, 1985; Ragnarok (with John Gribbin), 1991; Normansland, 1992; Stammering, 1993; Justice City, 1994; Back of Town Blues, 1996. *Literary Agent:* David Higham Associates, 5–8 Lower John Street, Golden Square, London W1F 9HA, England.

CONDÉ, Maryse, PhD; Guadeloupe author, dramatist and academic; *Professor Emerita, Columbia University, New York*; b. 11 Feb. 1937, Pointe-à-Pitre; m. 1st Mamadou Condé 1958 (divorced 1981); three c.; m. 2nd Richard Philcox 1982; one c. *Education:* Sorbonne, Univ. of Paris. *Career:* Programme Prod., French Services, BBC, London 1968–70, France Culture, Radio France Internationale, Paris 1980–85; Asst, Jussieu 1970–72, Lecturer, Nanterre 1973–80, Chargé de cours, Sorbonne 1980–85, Univ. of Paris; Prof. of French, Univ. of California at Berkeley 1989–92, Univ. of Maryland at Coll. Park 1992–95, Columbia Univ. 1995– (now Emer.); Visiting Prof., California Inst. of Technology 1989, Univ. of Virginia 1993–95, Harvard Univ. 1995; many visiting lectureships. *Publications:* fiction: Heremakhonon, 1976, English trans., 1982; Une Saison à Rihata, 1981, English trans. as A Season in Rihata, 1988; Ségou: Les murailles de terre, 1984, English trans. as Segu, 1987; Ségou II: La terre en miettes, 1985, English trans. as The Children of Segu, 1989; Pays Melé, suivi de, Nanna-ya, 1985, English trans. as Land of Many Colors, and Nanny-ya, 1999; Moi, Tituba, sorcière noire, 1986, English trans. as I, Tituba, Black Witch of Salem, 1992; La Vie scelerate, 1987, English trans. as Tree of Life: A Novel of the Caribbean, 1992; Antan Révolysion, 1989; Traversée de la mangrove, 1990, English trans. as Crossing the Mangrove, 1995; Les derniers rois mages, 1992, English trans. as The Last of the African Kings, 1997; La colonie du nouveau monde, 1993; La migration des coeurs, 1995, English trans. as Windward Heights, 1998; Desirada, 1997, English trans., 2000; La Belle Créole, 2001. Plays: Dieu nous l'a donne, 1972; Mort d'Oluwemi d'Ajumako, 1973; Le Morne de Massabielle, 1974, English trans. as The Hills of Massabielle, 1991; Pension les Alizes, 1988, English trans. as The Tropical Breeze Hotel, 1994; Comédie d'amour, 1993. Other: Anthologie de la littérature africaine d'expression française (ed.), 1966; La Poesie antillaise (ed.), 1977; Le Roman antillais (ed.), 1977; La Civilisation du bossale, 1978; Le profil d'une oeuvre: Cahier d'un retour au pays natal, 1978; La Parole des femmes: Essai sur des romancieres des Antilles de langue française, 1979; Bouquet de voix pour Guy Tirolien (ed.), 1990; Hugo le terrible, 1991; L'heritage de Caliban (ed. with others), 1992; Penser la creolite (with Madelaine Cottenet-Hage), 1995; Conversations with Maryse Condé (with Françoise Pfaff), 1996; Nouvelles d'Amérique (ed. with Lise Gauvin), 1998; Le Coeur à Rire et à Pleurer: Contes vrais de mon enfance, 1998, English trans.

as Tales from the Heart, 2000; Celanire cou-coupé: Roman fantastique, 2000; La belle Créole, 2001; Oratorio Créole, 2001, Histoire de la femme cannibale (trans. as The Story of the Cannibal Woman) 2004, Victoire, les saveurs et les mots 2006; contrib. to anthologies and journals. *Honours:* Commdr, Ordre des Arts et des Lettres 2001, Commdr Légion d'honneur 2004; Dr hc (Occidental Coll.) 1986, (Lehman Coll., CUNY) 1994; Fulbright Scholar 1985–86, Prix littéraire de la Femme 1986, Prix Alain Boucheron 1986, Guggenheim Fellowship 1987–88, Académie Française Prize 1988, Prix Carbet de la Caraibe 1997, Marguerite Yourcenar Prize 1999, Lifetime Achievement Award, New York University 1999, Prix Tropiques 2007. *Address:* 456 Riverside Drive, Apt 6B, New York, NY 10027, USA (home). *E-mail:* mc363@columbia.edu (home).

CONKIN, Paul Keith, BA, MA, PhD; American historian and writer; *Distinguished Research Professor, Vanderbilt University*; b. 25 Oct. 1929, Chuckey, TN; m. Dorothy L. Tharp 1954; one s. two d. *Education:* Milligan College, Vanderbilt University. *Career:* Asst Prof. of Philosophy and History, University of Southwestern Louisiana, 1957–59; Asst Prof., 1959–61, Assoc. Prof., 1961–66, Prof. of History, 1966–67, University of Maryland at College Park; Prof. of History, 1967–76, Merle Curti Prof. of History, 1976–79, University of Wisconsin at Madison; Distinguished Prof. of History, 1979–2000, Distinguished Research Prof., 2000–, Vanderbilt University; mem. American Historical Asscn; Organization of American Historians; Southern Historical Asscn, pres., 1996–97. *Publications:* Tomorrow a New World: The New Deal Community Program, 1959; Two Paths to Utopia: The Hutterites and the Llano Colony, 1964; F. D. R. and the Origins of the Welfare State, 1967, also published as The New Deal, 1967; Puritans and Pragmatists: Eight Eminent American Thinkers, 1968; The Heritage and Challenge of History (with Roland N. Stromberg), 1971; Self-evident Truths, 1974; A History of Recent America (with David Burner), 1974; New Directions in American Intellectual History (ed. with John Higham), 1979; Prophets of Prosperity: America's First Political Economists, 1980; TVA: Fifty Years of Grass-Roots Bureaucracy (ed. with Erwin C. Hargrove), 1983; Gone with the Ivy: A Biography of Vanderbilt University (with Henry Lee Swint and Patricia S. Miletich), 1985; Big Daddy from the Padernales: Lyndon Baines Johnson, 1986; The Southern Agrarians, 1988; Heritage and Challenge: The History and Theory of History (with Roland N. Stromberg), 1989; Cane Ridge, America's Pentecost, 1990; The Four Foundations of American Government: Consent, Limits, Balance, and Participation, 1994; The Uneasy Center: Reformed Christianity in Antebellum America, 1995; American Originals: Homemade Varieties of Christianity, 1997; When All Gods Trembled: Darwinism, Scopes, and American Intellectuals, 1998; A Requiem for the American Village, 2000. Contributions: scholarly books and journals. *Honours:* Albert J. Beveridge Award in American History, 1958; Guggenheim Fellowship, 1966–67; National Endowment for the Humanities Senior Fellowship, 1972–73, University Fellowship, 1990. *Address:* 1003 Tyne Blvd, Nashville, TN 37220, USA.

CONLEY, Robert Jackson, BA, MA; American writer and poet; b. 29 Dec. 1940, Cushing, OK; m. Evelyn Snell 1978. *Education:* Midwestern State University. *Career:* Instructor in English, Northern Illinois University, 1968–71; Southwest Missouri State University, 1971–74; Co-ordinator of Indian Culture, Eastern Montana College, 1975–77; Dir of Indian Studies, 1979–86, Assoc. Prof. of English, 1986–90, Morningside College; mem. International Poetry Society; Western Writers of America. *Publications:* Twenty-One Poems, 1975; Adawosgi: Swimmer Wesley Snell, A Cherokee Memorial, 1980; Echoes of Our Being (ed.), 1982; The Rattlesnake Band and Other Poems, 1984; Back to Malachi, 1986; The Actor, 1987; Killing Time, 1988; Wilder and Wilder, 1988; The Witch of Goingsnake and Other Stories, 1988; Colfax, 1989; The Saga of Henry Starr, 1989; Quitting Time, 1989; Go-ahead Rider, 1990; Ned Christie's War, 1990; Strange Company, 1991; Mountain Windsong: A Novel of the Trail of Tears, 1992; The Way of the Priests, 1992; Nickajack, 1992; Border Line, 1993; The Dark Way, 1993; The Long Trail North, 1993; The White Path, 1993; The Long Way Home, 1994; Geronimo: An American Legend (with John Milius and Larry Gross), 1994; To Make a Killing, 1994; Crazy Snake, 1994; The Way South, 1994; Zeke Proctor: Cherokee Outlaw, 1994; The Dark Island, 1995; Captain Dutch, 1995; Outside the Law, 1995; The War Trail North, 1995; War Woman: A Novel of the Real People, 1997; The Meade Solution, 1998; The Peace Chief: A Novel of the Real People, 1998; Incident at Buffalo Crossing, 1998; Brass, 1999; Cherokee Dragon: A Novel of the Real People, 2000; Barjack, 2000; Fugitive's Trail, 2000; Broke Loose, 2000; The Gunfighter, 2001; A Cold Hard Trail, 2001; Spanish Jack: A Novel of the Real People, 2001. Contributions: anthologies and periodicals. *Honours:* Spur Awards, Western Writers of America, 1992, 1995; Inducted, Oklahoma Professional Writers Hall of Fame, 1996; Oklahoma Writer of the Year, University of Oklahoma Professional Writing Program, 1999; Cherokee Medal of Honor, Cherokee Honor Society, 2000.

CONLEY, Tom Clark, BA, MA, PhD; American academic and writer; *Professor of French, Harvard University*; b. 7 Dec. 1943, New Haven, CT; m. Verena Conley; one s. one d. *Education:* Lawrence Univ. of Wisconsin, Columbia Univ., Sorbonne, Univ. of Paris, Univ. of Wisconsin, Madison. *Career:* Asst Prof., Assoc. Prof., Prof. of French 1971–95, Head Dept of French and Italian 1983–88, Univ. of Minnesota, Twin Cities; Prof. of French, Harvard Univ. 1995–; several visiting positions; mem. Int. Asscn of Philosophy and Literature, MLA of America, Midwest MLA, Société française des seiziémistes. *Publications:* Su realismo: Lectura de Buñuel 1988, Film Hieroglyphics: Ruptures in Classical Cinema 1991, The Graphic Unconscious in Early Modern French Writing 1992, The Self-Made Map: Cartographic Writing in Early Modern France 1996, L'Inconscient graphique 2000, Cartographies of Cinema 2006; also translations of seven vols, contrib. to books and numerous articles and reviews to periodicals. *Honours:* Woodrow Wilson Fellow 1965–66, Fulbright Fellow 1968–69, ACLS Fellow 1975–76, Nat. Endowment for the Humanities grants 1975, and Summer Fellow 1988, Newberry Library Quintennial Fellow 1988–89, Newberry Library Hermon Dunlap Smith Fellow 1992, Ville de Tours Medal of Honour 1990, Fellow Inst. for Research in the Humanities, Univ. of Wisconsin, Madison 1990–91, Guggenheim Fellow 2003–04. *Address:* 85 Dunster Street, Cambridge, MA 02138, USA. *E-mail:* tconley@fas.harvard.edu. *Website:* www.fas.harvard .edu/~rll.

CONLON, Kathleen (see Lloyd, Kathleen Annie)

CONN, Stewart; Scottish poet and playwright; b. 5 Nov. 1936, Glasgow. *Career:* radio producer, BBC, Glasgow 1962–77, Head of Radio Drama, Edinburgh 1977–92; literary adviser, Royal Lyceum Theatre, Edinburgh 1972–75; appointed to Edinburgh's poet laureateship, the Edinburgh Makar 2002–; Fellow Royal Scottish Acad. of Music and Drama; mem. Knight of Mark Twain, Shore Poets (pres.), Scottish Soc. of Playwrights. *Publications:* poetry: Thunder in the Air 1967, The Chinese Tower 1967, Stoats in the Sunlight (aka Ambush and Other Poems) 1968, An Ear to the Ground 1972, PEN New Poems 1973–74 (ed.) 1974, Under the Ice 1978, In the Kibble Palace: New and Selected Poems 1987, The Luncheon of the Boating Party 1992, In the Blood 1995, At the Aviary 1995, The Ice Horses (ed.) 1996, Stolen Light: Selected Poems 1999; plays: The Aquarium and Other Plays 1976, Thistlewood 1979, The Burning in Scots Plays of the 70s 2000, prose and poetry: Distances 2001, Ghosts at Cockcrow 2005; contrib. to anthologies, journals, radio. *Honours:* E. C. Gregory Award 1964, Scottish Arts Council Awards and Poetry Prize 1968, 1978, 1992, English-Speaking Union Travel Scholarship 1984, Scottish Arts Council Playwrights Bursary 1995, Soc. of Authors Travel Bursary 1996. *Literary Agent:* Lemon Unna & Durbridge Ltd, 24 Pottery Lane, Holland Park, London, W11 4LZ, England. *Address:* 1 Fettes Row, Edinburgh, EH3 6SF, Scotland. *E-mail:* stewart@jsconn.freeserve.co.uk.

CONNELL, Evan Shelby, Jr, BA; American author and poet; b. 17 Aug. 1924, Kansas City, MO. *Education:* Dartmouth College, University of Kansas, Stanford University, Columbia University, San Francisco State College. *Career:* Ed., Contact magazine, 1960–65; mem. American Acad. of Arts and Letters. *Publications:* fiction: The Anatomy Lesson and Other Stories, 1957; Mrs Bridge, 1959; The Patriot, 1960; At the Crossroads: Stories, 1965; The Diary of a Rapist, 1966; Mr Bridge, 1969; The Connoisseur, 1974; Double Honeymoon, 1976; St Augustine's Pigeon, 1980; The Alchymist's Journal, 1991; The Collected Stories of Evan S. Connell, 1995; Deus Lo Volt!: Chronicle of the Crusades, 2000. Poetry: Notes From a Bottle Found on the Beach at Carmel, 1963; Points for a Compass Rose, 1973. Non-Fiction: A Long Desire, 1979; The White Lantern, 1980; Son of the Morning Star: Custer and the Little Bighorn, 1984; Mesa Verde, 1992; The Aztec Treasure House, 2001. Contributions: periodicals. *Honours:* Eugene F. Saxton Fellow, 1953; Guggenheim Fellowship, 1963; Rockefeller Foundation Grant, 1967; California Literature Silver Medal, 1974; Los Angeles Times Book Award, 1985; American Acad. of Arts and Letters Award, 1987; Lannan Foundation Lifetime Achievement Award, 2000. *Address:* c/o Fort Marcy 13, 320 Artist Road, Sante Fe, NM 87501, USA.

CONNELLY, Mark, BA, MA, PhD; American writer and teacher; b. 8 July 1951, Philadelphia, PA. *Education:* Carroll College, University of Wisconsin, Milwaukee. *Career:* Instructor, Milwaukee Area Technical College, 1986–; mem. Irish Cultural and Heritage Center of Wisconsin, vice-pres.; MLA. *Publications:* The Diminished Self: Orwell and the Loss of Freedom, 1987; The Sundance Reader, 1997; Orwell and Gissing, 1997; The Sundance Writer, 2000; Deadly Closets: The Fiction of Charles Jackson, 2001. Contributions: Short stories in Milwaukee Magazine; Wisconsin Review; Indiana Review. *Honours:* Milwaukee Magazine Fiction Award 1982.

CONNELLY, Michael; American novelist; b. 1956, Philadelphia, PA. *Education:* Univ. of Florida. *Career:* crime reporter for newspapers based in Daytona Beach and Fort Lauderdale, Florida and for the Los Angeles Times. *Television writing:* Level 9 (co-creator, writer and producer) 2000. *Publications:* novels: The Black Echo 1992, The Black Ice 1992, The Concrete Blonde 1994, The Last Coyote 1995, The Poet 1996, Trunk Music 1997, Angels Flight 1998, Blood Work 1998, Void Moon 1999, A Darkness More Than Night 2001, City of Bones 2002, Chasing the Dime 2002, Lost Light 2003, The Narrows 2004, The Closers 2005, The Lincoln Lawyer 2005, Echo Park 2006; other: Crime Beat (collected journalism) 2006; editor: The Best American Mystery Stories 2003. *Honours:* Anthony Award, Macavity Award, Nero Award, Barry Award, Ridley Award, Maltese Falcon Award (Japan), .38 Caliber Award (France), Grand Prix (France), Premio Bancarella Award (Italy), Edgar Award for Best First Novel. *Address:* c/o Orion Publishing Group Ltd, 5 Upper St Martin's Lane, London, WC2H 9EA, England. *Website:* www .michaelconnelly.com.

CONNOLLY, Ray, BSc; British writer; b. 4 Dec. 1940, St Helens, Lancashire, England. *Education:* LSE. *Career:* columnist, London Evening Standard 1967–73, 1983–84, The Times 1989–90; regular contrib. Daily Mail 1998–2005. *Publications and screenplays:* A Girl Who Came to Stay 1973, That'll Be the Day 1973, Stardust (Writers' Guild of Great Britain Best

Original British Screenplay) 1974, Trick or Treat? 1975, James Dean: The First American Teenager 1975, Newsdeath 1978, A Sunday Kind of Woman 1980, Honky Tonk Heroes 1980, John Lennon 1940–1980 1981, The Sun Place 1981, An Easy Game to Play 1982, Stardust Memories (anthology) 1983, Forever Young 1984, Lytton's Diary 1985, Defrosting the Fridge 1988, Perfect Scoundrels 1989, Sunday Morning 1992, Shadows on a Wall 1994, A Day To Remember 1994, In the Sixties (anthology) 1995, Lost Fortnight 1996, The Rhythm of Life 1997, Days of Clover 2003, Love Out of Season 2007. *Literary Agent:* Rogers, Coleridge & White Ltd, 20 Powis Mews, London, W11 1JN, England. *E-mail:* plumsay@aol.com (office).

CONNOR, Joan; American writer, poet and educator; *Professor of English, Ohio University;* b. 21 Jan. 1954, Holyoke, MA, USA; m. Nils Wessell (separated); one s. *Education:* BA cum laude, Mount Holyoke College, 1976; MA, Middlebury College, 1984; MFA, Vermont College, 1995. *Career:* Assoc. Fiction Ed., Chelsea, 1994–96; Visiting Prof., Ohio Univ., Athens, 1995–96, Prof. of English 1996–,; mem. Associated Writing Programs (AWP); Young Writers' Institute. *Publications:* Here on Old Route 7 1997, We Who Live Apart 2000, History Lessons 2003; Contributions: anthologies and periodicals. *Honours:* Fellow, Vermont Studio Colony, 1990, MacDowell Colony, 1992, Virginia Center for the Creative Arts, 1993, Yaddo Colony, 1993, AWP Award, Pushcart Prize, John Gilgun Award. *Address:* 328 Carroll Road, Athens, OH 45701, USA. *E-mail:* connor@oak.cats.ohiou.edu.

CONQUEST, (George) Robert (Acworth), CMG, OBE, MA, DLitt, FBA, FRSL; British/American writer, academic and fmr diplomatist; *Senior Research Fellow, Hoover Institution, Stanford University;* b. 15 July 1917, Malvern, England; s. of Robert F. W. Conquest and Rosamund A. Acworth; m. 1st Joan Watkins 1942 (divorced 1948); two s.; m. 2nd Tatiana Milhailova 1948 (divorced 1962); m. 3rd Caroleen Macfarlane 1964 (divorced 1978); m. 4th Elizabeth Neece 1979. *Education:* Winchester Coll., Univ. of Grenoble and Magdalen Coll., Oxford. *Career:* mil. service 1939–46; HM Foreign Service 1946–56; Sydney and Beatrice Webb Research Fellow, LSE 1956–58; Visiting Poet, Univ. of Buffalo 1959–60; Literary Ed. The Spectator 1962–63; Sr Fellow, Columbia Univ. Russian Inst. 1964–65; Fellow, Woodrow Wilson Int. Center, Washington, DC 1976–77; Sr Research Fellow, Hoover Inst., Stanford Univ. 1977–79, 1981–; Distinguished Visiting Fellow, Heritage Foundation 1980–81; Adjunct Fellow, Center for Strategic and Int. Studies 1983–. *Publications:* Common Sense About Russia 1960, Power and Policy in the USSR 1960, Soviet Deportation of Nationalities 1960, Courage of Genius: The Pasternak Affair 1961, Industrial Workers in the USSR 1967, Soviet Nationalities Policy in Practice 1967, Agricultural Workers in the USSR 1968, The Soviet Police System 1968, Religion in the USSR 1968, The Soviet Political System 1968, Justice and the Legal System in the USSR 1968, The Great Terror: Stalin's Purge of the Thirties 1968, The Nation Killers: The Soviet Deportation of Nationalities 1970, Where Marx Went Wrong 1970, Lenin 1972, Kolyma: The Arctic Death Camps 1978, Inside Stalin's Secret Police: NKVD Politics, 1936–1939 1985, The Harvest of Sorrow: Soviet Collectivization and the Terror-Famine 1986, New and Collected Poems 1988, Tyrants and Typewriters: Communiques in the Struggle for Truth 1989, Stalin and the Kirov Murder 1989, The Great Terror: A Reassessment 1990, Stalin: Breaker of Nations 1991, History, Humanity, and Truth 1993, Demons Don't 1999, Reflections on a Ravaged Century 1999, Dragons of Expectation: Reality and Delusion in the Course of History 2005. *Honours:* Alexis de Tocqueville Award 1992, Jefferson Lectureship 1993, Michael Braude Award for Light Verse, American Acad. of Arts and Letters 1997, Richard Weaver Award for Scholary Letters 1999, Fondazione Liberal Career Award 2004, Presidential Medal of Freedom 2005. *Address:* Hoover Institution, Stanford University, Stanford, CA 94305-6010; 52 Peter Coutts Circle, Stanford, CA 94305, USA (home). *Telephone:* (650) 723-1647. *Fax:* (650) 723-1687. *Website:* www.hoover.org/bios/conquest.html.

CONRAN, Shirley Ida, OBE; British designer and author; b. 21 Sept. 1932, d. of W. Thirlbey Pearce and Ida Pearce; m. 1st Sir Terence Conran (divorced 1962); two s.; m. 2nd; m. 3rd. *Education:* St Paul's Girls' School and Portsmouth Art Coll. *Career:* Press Officer, Asprey Suchy (jewellers) 1953–54; Publicity Adviser to Conran Group cos 1955; org. and designed several kitchen and design exhbns; ran Conran Fabrics Ltd 1957; started Textile Design Studio 1958; Home Ed., Daily Mail 1962, Women's Ed. 1968; Women's Ed. The Observer Colour Magazine and contrib. to Woman's Own 1964; Fashion Ed. The Observer 1967, columnist and feature writer 1969–70; columnist, Vanity Fair 1970–71, Over 21 1972; has made numerous TV and radio appearances. *Publications:* Superwoman 1974, Superwoman Yearbook 1975, Superwoman in Action 1977, Futures 1979, Lace 1982, The Magic Garden 1983, Lace 2 1984, Savages (novel) 1987, Down with Superwoman 1990, The Amazing Umbrella Shop 1990, Crimson 1991, Tiger Eyes 1994, The Revenge of Mimi Quinn 1998. *Address:* c/o Simon & Schuster UK Ltd, Africa House, 64–78 Kingsway, London, WC2B 6AH, England (office).

CONRAN, Anthony (Tony), BA, MA; Welsh poet, dramatist, translator and critic; b. 7 April 1931, Kharghpur, India. *Education:* Univ. of Wales. *Career:* Research Asst, 1957–66, Research Fellow and Tutor in English, 1966–80, University of Wales, Bangor; mem. Welsh Acad., 1970; British Pteridological Society; English Folk Dance and Song Society; SIEF Ballad commission; Welsh Union of Writers; Asscn for the Study of Welsh Writers in English. *Publications:* Formal Poems, 1960; Metamorphoses, 1961 Stalae, 1966; Poems 1951–67, 4 vols, 1965–67, combined edn, 1974; The Penguin Book of Welsh Verse, 1967; Claim, Claim, Claim, 1969; Spirit Level, 1974; Life Fund, 1979;

The Cost of Strangeness: Essays on the English Poets of Wales, 1982; Welsh Verse, 1987; Bloddeuwedd and Other Poems, 1989; Castles, 1993; The Angry Summer by Idris Davies (ed.), 1993; All Hallows: A Symphony in Three Movements, 1995; Visions and Praying Mantids: The Angelogical Notebooks, 1997; The Peacemakers, by Waldo Williams (trans.), 1997; Frontiers in Anglo Welsh Poetry, 1997; A Theatre of Flowers: Collected Pastorals, 1998; Eros Proposes a Toast, 1998; A Gwynedd Symphony, 1999; Ragbag for Folkies: Poems and Songs, 2001; Branwen and Other Dance Dramas and Plays, 2003. Contributions: numerous magazines and journals. *Honours:* Welsh Arts Council Prize, 1960, 1989; Second Prize, BBC Wales Writer of the Year Award, 1993; Welsh Union of Writers, Tony Conran Festival, Bangor, 1995; Hon. Fellow, Welsh Acad., 1995; Hon. DLitt, University of Wales, 1997. *Address:* Min Menai, Siliwen Road, Bangor, Gwynedd LL57 2BS, Wales.

CONROY, (Donald) Patrick (Pat), BA; American writer; b. 26 Oct. 1945, Atlanta, GA; s. of Col Donald Conroy and Frances (Peg) Dorothy Conroy; m. 1st Barbara Bolling 1969 (divorced 1977); m. 2nd Lenore Gurewitz 1981 (divorced 1995); one s. five d. *Education:* The Citadel. *Career:* mem. Authors' Guild of America, PEN, Writers Guild. *Film screenplays:* Invictus 1988, The Prince of Tides (with Becky Johnson) 1991, Beach Music 1997. *Publications:* non-fiction: The Boo 1970, The Water is Wide 1972; novels: The Great Santini 1976, The Lords of Discipline 1980, The Prince of Tides 1986, Beach Music 1995. *Honours:* Ford Foundation Leadership Devt Grant 1971, Nat. Endowment for the Arts Award for Achievement in Educ. 1974, SC Hall of Fame, Acad. of Authors 1988, Golden Plate Award, American Acad. of Achievement 1992, Ga Comm. on the Holocaust Humanitarian Award 1996, Lotos Medal of Merit for Outstanding Literary Achievement 1996 and many others. *Address:* c/o Doubleday, 1540 Broadway, New York, NY 10036, USA.

CONSTANT, Paule, DèsSc; French author; b. 25 Jan. 1944, Gan; d. of Yves Constant and Jeanne Tauzin; m. Auguste Bourgeade 1968; one s. one d. *Education:* Univ. of Bordeaux and Univ. of Paris (Sorbonne). *Career:* Asst Lecturer in French Literature, Univ. of Abidjan 1968–75; Maître-assistant, then Maître de Conférences in French Literature and Civilization, Univ. of Aix–Marseille III 1975–90, Inst. of French Studies for Foreign Students 1986–95; Prof. Université Aix–Marseille III 1995–; diarist, Revue des Deux Mondes, Paris. *Publications:* novels: Ouregano 1980, Propriété privée 1981, Balta 1983, White Spirit 1989, Le Grand Ghâpal 1991, La Fille du Gobernator 1994, Confidence pour confidence 1998; Un monde à l'usage des demoiselles (essay) 1987. *Honours:* Prix Valéry Larbaud 1980, Grand Prix de l'Essai, Acad. Française 1987, Prix François Mauriac 1990, Grand Prix du Roman, Acad. Française 1990, Prix Goncourt 1998, Prix France Télévision du roman 1998; Chevalier, Légion d'honneur, France; Ordre de l'Educ. Nat. de Côte d'Ivoire. *Address:* Institut d'études françaises pour étudiants étrangers, 23 rue Gaston de Saporta, 13100 Aix-en-Provence; 29 rue Cardinale, 13100 Aix-en-Provence, France. *Telephone:* (4) 42-38-45-08.

CONSTANTINE, David John, BA, PhD; British poet, writer and translator; *Co-Editor, Modern Poetry in Translation;* b. 4 March 1944, Salford, Lancs., England; m. Helen Frances Best 1966; one s. one d. *Education:* Wadham Coll., Oxford. *Career:* Lecturer to Sr Lecturer in German, Univ. of Durham 1969–81; Fellow in German, Queen's Coll., Oxford 1981–2000; Co-Ed. (with Helen Constantine), Modern Poetry in Translation magazine 2004–; mem. Poetry Soc., Soc. of Authors. *Publications:* poetry: A Brightness to Cast Shadows 1980, Watching for Dolphins 1983, Mappi Mundi 1984, Madder 1987, Selected Poems 1991, Caspar Hauser 1994, Sleeper 1995, The Pelt of Wasps 1998, Something for the Ghosts 2002, Collected Poems 2004, A Poetry Primer 2004; fiction: Davies 1985, Back at the Spike 1994, Under the Dam (short stories) 2005; non-fiction: The Significance of Locality in the Poetry of Friedrich Hölderlin 1979, Early Greek Travellers and the Hellenic Ideal 1984, Hölderlin 1988, Friedrich Hölderlin 1992, Fields of Fire: A Life of Sir William Hamilton 2001, A Living Language 2004; translator: Hölderlin: Selected Poems 1996, Henri Michaux: Spaced, Displaced (with Helen Constantine) 1992, Philippe Jaccottet: Under Clouded Skies/Beauregard (with Mark Treharne) 1994, Goethe: Elective Affinities 1994, Kleist: Selected Writings 1998, Hölderlin's Sophocles 2001, Hans Magnus Enzensberger: Lighter Than Air 2002; editor: German Short Stories 2 1972. *Honours:* Alice Hunt Bartlett Prize 1984, Runciman Prize 1985, Southern Arts Literature Prize 1987, European Poetry Translation Prize 1998. *Address:* Modern Poetry in Translation, The Queen's College, Oxford, OX1 4AW (office); 1 Hill Top Road, Oxford, OX4 1PB, England (home). *Telephone:* (1865) 244701 (office). *E-mail:* david.constantine@queens .ox.ac.uk. *Website:* www.mptmagazine.com.

CONSTANTINE, Helen Frances, MA, MLitt; British translator; *Co-Editor, Modern Poetry in Translation;* b. (Helen Frances Best), m. David Constantine 1966; one s. one d. *Education:* Lady Margaret Hall, Oxford. *Career:* Co-Ed. (with David Constantine) Modern Poetry in Translation magazine 2004–; *Publications:* translator: Henri Michaux: Spaced, Displaced (with David Constantine) 1992, Paris Tales: A Literary Tour of the City 2004, Théophile Gautier: Mademoiselle de Maupin 2005, Choderlos de Laclos: Dangerous Liaisons 2007. *Address:* Modern Poetry in Translation, The Queen's College, Oxford, OX1 4AW (office); 1 Hill Top Road, Oxford, OX4 1PB, England (home). *Telephone:* (1865) 244701 (home). *E-mail:* helenconstantine@btinternet.com (home). *Website:* www.mptmagazine.com.

CONSTANTINE, Storm; British writer; b. 12 Oct. 1956, England. *Publications:* The Enchantments of Flesh and Spirit, 1987; The Bewitchments of Love and Hate, 1988; The Fulfillments of Fate and Desire, 1989; The Monstrous Regiment, 1989; Hermetech, 1991; Aleph, 1991; Burying the Shadow, 1992; Sign for the Sacred, 1993; Calenture, 1994; Stalking Tender Prey, 1995; Scenting Hallowed Blood, 1996.

COOK, Christopher Paul, BA, MA; British artist and poet; b. 24 Jan. 1959, Great Ayton, N Yorks.; s. of E.P. Cook and J. Leyland; m. Jennifer Jane Mellings 1982; two s. *Education:* Univ. of Exeter, Royal Coll. of Art. *Career:* Italian Govt Scholar Accad. di Belle Arti, Bologna 1986–89; Fellow in Painting Exeter Coll. of Art 1989–90; guest artist Stadelschule, Frankfurt 1991; Visiting Fellow Ruskin School, Univ. of Oxford 1992–93; Distinguished Visiting Artist Calif. State Univ., Long Beach 1994; Visiting Artist to Banaras Hindu Univ., Varanasi, India 1994, 1996; Reader in Painting Univ. of Plymouth 1997–. *Solo exhibitions include:* Camden Arts Centre 1985, Cleveland Gallery, Middlesbrough 1989, Museum van Rhoon, Rotterdam 1992, Northern Centre for Contemporary Art 1993, Helmut Pabst Gallery, Frankfurt 1995, Haugesund Kunstforening, Norway 1997, De Beyerd Museum, Breda 1999, Heidelberger Kunstverein 1999, Bundanon Trust, NSW 2000, Hirschl Contemporary Art, London 2000, Ferens Gallery, Hull 2001, Towner Gallery, Eastbourne 2001, Koraalberg Gallery, Antwerp 2002, Europaïsche Zentral Galerie, Frankfurt 2003, Dibou Gallery, New Orleans 2004, Art Museum, Memphis 2004, California State University, Long Beach 2005, Yokohama Museum, Japan 2005. *Publications:* Dust on the Mirror 1997, For and Against Nature 2000, A Thoroughbred Golden Calf 2003. *Honours:* Prizewinner John Moores Liverpool XXI 1999, Arts Council of England Award 2000, British Council Award to Artists 2003. *Address:* c/o Mary Ryan Gallery, Inc., 24 West 57th Street, 2nd Floor, New York, NY 10019, USA. *Telephone:* (212) 397-0669. *Fax:* (212) 397-0766. *E-mail:* c1cook@ blueyonder.co.uk. *Website:* www.cookgraphites.com.

COOK, Christopher Piers, BA, MA, DPhil, FRHistS; British writer and historian; b. 20 June 1945, Leicester. *Education:* University of Cambridge, University of Oxford. *Career:* Ed., Pears Cyclopedia, 1976–. *Publications:* Sources in British Political History, 6 vols, 1975–84; The Slump (with John Stevenson), 1976; Dictionary of Historical Terms, second edn, 1989; World Political Almanac, 1989; Longman Handbook of World History Since 1914, 1991; Britain Since 1945 (with John Stevenson), 1995; What Happened Where (with Diccon Bewes), 1996; Longman Handbook of Modern American History 1763–1996 (with David Waller), 1997; Longman Handbook of Modern European History 1763–1997, 1998; Longman Handbook of the Modern World (with John Stevenson), 1998; European Political Facts of the Twentieth Century (with John Paxton), fifth edn, 2001; A Short History of the Liberal Party 1900–2001, 2002; Longman Handbook of Modern British History 1714–2001, 2002; Longman Handbook of Twentieth Century Europe (with John Stevenson), 2003; The Routledge Guide to British Political Archives 2006, The Routledge Companion to Early Modern Europe 1453–1763 (with Philip Broadhead) 2006; contrib. to Guardian, TLS, THES. *Address:* c/o Pears Cyclopedia, Penguin Books, 80 Strand, London, WC2R 0RL, England.

COOK, David; British actor and writer; b. 21 Sept. 1940, Preston, Lancs., England. *Education:* Royal Coll. of Dramatic Art. *Career:* professional actor 1961–; Writer-in-Residence, St Martin's Coll., Lancaster 1982–83; mem. Soc. of Authors. *Publications:* Albert's Memorial 1972, Happy Endings 1974, Walter 1978, Winter Doves 1979, Sunrising 1982, Missing Persons 1986, Crying Out Loud 1988, Walter and June 1989, Second Best 1991. *Honours:* E. M. Forster Award 1977, Hawthornden Prize 1978, Southern Arts Fiction Prize 1984, Arthur Welton Scholarship 1991, Oddfellows Social Concern Award 1992. *Literary Agent:* c/o Deborah Rogers, 20 Powis Mews, London, W11 1JN, England. *Address:* Flat 17 Ockham Court, 24 Bardwell Road, Oxford, OX2 6SR, England (home).

COOK, Glen Charles; American writer; b. 9 July 1944, New York, NY; m. Carol Ann Fritz 1971; three s. *Education:* Univ. of Missouri. *Publications:* The Heirs of Babylon 1972, Shadow of All Night Falling 1979, October's Baby 1980, All Darkness Met 1980, Shadowline 1982, Starfishers 1982, Stars' End 1982, The Swordbearer 1982, The Black Company 1984, The Fire in His Hands 1984, Shadows Linger 1984, Doomstalker 1985, A Matter of Time 1985, Passage at Arms 1985, Warlock 1985, The White Rose 1985, With Mercy Toward None 1985, Ceremony 1986, Reap the East Wind 1987, Sweet Silver Blues 1987, All Ill Fate Marshalling 1988, Bitter Gold Hearts 1988, Cold Copper Tears 1988, The Dragon Never Sleeps 1988, Old Tin Sorrows 1989, Shadow Games 1989, The Silver Spike 1989, The Tower of Fear 1989, Dread Brass Shadows 1990, Dreams of Steel 1990, Sung in Blood 1990, Red Iron Nights 1991, Deadly Quicksilver Lies 1993, Bleak Seasons 1996, Petty Pewter Gods 1996, She is the Darkness 1997, Water Sleeps 1999, Faded Steel Heat 2000, Soldiers Live 2000, Angry Lead Skies 2002, Whispering Nickel Idols 2005, The Tyranny of the Night 2005; contrib. to anthologies and periodicals. *Address:* 4106 Flora Place, St Louis, MO 63110, USA.

COOK, Lila (see Africano, Lillian)

COOK, Paul, BA, MA, PhD; American academic and writer; b. 12 Nov. 1950, Tucson, AZ. *Education:* Northern Arizona Univ., Arizona State Univ., Univ. of Utah. *Career:* Sr Lecturer in English, Arizona State Univ., Tempe 1987–. *Publications:* Duende Meadow, 1985; Halo, 1986; On the Rim of the Mandala, 1987; Fortress on the Sun, 1997. *Literary Agent:* Richard Curtis Associates Inc., 171 E 74th Street, Second Floor, New York, NY 10021, USA. *Website:* www.curtisagency.com. *Address:* 1108 W Cornel, Tempe, AZ 85283, USA. *E-mail:* pcook@dancris.com.

COOK, Petronelle Marguerite Mary, (Margot Arnold), BA, DipArch, MA; British writer and teacher; b. 16 May 1925, Plymouth, Devon, England; m. Philip R. Cook, 20 July 1949, two s. one d. *Education:* University of Oxford. *Career:* mem. New England Historic and Genealogical Soc., Cornwall Family History Soc., University of Oxford Archaeological Soc. (pres. 1945). *Publications:* The Officers' Woman 1972, The Villa on the Palatine 1975, Marie 1979, Exit Actors, Dying 1980, The Cape Cod Caper 1980, Death of a Voodoo Doll 1981, Zadok's Treasurer 1981, Affairs of State 1981, Love Among the Allies 1982, Lament for a Lady Laird 1982, Death on the Dragon's Tongue 1982, Desperate Measures 1983, Sinister Purposes 1985, The Menehune Murders 1989, Toby's Folly 1990, The Catacomb Conspiracy 1991, The Cape Cod Conundrum 1992, Dirge for a Dorset Druid 1994, The Midas Murders 1995, Survivors and Non-Survivors 2002, The Well Man Trilogy 2003–04, Murder, with Supporting Cast 2005; as Petronelle Cook: The Queen Consorts of England 1993; contributions: numerous short stories to magazines. *Honours:* National Writers Club Fiction Prize 1983. *Address:* 11 High School Road, Hyannis, MA 02601, USA. *Telephone:* (508) 790-9468 (home).

COOK, Robin, BA, MD; American physician and writer; b. 4 May 1940, New York, NY; m. Barbara Ellen Mougin, 18 July 1979. *Education:* Wesleyan Univ., Columbia Univ., Harvard Univ. *Career:* Resident in General Surgery, Queen's Hospital, Honolulu 1966–68; Resident in Ophthalmology 1971–75, staff 1975–, Massachusetts Eye and Ear Infirmary, Boston. *Publications:* fiction: The Year of the Intern 1972, Coma 1977, Sphinx 1979, Brain 1981, Harmful Intent 1982, Fever 1982, Godplayer 1983, Mindbend 1985, Outbreak 1987, Mortal Fear 1988, Mutation 1989, Vital Signs 1991, Blindsight 1992, Fatal Cure 1993, Terminal 1993, Acceptable Risk 1995, Contagion 1996, Chromosome Six 1997, Invasion 1997, Toxin 1998, Vector 1999, Shock 2001, Abduction 2002, Seizure 2003, Marker 2005. *Address:* c/o Berkley Publicity, 375 Hudson Street, New York, NY 10014, USA.

COOK, Stanley, BA; British lecturer (retd) and poet; b. 12 April 1922, Austerfield, Yorkshire, England; m. Kathleen Mary Daly, one s. two d. *Education:* Christ Church, Oxford. *Career:* Lecturer, Huddersfield Polytechnic, 1969–81; Ed., Poetry Nottingham, 1981–85. *Publications:* Form Photograph, 1971; Sign of Life, 1972; Staff Photograph, 1976; Alphabet, 1976; Woods Beyond a Cornfield, 1981; Concrete Poems, 1984; Barnsdale, 1986; Selected Poems, 1972–86, 1986; The Northern Seasons, 1988. Other: Children's poems. *Honours:* Cheltenham Festival Competition Prize 1972.

COOK, Stanton R., BS; American newspaper publisher; b. 3 July 1925, Chicago, Ill.; s. of Rufus M. Cook and Thelma M. Borgerson; m. Barbara Wilson 1950 (died 1994). *Education:* Northwestern Univ. *Career:* Dist sales rep. Shell Oil Co. 1949–51; Production Eng Chicago Tribune Co. 1951–60, Asst Production Man. 1960–65, Production Man. 1965–67, Production Dir 1967–70, Dir Operations 1970, Gen. Man. 1970–72, Publr 1973–90, Pres. 1972–74, Chief Officer 1974–76, Chair. 1974–81; Dir Tribune Co. Chicago 1972–96, Pres. and CEO 1974–88, Chair. 1989–91; Chair. Chicago Nat. League Ball Club (Chicago Cubs) 1990–94; Dir A.P. 1975–84; Deputy Chair. and Dir Fed. Reserve Bank of Chicago 1980–83, Chair. 1984–85; mem. Bd of Dirs. Robert R. McCormick Tribune Foundation 1990–; numerous trusteeships. *Address:* 224 Raleigh Road, Kenilworth, IL 60043-1209, USA.

COOK, Thomas H., BA, MA, MPhil; American writer; b. 19 Sept. 1947, Fort Payne, AL; m. Susan Terner 1978; one d. *Education:* Georgia State Coll., Hunter Coll., CUNY, Columbia Univ. *Career:* teacher of English and history, Dekalb Community Coll., Clarkston, GA 1978–81; Contributing Ed. and Book Review Ed., Atlanta magazine 1978–82; mem. Authors' Guild, Authors' League. *Publications:* fiction: Blood Innocents 1980, The Orchids 1982, Tabernacle 1983, Elena 1986, Sacrificial Ground 1988, Flesh and Blood 1989, Streets of Fire 1989, Night Secrets 1990, The City When It Rains 1991, Evidence of Blood 1991, Mortal Memory 1993, Breakheart Hill 1995, The Chatham School Affair 1996, Instruments of Night 1998, Places in the Dark 2000, The Interrogation 2002, Red Leaves 2006, The Murmur of Stones 2006; non-fiction: Early Graves: The Shocking True-Crime Story of the Youngest Woman Ever Sentenced to Death Row 1990, Blood Echoes: The True Story of an Infamous Mass Murder and its Aftermath 1992. *Honours:* Edgar Allan Poe Awards 1981, 1988, Int. Asscn of Crime Writers Hammett Prize 1995, MWA Award 1996. *Address:* c/o Random House Inc., 1745 Broadway, New York, NY 10019, USA.

COOKE, John Peyton; American editor and writer; b. 7 March 1967, Amarillo, TX. *Education:* University of Wisconsin at Madison. *Career:* Assoc. Ed., Scientific American Medicine periodical, New York, 1994–; mem. MWA. *Publications:* The Lake, 1989; Out for Blood, 1991; Torsos, 1993; The Chimney Sweeper, 1994; Haven, 1996; The Rape of Ganymede, 1998. Contributions: anthologies and periodicals. *Honours:* First Place, Wyoming Young Author, 1982. *Address:* c/o Mysterious Press/Warner Books, 1271 Avenue of the Americas, New York, NY 10020, USA.

COOLIDGE, Clark; American poet; b. 26 Feb. 1939, Providence, RI; m. Susan Hopkins; one d. *Education:* Brown Univ. *Publications:* Flag Flutter and US Electric 1966, Poems 1967, Ing 1969, Space 1970, The So 1971, Moroccan Variations 1971, Suite V 1973, The Maintains 1974, Polaroid 1975, Quartz Hearts 1978, Own Face 1978, Smithsonian Depositions, and Subjects to a Film 1980, American Ones 1981, A Geology 1981, Research 1982, Mine: The One That Enters the Stories 1982, Solution Passage: Poems, 1978–1981 1986, The Crystal Text 1986, Mesh 1988, At Egypt 1988, Sound as Thought: Poems, 1982–1984 1990, The Book of During 1991, Odes of Roba 1991, Baffling Means 1991, On the Slates 1992, Lowell Connector: Lines and Shots from Kerouac's Town 1993, Own Face 1994, Registers: (People in All) 1994, The ROVA Improvisations 1994, Heart of the Breath: Poems 1979–1992 1996, Now It's Jazz (writing on music) 1999, On the Nameways 2000, Alien Tatters 2000, Bomb (anthology, with Keith Waldrop) 2001. *Honours:* NEA grant 1966, New York Poets Foundation Award 1968. *Address:* c/o Atelos, PO Box 5814, Berkeley, CA 94705-0814, USA.

COONEY, Raymond George Alfred, OBE; British actor, dramatist and director; b. 30 May 1932, London, England; m. Linda Dixon 1962; two s. *Career:* mem. Dramatists' Club. *Publications:* plays, both solo and in collaboration with others: One for the Pot 1961, Chase Me, Comrade 1964, Charlie Girl 1965, Bang Bang Beirut 1966, Not Now, Darling 1967, My Giddy Aunt 1968, Move Over Mrs Markham 1969, Why Not Stay for Breakfast? 1970, There Goes the Bride 1974, Run For Your Wife 1984, Two Into One 1985, Wife Begins at Forty 1986, It Runs in the Family 1987, Out of Order 1990, Funny Money 1994, Caught in the Net 2000. *Address:* Laurence Fitch Ltd, Mezzanine, Quadrant House, 80–82 Regent Street, London, W1B 5AU, England. *Telephone:* (20) 7734-9911. *E-mail:* information@laurencefitch.com. *Website:* www.laurencefitch.com.

COOPER, Jilly, OBE; British writer; b. 21 Feb. 1937, Hornchurch, Essex; d. of Brig. W. B. Sallitt, OBE and Mary Elaine Whincup; m. Leo Cooper 1961; one s. one d. *Education:* Godolphin School, Salisbury. *Career:* reporter, Middx Ind. 1957–59; account exec.; copy writer; publr's reader; various temporary roles 1959–69; columnist The Sunday Times 1969–82, Mail on Sunday 1982–87. *Publications:* How to Stay Married 1969, How Survive from Nine to Five 1970, Jolly Super 1971, Men and Super Men 1972, Jolly Super Too 1973, Women and Super Women 1974, Jolly Superlative 1975, Emily 1975, Super Men and Super Women 1976, Bella 1976, Harriet 1976, Octavia 1977, Work and Wedlock 1977, Superjilly 1977, Imogen 1978, Prudence 1978, Class 1979, Intelligent and Loyal 1980, Supercooper 1980, Violets and Vinegar (ed with Tom Hartman) 1980, The British in Love (ed) 1980, Love and Other Heartaches 1981, Jolly Marsupial 1982, Animals in War 1983, Leo and Jilly Cooper on Rugby 1984, The Common Years 1984, Riders 1985, Hotfoot to Zabriskie Point 1985, How to Survive Christmas 1986, 1996, Turn Right at the Spotted Dog 1987, Rivals 1988, Angels Rush In 1990, Polo 1991, The Man Who Made Husbands Jealous 1993, Araminta's Wedding 1993, Apassionata 1996, Score! 1999, Pandora 2002, Wicked! 2006. *Honours:* British Book Awards Lifetime Achievement Award 1998. *Literary Agent:* c/o Vivienne Schuster, Curtis Brown Ltd, Fourth Floor, Haymarket House, 28–29 Haymarket, London, SW1Y 4SP, England. *Telephone:* (20) 7393-4400. *Fax:* (20) 7393-4401. *E-mail:* cb@curtisbrown.co.uk. *Website:* www.curtisbrown.co.uk.

COOPER, Richard Newell, PhD; American economist, academic and fmr public official; *Maurits C. Boas Professor of International Economics, Harvard University*; b. 14 June 1934, Seattle, Wash.; s. of Richard W. Cooper and Lucile Newell; m. 1st Carolyn Cahalan 1956 (divorced 1980); m. 2nd Ann Lorraine Hollick 1982 (divorced 1994); m. 3rd Jin Chen 2000; two s. two d. *Education:* Oberlin Coll., London School of Econs, UK, Harvard Univ. *Career:* Sr Staff Economist, Council of Econ. Advisers 1961–63; Deputy Asst Sec. of State for Monetary Affairs 1965–66; Prof. of Econs, Yale Univ. 1966–77, Provost 1972–74; Under-Sec. of State for Econ. Affairs 1977–81; Maurits C. Boas Prof. of Int. Econs, Harvard Univ. 1981–; Dir Rockefeller Bros Fund 1975–77, Schroders Bank and Trust Co. 1975–77, Warburg-Pincus Funds 1986–98, Center for Naval Analysis 1992–95, Phoenix Cos 1983–2005, Circuit City Stores 1983–2004, CNA Corpn 1997–, Inst. for Int. Econs 1983–, Fed. Reserve Bank of Boston 1987–92 (Chair. 1990–92); Chair. Nat. Intelligence Council 1995–97; consultant to US Treasury, Nat. Security Council, World Bank, IMF, USN; Marshall Scholarship (UK) 1956–58; Fellow American Acad. of Sciences 1974. *Publications:* The Economics of Interdependence 1968, Economic Policy in an Interdependent World 1986, The International Monetary System 1987, Stabilization and Debt in Developing Countries 1992, Boom, Crisis and Adjustment (co-author) 1993, Environment and Resource Policies for the World Economy 1994, Trade Growth in Transition Economies (ed.) 1997, What The Future Holds (ed.) 2002; more than 300 articles. *Honours:* Hon. LLD (Oberlin Coll.) 1958; Dr hc (Paris II) 2000; Nat. Intelligence Medal 1996. *Address:* Center for International Affairs, Harvard University, 1737 Cambridge Street, Cambridge, MA 02138 (office); 33 Washington Avenue, Cambridge, MA 02140, USA (home). *Telephone:* (617) 495-5076 (office). *Fax:* (617) 495-8292 (office). *E-mail:* rcooper@fas.harvard.edu (office). *Website:* www.economics.harvard.edu (office).

COOPER, Susan Mary, MA; British writer; b. 23 May 1935, Burnham, Buckinghamshire; m. 1st Nicholas J. Grant 1963 (divorced 1982); one s. one d.; m. 2nd Hume Cronyn 1996 (died 2003). *Education:* Somerville Coll., Oxford. *Career:* mem. Authors' Guild, Soc. of Authors, Writers' Guild of America. *Publications:* Mandrake 1964, Behind the Golden Curtain: A View of the USA 1965, Essays of Five Decades by J. B. Priestley (ed.) 1968, J. B. Priestley: Portrait of an Author 1970, Foxfire (play with Hume Cronyn) 1982, Dreams and Wishes: Essays on Writing for Children 1996; children's fiction: Over Sea, Under Stone 1965, Dawn of Fear 1970, The Dark is Rising 1973, Greenwitch 1973, The Grey King 1975, Silver on the Tree 1975, Jethro and the Jumbie 1979, Seaward 1983, The Selkie Girl 1986, The Silver Cow: A Welsh Tale 1983, Matthew's Dragon 1991, Tam Lin 1991, Danny and the Kings 1993, The Boggart 1993, The Boggart and the Monster 1997, King of Shadows 1999, Frog 2002, Green Boy 2002, The Magician's Boy 2005, Victory 2006; television screenplays; contrib. to periodicals and anthologies. *Honours:* Horn Book

Fanfares, 1967, 1971, 1974, 1976, 1987, 1994, 2000; Boston Globe-Horn Book Awards, 1974, 1999; Newbery Honor Book, 1974; Newbery Medal, 1976; Tir na n-Og Awards, Welsh Arts Council, 1976, 1977; Silver Hugo Award, 1984; Writers' Guild of America Awards, 1984, 1985; Christopher Award, 1985; Judy Lopez Memorial Award for Children's Literature, 1993; Children's Book Award, Scottish Arts Council, 1999; Five ALA Notable Children's Books; Two Carnegie Medal Honor Books; Humanitas Prize. *Address:* c/o Margaret K. McElderry Books, Simon & Schuster, 1230 Sixth Avenue, New York, NY 10020, USA. *Website:* www.thelostland.com.

COOVER, Robert Lowell, MA; American writer, dramatist, poet and teacher; b. 4 Feb. 1932, Charles City, IA; m. Maria del Pilar Sans-Mallagre 1959, one s. two d. *Education:* Southern Illinois University, Indiana University, University of Chicago. *Career:* Teacher, Bard College, 1966–67, University of Iowa, 1967–69, Princeton University, 1972–73, Brown University, 1980–; various guest lectureships and professorships; mem. American Acad. and Institute of Arts and Letters, American Acad. of Arts & Sciences, PEN International, Bd of Dirs The Electronic Literature Org., numerous adv. bds. *Publications:* The Origin of the Brunists, 1966; The Universal Baseball Asscn, J. Henry Waugh, Prop., 1968; Pricksongs & Descants (short fictions), 1969; A Theological Position (plays), 1972; The Public Burning, 1977; A Political Fable (The Cat in the Hat for President), 1980; Spanking the Maid, 1982; In Bed One Night & Other Brief Encounters (short fictions) 1983, Gerald's Party, 1986; A Night at the Movies, 1987; Whatever Happened to Gloomy Gus of the Chicago Bears?, 1987; Pinocchio in Venice, 1991; John's Wife, 1996; Briar Rose, 1997, Ghost Town 1998, The Grand Hotels (of Joseph Cornell) 2002, The Adventures of Lucky Pierre, 2002. Contributions: Plays, poems, fiction, trans, essays and criticism in numerous publications and anthologies. *Honours:* William Faulkner Award for Best First Novel 1966, Rockefeller Foundation Grant 1969, Guggenheim Fellowships 1971, 1974, Obie Awards 1972–73, American Acad. of Arts and Letters Award 1976, National Endowment of the Humanities Grant 1985, Rhode Island Gov.'s Arts Award 1988, Deutscher Akademischer Austauschdienst Fellowship, Berlin 1990, Rhode Island Pell Award 1999, Lannan Foundation Fellowship 2000. *Address:* c/o Department of English, Brown University, Providence, RI 02912, USA. *Telephone:* (401) 863-1152.

COPE, Robert Knox, (Jack Cope); South African writer, poet and editor; b. 3 June 1913, Mooi River, Natal; m. Lesley de Villiers, 4 June 1942, two s. *Career:* co-founder and Ed., Contrast, South African, literary magazine, 1960–80. *Publications:* Lyrics and Diatribes, 1948; Selected Poems of Ingrid Jonker (co-trans.), 1968; The Rain Maker, 1971; The Student of Zend, 1972; My Son Max, 1977. Editor: Penguin Book of South African Verse. Other: Stage, radio and television adaptations. Contributions: School textbooks and magazines. *Honours:* British Council Award, 1960; Carnegie Fellowship, 1966; CNA Prize, Argus Prize, and Gold Medallist for Literature, Veld Trust Prize, 1971; Hon. DLitt (Rhodes Univ.).

COPE, Wendy Mary, MA, FRSL; British writer; b. 21 July 1945, Erith, Kent; d. of Fred Stanley Cope and Alice Mary Cope (née Hand). *Education:* Farringtons School, St Hilda's Coll., Oxford, Westminster Coll. of Educ., Oxford. *Career:* primary school teacher, London 1967–86; freelance writer 1986–; mem. Soc. of Authors (man. cttee 1992–95). *Publications include:* Across the City 1980, Hope and the 42 1984, Making Cocoa for Kingsley Amis 1986, Poem from a Colour Chart of House Paints 1986, Men and Their Boring Arguments 1988, Does She Like Wordgames? 1988, Twiddling Your Thumbs 1988, The River Girl 1990, Serious Concerns 1992, If I Don't Know 2001; editor: Is That the New Moon? – Poems by Women Poets 1989, The Orchard Book of Funny Poems 1993, The Funny Side 1998, The Faber Book of Bedtime Stories 2000, Heaven on Earth – 101 Happy Poems 2001, George Herbert: Verse and Prose (a selection) 2002; contribs to newspapers and reviews. *Honours:* Hon. DLitt (Southampton), (Oxford Brookes) 2003; Cholmondeley Award for Poetry 1987, Michael Braude Award for Light Verse, American Acad. of Arts and Letters 1995. *Literary Agent:* PFD, Drury House, 34–43 Russell Street, London, WC2B 5HA, England.

COPELAND, Ann (see Furtwängler, Virginia Walsh)

COPLEY, Paul; British actor and writer; b. 25 Nov. 1944, Denby Dale, Yorkshire, England; m. Natasha Pyne 1972. *Education:* Northern Counties Coll. of Education. *Career:* mem. Writers' Guild. *Stage performances:* John Wilson's For King and Country (Mermaid Theatre) (Plays and Players Most Promising Actor) 1976, The Servant (Birmingham Rep.) (Martini/TMA Award for Best Actor in a Supporting Role) 1995. *Plays staged:* Pillion (Bush Theatre, London) 1977, Viaduct (Bush Theatre, London) 1979, Tapster (Stephen Joseph Theatre, Scarborough) 1981, Fire-Eaters (Tricycle Theatre, London) 1984, Calling (Stephen Joseph Theatre, Scarborough) 1986. *Plays broadcast:* On May-Day (BBC Radio 4 Sunday Play) 1986, Tipperary Smith (BBC Radio 4) 1994, King Street Junior (episodes, Radio 4) 1995–98, Words Alive (BBC Education Radio) 1996–2003. *Publications:* plays: Odysseus and the Cyclops 1998, Chaucer's The Pardoner's Tale (adaptation) 1999, Jennifer Jenks and her Excellent Day Out 2000, Loki the Mischief Maker 2000. *Honours:* Olivier Award for Actor of the Year in a New Play 1976. *Address:* Casarotto Ramsay Ltd, 60 Wardour Street, London, W1V 4ND, England. *Website:* www.mrcopley .com.

CORBEN, Beverly Balkum, AA, BA, MA; American educator (retd), poet, writer and artist; b. 6 Aug. 1926; m. Herbert Charles Corben 1957; one step-s. two step-d. *Education:* Santa Monica College, University of California, Los Angeles, Case Western Reserve University. *Career:* Teaching Asst, 1972–73, Dir of Writing Laboratory, 1973–78, 1980–82, Scarborough College, University of Toronto, Canada; Visiting Scholar, 1978–80, Scholar-in-Residence, 1982–88, Harvey Mudd College; mem. Mississippi Poetry Society; Gulf Coast Writers Asscn; Writers Unlimited, pres., 1991, 1992; Acad. of American Poets. *Publications:* On Death and Other Reasons for Living (poems), 1972. Contributions: Poetic Justice; Texas Review; Voices International; Prophetic Voices; Modern Haiku; Old Hickory Review. *Honours:* Cleveland State University Hon. Alumna, 1971; More than 60 awards for poetry and fiction nationwide, 1989–.

CORBIN, Alain, BA, MA, PhD; French academic and writer; b. 12 Jan. 1936, Courtomer; m. Annie Lagorce 1963, two s. *Education:* University of Caen. *Career:* Asst Lecturer, University of Limoges, 1968–69; Senior Lecturer, 1969–72, Asst Prof., 1973–85, Prof. of History, 1985–86, University of Tours; Prof. of History, University of Paris, 1987–. *Publications:* (in English trans.) The Foul and the Fragrant: Odor and the French Social Imagination, 1986; A History of Private Life, Vol. 4, From the Fires of Revolution to the Great War (with Michelle Perrot), 1990; The Village of Cannibals: Rage and Murder in France, 1870, 1991; Women for Hire: Prostitution and Sexuality in France After 1850, 1992; The Lure of the Sea, 1994; Time, Desire, and Horror, 1996; Village Bells: Sound and Meaning in the Nineteenth-Century Countryside, 1998. Contributions: scholarly books and journals.

COREN, Alan, MA; British editor, author and broadcaster; b. 27 June 1938, London; s. of Samuel Coren and Martha Coren; m. Anne Kasriel 1963; one s. one d. *Education:* East Barnet Grammar School, Wadham Coll., Oxford, Univ. of California, Berkeley and Yale Univ. *Career:* Asst Ed. Punch 1963–66, Literary Ed. 1966–69, Deputy Ed. 1969–77, Ed. 1977–87; Ed. The Listener 1988–89; TV critic, The Times 1971–78, Columnist 1988–; Daily Mail 1972–76, Mail on Sunday 1984–92, Sunday Express 1992–96; contrib. to Observer, Listener, Sunday Times, Atlantic Monthly, TV Guide, Tatler, Times Literary Supplement, London Review of Books, Daily Telegraph, The Spectator, Playboy, Guardian; Commonwealth Fellowship 1961–63; Rector St Andrew's Univ. 1973–76. *Publications:* The Dog it was that Died 1965, All Except the Bastard 1969, The Sanity Inspector 1974, The Collected Bulletins of Idi Amin 1974, Golfing for Cats 1975, The Further Bulletins of Idi Amin 1975, The Arthur Books (12 novellas) 1976–80, The Lady from Stalingrad Mansions 1977, The Peanut Papers 1977, The Rhinestone as Big as the Ritz 1979, Tissues for Men 1980, The Cricklewood Diet 1982, Bumf 1984, Something for the Weekend 1986, Bin Ends 1987, Seems Like Old Times 1989, More Like Old Times 1990, A Year in Cricklewood 1991, Toujours Cricklewood? 1993, Sunday Best 1993, Animal Passions 1994, A Bit on the Side 1995, The Alan Coren Omnibus 1996, The Cricklewood Dome 1998, The Cricklewood Tapestry 2000. *Honours:* Hon. DLitt (Nottingham) 1993, British Soc. of Magazine Eds. Ed. of the Year 1986. *Address:* c/o The Times, News International Ltd, 1 Virginia Street, London, E98 1SS, England.

CORK, Richard Graham, MA, PhD; British art critic, writer, broadcaster and exhibition organizer; b. 25 March 1947, Eastbourne; m. Vena Jackson 1970; two s. two d. *Education:* Trinity Hall, Cambridge. *Career:* art critic, Evening Standard 1969–77, 1980–83, The Listener 1984–90; Ed., Studio International 1975–79; Durning-Lawrence Lecturer, Univ. Coll. London 1987; Slade Prof. of Fine Art, Cambridge 1989–90; Chief Art Critic, The Times 1991–2002; Art Critic, The New Statesman 2003–06; Henry Moore Foundation Sr Fellow, Courtauld Inst. of Art, London 1992–95; mem. Arts Council Visual Arts Panel (Chair.), British Council Visual Arts Advisory Cttee, Contemporary Art Soc., South Bank Bd Visual Art Advisory Panel, Syndic of Fitzwilliam Museum, Cambridge, Paul Mellon Centre Advisory Council. *Publications:* Vorticism and Abstract Art in the First Machine Age (two vols) 1975–76, The Social Role of Art 1979, Art Beyond the Gallery in Early Twentieth Century England 1985, David Bomberg 1987, Architect's Choice 1992, A Bitter Truth: Avant-Garde Art and the Great War 1994, Bottle of Notes: Claes Oldenburg and Coosje van Bruggen 1997, Jacob Epstein 1999, Everything Seemed Possible: Art in the 1970s 2003, New Spirit, New Sculpture, New Money: Art in the 1980s 2003, Breaking Down the Barriers: Art in the 1990s 2003, Annus Mirabilis? Art in the Year 2000 2003, Michael Craig-Martin 2006; numerous essays for catalogues and contribs to art magazines and periodicals. *Honours:* John Llewelyn Rhys Memorial Prize 1976, Sir Banister Fletcher Award 1986, Nat. Art Collections Fund Award 1995. *Address:* 24 Milman Road, London, NW6 6EG, England.

CORKHILL, Annette Robyn, BA, DipEd, MA, PhD; Australian writer, poet and translator; b. (Annette Robyn Vernon), 10 Sept. 1955, Brisbane; m. Alan Corkhill 1977; two s. one d. *Career:* teacher of foreign languages; now self-employed translator from German 1994–. *Publications:* The Jogger: Anthology of Australian Poetry 1987, Destination, Outrider 1987, Mangoes Encounter – Queensland Summer 1987, Age 1, LINQ 1987, Two Soldiers of Tiananmen, Earth Against Heaven 1990, Australian Writing: Ethnic Writers 1945–1991 1994, The Immigrant Experience in Australian Literature 1995; contrib. to Outrider, Australian Literary Studies. *Honours:* hon. mention The Creativity Centre, Harold Kesteven Poetry Prize 1987. *Address:* 5 Wattletree Place, The Gap, Qld 4061, Australia (home). *Telephone:* (7) 3300-4878. *Fax:* (7) 3300-4878. *E-mail:* translation@uq.net.au. *Website:* www.germantranslation .com.au.

CORMAN, Avery, BS; American novelist; b. 28 Nov. 1935, New York, NY; m. Judith Lishinsky 1967, two s. *Education:* New York University. *Career:* mem.

PEN American Center; Writers Guild of America. *Publications:* Oh God!, 1971; Kramer Vs Kramer, 1977; The Bust-Out King, 1977; The Old Neighborhood, 1980; Fifty, 1987; Prized Possessions, 1991; The Big Hype, 1992.

CORN, Alfred, BA, MA; American poet, writer, critic and translator; b. 14 Aug. 1943, Bainbridge, GA; m. Ann Jones 1967 (divorced 1971). *Education:* Emory University, Columbia University. *Career:* Poet-in-Residence, George Mason University, 1980, Blaffer Foundation, New Harmony, IN, 1989, James Thurber House, 1990; Humanities Lecturer, New School for Social Research, New York City, 1988; Ellison Chair in Poetry, University of Cincinnati, 1989; Bell Distinguished Visiting Prof., University of Tulsa, 1992; Hurst Residency in Poetry, Washington University, St Louis, 1994; numerous college and university seminars and workshops; many poetry readings; mem. National Book Critics Circle; PEN; Poetry Society of America. *Publications:* Poetry: All Roads at Once, 1976; A Call in the Midst of the Crowd, 1978; The Various Light, 1980; Tongues on Trees, 1980; The New Life, 1983; Notes from a Child of Paradise, 1984; An Xmas Murder, 1987; The West Door, 1988; Autobiographies, 1992; Present, 1997. Novel: Part of His Story, 1997. Criticism: The Metamorphoses of Metaphor, 1987; Incarnation: Contemporary Writers on the New Testament (ed.), 1990; The Pith Helmet, 1992; A Manual of Prosody, 1997. Contributions: Books, anthologies, scholarly journals, and periodicals. *Honours:* Woodrow Wilson Fellow, 1965–66; Fulbright Fellow, Paris, 1967–68; Ingram Merrill Fellowships, 1974, 1981; National Endowment for the Arts Fellowships for Poetry, 1980, 1991; Gustav Davidson Prize, Poetry Society of America, 1983; American Acad. and Institute of Arts and Letters Award, 1983; New York Foundation for the Arts Fellowships, 1986, 1995; Guggenheim Fellowship, 1986–87; Acad. of American Poets Prize, 1987; Yaddo Corporation Fellowship in Poetry, 1989; Djerassi Foundation Fellowship in Poetry, 1990; Rockefeller Foundation Fellowship in Poetry, Bellagio, Italy, 1992; MacDowell Colony Fellowships in Poetry, 1994, 1996.

CORNWELL, Bernard, (Susannah Kells), BA; British writer; b. 23 Feb. 1944, London, England; m. Judy Acker 1980. *Education:* Univ. of London. *Publications:* Redcoat 1987, Wildtrack 1988, Sea Lord (aka Killer's Wake) 1989, Crackdown (aka Murder Cay) 1990, Stormchild 1991, Scoundrel 1992, Stonehenge 2000 BC 1999, The Archer's Tale 2001, Gallows Thief 2001, The Last Kingdom 2004, The Pale Horseman 2005, Lords of the North Country 2006; Starbuck Chronicles series: Rebel 1993, Copperhead 1994, Battle Flag 1995, The Bloody Ground 1996; Arthur series: The Winter King 1995, Enemy of God 1996, Excalibur 1997; Sharpe series: Sharpe's Eagle 1981, Sharpe's Gold 1981, Sharpe's Company 1982, Sharpe's Sword 1983, Sharpe's Enemy 1984, Sharpe's Honour 1985, Sharpe's Regiment 1986, Sharpe's Siege 1987, Sharpe's Rifles 1988, Sharpe's Revenge 1989, Sharpe's Waterloo 1990, Sharpe's Devil 1992, Sharpe's Battle 1995, Sharpe's Tiger 1997, Sharpe's Triumph 1998, Sharpe's Fortress 1999, Sharpe's Trafalgar 2000, Sharpe's Prey 2001, Sharpe's Skirmish (short story) 2002, Sharpe's Havoc 2003, Sharpe's Escape 2004, Sharpe's Fury 2006; Grail Quest series: Harlequin 2000, Vagabond 2002, Heretic 2003; as Susannah Kells: A Crowning Mercy 1983, The Fallen Angels 1984, Coat of Arms 1986, The Aristocrats 1987. *Literary Agent:* Toby Eady Associates Ltd, Third Floor, 9 Orme Court, London, W2 4RL, England. *Telephone:* (20) 7792-0092. *Fax:* (20) 7792-0879. *E-mail:* toby@tobyeady.demon.co.uk. *Website:* www.tobyeadyassociates.co.uk; www.bernardcornwell.net.

CORNWELL, David John Moore, (John le Carré), BA; British writer; b. 19 Oct. 1931, Poole, Dorset; s. of Ronald Thomas Archibald Cornwell and Olive Glassy; m. 1st Alison Ann Veronica Sharp 1954 (divorced 1971); three s.; m. 2nd Valerie Jane Eustace 1972; one s. *Education:* St Andrew's Preparatory School, Pangbourne, Sherborne School, Berne Univ., Switzerland and Lincoln Coll., Oxford. *Career:* teacher, Eton Coll. 1956–58; in Foreign Service (Second Sec., Bonn, then Political Consul Hamburg) 1959–64. *Publications:* Call for the Dead 1961, Murder of Quality 1962, The Spy Who Came in From the Cold 1963, The Looking Glass War 1965, A Small Town in Germany 1968, The Naive and Sentimental Lover 1971, Tinker, Tailor, Soldier, Spy 1974, The Honourable Schoolboy 1977, Smiley's People 1979, The Quest for Carla (collected edn of previous three titles) 1982, The Little Drummer Girl 1983, A Perfect Spy 1986, The Russia House 1989, The Secret Pilgrim 1991, The Night Manager 1993, Our Game 1995, The Tailor of Panama 1996, Single and Single 1999, The Constant Gardener (British Book Awards Play.com TV & Film Book of the Year 2006) 2000, Absolute Friends 2004, The Mission Song 2006. *Honours:* Hon. Fellow Lincoln Coll. Oxford 1984–; Commdr de l'Ordre des Arts et des Lettres 2005; Hon. DLitt (Exeter) 1990, (St Andrews) 1996, (Southampton) 1997, (Bath) 1998; Somerset Maugham Award 1963, MWA Edgar Allan Poe Award 1965, James Tait Black Award 1977, CWA Gold Dagger 1978, MWA 'Grand Master Award' 1986, Premio Malaparte 1987, CWA Diamond Dagger 1988, Nikos Kazantzakis Prize 1991, CWA 'Dagger of Daggers' 2005. *Literary Agent:* David Higham Associates, 5–8 Lower John Street, Golden Square, London, W1F 9HA, England. *Telephone:* (20) 7434-5900. *Fax:* (20) 7437-1072.

CORNWELL, Patricia Daniels, BA; American writer; b. 9 June 1957, Miami, FL. *Education:* Davidson Coll. (NC). *Career:* police reporter, Charlotte Observer, NC 1979–81; computer analyst, Office of the Chief Medical Examiner, Richmond, Va 1985–91; mem. Authors' Guild, Int. Asscn of Identification, Int. Crime Writers Asscn, Nat. Asscn of Medical Examiners. *Publications include:* non-fiction: A Time of Remembering: The Story of Ruth Bell Graham 1983 (re-issued as Ruth: a Portrait 1997); fiction: Postmortem (John Creasey Award, British Crime Writers' Asscn 1991, Anthony Award, Boucheron Award, World Mystery Convention, MacAvity Award, Mystery Readers Int) 1990, Body of Evidence 1991, All That Remains 1992, Cruel and Unusual 1993, The Body Farm 1994, From Potter's Field 1995, Cause of Death 1996, Hornet's Nest 1996, Unnatural Exposure 1997, Point of Origin 1998, Southern Cross 1999, Black Notice 1999, The Last Precinct 2001, Isle of Dogs 2001, Portrait of a Killer: Jack the Ripper 2002, Blow Fly 2003, Trace 2004, Predator 2005, At Risk 2006. *Honours:* Investigative Reporting Award, N Carolina Press Asscn 1980, Gold Medallion Book Award, Evangelical Christian Publishers Asscn 1985, Edgar Award 1990, Prix du Roman d'Aventure 1991, Gold Dagger Award 1993, Sherlock Holmes Award 1999. *Address:* c/o Don Congdon Associates Inc., 156 5th Avenue, Suite 625, New York, NY 10010-7002, USA; c/o Little, Brown & Co., Brettenham House, Lancaster Place, London, WC2E 7EN, England.

CORONEL, Sheila S.; Philippine journalist; *Executive Director, Philippine Center for Investigative Journalism. Career:* began as cub reporter for Philippine Panorama 1983; reporter for The Manila Times, Manila Chronicle; Co-founder Philippine Center for Investigative Journalism 1989, currently Exec. Dir. *Honours:* Ramón Magsaysay Award for Journalism 2003. *Address:* Philippine Center for Investigative Journalism, PO Box 13038, Ortigas Center, Pasig, Metro Manila, The Philippines (office). *E-mail:* scoronel@pcij.org (office). *Website:* www.pcij.org (office).

COSGRAVE, Patrick, BA, MA, PhD; Irish writer; b. 28 Sept. 1941, Dublin; m. 1st Ruth Dudley Edwards 1965 (divorced); m. 2nd Norma Alice Green 1974 (divorced); one d.; m. 3rd Shirley Ward 1981. *Education:* University College, Dublin, Peterhouse, Cambridge. *Career:* London Ed., Radio Telefis Eireann, 1968–69; Conservative Research Department, 1969–71; Political Ed., The Spectator, 1971–75; Features Ed., Telegraph Magazine, 1974–76; Special Adviser to Rt Hon. Mrs Margaret Thatcher, 1975–79; Managing Ed., Quartet Crime (Quartet Books), 1979–81. *Publications:* The Public Poetry of Robert Lowell, 1969; Churchill at War: Alone, 1974; Cheyney's Law (novel), 1976; Margaret Thatcher: A Tory and Her Party, 1978, second edn as Margaret Thatcher: Prime Minister, 1979; The Three Colonels (novel), 1979; R. A. Butler: An English Life, 1981; Adventure of State (novel), 1984; Thatcher: The First Term, 1985; Carrington: A Life and a Policy, 1985; The Lives of Enoch Powell, 1989; The Strange Death of Socialist Britain, 1992. Contributions: various journals and magazines.

ĆOSIĆ, Dobrica; Serbian writer and politician; b. 29 Dec. 1921, Velika Drenova; m. Božica Ćosić; one d. *Education:* Belgrade Univ., Higher Party School. *Career:* war service 1941–45; worked as journalist, then as freelance writer; corresp. mem. Serbian Acad. of Arts and Sciences 1970, mem. 1976; left League of Communists of Yugoslavia (LCY), prosecuted; resumed active political activity 1980s; Pres. of Repub. of Yugoslavia 1992–93. *Publications:* The Sun is Far 1951, Roots 1954, Sections 1961, Fairy Tale 1965, The Time of Death (Vols 1–4) 1972–79, The Time of Evil: Sinner (Vols 1–4) 1985, Apostate 1986, Believer 1990, The Time of Power 1995, Kosovo; studies and essays: Hope and Fear 2001, Real and Possible 2001, Serbian Question (Vols 1–4) 2002, Writer's Notes (Vols 1–4) 2002. *Address:* Serbian Academy of Sciences and Arts, Knez Mikhailova Str. 35, Belgrade (office); Branka Djonovića 6, Belgrade, Serbia (home). *Telephone:* (11) 3342400 (office); (11) 663437 (home). (11) 182825*E-mail:* sasapres@bib.sanu.ac.yu (office).

COSMOS, Jean; French playwright; b. (Jean Louis Gaudrat), 14 June 1923, Paris; s. of Albert Gaudrat and Maria Maillebuau; m. Alice Jarrousse 1948; one s. two d. *Education:* Inst. St Nicholas, Igny, Coll. Jean-Baptiste Say, Paris. *Career:* songwriter 1945–50, writer for radio 1952–60, for TV 1964–; mem. Comm. Soc. des auteurs dramatiques 1971–; co-librettist Goya 1996 (opera). *Plays:* author or adapter of numerous plays for the theatre including la Fille du roi 1952, Au jour le jour 1952, les Grenadiers de la reine 1957, Macbeth 1959, 1965, le Manteau 1963, la Vie et la Mort du roi Jean 1964, Arden de Faversham 1964, Monsieur Alexandre 1965, la Bataille de Lobositz 1969, Major Barbara 1970, le Marchand de Venise 1971, Sainte Jeanne des Abattoirs 1972, Ce sacré Bonheur 1987; author of numerous TV plays including les Oranges (Albert Ollivier prize) 1964, le Pacte 1966, Un homme, un cheval 1968, la Pomme oubliée (after Jean Anglade), l'Ingénu (after Voltaire), Bonsoir Léon, la Tête à l'envers, le Trêve, le Coup Monté, Aide-toi, Julien Fontanes, magistrat (TV Series 1980–89), La Dictée 1984; with Jean Chatenêt: 16 à Kerbriant, Ardéchois coeur fidèle (Critics' choice) 1975, Les Yeux Bleus, la Lumière des Justes (after Henri Troyat); with Gilles Perrault: le Secret des dieux, la Filière, Fabien de la Drôme, seven-part serial of Julien Fontanes, Magistrat, regular contrib. to les Cinq dernières minutes. *Films include:* Bonjour toubib 1959 La vie et rien d'autre 1989, Le Colonel Chabert 1994, La fille de d'Artagnan 1994, Capitaine Conan 1996, Le bossu 1997, Laissez-passer 2002, Effroyables jardins 2003. *Honours:* TV, Soc. des auteurs et compositeurs prizes 1970; Chevalier Légion d'honneur, Officier des Arts et des Lettres. *Address:* c/o Artmédia, 20 avenue Rapp, 75007 Paris (office); 57 rue de Versailles, 92410 Ville d'Avray, France (home).

COSSERY, Albert; French writer and poet; b. 1913, Cairo, Egypt. *Career:* fmrly in Egyptian merchant navy; emigrated to Paris 1945. *Publications:* poetry: Les Morsures 1931; fiction: Les hommes oubliés de Dieu (trans. as Men God Forgot) 1942, La maison de la mort certaine (trans. as The House of Certain Death) 1942, Les fainéants dans la vallée fertile (trans. as The Lazy Ones) 1947, Mendiants et orgueilleux (trans. as If All Men were Beggars, aka A Room in Cairo, Proud Beggars) 1945, La violence et la derision 1964, Un complot de saltimbanques 1973, Une ambition dans le désert 1984, Les couleurs d'infamie 1999. *Address:* c/o Hotel La Louisiane, 60 rue de Seine, 75006 Paris, France.

COSTANZA, Mary Scarpone, BFA, BS; American artist, writer, poet and lecturer; b. 14 May 1927, Berwyn, PA; m. John Costanza 1951; one s. one d. *Education:* Tyler School of Fine Arts, Temple University. *Career:* Dir, Costanza Art Gallery; Painting exhibitions; mem. American-Italian Historical Asscn; Authors' Guild; Holocaust Memorial Museum. *Publications:* Kaddish/ Six Million, 1978; The Living Witness: Art in the Concentration Camps and Ghettos, 1982; Shoah (poems), 1997; Country Cousins (short stories), 1999. *Honours:* grants and awards. *Address:* 737 Polo Road, Bryn Mawr, PA 19010, USA.

COTTA, Michèle, LèsL, DrèsScPol; French journalist; *Director General, France 2*; b. 15 June 1937, Nice; d. of Jacques Cotta and Helène Scoffier; m. 1st Claude Tchou (divorced); one s. (deceased) one d.; m. 2nd Phillipe Barret 1992. *Education:* Lycée de Nice, Faculté de Lettres de Nice and Inst. d'études politiques de Paris. *Career:* journalist with L'Express 1963–69, 1971–76; Europ I 1970–71, 1986; political diarist, France-Inter 1976–80; Head of political service, Le Point 1977–80, Reporter 1986; Chief Political Ed. RTL 1980–81; Pres. Dir-Gen. Radio France 1981–82; Pres. Haute Autorité de la Communication Audiovisuelle 1982–86; Producer Faits de Soc. on TF1 1987, Dir of Information 1987–92, Pres. Sofica Images Investissements 1987; producer and presenter La Revue de presse, France 2 1993–95; political ed. Nouvel Economiste 1993–96; producer and presenter Polémiques, France 2 1995–99, Dir-Gen. France 2 1999–; editorial writer, RTL 1996–99; mem. Conseil économique et social. *Publications:* La collaboration 1940–1944, 1964, Les elections présidentielles 1966, Prague, l'êté des Tanks 1968, La Vième République 1974, Les miroirs de Jupiter 1986, Les Secrets d'une Victoire 1995. *Honours:* Chevalier, Légion d'honneur, Officier, Ordre nat. du mérite. *Address:* 70 boulevard Port Royal, 75005 Paris, France (home). *Telephone:* 1-49-22-20-16 (office); 1-49-22-20-17 (office); 6-09-48-10-00. *E-mail:* michele .cotta@groupe-ab.fr (office); mcotta@noos.fr (home). *Website:* www.france2.fr (office).

COULOMBE, Charles Aquila; American writer; b. 8 Nov. 1960, New York, NY; s. of the late Guy Coulombe and of Patricia Coulombe. *Education:* New Mexico Military Inst., Roswell. *Career:* mem. Authors' Guild, Catholic Writers' Guild of Great Britain. *Publications:* Everyman Today Call Rome 1987, The White Cockade 1990, Puritan's Progress 1996, The Muse in the Bottle 2002, Classic Horror Tales 2003, Vicars of Christ 2003, Rum 2004, Haunted Places in America 2004, Haunted Castles Around the World 2005; contrib. to periodicals. *Honours:* Christian Law Inst. Christ the King Award 1992, Knight Commdr of St Sylvester. *Literary Agent:* Wieser & Elwell, 80 Fifth Avenue, Suite 1101, New York, NY 10011, USA. *Address:* PO Box 660771, Arcadia, CA 91066, USA (office). *Telephone:* (626) 357-7236 (office). *E-mail:* ccoulomb@charlesacoulombe.com (office). *Website:* www.charlesacoulombe .com.

COULTER, Harris Livermore, BA, PhD; American writer and translator; b. 8 Oct. 1932, Baltimore, MD; m. Catherine Nebolsine 1960, two s. two d. *Education:* Yale University, Columbia University. *Publications:* Divided Legacy: A History of the Schism in Medical Thought, Vol. I: The Patterns Emerge, 1975, Vol. II: The Origins of Modern Western Medicine, 1977, Vol. III: Homeopathy and the American Medical Asscn, 1981, Vol. IV: Twentieth-Century Medicine: The Bacteriological Era, 1994; Homeopathic Science and Modern Medicine, 1981; DPT: A Shot in the Dark (with Barbara Fisher), 1985; Vaccination, Social Violence, and Criminality, 1990; The Controlled Clinical Trial: An Analysis, 1991; Aids and Syphilis: The Hidden Link. *Honours:* Hahnemann Prize, Société Royale Belge d'Homéopathie, 1985; La Medalla d'Or del Centenari, Academia Medico-Homepatica de Barcelona, 1990.

COUPER, Heather Anita, CBE, BSc, PhD, CPhys, FInstP, FRAS; British science broadcaster and writer; b. 2 June 1949, d. of George and the late Anita (née Taylor) Couper. *Education:* St Mary's Grammar School (Northwood) and Univs of Leicester and Oxford. *Career:* man. trainee Peter Robinson Ltd 1967–69; Research Asst Cambridge Observatories 1969–70; Lecturer Greenwich Planetarium, Old Royal Observatory 1977–83; Gresham Prof. of Astronomy 1993–96; mem. Millennium Commission 1994–; co-founder and Dir Pioneer Productions 1988–99; Pres. British Astronomy Asscn 1984–86; presenter numerous TV and radio programmes; columnist The Independent. *Television includes:* Heavens Above 1981, Spacewatch 1983, The Planets (series, Channel 4) 1985, The Stars (series, Channel 4) 1988, The Neptune Encounter (ITV) 1989, A Close Encounter of the Second Kind (BBC, Horizon) 1992, ET – Please Call Earth (Channel 4) 1992, Space Shuttle Discovery (Channel 4) 1993, Arthur C. Clarke: Visionary (Discovery Channel Europe) 1995, Electric Skies (Channel 4) 1996, The Science Behind Science Fiction (series, Channel 4) 1996, On Jupiter 1996, Black Holes 1997, Raging Planet (series, Channel 4) 1997–98, The Caspian Sea Monster (Channel 4) 1998, Killer Earth (series, Channel 4) 1998, Stormforce (series, Channel 4) 1999, Stephen Hawking: A Profile (BBC) 2002, Space Shuttle: Human Time Bomb? (Channel 4) 2003. *Radio includes:* Science Now 1983, Cosmic Pursuits 1985, Seeing Stars 1991–2001, ET on Trial 1993, Starwatch (series, BBC Radio 4) 1996, Sun Science 1999, The Essential Guide to the 21st Century (series, BBC World Service) 2000, Worlds Beyond (series, BBC Radio 4), Red Planet (series, BBC Radio 4), Naming the Universe (series, BBC Radio 4), The Modern Magi

(BBC Radio 4), Down Your Way (BBC Radio 4), With Great Pleasure (BBC Radio 4); numerous guest broadcasts, interviews, etc. *Publications:* Exploring Space 1980, Heavens Above (with Terence Murtagh) 1981, Journey into Space 1984, Starfinder (co-author) 1984, The Halley's Comet Pop-Up Book (with Patrick Moore) 1985, The Universe: A 3-Dimensional study (with David Pelham) 1985, Space Scientist (series) 1985–87, Comets and Meteors: The Planets, The Stars, The Sun (co-author), The Moon (co-author), Galaxies and Quasars (co-author), Satellites and Spaceprobes (co-author), Telescopes and Observatories (co-author), The Space Atlas (with Nigel Henbest) 1992, The Guide to the Galaxy (with Nigel Henbest) 1994, How the Universe Works (with Nigel Henbest) 1994, Black Holes (co-author) 1996, Big Bang (co-author) 1997, Is Anybody Out There? (co-author) 1998, To the Ends of the Universe (with Nigel Henbest) 1998, Space Encyclopedia (with Nigel Henbest) 1999, Universe (with Nigel Henbest) 1999, Mars: The Inside Story of the Red Planet (co-author) 2001, Extreme Universe (with Nigel Henbest) 2001, Mars: The Inside Story of the Red Planet (with Nigel Henbest) 2001, Philip's Stargazing 2005 (with Nigel Henbest) 2004. *Honours:* Hon. DLitt (Loughborough) 1991, Hon. DSc (Hertfordshire) 1994, (Leicester) 1994; Times Educational Supplement Sr Information Book Award 1987, New York TV Awards Gold Medal 1994, 1996, Banff Rockie Award 1995, New York Festivals Grand Award 1997 and Gold Medal 1998. *Literary Agent:* c/o Anthony Goff, David Higham Associates, 5–8 Lower John Street, Golden Square London, W1R 4HA, England. *E-mail:* heather@hencoup.com. *Website:* www.hencoup.com/ Heather.htm.

COUPLAND, Douglas Campbell; Canadian writer and artist; b. 30 Dec. 1961, Baden-Solingen, Germany. *Education:* Emily Carr Inst. for Art and Design, Vancouver, also studied in Japan and Italy. *Publications:* Generation X: Tales for an Accelerated Culture 1991, Shampoo Planet 1992, Life After God 1994, Microserfs 1995, Polaroids from the Dead (non-fiction) 1996, Girlfriend in a Coma 1997, Miss Wyoming 1999, City of Glass (non-fiction) 2000, God Hates Japan 2001, All Families are Psychotic 2001, Souvenir of Canada (non-fiction) 2002, School Spirit (non-fiction) 2002, Hey Nostradamus! 2003, September 10 (play) 2004, Souvenir of Canada 2 (non-fiction) 2004, Eleanor Rigby 2004, JPod 2006; contrib. to Art Forum, New Republic, New York Times, Wired. *Address:* c/o Fiona McMorrough, Flamingo, HarperCollinsPublishers, 77–85 Fulham Palace Road, Hammersmith, London, W6 8JB, England. *E-mail:* fionam@fmcm.co.uk. *Address:* c/o Writer's Union of Canada, 40 Wellington Street E, Third Floor, Toronto, ON M5E 1C7, Canada. *Website:* www.coupland.com.

COUR, Ajeet, MEcons; Indian writer; *Chairman, Academy of Fine Arts and Literature*; b. 16 Nov. 1934, Lahore, Pakistan; d. of M. S. Bajaj and Jaswant Kaur; m. Rajinder Singh 1953 (deceased); one d. (Arpana Caur). *Education:* Univ. of Delhi. *Career:* writer 1961–, accredited journalist 1963–; Chief Ed. Rupee Trade 1963–; Chair. Acad. of Fine Arts and Literature 1975–; Vice-Chair. Indian Council of Poverty Alleviation 1991; Writer-Del. Int. Women's Congress (Moscow, Russian Fed.) 1987; many works have been made into TV films, including Doosra Kewal (13 episodes). *Publications include:* Directory of Indian Women Today (ed.), Directory of Trade Between India and East European Countries; short stories: Gul Bano 1962, Mahik Di Maut, But Shikan, Faltu Aurat, Saviyan Chirian, Maut Ali Babe Dee, Na Maaro, Guari; Novellas: Dhupp Wala Shehar, Post Mortem, Pebbles in a Tin Drum 1997; Autobiography: Khaana Badosh (Sahitya Akademi Award 1986); Translations and adaptations: Portrait of a Lady (Henry James), Return of the Red Rose (K. A. Abbas), The Scarlet Letter (Hawthorne), The Sikhs (Khushwant Singh). *Honours:* numerous awards, including Shiromani Sahitkar of the Year 1979, Punjabi Sahitya Samikhta Bd 1979, one of Nine Distinguished Punjabi Writers and Artists, Punjab Govt 1979, Int. IATA Award 1984, Sahitya Akademi Award 1985, Bharatiya Bhasha Parishad (Calcutta) Award 1989, Punjabi Sahitya Sabha Award 1989, Dhaliwal Award 1990. *Address:* 166 SFS Flats, Mount Kallash, opp Delhi Public School, New Delhi 110 065, India (home). *Telephone:* (11) 6438070.

COURTEMANCHE, Gil; Canadian journalist and writer; b. Montréal, QC. *Film:* The Gospel of AIDS. *Publications:* Douces colères 1989, Trente artistes dans un train 1989, Chroniques internationales 1991, Québec (non-fiction) 1998, Nouvelles douces colères (non-fiction) 1999, Un Dimanche à la piscine à Kigali (novel, trans. as A Sunday at the Pool in Kigali) 2000. *Honours:* Prix des Libraires 2000. *Address:* c/o Canongate Books, 14 High Street, Edinburgh, EH1 1TE, Scotland.

COURTER, Gay, AB; American writer and film-maker; b. 1 Oct. 1944, Pittsburgh, PA; m. Philip Courter 1968, two s. *Education:* Antioch College, OH. *Career:* mem. Authors' Guild; Writers Guild of America East; Guardian Ad Litem; International Childbirth Asscn. *Publications:* The Bean Sprout Book, 1974; The Midwife, 1981; River of Dreams, 1984; Code Ezra, 1986; Flowers in the Blood, 1990; The Midwife's Advice, 1992; I Speak for This Child, 1995. *Contributions:* Parents; Women's Day; Publishers Weekly; Others.

COURTNEY, Dayle (see Goldsmith, Howard)

COURTNEY, Nicholas Piers; British author; b. 20 Dec. 1944, Berkshire, England; m. Vanessa Hardwicke 1980. *Education:* Nautical College, Berkshire, 1966; Royal Agricultural College, Cirencester; MRICS, MRAC. *Career:* mem. Brook's. *Publications:* Shopping and Cooking in Europe, 1980; The Tiger: Symbol of Freedom, 1981; Diana: Princess of Wales, 1982; Royal Children, 1982; Prince Andrew, 1983; Sporting Royals, 1983; Diana, Princess of Fashion, 1984; Queen Elizabeth, The Queen Mother, 1984; The Very Best of British, 1985; In Society: The Brideshead Years, 1986; Princess Anne, 1986; Luxury Shopping in London, 1987; Sisters in Law, 1988; A Stratford Kinshall, 1989; The Mall, 1990; Windsor Castle, 1991; A Little History of Antiques, 1995; Gale Force 10: The Life and Legacy of Admiral Beaufort, 2002. Contributions: Times; Redbook; Spectator; Independent; House and Garden.

COUSINEAU, Philip Robert, BA; American writer; b. 26 Nov. 1952, Columbia, SC, USA. *Education:* University of Detroit. *Publications:* The Hero's Journey: Joseph Campbell on His Life and Work, 1990; The Soul of the World, 1991; Deadlines: A Rhapsody on a Theme of Famous Last Words, 1991; Soul: An Archaeology: Readings from Socrates to Ray Charles, 1994; Prayers at 3am, 1995; Design Outlaws (with Christopher Zelov), 1996. Contributions: Parabola Magazine; Paris Magazine. *Address:* PO Box 330098, San Francisco, CA 94133, USA. *Website:* www.philcousineau.net.

COUSINS, Lucy, BA; British children's writer and illustrator; b. 1964; m.; four c. *Education:* Canterbury Coll., RCA. *Publications include:* Maisy the Mouse series: Maisy's House (Bologna Ragazzi Prize 1997) 1995, Where is Maisy? 1999, Where Does Maisy Live? 2000, At Home with Maisy 2002, Maisy's Year 2002, 1, 2, 3, What is Maisy Doing? 2003, Go Maisy Go 2003, How Will You Get There, Maisy? 2004, Maisy by the Sea 2004, Maisy Goes Camping 2004, Good Night Maisy 2004, Maisy, Charley and the Wobbly Tooth 2006; other books: Around the House 1992, Around the Farm 1992, Noah's Ark 1995, Katy Cat and Beaky Boo 2001, Jazzy in the Jungle (Smarties Book Prize) 2002, Za-za's Baby Brother 2003, Farm Animals 2004, What Can Rabbit Hear? 2005, Hooray for Fish! 2005. *Address:* c/o Walker Books, 87 Vauxhall Walk, London, SE11 5HJ, England (office). *E-mail:* editorial@walker.co.uk (office). *Website:* www.walkerbooks.co.uk/Lucy-Cousins.

COUSINS, Mark; British writer on film, producer and director; *Director, 4Way Pictures. Education:* Univ. of Stirling. *Career:* programmer, then Dir Edinburgh Film Festival 1991–96; has presented Moviedrome (BBC 2); f. 4Way Pictures film co. (with Antonia Bird and Robert Carlyle) 1998–; currently staff mem. for MSc in Film Studies Univ. of Edinburgh; f. charity Scottish Kids Are Making Movies, now Chair. *Television:* Scene by Scene (creator, presenter, dir, BBC). *Films include:* Dear Mr Gorbachev (assoc. dir). *Publications:* Imagining Reality: Faber Book of the Documentary (ed., with Kevin Macdonald) 1997, Scene by Scene 2002, The Story of Film 2004; contrib. to newspapers and magazines, including Prospect, The Times, Evening Standard, Scotland on Sunday, Sight and Sound, The Scotsman. *Honours:* Hon. Lecturer Univ. of Stirling. *Address:* School of Literatures, Languages and Cultures, University of Edinburgh, 12.16 David Hume Tower, George Square, Edinburgh, EH8 9JX, Scotland.

COUTO, Mia; Mozambican writer and journalist; b. 1955, Beira. *Career:* fmr Dir Mozambique Information Agency; columnist Notícias daily newspaper, Tempo magazine. *Publications:* Raiz d'orvalho (poems) 1983, Vozes Anoiteci-das (trans. as Voices Made Night) 1986, Cada homem e uma raca 1991 (trans. as Every Man is a Race 1994), Terra Sonambula 1992, Under the Frangipani, The Last Flight of the Flamingo 2005, and collections of short stories. *Honours:* Latin Union Prize for Literature 2007. *Address:* c/o Notícias, Rua Joaquim Lapa 55, CP 327, Maputo, Mozambique (office).

COUZYN, Jeni, BA; Canadian poet, psychotherapist, lecturer and broad-caster; b. 26 July 1942, South Africa. *Education:* University of Natal. *Career:* Writer-in-Residence, University of Victoria, BC 1976; founder and Dir, Bethesda Arts Centre, Nieu Bethesda, South Africa 1999–; mem. Guild of Psychotherapists, Poetry Soc. (general council 1968–75). *Publications:* Flying, 1970; Monkeys' Wedding, 1972; Christmas in Africa, 1975; House of Changes, 1978; The Happiness Bird, 1978; Life by Drowning, 1983; In the Skin House, 1993; Homecoming, 1998; A Time to Be Born, 1999; Selected Poems, 2000. Editor: Bloodaxe Book of Contemporary Women Poets, 1985; Singing Down the Bones, 1989. Other: Children's books and edns of poetry. *Honours:* Arts Council of Great Britain grants 1971, 1974, Canada Council grants 1977, 1983. *Literary Agent:* Andrew Mann, 1 Old Compton Street, London W1V 5PH, England. *Address:* c/o Bloodaxe Books Ltd, Highgreen, Tarset, North-umberland NE48 1RP, England.

COVARRUBIAS ORTIZ, Miguel, LicenLet, MLit; Mexican writer, poet and academic; b. 27 Feb. 1940, Monterrey; m. Silvia Mijares 1967; two d. *Education:* Universidad Autónoma de Nuevo León, Monterrey. *Career:* Dir Postgraduate Studies Division, Universidad Autónoma de Nuevo León, Monterrey 1973–76, Dir Centre for Literary and Linguistic Research 1976–79, Dir Inst. of Fine Arts 1976–79, Co-ordinator Creative Writing Workshop 1981–2001, Dean of the Faculty of Philosophy and Letters 2000–01; mem. Deslinde cultural review (dir 1985–2000), Sociedad General de Escritores de México. *Publications:* fiction: La raíz ausente 1962, Custodia de silencios 1965, Minusculario 1966; poetry: El poeta 1969, El segundo poeta 1977, Pandora 1987, Sombra de pantera 1999, Antología o tiranía 2003; essays: Papelería 1970, Olavide o Sade 1975, Nueva papelería 1978, Papelería en trámite 1997; translations:: El traidor (French and German contemporary poetry) 1993, Poemas de Schwitters/Cendrars 2003; conversations: Junto a una taza de café 1994, El rojo caballo de tu sonrisa 1997; contrib. to various publs and anthologies, including Antología de autores contemporáneos (fiction) 1972, Antología de autores contemporáneos (drama) 1980, Desde el Cerro de la Silla (Arts & Literature of Nuevo Léon) 1992. *Honours:* Xalapa Arts Festival Second Place for Story 1962, Universidad Autónoma de Nuevo León Arts Prize for Literature 1989, Gobierno del Estado du Nuevo León

Medal of Civic Merit in Literature and Arts 1993, Nat. Inst. of Fine Arts Poetry Translation Prize 1994. *Address:* Kant 2801, Contry/La Silla, Guadalupe, NL 67173, México.

COVINGTON, Vicki, BA, MSW; American writer; b. 22 Oct. 1952, Birming-ham, AL; m. Dennis Covington 1977, two d. *Education:* University of Alabama. *Publications:* Gathering Home, 1988; Bird of Paradise, 1990; Night Ride Home, 1992; The Last Hotel for Women, 1996. *Honours:* National Endowment for the Arts Fellowship 1988.

COWASJEE, Saros, MA, PhD; Canadian (b. Indian) academic, writer and editor; *Professor Emeritus, University of Regina;* b. 12 July 1931, Secundra-bad, India. *Education:* St John's Coll., Agra, Agra Univ. and Univ. of Leeds, UK. *Career:* Asst Ed. Times of India Press, Mumbai 1961–63; teacher, Univ. of Regina, Canada 1963–71, Prof. of English 1971–95, Prof. Emer. 1995–; Gen. Ed. Literature of the Raj series, Arnold Publrs, New Delhi 1984–2000; mem. Cambridge Soc., Asscn of Commonwealth Literature and Language Studies. *Publications:* Sean O'Casey: The Man Behind the Plays 1963, Sean O'Casey 1966, Stories and Sketches 1970, Goodbye to Elsa (novel) 1974, Coolie: An Assessment (criticism) 1976, So Many Freedoms: A Study of the Major Fiction of Mulk Raj Anand 1977, Nude Therapy (short stories) 1978, The Last of the Maharajas (screenplay) 1980, Studies in Indian and Anglo-Indian Fiction 1993, The Assistant Professor (novel) 1996, Strange Meeting and Other Stories (short stories) 2006; editor: fiction anthologies, including Stories from the Raj 1982, More Stories from the Raj and After 1986, Women Writers of the Raj 1990, The Best Short Stories of Flora Annie Steel 1995, Orphans of the Storm: Stories on the Partition of India 1995, The Oxford Anthology of Raj Stories 1998, The Mulk Raj Anand Omnibus 2004, A Raj Collection 2005, Selected Short Stories of Mulk Raj Anand 2006; contrib. to reviews and journals. *Honours:* four Canada Council and SSHRC Leave Fellowships, J.N. Tata Scholarship to research PhD at Univ. of Leeds. *Address:* Suite 308, 3520 Hillside Street, Regina, SK S4S 5Z5, Canada (home). *Telephone:* (306) 586-3896 (home). *E-mail:* saros.cowasjee@uregina.ca.

COWDREY, Herbert Edward John, MA, DD, FBA; British historian and writer; b. 29 Nov. 1926, Basingstoke, Hants.; m. Judith Watson Davis 1959 (died 2004); one s. two d. *Education:* Univ. of Oxford. *Career:* Deacon 1952; Priest 1953; Tutor and Chaplain St Stephen's House, Oxford 1952–56; Fellow and Tutor in Modern History 1956–87, Sr Research Fellow in Modern History 1987–94, Emeritus Fellow 1994–, St Edmund Hall, Oxford; Leverhulme Emeritus Fellow 1996–98. *Publications:* The Cluniacs and the Gregorian Reform 1970, The Epistolae Vagantes of Pope Gregory VII 1972, Two Studies in Cluniac History 1978, The Age of Abbot Desiderius 1983, Popes, Monks and Crusaders 1984, Pope Gregory VII 1998, The Crusades and Latin Monasti-cism 1999, Popes and Church Reform in the 11th Century 2000, The Register of Pope Gregory VII: An English Translation 2002, Lanfranc: Scholar, Monk and Archbishop 2003; contrib. to scholarly journals. *Address:* 19 Church Lane, Old Marston, Oxford, OX3 0NZ, England (home). *Telephone:* (1865) 794486 (home).

COWELL, Stephanie; American writer; b. 25 July 1943, New York, NY; m. Russell O'Neal Clay 1995, two s. *Career:* mem. Authors' Guild. *Publications:* Nicholas Cooke (actor, soldier, physician, priest) 1993, The Physician of London 1995, The Players: Shakespeare 1997, Marrying Mozart 2004. *Honours:* American Book Award 1996. *Address:* 585 West End Avenue, New York, NY 10024, USA.

COX, (Charles) Brian, CBE, BA, MA, MLitt, FRSL; British academic, writer, poet and editor; b. 5 Sept. 1928, Grimsby, Lincolnshire, England; s. of Hedley Cox and Rose Thompson; m. Jean Willmer 1954; one s., two d. *Education:* Pembroke Coll., Cambridge. *Career:* Lecturer, Senior Lecturer, University of Hull, 1954–66; Co-Ed., Critical Quarterly, 1959–; Prof. of English Literature, 1966–93, Prof. Emeritus, 1993–, Pro-Vice-Chancellor, 1987–91, University of Manchester; Visiting Prof., King's College, London, 1994; Hon. Fellow, Westminster College, Oxford, 1994; Mem., Arts Council, 1996–98; mem. Chair, North West Arts Board, 1994–2000. *Publications:* The Free Spirit, 1963; Modern Poetry (with A. E. Dyson), 1963; Conrad's Nostromo, 1964; The Practical Criticism of Poetry (with A. E. Dyson), 1965; Poems of This Century (ed. with A. E. Dyson), 1968; Word in the Desert (ed. with A. E. Dyson), 1968; The Waste Land: A Casebook (ed. with A. P. Hinchliffe), 1968; The Black Papers on Education (ed. with A. E. Dyson), 1971; The Twentieth Century Mind (ed. with A. E. Dyson), 3 vols, 1972; Conrad: Youth, Heart of Darkness and The End of the Tether (ed.), 1974; Joseph Conrad: The Modern Imagination, 1974; Black Paper 1975 (ed. with R. Boyson), 1975; Black Paper 1977 (ed. with R. Boyson), 1977; Conrad, 1977; Every Common Sight (verse), 1981; Two Headed Monster (verse), 1985; Cox on Cox: An English Curriculum for the 1990s, 1991; The Great Betrayal: Autobiography, 1992; Collected Poems, 1993; The Battle for the English Curriculum, 1995; African Writers (ed.), 1997; Literacy is Not Enough (ed.), 1998; Emeritus (poems), 2001. *Honours:* Hon. DLitt, De Montfort University, 1999. *Address:* 20 Park Gates Drive, Cheadle Hulme, Stockport SK8 7DF, England (home). *Telephone:* (161) 485-2162 (home).

COX, Richard, (R. W. Heber), TD, MA; British writer; b. 8 March 1931, Winchester, Hampshire, England; m. 1963 (divorced); two s. one d. *Education:* St Catherine's Coll., Oxford. *Career:* staff correspondent, Daily Telegraph 1966–72; mem. States of Alderney 2002–, Guernsey States 2003–06, Guernsey Overseas Aid Comm. 2004–, CARE Int. Council of Patrons 2006–. *Publica-tions:* Operation Sealion 1974, Sam7 1976, Auction 1978, KGB Directive 1981,

Ground Zero 1985, The Columbus Option 1986, An Agent of Influence 1988, Park Plaza 1991, Eclipse 1996, Murder at Wittenham Park (as R. W. Heber) 1998, How to Meet a Puffin (juvenile) 2004; contrib. to periodicals. *Address:* 18 Hauteville, Alderney, GY9 3UA, Channel Islands. *Telephone:* (1481) 823128 (office). *Fax:* (1481) 823128 (office).

COX-JOHNSON, Ann (see Saunders, Ann Loreille)

COYLE, Harold, BA; American writer; b. 6 Feb. 1952, New Brunswick, NJ; m. Patricia A. Bannon 1974, two s. one d. *Education:* Virginia Military Institute. *Career:* Commissioned Officer, US Army, 1974–91; mem. Asscn of Civil War Sites; Reserve Officers Asscn. *Publications:* Team Yankee, 1987; Sword Point, 1988; Bright Star, 1991; Trial by Fire, 1992; The Ten Thousand, 1993; Code of Honor, 1994.

COZ, Steve; American editor and publishing executive; b. 26 March 1957, Grafton, Mass.; s. of Henry Coz and Mary Coz; m. Valerie Virga 1987. *Education:* Harvard Univ. *Career:* freelance writer various US publs 1979–82; reporter Nat. Enquirer, Fla 1982–95, Ed.-in-Chief 1995, Editorial Dir American Media Inc.; American celebrity analyst BBC Radio 1995–96. *Honours:* Edgar Hoover Memorial Award for Distinguished Public Service 1996; Haven House Award of Excellence for Outstanding Reporting on Domestic Violence Issues 1996. *Address:* American Media Inc., 1000 American Media Way, Boca Raton, FL 33431-1000, USA (office). *Telephone:* (561) 997-7733 (office). *Fax:* (561) 272-8411 (office).

COZARINSKY, Edgardo; Argentine film director and writer; b. 13 Jan. 1939, Buenos Aires. *Career:* founder of film magazine, Flashback; film critic 1960s–70s; exiled in Paris, France 1974. *Films:* ... (Puntos suspensivos) (dir) 1970, Les apprentis-sorciers (dir) 1977, La memoire courte (writer) 1979, Not in Vain (dir) 1980, La guerre d'un seul homme (dir-ed.) 1981, Memoire: Marie MacCarthy (TV, dir) 1982, Autoportrait d'un inconnu: Jean Cocteau (dir) 1983, Haute Mer (dir) 1984, Sarah (dir) 1988, Guerriers et captives (writer, co-dir) 1989, Boulevard des crépuscules (dir) 1992, Citizen Langlois (dir) 1994, Tango deseo (writer, dir) 2002, La quimera de los héroes (writer) 2003, Ronda nocturna (writer, dir) 2004. *Publications:* El laberinto de la apariencia (essay) 1964, Borges y el cine (ed., collection of Borges' criticism, trans. as Borges in/and/on Film) 1970, El relato indefendible (essay) (La Nación essay prize) 1979, Vudú Urbano (short stories, trans. as Urbano Voodoo) 1985, El pase del testigo (essays, trans. as The Witness' Pass) 2001, La novia de Odessa (novel, trans. as The Bride from Odessa) 2001. *Address:* c/o Farrar, Straus and Giroux, 19 Union Square West, New York, NY 10003, USA. *E-mail:* fsg.publicity@fsgbooks.com.

COZZARELLI, Nicholas R.; American editor and academic; *Editor-in-Chief, Proceedings of the National Academy of Sciences. Career:* elected Ed.-in-Chief, Proceedings of the National Academy of Sciences 1989–; Prof. of Biochemistry and Molecular Biology, Univ. of California at Berkeley. *Publications:* editor: Mechanisms of Deoxyribonucleic Acid Replication and Recombination 1984, DNA Topology and its Biological Effects: Monograph 20 (with others) 1990; numerous research papers. *Address:* National Academy of Sciences, 500 Fifth Street NW, Washington, DC 20001, USA. *Website:* www.pnas.edu. *Address:* University of California, Berkeley Department of Molecular & Cell Biology, 61A Koshland Hall, Berkeley, CA 94720-3204, USA (office). *Telephone:* (510) 642-5266 (office). *Fax:* (510) 643-1079 (office). *E-mail:* ncozzare@socrates.berkeley.edu (office). *Website:* mcb.berkeley.edu/labs/cozzarelli (office).

CRACE, Jim, BA; British writer and dramatist; b. 1 March 1946, Brocket Hall, Lemsford, Hertfordshire, England; m. Pamela Ann Turton 1975; one s. one d. *Education:* Birmingham Coll. of Commerce, Univ. of London. *Publications:* Continent 1986, The Gift of Stones 1988, Arcadia 1992, Signals of Distress 1994, The Slow Digestions of the Night 1995, Quarantine 1997, Being Dead 1999, The Devil's Larder 2001, Genes 2001, Six 2003, Genesis 2003, The Pesthouse 2007; short stories: Refugees 1977, Annie, California Plates 1977, Helter Skelter, Hang Sorrow, Care'll Kill a Cat 1977, Seven Ages 1980; other: radio plays. *Honours:* Dr hc (Univ. of Central England) 2000; David Higham Award 1986, Guardian Prize for Fiction 1986, Whitbread Awards 1986, 1997, Antico Fattore Prize, Italy 1988, GAP Int. Prize for Literature 1989, Soc. of Authors Travel Award 1992, RSL Winifred Holtby Memorial Prize 1995, E. M. Forster Award 1996, Nat. Critics' Circle Award, USA 2001. *Address:* David Godwin Associates, 55 Monmouth Street, London, WC2H 9DG, England (office).

CRAFT, Robert Lawson, BA; American conductor and writer on music; b. 20 Oct. 1923, Kingston, NY. *Education:* Juilliard School of Music, New York, Berkshire Music Center, Tanglewood, studied conducting with Pierre Monteux. *Career:* conductor, Evenings-on-the-Roof and Monday Evening Concerts, Los Angeles 1950–68; asst to, later close assoc. of Igor Stravinsky 1948–71; numerous collaborations with Stravinsky; conducted first performances of various later works by Stravinsky; conducted works ranging from Monteverdi to Boulez; US premiere of Berg's Lulu (two-act version) Santa Fe 1963. *Recordings include:* works of Stravinsky, Webern and Schoenberg 1998. *Publications:* Conversations with Igor Stravinsky 1959, Memories and Commentaries 1960, Expositions and Developments 1962, Dialogues and a Diary 1963, Themes and Episodes 1967, Retrospections and Conclusions 1969, Chronicle of a Friendship 1972, Prejudices in Disguise 1974, Stravinsky in Photographs and Documents (with Vera Stravinsky) 1976, Current Convictions: Views and Reviews 1977, Present Perspectives 1984, Stravinsky's

Selected Correspondence (trans. and ed., two vols) 1982, 1984, Stravinsky: Glimpses of a Life 1992, The Moment of Existence: Music, Literature and the Arts 1996, An Improbable Life 2003, Down a Path of Wonder (memoirs) 2006; contrib. articles to various journals and other publications. *Address:* 1390 S Ocean Blvd, Pompano Beach, FL 33062, USA.

CRAGGS, Stewart Roger, MCLIP, FCLIP, MA, PhD; British academic librarian and writer; b. 27 July 1943, Ilkley, West Yorkshire, England; m. Valerie J. Gibson 28 Sept. 1968; one s. one d. *Education:* Leeds Polytechnic, Univ. of Strathclyde. *Career:* Teesside Polytechnic 1968–69; JA Jobling 1970–72; Sunderland Polytechnic, later Univ. 1973–95; Prof. of Music Bibliography, Univ. of Sunderland 1993; consultant, William Walton Edition, OUP 1995–. *Publications:* William Walton: A Thematic Catalogue 1977, Arthur Bliss: A Bio-Bibliography 1988, William Walton: A Catalogue 1990, Richard Rodney Bennett: A Bio-Bibliography 1990, John McCabe: A Bio-Bibliography 1991, William Walton: A Source Book 1993, John Ireland: A Catalogue, Discography and Bibliography 1993, Alun Hoddinott: A Bio-Bibliography 1993, Edward Elgar: A Source Book 1995, William Mathias: A Bio-Bibliography 1995, Arthur Bliss: A Source Book 1996, Soundtracks: An International Dictionary of Composers for Films 1998, Malcolm Arnold: A Bio-Bibliography 1998, William Walton: Music and Literature 1999, Lennox Berkeley: A Source Book 2000, Benjamin Britten: A Bio-Bibliography 2001, Arthur Bliss: Music and Literature 2002, Peter Maxwell Davies: A Source Book 2002. *Honours:* Library Asscn McColvin Medal for Best Reference Book 1990. *Address:* 106 Mount Road, High Barnes, Sunderland SR4 7NN, England. *E-mail:* stewcraggs@aol.com.

CRAIG, Amanda Pauline; British novelist and journalist; b. 22 Sept. 1959, South Africa; m. Robin John Cohen 1988, one s. one d. *Education:* Clare College, Cambridge. *Career:* mem. Society of Authors (management cttee 2000). *Publications:* Foreign Bodies, 1990; A Private Place, 1991; A Vicious Circle, 1996; In a Dark Wood, 2000; Love in Idleness, 2003. Contributions: periodicals. *Honours:* Young Journalist of the Year, 1996; Catherine Pakenham Award, 1998. *Literary Agent:* Curtis Brown Ltd, Haymarket House, 28–29 Haymarket, London, SW1Y 4SP, England. *Telephone:* (20) 7393-4400. *Fax:* (20) 7393-4401. *E-mail:* info@curtisbrown.co.uk. *Website:* www.curtisbrown.co.uk; www.amandacraig.com.

CRAIG, George; American publishing executive. *Career:* Dir Production, Honeywell Computers Scotland 1965–74; Vice-Chair. and Group Man. Dir William Collins, UK 1974–87; Pres. and CEO Harper & Row Publrs Inc. (now HarperCollins Publrs), New York 1987–96; mem. Bd of Dirs The News Corpn Ltd; mem. Editorial Advisory Bd Publrs Weekly Int. *Address:* c/o HarperCollins Publishers, 10 East 53rd Street, New York, NY 10022, USA. *Telephone:* (212) 207-7000. *Fax:* (212) 207-7759.

CRAIK, Elizabeth Mary, MA, MLitt; British academic, writer and editor; b. 25 Jan. 1939, Portmoak, Scotland; m. Alexander Craik 1964; one s. one d. *Education:* University of St Andrews, Girton College, Cambridge. *Career:* Research Fellow in Greek, University of Birmingham, 1963–64; Asst Lecturer to Senior Lecturer in Greek, University of St Andrews, 1964–97; fmr Prof. of Classics, Kyoto University, Japan, 1997; mem. Classical Society of Japan; Cambridge Philological Society; Hellenic Society. *Publications:* The Dorian Aegean, 1980; Marriage and Property (ed.), 1984; Euripides: Phoenician Women, 1988; Owls to Athens (ed.), 1990; Hippocrates: Places in Man, 1998; Stobaeus: The Seven Deadly Sins, 1998. Contributions: scholarly journals. *Honours:* British Acad. Awards, 1981, 1986; Carnegie Trust Award, 1986; Hon. DLitt, University of St Andrews, 2000.

CRAIK, Thomas Wallace, BA, MA, PhD; British academic, writer and editor; *Professor of English Emeritus, University of Durham;* b. 17 April 1927, Warrington, England; m. Wendy Ann Sowter 1955 (divorced 1975); one s. *Education:* Christ's Coll., Cambridge. *Career:* Asst Lecturer 1953, Lecturer 1954–65, Univ. of Leicester; Lecturer 1965–67, Sr Lecturer 1967–73, Univ. of Aberdeen; Prof. of English, Univ. of Dundee 1973–77; Prof. of English 1977–89, Prof. of English Emeritus 1989–, Univ. of Durham; mem. Int. Shakespeare Asscn. *Publications:* The Tudor Interlude 1958, The Comic Tales of Chaucer 1964; editor: Marlowe: The Jew of Malta 1966, Shakespeare: Twelfth Night 1975, Beaumont and Fletcher: The Maid's Tragedy 1988, Shakespeare: The Merry Wives of Windsor 1989, Shakespeare: King Henry V 1995; contrib. to scholarly journals and British Acad. Shakespeare Lecture 1979. *Address:* 8 Little Dene, Lodore Road, Newcastle upon Tyne, NE2 3NZ, England (home).

CRAMER, Richard Ben, BA, MS; American journalist and writer; b. 12 June 1950, Rochester, NY. *Education:* Johns Hopkins Univ., Columbia Univ. *Publications:* Ted Williams: The Season of the Kid 1991, What It Takes: The Way to the White House 1992, How Israel Lost: The Four Questions 2004; contrib. to periodicals. *Honours:* journalism awards. *Literary Agent:* Sterling Lord Literistic Inc, 65 Bleecker Street, New York, NY 10012, USA.

CRANE, Hamilton (see Mason, Sarah J.)

CRANE, Richard Arthur, BA, MA; British writer; b. 4 Dec. 1944, York, England; m. Faynia Williams 1975; two s. two step-d. *Education:* Jesus Coll., Cambridge. *Career:* Fellow in Theatre, Univ. of Bradford 1972–74; Resident Dramatist, Nat. Theatre 1974–75; Fellow in Creative Writing, Univ. of Leicester 1976; Literary Man., Royal Court Theatre 1978–79; Assoc. Dir, Brighton Theatre 1980–85; Dramaturg, Tron Theatre, Glasgow 1983–84; Visiting Writers Fellowship, Univ. of East Anglia 1988; writer-in-residence,

Birmingham Polytechnic 1990–91, HM Prison Bedford 1993; Lecturer in Creative Writing, Univ. of Sussex 1994–. *Stage plays:* The Tenant 1971, Crippen 1971, Decent Things 1972, Secrets 1973, The Quest 1974, Clownmaker 1975, Venus and Superkid 1975, Bloody Neighbours 1975, Satan's Ball 1977, Gogol 1979, Vanity 1980, Brothers Karamazov 1981, The Possessed 1985, Mutiny! (with David Essex) 1985, Soldier Soldier (with Tony Parker) 1986, Envy (with Donald Swann) 1986, Pushkin 1987, Red Magic 1988, Rolling the Stone 1989, Phaedra (with Michael Glenny) 1990, Baggage and Bombshells 1991, Under the Stars 1993, The Quiz 2005, Fool in the Night 2005. *Television plays:* Rottingdean 1980, The Possessed 1985. *Radio:* Gogol 1980, Decent Things 1984, Optimistic Tragedy 1986, Anna and Marina 1991, Understudies 1992, Vlad the Impaler 1992, The Sea The Sea (classic serial) 1993, Plutopia (with Donald Swann) 1994, Eugene Onegin 1999. *Publications:* Thunder 1976, Gunslinger 1979, Crippen 1993, Under the Stars 1994; editor: Poems from the Waiting Room 1993, The Last Minute Book 1995, Pandora's Books 1997; contrib. to Edinburgh Fringe, Guardian, Independent Stage, Index on Censorship, TLS. *Honours:* Edinburgh Fringe First Awards 1973, 1974, 1975, 1977, 1980, 1986, 1987, 1988, 1989. *Address:* c/o Micheline Steinberg, Fourth Floor, 104 Great Portland Street, London, W1W 6PE, England. *Telephone:* (20) 7631-1310. *E-mail:* miceline@steinplays.com.

CRAWFORD, John William, AA, BA, BSE, MSE, DEd; American poet, writer and academic; *Professor of English Emeritus, Henderson State University;* b. 2 Sept. 1936, Ashdown, AR; m. Kathryn Bizzell 1962; one s. one d. *Education:* Texarkana Coll., Ouachita Baptist Coll., Drake Univ., Oklahoma State Univ. *Career:* Instructor in English, Clinton Community Coll. 1962–66; Asst Prof. 1967–68, Assoc. Prof. 1968–73, Prof. of English 1973–97, Chair Dept of English 1977–86, Prof. Emeritus 1997–, Henderson State Univ.; mem. Arkansas Philological Asscn, Coll. English Asscn, Poets' Roundtable of Arkansas, South Central MLA. *Publications:* poetry: Making the Connection 1989, I Have Become Acquainted with the Rain 1997; non-fiction: Shakespeare's Comedies: A Guide 1968, Shakespeare's Tragedies: A Guide 1968, Steps to Success: A Study Skills Handbook 1976, Discourse: Essays on English and American Literature 1978, Romantic Criticism of Shakespearean Drama 1978, Early Shakespearian Actresses 1984, The Learning, Wit and Wisdom of Shakespeare's Renaissance Women 1997; contrib. to anthologies, reviews, quarterlies, journals, etc. *Honours:* Sybil Nash Abrams Prizes 1982, 1995, Poets' Roundtable of Arkansas Merit Award 1988, Arkansas Haiku Soc. Award 1998. *Address:* 1813 Walnut, Arkadelphia, AR 71923, USA (home). *Telephone:* (501) 767-1328 (office). *E-mail:* jwcraw@cablelynx.com.

CRAWFORD, Robert, MA, DPhil; British academic, writer and poet; *Professor of Modern Scottish Literature, University of St Andrews;* b. 23 Feb. 1959, Bellshill, Scotland; m. Alice Wales 1988; one s. one d. *Career:* Elizabeth Wordsworth Jr Research Fellow, Oxford 1984–87; British Acad. Postdoctoral Fellow, Univ. of Glasgow 1987–89; Lecturer in Modern Scottish Literature, Univ. of St Andrews 1989–95, Prof. of Modern Scottish Literature 1995–; Founding Ed. Verse poetry magazine 1984–95; gave Smithies Lectures, Balliol Coll., Oxford 2004; mem. English Asscn, Royal Soc. of Edinburgh. *Publications:* poetry: A Scottish Assembly 1990, Sharawaggi (with W. N. Herbert) 1990, Talkies 1992, Masculinity 1996, Spirit Machines 1999, The Tip of My Tongue 2003, Selected Poems 2005, Apollos of the North 2006; prose: The Savage and the City in the Work of T. S. Eliot 1987, Devolving English Literature 1992, Identifying Poets: Self and Territory in Twentieth-Century Poetry 1993, Literature in Twentieth-Century Scotland: A Select Bibliography 1995, The Modern Poet 2001; editor: Other Tongues: Young Scottish Poets in English, Scots, and Gaelic 1990, About Edwin Morgan (with Hamish Whyte) 1990, The Arts of Alasdair Gray (with Thom Naim) 1991, Reading Douglas Dunn (with David Kinloch) 1992, Liz Lochhead's Voices (with Anne Varty) 1994, Talking Verse: Interviews with Poets (with Henry Hart, David Kinloch, Richard Price) 1995, Penguin Modern Poets 9 (with John Burnside and Kathleen Jamie) 1996, Robert Burns and Cultural Authority 1997, Launch-site for English Studies: Three Centuries of Literary Studies at the University of St Andrews 1997, The Penguin Book of Poetry from Britain and Ireland since 1945 (with Simon Armitage) 1998, The Scottish Invention of English Literature 1998, The New Penguin Book of Scottish Verse (with Mick Imlah) 2000, Scottish Religious Poetry (with Meg Bateman and James McGonigal) 2000, Heaven-Taught Fergusson: Robert Burns's Favourite Scottish Poet 2003, The Book of St Andrews 2005, Contemporary Poetry and Contemporary Science 2006, Scotland's Books, The Penguin History of Scottish Literature 2007. *Honours:* Eric Gregory Award 1988, selected for Arts Council of GB New Generation Poets 1994, two Scottish Arts Council Book Awards. *Address:* School of English, University of St Andrews, Fife, KY16 9AL, Scotland (office). *Telephone:* (1334) 462666 (office). *Fax:* (1334) 462655 (office). *E-mail:* robert.crawford@st-and.ac.uk (office). *Website:* www.st-andrews.ac.uk/english/crawford/home.html (office).

CRAWFORD, Robert (see Rae, Hugh Crauford)

CRAWFORD, Thomas, MA; British academic and writer; b. 6 July 1920, Dundee, Scotland; m. Jean Rennie McBride 1946, one s. one d. *Education:* University of Edinburgh, University of Auckland. *Career:* Lecturer, 1953–60, Senior Lecturer, 1961–62, Assoc. Prof. of English, 1962–65, University of Auckland; Lecturer in English, University of Edinburgh, 1965; Commonwealth Research Fellow, McMaster University, Hamilton, Ontario, Canada, 1966–67; Reader in English, 1967–85, Hon. Reader in English, 1985–, University of Aberdeen; Ed., Scottish Literary Journal, 1974–84; mem. Asscn for Scottish Literary Studies, pres., 1984–88; Saltire Society; Scots Language

Society; Scottish Text Society. *Publications:* Burns: A Study of the Poems, 1960; Scott, 1965; Sir Walter Scott: Selected Poems (ed.), 1972; Love, Labour, and Liberty, 1976; Society and the Lyric, 1979; Longer Scottish Poems 1650–1830, 1987; Boswell, Burns and the French Revolution, 1989; The Correspondence of James Boswell and William Johnson Temple 1756–1795: Vol. I, 1756–1777 (ed.), 1997. Contributions: scholarly journals.

CRAY, Robert (see Emerson, Ru)

CRECY, Jeanne (see Williams, Jeanne)

CREECH, Sharon, BA, MA; American children's writer; b. 29 July 1945, Cleveland, OH; m.; one s. one d. *Education:* Hiram Coll., George Mason Univ. *Career:* fmr teacher, editorial asst, indexer, researcher. *Publications:* Absolutely Normal Chaos 1990, Walk Two Moons 1994, Pleasing the Ghost 1995, The Ghost of Uncle Arvie 1996, Chasing Redbird 1997, Bloomability 1998, The Wanderer 2000, Fishing in the Air 2000, A Fine Fine School 2001, Love That Dog 2001, Granny Torrelli Makes Soup 2003, Ruby Holler 2002, Heartbeat 2004. *Honours:* US Newbery Medal 1995, 2001, Claudia Lewis Poetry Award 2002, Christopher Award 2002, Mitten Award 2002, Carnegie Award. *Address:* c/o Bloomsbury Publishing PLC, 38 Soho Square, London, W1V 5DF, England. *Telephone:* (20) 7494-2111. *Fax:* (20) 7434-0151. *Website:* www.bloomsbury.com.

CREGIER, Don Mesick, BA, MA, PhD; American historian and writer; b. 28 March 1930, Schenectady, NY; m. Sharon Kathleen Ellis 1965. *Education:* Union Coll., New York, Univ. of Michigan, Columbia Pacific Univ. *Career:* Asst Instructor, Clark Univ., Worcester, Mass 1952–54; Instructor, Univ. of Tennessee, Martin 1956–57; Asst Prof., Baker Univ., Baldwin, Kan. 1958–61; Asst Prof., Keuka Coll., Keuka Park, NY 1962–64; Visiting Asst Prof., St John's Univ., Collegeville, Minn. 1964–65; Sr Fellow and Tutor, Mark Hopkins Coll., Brattleboro, Vt 1965–66; Assoc. Prof., St Dunstan's Univ., Charlottetown, PEI 1966–69; Assoc. Prof., Univ. of Prince Edward Island 1969–85, Prof. of History 1985–96, Adjunct Prof. 1996–2002; Abstractor, ABC/Clio Information Services 1978–; Foreign Book Review Ed., Canadian Review of Studies in Nationalism 1996–98; mem. Historical Soc., American Historical Asscn, Soc. for Academic Freedom and Scholarship, Canadian Asscn of Univ. Teachers, Mark Twain Soc., North American Conf. on British Studies. *Publications:* Bounder from Wales: Lloyd George's Career Before the First World War 1976, Novel Exposures: Victorian Studies Featuring Contemporary Novels 1979, Chiefs Without Indians: Asquith, Lloyd George, and the Liberal Remnant, 1916–1935 1982, The Decline of the British Liberal Party: Why and How? 1985, Freedom and Order: The Growth of British Liberalism Before 1868 1988, The Rise of the Global Village (co-author) 1988; contribs to reference works and professional journals. *Honours:* Mark Hopkins Fellow 1965, Canada Council Fellow 1972, Research Grant, Social Sciences and Humanities Research Council of Canada 1984–86. *Address:* PO Box 1100, Montague, PE COA 1RO, Canada. *E-mail:* dcregier@upei.ca. *Website:* www.cheironscourt.ca (office).

CREMISI, Teresa Emiliana Jacqueline, DipLit; Italian publisher; *President and Chief Operating Officer, Flammarion press;* b. 7 Oct. 1945, Alexandria, Egypt; d. of Vittorio Cremisi and Gabrielle Helou; m. Giovanni Pinna 1967; two c. *Education:* Notre-Dame de Sion, Alexandria, Lycée Marcelline and Univ. of Bocconi, Milan, Italy. *Career:* moved to Italy 1956; lexicographer, Garzanti press, Milan 1963–66, head of education dept 1966–72, Dir of Production 1972–79, Literary Dir 1979–85, co-Dir-Gen. 1985–89; contrib. to radio and TV co., Rai 1972–80, to cultural pages of l'Espresso and la Stampa 1979–89; Editorial Dir, Gallimard 1989–96, Publishing Dir 1996–2005; Pres. and COO, Flammarion press (part of Rizzoli-Corriere della Sera—RCS MediaGroup) 2005–, and Dir in charge of European strategy for RCS Libri 2005–. *Honours:* Officier, Ordre des Arts et des Lettres 1994, Chevalier, Légion d'honneur 2004. *Address:* Flammarion, 87 quai Panhard et Levasson, Paris 75013, France. *Website:* www.flammarion.com.

CREMONA, Hon. John Joseph, KM, LLD, DLitt, PhD, DJur; Maltese jurist, historian and writer; b. 6 Jan. 1918, Gozo; s. of Dr Antonio Cremona and Anne Camilleri; m. Beatrice Barbaro Marchioness of St George 1949; one s. two d. *Education:* Malta, Rome, London, Cambridge and Trieste Univs. *Career:* Crown Counsel 1947; Lecturer in Constitutional Law, Royal Univ. of Malta 1947–65; Attorney Gen. 1957–64; Prof. of Criminal Law, Univ. of Malta 1959–65; Prof. Emer. 1965–; Pres. of Council 1972–75; Crown Advocate-Gen. 1964–65; Vice Pres. Constitutional Court and Court of Appeal 1965–71; Judge, European Court of Human Rights 1965–92, Vice-Pres. 1986–92; Pro-Chancellor, Univ. of Malta 1971–74; Chief Justice of Malta, Pres. of the Constitutional Court, the Court of Appeal and the Court of Criminal Appeal 1971–81; mem. UN Cttee on Elimination of Racial Discrimination 1984–88, Chair. 1986–88; Judge, European Tribunal in Matters of State Immunity 1986–92, Vice-Pres. 1986–92; fmr Acting Gov.-Gen., Acting Pres. of Malta; Chair. Human Rights Section, World Asscn of Lawyers; Chair. Public Broadcasting Services Ltd 1996–98; Pres. Malta Human Rights Asscn; Vice-Pres. Int. Inst. of Studies Documentation and Information for the Protection of the Environment 1980–; mem. Int. Inst. of Human Rights 1992; mem. Editorial Bd several human rights journals in Europe and America; Fellow, Royal Historical Soc.; Hon. Fellow LSE; Hon. mem. Real Academia de Jurisprudencia y Legislación, Madrid. *Publications include:* The Treatment of Young Offenders in Malta 1956, The Malta Constitution of 1835 1959, The Legal Consequences of a Conviction in the Criminal Law of Malta 1962, The

Constitutional Development of Malta 1963, From the Declaration of Rights to Independence 1965, Human Rights Documentation in Malta 1966, Selected Papers (1946–89) 1990, The Maltese Constitution and Constitutional History 1994, Malta and Britain: The Early Constitutions 1996; three volumes of poetry; articles in French, Italian, German, Portuguese and American law reviews. *Honours:* Kt of Magisterial Grace, Sovereign Mil. Order of Malta; Kt Grand Cross Order of Merit (Italy); Kt Grand Cross, Constantine St George; Kt Order of St Gregory the Great; Kt Most Venerable Order of St John of Jerusalem; Companion of the Nat. Order of Merit (Malta); Chevalier, Légion d'honneur. *Address:* Villa Barbaro, Main Street, Attard, Malta. *Telephone:* 440818.

CRESSWELL, Jasmine Rosemary, BA, MA; American writer; b. 14 Jan. 1941, Dolgelly, Wales; m. Malcolm Candlish 1963; one s. three d. *Education:* Univ. of Melbourne, Macquarie Univ., Case Western Reserve Univ. *Career:* mem. Authors' Guild, Colorado Authors' League, Novelists Inc. (founder and past pres.), Rocky Mountain Fiction Writers. *Publications include:* Nowhere to Hide 1992, Keeping Secrets 1993, Eternity 1994, Desires and Deceptions 1995, No Sin Too Great 1996, Secret Sins 1997, The Daughter 1998, The Disappearance 1999, The Conspiracy 2001, The Third Wife 2002, Dead Ringer 2002, Decoy 2003, Full Pursuit 2004, Final Justice 2005. *Honours:* Colorado Romance Writer of the Year Awards 1986, 1989. *Literary Agent:* Dominick Abel Literary Agency Inc., 146 W 82nd Street, No. 1B, New York, NY 10024, USA.

CREWE, Quentin Hugh, FRSL; British author and journalist; b. 14 Nov. 1926, London, England; two s. three d. *Education:* Eton College, Trinity College, Cambridge. *Publications:* A Curse of Blossom, 1960; The Frontiers of Privilege, 1961; Great Chefs of France, 1978; International Pocket Book of Food, 1980; In Search of the Sahara, 1983; The Last Maharaja, 1985; Touch the Happy Isles, 1987; In the Realms of Gold, 1989–; Well I Forget the Rest (autobiog.), 1991; Foods from France, 1993; Crewe House, 1995; Letters from India, 1998. Contributions: Queen; Vogue; Spectator; Daily Mail; Times; Evening Standard.

CREWS, Frederick Campbell, BA, PhD; American academic and writer; *Professor Emeritus, University of California at Berkeley;* b. 20 Feb. 1933, Philadelphia, PA; m. Elizabeth Peterson 1959; two d. *Education:* Yale Univ., Princeton Univ. *Career:* Instructor, Univ. of California at Berkeley 1958–60, Asst Prof. 1960–62, Assoc. Prof. 1962–66, Prof. of English 1966–94, Prof. Emeritus 1994–; Fulbright Lecturer, Turin 1961–62; Ward-Phillips Lecturer, Univ. of Notre Dame 1974–75; Dorothy T. Burstein Lecturer, Univ. of California at Los Angeles 1984; Frederick Ives Carpenter Visiting Prof., Univ. of Chicago 1985; Nina Mae Kellogg Lecturer, Portland State Univ., Oregon 1989; David L. Kubal Memorial Lecturer, California State Univ., Los Angeles 1994; Fellow American Acad. of Arts and Sciences; mem. Cttee for Scientific Inquiry (advisory bd). *Publications:* The Tragedy of Manners 1957, E. M. Forster: The Perils of Humanism 1962, The Pooh Perplex 1963, The Sins of the Fathers 1966, Starting Over (ed.) 1970, Psychoanalysis and Literary Process (ed.) 1970, The Random House Handbook 1974, The Random House Reader (ed.) 1981, Out of My System 1975, The Borzoi Handbook for Writers (co-author) 1985, Skeptical Engagements 1986, The Critics Bear it Away 1992, The Memory Wars (co-author) 1995, Unauthorized Freud (ed.) 1998, Postmodern Pooh 2001, Follies of the Wise 2006; contrib. to scholarly journals and to magazines. *Honours:* ACLS Fellow 1965–66, Center for Advanced Study in the Behavioral Sciences Fellow 1965–66, Guggenheim Fellowship 1970–71, Univ. of California at Berkeley Distinguished Teaching Award 1985, Spielvogel Diamonstein PEN Prize 1992. *Address:* 636 Vincente Avenue, Berkeley, CA 94707, USA (home).

CREWS, Harry Eugene, BA, MSEd; American academic and writer; b. 6 June 1935, Alma, GA; m. Sally Thornton Ellis 1960 (divorced); two s. *Education:* University of Florida. *Career:* Teacher of English, Broward Junior College, Fort Lauderdale, 1962–68; Assoc. Prof., 1968–74, Prof. of English, 1974–, University of Florida, Gainesville. *Publications:* The Gospel Singer, 1968; Naked in Garden Hills, 1969; This Thing Don't Lead to Heaven, 1970; Karate is a Thing of the Spirit, 1971; Car, 1972; The Hawk is Dying, 1973; The Gypsy's Curse, 1974; A Feast of Snakes, 1976; A Childhood: The Biography of a Place, 1978; Blood and Grits, 1979; The Enthusiast, 1981; Florida Frenzy, 1982; A Grit's Triumph, 1983; Two, 1984; All We Need of Hell, 1987; The Knockout Artist, 1988; Body, 1990; Scar Lover, 1992; Celebrations, 1998.

CRICHTON, (John) Michael, (Michael Douglas, Jeffrey Hudson, John Lange), AB, MD; American writer, film director and fmr physician; b. 23 Oct. 1942, Chicago; s. of John Henderson Crichton and Zula Miller. *Education:* Harvard Univ., Harvard Medical School. *Career:* Lecturer in anthropology Cambridge Univ. 1965; Post-Doctoral Fellow Salk Inst., La Jolla 1969–70; Visiting Writer MIT 1988; mem. Acad. of Motion Picture Arts and Sciences, Author's Guild, Writers' Guild of America, Bd of Trustees Western Behavioral Sciences Inst., La Jolla 1986–91, Bd of Overseers, Harvard Univ. 1990–96, Author's Guild Council 1995–. *Television:* creator and exec. producer ER 1994–. *Film screenplays:* The Andromeda Strain 1971, Westworld (also dir) 1973, Terminal Man 1974, Coma (also dir) 1977, The Great Train Robbery (also dir) 1978, Looker (also dir) 1981, Runaway (also dir) 1984, Rising Sun (co-writer) 1993, Jurassic Park (co-writer) 1993, Disclosure 1995, Congo 1995, Twister (co-writer) 1996, The Lost World 1997, Sphere 1997, Thirteenth Warrior (also dir and producer) 1999, Jurassic Park III 2001,. *Publications:* fiction: The Andromeda Strain 1969, The Terminal Man 1972, The Great

Train Robbery 1975, Eaters of the Dead 1976, Congo 1980, Sphere 1987, Jurassic Park 1990, Rising Sun 1992, Disclosure 1993, The Lost World 1995, Airframe 1996, Timeline 1999, Prey 2002, State of Fear 2004, Next 2006; as Michael Douglas, with Douglas Crichton: Dealing, or Berkeley-to-Boston Forty-Brick Lost-Bag Blues 1971; as Jeffery Hudson: A Case of Need 1968; as John Lange: Odds On 1966, Scratch One 1967, Easy Go 1968, The Venom Business 1969, Zero Cool 1969, Grave Descend 1970, Drug of Choice 1970, Binary 1972; non-fiction: Five Patients: The Hospital Explained 1970, Jasper Johns 1977, Electronic Life: How to Think About Computers 1983, Travels 1988. *Honours:* MWA Edgar Allan Poe Awards 1968, 1980, Asscn of American Medical Writers Award 1970, Acad. of Motion Picture Arts and Sciences Technical Achievement Award 1995, George Foster Peabody Award, Writers' Guild of America Award 1995, Emmy Award for Best Dramatic Series 1996, Ankylosaur named Bienosaurus crichtoni 2000. *Literary Agent:* International Creative Management, 40 West 57th Street, New York, NY 10025, USA. *Address:* Constant Productions, 2118 Wilshire Blvd, Suite 433, Santa Monica, CA 90403, USA. *E-mail:* info@crichton-official.com. *Website:* www.crichton -official.com.

CRICK, Bernard; British academic and writer; b. 16 Dec. 1929, London. *Education:* Univ. Coll. London. *Career:* political writer, biographer, journalist and adviser; Literary Ed., Political Quarterly; Prof. of Politics, Birkbeck Coll., London, 1971–84; Emer. Prof., Univ. of London, 1993–; Adviser on Citizenship to DFES 1997–2003, to Home Office 2003–05. *Publications:* The American Science of Politics 1958, In Defence of Politics 1962, The Reform of Parliament 1964, Theory and Practice: Essays in Politics 1972, Basic Forms of Government 1973, Crime, Rape and Gin: Reflections on Contemporary Attitudes to Violence, Pornography and Addiction 1977, Political Education and Political Literacy (co-ed.) 1978, George Orwell: A Life 1980, Orwell Remembered (co-ed.) 1984, Socialism 1987, Politics and Literature 1987, Political Thoughts and Polemics 1990, National Identities (ed.) 1991, Essays on Citizenship 2000, Democracy. *Honours:* Hon. Fellow, Birkbeck Coll., Univ. Coll. London; Dr hc (Queens Univ., Belfast, Univs of Sheffield, East London, Kingston). *Address:* 8A Bellevue Terrace, Edinburgh, EH7 4DT, Scotland. *E-mail:* Bernard.Crick@ed.ac.uk.

CRICK, Donald Herbert; Australian writer; b. 16 July 1916, Sydney, NSW; m. 1943; one d. *Career:* mem. Australian Soc. of Authors (bd of management). *Screenplays:* The Veronica 1983, A Different Drummer 1985, The Moon to Play With 1987. *Publications:* fiction: Bikini Girl 1963, Martin Place 1964, Period of Adjustment 1966, A Different Drummer 1972, The Moon to Play With 1981; contrib. to Sydney Morning Herald, The Australian, Overland, The Australian Author. *Honours:* Mary Gilmore Centenary Award for Novel 1966, Rigby Anniversary Award for Novel 1980, Awgie Screenplay Award 1983–85. *Address:* 1/1 Elamang Avenue, Kirribilli, NSW 2061, Australia.

CRISCUOLO, Anthony Thomas, (Tony Crisp); British writer, journalist, broadcaster, psychotherapist and teacher (retd); b. 10 May 1937, Amersham, Bucks., England; s. of Alfred Criscuolo and Elizabeth Banning; m. 1st Brenda Crisp (divorced 1978); m. 2nd Hyone Criscuolo 1982; four s. one d. *Education:* London Polytechnic, Ruskin Coll., Oxford. *Career:* left school aged 15 without qualifications to work in Fleet Street as a photographer; started own business as freelance photo-journalist 1953; Nat. Service, RAF 1955–57; trained as male nurse; worked as photographer 1958–68; a Dir Landseer Studios and Photo Repro Co.; ran The Arcane Library in spare time, specializing in popular psychology, meditation, dreams, spiritual philosophy, sold to Helios Books 1969; began the study of dreams 1962; taught relaxation, yoga, meditation classes throughout Bucks. and at London Dance Centre; Founding mem. The British Wheel of Yoga; worked at Tyringham Naturopathic Clinic, Bucks. moved to Devon and helped his wife run a vegetarian wholefood guest-house 1970–71; started Ashram, Combe Martin, Devon (one of the first growth centres in UK) 1972–80; worked as dream corresp. for The Daily Mail and She magazine 1982–83; regularly worked as teacher and sometimes Dir Atsitsa holistic holiday community on the Greek island of Skyros and at the Skyros Inst. 1983–; taught dream work and self-regulation in Montreal, Canada and in Iceland; worked as dream interpreter with Teletext, UK 1993–95; lived in Melbourne, Australia 1995; worked for New Zealand Teletext producing a dream page 1995; currently living nr Swansea, S Wales. *Publications:* Yoga and Relaxation 1970, Do You Dream? 1971, Yield 1974, Yoga and Childbirth 1975, The Instant Dream Book 1984, Mind and Movement 1987, Dream Dictionary 1990, Liberating the Body 1992, The New Dream Dictionary 1994, The Hand Book 1994, Superminds 1998, Dreams and Dreaming 1999, Coincidences 2000, Dream Power 2003, Your Dream Interpreter 2004, Lucid Dreaming 2005; contrib. to newspapers, journals, radio and TV. *Address:* 1 Troedyrhiw, Caerlan, Abercrave, Swansea, SA9 1SX, Wales (home). *Telephone:* (1639) 731091. *E-mail:* tonycrisp@yahoo.com (home). *Website:* www .dreamhawk.com.

CRISP, Clement Andrew, OBE, BA; British dance critic. *Career:* Dance Critic, The Financial Times 1970–, The Spectator; Assoc. Prof. Univ. of Notre Dame, London campus 1993. *Publications:* Making a Ballet 1975, Ballerina: Portraits and Impressions of Nadia Nerina (ed.) 1975, Fifty Years of the Ballet Rambert, 1926–76 (ed.) 1976, The Colourful World of Ballet 1977, Lynn Seymour (jtly) 1980, Ballet Rambert: 50 Years and On 1981, Rambert: A Celebration – A Survey of the Company's First Seventy Years (jtly) 1996; with Mary Clarke: Understanding Ballet 1976, Ballet in Art 1978, Introducing Ballet 1978, Ballet Art: From the Renaissance to the Present 1978, Design for Ballet 1978, Ballet Goer's Guide 1981, The History of Dance 1983, Dancer:

Men in Dance 1986, How to Enjoy Ballet 1987, Ballerina: The Art of Women in Classical Ballet 1989, London Contemporary Dance Theatre: The First 21 Years 1989, Ballet: An Illustrated History 1992; with Peter Brinson: Ballet for All 1972, Ballet and Dance: A Guide to the Repertory 1981. *Honours:* Knight of the Order of Dannebrog (Denmark) 1992; Queen Elizabeth II Award Royal Acad. of Dancing 1992. *Address:* c/o The Financial Times, One Southwark Bridge, London, SE1 9HL, England. *Website:* news.ft.com/arts/arts.

CRISP, Tony (see Criscuolo, Anthony Thomas)

CRISPIN, Suzy (see Cartwright, Justin)

CRITCHLOW, Donald T., BA, MA, PhD; American historian, writer and editor; b. 18 May 1948, Pasadena, CA; m. Patricia Critchlow 1978, two d. *Education:* San Francisco State University, University of California at Berkeley. *Career:* Teaching Asst, 1974, Research Asst, Institute of Industrial Relations, 1975, Acting Instructor in Environmental Studies, 1977, University of California at Berkeley; Acting Instructor in History, San Francisco State University, 1976; Asst Prof. of History, North Central College, Napierville, IL, 1978–81, University of Dayton, 1981–83; Asst Prof., then Assoc. Prof. of History, University of Notre Dame, 1983–91; Ed., Journal of Policy History; Series Ed., Critical Issues in European and American History. *Publications:* The Brookings Institution, 1916–1952: Expertise and the Public Interest in a Democratic Society, 1985; Socialism in the Heartland: The Midwestern Experience, 1890–1920 (ed.), 1986; Federal Social Policy: The Historical Dimension (co-ed.), 1989; Poverty and Public Policy in Modern America (co-ed.), 1989; America! A Concise History (co-author), 1995; Studebaker: The Life and Death of an American Corporation, 1996; The Politics of Abortion and Birth Control in Historical Perspective (ed.), 1996; The Serpentine Way: Family Planning Policy in Postwar America: Elites, Agendas, and Political Mobilization, 1997.

CROCETTI, Nicola; Greek editor, journalist and translator; *Editor, Poesia magazine;* b. 1940, Patrasso. *Career:* lives in Italy; founder Crocetti Editore poetry publisher 1981–; Ed. and Dir Poesia magazine 1988–. *Honours:* Albo d'Oro 1999. *Address:* Crocetti Editore Srl, Via E. Falck 53, 20151 Milan, Italy. *Website:* www.crocettieditore.com.

CROFT, Andy, BA, PhD; British poet and writer; b. 13 June 1956, Handforth, Cheshire, England; m. Nikki Wray, four s. two d. *Education:* University of Nottingham. *Career:* full-time Lecturer, University of Leeds 1983–96; Writer-in-Residence, Great North Run 2000, HMP Holme House 2000–04; mem. Chair., Artistic Dir, Write Around Festival 1989–99. *Publications:* Red Letter Days 1994, Out of the Old Earth 1994, The Big Meeting 1994, Nowhere Special 1996, Gaps Between Hills 1996, A Weapon in the Struggle 1998, Selected Poems of Randall Swingler 2000, Just as Blue 2001, Great North 2001, Headland 2001, Comrade Heart 2003, Heart Laughter 2004; contrib. to The Guardian, The Independent, London Magazine, Marxism Today, Labour History Review, The Listener, The New Statesman. *Address:* c/o Tees Valley Arts, Gurney House, Gurney Street, Middlesbrough, TS1 1JL, England.

CROFT, Julian Charles Basset, BA, MA; Australian academic and writer; *Professor, University of New England, Armidale;* b. 31 May 1941, Newcastle, NSW; m. 1st Loretta De Plevitz 1967; one s.; m. 2nd Caroline Ruming 1987; one s. *Education:* Univ. of New South Wales, Univ. of Newcastle, NSW. *Career:* Lecturer, Univ. of Sierra Leone 1968–70; Assoc. Prof. 1970–94, Prof. 1994–, Univ. of New England, Armidale; mem. Asscn for the Study of Australian Literature. *Publications:* T. H. Jones 1975, The Collected Poems of T. Harri James (ed. with Don Dale-Jones) 1976, Breakfasts in Shanghai (poems) 1984, Their Solitary Way (novel) 1985, The Portable Robert D. FitzGerald (ed.) 1987, Confessions of a Corinthian 1991, The Life and Opinions of Tom Collins 1991, After a War (Any War) 2002. *Address:* Department of English, University of New England, Armidale 2351, Australia.

CROGGON, Alison; Australian poet, novelist and dramatist; b. 1962, South Africa; m. Daniel Keene. *Career:* theatre critic, The Bulletin, Melbourne 1989–92; Poetry Ed., Overland Extra 1992, Modern Writing 1992–94, Voices 1996; founder Ed. of online arts journals, Masthead and Theatre Notes; Australia Council Writer-in-Residence, Univ. of Cambridge, UK 2000; Australian co-ordinator, Poets Against the War 2003; mem. of artistic council, Malthouse Theatre. *Plays:* Lenz 1996, Samarkand 1997, The Famine 1998, Blue 2001, Monologues for an Apocalypse (radio text) 2001; music theatre: Confidentially Yours 1998, The White Army. *Libretti:* The Burrow 1995, Gauguin 2000. *Publications:* poetry: This is the Stone (Anne Elder Prize, Dame Mary Gilmore Prize) 1991, The Blue Gate 1997, Mnemosyne (chapbook) 2001, Attempts at Being 2002, The Common Flesh 2003, November Burning 2004; novels: The Gift (aka The Naming) 2002, The Riddle 2004, The Crow 2006. *Honours:* four Australia Council Fellowships. *E-mail:* ajcroggon@bigpond.com. *Website:* www.alisoncroggon.com.

CRONENBERG, David; Canadian film director and screenwriter; b. 15 March 1943, Toronto. *Education:* Univ. of Toronto. *Career:* fmr cinematographer and film editor; has directed fillers and short dramas for TV. *Films:* Transfer (writer, dir, prod.) 1966, From the Drain (writer, dir) 1967, Stereo (writer, dir, prod.) 1969, Crimes of the Future (writer, dir, prod.) 1970, The Victim (dir) 1974, Shivers (writer, dir) 1974, Rabid (writer, dir) 1976, Fast Company (writer, dir) 1979, The Brood (writer, dir) 1979, Scanners (writer, dir) 1980, Videodrome (writer, dir) 1982, The Dead Zone (dir) 1983, Into the Night (actor) 1985, The Fly (writer, dir, actor) 1986, Dead Ringers (writer, dir,

prod.) 1988, Nightbreed (actor) 1990, Naked Lunch (writer, dir) 1991, Blue (actor) 1992, M. Butterfly (dir) 1993, Henry & Verlin (actor) 1994, Boozecan (actor) 1994, Trial by Jury (actor) 1994, To Die For (actor) 1995, Blood & Donuts (actor) 1995, Crash (writer, dir, prod.) (Cannes Jury Special Prize 1997) 1996, The Stupids (actor) 1996, Extreme Measures (actor) 1996, I'm Losing You (exec. prod.) 1998, Last Night (actor) 1998, Resurrection (actor) 1999, eXistenZ (writer, dir, prod.) (Silver Berlin Bear 1999) 1998, Camera (writer, dir) 2000, Jason X (actor) 2001, Spider (dir, prod.) 2002, A History of Violence (dir, prod.) 2005. *Television:* Programme X (dir episode: Secret Weapons) 1970, Tourettes (film dir, writer) 1971, Letter from Michelangelo (film dir, writer) 1971, Jim Ritchie Sculptor (film dir, writer, prod.) 1971, Winter Garden (film dir, writer) 1972, Scarborough Bluffs (film dir, writer) 1972, Lakeshore (film dir, writer) 1972, In the Dirt (film dir, writer) 1972, Fort York (film dir, writer) 1972, Don Valley (film dir, writer) 1972, Peep Show (dir episodes: The Lie Chair, The Victim) 1975, Teleplay (writer, dir episode: The Italian Machine) 1976, Friday the 13th (dir episode: Faith Healer) 1987, Scales of Justice (dir episode: Regina vs Horvath) 1990, Moonshine Highway (actor) 1996, The Judge (actor) 2001. *Publications:* Crash 1996, Cronenberg on Cronenberg 1996. *Address:* David Cronenberg Productions Ltd, 217 Avenue Road, Toronto, ON M5R 2J3, Canada (office); c/o John Burnham, William Morris Agency, 151 South El Camino Drive, Beverly Hills, CA 90212, USA (office).

CRONIN, Anthony; Irish author; b. 23 Dec. 1928, Co. Wexford; s. of John Cronin and Hannah Barron; m. 1st Thérèse Campbell 1955; two d.; m. 2nd Anne Haverty 2003. *Education:* Blackrock Coll., Univ. Coll., Dublin and Kings Inns, Dublin. *Career:* Assoc. Ed. The Bell 1952–54; Literary Ed. Time and Tide 1956–58; Visiting Lecturer in English, Univ. of Montana, USA 1966–68; Writer-in-Residence, Drake Univ., Ia 1968–70; columnist, Irish Times 1973–80; cultural and artistic adviser to the Prime Minister of Ireland 1980–83, 1987–92. *Publications:* Poems 1958, The Life of Riley 1964, A Question of Modernity 1966, Dead as Doornails 1976, Identity Papers 1980, New and Selected Poems 1982, Heritage Now 1982, An Irish Eye 1985, No Laughing Matter, The Life and Times of Flann O'Brien 1989, The End of the Modern World 1989, Relationships 1994, Samuel Beckett: The Last Modernist 1996, The Minotaur and Other Poems 1999, Anthony Cronin's Personal Anthology 2000, Collected Poems 2004. *Honours:* DLitt (Trinity Coll., Dublin, Univ. of Ulster); Martin Toonder Award for contrib. to Irish literature 1983. *Address:* 30 Oakley Road, Dublin 6, Ireland. *Telephone:* (1) 4970490. *Fax:* (1) 4970490.

CRONIN, Jeremy, MA; South African poet and politician; b. 12 Sept. 1949. *Education:* Univ. of Cape Town and Sorbonne, Univ. of Paris. *Career:* Lecturer in Philosophy and Political Science, Univ. of Cape Town 1974–76; imprisoned for seven years for his involvement with the African Nat. Congress (ANC) 1976; fmr Educ. Officer, United Democratic Front; spent time in exile in England and Zambia; mem. cen. cttee South African Communist Party 1989–, currently Deputy Sec.-Gen.; mem. Nat. Exec. Cttee, ANC 1991–; Mem. of Parl. 1999–, Chair. Standing Cttee on Transport; Ed. African Communist, Umsebenzi. *Publications:* poetry: Inside (Ingrid Jonker Prize) 1983, Even the Dead 1997, Inside and Out 1999, More Than a Casual Contact 2006; nonfiction: Ideologies of Politics (co-ed.) 1976, 30 Years of the Freedom Charter (with R. Suttner) 1986. *Address:* POB 1027, 2000 Johannesburg, South Africa. *E-mail:* sacp@wn.apc.org.

CRONIN, Vincent Archibald Patrick, BA; British author; b. 24 May 1924, Tredegar, Wales; m. Chantal de Rolland 1949, two s. three d. *Education:* Harvard University, Trinity College, Oxford. *Publications:* The Golden Honeycomb, 1954; The Wise Man from the West, 1955; The Last Migration, 1957; A Pear to India, 1959; The Letter after Z, 1960; Louis XIV, 1964; Four Women in Pursuit of an Ideal, 1965; The Florentine Renaissance, 1967; The Flowering of the Renaissance, 1970; Napoleon, 1971; Louis and Antoinette, 1974; Catherine, Empress of all the Russias, 1978; The View from Planet Earth, 1981; Paris on the Eve, 1989; Paris: City of Light 1919–1939, 1995.

CRONON, William John, BA, MA, MPhil, PhD, DPhil; American academic and writer; *Frederick Jackson Turner and Vilas Research Professor of History, Geography and Environmental Studies, University of Wisconsin at Madison;* b. 11 Sept. 1954, New Haven, CT; m. Nancy Elizabeth Fey 1977; one s. one d. *Education:* Univ. of Wisconsin at Madison, Yale Univ., Univ. of Oxford. *Career:* Asst Prof. 1981–86, Assoc. Prof. 1986–91, Prof. of History 1991–92, Yale Univ.; Frederick Jackson Turner and Vilas Research Prof. of History, Geography and Environmental Studies, Univ. of Wisconsin at Madison 1992–; mem. Agricultural History Soc., American Anthropological Asscn, American Antiquarian Soc., American Historical Asscn, American Soc. for Environmental History, American Soc. for Ethnohistory, American Studies Asscn, Asscn of American Geographers, Ecological Soc. of America, Economic History Asscn, Forest History Soc., Organization of American Historians, Soc. of American Historians, Urban History Asscn. *Publications:* Changes in the Land: Indians, Colonists, and the Ecology of New England 1983, Nature's Metropolis: Chicago and the Great West 1991, Under an Open Sky: Rethinking America's Western Past (co-ed. with George Miles and Jay Gitlin) 1992, Uncommon Ground: Toward Reinventing Nature (ed.) 1995; contrib. to books and scholarly journals. *Honours:* Rhodes Scholarship 1976–78, Francis Parkman Prize 1984, Bancroft Prize 1992, American Soc. for Environmental History George Perkins Marsh Prize 1992, Forest History Soc. Charles A. Weyerhaeuser Award 1993, Guggenheim Fellowship 1995. *Address:* c/o Department of History, 3211 Humanities Building, 455 N Park Street,

University of Wisconsin, Madison, WI 53706, USA. *Telephone:* (608) 265-6023 (office). *E-mail:* wcronon@wisc.edu (office). *Website:* history.wisc.edu/cronon (office).

CROOK, Joseph Mordaunt, CBE, BA, MA, DPhil, FBA, FSA; British academic and writer; *Emeritus Professor of Architectural History, Royal Holloway and Bedford New College*; b. 27 Feb. 1937, London, England; m. 1st Margaret Mullholland 1964; m. 2nd Susan Mayor 1975. *Education:* Wimbledon Coll., Univ. of Oxford. *Career:* Asst Lecturer, Univ. of Leicester 1963–65; Lecturer 1965–75, Reader in Architectural History 1975–81, Bedford Coll., London; Ed., Architectural History 1967–75; Slade Prof. of Fine Art, Univ. of Oxford 1979–80; Visiting Fellow, Brasenose Coll., Oxford 1979–80, Humanities Research Centre, Australian Nat. Univ., Canberra 1985, Gonville and Caius Coll., Cambridge 1986; Prof. of Architectural History 1981–99, Emeritus Prof. 1999–, Dir Victorian Studies Centre 1990–99, Royal Holloway and Bedford New Coll.; Waynflete Lecturer and Visiting Fellow, Magdalen Coll., Oxford 1984–85; Public Orator, Univ. of London 1988–90; Humanities Fellow, Princeton Univ. 1990; Supernumerary Fellow, Brasenose Coll., Oxford 2002–; Vice-Chair. Westminster Abbey Fabric Comm. 2001–; mem. council British Acad. 1989–92; mem. Historic Buildings Council for England 1974–80, Soc. of Architectural Historians of Great Britain (exec. cttee 1964–77, pres. 1980–84), Victorian Soc. (exec. cttee 1970–77, council 1978–88). *Publications:* The Greek Revival 1968, Victorian Architecture: A Visual Anthology 1971, The British Museum 1972, The Greek Revival: Neo-Classical Attitudes in British Architecture 1760–1870 1973, The Reform Club 1973, The History of the King' Works (co-author), Vol. VI 1973, Vol. V 1976, William Burges and the High Victorian Dream 1981, Axel Haig and the Victorian Vision of the Middle Ages (co-author) 1984, The Dilemma of Style: Architectural Ideas from the Picturesque to the Post-Modern 1987, John Carter and the Mind of the Gothic Revival 1995, The Rise of the Nouveaux Riches: Style and Status in Victorian and Edwardian Architecture 1999, The Architect's Secret: Victorian Critics and the Image of Gravity 2003; editor: Eastlake: A History of the Gothic Revival 1970, Kerr: The Gentleman's House 1972, The Strange Genius of William Burges 1981, Clark: The Gothic Revival 1995; contrib. to books and scholarly journals. *Honours:* Hon. DLit 2004; Freeman 1979, Liveryman 1984, Worshipful Co. of Goldsmiths; Hitchcock Medallion 1974. *Address:* 55 Gloucester Avenue, London, NW1 7BA, England.

CROOKER, Barbara Poti, BA, MS; American educator, writer and poet; b. 21 Nov. 1945, Cold Spring, NY; m. Richard McMaster Crooker 1975; one s. three d. *Education:* Douglass Coll., Rutgers Univ., Elmira Coll. *Career:* instructor, County Coll. of Morris 1978–79, Women's Center, Cedar Crest Coll. 1982–85, Lehigh Community Coll. 1993, Cedar Crest Coll. 1999–; Asst Prof., Northampton Co. Area Community Coll. 1980–82; Artist-in-Educ. (poet in the schools) 1989–93; mem. Poetry Soc. of America, Acad. of American Poets. *Publications:* Writing Home 1983, Starting from Zero 1987, Looking for the Comet Halley 1987, The Lost Children 1989, Obbligato 1992, Moving Poems, In the Late Summer Garden 1998, Ordinary Life 2001, The White Poems 2001, Paris 2002, Greatest Hits 1980–2000 2003, Impressionism 2004, Radiance 2005; contrib. to anthologies, reviews, quarterlies, journals and magazines. *Honours:* Pennsylvania Council on the Arts Fellowships 1985, 1989, 1993, winner Passages North and Nat. Endowment for the Arts Emerging Writers Competition 1987, Phillips Award, Stone Country 1988, Virginia Center for the Creative Arts Fellowships 1990, 1992, 1994, 1995, 1997, 1998, 2000, 2001, 2003, First Prize, Karamu Poetry Contest 1997, First Place, New Millennium Writings Y2K Writing Prize 2000, Grand Prize Winner Dancing Poetry Contest 2000, Winner Byline Chapbook Competition 2001, Winner April is the Cruelest Month competition 2003, Winner Thomas Merton Poetry of the Sacred Award 2003, Winner Grayson Books Chapbook Competition 2004, W.B. Yeats Soc. of NY Poetry Prize 2004, Winner Pennsylvania Center for the Book Poster Competition 2004, Winner TallGrass Writers' Guild Poetry Prize 2004, Winner Word Press First Book Award 2004. *Address:* 7928 Woodsbluff Run, Fogelsville, PA 18051, USA (office). *Telephone:* (610) 395-5845 (office). *E-mail:* bcrooker@ix.netcom.com (office). *Website:* www.barbaracrooker.com.

CROSBY, Harry Clifton, (Christopher Anvil); American writer; b. 1925; m. Joy Dolores Douglas 1949, one s. one d. *Education:* Williams College, Juniata College. *Publications:* Mind Partner, 1960; The Day the Machines Stopped, 1964; Strangers in Paradise, 1969; Pandora's Planet, 1972; Warlord's World, 1975; The Steel, the Mist, and the Blazing Sun, 1980; Pandora's Legions, 2002; Interstellar Patrol, 2003. Contributions: magazines and journals.

CROSLAND, Margaret McQueen, BA; British writer and translator; b. 17 June 1920, Bridgnorth, Shropshire; d. of Leonard Crosland and Beatrice Crosland (née Wainwright); m. Max Denis (divorced); one s. *Education:* Royal Holloway Coll., Univ. of London. *Career:* temp. civil servant and researcher, then worked in antiquarian book trade; now writer and translator. *Publications include:* Madame Colette 1953, Jean Cocteau 1955, Louise of Stolberg 1962, Colette, The Difficulty of Loving 1973, Women of Iron and Velvet 1976, Beyond the Lighthouse 1981, Piaf 1985, Simone de Beauvoir 1992, The Enigma of Giorgio de Chirico 1999, Madame de Pompadour 2000, The Marquis de Sade Reader: The Passionate Philosopher (ed.) 2001, Meeting & Parting (poems) 2004, The Life and Legend of Jane Shore 2006. *Honours:* Prix de Bourgogne (France) 1973–74, Enid McLeod Literary Prize 1993. *Address:* 25 Thornton Meadow, Wisborough Green, Billingshurst, West Sussex, RH14 0BW, England. *Telephone:* (1403) 700652. *Fax:* (1403) 700652. *E-mail:* crosland.denis@virgin.net. *Website:* www.margaretcrosland.co.uk.

CROSS, Anthony Glenn, BA, MA, PhD, LittD, DLitt, FBA; British academic, writer and editor; *Professor Emeritus of Slavonic Studies, University of Cambridge*; b. 21 Oct. 1936, Nottingham, England; m. Margaret Elson 1960; two d. *Education:* Trinity Hall, Cambridge, Harvard Univ., Univ. of East Anglia, Fitzwilliam Coll., Cambridge. *Career:* Lecturer, Univ. of East Anglia 1964–69, Sr Lecturer 1969–72, Reader in Russian 1972–81; Visiting Fellow, Univ. of Illinois 1969–70, All Souls Coll., Oxford 1977–78; Reviews Ed. Journal of European Studies 1971–; Ed. Study Group on Eighteenth-Century Russia Newsletter 1973–; Roberts Prof. of Russian, Univ. of Leeds 1981–85; Chair. British Academic Cttee for Liaison with Soviet Archives 1983–95, Academia Rossica 2000–05; Prof. of Slavonic Studies, Univ. of Cambridge 1985–2004, Fellow, Fitzwilliam Coll. 1986–2004, retired Professorial Fellow 2004–, Prof. Emer. of Slavonic Studies 2004–; Frank Knox Fellow, Harvard Univ. 1960–61; mem. British Universities Asscn of Slavists (Pres. 1982–84). *Publications:* N. M. Karamzin 1971, Russia Under Western Eyes 1517–1825 1971, Russian Literature in the Age of Catherine the Great (ed.) 1976, Anglo-Russian Relations in the Eighteenth Century 1977, Great Britain and Russia in the Eighteenth Century (ed.) 1979, By the Banks of the Thames 1980, Russia and the West in the Eighteenth Century (ed.) 1981, The Tale of the Russian Daughter and her Suffocated Lover 1982, Eighteenth Century Russian Literature, Culture and Thought: A Bibliography (co-ed.) 1984, The Russian Theme in English Literature 1985, Russia and the World of the Eighteenth Century (co-ed.) 1988, An English Lady at the Court of Catherine the Great (ed.) 1989, Anglophilia on the Throne: The British and the Russians in the Age of Catherine II 1992, Engraved in the Memory: James Walker, Engraver to Catherine the Great and his Russian Anecdotes (ed.) 1993, Anglo-Russica: Aspects of Anglo-Russian Cultural Relations in the Eighteenth and Early Nineteenth Centuries 1993, Literature, Lives and Legality in Catherine's Russia (co-ed.) 1994, By the Banks of the Neva: Chapters From the Lives of the British in Eighteenth-Century Russia 1996, Russia in the Reign of Peter the Great: Old and New Perspectives (ed.) 1998, Britain and Russia in the Age of Peter the Great: Historical Documents (co-ed.) 1998, Peter the Great through British Eyes: Perceptions and Representations of the Tsar since 1698 2000, Catherine the Great and the British: A Pot-Pourri of Essays 2001, St Petersburg 1703–1825 (ed.) 2003, Anglo-Russian Cultural Encounters and Collisions (ed.) 2005; contrib. to scholarly journals. *Honours:* Academician Russian Acad. of the Humanities 1995, Antsiferov Prize, St Petersburg 1998, Nove Prize 1998, Dashkova Medal, Moscow 2003. *Address:* Fitzwilliam College, Storey's Way, Cambridge, CB3 0DG, England (office). *Telephone:* (1223) 332046 (office). *E-mail:* agc28@cus.cam.ac.uk (office).

CROSS, Gillian, MA, DPhil; British children's writer; b. 24 Dec. 1945, London; m. Martin Cross 1967; two s. two d. *Education:* Univ. of Oxford, Univ. of Sussex. *Publications:* The Runaway 1979, The Iron Way 1979, Revolt at Ratcliff's Rags 1980, Save Our School 1981, A Whisper of Lace 1981, The Dark Behind the Curtain 1982, The Demon Headmaster 1982, The Mintyglo Kid 1983, Born of the Sun 1983, On the Edge 1984, The Prime Minister's Brain 1985, Swimathon! 1986, Chartbreak 1986, Roscoe's Leap 1987, A Map of Nowhere 1988, Rescuing Gloria 1989, Twin and Super-Twin 1990, Wolf 1990, The Monster from Underground 1990, Gobbo the Great 1991, Rent-A-Genius 1991, New World 1992, The Great Elephant Chase (aka The Great American Elephant Chase) 1992, Beware Olga 1993, The Tree House 1993, The Furry Maccaloo 1993, The Revenge of the Demon Headmaster 1994, What Will Emily Do? 1994, The Crazy Shoe Shuffle 1995, Posh Watson 1995, The Roman Beanfeast 1996, Pictures in the Dark 1996, The Demon Headmaster Strikes Again 1996, The Demon Headmaster Takes Over 1997, The Goose Girl 1998, Tightrope 1999, Down With the Dirty Danes 2000, Calling a Dead Man (aka Phoning a Dead Man) 2001, The Treasure in the Mud 2001, Facing the Demon Headmaster 2002, Beware of the Demon Headmaster 2002, The Dark Ground 2004, The Black Room 2005. *Honours:* Library Asscn Carnegie Medal 1990, Whitbread Children's Novel Award 1992, Smarties Prize 1992. *Address:* c/o Oxford Children's Books, Oxford University Press, Great Clarendon Street, Oxford, OX2 6DP, England. *E-mail:* gillian@gilliancross.co.uk. *Website:* www.gillian-cross.co.uk.

CROSS, Victor (see Coffman, Virginia Edith)

CROSSAN, John Dominic, DD; Irish/American theologian, writer and academic; b. 17 Feb. 1934, Nenagh, County Tipperary, Ireland; m. Sarah Crossan. *Education:* Stonebridge Priory, Lake Bluff, IL, Maynooth Coll., Kildare, Ireland, Pontifical Biblical Inst., Rome, Ecole Biblique, Jerusalem. *Career:* mem., Servites religious order 1950–69; ordained Roman Catholic Priest 1957–69; Asst Prof. of Biblical Studies, Stonebridge Priory, Lake Bluff, IL 1961–65, Mundelein Seminary, IL 1967–68, Catholic Theological Union, Chicago 1968–69; Assoc. Prof. 1969–73, Prof. of Religious Studies 1973–95, Prof. Emeritus 1995–, DePaul Univ., Chicago; Chair. Parables Seminar 1972–75; Ed., Semeia: An Experimental Journal for Biblical Criticism 1980–86; Co-Chair. Jesus Seminar 1985–96; Croghan Bicentennial Visiting Prof. of Religion, Williams Coll., Williamstown, MA 1996; mem. American Acad. of Religion, Catholic Biblical Asscn, Chicago Soc. of Biblical Research (pres. 1978–79), Soc. of Biblical Literature, Studiorum Novi Testamenti Societas. *Publications:* Scanning the Sunday Gospel 1966, The Gospel of Eternal Life 1967, In Parables: The Challenge of the Historical Jesus 1973, The Dark Interval: Towards a Theology of Story 1975, Raid on the Articulate: Comic Eschatology in Jesus and Borges 1976, Finding Is the First Act: Trove Folktales and Jesus' Treasure Parable 1979, Cliffs of Fall: Paradox and Polyvalence in the Parables of Jesus 1980, A Fragile Craft: The Work of Amos

Niven Wilder 1981, In Fragments: The Aphorisms of Jesus 1983, Four Other Gospels: Shadows on the Contours of Canon 1985, Sayings Parallels: A Workbook for the Jesus Tradition 1986, The Cross that Spoke: The Origins of the Passion Narrative 1988, The Historical Jesus: The Life of a Mediterranean Jewish Peasant 1991, Jesus: A Revolutionary Biography 1994, The Essential Jesus: Original Sayings and Earliest Images 1994, Who Killed Jesus?: Exposing the Roots of Anti-Semitism in the Gospel Story of the Death of Jesus 1995, Who is Jesus?: Answers to Your Questions about the Historical Jesus 1996, The Birth of Christianity 1998, In Search of Paul (with Jonathan L. Reed) 2005; contrib. to many scholarly books and journals. *Honours:* American Acad. of Religion Award for Excellence in Religious Studies 1989, DePaul Univ. Via Sapientiae Award 1995. *Address:* c/o HarperCollins, 1350 Avenue of the Americas, New York, NY 10019, USA. *Website:* www.johndcrossan.com.

CROSSLEY-HOLLAND, Kevin John William, MA, FRSL; British academic, poet, writer, editor and translator; b. 7 Feb. 1941, Mursley, Buckinghamshire, England; m. 1st Caroline Fendall Thompson 1963; two s.; m. 2nd Ruth Marris 1972; m. 3rd Gillian Paula Cook 1982; two d.; m. 4th Linda Marie Waslien 1999. *Education:* St Edmund Hall, Oxford. *Career:* Fiction and Poetry Ed. Macmillan & Co. 1962–69; Lecturer in English, Tufts-in-London Programme 1967–78; Gregory Fellow in Poetry, Univ. of Leeds 1969–71; Talks Producer, BBC 1972; Editorial Dir, Victor Gollancz 1972–77; Lecturer in English Language and Literature, Univ. of Regensburg 1979–80; Editorial Consultant, Boydell and Brewer 1983–89; Arts Council Fellow in Writing, Winchester School of Art 1983, 1984; Visiting Prof. of English and Fulbright Scholar-in-Residence, St Olaf Coll., MN 1987–89; Endowed Chair in Humanities and Fine Arts, Univ. of St Thomas, St Paul, MN 1991–95; Dir, Minnesota Composers' Forum 1993–97; mem. steering cttee King's Lynn Festival 1997; co-founder and Chair., Poetry-next-to-the-Sea 1997–; Patron, Thomas Lovell Beddoes Soc. 2000, Soc. of Storytelling 2003. *Opera:* with Nicola Le Fanu: The Green Children, The Wildman. *Drama:* The Wufflings (with Ivan Cutting). *Publications:* poetry: The Rain-Giver 1972, The Dream-House 1976, Between My Father and My Son 1982, Time's Oriel 1983, Waterslain 1986, The Painting-Room 1988, East Anglian Poems 1989, New and Selected Poems 1991, The Language of Yes 1996, Poems from East Anglia 1997, Selected Poems 2001; children's fiction: Havelok the Dane 1964, King Horn 1965, The Green Children 1966, The Callow Pit Coffer 1968, Wordhoard (with Jill Paton Walsh) 1969, The Pedlar of Swaffham 1971, The Sea Stranger 1973, Green Blades Rising 1974, The Fire-Brother 1974, The Earth-Father 1976, The Wildman 1976, The Dead Moon 1982, Beowulf 1982, The Mabinogion (with Gwyn Thomas) 1984, Axe-Age, Wolf-Age 1985, Storm 1985, The Fox and the Cat: Animal Tales from Grimm (with Susanne Lugert) 1985, British Folk Tales 1987, The Quest for the Olwen (with Gwyn Thomas) 1988, Boo!: Ghosts and Graveyards 1988, Dathera Dad: Fairy Tales 1988, Small Tooth Dog: Wonder Tales 1988, Piper and Pooka: Boggarts and Bogles 1988, Wulf 1988, Under the Sun and Over the Moon 1989, Sleeping Nanna 1989, Sea Tongue 1991, Tales from Europe 1991, Long Tom and the Dead Hand 1992, The Tale of Taliesin (with Gwyn Thomas) 1992, The Labours of Herakles 1993, The Old Stories: Tales From East Anglia and the Fen Country 1997, Short! 1998, The King Who Was and Will Be 1998, Arthur: The Seeing Stone 2000, Enchantment 2000, The Ugly Duckling 2001, Arthur: At the Crossing Places 2001, Viking! 2002, Arthur: King of the Middle March 2003, How Many Miles to Bethlehem? 2004, King Arthur's World 2004, Outsiders 2005, Gatty's Tale 2006; non-fiction: Pieces of Land: A Journey to Eight Islands 1972, The Norse Myths 1980, The Stones Remain (with Andrew Rafferty) 1989; editor: Running to Paradise 1967, Winter's Tales for Children 3 1967, Winter's Tales 14 1968, New Poetry 2 (with Patricia Beer) 1976, The Faber Book of Northern Legends 1977, The Faber Book of Northern Folk-Tales 1980, The Riddle Book 1982, Folk-Tales of the British Isles 1985, The Oxford Book of Travel Verse 1986, Northern Lights 1987, Medieval Lovers 1988, Medieval Gardens 1990, Peter Grimes by George Crabbe 1990, The Young Oxford Book of Folk-Tales 1998, The New Exeter Book of Riddles (with Lawrence Sail) 1999, Light Unlocked (with Lawrence Sail); drama: The Wuffings (with Ivan Cutting) 1997; individual poems, translations from Old English, opera libretti, programmes for television and radio; contribs to numerous journals and magazines. *Honours:* Arts Council Award for Best Book for Young Children 1966–68, Poetry Book Soc. Choice 1976, and Recommendation 1986, Carnegie Medal 1986, Nestlé Smarties Prize Bronze Medal 2000, Guardian Children's Fiction Award 2001, Tir na n-Og Award 2001, Spoken Awards Silver Medal 2001, Hon. Fellow St Edmund Hall, Oxford 2001. *Literary Agent:* Rogers, Coleridge & White Ltd, 20 Powis Mews, London, W11 1JN, England. *Address:* Chalk Hill, Ringstead Road, Burnham Market, Norfolk PE31 8JR, England (home). *Telephone:* (1328) 730167 (office). *Fax:* (1328) 730169 (office). *E-mail:* kevin@crossley-holland.com (office).

CROWE, Thomas Rain, BA; American writer, poet, editor, publisher and translator; b. 23 Aug. 1949, Chicago, IL; pnr Nan Watkins; one s. *Education:* Furman Univ. *Career:* Ed., Beatitude magazine and Press, San Francisco, CA 1974–78; Founder-Dir, San Francisco Int. Poetry Festival 1976; Founder-Ed., Katuah Journal, Asheville, NC 1983–87; Publisher, New Native Press, Cullowhee, NC 1988–; masterclass instructor, South Carolina Gov.'s School for the Arts 1989, 1990; Ed.-at-Large, Asheville Poetry Review 1994–2001; Founder-Prod., Fern Hill Records 1994–; Founder-Performer, The Boatrockers 1996; mem. Amnesty Int., Foundation for Global Sustainability. *Opera:* The Eyes of the Butterfly (writer and dir) 1987. *Publications:* Learning to Dance (poems) 1985, Poems of Che Guevara's Dream 1991, The Sound of Light (poems and music) 1991, Night Sun (poems, three vols) 1993, The

Laugharne Poems 1997, Writing the Wind: A Celtic Resurgence (co-ed. and trans.) 1997, In Wineseller's Street: Poems of Hafiz (trans.) 1998, Drunk on the Wine of the Beloved: 100 Poems of Hafiz (trans.) 2001, Zoro's Field: My Life in the Appalachian Woods (memoir) 2005, The Baby Beats and the Second San Francisco Renaissance (ed., anthology) 2005; several translations 1991–2001. *Honours:* Thomas E. McDill Poetry Prize 1980, Atlanta Review Int. Merit Award 1996, Appalachian Writers Asscn Publishers' Book of the Year Award 1997. *Address:* 407 Canada Road, Tuskaseegee, NC 28783, USA. *E-mail:* newnativepress@hotmail.com.

CROWLEY, John, BA; American writer; b. 1 Dec. 1942, Presque Isle, ME. *Education:* Indiana University. *Publications:* The Deep, 1975; Beasts, 1976; Engine Summer, 1979; Little Big, 1981; Ægypt, 1987; Novelty (short stories), 1989; Great Work of Time, 1991; Antiquities: Seven Stories, 1993; Love & Sleep, 1994; Dæmonomania, 2000; The Translator, 2002. Other: Film Scripts; Television scripts, including America Lost and Found, The World of Tomorrow, and No Place to Hide. Contributions: periodicals. *Honours:* World Fantasy Award, 1982; American Film Festival Award, 1982; American Acad. and Institute of Arts and Letters Award in Literature, 1992.

CROZIER, Andrew, MA, PhD; British poet and lecturer; b. 1943, England. *Education:* Univ. of Cambridge, Univ. of Essex. *Career:* Sr Lecturer in English, Univ. of Sussex. *Publications:* poetry: Love Litter of Time Spent, 1967; Train Rides: Poems from '63 and '64, 1968; Walking on Grass, 1969; In One Side and Out the Other (with John James and Tom Phillips), 1970; Neglected Information, 1973; The Veil Poem, 1974; Printed Circuit, 1974; Seven Contemporary Sun Dials (with Ian Potts), 1975; Pleats, 1975; Duets, 1976; Residing, 1976; High Zero, 1978; Were There, 1978; Utamaro Variations, 1982; All Where Each Is, 1985; Ghosts in the Corridor (with Donald Davie and C. H. Sisson), 1992; prose: A Various Art (ed. with Tim Longville), 1987.

CROZIER, Brian Rossiter, (John Rossiter); British writer and journalist; b. 4 Aug. 1918, Kuridala, Queensland, Australia; s. of R. H. Crozier and Elsa Crozier (née McGillivray); m. 1st Mary Lillian Samuel 1940 (died 1993); one s. three d.; m. 2nd Jacqueline Marie Mitchell 1999. *Education:* Lycée, Montpellier, Peterborough Coll., Harrow, Trinity Coll. of Music, London. *Career:* music and art critic, London 1936–39; reporter and sub-ed., Stoke-on-Trent, Stockport, London 1940–41; aeronautical inspection 1941–43; sub-ed., Reuters 1943–44, News Chronicle 1944–48, sub-ed. and writer Sydney Morning Herald, Australia 1948–51; corresp., Reuters-AAP 1951–52; Features Ed., Straits Times, Singapore 1952–53; leader writer and corresp., The Economist 1954–64; BBC commentator, English, French and Spanish overseas services 1954–66, Chair. Forum World Features 1965–74; Ed., Conflict Studies 1970–75; Co-founder and Dir Inst. for the Study of Conflict 1970–79, Consultant 1979–; Columnist, Now!, London 1980–81, Nat. Review, New York 1978–90 (contributing ed. 1982–), The Times 1982–84, The Free Nation, London 1982–89; Adjunct Scholar, The Heritage Foundation 1983–95; Distinguished Visiting Fellow, Hoover Inst., Stanford, Calif., USA 1996–2001. *Art Exhibitions:* London 1948, Sydney 1949–50. *Publications:* The Rebels 1960, The Morning After 1963, Neo-Colonialism 1964, South-East Asia in Turmoil 1965, The Struggle for the Third World 1966, Franco 1967, The Masters of Power 1969, The Future of Communist Power (in USA: Since Stalin) 1970, De Gaulle (vol. I) 1973, (vol. II) 1974, A Theory of Conflict 1974, The Man Who Lost China (Chiang Kai-shek) 1977, Strategy of Survival 1978, The Minimum State 1979, Franco: Crepúsculo de un hombre 1980, The Price of Peace 1980, Socialism Explained (co-author) 1984, This War Called Peace (co-author) 1984, The Andropov Deception (novel) (under pseudonym John Rossiter) 1984, The Grenada Documents (ed.) 1987, Socialism: Dream and Reality 1987, The Gorbachev Phenomenon 1990, Communism: Why Prolong its Death Throes? 1990, Free Agent: The Unseen War 1993, The KGB Lawsuits 1995, Le Phénix rouge (co-author) 1995, The Rise and Fall of the Soviet Empire 1999 and contribs to journals in numerous countries. *Address:* 18 Wickliffe Avenue, Finchley, London, N3 3EJ, England (home). *Telephone:* (20) 8346-8124 (home). *Fax:* (20) 8346-4599.

CROZIER, Lorna, MA; Canadian poet and academic; *Distinguished Professor of Poetry, University of Victoria*; b. 24 May 1948, Swift Current, Saskatchewan; d. of Emerson Crozier and Peggy Crozier (née Ford); m. Patrick Lane 1978. *Education:* Univs of Saskatchewan, Regina and Alberta. *Career:* English teacher 1966–73; Special Lecturer, Univ. of Saskatchewan 1986–91; Writer-in-Residence, Univ. of Toronto, Ont. 1989–90; apptd Assoc. Prof. Dept of Writing, Univ. of Victoria, BC 1991, now Distinguished Prof. of Poetry and Chair Dept of Writing; guest at int. poetry festivals in Faenza, Italy, Cheltenham, UK, Toronto and Vancouver; mem. Saskatchewan Writers' Guild. *Publications include:* Inside is the Sky 1976, Crow's Black Joy 1978, No Longer Two People (with Patrick Lane) 1979, Animals of Fall 1979, Humans and Other Beasts 1980, The Weather 1981, The Garden Going On Without Us 1983, Angels of Flesh, Angels of Silence 1988, Inventing the Hawk (Gov.-Gen.'s Award for Poetry 1992) 1992, Everything Arrives at the Light 1995, A Saving Grace: The Collected Poems of Mrs Bentley 1996, The Transparency of Grief: 5 New Poems 1996, What the Living Won't Let Go (poetry) 1999, Apocrypha of Light 2002; editor: A Sudden Radiance 1987, Breathing Fire: The New Generation of Canadian Poets (with Patrick Lane) 1995, Desire in Seven Voices (essays) 1999, Addicted: Notes from the Belly of the Beast (essays) (with Patrick Lane) 2001, Bones in their Wings: Ghazals 2004, Whetstone (poetry) 2005, Breathing Fire 2 (with Patrick Lane) 2005. *Honours:* Prize of CBC Literary Competition 1987, Pat Lowther Award for Poetry 1992,

1996, Award for Poetry, Canadian Authors' Asscn 1992, Nat. Magazine Award Gold Medal 1996, Dorothy Livesay Poetry Prize, the Pat Lowther Poetry Award, Monday Magazine Award for Best Book of Poetry 2006. *Literary Agent:* McClelland & Stewart Inc., 481 University Avenue, Suite 900, Toronto, ON M5G 2E9, Canada. *Address:* Department of Writing, University of Victoria, PO Box 1700, STN CSC, Victoria, BC V8W 2Y2 (office); 1886 Cuttra Avenue, Saanichton, BC V8M 1L7, Canada (home). *Telephone:* (250) 721-7306 (office); (604) 652-3956 (home). *Fax:* (604) 652-1430 (home). *E-mail:* lcrozier@ finearts.uvic.ca (office). *Website:* www.finearts.uvic.ca/~lcrozier (office); www .lornacrozier.ca.

CRUMEY, Andrew David William Bernard, BSc, PhD; British writer; *Literary Editor, Scotland on Sunday;* b. 12 Oct. 1961, Glasgow, Scotland. *Education:* Imperial College, London, St Andrews Univ. *Career:* care worker, 1987–88; Research Assoc., Imperial College and Leeds University, 1989–92; school teacher, Newcastle upon Tyne, 1992–96; writer, 1996–; Literary Ed., Scotland on Sunday 2000–. *Publications:* novels: Music in a Foreign Language 1994, Pfitz 1995, D'Alembert's Principle 1996, Mr Mee 2000; Mobius Dick 2004. *Honours:* Saltire Society Award for Best First Book, 1994; Arts Council Writer's Award; Scottish Arts Council Book Award. *Literary Agent:* A. M. Heath & Co Ltd, 79 St Martin's Lane, London WC2N 4RE, England.

CRYSTAL, David, OBE, BA, PhD, FRCST, FBA; British writer and editor; b. 6 July 1941, Lisburn, County Antrim, Northern Ireland; m. 1st Molly Stack 1964 (died 1976); two s. two d.; m. 2nd Hilary Norman 1976; one s. *Education:* Univ. Coll. London. *Career:* Asst Lecturer, Univ. Coll. of North Wales 1963–65; Lecturer and Reader 1965–76, Prof. of Linguistic Science 1976–85, Univ. of Reading; Hon. Prof., Univ. of Wales, Bangor 1985–; Ed., Child Language Teaching and Therapy 1985–96, Linguistics Abstracts 1985–96; Consultant Ed., English Today 1986–94. *Publications:* Linguistics, Language and Religion 1965, What Is Linguistics? (third edn) 1974, The English Tone of Voice 1975, Child Language, Learning and Linguistics 1976, Working with LARSP 1979, Eric Partridge: In His Own Words 1980, A Dictionary of Linguistics and Phonetics 1980, Introduction to Language Pathology 1980, Clinical Linguistics 1981, Directions in Applied Linguistics 1981, Linguistic Controversies 1981, Profiling Linguistic Disability 1982, Linguistic Encounters with Language Handicap 1984, Language Handicap in Children 1984, Who Cares About English Usage? 1984, Listen to Your Child 1986, The English Language 1988, Cambridge Encyclopedia of Language 1987, Rediscover Grammar 1988, The Cambridge Encyclopedia 1990, Language A–Z 1991, Nineties Knowledge 1992, An Encyclopedic Dictionary of Language and Languages 1992, The Cambridge Factfinder 1993, The Cambridge Biographical Encyclopaedia 1994, The Cambridge Encyclopedia of the English Language 1995, Discover Grammar 1996, English as a Global Language 1997, Language Play 1998, Words on Words (with Hilary Crystal) 2000, Language Death 2000, John Bradburne's Mutemwa 2000, Language and the Internet 2001, Shakespeare's Words (with Ben Crystal) 2002, The New Penguin Encyclopedia 2002, The New Penguin Factfinder 2003, The Penguin Concise Encyclopedia 2003, The Stories of English 2004, The Language Revolution 2004, Making Sense of English Grammar 2004, A Glossary of Textspeak and Netspeak 2004, Pronouncing Shakespeare 2005, The Shakespeare Miscellany (with Ben Crystal) 2005, Dr Johnson's Dictionary 2005, How Language Works 2006, Words, Words, Words 2006, The Fight for English 2006, By Hook or By Crook: a journey in search of English 2007; also children's non-fiction books. *Honours:* Wheatley Medal 2001. *Address:* Akaroa, Gors Avenue, Holyhead, Anglesey LL65 1PB, Wales. *E-mail:* crystal@dial.pipex.com. *Website:* www .davidcrystal.com; www.crystalreference.com.

CSOÓRI, Sándor; Hungarian poet and writer; b. 3 Feb. 1930, Zámoly, Co. Fejér. *Education:* Lenin Inst., Budapest. *Career:* contrib. to Irodalmi Ujság (monthly) 1954–55, Új hang (monthly) 1955–56; drama critic Mafilm Studio 1968; joined opposition movt 1980; participated in political discussions of Monor 1985 and Lakitelek 1987; Founding mem. Hungarian Democratic Forum 1987, presidium mem. 1988–92; Chair. Illyés Gyula Foundation 1990–94; Pres. World Fed. of Hungarians 1991–2000. *Publications:* selected poems: Fölröppen a madár (The Bird Takes Wing) 1954, Ördögpille (Demon Butterfly) 1957, Menekülés a magányból (Escape from Loneliness) 1962, Elmaradt lázálom (Postponed Nightmare) 1980, Knives and Nails 1981, Hóemléke (Memory of Snow) 1983, Várakozás a tavaszban (Waiting in the Spring) 1983, Hattyúkkal ágyútűzben (In Cannon Fire with Swans) 1995, Ha volna életem (If I Had a Life) 1996, Quiet Vertigo 2001, Before and After the Fall 2004; sociographies: Tudósítás a toronyból (Report From the Tower) 1963, Kubai utinapló (Cuban Travel Diary) 1965; essay volumes: Faltól falig (From Wall to Wall) 1968, Nomád napló (Nomadic Diary) 1979, Félig bevallott élet (Half Confessed Life) 1984, Készülődés a számadásra (Preparation for Final Reckoning) 1987, Nappali hold (Daytime Moon) 1991, Tenger és diólevél I. II. (The Sea and Nut Leaves) 1994, Száll a alá poklokra (Descent into Hell) 1997; film scripts: Tízezer nap (Ten thousand days), Földobott kő (The thrown-up stone), 80 huszár (Eighty Hussars), Tüske a köröm alatt (A Thorn under the Fingernail), Hószakadás (Snow-Storm), Nincs idö (No Time Left). *Honours:* Attila József Prize 1954, Cannes Film Festival Prize 1964, 1968, Herder Prize 1981, Kossuth Prize 1990, Eeva Joenpelto Prize 1995, The Hungarian Book of the Year Award 1995, Karoli Gaspar Award, Hungarian Heritage Award. *Address:* Benczúr u. 15, 1068 Budapest, Hungary.

CUECO, Henri Aguilella; French artist and writer; b. 19 Oct. 1929, Uzerche, Corrèze; s. of Vincent Aguilella Cueco and Jeanne Aguilella Cueco (née Lagrange); m. Andrée Laval 1956; two s. *Education:* Coll. Moderne d'Uzerche. *Career:* f. mem. Coopérative des Malassis; teacher Faculté de Vincennes and Paris I; Prof. Ecole Nat. Supérieure des Beaux-Arts, Paris; numerous radio and TV broadcasts. *Art exhibitions:* Musée d'Art moderne Arc 1, Paris 1970, Arc 2 1982, Ecole Nat. Supérieure des Beaux Arts 1993; also in Japan; numerous group exhbns in France and Italy. *Major works:* Les Hommes rouges 1968–70, Le Grand méchoui 1972, Onze variations sur le thème du Radeau de la Méduse 1974, Les Chiens 1975, Murs et Claustras 1975–76, Les Herbes 1977–87, Les Chiens de Saqqarah 1990, Sols d'Afrique 1992, Les Pommes de terre 1987–93, Peintures d'après Poussin et Philippe de Champaigne 1995–97, murals and mosaics; theatre sets for Comédie française, Karlsruhe Opera. *Publications:* Le Journal d'une pomme de terre 1993, Le Collectionneur de collections 1995, Cueco (monograph) 1997, Le Volcan 1998, Le Troubadour à plumes 1999, Dialogue avec mon jardinier (trans. as Conversations with my Gardener) 2000, La Petite peinture 2001. *Honours:* Prix de la Fondation Félix Fénéon, Prix du Salon de la Jeune Peinture. *Address:* 88 rue Carnot, 95360 Montmagny (office); Le Pouget, 19410 Vigeois, France (home).

CULLINAN, Patrick; South African poet; b. 1932, Pretoria; m.; three c. *Education:* Charterhouse and Magdalen Colls, Oxford. *Career:* fmr farmer, sawmill worker, publisher and univ. lecturer; Ed., The Bloody Horse 1980–81. *Publications:* poetry: The Horizon Forty 1963, Today is Not Different 1978, The White Hail in the Orchard 1984, I Sing Where I Stand 1985, Selected Poems 1961–91 1992, Selected Poems 1961–94 1991, Transformations 1999; novel: Matrix 2002; non-fiction: Robert Jacob Gordon 1743–1795: The Man and his Travels at the Cape 1992, Imaginative Trespasser 2005. *Honours:* Cavaliere, Italy 2003; Olive Schreiner Prize 1980, three Pringle Awards, Slug Award, Sanlam Literary Award, Cape Town Historical Soc. Merit Award. *Address:* c/o Wits University Press, PO Wits, Johannesburg 2050, South Africa. *E-mail:* klippv@wup.wits.ac.za.

CULP, Marguerite (see Kearns, Marguerite)

CULVER, Timothy J. (see Westlake, Donald Edwin)

CUMMING, Peter E., BA, DipEd, MA; Canadian writer, dramatist and teacher; b. 23 March 1951, Brampton, ON; m. Mary Shelleen Nelson 1970. *Career:* Resident Artist in Drama, Wilfrid Laurier University, 1972–73; Exec. Dir, Atlantic Publishers Asscn, 1984–85; mem. Playwrights Union of Canada; Writers Union of Canada; Canadian Society of Children's Authors, Illustrators, and Performers; Asscn of Canadian College and University Teachers of English. *Publications:* Snowdreams, 1982; Ti-Jean, 1983; A Horse Called Farmer, 1984; Mogul and Me, 1989; Out on the Ice in the Middle of the Bay, 1993; contributing ed., Quill and Quire 1982–84. *Honours:* First Prize, Children's Prose, 1980, First Prize, Adult Fiction, 1981, Writers Federation of Nova Scotia; Toronto Board of Education Canada Day Playwriting Competition, 1981; Our Choice, Children's Book Centre, 1984, 1989, 1993; Hilroy Award for Innovative Teaching, 1990; George Wicken Prize in Canadian Literature, 1994; Tiny Torgi Award, 1995.

CUMMINGS, David Alexander; British musician (guitar) and screenwriter; b. 26 Nov. 1959. *Education:* Univ. of East Anglia. *Career:* mem., The Higsons 1980–81, Lloyd Cole & The Commotions 1987, Del Amitri 1987–95; writer for television and film comedy 1994–, collaborators include Harry Enfield, Paul Whitehouse and Alexei Sayle. *Recordings include:* with Del Amitri: albums: Waking Hours 1989, Change Everything 1992, Twisted 1995, Hatful Of Rain: The Best Of 1998; singles: Always The Last To Know 1992, Be My Downfall 1992, Just Like A Man 1992, When You Were Young 1993, Here And Now 1995, Driving With The Breaks On 1995, Roll To Me 1995, Tell Her This 1995. *Writing for film:* The Last Seduction II 1999, Kevin and Perry Go Large 2000. *Writing for television:* The Fast Show (BBC) 1994–2000, Harry Enfield & Chums (Tiger Aspect/BBC) 1994–98, Alexei Sayle's Merry-Go-Round (BBC) 1998, Happiness (BBC) 2001–03, Spine Chillers: Goths (BBC) 2003. *Publications:* The Fast Show Book (with Paul Whitehouse and Charlie Higson) 1996. *Honours:* Writers' Guild of Great Britain Award (jt winner, for Harry Enfield & Chums) 1997. *Address:* c/o Comedy Department, BBC Television Centre, Wood Lane, London, W12 7RJ, England (office).

CUMMINS, Walter Merrill, BA, MA, MFA, PhD; American academic, writer and editor; *Professor Emeritus, Farleigh Dickinson University;* b. 6 Feb. 1936, Long Branch, NJ; m. 1st Judith Gruenberg 1957 (divorced 1981); m. 2nd Alison Cunningham 1981; two d. *Education:* Rutgers Univ., Univ. of Iowa. *Career:* Instructor, Univ. of Iowa 1962–65; Asst Prof. 1965–69, Assoc. Prof. 1969–74, Prof. of English 1974–2002, Prof. Emeritus 2002–, Fairleigh Dickinson Univ.; Assoc. Ed. 1978–83, Ed.-in-Chief 1983–2002, Ed. Emer. 2002–, The Literary Review; Distinguished Retiring Ed., Council of Editors of Learned Journals 2002. *Publications:* A Stranger to the Deed (novel) 1968, Into Temptation (novel) 1968, The Other Sides of Reality: Myths, Visions and Fantasies (co-ed.) 1972, Student Writing Guide (co-ed.) 1973, Witness (short stories) 1975, Managing Management Climate (with George G. Gordon) 1979, Where We Live (short stories) 1983, Shifting Borders: East European Poetry of the Eighties (ed.) 1993, The Literary Traveler 2005, Programming Our Lives: Television and the Change in American Identity 2006; contrib. of stories, articles and reviews in many publs. *Honours:* New Jersey State Council on the Arts Fellowship 1982–83, Nat. Endowment for the Arts grants 1987–88, 1990–91. *Address:* 6 Hanover Road, Florham Park, NJ 07932, USA. *E-mail:* wcummins@att.net. *Website:* www.waltercummins.com.

CUMPER, Patricia (Pat); British playwright; b. 1955, Jamaica. *Education:* Univ. of Cambridge. *Radio contributions:* Another Country (BBC Radio 3), A Caribbean Blue (BBC Radio 4), Home Truths (BBC Radio 4), Something Understood (BBC Radio 4). *Television plays:* Doctors (BBC1). *Plays:* Fallen Angel and the Devil Concubine 1989, The Key Game 2002; musicals: Fabula Urbis (with Simon Deacon) 2002, Elysium. *Publication:* One Bright Child (novel). *Literary Agent:* Bill McLean Personal Management Ltd, 23B Deodar Road, London, SW15 2NP, England. *Telephone:* (20) 8789-8191.

CUNLIFFE, Sir Barrington (Barry) Windsor, Kt, CBE, BA, MA, PhD, LittD, FBA, FSA; British archaeologist and writer; *Professor of European Archaeology, Keble College, Oxford;* b. 10 Dec. 1939, Portsmouth, Hampshire, England; m. Margaret Herdman 1979; one s. one d. *Education:* St John's Coll., Cambridge. *Career:* Lecturer in Classics, Univ. of Bristol 1963–66; Prof. of Archaeology, Univ. of Southampton 1966–72; Prof. of European Archaeology and Fellow, Keble Coll., Oxford 1972–; Commr, Historic Buildings and Monuments Comm. for England 1987–2006; Gov., Museum of London 1995–97; Trustee, British Museum 2000–; mem. Medieval Soc., Prehistoric Soc., Royal Archaeological Inst., Soc. of Antiquaries (Vice-Pres. 1982–86, Pres. 1994–95). *Publications:* Excavations at Richborough, Vol. 5 1968, Roman Bath (ed.) 1969, Excavations at Fishbourne 1961–69 (two vols) 1971, Fishbourne: A Roman Palace and its Gardens 1971, Roman Baths Discovered 1971, Guide to the Roman Remains of Bath 1971, The Cradle of England 1972, The Making of the English 1973, The Regni 1974, Iron Age Communities in Britain: An Account of England, Scotland, and Wales from the Seventh Century BC until the Roman Conquest 1974, Excavations at Porchester Castle, Hants (five vols) 1975, 1976, 1977, 1985, 1994, Rome and the Barbarians 1975, Oppida: The Beginnings of Urbanisation in Barbarian Europe (with Trevor Rowley) 1976, Hengistbury Head 1978, Rome and her Empire 1978, The Celtic World 1979, Excavating Bath 1950–75 (ed.) 1979, Coinage and Society in Britain and Gaul: Some Current Problems (ed.) 1981, Antiquity and Man (ed.) 1982, Danebury: Anatomy of an Iron Age Hillfort 1983, Aspects of the Iron Age in Central Southern Britain (ed. with David Miles) 1984, Danebury: An Iron Age Hillfort in Hampshire, Vols 1 and 2 1984, Vols 4 and 5 1991, Vol. 6 1995, Heywood Sumner's Wessex 1985, Temple of Sulis Minerva at Bath Vol. I (with Peter Davenport) 1985, The City of Bath 1986, Hengistbury Head, Darcet, Vol. I 1987, Origins: The Roots of European Civilisation (ed.) 1987, Mount Batten, Plymouth: A Prehistoric and Roman Port 1988, Greeks, Romans & Barbarians: Spheres of Interaction 1988, Wessex to AD 1000 1993, The Oxford Illustrated Prehistory of Europe (ed.) 1994, Social Complexity and the Development of Towns in Iberia (ed. with S. Keay) 1995, The Ancient Celts 1997, Science and Stonehenge (ed. with C. Renfrew) 1997, The Guadajoz Project, Andalucia in the First Millennium BC (with M.-C. Fernandez Castro) 1999, The Danebury Environs Programme, Vols 1 and 2 2000, Facing the Ocean: The Atlantic and Its People (Wolfson Foundation History Prize) 2001, The Extraordinary Voyage of Pytheas the Greek 2001, The Celts 2003, Mediterranean Urbanization 800–600 BC (ed with R. Osborne), England's Landscape: The West (ed.) 2006; contribs to periodicals and archaeological journals. *Honours:* Dr hc (Univ. of Sussex), (Univ. of Bath), (Open Univ.); American Historical Asscn James Henry Breasted Prize 2001, Wolfson History Prize 2001, Grahame Clark Medal 2004, Gold Medal of the Soc. of Antiquaries. *Address:* Institute of Archaeology, University of Oxford, 36 Beaumont Street, Oxford, OX1 2PG, England (office). *Telephone:* (1865) 278240 (office). *Fax:* (1865) 278254 (office). *E-mail:* barry.cunliffe@arch.ox.ac.uk (office). *Website:* www.arch.ox.ac.uk (office).

CUNLIFFE, John; British children's writer and poet. *Career:* worked as a teacher and librarian before becoming a full-time writer; creator of the popular characters, Postman Pat, and Rosie and Jim. *Publications include:* Farmer Barnes series: numerous publs 1964–; Riddles and Rhymes and Rigmaroles 1971, The Giant Who Stole the World 1971, Giant Kippernose and Other Stories 1972, The King's Birthday Cake 1973, The Great Dragon Competition and Other Stories 1973, Small Monkey Tales 1974, Giant Brog and the Motorway 1976, Mr Gosling and the Runaway Chair 1978, Mr Gosling and the Great Art Robbery 1979, Our Sam: The Daftest Dog in the World 1980, Sara's Giant and the Upside-down House 1981, Fog Lane School and the Great Racing Car Disaster 1989, The Minister's Cat 1989, Big Jim and Little Jim 1990; Postman Pat series: numerous publs 1981–, including Postman Pat's Treasure Hunt, Postman Pat and the Mystery Thief, Postman Pat's Secret, Postman Pat's Rainy Day, Postman Pat's Foggy Day, Postman Pat's Difficult Day, Postman Pat's Tractor Express, Postman Pat Takes a Message, Postman Pat's Thirsty Day, Postman Pat's Letters on Ice, Postman Pat's A.B.C. Story, Postman Pat's 1, 2, 3 Story, Postman Pat to the Rescue, Postman Pat Plays for Greendale, Postman Pat's Safari, Postman Pat's Winter Storybook, Postman Pat and the Christmas Puddings, Postman Pat and the Greendale Ghost, Postman Pat Goes to Town, Postman Pat and the Toy Soldiers, Postman Pat's House, Postman Pat Gets a Pet, Postman Pat's Three Wishes, Postman Pat Gets Fat, Postman Pat and the Suit of Armour, Postman Pat's Christmas, Postman Pat Goes Football Crazy, Postman Pat and the Ice Cream Machine, Postman Pat and the Job Well Done; Rosie and Jim series: numerous publs 1991–, including Rosie and Jim and the Water Wizard, Rosie and Jim and the Rainbow, Rosie and Jim and the Man in the Wind, Rosie and Jim and the Drink of Milk, A Family for Duck, Jim Gets Lost, Rosie and Jim at the Seaside; poetry: Dare You Go 1992, Fizzy Whizzy Poetry Book 1995. *Literary Agent:* c/o Anthony Goff, David Higham Associates, 5–8 Lower John Street, Golden Square, London, W1F 9HA, England. *Telephone:* (20) 7434-5900. *Fax:* (20) 7437-1072. *E-mail:* anthonygoff@davidhigham.co.uk. *Website:* www.davidhigham.co.uk. *E-mail:* john.cunliffe@metronet.co.uk (home).

CUNNINGHAM, Michael, MA, MFA; American novelist; b. 6 Nov. 1952, Cincinnati. *Education:* Stanford Univ., Univ. of Iowa. *Career:* fmr bartender; joined Univ. of Ia Writers' Workshop 1978; writer for Carnegie Corpn; now Adjunct Asst Prof., Columbia Univ.; Guggenheim Fellowship 1993. *Publications:* Golden States 1984, A Home at the End of the World 1990, Flesh and Blood 1995, The Hours (Pulitzer Prize, PEN/Faulkner Award for Fiction 1999) 1998, Specimen Days 2005. *Honours:* Lambda Literary Award for Gay Men's Fiction 1995. *Literary Agent:* Steven Barclay Agency, 12 Western Avenue, Petaluma, CA 94952, USA. *Telephone:* (707) 773-0654. *Fax:* (707) 778-1868. *Website:* www.barclayagency.com. *Address:* Columbia University, Creative Writing Center, Room 415, 2970 Broadway, New York, NY 10027-6939, USA (office).

CUOMO, Mario Matthew, LLB; American fmr state governor and lawyer; *Of Counsel, Wilkie Farr & Gallagher LLP;* b. 15 June 1932, Queen's County NY; s. of Andrea and Immaculata Cuomo; m. Matilda Raffa; two s. (including Andrew Cuomo) three d. *Education:* St John's Coll. and St John's Univ. *Career:* admitted to NY Bar 1956, Supreme Court Bar 1960; Confidential Legal Asst to Hon. Adrian P. Burke, NY State Court of Appeals 1956–58; Assoc., Corner, Weisbrod, Froeb and Charles, Brooklyn 1958–63; partner 1963–75; Sec. of State, NY 1975–79; Lt-Gov. of New York State 1979–82, Gov. 1983–95; partner Wilkie Farr and Gallagher LLP 1995–; mem. faculty St John's Univ. Law School 1963–75; counsel to community groups 1966–72; fmr Co-Chairman and mem. Bd of Dirs Partnership for a Drug-Free America; Democrat. *Publications:* Forest Hills Diary: The Crisis of Low-Income Housing 1974, Maya 1984, Lincoln on Democracy (jtly) 1990, The New York Idea 1994, Common Sense 1995, Reason to Believe 1995, The Blue Spruce 1999, Why Lincoln Matters Today More Than Ever 2004; articles in legal journals. *Honours:* NY Rapallo Award, Columbia Lawyers' Asscn 1976, Dante Medal, Italian Govt./American Asscn of Italian Teachers 1976, Silver Medallion, Columbia Coalition 1976, Public Admin. Award, C.W. Post Coll. 1977. *Address:* Wilkie, Farr and Gallagher LLP, 787 7th Avenue, New York, NY 10019-6099 (office); 50 Sutton Place South, New York, NY 10022, USA. *Telephone:* (212) 728-8260 (office). *Fax:* (212) 728-9260 (office). *E-mail:* mcuomo@willkie.com (office). *Website:* www.willkie.com (office).

CUPITT, Rev. Don, MA; British ecclesiastic and university lecturer; b. 22 May 1934, Oldham; s. of Robert Cupitt and Norah Cupitt; m. Susan Marianne Day 1963; one s. two d. *Education:* Charterhouse, Trinity Hall, Cambridge, Westcott House, Cambridge. *Career:* ordained 1959; Curate, St Philip's Church, Salford 1959–62; Vice-Prin. Westcott House, Cambridge 1962–65; Fellow, Emmanuel Coll., Cambridge 1965–96, Dean 1966–91, Life Fellow 1996–; Asst Lecturer, Univ. of Cambridge 1968–73, Lecturer in Divinity 1973–96; Fellow of the Jesus Seminar, Westar Inst., Calif., USA 2001. *Television documentaries:* Who Was Jesus? 1977, The Sea of Faith (series) 1984. *Publications:* Christ and the Hiddenness of God 1971, Crisis of Moral Authority 1972, The Leap of Reason 1976, The Worlds of Science and Religion 1976, Who Was Jesus? (with Peter Armstrong) 1977, The Nature of Man 1979, Explorations in Theology 1979, The Debate about Christ 1979, Jesus and the Gospel of God 1979, Taking Leave of God 1980, The World to Come 1982, The Sea of Faith 1984, Only Human 1985, Life Lines 1986, The Long-Legged Fly 1987, The New Christian Ethics 1988, Radicals and the Future of the Church 1989, Creation out of Nothing 1990, What is a Story? 1991, The Time Being 1992, After All 1994, The Last Philosophy 1995, Solar Ethics 1995, After God: The Future of Religion 1997, Mysticism after Modernity 1997, The Religion of Being 1998, The Revelation of Being 1998, The New Religion of Life in Everyday Speech 1999, The Meaning of It All in Everyday Speech 1999, Kingdom Come in Everyday Speech 2000, Philosophy's Own Religion 2000, Reforming Christianity 2001, Emptiness and Brightness 2001, Is Nothing Sacred? 2002, Life, Life 2003, The Way to Happiness: A Theory of Religion 2005, The Great Questions of Life 2006, The Old Creed and the New 2006, Radical Theology 2006. *Honours:* Hon. DLitt (Bristol) 1985. *Address:* Emmanuel College, Cambridge, CB2 3AP, England. *Telephone:* (1223) 334200. *Fax:* (1223) 334426. *E-mail:* susancupitt@waitrose.com (home). *Website:* www.doncupitt.com.

CURREY, Richard; American writer; b. 19 Oct. 1949, West Virginia. *Education:* West Virginia University, Howard University. *Career:* writer 1972–; Visiting Prof., University of New Mexico, 1993; Distinguished Writer-in-Residence, Wichita State University, 1993; Mem., Writers Film Project, Chesterfield Film Company, 1996–97; Gives readings from his works. *Publications:* Fatal Light, 1988; The Wars of Heaven, 1990; Crossing Over: The Vietnam Stories, 1993; Lost Highway, 1997. *Honours:* D. H. Lawrence Fellow in Literature, 1981; Fellow, National Endowment for the Arts, 1982, 1987; Short Fiction Prize, Associated Writing Programs, 1984; O. Henry Award, 1988; Special Citation, Hemingway Foundation, 1989; Excellence in the Arts Award, Vietnam Veterans of America, 1989; Pushcart Prize, 1990; Fellow, Western States Arts Federation, 1993; Writer-in-Residence, State of West Virginia, 1994; Daugherty Award in the Humanities, 1997.

CURRIE JONES, Edwina, MA, MSc; British politician, writer and broadcaster; b. 13 Oct. 1946, Liverpool; d. of the late Simon Cohen; m. 1st Raymond F. Currie 1972 (divorced 2001); two d.; m. 2nd John Jones 2001. *Education:* Liverpool Inst. for Girls, St Anne's Coll., Oxford, London School of Econs. *Career:* teacher and lecturer in econs, econ. history and business studies

1972–81; mem. Birmingham City Council 1975–86; Conservative MP for Derbyshire S 1983–97; Parl. Pvt. Sec. to Sec. of State for Educ. and Science 1985–86; Parl. Under-Sec. of State for Health 1986–88; mem. Parl. Select Cttee on Social Services 1983–86; Jt Chair. Conservative Group for Europe 1995–97; Vice-Chair. European Movt 1995–99; Jt Chair. Future of Europe Trust 1995–97; contrib. to radio and TV including Winner Celebrity Mastermind 2004. *Radio presenter:* Late Night Currie, BBC 1998–2003. *Publications:* Life Lines 1989, What Women Want 1990, Three Line Quips 1992, A Parliamentary Affair (novel) 1994, A Woman's Place (novel) 1996, She's Leaving Home (novel) 1997, The Ambassador (novel) 1998, Chasing Men (novel) 2000, This Honourable House (novel) 2001, Diaries 1987–92 2002, Diaries 1992–97 2004. *Honours:* Speaker of the Year, Asscn of Speakers' Clubs 1990, 1994 Campaigner of the Year, The Spectator/Highland Park Parliamentarian of the Year Awardsc. *Literary Agent:* c/o Curtis Brown, Haymarket, London, SW1Y 4SP, England. *Telephone:* (20) 7396-6600. *Address:* c/o Little, Brown (UK) Ltd, Brettenham House, Lancaster Place, London, WC2E 7EN, England.

CURTEIS, Ian Bayley; British dramatist; b. 1 May 1935, London; m. 1st Dorothy Joan Armstrong 1964; two s.; m. 2nd Joanna Trollope (q.v.) 1985; two step-d.; m. 3rd Lady Grantley; two step-s. *Education:* Univ. of London. *Career:* dir and actor in theatres throughout UK and BBC TV script reader 1956–63; BBC and ATV staff dir (drama) 1963–67; Chair. Cttee on Censorship, Writers' Guild of Great Britain 1981–85, Pres. of Guild 1998–2001. *Plays for TV:* Beethoven, Sir Alexander Fleming (BBC entry, Prague Festival 1973), Mr. Rolls and Mr. Royce, Long Voyage Out of War (trilogy), The Folly, The Haunting, Second Time Round, A Distinct Chill, The Portland Millions, Philby, Burgess and Maclean (British entry, Monte Carlo Festival 1978), Hess, The Atom Spies, Churchill and the Generals (Grand Prize for Best Programme of 1981, New York Int. Film and TV Festival), Suez 1956, Miss Morison's Ghosts (British entry Monte Carlo Festival), BB and Lord D.; writer of numerous TV series; screenplays: La Condition humaine (André Malraux), Lost Empires (adapted from J. B. Priestley), Eureka, Graham Greene's The Man Within (TV) 1983, The Nightmare Years (TV) 1989, The Zimmerman Telegram 1990, Yalta 1991, The Choir (BBC 1), The Falklands Play 2002, More Love 2003, Yet More Love 2004, Miss Morrison's Ghosts 2004, The Bargain 2007; numerous articles and speeches on the ethics and politics of broadcasting. *Plays for radio:* Eroica 2000, Love 2001, After the Break, The Falklands Play 2002. *Publications:* Long Voyage Out of War (trilogy) 1971, Churchill and the Generals 1980, Suez 1956, 1980, The Falklands Play 1987. *Address:* Markenfield Hall, North Yorks., HG4 3AD; 2 Warwick Square, London, SW1V 2AA, England. *Telephone:* (1765) 603411 (office); (20) 7821-8606 (home). *Fax:* (1765) 607195 (office).

CURTIS, Anthony Samuel, BA, MA, FRSA; British journalist, editor and writer; b. 12 March 1926, London, England; m. Sarah Curtis 1960; three s. *Education:* Merton Coll., Oxford. *Career:* Deputy Ed., TLS 1959–60; Literary Ed., Sunday Telegraph 1960–70, Financial Times 1970–90; mem. Royal Literary Fund (treasurer 1975–98), Soc. of Authors (pension fund trustee), Literary Soc. *Publications:* The Pattern of Maugham 1974, Somerset Maugham: The Critical Heritage (with John Whitehead) 1987, Lit Ed: On Reviews and Reviewing 1998, Before Bloomsbury: The 1890s Diaries of Three Kensington Ladies 2002, Virginia Woolf: Bloomsbury and Beyond 2006, Golden Opportunities (play adaptation) 2006; contrib. to periodicals and radio. *Honours:* Harkness Fellowship in Journalism, USA 1958–59. *Address:* 9 Essex Villas, London, W8 7BP, England. *E-mail:* anticurtis@aol.com.

CURTIS, Jamie Lee, Lady Haden-Guest; American actress and author; b. 22 Nov. 1958, Los Angeles, Calif.; d. of Tony Curtis and Janet Leigh; m. Christopher Guest; one s. one d. *Education:* Choate School, Conn., Univ. of the Pacific, Calif. *Films include:* Halloween, The Fog, Terror Train, Halloween II, Road Games, Prom Night, Love Letters, Trading Places, The Adventures of Buckaroo Banzai: Across the 8th Dimension, Grandview, USA, Perfect, 8 Million Ways to Die, Mother's Boys, Drowning Mona, Amazing Grace and Chuck, A Man in Love, Dominick and Eugene, A Fish Called Wanda, Blue Steel, My Girl, Forever Young, My Girl 2, True Lies 1994 (Golden Globe Award for Best Actress in a musical or comedy), House Arrest 1996, Fierce Creatures 1996, Halloween H20 1998, Virus 1999, The Tailor of Panama 2000, Daddy and Them 2001, Halloween: Resurrection 2002, True Lies 2 2003, Freaky Friday 2003, Skipping Christmas 2004. *Television includes:* She's In The Army Now, Dorothy Stratten: Death of a Centrefold, Operation Petticoat, The Love Boat, Columbo, Quincy, Charlie's Angels, Anything but Love (dir), Money on the Side, As Summers Die, Anything but Love, Actor, The Heidi Chronicles, Nichoas' Gift. *Publications:* When I Was Little, A Four-Year-Old's Memoir of her Youth 1993, Tell Me Again About the Night I Was Born 1996, Today I Feel Silly and Other Moods That Make My Day 1999, Where Do Balloons Go? An Uplifting Mystery 2000, I'm Gonna Like Me Letting Off a Little Self-Esteem 2002, It's Hard To Be Five, Learning How To Work My Control Panel 2004. *Address:* c/o Rick Kurtzman, CAA, 9830 Wilshire Blvd, Beverly Hills, CA 90212, USA (office). *Telephone:* (310) 288-4545 (office).

CURTIS, Richard Whalley Anthony, CBE, BA; British screenwriter, film director and film producer; b. 8 Nov. 1956, New Zealand; s. of Anthony J. Curtis and Glynness S. Curtis; two s. one d. by Emma Vallencey Freud. *Education:* Harrow School, Christ Church, Oxford. *Career:* Co-founder and Producer Comic Relief 1985–2000. *Films:* Dead On Time 1983, The Tall Guy (writer) 1988, Four Weddings and a Funeral (writer, exec. producer) 1994, Bean (writer, exec. producer) 1997, Notting Hill (writer, exec. producer) 1999,

Bridget Jones's Diary (screenplay) 2001, Love Actually (writer, dir) 2003, Bridget Jones: The Edge of Reason (screenplay) 2004. *Television:* Not the Nine O'Clock News (series writer) 1979–82, The Black Adder (series writer) 1983, Spitting Image (series writer) 1984, Blackadder II (series writer) 1986, Blackadder the Third (series writer) 1987, Blackadder's Christmas Carol (writer) 1988, Blackadder: The Cavalier Years (writer) 1988, Blackadder Goes Forth (series writer) 1989, The Robbie Coltrane Special (contrib.) 1989, Mr Bean (series writer) 1989–95, Bernard and the Genie (writer) 1991, Merry Christmas Mr Bean (writer) 1992, Rowan Atkinson Live (contrib.) 1992, The Vicar of Dibley (series writer, exec. producer) 1994–, Hooves of Fire (writer) 1999, French & Saunders Live (contrib.) 2000, Legend of the Lost Tribe (exec. producer) 2002, The Girl in the Café (writer and exec. producer) (Humanitas Prize 2006) 2005. *Honours:* BAFTA Fellowship 2007. *Literary Agent:* c/o Anthony Jones, PFD, Drury House, 34–43 Russell Street, London, WC2B 5HA, England. *Telephone:* (20) 7344-1000. *Website:* www.pfd.co.uk.

CURTIS, Tony, MFA, DLitt, FRSL; British academic and poet; *Professor of Poetry, University of Glamorgan;* b. 26 Dec. 1946, Carmarthen, Wales; m. Margaret Blundell 1970; one s. one d. *Education:* Univ. Coll. of Swansea, Goddard Coll., Vermont, Univ. of Glamorgan. *Career:* Prof. of Poetry Univ. of Glamorgan. *Publications:* poetry: Walk Down a Welsh Wind 1972, Home Movies 1973, Album 1974, The Deerslayers 1978, Carnival 1978, Preparations: Poems 1974–79 1980, Letting Go 1983, Selected Poems 1970–85 1986, The Last Candles 1989, Taken for Pearls 1993, Heaven's Gate 2001; other: Islands (radio play) 1975, Out of the Dark Wood: Prose Poems, Stories 1977, Dannie Abse 1985, The Art of Seamus Heaney (ed.) 1986, The Poetry of Snowdonia 1989, The Poetry of Pembrokeshire (ed.) 1989, How to Study Modern Poetry 1990, How Poets Work (ed.) 1996, Welsh Painters Talking (ed.) 1996, Welsh Artists Talking (ed.) 2001, Coal 1997, Love from Wales 1993. *Honours:* Nat. Poetry Competition Winner 1984, Dylan Thomas Prize 1993, Cholmondeley Award 1997. *Address:* Pentwyn, 55 Colcot Road, Barry, Vale of Glamorgan CF62 8DC, Wales.

CURTIS, Wade (see Pournelle, Jerry Eugene)

CUSK, Rachel, BA; British writer; b. 8 Feb. 1967, Canada; d. of Peter Cusk and Carolyn Cusk; m. Adrian Clarke; two d. *Education:* St Mary's Convent, Cambridge and New Coll., Oxford. *Career:* writer 1992–. *Publications:* novels: Saving Agnes (Whitbread First Novel Award 1993) 1992, The Temporary 1995, The Country Life (Somerset Maugham Award) 1997, The Lucky Ones 2003, In the Fold 2005, Arlington Park 2006; non-fiction: A Life's Work 2001. *Address:* The Dower House, Nettlecombe, Williton, Somerset, TA4 4HS, England.

CUSSLER, Clive Eric, PhD; American novelist; b. 15 July 1931, Aurora, IL; s. of Eric Cussler and Amy Hunnewell; m. Barbara Knight 1955; three c. *Education:* Pasadena City Coll., Orange Coast Coll., California State Univ. *Career:* Owner Bestgen & Cussler Advertising, Newport Beach, Calif. 1961–65; Copy Dir Darcy Advertising, Hollywood, Calif. and Instr. in Advertising Communications, Orange Coast Coll. 1965–67; Advertising Dir Aquatic Marine Corpn, Newport Beach, Calif. 1967–79; Vice-Pres. and Creative Dir of Broadcast, Meffon, Wolff and Weir Advertising, Denver, Colo 1970–73; Chair. Nat. Underwater and Marine Agency; Fellow, New York Explorers Club, Royal Geographical Soc. *Publications:* The Mediterranean Caper 1973, Iceberg 1975, Raise the Titanic 1976, Vixen O-Three 1978, Night Probe 1981, Pacific Vortex 1982, Deep Six 1984, Cyclops 1986, Treasure 1988, Dragon 1990, Sahara 1992, Inca Gold 1994, Shock Wave 1995, Sea Hunters 1996, Flood Tide 1997, Clive Cussler and Dirk Pitt Revealed 1997, Serpent 1998, Atlantis Found 1999, Blue Gold 2000, Valhalla Rising 2001, Fire Ice (with Paul Kemprecos) 2002, Sea Hunters II 2002, The Golden Buddha (with Craig Dirgo) 2003, White Death 2003, Trojan Odyssey 2003, Black Wind (with Dirk Cussler) 2004, Sacred Stone 2005, Lost City (with Paul Kemprecos) 2006, Treasure of Khan (with Dirk Cussler) 2006, Dark Watch (with Jack Du Brul) 2007. *Honours:* Lowel Thomas Award, New York Explorers Club. *Address:* c/o Putnam Publishing Group, 200 Madison Avenue, New York, NY 10016, USA.

CUTTS, Simon; British artist, poet and publisher; b. 30 Dec. 1944, Derby; s. of George Tom Cutts and Elizabeth Purdy; m. 1st Annira Uusi-Illikainen (divorced 1973); one s.; m. 2nd Margot Hapgood (died 1985). *Education:* Herbert Strutt Grammar School, Belper, Derbyshire, Nottingham Coll. of Art, Trent Polytechnic. *Career:* travel and miscellaneous employment including The Trent Bookshop, Nottingham 1962–69; Jt Ed. Tarasque Press 1964–72; publishing, lecturing and writing 1972–74; Dir and Co-Partner Coracle Press Books (now Coracle Production and Distribution) 1975–87; Dir, Coracle Press Gallery 1983–86; Dir Victoria Miro Gallery 1985–; org. of exhbns in Europe and New York. *Publications:* numerous publs, including Quelques Pianos 1976, Pianostool Footnotes 1983, Petits-Airs for Margot 1986, Seepages 1988. *Address:* Victoria Miro, 21 Cork Street, London, W1 (office); 4/16 Courtfield Gardens, London, SW5, England (home). *Telephone:* (20) 7734-5082 (office); (20) 7370-4301 (home).

CZERNEDA, Julie Elizabeth, BSc; Canadian writer and editor; b. 11 April 1955, Exeter, ON; m. Roger Henry Czerneda 1976; one s. one d. *Education:* University of Waterloo, University of Saskatchewan, Queen's University, Kingston, ON. *Career:* Pres., Czerneda Publishing Inc 1991–98. *Publications:* Fiction: A Thousand Words for Stranger, 1997; Beholder's Eye, 1998; Ties of Power, 1999; Changing Vision, 2000. Other: many non-fiction books, 1986–99. Contributions: anthologies. *E-mail:* julie.czerneda@sff.net.

D

DABYDEEN, Cyril, BA, MA, MPA; Guyanese/Canadian poet, author, editor and essayist; *Lecturer in English, University of Ottawa*; b. 15 Oct. 1945, Guyana; s of the late Abel Dabydeen and of Hilda Persaud (née Oudit); previously married. *Education:* Lakehead Univ., Thunder Bay, Queen's Univ., Kingston. *Career:* juror, Neustadt Int. Prize for Literature 2000, Gov.-Gen.'s Award for Literature 2000; speaker, reader across Canada, USA, UK, Europe, India, Cuba, Caribbean and South America; currently Lecturer in English, Univ. of Ottawa; mem. US Asscn of Commonwealth Language and Literature Studies, International PEN. *Publications:* poetry: Distances 1977, Goatsong 1977, Heart's Frame 1979, This Planet Earth 1980, Islands Lovelier Than a Vision 1988, Coastland: New and Selected Poems 1989, Dark Swirl 1989, Stoning the Wind 1994, Born in Amazonia 1996, Discussing Columbus 1997, Hemisphere of Love 2003, Imaginary Origins: Selected Poems 2004; fiction: Still Close to the Island 1980, To Monkey Jungle 1986, The Wizard Swami 1989, Dark Swirl 1989, Jogging in Havana 1992, Sometimes Hard 1994, Berbice Crossing (short stories) 1996, Black Jesus and Other Stories 1997, My Brahmin Days and Other Stories 2000, North of the Equator (short stories) 2001, Play a Song, Somebody (short stories) 2004, Drums of my Flesh 2005; editor: A Shapely Fire: Changing the Literary Landscape 1987, Another Way to Dance: Contemporary Asian Poetry from Canada and the US 1996; contrib. to Canadian Forum, Canadian Fiction Magazine, Fiddlehead, Dalhousie Review, Antigonish Review, World Literature Today, Atlanta Review, The Critical Quarterly, Wascana Review, Literary Review, Globe and Mail, Caribbean Quarterly, Kunapipi. *Honours:* Sandbach Parker Gold Medal, A. J. Seymour Lyric Poetry Prize, Poet Laureate of Ottawa, Okanagan Fiction Award, recipient Canada Council, Ontario Arts Council, Ottawa-Carleton Region Literary Awards, Certificate of Merit for the Arts, honoured for work in race relations by City of Ottawa and the Fed. of Canadian Municipalities. *Address:* 295 Somerset Street E, Ottawa, ON K1N 6V9, Canada (home). *Telephone:* (613) 230-7854 (office). *E-mail:* cdabydeen@ncf.ca (home).

DABYDEEN, David, BA, PhD, FRSL; Guyanese/British poet, writer and academic; *Professor of Literature, Warwick University*; b. 9 Dec. 1955, Guyana. *Education:* University of Cambridge, University of London. *Career:* Junior Research Fellow, University of Oxford, 1983–87; Prof. of Literature, Warwick University, 1987–; mem. Arts Council of Great Britain, literature panel, 1985–89; Guyana's Ambassador to UNESCO, 1997. *Publications:* Slave Song, 1984; Coolie Odyssey, 1988; The Intended, 1991; Disappearance, 1993; Turner, 1994; The Counting House, 1996; Across the Dark Waters: Indian Identity in the Caribbean, 1996; A Harlot's Progress, 1999; Our Lady of Demerara 2004, Slave Song 2005; Contributions: various periodicals. *Honours:* Commonwealth Poetry Prize, 1984; Guyana Literature Prize, 1992. *Address:* c/o Warwick University, Coventry CV4 7AL, England.

DACEY, Philip, BA, MA, MFA; American poet and teacher; b. 9 May 1939, St Louis, MO; m. Florence Chard 1963 (divorced 1986); two s. one d. *Education:* St Louis University, Stanford University, University of Iowa. *Career:* Instructor in English, University of Missouri at St Louis, 1967–68; Faculty, Dept of English, Southwest State University, Marshall, Minnesota, 1970–; Distinguished Writer-in-Residence, Wichita State University, 1985. *Publications:* Poetry: The Beast with Two Backs, 1969; Fist, Sweet Giraffe, The Lion, Snake, and Owl, 1970; Four Nudes, 1971; How I Escaped from the Labyrinth and Other Poems, 1977; The Boy Under the Bed, 1979; The Condom Poems, 1979; Gerard Manley Hopkins Meets Walt Whitman in Heaven and Other Poems, 1982; Fives, 1984; The Man with Red Suspenders, 1986; The Condom Poems II, 1989; Night Shift at the Crucifix Factory, 1991. Editor: I Love You All Day: It is That Simple (with Gerald M. Knoll), 1970; Strong Measures: Contemporary American Poetry in Traditional Forms (with David Jaus), 1986. *Honours:* Woodrow Wilson Fellowship, 1961; New York YM-YWHA Discovery Award, 1974; National Endowment for the Arts Fellowships, 1975, 1980; Minnesota State Arts Board Fellowships, 1975, 1983; Bush Foundation Fellowship, 1977; Loft-McKnight Fellowship, 1984; Fulbright Lecturer, 1988.

DACRE, Paul Michael, BA; British newspaper editor; *Editor-in-Chief, Associated Newspapers*; b. 14 Nov. 1948, London; s. of Peter Dacre and Joan Dacre (née Hill); m. Kathleen Thomson 1973; two s. *Education:* Univ. Coll. School, London, Leeds Univ. *Career:* reporter, feature writer, Assoc. Features Ed., Daily Express 1970–76, Washington and New York Corresp. 1976–79; New York Bureau Chief, Daily Mail 1980, News Ed., London 1981–85, Asst Ed. (News and Foreign) 1986, Asst Ed. (Features) 1987, Exec. Ed. 1988, Assoc. Ed. 1989–91, Ed. 1992–, Ed.-in-Chief Assoc. Newspapers 1998–; Ed. Evening Standard 1991–92; Dir Associated Newspaper Holdings 1991–, Daily Mail & General Trust PLC 1998–, Teletext Holdings Ltd 2000–; mem. Press Complaints Comm. 1998–. *Address:* Daily Mail, Northcliffe House, 2 Derry Street, London, W8 5TT, England. *Telephone:* (20) 7938-6000. *Fax:* (20) 7937-7977.

DAENINCKX, Didier; French novelist and essayist; b. 1949, Saint-Denis. *Film screenplay:* Lumière Noire 1994. *Television writing:* Meurtres pour mémoire (TF1/Hamster) 1985, La Rançon de la gloire (FR3/Vamp) 1988, La Cicatrice (INA/La Sept/Coup d'œil) 1989, Novacek (France 2/Tanaïs) 1994, Le Premier qui dit non (France 2/VF Prod.) 1997, Chacun son Tour (France 2/Tanaïs) 1997. *Publications:* novels: Meurtres pour mémoire (Prix Paul Vaillant Couturier 1984, Grand Prix de Littérature Policière 1985) 1984, Le

Géant inachevé (Prix du Roman Noir 1985) 1984, Le Der des ders 1985, Métropolice 1985, Play-Back (Prix Mystère de la Critique 1987) 1986, Le Bourreau et son double 1986, Lumière Noire 1987, La Mort n'oublie personne 1989, Le Facteur fatal (Prix Populiste 1990) 1990, À louer sans commission 1991, Hors-limites 1992, Zapping (Prix Louis Guilloux 1993) 1992, Autres lieux 1993, Main courante 1994, En Marge 1994, Un Château en Bohême 1994, Les Figurants 1995, Nazis dans le métro 1996, À nous la vie 1996, Le Goût de la vérité 1997, Mort au premier tour 1997, Écrire en contre 1997, La Couleur du noir 1998, Passages d'enfer 1998, Cannibale 1998, Belleville Ménilmontant 1999, Banlieue nord 1999, La Repentie 1999, Éthique en toc 2000, Le Dernier Guérillero 2000, 12, rue Meckert 2001, Ceinture rouge 2001, La mort en dédicace 2001, Corvée de bois 2002, Le Retour d'Ataï 2002, Les Corps râlent 2003, Raconteur d'histoires 2003, La Route du rom 2003, Je tue il 2003, Le Crime de Sainte-Adresse 2004, Cités perdues 2005; children's books: La Fêtes des mères 1986, Le Chat de Tigali (Prix Polar Jeunes 1988) 1988, Le Papillon de toutes les couleurs (Premier Prix Goncourt du Livre de Jeunesse) 1998, La Péniche aux enfants 1999, Il faut désobéir 2002, Un Violon dans la nuit 2003, Viva la liberté 2004, L'Enfant du zoo 2004; essays: Jirinovski, le Russe qui fait trembler le monde (with Pierre Drachline) 1994, Négation-nistes, les chiffonniers de l'Histoire 1997, Paroles à la bouche du présent 1997, Le jeune poulpe contre la Vieille Taupe 1997, Au nom de la loi (with Valère Staraselski) 1998. *Honours:* Société des Gens de Lettres Prix Paul Féval de Littérature Populaire 1994. *Address:* c/o Éditions Verdier, 234 rue du Faubourg-Saint-Antoine, 75012 Paris, France (office). *Website:* www.daeninckx.net.

D'AGUIAR, Fred, BA, RMN; British poet, novelist, dramatist, essayist and academic; *Professor, Virginia Polytechnic Institute and State University*; b. 2 Feb. 1960, London, England. *Education:* Maudsley Hosp., Univ. of Kent. *Career:* writer-in-residence, London Borough of Lewisham 1986–87, Birmingham Polytechnic 1988–89; instructor in writing, Arvon Foundation 1986–; Judith Wilson Visiting Fellow, Univ. of Cambridge 1989–90; Northern Arts Literary Fellow, Newcastle and Durham Univs 1990–92; Visiting Writer, Amherst Coll., Massachusetts 1992–94; Asst Prof. of English, Bates Coll., Lewiston, ME 1994–95; Prof. of English, Univ. of Miami 1995–2003; Prof. and Dir Creative Writing, Virginia Polytechnic Inst. and State Univ. 2003–. *Television:* Sweet Thames 1992, Rwanda Stories 1995, The Longest Memory 1998. *Play:* A Jamaican Airman Foresees his Death 1995. *Publications:* poetry: Mama Dot 1985, Airy Hall 1989, British Subjects 1993, Bill of Rights 1998, Bloodlines (verse novel) 2000, An English Sampler, New and Selected Poems 2001; fiction: The Longest Memory 1994, Dear Future 1996, Feeding the Ghosts 1998, Bethany Bettany 2003; co-editor: The New British Poetry 1989; selected essays in The Age of Anxiety 1996, Black British Culture and Society 1999, Best American Essays 2000. *Honours:* Guyana Poetry Award 1987, BBC Race in the Media Award 1992, BFI Most Innovative Film Award 1993, Whitbread First Novel Award 1995, David Higham First Novel Award 1995, Guyana Fiction Award 1996. *Literary Agent:* David Higham Associates, 5 Lower John Street, London, W1, England. *Telephone:* (20) 7393-4400. *Fax:* (20) 7393-4401. *Website:* www.davidhigham.co.uk/html/Clients/Fred_DAguiar. *E-mail:* fredd@vt.edu.

DAHLEN, Beverly Jean, BA; American poet and teacher; b. 7 Nov. 1934, Portland, OR; m. Richard Pervier, 1957, divorced 1966. *Education:* California State University, Humboldt, California State University at San Francisco. *Career:* Asst Sec., Poetry Center, California State University, San Francisco, 1967–73; Creative Writing Teacher, California Poetry-in-the-Schools Project, 1970–74; Creative Writing Teacher, East Bay Community Arts Project, 1974–80; Adult Learning Center, City College of San Francisco, 1980–; Creative Writing Teacher, College of Marin, San Francisco State University; Teacher, summer writing workshops, Foothill College, Los Altos, CA, Lake Placid Art Center, Lake Place, New York, Naropa Institute, Boulder, CO; founder, HOWever. *Publications:* poetry: Out of the Third, 1974; A Letter at Easter: To George Stanley, 1976; The Egyptian Poems, 1983; A Reading, 1–7, 1985; A Reading, 11–17, 1989; A Reading, 9–10, 1992. Contributions: periodicals including: Shocks Magazine; Room; Bed; Isthmus; Transfer; Feminist Studies; Ironwood; Poetics Journal; Sagetrieb; Conjunctions; Acts; Hambone; HOW(ever). *Honours:* Residency, Briarcombe, Bolinas, CA, 1983; Residency, Djerrasi Foundation, Woodside, CA, 1984. *Address:* c/o Chax Press, 101 W Sixth Street, Tucson, AZ 85701, USA (office).

DAIF, Rachid al-; Lebanese writer. *Career:* teacher of Arabic literature, Lebanese Univ. *Publications include:* (in translation) Dear Mr Kawabata (novel) 1998, Passage to Dusk 2001, This Side of Innocence 2001. *Address:* PO Box 13-5991, Chourane, Beirut, Lebanon. *E-mail:* ounsi@rachid-el-daif.com. *Website:* www.rachid-el-daif.com/en.

DALAI LAMA, The, temporal and spiritual head of Tibet; Fourteenth Incarnation (Tenzin Gyatso); Tibetan; b. 6 July 1935, Taktser, Amdo Prov., NE Tibet; s. of Chujon Tsering and Tsering Dekyi. *Career:* born of Tibetan peasant family in Amdo Prov.; enthroned at Lhasa 1940; rights exercised by regency 1934–50; assumed political power 1950; fled to Chumbi in S Tibet after abortive resistance to Chinese State 1950; negotiated agreement with China 1951; Vice-Chair. Standing Cttee CPPCC, mem. Nat. Cttee 1951–59; Hon. Chair. Chinese Buddhist Ass200 1953–59; Del. to Nat. People's Congress

1954–59; Chair. Preparatory Cttee for the 'Autonomous Region of Tibet' 1955–59; fled Tibet to India after suppression of Tibetan national uprising 1959; Dr of Buddhist Philosophy (Monasteries of Sera, Drepung and Gaden, Lhasa) 1959; Supreme Head of all Buddhist sects in Tibet (Xizang); Presidential Distinguished Prof., Emory Univ., USA 2007–. *Publications:* My Land and People 1962, The Opening of the Wisdom Eye 1963, The Buddhism of Tibet and the Key to the Middle Way 1975, Kindness, Clarity and Insight 1984, A Human Approach to World Peace 1984, Freedom in Exile (autobiog.) 1990, My Tibet 1990, The Way to Freedom 1995, The Good Heart 1996, Beyond Dogma 1996, Ethics for the New Millennium 1998, Violence and Compassion 1998, Art of Happiness (co-author) 1999, Ancient Wisdom, Modern World 1999, The Path to Tranquility: Daily Wisdom 1999, Transforming the Mind: Eight Verses on Generating Compassion and Transforming Your Life 2000, A Simple Path: Basic Buddhist Teachings by His Holiness the Dalai Lama 2000, The Art of Living: A Guide to Contentment, Joy and Fulfillment 2001, Stages of Meditation: Training the Mind for Wisdom 2001, Compassionate Life 2001, His Holiness the Dalai Lama: In My Own Words 2001, Essence of the Heart Sutra 2002, How to Practice 2002, The Spirit of Peace 2002, How to See Yourself As You Really Are 2007, Comfort, Ease and Enlightenment: Living the Great Perfection 2007. *Honours:* Memory Prize 1989, Congressional Human Rights Award 1989, Nobel Peace Prize 1989, Freedom Award (USA) 1991. *Address:* Thekchen Choeling, McLeod Ganj 176219, Dharamsala, Himachal Pradesh, India.

DALE, Peter John, BA; British poet, writer and translator; b. 21 Aug. 1938, Addlestone, Surrey, England; m. Pauline Strouvelle 1963; one s. one d. *Education:* St Peter's Coll., Oxford. *Career:* secondary school teacher 1963–93; Co-Ed. Agenda 1972–96; Editorial Dir Between the Lines 1997–; Poetry Ed. Oxford Today 1999–; mem. Soc. of Authors, Translation Asscn. *Publications:* poetry: Walk from the House 1962, The Storms 1968, Mortal Fire 1976, One Another (sonnet sequence) 1978, Too Much of Water 1983, A Set of Darts (epigrams with W. S. Milne and Robert Richardson) 1990, Earth Light: New Poems 1991, Edge to Edge: Selected Poems 1996, Da Capo (poem sequence) 1997, Under the Breath 2002, Eight by Five 2007; prose: Michael Hamburger in Conversation with Peter Dale 1998, An Introduction to Rhyme 1998, Anthony Thwaite in Conversation with Peter Dale and Ian Hamilton 1999, Richard Wilbur in Conversation with Peter Dale 2000, Peter Dale in Conversation with Cynthia Haven 2003; translator: Selected Poems of François Villon 1978, Poems of Jules Laforgue 1986, The Divine Comedy, terza rima version 1996, Poems of Jules Laforgue 2001, Poems of François Villon 2001, Tristan Corbière: Wry-Blue Loves and Other Poems (Les Amours jaunes) 2005; contrib. to journals and periodicals. *Honours:* Arts Council bursary 1970. *Address:* 10 Selwood Road, Sutton, Surrey, SM3 9JU, England. *Telephone:* (20) 8296-9670 (office). *E-mail:* btluk@aol.com (office). *Website:* www.interviews-with-poets.com (office).

DALESKI, Hillel Matthew; South African academic and writer; b. 19 July 1926, Johannesburg; m. 1st Aviva Prop 1950 (divorced); four c.; m. 2nd Shirley Kaufman 1974. *Education:* BA 1947, BA (Hons) 1949, MA 1952, University of the Witwatersrand; PhD, Hebrew University, Jerusalem 1963. *Career:* Asst Lecturer to Assoc. Prof. 1958–76, Prof. of English 1976–, Chair., Dept of English 1968–70, 1984–85, Provost, School of Overseas Students 1973–76, Hebrew University, Jerusalem; mem. Dickens Society, pres. 1985. *Publications:* The Forked Flame: A Study of D. H. Lawrence 1965, Dickens and the Art of Analogy 1970, Joseph Conrad: The Way of Dispossession 1977, The Divided Heroine: A Recurrent Pattern in Six English Novels 1984, Unities: Studies in the English Novel 1985, Thomas Hardy and Paradoxes of Love 1997. *Honours:* Israel Acad. of Sciences and Humanities 1993; Hon. Foreign Mem., American Acad. of Arts and Sciences 1999; Israel Prize Laureate 2000, Distinguished Scholar Award in Lawrence Studies 2002. *Address:* Dept of English, Hebrew University, Jerusalem, Israel.

DALLAS, Ruth, CBE; New Zealand poet and children's writer; b. (Ruth Mumford), 29 Sept. 1919, Invercargill; d. of the late Francis Mumford and Minnie Jane Mumford. *Career:* worked for journal, Landfall 1962–68; Robert Burns Fellowship, Otago Univ. 1968; mem. PEN New Zealand. *Publications:* poetry: Country Road and Other Poems 1953, The Turning Wheel 1961, Experiment in Form 1964, Day Book: Poems of a Year 1966, Shadow Show 1968, Song for a Guitar 1976, Walking on Snow (New Zealand Book Award for Poetry 1977) 1976, Steps of the Sun 1979, Collected Poems 1987, Collected Poems 2000, The Joy of a Ming Vase (poems) 2006; children's fiction: The Children in the Bush 1969, Ragamuffin Scarecrow 1969, A Dog Called Wig 1970, The Wild Boy in the Bush 1972, The House on the Cliffs 1975, Shining Rivers 1979, Holiday Time in the Bush 1983; other: Sawmilling Yesterday 1958, Curved Horizon (autobiog.) 1991, The Black Horse and Other Stories 2000; contrib. to Southland Times, New Zealand Listener, Landfall (New Zealand Quarterly), Meanjin (Australian Quarterly), Poetry Australia, Review Magazine of Otago Univ. *Honours:* Hon. DLitt (Univ. of Otago) 1978; jt winner New Zealand Literary Fund Achievement Award 1963, Buckland Literary Award 1977, Blind Achievers Award for Literature 1999. *Address:* c/o Otago University Press, PO Box 56, Dunedin, New Zealand.

DALLEK, Robert, BA, MA, PhD; American writer, biographer and academic; b. 16 May 1934, New York, NY; m. 1st Ilse F. Shatzkin 1959 (died 1962); m. 2nd Geraldine R. Kronmal 1965; one s. one d. *Education:* Univ. of Illinois, Columbia Univ. *Career:* Instructor in History, Columbia Univ. 1960–64; Asst Prof. to Prof. of History, Univ. of California at Los Angeles 1964–94; Research Assoc., Southern California Psychoanalytic Inst. 1981–85; Commonwealth Fund Lecturer, Univ. Coll. London 1984; Thompson Lecturer, Univ. of Wyoming 1986; Charles Griffin Lecturer, Vassar Coll. 1987; Visiting Prof., California Inst. of Technology 1993, LBJ School of Public Affairs, Univ. of Texas 1996; Harmsworth Visiting Prof., Univ. of Oxford 1994–95; Prof. of History, Boston Univ. 1996; Marjorie Harris Weiss Lecturer, Brown Univ. 1998; Herbert Marcuse Lecturer, Brandeis Univ. 1999; Harry Seigle Lecturer, Washington Univ., St Louis 2001; Charles Grant Lecturer, Middlebury Coll. 2001; George Bancroft Lecturer, US Naval Acad. 2001; Montgomery Fellow and Visiting Prof. Dartmouth Coll. 2004–05; Fellow, American Acad. of Arts and Sciences, Soc. of American Historians (Pres. 2004–05), ACLS 1984–85; mem. American Psychoanalytic Asscn, Soc. of Historians of American Foreign Relations (pres. 1995). *Publications:* Democrat and Diplomat: The Life of William E. Dodd 1968, Western Europe: Vol. I of The Dynamics of World Power: A Documentary History of United States Foreign Policy 1945–1973 (ed.) 1973, Franklin D. Roosevelt and American Foreign Policy 1932–1945 1979, The American Style of Foreign Policy: Cultural Politics and Foreign Affairs 1983, Ronald Reagan: The Politics of Symbolism 1984, The Great Republic: A History of the American People (co-author) third edn 1985, Lone Star Rising: Lyndon Johnson and his Times 1908–1960 1991, The Encyclopedia of 20th-Century American History (assoc. ed. with others, four vols) 1995, Hail to the Chief: The Making and Unmaking of American Presidents 1996, Flawed Giant: Lyndon Johnson and his Times 1961–1973 1998, John F. Kennedy: An Unfinished Life 1917–1963 2003, Nixon and Kissinger 2007; contrib. to scholarly books and journals. *Honours:* Guggenheim Fellowship 1973–74, Sr Fellow, Nat. Endowment for the Humanities 1976–77, Bancroft Prize 1980, Rockefeller Foundation Humanities Fellow 1981–82, New York Times Book Review Notable Book Citations 1983, 1991, 1998, Lyndon B. Johnson Foundation research grants 1984–85, 1988–89. *Address:* 2138 Cathedral Avenue NW, Washington, DC 20008, USA. *Telephone:* (202) 588-8963. *Fax:* (202) 588-8964. *E-mail:* rdallek@aol.com.

DALMAS, John, BSc, PhD; American writer; b. 3 Sept. 1926, Chicago, IL; m. Gail Hill 1954; one s. one d. *Education:* Michigan State Coll., Univ. of Minnesota, Colorado State Univ. *Career:* mem. SFWA, Vasa Order of America. *Publications:* The Yngling 1969, The Varkaus Conspiracy 1983, Touch the Stars: Emergence (with Carl Martin) 1983, Homecoming 1984, The Scroll of Man 1985, Fanglith 1985, Aspen: Its Ecology and Management in the Western United States (sr author) 1985, The Reality Matrix 1986, The Walkaway Clause 1986, The Regiment 1987, The Playmasters (with Rodney Martin) 1987, Return to Fanglith 1987, The Lantern of God 1987, The General's President 1988, The Lizard War 1989, The White Regiment 1990, The Kalif's War 1991, The Yngling and the Circle of Power 1992, The Orc Wars (collection) 1992, The Regiment's War 1993, The Yngling in Yamato 1994, The Lion of Farside 1995, The Bavarian Gate 1997, The Three Cornered War 1999, The Lion Returns 1999, Soldiers 2001, The Puppet Master 2001, Otherwhens, Otherwheres (collection) 2003, The Second Coming 2004, The Regiment: A Trilogy (collection) 2004; contrib. to professional journals, fiction magazines and themed anthologies. *Address:* 1425 W Glass Avenue, Spokane, WA 99206; 7308 Country Meadow Lane, Plain City, OH 43064, USA (home). *Telephone:* (614) 873-5862 (home). *E-mail:* dalmas@earthlink.net. *Website:* www.sfwa .org/members/dalmas.

DALRYMPLE, Theodore; British physician, psychiatrist and essayist; b. (Anthony Daniels), 1949, London. *Career:* works in a British prison; Contributing Ed., City Journal, New York; columnist, The Spectator, London. *Publications:* Life at the Bottom: The Worldview that Makes the Underclass 2003, Our Culture – What's Left Of It (essays) 2005; contrib. to The Spectator, The Times, The Daily Telegraph, New Statesman, New Criterion, National Review, Wall Street Journal. *Address:* City Journal, Manhattan Institute for Policy Research, 52 Vanderbilt Avenue, New York, NY 10017, USA. *E-mail:* cj@city-journal.org. *Website:* www.city-journal.org.

DALRYMPLE, William Benedict Hamilton, MA, DLit, FRSL, FRGS, FRAS; British writer and historian; b. 20 March 1965, Edinburgh, Scotland; s. of Sir Hew Hamilton-Dalrymple and Lady Anne-Louise Hamilton-Dalrymple; m. Olivia Fraser; two s. one d. *Education:* Ampleforth Coll., Trinity Coll., Cambridge. *Radio:* Three Miles an Hour 2002, The Long Quest 2002. *Television:* Stones of the Raj 1997, Indian Journeys 1998, Sufi Soul 2005. *Publications:* In Xanadu 1989, City of Djinns 1993, From the Holy Mountain 1997, The Age of Kali (Prix de l'Astrobale-Etonnants voyageurs, France 2005) 1998, White Mughals: Love and Betrayal in Eighteenth-Century India 2002, Begums, Thugs and White Moghuls 2003, The Last Mughal 2006; contrib. to TLS, Guardian, New York Times, New York Review of Books, New Statesman. *Honours:* Yorkshire Post Best First Work Award 1990, Scottish Arts Council Award 1990, Thomas Cook Travel Book Award 1994, Sunday Times Young British Writer of the Year 1994, Scottish Arts Council Autumn Book Award 1997, BAFTA Grierson Award for Best Documentary 2002 Mungo Park Medal, Royal Scottish Geographical Soc. 2002, Stanford St Martin Religious Broadcasting Prize 2002, Wolfson History Prize 2003, Scottish Book of the Year 2003, Prix d'Astrolabe 2005, RSAA Percy Sykes Award 2005, FPA Media Award for Print Artist of the Year 2005. *Literary Agent:* c/o David Godwin Associates, 55 Monmouth Street, London, WC2H 9DG, England. *Telephone:* (20) 7240-9992. *Fax:* (20) 7395-6110. *E-mail:* sophie@davidgodwinassociates .co.uk. *Website:* www.davidgodwinassociates.co.uk. *Address:* 1 Pages' Yard, Church Street, London, W4 2PA, England (home). *E-mail:* wdalrymple1@aol .com (home). *Website:* www.williamdalrymple.com.

DALTON, Amanda; British writer; b. 1957, Coventry, Warwickshire. *Career:* teacher; fmr Centre Dir Arvon Foundation in Lumb Bank; Educ. Dir Royal Exchange Theatre, Manchester. *Radio:* original dramas broadcast on BBC Radio 3 and 4 include: No Harm 2004, Strike 2006. *Theatre:* works include: Mulgrave (Royal Exchange, Manchester), Dog Boy (Royal Exchange, Manchester), Mapping the Edge (Sheffield Theatres/WilsonWilson Co.). *Publications:* The Dad Baby 1994, Room of Leaves (adapted for BBC Radio 4 1998) 1996, How to Disappear 1999; contrib. to Comma: Anthology of Short Stories 2002; numerous poetry anthologies. *Honours:* PBS/Guardian Next Generation Poet 2004. *Address:* c/o Bloodaxe Books Ltd, Highgreen, Tarset, Northumberland NE48 1RP, England. *Telephone:* (1422) 844442 (home). *E-mail:* amandadalton@tiscali.co.uk (home). *Website:* www.bloodaxebooks.com.

DAMLUJI, Maysoon Salem ad-, RIBA; Iraqi government official and architect; *Senior Deputy Minister of Culture;* b. 1962, Baghdad. *Career:* worked as architect, London 1984, various positions internationally, including architectural designer and site architect; Mem. of Parliament; Sr Deputy Minister of Culture 2003–06; f. Iraqi Artists Asscn, UK (mem. exec. cttee); Founder-Pres. Iraqi Ind. Women's Group 2003–; Ed.-in-Chief of monthly magazine for women published in Iraq, NOON; founding mem. Studio of the Actor, London, UK 1994–; mem. Asscn of Iraqi Independent Democrats 2003–. *Address:* Ministry of Culture, Baghdad, Iraq (office). *E-mail:* aldamluji@aol.com (office).

DAN, Zeng; Chinese politician, journalist and writer; *Vice-General Manager, Chinese Centre for Tibet Research;* b. 1946, Tibet. *Education:* Fudan Univ., Shanghai. *Career:* began publishing career 1980; reporter, Tibet Daily, later Assoc. Chief Ed.; Dir Bureau of Culture, Tibet Autonomous Region, Vice-Sec. CCP Tibet Autonomous Region Cttee; Vice-Chair. China Fed. of Literary and Arts Circles, Vice-Chair. Chinese Writers' Asscn; Alt. mem. 12th CCP Cen. Cttee. 1982–87, 13th CCP Cen. Cttee. 1987–92, 14th CCP Cen. Cttee. 1992–97, 15th CCP Cen. Cttee. 1997–2002; currently Vice-Gen. Man. Chinese Centre for Tibet Research. *Publications include:* Report from the Roof of the World, The Blessing of the Deity. *Honours:* Tibet Autonomous Region Newspaper of the Year Award 1979, Tibet Autonomous Region Best Short Story Award 1980. *Address:* c/o Chinese Communist Party Tibetan Autonomous Region Committee, Lhasa, Tibet, People's Republic of China (office).

DANA, Robert Patrick, AB, MA; American academic and poet; b. 2 June 1929, Allston, MA; m. 1st Mary Kowalke 1951 (divorced 1973); three c.; m. 2nd Margaret Sellen 1974. *Education:* Drake University, University of Iowa. *Career:* Asst Prof., Assoc. Prof., Prof. of English, Cornell College, Mount Vernon, IA, 1953–94; Distinguished Visiting Poet, University of Florida, 1975–76, Wayne State University, 1978–79, University of Idaho, 1980, Wichita State University, 1982, Stockholm University, 1996; Ed., Hillside Press, Mount Vernon, 1957–67; Ed., 1964–68, Contributing Ed., 1991–, North American Review; Contributing Ed., American Poetry Review, 1973–88, New Letters, 1980–83; mem. Acad. of American Poets; PEN; Associated Writing Programs; Poetry Society of America. *Publications:* My Glass Brother and Other Poems, 1957; The Dark Flags of Waking, 1964; Journeys from the Skin: A Poem in Two Parts, 1966; Some Versions of Silence: Poems, 1967; The Power of the Visible, 1971; In a Fugitive Season, 1980; What the Stones Know, 1984; Blood Harvest, 1986; Against the Grain: Interviews with Maverick American Publishers, 1986; Starting Out for the Difficult World, 1987; What I Think I Know: New and Selected Poems, 1990; Wildebeest, 1993; Yes, Everything, 1994; Hello, Stranger: Beach Poems, 1996; A Community of Writers: Paul Engle and The Iowa Writers' Workshop, 1999; Summer, 2000; The Morning of the Red Admirals, 2004. Contributions: New Yorker; New York Times; Poetry; Georgia Review; Manoa. *Honours:* Rainer Maria Rilke Prize, 1984; National Endowment for the Arts Fellowships, 1985, 1993; Delmore Schwartz Memorial Poetry Award, 1989; Carl Sandburg Medal for Poetry, 1994; Pushcart Prize, 1996.

D'ANCONA, Matthew; British journalist and writer; *Editor, The Spectator;* b. 1968, London; m. Sarah Schaefer; two s. *Education:* St Dunstan's Coll., Magdalen Coll., Oxford. *Career:* fmrly worked for human rights magazine, Index on Censorship, trainee, news reporter, education correspondent The Times 1991–94, Asst Ed. 1994–95; Deputy Ed. comment section and political columnist The Sunday Telegraph 1996–98, Deputy Ed. 1998–2006; Ed. The Spectator 2006–; political columnist GQ magazine 2006–; mem. Millennium Commission 2001–; Fellow All Souls, Oxford 1989–96. *Publications:* The Jesus Papyrus (non-fiction, with Carsten Peter Thiede) 1997, The Quest for the True Cross (non-fiction, with Carsten Peter Thiede) 2002, Going East (novel) 2004, Tabatha's Code (novel) 2006. *Honours:* British Press Award for Political Journalist of the Year 2004. *Address:* The Spectator, 56 Doughty Street, London, WC1N 2LL, England (office). *Website:* www.spectator.co.uk.

DANGAREMBGA, Tsitsi; Zimbabwean novelist, playwright and film-maker; b. 1959, Mutoko, Southern Rhodesia. *Education:* Univ. of Cambridge, Univ. of Zimbabwe, Deutsche Film and Fernseh Akademie, Berlin. *Films:* Neria 1992, Everyone's Child 1996. *Publications:* The Lost of the Soil (play) 1983, The Letter (short story) 1985, She No Longer Weeps (play) 1987, Nervous Conditions (novel) 1988. *Honours:* Commonwealth Writers' Prize 1989.

DANGOR, Achmat; South African poet and novelist; b. 1948, Newclare, Johannesburg; m. Audrey Dangor. *Career:* mem., Black Thoughts 1970s, Congress of South African Writers (COSAW) 1980s; banned from publication

1973–79. *Play:* Majiet 1986. *Publications:* poetry: Bulldozer 1983, Private Voices 1992; fiction: Waiting for Leila 1978, The Z Town Trilogy (novel) 1989, Kafka's Cure: A Novella and Three Other Stories 1997, Bitter Fruit (novel) 2003; co-editor: Voices from Within: Black Poetry from South Africa 1986; contrib. to The Return of the Amasi Bird 1982, Modern South African Poetry 1984, New Nation, Staffrider. *Honours:* Mofolo-Plomer Prize, BBC Prize for African Poetry. *Address:* c/o Random House UK Ltd, 20 Vauxhall Bridge Road, London, SW1V 2SA, England. *Website:* www.randomhouse.co.uk.

DANIEL, Colin (see Windsor, Patricia)

DANIEL, Jean, LèsL; French (b. Algerian) journalist and writer; *Editor-in-Chief, Editorial Director and Director, Le Nouvel Observateur;* b. 21 July 1920, Blida, Algeria; s. of Jules Bensaïd and Rachel Bensimon; m. Michèle Bancilhon 1965; one d. *Education:* Sorbonne, Paris. *Career:* Cabinet of Félix Gouin, Pres. Council of Ministers 1946; Founder and Dir Caliban (cultural review) 1947–51; Prof. of Philosophy, Oran 1953; Asst Ed.-in-Chief, subsequently Ed.-in-Chief, L'Express 1955–64; Corresp., New Repub., Washington 1956–65; Assoc., Le Monde 1964; Ed.-in-Chief Le Nouvel Observateur 1964–, Ed. Dir 1965–, Dir 1978–; Admin. Louvre Museum 1992–99; Dir Monde des débats 2001; mem. Comité Nat. d'Ethique. *Publications:* L'Erreur 1953, Journal d'un journaliste, Le Temps qui reste 1973, Le Refuge et la source 1977, L'Ere des ruptures 1979, De Gaulle et l'Algérie 1985, Les religions d'un président 1988, Cette grande lueur à l'Est 1989, La Blessure 1992, Le Temps qui vient 1992, L'ami anglais 1994, Voyage au bout de la Nation (essay) 1995, Dieu, est-il fanatique? 1996, Avec le temps. Carnets 1970–1998 1998 (Prix Méditerranée 1999), Soleils d'Hiver 2001. *Honours:* Officier, Légion d'honneur, Croix de Guerre, Commdr Arts et Lettres, Commdr Ordre Nat. du Mérite; Prince of Asturias Award for Communication and the Humanities 2004. *Address:* Le Nouvel Observateur, 10–12 place de la Bourse, 75081 Paris Cedex 02, France (office). *Telephone:* 1-44-88-34-10 (office). *Fax:* 1-44-88-37-34 (office). *Website:* www.nouvelobs.com (office).

DANIEL, Wayne Wendell, BSEd, MPH, PhD; American academic and writer; b. 14 Feb. 1929, Tallapoosa, GA; m. Mary Yarbrough 1956; one s. two d. *Education:* University of Georgia, University of North Carolina, University of Oklahoma. *Career:* Statistical Research Asst, 1957–58, Research Statistician, 1959–60, Biostatistical Analyst, 1960–63, Chief, Mental Health Statistics Section, Biostatistics Service, 1965–67, Dir, Biostatistics Service, 1967–68, Chief Statistician, 1968, Georgia Dept of Public Health; Asst Prof. to Prof. of Decision Sciences, 1968–91, Prof. Emeritus, 1991–, Georgia State University; mem. American Public Health Asscn, fellow. *Publications:* Biostatistics: A Foundation for Analysis in the Health Sciences, 1974; Business Statistics for Management and Economics (with James C. Terrell), 1975; Introductory Statistics with Applications, 1977; Applied Nonparametric Statistics, 1978; Essentials of Business Statistics, 1984; Pickin' on Peachtree: A History of Country Music in Atlanta, 1990. Contributions: numerous journals and periodicals. *Address:* 2943 Appling Drive, Chamblee, GA 30341-5113, USA.

DANIELS, Dorothy, (Danielle Dorsett, Angela Gray, Cynthia Kavanaugh, Helaine Ross, Suzanne Somers, Geraldine Thayer, Helen Gray Weston); American writer; b. 1 July 1915, Waterbury, CT; m. 1937. *Education:* Normal School, New Brittain, CT. *Career:* mem. Authors' Guild; National League of American Pen Women, hon. mem.; Ventura County Writers. *Publications:* The Magic Ring, 1978; Purple and the Gold, 1978; Yesterday's Evil, 1980; Veil of Treachery, 1980; Legend of Death, 1980; Valley of Shadows, 1980; Monte Carlo, 1981; Saratoga, 1981; Sisters of Valcour, 1981; For Love and Valcour, 1983; Crisis at Valcour, 1985; Illusion of Haven's Edge, 1990.

DANIELS, Max (see Gellis, Roberta Leah)

DANIELS, Olga (see Sinclair, Olga Ellen)

DANIS, Daniel; Canadian playwright; b. 1962, Rouyn-Noranda, Québec. *Career:* lay missionary in Haiti 1980; assoc. playwright Théâtre de la Colline, Paris 2003–04; plays performed in Québec, Toronto, Vancouver, Calgary, Edmonton and in Scotland, Ireland, Belgium, France and Germany. *Plays:* Celle-là (Théâtre Ouvert 1993) (Prix de la Critique de Montréal, Prix du Gouverneur-général de Toronto 1993, Prix de la meilleure création en langue française, Syndicat Professionnel de la Critique Dramatique et Musicale 1995), Cendres de cailloux (Théâtre Espace Go, Montréal 1993) (Prix du meilleur texte original Soirée des Masques, Premier Prix Concours Int. de Manuscrits Festival de Maubeuge, Prix Radio France Int.), Le pont de pierres et la peau d'images 1992, Le chant du dire-dire (Théâtre Espace Go 1998) (Théâtre Nat. de la Colline, Paris 1999, Prix de la meilleure création en langue française, Syndicat Professionnel de la Critique Dramatique et Musicale), Le Langue-à-langue des chiens de roche (Théâtre de la Colline, Paris 1999) (Prix littéraire du Gouverneur-général 2002) 2005. *Address:* c/o L'Arche Editeur, 86 rue Bonaparte, 75006 Paris, France.

DANN, Colin Michael; British writer; b. 10 March 1943, Richmond, Surrey, England; m. Janet Elizabeth Stratton 1977. *Career:* mem. Soc. of Authors. *Publications:* The Animals of Farthing Wood 1979, In the Grip of Winter 1981, Fox's Feud 1982, The Fox Cub Bold 1983, The Siege of White Deer Park 1985, The Ram of Sweetriver 1986, King of the Vagabonds 1987, The Beach Dogs 1988, The Flight from Farthing Wood 1988, Just Nuffin 1989, In the Path of the Storm 1989, A Great Escape 1990, A Legacy of Ghosts 1991, The City Cats 1991, Battle for the Park 1992, The Adventure Begins 1994, Copycat 1998, Nobody's Dog 1999, Journey to Freedom 1999, Lion Country 2000, Pride of the

Plains 2002. *Honours:* Arts Council Nat. Award for Children's Literature 1980. *Address:* Castle Oast, Ewhurst Green, East Sussex, England.

DANN, Jack, BA; American writer, lecturer and editor; *Principal Partner, Alverson & Dann*; b. 15 Feb. 1945, Johnson City, NY; s. of Murray I. Dann and Edith Nash; m. 1st Jeanne Van Buren 1983 (divorced 1994); one step-s. one d.; m. 2nd Janeen Suzanne Webb 1995. *Education:* State Univ. of NY at Binghamton, St John's Law School. *Career:* Man. Ed. SFWA Bulletin 1970–75; Instructor of Writing, Science Fiction, Broome Community Coll., Binghamton 1972, 1990, 1991; Asst Prof., Cornell Univ., Ithaca, NY 1973; mem. Bd Dirs National Home Life Assurance Co., New York; Prin. Partner, Aultman Robertson & Assocs (advertising and public relations firm), Alverson & Dann (advertising and public relations firm); mem. SFWA. *Publications:* Starhiker: A Novel 1977, Christs and Other Poems 1978, Timetipping (short stories) 1980, Junction 1981, The Man Who Melted 1984, Slow Dancing In Time (short stories with Gardner Dozois, Michael Swanwick, Susan Casper, Jack L. Haldeman II) 1990, Echoes of Thunder (short novel, with Jack L. Haldeman II) 1991, High Steel (with Jack C. Haldeman II) 1993, The Memory Cathedral: A Secret History of Leonardo da Vinci 1995, The Silent 1998, Jubilee: The Essential Jack Dann 2001, Da Vinci Rising 2001, Counting Coup 2001, The Rebel: An Imagined Life of James Dean 2004, The Fiction Factory (short stories with Susan Casper, Gardner Dozois, Gregory Frost, Jack L. Haldeman II et al.) 2005; editor or co-editor: Wandering Stars: An Anthology of Jewish Fantasy and Science Fiction 1974, Faster Than Light: An Anthology of Stories about Interstellar Travel (with George Zenrowski) 1976, Immortal 1977, More Wandering Stars 1981, In the Field of Fire (with Jeanne Van Buren Dann) 1987, Three in Time: White Wolf Rediscovery Trio, Vol. 1 (with Pamela Sargent and George Zebroeski) 1998, Avram Davidson's Everybody has Somebody in Heaven: Essential Jewish Tales of the Spirit (with Grania Davis) 2000, Dreaming Down-Under (with Janeen Webb) 2001, Gathering the Bones (with Ramsey Campbell and Dennis Etchinson) 2003, Nebula Awards Showcase 2005; co-editor with Gardner Dozois: Future Power 1976, Aliens! 1980, Unicorns! 1982, Magicats! 1984, Bestiary! 1985, Mermaids! 1985, Sorcerers! 1986, Bestiary 1986, In the Field of Fire 1987, Demons! 1987, Dogtails!, Seaserpents! 1989, Dinosaurs! 1990, Little People 1991, Magicats II 1991, Unicorns II 1992, Dragons 1993, Invaders 1993, Horses! 1994, Angels 1995, Dinosaurs II 1995, Hackers 1996, Timegates 1997, Clones 1998, Nanotech 1998, Future War 1999, Armageddons 1999, Aliens Among Us 2000, Space Soldiers 2001, Genometry 2001, Future Sports 2002, Beyond Flesh 2002, Future Crimes 2003, AIs 2004, Robots 2005, Beyond Singularity 2005, Escape From Earth: New Adventures in Space (young adult volume) 2006, Futures Past 2006; contrib. to New Dimensions, Orbit, New Worlds, Asimov's Science Fiction Magazines, Fiction Writers' Handbook, Arbor House Treasury of Horror and the Supernatural, Playboy, Writer's Digest, Omni, SciFi.Com, Washington Post, Penthouse, Polyphony, Postscripts. *Honours:* Esteemed Kt, Mark Twain Soc. 1975–, Co-Winner Gilgamesh Award 1986, Nebula Award for Best Novella 1996, Co-Winner Aurealis Award for Best Science Fiction Story 1997, Ditmar Awards for Best Science Fiction Story 1997, for Best Anthology 1999, for Best Short Fiction 2002, Co-Winner World Fantasy Award for Best Anthology 1999, Peter McNamara Achievement Award 2004, Darrell Award for Best MidSouth Novel 2005. *Literary Agent:* Writers House Inc., 21 W 26 Street, New York, NY 10010, USA. *Telephone:* (212) 685-2400. *Fax:* (212) 685-1781. *Address:* PO Box 101, Foster, Vic. 3960, Australia. *E-mail:* jackdann@jackdann.com (office). *Website:* www.jackdann.com.

DANTICAT, Edwidge, BA, MFA; American writer; b. 19 Jan. 1969, Port-au-Prince, Haiti; m. Faidherbe Boyer 2002. *Education:* Clara Barton High School, New York, Barnard Coll., New York and Brown Univ., Rhode Island. *Career:* documentary film work with Jonathan Demme 1993–95; teacher at univs in Miami, New York and Texas. *Films as associate producer:* Courage and Pain 1996, The Agronomist 2003. *Publications:* fiction: Breath, Eyes, Memory 1994, Krik? Krak! (short stories) 1995, The Farming of Bones 1998, Behind the Mountains 2002, The Dew Breaker 2004; non-fiction: Odillon Pierre, Artist of Haiti (with Jonathan Demme) 1999, The Beacon Best of 2000: Great Writing by Women and Men of All Colors and Cultures (ed.) 2000, The Butterfly's Way: Voices from the Haitian Dyaspora in the United States (ed.) 2001, After the Dance 2002. *Honours:* Pushcart Short Story Prize 1995, Granta's Best of American Novelists Citation 1996, American Book Award 1998. *Address:* c/o Soho Press, 853 Broadway, No. 1903, New York, NY 10003, USA.

DANTO, Arthur Coleman, BA, MA, PhD; American academic, writer and editor; *Professor Emeritus, Columbia University*; b. 1 Jan. 1924, Ann Arbor, MI; m. 1st Shirley Rovetch 1946 (died 1978); two d.; m. 2nd Barbara Westman 1980. *Education:* Wayne State Univ., Columbia Univ., Univ. of Paris, France. *Career:* teacher 1952–72, Johnsonian Prof. of Philosophy 1972–92, Chair Philosophy Dept 1979–87, Prof. Emeritus 1992–, Columbia Univ.; Ed., Journal of Philosophy 1975–; Distinguished Fulbright Prof. to Yugoslavia 1976; art critic, The Nation 1984–. *Publications:* Analytical Philosophy of History 1965, Nietzsche as Philosopher 1965, Analytical Philosophy of Knowledge 1968, What Philosophy Is 1968, Mysticism and Morality 1972, Analytical Philosophy of Action 1973, Jean-Paul Sartre 1975, The Transfiguration of the Commonplace 1981, Narration and Knowledge 1985, The Philosophical Disenfranchisement of Art 1986, The State of the Art 1987, Connections to the World 1989, Encounters and Reflections 1990, Beyond the Brillo Box 1992, Embodied Meaning 1994, Playing with the Edge 1995, After the End of Art 1996, The Madonna of the Future 2000, The Abuse of Beauty

2003, Unnatural Wonders 2005; contrib. articles and reviews in many publications. *Honours:* Fulbright Scholarship 1949–50, Guggenheim Fellowships 1969, 1982, Lionel Trilling Book Prize 1982, George S. Polk Award for Criticism 1985, Nat. Book Critics Circle Award in Criticism 1990, New York Public Library Literary Lion 1993, College Art Asscn Frank Jewett Mather Prize in Criticism 1996, Prix Philosophie 2003. *Address:* 420 Riverside Drive, New York, NY 10025, USA. *Telephone:* (212) 666-3588 (office). *Fax:* (212) 666-1016 (office). *E-mail:* acd1@columbia.edu.

DAOUD, Hassan; Lebanese writer and editor; b. (Hassan Zebib), 1950. *Education:* Beirut Univ. *Career:* Chief Ed. of Nawafez cultural supplement, al-Mustaqbal Beirut daily newspaper; cultural ed. and contributor to Lebanese nat. newspapers and journals. *Publications include:* novels: The House of Mathilde 1983, The Penguin's Song, Added Days, The Promenade of the Angels, The Automatic Year. *Address:* c/o Granta Books, 2–3 Hanover Yard, Noel Road, London, N1 8BE, England (office).

DAOUST, Jean-Paul, MA; Canadian writer, poet, teacher and editor; b. 30 Jan. 1946, Valleyfield, QC. *Education:* University of Montréal. *Career:* Prof., Cegep Edouard-Montpetit, Québec; Mem., Editorial Board, magazine Estuaire; mem. Union des écrivaines et des écrivains québécois. *Publications:* Poetry: Oui, cher: Récit, 1976; Chaises longues, 1977; Portrait d'intérieur, 1981; Poèmes de Babylone, 1982; Taxi, 1984; Dimanche après-midi, 1985; La peau du coeur et son opéra, 1985; Les garçons magiques, 1986; Suite contemporaine, 1987; Les Cendres bleues, 1990; Rituels d'Amérique, 1990; Les Poses de la lumière, 1991; Du Dandysme, 1991; L'Amérique, 1993; Poèmes faxés (co-author), 1994; 111, Wooster Street, 1996; Taxi pour Babylone, 1996; Les Chambres de la Mer, 1991; Les Saisons de L'Ange, Tome I, 1997, Tome II, 1999; Blue Ashes, 1999; Les versets amoureux, 2001; Lèvres ouvertes, 2001; Roses labyrinthes, 2002. Other: Soleils d'acajou (novel), 1983; Le Désert Rose (novel), 2000. *Honours:* Gov.-Gen.'s Literary Award in Poetry, 1990.

DARBY, John, OBE, BA, DipEd, DPhil; Northern Irish academic and writer; *Research Director, Joan B. Kroc Institute for International Peace Studies, University of Notre Dame*; b. 18 Nov. 1940, Belfast; m. Marie Darby 1966; two s. *Education:* Queen's Univ., Belfast, St Joseph's Coll. of Education, Belfast, Univ. of Ulster. *Career:* teacher of history, St Malachy's Coll., Belfast 1963–71; Research and Publications Officer, Northern Ireland Community Relations Commission, Belfast 1971–74; Lecturer in Social Administration, New Univ. of Ulster 1974–85; Assoc. in Education, Graduate School of Education, Harvard Univ. 1980; Dir, Centre for the Study of Conflict 1985–91, Prof. of Ethnic Studies 1985–98, Univ. of Ulster; Visiting Prof., Center for Int. Studies, Duke Univ. 1988; Dir, Ethnic Studies Network 1991–, INCORE (Initiative on Conflict Resolution and Ethnicity), Univ. of Ulster and United Nations Univ., Japan 1992–97; Visiting Prof., Univ. of Notre Dame, IN 1999–2001, Prof. of Comparative Ethnic Studies 2000–, Research Dir Joan B. Kroc Inst. for Int. Peace Studies 2004–. *Publications:* Conflict in Northern Ireland 1976, Northern Ireland: Background to the Conflict (ed.) 1983, Dressed to Kill: Cartoonists and the Northern Irish Conflict 1983, Intimidation and the Control of Conflict in Northern Ireland 1986, Political Violence (ed. with N. Dodge and A. C. Hepburn) 1990, Scorpions in a Bottle 1997, The Management of Peace Processes (ed. with R. MacGinty) 2000, The Effects of Violence on Peace Processes 2001, Guns and Government: The Management of the Northern Ireland Peace Process 2002, Contemporary Peacekeeping (ed. with Roger MacGinty) 2003, Violence and Reconstruction 2005; contrib. to many books and journals. *Honours:* Outstanding Academic Book Citation, Choice 1977, Visiting Scholar Rockefeller Centre, Bellagio, Italy 1990, Guest Fellow Woodrow Wilson Center, Washington, DC 1992, Hon. Prof., Univ. of Sunderland 1997, Jennings Randolph Sr Fellow US Inst. of Peace, Washington, DC 1998, Fellow Fulbright New Century Scholars Program 2003. *Address:* 61 Strand Road, Portstewart, BT55 7LU, Northern Ireland. *Telephone:* (28) 7083-3098. *E-mail:* john.darby.3@nd.edu.

D'ARCY, Margaretta; Irish playwright and writer; m. John Arden (q.v.) 1957; five s. (one deceased). *Career:* Artistic Dir Corrandulla Arts and Entertainment Club 1973, Galway Women's Entertainment 1982, Galway Women's Sceal Radio, Radio Pirate-Woman 1986, Women in Media and Entertainment 1987; mem. Aosdána 1982. *Plays produced:* The Happy Haven 1961, Business of Good Government 1962, Ars Longa Vita Brevis 1964, The Royal Pardon 1966, Friday's Hiding 1967, The Hero Rises Up 1969, The Island of the Mighty 1974, The Non-Stop Connolly Show 1975, Vandaleur's Folly 1978, The Little Gray Home in the West 1978, The Making of Muswell Hill 1979 (all with John Arden), A Pinprick of History 1977. *Radio includes:* Keep Those People Moving 1972, The Manchester Enthusiasts 1984, Whose Is the Kingdom? 1988, A Suburban Suicide 1994 (all with John Arden). *Television documentary:* Profile of Sean O'Casey (with John Arden) 1973. *Films:* Circus Exposé 1987, Big Plane Small Axe (the Mis-Trials of Mary Kelly) 2005, Shell Hell 2005. *Publications:* Tell Them Everything (Prison Memoirs) 1981, Awkward Corners (with John Arden) 1988, Galway's Pirate Women, a Global Trawl 1996, Loose Theatre (Memoirs of a Guerrilla Theatre Activist) 2005. *Honours:* Arts Council Playwriting Award (with John Arden) 1972, Women's Int. Newsgathering Service, Katherine Davenport Journalist of the Year Award 1998, Documentary Award Galway Film Fleadh 2005. *Address:* c/o Casarotto Ramsay, 60–66 Wardour Street, London, W1V 3HP, England. *Telephone:* (20) 7287-4450. *Fax:* (20) 7287-9128.

D'ARGY SMITH, Marcelle; British journalist and magazine editor; b. 1947. *Career:* writer, Cosmopolitan magazine 1983–89, Ed. 1989–95; freelance journalist and broadcaster 1995–97; Ed. Woman's Journal 1997–99; stood as Pro Euro Conservative cand. in European elections 1999. *Publication:* The Lovers' Guide: What Women Really Want 2002. *Honours:* Women's Magazine Ed. of the Year 1991. *Address:* c/o Woman's Journal, Kings Reach Tower, Stamford Street, London, SE1, England.

DARKE, Marjorie Sheila; British children's writer; b. 25 Jan. 1929, Birmingham, England; m. 1952; two s. one d. *Education:* Leicester Coll. of Art, Central School of Art, London. *Career:* mem. Soc. of Authors, Int. PEN. *Publications:* for young adults: Ride the Iron Horse 1973, The Star Trap 1974, A Question of Courage 1975, The First of Midnight 1977, A Long Way to Go 1978, Comeback 1981, Tom Post's Private Eye 1982, Messages and Other Shivery Tales 1984, A Rose from Blighty 1990; for beginner readers: Mike's Bike 1974, What Can I Do? 1975, The Big Brass Band 1976, My Uncle Charlie 1977, Carnival Day 1979; children's: Kipper's Turn 1976, Kipper Skips 1979, Imp 1985, The Rainbow Sandwich 1989, Night Windows 1990, Emma's Monster 1992, Just Bear and Friends 1996. *Address:* Rogers, Coleridge & White, 20 Powis Mews, London, W11 1JN, England (office).

DARKO, Amma, BA; Ghanaian novelist; b. 1956, Ghana; m.; three c. *Education:* Univ. of Science and Technology, Kumasi. *Career:* tax inspector; Fellow, Cambridge Seminar, IWP-Iowa, Akad. Solitude Germany. *Publications:* Beyond the Horizon 1991, The Housemaid 1998, Faceless 2003, Not Without Flowers 2007. *Honours:* Ghana Book Award. *Address:* c/o Sub-Saharan Publishers, POB 358, Legon, Accra, Ghana (office). *Telephone:* (21) 404954 (home). *E-mail:* mmafoko@yahoo.com (home). *Website:* www.ammadarko.de.

DARNTON, Robert Choate, DPhil; American historian and academic; *Carl H. Pforzheimer Professor and Director of the University Library, Harvard University*; b. 10 May 1939, New York; s. of the late Byron Darnton and Eleanor Darnton; m. Susan Lee Glover 1963; one s. two d. *Education:* Harvard Univ., Oxford Univ., UK. *Career:* reporter, The New York Times 1964–65; Jr Fellow, Harvard Univ., 1965–68; Asst Prof., subsequently Assoc. Prof., Prof., Princeton Univ. 1968–, Shelby Cullom Davis Prof. of European History 1984–2007, Dir Program in European Cultural Studies 1987–95; Carl H. Pforzheimer Prof. and Dir of Univ. Library, Harvard Univ. 2007–; fellowships and visiting professorships including: Ecole des Hautes Etudes en Sciences Sociales, Paris 1971, 1981, 1985, Netherlands Inst. for Advanced Study 1976–77, Inst. for Advanced Study, Princeton 1977–81, Oxford Univ. (George Eastman Visiting Prof.) 1986–87, Collège de France, Wissenschafts-Kolleg zu Berlin 1989–90, 1993–94; Pres. Int. Soc. for Eighteenth-Century Studies 1987–91, American Historical Asscn 1999–2000; mem. Bd of Dirs, Voltaire Foundation, Oxford, Social Science Research Council 1988–91; mem. Bd of Trustees Center for Advanced Study in the Behavioral Sciences 1992–96, Oxford Univ. Press, USA 1993–, The New York Public Library 1994–; mem. various editorial bds; Fellow American Acad. of Arts and Sciences, American Philosophical Soc., American Antiquarian Soc.; Adviser, Wissenschafts-Kolleg zu Berlin 1994–; Foreign mem. Academia Europaea, Acad. Royale de Langue et de Littérature Françaises de Belgique; Guggenheim Fellow 1970; Corresp. Fellow British Acad. 2001. *Television series:* Démocratie (co-ed.), France 1999. *Publications:* Mesmerism and the End of the Enlightenment in France 1968, The Business of Enlightenment 1979, The Literary Underground of the Old Regime 1982, The Great Cat Massacre 1984, The Kiss of Lamourette 1989, Revolution in Print (co-ed.) 1989, Edition et sédition 1991, Berlin Journal, 1989–1900 1991, Gens de lettres, gens du livre 1992, The Forbidden Best-Sellers of Pre-Revolutionary France 1995, The Corpus of Clandestine Literature 1769–1789 1995, Démocratie (co-ed.) 1998, J.-P. Brissot: His Career and Correspondence 1779–1787 2001, Poesie und Polizei 2002, Pour les Lumières 2002, George Washington's False Teeth: An Unconventional Guide to the 18th Century 2003. *Honours:* Officier Ordre des Arts et des Lettres 1995, Chevalier Légion d'Honneur 2000; Dr hc (Neuchâtel) 1986, (Lafayette Coll.) 1989, (Univ. of Bristol) 1991, (Univ. of Warwick) 2001, (Univ. of Bordeaux) 2005; Leo Gershoy Prize, American Historical Asscn 1979, MacArthur Prize 1982, Los Angeles Times Book Prize 1984, Prix Médicis 1991, Prix Chateaubriand 1991, Nat. Book Critics Circle Award 1996, Gutenberg Prize 2004. *Address:* Office of the Director, Harvard University Library, Wadsworth House, 1341 Massachusetts Avenue, Cambridge, MA 02138 (office); 6 McCosh Circle, Princeton, NJ 08540, USA (home). *Telephone:* (617) 495-3650 (office); (609) 924-6905 (home). *Fax:* (617) 495-0370 (office). *E-mail:* administration@hulmail.harvard.edu (office). *Website:* hul.harvard.edu (office).

DARRIEUSSECQ, Marie; French writer; b. 3 Jan. 1969, Bayonne; m. *Education:* Ecole normale supérieure, Paris. *Career:* fmr teacher, Lille Univ. *Publications:* Truismes (novel, trans. as Pig Tales) 1996, Naissance des fantômes (novel, trans. as My Phantom Husband) 1998, Le Mal de mer (novel, trans. as Undercurrents, aka Breathing Underwater) 1999, Précisions sur les vagues (novel) 1999, Bref séjour chez les vivants (novel, trans. as A Brief Stay With the Living) 2001, Le Bébé (non–fiction) 2002, White (novel) 2003. *Address:* c/o Faber and Faber Ltd, 3 Queen Square, London, WC1N 3AU, England.

DARUWALLA, Keki Nasserwanji, MA; Indian poet, writer and fmr government official; b. 24 Jan. 1937, Lahore; m. Khorshed Keki Daruwalla 1965 (died 2000); two d. *Education:* Punjab Univ. *Career:* Special Asst to Prime Minister 1979; Chair. Jt Intelligence Cttee –1995; Visiting Fellow, Queen Elizabeth House, Oxford 1980–81; mem. Sahitya Akademi (advisory bd for English 1983–87, convenor 2003–). *Publications:* poetry: Under Oion 1970, Apparition in April 1971, Crossing of Rivers 1976, Winter Poems 1980, The Keeper of the Dead 1982, Landscapes 1987, Night River 2000, The Map Maker 2002, The Scarecrow and the Ghost (children's verse) 2004; fiction: Sword and Abyss 1979, A House in Ranikhet (short stories) 2003; editor: Two Decades of Indian Poetry, 1960–80 1981, The Minister for Permanent Unrest 1996; contrib. to anthologies, journals and periodicals. *Honours:* Sahitya Akademi Award 1984, Commonwealth Poetry Award (Asia Region) 1987. *Address:* 79 Mount Kailash, Pocket-A, SFS Apartments, New Delhi 110065, India (home). *Telephone:* (11) 26441574 (home). *E-mail:* kekid@del2.vsnl.net.in (home).

DARVILL, Timothy Charles, BA, PhD, DSc, FSA, FSA (Scot); British archaeologist and academic; *Professor of Archaeology, University of Bournemouth*; b. 22 Dec. 1957, Cheltenham, England. *Education:* Univ. of Southampton. *Career:* Dir Timothy Darvill Archaeological Consultants 1985–91; Prof. of Archaeology, Univ. of Bournemouth 1991–; mem. Cotswold Archaeological Trust (Chair. 1992–), Council for British Archaeology, Inst. of Field Archaeologists (Chair. 1989–91), Council of the National Trust 1988–97; Co-ordinator Neolithic Studies Group 1983–; Chair. Subject Cttee for Archeaology 2000–03. *Publications:* Megalithic Chambered Tombs of the Cotswold-Severn Region 1982, The Archaeology of the Uplands 1986, Prehistoric Britain 1987, Ancient Monuments in the Countryside 1987, Prehistoric Gloucestershire 1987, Neolithic Houses in Northwest Europe and Beyond (ed. with Julian Thomas) 1996, Prehistoric Britain from the Air 1996, The Concise Oxford Dictionary of Archaeology 2002, Long Barrows of the Cotswolds 2004; contribs to scholarly books and journals. *Address:* School of Conservation Sciences, University of Bournemouth, Poole House, Talbot Campus, Fern Barrow, Poole, Dorset, BH12 5BB, England (office). *Telephone:* (1202) 965536 (office). *E-mail:* tdarvill@bournemouth.ac.uk (office).

DARWISH, Mahmoud; Palestinian poet, politician and journalist; b. 1942, Birwa. *Education:* schools in Galilee, Moscow Univ., USSR. *Career:* journalist in Haifa, Israel; mem. Israeli Communist Party (Rakah) 1961–71; founder and fmr Chief Ed. al-Karmel literary magazine 1981; fmr Chief Ed. Al-Ittihad newspaper; left Israel for exile in Lebanon 1971; Ed. Shu'un Filistiniyya (Palestinian Affairs) 1972; Dir Palestinian Liberation Org. (PLO) Research Centre, Beirut 1975–82; mem. PLO Exec. 1987–93. *Publications:* Asafir Bila Ajniha (Bird Without Wings) 1960, Awraq al-Zaytun (Olive Leaves) 1964, Ashiq Min Filastin (A Lover from Palestine) 1966, Uhibbuki aw la Uhibikki (I Love You, I Love You Not) 1972, Qasidat Bayrut (Ode to Beirut) 1982, Madih al-Zill al-Ali (A Eulogy for the Tall Shadow) 1983, Sareer El Ghariba (Bed of a Stranger) 1988, Why Did You Leave the Horse Alone? 1994. *Honours:* Lotus Prize, Union of Afro-Asian Writers 1969, Mediterranean Prize 1980, Ibn Sina Prize 1982, Lenin Peace Prize 1983, Lannan Prize for Cultural Freedom 2001. *Address:* c/o Kegan Paul, PO Box 256, London, WC1B 3SW, England (office).

D'ARZILLE, Juliette; Swiss writer; b. 23 Nov. 1932, La Neuveille; m. Walter Friedemann 1955; one s. one d. *Education:* music and autodidactical literary education. *Career:* mem., Literature Committee, Canton of Neuchâtel, 1993–; mem. PEN International; Swiss Society of Writers; AENJ. *Publications:* Le deuxieme soleil, 1973; Identite suivi de les embellies, 1976; Une innocence verte, 1982; Nocturne, 1984; Esquisses et propos, 1986; D'ici et d'ailleurs, 1989; Hommage pluriel, 1998; Alentour, 1998; Acqua serena, 1998. Contributions: newspapers and magazines. *Honours:* French Literature Award, Canton of Bern, 1982. *Address:* En Arzille, 1788 Praz, Switzerland.

DAS, Kamala, (Madhavi Kutty, Kamala Suraiya); Indian poetry editor, poet, writer and painter; *President, Lokseva Trust International*; b. 31 March 1934, Malabar; m. K. Madhava Das 1949; three s. *Career:* Poetry Ed., Illustrated Weekly of India, Mumbai 1971–79; Chair. Kerala Forestry Bd; Pres. Lokseva Trust Int. *Art exhibitions:* paintings in various public and private collections. *Publications:* poetry: Summer in Calcutta: Fifty Poems 1965, The Descendants 1967, The Old Playhouse and Other Poems 1973, Tonight This Savage Rite: The Love Poetry of Kamala Das and Pritish Nandy 1979, Collected Poems 1987, Only the Soul Knows How to Sing, Ya Allah; fiction: Alphabet of Lust 1977, Manomi 1987, The Sandalwood Tree 1988; non-fiction: My Story (autobiog.), Path of the Columnist. *Honours:* Hon. DLit; Kerala Sahitya Acad. Award for Fiction 1969, Asian World Prize for Literature 1985, PEN Poetry Prize, Vayatar Award, Ezhuthachan Prize. *Address:* Royal Stadium Mansion, Cochin 20, India. *Telephone:* (484) 2204562 (office); (484) 2204330 (home). *E-mail:* suraiyabegum@sify.com (office); kamala52@hotmail.com (home).

DASHKOVA, Polina Victorovna; Russian writer; b. (Tatyana Polyachenko), 14 July 1960, Moscow; d. of Vitaly Vassiliyevich Polyachenko and Tatyana Leonidovna Polyachenko; m. Alexei Vitalyevich Shishov; two d. *Education:* Moscow Literary Inst. *Career:* freelance writer, began career as poet and trans. 1976–; journalist, Selskaya Molodezh magazine 1980–88; Head, Div. of Literature, Russian-American magazine Russian Courier 1988–93. *Publications include:* Blood of the Unborn 1996, Chechen Puppet 1996, Light Steps of Craziness 1997, No One Will Cry 1997, A Place Under the Sun 1998, Image of the Enemy, Golden Sand 1999, Time on Air 1999, Nursery 2000, Cherub 2001, Russian Orchid. *Telephone:* (22) 144 4254 (agent: Galina Dursthoff, Astrel, Germany); (22) 1460053*Address:* Maly Tishinsky pe 11/12, Apt 10, 123056 Moscow, Russia. *Telephone:* (095) 253-17-39.

DATHORNE, Oscar Ronald, BA, DipEd, MBA, MPA, MA, PhD; Guyanese academic, writer and poet; b. 19 Nov. 1934, Georgetown. *Education:* University of Sheffield, University of London, University of Miami. *Career:* Assoc. Prof., Ahmadu Bello University, Zaria, 1959–63, University of Ibadan,

1963–66; UNESCO Consultant to the Government of Sierra Leone, 1967–68; Prof. of English, Njala University College, University of Sierra Leone, 1968–69; Prof. of African Literature, Howard University, 1970; Prof. of Afro-American Literature, University of Wisconsin, Madison, 1970–71; Prof. of English and Black Literature, Ohio State University, 1977–. *Publications:* Dumplings in the Soup (novel), 1963; The Scholar Man (novel), 1964; Carribean Narrative (ed.), 1965; Carribean Verse (ed.), 1967; Africa in Prose, 1969; The Black Mind, 1975; African Literature in the Twentieth Century, 1976; Dark Ancestor, 1981; Dele's Child, 1985; Imagining the World: Typical Belief vs Reality in Global Encounters, 1994. *Address:* Department of English, University of Miami, Coral Gables, FL 33124, USA.

DAUGHARTY, Janice; American writer; b. 24 Oct. 1944, Valdosta, GA; m. Seward Daugharty 1963; one s. two d. *Education:* Valdosta State University. *Publications:* Dark of the Moon, 1994; Going through the Change, 1994; Necessary Lies, 1995; Pawpaw Patch, 1996; Earl in the Yellow Shirt, 1997; Whistle, 1998; Like a Sister, 1999. *Website:* www.janicedaugharty.com.

DAUNTON, Martin James, BA, PhD, LittD, FBA; British college principal, economic historian and academic; *Master of Trinity Hall and Professor of Economic History, University of Cambridge;* b. 7 Feb. 1949, Cardiff, Wales; m. Claire Gobbi 1984. *Education:* Univ. of Nottingham, Univ. of Kent, Univ. of Cambridge. *Career:* Lecturer, Univ. of Durham 1973–79; Lecturer, Univ. Coll. London 1979–85, Reader 1985–89, Prof. of History 1989–97; Convenor Studies in History series, Royal Historical Soc. 1995–2000; Prof. of Economic History, Univ. of Cambridge 1997–, Chair. Faculty of History 2001–03, Chair. School of Humanities and Social Sciences 2003–05, Master of Trinity Hall 2004–; Trustee, Nat. Maritime Museum 2002–; mem. Royal Historical Soc. (Pres. 2004–). *Publications:* Coal Metropolis: Cardiff, House and Home in the Victorian City 1850–1914, Royal Mail: The Post Office Since 1840, A Property Owning Democracy?, Progress and Poverty, Trusting Leviathan, Just Taxes; contrib. to Economic History Review, Past & Present, Business History, Historical Research, Journal of Urban History, Charity, Self-Interest and Welfare in the English Past, English Historical Review, Twentieth Century British History, Empire, Organisation of Knowledge in Victorian Britain 2005. *Honours:* Hon. LitD (London). *Address:* Trinity Hall, Trinity Lane, Cambridge, CB2 1TJ, England (office). *Telephone:* (1223) 332540 (office). *E-mail:* mjd42@cam.ac.uk (office). *Website:* www.trinhall.cam.ac.uk (office).

DAVERIO, John; American musicologist, writer and academic; b. 19 Oct. 1954, Sharon, Pennsylvania. *Education:* Fellow, Tanglewood Music Center, 1971–73; BM, 1975, MM, 1977, PhD, 1983, Boston University. *Career:* Lecturer, Longy School of Music, 1981–83; Asst Prof., 1983–89, Chair, Dept of Musicology, 1987–, Assoc. Prof., 1989–98, Prof. of Music, 1998–, Boston University; mem. Board of Dirs, American Musicological Society, 2000–02. *Publications:* Nineteenth-Century Music and the German Romantic Ideology, 1993; Robert Schumann: Herald of a 'New Poetic Age', 1997. Contributions: Journal of the American Musicological Society; 19th Century Music; Acta Musicologica; Journal of Musicology; Musical Quarterly; Music and Letters; Journal of Musicological Research; Il Saggiatore Musicale; The New Grove Dictionary of Music and Musicians, revised edn, 2001. *Honours:* Alfred Einstein Prize, 1988; Outstanding Academic Book Citation, Choice, 1997. *Address:* c/o Boston University College of Fine Arts, School of Music, 855 Commonwealth Avenue, Boston, MA 02215, USA. *E-mail:* daverio@bu.edu.

DAVEY, Frankland Wilmot, BA, MA, PhD; Canadian writer, poet and editor; *Carl F. Klinck Professor of Canadian Literature, University of Western Ontario;* b. 19 April 1940, Vancouver, BC; m. 1st Helen Simmons 1962 (divorced 1969); m. 2nd Linda McCartney 1969; one s. one d. *Education:* University of British Columbia, Vancouver, University of Southern California at Los Angeles. *Career:* Lecturer, 1963–67, Asst Prof., 1967–69, Royal Roads Military College, Victoria, BC; Writer-in-Residence, Sir George Williams University, Montréal, 1969–70; Asst Prof., 1970–72, Assoc. Prof., 1972–80, Prof. of English, 1980–90, Chair, Dept of English, 1985–88, 1989–90, York University, Toronto; Carl F. Klinck Prof. of Canadian Literature, University of Western Ontario, London, 1990–; mem. Asscn of Canadian College and University Teachers of English, pres., 1994–96. *Publications:* Poetry: D-Day and After, 1962; City of the Gulls and Sea, 1964; Bridge Force, 1965; The Scarred Hill, 1966; Four Myths for Sam Perry, 1970; Weeds, 1970; Griffon, 1972; King of Swords, 1972; L'An Trentiesme: Selected Poems 1961–70, 1972; Arcana, 1973; The Clallam, 1973; War Poems, 1979; The Arches: Selected Poems, 1981; Capitalistic Affection!, 1982; Edward and Patricia, 1984; The Louis Riel Organ and Piano Company, 1985; The Abbotsford Guide to India, 1986; Postcard Translations, 1988; Popular Narratives, 1991; Cultural Mischief: A Practical Guide to Multiculturalism, 1996. Criticism: Five Readings of Olson's 'Maximus', 1970; Earle Birney, 1971; From There to Here: A Guide to English-Canadian Literature Since 1960, 1974; Louis Dudek and Raymond Souster, 1981; The Contemporary Canadian Long Poem, 1983; Surviving the Paraphrase: 11 Essays on Canadian Literature, 1983; Margaret Atwood: A Feminist Poetics, 1984; Reading Canadian Reading, 1988; Post-National Arguments: The Politics of the Anglophone-Canadian Novel Since 1967, 1993; Reading 'KIM' Right, 1993; Canadian Literary Power: Essays on Anglophone-Canadian Literary Conflict, 1994; Karla's Web: A Cultural Examination of the Mahaffy-French Murders, 1994. Contributions: Books and journals. *Honours:* Macmillan Prize, 1962; Dept of Defence Arts Research Grants, 1965, 1966, 1968; Canada Council Fellowships, 1966, 1974; Humanities Research Council of Canada Grants, 1974, 1981; Canadian Federation

for the Humanities Grants, 1979, 1992; Social Sciences and Humanities Research Council Fellowship, 1981. *Address:* 499 Dufferin Avenue, London, ON N6B 2A1, Canada.

DAVEY, William; American poet and writer; b. 20 March 1913, New York, NY; m. 7th Susan Steenrod 1965. *Education:* Princeton Univ., NJ, Univ. of California, Berkeley, New York Univ., Univ. of Paris (Sorbonne), France. *Career:* Commando, First Special Service Force, Canadian-American Elite Unit, World War II; Contributing and Foreign Language Ed. The Long Story magazine 1991–2007; mem. Poetry Soc. of America, Poetry Soc. of Virginia, World Congress of Poets. *Publications:* Dawn Breaks the Heart (novel) 1932, Arms, Angels, Epitaphs (poems), The Angry Dust (novel, in Chinese) 1995, (in English) 2006, Trial of Pythagoras and Other Poems 1996, (in Greek 1998), Lost Adulteries and Other Stories 1998, Bitter Rainbow and Other Poems 1999, (in Greek) 2003; contrib. to anthologies, periodicals and magazines world-wide. *E-mail:* daveywdsd@aol.com (home). *Website:* www.williamdavey.com.

DAVIDSON, Basil Risbridger, MC; British historian and academic; b. 9 Nov. 1914, Bristol; s. of Thomas Davidson and Jessie Davidson; m. Marion Ruth Young 1943; three s. *Career:* served British Army 1940–45, Lt-Col 1945; journalist with The Economist, The Star, The Times, New Statesman, Daily Herald, Daily Mirror, 1938–62; Visiting Prof. in African History, Univ. of Ghana 1964, UCLA 1965; Regent's Lecturer in African History, UCLA 1971; Montague Burton Visiting Prof. of Int. Relations, Univ. of Edin. 1972; Simon Sr Research Fellow, Univ. of Manchester 1975–76; Agnelli Visiting Prof., Univ. of Turin 1990. *Publications:* principal works: Old Africa Rediscovered 1959, Black Mother—The African Slave Trade 1961 (revised 1980), The African Past 1964, History of West Africa to 1800 1965, History of East and Central Africa to the Late Nineteenth Century 1967, Africa in History: Themes and Outlines 1967, The Africans: A Cultural History 1969, The Liberation of Guiné 1969 (revised 1981), In the Eye of the Storm: Angola's People 1972, Black Star 1973, Can Africa Survive? 1975, Africa in Modern History, The Search for a New Society 1978, Special Operations Europe – Scenes from the Anti-Nazi War 1980, The People's Cause: A History of Guerrillas in Africa 1981, Modern Africa 1982, Africa (TV series) 1984, The Story of Africa 1984, The Fortunate Isles 1988, The Black Man's Burden 1992, The Search for Africa—History, Politics, Culture 1994, West Africa Before the Colonial Era: A History to 1850 1998. *Honours:* Freeman City of Genoa 1945; Hon. Research Fellow, Univ. of Birmingham 1974; Hon. Fellow, SOAS (Univ. of London) 1989; Mil. Cross, Bronze Star, US Army, Zasluge za Narod, Yugoslav Army, Grand Officer, Order of Prince Henry the Navigator (Portugal) 2002; Hon. DLitt (Univ. of Ibadan) 1975, (Dar es Salaam) 1985, (Univ. of Western Cape, SA) 1997; Hon. DUniv (Open Univ.) 1980, (Edin.) 1981, (Bristol) 1999; Haile Selassie Award for African Research 1970, Medalha Amílcar Cabral 1976. *Address:* 21 Deanery Walk, Avonpark Village, Limpley Stoke, Bath, BA2 7JQ, England (home).

DAVIDSON, Lionel, (David Line); British writer; b. 31 March 1922, Hull, Yorks., England; m. 1st Fay Jacobs 1949 (died 1988); two s.; m. 2nd Frances Ullman 1989. *Publications:* The Night of Wenceslas 1960, The Rose of Tibet 1962, A Long Way to Shiloh 1966, Run for Your Life (as David Line) 1966, Making Good Again 1968, Smith's Gazelle 1971, Mike and Me (as David Line) 1974, The Sun Chemist 1976, The Chelsea Murders 1978, Under Plum Lake 1980, Screaming High (as David Line) 1985, Kolymsky Heights 1994. *Honours:* Authors Club Silver Quill Award 1961, CWA Gold Dagger Awards 1961, 1967, 1979, and Cartier Diamond Dagger Award for Lifetime Achievement 2001. *Literary Agent:* c/o Sinclair-Stevenson, 3 South Terrace, London, SW7 2TB, England. *Telephone:* (20) 7581-2550. *Fax:* (20) 7581-2559.

DAVIDSON, Michael, BA, PhD; American academic, poet and writer; b. 18 Dec. 1944, Oakland, CA; m. 1st Carol Wikarska 1970 (divorced 1974); m. 2nd Lois Chamberlain 1988, two c. *Education:* San Francisco State University, SUNY at Buffalo, University of California at Berkeley. *Career:* Visiting Lecturer, San Diego State University, 1973–76; Curator, Archive for New Poetry, 1975–85, Prof. of Literature, 1977–, University of California at San Diego. *Publications:* poetry: Exchanges, 1972; Two Views of Pears, 1973; The Mutabilities, and the Foul Papers, 1976; Summer Letters, 1976; Grillwork, 1980; Discovering Motion, 1980; The Prose of Fact, 1981; The Landing of Rochambeau, 1985; Analogy of the Ion, 1988; Post Hoc, 1990. Other: The San Francisco Renaissance: Poetics and Community at Mid-Century, 1989. Contributions: periodicals. *Honours:* National Endowment for the Arts grant 1976.

DAVIES, Andrew Wynford, BA; British screenwriter; b. 20 Sept. 1936, Rhiwbina, Cardiff, Wales; m. Diana Huntley 1960; one s. one d. *Education:* Whitchurch Grammar School, Cardiff, Univ. Coll., London. *Career:* teacher, St Clement Danes Grammar School, London 1958–61, Woodberry Down Comprehensive School, London 1961–63; Lecturer, Coventry Coll. of Education 1963–71, Univ. of Warwick, Coventry 1971–87; full-time writer 1987–, also adapting numerous classics for television and film. *Television series:* Look and Read (episode 'Badgergirl') 1967, Bedtime Stories 1974, To Serve Them All My Days 1980, Educating Marmalade 1981, Danger: Marmalade at Work 1984, Badger Girl 1984, A Very Peculiar Practice 1986, Mother Love 1989, Alfonso Bonzo 1990, House of Cards 1990, The Old Devils 1992, To Play the King 1993, Middlemarch 1994, Game On (with Bernadette Davis) 1995, Pride and Prejudice 1995, Vanity Fair 1998, Wives and Daughters 1999, The Way We Live Now 2001, Doctor Zhivago 2002, He Knew He Was Right 2004, Bleak

House (series) 2005. *Television plays:* Who's Going to Take Me On? 1967, Is That Your Body Boy? 1970, No Good Unless It Hurts 1973, The Water Maiden 1974, Grace 1975, The Imp of the Perverse 1975, The Signalman 1976, A Martyr to the System 1976, Eleanor Marx 1977, Happy in War 1977, Velvet Glove 1977, Fearless Frank 1978, Renoir My Father 1978, The Legend of King Arthur 1979, Bavarian Night 1981, Heartattack Hotel 1983, Diana 1984, Pythons on the Mountain 1985, Inappropriate Behaviour 1987, Lucky Sunil 1988, Baby, I Love You 1988, Ball-Trap on the Cote Sauvage 1989, A Private Life 1989, Filipina Dreamers 1991, The Old Devils 1992, Harnessing Peacocks 1992, Anglo-Saxon Attitudes 1992, A Very Polish Practice 1992, Anna Lee 1993, A Few Short Journeys of the Heart 1994, The Final Cut 1995, Wilderness 1996, The Fortunes and Misfortunes of Moll Flanders 1996, Emma 1996, Getting Hurt 1998, A Rather English Marriage 1998, Take a Girl Like You 2000, Othello 2001, Tipping the Velvet 2002, Daniel Deronda 2002, Falling 2005, The Chatterley Affair 2006, The Line of Beauty 2006, Northanger Abbey 2007, The Diary of A Nobody 2007, A Room With A View 2007. *Radio plays:* The Hospitalization of Samuel Pellett 1964, Getting the Smell of It 1967, A Day in Bed 1967, Curse on Them, Astonish Me! 1970, Steph and the Man of Some Distinction 1971, The Innocent Eye 1971, The Shortsighted Bear 1972, Steph and the Simple Life 1972, Steph and the Zero Structure Lifestyle 1976, Accentuate the Positive 1980, Campus Blues 1984. *Films:* Time After Time 1985, Consuming Passions 1988, Circle of Friends 1995, The Tailor of Panama (screenplay) 2001, Bridget Jones's Diary (screenplay) 2001, Boudica 2003, Bridget Jones: The Edge of Reason (screenplay) 2004, Brideshead Revisited (screenplay) 2006. *Stage productions:* Can Anyone Smell the Gas? 1972, The Shortsighted Bear 1972, Filthy Fryer and the Woman of Mature Years 1974, What Are Little Girls Made Of? 1975, Rohan and Julia 1975, Randy Robinson's Unsuitable Relationship 1976, Teacher's Gone Mad 1977, Going Bust 1977, Fearless Frank 1978, Brainstorming with the Boys 1978, Battery 1979, Diary of a Desperate Woman 1979, Rose 1980, Prin 1990. *Publications include:* The Fantastic Feats of Doctor Boox 1972, Conrad's War 1978, Marmalade and Rufus 1980, Poonam's Pets (with Diana Davies) 1990, Getting Hurt 1990, B. Monkey 1992. *Honours:* Dr hc (Cardiff, Coventry, De Montfort, Open Univ., Warwick, Univ. Coll. London); Guardian Children's Fiction Award 1979, Boston Globe-Horn Book Award 1980, Broadcast Press Guild Award 1980, 1990, Pye Colour TV Award 1981, Royal Television Soc. Award 1987, 2006, BAFTA Award 1989, 1993, 2002, 2006, BAFTA Fellowship 2002, Writers' Guild Award 1991, 1992, Emmy Award 1991. *Literary Agent:* c/o Lemon, Unna and Durbridge, 24 Pottery Lane, London, W11 4LZ, England. *Telephone:* (20) 7727-1346.

DAVIES, (Edward) Hunter, BA, DipEd; British writer; b. 7 Jan. 1936, Renfrew, Scotland; m. Margaret Forster 1960; one s. two d. *Education:* Univ. Coll., Durham, England. *Publications include:* Here We Go Round the Mulberry Bush 1965, The Beatles 1968, The Glory Game 1972, A Walk Along the Wall 1974, A Walk Around the Lakes 1979, In Search of Columbus 1991, Wainwright: The Biography 1998, The Eddie Stobart Story 2001, Gazza: My Story 2004, Being Gazza: My Journey to Hell and Back 2006, The Beatles, Football and Me (autobiog.) 2006, My Story So Far (with Wayne Rooney) 2006, The Bumper Book of Football 2007; contrib. to Sunday Times 1960–84, Punch 1979–89, Independent (London) 1990–2000, New Statesman 1998–. *Address:* 11 Boscastle Road, London, NW5, England.

DAVIES, (Ivor) Norman Richard, CMG, MA, PhD, FBA, FRHistS; British academic and writer; b. 8 June 1939, Bolton, England; m. 1st Maria Zielińska 1966; one s.; m. 2nd Maria Korzeniewicz 1984; one s. *Education:* Univ. of Grenoble, Magdalen Coll., Oxford, Univ. of Sussex, Jagiellonian Univ. *Career:* Alistair Horne Research Fellow, St Antony's Coll., Oxford 1969–71; Lecturer 1971–84, Reader 1984–85, Prof. of Polish History 1985–96, Prof. Emeritus 1996–, Univ. of London; Visiting Prof., Columbia Univ. 1974, McGill Univ. 1977–78, Hokkaido Univ. 1982–83, Stanford Univ. 1985–86, Harvard Univ. 1991; Sr Research Assoc., Univ. of Oxford 1997–; Supernumerary Fellow Wolfson Coll. 1999–2006; Eleminasator Principalis, UNESCO Chair. Jagiellonian Univ. 2003–; Visiting Research Fellow, Clare Hall, Cambridge 2006–. *Publications:* White Eagle, Red Star: The Polish–Soviet War of 1919–1920 1972, God's Playground: A History of Poland (two vols) 1981, Heart of Europe: A Short History of Poland 1984, Europe: A History 1996, The Isles: A History 1999, Microcosm: Portrait of a Central European City (with Roger Moorehouse) 2002, Rising '44: The Battle for Warsaw 2004, Europe at War 1939–1945: No Simple Victory 2006, Europe East and West 2006; contrib. to scholarly books and journals. *Honours:* Dr hc (UMCS) 1993, (Gdańsk) 1997, (Kraków) 2004, (Sussex) 2006, (Warsaw) 2007; Knight Cross, Order of Polonia Restituta, Poland 1984, Commander Cross, Order of Merit, Poland 1992, Grand Cross, Order of Merit, Poland 1999. *Literary Agent:* DGA, 55 Monmouth Street, London, WC2, England. *Telephone:* (20) 7240-9992.

DAVIES, Paul Charles William; British theoretical physicist, cosmologist, writer and broadcaster; *Professor of Natural Philosophy, Australian Centre for Astrobiology; College Professor and Head, Centre for New Questions in Science, Arizona State University*; b. 22 April 1946, London, England. *Career:* fmrly at Univ. of Cambridge, Imperial Coll. London, Univ. of Newcastle upon Tyne; fmr Visiting Prof., Univ. of Queensland, Brisbane, Australia; moved to Australia 1990; fmrly at Univ. of Adelaide; currently Prof. of Natural Philosophy, Australian Centre for Astrobiology, Macquarie Univ.; took up Chair of SETI: Post-Detection Science and Tech. Taskgroup, Int. Acad. of Astronautics 2005–; Coll. Prof. and Head of Centre for New Questions in Science, Arizona State Univ., USA 2006–; mem. Editorial Advisory Bd Cosmos Magazine 2006–. *Television includes:* The Big Questions (six-part series for Australian SBS TV) 1995, More Big Questions (series for SBS TV) 1998, The Cradle of Life (BBC documentary) 2002. *Radio includes:* documentary on the wire telegraph for BBC Radio 4, series of 45-minute documentaries (including Desperately Seeking Superstrings) for BBC Radio 3, series of 30-minute documentaries for BBC World Service, The Genesis Factor (three-part BBC Radio 4 series on the origin of life) 2000. *Publications:* The Physics of Time Asymmetry 1974, Space and Time in the Modern Universe 1977, The Runaway Universe 1978, The Forces of Nature 1979, Other Worlds 1980, The Search for Gravity Waves 1980, The Edge of Infinity 1981, The Accidental Universe 1982, Quantum Fields in Curved Space (with N. D. Birrell) 1982, God and the New Physics 1983, Superforce 1984, Quantum Mechanics 1984, The Ghost in the Atom (with J. R. Brown) 1986, Fireball 1987, The Cosmic Blueprint 1987, Superstrings: A Theory of Everything? (with J. R. Brown) 1988, The New Physics (ed.) 1989, The Matter Myth (with J. Gribbin) 1991, The Mind of God 1992, The Last Three Minutes 1994, About Time: Einstein's Unfinished Revolution 1995, Are We Alone? The Philosophical Basis of the Search for Extraterrestrial Life 1995, The Big Questions (with Phillip Adams) 1996, One Universe or Many Universes? 1998, More Big Questions (with Phillip Adams) 1998, The Fifth Miracle: The Search for the Origin of Life (aka The Origin of Life) 1998, How to Build a Time Machine 2001, Science and Ultimate Reality (co-ed. with John D. Barrow & Charles Harper) 2004, The Goldilocks Enigma: Why is the Universe Just Right for Life? 2006; contrib. numerous articles to journals, newspapers and other publs, including The Economist, The Guardian, The New York Times, The Australian, The Sydney Morning Herald, The Age, The Bulletin, New Scientist. *Honours:* Glaxo Science Writers Fellowship, Templeton Prize 1995, the asteroid 1992 OG was officially named (6870) Pauldavies in his honour 1999, Kelvin Medal and Prize, Inst. of Physics (UK) 2001, Royal Soc. Michael Faraday Prize 2002, Advance Australia Award, two Eureka Prizes. *Address:* Australian Centre for Astrobiology, Macquarie University, NSW 2109, Australia (office); College of Liberal Arts and Sciences, MC 6505, Arizona State University, Tempe, AZ 85287, USA. *Telephone:* (2) 98509256 (Australia) (office); (480) 965-9011 (USA) (office). *Fax:* (2) 98508248 (office). *E-mail:* pdavies@els.mq.edu.au (office); Paul.Davies@asu.edu (office). *Website:* aca.mq.edu.au/PaulDavies/pdavies.html (office); www.asu.edu (office).

DAVIES, Peter Ho, BS, BA, MA; British writer; b. 1966, Coventry, England; m. *Education:* Manchester Univ., Univ. of Cambridge, Boston Univ., USA. *Career:* Business Man., Varsity magazine; Dir of MFA creative writing programme, Univ. of Michigan. *Publications:* The Ugliest House in the World (short stories) (John Llewellyn Rhys Prize, PEN Macmillan Prize 1999) 1998, Equal Love (short stories) 2000, The Welsh Girl (novel) 2007; contrib. short stories to Atlantic, Granta, Best American Short Stories 1995, 1996, 2001. *Honours:* H. L. Davis Oregon Book Award 1997, O. Henry Award 1998, New York Times Notable Book of the Year 2000. *Address:* Abner Stein Agency, 10 Roland Gardens, London, SW7 3PH, England (office). *E-mail:* abner@abnerstein.co.uk (office).

DAVIES, Peter Joseph, MB, MD, MRCP, FRACP; Australian physician and writer; b. 15 May 1937, Terang, Vic.; m. Clare Loughnan 1960; one d. *Career:* mem. Gastro-Enterological Soc. of Australia, Royal Musical Asscn, American Musicological Soc., Friends of Mozart (New York), Friends Int. Stiftung Mozareum (Salzburg). *Publications:* Mozart in Person: His Character and Health 1989, Mozart's Health, Illnesses and Death 1993, The Cause of Beethoven's Deafness 1996, Beethoven in Person: His Deafness, Illnesses and Death 2001, The Character of a Genius: Beethoven in Perspective 2002; contrib. to Journal of Medical Biography 1995. *Address:* 14 Hamilton Street, East Kew, Vic. 3102, Australia.

DAVIES, Piers Anthony David, ONZM, LLB, DipECL; New Zealand barrister, solicitor, screenwriter and poet; b. 15 June 1941, Sydney, NSW, Australia; m. Margaret Elaine Haswell 1973; one d. *Education:* Univ. of Auckland, City of London Coll. *Career:* Barrister and Solicitor, Wackrow, Williams and Davies, Auckland, New Zealand; Chair., Short Film Fund, New Zealand Film Comm. 1987–91; mem. Int. Law Asscn (cultural heritage law cttee 1997–). *Writing for film:* screenplays: The Life and Flight of Rev Buck Shotte (with Peter Weir) 1969, Homesdale (with Peter Weir) 1971, The Cars That Ate Paris (with Peter Weir) 1973, Skin Deep 1978, The Lamb of God 1985, A Fair Hearing 1995; documentary: R. v. Huckleberry Finn 1979, Olaf's Coast 1982. *Publications:* East and Other Gong Songs 1967, Day Trip from Mount Meru 1969, Diaspora 1974, Bourgeois Homage to Dada 1974, Central Almanac (ed.) 1974, Jetsam 1984; contrib. to anthologies and periodicals, chapters in Law Stories 2003, The Protection of the Underwater Cultural Heritage 2006, Encyclopaedia of New Zealand Forms and Precedents (ongoing). *Address:* 16 Crocus Place, Remuera, Auckland 5, New Zealand (home). *Telephone:* 9-5246927 (home).

DAVIES, Stephanie (Stevie), BA, MA, PhD, FRSL; Welsh writer and lecturer; *Director of Creative Writing, University of Wales, Swansea*; b. 2 Dec. 1946, Swansea; three c. *Education:* Univ. of Manchester. *Career:* Lecturer in English Literature, Victoria Univ. of Manchester 1971–84, Salford Univ. 1989–90; Sr Research Fellow in English Literature, Univ. of Surrey 1994–2001; Dir of Creative Writing, Univ. of Wales, Swansea 2004–; Royal Literary Fund Writing Fellow, Univ. of Wales, Swansea 2001–03; Fellow Welsh Acad. *Publications:* fiction: Boy Blue 1987, Primavera 1990, Arms and the Girl 1992, Closing the Book 1994, Four Dreamers and Emily 1996, The Web of Belonging 1997, Impassioned Clay 1999, The Element of Water 2001, Kith and Kin 2003; non-fiction: Renaissance Views of Man 1978, Images of

Kingship in 'Paradise Lost': Milton's Politics and Christian Liberty 1983, Emily Brontë: The Artist as a Free Woman 1983, The Idea of Woman in Renaissance Literature: The Feminine Reclaimed 1987, Emily Brontë 1988, Virginia Woolf's 'To the Lighthouse' 1989, John Milton 1991, Shakespeare's 'Twelfth Night' 1993, Emily Brontë: Heretic 1994, John Donne 1994, Henry Vaughan 1995, Shakespeare's 'The Taming of the Shrew' 1995, Emily Brontë 1998, Unbridled Spirits: Women of the English Revolution 1640–1660 1998, The Eyries 2007 contrib. to reference books, anthologies, quarterlies, reviews and journals. *Honours:* Fawcett Soc. Book Prize 1989, Arts Council of Wales Book of the Year 2002, Soc. of Authors travel grant 1999. *Address:* 9 Oystermouth Court, Castle Road, Mumbles, Swansea, SA3 5TD, Wales. *E-mail:* steviedavies@spirit.plus.com.

DAVIES, William Thomas Pennar, BA, BLitt, PhD; British author and poet; b. 12 Nov. 1911, Aberpennar, Glamorgan, Wales; m. Rosemarie Wolff 1943, four s. one d. *Education:* University of Wales, University of Oxford, Yale University. *Publications:* Fiction: Anadl o'r Uchelder, 1958; Caregel Nwyf, 1966; Meibion Darogan, 1968; Llais y Durtur, 1985. Poetry: Cinio'r Cythraul, 1946; Naw Wfft, 1957; Yr Efrydd o lyn Cynon, 1961; Y Tlws yn y Lotws, 1971; Llef, 1987. Non-Fiction: Cudd fy Meiau, 1957; Rhwng Chwedl a Chredo, 1966. Contributions: Reviews and periodicals. *Honours:* Commonwealth Fund Fellow, 1936–38; Fellow, 1938–40, Fellow hc, 1986, Hon. DD, 1987, University of Wales; Hon. Fellow, Welsh Acad., 1989.

DAVIS, Albert Joseph, Jr, (Albert Belisle Davis), BA, MA, PhD; American academic, writer and poet; *Alcee Fortier Distinguished Professor, Nicholls State University*; b. 23 June 1947, Houma, LA; m. 1st Carol Anne Campbell 1968 (divorced 1992); one s.; m. 2nd Mary Archer Freet 1994; one d. *Education:* Nicholls State Univ., Colorado State Univ., Univ. of Louisiana at Lafayette. *Career:* novelist-in-residence 1991–, Distinguished Service Prof. of Languages and Literature 1994–, Assoc. Dean Coll. of Arts and Sciences 1999–2001, Alcee Fortier Distinguished Prof. 2003–, Dean Univ. Coll. 2005–, Nicholls State Univ.; mem. Acad. of American Poets, Associated Writing Programs, Louisiana Asscn of Educators, Louisiana Division of the Arts (literary panel 1995–97), Nat. Education Asscn, PEN American Center. *Publications:* What They Wrote on the Bathhouse Walls (poems) 1989, Leechtime (novel) 1989, Marquis at Bay (novel) 1992, Virginia Patout's Parish (poems) 1999; contrib. to anthologies and literary journals. *Honours:* Ione Burden Award for the Novel 1983, John Z. Bennet Award for Poetry 1984, Louisiana Division of the Arts Creative Writing Fellowship 1989. *Address:* c/o Department of General Studies, Nicholls State University, PO Box 2106, Thibodaux, LA 70310, USA. *Telephone:* (985) 448-4090 (home). *E-mail:* albert.davis@nicholls.edu. *Website:* www.nicholls.edu.

DAVIS, Burke, AB; American historian and biographer; b. 24 July 1913, Durham, NC; m. 1st Evangeline McLennan 1940 (divorced 1980); one s. one d.; m. 2nd Juliet H. Burnett 1982. *Education:* Duke University, Guilford College, University of North Carolina. *Career:* Ed., Feature Writer and Sports Ed., Charlotte News, NC, 1937–47; Reporter, Baltimore Evening Sun, MD, 1947–52, Greensboro News, NC, 1951–60; Writer and Historian, Colonial Williamsburg, Virginia, 1960–78; Biography Juror, Pulitzer Prizes, 1980s. *Publications:* Whisper My Name, 1949; The Ragged Ones, 1951; Yorktown, 1952; They Called Him Stonewall, 1954; Gray Fox: Robert E. Lee and the Civil War, 1956; Jeb Stuart, The Last Cavalier, 1957; To Appomattox, 1959; Our Incredible Civil War, 1960; Marine! The Life of Chesty Puller; The Cowpens-Guilford Courthouse Campaign, 1962; America's First Army, 1962; Appomattox: Closing Struggle of the Civil War, 1963; The Summer Land, 1965; A Rebel Raider (co-author), 1966; The Billy Mitchell Affair, 1967; A Williamsburg Galaxy, 1967; The World of Currier & Ives (co-author), 1968; Get Yamamoto, 1969; Yorktown: The Campaign that won America, 1969; Billy Mitchell Story, 1969; Black Heroes of the American Revolution, 1971; Jamestown, 1971; Thomas Jefferson's Virginia, 1971; Amelia Earhart, 1972; Biography of a Leaf, 1972; Three for Revolution, 1975; Biography of a Kingsnake, 1975; George Washington and the American Revolution, 1975; Newer and Better Organic Gardening, 1976; Biography of a Fish Hawk, 1976; Old Hickory: A Life of Andrew Jackson, 1977; Mr Lincoln's Whiskers, 1978; Sherman's March, 1980; The Long Surrender, 1985; The Southern Railway, 1985; War Bird: The Life and Times of Elliott White Springs, 1986; Civil War: Strange and Fascinating Facts, 1989.

DAVIS, David Brion, AB, AM, PhD; American academic and writer; *Sterling Professor Emeritus of History, Yale University*; b. 16 Feb. 1927, Denver, Colo; m. 1st; one s. two d.; m. 2nd Toni Hahn Davis 1971; two s. *Education:* Dartmouth Coll., Harvard Univ. *Career:* Instructor, Dartmouth Coll. 1953–54; Asst Prof., Cornell Univ. 1955–58, Assoc. Prof. 1958–63, Prof. and Ernest I. White Prof. of History 1963–69; Fulbright Sr Lecturer, American Studies Research Centre, Hyderabad, India 1967; Harmsworth Prof., Univ. of Oxford, UK 1969–70; Prof. and Farnam Prof. of History, Yale Univ. 1969–78, Sterling Prof. of History 1978–2001, Sterling Prof. Emer. of History 2001–; Fellow, Center for Advanced Study in the Behavioral Sciences, Stanford 1972–73; Fulbright Lecturer, Univs of Guyana and the West Indies 1974; French-American Foundation Chair in American Civilization, École des Hautes Études en Sciences Sociales, Paris 1980–81; Gilder-Lehrman Inaugural Fellow 1996–97; Dir The Gilder-Lehrman Center at Yale for the Study of Slavery, Resistance and Abolition 1998–2004; Corresp. Fellow, British Acad.; mem. American Acad. of Arts and Sciences, American Antiquarian Soc., American Philosophical Soc., Inst. of Early American History and Culture, Org. of American Historians (Pres. 1988–89). *Publications:* Homicide in American Fiction, 1798–1860: A Study in Social Values 1957, The Problem of Slavery in Western Culture 1966, Ante-Bellum Reform (ed.) 1967, The Slave Power Conspiracy and the Paranoid Style 1969, Was Thomas Jefferson an Authentic Enemy of Slavery? 1970, The Fear of Conspiracy: Images of un-American Subversion from the Revolution to the Present (ed.) 1971, The Problem of Slavery in the Age of Revolution, 1770–1823 1975, The Great Republic (co-author) 1977, Antebellum American Culture: An Interpretive Anthology 1979, The Emancipation Moment 1984, Slavery and Human Progress 1984, Slavery in the Colonial Chesapeake 1986, From Homicide to Slavery: Studies in American Culture 1986, Revolutions: Reflections on American Equality and Foreign Liberations 1990, The Antislavery Debate: Capitalism and Abolitionism as a Problem in Historical Interpretation (with Thomas Bender) 1992, Challenging the Boundaries of Slavery 1993, The Boisterous Sea of Liberty: A Documentary History of America from Discovery Through the Civil War (with Steven Mintz) 1998, In the Image of God: Religion, Moral Values, and Our Heritage of Slavery 2001, Challenging the Boundaries of Slavery 2003, Inhuman Bondage: The Rise and Fall of Slavery in the New World 2006. *Honours:* Hon. LittD (Dartmouth Coll.) 1977, (Columbia Univ.) 1999; Hon. LHD (Univ. of New Haven) 1986; Guggenheim Fellowship 1958–59, Pulitzer Prize in General Non-Fiction 1967, Anisfield-Wolf Award 1967 Albert J. Beveridge Award, American Historical Asscn 1975, Nat. Book Award 1976 Bancroft Prize, Columbia Univ. 1976 Presidential Medal for Outstanding Leadership and Achievement, Dartmouth Coll. 1991, Bruce Catton Award for Lifetime Achievement, Soc. of American Historians 2004, Kidger Award, New England History Teachers Asscn 2004, Award for Scholarly Distinction, American Historical Asscn 2006. *Address:* c/o Gilder Lehrman Center, Yale University, PO Box 208206, New Haven, CT 06520-8206, USA (office). *E-mail:* david.b.davis@yale.edu (office).

DAVIS, Richard (Dick), BA, MA, PhD, FRSL; British academic and poet; *Professor of Persian, Ohio State University*; b. 18 April 1945, Portsmouth, Hampshire, England; m. Afkham Darbandi 1974; two d. *Education:* King's Coll., Cambridge, Univ. of Manchester. *Career:* fmrly teacher in Greece, Italy and Iran; teacher, Univs of Tehran, Iran 1970–78, Durham, Newcastle, California at Santa Barbara, USA; freelance writer, translator and reviewer 1978–84; poetry critic, The Listener 1980–86; Contributing Ed., PN Review 1983–89; Asst Prof., Dept of Near Eastern Languages and Cultures, Ohio State Univ. 1988–93, Assoc. Prof. of Persian 1993, currently Prof. of Persian and Chair. *Publications:* Shade Mariners (poems, chapbook) 1970, In the Distance (poems) 1975, Seeing the World (poems) (Heinemann Award 1981) 1980, Selected Writings of Thomas Traherne (ed.) 1980, Visitations (poems, chapbook) 1983, Wisdom and Wilderness: The Achievement of Yvor Winters (criticism) 1983, What the Mind Wants (poems, chapbook) 1984, The Conference of the Birds (trans. from the Persian of Attar, with Afkham Darbandi) (American Institute of Iranian Studies Translation Prize 2001) 1984, The Covenant (poems) 1984, The Little Virtues (trans. of Le Piccole Virtu by Natalia Ginzburg) 1985, The City and The House (trans. of La Citta e la Casa by Natalia Ginzburg) 1986, Lares (poems, chapbook) 1986, The Rubaiyat of Omar Khayyam, trans. by Edward Fitzgerald (ed.) 1989, Devices and Desires: New and Selected Poems (The Times and The Daily Telegraph Book of the Year) 1989, A Kind of Love: New & Selected Poems (Ingram Merrill Award 1993) 1991, The Legend of Seyavash (trans. of part of The Shahnameh by Ferdowsi) 1992, Epic and Sedition: the Case of Ferdowsi's Shahnameh (Persian Heritage Foundation Award) 1993, My Unce Napoleon (trans. of Dai Jan Napoleon by Iraj Pezeshkzad) (American Institute of Iranian Studies Translation Prize 2000) 1996, Touchwood: Poems 1991–1995 1996, Medieval Persian Epigrams (trans.) (Poetry Soc. of Great Britain recommendation) 1996, The Lion and the Throne: Stories from the Shahnameh of Ferdowsi (vol. one) 1998, Fathers and Sons: Stories from the Shahnameh of Ferdowsi (vol. two) 2000, Belonging (poems) (Economist Book of the Year) 2002, Panthea's Children: Hellenistic Novels and Medieval Persian Romances 2002; contrib. poems to numerous magazines and journals, including TLS, The Listener, The Spectator, Critical Quarterly, Poetry Review, Poetry Nation Review, Paris Review, Southern Review, Sequoia, Spectrum, The Hudson Review, Drastic Measures, Numbers, Helix, Other Poetry, Rialto, Agenda, Poetry Durham, TriQuarterly, Cambridge Review, Sewanee Review, Threepenny Review, Yale Review, New Criterion, Hellas, The Epigrammatist, la fontana, Dark Horse; contrib. articles and reviews to TLS, Journal of American Oriental Studies, International Journal of Middle Eastern Studies, Iranian Studies, Encyclopaedia Iranica, Encyclopaedia of Islam, Threepenny Review, New York Review of Books. *Honours:* Arts Council of Great Britain Writers' Award 1979, British Inst. of Persian Studies Award 1981, Fulbright Travel Award 1987, Guggenheim Fellow 1999–2000, Nat. Endowment for the Humanities Fellow 2001, Encyclopaedia Iranica Ferdowsi Award for Services to Persian Poetry 2001, Ohio State Univ. Distinguished Scholar Award 2002. *Address:* Department of Near Eastern Languages and Cultures, Ohio State University, 207E Jennings Hall, 1735 Neil Avenue, Columbus, OH 43210, USA (office). *Telephone:* (614) 292-5643 (office). *Fax:* (614) 292-1262 (office). *E-mail:* davis.77@osu.edu (office). *Website:* nelc.ohio-state.edu/people/person.cfm?ID=190.

DAVIS, Dorothy Salisbury, AB; American writer; b. 26 April 1916, Chicago, IL; m. Harry Davis 1946. *Education:* Barat College, Lake Forest, IL. *Career:* mem. MWA, CWA, Authors' Guild. *Publications:* A Gentle Murderer, 1951; Men of No Property, 1956; The Evening of the Good Samaritan, 1961; Enemy and Brother, 1967; Where the Dark Streets Go, 1969; The Little Brothers, 1974; A Death in the Life, 1976; Scarlet Night, 1980; Lullaby of Murder, 1984;

Tales for a Stormy Night, 1985; The Habit of Fear, 1987; A Gentleman Called, 1989; Old Sinners Never Die, 1991; Black Sheep, White Lambs, 1993. Contributions: New Republic. *Honours:* MWA Grand Master's Award 1985, Bouchereon XX Lifetime Achievement Award 1989.

DAVIS, Jack Leonard; Australian poet, dramatist and writer; b. 11 March 1917, Perth, WA; m. Madelon Jantine Wilkens 1987; one d. *Career:* writer-in-residence, Murdoch Univ. 1982; mem. Aboriginal Writers Oral Literature and Dramatists Asscn; Australian Writers Guild; PEN International. *Publications:* The First Born and Other Poems, 1968; Jagardoo Poems from Aboriginal Australia, 1978; The Dreamers (play), 1983; Kullark (play), 1983; John Pat and Other Poems, 1988; Burungin (Smell the Wind) (play), 1989; Plays From Black Australia, 1989. Contributions: Identity. *Honours:* Human Rights Award, 1987; BHP Award, 1988; Australian Artists Creative Fellowship, 1989; Hon. doctorates. *Address:* 3 Little Howard Street, Fremantle, WA, Australia.

DAVIS, James Madison, Jr, BA, MA, PhD; American writer and academic; *Professor, Gaylord College of Journalism, University of Oklahoma;* b. 10 Feb. 1951, Charlottesville, Va; s. of James Madison Davis and Alma Luci; m. 1st Simonne Evelyn Eck 1977 (divorced); two s.; m. 2nd Melissa Anne Haymes 1997; one s. *Education:* George Washington Univ., Franklin and Marshall Coll., Univ. of Maryland at College Park, Johns Hopkins Univ., Univ. of Southern Mississippi. *Career:* Instructor of English and journalism, Allegany Community Coll., Cumberland, Md 1975–77; instructor, part-time instructor and teaching asst, Univ. of Southern Mississippi 1977–79; Asst Prof. of English Composition, Pennsylvania State Univ., Erie 1979–84, Assoc. Prof. of English 1984–90, Prof. of English 1990–91; Writer-in-Residence, Mercyhurst Coll. 1989, 1990; Prof. on the Professional Writing Program, Gaylord Coll. of Journalism, Univ. of Oklahoma, Norman 1991–; mem. Int. Asscn of Crime Writers N America Br. (Pres. 1993–97, Sec. 1997–2001). *Publications:* fiction: The Murder of Frau Schütz 1988, White Rook 1990, Bloody Marko 1991, Red Knight 1992, And the Angels Sing 1996; non-fiction: Intro 14 (co-ed.) 1984, Critical Essays on Edward Albee (with Philip C. Kolin) 1986, Dick Francis 1989, Conversations with Robertson Davies 1989, Stanislaw Lem 1990, The Shakespeare Name Dictionary (with A. Daniel Frankforter, aka The Shakespeare Name and Place Dictionary) 1995, Murderous Schemes (contributing co-ed. with Donald Westlake) 1996, The Novelist's Essential Guide to Creating Plot 2000, Alfred Hitchcock in the Vertigo Murders 2000, Law and Order: Deadline 2004, The Van Gogh Conspiracy 2005; contrib. to books, newspapers, reviews, quarterlies and journals. *Honours:* Resident Fellow in Prose 1974, Resident Fellow in Fiction 1981, Fellowship 1988, Virginia Center for the Creative Arts, Contemporary Best Fiction Prize 1978, Resident Fellow in Fiction, Ragdale Foundation 1982, Hambridge Center for Creative Arts and Sciences 1982, Pennsylvania Council of the Arts Fellowship in Fiction 1984, MWA Edgar Allan Poe Scroll Award 1988. *Literary Agent:* c/o Peter Rubie Literary Agency, 240 W 35th Street, Suite 500, New York, NY 10001, USA. *Telephone:* (212) 279-1776. *Fax:* (212) 279-0927. *E-mail:* prubie@prlit.com. *Website:* www.prlit.com. *Address:* 1713 Asbury Court, Norman, OK 73071, USA. *Telephone:* (405) 321-5033. *E-mail:* jmadisondavis@ou.edu (office). *Website:* jmc.ou.edu/faculty/facultypages/davis.html (office).

DAVIS, Jon Edward, BA, MFA; American poet, writer and academic; *Professor of Creative Writing and Literature, Institute of American Indian Arts;* b. 28 Oct. 1952, New Haven, CT; m. Terry Lynne Layton 1978; one d. *Education:* University of Bridgeport, University of Montana. *Career:* Ed., CutBank 1982–85; Managing Ed., Shankpainter 1986–87; Fellow 1986–87, Co-ordinator, Writing Program 1987–88, Fine Arts Work Center, Provincetown, MA; Visiting Asst Prof., Salisbury State University, MD 1988–90; Prof. of Creative Writing and Literature, Inst. of American Indian Arts, Santa Fe, NM 1990–; Co-Ed., Countermeasures 1993–. *Publications:* poetry: West of New England 1983, Dangerous Amusements 1987, The Hawk, The Road, The Sunlight After Clouds 1995, Local Color 1995, Scrimmage of Appetite 1995; contrib. to anthologies, reviews, quarterlies and journals. *Honours:* Connecticut Poetry Circuit Competition winner 1980, Acad. of American Poets Prize 1985, INTRO Award for Fiction 1985, Nat. Endowment for the Arts Fellowship 1986, Richard Hugo Memorial Award, CutBank 1988, Maryland Arts Council Fellowship 1990, Owl Creek Press Chapbook Contest winner 1994, Palanquin Press Chapbook Contest winner 1995. *Address:* Faculty in Creative Writing, Institute of American Indian Arts, 83 A Van Nu Po Road, Santa Fe, NM, USA. *E-mail:* jdavis@iaia.edu.

DAVIS, Margaret Thomson; Scottish writer; b. 24 May 1926, Bathgate, West Lothian; m. (divorced); one s. *Education:* Albert Secondary Modern School, Glasgow. *Career:* mem. PEN, Scottish Labour History Society, Soc. of Authors. *Publications:* The Breadmakers 1972, A Baby Might Be Crying 1973, A Sort of Peace 1973, The Prisoner 1974, The Prince and the Tobacco Lords 1976, Roots of Bondage 1977, Scorpion in the Fire 1977, The Dark Side of Pleasure 1981, The Making of a Novelist 1982, A Very Civilized Man 1982, Light and Dark 1984, Rag Woman, Rich Woman 1987, Mothers and Daughters 1988, Wounds of War 1989, A Woman of Property 1991, A Sense of Belonging 1993, Hold Me Forever 1994, Kiss Me No More 1995, A Kind of Immortality 1996, Burning Ambition 1997, Gallaghers 1998, The Glasgow Belle 1998, A Tangled Web 1999, The Clydesiders 2000, The Gourlay Girls 2001, Strangers in a Strange Land 2001, The Clydesiders at War 2002, A Darkening of the Heart 2004, A Deadly Deception 2005, Write from the Heart (autobiog.) 2006; contrib. some 200 short stories to various periodicals.

Literary Agent: Heather Jeeves Literary Agency, 9 Kingsfield Crescent, Witney, Oxon OX28 2JB, England.

DAVIS, William Virgil, AB, MA, MDiv, PhD; American academic, writer and poet; *Professor of English, Baylor University;* b. 26 May 1940, Canton, OH; m. Carol Demske 1971; one s. *Education:* Ohio Univ., Pittsburgh Theological Seminary. *Career:* Teaching Fellow, Ohio Univ. 1965–67, Asst Prof. of English 1967–68, Consultant, Creative Writing Program 1992–98; Asst Prof. of English, Central Connecticut State Univ. 1968–72, Univ. of Illinois, Chicago 1972–77; Assoc. Prof. of English, Baylor Univ. 1977–79, Prof. of English and Writer-in-Residence 1979–, Centennial Prof. 2002–03; Guest Prof., Univ. of Vienna, Austria 1979–80, 1989–90, 1997, Univ. of Copenhagen 1984; Visiting Scholar-Guest Prof., Univ. of Wales, Swansea, UK 1983; Writer-in-Residence, Univ. of Montana 1983; Adjunct MFA Faculty, Southwest Texas State Univ. 1990–98; Adjunct mem. Grad. Faculty, Texas Christian Univ. 1992–96; mem. Acad. of American Poets, International Asscn of Univ. Profs of English, MLA, PAMLA, SCMLA, Poetry Soc. of America, Poets and Writers, Texas Asscn of Creative Writing Teachers; Councillor, Texas Inst. of Letters 1993–97; Ordained Minister, Presbyterian Church in the USA 1971. *Publications:* George Whitefield's Journals, 1737–1741 (ed.) 1969, Theodore Roethke: A Bibliography (contributing ed.) 1973, One Way to Reconstruct the Scene 1980, The Dark Hours 1984, Understanding Robert Bly 1988, Winter Light 1990, Critical Essays on Robert Bly (ed.) 1992, Miraculous Simplicity: Essays on R. S. Thomas (ed.) 1993, Robert Bly: The Poet and His Critics 1994; contrib. of articles to scholarly journals and poems in numerous anthologies and other publs; three books of poetry and over 900 poems in periodicals. *Honours:* Scholar in Poetry 1970, John Atherton Fellow in Poetry 1980, Bread Loaf Writers' Conf., Yale Series of Younger Poets Award 1979, Lilly Foundation Grant 1979–80, Calliope Press Chapbook Prize 1984, Outstanding Faculty Mem., Baylor Univ. 1989, James Sims Prize in American Literature 2002, Fellowship in Creative Writing, Poetry, Writers' League of Texas 2002. *Address:* 2633 Lake Oaks Road, Waco, TX 76710, USA (home). *Telephone:* (254) 772-3198 (office). *Fax:* (254) 710-6878 (office). *E-mail:* william_davis@baylor.edu (office).

DAVIS-GARDNER, Angela; American writer and academic; b. 21 April 1942, Charlotte, NC; one s. *Education:* BA, Duke University, 1963; MFA, University of North Carolina at Greensboro, 1965. *Career:* mem. Authors' Guild; Poets and Writers. *Publications:* Felice, 1982; Forms of Shelter, 1991. Contributions: Short stories in: Kansas Quarterly, Carolina Quarterly; Crescent Review; Greensboro Review; other literary quarterlies. *Honours:* Artists Fellowship, North Carolina Arts Council, 1981–82; Sir Walter Raleigh Award, 1991; Best Novel by North Carolinian. *Address:* Dept of English, North Carolina State University, Box 8105, Raleigh, NC 27695, USA.

DAVIS-GOFF, Annabel Claire; Irish writer; b. 19 Feb. 1942, Dublin; one s. one d. *Career:* Teacher of Literature, Bennington Coll., Vermont. *Publications:* Walled Gardens 1989, The Literary Companions to Gambling 1996, The Dower House 1998, This Cold Country 2002, The Fox's Walk 2003. *Literary Agent:* Sterling Lord Literistic Inc., 65 Bleeker Street, New York, NY 10012, USA.

DAVISON, Geoffrey Joseph, TD, FRICS; British writer; b. 10 Aug. 1927, Newcastle upon Tyne, England; m. Marlene Margaret Wilson 1956; two s. *Career:* mem. Pen and Palette Club. *Publications:* The Spy Who Swapped Shoes 1967, Nest of Spies 1968, The Chessboard Spies 1969, The Fallen Eagles 1970, The Honorable Assassins 1971, Spy Puppets 1973, The Berlin Spy Trap 1974, No Names on Their Graves 1978, The Bloody Legionnaires 1981, The Last Waltz (Vienna May 1945) 2001, The Colombian Contract 2001, The Dead Island 2001. *Address:* 95 Cheviot View, Ponteland, Newcastle upon Tyne, NE20 9BH, England (home). *Telephone:* (1661) 822347 (home). *E-mail:* davipont@onetel.com.

DAVISON, Liam; Australian writer and educator; b. 29 July 1957, Melbourne, Vic.; m. Francesca White 1983; one s. one d. *Education:* BA, Melbourne State College, 1970. *Career:* Instructor in Creative Writing, Peninsular College of Technical and Further Education; freelance writer 1988–. *Publications:* The Velodrome, novel, 1988; The Shipwreck Party, short stories, 1989; Soundings, novel, 1993; The White Woman, novel, 1994. *Honours:* Australia Council-Literature Board Fellowships, 1989, 1991; Marten Bequest Travelling Scholarship for Prose, 1992; National Book Council Banjo Award for Fiction, 1993.

DAWE, Donald Bruce, AO, MLitt, PhD; Australian writer; b. 15 Feb. 1930, Geelong; s. of Alfred John Dawe and Mary Ann Amelia Dawe; m. Gloria Desley Dawe (née Blain) 1964 (died 1997); two s. two d. *Education:* Northcote High School, Univs of Melbourne, New England and Queensland. *Career:* Educ. Section, RAAF 1959–68; teacher, Downlands Sacred Heart Coll., Toowoomba, Queensland 1969–71; Lecturer, Sr Lecturer, Assoc. Prof., Faculty of Arts, Univ. of Southern Queensland 1971–93. *Publications:* Condolences of the Season: Selected Poems 1971, Over Here, Hark! and Other Stories 1983, Essays and Opinions 1990, Mortal Instruments 1995, Sometimes Gladness: Collected Poems 1954–97 1997, A Poet's People 1999. *Honours:* Hon. DLitt (Univ. of Southern Queensland) 1995, (Univ. of NSW) 1997; Ampol Arts Award 1967, Patrick White Award 1980; Philip Hodgins Memorial Medal for Literary Excellence 1997. *Address:* 30 Cumming Street, Toowoomba, Queensland 4350, Australia. *Telephone:* (7) 4632-7525.

DAWE, Gerald Chartres, BA, MA; Irish poet and college lecturer; *Director Oscar Wilde Centre for Irish Writing, Trinity College, Dublin*; b. 22 April 1952, Belfast, Northern Ireland; m. Dorothea Melvin 1979; one s. one d. *Education:* Univ. of Ulster, Univ. Coll., Galway. *Career:* Tutor in English, Asst Lecturer, Univ. Coll., Galway 1978–87; Lecturer, Trinity Coll., Dublin 1987–, Dir MPhil in Creative Writing 1997–, Lecturer in English and Dir of the Oscar Wilde Centre for Irish Writing 1999–, Fellow, Trinity Coll. Dublin 2004; Fellow, English Asscn 2003; Burns Visiting Prof., Boston Coll. 2005; mem. Int. Asscn for the Study of Irish Literature, Irish Writers' Union, Poetry Ireland; readings and lectures in many parts of the world. *Publications:* poetry: Sheltering Places 1978, The Lundys Letter 1985, Sunday School 1991, Heart of Hearts 1995, The Morning Train 1999, Lake Geneva 2003; criticism: Across a Roaring Hill: The Protestant Imagination in Modern Ireland, with Edna Longley 1985, How's the Poetry Going?: Literary Politics and Ireland Today 1991, The Poet's Place, with John Wilson Foster 1991, Against Piety: Essays in Irish Poetry 1995, The Rest is History 1998, Stray Dogs and Dark Horses (selected essays) 2000; editor: The Younger Irish Poets 1982, 1991, Krino (anthology with Jonathan Williams) 1986–96, The Ogham Stone (anthology with Michael Mulreany) 2001, The Writer Fellow (anthology with Terence Brown) 2004), The Proper Word: Collected Criticism 2007; contrib. to newspapers, reviews, journals and radio. *Honours:* Hon. MA (Dublin) 2005; Major State Award 1974–77, Arts Council Bursary for Poetry 1980, 2005, Macaulay Fellowship in Literature 1984, Hawthornden Int. Writers' Fellowship 1988, Ledwig-Rowholt Fellowship 1999, Ulster Titanic Soc. Lifetime Achievement Award 2002. *Address:* Oscar Wilde Centre, School of English, Trinity College, Dublin 2, Ireland (office). *Telephone:* (1) 896-2897 (office). *Fax:* (1) 896-2886 (office). *E-mail:* gdawe@tcd.ie (office). *Website:* www.tcd.ie/oscarwildecentre (office); www.gallerypress.com; www.poetryireland.ie.

DAWES, Kwame Senu Neville, BA, PhD; Ghanaian/Jamaican poet, playwright and critic; b. 28 July 1962, Accra, Ghana; m. Lorna Marie; three c. *Education:* Univ. of the West Indies, Univ. of New Brunswick. *Career:* moved to Jamaica 1971; Chair. of the Division of Arts and Letters 1993–96; Asst Prof. in English Univ. of South Carolina at Sumter 1992–96, guest lecturer Univ. of South Carolina at Columbia 1994, Assoc. Prof. of English Univ. of South Carolina 1996–, Dir of MFA/Creative Writing programme 2001–; Series Ed. Caribbean Play Series, Peepal Tree Books, UK 1999–; Criticism Ed. Obsidian II literary journal, Raleigh, NC 2000–; programmer of annual Calabash Int. Literary Festival, Jamaica 2000–; Dir, USC English Dept Spring Writers Festival 2002–; South Carolina Arts Commission Individual Artist Fellowship 1996; Assoc. Fellow Univ. of Warwick 1996; mem. Nat. Book Critics' Circle, South Carolina Humanities Council (bd mem.), South Carolina Book Festival (mem. advisory bd). *Plays:* In the Warmth of the Cold, And the Gods Fell, In Chains of Freedom, The System, The Martyr, It Burns and it Stings, Charity's Come, Even Unto Death, Friends and Almost Lovers, Dear Pastor, Confessions, Brown Leaf, Coming in from the Cold, Song of an Injured Stone (musical), In My Garden, Charades, Passages, A Celebration of Struggle, Stump of the Terebinth, Valley Prince, One Love 2001. *Writing for radio:* Salut Haiti (poem/drama), Samaritans (play), New World A-Comin' (play). *Publications:* poetry: Progeny of Air 1994, Resisting the Anomie 1995, Prophets 1995, Jacko Jacobus 1996, Requiem 1996, Shook Foil 1998, Wheel and Come Again: Reggae Anthology (ed.) 1998, Mapmaker (chapbook) 2000, Midland 2001, Selected Poems 2002; fiction: A Place to Hide (short stories) 2002, Bivouac (novel) 2003; non-fiction: Natural Mysticism: Towards a New Reggae Aesthetic (literary criticism) 1998, Talk Yuh Talk: Interviews with Caribbean Poets 2000, Bob Marley: Lyrical Genius 2002; contrib. to numerous journals and periodicals, including Beat Magazine, Black Issues, Black Warrior Review, Bristol Evening Post, Calabash, Caribbean Writer, Dagens Nyheter (Sweden), Globe and Mail, Impact, Library Journal, Lines, Morning Star, Poetry London Newsletter, Poetry Review, Publishers Weekly, The Atlanta Journal/Constitution, The Brunswickan, The Courier, The Daily Gleaner, The Daily News, The English Review, The Guardian, The Herald, The London Times, The Observer, The State, The Sumter Item, The Telegraph Journal, The Voice, Time Out London, Venue, Wasafiri, Western Daily Press, World Literature Today, World Literature Written in English. *Honours:* Hon. Fellow Univ. of Iowa Int. Writing Program 1986; Forward Poetry Prize for Best First Collection 1994, winner Poetry Business Chapbook Competition 2000, Ohio Univ. Press Hollis Summers Poetry Prize 2000, Pushcart Prize 2001. *Address:* c/o English Department, University of South Carolina, Columbia, SC 29208, USA (office); 4 Doral Court, Columbia, SC 29229, USA (home). *E-mail:* dawesk@gwm.sc.edu. *Website:* www.kwamedawes.com.

DAWKINS, (Clinton) Richard, MA, DSc, FRS, FRSL; British biologist and author; *Charles Simonyi Professor of the Public Understanding of Science, University of Oxford*; b. 26 March 1941, Nairobi, Kenya; s. of Clinton John Dawkins and Jean Mary Vyvyan Dawkins (née Ladner); m. 1st Marian Stamp 1967 (divorced 1984); m. 2nd Eve Barham 1984; one d.; m. 3rd Hon. Lalla Ward 1992. *Education:* Balliol Coll., Oxford. *Career:* Asst Prof. of Zoology, Univ. of Calif., Berkeley, USA 1967–69; Lecturer, Univ. of Oxford 1970–89, Reader in Zoology 1989–96, Charles Simonyi Reader in the Public Understanding of Science 1995–96, Charles Simonyi Prof. 1996–; Ed. Animal Behaviour 1974–78, Oxford Surveys in Evolutionary Biology 1983–86; Fellow New College, Oxford 1970–; Gifford Lecturer Univ. of Glasgow 1988, Sidgwick Memorial Lecturer Newnham Coll., Cambridge 1988; Kovler Visiting Fellow Univ. of Chicago 1990; Nelson Lecturer Univ. of Calif. at Davis 1990. *Television includes:* Nice Guys Finish First, BBC 1985, The Blind Watch-maker, BBC 1986, Break the Science Barrier, Channel 4 1994, Royal Institution Christmas Lectures, BBC 1992, Big Ideas in Science, Channel 5 2004, The Root of All Evil?, Channel 4 2005. *Publications include:* The Selfish Gene 1976, The Extended Phenotype 1982, The Blind Watchmaker (RSL Prize 1987, LA Times Literature Prize 1987) 1986, The Tinbergen Legacy (ed with M. Dawkins and T. R. Halliday) 1991, River Out of Eden 1995, Climbing Mount Improbable 1996, Unweaving the Rainbow: Science, Delusion and the Appetite for Wonder 1998, A Devil's Chaplain (essays) 2003, The Ancestor's Tale: A Pilgrimage to the Dawn of Life 2004, The God Delusion 2006; numerous articles in scientific journals. *Honours:* Hon. Fellow Regent's Coll., London 1988, Balliol Coll. 2004, Hon. Patron, Philosophical Soc., Trinity Coll. Dublin 2004; Hon. DLitt (St Andrews) 1995, (ANU Canberra) 1996; Hon. DSc (Westminster) 1997, (Hull) 2001, (Sussex) 2005, (Durham) 2005, (Brussels) 2005; Hon. DUniv (Open Univ.) 2003; numerous awards including Silver Medal, Zoological Soc. 1989, Michael Faraday Award, Royal Soc. 1990, Nakayama Prize 1994, Int. Cosmos Prize 1997, Kistler Prize 2001, Bicentennial Kelvin Medal, Royal Soc. of Glasgow 2002, Shakespeare Prize for contribution to British Culture, Hamburg 2005, British Book Award for Author of the Year 2007. *Address:* University Museum of Natural History, Parks Road, Oxford, OX1 3PW, England (office). *E-mail:* simonyi.professor@oum.ox.ac.uk (office).

DAWNAY, Caroline Margaret; British literary agent; b. 22 Jan. 1950, Reading; d. of Oliver Dawnay and Margaret Boyle; one s. *Education:* St Mary's School, Wantage, Oxon., Univ. per Stranieri, Florence, Italy and Alliance Française, Paris. *Career:* Noel Gay Artists 1968–70, Michael Joseph publishers, London 1971–77; Dir A.D. Peters & Co. Ltd 1977–88, Peters Fraser & Dunlop Group Ltd (PFD) 1988–; Dir June Hall Literary Agency; Treas. Asscn of Authors' Agents 1991–94, Pres. 1994–97. *Address:* PFD, Drury House, 34–43 Russell Street, London, WC2B 3HA, England (office). *Telephone:* (20) 7344-1054 (office). *Fax:* (20) 7836-9539 (office). *E-mail:* jedelstein@pfd.co.uk (office). *Website:* www.pfd.co.uk (office).

DAWSON, Clay (see Levinson, Leonard)

DAWSON, Janet, BS, MA; American writer and fmr journalist; b. 31 Oct. 1949, Purcell, Oklahoma. *Education:* University of Colorado at Boulder, California State University at Hayward. *Career:* mem. MWA; Sisters in Crime; Private Eye Writers of America; American Crime Writers League; Authors' Guild; Mystery Readers International. *Publications:* Kindred Crimes, 1990; Till the Old Men Die, 1993; Take a Number, 1993; Don't Turn Your Back on the Ocean, 1994; Nobody's Child, 1995; A Credible Threat, 1996; Witness to Evil, 1997; Where the Bodies are Buried, 1998. Short Stories: By the Book; Little Red Corvette; Invisible Time; Witchcraft; Mrs Lincoln's Dilemma; What the Cat Dragged In. *Honours:* Award for Best First Private Eye Novel, St Martin's Press-Private Eye Writers Asscn, 1990. *Literary Agent:* Charlotte Sheedy Literary Agency, 65 Bleecker Street, 12th Floor, New York, NY 10012, USA.

DAWSON, Jill Dianne, BA, MA; British writer, poet, editor and teacher; b. 1962, Durham, England; pnr Meredith Bowles; two s. *Education:* Univ. of Nottingham, Sheffield Hallam Univ. *Career:* mem. Nat. Asscn of Writers in Education, Soc. of Authors. *Publications:* School Tales (ed.) 1990, How Do I Look? (non-fiction) 1991, Virago Book of Wicked Verse (ed.) 1992, Virago Book of Love Letters (ed.) 1994, Wild Ways (ed. with Margo Daly), White Fish with Painted Nails (poems) 1994, Trick of the Light (novel) 1996, Magpie (novel) 1998, Fred and Edie (novel) 2001, Gas & Air (ed. with Margo Daly), Wild Boy (novel) 2003, Watch Me Disappear 2006; contrib. to anthologies and periodicals. *Honours:* Eric Gregory Award 1992, second prize, London Writers Short Story Competition 1994, Blue Nose Poet of the Year 1995, London Arts Board New Writers 1998. *Literary Agent:* PFD, Drury House 34–43 Russell Street, London, WC2B 5HA, England. *Telephone:* (20) 7836-9539. *E-mail:* aelam@pfd.co.uk. *Website:* www.jilldawson.co.uk.

DAYAN, Yael; Israeli politician, writer and journalist; *Deputy Mayor of Tel-Aviv–Jaffa*; b. 12 Feb. 1939, Nahalal; d. of the late Gen. Moshe Dayan and of Ruth Dayan; m. Dov Sion; one s. one d. *Education:* Hebrew Univ. of Jerusalem Biology, Open Univ. of Israel. *Career:* Captain in Israeli Defense Forces Spokesman's Office; mem. (Labour Party) Knesset (Parl.) 1992–2003, founder and Chair. Cttee for the Advancement of the Status of Women, Chair. Sub-Cttee for Admin of the Occupied Territories; fmr mem. Cttee for Defence and Foreign Affairs, Cttee for Constitution, Law and Justice, Sub-Cttee for Gay and Lesbian Rights, Sub-Cttee for Violence Against Women; currently Deputy Mayor of Tel-Aviv–Jaffa (Mezet Party). *Publications include:* fiction: New Face in the Mirror 1959, Envy the Frightened 1961, Dust 1963, Death Had Two Sons 1967, Three Weeks in the Fall 1979; non-fiction: The Promised Land – Memoirs of Shmuel Dayan (ed.) 1961, A Soldier's Diary 1967, My Father, His Daughter 1985; political commentaries for Hebrew and foreign press. *Honours:* Bruno Kreisky Human Rights Award 1991, Olof Palme Award for Peace 1998, selected by L'Express magazine as one of 100 Women Who Make the World Move 1995, State of the World Forum's Women Redefining Leadership Award 1997. *Address:* Office of the Deputy Mayor, Rabin Square, Municipality of Tel-Aviv–Jaffa, Tel-Aviv (office); 10 Rupin Street, Tel-Aviv, Israel. *Telephone:* (3) 5218250 (office); (3) 5272611 (home). *Fax:* (3) 5216052 (office); (3) 5232004 (home). *E-mail:* yaeld@tel-aviv.gov.il (office); yael.d@banak.net.il (home).

DAYIOĞLU, Gülten; Turkish writer; b. 15 May 1935, Emet, Kütahya; d. of Lüftü and Emine Uyan; m. Ceudet Dayioğlu 1958; two s. *Education:* Atatürk

Girls' School, Istanbul and Istanbul Univ. *Career:* primary school teacher 1962–77; journalist, Cumhuriyet 1965–67, Milliyet 1967; writer from 1977, has written TV and radio plays, novels, short stories, travel books for children, series of children's books and research works on Turkish educ. system. *Publications include:* (titles in translation) adult fiction: Offspring (short stories, Yunus Nadi Story Award 1964–65), Those Left Behind (short stories), Back Home, Green Cherry (novel), Green Cherry II, The Eight Colour, Mo's Secret, Flowers of the Doomsday, Birds of the Twilight, Mystical Powers of Yada; children's books: Fadiş, Brothers and Sisters, Suna's Sparrows, When I Grow Up, Smart Fleas, Children of the Radiation Era, The Immortal Queen, A Bird flew Over the Danube, Purple Clouds in the Sky, Ganga, If Only the World Belonged to Children, They Were Four Siblings, The Stork in the Snow (Children's Literature Story Award, Arkin Bookstore 1974–75), The Beautiful Lady (Children's Literature Tale Award, Arkin Bookstore 1974–75), Gül The Bride (Story Award, Turkish Family Planning Foundation) 1987, Journey to the Back of the Mountain Kaf (Children's Literature Award, Ministry of Culture and Tourism) 1988, Mystery of the Parbat Mountain (İzmir Metropolitan Municipality Children's Novel Award) 1989, Trip to a Totally Different World: America 1990, Trip to The Country of Legends; China 1990, A Trip to the World of Kangaroos: Australia, The Eyes of the Midos Eagle (Altin Kitap Odülü Golden Books Award) 1991. *Address:* Nişantaşi Ihlamuryolu 45, Çatalkaya Apt Daire 9, 80200 Nişantaşi, Istanbul, Turkey. *Telephone:* (1) 1483087. *Fax:* (1) 1483087. *E-mail:* gulten@gultendayioglu.com. *Website:* www.gultendayioglu.com.

DÉ, Shobha; Indian writer and journalist; b. 7 Jan. 1948, Satara, India; m. 1st (divorced); m. 2nd Dilip Dé 1984; four d. two s. *Education:* Queen Mary's School, Bombay. *Career:* fmr model; later copy-writer; launched India's first gossip magazine Stardust; also launched magazines Society, Celebrity and TV soap-opera Swabhimaan 1995. *Publications include:* Socialite Evenings 1989, Strange Obsessions 1993, Shooting From the Hip: Selected Writings 1994, Snapshots 1995, Small Betrayals (short stories) 1995, Second Thoughts 1996, Selective Memory: Stories From My Life 1998; articles and columns in newspapers and magazines. *Address:* c/o Penguin Books India, 11 Community Centre, Panchsheel, Park, New Delhi 110017, India. *Telephone:* (11) 6494401. *Fax:* (11) 6494403.

DE ARAUGO, Sarah Therese (Tess); Australian writer; b. 26 May 1930, Lismore, Vic.; d. of Ivor O'Mullane and Rose Ryan; m. Maurice De Araugo 1950; two s. two d. *Education:* Notre Dame de Sion Coll., Warragal, Vic., Stotts Business Coll., Melbourne. *Career:* proprietor various businesses 1954–2002; Publisher, Rose Publishing House 1993–2002; mem. Australian Soc. of Authors, Fellowship of Australian Writers, Royal Historical Soc. of Victoria, Women Writers of Australia, Nepean Historical Soc. *Publications:* You Are What You Make Yourself To Be 1980, The Kurnai of Gippsland 1985, Boonorong on the Mornington Peninsula 1993, Dear Feathers 2000, Short Stories 1997–2005; contrib. to encyclopaedias and periodicals. *Honours:* New South Wales Premier's Award for Australian Literature 1985, Nat. Book Council Banjo Award in Australian Literature 1985, Australian Literature Bd Fellowship 1987, and writer's grant 1989, PEN Int. Short Story Award, Australia 1991. *Address:* 161 Sixth Avenue, Rosebud, Vic. 3939, Australia (home). *Telephone:* (59) 865632 (home).

DE BELOT, Jean Marie Louis, MA; French journalist and editor; *Editorial Director, Le Figaro*; b. 15 Dec. 1958, Neuilly-sur-Seine; s. of Philippe de Belot and Claude de Belot (née Vimal-Dessaignes); m. Frédérique Brunet 1983; two s. three d. *Education:* Univ. of Paris II-Panthéon Assas. *Career:* journalist, La Tribune de l'economie 1984; journalist then Chief Econ. Reporter, Le Figaro 1985, Chief Reporter, Expansion Group 1987, Chief of Financial Services 1990, Editorial Dir 2000–; Jt Chief Ed. Les Echos 1992, Chief Econ. Ed. 1998. *Address:* Le Figaro, 37 rue de Louvre, 75002 Paris, France (office). *Telephone:* (1) 42-21-62-00 (office). *Fax:* (1) 42-21-64-05 (office). *E-mail:* jde.belot@lefigaro.fr (office).

DE BENOIST, Alain, (Fabrice Laroche, Robert de Herte); French journalist, essayist and lecturer; b. 11 Dec. 1943, Saint-Symphorien; s. of Alain de Benoist and Germaine de Benoist (née Langouet); m. Doris M. Christians 1972; two s. *Education:* Lycées Montaigne et Louis-le-Grand, Paris, Sorbonne, Paris. *Career:* Ed.-in-Chief L'Observateur européen 1964–68, Nouvelle Ecole 1969–, Midi-France 1970–71; journalist, L'Echo de la presse et de la publicité 1968, Courrier de Paul Dehème 1969–76; critic, Valeurs actuelles and Spectacle du monde 1970–82, Figaro-Magazine 1977–92; Dir Krisis 1988–; mem. several socs, research groups, etc. *Publications:* Les Indo-Européens 1966, L'Empirisme logique et la Philosophie du Cercle de Vienne 1970, Avec ou sans Dieu 1970, Morale et Politique de Nietzsche 1974, Vu de droite: Anthologie critique des idées contemporaines 1977, Les Idées a l'endroit 1979, Guide pratique des prénoms 1980, Comment peut-on etre paien? 1981, Feter Noël 1982, Orientations pour des années décisives 1982, Traditions d'Europe 1983, Démocratie: Le problème 1985, Europe, Tiers monde, même combat 1986, Le Grain de sable 1994, La Ligne de mire 1995, L'Empire intérieur 1995, Céline et l'Allemagne 1996, Famille et société 1996, Ernst Jünger 1997, L'écume et les galets 2000, Dernière année 2002, Critiques-Théoriques 2003, Au-delà des droits de l'homme 2004, Bibliographie Carl Schmitt 2004, Bibliographie générale des droites françaises 2004–05; contribs to various publs. *Honours:* Grand prix de l'essai de l'Acad. française 1978. *Address:* 5 rue Carrière-Mainguet, 75011 Paris, France (office). *Telephone:* 1-40-24-25-11 (office). *Fax:* 1-40-24-25-11 (office). *E-mail:* alain.de.benoist@free.fr. *Website:* www.alaindebenoist.com.

DE BERNIÈRES, Louis, MA; British writer; b. (Louis Henry Piers de Bernière-Smart), 8 Dec. 1954, London; s. of Maj. Reginald Piers Alexander de Bernière-Smart. *Education:* Bradfield Coll., Berkshire, Univ. of Manchester, Leicester Polytechnic, Inst. of Educ., Univ. of London. *Career:* landscape gardener 1972–73; teacher and rancher, Colombia 1974; philosophy tutor 1977–79; car mechanic 1980; English teacher 1981–84; bookshop asst 1985–86; supply teacher 1986–93; mem. Antonius Players 2003–; mem. PEN. *Publications:* The War of Don Emmanuel's Nether Parts 1990, Señor Vivo and the Coca Lord 1991, The Troublesome Offspring of Cardinal Guzman 1992, Captain Corelli's Mandolin 1994, Labels 1997, The Book of Job 1999, Gunter Weber's Confession 2001, Sunday Morning at the Centre of the World 2001, Red Dog 2001, Birds Without Wings 2004; contrib. to Second Thoughts, Granta. *Honours:* Hon. Fellow, Trinity Coll. of Music; Dr hc (Univ. of East Anglia, Deree Univ. of Athens, Univ. of Aberdeen); Granta Best of Young British Novelists 1994, Author of the Year Award 1997, Whittaker Platinum Award, Millepages Prize for Best Foreign Novel (France) 2006. *Literary Agent:* Lavinia Trevor Agency, 7 The Glasshouse, 49A Goldhawk Road, London, W12 8QP, England. *Telephone:* (1986) 788665 (office).

DE BOISSIÈRE, Ralph Anthony Charles; Australian writer; b. 6 Oct. 1907, Port-of-Spain, Trinidad; m. Ivy Alcantara 1935; two d. *Publications:* Crown Jewel (novel) 1952, Calypso Isle (play) 1955, Rum and Coca-Cola (novel) 1956, No Saddles for Kangaroos (novel) 1964, The Call of the Rainbow (novel) 2007, Homeless in Paradise (novel) 2007, A Trinidadian Quartet 2006, Autobiography 2007. *Address:* 10 Vega Street, North Balwyn, Vic. 3104, Australia (home). *Telephone:* (3) 9859-5715 (home). *E-mail:* rdeboissiere@westnet.com.au (home).

DE BONO, Edward Francis Charles Publius, DPhil, PhD; British author and academic; b. 19 May 1933, s. of the late Prof. Joseph de Bono and of Josephine de Bono (née O'Byrne); m. Josephine Hall-White 1971; two s. *Education:* St Edward's Coll., Malta, Royal Univ. of Malta and Christ Church, Oxford. *Career:* Research Asst, Univ. of Oxford 1958–60, Jr Lecturer in Medicine 1960–61; Asst Dir of Research, Dept of Investigative Medicine, Univ. of Cambridge 1963–76, Lecturer in Medicine 1976–83; Dir Cognitive Research Trust, Cambridge 1971–; Sec.-Gen. Supranational Independent Thinking Org. 1983–; f. Edward de Bono Nonprofit Foundation; Chair. Council, Young Enterprise Europe 1998–; creator of two TV series: The Greatest Thinkers 1981, de Bono's Thinking Course 1982. *Publications:* The Use of Lateral Thinking 1967, The Five-Day Course in Thinking 1968, The Mechanism of Mind 1969, Lateral Thinking: A Textbook of Creativity 1970, The Dog Exercising Machine 1970, Technology Today 1971, Practical Thinking 1971, Lateral Thinking for Management 1971, Children Solve Problems 1972, Po: Beyond Yes and No 1972, Think Tank 1973, Eureka: A History of Inventions 1974, Teaching Thinking 1976, The Greatest Thinkers 1976, Wordpower 1977, The Happiness Purpose 1977, The Case of the Disappearing Elephant 1977, Opportunities: A Handbook of Business Opportunity Search 1978, Future Positive 1979, Atlas of Management Thinking 1981, de Bono's Thinking Course 1982, Conflicts: A Better Way to Resolve Them 1985, Six Thinking Hats 1985, Letter to Thinkers 1987, I Am Right You Are Wrong 1990, Positive Revolution for Brazil 1990, Six Action Shoes 1991, Serious Creativity 1992, Teach Your Child to Think 1992, Water Logic 1993, Parallel Thinking 1994, Teach Yourself to Think 1995, Mind Pack 1995, Edward de Bono's Textbook of Wisdom 1996, How to be More Interesting 1997, Simplicity 1998, New Thinking for the New Millennium 1999, Why I Want to be King of Australia 1999, The Book of Wisdom 2000, The de Bono Code 2000, H+ (Plus) A New Religion 2006, Tactics: The Art and Science of Success 2007, How to Have Creative Ideas 2007; numerous publs in Nature, Lancet, Clinical Science, American Journal of Physiology. *Honours:* Hon. Registrar St Thomas' Hosp. Medical School, Harvard Medical School; Hon. Consultant Boston City Hosp. 1965–66; planet DE73 named edebono after him. *Address:* Cranmer Hall, Fakenham, Norfolk, NR21 9HX, England (home); L2 Albany, Piccadilly, London, W1V 9RR. *Website:* www.edwarddebono.com (office).

DE BORTOLI, Ferruccio; Italian journalist; *CEO, Reslisi*; b. 20 May 1953, Milan; s. of Giovanni De Bortoli and Giancarla Soresini; m. Elisabetta Cordani 1982; one s. one d. *Education:* Univ. of Milan. *Career:* journalist 1973–; mem. editorial staff, Corriere d'Informazione 1975–78; Econs Corresp. Corriere della Sera 1978–85; Ed.-in-Chief, L'Europeo (magazine) 1985–86; Ed.-in-Chief, Econs Section, Corriere della Sera 1987–93; Deputy Ed. Corriere della Sera 1993–96, Ed. 1997–2003; CEO Reslisi 2003–; Pres. Flammarion 2003–. *Address:* Via Solferino 28, 20122 Milan (office); Via Donatello 36, 20131 Milan, Italy (home). *Telephone:* 0262827560 (office). *Fax:* 0229009705 (office). *E-mail:* fdebortoli@corriere.it (office). *Website:* www.corriere.it (office).

DE BOTTON, Alain; Swiss writer; b. 20 Dec. 1969, Zürich. *Education:* Gonville and Caius Coll., Cambridge. *Publications:* Essays in Love (aka On Love) 1993, The Romantic Movement: Sex, Shopping, and the Novel 1994, Kiss and Tell 1995, How Proust Can Change Your Life: Not a Novel 1997, The Consolations of Philosophy 2000, The Art of Travel (Charles Veillon European Essay Prize, Switzerland 2003) 2002, Status Anxiety 2004; The Architecture of Happiness 2006; contrib. articles, book and television reviews to various periodicals. *Honours:* Chevalier, Ordre des Arts et des Lettres 2003. *Literary Agent:* PFD, Drury House, 34–43 Russell Street, London, WC2B 5HA, England. *Telephone:* (20) 7344-1000. *Fax:* (20) 7352-7356. *E-mail:* cdawnay@pfd.co.uk. *Website:* www.pfd.co.uk. *Address:* 73 Sterndale Road, London, W14 OHU, England. *E-mail:* adb@netcomuk.co.uk. *Website:* www.alaindebotton.com.

DE BRUYN, Günter; German writer; b. 1 Nov. 1926, Berlin; one s. *Education:* studied in Berlin. *Career:* mem. Akademie der Künste, Berlin; Deutsche Akademie für Sprache und Dichtung e. v., Darmstadt. *Publications:* Der Hohlweg 1963, Buridans Esel 1968, Preisverleihung 1972, Das Leben des Jean Paul Richter 1975, Tristan und Isolde 1975, Märkische Forschungen: Erzahlung für Freunde der Literaturgeschichte 1978, Im Querschnitt 1979, Babylon 1980, Neue Herlichkeit 1984, Rahels erste Liebe: Rahel Levin und Karl Graf von Finckenstein in ihren Briefen 1985, Frauendienst 1986, Lesefreuden: Uber Bücher und Menschen 1986, Jubelschreie, Trauergesänge: Deutsche Befindlichkeiten 1991, Zwischenbilanz: Eine Jugen in Berlin 1992, Vierzig Jahre: Ein Lebensbericht 1996, Mein Brandenburg 1997, Die Finckensteins 1999, Preußens Luise 2000, Unter den Linden 2003. *Honours:* Heinrich Mann Prize 1965, Lion Feuchtwanger Prize 1980, Thomas Mann Prize 1990, Heinrich Böll Prize 1990, Grant Cross of Merit, Federal Republic of Germany 1994, Konrad Adenauer Foundation Prize for Literature 1996, two honorary doctorates. *Address:* Blabber 1, 15848 Tauche, Germany. *E-mail:* gdebruyn@web.de.

DE CUENCA Y CUENCA, Luis Alberto; Spanish philologist, poet, translator and writer; b. 1950, Madrid. *Education:* Universidad Autónoma de Madrid. *Career:* Prof. Philology Inst. of Council for Scientific Research, then Publs Dir; literary critic for several publs including El País; Dir Biblioteca Nacional (Nat. Library) 1996–2000; Premio Nacional de Literatura Infantil y Juvenil 1989. *Publications include:* El cantar de Valtario (trans. as The Song of Valtario), El héroe y sus máscaras (trans. as The Hero and his Masks). *Address:* c/o Biblioteca Nacional, Paseo de Recoletos 20, 28071 Madrid, Spain. *Telephone:* (1) 5807800. *Fax:* (1) 5775634.

DE GRASSE TYSON, Neil, BA, PhD; American astrophysicist and writer; b. New York, NY; m.; two c. *Education:* Bronx High School of Science, Univ. of Harvard, Columbia Univ. *Career:* full-time research scientist at Princeton Univ., NJ; essayist for Natural History magazine 1995–; part of cttee studying the future of the US Aerospace Industry 2001, and the Implementation of the US Space Exploration Policy 2004; currently Dir of Hayden Planetarium, NY; astrophysicist at American Museum of Natural History. *Publications include:* non-fiction: Merlin's Tour of the Universe 1989, Universe Down to Earth 1994, Just Visiting This Planet 1998, The Sky is Not the Limit: Adventures of an Urban Astrophysicist 2000, One Universe: at Home in the Cosmos 2000, Cosmic Horizons: Astronomy at the Cutting Edge (ed.) 2001, Origins: Fourteen billion years of cosmic evolution (with Donald Goldsmith) 2005. *Address:* Department of Astrophysics, American Museum of Natural History, Central Park West at 79th Street, New York, NY 10024, USA. *Telephone:* (212) 769-5912. *Fax:* (212) 769-5934. *E-mail:* tyson@amnh.org. *Website:* research.amnh.org/~tyson.

DE GROEN, Alma; New Zealand playwright and screenwriter; b. 1941, Foxton Beach; d. of Archibald Mathers and Eileen Mathers; m. Geoffrey De Groen (divorced); one d. *Career:* moved to Australia 1964; became playwright 1970; Writer-in-Residence, West Australia Inst. of Tech. 1986, Queensland Univ. 1989, Rollins Coll., Fla, USA 1989; dramaturg, Griffin Theatre Co. 1987. *Plays include:* The Joss Adams Show 1970, Perfectly All Right (aka Sweatproof Boy) 1972, The After-Life of Arthur Cravan 1973, Chidley 1977, Going Home 1976, Vocations (also screenplay) 1981, The Rivers of China 1986, The Girl Who Saw Everything 1991, The Woman in the Window 1999, Wicked Sisters 2003. *Television writing:* Man of Letters (ABC) 1985, Singles, After Marcuse (ABC), Rafferty's Rules: The Women (Channel 7) 1988. *Radio writing:* Available Light (ABC) 1991, Stories in the Dark (with Ian D. MacKenzie). *Honours:* Australian Writers' Guild Award for Best TV Adaptation 1985, for Best Stage Play 1993, Premier's Literary Award for Drama in New South Wales and Victoria 1988, Patrick White Literary Award 1998. *Literary Agent:* c/o RGM Associates, PO Box 128, Surry Hills, NSW 2010, Australia. *Telephone:* (2) 9281-3911. *Fax:* (2) 9281-4705. *E-mail:* info@rgm.com.au. *Website:* www.rgm.com.au.

DE GROOT, Albert; Dutch publisher; b. 3 May 1945, Rotterdam; s. of Albertus A. De Groot and Cornelia A. Hess; m. Janetta C. Pasman 1964; one s. one d. *Career:* no formal educ.; Production Man. Rotterdam Univ. Press 1963, Sales Man. 1967; Ed., Elsevier Nederland 1969, Ed.-in-Chief 1972, Vice-Man. 1974; Man. Dir Veen, Luitingh-Sijthoff, Kosmos, Contact 1979, Uitgeverij L. J. Veen BV; now Dir Veen Uitgevers Groep. *Address:* Veen Uitgevers Groep, St Jacobsstraat 125, PO Box 14095, 3508 SC Utrecht, Netherlands.

DE GRUCHY, John Wesley, BA, BD, MTh, DTh, DSocSci; South African academic, writer and editor; *Professor Emeritus of Christian Studies, University of Cape Town;* b. 18 March 1939, Pretoria; m. Isobel Dunstan; two s. one d. *Education:* Rhodes Univ., Chicago Theological Seminary, Univ. of S Africa, Univ. of Cape Town. *Career:* ordained Minister, United Congregational Church 1961; Pastor, Durban, 1961–68, Johannesburg 1968–73; Dir S African Council of Churches, 1968–73; Lecturer, Univ. of Cape Town 1973–75, Sr Lecturer 1975–80, Assoc. Prof. 1980–86, Robert Selby Taylor Prof. of Christian Studies 1986–2004, Prof. Emer. 2004–, Dir Grad. School in Humanities 2000–03, Sr Research Scholar 2003–; Founder-Ed. Journal of Theology for Southern Africa 1973–; Pres. United Congregational Church 1980–81. *Publications:* The Church Struggle in South Africa 1979, Apartheid is a Heresy (co-ed. with Charles Villa-Vicencio) 1983, Bonhoeffer and South Africa 1985, Resistance and Hope: South African Essays in Honour of Beyers Naude (co-ed. with Charles Villa-Vicencio) 1985, Cry Justice! Prayers, Meditations, and Readings from South Africa 1986, Theology and Ministry in Context and Crisis: A South African Perspective 1987, Dietrich Bonhoeffer: Witness to Jesus Christ 1987, Reinhold Niebuhr (co-ed. with Larry Rasmussen) 1988, Karl Barth: Theologian of Freedom (co-ed. with Clifford Green) 1989, Karl Rahner: Theologian of the Graced Search for Meaning (co-ed. with Geoffrey Kelly) 1989, Adolf von Harnack: Liberal Theology at Its Height (co-ed. with H. Martin Rumscheidt) 1989, A Southern African Guide to World Religions (co-ed. with Martin Prozesky) 1991, In Word and in Deed: Towards a Practical Theology of Social Transformation: A Framework for Reflection and Training (with Jim Cochrane and Robin Petersen) 1991, Liberating Reformed Theology: A South African Contribution to an Ecumenical Debate 1991, Doing Ethics in Context: South African Perspectives (co-ed. with Charles Villa-Vicencio) 1994, Religion and the Reconstuction of Civil Society (co-ed. with Stephen Martin) 1995, Living Faiths in South Africa (co-ed. with Martin Prozesky) 1995, Christianity and Democracy 1995, Bonhoeffer for a New Day: Theology in a Time of Transition (co-ed.) 1997, The Cambridge Companion to Dietrich Bonhoeffer 1999, Facing the Truth: South African Faith Communities and the Truth and Reconciliation Commission (co-ed. with Jim Cochrane and Stephen Martin) 1999, The London Missionary Society in Southern Africa: Historical Essays in Celebration of the Bicentenary of the LMS in Southern Africa, 1799–1999 (co-ed.) 2000, Christianity, Art, and Transformation 2001, Reconciliation (monograph) 2002; contribs to scholarly journals. *Honours:* Hon. DLitt (Chicago Theological Seminary) 2002, (Rhodes Univ.) 2004. *Address:* Research Office, University of Cape Town, Post Bag Rondebosch 7701, Cape Town (office); PO Box 130, Hermanus 7200, South Africa (home). *Telephone:* (28) 3130844 (home). *Fax:* (28) 3130844 (home). *E-mail:* jwdeg@global.co.za (home).

DE KRETSER, Michelle, MA; Australian writer; b. Colombo, Sri Lanka. *Education:* Melbourne Univ., Univ. of the Sorbonne, Paris. *Career:* moved to Australia aged 14; fmrly teacher in Montpellier, ed. for Lonely Planet, freelance ed. *Publications:* fiction: The Rose Grower 1999, The Hamilton Case (Commonwealth Writers Prize, SE Asia and South Pacific Region 2004) 2003; editor: Brief Encounters: Stories of Love, Sex and Travel 1998. *Address:* c/o Random House Australia, 20 Alfred Street, Milson's Point, NSW 2061, Australia.

DE LA BILLIÈRE, Gen. Sir Peter (Edgar de la Cour), Kt, KCB, KBE, DSO, MC, DL; British army officer (retd) and banker (retd); b. 29 April 1934, Plymouth; s. of Surgeon Lt-Commdr Claude Dennis Delacour de Labillière and Frances Christing Wright Lawley; m. Bridget Constance Muriel Goode 1965; one s. two d. *Education:* Harrow School, Staff Coll., Royal Coll. of Defence Studies. *Career:* joined King's Shropshire Light Infantry 1952; commissioned, Durham Light Infantry; served Japan, Korea, Malaya (despatches 1959), Jordan, Borneo, Egypt, Aden, Gulf States, Sudan, Oman, Falkland Islands; Commdg Officer, 22 Special Air Service (SAS) Regt 1972–74; Gen. Staff Officer 1 (Directing Staff), Staff Coll. 1974–77; Commdr British Army Training Team, Sudan 1977–78; Dir SAS and Commdr SAS Group 1978–83; Commdr British Forces, Falkland Islands and Mil. Commr 1984–85; Gen. Officer Commdg Wales 1985–87; Col Comdt. Light Div. 1986–90; Lt-Gen. Officer commanding SE Dist 1987–90; Commdr British Forces in Middle East Oct. 1990–91; rank of Gen. 1991 after Gulf War, Ministry of Defence Adviser on Middle East 1991–92; retd from army June 1992; Pres. SAS Asscn 1991–96, Army Cadet Force 1992–99; mem. Council Royal United Services Inst. 1975–77; Chair. Jt Services Hang Gliding 1986–88; Cdre Army Sailing Asscn 1989–90; Commr Duke of York's School 1988–90; Freeman City of London 1991; Hon. Freeman Fishmongers' Co. 1991; Pres. Harrow School Asscn 2002–; Trustee Imperial War Museum 1992–99; Dir (non-exec.), Middle East and Defence Adviser, Robert Fleming Holdings 1992–99; Chair. Meadowland Meats 1994–2002; Jt Chair. Dirs FARM Africa 1995–2001 (mem. Bd 1992–2001); DL Hereford and Worcester 1993; Trustee Naval and Mil. Club 1999–2003, mem. Bd 1999–2003; Pres. Friends of Imperial War Museum 2003; Pres. Harrow Asscn 2002–. *Television:* Discovery: Clash of the Generals 2004. *Publications:* Storm Command: a personal story of the Gulf War 1992, Looking for Trouble (autobiog.) 1994, Supreme Courage: Heroic Stories from 150 Years of the Victoria Cross 2004. *Honours:* Hon. DSc (Cranfield) 1992; Hon. DCL (Durham) 1993; Legion of Merit Chief Commdr (USA), Order of Abdul Aziz 2nd Class (Saudi Arabia), Meritorious Service Cross (Canada), Kuwait Decoration of the First Class, Order of Qatar Sash of Merit.

DE LA MARTINIÈRE, Hervé; French publisher; *President and CEO, Groupe La Martinière. Career:* fmrly in sales, Hachette; fmr Ed., Hachette Littérature, Hachette-Réalités, Nathan; f. Editions La Martinière 1992–, currently Pres. and CEO Groupe La Martinière; CEO Editions du Seuil 2005–06. *Address:* 2 rue Christine, 75006, Paris, France. *Telephone:* 1-40-51-52-00. *Fax:* 1-40-51-52-05. *Website:* www.lamartiniere.fr.

DE LANGE, Nicholas Robert Michael, DPhil, PhD, DD; British scholar and translator; b. 7 Aug. 1944, Nottingham, England. *Education:* Christ Church, Oxford, Univ. of Cambridge. *Career:* Fellow, Wolfson Coll., Cambridge; mem. British Asscn of Jewish Studies, Soc. of Authors, Translation Asscn. *Publications:* Apocrypha 1978, Atlas of the Jewish World 1984, Judaism 1986, Illustrated History of the Jewish People 1997, An Introduction to Judaism 2000, Ignaz Maybaum: A Reader 2001; many trans.; contrib. to Tel-Aviv Review, Jerusalem Review. *Honours:* George Webber Prize for Trans. 1990, TLS/Porjes Prize for Trans. 2001, 2004. *Address:* Faculty of Divinity, West Road, Cambridge, CB3 9BS, England (office). *E-mail:* nrml1@cam.ac.uk (office).

DE LINT, Charles Henri Diederick Hoefsmit, (Samuel M. Key); Canadian writer, musician and artist; b. 22 Dec. 1951, Bussum, The Netherlands; m. MaryAnn Harris 1980. *Career:* owner and Ed., Triskell Press; writer-in-residence, Ottawa and Gloucester Public Libraries 1995; mem. SFWA, Science Fiction Writers of Canada. *Publications:* De Grijze Roos 1983, The Riddle of the Wren 1984, Moonheart: A Romance 1984, The Harp of the Grey Rose 1985, Mulengro: A Romany Tale 1985, Yarrow: An Autumn Tale 1986, Ascian in Rose 1987, Jack the Giant-Killer (Canadian SF/Fantasy Award for Best Work in English 1988) 1987, Greenmantle 1988, Wolf Moon 1988, Svaha 1989, The Valley of Thunder (Philip José Farmer's The Dungeon Vol. 3) 1989, Berlin 1989, Westlin Wind 1989, The Hidden City (Philip José Farmer's The Dungeon Vol. 5) 1990, The Fair in Emain Macha 1990, Drink Down the Moon 1990, Ghostwood 1990, Angel of Darkness (as Samuel M. Key) 1990, The Dreaming Place 1990, The Little Country (New York Public Library's Best Books for the Teen Age 1992, Homer Award for Best Fantasy Novel 1992) 1991, Uncle Dobbin's Parrot Fair 1991, Ghosts of Wind and Shadow 1991, Death Leaves an Echo 1991, Hedgework and Guessery 1991, Our Lady of the Harbour 1991, Paperjack 1991, Spiritwalk 1992, Merlin Dreams in the Mondream Wood 1992, From a Whisper to a Scream (as Samuel M. Key) 1992, I'll Be Watching You (as Samuel M. Key) 1992, Dreams Underfoot 1993, The Wishing Well 1993, Into the Green 1993, The Wild Wood 1994, Memory & Dream 1994, The Ivory and the Horn 1995, Jack of Kinrowan (YALSA Popular Paperbacks for Young Adults 2003) 1997, Trader (YALSA Best Books for Young Adults 1999) 1997, Someplace to be Flying 1998, Moonlight and Vines (World Fantasy Award for Best Collection 2000) 1999, The Newford Stories 1999, The Buffalo Man 1999, Forests of the Heart 2000, Triskell Tales 2000, The Road to Lisdoonvarna 2001, The Onion Girl 2001, Seven Wild Sisters (YALSA Best Books for Young Adults 2003) 2002, Waifs and Strays 2002, Tapping the Dream Tree 2002, A Circle of Cats 2003, A Handful of Coppers 2003, Spirits in the Wires 2003, Refinerytown 2003, Medicine Road 2004, The Blue Girl (YALSA Best Books for Young Adults 2005, Ontario Library Asscn White Pine Award for Best Canadian young adult fiction 2006, Great Lakes Great Books Award 2007) 2004, Quicksilver & Shadow 2005, The Hour Before Dawn 2005, Make A Joyful Noise 2006, Triskell Tales 2 2006, Widdershins 2006, Promises to Keep 2007, Old Man Crow 2007, Little (Grrl) Lost 2007. *Honours:* Small Press and Artists Organization Award for Fiction 1982, Int. Asscn for the Fantastic in the Arts William L. Crawford Award for Best New Fantasy Author 1984, Readercon Small Press Award for Best Short Work 1989, Reality 1 Commendations Best Fantasy Author Award (for The Drowned Man's Reel) 1991, Prix Ozone for Best Foreign Fantasy Short Story (for Timeskip) 1997. *Address:* PO Box 9480, Ottawa, ON K1G 3V2, Canada (office). *E-mail:* cdl@cyberus.ca (office). *Website:* www.charlesdelint.com.

DE LUCA, Erri; Italian writer and journalist; b. 1950, Naples. *Career:* self-taught ancient Hebrew, has translated several sections of the Bible. *Publications:* Non ora, non qui 1989, Variazioni sopra una nota sola – Lettere a Francesca 1990, Una nuvola come tappeto 1991, Aceto, arcobaleno 1993, In alto a sinistra 1994, Pianoterra 1995, Ora prima 1997, Alzaia 1997, Tu, mio 1999, L'urgenza della libertà 1999, Cattività 1999, Tre cavalli 2000, Un papavero rosso all'occhiello senza coglierne il fiore 2000, Elogio del massimo timore 2000, Altre prove di risposta 2000, Montedidio (Prix Femina étranger 2003) 2001, Lettere da una città bruciata 2002, Opera sull'acqua e altre poesie (poems) 2002, Nocciolo d'oliva 2002, L'ultimo viaggio di Sindbad 2003, Il contrario di uno 2003, Immanifestazione 2003, Mestieri all'aria aperta 2004, Morso di luna nuova (written in Neapolitan dialect) 2004, Precipitazioni 2004, Solo andata. Righe che vanno troppo spesso a capo (poems) 2005, Chisciottimista 2005, Sulla traccia di Nives 2005. *Address:* c/o Giangiacomo Feltrinelli Editore s.r.l., via Andegari 6, 20121 Milan, Italy. *E-mail:* scrivimi@feltrinelli.it.

DE MADARIAGA, Isabel, PhD, FBA, FRHistS; British academic; *Professor Emerita of Russian Studies, School of Slavonic and East European Studies, University of London*; b. 27 Aug. 1919, Glasgow, Scotland; d. of Salvador de Madariaga and Constance Archibald; m. Leonard B. Schapiro 1943 (divorced 1976). *Education:* Ecole Internationale, Geneva, Switzerland, Headington School for Girls, Oxford, Instituto Escuela, Madrid, Univ. of London. *Career:* BBC Monitoring Service 1940–43; Cen. Office of Information London 1943–47; Econ. Information Unit, Treasury 1947–48; Editorial Asst, Slavonic and East European Review 1951–64; Part-time Lecturer in History, LSE 1953–66; Lecturer in History, Univ. of Sussex 1966–68; Sr Lecturer in Russian History, Univ. of Lancaster 1968–71; Reader in Russian Studies, School of Slavonic and East European Studies, Univ. of London 1971–81, Prof. 1981–84, Prof. Emer. 1984–; Corresp. mem. Royal Spanish Acad. of History. *Publications:* Britain, Russia and the Armed Neutrality of 1780 1963, Opposition (with G. Ionescu) 1965, Russia in the Age of Catherine the Great 1981, Catherine II: A Short History 1990, Politics and Culture in Eighteenth-Century Russia 1998, Ivan the Terrible 2005; books translated into many languages including Turkish and Russian; many scholarly articles. *Address:* 25 Southwood Lawn Road, London, N6 5SD, England (home). *Telephone:* (20) 8341-0862 (home).

DE MOOR, Margriet; Dutch novelist; b. 21 Nov. 1941. *Career:* fmr singer; started writing 1988. *Publications:* Op de rug gezien (short stories, trans. as Seen From Behind) 1988, Dubbelportret (short stories, trans. as Double Portrait) 1989, Eerst grijs dan wit dan blauw (novel, trans. as First Grey Then White Then Blue) (Ako Literature Prize) 1991, De virtuoos (novel, trans. as The Virtuoso) 1993, Ik droom dus (short stories) 1995, Hertog van Egypte (novel, trans. as The Duke of Egypt) 1996, Zee-Binnen (novel, trans. as Sea Island) 1999, Verzamelde verhalen (collection) 2000, Kreutzersonate (novel, trans. as The Kreutzer Sonata) 2005. *Honours:* Lucy B. and C. W. van der Hoogt Prize 1990. *Address:* c/o Pan MacMillan Ltd, 20 New Wharf Road, London, N1 9RR, England.

DE NAPOLI, Francesco, DScS; Italian writer, poet and librarian; b. 15 June 1954, Potenza; m. Assunta Cardile 1987; two d. *Career:* Dir, Istituto 'A. Labriola', Cassino; Pres. Giuria Premio Letterario Internazionale 'Succisa Virescit'. *Publications:* poetry: Noùmeno e realtà 1979, Fernfahrplan 1980, La dinamica degli eventi 1983, L'attesa 1987, Il pane di Siviglia 1989, Urna d'amore 1992, Dialogo serale 1993, Poesie per Urbino 1996, Nel tempo a Zenja 1998, Carte da gioco 1999, La Casa del Porto 2002, La dimensione del noùmeno 2003; contrib. to anthologies: Dossier poesia 1993, Poeti di Paideia 1994, Ciò che non siamo. Omaggio a Eugenio Montale nel centenario della nascita 1996, Il fiore del deserto 1998, Ritmo Cassinese 2000, Rocco Scotellaro Oltre il Sud 2003; prose: Contagi 1990, Banalità 1994, Animatore d'ombre 1996, Giogo/forza 2000; essay collections: La letteratura di protesta del Novecento in Europa e in America 1990, Breve profilo della poesia Italiana del secondo Novecento 1993, Del mito, del simbolo e d'altro. Cesare Pavese e il suo tempo 2000, Graffiti poetici 2000, Evgenij Evtushenko cantore dei mali del mondo 2002, Per una cultura del libro 2003; contrib. to various publications. *Honours:* Hon. PhD (Paris) 1994, (Massachusetts) 1995; Hon. Prof. of Italian Literature, Brussels 1993; Premio Città di Valletta, Premio David, Premio Albatros, Premio Cultura della Presidenza del Consiglio dei Ministri 1982, Premio Monferrato 1982, Premio Firenze Capitale Europea della Cultura 1986, Premio Casentino 1990, Premio Goffredo Parise 1998, Premio Luci de Ciociaria 1998, Premio Eugenio Montale 1998. *Address:* Via Belvedere 21, Località Foresta, 03044 Cervaro (FR), Italy (home). *E-mail:* fdenapoli@libero.it (home). *Website:* www.francescodenapoli.it.

DE PALCHI, Alfredo; Italian poet and editor; b. 13 Dec. 1926, Verona; m. 1st Sonia Raiziss 1952 (deceased); one d.; m. 2nd Rita Di Pace 1988. *Career:* Ed., Chelsea Publications Inc. *Publications:* Modern European Poetry, Italian section (co-ed.), 1966; Sessioni con l'analista (poems), 1967, in English as Sessions with My Analyst, 1970; Mutazioni (poems), 1988; The Scorpion's Dark Dance (poems), 1993; Costellazione Anonima (poems), 1998, in English as Anonymous Constellation, 1997; The Metaphysical Streetcar Conductor: Sixty Poems by Luciano Erba, 1998; Addictive Aversions (poems), 1999; Paradigma (poems), 2001, Paradigma, Tutte le poesie: 1947–2005 (poems) 2006. *Honours:* Premio Nazionale di Poesia, Città di S. Vito al Tagliamento 1988. *Address:* 33 Union Square W, New York, NY 10003, USA.

DE POSADAS, Carmen; Uruguayan writer; b. 13 Aug. 1953, Montevideo; d. of Luis de Posadas and Sara de Posadas; m. 1st (divorced); two d.; m. 2nd Mariano Rubio (died 1979). *Education:* British Schools in Uruguay and Madrid, Spain and St Julian's Convent, Oxford, UK. *Publications include:* Mr North Wind (Ministry of Culture Prize) 1984, Cinco moscas azules 1996, Liliana Broja 1997 (Special Mention, Bologna Fook Fair), Nada es lo que parece 1997, Pequeñas Infamias (Planeta Prize) 1998, Un verano llamado amor 1999, La Belle Oleo (biog.), The Good Servant (novel); 20 works for children, two screenplays; works translated into 22 languages including Japanese. *Address:* c/o Editorial Planeta, Jovellanos No. 5, 280141 Madrid, Spain. *Telephone:* (91) 5213860. *Fax:* (91) 5217190. *E-mail:* visiortega@hotmail.com.

DE RIVOYRE, Christine Berthe Claude Denis, LèsL; French writer and journalist; b. 29 Nov. 1921, Tarbes, Hautes-Pyrénées; d. of François de Rivoyre and Madeleine Ballande. *Education:* Instituts du Sacré-Coeur of Bordeaux and Poitiers, Faculté des Lettres de Paris and School of Journalism, Syracuse Univ., NY, USA. *Career:* journalist with Le Monde 1950–55; Literary Ed. of Marie-Claire 1955–65; mem. Haut comité de la langue française 1969–, Jury of Prix Médicis 1970–. *Publications:* L'alouette au miroir 1956, La mandarine 1957, La tête en fleurs 1960, La glace à l'ananas 1962, Les sultans 1964, Le petit matin (Prix Interallié 1968) 1968, Le seigneur des chevaux (with Alexander Kalda) 1969, Fleur d'agonie 1970, Boy (Prix des Trois Couronnes 1973) 1973, Le voyage à l'envers 1977, Belle alliance 1982, Reine-mère 1985, Crépuscule taille unique 1989, Racontez-moi les flamboyants 1995. *Honours:* Officier, Légion d'honneur; Officier, Ordre des Arts et des Lettres; Grand Prix de la ville de Bordeaux 1973, Grand Prix littéraire Prince Rainier de Monaco 1982, Prix Paul Morand 1984, Prix Saint-Simon 1995. *Address:* c/o Editions Grasset, 61 rue des Saints-Péres, 75006 Paris (office); Onesse-Laharie, 40110 Morcenx, France.

DE ROO, Anne Louise, BA; New Zealand writer; b. 1931, Gore. *Education:* University of Canterbury, Christchurch. *Publications:* Children's Fiction: The Gold Dog, 1969; Moa Valley, 1969; Boy and the Sea Beast, 1971; Cinnamon and Nutmeg, 1972; Mick's Country Cousins, 1974; Scrub Fire, 1977; Traveller, 1979; Because of Rosie, 1980; Jacky Nobody, 1983; The Bat's Nest, 1986; Friend Troll, Friend Taniwha, 1986; Mouse Talk, 1990; The Good Cat, 1990; Hepzibah Mouse's ABC, 1991; Sergeant Sal, 1991; Hepzibah's Book of Famous Mice, 1993. Fiction: Hope Our Daughter, 1990; Becoming Fully Human, 1991; And We Beheld His Glory, 1994. Plays: The Dragon Master, 1978; The Silver Blunderbuss, 1984. *Honours:* ICI bursary 1981.

DE SOUZA, Carl; Mauritian writer; b. 1949, Rose Hill. *Education:* Royal Coll., Port Louis, Royal Coll., Curepipe and Univ. of London. *Career:* teacher, St Esprit Coll. –1995; Rector St Mary's Coll., Rose Hill 1995–; played badminton for nat. team, later becoming man. of nat. team; fmr Pres.

Mauritius Badminton Fed. and Sec.-Gen. African Badminton Fed. *Publications:* novels: Le Sang de l'Anglais (Prix de l'ACCT) 1993, La Maison qui marchait vers la large (Prix des Mascareignes) 1996, Les Jours Kaya 2000, Ceux qu'on jette à la mer 2001; short stories: La Comète de Halley (Prix Pierre Renaud) 1986, Le Raccourci 1993. *Honours:* Chevalier, Ordre des Arts et des Lettres. *Address:* c/o Editions de l'Olivier, 27 rue Jacob, Paris 75006, France (office).

DE SOUZA, Eunice, BA, PhD; Indian poet and writer; b. 1 Aug. 1940, Poona. *Education:* Univ. of Mumbai. *Career:* Reader in English 1969–, Head Dept of English 1990–, St Xavier's Coll., Mumbai. *Publications:* Folk Tales from Gujarat 1975, Himalayan Tales 1978, Fix 1979, Women in Dutch Painting 1988, Ways of Belonging: Selected Poems 1990, Selected and New Poems 1994, Nine Indian Women Poets (ed.) 1997, Talking Poems 1999, Women's Voices (with Lindsay Pereira) 2002, Purdah 2004; several children's books. *Honours:* Poetry Book Soc. Recommendation 1990. *Address:* c/o Department of English, St Xavier's College, Mumbai 400 001, India.

DE WAARD, Elly; Dutch poet; b. 8 Sept. 1940, Bergen. *Education:* Murmellius Gymnasium, Alkmaar and Univ. of Amsterdam. *Career:* teacher of poetry at Amazone 1983–; Founder-mem. Anna Bijns Foundation and Anna Bijns Prijs (prize for women writers) 1985, De Nieuwe Wilden (The New Wild Ones, group of young female poets) 1988. *Publications:* Afstand (Distance) 1978, Luwte (Shelter) 1979, Furie (Fury) 1981, Strofen 1983, Een wildernis van verbindingen 1986, Onvoltooiing 1988, Eenzang 1992, Anderling 1998, Zestig 2000, Van cadmium lekken de bossen 2001. *Address:* Vogelwater, Staringweg, 1935 MZ, Egmond-Binnen, Castricum, Netherlands.

DE WEESE, Thomas Eugene (Gene), (Jean DeWeese, Thomas Stratton, Victoria Thomas); American writer; b. 31 Jan. 1934, Rochester, IN; m. Beverly Amers 1955. *Education:* Valparaiso Technical Institute, IN, Indiana University, Kokomo, University of Wisconsin, Milwaukee, Marquette University, Milwaukee. *Publications:* Fiction: Jeremy Case, 1976; The Wanting Factor, 1980; A Different Darkness, 1982; Something Answered, 1983; Chain of Attack, 1987; The Peacekeepers, 1988; The Final Nexus, 1988; Renegade, 1991; Into the Nebula, 1995; King of the Dead, 1996; Lord of the Necropolis, 1997. (Wth Robert Coulson): The Invisibility Affair, 1967; The Mind-Twisters Affair, 1967; Gates of the Universe, 1975; Now You See It/Him/Them. . ., 1976; Charles Fort Never Mentioned Wombats, 1977; Nightmare Universe, 1985.(As Jean DeWeese): The Reimann Curse, 1975; The Moonstone Spirit, 1975; The Carnelian Cat, 1975; Cave of the Moaning Wind, 1976; Web of Guilt, 1976; The Doll With Opal Eyes, 1976; Nightmare in Pewter, 1978; Hour of the Cat, 1980; The Backhoe Gothic, 1981. (As Victoria Thomas): Ginger's Wish (with Connie Kugi), 1987. Other: Black Suits From Outer Space; several other science fiction novels for children. Non-Fiction: Fundamentals of Space Navigation, 1968; Fundamentals of Digital Computers, 1972; Fundamentals of Integrated Circuits, 1972; Making American Folk Art Dolls (with Gini Rogowski), 1975; Computers in Entertainment and the Arts, 1984. Contributions: anthologies and magazines. *Honours:* Best Novel Awards, 1976, 1982, Best Juvenile Book Award, 1979, Council for Wisconsin Writers; Notable Science Book of the Year, NSTA, 1984. *Address:* 2718 N Prospect, Milwaukee, WI 53211, USA.

DEAMBROSIS, Mercedes; Spanish/Greek novelist; b. 1 Oct. 1955, Madrid, Spain. *Publications include:* Milagrosa (novel) 2002. *Address:* c/o Dedalus Ltd, Langford Lodge, St Judith's Lane, Sawtry, Cambridgeshire PE28 5XE, England. *E-mail:* info@dedalusbooks.com. *Website:* www.dedalusbooks.com.

DEAN, Winton Basil, MA, FBA; British musicologist and author; b. 18 March 1916, Birkenhead; s. of Basil Dean and Esther (née Van Gruisen) Dean; m. Hon. Thalia Mary Shaw 1939 (died 2000); one s. (two d. deceased) one adopted d. *Education:* Harrow, King's Coll., Cambridge. *Career:* mem. Music Panel, Arts Council of GB 1957–60; Ernest Bloch Prof. of Music, Univ. of Calif., Berkeley, USA 1965–66, Regent's Lecturer 1977; mem. Council, Royal Musical Asscn 1965–98 (Vice-Pres. 1970–98, Hon. mem. 1998–); mem. Vorstand, GF Händel-Gesellschaft, Halle 1980– (Vice-Pres. 1991–99, Hon. mem. 1999), Kuratorium, Göttinger Händel-Gesellschaft 1982–97, Hon. mem. 1997–; Hon. mem. RAM; Corresp. mem. American Musicological Soc. *Publications:* Bizet 1948, Carmen 1949, Handel's Dramatic Oratorios and Masques 1959, Shakespeare and Opera 1964, Georges Bizet, his Life and Work 1965, Handel and the Opera Seria 1969, The New Grove Handel 1982, Handel's Operas 1704–1726 (with J. M. Knapp) 1987, Essays on Opera 1990, (co-ed.) Handel's Opera Giulio Cesare in Egitto 1999, Handel's Operas 1726–1741 2007; maj. contribs to New Oxford History of Music, vol. VIII 1982 and Grove's Dictionary of Music and Musicians, 5th and 6th edns 1954, 1980. *Honours:* Hon. MusDoc (Cambridge) 1996; City of Halle Handel Prize 1995. *Address:* Hambledon Hurst, Godalming, Surrey GU8 4HF, England (home). *Telephone:* (1428) 682644 (home). *E-mail:* dean584@aol.com (home).

DEANE, John F.; Irish poet, writer and translator; b. 1943, Achill Island, Co. Mayo. *Education:* Mungret and Univ. Coll. Dublin. *Career:* teacher; re-founded Poetry Ireland and Poetry Ireland Review 1979; Ed., The Dedalus Press. *Publications:* poetry: Stalking After Time 1977, High Sacrifice 1981, Winter in Meath 1984, Road with Cypress and Star 1988, The Stylized City: Selected and New Poems 1991, Walking on Water 1994, Toccata and Fugue 2001, Manhandling the Deity 2003; novels: One Man's Place 1994, Flightlines 1996, Undertow 2002; short story collections: Free Range 1994, The Coffin Master and Other Stories 2000; translator of works by Marin Sorescu, Tomas Tranströmer and Jacques Rancourt. *Honours:* Robert Penn Warren Prize 2000, Howard Nemerov Sonnet Award 2001, Firman Houghton Award 2002, Robert Frost Award 2002, New Criterion Poetry Prize 2004. *Address:* The Dedalus Press, 24 The Heath, Cypress Downs, Dublin, 6W, Ireland. *Fax:* (353) 1 490 2582. *E-mail:* deanejohn@hotmail.com. *Website:* homepage.tinet.ie/~johndeane/.

DEANE, Seamus Francis, PhD; Irish professor of English and American literature; b. 9 Feb. 1940, s. of Winifred Deane and Frank Deane; m. Marion Treacy 1963; three s. one d. *Education:* Queen's Univ., Belfast, Univ. of Cambridge. *Career:* Fulbright and Woodrow Wilson Scholar, Visiting Lecturer, Reed Coll., Portland, Ore. 1966–67; Visiting Lecturer, Univ. of Calif., Berkeley 1967–68, Visiting Prof. 1978; Lecturer, Univ. Coll., Dublin 1968–77, Sr Lecturer 1978–80, Prof. of English and American Literature 1980–93; Visiting Prof., Univ. of Notre Dame, Indiana 1977, Keough Prof. of Irish Studies 1993–; Walker Ames Prof., Univ. of Washington, Seattle 1987, Jules Benedict Distinguished Visiting Prof., Carleton Coll., Minn. 1988; Dir Field Day Theatre Co. 1980–; mem. Royal Irish Acad. 1982. *Publications:* Celtic Revivals 1985, Short History of Irish Literature 1986, Selected Poems 1988, The French Revolution and Enlightenment in England 1789–1832 1988, Field Day Anthology of Irish Writing 550–1990 1991, Reading in the Dark 1996, Strange Country 1997, Foreign Affections: Essays on Edmund Burke 2005. *Honours:* Hon. DLitt (Ulster) 1999; AE Memorial Award for Literature 1972; Ireland/America Fund Literary Award 1988; Guardian Fiction Prize 1996; Irish Times Int. Fiction Prize 1997, Irish Times Irish Literature Prize 1997; Ruffino Antico Fattore Int. Literary Award (Florence, Italy) 1998. *Address:* Institute of Irish Studies, 1145 Flanner Hall, University of Notre Dame, IN 46556, USA.

DEAR, Nick, BA; British playwright; b. 11 June 1955, Portsmouth, England; partner, Penny Downie; two s. *Education:* Univ. of Essex. *Career:* Playwright-in-Residence, Univ. of Essex 1985, Royal Exchange Theatre 1987–88; mem. Writer's Guild of Great Britain. *Film screenplays:* The Monkey Parade 1983, The Ranter 1988, Persuasion 1995, The Gambler 1997, The Turn of the Screw 1999, Cinderella 2000, Byron 2003, Eroica 2003, The Hollow 2004, Cards on the Table 2006. *Opera libretti:* A Family Affair 1993, Siren Song 1994, The Palace in the Sky 2000. *Publications:* Temptation 1984, The Art of Success 1986, Food of Love 1988, A Family Affair (after Ostrovsky) 1988, In the Ruins 1989, The Last Days of Don Juan (after Tirso) 1990, Le Bourgeois Gentilhomme (after Molière) 1992, Pure Science 1994, Zenobia 1995, Summerfolk (after Gorky) 1999, The Villains' Opera 2000, The Promise (after Arbuzov) 2002, Power 2003, Lunch in Venice 2005; several radio plays. *Honours:* John Whiting Award 1987, BAFTA Award 1996, Broadcasting Press Guild Award 1996, South Bank Show Theatre Award 1999, Prix Italia 2004. *Address:* c/o Rosica Colin Ltd, 1 Clareville Grove Mews, London, SW7 5AH, England.

DEARDEN, James Shackley; British writer and editor; b. 9 Aug. 1931, Barrow-in-Furness, England. *Education:* Bembridge School. *Career:* Curator Ruskin Galleries, Bembridge School, Isle of Wight and Brantwood Coniston 1957–96; mem. Ruskin Soc., Turner Soc., Companion of the Guild of St George (master), Old Bembridgians Asscn (past pres.), Isle of Wight Foot Beagles (fmr master and pres.), Friends of Ruskin's Brantwood (hon. life mem. and vice-pres.). *Publications:* The Professor: Arthur Severn's Memoir of Ruskin 1967, A Short History of Brantwood 1967, Iteriad by John Ruskin (ed.) 1969, Facets of Ruskin 1970, Ruskin and Coniston (with K. G. Thorne) 1971, John Ruskin 1973, revised edn 2004, Turner's Isle of Wight Sketch Book 1979, John Ruskin e Les Alpi 1989, John Ruskin's Camberwell 1990, A Tour to the Lakes in Cumberland: John Ruskin's Diary for 1830 (ed.) 1990, John Ruskin and Victorian Art 1993, Ruskin, Bembridge and Brantwood 1994, Hare Hunting on the Isle of Wight 1996, John Ruskin, A Life in Pictures 1999, King of the Golden River by John Ruskin (ed.) 1999, John Ruskin, An Illustrated Life 2004, Further Facets of Ruskin 2007; contrib. to Book Collector, Connoisseur, Apollo, Burlington, Bulletin of John Rylands Library, Country Life, Ruskin Newsletter (ed.), Ruskin Research Series (gen. ed.), Journal of Pre-Raphaelite Studies (editorial advisory bd), Whitehouse Edition of Ruskin's Works (jt gen. ed.). *Honours:* Hon. DLitt (Univ. of Lancaster) 1998. *Address:* 4 Woodlands, Foreland Road, Bembridge, Isle of Wight, England (home).

DEARY, Terry; British children's writer; b. 3 Jan. 1946, Sunderland; m. Jenny Deary 1975; one d. *Career:* fmr actor, theatre dir and drama teacher; Patron Single Homeless Action Initiative in Derwentside, Macmillan Cancer Relief Sunderland Appeal, Grace House Children's Hospice Appeal, Burnhope Asscn of Rural Crafts. *Radio:* Terrible Tales of Wales (series, BBC Radio Wales) 2005. *Theatre:* The Terry Deary History Roadshow (one-man show). *Publications include:* juvenile fiction: Calamity Kate 1980, Hope Street 1980, The Lambton Worm 1981, Twist of the Knife 1981, The Custard Kid 1982, The Wishing Well Ghost 1983, The Silent Scream 1984, The Windmill of Nowhere 1984, I Met her on a Rainy Day 1985, A Witch in Time 1986, Treasure of Skull Island 1986, Spine Chilling Stories 1987, The Ghosts of Batwing Castle 1988, The Dream Seller 1988, Bad Bart and Billy the Brave 1989, Magic of the Mummy 1990, Treasure of Grey Manor 1990, Two in to One Won't Go 1991, The Great Father Christmas Robbery 1991, Shadow Play 1992, Ghost Town 1992, Durham Tales 1993, The Spark Files (series) 1998–, Ghost for Sale 1999, Hat Trick 2000, Pitt Street Pirates 2001, Footsteps in the Fog 2003, War Games 2004, Dirty Little Imps 2004, Egyptian Tales (series) 2004–, The Boy who Haunted Himself 2004, The Last Viking 2005, The Fire Thief 2005, Flight of the Fire Thief 2006; juvenile non-fiction: True Monster Stories 1992, True Horror Stories 1993, True Shark Stories 1995, Shivers: Mysteries 1995, Terror

1995, Disasters 1995, Spooks 1995, The Magic of the Mummy 1995, The Truth About Guy Fawkes? 1996, True Detective Stories 1996, Who Killed Kit Marlowe? 1996, The Real Joan of Arc? 1996, Who Shot Queen Victoria? 1996, Encounter on the Moon 1996, The Philadelphia Experiment 1996, The Discovery at Roswell 1996, Alien Landing 1996, Vanished! 1996, Break Out! 1996, The Nuclear Winter Man 1996, True UFO Stories 1997, Explorers 1997, Inventors 1997, Scientists 1997, Writers 1997, Tudor Terror (series) 1997–, True War Stories 1998, Top Ten Shakespeare Stories 1998, Top Ten Greek Legends 1998, Bloody Scotland 1998, True Disaster Stories 1999, Potty Politics 1999, The Time Detectives (series) 2000–, Read-It! Chapter Books: Historical Tales (series) 2005–, Terry Deary's Terribly True Stories (series) 2006–; Horrible Histories series: The Terrible Tudors (Blue Peter Book Award 2001) 1993, The Awesome Egyptians 1993, The Vile Victorians 1994, The Rotten Romans (Blue Peter Book Award 2002) 1994, The Vicious Vikings 1994, The Blitzed Brits 1995, Cruel Kings and Mean Queens 1995, The Groovy Greeks 1995, The Slimy Stuarts 1996, Wicked Words 1996, Dreadful Diary 1996, The Twentieth Century 1996, The Measly Middle Ages 1996, Poisonous Postcards 1997, Cut-throat Celts 1997, Dark Knights and Dingy Castles 1997, The Angry Aztecs 1997, The Gorgeous Georgians 1998, Even More Terrible Tudors 1998, The Frightful First World War 1998, Rowdy Revolutions 1999, Mad Millennium Play 1999, The Savage Stone Age 1999, The Woeful Second World War 1999, The Smashing Saxons 2000, Ireland 2000, The Incredible Incas 2000, Horrible Christmas 2000, The Stormin' Normans 2001, The USA 2001, The Barmy British Empire 2002, France 2002, Cruel Crimes and Painful Punishments 2002, Ruthless Romans 2003, The Wicked History of the World 2003, The Mad Miscellany 2004, Loathsome London 2005, Rotten Rulers 2005, Edinburgh 2005, York 2005, Dublin 2006, Stratford-Upon-Avon 2006, Pirates 2006, Awesome Annual 2006, Monstrous Miscellany 2006, Knights 2006, The Horrible History of the World 2006, Oxford 2007. *Honours:* Hon. DEduc (Sunderland) 2000; Books for Keeps magazine Outstanding Children's Non-Fiction Author of the 20th Century 1999. *Address:* Terry-Deary.net Ltd, The Board Inn, Burnhope, County Durham DH7 0DP, England (office). *E-mail:* teryy@terry-deary.net. *Website:* www.terry-deary.net.

DE'ATH, Richard (see Haining, Peter Alexander)

DEAVER, Jeffery Wilds, DJur; American novelist; b. 6 May 1950, Chicago. *Education:* Univ. of Missouri, Fordham Law School. *Career:* magazine journalist, lawyer, full-time writer 1990–. *Publications:* fiction: Voodoo 1987, Manhattan is My Beat 1988, Death of a Blue Movie Star 1990, Hard News 1991, Shallow Graves 1992, Mistress of Justice 1992, Bloody River Blues 1993, The Lesson of her Death 1993, Praying for Sleep 1994, A Maiden's Grave 1995, The Bone Collector 1997, The Coffin Dancer 1998, The Devil's Teardrop 1999, The Empty Chair (WHSmith Thumping Good Read Award 2001) 2000, Speaking in Tongues 2000, Hell's Kitchen 2001, The Blue Nowhere 2001, The Stone Monkey 2002, The Vanished Man 2003, Twisted 2004, Garden of Beasts 2004, The Cold Moon 2006, More Twisted 2007, The Sleeping Doll 2007; editor: A Century of Great Suspense Stories 2001, A Hot and Sultry Night for Crime 2003; non-fiction: The Complete Law School Companion 1992; contrib. to Crimes of the Heart 1995, The Best of the Best 1997, Irreconcilable Differences 1999, The World's Finest Mystery and Crime Stories vols 1, 3 and 4 (2000–03), A Confederacy of Crime 2000, Opening Shots 2 2001, Much Ado About Murder 2002, Men from Boys 2003. *Address:* c/o Hodder & Stoughton, 338 Euston Road, London, NW1 3BH, England. *E-mail:* info@jefferydeaver.com. *Website:* www.jefferydeaver.com.

DEBELJAK, Aleš, PhD; Slovenian poet, writer and translator; *Director Cultural Studies Department, University of Ljubljana*; b. 1961, Ljubljana; m. Erica Johnson; three c. *Education:* Univ. of Ljubljana and Syracuse Univ., USA. *Career:* Dir Cultural Studies Dept, Univ. of Ljubljana; Visiting Prof. in European Advanced Interdisciplinary Studies, Coll. of Europe, Warsaw; Gen. Ed., Terra Incognita: Writings from Central Europe book series; Contributing Ed., Trafika: An International Literary Review; mem. advisory bd Davies Publishing Group. *Publications:* poetry: Zamenjave, zamenjave 1982, Imena smrti 1985, Slovar tišine (Dictionary of Silence) 1987, Minute strahu (Anxious Moments) 1992, Mesto in otrok (The City and the Child) 1996; contrib. numerous poems to anthologies and journals; non-fiction: Twilight of the Idols: Recollections of a Lost Yugoslavia 1994, Reluctant Modernity: The Institution of Art and its Historical Forms 1998, The Hidden Handshake: National Identity and Europe in the Post Communist World 2004, Auf der Suche nach dem verlorenen Paradies (essays) 2004, Evropa brez Evropejcev 2004, Na dnu predala 2005, Ustvariti Evropejce/Fare gli Europei 2006; editor: Ameriška metafikcija 1988, Shifting Borders: East European Poetries in the Eighties 1993, Prisoners of Freedom: Contemporary Slovenian Poetry 1994, Selected Poems of Edvard Kocbek 1995, The Imagination of Terra Incognita: Slovenian Writing 1945–95 1997. *Honours:* Slovenian Ambassador of Science 2001; Fellow Inst. of Advanced Study, Collegium Budapest 1996, Sr Fulbright Fellow Univ. of California at Berkeley 1997; Hayden Carruth Poetry Prize 1989, Kristal Vilenica Poetry Award 1990, Preseren Foundation Prize (nat. book award) 1990, Miriam Lindberg Israel Poetry for Peace Prize, Tel-Aviv 1996, Chiqyu Poetry Prize, Tokyo 2000, Civitella Ranieri Fellowship, Umbertide, Italy 2002. *Address:* Department of Cultural Studies, School of Social Sciences, University of Ljubljana, Kardeljeva pl. 5, Ljubljana 1000 (office); Zvezna 41, Ljubljana 1000, Slovenia (home). *E-mail:* ales.debeljak@fdv.uni-lj.si (office); ales.debeljak@guest.arnes.si (home). *Website:* www.fdv.uni-lj.si (office); www.fdv-kulturologija.si.

DEBRAY, (Jules) Régis; French writer and government official; b. 2 Sept. 1940, Paris; s. of Georges Debray and Janine Alexandre; m. Elisabeth Burgos 1968; one d. *Education:* Ecole normale supérieure de la rue d'Ulm. *Career:* colleague of Che Guevara, imprisoned in Bolivia 1967–70; Co-Ed., Comité d'études sur les libertés 1975; adviser on foreign affairs to François Mitterrand; responsible for Third World Affairs, Secr.-Gen. of Presidency of Repub. 1981–84; Office of Pres. of Repub. 1984–85, 1987–88; Maître des requêtes, Conseil d'Etat 1985–93; Sec.-Gen. Conseil du Pacifique Sud 1986–. *Publications:* La Critique des armes 1973, La Guerilla du Che 1974, Entretiens avec Allende 1971, Les Epreuves du fer 1974, L'Indésirable 1975, La Neige brûle 1977, Lettre aux communistes français et á quelques autres 1978, Le Pouvoir intellectuel en France 1979, Le Scribe 1980, Critique de la raison politique 1981, La Puissance et les rêves 1984, Les Empires contre l'Europe 1985, Comète, ma comète 1986, Eloges 1986, Les Masques 1987, Que vive la République 1988, A demain de Gaulle 1990, Cours de médiologie générale 1991, Christophe Colomb, le visiteur de l'aube: les traités de Tordesillas 1992, Vie et mort de l'image: une histoire du regard en Occident 1992, Contretemps: Eloge des idéaux perdus 1992, Ledannois 1992, L'Etat séducteur 1993, L'Oeil naïf 1994, Manifestes médiologiques 1994, Par amour de l'art 1998, L'Abus monumental 1999, Croire, voir, faire 1999, L'Emprise 2000, i.f. suite et fin 2000, Introduction à la médiologie 2000, Loués soient les seigneurs 2000, L'Enseignement du fait religieux dans l'école laïque 2002, L'Edit de Caracalla ou plaidoyer pour les Etats-Unis d'occident 2002, L'Ancien Testament à travers 100 chefs-d'œuvre de la peinture 2003, Le Nouveau Testament à travers 100 chefs-d'œuvre de la peinture 2003, Dieu, un itinéraire 2003, Haïti et la France: Rapport à Dominique de Villepin, ministre des Affaires étrangères 2004, Le siecle et la règle 2004, Ce que nous voile le voile 2004, La Mythologie gréco-latine à travers 100 chefs-d'oeuvres de la peinture 2004, L'Histoire ancienne à travers 100 chefs-d'oeuvres de la peinture 2004, Chroniques de l'idiotie triomphante 2004. *Honours:* Prix Fémina 1977. *Address:* Editions Gallimard, 5 rue Sébastien Bottin, 75007 Paris, France.

DECAUX, Alain; French historian and television producer; b. 23 July 1925, Lille; s. of Francis Decaux and Louise Tiprez; m. 1st Madeleine Parisy 1957; one d.; m. 2nd Micheline Pelletier 1983; one s. one d. *Education:* Lycée Faidherbe, Lille, Lycée Janson-de-Sailly, Paris and Univ. of Paris. *Career:* journalist 1944–; historian 1947–; cr. radio programme La tribune de l'histoire with André Castelot, Colin-Simard and later Jean-François Chiappe 1951; cr. TV programmes: La caméra explore le temps, with Stellio Lorenzi and André Castelot 1956, Alain Decaux raconte 1969, L'histoire en question 1981, Le dossier d'Alain Decaux 1985; f. magazine L'histoire pour tous 1960; Pres. Groupement syndical des auteurs de télévision 1964–66, 1971–72; Vice-Chair. Société des auteurs et compositeurs dramatiques 1965–67, 1969–71, Chair. 1973–75; Dir Société Técipress 1967–91; Vice-Chair. Syndicat nat. des auteurs et compositeurs 1968–73; Admin. Librairie Plon 1969–72; Dir Historia Magazine 1969–71; worked on various periodicals, including Les nouvelles littéraires, Le Figaro littéraire, Historia, Histoire pour tous, Miroir de l'histoire, Lecture pour tous; Chair. Centre d'animation culturelle des Halles et du Marais (Carré Thorigny) 1971–73; mem. Conseil supérieur des lettres 1974; mem. Man. Cttee, Centre nat. des lettres 1974–75; Minister of Francophone Affairs 1988–91; Policy Co-ordinator, French Overseas TV 1989; elected to Académie Française 1979; Chair. Centre d'action culturelle de Paris 1981–; Chair. Société des amis d'Alexandre Dumas 1971; Pres. Coll. des conservateurs du Château de Chantilly 1998–. *Publications:* Louis XVII 1947, Letizia, mère de l'empereur 1949, La conspiration du général Malet 1952, La Castiglione, dame de cœur de l'Europe 1953, La belle histoire de Versailles 1954, De l'Atlantide à Mayerling 1954, Le prince impérial 1957, Offenbach, roi de Second Empire 1958, Amours Second Empire 1958, L'énigme Anastasia 1960, Les heures brillantes de la Côte d'Azur, Les grands mystères du passé 1964, Les dossiers secrets de l'histoire 1966, Grands secrets, grandes énigmes 1966, Nouveaux dossiers secrets 1967, Les Rosenberg ne doivent pas mourir (play) 1968, Grandes aventures de l'histoire 1968, Histoire des Françaises (2 vols) 1972, Histoire de la France et des Français (with André Castelot, 13 vols) 1970–74, Le cuirassé Potemkine (co-writer, play) 1975, Blanqui 1976, Les face à face de l'histoire 1977, Alain Decaux raconte (4 vols) 1978, 1979, 1980, 1981, L'Histoire en question (2 vols) 1982–83, Notre-Dame de Paris (co-writer, play) 1978, Danton et Robespierre (co-writer, play) 1979, Un homme nommé Jésus (co-writer, play) 1983, Victor Hugo (biog.) 1984, Les Assassins 1986, Le Pape pèlerin 1986, Destins fabuleux 1987, Alain Decaux raconte l'Histoire de France aux enfants 1987, L'Affaire du Courrier de Lyon 1987, Alain Decaux raconte la Révolution Française aux enfants 1988, La Liberté ou la mort (co-writer) 1988, La Révolution racontée aux enfants 1988, Alain Decaux raconte Jésus aux enfants 1991, Jésus était son nom 1991 (play), Le Tapis rouge 1992, Je m'appelais Marie-Antoinette (co-writer, play) 1993, Histoires Extraordinaires 1993, Nouvelles histoires extraordinaires 1994, L'abdication 1995, C'était le XXe siècle 1996, Alain Decaux raconte la Bible aux enfants 1996, Monaco et ses princes 1997, La course à l'abîme 1997, La Guerre absolue 1998, De Staline à Kennedy 1999, De Gaulle, celui qui a dit non (co-writer) 1999, Morts pour Vichy 2000, L'Avorton de Dieu: une vie de Saint Paul 2003, Tous les personnages sont vrais (Prix Saint-Simon 2005) 2004. *Honours:* Prix d'histoire, Académie Française 1950, Grande médaille d'or, Ville de Versailles 1954, Grand prix du disque for Révolution française 1963, Prix Plaisir de lire 1968, Oscar de la télévision et de la radio 1968, 1973, Prix de la Critique de Télévision 1972, médaille de vermeil de la Ville de Paris 1973, Prix littéraire de la Paulée de Meursault 1973; Grand Officier, Légion d'honneur, Grand

Croix, Ordre National du Mérite, Commdr Ordre des Arts et des Lettres. *Address:* 86 boulevard Flandrin, 75116 Paris, France. *Telephone:* (1) 44059095 (office).

DECLEMENTS, Barthe, BA, MEd; American writer; b. 8 Oct. 1920, Seattle, WA; m. 1st Don Macri (divorced); m. 2nd Gordon Greimes (divorced); four c. *Education:* Western Washington College, University of Washington, Seattle. *Career:* school teacher 1944–46, 1961–78; high school counselor 1978–83. *Publications:* Nothing's Fair in Fifth Grade, 1981; How Do You Lose Those Ninth Grade Blues?, 1983; Seventeen and In-Between, 1984; Sixth Grade Can Really Kill You, 1985; I Never Asked You to Understand Me, 1986; Double Trouble (with Christopher Greimes), 1987; No Place For Me, 1987; The Fourth Grade Wizards, 1988; Five-Finger Discount, 1989; Monkey See, Monkey Do, 1990; Wake Me at Midnight, 1991; Breaking Out, 1991; The Bite of the Gold Bug, 1992; The Pickle Song, 1993; Tough Loser, 1994; Spoiled Rotten, 1996; Liar, Liar, 1998. Contributions: periodicals. *Honours:* over 25 awards.

DEEDES, Baron (Life Peer), cr. 1986, of Aldington in the County of Kent; **William Francis Deedes,** KBE, PC, MC, DL; British politician and newspaper editor; b. 1 June 1913, Aldington, Kent; s. of (Herbert) William Deedes; m. Evelyn Hilary Branfort 1942 (died 2004); two s. (one deceased) three d. *Education:* Harrow School. *Career:* journalist with Morning Post 1931–37; war corresp. on Abyssinia 1935; served in World War II 1939–45, Queen's Westminsters (12 King's Royal Rifle Corps); MP (Conservative) for Ashford Div. of Kent 1950–74; Parl. Sec., Ministry of Housing and Local Govt 1954–55; Parl. Under-Sec. Home Dept 1955–57; DL, Kent 1962; Minister without Portfolio (Information) 1962–64; mem. Advisory Cttee on Drug Dependence 1967–74; Chair. Select Cttee on Immigration and Race Relations 1970–74; Ed. Daily Telegraph 1974–86, mem. editorial staff 1986–; Amb. for UNICEF 1998–. *Publications:* Dear Bill: W. F. Deedes Reports (autobiog.) 1997, At War With Waugh 2003, Brief Lives 2004, Dear Bill: W. F. Deedes Reports 2005, Words and Deeds: Selected Journalism 1931–2006 2006. *Honours:* Hon. DCL (Kent) 1988; Special Award, British Press Awards 1992. *Address:* New Hayters, Aldington, Kent, TN25 7DT, England (home). *Telephone:* (1233) 720269 (home).

DEFORD, Frank, BA; American writer and editor; b. 16 Dec. 1938, Baltimore, MD; m. Carol Penner 1965; one s. two d. *Education:* Princeton Univ. *Career:* Contributing Ed., Sports Illustrated 1962–69, 1998–, Vanity Fair 1993–96; writer and commentator, Cable News Network 1980–86, Nat. Public Radio 1980–89, 1991–, NBC 1986–89, ESPN 1992–96, HBO 1996–; Ed.-in-Chief, The National 1989–91; writer, Newsweek Magazine 1991–93, 1996–98. *Film screenplays:* Trading Hearts 1986, Four Minutes 2005. *Publications:* Five Strides on the Banked Track 1969, Cut 'N' Run 1971, There She Is 1972, The Owner 1974, Big Bill Tilden: The Triumphs and the Tragedy 1977, Everybody's All-American 1981, Alex: The Life of a Child 1982, Spy in the Deuce Court 1987, World's Tallest Midget 1988, Casey on the Loose 1989, Love and Infamy 1993, The Other Adonis 2001, An American Summer 2002, The Old Ball Game 2005; contrib. to numerous magazines. *Honours:* Nat. Asscn of Sportswriters and Sportscasters Sportswriter of the Year 1982–88, Emmy Award 1988, Cable Ace 1996, Peabody Award 1999. *Address:* PO Box 1109, Greens Farms, CT 06838, USA. *Telephone:* (203) 259-1787. *E-mail:* frankbde@aol.com. *Literary Agent:* Sterling Lord Literistic Inc., 65 Bleecker Street, New York, NY 10012, USA. *Address:* PO Box 1109, Greens Farms, CT 06838, USA. *E-mail:* frankbde@aol.com.

DEFORGES, Régine Marie Léone, Princess Wiazemsky; French writer and publisher; b. 15 Aug. 1935, Montmorillon; d. of Clément and Bernadette (née Peyon) Deforges; one s. one d.; m. 2nd Pierre Wiazemsky 1984; one d. *Education:* Inst St-Martial, Montmorillon. *Career:* bookseller 1960–76; Founder and Chair. Editions l'Or du Temps 1968 (Editions Régine Deforges from 1984); Rep. to Ministry of Culture 1982–83; mem. Comité consultatif de la langue française, PEN-Club; mem. judging panel Prix Femina 1984–; Chair. Soc. des Gens de Lettres de France 1988–, Éditions Ramsay & Régine Deforges 1989–92. *Publications:* O m'a dit 1975, Blanche et Lucie 1977, Le cahier volé 1978, Contes pervers, Lola et quelques autres 1979, La révolte des nonnes 1981, La bicyclette bleue (three vols) 1982–86, Les enfants de Blanche 1983, Léa aux pays des dragons 1983, 101 avenue Henri Martin 1984, Le diable en rit encore 1985, L'Apocalypse 1985, Pour l'amour de Marie Salat 1986, Le livre du point de croix 1986, Sous le ciel de Novgorod 1988, Ma cuisine 1989, Juliette Gréco 1990, Noir Tango 1990, Rue de la Soie 1994, Roger Stéphane ou la passion d'admirer 1995, La dernière colline 1996, L'orage 1996, Pêle-mêle. Chroniques de l'Humanité 1998, 1999, 2000, Paris Chansons 1998, Cuba libre! 1999, Camilo 1999, Alger, ville blanche 2003, Journal de l'année 2003, Les Généraux du Crepuscule 2004, Le collier de perles 2004, Les poètes et les putains 2004, La hire ou la colère de Jehanne 2005. *Honours:* Officier, Légion d'Honneur 1992, Officier, Ordre Nat. du Mérite, Officer, Ordre Nat. des Arts et des Lettres 2006; Maisons de la Presse Award 1981. *Address:* 58 rue St André des Arts, 75006 Paris, France. *Telephone:* (1) 43-54-39-16. *Fax:* (1) 43-54-39-16. *E-mail:* rdeforgessec@netcourrier.com.

DEGRADA, Francesco, DipMus, BA; Italian musicologist, academic, writer and music editor; *Professor of Music History, University of Milan*; b. 23 May 1940, Milan. *Education:* Milan Conservatory, Univ. of Milan. *Career:* teacher, Bolzano Conservatory, Brescia Conservatory; Lecturer 1964–76, Prof. of Music History 1976–, Dir of the Arts Dept 1983–, Univ. of Milan; teacher, Milan Conservatory 1966–73; founder-Dir and harpsichordist, Complesso Barocco di Milano 1967–76; Consultant to the Publisher, G. Ricordi 1971–; mem. editorial bds of critical edns of Vivaldi, Pergolesi and Verdi; mem. Accademia Nazionale di Santa Cecilia, Roma, Academia Europaea, London. *Publications:* Al Gran Sole Carico d'Amore, Per Un Nuovo Teatro Musicale 1974, Sylvano Bussotti e il Suo Teatro 1976, Antonio Vivaldi da Venezia all'Europa 1977, Il Palazzo Incantato, Studi Sulla Tradizione del Melodramma dal Barocco al Romanticismo (two vols) 1979, Vivaldi Veneziano Europeo 1980, Illusione e disincanto. Mozart e altri percorsi settecenteschi 2000; editor: Studi Pergolesiani/Pergolesi Studies (four vols) 1986, 1988, 1999, 2000, Andrea Gabrieli e il Suo Tempo 1988; contrib. many articles to scholarly journals. *Address:* c/o Università degli Studi di Milano, Via Festa del Perdono 7, 20122 Milan (office); Via Gaudenzio Ferrari 3, 20123 Milan, Italy.

DEGUY, Michel; French poet, writer and editor; *Professor Emeritus, Université de Paris*; b. 23 May 1930, Paris. *Education:* studied in Paris. *Career:* Ed. Poésie 1972–; Univ. Prof., Paris; currently Prof. Emer., Université de Paris; Pres. Collège Int. de Philosophie, Paris. *Publications:* Les Meurtrières 1959, Fragments du cadastre 1960, Poèmes de la presqu'île 1961, Approche de Hölderlin 1962, Le Monde de Thomas Mann 1963, Biefs 1964, Actes 1966, Oui-dire 1966, Histoire des rechutes 1968, Figurations 1969, Tombeau de Du Bellay 1973, Poèmes 1960–1970 1973, Reliefs 1975, Jumelages suivi de Made in U.S.A. 1978, Donnant, donnant 1981, La Machine matriomoniale ou Marivaux 1982, René Girard et le problème du mal (with J.-P. Dupuy) 1982, Gisants 1985, Poèmes II 1970–1980 1986, Brevets 1986, Choses de la poésie et affaire culturelle 1986, Le Comité: Confessions d'un lecteur de grande maison 1988, La Poésie n'est pas seule: Court traité de Poétique 1988, Arrets fréquents 1990, Aux heures d'affluence 1993, A ce qui n'en finit pas 1995, L'Energie du Desespoir 1998, La Raison Poétique 2000, L'Impair 2000, Spleen de Paris 2001, Poèmes en pensée 2001, Sans Retour 2004, Au Juge 2004. *Honours:* Officier du Mérite, Commdr, Ordre des Arts et des Lettres; Grand Prix nat. de Poésie 1989, Grand Prix de Poésie de l' Acad. française 2004. *Address:* 8 rue de l'Abbide, Paris 75005, France. *Fax:* 1-47-05-70-37 (office). *E-mail:* r.martin@maison-des-ecrivains.asso.fr (office).

DEIGHTON, Len; British writer; b. 1929, London. *Publications:* The Ipcress File 1962 (also film), Horse under Water 1963, Funeral in Berlin 1964 (also film), Où est le Garlic 1965, Action Cook Book 1965, Cookstrip Cook Book (USA) 1966, Billion Dollar Brain 1966 (also film), An Expensive Place to Die 1967, Len Deighton's London Dossier (guide book) 1967, The Assassination of President Kennedy (co-author) 1967, Only When I Larf 1968 (also film), Bomber 1970 (also radio dramatization), Declarations of War (short stories) 1971, Close-Up 1972, Spy Story 1974 (also film), Yesterday's Spy 1975, Twinkle, Twinkle, Little Spy 1976, Fighter: the True Story of the Battle of Britain 1977, SS-GB 1978, Airshipwreck (co-author) 1978, Blitzkrieg 1979, Battle of Britain (co-author) 1980, XPD 1981, Goodbye Mickey Mouse 1982, Berlin Game 1983, Mexico Set 1984, London Match 1985, Winter: a Berlin Family 1899–1945 1987, Spy Hook 1988, ABC of French Food 1989, Spy Line 1989, Spy Sinker 1990, Basic French Cookery Course 1990, Mamista 1991, City of Gold 1992, Violent Ward 1993, Blood, Tears and Folly 1993, Faith 1994, Hope 1995, Charity 1996. *Address:* c/o Jonathan Clowes Ltd, 10 Iron Bridge House, Bridge Approach, London, NW1 8BD, England. *Telephone:* (20) 7722-7674 (office). *E-mail:* jonathanclowes@aol.com (office).

DEL DUCA, Simone; French publisher and foundation executive; b. 18 July 1912, Saint-Maur-des-Fossés; d. of Henri and Ga ëtane Nirouet; m. Cino del Duca (deceased). *Career:* Dir del Duca group 1967–80, Pres. Dir-Gen. del Duca printing and publishing 1967–80; Dir Paris-Jour newspaper 1967–72; Admin. La Vie des Métiers and Gallia-Publicité; literary Publr, Publr of Modes de Paris, Nous-Deux, Intimité, Télé-Poche magazines; Pres. Industrie Grafiche Cino del Duca, Milan, Italy; Founder, Pres. Fondation Simone et Cino del Duca 1975; Corresp. mem. Inst. de France (Acad. des Beaux-Arts) 1994–. *Honours:* Commdr de la Légion d'Honneur; Officier de l'Ordre Nat du Mérite; Chevalier des Arts et Lettres; Grand Officier du Mérite (Italy); Commdr de la Stella della Solidarieta Italiana (Italy); decorations from Malta and Monaco; Dr hc (Paris and Urbino, Italy); numerous awards. *Address:* Fondation Simone et Cino del Duca, 10 rue Alfred de Vigny, 75008 Paris, France.

DEL PASO, Fernando; Mexican writer, poet and artist; b. 1 April 1935, Mexico City, DF. *Education:* Universidad Nacional Autónoma de México. *Career:* fmrly worked on Int. Writing Program, Univ. of Iowa City, USA for two years, worked for BBC in London, England for 14 years, worked for Radio France Internationale, then as Consul General Mexico, both in France for eight years; mem. El Colegio Nacional. *Art exhibitions include:* works exhibited in Museo de Arte Moderno and Museo Carrillo Gil in Mexico City, Hospicio Cabañas in Guadalajara, and in the UK, USA, Spain and France. *Publications:* Sonetos del amor y de lo diario (poems) 1958, De la A a la Z por un poeta (poems for children), Paleta de diez colores (poems for children), José Trigo (novel) 1966, Palinuro de México (novel) (Premio Novela México 1976, Premio Internacional Rómulo Gallegos 1982, Premio a la Mejor Novela Publicada en Francia 1985) 1976, Noticias del imperio (novel) 1986, Linda 67: Historia de un crimen (novel) 1995, La muerte se va a Granada (play) 1998, Memoria y olvido. Vida de Juan José Arreola (non-fiction) 2003. *Honours:* Premio Xavier Villaurrutia 1966, Premio Nacional de Letras y Artes 1991. *Address:* c/o El Colegio Nacional, Luis González Obregón 23, Centro Histórico, Mexico City 06020 DF, Mexico (office).

DELANEY, Francis (Frank) James Joseph; Irish broadcaster and writer; b. 24 Oct. 1942, Tipperary. *Career:* television and radio broadcaster, journalist, RTE News Dublin, BBC Northern Ireland, BBC TV and BBC Radio 4;

mem. Athenaeum, Chelsea Arts. *Publications:* James Joyce's Odyssey 1981, Betjeman Country 1983, The Celts 1986, A Walk in the Dark Ages 1988, My Dark Rosaleen (novella) 1989, Legends of the Celts 1989, The Sins of the Mothers 1992, A Walk to the Western Isles 1993, Telling the Pictures 1993, A Stranger in Their Midst 1995, The Amethysts 1997, Desire and Pursuit 1998, Pearl 1999, At Ruby's 2001, Jim Hawkins and the Curse of Treasure Island (as Francis Bryan) 2001, Ireland: A Novel 2004. *Address:* c/o HarperCollins Publishers, 77–85 Fulham Palace Road, Hammersmith, London, W6 8JB, England. *E-mail:* authors@harpercollins.co.uk. *Website:* www.harpercollins .co.uk.

DELANEY, Lawrence (Larry); Canadian newspaper editor and publisher; b. 30 Aug. 1942, Eastview, ON; m. Joanne Bonell 1964; one s. one d. *Career:* co-founder, Ed. and publisher, Country Music News, Canada's national music newspaper 1980–, providing international exposure and profile for Canadian country music artists and industry; mem. Canadian Country Music Asscn, CMA, CPPA. *Honours:* received CCMA Country Music Person of the Year citation 11 times; inducted into Canadian Country Music Hall of Fame 1989, Ottawa Valley Country Music Hall of Fame 1993, CCMA Hall of Honour 1996. *Address:* Country Music News, PO Box 7323 Vanier Terminal, Ottawa, ON K1L 8E4, Canada (office). *E-mail:* Larry@CountryMusicNews.ca. *Website:* www.countrymusicnews.ca.

DELANEY, Shelagh; British playwright; b. 1939, Salford; one d. *Education:* Broughton Secondary School. *Career:* has written numerous plays, films, radio plays and TV series. *Plays include:* A Taste of Honey (Charles Henry Foyle New Play Award, Arts Council Bursary, New York Drama Critics' Award) 1958, The Lion in Love 1960. *Films include:* A Taste of Honey (BFA Award, Robert Flaherty Award) 1961, The White Bus 1966, Charlie Bubbles (Writers' Guild Award) 1968, Dance with a Stranger (Prix Film Jeunesse-Etranger, Cannes) 1985. *TV includes:* St Martin's Summer 1974, The House that Jack Built (series) 1977, Find Me First 1979. *Radio plays:* So Does the Nightingale 1980, Don't Worry About Matilda 1983. *Publications include:* A Taste of Honey 1959, The Lion in Love 1961, Sweetly Sings the Donkey 1963. *Address:* c/o Sayle Screen Ltd, 11 Jubilee Place, London, SW3 3TE, England (office).

DELANY, Samuel Ray; American writer and academic; *Professor of Comparative Literature, University of Massachusetts, Amherst;* b. 1 April 1942, New York, NY; m. 1961 (divorced 1980); one s. one d. *Education:* City College, CUNY. *Career:* Ed., Wuark, 1970–71; Senior Fellow, Center for 20th Century Studies, University of Wisconsin, Milwaukee, 1977; Society for the Humanities, Cornell University, 1987; Prof. of Comparative Literature, University of Massachusetts, Amherst, 1988–. *Publications:* The Jewels of Aptor, 1962; The Fall of the Towers, Vol. 1, Captives of the Flames, 1963, as Out of the Dead City, 1968, Vol. 2, The Towers of Toron, 1964, Vol. 3, City of a Thousand Suns, 1965; The Ballad of Beta-2, 1965; Empire Star, 1966; Babel-17, 1966; The Einstein Intersection, 1967; Nova, 1968; Driftglass: Ten Tales of Speculative Fiction, 1971; Dhalgren, 1975; Triton, 1976; The Jewel-Hinged Jaw: Notes on the Language of Science Fiction, 1977; The American Shore, 1978; Empire, 1978; Nebula Award Winners 13 (ed.), 1979; Distant Stars, 1981; Stars in My Pocket Like Grains of Sand, 1984; Starboard Wine: More Notes on the Language of Science Fiction, 1984; The Splendour and Misery of Bodies, 1985; Flight from Neveryon, 1985; They Fly at Ciron, 1992; Neveryon, 1993; Tales of Neveryon, 1993; The Mad Man, 1994; Aye, and Gomorrah, 2003. *Literary Agent:* Henry Morrison, Box 234, Bedford Hills, NY 10507, USA. *Address:* c/o Bantam Books, 666 Fifth Avenue, New York, NY 10019, USA.

DELBANCO, Andrew Henry, AB, AM, PhD; American academic and writer; b. 20 Feb. 1952, White Plains, NY; m. Dawn Ho Delbanco 1973; one s. one d. *Education:* Harvard University. *Career:* Asst Prof., Harvard University, 1981–85; Assoc. Prof., 1985–87, Prof., 1987–, Julian Clarence Levi Prof. in the Humanities, 1995–, Columbia University; Adjunct Prof., Yale University, 1989; mem. Society of American Historians. *Publications:* William Ellery Channing: An Essay on the Liberal Spirit in America, 1981; The Puritan Ordeal, 1989; The Death of Satan: How Americans Have Lost the Sense of Evil, 1995; Required Reading: Why Our American Classics Matter Now, 1997. Editor: The Puritans in America: A Narrative Anthology (with Alan Heimert), 1985; The Sermons of Ralph Waldo Emerson, Vol. II (with Teresa Toulouse), 1990; The Portable Abraham Lincoln, 1992. Contributions: Professional journals and to general periodicals. *Honours:* Guggenheim Fellowship; ACLS Fellowship; National Endowment for the Humanities Fellowship; National Humanities Center Fellowship. *Address:* c/o Dept of English and Comparative Literature, Columbia University, 1150 Amsterdam Avenue, New York, NY 10027, USA.

DELBANCO, Nicholas Franklin, BA, MA; American writer and academic; *Professor, University of Michigan at Ann Arbor;* b. 27 Aug. 1942, London, England; m. Elena Carter Greenhouse 1970; two d. *Education:* Harvard Univ., Columbia Univ. *Career:* Faculty, Language and Literature Division, Bennington Coll. 1966–85; Founder-Dir, Bennington Coll. Writing Workshops 1977–85; Visiting Lecturer, Iowa Writers Program, Univ. of Iowa 1979; Adjunct Prof. School of the Arts, Columbia Univ. 1979, 1996, 1997; Visiting writer-in-residence, Trinity Coll. 1980; M. Scott Bundy Visiting Prof. of English, Williams Coll. 1982, 1985; staff Bread Loaf Writers' Conference 1984–94; Prof. of English, Skidmore Coll. 1984–85; Prof., Univ. of Michigan at Ann Arbor 1985–; Robert Frost Distinguished Univ. Professorship 2006–; mem. Associated Writing Programs, Authors' League, Authors' Guild, Signet Soc., New York State Writers' Inst., PEN. *Publications:* The Martlet's Tale

(novel) 1966, Grasse 3/23/66 (novel) 1968, Consider Sappho Burning (novel) 1969, News (novel) 1970, In the Middle Distance (novel) 1971, Fathering (novel) 1973, Small Rain (novel) 1975, Possession (novel) 1977, Sherbrookes (novel) 1978, Stillness (novel) 1980, Group Portrait: Conrad, Crane, Ford, James, and Wells 1982, About My Table and Other Stories 1983, The Beaux Arts Trio: A Portrait 1985, Running in Place: Scenes from the South of France 1989, The Writers' Trade, and Other Stories 1990, Speaking of Writing: Selected Hopwood Lectures (ed.) 1990, Writers and Their Craft: Short Stories and Essays on the Narrative (ed. with Laurence Goldstein) 1991, In the Name of Mercy (novel) 1995, Talking Horse: Bernard Malamud on Life and Art (ed. with Alan Cheuse) 1996, Old Scores (novel) 1997, The Lost Suitcase: Reflections on the Literary Life 2000, What Remains (novel) 2000, The Writing Life: Further Hopwood Lectures (ed.) 2000, The Countess of Stanlein Restored: A History of the Paganini Stradivarius Violoncello of 1707 2002, The Vagabonds (novel) 2004, Anywhere Out of The World (essays) 2005, Spring and Fall (novel) 2006; contrib. to periodicals, anthologies, quarterlies, reviews and journals. *Honours:* Nat. Endowment for the Arts Creative Writing Fellowships 1973, 1982, Guggenheim Fellowship 1980, Nat. Endowment for the Arts/PEN Syndicated Fiction Awards 1983, 1985, 1989, MacDowell Colony Fellowship 1985, Yaddo Fellowships 1987, 1989, 1994, Robert Frost Collegiate Professorship Univ. of Michigan 1998, Michigan Author of the Year 2002. *Literary Agent:* Brandt & Hochman Literary Agents Inc., 1501 Broadway, New York, NY 10036, USA. *Address:* c/o The Hopwood Room, 1186 Angell Hall, University of Michigan at Ann Arbor, Ann Arbor, MI 48109, USA (office). *Telephone:* (734) 764-6296 (office).

DELEHANTY, Randolph, BA, MA, PhD; American author, lecturer and exhibition curator; *Historian, Presidio Trust;* b. 5 July 1944, Memphis, Tenn. *Education:* Georgetown Univ., Univ. of Chicago and Harvard Univ. *Career:* author of historical and architectural books; curator of major art, nature and history exhbns; Founding Dir Ogden Museum of Southern Art, Univ. of New Orleans 1995–99; Historian for Presidio Trust, Golden Gate Nat. Parks, San Francisco 2000–. *Exhibitions:* Plants + Insects/Art + Science 2006, From Above – A Robert Cameron Retrospective 2005, Birds of the Pacific Slope 2004, Japan at the Dawn of the Modern Age Woodblock Prints from Meiji Era 2002. *Publications:* San Francisco: Walks and Tours in the Golden Gate City 1980, California: A Guidebook 1984, Preserving the West 1985, In the Victorian Style 1991, New Orleans: Elegance and Decadence 1993, San Francisco: The Ultimate Guide 1995, Classic Natchez 1996, Art in the American South 1996, Randolph Delehanty's Ultimate Guide to New Orleans 1998, San Francisco Victorians 2000, A Guide to San Francisco Recreation and Parks 2000, Treasure Houses: Louisiana Museums for a New Millennium 2000, New Guardians for the Golden Gate: How America got a Great National Park (with Amy Meyer) 2006; contrib. to The Companion to Southern Literature 2002. *Address:* 2004 Gough Street, San Francisco, CA 94109-3418, USA. *E-mail:* randolph_delehanty@post.harvard.edu.

DeLILLO, Don, BA; American writer; b. 20 Nov. 1936, New York, NY; m. Barbara Bennett 1975. *Education:* Cardinal Hayes High School, Fordham Coll., New York. *Career:* fmr advertising copywriter Ogilvy, Benson & Mather. *Plays:* The Day Room 1987, Valparaiso 1999. *Publications:* Americana 1971, End Zone 1972, Great Jones Street 1973, Ratner's Star 1976, Players 1977, Running Dog 1978, The Names 1982, White Noise 1985 (Nat. Book Award 1985), Libra 1988 (Irish Times Fiction Prize 1989), Mao II 1991 (PEN/ Faulkner Award 1992), Underworld 1997, The Body Artist 2000, Cosmopolis 2003, Falling Man 2007. *Honours:* American Acad. of Arts and Letters Award in Literature 1984, Jerusalem Prize for the Freedom of the Individual in Soc. 1999, William Dean Howells Medal 2000. *Literary Agent:* Wallace Literary Agency, 177 E 70th Street, New York, NY 10021, USA.

DEMARIA, Robert, BA, MA, PhD; American academic, writer and poet; *Professor Emeritus of English, Dowling College;* b. 28 Sept. 1928, New York, NY; m. 1st Maddalena Buzeo; m. 2nd Ellen Hope Meyer; three s. one d. *Education:* Columbia Univ. *Career:* instructor, Univ. of Oregon 1949–52; Asst Prof., Hofstra Univ. 1952–61; Assoc. Dean, New School for Social Research, New York 1961–64; Prof. of English, Dowling Coll. 1965–97, Prof. Emer. 1997–; Ed. and Publr The Mediterranean Review 1969–73; Publr The Vineyard Press 1998–. *Publications:* fiction: Carnival of Angels 1961, Clodia 1965, Don Juan in Lourdes 1966, The Satyr 1972, The Decline and Fall of America 1973, To Be a King 1976, Outbreak 1978, Blowout 1979, The Empress 1980, Secret Places 1981, A Passion for Power 1983, Sons and Brothers (two vols) 1985, Stone of Destiny 1986, That Kennedy Girl 1999, The White Road 2000, Blood of the Hunter 2005, My Secret Childhood: Growing Up in New York (memoir) 2005; non-fiction (textbooks): The College Handbook of Creative Writing 1991, A Contemporary Reader for Creative Writing 1995; contrib. of fiction, poetry and articles in numerous publs. *Address:* 106 Vineyard Place, Port Jefferson, NY 11777, USA. *Telephone:* (631) 928-3460 (home). *E-mail:* debobaria@optonline.net. *Website:* www.thevineyardpress .com.

DEMERS, Patricia, MA, PhD; Canadian academic; *President, Royal Society of Canada. Education:* McMaster and Ottawa Univs. *Career:* currently Prof., Dept of English, Univ. of Alberta, Chair of Dept 1995–98; specialisation in early modern and contemporary women's writing, Elizabethan and Jacobean drama, 17th century poetry, biblical literature, children's literature; Vice-Pres. Social Sciences and Humanities Research Council (SSHRC) 1998–2002; inducted into Royal Soc. of Canada 2000, Hon. Ed., Exec. mem., elected Pres. (first woman in position) 2005–(07). *Publications:* From Instruction to Delight:

Children's Literature to 1850 (ed.) 2nd Edn 2004, A Garland from the Golden Age, Women's Writing in English 2005; contrib. numerous articles in professional journals including Mosaic, English Studies in Canada, Semeia, Sixteenth Century Journal, Huntington Library Quarterly, Renaissance and Reformation, Bunyan Studies, Literature and Theology and Topia. *Address:* The Royal Society of Canada, 283 Sparks Street, Ottawa, Ont. K1R 7X9 (office); Department of English, University of Alberta, 3–5 Humanities Centre, Edmonton, Alberta T6G 2E5, Canada (office). *Telephone:* (613) 991-6990 (office); (780) 492-3258 (office). *Fax:* (613) 991-6996 (office); (780) 492-8142 (office). *E-mail:* adminrsc@rsc.ca (office); patricia.demers@ualberta.ca (office). *Website:* www.rsc.ca (office); www.ualberta.ca (office).

DEMETILLO, Ricaredo, AB, MFA; Philippine academic, poet and writer; b. 2 June 1920, Dumangas. *Education:* Silliman University, University of Iowa. *Career:* Asst Prof., 1959–70, Chair., Dept of Humanities, 1961–62, Assoc. Prof., 1970–75, Prof. of Humanities, 1975–86, University of the Philippines. *Publications:* Poetry: No Certain Weather, 1956; La Via: A Spiritual Journey, 1958; Daedalus and Other Poems, 1961; Barter in Panay, 1961; Masks and Signature, 1968; The Scare-Crow Christ, 1973; The City and the Thread of Light, 1974; Lazarus, Troubadour, 1974; Sun, Silhouttes and Shadow, 1975; First and Last Fruits, 1989. Novel: The Genesis of a Troubled Vision, 1976. Play: The Heart of Emptiness is Black, 1973. Non-Fiction: The Authentic Voice of Poetry, 1962; Major and Minor Keys, 1986.

DEMOS, John Putnam, BA, MA; American academic and writer; b. 2 May 1937, Cambridge, MA; m. Elaine Virginia Damis 1963, two c. *Education:* Harvard University, University of Oxford, University of California at Berkeley. *Career:* Teaching Fellow, Harvard University, 1966–68; Asst Prof., 1968–72, Prof. of History, 1972–86, Brandeis University; Prof. of History, Yale University, 1986–; mem. American Historical Asscn. *Publications:* A Little Commonwealth: Family Life in Plymouth Colony, 1970; Remarkable Providences, 1600–1760 (ed.), 1972; Turning Points: Historical and Sociological Essays on the Family (ed. with Sarane Boocock), 1978; Entertaining Satan: Witchcraft and the Culture of Early New England, 1982; Past, Present, and Personal, 1986; The Unredeemed Captive, 1994. Contributions: scholarly journals and other publications. *Honours:* Bancroft Prize in American History, Columbia University, 1983; Francis Parkman Prize, 1995; Ray Allen Billington Prize, 1995.

DEMPSEY, Gaylene Katharan; Canadian editor; b. 1 Aug. 1960, Winnipeg, MB; m. David Sherman 1993. *Career:* Ed. monthly entertainment paper, Circuit 1989–; Ed.-in-Chief monthly entertainment paper, The Insider 1990–; Ed., Jazz Winnipeg Festival Programme 1990–; volunteer, Winnipeg Folk Festival 1990–; Exec. Dir, Manitoba Audio Recording Industry Asscn (MARIA) 1991–; represents the Manitoba Music Industry from songwriters to labels; freelance work; mem. FACTOR Nat. Advisory Bd, Artspace (exec. mem.). *Publications:* contrib. several articles to SOCAN Words and Music, Grafitti Magazine. *Address:* 242 Spence Street, Suite 1, Winnipeg, Manitoba, R3C 1Y4, Canada.

DENBY, Joolz; British writer and performance artist. *Career:* has performed at numerous UK arts festivals, including five Edinburgh Fringe Festivals, two Edinburgh Book Festivals, 20 Glastonbury Festivals, also in Canada, the Netherlands, Germany, Norway, Israel, Poland, Slovakia; readings and seminars worldwide; mem. Red Sky Coven cult performance group; regular broadcasts on radio and TV. *Recordings:* War of Attrition (poems, with music) 1983, The Kiss (poems, with music) 1984, Never Never Land (spoken word) 1984, Love Is Sweet Romance (poems, with music) 1985, Mad, Bad, & Dangerous to Know (poems, with music) 1986, Hex (poems, with music) 1990, Weird Sister (poems, with music) 1991, Joolz 1983–85, True North (poems, with music) 1997. *Publications:* fiction: The Quick & the Dead 2 (short story), Trouble (short story), Stone Baby (novel) (The Crimewriter's Asscn New Crime Writer of the Year Award) 2000, Corazon (novel) 2001, Billie Morgan (novel) (Orange Prize for Fiction) 2005, Borrowed Light 2006; poetry: Mad, Bad, & Dangerous to Know 1986, Emotional Terrorism 1990, The Pride of Lions 1994, Errors of the Spirit 2000. *Address:* The Office, POB 162, Bradford, BD3 8PY, England. *Fax:* (1274) 667974. *E-mail:* postmaster@joolz.net. *Website:* www.joolz.net.

DENEZHKINA, Irina; Russian writer; b. 1984. *Publications:* Give Me (Songs for Lovers) (short stories, in trans.) (Nat. Bestseller Award, Russia) 2002. *Address:* c/o Chatto & Windus, Random House, 20 Vauxhall Bridge Road, London, SW1V 2SA, England.

DENG, Xiaohua, (Can Xue); Chinese writer; b. 30 May 1953, Changsha, Hunan; d. of Deng Jun Hong and Li Ying; m. Lu Rong 1979; one s. *Career:* parents were condemned as ultra-rightists in 1957, forced to leave school aged 13; factory worker 1970–80; tailor 1980–85; professional writer 1985–. *Publications include:* Soap Bubbles on Dirty Water, Dialogues in Paradise 1989, Yellow Mud Street, Dating, Old Floating Cloud 1989, Apple Tree in the Corridor, The Instant when the Cuckoo Sings 1991, The Embroidered Shoes 1997, Castle of the Soul (essays on Kafka) 1999; works on Borges and Shakespeare. *Honours:* Hon. mem. Int. Writing Program, Univ. of Iowa, USA. *Address:* c/o 3-3 Building, No. 904, He Xi, Changsha, Hunan, People's Republic of China.

DENGLER, Sandy, BS, MS, PhD; American writer; *Managing Editor, Journal of Paleontology;* b. 8 June 1939, Newark, OH; m. William F. Dengler 1963; two d. *Education:* Bowling Green State Univ., OH, Arizona State Univ., Univ. of

Oklahoma. *Career:* mem. MWA, Soc. of Vertebrate Palaeontologists, Writers' Guild. *Publications:* non-fiction: Fanny Crosby 1985, John Bunyan 1986, D. L. Moody 1987, Susanna Wesley 1987, Florence Nightingale 1988; fiction: Barn Social 1978, Yosemite's Marvellous Creatures 1979, Summer of the Wild Pig 1979, Melon Hound 1980, The Horse Who Loved Picnics 1980, Mystery at McGehan Ranch 1982, Chain Five Mystery 1984, Summer Snow 1984, Winterspring 1985, This Rolling Land 1986, Jungle Gold 1987, Code of Honor 1988, Power of Pinjarra 1989, Taste of Victory 1989, East of Outback 1990, Death Valley 1993, Cat Killer 1993, Dublin Crossing 1993, Mouse Trapped 1993, Gila Monster 1994, Last Dinosaur 1994, Murder on the Mount 1994, Shamrock Shore 1994, Emerald Sea 1994, The Quick and the Dead 1995, King of the Stars 1995, Hyaenas 1998, African Adventure 2003; contrib. to journals and magazines. *Honours:* Warm Beach Writer of the Year 1986, Romance Writers of America Golden Medallion 1987. *Address:* 2563 Highland Loop, Port Townsend, WA 98368, USA. *E-mail:* sdengler@ou.edu.

DENKER, Henry, LLB; American writer and playwright; b. 25 Nov. 1912, New York, NY. *Education:* New York University. *Career:* mem. Dramatists Guild, council, 1970–73; Authors' Guild; Authors League, council; Writers Guild of America East. *Publications:* I'll Be Right Home, Ma, 1947; My Son, the Lawyer, 1949; Salome: Princess of Galilee, 1951; The First Easter, 1951; The Child is Mine, 1955; The Director, 1970; The Kingmaker, 1972; A Place for the Mighty, 1974; The Physicians, 1975; The Experiment, 1976; The Starmaker, 1977; The Scofield Diagnosis, 1977; The Actress, 1978; Error of Judgement, 1979; Horowitz and Mrs Washington, 1979, as play, 1980; The Warfield Syndrome, 1981; Outrage, 1982, as play, 1983, as film, 1985; The Healers, 1983; Kincaid, 1984; Robert, My Son, 1985; Judge Spence Dissents, 1986; The Choice, 1987; The Retreat, 1988; A Gift of Life, 1989; Payment in Full, 1990; Doctor on Trial, 1991; Mrs Washington and Horowitz, too, 1992; Labyrinth, 1994; This Child is Mine, 1995; To Marcy, With Love, 1996; Benjie, 1999; Class Action, 2002. Plays: Time Limit, 1957; A Far Country, 1961; A Case of Libel, 1963; What Did We Do Wrong?, 1967; The Headhunters, 1976; The Second Time Around, 1977; Outrage, 1987; Tea With Madam Bernhardt, 1991; Curtain Call, 1999. *Address:* 241 Central Park W, New York, NY 10024, USA.

DENNETT, Daniel Clement, DPhil; American philosopher, academic and author; *University Professor and Director, Center for Cognitive Studies, Tufts University;* b. 28 March 1942, Beirut; s. of Daniel C. Dennett, Jr and Ruth M. Leck; m. Susan Bell 1962; one s. one d. *Education:* Phillips Exeter High School, Wesleyan Univ., Harvard Univ., Oxford Univ. *Career:* Asst Prof. of Philosophy, Univ. of Calif., Irvine 1965–70, Assoc. Prof. 1971; Assoc. Prof., Tufts Univ. 1971–75, Prof. 1975–85, Distinguished Arts and Sciences Prof. 1985–2000, Dir Center for Cognitive Studies, Tufts 1985–, Univ. Prof. 2000–, also now Austin B. Fletcher Prof. of Philosophy; Visiting Prof., Harvard 1973–74, Pittsburgh 1975, Oxford 1979, Ecole Normale Supérieure, Paris 1985; Visiting Fellow, All Souls Coll. Oxford 1979; John Locke Lecturer, Oxford 1983, Gavin David Young Lecturer, Adelaide, Australia 1984; Woodrow Wilson Fellow 1963, Guggenheim Fellow 1973, 1986, Fulbright Fellow 1978; Fellow Center for Advanced Study in Behavioral Sciences 1979, American Acad. of Arts and Sciences 1987. *Publications:* Content and Consciousness 1969, Brainstorms 1978, The Mind's I (with Douglas Hofstadter) 1981, Elbow Room 1984, The Intentional Stance 1987, Consciousness Explained 1991, Darwin's Dangerous Idea 1995, Kinds of Minds 1996, Brainchildren 1998, Freedom Evolves 2003, Breaking the Spell: Religion as a Natural Phenomenon 2006; numerous articles in professional journals. *Address:* Center for Cognitive Studies, Tufts University, Medford, MA 02155-7059, USA (office). *Telephone:* (617) 627-3297 (office). *Fax:* (617) 627-3952 (office). *E-mail:* ddennett@tufts.edu (office). *Website:* ase.tufts.edu/cogstud/~ddennett.htm (office).

DENNIS, Carl, BA, PhD; American poet, writer and academic; b. 17 Sept. 1939, St Louis, MO. *Education:* Oberlin College, University of Chicago, University of Minnesota, University of California at Berkeley. *Career:* Prof. of English, SUNY at Buffalo, 1966–; Sometime faculty mem., Writing Program, Warren Wilson College; mem. PEN. *Publications:* Poetry: A House of My Own, 1974; Climbing Down, 1976; Signs and Wonders, 1979; The Near World, 1985; The Outskirts of Troy, 1988; Meetings with Time, 1992; Ranking the Wishes, 1997; Practical Gods, 2001; New and Selected Poems 1974–2004, 2004. Other: Poetry as Persuasion, 2001. Contributions: many anthologies, quarterlies, reviews and journals. *Honours:* Guggenheim Fellowship; National Endowment for the Arts Fellowship; Fellow, Rockefeller Study Center, Bellagio, Italy; Ruth Lilly Prize, 2000; Pulitzer Prize in Poetry, 2002. *Address:* 49 Ashland Avenue, Buffalo, NY 14222, USA. *E-mail:* cedennis@buffalo.edu.

DENNIS, Everette Eugene, Jr, BS, MA, PhD; American foundation executive, educator and author; b. 15 Aug. 1942, Seattle, WA; m. Emily J. Smith 1988. *Education:* University of Oregon, Syracuse University, University of Minnesota. *Career:* Asst Prof., Journalism, Mass Communication, Kansas State University, Manhattan, 1968–72; Instructor, Asst Prof., Assoc. Prof., School of Journalism and Mass Communication, University of Minnesota, 1972–81; Visiting Prof., Medill School of Journalism, Northwestern University, 1976–77; Dean, Prof., School of Journalism, University of Oregon, 1981–84; Exec. Dir, The Freedom Forum Media Studies Center, Columbia University; Senior Vice-Pres., The Freedom Forum, Arlington, Virginia; Ed.-in-Chief, Media Studies Journal; mem. International Communication Asscn; Eastman House International Museum of Photographs; American Antiquarian Society; Asscn for Education in Journalism and Mass

Communication; International Press Institute; Society of Professional Journalists. *Publications:* Other Voices: The New Journalism in America, 1973; The Media Society, 1978; The Economics of Libel, 1986; Understanding Mass Communication (ed.), 1988; Demystifying Media Technology, 1993; America's Schools and the Mass Media, 1993; The Culture of Crime, 1995; Radio, The Forgotten Medium, 1995; American Communication Research, 1996. Contributions: hundreds of articles to popular, professional and scholarly periodicals. *Honours:* Harvard University Fellowships, 1978–79, 1980, 1981; Other fellowships; various writing prizes and awards.

DENNISTON, Rev. Robin Alastair, MA, MSc, PhD; British publisher and ecclesiastic; b. 25 Dec. 1926, London; s. of the late Alexander Guthrie Denniston and Dorothy Mary Gilliat; m. 1st Anne Alice Kyffin Evans 1950 (died 1985); one s. two d.; m. 2nd Dr Rosa Susan Penelope Beddington 1987 (died 2001). *Education:* Westminster School and Christ Church, Oxford. *Career:* Ed. Collins 1950–59; Man. Dir Faith Press 1959–60; Ed. Prism 1959–61; Promotion Man. Hodder & Stoughton Ltd 1960–64, Editorial Dir 1966, Man. Dir 1968–72, also Dir Mathew Hodder Ltd and subsidiary cos; Deputy Chair. George Weidenfeld & Nicolson (and subsidiary cos) 1973; Chair. (non-exec.) A. R. Mowbray & Co. 1974–88; Chair. Sphere Books 1975–76, Thomas Nelson & Sons (and subsidiary cos) 1975, Michael Joseph Ltd 1975, George Rainbird Ltd 1975; Dir Thomson Publs Ltd 1975, Hamish Hamilton Ltd 1975, W. W. Norton 1989–; Academic Publr, Oxford Univ. Press 1978, Sr Deputy Sec. to the Dels. 1984–88, Oxford Publr 1984–88; Student of Christ Church 1978; ordained Deacon 1978, Priest 1979; Hon. Curate, Parish of Clifton-on-Teme 1978, New with S Hinksey 1985; Non-Stipendiary Minister, Great with Little Tew 1987–90, St Serfs, Burntisland and St Columba's Aberdour, Fife 1990–93; Priest-in-Charge, Great with Little Tew and Over Worton with Nether Worton 1995–2002. *Publications:* The Young Musicians 1956, Partly Living 1967, Part Time Priests? (ed.) 1960, Anatomy of Scotland (co-ed.) 1992, Churchill's Secret War: Diplomatic Decrypts, the Foreign Office and Turkey 1942–4 1997, Trevor Huddleston: A Life 1999, Thirty Secret Years: A. G. Denniston's Work in Signals Intelligence 1914–44 2007. *Address:* 25 Pyndar Court, Newland, Malvern, Worcs., WR13 5AX, England (home). *Telephone:* (1684) 573141 (home).

DENNY, Neill; British editor; *Editor-in-Chief, The Bookseller*; b. 1966, London; m.; two c. *Career:* worked at Haymarket and Centaur on magazines including Marketing, Marketing Direct and Precision Marketing; Ed. Marketing Direct 1995–98, Retail Week 1999–2004; Ed.-in-Chief The Bookseller 2004–. *Address:* The Bookseller, Fifth Floor, Endeavour House, Shaftesbury Avenue, London, WC2H 8TJ, England. *E-mail:* neill.denny@bookseller.co.uk. *Website:* www.thebookseller.com.

DEPESTRE, René; French poet and writer; b. 29 Aug. 1926, Jacmel, Haiti; m. Nelly Campano 1962. *Education:* Sorbonne, Univ. of Paris. *Career:* Attaché, Office of Culture, UNESCO, Paris 1978–86, mem. Cabinet of Dir-Gen. 1978–82, Section de la Création Artistique 1982–86. *Publications:* poetry: Etincelles 1945, Gerbe de sang 1946, Minerai noir 1956, Un arc-en-ciel pour l'occident chrétien 1967, Journal d'un animal marin (selected poems, 1956–90) 1990, Au matin de la négritude 1990, Anthologie personnelle 1993, Rage de Vivre, poesies completes 2007; fiction: Alléluia pour une femme jardin 1973, Le Mat de cocagne 1979, Hadriana dans tous mes reves 1988, Eros dans un train chinois: Neuf histories d'amour et un conte sorcier 1990; non-fiction: Pour la révolution, pour la poésie 1969, Bonjour et adieu a la négritude 1980, Le Métier à métisser 1998, Encore une mer á traverser 2004, Non-assistance á poètes en danger 2005. *Honours:* Prix Goncourt 1982, Prix Renaudot 1988, Prix Antigone, Montpellier, Prix de la Société des Gens de Lettres, Prix du Roman de l'Académie royale de langue et de littérature françaises de Belgique, Prix Grisane, Italy. *Address:* 31 bis, Route de Roubia, 11200 Lezignan-Corbières, France (home). *Telephone:* (4) 68-27-54-84 (home). *Fax:* (4) 68-27-53-57 (home).

DERFLER, (Arnold) Leslie; American academic and writer; b. 11 Jan. 1933, New York, NY; m. Gunilla Derfler 1962; four d. *Education:* BA, City College, CUNY, 1954; University of Chicago, 1956; University of Paris, 1960; MA, 1957, PhD, 1962, Columbia University. *Career:* Faculty, City College, CUNY, 1959–62, Carnegie Mellon University, 1962–68, University of Massachusetts, Amherst, 1968–69; Prof. of History, Florida Atlantic University, 1969–; Visiting Prof., London Center, Florida State University, 1985. *Publications:* The Dreyfus Affair: Tragedy of Errors, 1963; The Third French Republic, 1870–1940, 1966; Socialism Since Marx, 1973; Alexandre Millerand: The Socialist Years, 1977; President and Parliament: A Short History of the French Presidency, 1984; An Age of Conflict: Readings in 20th Century European History, 1990; Paul Lafargue and the Founding of French Marxism, 1842–1882, 1991; Paul Lafargue and the Flowering of French Socialism, 1882–1911, 1998. *Honours:* American Philosophical Society Grants, 1967, 1976, 1981, 1991; Distinguished Scholar Award, Florida Atlantic University, 1982; National Endowment for the Humanities Fellowship, 1984–85. *Address:* c/o Department of History, Florida Atlantic University, Boca Raton, FL 33431, USA.

DERIEX, Suzanne, LicMathSc, Semi-licTheol; Swiss novelist; b. (Suzanne Piguet-Cuendet), 16 April 1926, Yverdon; m. Jean-François Piguet 1949; three s. *Education:* Univ. of Lausanne. *Publications:* Corinne 1961, San Domenico 1964, L'enfant et la mort 1968, Pour dormir sans rêves 1980, L'homme n'est jamais seul 1983, Les sept vies de Louise Croisier née Moraz 1996, Un arbre de vie 1995, Exils 1999, La Tourmente 2001, Graines de ciel

2004. *Honours:* Jubilé de Lyceum Club de Suisse prize 1963, Prix Veillon 1968, Prix Pro Helvetia 1983, Prix Alpes-Jura 1988, Prix des Murailles 1988, Prix du Livre vaudois 1990. *Address:* Rte de Lausanne 11, 1096 Cully, Switzerland. *Telephone:* (21) 799-15-03. *Fax:* (21) 799-41-47. *E-mail:* suzannederiex@freesurf.ch.

DERR, Mark, AB, MA; American writer; b. (Mark Burgess Derr), 20 Jan. 1950, Baltimore, Md; m. Gina L. Maranto 1982. *Education:* Johns Hopkins Univ., Baltimore. *Publications:* Some Kind of Paradise: A Chronicle of Man and the Land in Florida 1989, Over Florida 1992, The Frontiersman: The Real Life and the Many Legends of Davy Crockett 1993, Dog's Best Friend: Annals of the Dog-Human Relationship 1997, A Dog's History of America: How Our Best Friend Explored, Conquered and Settled A Continent 2004; contrib. to The Atlantic, Audubon Society, Natural History, New York Times. *Address:* 4245 Sheridan Avenue, Miami Beach, FL 33140, USA (home). *Telephone:* (305) 534-2604 (office). *E-mail:* mark.derr@gmail.com (office). *Website:* mbdog.blogspot.com.

DERSHOWITZ, Alan Morton, LLB; American lawyer and academic; *Felix Frankfurter Professor of Law, Harvard University*; b. 1 Sept. 1938, New York, NY; s. of Harry Dershowitz and Claire Ringel; m. Carolyn Cohen; two s. one d. *Education:* Brooklyn Coll. and Yale Univ. *Career:* admitted to DC Bar 1963, Mass Bar 1968, US Supreme Court 1968; law clerk to Chief Judge David Bazelon, US Court of Appeal 1962–63, to Justice Arthur Goldberg, US Supreme Court 1963–64; mem. Faculty, Harvard Coll. 1964–, Prof. of Law 1967–, Felix Frankfurter Prof. of Law 1993–; Fellow, Center for Advanced Study of Behavioral Sciences 1971–72; consultant to Dir Nat. Inst. for Mental Health 1967–69, Pres.'s Comm. on Civil Disorders 1967, Pres.'s Comm. on Causes of Violence 1968, Nat. Asscn for Advancement of Colored People Legal Defense Fund 1967–68, Pres.'s Comm. on Marijuana and Drug Abuse 1972–73, Ford Foundation Study on Law and Justice 1973–76; rapporteur, Twentieth Century Fund Study on Sentencing 1975–76; Guggenheim Fellow 1978–79; mem. Comm. on Law and Social Action, American Jewish Congress 1978; Dir American Civil Liberties Union 1968–71, 1972–75, Asscn of Behavioral and Social Sciences, NAS 1973–76; Chair. Civil Rights Comm. New England Region, Anti-Defamation League, B'nai B'rith 1980. *Publications:* Psychoanalysis, Psychiatry and the Law (with others) 1967, Criminal Law: Theory and Process 1974, The Best Defense 1982, Reversal of Fortune: Inside the von Bülow Case 1986, Taking Liberties: A Decade of Hard Cases, Bad Laws and Bum Raps 1988, Chutzpah 1991, Contrary to Popular Opinion 1992, The Abuse Excuse 1994, The Advocate's Devil 1994, Reasonable Doubt 1996, The Vanishing American Jew 1997, Sexual McCarthyism 1998, Just Revenge 1999, The Genesis of Justice 2000, Supreme Injustice: How the High Court Hijacked Election 2000 2001, Letters to a Young Lawyer 2001, Shouting Fire: Civil Liberties in a Turbulent Age 2002, Why Terrorism Works 2002, America Declares Independence 2003, The Case for Israel 2003, America on Trial 2004, Preemption: A Knife That Cuts Both Ways 2006; contrib. articles to legal journals. *Honours:* Hon. MA (Harvard Coll.) 1967; Hon. LLD (Yeshiva) 1989. *Address:* Harvard University Law School, Hauser 520, 1575 Massachusetts Avenue, Cambridge, MA 02138-2801, USA (office). *Telephone:* (617) 495-4617 (office). *Fax:* (617) 495-7855 (office). *E-mail:* dersh@law.harvard.edu (office). *Website:* www.law.harvard.edu (office).

DESAI, Anita, BA, FRSL; Indian writer and academic; *John E. Burchard Professor Emerita of Humanities, Massachusetts Institute of Technology*; b. 24 June 1937, Mussoorie; d. of Toni Nimé and D. N. Mazumdar; m. Ashvin Desai 1958; two s. two d. *Education:* Queen Mary's School, Delhi and Miranda House, Univ. of Delhi. *Career:* Elizabeth Drew Visiting Prof., Smith Coll., Mass, USA 1987–88; Purington Prof. of English, Mount Holyoke Coll. 1988–92; John E. Burchard Prof. of Humanities, MIT, Cambridge, Mass 1993–2002, now Prof. Emer.; Gildersleeves Prof., Barnard Coll.; Visiting Scholar, Rockefeller Foundation, Bellagio, Italy; Sidney Harman Visiting Prof. and Writer-in-Residence, Baruch Coll. 2003; mem. American Acad. of Arts and Letters, PEN, Sahitya Akademi, India. *Film screenplay:* In Custody 1994. *Television:* The Village By The Sea (BBC) 1994. *Publications:* Cry, The Peacock 1963, Voices in the City 1965, Bye-Bye, Blackbird 1971, Where Shall We Go This Summer? 1973, Fire on the Mountain 1978, Games at Twilight 1979, Clear Light of Day 1980, The Village by the Sea 1983, In Custody 1984, Baumgartner's Bombay 1988, Journey to Ithaca 1995, Fasting, Feasting 1999, Diamond Dust and Other Stories 2000, The Zigzag Way 2004; children's books: The Peacock Garden, Cat on a Houseboat. *Honours:* Hon. Fellow, Girton Coll., Cambridge 1988, Clare Hall, Cambridge 1991, Hon. mem. American Acad. of Arts and Letters; Royal Soc. of Literature Winifred Holtby Prize 1978, Sahitya Acad. Prize 1978, Fed. of Indian Publishers Award 1978, Guardian Prize for Children's Fiction 1983, Hadassah Prize, New York 1988, Literary Lion, NY Public Library 1993, Alberto Moravia Prize for Literature, Italy 1999, Padma Sri 1989, Scottish Arts Council Neil Gunn Award for Int. Writing 1994. *Literary Agent:* Rogers, Coleridge & White Ltd, 20 Powis Mews, London, W11 1JN, England. *Telephone:* (20) 7221-3717 (office). *Fax:* (20) 7229-9084 (office).

DESAI, Kiran; Indian novelist; b. 3 Sept. 1971, India; d. of Anita Desai. *Education:* Bennington Coll., Hollins Univ. and Columbia Univ. *Publications:* novels: Hullabaloo in the Guava Orchard (Betty Trask Award) 1998, The Inheritance of Loss (Man Booker Prize) 2006. *Address:* c/o Hamish Hamilton, 80 Strand, London, WC2 0RL, England (office).

DESCÔTEAUX, Bernard; Canadian journalist and publisher; *Chief Editor, Le Devoir;* b. 16 Sept. 1947, Sainte-Monique, Quebéc; two c. *Education:* Univ. of Toronto, University of Montréal in Québec (UQAM), Univ. of Montréal. *Career:* journalist La Voix de l'est (The Voice of the East) 1969–70; information officer, Canadian Industries Ltd. 1970–71; travel co-ordinator, Tourbec Inc. 1972–73; information officer, Information Canada 1973–74; Municipal Chronicler, Le Devoir newspaper 1974–76, Parl. Corresp. to French Nat. Ass. 1976–83, 1987–90, Parl. Corresp. to Fed. Govt., Ottawa 1983–87, Chief Ed. and Dir of Information 1990–92, Chief Ed. 1992–. *Address:* Le Devoir, 2050 rue de Bleury, Ninth Floor, Montréal, QC H3A 3M9, Canada (office). *E-mail:* redaction@ledevoir.com (office). *Website:* www.ledevoir.com (office).

DESHPANDE, Shashi, BA, MA, BL; Indian writer; b. 19 Aug. 1938, Dharwad; d. of Adya Rangacharya and Sharada Adya; m. D. H. Deshpande 1962; two s. *Education:* Univs of Mumbai and Mysore. *Career:* fmrly worked for a law journal and magazine; full-time writer 1970–; mem. Sahitya Akademi Bd for English 1989–94. *Film script:* Drishti 1990. *Publications:* The Dark Holds no Terrors 1980, If I Die Today 1982, Come Up and Be Dead 1982, Roots and Shadows 1983, That Long Silence 1988, The Binding Vine 1993, A Matter of Time 1996, Small Remedies 2000; short stories: The Legacy and Other Stories 1978, It Was Dark 1986, The Miracle and Other Stories 1986, It Was the Nightingale 1986, The Intrusion and Other Stories 1994, The Stone Women 2000, Collected Stories, Vol. I 2003, Vol. II 2004, Moving On 2004; non-fiction: Writing from the Margin and other essays 2003. *Honours:* Thirumathi Rangammal Prize 1984, Sahitya Akademi Award for a Novel 1990, Nanjangud Thirumalamba Award 1991. *Literary Agent:* Alison M. Bond Agency, 155 W 72nd Street, New York, NY 10023, USA. *Address:* 409 41st Cross, Jayanagar V Block, Bangalore 560041, India (home). *Telephone:* (80) 26636228 (home). *Fax:* (80) 26641137 (home). *E-mail:* shashid@vsnl.com (home).

DESMÉE, Gilbert Georges, Dip; French writer, editor and educator; b. 29 Jan. 1951, Suresnes; m. Maria Desmée 1952. *Education:* University of Cachan, University of Versailles. *Career:* Dir, Sapriphage literary review 1988–2001; mem. ELVIR. *Publications:* Le Schiste Métamorphique, 1990; L'Infini pour respirer in Histoire de livres d'artistes, 1991; Un Magdalénien Contemporain in Robert Pérot, 1994; En écho des corps d'écriture, 1995; Je m'en dit tu, 1996; Seul le geste serait fécond, 1997. Contributions: anthologies, including: Le Bel Aujourd'hui; Boris Lejeune; journals, including: Encres Vives; Sapriphage; Agone; Contre-Vox; L'Estracelle; Textuerre; Présage; L'Arbre à Paroles; Le Cri d'Os.

DESMOND, Richard Clive; British publishing and media executive; *Chairman, Northern & Shell PLC;* b. 8 Dec. 1951, s. of Cyril Desmond and Millie Desmond; m. Janet Robertson 1983; one s. *Career:* Advertisement Exec. Thomson Newspapers 1967–68; Group Advertisement Man. Beat Publs Ltd 1968–74; f. Northern & Shell Network 1974 (later Northern & Shell PLC) Chair. 1974–; launched Int. Musician (magazine) 1974; Demonde Advertising 1976–89; Publr Next, Fitness, Cook's Weekly, Venture, Penthouse, Bicycle, Stamps, Electric Blue, Rock CD, Guitar, For Woman, Attitude, Arsenal, Liverpool; f. Fantasy Channel 1995, OK! Magazine 1993–, OK! TV 1999–; owner Express Newspapers 2000–. *Address:* Northern & Shell PLC, Ludgate House, 245 Blackfriars Road, London, SE1 9UX, England (office). *Telephone:* (20) 7928-8000 (office). *Fax:* (20) 7922-7789 (office). *E-mail:* ed98@cityscape.co .uk (office).

DeSOTO, Lewis, MFA; South African writer and artist; b. 1952, Bloemfontein; m. Gunilla Josephson. *Education:* Univ. of British Columbia. *Career:* moved to Canada 1967; fmr Ed., Literary Review of Canada. *Exhibitions:* paintings in public and private galleries across Canada. *Publications:* A Blade of Grass 2004; contrib. to numerous literary journals. *Honours:* Books in Canada/Writers' Trust Short Prose Award. *Address:* c/o The Maia Press Ltd, 82 Forest Road, London, E8 3BH, England (office).

DETHERIDGE, Andrew John, BA, MA, PGCE; British writer, poet and lecturer; b. 11 April 1969, Stourport, Worcestershire, England; s. of Colin Detheridge and Barbara Norris; m. Alexandra Jayne Cope; one d. *Education:* Univ. of Nottingham, Univ. of Wolverhampton. *Career:* English/History Teacher, St Peter's School 1994–95; English Teacher, George Dixon School 1995–96, Castle High School 1996–99; Lecturer and Poet-in-Residence, Sandwell Coll., West Midlands 1999–2004, Castle High School 2005–; mem. Equity. *Publications:* Naked 1999, In the Light of Dreams 2000, Ocean's Spray 2001, In Character 2001, The City of the Dead 2002, The World Spins Darkly 2002, Vast Skies 2002, Travelling Through Life 2003, Snow Falls from the Branch 2005, The Break-dancing Spider 2005, Away with Words 2006; contrib. poetry, short stories, haiku, senryu in numerous magazines and anthologies. *Honours:* Forward Press one of the top 100 poets of the year 1999, 2003, Partners in Poetry Open Competition winner 1999, second prize 2000, jt first prize East Barnet Festival Competition 2001, haiku in Museum of Haiku Literature, award winner Hoshi-to-Mori Int. Tanka Contest 2004, runner-up Ragged Raven Poetry Competiton 2004. *Address:* Haden House, 188b Cradley Road, Netherton, Dudley, West Midlands DY2 9TE, England (home). *Telephone:* (1384) 416988 (home). *E-mail:* adetheridge@castle.dudley.gov.uk (office).

DEVANE, Terry (see Healy, Jeremiah)

DEVENNE, François, PhD; French writer; b. 1964, Nantes. *Career:* wrote student thesis on geography and agriculture of Kilimanjaro; fmr course co-ordinator Univ. d'Artois; worked at Inst. Français de Recherche en Afrique (IFRA), Nairobi, Kenya; now lives in Paris. *Publications:* Kilimandjaro montagne, mémoire, modernité (co-ed., essays and photographs) 2003, Trois rêves au Mont Mérou (novel) 2003, La Traversée des contes (novel) 2006. *Address:* c/o Actes Sud, 18 rue Séguier, 75006 Paris, France. *E-mail:* accueil .paris@actes-sud.fr.

DEVEREAUX, Emily (see Lewis-Smith, Anne Elizabeth)

DEVERELL, Rex Johnson, BA, BD, STM; Canadian playwright; b. 17 July 1941, Toronto, ON; m. Rita Joyce Shelton 1967, one s. *Education:* McMaster University, Union Theological Seminary. *Career:* Resident Playwright, Globe Theatre, Regina, 1975–91; Pres., Playwrights Union of Canada, 1991–93; mem. Saskatchewan Writers Guild; Playwrights Union of Canada; Saskatchewan Playwrights Centre; Amnesty International. *Publications:* Boiler Room Suite, 1978; Superwheel, 1979; Drift, 1981; Black Powder, 1981. Other: Deverell of the Globe (anthology), television and radio scripts, opera libretti and children's plays. Contributions: Canadian Theatre Review; Canadian Children's Literature; Canadian Drama; Prairie Fire; Grain. *Honours:* McMaster University Honour Society, 1963; Ohio State Award, 1974; Canadian Authors Asscn Medal, 1978; Major Armstrong Award, 1986.

DEVERELL, William Herbert, BA, LLB; Canadian writer; b. 4 March 1937, Regina, Sask.; m. Tekla Melnyk; one s. one d. *Education:* Univ. of Saskatchewan. *Career:* on staff, Saskatoon Star-Phoenix 1956–60, Canadian Press, Montréal 1960–62, Vancouver Sun, 1963; partner in law firm, Vancouver 1964–79; writer 1979–; mem. British Columbia Bar Asscn, British Columbia Civil Liberties Asscn, Crime Writers' Asscn, Crime Writers of Canada, Writers Union of Canada (Chair. 1994–95). *Publications:* fiction: Needles 1979, High Crimes 1979, Mecca 1983, Dance of Shiva 1984, Platinum Blues 1988, Mindfield 1989, Kill All the Lawyers 1994, Slander 1999, Laughing Falcon 2001, Mind Games 2003, April Food 2005; non-fiction: Fatal Cruise: The Trial of Robert Frisbee 1991, Street Legal – The Betrayal 1995, Trial of Passion 1997. *Honours:* McClelland and Stewart/Seal First Novel Award 1979, Book of the Year Award, Periodical Distributors Asscn of Canada 1980, Arthur Ellis Canadian Crime Writer Award 1998, Dashiell Hammett Int. Asscn of Crime Writers Award 1998. *Address:* Box 14, Rural Route 1, North Pender Island, BC V0N 2M0, Canada. *E-mail:* william@deverell.com. *Website:* www.deverell.com.

DEVEREUX, Eve (see Barnett, Paul Le Page)

DEVI, Ananda, PhD; Mauritian novelist. *Career:* currently living in France. *Publications:* novels: Rue la Poudrière 1989, Le Voile de Draupadi 1993, L'Arbre fouet 1997, Moi, l'interdite 2000, Pagli 2001, Soupir 2002, Le Long désir 2003, La Vie de Joséphin le Fou 2003; short stories: Solstices 1977, Le Poids des êtres 1987. *Address:* c/o Éditions Gallimard, 5 rue Sébastien-Bottin, Paris 75328, France (office).

DEVLIN, Polly, OBE; Irish writer, journalist, broadcaster, film-maker and art critic; b. Co. Tyrone; m. Adrian Garnett; three d. *Education:* Nat. Film School. *Career:* Features Ed. Vogue magazine; columnist, New Statesman, London Evening Standard; journalist with Vogue (American edn), Sunday Times, the Observer; hosted series of talks and interviews on TV for BBC Northern Ireland 1980s, has broadcast numerous talks and has written a radio play for BBC, London, mem. Northern Ireland team, Round Britain Quiz, BBC Radio 4; art critic for The International Herald Tribune 1990–91; mem. judging panel Booker Prize, UK, Irish Times-Aer Lingus Irish Literature Prizes 1992. *Film:* The Daisy Chain (documentary, also writer and dir. *Publications:* Vogue Book of Fashion Photography 1979, The Far Side of the Lough 1983, All of Us There 1983, Dora or the Shifts of the Heart 1990, Mitchell Beazley Guide Book to Dublin, Only Sometimes Looking Sideways (essays) 1998. *Honours:* winner Vogue talent competition 1964. *Website:* www .pollydevlin.co.uk.

DEW, Robb (Reavill) Forman; American writer; b. 26 Oct. 1946, Mount Vernon, OH; m. Charles Burgess Dew 1968, two s. *Education:* Louisiana State Univ. *Career:* Fellow Iowa Writers' Workshop 1984. *Publications:* Dale Loves Sophie to Death (American Book Award) 1982, The Time of Her Life 1984, Fortunate Lives 1991, A Southern Thanksgiving: Recipes and Musings for a Manageable Feast 1992, The Family Heart: A Memoir of When Our Son Came Out 1994, The Evidence Against Her 2001, The Truth of the Matter 2005. *Honours:* Guggenheim grant 1983. *Literary Agent:* Miriam Altshuler Literary Agency, 53 Old Post Road North, Red Hook, NY 12571, USA. *Telephone:* (845) 758-9408. *Fax:* (845) 758-3118. *E-mail:* malalit@ulster.net. *Address:* 218 Buckley Street, Williamstown, MA 01267, USA (home). *Telephone:* (413) 458-3477 (home). *Fax:* (413) 458-5171 (home). *E-mail:* robbformandew@aol.com.

DEWDNEY, Christopher; Canadian poet and writer; b. 9 May 1951, London, ON; m. 1st Suzanne Dennison 1971 (divorced 1975); one d.; m. 2nd Lise Downe 1977 (divorced 1990); one s.; m. 3rd Barbara Gowdy. *Education:* South and Westminster Collegiate Institutes, London, ON, H. B. Beal Art Annex, London, ON. *Career:* Assoc. Fellow, Winters College, York University, Toronto, 1984; Poetry Ed., Coach House Publishing, Toronto, 1988; Academic Adviser, Columet College, York University, 1997–. *Publications:* Poetry: Golders Green, 1972; A Paleozoic Geology of London, Ontario, 1973; Fovea Centralis, 1975; Spring Trances in the Control Emerald Night, 1978; Alter Sublime, 1980; The Cenozoic Asylum, 1983; Predators of the Adoration: Selected Poems 1972–1982, 1983; Permugenesis, 1987; The Radiant Inventory, 1988; Demon Pond, 1994. Other: The Immaculate Perception, 1986; Recent Artifacts from the Institute of Applied Fiction, 1990; Concordant

Proviso Ascendant: A Natural History of Southwestern Ontario, Book III, 1991; The Secular Grail, 1993; Demon Pond, 1994; Last Flesh, 1998; Signal Fires, 2000; The Natural History, 2002. Contributions: periodicals. *Honours:* Design Canada Award, 1974; CBC Prize, 1986; Fellow, Columet College, York University; Fellow, McLuhen Program in Culture and Technology.

DEWEESE, Jean (see De Weese, Thomas Eugene (Gene))

DEWHIRST, Ian, MBE, BA; British librarian (retd), writer and poet; b. 17 Oct. 1936, Keighley, Yorkshire; s. of Harold Dewhirst and Mary E. Dewhirst. *Education:* Victoria Univ. of Manchester. *Career:* staff, Keighley Public Library 1960–91; mem. Yorkshire Dialect Soc., Edward Thomas Fellowship. *Publications:* The Handloom Weaver and Other Poems 1965, Scar Top and Other Poems 1968, Gleanings from Victorian Yorkshire 1972, A History of Keighley 1974, Yorkshire Through the Years 1975, Gleanings from Edwardian Yorkshire 1975, The Story of a Nobody 1980, You Don't Remember Bananas 1985, Keighley in Old Picture Postcards 1987, In the Reign of the Peacemaker 1993, Down Memory Lane 1993, Images of Keighley 1996, A Century of Yorkshire Dialect (co-ed.) 1997, Keighley in the Second World War 2005; contrib. to Yorkshire Ridings Magazine, Lancashire Magazine, Dalesman, Cumbria, Pennine Magazine, Transactions of the Yorkshire Dialect Society, Yorkshire Journal, Down Your Way. *Honours:* Hon. DLitt (Univ. of Bradford) 1996. *Address:* 14 Raglan Avenue, Fell Lane, Keighley, West Yorkshire BD22 6BJ, England (home). *Telephone:* (1535) 662268 (home).

DEWHURST, Eileen Mary, MA; British writer; b. 27 May 1929, Liverpool, England; m. (divorced). *Education:* St Anne's Coll., Oxford. *Career:* mem. CWA, Soc. of Authors. *Publications:* crime novels: Death Came Smiling 1975, After the Ball 1976, Curtain Fall 1977, Drink This 1980, Trio in Three Flats 1981, Whoever I Am 1982, The House That Jack Built 1983, There Was a Little Girl 1984, Playing Safe 1985, A Private Prosecution 1986, A Nice Little Business 1987, The Sleeper 1988, Dear Mr Right 1990, The Innocence of Guilt 1991, Death in Candie Gardens 1992, Now You See Her 1995, The Verdict on Winter 1996, Alias the Enemy 1997, Roundabout 1998, Death of a Stranger 1999, Double Act 2000, Closing Stages 2001, No Love Lost 2001, Easeful Death 2003, Naked Witness 2003; contrib. to Ellery Queen's Mystery Magazine, CWA Annual Anthologies. *Literary Agent:* c/o Gregory and Co., 3 Barb Mews, London, W6 7PA, England.

DEWHURST, Keith, BA; British writer; b. 24 Dec. 1931, Oldham, England; m. 1st Eve Pearce 1958 (divorced 1980); one s. two d.; m. 2nd Alexandra Cann 1980. *Education:* Peterhouse, Cambridge. *Career:* sports writer, Evening Chronicle, Manchester 1955–59; presenter, Granada TV 1968–69, BBC2 TV, London 1972; arts columnist, The Guardian, London 1969–72; writer-in-residence, Western Australia APA, Perth 1984. *Publications:* Lark Rise to Candleford (two plays) 1980, Captain of the Sands (novel) 1981, Don Quixote (play) 1982, McSullivan's Beach (novel) 1986, Black Snow (play) 1992, War Plays (plays) 1997, Philoctetes (trans. of play) 2000. *Address:* 12 Abingdon Road, London, W8 6AF, England.

DEXTER, (Norman) Colin, OBE, MA (Cantab.), MA (Oxon.); British author; b. 29 Sept. 1930, Stamford, Lincs.; s. of Alfred Dexter and Dorothy Dexter (née Towns); m. Dorothy Cooper 1956; one s. one d. *Education:* Stamford School, Christ's Coll., Cambridge. *Career:* nat. service (Royal Signals) 1948–50; taught Classics 1954–66; Sr Asst Sec. Oxford Delegacy of Local Examinations 1966–88; Fellow, St Cross Coll., Oxford. *Publications:* Last Bus to Woodstock 1975, Last Seen Wearing 1977, The Silent World of Nicholas Quinn 1977, Service of All the Dead 1979, The Dead of Jericho 1981, The Riddle of the Third Mile 1983, The Secret of Annexe 3 1986, The Wench is Dead 1989, The Jewel that was Ours 1991, The Way through the Woods 1992, Morse's Greatest Mystery and Other Stories 1993, The Daughters of Cain 1994, Death is Now my Neighbour 1996, The Remorseful Day 1999. *Honours:* Gold Dagger, Crime Writers' Assocn (twice), Silver Dagger (twice), Cartier Diamond Dagger, Freedom of the City of Oxford 2001. *Address:* 456 Banbury Road, Oxford, OX2 7RG, England.

DEXTER, Peter (Pete) Whittemore, BA; American columnist and writer; b. 22 July 1943, Pontiac, MI; m. Dian McDonough; one c. *Education:* Univ. of South Dakota. *Career:* columnist, Philadelphia Daily News 1976–86, Esquire magazine 1985–86, Sacramento Bee 1986–90s. *Film screenplays:* Rush 1991, Mulholland Falls 1996, Michael 1996, Shortcut to Happiness 2003. *Publications:* God's Pocket 1983, Deadwood (also screenplay, as Wild Bill) 1986, Paris Trout (also screenplay) (Nat. Book Award) 1988, Brotherly Love 1991, The Paperboy 1994, Train 2003, Paper Trails 2007. *Honours:* Associated Press (California-Nevada) Mark Twain Award 1987, Penn West Award, Los Angeles 1988, Bay Area Book Reviewers Award 1988. *Address:* c/o Ecco Press, HarperCollins Publishers, 10 East 53rd Street, New York, NY 10022, USA.

DHALIWAL, Daljit, MA; British journalist; *Anchor, Wide Angle;* b. London; m. Lee Patrick Sullivan. *Education:* Univ. of East London, Univ. of London. *Career:* reporter BBC, London 1990, NI Corresp. and Anchor, BBC World – 1995; reporter ITN, London 1995, Anchor World News for Public TV, Channel 4 News and World Focus –2001; Anchor Your World Today and World Report CNN (Cable Network News) Int. (CNNI), Atlanta, Ga USA 2002–04; Anchor, Wide Angle (Public Broadcasting System), New York, 2002, 2006–; reported on Balkans conflict, genocide in Rwanda, US war against terror, tensions in Middle East, war in Iraq; interviews with Gerry Adams, Benazir Bhutto, Yasser Arafat, Jack Straw; moderator and host UN Confs in New York and The Hague; Judge, Amnesty Int. Media Awards, BAFTA Awards. *Honours:* Dr

hc (Univ. of East London). *Address:* Wide Angle, c/o Thirteen/WNET, 450 West 33rd Street, New York, NY 10001, USA (office). *Telephone:* (212) 560-1313 (office). *Fax:* (212) 560-1314 (office). *Website:* www.pbs.org/wnet/wideangle (office).

DI BLASI, Debra, BFA; American educator and writer; b. 27 May 1957, Kirksville, MO; m. Carlos Roberto di Blasi 1984 (divorced 1989). *Education:* University of Missouri, Columbia, Kansas City Art Institute, San Francisco State University. *Career:* Advertising Man., Robert Half of Northern California, San Francisco, 1986–89; Advertising Production Man., MacWeek, San Francisco, 1989; Asst to the Exec. Dir, Accessible Arts Inc, Kansas City, MO, 1990–92; Senior Secretary, International Network Design and Engineering Dept, Spring Communications, Kansas City, MO, 1992–95; Writing Tutor, 1994, Learning Specialist, 1995–, Kansas City Art Institute, Kansas City, MO; Judge, River of Words National Poetry Competition, 1997; Assoc. Guest Ed., SOMA; Lectures, readings from her works; mem. National Geographic Society; Writers Place; Kansas City Art Institute Alumni Circle. *Publications:* The Season's Condition (screenplay), 1993; Drought (screenplay), 1997; Drought and Say What You Like (novellas), 1997; Prayers of an Accidental Nature (novellas), 1999. Contributions: short stories in anthologies, incl.: Lovers: Writings by Women, 1992; Exposures: Essays by Missouri Women, 1997; short stories in periodicals, incl.: Moondance; Cottonwood; Potpourri; New Letters; Sou'wester; New Delta Review; AENE; Colorado-North Review; Transfer; Essays, articles and reviews to periodicals, incl.: SOMA; New Art Examiner. *Honours:* Eyster Prize for Fiction, for short story An Interview with My Husband, New Delta Review, 1991.

DI CICCO, Pier Giorgio, BA, BEd, MDiv, BSTheol; Canadian poet and priest; b. 5 July 1949, Arezzo, Italy. *Education:* University of Toronto, St Paul's University. *Career:* founder and Poetry Ed., Poetry Toronto Newsletter, 1976–77; Assoc. Ed., Books in Canada, 1976–79; Co-Ed., 1976–79, Poetry Ed., 1980–82, Waves; Ordained Roman Catholic Priest and Assoc. Pastor, St Anne's Church, Brampton, Ontario, 1993–; Poet Laureate of Toronto 2007–07. *Publications:* We Are the Light Turning, 1975; The Sad Facts, 1977; The Circular Dark, 1977; Dancing in the House of Cards, 1977; A Burning Patience, 1978; Roman Candles: An Anthology of 17 Italo-Canadian Poets (ed.), 1978; Dolce-Amaro, 1979; The Tough Romance, 1979; A Straw Hat for Everything, 1981; Flying Deeper into the Century, 1982; Dark to Light: Reasons for Humanness: Poems 1976–1979, 1983; Women We Never See Again, 1984; Twenty Poems, 1984; Post-Sixties Nocturne, 1985; Virgin Science: Hunting Holistic Paradigms, 1986; The City of Hurried Dreams, 1993. *Honours:* Canada Council Awards, 1974, 1976, 1980; Carleton University Italo-Canadian Literature Award, 1979.

DI MICHELE, Mary, MA; Canadian poet, writer and academic; b. 6 Aug. 1949, Lanciano, Italy; m. (divorced); one d. *Education:* Univ., Univ. of Windsor. *Career:* Poetry Ed., Toronto Life, 1980–81, Poetry Toronto, 1982–84; Writer-in-Residence, Univ. of Toronto, 1985–86, Metro Reference Library, Toronto, 1986, Regina Public Library, 1987–88; Writer-in-Residence, 1990, then Assoc. Prof., Creative Writing Programme, Concordia Univ.; mem. Italian-Canadian Writers Asscn; Writers Union. *Publications:* Poetry: Tree of August, 1978; Bread and Chocolate, 1980; Mimosa and Other Poems, 1981; Necessary Sugar, 1984; Immune to Gravity, 1986; Luminous Emergencies, 1990; Stranger in You: Selected Poems & New, 1995; Debriefing the Rose, 1998. Novels: Under My Skin, 1994; Tenor of Love, 2005. Editor: Anything is Possible, 1984. Contributions: anthologies and periodicals. *Honours:* First Prize for Poetry, CBC Literary Competition, 1980; Silver Medal, DuMaurier Poetry Award, 1982; Air Canada Writing Award, 1983. *Address:* c/o Dept of English, Concordia University, 1455 de Maisonneuve Blvd W, Montréal, QC H3G 1M8, Canada.

DI PRIMA, Diane; American poet, writer, dramatist, translator and publisher and artist; b. 6 Aug. 1934, New York, NY; m. 1st Alan S. Marlowe 1962 (divorced 1969); m. 2nd Grant Fisher 1972 (divorced 1975); two s. three d. *Education:* Swarthmore Coll. *Career:* co-founder, New York Poets Theater, 1961–65; Co-Ed. (with LeRoi Jones), 1961–63, Ed., 1963–69, Floating Bear magazine; Publisher, Poets Press, 1964–69, Eidolon Editions, 1974–; Faculty, Naropa Institute, 1974–97, New College of California, San Francisco, 1980–87; Co-Founder, San Francisco Institute of Magical and Healing Arts, 1983–91; Senior Lecturer, California College of Arts and Crafts, Oakland, 1990–92; Visiting Faculty, San Francisco Art Institute, 1992; Adjunct Faculty, California Institute of Integral Studies, 1994–95; Master Poet-in-Residence Columbia College Chicago 2000. *Publications:* This Kind of Bird Flies Backward, 1958; Ed., Various Fables from Various Places, 1960; Dinners and Nightmares, 1961, 1998; The New Handbook of Heaven, 1962; Translator, The Man Condemned to Death, 1963; Poets Vaudeville, 1964; Seven Love Poems from the Middle Latin, 1965; Haiku, 1966; New Mexico Poem, 1967; Earthsong, 1968; Hotel Albert, 1968; Ed., War Poems, 1968; Memoirs of a Beatnik, 1969, 1988; LA Odyssey, 1969; The Book of Hours, 1970; Kerhonkson Journal 1966, 1971; Revolutionary Letters, 1971; The Calculus of Variation, 1972; Loba, Part 1, 1973; Ed., The Floating Bear: a Newsletter, 1973; Freddie Poems, 1974; Brass Furnace Going Out, 1975; Selected Poems 1956–1975, 1975; Loba, Part 2, 1976; Loba as Eve, 1977; Loba, Parts 1–8, 1978; Wyoming Series, 1988; The Mysteries of Vision, 1988; Pieces of a Song: Selected Poems, 1990; Seminary Poems, 1991; The Mask is the Path of the Star, 1993; Loba, Parts 9–16, 1998; Recollections of My Life as a Woman, 2001, Fun with Forms 2001, Towers Down (with Clive Matson) 2002, The Ones I Used to Laugh With 2003; work trans. into over 20 languages. Contributions: Over 300 literary and popular magazines and newspapers; Work appeared in over 100 anthologies. *Honours:* National Endowment for the Arts Grants, 1966, 1973; Co-ordinating Council of Little Magazines Grants, 1967, 1970; Lapis Foundation Awards, 1978, 1979; Institute for Aesthetic Development Award, 1986; Lifetime Service Award, National Poetry Asscn. 1993; Hon. DLitt, St Lawrence University, Canton, New York, 1999. *Address:* 78 Niagara Avenue, San Francisco, CA 94112, USA.

DI ROSA, Antonio, BSc; Italian journalist; *Editor, La Gazzetta;* b. 17 April 1951, Messina; s. of Calogero Rossetti and Anna Rossetti; partner; one s. two d. *Career:* began career at Giornale di Calabria 1974–78; moved to Gazzetta del Popolo 1978, Deputy Head Home News 1979–81, Head 1981–84; joined La Stampa 1984, Head Home News April–July 1988; Deputy Cen. Ed.-in-Chief Corriere della Sera 1988–93, Cen. Ed.-in-Chief 1993–96, Deputy Ed. 1996–2000; Ed. Il Secolo XIX 2000; Ed. La Gazzetta dello Sport 2004–. *Honours:* Premio Senigallia 1983. *Address:* Gazzetta dello Sport, Via Solferino 28, 20121 Milan (office); Via G. Morelli 1, Milan, Italy (home). *Telephone:* (02) 62828024 (office). *Fax:* (02) 62827917 (office). *E-mail:* adirosa@rcs.it (office). *Website:* www.gazzetta.it (office).

DIAMOND, Jared Mason, BA, PhD; American physiologist and academic; *Professor of Geography and Physiology, David Geffen School of Medicine, UCLA;* b. 10 Sept. 1937, Boston; s. of Louis K. Diamond and Flora K. Diamond; m. Marie M. Cohen 1982. *Education:* Harvard Univ., Univ. of Cambridge, UK. *Career:* Fellow Trinity Coll., Cambridge 1961–65, Jr Fellow Soc. of Fellows, Harvard Univ. 1962–65; Assoc. in Biophysics, Harvard Medical School 1965–66; Assoc. Prof. of Physiology, Univ. of Calif. Medical School, Los Angeles 1966–68, Prof. 1968–; Research Assoc. Dept of Ornithology American Museum of Natural History 1973–; mem. NAS; Fellow American Acad. of Arts and Sciences, American Physiological Soc., Biophysics Soc., American Philosophical Soc., American Soc. of Naturalists, Fellow American Ornithologists Union. *Publications:* The Avifauna of the Eastern Highlands of New Guinea 1972, Ecology and Evolution of Communities (co-ed.) 1975, Birds of Karkar and Bagabab Islands, New Guinea (co-author) 1979, Community Ecology (co-author) 1985, The Third Chimpanzee: The Evolution and Future of the Human Animal 1992, Guns, Germs and Steel: The Fates of Human Societies (Pulitzer Prize, Cosmos Prize) 1998, Why is Sex Fun? 1998, The Birds of Northern Melanesia 2001, Collapse: How Societies Choose to Fail or Survive 2004; several hundred research papers on physiology, ecology and ornithology; contribs to Discover, Natural History, Nature. *Honours:* Burr Award of Nat. Geographical Soc. 1979, Los Angeles Times Book Prize 1992, Science Book Prize, New Scientist London 1992, Nat. Medal of Sciences 1999, Tyler Prize 2001. *Address:* Department of Physiology, David Geffen School of Medicine, 1251A Bunche Hall, University of California at Los Angeles, Los Angeles, CA 90095-1524, USA (office). *Telephone:* (310) 825-6177 (office). *E-mail:* jdiamond@geog.ucla.edu (office). *Website:* 149.142.237.180/faculty/diamond.htm (office).

DIAZ, Junot, BA, MFA; American writer; b. 1968, Santo Domingo, Dominican Republic. *Education:* Rutgers University, Cornell University. *Publications:* Drown 1996, Negocios 1997; contrib. to New Yorker, Paris Review, African Verse, anthologies. *Address:* c/o Riverhead Books, 375 Hudson Street, New York, NY 10014, USA.

DICKEY, Christopher, BA, MS; American journalist and writer; b. 31 Aug. 1951, Nashville, TN; m. 1st Susan Tuckerman 1969 (divorced 1979); m. 2nd Carol Salvatore 1980, one s. *Education:* University of Virginia, Boston University. *Career:* staff, Washington Post, 1974–86; Cairo Bureau Chief, 1986–88, Paris Bureau Chief, 1988–93, 1995–, Middle East Regional Ed., 1993–, Newsweek; mem. Council on Foreign Relations. *Publications:* With the Contras: A Reporter in the Wilds of Nicaragua, 1986; Expats: Travels in Arabia, from Tripoli to Teheran, 1990; Innocent Blood (novel), 1997; Summer of Deliverance: A Memoir of Father and Son 1998, The Sleeper (novel) 2004; contrib. to periodicals. *Honours:* Interamerican Press Asscn Award, 1980; Mary Hemingway Award, Overseas Press Club, 1983; Edward Weintal Award for Diplomatic Reporting, Georgetown University. *Address:* c/o Newsweek, 251 W 57th Street, New York, NY 10019, USA (office). *Website:* www.christopherdickey.com (home).

DICKIE, Margaret, AB, PhD; American academic and writer; b. 13 Sept. 1935, Bennington, Vermont; m. Benjamin Uroff 1961 (divorced 1978); two d. *Education:* Middlebury College, Brown University. *Career:* Asst Prof., then Prof. of English, 1967–87, Dept Head, 1983–87, University of Illinois at Urbana-Champaign; Helen S. Lancer Distinguished Prof., University of Georgia, Athens, 1987–; Mem., Board of Trustees, University of Georgia Foundation; mem. MLA of America; American Studies Asscn. *Publications:* Hart Crane: The Patterns of His Poetry, 1975; Sylvia Plath and Ted Hughes, 1979; On the Modernist Long Poem, 1986; Lyric Contingencies: Emily Dickinson and Wallace Stevens, 1991; Gendered Modernisms: Women Poets and Their Readers (co-ed.), 1996; Stern, Bishop, and Rich: Lyrics of Love, War, and Place, 1997. *Honours:* Distinguished Alumni Award, Middlebury College. *E-mail:* mmdickie@parallel.park.uga.edu.

DICKINSON, Donald Percy, BA, MFA; Canadian writer and teacher; b. 28 Dec. 1947, Prince Albert, SK; m. Chellie Eaton 1970; two s. one d. *Education:* Univ. of Saskatchewan, Univ. of British Columbia. *Career:* Fiction Ed., Prism International 1977–79; teacher of English, Lillooet Secondary School 1981–2003; mem. Oldtimers' Hockey Asscn, Writers' Union of Canada. *Publications:* novels: The Crew 1993, Robbiestime 2000; short stories: Third

Impressions 1982, Fighting the Upstream 1987, Blue Husbands 1991; contrib. to Best Canadian Short Fiction 1984, Words We Call Home 1990, The New Writers 1992, The Porcupine Quill Reader 1996. *Honours:* Bankson Award 1979, Ethel Wilson Fiction Prize 1991. *Address:* 554 Victoria Street, Box 341, Lillooet, BC V0K 1V0, Canada.

DICKINSON, Margaret (see Muggeson, Margaret Elizabeth)

DICKINSON, Peter, MA, DMus, LRAM, ARCM, FRCO; British composer, pianist and writer; *Emeritus Professor, Keele University and Goldsmiths' College, London;* b. 15 Nov. 1934, Lytham, Lancashire, England; m. Bridget Jane Tomkinson; two s. *Education:* Queens' Coll., Cambridge and Juilliard School of Music, New York, USA. *Career:* various teaching posts in New York, London and Birmingham; First Prof. of Music, Keele Univ. 1974–84, Prof. Emeritus 1984–; Prof., Goldsmiths' Coll., London 1991–97, Emeritus Prof. 1997–; Head of Music, Inst. of United States Studies, Univ. of London 1997–2004; performances, broadcasts and recordings as pianist, mostly with sister, mezzo-soprano Meriel Dickinson. *Compositions include:* Transformations for orchestra 1970, Organ Concerto 1971, Piano Concerto 1984, Merseyside Echoes for orchestra 1985, Violin Concerto 1986, chamber music, choral works, songs, keyboard music, church music. *Recordings include:* Piano Concerto, Outcry, Organ Concerto, Song Cycles (Auden, Dylan Thomas, Cummings, Heath-Stubbs, Lord Berners, Philip Larkin), Rags, Blues and Parodies (Burns, Corso, Lord Byron, Stevie Smith, Satie), American Trio, organ and piano works. *Publications:* 20 British Composers (ed.) 1975, The Complete Songs and The Complete Piano Music of Lord Berners (ed., two vols) 1982, Collected Works for Solo Piano of Lennox Berkeley (ed.) 1989, Marigold: The Music of Billy Mayerl 1999, Copland Connotations: Studies and Interviews 2002, The Music of Lennox Berkeley 2003, Cage Talk: Historic Interviews With and About John Cage 2006; contrib. to various books and journals, incl. book chapters and dictionaries. *Honours:* Hon. DMus (Keele Univ.) 1999; Hon. FTCL. *Address:* c/o Novello & Company, 8–9 Frith Street, London, W1V 5TZ, England.

DICKSON, Mora Agnes, DipArt; British author and artist; b. 20 April 1918, Glasgow, Scotland. *Education:* Edinburgh College of Art, Byam Shaw School of Drawing and Painting, London. *Publications:* New Nigerians, 1960; Baghdad and Beyond, 1961; A Season in Sarawak, 1962; A World Elsewhere, 1964; Israeli Interlude, 1966; Count Us In, 1968; Longhouse in Sarawak, 1971; Beloved Partner, 1974; A Chance to Serve (ed.), 1977; The Inseparable Grief, 1977; Assignment in Asia, 1979; The Powerful Bond, 1980; Nannie, 1988.

DICKSON, Peter George Muir, DLitt, FBA; British historian and academic; *Professor Emeritus, University of Oxford;* b. 26 April 1929, London; s. of William Muir Dickson and Regina Dowdall-Nicolls; m. Ariane Flore Faye 1964; one d. *Education:* St Paul's School, London, Worcester Coll., Oxford. *Career:* Fellow Nuffield Coll., Oxford 1954–56; Tutor, St Catherine's Soc., Oxford 1956–60, Fellow St Catherine's Coll. 1960–96, Emer. Fellow 1996–, Univ. Reader in Modern History 1978–89, Prof. of Early Modern History 1989–96, Emer. Prof. 1996–. *Publications:* The Sun Insurance Office 1710–1960 1960, The Financial Revolution in England 1688–1756 1967, Finance and Government under Maria Theresia 1740–1780 1987. *Address:* Field House, Iffley, Oxford, OX4 4EG, England (home). *Telephone:* (1865) 271757 (office); (1865) 779599 (home).

DIDION, Joan, BA; American writer; b. 5 Dec. 1934, Sacramento, Calif.; d. of Frank Reese Didion and Eduene (née Jerrett) Didion; m. John Gregory Dunne 1964 (died 2003); one d. (died 2005). *Education:* Univ. of Calif., Berkeley. *Career:* Assoc. Features Ed. Vogue magazine 1956–63; fmr columnist Esquire, Life, Saturday Evening Post, fmr contributor Nat. Review; freelance writer 1963–; mem. American Acad. of Arts and Letters, American Acad. of Arts and Sciences, Council on Foreign Relations. *Screenplays:* The Panic in Needle Park 1971, Play It as It Lays 1972, A Star is Born 1976, True Confessions 1981, Hills Like White Elephants 1991, Broken Trust 1995, Up Close and Personal 1996. *Publications include:* novels: Run River 1963, Play It as It Lays 1970, A Book of Common Prayer 1977, Telling Stories 1978, Democracy 1984, The Last Thing He Wanted 1996; essays: Slouching Towards Bethlehem 1969, The White Album 1978, After Henry 1992; non-fiction: Salvador 1983, Miami 1987, After Henry 1992, Political Fictions 2001, Where I Was From: A Memoir 2003, The Year of Magical Thinking (Nat. Book Award for Non-fiction) 2005. *Honours:* First Prize Vogue's Prix de Paris 1956, American Acad. of Arts and Letters Morton Dauwen Zabel Prize 1978, Edward McDowell Medal 1996, George Polk Award 2001. *Literary Agent:* Janklow & Nesbit, 445 Park Avenue, New York, NY 10022-2606, USA.

DIEKMANN, Kai; German newspaper executive; *Editor-in-Chief, Bild;* b. 1965. *Career:* corresp. Bild and Bild am Sonntag, Bonn 1987; chief reporter Illustrierten Bunte, Munich 1989–91; Chief Ed. Bild-Zeitung, Berlin 1991–92, Chief Ed. and Chief Political Corresp. Bild-Zeitung, Hamburg 1992–97, Chief Corresp. Bild and Bild am Sonntag, Bonn 1987; Chief Reporter Illustrierten Bunte, Munich 1989–91; Chief Ed. Welt am Sonntag 1998–2000, Ed.-in-Chief Bild and Publr Bild and Bild am Sonntag 2001–. *Publications include:* (co-author) Rita Süssmuth im Gespräch 1994, Die neue Bundespräsident im Gespräch 1994, Helmut Kohl: Ich wollte Deutschlands Einheit 1996. *Address:* Bild, Axel-Springer-Platz 1, 20355 Hamburg, Germany (office). *Telephone:* (40) 34700 (office). *Fax:* (40) 345811 (office). *Website:* www.bild.de (office).

DIENSTBIER, Jiří; Czech politician, journalist and writer; *Ambassador-at-Large and Director and Trustee, Reuters Founders Share Company;* b. 20 April

1937, Kladno; s. of Jiří Dienstbier and Anna Dienstbierová; m. 4th J. Melenová 1999; one s. three d. *Education:* Charles Univ., Prague. *Career:* Czechoslovak Broadcasting 1959, foreign correspondent in Far East, USSR, Germany, France, UK, Yugoslavia 1960–68, USA 1968–69; dismissed from broadcasting 1970; worked in archives of an eng company; expelled from Czechoslovak CP and Journalists' Union 1969; signed Charter 1977, spokesman 1979; sentenced to three years in prison 1979–82; boilerman 1982–89; spokesman for Charter 77 1985–86; ed. of Čtverec (The Square), a periodical on int. politics 1979–; Co-Founder of Lidové Noviny (The People's Newspaper) 1988–; Czechoslovak Minister for Foreign Affairs 1989–92; mem. Council of State 1990–92, Deputy Prime Minister CFSR 1990–92, Deputy to House of People Fed. Ass. 1990–92, Chair. Council of the Civic Movt 1991–; Chair. Free Democrats Party (fmrly Civic Movt) 1993–95 (merged with Liberal Nat. Social Party 1995); Chair. Liberal Nat. Social Party 1995–96 (left Party 1997); Chair. Czech Council on Foreign Relations; mem. Comm. on Global Governance; mem. UN Cttee for Solving Global Problems 1995–; Special Envoy to Gen. Ass. of UN 1995; lecturer 1998–; Special Rapporteur of the UN Comm. on Human Rights for Bosnia and Herzegovina, Croatia and Yugoslavia 1998–2001; Dir and Trustee, Reuters Founders Share Co. 2005–; Visiting Prof., Claremont Grad. Univ., Calif. 1997–98, Univ. of North Carolina, Chapel Hilll 1999, Charles Univ., Prague 2001, 2003, Watson Inst., Brown Univ. 2003. *Publications include:* The Night Began at Three in the Morning 1967, Before We Roast Young Pigs 1976, Christmas Present 1977, Guests 1978, Charter 77 – Human Rights and Socialism 1981, Radio Against Tanks 1988, Dreaming of Europe 1990, From Dreams to Reality 1999; Kosovo Shades over Balkans 2002, Tax on Blood 2002, stage plays, articles and essays in Samizdat. *Honours:* Grand Cross of Order for Merit (Order of Kts of Malta) 1990; Das Grosse Verdienstkreuz mit Stern und Schulterband (Germany) 2002, Officier Légion d'honneur 2005; Dr hc (Univ. de Bourgogne) 1993; Humanist of the Year (USA) 1979, Francesco Cossiga Medal (Italy) 1991, Pro Merito Medal, Parl. Ass. Council of Europe 1991, Hero of Freedom of the Press in the World, IPI (Boston, USA) 2000. *Address:* Rytířská 31, 11000 Prague (office); Apolinářská 6, 12800 Prague 2, Czech Republic (home). *Telephone:* (2) 2161-0109; (2) 2492-3321 (home). *E-mail:* jiri_dienstbier@mzv.cz (office); j@dienstbier.cz (home).

DIEZ, Rolo; Argentine novelist, screenwriter and journalist; b. 1940, Buenos Aires. *Publications:* Los compañeros 1987, Una baldosa en el valle de la muerte 1992, La Vida que me doy (Flauta Magica) 2001, Papel Picado 2003, Tequila Blue 2004. *Address:* c/o Bitter Lemon Press, 37 Arundel Gardens, London, W11 2LW, England. *E-mail:* books@bitterlemonpress.com. *Website:* www.bitterlemonpress.com.

DIFORIO, Robert G., BA; American publishing executive; *Principal, D4EO Literary Agency*; b. 19 March 1940, Mamaroneck, NY; s. of Richard John Diforio Sr and Mildred Kuntz; m. Birgit Rasmussen 1983; one s. one d. *Education:* Williams Coll., Mass and Harvard Business School's Advanced Man. Program. *Career:* Vice-Pres. Kable News Co. 1970; Vice-Pres. and Sales Man. New American Library (NAL) 1972, Sr Vice-Pres. and Marketing Dir 1976, Pres. and Publr 1980–81, CEO and Chair. Bd NAL/E. P. Dutton 1983–89; Prin. D4EO Literary Agency 1991–. *Address:* 7 Indian Valley Road, Weston, CT 06883, USA (office). *Telephone:* (203) 544-7180 (office); (203) 544-7182 (home). *Fax:* (203) 544-7160 (office). *E-mail:* d4eo@optonline.net (office). *Website:* www.publishersmarketplace.com/members/d4eo (office).

DIGGINS, John Patrick, BA, MA, PhD; American academic and writer; *Distinguished Professor of History, City University of New York*; b. 1 April 1935, San Francisco, CA; m. Jacy Battles 1960 (divorced 1977); one s. one d. *Education:* Univ. of California at Berkeley, San Francisco State Coll., Univ. of Southern California at Los Angeles. *Career:* Assoc. Prof., later Prof. of History, Univ. of California at Irvine; Distinguished Prof. of History, CUNY; mem. ACLS, American Historical Asscn, American Philosophical Soc., American Studies Asscn. *Publications:* Mussolini and Fascism: The View from America 1972, The American Left in the Twentieth Century 1973, Up from Communism: Conservative Odysseys in American History 1975, The Bard of Savagery: Thornstein Veblen and Modern Social Theory 1978, The Problem with Authority in America (ed. with Mark E. Kahn) 1981, The Lost Soul of American Politics: Virtue, Self-Interest, and the Foundations of Liberalism 1984, The Proud Decades: America in War and Peace, 1941–1960 1988, The Rise and Fall of the American Left 1992, The Promise of Pragmatism: Modernism and the Crisis of Knowledge and Authority 1994, Max Weber: Politics and the Spirit of Tragedy 1996, The Liberal Persuasion: Arthur Schlesinger Jr and the Challenge of the American Past 1997, On Hallowed Ground: Abraham Lincoln and the Foundations of American History 2000, Ronald Reagan: Fate, Freedom and the Making of History 2007; contrib. to scholarly books and journals. *Honours:* Nat. Endowment for the Humanities Fellowship 1972–73, American Historical Asscn John H. Dunning Award 1973, Guggenheim Fellowship 1975–76. *Address:* c/o Graduate School and University Center, City University of New York, 365 Fifth Avenue, New York, NY 10016, USA. *E-mail:* jdiggins@gc.cuny.edu.

DILKS, David Neville, BA, FRSL, FCGI; British historian, academic and university administrator; b. 17 March 1938, Coventry; s. of Neville Ernest and Phyllis Dilks; m. Jill Medlicott 1963; one s. *Education:* Royal Grammar School, Worcester, Hertford Coll. and St Antony's Coll., Oxford. *Career:* Asst Lecturer, Lecturer LSE 1962–70; Prof. of Int. History, Univ. of Leeds 1970–91, Chair. School of History 1974–79, Dean Faculty of Arts 1975–77; Vice-Chancellor Univ. of Hull 1991–99; Visiting Fellow, All Souls' Coll., Oxford 1973; Chair. and Founder Commonwealth Youth Exchange Council 1968–73; mem. Advisory Council on Public Records 1977–85, Inst. of Contemporary British History 1986–, Univs Funding Council 1988–91; Trustee Edward Boyle Memorial Trust 1982–96, Imperial War Museum 1983–91, Lennox-Boyd Trust 1984–91, Royal Commonwealth Soc. Library Trust 1987–91; Pres. Int. Cttee for the History of the Second World War 1992–2000; Freeman, Goldsmiths' Co. 1979, Liveryman 1984; Fellow, City and Guilds of London Inst. *Television:* historical adviser, The Gathering Storm (HBO/BBC) 2002. *Publications:* Curzon in India (Vols 1 & 2) 1969, 1970, The Diaries of Sir Alexander Cadogan (ed.) 1971, Retreat from Power (two vols, ed.) 1981, The Missing Dimension: Government and Intelligence Communities in the Twentieth Century (ed.) 1984, Neville Chamberlain: Pioneering & Reform, 1869–1929 1984, Barbarossa 1941, The Axis, The Allies and World War: Retrospect, Recollection, Revision (jtly), Grossbritannien und der deutsche Widerstand (jtly) 1994, The Great Dominion: Winston Churchill in Canada 1900–1954 2005; and numerous articles in learned journals. *Honours:* Dr hc (Russian Acad. of Sciences) 1996; Curzon Prize, Univ. of Oxford 1960, Prix du rayonnement de la langue française 1994, Médaille de Vermeil, Acad. Française 1994. *Address:* Wits End, Long Causeway, Leeds, LS16 8EX, West Yorks., England (home). *Telephone:* (113) 267-3466 (home). *Fax:* (113) 261-1240 (home).

DILLARD, Annie, MA; American author; b. 30 April 1945, Pittsburgh, Pa; d. of Frank Doak and Gloria Lambert; m. 1st R. H. W. Dillard 1965; m. 2nd Gary Clevidence 1979 (divorced); m. 3rd Robert D. Richardson, Jr 1988; one d. two step-d. *Education:* Hollins College. *Career:* contributing editor, Harper's Magazine 1974–85; Distinguished Visiting Prof. Wesleyan Univ. 1979–83, Adjunct Prof. 1983–, writer in residence 1987–; mem. Bd of Dirs Writers' Conf. 1984– (Chair. 1991–); mem. Nat. Cttee on US –China Relations 1982–. *Publications:* Tickets for a Prayer Wheel (poetry), Pilgrim at Tinker Creek (prose) 1974, Holy the Firm 1978, Living by Fiction 1982, Teaching a Stone to Talk 1982, Encounters with Chinese Writers 1984, An American Childhood 1987, The Writing Life 1989, The Living (novel) 1992, The Annie Dillard Reader 1994, Mornings Like This (poetry) 1995, For the Time Being 1999, The Maytrees (prose) 2007. *Honours:* Pulitzer Prize (for Pilgrim at Tinker Creek) 1975, Nat. Endowment for the Arts (Literature) Grant 1981, John Simon Guggenheim Memorial Grant 1985, Gov. of Conn.'s Award 1993, The Campion Award 1994, The Milton Prize 1994, American Arts and Letters Award in Literature 1998. *Address:* c/o Timothy Seldes, Russell and Volkening, 50 W 29th New York, NY 10001-4227, USA.

DILLARD, Richard Henry Wilde; American academic, writer, poet and editor; b. 11 Oct. 1937, Roanoke, Virginia; m. 1st Annie Doak 1965 (divorced 1972); m. 2nd Cathy Hankla 1979. *Education:* BA, Roanoke College, Salem, Virginia, 1958; MA, 1959, PhD, 1965, University of Virginia. *Career:* Instructor, Roanoke College, 1961, University of Virginia, 1961–64; Asst Prof., 1964–68, Assoc. Prof., 1968–74, Prof. of English, 1974–, Hollins College, Virginia; Contributing Ed., Hollins Critic, 1966–77; Ed.-in-Chief, Children's Literature, 1992–. *Publications:* Fiction: The Book of Changes, 1974; The First Man on the Sun, 1983; Omniphobia, 1995. Poetry: The Day I Stopped Dreaming About Barbara Steele and Other Poems, 1966; News of the Nile, 1971; After Borges, 1972; The Greeting: New and Selected Poems, 1981; Just Here, Just Now, 1994. Non-Fiction: Horror Films, 1976; Understanding George Garrett, 1988. Editor: The Experience of America: A Book of Readings (with Louis D. Rubin Jr), 1969; The Sounder Few: Essays from 'The Hollins Critic' (with George Garrett and John Rees Moore), 1971. Contributions: periodicals. *Honours:* Acad. of American Poets Prize, 1961; Ford Foundation Grant, 1972; O. B. Hardison Jr Poetry Award, Folger Shakespeare Library, Washington, DC, 1994. *Address:* PO Box 9671, Hollins College, CA 24020, USA.

DILLINGHAM, William Byron, BA, MA, PhD; American academic and writer; *Charles Howard Candler Professor Emeritus, Emory University*; b. 7 March 1930, Atlanta, Ga; s. of Cornelius Howard Dillingham and Emerald Storey; m. Elizabeth Joiner 1952; one s. two d. *Education:* Emory Univ., Univ. Pennsylvania. *Career:* Instructor, Emory Univ. 1956–58, Asst Prof., Assoc. Prof., Prof., Charles Howard Candler Prof. of American Literature 1959–96, Prof. Emer. 1996–; mem. Advisory Bds Nineteenth-Century Literature, South Atlantic Bulletin. *Publications:* Humor of the Old Southwest 1965, Frank Norris: Instinct and Art 1969, An Artist in the Rigging: The Early Work of Herman Melville 1972, Melville's Short Fiction, 1853–1856 1977, Melville's Later Novels 1986, Practical English Handbook (10th edn) 1996, Melville and his Circle: The Last Years 1996, Rudyard Kipling: Hell and Heroism 2005; contrib. of numerous articles and reviews to scholarly journals. *Honours:* Emory Univ. Scholar/Teacher of the Year 1984, Emory Univ. Award of Distinction 2000, Distinguished Emer. Award 2004, numerous fellowships. *Address:* 1416 Vistaleaf Drive, Decatur, GA 30033 (home); 3258 Esperanza Avenue, Daytona Beach Shores, FL 32108 USA (home). *Telephone:* (404) 636-4486 (Decatur) (home). *E-mail:* wdillin@emory.edu.

DILLON, Millicent Gerson, BA, MA; American writer; b. 24 May 1925, New York, NY; m. 1st Murray Lesser 1948 (divorced 1959); two d. *Education:* Hunter College, CUNY, San Francisco State University. *Career:* mem. PEN, Authors' Guild. *Publications:* Baby Perpetua and Other Stories, 1971; The One in the Back is Medea (novel), 1973; A Little Original Sin: The Life and Work of Jane Bowles, 1981; After Egypt, 1990; The Dance of the Mothers (novel), 1991; You Are Not I: A Portrait of Paul Bowles, 1998; Harry Gold: A Novel, 2000. Contributions: Southwest Review; Witness; Threepenny Review;

The New Yorker; Raritan. *Honours:* Five O. Henry Short Story Awards; Best American Short Stories, 1992; Guggenheim Fellowship; National Endowment for the Humanities Fellowship. *Literary Agent:* Ira Silverberg, Donadio and Olson, 121 W 27th Street, New York, NY 10001, USA. *Address:* 83 Sixth Avenue, San Francisco, CA 94118, USA.

DILSAVER, Paul, BA, BS, MA, MFA; American poet, writer and editor; b. 8 Dec. 1949, Colorado. *Education:* University of Southern Colorado, Colorado State University, Bowling Green State University, Ohio, SUNY. *Career:* Instructor, Laramie County Community College, Cheyenne, WY, 1973–74, Casper College, WY, 1974–77, Western Illinois University, Macomb, 1979–81; Poetry Ed., Rocky Mountain Creative Arts Journal and Chapbook Series, 1974–78; Poet-in-Residence, Wyoming Arts Council, 1977–78; Ed., Blue Light Books, 1979–, Blue Light Review, 1983–91; Asst Prof. of English, Carroll College, Helena, Montana, 1981–84; Lecturer in English, University of Southern Colorado, 1986–91; Visiting Instructor of English, Anoka-Ramsey College, Coon Rapids, Minnesota, 1991–92. *Publications:* Malignant Blues (poems), 1976; Words Wyoming (anthology), 1976; A Brutal Blacksmith: An Anvil of Bruised Tissue (poems), 1979; Encounters with the Antichrist (prose poems), 1982; Character Scatology (poems), 1984; Stories of the Strange (fiction), 1985; Nurtz! Nurtz! (novel), 1989; A Cure for Optimism (poems), 1993; The Toilet Papers (anthology), 1994; Medi-Phoria, 1999; Hardcore Haiku, 2000. Contributions: various anthologies and periodicals.

DIMARCO, Cris, BA, MAT; American editor and writer; b. (Cris Newport), 14 July 1960, Melrose Park, IL; m.; two c. *Education:* Univ. of Massachusetts at Boston, Tufts Univ. *Career:* Asst Prof. of English 1991, Assoc. Prof. of English 1994, New Hampshire Technical Inst.; Sr Ed., Windstorm Creative 1997–. *Publications:* Sparks Might Fly 1994, The White Bones of Truth 1994, Queen's Champion: The Legend of Lancelot Retold 1997, 1001 Nights: Exotica 1 1999, Exotica 2 2002, Kresh: The Golton Box 2004; contrib. to periodicals. *Address:* PO Box 28, Port Orchard, WA 98366, USA. *E-mail:* crisdimarco@windstormcreative.com.

DIMBLEBY, David, MA; British broadcaster and journalist; b. 28 Oct. 1938, London; s. of the late Richard Dimbleby and of Dilys Thomas; m. 1st Josceline Gaskell 1967 (divorced 2000); one s. two d.; m. 2nd Belinda Giles 2000; one s. *Education:* Charterhouse, Christ Church, Oxford, Univs of Paris and Perugia. *Career:* presenter and interviewer, BBC Bristol 1960–61; Chair. Dimbleby and Sons Ltd 1986–2001, fmrly Man. Dir 1967. *Broadcasts include:* Quest (religious programme), What's New? (children's science), People and Power 1982–83; General Election Results Programmes 1979, 1983, 1987, 2001, various programmes for the Budget, by-elections, local elections etc.; presenter Question Time BBC 1993–. *Documentary films include:* Ku-Klux-Klan, The Forgotten Million, Cyprus: The Thin Blue Line 1964–65, South Africa: The White Tribe (Royal TV Soc. Supreme Documentary Award) 1979, The Struggle for South Africa (US Emmy Award, Monte Carlo Golden Nymph) 1990, US–UK Relations: An Ocean Apart 1988, David Dimbleby's India 1997; live commentary on many public occasions including: State Opening of Parliament, Trooping the Colour, Wedding of HRH Prince Andrew and Sarah Ferguson, HM The Queen Mother's 90th Birthday Parade (Royal TV Soc. Outstanding Documentary Award), Funeral of Diana, Princess of Wales 1997, Memorial services including Lord Olivier (Royal TV Soc. Outstanding Documentary Award), How We Built Britain (and book) 2007. *Publication:* An Ocean Apart (with David Reynolds) 1988. *Honours:* Richard Dimbleby Award, BAFTA 1998. *Literary Agent:* c/o Rosemary Scoular, PFD, Drury House, 34-43 Russell Street, London, WC2B 5HA, England. *Telephone:* (20) 7344-1084. *Fax:* (20) 7836-9539.

DIMBLEBY, Jonathan, BA; British broadcaster, journalist and writer; b. 31 July 1944, Aylesbury, Bucks.; s. of the late Richard Dimbleby and of Dilys Thomas; m. Bel Mooney 1968 (divorced); one s. one d. *Education:* Univ. Coll. London. *Career:* reporter BBC Bristol 1969–70, World at One (BBC Radio) 1970–71, This Week (Thames TV) 1972–78, 1986–88, TV Eye 1979, Jonathan Dimbleby in Evidence series (Yorkshire TV) 1980–84; Assoc. Ed./Presenter First Tuesday 1982–86; Presenter/Ed. Jonathan Dimbleby on Sunday (TV-am) 1985–86, On the Record (BBC TV) 1988–93, Charles: the Private Man, the Public Role (Central TV) 1994, weekly political programme Jonathan Dimbleby (ITV) 1995–; presenter Any Questions? and Any Answers? (both BBC Radio 4) 1987–; main presenter of Gen. Election coverage (ITV); Pres. Voluntary Service Overseas 1999–, Soil Asscn 1997–, Royal Soc. for the Protection of Birds 2001–04, Bath Festivals Trust 2003–06; Vice-Pres. Council for Protection of Rural England 1997–; Trustee Richard Dimbleby Cancer Fund, Dimbleby Cancer Care and the Susan Chilcott Scholarship. *Publications:* Richard Dimbleby 1975, The Palestinians 1979, The Prince of Wales: A Biography 1994, The Last Governor 1997. *Honours:* Richard Dimbleby Award 1974. *Literary Agent:* David Higham Associates, Ltd, 5 Lower John Street, Golden Square, London, W1R 4HA, England. *Telephone:* (20) 7437-7888 (office).

DINNERSTEIN, Leonard, BA, MA, PhD; American academic and writer; *Professor Emeritus of American History, University of Arizona, Tucson;* b. 5 May 1934, New York, NY; m. Myra Anne Rosenberg 1961; one s. one d. *Education:* City Coll., CUNY, Columbia Univ., New York. *Career:* Instructor, New York Inst. of Tech. 1960–65; Asst Prof., Fairleigh Dickinson Univ. 1967–70; Assoc. Prof., Univ. of Arizona, Tucson 1970–72, Prof. of American History 1972–2003, Prof. Emer. 2003–. *Publications:* The Leo Frank Case 1968, The Aliens (with F. C. Jaher, aka Uncertain Americans) 1970, American

Vistas (with K. T. Jackson) 1971, Antisemitism in the United States 1971, Jews in the South (with M. D. Palsson) 1973, Decisions and Revisions (with J. Christie) 1975, Ethnic Americans: A History of Immigration and Assimilation (with D. M. Reimers) 1975, Natives and Strangers (with R. L. Nichols and D. M. Reimers) 1979, America and the Survivors of the Holocaust 1982, Uneasy at Home 1987, Antisemitism in America 1994. *Address:* 1981 Miraval Cuarto, Tucson, AZ 85718, USA (home). *Telephone:* (520) 615-8585 (home). *Fax:* (520) 615-8586 (home). *E-mail:* dinnerst@u.arizona.edu (home).

DIONNE, Joseph Lewis, BA, MS; American publisher; b. 29 June 1933, Montgomery, Ala; s. of Antonio Ernest Joseph Dionne and Myrtle Mae (Armstrong) Dionne; m. Joan F. Durand 1954; two s. one d. *Education:* Hofstra Univ., Columbia Univ. *Career:* Guidance Counsellor, LI public schools 1956–61; Asst Prof., Hofstra Univ., Hempstead, NY 1962–63; Dir of Instruction, Project Dir Ford Foundation School Improvement, Brentwood, NY public schools 1963–66; Vice-Pres. (Research and Devt) Educational Devt Labs, Huntington, NY 1966–68; Vice-Pres. and Gen. Man. CTB/McGraw-Hill, Monterey, Calif. 1968–73; Sr Vice-Pres. (Corp. Planning) McGraw-Hill Inc., New York 1973–77, Pres. McGraw-Hill Information Systems Co., New York 1977–79, Exec. Vice-Pres. (Operations) McGraw Hill Inc. 1979–81, Pres. 1981–93, CEO 1983–98, Chair. 1988–98; mem. Bd of Dirs, Equitable Life Insurance Co. of America, United Telecommunications Inc.; Trustee Harris Corpn, Teachers' Coll., Columbia Univ., Hofstra Univ.

DIRIE, Waris; Somali writer and model; b. 1964. *Career:* emigrated to London 1978; maid to Somalian amb., janitor McDonald's, model; f. Desert Dawn; UNFPA Special Amb. for Women's Rights in Africa 1997–; Founder Waris Dirie Foundation (to campaign against Female Genital Mutilation). *Publications:* Desert Flower 1998, Desert Dawn 2002, Desert Children 2005. *Honours:* Hon. mem. Club of Budapest. *Address:* c/o Virago Press, Brettenham House, Lancaster Place, London, WC2E 7EN, England. *Telephone:* (20) 7911-8000. *Fax:* (20) 7911-8100. *Website:* www.waris-dirie-foundation.com.

DISCH, Thomas Michael, (Leonie Hargrave, Dobbin Thorpe); American writer, poet, dramatist, librettist and lecturer; b. 2 Feb. 1940, Des Moines, IA. *Education:* Cooper Union, New York, New York University. *Career:* lecturer at colleges and universities; Artist-in-Residence, College of William and Mary, 1996; mem. National Book Critics Circle; PEN; Writers Guild. *Publications:* Fiction: The Genocides, 1965; Mankind Under the Leash, 1966; The House That Fear Built (with John Sladek), 1966; Echo Round His Bones, 1967; Black Alice (with John Sladek), 1968; Camp Concentration, 1968; The Prisoner, 1969; 334, 1974; Clara Reeve, 1975; On Wings of Song, 1979; Triplicity, 1980; Neighboring Lives (with Charles Naylor), 1981; The Businessman: A Tale of Terror, 1984; Amnesia 1985; The M.D.: A Horror Story, 1991; The Priest: A Gothic Romance, 1995. Poetry: The Right Way to Figure Plumbing, 1972; ABCDEFG HIJKLM NOPQRST UVWXYZ, 1981; Orders of the Retina, 1982; Burn This, 1982; Here I Am, There You Are, Where Were We, 1984; Yes, Let's: New and Selected Poetry, 1989; Dark Verses and Light, 1991; The Dark Old House, 1995. Criticism: The Castle of Indolence, 1995; The Dreams Our Stuff is Made of: How Science Fiction Conquered the World, 1998. Other: Short story collections; plays; opera libretti; Children's books. Contributions: many anthologies and periodicals. *Honours:* O. Henry Prizes, 1975, 1979; John W. Campbell Memorial Award, 1980; BSFA Award, 1981. *Address:* Box 226, Barryville, NY 12719, USA.

DISIPIO, Rocco Thomas, BSc; American writer; b. 17 Dec. 1949, Philadelphia, PA; m. Jane Heeres Newell 1974 (divorced). *Education:* Michigan State University. *Publications:* Arcadia Ego, 1995; Darkness Paradise, 1998. Contributions: Exile; Canadian Literary Journal. *Honours:* USA Today Award 1998.

DISKI, Jenny, FRSL; British writer; b. 1947, London. *Education:* Univ. Coll. London. *Career:* teacher 1970s–early 1980s. *Television writing:* A Fair and Easy Passage, The Ultimate Object of Desire, Murder in Mind. *Publications:* novels: Nothing Natural 1986, Rainforest 1987, Then Again 1990, Happily Ever After 1991, Monkey's Uncle 1994, The Dream Mistress 1996, Only Human: A Comedy 2000, After These Things 2004; short stories: The Vanishing Princess 1995; essay collections: Don't 1998, A View from the Bed 2001; travel writing: Stranger on a Train: Daydreaming and Smoking Around America with Interruptions 2002, On Trying to Keep Still 2006; autobiography: Skating to Antarctica 1997; contrib. to The Observer, The Guardian, The Telegraph, The Independent, LRB. *Honours:* Mind Prize 1997, Thomas Cook Travel Book Award 2003, J. R. Ackerley Prize for Autobiography 2003. *Address:* c/o Little, Brown & Co., Time Warner Book Group, Brettenham House, Lancaster Place, London, WC2E 7EN, England.

DIVINE, Robert Alexander, BA, MA, PhD; American academic and writer; *Professor Emeritus of American History, University of Texas at Austin;* b. 10 May 1929, New York, NY; m. 1st Barbara Christine Renick 1955; three s. one d. (died 1993); m. 2nd Darlene S. Harris 1996 (died 2003). *Education:* Yale Univ. *Career:* Instructor, Univ. of Texas at Austin 1954–57, Asst Prof. 1957–61, Assoc. Prof. 1961–63, Prof. 1963–80, George W. Littlefield Prof. of American History 1981–96, Prof. Emer. 1996–; Fellow, Center for Advanced Study in the Behavioural Sciences, Stanford 1962–63; Albert Shaw Lecturer, Johns Hopkins Univ. 1968; mem. Soc. for Historians of American Foreign Relations. *Publications:* American Immigration Policy 1924–1952 1957, The Illusion of Neutrality 1962, The Reluctant Belligerent: American Entry into World War II 1965, Second Chance: The Triumph of Internationalism in America During World War II 1967, Roosevelt and World War II 1969, Foreign

Policy and US Presidential Elections 1940–1960 (two vols) 1974, Since 1945: Politics and Diplomacy in Recent American History 1975, Blowing on the Wind 1978, Eisenhower and the Cold War 1981, America: Past and Present (with T. H. Breen, George Fredrickson and R. Hal Williams) 1984, The Sputnik Challenge 1993, Perpetual War for Perpetual Peace 2000; editor: American Foreign Policy 1960, The Age of Insecurity: America 1920–1945 1968, Twentieth-Century America: Contemporary Documents and Opinions (with John A. Garraty) 1968, American Foreign Policy Since 1945 1969, Causes and Consequences of World War II 1969, The Cuban Missile Crisis 1971, Exploring the Johnson Years 1981, The Johnson Years: Vol. Two, Vietnam, the Environment and Science 1987, The Johnson Years: Vol. Three, LBJ at Home and Abroad 1994; contrib. to scholarly books and journals. *Honours:* Rockefeller Humanities Fellowship 1976–77, Univ. of Texas Grad. Teaching Award 1986, Eugene E. Emme Astronautical Literature Award 1993. *Address:* 10617 Sans Souci Place, Austin, TX 78759, USA. *E-mail:* rdivine@austin.rr.com.

DIXON, Roger, (John Christian, Charles Lewis); British author and playwright; b. 6 Jan. 1930, Portsmouth, England; m. Carolyn Anne Shepheard 1966, two s. four d. *Publications:* Noah II, 1970; Christ on Trial, 1973; The Messiah, 1974; Five Gates to Armageddon (as John Christian), 1975; The Cain Factor (as Charles Lewis), 1975; Going to Jerusalem, 1977; Georgiana, 1984; Return to Nebo, 1991. Musical: The Commander of New York (with Phil Medley and Basil Bova), 1987. Other: Over 50 radio plays and series.

DIXON, Stephen; American writer and university teacher; *Professor, Johns Hopkins University*; b. 6 June 1936, New York, NY, USA; m. Anne Frydman, 17 Jan. 1982, two d. *Education:* BA City College, CUNY 1958. *Career:* Prof. Johns Hopkins Univ. 1980–2007. *Publications:* No Relief 1976, Work 1977, Too Late 1978, Quite Contrary 1979, 14 Stories 1980, Movies 1983, Time to Go 1984, Fall and Rise 1985, Garbage 1988, Love and Will 1989, The Play and Other Stories 1989, All Gone 1990, Friends 1990, Frog 1991, Long Made Short 1993, The Stories of Stephen Dixon 1994, Interstate 1995, Man on Stage 1996, Gould 1997, Sleep 1999, 30 1999, Tisch 2000, I. 2002, Old Friends 2004, Phone Rings 2005, End of I. 2006, Meyer (novel) 2007; contrib. to anthologies and periodicals. *Honours:* Stegner Fiction Fellowship, Stanford Univ. 1964–65; National Endowment of the Arts Grants 1974–75, 1990–91; American Acad. and Institute of Arts and Letters Award 1983; John Train Prize, Paris Review 1984; Guggenheim Fellowship 1985–86, two Pushcart Prizes, three Bestamerican Prizes, three O'Henry Prizes, Best Story from the South. *Address:* 1315 Boyce Ave, Baltimore, MD 21204, USA. *Telephone:* (410) 516-5274 (office); (410) 825-8038 (home). *Fax:* (410) 516-6828 (office).

DJEBAR, Assia; Algerian novelist, poet, dramatist, film maker and academic; *Silver Chair Professor of Francophone Literature and Civilization, New York University*; b. (Fatima-Zohra Imalhayène), June 1936, Cherchell; d. of the late Tahar Imalhayène and Bahia Sahraoui; m. 1st Ahmed Ould-Rouïs 1958 (divorced 1975); m. 2nd Malek Alloula 1981. *Education:* Lycée Fénélon, Paris and École Normale Supérieure de Sèvres, France. *Career:* taught history at Univ. of Algiers 1962–65, 1974–84; Foundation Distinguished Prof. and Dir, Center for French and Francophone Studies, Louisiana State Univ. 1995–2001; Silver Chair Prof. of Francophone Literature and Civilization, New York Univ. 2002–; mem. Acad. Royale de Langue Française de Belgique, Acad. Française 2005. *Films:* La Nouba des femmes du Mont Chenoua 1979, La Zerda ou les chants d'oubli 1982. *Publications:* La Soif (trans. as The Mischief) 1957, Les Impatients 1958, Women of Islam 1961, Les Enfants du nouveau monde 1962, Les Alouettes naïves 1967, Poèmes pour l'Algérie heureuse 1969, Rouge l'aube (with Walid Garn) 1969, La Nouba des femmes du Mont Chenoua 1969, Les Femmes d'Alger dans leur appartement (trans. as Women of Algiers in their Apartment) 1980, L'Amour la fantasia (trans. as Fantasia: An Algerian Cavalcade) 1985, Ombre sultane (trans. as A Sister to Scheherazade) 1987, Loin de Médine (trans. as Far from Medina) 1991, Chronique d'un été algérien 1993, Le Blanc de l'Algérie (trans. as Algerian White) 1995, Vaste est la prison (trans. as So Vast the Prison) 1995, Oran, langue morte 1997, Les Nuits de Strasbourg 1997, Ces voix qui m'assiègent 1999, Filles d'Ismaël dans le vent et la tempête (musical drama in five acts) 2002, La Femme sans sepulture 2002, La Disparation de la langue française 2004. *Honours:* Dr hc (Concordia Univ., Montréal) 2002, (Osnabrück Univ.) 2005; Venice Film Festival Int. Critics' Prize 1979, Prix Maurice Maeterlinck 1995, Neustadt Int. Prize for Literature 1996, Yourcenar Prize 1997, Friedenspreis des Deutschen Buchhandels 2000, Pablo Neruda Prize, Italy 2005, Grinzane Cavour Prize, Italy 2006. *Address:* Department of French, New York University, 13 University Place, Office 621, New York, NY 10003-4556, USA (office). *Telephone:* (212) 992-9509 (office). *E-mail:* assia.djebar@nyu.edu (office). *Website:* french.as.nyu.edu/object/assiadjebar.html (office); www.assiadjebar.net.

DJEDIDI, Hafedh; Tunisian poet, novelist and journalist; b. 1954. *Publications:* Rien que le fruit pour toute bouche (poems) (Prix de l'ACTT, Paris) 1985, Chassés/croisés (novel, with Guy Coissard) 1986, Intempéries 1987, Le Cimeterre ou le Souffle du Vénérable (Prix de l'ACTT, Paris) 1987, Les sept grains du chapelet, Les vents de la nostalgie, Fièvres dans Hach-Médine. *Address:* c/o L'Harmattan, 16 rue des Ecoles, 75005 Paris, France.

DJEMAÏ, Abdelkader; Algerian novelist, journalist and dramatist; b. 16 Nov. 1948, Oran. *Career:* exiled in France 1993–; freelance journalist for publs, including La République, Algérie-Presse-Service, El Moudjahid, Algérie Actualité, Le Matin, Ruptures, Le Monde Diplomatique, Les Temps Modernes, Machrek-Maghreb, Qantara, France Culture; mem. Soc. des Gens de Lettres. *Plays:* L'affaire R.D., Paroles de quartier, Histoires parallèles. *Publications:* novels: Saison de pierres 1986, Mémoires de nègre 1991, Un Été en cendres (Prix Découverte Albert Camus, Prix Tropiques) 1995, Sable rouge 1996, 31 rue de l'aigle 2000, Camping (Prix Amerigo Vespucci) 2002, Gare du Nord 2003, Le Nez sur la vitre (Lauréat du Prix littéraire de la Ville d'Ambronay 2005) 2004; non-fiction: Camus à Oran 1995, Histoire d'un amour 1997, Le Caire qui bat 2006, Pain, adour et fantaisies 2006; contrib. to Petites agonies urbaines 2006. *Honours:* Chevalier, Ordre des Arts et des Lettres.

DJERASSI, Carl, AB, PhD; American chemist, academic and author; *Professor Emeritus of Chemistry, Stanford University*; b. 29 Oct. 1923, Vienna; s. of Dr Samuel Djerassi and Dr Alice Friedmann; m. 1st Virginia Jeremiah (divorced 1950); m. 2nd Norma Lundholm (divorced 1976); one s. one d. (deceased); m. 3rd Diane W. Middlebrook 1985. *Education:* Kenyon Coll. and Univ. of Wisconsin. *Career:* Research Chemist, Ciba Pharmaceutical Co., Summit, NJ 1942–43, 1945–49; Assoc. Dir of Research, Syntex, SA, Mexico City 1949–51, Research Vice-Pres. 1957–60, Pres. Syntex Research 1968–72; Assoc. Prof. of Chem., Wayne State Univ., Detroit 1952–54, Prof. 1954–59; Prof. of Chem., Stanford Univ. 1959–2002, Prof. Emer. 2002–; Pres. Bd Zoecon Corpn (renamed Sandoz Crop Protection Corpn) 1968–83, Chair. 1968–88; f. Djerassi Foundation Resident Artists Program; Royal Chemical Soc. Centenary Lecturer 1964; Royal Swedish Acad. of Eng Sciences thirteenth Chemical Lecturer 1969; Swedish Pharmaceutical Soc. Scheele Lecturer 1972; mem. Editorial Bd Journal of the American Chemical Society 1968–76, Journal of Organic Chemistry 1955–58, Tetrahedron 1958–92, Steroids 1963–, Proceedings of NAS 1964–70; mem. NAS Bd on Science and Tech. for Int. Devt 1967–76, Chair. 1972–76; mem. American Pugwash Cttee 1967–1981; mem. NAS, NAS Inst. of Medicine, Brazilian Acad. of Sciences, American Acad. of Arts and Sciences; Foreign mem. German Acad. of Natural Scientists (Leopoldina), Royal Swedish Acad. of Sciences 1973, Bulgarian Acad. of Sciences 1979, Royal Swedish Acad. of Eng Sciences 1984, Acad. Europaea. *Plays:* An Immaculate Misconception 1998, Oxygen (with Roald Hoffman) 2000, Calculus 2003, EGO 2003, Three on a Couch 2004, Phallacy 2005; numerous broadcasts. *Publications:* (author or co-author) Optical Rotatory Dispersion 1960, Steroid Reactions 1963, Interpretation of Mass Spectra of Organic Compounds 1964, Structure Elucidation of Natural Products by Mass Spectrometry (two vols) 1964, Mass Spectrometry of Organic Compounds 1967, The Politics of Contraception 1979, 1981, The Futurist and Other Stories (fiction) 1988, Cantor's Dilemma (novel) 1989, Steroids Made It Possible (autobiog.) 1990, The Clock Runs Backward (poetry) 1991, The Pill, Pygmy Chimps and Degas' Horse (autobiog.) 1992, Bourbaki Gambit (novel) 1994, From the Lab into the World (collected essays) 1994; Marx, deceased (novel) 1996, Menachem's Seed (novel) 1997, NO (novel) 1998, This Man's Pill (memoir) 2001, Newton's Darkness: Two Dramatic Views (with David Pinner) 2003; numerous scientific articles, also poems, memoirs and short stories. *Honours:* Hon. Fellow, Royal Chemical Soc. 1968, American Acad. of Pharmaceutical Science; Austrian Cross for Culture and Science 1999, Great Merit Cross of Germany 2003; numerous hon. degrees; Award in Pure Chem. 1958, Baekeland Medal 1959, Fritzsche Medal 1960, Creative Invention Award 1973, Award in the Chem. of Contemporary Technological Problems 1983, Esselen Award for Chem. in the Public Interest 1989, ACS; Intra-Science Research Award 1969, Freedman Foundation Patent Award 1971, Chemical Pioneer Award 1973, Perkin Medal 1975, American Inst. of Chemists; Nat. Medal of Science 1973 (for synthesis of first oral contraceptive), Wolf Prize in Chem. 1978, Bard Award in Medicine and Science 1983, Roussel Prize (Paris) 1988, NAS Award for the Industrial Application of Science 1990, Nat. Medal of Tech. 1991, Priestley Medal (ACS) 1992, Nevada Medal 1992, Thomson Gold Medal (Int. Mass Spectrometry Soc.) 1994, Prince Mahidol Award (Thailand) 1996, Willard Gibbs Medal 1997, Othmer Gold Medal, Chem. Heritage Foundation 2000, Erasmus Medal, Academia Europaea 2003, Gold Medal, American Inst. of Chemists 2004, on postage stamp, Austrian Post Office 2005. *Address:* Department of Chemistry, Stanford University, Stanford, CA 94305-5080, USA (office). *Telephone:* (650) 723-2783 (office). *E-mail:* djerassi@stanford.edu (office). *Website:* www.djerassi.com (office); www.stanford.edu/dept/chemistry (office).

DOBAI, Péter, DipEd; Hungarian writer, poet and screenwriter; b. 12 Aug. 1944, Budapest; m. 1st Donatella Failioni 1972; m. 2nd Maria Mate 1992. *Education:* Univ. of Budapest. *Career:* mem. Hungarian Acad. of Artists, Hungarian Writers' Assscn (mem. Exec. Bd), PEN Club, Hungary. *Publications:* fiction: Csontmolnárok 1974, Tartozó élet 1975, Lavina 1980, Vadon 1982, Háromszögtan 1983, A birodalom ezredese 1985, Iv 1988, Lendkerék 1989; short story collections: Játék a szobákkal 1976, Sakktábla két figurával 1978; poetry: Kilovaglás egy öszi erödböl 1973, Egy arc módosulásai 1976, Hanyatt 1978, Az éden vermei 1985, Válogatott versek 1989, Vitorlák emléke 1994, Önmúltszázad 1996, Versek egyelnémult klavírra 2002, Ma könnyebb. Holnap messzebb 2004, Barth hadapród, becsületszavamra, visszatér a nyár 2005; essays: Augyali agresszió 2002; 15 screenplays 1971–95. *Honours:* J ózsef Attila Prize 1976, several awards, Hungarian Literary Foundation and Minister of Culture, various screenplay awards, including Cannes Film Festival 1981. *Address:* Közraktár u 12/B, 1093 Budapest, Hungary (home).

DOBBS, Michael John, PhD, MALD, MA; British writer; b. 14 Nov. 1948; m. Rachel Dobbs; four s. *Education:* Christ Church, Oxford and Fletcher School of Law and Diplomacy, USA. *Career:* UK Govt Special Adviser 1981–87; Chief of Staff, UK Conservative Party 1986–87, Jt Deputy Chair. 1994–95; Deputy

Chair. Saatchi & Saatchi 1983–91; BBC TV presenter 1999–2001. *Publications:* House of Cards 1989, Wall Games 1990, Last Man to Die 1991, To Play the King 1992, The Touch of Innocents 1994, The Final Cut 1995, Goodfellowe MP 1997, The Buddha of Brewer Street 1998, Whispers of Betrayal 2000, Winston's War 2002, Never Surrender 2003, Churchill's Hour 2004, Churchill's Triumph 2005, First Lady 2006. *Address:* Newton House, Wylye, Wilts. BA12 0QS, England (office). *Telephone:* 7836 201967 (mobile). *E-mail:* michldobbs@aol.com (office).

DOBSON, Andrew Nicholas Howard, BA, DPhil; British academic and writer; *Professor of Politics, Keele University*; b. 15 April 1957, Doncaster, England. *Education:* Reading Univ., Univ. of Oxford. *Career:* Editorial Bd, Environmental Values 1991–2004, Environmental Politics 1991– (chair. editorial bd), Anarchist Studies 1991–2000; Lecturer in Politics, Keele Univ. 1983–93, Chair of Politics 1993–2001; Chair of Politics, Open Univ. 2002–06; Chair of Politics Keele Univ. 2006–. *Publications:* An Introduction to the Politics and Philosophy of José Ortega y Gasset 1989, Green Political Thought 1990, The Green Reader: Essays Toward a Sustainable Society (ed.) 1991, The Politics of Nature: Explorations in Green Political Theory (ed. with Paul Lucardie) 1993, Jean-Paul Sartre and the Politics of Reason: A Theory of History 1993, Justice and the Environment: Conceptions of Environmental Sustainability and Theories of Distributive Justice 1998, Fairness and Futurity: Essays on Environmental Sustainability and Social Justice 1999, Citizenship and the Environment 2003, Citizenship, Environment, Economy (ed. with Angel Valencia) 2005, Environmental Citizenship (ed. with Derek Bell) 2005, Political Theory and the Ecological Challenge (ed. with Robyn Eckerlsey) 2006; contrib. numerous articles and book reviews to magazines and journals. *Honours:* Spanish Government Scholar 1983–84, Postdoctoral Fellow Economic and Social Science Research Council 1984–87. *Address:* School of Politics, International Relations and Philosophy, Keele University, Keele, Staffordshire, ST5 5BG, England (office). *Telephone:* (1908) 652022 (office). *E-mail:* a.n.h.dobson@keele.ac.uk (office).

DOBSON, Joanne; American writer and academic; b. 27 March 1942, New York, NY; m. David Eugene Dobson 1963; one s. two d. *Education:* BA, King's College, Briarcliff Manor, New York, 1963; MA, SUNY at Albany, 1977; PhD, University of Massachusetts at Amherst, 1985. *Career:* Founding Mem., 1983–93, Mem., Editorial Board, 1993–96, Legacy: Journal of American Women Writers; General Co-ed., American Women Writers reprint series, Rutgers University Press, 1984–92; Visiting Prof. of English and American Studies, Amherst College, Amherst, Massachusetts, 1985–86; Visiting Asst Prof. of English, Tufts University, Medford, Massachusetts, 1986–87; Asst Prof., 1987–92, Assoc. Prof. of English, 1992–, Fordham University, Bronx, New York; Mem., Editorial Board, American Literature, 1995–97; mem. Founding Mem., Emily Dickinson International Society, Mem., Board of Dirs, 1988–91. *Publications:* The Hidden Hand (ed.), 1988; Dickinson and the Strategies of Reticence: The Woman Writer in Nineteenth-Century America, 1989; Quieter than Sleep (novel), 1997; The Northbury Papers (novel), 1998; The Raven and the Nightingale (novel), 1999; Cold and Pure and Very Dead (novel), 2000. Contributions: periodicals including American Quarterly. *Literary Agent:* Deborah Schneider, Gelfman Schneider, 250 W 57th Street, New York, NY 10107, USA. *Address:* Department of English, Fordham University, Bronx, NY 10458, USA. *E-mail:* dedcons@aol.com.

DOBSON, Rosemary, AO; Australian writer, poet and editor; b. 18 June 1920, Sydney, NSW; d. of Austin A. G. Dobson and Marjorie Dobson (née Caldwell); m. Alexander Thorley Bolton 1951; two s. one d. *Education:* Frensham School, Mittagong, NSW and Univ. of Sydney. *Career:* teacher of art; mem. Editorial Dept Angus and Robertson Publrs, Sydney; freelance writer 1951–; mem. Australian Soc. of Authors. *Publications:* In a Convex Mirror 1944, The Ship of Ice and Other Poems (Sydney Morning Herald Award for Poetry 1948) 1948, Child with a Cockatoo and Other Poems 1955, Australian Poets: Rosemary Dobson 1963, Cock Crow 1965, Songs for all Seasons 1968, Focus on Ray Crooke (prose) 1971, Selected Poems 1973, Moscow Trefoil (co-author) 1975, Greek Coins: A Sequence of Poems 1977, Australian Voices (ed.) 1978, Over the Frontier 1978, Seven Russian Poets (co-author) 1979, Selected Poems 1980, The Three Fates and Other Poems (Grace Leven Prize for Poetry 1984, Victoria Premier's Literary Awards for Poetry (jtly) 1985) 1984, Summer Press 1987, Collected Poems 1991, Untold Lives: A Sequence of Poems 1992, Untold Lives and Later Poems 2000. *Honours:* Hon. Life mem. Asscn for the Study of Australian Literature 1985; Hon. DLit (Sydney) 1996; FAW Christopher Brennan Award 1978, Robert Frost Prize 1979, Sr Literary Fellowship, Australia Council 1980, Patrick White Award for Literature 1984, Emer. Fellowship, Literature Bd of Australia Council 1996, Age Book of the Year Award 2000, NSW Premier's Literary Award Special Award 2006, NSW Soc. of Women Writers Alice Award 2006. *Literary Agent:* Curtis Brown Pty Ltd, POB 19, Paddington, NSW 2021, Australia. *Address:* 61 Stonehaven Crescent, Deakin, ACT 2600, Australia (home). *Telephone:* (2) 6281-1436 (home). *Fax:* (2) 6281-5842 (home). *E-mail:* rdobsonbolton@gmail.com (home).

DOBSON, Sue, BA; British magazine editor, travel writer and photographer; *Travel Editor, Choice magazine*; b. 31 Jan. 1946, Maidstone, Kent; d. of Arthur and Nellie Henshaw; m. Michael Dobson 1966 (divorced 1974). *Education:* Holy Family Convent and Assumption Convent (Ramsgate), Ursuline Convent (Westgate-on-Sea) and Polytechnic of North-East London. *Career:* Ed. Small Trader, London 1964; Fashion, Cookery and Beauty Ed. Femina, SA 1965–69; Contributing Ed. Fair Lady, SA 1969–71; Ed. S Africa Inst. of Race

Relations 1972–74, Wedding Day and First Home, London 1978–81, Successful Slimming, London 1981–82, Woman and Home, London 1982–94; Ed.-in-Chief Choice magazine 1994–2002, Travel Ed. 2002–. *Publication:* The Wedding Day Book (2nd edn) 1989. *Honours:* Travel Writing Award 2001, 2004. *E-mail:* sue@choice-magazine.com (office).

DOBYNS, Stephen, BA, MFA; American academic, poet and writer; b. 19 Feb. 1941, Orange, NJ; m.; three c. *Education:* Shimer College, Mount Carroll, IL, Wayne State University, University of Iowa. *Career:* Instructor, SUNY at Brockport, 1968–69; Reporter, Detroit News, 1969–71; Visiting Writer, University of New Hampshire, 1973–75, University of Iowa, 1977–79, Boston University, 1978–79, 1980–81, Syracuse University, 1986; Faculty, Goddard College, Plainfield, Vermont, 1978–80, Warren Wilson College, Swannanoa, NC, 1982–87; Prof. of Creative Writing, Syracuse University, New York, 1987–. *Publications:* Poetry: Concurring Beasts, 1972; Griffon, 1976; Heat Death, 1980; The Balthus Poems, 1982; Black Dog, Red Dog, 1984; Cemetery Nights, 1987; Body Traffic, 1991; Velocities: New and Selected Poems, 1966–1992, 1994; Common Carnage, 1996; Pallbearers Envying the One Who Rides, 1999. Fiction: A Man of Little Evils, 1973; Saratoga Longshot, 1976; Saratoga Swimmer, 1981; Dancer with One Leg, 1983; Saratoga Headhunter, 1985; Cold Dog Soup, 1985; Saratoga Snapper, 1986; A Boat Off the Coast, 1987; The Two Deaths of Señora Puccini, 1988; Saratoga Bestiary, 1988; The House of Alexandrine, 1989; Saratoga Hexameter, 1990; After Shocks/Near Escapes, 1991; Saratoga Haunting, 1993; The Wrestler's Cruel Study, 1993; Saratoga Backtalk, 1994; Saratoga Fleshpot, 1995; Saratoga Trifecta, 1995; The Church of Dead Girls, 1997; Saratoga Strongbox, 1998; Boy in the Water, 1999; Eating Naked, 2000. *Honours:* Lamont Poetry Selection Award, 1971; MacDowell Colony Fellowships, 1972, 1976; Yaddo Fellowships, 1972, 1973, 1977, 1981, 1982; National Endowment for the Arts Grants, 1974, 1981; Guggenheim Fellowship, 1983; National Poetry Series Prize, 1984.

DOCHERTY, John (see Sills-Docherty, Jonathan John)

DOCTOROW, Edgar Lawrence (E.L.), AB; American novelist, dramatist and academic; *Lewis and Loretta Gluckman Professor of American and English Letters, New York University*; b. 6 Jan. 1931, New York; s. of David Richard and Rose Doctorow (née Levine); m. Helen Esther Setzer 1954; one s. two d. *Education:* Kenyon Coll., Gambier, Ohio, Columbia Univ. *Career:* served in US army 1953–55; script reader, Columbia Pictures 1959; Ed. New American Library, New York 1960–64; Ed.-in-Chief Dial Press., New York 1964–69, Publr 1969; Writer-in-Residence, Univ. of Calif., Irvine 1969–70; mem. faculty, Sarah Lawrence Coll., Bronxville, NY 1971–78; Creative Writing Fellow, Yale School of Drama 1974–75; Creative Artists Program Service Fellow 1973–74; Visiting Sr Fellow, Council on Humanities, Princeton Univ. 1980–81, Prof. of English 1982–87; Lewis and Loretta Gluckman Prof. of American and English Letters, New York Univ. 1987–; mem. Authors Guild (dir), American PEN, Writers Guild of America East, Century Asscn; Guggenheim Fellow 1973. *Publications:* Welcome to Hard Times 1960, Big as Life 1966, The Book of Daniel 1971, Ragtime 1975, Drinks before Dinner (play) 1975, Loon Lake 1980, Lives of the Poets: Six Stories and a Novella 1984, World's Fair 1985, Billy Bathgate 1988, Jack London, Hemingway and the Constitution: Selected Essays 1977–92 1993, The Waterworks 1994, Poets and Presidents: Selected Essays 1994, The Best American Short Stories (ed. with Katrina Kenison) 2000, City of God 2000, Sweet Land Stories 2004, Reporting the Universe 2004, The March 2006, Creationists: Selected Essays 1993–2006 2006. *Honours:* Hon. LHD (Kenyon Coll.) 1976, (Hobart Coll.) 1979; Hon. DLitt (William Smith Coll.) 1979; Hon. DHL (Brandeis Univ. 1989; Arts and Letters Award (American Acad. and Nat. Inst. of Art) 1976, Nat. Book Critics Circle Award 1976, 1990, 2005, Guggenheim Fellow 1973, Nat. Book Award 1986, William Dean Howells Medal, American Acad. of Arts and Letters 1990, PEN/Faulkner Prize 1990, 2005, Nat. Humanities Medal 1998, Commonwealth Award 2000. *Literary Agent:* c/o International Creative Management, 825 8th Avenue, New York, NY 10019, USA. *Address:* English Department, New York University, 19 University Place, Second Floor, New York, NY 10003; c/o Random House Publishers, 1745 Broadway, New York, NY 10019, USA (office). *E-mail:* eld1@nyu.edu.

DODD, Wayne Donald, BA, MA, PhD; American poet, writer, editor and academic; *Distinguished Professor Emeritus, Ohio University*; b. 23 Sept. 1930, Clarita, OK; m. 1st Betty Coshow 1958 (divorced 1980); m. 2nd Joyce Barlow 1981; two c. *Education:* Univ. of Oklahoma. *Career:* Instructor 1960–64, Asst Prof. of English 1964–68, Univ. of Colorado at Boulder; Fellow Center for Advanced Studies, Wesleyan Univ. 1964; Assoc. Prof. 1968–73, Prof. of English 1973–94, Edwin and Ruth Kennedy Distinguished Prof. of Poetry 1994–2001, Distinguished Prof. Emeritus 2001–, Ohio Univ.; Ed., Ohio Review 1971–2001; mem. Associated Writing Programs. *Publications:* poetry: We Will Wear White Roses 1974, Made in America 1975, The Names You Gave It 1980, The General Mule Poems 1981, Sometimes Music Rises 1986, Echoes of the Unspoken 1990, Of Desire and Disorder 1994, The Blue Salvages 1998, Is 2003; fiction: A Time of Hunting 1975; other: Poets on the Line (ed.) 1987, Toward the End of the Century: Essays into Poetry 1992, Art and Nature: Essays by Contemporary Writers (ed.) 1993, Mentors (ed.) 1994; contrib. to anthologies, reviews, quarterlies and journals. *Honours:* ACLS Fellowship 1964–65, Ohio Arts Council Fellowships 1980, 1989, 1998, NEA Fellowship in Poetry 1982, Ohioana Library Foundation Krout Award for Lifetime Achievement in Poetry 1991, Rockefeller Foundation Fellowship 1995, Ohio

Gov.'s Award for the Arts 2001. *Address:* 11292 Peach Ridge Road, Athens, OH 45701, USA. *E-mail:* doddw@ohio.edu. *Website:* www.waynedodd.com.

DOHERTY, Berlie, BA; British writer, dramatist and poet; b. 6 Nov. 1943, Liverpool, England; m. Gerard Doherty 1966 (divorced 1996); one s. two d. *Education:* Durham Univ., Liverpool Univ., Sheffield Univ. *Career:* mem. Arvon Foundation, Lumb Bank (Chair. 1988–93). *Publications:* fiction: Requiem 1991, The Vinegar Jar 1994, Abela 2007; children's books: How Green You Are 1982, The Making of Fingers Finnigan 1983, White Peak Farm 1984, Children of Winter 1985, Granny Was a Buffer Girl 1986, Tilly Mint Tales 1986, Tilly Mint and the Dodo 1988, Paddiwak and Cosy 1988, Tough Luck 1988, Spellhorn 1989, Dear Nobody 1990, Snowy 1992, Big, Bulgy, Fat Black Slug 1993, Old Father Christmas 1993, Street Child 1993, Walking on Air (poems) 1993, Willa and Old Miss Annie 1994, The Snake-Stone 1995, The Golden Bird 1995, Dear Nobody (play) 1995, The Magical Bicycle 1995, Our Field 1996, Morgan's Field (play) 1996, Daughter of the Sea 1996; Contributions: periodicals. *Honours:* Boston Globe-Horn Book Award 1987, Burnley Children's Book of the Year Award 1987, Carnegie Medals 1987, 1991, Writer's Guild of Great Britain Children's Play Award 1994. *Literary Agent:* c/o Veronique Baxter, David Higham Associates, 5-8 Lower John Street, Golden Square, London W1R 4HA, England. *E-mail:* veroniquebaxter@davidhigham.co.uk. *Website:* www.berliedoherty.com.

DOLIS, John, BA, MA, PhD; American academic, writer and poet; *Associate Professor of English, Pennsylvania State University*; b. 25 April 1945, St Louis, MO. *Education:* St Louis Univ., Loyola Univ., Chicago. *Career:* Teaching Asst 1967–69, 1970–73, Lecturer 1974–75, 1978–80, Loyola Univ., Chicago; Instructor, Columbia Coll. 1970–71, Northeastern Illinois Univ. 1978–80, Univ. of Kansas 1981–85; Fulbright Lecturer, Univ. of Turin 1980–81; Asst Prof. 1985–92, Assoc. Prof. 1992–, Pennsylvania State Univ., Scranton; Sr Fulbright Lecturer, Univ. of Bucharest 1989–90; Visiting Prof. of American Culture and Literature, Bilkent Univ., Ankara 1995–96; mem. editorial bd, Antemnae, Arizona Quarterly, Nathaniel Hawthorne Review; mem. American Culture Asscn, American Literature Asscn, American Philosophical Asscn, Asscn for Applied Psychoanalysis, Int. Asscn for Philosophy and Literature, Int. Husserl and Phenomenological Research Soc., Int. Soc. for Phenomenology and the Human Sciences, Int. Soc. for Phemomenology and Literature, MLA, Nathaniel Hawthorne Soc., Nat. Social Science Asscn, Soc. for the Advancement of American Philosophy, Soc. for Phenomenology and Existential Philosophy, Soc. for Philosophy and Psychiatry, Soc. for Romanian Studies, Thoreau Soc., World Phenomenology Inst. *Publications:* The Style of Hawthorne's Gaze: Regarding Subjectivity 1993, Bl( )nk Space 1993, Time Flies: Butterflies 1999, Tracking Thoreau: Double-Crossing Nature and Technology 2005; contrib. articles in scholarly journals, poems in anthologies and magazines. *Honours:* Nat. Endowment for the Humanities Fellowships 1979, 1988, Pharmakon Research Int. Award for Excellence in Scholarly Activities, Pennsylvania State Univ. 1991, various grants. *Address:* 711 Summit Pointe, Scranton, PA 18508, USA. *E-mail:* jjd3@psu.edu.

DOLL, Mary Aswell, BA, MA, PhD; American academic; b. 4 June 1940, New York, NY; m. William Elder Doll Jr 1966 (divorced 1994); one s. *Education:* Connecticut College, New London, Johns Hopkins University, Syracuse University. *Career:* Asst Prof., SUNY at Oswego, 1978–84; Lecturer, University of Redlands, CA, 1985–88; Asst Prof., Loyola University, 1988; Visiting Asst Prof., Tulane University, 1988; Assoc. Prof. Our Lady of Holy Cross College 1989–93, Prof. 1993–99; Prof., Savannah College of Art and Design 2000–; mem. MLA; Thomas Wolfe Society. *Publications:* Rites of Story: The Old Man at Play, 1987; Beckett and Myth: An Archetypal Approach, 1988; In the Shadow of the Giant: Thomas Wolfe, 1988; Walking and Rocking, 1989; Joseph Campbell and the Power of the Wilderness, 1992; Stoppard's Theatre of Unknowing, 1993; To the Lighthouse and Back, 1996; Like Letters in Running Water: A Mythopoetics of Curriculum, 2000, Triple Takes On Curricular Worlds 2006; contribs to periodicals. *Honours:* Outstanding Book Citation Choice, 1989; Sears-Roebuck Teaching Excellence Award. *Address:* 527 E 56th Street, Savannah, GA 31405, USA.

DOLLIMORE, Jonathan, BA, PhD; British academic and writer; b. 31 July 1948, Leighton Buzzard, England. *Education:* University of Keele, University of London. *Career:* Lecturer, 1976–89, Senior Lecturer, 1989–90, Reader, 1990–93, Prof. of English, 1993–95, School of English and American Studies, Prof., Graduate Research Centre for the Humanities, 1995–99, University of Sussex; Visiting Fellow, Humanities Research Centre, Canberra, 1988, Human Sciences Research Council of South Africa, 1996; Mellon Fellow, National Humanities Center, NC, 1988–89; Scholar-in-Residence, Centre for Renaissance and Baroque Studies, University of Maryland, 1991–92; Cecil and Ida Green Visiting Prof., University of British Columbia, 1997; Prof. of English, University of York, 1999–; Visiting Prof., LeHigh University, University of Oregon and University of Tel-Aviv, 2002. *Publications:* The Selected Plays of John Webster (ed. with Alan Sinfield), 1983; Radical Tragedy: Religion, Ideology and Power in the Drama of Shakespeare and his Contemporaries, 1984; Political Shakespeare: New Essays in Cultural Materialism (ed. with Alan Sinfield), 1985; Sexual Dissidence: Augustine to Wilde, Freud to Foucault, 1991; Death, Desire and Loss in Western Culture, 1998; Sex, Literature and Censorship, 2001. Contributions: many scholarly books and journals.

DOMÍNGUEZ, Carlos María; Argentine writer, journalist and literary critic; b. 1955, Buenos Aires. *Publications:* fiction: Pozo de Vargas 1985, Mares baldíos (short stories), Bicicletas negras 1991, La Mujer Hablada (Bartolomé Hidalgo Prize) 1998, La Casa de papel (trans. as The Paper House) (Premio de la Fundación Lolita Rubial, Vienna's Jury of Young Readers Prize) 2001, Tres Muescas en mi carabina (Juan Carlos Onetti Prize) 2003; non-fiction: Construcción de la noche: la vida de Juan Carlos Onetti (biog., with María Esther Gilio) 1993, El Bastardo: la vida de Roberto de las Carreras y su madre Clara (biog.) 1997, Delitos de amores crueles: las mujeres uruguayas frente a la justicia 1865–1911 2001, Tola Invernizzi: la rebelión de la ternura (biog.) 2001, Historia de un dictador (biog.), Escritos en el agua (Premio del Ministerio de Educación y Cultura de Uruguay), El norte profundo, El compás de oro (collected articles), Historias del polvo y el camino (collected articles); plays: La incapaz, Polski (with Jorge Boccanera). *Address:* c/o Publicity Department, Random House, 20 Vauxhall Bridge Road, London, SW1V 2SA, England (office).

DOMMISSE, Ebbe, BA, MSc; South African newspaper editor; b. 14 July 1940, Riversdale; s. of Jan Dommisse and Anna Dommisse; m. Daléne Laubscher 1963; two s. one d. *Education:* Paarl Boys High School, Univ. of Stellenbosch and Grad. School of Journalism, Columbia Univ., New York, USA. *Career:* reporter, Die Burger, Cape Town 1961, Chief Sub-Ed. 1968, News Ed. 1971; Asst Ed. and Political Commentator, Beeld, Johannesburg (Founder-mem. of new Johannesburg daily) 1974; Asst Ed. Die Burger 1979, Sr Asst Ed. 1984, Ed. 1990–; Exec. mem. Nasionale Koerante; Trustee Helpmekaarfonds; mem. Akad. vir Wetenskap en Kuns; Nieman Travel Fellowship 1987. *Publications:* with Alf Ries: Broedertwis 1982, Leierstryd 1990. *Address:* Die Burger, 40 Heerengracht, PO Box 692, Cape Town 8000, South Africa (office). *Telephone:* (21) 4062222.

DONALD, David Herbert, AB, MA, PhD; American academic and author; b. 1 Oct. 1920, Goodman, MI; m. Aida DiPace 1955, one s. *Education:* Millsaps College, Jackson, MI, University of North Carolina, University of Illinois. *Career:* Instructor, 1947–49, Asst Prof., 1951–52, Assoc. Prof., 1952–57, Prof. of History, 1957–59, Columbia University; Assoc. Prof. of History, Smith College, 1949–51; Visiting Assoc. Prof., Amherst College, 1950; Fulbright Lecturer in American History, University College of North Wales, 1953–54; Mem., Institute for Advanced Study, 1957–58; Harmsworth Prof. of American History, University of Oxford, 1959–60; Prof. of History, Princeton University, 1959–62; Harry C. Black Prof. of American History and Dir of the Institute of Southern History, Johns Hopkins University, 1962–73; Charles Warren Prof. of American History and Prof. of American Civilization, 1973–91, Prof. Emeritus, 1991–, Harvard University; mem. American Acad. of Arts and Sciences, fellow; American Antiquarian Society; American Historical Asscn; Massachusetts Historical Asscn; Organization of American Historians; Southern Historical Asscn, pres., 1969; Hon. doctorates. *Publications:* Lincoln's Herndon, 1948; Divided We Fought: A Pictorial History of the War, 1861–1865, 1952; Inside Lincoln's Cabinet: The Civil War Diaries of Salmon P. Chase, 1954; Lincoln Reconsidered: Essays on the Civil War Era, 1956; Charles Sumner and the Coming of the Civil War, 1960; Why the North Won the Civil War, 1960; The Civil War and Reconstruction (with J. G. Randall), second edn, 1961; The Divided Union, 1961; The Politics of Reconstruction, 1863–1867, 1965; The Nation in Crisis, 1861–1877, 1969; Charles Sumner and the Rights of Man, 1970; The South Since the War (with Sidney Andrews), 1970; Gone for a Soldier: The Civil War Memoirs of Private Alfred Bellard, 1975; The Great Republic: A History of the American People (with others), 1977; Liberty and Union: The Crisis of Popular Government, 1830–1890, 1978; Look Homeward: A Life of Thomas Wolfe, 1987; Lincoln, 1995. Contributions: scholarly journals. *Honours:* Pulitzer Prizes in Biography, 1960, 1988; Guggenheim Fellowships, 1964–65, 1985–86; C. Hugh Holman Prize, MLA, 1988; Distinguished Alumnus Award, University of Illinois, 1988; Benjamin L. C. Wailes Award, Mississippi Historical Society, 1994; Lincoln Prize, 1996; Christopher Award, 1996; Distinguished Non-Fiction Award, American Library Asscn, 1996.

DONALDSON, (Charles) Ian Edward; Australian academic and writer; b. 6 May 1935, Melbourne, Vic.; m. 1st Tasmin Jane Procter 1962 (divorced 1990); one s. one d.; m. 2nd Grazia Maria Therese Gunn 1991. *Education:* BA, University of Melbourne, 1958; BA, 1960, MA, 1964, Magdalen College, Oxford. *Career:* Senior Tutor in English, 1958, Visiting appointment, 1991, University of Melbourne; Harmsworth Senior Scholar, Merton College, Oxford, 1960–62; Fellow and Lecturer in English, Wadham College, Oxford, 1962–69; CUF Lecturer in English, University of Oxford, 1963–69; Visiting appointments, University of California at Santa Barbara, 1967–68; Gonville and Caius College, Cambridge, 1985, Cornell University, 1988, Folger Shakespeare Library, Washington, DC, 1988; Prof. of English, 1969–91, Foundation Dir, Humanities Research Centre, 1974–90, Australian National University, Canberra, Interim Dir 2004–; Regius Prof. of Rhetoric and English Literature, University of Edinburgh, 1991–95; Grace I Prof. of English King's College Cambridge 1995–2002, Dir Centre for Research in the Arts, Social Sciences and Humanities 2001–03, Fellow 1995–2004. *Publications:* The World Upside Down: Comedy From Jonson to Fielding, 1970; Ben Jonson: Poems (ed.), 1975; The Rapes of Lucretia: A Myth and its Transformations, 1982; Jonson and Shakespeare (ed.), 1983; Transformations in Modern European Drama (ed.), 1983; Seeing the First Australians (ed. with Tasmin Donaldson), 1985; Ben Jonson, 1985; Shaping Lives: Reflections on Biography (co-ed.), 1992; Jonson's Walk to Scotland, 1993; The Death of the Author and the Life of the Poet, 1995; Ben Jonson: Selected Poems (ed.), 1995; Jonson's Magic Houses, 1997. Contributions: scholarly journals. *Honours:* Fellow

Australian Acad. of the Humanities 1975; Fellow British Acad. 1993 (Corresponding Fellow 1987); Fellow Royal Society of Edinburgh 1993. *Address:* 11 Grange Road, Cambridge CB3 9AS, England.

DONALDSON, Julia; British children's writer and teacher; b. 1948, London. *Education:* Univ. of Bristol. *Career:* children's songwriter for BBC TV and radio. *Plays:* All Aboard 1995, Problem Page 2000, High Impact 2000, Bombs and Blackberries 2003. *Publications:* juvenile fiction: A Squash and a Squeeze 1993, The Magic Twig 1995, Mr Snow 1996, Spacegirl Sue 1996, Storyworlds 1997, Books and Crooks 1998, Waiter! Waiter! 1998, The Brownie King 1998, The Gruffalo 1999, Rabbit's Nap 2000, Hide and Seek Pig 2000, Fox's Socks 2000, Monkey Puzzle 2000, Postman Bear 2000, Blue Banana 2002, Night Monkey Day Monkey 2002, Room on the Broom 2002, Spinderella 2002, The Dinosaur's Diary 2002, Princess Mirror-Belle 2003, The Smartest Giant in Town 2003, The Spiffiest Giant in Town 2003, Chameleons: Brick-a-Breck 2003, Conjuror Cow 2003, The Magic Paintbrush 2003, The Snail and the Whale 2003, The Wrong Kind of Bark 2004, One Ted Falls Out of Bed 2004, Crazy Mayonnaisy Mum 2004, Sharing a Shell 2004, The Gruffalo's Child (British Book Award for Children's Book of the Year 2005) 2004, Wriggle and Roar!: Rhymes to Join in With 2004, Rose's Hat 2005, Princess Mirror-Belle 2 2005, Chocolate Mousse for Greedy Goose 2005, Hippo Has a Hat 2005, Charlie Cook's Favourite Book 2005, Follow the Swallow 2007, Tyrannosaurus Drip 2007. *Address:* Pan Macmillan Publishers, 20 New Wharf Road, London, N1 9RR, England. *Website:* www.panmacmillan.com.

DONALDSON, Samuel (Sam) Andrew, BA; American journalist; b. 11 March 1934, El Paso, Tex.; s. of Samuel A. Donaldson and Chloe Hampson; m. 1st Billie K. Butler 1963; three s. one d.; m. 2nd Janice C. Smith 1983. *Education:* Univ. of Texas, El Paso and Univ. of Southern Calif. *Career:* radio/TV news reporter/anchorman, WTOP, Washington, DC 1961–67; Capitol Hill/corresp., ABC News, Washington, DC 1967–77, White House Corresp. 1977–89, Chief White House Corresp. 1998–99, Anchor, Prime Time Live 1989–98; Co-anchor 20/20 Live, ABC 1998; Anchor, SamDonaldson@abc-news.com 1999, The Sam Donaldson Show, ABC Radio Network 2001–; panellist, This Week With David Brinkley 1981–96; Co-anchor, This Week With Sam Donaldson and Cokie Roberts 1996–2002; currently panelist This Week and co-host Politics Live, ABC News Now. *Publication:* Hold on Mr President 1987. *Honours:* Broadcaster of the Year Award, Nat. Press Foundation 1998 and numerous other awards. *Address:* ABC, 1717 Desales Street, NW, Washington, DC 20036, USA (office). *E-mail:* samdonaldson@abcnews.com (office).

DONALDSON, Stephen Reeder, (Reed Stephens), BA, MA; American writer; b. 13 May 1947, Cleveland, OH; m. 1st (divorced); m. 2nd Stephanie 1980; one s. one d. *Education:* Coll. of Wooster, Kent State Univ. *Career:* Assoc. Instructor, Ghost Ranch Writers' Workshops 1973–77; Contributing Ed., Journal of the Fantastic in the Arts; mem. Int. Asscn for the Fantastic in the Arts. *Publications:* Thomas Covenant series: The Chronicles of Thomas Covenant the Unbeliever, Vol. I Lord Foul's Bane 1977, Vol. 2 The Illearth War 1977, Vol. 3 The Power that Preserves 1977; The Second Chronicles of Thomas Covenant, Vol. 1 The Wounded Land 1980, Vol. 2 The One Tree 1982, Vol. 3 White Gold Wielder 1983; The Last Chronicles of Thomas Covenant, Vol. I The Runes of the Earth 2004; Mordant's Need, Vol. 1 The Mirror of Her Dreams 1986, Vol. 2 A Man Rides Through 1987; the Gap sequence: The Gap Into Conflict: The Real Story 1991, The Gap Into Vision: Forbidden Knowledge 1991, The Gap Into Power: A Dark and Hungry God Arises 1992, The Gap Into Madness: Chaos and Order 1994, The Gap Into Ruin: This Day All Gods Die 1996; other novels: Gilden-Fire 1982, Daughter of Regals and Other Tales 1984, Reave the Just and Other Tales 1999, The Man Who Fought Alone 2001; as Reed Stephens: The Man Who Killed His Brother 1980, The Man Who Risked His Partner 1984, The Man Who Tried to Get Away 1990; editor: Strange Dreams: Unforgettable Fantasy Stories 1993; contrib. to magazines. *Honours:* Hon. DLitt (Coll. of Wooster) 1993; British Fantasy Soc. Best Novel Award 1978, World Science Fiction Convention John W. Campbell Award 1979, Balrog Awards 1981, 1983, 1985, Saturn Award 1983. *Literary Agent:* Howard Morhaim Literary Agency, 841 Broadway, Suite 604, New York, NY 10003, USA. *Website:* www.stephendonaldson.com.

DONALDSON, William, MA, PhD; British teacher and writer; b. 19 July 1944, Ellon, Scotland; two s. one d. *Education:* Univ. of Aberdeen. *Career:* Registrar of the North East Survey; teacher of English; Assoc. Lecturer, Open Univ. *Publications:* Popular Literature in Victorian Scotland 1986, The Jacobite Song 1988, The Language of the People 1989, The Highland Pipe and Scottish Society 2000, Pipers: A Guide to the Players and Music of the Highland Bagpipe 2005. *Honours:* Blackwell Prize 1988, Scottish Arts Council Book Award 1989, Piper & Drummer Online Award 2000. *Address:* The Open University in Scotland, 10 Drumsheugh Gardens, Edinburgh, EH3 7QJ, Scotland (office).

DONGLI JIEFU (see Zhang Changxin)

DONLEAVY, James Patrick; Irish author; b. 23 April 1926, New York City; s. of Patrick Donleavy and Margaret Donleavy; m. 1st Valerie Heron (divorced 1969); one s. one d.; m. 2nd Mary Wilson Price (divorced 1989); one s. one d. *Education:* Preparatory School, New York and Trinity Coll., Dublin. *Career:* served in USN during World War II. *Publications:* (novels) The Ginger Man 1955, A Singular Man 1963, The Beastly Beatitudes of Balthazar B 1968, The Onion Eaters 1971, A Fairy Tale of New York 1973, The Destinies of Darcy Dancer, Gentleman 1977, Schultz 1979, Leila 1983, Wrong Information is Being Given Out at Princeton 1998; (short stories and sketches) Meet My Maker the Mad Molecule 1964, An Author and His Image 1997; (novella) The Saddest Summer of Samuel S. 1966; also: The Unexpurgated Code: A Complete Manual of Survival and Manners 1975, De Alfonce Tennis, The Superlative Game of Eccentric Champions. Its History, Accoutrements, Rules, Conduct and Regimen. A Legend 1984, J. P. Donleavy's Ireland: In All Her Sins and in Some of Her Graces 1986, A Singular Country 1989, The History of the Ginger Man 1993, The Lady Who Liked Clean Rest Rooms 1995; (plays) The Ginger Man 1959, Fairy Tales of New York 1960, A Singular Man 1964, The Saddest Summer of Samuel S. 1968, The Plays of J. P. Donleavy 1972, The Beastly Beatitudes of Balthazar B. 1981, Are You Listening Rabbi Löw? 1987, That Darcy, That Dancer, That Gentlemen 1990. *Honours:* Evening Standard Drama Award 1960, Brandeis Univ. Creative Arts Award 1961–62, Citation, American Acad. and Nat. Inst. of Arts and Letters 1975, Worldfest Houston Gold Award 1992, Cine Golden Eagle Writer and Narrator 1993. *Address:* Levington Park, Mullingar, Co. Westmeath, Ireland. *Telephone:* (44) 9348903. *Fax:* (44) 9348351.

DONNELLY, Jennifer; American writer; b. Portchester, NY; m. *Education:* Univ. of Rochester. *Career:* fmr antiques dealer, reporter, copywriter. *Publications:* fiction: The Tea Rose 2002, The Winter Rose 2006; juvenile: Humble Pie 2002, A Gathering Light (aka A Northern Light) (Carnegie Medal 2004) 2003. *Honours:* CILIP Carnegie Medal, Printz Honor Award, Borders Original Voices Young Adult Prize, Los Angeles Times Book Prize. *Address:* c/o Bloomsbury Publishing PLC, 38 Soho Square, London, W1D 3HB, England. *E-mail:* jen@jenniferdonnelly.com. *Website:* www.jenniferdonnelly.com.

DONNER, Jörn Johan, BA; Finnish film director, writer, politician and diplomatist; b. 5 Feb. 1933, Helsinki; s. of Dr Kai Donner and Greta von Bonsdorff; m. 1st Inga-Britt Wik 1954 (divorced 1962); m. 2nd Jeanette Bonnier 1974 (divorced 1988); m. 3rd Bitte Westerlund 1995; five s. one d. *Education:* Helsinki Univ. *Career:* worked as writer and film dir in Finland and Sweden, writing own film scripts; contrib. and critic to various Scandinavian and int. journals; CEO Jörn Donner Productions 1966–; Dir Swedish Film Inst., Stockholm 1972–75, Exec. Producer 1975–78, Man. Dir 1978–82; Chair. Bd Finnish Film Foundation, 1981–83, 1986–89, 1992–95; mem. Bd Marimekko Textiles and other cos; mem., Helsinki City Council 1969–1972, 1984–92; mem. Parl. 1987–95; Vice-Chair. Foreign Affairs Cttee 1991–95; Chair. Finnish EFTA Parliamentarians 1991–95; Consul-Gen. of Finland, Los Angeles 1995–96; mem. European Parl. 1996–99. *Films:* A Sunday in September 1963, To Love 1964, Adventure Starts Here 1965, Rooftree 1967, Black on White 1968, Sixty-nine 1969, Portraits of Women 1970, Anna 1970, Images of Finland 1971, Tenderness 1972, Baksmalla 1974, Three Scenes (with Ingmar Bergman), The Bergman File 1975–77, Men Can't Be Raped 1978, Dirty Story 1984, Letters from Sweden 1987, Ingmar Bergman, a Conversation 1998, The President 2000. *Television:* host of talk show (Sweden and Finland) 1974–95. *Publications:* 52 books including: Report from Berlin 1958, The Personal Vision of Ingmar Bergman 1962. *Honours:* Opera Prima Award Venice Film Festival 1963, Vittorio de Sica Prize, Sorrento 1978, Acad. Award for Producer of Best Foreign Language Picture (Fanny and Alexander) 1984. *Address:* POB 214, 00171 Helsinki (office); Pohjoisranta 12, 00170 Helsinki, Finland (home). *Telephone:* (9) 1356060 (office); (9) 1357112 (home). *Fax:* (9) 1357568 (office). *E-mail:* j.donner@surfnet.fi (home).

DONOGHUE, Denis, PhD; Irish literary critic; b. 1 Dec. 1928. *Education:* Univ. Coll., Dublin. *Career:* Admin. Office, Irish Dept of Finance 1951–54; Asst Lecturer, Univ. Coll., Dublin 1954–57, Coll. lecturer 1957–62, 1963–64, Prof. of Modern English and American Literature 1965–79; Visiting Scholar, Univ. of Pa 1962–63; Univ. Lecturer, Cambridge Univ. and Fellow, King's Coll. 1964–65; Henry James Prof. of Letters, New York Univ. 1979–; mem. Int. Cttee of Asscn of Univ. Profs of English; BBC Reith Lecturer 1982. *Publications:* The Third Voice 1959, Connoisseurs of Chaos 1965, The Ordinary Universe 1968, Emily Dickinson 1968, Jonathan Swift 1969, Yeats 1971, Thieves of Fire 1974, Sovereign Ghost: Studies in Imagination 1978, Ferocious Alphabets 1981, The Arts Without Mystery 1983, We Irish: Essays on Irish Literature and Society 1987, Walter Pater: Lover of Strange Souls 1995, The Practice of Reading 1998, Words Alone: The Poet T. S. Eliot 2000, Adam's Curse: Reflections on Literature and Religion 2001, The American Classics: A Personal Essay 2005; contribs to reviews and journals and ed. of three vols. *Honours:* Hon. DLitt. *Address:* English Department, New York University, 726 Broadway (7th Floor), New York, NY 10003, USA; Gaybrook, North Avenue, Mount Merrion, Dublin, Ireland. *E-mail:* dd1@nyu.edu (office).

DONOGHUE, Emma, BA, PhD; Irish/Canadian writer and dramatist; b. 24 Oct. 1969, Dublin, Ireland; d. of Denis and Frances Donoghue; partner, Christine Roulston; one s. *Education:* Univ. Coll., Dublin, Univ. of Cambridge, UK. *Career:* mem. Authors' Soc., Writers' Union of Canada. *Plays:* I Know My Own Heart (Dublin) 1993, Ladies and Gentlemen (Dublin) 1993, Kissing the Witch (San Francisco) 2000. *Radio:* plays: Trespasses (RTE) 1996, Don't Die Wondering (BBC Radio 4) 2000, Mix (BBC Radio 3) 2003; series: Exes (BBC Radio 4) 2001, Humans and Other Animals (BBC Radio 4) 2003. *Publications:* Passions Between Women 1993, Stir-Fry (novel) 1994, Hood (novel) 1995, Kissing the Witch (short stories) 1997, What Sappho Would Have Said (aka Poems Between Women, anthology) 1997, We Are Michael Field (biog.) 1998, Ladies and Gentlemen (play) 1998, The Mammoth Book of Lesbian Short Stories (anthology) 1999, Slammerkin (novel) 2000, The Woman Who Gave

Birth to Rabbits (short stories) 2002, Life Mask (novel) 2004, Touchy Subjects: Stories 2006. *Honours:* Gay, Lesbian and Bisexual Book Award, American Library Asscn 1997, Ferro-Grumley Fiction Award 2002. *Address:* c/o Caroline Davidson, 5 Queen Anne's Gardens, London, W4 1TU, England (office); 131 Langarth Street East, London, Ont., N6C 1Z4, Canada (home). *E-mail:* emma@emmadonoghue.com. *Website:* www.emmadonoghue.com.

DONOVAN, Anne; Scottish writer. *Publications:* Hieroglyphics and Other Stories 2001, Buddha Da (novel) 2003. *Honours:* Macallan/Scotland on Sunday Short Story Competition 1997, Canongate Prize 2000, Scottish Arts Council Award 2004, Le Prince Maurice Award (Mauritius) 2004. *Address:* c/o Canongate Books, 14 High Street, Edinburgh, EH1 1TE, Scotland. *E-mail:* info@canongate.co.uk. *Website:* www.canongate.co.uk.

DONOVAN, Gerard; Irish poet and novelist; b. Wexford. *Education:* Johns Hopkins Univ. *Career:* frmly taught at Johns Hopkins Univ., Univ. of Arkansas; currently Adjunct Assoc. Prof. of English, Southampton Coll., New York, USA. *Publications:* Columbus Rides Again (poems) 1992, Kings and Bicycles (poems) 1995, The Lighthouse (poems) 2000, Schopenhauer's Telescope (novel) 2003, Doctor Salt (novel) 2005; short stories, contrib. to The Sewanee Review, New Statesman, Stand, Irish Times, Poetry Ireland Review, The Salmon, Writing in the West, Paris Review. *Address:* c/o Salmon Publishing, Knockeven, Cliffs of Moher, County Clare, Ireland.

DONOVAN, Paul James Kingsley, MA; British author and journalist; b. 8 April 1949, Sheffield, Yorks., England; m. Hazel Case 1979, one s. two d. *Education:* Oriel Coll., Oxford. *Career:* reporter and TV Critic, Daily Mail 1978–85; Showbusiness Ed. and Critic, Today 1986–88; radio columnist, Sunday Times 1988–. *Publications:* Roger Moore 1983, Dudley 1988, The Radio Companion 1991, All Our Todays 1997; contribs to The Times, Sunday Times, Observer, Guardian, The Author; several articles to Oxford Dictionary of National Biography. *Address:* 11 Stile Hall Gardens, London, W4 3BS, England. *Telephone:* (20) 8994-5316. *Fax:* (20) 8747-4850. *E-mail:* pauldon@scribbler.freeserve.co.uk.

DOODY, Margaret Anne, BA, MA, PhD; Canadian academic and writer; *John and Barbara Glynn Family Professor of Literature, University of Notre Dame*; b. 21 Sept. 1939, St John, NB; d. of Rev. Hubert Doody and Anne Ruth Cornwall. *Education:* Centreville Regional High School, NB, Dalhousie Univ., Halifax, Lady Margaret Hall, Oxford, UK. *Career:* Instructor in English 1962–64; Asst Prof., English Dept, Vic. Univ. 1968–69; Lecturer, Univ. Coll. of Swansea, UK 1969–77; Visiting Assoc. Prof. of English, Univ. of California, Berkeley 1976–77, Assoc. Prof. 1977–80; Prof. of English, Princeton Univ., NJ 1980–89; Andrew W. Mellon Prof. of Humanities and Prof. of English, Vanderbilt Univ., Nashville, Tenn. 1989–99, Dir Comparative Literature 1992–99; John and Barbara Glynn Family Prof. of Literature, Univ. of Notre Dame, Ind. 2000–; Commonwealth Fellowship 1960–62; Canada Council Fellowship 1964–65; Imperial Oil Fellowship 1965–68; Guggenheim Foundation Fellowship 1978; Nat. Endowment for the Humanities Fellowship 2007. *Play:* Clarissa (co-writer), New York 1984. *Publications:* non-fiction: A Natural Passion: A Study of the Novels of Samuel Richardson 1974, Aristotle Detective 1978, The Daring Muse 1985, Frances Burney: The Life in the Works 1988, Samuel Richardson: Tercentenary Essays (ed. with Peter Sabor) 1989, The True Story of the Novel 1996, Anne of Green Gables (co-ed. with Wendy Barry and Mary Doody Jones) 1997, Tropic of Venice 2007; Aristotle detective series: Aristotle Detective 1978, Aristotle and the Fatal Javelin (short story) 1980, Aristotle and the Poetic Justice 2002, Aristotle and the Secrets of Life 2003; other fiction: The Alchemists (novel) 1980, Poison in Athens (novel) 2004, Mysteries of Eleusis (novel) 2005, Annello di Bronzo (novella). *Honours:* Hon. LLD (Dalhousie) 1985; Rose Mary Crawshay Prize 1986. *Address:* English Department, 356 O'Shaughnessy Hall, University of Notre Dame, Notre Dame, IN 46556 (office); 435 Edgewater Drive, Mishawaka, IN 46545, USA (home). *Telephone:* (574) 631-0465 (office); (574) 257-7927 (home). *E-mail:* mdoody@nd.edu (office); margaret.doody.1@nd.edu (office). *Website:* www.nd.edu/~mdoody (office).

DÖPFNER, Mathias, MA; German publishing executive; *CEO and Head of Newspapers Division, Axel Springer AG*; b. 15 Jan. 1963, Bonn; m. *Career:* journalist, Frankfurter Allgemeine Zeitung 1982; dir public relations agency 1988–90; fmr Asst to CEO, Gruner & Jahr, Hamburg; Ed.-in-Chief Wochenpost, Berlin 1994–96, Hamburger Morgenpost 1996–98; joined Axel Springer AG 1998, fmr Ed.-in-Chief Die Welt, mem. Man. Bd, Multimedia Div. 2000–, Head of Newspapers Div. 2000–, CEO 2002–; mem. Bd of Dirs Time Warner 2006–. *Address:* Axel Springer Verlag AG, Axel-Springer-Platz 1, 20350 Hamburg, Germany (office). *Telephone:* (40) 34722370 (office). *Fax:* (40) 34729037 (office). *Website:* www.asv.de (office).

DOR, Moshe, BA; Israeli poet, journalist and editor; b. 9 Dec. 1932, Tel-Aviv; m. Ziona Dor 1955, two s. *Education:* Hebrew University of Jerusalem, University of Tel-Aviv. *Career:* Counsellor for Cultural Affairs, Embassy of Israel, London, England 1975–77; Distinguished Writer-in-Residence, American University, Washington, DC 1987; mem. Asscn of Hebrew Writers, Israel, National Federation of Israel Journalists, Israel PEN Centre (pres. 1988–90). *Publications:* From the Outset, 1984; On Top of the Cliff (in Hebrew), 1986; Crossing the River, 1989; From the Outset (selected poems in Dutch trans.), 1989; Crossing the River (selected poems in English trans.), 1989; Love and Other Calamities (poems in Hebrew), 1993; Khamsin (memoirs and poetry in English trans.), 1994; The Silence of the Builder (poems in Hebrew), 1996; co-ed., English anthologies of Israeli Hebrew poetry: The Burning Bush, 1977; The Stones Remember, 1991; After the First Rain, 1997; books of poetry, children's verse, literary essays, interviews with writers, trans of poetry and literature from English into Hebrew. *Honours:* Honourable Citation, International Hans Christian Andersen Prize for Children's Literature, 1975; Holon Prize for Literature, 1981; Prime Minister's Award for Creative Writing, 1986; Bialik Prize for Literature, 1987.

DORESKI, William, BA, MA, PhD; American academic, writer and poet; *Professor of English, Keene State College*; b. 10 Jan. 1946, Stafford, CT; m. Carole Doreski 1981. *Education:* Goddard Coll., Boston Univ., Princeton Univ., Dartmouth Coll. *Career:* Writer-in-Residence, Emerson Coll. 1973–75; Instructor in Humanities, Goddard Coll. 1975–80; Asst Prof., Keene State Coll., NH 1982–87, Assoc. Prof. 1988–91, Prof. of English 1992–; mem. American Studies Asscn, Associated Writing Programs, Asscn of Scholars and Critics, MLA, New Hampshire Writers' Project, Robert Frost Soc., Wallace Stevens Soc. *Publications:* The Testament of Israel Potter 1976, Half of the Map 1980, Earth That Sings: The Poetry of Andrew Glaze 1985, How to Read and Interpret Poetry 1988, The Years of Our Friendship: Robert Lowell and Allen Tate 1990, Ghost Train 1991, The Modern Voice in American Poetry 1995, Sublime of the North and Other Poems 1997, Pianos in the Woods 1998, Shifting Colors: The Public and the Private in the Poetry of Robert Lowell 1999, My Shadow Instead of Myself 2004, Sacra Via 2005; contrib. to books, journals, reviews, quarterlies and magazines. *Honours:* Poet Lore Trans. Prize 1975, Black Warrior Prize 1979, Nat. Endowment for the Humanities grants 1987, 1995, Whiting Foundation Fellowship 1988, Clay Potato Fiction Prize 1997, Frith Press Poetry Award 1997. *Address:* Department of English, Keene State College, Keene, NH 03435, USA (office). *Telephone:* (603) 358-2698 (office); (603) 924-7987 (home). *Fax:* (603) 358-2773 (office). *E-mail:* wdoreski@keene.edu (office).

DORET, Michel, BA, BS, MA, MPhil, PhD; American architect, artist, writer and poet; b. 5 Jan. 1938, Petion-Ville, Haiti; m. Liselotte Bencze 1970. *Education:* Pace Univ., New York Univ., SUNY, George Washington Univ. *Career:* founder and Dir, Les Editions Amon Ra 1982–97; founder-producer Michel's Video Studios New York 2000–; three art collections displayed in over 30 group and solo exhibitions in Europe, the USA and on the intenet; festivals; mem. several literary organizations. *Videos as producer:* 150 films in three series, 30 shown on Channel 20 Public Access Long Island Broadcasting Station. *Publications:* Isolement 1979, La Poésie francophone (eight vols) 1980, Panorama de la poésie feminine Suisse Romande 1982, Panorama de la poésie feminine francophone 1984, La negritude dans la poésie haitienne 1985, Poétesses Genevoises francophones 1985, Haiti en Poésie 1990, Les Mamelles de Lutèce 1991, Lyrisme du Moi 1992, The History of the Architecture of Ayiti (two vols) 1995; contrib. to numerous books, journals, reviews and other publications. *Honours:* various medals, diplomas, and hon. mentions. *Address:* 26 Mellow Lane, Westbury, NY 11590, USA. *E-mail:* mdor26@aol.com. *Website:* www.micheldoret.com.

DORFMAN, (Vladimiro) Ariel; Chilean writer and academic; *Walter Hines Page Research Professor of Literature and Latin American Studies, Duke University*; b. 6 May 1942, Buenos Aires, Argentina; m. Angélica 1966; two s. *Education:* Univ. of Chile, Santiago. *Career:* Teaching Asst Univ. of Chile 1963–65, Asst Prof. of Spanish Literature and Journalism 1965–68, Assoc. Prof. 1968–70, Prof. 1970–73; exiled after Chilean coup 1973; Maître des Conférences Spanish-American Literature, Sorbonne Paris IV 1975–76; Head Scientific Research, Spanns Seminarium, Univ. of Amsterdam 1976–80; Visiting Prof. Univ. of Maryland 1983; Post-Doctoral Fellow and Consultant Latin American Council, Duke Univ., NC 1984, Visiting Prof. of Literature and Latin American Studies 1985–89, Research Prof. of Literature and Latin American Studies, 1989–96, Walter Hines Page Distinguished Prof. of Literature and Latin American Studies, Center for Int. Studies and Romance Studies 1996–; Research Scholar Univ. of Calif. at Berkeley 1968–69; Friedrich Ebert Stiftugn Research Fellow 1974–76; Fellowship at Woodrow Wilson Int. Center for Scholars 1980–81; Visiting Fellow Inst. for Policy Studies 1981–84; Fellow American Acad. of Arts and Sciences. *Plays:* Widows (Kennedy Center New American Plays Award) 1988, Death and the Maiden (Olivier Award for Best Play, London 1992) 1991, Reader (Kennedy Center Roger L. Stevens Award) 1992, Who's Who (with Rodrigo Dorfman) 1998, Speak Truth to Power: Voices from Beyond the Dark 2000, The Other Side 2004, Manifesto from Another World: Voices from Beyond the Dark 2004, Purgatorio 2005, Picasso Lost and Found 2005. *Film screenplays:* Death and the Maiden 1994, Prisoners in Time 1995, My House is on Fire 1997. *Publications:* fiction: Hard Rain 1973, My House is On Fire 1979, Widows 1983, Dorando la pildora 1985, Travesía 1986, The Last Song of Manuel Sendero 1987, Máscara 1988, Konfidenz 1995, The Nanny and the Iceberg 1999, Blake's Therapy 2001, The Rabbit's Rebellion 2001, The Burning City (with Joaquin Dorfman) 2003; poetry: Missing 1982, Last Waltz in Santiago and Other Poems of Exile and Disappearance 1988, In Case of Fire in a Foreign Land: New and Collected Poems from Two Languages 2002; non-fiction: How to Read Donald Duck (with Armand Mattelart) 1971, The Empire's Old Clothes 1983, Some Write to the Future 1991, Heading South, Looking North: A Bilingual Journey 1998, Exorcising Terror: The Incredible Ongoing Trial of General Augusto Pinochet 2002, Desert Memories: Journeys Through the Chilean North 2004, Other Septembers, Many Americas: Selected Provocations, 1980–2004 2004. *Honours:* Dr hc (Ill. Wesleyan Univ.) 1989, (Wooster Coll.) 1991, (Bradford Coll.) 1993, (American Univ.) 2001,; Time Out Award 1991, New York Public Library Literary Lion 1992,

Dora Mavor Award 1994, Int. Poetry Forum Charity Randall Citation 1995, Writers' Guild of Great Britain Best Film for Television 1995, ALOA Prize, Denmark 2002, Lowell Thomas Silver Award for Travel Book 2004. *Address:* c/o Center for International Studies, Duke University, PO Box 90404, Durham, NC 27708, USA. *Fax:* (919) 684-8749 (office). *E-mail:* adorfman@ duke.edu (office). *Website:* www.adorfman.duke.edu (office).

DORIN, Françoise Andrée Renée; French actress, novelist and playwright; b. 23 Jan. 1928, Paris; d. of late René Dorin and of Yvonne Guilbert; m. Jean Poiret (b. Poiré) (divorced); one d. *Career:* at Théâtre des Deux-Ânes, then du Quartier Latin (Les Aveux les plus doux 1957), then La Bruyère (Le Chinois 1958); Presenter TV programme Paris-Club 1969; playwright and author 1967–. *Songs include:* Que c'est triste Venise, N'avoue jamais, Faisons l'humour ensemble, Les miroirs truqués 1982. *Plays include:* Comme au théâtre 1967, La Facture 1968, Un sale égoiste, Les Bonshommes 1970, Le Tournant 1973, Le Tube 1974, L'Autre Valse 1975, Si t'es beau, t'es con 1976, Le Tout pour Le tout 1978, L'Intoxe 1980, Les Cahiers Tango 1987, Et s'il n'en restait qu'un 1992; lyrics for Vos gueules les mouettes 1971, Monsieur Pompadour 1972, L'Etiquette 1983, Les jupes-culottes 1984, La valise en carton (musical comedy) 1986, L'âge en question 1986, La Retour en Toupaine 1993, Monsieur de Saint-Futile (Vaudeville) 1996, Soins intensifs 2001. *Publications:* novels include Virginie et Paul, La Seconde dans Rome, Va voir Maman, Papa travaille 1976, Les lits à une place 1980, Les miroirs truqués 1982, Les jupes-culottes 1984, Les corbeaux et les renardes 1988, Nini patte-en-l'air 1990, Au nom du père et de la fille 1992, Pique et Coeur 1993, La Mouflette 1994, Les Vendanges tardives 1997, La Courte paille 1999, Les Julottes 2001. *Honours:* Chevalier, Légion d'honneur, Officier, Ordre nat. du Mérite, Arts et Lettres; trophée Dussane 1973, Grand Prix du théâtre (for L'Etiquette) 1981. *Address:* c/o Artmédia, 20 avenue Rapp, 75007 Paris, France.

DORMANN, Geneviève; French writer and journalist; b. 24 Sept. 1933, Paris; d. of Maurice Dormann and Alice Dormann; m. 1st Philippe Lejeune (divorced); three d.; m. 2nd Jean-Loup Dabadie (divorced); one d. *Education:* Lycée La Fontaine, Paris. *Career:* writer and journalist, Le Figaro newspaper. *Screenplays:* Der Fangschuß (aka Coup de grâce) 1976, Mont-Oriol (TV adaptation) 1980, Quatre femmes, quatre vies: Des chandails pour l'hiver 1981. *Publications:* Novels: La Fanfaronne 1959, Le chemin des dames 1964, La passion selon saint Jules 1967, Je t'apporterai des orages (Prix des Quatre Jurys) 1971, Le bateau du courrier (Prix des Deux Magots 1975) 1974, Mickey, l'ange 1977, Fleur de péché 1980, Le roman de Sophie Trébuchet (Prix Kléber Haedens, Prix de la Ville de Nantes) 1982, Amoureuse Colette 1984, Le livre du point de croix 1986, Le bal du Dodo (Grand Prix du Roman, Acad. française) 1989, Paris est une ville pleine de lions 1991, La petite main 1993, La gourmandise de Guillaume Apollinaire 1994, Adieu phénomène (Prix Genevois) 1999; Short stories: La première pierre 1957. *Honours:* Grand Prix du Roman, Ville de Paris 1981. *Address:* 9 rue de Poitiers, 75007 Paris, France.

DORMER, Richard; Irish actor and playwright; b. 11 Nov. 1969, Armagh; m. Rachel O'Riordan. *Education:* RADA, London. *Career:* co-founder and writer-in-residence, Ransom Productions 2002–. *Plays:* Hurricane 2002, The Half 2005. *Film:* Middletown 2006. *Honours:* The Stage Best Actor Award, BBC Stewart Parker Award. *Address:* Ransom Productions, 15 Church Street, Belfast, BT1 1PG (office); 60 Fernwood Street, Belfast, BT7 3BQ, Northern Ireland (home). *Telephone:* (28) 9096-4320. *E-mail:* ransomproduction@ btconnect.com. *Website:* www.ransomproductions.co.uk.

DORNER, Majorie, BA, MA, PhD; American academic and writer; b. 21 Jan. 1942, Luxemburg, WI; two d. *Education:* St Norbert College, Marquette University, Purdue University. *Career:* Prof. of English Literature, Winona State University, Minnesota, 1971–. *Publications:* Nightmare, 1987; Family Closets, 1989; Freeze Frame, 1990; Winter Roads, Summer Fields, 1992; Blood Kin, 1992. Contributions: various publications. *Honours:* Minnesota Book Awards 1991, 1993.

DORR, James Suhrer, BS, MA; American writer and poet; b. 12 Aug. 1941, Pensacola, Fla; s. of Frank J. Dorr and Betty S. Dorr; m. Ruth Michelle Clark 1975 (divorced 1982). *Education:* Massachusetts Inst. of Tech., Indiana Univ. *Career:* tech. writer, Ed., Wrubel Computing Center, Bloomington, Ind. 1969–81; writer, Marketing Consultant, The Stackworks 1982; Assoc. Ed., Bloomington Area Magazine 1983–86; freelance writer 1982–; mem. SFWA, Horror Writers Asscn, Science Fiction Poetry Asscn, Short Mystery Fiction Soc. *Publications:* Towers of Darkness (poems) 1990, Strange Mistresses (short fiction) 2001, Darker Loves (short fiction) 2007; contrib. Borderlands II 1991, Grails 1992, Dark Destiny I and II 1994–95, Dante's Disciples 1996, Darkside: Horror for the Next Millennium 1996, Dark Tyrants 1997, Gothic Ghosts 1997, Asylums and Labyrinths 1997, The Best of Cemetery Dance 1998, New Mythos Legends 1999, Children of Cthulhu 2002, The Darker Side: Generations of Horror 2002, Spooks! 2004; also to anthologies, periodicals, journals, reviews, magazines, quarterlies and newspapers. *Honours:* Rhysling Hon. Mention 1993, 1995, 1996, 1997, 2001. *Address:* 1404 E Atwater, Bloomington, IN 47401, USA.

DORSETT, Danielle (see Daniels, Dorothy)

DORSEY, Candas Jane, BA, BSW; Canadian writer, poet and editor; b. 16 Nov. 1952, Edmonton, AB. *Education:* University of Alberta, University of Calgary. *Career:* freelance writer and ed., Edmonton Bullet, Edmonton, AB,

1980; has also worked in theatre and as social worker. *Publications:* This Is for You (poems), 1973; Orion Rising (poems), 1974; Results of the Ring Toss (poems), 1976; Hardwired Angel (novel, co-author), 1987; Machine Sex and Other Stories, 1988; Tesseracts Three: Canadian Science Fiction (co-ed.), 1990; Leaving Marks (poems), 1992; Dark Earth Dreams (novel, co-author), 1995; Black Wine, 1997. Contributions: short fiction to books including: Getting Here; Tesseracts. *Honours:* First Prize, shared with co-author, for Hardwired Angel, Ninth Annual Pulp Press International 3-Day Novel Competition, 1987. *Address:* c/o Porcepic Books, 4252 Commerce Circle, Victoria, BC V8Z 4M2, Canada.

DORST, Tankred; German writer; b. 19 Dec. 1925, Sonneberg; s. of Max Dorst and Elisabeth Dorst; m. Ursula Ehler-Dorst. *Career:* dir production of Ring, Bayreuth Festival 2006; mem. German PEN Centre, Bayerische Akad. der schönen Künste, Deutsche Akad. der darstellenden Künste, Deutsche Akad. für Sprache und Dichtung. *Film as director and screenwriter:* Eisenhans. *Plays:* around 40 plays including Toller, Eiszeit, Merlin oder das wüste Land, Herr Paul, Was sollen wir tun, Fernando Krapp hat mir diesen Brief geschrieben, Die Legende vom Armen Heinrich; Karlos, Korbes; several opera libretti; four plays for children. *TV films (writer and director):* Klaras Mutter, Mosch, Eisenhaus. *Publications:* Plays (Vols 1–7), Merlins Zauber, Die Reise nach Stettin: Der schöne Ort. *Honours:* several prizes including Gerhart Hauptmann Prize, Georg-Büchner Prize 1990. *Address:* Karl Theodor Strasse 102, 80796 Munich, Germany (home). *Fax:* (89) 3073256.

DOTTO, Lydia Carol; Canadian science writer; b. 29 May 1949, Cadomin, Alberta; d. of August Dotto and Assunta Dotto. *Education:* Carleton Univ., Ont. *Career:* joined Edmonton Journal 1969, Toronto Star 1970, 1971; science writer, Toronto Globe and Mail 1972–78; has covered space missions 1972–; freelance writer 1978–; Exec. Ed. Canadian Science News Service 1982–92; two dives under arctic ice, Resolute Bay, NWT 1974; participant zero-gravity training flight, Johnson Space Center, Houston, Tex., USA 1983; Co-Dir SpaceNet Canada 1995–. *Publications include:* The Ozone War (co-author) 1978, Thinking the Unthinkable: Civilization and Rapid Climate Change 1988, Canada in Space 1987, Planet Earth in Jeopardy: The Environmental Consequences of Nuclear War 1986, Asleep in the Fast Lane: The Impact of Sleep on Work 1990, Asleep in the Fast Lane – How Your Sleeping Habits Affect Your Life 1990, Losing Sleep: How Your Sleeping Habits Affect Your Life 1990, Blue Planet – A Portrait of Earth 1991, Ethical Choices and Global Greenhouse Warming 1993, The Astronauts: Canada's Voyageurs in space 1993, Storm Warning – Gambling with the Climate of our Planet 1999. *Honours:* Canadian Science Writers' Awards for newspaper and magazine articles 1974, 1981, 1984, 1994, Canadian Meteorological Soc. Award 1975, Stanford Fleming Medal, Royal Canadian Inst. 1982–83. *Address:* 599 Gilmour Street, Peterborough, Ontario, K9H 2K3, Canada. *E-mail:* ldotto@ sympatico.ca.

DOTY, Mark, BA, MFA; American poet and academic; *John and Rebecca Moores Professor, University of Houston;* b. 10 Aug. 1953, Maryville, TN. *Education:* Drake Univ., Goddard Coll. *Career:* faculty, MFA Writing Program, Vermont Coll. 1981–94, Writing and Literature, Goddard Coll. 1985–90; guest faculty, Sarah Lawrence Coll. 1990–94, 1996; Fannie Hurst Visiting Prof., Brandeis Univ. 1994; visiting faculty, Univ. of Iowa 1995, 1996, Columbia Univ. 1996; Prof., Creative Writing Program, Univ. of Utah 1997–98; John and Rebecca Moores Prof. of English, Univ. of Houston. *Publications:* Turtle, Swan 1987, Bethlehem in Broad Daylight 1991, My Alexandria 1993, Atlantis 1995, Heaven's Coast (memoir) 1996, Firebird (memoir) 1999, Source 2001, School of Arts (poems) 2005; contrib. to many anthologies and journals. *Honours:* Theodore Roethke Prize 1986, NEA Fellowships in Poetry 1987, 1995, Pushcart Prizes 1987, 1989, Los Angeles Times Book Prize 1993, Ingram Merrill Foundation Award 1994, National Book Critics Circle Award 1994, Guggenheim Fellowship 1994, Whiting Writers Award 1994, Rockefeller Foundation Fellowship, Bellagio, Italy 1995, New York Times Notable Book of the Year citations 1995, 1996, American Library Asscn Notable Book of the Year 1995, T. S. Eliot Prize 1996, Bingham Poetry Prize 1996, Ambassador Book Award 1996, Lambda Literary Award 1996. *Address:* English Department, Room 232D C, University of Houston, 4800 Cullen Boulevard, Houston, TX 77204-3013, USA (office). *Telephone:* (713) 743-2907 (office). *Website:* www.hfac.uh.edu/English (office).

DOUGHTY, Louise, BA, MA; British novelist and playwright; b. 4 Sept. 1963, Melton Mowbray, England. *Education:* Leeds Univ., Univ. of East Anglia. *Career:* Chair of judges Orange Award for New Writers; mem. Society of Authors 1998–. *Publications:* fiction: Crazy Paving 1995, Dance With Me 1996, Honey-Dew 1998, Fires in the Dark 2003, Stone Cradle 2006; radio plays: Maybe 1991, The Koala Bear Joke 1994, Nightworkers 1999. *Honours:* Radio Times Drama Award 1991, Ian St James Award 1991. *Literary Agent:* c/o Antony Harwood Ltd, Office 109, Riverbank House, 1 Putney Bridge Approach, London SW6 3JD, England.

DOUGLAS, Garry (see Kilworth, Garry Douglas)

DOUGLAS, Michael (see Crichton, (John) Michael)

DOUTINÉ, Heike, PhD; German writer; b. 1946, Hamburg. *Education:* Univ. of Hamburg/Cologne. *Career:* numerous novels, short stories and poems; Guest Prof. Univ. of Los Angeles and Ford Foundation, USA. *Publications include:* novels: Wanke nicht, mein Vaterland, Berta, Wir Zwei, Die Meute, Der Hit, Im Lichte Venedigs (jtly) 1987, Blutiger Mund – Die Tage des Mondes

1991; poetry: In tiefer Trauer, Das Herz auf dem Lanze, Blumen begießen, bevor es anfängt zu regnen (also short stories) 1986, Lieder und Canones 1995, Roses and Other Songs 2001; short stories: Deutscher Alltag – Meldungen über Menschen; librettos for Peace Cantata by Norbert Linke 1996, Desire by Ali Sadé 2003, Peace Oratorio by Linke, Oratorio of the Roses. *Honours:* Prize for Novel, Neue Literarische Gesellschaft, Villa Massimo Prize, Italy 1973–74, Prix de Rome. *Address:* Ohnhorststr. 26, 22609 Hamburg, Germany.

DOVE, Rita Frances, BA, MFA; American writer, poet and academic; *Commonwealth Professor, University of Virginia;* b. 28 Aug. 1952, Akron, OH; d. of Ray Dove and Elvira Dove (née Hord); m. Fred Viebahn 1979; one d. *Education:* Miami Univ., Ohio, Univ. of Tübingen, Germany and Univ. of Iowa. *Career:* Asst Prof., Ariz. State Univ., Tempe 1981–84, Assoc. Prof. 1984–87, Prof. of English 1987–89; Prof., Univ. of Va, Charlottesville 1989–93, Commonwealth Prof. of English 1993–; Poet Laureate of the USA 1993–95, of the Commonwealth of Virginia 2004–06; Consultant in Poetry, Library of Congress 1993–95; Assoc. Ed., Callaloo 1986–; adviser and Contributing Ed. Gettysburg Review 1987–, TriQuarterly 1988–, Ploughshares 1992–, Georgia Review 1994–, Bellingham Review 1996–, Poetry Int. 1996–, Mid-American Review 1998–, Hunger Mountain 2003–; Writer-in-Residence, Tuskegee Inst., Ala 1982; poetry panellist, Nat. Endowment for Arts, Washington, DC 1984–86 (Chair. 1985); judge, Pulitzer Prize in Poetry 1991 (Chair. of Jury 1997); mem. jury Anisfield-Wolf Book Awards; Chancellor The Acad. of American Poets 2006–; mem. Acad. of American Poets, Associated Writing Programs, Poetry Soc. of America, Poets and Writers; Fulbright Fellow 1974–75, Nat. Endowment for the Arts grants 1978, 1989, Portia Pittman Fellow, Tuskegee Inst. 1982, Guggenheim Fellowship 1984, Rockefeller Foundation Residency in Bellagio, Italy 1988, Mellon Fellow, Nat. Humanities Center 1989, Fellow, Center for Advanced Studies, Univ. of Virginia 1989–92. *Publications:* poetry: Ten Poems 1977, The Only Dark Spot in the Sky 1980, The Yellow House on the Corner 1980, Mandolin 1982, Museum 1983, Thomas and Beulah (Pulitzer Prize in Poetry 1987) 1986, The Other Side of the House 1988, Grace Notes 1989, Selected Poems 1993, Lady Freedom Among Us 1994, Mother Love 1995, Evening Primrose 1998, On the Bus with Rosa Parks 1999, Best American Poetry (ed.) 2000, American Smooth 2004; prose: Fifth Sunday (short stories) 1985, Through the Ivory Gate (novel) 1992, The Darker Face of Earth (verse play) 1994, The Poet's World (essays) 1995. *Honours:* numerous hon. degrees; Acad. of American Poets Peter I. B. Lavan Younger Poets Award 1986, General Electric Foundation Award for Younger Writers 1987, Ohio Gov.'s Award 1988, Nat. Book Award in Poetry 1991, NAACP Great American Artist Award 1993, American Acad. of Achievement Golden Plate Award 1993, Folger Shakespeare Library Renaissance Forum Award 1994, Charles Frankel Prize/Nat. Humanities Medal 1996, Heinz Award in the Arts and Humanities 1996, Sara Lee Frontrunner Award 1997, Barnes and Noble Writers Award 1997, Levinson Prize 1998, Ohioana Library Book Award 2000, New York Public Library Literary Lion 2000, Duke Ellington Lifetime Achievement Award in the Literary Arts, Ellington Fund in Washington, DC 2001. *Address:* Department of English, University of Virginia, POB 400121, Charlottesville, VA 22904-4121, USA. *Telephone:* (434) 924-6618 (office). *E-mail:* rfd4b@virginia.edu (office). *Website:* www.people.virginia.edu/~rfd4b (office).

DOVRING, Karin Elsa Ingeborg, MA, PhD, PhilLic; American writer, poet and dramatist; *Research Professor of Communications and Media Studies, University of Illinois;* b. 5 Dec. 1919, Stenstorp, Sweden; m. Folke Dovring 1943 (died 1998). *Education:* Coll. of Commerce, Göteborg, Lund Univ., Göteborg Univ. *Career:* journalist 1940–60; Research Assoc., Harold D. Lasswell, Yale Univ. 1953–78, Univ. of Illinois at Urbana-Champaign 1968–69; Visiting Lecturer, many univs and colls; Research Prof. of Communications and Media Studies, Univ. of Illinois 2000–; mem. Int. Soc. of Poets, USA, Acad. of American Poets (elected mem. 2002), Entertainer Independent Asscn, Nashville, Tenn. *Radio and TV plays:* Plot of Generation, Open House, Lady of the Jury. *Publications:* Songs of Zion 1951, Road of Propaganda 1959, Land Reform as a Propaganda Theme (third edn) 1965, Optional Society 1972, Frontiers of Communication 1975, No Parking This Side of Heaven (short stories) 1982, Harold D. Lasswell: His Communication with a Future 1987, Heart in Escrow (novel) 1990, Faces in a Mirror (poems) 1995, Shadows on a Screen (poems) 1996, Whispers on a Stage (poems) 1996, English as Lingua Franca 1997, In the Service of Persuasion: English as Lingua Franca across the Globe 2001, Propaganda is the Poetry of Politics 2002, Propagandists: Artists in Action 2004, Changing Scenery (poems) 2003; contrib. to anthologies, including 'Life Expectancy' poem in Our 100 Most Famous Poets – The Brief Chroniclers of Our Time 2004; contrib. to professional journals. *Honours:* hon. lifetime mem. Société Jean Jacques Rousseau, Geneva 1947, life mem. Pres.'s Council, Univ. of Ill.; Int. Poet of Merit Award 2002, Ed.'s Choice Award for Outstanding Achievement in Poetry 2003. *Address:* 613 W Vermont Avenue, Urbana, IL 61801 (home); c/o College of Communications, University of Illinois, 119 Gregory Hall MC-462, 810 S Wright Street, Urbana, IL 61801, USA (office). *Telephone:* (217) 344-6750 (home); (217) 333-2350 (office).

DOWLING, Vincent; American (b. Irish) actor, director, producer and playwright; *Founding Director and President-for-Life, Miniature Theatre of Chester;* b. 7 Sept. 1929, Dublin; s. of Mai Kelly Dowling and William Dowling; m. 1st Brenda Doyle 1952 (deceased); m. 2nd Olwen Patricia O'Herlihy 1975; one s. four d. *Education:* St Mary's Coll., Rathmines, Dublin, Rathmines School of Commerce, Brendan Smith Acad. of Acting. *Career:* with Standard Life Insurance Co., Dublin 1946–50; Brendan Smith Productions, Dublin 1950–51; Roche-David Theatre Productions 1951–53; actor, Dir, Deputy Artistic Dir, Lifetime Assoc., Abbey Theatre, Dublin 1953–76, Artistic Dir 1987–89; Producing Dir Great Lakes Shakespeare Festival, Cleveland, Ohio 1976–84; Artistic and Producing Dir Solvang Theaterfest 1984–86; Prof. of Theatre, Coll. of Wooster, Ohio 1986–87; Producing Dir, Abbey Theatre 1989–90; Founding Dir and Pres.-for-Life, Miniature Theatre of Chester 1990–; residency Tyrone Guthrie Arts Centre, Annamackerrig, Ireland 2005; host Shooting from the Hip WXOT Northampton Valley Free Radio 2005–06; Co-Founder, Jacob's Ladder Trail Business Asscn; several distinguished visiting professorships at univs in USA. *Film appearances:* My Wife's Lodger 1953, Boyds Shop 1959, Johnny Nobody 1963, Young Cassidy 1965. *Original plays:* The Fit-Ups 1978, Acting is Murder 1986, A Day in the Life of an Abbey Actor 1990, Wilde About Oscar, Another Actor at the White House (one-man show), The Upstart Crow (A Two-Person Play about Will Shakespeare) 1995, 4 P's (one-man autobiographical), The Miraculous Revenge (adapted; played, produced and co-directed) 2004. *Plays:* as producer: Arthur Miller's The Price 2005, Solomon 2005. *Radio:* role of Christy Kennedy (for 17 years) in The Kennedys of Castlerosse, Radio Éireann; writer, narrator Festival Scrapbook, Radio WCLV, Cleveland, Ohio 1980-84. *Television:* dir and producer The Playboy of the Western World (Emmy Award) Public Broadcasting Service, USA 1983, One Day at a Time, ABC Television 1998. *Publication:* Astride the Moon (autobiog.) 2000, My Abbey (Theatre), articles for Irish Echo Newspaper, 75th Anniversary Issue, Irish Sunday Independent Magazine. *Honours:* Hon. DFA (Westfield State Coll., Mass. John Carroll Univ., Cleveland, Ohio, Coll. of Wooster, Ohio 1999), DHumLitt (Kent State Univ.) 2003; European Artist's Prize, Loyola Univ. 1969; Outstanding Producer, Cleveland Critics Circle Award 1982 for The Life and Adventures of Nicholas Nickelby; Irishman of the Year 1982; Wild Geese Award 1988, Loyola Mellon Humanitarian Award 1989, Walks of Life Award, Irish American Archives Soc. of Cleveland 2000, Amb. (of Ireland to USA) Award 2005. *Address:* 322 East River Road, Huntington, MA 01050, USA (home). *Telephone:* (413) 667-3906 (home). *Fax:* (413) 667-3906 (home). *E-mail:* newlo@compuserve.com (home). *Website:* www.miniaturetheatre.org (office).

DOWNES, David Anthony, (David Anton), BA, MA, PhD; American academic and writer; *Professor of English Emeritus, California State University, Chico;* b. 17 Aug. 1927, Victor, CO; m. Audrey Romaine Ernst 1949; one s. three d. *Education:* Regis Univ., Marquette Univ., Univ. of Washington. *Career:* Asst Prof., Prof. and Chair of Dept, Univ. of Seattle 1953–68; Prof. of English and Dean of Humanities and Fine Arts 1968–72, Dir of Educational Development Projects 1972–73, Dir of Humanities Programme 1973–74, Dir of Graduate English Studies 1975–78, Chair of Dept 1978–84, Prof. Emeritus 1991, California State Univ., Chico; Consultant, Cowles Rare Book Library, Gonzaga Univ. 1997. *Publications:* Gerard Manley Hopkins: A Study of his Ignatian Spirit 1959, Victorian Portraits: Hopkins and Pater 1965, Pater, Kingsley and Newman 1972, The Great Sacrifice: Studies in Hopkins 1983, Ruskin's Landscape of Beatitude 1984, Hopkins' Sanctifying Imagination 1985, The Ignatian Personality of Gerard Manley Hopkins 1990, The Belle of Cripple Creek (novel) 2001, Hopkins' Achieved Self 2002, The Hopkins' Society: The Making of a World-Class Poet 2005, The Angel in Wax 2005, Sailing: Inside Passage 2006; contrib. scholarly books and journals. *Honours:* Hon. DJur (Gonzaga Univ.) 1997; Exceptional Merit Awards for Scholarship 1984, 1988, 1990, 1992. *Address:* 1076 San Ramon Drive, Chico, CA 95973, USA (office). *Telephone:* (530) 345-2297 (office). *E-mail:* ddownes@csuchico.edu (office).

DOWNIE, Leonard, Jr, MA; American newspaper editor; *Executive Editor, The Washington Post;* b. 1 May 1942, Cleveland, Ohio; s. of Leonard Downie Sr and Pearl Evenheimer; m. 1st Barbara Lindsey 1960 (divorced 1971); two s.; m. 2nd Geraldine Rebach 1971 (divorced 1997); one s. one d.; m. 3rd Janice Galin 1997. *Education:* Ohio State Univ. *Career:* joined The Washington Post 1964, became investigative reporter in Washington, specializing in crime, housing and urban affairs; helped to supervise coverage of Watergate affair; Asst Man. Ed. Metropolitan News 1974–79; London Corresp. Washington Post 1979–82, Nat. Ed. 1982–84, Man. Ed. 1984–91; Exec. Ed. 1991–; Dir LA Times–Washington Post News Service 1991–, Int. Herald Tribune 1996–2002; Alicia Patterson Foundation Fellow 1971–72. *Publications:* Justice Denied 1971, Mortgage on America 1974, The New Muckrakers 1976, The News About the News (with Robert G. Kaiser) 2002. *Honours:* Hon. LLD, Ohio State Univ.; two Washington-Baltimore Newspaper Guild Front Page Awards, American Bar Asscn Gavel Award for legal reporting, John Hancock Award for business and financial writing. *Address:* The Washington Post, 1150 15th Street, NW, Washington, DC 20071, USA (office). *Telephone:* (202) 334-7512 (office). *Website:* www.washingtonpost.com.

DOWNIE, Mary Alice Dawe, BA; Canadian writer; b. (Mary Alice Dawe Hunter), 12 Feb. 1934, Alton, Ill., USA; m. John Downie 1959; three d. *Education:* Trinity Coll., Univ. of Toronto. *Career:* Book Review Ed., Kingston Whig-Standard 1973–78; mem. Writers' Union of Canada, PEN. *Publications:* The Wind Has Wings: Poems from Canada (with Barbara Robertson) 1968, Honor Bound (with John Downie) 1971, Scared Sarah 1974, The Magical Adventures of Pierre 1974, Dragon on Parade 1974, The Witch of the North: Folktales from French Canada 1975, The King's Loon 1979, And Some Brought Flowers: Plants in a New World (with Mary Hamilton) 1980, The Last Ship 1980, Jenny Greenteeth 1981, Seeds and Weeds: A Book of Country Crafts (with Jillian Gilliland) 1981, A Proper Acadian (with George Rawlyk)

1982, The Wicked Fairy-Wife 1983, Alison's Ghost (with John Downie) 1984, Stones and Cones (with Jillian Gilliland) 1984, The New Wind Has Wings: Poems from Canada (with Barbara Robertson) 1984, The Window of Dreams: New Canadian Writing for Children 1986, The Well-Filled Cupboard (with Barbara Robertson) 1987, How the Devil Got his Cat 1988, The Buffalo Boy and the Weaver Girl (with Mann Hwa Huang-Hsu) 1989, Doctor Dwarf and Other Poems for Children, by A. M. Klein (with Barbara Robertson) 1990, Cathal the Giant-Killer and the Dun Shaggy Filly 1991, Written in Stone: A Kingston Reader (with M. A. Thompson) 1993, The Cat Park 1993, Snow Paws 1996, Bright Paddles 1999, Danger in Disguise (with John Downie) 2000, A Song for Acadia/Une Chanson pour l'Acadie 2004, A Pioneer ABC 2005; contrib. to Hornbook Magazine, Pittsburgh Press, Kingston Whig-Standard, Ottawa Citizen, Globe and Mail, Montréal Gazette, OWL Magazine, Chickadee, Crackers. *Address:* 190 Union Street, Kingston, ON K7L 2P6, Canada. *Telephone:* (613) 542-3464. *Fax:* (613) 542-3464. *E-mail:* downiej@post.queensu.ca.

DOWNING, Michael Bernard, AB; American academic, writer, poet and editor; b. 8 May 1958, Pittsfield, Massachusetts. *Education:* Harvard Univ. *Career:* Sr Ed., Oceanus periodical, Woods Hole, Massachusetts 1983–84, FMR periodical, Milan, Italy 1984–86; Instructor in English, Bentley Coll., Waltham, Massachusetts 1987–88; Instructor 1988–91, Asst Prof. of Humanities, Dir of Writing Programme 1992–, Wheelock Coll., Boston, Massachusetts; mem. PEN, Authors' Guild, Authors' League of America, Share Our Strength (writers' cttee). *Publications:* A Narrow Time (novel), 1987; Mother of God (novel), 1990; The Last Shaker (play, produced 1995); Perfect Agreement (novel), 1997. Contributions: anthologies including Louder than Words; Stories, poems, essays and reviews to periodicals including: America; Commonweal; Harvard; Salopian. *Honours:* Harvard-Shrewsbury Fellow, Shropshire, England, 1980–81; Best Book Citation, Newsday, 1997. *E-mail:* downing58@aol.com.

DOWRICK, Stephanie Barbara; New Zealand fmr publishing executive, writer, psychotherapist and minister; b. 2 June 1947, d. of Harold Dowrick and Mary Dowrick (née Brisco); one s. one d. *Education:* Sacred Heart Coll., Lower Hutt and Univ. of Wellington, New Seminary, New York, USA, Univ. of Western Sydney, Australia. *Career:* Co-Founder The Women's Press, London 1977, Man. Dir 1977–82, Chair. 1991; moved to Sydney, Australia 1983; Fiction Publr, Allen and Unwin, NSW; columnist, Good Weekend magazine 2001–; regular guest on ABC Radio; gives talks and conducts retreats and workshops on various spiritual, psychological and ethical issues. *Publications include:* non-fiction: Every Day a New Beginning, Daily Acts of Love, Land of Zeus 1975, Why Children? (co-ed.) 1982, Intimacy and Solitude 1991, The Intimacy & Solitude Workbook, The Intimacy & Solitude Self-Therapy Book, Speaking With the Sun (co-ed.) 1991, After the Gulf War: For Peace in the Middle East 1991, The Intimacy and Solitude Workbook 1993, Forgiveness and Other Acts of Love 1997, The Universal Heart 2000, Free Thinking 2004; audio: Accepting Yourself & Loving Others (two CDs), Guided Meditations: Grace & Courage, The Art of Acceptance – Living in an Imperfect world, Living with Change, The Human Virtues; fiction: Tasting Salt, Running Backwards Over Sand 1985, Katherine Rose Says NO (children's fiction). *Address:* Andrew Hawkins, Allen and Unwin Pty Ltd, 83 Alexander Street, Crows Nest, NSW 2065, Australia (office). *Telephone:* (2) 9810-3277 (office). *E-mail:* AndrewH@allenandunwin.com (office); stephanie@stephaniedowrick.com. *Website:* www.stephaniedowrick.com.

DOYLE, Charles Desmond, (Mike Doyle), DipEd, BA, MA, PhD; Canadian academic, writer and poet; *Professor Emeritus, University of Victoria*; b. 18 Oct. 1928, Birmingham, England; m. 1st Helen Merlyn Lopdell 1952 (deceased); m. 2nd Doran Ross Smithells 1959 (divorced); three s. one d. *Education:* Univ. of New Zealand, Univ. of Auckland. *Career:* Lecturer, Univ. of Auckland 1961–66, Sr Lecturer 1966–68; Assoc. Prof., Univ. of Victoria, BC 1968–76, Prof. of English 1976–93, Prof. Emeritus 1993–; mem. New Canterbury Literary Soc., Writers' Union of Canada, PEN Canada. *Publications:* A Splinter of Glass 1956, The Night Shift: Poems on Aspects of Love (with others) 1957, Distances 1963, Messages for Herod 1965, A Sense of Place 1965, Quorum-Noah 1970, Abandoned Sofa 1971, Earth Meditations 1971, Earthshot 1972, Preparing for the Ark 1973, Pines (with P. K. Irwin) 1975, Stonedancer 1976, A Month Away from Home 1980, A Steady Hand 1982, The Urge to Raise Hats 1989, Separate Fidelities 1991, Intimate Absences: Selected Poems 1954–1992 1993, Trout Spawning at the Lardeau River 1997, Living Ginger 2004; non-fiction: R. A. K. Mason 1970, James K. Baxter 1976, William Carlos Williams and the American Poem 1982, William Carlos Williams: The Critical Heritage (ed.) 1982, The New Reality (co-ed.) 1984, Wallace Stevens: The Critical Heritage (ed.) 1985, After Bennett (co-ed.) 1986, Richard Aldington: A Biography 1989, Richard Aldington: Reappraisals (ed.) 1990; contrib. to journals, reviews and periodicals. *Honours:* UNESCO Creative Arts Fellowship 1958–59, ACLS Fellowship 1967–68. *Address:* 641 Oliver Street, Victoria, BC V8S 4W2, Canada (home). *Telephone:* (250) 595-5006 (home). *E-mail:* doylec@uvic.ca (home).

DOYLE, Roddy; Irish writer and playwright; b. 1958, Dublin; m. Belinda Doyle; two s. *Career:* lecturer at universities. *Play:* Brown Bread 1992, USA 1992. *Publications:* The Commitments 1987, screenplay (with Dick Clement and Ian La Frenais) 1991, The Snapper 1990, screenplay 1992, The Van 1991, Paddy Clarke Ha Ha Ha (Booker Prize) 1993, The Woman Who Walked into Doors 1996, A Star Called Henry 1999, The Giggler Treatment 2000, Rory and Ita 2002, Oh, Play That Thing 2004, Paula Spencer 2006. *Address:* c/o Patti Kelly, Viking Books, 375 Hudson Street, New York, NY 10014, USA (office).

DRAAISMA, Douwe; Dutch psychologist and writer; *Professor of History of Psychology, University of Gröningen*; b. 1953. *Education:* Univ. of Gröningen. *Career:* Prof. of History of Psychology Univ. of Gröningen, Univ. of Utrecht; mem. Heymans Inst. for Fundamental Psychological Research, Research School Science, Technology and Modern Culture, European Soc. for the History of the Human Sciences. *Publications:* Het verborgen raderwerk: Over tijd, machines en bewustzijn 1990, De metaforenmachine: Een geschiedenis van het geheugen (trans. as Metaphors of Memory: A History of Ideas About the Mind) 1993, Een droevige zaak: Damasio over Descartes, Hersenen en Emoties, The Age of Precision: F. C. Donders and the Measurement of Mind 2002, Waarom het leven sneller gaat als je ouder wordt: Over het autobiografisch geheugen (trans. as Why Life Speeds Up As You Get Older: How Memory Shapes Our Past) 2002; contrib. chapters to books and articles to journals, including Feit en Fictie, History of the Human Sciences, Nature, Annals of Science, Arts, lettres et cultures de Flandres et des Pays-Bas, Psychological Medicine. *Honours:* Heymans Award Dutch Psychological Asscn 1990. *Address:* Heymans Institute (DPMG), University of Groningen, Grote Kruisstraat 2/1, 9712 TS Gröningen, The Netherlands (office). *Telephone:* (50) 363-6364. *Fax:* (50) 363-6304. *E-mail:* draaisma@douwedraaisma.nl. *Website:* www.douwedraaisma.nl.

DRABBLE, Margaret, CBE, BA; British author; b. 5 June 1939, Sheffield; d. of the late J. F. Drabble and Kathleen Drabble (née Bloor); sister of A. S. Byatt; m. 1st Clive Swift 1960 (divorced 1975); two s. one d.; m. 2nd Michael Holroyd (q.v.) 1982. *Education:* Newnham Coll., Cambridge. *Career:* Chair., Nat. Book League 1980–82; Ed. The Oxford Companion to English Literature 1979–2000; Vice-Patron, Child Psychotherapy Trust 1987–. *Publications:* fiction: A Summer Bird-Cage 1963, The Garrick Year 1964, The Millstone (John Llewelyn Rhys Memorial Prize 1966) 1965, Jerusalem the Golden 1967, The Waterfall 1969, The Needle's Eye 1972, The Realms of Gold 1975, The Ice Age 1977, The Middle Ground 1980, The Radiant Way 1987, A Natural Curiosity 1989, The Gates of Ivory 1991, The Witch of Exmoor 1996, The Peppered Moth 2001, The Seven Sisters 2002, The Red Queen 2004, The Sea Lady 2006; plays: Laura 1964, Isadora 1968, Thank You All Very Much 1969, Bird of Paradise 1969; non-fiction: Wordsworth 1966, Arnold Bennett: A Biography 1974, The Genius of Thomas Hardy (ed.) 1976, For Queen and Country: Britain in the Victorian Age 1978, A Writer's Britain 1979, The Oxford Companion to English Literature (co-ed.) 1985, 2000, The Concise Oxford Companion to English Literature (co-ed. with Jenny Stringer) 1987, Angus Wilson: A Biography 1995. *Honours:* Hon. Foreign mem. American Acad. of Arts and Letters 2002; Hon. Fellow, Sheffield City Polytechnic 1989; Hon. DLitt (Sheffield) 1976, (Bradford) 1988, (Hull) 1992, Hon. doctorates (Manchester) 1987, (Keele) 1988, (East Anglia) 1994, (York) 1995; James Tait Black Memorial Prize 1968, Book of the Year Award, Yorkshire Post 1972, E. M. Forster Award, American Acad. of Arts and Letters 1973, St Louis Literary Award 2003. *Literary Agent:* PFD, Drury House, 34–43 Russell Street, London, WC2B 5HA, England. *Telephone:* (20) 7344-1000.

DRACKETT, Philip (Phil) Arthur, (Paul King); British writer and broadcaster; b. 25 Dec. 1922, Finchley, Middlesex, England; m. Joan Isobel Davies 1948. *Education:* Woodhouse School, Univ. of Cambridge, Univ. of London. *Career:* mem. Sports Writers Asscn, Guild of Motoring Writers, Friends of Mundesley Library. *Publications:* Fighting Days 1942, Come Out Fighting (with Matt Wells) 1944, Speedway 1951, Motor Racing 1952, Motoring 1955, You and Your Car (with Leslie Webb) 1958, Great Moments in Motoring 1958, You and Your Motor Cycle (with Aubrey Thompson) 1959, Automobiles Work Like This 1960, Veteran Cars 1961, Motor Rallying 1963, Passing the Test 1964, Young Car Drivers Companion (as Paul King) 1964, Taking Your Car Abroad 1965, Let's Look at Cars 1966, Slot Car Racing 1968, International Motor Racing (ed., four vols) 1969–72, Like Father Like Son 1969, Rally of the Forests 1970, Car Care Tips 1973, Motor Racing Champions (ed., two vols) 1973–74, Book of the Veteran Car 1973, Purnell Book of Great Disasters 1978, Purnell Book of Dangermen 1979, Encyclopaedia of the Motor Car (ed.) 1979, Wonderful World of Cars 1979, Inns and Harbours of North Norfolk 1980, The Car Makers 1980, The Story of the RAC International Rally 1980, Vintage Cars 1981, The Classic Mercedes-Benz 1983, Brabham, Story of a Racing Team 1985, Flashing Blades, The Story of British Ice Hockey 1987, They Call it Courage: The Story of the Segrave Trophy 1990; Benetton–Ford: A Racing Partnership 1990, Vendetta on Ice 1993, Just Another Incident (with Jack Kemsley) 1994, Ice Hockey Films 1995, Total Ice Hockey Encyclopedia (contrib.) 1998, Champions on Ice (with Dennis Fill) 2000; contrib. to newspapers and magazines. *Honours:* first hon. life mem. British Ice Hockey Writers Asscn . *Address:* 9 Victoria Road, Mundesley, Norfolk NR11 8RG, England.

DRAKE, Barbara Ann, BA, MFA; American academic, poet and writer; *Professor of English, Linfield College*; b. 13 April 1939, Abilene, KS; m. 1st Albert Drake 1960 (divorced 1985); one s. two d.; m. 2nd William Beckman 1986. *Education:* Univ. of Oregon. *Career:* Instructor, Michigan State Univ. 1974–83; Prof. of English, Linfield Coll. 1983–. *Publications:* poetry: Narcissa Notebook 1973, Field Poems 1975, Love at the Egyptian Theatre 1978, Life in a Gothic Novel 1981, What We Say to Strangers 1986, Bees in Wet Weather 1992, Space Before A 1996, Small Favors 2003; prose: Peace at Heart: An Oregon Country Life (memoir) 1998; contrib. to many books, anthologies, reviews, quarterlies and journals. *Honours:* Northwest Arts Foundation grant

1985, NEA Fellowship 1986, Linfield Coll. Edith Green Distinguished Prof. Award 1993. *Address:* c/o Linfield College, 900 SE Baker Street, McMinnville, OR 97128 (office); 6104 NW Lilac Hill Road, Yamhill, OR 97148, USA (home). *Telephone:* (503) 883-2288 (office). *E-mail:* bdrake@linfield.edu (office).

DRAKE, Nick; British poet and translator; b. 1961. *Education:* Magdalene Coll., Cambridge. *Play produced:* To Walk the Clouds, Nottingham Playhouse 2006. *Screenplay:* Romulus My Father, directed by Richard Roxburgh 2007. *Radio:* Mr Sweet Talk (writer) 2006. *Publications:* poetry: Chocolate and Salt (pamphlet) 1990, The Man in the White Suit (Forward Prize for Best First Collection) 1999, From the Word Go 2007; play: To Walk the Clouds 2006; non-fiction: The Poetry of W. B. Yeats 1991, Nefertiti: The Book of the Dead 2006; translator: Peribañez and Comendador of Ocaña, by Lope de Vega 1998. *Honours:* Eric Gregory Award 1990. *Literary Agent:* c/o Julia Kreitman, The Agency, 24 Pottery Lane, Holland Park, London, W11 4 LZ, England. *Telephone:* (20) 7727-1346. *Fax:* (20) 7727-9037. *E-mail:* info@theagency.co.uk. *Website:* www.theagency.co.uk. *E-mail:* nickfdrake@hotmail.com.

DRAKULIĆ, Slavenka; Croatian journalist and writer; b. 1949. *Career:* contribs to newspapers and magazines, including The New Republic, La Stampa, Dagens Nyheter, Frankfurter Rundechau and The Observer. *Publications include:* How We Survived Communism and Even Laughed, Balkan Express, Café Europa, Holograms of Fear, Marble Skin, The Taste of a Man 1997, S: A Novel About the Balkans 1999, As if I am Not There 1999, They Would Never Hurt a Fly 2005. *Address:* c/o Abacus, Brettenham House, Lancaster Place, London, WC2E 7EN, England.

DRAPER, Alfred Ernest; English author; b. 26 Oct. 1924, London; m. Barbara Pilcher 1951, two s. *Education:* North West London Polytechnic. *Career:* mem. National Union of Journalists, life mem. *Publications:* Swansong for a Rare Bird, 1969; The Death Penalty, 1972 (made into a French Film); Smoke Without Fire, 1974; The Prince of Wales, 1975; The Story of the Goons, 1976; Operation Fish, 1978; Amritsar, 1979; Grey Seal, 1981; Grey Seal: The Restless Waves, 1983; The Raging of the Deep, 1985; Storm over Singapore, 1986; The Con Man, 1987; Dawns Like Thunder, 1987; The Great Avenging Day, 1989; A Crimson Splendour, 1991; Operation Midas, 1993. Contributions: numerous periodicals. *Address:* 11 Thelusson Court, Woodfield Road, Radlett, Hertfordshire WD7 8JF, England (home).

DRAPER, Hastings (see Jeffries, Roderic Graeme)

DRAPER, Ronald Philip, BA, PhD; British academic (retd) and writer; *Professor Emeritus, University of Aberdeen*; b. 3 Oct. 1928, Nottingham, England; m. Irene Margaret Aldridge 1950; three d. *Education:* Univ. of Nottingham. *Career:* Lecturer in English, Univ. of Adelaide, Australia 1955–56; Lecturer, Univ. of Leicester 1957–68, Sr Lecturer 1968–73; Prof., Univ. of Aberdeen 1973–86, Regius Chalmers Prof. of English 1986–94, Prof. Emer. 1994–. *Publications:* D. H. Lawrence 1964, D. H. Lawrence: The Critical Heritage (ed.) 1970, Hardy: The Tragic Novels (ed.) 1975, George Eliot, The Mill on the Floss and Silas Marner (ed.) 1977, Tragedy, Developments in Criticism (ed.) 1980, Lyric Tragedy 1985, The Winter's Tale: Text and Performance 1985, Hardy: Three Pastoral Novels (ed.) 1987, The Literature of Region and Nation (ed.) 1989, An Annotated Critical Bibliography of Thomas Hardy (with Martin Ray) 1989, The Epic: Developments in Criticism (ed.) 1990, A Spacious Vision: Essays on Hardy (co-ed.) 1994, An Introduction to Twentieth-Century Poetry in English 1999, Shakespeare: The Comedies 2000; contrib. to books and scholarly journals. *Address:* Maynestay, Chipping Campden, Glos., GL55 6DJ, England (home). *Telephone:* (1386) 840796 (home). *E-mail:* rpdraper@tiscali.co.uk (home).

DRAŠKOVIĆ, Vuk; Serbian politician, journalist and writer; *President, Serbian Renewal Movement*; b. 29 Nov. 1946, Central Banat Region, Vojvodina; m. Danica Drašković (née Bošković). *Education:* Belgrade Univ. *Career:* moved to Herzegovina; as student took part in demonstrations 1968; mem. staff Telegraph Agency of Yugoslavia TANJUG 1969–78, worked in Lusaka, Zambia; dismissed from post of correspondent for disinformation 1978; Adviser Council of Trade Unions of Yugoslavia 1978–80; Ed. Rad (newspaper) 1980–85; freelance journalist and writer 1985–; Founder and Pres. Serbian Renewal Movt (Srpslei pokret obnove) 1990–; candidate for Presidency of Yugoslavia 1990, 1992, of Serbia 1997; mem. Nat. Ass.; detained, released from detention July 1993; leader of mass protests against Pres. Milošević from Nov. 1996; Vice-Prime Minister of Yugoslavia 1998–99 (resgnd); Minister of Foreign Affairs 2004–06. *Publications include:* novels: Judge, Knife, Prayer 1, Prayer 2, Russian Consul, Night of the General, Polemics, Answers; numerous articles and collections of articles. *Address:* Serbian Renewal Movement (Srpski pokret obnove), 11000 Belgrade, Kneza Mihailova 48, Serbia (office). *Telephone:* (11) 635281 (office). *Fax:* (11) 628170 (office). *E-mail:* vuk@spo.org.yu (office). *Website:* www.spo.org.yu (office).

DRAZEN, Jeffrey M., BS, MD; American writer; *Editor-in-Chief, New England Journal of Medicine*; b. 19 May 1946, St Louis, MO. *Career:* Prof. in the Dept of Environmental Health, Harvard School of Public Health; Parker B. Francis Prof. of Medicine, Dept of Medicine, Brigham and Women's Hospital; Ed.-in-Chief, New England Journal of Medicine. *Publications:* Five Lipoxygenase Products in Asthma (ed.) 1998; contrib. to Genomic Medicine: Articles from the New England Journal of Medicine 2001. *Address:* New England Journal of Medicine, 10 Shattuck Street, Boston, MA 02115-6094, USA. *Telephone:* (617) 734-9800. *Fax:* (617) 739-9864. *E-mail:* jmdrazen@nejm.org. *Website:* www.nejm.org.

DREW, Bettina, BA, MA,; American writer, poet and teacher; b. 23 April 1956, New York, NY. *Education:* University of California, Berkeley, City College, CUNY, Yale University. *Career:* Lecturer in English, College of New York; Lecturer in Humanities, New York University, 1990–93; Part-time Acting Instructor, Yale University, 1995–97; mem. PEN American Center; Biography Seminar, New York University. *Publications:* Nelson Algren: A Life on the Wild Side, 1989; The Texas Stories of Nelson Algren (ed.), 1995; Crossing the Expendable Landscape, 1997. Contributions: Boulevard; The Writer; Chicago Tribune; Threepenny Review; Washington Post Book World; Chicago Tribune Book World; Ms; Black American Literature Forum; Michigan Quarterly Review; poems to various magazines.

DREWE, Robert Duncan; Australian writer and dramatist; b. 9 Jan. 1943, Melbourne, Vic.; m. 3rd Candida Baker; four s. two d. *Education:* Hale School, Perth, WA. *Career:* Literary Ed., The Australian 1972–75; writer-in-residence, Univ. of Western Australia, Nedlands 1979, La Trobe Univ., Bundoora, Vic. 1986; columnist, Mode, Sydney, and Sydney City Monthly 1981–83; mem. Australian Soc. of Authors. *Publications:* The Savage Crows 1976, A Cry in the Jungle Bar 1979, Fortune 1986, Our Sunshine 1991, The Picador Book of the Beach (ed.) 1993, The Drowner (novel) 1996, The Penguin Book of the City (ed.) 1997, Walking Ella (non-fiction) 1998, The Shark Net: Memories and Murder 2000, Grace 2005; short stories: The Bodysurfers 1983, The Bay of Contented Men 1989; plays: The Bodysurfers 1989, South American Barbecue 1991; contrib. to The Bulletin, The Australian, TLS, Granta. *Honours:* Hon. DLitt (Univ. of Queensland) 1997; Nat. Book Council Award 1987, Commonwealth Writers' Prize 1990, Australian Creative Artists' Fellowship 1993–96, New South Wales, Victoria, West Australia and South Australia Premiers' literary prizes 1997, Book of the Year 1997, Adelaide Festival Prize for Literature 1998. *Literary Agent:* Hickson Associates, 128 Queen Street, Woolahra, NSW 2025, Australia.

DREYER, Inge, Rektorin i.R.; German poet; b. 12 June 1933, Berlin; d. of Curt Ganswindt and Katharina Ganswindt. *Education:* Univ. of Berlin Coll. of Educ. *Career:* teacher, Fritz-Karsen-Schule, Berlin 1956–68; Headmistress Walt-Disney-Schule, Berlin 1968–78; retd from teaching 1978; professional writer 1978–; works with Project Märchen zaubern Brot für Kinder in co-operation with Berliner Märchentage, UNICEF etc. 2003–. *Publications:* Achtung Stolperstelle 1982, Schule mit Dachschaden 1985, Tönende Stille 1985, Die Streuner von Pangkor 1987, Die Blütenkrone 2002, Der Schatz des goldenen Bären 2002, Der Federfächer 2002, Die Schattenschwingen 2002, Die Himmelsschlange 2003, Die goldene Heuschrecke 2003, Muckepuck und Klitzerlitzchen 2003; Märchen für einen kleinen Wolf 2003; Die klingende Krone 2003; Das Weihnachtsgespenst 2003; Das stille Licht 2003; Die Nikolausvögel 2003; Die Tochter des Berggeistes 2003; Der Mondschein-Bubu 2004; König Brummelmax 2004; Die hölzernen Flügel 2004; Das Diamantenherz 2004; Der goldene Käfig 2004; Die Zaubertrommel 2004; contribs to several anthologies and literary journals. *Honours:* Hon. Prof. of Literature Paris 1992–; Hon. DLitt (London) 1992; Golden Crown World Poets' Award 1990, Int. Cultural Diploma of Honour 1995, ABI Woman of the Year 1997. *Address:* Winkler Str. 4A, 14193 Berlin, Germany (home). *Telephone:* (30) 8915783 (home).

DRISCOLL, F. Paul; American opera director and writer; *Editor-in-Chief, Opera News*; b. 23 Aug. 1954, New York. *Education:* Regis High School, Manhattan and Coll. of the Holy Cross, Worcester, Mass. *Career:* fmr actor, Foothills Theater, Worcester; freelance dir and designer for theatre; worked at dept store, Lord & Taylor in various roles 1978–85; Product Development Man., Metropolitan Opera Guild retail programme 1985–90; freelance writer and dir from 1990, contributing reviews, stories and essays to publs, including Chamber Music, Musical America, Opera News, Stagebill; Picture Ed., Opera News, then Man. Ed. from 1998, later Exec. Ed., now Ed.-in-Chief; Dir of some 20 musicals and operettas, Coll. Light Opera Co., Falmouth, MA until 1998; Artistic Dir, Scarsdale Summer Music Theater for two years; Dir, Working, by the Washington Chamber Symphony, Kennedy Center; Dramatic Dir, Blue Hill Troupe 1998–2004. *Television:* host Opera New York, WNYE 2002–04TV. *Publications:* 25 years at Highfield: A History of the College Light Opera Company 1992, Fantastic Opera (with artist, John Martinez) 1997. *Address:* Opera News, 70 Lincoln Center Plaza, New York, NY 10023, USA. *E-mail:* info@operanews.com. *Website:* www.metoperafamily.org/operanews.

DRISCOLL, Peter John, BA; British writer and journalist; b. 4 Feb. 1942, London, England; m. Angela Hennessy 1967, one s. one d. *Education:* University of the Witwatersrand. *Career:* reporter, Rand Daily Mail, Johannesburg, South Africa, 1959–67; Sub-ed., Scriptwriter, ITV News, London, 1969–73. *Publications:* The White Lie Assignment, 1971; The Wilby Conspiracy, 1972; In Connection with Kilshaw, 1974; The Barboza Credentials, 1976; Pangolin, 1979; Heritage, 1982; Spearhead, 1987; Secrets of State, 1991.

DRIVER, Charles Jonathan (Jonty), BA, BEd, MPhil, FRSA; British writer, poet and schools consultant; b. 19 Aug. 1939, Cape Town, South Africa; m. Ann Elizabeth Hoogewerf 1967; two s. one d. *Education:* Univ. of Cape Town, Trinity Coll., Oxford. *Career:* Housemaster, Int. Sixth Form Centre, Sevenoaks School 1968–73; Dir of Sixth Form, Matthew Humberstone Comprehensive School 1973–78; Research Fellow, Univ. of York 1976; Principal, Island School, Hong Kong 1978–83; Headmaster, Berkhamsted School 1983–89; The Master, Wellington Coll., Crowthorne, Berkshire 1989–2000; Ed., Conference and Common Room 1993–2000. *Publications:*

novels: Elegy for a Revolutionary 1968, Send War in Our Time, O Lord 1970, Death of Fathers 1972, A Messiah of the Last Days 1974, Shades of Darkness 2004; poetry: I Live Here Now 1979, Occasional Light (with Jack Cope) 1979, Hong Kong Portraits 1985, In the Water-Margins 1994, Holiday Haiku 1996, Requiem 1998, So Far: Selected Poems 1960–2004 2004; non-fiction: Patrick Duncan (biog.) 1980; contrib. to numerous magazines and journals. *Address:* Apple Yard Cottage, Mill Lane, Northiam, nr Rye, Sussex TN31 6JU, England (home). *Telephone:* (1797) 253289 (home). *E-mail:* jontydriver@hotmail.com (home).

DRIVER, Paul William, MA; British music critic and writer; b. 14 Aug. 1954, Manchester, England. *Education:* Univ. of Oxford. *Career:* music critic, The Boston Globe 1983–84, Sunday Times 1985–; mem. Editorial Bd Contemporary Music Review; mem. Critics Circle; Patron, Manchester Musical Heritage Trust. *Radio:* Ear to the Ground (series of conversations with composers, BBC Radio 4) 2004. *Publications:* A Diversity of Creatures (ed.) 1987, Music and Text (ed.) 1989, Manchester Pieces 1996, Penguin English Verse (ed., Vols 1–6) 1995, Penguin Popular Poetry (ed., Vols 1–6) 1996; contrib. to Sunday Times, Financial Times, Tempo, London Review of Books, Opera, New York Times, Gramophone, TLS and numerous others. *Address:* Louise Greenberg Books Ltd, The End House, Church Crescent, London, N3 1BG, England (office). *Telephone:* (20) 7624-4501 (office). *E-mail:* paul@driver4044.freeserve .co.uk.

DRUMMOND, June, BA; South African author; b. 15 Nov. 1923, Durban. *Education:* University of Cape Town. *Career:* mem. Soroptimist International; Writers Circle of South Africa. *Publications:* Slowly the Poison, 1975; The Patriots, 1979; The Trojan Mule, 1982; The Bluestocking, 1985; Junta, 1989; The Unsuitable Miss Pelham, 1990.

DRUON, Maurice Samuel Roger Charles; French writer; b. 23 April 1918, Paris; s. of René Druon and Léonilla Samuel-Cros; m. Madeleine Marignac 1968. *Education:* Lycée Michelet, Ecole des Sciences Politiques, Faculté des Lettres de Paris. *Career:* war corresp., Allied Armies 1944–45; mem. Acad. française 1966, Perm. Sec. 1986–99; Minister for Cultural Affairs 1973–74; mem. French Parl. 1978–81, Ass. of Council of Europe 1978–81, European Parl. 1979–80; mem. Franco-British Council 1972–90; Pres. Franco-Italian Asscn 1985–91; mem. Dialogue Franco-Russe 2004, Acad. of Morocco 1980, Athen's Acad. 1981, Brazilian Acad. of Letters 1995, Russian Acad. of Science 2006. *Film script:* Les grandes familles 1958, Le Baron de l'écluse 1960. *Television scripts:* Les rois maudits 1972, 2005, Les grandes familles 1991. *Publications:* Lettres d'un Européen 1943, Le chant des partisans 1943, La dernière brigade 1946, La fin des hommes (three vols Les grandes familles (Prix Goncourt 1948) 1948, La chute des corps 1950, Rendez-vous aux enfers 1951), La volupté d'être 1954, Les rois maudits 1955–77 (seven vols Le roi de fer, La reine étranglée, Les poisons de la couronne, La loi des mâles, La louve de France, Le lis et le lion, Quand un Roi perd la France), Tistou les pouces verts 1957, Alexandre le Grand 1958, Des seigneurs de la plaine à l'hôtel de Mondez 1962, Les mémoires de Zeus (two vols L'aube des dieux 1963, Les jours des hommes 1967), Bernard Buffet 1964, Paris, de César à St Louis 1964, Le pouvoir 1965, Les tambours de la mémoire 1965, Le bonheur des uns . . . 1967, Discours de réception à l'Académie française 1968, L'avenir en désarroi 1968, Vézelay, colline éternelle 1968, Nouvelles lettres d'un européen 1943–70, Une église qui se trompe de siècle 1972, La parole et le pouvoir 1974, Oeuvres complètes 1974–79, Attention la France 1981, Réformer la démocratie 1982, La culture et l'état 1985, Lettre aux français sur leur langue et leur âme 1994, Circonstances (Prix Saint-Simon) 1997, Circonstances Politiques 1998, Circonstances Politiques II 1999, Le bon français (Prix Agrippa d'Aubigné 2000) 1999, La France aux ordres d'un cadavre, Ordonnances pour un Etat malade 2002, Le Franc-Parler 2003; plays: Mégarée 1942, Un voyageur 1953, La Contessa 1962. *Honours:* Hon. mem. Romanian Acad. 1996; Hon. KBE; Grand-Croix, Légion d'honneur, Commdr des Arts et Lettres, Commdr, Order of Phoenix (Greece), Commdr Ordre de la République de Tunisie, Grand Cross of Merit (Italy), Grand Officier, Ordre du Lion du Sénégal, Grand Cross of the Aztec Eagle (Mexico), Grand Officer, Order of Merit (Malta), Ordre du Mérite culturel (Monaco), Ordre de Saint-Charles (Monaco), Grand Officier, Ordre de l'Honneur de Grèce, du Ouissam Alaouite, Grand Cross of the Christ (Portugal), Grand Officier, Orden de Mayo (Argentina), Ordre de l'Étoile de Roumanie, Grand Officier, Ordre de Rio Branco (Brazil); Hon. DLitt (York Univ., Ont.) 1987, (Boston) 1997, (Tirana); Prix Goncourt 1948, Prix Prince Pierre de Monaco 1966, Prix Saint Simon 1998, Prix Agrippa d'Aubigné 2000. *Literary Agent:* c/o Agence Hoffman, 77 Boulevard Saint-Michel, 75005 Paris, France. *Telephone:* 1-43-26-56-94. *Fax:* 1-43-26-34-07. *Address:* Académie Française, 23 quai Conti, 75006 Paris (office); 81 rue de Lille, 75007 Paris (home); Abbaye de Faise, 33570 Les Artigues de Lussac, France (home).

DRYSDALE, Helena Claire, MA, FRSL; British writer; b. 6 May 1960, London; m. Richard Pomeroy 1987, two d. *Education:* Trinity Coll., Cambridge. *Career:* mem. RGS, Soc. of Authors, London Library, Pro Patrimonio. *Television:* Dancing with the Dead (Granada/WNet). *Publications:* Alone Through China and Tibet 1986, Dancing with the Dead 1991, Looking for Gheorghe: Love and Death in Romania (aka Looking for George) 1995, Mother Tongues: Travels Through Tribal Europe 2002, Strangerland 2006; contrib. to Vogue, Marie Claire, Independent, Independent on Sunday, Sunday Times, Daily Telegraph, Harpers and Queen, Cosmopolitan, World, New Statesman. *Honours:* exhibitioner Trinity Coll., PEN/J. R. Ackerley Award for Autobiography 1995, Esquire/Waterstones/Apple Award for Autobiography 1995. *Literary Agent:* AP Watt Ltd, 20 John Street, London, WC1N 2DR, England. *Website:* www.helenadrysdale.com.

DU, Daozheng; Chinese journalist; b. Nov. 1923, Dingxiang Co., Shanxi Prov.; s. of Du Xixiang and Qi Luaying; m. Xu Zhixian 1950; one s. four d. *Education:* Middle School, Dingxiang, Shanxi and Beijing Marx-Lenin Coll. *Career:* joined CCP 1937; Chief of Hebei and Guangdong Bureau, Xinhua News Agency 1949–56; Ed.-in-Chief Yangchen Wanbao 1956–69; Dir Home News Dept, Xinhua News Agency 1977–82; Ed.-in-Chief Guangming Daily 1982; Dir Media and Publs Office 1987–88; Deputy 7th NPC 1988–; Dir State Press and Publs Admin. 1988–89. *Publications:* Explore Japan (co-author), Interviews with Famous Chinese Journalists. *Honours:* Hon. Pres. Newspaper Operation and Man. Asscn 1988–; Nat. News Prize 1979.

DU VAUL, Virginia (see Coffman, Virginia Edith)

DUBE, Marcel, BA; Canadian dramatist, author, poet and translator; b. 3 Jan. 1930, Montréal, QC; m. Nicole Fontaine 1956. *Education:* Collège Sainte-Marie, University of Montréal, theatre schools in Paris. *Career:* mem. Académie canadienne-française, fellow; Federation of Canadian Authors and Artists, pres., 1959; Royal Society of Canada, fellow. *Publications:* Over 30 plays, including: Zone, 1955, English trans., 1982; Un simple soldat, 1958; Le temps des lilas, 1958, English trans. as Time of the Lilacs, 1990; Florence, 1958; Bilan, 1968; Les beaux dimanches, 1968; Au retour des oies blanches, 1969, English trans. as The White Geese, 1972; Hold-up! (with Louis-George Carrier), 1969; Un matin commes les autres, 1971; Le neufrage, 1971; De l'autre coté du mur, 1973; L'impromptu de Québec, ou Le testament, 1974; L'été s'appelle Julie, 1975; Le réformiste, ou L'honneur des hommes, 1977; Le trou, 1986; L'Amérique a sec, 1986. Other: Television series. Poetry: Poèmes de sable, 1974. Non-Fiction: Textes et documents, 1968; La tragédie est un acte de foi, 1973; Jean-Paul Lemieux et le livre, 1988; Andrée Lachapelle: Entre ciel et terre, 1995. *Honours:* Prix Victor-Morin, Saint-Jean-Baptiste Society, 1966; Prix David, Québec, 1973; Molson Prize, Canada Council, 1984; Académie canadienne-française Medal, 1987.

DUBERMAN, Martin Bauml, BA, MA, PhD; American academic and writer; b. 6 Aug. 1930, New York, NY. *Education:* Yale Univ., Harvard Univ. *Career:* Teaching Fellow, Harvard Univ. 1955–57; Instructor, Yale Univ. 1957–61, Morse Fellow 1961–62; Bicentennial Preceptor and Asst Prof., Princeton Univ. 1962–65, Assoc. Prof. 1965–67, Prof. 1967–71; Distinguished Prof. of History, Lehman Coll. and Graduate School and Univ. Center, CUNY 1972– (now Prof. Emeritus); founder-Dir, Center for Lesbian and Gay Studies, Graduate School and Univ. Center, CUNY 1991–; Visiting Randolph Distinguished Prof., Vassar Coll. 1992; Assoc. Ed., Journal of the History of Sexuality 1993–, Masculinities: Interdisciplinary Studies on Gender 1993–, Journal of Gay and Lesbian Psychotherapy 2000–. *Publications:* Charles Francis Adams, 1807–1886 1960, In White America 1964, The Antislavery Vanguard: New Essays on the Abolitionists (ed.) 1965, James Russell Lowell 1966, The Uncompleted Past 1969, The Memory Bank 1970, Black Mountain: An Exploration in Community 1972, Male Armor: Selected Plays, 1968–1974 1975, Visions of Kerouac 1977, About Time: Exloring the Gay Past 1986, Hidden from History: Reclaiming the Gay and Lesbian Past (co-ed.) 1989, Paul Robeson 1989, Cures: A Gay Man's Odyssey 1991, Mother Earth: An Epic Play on the Life of Emma Goldman 1991, Stonewall 1993, Midlife Queer 1996, A Queer World: The Center for Lesbian and Gay Studies Reader (ed.) 1997, Queer Representations: Reading Lives, Reading Cultures (ed.) 1997, Left Out: The Politics of Exclusion (essays) 1999, The Worlds of Lincoln Kirstein 2007; contrib. to journals and newspapers. *Honours:* Bancroft Prize 1961, Vernon Rice/Drama Desk Award 1965, Borough of Manhattan Pres.'s Gold Medal in Literature 1988, two Lambda Book Awards 1990, Asscn of Gay and Lesbian Psychiatrists Distinguished Service Award 1996, Key to the City of Cambridge, MA 1994, Legal Public Service Award 1995, NOMAS Men's Studies Award 1998, GALA Award 1998. *Address:* c/o Department of History, Lehman College, CUNY, 202c Carman Hall, 250 Bedford Park Blvd West, Bronx, New York, NY 10468, USA (office).

DUBERSTEIN, Larry, BA, MA; American writer and cabinet maker; b. 18 May 1944, New York, NY; three d. *Education:* Wesleyan Univ., Harvard Univ. *Publications:* Nobody's Jaw 1979, The Marriage Hearse 1983, Carnovsky's Retreat 1988, Postcards from Pinsk 1991, Eccentric Circles 1992, The Alibi Breakfast 1995, The Handsome Sailor 1998, The Mt Monadnock Blues 2003, The Day The Bozarts Died 2006; contribs include articles, essays, poems, reviews in Saturday Review, Boston Review, The National, The Phoenix, New York Times Book Review, Boston Globe. *Honours:* New American Writing Awards 1987, 1991, New York Times Notable Book 1998, Book Sense Notable Book 2007. *Address:* 117 Hamilton Street, Cambridge, MA 02139, USA.

DUBIE, Norman Evans, Jr, BA, MFA; American academic, writer and poet; b. 10 April 1945, Barre, VT. *Education:* Goddard College, University of Iowa. *Career:* teaching asst, Goddard College 1967–69; teaching asst, 1969–70, Writing Fellow, 1970–71, Distinguished Lecturer and Mem. of the Graduate Faculty, 1971–74, University of Iowa; Poetry Ed., Iowa Review, 1971–72, Now Magazine, 1973–74; Asst Prof., Ohio University, 1974–75; Lecturer, 1975–76, Dir, Creative Writing, 1976–77, Assoc. Prof., 1978–81, Prof. of English, 1982–, Arizona State University. *Publications:* The Horsehair Sofa, 1969; Alehouse Sonnets, 1971; Indian Summer, 1973; The Prayers of the North American Martyrs, 1975; Popham of the New Song, 1975; In the Dead of Night, 1975; The Illustrations, 1977; A Thousand Little Things, 1977; Odalisque in White, 1978; The City of the Olesha Fruit, 1979; Comes Winter, the Sea Hunting,

1979; The Everlastings, 1980; The Window in the Field, 1982; Selected and New Poems, 1983; The Springhouse, 1986; Groom Falconer, 1989; Radio Sky, 1991; The Clouds of Magellan, 1991; The Choirs of June and January, 1993. Contributions: anthologies and periodicals. *Honours:* Bess Hokin Prize, 1976; Guggenheim Fellowship, 1977–78; Pushcart Prize, 1978–79; National Endowment for the Arts grant, 1986; Ingram Merrill Grant, 1987. *Address:* c/o Department of English, Arizona State University, Tempe, AZ 85281, USA.

DUBOIS, Jean-Paul; French writer; b. 1950, Toulouse. *Career:* journalist, Le Nouvel Observateur. *Publications:* Tous les matins je me lève (novel) 1988, La vie me fait peur (novel) 1994, Kennedy et Moi (novel) (Prix France Télévision) 1996, L'Amérique m'inquiète 1996, Prends soin de moi 1997, Je pense à autre chose 1997, Si ce livre pouvait me rapprocher de toi 1999, Les poissons me regardent 2001, Jusque-là tout allait bien en Amérique 2002, Une vie française (Prix du Roman FNAC, Prix Femina) (trans. as A French Life 2007) 2004. *Address:* c/o Le Nouvel Observateur, 10–12 place de la Bourse, 75002 Paris, France.

DUBOIS, M. (see Kent, Arthur William Charles)

DUCHARME, Réjean; Canadian novelist, dramatist, screenwriter, sculptor and painter; b. 12 Aug. 1941, Saint-Félix-de-Valois, QC. *Education:* Ecole Polytechnique, Montréal. *Publications:* Fiction: L'avalée des avalés, 1966; English trans. as The Swallower Swallowed, 1968; Le nez qui voque, 1967; L'océantume, 1968; La fille de Christophe Colomb, 1969; L'huver de force, 1973; Les enfantomes, 1976; Dévadé, 1990; Va savoir, 1994. Plays: Le Cid maghané, 1968; Le marquis qui perdit, 1970; Inès Pérée et Inat Tendu, 1976; HA! ha!..., 1982. Screenplays: Les bons débarras (with Francis Manckiewicz), 1979; Les beaux souvenirs (with Francis Manckiewicz), 1981. *Honours:* Governor-General's Awards for Fiction 1966, Drama 1982.

DUCKWORTH, Marilyn, OBE; New Zealand writer; b. (Marilyn Rose Adcock), 10 Nov. 1935, Auckland; d. of Cyril John Adcock and Irene Robinson; sister of Fleur Adcock (q.v.); m. 1st Harry Duckworth 1955 (divorced 1964); m. 2nd Ian Macfarlane 1964 (divorced 1972); m. 3rd Daniel Donovan 1974 (died 1978); m. 4th John Batstone 1985; four d. *Education:* Queen Margaret Coll., Wellington and Victoria Univ., Wellington. *Career:* 10 writers' fellowships 1961–96 including Katherine Mansfield Fellowship, Menton 1980, Fulbright Visiting Writer's Fellowship, USA 1987, Victoria Univ. Writing Fellowship 1990, Hawthornden Writing Fellowship, Scotland 1994, Sargeson Writing Fellowship, Auckland 1995, Auckland Univ. Literary Fellowship 1996. *Plays:* Home to Mother, Feet First. *Publications:* fourteen novels including A Gap in the Spectrum 1959, A Barbarous Tongue 1963, Disorderly Conduct 1984, Married Alive 1985, Pulling Faces 1987, A Message from Harpo 1989, Unlawful Entry 1992, Seeing Red 1993, Leather Wings 1995, Studmuffin 1997, Swallowing Diamonds 2003; short stories: Explosions on the Sun 1989; poems: Other Lovers' Children 1975; memoir: Camping on the Faultline 2000. *Honours:* NZ Literary Fund Award for Achievement 1963, NZ Book Award for Fiction 1985. *Address:* 41 Queen Street, Mt Victoria, Wellington 6001, New Zealand. *Telephone:* (4) 384-9990 (home). *Fax:* (4) 384-9990 (home). *E-mail:* marilynduckworth@paradise.net.nz (home).

DUCORNET, Erica (Rikki) Lynn; American writer, artist and teacher; b. 19 April 1943, New York, NY; one s. *Education:* Bard College. *Career:* Novelist-in-Residence, University of Denver, 1988–; Visiting Prof., University of Trento, Italy, 1994; mem. PEN. *Publications:* The Stain, 1984; Entering Fire, 1986; The Fountains of Neptune, 1989; Eben Demarst, 1990; The Jade Cabinet, 1993; The Butcher's Tales, 1994; Phosphor in Dreamland, 1995; The Word 'Desire', 1997; The Fan-Maker's Inquisition, 1999. Contributions: periodicals. *Honours:* Critics Choice Award, 1995; Charles Flint Kellogg Award in Arts and Letters, 1998.

DUDA, Virgil; Romanian novelist; b. 25 Feb. 1939, Barlad. *Education:* Coll. of Juridicial Sciences, Bucharest. *Career:* emigrated to Israel 1988; fmr Ed. Ultima ora newspaper; fmr vice-pres. Asscn of Israeli Writers in the Romanian Language. *Publications:* novels: Povestiri din provincie 1967, Catedrala 1969, Anchetatorul penal 1972, Deruta 1973, Al doilea pasaj 1976, Cora 1977, Mastile 1979, Razboiul amintirilor 1981, Hartuiala 1984, Oglinda salvata 1986, Alvis si destinul 1993, Romania, sfarsit de Decembrie 1994, To Live in Sin 1996; short stories: Anchetatorul apatic. *Honours:* Arcadia Literature Prize 1992, Sion Prize 2001.

DUDEN, Anne; German writer; b. 1 Jan. 1942, Oldenburg. *Education:* West Berlin. *Career:* trained as bookseller, studied literature and sociology, had various jobs, then worked in publishing; co-founder Rotbuch Verlag (Publrs), Berlin 1973, mem. staff 1973–78; freelance writer, London 1978–. *Publications include:* Übergang (short stories) 1982, Das Judasschaf 1985, Steinschlag (poems) 1993, Wimpertier (mixed prose pieces and poems) 1995, Der wunde Punkt im Alphabet (essays, sketches and commentaries on painting) 1995, Hingegend (poems) 2001, Heimaten 2001. *Honours:* Krahichsteiner Literaturpreis 1986, Heinreich Boell Prize 2003.

DUDLEY, Helen (see Hope-Simpson, Jacynth Ann)

DUEMER, Joseph, BA, MFA; American academic, poet and writer; *Professor of Humanities, Clarkson University;* b. 31 May 1951, San Diego, CA; m. Carole A. Mathery 1987. *Education:* Univ. of Washington, Univ. of Iowa. *Career:* Lecturer, Western Washington Univ. 1981–83, San Diego State Univ. 1983–87; Assoc. Prof. of Humanities, Clarkson Univ. 1987–2002, Prof. 2002–; Poet-in-Residence, St Lawrence Univ. 1990; Fulbright Sr Research Fellow, Viet Nam 2000–01; mem. Associated Writing Programs (bd of dirs 1998–2002). *Publications:* poetry: Fool's Paradise 1980, The Light of Common Day 1985, Customs 1987, Static 1996, Primitive Alphabets 1998, Magical Thinking 2001; editor: Dog Music (with Jan Simmerman) 1996; contrib. to reference books, anthologies, reviews, journals, magazines and radio. *Honours:* NEA Creative Writing Fellowships 1984, 1992, Nat. Endowment for the Humanities grants 1985, 1995. *Address:* c/o Clarkson University, Potsdam, NY 13699, USA (office).

DUFF, Alan; New Zealand columnist and writer; b. 26 Oct. 1950, Rotorua; m. Joanna Robin Harper 1990. *Career:* syndicated newspaper columnist 1971–. *Publications:* Once Were Warriors 1994, One Night Out Stealing 1995, Out of the Mist and Steam 1999, Szabad 2001, Jake's Long Shadow 2002.

DUFF-WARE, Freddie (see Barnett, Paul Le Page)

DUFFY, Carol Ann, CBE, BA, FRSL; British poet and dramatist; b. 23 Dec. 1955, Glasgow, Scotland; d. of Frank Duffy and May Black; one d. *Education:* St Joseph's Convent, Stafford and Univ. of Liverpool. *Career:* Poetry Ed. Ambit 1983–; Lecturer in Creative Writing, Manchester Metropolitan Univ. 1996–; mem. Poetry Soc. (Vice-Pres.). *Plays:* Take My Husband 1984, Cavern Dreams 1986, Grimm Tales 1994, More Grimm Tales 1997. *Publications:* poetry: Fleshweathercock 1973, Standing Female Nude (Scottish Arts Council Award) 1985, Selling Manhattan (Scottish Arts Council Award, Somerset Maugham Award 1988) 1987, Home and Away 1988, The Other Country (Dylan Thomas Award) 1990, Mean Time (Whitbread Poetry Award, Forward Poetry Prize, Scottish Arts Council Book Award) 1993, Selected Poems 1994, The Pamphlet 1998, The World's Wife 1999, Time's Tidings 1999, Feminine Gospels 2001, Underwater Farmyard 2002, Out of Fashion (ed.) 2004, Rapture (T. S. Eliot Prize 2006) 2005, Another Night Before Christmas 2005, Selected Poems 2006, The Lost Happy Endings (with Jane Ray) 2006, The Hat (for children) 2007. *Honours:* C. Day-Lewis Fellowships 1982–84, Eric Gregory Award 1985, Cholmondeley Award 1992, Lannan Award (USA) 1995, Signal Poetry Award 1997. *Address:* c/o Pan Macmillan Ltd, 20 New Wharf Road, London, N1 9RR, England.

DUFFY, Eamon, PhD, DD, FBA, FSA; Irish writer and academic; *Professor of the History of Christianity, University of Cambridge;* b. 1947, Dundalk; m. Jennifer Elizabeth Browning; one s. two d. *Education:* Hull Univ., Selwyn Coll., Cambridge. *Career:* Prof. of the History of Christianity, Univ. of Cambridge. *Publications:* Challoner and his Church: Catholic Bishop in Georgian England 1981, What Catholics Believe About Mary 1989, The Stripping of the Altars: Traditional Religion in England 1400–1580 1992, The Creed in the Catechism: The Life of God for Us 1996, Saints and Sinners: A History of the Popes 1997, The Voices of Morebath: Reformation and Rebellion in an English Village 2001, Faith of our Fathers 2004, Marking the Hours: English People and Their Prayers 1240–1570 2006, Walking to Emmaus 2006; contrib. to New York Review of Books. *Honours:* Longman's History Today prize 1994, Hawthornden Prize 2002. *Address:* c/o Yale University Press London, 47 Bedford Square, London, WC1B 3DP, England (office). *Telephone:* (1223) 332144 (office).

DUFFY, Maureen Patricia, BA, FRSL, FKC; British writer and poet; b. 21 Oct. 1933, Worthing, Sussex, England; d. of Grace Rose Wright. *Education:* Trowbridge High School for Girls, Sarah Bonnell High School for Girls, King's Coll., London. *Career:* staged pop art exhbn with Brigid Brophy 1969; Chair. Greater London Arts Literature Panel 1979–81, Authors Lending and Copyright Soc. 1982–94, Copyright Licensing Agency 1996–99 (Vice-Chair. 1994–96); Pres. Writers' Guild of GB 1985–88 (Jt Chair. 1977–78); Co-founder Writers' Action Group 1972–79; Vice-Pres. European Writers Congress 1992–2003 (Pres. 2003–05), Beauty without Cruelty 1975–, British Copyright Council 1998–2003 (Vice-Chair. 1981–86, Chair. 1989–98, Hon. Pres. 2003); Fellow, King's Coll., London 2002. *Radio:* The Passionate Shepherdess, Only Goodnight. *Television:* Upstairs Downstairs (Episode 11). *Plays:* Pearson (London Playwrights' Award), Rites (Nat. Theatre) 1969, A Nightingale in Bloomsbury Square (Hampstead Theatre) 1974, The Masque of Henry Purcell (Southwark Theatre) 1995. *Publications:* That's How It Was 1962, The Single Eye 1964, The Microcosm 1966, The Paradox Players 1967, Lyrics for the Dog Hour (poems) 1968, Wounds 1969, Love Child 1971, The Venus Touch 1971, The Erotic World of Faery 1972, I Want to Go to Moscow 1973, Capital 1975, Evesong (poems) 1975, The Passionate Shepherdess 1977, Housespy 1978, Memorials of the Quick and the Dead (poems) 1979, Inherit the Earth 1980, Gorsaga 1981, Londoners: An Elegy 1983, Men and Beasts 1984, Collected Poems 1949–84 1985, Change 1987, A Thousand Capricious Chances: Methuen 1889–1989 1989, Illuminations 1991, Occam's Razor 1992, Henry Purcell (biog.) 1994, Restitution 1998, England: The Making of a Myth from Stonehenge to Albert Square 2001, Alchemy 2004. *Honours:* Hon. Pres. Authors Lending and Copyright Soc. 2002; CISAC Gold Medal for Literature 2002, Benson Medal RSL 2004. *Address:* 18 Fabian Road, London, SW6 7TZ, England. *Telephone:* (20) 7385-3598. *Fax:* (20) 7385-2468.

DUFFY, Stella, BA; British/New Zealand writer and performer; b. 1963, London; partner, Shelley Silas. *Education:* Victoria Univ. *Career:* raised in NZ, returned to England 1986. *Plays:* The Tedious Predictability of Falling in Love (Oval House) 1990, The Hand (Bristol Old Vic and tour) 1995, Close to You (Hen and Chickens Theatre) 1996, Crocodiles and Bears (BAC) 1999, Immaculate Conceit (Lyric Hammersmith) 2003, Breaststrokes (BAC) 2004, Cell Sell (Nat. Youth Theatre, Soho Theatre) 2005. *Publications:* novels: Calendar Girl 1994, Wavewalker 1996, Beneath the Blonde 1997, Singling

Out the Couples 1998, Fresh Flesh 1999, Eating Cake 1999, Immaculate Conceit 2000, State of Happiness 2004, Parallel Lies 2005, Mouths of Babes 2005; editor: Tart Noir (with Lauren Henderson). *Honours:* CWA Short Story Dagger 2002. *Literary Agent:* William Morris Agency (UK) Ltd, 52–53 Poland Street, London, W1F 7LX, England. *Website:* www.wma.com/0/locations/london. *Address:* c/o Virago Press, Brettenham House, Lancaster Place, London, WC2E 7EN, England. *Telephone:* (20) 7911-8000. *Website:* www.tartcity.com.

DUFOSSÉ, Christophe; French writer; b. 1963, Paris. *Career:* literature teacher. *Publications:* novels: L'Heure de la sortie (trans. as School's Out) (Prix du Premier Roman 2002) 2002, La Diffamation 2004, Dévotion 2006. *Address:* c/o Éditions Denoël, 9 rue du Cherche-Midi, 75278 Paris cédex 06, France.

DUGGAN, Christopher, BA; British lecturer and writer; b. 11 April 1957, London, England; m. Jennifer Virginia Mundy 1987. *Education:* Merton College, Oxford. *Career:* Junior Research Fellow, Wolfson College, Oxford, 1983–85; Fellow, All Soul's College, Oxford, 1985; Lecturer in Italian History, Dir of Centre for the Advanced Study of Italian Society, University of Reading, 1987–. *Publications:* A History of Sicily (co-author), 1986; Fascism and the Mafia, 1989; A Concise History of Italy, 1994; Francisco Crispi, 2003. Contributions: articles and reviews to various journals and newspapers.

DUGGAN, Laurence (Laurie), BA, PhD; Australian poet and teacher; b. 1949, Melbourne. *Education:* Monash Univ. and Melbourne Univ. *Career:* media studies teacher, Swinburne 1976, Canberra Coll. 1983; taught at Victoria Univ. of Tech. 1994, Univ. of Western Sydney 1999; film scriptwriter 1978–83; Poetry Ed. Meanjin 1994–97; poetry reviewer, Times on Sunday 1986; columnist, Australian Book Review 1992–94; Hon. Research Adviser, Australian Studies Centre, Univ. of Queensland 2002–06; Sr Lecturer and Writer-in-Residence, Griffith Univ. –2006; freelance 2006–. *Publications:* poetry: The Ash Range (Victorian Premier New Writing Award) 1987, The Epigrams of Martial (Wesley Michael Wright Award), Mangroves (Age Poetry Book of the Year 2003, ASAL Gold Medal 2004) 2003, Compared to What: Selected Poems 1971–2003 2005, Let's Get Lost (with Pam Brown and Ken Bolton) 2005, The Passenger 2006; non-fiction: Ghost Nation: Imagined Space and Australian Visual Culture 1901–39 2001; contrib. of numerous poems to anthologies and journals. *E-mail:* laurieduggan@btinternet.com.

DUKE, Elizabeth (see Wallington, Vivienne Elizabeth)

DUKORE, Bernard Frank, BA, MA, PhD; American academic and writer; *University Distinguished Professor Emeritus of Theatre Arts and Humanities, Virginia Polytechnic Institute and State University, Blacksburg;* b. New York, NY; one s. two d. *Education:* Brooklyn Coll., CUNY, Ohio State Univ., Univ. of Illinois. *Career:* Instructor, Hunter Coll., CUNY 1957–60; Asst Prof., Univ. of Southern California, Los Angeles 1960–62; Asst to Assoc. Prof., California State Univ., Los Angeles 1962–66; Assoc. Prof. to Prof. of Theatre, CUNY 1966–72; Prof. of Drama and Theatre, Univ. of Hawaii 1972–86; Univ. Distinguished Prof. of Theatre Arts and Humanities, Virginia Polytechnic Inst. and State Univ., Blacksburg 1986–97, Univ. Distinguished Prof. Emer. 1997–; Hoffman Eminent Scholar Chair in Theatre, Florida State Univ. 1997; Fellow, American Theatre Asscn; mem. Pinter Soc., Int. Shaw Soc. *Publications:* Bernard Shaw, Director 1971, Bernard Shaw, Playwright 1973, Dramatic Theory and Criticism 1974, Where Laughter Stops: Pinter's Tragicomedy 1976, Collected Screenplays of Bernard Shaw 1980, Money and Politics in Ibsen, Shaw and Brecht 1980, The Theatre of Peter Barnes 1981, Harold Pinter 1982, Alan Ayckbourn: A Casebook 1991, The Drama Observed (ed. and annotator, four vols) 1992–93, Shaw and the Last Hundred Years (ed.) 1994, Barnestorm: The Plays of Peter Barnes 1995, Bernard Shaw and Gabriel Pascal 1996, Not Bloody Likely: The Columbia Book of Bernard Shaw Quotations 1997, Shaw on Cinema (ed. and annotator) 1997, Sam Peckinpah's Feature Films 1999, Shaw's Theatre 2000. *Honours:* Guggenheim Fellowship 1969–70, Nat. Endowment for the Humanities Fellowships 1976–77, 1984–85, 1990, Fulbright Research Scholarship, UK and Ireland 1991–92. *Address:* School of the Arts, Virginia Polytechnic Institute and State University, Blacksburg, VA 24061-0141 (office); 2510 Plymouth Street, Blacksburg, VA 24060, USA (home). *Telephone:* (540) 961-6999 (home). *E-mail:* bdukore@vt.edu.

DUMMETT, Sir Michael Anthony Eardley, Kt, MA, DLitt; British academic; b. 27 June 1925, London; s. of George Herbert Dummett and Mabel Iris Dummett (née Eardley-Wilmot); m. Ann Chesney 1951; three s. two d. *Education:* Sandroyd School, Winchester Coll., Christ Church, Oxford. *Career:* mil. service 1943–47; Asst Lecturer in Philosophy, Univ. of Birmingham 1950–51; Prize Fellow, All Souls Coll., Oxford 1950–57, Research Fellow 1957–61; Harkness Foundation Fellow, Univ. of Calif., Berkeley 1955–56; Reader in Philosophy of Mathematics, Univ. of Oxford 1961–74; Sr Research Fellow, All Souls Coll., Oxford 1974–79, Sub-Warden 1974–76; Visiting Lecturer, Univ. of Ghana 1958, Stanford Univ., Calif., USA 1960–66, Univ. of Minn. 1968, Princeton Univ. 1970, Rockefeller Univ., New York 1973; William James Lecturer in Philosophy, Harvard Univ. 1976; Wykeham Prof. of Logic, Univ. of Oxford 1979–92; Fellow, New College, Oxford 1979–92, Emer. Fellow 1992–98, Hon. Fellow 1998–; Fellow, British Acad. 1967–84 (resgnd) Sr Fellow 1995–; Emer. Fellow, All Souls College, Oxford 1979–; Chair. Jt Council for the Welfare of Immigrants 1970–71; mem. unofficial cttee of inquiry into events in Southall, 1979–80, Shadow Bd Barclays Bank 1981; Foreign Hon. mem. American Acad. of Arts and Sciences. *Publications:* Frege:

Philosophy of Language 1973, The Justification of Deduction 1973, Elements of Intuitionism 1977, Truth and other Enigmas 1979, Immigration: Where the Debate Goes Wrong 1978, Catholicism and the World Order 1979, The Game of Tarot 1980, Twelve Tarot Games 1980, The Interpretation of Frege's Philosophy 1981, Voting Procedures 1984, The Visconti-Sforza Tarot Cards 1986, Ursprünge der Analytischen Philosophie 1988, The Logical Basis of Metaphysics 1991, Frege and other Philosophers 1991, Frege: Philosophy of Mathematics 1991, Grammar and Style 1993, The Seas of Language 1993, Origins of Analytical Philosophy 1993, Il Mondo e l'Angelo 1993, I Tarocchi Siciliani 1995, A Wicked Pack of Cards 1996, Principles of Electoral Reform 1997, La Natura e il Futuro della Filosofia 2001, On Immigration and Refugees 2001, A History of the Occult Tarot 1870–1970 2002, Truth and the Past 2004, A History of Games Played with the Tarot Pack (with J. McLean) 2003, Thought and Reality 2006. *Honours:* Dr hc (Nijmegen) 1983, Hon. DLitt (Caen) 1993, (Aberdeen) 1993, (Stirling) 2003, (Athens) 2005, Hon. DUniv (Stirling) 2002; Lakatos Award 1994, Rolf Schock Prize in Philosophy and Logic 1995. *Address:* 54 Park Town, Oxford, OX2 6SJ, England (home). *Telephone:* (1865) 558698 (home). *Fax:* (1865) 558698 (home).

DUMONT, André, BA, BEd; Canadian writer; b. 12 April 1929, Campbellton, NB; m. Germaine Richard 1958, two s. two d. *Publications:* Français Renouvele I, 1964, II, 1966; Le Parti Acadien (co-author), 1972; Jeunesse Mouvementée, 1979; Quand Je Serai Grand, 1989; Pour un Français Moderne, 1990; Avancez en Arrière, 1996. Contributions: Over 100 articles on different topics, mostly political.

DUNANT, Peter (see Dunant, Sarah)

DUNANT, Sarah, (Peter Dunant), BA; British broadcaster and writer; b. 8 Aug. 1950, London; d. of David and Estelle (née Joseph) Dunant; pnr Ian David Willox; two d. *Education:* Godolphin and Latymer School and Newnham Coll., Cambridge. *Career:* actress 1972–73; teacher (Japan) 1973–74; travelling (Asia) 1973–74, (S and Cen. America) 1976–77; Producer BBC Radio 1974–76; freelance journalist, novelist, scriptwriter, radio and TV presenter 1977–; sometime Presenter Woman's Hour, BBC Radio Four 1986–, The Late Show BBC 2 TV 1989–95, Night Waves BBC Radio 3 1997–. *Publications:* as Sarah Dunant: Snow Storms in a Hot Climate 1988, Birth Marks 1991, Fatlands (CWA Silver Dagger Award) 1993, The War of the Words: Essays on Political Correctness (ed.) 1994, Under My Skin 1995, The Age of Anxiety (ed.) 1996, Transgressions 1997, The Age of Anxiety (ed.) 1998, Mapping the Edge 1999, The Birth of Venus 2002, In the Company of the Courtesan 2006; as Peter Dunant: Exterminating Angels (co-author) 1983, Intensive Care (co-author) 1986; contrib. to various London magazines, Listener, Guardian. *Literary Agent:* Aitken Alexander Associates Ltd, 18–21 Cavaye Place, London, SW10 9PT, England. *Telephone:* (20) 7373-8672. *Fax:* (20) 7373-6002. *E-mail:* reception@aitkenalexander.co.uk. *Website:* www.aitkenalexander.co.uk. *Address:* 1A (Highwood Road, London, N19 4PN, England (home). *Telephone:* (20) 7281-1555 (home). *Fax:* (20) 7272-4147 (home).

DUNCAN, Lois, BA; American writer; b. 28 April 1934, Philadelphia, PA; m. Donald W. Arquette 1965, two s. three d. *Education:* Duke University, University of New Mexico. *Publications:* Ransom, 1966; A Gift of Magic, 1971; I Know What You Did Last Summer, 1973; Down a Dark Hall, 1974; Summer of Fear, 1976; Killing Mr Griffin, 1978; Daughters of Eve, 1979; Stranger With My Face, 1981; My Growth as a Writer, 1982; The Third Eye, 1984; Locked in Time, 1985; Horses of Dreamland, 1986; The Twisted Window, 1987; Songs From Dreamland, 1989; The Birthday Moon, 1989; Don't Look Behind You, 1989; Who Killed My Daughter?, 1992; The Circus Comes Home, 1993; Psychic Connections: A Journey into the Mysterious World of Psi (co-author William Roll), 1995; The Magic of Spider Woman, 1996; Gallows Hill, 1997; Night Terrors (edited anthology), 1997; Trapped (edited anthology), 1998.

DUNCAN-JONES, Katherine Dorothea, BLitt, MA, FRSL; British academic and editor; *Senior Research Fellow, Somerville College, Oxford;* b. 13 May 1941; m. Andrew N. Wilson 1971 (divorced 1990); two d. *Education:* King Edward VI High School for Girls, Birmingham and St Hilda's Coll., Oxford. *Career:* Fellow and Tutor in English Literature, Somerville Coll., Oxford 1966–, Sr Research Fellow 2001–; Prof. of English Literature, Univ. of Oxford 1998–2001. *Publications include:* biography: Sir Philip Sidney: Courtier Poet 1991, Ungentle Shakespeare 2001; editor: Miscellaneous Prose of Sir Philip Sidney 1977, Sir Philip Sidney 1989, Shakespeare's Sonnets 1997; contrib. to Review of English Studies, TLS and other journals. *Honours:* Mary Ewart Research Fellow, Somerville Coll. 1963–65, Fellow, New Hall, Cambridge 1965–66, Hon. Research Fellow, Univ. Coll. London 2000; Ben Jonson Discoveries Prize 1996. *Address:* c/o Somerville College, Oxford, OX2 6HD, England. *Telephone:* (1865) 281267 (office). *E-mail:* katherine.duncan-jones@some.ox.ac.uk.

DUNCKER, Patricia, MA, DPhil; British writer; *Professor of Creative Writing, University of East Anglia;* b. 29 June 1951, Kingston, Jamaica. *Education:* Univ. of Cambridge, Univ. of Oxford. *Career:* Lecturer, Roehampton Inst. 1978–80, Oxford Polytechnic 1980–86, Univ. of Poitiers, France 1987–91, Univ. of Wales, Aberystwyth 1991–2002; Prof. of Creative Writing, Univ. of East Anglia 2002–; mem. Soc. of Authors, Yr Academi Gymreig (The Welsh Acad.), PEN, RSA. *Publications:* Sisters and Strangers: An Introduction to Contemporary Feminist Fiction 1992, Hallucinating Foucault 1996, Cancer Through the Eyes of Ten Women 1996, Monsieur Shoushana's Lemon Trees 1997, James Miranda Barry (aka The Doctor) 1999, The Deadly Space

Between 2002, Writing on the Wall 2002, Seven Tales of Sex and Death 2003, Miss Webster and Chérif 2006; contrib. to Critical Quarterly, Stand Magazine, Women: A Cultural Review. *Honours:* Dillons First Fiction Award, McKitterick Prize. *Literary Agent:* c/o Victoria Hobbs, A. M. Heath & Co Ltd, 79 St Martin's Lane, London, WC2N 4RE, England. *Address:* School of English and American Studies, University of East Anglia, Norwich, Norfolk NR4 7TJ, England (office). *E-mail:* p.duncker@uea.ac.uk (office).

DUNHAM, William Wade, BS, MS, PhD; American academic and writer; *Truman Koehler Professor of Mathematics, Muhlenberg College*; b. 8 Dec. 1947, Pittsburgh, PA; m. Penelope Higgins 1970; two s. *Education:* Univ. of Pittsburgh, Ohio State Univ. *Career:* Truman Koehler Prof. of Mathematics, Muhlenberg Coll. 1992–; mem. Mathematical Asscn of America, Nat. Council of Teachers of Mathematics. *Publications:* Journey Through Genius: The Great Theorems of Mathematics 1990, The Mathematical Universe 1994, Euler: The Master of Us All 1999, The Calculus Gallery 2005, The Genius of Euler 2007 (ed.) 2007; contrib. to American Mathematical Monthly, Mathematics Magazine, College Mathematics Journal, Mathematics Teacher. *Honours:* Univ. of Pittsburgh M. M. Culver Award 1969, Hanover Coll. Master Teacher Award 1981, Nat. Endowment for the Humanities Summer Seminars on Great Theorems 1988–96, Indiana Humanities Council Humanities Achievement Award for Scholarship 1991, Mathematical Asscn of America George Pólya Award 1993, Mathematical Asscn of America Trevor Evans Award 1997, Muhlenberg Coll. Lindback Teaching Award 2001, Mathematical Asscn of America Lester R. Ford Award 2006. *Address:* Department of Mathematics, Muhlenberg College, Allentown, PA 18104, USA.

DUNKERLEY, James, BA, BPhil, PhD; British academic and writer; *Professor in Politics and History, Queen Mary and Westfield College, London*; b. 15 Aug. 1953, Wokingham, England. *Education:* University of York, Hertford College, Oxford, Nuffield College, Oxford. *Career:* researcher, Latin America Bureau, London 1979–80, 1983–84; Research Fellow, Institute for Latin American Studies, University of London 1981–82, Centre for Latin American Studies, University of Liverpool 1982–83; Fellow, Kellogg Institute, University of Notre Dame, IN 1985; Reader in Politics, Queen Mary and Westfield College, London 1986–, Prof. in Politics and History 1990–; Dir Inst. of Latin American Studies London 1998–; Dir Inst. for the Study of the Americas 2004–. *Publications:* Unity is Strength: Trade Unions in Latin America (with C. Whitehouse), 1980; Bolivia: Coup d'Etat, 1980; The Long War: Dictatorship and Revolution in El Salvador, 1982; Rebellion in the Veins: Political Struggle in Bolivia, 1952–1982, 1984; Granada: Whose Freedom? (with F. Amburseley), 1984; Origenes del poder militar en Bolivia 1879–1935, 1987; Power in the Isthmus: A Political History of Central America, 1988; Political Suicide in Latin America and Other Essays, 1992; The Pacification of Central America, 1994, Warriors and Scribes 2000; Americana, The Americas in the World, around 1850 2000. Contributions: scholarly journals, newspapers, and magazines. *Address:* Institute for the Study of the Americas, Senate House, Malet Street, London, WC1E 7HU, England (office). *Telephone:* (20) 7862-8870 (office). *Fax:* (20) 7862-8886 (office). *E-mail:* americas@sas.ac.uk (office). *Website:* www.americas.ac.uk (office).

DUNLAP, Susan, BA, MAT; American writer; b. 20 June 1943, Kew Gardens, NY; m. Newell Dunlap 1970. *Education:* Bucknell University, University of North Carolina. *Career:* founding mem., Sisters in Crime (pres. 1990–91). *Publications:* An Equal Opportunity Death, 1984; Karma, 1984; As a Favor, 1984; Not Exactly a Brahmin, 1985; The Bohermian Connection, 1986; The Last Annual Slugfest, 1986; Too Close to the Edge, 1987; A Dinner to Die For, 1987; Pious Deception, 1989; Diamond in the Buff, 1990; Rogue Wave, 1991; Death and Taxes, 1993; Time Expired, 1993; High Fall, 1994; Sudden Exposure, 1995; Cop Out, 1997. Other: Deadly Allies II: Private Eye Writers of America and Sisters in Crime Collaborative Anthology (co-ed.), 1994. Contributions: numerous short stories to periodicals including: Ellery Queen's Mystery Magazine; Alfred Hitchcock's Mystery Magazine.

DUNMORE, Helen, BA; British poet and novelist; b. 1952, Yorkshire; m.; one s. one d. one step-s. *Education:* York Univ. *Career:* cttee mem. Soc. of Authors (Chair. 2005–). *Publications include:* poetry: The Apple Fall 1983, The Sea Skater (Poetry Soc. Alice Hunt Bartlett Award) 1986, The Raw Garden (Poetry Book Soc. Choice) 1988, Short Days, Long Nights: New & Selected Poems 1991, Secrets (Signal Poetry Award 1995) 1994, Recovering a Body 1994, Bestiary 1997, Out of the Blue: New and Selected Poems 2001; fiction: Going to Egypt 1992, Zennor in Darkness (McKitterick Prize 1994) 1993, In the Money 1993, Burning Bright 1994, A Spell of Winter (Orange Prize for Women Writers of Fiction 1996) 1995, Talking to the Dead 1996, Your Blue-Eyed Boy 1998, With Your Crooked Heart 1999, The Siege 2001, The Silver Bead 2003, Ingo 2005, House of Orphans 2006, The Tide Knot 2006; short stories: Love of Fat Men 1997, Ice Cream 2000, Mourning Ruby 2003. *Honours:* Hon. FRSL . *Literary Agent:* Caradoc King, A. P. Watt Ltd, 20 John Street, London, WC1N 2DR, England. *Telephone:* (20) 7405-6774. *Fax:* (20) 7831-2154. *Website:* helendunmore.com.

DUNMORE, John, BA, PhD; New Zealand academic and writer; *Professor Emeritus, Massey University*; b. 6 Aug. 1923, Trouville, France; m. Joyce Megan Langley 1946; one s. one d. *Education:* Univ. of London, UK, Univ. of New Zealand. *Career:* Lecturer, Sr Lecturer, Prof., Dean, Massey Univ. 1961–83, Prof. Emer. 1984–; mem. Australasian Language and Literature Asscn (Pres. 1980–82). *Publications:* French Explorers in the Pacific 1966–69, The Fateful Voyage of the St Jean Baptiste 1969, Norman Kirk: A Portrait 1972, Pacific Explorer 1985, New Zealand and the French 1990, The French and the Maoris 1992, Who's Who in Pacific Navigation 1992, The Journal of La Perouse 1994–95, I Remember Tomorrow 1998, Monsieur Baret: First Woman Around the World 2002, The Pacific Journal of Bougainville 2003, Storms and Dreams 2005, Where Fate Beckons 2006, Wild Cards 2006, Mrs Cook's Book of Recipes 2006; contrib. to numerous learned journals and periodicals. *Honours:* Chevalier de la Légion d'honneur 1976, Officier 2007; NZ Commemoration Medal 1990, Companion NZ Order of Merit 2001; Hon. DLitt 2006; New Zealand Book of the Year 1970, Academic Palms 1986, Massey Medal 1993. *Address:* 89/65 Guildford Drive, Paraparaumu 5032, New Zealand.

DUNN, Douglas Eaglesham, OBE, BA, FRSL; Scottish poet; *Professor of Creative Writing, University of St Andrews*; b. 23 Oct. 1942, Inchinnan; s. of William D. Dunn and Margaret McGowan; m. 1st Lesley B. Wallace 1964 (died 1981); m. 2nd Lesley Jane Bathgate 1985; one s. one d. *Education:* Univ. of Hull. *Career:* full-time writer 1971–91; Writer-in-residence Duncan of Jordanstone Coll. of Art and Dundee Dist Libraries 1986–88; Fellow in Creative Writing, Univ. of St Andrews 1989–91, Prof. 1991–, Head School of English 1994–99; Dir St Andrews Scottish Studies Inst. 1992–; Hon. Visiting Prof. Dundee Univ. 1987–89; mem. Scottish PEN. *Publications:* Terry Street 1969 (Somerset Maugham Award 1972), The Happier Life 1972, New Poems 1972–73 (ed.) 1973, Love or Nothing 1974 (Faber Memorial Prize 1976), A Choice of Byron's Verse (ed.) 1974, Two Decades of Irish Writing (criticism) 1975, The Poetry of Scotland (ed.) 1979, Barbarians 1979, St Kilda's Parliament 1981 (Hawthornden Prize 1982), Europa's Lover 1982, A Rumoured City: New Poets from Hull (ed.) 1982, To Build a Bridge: A Celebration of Humberside in Verse (ed.) 1982, Elegies 1985 (Whitbread Poetry Award and Whitbread Book of the Year 1986), Secret Villages (short stories) 1985, Selected Poems 1986, Northlight 1988, New and Selected Poems 1989, Poll Tax: The Fiscal Fake 1990, Andromache 1990, The Essential Browning (ed.) 1990, Scotland. An Anthology (ed.) 1991, Faber Book of Twentieth Century Scottish Poetry (ed.) 1992, Dante's Drum-Kit 1993, Boyfriends and Girlfriends (short stories) 1995, Oxford Book of Scottish Short Stories (ed.) 1995, The Donkey's Ears, The Year's Afternoon 2000, 20th Century Scottish Poems (ed.) 2000. *Honours:* Hon. Fellow, Humberside Coll. 1987; Hon. LLD (Dundee) 1987; Hon. DLitt (Hull) 1995; Cholmondeley Award 1989. *Address:* School of English, The University, St Andrews, Fife, KY16 9AL, Scotland (office). *Telephone:* (1334) 462666 (office). *Fax:* (1334) 462655 (office). *E-mail:* ded@st-andrews.ac.uk (office).

DUNN, John Montfort, BA, FBA, FSA; British political theorist; *Professor of Political Theory, University of Cambridge*; b. 9 Sept. 1940, Fulmer; s. of Brig. Henry G. M. Dunn and Catherine M. Kinloch; m. 1st Susan D. Fyvel 1965; m. 2nd Judith F. Bernal 1971; m. 3rd Ruth Ginette Scurr 1997; two s. (one deceased) two d. *Education:* Winchester Coll., Millfield School, King's Coll., Cambridge and Harvard Univ., USA. *Career:* Grad. School of Arts and Sciences; Official Fellow in History, Jesus Coll., Cambridge 1965–66; Fellow, King's Coll., Cambridge 1966–, Coll. Lecturer, Dir of Studies in History 1966–72; Lecturer in Political Science, Univ. of Cambridge 1972–77, Reader in Politics 1977–87, Prof. of Political Theory 1987–; Visiting Lecturer, Univ. of Ghana 1968–69; Chair. Section P. (Political Studies), British Acad. 1994–97, Bd of Consultants, Kim Dae-Jung Peace Foundation for the Asia-Pacific Region 1994–; Distinguished Visiting Prof., Univs of Tulane, Minnesota, Yale; mem. Council of British Acad. 2004–07. *Publications:* The Political Thought of John Locke 1969, Modern Revolutions 1972, Dependence and Opportunity (with A. F. Robertson) 1973, Western Political Theory in the Face of the Future 1979, Political Obligation in its Historical Context 1980, Locke 1984, The Politics of Socialism 1984, Rethinking Modern Political Theory 1985, The Economic Limits to Modern Politics (ed.) 1990, Interpreting Political Responsibility 1990, Storia delle dottrine politiche 1992, Democracy: The Unfinished Journey (ed.) 1992, Contemporary Crisis of the Nation State? (ed.) 1994, The History of Political Theory 1995, Great Political Thinkers (21 vols, co-ed.) 1997, The Cunning of Unreason 2000, Pensare la Politica 2002, Locke: A Very Short Introduction 2003, Setting the People Free: The Story of Democracy 2005. *Honours:* hon. foreign mem. American Acad. of Arts and Sciences 1991. *Address:* King's College, Cambridge, CB2 1ST (office); The Merchant's House, 31 Station Road, Swavesey, Cambridge, CB4 5QJ, England (home). *Telephone:* (1223) 331258 (office); (1954) 231451 (home). *Fax:* (1223) 331315 (office). *E-mail:* jmd24@cam.ac.uk (office).

DUNN, Stephen, BA, MA; American poet and writer; b. 24 June 1939, New York, NY; m. 1st Lois Kelly 1964 (divorced); two d.; m. 2nd Barbara Hurd 2003. *Education:* Hofstra Univ., New School for Social Research, New York, Syracuse Univ. *Career:* Asst Prof., Southwest Minnesota State College, Marshall, 1970–73; Visiting Poet, Syracuse Univ., 1973–74, Univ. of Washington at Seattle, 1980; Assoc. Prof. to Prof., 1974–90, Distinguished Prof., Richard Stockton College of NJ; Adjunct Prof. of Poetry, Columbia Univ., 1983–87. *Publications:* Poetry: Five Impersonations, 1971; Looking for Holes in the Ceiling, 1974; Full of Lust and Good Usage, 1976; A Circus of Needs, 1978; Work and Love, 1981; Not Dancing, 1984; Local Time, 1986; Between Angels, 1989; Landscape at the End of the Century, 1991; New and Selected Poems, 1974–1994, 1994; Loosestrife, 1996; Riffs and Reciprocities, 1998; Different Hours, 2000; Local Visitations, 2003, The Insistence of Beauty 2006. Other: Walking Light: Essays and Memoirs, 1993. Contributions: periodicals. *Honours:* Acad. of American Poets Prize, 1970; National Endowment for the Arts Fellowships, 1973, 1982, 1989; Bread Loaf Writers

Conference Robert Frost Fellowship, 1975; Theodore Roethke Prize, 1977; New Jersey Arts Council Fellowships, 1979, 1983; Helen Bullis Prize, 1982; Guggenheim Fellowship, 1984; Levinson Prize, 1988; Oscar Blumenthal Prize, 1991; James Wright Prize, 1993; American Acad. of Arts and Letters Award, 1995; Pulitzer Prize in Poetry, 2001.

DUNNE, Dominick, BA; American novelist and essayist; b. 29 Oct. 1925, Hartford, CT; m. Ellen Griffin 1952 (divorced); two s. one d. (deceased). *Education:* Williams College. *Career:* television and film producer; co-founder, Dunne-Didion-Dunne film production company. *Publications:* The Winners: Part II of Joyce Haber's 'The Users', 1982; The Two Mrs Grenvilles, 1985; Fatal Charms, and Other Tales of Today, 1986; People Like Us, 1988; An Inconvenient Woman, 1990; The Mansions of Limbo, 1991; A Season in Purgatory, 1993; Another City, Not My Own: A Novel in the Form of a Memoir, 1997; The Way We Lived Then: Recollections of a Well-Known Name Dropper, 1999; Justice: Crimes, Trials and Punishments, 2001.

DuNOUR, Shlomo; Israeli writer and teacher; b. 1921, Łodz, Poland; m. Mirian DuNour. *Career:* moved to Palestine 1938; leader of the Aliyat Ha Noar Movement; teacher, Dept of History, Hebrew Univ., Univ. of Haifa. *Publications include:* novels: Yet Another 1978, Adiel 2001. *Honours:* Newman Prize 1978, Jerusalem Prize for Literature 1999. *Address:* c/o The Toby Press, PO Box 8531, New Milford, CT 06776-8531, USA. *Website:* www .tobypress.com.

DUQUESNE, Jacques Henri Louis, LenD; French journalist and writer; b. 18 March 1930, Dunkerque; s. of Louis Duquesne and Madeleine Chevalier; m. Edith Dubois 1954; one s. one d. *Education:* Coll. Jean-Bart, Dunkirk and Faculté de Droit, Paris. *Career:* reporter, La Croix 1957–64; Deputy Dir Panorama Chrétien 1964–70, head of investigations 1967; Asst Ed.-in-Chief, L'Express 1970–71; Co-founder and Asst Ed.-in-Chief, Le Point 1972–74, Ed.-in-Chief 1974–77, Pres.-Dir-Gen. 1985–90; Dir-Gen. La Vie Catholique group of publs 1977–79; news reporter, Europe No. 1 1969–97, La Croix 1983–, Midi Libre 1997–; Chair. Bd L'Express 1997–2005; mem. Jury, Prix Interallié 1986–. *Publications:* L'Algérie ou la guerre des mythes 1959, Les 16–24 ans 1964, Les prêtres 1965, Les catholiques français sous l'occupation 1966, Demain une Eglise sans prêtres 1968, Dieu pour l'homme d'aujourd'hui 1970, La gauche du Christ 1972, Les 13–62 ans 1974, La grande triche 1977, Une voix, la nuit 1979, La rumeur de la ville 1981, Maria Vadamme 1983, Alice Van Meulen 1985, Saint-Eloi 1986, Au début d'un bel été 1988, les Vents du Nord m'ont dit 1989, Catherine Courage 1990, Jean Bart 1992, Laura C. 1994, Jésus 1994, Théo et Marie 1996, les Années Jean-Paul II 1996 (jtly), Le Dieu de Jésus 1997, Le Bonheur en 36 vertus, Romans du Nord 1999, Les Héritières 2000, Pour comprendre la guerre d'Algérie 2001, Et pourtant nous étions heureux 2003, Marie 2004, Dieu malgré tout 2005. *Honours:* Chevalier, Légion d'honneur. *Address:* 13 rue de Poissy, 75005 Paris, France (home). *Telephone:* 1-43-54-32-41.

DURAN COHEN, Ilan, MFA; French film director, screenwriter and novelist; b. 1963. *Education:* New York Univ. Film School, USA. *Career:* lives and works in Paris, France. *Films:* Lola Zipper (writer, dir) 1991, La confusion des genres (writer, dir, producer) 2000, Les petits fils (writer, dir, producer) 2004, Les amants du Flore (dir) 2006. *Radio:* Reality Zoo (France Culture). *Publications:* novels: Chronique alicienne 1997, Le Fils de la sardine 1999, Mon cas personnel 2002. *Honours:* Horizon Prize, Venice Film Festival 2004. *Literary Agent:* c/o Artmédia, 20 avenue Rapp, 75007 Paris, France. *Telephone:* 1-43-17-33-00. *Fax:* 1-44-18-34-60. *E-mail:* info@artmedia.fr. *Website:* www.artmedia.fr. *Address:* Fugitive Productions, 64 rue Pierre Charron, 75008 Paris, France (office). *Telephone:* 1-45-61-27-97 (office). *E-mail:* fugitiveprod@wanadoo.fr (office).

DURAND, Claude; French publisher; b. 9 Nov. 1938, Livry-Gargan (Seine-et-Oise); s. of Félix Durand and Suzanne Durand (née Thuret); m. Carmen Perea 1965; two s. *Education:* Ecole normale d'instituteurs de Versailles. *Career:* fmr schoolteacher; Literary Dir Editions du Seuil 1965–78; Gen. Man. Editions Grasset 1978–80; Chair. and CEO Librairie Arthème Fayard 1980–, Librairie Stock 1991–98; Chair. Bd of Dirs Inst. Mémoire de l'édition contemporaine 1990–93, Deputy Chair. 1993–. *Publication:* La Nuit zoologique (novel, Prix Médicis) 1979. *Honours:* Officier, Légion d'honneur, Chevalier, Ordre nat. du Mérite, Commdr des Arts et des Lettres. *Address:* Librairie Fayard, 75 rue des Saints-Pères, 75006 Paris (office); 46 rue de Naples, 75008 Paris, France (home).

DURBAN, (Rosa) Pam; American academic and writer; b. 4 March 1947, Aiken, SC; m. Frank H. Hunter 1983. *Education:* BA, University of North Carolina at Greensboro, 1969; MFA, University of Iowa, 1979. *Career:* Ed., Atlanta Gazette, 1974–75; Visiting Asst Prof. of Creative Writing, SUNY at Geneseo, 1979–80; Asst Prof. of Creative Writing, Murray State University, 1980–81; Assoc. Prof. of Creative Writing, Ohio University, 1981–86; Prof. of English and Creative Writing, Georgia State University, 1986–. *Publications:* All Set about with Fever Trees and Other Stories, 1985; The Laughing Place, 1993; So Far Back, 2000. Contributions: anthologies and periodicals. *Honours:* James A. Michener Fellowship, University of Iowa, 1982–83; Rinehart Award in Fiction, Rinehart Foundation, 1984; Ohio Arts Council Fellowships, 1983–84, 1986–87; Whiting Writer's Award, 1987; National Endowment for the Arts Creative Writing Fellowship, 1998. *Address:* c/o Department of English, Georgia State University, Atlanta, GA 30303, USA.

DURBEN, Maria-Magdalena; German writer; b. 8 July 1935, d. of Bernhard Block and Eva Block (née Klein); m. 2nd Wolfgang Durben 1967. *Education:* studied in Erfurt and Berlin. *Career:* writes in collaboration with Wolfgang Durben. *Publications:* Ein Stückchen von Gott, Gruß an Taiwan, Wenn der Schnee fällt, Da schrie der Schatten fürchterlich, Schaukle am blauen Stern, Unterm Glasnadelzelt: Gedichte 1976, Roter Rausch und weiße Haut, Wenn das Feuer fällt, Wenn die Asche fällt 1977, Lichtrunne, Zwischen Knoblauch und Chrysanthemen 1979, Haiku mit Stäbchen: Japan-Abenteuer, Reise auf einer Teewolke 1980. *Honours:* Dr hc (Gdańsk, Poland) 1977, (New York); Hon. DLitt (Karachi) 1978, (World Acad. of Languages and Literature, São Paulo, Brazil) 1978, (World Acad. of Arts and Culture, Taipei) 1979; numerous awards. *Address:* Schulstr. 8–10, 66701 Beckingen, Germany.

DURKIN, Barbara Rae Wernecke, AA, BS; American writer; b. 13 Jan. 1944, Baltimore, MD; m. William J. Durkin 1973, two s. *Education:* Essex Community College, Towson State College, Morgan State College, John Hopkins University. *Career:* mem. American PEN Women; International Women's Writing Guild. *Publications:* Oh, You Dundalk Girls, Can't You Dance the Polka?, 1984; Visions and Viewpoints (ed.), 1993. *Honours:* American Library Asscn Best of 1984 List 1984.

DÜRR, Alfred, PhD; German musicologist and editor; b. 3 March 1918, Charlottenburg. *Education:* Univ. of Göttingen. *Career:* mem. 1951–83, Asst Dir 1962–81, Johann-Sebastian-Bach-Inst., Göttingen; Ed., Bach-Jahrbuch 1953–74; ed. of works for Bach Neue Ausgabe sämtlicher Werke; mem. Akademie der Wissenschaften, Göttingen 1976–; corresponding mem. American Musicological Soc. 1988–. *Publications:* Studien über die frühen Kantaten Johann Sebastian Bachs 1951, Zur Chronolgie der Leipzigir Vokalwerke J. Bachs (revised reprint from Bach-Jahrbuch 1957) 1976, Johann Sebastian Bach, Weihnachts Oratorium 1967, Die Kantaten von Johann Sebastian Bach 1971, Johann Sebastian Bach: Seine Handschrift-Abbild seines Schaffens 1984, Im Mittelpunkt Bach: Ausgewählte Aufsätze und Vorträge 1988, Die Johannes-Passion von Johann Sebastian Bach: Entstehung, Überlieferung, Werkeinführung 1988, Bachs Werk vom Einfall bis zur Drucklegung 1989, Johann Sebastian Bach – Das Wohltemperierte Klavier 1998; contrib. articles in scholarly journals. *Honours:* Dr hc (Baldwin-Wallace Coll., Berea, OH) 1982, (Oxford) 1995; Festschrift published in honour of 65th birthday 1983. *Address:* Charlottenburger Strasse 19, 37085 Göttingen, Germany. *Telephone:* (551) 7992817.

DURRANI, Tehmina; Pakistani writer; d. of S. U. Durrani; m. 1st Maj. (retd) Anees; m. 2nd Ghulam Mustafa Khar (divorced); two d.; m. 3rd Mian Shahbaz Sharif (Pres. Pakistan Muslim League-Nawaz and fmr Chief Minister of Punjab) 2005. *Career:* controversial writer; wrote autobiography after split with notorious fmr feudal landlord Ghulam Mustafa Khar; currently associated with NGO that works for the rehabilitation of battered wives. *Publications:* My Feudal Lord (autobiog.), Mirror to the Blind 1996, Blasphemy 1998. *Address:* c/o Viking Penguin, 27 Wright's Lane, London, W8, England.

DÜRRSON, Werner, PhD; German poet, writer, dramatist and translator; b. 12 Sept. 1932, Schwenningen am Neckar. *Education:* Trossingen, Tübingen, Munich. *Career:* has taught at several univs in France and Germany; mem. Asscn Internationale des Critiques littéraires, Paris, Asscn of German Writers, PEN. *Publications:* Dreizehn Gedichte (poems) 1965; Schatten=geschlecht (poems) 1966; Drei Dichtungen (poems) 1970; Schubart (play) 1980, Stehend bewegt (poem) 1980, Der Luftkünstler (prose) 1983, Wie ich lese? (essay) 1986, Ausleben (selection of poems) 1988, Abbreviaturen (aphorisms) 1989, Werke (poetry and prose, four vols) 1992, Ausgewählte Gedichte (poems) 1995, The Kattenhorn Silence (trans. by Michael Hamburger) 1995, Stimmen aus der Gutenberg-Galaxis (literary essays) 1997, Der verkaufte Schatten 1997, Wasserspiele (poems) 1999, Pariser Spitzen (poems) 2001, Aufgehobene Zeit 2002, Schillerknochen (poem) 2005; several works in co-operation with painters, including Klaus Staeck, Erich Heckel, HAP Grieshaber, Jonny Friedlaender, and musicians, including Klaus Fessmann; trans of authors, including Guillaume d'Aquitaine, Marguerite de Navarre, Stéphane Mallarmé, Arthur Rimbaud, Yvan Goll, René Char and Henri Michaux; contrib. to anthologies and radio. *Honours:* South West German Press Lyric Poetry Prize 1953, German Awards for Short Stories 1973, 1983, Literary Prize, Stuttgart 1978, Literary Prize, Überlingen 1985, Bundesverdienstkreuz 1993, Prize of the Schiller Foundation, Weimar 1997, Eichendorff Literary Prize 2001, Villa Massimo, Rome 2004. *Address:* Schloss Neufra, 88499 Riedlingen/Donau, Germany. *Telephone:* 73714242. *E-mail:* wernerdurrson@aol.com.

DURST, Paul; American writer; b. 23 April 1921, Archbald, PA. *Education:* Colorado State College, Northwest Missouri State College. *Publications:* Die! Damn You, 1952; Bloody River, 1953; Trail Herd North, 1953; Guns of Circle 8 (as Jeff Cochran), 1954; Along the Yermo Rim (as John Shane), 1954; My Deadly Angel (as John Chelton), 1955; Showdown, 1955; Justice, 1956; Kid From Canadian, 1956; Prairie Reckoning, 1956; Sundown in Sundance (as John Shane), 1956; Six-Gun Thursday (as John Shane), 1956; Gunsmoke Dawn (as John Shane), 1957; John Law, Keep Out, 1957; Ambush at North Platte, 1957; The River Flows West, 1957; If They Want Me Dead (as Peter Bannon), 1958; If I Should Die (as Peter Bannon), 1958; Kansas Guns, 1958; Dead Man's Range, 1958; The Gun Doctor, 1959; Johnny Nation, 1960; Whisper Murder Softly (as Peter Bannon), 1963; Backlash, 1967; Badge of Infamy, 1968; Intended Treason: What Really Happened to the Gunpowder

Plot, 1970; A Roomful of Shadows (autobiog.), 1975; The Florentine Table, 1980; Paradiso Country, 1985.

DUVAL, Jeanne (see Coffman, Virginia Edith)

DUY, Nguyen; Vietnamese poet, writer and dramatist; b. 12 Dec. 1948, Dong Ve, Thanh Hoa. *Education:* Univ. of Hanoi. *Career:* served as militia squad leader defending Ham Rong-Thanh Hoa 1965–67; staff mem., Van Nghe Giai Phong (Liberation Literature and Arts) newspaper 1967–77; representative of Van Nghe (Literature and Arts) in the South 1977–. *Publications:* ten poetry collections incl.: Anh trang (Moonlight), Qua Tang (The Gift), Ve (Returning), Distant Road: Selected Poems 1999; also three memoir collections, one novel. *Honours:* Van Nghe Poetry Prize 1973, Viet Nam Writers' Association Poetry Prize 1985. *Address:* c/o Van Nghe, 17 Tran Quoc Toan, Hanoi, Viet Nam.

DWORKIN, Ronald Myles, FBA; American legal scholar, philosopher and writer; *Professor of Law, New York University*; b. 11 Dec. 1931, s. of David Dworkin and Madeline Talamo; m. Betsy Celia Ross 1958 (died 2000); one s. one d. *Education:* Harvard Coll., Oxford Univ., UK, Harvard Law School. *Career:* Legal Sec. to Judge Learned Hand 1957–58; Assoc., Sullivan & Cromwell, New York 1958–62; Assoc. Prof. of Law, Yale Law School 1962–65, Prof. 1965–68, Wesley N. Hohfeld Prof. of Jurisprudence 1968–69; Prof. of Jurisprudence, Oxford Univ. 1969–98, now Emer., Fellow Univ. Coll. 1969–98, now Emer.; Quain Prof. of Jurisprudence, Univ. Coll., London 1998–2004, Bentham Prof. of Law and Philosophy 2004–; Visiting Prof. of Philosophy, Princeton Univ. 1974–75; Prof. of Law, New York Univ. Law School 1975–; Prof.-at-Large, Cornell Univ. 1976–80; Visiting Prof. of Philosophy and Law, Harvard Univ. 1977, of Philosophy 1979–82; mem. Council, Writers and Scholars Educational Trust 1982–, Programme Cttee, Ditchley Foundation 1982–; Co-Chair. US Democratic Party Abroad 1972–76; Fellow American Acad. of Arts and Sciences 1979. *Publications:* Taking Rights Seriously 1977, The Philosophy of Law (Ed.) 1977, A Matter of Principle 1985, Law's Empire 1986, Philosophical Issues in Senile Dementia 1987, A Bill of Rights for Britain 1990, Life's Dominion 1993, Freedom's Law 1996, Sovereign Virtue 2000, Justice in Robes 2006; articles in legal and philosophical journals. *Honours:* Hon. Queen's Counsel; Hon. LLD (Williams Coll.) 1981, (John Jay Coll. of Criminal Justice) 1983, (Claremont Coll.) 1987, (Kalamazoo Coll.) 1987. *Address:* New York University School of Law, 4111 Vanderbilt Hall, 40 Washington Square South, New York, NY 10012, USA (office); 17 Chester Row, London, SW1W 9JF, England. *Telephone:* (212) 998-6248 (office). *Fax:* (212) 995-4526 (office). *E-mail:* ronald.dworkin@nyu.edu (office). *Website:* www.nyu.edu/gsas/dept/philo/faculty/dworkin (office).

DWYER, Deanna (see Koontz, Dean Ray)

DWYER, K. R. (see Koontz, Dean Ray)

DYBEK, Stuart, BS, MA, MFA; American poet, writer and academic; *Professor of English, Western Michigan University*; b. 10 April 1942, Chicago, Ill.; m. Caren Bassett 1966; one s. one d. *Education:* Loyola Univ., Univ. of Iowa. *Career:* teaching asst, Univ. of Iowa 1970–72, Teaching and Writing Fellow 1972–73; Prof. of English, Western Michigan Univ. 1973–; Guest Writer and Teacher, Michigan Council for the Arts' Writer in the Schools Program 1973–92; Faculty, Warren Wilson MFA Program in Creative Writing 1985–89; Visiting Prof. of Creative Writing, Princeton Univ. 1990, Univ. of California, Irvine 1995; Univ. of Iowa Writers' Workshop 1998; Writer-in-Residence, Northwestern Univ. 2001–02; numerous readings, lectures and workshops. *Publications:* Brass Knuckles (poems) 1979, Childhood and Other Neighbourhoods (short stories) 1980, The Coast of Chicago (short stories) 1990, The Story of Mist (short stories and prose poems) 1994, I Sailed with Magellan (novel) 2003, Streets in Their Own Ink (poems); contrib. to many anthologies and magazines. *Honours:* Soc. of Midwest Authors Award for Fiction 1981, 2004, Friends of American Literature Cliffdwellers Award for Fiction 1981, special citation PEN/Hemingway Prize Cttee 1981, Michigan Council for the Arts grants 1981, 1992, Guggenheim Fellowship 1982, Nat. Endowment for the Arts Fellowships 1982, 1994, Pushcart Prize 1985, O. Henry Prize 1985, Nelson Algren Prize 1985, Whiting Writers Award 1985, Arts Foundation of Michigan Arts Award 1986, American Acad. of Arts and Letters Award for Fiction 1994, PEN/Malamud Award 1995, Rockefeller Residency, Bellagio, Italy 1996, Lannan Writers Award 1998, Soc. of Midland Authors Award in Fiction 2003. *Address:* 320 Monroe, Kalamazoo, MI 49006, USA. *E-mail:* sdybek@earthlink.net.

DYER, Charles; British playwright, actor and director; b. 17 July 1928, Shrewsbury, England; m. Fiona 1960; three s. *Career:* acted in 250 plays. *Plays as writer:* Time, Murderer, Please 1956, Wanted – One Body! 1956, Prelude to Fury 1959, Red Cabbage and Kings 1960, Rattle of a Simple Man (also dir, Garrick, London, Booth Theatre, Broadway) 1962, Staircase (also dir, RSC, Aldwych, London, Biltmore Theatre, Broadway) 1966, Mother Adam (also dir, Royal Shakespeare Theatre, Stratford-upon-Avon, Arts Theatre, London) 1971, A Hot Godly Wind 1973, Futility Rites 1980, Lovers Dancing (Albery Theatre, London) 1982. *Film appearances:* The Loneliness of the Long-Distance Runner 1962, Rattle of a Simple Man 1964, The Knack 1965, How I Won the War 1967. *Film screenplays:* Rattle of a Simple Man 1964, Staircase 1969. *Publications:* Turtle in the Soup 1948, Who On Earth 1950, Poison in Jest 1952, Jovial Parasite 1955, Red Cabbage and Kings 1958, Rattle

of a Simple Man (novel, play) 1962, Staircase (novel, play) 1966, Mother Adam 1970, Lovers Dancing 1982; Those Old Trombones (autobiographical novel) 2006. *Address:* Old Wob, Gerrards Cross, Buckinghamshire SL9 8SF, England.

DYER, Geoff; British writer; b. 5 June 1958, Cheltenham, England. *Education:* Corpus Christi Coll., Oxford. *Publications:* Ways of Telling (criticism) 1986, The Colour of Memory (novel) 1989, But Beautiful (novel) 1991, The Search (novel) 1993, The Missing of the Somme (non-fiction) 1994, Out of Sheer Rage (literary essay) 1997, Paris Trance (novel) 1998, Anglo-English Attitudes (essays) 1999, Yoga for People Who Can't be Bothered to Do It (essays) 2003, The Ongoing Moment (non-fiction) 2005; contrib. to Granta, LA Weekly, Nerve, The Observer. *Honours:* Somerset Maugham Prize 1992. *Address:* c/o Little, Brown, Brettenham House, Lancaster Place, London, WC2E 7EN, England.

DYER, James Frederick, MA; British writer; b. 23 Feb. 1934, Luton, England. *Education:* Leicester Univ. *Career:* writer on archaeology and local history; Ed. Shire Archaeology 1974–; mem. Soc. of Authors, Royal Archaeological Inst., Soc. of Antiquaries. *Publications:* Southern England: An Archaeological Guide 1973, Penguin Guide to Prehistoric England and Wales 1981, Discovering Archaeology in England and Wales 1985, Discovering Prehistoric England 1993, Ancient Britain 1995, The Stopsley Book 1998, The Stopsley Picture Book 1999, Rhubarb and Custard: The History of Luton Modern School 2004. *Honours:* Hon. DArts (Univ. of Luton) 1999. *Address:* 6 Rogate Road, Luton, Bedfordshire LU2 8HR, England (home). *Telephone:* (1582) 724808 (home).

DYSON, Anthony Edward, MA, MLitt; British writer; b. 28 Nov. 1928, London, England. *Education:* Pembroke College, Cambridge. *Career:* Lecturer, University College of Wales, Bangor 1955–63. Co-Founder, Dir, Critical Quarterly Society, 1960–84; Visiting Prof., Concordia University, Montréal, Canada, 1967, 1969, University of Connecticut, USA, 1976; General Ed., Macmillan Casebooks, England, 1968–; Dir, Norwich Tapes Ltd, England, 1979–; Hon. Fellow, former Reader in English, University of East Anglia, Norwich, 1963–1982. *Publications:* Modern Poetry (with C. B. Cox), 1963; The Crazy Fabric: Essays in Irony, 1965; The Practical Criticism of Poetry (with C. B. Cox), 1965; Modern Judgements on Dickens, 1968; Word in the Desert (with C. B. Cox), 1968; Casebook on Bleak House, 1969; Black Papers on Education, 3 vols, 1969–70; The Inimitable Dickens, 1970; Between Two Worlds: Aspects of Literary Form, 1972; Twentieth Century Mind (with C. B. Cox), 3 vols, 1972; English Poetry: Select Bibliographical Guides, 1973; English Novel: Select Bibliographical Guides, 1974; Casebook on Paradise Lost (with Julian Lovelock), 1974; Education and Democracy (with Julian Lovelock), 1975; Yeats, Eliot and R. S. Thomas: Riding the Echo, 1981; Poetry Criticism and Practice, 1986; Thom Gunn, Ted Hughes and R. S. Thomas, 1990; The Fifth Dimension, 1996. Contributions: numerous journals. *Address:* c/o Macmillan Publishers, Hampshire RG21 2XS, England.

DYSON, Freeman John, FRS; American physicist and academic; *Professor Emeritus of Physics, Institute for Advanced Study*; b. 15 Dec. 1923, Crowthorne, England; s. of late Sir George Dyson and Lady Mildred (Atkey) Dyson; m. 1st Verena Huber 1950 (divorced 1958); m. 2nd Imme Jung 1958; one s. five d. *Education:* Cambridge and Cornell Univs. *Career:* Fellow of Trinity Coll., Cambridge 1946; Warren Research Fellow, Birmingham Univ. 1949; Prof. of Physics, Cornell Univ. 1951–53; Prof., Inst. for Advanced Study, Princeton 1953–94, Prof. Emer. 1994–; Chair. Fed. of American Scientists 1962; mem. NAS 1964–; Foreign Assoc. Acad. des Sciences, Paris 1989. *Publications:* Disturbing the Universe 1979, Weapons and Hope 1984, Origins of Life 1986, Infinite in All Directions 1988, From Eros to Gaia 1992, Imagined Worlds 1997, The Sun, The Genome and the Internet 1999, The Scientist as Rebel 2006, A Many-colored Glass 2006; papers in The Physical Review, Journal of Mathematical Physics, etc. *Honours:* Hon. DSc (City Univ., UK) 1981 (Oxford) 1997; Gifford Lecturer, Aberdeen 1985; Heineman Prize, American Inst. of Physics 1965, Lorentz Medal, Royal Netherlands Acad. 1966, Hughes Medal, Royal Soc. 1968, Max Planck Medal, German Physical Soc. 1969, Harvey Prize, Israel Inst. of Tech. 1977, Wolf Prize (Israel) 1981, Matteucci Medal, Rome 1990, Fermi Award (USA) 1994, Templeton Prize 2000. *Address:* Institute for Advanced Study, Princeton, NJ 08540 (office); 105 Battle Road Circle, Princeton, NJ 08540, USA. *Telephone:* (609) 734-8055 (office). *Fax:* (609) 951-4489 (office). *E-mail:* dyson@ias.edu (office). *Website:* www.sns.ias.edu/~dyson (office).

DZHAGAROV, Georgi; Bulgarian poet, playwright and politician; b. 1925, Byala, Sliven. *Education:* Maxim Gorky Literary Inst., Moscow. *Career:* Vice-Pres. State Council 1971–89; mem. Union of Bulgarian Writers (chair. 1966–72). *Plays include:* Prokurorat (The Public Prosecutor) 1964, Slanchev udar 1977. *Publications:* Moite Pesni (My Songs) 1954, Lirika (Lyrics) 1956, V minuti na mulchanie (During Moments of Silence) 1969, Stikhotvoreniya (Poems) 1969, Izpoved (Confession) 1984, Ptitsi sreshtu vyatura (Birds Against the Wind) 1985. *Honours:* Académie Française special prize for world poetry 1982. *Address:* c/o Sajuz na Balgarskite Pisateli, ul. A. Kancev 5, 1040 Sofia, Bulgaria.

E

EADY, F. R. (see Kerner, Fred)

EAGLETON, Terence (Terry) Francis, PhD, FBA; British academic; *John Edward Taylor Professor of English Literature, University of Manchester*; b. 22 Feb. 1943, Salford, Lancs.; s. of Francis Paul Eagleton and Rosaleen Riley; m. 1st Elizabeth Rosemary Galpin 1966 (divorced 1976); two s.; m. 2nd Willa Murphy 1996; one s. one d. *Education:* Trinity Coll., Cambridge. *Career:* Fellow in English, Jesus Coll., Cambridge 1964–69; Tutorial Fellow, Wadham Coll., Oxford 1969–89; Lecturer in Critical Theory and Fellow of Linacre Coll., Oxford 1989–92; Thomas Warton Prof. of English Literature and Fellow of St Catherine's Coll., Oxford 1992–2001; fmr Prof. of Cultural Theory, Univ. of Manchester, currently John Edward Taylor Prof. of English Literature. *Film:* screenplay for Wittgenstein. *Plays:* St Oscar 1989, Disappearances 1998. *Publications:* Criticism and Ideology 1976, Marxism and Literary Criticism 1976, Literary Theory: an Introduction 1983, The Function of Criticism 1984, The Rape of Clarissa 1985, Against the Grain 1986, William Shakespeare 1986, The Ideology of the Aesthetic 1990, Ideology: An Introduction 1993, The Crisis of Contemporary Culture 1993, Heathcliff and the Great Hunger 1995, The Illusions of Postmodernism 1996, Literary Theory 1996, Crazy John and the Bishop and Other Essays on Irish Culture 1998, Scholars and Rebels in Ireland 1999, The Idea of Culture 2000, The Gatekeeper (autobiog.) 2001, Sweet Violence: The Idea of the Tragic 2002, Figures of Dissent (essays) 2003, After Theory 2003, The English Novel: An Introduction 2004, Holy Terror 2005, The Meaning of Life 2007; contribs to periodicals incl. London Review of Books. *Honours:* Hon. DLitt (Salford) 1994; Dr hc (Nat. Univ. of Ireland) 1995, (Santiago di Compostela) 1997; Irish Sunday Tribune Arts Award 1990. *Address:* Department of English and American Studies, University of Manchester, Manchester, M13 9PL, England (office). *Telephone:* (161) 275-3146 (office). *Fax:* (161) 275-3256 (office). *E-mail:* english@man.ac.uk (office). *Website:* www.art.man.ac.uk/english (office).

EARLEY, Tony, BA, MFA; American writer; *Samuel Milton Fleming Chair in English, Vanderbilt University*; b. 1961, San Antonio, TX; m. Sarah Earley. *Education:* Warren Wilson Coll., Univ. of Alabama at Tuscaloosa. *Career:* fmrly reporter The Thermal Belt News Journal, Columbus, sports ed. and features writer The Daily Courier, Forest City; fmr instructor, Carnegie-Mellon Univ., Univ. of Alabama; Asst Prof., Vanderbilt Univ. 1997–, now Samuel Milton Fleming Chair in English. *Publications:* Charlotte (short story, in Harper's) 1992, The Prophet from Jupiter (short story, in Harper's) 1993, Here We Are in Paradise (short story collection) 1994, Jim the Boy (novel) 2000, Somehow Form a Family: Stories That are Mostly True (essays) 2001; contrib. to journals, including The New Yorker, Harper's, Esquire, and anthologies, including Best American Short Stories. *Honours:* PEN Syndicated Fiction Award 1993, Granta Best of Young American Novelists citation 1996. *Address:* c/o English Department, Vanderbilt University, 413 Benson Hall, Nashville, TN 37235, USA. *E-mail:* tony.l.earley@vanderbilt.edu.

EARLS, Nick, MBBS; Australian writer, editor and physician; b. 8 Oct. 1963, Newtownards, Northern Ireland; m. Sarah Garvey 1991. *Education:* Univ. of Queensland. *Career:* medical practitioner, Brisbane, Qld, Australia 1987–94; freelance writer 1988–; continuing Medical Education Ed., Medical Observer, Qld 1994–. *Publications:* Passion (short stories) 1992, After January (young adult novel) (3M Talking Book of the Year Award, Young People's Category 1996, CBE-International Youth Library Notable Book, Munich 1997) 1996, Zigzag Street (novel) 1996; contrib. short fiction to anthologies, including Nightmares in Paradise. *E-mail:* nickearls@mpx.com.au. *Website:* www .nickearls.com.

EARLY, Gerald; American academic, writer and poet; b. 21 April 1952, Philadelphia, PA; m. Ida Haynes 1977; two d. *Education:* BA cum laude, English, University of Pennsylvania, 1974; MA, English, 1980, PhD, English, 1982, Cornell University. *Publications:* Tuxedo Junction: Essays on American Culture, 1990; My Soul's High Song, 1991; Lure and Loathing, 1993; Daughters: One Family and Fatherhood, 1994; Culture of Bruising, 1994; How the War in the Streets is Won, 1995. *Contributions:* Essays, reviews and poetry to many journals including: American Poetry Review; Northwest Review; Tar River Poetry; Raccoon; Seneca Review; Obsidian ll; Black American Literature Forum. *Honours:* Whiting Foundation Writers' Award, 1988; CCLM-General Electric Foundation Award for Younger Writers, 1988; several Fellowships. *Address:* Washington University, Campus Box 1109, One Brookings Drive, St Louis, MO 63130, USA.

EASTAUGH, Kenneth; British critic and writer; b. 30 Jan. 1929, Preston, England. *Career:* television critic, 1965–67, show business writer, 1967–70, Daily Mirror, London; Chief Show Business Writer, The Sun, London, 1970–73; TV Columnist, The Times, London, 1977; Film Critic, Prima Magazine, 1976–; Music Critic, Classical Music Weekly, 1976–; Chief Show Business Exec., Daily Star, London, 1978–83. *Publications:* The Event (television play), 1968; Better Than a Man (television play), 1970; Dapple Downs (radio serial), 1973–74; Awkward Cuss (play), 1976; Havergal Brian: The Making of a Composer (biog.), 1976; Coronation Street (television series), 1977–78; The Carry On Book (cinema), 1978; Havergal Who? (television documentary), 1980; Mr Love (novel, screenplay), 1986; Dallas (television serial), 1989; Embers (play), 1998; The New Carry On Book, 1998. *Literary*

Agent: Curtis Brown Ltd, Haymarket House, 28–29 Haymarket, London, SW1Y 4SP, England. *Telephone:* (20) 7393-4400. *Fax:* (20) 7393-4401. *E-mail:* info@curtisbrown.co.uk. *Website:* www.curtisbrown.co.uk.

EASTHOPE, Antony Kelynge Revington, BA, MA, MLitt; British academic and writer; b. 14 April 1939, Portsmouth, England; m. Diane Garside 1972; one s. two d. *Education:* Christ's Coll., Cambridge. *Career:* Brown Univ., RI, USA 1964–66; Warwick Univ., England 1967–68; Manchester Metropolitan Univ. 1969–. *Publications:* Poetry as Discourse, 1983; What a Man's Gotta Do, 1986; British Post-Structuralism, 1988; Poetry and Phantasy, 1989; Literary into Cultural Studies, 1991; Wordsworth, Now and Then, 1993; Englishness and National Culture, 1999. Contributions: numerous magazines and journals. *Honours:* Charter Fellow, Wolfson College, Oxford, 1985–86; Visiting Fellow, University of Virginia, 1990. *Address:* 27 Victoria Ave, Didsbury, Manchester M20 8QX, England.

EASTON, Robert Olney, BS, MA; American writer; b. 4 July 1915, San Francisco, CA; m. Jane Faust 1940, four d. *Education:* Stanford University, Harvard University, University of California. *Publications:* The Happy Man, 1943; Lord of Beasts (co-author), 1961; The Book of the American West (co-author), 1963; The Hearing, 1964; Californian Condor (co-author), 1964; Max Brand, 1970; Black Tide, 1972; This Promised Land, 1982; China Caravans, 1982; Life and Work (co-author), 1988; Power and Glory, 1989; Love and War (co-author), 1991. Contributions: Magazines.

EATON, Charles Edward, BA, MA; American poet and writer; b. 25 June 1916, Winston-Salem, NC; m. Isabel Patterson 1950. *Education:* Duke University, University of North Carolina at Chapel Hill, Princeton University, Harvard University. *Career:* Instructor in Creative Writing, University of Missouri, 1940–42; Vice-Consul, American Embassy, Rio de Janeiro, 1942–46; Prof. of Creative Writing, University of North Carolina, 1946–52; mem. American Acad. of Poets. *Publications:* Poetry: The Bright Plain, 1942; The Shadow of the Swimmer, 1951; The Greenhouse in the Garden, 1956; Countermoves, 1963; On the Edge of the Knife, 1970; The Man in the Green Chair, 1977; Colophon of the Rover, 1980; The Thing King, 1983; The Work of the Wrench, 1985; New and Selected Poems 1942–1987, 1987; A Guest on Mild Evenings, 1991; The Country of the Blue, 1994; The Fox and I, 1996; The Scout in Summer, 1999; The Jogger by the Sea, 2000; Between the Devil and the Deep Blue Sea, 2003. Fiction: A Lady of Pleasure, 1993. Short Stories: Write Me From Rio, 1959; The Girl From Ipanema, 1972; The Case of the Missing Photographs, 1978; New and Selected Stories 1959–1989, 1989. Other: The Man From Buena Vista, New and Selected Non-Fiction, 2001. Contributions: Magazines and journals. *Honours:* Bread Loaf Writers' Conference Robert Frost Fellowship, 1941; Ridgely Torrence Memorial Award, 1951; Gertrude Boatwright Harris Award, 1955; Arizona Quarterly Awards, 1956, 1975, 1977, 1979, 1982; Roanoke-Chowan Awards, 1970, 1987, 1991; Oscar Arnold Young Award, 1971; O. Henry Award, 1972; Alice Faye di Castagnola Award, 1974; Arvon Foundation Award, 1980; Hollins Critic Award, 1984; Brockman Awards, 1984, 1986; Kansas Quarterly Awards, 1987; North Carolina Literature Award, 1988; Fortner Award, 1993; Hon. DLitt, St Andrews College, NC, 1998.

EATWELL, Baron (Life Peer), cr. 1992, of Stratton St Margaret in the County of Wiltshire; **John Leonard Eatwell,** PhD; British academic; *Professor of Financial Policy, University of Cambridge*; b. 2 Feb. 1945, s. of Harold Jack Eatwell and Mary Eatwell; m. Hélène Seppain 1970 (divorced); two s. one d. *Education:* Headlands Grammar School, Swindon, Queens' Coll. Cambridge, Harvard Univ., USA. *Career:* Teaching Fellow, Grad. School of Arts and Sciences, Harvard Univ. 1968–69; Research Fellow, Queens' Coll. Cambridge 1969–70; Fellow, Trinity Coll. Cambridge 1970–96, Asst Lecturer, Faculty of Econs and Politics, Cambridge Univ. 1975–77, Lecturer 1977, currently Prof. of Financial Policy, Pres. Queens' Coll. 1997–; Visiting Prof. of Econs, New School for Social Research, New York 1982–96; Econ. Adviser to Neil Kinnock, Leader of Labour Party 1985–92; Opposition Spokesman on Treasury Affairs and on Trade and Industry, House of Lords 1992–93, Prin. Opposition Spokesman on Treasury and Econ. Affairs 1993–97; Trustee Inst. for Public Policy Research 1988–95, Sec. 1988–97, Chair. 1997–; Dir (non-exec.) Anglia TV Group 1994–2001, Cambridge Econometrics Ltd 1996–; Chair. Extemporary Dance Theatre 1990, Crusaid 1993–98, British Screen Finance Ltd 1997–2000 and assoc. cos; Gov. Contemporary Dance Trust 1991–95; Dir Arts Theatre Trust, Cambridge 1991–98, Bd, Securities and Futures Authority 1997–; mem. Bd Royal Opera House 1998–; Chair. Royal Ballet 1998–2001, Commercial Radio Cos Asscn 2000–04, British Library Bd 2001–; mem. Regulatory Decisions Cttee, FSA 2001–05; Dir Cambridge Endowment for Research in Finance 2002–; Gov. Royal Ballet School 2003–; Dir (non-exec.) Rontech Ltd 2003–. *Publications:* An Introduction to Modern Economics (with Joan Robinson) 1973, Whatever Happened to Britain? 1982, Keynes's Economics and the Theory of Value and Distribution (ed. with Murray Milgate) 1983, The New Palgrave: A Dictionary of Economics, 4 Vols 1987, The New Palgrave Dictionary of Money and Finance, 3 Vols 1992 (both with Murray Milgate and Peter Newman), Transformation and Integration: Shaping the Future of Central and Eastern Europe (jtly) 1995, Global Unemployment: Loss of Jobs in the '90s (ed.) 1996, Not "Just Another Accession": The Political Economy of EU Enlargement to the East (jtly) 1997,

Global Finance at Risk: Case for International Regulation (with L. Taylor) 2000, Hard Budgets, Soft States 2000, Social Policy Choices in Central and Eastern Europe 2002, International Capital Markets (with L. Taylor) 2002; articles in scientific journals. *Address:* The President's Lodge, Queens' College, Cambridge, CB3 9ET, England. *Telephone:* (1223) 335556. *Fax:* (1223) 335555. *E-mail:* president@quns.cam.ac.uk (office).

EAVES, Will; British writer and editor; *Arts Editor, The Times Literary Supplement*; b. 1967, Bath. *Education:* King's Coll., Cambridge. *Career:* currently Arts Ed. The Times Literary Supplement. *Publications:* The Oversight (novel) 2001, Nothing To Be Afraid Of (novel) 2005, Small Hours (poems) 2006. *Address:* The Times Literary Supplement, Times House, 1 Pennington Street, London, E9B 1BS, England. *Website:* www.the-tls.co.uk.

EBADI, Shirin; Iranian lawyer, human rights activist and academic; b. 1947, Hamadan; d. of Mohammad Ali Ebadi; m.; two d. *Education:* Univ. of Tehran. *Career:* apptd Judge (first and only woman) and Pres. of Tehran City Court 1974, forced to step down from bench after 1979 revolution, retd 1984; currently runs own law practice, specializing in human rights; arrested on charges of "disturbing public opinion" 2000, received suspended sentence Sept. 2000; mem. Cttee for the Defence of Rights of the Victims of Serial Murders; Founder Asscn for Support of Children's Rights in Iran, Centre for Defence of Human Rights; Lecturer in Law, Univ. of Tehran. *Publications include:* The Rights of the Child: A Study of Legal Aspects of Children's Rights in Iran 1994, History and Documentation of Human Rights in Iran 2000, Iran Awakening 2006; numerous other books and journal articles. *Honours:* Hon. LLD (Brown Univ.) 2004, (Univ. of British Columbia) 2004; Dr hc (Univ. of Maryland, College Park) 2004, (Univ. of Toronto) 2004, (Simon Fraser Univ.) 2004, (Univ. of Akureyri) 2004, (Australian Catholic Univ.) 2005, (Univ. of San Francisco) 2005, (Concordia Univ.) 2005, (Univ. of York) 2005, (Université Jean Moulin, Lyon) 2005; Human Rights Watch Award 1996, Rafto Prize 2001, Nobel Peace Prize (first Iranian and first Muslim woman) 2003, International Democracy Award 2004, Lawyer of the Year Award 2004, ranked 99th by Forbes magazine amongst 100 Most Powerful Women 2004, UCI Citizen Peacebuilding Award 2005, The Golden Plate Award, Academy of Achievement 2005. *Address:* c/o University of Tehran, Enghelab Avenue, Tehran 14174, Iran. *Website:* www.shirinebadi.ir.

EBERT, Alan, BA, MA; American author; b. 14 Sept. 1935, New York, NY. *Education:* Brooklyn College, CUNY, Fordham University. *Career:* mem. American Society of Journalists and Authors. *Publications:* The Homosexuals, 1977; Every Body is Beautiful (with Ron Fletcher), 1978; Intimacies, 1979; Traditions (novel), 1981; The Long Way Home (novel), 1984; Marriages (novel), 1987. Contributions: Family Circle; Essence; Look; Us; Good Housekeeping.

EBERT, Roger Joseph, BS; American film critic, writer and lecturer; b. 18 June 1942, Urbana, IL; m. Chaz Hammelsmith 1992. *Education:* University of Illinois, University of Cape Town, University of Chicago. *Career:* Reporter, News Gazette, Champaign-Urbana, IL, 1958–66; Instructor, Chicago City College, 1967–68; Film Critic, Chicago Sun-Times, 1967–, US Magazine, 1978–79, WMAQ-TV, Chicago, 1980–83, WLS-TV, Chicago, 1984–, New York Post, 1986–88, New York Daily News, 1988–92, Compu Serve, 1991–, Microsoft Cinemania, 1994–97; Lecturer, University of Chicago, 1969–; Co-Host, Sneak Previews, WTTW-TV, Chicago, 1977–82; At the Movies, syndicated television programme, 1982–86; Siskel and Ebert, syndicated television programme, 1986–99; Ebert and Roeper and the Movies, syndicated television programme, 1999–; mem. Acad. of London; American Newspaper Guild; National Society of Film Critics; Writers' Guild of America. *Publications:* An Illini Century, 1967; A Kiss is Still a Kiss, 1984; Roger Ebert's Movie Home Companion (annual vols), 1986–93, subsequently Roger Ebert's Video Companion, 1994–98; The Perfect London Walk (with Daniel Curley), 1986; Two Weeks in the Midday Sun: A Cannes Notebook, 1987; The Future of the Movies: Interviews with Martin Scorsese, Steven Spielberg, and George Lucas (with Gene Siskel), 1991; Behind the Phantom's Mask, 1993; Ebert's Little Movie Glossary, 1994; The Future of the Movies: The Computer Insectiary (co-author), 1994; Roger Ebert's Book of Film, 1996; Questions for the Movie Answer Man, 1997; Roger Ebert's Movie Yearbook, 1998–; Ebert's Bigger Little Movie Glossary, 1999; I Hated, Hated, Hated This Movie, 2000. Contributions: newspapers and magazines. *Honours:* Overseas Press Club Award, 1963; Rotary Fellow, 1965; Pulitzer Prize for Criticism, 1975; Chicago Emmy Award, 1979; Hon. Doctorate, University of Colorado, 1993; Kluge Fellow in Film Studies, University of Virginia, 1995–96.

EBERT, Tibor, BA; Hungarian writer, poet and dramatist; b. 14 Oct. 1926, Bratislava, Czechoslovakia; m. Eva Gati 1968; one d. *Education:* Ferenc Liszt Acad. of Music, Eötvös Lórand Univ., Budapest. *Career:* Dramaturg József Attila Theatre, Budapest 1984–85; Ed.-in-Chief Agora Publrs, Budapest 1989–92; Ed. Hirvivo Literary Magazine 1990–92; mem. PEN Club, Asscn of Hungarian Writers, Literary Asscn Berzsenyi. *Plays:* Les Escaliers, Musique de Chambre, Demosthenes, Esterhaźy, Bartók, Attila, Le Rout Casimir et Olivier, Le Tableau. *Publications:* Mikrodrámák 1971, Rosarium 1987, Kobayashi 1989, Legenda egy fúvószenekarról 1990, Jób könyve 1991, Fagyott Orpheusz (poems) 1993, Esö 1996, Egy város glóriája 1997, Bartók 1997, Eredök 1998, Éltem 1998, Drámák 2000, Bolyongás 2001, Vecseruye 2001, Kaleidoszkóp 2002, Álmomban 2002, Feljegyzcsék 2004, Tüzfalau 2006, Vár 2006; contrib. numerous short stories, poems, dramas and essays to several leading Hungarian literary journals and magazines. *Honours:* Hon. mem. Franco-Hungarian Soc. 1980–; Order of Hungarian Republic 1996; Bartók Prize 1987, Commemorative Medal, City of Pozsony-Pressburg-Bratislava 1991, Esterházy Prize 1993. *Address:* Csévi u 15c, 1025 Budapest, Hungary.

ECHENOZ, Jean Maurice Emmanuel; French writer; b. 26 Dec. 1947, Orange, Vaucluse; s. of Marc Echenoz and Annie Languin; one s. *Education:* Univ. of Aix-en-Provence, Sorbonne and Univ. of Paris. *Career:* professional writer 1979–. *Publications:* Le Méridien de Greenwich (Prix Fénéon 1980) 1979, Cherokee (Prix Médicis Étranger) 1983, L'Equipée malaise (trans. as Double Jeopardy) 1986, L'Occupation des sols 1988, Lac (Grand Prix du Roman de la Société des Gens de Lettres 1990, European Literature Prize, Glasgow 1990) 1989, Nous trois 1992, Les Grandes blondes (trans. as Big Blondes) (Prix Novembre) 1995, Un An 1997, Je m'en vais (trans. as I'm Gone) (Prix Goncourt) 1999, Jérôme Lindon 2001, Samuel (trans. of bible, jtly) 2001, Au piano (trans. as Piano) 2003. *Honours:* Prix Georges Sadoul 1980, Prix Fénéon 1980, Prix Médicis 1983, Grand Prix Soc. des gens et lettres 1990, European Literature Prize, Glasgow 1990, Prix Novembre 1995, Grand Prix du roman de la Ville de Paris 1997, Prix Goncourt 1999. *Address:* c/o Editions de Minuit, 7 rue Bernard-Palissy, 75006 Paris, France.

ECO, Umberto, PhD; Italian writer and academic; *Professor, University of Bologna*; b. 5 Jan. 1932, Alessandria, Piedmont; s. of Giulio Eco and Giovanna Bisio; m. Renate Ramge 1962; one s. one d. *Education:* Liceo Plana, Alessandria, Univ. degli Studi, Turin. *Career:* cultural ed. Italian TV (RAI), Milan 1954–59; mil. service 1958–59; Sr Non-fiction Ed., Bompiani, Milan 1959–75; Asst Lecturer in Aesthetics, Univ. of Turin 1956–63, Lecturer 1963–64; Lecturer, Faculty of Architecture, Univ. of Milan 1964–65; Prof. of Visual Communications, Univ. of Florence 1966–69; Prof. of Semiotics, Milan Polytechnic 1970–71; Assoc. Prof. of Semiotics, Univ. of Bologna 1971–75, Prof. 1975–, Dir Inst. of Communications Disciplines 1993–, f. School of Arts 2000; Visiting Prof. New York Univ. 1969–70, 1976, Northwestern Univ. 1972, Yale Univ. 1977, 1980, 1981, Columbia Univ. 1978, 1984; Columnist on L'Espresso 1965; Ed. VS 1971–; mem. Academia Europaea 1998–. *Publications:* Il Problema Estetico in San Tommaso (trans. as The Aesthetics of Thomas Aquinas) 1956, Sviluppo dell'Estetica Medioevale (trans. as Art and Beauty in the Middle Ages) 1959, Opera Aperta 1962, Diario Minimo 1963, Apocalittici e Integrati 1964, L'Oeuvre Ouverte 1965, La Struttura Assente 1968, Il Costume di Casa 1973, Trattato di Semiotica Generale 1975, A Theory of Semiotics 1976, The Role of the Reader 1979, Il Nome della Rosa (novel, trans. as The Name of the Rose) 1981, Semiotics and the Philosophy of Language 1984, Sette anni di desiderio 1977–83 1984, Faith in Fakes 1986, Il pendolo di Foucault 1988, The Open Work 1989, The Limits of Interpretation 1990, Misreadings 1993, How to Travel with a Salmon and Other Essays 1994, L'isola del giorno prima (novel, trans. as The Island of the Day Before) 1995, The Search for the Perfect Language 1995, Serendipities 1997, Kant and the Platypus 1999, Baudolino (novel) 2000, Experiences in Translation 2000, Five Moral Pieces 2001, Mouse or Rat?: Translation as Negotiation 2003, On Beauty: A History of a Western Idea (ed.) 2004, The Mysterious Flame of Queen Loana 2005, Turning Back the Clock: Hot Wars and Media Populism (essays) 2007. *Honours:* Chevalier de la Légion d'honneur, Ordre pour le Mérite, Cavaliere di Gran Croce (Italy); Hon. DLitt (Glasgow) 1990, (Kent) 1992 and numerous other hon. degrees; Medici Prize 1982, McLuhan Teleglobe Prize 1985, Crystal Award (World Econ. Forum) 2000; Prince of Asturias Prize for Communication and the Humanities 2000. *Address:* Scuola Superiore Studi Umanistici, Via Marsala 26, Bologna, Italy. *Telephone:* (051) 2917111 (office). *E-mail:* sssub@dsc.unibo.it (office).

EDDINGS, David, BA, MA; American writer; b. 7 July 1931, Spokane, WA; m. Judith Leigh Schall 1962. *Education:* Reed Coll., Univ. of Washington, Seattle. *Career:* served in the US Army 1954–56; fmr sales clerk, Boeing Co.; fmr coll. English teacher. *Publications:* High Hunt 1973, Pawn of Prophecy 1982, Queen of Sorcery 1982, Magician's Gambit 1983, Castle of Wizardry 1984, Guardians of the West 1987, King of the Margos 1988, Demon Lord of Karanda 1988, The Diamond Throne 1989, The Sorceress of Darshiva 1989, The Ruby Knight 1990, The Seeress of Kell 1991, The Losers 1992, The Sapphire Rose 1992, Domes of Fire 1993, The Hidden City 1994, The Shining Ones 1994; with Leigh Eddings: Belgarath the Sorcerer 1995, Polgara the Sorceress 1997, The Rivan Codex 1998, The Redemption of Althalus 2000, Regina's Song 2002, The Elder Gods 2003, The Treasured One 2004, The Crystal Gorge 2005, The Younger Gods 2006. *Address:* c/o Ballantine Books Inc, 201 E 50th Street, New York, NY 10022, USA.

EDGAR, David Burman, BA; British writer; b. 26 Feb. 1948, Birmingham; s. of Barrie Edgar and Joan Edgar (née Burman); m. Eve Brook 1979 (died 1998); two step-s.; pnr Stephanie Dale. *Education:* Oundle School, Manchester Univ. *Career:* Fellow in Creative Writing, Leeds Polytechnic 1972–74; Resident Playwright, Birmingham Repertory Theatre 1974–75, Bd mem. 1985–; Lecturer in Playwriting, Univ. of Birmingham 1975–78, Dir of Playwriting Studies 1989–, Prof. 1995–99; Founder Writers' Union 1970s; UK/US Bicentennial Arts Fellow resident in USA 1978–79; Literary Consultant, RSC 1984–88; Fellow Birmingham Polytechnic 1991, Judith E. Wilson Fellow, Clare Hall, Cambridge 1996. *Plays:* Two Kinds of Angel 1970, Rent or Caught in the Act 1972, State of Emergency 1972, The Dunkirk Spirit 1974, Dick Deterred 1974, O Fair Jerusalem 1975, Saigon Rose 1976, Blood Sports 1976, Destiny (for RSC) 1976, Wreckers 1977, The Jail Diary of Albie Sachs (for RSC) 1978, Mary Barnes 1978–79, Teendreams 1979, The Adventures of Nicholas Nickleby (adaptation for RSC) 1980, Maydays (for RSC) 1983, Entertaining Strangers 1985, That Summer 1987, The Shape of the Table

1990, Dr Jekyll and Mr Hyde (adaptation for RSC) 1991, Pentecost 1994, Other Place 1994, Young Vic 1995, Albert Speer (adaptation for Nat. Theatre) 2000, The Prisoner's Dilemma 2001, Continental Divide 2003, Playing with Fire (Nat. Theatre, London) 2005. *TV Plays:* I Know What I Meant 1974, Baby Love 1974, Vote for Them 1989, Buying a Landslide 1992, Citizen Locke 1994. *Radio:* Ecclesiastes 1977, A Movie Starring Me 1991. *Film:* Lady Jane 1986. *Publications:* Destiny 1976, Wreckers 1977, Teendreams 1979, Maydays 1983, Plays One 1987, The Second Time as Farce 1988, Heartlanders 1989, Plays Two 1990, Plays Three 1991, Pentecost 1995, State of Play (ed.) 1999, Albert Speer 2000, The Prisoner's Dilemma 2001, Continental Divide 2004, Playing With Fire 2005. *Honours:* Hon. Sr Research Fellow, Univ. of Birmingham 1988–92, Hon. Prof. 1992–; Hon. MA (Bradford) 1986; DUniv (Surrey) 1993, (Birmingham) 2002; Soc. of West End Theatres Best Play Award 1980, Tony Award for Best Play 1981, Plays and Players Award for Best Play 1983, Evening Standard Award for Best Play 1995. *Literary Agent:* 6th Floor, Fairgrove House, New Oxford Street, London, WC1A 1HB, England. *Telephone:* (20) 7079-7990 (office). *Fax:* (20) 7079-7999 (office).

EDGECOMBE, Jean Marjorie, AM, BA; Australian writer; b. 28 Feb. 1914, Bathurst, NSW; d. of Edwin Ray and Katie Helen (née Hazlewood) Ray; m. Gordon Henry Edgecombe 1945; two d. two s. *Education:* Sydney Univ., Metropolitan Business Coll., Sydney. *Career:* mem. Australian Conservation Foundation, The Australian Museum Soc., Australian Soc. of Authors, Hornsby Shire Historical Soc., Nat. Trust of Australia (NSW), State Library of NSW Foundation, Wildlife Preservation Soc. Queensland, The Coast and Mountain Walkers of NSW. *Publications:* Discovering Lord Howe Island (with Isobel Bennett) 1978, Discovering Norfolk Island (with Isobel Bennett) 1983, Flinders Island, the Furneaux Group 1985, Flinders Island and Eastern Bass Strait 1986, Lord Howe Island, World Heritage Area 1987, Phillip Island and Western Port 1989, Norfolk Island, South Pacific: Island of History and Many Delights 1991, Discovering Flinders Island 1992, Discovering King Island, Western Bass Strait 1993; contrib. articles and poems to various publications. *Address:* 7 Oakleigh Avenue, Thornleigh, 2120 NSW, Australia.

EDRIC, Robert (see Armitage, Gary Edric)

EDSON, Russell; American poet and writer; b. 9 April 1935; m. Frances Edson. *Education:* Art Students' League, New York, New School for Social Research, New York, Columbia University, Black Mountain College, NC. *Publications:* poetry: Appearances: Fables and Drawings, 1961; A Stone is Nobody's: Fables and Drawings, 1964; The Boundary, 1964; The Very Thing That Happens: Fables and Drawings, 1964; The Brain Kitchen: Writings and Woodcuts, 1965; What a Man Can See, 1969; The Childhood of an Equestrian, 1973; The Calm Theatre, 1973; A Roof with Some Clouds Behind It, 1975; The Intuitive Journey and Other Works, 1976; The Reason Why the Closet-Man is Never Sad, 1977; Edson's Mentality, 1977; The Traffic, 1978; The Wounded Breakfast: Ten Poems, 1978; With Sincerest Regrets, 1981; Wuck Wuck Wuck!, 1984; The Wounded Breakfast, 1985; Tick Tock, 1992; The Tunnel: Selected Poems, 1994. Fiction: Gulping's Recital, 1984; The Song of Percival Peacock, 1992. *Honours:* Guggenheim Fellowship, 1974; National Endowment for the Arts Grant, 1976, and Fellowship, 1982; Whiting Foundation Award, 1989.

EDWARDS, Anne; American writer; b. 20 Aug. 1927, Porchester, NY; m. Stephen Citron; one s. one d. *Education:* UCLA, Southern Methodist Univ. *Career:* Pres. Authors' Guild of America 1982–86; Bd Emerita Authors' Guild 1986–2005. *Publications:* A Child's Bible (adaptation) 1967, The Survivors 1968, Miklos Alexandrovitch is Missing 1969, Shadow of a Lion 1970, The Hesitant Heart 1974, Judy Garland: A Biography 1974, Haunted Summer 1974, The Inn and Us (with Stephen Citron) 1975, Child of Night 1975, P. T. Barnum 1976, The Great Houdini 1977, Vivien Leigh: A Biography 1977, Sonya: The Life of the Countess Tolstoy 1981, The Road to Tara: The Life of Margaret Mitchell 1983, Matriarch: Queen Mary and the House of Windsor 1984, A Remarkable Woman: Katherine Hepburn 1985, Early Reagan: The Rise to Power 1986, The Demilles: An American Dynasty 1987, American Princess: A Biography of Shirley Temple 1988, Royal Sisters: Queen Elizabeth and Princess Margaret 1990, Wallis: The Novel 1991, The Grimaldis of Monaco: Centuries of Scandals, Years of Grace 1992, La Divina 1994, Throne of Gold: The Lives of the Aga Khans 1995, Streisand: It Only Happens Once 1996, Diana: The Life She Led 1999, Maria Callas: An Intimate Biography 2001, The Reagans: Portrait of a Marriage 2003; contrib. to Architectural Digest magazine. *Honours:* Birmingham Coll. Woman of Achievement Award, Birmingham, AL 2002. *Literary Agent:* Curtis Brown Ltd, 10 Astor Place, New York, NY 10003, USA.

EDWARDS, F. E. (see Nolan, William Francis)

EDWARDS, (James) Griffith, CBE, FMedSci; British psychiatrist and academic; *Emeritus Professor of Addiction Behaviour, Institute of Psychiatry, University of London;* b. 3 Oct. 1928, India; s. of the late J. T. Edwards and Constance Amy Edwards (née McFadyean); m. 1st 1969 Evelyn Morrison (divorced 1981); one s. two d. (one deceased); m. 2nd Frances Susan Stables 1981. *Education:* Andover Grammar School, Balliol Coll., Univ. of Oxford. *Career:* served RA 2nd Lt 1948–49; Jr Hosp. appointments, King George Ilford, St Bartholomew's, the Maudsley Hosp. 1956–62; worker 1962, Lectr 1966, Sr Lectr 1967 Inst. of Psychiatry; Dir Addiction Research Unit 1967–94; fmrly Chair. Nat. Addiction Centre; Prof. of Addiction Behaviour, Inst. of Psychiatry, Univ. of London 1979–94, Emer. Prof. 1994–; Ed. Addiction (formerly British Journal of Addiction) 1978–96, Ed.-in-Chief 1996–2004,

Commissioning Ed. 2005–; Series Ed. Int. Monographs on the Addictions 1995–; Hon. Prof. Univ. of Chile 1992–. *Publications:* Alcohol: the Ambiguous Molecule 2000, Matters of Substance: Drugs and Why We Use Them 2004; papers on scientific and clinical aspects of addiction. *Honours:* Jellinek Memorial Prize (international award for alcohol research) 1981, Nathan B. Eddy Gold Medal (international award for drug misuse research) 1996, Auguste Forrell Prize (European award for alcohol research) 1998. *Address:* c/o National Addiction Centre, Institute of Psychiatry, King's College London, De Crespigny Park, London, SE5 8AF (office); 32 Crooms Hill, London, SE10 8ER, England (home). *Telephone:* (20) 8858-5631 (home). *E-mail:* p.davis@iop .kcl.ac.uk (office); grifsu@crooms.freeserve.co.uk (home).

EDWARDS, Jorge; Chilean writer and diplomatist; b. 29 July 1931, Santiago. *Education:* Univ. of Chile, Princeton Univ., USA. *Career:* diplomatist 1957–73, Amb. to Cuba 1970, Advisory Minister in Paris 1971–73. *Publications:* (novels) El patio 1952, Gente de la ciudad 1962, Las máscaras 1967, Temas y variaciones 1969, Fantasmas de carne y hueso 1992, El peso de la noche 1965, Los convidados de piedra 1978, El museo de cera 1981, La mujer imaginaria 1985, El anfitrión 1988, El origen del mundo 1996, Persona non grata 2006. *Honours:* Literary Prize of the City of Santiago 1961, 1991, Atenea Prize of Univ. of Concepción (Chile), Essay Prize of the City of Santiago 1991, Cervantes Prize for Literature 2000. *Address:* c/o Alfaguara, Torrelaguna 60, 28043 Madrid, Spain.

EDWARDS, Josh (see Levinson, Leonard)

EDWARDS, Norman (see Carr, Terry Gene)

EDWARDS, Philip Walter, PhD, FBA; British academic; b. 7 Feb. 1923, Barrow-in-Furness; s. of the late R. H. Edwards and B. Edwards; m. 1st Hazel Valentine 1947 (died 1950); m. 2nd Sheila Wilkes 1952; three s. one d. *Education:* King Edward's High School, Birmingham, Univ. of Birmingham. *Career:* Lecturer in English, Univ. of Birmingham 1946–50; Prof. of English Literature, Trinity Coll. Dublin 1960–66; Visiting Prof., Univ. of Mich. 1964–65; Prof. of Literature, Univ. of Essex 1966–74; Visiting Prof., Williams Coll., Mass. 1969; Visiting Fellow, All Souls Coll., Oxford 1970–71; King Alfred Prof. of English Literature, Univ. of Liverpool 1974–90; Visiting Prof., Univ. of Otago, New Zealand 1980, Int. Christian Univ., Tokyo 1989. *Publications:* Sir Walter Ralegh 1953, The Spanish Tragedy (ed.) 1959, Shakespeare and the Confines of Art 1968, Massinger, Plays and Poems (ed. with C. Gibson) 1976, Pericles Prince of Tyre (ed.) 1976, Threshold of a Nation 1979, Hamlet Prince of Denmark (ed.) 1985, Shakespeare: A Writer's Progress 1986, Last Voyages 1988, The Story of the Voyage 1994, Sea-Mark: The Metaphorical Voyage, Spenser to Milton 1997, The Journals of Captain Cook (ed.) 1999, Pilgrimage and Literary Tradition 2005. *Address:* High Gillinggrove, Gillinggate, Kendal, Cumbria, LA9 4JB, England (home). *Telephone:* (1539) 721298 (home).

EDWARDS, Robert John, CBE; British journalist; b. 26 Oct. 1925, Farnham, Surrey; s. of Gordon Edwards and Margaret Edwards (née Grain); m. 1st Laura Ellwood 1952 (dissolved 1972); two s. two d.; m. 2nd Brigid Segrave 1977. *Education:* Ranelagh School. *Career:* Ed. Tribune 1951–55; Deputy Ed. Sunday Express 1957–59; Ed. Daily Express 1961–62, 1963–65; Ed. Evening Citizen (Glasgow) 1962–63; Ed. Sunday People (fmrly The People) 1966–72; Ed. Sunday Mirror 1972–84; Dir Mirror Group Newspapers 1976–86, Sr Group Ed. 1984–85, Deputy Chair. (non-exec.) 1985–86; Chair. London Press Club Scoop of the Year Awards Panel 1990–2003; Ombudsman to Today newspaper 1990–95. *Publication:* Goodbye Fleet Street 1988. *Address:* Tregeseal House, Nancherrow, St Just, Penzance, TR19 7PW, England (home). *Telephone:* (1736) 787060 (home). *Fax:* (1736) 786617 (home). *E-mail:* edwardsrj@aol.com (home).

EGAN, Gregory Mark, BSc; Australian writer; b. 20 Aug. 1961, Perth, WA. *Education:* University of Western Australia. *Publications:* Fiction: An Unusual Angle, 1983; Quarantine, 1992; Permutation City, 1994; Distress, 1995; Diaspora, 1997; Teranesia, 1999. Short Stories: Axiomatic, 1995; Luminous, 1998. Contributions: Interzone Magazine; Asimov's Science Fiction Magazine. *Honours:* John W. Campbell Memorial Award, 1995; Hugo Award, 1999. *Literary Agent:* Curtis Brown Ltd, Haymarket House, 28–29 Haymarket, London, SW1Y 4SP, England. *Telephone:* (20) 7393-4400. *Fax:* (20) 7393-4401. *E-mail:* info@curtisbrown.co.uk. *Website:* www .curtisbrown.co.uk.

EGGERS, Dave; American writer; m. Vendela Vida 2003. *Career:* Ed. Might magazine 1994–97, Timothy McSweeney's Quarterly Concern, or 'McSweeney's,' journal and publishers 1998–. *Publications:* A Heartbreaking Work of Staggering Genius (memoir) 2000, You Shall Know Our Velocity (novel) 2003, The Future Dictionary of America (with Jonathan Safran Foer and Nicole Krauss) 2004, The Best of McSweeney's: Volume 1 (ed.) 2004, Volume 2 (ed.) 2005, How We Are Hungry 2005, What is the What: The Autobiography of Valentino Achak Deng: A Novel 2006; contrib. to periodicals. *Address:* McSweeney's, 826 Valencia Street, San Francisco, CA 94110, USA (office). *E-mail:* letters@mcsweeneys.net (office). *Website:* www.mcsweeneys.net.

EGLETON, Clive Frederick William; British writer, retd army officer and retd civil servant; b. 25 Nov. 1927; m. Joan Evelyn Lane 1949 (died 1996); two s. *Education:* Staff Coll., Camberley. *Career:* mem. CWA, Soc. of Authors. *Publications:* A Piece of Resistance 1970, Last Post for a Partisan 1971, The Judas Mandate 1972, Seven Days to a Killing 1973, The October Plot 1974, Skirmish 1975, State Visit 1976, The Mills Bomb 1978, Backfire 1979, The Winter Touch 1981, A Falcon for the Hawks 1982, The Russian Enigma 1982,

A Conflict of Interests 1983, Troika 1984, A Different Drummer 1985, Picture of the Year 1987, Gone Missing 1988, Death of a Sahib 1989, In the Red 1990, Last Act 1991, A Double Deception 1992, Hostile Intent 1993, A Killing in Moscow 1994, Death Throes 1994, A Lethal Involvement 1995, Warning Shot 1996, Blood Money 1997, Dead Reckoning 1999, The Honey Trap 2000, One Man Running 2001, Cry Havoc 2002, Assassination Day 2003, The Renegades 2005. *Address:* Dolphin House, Beach House Lane, Bembridge, PO35 5TA, Isle of Wight (office). *Telephone:* (1983) 873893 (office). *Fax:* (1983) 872151 (office).

EGNER, Eugen; German writer and draughtsman; b. 10 Oct. 1951, Ingelfingen. *Career:* contributed cartoons to Titanic and Die Rabe, short stories to Die Rabe, Frankfurter Rundschau. *Publications include:* novels: Tagebuch eines Trinkers (trans. as From the Diary of an Alcoholic) 1991, Der künstliche Mann (trans. as The Artificial Man) 1992, Die Tagebücher des W. A. Mozart (trans. as The Diaries of W. A. Mozart) 1998, Androiden auf Milchbasis (trans. as Androids from Milk) 2002. *Address:* c/o Dedalus Ltd, Langford Lodge, St Judith's Lane, Sawtry, Cambridgeshire PE28 5XE, England. *E-mail:* info@dedalusbooks.com. *Website:* www.dedalusbooks.com.

EHLE, John Marsden, Jr, BA; American writer; b. 13 Dec. 1925, Asheville, NC; m. 1st Gail Oliver 1952 (divorced 1967); m. 2nd Rosemary Harris 1967; one d. *Education:* University of North Carolina at Chapel Hill. *Career:* Faculty, University of North Carolina at Chapel Hill, 1951–63; Special asst to Gov. Terry Sanford, NC, 1963–64; Programme Officer, Ford Foundation, New York, 1964–65; Mem., White House Group for Domestic Affairs, 1964–66; Special Consultant, Duke University, 1976–80; mem. Authors' League; PEN; State of North Carolina Awards Commission, 1982–93. *Publications:* Fiction: Move Over, Mountain, 1957; Kingstree Island, 1959; Lion on the Hearth, 1961; The Land Breakers, 1964; The Road, 1967; Time of Drums, 1970; The Journey of August King, 1971; The Changing of the Guard, 1975; The Winter People, 1981; Last One Home, 1983; The Widows Trial, 1989. Non-Fiction: The Free Men, 1965; The Survivor, 1968; Trail of Tears: The Rise and Fall of the Cherokee Nation, 1988; Dr Frank: Living with Frank Porter Graham, 1993. Screenplay: The Journey of August King, 1995. *Honours:* Walter Raleigh Prizes for Fiction, North Carolina Dept of Cultural Affairs, 1964, 1967, 1970, 1975, 1984; Mayflower Society Cup, 1965; State of North Carolina Award for Literature, 1972; Gov.'s Award for Distinguished Meritorious Service, NC, 1978; Lillian Smith Prize, Southern Regional Council, 1982; Distinguished Alumnus Award, University of North Carolina at Chapel Hill, 1984; Thomas Wolfe Memorial Award, Western North Carolina Historical Asscn, 1984; W. D. Weatherford Award, Berea College, 1985; Caldwell Award, North Carolina Humanities Council, 1995. *Address:* 125 Westview Drive NW, Winston-Salem, NC 27104, USA.

EHRENREICH, Barbara, PhD; American writer; b. 26 Aug. 1941. *Education:* Reed Coll., Rockefeller Univ., New York. *Career:* columnist, Time 1991–97, The Progressive; teacher of essay-writing, Graduate School of Journalism, Univ. of California at Berkeley 1998, 2000; guest columnist, New York Times 2004; Guggenheim Fellowship 1987–88; John D. and Catherine T. MacArthur Foundation grant for research and writing 1995. *Publications:* non-fiction: The American Health Empire: Power, Profits and Politics (with John Ehrenreich) 1971, Witches, Midwives and Nurses: A History of Women Healers (with Diedre English) 1972, For Her Own Good: 150 Years of the Experts' Advice to Women (with Deirdre English) 1978, The Hearts of Men: American Dreams and the Flight from Commitment 1983, Re-Making Love: The Feminization of Sex (with Elizabeth Hess and Gloria Jacobs) 1986, The Mean Season: The Attack on Social Welfare (with Frances Fox Piven, Richard Cloward and Fred Block) 1987, Fear of Falling: The Inner Life of the Middle Class 1989, The Worst Years of Our Lives: Irreverent Notes from a Decade of Greed (essays) 1990, Complaints and Disorders: The Sexual Politics of Sickness (with Diedre English) 1991, Blood Rites: Origins and History of the Passions of War 1991, The Snarling Citizen 1995, Nickel and Dimed (Sydney Hillman Award for Journalism 1999, Brill's Content Hon. Mention 1999 for chapter that appeared in Harper's Jan. 1999) 2002, Global Woman: Nannies, Maids and Sex Workers in the New Economy (essays, ed. with Arlie Russell Hochschild) 2002, Bait and Switch: The Futile Pursuit of the Corporate Dream 2006, Dancing in the Streets: A History of Collective Joy 2007; fiction: Kipper's Game 1993; contrib. essay, Maid to Order, to Harper's 2000, essay to Welcome to Cancerland 2003; contrib. to magazines, including Ms., Harper's, The Nation, The Progressive, The New Republic, The Atlantic Monthly and the New York Times Magazine. *Honours:* Dr hc (Reed Coll.), (State Univ. of New York at Old Westbury), (Coll. of Wooster in Ohio), (John Jay Coll.), (UMass-Lowell), (La Trobe Univ., Melbourne, Australia); Nat. Magazine Award for Excellence in Reporting (jtly) 1980, Ford Foundation Award for Humanistic Perspectives on Contemporary Soc. 1982. *Address:* The New York Times, 229 W 43rd Street, New York, NY 10036, USA. *Website:* www.nytimes.com.

EHRET, Terry, BA, MA; American poet and lecturer; b. 12 Nov. 1955, San Francisco, CA; m. Donald Nicholas Moe 1979, three c. *Education:* Stanford University, Chapman College, San Francisco State University. *Career:* Instructor in English, Santa Rosa Junior College, 1991–; Lecturer in Poetry, Sonoma State University, 1994–, San Francisco State University, 1995–99; founding Ed., Sixteen Rivers Press, 1999–; many poetry readings and lectures; mem. Acad. of American Poets; Associated Writing Programs; California Poets in the Schools; Poets and Writers. *Publications:* Suspensions (with Steve Gilmartin and Susan Herron Sibbet), 1990; Lost Body, 1993; Travel/How We Go on Living, 1995; Translations from the Human Language, 2001. Contributions: Reviews and journals. *Honours:* National Poetry Series Award, 1992; California Commonwealth Club Book Award for Poetry, 1994; Pablo Neruda Poetry Prize, Nimrod magazine, 1995.

EHRLICH, Eugene, BS, MA; American lexicographer and writer; b. 21 May 1922, New York, NY. *Education:* City College, CUNY, Columbia University. *Career:* Asst Prof., Fairleigh Dickinson University, 1946–48; Assoc. in English, Columbia University, 1949–87. *Publications:* How to Study Better, 1960; The Art of Technical Writing (with D. Murphy), 1962; Researching and Writing Term Papers and Reports (with D. Murphy), 1964; College Developmental Reading (with D. Murphy and D. Pace), 1966; Basic Grammar for Writing (with D. Murphy), 1970; Concise Index to English (with D. Murphy), 1974; Basic Vocabulary Builder, 1975; English Grammar, 1976; Punctuation, Capitalization and Spelling, 1977; Oxford American Dictionary (with others), 1980; The Oxford Illustrated Literary Guide to the United States (with Gorton Carruth), 1982; Speak for Success, 1984; Amo, Amas, Amat and More, 1985; The Bantam Concise Handbook of English, 1986; Harper's Dictionary of Foreign Terms, no. three, 1990; Collins Gem Dictionary, 1990; Collins Gem Thesaurus, 1990; Choose the Right Word (with S. I. Hayakawa), 1994; Veni, Vidi, Vici, 1995; The Highly Selective Dictionary for the Extraordinarily Literate, 1997; Les Bons Mots, 1997.

EHRLICH, Paul Ralph, MA, PhD; American population biologist and academic; *Bing Professor of Population Studies, Stanford University*; b. 29 May 1932, Philadelphia, Pa; s. of William Ehrlich and Ruth Ehrlich (née Rosenberg); m. Anne Fitzhugh Howland 1954; one d. *Education:* Univs of Pennsylvania and Kansas. *Career:* Assoc. Investigator, USAF research project, Alaska and Univ. of Kansas 1956–57; Research Assoc., Chicago Acad. of Sciences and Univ. of Kansas Dept of Entomology 1957–59; mem. Faculty, Stanford Univ. 1959, Prof. of Biology 1966–, Bing Prof. of Population Studies 1976–; Pres. Center for Conservation Biology 1988–; Corresp. NBC News 1989–92; Fellow, AAAS; mem. NAS, European Acad. of Sciences and Arts 1992. *Publications:* How to Know the Butterflies 1961, Population Resources, Environment (both with A. H. Ehrlich) 1970, 1972, The Population Bomb 1968, 1971, How to be a Survivor (with R. L. Harriman) 1971, co-ed.: Man and the Ecosphere (with J. P. Holdren and R. W. Holm) 1971, Global Ecology (with J. P. Holdren) 1971, Human Ecology (with A. H. Ehrlich and J. P. Holdren) 1973, Ark II (with D. Pirages) 1974, The Process of Evolution (with R. W. Holm and D. R. Parnell) 1974, The End of Affluence (with A. H. Ehrlich) 1974, Biology and Society (with R. W. Holm and I. Brown) 1976, The Race Bomb (with S. Feldman) 1977, Ecoscience: Population, Resources, Environment (with A. H. Ehrlich and J. P. Holdren) 1977, Introduction to Insect Biology and Diversity (with H. V. Daly and J. T. Doyen) 1978, The Golden Door: International Migration, Mexico and the U.S. (with D. L. Bilderback and A. H. Ehrlich) 1979, Extinction: The Causes and Consequences of the Disappearance of Species (with A. H. Ehrlich) 1981, Machinery of Nature 1986, Earth (with A. H. Ehrlich) 1987, The Birder's Handbook (with D. Dobkin and D. Wheye) 1988, New World/New Mind (with R. Ornstein) 1989, The Population Explosion (with A. H. Ehrlich) 1990, Healing the Planet (with A. H. Ehrlich) 1991, Birds in Jeopardy 1992, The Stork and the Plow (with A. H. Ehrlich and G. C. Daily) 1995, Betrayal of Science and Reason (with A. H. Ehrlich) 1996, Human Natures 2000, Wild Solutions 2001, One With Nineveh, and other books; over 800 scientific and popular articles. *Honours:* Hon. mem. Int. Soc. for Philosophical Enquiry 1991; Hon. DHumLitt (Univ. of the Pacific) 1970; Crafoord Prize, Royal Swedish Acad. of Sciences 1990, UNEP Sasakawa Environment Prize 1994, Blue Planet Prize, Asahi Glass Foundation 1999 and many other awards for work in ecology, evolution and conservation. *Address:* Department of Biological Sciences, HERRIN 409, Stanford University, Stanford, CA 94305-5020, USA. *Telephone:* (650) 723-3171. *Website:* www.stanford.edu/group/CCB/Staff/Ehrlich.html.

EISEN, Cliff, BA, MA, PhD; Canadian musicologist; *Reader in Historical Musicology, King's College London*. *Education:* Univ. of Toronto and Cornell Univ. *Career:* Assoc. Ed., New Köchel Catalogue; Gen. Ed., Oxford Companion to Mozart; served as musicological adviser to Robert Levin, Christopher Hogwood and the Acad. of Ancient Music for recordings of the Mozart's piano concertos. *Publications:* Mozart Studies (ed. and contrib.) 1991, New Mozart Documents 1991, Wolfgang Amadeus Mozart, Symphony K. 425 ('Linz') 1992, Mozarts Streichquintette: Beiträge zum musikalischen Satz, zum Gattungskontext und zu Quellenfragen. (ed. with W. D. Seiffert, also contrib.) 1994, Orchestral Music in Salzburg, 1750–1780 (jtly) 1994, Mozart Studies 2 (ed. and contrib.) 1997, Four Viennese String Quintets 1998, A Companion to Mozart's Piano Concertos (with Arthur Hutchings) 1998, The New Grove Mozart (with Stanley Sadie) 2000, W. A. Mozart: Piano Concerto in E-flat, KV 271 (with Robert Levin) 2000, Mozart: A Life in Letters (with Stewart Spencer) 2006, The Cambridge Mozart Encyclopedia (with Simon P. Keefe) 2006; contribs to Journal of the Royal Musical Asscn, Early Music, numerous chapters in academic works. *Address:* Department of Music, King's College London, Strand, London, WC2R 2LS, England (office). *Telephone:* (20) 7848-2029 (office). *Fax:* (20) 7848-2326 (office). *E-mail:* cliff.eisen@kcl.ac.uk. *Website:* www.kcl.ac.uk/kis/schools/hums/music (office).

EISENBERG, Deborah, BA; American writer; b. 20 Nov. 1945, Chicago, IL; pnr Wallace Shawn. *Education:* Marlboro Coll., Vermont, New School Coll., New School for Social Research. *Career:* teacher MFA Creative Writing Program, Univ. of Virginia. *Plays:* Pastorale (play) 1982. *Publications:* Transactions in a Foreign Currency (short stories) 1986, Under the 82nd Airborne (short stories) 1992, Air, 24 Hours: Jennifer Bartlett (monograph) 1994, The Stories (So Far) of Deborah Eisenberg 1996, All Around Atlantis

1997, Twilight of the Superheroes (short stories) 2006. *Honours:* O. Henry Awards 1986, 1995, 1997, 2002, Whiting Writer's Award 1987, Guggenheim Fellowship 1987, Deutscher Akademischer Austauschdienst Fellowship, Berlin 1991, Friends of American Writers Award 1993, Ingram Merrill Foundation Award 1993, American Acad. of Arts and Letters Award for Literature 1993, Smart Foundation Prize for Best Story in Yale Review 1996, The Rea Award for the Short Story 2000, Lannon Foundation Fellowship 2003. *Literary Agent:* Janklow & Nesbit Associates, 445 Park Avenue, New York, NY 10022, USA.

EKINS, Paul Whitfield, BSc, MSc, MPhil, PhD; British economist and writer; *Professor of Sustainable Development, University of Westminster;* b. 24 July 1950, Jakarta, Indonesia; m. Susan Anne Lofthouse 1979; one s. *Education:* Imperial Coll., London, Birkbeck Coll., London, Univ. of Bradford. *Career:* Research Fellow, School of Peace Studies, Univ. of Bradford 1987–90; Research Assoc., Dept of Applied Econs, Univ. of Cambridge 1991–98; Sr Lecturer, School of Politics, Int. Relations and the Environment, Keele Univ. 1996–98, Reader 1998–2000, Prof. 2000–02; Prof. of Sustainable Devt, Univ. of Westminster 2002–, Head Environment Group Policy Studies Inst. 2002–; mem. Global 500 Forum, Int. Soc. for Ecological Econs, Royal Comm. on Environmental Pollution 2002–; Hon. Fellow, Centre for Social and Environmental Accounting Research, Univ. of Dundee 1992–. *Publications:* The Living Economy: A New Economics in the Making (ed.) 1986, A New World Order: Grassroots Movements for Global Change 1992, Wealth Beyond Measure: An Atlas of New Economics (with Mayer Hillman and Robert Hutchison) 1992, Real Wealth: Green Economics in the Classroom (with Ken Webster) 1994, Global Warming and Energy Demand (ed. with Terry Barker and Nick Johnstone) 1995, Economic Growth and Environmental Sustainability 2000; contrib. to books, journals, reviews and newspapers. *Honours:* UNEP Global 500 Award for Environmental Achievement 1994. *Address:* c/o Policy Studies Institute, 50 Hanson Street, London, W1W 6UP, England (office). *Telephone:* (20) 7911-7516 (office). *Fax:* (20) 7911-7501 (office). *E-mail:* p.ekins@psi.org.uk (office). *Website:* www.psi.org.uk (office).

EKLUND, Gordon Stewart; American writer; b. 24 July 1945, Seattle, WA; one d. *Education:* Contra Costra College. *Career:* mem. SFWA. *Publications:* The Eclipse of Dawn, 1971; A Trace of Dreams, 1972; Beyond the Resurrection, 1973; All Times Possible, 1974; Serving in Time, 1975; Falling Toward Forever, 1975; If the Stars are Gods, 1976; The Dance of the Apocalypse, 1976; The Grayspace Beast, 1976; Find the Changeling, 1980; The Garden of Winter, 1980; Thunder on Neptune, 1989. Contributions: Analog; Galaxy; If Science Fiction; Fantasy and Science Fiction; Universe; New Dimensions; Amazing Stories; Fantastic. *Honours:* Nebula Award 1975.

EKWENSI, Cyprian; Nigerian author and pharmacist; b. 26 Sept. 1921, Minna, Northern Nigeria. *Education:* Govt Coll., Ibadan, Achimota Coll., Ghana, School of Forestry, Ibadan, Higher Coll., Yaba, Chelsea School of Pharmacy, Univ. of London, Iowa Univ. *Career:* Lecturer in Biology, Chem. and English, Igbobi Coll., Lagos 1947–49; Lecturer, School of Pharmacy, Lagos 1949–56; Pharmacist, Nigerian Medical Service 1956; Head of Features, Nigerian Broadcasting Corpn 1956–61; Dir of Information, Fed. Ministry of Information, Lagos 1961–66; Dir of Information Services, Enugu 1966; Chair. East Cen. State Library Board, Enugu 1971–75; Man. Dir Star Printing and Publishing Co. Ltd 1975–79, Niger Eagle Press 1981–; Visiting Lecturer, Iowa Univ.; mem. Pharmaceutical Socs of GB and Nigeria, Nigerian Arts Council, Soc. of Nigerian Authors, Inst. Public Relations Nigeria and UK. *Publications:* When Love Whispers, Ikolo the Wrestler 1947, The Leopard's Claw 1950, People of the City 1954, Passport of Mallam Ilia, The Drummer Boy 1960, Jagua Nana 1961, Burning Grass, An African Night's Entertainment, Yaba Round about Murder 1962, Beautiful Feathers 1963, Great Elephant Bird, Rainmaker 1965, Lokotown, Juju Rock, Trouble in Form VI, Iska, Boa Suitor 1966, Coal Camp Boy 1973, Samankwe in the Strange Forest 1974, Samankwe and the Highway Robbers, Restless City, Christmas Gold 1975, Survive the Peace 1976, Divided We Stand 1980, Motherless Baby 1980, Jaguanana's Daughter 1986, For a Roll of Parchment 1986, Beneath the Convent Wall 1987, Restless City and Xmas Gold, Behind the Convent Wall 1988, Death at Mile Two 1988, Lagos Love Deal 1988, Masquerade Time 1991, King Forever 1992. *Honours:* Dag Hammarskjöld Int. Award for Literary Merit 1968. *Address:* Hillview Crescent, Independence Layout, P.O. Box 317, Enugu, Nigeria (home).

ELDER, Karl, BS, MS, MFA; American poet, writer, editor and academic; *Jacob and Lucile Fessler Professor of Creative Writing, Lakeland College;* b. 7 July 1948, Beloit, WI; m. Brenda Kay Olson 1969; two s. *Education:* Northern Ill. Univ., Wichita State Univ. *Career:* instructor, Southwest Missouri State Univ. 1977–79; Faculty, Lakeland Coll. 1979–89, Jacob and Lucile Fessler Prof. of Creative Writing and poet-in-residence 1990–. *Publications:* poetry: Can't Dance an' it's Too Wet to Plow 1975, The Celibate 1982, Phobophobia 1987, What Is the Future of Poetry? (ed.) 1991, A Man in Pieces 1994, The Geocryptogrammatist's Pocket Compendium of the United States 2001, Mead: Twenty-six Abecedariums 2005, The Minimalist's How-to Handbook 2005; contrib. to many anthologies, reviews, quarterlies and journals. *Honours:* Lucien Stryk Award for Poetry 1974, Illinois Arts Council Award 1975, and grant 1977, Lakeland Coll. Outstanding Teacher Award 1987, Robert Schuricht Endowment 1993, Pushcart Prize 2000, Mikrokosmos Prize for Poetry 2002. *Address:* c/o Creative Arts Division, Lakeland College, PO Box 359, Sheboygan, WI 53082-0359, USA. *Telephone:* (920) 565-1276. *E-mail:* kelder@excel.net. *Website:* www.greatlakeswritersfestival.org; www1.lakeland.edu/seems/.

ELDERKIN, Susan, MA; British novelist; b. 1968, Crawley, Surrey, England. *Education:* Univ. of Cambridge, Univ. of East Anglia. *Publications:* Sunset Over Chocolate Mountains 2000, The Voices 2003. *Honours:* Betty Trask Award 2000, one of Granta's 20 Best Young British Novelists of the Decade 2003. *Literary Agent:* Aitken Alexander Associates, 18–21 Cavaye Place, London, SW10 9PT, England. *Telephone:* (20) 7373-8672. *Fax:* (20) 7373-6002. *E-mail:* clare@aitkenalexander.co.uk. *Website:* www.aitkenalexander.co.uk; www.susanelderkin.com.

ELDRED-GRIGG, Stevan Treleaven, MA, PhD; New Zealand writer and historian; b. 5 Oct. 1952, Grey Valley; m. Lauree Arlene Hunter 1976 (divorced 1994); three s. *Education:* Univ. of Canterbury, Australian Nat. Univ. *Career:* Postdoctoral Fellow, Univ. of Canterbury, Christchurch 1981; Judge, New Zealand Book Awards 1984; Writing Fellow, Victoria Univ. 1986; Arts Council of NZ Scholar-in-Letters 1991; New Zealand Writing Fellow, Iowa Univ., USA; Prof. of Literature Shanghai Int. Studies Univ., China 2003–04; Wellington Branch Pres. NZ Soc. of Authors 1995–98, Nat. Vice-Pres. 1998–99; mem. PEN New Zealand Centre, Canterbury Provincial Committee; Trustee Chirstchurch Book Festival Trust 1996–2000. *Publications:* fiction: Oracles and Miracles 1987, adapted as radio play 1989, stage play 1990, The Siren Celia 1989, The Shining City 1991, Gardens of Fire 1993, My History, I Think 1994, Mum 1995, Blue Blood 1997, Kaput! 2001, Sheng Xian Qi Ji 2002; non-fiction: A Southern Gentry: New Zealanders Who Inherited the Earth 1980, A New History of Canterbury 1982, Pleasures of the Flesh 1984, New Zealand Working People 1890–1990 1990, The Rich 1996; contribs short stories to periodicals, including Island, Landfall, New Zealand Listener; historical essays to periodicals, including New Zealand Journal of History, Journal of the Royal Australian Historical Society, New Zealand Geographic; literary and critical essays to Landfall, Sites, Island, Ming Dao Literature and Arts, New Zealand Books. *Honours:* A. V. Reed Memorial Book Award 1984, second prize Book Publishers' Asscn of New Zealand Goodman Fielder Wattie Award 1988, Commonwealth Writers Prize for South-East Asia and the South Pacific 1988, Trust Bank Canterbury Community Trust Arts Excellence Award 1996. *Literary Agent:* Sayer Literary Agency, PO Box 78–199, Grey Lynn, Auckland, New Zealand. *E-mail:* susan.sayer@xtra.co.nz. *Website:* www.eldred-grigg.com.

ELDRIDGE, Colin Clifford, BA, PhD, FRHistS; British academic and writer; *Professor of History, University of Wales;* b. 16 May 1942, Walthamstow, England; m. Ruth Margaret Evans 1970 (died 2003); one d. *Education:* Univ. of Nottingham. *Career:* Postdoctoral Fellow in the Arts and Social Sciences, Univ. of Edinburgh 1966–68; Lecturer, Univ. of Wales, Lampeter 1968–75, Sr Lecturer in History 1975–92, Reader 1992–98, Prof. of History 1998–; mem. Historical Asscn, Asscn of History Teachers in Wales, British Asscn of Canadian Studies, British Australian Studies Asscn. *Publications:* England's Mission: The Imperial Idea in the Age of Gladstone and Disraeli 1973, Victorian Imperialism 1978, Essays in Honour of C. D. Chandaman 1980, British Imperialism in the 19th Century 1984, Empire, Politics and Popular Culture 1989, From Rebellion to Patriation: Canada and Britain in the Nineteenth and Twentieth Centuries 1989, Disraeli and the Rise of a New Imperialism 1996, The Imperial Experience: From Carlyle to Forster 1996, The Zulu War, 1879 1996, Kith and Kin: Canada, Britain and the United States form the Revolution to the Cold War 1997; contrib. to various learned journals. *Address:* History Department, University of Wales, Lampeter, Ceredigion SA48 7ED (office); Tanerdy, Ciliau Aeron, Lampeter, Ceredigion SA48 8DL, Wales (home). *Telephone:* (1570) 424744 (office); (1570) 470667 (home). *Fax:* (1570) 424998 (office). *E-mail:* c.eldridge@lamp.ac.uk (office). *Website:* www.lamp.ac.uk/history (office).

ELDRIDGE, David; British playwright; b. 1974. *Education:* Univ. of Exeter. *Plays:* Serving it Up 1996, Under the Blue Sky 2001, Festen 2004, M.A.D. 2004, Incomplete and Random Acts of Kindness 2005. *Television:* Our Hidden Lives 2005. *Literary Agent:* c/o A & C Black Publisher Ltd., 38 Soho Square, London, W1D 3HB, England. *Telephone:* (20) 7758-0200. *Website:* www.acblack.com.

ELEGANT, Robert Sampson, BA, MA, MS; British author and journalist; b. 7 March 1928, New York, NY, USA; m. 1st Moira Clarissa Brady 1956 (died 1999); one s. one d.; m. 2nd Ursula Rosemary Righter (née Douglas) 2003. *Education:* University of Pennsylvania, US Army Language School, Yale University, Columbia University. *Career:* War, Southeast Asia Correspondent, various agencies 1951–61; Central European Bureau, Newsweek 1962–64; Los Angeles Times, Washington Post 1965–70; Foreign Affairs Columnist 1970–76; Visiting Prof. Univ. of S Carolina 1976, Boston Univ. 1994–95; mem. Authors' League of America; Hong Kong Foreign Correspondents' Club (Pres. 1960). *Publications:* China's Red Masters 1951, The Dragon's Seed 1959, The Centre of the World 1961, Mao v Chiang: The Battle for China 1972, The Great Cities, Hong Kong 1977, Pacific Destiny 1990; fiction: A Kind of Treason 1966, The Seeking 1969, Dynasty 1977, Manchu 1980, Mandarin 1983, White Sun, Red Star 1987 (publ. in US as From a Far Land 1988), Bianca 1992, The Everlasting Sorrow 1994, Last Year in Hong Kong 1997, The Big Brown Bears 1998, Bianca 2000, Cry Peace 2005; contribs to newspapers and periodicals. *Honours:* Vietnam, Korea, Matuya service medals (USA and British), World War II; Pulitzer Fellow 1951–52; Ford Foundation Fellowship 1954–55; Overseas Press Club Awards 1963,

1966, 1967, 1972; Sigma Delta Chi Award 1966, Edgar Allan Poe Award 1967; Fellow, American Enterprise Institute for Public Policy Research, Washington, DC 1976–78; Senior Fellow, Institute for Advanced Study, Berlin 1993–94. *Literary Agent:* Christopher Sinclair-Stevenson, 3 South Terrace, London, SW7 2TB, England. *Address:* 10 Quick Street, London, N1 8HL, England (office). *Telephone:* (20) 7837-1009 (office). *Fax:* (20) 7837-1009 (office). *E-mail:* relegant@yahoo.com (home).

ELFYN, Menna, BA; British poet; *Director of Creative Writing, Trinity College, Camarthen and Royal Literary Fund Fellow, Aberystwyth University*; b. 1951, S Wales; d. of Rev. T. Elfyn Jones and Rachel Maria Jones; m. Wynnford James 1974; two c. *Education:* Univs of Swansea and Aberystwyth. *Career:* Lecturer, St David's Coll., Lampeter 1979–86; Lecturer in Educ., Univ. of Swansea 1989–92; Co-Dir of Creative Writing, Trinity Coll., Carmarthen 1997, Dir 1998–; Royal Literary Fund Fellow Aberystwyth Univ. 2002–; columnist, Western Mail 1996–; Artist-in-Residence at various schools, colls and hosps, UK and USA; readings worldwide at festivals and for British Council in Sri Lanka, Philippines, Zimbabwe, Macedonia, Estonia, Poland, Romania; work trans. into 14 languages; has presented TV documentaries; Writing Fellow Univ. of Wales 1984; mem. Gorsedd of Bards 1993. *Plays:* seven stage plays, two for television; 4 plays for BBC Radio 2002–06. *Music:* co-writer choral symphony Garden of Light for New York Philharmonic Orchestra. *Publications include:* Aderyn Bach Mewn Llaw (Welsh Arts Council Prize) 1990, Eucalyptus: Detholiad o Gerddi 1995, Cell Angel 1996, Cusan Dyn Dall/Blind Man's Kiss 2000, Modern Welsh Poetry (ed. with John Rowlands) 2003; other vols of poetry; two novels for teenagers; various works for music, produced as librettist for four US composers; Perffaith Nam (Perfect Flaw) 2005. *Honours:* many poetry prizes including Best Vol. of Eisteddfod 1977, Welsh Arts Council Best Book of the Year 1990–2003, Poet Laureate for the Children of Wales 2002–03. *Address:* Cysgod y Craig, Stryd y Gwynt, Llandysul, Ceredigion, Wales (home). *Telephone:* (1559) 362122. *E-mail:* m.elfyn@trinity-cm.ac.uk (office); menna@elfyn.fsnet .co.uk (home). *Website:* www.menna.elfyn.co.uk (home). *Address:* c/o Bloodaxe Books Ltd, Highgreen, Tarset, Northumberland NE48 1RP, England.

ELIOT, Karen (see Home, Stewart Ramsay)

ELISHA, Ron, MB, BS; Australian medical practitioner and playwright; b. 19 Dec. 1951, Jerusalem, Israel; m. Bertha Rita Rubin 1981; one s. one d. *Education:* Melbourne Univ. *Career:* self-employed Gen. Practitioner; mem. Australian Writers' Guild. *Publications:* In Duty Bound 1983, Two 1985, Einstein 1986, The Levine Comedy 1987, Pax Americana 1988, Safe House 1989, Esterhaz 1990, Impropriety 1993, Choice 1994, Pigtales 1994, Unknown Soldier 1996, Too Big 1997, The Goldberg Variations 2000, A Tree, Falling 2003, Ladies & Gentlemen 2005, Wrongful Life 2005, Controlled Crying 2006, Renaissance 2006, Ten Minutes 2007; contribs to Business Review Weekly, The Age, Vogue Australia, Generation Magazine, Australian Book Review, Centre Stage Magazine, Melbourne Jewish Chronicle, The Westerly, Medical Observer. *Honours:* Best Stage Play 1982, 1984, Major Award 1982, Gold Award, Best Screenplay, Houston Int. Film Festival 1990, Best TV Feature, Australian Writers' Guild Award 1992, Mitch Mathews Award 2006. *Literary Agent:* c/o Marea Jablonski, BGM, 28 Rupert Street, Collingwood, Vic., Australia. *Telephone:* (3) 9419-7133. *E-mail:* marea@bgange.com.au. *Address:* 2 Malonga Court, North Caulfield, Vic. 3161, Australia (home). *Telephone:* (3) 9571-9933 (office). *Fax:* (3) 9571-3604 (office). *E-mail:* relisha@bigpond.net.au (home).

ELKINS, Aaron, BA, MA, EdD; American writer; b. 24 July 1935, New York, NY; m. 1st Toby Siev 1959 (divorced 1972); two s.; m. 2nd Charlotte Trangmar 1972. *Education:* Hunter Coll., CUNY, Univ. of Wisconsin, Madison, Univ. of Arizona, California State Univ., Los Angeles, Univ. of California, Berkeley. *Career:* Dir Man. Devt, Contra Costa Co. Govt 1971–76, 1980–83; Lecturer, Univ. of Maryland, College Park, European Div. 1976–78, 1984–85; man. analyst, US Office of Personnel Man., San Francisco 1979–80; author 1982–. *Publications:* Fellowship of Fear 1982, The Dark Place 1983, Murder in the Queen's Armes 1985, A Deceptive Clarity 1987, Old Bones (MWA Edgar Allan Poe Award 1988) 1987, Curses 1989, Icy Clutches 1990, A Glancing Light 1991, Make No Bones 1991, Old Scores 1993, Dead Men's Hearts 1994, Twenty Blue Devils 1997, Loot 1999, Skeleton Dance 2000, Turncoat 2002, Good Blood 2004, Where There's A Will 2005, Unnatural Selection 2006, Little Tiny Teeth 2007; with Charlotte Elkins: A Wicked Slice 1989, Rotten Lies 1995, Nasty Breaks 1998, Where Have All the Birdies Gone? 2004, On the Fringe 2005. *Honours:* Agatha Award (jtly) 1992, Nero Wolfe Award 1994. *Literary Agent:* c/o Lisa Erbach Vance, The Aaron Priest Agency Inc., 708 Third Avenue, 23rd Floor, New York, NY 10017, USA. *Website:* www.aaronelkins.com.

ELKINS, Caroline, PhD; American academic and author; *Hugo K. Foster Associate Professor of African Studies, Harvard University*; b. 1969. *Education:* Princeton Univ., Harvard Univ. *Career:* Hugo K. Foster Assoc. Prof. of African Studies and Policy Fellow Kennedy School of Govt in the Carr Centre for Human Rights Policy, Harvard Univ.; has travelled and worked in rural Africa; speaks Swahili and some Kikuyu. *Television and radio broadcasts include:* All Things Considered (NPR), The World (BBC), Charlie Rose (PBS). *Publications:* Imperial Reckoning: The Untold Story of Britain's Gulag in Kenya (Pulitzer Prize in General Non-Fiction) 2005, Settler Colonialists in the 20th Century: Projects, Practices, Legacies (ed. with Susan Pedersen) 2005; contrib. to The New York Times Book Review, The Atlantic, The New Republic and to academic journals. *Address:* c/o Department of History, Harvard

University, Robinson Hall, 35 Quincy Street, Cambridge, MA 02138, USA (office). *Telephone:* (617) 495-2568 (office). *E-mail:* elkins@fas.harvard.edu (office).

ELLIOT, Alistair, BA, MA; British poet, translator, editor and librarian (retd); b. 13 Oct. 1932, Liverpool, Lancashire, England; m. 1956, two s. *Education:* Fettes College, Edinburgh, Christ Church, Oxford. *Career:* Librarian, Kensington Public Library, London, 1959–61, Keele University, 1961–65, Pahlavi University, Iran, 1965–67, Newcastle University, 1967–82. *Publications:* Air in the Wrong Place, 1968; Contentions, 1977; Kisses, 1978; Talking to Bede, 1982; Talking Back, 1982; On the Appian Way, 1984; My Country: Collected Poems, 1989; Turning the Stones, 1993; Facing Things, 1997. Editor: Poems by James I and Others, 1970; Virgil, The Georgics with John Dryden's Translation, 1981. Editor and Translator: French Love Poems (bilingual), 1991; Italian Landscape Poems (bilingual), 1993; Roman Food Poems, 2003. Translator: Alcestis, by Euripides, 1965; Peace, by Aristophanes, 1965; Femmes Hombres, by Paul Verlaine, 1979; The Lazarus Poems, by Heinrich Heine, 1979; Medea, by Euripides, 1993; La Jeune Parque, by Paul Valéry, 1997. Contributions: many journals, reviews and magazines. *Honours:* Arts Council of Great Britain Grant, 1979; Ingram Merrill Foundation Fellowships, 1983, 1989; Prudence Farmer Awards, New Statesman, 1983, 1991; Djerassi Foundation Fellowship, 1984; Cholmondeley Award, Society of Authors, 2000. *Address:* 27 Hawthorn Road, Newcastle upon Tyne, NE3 4DE, England.

ELLIOT, Bruce (see Field, Edward)

ELLIOTT, Sir John Huxtable, Kt, FBA; British historian and academic; b. 23 June 1930, Reading, Berks.; s. of Thomas Charles Elliott and Janet Mary Payne; m. Oonah Sophia Butler 1958. *Education:* Eton Coll. and Trinity Coll., Cambridge. *Career:* Asst Lecturer in History, Univ. of Cambridge 1957–62, Lecturer 1962–67; Prof. of History, King's Coll., Univ. of London 1968–73; Prof., School of Historical Studies, Inst. for Advanced Study, Princeton, NJ 1973–90; Regius Prof. of Modern History, Univ. of Oxford and Fellow, Oriel Coll., Oxford 1990–97; Fellow, Trinity Coll., Cambridge 1954–67, Fellow, Royal Acad. of History, Madrid, American Acad. of Arts and Sciences, American Philosophical Soc, King's Coll., Univ. of London 1998, Accad. Naz. dei Lincei 2003; mem. Scientific Cttee, Prado Museum 1996. *Publications:* Imperial Spain, 1469–1716 1963, The Revolt of the Catalans 1963, Europe Divided, 1559–1598 1968, The Old World and the New, 1492–1650 1970, The Diversity of History (co-ed. with H. G. Koenigsberger) 1970, A Palace for a King (with J. Brown) 1980 (revised edn 2003), Memoriales y Cartas del Conde Duque de Olivares 1978–80, Richelieu and Olivares 1984, The Count-Duke of Olivares 1986, Spain and Its World 1500–1700 1989, The Hispanic World (ed.) 1991, The World of the Favourite (co-ed.) 1999, The Sale of the Century (with J. Brown) 2002, Empires of the Atlantic World 2006. *Honours:* Hon. Fellow, Trinity Coll., Cambridge 1991, Oriel Coll., Oxford 1997; Commdr, Order of Alfonso X El Sabio 1984, Commdr, Order of Isabel la Católica 1987, Grand Cross of Order of Alfonso X, El Sabio 1988, Grand Cross of Order of Isabel la Católica 1996, Cross of Sant Jordi (Catalonia) 1999; Dr hc (Universidad Autónoma de Madrid) 1983, (Genoa) 1992, (Portsmouth) 1993, (Barcelona) 1994, (Warwick) 1995, (Brown) 1996, (Valencia) 1998, (Lleida) 1999, (Madrid Complutense) 2003, (Coll. of William and Mary) 2005; Visitante Ilustre of Madrid 1983, Leo Gershoy Award, American Historical Asscn 1985, Wolfson Literary Award for History and Biography 1986, Medal of Honour, Universidad Int. Menéndez y Pelayo 1987, Gold Medal for Fine Arts (Spain) 1991, Eloy Antonio de Nebrija Prize (Univ. of Salamanca) 1993, Prince of Asturias Prize in Social Sciences 1996, Gold Medal, Spanish Inst., New York 1997, Balzan Prize for History 1500–1800 1999. *Address:* 122 Church Way, Iffley, Oxford, OX4 4EG, England. *Telephone:* (1865) 716703.

ELLIOTT, Osborn, AB; American journalist; b. 25 Oct. 1924, New York City; s. of John and Audrey N. (Osborn) Elliott; m. 1st Deirdre M. Spencer 1948 (divorced 1972); three d.; m. 2nd the fmr Mrs. Inger A. McCabe; one step s. two step d. *Education:* The Browning School (NY), St Paul's School (Concord) and Harvard Univ. *Career:* served with USNR 1944–46; Reporter NY Journal of Commerce 1946–49; Contributing Ed. Time 1949–52, Assoc. Ed. 1952–55; Senior Business Ed. Newsweek 1955–59, Man. Ed. 1959–61, Ed., Editor-in-Chief, Pres., CEO, Chair. of Bd 1961–76; Deputy Mayor for Econ. Devt, New York 1976–77; Dean Graduate School of Journalism, Columbia Univ., New York 1979–86; Prof. Columbia Univ. 1979–94; fmr Dir Washington Post Co.; fmr Trustee, American Museum of Natural History, Asia Soc., Lincoln Center Theatre, New York Public Library, St Paul's School, Winston Churchill Foundation of the US Ltd; mem. Council on Foreign Relations, Pulitzer Prize Bd 1979–86; mem. Bd of Overseers of Harvard Coll. 1965–71; Chair. Citizens' Cttee for New York City 1975–80, 1990–; mem. Bd New Yorkers for Children 1999–; Organizer Save Our Cities! Save Our Children! march, Washington, DC May 1992; Fellow American Acad. of Arts and Sciences. *Publications:* Men at the Top 1959, The World of Oz 1980, The Negro Revolution in America (ed.) 1964. *Honours:* numerous awards and hon. degrees. *Address:* 84 Water Street, Stonington, CT 06378, USA. *Telephone:* (860) 535-5999 (home). *Fax:* (860) 535-4970 (home).

ELLIOTT, Sir Roger James, Kt, MA, DPhil, FRS; British physicist and publisher; b. 8 Dec. 1928, Chesterfield; s. of James Elliott and Gladys Elliott (née Hill); m. Olga Lucy Atkinson 1952; one s. two d. *Education:* Swanwick Hall School, Derbyshire and New Coll., Oxford. *Career:* Research Assoc. Univ. of Calif., Berkeley 1952–53; Research Fellow, Atomic Energy Research Est.,

Harwell 1953–55; Lecturer, Univ. of Reading 1955–57; Lecturer, Univ. of Oxford 1957–65, Reader 1965–74, Fellow, St John's Coll. 1957–74 (now Hon. Fellow), New Coll. 1974–96 (now Hon. Fellow), Wykeham Prof. of Physics 1974–89, Prof. of Physics 1989–96, Prof. Emer. 1996–; Del. Oxford Univ. Press 1971–88, Sec. to Dels and Chief Exec. 1988–93, Chair. Computer Bd 1983–87; mem. Bd Blackwell Ltd 1996–, Chair. 1999–2002; Visiting Prof., Univ. of Calif., Berkeley 1960–61; Miller Visiting Prof., Univ. of Ill., Urbana 1966; Visiting Distinguished Prof., Fla State Univ. 1981, Mich. State Univ. 1997–2000; Physical Sec. and Vice-Pres. Royal Soc. (London) 1984–88; Treas. Publrs Asscn 1990–92, Pres. 1992–93; Chair. ICSU Press 1997–2002, Disability Information Trust 1998–2001; mem. Bd (part-time) UKAEA 1988–94, British Council 1990–98, Mexican Acad. of Science 2003; Fellow, Inst. of Physics; Treas. ICSU 2002. *Publications:* Magnetic Properties of Rare Earth Metals 1972, Solid State Physics and its Applications 1973; articles in learned journals. *Honours:* Hon. DSc (Paris) 1983, (Bath) 1991, (Essex) 1993; Maxwell Medal (Physical Soc.) 1968, Guthrie Medal 1989. *Address:* 11 Crick Road, Oxford, OX2 6QL, England (home). *Telephone:* (1865) 273997. *Fax:* (1865) 273947. *E-mail:* r.elliott1@physics.ox.ac.uk (office).

ELLIS, Bret Easton, BA; American writer; b. 7 March 1964, Los Angeles. *Education:* Bennington Coll. *Career:* mem. Authors' Guild. *Publications:* Less Than Zero 1985, The Rules of Attraction 1987, American Psycho 1989, The Informers 1994, Glamorama 1998, Lunar Park 2005; contrib. to Rolling Stone, Vanity Fair, Elle, Wall Street Journal, Bennington Review. *Literary Agent:* c/o Amanda Urban, International Creative Management, 40 W 57th Street, New York, NY 10019, USA.

ELLIS, Charles Richard, MA; American publishing executive; b. 20 July 1935, New York; s. of Charles Ellis and Ruth Allen; m. 1st Nathalie Likwas 1957 (divorced 1963); one s.; m. 2nd Jeanne Laurent 1963; four step-s. *Education:* Princeton and Columbia Univs. *Career:* teacher, Barnard School, New York 1958–63; Man. Scientific Research Assocs Chicago 1963–68; Exec. Ed. DC Heath, Boston 1968–70; Chair. and Man. Dir DC Heath Ltd, UK 1970–75; Co-Man. Dir Pergamon Press, UK 1975–78; Marketing Dir Elsevier Publishing, Amsterdam 1978–81; Pres. Elsevier Scientific Publishing Co. New York 1981–88; Exec. Vice-Pres. John Wiley & Sons, New York 1988–90, Pres., CEO 1990–97, Sr Adviser 1998–; Pres. Bd of Trustees, Princeton Univ. Press. 1987–; Chair. Asscn of American Publrs 1992–94; Vice-Chair. Int. Publrs Asscn 1996–. *Honours:* Chevalier des Arts et des Lettres. *Address:* 300 East 54th Street, New York, NY 10022 (home); c/o John Wiley & Sons, 605 Third Avenue, New York, NY 10158, USA (office).

ELLIS, David George, MA, PhD; British academic, writer and translator; b. 23 June 1939, Swinton, Lancashire, England; m. 1966; two d. *Education:* Univ. of Cambridge. *Career:* Lecturer, La Trobe University, Melbourne, Vic., Australia, 1968–72; Lecturer, Senior Lecturer, Prof., University of Kent at Canterbury, England, 1972–. *Publications:* Stendhal, Memoirs of an Egotist (trans.), 1975; Wordsworth, Freud and the Spots of Time: Interpretation in 'The Prelude', 1985; D. H. Lawrence's Non-Fiction: Art, Thought and Genre (with Howard Mills), 1988; Imitating Art: Essays in Biography (ed.), 1993; Dying Game, vol. three, New Cambridge Biography of D. H. Lawrence, 1998; Literary Lives: Biography and the Search for Understanding, 2000. *Address:* English School, University of Kent at Canterbury, Canterbury CT2 7NX, England.

ELLIS, Gavin Peter; New Zealand journalist; *Editor-in-Chief, New Zealand Herald*; b. 6 March 1947, Auckland; s. of Peter Fisher Dundass Ellis and Catherine Ellis (née Gray); m. 1st Janine Laurette Sinclair 1969; m. 2nd Jennifer Ann Lynch 1991; one s. *Education:* Mount Roskill Grammar School and Auckland Univ. *Career:* on staff of Auckland Star paper 1965–70; public relations consultant 1970–71; joined New Zealand Herald 1972, Asst Ed. 1987–96, Ed. 1996–99, Ed.-in-Chief 1999–; Harry Brittain Memorial Fellow 1980; Chair. NZ Section, Commonwealth Press Union; mem. New Zealand Knowledge Wave Trust; mem. NZ Council for Security Co-operation Asia-Pacific. *Address:* 46 Albert Street, Auckland, New Zealand. *Telephone:* (9) 379-5050. *Fax:* (9) 373-6406. *E-mail:* gavin_ellis@herald.co.nz (office); gavin.ellis@xtra.co.nz (home). *Website:* www.nzherald.co.nz (office).

ELLIS, John Martin, BA, PhD; American academic; *Professor Emeritus of German Literature, University of California, Santa Cruz*; b. 31 May 1936, London, England; s. of John Albert Ellis and Emily Ellis; m. Barbara Rhoades 1978; two s. two d. one step-d. *Education:* City of London School and Univ. Coll., London. *Career:* Royal Artillery 1954–56; Tutorial Asst in German, Univ. of Wales, Aberystwyth 1959–60; Asst Lecturer in German, Univ. of Leicester 1960–63; Asst Prof. of German, Univ. of Alberta, Canada 1963–66; Assoc. Prof. of German Literature, Univ. of Calif., Santa Cruz 1966–70, Prof. 1970–94, Prof. Emer. 1994–, Dean Graduate Div. 1977–86; Literary Ed. Heterodoxy 1992–2000; Sec.-Treas. Asscn of Literary Scholars and Critics 1994–2001; Pres. Calif. Asscn of Scholars 2007–; Guggenheim Fellowship, Nat. Endowment for the Humanities Sr Fellowship. *Publications include:* Narration in the German Novelle 1974, The Theory of Literary Criticism: A Logical Analysis 1974, Heinrich von Kleist 1979, One Fairy Story Too Many: The Brothers Grimm and Their Tales 1983, Against Deconstruction 1989, Language, Thought and Logic 1993, Literature Lost: Social Agendas and the Corruption of the Humanities 1997. *Honours:* Nat. Asscn of Scholars' Peter Shaw Memorial Award (for Literature Lost). *Address:* 144 Bay Heights, Soquel, CA 95073, USA. *Telephone:* (831) 476-1144. *Fax:* (831) 476-1188. *E-mail:* john.ellis@earthlink.net (office).

ELLIS, Peter Berresford, (Peter MacAlan, Peter Tremayne); British writer; b. 10 March 1943, Coventry, Warwickshire, England; m. Dorothea Cheesmur 1966. *Education:* Brighton College of Art, University of East London. *Career:* mem. Celtic League, international chair., 1988–90; CWA; Irish Literary Society; London Asscn for Celtic Education, chair., 1989–90, vice-pres., 1990–96; FRHistS; Royal Society of Antiquaries of Ireland, fellow; Society of Authors. *Publications:* Wales – A Nation Again!: The Nationalist Struggle for Freedom, 1968; The Creed of the Celtic Revolution, 1969; The Scottish Insurrection of 1820 (with Seumas Mac a'Ghobhainn), 1970; The Problem of Language Revival (with Seumas Mac a'Ghobhainn), 1971; A History of the Irish Working Class, 1972; The Cornish Language and Its Literature, 1974; Hell or Connaught!: The Cromwellian Colonisation of Ireland, 1652–1660, 1975; The Boyne Water: The Battle of the Boyne, 1690, 1976; The Great Fire of London: An Illustrated Account, 1976; Caesar's Invasion of Britain, 1978; A Voice From the Infinite: The Life of Sir Henry Rider Haggard, 1856–1925, 1978; MacBeth: High King of Scotland, 1040–57 AD, 1979; By Jove, Biggles!: The Life of Captain W. E. Johns (with Piers Williams), 1981; The Liberty Tree, 1982; The Last Adventurer: The Life of Talbot Mundy, 1879–1940, 1984; Celtic Inheritance, 1985; The Celtic Revolution: A Study in Anti-Imperialism, 1985; The Rising of the Moon: A Novel of the Fenian Invasion of Canada, 1987; A Dictionary of Irish Mythology, 1987; The Celtic Empire: The First Millennium of Celtic History, c. 1000 BC–51 AD, 1990; A Guide to Early Celtic Remains in Britain, 1991; A Dictionary of Celtic Mythology, 1992; Celt and Saxon: The Struggle for Britain AD 410–937, 1993; The Celtic Dawn: A History of Pan Celticism, 1993; The Book of Deer, 1994; The Druids, 1994; Celtic Women: Women in Celtic Society and Literature, 1996; Celt and Greek: Celts in the Hellenic World, 1997; Celt and Roman: The Celts of Italy, 1998; The Chronicles of the Celts: New Tellings of Their Myths and Legends, 1999; Erin's Blood Royal: The Gaelic Noble Dynasties of Ireland, 2001. As Peter MacAlan: The Judas Battalion, 1983; Airship, 1984; The Confession, 1985; Kitchener's Gold, 1986; The Valkyrie Directive, 1987; The Doomsday Decree, 1988; Fireball, 1991; The Windsor Protocol, 1993. As Peter Tremayne: The Hound of Frankenstein, 1977; Dracula Unborn, 1977; The Vengeance of She, 1978; The Revenge of Dracula, 1978; The Ants, 1979; The Curse of Loch Ness, 1979; The Fires of Lan-Kern, 1978; Dracula, My Love, 1980; Zombie!, 1981; The Return of Raffles, 1981; The Morgow Rises!, 1982; The Destroyers of Lan-Kern, 1982; The Buccaneers of Lan-Kern, 1983; Snowbeast!, 1983; Raven of Destiny, 1984; Kiss of the Cobra, 1984; Swamp!, 1985; Angelus!, 1985; My Lady of Hy-Brasil and Other Stories, 1987; Nicor!, 1987; Trollnight!, 1987; Ravenmoon, 1988; Island of Shadows, 1991; Aisling and Other Irish Tales of Terror, 1992; Murder by Absolution, 1994; Shroud for the Archbishop, 1995; Suffer Little Children, 1995; The Subtle Serpent, 1996; The Spider's Web, 1997; The Un-Dead: The Legend of Bram Stoker and Dracula (with Peter Haining), 1997; Valley of the Shadow, 1998; The Monk Who Vanished, 1999; Act of Mercy, 1999; Hemlock at Vespers, 2000; Our Lady of Darkness, 2000. Contributions: anthologies, newspapers and magazines. *Honours:* Bard of the Cornish Gorsedd, 1987; Irish Post Award, 1988.

ELLIS, Richard J., BA, MA, PhD; British academic and writer; *Mark O. Hatfield Professor of Politics, Willamette University*; b. 27 Nov. 1960, Leicester, England; m. Juli Takenaka 1987. *Education:* University of California, Santa Cruz, University of California at Berkeley. *Career:* Asst Prof. Willamette University, Salem, Oregon 1990–95, Assoc. Prof. 1995–99, Mark O. Hatfield Prof. of Politics 1999–; mem. American Political Science Asscn; Organization of American Historians. *Publications:* Dilemmas of Presidential Leadership (co-author), 1989; Cultural Theory (co-author), 1990; American Political Cultures, 1993; Presidential Lightning Rods: The Politics of Blame Avoidance, 1994; Politics, Policy and Culture (co-ed.), 1994; Culture Matters: Essays in Honor of Aaron Wildavsky (co-ed.), 1997; The Dark Side of the Left: Illiberal Egalitarianism in America, 1997; Speaking to the People: The Rhetorical Presidency in Historical Perspective, 1998; The Founding of the American Presidency, 1999; Democratic Delusions; The Initiative Process in America, 2002, To The Flag: The Unlikely History of the Pledge of Allegiance 2005; contrib. to Comparative Studies in Society and History; Journal of Behavioural Economics; Presidential Studies Quarterly; Journal of Theoretical Politics: Studies in American Political Development; Review of Politics; Polity; Western Political Quarterly; Critical Review; American Political Science Review. *Honours:* Regents Fellowship, University of California, 1983–85; I. G. S. Harris Fellowship, 1986–88; Summer Stipend, National Endowment for the Humanities, 1991, 2003; Fellowship, George and Eliza Howard Foundation, 1993–94; Oregon Council for the Humanities Research Grant 1994, 2003, Arnold L. and Lois S. Graves Award in the Humanities 1998, Lawrence D. Cress Award for Excellence in Faculty Scholarship 2003. *Address:* Willamette University, Salem, OR 97301, USA.

ELLIS, (Christopher) Royston George, (Richard Tresillian); British writer, lecturer and poet; b. 10 Feb. 1941, Pinner, Middx; one s. *Career:* Asst Ed., Jersey News and Features Agency 1961–63; Assoc. Ed. Canary Islands Sun, Las Palmas 1963–66; Ed. The Educator, Dir Dominica Broadcasting Services and Reuters, Cana Corresp. 1974–76; Man. Ed., Wordsman Features Agency 1977–86; Editorial Consultant, Explore Sri Lanka 1990–2005; Travel and Colonial Property Corresp., Sunday Times, Colombo 1991–; mem. Inst. of Rail Transport (India), Royal Commonwealth Soc. *Publications:* Jiving to Gyp 1959, Rave 1960, The Big Beat Scene 1961, The Rainbow Walking Stick 1961, Rebel 1962, Burn Up 1963, The Mattress Flowers 1963, The Flesh Merchants 1966, The Rush at the End 1967, The Bondmaster Series (seven books) 1977–83, The Fleshtrader Series (three books) 1984–85, The Bloodheart

Series (three books) 1985–87, Giselle 1987, Guide to Mauritius 1988–98, India By Rail 1989–97, Sri Lanka By Rail 1994, Bradt Guide to the Maldives 1995–2006, A Maldives Celebration (with Gemunu Amarasinghe) 1997, A Man For All Islands 1998, Festivals of the World: Madagascar, Trinidad 1999, A Hero In Time 2001, Bradt Guide to Sri Lanka 2002–06; contribs to newspapers and magazines. *Honours:* Dominica Nat. Poetry Awards 1967, 1971. *Address:* Horizon Cottage, Kaikawala-Induruwa, Sri Lanka. *Website:* www.roystonellis.com.

ELLISON, Harlan Jay; American author; b. 27 May 1934, Cleveland, OH; s. of Louis Laverne Ellison and Serita (née Rosenthal) Ellison; m. 1st Charlotte Stein 1956 (divorced 1959); m. 2nd Billie Joyce Sanders 1961 (divorced 1962); m. 3rd Lory Patrick 1965 (divorced 1965); m. 4th Lori Horwitz 1976 (divorced 1977); m. 5th Susan Toth 1986. *Education:* Ohio State Univ. *Career:* part-time actor, Cleveland Playhouse 1944–49; f. Cleveland Science-Fiction Soc. 1950 and Science-Fantasy Bulletin; served US Army 1957–59; ed. Rogue magazine, Chicago 1959-60, Regency Books, Chicago 1960–61; lecturer at colls and univs; voice-overs for animated cartoons; book critic, LA Times 1969–82; Editorial Commentator Canadian Broadcasting Co. 1972–78; Instructor Clarion Writers Workshop, Michigan State Univ. 1969–77; Pres. The Kilimanjaro Corpn 1979–; TV writer for Alfred Hitchcock Hour, Outer Limits, The Man from U.N.C.L.E., Burke's Law; film writer for The Dream Merchants, The Oscar, Nick the Greek, Best By Far, Harlan Ellison's Movie; scenarist: I, Robot 1978, Bug Jack Barron 1982–83; creative consultant, writer and dir The Twilight Zone 1984–85; conceptual consultant, Babylon 5 1993–98; mem. American Writers' Guild and American Science Fiction Writers. *Publications include:* Dangerous Visions (ed.) 1967, The Glass Teat 1970, The Other Glass Teat 1975, A Boy and His Dog (novella) 1975, Strange Wine 1978, Stalking the Nightmare 1982, An Edge in My Voice 1985, The Essential Ellison 1987, Angry Candy (short stories) 1988, Harlan Ellison's Watching 1989, The Harlan Ellison Hornbook 1990, Harlan Ellison's Movie 1990, Mefisto in Onyx 1993, Mind Fields (33 stories inspired by the art of Jacek Yerka) 1994, Robot: The Illustrated Screenplay 1994, City on the Edge of Forever (screenplay) 1995, Slippage 1996, Edgeworks: The Collected Ellison (four vols) 1996–97, Repent, Harlequin 1997, Troublemakers 2001. *Honours:* Hugo Awards 1967, 1968, 1973, 1974, 1975, 1977, 1986, Special Achievement Awards 1968–72, Certificate of Merit, Trieste Film Festival 1970, Edgar Allan Poe Award, Mystery Writers 1974, 1988, American Mystery Award 1988, Bram Stoker Award, Horror Writers Asscn 1988, 1990, 1994; World Fantasy Award 1989, Georges Méliès Award for cinematic achievement 1972, 1973, PEN Award for journalism 1982; Americana Annual American Literature: Major Works 1988, World Fantasy 1993 Life Achievement Award, two Audie Awards, Audio Publishers Asscn 1999 and numerous other awards. *Address:* c/o HERC, PO Box 55548, Sherman Oaks, CA 91413-0548, USA.

ELLMANN, Lucy, MA; American/British writer, screenwriter and critic; b. 18 Oct. 1956, Evanston, IL; d. of Richard Ellmann and Mary Ellmann (née Donahue); m. Todd McEwen; one d. *Education:* Falmouth School of Art, Cornwall, Univ. of Essex and Courtauld Inst., London, UK. *Career:* mem. judging panel Irish Times-Aer Lingus Int. Fiction Prize 1992; Hawthornden Fellow 1992, Royal Literary Fund Fellow 2005. *Publications:* novels: Sweet Desserts (Guardian Fiction Prize) 1988, Varying Degrees of Hopelessness 1991, Man or Mango 1998, Dot in the Universe 2003, Doctors & Nurses 2006; contrib. to various periodicals and newspapers, including New Statesman, TLS, Guardian, Independent on Sunday, Observer, Washington Post, New York Times Book Review. *Address:* c/o Bloomsbury Publishing, 37 Soho Square, London, W1D 3HB, England.

ELLROY, James; American writer; b. (Lee Earle Ellroy), 4 March 1948, Los Angeles, Calif.; m. 1st Mary Doherty 1988 (divorced 1991); m. 2nd Helen Knode 1991. *Education:* John Burroughs Junior High School and Fairfax High School, Los Angeles. *Publications:* Brown's Requiem 1981, Clandestine 1982, Blood on the Moon (Lloyd Hopkins series) 1983, Because the Night (Lloyd Hopkins series) 1984, Killer on the Road 1986, Silent Terror 1986, Suicide Hill (Lloyd Hopkins series) 1986, The Black Dahlia (LA series) 1987, The Big Nowhere (LA series) 1988, LA Confidential (LA series) 1990, White Jazz (LA series) 1992, Hollywood Nocturnes (essays and stories) 1994, American Tabloid (Underworld USA series) (Time Magazine Novel of the Year) 1995, My Dark Places (memoir) (Salon.com Book of the Year) 1996, LA Noir 1998, Crime Wave (essays and stories) 1999, The Cold Six Thousand (Underworld USA series) 2001, Destination: Morgue (essays and stories) 2003. *Literary Agent:* Sobel Weber Associates Inc, 146 East 19th Street, New York, NY 10003, USA. *Address:* c/o Warner Books Publicity Dept, 1271 Avenue of the Americas, New York, NY 10020, USA (office).

ELMSLIE, Kenward Gray, (Lavinia Sanchez), BA; American poet, librettist, writer and performance artist; b. 27 April 1929, New York, NY. *Education:* Harvard Univ. *Career:* mem. American Soc. of Composers, Authors and Publishers. *Publications:* poetry: The Champ 1968, Album 1969, Circus Nerves 1971, Motor Disturbance 1971, Tropicalism 1976, The Alphabet Work 1977, Communications Equipment 1979, Moving Right Along 1980, Sung Sex 1989, Pay Dirt (with Joe Brainard) 1992, Champ Dust 1994, Girl Machine, White Attic, Routine Disruptions: Selected Poems and Lyrics 1998, Cyberspace (with Trevor Winkfield) 2000, Blast from the Past 2000, Nite Soil 2000, Snippets 2002, Agenda Melt 2004; musical theatre: Lizzie Borden 1966, Miss Julie 1966, The Sweet Bye and Bye 1973, The Seagull 1974, Washington Square 1976, Three Sisters 1986; musical plays: The Grass Harp 1971, Lola 1982, Postcards on Parade 1993; fiction: The Orchid Stories 1972, Bimbo Dirt

1981, 26 Bars 1986; other: City Junket (play) 1987, Bare Bones (memoir) 1995, LingoLand (musical revue) 2005; contrib. to many anthologies, reviews and journals. *Honours:* Frank O'Hara Poetry Award 1971. *Address:* PO Box 38, Calais, VT 05648, USA (office). *Fax:* (212) 929-5166 (office). *Website:* www .kenwardelmslie.com.

ELSOM, John Edward, BA, PhD; British dramatist, journalist, broadcaster and lecturer; b. 31 Oct. 1934, Leigh on Sea, Essex, England; m. Sally Mays 1956, two s. *Education:* City Univ., London. *Career:* script adviser, Paramount Pictures 1960–68; theatre critic, London Magazine 1963–68, The Listener 1972–82; correspondent, Contemporary Review 1978–88; Lecturer and Course Leader in Arts Criticism, City Univ., London 1986–96; consultant, South Bank Univ. 1996–97, School for Oriental and African Studies, Univ. of London 1997; Dir of arts management consultancy, Arts Interlink; mem. Liberal Party of Great Britain Art and Broadcasting Cttee (chair. and convenor 1978–88), Int. Asscn of Theatre Critics (hon. pres.). *Publications:* Theatre Outside London 1969, Erotic Theatre 1972, Post-War British Theatre 1976, The History of the National Theatre 1978, Change and Choice 1978, Post-War British Theatre Criticism (ed.) 1981, Is Shakespeare Still Our Contemporary? (ed.) 1989, Cold War Theatre 1992, Missing the Point 1998; also plays; contrib. to Observer, Mail on Sunday, Encounter, TLS, The World and I, Sunday Telegraph, Plays International, Plays & Players, San Diego Union and others. *Address:* 14 Homersham Road, Kingston-upon-Thames, Surrey KT1 3PN, England.

ELTIS, Walter Alfred, MA, DLitt; British economist; *Fellow Emeritus, Exeter College, Oxford;* b. 23 May 1933, Warnsdorf, Czechoslovakia; s. of Rev. Martin Eltis and Mary Schnitzer; m. Shelagh M. Owen 1959; one s. two d. *Education:* Wycliffe Coll., Emmanuel Coll. Cambridge and Nuffield Coll. Oxford. *Career:* Research Fellow in Econs, Exeter Coll., Oxford 1958–60; Lecturer in Econs, Univ. of Oxford 1961–88; Fellow and Tutor in Econs, Exeter Coll. Oxford 1963–88, Fellow Emer. 1988–; Econ. Dir Nat. Econ. Devt Office 1986–88, Dir-Gen. 1988–92; Chief Econ. Adviser to the Pres. of Bd of Trade 1992–95; Visiting Reader in Econs, Univ. of Western Australia 1970–71; Visiting Prof., Univ. of Toronto 1976–77, European Univ. Florence 1979, Univ. of Reading 1992–2004; Gresham Prof. of Commerce, Gresham Coll. London 1993–96; mem. Reform Club (Chair. 1994–95), Political Economy Club, Royal Automobile Club, European Soc. for the History of Econ. Thought (Vice-Pres. 2000–04). *Publications:* Growth and Distribution 1973, Britain's Economic Problem: Too Few Producers (with R. Bacon) 1976, The Classical Theory of Economic Growth 1984, Keynes and Economic Policy (with P. Sinclair) 1988, Classical Economics, Public Expenditure and Growth 1993, Britain's Economic Problem Revisited 1996, Condillac: Commerce and Government (co-ed. with S. M. Eltis) 1998, Britain, Europe and EMU 2000. *Address:* Danesway, Jarn Way, Boars Hill, Oxford, OX1 5JF, England (home). *Telephone:* (1865) 735440 (home).

ELTON, Benjamin (Ben) Charles, BA; British writer and performer; b. 3 May 1959, s. of Prof. Lewis Richard Benjamin Elton and Mary Elton (née Foster); m. Sophie Gare 1994. *Education:* Godalming Grammar School, S Warwicks. Coll. of Further Educ., Univ. of Manchester. *Career:* first professional appearance Comic Strip Club 1981; numerous tours as stand-up comic 1986–. *Film:* Maybe Baby (writer and dir) 2000, Much Ado About Nothing (actor) 1993. *Television:* writer: Alfresco 1982–83, The Young Ones (jtly) 1982–84, Happy Families 1985, Filthy Rich and Catflap 1986, Black-adder II (jtly) 1986, Blackadder the Third (jtly) 1987, Blackadder Goes Forth (jtly) 1989, The Thin Blue Line (jtly) 1995–96; writer and performer: South of Watford (jtly, documentary series) 1984–85, Friday Night Live 1988, Saturday Live 1985–87, Ben Elton Live 1989, 1993, 1997, The Man from Auntie 1990, 1994, Stark 1993, The Ben Elton Show (jtly) 1998. *Theatre:* Gasping 1990, Silly Cow 1991, Popcorn 1996, Blast from the Past 1998, The Beautiful Game (musical, book and lyrics) 2000, We Will Rock You (story to musical) 2002, Tonight's the Night (story to musical) 2003. *Recordings:* albums: Motormouth 1987, Motorvation 1989. *Publications:* novels: Bachelor Boys 1984, Stark 1989, Gridlock 1992, This Other Eden 1993, Popcorn 1996, Blast from the Past 1998, Inconceivable 1999, Dead Famous 2001, High Society 2002, Past Mortem 2004, The First Casualty 2005, Chart Throb 2006. *Honours:* British Acad. Best Comedy Show Awards 1984, 1987, Best New Comedy Laurence Olivier Award 1998. *Literary Agent:* c/o Phil McIntyre, Second Floor, 35 Soho Square, London, W1D 3QX, England.

EMECHETA, (Florence Onye) Buchi, BSc; Nigerian/British writer and lecturer; b. 21 July 1944, Lagos, Nigeria; d. of Jeremy Nwabudike Emecheta and Alice Okwuekwu Emecheta; m. Sylvester Onwordi 1960; two s. three d. *Education:* Methodist Girls' High School, Lagos and Univ. of London. *Career:* fmr librarian and community worker; Sr Research Fellow, Visiting Prof. of English, Univ. of Calabar 1980–81; Lecturer, Yale Univ., USA 1982, Univ. of London 1982; numerous visiting professorships at univs in USA; Propr Ogwugwn Afo Publishing Co.; mem. Home Sec.'s Advisory Council on Race 1979, Arts Council 1982–83, PEN International; contrib. to newspapers and periodicals, including New Statesman, New Society, New International, Sunday Times Magazine, Times Literary Supplement, Guardian. *Publications:* In the Ditch 1972, Second Class Citizen 1975, The Bride Price 1976, The Slave Girl (New Statesman Jock Campbell Award for Commonwealth Writers 1979) 1977, The Joys of Motherhood 1979, Naira Power 1981, On Our Freedom 1981, Destination Biafra 1982, Double Yoke 1982, Adah's Story 1983, A Land of Marriage 1983, The Rape of Shavi 1983, Head Above Water (autobiog.) 1984, Family Bargain 1987, Gwendolen 1990, Kehinde 1994, The

New Tribe 2000; children's books: Titch the Cat 1979, Nowhere to Play 1980, The Moonlight Bride 1980, The Wrestling Match 1980. *Honours:* Jack Campbell Award, New Statesman 1979, one of Best Young British Writers 1983.

EMERSON, Ru, (Robert Cray), LLB; American writer; b. 15 Dec. 1944, Monterey, CA. *Education:* Univ. of Montana, LA Co. Bar Asscn. *Career:* mem. SFWA. *Publications:* Princess of Flames 1986, To the Haunted Mountains 1987, In the Caves of Exile 1988, On the Seas of Destiny 1989, SpellBound 1990, Beauty and the Beast 1990, Trilogy: Night Threads (The Calling of the Three 1990, The Two in Hiding 1991, One Land, One Duke 1993), The Bard's Tale: Fortress of Frost and Fire (with Mercedes Lackey) 1993, The Sword and the Lion 1993, Trilogy: Night Threads (The Craft of Light 1993, The Art of the Sword 1994, The Science of Power 1995), Xena: Warrior Princess The Empty Throne 1996, Xena: Warrior Princess The Huntress and the Sphynx 1997, Xena: Warrior Princess The Thief of Hermes 1997, Voices of Chaos (with A. C. Crispin) 1998, Against the Giants 1999, Trilogy: Xena: Warrior Princess (Go Quest, Young Man 1999, Questward Ho! 2000, How the Quest Was Won 2000), Keep on the Borderland 2001; contrib. to anthologies and magazines. *Address:* 2600 Reuben Boise Road, Dallas, OR 97338, USA. *E-mail:* ruemerson@aol.com.

EMMETT, Nicholas; Irish writer and translator; b. 22 July 1935, Dublin; m. Anne Brit Emmett 1965. *Education:* Univ. of Oslo, Univ. of Galway. *Career:* left school at 14 to work in tobacco factory; short stories published England, USA, Ireland, Norway 1970–2004; taxi-owner and driver six years; interpreter-translator, Indian Embassy, Oslo, Norway 1973; founding Co-Ed., Ragtime, English cultural magazine, Norway; mem. The Irish Writers' Union, Soc. of Authors. *Publications:* The Cave (novel) 1987, The Red Mist and Other Stories 1988; short stories include Brains on the Dump 1991, An Empty Glass House, A Pale Green Moon; contrib. 87 short stories and articles in newspapers, anthologies and magazines, England, USA, Ireland, Norway; 23 stories broadcast on BBC and Irish National Radio. *Honours:* Irish Arts Council writing grant 1976. *Address:* Rathcoffey North, Donadea, Co. Kildare, Ireland. *Telephone:* (86) 366-8426 (home).

EMMOTT, William (Bill) John, BA; British journalist; b. 6 Aug. 1956, s. of Richard Emmott and Audrey Emmott; m. 1st Charlotte Crowther 1982 (divorced); m. 2nd Carol Barbara Mawer 1992. *Education:* Latymer Upper School, Hammersmith and Magdalen and Nuffield Colls, Oxford. *Career:* Brussels Corresp., The Economist 1980–82, Econs Corresp. 1982–83, Tokyo Corresp. 1983–86, Finance Ed. 1986–89, Business Affairs Ed. 1989–93, Ed.-in-Chief 1993–2006, Editorial Dir Economist Intelligence Unit May–Dec. 1992. *Publications:* The Pocket Economist (with R. Pennant-Rea) 1983, The Sun Also Sets 1989, Japanophobia 1993, Kanryo no Taizai 1996, 20:21 Vision: The Lessons of the 20th Century for the 21st 2003. *Honours:* Hon. Fellow, Magdalen Coll., Oxford 2002; Hon. LLD (Warwick) 1999; Hon. DLitt (City) 2001. *Address:* c/o The Economist, 25 St James's Street, London, SW1A 1HG, England (office).

ENAHORO, Chief Anthony, C.FR.; Nigerian politician, journalist, newspaper publisher and company director; b. 22 July 1923, Uromi Ishan, Bendel State; s. of late Chief Okotako Enahoro and Princess Inibokun Okoje; m. Helen Ediae 1954; four s. one d. *Education:* Govt Schools Uromi and Owo, King's Coll. Lagos. *Career:* journalist 1942–52; Ed. Southern Nigerian Defender 1944–45, Daily Comet 1945–49; Assoc. Ed. West African Pilot; Ed.-in-Chief Nigerian Star 1950–52; foundation mem. Action Group Party, later Acting Gen. Sec. and Fed. Vice-Pres.; Chair. Uromi Dist Council and Ishan Div. Council; mem. Western House of Assembly and Fed. House of Reps and Party Chief Whip 1951–54; Dir Nat. Coal Bd 1953–56; Minister of Home Affairs, Transport, Information and Midwest Affairs and Leader of the House (Western Region) 1954–59; Fed. MP and Opposition Spokesman on Foreign Affairs, Internal Affairs and Legislature Affairs 1959–63; moved motion for self-govt and attended all constitutional talks preceding independence in 1960; detained during Emergency period Western Region 1962, fled to Britain, extradited and imprisoned in Nigeria for treasonable felony; released by mil. govt 1966; Leader, Midwest State del. to Constitutional Conf. and mem. Constitutional Cttee 1966; Fed. Commr for Information, Culture, Youth, Sports, Co-operatives and Labour 1967–75; mem. Nat. Democratic Coalition (NADECO); Fed. Commr for Special Duties 1975; Pres. World Black and African Festival of Arts and Culture 1972–75; State Chair. Nat. Party of Nigeria 1978–80; Chair. Cttees Edo State Movt 1981–, Nigerian Shippers Council 1982; detained Aug.–Dec. 1994. *Publication:* Fugitive Offender (autobiog.). *Honours:* Hon. DSc (Benin) 1972. *Address:* Rainbow House, 144 Upper Mission Road, P.M.B. 1425, Benin City, Nigeria. *Telephone:* 200803 (office); 243770 (home).

ENG, Stephen Richard, BA, MS; American biographer, poet and literary journalist; b. 31 Oct. 1940, San Diego, CA; m. Anne Jeanne Kangas 1969, two s. two d. *Education:* George Washington University, Washington, DC, Portland State University, Oregon. *Career:* Poetry Ed., The Diversifier, 1977–78; Assoc. Ed., Triads, 1985; Dir and Ed., Nashville House, 1991–; Staff Book Reviewer, Nashville Banner, 1993–98; mem. Broadcast Music Inc, 1972–; Syndic, F. Marion Crawford Memorial Society, 1978–; Country Music Asscn, 1990–; Science-Fiction Poetry Asscn, 1990–. *Publications:* Elusive Butterfly and Other Lyrics (ed.), 1971; The Face of Fear and Other Poems (ed.), 1984; The Hunter of Time: Gnomic Verses (ed.), 1984; Toreros: Poems (ed.), 1990; Poets of the Fantastic (co-ed.), 1992; A Satisfied Mind: The Country Music Life of Porter Wagoner, 1992; Jimmy Buffett: The Man From Margaritaville Revealed, 1996; Yellow Rider and Other Lyrics, 2000. Contributions: Lyric; Night Cry; Journal of Country Music; Tennessee Historical Quarterly; Bookpage; Nashville Banner; Music City Blues; Space & Time. *Honours:* American Poets' Fellowship Society Certificate of Merit, 1973; Co-Winner, Rhysling Award, Science Fiction Poetry Asscn, 1979; Best Writer, 1979, 1983, Special Achievement, 1985, Small Press Writers and Artists Organization.

ENGEL, Howard, BA; Canadian writer; b. 2 April 1931, Toronto, Ont.; m. 1st Marian Ruth Passmore 1962 (divorced); one s. one d.; m. 2nd Janet Evelyn Hamilton 1978 (deceased); one s. *Education:* St Catharine's Collegiate Inst., McMaster Univ., Ontario Coll. of Educ. *Career:* Writer-in-Residence, Hamilton Public Library 1989; Barker Fairley Distinguished Visitor in Canadian Culture, Univ. Coll., Univ. of Toronto 1995–96; mem. Crime Writers of Canada (Chair. 1986–87), Int. Asscn of Crime Writers, MWA, Writers' Guild of Canada. *Publications:* The Suicide Murders 1980, The Ransom Game 1981, Murder on Location 1982, Murder Sees the Light 1984, A City Called July 1986, A Victim Must Be Found 1988, Dead and Buried 1990, Murder in Montparnasse 1992, Criminal Shorts: Mysteries by Canadian Crime Writers (co-ed. with Eric Wright) 1992, There was an Old Woman 1993, Getting Away With Murder 1995, Lord High Executioner: An Unashamed Look at Hangmen, Headsmen, and Their Kind 1996, Mr Doyle and Dr Bell 1997, A Child's Christmas in Scarborough 1997, The Cooperman Variations 2001, Memory Book 2005; contrib. to radio and TV. *Honours:* Hon. LLD (Brock Univ.) 1994; Arthur Ellis Award for Crime Fiction 1984, Harbourfront Festival Prize 1990, Matt Cohen Literary Award for a body of work 2005. *Literary Agent:* c/o Beverley Slopen Literary Agency, 131 Bloor Street W, Suite 711, Toronto, ON M5S 1S3, Canada. *Telephone:* (416) 964-9598. *Fax:* (416) 921-7726. *E-mail:* beverley@slopenagency.ca. *Website:* www.slopenagency.ca. *Address:* 281 Major Street, Toronto, ON M5S 2L5, Canada.

ENGEL, Johannes K.; German journalist and editor; b. 29 April 1927, Berlin; s. of Karl and Anna (née Helke) Engel; m. Ruth Moter 1951; one s. one d. *Career:* journalist, Int. News Service and Der Spiegel magazine 1946–, office man., Frankfurt am Main 1948, Dept Head 1951, Ed.-in-Chief, Hamburg 1961, co-Ed.-in-Chief Der Spiegel (with Erich Böhme) 1973–86. *Address:* Kirchenredder 7, 22339 Hamburg, Germany. *Telephone:* 30071 (office).

ENGELL, Hans; Danish politician and newspaper editor; *Editor-in-Chief, Ekstra Bladet;* b. 8 Oct. 1948, Copenhagen; s. of Knud Engell Andersen. *Education:* Coll. of Journalism. *Career:* journalist for Berlingske newspaper consortium 1968–78; Head of Press Service of Conservative People's Party 1978–82; mem. Parl. 1984–, Minister for Defence 1982–87, of Justice 1989–93; Chair. Conservative Parl. Group 1987–89; Leader Conservative People's Party 1995–97; Ed.-in-Chief Ekstra Bladet 2000–. *Address:* Ekstra Bladet, Rådhuspladsen, 1785 Copenhagen (office); Puggaardsgade 13, 1573 Copenhagen, Denmark. *Telephone:* 33-47-23-02 (office). *Fax:* 33-47-14-10-00 (office). *E-mail:* hans.engell@eb.dk (office).

ENGELS, John David, BA, MFA; American academic, poet and writer; b. 19 Jan. 1931, South Bend, IN; m. Gail Jochimsen 1957, four s. two d. *Education:* University of Notre Dame, University College, Dublin, University of Iowa. *Career:* Instructor, Norbert College, West De Pere, Wisconsin, 1957–62; Asst Prof., 1962–70, Prof. of English, 1970–, St Michael's College, Winooski Park, Vermont; Visiting Lecturer, University of Vermont, 1974, 1975, 1976; Slaughter Lecturer, Sweet Briar College, 1976; Writer-in-Residence, Randolph Macon Women's College, 1992. *Publications:* Poetry: The Homer Mitchell Place, 1968; Signals from the Safety Coffin, 1975; Blood Mountain, 1977; Vivaldi in Early Fall, 1981; The Seasons in Vermont, 1982; Weather-Fear: New and Selected Poems 1958–1982, 1983; Cardinals in the Ice Age, 1987; Walking to Cootehill: New and Selected Poems 1958–1992, 1993; Big Water, 1995. Other: Writing Techniques (with Norbert Engels), 1962; Experience and Imagination (with Norbert Engels), 1965; The Merrill Checklist of William Carlos Williams (ed.), 1969; The Merrill Studies in Paterson (ed.), 1971. *Honours:* Bread Loaf Writers' Conference Scholarship, 1960, and Robert Frost Fellowship, 1976; Guggenheim Fellowship, 1979.

ENGLADE, Kenneth (Ken) Francis, BA; American writer and fmr journalist; b. 7 Oct. 1938, Memphis, TN; m. 1st Sharon Flynn 1960 (divorced); two s. one d.; m. 2nd Sara Elizabeth Crewe 1980 (divorced 1991); m. 3rd Heidi Hizel 1997. *Education:* Louisiana State University. *Career:* mem. American Society of Journalists and Authors; Authors' Guild; Southwest Writers. *Publications:* Non-Fiction: Cellar of Horror, 1989; Murder in Boston, 1990; Beyond Reason: The True Story of a Shocking Double Murder, a Brilliant and Beautiful Virginia Socialite, and a Deadly Psychotic Obsession, 1990; Deadly Lessons, 1991; A Family Business, 1992; To Hatred Turned: A True Story of Love and Death in Texas, 1992; Blood Sister, 1994; Hot Blood: The Millionairess, the Money, and the Horse Murders, 1996. Fiction: People of the Plains, 1996; The Tribes, 1996; The Soldiers, 1996; Battle Cry, 1996. *Address:* c/o St Martin's Press, 175 Fifth Avenue, New York, NY 10010, USA.

ENGLE, Margarita; American novelist and poet; b. 2 Sept. 1951, Pasadena, CA; m. Curtis Engle, 18 April 1978, one s. one d. *Education:* BS, Agronomy, California Polytechnic University, Pomona, 1974; MS, Botany, Iowa State University, Ames, 1977. *Career:* mem. PEN USA West. *Publications:* Singing to Cuba, 1993; Skywriting, 1995. *Honours:* Cintas Fellowship, San Diego Book Award. *Literary Agent:* Julie Castiglia, 1155 Camino Del Mar, Suite 510, Del Mar, CA 92014, USA.

ENQUIST, Anna; Dutch writer, poet, psychoanalyst and musician; b. 19 July 1945, Amsterdam; m. B. E. Widlund. *Education:* Univ. of Leiden, The Hague Conservatory. *Career:* pianist, psychology teacher, school psychologist; staff, Netherlands Psychoanalytical Inst. 1987–2000. *Publications:* poetry: Soldatenliederen 1991, Jachtscènes 1992, Een nieuw afscheid 1994, Klaarlichte dag 1996, De tweede helft 2000, Hier was vuur (The Fire Was Here) 2003, De tussentijd 2004; novels: Het meesterstuk (The Masterpiece) 1994, Het geheim (The Secret) 1997, De ijsdragers (The Ice Carriers) 2002, De thuiskomst 2005; short stories: De kwetium (The Injury) 1999; monologues: De sprong 2003. *Honours:* Debuut Prize 1994, Trouw Publiekprize 1997. *Literary Agent:* De Arbeiderspers, Herengracht 370–372, Amsterdam, The Netherlands. *Telephone:* 20-5247500 (office). *Fax:* 20-6224937 (office). *E-mail:* info@arbeiderspers.nl (office).

ENQUIST, Lynn W.; American editor and writer. *Career:* Ed.-in-Chief, Journal of Virology, American Soc. for Microbiology. *Publications:* contrib. to Experiments with Gene Fusions 1984, Principles of Virology: Molecular Biology, Pathogenesis and Control 1999. *Address:* Journal of Virology, American Society for Microbiology, 1752 North Street NW, Washington, DC 20036-2904, USA. *Website:* www.jvi.asm.org.

ENQUIST, Per Olov, MA; Swedish novelist, playwright, journalist and poet; b. 1934, Hjoggböle; m. 2nd Lone Bastholm. *Education:* Univ. of Uppsala. *Career:* Visiting Prof. UCLA 1973. *Publications:* Kristallögat 1961, Färdvägen 1963, Magnetisörens Femte Vinter 1964, Bröderna Casey 1964, Hess 1966, Sextiotalskritik 1966, Legionärerna 1968, Sekonden 1971, Katedralen i München 1972, Berättelser Från de Inställda Upprorens Tid (short stories) 1974, Tribadernas Natt 1975, Chez Nous (with Anders Ehnmark) 1976, Musikanternas Uttåg 1978, Mannen På Trottoaren 1979, Till Fedra 1980, Från Regnormarnas Liv 1981, En Triptyk 1981, Doktor Mabuses Nya Testamente (with Anders Ehnmark) 1982, Strindberg Ett Liv 1984, Nedstörtad Ängel 1985, Två Reportage om Idrott 1986, I Lodjurets Timma 1988, Kapten Nemos Bibliotek 1991, Hamsun (screenplay) 1996, Bildmakarna (play) 1998, Livläkarens Besök 1999, Systrarna (play) 2000, Lewis Resa 2001; contrib. to literary criticism in newspapers, including Uppsala Nya Tidning, Svenska Dagbladet, Expressen. *Honours:* Nordic Council literary prize 1968, August Award 1999, Independent Foreign Fiction Prize 2003. *Address:* c/o Vintage, Random House, 20 Vauxhall Bridge Road, London, SW1V 2SA, England.

ENSLIN, Theodore Vernon; American poet and writer; b. 25 March 1925, Chester, PA; m. 1st Mildred Marie Stout 1945 (divorced 1961); one s. one d.; m. 2nd Alison Jane Jose 1969; one s. *Education:* studied with Nadia Boulanger. *Career:* columnist, The Cape Codder, Orleans, MA 1949–56. *Publications:* Poetry: The Work Proposed, 1958; New Sharon's Prospect, 1962; The Place Where I Am Standing, 1964; To Come to Have Become, 1966; The Diabelli Variations and Other Poems, 1967; 2/30–6/31: Poems 1967, 1967; The Poems, 1970; Forms, five vols, 1970–74; The Median Flow: Poems 1943–73, 1974; Ranger, Ranger 2, two vols, 1979, 1980; Music for Several Occasions, 1985; Case Book, 1987; Love and Science, 1990; A Sonare, 1994. Fiction: 2 + 12 (short stories), 1979. Play: Barometric Pressure 29.83 and Steady, 1965. Other: Mahler, 1975; The July Book, 1976. *Honours:* Nieman Award for Journalism 1955, National Endowment for the Arts grant 1976.

ENZENSBERGER, Hans Magnus, (Andreas Thalmayr), DPhil; German poet and writer; *Artistic Director, Renaissance Theatre Berlin;* b. 11 Nov. 1929, Kaufbeuren; m. 1st Dagrun Averaa Christensen; one d.; m. 2nd Maria Alexandrowna Makarowa 1986; m. 3rd Katharina Bonitz; one d. *Education:* Univs of Erlangen, Freiburg im Breisgau, Hamburg and Paris. *Career:* Third Programme Ed., Stuttgart Radio 1955–57; Lecturer, Hochschule für Gestaltung, Ulm 1956–57; Literary Consultant to Suhrkamp's (publrs), Frankfurt 1960–; mem. 'Group 47', Ed. Kursbuch (review) 1965–75, Publr 1970–90; Ed. TransAtlantik (monthly magazine) 1980–82; Publr and Ed., Die Andere Bibliothek 1985–2005; Artistic Dir Renaissance Theatre Berlin 1995–. *Publications:* poetry: Verteidigung der Wölfe 1957, Landessprache 1960, Blindenschrift 1964, Poems for People Who Don't Read Poems (English edn) 1968, Gedichte 1955–1970 1971, Mausoleum 1975; essays: Clemens Brentanos Poetik 1961, Einzelheiten 1962, Politik und Verbrechen 1964; also: Deutschland, Deutschland unter Anderen 1967, Das Verhör von Habana (play) 1970, Freisprüche 1970, Der kurze Sommer der Anarchie (novel) 1972, Gespräche mit Marx und Engels 1973, Palaver 1974; Ed. Museum der Modernen Poesie 1960, Allerleirauh 1961, Andreas Gryphius Gedichte 1962, Edward Lears kompletter Nonsense (trans.) 1977, Raids and Reconstruction (essays, English edn), Der Untergang der Titanic (epic poem) 1978, Die Furie des Verschwindens 1980, Politische Brosamen 1982, Critical Essays 1982, Der Menschenfreund 1984, Ach Europa! 1987, Mittelmass und Wahn 1988, Requiem für eine romantische Frau 1988, Der Fliegende Robert 1989, Zukunftsmusik (poems) 1991, Die grosse Wanderung 1992, Aussichten auf den Bürgerkrieg 1993, Diderots Schatten 1994, The Palace (libretto) 1994, Civil War (English edn) 1994, Selected Poems (English edn) 1994, Kiosk (poems) 1995 (English edn 1997), Voltaires Neffe (play) 1996, Der Zahlenteufel 1997, The Number Devil (English edn) 1998, Zickzack 1997, Wo warst du, Robert? (novel) 1998, Where were you, Robert? (English edn) 2000, Leichter als Luft (poems) 1999 (English edn 2001), Mediocrity and Delusion (English edn) 1992, Die Elixiere der Wissenschaft (essays and poems) 2002, Nomaden im regal (essays) 2003, Die Geschichte der Wolken (poems) 2003, Dialoge (prose) 2005; as Andreas Thalmayr: Heraus mit der Sprache 2005. *Honours:* Ordre pour le Mérite 2000; Hugo Jacobi Prize 1956, Kritiker Prize 1962, Georg

Büchner Prize 1963, Premio Pasolini 1982, Heinrich Böll Prize 1985, Kultureller Ehrenpreis der Stadt München 1994, Heinrich Heine Prize, Düsseldorf 1997, Príncipe de Asturias 2002, and others. *Address:* c/o Suhrkamp-Verlag, Lindenstr. 29, 60325 Frankfurt am Main, Germany.

EPHRON, Delia; American author, scriptwriter and producer; b. 1945, Beverly Hills, Calif.; d. of the late Henry Ephron and of Phoebe Ephron (née Wolkind); sister of Nora Ephron (q.v.); m. Jerome Kass. *Career:* began career as journalist, New York Magazine and New York Times; co-writer of screenplays with sister, Nora Ephron. *Screenplays include:* This is My Life 1992, Sleepless in Seattle (assoc. producer) 1993, Mixed Nuts (also exec. producer) 1994, Michael (also exec. producer and composer of song, Lips Like a Blowfish) 1996, You've Got Mail (also exec. producer) 1998, Lucky Numbers 1999, Hanging Up (also exec. producer) 2000, The Sisterhood of the Traveling Pants 2005, Bewitched 2005. *Publications include:* How to Eat Like A Child, Teenage Romance or How to Die of Embarrassment, Big City Eyes 2000; numerous children's books. *Literary Agent:* International Creative Management, 40 West 57th Street, New York, NY 10019, USA.

EPHRON, Nora, BA; American writer and scriptwriter; b. 19 May 1941, New York; d. of Henry Ephron and Phoebe (née Wolkind) Ephron; sister of Delia Ephron (q.v.); m. 1st Dan Greenburg (divorced); m. 2nd Carl Bernstein (divorced); two s.; m. 3rd Nicholas Pileggi. *Education:* Wellesley Coll. *Career:* reporter, New York Post 1963–68; freelance writer 1968–; Contributing Ed. and columnist, Esquire Magazine 1972–73, Sr Ed. 1974–78; Contributing Ed., New York Magazine 1973–74; mem. American Writers' Guild, Authors' Guild, PEN, Acad. of Motion Picture Arts and Sciences. *Film appearances:* Crimes and Misdemeanors, Husbands and Wives. *Screenplays:* Silkwood (with Alice Arlen) 1983, Heartburn 1986, When Harry Met Sally... 1989, Cookie 1989 (co-exec. producer, co-screenwriter), My Blue Heaven 1990, This is My Day 1992 (dir, screenwriter, with Delia Ephron), Sleepless in Seattle (also dir) 1993, Mixed Nuts (also dir), Michael (also dir) 1996, You've Got Mail (also dir) 1998, Red Tails in Love: a Wildlife Drama in Central Park (also producer and dir) 2000, Lucky Numbers 1999, Hanging Up (also producer) 2000, Bewitched (also dir) 2005. *Publications:* Wallflower at the Orgy 1970, Crazy Salad 1975, Scribble, Scribble 1978, Heartburn 1983, Nora Ephron Collected 1991, Big City Eyes 2000, I Feel Bad About My Neck 2006. *Honours:* BAFTA for Best Screenplay 1989. *Literary Agent:* c/o Sam Cohn, International Creative Management, 40 West 57th Street, New York, NY 10019, USA.

EPSTEIN, Joseph, BA; American editor, writer and lecturer; b. 9 Jan. 1937, Chicago, IL; m. Barbara Maher 1976; one s. *Education:* Univ. of Chicago. *Career:* Assoc. Ed., The New Leader 1962–63; Sr Ed., Encyclopaedia Britannica 1965–69, Quadrangle/New York Times Books 1969–70; Lecturer, Northwestern Univ. 1974–; Ed., The American Scholar from 1975. *Publications:* Divorced in America 1975, Ambition 1979, Familiar Territory 1980, The Middle of My Tether 1983, Plausible Prejudices 1985, Once More Around the Block 1987, Partial Payments 1989, A Line Out for a Walk 1991, The Golden Boys: Stories 1991, Pertinent Players 1993, With My Trousers Rolled 1995, Life Sentences 1997, Narcissus Leaves the Pool 1999, Snobbery: The American Version 2002, Friendship: An Exposé 2006, Alexis de Tocqueville: Democracy's Guide 2007; editor: Masters: Portraits of Teachers 1980, Best American Essays 1993, Norton Book of Personal Essays 1997; contrib. to books, and to journals, including Atlantic Monthly, Harper's Magazine, The New Yorker. *Address:* c/o Houghton Mifflin Company, Trade Division, Adult Editorial, Eighth Floor, 222 Berkeley Street, Boston, MA 02116-3764, USA.

EPSTEIN, Leslie, DipAnthro, MA, DFA; American writer; b. 1938, Los Angeles, CA; one s. *Education:* Yale, Merton Coll., Oxford, UCLA. *Career:* Dir of Creative Writing Programme, Univ. of Boston; Ed., Tikkun; writer-in-residence, Rockefeller Inst., Bellagio, Italy. *Publications:* P. D. Kimerakov 1975, The Steinway Quintet Plus Four 1976, King of the Jews 1978, The Elder 1979, Regina 1982, Goldkorn Tales 1986, Pinto and Sons 1990, Pandaemonium 1997, Ice Fire Water: A Leib Goldkorn Cocktail, San Remo Drive: a Novel from Memory 2003; contrib. to numerous magazines and newspapers. *Honours:* Rhodes scholar 1960–72, Fulbright scholar, NEA fellow 1972, 1981–82, Guggenheim fellow 1977–78; Award for Distinction in Literature, American Acad. and Inst. of Arts and Letters. *Address:* c/o Department of English, Boston University, 236 Bay Road, Boston, MA 02215, USA. *Telephone:* (617) 3532506. *E-mail:* leslieep@bu.edu.

EPSTEIN, Seymour (Sy); American writer and academic; b. 2 Dec. 1917, New York, NY; m. Miriam Kligman 1956; two s. *Career:* mem. Authors' Guild, PEN. *Publications:* Pillar of Salt, 1960; Leah, 1964; Caught in That Music, 1967; The Dream Museum, 1971; Looking for Fred Schmidt, 1973; A Special Destiny, 1986; September Faces, 1987; Light, 1989. Contributions: periodicals. *Honours:* Edward Lewis Wallant Memorial Award, 1965; Guggenheim Fellowship, 1965.

ERBA, Luciano, PhD; Italian poet, translator, writer and retd academic; b. 18 Sept. 1922, Milan. *Education:* Catholic Univ., Milan. *Career:* Prof. of Comparative Literature, Rutgers Univ., NB, USA 1964–65; Prof. of Italian and French Literature, Univ. of Washington at Seattle, USA 1965–66; Prof. of French Literature, Univ. of Padua 1973–82, Univ. of Verona 1982–87, Catholic Univ., Milan 1987–97. *Publications:* Linea K 1951, Il bel paese 1956, Il prete di Ratanà 1959, Il male minore 1960, Il prato più verde 1977, Il nastro di Moebius 1980, Il cerchio aperto 1983, L'ippopotamo 1989, L'ipotesi circense 1995, Negli spazi intermedi 1998, Nella terra di mezzo 2000; other: Françoise (novel) 1982, radio plays, translations. *Honours:* Viareggio Prize

1980, Bagutta Prize 1988, Librex-Guggenheim Eugenio Montale Prize 1989, Italian PEN Club Prize 1995. *Address:* Via Giason del Maino 16, 20146 Milan, Italy.

ERBSEN, Claude Ernest, BA; American journalist; b. 10 March 1938, Trieste, Italy; s. of Henry M. Erbsen and Laura Erbsen; m. 1st Jill J. Prosky 1959; m. 2nd Hedy M. Cohn 1970; two s. one d. *Education:* Amherst Coll. Mass. *Career:* reporter and printer, Amherst Journal Record 1955–57; staff reporter, El Tiempo, Bogotá 1960; with Associated Press (AP) in New York and Miami 1960–65; reporter to Chief of Bureau, AP Brazil 1965–69; Exec. Rep. for Latin America, AP 1969–70; Business Man. and Admin. Dir AP–Dow Jones Econ. Report, London 1970–75; Deputy Dir AP World Services, New York 1975–80, Vice-Pres., Dir 1987–; Vice-Pres., Dir AP–Dow Jones News Services 1980–87; mem. Bd Dirs World Press Inst. St Paul; mem. Int. Press Inst., Council on Foreign Relations. *Honours:* San Giusto d'Oro award, City of Trieste 1995. *Address:* Associated Press, 50 Rockefeller Plaza, New York, NY 10020-1605 (office); 27 Stratton Road, Scarsdale, NY 10583-7556, USA (home). *Telephone:* (212) 621-1750 (office).

ERDRICH, (Karen) Louise, MA; American writer and poet; b. 7 June 1954, Little Falls, MN; d. of Ralph Louis Erdrich and Rita Joanne (Gourneau) Erdrich; m. Michael Anthony Dorris 1981 (died 1997); six c. (one s. deceased). *Education:* Dartmouth Coll., Johns Hopkins Univ. *Career:* Visiting Poetry Teacher, ND State Arts Council 1977–78; Teacher of Writing, Johns Hopkins Univ., Baltimore 1978–79; Communications Dir, Ed., Circle-Boston Indian Council 1979–80; Textbook Writer Charles Merrill Co. 1980; mem. PEN (mem. Exec. Bd 1985–90); Guggenheim Fellow 1985–86. *Publications:* fiction: Love Medicine (Nat. Book Critics' Circle Award for best work of fiction) 1984, The Beet Queen 1986, Tracks 1988, The Crown of Columbus (with Michael Anthony Dorris) 1991, The Bingo Palace 1994, The Bluejay's Dance 1995, Tales of Burning Love 1996, The Antelope Wife 1998, The Birchbark House 1999, The Last Report on the Miracles at Little No Horse 2001, The Master Butcher's Singing Club 2003, Four Souls 2004, The Painted Drum 2005; poetry: Jacklight 1984, Baptism of Desire 1989; non-fiction: Imagination (textbook) 1980; contrib. short stories, children's stories, essays and poems to anthologies and journals, including American Indian Quarterly, Atlantic, Frontiers, Kenyon Review, Ms, New England Review, New York Times Book Review, New Yorker, North American Review, Redbook. *Honours:* Nelson Algren Award 1982, Pushcart Prize 1983, Nat. Magazine Fiction Award 1983, 1987, First Prize O. Henry Awards 1987. *Literary Agent:* The Wylie Agency, 250 West 57th Street, Suite 2114, New York, NY 10107-2199, USA. *Telephone:* (212) 246-0069. *Fax:* (212) 586-8953 (office). *E-mail:* mail@wylieagency.com (office).

ERENUS, Bilgesu, BA; Turkish playwright; b. 13 Aug. 1943, Bilecik; d. of Avni Duru and Aliye Duru; m. M. Erenus 1967 (divorced 1990); one s. *Education:* Kadiköy High School for Girls, Istanbul, Istanbul Conservatory of Music and Univ. of Istanbul. *Career:* scriptwriter, Türkiye Radyo Televizyon Kurumu (TRT—Turkish Radio-Television Corpn) 1965–73; playwright 1973–, 13 plays performed in Turkey, six published, several translated into French and German, one performed in Paris; social activist under mil. regime 1980–83, prosecuted by martial courts and held in solitary confinement. *Plays include:* Red Black Tree 2003. *Publications include:* L'Invité 1984, İkili Oyun (film script) 1989, Devlerin Ölümü (film script) 1990, Gece 1996, Aydinlik Zindan (co-author) 2002. *Honours:* First Prize, World Children's Year Play Competition 1976, named Best Playwright in Turkey 1978. *Address:* Ayazpaşa Cami Sok, Saray Apt 10/12, Taksim, Istanbul, Turkey. *Telephone:* (1) 1432112.

ERICKSON, Stephen (Steve) Michael, BA, MA; American novelist; b. 20 April 1950, Santa Monica, CA. *Education:* University of California, Los Angeles. *Career:* Arts Ed., 1989–91, Film Ed., 1992–93, L.A. Weekly; Instructor, California Institute of the Arts, 2000–. *Publications:* Days Between Stations, 1985; Rubicon Beach, 1986; Tours of the Black Clock, 1989; Leap Year, 1989; Arc d'X, 1993; Amnesiascope, 1996; American Nomad, 1997; The Sea Came in at Midnight, 1999. Contributions: New York Times; Esquire; Rolling Stone; Details; Elle; Los Angeles Times; Los Angeles Magazine; LA Weekly; LA Style; San Francisco Magazine; Salon; Conjunctions. *Honours:* Samuel Goldwyn Award, 1972; National Endowment for the Arts Fellowship, 1987.

ERNAUX, Annie; French writer; b. (Annie Duchesne), 1 Sept. 1940, Lillebonne, Seine-Maritime; d. of the late Alphonse Duchesne and Blanche Dumenil; m. Philippe Ernaux 1964 (divorced); two s. *Education:* Lycée Jeanne-d'Arc, Rouen, Univs of Rouen, Bordeaux and Grenoble. *Career:* teacher of literature 1966–2000. *Publications:* Les armoires vides 1974, Ce qu'ils disent ou rien 1977, La femme gelée 1981, La place 1984, Une femme 1988, Passion simple 1992, Journal du dehors 1993, La honte 1997, Je ne suis pas sortie de ma nuit 1997, L'événement 2000, La Vie Extérieure 2000, Se perdre 2001, L'occupation 2002, L'écriture comme un couteau 2003, L'usage de la photo 2005. *Honours:* Prix Renaudot 1984. *Address:* 23 rue des Lozères, 95000 Cergy, France (home). *E-mail:* annie.ernaux@tiscali.fr (home).

ERSKINE, Barbara, MA; British writer; b. 10 Aug. 1944, Nottingham, England; m.; two s. *Education:* Univ. of Edinburgh. *Career:* mem. Soc. of Authors, Scientific and Medical Network. *Publications:* Lady of Hay 1986, Kingdom of Shadows 1988, Encounters 1990, Child of the Phoenix 1992, Midnight is a Lonely Place 1994, House of Echoes 1996, Distant Voices 1996, On the Edge of Darkness 1998, Whispers in the Sand 2000, Hiding from the

Light 2002, Sands of Time 2003, Daughters of Fire 2006; contrib. of numerous short stories to magazines and journals. *Address:* c/o Blake Friedmann, 122 Arlington Road, London, NW1 7HP, England.

ESBER, Ali Ahmad Said, (Adonis), PhD; Syrian poet and academic; b. 1930, Oassabin. *Education:* Univ. of Damascus, Univ. of St Joseph, Beirut. *Career:* Prof. of Arabic Literature, Lebanese Univ., Beirut 1971–85; PhD Adviser, Univ. of St Joseph, Beirut 1971–85; Visiting Lecturer, Collège de France, Paris 1983, Georgetown Univ., Washington, DC 1985; Assoc. Prof. of Arab Poetry, Univ. of Geneva 1989–95; mem. Acad. Stéphane Mallarmé, Paris, Haut Conseil de Réflexion du Collège Int. de Philosophie, Paris. *Publications:* poetry in French: Chants de Mihyar le Damascene 1983, Tombeau pour New York suivi de Prologue a l'histoire des rois des ta'ifa et de Ceci est mon nom 1986, Le Temps les Villes 1990, Célébrations 1991, Chronique des branches 1991, Mémoire du vent (anthology) 1991, Soleils Seconds 1994, Singuliers 1995; in English: An Introduction to Arab Poetics 1990, The Pages of Day and Night 1994; also poetry in Arabic. *Honours:* Officier, Ordre des Arts et des Lettres 1993; Prix des Amis du Livre, Beirut 1968, Syria-Lebanon Award, Int. Poetry Forum 1971, Nat. Prize for Poetry, Lebanon 1974, Grand Prix des Biennales Internationales de la Poésie de Liège, Belgium 1986, Prix Jean Malrieu-Etranger, Marseille 1991, Feronia-Cita di Fiano, Rome 1993, Nazim Hikmat Prize, Istanbul 1994, Prix Méditerranée-Etranger, France 1995. *Address:* 1 Square Henri Regnault, 92400 Courbevoie, France.

ESCANDELL, Noemi, BLitt, BA, MA, PhD; Cuban academic and poet; b. 27 Sept. 1936, Havana; m. Peter Knapp 1957 (divorced 1972); two s. two d. *Education:* Instituto de la Vibora, Queens Coll., CUNY, Harvard Univ. *Career:* Asst Prof., Bard Coll. 1976–83; Language Programme Dir, Nuevo Instituto de Centroamerica, Esteli, Nicaragua 1987–88; Prof. of Spanish, Westfield State Coll. 1983–93; Dir Afterschool Programme, Ross School, Washington, DC 1995–96; Poet-in-Residence, Millay Colony for the Arts, Austerlitz, New York 1983, 1991; mem. Acad. Iberoamericana de Poesía (Washington, DC chapter). *Publications:* Cuadros 1982, Ciclos 1982, Palabras/Words 1986; contrib. to anthologies and periodicals. *Honours:* special mention Certamen Poetico Federico García Lorca Poetry Contest 1995, first prize in poetry Certamen Literario International Odon Betanzos Palacio 1996.

ESENOV, Rahim; Turkmenistan journalist and writer. *Career:* freelance reporter for Radio Free Europe/Radio Liberty. *Publications include:* Ventsenosny Skitalets (The Crowned Wanderer, novel) 2003. *Honours:* PEN/Barbara Goldsmith Freedom to Write Award, USA. *Address:* c/o Radio Free Europe/Radio Liberty, Vinohradska 1, 110 00 Prague 1, Czech Republic (office). *E-mail:* rausova@rferl.org.

ESHLEMAN, (Ira) Clayton, BA, MAT; American academic, poet, writer and translator; b. 1 June 1935, Indianapolis, IN; s. of Ira Clayton and Gladys Maine Eshleman; m. 1st Barbara Novak 1961 (divorced 1967); one s.; m. 2nd Caryl Reiter 1970. *Education:* Indiana Univ. *Career:* Ed., Folio (three issues) 1959–60, Quena (one issue) 1966; Instructor in English, Univ. of Maryland Eastern Overseas Division 1961–62; English-language instructor, Matsushita Electric Corporation, Kobe, Japan 1962–64; Instructor, New York Univ. American Language Inst. 1966–68; Publisher, Caterpillar Books 1966–68; founder-Ed. and Publisher, Caterpillar magazine 1967–73; faculty mem. School of Critical Studies, California Inst. of the Arts, Valencia 1970–72; teacher of American poetry, American Coll., Paris, France 1973–74; Dreyfuss Poet-in-Residence and Lecturer in Creative Writing, California Inst. of Technology, Pasadena 1979–84; Visiting Lecturer in Creative Writing, Univ. of California at San Diego, Los Angeles, Santa Barbara, and Riverside 1979–86; reviewer, Los Angeles Times Book Review 1979–86; founder-Ed., Sulfur magazine 1981–2000; Prof. of English, Eastern Michigan Univ., Ypsilanti 1986–2003, Prof. Emeritus 2003–; Regents Lecturer, UCLA 2007; numerous residencies, lecture programmes, workshops, readings across the USA and abroad. *Publications:* poetry and prose: Mexico & North 1962, The Chavin Illumination 1965, Lachrymae Mateo: Three Poems for Christmas 1966, Walks 1967, The Crocus Bud 1967, Cantaloups and Splendour 1968, Brother Stones 1968, T'ai 1969, Indiana 1969, The House of Ibuki 1969, The House of Okumura 1969, The Yellow River Record 1969, A Pitch-blende 1969, A Caterpillar Anthology: A Selection of Poetry and Prose from Caterpillar Magazine (ed.) 1971, Altars 1971, The Wand 1971, Bearings 1971, The Sanjo Bridge 1972, The Last Judgment: For Caryl on her Thirty-first Birthday, for the End of her Pain 1973, Coils 1973, Human Wedding 1973, Realignment 1974, Aux Morts 1974, Grotesca 1975, Portrait of Francis Bacon 1975, The Gull Wall 1975, The Woman Who Saw through Paradise 1976, Cogollo 1976, The Name Encanyoned River 1977, On Mules Sent from Chavin: A Journal and Poems 1977, Core Meander 1977, What She Means 1978, Nights We Put the Rock Together 1980, Hades in Manganese 1981, Fracture 1983, The Name Encanyoned River: Selected Poems 1960–85 1986, The Parallel Voyages (co-ed.) 1987, Hotel-Cro-Magnon 1989, Novices: A Study of Poetic Apprenticeship 1989, Antiphonal Swing: Selected Prose 1962–87 1989, Under World Arrest 1994, Nora's Roar 1996, From Scratch 1998, Erratics 2000, A Cosmogonic Collage: Sections I, II and V 2000, Jisei 2000, Companion Spider (essays) 2002, Sweetheart 2002, Everwhat 2002, Juniper Fuse: Upper Paleolithic Imagination & the Construction of the Underworld 2003, My Devotion 2004, Reciprocal Distillations 2006, A Shade of Paden 2006, An Alchemist with One Eye on Fire 2006; translator of various works by Antonin Artaud, Bernard Bador, Aimé Césaire, Michel Deguy, Pablo Neruda and César Vallejo; contrib. poems, essays, reviews and translations to periodicals, including Agni, American Poetry Review, Antaeus, Big Table, Boxkite (Australia),

Brooklyn Rail, Chicago Review, Conjunctions, Denver Quarterly, Evergreen Review, Exquisite Corpse, Facture, Fence, Grand Street, Harpers, House Organ, Hunger, Kenyon Review, Los Angeles Times Book Review, Mandorla (Mexico City), Montemora, New American Writing, New Directions Annual, New York Times Sunday Book Review, Origin, Paris Review, Parnassus, Partisan Review, PoeSie (Paris), Poetry (Chicago), Rehauts (Paris), Sugar Mule, Tri-Quarterly, Ur Vox, Verse; contrib. to anthologies. *Honours:* Hon. DLitt (SUNY) 2000; Organization of American States grant 1964–65, Nat. Translation Center Award (for translation of Poemas Humanos) 1967, Poetry magazine award (for Five Poems) 1968, Nat. Translation Center grants 1968, 1969, Co-ordinating Council of Literary Magazines grants (for Caterpillar) 1968–70, Fels Non-fiction Award 1975, Carnegie Author's Fund Award 1977, PEN Translation Prize 1977, California Arts Council grants 1977–78, Guggenheim Fellowship (for research on Upper Paleolithic cave art) 1978, Nat. Book Award in Translation 1979, NEA Poetry Fellowship 1979, grant 1983–96, and Translation Fellowship 1988, Nat. Endowment for the Humanities grant (for research on Upper Paleolithic cave art) 1980, and Translation Fellowship 1981, Witter Bynner translation grant 1981, Soros Foundation travel grant to Hungary 1986, Cooper Fellow Swarthmore Coll. 1987, Michigan Arts Council grant 1988, USIA Mexican Translation Project academic specialist grant 1992, Arts Foundation of Michigan Artists Award 1992, Council of Literary Magazines and Presses editorial fellowship (for Sulfur) 1992, American Acad. of Poets Landon Translation Prize (for Trilce), Eastern Michigan Univ. Distinguished Faculty Research/Creativity Award 1989, research grants 1997, 1999, 2001, Research Fellowship 2002, and scholarship recognition (for Companion Spider) 2002, San Diego State Univ. Alfonse X. Sabio Award for Excellence in Literary Translation 2002, residency Rockefeller Study Center, Bellagio, Italy 2004. *Address:* 210 Washtenaw Avenue, Ypsilanti, MI 48197, USA. *E-mail:* ceshleman@comcast.net. *Website:* www.claytoneshleman.com.

ESLER, Gavin William James, BA, MA, FRSA; British broadcaster and writer; *Presenter, Newsnight;* b. 27 Feb. 1953, Glasgow, Scotland; m. Patricia Warner; one s. one d. *Education:* Univs of Kent and Leeds. *Career:* Presenter on BBC TV News and Radio (including Newsnight BBC 2, Dateline London BBC World, Four Corners BBC Radio 4); newspaper columnist. *Publications:* fiction: Loyalties 1990, Deep Blue 1992, The Blood Brother 1995; non-fiction: The United States of Anger 1997; contrib. to anthologies, journals, periodicals, quarterlies, newspapers and magazines. *Honours:* Hon. MA (Univ. of Kent); Hon. DCL; Royal Television Soc. Award. *Literary Agent:* Curtis Brown Ltd, Haymarket House, 28–29 Haymarket, London, SW1Y 4SP, England. *Telephone:* (20) 7393-4400. *Fax:* (20) 7393-4401. *E-mail:* info@curtisbrown.co .uk. *Website:* www.curtisbrown.co.uk. *Address:* BBC Newsnight, Room G680, BBC TV Centre, Wood Lane, London, W12 7RJ, England (office). *E-mail:* gavin.esler@bbc.co.uk (office). *Website:* news.bbc.co.uk/1/hi/programmes/newsnight (office).

ESMENARD, Francis; French publisher; b. 8 Dec. 1936, Paris; s. of Robert Esmenard and Andrée Michel; one s. *Career:* Pres., Dir-Gen. Editions Albin Michel 1982–, Paris; Vice-Pres. Nat. Publishing Syndicat 1979–; Prés. du Directoire 1999–. *Address:* Editions Albin Michel, 22 rue Huyghens, 75014 Paris, France (office). *Telephone:* 1-42-79-10-00. *Fax:* 1-43-27-21-58.

ESMOND, Harriet (see Burke, John Frederick)

ESPADA, Martin, BA, JD; American poet and educator; b. 1957, Brooklyn, NY; m.; one s. *Education:* Univ. of Wisconsin, Northeastern Univ., Boston, MA. *Career:* Assoc. Prof. of English, Univ. of Massachusetts-Amherst; Poet Laureate of Northampton, MA. *Publications:* poetry: Trumpets From the Islands of their Eviction 1987, Rebellion is the Circle of a Lover's Hands 1990, City of Coughing and Dead Radiators 1993, A Mayan Imagine the Angels of Bread 1996, Astronomer in Hell's Kitchen 2000, Alabanza: New and Selected Poems 1982–2002 2003; editor: Poetry Like Bread: Poets of the Political Imagination 1994, El Coro: A Chorus of Latino and Latina Poets 1997; other: Zapata's Disciple: Essays 1998; contrib. to publications, including New York Times Book Review, Harpers, The Nation, The Best American Poetry. *Honours:* Nat. Endowment for the Arts Fellowships, PEN/Revson Fellowship, Massachusetts Artists Foundation Fellowship; American Book Award, PEN/Voelker Award for Poetry, Paterson Poetry Prize, Independent Publisher Book Award. *Address:* c/o University of Massachusetts, Amherst, MA 01003, USA. *E-mail:* martin@martinespada.net. *Website:* www.martinespada.net.

ESPOSITO, Nancy Giller, BA, MA; American poet, writer, editor and academic; *Senior Lecturer, Bentley College;* b. 1 Jan. 1942, Dallas, TX. *Education:* Univ. of Wisconsin, New York Univ. *Career:* Assoc. Prof., Illinois Central Coll., East Peoria 1968–70; Instructor, Harvard Univ. 1976–80, 1981–84, Wellesley Coll. 1980; Lecturer, Tufts Univ. 1986–93, Boston Coll. 1994; Sr Lecturer, Bentley Coll. 1986–; CIEE Seminar, Viet Nam 2002; mem. Acad. of American Poets, Associated Writing Programs, Poetry Soc. of America, Poets and Writers, PEN. *Publications:* Changing Hands 1984, Mêm' Rain 2002, Greatest Hits 1978–2001 2003; contrib. to anthologies, including Two Decades of New Poets 1984, Ixok-Amar-Go 1987, Quarterly Review of Literature 50th Anniversary Anthology 1993, Poetry from Sojourner 2004, and to reviews, journals and periodicals. *Honours:* Discovery/The Nation Award 1979, Virginia Center for the Creative Arts Fellow 1979–80, 1981, 1990, 2003–04, Yaddo Fellow 1981, Colladay Award 1984, MacDowell Colony Fellow 1986–87, Gordon Barber Memorial Award, Poetry Soc. of America 1987, Fulbright-Hays Grant, Egypt 1988, Publishing Award

1988, Faculty Development Fund Grants, Bentley Coll. 1997, 1999, 2003, Ragdale Foundation Fellow 1990, Bentley Coll. Faculty Grant, Viet Nam 1999–2000. *Address:* 34 Trowbridge Street, Belmont, MA 02478, USA.

ESQUIVEL, Laura; Mexican novelist; b. 30 Sept. 1950, México, DF; m. 1st Alfonso Arau (divorced); m. 2nd Javier Valdez. *Publications:* Como agua para chocolate (trans. as Like Water for Chocolate, novel) 1990, La ley del amor (The Law of Love) 1996, Íntimas suculencias (trans. as Between Two Fires: Intimate Writings on Life, Love, Food and Flavour) 1998, Estrellita Marinera 1999, El libro de las emociones: son de la razón sin corazón 2000, Tan veloz como el deseo (Swift as Desire) 2001, Malinche 2006. *Honours:* American Booksellers Association ABBY Award 1994. *Address:* c/o Simon & Schuster Ltd, Africa House 64–78 Kingsway, London, WC2B 6AH, England.

ESSOP, Ahmed, BA; South African/Indian writer; b. 1 Sept. 1931, Dabhel, India; m. 1960; one s. three d. *Education:* Univ. of South Africa. *Publications:* The Hajii and Other Stories 1978, The Visitation 1980, The Emperor 1984, Noorjehan and Other Stories 1990, The King of Hearts and Other Stories 1997, Narcissus and Other Stories 2002, Suleiman M. Nana: A Biographical and Historical Record of His Life and Times 2002, The Third Prophecy 2004. *Honours:* Olive Schreiner Award, English Acad. of Southern Africa 1979. *Address:* PO Box 1747, Lenasia 1820, Johannesburg, South Africa. *Telephone:* (11) 854-4267 (home).

ESTERER-WANDSCHNEIDER, Ingeborg Charlotte Martha Katharina, DrPhil; German journalist; b. 18 Feb. 1926, Mainz; d. of Jakob-Ernst Günther and Charlotte Günther; m. 1st Rainer Esterer 1951; m. 2nd Hajo Wandschneider 1972; one s. one d. *Education:* high schools in Mainz and Berlin and Univs of Berlin and Hamburg. *Career:* freelance journalist 1948–51, 1990–; Sec. Inst. français, Hamburg 1951–53; Ed. Kristall (entertainment and science magazine) 1954–60; freelance radio journalist and trans. of French and English books 1960–70; Public Relations Officer, Amnesty International (German Section) 1968–70; Leading Ed. Vital (health and fitness magazine) 1970–83, Für Sie (women's magazine) 1983–90. *Honours:* First Prize (Medical Journalism—Ophthalmology) 1989. *Address:* Cranachstrasse 39, 2000 Hamburg 52, Germany. *Telephone:* (40) 893154.

ESTERHÁZY, Péter; Hungarian writer and essayist; b. 14 April 1950, s. of Mátyás Esterházy and Lili Mányoky; m. Gitta Reén; two s. two d. *Education:* Budapest Univ. *Career:* worked as a system supervisor; full-time writer 1978–. *Publications:* short stories: Pápai vizeken ne kalózkodj! 1977; novels: Fancsikó és Pinta 1976, Termelési regény 1979, Függő 1981, Ki szavatol a lady biztonságáért? 1982, Kis magyar pornográfia (translated as A Little Hungarian Pornography) 1984, A sziv segédigéi 1985, Bevezetés a szépirodalomba 1986, Tizenhét hattyúk (as Csokonai Lili) 1987, Hrabal könyve (translated as The Book of Hrabal) 1990, Hahn-Hahn grófnő pillantása (The Glance of Countess Hahn-Hahn Down the Danube) 1991, Egy nő (She Loves Me) 1995, Harmonia caelistis (translated as Celestial Harmonies) 2000; essays: A kitömött hattyú 1988, Az elefántcsonttoronyból 1991, A halacska csodálatos élete 1991, Egy kékharisnya följegyzéseiből 1994, Egy kék haris 1996. *Honours:* Füst Milán, Déry, Kossuth Prize 1996, József Attila, Krúdy, Aszu, Márai, Magyar Irodalini Díj, Vilenica awards, Österreichische Staatspreis für europäische Literatur, Frankfurt Book Fair Peace Prize 2004. *Address:* c/o Hungarian Writers' Federation, Bajza-utca 18, 1062 Budapest, Hungary. *Telephone:* (1) 322-8840.

ESTÉVEZ, Abilio, BLit, DPhil; Cuban writer; b. 7 Jan. 1954, Havana. *Education:* Havana Univ. *Career:* Ed. literary journal, El Caimán Barbudo 1987–88; Ed.-in-Chief literary journal, Conjunto (in Drama Dept., Casa de las Américas) 1988; Visiting Prof. of Hispanoamerican Literature, Sassari Univ., Italy 1989; Prof. of Drama, Escuela Nacional de Teatro Alvaro de Rosson, Venezuela 1991; Prof., Casa de las Américas, Havana 1992; Head of Drama Dept., Ollantay Organization, New York, USA 1993; fmr Arts Ed., literary journals, Quimera de España, Dialog de Polonia, Casa de las Américas, Unión, Tablas, Revolución y Cultura; mem. editorial bd of literary journal, La Gaceta de Cuba. *Plays include:* La verdadera culpa de Juan Clemente Zenea (Premio de la Crítica 1987, Festival de Teatro de La Habana Premio Santiago Pita 1991) 1987, Yo tuve un sueño feliz (Premio de la Crítica 1991) 1989, Perla marina 1993, La Noche (Instituto de Cooperación Iberoamericana Premio Teatral Tirso de Molina, Madrid 1994) 1994, Santa Cecilia 1995. *Publications:* Juego con Gloria (short stories) 1982, Manual de tentaciones (poems) (Premio Luis Cernuda, Spain 1989) 1989, Premio de Crítica Cubana 1989) 1989, Regreso a Cyterea (short story) 1990, Muerte y transfiguración (poem) 1995, Tuyo es el reino (novel, trans. as Thine Is the Kingdom) (Premio de la Crítica Cubana 1999) 1997, El horizonte y otros regresos (short stories) 1998, Los palacios distantes (novel, trans. as Distant Palaces) (Premio Internacional de Novela Rómulo Gallegos 2003) 2002. *Honours:* Unión de Escritores y Artistas de Cuba Premio José Antonio Ramos 1984. *Address:* c/o Arcade Publishing, 141 Fifth Avenue, Eighth Floor, New York, NY 10010, USA. *E-mail:* publicity@ arcadepub.com.

ESTLEMAN, Loren Daniel, BA; American writer; b. 15 Sept. 1952, Ann Arbor, Mich.; s. of Leauvett C. Estleman and Louise A. Estleman; m. Deborah Ann Green 1993; one step-s. one step-d. *Education:* Eastern Mich., Univ. *Career:* police reporter, Ypsilanti Press 1972–73; Ed.-in-Chief, Community Foto News 1975–76; Special Writer, Ann Arbor News 1976; staff writer, Dexter Leader 1977–80; full-time novelist 1980–; Vice-Pres. Western Writers of America 1998–2000, Pres. 2000–02. *Publications:* novels: The Oklahoma Punk 1976, The Hider, Sherlock Holmes vs. Dracula 1978, The High Rocks

1979, Dr. Jekyll and Mr. Holmes, Stamping Ground, Motor City Blue 1980, Aces and Eights, Angel Eyes, The Wolfer 1981, Murdock's Law, The Midnight Man 1982, Mister St John, The Glass Highway 1983, This Old Bill, Sugartown, Kill Zone, The Stranglers 1984, Every Brilliant Eye, Roses Are Dead, Gun Man 1985, Any Man's Death 1986, Lady Yesterday 1987, Bloody Season, Downriver 1988, Silent Thunder, Peeper 1989, Sweet Women Lie, Whiskey River 1990, Sudden Country, Motown 1991, King of the Corner 1992, City of Widows 1994, Edsel 1995, Stress 1996, Never Street, Billy Gashade 1997, The Witchfinder, Journey of the Dead, Jitterbug 1998, The Rocky Mountain Moving Picture Association 1999, The Hours of the Virgin 1999, White Desert 2000, The Master Executioner 2001, Sinister Heights 2002, Something Borrowed, Something Black 2002, Black Powder, White Smoke 2002, Poison Blonde 2003, Port Hazard 2004, Retro 2004, Little Black Dress 2005, The Undertaker's Wife 2005; non-fiction: The Wister Trace 1987, Writing the Popular Novel 2004; collections: General Murders 1988, The Best Western Stories of Loren D. Estleman 1989, People Who Kill 1993; anthologies: P.I. Files 1990, Deals with the Devil 1994, American West 2001. *Honours:* Western Writers of America Spur Award, Best Historical Novel 1981, Spur Award, Best Short Fiction 1986, 1996, Private Eye Writers of America Shamus Award, Best Novel 1984, Shamus Award, Best Short Story 1985, 1988, Mich. Foundation of the Arts Award for Literature 1987, Mich. Library Asscn Authors Award 1997, Spur Award, Best Western Novel 1999, Western Heritage Award, Outstanding Western Novel 1998, 2001, Western Heritage Award, Outstanding Short Story 2000, Western Heritage Award for Outstanding Western Novel 2001, Shamus Award for Best Short Story 2003; Dr hc of Humane Letters, Eastern Mich. Univ. 2002. *Address:* 5552 Walsh Road, Whitmore Lake, MI 48189, USA. *Website:* www.lorenestleman.com (office).

ESZTERHAS, Joseph (Joe) A.; American scriptwriter; b. 23 Nov. 1944, Csakanydoroszlo, Hungary; s. of Stephen Eszterhas and Maria Biro; m. 1st Geraldine Javer 1972 (divorced 1994); one s. one d.; m. 2nd Naomi Baka 1994; one s. *Education:* Ohio State Univ. *Career:* reporter, Plain Dealer, Cleveland; staff writer, Man. Ed. Rolling Stone, San Francisco 1971–75; screenwriter 1975–; writer and producer, Checking Out 1980, Betrayed 1989. *Film screenplays:* FIST 1978, Flashdance 1983, Jagged Edge 1985, Big Shots 1987, Betrayed 1988, Checking Out 1989, Music Box 1990, Hearts of Fire 1990, Basic Instinct 1992, Nowhere to Run 1993, Sliver 1993, Showgirls 1995, Jade 1995, Telling Lies in America 1997, An Alan Smithee Film: Burn Hollywood Burn 1997, Basic Instinct 2 2006, Szabadság, szerelem 2006. *Publications:* novels: Thirteen Seconds: Confrontation at Kent State 1970, Charlie Simpson's Apocalypse 1974, Nark! 1974, Fist 1977; non-fiction: Hollywood Animal: A Memoir 2004, The Devil's Guide to Hollywood: The Screenwriter as God! 2006. *Honours:* recipient of various awards. *Address:* c/o St Martin's Press, 175 Fifth Avenue, New York, NY 10010, USA. *Website:* www.joeeszterhas.com.

ETCHEMENDY, Nancy Howell, BA; American writer and poet; b. 19 Feb. 1952, Reno, NV; m. John W. Etchemendy 1973, one s. *Education:* University of Nevada, Reno. *Career:* mem. Treasurer, 1996–97, Trustee, 1997–98, Horror Writers' Asscn; Society of Children's Book Writers; SFWA. *Publications:* The Watchers of Space, 1980; Stranger from the Stars, 1983; The Crystal City, 1985; The Power of UN, 2000. Contributions: numerous short stories, essays and individual poems to magazines and journals. *Honours:* Bram Stoker Award 1998. *Literary Agent:* Curtis Brown Ltd, 10 Astor Place, New York, NY 10003, USA. *E-mail:* etchemendy@sff.net.

ETTER, David (Dave) Pearson, BA; American fmr poet, writer and editor; b. 18 March 1928, Huntington Park, CA; m. Margaret A. Cochran 1959; one s. one d. *Education:* Univ. of Iowa. *Career:* Promotion Dept, Indiana Univ. Press 1959–60; Rand McNally Publishing Co. 1960–61; Ed., Northwestern Univ. Press 1962–63; Asst Ed., Encyclopaedia Britannica, Chicago 1964–73; Ed., Northern Illinois Univ. Press 1974–80; freelance writer, poet and ed. 1981–87; teacher of creative writing and other jobs 1988–97. *Publications:* Go Read the River 1966, The Last Train to Prophetstown 1968, Well You Needn't 1975, Central Standard Time 1978, Open to the Wind 1978, Riding the Rock Island Through Kansas 1979, Cornfields 1980, West of Chicago 1981, Boondocks 1982, Alliance, IL 1983, Home State 1985, Live at the Silver Dollar 1986, Selected Poems 1987, Midlanders 1988, Electric Avenue 1988, Carnival 1990, Sunflower County 1994, How High the Moon 1996, The Essential Dave Etter 2001, Greatest Hits 1960–2000 2002, Looking for Sheena Easton 2004; contrib. to Poetry, Nation, Chicago Review, Kansas Quarterly, Prairie Schooner, Poetry Northwest, TriQuarterly, Massachusetts Review, North American Review, Ohio Review, New Letters, Shenandoah, Beloit Poetry Journal, El Corno Emplumado, San Francisco Review, New Mexico Quarterly, Mark Twain Journal, Slow Dancer (England), among others. *Honours:* Soc. of Midland Authors Poetry Prize 1967, Friends of Literature Poetry Prize 1967, Bread Loaf Writers' Conference Fellowship in Poetry 1967, Illinois Sesquicentennial Poetry Prize 1968, Theodore Roethke Poetry Prize 1971, Carl Sandburg Poetry Prize 1982. *Address:* 628 E Locust Street, Lanark, IL 61046, USA (home). *Telephone:* (815) 493-6778 (home).

ETZIONI, Amitai, BA, MA, PhD; American sociologist, academic and writer; *Professor, George Washington University;* b. 4 Jan. 1929, Cologne, Germany; m. 1st Minerva Morales 1965 (died 1985); five s.; m. 2nd Patricia Kellogg 1992. *Education:* Hebrew Univ., Jerusalem, Univ. of California at Berkeley. *Career:* Faculty 1958–67, Prof. of Sociology 1967–78, Chair Dept of Sociology 1969–78, Columbia Univ.; Fellow, Center for Advanced Study in the Behavioral

Sciences 1965–66; Founder-Dir, Center for Policy Research 1968–; Guest Scholar, Brookings Institution 1978–79; Sr Adviser, White House, Washington, DC 1979–80; Univ. Prof. 1980–, Dir Center for Communitarian Studies 1995–, George Washington Univ.; Thomas Henry Carroll Ford Foundation Visiting Prof., Graduate School of Business, Harvard Univ. 1987–89; Ed., The Responsive Community: Rights and Responsibilities quarterly 1990–; Founder-Dir, The Communitarian Network 1993–; mem. American Sociological Asscn (pres. 1995), Soc. for the Advancement of Socio-Economics (founder-pres. 1989–90, hon. fellow). *Publications:* A Comparative Analysis of Complex Organizations 1961, Modern Organizations 1964, Political Unification: A Comparative Study of Leaders and Forces 1965, Studies in Social Change 1966, The Active Society 1968, Genetic Fix 1973, Social Problems 1975, An Immodest Agenda 1982, Capital Corruption 1984, The Moral Dimension 1988, The Spirit of Community: Rights, Responsibilities and the Communitarian Agenda 1993, The New Golden Rule: Community and Morality in a Democratic Society 1996, The Limits of Privacy 1999, My Brother's Keeper 2004, The Common Good 2004, From Empire to Community: A New Approach to International Relations 2004, How Patriotic is the Patriot Act? Freedom versus Security in the Age of Terrorism 2004; contrib. to scholarly journals, newspapers, periodicals and television. *Honours:* Social Science Research Council Fellowship 1960–61, Guggenheim Fellowship 1968–69, American Revolution Bicentennial Commission Certificate of Appreciation 1976, Simon Wiesenthal Center Tolerance Book Award 1997, hon. doctorates. *Address:* c/o The Gelman Library, George Washington University, Suite 703, 2130 H Street NW, Washington, DC 20052, USA. *Telephone:* (202) 994-8190 (office). *Fax:* (202) 994-1606 (office). *E-mail:* etzioni@gwv.edu (office). *Website:* www .communitariannetwork.org (office).

EUGENIDES, Jeffrey, BA, MA; American novelist; b. 1960, Detroit, Mich.; m.; one d. *Education:* Brown Univ., Stanford Univ. *Career:* Fellow, Berliner Künstlerprogramm 2002; Guggenheim Foundation Fellowship, Nat. Foundation for the Arts Fellowship, American Acad. in Berlin Prize Fellowship 2000–01; teacher in Creative Writing Program, Princeton Univ. 1999–2000, 2007–. *Publications:* The Virgin Suicides 1993, Middlesex (Pulitzer Prize for Fiction 2003) 2002; contrib. to The New Yorker, The Paris Review, The Yale Review, The Gettysburg Review, Best American Short Stories, Granta's Best of Young American Novelists. *Honours:* Whiting Writers' Award, American Acad. of Arts and Letters Harold D. Vursell Memorial Award. *Address:* Creative Writing Program, Princeton University, 185 Nassau Street, Princeton, NJ 08544, USA. *Telephone:* (609) 258-8561. *Fax:* (609) 258-2230. *Website:* www.princeton.edu/~visarts/cwr.

EULO, Ken; American playwright, stage director and novelist; b. 17 Nov. 1939, Newark, NJ; m.; one s. *Education:* University of Heidelberg. *Career:* Artistic Dir, Courtyard Playhouse, New York; Staff Writer, Paramount; mem. Dramatists' Guild; Italian Playwrights of America; Writers' Guild of America. *Publications:* Plays: Bang?, 1969; Zarf, I Love You, 1969; SRO, 1970; Puritan Night, 1971; Billy Hofer and the Quarterback Sneak, 1971; Black Jesus, 1972; The Elevator, 1972; 48 Spring Street, 1973; Final Exams, 1975; The Frankenstein Affair, 1979; Say Hello to Daddy, 1979. Fiction: Bloodstone, 1982; The Brownstone, 1982; The Deathstone, 1982; Nocturnal, 1983; The Ghost of Veronica, 1985; House of Caine, 1988. Other: Television scripts. Contributions: Magazines and newspapers.

EVANS, Aled Lewis, BA, BTh; Welsh poet, teacher, preacher and broadcaster; b. 9 Aug. 1961, Machynlleth. *Education:* Univ. Coll. of North Wales, Bangor and Univ. of Wales, Aberystwyth. *Career:* teacher bilingual creative writing classes, Wrexham Library, Rhyl Library; mem. Gorsedd of Bards, Chester Poets. *Theatre includes:* The Cafe, Wrexham Festival 2004, Mari'r Golay (to commemorate Welsh religious revival), Deufor Gyfarfod (to commemorate Welsh hymn writer, Ann Griffiths). *Publications:* poetry: Tonnau 1989, Ga'i ddarn o awyr las heddiw? 1991, Sglefrfyrddio 1994, Wavelengths (in trans.) 1995, Bro Maelor 1996, Mendio Gondola 1997, Llyfr Erchwyn Gwely 1998, Troeon 1998, Mixing the Colours (in trans.) 1999; novels: Rhwng Dau Lanw Medi (Between Two September Tides) 1994, Y Caffi (The Cafe) 2002; also short stories; contrib. to Barn, Golwg, Y Traethodydd, Poetry Wales and other Welsh periodicals; to anthologies, including A White Afternoon 1998, The Bloodaxe Book of Modern Welsh Poetry 2003. *Honours:* Nat. Eisteddfod of Wales literary awards 1991, 1998, 1999. *Address:* 28 Jubilee Road, Pentrefelin, Wrexham, Wrexham County LL13 7NN, Wales.

EVANS, C. Stephen, BA, PhD; American philosopher and writer; b. 26 May 1948, Atlanta, GA; m. Jan Walter 1969, one s. two d. *Education:* Wheaton College, Yale University. *Career:* Asst Prof., 1974–78, Assoc. Prof., 1978–82, Prof., 1982–84, Wheaton College, IL; Prof., Philosophy, Psychology, Kierkegaard Library Curator, 1986–94, Division Chair, 1991–93, St Olaf College, Northfield, MN; Prof. of Philosophy, 1994–, William Spoelhof Teacher-Scholar, 1994–96, Calvin College, Grand Rapids, MI; Visiting positions; Lectures; mem. American Philosophical Asscn; Kierkegaard Society, pres., 1991; Society of Christian Philosophers. *Publications:* Despair: A Moment or a Way of Life?, 1971; Preserving the Person: A Look at the Human Sciences, 1977; Subjectivity and Religious Belief: An Historical Critical Study, 1978; Kierkegaard's Fragments, and Postscripts: The Religious Philosophy of Johannes Climacus, 1983; Contours of Christian Philosophy, Vol. IV: Philosophy of Religion: Thinking about Faith, 1985; The Quest for Faith: Reason and Mystery as Pointers to God, 1986; Wisdom and Humanness in Psychology, 1989; Søren Kierkegaard's Christian Psychology, 1990; Passionate Reason: Making Sense of Kierkegaard's Philosophical Fragments, 1992;

Foundation of Kierkegaard's Vision of Community: Religion, Ethics, and Politics in Kierkegaard, 1992; The Historical Christ and the Jesus of Faith: The Incarnational Narrative as History, 1996; Faith Beyond Reason, 1998. Contributions: articles and reviews to journals. *Honours:* George C. Marshall Fellow, 1977–78; National Endowment for the Humanities Fellowships, 1988–89, 2000–01; Fellow, Center for Faith Development, Emory University, 1988–89; Pew Evangelical Senior Scholar, 1991–94. *Address:* 2600 Golfridge Drive SE, Grand Rapids, MI 49546, USA. *E-mail:* sevans@calvin.edu.

EVANS, George, BA, MA; American writer, poet, translator and editor; b. Pittsburgh, PA. *Education:* Johns Hopkins Univ., Carnegie-Mellon Univ. *Career:* medical corpsman and sergeant in the US Air Force 1967–70; founder ed., Streetfare Journal project. *Publications include:* poetry: Wrecking, Nightvision, Eye Blade, Sudden Dreams: New & Selected Poems; editor: Charles Olson and Cid Corman: Complete Correspondence 1950–64. *Honours:* Lanann Foundation Fellowship, National Endowment of the Arts Fellowship, California Arts Fellowship, Monbusho Fellowship from the Japanese Ministry of Education. *Address:* c/o Curbstone Press, 321 Jackson Street, Willimantic, CT 06226-1738, USA. *E-mail:* info@curbstone.org. *Website:* www.curbstone .org.

EVANS, Sir Harold Matthew, Kt, MA; American (b. British) publisher and fmr newspaper editor and writer; *Editor at Large, The Week and Contributing Editor, US News & World Report;* b. 28 June 1928, Manchester, England; s. of the late Frederick and Mary Evans; m. 1st Enid Parker 1953 (divorced 1978); one s. two d.; m. 2nd Tina Brown (q.v.) 1982; one s. one d. *Education:* Durham Univ. *Career:* Commonwealth Fund Fellow, Univ. of Chicago 1956–57; Ed. Sunday Times, London 1967–81, The Times 1981–82; mem. Bd Times Newspapers Ltd, Dir 1978–82; Int. Press Inst. 1974–80; Dir Goldcrest Films and Television 1982–85; Ed.-in-Chief Atlantic Monthly 1984–86, Contributing Ed. 1986–, Editorial Dir and Vice-Chair. 1998–; Ed. Dir U.S. News and World Report 1984–86, Contributing Ed. 1986–, Editorial Dir and Vice-Chair. 1998–; Vice-Pres. and Sr Ed. Weidenfeld and Nicolson 1986–87; Adviser to Chair. Condé Nast Publications 1986–; Founding Ed.-in-Chief, Condé Nast Traveler 1986–90; Pres. and Publr Random House Adult Trade Group 1990–97; Editorial Dir Mortimer Zuckerman's media properties 1997–; Editorial Dir and Vice-Chair. New York Daily News Inc. 1998–99, Fast Co. 1998–; author Little, Brown and Co., NY 2000–; writer and presenter A Point of View (BBC Radio 4) 2005–; Fellow, Soc. Industrial Artists, Inst. of Journalists; Hon. Visiting Prof. of Journalism City Univ. 1978–; Hon. DCL (Durham) 1998. *Publications:* Active Newsroom 1964, Editing and Design, Newsman's English 1970, Newspaper Design 1971, Newspaper Headlines 1973, Newspaper Text 1973, We Learned to Ski (co-author) 1974, Freedom of the Press 1974, Pictures on a Page 1978, Suffer the Children (co-author), How We Learned to Ski 1983, Good Times, Bad Times 1983, Front Page History 1984, The American Century 1998, They Made America 2004. *Honours:* Dr hc (Stirling) 1982, (Teesside, London Inst.), Hon. DCL (Durham) 1998; Journalist of the Year Prize 1973, Int. Ed. of the Year Award 1975, Inst. of Journalists Gold Medal Award 1979; Design and Art Dir, Pres.'s Award 1981, Ed. of Year Award, Granada 1982, Hood Medal, Royal Photographic Soc. 1981, Press Photographers of GB Award 1986; Gold Award for Achievement, British Press Awards 2000, World Press Freedom Hero, Int. Press Inst. 2000. *Address:* Little, Brown and Co., 1271 Avenue of the Americas, New York, NY 10020, USA (office). *Telephone:* (212) 302-9671 (office); (212) 371-1193 (home). *Fax:* (212) 302-9671 (office); (212) 754-4273 (home). *E-mail:* cindyquillinan@gmail .com (office); harold371@aol.com (home).

EVANS, Jonathan (see Freemantle, Brian Harry)

EVANS, Joni; American publishing executive; *Senior Vice-President, Literary Department, William Morris Agency.* *Career:* Publr Linden Press, Simon & Schuster 1979–85, Pres. Simon & Schuster Trade Div. 1985–87; Publr Random House imprint 1987–90, Pres., Publr own imprint, apptd Exec. Vice-Pres. Random House Inc. 1990; Sr Vice-Pres. William Morris Agency Literary Dept 1993–. *Honours:* named one of the 101 Most Powerful People in Entertainment, Entertainment Weekly 1990. *Address:* William Morris Agency, 1325 Avenue of the Americas, New York, NY 10019, USA (office). *Telephone:* (212) 586-5100 (office). *Fax:* (212) 246-3583 (office). *E-mail:* jevans@wma.com (office). *Website:* www.wma.com.

EVANS OF TEMPLE GUITING, Baron (Life Peer), cr. 2000, of Temple Guiting in the County of Gloucestershire; **Matthew Evans,** CBE, BSc Econs, FRSA; British publishing executive; b. 7 Aug. 1941, s. of the late George Ewart Evans and Florence Ellen Evans; m. 1st Elizabeth Amanda Mead 1966 (divorced 1991); two s.; m. 2nd Caroline Michel 1991; two s. one d. *Education:* Friends' School, Saffron Walden and LSE. *Career:* bookselling 1963–64; with Faber & Faber 1964–, Man. Dir 1972–93, Chair. 1981–; Chair. Nat. Book League 1982–84, English Stage Co. 1984–90; mem. Council, Publishers' Asscn 1978–84; Gov. BFI 1982–87, Vice-Chair. 1996–97; Chair. Library and Information Comm. 1995–99; Chair. Museums, Libraries and Archives Council 2000–02; Dir Which? Ltd 1997–; mem. Arts Council Nat. Lottery Advisory Panel 1997–99, Univ. for Industry Advisory Group 1997, Royal Opera House Working Group 1997, Arts and Humanities Research Bd 1998–; mem. Franco-British Soc. 1981–; founder mem. Groucho Club (Dir 1982–97). *Honours:* Hon. FRCA 1999; Hon. FLA 1999. *Address:* Faber & Faber, 3 Queen Square, London, WC1N 3AU, England. *Telephone:* (20) 7465-0045. *Fax:* (20) 7465-0034.

EVANS, Max; American writer and painter; b. 29 Aug. 1925. *Publications:* Southwest Wind (short stories), 1958; Long John Dunn of Taos, 1959; The Rounders, 1960; The Hi Lo Country, 1961; Three Short Novels: The Great Wedding, The One-Eyed Sky, My Pardner, 1963; The Mountain of Gold, 1965; Shadow of Thunder, 1969; Three West: Conversations with Vardis Fisher, Max Evans, Michael Straight, 1970; Sam Peckinpah, Master of Violence, 1972; Bobby Jack Smith, You Dirty Coward!, 1974; The White Shadow, 1977; Xavier's Folly and Other Stories, 1984; Super Bull and Other True Escapades, 1985.

EVANS, Nicholas, BA; British author; b. Bromsgrove, Worcestershire; m. 2nd Charlotte Gordon Cumming; three s. one d. *Education:* Univ. of Oxford. *Career:* previously journalist Evening Chronicle, Newcastle upon Tyne and producer documentaries for London Weekend TV, writer and producer films for TV and cinema; now novelist. *Publications:* The Horse Whisperer 1995, The Loop 1998, The Smoke Jumper 2001, The Divide 2005. *Literary Agent:* AP Watt, 20 John Street, London, WC1N 2DR, England. *E-mail:* nicholas@ nicholasevans.com (office). *Website:* www.nicholasevans.com.

EVANS, Richard John, MA, DPhil, LittD, FBA, FRSL; British historian and academic; *Professor of Modern History, University of Cambridge;* b. 29 Sept. 1947, Woodford, Essex; s. of the late Ieuan Trefor Evans and of Evelyn Evans (née Jones); m. 1st Elín Hjaltadóttir 1976 (divorced 1993); m. 2nd Christine L. Corton 2004; two s. *Education:* Forest School, London, Jesus Coll., Oxford, St Antony's Coll., Oxford. *Career:* Lecturer in History, Stirling Univ. 1972–76; Lecturer in European History, Univ. of E Anglia 1976–83, Prof. 1983–89; Prof. of History, Birkbeck Coll., Univ. of London 1989–98; Vice-Master Birkbeck Coll. Univ. of London 1993–98, Acting Master 1997; Prof. of Modern History, Cambridge Univ. 1998–; Fellow Gonville and Caius Coll., Cambridge 1998–; Visiting Assoc. Prof. of European History, Columbia Univ., New York 1980; Fellow Royal Historical Soc.; Fellow Alexander von Humboldt Foundation, Free Univ. of Berlin 1981; Fellow Humanities Research Centre, ANU, Canberra, Australia 1986. *Publications:* The Feminist Movement in Germany 1894–1933 1976, The Feminists 1977, Society and Politics in Wilhelmine Germany (ed.) 1978, Sozialdemokratie und Frauenemanzipation im deutschen Kaiserreich 1979, The German Family (co–ed.) 1981, The German Working Class (co–ed.) 1982, The German Peasantry (co–ed.) 1986, The German Unemployed (co–ed.) 1987, Death in Hamburg 1987, Comrades and Sisters 1987, Rethinking German History 1987, In Hitler's Shadow 1989, Kneipengespräche im Kaiserreich 1989, Proletarians and Politics 1990, Rituals of Retribution 1996, Rereading German History 1997, In Defence of History 1997, Tales from the German Underworld 1998, Lying about Hitler 2001, The Coming of the Third Reich 2003, The Third Reich in Power 2005; contrib. to scholarly journals, newspapers, magazines, radio and TV. *Honours:* Hon. Fellow Jesus Coll., Oxford 1998, Birkbeck Coll. 1999; Stanhope Historical Essay Prize 1969, Wolfson Literary Award for History 1987, William H. Welch Medal, American Asscn for the History of Medicine 1988, Hamburg Civic Medal for Arts and Sciences 1993, Fraenkel Prize in Contemporary History 1994. *Address:* Gonville and Caius College, Cambridge, CB2 1TA, England (office). *Telephone:* (1223) 332495 (office). *E-mail:* rje36@cam.ac.uk (office). *Website:* www.richardjevans.com (office).

EVANS, Robert John Weston, PhD, FBA; British historian and academic; *Regius Professor of Modern History, University of Oxford;* b. 7 Oct. 1943, Leicester; s. of T. F. Evans and M. Evans; m. Kati Robert 1969; one s. one d. *Education:* Dean Close School, Cheltenham and Jesus Coll., Cambridge. *Career:* Research Fellow, Brasenose Coll. Oxford 1968–97; Univ. Lecturer in Modern History of East-Central Europe, Univ. of Oxford 1969–90, Reader 1990–92, Prof. of European History 1992–97, Regius Prof. of Modern History 1997–; Ed. English Historical Review 1985–95; Fellow Austrian Acad. of Sciences 1997; Fellow, Learned Soc. of Czech Repub. 2004. *Publications:* Rudolf II and His World 1973; The Wechel Presses 1975, The Making of the Habsburg Monarchy 1979, The Coming of the First World War (co-ed) 1988, Crown, Church and Estates (co-ed) 1991, The Revolutions in Europe 1848–9 (ed.) 2000. *Honours:* Hon. Fellow Hungarian Acad. of Sciences 1995; Wolfson Literary Award for History 1980, Anton Gindely-Preis (Austria) 1986, František Palacký Medal (Czechoslovakia) 1991. *Address:* Oriel College, Oxford, OX1 4EW (office); Rowan Cottage, 45 Sunningwell, Abingdon, Oxon., OX13 6RD, England (home). *Telephone:* (1865) 277265 (office). *E-mail:* robert .evans@mohist.ox.ac.uk (office). *Website:* www.history.ox.ac.uk (office).

EVARISTO, Bernardine, FRSL; British writer; b. 1959, London. *Career:* trained as an actor and worked in theatre; has also written for theatre, radio and print media; int. readings and teaching residencies, including Visiting Prof. Barnard Coll./Columbia Univ., writer-in-residence Univ. of the Western Cape, Cape Town, Writing Fellow Univ. of East Anglia, and several British Council workshops; Dir Spread the Word Literature Devt Agency 1995–99; Special Adviser (Literature) Arts Council, London 2001–; Literature Adviser British Council 2003–; mem. Advisory Bd MA Creative Writing, City Univ. 2004–; mem. The Poetry Soc. (gen. council 2001–04, chair. 2003–04), Museum of London (advisory cttee 2004–). *Plays:* Moving Through (Royal Court Theatre Upstairs, London), Mapping the Edge (co-writer, WilsonWilson Co. and Sheffield Crucible Theatre, and BBC Radio 3) 2002, Madame Bitterfly and The Stockwell Diva (BBC Radio 4) 2003, Cityscapes (multi-media collaboration with saxophonist Andy Sheppard and pianist Joanna MacGregor for City of London Festival) 2003. *Publications:* Island of Abraham (poems) 1994, Lara (verse novel) (BT Ethnic and Multicultural Media Award for Best Book/Novel 1999) 1997, The Emperor's Babe (verse novel) 2001, Soul Tourists (verse novel) 2005. *Honours:* Arts Council Writers' Award 2000, Nat. Endowment for Science, Technology and the Arts Award 2003. *Literary Agent:* Curtis Brown Agency, Haymarket House, 28–29 Haymarket, London, SW1Y 4SP, England. *E-mail:* camillah@curtisbrown.co.uk. *Address:* c/o Hamish Hamilton/Penguin, 80 Strand, London, WC2R 0RL, England. *E-mail:* bernardine_evaristo@ hotmail.com. *Website:* www.bevaristo.net.

EVDOKIMOV, Aleksei; Latvian journalist; b. 1975. *Career:* journalist in Riga. *Publication:* Headcrusher (novel, in trans., with Alexander Garros) (Nat. Bestseller Prize, Russia) 2003. *Address:* c/o Chatto & Windus, Random House, 20 Vauxhall Bridge Road, London, SW1V 2SA, England.

EVENO, Bertrand; French publishing executive; b. 26 July 1944, Egletons; s. of Jean-Jacques Eveno and Suzanne Gavoille; m. 2nd Brigitte Pery 1984; five d. (three d. from previous m.). *Education:* Lycée Condorcet and Law Faculty, Paris. *Career:* Treasury Inspector 1973–77; Tech. Consultant to Health Minister 1977–78; Cabinet Dir for Minister of Culture and Communication 1978–81; mem. Atomic Energy Comm. Control Bd 1981–83; Deputy Gen. Man. André Shoe Co. 1984–86; Chair. Editions Fernand Nathan 1987–2000; Pres. Conseil d' admin., Fondation nationale de la photographie 1981–95, Gens d'Image 1986–2000; Chair. Larousse-Nathan Int. 1988–90, Le Robert dictionaries 1989–2000, Editions Masson 1995–98; Dir-Gen. Groupe de la Cité 1988–2000, Presses de la Cité 1991–95; Pres., Dir-Gen. Larousse-Bordas 1996–2000; Pres., Dir-Gen. Havas Educ. et Référence 1999–; Dir Anaya Groupe 1999–2000; Pres. Agence France Presse 2000–; Zellidja Scholarship 1961. *Publication:* monograph on Willy Ronis in Les grands photographes 1983. *Address:* Agence France Presse, 11–25 place de la Bourse, BP 20, 75061 Paris Cédex 02 (office); 80 rue de Rennes, 75006 Paris, France (home). *Telephone:* 1-40-41-46-46. *Fax:* 1-40-41-46-32. *Website:* www.afp.com (office).

EVENSON, Brian, BA, MA, PhD; American academic, writer and editor; b. 12 Aug. 1966, Ames, IA; m. Connie Joyce Evenson 1989; two d. *Education:* Brigham Young University, University of Washington. *Career:* Asst Prof., English, Brigham Young University, 1994–96; Asst Prof., English, Oklahoma State University, 1996–; Fiction Ed., Cimarron Review, 1996–; Ed., Conjunctions, 1997–. *Publications:* Altmann's Tongue, 1994; The Din of Celestial Birds, 1997; Prophets and Brothers, 1997; Father of Lies, 1998. *Honours:* National Endowment for the Arts Grant, 1995.

EVERDELL, William Romeyn, BA, MA, PhD; American educator and writer; *Dean of Humanities, St Ann's School;* b. 25 June 1941, New York, NY; m. Barbara Scott 1966; two s. *Education:* Princeton Univ., Univ. of Paris, New York Univ. *Career:* Chair. of History Dept, St Ann's School 1972–73, Head of Upper School 1973–75, Co-Chair. of History Dept 1975–84, Dean of Humanities 1984–; Adjunct Instructor, New York Univ. 1984–89; mem. Int. Soc. for Intellectual History, New York Acad. of Sciences, Soc. for Eighteenth-Century Studies, Soc. of French Historical Studies. *Publications:* Rowboats to Rapid Transit (co-author) 1974, The End of Kings: A History of Republics and Republicans 1983, Christian Apologetics in France, 1730–1790: The Roots of Romantic Religion 1987, The First Moderns: Profiles in the Origins of Twentieth-Century Thought 1997; contrib. to periodicals. *Honours:* Woodrow Wilson Fellowships 1964, 1970, Nat. Endowment for the Humanities Fellowships 1985, 1990, Nat. Endowment for the Humanities/Wallace Foundation Teacher-Scholar 1990–91, honoree New York Public Library Books to Remember 1998. *Address:* St Ann's School, 129 Pierrepont Street, New York, NY 11201, USA (office). *Telephone:* (718) 522-1660 (office). *E-mail:* weverdell@earthlink.net (home).

EVERETT, Graham, BA, MA, PhD; American academic, poet, writer, painter and producer; *Producer, Street Productions;* b. 23 Dec. 1947, Oceanside, NY; s. of James Harvey Everett and Jacqueline Vaughan; m. Elyse Arnow 1981; one s. *Education:* Canisius Coll., State Univ. of NY at Stony Brook. *Career:* Ed. and Publr Street Press and Magazine 1972–86; Prof. 1986–. *Exhibition:* Constructions 2006. *Films:* Artist@Work Series. *Music:* Multiverses by Middleclass Poetry Band. *Publications:* Trees 1978, Strange Coast 1979, Paumanok Rising: An Anthology of Eastern Long Island Aesthetics (co-ed.) 1981, Sunlit Sidewalk 1985, Minus Green 1992, Minus Green Plus 1995, Corps Calleux 2000, Multiverses 2003, That Nod Toward Love 2006; contribs to anthologies, reviews, quarterlies and journals. *Address:* PO Box 772, Sound Beach, NY 11789, USA. *Telephone:* (516) 877-3447 (office). *E-mail:* tgle47@yahoo.com (home).

EVERETT, Percival, BA, MA; American writer and academic; *Professor, University of Southern California at Los Angeles;* b. 22 Dec. 1956, Fort Gordon, GA. *Education:* Univ. of Miami, Univ. of Oregon, Brown Univ. *Career:* Assoc. Prof., Univ. of Kentucky, Lexington 1985–89, Univ. of Notre Dame, IN 1989–92; Prof., Univ. of California at Riverside 1992–99, Univ. of Southern California at Los Angeles 1999–; mem. MLA, Writers' Guild of America. *Publications:* Suder 1983, Walk Me to the Distance 1985, Cutting Lisa 1986, The Weather and Women Treat Me Fair 1989, Zulus 1989, For her Dark Skin 1989, The One That Got Away 1992, God's Country 1994, The Body of Martin Aguilera 1994, Big Picture 1996, Watershed 1996, Frenzy 1996, Glyph 1999, Erasure 2001, Damned If I Do 2005, American Desert 2005, Wounded 2007; contrib. to anthologies and periodicals. *Address:* c/o Department of English, University of Southern California at Los Angeles, Los Angeles, CA 90089, USA.

EXTON, Clive; British screenwriter and playwright; b. 11 April 1930, London, England; m. 1st Patricia Fletcher Ferguson 1951, two d.; m. 2nd Margaret Josephine Reid 1957, one s. two d. *Education:* Christ's Hospital. *Career:* writer of television plays, television series, screenplays and stage plays. *Plays include:* Barking in Essex, The Boundary 1971, Have You Any Dirty Washing Mother Dear? 1971, Twixt 1990, Murder is Easy (adaptation) 1993. *Film and television screenplays:* episodes of: The World of Tim Frazer 1960, Kipps 1960, Out of This World 1962, Armchair Theatre 1960–64, Theatre 625 1965, The Wednesday Play 1966, Thirteen Against Fate 1966, Play of the Month 1967, Out of the Unknown 1969, ITV Playhouse 1969, Conceptions of Murder 1970, Survivors 1975, Shades of Greene 1976, Killers 1976, The Crezz 1977, Dick Barton: Special Agent 1979, Ruth Rendell Mysteries 1987, Jeeves and Wooster 1990–93, Anna Lee 1994, Poirot 1989–2001, The Infinite Worlds of H.G. Wells 2001, Rosemary & Thyme 2003–06; screenplays for: I'll Have You to Remember 1961, Utan fast bostad 1961, Hold My Hand, Soldier 1963, A Place to Go 1963, Night Must Fall 1964, The Close Prisoner 1964, Land of My Dreams 1965, The Big Eat 1965, Prenociste 1966, Ohne festen Wohnsitz 1966, Unruhiger Tag, Ein 1966, The Human Voice 1966, Isadora 1968, Entertaining Mr Sloane 1970, 10 Rillington Place 1971, Jeg lar deg ikke glemme 1971, Doomwatch 1972, The House in Nightmare Park 1973, Stigma 1977, Casting the Runes (adaptation) 1979, The Awakening 1980, Red Sonja 1985, A Guilty Thing Surprised 1988, Shake Hands Forever 1988. *Honours:* Writers' Guild Award 1994. *Address:* Rochelle Stevens & Co., 2 Terrets Place, Upper Street, Islington, London, N1, England (office).

EYNON, Robert (Bob), BA; British academic and writer; b. 20 March 1941, Tynewydd, Rhondda, Wales. *Education:* Univ. of London. *Publications:* Bitter Waters 1988, Texas Honour 1988, Johnny One Arm 1989, Gunfight at Simeons Ridge 1991, Gun Law Legacy 1991, Sunset Reckoning 1993, Anderton Justice 1997, Pecos Vengeance 1998, Brothers Till Death 1999, Dol Rhydian 1999, Lladd Akamuro 2000, Arizona Payback 2001, Poison Valley 2003, The Reluctant Lawman 2005; also Welsh novels and short stories for learners, including Perygl Yn Sbaen 1987, Yr Asiant Cudd 1997. *Address:* 5 Troedyrhiw Terrace, Treorchy, Rhondda CF42 6PG, Wales.

FABEND, Firth Haring, (Firth Haring), BA, PhD; American writer and historian; b. 12 Aug. 1937, Tappan, NY; m. Carl Fabend 1966, two d. *Education:* Barnard Coll., New York Univ. *Career:* Fellow Holland Soc. of New York 1993; Fellow New Netherland Project 1996. *Publications:* as Firth Haring: The Best of Intentions, 1968; Three Women, 1972; A Perfect Stranger, 1973; The Woman Who Went Away, 1981; Greek Revival, 1985. As Firth Haring Fabend: A Dutch Family in the Middle Colonies, 1660–1800. Contributions: de Halve Maen; New York History. *Honours:* New York State Historical Asscn Ms Award 1989, Hendricks Prize 1989.

FABER, Michel; Australian writer; b. 1959, Netherlands; m. 2nd Eva Youren; two step-s. *Education:* Melbourne Univ. *Career:* emigrated to Australia 1967; now lives in Scotland. *Publications:* Fish (short story), Some Rain Must Fall (short stories) 1996, Under the Skin (novel) 1999, The 199 Steps (short story), The Courage Consort (short story), The Crimson Petal and the White (novel) 2002, The Fahrenheit Twins (short stories) 2005, The Apple (short stories) 2006; contrib. to The Guardian. *Honours:* Macallan short story award, Saltire First Book of the Year Award 1999. *Address:* c/o Canongate Books, 14 High Street, Edinburgh, EH1 1TE, Scotland.

FADIMAN, Anne; American writer, essayist, editor and academic; *Francis Writer-in-Residence, Yale University;* b. 1953, New York, NY; d. of Clifton Fadiman and Annalee Whitmore Jacoby; m. George Howe Colt; two c. *Education:* Harvard Univ. *Career:* undergraduate columnist, Harvard Magazine; worked Nat. Outdoor Leadership School, Wyoming; fmr staff writer Life magazine; Founding Ed. Civilization magazine; fmr teacher of non-fiction writing, Smith Coll.; Ed. The American Scholar quarterly 1997–2004; Francis Writer-in-Residence, Yale Univ. 2005–. *Publications:* non-fiction: The Spirit Catches You and You Fall Down (Nat. Book Critics Circle Award, Salon Book Award, Los Angeles Times Book Prize, Boston Book Review Ann Rea Jewell Award) 1997, Ex Libris: Confessions of a Common Reader 1998, Best American Essays (ed.) 2003, Rereadings (ed.) 2005, At Large and At Small 2007; contrib. numerous articles and essays to newspapers, magazines and journals, including Harper's, New Yorker, New York Times, Washington Post. *Honours:* Stanford Univ. John S. Knight Fellowship 1991–92, Nat. Magazine Award for Reporting, Nat. Magazine Award for Essays. *Literary Agent:* c/o Robert Lescher (literary agent), Lescher & Lescher, 47 E 19th Street, New York, NY 10003; c/o Steven Barclay Agency (lecture agent), 12 Western Avenue, Petaluma, CA 94952, USA. *Telephone:* (707) 773-0654 (Petaluma). *Fax:* (707) 778-1868 (Petaluma). *E-mail:* rl@lescherltd.com; steven@barclayagency.com. *Website:* www.barclayagency.com. *Address:* Department of English, Yale University, New Haven, CT 06520, USA (office). *Website:* www.yale.edu/english/Profiles/fadiman.htm (office).

FAECKE, Peter; German journalist and writer; b. 3 Nov. 1940, Grunwald. *Publications:* Die Brandstifter (novel) 1962, Der Rote Milan (novel) 1965, Postversand (novel) (with Wolf Vostell) 1970, Gemeinsam gegen Abriss: Ein Lesebuch aus Arbeitersiedlungen 1974, Das Unaufhaltsame Glück der Kowalskis 1982, Flug ins Leben 1988, Der Mann mit den besonderen Eigenschaften (novel) 1990, Grabstein für Fritz (documentary film) 1993, Als Elizabeth Arden Neunzehn war (novel) 1994, Eine Liebe zum Land (film script) 1994, Ankunft eines Schüchternen in Himmel (novel) 2000, Das Kreuz des Südens (reports) 2001, Von Überfliessen der Anden, Reportagen aus Peru 2001, Hochzeitsvorbereitungen auf dem Lande (novel) 2003, Die geheimen Videos des Herrn Vladimiro (novel) 2004, Lima die Schöne-Lima die Schreckliche (reports) 2005, Wenn bei uns ein Gratis stirbt (reports) 2005. *Honours:* awards include stipend of Villa Massimo, Rome and literature prizes of Lower Saxony, North-Rhine-Westphalia and City of Cologne. *Address:* Mevissenstrasse 16, 50668 Cologne, Germany. *Telephone:* (221) 726207. *Fax:* (221) 723259. *E-mail:* edition@peterfaecke.de (office); peterfaecke@t-online.de (home). *Website:* www.peterfaecke.de.

FAES, Urs, MA, DrPhil; Swiss writer, poet and dramatist; b. 13 Feb. 1947, Aarau. *Education:* Univ. of Zürich. *Career:* journalist 1979–81, dramatist 1982–86, writer 1982–; mem. Auteurs de Suisse, PEN. *Publications:* Eine Kerbe im Mittag (poems) 1975, Heidentum und Aberglaube (essay) 1979, Regenspur (poems) 1979, Webfehler (novel) 1983, Zugluft (play) 1983, Der Traum vom Leben (short stories) 1984, Kreuz im Feld (play) 1984, Bis ans Ende der Erinnerung (novel) 1986, Wartzimmer (play) 1986, Partenza (radio play) 1986, Sommerwende (novel) 1989, Alphabet des Abschieds 1991, Eine andere Geschichte (radio play) 1993, Augenblicke im Paradies (novel) 1994, Ombra (novel) 1997, Und Ruth (novel) 2001, Als hätte die Stille Türen (novel) 2005. *Honours:* City of Zürich Prize 1986, Prize for Literature 1991, Kanton Solothurn Literary Prize 1999, Schiller Prize 2001, Werkjahr auszeichnung Kantou Zürich 2005. *Address:* Sirius Str 4, 8044 Zürich, Switzerland (office). *Telephone:* (43) 244 9063 (office); (79) 261 3053 (home). *E-mail:* urs.faes@bluewin.ch (office).

FAGAN, Brian Murray, BA, MA, PhD; British academic and writer; b. 1 Aug. 1936, Birmingham, England; m. Lesley Ann Newhart 1985; two c. *Education:* Pembroke Coll., Cambridge. *Career:* Keeper of Prehistory, Livingstone Museum, Zambia 1959–65; Visiting Assoc. Prof., University of Illinois 1965–66; Assoc. Prof. 1967–69, Prof. of Anthropology 1969–, University of California at Santa Barbara. *Publications:* Victoria Falls Handbook, 1964;

Southern Africa During the Iron Age (ed.), 1966; Iron Age Cultures in Zambia (with S. G. H. Daniels and D. W. Phillipson), 2 vols, 1967, 1969; A Short History of Zambia, 1968; The Hunter-Gatherers of Gwisho (with F. Van Noten), 1971; In the Beginning, 1972; People of the Earth, 1974; The Rape of the Nile, 1975; Elusive Treasure, 1977; Quest for the Past, Archaeology: A Brief Introduction, 1978; Return to Babylon, 1979; The Aztecs, Clash of Cultures, 1984; Adventures in Archaeology, Bareboating, Anchoring, 1985; The Great Journey, 1987; The Journey From Eden, 1990; Ancient North America, 1991; Kingdoms of Jade, Kingdoms of Gold, 1991; Time Detectives, 1995; Oxford Companion to Archaeology, 1996; Into the Unknown, 1997; From Black Land to Fifth Sun, 1998; Floods, Famines and Emperors, 1999; The Long Summer: How Climate Changed Civilisation 2004. *Address:* Department of Anthropology, University of California at Santa Barbara, CA 93106, USA.

FAGLES, Robert, AB, MA, PhD; American academic, translator and poet; b. 11 Sept. 1933, Philadelphia, Pa; m. Marilyn Duchovnay 1956; two c. *Education:* Amherst Coll., Yale Univ. *Career:* Instructor, Yale Univ. 1959–60; Instructor, Princeton Univ. 1960–62, Asst Prof. 1962–65, Assoc. Prof. 1965–70, Dir Program in Comparative Literature 1966–75, Prof. 1970–2002, Chair. Dept of Comparative Literature 1975–94, Arthur W. Marks Prof. of Comparative Literature, Emer. 2002–; mem. American Acad. of Arts and Letters, American Acad. of Arts and Sciences, American Philosophical Soc. *Publications:* translator: Complete Poems, by Bacchylides 1961, The Oresteia, by Aeschylus 1975, The Three Theban Plays, by Sophocles 1984, The Iliad, by Homer 1990, The Odyssey, by Homer 1996, The Aeneid, by Virgil 2006; poetry: I, Vincent: Poems from the Pictures of Van Gogh 1978; co-editor: Homer: A Collection of Critical Essays 1962, Pope's Iliad and Odyssey 1967; contrib. to books and journals. *Honours:* Commdr, Order of the Phoenix (Hellenic Repub.) 1999; Dr hc (Amherst Coll.) 1990, (Bowdoin Coll.) 2000, (Yale Univ.) 2002; Harold Morton Landon Trans. Award Acad. of American Poets 1991, American Acad. of Arts and Letters Award in Literature 1996, PEN/Ralph Manheim Medal for Life-time Achievement in Trans. 1997. *Address:* Department of Comparative Literature, Princeton University, Princeton, NJ 08544, USA (office). *E-mail:* fagles@princeton.edu (office).

FAHRNER, Martin; Czech playwright, writer and poet; b. 1964, Jablonec nad Nisou. *Education:* DAMU Prague Theatre School. *Publications:* Steiner aneb Co jsme delali (novel) 2001, Pošetilost doktora vinnetouologie (novel) 2004. *Literary Agent:* Dana Blatná Literary Agency, Jináčovice 3, 66434 Kuřim, Czech Republic. *E-mail:* dblatna@volny.cz.

FAINLIGHT, Ruth; American poet, writer, translator and librettist; b. 2 May 1931, New York, NY; m. Alan Sillitoe 1959; one s. one d. *Education:* Coll. of Arts and Crafts, Birmingham, Brighton. *Career:* poet-in-residence, Vanderbilt Univ. 1985, 1990; mem. PEN, Writers in Prison Cttee, Soc. of Authors Writing Tutor; libretti for Performing Arts Lab (Opera & Music Theatre) 1997–99. *Publications:* poetry: Cages 1966, To See the Matter Clearly 1968, The Region's Violence 1973, Another Full Moon 1976, Sibyls and Others 1980, Climates 1983, Fifteen to Infinity 1983, Selected Poems 1987, The Knot 1990, Sibyls 1991, This Time of Year 1994, Selected Poems (expanded 2nd edn) 1995, Sugar-Paper Blue 1997, Burning Wire 2002, Moon Wheels 2006; translations: All Citizens Are Soldiers, from Lope de Vega (with Alan Sillitoe) 1969, Navigations 1983, Marine Rose: Selected Poems of Sophia de Mello Breyner 1988, The Theban Plays of Sophocles (with Robert Littman) 2007; short stories: Daylife and Nightlife 1971, Dr Clock's Last Case 1994; libretti: The Dancer Hotoke 1991, The European Story 1993, Bedlam Britannica 1995; contrib. to Atlantic Monthly, Critical Quarterly, English, Hudson Review, Lettre Internationale, London Magazine, London Review of Books, New Yorker, Poetry Review, Threepenny Review, TLS. *Honours:* Cholmondeley Award for Poetry 1994, Hawthornden Award for Poetry 1994. *Address:* 14 Ladbroke Terrace, London, W11 3PG, England (home). *E-mail:* ruth.fainlight@googlemail.com (office).

FAIRBAIRNS, Zoe Ann, MA; British writer; b. 20 Dec. 1948, England. *Education:* University of St Andrews, Scotland. *Career:* C. Day-Lewis Fellowship, Rutherford School, London, 1977–78; Writer-in-Residence, Deakin University, Australia, 1983, Sunderland Polytechnic, 1983–85; mem. Writer's Guild. *Publications:* Live as Family 1968, Down 1969, Benefits 1979, Stand We at Last 1983, Here Today 1984, Closing 1987, Daddy's Girls 1991, Other Names 1998, How Do You Pronounce Nulliparous? 2004. Contributions: New Scientist, Guardian, Women's Studies International Quarterly, Spare Rib, Arts Express. *Honours:* Fawcett Book Prize 1985. *Website:* www.zoefairbairns.co.uk.

FAIRBURN, Eleanor M., (Catherine Carfax, Emma Gayle, Elena Lyons); Irish writer; b. 23 Feb. 1928; m. Brian Fairburn; one d. *Career:* tutor in practical writing, Univ. of Leeds Adult Educ. Centre (retd); mem. Middlesbrough Writers Group (Pres. 1988–90). *Publications:* The Green Popinjays 1962, The White Seahorse 1964, The Golden Hive 1966, Crowned Ermine 1968, The Rose in Spring 1971, White Rose, Dark Summer 1972, The Rose at Harvest End 1975, Winter's Rose 1976, Edith Cavell (biog.) 1985, Mary Hornbeck Glyn (biog.) 1987, Grace Darling (biog.) 1988; as Catherine Carfax: A Silence with Voices 1969, The Semper Inheritance 1972, To Die a Little 1972, The Sleeping Salamander 1973; as Emma Gayle: Cousin Caroline 1980,

Frenchman's Harvest 1980; as Elena Lyons: The Haunting of Abbotsgarth 1980, A Scent of Lilacs 1982. *Literary Agent:* c/o S. Cashman, Wolfhound Press, Mountjoy Square, Dublin 1, Ireland. *Address:* 27 Minsterley Drive, Acklam, Middlesbrough, Cleveland, TS5 8QU, England (home). *Telephone:* (1642) 821550. *E-mail:* eleanorfairburn@aol.com.

FAIRCLOUGH, Troy Andrew; British playwright; b. 1976, Brixton, London. *Plays:* You Don't Kiss 2001, Justin Fashanu woz 'ere 2004. *Honours:* Newham Writing Out Award 2001. *Address:* c/o Oval House Theatre, 52–54 Kennington Oval, London, SE11 5SW, England. *Telephone:* (20) 7582-0080. *Website:* www.ovalhouse.com.

FAIRFAX, John; British writer and poet; b. 9 Nov. 1930, London, England; two s. *Career:* co-founder and mem. of council of management, Arvon Foundation 1968; Dir, Phoenix Press, Arts Workshop, Newbury; Poetry Ed., Resurgence. *Publications:* The Fifth Horseman of the Apocalypse 1969, Double Image 1971, Adrift on the Star Brow of Taliesin 1974, Bone Harvest Done 1980, Wild Children 1985, The Way to Write 1981, Creative Writing 1989, Spindrift Lp 1981, 100 Poems 1992, Zuihitsu 1996, Poem Sent to Satellite E2F3 1997, Poem on Sculpture 1998, Poem in Hologram 1998; commissioned poems: Boots Herbal Garden (engraved on glass for several insts) 1999, 2003, Poems for dance and art films 2001–03, Poems in Virtual Reality 2003–04; contrib. to most major literary magazines. *Address:* The Thatched Cottage, Eling, Hermitage, Newbury, Berkshire RG16 9XR, England (home). *Telephone:* (1635) 200585 (home).

FAIRLEY, John Alexander, MA; British broadcasting executive and writer; b. 15 April 1939, Liverpool, England; three d. *Education:* Queen's College, Oxford. *Career:* journalist, Bristol Evening Post, 1963, London Evening Standard, 1964; Producer, BBC Radio, 1965–68; Producer, 1968–78, Dir of Programmes, 1984–92, Managing Dir, 1992–95, Yorkshire TV; Chair., ITV Broadcast Board, 1995–. *Publications:* The Coup, 1975; The Monocled Mutineer (with W. Allison), 1975; Arthur C. Clarke's Mysterious World, 1980; Great Racehorses in Art, 1984; Chronicles of the Strange and Mysterious, 1987; Racing in Art, 1990; The Cabinet of Curiosities, 1991; A Century of Mysteries, 1993; The Art of the Horse, 1995.

FAIRSTEIN, Linda; American lawyer and writer; b. 1947; m. Justin N. Feldman 1986. *Career:* lawyer, Office of the District Attorney, Manhattan, New York 1972, Head, Sex Crimes Unit 1974–2002; provided training for police, prosecution and medical staff, and rape counsellors; writer 1993–. *Publications:* Sexual Violence: Our War Against Rape (non-fiction) 1993, Final Jeopardy 1996, Likely to Die 1997, Cold Hit 1999, The Deadhouse 2001, The Bonevault 2003, The Kills 2004, Entombed 2005, Death Dance 2006, Bad Blood 2007. *Address:* c/o Simon & Schuster, 1230 Avenue of the Americas, New York, NY 10020, USA.

FAKHOURY, Tamirace, BA, MA, PhD; Lebanese writer and poet; b. 26 Nov. 1974, Beit Chabab. *Education:* Lebanese American Univ., Beirut and Univ. of Freiburg, Germany. *Career:* Asst, Hon. Consulate of Ghana, Lebanon 1995–96; teacher, Int. Coll., Beirut 1996–2002; Lecturer, American Univ. of Science and Technology, Beirut 1999–2002; currently researcher, Arnold Bergstraesser Institut, Germany; freelance journalist, al-Anwar daily newspaper, Beirut. *Publications:* poetry: Le pays de l'Empereur et de l'Enfant perdu 1983, Aubades 1996, Contre-Marées 2000, Poème absent 2004; prose: Ethnic Conflict and the Methods of its Regulation (conference report for UNESCO) 2004, International Relations in an Uncertain Hegemonial World System (conference report for UNESCO) 2005; contrib. poems and articles to Lebanese and French journals and magazines. *Address:* Arnold Bergstraesser Institut, Windausstr. 16, 79110 Freiburg i Brsg, Germany (office).

FALCK, (Adrian) Colin, BA, MA, PhD; British academic, writer and poet; b. 14 July 1934, London, England; one d. one s. *Education:* University of Oxford, University of London. *Career:* Lecturer in Sociology LSE 1961–62; Assoc. Ed. The Review 1962–72; Lecturer in Literature Chelsea College 1964–84; Poetry Ed. The New Review 1974–78; Assoc. Prof. York College, Pennsylvania 1989–99. *Publications:* The Garden in the Evening 1964, Promises 1969, Backwards into the Smoke 1973, Poems Since 1900: An Anthology (ed. with Ian Hamilton) 1975, In This Dark Light 1978, Robinson Jeffers: Selected Poems (ed.) 1987, Myth, Truth and Literature 1989, Edna St Vincent Millay: Selected Poems (ed.) 1991, Memorabilia 1992, Post-Modern Love 1997, American and British Verse in the Twentieth Century 2004. Contributions: many professional journals and general periodicals. *Literary Agent:* Johnson & Alcock Ltd, Clerkenwell House, 45–47 Clerkenwell Green, London, EC1R 0HT, England. *Address:* 20 Thurlow Road, London, NW3 5PP, England (home). *Telephone:* (20) 7435-6806. *Fax:* (20) 7435-6806.

FALCONER, Lee N. (see May, Julian)

FALK, Richard A., BS, JSD, LLB; American academic; *Senior Research Fellow, Princeton University;* b. 13 Nov. 1930, New York. *Education:* Wharton School, Univ. of Pennsylvania, Harvard Law School, Yale Law School. *Career:* Asst Prof., later Assoc. Prof., Coll. of Law, Ohio State Univ. 1955–61; Ford Foundation Fellow, Harvard Law School 1958–59; Visiting Assoc. Prof., Princeton Univ. 1961–62, Assoc. Prof. of Int. Law 1962–65, Albert G. Milbank Prof. of Int. Law and Practice 1965–2001, Sr Research Fellow 2002–; Acting Dir, Center of Int. Studies 1975, 1982; Fellow, Center for Advanced Study in the Behavioral Sciences, Stanford, CA 1968–69; visiting prof. at numerous univs including Stockholm, American Univ. in Cairo, Univ. of Wales, Univ. of Calif., Santa Barbara; Chair. Nuclear Age Peace Foundation; mem. Editorial Bd numerous publs including The Nation, The Progressive, World Politics, Foreign Policy Magazine, Peace Forum; fmr mem. several int. panels of judges; participation in numerous int. and govt comms, including Ind. World Comm. on the Oceans 1995–2000, Ind. Int. Comm. on Kosovo 1999–2001. *Publications include:* Law, War and Morality in the Contemporary World 1963, Legal Order in a Violent World 1968, Crimes of War (jt ed.) 1971, A Global Approach to National Policy 1975, Human Rights and State Sovereignty 1981, Reviving the World Court 1986, Revitalizing International Law 1989, International Law and World Order (jt author) 1997, Human Rights Horizons 2001, Religion and Humane Global Governance 2002, The Great Terror War 2003, Unlocking the Middle East 2005; numerous articles in learned journals. *Honours:* hon. mem. Bd of Eds American Journal of International Law; hon. degrees from Monmouth Coll. 1987, City Univ. of NY 1999, John Jay Coll., York Univ. 2004. *Address:* 723 Alston Road, Santa Barbara, CA 93108, USA (home). *Telephone:* (805) 893-7860 (office). *Fax:* (805) 893-8003 (office). *E-mail:* falk@global.ucsb.edu.

FALKIRK, Richard (see Lambert, Derek William)

FALLON, Ivan Gregory, FRSA; Irish journalist; b. 26 June 1944, s. of Padraic Fallon and Dorothea Maher; m. 1st Susan Mary Lurring 1967 (divorced 1997); one s. two d.; m. 2nd Elizabeth Rees-Jones 1997. *Education:* St Peter's Coll., Wexford, Trinity Coll. Dublin. *Career:* on staff of Irish Times 1964–66, Thomson Prov. Newspapers 1966–67, Daily Mirror 1967–68, Sunday Telegraph 1968–70; Deputy City Ed., Sunday Express 1970–71, Sunday Telegraph 1971–84, City Ed. 1979–84; Deputy Ed. Sunday Times 1984–94; Group Editorial Dir, Argus Group, SA 1994–; Chief Exec. Ind. Newspapers Holdings Ltd, South Africa 1997–; Exec. Chair. iTouch PLC 2000–; mem. Council, Univ. of Buckingham 1982–; Council of Govs, United Medical and Dental Schools of Guy's and St Thomas' Hosps 1985–94; Trustee Project Trust 1984–94, Generation Trust, Guy's Hosp. 1985–; Dir N. Brown Holdings 1994–. *Publications:* DeLorean: The Rise and Fall of a Dream-maker (with James L. Srodes) 1983, Takeovers 1987, The Brothers: The Rise of Saatchi and Saatchi 1988, Billionaire: The Life and Times of Sir James Goldsmith 1991, The Player: The Life of Tony O'Reilly 1994. *Address:* Prospect House, Klein Constantia Road, Constantia, Cape Town, South Africa. *Telephone:* (11) 6332115. *Fax:* (11) 8342881.

FALLON, Martin (see Patterson, Harry)

FALLON, Peter, BA, HDipEd, MA; Irish editor and poet; b. 26 Feb. 1951, Osnabrück, Germany; two c. *Education:* Trinity College, Dublin. *Career:* Founder, Ed., Gallery Press, Dublin, 1970–; Poet-in-Residence, Deerfield Acad., MA, 1976–77, 1996–97; International Writer-in-Residence at various Indiana Schools, 1979; Fiction Ed., O'Brien Press, Dublin, 1980–85; Teacher, Contemporary Irish Poetry, School of Irish Studies, Dublin, 1985–89; Writing Fellow, Poet-in-Residence, Trinity College, Dublin, 1994; Heimbold Prof. of Irish Studies, Villanova University, PA. *Publications:* poetry: Among the Walls 1971, Co-incidence of Flesh 1972, The First Affair 1974, Finding the Dead 1978, The Speaking Stones 1978, Winter Work 1983, The News and Weather 1987, The Penguin Book of Contemporary Irish Poetry (ed. with Derek Mahon) 1990, The Georgics of Virgil (trans.) 2004; other: Eye to Eye 1992, News of the World: Selected and New Poems 1998, 1999; contrib. to poetry anthologies, periodicals and journals. *Honours:* Irish Arts Council Bursary, 1981; National Poetry Competition, England, 1982; Meath Merit Award, Arts and Culture, 1987; O'Shaughnessy Poetry Award, 1993. *Address:* Gallery Press, Loughcrew, Oldcastle, County Meath, Ireland.

FALLOWELL, Duncan Richard; British writer; b. 26 Sept. 1948, London, England. *Education:* Magdalen Coll., Oxford. *Opera libretto:* Gormenghast 1998. *Publications:* Drug Tales 1979, April Ashley's Odyssey 1982, Satyrday 1986, The Underbelly 1987, To Noto 1989, Twentieth Century Characters 1994, One Hot Summer in St Petersburg 1994, A History of Facelifting 2003. *Address:* 44 Leamington Road Villas, London, W11 1HT, England.

FALLOWS, David Nicholas, BA, MMus, PhD, FBA; British musicologist; *Professor of Musicology, University of Manchester;* b. 20 Dec. 1945, Buxton, England; m. Paulène Oliver 1976 (separated); one s. one d. *Education:* Jesus Coll., Cambridge, King's Coll., London, Univ. of California at Berkeley. *Career:* Asst, Studio der Frühen Musik, Munich 1967–70; Lecturer in Music, Univ. of Wisconsin at Madison 1973–74; Lecturer in Music, Univ. of Manchester 1976–82, Sr Lecturer 1982–92, Reader in Music 1992–97, Prof. of Musicology 1997–; Reviews Ed., Early Music 1976–95, 1999–2000; Visiting Assoc. Prof., Univ. of N Carolina at Chapel Hill 1982–83; founder and Gen. Ed., Royal Musical Asscn Monographs 1982–98; Visiting Prof. of Musicology, École Normale Supérieure, Paris 1993; corresponding mem. American Musicological Soc. 1999–; mem. Int. Musicological Soc. (vice-pres. 1997–2002, pres. 2002–07), Royal Musical Asscn (vice-pres. 2000–). *Publications:* Dufay 1982, Chansonnier de Jean de Montchenu (co-author) 1991, Companion to Medieval and Renaissance Music (ed. with T. Knighton) 1992, The Songs of Guillaume Dufay 1995, Oxford Bodleian Library MS Canon Misc. 213: Late Medieval and Early Renaissance Music in Facsimile, Vol. 1 (ed.) 1995, Songs and Musicians in the Fifteenth Century 1996, The Songbook of Fridolin Sicher 1996, A Catalogue of Polyphonic Songs 1415–1480 1999; contrib. to reference works, scholarly books and professional journals, including Gramophone, The Guardian, Early Music, New Grove Dictionary of Music and Musicians 1980, 2001. *Honours:* Ingolf Dahl Prize in Musicology 1971, Dent Medal 1982; Chevalier, Ordre des Arts et des Lettres 1994. *Address:* 10 Chatham Road, Manchester, M16 0DR, England (home).

Telephone: (161) 881 1188 (office). E-mail: david.fallows@manchester.ac.uk (home).

FALUDI, Susan C.; American journalist and writer; b. 18 April 1959, Yorktown Heights, NY. Education: Harvard Univ., Radcliffe Coll. Career: Man. Ed. Harvard Crimson student newspaper; copy clerk, New York Times 1981–86; reporter Miami Herald, Atlanta Constitution 1981–86, San José Mercury News 1986–88; reporter, San Francisco bureau, Wall Street Journal 1990–; contribs to Ms and Mother Jones magazines; mem. Advisory Bd Fairness and Accuracy in Reporting 1992–; mem. Nat. Writers Guild 1994–99. Publications: Backlash: The Undeclared War Against American Women (Nat. Book Critics' Circle Award for Gen. Non-fiction 1992) 1991, Stiffed: The Betrayal of the American Man 2000. Honours: Pulitzer Prize for Explanatory Journalism 1991 for a report on the leveraged buy-out of Safeway Stores, Inc.. Literary Agent: Sandra Dijkstra Literary Agency, 1155 Camino del Mar, Suite 515, Del Mar, CA 92014, USA.

FAN, Jingyi; Chinese journalist; President, China Society of News Photography; b. 1931, Suzhou City, Jiangsu Prov. Education: St John's University, Shanghai. Career: joined CCP 1978; Ed., later Ed.-in-Chief, Deputy Dir, later Dir and mem. Editorial Bd Liaoning Daily 1979–84; Dir Foreign Languages Publ. and Distribution Bureau 1984–86; Ed.-in-Chief Economic Daily 1986–93, People's Daily 1993–98; Del., 13th CCP Nat. Congress 1987–92, 14th CCP Nat. Congress 1992–97; mem. 8th CPPCC Nat. Cttee 1993–98 (Vice-Chair. Economy Cttee); mem. Standing Cttee of 9th NPC 1998–2003 (Vice-Chair. Educ., Science, Culture and Public Health Cttee); Pres. China Soc. of News Photography 1995–. Honours: Hon. Pres. Photo-Journalism Soc. 1994–; honoured as one of the excellent journalists of China 1991. Address: c/o Standing Committee of the National People's Congress, Beijing, People's Republic of China.

FANTHORPE, Robert Lionel, BA, FRSA, FCMI; British priest, writer, broadcaster, academic and consultant; Director of Media Studies, Cardiff Academy; b. 9 Feb. 1935, Dereham, Norfolk, England; m. Patricia Alice Tooke 1957; two d. Education: FCP, teaching certificate with advanced mains distinction, Anglican ordination certificate. Career: consultant and Festival Co-ordinator, UK Year of Literature and Writing 1995; Dir of Media Studies, Cardiff Acad. 2002–; mem. MENSA, Equity, Soc. of Authors, Welsh Acad.; patron Jumbo motorcyclists' charity; Pres. ASSAP 1999; Pres. BUFORA 2000; guest celebrity poet Margate Poetry Festival 2000. Television and Radio: presenter, Fortean TV (Channel 4) 1997, The Real Nostradamus (Channel 4), Stranger than Fiction (Westcountry TV), Stations of the Cross (HTV), Holy Quiz (HTV) 2000, Three Wise Men (BBC Radio Wales) 2000, Talking Stones 2002, 2003, Real Radio Reverend slot (Real Radio 105FM), role of Regression Detective This Morning (Granada TV). Publications: The Black Lion 1979, The Holy Grail Revealed 1982, Life of St Francis 1988, God in All Things 1988, Thoughts and Prayers for Troubled Times 1989, Birds and Animals of the Bible 1990, Thoughts and Prayers for Lonely Times 1990, The First Christmas 1990, Rennes-le-Château 1992, The Oak Island Mystery 1995, The Abbot's Kitchen 1995, The World's Greatest Unsolved Mysteries 1997, The World's Most Mysterious People 1998, The World's Most Mysterious Places 1998, Mysteries of the Bible 1999, Death, the Final Mystery 2000, The World's Most Mysterious Objects 2002, The World's Most Mysterious Murders 2003, Talking Stones (book of TV series) 2003, Unsolved Mysteries of the Sea 2004. Honours: Electrical Development Assen Diploma 1958, holder of seven World Championships for Professional Authors: Prose, Drama, Poetry and Autobiography, Grand Chaplain Gen. Knights Templar Priory of the Holy Lands 2002–04. Address: Rivendell, 48 Claude Road, Roath, Cardiff, Wales. Telephone: (2920) 498368 (office). Fax: (2920) 496832. E-mail: Fanthorpe@aol .com. Website: www.lionel-fanthorpe.com.

FANTHORPE, Ursula Askham, CBE, MA, FRSA, FRSL; British poet and writer; b. 22 July 1929, Kent; d. of the late Richard Fanthorpe and Winifrid Elsie Askham Redmore; pnr R. V. Bailey. Education: St Catherine's School, Bramley, St Anne's Coll., Oxford, London Inst. of Educ., Univ. of Swansea. Career: Asst Mistress Cheltenham Ladies' Coll. 1954–62, Head of English 1962–70; English teacher Howells School, Llandaff 1972–73; temporary clerical work Bristol 1973–74; clerk/receptionist, Burden Neurological Hosp. Bristol 1974–89; Arts Council writer-in-residence St Martin's Coll., Lancaster 1983–85; Northern Arts Literary Fellow Univs of Durham and Newcastle 1987–88; freelance writer 1989–; various workshops and collaborations with artists and musicians; mem. Nat. Trust, Wildlife and Wetlands Trust, Council for the Protection of Rural England, Compassion in World Farming, Medical Foundation, Religious Soc. of Friends, PEN, Soc. of Authors. Publications: Side Effects 1978, Standing To 1982, Voices Off 1984, Selected Poems 1986, A Watching Brief 1987, Neck-Verse 1992, Safe as Houses 1995, Consequences 2000, Christmas Poems 2002, Queueing for the Sun 2003, Collected Poems 2005, Homing In 2006; contrib. to anthologies, including Selected Poems 1986, Penguin Modern Poets 6 1996, Double Act (audiobook with R. V. Bailey) 1997, Poetry Quartets 5 (audiobook) 1999; contrib. to radio and TV programmes and to numerous journals and periodicals. Honours: Hon. Fellow Cheltenham & Gloucester Coll. of Higher Educ. 1995, St Anne's Coll., Oxford 2003, Sarum Coll., Salisbury 2004; Hon. DLitt (West of England) 1995, (Bath) 2006, Dr hc (Gloucestershire) 2000; Soc. of Authors Travelling Fellowship 1983, Hawthornden Fellowships 1987, 1997, 2002, Arts Council Writers' Award 1994, Soc. of Authors Cholmondeley Award 1995, Queen's Gold Medal for Poetry 2003. Address: Culverhay House, Wotton-under-Edge, Gloucestershire

GL12 7LS, England (home). Fax: (1453) 843105 (home). E-mail: fanthorpe .bailey@virgin.net.

FARAH, Nuruddin; Somali novelist; b. 24 Nov. 1945, Baidoa; s. of Farah Hassan and Fatuma Aleli; m. Amina Mama 1992; one s. one d. Education: Panjab Univ., Chandigarh, India, Univs of London and Essex, UK. Career: Lecturer, Nat. Univ. of Somalia, Mogadishu 1971–74; Assoc. Prof., Univ. of Jos, Nigeria 1981–83; Writer-in-Residence, Univ. of Minn. 1989, Brown Univ. 1991; Prof., Makerere Univ., Kampala 1990; Rhodes Scholar St Antony's Coll., Oxford 1996; Visiting Prof., Univ. of Texas at Austin 1997; now full-time novelist; mem. Union of Writers of the African People, PEN Int., Somali-Speaking PEN Centre. Plays include: The Offering 1976, Yussuf and his Brothers 1982. Publications: From a Crooked Rib 1970, A Naked Needle 1976, Sweet and Sour Milk 1979, Sardines 1981, Close Sesame 1983, Maps 1986, Gifts 1992, Secrets 1998, Yesterday, Tomorrow: Voices from the Somali Diaspora 1999, Links 2004, Knots 2007; contrib. to Guardian, New African, Transition Magazine, New York Times, Observer, TLS, London Review of Books. Honours: Hon. DLitt (Univ. of Kent at Canterbury) 2000; English-speaking Union Literary Prize 1980, Tucholsky Award 1991, Premio Cavour Award 1992, Zimbabwe Annual Award 1993, Neustadt Int. Literary Prize 1998, Festival Étonnant Voyageur St Malo, France 1998. Address: c/o Deborah Rogers, Rogers, Coleridge & White, 20 Powis Mews, London, W11 1JN, England (office).

FARELY, Alison (see Poland, Dorothy Elizabeth Hayward)

FARHI, (Musa) Moris, MBE, BA, FRSL, FRGS; Turkish novelist and poet; b. 5 July 1935, Ankara; m. Nina Ruth Gould 1978; one step-d. Education: Istanbul American Coll., RADA London. Career: mem. Soc. of Authors, Writers Guild, PEN, Int. PEN (vice-pres.). Television: various scripts 1960–80. Publications: The Pleasure of Death 1972, The Last of Days 1983, Journey Through the Wilderness 1989, Children of the Rainbow 1999, Young Turk (novel) 2004; contrib. to Menard Press, Voices Within the Art: The Modern Jewish Poets, Men Cards, European Judaism, Modern Poetry in Translation, Frank, Jewish Quarterly, Steaua (Romania), Confrontation (USA), North Atlantic Review (USA), Reflections on the Universal Declaration of Human Rights. Honours: Associazione Thema Romano (Italy) 2002, Romani Acad. of Arts and Sciences Special Prize, Berlin 2003, Alberto Benveniste Prize for Literature, Paris 2007. Address: 11 North Square, London, NW11 7AB, England. E-mail: farhi@ clara.net.

FARICY, Robert, BS, PhL, MA, STL, STD, SJ; American academic and writer; Professor Emeritus, Pontifical Gregorian University; b. 29 Aug. 1926, St Paul, MN. Education: US Naval Acad., St Louis Univ., Lyon-Fourvière Seminaire des Missions, Catholic Univ. of America. Career: Asst Prof., Catholic Univ. of America 1965–71; Prof. of Spiritual Theology, Pontifical Gregorian Univ., Rome, Italy 1971–96, Prof. Emer. 1996–; Visiting Prof., Pontifical Urbaniana Univ., Rome 2000–02; Visiting Prof., Regina Mundi Inst., Rome 2000–05. Publications: Seeking Jesus in Contemplation and Discernment 1983, Medjugorje Up Close: Mary Speaks to the World (with L. Rooney) 1985, Contemplating Jesus (with R. Wicks) 1986, The Contemplative Way of Prayer (with L. Rooney) 1986, The Healing of the Religious Life (with S. Blackborow) 1986, Lord, Teach Us to Pray (with L. Rooney) 1986, Wind and Sea Obey Him: Approaches to a Theology of Nature 1986, Medjugorje Journal (with L. Rooney) 1987, Lord Jesus, Teach Me to Pray (with L. Rooney) 1988, The Lord's Dealing 1988, Mary Among Us 1989, Medjugorje Retreat (with L. Rooney) 1989, Pilgrim's Journal 1990, Our Lady Comes to Scottsdale (with L. Rooney) 1991, Return to God (with L. Rooney) 1993, Knowing Jesus in the World (with L. Rooney) 1996, Your Wounds I Will Heal (with L. Rooney) 1998, Praying with Mary 2000; contrib. to numerous theological and philosophical journals. Address: Pontifical Gregorian University, Piazza della Pilotta 4, 00187 Rome, Italy (office); 1404 W Wisconsin Avenue, Milwaukee, WI 53233, USA (home). Telephone: (6) 5504098 (office); (414) 288-5000 (home). Fax: (339) 152-4263 (office). E-mail: bobfaricy@yahoo.com (home). Website: www.robertfaricy.org.

FARLEY, Carol, BA, MA; American children's writer; b. 20 Dec. 1936, Ludington, MI; m. 1954; one s. three d. Education: Western Michigan Univ., Michigan State Univ., Central Michigan Univ. Career: mem. MWA, Authors' Guild, Children's Book Guild, Soc. of Children's Book Writers, Chicago Children's Reading Round Table. Publications: Mystery of the Fog Man 1974, The Garden is Doing Fine 1976, Mystery in the Ravine 1976, Mystery of the Melted Diamonds 1985, Case of the Vanishing Villain 1986, Case of the Lost Look Alike 1988, Korea, Land of the Morning Calm 1991, Mr Pak Buys a Story 1997; contrib. to The Writer, Soc. of Children's Book Writer's Bulletin, Cricket, Disney Adventures, Challenge, Spider, Pockets, Appleseeds. Honours: Child Study Assen Best Book of Year 1976, Friends of the Writer Best Juvenile Book by Mid-West Writer 1978, IRA/CBC Children's Choice Book 1987. Address: 5448 Desert Paradise Drive, Las Vegas, NV 89130, USA.

FARLEY, Paul; British poet; Reader in Poetry, Lancaster University; b. 1965, Liverpool, England. Education: Chelsea School of Art. Career: fmr writer-in-residence with the Wordsworth Trust; Reader in Poetry, Lancaster Univ. 2006–. Publications: The Boy from the Chemist is Here to See You (Forward Prize for Best First Collection) 1998, The Ice Age: Poems (Whitbread Book Award for best poetry collection 2003) 2002, Distant Voices, Still Lives 2006, Tramp in Flames 2006. Honours: Somerset Maugham Award, Sunday Times Young Writer of the Year award, Royal Literary Fund Fellow, Liverpool Hope Univ. College 2000/01, 2001/02, Forward Prize for the Best Single Poem (for Liverpool Disappears for a Billionth of a Second) 2005. Literary Agent: c/o

Peter Straus, Rogers, Coleridge and White, 20 Powis Mews, London W11, England. *Telephone:* (20) 7221-3717. *Address:* c/o Department of Creative Writing, Lancaster University, Bailrigg, Lancaster, LA1 4YW, England. *E-mail:* p.j.farley@lancaster.ac.uk.

FARMER, Beverley Anne, BA; Australian writer; b. 1941, Melbourne; one s. *Education:* Univ. of Melbourne. *Publications:* Alone 1980, Milk 1983, Home Time 1985, A Body of Water: A Year's Notebook 1990, Place of Birth 1990, The Seal Woman 1992, The House in the Light 1995, Collected Stories 1996, The Bone House 2005. *Honours:* NSW Premier's Prize for Fiction (for Milk) 1984.

FARMER, David Hugh, BLitt, FRHistS, FSA; British lecturer and writer; b. 30 Jan. 1923, Ealing, London, England; m. Pauline Ann Widgery 1966 (died 1999); two s. *Education:* Linacre Coll., Oxford. *Career:* Lecturer, Reading Univ. 1967–77, Reader 1977–88; also lectured in Denmark, Italy. *Publications:* Life of St Hugh of Lincoln 1961, The Monk of Farne 1962, The Rule of St Benedict 1968, The Oxford Dictionary of Saints 1978, Benedict's Disciples 1980, The Age of Bede 1983, St Hugh of Lincoln 1985, Bede's Ecclesiastical History 1990, Christ Crucified and Other Meditations 1994; contrib. to St Augustine's Abbey (English Heritage) 1997, Benedictines in Oxford 1997, The Story of Christian Spirituality 2001, Dictionnaire d'Histoire Ecclesiastique, New Catholic Encyclopedia, Bibliotheca Sanctorum, Lexikon der Christlichen Ikonographie, Studia Monastica, Studia Anselmiana, Journal of Ecclesistical History, English Historical Review, The Tablet. *Address:* 23 Hartslock Court, Shooters Hill, Pangbourne, Berkshire RG8 7BJ, England (home).

FARMER, Penelope Jane, BA, DipSoc; British writer; b. 14 June 1939, Westerham, Kent; m. 1st Michael John Mockridge 1962 (divorced 1977); one s. one d.; m. 2nd Simon Shorvon 1984 (divorced 1996). *Education:* St Anne's College, Oxford, Bedford College, London. *Career:* mem. PEN; Society of Authors. *Publications:* Fiction: Standing in the Shadow, 1984; Eve: Her Story, 1985; Away from Home, 1987; Glasshouses, 1988; Snakes and Ladders, 1993. Children's Books: The China People, 1960; The Summer Birds, 1962; The Magic Stone, 1964; The Saturday Shillings, 1965; The Seagull, 1965; Emma in Winter, 1966; Charlotte Sometimes, 1969; Dragonfly Summer, 1971; A Castle of Bone, 1972; William and Mary, 1974; Heracles, 1975; August the Fourth, 1975; Year King, 1977; The Coal Train, 1977; Beginnings: Creation Myths of the World (ed.), 1979; The Runaway Train, 1980; Thicker Than Water, 1989; Stone Croc, 1991; Penelope, 1994; Twin Trouble, 1996. Other: Anthology: Two: The Book of Twins and Doubles, 1996, Sisters 1998, Grandmothers 2000; Short stories; Radio and television scripts. Contributions: periodicals. *Honours:* American Library Asscn Notable Book, 1962; Carnegie Medal Commendation, 1963. *Literary Agent:* c/o Conville & Walsh, 2 Cranton Street, London, W1, England. *E-mail:* clare@office.convilleandwalsh.com.

FARRINGTON, David Philip, OBE, MA, PhD, FBA, FMedSci; British psychologist, academic and criminologist; *Professor of Psychological Criminology, Institute of Criminology, University of Cambridge;* b. 7 March 1944, Ormskirk, Lancs.; s. of William Farrington and Gladys Holden Farrington; m. Sally Chamberlain 1966; three d. *Education:* Univ. of Cambridge. *Career:* mem. staff, Inst. of Criminology, Univ. of Cambridge 1969–, Prof. of Psychological Criminology 1992–; Pres. European Asscn of Psychology and Law 1997–99; Visiting Fellow, US Nat. Inst. of Justice 1981; Chair. Div. of Criminological and Legal Psychology, British Psychological Soc. 1983–85; mem. Parole Bd for England and Wales 1984–87; Vice-Chair. US Nat. Acad. of Sciences Panel on Violence 1989–92; Visiting Fellow US Bureau of Justice Statistics 1995–98; Co-Chair. US Office of Juvenile Justice and Delinquency Prevention Study Group on Serious and Violent Juvenile Offenders 1995–97; Pres. British Soc. of Criminology 1990–93, Pres. American Soc. of Criminology 1998–99; Co-Chair. US Office of Juvenile Justice and Delinquency Prevention Study Group on Very Young Offenders 1998–2000; Chair. UK Dept of Health Advisory Cttee for the Nat. Programme on Forensic Mental Health 2000–03; mem. Bd of Dirs Int. Soc. of Criminology 2000–; Pres. Acad. of Experimental Criminology 2001–03; Co-Chair. Campbell Collaboration Crime and Justice Group 2000–. *Publications:* 27 books and over 420 articles on criminology and psychology. *Honours:* Sellin-Glueck Award of American Soc. of Criminology 1984, Sutherland Award of American Soc. of Criminology 2002, Joan McCord Award, Acad. of Experimental Criminology 2005, Beccaria Gold Medal, Criminology Soc. of German-Speaking Countries 2005. *Address:* Institute of Criminology, University of Cambridge, Sidgwick Avenue, Cambridge, CB3 9DT (office); 7 The Meadows, Haslingfield, Cambridge, CB3 7JD, England (home). *Telephone:* (1223) 335360 (office); (1223) 872555 (home). *Fax:* (1223) 335356 (office). *E-mail:* enquiries@crim.cam.ac.uk (office). *Website:* www.crim .cam.ac.uk (office).

FARROW, James S. (see Tubb, Edwin Charles)

FARROW, John (see Ferguson, Trevor)

FASQUELLE, Jean-Claude; French publisher; *Chairman of the Board, Éditions Grasset et Fasquelle;* b. 29 Nov. 1930, Paris; s. of Charles Fasquelle and Odette Cyprien-Fabre; m. 1st Solange de la Rochefoucauld; one d.; m. 2nd Nicola Jegher 1966. *Education:* Ecole des Roches, Verneuil-sur-Avre, Sorbonne and Faculté de Droit, Paris. *Career:* Pres.-Dir-Gen. Société des Editions Fasquelle 1953–60, Editions du Sagittaire 1958–; Admin.-Dir-Gen. Editions Grasset et Fasquelle 1960, Pres.-Dir-Gen. 1980–2000, Chair. of Bd 2000–; Dir Le Magazine littéraire (monthly) 1970–2004. *Address:* Éditions Grasset et Fasquelle, 61 rue des Saints-Pères, 75006 Paris (office); 13 Square

Vergennes, 75015 Paris, France (home). *Telephone:* 1-44-39-22-00 (office). *Fax:* 1-44-39-22-18 (office).

FATCHEN, Maxwell Edgar, AM; Australian author and poet; b. 3 Aug. 1920, Adelaide, SA; m. Jean Wohlers 1942, two s. one d. *Career:* journalist and feature writer, Adelaide News 1946–55; special writer, The Advertiser 1955, 1981–84, Literary Ed. 1971–81; mem. Australian Soc. of Authors, Australian Fellowship of Writers, South Australian Writers' Centre, Media Alliance. *Publications:* The River Kings, 1966; Conquest of the River, 1970; The Spirit Wind, 1973; Chase Through the Night, 1977; Closer to the Stars, 1981; Wry Rhymes, 1987; A Country Christmas, 1990; Tea for Three, 1994. Contributions: Denver Post; Sydney Sun; Regional South Australian Histories. *Honours:* Advance Australia Award for Literature 1991, AMP-Walkley Award for Journalism 1996, SA Great Award for Literature 1999.

FAULCON, Robert (see Holdstock, Robert)

FAULKS, Sebastian, CBE, MA, FRSL; British writer; b. 20 April 1953, Newbury, Berks.; s. of Peter Faulks and Pamela Lawless; m. Veronica Youlten 1989; two s. one d. *Education:* Wellington Coll. and Emmanuel Coll., Cambridge. *Career:* reporter Daily Telegraph newspaper 1979–83, feature writer Sunday Telegraph 1983–86; Literary Ed. The Independent 1986–89, Deputy Ed. The Independent on Sunday 1989–90, Assoc. Ed. 1990–91; columnist The Guardian 1992–97, Evening Standard 1997–99, Mail on Sunday 1999–2000. *Television:* Churchill's Secret Army 2000. *Publications:* A Trick of the Light 1984, The Girl at the Lion d'Or 1989, A Fool's Alphabet 1992, Birdsong 1993, The Fatal Englishman 1996, Charlotte Gray 1998, On Green Dolphin Street 2001, Human Traces 2005, Pistache 2006, Engleby 2007. *Literary Agent:* Aitken Alexander Associates Ltd, 18–21 Cavaye Place, London, SW10 9PT, England. *Telephone:* (20) 7373-8672. *Fax:* (20) 7373-6002. *E-mail:* reception@aitkenalexander.co.uk. *Website:* www.aitkenalexander.co .uk.

FAURE, Roland; French journalist; b. 10 Oct. 1926, Montelimar; s. of Edmond Faure-Geors and Jeanne Gallet; m. Véra Hitzbleck 1956; three s. *Education:* Enclos Saint-François, Montpellier and Faculté de Droit, Aix-en-Provence. *Career:* journalist, Méridional-la France, Marseilles 1947; del. in America, Asscn de la presse latine d'Europe et d'Amerique 1951, Sec.-Gen. 1954–; Founder and Ed.-in-Chief, Journal français du Brésil, Rio de Janeiro 1952–53; Diplomatic Ed. L'Aurore 1954, Head of Diplomatic Service 1959, Ed.-in-Chief 1962, Dir and Ed.-in-Chief 1968–78; attached to Cabinet of Minister of Public Works 1957–58; Dir Toutes les nouvelles de Versailles 1954–86; mem. Admin. Bd Antenne 2 1975–79; Dir of Information, Radio-France 1979–81; Founder and Dir Radio CVS 1982; Pres. Dir-Gen. Société Nat. de programme Radio France 1986–89, Société Nat. de Radiodifffusion; Pres. Université radiophonique et télévisuelle int. (URTI) 1987–97, Communauté des radios publiques de langue française (CRPLF) 1987; Pres. Admin. Council Fondations Marguerite Long-Jacques Thibaud 1991–; Pres. Club DAB 1991–; mem. Conseil Supérieur de l'Audiovisuel (CSA) 1989–97, mem. numerous professional asscns. etc. *Publications:* Brésil dernière heure 1954; articles in newspapers and journals. *Honours:* Officier, Légion d'honneur; Officier, Ordre Nat. du Mérite, des Arts et des Lettres. *Address:* La Radio numérique, 40 rue Guynemer, 92130 Issy-les-Moulineaux (office); 94 boulevard de la Tour Maubourg, Paris 7e, France (home). *Telephone:* 1-49-55-01-15 (office).

FAWKES, Richard Brian, BA; British writer, dramatist and film director; b. 31 July 1944, Camberley, Surrey, England; m. Cherry Elizabeth Cole 1971, two s. one d. *Education:* St David's Univ. Coll. *Career:* mem. Soc. of Authors, Soc. for Theatre Research. *Publications:* The Last Corner of Arabia (with Michael Darlow), 1976; Fighting for a Laugh, 1978; Dion Boucicault: A Biography, 1979; Notes from a Low Singer (with Michael Langdon), 1982; Welsh National Opera, 1986. Other: Plays for stage, radio, and television; Documentary film scripts. Contributions: journals and magazines including, BBC Music Magazine, Opera Now, Classical Music and Daily Telegraph. *Honours:* West Midlands Arts Asscn Bursary 1978.

FEDER, Kenneth, BA, MA, PhD; American archaeologist and writer; *Professor of Anthropology, Central Connecticut State University;* b. 1 Aug. 1952, New York, USA; m. Melissa Jean Kalogeros 1981; two s. *Education:* State Univ. of New York, Univ. of Connecticut. *Career:* Prof. of Anthropology, Central Connecticut State Univ. 1977–. *Publications:* Human Antiquity (with Michael Park) 1989, Frauds, Myths and Mysteries: Science and Pseudoscience in Archaeology 1990, A Village of Outcasts: Historical Archaeology and Documentary Research at the Lighthouse 1994, The Past In Perspective: An Introduction to Human Prehistory 1996, Field Methods in Archaeology (with Tom Hester and Harry Shafer) 1997, Lessons From the Past 1999, Dangerous Places: Health and Safety in Archaeology (co-ed. with David Poirier) 2001, Atlantis: Fact or Fiction, The Trojan War, Theseus and the Minotaur, Jason and the Argonauts (contribs to The Seventy Great Mysteries of the Ancient World, co-ed. by Brian Fagan) 2001, Linking to the Past 2004, Skeptics, Fencesitters and True Believers in Archaeological Fantasies 2005 (co-ed. Garrett Fagan); contrib. to Encyclopedia of Anthropology 2006. *Honours:* Fellow Cttee for the Scientific Investigation of Claims of the Paranormal, Excellence in Teaching Central Connecticut State Univ. *Address:* Department of Anthropology, Central Connecticut State University, New Britain, CT 06050, USA (office). *Telephone:* (860) 832-2615 (office). *E-mail:* feder@ccsu .edu.

FEDERMAN, Raymond; American academic and writer; b. 15 May 1928, Paris, France; m. Erica Hubscher 1960; one d. *Education:* Univ. Calif. at Los Angeles and Columbia Univ. *Career:* Asst Prof., Univ. of California at Santa Barbara 1959–64; Assoc. Prof., State Univ. of NY, Buffalo 1964–68, Prof. 1968–90, Distinguished Prof. of Literature 1990–99, Melodia E. Jones Distinguished Prof. 1992–99; Guggenheim Fellow 1966–67, Nat. Endowment for the Arts Fellow 1986. *Publications:* novels: Double or Nothing 1971, Take It or Leave It 1976, The Voice in the Closet 1979, The Twofold Vibration 1982, Smiles on Washington Square 1985, To Whom It May Concern 1990; essays: Journey to Chaos 1965, Surfiction 1976, Critifiction 1992, The Supreme Indecision of the Writer 1996, La Fourrure de Ma Tante Rachel 1996, Loose Shoes 1999, The Precipice and Other Catastrophes 1999. *Honours:* American Book Award 1987. *Address:* c/o Department of English, State University of New York, Clemens Hall, Buffalo, NY 14620, USA (office).

FEI MA (see Marr, William Wei-Yi)

FEIFFER, Jules Ralph; American cartoonist, writer and dramatist; b. 26 Jan. 1929, New York, NY; s. of David Feiffer and Rhoda Davis; m. 1st Judith Sheftel 1961 (divorced 1983); one d.; m. 2nd Jennifer Allen 1983; two c. *Education:* Art Students' League, Pratt Inst. *Career:* asst to syndicated cartoonist Will Eisner 1946–51; cartoonist, author, syndicated Sunday page, Clifford, engaged in various art jobs 1953–56; contributing cartoonist Village Voice, New York 1956–97; cartoons published weekly in The Observer (London) 1958–66, 1972–82, regularly in Playboy (magazine); sponsor Sane; US Army 1951–53; mem. Dramatists' Guild (council 1970); currently Adjunct Prof., Program in Writing and Literature, Stony Brook Southampton Coll.; fmr teacher Yale School of Drama, Northwestern Univ.; fmr Sr Fellow, Columbia Univ. Nat. Arts Journalism Program; mem. American Acad. of Arts and Letters. *Plays:* Crawling Arnold 1961, Little Murders 1966, God Bless 1968, The White House Murder Case 1970, Feiffer on Nixon: The Cartoon Presidency 1974, Knock Knock 1975, Grown Ups 1981, A Think Piece 1982, Carnal Knowledge 1988, Anthony Rose 1989, Feiffer The Collected Works (vols 1, 2, 3) 1990, A Bad Friend 2003. *Screenplays:* Little Murders 1971, Carnal Knowledge 1971, Popeye 1980, I Want to Go Home (Best Screenplay, Venice Film Festival) 1989, I Lost My Bear 1998, Bark, George 1999. *Publications:* Sick, Sick, Sick 1959, Passionella and Other Stories 1960, The Explainers 1961, Boy, Girl, Boy, Girl, 1962, Hold Me! 1962, Harry, The Rat With Women (novel) 1963, Feiffer's Album 1963, The Unexpurgated Memoirs of Bernard Mergendeiler 1965, The Great Comic Book Heroes 1967, Feiffer's Marriage Manual 1967, Pictures at a Prosecution 1971, Ackroyd (novel) 1978, Tantrum 1980, Jules Feiffer's America: From Eisenhower to Reagan 1982, Marriage is an Invasion of Privacy 1984, Feiffer's Children 1986, Ronald Reagan in Movie America 1988, Elliott Loves (also play) 1990, The Man in the Ceiling (juvenile) 1993, A Barrel of Laughs, A Vale of Tears (juvenile) 1995. *Honours:* Hon. Fellow, Inst. for Policy Studies 1987; Dr hc (Southampton Coll., Long Island Univ.) 1999 Acad. Award for Animated Cartoon (for Munro) 1961, Special George Polk Memorial Award 1962, Best Foreign Play, English Press (for Little Murders) 1967, Outer Critics Circle Award (Obie) 1969, (The White House Murder Case) 1970, Pulitzer Prize, Editorial Cartooning 1986, Writers Guild of America, East's Ian McLellan Hunter Award for Lifetime Achievement in Writing 2004, Nat. Cartoonist Soc. Milton Caniff Lifetime Achievement Award 2004, Benjamin Franklin Creativity Laureate Award 2006. *Address:* c/o Program in Writing and Literature, Stony Brook Southampton, 239 Montauk Highway, Southampton, NY 11968, USA.

FEINSTEIN, (Allan) David, BA, MA, PhD; American psychologist and writer; b. 22 Dec. 1946, New York, NY; m. Donna Eden 1984. *Education:* Whittier Coll., US Int. Univ., Union Inst. *Career:* mem. American Psychological Asscn, Asscn for Humanistic Psychology. *Publications:* Personal Mythology, 1988; Rituals for Living and Dying, 1990; The Mythic Path, 1997; Energy Medicine, 1999; Energy Psychology Interactive, 2003. Contributions: The Futurist; Common Boundary; Psychotherapy; American Journal of Hypnosis; American Journal of Orthopsychiatry. *Honours:* William James Award, Whittier Coll. 1968, Outstanding Contribution Award, Asscn for Comprehensive Energy Psychology 2002. *Address:* 777 E Main Street, Ashland, OR 97520, USA. *Telephone:* (541) 482-1800 (office). *Fax:* (541) 488-1739 (office).

FEINSTEIN, Elaine Barbara, FRSL; British poet and writer; b. 24 Oct. 1930, Bootle, Lancashire, England; three s. *Education:* Newnham Coll., Cambridge. *Career:* editorial staff, Cambridge Univ. Press 1960–62; Lecturer, Bishops Stortford Coll. 1963–66; Asst Lecturer, Univ. of Essex 1967–70. *Radio plays:* Echoes 1980, A Late Spring 1981, A Day Off 1983, Marina Tsvetayeva: A Life 1985, If I Ever Get On My Feet Again 1987, The Man in her Life 1990, Foreign Girls, a trilogy 1993, A Winter Meeting 1994, Lady Chatterley's Confession (adaptation) 1996. *Television screenplays:* Breath 1975, Lunch 1981, The Edwardian Country Gentlewoman's Diary 12-part series) 1984, A Brave Face 1985, The Chase (episode four) 1988, A Passionate Woman (six-part series on life of Marie Stopes) 1990, The Brecht Project (three parts of series). *Publications:* poetry: In a Green Eye 1966, The Magic Apple Tree 1971, At the Edge 1972, The Celebrants and Other Poems 1973, Some Unease and Angels: Selected Poems 1977, Selected Poems 1977, The Feast of Eurydice 1980, Badlands 1987, City Music 1990, Selected Poems 1994, Daylight 1997, Gold 2000, Collected Poems and Translations 2002, Talking to the Dead 2007; biographies: Bessie Smith 1985, A Captive Lion: The Life of Marina Tsvetayeva 1987, Lawrence's Women (aka Lawrence and the Women) 1993, Pushkin 1998, Ted Hughes: The Life of a Poet 2001, Anna of All the Russias: the Life of Anna Akhmatova 2005; novels: The Circle 1970, The Amberstone Exit 1972, The Glass Alembic (aka The Crystal Garden) 1973, Children of the Rose 1975, The Ecstasy of Dr Miriam Garner 1976, The Shadow Master 1978, The Survivors 1982, The Border 1984, Mother's Girl 1988, All You Need 1989, Loving Brecht 1992, Dreamers 1994, Lady Chatterley's Confession 1996, Dark Inheritance 2001; short stories: Matters of Chance 1972, The Silent Areas 1980. *Honours:* Hon. DLitt (Leicester Univ.) 1990; Arts Council Grant/Award for Translation 1970, 1979, 1981, 2004, Daisy Miller Prize 1971, Chomondeley Award 1990. *Literary Agent:* Rogers, Coleridge & White Ltd, 20 Powis Mews, London, W11 1JN, England. *Address:* c/o Carcanet Press, Fourth Floor, Alliance House, Cross Street, Manchester, M2 7AP, England (office).

FEIST, Raymond E., BA; American writer; b. 1945, Los Angeles, CA; m. Kathleen Starbuck; one c. *Education:* Univ. of California, San Diego, CA. *Publications include:* novels: Magician 1982, Silverthorn 1985, A Darkness at Sethanon 1986, Magician's Apprentice 1986, Master 1986, Daughter of the Empire 1987, Faerie Tale 1988, Prince of the Blood 1989, Servant of the Empire 1990, Mistress of the Empire 1992, The King's Buccaneer 1992, Shadow of a Dark Queen 1994, Rise of a Merchant Prince 1995, Rage of a Demon King 1997, Shards of a Broken Crown 1998, The Betrayal 1998, The Assassins 1999, Tear of the Gods 2000, The Atlas of Midkemia 2000, Krondor 2001, Murder in Lamut 2002, Birthright: The Book of Man 2002, Honoured Enemy 2002, Talon of the Silver Hawk 2002, King of Foxes 2003, Jimmy the Hand 2003, Exile's Return 2004, Flight of the Nighthawks 2005, Into a Dark Realm 2006. *Address:* c/o Voyager, Harper Collins Publishing, 10 E 53rd Street, New York, NY 10022, USA. *Website:* www.raymondfeistbooks.com.

FEKETE, John, BA, MA, PhD; Canadian academic and writer; *Distinguished Research Professor, Centre for Theory, Culture and Politics, Trent University*; b. 7 Aug. 1946, Budapest, Hungary. *Education:* McGill Univ., Montreal, Univ. of Cambridge, UK. *Career:* Visiting Asst Prof. of English, McGill Univ. 1973–74; Assoc. Ed. Telos 1974–84; Visiting Asst Prof. of Humanities, York Univ., Toronto, Ont. 1975–76; Asst Prof., Trent Univ., Peterborough, Ont. 1976–78, Assoc. Prof. 1978–84, Prof. of English and Cultural Studies 1984–, Distinguished Research Prof. Centre for Theory, Culture and Politics 1990–. *Publications:* The Critical Twilight: Explorations in the Ideology of Anglo-American Literary Theory from Eliot to McLuhan 1978, The Structural Allegory: Reconstructive Encounters With the New French Thought 1984, Life After Postmodernism: Essays on Culture and Value 1987, Moral Panic: Biopolitics Rising 1994; contrib. to Canadian Journal of Political and Social Theory, Canadian Journal of Communications, Science-Fiction Studies, Sexuality and Culture. *Honours:* Distinguished Research Award, Trent Univ. 1990. *Address:* Trent University, 1600 West Bank Drive, Peterborough, ON K9J 7B8 (office); 1818 Cherryhill Road, Apt 406, Peterborough, ON K9K 1S6, Canada (home). *Telephone:* (705) 748-1771 (office). *E-mail:* jfekete@trentu.ca (office). *Website:* www.trentu.ca/culturalstudies (office); www.trentu.ca/english (office).

FELDMAN, Alan Grad, AB, MA, PhD; American writer, poet and teacher; b. 16 March 1945, New York, NY; m. Nanette Hass 1972; one s. one d. *Education:* Columbia Coll., Columbia Univ., State Univ. of NY at Buffalo. *Publications:* The Household 1966, The Happy Genius 1978, Frank O'Hara 1978, The Personals 1982, Lucy Mastermind 1985, Anniversary 1992, A Sail to Great Island 2004; contribs to The New Yorker, Atlantic, Kenyon Review, Mississippi Review, Ploughshares, North American Review, Threepenny Review, Boston Review, Tendril, College English. *Honours:* Award for Best Short Story in a Coll. Literary Magazine, Saturday Review-Nat. Student Asscn 1965, Elliston Book Award for Best Book of Poems by a Small Press in USA 1978, Felix Pollak Prize for Poetry 2004. *Address:* 399 Belknap Road, Framingham, MA 01701, USA.

FELDMAN, Gerald Donald, BA, MA, PhD; American academic and writer; *Professor of History, University of California at Berkeley*; b. 24 April 1937, New York, NY; m. 1st; one s. one d.; m. 2nd Norma von Ragenfeld 1983. *Education:* Columbia Coll., Harvard Univ. *Career:* Asst Prof., Univ. of California, Berkeley 1963–68, Assoc. Prof. 1968–70, Prof. of History 1970–, Dir Center for German and European Studies 1994–, Chancellor's Professorship 1997–2000, Dir Inst. of European Studies 2000–; Karl W. Deutsch Guest Prof., Wissenschaftszentrum Berlin, Oct.–Dec. 1997; Berlin Prize Fellow, American Acad. in Berlin 1998–99; mem. Exec. Cttee, Friends of the German Historical Inst., Washington, DC 1990–2002, Pres. and Chair. 2002–, mem. scientific advisory bd 2003–; Chair. Historical Comm. of the Bank of Austria 2000–; mem. Bd of Dirs, Historical Soc. of the Deutsche Bank 1991–; mem. Advisory Bd Centre de Recherche, Historial de la Grand Guerre, Peronne, Historical Comm. of the Dresdener Bank 2001–; mem. Advisory Bd European Asscn for Banking History 1991–2004, Chair. Advisory Bd 2005–; corresponding mem. Historische Kommission zu Berlin 1980–, Bavarian Acad. of Sciences 2004–; mem. editorial or advisory bds, Geschichte und Gesellschaft 1974–, German Yearbook on Business History 1982–, Contemporary European History 1991–, German Politics and Soc. 1995–. *Publications:* Army, Industry and Labor in Germany, 1914–1918 1966, German Imperialism, 1914–1918 1972, A Documentary History of Modern Europe (with Thomas G. Barnes, four vols) 1972, Iron and Steel in the German Inflation, 1916–1923 1977, Historische Prozesse der Deutschen Inflation 1914–1924 (with Otto Büsch) 1978, The German Inflation Reconsidered: A Preliminary Balance (with Carl-Ludwig Holtfrerich, Gerhard A. Ritter and Peter-Christian Witt) 1982, The Experience of Inflation: International Comparative Studies (with Carl-Ludwig Holtfrerich, Gerhard A. Ritter and Peter-Christian Witt) 1984, Die Anpassung and die Inflation/The Adaption to Inflation (with Carl-Ludwig

Holtfrerich, Gerhard A. Ritter and Peter-Christian Witt) 1986, Konsequenzen der Inflation/Consequences of Inflation (with Carl-Ludwig Holtfrerich, Gerhard A. Ritter and Peter-Christian Witt) 1989, Arbeiter, Unternehmer und Staat im Bergbau: Industrielle Beziehungen im internationalen Vergleich (with Klaus Tenfelde, trans. as Workers, Owners and Politics in Coal Mining: An International Comparison of Industrial Relations) 1989, Great Disorder: Politics, Economics, and Society in the German Inflation, 1916–1924 1993, The Evolution of Financial Institutions and Markets in Twentieth-Century Europe (with Youssef Cassis and Ulf Olsson) 1995, How to Write the History of a Bank (with Martin M. G. Fase and Manfred Pohl) 1995, Hugo Stinnes: Biographie eines Industriellen, 1870–1914 1998, The Treaty of Versailles: A Reassessment after 75 Years (co-ed. with Manfred F. Boemeke and Elisabeth Glaser) 1998, Allianz and the German Insurance Business, 1933–1945 (co-winner Hagley Prize for Best Book in Business History 2002) 2001, August Thyssen und Hugo Stinnes: Ein Briefwechsel 1898–1922 2003, Networks of Persecution: Business, Bureaucracy and the Organization of the Holocaust 2005; contrib. to many scholarly books and journals. *Honours:* Commdr's Cross, Order of Merit (Germany) 2000; ACLS Fellowships 1966–67, 1970–71, Guggenheim Fellowship 1973–74, Business History Review Newcomen Prize for Best Essay 1975, Nat. Endowment for the Humanities Fellowship 1977–78, German Marshall Fund Fellow 1981–82, Rockefeller Foundation Center Residency, Bellagio, Italy 1987, Woodrow Wilson Center Fellow 1991–92, American Historical Asscn Conference Group for Central European History book prize 1995, German Studies Asscn DAAD Book Prize 1995, co-winner Financial Times/Booz-Allen & Hamilton Business Book Award 1995, Alexander von Humboldt Research Prize Fellow 2002–03. *Address:* University of California at Berkeley, Department of History, Berkeley, CA 94720, USA (office). *Telephone:* (510) 642-2518 (office). *Fax:* (510) 643-5323 (office).

FELDMAN, Irving Mordecai, BS, MA; American academic and poet; b. 22 Sept. 1928, New York, NY; m. Carmen Alvarez del Olmo 1955; one s. *Education:* City College, CUNY, Columbia University. *Career:* Teacher, Univ. of Puerto Rico, Rio Piedras, 1954–56, Univ. of Lyons, France, 1957–58, Kenyon College, Gambier, Ohio, 1958–64; Prof. of English, SUNY at Buffalo, 1964–. *Publications:* Poetry: Work and Days and Other Poems, 1961; The Pripet Marshes and Other Poems, 1965; Magic Papers and Other Poems, 1970; Lost Originals, 1972; Leaping Clear, 1976; New and Selected Poems, 1979; Teach Me, Dear Sister, and Other Poems, 1983; All of us Here and Other Poems, 1986; Beautiful False Things, 2000; The Life and Letters, 1994; Beautiful False Things, 2000; Collected Peoms 1954–2004, 2004. *Honours:* Kovner Award, Jewish Book Council of America, 1962; Ingram Merrill Foundation Grant, 1963; American Acad. of Arts and Letters Grant, 1973; Guggenheim Fellowship, 1973; Creative Artists Public Service Grant, 1980; Acad. of American Poets Fellowship, 1986; John D. and Catherine T. MacArthur Foundation Fellowship, 1992. *Address:* c/o Department of English, State University of New York at Buffalo, Buffalo, NY 14260, USA. *E-mail:* feldman@buffalo.edu.

FELDMAN, Paula R., BA, MA, PhD; American academic and writer; *C. Wallace Martin Professor of English and Louise Fry Scudder Professor of Liberal Arts, University of South Carolina, Columbia;* b. 4 July 1948, Washington, DC; d. of Samuel Feldman and Selma Leon Feldman; m. Peter Mugglestone; one c. *Education:* Bucknell Univ., Northwestern Univ. *Career:* Asst Prof. of English, Univ. of South Carolina, Columbia 1974–79, Assoc. Prof. 1979–89, Prof. of English 1989–, Dir Grad. Studies in English 1991–93, C. Wallace Martin Prof. of English 1999–, Louise Fry Scudder Prof. of Liberal Arts 2000–. *Publications:* The Microcomputer and Business Writing (with David Byrd and Phyllis Fleishel) 1986, The Journals of Mary Shelley (co-ed. with Diana Scott-Kilvert, two vols) 1987, The Wordworthy Computer: Classroom and Research Applications in Language and Literature (with Buford Norman) 1987, Romantic Women Writers: Voices and Countervoices (co-ed. with Theresa Kelley) 1995, British Women Poets of the Romantic Era: An Anthology 1997, A Century of Sonnets: The Romantic Era Revival 1750–1850 (co-ed. with Daniel Robinson) 1999, Records of Woman (ed.) 1999, The Keepsake for 1829 (ed.) 2006; contrib. to Studies in English Literature 1980, Keats-Shelley Journal 1997, 2006, Papers of the Bibliographical Society of America 1978, ADE Bulletin 1995, New Literary History 2002, Approaches to Teaching Shelley's Frankenstein 1990, Blake: An Illustrated Quarterly 1994, Approaches to Teaching the Women Romantic Poets 1997, Romanticism and Women Poets 1997, Cambridge Guide to Women's Writing 1999. *Address:* Department of English, University of South Carolina, 1620 College Street, Columbia, SC 29208, USA (office). *Telephone:* (803) 777-4204 (office). *Fax:* (803) 777-9064 (office). *E-mail:* feldmanp@gwm.sc.edu (office). *Website:* www.paulafeldman.com (office).

FELL, Alison; Scottish writer and poet; *Research Fellow in Creative Arts, Middlesex University;* b. 4 June 1944, Dumfries; m. Roger Coleman 1964, divorced 1966, one s. *Education:* Diploma in Sculpture, Edinburgh College of Art 1967; Postgraduate Certificate in Education, English, Media Studies, University of London, Institute of Education 1981; National Film School 1992. *Career:* Co-founder Welfare State Theatre Leeds-Bradford 1970, Women's Street Theatre London 1971; Journalist Underground Press 1971–75; Fiction Ed. Spare Rib 1975–79; C. Day-Lewis Fellow and Writer-in-Residence London Borough of Brent 1978; Writer-in-Residence London Borough of Walthamstow 1981–82, New South Wales Institute of Technology, Australia 1986; Guest Writer Female Eye Conference Huddersfield, England 1996; Writing Fellow University of East Anglia 1998; British Council tours to Germany, Canada and USA 1996–97, 2000; Co-Judge Presenter New Blood Competition, Institute of Contemporary Arts 1996; Royal Literary Fund Fellow University College London 2002–03; Research Fellow Middlesex Univ. 2003–(06); Royal Literary Fund Fellow, Courtauld Inst. of Art 2006–; has led writing workshops; readings from her works; mem. Soc. of Authors, RSL. *Publications:* fiction: The Grey Dancer 1981, Every Move You Make 1984, The Bad Box 1987, Mer de Glace 1991, The Pillow Boy of the Lady Onogoro 1994, The Mistress of Lilliput 1999, Tricks of the Light 2003; poetry: Kisses for Mayakovsky 1984, The Crystal Owl 1988, Dreams, like heretics 1997, Lightyear 2005; other: The Shining Mountain 1989, Dionysus Day (prose poem) 1992, The Weaver (feature film) 1993, Whispers in the Dark 1995, Medea: Mapping the Edge (play) 2001; contrib. to books and magazines. *Honours:* Alice Hunt Bartlett Prize, National Poetry Society 1984, Boardman Tasker Award for Mountain Literature 1991. *Literary Agent:* Peake Associates, 14 Grafton Crescent, London, NW1 8SL, England.

FELLOWES, Julian Alexander; British novelist, screenwriter, actor and producer; b. 6 Aug. 1949, Egypt; m. Emma Kitchener-Fellowes 1990; one s. *Education:* Magdalene Coll., Cambridge. *Career:* numerous television and film appearances. *Screenplays:* Little Lord Fauntleroy (Emmy Award) 1995, The Prince and the Pauper (also prod.) 1996, Gosford Park (also prod.) (New York Film Critic's Circle Best Screenplay, Nat. Soc. of Film Critics Best Screenplay, Acad. Award for Best Original Screenplay) 2001, Vanity Fair 2004. *Film:* Separate Lies (dir) (Nat. Bd of Review Best Directorial Debut) 2005. *Television:* host of quiz, Never Mind the Full Stops (BBC4) 2006. *Publications:* novel: Snobs: A Novel 2004; other: A Viewer's Guide to Aristocrats 1999; fiction as Rebecca Greville: Poison Presented 1975, Court in the Terror 1976. *Address:* c/o Weidenfeld & Nicholson, Orion House, 5 Upper St Martin's Lane, London, WC2H 9EA, England.

FENBY, Jonathan Theodore Starmer, CBE; British writer and journalist; *Editor-in-Chief and China Editor, Trusted Sources;* b. 11 Nov. 1942, London; s. of the late Charles Fenby and June Fenby (née Head); m. Renée Wartski 1967; one s. one d. *Education:* King Edward's School, Birmingham, Westminster School and New Coll. Oxford. *Career:* corresp. and ed. Reuters World Service, Reuters Ltd 1963–77; corresp. (France and Germany), The Economist 1982–86; Home Ed. and Asst Ed. The Independent 1986–88; Deputy Ed. The Guardian 1988–93; Ed. The Observer 1993–95; Dir Guardian Newspapers 1990–95; Ed. South China Morning Post 1995–99; Ed. Netmedia Group; Assoc. Ed. Sunday Business 2000–01; Ed. Business Europe 2000–01; Ed. www.earlywarning.com 2004–06; currently Ed.-in-Chief and China Ed., Trusted Sources; mem. Bd European Journalism Centre, Belgian–British Colloquium. *Radio:* broadcasts on BBC, CBC and French and Swiss radio. *Television:* broadcasts on BBC, CNN, CNBC, Channel Four and FR2. *Publications:* The Fall of the House of Beaverbrook 1979, Piracy and the Public 1983, The International News Services 1986, On the Brink: The Trouble with France 1998 (new edn 2002), Comment peut-on être Français? 1999, Dealing With the Dragon: A Year in the New Hong Kong 2000, Generalissimo: Chiang Kai-shek and the China He Lost 2003, The Sinking of the Lancastria 2005, Alliance: The Inside Story of How Roosevelt, Stalin and Churchill Won One War and Began Another 2007; contrib. to newspapers and magazines in Europe, USA, Asia. *Honours:* Chevalier, Ordre du Mérite (France) 1992. *Address:* Trusted Sources, 48 Charlotte Street, London, W1T 2NS (office); 101 Ridgmount Gardens, Torrington Place, London, WC1E 7AZ, England (home). *Telephone:* (20) 3008-5764 (office). *E-mail:* jtfenby@hotmail.com (home). *Website:* www.trustedsources.co.uk (office).

FENDRICH, James Max, BA, MA, PhD; American sociologist and writer; b. 31 Oct. 1938, Salem, SD; m. 1st Judith Curtin-Ausman 1963 (divorced 1983); m. 2nd Mary E. Bryant 1985, two s. two d. *Education:* Seattle Univ., Univ. of Notre Dame, Michigan State Univ. *Career:* Asst Prof., 1965–68, Assoc. Prof., 1968–74, Prof. of Sociology, 1974–94, Florida State University, Tallahassee; Consulting; mem. American Sociological Asscn; Southern Sociological Asscn; Society for the Study of Social Problems. *Publications:* Leadership in American Society: A Case Study of Black Leadership (co-author), 1969; Ideal Citizens: The Legacy of the Civil Rights Movement, 1993.

FENNARIO, David; Canadian playwright; b. 26 April 1947, Verdun, QC; m. Elizabeth Fennario 1976, one c. *Education:* Dawson Coll., Montréal. *Career:* Playwright-in-Residence, Centaur Theatre, Montréal 1973–; co-founder, Cultural Workers Asscn; mem. International Socialist. *Publications:* plays: On the Job, 1976; Nothing to Lose, 1977; Without a Parachute, 1978; Balconville, 1980; Changes, 1980; Moving, 1983; Joe Beef, 1991; Doctor Thomas Weill Cream, 1994; Placeville Marie, 1996. *Honours:* Canada Council grant 1973, Chalmers Awards 1976, 1979, Prix Pauline Julien 1986.

FENNELLY, Antonia (Tony), BA; American author; b. 25 Nov. 1945, Orange, NJ; m. James Richard Catoire 1972. *Education:* Univ. of New Orleans. *Career:* mem. MWA, Authors' Guild, International Asscn of Crime Writers, Sisters in Crime. *Publications:* The Glory Hole Murders, 1985; The Closet Hanging, 1987; Kiss Yourself Goodbye, 1989; Der Hippie in Der Wand, 1992; Hurenglanz, 1993; 1(900) D-E-A-D, 1997. *Honours:* MWA Edgar Allan Poe Special Award 1986.

FENNER, Carol Elizabeth; American children's writer and illustrator; b. 30 Sept. 1929, Almond, NY; m. Jiles B. Williams 1965. *Career:* mem. Soc. of Children's Book Writers and Illustrators. *Publications:* Tigers in the Cellar, 1963; Christmas Tree on the Mountain, 1966; Lagalag, the Wanderer, 1968;

Gorilla, Gorilla, 1973; The Skates of Uncle Richard, 1978; Saving Amelia Earhart, 1982; A Summer of Horses, 1989; Randall's Wall, 1991; Yolonda's Genius, 1995; The King of Dragons, 1998. Contributions: Magazines. *Honours:* Notable Book Citations, 1963, 1973, Newbery Honor Book, 1996, American Library Asscn; Christopher Medal, 1973; Library of Congress Book of the Year, 1973; Michigan Council for the Arts Literature Grant, 1982; Readers' Choice Master Lists Citations, 1991–92; Maryland Children's Book Award, 1997; Patterson Prize, 1999.

FENNER, James R. (see Tubb, Edwin Charles)

FENNO, Jack (see Calisher, Hortense)

FENTON, James Martin, MA, FRSL, FRSA; British poet, writer and journalist; b. 25 April 1949, Lincoln; s. of Rev. Canon J. C. Fenton and Mary Hamilton Ingoldby. *Education:* Durham Choristers School, Repton School, Magdalen Coll. Oxford. *Career:* Asst Literary Ed., New Statesman 1971, Editorial Asst 1972, Political Columnist 1976–78; freelance corresp. in Indo-China 1973–75; German Corresp., The Guardian 1978–79; Theatre Critic, Sunday Times 1979–84; Chief Book Reviewer, The Times 1984–86; Far East Corresp. The Independent 1986–88, columnist 1993–95; Prof. of Poetry, Oxford Univ. 1994–99, Trustee Nat. Gallery London 2002, Visitor Ashmolean Museum 2003. *Publications include:* Our Western Furniture 1968, Terminal Moraine 1972, A Vacant Possession 1978, A German Requiem 1980, Dead Soldiers 1981, The Memory of War 1982, You Were Marvellous 1983, Children in Exile 1984, Poems 1968–83 1985, The Fall of Saigon (in Granta 15) 1985, The Snap Revolution (in Granta 18) 1986, Cambodian Witness: The Autobiography of Someth May (ed.) 1986, Partingtime Hall (poems, with John Fuller) 1987, All the Wrong Places: Adrift in the Politics of Asia 1989, Manila Envelope 1989, Underground in Japan, by Rey Ventura (ed.) 1992, Out of Danger (poems) 1993, Collected Stories by Ernest Hemingway (ed.) 1995, Leonardo's Nephew: Essays on Art and Artists 1998, The Strength of Poetry, Oxford Lectures, An Introduction to English Poetry 2002, A Garden from a Hundred Packets of Seed, The Love Bomb & Other Musical Pieces 2003, Selected Poems 2006; trans.: Verdi's Rigoletto 1982, Simon Boccanegra 1985. *Honours:* Hon. Fellow, Magdalen Coll., Oxford 1999; Antiquary to the RA 2002. *Address:* c/o Peters, Fraser & Dunlop, Drury House, 34–43 Russell Street, London, WC2B 5HA, England (office).

FÉRAL, Josette, PhD; Canadian critic and theatre scholar; *Chair, École Supérieure de Théâtre, Université du Québec. Education:* Université de Paris. *Career:* Prof., Univ. of Toronto 1978–81; Titular Prof., École Supérieure de Théâtre de l'Université du Québec 1981, Montréal, currently Dir; Vice-Pres. Int. Federation for Theatre Research (FIRT) 1995–99, Pres. 1999–2003. *Publications:* non-fiction: La Culture contre l'art 1990, Dresser un monument à l'éphémère 1995, Mise en scène et Jeu de l'acteur (two vols) 1997–98, Trajectoires du soleil 1998, Les Chemins de l'acteur, Acerca de la teatralidad 2004, Teatro, Teorica y practica: mas alla de las fronteras 2004; editor: Théâtralité, écriture et mise en scène 1985, Substance 98/99 2002, L'école du jeu 2003, Ariane Mnouchkine und Das Théâtre du Soleil 2003; contribs. to numerous books and journals. *Honours:* Prix Jean Beraud 1989–90. *Address:* École Supérieure de Théâtre, Université du Québec à Montréal, CP 8888, succursale Centre-Ville, Montréal, H3C 3P8, Canada (office). *Telephone:* (514) 987 4116 (office). *Fax:* (514) 987 7881 (office). *E-mail:* feral.josette@uqam.ca (office). *Website:* josette-feral.org (home).

FERDINANDY, György (Georges), DèsL; American academic and writer; b. 11 Oct. 1935, Budapest, Hungary; m. 1st Colette Peyrethon 1958; m. 2nd Maria Teresa Reyes-Cortes 1981; three s. one d. *Education:* Univ. of Strasbourg, France. *Career:* freelance literary critic, Radio Free Europe, 1977–86; Prof., University of Puerto Rico, Cayey, Puerto Rico 1964–2001; mem. Société des Gens de Lettres, France; Hungarian Writers' Asscn; International PEN. *Publications:* in French: L'ile sous l'eau 1960, Famine au Paradis 1962, Le seul jour de l'année 1967, Itinéraires 1973, Chica, Claudine, Cali 1973, L'oeuvre hispanoaméricaine de Zs Remenyik 1975, Fantomes magnétiques 1979, Youri 1983, Hors jeu 1986, Mémoires d'un exil terminé 1992, Entre chien et loup 1996; in Hungarian: Latoszemueknek 1962, Tizenharom Töredék 1964, Futoszalagon 1965, Nemezio Gonzalex 1970, Valencianal a tenger 1975, Mammuttemetö 1982, A Mosoly Albuma 1982, Az elveszett gyermek 1984, A Vadak Utjan 1986, Szerecsenségem Története 1988, Furcsa, idegen szerelem 1990, Uzenöfüzet 1991, Szomorü Szigetek 1992, A Francia Völegény 1993, Ta'vlattan 1994, Az Amerikai telefon 1996; in Spanish: Saldo a medio camino 1976, Hambre en el Paraiso 1998, Exilio 2000, Regreses 2004, Cielo vacios 2006; contributions: Le Monde, NRF, Europe, Elet és Irodalom, Kortars, Uj Hold, Magyar Naplo. *Honours:* Del Duca Prix 1961, St Exupéry Literary Award 1964, Book of the Year 1993, Prize Jòzsef Attila, Budapest 1995, Prize Ma'rai Sàndor, Budapest 1997, Prize Gyula Krudy 1999, PEN Club Int. Prize 2001, Alföld Prize 2004, MAOE Grand Prize 2006. *Address:* 1481 SW, 124 CT-D, Miami, FL 33184, USA (home). *Telephone:* (305) 485-5527 (home).

FERGUSON, Gillian K.; British poet and journalist; b. Edinburgh, Scotland. *Education:* Univ. of Edinburgh. *Career:* jewellery maker, artist; columnist, The Scotsman; fmr TV critic, Scotland on Sunday; currently columnist, The Herald newspaper, Financial Times weekend magazine. *Publications:* poetry: Air for Sleeping Fish 1997, Baby 2000; contrib. to anthologies and journals. *Honours:* three Writers' Bursaries from the Scottish Arts Council; prizewinner Daily Telegraph Arvon Int. Poetry Competition. *Address:* c/o The Herald, 200 Renfield Street, Cowcaddens, Glasgow, G2 3QB, Scotland (office).

FERGUSON, Joseph Francis, BA; American critic, writer and poet; b. 11 Feb. 1952, Yonkers, NY; m. Janice Robinson 1986; one s. *Education:* SUNY at New Paltz, Pace University. *Career:* critic for various publications. *Publications:* Contributions: fiction and poetry in many anthologies and other publications; Articles and columns in numerous publications. *Honours:* Honorable mention, American Poetry Asscn Contest, 1989; Honorable mention, World of Poetry Contest, 1990; Golden Poet, World of Poetry, 1990; Distinguished Poet of America, 1993.

FERGUSON, Niall Campbell Douglas, MA, DPhil; British historian, writer and academic; *Laurence A. Tisch Professor of History, Harvard University;* b. 18 April 1964, Glasgow, Scotland; s. of James Campbell Ferguson and Molly Hamilton; m. Susan M. Douglas 1994; two s. one d. *Education:* Univ. of Oxford, Univ. of Hamburg. *Career:* Fellow, Christ's Coll., Cambridge 1989–90, Peterhouse, Cambridge 1990–92, Jesus Coll., Oxford, 1992–; Prof. of Political and Financial History, Univ. of Oxford 2000–02, Herzog Prof. of Financial History, Stern School of Business, New York Univ. 2002–04; Laurence A. Tisch Prof. of History, Harvard Univ. 2004–; Sr Fellow, Hoover Inst., Stanford Univ. 2003–; William Ziegler Prof. of Business Admin, Harvard Business School 2006–. *Television:* Empire: How Britain Made the Modern World 2003, American Colossus 2004, War of the World 2006. *Publications:* Paper and Iron: Hamburg Business and German Politics in the Era of Inflation 1897–1927 1995, (ed.) Virtual History: Alternatives and Counterfactuals 1997, The World's Banker: A History of the House of Rothschild, The Pity of War 1998, The Cash Nexus: Money and Power in the Modern World 1700–2000 2001, Empire: How Britain Made the Modern World 2003, Colossus: the Price of America's Empire 2004, The War of The World: History's Age of Hatred 2006. *Honours:* Wadsworth Prize for Business History 1998. *Address:* Harvard University, Minda de Gunzberg Center for European Studies, Adolphus Busch Hall, 27 Kirkland Street, Cambridge, MA 02138, USA (office). *Telephone:* (617) 495-4303 (ext. 203) (office). *Fax:* (617) 496-9594 (office). *E-mail:* nfergus@fas.harvard.edu (office). *Website:* www.ces.fas .harvard.edu (office); www.niallferguson.org (home).

FERGUSON, Robert Thomas, BA; British writer; b. 2 June 1948, Stoke on Trent, England; m. 1987. *Education:* Univ. Coll. London. *Publications:* Enigma: The Life of Knut Hamsun 1987, Henry Miller: A Life 1991, Henrik Ibsen: A New Biography 1996, Dr Ibsens Gjengangere (in Norwegian, Dr Ibsen's Ghosts, radio play) 1999, Siste Kjaerlighet (in Norwegian, Last Love, novel) 2002, The Short Sharp Life of T. E. Hulme 2002, Fleetwood (in Norwegian, novel) 2004; contrib. to Best Radio Drama 1984, Best Radio Drama 1986. *Honours:* BBC Methuen Giles Cooper Awards 1984, 1986, J. G. Robertson Prize 1985–87. *Address:* Trudvagvn 25, 0363 Oslo, Norway. *E-mail:* robert.ferguson@c2i.net.

FERGUSON, Trevor, (John Farrow); Canadian novelist, playwright and screenwriter; b. 11 Nov. 1947, Seaforth, Ont.; s. of the late Rev. P. A. Ferguson and M. V. Joyce (Jo) Ferguson (née Sanderson). *Career:* mem. Writers' Union of Canada, Chair. 1990–91. *Plays produced:* Long Long Short Long (Montreal) 2002, Beach House, Burnt Sienna (Hudson, QC) 2002, Barnacle Wood (Montreal) 2004, Zarathustra Said Some Things, No? (New York) 2006. *Publications:* novels: High Water Chants 1977, Onyx John 1985, The Kinkajou 1989, The True Life Adventures of Sparrow Drinkwater 1993, The Fire Line 1995, The Timekeeper 1995; as John Farrow: City of Ice 1999, Ice Lake 2001, The Earth In Its Devotion 2007; drama: Long Long Short Long 2006. *Honours:* Hugh MacLennan Award for Fiction, Québec Writers' Fed. 1996, Nat. Magazine Awards Foundation Gold Award. *Literary Agent:* c/o Anne McDermid and Associates, 92 Willcocks Street, Toronto, ON M5S 1C8, Canada. *Telephone:* (416) 324-8845.

FERGUSON, William Rotch; American academic, writer and poet; b. 14 Feb. 1943, Fall River, MA; m. Nancy King 1983. *Education:* BA, 1965, MA, 1970, PhD, 1975, Harvard University. *Career:* Instructor, 1971–75, Asst Prof., 1975–77, Boston University; Visiting Prof., 1977–79, Asst Prof., 1979–83, Assoc. Prof. of Spanish, 1983–, Adjunct Prof. of English, 1989–, Chair., Foreign Languages, 1990–98, Clark University, Worcester, Massachusetts; Visiting Lecturer in Spanish Renaissance Literature, University of Pennsylvania, 1986–87; Assoc. Ed., Hispanic Review, 1986–87; mem. American Asscn of University Profs; International Institute in Spain; MLA. *Publications:* Dream Reader (poems), 1973; Light of Paradise (poems), 1973; La versificación imitativa en Fernando de Herrera, 1981; Freedom and Other Fictions (short stories), 1984. Contributions: scholarly journals, anthologies, periodicals and magazines. *Address:* 1 Tahanto Road, Worcester, MA 01602, USA.

FERLINGHETTI, Lawrence, MA, DUniv, PhD; American writer and painter; b. 24 March 1920, Yonkers, New York; s. of Charles Ferlinghetti and Clemence Mendes-Monsanto; m. 1951; one s. one d. *Education:* Columbia Univ., Univ. of Paris. *Career:* served as Lt Commdr USNR in World War II; f. (with Peter D. Martin) one of the first all-paperback bookshops in USA, City Lights Bookstore, San Francisco 1953; f. City Lights publishing co. 1955; arrested on obscenity charges following publ. of Allan Ginsberg's 'Howl' 1956 (later acquitted); participant One World Poetry Festival, Amsterdam 1980, World Congress of Poets, Florence 1986; First Poet Laureate of San Francisco 1998–99; mem. Nat. Acad. of Arts and Letters 2003. *One-man exhibitions:* Ethel Guttman Gallery, San Francisco 1985, Peter Lembcke Gallery, San Francisco 1991, Butler Inst., Youngstown OH 1993, Retrospective Exhbn, Palazzo delle Esposizioni, Rome 1996, George Krevsky Fine Arts, San Francisco 2004. *Publications include:* Pictures of the Gone World (poems)

1955, Selections from Paroles by Jacques Prévert, A Coney Island of the Mind (poems) 1958, Berlin 1961, Her (novel), Starting from San Francisco (poems) 1961, Where is Vietnam? 1965, An Eye on the World 1967, After the Cries of the Birds 1967, Unfair Arguments with Existence (7 plays), Routines (plays), The Secret Meaning of Things (poems) 1969, Tyrannus Nix? (poem) 1969, The Mexican Night (travel journal) 1970, Back Roads to Far Places (poems) 1971, Open Eye, Open Heart (poems) 1973, Who Are We Now? 1976, Northwest Ecolog 1978, Landscapes of Living and Dying (poems) 1979, Literary San Francisco: A Pictorial History from the Beginnings to the Present (with Nancy J. Peters) 1980, Leaves of Life: Drawings from the Model 1983, The Populist Manifestos 1983, Over All the Obscene Boundaries (poems) 1984, Endless Life: Selected Poems 1984, Seven Days in Nicaragua Libre 1984, Inside the Trojan Horse 1987, Love in the Days of Rage (novel) 1988, When I Look at Pictures (poems and paintings) 1990, These Are My Rivers; New and Selected Poems 1993, A Far Rockaway of the Heart 1997, How to Paint Sunlight: New Poems 2001, Americus Book One (poems) 2004; Ed. City Lights Books; also translations, film-scripts and phonograph records. *Honours:* Poetry Prize, City of Rome 1993, Premio Internazionale Flaiano, Italy 1999, Premio Internazionale di Camaiore, Italy 1999, Premio Cavour, Italy 2000, LA Times Book Festival Lifetime Achievement Award 2001, Poetry Soc. of America Robert Frost Medal 2003, Nat. Book Foundation Literarian Award 2005. *Address:* c/o City Lights Bookstore, 261 Columbus Avenue, San Francisco, CA 94133-4519, USA (office). *Telephone:* (415) 362-1901. *Fax:* (415) 362-4921. *E-mail:* staff@citylights.com (office).

FERLITA, Ernest Charles, BS, STL, DFA; American writer and priest; *Emeritus Professor of Drama, Loyola University*; b. 1 Dec. 1927, Tampa, FL. *Education:* Spring Hill College, St Louis University, Yale University. *Career:* Jesuit priest; Prof. Emer. of Drama Loyola Univ.; mem. Dramatists Guild, Int. Hopkins Soc. *Publications:* The Theatre of Pilgrimage 1971, Film Odyssey (co-author) 1976, The Way of the River 1977, The Parables of Lina Wertmuller (co-author) 1977, Religion in Film (contributor) 1982, Gospel Journey 1983, The Mask of Hiroshima in Best Short Plays 1989, The Uttermost Mark 1990, The Paths of Life, Cycles A, B, C 1992, 1993, 1994, The Road to Bethlehem 1997, Two Cities 1999, In the Light of the Lord 2002. *Honours:* First Prize Christian Theatre Artists Guild 1971, American Radio Scriptwriting Contest 1985, Miller Award 1986, Second Prize International Competition of Religious Drama 2000, Winner Catholic Univ. One-Act Play Competition 2004, Hon. Mention Catholic Univ. of America 2004. *Address:* 6363 St Charles Avenue, New Orleans, LA 70118, USA (home).

FERLOSIO, Rafael Sanchez; Spanish/Italian writer; b. 1927, Rome, Italy. *Publications:* The Adventures of the Ingenious Alfanhui 1951, The Jarama 1956, Mientrasno cambien los dioses, nada ha cambiado 1986, Ensayos y articulos 1992. *Honours:* Spanish National Critics' Prize. *Address:* c/o Dedalus Ltd, Langford Lodge, St Judith's Lane, Sawtry, Cambridgeshire PE28 5XE, England. *E-mail:* info@dedalusbooks.com. *Website:* www.dedalusbooks.com.

FERMOR, Sir Patrick Michael Leigh, Kt, DSO, OBE, CLit; British writer; b. 11 Feb. 1915, London; s. of the late Sir Lewis Leigh Fermor and Muriel Eileen Fermor (née Ambler); m. Hon. Joan Eyres-Monsell 1968 (died 2003). *Education:* King's School, Canterbury. *Career:* travelled for four years in Cen. Europe, Balkans and Greece in 1930s; enlisted in Irish Guards 1939; 'I' Corps 1940; Lt British Mil. Mission, Greece 1940; Liaison Officer, Greek GHQ, Albania; with Cretan Resistance for two years in German-occupied Crete; Team-Commdr Special Allied Airborne Reconnaissance Force, N Germany 1945; Deputy Dir British Inst. Athens 1945–46; travelled in Caribbean and Cen. America 1947–48; Corresp. mem. Athens Acad. 1980. *Publications:* The Traveller's Tree (Heinemann Foundation Prize for Literature 1950, Kemsley Prize 1951) 1950, Colette's Chance Acquaintances (trans.) 1952, A Time to Keep Silence 1953, The Violins of Saint Jacques 1953, The Cretan Runner (trans.) 1955, Mani (Duff Cooper Prize) 1958, Roumeli 1966, A Time of Gifts (WHSmith Award 1978) 1977, Between the Woods and the Water (Thomas Cook Award) 1986, Three Letters from the Andes 1991, Words of Mercury 2003. *Honours:* Hon. Citizen of Heraklion, Crete 1947, Gytheion, Laconia 1966, Kardamyli, Messenia 1967; Chevalier, Ordre des Arts et des Lettres (France) 1995; Hon. DLitt (Kent) 1991, (American School of Greece) 1993, (Warwick) 1996; Int. PEN/Time Life Silver Pen Award 1986, Municipality of Athens Gold Medal of Honour 1988, Prix Jacques Audiberti, Ville d'Antibes 1992, British Guild of Travel Writers Lifetime Achievement Award 2004.

FERNANDEZ, Dominique, DèsSc; French writer; b. 25 Aug. 1929, Neuilly-sur-Seine; s. of Ramon Fernandez and Liliane Chomette; m. Diane Jacquin de Margerie (divorced); one s. one d. *Education:* Lycée Buffon, Paris and Ecole Normale Supérieure. *Career:* Prof. Inst. Français, Naples 1957–58; Prof. of Italian, Univ. de Haute-Bretagne 1966–89; literary critic, L'Express 1959–84, Le Nouvel Observateur 1985–; music critic, Diapason 1977–85, Opera International 1978; elected mem. Académie française 2007; mem. Reading Cttee, Editions Bernard Grasset 1959–. *Publications:* Le roman italien et la crise de la conscience moderne 1958, L'écorce des pierres 1959, L'aube 1962, Mère Méditerranée 1965, Les Evènements de Palerme 1966, L'échec de Pavèse 1968, Lettre à Dora 1969, Les enfants de Gogol 1971, Il Mito dell'America 1969, L'arbre jusqu'aux racines 1972, Porporino 1974, Eisenstein 1975, La rose des Tudors 1976, Les Siciliens 1977, Amsterdam 1977, L'étoile rose 1978, Une fleur de jasmin à l'oreille 1980, Le promeneur amoureux 1980, Signor Giovanni 1981, Dans la main de l'ange 1982, Le volcan sous la ville 1983, Le banquet des anges 1984, L'amour 1986, La gloire du paria 1987, Le rapt de Perséphone (opera libretto) 1987, Le radeau de la Gorgone 1988, Le rapt de Ganymede 1989, L'Ecole du Sud 1991, Porfirio et Constance 1992, Séville 1992, L'Or des Tropiques 1993, Le Dernier des Médicis 1993, la Magie Blanche de Saint-Pétersbourg 1994, Prague et la Bohême (jtly) 1995, la Perle et le croissant 1995, le Musée idéal de Stendhal 1995, Saint-Pétersbourg 1996, Tribunal d'honneur 1997, Le musée de Zola 1997, Le voyage d'ltalie 1998, Rhapsodie roumaine 1998, Palerme et la Sicile 1998, Le loup et le chien 1999, Les douze muses d'Alexandre Dumas 1999, Bolivie 1999, Nicolas 2000, Errances solaires 2000, L'amour qui ose dire son nom 2001, Syrie 2002, La Course à l'abîme 2002, Dictionnaire amoureux de la Russie 2004, Rome 2004. *Honours:* Chevalier, Légion d'honneur, Commdr, Ordre Nat. du Mérite; Commdr Cruzeiro do Sul (Brazil); Prix Médicis 1974, Prix Goncourt 1982, Grand Prix Charles Oulmont 1986, Prix Prince Pierre de Monaco 1986, Prix Méditerranée 1988, Prix Oscar Wilde 1988. *Address:* 14 rue de Douai, 75009 Paris (home); c/o Editions Bernard Grasset, 61 rue des Saints-Pères, 75006 Paris, France (office).

FERNÁNDEZ-ARMESTO, Felipe Fermín Ricardo, BA, MA, DPhil, FRHistS; British historian; *Prince of Asturias Chair of Spanish Civilization, Tufts University, Boston*; b. 6 Dec. 1950, London, England; m. Lesley Patricia Hook 1977; two s. *Education:* Magdalen Coll., Oxford. *Career:* journalist, The Diplomatist 1972–74; Sr Visiting Fellow, John Carter Brown Library, Brown Univ., USA 1997–99; Professorial Fellow, Queen Mary Univ. of London 2000–; Prince of Asturias Chair of Spanish Civilization, Tufts Univ., Boston 2005–; mem. Hakluyt Soc., Soc. of Authors, PEN, Athenaeum, Historical Asscn, Asscn of Hispanists, American Historical Asscn; Fellow, Soc. of Antiquaries, Netherlands Inst. *Publications:* The Canary Islands after the Conquest 1982, Before Columbus 1987, The Spanish Armada 1988, Barcelona 1991, The Times Atlas of World Exploration (general ed.) 1991, Columbus 1991, Edward Gibbon's Atlas of the World 1992, Millennium 1995, The Times Guide to the People of Europe 1995, The Times Illustrated History of Europe 1995, Reformation (with Derek Wilson) 1996, Truth 1997, Religion 1997, Civilizations 2000, The Americas: A History of the Continents 2003, So You Think You're Human 2004, Amerigo 2006, Pathfinders 2006; contrib. to scholarly books, newspapers and periodicals. *Honours:* Hon. DLitt (La Trobe Univ., Australia) 1997; Arnold Modern History Prize 1971, Leverhulme Research Fellowship 1981, Library Asscn commendation 1992, Nat. Maritime Museum Caird Medal 1997, John Carter Brown Medal 1999. *Literary Agent:* David Higham Associates, 5–8 Lower John Street, Golden Square, London, W1F 9HA, England.

FERNIOT, Jean; French journalist; b. 10 Oct. 1918, Paris; s. of Paul Ferniot and Jeanne Ferniot (née Rabu); m. 1st Jeanne Martinod 1942 (divorced); one s. two d.; m. 2nd Christiane Servan-Schreiber 1959 (divorced); two s.; m. 3rd Béatrice Lemaître 1984. *Education:* Lycée Louis-le-Grand. *Career:* Head, Political Dept, France-Tireur 1945–57; Political Columnist, L'Express 1957–58; Chief Political Correspondent France-Soir 1959–63; Ed. L'Express 1963–66; with Radio Luxembourg 1967–83; Political Commentator France-Soir 1967–70, Asst Chief Ed. 1969–70; Dir at Éditions Grasset, in charge of Collection Humeurs 1978–83; Dir then Adviser Cuisine et Vins de France 1981; Pres. Fondation Communication Demain 1980–89, Terminology Comm., Nat. Council for Tourism 1991–97; Pres. (Supervisory Council) Evénement du Jeudi 1992; mem. jury, Prix Interallié 1970–. *Publications:* Les ides de mai 1958, L'ombre porté 1961, Pour le pire 1962, Derrière la fenêtre 1964, De Gaulle et le 13 mai 1965, Mort d'une révolution 1968, Paris dans mon assiette 1969, Complainte contre X 1973, De de Gaulle à Pompidou 1972, Ça suffit! 1973, Pierrot et Aline 1973, La petite légume 1974, Les vaches maigres (with Michel Albert) 1975, Les honnêtes gens 1976, C'est ça la France 1977, Vous en avez vraiment assez d'être français 1979, Carnet de croûte 1980, Le Pouvoir et la sainteté 1982, Le Chien-loup 1983, Saint Judas 1984, Un mois de juin comme on les aimait 1986, Soleil orange 1988, Miracle au village 1989, Je recommencerais bien 1991, L'Europe à Table 1993, La France des Terroirs Gourmands 1993, Jérusalem, nombril du monde 1994, La Mouffe 1995, Morte saison 1996, Un temps pour aimer, un temps pour haïr 1999, Ce soir ou jamais 2002, Noces de Nuit 2003, C'était ma France 2004, L'enfant du miracle 2006. *Honours:* Commdr des Arts et des Lettres, Croix de Guerre, Chevalier du Mérite Agricole, Commdr du Mérite (Italy); Prix Interallié 1961. *Address:* 11 bis rue d'Orléans, 92200 Neuilly-sur-Seine, France. *Telephone:* 1-46-24-25-30 (home).

FERRANTI, Marie; French writer; b. 1964, Corsica. *Career:* fmr teacher in literature before becoming full-time novelist. *Publications include:* Les Femmes de San Stefano (Prix François Mauriac) 1995, La Chambre des Défunts 1996, La Fuite aux Agriates 2000, Le Paradoxe de l'Ordre 2002, La Princess de Mantoue (Grand Prix du Roman, Acad. Française) 2002. *Address:* c/o Editions Gallimard, 5 rue Sébastian-Bottin, 75328 Paris Cedex 7, France (office).

FERRÉ, Rosario, MA, PhD; American writer; b. 28 July 1942, Ponce, Puerto Rico; m. Benigno Trigo 1960 (divorced); two s. one d. *Education:* University of Puerto Rico, University of Maryland. *Career:* founder-Dir, Zona de carga y descarga, Puerto Rican literary journal. *Publications:* (in English) The Youngest Doll, 1991; The House on the Lagoon, 1995; Sweet Diamond Dust and Other Stories, 1996; Flight of the Swan, 2001. Contributions: anthologies.

FERRIS, Paul Frederick; British writer and dramatist; b. 15 Feb. 1929, Swansea, Wales. *Publications:* A Changed Man 1958, The City 1960, Then We Fall 1960, The Church of England 1962, A Family Affair 1963, The Doctors 1965, The Destroyer 1965, The Nameless: Abortion in Britain Today 1966, The

Dam 1967, Men and Money: Financial Europe Today 1968, The House of Northcliffe 1971, The New Militants 1972, The Detective 1976, Talk to Me about England 1979, Richard Burton 1981, A Distant Country 1983, Gentlemen of Fortune 1984, Children of Dust 1988, Sex and the British 1993, Caitlin 1993, The Divining Heart 1995, Dr Freud: A Life 1997, Dylan Thomas: The Biography 1999, Infidelity 1999, New Collected Letters of Dylan Thomas 2000, Cora Crane 2003, Vendetta 2005; TV plays: The Revivalist 1975, Dylan 1978, Nye 1982, The Extremist 1983, The Fasting Girl 1984. *Literary Agent:* Curtis Brown Ltd, Haymarket House, 28–29 Haymarket, London, SW1Y 4SP, England. *Telephone:* (20) 7393-4400. *Fax:* (20) 7393-4401. *E-mail:* info@curtisbrown.co.uk. *Website:* www.curtisbrown.co.uk.

FERRON, Madeleine; Canadian writer; b. 24 July 1922, Louiseville, QC; m. Robert Cliche 1945, two s. one d. *Publications:* short stories: Coeur de Sucre, 1966; Le Chemin des Dames, 1977; Histoires Edifiantes, 1981; Un Singulier Amour, 1987; Le Grand Theatre, 1989. Fiction: La Fin des Loups-Garous, 1966; Le Baron Ecarlate, 1971; Sur le Chemin Craig, 1982; essays: Quand le Peuple fait la loi, 1972; Les Beaucerons, ces insoumis, 1974; Adrienne, une saga familiale, 1993. *Honours:* Chevalier, Ordre nat. du Québec 1992.

FERRY, David Russell, BA, MA, PhD; American academic, poet, writer and translator; b. 5 March 1924, Orange, NJ; s. of Robert Edward Ferry and Elsie Ferry (née Russell); m. Anne Elizabeth Davidson 1958 (died 2006); one s. one d. *Education:* Amherst Coll., Harvard Univ. *Career:* Instructor, Wellesley Coll. 1952–55, Asst Prof. 1955–61, Assoc. Prof. 1961–67, Prof. of English 1967–71, Sophie Chautal Hart Prof. of English 1971–89, Prof. Emer. 1989–; Fannie Hurst Visiting Poet, Washington Univ., St Louis 1999; Fellow, Acad. of American Poets 1994, American Acad. of Arts and Sciences 1998. *Publications:* The Limits of Mortality: An Essay on Wordsworth's Major Poems 1959, On the Way to the Island (poems) 1960, British Literature (co-ed., two vols) 1974, Strangers: A Book of Poems 1983, Gilgamesh: A New Rendering in English Verse 1992, Dwelling Places: Poems and Translations 1993, The Odes of Horace: A Translation 1997, The Eclogues of Virgil: A Translation 1999, Of No Country I Know: New and Selected Poems and Translations 1999, The Epistles of Horace: A Translation 2001; contribs to literary journals. *Honours:* Hon. Fellow, Acad. of American Poets 1995; Hon. DLitt (Amherst Coll.) 2006; Pushcart Prize 1988, Ingram Merrill Award for Poetry and Trans. 1993, Teasdale Prize for Poetry 1995, Guggenheim Fellowship 1996–97, William Arrowsmith Trans. Prize, AGNI 1999, Bingham Poetry Prize, Boston Book Review 2000, Lenore Marshall Poetry Prize 2000, Rebekah Johnson Bobbitt Nat. Prize for Poetry, Library of Congress 2000, American Acad. of Arts and Letters Award for Literature 2001, Harold Morton Landon Trans. Prize, Acad. of American Poets 2002. *Address:* 49 Cypress Street #2, Brookline, MA 02138, USA (home). *Telephone:* (617) 232-5111 (office). *E-mail:* dferry@wellesley.edu (office); david_ferry@hotmail.com (home).

FERRY, Luc, Dr rer. pol; French philosopher, politician and academic; b. 3 Jan. 1951, Colombes; s. of Pierre Ferry and Monique Faucher; m. Marie-Caroline Becq de Fouquières 1999; three d. (one from previous marriage). *Education:* Lycée Saint-Exupéry, Centre nat. de télé-enseignement, Sorbonne, Univ. of Heidelberg. *Career:* lecturer, Teacher Training Coll., Arras, Asst Lecturer, Univ. of Reims 1977–79; Asst Lecturer, Ecole Normale Supérieure, Paris 1977–79, 1980–82; Research Attaché Nat. CNRS 1980–82; Asst Lecturer, Univ. of Paris I-Panthéon Sorbonne and Paris X-Nanterre 1980–88; Prof. of Political Sciences, Inst. of Political Studies, Univ. of Lyon II-Lumière 1982–88; Prof. of Philosophy, Univ. of Caen 1989–97; Asst Lecturer, Paris I 1989; Prof. of Philosophy, Univ. of Paris VI-Jussieu 1996–; Founder-mem., Sec. Gen. College of Philosophy 1974–; responsible for Ideas section then Editorial Adviser, L'Express 1987–94; Pres. Nat. Curriculum Council (CNP) 1994–2002; Minister for Nat. Educ., Research and Technology 1997–2002; Minister of Youth, Nat. Educ. and Research 2002–04; mem. Comm. for UNESCO 1997–2002; Dir Editions Grasset collection of Coll. of Philosophy; fmr mem. Saint-Simon Foundation; columnist for Le Point 1995–. *Publications include:* Philosophie politique (3 vols 1984–85), la Pensée 68, le Nouvel ordre écologique: l'arbre, l'animal et l'homme (Prix Jean-Jacques Rousseau) 1992, Homo aestheticus – L'Intervention du goût à l'âge démocratique 1990 (Prix Médicis 1992), l'Homme Dieu ou le sens de la vie (Prix Littéraire des Droits de l'Homme)1996, La Sagesse des Modernes 1998, Le Sens du Beau 1998, Philosopher à dix-huit ans (jtly) 1999, Qu'est-ce que l'homme? (jtly) 2000, Qu'est-ce qu-une vie réussie 2002, numerous articles on philosophy. *Honours:* Chevalier Légion d'honneur, Ordre des Arts et des Lettres. *Address:* c/o Ministry of Youth, National Education and Research, 110 rue de Grenelle, 75357 Paris, France (office).

FFORDE, Jasper; British novelist; b. 1961, London, England. *Education:* Dartington Hall School. *Career:* fmrly worked in the film industry. *Publications:* The Eyre Affair 2001, Lost in a Good Book 2002, The Well of Lost Plots (Bollinger Everyman Wodehouse Prize for Comic Writing 2004) 2003, Something Rotten 2004, The Big Over Easy 2005, The Fourth Bear 2006, First Among Sequels 2007. *Honours:* Sherlock Award for Best Comic Detective 2002. *Literary Agent:* Janklow & Nesbit UK, 29 Adam & Eve Mews, London, W8 6UG, England. *E-mail:* wizardwheeze@jasperfforde.com. *Website:* www.jasperfforde.com.

FICKERT, Kurt Jon, BA, MA, PhD; German academic and writer; b. 19 Dec. 1920, Pausa; m. Lynn Barbara Janda 1946, two s. one d. *Education:* Hofstra Univ., New York Univ. *Career:* Instructor, Hofstra Univ. 1947–52; Asst Prof., Florida State Univ. 1953–54, Kansas State Univ. 1954–56; Asst Prof.,

Wittenberg Univ., Assoc. Prof., Prof. 1956–86, Prof. Emeritus 1986–; mem. Ohio Poetry Day Asscn (pres. 1970–75). *Publications:* To Heaven and Back, 1972; Hermann Hesse's Quest, 1978; Kafka's Doubles, 1979; Signs and Portents, 1980; Franz Kafka: Life, Work, Criticism, 1984; Neither Left nor Right: The Politics of Individualism in Uwe Johnson's Work, 1987; End of a Mission, 1993; Dialogue With the Reader, 1995. Contributions: journals and magazines.

FIDO, Martin Austin, BA, BLitt; British academic and writer; *Writing Instructor, Boston University*; b. 18 Oct. 1939, Penzance, Cornwall, England; m. 1st Judith Mary Spicer 1961 (divorced 1972); m. 2nd Norma Elaine Wilson 1972 (divorced 1984); m. 3rd Karen Lynn Sandel 1994; one s. two d. *Education:* Lincoln College, Oxford. *Career:* Andrew Bradley Junoir Research Fellow, Balliol College, Oxford, 1963–66; Lecturer in English, University of Leeds, 1966–72; Visiting Assoc. Prof., Michigan State University, 1971–72; Reader in English and Head, Dept of English and Linguistics, University of the West Indies, Barbados, 1973–83; Writing Instructor, Boston University, 2001–; Actor, Hoevec Investors Ltd, Barbados, 1981–83; Courier, Guide-Lecturer: Footprints Walks, City Walks, King Arthur Land Tours, 1983–2001; Broadcaster, BBC Radio 2, 1992, LBC Radion, 1987–. *Publications:* Charles Dickens: An Authentic Account of His Life and Times, 1970; Oscar Wilde, 1973; Rudyard Kipling, 1974; Shakespeare, 1978; Murder Guide to London, 1986; The Crimes, Detection and Death of Jack the Ripper, 1987; Body-snatchers: A History of the Resurrectionists, 1742–1832, 1989; Murders after Midnight, 1990; The Peasenhall Murder (co-author), 1990; The Jack the Ripper A to Z (co-author), 1991; The Chronicle of Crime: The Infamous Felons of Modern History and Their Hideous Crimes, 1993; Deadly Jealousy, 1993; Great Crimes and Trials of the Twentieth Century (co-author), 1994; Twentieth Century Murder, 1995; The World's Worst Medical Mistakes (co-author), 1996; Our Family (co-author), 1997; The World of Charles Dickens, 1997; The World of Sherlock Holmes, 1998; The World of Agatha Christie, 1999; The Official Encyclopedia of Scotland Yard (co-author), 1999; The Krays: Unfinished Business, 2000; To Kill and Kill Again, 2000, US edn as A History of British Serial Killers, 2001. Other: Writer and reader of audiotapes dealing with criminals and true crime stories. Contributions: Essays in Criticism; Notes and Queries; English Language Studies; Modern Language Review; Dutch Opera Yearbook; Ripperologist; Ripperana; Reviews to periodicals including: Times Educational Supplement; TLS; Oxford Review; Oxford Magazine. *Honours:* Ripperana Award 1999. *Literary Agent:* c/o Richard Jeffs, Communications Consultants, 52 Warwick Crescent, Edgbaston, Birmingham, B15 2LH, England. *Address:* 34 Streeter Hill Road, North Falmouth, MA 02556 (home); c/o CAS Writing Center, Boston University, 730 Commonwealth Avenue, Boston, MA 02215, USA (office). *Telephone:* (508) 540-5101 (home); (617) 358-1513 (office). *E-mail:* fido@bu.edu (office).

FIELD, Edward, (Bruce Elliot); American writer and poet; b. 7 June 1924, New York, NY. *Education:* New York Univ. *Career:* Fellow, American Acad. of Rome. *Publications:* Stand Up, Friend, With Me 1963, Variety Photoplays 1967, Eskimo Songs and Stories 1973, A Full Heart 1977, A Geography of Poets (ed.) 1979, revised edn as A New Geography of Poets 1992, New and Selected Poems 1987, Counting Myself Lucky 1992, A Frieze for a Temple of Love 1998, Magic Words 1998, The Villagers 2000, The Man Who Would Marry Susan Sontag, and Other Intimate Literary Portraits of the Bohemian Era 2005; contrib. to reviews, journals and periodicals. *Honours:* Lamont Award 1963, Shelley Memorial Award 1978, Lambda Award 1993, Bill Whitehead Lifetime Achievement Award, W. H. Auden Award. *Address:* 463 West Street, A323, New York, NY 10014, USA. *E-mail:* fieldinski@yahoo.com. *Website:* www.edwardfield.com.

FIELDING, Helen; British author and journalist; b. 19 Feb. 1958, Morley, W Yorks.; pnr Kevin Curran; one s. *Education:* Univ. of Oxford. *Career:* began career working for BBC; fmr columnist, The Independent. *Publications:* Cause Celeb 1994, Bridget Jones's Diary 1996, Bridget Jones: The Edge of Reason 2000, Bridget Jones's Guide to Life (for Comic Relief charity) 2001, Olivia Joules and the Overactive Imagination 2004. *Honours:* Nielsen BookScan and The Times Platinum Book Award, British Book Awards 2002, listed in The Observer as one of the 50 funniest acts in British comedy 2003. *Address:* c/o Picador, Pan Macmillan Publishers, 20 New Wharf Road, London, N1 9RR, England.

FIENNES, Sir Ranulph Twisleton-Wykeham-, 3rd Bt, cr. 1916, OBE, DLitt; British travel writer, lecturer and explorer; b. 7 March 1944, Windsor; s. of Lt-Col Sir Ranulph Twisleton-Wykeham-Fiennes, DSO, 2nd Bt and Audrey Newson; m. 1st Virginia Pepper 1970 (died 2004); m. 2nd Louise Millington 2005. *Education:* Eton. *Career:* Lt Royal Scots Greys 1966, Capt. 1968, retd 1970; attached 22 SAS Regt 1966, Sultan of Muscat's Armed Forces 1968; Leader, British Expeditions to White Nile 1969, Jostedalsbre Glacier 1970, Headless Valley, BC 1971, (Towards) North Pole 1977; Leader, Transglobe Expedition (1st polar circumnavigation of world on its polar axis) 1979–82; led first unsupported crossing of Antarctic continent and longest unsupported polar journey in history Nov. 1992–Feb. 1993; discovered lost city of Ubar in Oman 1993; ran seven marathons on six continents in seven days 2003; Exec. Consultant to Chair. of Occidental Petroleum Corpn 1984–90. *Publications:* A Talent for Trouble 1970, Ice Fall in Norway 1972, The Headless Valley 1973, Where Soldiers Fear to Tread 1975, Hell on Ice 1979, To the Ends of the Earth 1983, Bothie – The Polar Dog (with Virginia Twisleton-Wykeham-Fiennes) 1984, Living Dangerously 1987, The Feather Men 1991, Atlantis of the Sands 1992, Mind over Matter 1993, The Sett 1996, Fit for Life 1998, Beyond the

Limits 2000, The Secret Hunters 2001, Captain Scott 2003. *Honours:* Hon. DSc (Loughborough Coll.) 1986; Hon. DUniv (Univ. of Cen. England in Birmingham) 1995, (Univ. of Portsmouth) 2000; Hon. DLitt (Glasgow Caledonian); Dhofar Campaign Medal 1969, Sultan's Bravery Medal 1970, Livingstone Medal, Royal Scottish Geographical Soc., Royal Inst. of Navigation 1977, Gold Medal of Explorers Club of NY 1983, Founders Medal Royal Geographical Soc. 1984, Polar Medal for Arctic and Antarctic, with Bars 1985, with clasp 1995, ITN Award for Int. Exploit of the Decade 1989, Explorers Club Millennium Award for Polar Exploration 2000. *Address:* Greenlands, Exford, Minehead, West Somerset, TA24 7NU, England. *Telephone:* (1643) 831350.

FIFIELD, Christopher George, MusB, ARCO, ARMCM; British conductor and writer on music; *Music Director, Lambeth Orchestra*; b. 4 Sept. 1945, Croydon, Surrey, England; m. Judith Weyman 1972 (divorced); three c. *Education:* Manchester Univ., Royal Manchester Coll. of Music, Guildhall School, Cologne Musikhochschule. *Career:* fmrly Asst Dir of Music Capetown Opera, music staff Glyndebourne for 12 years, Music Dir London Contemporary Dance Theatre, Dir Northampton Symphony Orchestra, Central Festival Opera, Reigate and Redhill Choral Soc. and Jubilate Choir; frequent conductor at Trinity Coll. of Music; Dir of Music, Univ. Coll. London 1980–90; fmrly chorus master Chelsea Opera Group; currently Music Dir and Conductor, Lambeth Orchestra. *Publications:* Max Bruch: his Life and Works 1988, Wagner in Performance 1992, True Artist and True Friend: A Biography of Hans Richter 1993, Letters and Diaries of Kathleen Ferrier 2003, Ibbs and Tillett: the Rise and Fall of a Musical Empire 2005; contrib. to reference books and journals, including Viking Opera Guide, International Opera Guide, New Grove Dictionary of Opera 1992, Grove 7, Dictionary of National Biography, Oxford Companion to Music. *Address:* 162 Venner Road, London, SE26 5JQ, England. *Telephone:* (7752) 273558. *E-mail:* christopherfifield@ntlworld.com. *Website:* www.lambeth-orchestra.org.uk.

FIGES, Eva, BA; British writer; b. 15 April 1932, Berlin; d. of Emil Unger and Irma Unger; m. John Figes 1954 (divorced 1963); one s. one d. *Education:* Kingsbury Co. School, Queen Mary Coll., Univ. of London. *Publications include:* Winter Journey 1967, Patriarchal Attitudes 1970, B 1972, Nelly's Version 1977, Little Eden 1978, Waking 1981, Sex and Subterfuge 1982, Light 1983, The Seven Ages 1986, Ghosts 1988, The Tree of Knowledge 1990, The Tenancy 1993, The Knot 1996, Tales of Innocence and Experience 2003. *Honours:* Guardian Fiction Prize 1967. *Address:* Rogers, Coleridge & White Ltd, 20 Powis Mews, London, W11 1JN, England (office). *Telephone:* (20) 7221-3717 (office). *Fax:* (20) 7229-9084 (office).

FIGES, Orlando, PhD; British historian, academic and writer; *Professor of History, Birkbeck College, London*; b. 20 Nov. 1959, s. of John Figes and Eva Figes (née Unger); m. Stephanie Palmer 1990; two d. *Education:* Gonville and Caius Coll., Cambridge, Trinity Coll., Cambridge. *Career:* Fellow Trinity Coll., Cambridge 1984–89, Dir of Studies in History 1988–98, Lecturer in History, Univ. of Cambridge 1987–99; Prof. of History, Birkbeck Coll., Univ. of London 1999–. *Publications include:* Peasant Russia, Civil War: the Volga Countryside in Revolution 1917–21 1989, A People's Tragedy: the Russian Revolution 1891–1924 (Wolfson History Prize, WHSmith Literary Award, NCR Book Award, Los Angeles Times Book Prize) 1996, Interpreting the Russian Revolution (co-author) 1999, Natasha's Dance: a Cultural History of Russia 2002, The Whisperers: Private Lives in Stalin's Russia 2007; numerous review articles and contribs to other published books. *Address:* School of History, Classics and Archaeology, Birkbeck College, Malet Street, London, WC1E 7HX, England (office). *Telephone:* (20) 7631-6299 (office). *Fax:* (20) 7631-6552 (office). *E-mail:* orlando.figes@ntlworld.com (office). *Website:* www.bbk.ac.uk/hca/staff/figes.shtml; www.bbk.ac.uk (office).

FILIMON, Valeria; Romanian journalist; b. 29 May 1949, Butimanu; d. of Ion Dumitrescu and Maria Dumitrescu; m. Vasile Filimon 1984. *Education:* Univ. of Bucharest. *Career:* freelance journalist for various Romanian dailies and literary magazines 1967–90; Assoc. Prof. 1970–90; journalist 1990–93; Ed.-in-Chief Femeia Moderna (magazine) 1993–98, Regala 1998–, Olimp 1999–; Project Co-ordinator in Romania, Int. Fed. of Journalists 1996–; Vice-Pres. Asscn of Romanian Journalists. *Publications:* co-author of critical edn of Romanian novelist Liviu Rebreanu 1968–75; Lyceum (collection of literary criticism in two vols) 1974. *Honours:* Romanian Writers' Union Prize. *Address:* Societatea Ziaristilor din Romania, Piata Presei Libere 1, Oficial Postal 33, 71341 Bucharest (office); Bd Pache Protopopescu No. 11, Sector 2, 70311 Bucharest, Romania. *Telephone:* (21) 2223346 (office); (21) 3152482. *Fax:* (21) 2224266 (office); (21) 3130675.

FILIPACCHI, Daniel; French journalist and publisher; *Honorary President, Hachette Filipacchi Médias*; b. 12 Jan. 1928, Paris; s. of Henri Filipacchi and Edith Besnard. *Career:* typographer, Paris-Match 1944, photographer 1948, head of information and dir of photographic service 1953; fashion photographer, Marie-Claire 1957; producer of radio transmissions, Europe No. 1 1955, 1960; Owner and Dir Jazz Magazine 1955, Cahiers du cinéma 1961–70; Founder and Dir Salut les copains (became Salut 1976) 1961, Lui, Mlle Age tendre (became OK Age tendre 1976), Pariscope 1965, Photo 1967, Le Monde des Grands Musées 1968, Ski 1969, Union 1972, Playboy France 1973–84, Girls 1982; editorial adviser to Newlook 1982, Penthouse 1984; Pres.-Dir-Gen. WEA Filipacchi Music SA 1971–84, Cogedipresse; Owner and fmr Dir Paris-Match 1976; mem. editorial Cttee Elle 1981; Vice-Pres. Hachette 1981–93, Pres.-Dir-Gen. Hachette Magazines Inc. (USA) 1990; Pres.-Dir-Gen. Filipac-

chi Médias SA 1993–97; Jt Man. Cogédipresse 1994–97; Admin. and Hon. Pres. Hachette Filipacchi Médias 1997–. *Address:* Hachette Filipacchi Médias, Immeuble Europa, 149–151 rue Anatole-France, 92534 Levallois-Perret cedex, France.

FILIPETTI, Aurélie; French novelist; b. 1973, Lorraine. *Publications:* novel: Les derniers jours de la classe ouvrière 2003. *Address:* c/o Stock, 27 rue Cassette, 75006 Paris, France (office).

FILIPPINI, Serge; French novelist, critic and philosopher; b. 1950, Pontarlier. *Publications:* L'Aquarium 1980, Angele 1986, La Vie en double 1987, L'Homme incendié (trans. as The Man in Flames) 1990, Comedia 1992, Haut mal 1993, LeRoi de Sicile 1998, L'Amant absolu 1999, Un Amour de Paul 2000, Érotique du mensonge 2003. *Address:* c/o Dedalus Ltd, Langford Lodge, St Judith's Lane, Sawtry, Cambridgeshire PE28 5XE, England. *E-mail:* info@dedalusbooks.com. *Website:* www.dedalusbooks.com.

FINCH, Peter; British poet and writer; *Chief Executive, Academi*; b. 6 March 1947, Cardiff, Wales; two s. one d. *Education:* Glamorgan Polytechnic. *Career:* Ed. Second Aeon 1966–75; Chief Exec. Academi Welsh Nat. Literature Promotion Agency and Soc. for Writers; mem. Welsh Acad., Welsh Union of Writers. *Publications:* Wanted 1967, Pieces of the Universe 1968, How to Learn Welsh 1977, Between 35 and 42 (short stories) 1982, Some Music and a Little War 1984, How to Publish Your Poetry 1985, Reds in the Bed 1986, Selected Poems 1987, How to Publish Yourself 1988, Make 1990, Poems for Ghosts 1991, Five Hundred Cobbings 1994, The Spe Ell 1995, The Poetry Business 1995, Antibodies 1997, Useful 1997, Food 2001, Real Cardiff 2002, Vizet/Water 2003, Real Cardiff Two 2004, The Big Book of Cardiff (ed.) 2005, The Welsh Poems 2006; contrib. to magazines and journals. *Address:* 19 Southminster Road, Roath, Cardiff, CF23 5AT, Wales. *E-mail:* peter@peterfinch.co.uk. *Website:* www.peterfinch.co.uk.

FINCKE, Gary William, BA, MA, PhD; American academic, poet and writer; *Professor of English and Creative Writing, Susquehanna University*; b. 7 July 1945, Pittsburgh, PA; m. Elizabeth Locker 1968; two s. one d. *Education:* Thiel Coll., Miami Univ., Kent State Univ. *Career:* Instructor in English, Pennsylvania State Univ. of Monaca 1969–75; Chair. Dept of English, LeRoy Central School, New York 1975–80; Admin. Susquehanna Univ. 1980–93, Prof. of English and Dir of the Writers' Inst. 1993–; Ed. The Apprentice Writer 1982–2005; syndicated columnist 1996–. *Publications:* poetry: Breath 1984, The Coat in the Heart 1985, The Days of Uncertain Health 1988, Handing the Self Back 1990, Plant Voices 1991, The Public Talk of Death 1991, The Double Negatives of the Living 1992, Inventing Angels 1994, The Technology of Paradise 1998, The Almanac for Desire 2000; fiction: For Keepsies 1993, Emergency Calls 1996, The Inadvertent Scofflaw 1999, Blood Ties 2002, Writing Letters for the Blind 2003, The Stone Child 2003, Amp'd: A Father's Backstage Pass 2004, Sorry I Worried You 2004, Standing Around the Heart 2005; contrib. to many anthologies, reviews, quarterlies, journals and magazines. *Honours:* various grants and fellowships; Beloit Fiction Journal Short Story Prize 1990, Bess Hokin Prize Poetry Magazine 1991, Book-of-the-Month Vietnam Veteran's Magazine 1993, Notable Fiction Book of the Year Dictionary of Literary Biography 1993, Pushcart Prize 1995, 2000, Rose Lefcowitz Prize Poet Lore 1997, Ohio State Univ. Press/The Journal Poetry Prize 2003, Flannery O'Connor Award for Short Fiction 2003, George Garrett Fiction Prize 2003. *Address:* 3 Melody Lane, Selinsgrove, PA 17870, USA.

FINE, Anne, OBE, BA, FRSL; British writer; b. (Anne Laker), 7 Dec. 1947, Leicester; d. of Brian Laker and Mary Baker; m. Kit Fine 1968 (divorced 1991); two d. *Education:* Northampton High School for Girls and Univ. of Warwick. *Career:* Children's Laureate 2001–03; mem. Soc. of Authors. *Publications:* for older children: The Summer House Loon 1978, The Other Darker Ned 1978, The Stone Menagerie 1980, Round Behind the Icehouse 1981, The Granny Project 1983, Madame Doubtfire 1987, Goggle-Eyes (Guardian Children's Fiction Prize, Carnegie Medal 1990) 1989, The Book of the Banshee 1991, Flour Babies (Whitbread Children's Book of the Year, Carnegie Medal 1993) 1992, Step by Wicked Step 1995, The Tulip Touch (Whitbread Children's Book of the Year) 1996, Very Different (short stories) 2001, Up on Cloud Nine 2002, Frozen Billy 2004, The Road of Bones 2006; for younger children: Scaredy-Cat 1985, Anneli the Art Hater 1986, Crummy Mummy and Me 1988, A Pack of Liars 1988, Stranger Danger 1989, Bill's New Frock (Smarties Prize 1990) 1989, The Country Pancake 1989, A Sudden Puff of Glittering Smoke 1989, A Sudden Swirl of Icy Wind 1990, Only a Show 1990, Design-a-Pram 1991, A Sudden Glow of Gold 1991, The Worst Child I Ever Had 1991, The Angel of Nitshill Road 1991, Poor Monty (picture book) 1991, The Same Old Story Every Year 1992, The Chicken Gave It to Me 1992, The Haunting of Pip Parker 1992, The Diary of a Killer Cat 1994, Press Play 1994, How to Write Really Badly 1996, Countdown 1996, Jennifer's Diary 1996, Care of Henry 1996, Loudmouth Louis 1998, Charm School 1999, Roll Over Roly 1999, Bad Dreams 2000, Ruggles (picture book) 2001, Notso Hotso 2001, The Jamie and Angus Stories 2002, How to Cross the Road and Not Turn Into a Pizza 2002, The More the Merrier 2003; adult fiction: The Killjoy 1986, Taking the Devil's Advice 1990, In Cold Domain 1994, Telling Liddy 1998, All Bones and Lies 2001, Raking the Ashes 2005; adult non-fiction: Telling Tales: an Interview with Anne Fine 1999. *Honours:* Dr hc; Scottish Arts Council Writer's Bursary 1986, Scottish Arts Council Book Award 1986, Guardian Children's Fiction Award 1990, Carnegie Medal 1990, 1993, Publishing News' British Book Awards Children's Author of the Year 1990, 1993, Whitbread Children's Novel Award 1993, 1997, Nasen Special Educational Needs Book Award 1996, Prix

Sorcière 1998, Prix Versele 1999, 2000, Boston Globe Horn Book Award 2003. *Literary Agent:* c/o David Higham Associates, 5–8 Lower John Street, London, W1R 4HA, England. *Telephone:* (20) 7434-5900. *Website:* www.annefine.co.uk. *Fax:* (1833) 690519 (home).

FINK, Gerald R., PhD; American geneticist and academic; *American Cancer Society Professor of Genetics, Massachusetts Institute of Technology*; b. 1 July 1940, Brooklyn, New York; s. of Rebecca Fink and Benjamin Fink; m. Rosalie Lewis 1961; two d. *Education:* Amherst Coll., Yale Univ. *Career:* Postdoctoral Fellow, NIH 1965–66, 1966–67; Instructor, NIH Grad. Program 1966; Instructor, Cold Spring Harbor Summer Program 1970–; Asst Prof. of Genetics Cornell Univ. 1967–71, Assoc. Prof. 1971–76, Prof. 1976–79, Prof. of Biochem. 1979–82; Prof. of Molecular Genetics, MIT 1982–; American Cancer Soc. Prof. of Genetics 1979–; mem. Whitehead Inst. for Biomedical Research 1982–, Dir 1990–; Sec. Genetics Soc. of America 1977–80, Vice-Pres. 1986–87, Pres. 1988–89; mem. NAS, American Acad. of Arts and Sciences. *Publications:* numerous scientific publs. *Honours:* Hon. DSc (Amherst Coll.) 1982; NAS-US Steel Prize in Molecular Biology 1981, Genetics Soc. of America Medal 1982, Yale Science and Eng Award 1984, Emil Christian Hansen Foundation Award for Microbiological Research 1986. *Address:* Whitehead Institute for Biomedical Research, 9 Cambridge Center, Cambridge, MA 02142, USA (office). *Telephone:* (617) 258-5215 (office). *E-mail:* gfink@wi.mit.edu (office). *Website:* www.wi.mit.edu/far/far_fink_bio.html (office); web.mit.edu/biology/www/facultyareas/facresearch/fink.shtml (office).

FINKEL, Donald, BA, MA; American poet and academic; b. 21 Oct. 1929, New York, NY; m. Constance Urdang 1956, one s. two d. *Education:* Columbia University. *Career:* teacher, University of Iowa, 1957–58, Bard College, 1958–60; Faculty, 1960–92, Poet-in-Residence, 1965–92, Poet-in-Residence Emeritus, 1992–, Washington University, St Louis; Visiting Lecturer, Bennington College, 1966–67, Princeton University, 1985, University of Missouri-St Louis, 1998–99, Webster University, 1999–2000. *Publications:* The Clothing's New Emperor and Other Poems, 1959; Simeon, 1964; A Joyful Noise, 1966; Answer Back, 1968; The Garbage Wars, 1970; Adequate Earth, 1972; A Mote in Heaven's Eye, 1975; Going Under, and Endurance: An Arctic Idyll: Two Poems, 1978; What Manner of Beast, 1981; The Detachable Man, 1984; Selected Shorter Poems, 1987; The Wake of the Electron, 1987; Beyond Despair, 1994; A Question of Seeing, 1998. *Honours:* Helen Bullis Prize, 1964; Guggenheim Fellowship, 1967; National Endowment for the Arts Grants, 1969, 1973; Ingram Merrill Foundation Grant, 1972; Theodore Roethke Memorial Prize, 1974; Morton Dauwen Zabel Award, American Acad. of Arts and Letters, 1980; Dictionary of Literary Biography Yearbook Award, 1994.

FINLAY, Mary Louise, BA; Canadian journalist, broadcaster and writer; b. 29 March 1947, Ottawa, Ont.; d. of John Francis and Helen B. Finlay; one s. *Education:* Univ. of Ottawa and Harvard Univ., USA. *Career:* Historical Researcher, Trans. Canadian War Museum 1967–70; Current Affairs Interviewer, Producer 1970–75; Presenter Take 30 1975–77; Presenter, writer Finlay and Company 1976; contrib. As It Happens (radio) 1977–78, 90 Minutes Live 1977–78; Presenter, Producer Live It Up 1978–81; Co-Presenter The National Driving Test 1980; Co-Presenter, Producer The Journal 1981–88; Presenter Sunday Morning 1988–94; Presenter Now The Details 1994–97; Nieman Fellow, Harvard Univ. 1986; mem. Canadian Civil Liberties Union. *TV documentaries scripted:* The Railroad Show 1974, The Mackenzie Valley Pipeline Inquiry 1976, All is Calm 1983, Timothy Findley's War 1983, Taking a Chance on Faro 1984, The Right to Die 1984, The Death of Clarence Warren 1985, Congress and the Contras 1985. *Address:* Box 500, Station A, Toronto, ON, M5W 1E6 (office); 100 Edith Drive, Toronto, ON M4R 1Z2, Canada (home).

FINLAY, William (see Mackay, James Alexander)

FINN, Pavel Konstantinovich; Russian scriptwriter; b. (Pavel Finn-Halfin), 28 June 1940, Moscow; m. Irina Chernova-Finn; one s. *Education:* All-Union State Inst. of Cinematography. *Career:* fmr journalist, documentary maker; freelance script writer 1968–; Head of Higher Workshop Course of Scriptwriters; Chair. Cinema Dramaturgy Council, Moscow Union of Cinematographers 2001; First Deputy Chair. Russian Union of Cinematographers 2001–. *Films include:* Headless Horse Rider 1973, Armed and Very Dangerous 1977, 26 Days of Dostoyevsky's Life 1980, Icicle in a Warm Sea 1983, Witness 1985, Lady Macbeth of Mtsensk Region 1989, Accidental Waltz 1989, Sunset 1990, Myth about Leonid 1991, A Big Concert of Peoples 1991, Shylock 1993, Jester's Revenge 1994, For What 1995, Career of Arthur Whui 1996, Break Point, We Are Your Kids, Moscow, Eve's Gates, Death of Tairov or Princess Brambilla, Secrets of Court Coups. *Address:* Union of Cinematographers, Vassil'yevskaya str. 13, 123825 Moscow (office); 4th Rostovsky per. 2/1, apt 9, 119121 Moscow, Russia (home). *Telephone:* (495) 248-53-28 (home); (495) 334-59-34 (home). *Fax:* (495) 251-51-06 (office). *E-mail:* pavelfinn@mtu-net.ru (home).

FINNIGAN, (Helen) Joan, BA; Canadian poet, playwright and oral historian; b. 23 Nov. 1925, Ottawa, ON; d. of Frank Finnigan and Maye Finnigan (née Horner); m. Charles Grant MacKenzie 1949 (died 1965); two s. one d. *Education:* Lisgar Collegiate, Ottawa, Carleton and Queen's Univs. *Career:* gen. reporter, Ottawa Journal; freelance journalist 1949–67; research, scriptwriting, idea production, interviewing Canadian Nat. Film Bd 1969–1976; scriptwriter CBC Radio 1976–84; four photography exhibitions, guest lectures, radio and TV appearances; mem. Writers' Union of Canada, League of Canadian Poets. *Plays:* A Prince of Good Fellows 1976, Up the Vallee! 1978, Songs from Both Sides of the River 1987. *Screenplay:* The Best Damn Fiddler from Calabogie to Kaladar (nine Genie Awards, Canadian Film Award for Best Screenplay) 1969. *Radio plays:* Songs for the Bible Belt, May Day Rounds, Children of the Shadows, There's No Good Time Left – None at All. *Publications:* poetry: Through the Glass, Darkly 1963, A Dream of Lilies 1965, Entrance to the Greenhouse (Centennial Award for Poetry 1969) 1968, It Was Warm and Sunny When We Set Out 1970, In the Brown Cottage on Loughborough Lake 1970, Living Together 1976, A Reminder of Familiar Faces 1978, This Series Has Been Discontinued 1980, The Watershed Collection 1988, Wintering Over 1992, Second Wind, Second Sight 1998; prose: Some of the Stories I Told You Were True (oral history) 1981, Legacies, Legends and Lies (Ottawa-Carleton Literary Award) 1985, Tell Me Another Story (oral history) 1988, The Dog Who Wouldn't Be Left Behind (juvenile) 1989, Old Scores: New Goals, History of Ottawa Senators 1891–1992 1992, A History of Lisgar Collegiate, 1843–1993 1993, Witches, Ghosts and Loups-Garous 1994, Dancing at the Crossroads 1995, Down the Unmarked Roads 1997, Tallying the Tales of the Old-Timers (oral/social history) 1998, Life Along the Opeongo Line 2004. *Honours:* Pres.'s Medal for Poetry, Univ. of Western Ontario 1969; Philemon Wright Award 1983, Award for Community Service in Arts and Culture, West Quebecers Awards 2005. *Address:* Moore Farm, Hartington, ON K0H 1W0, Canada (home).

FINNIS, John Mitchell, LLB, DPhil, FBA; Australian/British academic and barrister; *Professor of Law and Legal Philosophy, University of Oxford*; b. 28 July 1940, Adelaide; s. of the late Maurice M. S. Finnis and of Margaret McKellar Stewart; m. Marie Carmel McNally 1964; three s. three d. *Education:* St Peter's Coll., Adelaide, Univ. of Adelaide, Oxford Univ. *Career:* Fellow and Praelector in Jurisprudence, Univ. Coll., Oxford 1966–, Stowell Civil Law Fellow 1973–, Vice-Master 2001–; Lecturer in Law, Oxford Univ. 1966–72, Rhodes Reader in the Laws of the Commonwealth and the United States 1972–89, Prof. of Law and Legal Philosophy 1989–, mem. Philosophy Sub-Faculty 1984–, Chair. Bd of Faculty of Law 1987–89; Prof. and Head of Dept of Law, Univ. of Malawi 1976–78; Biolchini Family Prof. of Law, Univ. of Notre Dame, Ind., USA 1995–, Adjunct Prof. of Philosophy 1999–; barrister, Gray's Inn 1970–; Gov., Plater Coll., Oxford 1972–92; Consultor, Pontifical Commission Iustitia et Pax 1977–89, mem. 1990–95; Special Adviser, Foreign Affairs Cttee, House of Commons, on role of UK Parl. in Canadian Constitution 1980–82; mem. Catholic Bishops' Jt Cttee on Bio-ethical Issues 1981–89, Int. Theological Comm. (Vatican) 1986–92; Gov. Linacre Centre for Medical Ethics 1981–96, 1998– (Vice-Chair. 1987–96, 1998–); Huber Distinguished Visiting Prof., Boston Coll. Law School 1993–94; mem. Pontifical Acad. Pro Vita 2001–. *Publications:* Halsbury's Laws of England (fourth edn), Vol. 6 (Commonwealth and Dependencies) 1974, 1990, 2003, Natural Law and Natural Rights 1980, Fundamentals of Ethics 1983, Nuclear Deterrence, Morality and Realism (with Joseph Boyle and Germain Grisez) 1987, Moral Absolutes 1991, Aquinas: Moral, Political and Legal Theory 1998; articles on constitutional law, legal philosophy, ethics, moral theology and late sixteenth-century history. *Address:* University College, Oxford, OX1 4BH, England (office); Notre Dame Law School, South Bend, IN 46556, USA (office). *Telephone:* (1865) 276641 (UK) (office); (574) 631-5989 (USA) (office); (1865) 558660 (UK) (home).

FINSCHER, Ludwig, PhD; German musicologist, lexicographer and academic (retd); b. 14 March 1930, Kassel. *Education:* Univs of Göttingen and Saarbrücken. *Career:* Asst Lecturer, Univ. of Kiel 1960–65, Univ. of Saarbrücken 1965–68; Ed. Die Musikforschung 1961–68, Co-Ed. 1968–74; Prof. of Musicology, Univ. of Frankfurt am Main 1968–81, Univ. of Heidelberg 1981–95; mem. Akad. der Wissenschaften, Heidelberg, Akad. der Wissenschaften und der Literatur, Mainz, Academia Europaea; Corresp. mem. American Musicological Soc. *Publications:* Collected Works of Gaffurius (ed., two vols) 1955, 1960, Collected Works of Compère (ed., five vols) 1958–72, Loyset Compère (*c.* 1450–1518): Life and Works 1964, Geschichte der Evangelischen Kirchenmusik (co-ed., second edn) 1965, Studien zur Geschichte des Streichquartetts: I, Die Entstehung des klassischen Streichquartetts: Von den Vorformen zur Grundlegung durch Joseph Haydn 1974, Collected Works of Hindemith (co-ed. with K. von Fischer) 1976–, Renaissance-Studien: Helmuth Osthoff zum 80. Geburtstag (ed.) 1979, Quellenstudien zu Musik der Renaissance (ed., two vols) 1981, 1983, Ludwig van Beethoven (ed.) 1983, Claudio Monteverdi: Festschrift Reinhold Hammerstein zum 70. Geburtstag (ed.) 1986, Die Musik des 15. und 16. Jahrhunderts: Neues Handbuch der Musikwissenschaft (ed., Vol. 3/1–2) 1989–90, Die Mannheimer Hofkapelle im Zeitalter Carl Theodors (ed.) 1992, Die Musik in Geschichte und Gegenwart (ed., second edn, 26 vols) 1994–, Bach's Posthumous Role in Music History 1998, Joseph Haydn 2000; contrib. editorially to the complete works of Mozart and Gluck, contrib. to scholarly books and journals. *Honours:* Hon. Mem. Int. Musicological Soc., Gesellschaft für Musikforschung; Hon. Foreign Mem. Royal Musical Assen, London 1978–; Chevalier, Ordre nat. du Mérite 1994, Grand Order of Merit (Germany) 1997; Dr hc (Athens) 2002, (Zürich) 2003; Akademie der Wissenschaften Prize, Göttingen 1968, Balzan 2006. *Address:* Am Walde 1, 38302 Wolfenbüttel, Germany (home). *Telephone:* (5331) 32713 (home). *Fax:* (5331) 33276 (home).

FINSTAD, Suzanne, BA, JD; American author and attorney; b. 14 Sept. 1955, Minneapolis, MN. *Education:* Univ. of Texas, Austin, Univ. of Houston, Univ. of Grenoble, France, Bates Coll. of Law, LSE. *Publications:* Heir Not Apparent 1984, Ulterior Motives 1987, Sleeping with the Devil 1991, Warren Beatty: A Private Man 2005; contrib. to magazines. *Honours:* Order of the Barons 1980;

American Jurisprudence Award in Criminal Law, Bancroft-Whitney Publishing Co 1979, Frank Wardlaw Award 1985. *Address:* c/o Joel Gotler, 152 N La Peer Drive, Beverly Hills, CA 90048, USA.

FINZI, Sergio, BPhil; Italian psychoanalyst and writer; b. 15 May 1936, Brescia; m. Virginia Finzi Ghisi. *Education:* Univ. of Pavia, École Freudienne de Paris. *Publications:* with Virgina Finzi: Un saggio in famiglia 1971, Il principe splendente 1973, Lavoro dell' inconscio e comunismo 1975, Nevrosi di guerra in tempo di pace 1989, Gli effetti dell' amore 1995, La scienza dei Vincoli 2000, Sul Monte della Preda 2004, L'Ombra del Grillo Parlante 2005; contribs to Il piccolo Hans 1974–95, Il Cefalopodo, Ambulatorio. *Address:* Via Rubens 9, 20148 Milan, Italy. *Telephone:* (02) 4046238 (office); (335) 5899367 (home). *Fax:* (02) 4046238 (office).

FIRER, Susan, BA, MA; American academic and poet; b. 14 Oct. 1948, Milwaukee, WI; one s. two d. *Education:* Univ. of Wisconsin at Milwaukee. *Career:* Teaching Asst, 1981–82, Lecturer, 1982, Adjunct Asst Prof. of English, 1988–, University of Wisconsin at Milwaukee. *Publications:* My Life with the Tsar and Other Poems, 1979; The Underground Communion Rail, 1992; The Lives of the Saints and Everything, 1993. Contributions: numerous anthologies, reviews, journals, and magazines. *Honours:* Acad. of American Poets Prize, University of Wisconsin at Milwaukee, 1977; Best American Poetry, 1992; Cleveland State University Poetry Center Prize, 1992; Wisconsin Council of Writers Posner Poetry Award, 1993; First Place, Writer's Place Literary Awards, 1995; Milwaukee County Artist Fellowship, 1996; Work included in Midwest Express Center, 1998.

FIRST, Philip (see Williamson, Philip G.)

FISCHER, August A.; Swiss fmr publishing executive; b. 7 Feb. 1939, Zürich; m. Gillian Ann Fischer 1961; one s. one d. *Career:* various positions E.I. Du Pont de Nemours & Co. 1962–78; Man. Dir European subsidiary of Napp Systems Inc. 1978–81, Exec. Vice-Pres., then Pres. and COO Napp Systems Inc., San Diego, Calif. 1981–89; Gen. Man. Devt, News Int. PLC 1989–90, Man. Dir 1990–95, mem. Bd and COO News Corpn Ltd 1991–95, Chief Exec. News Int. PLC (UK subsidiary of News Corpn) 1993–95; mem. Supervisory Bd Ringier AG, Zürich, consultant 1995–97; Chair. Bd and CEO Axel Springer Verlag AG 1998–2001; mem. American Man. Asscn, The Pres.'s Asscn; Trustee St Katharine and Shadwell Trust. *Address:* c/o Axel Springer Verlag AG, Axel-Springer-str. 65, 10117 Berlin, Germany (office).

FISCHER, David Hackett, AB, PhD; American historian and academic; *Warren Professor of History, Brandeis University;* b. 2 Dec. 1935, Baltimore, MD. *Education:* Princeton Univ., Johns Hopkins Univ. *Career:* currently Univ. Prof. and Warren Prof. of History, Brandeis Univ.; Co-Ed., Pivotal Moments in American History series. *Publications include:* Albion's Seed: Four British Folkways in America 1989, Paul Revere's Ride 1994, The Great Wave: Price Movements in Modern History 1996, Bound Away: Virginia and the Westward Movement 2000, Washington's Crossing (Pulitzer Prize for History 2005) 2004. *Address:* Department of History, Brandeis University, MS 036, 415 South Street, Waltham, MA 02454, USA.

FISCHER, Tibor; British journalist and novelist; b. 15 Nov. 1959, Stockport, England. *Education:* Univ. of Cambridge. *Publications:* Under the Frog (aka Under the Frog: A Black Comedy) 1992, The Thought Gang 1994, The Collector Collector 1997, Don't Read This Book if You're Stupid (short stories, aka I Like Being Killed) 2000, Voyage to the End of the Room 2003. *Honours:* Betty Trask Award 1992, one of Granta's Best of Young British Novelists 1993. *Literary Agent:* c/o William Morris, 52 Poland Street, London, W1F 7LX, England.

FISCHEROVÁ, Sylva; Czech poet; b. 5 Nov. 1963, Prague; d. of Josef Ludvík and Jarmila Fischerová. *Education:* Olomouc Grammar School and Charles Univ. *Career:* teaching asst, Dept of Classical Studies, Charles Univ., Prague. *Publications:* Zvláštní znamení (anthology) 1985, Chvění závodních koní 1986, Velká zrcadla 1990, The Tremor of the Racehorses 1990. *Address:* Dukelská 19, 772 00 Olomouc, Czech Republic. *Telephone:* (68) 259454.

FISH, Joe (see Williamson, Philip G.)

FISH, Stanley Eugene, BA, MA, PhD; American academic and writer; *Davidson-Kahn Distinguished Professor of Law and Humanities, Florida International University;* b. 19 April 1938, Providence, RI; m. 1st Adrienne Aaron 1959 (divorced 1980); one d.; m. 2nd Jane Parry Tompkins 1982. *Education:* Univ. of Pennsylvania, Yale Univ. *Career:* Asst Prof. 1963–67, Assoc. Prof. of English 1967–69, Prof. of English 1969–74, Univ. of California at Berkeley; Visiting Asst Prof., Washington Univ., St Louis 1967; Visiting Prof., Sir George Williams Univ. 1969, Linguistics Inst., SUNY 1971, Columbia Univ. 1983–84; Visiting Prof. 1971, Prof. of English 1974–78, William Kenan Jr Prof. of English and Humanities 1978–85, Chair Dept of English 1983–85, Johns Hopkins Univ.; Visiting Bing Prof. of English, Univ. of Southern California at Los Angeles 1973–74; Adjunct Prof., Univ. of Maryland Law School 1976–85; Arts and Sciences Prof. of English and Prof. of Law, Duke Univ. 1985–98; Exec. Dir, Duke Univ. Press 1993–98; Dean Coll. of Liberal Arts and Sciences, Univ. of Illinois at Chicago 1999–2005; Distinguished Visiting Prof., John Marshall Law School 2000–02; Fellow, Humanities Research Inst., Univ. of California at Irvine 1989; Davidson-Kahn Distinguished Prof. of Law and Humanities, Florida Int. Univ. 2005–; mem. American Acad. of Arts and Sciences, Milton Soc. of America (pres. 1980). *Publications:* John Skelton's Poetry 1965, Surprised by Sin: The Reader in

Paradise Lost 1967, Seventeenth Century Prose: Modern Essays in Criticism (ed.) 1971, Self-Consuming Artifacts: The Experience of Seventeenth Century Literature 1972, The Living Temple: George Herbert and Catechizing 1978, Is There a Text in This Class?: The Authority of Interpretive Communities 1980, Doing What Comes Naturally: Change, Rhetoric, and the Practice of Theory in Literary and Legal Studies 1989, There's No Such Thing as Free Speech, and It's a Good Thing, Too 1994, Professional Correctness: Literary Studies and Political Change 1995, The Stanley Fish Reader (ed. by H. Aram Veeser) 1998, The Trouble with Principle 1999, How Milton Works 2001; contrib. to scholarly books and journals. *Honours:* ACLS Fellowship 1966, Univ. of California at Berkeley Humanities Research Professorship 1966, 1970, second place Explicator Prize 1968, Guggenheim Fellowship 1969–70, Milton Soc. of America Honored Scholar 1991, PEN/Spielvogel-Diamonstein Award 1994, Hanford Book Award 1998. *Address:* Florida International University, School of Law, GL 495, 11200 SW Eighth Street, Miami, FL 33199, USA (office). *Telephone:* (305) 348-7820 (office). *E-mail:* fishs@fiu.edu.

FISHER, Allen, BA, MA; British painter, poet and art historian; *Professor of Poetry and Art, Manchester Metropolitan University;* b. 1 Nov. 1944, Norbury, Surrey, England. *Education:* Univ. of London, Univ. of Essex. *Career:* fmr Prof. of Poetry and Art, Roehampton Univ.; currently Head Dept of Contemporary Arts and Prof. of Poetry and Art, Manchester Metropolitan Univ. *Public collections:* Tate Gallery, London, King's Coll. Archive, Univ. of London, Hereford City Museum, Living Museum, Reykjavik, Iceland. *Exhibitions:* solo shows: King's Archives London 2003, Lulham Gallery, London 1998, 2002, King's Manor Gallery, York 1993, Old Mayor's Parlour, Hereford 1991; two-man retrospective exhbn: Hereford City Museum 1994. *Publications include:* Place Book One 1974, Brixton Fractals 1985, Unpolished Mirrors 1985, Stepping Out 1989, Future Exiles 1991, Fizz 1994, Civic Crime 1994, Breadboard 1994, Now's the Time 1995, The Topological Shovel (essays) 1999, Watusi 2000, Ring Shout 2001, Sojourns 2001, Gravity 2004, Entanglement 2004, Place 2005; contrib. to various magazines and journals. *Honours:* Alice Hunt Bartlett Award (jtly) 1975. *Address:* Department of Contemporary Arts, Manchester Metropolitan University, Hassall Road, Alsager, Cheshire, ST7 2HL (office); 14 Hopton Road, Hereford, HR1 1BE, England (home). *Telephone:* (161) 247-5301 (office). *Fax:* (161) 247-6377 (office). *E-mail:* allen.fisher@mmu.ac.uk (office). *Website:* www.cheshire.mmu .ac.uk/dca (office); www.eri.mmu.ac.uk/staff/profile.php?id=58 (office); www .allenfisher.co.uk.

FISHER, Carrie; American actress and author; b. 21 Oct. 1956, Beverly Hills; d. of Eddie Fisher and Debbie Reynolds; m. Paul Simon 1983 (divorced 1984); one d. *Education:* Beverly Hills High School and Cen. School of Speech and Drama, London. *Career:* appeared with her mother in nightclub act aged 13; appeared in chorus of Broadway production of Irene, starring Debbie Reynolds, aged 15; Broadway stage appearances in Censored Scenes from King Kong, Agnes of God; several TV credits; film début in Shampoo (Photoplay Award as Best Newcomer of the Year) 1974. *Films include:* Shampoo 1974, Star Wars 1977, The Empire Strikes Back 1980, The Blues Brothers 1980, Return of the Jedi 1983, Under the Rainbow, Garbo Talks, The Man With One Red Shoe 1985, Hannah and Her Sisters 1986, Amazing Women on the Moon 1987, Appointment With Death 1988, The 'Burbs 1989, Loverboy 1989, She's Back 1989, When Harry Met Sally… 1989, The Time Guardian 1990, Sibling Rivalry 1990, Drop Dead Fred 1991, Soapdish 1991, This is My Life 1992, Austin Powers: International Man of Mystery 2000, Scream 3 2000, Famous 2000, Heartbreakers 2001, Jay and Silent Bob Strike Back 2001, A Midsummer Night's Rave 2002. *Publications:* Postcards From the Edge (novel and screenplay, PEN Award for first novel 1987) 1987, Surrender the Pink 1990, Delusions of Grandma 1994 (novels), The Best Awful There Is 2003; short stories. *Literary Agent:* c/o William Morris Agency, 1 William Morris Place, Beverly Hills, CA 90212, USA.

FISHER, Leonard Everett, BFA, MFA; American painter, illustrator and writer; b. 24 June 1924, New York, NY; s. of Benjamin M. Fisher and Ray M. Fisher; m. Margery Meskin 1952; one s. two d. *Education:* Yale Univ. *Career:* Dean, Whitney School of Art, New Haven, Conn. 1951–53; Academic Dean, Paier Coll. of Art, Hamden, Conn., now Dean Emer.; mem. PEN, Authors' Guild, Soc. of Illustrators, Soc. of Children's Book Authors and Illustrators; Life Mem. Silvermine Guild of Artists, New Haven Paint and Clay Club; mem. Advisory Bd MFA Program, Western Connecticut Univ., Lowe Cttee New Britain Museum of American Art. *Art:* illustrations and paintings in collections including Library of Congress, Smithsonian Inst., Union Coll., Schenectady, Mt Holyoke Coll., New Britain Museum of American Art, Butler Art Inst., New York Public Library, and Univs of Minnesota, Southern Mississippi, Brown, Oregon, Connecticut. *Publications include:* non-fiction: Colonial Americans (19 vols) 1964–76, Ellis Island 1986, Look Around 1987, The Tower of London 1987, Galileo 1992, Tracks Across America 1992, Stars and Stripes 1993, Marie Curie 1994, Moses 1995, Gandhi 1995, Niagara Falls 1996, Anasazi 1997; fiction: Death of Evening Star 1972, Across the Sea from Galway 1975, Sailboat Lost 1991, Cyclops 1991, Kinderdike 1994, William Tell 1996, The Jetty Chronicles 1997, Gods and Goddesses of the Ancient Maya 2000, Sky, Sea, the Jetty and Me 2001, Gods and Goddesses of the Ancient Norse 2001; illustrator of around 160 books by other authors. *Honours:* hon. degree (Paier Coll. of Art); Premio Grafico Fiera di Bologno (Italy) 1968, Univ. of Southern Mississippi Medallion 1979, Christopher Medal 1980, Nat. Jewish Book Award for Children's Literature 1981, Children's Book Guild Washington Post Non-Fiction Award 1989, Catholic Library Asscn Regina Medal 1991,

Univ. of Minnesota Kerlan Award 1991, American Library Asscn Arbuthnot Honour Lecture Citation 1994. *Literary Agent:* c/o William B. R. Reiss, John Hawkins and Associates, New York, NY 10010, USA. *Address:* 7 Twin Bridge Acres Road, Westport, CT 06880 (home); c/o Cavalier Galleries, 405 Greenwich Avenue, Greenwich, CT 06830, USA. *Telephone:* (203) 227-0133 (home). *Fax:* (203) 227-0133 (home). *E-mail:* l.e.fisher@sbcglobal.net (home).

FISHER, Roy, BA, MA, FRSL; British poet and musician; b. 11 June 1930, Birmingham, England. *Education:* Univ. of Birmingham. *Career:* mem. Musicians' Union, Soc. of Authors. *Publications:* City 1961, Interiors 1966, The Ship's Orchestra 1967, The Memorial Fountain 1968, Matrix 1971, The Cut Pages 1971, Metamorphoses 1971, The Thing About Joe Sullivan 1978, A Furnace 1986, The Left-Handed Punch 1987, Poems 1955–1987 1988, Birmingham River 1994, The Dow Low Drop: New and Selected Poems 1996, Interviews Through Time 2000, The Long and the Short of It: Poems 1955–2005 2005; contrib. to numerous journals and magazines. *Honours:* Hon. Poet of the City of Birmingham 2003; Hon. DLitt (Keele) 1999; Andrew Kelus Prize 1979, Cholmondeley Award 1981, Hamlyn Award 1997;. *Address:* Four Ways, Earl Sterndale, Buxton, Derbyshire SK17 0EP, England. *Telephone:* (1298) 83279 (home). *E-mail:* fourways.ear@virgin.net.

FISHKIN, Shelley Fisher, BA, MA, MPhil, PhD; American academic, writer and editor; b. 9 May 1950, New York, NY; m. James Steven Fishkin 1973, two s. *Education:* Swarthmore Coll., Yale Univ. *Career:* Visiting Lecturer, Yale University, 1981–84; Senior Lecturer, 1985–89, Assoc. Prof., 1989–92, Prof. of American Studies, 1993–, Prof. of American Studies and English, 1994–, University of Texas at Austin; Assoc. Ed., American National Biography, 1989–; mem. American Literature Asscn; American Studies Asscn; Authors' Guild; Charlotte Perkins Gilman Society, co-founder and exec. dir, 1990–; International Theodore Dreiser Society; Mark Twain Circle of America, pres., 1997–; MLA; Research Society for American Periodicals, board of dirs, 1991–94. *Publications:* From Fact to Fiction: Journalism and Imaginative Writing in America, 1985; Was Huck Black?: Mark Twain and African-American Voices, 1993; Listening to Silences: New Essays in Feminist Criticism (ed. with Elaine Hedges), 1994; The Oxford Mark Twain (ed.), 29 vols, 1996; Lighting Out for the Territory: Reflections on Mark Twain and American Culture, 1997. Contributions: Books, journals, newspapers and periodicals. *Honours:* Mellon Fellow, 1979, Rockefeller Humanist Fellow, 1984, Aspen Institute; Frank Luther Mott-Kappa Tau Alpha Research Book Award, National Journalism Scholarship Society, 1986; ACLS Fellowship, 1987–88; Humanities Scholar, Connecticut Humanities Council, 1987, 1989–91; Visiting Fellow, 1992–93; Life Mem., 1993–, Clare Hall, Cambridge; Outstanding Academic Book Citation, Choice, 1994.

FISHLOCK, Trevor; British journalist and writer; b. 21 Feb. 1941, Hereford, England; m. Penelope Symon 1978. *Career:* Portsmouth Evening News 1957–62; freelance news agency reporter 1962–68; staff correspondent, Wales and W England 1968–77, South Asia correspondent 1980–83, New York correspondent 1983–86, Times; roving foreign correspondent 1986–89, 1993–96, Moscow correspondent 1989–91, Daily Telegraph; roving foreign correspondent, Sunday Telegraph 1991–93; mem. Travellers' Club, Soc. of Authors, World Press Inst. *Publications:* Wales and the Welsh 1972, Discovering Britain: Wales 1975, Talking of Wales 1975, Americans and Nothing Else 1980, India File 1983, The State of America 1986, Indira Gandhi (juvenile) 1986, Out of Red Darkness 1992, My Foreign Country 1997, Wild Tracks 1998, Cobra Road 1999, More Wild Tracks 2000, Fishlock's Sea Stories 2003, Conquerors of Time: Exploration and Invention in the Age of Daring 2004, More Fishlock's Sea Stories 2005. *Honours:* David Holden Award for Foreign Reporting 1983, Int. Reporter of the Year 1986, British Press Awards. *Address:* 7 Teilo Street, Pontcanna, Cardiff CF11 9JN, Wales.

FISHMAN, Charles Munroe, (Charles Adés Fishman), BA, MA, DA; American academic, poet and writer; b. 10 July 1942, Oceanside, NY; s. of Morris (Murray) Fishman and Naomi (Toby) Ades; m. Ellen Marci Haselkorn 1967; two d. *Education:* Hofstra Univ., Stony Brook Univ., State Univ. of NY (SUNY) at Albany. *Career:* Founder-Dir Visiting Writers Program, SUNY at Farmingdale 1979–97, Distinguished Service Prof. 1989–, Prof. Emeritus 1997–, Founder-Dir Distinguished Speakers Program 2001–07; Founder-Ed. Xanadu 1975–78; Poetry Ed. Gaia 1993–95; Cistercian Studies Quarterly 1998–99, Journal of Genocide Research 1999; Assoc. Ed. The Drunken Boat 1999–2005; Poetry Ed. New Works Review 2003–; past mem. Associated Writing Programs, Authors' Guild, Poetry Soc. of America, Poets and Writers; mem. Bd Walt Whitman Birthplace Asscn 2007–. *Publications:* An Index to Women's Magazines and Presses (ed.) 1977, Mortal Companions 1977, The Death Mazurka 1987, Zoom 1990, Catlives (by Sarah Kirsch; trans. with Marina Roscher) 1991, Blood to Remember: American Poets on the Holocaust (ed.) 1991, (revised edn) 2007, As the Sun Goes Down in Fire 1992, Nineteenth-Century Rain 1994, The Firewalkers 1996, An Aztec Memory 1997, Time Travel Reports 2002, Country of Memory 2004, 5,000 Bells 2004, Chopin's Piano 2006; contrib. to many anthologies and over 300 periodicals. *Honours:* Poetry Soc. of America Gertrude B. Claytor Memorial Award 1987, American Library Asscn Outstanding Academic Book of the Year 1989, New York State/United Univ. Professions Excellence Award 1990, New England Poetry Club Firman Houghton Poetry Award 1995, New York Foundation for the Arts Fellowship in Poetry 1995, winner, Anabiosis Press Chapbook Competition 1996, Southern California Anthology Ann Stanford Poetry Prize 1996, Eve of St Agnes Poetry Prize 1999, George M. Estabrook Award for Distinguished Service 2000, Harvard School of Educ.'s Applaud an Educator

Award 2005, Long Island Poet of the Year 2006. *Address:* Horton Hall, Farmingdale State College, Farmingdale, NY 11735, USA (office). *Telephone:* (631) 420-2687 (office). *Fax:* (631) 420-2753 (office). *E-mail:* carolus@optonline.net (office). *Website:* www.charlesfishman.com.

FISK, Pauline; British writer; b. 27 Sept. 1948, London, England; m. David Davies 1972; two s. three d. *Publications:* Midnight Blue 1990, Telling the Sea 1992, Tyger Pool 1994, Beast of Whixall Moss 1997, The Candle House 1999, Sabrina Fludde 2001, The Red Judge 2005, The Mrs Morridge Project 2005; contribs to Homes and Gardens 1989 and anthologies, including Something to Do With Love 1996, Heading Out 2003, Hubble Bubble 2003, Love, Hate and My Best Mate 2004. *Honours:* Smarties Grand Prix Prize 1990. *Address:* c/o Laura Cecil, 17 Alwyne Villas, London, N1 2HG, England.

FITZGERALD, Frances; American writer; b. 1940, d. of Desmond Fitzgerald and Marietta Peabody Fitzgerald Tree. *Education:* Radcliffe Coll. *Career:* author of series of profiles for Herald Tribune magazine; freelance author of series of profiles, Vietnam 1966; frequent contrib. to The New Yorker; Vice-Pres. PEN; mem. Editorial Bds The Nation, Foreign Policy. *Publications include:* Fire in the Lake – The Vietnamese and the Americans in Vietnam (Pulitzer Prize 1973, Nat. Book Award 1973) 1972, America Revised – History Schoolbooks in the Twentieth Century 1979, Cities on a Hill – A Journey Through Contemporary American Cultures 1986, Way Out There in the Blue – Reagan, Star Wars and the End of the Cold War (New York Times Ed.'s Choice, New York Public Library Helen Bernstein Award) 2000; contribs to The New York Review of Books, The New York Times Magazine, Esquire, Architectural Digest, Islands, Rolling Stone. *Honours:* Overseas Press Club Award 1967, Nat. Inst. of Arts and Letters Award 1973, Sydney Hillman Award 1973, George Polk Award 1973, Bancroft Award for History 1973. *Address:* c/o Simon and Schuster Inc., 1230 Avenue of the Americas, New York, NY 10020, USA.

FITZGERALD, Judith Ariana, MA, PhD; Canadian poet, columnist and academic; b. 11 Nov. 1952, Toronto, Ont. *Education:* York Univ., Ont. and Univ. of Toronto. *Career:* teacher, Erindale Coll. 1978–81; Asst Prof., Laurentian Univ., Ont. 1981–83; Poetry Ed. Black Moss Press 1981–87; entertainment reporter, The Globe 1983–84; critic, The Toronto Star 1984–88, columnist 1987, 1992–93, 1997–99; Ed. Countrywave 1995–1996; creator and Sr Writer, Today's Country 1992–1998; numerous writer-in-residencies; juror, Gov.-Gen.'s Poetry Award 1998. *Publications:* poetry: City Park 1972, Journal Entries 1975, Victory 1975, Lacerating Heartwood 1977, Easy Over: Poems 1981, Un Dozen: thirteen Canadian Poets (ed.) 1982, Split/Level 1983, Heart Attacks 1984, Beneath the Skin of Paradise: The Piaf Poems 1984, My Orange Gorange (juvenile) 1985, Given Names: New and Selected Poems, 1972–1985 (Writers' Choice Award 1986) 1985, Whale Waddleby (juvenile) 1986, SP/ELLES: Poetry by Canadian Women/Poésie de femmes canadiennes (ed.) 1986, Diary of Desire 1987, First Person Plural (ed.) 1987, Rapturous Chronicles 1991, Ultimate Midnight 1992, Habit of Blues: Rapturous Chronicles II 1993, Walkin' Wounded 1993, River 1995, AKA Paradise 1996, Building a Mystery: the Story of Sarah McLachlan and Lilith Fair 1997, Twenty-Six Ways Out of This World 1999, Sarah McLachlan: Building a Mystery 2000, Adagios 2000, Marshall McLuhan: Wise Guy 2001, Book One of the Adagios Quartet: Iphigenia's Song 2003, Book Two of the Adagios Quartet: Orestes' Lament 2004, The Spirit of Indian Women 2005; criticism and poetry in anthologies, journals and newspapers. *Honours:* Canada Council Arts Grant A 1988, 1990, 1991, 1993, Professional Writers' Grant 2000, Fiona Mee Award 1983, Silver Medal, New York Int. Radio Festival 1995, 1996, 1997, Gold 1998. *Address:* PO Box 876 Sundridge, Ontario, P0A 1Z0, Canada. *Website:* www.judithfitzgerald.ca.

FITZGERALD, Niall, KBE, FRSA, BComm; Irish business executive; *Chairman, Reuters Group PLC;* b. 13 Sept. 1945; m.; two s. two d. *Education:* Univ. Coll., Dublin. *Career:* joined Unilever 1967, various man. roles including CEO, Unilever Food Div., S Africa, early 1980s, later Treasurer, Unilever, London, Dir Unilever PLC and Unilever NV 1987–2004, Financial Dir 1987–89, Co-ordinator, Edible Fats and Dairy 1989–90, mem. Foods Exec. 1989–91, Co-ordinator, Detergents 1991–95, Vice-Pres. Unilever PLC 1994–96, Chair. 1996–2004, also becoming Vice-Chair. Unilever NV 1996–2004; Dir Reuters Group 2003–, Chair. 2004–; Pres. Advertising Asscn, S Africa Int. Investment Advisory Council, Shanghai Major's Int. Business Leaders' Council; Vice-Chair. The Conf. Bd; mem. World Econ. Forum, Int. Advisory Bd, Council on Foreign Relations, Trilateral Comm., EU–China Cttee, US Business Council; Gov. Nat. Inst. of Econ. and Social Research; Trustee, Leverhulme Trust; fmr Dir Merck, Ericsson, Bank of Ireland, Prudential Corpn. *Address:* Reuters Group PLC, Reuters Building, Canary Wharf, London, E14 5EP, England (office). *Telephone:* (20) 7250-1122 (office). *Fax:* (20) 7542-4064 (office). *Website:* www.reuters.com (office).

FITZMAURICE, Gabriel John; Irish teacher and poet; *Principal Teacher, Moyvane National School;* b. 7 Dec. 1952, Moyvane, Co. Kerry; m. Brenda Downey 1981; one s. one d. *Education:* St Michael's Coll., Listowel, Co. Kerry, Mary Immaculate Coll., Limerick. *Career:* Asst Teacher, Avoca Nat. School, Co. Wicklow 1972–74; Teacher, Christ the King Nat. School, Limerick City 1974–75; Prin. Teacher, Moyvane Nat. School, Co. Kerry 1975–; represented Ireland, Europees Poeziefestival, Leuven, Belgium 1987, 1991. *Publications:* Poetry in English: Rainsong 1984, Road to the Horizon 1987, Dancing Through 1990, The Father's Part 1992, The Space Between: New and Selected Poems 1984–92 1993, The Village Sings 1996, A Wrenboy's Carnival: Poems

1980–2000 2000, I and the Village 2002, The Boghole Boys 2005. Poetry in Irish: Nocht 1989, Ag Síobhsíul Chun An Rince 1995, Giolla na nAmhrán: Dánta 1988–1998 1998. Essays: Kerry on My Mind 1999; other: Children's poetry in English and Irish; translator: The Purge, by Mícheál Ó hAirtnéide 1989, Poems I Wish I'd Written 1996, Poems from the Irish: Collected Translations 2004. Editor: The Flowering Tree 1991, Between the Hills and Sea: Songs and Ballads of Kerry 1991, Con Greaney: Traditional Singer 1991, Homecoming/An Bealach 'na Bhaile: Selected Poems of Cathal Ó Searcaigh (Cló Iar-Chonnacnta 1993, Irish Poetry Now: Other Voices 1993, Kerry Through Its Writers 1993, The Listowel Literary Phenomenon: North Kerry Writers – A Critical Introduction 1994, Rusty Nails and Astronauts: A Wolfhound Poetry Anthology 1999, 'The Boro' and 'The Cross': The Parish of Moyvane-Knockanure (with Áine Cronin and John Looney) 2000, The Kerry Anthology 2000, Come and Good Men and True 2004, The Woold of Bryan Mac Mahon 2005; contribs to newspapers, reviews, and journals. *Honours:* Award Winner, Gerard Manley Hopkins Centenary Poetry Competition 1989. *Address:* Applegarth, Moyvane, Co. Kerry, Ireland (home).

FITZSIMMONS, Thomas, BA, MA; American poet, writer, translator, editor and publisher and academic; *Professor Emeritus of English and Comparative Literature, Oakland University;* b. 21 Oct. 1926, Lowell, Mass; m. Karen Hargreaves; two s. *Education:* Fresno State Coll., Sorbonne and Institut de Sciences Politiques, Paris, Stanford Univ., Calif., Columbia Univ., New York. *Career:* writer and Ed. The New Republic magazine 1952–55; research team Chair. 1955–56, Dir of Research for Publ. 1956–58, Dir and Ed. 1958–59, HRAF Press, Yale Univ.; Asst Prof., Oakland Univ., Rochester, Mich. 1959–61, Assoc. Prof. 1961–66, Prof. of English and Comparative Literature 1966–89, Prof. Emer. 1989–; Fulbright Lecturer, Tokyo Univ. of Educ. 1962–64, Tsuda Univ., Tokyo 1962–64, Univ. of Bucharest 1967–68, Univ. of Nice 1968; Visiting Lecturer, Japan Nat. Women's Univ., Tokyo 1973–75, Keio Univ., Tokyo 1973–75, Detroit Inst. of Arts 1986; Visiting Prof., Tokyo Univ. of Educ. 1973–75, Kyushu Nat. Univ., Fukuoka 1979; Visiting Poet and Scholar, Sophia Univ., Tokyo 1988–89; Ed.-Publr Katydid Books. *Publications:* poetry: This Time This Place 1969, Mooning 1971, Meditation Seeds 1971, With the Water 1972, Playseeds 1973, The Big Huge 1975, The Nine Seas and the Eight Mountains 1981, Rocking Mirror Daybreak 1982, Water Ground Stone (poems and essays) 1994, The Dream Machine 1996, Fencing the Sky 1998, Iron Harp 1999, Build Me Ruins 2002, Is Two :: Becomes One 2005; other: author, ed. or trans. of more than 60 vols 1955–2004. *Honours:* Nat. Endowment for the Arts Fellowships 1967, 1982, 1989–90, and Grants 1984, 1986, Oakland Univ. Research Fellowship 1982, Japan-US Friendship Foundation Grant 1983, Michigan Council for the Arts Award 1986, Fulbright Research Fellowship, Japan 1988–89. *Address:* 1 Balsa Road, Santa Fe, NM 87508, USA. *Website:* www.katydidbooks.com.

FITZSIMONS, Sheila, BA, PGCE; British editor; *Executive Editor, The Guardian. Education:* Coloma Convent School, Somerville Coll., Oxford and Worcester Coll. of Higher Education. *Career:* economics and business studies teacher 1984–90; Deputy Ed. of Education, The Guardian 1990–92, Ed. of Education 1992–94, Asst News Ed. 1994–96; Business News Ed., The Observer 1996–98; special projects and editorial development, The Guardian 1998–99, Exec. Ed. 1999–. *Address:* Guardian Newspapers Ltd, 119 Farringdon Road, London, EC1R 3ER, England (office). *Website:* www .guardian.co.uk.

FLAGG, Fannie; American writer and actress; b. 21 Sept. 1941, Birmingham, AL. *Education:* Univ. of Alabama, Pittsburgh Playhouse, Town and Gown Theatre. *Career:* fmr television news anchor; fmr co-host 'Candid Camera'. *Films include:* Five Easy Pieces 1970, Some of My Best Friends Are 1971, Stay Hungry 1976, Grease 1978, Rabbit Test 1978, My Best Friend is a Vampire 1988, Crazy in Alabama 1999. *Television appearances include:* The New Dick Van Dyke Show 1971–73, The New Original Wonder Woman 1975, Sex and the Married Woman 1977, Harper Valley P.T.A. 1981. *Theatre includes:* Patio Porch, Come Back to the Five and Dime, Jimmy Dean, Jimmy Dean, The Best Little Whorehouse in Texas. *Publications:* Daisy Fay and the Miracle Man, Coming Attractions: A Wonderful Novel 1981, Fried Green Tomatoes at the Whistle Stop Cafe (also screenplay, with Jon Avnet) 1987, Welcome to the World, Baby Girl! 1988, Standing in the Rainbow 2002, A Redbird Christmas 2004, Can't Wait to Get to Heaven 2006; contrib. to magazines and newspapers. *Address:* c/o Random House Inc., 201 E 50th Street, New York, NY 10022, USA.

FLAM, Jack Donald, BA, MA, PhD; American academic and writer; *Distinguished Professor of Art and Art History, Brooklyn College, CUNY;* b. 2 April 1940, Paterson, NJ; m. Bonnie Burnham 1972; one d. *Education:* Rutgers Univ., Columbia Univ., New York Univ. *Career:* Instructor in Art, Newark Coll. of Arts and Sciences, Rutgers Univ. 1962–66; Asst Prof. of Art 1966–69, Assoc. Prof. of Art 1969–72, Univ. of Florida; Assoc. Prof. of Art 1975–79, Prof. of Art 1980–91, Distinguished Prof. of Art 1991–, Brooklyn Coll., CUNY; Assoc. Prof. of Art History 1979–80, Prof. of Art History 1980–91, Distinguished Prof. of Art History 1991–, Grad. School and Univ. Center, CUNY; art critic, The Wall Street Journal 1984–92; mem. Int. Asscn of Art Critics, PEN. *Publications:* Matisse on Art 1973, Zoltan Gorency 1974, Bread and Butter 1977, Henri Matisse Paper Cut-Outs (co-author) 1977, Robert Motherwell (co-author) 1983, Matisse: The Man and His Art 1869–1918 1986, Fernand Léger 1987, Matisse: A Retrospective 1988, Motherwell 1991, Richard Diebenkorn: Ocean Park 1992, Matisse: The Dance 1993, Western Artists/African Art 1994, The Paine Webber Art Collection (co-author) 1995,

Robert Smithson: The Collected Writings (ed.) 1996, Judith Rotheschild an Artist's Search 1998, Les Peintures de Picasso: Un Théâtre Mentale 1998, The Modern Drawing 1999, Matisse and Picasso: The Story of Their Rivalry and Friendship 2003, Primitivism and Twentieth-Century Art: A Documentary History 2003, Matisse, his Art and his Textiles (co-author) 2004, Matisse–Derain, Collioure 1905, un été fauve (co-author) 2005, Matisse in Transition: Around Laurette 2006, Hungarian Fauves: From Paris to Nagybáná (co-author) 2006; contrib. to Apollo, Art in America, Art News, New York Review of Books. *Honours:* Guggenheim Fellowship 1979–80, Nat. Endowment for the Humanities Fellowship 1987–88. *Address:* c/o Georges Borchardt Inc., 136 E 57th Street, New York, NY 10022, USA.

FLAMMARION, Charles-Henri, LèsL, LèsLet, MBA; French publishing executive; b. 27 July 1946, Boulogne-Billancourt; s. of the late Henri Flammarion and of Pierrette Chenelot; m. Marie-Françoise Mariani 1968; one s. two d. *Education:* Lycée de Sèvres, Sorbonne, Paris, Institut d'Etudes Politiques, Paris and Columbia Univ., USA. *Career:* Asst Man. Editions Flammarion 1972–81, Gen. Man. 1981–85, Pres. Flammarion SA 1985–; Pres. Editions J'ai Lu 1982–, Audie-Fluide Glacial 1990–; mem. Bureau du Syndicat Nat. de l'Édition 1978–88, 1996–; Vice-Pres. Cercle de la Librairie 1988–94, Pres. 1994–2003; Pres. Casterman 1999–. *Address:* Flammarion SA, 26 rue Racine, 75006 Paris (office); 5 avenue Franco-Russe, 75007 Paris, France (home).

FLANAGAN, Mary, BA, MA; American novelist and critic; b. 20 May 1943, Rochester, NH. *Education:* Brandeis Univ., Waltham. *Career:* creative writing seminars (two terms), Univ. of East Anglia, England; mem. PEN, Society of Authors. *Publications:* Bad Girls, 1984; Trust, 1987; Rose Reason, 1991; The Blue Woman, 1994; Adèle, 1997.

FLANAGAN, Richard; Australian writer and film director; b. 1961, Tasmania. *Education:* Univ. of Oxford, UK. *Career:* fmr river guide; scriptwriter, author of history books, novelist. *Film:* The Sound of One Hand Clapping (dir). *Publications include:* non-fiction: A Terrible Beauty: A History of the Gordon River County, Codename Iago: The Story of John Friedrich, Parish-Fed Bastards: A History of the Politics of the Unemployed in Britain 1884–1939 1994; novels: Death of a River Guide (Victorian Premier's Award for Fiction) 1995, The Sound of One Hand Clapping 1998, Gould's Book of Fish (Commonwealth Writer's Prize) 2002, The Unknown Terrorist 2007. *Honours:* Rhodes Scholar. *Address:* Atlantic Books, Ormond House, 26–27 Boswell Street, London, WC1N 3JZ, England (office).

FLANAGIN, Annette, RN, MA; American; *Managing Senior Editor, Journal of the American Medical Association. Education:* Georgetown Univ., Washington DC. *Career:* fmr pres., Council of Science Eds; Managing Sr Ed., Journal of the American Medical Asscn; Distinguished Lecturer Sigma Theta Tau Int. 1994–2001, Distinguished Writer 1998–2001, 2004–; Fellow American Acad. of Nursing; mem. Council of Science Eds 1989–. *Publications:* AMA Manual of Style (co-author), 9th edn 1998; over 60 articles. *Honours:* Frances Larsen Memorial Award for Excellence in Medical Writing AMWA 1994. *Address:* Journal of the American Medical Association (JAMA), 515 North State Street, Chicago, IL 60610, USA. *Telephone:* (342) 464-2432. *E-mail:* annette_flanagin@ama-assn.org. *Website:* jama.ama-assn.org.

FLEISCHER, Ezra; Israeli poet and academic; *Professor of Medieval Hebrew Poetry, Hebrew University of Jerusalem;* b. 7 Aug. 1928, Romania; m. Anat Rappaport 1955; one s. one d. *Education:* Univ. of Bucharest and Hebrew Univ., Jerusalem. *Career:* political prisoner in Romania 1952–55; emigrated to Israel 1960; Dir Geniza Research Inst. for Hebrew Poetry, Israel Nat. Acad. of Sciences and Humanities 1967–; Prof. of Medieval Hebrew Poetry, Hebrew Univ. of Jerusalem 1973–; mem. Israel Acad. of Sciences and Humanities 1984–; Corresp. Fellow, American Acad. for Jewish Research; Pres. World Union of Jewish Studies 1989–93. *Publications:* poetry: Fables 1957, The Burden of Gog 1959, At Midnight 1961; research: The Poems of Shelomo Ha-Bavli 1973, The Pizmonim of Anonymus 1974, Hebrew Liturgical Poetry in the Middle Ages 1975, The Yozer, its Emergence and Development 1984, Eretz Israel Prayer and Prayer Rituals as Portrayed in the Geniza Documents 1988, The Proverbs of Sa'id Ben Bābshād 1990, The History of Hebrew Poetry in Muslim Spain (jtly) 1995, The History of Hebrew Poetry in Christian Spain and Southern France (jtly) 1997, Yehuda ha-Levi and his Circle (jtly) 2001; numerous articles in periodicals. *Honours:* Hon. DHL (Hebrew Union Coll., Jerusalem, Jewish Theological Seminary, New York); Israel Prize for Poetry 1959, Bialik Prize for Judaic Studies 1986, Rothschild Prize for Jewish Studies 1992. *Address:* Hebrew University of Jerusalem, Mount Scopus, 91905 Jerusalem; 14/8 Gelber Street, 96755 Jerusalem, Israel.

FLEISCHMAN, Paul, BA; American children's writer and poet; b. 5 Sept. 1952, Monterey, CA; m. Becky Mojica 1978, two s. *Education:* University of California at Berkeley, University of New Mexico. *Career:* mem. Authors' Guild; Society of Children's Book Writers. *Publications:* The Birthday Tree, 1979; The Half-a-Moon Inn, 1980; Graven Images, 1982; Path of the Pale Horse, 1983; Finzel the Farsighted, 1983; Coming-and-Going Men, 1985; I Am Phoenix: Poems for Two Voices, 1985; Rondo in C, 1988; Joyful Noise: Poems for Two Voices, 1989; Saturnalia, 1990; Shadow Play, 1990; The Borning Room, 1991; Time Train, 1991. *Honours:* Silver Medal, Commonwealth Club of California, 1980; Newberry Medals, American Library Asscn, 1983, 1989; Parents Choice Award, 1983; numerous citations by Society of Children's Book Writers, American Library Asscn, New York Times.

FLEISCHMAN, (Albert) Sidney, BA; American writer; b. 16 March 1920, New York, NY. *Education:* San Diego State Univ. *Publications:* 10 adult novels 1948–63, over 40 children's books 1962–. *Honours:* Newbery Award 1987. *Address:* 305 10th Street, Santa Monica, CA 90402, USA. *Website:* www .sidfleischman.com.

FLEISSNER, Robert F., (Archibald Harris), MA, PhD; American academic and writer; b. 17 Oct. 1932, Auburn, NY; m. Judith Gerber 1966 (divorced 1967). *Education:* Hamilton Coll., Cornell Univ., Catholic Univ. of America, Middlebury Coll., Univ. of North Carolina at Chapel Hill, Ohio State Univ., New York Univ. *Career:* Instructor in English, Speech and Drama, Spring Hill Coll., Mobile, AL 1958–59; Asst Instructor in English, Ohio State Univ. 1960–61; Lecturer in English, City Coll., CUNY 1962–64; Asst Prof. of English, Dominican Coll., Blauvelt, NY 1964–66; Instructor in English, Univ. of New Mexico, Albuquerque 1966–67; Asst Prof., then Assoc. Prof. of English, Central State Univ., Wilberforce, OH 1967–2005; mem. MLA of America, T. S. Eliot Soc., Shakespeare Asscn of America. *Publications:* Dickens and Shakespeare: A Study in Histrionic Contrasts 1969, Resolved to Love: The 1592 Edition of Henry Constable's 'Diana' Critically Considered 1980, The Prince and the Professor: The Wittenberg Connection in Marlowe, Shakespeare, Goethe and Frost – A Hamlet-Faust(us) Analogy 1986, Ascending the Prufrockian Stair: Studies in a Dissociated Sensibility 1988, A Rose by Another Name: A Survey of Literary Flora from Shakespeare to Eco 1989, Shakespeare and the Matter of the Crux 1991, T. S. Eliot and the Heritage of Africa 1992, Frost's Road Taken 1996, Sources, Meaning, and Influences of Coleridge's 'Kubla Khan' 2000, Names, Titles and Characters by Literary Writers: Shakespeare, 19th- and 20th-Century Authors 2001, The Master Sleuth on the Trail of 'Edwin Drood': Sherlock Holmes and the Jasper Syndrome (as Archibald W. Harris) 2001, Shakespearean and Other Literary Investigations with the Master Sleuth (and Conan Doyle): Homing in on Holmes 2003; Shakespeare and Africa: The Dark Lady of his Sonnets Revamped and Other Africa-Related Associations 2005; contrib. to books and journals. *Address:* 367 E Cassilly Street, Springfield, OH 45503, USA (home). *Telephone:* (937) 324-7533 (home).

FLEMING, Laurence William Howie; British author, artist and landscape designer; b. 8 Sept. 1929, Shillong, Assam, India. *Education:* The New School, Darjeeling, India, Repton School, Derbyshire, St Catharine's College, Cambridge. *Career:* Royal Air Force 1947–49; mem. International PEN; Writers Guild; Anglo-Brazilian Society. *Publications:* A Diet of Crumbs, 1959; The English Garden, 1979; The One Hour Garden, 1985; Old English Villages, 1986; Roberto Burle Marx: A Portrait, 1996. Contributions: journals.

FLETCHER, John Walter James, (Jonathan Fune), BA, MA, MPhil, PhD; British academic, writer and translator; *Professor Emeritus, University of East Anglia;* b. 23 June 1937, Barking, Essex, England; m. Beryl Sibley Connop 1961; two s. one d. *Education:* Univ. of Cambridge, Univ. of Toulouse. *Career:* Lecturer Univ. of Toulouse 1961–64, Univ. of Durham 1964–66; Lecturer in French 1966–68, Reader in French 1968–69, Prof. of Comparative Literature 1969–89, Prof. of European Literature 1989–98, Prof. Emeritus 1998–, Univ. of East Anglia; Hon. Sr Research Fellow Univ. of Kent at Canterbury 1997–; mem. Asscn of Univ. Teachers, Soc. of Authors, Translators' Asscn. *Publications:* The Novels of Samuel Beckett 1964, Samuel Beckett's Art 1967, A Critical Commentary on Flaubert's Trois Contes 1968, New Directions in Literature: Critical Approaches to a Contemporary Phenomenon 1968, Samuel Beckett: Fin de Partie (ed. with Beryl S. Fletcher) 1970, Samuel Beckett: His Works and his Critics, An Essay in Bibliography (with Raymond Federman) 1970, Beckett: A Study of his Plays (with John Spurling) 1972, Claude Simon and Fiction Now 1975, Novel and Reader 1980, Alain Robbe-Grillet 1983, The Nouveau Roman Reader (ed. with John Calder) 1986, Iris Murdoch: A Primary and Secondary Bibliography (with Cheryl Bove) 1994, Faber Critical Guide: Samuel Beckett 2000, About Beckett: The Playwright and the Work 2003; contrib. to scholarly journals, newspapers and periodicals. *Honours:* Scott Moncrieff Prize 1990, hon. mention Florence Gould Foundation Trans. Prize 1990. *Address:* SECL, University of Kent, Canterbury, CT2 7NF, England (office). *Telephone:* (1227) 827121 (office). *Fax:* (1227) 823641 (office). *E-mail:* j.w.j.fletcher@kent.ac.uk (office).

FLETCHER, Susan; British novelist; b. 1979, Birmingham. *Education:* Univ. of East Anglia. *Publication:* Eve Green (novel) (Whitbread First Novel Award 2004, Betty Trask Prize 2005) 2004, Oystercatchers 2007. *Literary Agent:* Curtis Brown Group Ltd, Haymarket House, 28–29 Haymarket, London, SW1Y 4SP, England. *Telephone:* (20) 7393-4400. *Fax:* (20) 7393-4401. *E-mail:* info@curtisbrown.co.uk. *Website:* www.curtisbrown.co.uk.

FLETT, Kathryn Alexandra; British journalist; b. 1 April 1964, Herts.; d. of Douglas J. Flett and Patricia Jenkins; two s. *Education:* Notting Hill and Ealing High School, Hammersmith and West London Coll., King's Coll. London. *Career:* staff writer, I-D magazine 1985–87; Fashion Ed., Features Ed. The Face magazine 1987–89; freelance contrib. to many int. publs including The Times, The Sunday Times, The Observer, The Guardian, The Face, Arena, Elle, Harpers Bazaar, etc. 1989–92; Contributing Ed. Arena Magazine 1991–92, Ed. 1992–95; Ed. Arena Homme Plus 1993–95; columnist (currently television critic) The Observer 1994–, Assoc. Ed. Observer Life 1995–98. *Publication:* The Heart-Shaped Bullet 1999. *Address:* c/o The Observer, 3–7 Herbal Hill, London, EC1R 5EJ, England (office). *E-mail:* kathryn.flett@observer.co.uk (office).

FLINT, James; British writer; b. 1968, Stratford-upon-Avon. *Education:* Univ. of East Anglia. *Career:* fmr ed., Wired UK and mute magazines, journalist for Daily Telegraph. *Publications:* novels: The Nuclear Train (short story), Mute 2 1995, Habitus 1998, 52 Ways to Magic America (Amazon.co.uk Bursary Award 2000) 2002, The Book of Ash 2004, Soft Apocalyse: Twelve Tales from the Turn of the Millennium 2004; contrib. short stories to collections, and to the Daily Telegraph and various magazines. *Address:* c/o Viking, 375 Hudson Street, New York, NY 10014, USA. *Website:* www .jamesflint.com.

FLINT, John (see Wells, Peter Frederick)

FLORA, Joseph Martin, BA, MA, PhD; American academic, writer and editor; *Atlanta Professor of Southern Culture, University of North Carolina, Chapel Hill;* b. 9 Feb. 1934, Toledo, OH; m. Glenda Christine Flora 1959; four s. *Education:* Univ. of Michigan. *Career:* Teaching Fellow to Instructor, Univ. of Michigan 1957–62; Instructor 1962–64, Asst Prof. 1964–66, Assoc. Prof. 1966–77, Prof. 1977–2001, Atlanta Prof. of Southern Culture 2001–, Univ. of North Carolina at Chapel Hill; Visiting Prof., Univ. of New Mexico 1976, 1996; Sr Ed. American Literature 1915–1945, Twayne Publishers 1989–; mem. American Literature Asscn, James Branch Cabell Soc., Hemingway Soc., MLA, Soc. for the Study of Southern Literature, South Atlantic MLA (pres. 1998–99), Thomas Wolfe Soc. (pres. 1995–97), Western Literature Asscn (pres. 1992). *Publications:* Vardis Fisher 1965, William Ernest Henley 1970, Frederick Manfred 1974, Southern Writers: A Biographical Dictionary (ed. with Robert Bain and Louis D. Rubin Jr) 1979, Hemingway's Nick Adams 1982, The English Short Story 1880–1945: A Critical History (ed.) 1985, Fifty Southern Writers After 1900 (ed. with Robert Bain) 1987, Fifty Southern Writers Before 1900 (ed. with Robert Bain) 1987, Ernest Hemingway: A Study of the Short Fiction 1989, Contemporary Fiction Writers of the South (ed. with Robert Bain) 1993, Contemporary Poets, Dramatists, Essayists, and Novelists of the South (ed. with Robert Bain) 1994, Rediscovering Vardis Fisher: Centennial Essays 2000, The Companion to Southern Literature (ed. with Lucinda MacKethan) 2002, Southern Writers (ed. with Amber Vogel) 2006; contrib. to books and journals. *Honours:* Kenan Research Award 1978, North Carolina Literary and Historical Asscn Mayflower Award 1982, Jules and Frances Landry Award 2006. *Address:* 505 Caswell Road, Chapel Hill, NC 27514, USA. *Telephone:* (919) 962-2503 (office); (919) 942-4902 (home). *Fax:* (919) 662-3520 (office). *E-mail:* jflora@email.unc.edu (office).

FLORENCE, Peter Kenrick, MBE; British; *Director, The Hay Festival.* *Career:* co-founder and Dir of literary festival, The Guardian Hay Festival 1988–. *Address:* Hay Festival, The Drill Hall, 25 Lion Street, Hay-on-Wye, HR3 5AD, England. *Website:* www.hayfestival.com.

FLUSFEDER, David, BA, MA; American writer; b. Nov. 1960, Summit, NJ; m. Susan Swift 1990; one s. one d. *Education:* Sussex Univ., Univ. of East Anglia. *Publications:* novels: Man Kills Woman, 1993; Like Plastic, 1996; Morocco, 2000; The Gift, 2003; contribs to short stories in anthologies, incl. New Writing 8, Fatherhood, The Agony and the Ecstasy; magazines and newspapers incl. Erotic Review, Arena, Esquire, Jewish Quarterly, The Times, Guardian, TLS, GQ, Frankfurter Allgemeine Zeitung, Literaturen, Jewish Chronicle, Daily Telegraph. *Honours:* Encore Award 1997. *Address:* c/o Fourth Estate, 77–85 Fulham Palace Road, London, W6 8JB, England.

FLYNN, Robert Lopez; American academic and writer; b. 12 April 1932, Chillicothe, TX; m. Jean Sorrels 1953; two d. *Career:* Asst Prof. Baylor Univ., Waco, TX 1959–63; Novelist-in-Residence, Trinity Univ., San Antonio, TX 1963–2001. *Publications:* North to Yesterday 1967, In the House of the Lord 1969, The Sounds of Rescue, The Signs of Hope 1970, Seasonal Rain and Other Stories 1986, Wanderer Springs 1987, A Personal War in Vietnam 1989, When I Was Just Your Age 1992, The Last Klick 1994, Living with the Hyenas 1996, The Devil's Tiger 2000, Tie-Fast Country 2001, Growing Up a Sullen Baptist, and Other Lies 2001, Slouching Toward Zion, and Other Lies 2004. *Address:* 101 Cliffside Drive, San Antonio, TX 78231, USA.

FO, Dario; Italian playwright, clown, actor and painter; b. 24 March 1926, San Giano; m. Franca Rame 1954; one c. *Education:* Acad. of Fine Arts, Milan. *Career:* comedian, Teatro di Rivista; co-founder theatre groups, Fo-Rame Co. 1957–68, Associazione Nuova Scena 1968–69, Collettivo Teatrale la Comune 1970–; cand. for Mayor of Milan 2006. *Film scripts:* Lo Svitato 1956, Musica per vecchi animali 1989. *Plays include:* Il dito nell'occhio (with Franco Parenti and Giustino Durano) 1953, I sani da legare (with Parenti and Durano) 1954, Ladri, manichini e donne nude 1957, Comica finale 1958, Gli arcangeli non giocano a flipper 1959, La storia vera di Piero d'Angera, che alla crociata non c'era 1960, Aveva due pistole con gli occhi bianchi e neri 1960, Chi ruba un piede è fortunato in amore 1961, Isabella, tre caravelle e un cacciaballe 1963, Settimo: ruba un po' meno 1964, La colpa è sempre del diavolo 1965, La signora è da buttare 1967, Grande pantomima per pupazzi piccoli, grandi e medi 1968, L'operaio conosce 300 parole, il padrone 1000, per questo lui è il padrone 1969, Legami pure, tanto spacco tutto lo stesso 1969, Il funeral e del padrone 1969, Mistero buffo 1969, Morte accidentale di un anarchico 1970, Fedayin 1971, Basta con i fascisti 1973, Ci ragiono e canto N.3 1973, Guerra di popolo in Cile 1973, Non si paga, non si paga! 1974, Fanfani rapito 1975, La marijuana della mamma è la più bella 1975, Tutta casa, letto e chiesa 1977, La tragedia di Aldo Moro 1979, Storia della tigre e altre storie 1979, Una madre (with Franca Rame) 1981, Clacson, trombette e pernacchi 1981, L'Opera dello sghignazzo 1982, Il fabulazzo osceno 1982, Coppia aperta 1982, Patapunfete 1983, Quasi per caso una donna: Elisabetta 1983, Dio li fa poi li accoppa 1983,

Lisistrata romana 1983, Hellequin, Harlekin, Arlecchino 1985, Diario di Eva 1985, Parti femminili (with Franca Rame) 1986, Il ratto della Francesca 1986, La rava e la fava (aka La parte del leone) 1987, Lettera dalla Cina 1989, Il braccato 1989, Il papa e la strega 1989, Zitti! Stiamo precipitando! 1990, Johan Padan a la descoverta de le Americhe 1991, Parliamo di donne (two one-act pieces, L'Eroina and Grassa è bello) 1991, Settimo: ruba un po' meno! n. 2 1992, Dario Fo incontra Ruzzante 1993, Mamma! I sanculotti! 1993, Un palcoscenico per le donne 1994, Sesso? Grazie, tanto per gradire! 1994, Bibbia dei villani 1996, Il diavolo con le zinne 1996, Lu Santo Jullare Francesco 1999, My First Seven Years (Plus a Few More) (memoir) 2005, L'Anomalo Bicefalo (on the Premier Silvio Berlusconi) 2006. *Radio:* Poer Nano 1950, Chicchirichì, Cocoricò, Ragazzi in Gamba, Non si vive di solo pane 1951. *Television:* Canzonissima 1962, Il teatro di Dario Fo 1976, Buona sera con Franca Rame 1980, Trasmissione forzata 1987. *Honours:* Hon. DLitt (Westminster) 1997; Dr hc (Univ. La Sapienza, Rome) 2006; Univ. of Copenhagen Sonning Prize 1981, Associazione Torre Nat. Award Against Violence and the Camorra 1986, Obie Prize 1986, Campione d'Italia Agro Dolce Prize 1987, Nobel Prize for Literature 1997. *Address:* C. So di Porta Romana 132, 20122 Milan, Italy (office). *Telephone:* (02) 58430506 (office). *E-mail:* francarame@iol.it (office). *Website:* www.francarame.it (office).

FOER, Jonathan Safran; American writer; b. 1977, Washington, DC; m. Nicole Krauss. *Education:* Princeton Univ. *Publications:* A Convergence of Birds: Original Fiction and Poetry Inspired by the Work of Joseph Cornell (ed.) 2001, 2006, Everything is Illuminated (novel) 2002, Amelia Bedelia, Bookworm 2003, I'm OK 2004, The Future Dictionary of America (with Dave Eggers and Nicole Krauss) 2004, Extremely Loud and Incredibly Close 2005; contrib. to Paris Review, Conjunctions, New Yorker. *Honours:* Zoetrope: All Story Fiction Prize 2000, Nat. Jewish Book Award, Guardian First Book Award 2002. *Literary Agent:* The Marsh Agency, 11 Dover Street, London, W1S 4LJ, England. *Telephone:* (20) 7399-2800. *Fax:* (20) 7399-2801. *Website:* www.marsh-agency.co.uk. *Address:* c/o Houghton Mifflin Co, Trade Division, Adult Editorial, Eighth Floor, 222 Berkeley Street, Boston, MA 02116-3764, USA.

FOERSTER, Richard Alfons, BA, MA; American editor, writer and poet; b. 29 Oct. 1949, New York, NY; s. of Alfons Foerster and Elizabeth Foerster; m. Valerie Elizabeth Malinowski 1972 (divorced 1985). *Education:* Fordham Univ., Univ. of Virginia, Manhattanville Coll. *Career:* Asst Ed., Clarence L. Barnhart Inc. 1973–75; Ed., Prentice Hall Inc. 1976–78; Assoc. Ed. 1978–94, Ed. 1994–2001, Chelsea Magazine; Hobart City Int. Writer-in-Residence 2002; Ed., Chautauqua Literary Journal 2003–; mem. Acad. of American Poets, Maine Writers and Publishers Alliance, Poetry Soc. of America, Soc. for the Arts, Religion and Contemporary Culture, PEN, Poets' Prize Cttee, Book Critics Circle. *Publications:* Transfigured Nights 1990, Sudden Harbor 1992, Patterns of Descent 1993, Trillium 1998, Double Going 2002, The Burning of Troy 2006; contrib. to Best American Poetry, Boulevard, Epoch, Kenyon Review, Nation, New Criterion, Paris Review, Poetry, Shenandoah, Southern Review, Southwest Review, Tri-Quarterly. *Honours:* Discovery/The Nation Award 1985, Bess Hokin Prize 1992, Hawthornden Fellow 1993, NEA Creative Writing Fellowship 1995, Maine Arts Commission Individual Artist Fellowship 1997, Amy Lowell Poetry Travelling Scholarship 2000–01. *Address:* PO Box 1040, York Beach, ME 03910, USA.

FOGEL, Robert William, PhD, FAAS; American historian, academic, economist and biodemographer; *Charles R. Walgreen Distinguished Service Professor and Director, Center for Population Economics, University of Chicago;* b. 1 July 1926, New York, NY; s. of Harry Gregory and Elizabeth (Mitnik) Fogel; m. Enid Cassandra Morgan 1949; two s. *Education:* Cornell, Columbia, Cambridge, Harvard and Johns Hopkins Univs. *Career:* Instructor, Johns Hopkins Univ. 1958–59; Asst Prof., Univ. of Rochester 1960–64; Assoc. Prof., Univ. of Chicago 1964–65, Prof. of Economics 1965–75, Prof. of Economics and History 1970–75; Prof., Harvard Univ. 1975–81; Charles R. Walgreen Distinguished Service Prof. of American Insts, Univ. of Chicago 1981–, Dir Center for Population Econs 1981–; Chair. History Advisory Cttee of the Math. Social Science Bd 1965–72; Pres. Econ. History Asscn 1977–78; Social Science History Asscn 1980–81; American Econ. Asscn 1998; Nat. Bureau of Econ. Research Assoc.; Fellow Econ. Soc., American Acad. of Arts and Sciences, NAS, Royal Historical Soc., AAAS, American Philosophical Soc. *Publications:* The Union Pacific Railroad: A Case in Premature Enterprise 1960, Railroads and American History (co-author) 1971, The Dimensions of Quantitative Research in History (co-author) 1972, Time on the Cross: The Economics of American Negro Slavery (with S. L. Engerman) 1974, Ten Lectures on the New Economic History 1977, Which Road to the Past? Two Views of History (with G. R. Elton) 1983, Without Consent or Contract: The Rise and Fall of American Slavery (co-author), Vol. I 1989, Vols II–IV 1992, The Political Realignment of the 1850s: A Socioeconomic Analysis 1996, The Fourth Great Awakening and the Future of Egalitarianism 2000, The Escape from Hunger and Premature Death 1700–2100: Europe, America and the Third World 2004, The Slavery Debates 1952–1990: a retrospective 2003; contrib. to numerous books and scholarly journals. *Honours:* several hon. degrees, Nat. Science Foundation grants 1967, 1970, 1972, 1975, 1978, 1992–96, Fulbright Grant 1968; Arthur H. Cole Prize 1968, Schumpeter Prize 1971, Bancroft Prize in American History 1975, Gustavus Myers Prize 1990, shared Nobel Prize in Econs 1993. *Address:* Center for Population Economics, University of Chicago, Graduate School of Business, 5807 South Woodlawn Avenue, Chicago, IL 60637-1511 (office); 5321 S University Avenue, Chicago,

IL 60615, USA (home). *Telephone:* (773) 702-7709 (office). *Fax:* (773) 702-2901 (office). *E-mail:* rwf@cpe.uchicago.edu (office). *Website:* www.cpe.uchicago.edu (office); gsb.uchicago.edu (office).

FOIS, Marcello; Italian novelist and playwright; b. 1960, Nuoro, Sardinia; m.; two c. *Education:* Univ. of Bologna. *Television screenplays:* Distretto di Polizia (series) 2000–. *Film screenplays:* Ilaria Alpi – Il più crudele dei giorni 2002, Certi bambini 2004. *Plays:* L'ascesa degli angeli ribelli, Di profilo, Stazione, Terra di nessuno, Cinque favole sui bambini. *Publications:* Ferro Recente 1992, Picta (Premio Calvino) 1992, Meglio Morti 1993, Falso gotico nuorese 1993, Il silenzio abitato delle case 1996, Gente del libro 1996, Sheol 1997, Nulla (Premio Dessi) 1997, Sempre caro (Premio Scerbanenco) 1998, Gap 1999, Sangue dal cielo 1999, Radiofavole 1999, Sola andata 1999, Dura madre 2001, Piccole storie nere 2002, L'altro mondo 2002, Materiali 2002, Tamburini. Cantata per voce sola 2004. *Address:* c/o Vintage, 20 Vauxhall Bridge Road, London, SW1V 2SA, England.

FOLEY, John (Jack) Wayne Harold, BA, MA; American poet, writer, editor and broadcaster; b. 9 Aug. 1940, Neptune, NJ; m. Adelle Joan Abramowitz 1961, one s. *Education:* Cornell University, University of California, Berkeley. *Career:* Host, Exec. Producer in charge of Poetry Programme, KPFA-FM, Berkeley, CA, 1988–; Guest Ed., Poetry: San Francisco, 1988–89; Ed.-in-Chief, Poetry USA, Oakland, CA, 1990–95; Contributing Ed., Poetry Flash, 1992–; Resident Artist, Djerassi Program, 1994; Performs poetry with wife; mem. MLA; Poets and Writers; National Poetry Asscn; PEN, Oakland, CA, Programme Dir, 1990–97. *Publications:* Poetry: Letters/Lights – Words for Adelle, 1987; Gershwin, 1991; Adrift, 1993; Exiles, 1996; Bridget, 1997; New Poetry from California: Dead/Requiem (with Ivan Argüelles), 1998; Some Songs by Georges Brassens (trans.), 2002. Prose: Inciting Big Joy, monograph, 1993; O Her Blackness Sparkles! – The Life and Times of the Batman Art Gallery, San Francisco, 1960–63, 1995; O Powerful Western Star (criticism), 2000; Foley's Books (criticism), 2000; The 'Fallen Western Star' Wars (criticism, ed.), 2001. Contributions: journals, including: Barque; Beloit Poetry Journal; Berkeley Poetry Review; Blue Beetle Press Magazine; Cafe Review; The Experioddicist; Exquisite Corpse; Galley Sail Review; Inkblot; MaLLife; Malthus; Meat Epoch; New York Quarterly; NRG; Outre; Talisman; Tight; Transmog; Wet Motorcycle; ELH; Heaven Bone; Konch; Linden Lane Magazine; Lower Limit Speech; Multicultural Review; Open Letter; Poetry Flash; Prosodia; Seattle Literary Quarterly; W'Orcs; Bright Lights; Journal of Popular Film; Artweek; East Bay Express; Poetry Flash; Anthologies, including: Poly: New Speculative Writing; The Love Project; Online column (criticism) at The Alsop Review (www.alsopreview.com). *Honours:* Full Scholarship to Cornell University, 1958–63; Woodrow Wilson Fellowship, University of California, 1963–65; Yang Poetry Prize, University of California at Berkeley, 1971; Poetry Grantee, Oakland Arts Council, 1992–95; The Artists Embassy Literary/Cultural Award, 1998–2000. *Address:* 2569 Maxwell Avenue, Oakland, CA 94601-5521, USA. *E-mail:* jasfoley@aol.com.

FOLEY, Johanna (Jo) Mary, BA; British magazine editor; b. 8 Dec. 1945, Co. Kerry, Ireland; d. of the late John Foley and Mary Foley; m. Desmond Francis Conor Quigley 1973. *Education:* St Joseph's Convent, Kenilworth and Manchester Univ. *Career:* reporter, Birmingham Post 1970; Beauty Ed. Woman's Own 1972–73, Sr Asst Ed. 1978; Launch Ed. Successful Slimming 1976; Woman's Ed. The Sun 1980; Ed. Woman 1982, Observer Magazine 1986, Options 1988–91; Exec. Ed. The Times 1984–85; freelance journalist and media consultant 1991–; Magazine Ed. of the Year 1983. *Address:* The Reform Club, Pall Mall, London SW1, England.

FOLEY, (Mary) Louise Munro, BA; American novelist; b. 22 Oct. 1933, Toronto, ON, Canada; m. Donald J. Foley 1957; two s. *Education:* University of Western Ontario, Ryerson Institute of Technology, California State University, Sacramento. *Career:* Columnist, News-Argus, Goldsboro, NC, 1971–73; Ed. of Publications, Institute for Human Service Management, California State University, Sacramento, 1975–80; mem. Authors' Guild; California Writers Club; National League of American Pen Women; Society of Children's Book Writers and Illustrators; Novelists Inc. *Publications:* The Caper Club, 1969; No Talking, 1970; Sammy's Sister, 1970; A Job for Joey, 1970; Somebody Stole Second, 1972; Stand Close to the Door (ed.), 1976; Tackle 22, 1978; Women in Skilled Labor (ed.), 1980; The Train of Terror, 1982; The Sinister Studies of KESP-TV, 1983; The Lost Tribe, 1983; The Mystery of the Highland Crest, 1984; The Mystery of Echo Lodge, 1985; Danger at Anchor Mine, 1985; The Mardi Gras Mystery, 1987; Mystery of the Sacred Stones, 1988; Australia! Find the Flying Foxes, 1988; The Cobra Connection, 1990; Ghost Train, 1991; Poison! Said the Cat, 1992; Blood! Said the Cat, 1992; Thief! Said the Cat, 1992; In Search of the Hidden Statue, 1993; Moving Target, 1993; Stolen Affections, 1995; Running Into Trouble, 1996; The Vampire Cat Series: My Substitute Teacher's Gone Baity, 1996, The Bird-Brained Fiasco, 1996, The Phoney Baloney Professor, 1996, The Cat-Nap Cat-Astrophe, 1997. *Address:* 5010 Jennings Way, Sacramento, CA 95819, USA.

FOLLETT, Kenneth (Ken) Martin, BA; British writer; b. 5 June 1949, Cardiff, Wales; s. of Martin D. Follett and Veenie Evans; m. 1st Mary Elson 1968 (divorced 1985); one s. one d.; m. 2nd Barbara Broer 1985; one step-s. two step-d. *Education:* Univ. Coll. London. *Career:* trainee reporter, South Wales Echo, Cardiff 1970–73; reporter, London Evening News 1973–74; Editorial Dir Everest Books, London 1974–76, Deputy Man. Dir 1976–77; full-time writer 1977–; Fellow Univ. Coll. London 1994; mem. Council, Nat. Literary Trust 1996–; Chair. Nat. Year of Reading 1998–99; Pres. Dyslexia Inst. 1998–; Vice-

Pres. Stevenage Borough Football Club 2000–, Stevenage Community Trust 2002–; Patron, Stevenage Home-Start 2000–; Chair. Govs, Roebuck Primary School and Nursery 2001–; Chair. of the Advisory Cttee, Reading is Fundamental UK 2003–; Bd mem., Nat. Acad. of Writing 2003–; Dir, Stevenage Leisure Ltd 1999–2004. *Publications:* The Shakeout 1975, The Bear Raid 1976, The Modigliani Scandal 1976, The Power Twins and the Worm Puzzle 1976, The Secret of Kellerman's Studio 1976, Paper Money 1977, Eye of the Needle (MWA Edgar Award 1979) 1978, Triple 1979, The Key to Rebecca 1980, The Man from St Petersburg 1982, On Wings of Eagles 1983, Lie Down with Lions 1986, The Pillars of the Earth 1989, Night Over Water 1991, A Dangerous Fortune 1993, A Place Called Freedom 1995, The Third Twin 1996, The Hammer of Eden 1998, Code to Zero 2000, Jackdaws (Corine Readers' Award, Germany 2003) 2001, Hornet Flight 2003, Whiteout 2004, World Without End 2007; screenplays; contrib. to book reviews and essays. *Address:* PO Box 4, Knebworth, Hertfordshire SG3 6UT, England (office). *Telephone:* (1438) 810400 (office). *Fax:* (1438) 810444 (office). *E-mail:* ken@ken-follett.com (office). *Website:* www.ken-follett.com (office).

FONER, Eric, BA, PhD; American academic and writer; *Professor of History, Columbia University*; b. 7 Feb. 1943, New York, NY; m. Lynn Garafola 1980; one d. *Education:* Columbia Coll., Oriel Coll., Oxford, UK, Columbia Univ., New York. *Career:* Prof., City Coll. and Grad. School and Univ. Center, CUNY 1973–82; Pitt Prof. of American History and Institutions, Univ. of Cambridge, UK 1980–81; Prof., Columbia Univ. 1982–88, DeWitt Clinton Prof. of History 1988–; Fulbright Prof. of American History, Moscow State Univ. 1990; Harmsworth Prof. of American History, Univ. of Oxford 1993–94; Corresp. Fellow, British Acad.; mem. American Acad. of Arts and Sciences, Org. of American Historians (Pres. 1993–94), American Historical Asscn (Pres. 2000). *Publications:* Free Soil, Free Labor, Free Men: The Ideology of the Republican Party Before the Civil War 1970, Nat Turner 1971, Tom Paine and Revolutionary America 1976, Politics and Ideology in the Age of the Civil War 1980, Nothing But Freedom: Emancipation and its Legacy 1983, Reconstruction: America's Unfinished Revolution 1863–1877 1988, A Short History of Reconstruction 1990, A House Divided: America in the Age of Lincoln (with Olivia Mahoney) 1990, Freedom's Lawmakers: A Directory of Black Officeholders During Reconstruction 1993, Thomas Paine 1995, America's Reconstruction: People and Politics After the Civil War (with Olivia Mahoney) 1995, The Story of American Freedom 1998, Who Owns History? 2002, Give Me Liberty!: An American History 2004, Forever Free 2005; contrib. to scholarly journals and periodicals. *Honours:* ACLS Fellowship 1972–73, Guggenheim Fellowship 1975–76, Nat. Endowment for the Humanities Sr Fellowships 1982–83, 1996–97, Los Angeles Times Book Award for History 1989, Bancroft Prize 1989, Parkman Prize 1989, Lionel Trilling Award 1989, Owsley Prize 1989, American Historical Asscn James Harvey Robinson Prize 1991, New York Public Library Literary Lion 1994, New York Council for the Humanities Scholar of the Year Award 1995. *Address:* 606 W 116th Street, New York, NY 10027, USA. *Telephone:* (212) 854-5253 (office). *Fax:* (212) 961-1903 (office). *E-mail:* ef17@columbia.edu (office). *Website:* www.ericfoner.com (office).

FONSECA, Rubem; Brazilian writer; b. 11 May 1925, Juiz de Fora, MG. *Education:* Escola de Policia, Rio de Janeiro, Fundação Getúlio Vargas, New York Univ. *Career:* commissioner of police, São Cristóvão (RJ) 1952. *Screenplays include:* Relatório de um homen casado, Stelinha, A grande arte. *Publications:* Os prisioneiros 1963, A coleira do cão 1965, Lucía McCartney 1967, O caso Morel 1973, O homen de fevereiro ou março 1973, Felis ano novo 1975, O cobrador (Prêmio Estácio de Sá) 1979, A grande arte (trans. as High Art) (Prêmio Goethe, Prêmio Jabuti) 1983, Buffo & Spallanzani 1986, Vastas emoções e pensamentos imperfeitos (Prêmio Pedro Nava) 1988, Agosto 1990, Romance negro e outras histórias 1992, Contos reunidos 1994, O selvagem da opera 1994, O buraco na parede (Prêmio Jabuti) 1995, Romance negro, Felis ano novo e outras histórias 1996, Histórias de amor 1997, E do meio do mundo prostitute só amores guardei ao meu charuto (Prêmio Machado de Assis) 1997, Confraria dos espadas (Prêmio Eça de Queiroz) 1998, O doente Molière (Prêmio de melhor romance do ano, Associação Paulista de Críticos de Arte) 2000, Secreções, excreções, desatinos 2001, Pequenas criaturas 2002, Diário de um fescenino 2003, 64 contos de Rubem Fonseca 2004; contrib. to numerous anthologies. *Honours:* Prêmio Luis de Camões 2003, Premio Juan Rulfo 2003. *Address:* c/o Companhia das Letras, Rua Bandeira Paulista 702 cj. 32, 04532-002 São Paulo, SP, Brazil. *Telephone:* (11) 3707-3500. *Fax:* (11) 3707-3501. *Website:* www.ciadasletras.com.br.

FONTAINE, André; French journalist; b. 30 March 1921, Paris; s. of Georges Fontaine and Blanche Rochon-Duvigneaud; m. Isabelle Cavaillé 1943; two s. one d. *Education:* Coll. Ste. Marie de Monceau, Paris, Sorbonne and Faculty of Law, Paris Univ. *Career:* journalist 1946–; joined Le Monde 1947, Foreign Ed. 1951–69, Chief Ed. 1969–85, Ed.-in-Chief and Dir 1985–91, Consultant to Dir 1991–; mem. Bd French Inst. of Int. Relations –1992, Bank Indosuez 1983–85; Chair. Group on Int. Strategy for the Ninth French Plan 1982; Vice-Chair. Franco-British Council (French section) 1999–2002. *Publications:* L'alliance atlantique à l'heure du dégel 1960, History of the Cold War (two vols) 1965, 1967, La guerre civile froide 1969, Le dernier quart du siècle 1976, La France au bois dormant 1978, Un seul lit pour deux rêves 1981, Sortir de l'hexagonie (with others) 1984, L'un sans l'autre 1991, Après eux le déluge 1995, La tache rouge 2004. *Honours:* Atlas Int. Ed. of the Year 1976. *Address:* Le Monde, 80 boulevard Auguste-Blanqui, 75707 Paris Cedex 13, France (office). *Telephone:* 1-57-28-20-00 (office). *Fax:* 1-57-28-21-21 (office). *E-mail:* a.fontaine@lemonde.fr (office). *Website:* www.lemonde.fr (office).

FONTENEAU, Pascale; Belgian writer; b. 1963, Fougères, Ille-et-Vilaine. *Education:* Université libre de Bruxelles. *Career:* broadcast first story Chronique des polars on campus radio, Université libre de Bruxelles; writer of novels for Série noire, Gallimard 1992–; contrib. to Le Monde newspaper, Paris 2003–. *Publications include:* Confidences sur l'escalier 1992, Etats de lame 1993, Les Fils perdus de Sylvie Derijke 1995, Les Damnés de l'artère 1996, Otto 1997, La Puissance du désordre 1997, La Vanité des pions 2000. *Address:* c/o Éditions Gallimard, 5, rue Sébastien-Bottin, Paris 75328, France (office).

FOOT, Rt Hon. Michael Mackintosh, PC, MP; British politician and journalist; b. 23 July 1913, Plymouth, Devon; s. of the late Isaac Foot; (brother of the late Lord Caradon); m. Jill Craigie 1949 (died 1999). *Education:* Forres School, Swanage, Leighton Park School, Reading and Wadham Coll., Oxford. *Career:* Pres. Oxford Union 1933; contested Monmouth 1935; Asst Ed. Tribune 1937–38, Jt Ed. 1948–52, Ed. 1952–59, Man. Dir 1952–74; mem. staff Evening Standard 1938, Acting Ed. 1942–44; political columnist Daily Herald 1944–64; MP (Labour) for Plymouth, Devonport 1945–55, for Ebbw Vale 1960–83, for Blaenau Gwent 1983–92; fmr Opposition Spokesman on European Policy; Sec. of State for Employment 1974–76; Lord Pres. of Council, Leader of House of Commons 1976–79, Shadow Leader 1979–80; Deputy Leader of Labour Party 1976–80, Leader 1980–83. *Publications:* Armistice 1918–1939 1940, Trial of Mussolini 1943, Brendan and Beverley 1944, part author Guilty Men 1940 and Who Are the Patriots? 1949, Still At Large 1950, Full Speed Ahead 1950, The Pen and the Sword 1957, Parliament in Danger 1959, Aneurin Bevan Vol. I 1962, Vol. II 1973, Harold Wilson: A Pictorial Biography 1964, Debts of Honour 1980, Another Heart and Other Pulses 1984, Loyalists and Loners 1986, The Politics of Paradise 1988, H.G.: The History of Mr. Wells 1995, Aneurin Bevan 1897–1960 1997, Dr. Strangelove I Presume 1999, The Uncollected Michael Foot 2003. *Honours:* Hon. Fellow, Wadham Coll., Oxford 1969; Hon. mem. Nat. Union of Journalists 1985; Spanish Republican Order of Liberation 1973; Hon. DLitt (Univ. of Wales) 1985, (Nottingham) 1990, (Plymouth) 1993; Hon. LLD (Exeter) 1990. *Address:* c/o Tribune, 9 Arkwright Road, London, NW3 6AN, England.

FOOT, Philippa Ruth, MA, FBA; British academic; *Griffin Professor Emerita, University of California, Los Angeles*; b. 3 Oct. 1920, Owston Ferry, Lincs.; d. of W. S. B. Bosanquet and Esther Cleveland Bosanquet; m. M. R. D. Foot 1945 (divorced 1960). *Education:* Somerville Coll., Oxford. *Career:* Lecturer in Philosophy, Somerville Coll. Oxford 1947–50, Fellow and Tutor 1950–69, Vice-Prin. 1967–69, Sr Research Fellow 1970–88, Hon. Fellow 1988–; Prof. of Philosophy, UCLA 1974–91, Griffin Prof. 1988–91, Prof. Emer. 1991–; fmr Visiting Prof., Cornell Univ., MIT, Univ. of California, Berkeley, Princeton Univ., City Univ. of New York; Pres. Pacific Div. American Philosophical Asscn 1983–84; mem. American Acad. of Arts and Sciences. *Publications:* Theories of Ethics (ed.) 1967, Virtues and Vices 1978, Natural Goodness 2001, Moral Dilemmas 2002; articles and reviews in professional journals. *Honours:* Dr hc (Sofia Univ., Bulgaria) 2000. *Address:* 15 Walton Street, Oxford, OX1 2HG, England. *Telephone:* (1865) 557130.

FOOTE, (Albert) Horton, Jr; American dramatist and scriptwriter; b. 14 March 1916, Wharton, TX; m. Lillian Valish 1945; two s. two d. *Education:* Pasadena Playhouse School Theatre, CA, 1933–35; Tamara Daykarhanova School Theatre, New York City, 1937–39. *Career:* Actor, American Actors Theatre, New York City, 1939–42; Theatre Workshop Dir and Producer, King-Smith School of Creative Arts, Washington, DC, 1944–45; Man., Productions Inc, Washington, DC, 1945–48; mem. American Acad. of Arts and Letters. *Publications:* Novel: The Chase, 1956. Plays: Texas Town, 1942; Out of My House, 1942; Only the Heart, 1944; Celebration, 1948; The Chase, 1952; The Trip to Bountiful, 1953; The Midnight Caller, 1953; A Young Lady of Property, 1954; The Traveling Lady, 1955; The Roads to Home, 1955; Tomorrow, 1960; Roots in a Parched Ground, 1962; The Road to the Graveyard, 1985; Blind Date, 1986; Habitation of Dragons, 1988; Dividing the Estate, 1989; Talking Pictures, 1990; The Young Man from Atlanta, 1994; Night Seasons, 1994; Laura Dennis, 1994. Screenplays: Storm Fear, 1956; To Kill a Mockingbird, 1962; Baby, the Rain Must Fall, 1965; Hurry Sundown, 1966; Tomorrow, 1971; Tender Mercies, 1983; 1918, 1984; On Valentine's Day, 1985; The Trip to Bountiful, 1985; Spring Moon, 1987; Convicts, 1991; Of Mice and Men, 1992. Other: Farewell: A Memoir of a Texas Childhood, 1999; Beginnings (memoir), 2001; many television scripts. *Honours:* Acad. Awards, 1962, 1983; Writers Guild of America Awards, 1962, 1989; Pulitzer Prize in Drama, 1995; American Acad. of Arts and Letters Gold Medal, 1998.

FORAN, Charles William, BA, MA; Canadian writer; b. 2 Aug. 1960, North York, ON; m. Mary, two d. *Education:* University of Toronto, University College, Dublin. *Career:* Librarian and Freelance Journalist, New York State 1985–88; Teacher Beijing College 1988–90; Freelance Writer and Journalist 1990–; mem. PEN Canada; Writers Union of Canada. *Publications:* Coming Attractions (5 short stories) 1987, Sketches in Winter (non-fiction) 1992, Kitchen Music (novel) 1994, The Last House of Ulster (non-fiction) 1995, Butterfly Lovers (novel) 1996, The Story of My Life (So Far) (non-fiction) 1998, House on Fire (novel) 2001; contrib. to Globe and Mail, The Walrus, Saturday Night Magazine. *Honours:* QSpell Award, Fiction 1990, 1998, Non-Fiction 1995. *Address:* 298 Boswell Avenue, Peterborough, ON K9J 5G3, Canada.

FORBES, Bryan, CBE; British film industry executive, film director, screenwriter and novelist; b. 22 July 1926, Stratford, London; m. Nanette Newman 1955; two d. *Education:* West Ham Secondary School, RADA. *Career:* first stage appearance 1942; served in Intelligence Corps 1944–48; entered films as actor 1948; Head of Production, Assoc. British Picture Corpn 1969–71, subsequently became EMI Film Productions Ltd; mem. Gen. Advisory Council of BBC 1966–69, Experimental Film Bd of British Film Acad.; Govt Nominee BBC Schools Broadcasting Council 1972; mem. Beatrix Potter Soc. (pres. 1982–96, now patron), Nat. Youth Theatre (pres. 1984–2005), Writers Guild of GB (pres. 1988–91); founder and fmr Dir Capital Radio Ltd. *Films:* wrote and co-produced The Angry Silence (British Film Acad. Award) 1959; dir Whistle Down the Wind 1961; writer and dir The L-Shaped Room (UN Award) 1962, Seance on a Wet Afternoon (Best Screenplay Award) 1963, King Rat 1964; writer Only Two Can Play (Best Screenplay Award) 1964; producer and dir The Wrong Box 1965; writer, producer and dir The Whisperers 1966, Deadfall 1967, The Madwoman of Chaillot 1968, The Raging Moon (Long Ago Tomorrow in USA) 1970; dir Macbeth 1980, Killing Jessica 1986, Star Quality 1986, The Living Room 1987, One Helluva Life 2002; writer, producer and dir filmed biography of Dame Edith Evans for Yorkshire TV 1973; filmed documentary on lifestyle of Elton John for ATV 1974; wrote and dir The Slipper and the Rose 1975, Jessie (BBC) 1977, Ménage à trois (Better Late than Never in USA) 1981, The Endless Game 1989 (for Channel 4 TV); dir British segment of The Sunday Lovers 1980; dir The King in Yellow (for LWT Television) 1982, The Naked Face 1983; produced, wrote and dir International Velvet 1977. *Publications:* Truth Lies Sleeping (short stories) 1951, The Distant Laughter (novel) 1972, Notes for a Life (autobiog.) 1974, The Slipper and the Rose 1976, Ned's Girl (biog. of Dame Edith Evans) 1977, International Velvet (novel) 1978, Familiar Strangers (novel, aka Stranger) 1979, That Despicable Race – A History of the British Acting Tradition 1980, The Rewrite Man (novel) 1983, The Endless Game (novel) 1986, A Song at Twilight (novel) 1989, A Divided Life (autobiog.) 1992, The Twisted Playground (novel) 1993, Partly Cloudy (novel) 1995, Quicksand (novel) 1996, The Memory of All That 1999. *Honours:* Hon. DLitt (Council for Nat. Academic Awards) 1987, (Sussex) 1999; many film festival prizes. *Literary Agent:* Curtis Brown Ltd, Haymarket House, 28–29 Haymarket, London, SW1Y 4SP, England. *Telephone:* (20) 7393-4400. *Fax:* (20) 7393-4401. *E-mail:* info@curtisbrown.co.uk.

FORBES, Calvin, MFA; American poet, writer and academic; *Professor, School of the Art Institute of Chicago*; b. 6 May 1945, Newark, NJ. *Education:* New School for Social Research, Rutgers Univ., Brown Univ. *Career:* Asst Prof. of English, Emerson Coll. 1969–73, Tufts Univ. 1973–74, 1975–77; Asst Prof. of Creative Writing, Washington Coll. 1988–89; Assoc. Prof., then Prof. and Chair. of Writing Program, School of the Art Inst. of Chicago 1991–; mem. Coll. Language Asscn, MLA of America. *Performance:* musical suite based on his poems, Rochester NY 2003. *Publications:* poetry: Blue Monday 1974, From the Book of Shine 1979, The Shine Poems 2001; contrib. to many anthologies. *Honours:* Bread Loaf Writers' Conf. Fellowship 1973, Fulbright to teach at Univ. of Copenhagen, Denmark 1975–76, Yaddo Residency 1976–77, Nat. Endowment for the Arts Fellowship 1982–83, DC Comm. on the Arts Fellowship 1984, Illinois Arts Council Fellowship 1999. *Address:* School of the Art Institute of Chicago, 37 S Wabash Avenue, Chicago, IL 60603, USA (office). *E-mail:* cforbes777@msn.com (home).

FORBES, John, BA; Australian poet and writer; b. 1 Sept. 1950, Melbourne, Vic. *Education:* Univ. of Sydney. *Career:* Ed., Surfer's Paradise 1974–83; mem. Australian Soc. of Authors. *Publications:* Tropical Skiing 1976, On the Beach 1977, Drugs 1980, Stalin's Holidays 1981, The Stunned Mullet and Other Poems 1988, New and Selected Poems 1992; contrib. to newspapers and magazines. *Honours:* New Poetry Prize 1973, Southerly Prize 1976, Grace Leverson Prize 1993. *Address:* 91 Prospect Road, Summer Hill, 2130 NSW, Australia.

FORBES, Leonie Evadne; Jamaican actress, broadcaster and playwright; b. 14 June 1937, Kingston; d. of Jonathan and Gladys Forbes; m. 1st Ludlow Galloway (divorced 1963); one s.; m. 2nd Keith Amil 1963 (divorced 1975); two d. one s.; m. 3rd Paul Harvey 1978 (divorced 1987). *Education:* Kingston Sr School, Excelsior High School, Durham Coll. and Royal Acad. of Dramatic Arts (London). *Career:* Sec. Extra Mural Dept, Univ. of West Indies 1955–60; studies and work in UK 1961–66; Announcer Jamaica Broadcasting Corpn 1960–61, Producer, Presenter Radio and TV 1966–68, Producer, Presenter TV 1970–72, Head FM Radio 2 1972–75, Dir of Broadcasting 1976–77, Head Dept of Theatre 1978–79; Librarian Radio and TV, Australian Broadcasting Corpn 1968–70; Officer of the Order of Distinction 1980; Bronze Musgrave Medal 1974, Silver 1987; Award of Excellence (Caribbean Acad. of Arts and Culture) 1991; Centenary Medal (Inst of Jamaica) 1991. *Plays and films include:* Miss Unusual, Sea Mama, The Rope and The Cross, Old Story Time, Champagne and Sky Juice – Children of Babylon, I Marcus Garvey, Milk and Honey, Passion and Paradise, Whiplash. *TV appearances include:* I Is a Long Memoried Woman, Orchid House, Songs of Praise, South of the Border, Dixon of Dock Green, Hugh and I, Martin. *Publications include:* Moments by Myself 1988, Re-entry into Sound, Part IV (jtly) 1989; plays: Let's Say Grace, What's Good for the Goose, The Baby Born. *Address:* 6 Barbican Close, Kingston 6, Jamaica. *Telephone:* 927-3584.

FORBES, Malcolm Stevenson (Steve), Jr, LHD; American publishing executive; *President and CEO, Forbes Inc.*; b. 18 July 1947, Morristown, NJ; s. of Malcolm Forbes and Roberta Laidlaw; m. Sabina Beekman 1971. *Education:* Princeton Univ. and Lycoming Coll. Jacksonville Univ. *Career:* with Forbes Inc., New York 1970–, Pres. and COO 1980–90, Deputy Ed.-in-Chief 1982–90, Ed.-in-Chief, Forbes Magazine and Pres. and CEO 1990–; Chair. Forbes Newspapers 1989–; mem. Bd for Int. Broadcasting 1983–93, Chair. 1985–93; mem. Advisory Council, Dept of Econs Princeton Univ. 1985–. *Wrote:* Some Call It Greed (film script) 1977. *Publication:* Fact and Comment (ed.) 1974. *Honours:* several hon. degrees. *Address:* Forbes Inc., 60 Fifth Avenue, New York, NY 10011, USA (office). *Telephone:* (212) 620-2200 (office). *Fax:* (212) 620-2245 (office). *Website:* www.forbesinc.com (office).

FORD, David (see Harknett, Terry)

FORD, Kirk (see Spence, William John Duncan)

FORD, Peter; British author and editor; b. 3 June 1936, Harpenden, Hertfordshire, England; m. (divorced); two s. one d. *Education:* St George's School. *Career:* Ed., Cassell, 1958–61; Senior Copy Ed., Penguin Books, 1961–64; Senior Ed., Thomas Nelson, 1964–70; mem. Society of Authors; New York Acad. of Sciences; Folklore Society. *Publications:* The Fool on the Hill, 1975; Scientists and Inventors, 1979; The True History of the Elephant Man, 1980; Medical Mysteries, 1985; The Picture Buyer's Handbook, 1988; A Collector's Guide to Teddy Bears, 1990; Rings and Curtains: Family and Personal Memoirs, 1992; The Monkey's Paw and Other Stories by W. W. Jacobs, 1994; A Willingness to Die: Memoirs of Brian Kingcome, 1999.

FORD, Richard, BA, MFA; American writer; b. 16 Feb. 1944, Jackson, Miss.; m. Kristina Hensley Ford 1968. *Education:* Mich. State Univ., Univ. of Calif., Irvine. *Career:* lecturer, Univ. of Mich., Ann Arbor 1974–76; Asst Prof. of English, Williams Coll., Williamstown, Mass 1978–79; lecturer, Princeton Univ. 1980–81; Guggenheim Fellowship 1977–78; Nat. Endowment for the Arts Fellowships 1979–80, 1985–86; mem. American Acad. of Arts and Letters, PEN, Writers' Guild, American Acad. of Arts and Sciences. *Screenplays:* American Tropical 1983, Bright Angel 1991. *Publications:* A Piece of My Heart (novel) 1976, The Ultimate Good Luck (novel) 1981, The Sportswriter (novel) 1986, Rock Springs (short stories) 1987, My Mother in Memory (ed.) 1988, The Best American Short Stories (ed., with Shannon Ravenal) 1990, Wildlife (novel) 1990, The Granta Book of the American Short Story (ed.) 1992, Independence Day (novel) (Pulitzer Prize for Fiction 1996, PEN/Faulkner Award for Fiction 1996) 1995, Women with Men (short stories) 1997, The Granta Book of the American Long Story (ed.) 1999, A Multitude of Sins (short stories) 2002, The Lay of the Land (novel) 2006. *Honours:* Dr hc (Rennes, France, Michigan); Miss. Acad. of Arts and Letters Literature Award 1987, American Acad. and Inst. of Arts and Letters Award for Literature 1989, American Acad. of Arts and Letters Award in Merit for the Novel 1997, PEN-Malamud Award for Short Fiction 2001; Officier, Ordre des Arts et des Lettres. *Literary Agent:* International Creative Management, 40 West 57th Street, New York, NY 10019, USA. *Telephone:* (212) 556-5764.

FOREMAN, Amanda, BA, PhD, FRSA; British historian and writer; b. 1968, London; d. of Carl Foreman; m.; one s. two d. *Education:* Sarah Lawrence Coll., Bronxville, NY, Columbia Univ., New York and Lady Margaret Hall, Oxford. *Career:* Henrietta Jex Blake Sr Scholarship, Univ. of Oxford 1998; TV and radio presenter 1998–; freelance contrib. to newspapers in the UK and USA. *Publications:* Georgiana: Duchess of Devonshire (Whitbread Award for Biography of the Year) 1998, Georgiana's World 2001, Our American Cousins 2007. *Literary Agent:* The Wylie Agency, 17 Bedford Square, London, WC1B 3JA, England. *E-mail:* mail@wylieagency.co.uk. *Website:* www.wylieagency.co.uk; www.amanda-foreman.com.

FOREMAN, Richard, BA, MFA; American dramatist and theatre director; b. 10 June 1937, New York, NY; m. 1st Amy Taubin 1961 (divorced 1972); m. 2nd Kate Manhelm 1986. *Education:* Brown Univ., Yale Univ. *Career:* Artistic Dir Ontological-Hysteric Theatre, New York 1968–, Theatre O H, Paris 1973–85; Dir-in-Residence, New York Shakespeare Festival 1975–76; Dir Broadway and off-Broadway plays; mem. Dramatists Guild, PEN, Soc. of Stage Dirs. *Publications:* Dr Selavy's Magic Theater 1972, Rhoda in Potatoland 1976, Theatre of Images 1977, Reverberation Machines 1985, Film is Evil: Radio is Good 1987, Unbalancing Acts: Foundations for a Theater 1992, My Head Was a Sledgehammer 1995, Paradise Hotel 2001, Bad Boy Nietzsche 2006. *Honours:* Hon. DArts (Brown Univ.) 1993; Officier, Orde des Artes et des Lettres 2004; New York State Arts Council Creative Artists Public Service Fellow 1971, 1974, Guggenheim Fellowship 1972, Rockefeller Foundation Fellow 1974, Nat. Endowment for the Arts Lifetime Achievement Award 1990, American Acad. of Arts and Letters Prize in Literature 1992, John D. and Catherine T. MacArthur Foundation Fellow 1995–2000, PEN Master American Dramatist Award 2001. *Address:* 152 Wooster Street, New York, NY 10012, USA. *E-mail:* mmeedwarda@earthlink.net.

FORKER, Charles Rush, AB, BA, MA, PhD; American academic and writer; *Professor of English Emeritus, University of Indiana*; b. 11 March 1927, Pittsburgh, PA. *Education:* Bowdoin College, Merton College, Oxford, Harvard University. *Career:* Instructor, University of Wisconsin, 1957–59; Instructor, 1959–61, Asst Prof., 1961–65, Assoc. Prof., 1965–68, Prof., 1968–92, Prof. Emeritus, 1992–, Indiana University; Visiting Prof., University of Michigan, 1969–70, Dartmouth College, 1982–83, Concordia University, Montréal, 1989; mem. American Asscn of University Profs; Guild of Anglican Scholars, pres., 1993–94; International Shakespeare Asscn; Malone Society; Marlowe Society; MLA; Renaissance Society of America; Shakespeare Society of America; World Centre for Shakespeare Studies, advisory board. *Publications:* James Shirley: The Cardinal (ed.), 1964;

William Shakespeare: Henry V (ed.), 1971; Edward Phillips's 'History of the Literature of England and Scotland': A Translation from the 'Compendiosa Enumeratio Poetarum' with an Introduction and Commentary (with Daniel G. Calder), 1973; Visions and Voices of the New Midwest (assoc. ed.), 1978; Henry V: An Annotated Bibliography (with Joseph Candido), 1983; Skull Beneath the Skin: The Achievement of John Webster, 1986; Fancy's Images: Contexts, Settings, and Perspectives in Shakespeare and His Contemporaries, 1990; Christopher Marlowe: Edward the Second (ed.), 1994; Richard II: The Critical Tradition, 1998; William Shakespeare: Richard II (ed.), 2002. Contributions: scholarly books and journals. Honours: Fulbright Fellowship, England, 1951–53; Folger Fellow, 1963; Huntington Library Fellow, 1969; National Endowment for the Humanities Senior Research Fellow, 1980–81. Address: 1219 E Maxwell Lane, Bloomington, IN 47401, USA. Telephone: (812) 332-6564 (home). E-mail: forker@indiana.edu (office).

FORMAN, Robert Kraus Conrad, BA, MA, MPhil, PhD; American academic and writer; President, The Forge Institute; b. 3 Aug. 1947, Baltimore, Md; m. Yvonne Forman 1975; two c. Education: Univ. of Chicago, Columbia Univ., New York. Career: Adjunct Prof., New School for Social Research, New York City 1985–88; Instructor, Union Theological Seminary, New York City 1987; Visiting Asst Prof., Vassar Coll. 1989–90; Assoc. Prof. of Religion, Hunter Coll., CUNY 1990–2001; Sr Fellow, Columbia Univ. Writing Program 1993, Otto Friedrich Schoolhuset 2004–; Founder-Exec. Ed. Journal of Consciousness Studies: Controversies in Science and the Humanities 1991–; mem. American Acad. of Religion, Asscn for Asian Studies, Asscn for Transpersonal Psychology, Inst. for Noetic Sciences, Sankat Mocan (Save the Ganges) Foundation; Founder CBO, The Forge Inst., The Forge Guild. Publications: The Problem of Pure Consciousness (ed.) 1990, Meister Eckhart: Mystic as Theologian: An Experiment in Methodology 1991, The Religions of Asia, third edn (gen. ed.) 1993, Religions of the World, third edn (gen. ed.) 1993, The Innate Capacity (ed.) 1997, Mysticism, Mind, Consciousness 2001, Grass Roots Spirituality: What It Is, Why It Is Here, Where It Is Going 2004; contrib. to more than 30 scholarly books and journals. Honours: New World Foundation Grants 1992, 1993, 1994, CUNY Research Grant 1996, Fetzer Institute Grants 1997, 2001, 2002, 2007, Bross Prize for Manuscript in Religion 2000, Inner Guidance Foundation Grant 2000, 2004, Jonas Foundation Grant, Jameson Grant, Angell Foundation Grant, Medal, Helsinki University, Finland. Address: 383 Broadway, Hastings-on-Hudson, NY 10706, USA (home). Telephone: (914) 478-7802 (office). E-mail: forman@theforge.org (office). Website: www.theforge.org (office).

FORNA, Aminatta, LLB; Sierra Leone/British writer; b. 1965, Scotland; d. of Mohamed Sorie Forna and Maureen Christison; m. Simon Westcott 1994. Education: Univ. Coll., London. Career: BBC TV documentary producer and journalist 1989–99; Harkness Fellow, Univ. of California, Berkeley, USA 1996; mem. Bd Index on Censorship Bd Caine Prize for Africa. Publications: The Devil That Danced on the Water: A Daughter's Memoir 2002, Ancestor Stones (novel) 2006. Literary Agent: c/o DGA, 55 Monmouth Street, London, WC2H 9DG, England. Telephone: (20) 7240-9992. E-mail: assistant@davidgodwinassociates.co.uk.

FORNÉS, María Irene; Cuban/American playwright; b. 1931, Havana. Career: Man. Dir New York Theatre Strategy 1973–79; fmr TCG (Theatre Communications Group)/Pew Artist-in-Residence, Women's Project and Productions; contrib. to Performing Arts Journal and numerous anthologies. Plays (many unpublished): The Widow 1961, Tango Palace (aka There! You Died) 1963, The Office 1964, Promenade 1965, The Successful Life of 3 1965, The Annunciation 1967, A Vietnamese Wedding 1967, The Red Burning Light (aka Mission XQ3) 1968, Dr Kheal 1968, Molly's Dream 1968, Baboon!!! 1972, Aurora 1974, Cap-a-Pie 1975, Washing 1976, Fefu and Her Friends 1977, In Service 1978, Evelyn Brown 1979, Eyes on the Harem 1979, A Visit 1981, Sarita 1982, The Danube 1982, The Curse of the Langston House 1983, Mud 1983, Abingdon Square 1984, The Conduct of Life 1985, Drowning 1985, The Trial of Joan of Arc on a Matter of Faith 1986, Lovers and Keepers 1986, The Mothers 1986, Oscar and Bertha 1987, Hunger 1988, And What of the Night? 1989, Enter the Night, The Summer in Gossensass, Letters from Cuba 1999. Honours: nine Obie awards; NEA (National Endowment for the Arts) awards, including Distinguished Artists Award; Rockefeller Foundation grants; Guggenheim grant; American Acad. and Inst. of Arts and Letters Award; NY State Governor's Arts Award; PEN/Nabokov Award 2002. Address: c/o Performing Arts Journal, The MIT Press, Five Cambridge Center, Cambridge, MA 02142–1493, USA (office).

FORRESTER, Helen; British writer; b. 6 June 1919, Hoylake, Cheshire. Education: privately. Career: resident in Canada 1953–; writer-in-residence, Lethbridge Community Coll. 1980, Edmonton Public Library 1990; mem. Writers' Union of Canada, Soc. of Authors, London, Canadian Asscn of Children's Authors, The Authors' Lending and Copyrights Soc. Ltd, London; Patron Chester Library Festival. Publications include: Thursday's Child 1959, Twopence to Cross the Mersey (autobiog.) 1974, Minerva's Stepchild (autobiog.) 1979, Liverpool Daisy (Hudson's Bay Beaver Award) 1979, By the Waters of Liverpool (autobiog.) 1981, Liverpool Miss 1982, Lime Street at Two (autobiog.) (Alberta Culture's Literary Award 1984) 1985, The Moneylenders of Shahpur (Hudson's Bay Beaver Award for best unpublished manuscript 1970) 1987, Yes, Mama (Writers' Guild Fiction Award 1989) 1987, The Lemon Tree 1991, The Liverpool Basque 1993, Mourning Doves 1996, Madame Barbara 1999, A Cuppa Tea and an Aspirin 2003; numerous short stories, book reviews and contribs to journals. Honours: Hon. DLitt (Liverpool) 1988;

Hon. LittD (Alberta) 1993; Govt of Alberta Achievement Award for Literature 1979, YMCA Woman of the Arts 1987. Address: c/o Writers' Union of Canada, 24 Ryerson Avenue, Toronto, Ontario, M5T 9Z9, Canada. Website: www.helenforrester.com.

FORRESTER, Viviane; French writer and critic; b. 29 Sept. 1925, Paris; d. of Edgar Dreyfus and Yvonne Dreyfus (née Hirsch); m. 1st Simon Stolof (divorced); two s.; m. 2nd; m. 3rd John Forrester 1967. Career: literary critic La Quinzaine Littéraire 1974, 1994–, Nouvel Observateur 1975, Le Monde 1994–; mem. Jury Prix Fémina. Publications include: Ainsi des Exilés 1970, Le Grand festin 1971, Virginia Woolf 1973, Le Corps entier de Marigda 1975, Violence ou calme 1980, Les Allées cavalières 1982, Van Gogh ou l'enterrement dans les blés (Prix Fémina-Vacaresco) 1983, L'Oeil de la nuit 1987, Ce soir, après la guerre (Prix de l'Académie française) 1992, L'Horreur économique (Prix Médicis essai) 1996, Une Étrange dictature 2000, Au Louvre avec Viviane Forrester: Leonardo da Vinci 2001, Le Crime occidental 2004, Mes Passions de Toujours 2006. Honours: Chevalier, Légion d'Honneur, Officier, Ordre Nat du Mérite, Commdr, Ordre des Arts et des Lettres. Address: 40 rue du Bac, 75007 Paris, France (home). Telephone: (1) 42-22-65-36 (home).

FORSTER, Margaret, BA, FRSL; British writer; b. 25 May 1938, Carlisle; d. of Arthur Gordon Forster and Lilian Forster (née Hind); m. Edward Hunter Davies 1960; one s. two d. Education: Carlisle Co. High School and Somerville Coll., Oxford. Career: chief non-fiction reviewer London Evening Standard 1977–80; mem. Arts Council Literary Panel 1978–81. Publications: non-fiction: The Rash Adventurer: The Rise and Fall of Charles Edward Stuart 1973, William Makepeace Thackeray: Memoirs of a Victorian Gentleman 1978, Significant Sisters: Grassroots of Active Feminism 1839–1939 1984, Elizabeth Barrett Browning: A Biography 1988, Elizabeth Barrett Browning: Selected Poems (ed.) 1988, Daphne du Maurier: The Authorised Biography 1993, Hidden Lives: A Family Memoir 1995, Rich Desserts and Captains Thin: A Family and Their Times 1831–1931 1997, Precious Lives (memoir) 1997, Good Wives?: Mary, Fanny, Jennie and Me 1845–2001 2001; novels: Dame's Delight 1964, Georgy Girl (filmscript with Peter Nichols 1966) 1963, The Bogeyman 1965, The Travels of Maudie Tipstaff 1967, The Park 1968, Miss Owen-Owen is at Home 1969, Fenella Phizackerley 1970, Mr Bone's Retreat 1971, The Seduction of Mrs Pendlebury 1974, Mother, Can You Hear Me? 1979, The Bride of Lowther Fell 1980, Marital Rites 1981, Private Papers 1986, Have the Men had Enough? 1989, Lady's Maid 1990, The Battle for Christabel 1991, Mothers' Boys 1994, Shadow Baby 1996, The Memory Box 1999, Diary of an Ordinary Woman 1914–1995 2003, Is There Anything You Want? 2005, Keeping the World Away 2006, Over 2007. Honours: RSL Award 1988, Fawcet Soc. Prize 1993. Literary Agent: The Sayle Literary Agency, Bickerton House, 25–27 Bickerton Road, London, N19 5JT, England. Telephone: (20) 7263-8681. Fax: (20) 7561-0529. Address: 11 Boscastle Road, London, NW5 1EE; Grasmoor House, Loweswater, nr Cockermouth, Cumbria, CA13 0RU, England. Telephone: (20) 7485-3785 (London); (1900) 85303 (Cumbria).

FORSYTH, Frederick, CBE; British writer; b. 25 Aug. 1938, Ashford, Kent; m. 1st Carole Cunningham 1973; two s.; m. 2nd Sandy Molloy. Education: Tonbridge School, Univ. of Granada, Spain. Career: with RAF 1956–58; reporter, Eastern Daily Press, Norfolk 1958–61; joined Reuters 1961, reporter, Paris 1962–63, Chief of Bureau, E Berlin 1963–64; radio and TV reporter, BBC 1965–66; Asst Diplomatic Corresp., BBC TV 1967–68; freelance journalist, Nigeria and Biafra 1968–69. Television appearances include: Soldiers (narrator) 1985, Frederick Forsyth Presents 1989. Publications: fiction: The Day of the Jackal 1971, The Odessa File 1972, The Dogs of War 1974, The Shepherd 1975, The Devil's Alternative 1979, No Comebacks (short stories) 1982, The Fourth Protocol 1984, The Negotiator 1988, The Deceiver 1991, Great Flying Stories (ed.) 1991, The Fist of God 1993, Icon 1996, The Phantom of Manhattan 1999, Quintet 2000, The Veteran and Other Stories 2001, Avenger 2003, The Afghan 2006; non-fiction: The Biafra Story 1969 (revised edn as The Making of an African Legend: The Biafra Story 1977), Emeka 1982, I Remember: Reflections on Fishing in Childhood 1995. Honours: MWA Edgar Allan Poe Award 1971. Address: c/o Bantam Books, 62–63 Uxbridge Road, London, W5 5SA, England.

FORTE, Allen, BA, MA; American musician and writer; Battell Professor Emeritus of the Theory of Music, Yale University New Haven; b. 23 Dec. 1926, Portland, OR; s. of M. Palmer and Marion Eastman Forte. Education: Columbia Univ. Career: Faculty, Teachers Coll., Columbia Univ. 1953–59, Manhattan School of Music 1957, Mannes Coll. of Music 1957–59; Instructor, Yale Univ. 1959–61, Asst Prof. 1961–64, Assoc. Prof. 1964–68, Prof. 1968–91, Battell Prof. of the Theory of Music from 1991, now Prof. Emer.; Ed., Journal of Music Theory 1960–67; Gen. Ed., Composers of the Twentieth Century 1980–; Fellow American Acad. of Arts and Sciences 1995; mem. American Musicological Soc., Soc. for Music Theory (pres. 1977–82). Publications: Contemporary Tone-Structure 1955, Schenker's Conception of Musical Structure 1959, Bartók's 'Serial' Composition 1960, The Compositional Matrix 1961, Tonal Harmony in Concept and Practice 1962, A Theory of Set-complexes for Music 1964, A Program for the Analytical Reading of Scores 1966, Computer-implemented Analysis of Musical Structure 1966, Music and Computing: The Present Situation 1967, The Structure of Atonal Music 1970, The Harmonic Organization of The Rite of Spring 1978, Introduction to Schenkerian Analysis (with S. Gilbert) 1982, The American Popular Ballad of the Golden Era 1924–1950 1995, The Atonal Music of Anton Webern 1998,

Olivier Messiaen as Serialist 2002, Listening to Classic American Popular Songs 2001, Toward a Theory of Intervallic Harmony 2004, Schoenberg's Opus 19, No. 4 2004, Songs of Yesterday for Today (pianist-arranger) 2005, Messiaen's Chords 2006, The Development of Diminutions in American Jazz 2006; contrib. to learned books and journals. *Honours:* Hon. PhD (Eastman School of Music) 1988; Sr Marshal Yale Univ. Commencement Ceremony 2004; WWII Victory Medal, Guggenheim Fellowship 1981, Festschrift published in his honour: Music Theory in Concept and Practice 1997. *Address:* c/o Department of Music, PO Box 208310, Yale University, New Haven, CT 06520 (office); 10 Mulberry Hill, Hamden, CT 06517, USA (home). *Telephone:* (203) 288-8888 (home). *E-mail:* allen.forte@yale.edu (home). *Website:* www .allenforte.com.

FORTEY, Richard Alan, PhD, ScD, FRS; British palaeontologist and writer; *Merit Researcher, Natural History Museum, London*; b. 15 Feb. 1946, London; s. of Frank Allen Fortey and Margaret Fortey (née Wilshin); m. 1st Bridget Elizabeth Thomas (divorced); one s.; m. 2nd Jacqueline Francis 1977; one. s. two d. *Education:* Ealing Grammar School for Boys, King's Coll. Cambridge. *Career:* Research Fellow, then Sr Scientific Officer, Natural History Museum, London 1970–77, Prin. Scientific Officer 1978–86, Sr Prin. Scientific Officer 1986–98, Merit Researcher 1998–; Howley Visiting Prof. Memorial Univ. of Newfoundland 1977–78; Visiting Prof. of Palaeobiology, Oxford Univ. 2000–; Collier Chair in Public Understanding of Science and Tech., Univ. of Bristol 2002–03; mem. Geological Soc. of London 1972–, British Mycological Soc. 1980–. *Publications:* The Roderick Masters Book of Money Making Schemes (as Roderick Masters) 1981, Fossils: The Key to the Past 1982, The Hidden Landscape 1993, Life: An Unauthorised Biography 1997, Trilobite! 2000, The Earth: An Intimate History 2004. *Honours:* Natural World Book of the Year Award 1994, Lyell Medal, Geological Soc. of London 1996, Frink Medal Zoological Soc. of London 2001, Lewis Thomas Prize Rockefeller Univ. 2003, Linnean Medal for Zoology 2006, Michael Faraday Prize Royal Soc. 2006. *Address:* Department of Palaeontology, Natural History Museum, Cromwell Road, London, SW7 5BD, England (office). *Telephone:* (20) 7942-5493 (office). *Fax:* (20) 7942-5546 (office). *E-mail:* r.fortey@nhm.ac.uk (office). *Website:* www .nhm.ac.uk/palaeontology (office).

FOSSE, Jon, Cand. philol; Norwegian writer, dramatist and poet; b. 29 Sept. 1959, Haugesund. *Education:* Univ. of Bergen. *Career:* teacher of creative writing Acad. of Writing, Bergen 1987–93; professional writer 1993–; mem. Norwegian Soc. of Authors, Norwegian Soc. of Dramatists. *Plays:* Og aldri skal vi skiljast 1994, Namnet 1995, Nokon kjem til å komme 1996, Barnet, Mor og barn, Sonen: Tre skodespel 1997, Natta syng sine songar, Ein sommars dag: To skodespel 1998, Draum om hausten 1999, Besak, Vinter, Ettermiddag. Tre skodespel 2000, Vakkert 2001, Dadsvariasjonar 2002, Jenta i sofaen 2003. *Publications:* fiction: Raudt, svart 1983, Stengd gitar 1985, Naustet 1989, Flaskesamlaren 1991, Bly og vatn 1992, Melancholia I 1995, Melancholia II 1996; shorter prose: Blod. Steinen er Forteljing 1987, To forteljingar 1993, Prosa frå ein oppvekst. Kortprosa 1994, Eldre kortare prosa 1997, Morgon og kveld 2000, Det er Ales; poetry: Engel med vatn i augene 1986, Hundens bevegelsar 1990, Hund og engel 1992, Nye dikt 1997, Ange i vind 2003; essays: Frå telling via showing til writing 1989, Gnostiske essays 1999; also books for children. *Honours:* Chevalier, Ordre Nat. du Mérite; hon. mem. Norwegian Actors' Soc.; Noregs Mållags Prize for Children's Books 1990, Andersson-Rysst Fondet 1992, Prize for Literature in New Norwegian 1993, 2003, Samlags Prize 1994, Ibsen Prize 1996, Sunnmoers Prize 1996, Melsom Prize 1997, Asshehoug Prize 1997, Dobloug Prize 1999, Gyldendal Prize 2000, Nordic Prize for Dramatists 2000, Nestroy Prize 2001, Scandinavian National Theatre Prize 2002, Norwegian Council of Culture Prize of Honour 2003, Norwegian Theatre Prize of Honour (Hedda) 2003, UBU Prize for best foreign play, Italy 2004. *Literary Agent:* Samlaget, Boks 4672 Sofienberg, 0506 Oslo, Norway; Colombine Teaterförlag, Gaffelgränd 1A, 11130 Stockholm, Sweden (office).

FOSTER, Cecil Adolphus, BA; Barbadian/Canadian writer and journalist; b. 26 Sept. 1954, Barbados; three s. *Education:* University of the West Indies, York University, Toronto. *Career:* mem. PEN Canada. *Publications:* No Man in the House, 1992; Sleep on Beloved, 1994; Caribana: The Greatest Celebration, 1995; A Place Called Heaven: The Meaning of Being Black, 1996; Slammin' Tar, 1998; Island Wing, 1998, Dry Bones Memories 2001, Where Race Does Not Matter: The New Spirit of Modernity 2004. *Honours:* Gordon Mantador Award 1997.

FOSTER, David Manning, BSc, PhD; Australian writer; b. 15 May 1944, Katoomba; m. 1st Robin Bowers 1964; one s. two d.; m. 2nd Gerda Busch 1975; one s. two d. *Education:* Univ. of Sydney, Australian Nat. Univ., Univ. of Pennsylvania. *Career:* professional fiction writer 1973–. *Publications:* novels: The Pure Land 1974, The Empathy Experiment 1977, Moonlite 1981, Plumbum 1983, Dog Rock: A Postal Pastoral 1985, The Adventures of Christian Rosy Cross 1986, Testostero 1987, The Pale Blue Crochet Coat-hanger Cover 1988, Mates of Mars 1991, Self Portraits (ed.) 1991, A Slab of Fosters 1994, The Glade Within the Grove 1996, The Ballad of Erinungarah 1997, Crossing the Blue Montain (contributor) 1997, In the New Country 1999, The Land Where Stories End 2001; short stories: North South West: Three Novellas 1973, Escape to Reality 1977, Hitting the Wall: Two Novellas 1989. *Honours:* The Age Award 1974, Australian Nat. Book Council Award 1981, NSW Premier's Fellowship 1986, Keating Fellowship 1991–94, James Joyce Foundation Award 1996, Miles Franklin Award 1997, Courier Mail Award 1999. *Address:* PO Box 57, Bundanoon, NSW 2578, Australia.

FOSTER, James Anthony (Tony); Canadian writer; b. 2 Aug. 1932, Winnipeg, Manitoba; m. 1964; one s. two d. *Education:* University of Brunswick. *Career:* mem. Canadian Authors Asscn; PEN; Writers Guild of America; Writers' Union of Canada. *Publications:* Zig Zag to Armageddon, 1978; By-Pass, 1982; The Money Burn, 1984; A coeur ouvert, 1985; Heart of Oak: A Pictorial History of the Royal Canadian Navy, 1985; Meeting of Generals, 1986; Sea Wings: A Pictorial History of Canada's Waterborne Defence Aircraft, 1986; Muskets to Missiles, 1987; Rue du Bac, 1987; For Love and Glory, 1989; The Bush Pilots: A Canadian Phenomena, 1990; Ransom for a God, 1990; The Sound and the Silence, 1990.

FOSTER, Jeanne (see Williams, Jeanne)

FOSTER, Linda Nemec, BA, MFA; American poet, writer and teacher; b. 29 May 1950, Garfield Heights, OH; m. Anthony Jesse Foster 1974; one s. one d. *Education:* Aquinas Coll., Grand Rapids and Goddard Coll., Plainfield, VT. *Career:* teacher of creative writing and poetry, Michigan Council for the Arts 1980–; Instructor of English Composition, Ferris State Univ. 1983–84; Dir of Literature Programming, Urban Inst. for Contemporary Arts, Grand Rapids 1989–96; founder, Contemporary Writers Series, Aquinas Coll. 1997, Lecturer in Poetry 1999–; guest lecturer and speaker at various schools, colls, and conferences; first Poet Laureate of Grand Rapids, MI 2003; mem. Acad. of American Poets, Detroit Women Writers, Poetry Resource Center of Michigan, Urban Inst. for Contemporary Arts, Poetry Soc. of America. *Publications:* A History of the Body 1987, A Modern Fairy Tale: The Baba Yaga Poems 1992, Trying to Balance the Heart 1993, Living in the Fire Nest 1996, Contemplating the Heavens 2001, Amber Necklace from Gdańsk 2001, Listen to the Landscape 2006; contrib. to reviews, journals and magazines. *Honours:* Michigan Council for the Arts Creative Artist grants in poetry 1984, 1990, 1996, American Poetry Asscn Grand Prize 1986, hon. mention Writers' Digest 1987, prizewinner McGuffin Poetry Contest 1987, 1994, Passages North Nat. Poetry Competition 1988, Poetry/Visual Art Selections, Sage Coll., New York 1994, 1995, Arts Foundation of Michigan Fellowship in Poetry 1996, National Writer's Voice Project Fellowship 1999, Art Serve Michigan grant in poetry 2001, first runner-up Nat. Poetry Review Laureate Prize 2006. *Address:* 2024 Wilshire Drive SE, Grand Rapids, MI 49506, USA. *Website:* www .lindanemecfoster.com.

FOSTER, Paul, BA, LLB; American dramatist and screenwriter; b. 15 Oct. 1931, Pennsgrove, NJ. *Education:* Rutgers University, New York University Law School. *Career:* mem. Dramatists Guild; Society of Composers and Dramatic Authors, France; Players Club, New York City. *Publications:* 25 books of plays including: Tom Paine, 1971; Madonna in the Orchard, 1971; Satyricon, 1972; Elizabeth I, 1972; Marcus Brutus, 1976; Silver Queen Saloon, 1976; Mellon and the National Art Gallery, 1980; A Kiss is Just a Kiss, 1984; 3 Mystery Comedies, 1985; The Dark and Mr Stone, 1985; Odon von Horvath's Faith, Hope and Charity, trans., 1987; Make Believe (with music by Solt Dome), musical book and lyrics, 1994. Films: Smile, 1980; Cop and the Anthem, 1982; When You're Smiling, 1983; Cinderella, 1984; Home Port, 1984. Contributions: Off-Off Broadway Book, 1972; Best American Plays of the Modern Theatre, 1975; New Stages magazine. *Honours:* Rockefeller Foundation Fellowship, 1967; British Arts Council Award, 1973; Guggenheim Fellowship, 1974; Theater Heute Award, 1977.

FOSTER, Robert Fitzroy (Roy), FBA; Irish historian, writer and academic; *Carroll Professor of Irish History, Hertford College, University of Oxford*; b. 16 Jan. 1949, Waterford. *Education:* Trinity Coll. Dublin. *Career:* Prof. of Modern British History, Birkbeck College, London 1989-91; Carroll Prof. of Irish History and Fellow, Hertford Coll., Oxford 1991–; visiting fellowships include St. Anthony's Coll., Oxford, Inst. for Advanced Study, Princeton, NJ, Princeton Univ.; Fellow, British Acad. 1989. *Publications:* biogs of Charles Stewart Parnell 1976 and Lord Randolph Churchill 1981, Modern Ireland 1600–1972 1988, The Oxford Illustrated History of Ireland 1989, Paddy and Mr Punch 1997, W. B. Yeats: A Life, Vol. I: The Apprentice Mage 1865–1914 2001, The Irish Story: Telling Tales and Making it Up in Ireland 2001 (Christian Gauss Award from Phi Beta Kappa 2003), W. B. Yeats: A Life, Vol. II: The Arch-Poet 1915–1939 2003, Conquering England: the Irish in Victorian London (with Fintan Cullen) 2005. *Honours:* Hon. DLitt (Aberdeen) 1997, (Queen's, Belfast) 1998, (Trinity Coll. Dublin) 2003, (Nat. Univ. of Ireland) 2004; Hon. Fellow, Birkbeck Coll., Univ. of London 2005. *Address:* Hertford College, Catte Street, Oxford, OX1 3BW, England (office). *Telephone:* (1865) 279400 (office). *E-mail:* roy.foster@hertford.ox.ac.uk (office). *Website:* www.hertford.ox.ac.uk (office).

FOTTORINO, Éric; French journalist and writer; b. 1960, Nice. *Career:* journalist, Le Monde. *Publications:* Le Festin de la terre 1988, La Piste blanche 1991, Rochelle 1991, Besoin d'afrique 1992, Homme de terre 1993, La France en friche 1994, Mille et un soleils 1995, Aventures industrielles 1996, Coeur d'afrique 1997, Les Éphémères 1994, Voyage au centre du cerveau 1998, Un Territoire fragile (Prix Europe, Prix des Bibliothécaires) 2000, Nordeste 2001, Je pars demain 2001, C'est mon tour 2003, Caresse de rouge (Prix François-Mauriac) 2004, Korsakov (Prix Roman France Télévision 2004, Prix des libraires 2005, Prix Nice-Baie des Anges 2005) 2004. *Address:* c/o Editions Gallimard, 5 rue Sébastien-Bottin, 75328 Paris Cédex 07, France.

FOUDA, Yosri; Egyptian journalist; b. 1964. *Education:* American Univ. in Cairo. *Career:* producer Arabic-language TV Service, BBC, London, UK – 1996; reporter, Al Jazeera London Bureau, UK 1996–, presenter 'Top Secret'

TV programme (interviewed April 2002 Khalid Shaikh Mohammed, Chief of Al-Qaeda Mil. Cttee, believed to have masterminded 9/11 US attacks).

FOULKE, Robert Dana, AB, MA, PhD; American academic, writer and travel writer; b. 25 April 1930, Minneapolis, Minn.; m. Patricia Ann Nelson 1953; one s. two d. *Education:* Princeton Univ., Univ. of Minnesota. *Career:* Instructor in English, Univ. of Minnesota 1956–59, 1960–61; Asst Prof. of English, Trinity Coll., Hartford 1961–66, Assoc. Prof. 1966–70; Prof. of English, Skidmore Coll. 1970–92, Chair. Dept 1970–80; Visiting Assoc. and Life Mem. Clare Hall, Cambridge, UK 1976–77, 1990–91; Visiting Fellow, Dept of English, Princeton Univ. 1988; Literary Ed. The Oxford Encyclopedia of Maritime History 1999–2006; mem. Coll. English Asscn, MLA, Joseph Conrad Soc., Melville Soc., American Soc. of Journalists and Authors, Soc. of American Travel Writers, Travel Journalists Guild (Co-Pres. 2004–06), Hakluyt Soc., Nat. Maritime Historical Soc., North American Soc. for Oceanic History (mem. Exec. Council 1995–), Soc. for Nautical Research. *Television:* Sailing with Confidence (three 30-minute programmes produced by WMHT, Troy, NY) 1990. *Publications:* An Anatomy of Literature (co-author and ed.) 1972, The Writer's Mind (co-ed.) 1983, The Sea Voyage Narrative 1997, 2002; travel guides: Europe Under Canvas 1980, Fielding's Motoring and Camping Europe 1986, Day Trips and Getaway Vacations in New England 1983, Day Trips and Getaway Vacations in Mid-Atlantic States 1986, Exploring Europe by Car 1991, Fielding's Great Sights of Europe 1994, Colonial America 1995, Romantic Weekends: New England 1998, Day Trips and Get Away Weekends: New England 1999, Day Trips and Get Away Weekends: Mid-Atlantic States 2000, Day Trips and Getaway Weekends: Connecticut, Rhode Island and Massachusetts 2002, Day Trips and Getaway Weekends: Vermont, New Hampshire and Maine 2002, An Adventure Guide to the Champkin and Hudson River Valleys 2003, A Visitor's Guide to Colonial and Revolutionary New England 2006; contribs to numerous articles in scholarly journals and some 500 travel articles in magazines and newspapers. *Honours:* Fulbright Fellow, Univ. of London, UK 1959–60, Alexander O. Vietor Fellow, John Carter Brown Library, Brown Univ. 1993. *Address:* 25 Dark Bay Lane, Lake George, NY 12845, USA (office). *E-mail:* rfoulke@skidmore.edu (office); .

FOUQUE, Antoinette, Dr rer. pol, DipLit; French psychoanalyst, feminist and publisher; b. 1 Oct. 1936, Marseilles; d. of Alexis and Vincente Grugnardi; m. René Fouque; one d. *Education:* Univ. of Aix-Marseille and Ecole des Hautes Etudes (Paris). *Career:* Literary Critic and Trans. 1964–68; co-founder Mouvement de Libération des Femmes (MLF) 1968; organizer Politique et Psychanalyse group 1968; founder, Dir Editions Des Femmes publrs 1973, founder three Des Femmes bookshops in Paris, Lyons and Marseilles 1974; Dir Le Quotidien des Femmes magazine 1974, Des Femmes en Mouvements magazine 1978–82; founder Inst. de Recherche en Sciences des Femmes, Coll. de Féminiologie 1978; founder talking book co. (books on cassette) 1980; Dir La Psychanalyste books 1983; founder, Pres. Alliance des Femmes pour la Démocratisation 1989; Rep. for the creation of a women's art museum to Sec. of State for the Rights of Women 1990; Ed. at Passages 1991; Pres. Alliance Française, San Diego (USA) 1986–88; Int. Pres. Women Int. Center, San Diego 1987–88; founder, Hon. Pres. Parité 2000 club 1992; founder mem. Women of Europe cttee 1993; MEP (Energie Radicale list) 1994–99, Vice-Pres. Comm. on the Rights of Women 1994, mem. official del. to UN Int. Conf. on Women, Beijing; teacher Univ. of Paris I (Panthéon-Sorbonne) 1990, Paris VIII (St Denis) 1992 (Dir of Research 1994). *Publications:* Women in Movements, Yesterday, Today, Tomorrow 1992, Il y a deux sexes 1995, If It Is a Woman: Toward a New Human Contact 1999. *Honours:* Officier, Légion d'honneur, Chevalier, Ordre des Arts et des Lettres; Living Legacy Award, San Diego, USA 1986, Leading Women in Europe Award, Milan, Italy 1989, Susan B. Antony Award, USA 1990. *Address:* Editions Des Femmes, 6 rue de Mézières, 75006 Paris, France.

FOWLER, Alastair David Shaw, MA, DPhil, DLitt, FBA; British academic, writer and editor; *Regius Professor Emeritus, University of Edinburgh*; b. 17 Aug. 1930, Glasgow, Scotland; m. Jenny Catherine Simpson 1950, one s. one d. *Education:* University of Edinburgh, University of Oxford. *Career:* Junior Research Fellow Queen's College, Oxford 1955–59; Instructor Indiana University 1957–58; Lecturer University College, Swansea 1959–61; Fellow and Tutor in English Literature Brasenose College, Oxford 1962–71; Visiting Prof. Columbia University 1964; Mem. Institute for Advanced Study, Princeton, NJ 1966, 1980; Visiting Prof. 1969, 1979, 1985–90, Prof. of English 1990–98, University of Virginia; Regius Prof. of Rhetoric and English Literature 1972–84, Prof. Emeritus 1984–, University Fellow 1985–87, University of Edinburgh; Advisory Ed. New Literary History 1972–2003; Visiting Fellow Council of the Humanities, Princeton University 1974, Humanities Research Centre, Canberra 1980, All Souls College, Oxford 1984; General Ed. Longman Annotated Anthologies of English Verse 1977–80; Mem. Editorial Board English Literary Renaissance 1978–2003, Word and Image 1984–91, 1992–97, The Seventeenth Century 1986–2003, Connotations 1990–99, English Review 1990–, Translation and Literature 1990–; mem. Agder Akademi 2003. *Publications:* De re poetica, by Richard Wills (ed. and trans.) 1958, Spenser and the Numbers of Time 1964, Spenser's Images of Life, by C. S. Lewis (ed.) 1967, The Poems of John Milton (ed. with John Carey) 1968, Triumphal Forms 1970, Silent Poetry (ed.) 1970, Topics in Criticism (ed. with Christopher Butler) 1971, Seventeen 1971, Conceitful Thought 1975, Catacomb Suburb 1976, Edmund Spenser 1977, From the Domain of Arnheim 1982, Kinds of Literature 1982, A History of English Literature 1987, The New Oxford Book of Seventeenth Century Verse (ed.) 1991, The Country House Poem 1994, Time's Purpled Masquers 1996, Milton: Paradise Lost (ed.) 1998, Renaissance Realism 2003, How to Write 2006; contrib. to scholarly books and journals. *Address:* 11 E Claremont Street, Edinburgh, EH7 4HT, Scotland (home). *Telephone:* (131) 556-0366 (home).

FOWLER, Don D., BA, PhD; American academic and writer; *Professor of Historic Preservation and Anthropology, University of Nevada*; b. 24 April 1936, Torrey, Utah; m. Catherine Sweeney 1963. *Education:* Weber State College, University of Utah, University of Pittsburgh. *Career:* Instructor, 1964–65, Asst Prof., 1965–67, Assoc. Prof. of Anthropology and Exec. Dir of Human Systems Center of the Desert Research Institute, 1968–71, Research Prof. and Exec. Dir of the Social Sciences Center of the Desert Research Institute, 1971–78, Mamie Kleberg Prof. of Historic Preservation and Anthropology, 1978–, Chair., Dept of Anthropology, 1990–98, University of Nevada, Reno; Visiting Postdoctoral Fellow, 1967–68, Research Assoc., 1970–, Smithsonian Institution, Washington, DC; Fellow, American Anthropological Asscn; mem. Soc. for American Archaeology (pres. 1985–87). *Publications:* Down the Colorado: John Wesley Powell's Diary of the First Trip Through the Grand Canyon (with Eliot Porter), 1969; The Anthropology of the Numa: John Wesley Powell's Manuscripts on Great Basin Indians, 1968–1980 (with C. S. Fowler), 1971; 'Photographed all the Best Scenery': Jack Hillers' Diary of the Powell Expedition, 1871–1875 (ed.), 1971; In Sacred Manner We Live: Edward S. Curtis' Indian Photographs, 1972; Material Culture of the Numa: The John Wesley Powell Collection, 1867–1880 (with J. F. Matley), 1979; American Archaeology Past and Future: A Celebration of the Society for American Archaeology, 1935–1985 (ed. with D. J. Meltzer and J. A. Sabloff), 1986; Anthropology of the Desert West: Essays in Honor of Jesse D. Jennings (ed. with Carol J. Condie), 1986; The Western Photographs of Jack Hillers, 'Myself in the Water', 1989; Others Knowing Others: Perspectives on Ethnographic Careers (ed. with Donald L. Hardesty), 1994; A Laboratory for Anthopology: Science and Romanticism in the American Southwest, 1946–1930, 2000, Philadelphia and the Development of Americanist Archaeology (ed. with D. R. Wilcox) 2003, Southwestern Archaeology in the Twentieth Century (ed. with L. Cordell) 2005; contrib. to many scholarly journals. *Honours:* many private and government grants; Distinguished Graduate Medal, University of Pittsburgh 1986; Lifetime Achievement Award, Society for American Archaeology 2003, Outstanding Researcher Univ. of Nevada, Reno 2003. *Address:* 1010 Foothill Road, Reno, NV 89511, USA. *Telephone:* (775) 853-3471.

FOWLER, Marian Elizabeth, BA, MA, PhD; Canadian writer; b. 15 Oct. 1929, Newmarket, ON; m. Dr Rodney Singleton Fowler 1953 (divorced 1977), one s. one d. *Education:* Univ. of Toronto. *Publications:* The Embroidered Tent: Five Gentlewomen in Early Canada 1982, Redney: A Life of Sara Jeannette Duncan 1983, Below the Peacock Fan: First Ladies of the Raj 1987, Blenheim: Biography of a Palace 1989, In a Gilded Cage: From Heiress to Duchess 1993, The Way She Looks Tonight: Five Women of Style 1996, Hope: Adventures of a Diamond 2003; contrib. to English Studies in Canada, University of Toronto Quarterly, Dalhousie Review, Ontario History, Dictionary of Canadian Biography, Oxford Companion to Canadian Literature, New Canadian Encyclopaedia. *Honours:* Gov.-Gen.'s Gold Medal in English 1951, Canadian Biography Award 1979. *Address:* Apt 503, 77 St Clair Avenue E, Toronto, ON M4T 1M5, Canada.

FOWLER, Rebecca, BSc; British newspaper editor; b. 1958; m. Niall Ferguson; one s. one d. *Education:* Univ. of Southampton. *Career:* freelance journalist; Medical Corresp., Mail on Sunday, then Features Ed.; journalist Daily Mail; Assoc. Ed. Sunday Times 1991, then Deputy Ed.; fmr Ed. Sunday Express. *Address:* c/o Sunday Express, Ludgate House, 245 Blackfriars Road, London, SE1 9UX, England.

FOX, Hugh Bernard, (Connie Fox), BS, MA, PhD; American academic, writer, poet and dramatist; b. 12 Feb. 1932, Chicago, IL; m. 1st Lucia Alicia Ungaro 1957 (divorced 1969); one s. two d.; m. 2nd Nona W. Werner 1970; one s. two d.; m. 3rd Maria Bernadette Costa 1988. *Education:* Loyola Univ., Chicago, Univ. of Illinois, Urbana-Champaign. *Career:* Prof. of American Literature Loyola Marymount Univ., Los Angeles 1958–68; Fulbright Prof., Mexico 1961, Venezuela 1964–66, Brazil 1978–80; Ed. Ghost Dance: The International Quarterly of Experimental Poetry 1968–95; Prof., Michigan State Univ. 1968–99, Prof. Emer.; Lecturer Spain, Portugal 1975–76. *Publications:* fiction: Honeymoon/Mom 1978, Leviathan 1980, Shaman 1993, The Last Summer 1995; poetry: The Face of Guy Lombardo 1975, Almazora 42 1982, Jamais Vu 1991, The Sacred Cave 1992, Once 1995, Techniques 1997; non-fiction: Henry James 1968, Charles Bukowski: A Critical and Bibliographical Study 1969, The Gods of the Cataclysm 1976, First Fire: Central and South American Indian Poetry 1978, Lyn Lifshin: A Critical Study 1985, The Mythological Foundations of the Epic Genre: The Solar Voyage as the Hero's Journey 1989, Stairway to the Sun 1996, Strata 1998, Back 1999, Slides 2000, The Angel of Death: O Ango da Morte 2001, Boston: A Long Poem 2002, Voices 2002, Hugh Fox: Greatest Hits 1968–2001 2003, The Book of Ancient Revelations 2004, The Home of the Gods 2005, Time and Other Poems 2005, Blood Cocoon: Selected Poetry (as Connie Fox) 2005, Collected Poetry 2006, Our Gang: The Last Act 2006; contrib. to many journals, reviews, quarterlies and periodicals. *Honours:* John Carter Brown Library Fellowship, Brown Univ. 1968, Organization of American States Grants, Argentina 1971, Chile 1986. *Address:* 333 Oxford Road, East Lansing, MI 48823-3153, USA. *Telephone:* (517) 337-2829. *E-mail:* hughfox8@aol.com.

FOX, Merrion (Mem) Frances; Australian writer; b. 5 March 1946, Melbourne, Vic.; m. Malcolm 1969; one d. *Education:* BA, Flinders University, 1978; BEd, Sturt College, 1979; Graduate Diploma, Underdale College, 1981. *Career:* mem. Australian Society of Authors; Australian Children's Book Council. *Publications:* Children's Books: Possum Magic, 1983; Wilfrid Gordon McDonald Partridge, 1984; How to Teach Drama to Infants, 1984; A Cat Called Kite, 1985; Zoo-Looking, 1986; Hattie and the Fox, 1986; Sail Away, 1986; Arabella, 1986; Just Like That, 1986; A Bedtime Story, 1987; The Straight Line Wonder, 1987; Goodnight Sleep Tight, 1988; Guess What?, 1988; Koala Lou, 1988; Night Noises, 1989; Shoes for Grandpa, 1989; Sophie, 1989; Memories, 1992; Tough Boris, 1994; Wombat Divine, 1995; Boo to a Goose, 1996; Feathers and Fools, 1996. Adult Books: Mem's the Word, 1990; Dear Mem Fox, I Have Read All Your Books, Even the Pathetic Ones, 1992. Co-Author: English Essentials: The Wouldn't-be-without-it Handbook on Writing Well, 1993; Radical Reflections: Passionate Opinions on Teaching, Learning, and Living, 1993. Contributions: Language Arts; Horn Book; Australian Journal of Language and Literacy; Reading Teacher; Reading and Writing Quarterly; Dragon Lode. *Honours:* New South Wales Premier's Literary Award, Best Children's Book, 1984; KOALA First Prize, 1987; Dromkeen Medal for Outstanding Services to Children's Literature, 1990; Advance Australia Award, 1990; AM, 1994; Alice Award, Fellowship of Australian Women Writers, 1994; Hon. Doctorate, University of Wollongong, 1996. *Literary Agent:* Australian Literary Management, 2A Booth Street, Balmain, NSW 2041, Australia.

FOX, Paula; American novelist; b. 22 April 1923, New York, NY; m. 1st Howard Bird 1940 (divorced); one d.; m. 2nd Richard Sigerson 1948 (divorced); two s.; m. 3rd Martin Greenberg 1962. *Education:* Columbia Univ. *Career:* mem. American Acad. of Arts and Letters. *Publications:* Novels: Poor George, 1967; Desperate Characters, 1970; The Western Coast, 1972; The Widow's Children, 1976; A Servant's Tale, 1984; The God of Nightmares, 1990. Children's Books: Maurice's Room, 1966; A Likely Place, 1967; Dear Prosper, 1968; The Stone-Faced Boy, 1968; The King's Falcon, 1969; Blowfish Live in the Sea, 1970; The Slave Dancer, 1973; The Little Swinehead and Other Tales, 1978; A Place Apart, 1980; One-Eyed Cat, 1984; The Moonlight Man, 1986; The Village by the Sea (aka In a Place of Danger), 1988; Monkey Island, 1991; Western Wind, 1993; The Eagle Kite (aka The Gathering Darkness), 1995; Amzat and His Brothers: Three Italian Tales, 1999. Other: Borrowed Finery (memoir), 2001. *Honours:* Hans Christian Andersen Medal for Children's Literature. *Address:* c/o Flamingo, 77–85 Fulham Palace Road, London, W6 8JB, England.

FRAILE, Medardo, PhD, DLitt; Spanish writer and academic; b. 21 March 1925, Madrid; m. Janet H. Gallagher; one d. *Education:* Univ. of Madrid. *Career:* mem. Gen. Soc. of Spanish Authors, Working Community of Book Writers, Asscn of Univ. Teachers. *Publications:* Cuentos con algún amor 1954, A la luz cambian las cosas 1959, Cuentos de verdad 1964, Descubridor de nada y otros cuentos 1970, Con los días contado 1972, Samuel Ros hacia una generación sin crítica 1972, La penúltima Inglaterra 1973, Poesía y Teatro españoles contemporáneos 1974, Ejemplario 1979, Autobiografía (novella) 1986, Cuento español de Posguerra 1986, El gallo puesto en hora 1987, Entre paréntesis 1988, Santa Engracia, número dos o tres 1989, Teatro español en un acto 1989, El rey y el país con granos 1991, Cuentos completos 1991, Claudina y los cacos 1992, La familia irreal inglesa 1993, Los brazos invisibles 1994, Documento nacional 1997, Contrasombras 1998, Ladrones del Paraíso 1999, Cuentos de verdad (anthology) 2000, Descontar y contar (México) 2000, La letra con sangre 2001, Años de aprendizaje (Venezuela) 2001, Escritura y Verdad, Cuentos completos 2004, Palabra en el tiempo 2005, En Madrid también se vive en Oruro (Bolivia) 2007; translator: El Weir de Hermiston by R. L. Stevenson 1995; contrib. to many publs. *Honours:* Colegiado de Honor del Colegio Heráldico de España y de las Indias 1965, Comendador con Placa de la Orden Civil de Alfonso X El Sabio 1999, Orden venezolana de Don Balthasar de León de Primera Clase; Sésamo Award 1956, Literary Grant, Fundación Juan March 1960, Critics' Book of the Year 1965, La Estafeta Literaria Award 1970, Hucha de Oro 1971, Research Grant, Carnegie Trust for Univs of Scotland 1975. *Address:* 24 Etive Crescent, Bishopbriggs, Glasgow, G64 1ES, Scotland.

FRAIN, Irène Marie Anne; French writer and journalist; b. 22 May 1950, Lorient; d. of Jean Le Pohon and Simone Le Pohon (née Martelot); m. François Frain 1969; one d. *Education:* high schools in Lorient and Rennes and Univ. of Paris IV (Paris-Sorbonne). *Career:* teacher, secondary schools, then Univ. of Paris III (Sorbonne-Nouvelle) 1971–86; first book published 1979; journalist on Paris Match magazine 1984–. *Publications:* Quand les Bretons peuplaient les mers 1979, Contes du cheval bleu les jours de grand vent 1980, Le Nabab (Prix des Maisons de la Presse) 1982, Modern Style 1984, Désirs (Prix des Ecrivains de l'Ouest) 1986, Secret de Famille (Prix Radio-Télé Luxembourg–RTL Grand Public) 1989, Histoire de Lou 1989, La guirlande de Julie 1991, Devi 1993, Quai des Indes 1993, Vive la mariée 1993, La vallée des hommes perdus 1994, L'homme fatal 1995, L'inimitable 1998, A jamais 1999, La maison de la source 2000, Pour que ne fleurisse le monde (with Jetsun Pema) 2002, Les Hommes, etc. 2003. *Honours:* Officier des Arts et Lettres 1989; Chevalier de la Légion d'honneur 1998; Officier de l'Ordre nat. du Mérite 2002. *Address:* c/o Editions Fayard, 75 rue des Saints-Pères, 75006 Paris, France. *Telephone:* (1) 43-06-06-71. *Fax:* (1) 43-06-06-81. *E-mail:* irene.frain@wanadoo.fr. *Website:* www.irenefrain.com.

FRAJLICH, Anna, MA, PhD; Polish poet and academic; b. 10 March 1942, Katta Taldyk, Kyrgyzstan; m. Władysław Zajac 1965; one s. *Education:* Warsaw Univ., New York Univ. *Career:* Lecturer, Dept of Slavic Languages, Columbia Univ. 1982–; mem. PEN Club, Center for Writers in Exile, USA, Asscn of Polish Writers. *Publications:* Indian Summer 1982, Który las 1986, Between Dawn and the Wind 1991, Ogrodem i ogrodzeniem (The Garden and the Fence) 1993, Jeszcze w drodze (Still on its Way) 1994, Wsłońcu listopada 2000, Znów szuka mnie wiatr 2001; contribs to Terra Poetica, Artful Dodge, The Polish Review, Wisconsin Review, Mr Cogito, The Jewish Quarterly, Poésie Première, World Literature Today; chapters in several books. *Honours:* Knight's Cross of the Order of Merit, Poland 2002; Koscielski Foundation Award, Switzerland 1981, Readers' Choice for Polish Book of the Month, Rzeczpospolita newspaper, Warsaw 2001, W. & N. Turzanski Foundation Literary Award, Canada 2003. *Address:* c/o Department of Slavic Languages, Columbia University, New York, NY 10027, USA.

FRAME, Ronald William Sutherland, MA, MLitt; British author; b. 23 May 1953, Glasgow, Scotland; s. of Alexander D. Frame and Isobel D. Frame (née Sutherland). *Education:* The High School of Glasgow, Univ. of Glasgow, Jesus Coll. Oxford. *Career:* full-time author 1981–; many recent Scottish-set short stories published in UK, N America and Australia; regular weekly 'Carnbeg' short story in The Herald (Scotland) 2007. *Publications:* Winter Journey 1984, Watching Mrs. Gordon 1985, A Long Weekend with Marcel Proust 1986, Sandmouth People 1987, Paris (TV play) 1987, A Woman of Judah 1987, Penelope's Hat 1989, Bluette 1990, Underwood and After 1991, Walking My Mistress in Deauville 1992, The Sun on the Wall 1994, The Lantern Bearers 1999, Permanent Violet 2002, Time in Carnbeg 2004. TV screenplays: Paris 1985, Out of Time 1987, Ghost City 1994, A Modern Man 1996, Four Ghost Stories for Christmas (adaptation) 2000, Darien: Disaster in Paradise 2003, Cromwell 2003, The Two Loves of Anthony Trollope (script contrib.) 2004. Radio scripts include: Winter Journey 1985, Twister 1986, Rendezvous 1987, Cara 1989, The Lantern Bearers 1997, The Hydro (serial) 1997–99, Havisham 1998, Maestro 1999, Pharos 2000, Don't Look Now (adaptation) 2001, Sunday at Sant' Agata 2001, Greyfriars 2002, The Servant (adaptation) 2005, The Razor's Edge (adaptation) 2005, A Tiger for Malgudi (adaptation) 2006 The Blue Room (adaptation) 2007. *Honours:* Betty Trask Prize (jt first recipient) 1984, Samuel Beckett Prize 1986, TV Industries' Panel's Most Promising Writer New to Television Award 1986, Saltire Scottish Book of the Year 2000, American Library Asscn's Barbara Gittings Honor Prize for Fiction 2003. *Literary Agent:* c/o Curtis Brown Ltd, Haymarket House, 28–29 Haymarket, London, SW1Y 4SP, England. *Telephone:* (20) 7393-4400. *Fax:* (20) 7393-4401. *E-mail:* info@curtisbrown.co.uk. *Website:* www.curtisbrown.co.uk.

FRANCE, (Evelyn) Christine, BA; Australian art historian; b. 23 Dec. 1939, Sydney, NSW; m. Stephen Robert Bruce France 1962; one d. *Education:* University of Sydney. *Publications:* Justin O'Brien: Image and Icon, 1987; Margaret Olley, 1990; Marea Gazzard: Form and Clay, 1994; Jean Appleton: A Lifetime with Art, 1998. Contributions: Art and Australia; Australian newspapers.

FRANCIS, Clare Mary, MBE, BSc; British writer and fmr yachtswoman; b. 17 April 1946, Thames Ditton, Surrey; d. of Owen Francis; m. Jacques Robert Redon 1977 (divorced 1985); one s. *Education:* Royal Ballet School and Univ. Coll. London. *Career:* crossed Atlantic Ocean singlehanded in 37 days, Falmouth (UK) to Newport (USA) 1973; competed in Round Britain Race 1974, Azores Race 1975, L'Aurore Race 1975, 1976; women's record Observer Transatlantic Singlehanded Race (29 days) 1976; first woman skipper Whitbread Round the World Race 1977–78; full-time novelist 1981–; Fellow, Univ. Coll. London 1979; Pres. Action for ME (charity). *TV Series:* The Commanding Sea (co-writer and presenter) 1981. *Publications:* non-fiction: Come Hell or High Water 1977, Come Wind or Weather 1978, The Commanding Sea 1981; novels: Night Sky 1983, Red Crystal 1985, Wolf Winter 1987, Requiem 1991, Deceit 1993 (televised 2000), Betrayal 1995, A Dark Devotion 1997, Keep Me Close 1999, A Death Divided 2001, Homeland 2004. *Honours:* Hon. Fellow, UMIST 1981. *Address:* c/o John Johnson Agency, 45–47 Clerkenwell Green, London, EC1R 0HT, England. *Website:* www.clarefrancis.com.

FRANCIS, Richard (Dick) Stanley, CBE, FRSL; British writer; b. 31 Oct. 1920, Tenby, S Wales; s. of George V. Francis and Catherine M. Francis; m. Mary M. Brenchley 1947 (died 2000); two s. *Career:* fighter and bomber pilot, RAF 1940–46; amateur steeplechase jockey (Nat. Hunt racing) 1946–48; professional steeplechase jockey 1948–57; champion steeplechase jockey 1953–54; racing columnist, Sunday Express 1957–73; author and novelist 1957–. *Publications:* fiction: Dead Cert 1962, Nerve 1964, For Kicks (CWA Silver Dagger Award 1966) 1965, Odds Against (Sid Halley series) 1965, Flying Finish 1966, Blood Sport 1967, Forfeit (Edgar Allan Poe Award 1970) 1968, Enquiry 1969, Rat Race 1970, Bonecrack 1971, Smokescreen 1972, Slayride 1973, Knockdown 1974, High Stakes 1975, In the Frame 1976, Risk 1977, Trial Run 1978, Whip Hand (Sid Halley series) (Edgar Allan Poe Award 1980, CWA Gold Dagger Award 1980) 1979, Reflex 1980, Twice Shy 1981, Banker 1982, The Danger 1983, Proof 1984, Break In (Kit Fielding series) 1985, Bolt (Kit Fielding series) 1986, Hot Money 1987, The Edge 1988, Straight 1989, Great Racing Stories (co-ed.) 1989, Longshot 1990, Comeback 1991, Driving Force 1992, Decider 1993, Wild Horses 1994, Come to Grief (Sid Halley series) (Edgar Allan Poe Award 1996) 1995, To The Hilt 1996, 10lb Penalty 1997, Field of Thirteen 1998, Second Wind 1999, Shattered 2000, Under Orders 2006; non-fiction: The Sport of Queens (autobiog.) 1957, Lester (biog. of Lester Piggott) 1986. *Honours:* Hon. DHumLitt (Tufts Univ., Mass., USA) 1991; Cartier Diamond Dagger Award for life's work 1990, named Grand Master by Mystery Writers of America 1996, three Edgar Awards. *Literary Agent:* c/o John Johnson, Johnson & Alcock Ltd, Clerkenwell House, 45–47 Clerkenwell Green, London, EC1R 0HT, England.

FRANCIS, Matthew, MA, PhD; British poet and novelist; *Lecturer in Creative Writing, University of Wales Aberystwyth;* b. 1956, Gosport, Hants.; s. of Leslie Francis and Marian Mary Francis (née Rennie); m. Creina Burford-Bowden 1986. *Education:* Univs of Cambridge and Southampton. *Career:* fmrly Lecturer in Creative Writing, Univ. of Glamorgan, S Wales; Lecturer in Creative Writing, Univ. of Wales Aberystwyth 2003–. *Publications:* poetry: Blizzard 1996, Dragons 2001, Whereabouts 2006; novel: WHOM 1989; criticism: Where the People Are: Language and Community in the Poetry of W. S. Graham 2004; editor: W. S. Graham, New Collected Poems 2004. *Honours:* Southern Arts Literature Prize 1997, Gathering Swallows Prize 1997, Hawthornden Fellowship 1998, MFCAP Prize 1999, TLS/Blackwells Prize 2000, Next Generation Poets List 2004. *Literary Agent:* c/o Faber and Faber Ltd, 3 Queen Square, London, WC1N 3AU, England. *Telephone:* (1970) 622469 (office). *Fax:* (1970) 622530 (office). *E-mail:* mwf@aber.ac.uk (office). *Website:* www.aber.ac.uk (office); www.7greenhill.freeserve.co.uk (home).

FRANCK, Dan; French writer and screenwriter; b. 17 March 1952, Paris; s. of Alain Franck and Marcelle Franck (née Refkolevsky); two s. *Education:* Lycée de la Celle-Saint-Cloud, Lycée de Rueil-Malmaison, Sorbonne Univ. *Films as writer:* Netchaïev est de retour 1991, Berlin Lady (TV) 1991, La Séparation 1994, Tykho Moon 1996, Les Parents modèles (TV) 1997, Jean Moulin (TV) 2002, Simon le juste (TV) 2003, Les Enfants 2005. *Film appearances:* Toujours seuls 1991, En compagnie d'Antonin Artaud 1993, Paddy 1999. *Publications:* Les Calendes grecques (Prix du Premier Roman) 1980, Apolline 1982, La Dame du soir 1984, Les Adieux 1987, Le Cimetière des fous 1989, La Séparation (Prix Renaudot) 1991, Une jeune fille 1994, Tabac 1995, Nu couché 1998, Bohèmes 1998, Un siècle d'amour (with Enki Bilal) 1999, Libertad! 2004; with Jean Vautrin: Les Aventures de Boro, reporter-photographe: La Dame de Berlin 1988, Le Temps des cerises 1990, Les Noces de Guernica 1994, Mademoiselle Chat 1996, Boro s'en va en guerre 2000; essays: Les Têtes de l'art 1983, Le Petit livre de l'orchestre et de ses instruments 1993, Le Carnet de la Californie 1999. *Address:* c/o Le Seuil, 27 rue Jacob, 75261 Paris Cédex 06, France.

FRANCK, Thomas Martin, BA, LLM, SJD; American academic and writer; *Murry and Ida Becker Professor of Law Emeritus, New York University School of Law;* b. 14 July 1931, Berlin, Germany. *Education:* University of British Columbia, Harvard Law School. *Career:* Asst Prof., University of Nebraska College of Law 1954–56; Assoc. Prof. New York University School of Law 1960–62, Prof. of Law 1962–, Dir, Center for International Studies 1965–2002, Murry and Ida Becker Professor of Law Emeritus 2002–; Visiting Prof., Stanford Law School 1963, University of East Africa Law School, Dar es Salaam 1963–66, Osgood Hall Law School, York University, Toronto 1972–76, Woodrow Wilson School, Princeton University 1979; Lecturer, The Hague Acad. of International Law 1993; Visiting Fellow, Trinity College, Cambridge 1996–97; mem. Africa Watch; American Society of International Law; Canadian Council on International Law; Council on Foreign Relations; French Society of International Law; German Society of International Law; Institut du Droit International; International Law Asscn, vice-pres. 1973–94, hon. vice-pres. 1994–; International Peace Acad.; Acad. of Arts and Sciences 2003. *Publications:* United States Foreign Relations Law: Documents and Sources (co-author), 5 vols 1980–84, The Tethered Presidency 1981, Human Rights in Third World Perspective, 3 vols 1982, Foreign Relations and National Security Law 1987, The Power of Legitimacy Among Nations 1990, Political Questions/Judicial Answers: Does the Rule of Law Apply to Foreign Affairs? 1992, Fairness in the International Legal and Institutional System 1993, Fairness in International Law and Institutions 1995, International Law Decisions in National Courts (co-ed.) 1996, The Empowered Self: Law and Society in the Age of Individualism 1999, Delegating State Powers, The Effect of Treaty Regimes on Democracy and Sovereignty 2000, Recourse to Force: State Action Against Threats and Armed Attacks 2002; contribs to scholarly journals. *Honours:* Hon. LLD (British Columbia) 1995, (Wales Aberystwyth) 2004, (Glasgow) 2004, Hon. DHL (Monterey Institute of International Studies) 2003; Guggenheim Fellowships 1973–74, 1982–83, Christopher Medal 1976, Certificates of Merit, American Society of International Law 1981, 1986, 1994, 1996, John E. Read Medal, Canadian Council on International Law 1994, Hudson Medal, American Society of International Law 2003. *Address:* c/o New York University School of Law, 40 Washington Square S, New York, NY 10012, USA (office). *Telephone:* (212) 998-6209 (office). *Fax:* (212) 995-4653 (office). *E-mail:* franckt@juris.law.nyu.edu (office).

FRANCO, Tomaso, DJur; Italian poet and writer; b. 23 May 1933, Bologna; m. (divorced); two s. *Education:* studied classics, law and art. *Publications:* poetry: Uno Scatto dell'Evoluzione 1984, Parole d'Archivio 1986, Il Libro dei Torti 1988, Casa di Frontiera 1990, Volavi Per Me 2000, In Un Luogo della Mente 2001, Nome Lontano 2004, plaguette, Esitante per Amore 2004; anthologies: Il Viaggiatore Indispensabile 2002; novels: Soldato dei Sogni 1995; short stories: I Muri della Casa 2005; essays: Sila-Torino 1961, Lettere a un Fuoruscito 1988, Antichità di Lavarone 2003; contrib. to various anthologies, newspapers, and journals. *Honours:* first prize Clemente Rèbora, Milan 1986, Gold Medal, City of Como 1990, first prize (National) Associazione

Promozione Cultura in Toscana 1992. *Address:* Via San Domenico 2, 36100 Vicenza, Italy.

FRANCO ESTADELLA, Antonio; Spanish journalist; *Editor, El Periódico de Catalunya;* b. 21 Jan. 1947, Barcelona; s. of Alfonso Franco and Lolita Estadella; m. Marie-Hélène Bigatá; one s. one d. *Career:* Ed. Sports Section Diario Barcelona 1970, Ed.-in-Chief 1973, Asst Dir 1975; Dir Siete Días (TV programme) 1977; f. El Periódico de Catalunya 1977, Ed. 1987–, Ed.-in-Chief; Jt Ed. El País 1982. *Honours:* Premio Ortega y Gasset (for journalism), Premio Godó (for journalism), Premio Luca de Tena (for journalism). *Address:* El Periódico de Catalunya, Consell de Cent 425–427, 08009 Barcelona, Spain. *Telephone:* (93) 2655353. *Fax:* (93) 4846517. *E-mail:* afranco@elperiodico.com (office). *Website:* www.elperiodico.es (office).

FRANCO RAMOS, Jorge; Colombian writer; b. 1964, Medellín. *Education:* London Int. Film School, England and Pontificia Universidad Javeriana, Bogotá. *Publications:* Maldito amor (short stories) (winner Concurso Nacional de Narrativa Pedro Gómez Valderrama) 1996, Mala noche (novel) (winner Concurso Nacional de Novela Ciudad de Pereira) 1997, Rosario Tijeras (novel) (Dashiell Hammett Prize 2000) 1999, Paraíso Travel (novel) 2001. *Honours:* Ministry of Culture nat. grant for novel 1999. *Address:* c/o Seven Stories Press, 140 Watts Street, New York, NY 10013, USA. *E-mail:* publicity@sevenstories .com. *Website:* www.jorge-franco.com.

FRANK, Elizabeth, MA, PhD; American writer and academic; *Joseph E. Harry Professor of Modern Languages and Literature, Center for Curatorial Studies, Bard College;* b. 1945, Los Angeles, CA. *Education:* Univ. of Calif., Berkeley. *Career:* Joseph E. Harry Prof. of Modern Languages and Literature, Center for Curatorial Studies, Bard Coll. 1982–. *Publications:* Jackson Pollock (biog.) 1983, Louise Bogan: A Portrait (biog.) (Pulitzer Prize for Biog. 1986) 1985, Esteban Vicente (biog.) 1995, Cheat and Charmer (novel) 2004; contrib. numerous articles to New York Arts Journal, Art in America, Journal of Modern Literature, Twentieth-Century Literature, ARTnews, Bennington Review, The Nation, Salmagundi, New York Times Book Review, Partisan Review. *Honours:* Ford Foundation Fellowship 1967–72, Temple Univ. Fellowship 1977, The Newbery Library Fellowship 1977, American Council of Learned Socs Fellowship 1977, Nat. Endowment for the Humanities Fellowship. *Address:* Center for Curatorial Studies, Bard College, Annandale-on-Hudson, NY 12504-5000, USA. *E-mail:* frank@bard.edu.

FRANK, Joseph Nathaniel; American academic and writer; b. 6 Oct. 1918, New York, NY; m. Marguerite J. Straus 1953; two d. *Education:* New York University, 1937–38; University of Wisconsin 1941–42; University of Paris, 1950–51; PhD, University of Chicago, 1960. *Career:* Ed., Bureau of National Affairs, Washington, DC, 1942–50; Asst Prof., Dept of English, University of Minnesota, 1958–61; Assoc. Prof., Rutgers University, 1961–66; Prof. of Comparative Literature, 1966–85, Dir of Christian Gauss Seminars, 1966–83, Princeton University; Visiting Mem., Institute for Advanced Study, 1984–87; Prof. of Comparative Literature and Slavic Languages and Literatures, 1985–89, Prof. Emeritus, 1989–, Stanford University; mem. American Acad. of Arts and Sciences, fellow. *Publications:* The Widening Gyre: Crisis and Mastery in Modern Literature, 1963; Dostoevsky: The Seeds of Revolt, 1821–1849, 1976; Dostoevsky: The Years of Ordeal, 1850–1859, 1983; Dostoevsky: The Stir of Liberation, 1860–1865, 1986; Selected Letters of Fyodor Dostoevsky (co-ed.), 1987; Through the Russian Prism, 1989; The Idea of Spatial Form, 1991; Dostoevsky: The Miraculous Years, 1865–1871, 1995. Contributions: Southern Review; Sewanee Review; Hudson Review; Partisan Review; Art News; Critique; Chicago Review; Minnesota Review; Russian Review; Le Contrat Social; Commentary; Encounter; New York Review. *Honours:* Fulbright Scholar, 1950–51; Rockefeller Fellow, 1952–53, 1953–54; Guggenheim Fellowships, 1956–57, 1975–76; Award, National Institute of Arts and Letters, 1958; Research Grants, ACLS, 1964–65, 1967–68, 1970–71; James Russell Lowell Prize, 1977; Christian Gauss Awards, 1977, 1996; Rockefeller Foundation Fellowships, 1979–80, 1983–84; National Book Critics Circle Award, 1984. *Address:* c/o Dept of Slavic Languages and Literatures, Stanford University, Stanford, CA 94305, USA.

FRANKE, William, BA, MA, PhD; American academic and poet; b. 1 April 1956, Milwaukee, Wisconsin. *Education:* Williams College, University of Oxford, University of California at Berkeley, Stanford University. *Career:* Adjunct Faculty Mem., Columbia College, 1984–86; Faculty Mem., 1991–96, Assoc. Prof. of Comparative Literature and Italian, 1996–, Vanderbilt University, Nashville, Tennessee; Lecturer, educational institutions including Stanford University, 1991, University of Tulsa, 1992, University of Reading, England, 1995. *Publications:* Dante's Interpretive Journey, 1996. Contributions: Books including Through a Glass Darkly: Essays in the Religious Imagination; Dante: Contemporary Perspectives, 1996; Articles and poems to journals including SEAMS: Cultural Arts Journal; California State Poetry Quarterly; Italian Quarterly; Religion and Literature; Yeats-Eliot Review; Symploke: Journal for the Intermingling of Literary, Cultural, and Theoretical Scholarship. *Honours:* John E. Moody Scholar, University of Oxford, 1978–80; Scholarship to W. B. Yeats International Summer School, Sligo, Ireland, 1979; Alexander von Humboldt Fellow, Germany, 1994–95; Grants, Istituto Italiano per gli studi filosifici, Naples, Italy, 1995, 1996; Robert Penn Warren Center for the Humanities Fellow, 1995–96. *Address:* c/o Vanderbilt University, PO Box 1709, Station B, Nashville, TN 37235, USA.

FRANKEL, Max, MA; American journalist; b. 3 April 1930, Gera, Germany; s. of Jacob A. Frankel and Mary (Katz) Frankel; m. 1st. Tobia Brown 1956 (died

1987); two s. one d.; m. 2nd Joyce Purnick 1988. *Education:* Columbia Univ., New York. *Career:* mem. staff, The New York Times 1952, Chief Washington Corresp. 1968–72, Sunday Ed. 1973–76, Editorial Pages Ed. 1977–86, Exec. Ed. 1986–94, 1994–95, also columnist New York Times magazine 1995–2000. *Publication:* The Time of My Life and My Life with the Times 1999, High Noon in the Cold War: Kennedy, Khrushchev and the Cuban Missile Crisis 2004. *Honours:* Pulitzer Prize for Int. Reporting 1973. *Address:* c/o The New York Times Co., 15 West 67th Street, New York, NY 10023-6226, USA.

FRANKEL, Naomi; Israeli poet and writer; *Address:* c/o Hebron University, PO Box 40, Hebron, West Bank, via Israel.

FRANKFURT, Harry Gordon, BA, MA, PhD; American writer and academic; *Professor Emeritus of Philosophy, Princeton University*; b. 29 May 1929, Langhorne, PA; m. Joan Gilbert. *Education:* Johns Hopkins Univ., Cornell Univ. *Career:* instructor, Ohio State Univ. 1956–59, Asst Prof. 1959–62; Assoc. Prof., SUNY at Binghamton 1962–63; Research Assoc., Rockefeller Univ., New York 1963–64, Assoc. Prof. 1964–71, Prof. of Philosophy 1971–76; Visiting Fellow, All Souls Coll., Oxford 1971–72; Visiting Prof., Vassar Coll. 1973–74, Univ. of Pittsburgh 1975–76, Univ. of California at Los Angeles 1990; Prof. of Philosophy, Yale Univ. 1976–89, Chair Dept of Philosophy 1978–87, John M. Schiff Prof. 1989; Prof. of Philosophy, Princeton Univ. 1990–2002, Prof. Emeritus 2002–; Fellow American Acad. of Arts and Sciences; mem. American Philosophical Asscn (Eastern Division) (pres. 1991–92). *Publications:* Demons, Dreamers, and Madmen: The Defense of Reason in Descartes's Meditations 1970, Leibniz: A Collection of Critical Essays (ed.) 1972, The Importance of What We Care About 1988, Necessity, Volition and Love 1999, The Reasons of Love 2004, On Bullshit 2005. *Honours:* Nat. Endowment for the Humanities Fellowships 1981–82, 1994, Guggenheim Fellowship 1993. *Address:* c/o 109 Marx Hall, Princeton University, Princeton, NJ 08544, USA.

FRANKLAND, (Anthony) Noble, DFC, CBE, CB, MA, DPhil; British historian and writer; b. 4 July 1922, Ravenstonedale, England; m. 1st Diana Madeline Fovargue Tavernor 1944 (died 1981); one s. one d.; m. 2nd Sarah Katharine Davies 1982. *Education:* Trinity College, Oxford. *Career:* served in Royal Air Force 1941–45, Bomber Command 1943–45, Air Historical Branch Air Ministry 1948–50; Official British Military Historian, Cabinet Office 1951–58; Deputy Dir of Studies, Royal Institute of International Affairs 1956–60; Dir, Imperial War Museum 1960–82; Lees Knowles Lecturer, Trinity College, Cambridge 1963. *Publications:* Documents on International Affairs 1958, 1959, 1960, Crown of Tragedy: Nicholas II 1960, The Strategic Air Offensive Against Germany 1939–45 (with Sir Charles Webster), 4 vols 1961, The Bombing Offensive Against Germany: Outlines and Perspectives 1965, Bomber Offensive: The Devastation of Europe 1970, The Politics and Strategy of the Second World War (co-ed.), eight vols 1974–78, Decisive Battles of the Twentieth Century: Land, Sea, Air (co-ed.) 1976, Prince Henry, Duke of Gloucester 1980, Encyclopedia of Twentieth Century Warfare (general ed. and contributor) 1989, Witness of a Century: Prince Arthur, Duke of Connaught 1850–1942 1993, History at War: The Campaigns of an Historian 1998, The Unseen War (novel); contributions: Encyclopaedia Britannica, TLS, The Times, Daily Telegraph, Spectator, Observer, military journals. *Address:* 26–27 Riverview Terrace, Abingdon, Oxfordshire, OX14 5AE, England (home). *Telephone:* (1235) 521624 (home).

FRANKLIN, Dan; British publisher; *Publishing Director, Jonathan Cape*. *Career:* currently Publishing Dir, Jonathan Cape. *Address:* Jonathan Cape Ltd, Random House, 20 Vauxhall Bridge Road, London, SW1V 2SA, England. *E-mail:* dfranklin@randomhouse.co.uk. *Website:* www.randomhouse.co.uk.

FRANKLIN, John Hope, AM, PhD; American writer, historian and academic; *James B. Duke Professor Emeritus of History, Duke University*; b. 2 Jan. 1915, Rentiesville, Okla; s. of Buck Colbert Franklin and Mollie Franklin (née Parker); m. Aurelia E. Whittington 1940 (died 1999); one s. *Education:* Fisk Univ., Harvard Univ. *Career:* Instructor in History Fisk Univ. 1936–38; Prof. of History St Augustine's Coll. 1939–43, NC Coll., Durham 1943–47, Howard Univ. 1947–56; Chair. Dept of History Brooklyn Coll. 1956–64; Prof. of American History Univ. of Chicago 1964–82, Chair. Dept of History 1967–70, John Matthews Manly Distinguished Service Prof. 1969–82; James B. Duke Prof. of History, Duke Univ. 1982–85, James B. Duke Prof. Emer. 1985–; Prof. of Legal History, Duke Law School 1985–92; Pitt Prof. of American History and Institutions Cambridge Univ. 1962–63; Visiting Prof. Harvard, Wis., Cornell, Hawaii, Calif. and Cambridge Univs and Salzburg Seminar; Chair. Bd of Foreign Scholarships 1966–69, Nat. Council on Humanities 1976–79; Chair. Pres.'s Initiative on Race 1997, Advisory Bd Nat. Park System 2000; Dir Ill. Bell Telephone Co. 1972–80; Edward Austin Fellow 1937–38, Rosenwald Fellow 1937–39, Guggenheim Fellow 1950–51, 1973–74; Pres.'s Fellow, Brown Univ. 1952–53, Center for Advanced Study in Behavioral Science 1973–74; Sr Mellon Fellow, Nat. Humanities Center 1980–82; Fulbright Prof., Australia 1960; Jefferson Lecturer in Humanities 1976; mem. Bd of Dirs Salzburg Seminar, Museum of Science and Industry 1968–80; mem. American Historical Asscn (Pres. 1978–79), Southern Historical Asscn (Pres. 1970–71), Org. of American Historians (Pres. 1970–75), Asscn for Study of Negro Life and History, American Studies Asscn, American Philosophical Soc., American Asscn of Univ. Profs; mem. Bd Duke Endowment 1994. *Television:* First Person Singular (PBS) 1997, Tutu and Franklin: Journey Towards Peace (PBS) 1999, Biographical Conversations (PBS) 2001. *Publications:* Free Negro in North Carolina 1943, From Slavery to Freedom: A History of Negro Americans 1947 (with A. A. Moss, Jr), 8th edn 2000, Militant South 1956, Reconstruction After the Civil War 1961, The Emancipation Proclamation 1963, Land of the Free (with others) 1966, Illustrated History of Black Americans 1970, A Southern Odyssey 1976, Racial Equality in America 1976, George Washington Williams: A Biography 1985, Race and History: Selected Essays 1938–88 1990, The Color Line: Legacy for the 21st Century 1993; Ed. Civil War Diary of James T. Ayers 1947, A Fool's Errand (by Albion Tourgee) 1961, Army Life in a Black Regiment (by Thomas Higginson) 1962, Color and Race 1968, Reminiscences of an Active Life (by John R. Lynch) 1970, African Americans and the Living Constitution (ed. with Gemma R. McNeil) 1995, Runaway Slaves: Rebels on the Plantation (with Loren Schwenirager) 1999. *Honours:* numerous hon. degrees; Jefferson Medal (American Philosophical Soc.) 1993, Presidential Medal of Freedom 1995, Spingarn Medal 1995, Skirball Award 2000, Harold Washington 2000, Lincoln Prize 2000. *Address:* 208 Pineview Road, Durham, NC 27707, USA (home). *Telephone:* (919) 489-7513 (office). *Fax:* (919) 490-9789.

FRANZEN, Jonathan, BA; American writer; b. 1959, Western Springs, IL; m. Valerie Cornell (divorced). *Education:* Swarthmore Coll., Free Univ. of Berlin, Germany. *Career:* fmrly worked in seismology lab., Harvard Univ. Dept of Earth and Planetary Sciences; currently full-time writer; columnist, The New Yorker, Harper's. *Publications:* The Twenty-Seventh City (Whiting Award) 1988, Strong Motion 1991, The Corrections (Nat. Book Award for Fiction, New York Times Ed.'s Choice, James Tait Black Memorial Prize for Fiction 2003) 2001, How to be Alone (essays) 2002, The Discomfort Zone: A Personal History 2006; contrib. to New Yorker, Harper's. *Honours:* American Acad. Berlin Prize 2000, Granta Best Young American Novelist. *Literary Agent:* Steven Barclay Agency, 12 Western Avenue, Petaluma, CA 94952, USA. *Telephone:* (707) 773-0654. *Fax:* (707) 778-1868. *Website:* www.barclayagency.com. *Address:* c/o Farrar, Straus and Giroux, 19 Union Square W, New York, NY 10003 (office); 875 Sixth Avenue, New York, NY 10001, USA. *Website:* www.jonathanfranzen.com.

FRASER, Lady Antonia, CBE, MA, FRSL; British writer; b. 27 Aug. 1932, London; d. of the late Earl and Countess of Longford; m. 1st Hugh Fraser 1956 (divorced 1977, died 1984); three s. three d.; m. 2nd Harold Pinter (q.v.) 1980. *Education:* Dragon School, Oxford, St Mary's Convent, Ascot and Lady Margaret Hall, Oxford. *Career:* mem. Cttee English PEN 1979–88 (Pres. 1988–89, Vice-Pres. 1990–), Crimewriters Asscn 1980–86, Writers in Prison Cttee, Chair. 1985–88, 1990. *TV plays:* Charades 1977, Mister Clay 1985. *Publications:* King Arthur 1954, Robin Hood 1955, Dolls 1963, History of Toys 1966, Mary, Queen of Scots 1969 (James Tait Black Memorial Prize), Cromwell: Our Chief of Men 1973, King James VI of Scotland and I of England 1974, Scottish Love Poems, A Personal Anthology 1974, Kings and Queens of England (ed.) 1975, Love Letters (anthology) 1976, Quiet as a Nun 1977, The Wild Island 1978, King Charles II 1979, Heroes and Heroines (ed.) 1980, A Splash of Red 1981, Cool Repentance 1982, Oxford In Verse (ed.) 1982, The Weaker Vessel 1984 (Wolfson History Prize), Oxford Blood 1985, Jemima Shore's First Case 1986, Your Royal Hostage 1987, Boadicea's Chariot: The Warrior Queens 1988, The Cavalier Case 1990, Jemima Shore at the Sunny Grave 1991, The Six Wives of Henry VIII 1992, Charles II: His Life and Times 1993, Political Death: A Jemima Shore Mystery 1994, The Gunpowder Plot (St Louis Literary Award 1996, CWA Non Fiction Gold Dagger 1996) 1996, The Lives of the Kings and Queens of England 1998, Marie Antoinette: the Journey 2001, Love and Louis XIV 2006; ed. The Pleasure of Reading 1992; television adaptations of Quiet as a Nun 1978, Jemima Shore Investigates 1983. *Honours:* Hon. DLitt (Hull) 1986, (Sussex) 1990, (Nottingham) 1993, (St Andrew's) 1994; Prix Caumont-La Force 1985, Norten Medlicott Medal, Historical Asscn 2000. *Literary Agent:* Curtis Brown Group Ltd., Haymarket House, 28/29 Haymarket, London, SW1Y 4SP, England. *Telephone:* (20) 7396-6600. *Fax:* (20) 7396-0110.

FRASER, Sir David William, OBE; British author; b. 30 Dec. 1920, Camberley, England; m. 1st Anne Balfour 1947 (divorced); one d.; m. 2nd Julia de la Hey 1957; two s. two d. *Education:* Christ Church, Oxford, British Army Staff College, Imperial Defence College. *Career:* Career Officer, British Army 1941–80, retiring with rank of Gen.; Vice-Lord-Lieutenant, Hampshire 1988–96. *Publications:* Alanbrooke, 1982; And We Shall Shock Them, 1983; The Christian Watt Papers, 1983; August 1988, 1983; A Kiss for the Enemy, 1985; The Killing Times, 1986; The Dragon's Teeth, 1987; The Seizure, 1988; A Candle for Judas, 1989; In Good Company, 1990; Adam Hardrow, 1990; Codename Mercury, 1991; Adam in the Breach, 1993; The Pain of Winning, 1993; Knight's Cross: A Life of Field Marshal Erwin Rommel, 1993; Will: A Portrait of William Douglas Home, 1995; Frederick the Great, 2000. *Honours:* Grand Cross 1980, Order of the Bath. *Address:* PFD, Drury House, 34–43 Russell Street, London, WC2B 5HA, England (office).

FRASER, George MacDonald, OBE, FRSL; British writer; b. 2 April 1925, Carlisle; s. of the late William Fraser and Anne Struth Donaldson; m. Kathleen Margarette Hetherington 1949; two s. one d. *Education:* Carlisle Grammar School, Glasgow Acad. *Career:* joined Army 1943, served as infantryman XIVth Army, Burma, later Lt Gordon Highlanders; journalist in England, Canada, Scotland 1947–65; Deputy Ed. Glasgow Herald 1965–69; author 1969–. *Film screenplays:* The Three Musketeers 1973, The Four Musketeers 1974, The Prince and the Pauper 1977, Octopussy 1981, Red Sonja 1985, Casanova 1987, The Return of the Musketeers 1989. *Publications include:* The General Danced at Dawn 1970, The Steel Bonnets 1971, McAuslan in the Rough 1974, Mr American 1980, The Pyrates 1983, The

Sheikh and the Dustbin 1988, The Hollywood History of the World 1988, Quartered Safe Out of Here 1992, The Candlemass Road 1993, Black Ajax 1997, The Light's on at Signpost (autobiog.) 2002; Flashman series: Flashman 1969, Royal Flash 1970, Flash for Freedom! 1971, Flashman at the Charge 1973, Flashman in the Great Game 1975, Flashman's Lady 1977, Flashman and the Redskins 1982, Flashman and the Dragon 1985, Flashman and the Mountain of Light 1990, Flashman and the Angel of the Lord 1994, Flashman and the Tiger 1999, Flashman on the March 2005. *Literary Agent:* Curtis Brown, 28–29 Haymarket, London, SW1Y 4SP, England. *Address:* Baldrine, Isle of Man.

FRASER, Helen Jean Sutherland, MA; British publishing executive; *Managing Director, Penguin UK*; b. 8 June 1949, London; d. of the late G. S. and of Paddy Fraser; m. Grant James McIntyre 1982; two d. two step-d. *Education:* St Anne's Coll., Oxford. *Career:* Ed. Methuen Academic Ltd 1972–74, Open Books Ltd 1974–76; Ed. Fontana non-fiction, then Editorial Dir William Collins 1977–87; Publr William Heinemann 1987–91; Publr Reed Trade Books 1991–96, Man. Dir 1996–97; Man. Dir Penguin Gen. Div. 1997–2001, Penguin UK 2001–. *Address:* Penguin Books Ltd, 80 Strand, London, WC2 0RL, England (office). *Telephone:* (20) 7010-3000 (office). *E-mail:* helen.fraser@penguin.co.uk (office). *Website:* www.penguin.co.uk (office).

FRASER, Jane (see Pilcher, Rosamunde)

FRASER, Kathleen Joy, BA; American academic, poet, publisher and editor; *Professor Emerita of Writing, San Francisco State University*; b. 22 March 1937, Tulsa, Okla; m. 1st Jack Marshall 1961 (divorced 1970); one s.; m. 2nd Arthur K. Bierman 1984. *Education:* Occidental Coll., Los Angles, Columbia Univ., New School for Social Research, New York. *Career:* Visiting Prof., Univ. of Iowa 1969–71; Writer-in-Residence, Reed Coll., Portland, Ore. 1971–72; Dir Poetry Center, San Francisco State Univ. 1972–75, Assoc. Prof. 1975–78, Prof. 1978–92, Prof. Emer. of Writing 1992–; Guest Writer, California Coll. of the Arts 2003–; Ed. How(ever); featured poet, Smerilliana (Italian trans.) 2006. *Exhibition:* text/image collaborative works with painter Hermine Ford, Pratt Inst. of Architecture, Rome. *Play:* Celeste & Sirius (produced for San Francisco Poets Theatre) 2003. *Publications:* poetry: Change of Address and Other Poems 1966, In Defiance of the Rains 1969, Little Notes to You from Lucas Street 1972, What I Want 1974, Magritte Series 1978, New Shoes 1978, Each Next 1980, Something (Even Human Voices) in the Foreground, A Lake 1984, Notes Preceding Trust 1987, Boundary 1988, Giotto, Arena 1991, When New Time Folds Up 1993, Wing 1995, Il Cuore: The Heart, New and Selected Poems 1970–95, 1997, hi dde violeth i dde violet 2003, Discrete Categories Into Coupling 2004, Witness 2007; prose: Feminist Poetics: A Consideration of Female Construction of Language (ed.) 1984, Translating the Unspeakable (essays) 1999. *Honours:* Dr hc (San Francisco State Univ.); YMM-YWHA Discovery Award 1964, Nat. Endowment for the Arts grant 1969, and Fellowship 1978, Guggenheim Fellowship in Poetry 1981. *Address:* 1936 Leavenworth Street, San Francisco, CA 94133, USA. *E-mail:* kfraser@sfsu .edu.

FRASER, Sylvia Lois, BA; Canadian writer; b. 8 March 1935, Hamilton, Ont.; d. of the late George Meyers and Gladys Meyers; m. Russell James Fraser 1959 (divorced 1978). *Education:* Univ. of Western Ontario. *Career:* feature writer, The Toronto Star Weekly 1952–68; writer 1968–; Guest Lecturer, Banff Centre 1973–79, 1985, 1987, 1988; Writer-in-Residence, Univ. of Western Ontario 1980; Instructor, Huron Coll. Writers' Workshop 2003. *Publications:* Pandora 1972, A Candy Factory 1975, A Casual Affair 1978, The Emperor's Virgin 1980, Berlin Solstice 1984, My Father's House (Canadian Authors' Assn Non-Fiction Book Award) 1987, The Book of Strange (also published as The Quest for The Fourth Monkey, American Library Assn Booklist Medal) 1992, The Ancestral Suitcase 1996, The Rope in the Water: a Pilgrimage to India 2001, The Green Labyrinth – Exploring the Mysteries of the Amazon 2003. *Honours:* Women's Press Club Medal 1967, 1968, Pres.'s Medal for Canadian Journalism 1968, Nat. Magazine Gold Medal 1994, 2004, 2005, Silver Medal 1996, 2002. *Address:* 701 King Street W No. 302, Toronto, ON M5V 2W7, Canada. *Telephone:* (416) 703-7030. *E-mail:* sylviafraser@ sympatico.ca. *Website:* www.sylviafraser.net.

FRAYLING, Sir Christopher John, Kt, PhD; British historian, organization official and broadcaster; *Chairman, Arts Council England*; b. 26 Dec. 1946; m. Helen Anne Snowdon. *Education:* Repton School, Churchill Coll. Cambridge. *Career:* lecturer Univ. of Bath, Univ. of Exeter 1970s; Prof. of Cultural History, RCA 1979–, f. Dept of Cultural History, Rector 1996–; mem. Arts Council England 1987–2000, Chair. 2004–; Chair. Design Council, Crafts Study Centre, Royal Mint Advisory Cttee; fmr Gov. BFI; mem. Arts & Humanities Research Bd; trustee Victoria & Albert Museum. *Television includes:* The Art of Persuasion (New York Film and Television Festival Gold Medal), The Face of Tutankhamun, Strange Landscape. *Radio includes:* The Rime of the Bounty (Sony Radio Award, Soc. of Authors Award). *Publications include:* Napoleon Wrote Fiction 1973, The Vampyre 1976, Spaghetti Westerns 1980, The Face of Tutankhamun 1992, Clint Eastwood: A Critical Biography 1993, Strange Landscape: A Journey through the Middle Ages 1995, Nightmare: The Birth of Horror 1996, Sergio Leone: Something to do with Death 2000, Ken Adam: The Art of Production Design 2005, Mad, Bad and Dangerous? The Scientist and Cinema 2006. *Address:* Arts Council England, 2 Pear Tree Court, London, EC1R 0DS, England (office). *Telephone:*

0845 300-6200 (office). *Fax:* (20) 7608-4100 (office). *Website:* www.artscouncil .org.uk (office).

FRAYN, Michael, BA, FRSL; British playwright and author; b. 8 Sept. 1933, London; s. of the late Thomas A. Frayn and Violet A. Lawson; m. 1st Gillian Palmer 1960 (divorced 1989); three d.; m. 2nd Claire Tomalin (q.v.) 1993. *Education:* Kingston Grammar School and Emmanuel Coll., Cambridge. *Career:* reporter, The Guardian 1957–59; columnist 1959–62; columnist, The Observer 1962–68. *Stage plays:* The Two of Us 1970, The Sandboy 1971, Alphabetical Order 1975 (Evening Standard Best Comedy of the Year 1975), Donkeys' Years 1976 (Laurence Olivier Award for Best Comedy 1976, Society of West End Theatre Comedy of the Year 1976), Clouds 1976, Balmoral 1978, Liberty Hall (new version of Balmoral) 1980, Make and Break 1980 (Evening Standard Best Comedy of the Year 1980), Noises Off (Evening Standard Best Comedy of the Year 1982, Laurence Olivier Award for Best Comedy 1982, Society of West End Theatre Comedy of the Year 1982) 1982, Benefactors (Laurence Olivier/BBC Award for Best New Play 1984) 1984, Look Look 1990, Here 1993, Now You Know 1995, Copenhagen (Evening Standard Award for Best Play of the Year 1998, West End Critics' Circle Best New Play Award 1998, Prix Molière Best New Play 1999, Tony Award for Best Play 2000) 1998, Alarms and Excursions 1998, Democracy (Evening Standard Theatre Award for Best Play, Critics' Circle Award for Best Play 2003) 2003. *TV includes:* plays: Jamie, on a Flying Visit (BBC) 1968, Birthday (BBC) 1969; documentary series: Second City Reports (with John Bird, Granada) 1964, Beyond a Joke (with John Bird and Eleanor Bron) 1972, Making Faces 1975; documentaries: One Pair of Eyes 1968, Laurence Sterne Lived Here 1973, Imagine a City Called Berlin 1975, Vienna: The Mask of Gold 1977, Three Streets in the Country 1979, The Long Straight (Great Railway Journeys of the World) 1980, Jerusalem 1984, Magic Lantern, Prague 1993, Budapest: Written in Water 1996 (all BBC documentaries); films: First and Last 1989, A Landing on the Sun 1994. *Cinema:* Clockwise 1986, Remember Me? 1997. *Plays translated include:* The Cherry Orchard, Three Sisters, The Seagull, Uncle Vanya, Wild Honey, The Sneeze (Chekhov), The Fruits of Enlightenment (Tolstoy), Exchange (Trifonov), Number One (Anouilh). *Publications:* novels: The Tin Men 1965 (Somerset Maugham Award 1966), The Russian Interpreter 1966 (Hawthornden Prize 1967), Towards the End of the Morning 1967, A Very Private Life 1968, Sweet Dreams 1973, The Trick of It 1989, A Landing on the Sun 1991 (Sunday Express Book of the Year), Now You Know 1992, Headlong 1999, Spies (Whitbread Award for Best Novel) 2002; non-fiction: Constructions (philosophy) 1974, Speak after the Beep 1995, Celia's Secret (with David Burke) 2000, The Human Touch: Our Part in the Creation of the Universe 2006; several vols of collections of columns, plays and translations. *Honours:* Hon. Fellow, Emmanuel Coll., Cambridge, Hon. DLitt (Cambridge) 2001; Order of Merit (Germany) 2004; Heywood Hill Literary Prize 2002, Golden PEN Award 2003, Saint Louis Literary Award 2006, McGovern Award 2006. *Address:* c/o Greene & Heaton Ltd, 37A Goldhawk Road, London, W12 8QQ, England.

FRAZER, Andrew (see Marlowe, Stephen)

FRAZEUR, Joyce Jaeckle, BA; American poet and writer; b. 17 Jan. 1931, Lewisburg, PA; m. Theodore C. Frazeur Jr 1954, one s. two d. *Education:* William Smith College. *Publications:* poetry: A Slip of Greenness, 1989; The Bovine Affliction, 1991; Flower Soup, 1993; Chirruping, 1994; Cycles, 1996; novel: By Lunar Light, 1995; contrib. to newspapers, reviews, magazines and journals.

FRAZIER, Charles, PhD; American writer; b. 4 Nov. 1950, Asheville, NC; m. Catherine Frazier; one d. *Education:* Univ. of North Carolina, Appalachian State Univ., Univ. of South Carolina. *Career:* fmr faculty mem., Univ. of Colo and North Carolina State Univ. *Publications:* Adventuring in the Andes: The Sierra Club Travel Guide to Ecuador, Peru, Bolivia, the Amazon Basin, and the Galapagos Islands (with Donald Secreast) 1985, Cold Mountain: Odyssey in North Carolina (novel, Nat. Book Award) 1997, Thirteen Moons (novel) 2006. *Address:* c/o Darhansoff, Verrill & Feldman, 236 West 26th Street, Suite 802, New York, NY 10001, USA; c/o Sceptre, 338 Euston Road, London, NW1 3BH, England.

FRÈCHES, José Vincent, PhD; French writer and publisher; b. 25 June 1950, Dax, Landes; s. of Claude-Henri Frèches and Nicole Frèches (née Menguy); m. Claire Thory 1973; two d. one s. *Education:* lycées in Brazil, Italy, Portugal and France, Univs of Aix-en-Provence and Paris VII, Ecole nat. d' Admin. *Career:* Curator Musée des Beaux Arts, Grenoble, Guimet 1971–72; Maitre de Confs Ecole du Louvre, Insp. of Provincial Museums, Musées de France 1974–75; Auditeur Cour des Comptes 1978, Rapporteur Comm. des Marchés de bâtiment 1979–82, Chargé de mission Commissariat au Plan and Office of First Pres. Cour des Comptes 1980–82, Conseiller Cour des Comptes 1982; Chargé de mission to Dir-Gen. of Information and Exterior Relations, Ville de Paris 1982–83, Rapporteur Gen. Comm. du câble 1983–85, Asst Dir of Communication 1985, Dir Vidéothèque de Paris 1985, Admin. Bibliothèque publique d'information 1982–; Rapporteur Gen. Comm. Communication demain du RPR 1986; Conseiller in the cabinet of Prime Minister Jacques Chirac 1986–88; Dir Havas 1988, Visicable +; Dir-Gen. Groupe Fabre 1990–98; Admin. Pierre Fabre SA 1994–98; Admin. Midi Libre 1996–2000, Pres. 1998–2000; Pres. du conseil de surveillance des laboratoires Dolisos; mem. du conseil artistique de la Réunion des musées nat. 1988–; jury mem. Prix Méditerranée. *Publications:* La Sinologie 1975, Les Musées de France 1980, L'ENA, voyage au centre de l'Etat 1981, La France socialiste 1983, Le

Coût d'Etat permanent 1984, La Télévision par câble 1985, La Guerre des images 1985, Modernissimots 1987, Voyage au centre du pouvoir 1989, Le Poisson pourrit par la tête (jtly) 1992, Toulouse-Lautrec (jtly) 1991, Le Caravage, peintre et assassin 1995, L'Arbre de la compassion 2004. *Honours:* Chevalier, Légion d'honneur. *Address:* Pierre Fabre SA, 45 place Abel Gance, 92100 Boulogne-Billancourt (office); 48 rue de Verneuil, 75007 Paris, France (home).

FREDERICKS, Frohm (see Kerner, Fred)

FREEBORN, Richard Harry, BA, MA, DPhil; British academic, writer and translator; *Professor Emeritus of Russian Literature, University of London*; b. 19 Oct. 1926, Cardiff, Wales; m. Anne Davis 14 Feb. 1954; one s. three d. *Education:* Univ. of Oxford. *Career:* Univ. Lecturer in Russian and Hulme Lecturer in Russian, Brasenose Coll., Oxford, 1954–64; Visiting Prof., UCLA 1964–65; Sir William Mather Chair of Russian Studies, Univ. of Manchester 1965–67; Prof. of Russian Literature, Univ. of London 1967–88, Prof. Emer. 1988–; Chair. Library Circle. *Publications:* fiction: Two Ways of Life 1962, The Emigration of Sergey Ivanovich 1963, Russian Roulette 1979, The Russian Crucifix 1987; non-fiction: Turgenev: A Study 1960, A Short History of Modern Russia 1966, The Rise of the Russian Novel 1974, Russian Literary Attitudes from Pushkin to Solzhenitsyn (ed.) 1976, Russian and Slavic Literature to 1917, Vol. I (co-ed. with Charles Ward) 1976, The Russian Revolutionary Novel: Turgenev to Pasternak 1982, Ideology in Russian Literature (co-ed. with Jane Grayson) 1990, Furious Vissarion: Belinski's Struggle for Literature, Love and Ideas 2003, Dostoevsky 2003; translator: Sketches from a Hunter's Album, by Turgenev 1967, Home of the Gentry, by Turgenev 1970, Rudin, by Turgenev 1974, Love and Death: Six Stories by Ivan Turgenev 1983, First Love and Other Stories, by Turgenev 1989, Fathers and Sons, by Turgenev 1991, A Month in the Country, by Turgenev 1991, An Accidental Family, by Dostoevsky 1994; editor: Anton Chekhov: The Steppe and Other Stories 1991, Ivan Goncharov: Oblomov 1992, Reference Guide to Russian Literature: Articles on the Classic Russian Novel, Gor'kii, Kuzmin, Pasternak *et al.* 1998, The Cambridge Companion to Tolstoy (contrib.) 2002, Solzhenitsyn (updated) – New Makers of Modern Culture 2007; contribs to various publs. *Honours:* Hon. DLitt (London) 1984. *Address:* 24 Park Road, Surbiton, Surrey, KT5 8QD, England.

FREEDMAN, David Noel, BA, BTh, PhD; American academic, writer and editor; *Endowed Chair in Hebrew Biblical Studies, University of California at San Diego*; b. 12 May 1922, New York, NY; m. Cornelia Anne Pryor 1944; two s. two d. *Education:* City College, CUNY, University of California at Los Angeles, Princeton Theological Seminary, Johns Hopkins University. *Career:* Ordained Minister, Presbyterian Church, USA, 1944; State Supply Minister, Acme and Deming, Washington, Presbyterian Churches, 1944–45; Teaching Fellow, 1946–47, Asst Instructor, 1947–48, Johns Hopkins University; Asst Prof. of Old Testament, 1948–51, Prof. of Hebrew and Old Testament, 1951–60, Western Theological Seminary, Pittsburgh; Assoc. Ed., 1952–54, Ed., 1955–59, Journal of Biblical Literature; Prof. of Hebrew and Old Testament, 1960–61, James A. Kelso Prof. of Hebrew and Old Testament, 1961–64, Pittsburgh Theological Seminary; Prof. of Old Testament, 1964–70, Dean of Faculty, 1966–70, Gray Prof. of Old Testament Exegesis, 1970–71, San Francisco Theological Seminary; Prof. of Old Testament, Graduate Theological Union, 1964–71; Vice-Pres., 1970–82, Dir of Publications, 1974–82, American Schools of Oriental Research; Ed., Biblical Archaeologist, 1976–82; Prof. of Biblical Studies, 1971–92, Dir, Program on Studies in Religion, 1971–91, Arthur F. Thurnau Prof. in Old Testament Studies, 1984–92, University of Michigan; Visiting Prof. in Old Testament Studies, 1985–86, Prof. in Hebrew Biblical Studies, 1987, Endowed Chair in Hebrew Biblical Studies, 1987–, University of California at San Diego; numerous visiting lectureships and professorships; mem. American Acad. of Religion; American Archaeological Institute; American Oriental Society; American Schools of Oriental Research; Explorers' Club; Society of Biblical Literature. *Publications:* God Has Spoken (with J. D. Smart), 1949; Studies in Ancient Yahwistic Poetry (with Frank M. Cross), 1950; Early Hebrew Orthography (with Frank M. Cross), 1952; The People of the Dead Sea Scrolls (with J. M. Allegro), 1958; The Secret Sayings of Jesus (with R. M. Grant), 1960; Ashdod I (with M. Dothan), 1967; The Published Works of W. F. Albright (with R. B. MacDonald and D. L. Mattson), 1975; William Foxwell Albright: Twentieth Century Genius (with L. G. Running), 1975; The Mountain of the Lord (with B. Mazar and G. Cornfeld), 1975; An Explorer's Life of Jesus (with W. Phillips), 1975; Hosea (Anchor Bible Series; with F. I. Andersen), 1980; Pottery, Poetry and Prophecy, 1981; The Paleo-Hebrew Leviticus Scroll (with K. A. Mathews), 1985; Amos (Anchor Bible Series; with F. I. Andersen), 1989; The Unity of the Hebrew Bible, 1991; Studies in Hebrew and Aramaic Orthography (with D. Forbes and F. I. Andersen), 1992; The Relationship Between Herodotus' History and Primary History (with Sara Mandell), 1993; Divine Commitment and Human Obligation 1997, Psalm 119 1999, Micah (with F. I. Andersen) 2000, The Nine Commandments 2000. Other: The Biblical Archaeologist Reader (co-ed.), four vols, 1961, 1964, 1970, 1982; Anchor Bible Series (co-ed.), 18 vols, 1964–72, 50 vols (gen. ed.), 1972–; Computer Bible Series (co-ed.), 18 vols, 1971–80; Anchor Bible Reference Library (general ed.), 16 vols, 1988–96; Anchor Bible Dictionary (ed.-in-chief), six vols, 1992, Eerdmans Critical Commentary Series (gen. ed.) 1999–; Bible in its World Series 2000–; Eerdmans Dictionary of the Bible (ed.-in-chief) 2000. *Honours:* Guggenheim Fellowship, 1958–59; AATS Fellowship, 1965;

Hon. doctorates. *Address:* c/o Department of History, No. 0104, University of California, San Diego, 9500 Gilman Drive, La Jolla, CA 92093-0104, USA.

FREEDMAN, Sir Lawrence David, Kt, KCMG, CBE, DPhil, FRSA, FRHistS, FBA, FKC; British academic; *Professor of War Studies and Vice-Principal (Research), King's College London*; b. 7 Dec. 1948, Tynemouth; s. of the late Lt-Commdr Julius Freedman and Myra Robinson; m. Judith Hill 1974; one s. one d. *Education:* Whitley Bay Grammar School and Univs of Manchester, Oxford and York. *Career:* Research Assoc., IISS 1975–76; Research Fellow, Royal Inst. of Int. Affairs 1976–78, Head of Policy Studies 1978–82; Fellow, Head Dept of War Studies, King's Coll. London 1978–, Prof. 1982–, Head School of Social Science and Public Policy 2001–, Vice-Principal (Research); mem. Council, IISS 1984–92, 1993–, School of Slavonic and E European Studies 1993–97; Chair. Cttee on Int. Peace and Security, Social Science Research Council (USA) 1993–98; occasional newspaper columnist; Trustee Imperial War Museum 2001–. *Publications:* US Intelligence and Soviet Strategic Threat 1978, Britain and Nuclear Weapons 1980, The Evolution of Nuclear Strategy 1981, 1989, Nuclear War and Nuclear Peace (co-author) 1983, The Troubled Alliance (ed.) 1983, The Atlas of Global Strategy 1985, The Price of Peace 1986, Britain and the Falklands War 1988, US Nuclear Strategy (co-ed.) 1989, Signals of War (with V. Gamba) 1989, Europe Transformed (ed.) 1990, Military Power in Europe (essays, ed.) 1990, Britain in the World (co-ed.) 1991, Population Change and European Security (co-ed.) 1991, War, Strategy and International Politics (essays, co-ed.) 1992, The Gulf Conflict 1990–91, Diplomacy and War in the New World Order (with E. Karsh) 1993, War: A Reader 1994, Military Intervention in Europe (ed.) 1994, Strategic Coercion (ed.) 1998, The Revolution in Strategic Affairs 1998, The Politics of British Defence Policy 1979–1998 1999, Kennedy's Wars 2000, The Cold War 2001, Superterrorism (ed.) 2002, Deterrence 2004, The Official History of the Falklands Campaign 2005; articles etc. *Honours:* Hon. Dir Centre for Defence Studies 1990–; Silver Medallist, Arthur Ross Prize, Council on Foreign Relations (USA) 2000, RUSI Chesney Gold Medal 2006. *Address:* King's College London, Office of the Principal, James Clerk Maxwell Building, 57 Waterloo Road, London, SE1 8WA, England (office). *Telephone:* (20) 7848-3984 (office); (20) 7848-3985 (office). *Fax:* (20) 7848-3668 (office). *E-mail:* lawrence.freedman@kcl.ac.uk (office); LFREED0712@aol.com (home).

FREEMAN, Gillian, (Elisabeth von Stahlenberg), BA; British writer; b. 5 Dec. 1929, London, England; m. Edward Thorpe 1955, two d. *Education:* University of Reading. *Career:* mem. Arts Council, Writers' Guild of Great Britain. *Publications:* The Liberty Man, 1955; Fall of Innocence, 1956; Jack Would be a Gentleman, 1959; The Story of Albert Einstein, 1960; The Leather Boys, 1961; The Campaign, 1963; The Leader, 1965; The Undergrowth of Literature, 1969; The Alabaster Egg, 1970; The Marriage Machine, 1975; The Schoolgirl Ethic: The Life and Work of Angela Brazil, 1976; Nazi Lady: The Diaries of Elisabeth von Stahlenberg, 1938–48, 1979; An Easter Egg Hunt, 1981; Lovechild, 1984; Life Before Man, 1986; Ballet Genius (with Edward Thorpe), 1988; Termination Rock, 1989; His Mistress's Voice, 2000. Other: Screenplays and adaptations; Ballet scenarios. Contributions: periodicals.

FREEMAN, Gwendolen, BA; British author; b. 4 April 1908, Ealing, London, England; one adopted s. *Education:* Girton College, Cambridge. *Career:* Women's Ed., Birmingham Post; Public Relations Office Birmingham Ministry of Labour; The Spectator. *Publications:* The Houses Behind 1947, Children Never Tell 1949, When You Are Old 1951, Between Two Worlds 1979, A Zeppelin in My Childhood 1989, United Family Record 1989, World of an Artist 1990, Alma Mater 1990, Scriptural Beasts 1991, Whys of Loving 1993, Flora at School 1994, The Dodona Oak 1995, Anna with Tristram 1995, Midland Thirties 1998, People of the Century 2000, Harriet Without Conclusions 2001, Queen Victoria and Ping Pong 2003; contrib. to newspapers. *Address:* c/o Brewin Books Ltd, Doric House, 56 Alcester Road, Studley, Warwickshire B80 7LG, England.

FREEMAN, James Montague, BA, MA, PhD; American academic and writer; *Professor Emeritus, San Jose State University*; b. 1 Dec. 1936, Chicago, IL; m. Patricia Ann Freeman 1968; one s. *Education:* Northwestern Univ., Harvard Univ. *Career:* Asst Prof. to Prof. of Anthropology, San Jose State Univ. 1966–2000, Prof. Emer. 2000–; mem. Aid to Refugee Children Without Parents 1988–95, and its successor, Aid to Children Without Parents Inc. (chair. of the bd 1995–99), Southwestern Anthropological Asscn (pres. 1991–92), Friends of Hue Foundation (chair. of bd) 2000–. *Publications:* Scarcity and Opportunity in an Indian Village 1977, Untouchable: An Indian Life History 1979, Hearts of Sorrow: Vietnamese-American Lives 1989, Changing Identities: Vietnamese Americans 1975–1995 1996, Voices from the Camps: Vietnamese Children Seeking Asylum (with Nguyen Dinh Huu) 2003; contrib. to scholarly books and journals. *Honours:* American Inst. of Indian Studies Fellowship 1971–72, Social Science Research Council grant 1976–77, 1979–80, Fellow Center for Advanced Study in Behavioral Sciences, Stanford 1976–77, Choice Outstanding Academic Book 1979, Nat. Endowment for the Humanities Fellowship 1983–84, San Jose State Univ. Pres.'s Scholar 1984, San Jose State Univ. Outstanding Prof. 1986, Before Columbus Foundation American Book Award 1990, Asscn for Asian-American Studies Outstanding Book Award 1990, Austin D. Warburton Award for Outstanding Scholarship 1991, Nat. Science Foundation grant (jtly) 1998–99, Alfred P. Sloan Foundation grant (jtly) 1998–2000. *Address:* c/o Department of Anthropology, San Jose State University, San Jose, CA 95192, USA.

FREEMAN, Judith; American writer and critic; b. 1 Oct. 1946, Ogden, UT; m. Anthony Hernandez 1986, one s. *Career:* Contributing Critic, Los Angeles Times Book Review; mem. PEN West. *Publications:* Family Attractions, 1988; The Chinchilla Farm, 1989; Set for Life, 1991; A Desert of Pure Feeling, 1996. *Honours:* Western Heritage Award for Best Western Novel, 1991.

FREEMANTLE, Brian Harry, (Harry Asher, Jonathan Evans, Richard Gant, Anrea Hart, John Maxwell, Jack Winchester); British writer; b. 10 June 1936, Southampton, England; m. Maureen Hazel Tipney 1957; three d. *Education:* secondary school, Southampton. *Career:* reporter, New Milton Advertiser 1953–58, Bristol Evening News 1958, Evening News, London 1959–61; reporter, Daily Express 1961–63, Asst Foreign Ed. 1963–69; Foreign Ed., Daily Sketch, London 1969–70, Daily Mail, London 1971–75. *Publications:* fiction: The Touchables 1968, Goodbye to an Old Friend 1973, Face Me When You Walk Away 1974, The Man Who Wanted Tomorrow 1975, The November Man 1976, Hell's Kitchen 1977, The Iron Cage 1980, Deaken's War 1982, Rules of Engagement 1984, Vietnam Legacy 1984, The Lost American 1984, The Laundryman 1986, The Kremlin Kiss 1986, The Bearpit 1988, O'Farrell's Law 1990, The Factory 1990, The Choice of Eddie Franks 1990, Betrayals 1991, Little Grey Mice 1992, The Button Man 1993, No Time for Heroes 1995, Mindreader 1998, The Profiler 1998, At Any Price 1999, The Watchmen 2002, Ice Age 2002, Two Women 2003, The Holmes Inheritance 2004, Triple Cross 2004, Dead End 2005, The Holmes Factor 2005, Time To Kill 2006, The Namedropper 2007, also 11 books in the Charlie Muffin mystery series; non-fiction: KGB 1982, CIA 1983, The Fix: Inside the World Drug Trade 1985, The Steal: Counterfeiting and Industrial Espionage 1987, The Octopus: Europe in the Grip of Organised Crime 1996; contrib. to periodicals. *Address:* c/o Jonathan Clowes, 10 Iron Bridge House, Bridge Approach, London, NW1 8BD, England.

FREI, Max; Russian writer. *Career:* pseudonym of Svetlana Martynchik and Igor Stepin, and also the protagonist of a number of novels. *Publications:* fiction: The Labyrinths of Echo series; non-fiction: The ABCs of Contemporary Art, A Book of Indecencies, A Book of Fantasy Worlds, Russian Heterogeneous Fairy Tale. *Website:* www.frei.ru.

FREIBERG, Stanley Kenneth, BA, MA, PhD; American fmr teacher, poet and writer; b. 26 Aug. 1923, Wis.; m. Marjorie Ellen Speckhard 1947; one s. one d. *Education:* Univ. of Wisconsin. *Career:* Chair. English Dept, Cottey Cottage, Nevada, Mo. 1954–58; Chair. Bd of Foreign Language Studies, Univ. of Baghdad, Iraq 1964–65. *Plays:* Mad Blake at Felpham (Open Space Theatre, Victoria, BC 1987), Blake and Beethoven in The Tempest (Univ. of Victoria 1992), Bush, Blake and Job in the Garden of Eden (St Anne's Acad., Victoria 2005). *Music:* words and music for Seven Tone Poems, premiered at Victoria Conservatory of Music 2002–06. *Publications:* The Baskets of Baghdad: Poems of the Middle East 1968, (reprinted with story and verse additions) 2006, Plumes of the Serpent: Poems of Mexico 1973, The Caplin-Crowded Seas: Poems of Newfoundland 1975, Nightmare Tales: Ten Stories of Nova Scotia 1980, Mad Blake at Felpham (play) 1987, The Hidden City: A Poem of Peru 1988, Blake and Beethoven in the Tempest (play) 1997, The Dignity of Dust: Poems from the Four Directions 1997, Sverre, King of Norway: Drama of 12th Century Norway 1999, Jahanara, Daughter of the Taj Mahal: Drama of the Mogul Empire 1631–1681 1999, Black Madonna of the Deluge: Drama of 17th Century Poland 2000, Anaho of the Southstars: Novella of Pyramid Lake, Nevada 2003, On Gravel Roads: Tales of Early Ontario 2004, Bush, Blake and Job in the Garden of Eden (play) 2005, Seven Tone Poems 2007; contrib. to Redlands Review, Christian Century, Dalhousie Review, Queen's Quarterly, Ariel, Parnassus of World Poets 1994. *Honours:* Canada Council Award 1978. *Address:* 202–268 Superior Street, Victoria, BC V8V 1T3, Canada. *Telephone:* (250) 382-9352. *Website:* www.stanfreiberg.com.

FREIREICH, Valerie J., BA, JD; American lawyer and writer; b. 14 July 1952, Chicago, IL; m. Jordan L. Kaplan 1980, one s. *Education:* University of Illinois at Champaign-Urbana. *Career:* lawyer, various law firms, 1977–84; Sole Practitioner in Small Business and Real Estate Law, 1984–; mem. American Bar Asscn; SFWA; American Asscn for the Advancement of Science; Illinois State Bar Asscn. *Publications:* fiction: Becoming Human, 1995; Testament, 1995; Beacon, 1996; Sensations of the Mind (short story). Contributions: short stories and novellas to periodicals including: Aboriginal Science Fiction; Asimov's Science Fiction; Tomorrow Speculative Fiction. *Honours:* Writers of the Future Quarterly prize, First Prize, for Short Story, 1990. *Address:* 2 Paddock, Lemont, IL 60439, USA.

FREISINGER, Randall Roy; American academic and poet; b. 6 Feb. 1942, Kansas City, MO; m.; two s. *Education:* BJ, Journalism, 1962, MA, English Literature, 1964, PhD, English Literature, 1975, University of Missouri. *Career:* Instructor, Jefferson College, 1964–68; Resident Lecturer, University of Maryland Overseas Program, 1968–69, 1975–76; Asst Prof., Columbia College, 1976–77; Asst, Assoc. Prof., 1977–93, Prof. of Rhetoric, Literature and Creative Writing, 1993–, Michigan Technological University; Assoc. Ed., Laurel Review, 1989–; mem. Associated Writing Programs; National Council of Teachers of English. *Publications:* Running Patterns, 1985; Hand Shadows, 1988; Plato's Breath, 1997. Contributions: anthologies, journals, reviews, and quarterlies. *Honours:* Winner, Flume Press National Chapbook Competition, 1985; May Swenson Poetry Award, 1996. *Address:* 200 Prospect Street, Houghton, MI 49931, USA.

FRENCH, Anne, MA; New Zealand poet, critic and publishing executive; b. 5 March 1956, Wellington; d. of Derek Lawrence and M. Olive French; one s.

Education: Wellington Girls' Coll., Victoria Univ. of Wellington and Auckland Teachers' Coll. *Career:* Ed. Oxford Univ. Press (NZ br.) 1979, then Literary Ed., apptd Publr 1982; Sec. NZ PEN 1980, 1981; Councillor Book Publishers' Asscn of NZ 1984; Man. Ed. Museum of New Zealand Te Papa Tongarewa 1995–; mem. Council Local Publishers' Forum 1991, jury Montana New Zealand Book Awards 2004; Queen Elizabeth II Arts Council Writers' Bursary 1990; Inaugural Writing Fellow, Massey Univ. 1993–. *Publications include:* poetry: All Cretans are Liars 1987, The Male as Evader 1988, Cabin Fever 1990, Seven Days on Mykonos 1993, Boys' Night Out 1998, Wild 2004. *Honours:* PEN Young Writers' Award 1973, 1974, NZ Book Award for Poetry 1988, PEN Best First Book Award 1988. *Address:* 53 Ngatiawa Street, One Tree Hill, Auckland 5, New Zealand. *Telephone:* (9) 636-8910. *Fax:* (9) 524-6723.

FRENCH, Linda (see Mariz, Linda Catherine French)

FRENCH, Marilyn, (Mara Solwoska), MA, PhD; American writer and critic; b. 21 Nov. 1929, New York, NY; d. of E. C. Edwards and Isabel Hazz; m. Robert M. French Jr 1950 (divorced 1967); one s. one d. *Education:* Hofstra Coll. and Harvard Univ. *Career:* secretarial and clerical work 1946–53; Lecturer, Hofstra Coll. 1964–68; professional writer 1967–; Asst Prof. Holy Cross Coll. Worcester, MA 1972–76; Mellon Fellow, Harvard Univ. 1976–77. *Television:* The Women's Room 1979. *Publications:* fiction: The Women's Room 1977, The Bleeding Heart 1980, Her Mother's Daughter 1987, Our Father: A Novel 1994, My Summer with George 1996; non-fiction: The Book as World—James Joyce's Ulysses 1976, Shakespeare's Division of Experience 1981, Beyond Power: On Women, Men and Morals 1985, The War Against Women 1992, A Season in Hell (memoir) 1998, From Eve to Dawn: A History of Women (three vols) 2002–04; contrib. to books and periodicals. *Honours:* New Options' Political Book Award 1986. *Literary Agent:* Charlotte Sheedy Literary Agency, 65 Bleecker Street, New York, NY 10012, USA. *E-mail:* mfrench189@aol.com (office).

FRENCH, Nicci (see French, Sean, and Gerrard, Nicci)

FRENCH, Philip Neville, BA; British writer, broadcaster and film critic; b. 28 Aug. 1933, Liverpool, England; m. Kersti Elisabet Molin 1957; three s. *Education:* Exeter Coll., Oxford and Indiana Univ. *Career:* reporter, Bristol Evening Post 1958–59; Producer, North American Service 1959–61, Talks Producer 1961–67, Sr Producer 1968–90, BBC Radio; theatre critic 1967–68, arts columnist 1967–72, New Statesman; film critic, The Observer 1978–. *Publications:* The Age of Austerity, 1945–51 (ed. with Michael Sissons) 1963, The Novelist as Innovator (ed.) 1966, The Movie Moguls 1969, Westerns: Aspects of a Movie Genre 1974, Three Honest Men: Portraits of Edmund Wilson, F. R. Leavis, Lionel Trilling 1980, The Third Dimension: Voices from Radio Three (ed.) 1983, The Press: Observed and Projected (ed. with Deac Rossell) 1991, Malle on Malle (ed.) 1992, The Faber Book of Movie Verse (ed. with Ken Wlaschin) 1993, Wild Strawberries (with Kersti French) 1995, Cult Movies (with Karl French) 1999, Westerns and Westerns Revisited 2005; contrib. to many anthologies and periodicals. *Honours:* Dr hc (Lancaster Univ.) 2006. *Address:* 62 Dartmouth Park Road, London, NW5 1SN, England (home). *Telephone:* (20) 7485-1711 (home). *E-mail:* pn.french@blueyonder.co.uk (home).

FRENCH, Sean, (Nicci French), BA; British writer; b. 28 May 1959, Bristol, England; m. Nicci Gerrard 1990; two s. two d. *Education:* Christ Church, Oxford. *Career:* Deputy Literary Ed., Sunday Times, London 1984–86; Deputy Ed., New Society 1986–87; columnist, New Statesman and Society 1987–2000; also writes with Nicci Gerrard, under joint pseudonym of Nicci French. *Publications:* Fatherhood (ed.) 1992, The French Brothers' Wild and Crazy Film Quiz Book (with Karl and Patrick French) 1992, The Imaginary Monkey (novel) 1993, Patrick Hamilton: A Life (biog.) 1993, Bardot (biog.) 1994, Dreamer of Dreams (novel) 1995, The Terminator (criticism) 1996, Jane Fonda (biog.) 1997, The Faber Book of Writers on Writers (ed.) 1999, Start from Here (novel) 2004; as Nicci French: The Memory Game 1997, The Safe House 1998, Killing Me Softly 1999, Beneath the Skin 2000, The Red Room 2001, Land of the Living 2003, Secret Smile 2004, Things We Knew Were True 2004, Catch Me When I Fall 2005, Losing You 2007. *Literary Agent:* PFD, Drury House, 34–43 Russell Street, London, WC2B 5HA, England. *Address:* The Old Rectory, Elmsett, Ipswich IP7 6NA, England (home). *E-mail:* seanicci@dircon.co.uk.

FRENCH, Warren Graham; American academic and writer; b. 26 Jan. 1922, Philadelphia, Pennsylvania. *Education:* BA, University of Pennsylvania, 1943; MA, 1948, PhD, American Literature 1954, University of Texas. *Career:* mem. International John Steinbeck Society; American Literature; MLA of America; American Studies Asscn; Western American Literature Asscn. *Publications:* John Steinbeck, 1961; Frank Norris, 1962; J. D. Salinger, 1963; The Social Novel at the End of an Era, 1966; Jack Kerouac, 1986; J. D. Salinger, Revisited, 1988; The San Francisco Poetry Renaissance, 1955–1960, 1991. Editor: The Thirties, 1967; The Forties, 1969; The Fifties, 1971; The South in Film, 1981; The Twenties, 1975. Contributions: numerous American academic journals. *Honours:* DHL, Ohio University, 1985. *Address:* 23 Beechwood Road, Uplands, Swansea, West Glamorgan SA2 0HL, Wales.

FRESÁN, Rodrigo; Argentine writer and journalist; b. 1963, Buenos Aires. *Career:* journalist 1984–; moved to Barcelona, Spain 1999–. *Publications:* Historia argentina (short stories) 1991, Vidas de santos (short stories) 1993, Trabajos manuales 1994, Esperanto (novel) 1995, La velocidad de las cosas (novel) 1998, Mantra 2001, Jardines de Kensington (novel, trans. as Kensington Gardens) 2004; contrib. to various publications, including Página 12. *Honours:* Premio Lateral de Narrativa 2004. *Address:* c/o Faber and Faber Ltd, 3 Queen Square, London, WC1N 3AU, England. *E-mail:* gapublicity@faber.co.uk.

FREUD, Esther Lea; British writer; b. 2 May 1963, London, England; pnr David Morrissey; two s. one d. *Education:* Drama Centre, London. *Career:* fmr actor; co-f. film production co., Tubedale Films. *Publications:* Hideous Kinky (novel) 1991, Peerless Flats (short stories) 1993, Gaglow 1997, The Wild 2000, The Sea House (novel) 2003, Love Falls 2007. *Literary Agent:* AP Watt Ltd, 20 John Street, London, WC1N 2DR, England. *Telephone:* (20) 7282-3106.

FREUDENBERGER, Nell; American writer; b. 1975, New York, NY. *Career:* English teacher in Bangkok and New Delhi. *Publications:* Lucky Girls (PEN/Malamud Award 2004) 2003, The Dissident 2006; contrib. to The New Yorker, Granta. *Honours:* Whiting Writers' Award 2005. *Address:* c/o Ecco, Harper Collins Publishing, 10 E 53rd Street, New York, NY 10022, USA (office).

FREWER, Glyn Mervyn Louis, (Mervyn Lewis), MA; British writer and scriptwriter; b. 4 Sept. 1931, Oxford, England; m. Lorna Townsend 1956; two s. one d. *Education:* St Catherine's Coll., Oxford. *Career:* Student Officer, British Council, Oxford 1955; copywriter for various agencies 1955–64; Advertising Agency Assoc. Dir 1975–85; Propr antiquarian/secondhand bookshop 1985–2001. *Scripts:* The Hitch-Hikers (BBC Radio play) 1957, also scripts for children's TV series, industrial films, etc.. *Publications:* children's fiction: Adventure in Forgotten Valley (Jr Literary Guild of America Choice 1964) 1962, Adventure in the Barren Lands 1964, The Last of the Wispies 1965, The Token of Elkin 1970, Crossroad 1970, The Square Peg 1972, The Raid 1976, The Trackers 1976; adult fiction: Death of Gold (as Mervyn Lewis) 1970; wildlife fiction: Tyto: The Odyssey of an Owl 1978, Bryn of Brockle Hanger 1980, Fox 1984, The Call of the Raven 1987; poetry: Shout to the Sky 2007; contrib. to Birds, Imagery, The Countryman. *Honours:* Freeman of the City of Oxford 1967. *Address:* Cottage Farm, Taston, Oxford, OX7 3JN, England (home).

FRIDAY, Nancy; American feminist and writer; b. 27 Aug. 1937, Pittsburgh, PA; m. Norman Pearlstine. *Education:* Wellesley Coll., Mass. *Career:* grew up in Charleston, SC; worked briefly as reporter for San Juan Island Times and as magazine ed. in New York, England, Italy and France before turning to full-time writing in 1963; has produced several books of 'pop psychology' since 1973. *Publications include:* My Secret Garden: Women's Sexual Fantasies 1973, Forbidden Flowers – More Women's Sexual Fantasies 1975, My Mother, My Self – The Daughter's Search for Identity 1977, Men in Love, Men's Sexual Fantasies – The Triumph of Love Over Rage 1980, Jealousy 1985, Women on Top – How Real Life Has Changed Women's Sexual Fantasies 1991, Self Exploration and Insatiable Lust 1991, The Power of Beauty 1996, To Be Seen 1996, The Power of Beauty 1996, The Mirrored Self 1997, Our Looks, Our Lives – Sex, Beauty, Power and the Need to be Seen 1999. *Address:* PO Box, 1371 Key West, FL 33041, USA. *Website:* www.nancyfriday.com.

FRIEDA, Leonie Harriet Elisabeth Natascha; Swedish historian and biographer; b. 1956, d. of Leo and Margareta Groth; m. Nigel Frieda 1986 (divorced 1998); one s. one d. *Education:* Moira House, Eastbourne, England, Rissen Gymnasium, Hamburg, Inst. of Linguists. *Career:* model, translator; Propr, MATRIX recording studios 1986–2001; also music business man. to various popstars, producers and engineers. *Publications:* Catherine de Medici: A Biography 2004. *Address:* c/o Weidenfeld & Nicholson, The Orion Publishing Group Ltd, Orion House, 5 Upper St Martin's Lane, London, WC2H 9EA, England. *Telephone:* (20) 7240-3444. *Fax:* (20) 7240-4822. *Website:* www.leoniefrieda.com.

FRIEDMAN, Alan Howard, BA, MA, PhD; American writer and academic; *Professor Emeritus, University of Illinois*; b. 4 Jan. 1928, New York City; m. 1st Leonore Ann Helman 1950 (divorced); one s.; m. 2nd Kate Miller Gilbert 1977; one s. *Education:* Harvard Coll., Columbia Univ., Univ. of California, Berkeley. *Career:* mem staff, Columbia Univ., Swarthmore Coll., Queens Coll.; Prof. Emer., Univ. of Illinois. *Publications:* The Turn of the Novel 1966, Hermaphrodeity (novel) 1972; contribs to Twentieth Century Mind, American Literary Anthology, Hudson Review, Mademoiselle, Partisan Review, New American Review, Paris Review, New York Times Book Review, Fiction International, Kansas Quarterly, Denver Quarterly, Raritan. *Honours:* D.H. Lawrence Fellowship 1974, Nat. Endowment for the Arts Award 1975, Pen Syndicated Fiction Award 1987, Grand Prize, Nat. Library of Poetry 1998, Best Actor Award, Asscn of Community Theatres 2001. *Address:* 3530 Monte Real, Escondido, CA 92029, USA. *E-mail:* alanfman@post.harvard.edu.

FRIEDMAN, Bruce Jay, BJ; American writer, dramatist and screenwriter; b. 26 April 1930, New York, NY; m. 1st Ginger Howard 1954 (divorced 1978); three s.; m. 2nd Patricia O'Donohue 1983; one d. *Education:* University of Missouri. *Career:* Editorial Dir, Magazine Management Co, New York City, 1953–64; mem. PEN. *Publications:* Stern, 1962; Far From the City of Class, and Other Stories, 1963; A Mother's Kisses, 1964; Black Humour (ed.), 1965; Black Angels, 1966; Pardon Me, Sir, But Is My Eye Hurting Your Elbow? (with others), 1968; The Dick, 1970; About Harry Towns, 1974; The Lonely Guys Book of Life, 1978; Let's Hear It for a Beautiful Guy, and Other Works of Short Fiction, 1984; Tokyo Woes, 1985; Violencia, 1988; The Current Climate, 1990; Collected Short Fiction of Bruce Jay Friedman, 1995; The Slightly Older Guy,

1995. Other: Plays and screenplays including Have You Spoken to Any Jews Lately, 1995; A Father's Kisses, 1996.

FRIEDMAN, Dennis, LRCP,; British psychiatrist and writer; b. 23 Feb. 1924, London, England; m. Rosemary Tibber 1949, four d. *Education:* Royal College of Physicians, London. *Career:* Fellow Royal College of Psychiatrists; mem. Royal Society of Medicine, Royal College of Surgeons. *Publications:* Inheritance: A Psychological History of the Royal Family, 1993; Darling Georgie: The Enigma of King George V, 1998; Ladies of the Bedchamber: The Role of the Royal Mistress, 2003. Contributions: books and other publications. *Address:* Apt 5, 3 Cambridge Gate, London, NW1 4JX, England. *Telephone:* (20) 7935-6252 (home). *Fax:* (20) 7486-2398 (home). *E-mail:* dennisfriedman@aol.com (home).

FRIEDMAN, Jane, BA; American publishing executive; *President and CEO, HarperCollins Worldwide*; b. Sept. 1945, Brooklyn, NY. *Education:* New York Univ. *Career:* dictaphone typist, publicity dept Alfred A. Knopf, subsidiary co of Random House 1968, later Assoc. Publr Alfred A. Knopf; Pres. Random House Audio 1985; Publr Vintage Books 1990; Exec. Vice-Pres. Knopf Publishing Group, Random House Inc. 1992; fmr mem. Random House Exec. Cttee; Pres., CEO HarperCollins Worldwide 1997–. *Address:* Harper-Collins, 10 East 53rd Street, New York, NY 10022-5299, USA (office). *Telephone:* (212) 207-7000 (office). *Fax:* (212) 207-7759 (office). *Website:* www.harpercollins.com (office).

FRIEDMAN, Lawrence J., BA, MA, PhD; American academic and writer; b. 8 Oct. 1940, Cleveland, OH. *Education:* University of California at Riverside, University of California at Los Angeles, Menninger Foundation Interdisciplinary Studies Program. *Career:* Asst Prof., Arizona State University 1967–71; Assoc. Prof. 1971–77, Prof. of History and American Studies 1977–91, Distinguished University Prof. 1991–93, Bowling Green State University; Visiting Scholar, Harvard University 1991, 2004; Prof. of History, Indiana University 1993–; Fulbright Distinguished Chair, Germany 2002–03; Visiting Prof. of History of Science Harvard Univ. 2005; mem. American Asscn of University Profs; American Historical Asscn; Cheiron; Organization of American Historians; Society of American Historians. *Publications:* The White Savage: Racial Fantasies in the Postbellum South 1970, Inventors of the Promised Land 1975, Gregarious Saints: Self and Community in American Abolitionism 1830–1870 1982, Menninger: The Family and the Clinic 1990, Identity's Architect: A Biography of Erik Erikson 1999, Charity, Philanthropy and Civility in American History 2003. Contributions: Books and professional journals. *Honours:* National Endowment for the Humanities Fellowships 1979–80, 1986–87, 1994–95, Ohioana Library Asscn Book Award in History 1983, Paul and Ruth Olscamp Distinguished Research Award 1989–92, John Adams Fellow, Institute of United States Studies, University of London, Writer of the Year, Int. Biographical Center at Cambridge 2003, Independent Sector Research Prize 2003, Asscn of Fundraising Professionals Research Prize 2003. *Address:* 3709 Tamarron Drive, Bloomington, IN 47408 (home); c/o Department of History, Indiana University, Bloomington, IN 47405, USA (office). *E-mail:* LJFriedm@indiana.edu.

FRIEDMAN, Lawrence Meir, AB, JD, MLL; American academic and writer; b. 2 April 1930, Chicago, IL; m. Leah Feigenbaum 1955, two d. *Education:* University of Chicago. *Career:* Asst to Assoc. Prof. 1957–61, Childress Memorial Lecturer 1987, St Louis University; Assoc. Prof. to Prof. of Law University of Wisconsin, Madison 1961–68; Prof. of Law 1968–76, Marion Rice Kirkwood Prof. of Law 1976–, Stanford University; David Stouffer Memorial Lecturer Rutgers University 1969; Fellow Center for Advanced Study in the Behavioral Sciences 1973–74, Institute for Advanced Study, Berlin 1985; Sibley Lecturer University of Georgia 1976; Wayne Morse Lecturer University of Oregon 1985; Jefferson Lecture University of California at Berkeley 1995; Ruston Lecture Cumberland School of Law 1997; Tucker Lecture Washington and Lee University 2000; Charter Lecture Univ. of Georgia 2004; Pres. Research Cttee Sociology of Law 2003–; mem. American Acad. of Arts and Sciences; Law and Society Asscn, pres.1979–81; American Society for Legal History, pres. 1990–91; Society of American Historians. *Publications:* Contract Law in America 1965, Government and Slum Housing: A Century of Frustration 1968, Law and the Behavioral Sciences (with Stewart Macaulay) 1969, A History of American Law 1973, The Legal System: A Social Science Perspective 1975, Law and Society: An Introduction 1978, The Roots of Justice: Crime and Punishment in Alameda County, CA, 1870–1910 1981, American Law 1984, Total Justice: What Americans Want from the Legal System and Why 1985, Your Time Will Come: The Law of Age Discrimination and Mandatory Retirement 1985, American Law and the Constitutional Order Historical Perspectives (ed. with Harry N. Schrieber) 1988, The Republic of Choice: Law, Authority and Culture 1990, Crime and Punishment in American History 1993, Law and Society: Readings on the Study of Law (co-ed.) 1995, Legal Culture and the Legal Profession (co-ed.) 1996, The Crime Conundrum (co-ed.) 1997, The Horizontal Society 1999, American Law in the 20th Century 2002, Law in America: A Short History 2002, Legal Culture in the Age of Globalization: Latin-America and Mediterranean Europe (co-ed.) 2003. *Honours:* Scribes Award 1974, Triennial Award Order of Coif 1976, Willard Hurst Prize 1982, Harry Kalven Prize 1992, Silver Gavel Award American Bar Asscn 1994; five hon. doctorates 1977–98. *Address:* c/o School of Law, Stanford University, Stanford, CA 94305, USA.

FRIEDMAN, (Eve) Rosemary, (Robert Tibber, Rosemary Tibber); British writer; b. 5 Feb. 1929, London, England; m. Dennis Friedman 1949; four d. *Education:* Queen's Coll., London, Univ. Coll., London. *Career:* mem. judging panel Authors' Club First Novel Award 1989, Betty Trask Fictioni Award 1991, Jewish Quarterly Literary Prizes 1993, Macmillan Silver Pen Award 1996, 1997; mem. PEN, RSL, Soc. of Authors, Writers' Guild of Great Britain, BAFTA. *Publications:* No White Coat 1957, Love on my List 1959, We All Fall Down 1960, Patients of a Saint 1961, The Fraternity 1963, The Commonplace Day 1964, Aristide 1966, The General Practice 1967, Practice Makes Perfect 1969, The Life Situation 1977, The Long Hot Summer 1980, Proofs of Affection 1982, A Loving Mistress 1983, Rose of Jericho 1984, A Second Wife 1986, Aristide in Paris 1987, To Live in Peace 1987, An Eligible Man 1989, Golden Boy 1994, Vintage 1996, The Writing Game 1999, Intensive Care 2001, Paris Summer 2004; others: Home Truths (play) 1997, Doctors (television) 2003, Change of Heart (play) 2004; contribs to Confrontations with Judaism 1966, Reviewer, Sunday Times, TLS, Guardian, Sunday Times, Jewish Quarterly. *Address:* Apt 5, 3 Cambridge Gate, London, NW1 4JX, England. *E-mail:* rosemaryfriedman@hotmail.com. *Website:* www.rosemaryfriedman.co.uk.

FRIEDMAN, Thomas L., MPhil; American journalist; *Foreign Affairs Columnist, New York Times*; b. 20 July 1953, Minneapolis; m. Ann Friedman; two d. *Education:* Brandeis Univ., St Antony's Coll. Oxford, UK. *Career:* joined The New York Times 1981, Beirut Bureau Chief 1982–84, Israel Bureau Chief 1984–88, Washington Chief Diplomatic Corresp., Chief White House Corresp., Chief Econs Corresp., Foreign Affairs Columnist 1995–. *Television:* documentaries: The Roots of 9/11 (New York Times TV), Straddling the Fence (Discovery Channel). *Publications include:* From Beirut to Jerusalem (Nat. Book Award for Non-Fiction, Overseas Press Club Award) 1989, The Lexus and the Olive Tree (Overseas Press Club Award for Best Non-Fiction Book on Foreign Policy) 2000, Longitudes and Latitudes: America in the Age of Terrorism 2002, The World is Flat (Financial Times/Goldman Sachs Business Book Award) 2005. *Honours:* Pulitzer Prize for Int. Reporting 1983, 1988, for Distinguished Commentary 2002. *Address:* The New York Times, 1627 Eye Street, NW, Suite 700, Washington, DC 20006, USA (office). *Telephone:* (202) 862-0300 (office). *Fax:* (202) 862-0340 (office). *Website:* www.nytimes.com (office).

FRIEDMANN, Patricia Ann, AB, MEd; American author; b. 29 Oct. 1946, New Orleans, LA; m. 1st Robert Skinner 1979 (divorced 1996); one s. one d.; m. 2nd Edward Muchmore 1999. *Education:* Smith Coll., Temple Univ., Univ. of Denver. *Career:* Managing Ed. Diplomat 1980–82; Ed. Jewish Times 1976–78; Adjunct Faculty, Loyola Univ. 1993–; Writer-in-Residence, Tulane Univ. 2001; mem. Authors' Guild, Int. Women Writers Guild, PEN America Center. *Publications:* Too Smart to Be Rich 1988, The Exact Image of Mother 1991, The Accidental Jew (part of Native Tongues stage production) 1994, Eleanor Rushing 1998, Lovely Rita (part of Native Tongues stage production) 2000, Odds (novel) 2000, Secondhand Smoke (novel) 2002, Side Effects (novel (2004); A Little Bit Ruined (novel) 2007; contrib. of short stories and essays to anthologies and periodicals, including Newsweek, Oxford American, Speakeasy New Orleans Noir, My New Orleans, New Orleans Review, Horn Gallery, Intersections. *Honours:* Discover Great New Writers, Original Voices, Book Sense 76 selection. *Literary Agent:* The Blythe Agency, 25 Washington Street, Suite 614, Brooklyn, NY 11201, USA. *Telephone:* (718) 781-6489. *E-mail:* rolph@blythe-agency.com. *Website:* www.blythe-agency.com. *Address:* 8330 Sycamore Place, New Orleans, LA 70118, USA (home). *E-mail:* pattyfriedmann@aol.com (office); afreelunch@aol.com (home). *Website:* www.pattyfriedmann.com (office).

FRIEDRICH, Paul William, BA, MA, PhD; American anthropologist, writer and poet; *Professor Emeritus, University of Chicago*; b. 22 Oct. 1927, Cambridge, MA; m. 1st Lore Bucher 1950 (divorced 1966); one s. two d.; m. 2nd Margaret Hardin 1966 (divorced 1974); m. 3rd Deborah Joanna Gordon 1975 (divorced 1996); two d.; m. 4th Domnica Radulescu 1996 (divorced 2004); one s. *Education:* Williams Coll., Harvard Coll., Harvard Univ., Yale Univ. *Career:* Asst Prof., Univ. of Pennsylvania 1959–62; Visiting Asst Prof., Univ. of Michigan 1960, 1961; Assoc. Prof., Univ. of Chicago 1962–67, Prof. of Anthropology, Linguistics, Social Thought 1967–94, Prof. Emer. 1994–; Visiting Prof., Indiana Univ. 1964, Georgetown Univ. 1998, 1999, 2000, Washington and Lee Univ. 1999, Univ. of Virginia 2002; mem. Acad. of American Poets, American Acad. of Arts and Sciences, American Anthropological Asscn, American Asscn for Teachers of Slavic and East European Languages, American Asscn for the Advancement of Science, Linguistic Soc. of America (life mem.), Linguistic Soc. of India (life mem.), Poetry Soc. of America. *Publications:* Proto-Indo-European Trees 1970, The Tarascan Suffices of a Locative Space: Meaning and Morphotactics 1971, A Phonology of Tarascan 1973, On Aspect Theory and Homeric Aspect 1974, Proto-Indo-European Syntax: The Order of Meaningful Elements 1975, Neighboring Leaves Ride This Wind (poems) 1976, The Meaning of Aphrodite 1978, Bastard Moons (poems) 1978, Language, Context, and the Imagination: Essays by Paul Friedrich (ed. by A. S. Dil) 1979, Redwing (poems) 1982, The Language Parallax: Linguistic Relativism and Poetic Indeterminacy 1986, The Princes of Naranja: An Essay in Anthrohistorical Method 1987, Sonata (poems) 1987, Russia and Eurasia: Encyclopedia of World Cultures, Vol. 6 (co-ed.) 1994, Music in Russian Poetry 1998 contrib. to books, journals and anthologies. *Honours:* Ford Foundation grant 1957, Social Science Research Council grant 1966–67, Nat. Endowment for the Humanities grant 1974–76, Guggenheim Fellowship 1982–83, Burlington Award for Excellence in Graduate Teaching 1999. *Address:* c/o Committee on Social Thought, University of Chicago, 1130 E 59th Street, Chicago, IL 60637, USA. *Telephone:* (773) 702-7004 (office). *Fax:* (773) 702-4503 (office). *E-mail:* pfriedri@uchicago.edu.

FRIEL, Brian, FRSL; Irish writer; b. 9 Jan. 1929, Omagh, Co. Tyrone; s. of Patrick Friel and Christina MacLoone; m. Anne Morrison 1954; one s. four d. *Education:* St Columb's Coll., Derry, St Patrick's Coll., Maynooth, St Joseph's Training Coll., Belfast. *Career:* taught in various schools 1950–60; full-time writer 1960–; mem. Irish Acad. of Letters, Aosdána 1983–, American Acad. of Arts and Letters, RSL. *Plays:* Philadelphia, Here I Come! 1965, The Loves of Cass McGuire 1967, Lovers 1968, The Mundy Scheme 1969, Crystal and Fox 1970, The Gentle Island 1971, The Freedom of the City 1973, Volunteers 1975, Living Quarters 1976, Aristocrats 1979, Faith Healer 1979, Translations (Ewart-Biggs Memorial Prize, British Theatre Asscn Award) 1981, Three Sisters (trans.) 1981, The Communication Cord 1983, Fathers and Sons 1987, Making History (Best Foreign Play, New York Drama Critics Circle 1989) 1988, A Month in the Country 1990, Dancing at Lughnasa 1990, The London Vertigo 1991, Wonderful Tennessee 1993, Selected Stories 1994, Molly Sweeney 1995, Give Me Your Answer, Do! 1997, Uncle Vanya (after Chekov) 1998, The Yalta Game 2001, The Bear (trans.) 2002, Afterplay 2002, Performances 2003, The Home Place 2005 (Evening Standard Award for Best Play 2005). *Publications:* The Last of the Name (ed.) 1988; collected stories: The Saucer of Larks 1962, The Gold in the Sea 1966. *Honours:* Hon. Fellow, Univ. Coll. Dublin; Hon. DLitt (Nat. Univ. of Ireland) 1983, (Queen's Univ., Belfast) 1992, (Georgetown Univ., Washington, DC, Dominican Coll., Chicago), (Trinity Coll., Dublin) 2004. *Address:* Drumaweir House, Greencastle, Co. Donegal, Ireland (home). *Telephone:* (74) 9381119 (home). *Fax:* (74) 9381408 (home).

FRIGGIERI, Oliver, BA, MA, PhD; Maltese academic, writer, poet and literary critic; *Professor of Maltese Literature, University of Malta*; b. 27 March 1947, Furjana, Malta; s. of Charles Friggieri and Mary Galea; m. Eileen Cassar; one d. *Education:* Univ. of Malta, Catholic Univ. of Milan. *Career:* Prof. of Maltese Literature, Univ. of Malta 1987–, Head of Dept of Maltese 1987–2004; founder mem. Academia Internationale Mihai Eminescu, Craiova 1995; mem. Asscn Int. des Critiques Litteraires, Paris; participant and guest speaker at 70 int. congresses throughout Europe; guest poet at numerous poetry recitals in maj. European cities; co-founder of Saghtar nat. student magazine 1971; Literary Ed. of In-Nazzjon 1971–82. *Achievements:* author of first oratorio in Maltese: Pawlu ta' Malta 1985, first poetry album recording in Maltese 1997, various cantatas and religious hymns. *Radio:* weekly cultural programme presenter (Radio Malta). *Television:* regular appearances on Maltese and other networks. *Publications:* novels: Il-Gidba 1977, L-Istramb 1980, Fil-Parlament ma Jikbrux Fjuri 1986, Gizimin li Qatt ma Jiftah 1998, It-Tfal Jigu bil-Vapuri 2000; short stories: Stejjer ghal Qabel Jidlam Vol. I 1979, Vol. II 1983 (combined, enhanced edn) 1986, Fil-Gżira Taparsi jikbru l-Fjuri 1991, Koranta and Other Short Stories from Malta 1994; poetry: Mal-Fanal Hemm Harstek Tixghel 1988, Rewwixta (play-poem) 1990, Poeziji 1998, Il-Kliem li Tghidlek Qalbek 2001, Il-Poeziji Migbura 2002; literary criticism: Kittieba ta' Zmienna 1970, Ir-Ruh fil-Kelma 1973, Il-Kultura Taljana f'Dun Karm 1976, Fl-Gharbiel 1976, Storja tal-Letteratura Maltija 1979, Saggi Kritici 1979, Ellul Mercer f'Leli ta' Haz-Zghir Mir-Realta' ghall-Kuxjenza 1983, Gwann Mamo Il'Kittieb tar-Riforma Socjali 1984, Dizzjunarju ta' Termini Letterarji 1986, L'Idea tal'Letteratura 1986, Mekkanizmi Metaforici f'Dun Karm 1988, Dun Karm 'Il-Jien u Lil hinn Minnu' 1988, Il-Kuxjenza Nazzjonali Maltija 1995, L-Istudji Kritici Migbura 1995, L'Istorja tal-Poezija Maltija 2001; numerous works translated into various languages, poems in anthologies and articles in academic journals and newspapers. *Honours:* Nat. Order of Merit 1999; First Prize for Literary Criticism XIV Concorso Silarus 1982, Premio Internazionale Mediterraneo, Palermo 1988, Malta Govt Literary Award 1988, 1996, 1997, 1999, Premio Sampieri per la Poesia 1995, Premio Internazionale Trieste Poesia 2002, Gold Medal Award Malta Soc. of Arts, Manufactures and Commerce 2003, Premio Faber (Italy) 2004. *Address:* Faculty of Arts, University of Malta, Msida, Malta (office).

FRIMAN, Alice Ruth, BA, MA; American academic, poet and writer; *Instructor of Creative Writing and Poetry, Georgia College and State University*; b. 20 Oct. 1933, New York, NY; m. 1st Elmer Friman 1955; two s. one d.; m. 2nd Marshall Bruce Gentry 1989. *Education:* Brooklyn Coll., CUNY, Indiana Univ., Butler Univ. *Career:* Lecturer in English, Indiana Univ.-Purdue Univ. of Indianapolis 1971–74; Faculty, Univ. of Indianapolis 1971–90, Prof. of English 1990–93, Prof. Emer. 1993–; Visiting Prof. of Creative Writing, Indiana State Univ. 1982, Ball State Univ. 1996; Writer-in-Residence, Curtin Univ., Perth, Australia 1989; Instructor of Creative Writing and Poetry and Assoc. Ed. of Arts and Letters, Georgia Coll. and State Univ., Milledgeville 2003–; mem. Associated Writing Programs, MLA, Poetry Soc. of America, Writers' Center of Indiana (Bd mem. 1984–89, Hon. Life Mem. 1993–). *Publications:* A Question of Innocence 1978, Song to My Sister 1979, Loaves and Fishes: A Book of Indiana Women Poets (ed.) 1983, Reporting from Corinth 1984, Insomniac Heart 1990, Driving for Jimmy Wonderland 1992, Inverted Fire 1997, Zoo 1999, The Book of the Rotten Daughter 2006; contrib. to several anthologies and numerous reviews, quarterlies and journals. *Honours:* Dr hc (Indianapolis) 2002; Virginia Center for the Creative Arts Fellowships 1983, 1984, 1993, 1996, 2000, Poetry Soc. of America Consuelo Ford Award 1988, Poetry Soc. of America Cecil Hemley Memorial Award 1990,

Soc. for the Study of Midwestern Literature Midwest Poetry Award 1990, New England Poetry Club Erika Mumford Prize 1990, Millay Colony for the Arts Fellowship 1990, Yaddo Fellowship 1991, Poetry Soc. of America Lucille Medwick Memorial Award 1993, Univ. of Indianapolis Teacher of the Year Award 1993, First Prize, Abiko Quarterly Int. Poetry Contest 1994, New England Poetry Club Firman Houghton Award 1996, Indiana Arts Comm. Individual Artist Fellowship 1996–97, Truman State Univ. Ezra Pound Poetry Award 1998, Arts Council of Indianapolis Creative Renewal Fellowship 1999–2000, New England Poetry Club Sheila Margaret Motton Prize 2001, Georgia Poetry Circuit 2001–02, Shenandoah James Boatwright Prize for Poetry 2002, Bernheim Writing Fellowship 2003–04, MacDowell Fellowship 2004. *Address:* Department of English, PO Box 44, Georgia College and State University, Milledgeville, GA 31061 (office); 109 Treanor Drive, Milledgeville, GA 31061, USA (home). *Telephone:* (478) 414-1364 (home). *Fax:* (478) 445-5961 (office). *E-mail:* alicefriman@alltel.net (home).

FRITZ, Walter Helmut; German writer; b. 26 Aug. 1929, Karlsruhe; s. of Karl T. Fritz and Hedwig Fritz. *Education:* Univ. of Heidelberg. *Career:* poetry teacher, Univ. of Mainz; has lectured in Europe, America and Africa; mem. Akad. der Wissenschaften und der Literatur, Mainz, Bayerische Akad. der Schönen Künste, Munich, Deutscher Akad. für Sprache und Dichtung, Darmstadt, PEN. *Publications:* poetry and prose, including: Achtsam sein 1956, Veränderte Jahre 1963, Umwege 1964, Zwischenbemerkungen 1965, Abweichung 1965, Die Verwechslung 1970, Aus der Nähe 1972, Die Beschaffenheit solcher Tage 1972, Bevor uns Horen und Sehen Vergeht 1975, Schwierige Überfahrt 1976, Auch jetzt und morgen 1979, Gesammelte Gedichte 1979, Wunschtraum Alptraum (poems) 1981, Werkzeuge der Freiheit (poems) 1983, Cornelias Traum, Aufzeichnungen 1985, Immer einfacher immer schwieriger (poems) 1987, Zeit des Sehens (prose) 1989, Mit einer Feder aus den Flügen des Ikarus, Ausgewählte Gedichte, Mit einem Nachwort von Harald Hartung 1989, Die Schlüssel sind vertauscht (poems) 1992, Gesammelte Gedichte 1979–1994 1994, Das offene Fenster 1997, Zugelassen im Leben (poems) 1999, Maskenzug (poems) 2003; contrib. to journals and peiodicals. *Honours:* City of Karlsruhe Literature Prize 1960, Grosser Literaturpreis Bayerische Akad. der Schönen Künste Prize 1962, 1995, Heine-Taler Lyric Prize 1966, Fed. of German Industry Culture Circle Prize 1971, Stuttgarter Literaturpreis 1986, Villa Massimo-Stipendium, Georg-Trakl-Preis 1992. *Address:* Kolbergerstrasse 2A, 76139 Karlsruhe, Germany. *Telephone:* (721) 683346.

FROHM, Frederika (see Kerner, Fred)

FROMME, Friedrich Karl, DPhil; German journalist; b. 10 June 1930, Dresden; s. of Prof. Dr Albert Fromme and Dr Lenka Fromme; m. 1st Traute Kirsten 1961 (died 1992); m. 2nd Brigitte Burkert 1997. *Education:* studies in science, politics and public law. *Career:* teaching Asst, Univ. of Tübingen 1957–62; Ed. Süddeutscher Rundfunk 1962–64, Frankfurter Allgemeine Zeitung (FAZ) 1964–68; Bonn corresp. FAZ 1968–73; Ed. responsible for internal politics and co-ordination, FAZ 1974–97; freelance writer. *Publications:* Von der Weimarer Verfassung zum Bonner Grundgesetz 1962, Der Parlamentarier–ein Freier Beruf? 1978, Gesetzgebung im Widerstreit 1980. *Honours:* Grosses Bundesverdienstkreuz 1995, Theodor Wolff Prize 1997. *Address:* Welt am Sonntag, 20350, Hamburg (office); Mohrengarten 60, 40822 Mettmann, Germany. *Telephone:* (2104) 958768.

FROST, Sir David Paradine, Kt, OBE, MA; British broadcast journalist and writer; b. 7 April 1939, Tenterden, Kent; s. of Rev. W. J. Paradine Frost; m. 1st Lynne Frederick 1981 (divorced 1982); m. 2nd Lady Carina Fitzalan Howard 1983; three s. *Education:* Gillingham and Wellingborough Grammar Schools, Gonville and Caius Coll., Cambridge. *Career:* appeared in BBC TV satire series That Was The Week That Was 1962–63, That Was The Year That Was 1962–63; other programmes with BBC included A Degree of Frost 1963, 1973, Not So Much A Programme More A Way Of Life 1964–65, The Frost Report 1966–67, Frost Over England 1967; appeared in The Frost Programme, ITA 1966–67, 1967–68, 1972; Chair. and CEO David Paradine Ltd 1966–; Jt Founder London Weekend Television 1967; Jt Deputy Chair. Equity Enterprises 1973–76 (Chair. 1972–73); Jt Founder and Dir TV-AM 1981–93, host of numerous programmes, including That Was The Week That Was (USA) 1964–65, Frost On Friday, Frost On Saturday, Frost On Sunday etc., David Frost Show (USA) 1969–72, David Frost Revue (USA) 1971–73, Frost Over Australia 1972–77, Frost Over New Zealand 1973–74, The Frost Interview 1974, We British 1975, The Sir Harold Wilson Interviews 1967–77, The Nixon Interviews 1976–77, The Crossroads of Civilisation 1977–78; David Frost Presents the Int. Guinness Book of World Records 1981–86, Frost over Canada 1982–83, The Spectacular World of Guinness Records 1987–88, Talking with David Frost 1991–; Presenter Sunday Breakfast with Frost 1993–2005; The Frost Programme 1993–; joined Al-Jazeera International 2005–, Host Frost Over the World; Pres. Lord's Taverners 1985, 1986; Companion TV and Radio Industries Club 1992. *Films produced:* The Rise and Rise of Michael Rimmer 1970, Charley One-Eye 1972, Leadbelly 1974, The Slipper and the Rose 1975, Dynasty 1975, The Ordeal of Patty Hearst 1978, The Remarkable Mrs Sanger 1979. *Publications:* That Was The Week That Was 1963, How to Live Under Labour 1964, Talking With Frost 1967, To England With Love (with Antony Jay) 1967, The Americans 1970, Whitlam and Frost 1974, I Gave Them a Sword 1978, I Could Have Kicked Myself 1982, Who Wants to Be a Millionaire? 1983, The Mid-Atlantic Companion (jtly) 1986, The Rich Tide (jtly) 1986, The World's Shortest Books 1987, David Frost An Autobiography: Part One 1993. *Honours:* Hon. Prof.

Thames Valley Univ. 1994; Hon. DCL (Univ. of East Anglia) 2004; Golden Rose, Montreux (for Frost over England) 1967, Royal TV Soc.'s Award 1967, Richard Dimbleby Award 1967, Emmy Award 1970, 1971, Religious Heritage of America Award 1970, Albert Einstein Award (Communication Arts) 1971, BAFTA Fellowship 2005. *Address:* David Paradine Ltd, 5 St Mary Abbots Place, Kensington, London, W8 6LS, England. *Telephone:* (20) 7371-1111. *Fax:* (20) 7602-0411.

FROST, Jason (see Obstfeld, Raymond)

FROST, Richard, BA, MA; American poet, writer and academic; b. 8 April 1929, Palo Alto, CA; m. 1st Frances Atkins 1951, one s. two d.; m. 2nd Carol Kydd 1969, two s. *Education:* San Jose State College. *Career:* Instructor in English, San Jose State College, 1956–57, Towson State College, 1957–59; Asst Prof., 1959–64, Assoc. Prof., 1964–71, Prof. of English, 1971–, SUNY at Oneonta. *Publications:* The Circus Villains, 1965; Getting Drunk With the Birds, 1971; Neighbor Blood, 1996. Contributions: Magazines, reviews, quarterlies and journals. *Honours:* Danforth Fellow, Bread Loaf Writers' Conference, 1961; Resident Fellow, Yaddo, 1979, 1981, 1983; Gustav Davidson Memorial Award, Poetry Society of America, 1982; National Endowment for the Arts Creative Writing Fellowship, 1992. *Address:* c/o Department of English, State University of New York at Oneonta, Oneonta, NY 13820, USA. *Telephone:* (607) 988-7170. *E-mail:* frostrq@oneonta.edu.

FROSTENSON, Katarina; Swedish poet, novelist and playwright; b. 5 March 1953, Brännkyrka. *Career:* Ed. Halifax (literary calendar) 1986–96; translated from French including Emanuel Bove, Marguerite Duras and Georges Bataille; mem. Swedish Acad. 1992, adjudication panel Nobel Prize for Literature. *Publications include:* verse collections: I mellan (Between) 1978, Rena land (Pure Countries) 1980, Den andra (The Other) 1982, I det gula (In the Yellow) 1985, Samtalet (The Conversation) 1987, Joner (Ions) 1991, Tankarna (The Thoughts) 1994, Korallen (The Choral) 1999; prose: Berättelser från dom (Tales From Them) 1992; drama: 4 monodramer (Four Monodramas) 1990, Traum (Dream) 1992, Sal P (Ward P) 1995, Staden (The City, libretto for opera by Sven-David Sandström) 1998, Kristallvägen (The Crystal Road) 2000, Safirgränd (Sapphire Lane) 2000; Raymond Chandler och filmen (Raymond Chandler and film) (essay) 1978. *Honours:* Great Prize of Soc. of Nine 1989, Bellman Prize 1994, Swedish Radio Prize for Lyrical Poetry 1996. *Address:* Swedish Academy, PO Box 2118, 103 13 Stockholm, Sweden.

FRY, Stephen John, MA; British actor, writer and director; b. 24 Aug. 1957, s. of Alan John Fry and Marianne Eve Fry (née Newman). *Education:* Uppingham School, Queens' Coll. Cambridge. *Career:* Columnist The Listener 1988–89, Daily Telegraph 1990–; wrote first play Latin, performed at Edin. Festival 1980; and at Lyric Theatre, Hammersmith 1983; appeared with Cambridge Footlights in revue The Cellar Tapes, Edinburgh Festival 1981; re-wrote script Me and My Girl, London, Broadway, Sydney 1984; mem. Amnesty Int., Comic Relief; Pres. Friends for Life Terrence Higgins Trust. *Plays:* Forty Years On, Chichester Festival and London 1984, The Common Pursuit, London 1988 (TV 1992). *Radio:* Loose Ends 1986–87, Whose Line Is It Anyway? 1987, Saturday Night Fry 1987, 1998. *TV series:* There's Nothing to Worry About 1982, Alfresco 1983–84, The Young Ones 1984, Happy Families 1985, Blackadder II 1985, Saturday Live 1986–87, A Bit of Fry and Laurie 1987–95, Blackadder's Christmas Carol 1988, Blackadder Goes Forth 1989, Jeeves and Wooster 1990–93, Stalag Luft 1993, Laughter and Loathing 1995, Gormenghast 2000, Absolute Power 2003, QI 2003–. *Films:* The Good Father, A Fish Called Wanda, A Handful of Dust, Peter's Friends 1992, IQ 1995, Wind in the Willows, Wilde 1997, Cold Comfort Farm 1997, A Civil Action 1997, Whatever Happened to Harold Smith? 2000, Relatives Values 2000, Discovery of Heaven 2001, Gosford Park 2002, Bright Young Things (writer, dir, exec. producer) 2003, Mirrormask 2004, A Cock and Bull Story 2005, V for Vendetta 2006, Stormbreaker 2006. *Publications:* Paperweight (collected essays) 1992, Stephen Fry Mixed Shrinkwrap 1993, X10 Hippopotamus Shrinkwrap 1993, The Liar (novel) 1993, The Hippopotamus 1994, A Bit of Fry and Laurie (with Hugh Laurie) 1994, 3 Bits of Fry and Laurie (with Hugh Laurie) 1994, Fry and Laurie 4 (with Hugh Laurie) 1994, Paperweight Vol. II (collected essays) 1995, Making History 1996, Moab is my Washpot (autobiog.) 1997, The Stars' Tennis Balls (novel) 2000, The Salmon of Doubt by Douglas Adams (ed.) 2002, Revenge (novel) 2002, Rescuing the Spectacled Bear (novel) 2002, Incomplete & Utter History of Classical Music (with Tim Lihoreau) 2005, The Ode Less Travelled: Unlocking the Poet Within 2005. *Honours:* Hon. LLD (Dundee) 1995, (East Anglia) 1999, Hon. DLit, Dr hc (Anglia Ruskin) 2005. *Literary Agent:* Hamilton Hodell Ltd, Fifth Floor, 66-68 Margaret Street, London, W1W 8SR, England; c/o Toni Howard, ICM, 8942 Wilshire Blvd, Beverly Hills, CA 90211, USA. *Telephone:* (20) 7636-1221. *Fax:* (20) 7636-1226. *Website:* www.stephenfry.com.

FRYE, Roland Mushat, AB, PhD; American academic and writer; b. 3 July 1921, Birmingham, AL; m. Jean Elbert Steiner 1947, one s. *Education:* Princeton University, Princeton Theological Seminary. *Career:* Emory University, 1952–61; L. P. Stone Foundation Lecturer, Princeton Theological Seminary, 1959; Faculty, 1965–83, Emeritus Prof., 1983–, National Phi Beta Kappa Visiting Scholar, 1985–86, University of Pennsylvania; Chair., 1989–91, Chair. Emeritus, 1991–, Center of Theological Inquiry, Princeton, NJ. *Publications:* God, Man and Satan: Patterns of Christian Thought and Life, 1960; Shakespeare and Christian Doctrine, 1963; Shakespeare's Life and Times: A Pictorial Record, 1967; Milton's Imagery and the Visual Arts: Iconographic Tradition in the Epic Poems, 1978; Is God a Creationist?: The

Religious Case Against Creation-Science, 1983; The Renaissance Hamlet: Issues and Responses in 1600, 1984. Contributions: scholarly journals.

FRYER, Jonathan, (G. L. Morton), BA, MA; British writer, broadcaster and academic; b. 5 June 1950, Manchester, England. *Education:* Diplôme D'Etudes Françaises, Université de Poitiers, France, St Edmund Hall, Oxford. *Career:* journalist, Reuters, London and Brussels 1973–74; Visiting Lecturer, School of Journalism, Univ. of Nairobi, Kenya 1976; Subject Teacher, SOAS, Univ. of London 1993–; Chair. Liberal International British Group; mem. English PEN, RSL, Soc. of Authors. *Publications:* The Great Wall of China 1975, Isherwood 1977, revised edn as Eye of the Camera 1993, Brussels as Seen by Naif Artists (with Rona Dobson) 1979, Food for Thought 1981, George Fox and the Children of the Light 1991, Dylan 1993, The Sitwells (with Sarah Bradford and John Pearson) 1994, André and Oscar 1997, Soho in the Fifties and Sixties 1998, Robbie Ross: Oscar Wilde's True Love 2000, Wilde 2005, Fuelling Kuwait's Development 2007; numerous political pamphlets, mainly on Third World themes; contribs to Economist, Tablet, Geographical Magazine, Guardian, London Magazine, Gay Times, Society Today, The Wildean, Liberator, The Liberal, and others. *Honours:* Chevalier, Ordre nat. du Mérite (Mauritania) 2000; Elizabeth Longford Historical Biography Award 2006. *Literary Agent:* Andrew Lownie, 38 Great Smith Street, London, SW1P 3BU, England. *Telephone:* (20) 7222-7574. *E-mail:* lownie@globalnet.co.uk. *Address:* 140 Bow Common Lane, London, E3 4BH, England (home). *Telephone:* (20) 8980-4382 (office). *E-mail:* jonathanfryer@hotmail.com (home).

FU, Tianlin; Chinese poet; b. 24 Jan. 1946, Zizhong Co., Sichuan Prov. *Education:* Chongqing Middle School, Electronic Tech. School. *Career:* worked in orchard Chongqing 1962–79; clerk, Beibei Cultural Centre 1980–82; Ed. Chongqing Publishing House 1982–. *Publications:* Green Musical Notes 1981, Between Children and the World 1983, Island of Music 1985, Red Strawberry 1986, Selected Poems of Seven Chinese Poets 1993. *Honours:* First Prize of Chinese Poetry 1983. *Address:* Chongqing Publishing House, 205 Changjiang 2 Road, 630050, Chongqing City, Sichuan, People's Republic of China.

FUENTES, Carlos; Mexican writer and diplomatist; b. 11 Nov. 1928, Mexico City; s. of Rafael Fuentes Boettiger and Berta Macías Rivas; m. 1st Rita Macedo 1957; one d.; m. 2nd Sylvia Lemus 1973; one s. one d. *Education:* Univ. of Mexico, Inst. des Hautes Etudes Internationales, Geneva. *Career:* mem. Mexican Del. to ILO, Geneva 1950–51; Asst Head, Press Section, Ministry of Foreign Affairs, Mexico 1954; Asst Dir Cultural Dissemination, Univ. de Mexico 1955–56; Head Dept of Cultural Relations, Ministry of Foreign Affairs 1957–59; Ed. Revista Mexicana de Literatura 1954–58, Co-Ed. El Espectador 1959–61, Ed. Siempre and Politica 1960–; Amb. to France 1974–77; Prof. of English and Romance Languages Univ. of Pennsylvania 1978–83; fmr Prof. of Spanish and Comparative Literature, Columbia Univ., New York; Prof. of Comparative Literature, Harvard Univ. 1984–86, Robert F. Kennedy Prof. of Latin American Studies 1987–89; Simon Bolivar Prof. Univ. of Cambridge 1986–87; Prof.-at-Large Brown Univ. 1995–; Pres. Modern Humanities Research Asscn 1989–; fmr Adjunct Prof. of English and Romance Languages, Univ. of Pennsylvania; Fellow, Woodrow Wilson Int. Center for Scholars, Washington, DC 1974; Fellow of the Humanities, Princeton Univ.; Virginia Gildersleeve Visiting Prof., Barnard Coll., New York; Edward Leroc Visiting Prof., School of Int. Affairs, Columbia Univ., New York; mem. American Acad. and Inst. of Arts and Letters, El Colegio Nacional, Mexico, Mexican Nat. Comm. on Human Rights. *Film and TV screenplays:* Pedro Paramo 1966, Tiempo de morir 1966, Los caifanes 1967, El espejo enterrado (The Buried Mirror, TV series) 1992. *Publications:* Los días enmascarados 1954, La región más transparente 1958, Las buenas conciencias 1959, La muerte de Artemio Cruz 1962, Aura 1962, The Argument of Latin America 1963, Cantar de ciegos 1964, Zona sagrada 1967, Cambio de piel (Biblioteca Breve Prize) 1967, Paris: la revolución de mayo 1968, Cumpleaños 1969, El mundo de José Luis Cuevas 1969, La nueva novela hispanoamericana 1969, Casa con dos puertas 1970, Todos los gatos son pardos (play) 1970, El tuerto es rey (play) 1970, Tiempo mexicano 1971, Poemas de amor 1971, Los signos en rotación y otros ensayos (ed.) 1971, Los reinos originarios 1971, Cuerpos y ofreadas 1972, Chac Mool y otros cuentos 1973, Cervantes o La crítica de la lectura 1974, Terra Nostra (Javier Villaurrutia Prize 1975, Rómulo Gallegos Prize 1977) 1975, La cabeza de la hidra 1978, Una familia lejana 1980, Agua quemada 1981, Orquídeas a la luz de la luna (play) 1982, High Noon in Latin America 1983, Juan Soriano y su obra 1984, On Human Rights: A Speech 1984, El gringo viejo (IUA Prize 1989) 1985, Latin America: At War with the Past 1985, Palacio Nacional (with Guillermo Tovar y de Teresa) 1986, Gabriel García Marquez and the Invention of America 1987, Cristóbal nonato (novel) (Miguel de Cervantes Prize) 1987, Myself with Others (essays) 1988, Valiante mundo nuevo 1990, La campaña (novel) 1990, Constancia y otras novelas para vírgenes 1990, El espejo enterrado 1992, Geografía de la novela (essays) 1993, Tres discursos para dos aldeas 1993, El naranjo (novellas) 1993, Nuevo tiempo mexicano 1994, Frontera de cristal 1995, Diana o la cazadora solitaria 1995, Por un progreso incluyente 1997, Retratos en el tiempo 1998, Los años con Laura Díaz 1999, Instinto de Inez 2000, Los cinco soles de México 2000, En esto creo 2002, La silla del águila 2003, This I Believe: An A–Z of a Writer's Life 2004, Contra Bush 2004, The Eagle's Throne 2006. *Honours:* Hon. Citizen of Santiago de Chile 1993, Buenos Aires 1993, Veracruz 1993; Order of Merit, Chile 1992; Légion d'honneur 1992; Order of the South Cross, Brazil 1997; French Order of Merit 1998; Dr hc (Harvard, Wesleyan, Essex, Cambridge, Salamanca, Ghent, Madrid); Biblioteca Breva Prize, Barcelona 1967, Rómulo Gallegos

Prize, Caracas 1975, Mexican Nat. Award for Literature 1984, Ruben Dario Prize 1988, Premio Principe de Asturias 1992, UNESCO Picasso Medal 1994, Grinzane-Cavour Award 1994, French and Brazilian Acads Latin Civilization Prize 1999, Mexican Senate Medal 2000, Los Angeles Public Library Award 2001, Commonwealth Award Delaware 2002, Giuseppe Acerbi literature prize, Italy 2004, Galileo Prize, Florence, Italy 2005, Blue Metropolis Award, Montreal 2005, Franklin Delano Roosevelt Freedom of Speech Award 2006. *Address:* c/o Brandt & Brandt, 1501 Broadway, New York, NY 10036, USA; c/o Balcells, Diagonal 580, Barcelona 08021, Spain. *Telephone:* (212) 840-5760 (USA); (93) 200 8933 (Spain). *Fax:* (212) 840-5776 (USA); (93) 200 7041 (Spain).

FUGARD, Athol; South African actor and playwright; b. 11 June 1932, s. of Harold David Fugard and Elizabeth Magdelene Potgiefer; m. Sheila Fugard 1956; one d. *Career:* leading role in Meetings with Remarkable Men (film) 1977, The Guest (BBC production) 1977; acted in and wrote script for Marigolds in August (film). *Plays:* The Blood Knot, Hello and Goodbye, People are Living Here, Boesman and Lena 1970, Sizwe Banzi is Dead 1973, The Island 1973, Statements After an Arrest Under the Immorality Act 1974, No Good Friday 1974, Nongogo 1974, Dimetos 1976, The Road to Mecca 1984, My Children, My Africa, The Guest (film script) 1977, A Lesson from Aloes 1979 (author and dir Broadway production 1980), Master Harold and the Boys 1981, A Place with the Pigs (actor and dir) 1988, Playland 1992, Sign of Hope 1992, Valley Song (actor and dir) 1996, The Captain's Tiger 1999, Sorrows and Rejoicings 2001. *Films include:* Marigolds in August 1981, The Guest 1984; acted in films Gandhi 1982, Road to Mecca 1991 (also co-dir). *Publications:* Notebooks 1960–77, Playland 1992; novel: Tsotsi 1980; plays: Road to Mecca 1985, A Place with the Pigs 1988, Cousins: A Memoir 1994. *Honours:* Hon. DLit (Natal and Rhodes Univs); Dr hc (Univ. of Cape Town, Georgetown Univ., Washington, DC, New York, Pennsylvania, City Univ. of New York); Hon. DFA (Yale Univ.) 1973; winner Silver Bear Award, Berlin Film Festival 1980, New York Critics Award for A Lesson From Aloes 1981, London Evening Standard Award for Master Harold and the Boys 1983, Commonwealth Award for Contrib. to American Theatre 1984. *Address:* P.O. Box 5090, Walmer, Port Elizabeth 6065, South Africa.

FUJINO, Chiya; Japanese novelist; b. 27 Feb. 1962, Fukuoka Prefecture, Kyushu. *Education:* Chiba Univ. *Career:* worked for a publishing co. –1995. *Publications:* novels: Gogo no jikanwari (Afternoon Schedule) (Kaien Prize for New Writers) 1995, Shonen to shojo no poruka (Boy's and Girl's Polka) 1996, Oshaberi kaidan (A Chatty Ghost Story) (Noma Literary Prize) 1998, Natsu no yakusoku (Summer Promise) (Akutagawa Prize) 1999, Ruuto 225 (Route 225) 2002, Bejitaburu haitsu (Vegetable Apartment) 2005; contrib. short stories to Tokyo Fragments 2004, Inside and Other Short Fiction 2006.

FUJISAWA, Shû; Japanese novelist. *Education:* Hôsei Univ. *Career:* Ed., Tosho Shimbun –1996. *Publications:* novels: Zonu o hidari ni magare (Turn Left at the Zone) 1993, Sotomawari, Saigon pikkuappu, Suna ti hikari, Shibō Yūgi, Satori, Solo et Saigon pikkuappu, Buenosu Airesu gozen reiji (Midnight in Buenos Aires) (Akutagawa Prize) 1998, Orenji ando tāru (Orange and Tar) 2000, Buyinuosiailisi wu ye ling dian 2000, Hakozaki Junction 2003. *Address:* c/o Kawade Shobo Shinsha Publishers, 2-32-2 Sendagaya, Shibuya-ku, Tokyo 151-0051, Japan. *E-mail:* info@kawade.co.jp.

FUKUYAMA, Francis, PhD; American writer and academic; *Bernard L. Schwartz Professor of International Political Economy, Paul H. Nitze School of Advanced International Studies, Johns Hopkins University*; b. New York. *Education:* Cornell and Harvard Univs. *Career:* fmrly a sr social scientist, RAND Corpn, Washington, DC and Deputy Dir State Dept's Policy Planning Staff; Hirst Prof. of Public Policy, George Mason Univ., Fairfax, Va; Dean of Faculty, Paul H. Nitze School of Advanced Int. Studies, Johns Hopkins Univ. 2002–04, now Bernard L. Schwartz Prof. of Int. Political Economy; mem. Pres.'s Council on Bioethics; mem. advisory Bd National Endowment for Democracy, The National Interest, Journal of Democracy, The New America Foundation; fmr mem. US delegation Egyptian-Israeli talks on Palestinian autonomy. *Publications:* The End of History and the Last Man 1992, Trust: The Social Virtues And the Creation of Prosperity 1996, The Great Disruption: Human Nature and the Reconstitution of the Social Order 1999, Our Posthuman Future 2002, State-Building: Governance and World Order in the 21st Century 2004, After the Neocons 2006, America at the Crossroads: Democracy, Power, and the Neoconservative Legacy 2006. *Address:* Paul H. Nitze School of Advanced International Studies, The Rome Building, Room 507, 1619 Massachusetts Avenue, NW, Washington, DC 20036, USA (office). *Telephone:* (202) 663-5765 (office). *Fax:* (202) 663-5769 (office). *E-mail:* fukuyama@jhu.edu (office). *Website:* www.francisfukuyama.com (office).

FULFORD, Robert Marshall Blount; Canadian journalist and writer; b. 13 Feb. 1932, Ottawa, ON; m. 1st Jocelyn Jean Dingman 1956 (divorced 1970); one s. one d.; m. 2nd Geraldine Patricia Sherman 1970; two d. *Education:* Malvern Collegiate, Toronto. *Career:* reporter, 1950–53, 1956–57, columnist, 1992–, Globe and Mail; Asst Ed., Canadian Homes and Gardens, 1955, Mayfair, 1956, Maclean's, 1962–64; Columnist, Toronto Star, 1958–62, 1964–68, 1971–87; Ed., Saturday Night, 1968–87; Barker Fairley Distinguished Visitor in Canadian Culture, University College, University of Toronto, 1987–88; Columnist and Contributing Ed., Financial Times, 1988–92; Chair, Banff Centre Program in Arts Journalism, 1989–91, Maclean Hunter Program in Communications Ethics, Ryerson Polytechnic Institute, Toronto, 1989–93; mem. Canadian Civil Liberties Asscn. *Publications:* This

Was Expo, 1968; Crisis at the Victory Burlesk, 1968; Marshall Delaney at the Movies, 1974; An Introduction to the Arts in Canada, 1977; Canada: A Celebration, 1983; Best Seat in the House: Memoirs of a Lucky Man, 1988; Accidental City: The Transformation of Toronto, 1995. *Honours:* Prix d'Honneur, Canadian Conference of the Arts, 1981; Officer of the Order of Canada, 1984; Hon. doctorates, McMaster University, 1986, York University, 1987, University of Western Ontario, 1988, University of Toronto, 1994.

FULLER, Charles; American dramatist; b. 5 March 1939, Philadelphia, PA; m. Miriam A. Nesbitt 1962, two s. *Education:* Villanova University, LaSalle College. *Career:* co-founder and Co-Dir, Afro-American Arts Theatre, Philadelphia, 1967–71; Writer and Dir, The Black Experience, WIP Radio, Philadelphia, 1970–71; Prof. of African-American Studies, Temple University, until 1993; mem. Dramatists Guild; PEN; Writers Guild of America. *Publications:* Plays: The Village: A Party, 1968, revised version as The Perfect Party, 1969; In My Names and Days, 1972; Candidate, 1974; In the Deepest Part of Sleep, 1974; First Love, 1974; The Lay Out Letter, 1975; The Brownsville Raid, 1976; Sparrow in Flight, 1978; Zooman and the Sign, 1981; A Soldier's Play, 1982; We: Part I, Sally, 1988, Part II, Prince, Part III, Jonquil, 1989, Part IV, Burner's Frolic, 1990; Songs of the Same Lion, 1991. Other: Screenplays and television series. *Honours:* National Endowment for the Arts Grant, 1976; Rockefeller Foundation Grant, 1976; Guggenheim Fellowship, 1977–78; Obie Award, 1981; Pulitzer Prize in Drama, 1982; New York Drama Critics Circle Award, 1982; Edgar Allan Poe Mystery Award, 1985.

FULLER, Cynthia Dorothy, BA, PGCE, MLitt; British poet and adult education tutor; b. 13 Feb. 1948, Isle of Sheppey, England; m. (divorced); two s. *Education:* Sheffield University, University of Oxford, Aberdeen University. *Career:* teacher of English, Redborne School, 1970–72; freelance in adult education, Depts at Durham, Leeds and Newcastle Universities, also Open University and Workers' Education Asscn. *Publications:* Moving Towards Light 1992, Instructions for the Desert 1996, Only a Small Boat 2001, Jack's Letters Home 2006 contrib. poems in various magazines, including Other Poetry, Iron, Poetry Durham, Literary Review. *Honours:* Northern Arts Financial Assistance.

FULLER, Jean Violet Overton, BA; British writer and poet; b. 7 March 1915, Iver Heath, Bucks; d. of Capt. John Henry Fuller and Violet Overton Fuller. *Education:* Brighton High School, RADA, University of London, University College London. *Career:* mem. Soc. of Authors. *Publications:* The Comte de Saint Germain 1988, Blavatsky and Her Teachers 1988, Dericourt: The Chequered Spy 1989, Sickert and the Ripper Crimes 1990, Cats and Other Immortals 1992, Espionage as a Fine Art 2002, Krishnamurti and the Wind 2003, Driven to It (autobiog.) 2007. *Honours:* Writers 1968. *Address:* Fuller D'Arch Smith Ltd, 37B New Cavendish Street, London, England.

FULLER, John Leopold, BA, BLitt, MA, FRSL; British poet and writer; *Emeritus Fellow, Magdalen College, Oxford;* b. 1 Jan. 1937, Ashford, Kent, England; m. Cicely Prudence Martin 1960; three d. *Education:* New Coll., Oxford. *Career:* Fellow and Tutor, Magdalen Coll., Oxford; Emeritus Fellow, Magdalen Coll., Oxford. *Publications:* Fairground Music 1961, The Tree That Walked 1967, Cannibals and Missionaries 1972, The Sonnet 1972, Epistles to Several Persons 1973, Penguin Modern Poets 22 1974, The Mountain in the Sea 1975, Lies and Secrets 1979, The Illusionists 1980, The Dramatic Works of John Gay (ed.) 1983, The Beautiful Inventions 1983, Flying to Nowhere 1983, The Adventures of Speedfall 1985, Selected Poems, 1954–82 1985, The Grey Among the Green 1988, Tell it Me Again 1988, The Burning Boys 1989, Partingtime Hall (with James Fenton) 1989, The Mechanical Body and Other Poems 1991, Look Twice 1991, The Worm and the Star 1993, The Chatto Book of Love Poetry 1994, Stones and Fires 1996, Collected Poems 1996, A Skin Diary 1997, W. H. Auden: A Commentary 1998, W. H. Auden: Poems Selected by John Fuller 2000, The Oxford Book of Sonnets (ed.) 2000, The Memoirs of Laetitia Horsepole 2001, Now and for a Time 2002, Ghosts 2004, Flawed Angel 2005, The Space of Joy 2006; contrib. to periodicals, reviews and journals. *Honours:* Newdigate Prize 1960, Richard Hillary Award 1962, E. C. Gregory Award 1965, Geoffrey Faber Memorial Prize 1974, Southern Arts Prize 1980, Whitbread Prize 1983, Forward Prize 1996. *Address:* 4 Benson Place, Oxford, OX2 6QH, England.

FULLER, Lawrence Robert, BJ; American newspaper publisher; b. 9 Sept. 1941, Toledo; s. of Kenneth Fuller and Marjory Rairdon; m. Suzanne Hovik 1967; one s. one d. *Education:* Univ. of Missouri. *Career:* reporter, Globe Gazette, Mason City, Ia 1963–67; reporter, later City Ed. Minneapolis Star 1967–75; Exec. Ed. Messenger-Inquirer, Owensborough, Ky 1975–77; Exec. Ed. Argus Leader, Sioux Falls, South Dakota 1977–78, Pres., Publr 1974–84, 1986–99; Pres. Gannett News Media, Washington, DC 1984–85; Dir Corp. Communications, Gannett Co. Inc. Washington 1985–86; Vice-Pres. Gannett/West Regional Newspaper Group 1986–97, The Honolulu Advertisers 1986–97; mem. American Newspaper Publishers' Asscn, American Soc. of Newspaper Eds etc. *Address:* 605 Kapiolani Boulevard, Honolulu, HI 96813, USA.

FULLER, Steve William, MPhil, PhD, FRSA; American sociologist and writer; *Professor of Sociology, University of Warwick;* b. 12 July 1959, New York; s. of Theodore Beardsley Fuller and Sylvia Malherbe Gonzalez; partner, Dolores Marie Byrnes. *Education:* Regis High School, New York, Columbia Univ., New York, Univ. of Cambridge, UK, Univ. of Pittsburgh. *Career:* Teaching Fellow in History and Philosophy of Science Univ. of Pittsburgh 1982–85; Asst Prof. of Philosophy Univ. of Colorado, Boulder 1985–88; Asst to Assoc. Prof. of Science and Tech. Studies, Virginia Tech. 1988–94; Assoc. Prof. of Rhetoric and Communication Univ. of Pittsburgh 1993–94; Prof. of Sociology and Social Policy Univ. of Durham, England 1994–99; Prof. of Sociology Univ. of Warwick, England 1999–; Visiting Prof. Netherlands, Germany, Sweden, Israel, Japan, USA, Denmark; Exec. Ed. Social Epistemology: A Journal of Knowledge, Culture and Policy 1987–97; Exec. Ed. Technoscience: The Newsletter of the Soc. for Social Studies of Science 1989–97; Pres. Acad. Bd Knowledge Man. Consortium Int. 1999; Fellow, Economic and Social Research Council (ESRC), UK 2000; mem. numerous editorial bds and prize cttees; mem. American Philosophical Asscn, Philosophy of Science Asscn, Soc. for the Social Studies of Science (4S) (mem. Council 1998–), European Asscn for the Study of Science and Tech. (mem. council 1994–98), American Sociological Asscn, British Sociological Asscn, History of Science Soc., American Asscn for the Rhetoric of Science and Tech. (Founding Vice-Pres. 1993–94), Business Processes Resources Centre Warwick Univ. (mem. advisory bd 1999–); UK Partner, EU Sixth Framework Project on Knowledge Politics of Converging Technologies 2006–08. *Publications:* Social Epistemology 1988, Philosophy of Science and its Discontents 1989, Philosophy, Rhetoric and the End of Knowledge: The Coming of Science and Technology Studies (revised second edn subtitled A New Beginning for Science and Technology Studies, with James H. Collier) 1993, Science 1997, The Governance of Science: Ideology and the Future of the Open Society 2000, Thomas Kuhn: A Philosophical History for Our Times 2000, Knowledge Management Foundations 2002, Kuhn vs Popper: The Struggle for the Soul of Science (named Book of the Month by Popular Science magazine (USA) Feb. 2005) 2003, The Intellectual: The Positive Power of Negative Thinking (named a Book of the Year by New Statesman magazine (UK) for 2005) 2005, The Philosophy of Science and Technology Studies 2006, The New Sociological Imagination 2006, New Frontiers in Science and Technology Studies 2007, The Knowledge Book: Key Concepts in Philosophy, Science and Culture 2007, Science vs Religion? Intelligent Design and the Problem of Evolution 2007; editor: The Cognitive Turn: Psychological and Sociological Perspectives on Science (with others) 1989, Controversial Science: From Content to Contention (with others) 1993, Social Psychology of Science (with William Shadish) 1994, Contemporary British and American Philosophy and Philosophers (with Ouyang Kang) 1998–2004; contrib. of numerous articles, book reviews, essays. *Honours:* NSF Post-Doctoral Fellowship in History and Philosophy of Science, Univ. of Iowa 1989, ESRC Fellow in Public Understanding of Science 1998; Kellett Fellowship, Clare Coll., Cambridge 1979–81, Andrew Mellon Pre-Doctoral Fellowship, Pittsburgh 1981–82, Apple Teaching Award 1985, Nat. Endowment for the Humanities Fellowship 1989, Ford Foundation Project grant 2002–03. *Address:* Department of Sociology, University of Warwick, 2.23 Ramphal Building, Gibbet Hill Road, Coventry, CV4 7AL, England (office). *Telephone:* (24) 7652-3940 (office). *Fax:* (24) 7652-3497 (office). *E-mail:* s.w .fuller@warwick.ac.uk (office). *Website:* www.warwick.ac.uk/~sysdt/Index .html (office).

FULLERTON, Alexander Fergus; British writer; b. 20 Sept. 1924, Saxmundham, Suffolk, England; m. Priscilla Mary Edelston 1956, three s. *Education:* Royal Naval Coll., Dartmouth, Univ. of Cambridge. *Career:* Home Sales Man. Heinemann 1959–61; Editorial Dir Peter Davies Ltd 1961–64; Gen. Man. Arrow Books 1964–67. *Publications:* Surface! 1953, A Wren Called Smith 1957, The White Men Sang 1958, The Blooding of the Guns 1976, Sixty Minutes for St George 1977, Patrol to the Golden Horn 1978, Storm Force to Narvik 1979, Last Lift from Crete 1980, All the Drowning Seas 1981, A Share of Honour 1982, The Torch Bearers 1983, The Gatecrashers 1984, Special Deliverance 1986, Special Dynamic 1987, Special Deception 1988, Bloody Sunset 1991, Look to the Wolves 1992, Love for an Enemy 1993, Not Thinking of Death 1994, Into the Fire 1995, Band of Brothers 1996, Return to the Field 1997, Final Dive 1998, In at the Kill 1999, Wave Cry 1999, The Floating Madhouse 2000, Single to Paris 2001, Flight to Mons 2003, Westbound, Warbound 2003, Stark Realities 2004, Non-Combatants 2005, Staying Alive 2006. *Honours:* mentioned in despatches 1945. *Literary Agent:* Johnson & Alcock Ltd, Clerkenwell House, 45–47 Clerkenwell Green, London, EC1R 0HT, England. *E-mail:* alexfullerton@tiscali.co.uk.

FULTON, Alice, BA, MFA; American academic and poet; b. 25 Jan. 1952, Troy, NY; m. Hank de Leo, 1980. *Education:* Empire State Coll., Albany, NY, Cornell Univ. *Career:* Asst Prof., 1983–86, Willam Willhartz Prof., 1986–89, Assoc. Prof., 1989–92, Prof. of English, 1992–, University of Michigan; Visiting Prof. of Creative Writing, Vermont College, 1987, University of California at Los Angeles, 1991. *Publications:* Anchors of Light, 1979; Dance Script with Electric Ballerina, 1983; Palladium, 1986; Powers of Congress, 1990; Sensual Math, 1995; Feeling as a Foreign Language: The Good Strangeness of Poetry, 1999; Felt, 2001. *Honours:* Macdowell Colony Fellowships, 1978, 1979; Millay Colony Fellowship, 1980; Emily Dickinson Award, 1980; Acad. of American Poets Prize, 1982; Consuelo Ford Award, 1984; Rainer Maria Rilke Award, 1984; Michigan Council for the Arts Grants, 1986, 1991; Guggenheim Fellowship, 1986–87; Yaddo Colony Fellowship, 1987; Bess Hokin Prize, 1989; Ingram Merrill Foundation Award, 1990; John D. and Catherine T. MacArthur Foundation Fellowship, 1991–96; Elizabeth Matchett Stover Award, 1994.

FULTON, Len, BA; American writer and publisher; *Publisher, Dust Books;* b. 15 May 1934, Lowell, MA; one s. one d. *Education:* University of Wyoming. *Career:* mem. Literary Advisory Panel, National Endowment for the Arts,

1976–78; mem. Advisory Board, Center for the Book, Library of Congress, 1978–80; Publisher, Dust Books; mem. PEN. *Publications:* The Grassman (novel) 1974, Dark Other Adam Dreaming (novel) 1976, (play) 1984, American Odyssey (travelogue) 1978, For the Love of Pete (play) 1988, Grandmother Dies (play) 1989, Headlines (play) 1990. *Address:* PO Box 100, Paradise, CA 95967, USA.

FULTON, Robin, MA, PhD; Scottish poet, writer, translator and editor; b. 6 May 1937, Arran, Scotland. *Education:* Univ. of Edinburgh. *Publications:* poetry: Instances 1967, Inventories 1969, The Spaces Between the Stones 1971, The Man with the Surbahar 1971, Tree-Lines 1974, Following a Mirror 1980, Selected Poems 1963–78 1980, Fields of Focus 1982, Coming Down to Earth and Spring is Soon 1990, Scottish Poetry (supplement) 2003; criticism: Contemporary Scottish Poetry: Individuals and Contexts 1974, The Way the Words are Taken, Selected Essays 1989; editor: Lines Review and assocd publs 1967–76, Iain Crichton Smith: Selected Poems 1955–80 1982, Robert Garioch: The Complete Poetical Works with Notes 1983, Robert Garioch: A Garioch Miscellany, Selected Prose and Letters 1986, Robert Garrioch, Collected Poems 2004; translator: An Italian Quartet 1966, Five Swedish Poets 1972, Lars Gustafsson, Selected Poems 1972, Gunnar Harding: They Killed Sitting Bull and Other Poems 1973, Tomas Tranströmer: Selected Poems 1974, Östen Sjöstrand: The Hidden Music & Other Poems 1975, Toward the Solitary Star: Selected Poetry and Prose 1988, Werner Aspenström: 37 Poems 1976, Tomas Tranströmer: Baltics 1980, Werner Aspenström: The Blue Whale and Other Prose Pieces 1981, Kjell Espmark: Béla Bartók Against the Third Reich and Other Poems 1985, Olav Hauge: Don't Give Me the Whole Truth and Other Poems 1985, Tomas Tranströmer: Collected Poems 1987, Stig Dagerman: German Autumn 1988, Pär Lagervist: Guest of Reality 1989, Preparations for Flight, and other Swedish Stories 1990, Four Swedish Poets (Kjell Espmark, Lennart Sjögren, Eva Ström & Tomas Tranströmer) 1990, Olav Hauge: Selected Poems 1990, Hermann Starheimsaeter: Stone-Shadows 1991, Five Swedish Poets (Werner Aspenström, Kjell Espmark, Lennart Sjögren, Eva Ström, Staffan Söderblom) 1997, Tomas Tranströmer, New Collected Poems 1997, revised 2006, Henrik Nordbrandt, My Life, My Dream 2002, Olav Hauge, Leaf-Huts and Snow-Houses 2003. *Honours:* Gregory Award 1967, Writers Fellowship, University of Edinburgh 1969, Scottish Arts Council Writers Bursary 1972, Arthur Lundquist Award for Trans. from Swedish 1977, Swedish Acad. Award 1978, 1998. *Address:* Postboks 467, Stavanger 4002 (office); Mjughaug Terrasse 8, Hafrsfjord 4048, Norway (home). *Telephone:* (51) 592346 (home).

FUNDER, Anna, BA, LLB, MA; Australian writer; b. 1966, Melbourne, Vic.; d. of Prof. John Funder and the late Dr Kathleen Funder; m.; two d. *Education:* Univ. of Melbourne, Free Univ. of Berlin, Germany. *Career:* Co-Ed. Melbourne Univ. Law Review 1991; int. lawyer, Office of Int. Law, Attorney-Gen.'s Dept 1993–95; researcher and trans., Deutsche Welle TV, Berlin; radio and TV producer, ABC, Australia; Writer-in-Residence, Australia Centre, Potsdam, Germany; has toured extensively internationally and spoken at many writers' festivals and special appearances; numerous radio and TV appearances. *Publications:* Stasiland: Stories from Behind the Berlin Wall (BBC 4 Samuel Johnson Prize 2004) 2002 (has been published in 15 countries and translated into 12 languages; chosen as BBC Book of the Week; has been adapted for radio and CD in Britain and Australia; currently being developed as a play by Royal Nat. Theatre, London). *Honours:* English Prize, Univ. of Melbourne, DAAD Scholarship, Australian-German Asscn Fellowship, Arts Victoria Literary Grant, Australia Council Literary Grant 2002, Felix Meyer Creative Writing Award, The Index Freedom of Expression Award 2004, Heinemann Award 2004. *Address:* c/o Granta, 2–3 Hanover Yard, Noel Road, London, N1 8BE, England. *Telephone:* (20) 7704-9776. *Fax:* (20) 7704-0474. *Website:* www.granta.com.

FUNE, Jonathan (see Fletcher, John Walter James)

FUNKE, Cornelia Caroline; German children's writer; b. 1958, Dorsten, Westphalia; m. Rolf Funke; one d. one s. *Education:* Hamburg Univ., Hamburg State Coll. of Design. *Career:* worked as designer of board games, illustrator of children's books; began writing/illustrating full-time aged 28; also works for ZDF state TV channel. *Publications:* Monstergeschichten 1993, Die Wilden Hühner 1993, Rittergeschichten 1994, Zwei wilde kleine Hexen 1994, Kein Keks für Kobolde 1994, Greta und Eule, Hundesitter 1995, Der Mondscheindrache 1996, Die Gespensterjäger auf eisiger Spur 1996, Die Wilden Hühner auf Klassenfahrt 1996, Hände weg von Mississippi 1997, Drachenreiter (trans. as Dragon Rider) 1997, Prinzessin Isabella (trans. as The Princess Knight) 1997, Tiergeschichten 1997, Das verzauberte Klassenzimmer 1997, Die Wilden Hühner Fuchsalarm 1998, Dachbodengeschichten 1998, Potilla und der Mützendieb 1998, Dicke Freundinnen 1998, Igraine Ohnefurcht 1998, Strandgeschichten 1999, Das Piratenschwein (trans. as Pirate Girl) 1999, Herr der Diebe (trans. as The Thief Lord) (Swiss Youth Literature Award, Zurich Children's Book Award, Venice House of Literature Book Award, Mildred L. Batchelder Award for the best trans. children's book of the year) 2000, Lilli und Flosse 2000, Mick und Mo im Wilden Westen (trans. as Mick and Mo in the Wild West) 2000, Die Wilden Hühner und das Glück der Erde 2000, Kleiner Werwolf 2001, Als der Weihnachtsmann vom Himmel fiel 2001, Dicke Freundinnen und der Pferdedieb 2001, Die Gespensterjäger im Feuerspuk 2001, Die Gespensterjäger in der Gruselburg 2001, Die Gespensterjäger in grosser Gefahr 2001, Der geheimnisvolle Ritter Namenlos 2001, Die Wilden Hühner Bandenbuch 2001, Emma und der blaue Dschinn 2002, Die schönsten Erstlesegeschichten 2002, Die Glücksfee 2003,

Hinter verzauberten Fenstern 2003, Käpten Knitterbart 2003, Tintenherz (trans. as Inkheart) 2003, Kribbel Krabbel Käferwetter 2003, Der wildeste Bruder der Welt 2003, Der verlorene Wackelzahn 2003, Die Wilden Hühner und die Liebe 2003, Die Wilden Hühner Tagebuch 2004, Tintenblut (trans. as Inkspell) 2005, When Santa Fell to Earth 2006. *Literary Agent:* Oliver G. Latsch, Literaturagentur, Novalisweg 5, 22303 Hamburg, Germany. *Telephone:* (40) 31-70-56-66. *Fax:* (40) 31-70-56-67. *E-mail:* info@oliverlatsch.com. *Address:* Cecilie Dressler Verlag, z.Hd. Cornelia Funke, Poppenbütteler Chaussee 53, 22397 Hamburg, Germany (office). *Website:* www.cornelia-funke.com.

FURSENKO, Aleksander Aleksandrovich; Russian historian; b. 11 Nov. 1927, s. of Alexander Vasilievich Fursenko and Vanda Vladislavovna Fursenko (née Rokitskaya); m. Natalia Lvovna Fursenko (Gol'dina) 1948; two s. *Education:* Leningrad State Univ. *Career:* researcher Leningrad br. of Inst. of History USSR (now Russian) Acad. of Sciences; fmr First Deputy Chair. Presidium Scientific Cen. Acad. of Sciences; Corresp. mem. USSR Acad. of Sciences 1987, mem. 1990, Acad.-Sec. Dept of History 1996–2002; with St Petersburg Inst. of History; research in history of USA, econ. history, int. relations. *Publications include:* Struggle for the Partition of China and the American Open Doors Doctrine 1956, Oil Trusts and World Politics 1880–1918 1965, Rockefellers' Dynasty 1970, American Revolution and Formation of USA 1978, The Battle for Oil: The Economics and Politics of International Corporate Conflict over Petroleum 1990, One Hell of a Gamble: Khrushchev, Kennedy and Castro 1958–64 (with Timothy Naftali) 1997, Khrushchev's Cold War (with Timothy Naftali) 2006. *Address:* 32A Leninskiy prospekt, Presidium of Academy of Sciences, Department of History, 117993 Moscow; 7 Petrozavodskaya ul., Institute of History, 197110 St Petersburg, Russia. *Telephone:* (495) 938-17-63 (Moscow); (812) 230-68-50 (St Petersburg); (812) 235-41-98 (St Petersburg). *Fax:* (495) 938-18-44 (Moscow); (812) 235-64-85 (St Petersburg). *E-mail:* fursenko@leontief.ru.

FURST, Alan, BA, MA; American writer; b. 20 Feb. 1941, New York, NY. *Education:* Oberlin Coll., Pennsylvania State Univ. *Career:* fmr Fulbright Teaching Fellow, Faculté des Lettres, Univ. of Montpellier, France; worked for City of Seattle Arts Comm.; fmr columnist in France for International Herald Tribune. *Publications:* Your Day in the Barrel 1976, The Paris Drop 1980, The Caribbean Account 1981, Shadow Trade 1983, Night Soldiers 1988, Dark Star 1991, The Polish Officer 1995, The World at Night 1996, Red Gold 1999, Kingdom of Shadows 2001, Blood of Victory 2002, Dark Voyage 2004, The Foreign Correspondent 2006; contrib. to periodicals. *Address:* c/o Random House Inc., 1745 Broadway, Third Floor, New York, NY 10019, USA. *E-mail:* alan@alanfurst.net. *Website:* www.alanfurst.net.

FURTWÄNGLER, Virginia Walsh, (Ann Copeland), BA, MA, PhD; American writer, teacher, pianist and accompanist; *Hallie Ford Chair Emerita of English, Willamette University, Salem;* b. 16 Dec. 1932, Hartford, CT; m. Albert Furtwängler 1968; two s. *Education:* Coll. of New Rochelle, Catholic Univ. of America, Cornell Univ. *Career:* Lecturer in English, Coll. of New Rochelle; Writer-in-Residence, Coll. of Idaho 1980, Linfield Coll. 1980–81, Univ. of Idaho 1982, 1986, Wichita State Univ. 1988, Mt Allison Univ. 1990, St Mary's Univ. 1993; Hallie Ford Chair of English, Willamette Univ. 1996, now Emer.; mem. Authors' Guild; has taught many writing workshops in USA and Canada. *Film:* Letter From Francis (winner of top TV Story Award for 1992). *Radio:* several stories read on CBC. *Publications:* At Peace 1978, The Back Room 1979, Earthen Vessels 1984, The Golden Thread 1989, Strange Bodies on a Stranger Shore 1994, The ABC's of Writing Fiction 1996, Season of Apples 1996, Musicking – A Memoir of Musical Time (memoir); contribs to anthologies and magazines. *Honours:* Kent Fellowship from Danforth Foundation, several Canada Council Awards, two Nat. Endowment for the Arts Writing Fellowships, Ingram Merrill Foundation Award. *Address:* 235 Oak Way NE, Salem, OR 97301, USA. *Telephone:* (503) 316-8011 (office). *E-mail:* vfurtwan@willamette.edu. *Website:* members.authorsguild.net/acopeland.

FUSSELL, Paul, MA, PhD; American writer and academic; *Professor Emeritus of English Literature, University of Pennsylvania;* b. 22 March 1924, Pasadena, Calif.; s. of Paul Fussell and Wilma Wilson Sill; m. 1st Betty Harper 1949 (divorced 1987); one s. one d.; m. 2nd Harriette Rhawn Behringer 1987. *Education:* Pomona Coll., Harvard Univ. *Career:* Instructor in English, Conn. Coll. 1951–54; Asst Prof. then Prof. of English, Rutgers Univ. 1955–76, John DeWitt Prof. of English Literature 1976–83; Donald T. Regan Prof. of English Literature, Univ. of Pa 1983–94, Emer. Prof. 1994–; Visiting Prof. King's Coll., London 1990–92; Consultant Ed. Random House 1963–64; Contributing Ed. Harper's 1979–83, The New Republic 1979–85. *Publications:* Theory of Prosody in 18th Century England 1954, Poetic Meter and Poetic Form 1965, The Rhetorical World of Augustan Humanism 1965, Samuel Johnson and the Life of Writing 1971, The Great War and Modern Memory 1975, Abroad: British Literary Travelling between the Wars 1980, The Boy Scout Handbook and Other Observations 1982, Class: A Guide through the American Status System 1983, Sassoon's Long Journey (ed.) 1983, The Norton Book of Travel (ed.) 1987, Thank God for the Atom Bomb and Other Essays 1988, Wartime: Understanding and Behaviour in the Second World War 1989, Killing in Verse and Prose and other essays 1990, The Norton Book of Modern War (ed.) 1991, BAD: or, The Dumbing of America 1991, The Bloody Game: An Anthology of Modern War 1992, The Anti-Egotist: Kingsley Amis, Man of Letters 1994, Doing Battle: The Making of a Skeptic 1996, Uniforms 2002, The Boys' Crusade 2004. *Honours:* Hon.

LittD (Pomona Coll.) 1980, (Monmouth Coll., NJ) 1985; James D. Phelan Award 1964, Lindback Foundation Award 1971, Sr Fellow Nat. Endowment for the Humanities 1973–74, Guggenheim Fellowship 1977–78, Rockefeller Foundation Fellow 1983–84, Nat. Book Award, Nat. Book Critics Circle Award, Emerson Award. *Address:* Apt 4-H, 2020 Walnut Street, Philadelphia, PA 19103, USA. *Telephone:* (215) 557-0144.

FYFIELD, Frances (see HEGARTY, Frances)

G

GAARDER, Jostein; Norwegian writer; b. 1952, Oslo; m.; two s. *Publications:* Diagnosen og andre noveller (trans. as The Diagnosis and Other Stories) 1986, Froskeslottet (trans. as The Frog Castle, children's book) 1988, Kabalmysteriet (trans. as The Solitaire Mystery) 1990, Sofies verden: Roman on filosofiens historie (trans. as Sophie's World: A Novel about the History of Philosophy) 1991, Julemysteriet (trans. as The Christmas Mystery) 1992, I et speil, i en gåte (trans. as Through a Glass, Darkly) 1993, Hallo? Er det noen her? (trans. as Hello? Is Anybody There?, children's book) 1996, Vita Brevis (trans. as That Same Flower, novella) 1996, Maya 1999, Sirkusdirektørens datter (trans. as The Ringmaster's Daughter) 2001, The Orange Girl (in trans.) 2004. *Honours:* Norwegian Literary Critics Award 1991, Norwegian Ministry of Cultural and Scientific Affairs Literary Prize 1991. *Address:* c/o H. Ashehoug & Co, Postboks 363 Sentrum, 0102 Oslo, Norway.

GADDIS, John Lewis, PhD; American historian and academic; *Robert A. Lovett Professor of History, Yale University;* b. 1942; m. (divorced); two s.; m. 2nd Toni Dorfman 1997. *Education:* Univ. of Texas, Austin. *Career:* Lecturer and later Prof., Dept of History, Ohio Univ. 1969–94, f. Contemporary History Inst., Ohio 1987; Sr Fellow, Hoover Inst. 2000–02; Robert A. Lovett Professor of History, Yale Univ. 1997–; fmr Lecturer, US Naval War Coll., Univ. of Helsinki, Finland, Princeton Univ., Univ. of Oxford, UK; George Eastman Visiting Prof., Balliol Coll., Oxford 2000–01; mem. Editorial Bd Foreign Affairs; mem. Advisory Bd Cold War Int. History Project; Fellow, American Acad. of Arts and Sciences 1995. *Publications:* The United States and the Origins of the Cold War 1941–47 1972, Russia, The Soviet Union and the United States: An Interpretive History 1978, Strategies of Containment: A Critical Appraisal of Postwar American National Security Policy 1982, The Long Peace: Inquiries into the History of the Cold War 1987, The United States and the End of the Cold War: Reconsiderations, Implications, Provocations 1992, We Now Know: Rethinking Cold War History 1997, The Landscape of History: How Historians Map the Past 2002, Surprise, Security, and the American Experience 2004, The Cold War 2006. *Address:* Department of History, Yale University, PO Box 208324, New Haven, CT 06520-8353, USA (office). *Telephone:* (203) 432-1374 (office). *Fax:* (203) 432-6520 (office). *E-mail:* john.gaddis@yale.edu (office). *Website:* www.yale.edu/history/faculty/gaddis .html (office).

GAGE, Elizabeth, BA; American writer; b. (Susan Libertson), 28 Dec. 1947, Chicago, Ill.; d. of Kenneth H. and Alices Falces Rusch; m. Joseph Libertson 1969; one d. *Education:* West Sr High, Madison, Wis. and Northwestern Univ., Evanston, Ill. *Publications:* Strange Emotion 1978, A Glimpse of Stocking 1988, Pandora's Box 1990, The Master Stroke 1991, Taboo 1992, The Ghosts of War 1993, Intimate 1995, Confession 1998, Against All Odds 1998, The Hourglass 1999. *Address:* 145 N Kihei Road, Kihei, Maui, HI 96753, USA.

GAGLIANO, Frank, BA, MFA; American playwright, screenwriter, novelist and academic; b. 18 Nov. 1931, New York, NY. *Education:* Queens College, CUNY, University of Iowa, Columbia University. *Career:* Playwright-in-Residence, RSC, London, 1967–69; Asst Prof. of Drama, Playwright-in-Residence, Dir of Contemporary Playwrights Center, Florida State University, Tallahassee, 1969–73; Lecturer in Playwriting, Dir of Conkie Workshop for Playwrights, University of Texas, Austin, 1973–75; Distinguished Visiting Prof., University of Rhode Island, 1975; Benedum Prof. of Theatre, West Virginia University, 1976–; Artistic Dir, Carnegie Mellon, Showcase of New Plays, 1986–99; Artistic Dir, University of Michigan's Festival of New Works, 2000–02. *Publications:* The City Scene (2 plays), 1966; Night of the Dunce, 1967; Father Uxbridge Wants to Marry, 1968; The Hide-and-Seek Odyssey of Madeline Gimple, 1970; Big Sur, 1970; The Prince of Peasantmania, 1970; The Private Eye of Hiram Bodoni (television play), 1971; Quasimodo (musical), 1971; Anywhere the Wind Blows (musical), 1972; In the Voodoo Parlour of Marie Laveau, 1974; The Commedia World of Lafcadio Beau, 1974; The Resurrection of Jackie Cramer (musical), 1974; Congo Square (musical), 1975, revised, 1989; The Total Immersion of Madelaine Favorini, 1981; San Ysidro (dramatic cantata), 1985; From the Bodoni County Songbook Anthology, Book I, 1986, musical version, 1989; Anton's Leap (novel), 1987; The Farewell Concert of Irene and Vernon Palazzo, 1994; My Chekhov Light, 1998.

GAGNON, Madeleine, BA, MA, PhD; Canadian writer and poet; *Writer, Académie des Lettres du Québec;* b. 27 July 1938, Amqui, QC; m. (divorced); two s. *Education:* Université Saint-Joseph du Nouveau-Brunswick, Univ. of Montréal, Université d'Aix-en-Provence. *Career:* teacher of literature, Université du Québec à Montréal 1969–82; various guest professorships and writer-in-residencies; currently Writer-in-Residence, Université du Québec à Rimouski; poetry retrospective 2007; mem. Union des écrivaines et des écrivains québécois, Acad. des Lettres du Québec, PEN Canada, Québec section. *Publications:* Les Morts-vivants 1969, Pour les femmes et tous les autres 1974, Poélitique 1975, La Venue à l'écriture (with Hélène Cixous and Annie Leclerc) 1977, Retailles (with Denise Boucher) 1977, Antre 1978, Lueur: Roman archéologique 1979, Au coeur de la lettre 1981, Autographie 1 and 2: Fictions 1982, Les Fleurs du catapla 1986, Toute écriture est amour 1989, Chant pour un Québec lointain 1991, La Terre est remplie de langage 1993, Les Cathédrales sauvages 1994, Le Vent majeur 1995, Le Deuil du soleil 1998, Rêve de Pierre 1999, Les Femmes et la guerre (translated as Women in a World at War) 2000, My Name is Bosnia 2006; contrib. to many periodicals. *Honours:* Journal de Montréal Grand Prize 1986, Gov.-Gen.'s Award for Poetry 1991, Québec Grand Prize Athanase-David 2002. *Address:* c/o Union des écrivaines et des écrivains québécois, La Maison des écrivains, 3492 avenue Laval, Montréal, QC H2X 3C8, Canada.

GAILLARD, Frye, BA; American journalist and author; b. 23 Dec. 1946, Mobile, AL; m. Nancy B. Gaillard, two d. *Education:* Vanderbilt University. *Publications:* Watermelon Wine: The Spirit of Country Music, 1978; Race, Rock and Religion, 1982; The Catawba River, 1983; The Unfinished Presidency: Essays on Jimmy Carter, 1986; The Dream Long Deferral, 1988; The Secret Diary of Mikhail Gorbachev, 1990; Southern Voices, 1991; Kyle at 200 MPH, 1993; Lessons from the Big House, 1994; The Way We See It, 1995; If I Were a Carpenter: Twenty Years of Habitat for Humanity, 1996; Mobile and the Eastern Shore, 1997; As Long as the Waters Flow: Native Americans in the South and East, 1998; The S21 All-Stars, 1999. Contributions: The Oxford American; Saturday Review; Parade; Southern Accents; Southern Magazine; New West. *Honours:* Gustavus Myers Award, 1989; Small Press Award, 1997; Library of Congress Legacies Recognition, 1999.

GAIMAN, Neil Richard; British writer and illustrator; b. 10 Nov. 1960, Portchester, Hants.; m.; three c. *Career:* creator and writer of Sandman comics (75 issues, collected in 10 vols); collaborations with Dave McKean, Terry Pratchett. *Television writing:* Neverwhere (BBC) 1996, Babylon 5 (episode) 1997. *Films:* Princess Mononoke (writer of English version) 1997, A Short Film About John Bolton (writer, dir) 2003, MirrorMask (writer) 2004, Beowulf (writer of adaptation, exec. prod.) 2007, Stardust (producer) 2007. *Publications:* novels: Ghastly Beyond Belief 1985, Don't Panic 1987, Violent Cases 1987, Black Orchid 1988, Good Omens 1990, Miracleman – The Golden Age 1992, Signal to Noise 1992, Death – The High Cost of Living 1993, Neverwhere 1997, Stardust 1998, Sandman – The Dream Hunters 1999, American Gods (Hugo, Nebula, SFX Stoker and Locus Awards 2001) 2001, Sandman – Endless Nights 2003, Anansi Boys (Mythopoeic Award 2007) 2005; juvenile fiction: The Day I Swapped My Dad for Two Goldfish 1997, Coraline (Hugo, Nebula and Locus Awards 2003) 2002, Elizabeth Burr/Worzalla Award 2003) 2002, The Wolves in the Walls (with Dave McKean) (BSFA Best Short Fiction, Liber Award 2003, Andersen Award 2004) 2003; short stories: A Study in Emerald (Hugo Award for Best Short Story 2005) 2003, Fragile Things 2006; anthologies: Angels and Visitations 1993, Smoke and Mirrors – Short Fictions and Illusions 1998; other: The Absolute Sandman 2006; ed.: Now We Are Sick 1991; contrib. to Time Out, The Sunday Times, Comic Relief, Punch, The Observer, The Face, BBC Radio 3. *Honours:* Int. Horror Critics' Guild Award for Best Collection, Eagle Award for Best Graphic Novel 1988, Best Writer of American Comics 1990, Will Eisner Comic Industry Award 1991–94, Diamond Distributors' Gem Award 1993, GLAAD Award for Best Comic 1996, Mythopoeic Award for Best Novel (France) 1999, Julia Verlanger Award 1999, Bram Stoker Award 1999, 4-11 Award for Best Children's Illustrated Book 2003, Eagle Award 2004. *Literary Agent:* Merrilee Heifetz, Writers House, 21 W 26th Street, New York, NY 10010, USA. *Telephone:* (212) 685-2400. *Website:* www.neilgaiman.com.

GAINES, Ernest James, BA; American writer and academic; *Professor of English, University of Louisiana, Lafayette;* b. 15 Jan. 1933, River Lake Plantation, Pointe Coupee Parish, La; m. Dianne Saulney. *Education:* San Francisco State Univ., Stanford Univ. *Career:* writer-in-residence, Denison Univ. 1971, Stanford Univ. 1981; Visiting Prof. 1983, writer-in-residence 1986, Whittier Coll.; Prof. of English and writer-in-residence, Univ. of La Lafayette (fmrly Univ. of Southwestern La) 1983–; Fellow American Acad. of Arts and Letters. *Publications:* Catherine Carmier 1964, Of Love and Dust 1967, Bloodline (short stories) 1968, The Autobiography of Miss Jane Pittman 1971, A Long Day in November 1971, In My Father's House 1978, A Gathering of Old Men 1983, A Lesson Before Dying (Nat. Book Critics Circle Award 1994, Southern Writers Conference Award 1994, La Library Asscn Award 1994) 1993. *Honours:* Fellow Stanford Univ. Creative Writing Program 1958, Nat. Endowment for the Arts grant 1967, Rockefeller Grant 1970, Guggenheim Fellowship 1971, John D. and Catherine T. MacArthur Foundation Fellowship 1993; Dr hc (Bard Coll.), (Brown Univ.), (Denison Univ.), (La State Univ.), (Loyola Univ.), (Savannah Coll. of Art and Design), (Tulane Univ.), (Univ. of Miami), (Univ. of the South, Sewanee), (Whittier Coll.); Black Acad. of Arts and Letters Award 1972, Commonwealth Club of Calif. Fiction gold medals 1972, 1984, American Acad. and Inst. of Arts and Letters Award 1987, La Humanist of the Year 1989, La Center for the Book Award 2000, Nat. Govs' Asscn Award for Distinguished Service in the Arts 2000, La Govs' Award for Lifetime Achievement 2000, La Writers' Award 2000; Chevalier, Ordre des Arts et des Lettres 1996, Nat. Humanities Medal 2000. *Literary Agent:* Tanya Bickley Enterprises Inc., PO Box 1656, New Canaan, CT 06840, USA. *Address:* c/o Department of English, University of Louisiana Lafayette, Griffin Hall, Room 221, Lafayette, LA 70504, USA.

GAINHAM, Sarah; British writer; b. 1 Oct. 1922, London, England; m. Kenneth Robert Ames 1964 (died 1975). *Publications:* Time Right Deadly, 1956; Cold Dark Night, 1957; The Mythmaker, 1957; Stone Roses, 1959; Silent Hostage, 1960; Night Falls on the City, 1967; A Place in the Country, 1968; Takeover Bid, 1970; Private Worlds, 1971; Maculan's Daughter, 1973; To the

Opera Ball, 1975; The Habsburg Twlight, 1979; The Tiger, Life, 1983; A Discursive Essay on the Presentation of Recent History in English, 1998. Contributions: Encounter; Atlantic; BBC.

GALA, Antonio, LicenDer, LicenFilyLetras, LicenCienciasPoliticasyEcon; Spanish writer; b. 2 Oct. 1936, Córdoba; s. of Luis Gala and Adoración Velasco. *Education:* Univs. of Seville and Madrid. *Publications include:* plays: Los Verdes Campos del Edén, Los Buenos Días Perdidos, Anillos Para Una Dama, La Vieja Señorita del Paraíso, El Cementerio de los Pájaros, Petra Regalada, El Hotelito, Carmen Carmen, Los Bellos Durmientes; novels: El Manuscrito Carmesí, La Pasión Turca, Más Allá del Jardín 1995, La Regla de Tres 1996, El Corazón Tardío 1998, Las Afuneras de Dios 1999; poetry: Enemigo Intimo, Sonetos de la Zubia, Testamento Andaluz; essays: Charlas con Troylo, La Soledad Sonora. *Honours:* Dr hc (Córdoba); Nat. Prize for Literature, Hidalgo Prize, Planeta Prize; many other literary and theatre awards. *Address:* Calle Macarena No. 16, 28016 Madrid, Spain. *Telephone:* (91) 3592037.

GALASSI, Jonathan White, MA; American publishing executive; *President, Farrar, Straus & Giroux Inc.*; b. 4 Nov. 1949, Seattle, Wash.; s. of Gerard Goodwin Galassi and Dorothea Johnston Galassi (née White); m. Susan Grace Galassi 1975; two d. *Education:* Harvard and Cambridge Univs. *Career:* Ed. Houghton Mifflin Co., Boston, New York 1973–81; Sr Ed. Random House, Inc., New York 1981–86; Exec. Ed. and Vice-Pres. Farrar, Straus & Giroux Inc., New York 1986–87, Ed.-in-Chief and Sr Vice-Pres. 1988–93, Exec. Vice-Pres. 1993–99, Publr 1999–, Pres. 2002–; Poetry Ed. Paris Review 1978–88; Guggenheim Fellow 1989; mem. Acad. of American Poets (Dir 1990–2002, Pres. 1994–99, Chair. 1999–2002, Hon. Chair. 2002–). *Publications:* Morning Run (poetry) 1988, The Second Life of Art: Selected Essays of Eugenio Montale (ed., trans.) 1982, Otherwise: Last and First Poems of Eugenio Montale (ed., trans.) 1986, Eugenio Montale, Collected Poems 1916–56 (ed., trans.) 1998, North Street (poetry) 2000, Eugenio Montale, Postumous Diary 2001. *Honours:* Fellow American Acad. of Arts and Sciences 2002; Roger Klein Award for Editing, PEN 1984, Award in Literature, American Acad. of Arts and Letters 2000. *Address:* Farrar, Straus & Giroux Inc., 19 Union Square W, New York, NY 10003 (office); 239 Sackett Street, Brooklyn, NY 11231, USA (home). *Telephone:* (212) 741-6900 (office). *Website:* www.fsgbooks.com (office).

GALEANO, Eduardo Hughes; Uruguayan author and journalist; b. 3 Sept. 1940, Montevideo; m. 1st Silvia Brando 1959, one d.; m. 2nd Graciela Berro 1962, one s. one d.; m. 3rd Helena Villagra 1976. *Career:* Ed.-in-Chief, Marcha, 1961–64, University Press, 1965–73, Montevideo; Dir, Época, Montevideo, 1964–66; Founder-Dir, Crisis, Buenos Aires, 1973–76. *Publications:* Los días siguientes, 1963; China 1964, 1964; Guatamala: Clave de Latinoamerica, 1967, English trans. as Guatemala: Occupied Country, 1969; Reportajes, 1967; Los fantasmas del día del léon, y otros relatos, 1967; Su majestad el fútbol, 1968; Las venas abiertas de América Latina, 1971, English trans. as The Open Veins of Latin America, 1973; Siete imágenes de Bolivia, 1971; Crónicas latinoamericanas, 1972; Vagamundo, 1973; La cancion de nosotros, 1975; Conversaciones con Ramón, 1977; Días y noches de amor y de guerra, 1978, English trans. as Days and Nights of Love and War, 2000; La piedra arde, 1980; Voces de nuestro tiempo, 1981; Memoria del fuego: Genesis, 1982, English trans. as Memory of Fire: Genesis, 1985; Memoria del fuego: Las caras y las máscaras, 1984, English trans. as Memory of Fire: Faces and Masks, 1987; Aventuras de los jóvenes dioses, 1984; Ventana sobre Sandino, 1985; Contraseña, 1985; Memoria del fuego: El siglo del viento, 1986, English trans. as Memory of Fire: Century of the Wind, 1988; El descubrimento de América que todavía no fue y otros escritos, 1986; El tigre azul y otros artículos, 1988; Entrevistas y artículos, 1962–1987, 1988; El libro de los abrazos, 1989, English trans. as The Book of Embraces, 1991; Nosostros decimos no, 1989, English trans. as We Say No, 1992; América Latina para entenderte mejor, 1990; Palabras: Antología personal, 1990; An Uncertain Grace: Essays by Eduardo Galeano and Fred Ritchin, 1990; Ser como ellos y otros artículos, 1992; Amares, 1993; Las palabras andantes, 1993, English trans. as Walking Woods, 1995; Uselo y tírelo, 1994; El fútbol a sol y sombra, 1995, English trans. as Football in Sun and Shadow, 1998; Patas arriba: La escuela del mundo al revés, 1998, English trans. as Upside Down: A Primer for the Looking-Glass World, 2000. *Honours:* Premio Casa de las Américas, 1975, 1978; American Book Award, 1989.

GALGUT, Damon; South African playwright and novelist; b. 1963, Pretoria. *Education:* Univ. of Cape Town. *Plays:* Echoes of Anger, Party for Mother, Alive and Kicking, The Green's Keeper. *Publications:* novels: A Sinless Season 1982, Small Circle of Beings 1988, The Beautiful Screaming of Pigs 1991, The Quarry 1995, The Good Doctor (Commonwealth Writers Prize Africa Region Best Book Award 2004) 2003. *Honours:* CNA Award 1992. *Literary Agent:* Peake Associates, 14 Grafton Crescent, London, NW1 8SL, England.

GALIN, Alexander; Russian playwright, actor and film and theatre director; b. (Aleksandr Mikhailovich Pourer), 10 Sept. 1947, Rosvovskya oblast (USSR); s. of Mikhail Pourer and Lubov Pourer; m. Galina Alekseyevna Pourer 1970; one s. *Education:* Inst. of Culture, Leningrad. *Career:* factory worker, later actor in puppet theatre; freelance writer 1978–. *Plays include:* The Wall 1971, Here Fly the Birds 1974, The Hole 1975, The Roof 1976, Retro 1979, The Eastern Tribune 1980, Stars in the Morning Sky 1982, The Toastmaster 1983, Jeanne 1986, Sorry 1990, The Title 1991, The Czech Photo 1993, The Clown and the Bandit 1996, The Anomaly 1996, Sirena and Victoria 1997, The Competition 1998; plays translated into several languages include Stars in the Morning Sky (selected plays translated into English) 1989, The Group 1995, Rendez-Vous in the Sea of Rain 2002, New Logic 2005. *Film:* (scriptwriter and dir) Casanova's Coat (The Delegation), (scriptwriter, actor and dir) Photo 2003; screenplays: My Last Will 2004, The Heathen 2005. *Publication:* Selected Plays 1989. *Honours:* Amb. of the Arts, Fla 1989. *Address:* Gorohowsky pereulok 15, Apt. 11, 103064 Moscow, Russia. *Telephone:* (495) 267-70-21. *Fax:* (495) 267-70-21. *E-mail:* agalin@online.ru. *Website:* www.webcenter.ru/~agalin.

GALINDO, Rosario Arias de, (Doña Mami); Panamanian publishing executive; b. 4 Jan. 1920, Panamá; d. of Harmodio Arias (Pres. of Panama 1932–36) and Rosario Guardia de Arias; m. Gabriel Galindo V. 1940; one s. two d. *Education:* Sacred Heart Convent, Santiago, Chile, schools in Brussels and Paris and Univ. studies in Geneva, Paris and Panamá. *Career:* mem. Bd Dirs Nat. Red Cross 1952–62, Cttee for Human Rights 1980–89, Nat. Ind. Union for Democratic Action 1981–89, Inter-American Press 1991; apptd Pres. Editora Panamá América, SA 1962–2002; Publr El Panamá América and Crítica Libre daily newspapers –2002; mem. Bd of Trustees Isthmian Foundation for Econ. and Social Studies 1991, Foundation for the Advancement of Women 1991; mem. Latin American Inst. for Advanced Studies, Panamanian Art Inst., Nat. Concert Asscn. *Film:* Códigos de silencio (as herself) 1995. *Publications include:* articles on Human Rights, freedom of the press and democracy in Panamanian and American newspapers including Freedom House (New York) and La Prensa (Panamá). *Honours:* Keys to the City of Panamá 1991; Manuel Amador Guerrero decoration 1991. *Address:* PO Box B-4, Vía Fernández de Córdoba (Vista Hermosa), Panamá 9A, Panama. *Telephone:* 61-2300. *Fax:* 61-3152.

GALIOTO, Salvatore, BA, MA; American academic (retd) and poet; b. 6 June 1925, Italy; m. Nancy Morris 1978, one s. *Education:* University of New Mexico, University of Denver, John Hay Fellow, Yale University, Catskill Area Project Fellow, Columbia University, University of New Haven. *Career:* mem. Long Island Historians' Society; Asian Society; California State Poetry Society; Poets and Writers of America; International Society of Poets. *Publications:* The Humanities: Classical Athens, Renaissance Florence and Contemporary New York, 1970; Bibliographic Materials on Indian Culture, 1972; Let Us Be Modern (poems), English, Italian, 1985; INAGO Newsletter (poems), 1988; Is Anybody Listening? (poems), English, 1990; Flap Your Wings (poems), 1992; Rosebushes and the Poor (poems), Italian, 1993. Contributions: anthologies and periodicals. *Honours:* Purple Heart, Bronze Star, 1944; John Hay Fellowship, 1958–59; Asian Studies Fellow, 1965–66; First Prize, Chapbook Competition, The Poet, 1985, 1986; Gold Medal, Istituto Carlo Capodieci, 1987; INAGO Newspaper Poet, 1989.

GALL, Henderson Alexander (Sandy), MA; British television journalist; b. 1 Oct. 1927, Penang, Malaysia; m. Aug. 1958, one s. three d. *Education:* Aberdeen University, Scotland. *Publications:* Gold Scoop, 1977; Chasing the Dragon, 1981; Don't Worry about the Money Now, 1983; Behind Russian Lines: An Afghan Journal, 1983; Afghanistan: Agony of a Nation, 1988; Salang, 1989; George Adamson: Lord of the Lions, 1991; News From the Front: The Life of a Television Reporter, 1994; The Bushmen of Southern Africa: Slaughter of the Innocent, 2001. *Honours:* Rector, 1978–81, Hon. LLD, 1981, Aberdeen University; Sitara-i-Pakistan, 1986; Lawrence of Arabia Medal, 1987; CBE, 1988. *Literary Agent:* Knight Ayton Management, 114 St Martin's Lane, London WC2N 4BE, England. *E-mail:* info@knightayton.co.uk. *Website:* www.knightayton.co.uk.

GALLAGHER, Tess, BA, MA, MFA; American poet and writer; b. 21 July 1943, Port Angeles, Wash.; m. 1st Lawrence Gallagher 1963 (divorced 1968); m. 2nd Michael Burkard 1973 (divorced 1977); m. 3rd Raymond Carver (died 1988); pnr Josie Gray 1994. *Education:* Univ. of Wash., Seattle and Univ. of Iowa. *Career:* Instructor, St Lawrence Univ., Canton, New York 1974–75; Asst Prof., Kirkland Coll., Clinton, New York 1975–77; Visiting Lecturer, Univ. of Montana 1977–78; Asst Prof., Univ. of Arizona, Tucson 1979–80; Prof. of English, Syracuse Univ. 1980–89; Visiting Fellow, Williamette Univ. 1981; Cockefair Chair and Writer-in-Residence, Univ. of Missouri, Kansas City 1994; Poet-in-Residence, Trinity Coll., Hartford, Conn. 1994; Edward F. Arnold Visiting Prof. of English, Whitman Coll., Walla Walla, Wash. 1996–97; Poet-in-Residence, Bucknell Univ. 1998; mem. Writers Union, PEN, American Poetry Soc., Poets and Writers. *Films:* consultant: Short Cuts, boxed set of Short Cuts, To Write, Keep Kind, Luck, Trust & Ketchup, I Remember Theodore Roethke 2005. *Publications:* poetry: Stepping Outside 1974, Instructions to the Double 1976, Under Stars 1978, Portable Kisses 1978, On Your Own 1978, Willingly 1984, Amplitude: New and Selected Poems 1987, Moon Crossing Bridge 1992, The Valentine Elegies 1993, Portable Kisses Expanded 1994, My Black Horse: New and Selected Poems 1995, Dear Ghosts 2006, Distant Rain, conversation with Jacucho Setonchi, Buddhist nun; short stories: The Lover of Horses 1986, At the Owl Woman Saloon 1997, various magazine publs of stories written with Irish storyteller Jose Gray; non-fiction: Instead of Dying, A Concert of Tenses: Essays on Poetry 1986, Soul Barnacles: Ten More Years with Ray 2000; translator (with Liliana Ursu and Adam Sorkin): The Sky Behind the Forest, by Liliana Ursu 1997, A New Path to the Ocean, by Liliana Ursu 2006; screenplay: Dostoevsky (with Raymond Carver) 1985, many introductions to the works of Raymond Carver 1988–2000, Introduction to Alfredo Arreguin, Patterns of Dreams and Nature, Preface in To Beyond Forgetting: Poems About Alzheimers 2006; contrib. to many anthologies. *Honours:* Hon. DHumLitt (Whitman Coll.), 1998, Hon. DLit (Hartford) 2004; Elliston Award 1976, NEA grants 1977, 1981, 1987, Guggenheim Fellowship 1978, American Poetry Review Award 1981, Wash.

State Governor's Awards 1984, 1986, 1987, 1993, New York State Arts grant 1988, Maxine Cushing Gray Foundation Award 1990, American Library Asscn Most Notable Book List 1993, Lyndhurst Prize 1993, Translation Award 1997, Pryor Award for Literary Excellence 1999, Univ. of Wash. Alumni of the Year Award 2004, Wash. State Humanities Profs John Terry Award for Excellence 2004, Wash. State Poets Asscn Lifetime Achievement Award 2004, Univ. of Wash. Alumnae of the Year Award 2004. *Literary Agent:* International Creative Management, 40 West 57th Street, New York, NY 10019, USA.

GALLAHER, John Gerard, MA, PhD; American academic and writer; *Professor Emeritus of History, Southern Illinois University at Edwardsville*; b. 28 Dec. 1928, St Louis, MO; m. C. Maia Hofacker 1956; one s. two d. *Education:* Univ. of Paris and Univ. of Grenoble, France, Washington Univ., St Louis Univ. *Career:* Univ. Research Fellow, Southern Illinois Univ. at Edwardsville 1978–79, then Prof. to Prof. Emer. of History; mem. Napoleonic Alliance, Pres. 2001–03. *Publications:* The Iron Marshal: A Biography of Louis N. Davout 1976, The Students of Paris and the Revolution of 1848 1980, Napoleon's Irish Legion 1993, General Alexandre Dumas: Soldier of the French Revolution 1997; contribs to reference works, books and scholarly journals. *Honours:* Chevalier, Ordre des palmes académiques, Int. Napoleonic Soc. Legion of Merit; Fulbright Research Scholar, France 1959–60. *Address:* 8461 SE 71st Street, Mercer Island, WA 98040, USA.

GALLAIRE, Fatima; Algerian/French playwright, director, novelist and writer; b. 1944, El Harrouch; m.; two c. *Education:* Univs of Algiers and Paris VIII (Vincennes, St-Denis) and Cinémathèque, Algiers. *Career:* worked for Nat. Film Centre in Algeria and directed several documentary films; Cowles Visiting Author Dept of French, Grinnell Coll., IA, USA 2000; mem. SACD (France); lives and works in France. *Plays include:* Princesses (Soc. des Auteurs Award) 1987, Les Co-épouses 1990, Témoignage contre un homme stérile (translated as Madame Bertin's Testimony), Des cailloux pour la soif (radio play translated as Pebbles for your Thirst), La Fête virile 1992, Molly des sables 1994, Au cœur, la brûlure 1994, Les Richesses de l'hiver 1996, Le Secret des vieilles 1996, La Beauté de l'icône 2003, Théâtre I (collection); numerous short stories and novels for children. *Honours:* Arletty Prize for Drama in French 1990, Acad. française AMIC Prize 1994. *Address:* 41 rue Dunois, Paris 75013, France. *E-mail:* fatima@gallaire.com. *Website:* www.gallaire.com.

GALLANT, Mavis, CC, OC, FRSL; Canadian writer and literary critic; b. 11 Aug. 1922, Montréal, QC. *Education:* schools in Montréal and New York, USA. *Career:* Employee Nat. Film Bd of Canada and Montréal Standard; emigrated to France 1950; short stories published The New Yorker 1951–; has written reviews and essays for New York Review of Books, The New York Times Book Review; Writer-in-Residence Univ. of Toronto 1983–84. *Publications:* short stories: The Other Paris 1956, My Heart is Broken 1964, The Pegnitz Junction 1973, The End of the World 1974, From the Fifteenth District 1978, Home Truths (Gov.-Gen. Award 1982) 1981, Overhead in a Balloon 1985, In Transit 1988, Across the Bridge 1993, Paris Notebooks 1997, The Selected Stories of Mavis Gallant 2004; novels: Green Water, Green Sky 1969, A Fairly Good Time 1970; play: What is to Be Done? 1984; non-fiction: Paris Journals: Selected Reviews and Essays 1986. *Honours:* Hon. mem. American Acad. and Inst. of Arts and Letters 1989; hon. degree (Univ. Sainte Anne), Pointe de Eglise, NS 1984; Hon. LLD (Queen's) 1991; Canada-Australia Literary Prize 1984, Canada Council Molson Prize for the Arts 1997; Tributee Int. Authors Festival, Harbourfront, Toronto 1993. *Address:* c/o McLelland & Stewart, Suite 900, 481 University Avenue, Toronto, Ontario, M5G 2E9, Canada.

GALLANT, Roy Arthur, BA, MS; American author and teacher; b. 17 April 1924, Portland, ME; m. Kathryn Dale 1952, two s. *Education:* Bowdoin College, Columbia University, Columbia University. *Career:* Managing Ed., Scholastic Teachers Magazine, 1954–57; Author-in-Residence, Doubleday, 1957–59; Editorial Dir, Aldus Books, London, 1959–62; Ed.-in-Chief, The Natural History Press, 1962–65; Consultant, The Edison Project, Israel Arts and Sciences Acad.; Dir, Southworth Planetarium, 1980–2000, Prof. Emeritus, 2001–, Univ. Southern Maine. *Publications:* Approximately 100 books, including: Our Universe, 1986; Private Lives of the Stars, 1986; Rainbows, Mirages and Sundogs, 1987; Before the Sun Dies, 1989; Ancient Indians, 1989; The Peopling of Planet Earth, 1990; Earth's Vanishing Forests, 1991; A Young Person's Guide to Science, 1993; The Day the Sky Split Apart, 1995; Geysers, 1997; Sand Dunes, 1997; Limestone Caves, 1998; Planet Earth, 1998; When the Sun Dies, 1998; Glaciers, 1999; The Ever-Changing Atom, 1999; Earth's Place in Space, 1999; Early Humans, 1999; Dance of the Continents, 1999; The Origins of Life, 2000; The Life Stories of Stars, 2000; Stars, 2000; Rocks, 2000; Minerals, 2000; Fossils, 2000; Comets and Asteroids, 2000; The Planets, 2000; Water, 2000; Space Station, 2000; Meteorite Hunter, 2002; Earth Structure, 2003; Earth History, 2003; Plate Tectonics, 2003; Natural Resources, 2003; Earth's Atmosphere, 2003; Earth's Water, 2003; Inheritance, 2003; Biodiversity, 2003. *Honours:* Thomas Alva Edison Foundation Mass Media Award, 1955; Distinguished Achievement Award, University of Southern Maine, 1981; John Burroughs Award for Nature Writing, 1995; Lifetime Achievement Award, Maine Library Asscn, 2001. *Address:* PO Box 228, Beaver Mountain Lake, Rangeley, ME 04970, USA (home). *Telephone:* (207) 864-5135 (home). *E-mail:* roygall@verizon.net (home).

GALLIMARD, Antoine; French publisher; *President and Director-General, Éditions Gallimard*; b. 1947, Paris. *Career:* fmr journalist; worked for family business, Éditions Gallimard 1972–81, Dir-Gen. 1981–, Pres. and Exec. Dir Galllimard 1988–. *Address:* Éditions Gallimard, 5 rue Sébastien-Bottin, 75328 Paris cédex 07, France. *Website:* www.gallimard.fr.

GALLO, Max Louis, DenH, DèsSc; French politician, writer and university teacher; b. 7 Jan. 1932, Nice; s. of Joseph Gallo and Mafalda Galeotti. *Education:* Univ. de Paris and Inst. d'Etudes Politiques. *Career:* teacher Lycée de Nice 1960–65; Sr Lecturer Univ. of Nice 1965–70; Gen. Ed. book series Ce Jour-là, l'Histoire que nous vivons, la Vie selon. . ., le Temps des révélations; contrib. to various newspapers; devised TV programme Destins du Siècle 1973; Deputy (Socialist) for Alpes-Maritimes 1981–83; jr minister and Govt spokesman 1983–84; Ed. Matin de Paris newspaper 1985–86; MEP 1984–94; Nat. Sec. (Culture) Parti Socialiste 1988–90. *Publications:* L'Italie de Mussolini 1964, La Grande Peur de 1989 (as Max Laugham) 1966, L'Affaire d'Ethiopie 1967, Maximilien Robespierre, Histoire d'une solitude 1968, Gauchisme, réformisme et révolution 1968, Histoire de l'Espagne franquiste 1969, Cinquième Colonne 1930–1940 1970, la Nuit des longs couteaux 1970, Tombeau pour la Commune, Histoire de l'Espagne franquiste 1971, Le Cortège des vainqueurs 1972, La Mafia, un pas vers la mer 1973, L'Affiche, miroir de l'Histoire (illustrated) 1973, L'Oiseau des origines 1974: La Baie des anges (Vol. I) 1975, Le Palais des fêtes (Vol. II) 1976, La Promenade des Anglais (Vol. III) 1976, Le Pouvoir à vif, Despotisme, démocratie et révolution, Que sont les siècles pour la mer 1977, Les hommes naissent tous le même jour: Aurore (Vol. I) 1978, Crépuscule (Vol. II) 1979, Une affaire intime 1979, L'Homme Robespierre: histoire d'une solitude 1978, Un crime très ordinaire 1982, Garibaldi 1982, La Demeure des puissants 1983, La Troisième alliance, pour un nouvel individualisme, Le Grand Jaurès 1984, Le Beau Rivage 1985, Lettre ouverte à Maximilien Robespierre sur les nouveaux Muscadins, Belle Epoque 1986, Que passe la justice du roi, la Route Napoléon 1987, Jules Vallès 1988, Une Affaire publique 1989, Les Clés de l'histoire contemporaine 1989, Manifeste pour une fin de siècle obscure 1989, La Gauche est morte, vive la gauche! 1990, Le Regard des femmes 1991, La Fontaine des innocents (Prix Carlton 1992), Une femme rebelle: Vie et mort de Rosa Luxembourg 1992, L'Amour au temps des solitudes 1993, Les Rois sans visage 1994, Le Condottiere 1994, Le Fils de Klara H. 1995, L'Ambitieuse 1995, La Part de Dieu 1996, Le Faiseur d'or 1996, La Femme derrière le miroir, Napoléon, Le chant du départ (biog., Vol. I) 1997, L'Immortel de Saint-Hélène (Vol. IV) 1997, De Gaulle: L'Appel du destin (Vol. I) 1998, La Solitude du combattant (Vol. II) 1998, Le Premier des Français (Vol. III) 1998, La Statue du Commandeur (Vol. IV) 1998, L'Amour de la France expliqué a mon fils, le Jardin des oliviers 1999, Bleu, blanc, rouge (Vol. I: Mariella) 2000, Les Patriotes (four vols) 2000–01. *Address:* Editions Robert Laffont, 24 avenue Marceau, 75008 Paris, France.

GALLOWAY, Janice, MA; British writer; b. 2 Dec. 1956, Ayrshire, Scotland; d. of the late James Galloway and Janet Clark McBride; one s. *Education:* Ardrossan Acad., Univ. of Glasgow, HNC in fine bookbinding. *Career:* singing waitress 1972–74; welfare rights worker 1976; teacher of English 1980–90; Creative Writing Dept, Univ. of Glasgow 2002–06; mem. Soc. of Authors. *Exhibition:* Roengarten (with Anne Bevan), Hunterian Gallery, Glasgow. *Play:* Fall 1998. *Music:* Monster (with Saly Beamish), Scottish Opera and Brighton Festival 2001. *Publications:* The Trick is to Keep Breathing 1990, Blood 1991, Foreign Parts 1994, Where You Find It 1996, Pipelines (with sculptor Anne Bevan) 2000, Monster (opera libretto for composer Sally Beamish) 2002, Clara 2002, boy book see 2003, Rosengarten (with Anne Bevan) 2004. *Honours:* MIND/Alan Lane Prize, Scottish Arts Council Award 1991, Scottish Arts Council Award 1994, McVitie's Prize 1994, American Acad. of Arts and Letters E. M. Forster Award 1994, Creative Scotland Award 2001, Saltire Book of the Year 2002. *Literary Agent:* c/o Derek Johns, AP Watt Ltd, 20 John Street, London, WC1N 2DR, England. *Telephone:* (20) 7405-6774. *Fax:* (20) 7831-2154. *E-mail:* djohns@apwatt.co.uk. *Website:* www.apwatt.co.uk (office); www.galloway.1to1.org.

GALVIN, Brendan, BS, MA, MFA, PhD; American academic and poet; b. 20 Oct. 1938, Everett, MA; m. Ellen Baer 1968, one s. one d. *Education:* Boston College, Northeastern University, University of Massachusetts. *Career:* Instructor, Northeastern University, 1964–65; Asst Prof., Slippery Rock State College, 1968–69; Asst Prof., 1969–74, Assoc. Prof., 1974–80, Prof. of English, 1980–, Central Connecticut State University; Visiting Prof., Connecticut College, 1975–76; Ed. (with George Garrett), Poultry: A Magazine of Voice, 1981–; Coal Royalty Chairholder in Creative Writing, University of Alabama, 1993. *Publications:* The Narrow Land, 1971; The Salt Farm, 1972; No Time for Good Reasons, 1974; The Minutes No One Owns, 1977; Atlantic Flyway, 1980; Winter Oysters, 1983; A Birder's Dozen, 1984; Seals in the Inner Harbour, 1985; Wampanoag Traveler, 1989; Raising Irish Walls, 1989; Great Blue: New and Selected Poems, 1990; Early Returns, 1992; Saints in Their Ox-Hide Boat, 1992; Islands, 1993; Hotel Malabar, 1998. *Honours:* National Endowment for the Arts Fellowships, 1974, 1988; Connecticut Commission on the Arts Fellowships, 1981, 1984; Guggenheim Fellowship, 1988; Sotheby Prize, Arvon International Foundation, 1988; Levinson Prize, Poetry magazine, 1989; O. B. Hardison Jr Poetry Prize, Folger Shakespeare Library, 1991; Charity Randall Citation, International Poetry Forum, 1994.

GANDER, Forrest; American academic, poet and editor; *Professor of English and Comparative Literature, Brown University*; b. 21 Jan. 1956, Barstow, CA; m. C. D. Wright 1983; one s. *Career:* Prof. of English and Comparative Literature, Brown Univ.; mem. Associated Writing Programs, PEN, Center for Art in Translation. *Publications:* Rush to the Lake 1988, Eggplants and Lotus Root 1991, Lynchburg 1993, Mouth to Mouth: Poems by 12

Contemporary Mexican Women (ed.) 1993, Deeds of Utmost Kindness 1994, Science & Steepleflower 1998, Torn Awake 2001, Immanent Visitor: Selected Poems of Jaime Saenz (trans. with Kent Johnson) 2001, Eye Against Eye 2005, A Faithful Existence: Reading, Memory and Transcendence (trans. with K. Johnson) 2006. *Honours:* Whiting Writers Award 1997, Pushcart Prize 2000, Howard Foundation Award 2005. *Address:* Literary Arts, PO Box 1923, Brown University, Providence, RI 02912 (office); 351 Nayatt Road, Barrington, RI 02806, USA (home). *E-mail:* forthgone@brown.edu. *Website:* www.brown.edu/departments/literary-arts/people/forrest.

GANNON, Lucy, MBE; British writer; b. 1948; m. (deceased); one d. *Career:* fmrly nurse, residential social worker and military policewoman; has devised and written numerous TV series and dramas; writer-in-residence, Royal Shakespeare Co. 1987. *Television includes:* Keeping Tom Nice (Richard Burton Award 1987, John Whiting Award 1990), Wicked Old Nellie 1989, Testimony of a Child 1989, A Small Dance (Prix Europa 1991) 1991, Soldier, Soldier 1991, Peak Practice 1993, Tender Loving Care 1993, Bramwell 1995, Trip Trap 1996, Bramwell IV 1998, Bramwell – Our Brave Boys 1998, The Gift 1998, Big Cat 1998, Hope and Glory 1999, Pure Wickedness 1999, Plain Jane 2002, Servants 2003, Blue Dove 2003, Dad (BAFTA Cymru) 2005. *Publications:* Keeping Tom Nice (theatre play), Raping the Gold (theatre play). *Literary Agent:* The Agency (London) Ltd, 24 Pottery Lane, Holland Park, London, W11 4 LZ, England. *Telephone:* (20) 7727-1346. *Fax:* (20) 7727-9037. *E-mail:* info@theagency.co.uk. *Website:* www.theagency.co.uk.

GANT, Richard (see Freemantle, Brian Harry)

GAO, Ertai; Chinese writer, artist and philosopher; b. 1935, Jiangsu Province; m. Gao Maya. *Career:* sent to a labour camp after publication of essay, On Beauty 1957; sentenced to hard labour 1966–72 (exonerated 1978); imprisoned for writing 1989; exiled in the USA; fmrly worked in Dunhuang Research Inst., Chinese Acad. of Social Sciences, Lanzhou Univ., Sichuan Normal Univ., Nankai Univ., Nanjing Univ.; currently Fellow Int. Inst. of Modern Letters; currently Visiting Scholar Univ. of Nevada, USA; writer-in-residence, City of Asylum, Las Vegas; mem. PEN America Center. *Art Exhibitions:* Newark Museum, New Jersey, Mulvane Art Museum, Washburn Univ., Kansas, Int. Inst. of Modern Letters, Univ. of Nevada. *Publications:* The Struggle of Beauty, Beauty, The Symbol of Freedom, In Search of My Homeland 2006; contrib. essays and articles to numerous journals and anthologies, including Fissures: Chinese Writing Today, Persimmon. *Honours:* Nat. Science Council State Expert with Distinguished Contributions 1985, Witness of the World Prize 1999. *Address:* University of Nevada, 4505 Maryland Parkway, Las Vegas, NV 89154-9900, USA (office).

GAO, Hongbo, (Xiang Chuan); Chinese poet; b. 1951, Kailu, Nei Monggol. *Education:* Peking Univ. *Career:* joined the PLA 1969; Vice-Chief News Section, Literature and Art Gazette; Vice-Dir Gen. Office of Chinese Writers' Asscn; Assoc. Ed. Chinese Writers'; Ed. Journal of Poetry; Sec. Secr. of Chinese Writers' Asscn. *Publications:* Elephant Judge, Geese, Geese, Geese, The Crocodile that Eats Stones, The Secret of the Shouting Spring, I Love You, Fox, The Fox that Grows Grapes, The Maid and the Bubble Gum, Flying Dragon and Magic Pigeon, I Wonder, Whisper (Nat. Award for Best Children's Literature). *Address:* Chinese Writers' Association, Beijing, People's Republic of China (office).

GAO, Xingjian, BA; French (b. Chinese) writer and dramatist; b. 4 Jan. 1940, Ganzhou, Jiangxi Prov., People's Republic of China. *Education:* Dept of Foreign Languages, Beijing. *Career:* translator China Reconstructs (magazine), later for Chinese Writers Asscn.; writer for People's Art Troupe; spent five years in 're-education' during Cultural Revolution; left China 1987 after work banned in 1985, living in Paris 1988–. *Publications:* plays: Wild Man 1990, Bus Stop, The Other Shore 1999, Fugitives 1993; novels: Soul Mountain 1999, Return to Painting 2001, One Man's Bible 2002; other: Snow in August (opera) 2002, Buying a Fishing Rod for my Grandfather (short stories) 2004. *Honours:* Chevalier des Arts et des Lettres 1992; Prix Communauté française de Belgium 1994, Prix du Nouvel An Chinois 1997, Nobel Prize for Literature 2000. *Address:* c/o HarperCollins, 77-85 Fulham Palace Road, London, W6 8JB, England.

GAO, Ying; Chinese author and poet; b. 25 Dec. 1929, Jiaozuo, Henan; s. of Gao Weiya and Sha Peifen; m. Duan Chuanchen 1954; one s. two d. *Career:* Vice-Chair. Sichuan Br. and mem. Council, Chinese Writers' Asscn; Deputy Dir Ed. Bd, Sichuan Prov. Broadcasting Station 1983–; mem. Sichuan Political Consultative Conf. *Publications:* The Song of Ding Youjun, Lamplights around the Three Gorges, High Mountains and Distant Rivers, Cloudy Cliff (novel), Da Ji and her Fathers (novel and film script), The Orchid (novel), Loving-Kindness of the Bamboo Storey (collection of prose), Mother in my Heart (autobiographical novel), Songs of Da Liang Mountains (poems), Frozen Snowflakes (poems), Reminiscences, Xue Ma (novel), Gao Ying (short stories). *Address:* Sichuan Branch of Chinese Association of Literary and Art Workers, Bu-hou-jie Street, Chengdu, Sichuan, People's Republic of China. *Telephone:* 66782836.

GARAFOLA, Lynn, AB, PhD; American dance critic, historian and teacher; *Professor of Dance, Barnard College*; b. 12 Dec. 1946, New York, NY; m. Eric Foner 1980; one d. *Education:* Barnard Coll., CUNY. *Career:* Ed., Studies in Dance History 1990–99; Adjunct Prof. Dept of Dance, Barnard Coll., New York 2003–; mem. Soc. of Dance History Scholars, Dance Critics Asscn. *Publications:* Diaghilev's Ballets Russes, André Levinson on Dance: Writings from

Paris in the Twenties (ed. with Joan Acocella), The Diaries of Marius Petipa (ed. and trans.), Jose Limon: An Unfinished Memoir (ed.), Dance for a City: Fifty Years of the New York City Ballet (ed.), The Ballets Russes and its World (ed.), Legacies of 20th-Century Dance; contrib. to Dance Magazine, Dance Research, Ballet Review, Nation, Women's Review of Books, TLS, New York Times Book Review. *Honours:* Torre de los Buenos Prize 1989, CORD Award for Outstanding Publication 1999, Kurt Weill Prize 2001. *Address:* Department of Dance, Barnard College, New York, NY 10027, USA. *E-mail:* lg97@columbia.edu.

GARCÍA MÁRQUEZ, Gabriel (Gabo) José; Colombian writer; b. 6 March 1928, Aracataca; s. of Gabriel Eligio García and Luisa Santiaga Márquez; m. Mercedes Barch March 1958; two s. *Education:* secondary school and Universidad Nacional de Colombia, Universidad de Cartagena. *Career:* began writing books 1946; lived in Baranquilla; corresp. El Espectador in Rome, Paris; first novel published while living in Caracas, Venezuela 1957; est. bureau of Prensa Latina (Cuban press agency) in Bogotá; worked for Prensa Latina in Havana, Cuba, then as Deputy Head of New York Office 1961; lived in Spain, contributing to magazines Mundo Nuevo, Casa de las Américas; went to Mexico; founder-Pres., Fundación Habeas 1979–; invited back to Colombia by Pres. 1982; Hon. Fellow, American Acad. of Arts and Letters; Hon. Pres. Latin America Solidarity Action Foundation (Alas) 2006–. *Publications:* fiction: La hojarasca (trans. as Leaf Storm and Other Stories) 1955, El coronel no tiene quien le escriba (trans. as No One Writes to the Colonel and Other Stories) 1961, La mala hora (trans. as In Evil Hour) 1962, Los funerales de la Mamá Grande (trans. as Funerals of the Great Matriarch) 1962, Cien años de soledad (trans. as One Hundred Years of Solitude) 1967, Isabel viendo llover en Macondo 1967, La incredíble y triste historia de la cándida Eréndira y su abuela desalmada (trans. as Innocent Erendira and Other Stories) 1972, El negro que hizo esperar a los angeles 1972, Ojos de perro azul 1972, El otoño del patriarca (trans. as The Autumn of the Patriarch) 1975, Todos los cuentos de Gabriel García Márquez: 1947–1972 1975, Crónica de una muerte anunciada (trans. as Chronicle of a Death Foretold) 1981, El rastro de tu sangre en la nieve: El verano feliz de la señora Forbes 1982, María de mi corazón (screenplay, with J. H. Hermosillo) 1983, Collected Stories 1984, El amor en los tiempos del cólera (trans. as Love in the Time of Cholera) 1984, El General en su laberinto (trans. as The General in his Labyrinth) 1989, Amores difíciles 1989, Doce cuentos peregrinos (trans. as Strange Pilgrims: Twelve Stories) 1992, Del amor y otros demonios (trans. as Of Love and Other Demons) 1994, La bendita manía de contar 1998, Memoria de mis putas tristes (trans. as Memories of my Melancholy Whores) 2004, Telling Tales (contrib. to charity anthology) 2004; non-fiction: La novela en América Latina: Diálogo (with Mario Vargas Llosa) 1968, Relato de un náufrago (trans. as The Story of a Shipwrecked Sailor) 1970, Cuando era feliz e indocumentado 1973, Crónicas y reportajes 1978, Periodismo militante 1978, De viaje por los países socialistas: 90 días en la 'cortina de hierro' 1978, Obra periodistica (four vols) 1981–83, El olor de la guayaba: Conversaciones con Plinio Apuleyo Mendoza (trans. as The Fragrance of Guava) 1982, Persecución y muerte de minorías: Dos perspectivas 1984, La aventura de Miguel Littín, clandestino en Chile: Un reportaje (trans. as Clandestine in Chile: The Adventures of Miguel Littín) 1986, Primeros reportajes 1990, Notas de prensa 1980–1984 1991, Elogio de la utopia: una entrevista de Nahuel Maciel 1992, Noticia de un secuestro (trans. as News of a Kidnapping) 1996, Vivir para contarla (memoir, vol. one, trans. as Living to Tell the Tale) 2002. *Honours:* Hon. LLD (Columbia Univ., New York) 1971; Colombian Asscn of Writers and Artists Award 1954, Premio Literario Esso (Colombia) 1961, Chianciano Award (Italy) 1969, Prix de Meilleur Livre Étranger (France) 1969, Books Abroad/Neustadt International Prize for Literature 1972, Rómulo Gallegos Prize (Venezuela) 1972, Nobel Prize for Literature 1982, Los Angeles Times Book Prize for Fiction 1988, Serfin Prize 1989, Premio Príncipe de Asturias 1999. *Literary Agent:* Agencia Literaria Carmen Balcelos, Diagonal 580, Barcelona, Spain.

GARCIA-ROZA, Luiz Alfredo; Brazilian writer and academic; *Professor of Philosophy, Universidade do Estado do Rio de Janeiro;* b. 1936, Rio de Janeiro. *Career:* currently Prof. of Philosophy, Universidade do Estado do Rio de Janeiro. *Publications in translation:* The Silence of the Rain (Nestlé and Jabuti Prizes, Brazil) 1997, December Heat 2004, Southwesterly Wind 2005, A Window in Copacabana 2005, Pursuit 2006. *Address:* c/o Institute of Psychology, Universidade do Estado do Rio de Janeiro, Campus Francisco Negrão de Lima, Pavilhão João Lyra Filho, Rua São Francisco Xavier 524, Maracanã, 20550-900 Rio de Janeiro, Brazil. *Website:* www.garcia-roza.com.

GARCÍA SÁNCHEZ, Javier; Spanish writer and poet; b. 1955, Barcelona. *Publications:* Lady of the South Wind 1990, La historia más triste 1991, La vida fosil 1998, Falta alma 2001, The Others 2002, Indurain: A Tempered Passion 2002, Dios se ha ido 2003. *Address:* c/o Dedalus Ltd, Langford Lodge, St Judith's Lane, Sawtry, Cambridgeshire PE28 5XE, England.

GARDAM, Jane Mary, BA, FRSL; British novelist; b. 11 July 1928, Coatham; d. of William Pearson and Kathleen Pearson (née Helm); m. David Hill Gardam 1954; two s. one d. *Education:* Saltburn High School for Girls, Bedford Coll. for Women, Univ. of London. *Career:* oo-ordinator UK Hosp. Libraries British Red Cross 1951–53; Literary Ed. Time and Tide 1952–54; mem. PEN. *Radio play:* The Tribute. *Publications:* juvenile fiction: A Long Way from Verona 1971, A Few Fair Days 1971, The Summer After the Funeral 1973, Bilgewater 1977; novels: God on the Rocks (Prix Baudelaire) 1978, The Hollow Land (Whitbread Literary Award 1983) 1981, Bridget and William 1981, Horse 1982, Kit 1983, Crusoe's Daughter 1985, Kit in Boots 1986, Swan

1987, Through the Doll's House Door 1987, The Queen of the Tambourine (Whitbread Novel Award) 1991, Faith Fox 1996, Tufty Bear 1996, The Green Man 1998, The Flight of the Maidens 2000, Old Filth 2004; short stories: Black Faces, White Faces (David Higham Award 1978, Winifred Holtby Award 1978) 1975, The Sidmouth Letters 1980, The Pangs of Love (Katherine Mansfield Award 1984) 1983, Showing the Flag 1989, Going into a Dark House 1994, Missing the Midnight 1997; non-fiction: The Iron Coast 1994. *Honours:* Hon. DLitt. *Address:* Haven House, Sandwich, Kent CT13 9ES; Throstlenest Farm, Crackpot, N Yorks; 34 Denmark Road, London, SW19, England. *Telephone:* (14304) 612680.

GARDEL, Louis; French publishing editor, novelist and screenwriter; b. 8 Sept. 1939, Algiers, Algeria; s. of Jacques Gardel and Janine Blasselle; m. 1st Béatrice Herr (deceased) 1963; m. 2nd Hélène Millerand 1990; two s. two d. *Education:* Lycée Bugeaud, Algiers, Lycée Louis-le-Grand, Paris and Institut d'Etudes Politiques, Paris. *Career:* Head of Dept Inst. des Hautes Etudes d'Outre-Mer 1962–64; Man. Soc. Rhône-Progil 1964–74; Head of Dept Conseil Nat. du Patronat 1974–80; Literary Consultant, Editions du Seuil 1980, Literary Ed. 1980–; mem. juries Prix Renaudot, Conseil Supérieur de la Langue Française. *Film screenplays:* Fort Saganne, Nocturne Indien, Indochine, La Marche de Radetzky 1996, Est.Ouest, Himalaya 1999, Princesse Marie 2005. *Publications:* L'Eté Fracassé 1973, Couteau de chaleur 1976, Fort Saganne 1980 (Grand Prix du Roman de l' Acad. française), Notre Homme 1986, Le Beau Rôle 1989, Darbaroud 1993. L'Aurore des Bien-Aimés 1997, Grand-Seigneur 1999, La Gare d'Alger 2007. *Honours:* Chevalier, Légion d'honneur. *Address:* 25 rue de la Cerisaie, 75004, Paris (home); Editions du Seuil, 27 rue Jacob, 75006 Paris, France (office). *Telephone:* 1-40-46-50-50 (office). *E-mail:* froumens@seuil.com (office).

GARDEN, Bruce (see Mackay, James Alexander)

GARDEN, Nancy, BFA, MA; American writer, editor and teacher; b. 15 May 1938, Boston, Mass. *Education:* Columbia University School of Dramatic Arts, Teachers College, Columbia University. *Career:* Actress, Lighting Designer, 1954–64; Teacher of Speech and Dramatics, 1961–64; Ed., educational materials, textbooks, 1964–76; Teacher of Writing, Adult Education, 1974; Correspondence School, 1974–; mem. Society of Children's Book Writers and Illustrators. *Publications:* What Happened in Marston, 1971; The Loners, 1972; Maria's Mountain, 1981; Fours Crossing, 1981; Annie on My Mind, 1982; Favourite Tales from Grimm, 1982; Watersmeet, 1983; Prisoner of Vampires, 1984; Peace, O River, 1986; The Door Between, 1987; Lark in the Morning, 1991; My Sister, the Vampire, 1992; Dove and Sword, 1995; My Brother, the Werewolf, 1995; Good Moon Rising, 1996; The Year They Burned the Books, 1999. The Monster Hunter series: Case No. 1, Mystery of the Night Raiders, 1987; Case No. 2: Mystery of the Midnight Menace, 1988; Case No. 3: Mystery of the Secret Marks, 1989; Case No. 4: Mystery of the Kidnapped Kidnapper, 1994; Case No. 5: Mystery of the Watchful Witches, 1995. Non-Fiction: Berlin: City Split in Two, 1971; Vampires, 1973; Werewolves, 1973; Witches, 1975; Devils and Demons, 1976; Fun with Forecasting Weather, 1977; The Kids' Code and Cipher Book, 1981. Contributions: Lambda Book Report.

GÄRDENFORS, Peter, PhD; Swedish academic; *Professor of Cognitive Science, Lund University;* b. 21 Sept. 1949, Degeberga; s. of Torsten Gärdenfors and Ingemor Gärdenfors (née Jonsson); m. Annette Wald 1975 (divorced 2002); three s. one d. *Education:* Lund Univ., Princeton Univ., USA. *Career:* Lecturer in Philosophy, Lund Univ. 1974–80, Reader in Philosophy of Science 1975–77, Reader in Philosophy 1980–88, Prof. of Cognitive Science, 1988–; Visiting Fellow, Princeton Univ., USA 1973–74, ANU 1986–87; Visiting Scholar, Stanford Univ., USA 1983–84; Visiting Prof., Univ. of Buenos Aires 1990; Ed. Theoria 1978–86, Journal of Logic, Language and Information 1991–96; mem. Royal Swedish Acad. of Letters, Academia Europaea, Deutsche Akad. für Naturforscher Leopoldina. *Publications:* Generalized Quantifiers (ed.) 1986, Knowledge in Flux 1988, Decision, Probability and Utility (with N.-E. Sahlin) 1988, Belief Revision (ed.) 1992, Blotta Tanken 1992, Fangslande Information 1996, Cognitive Semantics (with J. Allwood) 1998, Conceptual Spaces 2000, How Homo Became Sapiens 2003. *Honours:* Rausing Prize 1986. *Address:* Department of Philosophy, Kungshuset, Lundagard, 222 22 Lund, Sweden (office). *Telephone:* (46) 2224817 (office). *Fax:* (46) 2224424 (office). *E-mail:* peter.gardenfors@lucs.lu.se (office). *Website:* www.lucs.lu.se/people/Peter.Gardenfors (office).

GARDONS, S. S. (see Snodgrass, W. D.)

GARFINKEL, Patricia Gail, BA; American poet and writer; b. 15 Feb. 1938, New York, NY; divorced; two s. *Education:* New York Univ. *Career:* currently Head of Issues Policy Devt Group, Office of Legislative and Public Affairs, US Nat. Science Foundation; mem. Poets and Writers. *Publications:* Ram's Horn (poems) 1980, From the Red Eye of Jupiter (poems) 1990, Making the Skeleton Dance 2000; contrib. to numerous anthologies and other publications. *Honours:* Poetry in Public Places Award for New York State 1977, first prize Lip Service Poetry Competition 1990, Washington Writers Publishing House Book Competition 1990, winner Moving Words competition. *Address:* 900 N Stuart Street, Suite 1001, Arlington, VA 22203, USA (office). *Telephone:* (703) 292-7736 (office). *E-mail:* pgarfink@nsf.gov (office).

GARFITT, Roger, BA; British poet and writer; b. 12 April 1944, Melksham, Wiltshire, England. *Education:* Merton College, Oxford. *Career:* Arts Council Creative Writing Fellow, University College of North Wales, Bangor, 1975–77,

and Poet-in-Residence, Sunderland Polytechnic, 1978–80; Ed., Poetry Review, 1977–82; Welsh Arts Council Poet-in-Residence, Ebbw Vale, 1984; Poet-in-Residence, Pilgrim College, Boston, 1986–87, Blyth Valley Disabled Forum, 1992; mem. National Asscn of Writers in Education: Poetry Society; Welsh Acad. *Publications:* Caught on Blue, 1970; West of Elm, 1974; The Broken Road, 1982; Rowlstone Haiku (with Frances Horovitz), 1982; Given Ground, 1989; Border Songs, 1996. Contributions: journals, reviews, and magazines. *Honours:* Guinness International Poetry Prize, 1973; Gregory Award, 1974.

GARG, Mridula, MA; Indian writer; b. 25 Oct. 1938, Calcutta (now Kolkata); d. of Birendra Prasad and Ravi Kanta Jain; m. Anand Garg 1963; two c. *Education:* Delhi School of Econs. *Career:* Lecturer in Econs 1960–63; writer of short stories, novels and plays in Hindi, later English. *Publications:* novels: Uske Hisse Ki Dhoop (M. P. Sahitya Acad. Award) 1975, A Touch of Sun 1977, Chittcobra 1979, Anitya 1980, Main Aur Main 1984, Daffodils on Fire (short stories) 1990, Kathgulab (Country of Goodbyes) (Vyas Samman Award, K. K. Birla Foundation 2005) 1996, The Colour of My Being 1996; plays include: Ek Aur Ajnabi (All India Radio Award) 1978, Jadoo-ka-Kalen. *Honours:* Sahityakar Sanhan, Hindi Acad., Delhi 1988, Sahitya Bhushan, V.P. Hindi Sansthan 1999, Helamn-Hammett Grant, Human Rights Watch 2000, Vishna Hindi Sammelan San Man 2003. *Address:* E-118 Masjid Moth, Greater Kailash-3, New Delhi 110 048, India. *Telephone:* (98117) 66775 (office); (11) 29222140 (home). *Fax:* (11) 26673073 (office). *E-mail:* garg_anand@yahoo.com (office).

GARLAND, Alex, BA; British writer; b. 1970, London, England. *Education:* Univ. of Manchester. *Career:* occasionally works as an illustrator and a freelance journalist. *Publications:* The Beach (novel) 1996, The Tesseract (novel) 1999, 28 Days Later (screenplay) 2002, The Coma (novel) 2004. *Address:* c/o Faber and Faber Ltd, 3 Queen Square, London, WC1N 3AU, England.

GARLICK, Raymond, BA, DLitt; British poet and lecturer (retd); b. 21 Sept. 1926, London; m. Elin Jane Hughes 1948; one s. one d. *Education:* Univ. Coll. of North Wales, Bangor, Central Univ., Pella, IA. *Career:* Principal Lecturer, Trinity Coll., Carmarthen 1972–86; Fellow, Welsh Acad. *Publications:* poetry: Poems from the Mountain-House 1950, Requiem for a Poet 1954, Poems from Pembrokeshire 1954, The Welsh-Speaking Sea 1954, Blaenau Observed 1957, Landscapes and Figures: Selected Poems, 1949–63 1964, A Sense of Europe: Collected Poems, 1954–68 1968, A Sense of Time: Poems and Antipoems, 1969–72 1972, Incense: Poems, 1972–75 1975, Collected Poems, 1946–86 1987, Travel Notes: New Poems 1992, The Delphic Voyage 2003; other: An Introduction to Anglo-Welsh Literature 1970, Anglo-Welsh Poetry, 1480–1980 (ed.) 1982. *Honours:* Hon. Fellow, Trinity Coll., Carmarthen 1995, Univ. of Wales, Bangor 2006; Welsh Arts Council Prizes. *Address:* 26 Glannant House, College Road, Carmarthen, SA31 3EF, Wales (home). *Telephone:* (1267) 232587 (home).

GARNER, Alan, OBE; British writer; b. 17 Oct. 1934, Cheshire, England; s. of Colin Garner and Marjorie Garner (née Greenwood Stuart); m. 1st Ann Cook 1956 (divorced); one s. two d.; m. 2nd Griselda Greaves 1972; one s. one d. *Education:* Manchester Grammar School, Magdalen Coll., Oxford. *Career:* mil. service with rank of Lt, RA; mem. Editorial Bd Detskaya Literatura Publrs, Moscow. *Plays:* Holly from the Bongs 1965, Lamaload 1978, Lurga Lom 1980, To Kill a King 1980, Sally Water 1982, The Keeper 1983, Pentecost 1997, The Echoing Waters 2000. *Dance drama:* The Green Mist 1970. *Libretti:* The Bellybag 1971, Potter Thompson 1972, Lord Flame 1996. *Screenplays:* The Owl Service 1969, Red Shift 1978, Places and Things 1978, Images 1981 (First Prize, Chicago Int. Film Festival), Strandloper 1992. *Publications:* The Weirdstone of Brisingamen 1960, The Moon of Gomrath 1963, Elidor 1965, Holly from the Bongs 1966, The Old Man of Mow 1967, The Owl Service (Library Asscn Carnegie Medal 1967, Guardian Award 1968) 1967, The Book of Goblins (Ed.) 1969, Red Shift 1973, The Breadhorse 1975, The Guizer 1975, The Stone Book Quartet (Children's Book Asscn of USA Phoenix Award 1996) 1976–78, Tom Fobble's Day 1977, Granny Reardun 1977, The Aimer Gate 1978, Fairy Tales of Gold 1979, The Lad of the Gad 1980, A Book of British Fairy Tales (Ed.) 1984, A Bag of Moonshine 1986, Jack and the Beanstalk 1992, Once Upon a Time 1993, Strandloper 1996, The Little Red Hen 1997, The Voice That Thunders 1997, The Well of the Wind 1998, Thursbitch 2003. *Honours:* Lewis Carroll Shelf Award, USA 1970, Chicago Int. Film Festival Gold Plaque 1981. *Literary Agent:* c/o Kate Jones, ICM Books, 4–6 Soho Square, London, W1D 3PZ, England.

GARNER, Helen, BA; Australian teacher, novelist and journalist; b. 7 Nov. 1942, Geelong, Vic.; d. of Bruce Ford and Gweneth Ford (née Gadsden); m. 3rd Murray Bail 1992 (divorced 1998); one d. *Education:* Univ. of Melbourne. *Publications:* Monkey Grip, 1977; Honour, and Other People's Children, 1980; The Children's Bach, 1984; Postcards from Surfers, 1985; Cosmo Cosmolino, 1992; The Last Days of Chez Nous, 1993; The First Stone, 1995; True Stories, 1996, The Feel of Steel 2001, Joe Cinque's Consolation 2004. *Honours:* Hon. DLitt (Newcastle) 2003, Hon. LLD (Melbourne) 2003. *Address:* c/o Barbara Mobbs, PO Box 126, Edgecliff, NSW 2027, Australia. *Telephone:* (2) 9363-5323.

GARNETT, Richard Duncan Carey, BA, MA; British writer, publisher and translator; b. 8 Jan. 1923, London; m. (Mary Letitia) Jane Dickins 1954; two s. *Education:* King's Coll., Cambridge. *Career:* Production Man., Rupert Hart-Davis Ltd 1955–59, Dir 1957–66; Dir Adlard Coles Ltd 1963–66; Ed., Macmillan, London 1966–82, Dir 1972–82, Dir Macmillan Publishers

1982–87. *Publications:* Goldsmith: Selected Works (ed.) 1950, Robert Gruss: The Art of the Aqualung (trans.) 1955, The Silver Kingdom (aka The Undersea Treasure) 1956, Bernard Heuvelmans: On the Track of Unknown Animals (trans.) 1958, The White Dragon 1963, Jack of Dover 1966, Bernard Heuvelmans: In the Wake of the Sea-Serpents (trans.) 1968, Joyce (ed. with Reggie Grenfell) 1980, Constance Garnett: A Heroic Life 1991, Sylvia and David, The Townsend Warner/Garnett Letters (ed.) 1994, Rupert Hart-Davis Limited: A Brief History 2004. *Literary Agent:* AP Watt Ltd, 20 John Street, London, WC1N 2DR, England. *Telephone:* (20) 7405-6774. *Fax:* (20) 7831-2154. *E-mail:* apw@apwatt.co.uk. *Website:* www.apwatt.co.uk. *Address:* Hilton Hall, High Street, Hilton, Huntingdon, Cambs., PE28 9NE, England (home). *Telephone:* (1480) 830417 (home).

GARRÉTA, Anne F., PhD; French writer; *Lecturer, University of Rennes II*; b. 1962, Paris. *Education:* Princeton Univ., USA. *Career:* currently Lecturer, Univ. of Rennes II; Guest Lecturer, univs in USA; mem. L'Oulipo 2000–. *Publications include:* Sphinx 1986, Ciels liquides 1990, La Pyramide (short story) 1991, La Décomposition 1999, Pas un jour (Prix Médicis 2002) 2002; articles in literary reviews. *Address:* c/o Éditions Grasset & Fasquelle, 61 rue des Saints-Pères, 75006 Paris, France (office).

GARRETT, George Palmer, Jr, BA, MA, PhD; American academic, writer, poet and editor; b. 11 June 1929, Orlando, FL; m. Susan Parrish Jackson 1952, two s. one d. *Education:* Princeton University. *Career:* Asst Prof., Wesleyan University, 1957–60; US Poetry Ed., Transatlantic Review, 1958–71; Visiting Lecturer, Rice University, 1961–62; Assoc. Prof., 1962–67, Hoyns Prof. of English, 1984–, University of Virginia; Writer-in-Residence, Princeton University, 1964–65, Bennington College, Vermont, 1979, University of Michigan, 1979–80, 1983–84; Prof. of English, Hollins College, Virginia, 1967–71; Prof. of English and Writer-in-Residence, University of South Carolina, 1971–73; Senior Fellow, Council of the Humanities, Princeton University, 1974–78; Adjunct Prof., Columbia University, 1977–78; mem. Fellowship of Southern Letters; Cosmos Club. *Publications:* Fiction: The Finished Man, 1959; Which Ones Are the Enemy?, 1961; Do, Lord, Remember Me, 1965; Death of the Fox, 1971; The Succession: A Novel of Elizabeth and James, 1983; Poison Pen, or, Live Now and Pay Later, 1986; Entered from the Sun, 1990; The Old Army Game, 1994; The King of Babylon Shall Not Come Against You, 1996. Short Stories: King of the Mountain, 1958; In the Briar Patch, 1961; Cold Ground Was My Bed Last Night, 1964; A Wreath for Garibaldi and Other Stories, 1969; The Magic Striptease, 1973; To Recollect a Cloud of Ghosts: Christmas in England, 1979; An Evening Performance: New and Selected Short Stories, 1985. Poetry: The Reverend Ghost, 1957; The Sleeping Gypsy and Other Poems, 1958; Abraham's Knife and Other Poems, 1961; For a Bitter Season: New and Selected Poems, 1967; Welcome to the Medicine Show: Postcards, Flashcards, Snapshots, 1978; Luck's Shining Child: A Miscellany of Poems and Verses, 1981; The Collected Poems of George Garrett, 1984; Days of Our Lives Lie in Fragments, 1998. Other: James Jones, 1984; Understanding Mary Lee Settle, 1988; The Sorrows of Fat City, 1992; Whistling in the Dark, 1992; My Silk Purse and Yours, 1993; Bad Man Blues, 1998; Going to See the Elephant, 2002; Southern Excursions, 2003. Editor: 20 books, 1963–93. *Honours:* American Acad. in Rome Fellowship, 1958; Sewanee Review Fellowship in Poetry, 1958; Ford Foundation Grant, 1960; National Endowment for the Arts Grant, 1967; Guggenheim Fellowship, 1974; American Acad. of Arts and Letters Award, 1985; Cultural Laureate of Virginia, 1986; T. S. Eliot Award, 1989; PEN/Malamud Award for Short Fiction, 1989; Aiken Taylor Award for Poetry, 2000; Commonwealth of Virginia Gov.'s Award for the Arts, 2000; Poet Laureate of the Commonwealth of Virginia, 2002–04, Cleanth Brooks Medal 2005, Thomas Wolfe Prize 2006. *Address:* 1845 Wayside Place, Charlottesville, VA 22903, USA (home). *Telephone:* (434) 979-5366 (home). *E-mail:* gpg@virginia.edu (home).

GARRISON, Deborah, BA, MA; American editor and poet; b. 12 Feb. 1965, Ann Arbor, MI; m. Matthew C. Garrison 1986; one s. two d. *Education:* Brown Univ., New York Univ. *Career:* editorial staff, New Yorker 1986–2000; Poetry Ed., Alfred A. Knopf 2000–; Sr Ed., Pantheon Books 2000–. *Publications:* A Working Girl Can't Win and Other Poems 1998, The Second Child: Poems 2007; contribs to Slate, New York Times, New Yorker, Publisher's Weekly, Poets & Writers. *Address:* c/o Alfred A. Knopf, 1745 Broadway, New York, NY 10019-4305, USA (office).

GARROS, Alexander; Latvian journalist; b. 1975. *Career:* journalist in Riga. *Publication:* Headcrusher (novel, in trans., with Aleksei Evdokimov) (Nat. Bestseller Prize, Russia) 2003. *Address:* c/o Chatto & Windus, Random House, 20 Vauxhall Bridge Road, London, SW1V 2SA, England.

GARROW, David Jeffries; American writer and academic; b. 11 May 1953, New Bedford, Mass. *Education:* BA magna cum laude, Wesleyan University, 1975; MA, 1978, PhD, 1981, Duke University. *Career:* Senior Fellow, Twentieth Century Fund, 1991–93; Visiting Distinguished Prof., Cooper Union, 1992–93; James Pinckney Harrison Prof. of History, College of William and Mary, 1994–95; Distinguished Historian-in-Residence, American University, Washington, DC, 1995–96; Presidential Distinguished Prof., Emory University, 1997–. *Publications:* Protest at Selma, 1978; The FBI and Martin Luther King Jr, 1981; Bearing the Cross, 1986; The Montgomery Bus Boycott and the Women Who Started It (ed.), 1987; Liberty and Sexuality, 1994. Contributions: New York Times; Washington Post; Newsweek; Dissent; Journal of American History; Constitutional Commentary. *Honours:* Pulitzer Prize in Biography, 1987; Robert F. Kennedy Book Award, 1987; Gustavus Myers Human Rights Book Award, 1987. *Address:* Emory University Law School, Atlanta, GA 30322, USA.

GARTON ASH, Timothy John, CMG, MA, FRSA, FRHistS, FRSL; British writer and academic; *Fellow and Senior Research Fellow in Contemporary European History, University of Oxford*; b. 12 July 1955, London, England; m. Danuta Maria 1982; two s. *Education:* Exeter Coll., Oxford, St Antony's Coll., Oxford. *Career:* editorial writer The Times 1984–86; Foreign Ed. The Spectator 1984–90; Fellow Woodrow Wilson Int. Center for Scholars, Washington, DC 1986–87; Sr Assoc. mem., St Antony's Coll., Oxford 1987–89, Fellow and Sr Research Fellow in Contemporary European History 1990–; columnist The Independent 1988–90, The Guardian 2002–; Sr Fellow Hoover Inst., Stanford Univ. 2000–; Fellow Acad. of Sciences, Berlin-Brandenburg, European Acad. of Arts and Sciences; Corresp. Fellow Inst. for Human Sciences, Vienna; mem. PEN, Soc. of Authors. *Publications:* 'Und willst du nicht mein Bruder sein...': Die DDR heute 1981, The Polish Revolution: Solidarity 1983, The Uses of Adversity: Essays on the Fate of Central Europe 1989, We the People: The Revolution of '89 Witnessed in Warsaw, Budapest, Berlin and Prague 1990, In Europe's Name: Germany and the Divided Continent 1993, Freedom for Publishing for Freedom: The Central and East European Publishing Project (ed.) 1995, The File: A Personal History 1997, History of the Present 1999, Free World 2004; contribs to books, newspapers and magazines. *Honours:* Golden Insignia of the Order of Merit, Poland 1992, Kt's Cross of the Order of Merit, Germany 1995, Order of Merit, Czech Repub. 2000; Hon. DLitt (St Andrew's) 2004; Soc. of Authors Somerset Maugham Award 1984, Veillon Foundation Prix Européen de l'Essai 1989, David Watt Memorial Prize 1989, Granada Award for Commentator of the Year 1989, Friedrich Ebert Stiftung Prize 1991, Imre Nagy Memorial Plaque, Hungary 1995, Premio Napoli 1995, Orwell Prize for Journalism 2006. *Address:* St Antony's College, Oxford, OX2 6JF, England (office). *Telephone:* (1865) 274470 (office). *Fax:* (1865) 274478 (office). *E-mail:* european.studies@sant.ox.ac.uk (office). *Website:* www.sant .ox.ac.uk (office); www.timothygartonash.com.

GARWOOD, Julie; American writer; b. 26 Dec. 1946, Kansas City, MO; m. Gerald Garwood 1967 (divorced); two s. one d. *Education:* Avila Coll. *Publications:* Gentle Warrior 1985, Rebellious Desire 1986, Honor's Splendor 1987, The Lion's Lady 1988, The Bride 1989, Guardian Angel 1990, The Gift 1990, The Prize 1991, The Secret 1992, Castles 1993, Saving Grace 1993, Prince Charming 1994, For the Roses 1995, The Wedding 1996, One Pink Rose 1997, One White Rose 1997, One Red Rose 1997, Come the Spring 1997, The Clayborne Brides 1998, Ransom 1999, Heartbreaker 2000, Shadow Dance 2007. *Address:* PO Box 7574, Leawood, KS 66211, USA. *Website:* www .juliegarwood.com.

GASCOIGNE, John; British academic and writer; b. 20 Jan. 1951, Liverpool, England; m. Kathleen May Bock 1980; one s. one d. *Education:* BA, University of Sydney, 1972; MA, Princeton University, 1974; PhD, University of Cambridge, 1981. *Career:* Lecturer, St Paul's Teachers' College, Rabaul, 1973, University of Papua New Guinea, Port Moresby, 1977–78; Tutor, 1980–84, Lecturer, 1984–87, Senior Lecturer, 1987–96, Assoc. Prof. of History, 1997–2003, Prof. of History, 2003–, University of New South Wales; Reviews Ed., Journal of Religious History, 1996–. *Publications:* Cambridge in the Age of Enlightenment: Science, Religion and Politics from the Restoration to the French Revolution, 1988; Joseph Banks and the English Enlightenment: Useful Knowledge and Polite Culture, 1994; Science in the Service of Empire: Sir Joseph Banks and the British State in the Age of Revolution, 1998; Science, Politics and Universities in Europe 1600–1800, 1999; The Enlightenment and the Origins of European Australia, 2002. Contributions: scholarly books and journals. *Honours:* Hancock Prize, Australian Historical Society, 1991; FRHistS, London, 1992; Fellow, Australian Acad. of the Humanities. *Address:* c/o School of History, University of New South Wales, Sydney, NSW 2052, Australia.

GASH, Jonathan (see Grant, John)

GASKELL, Jane; British writer; b. 7 July 1941, Lancashire, England. *Career:* staff mem., Daily Express 1961–65, Daily Sketch 1965–71, Daily Mail 1971–84. *Publications:* Strange Evil, 1957; King's Daughter, 1958; Attic Summer, 1958; The Serpent, 1963; The Shiny Narrow Grin, 1964; The Fabulous Heroine, 1965; Atlan, 1965; The City, 1966; All Neat in Black Stockings, 1966 (filmed); A Sweet Sweet Summer, 1969; Summer Coming, 1974; Some Summer Lands, 1977; Sun Bubble, 1990. *Honours:* Somerset Maugham Award 1970.

GASKIN, Catherine Majella Sinclair; Irish/Australian writer; b. 2 April 1929, Co. Louth; d. of James Gaskin and Mary Gaskin (née Harrington); m. Sol Cornberg 1955 (died 1999). *Education:* Holy Cross Coll., Sydney and Sydney Conservatorium of Music, Australia. *Career:* published first novel aged 17; many titles translated into several European languages. *Publications include:* This Other Eden 1946, With Every Year 1947, Dust in Sunlight 1950, All Else is Folly 1951, Daughter of the House 1952, Sara Dane (serialized for TV) 1955, Blake's Reach 1958, Corporation Wife 1960, I Know My Love 1962, The Tilsit Inheritance 1963, The File on Devlin (adapted as TV film) 1965, Edge of Glass 1967, Fiona 1970, A Falcon for a Queen 1972, The Property of a Gentleman 1974, The Lynmara Legacy 1975, The Summer of the Spanish Woman 1977, Family Affairs 1980, Promises 1982, The Ambassador's Women 1985, The Charmed Circle 1988. *Address:* Villa 139, The Manors, 15 Hale Road, Mosman, NSW 2088, Australia. *Telephone:* (2) 9908-8089.

GASKIN, John Charles Addison, BLitt, MA, DLitt; British academic and writer; b. 4 April 1936, Hitchin, Herts.; m. Diana Dobbin 1972; one s. one d. *Education:* City of Oxford High School, St Peter's Coll., Oxford. *Career:* Lecturer, Trinity Coll., Dublin 1965–78, Fellow 1978–, Prof. of Philosophy 1982–97; mem. Hume Soc., Kildare St and University Club, Dublin, Northern Counties Club, Newcastle upon Tyne. *Publications:* Hume's Philosophy of Religion 1978, The Quest for Eternity: An Outline of the Philosophy of Religion 1984, Varieties of Unbelief From Epicurus to Sartre 1989, David Hume: Dialogues Concerning Natural Religion and the Natural History of Religion (ed.) 1993, The Epicurean Philosophers (ed.) 1994, Thomas Hobbes: Human Nature and the De Corpore (ed.) 1994, Hobbes: Leviathan 1996, The Dark Companion: Ghost Stories 2001, The Long Retreating Day: Tales of Twilight and Borderlands 2005; contribs to scholarly journals, periodicals, reference books and anthologies of stories. *Honours:* Hon. Tutor, Hatfield Coll., Durham 1997–. *Address:* Crook Crossing, by Netherwitton, Morpeth, Northumberland, NE61 4PY, England (home). *Telephone:* (1669) 620249 (home).

GASS, William Howard, AB, PhD; American academic, writer and critic; b. 30 July 1924, Fargo, ND; m. 1st Mary Pat O'Kelly 1952; two s. one d.; m. 2nd Mary Henderson 1969; two d. *Education:* Kenyon College, Cornell University. *Career:* Instructor in Philosophy, College of Wooster, 1950–54; Asst Prof., 1955–58, Assoc. Prof., 1960–65, Prof. of Philosophy, 1966–69, Purdue University; Visiting Lecturer in English and Philosophy, University of Illinois, 1958–59; Prof. of Philosophy, 1969–78, David May Distinguished Prof. in the Humanities, 1979–2001, Dir, International Writers Centre, 1990–2001, Washington University; mem. American Acad. of Arts and Letters; American Acad. of Arts and Sciences. *Publications:* Fiction: Omensetter's Luck, 1966; Willie Masters' Lonesome Wife, 1968; The Tunnel, 1995. Stories: In the Heart of the Heart of the Country, 1968; Cartesian Sonata, 1998. Essays: Fiction and the Figures of Life, 1971; On Being Blue, 1976; The World Within the Word, 1978; The Habitations of the Word, 1984; Finding a Form, 1996; Tests of Time, 2002. Editor: The Writer in Politics (with Lorin Cuoco), 1996; The Writer and Religion (with Lorin Cuoco) 2000; Literary St Louis (with Lorin Cuoco) 2000. Translator: Reading Rilke, 1999. Contributions: Essays, criticism, poems, stories, and trans in various publications. *Honours:* Longview Foundation Prize for Fiction, 1959; Rockefeller Foundation Grant, 1965–66; Guggenheim Fellowship, 1970–71; American Acad. and Institute of Arts and Letters Award, 1975, and Medal of Merit, 1979; Pushcart Prizes, 1976, 1983, 1987, 1992; National Book Critics Circle Awards, 1985, 1996, 2003; Getty Scholar, 1991–92; American Book Award, Before Columbus Foundation, 1996; Lannan Lifetime Achievement Award, 1997; PEN-Nabokov Prize, 2000; PEN Spielvogel Diamondstein Award 2003. *Address:* 6304 Westminster Place, St Louis, MO 63130, USA.

GATENBY, Greg, BA; Canadian artistic director and poet; b. 5 May 1950, Toronto, ON. *Education:* York Univ. *Career:* Ed., McClelland and Stewart, Toronto 1973–75; Artistic Dir, Harbourfront Reading Series and concomitant festivals 1975, Humber Coll. School of Creative Writing 1992–93; mem. PEN Canadian Centre, Writers' Union of Canada. *Publications:* Imaginative Work: Rondeaus for Erica 1976, Adrienne's Blessing 1976, The Brown Stealer 1977, The Salmon Country 1978, Growing Still 1981; contrib. to anthologies, including 52 Pickup 1977, Whale Sound 1977, Whales: A Celebration 1983, The Definitive Notes 1991, The Wild is Always There 1993, Toronto Literary Guide 1999; translator: Selected Poems, by Giorgio Bassani 1980, The Wild Is Always There Vol. 2 1995, The Very Richness of that Past 1995. *Honours:* City of Toronto Arts Award for Literature 1989, hon. lifetime mem. League of Canadian Poets 1991, Jack Award for Lifetime Promotion of Canadian Books 1994, E. J. Pratt Lifetime Fellow 1995. *Address:* c/o The League of Canadian Poets, 920 Yonge Street, Suite 608, Toronto, ON M4W 3C7, Canada.

GATES, Henry Louis, Jr, MA, PhD; American academic, author and editor; *W. E. B. Du Bois Professor of the Humanities and Director, W.E.B. DuBois Institute for African and African-American Research, Harvard University;* b. 16 Sept. 1950, Piedmont, W Va; s. of Henry-Louis Gates and Pauline Augusta Gates (née Coleman); m. Sharon Lynn Adams 1979; two d. *Education:* Yale Univ. and Clare Coll. Cambridge. *Career:* fmr European corresp. for Time magazine; lecturer in English, Yale Univ. 1976–79, Asst Prof. English and Afro-American Studies 1979–84, Assoc. Prof. 1984–85; Prof. of English, Comparative Literature and Africana Studies, Cornell Univ. 1985–90; John Spencer Bassett Prof. of English, Duke Univ. 1990–91; W. E. B. Du Bois Prof. of the Humanities and Chair. Dept of African and African-American Studies, Harvard Univ. 1991–, also Dir W. E. B. DuBois Inst. for African and African-American Research; Pres. Afro-American Acad. 1984–; ed. African American Women's Writings (Macmillan reprint series), Encyclopedia Africana; columnist, New Yorker, New York Times; mem. Pulitzer Prize Bd. *Publications include:* Figures in Black (literary criticism) 1987, The Signifying Monkey 1988, Loose Canons (literary criticism) 1992, Colored People (short stories) 1994, The Future of the Race (with Cornel West) 1996, Thirteen Ways of Looking at a Black Man., Africana (jtly) (TV documentary), Wonders of the African World 1999, The Curitas Enthology of African – American Slave Narratives, The African-American Century 2000; Co-Ed. Encarta Africana Encycloaedia 1999; Ed. The Bondswoman's Narrative 2002, America Behind the Color Line 2004. *Honours:* numerous hon. degrees; American Book Award for The Signifying Monkey; McArthur Foundation Award, Nat. Humanities Medal 1998, Zora Neale Hurston Society Award for Cultural Scholarship, Tikkun National Ethics Award, Hon. Citizenship of Benin 2001. *Address:* Department of African and African-American Studies, Barker Center, 2nd Floor, 12 Quincy Street, Cambridge, MA 02138, USA. *Telephone:* (617) 496-5468. *Fax:* (617) 495-9490. *Website:* www.fas.harvard.edu/~afroam; www.fas.harvard.edu/~du_bois.

GATHORNE-HARDY, Jonathan, BA; British writer; b. 17 May 1933, Edinburgh, Scotland; m. 1st Sabrina Tennant 1962; one s. one d.; m. 2nd Nicolette Sinclair Loutit 1985. *Education:* Trinity Coll., Cambridge. *Publications:* One Foot in the Clouds (novel) 1961, Chameleon (novel) 1967, The Office (novel) 1970, The Rise and Fall of the British Nanny 1972, The Public School Phenomenon 1977, Love, Sex, Marriage and Divorce 1981, Doctors 1983, The Centre of the Universe is 18 Baedeker Strasse (short stories) 1985, The City Beneath the Skin (novel) 1986, The Interior Castle: A Life of Gerald Brenan (biog.) 1992, Particle Theory (novel) 1996, Alfred C. Kinsey – Sex the Measure of All Things, A Biography 1998, Half an Arch (J R Ackerley Prize for Autobiography 2005); other: 11 novels for children; contrib. to numerous magazines and journals. *Address:* 31 Blacksmith's Yard, Binham, Fakenham, Norfolk, NR21 0AL, England. *Telephone:* (1328) 830400. *Fax:* (1328) 830400. *E-mail:* jonnygathorne@freenet.co.uk.

GATTEY, Charles Neilson; British author, playwright and lecturer; b. 3 Sept. 1921, London, England. *Education:* Univ. of London. *Career:* mem. Society of Civil Service Authors (pres. 1980), The Garrick. *Publications:* The Incredible Mrs Van Der Eist, 1972; They Saw Tomorrow, 1977; Queens of Song, 1979; The Elephant that Swallowed a Nightingale, 1981; Peacocks on the Podium, 1982; Foie Gras and Trumpets, 1984; Excess in Food, Drink and Sex, 1987; Prophecy and Prediction in the 20th Century, 1989; Luisa Tetrazzini, 1995; Crowning Glory: The Merits of the Monarchy, 2003. Other: Television Play: The White Falcon, 1955. Film: The Love Lottery, 1954.

GATTI, Armand; French playwright; b. 26 Jan. 1924, Monaco. *Education:* Seminary of Saint Paul, near Cannes. *Publications:* Le Poisson noir 1958, La crapaud-buffle 1959, Le Voyage de Grand Chou 1960, Chant public devant deux chaises électriques 1966, V comme Vietnam 1967, Le Passion du général Franco 1968, Un homme seul 1969, Petit manuel de guérilla urbaine 1971, La colonne Durutti 1974, Die Hälfte des Himmels und wir 1975, Le labyrinthe 1982, Opéra avec titre long 1987, Oeuvres théâtrales, 3 tomes regroupant 44 pièces de 1958 à 1990 1991, Ces empereurs aux ombrelles trouées 1991, Le chant d'amour des alphabets d'Auschwitz 1992, Gatti à Marseille 1993, Adam quoi? 1993, La journée d'une infirmière 1995, Notre tranchée de chaque jour 1996, L'Inconnu no. 5 1996, Les personnages de théâtre meurent dans la rue 1997, La Parole errante 1999, L'anarchie comme un battement d'ailes (4 vols) 2001, 2003. *Honours:* Commdr Ordre des Arts et des Lettres 2004, Chevalier de la Légion d'honneur 2000; Prix Fénéon 1959, Grand prix national du théâtre 1988, Médaille de vermeil Picasso UNESCO 1994. *Address:* La Parole Errante, 9 rue François-Debergue, 93100 Montreuil-sous-Bois, France.

GAUDÉ, Laurent; French novelist and playwright; b. 6 July 1972, Paris. *Plays include:* Combats de possédés 1999, Onysos le furieux 2000, Cendres sur les mains 2001, Pluie de cendres 2001, Le Tigre bleu de l'Euphrate 2002, Médéé Kali 2003, Salina 2003, Les Sacrifiées 2004. *Publications include:* novels: Cris 2001, La Mort du roi Tsongor (Prix Goncourt, Prix des Libraires 2003) 2002, Le Soleil des Scorta (Prix Goncourt) 2004. *Address:* c/o Actes Sud, BP 38, 13633 Arles Cédex, France.

GAUNT, Graham (see Grant, John)

GAY, Marie-Louise; Canadian designer, writer and illustrator; b. 17 June 1952, Québec City, QC; d. of Bernard Roland and Colette Gay; m. David Toby Homel; two s. *Education:* Institut des Arts Graphiques de Montréal, Montréal Museum of Fine Arts School, Acad. of Art Coll., San Francisco, USA. *Career:* Graphic Designer Perspectives and Décormag magazines 1974–76; Art Dir La Courte Echelle publrs 1980; Lecturer in Illustration, Univ. of Québec, Montréal 1981–, Ahuntsic Coll. 1984–85; Writer and Designer, Bonne Fête Willy 1989, Qui a peur de LouLou? 1993, Le jardin de Babel (children's puppet plays) 1999; Set Designer La Boîte, Nat. Film Bd of Canada animated film 1989; mem. Canadian Children's Book Centre, Ibby Canada, Communication-Jeunesse, PEN Canada. *Publications:* illustrator: Hou Ilva 1976, Dou Ilvien 1978, Hébert Luée 1980, Lizzy's Lion 1984, The Last Piece of Sky 1993, The Three Little Pigs 1994, When Vegetables Go Bad! 1994, The Fabulous Song 1996, Rumplestiltskin 1997, Dreams are More Real than Bathtubs 1998, The Christmas Orange 1998, How to Take Your Grandmother to the Museum 1998, Yuck, A Love Story 2000, Houndsley and Catina 2006, Houndsley and Catina and the Birthday Surprise 2006; writer and illustrator: De Zéro à Minuit 1981, La Sœur de Robert 1983, La Drôle d'Ecole 1984, Moonbeam on a Cat's Ear 1986, Rainy Day Magic 1987, Angel and the Polar Bear 1988, Fat Charlie's Circus 1989, Willy Nilly 1990, Mademoiselle Moon 1992, Rabbit Blue 1993, Midnight Mimi 1994, Princess Pistache 1998, Stella, Star of the Sea 1999, Sur mon île 1999, Stella, Queen of the Snow 2000, Stella, Fairy of the Forest 2002, Good Morning Sam 2003, Good Night Sam 2003, Stella, Princess of the Sky 2004, What Are You Doing, Sam? 2006, Travels With My Family (co-written with David Homel) 2006. *Honours:* numerous awards include two Canadian Council prizes 1985, Gov.-Gen.'s Award 1988, 2000, Mr Christie's Book Award 1997–2000, CBA's Libris Award 2000, two Ruth Schwartz Awards 2000, 2006, Torgi, Print Braille Award 2001, Elisabeth Mrazik Cleaver Award 2001, Vicky Metcalfe Body of Work Award 2006, Marilyn Baillie Picture Book Award 2006. *Address:* 773 Davaar, Montréal, QC H2V 3B3, Canada. *Telephone:* (514) 273-0368. *Fax:* (514) 273-5488.

GAY, Peter, PhD; American historian and academic; *Sterling Professor Emeritus of History, Yale University*; b. 20 June 1923, Berlin, Germany; s. of Morris Fröhlich and Helga Fröhlich; m. Ruth Slotkin 1959; three step-d. *Education:* Univ. of Denver and Columbia Univ. *Career:* left Germany 1939; Dept of Public Law and Govt, Columbia Univ. 1947–56, Dept of History 1956–69, Prof. of History 1962–69, William R. Shepherd Prof. 1967–69; Prof. of Comparative European Intellectual History, Yale Univ. 1969–, Durfee Prof. of History 1970–84, Sterling Prof. of History 1984–93, Sterling Prof. Emer. 1993–; Guggenheim Fellow 1967–68; Overseas Fellow, Churchill Coll., Cambridge, England 1970–71; Visiting Fellow, Inst. for Advanced Study, Berlin 1984; Dir Center for Scholars and Writers, New York Public Library 1997–; mem. American Historical Assn, French Historical Soc. *Publications:* The Dilemma of Democratic Socialism: Eduard Bernstein's Challenge to Marx 1951, Voltaire's Politics: The Poet as Realist 1959, Philosophical Dictionary 1962, The Party of Humanity: Essays in the French Enlightenment 1964, The Loss of Mastery: Puritan Historians in Colonial America 1966, The Enlightenment: An Interpretation, Vols I, II 1966, 1969, Weimar Culture: The Outsider as Insider 1969, The Bridge of Criticism: Dialogues on the Enlightenment 1970, The Question of Jean-Jacques Rousseau 1974, Modern Europe (with R. K. Webb) 1973, Style in History 1974, Art and Act: On Causes in History – Manet, Gropius, Mondrian 1976, Freud, Jews and Other Germans: Masters and Victims in Modernist Culture 1978, The Bourgeois Experience: Victoria to Freud, Vols I, II, III 1984, 1986, 1993, Freud for Historians 1985, Freud: A Life for Our Time 1988, A Freud Reader 1989, Reading Freud: Explorations and Entertainments 1990, The Cultivation of Hatred 1993, The Naked Heart 1995, Pleasure Wars 1998, My German Question: Growing Up in Nazi Berlin 1998, Mozart 1999, Schnitzler's Century 2001, Savage Reprisals 2002; also translations and anthologies. *Honours:* Hon. DHumLitt (Denver) 1970, (Md) 1979, (Hebrew Univ. Coll., Cincinnati) 1983, (Clark Univ., Worcester) 1985; Nat. Book Award 1967, Melcher Book Award 1967, Gold Medal for Historical Science, Amsterdam 1990, Geschwister Scholl Prize 1999. *Address:* 760 West End Avenue, Apt 15A, New York, NY 10025, USA (home). *Telephone:* (212) 930-9257 (office); (212) 865-0577 (home). *Fax:* (212) 930-0040 (office). *E-mail:* pgay@nypl.org.

GAYLE, Emma (see Fairburn, Eleanor M.)

GEBAUER, Phyllis, BS, MA; American novelist, writer and teacher; b. 17 Oct. 1928, Chicago, IL; m. Frederick A. Gebauer 1950 (deceased). *Education:* Northwestern Univ., Univ. of Houston, postgraduate studies at several univs. *Career:* workshop leader, Santa Barbara Writers' Conference 1980–2005; Instructor, Univ. of California at Los Angeles Extension Writers' Program 1989–; Lecturer, San Diego State Univ. Writers Conference 1995–; mem. PEN Center USA West, Dorothy L. Sayers Soc. *Publications:* The Pagan Blessing 1979, The Cottage 1985, The Final Murder of Monica Marlowe 1986, Criticism, The Art of Give and Take 1987. *Honours:* Santa Barbara City Coll. First Prize for Fiction 1972, First and Second Prizes for Fiction 1973, UCLA Extension Outstanding Teacher in Creative Writing 1993. *Address:* 515 West Scenic Drive, Monrovia, CA 91016-1511, USA.

GEBEYLI, Claire; Lebanese poet and journalist; b. 1935, Alexandria. *Career:* Assoc. Ed. and columnist, L'Orient-le Jour newspaper; Lecturer, St Joseph's Univ., Beirut. *Publications:* poetry: Poésies latentes 1968, Mémorial d'exil 1975, Cantate pour l'oiseau mort 1996; contrib. to La Corde Raide magazine, The Poetry of Arab Women: A Contemporary Anthology 2001. *Honours:* ACCT Prize 1980, Edgar Allen Poe Prize 1985. *Address:* L'Orient-le Jour, Société Générale de Presse et d'Édition SAL, Kantari - Imm Kantari Corner, Beirut 11-2488, Lebanon (office). *E-mail:* redaction@lorientlejour.com (office). *Website:* www.lorientlejour.com (office).

GÉBLER, Carlo, BA; Irish writer, filmmaker, prison teacher and academic; *Temporary Lecturer in Creative Writing, Queen's University, Belfast*; b. 21 Aug. 1954, Dublin; m. Tyga Thomason 1990; three s. two d. *Education:* Univ. of York, graduate of National Film and Television School. *Career:* part-time teacher of creative writing, HM Prison Maze, Co. Antrim 1993–95; Writer-in-Residence, HM Prison Maghaberry, Co. Antrim 1997; Temp. Lecturer in Creative Writing, Queen's Univ., Belfast 2006–; mem. Aosdána (Ireland) 1990; British Council Int. Writing Fellow, Trinity Coll., Dublin 2004, Arts Council Writing Fellow 2006. *Television:* Put to the Test (Royal Television Soc. Best Regional Documentary Award 1999). *Publications:* The Eleventh Summer 1985, August in July 1986, Work & Play 1987, Driving Through Cuba 1988, Malachy and His Family 1990, The Glass Curtain: Inside an Ulster Community 1991, Life of a Drum 1991, The Witch That Wasn't 1991, The Cure 1994, W9 and Other Lives 1998, How to Murder a Man 1998, Frozen Out 1998, The Base 1999, Father & I 2000, Dance of Death 2000, Caught on a Train (Bisto Merit Award 2001) 2001, 10 Rounds 2002, August '44 2003, The Siege of Derry 2005, The Bull Raid 2005, Silhouette (short play, in How Long is Never?) 2007, Darfur, a response 2007. *Literary Agent:* c/o Antony Harwood, 103 Walton Street, Oxford, OX2 6EB, England. *Telephone:* (1865) 559615; (1865) 513462. *Fax:* (1865) 310660. *E-mail:* ant@antonyharwood.com. *Website:* www.antonyharwood.com.

GEDDES, Gary, MA, PhD; Canadian writer, poet and fmr academic; b. 9 June 1940, Vancouver, BC; m. 1st Norma Joan Fugler 1963 (divorced 1969); one d.; m. 2nd Jan Macht 1973 (divorced 1998); two d. *Education:* Univ. of British Columbia, Univ. of Reading, Univ. of Toronto. *Career:* Lecturer, Carleton Univ., Ottawa, ON 1971–72, Univ. of Victoria, BC 1972–74; writer-in-residence 1976–77, Visiting Asst Prof. 1977–78, Univ. of Alberta, Edmonton; Assoc. Prof. 1978–79, Prof. of English 1979–98, Concordia Univ., Montréal, QC; Distinguished Prof. of Canadian Culture, Western Washington Univ. 1998–2001; writer-in-residence, Univ. of Ottawa 2004, Green Coll. 2005, Univ. BC 2005, Vancouver Public Library 2006; mem. League of Canadian Poets, Writers' Union of Canada, Playwright's Union of Canada. *Publications:* poetry: Poems 1971, Rivers Inlet 1972, Snakeroot 1973, Letter of the Master of Horse 1973, War and Other Measures 1976, The Acid Test 1980, The Terracotta Army 1984, Changes of State 1986, Hong Kong 1987, No Easy Exit/ Salida difícil 1989, Light of Burning Towers 1990, Girl By the Water 1994, Perfect Cold Warrior 1995, Active Trading: Selected Poems 1970–95, 1996, Flying Blind 1998, Skaldance 2004, Falsework 2007; short stories: The Unsettling of the West 1986; non-fiction: Letters from Managua: Meditations on Politics and Art 1990, Sailing Home: A Journey Through Time, Place and Memory 2001, Kingdom of Ten Thousand Things: An Impossible Journey from Kabul to Chiapas 2005; play: Les Maudits Anglais 1984; criticism: Conrad's Later Novels 1980; translation: I Didn't Notice the Mountain Growing Dark, by Li Bai and Du Fu (with George Liang) 1986; editor: 20th Century Poetry and Poetics 1969, 15 Canadian Poets (with Phyllis Bruce, aka 15 Canadian Poets x 3) 1970, Skookum Wawa: Writings of the Canadian Northwest 1975, Divided We Stand 1977, Chinada: Memoirs of the Gang of Seven 1983, The Inner Ear: An Anthology of New Canadian Poets 1983, Vancouver: Soul of a City 1986, Compañeros: Writings about Latin America (with Hugh Hazelton) 1990, The Art of Short Fiction: An International Anthology 1992. *Honours:* E. J. Pratt Medal, Canadian Authors Assn Nat. Poetry Prize, Commonwealth Poetry Competition America's Best Book Award 1985, Writers Choice Award, National Magazine Gold Award, Archibald Lampman Prize, Gabriela Mistral Prize 1996, Poetry Book Society Recommendation 1996. *Address:* 2750 Seaside Drive, RR 2, Sooke, BC V0S 1N0, Canada (home). *Telephone:* (250) 598-5361 (office); (250) 646-2460 (home). *E-mail:* gedworks@islandnet.com (office).

GEDDES, John M., MA; American newspaper editor; *Managing Editor, The New York Times*; b. 1952. *Education:* Univs. of RI and Wis. *Career:* reporter Ansonia Evening Sentinel, Ansonia, Conn. 1976; reporter Associated Press-Dow Jones News Service, NY 1976–78, Bonn, Germany 1978–79; econs corresp. The Times, Bonn 1979–80; joined Wall Street Journal 1980, various positions including Bureau Chief, Bonn, Deputy Man. Ed. then Man. Ed. European Edn, News Ed., Asst Man. Ed., Sr Ed. and Nat. News Ed. –1993; fmr Prin. Friday Holdings; CEO BIS Strategic Decisions (market research co.) 1993–94; Business and Financial Ed. New York Times 1994–97, Deputy Man. Ed. 1997–2003, Man. Ed. for News Operations 2003–. *Address:* The New York Times, 229 West 43rd Street, New York, NY 10036, USA (office). *Website:* www.nytco.com (office).

GEDGE, Pauline Alice; Canadian writer; b. 1945, Auckland, New Zealand; two s. *Education:* University of Manitoba, one year. *Publications:* Child of the Morning, 1977; The Eagle and the Raven, 1978; Stargate, 1982; The Twelfth Transforming, 1984; Mirage, 1990, in US as Scroll of Saqqara, 1990; The Covenant, 1992; House of Dreams, 1994, in US as Lady of the Reeds, 1995; House of Illusions, 1997. *Honours:* Jeanne Boujassy Award, Société des Gens de Lettres, France; Winner, New Novelist Competition, Alberta Culture, 1978. *Address:* c/o Penguin Group (Canada), 90 Eglinton Avenue East, Suite 700, Toronto, Ontario M4P 2Y3, Canada.

GEE, Maggie Mary, PhD, MA, BLitt, FRSL; British author, journalist and lecturer; *Visiting Professor in Creative Writing, Sheffield Hallam University*; b. 2 Nov. 1948, Poole, Dorset; d. of V. V. Gee and Aileen Gee (née Church); m. Nicholas Rankin 1983; one d. *Education:* Horsham High School, Somerville Coll., Oxford, Wolverhampton Polytechnic. *Career:* Research Asst, Wolverhampton Polytechnic 1975–79; Eastern Arts Writing Fellow, Univ. of E Anglia 1982; Visiting Fellow, Sussex Univ. 1986–96, Teaching Fellow 1996–; Writer-in-Residence Northern Arts 1996; Visiting Lecturer, Northumbria Univ. 1999–; Writer-in-Residence, Kingston Univ. 2003–; Visiting Prof. in Creative Writing, Sheffield Hallam Univ.; regular reviews in Daily Telegraph, Sunday Times; judge Booker Prize 1989; Fellow RSL (mem. of council 1998–, chair. of council 2004–); Hawthornden Fellow 1989; mem. Soc. of Authors (man. cttee 1991–94, council 1999–). *Publications:* fiction: Dying, in Other Words 1981, The Burning Book 1983, Light Years 1985, Grace 1988, Where are the Snows? 1991, Christopher and Alexandra 1992, Lost Children 1994, How May I Speak in my Own Voice 1995, The Ice People 1998, The White Family 2002, The Flood 2003, My Cleaner 2005, The Blue (short stories) 2006, NW15 (ed. with B. Evaristo) 2007. *Honours:* Best of Young British Novelists 1982. *Address:* c/o Anna Wilson, Saqi Books, 26 Westbourne Grove, London, W2 5RH (office); c/o Society of Authors, 84 Drayton Gardens, London, SW10 9SB, England (office). *Telephone:* (20) 7221-9347 (office). *Fax:* (20) 7229-7492 (office). *E-mail:* publicity@saqibooks.com (office). *Website:* www.saqibooks.com (office).

GEE, Maurice Gough, MA; New Zealand novelist; b. 22 Aug. 1931, Whakatane; m. Margaretha Garden 1970; one s. two d. *Education:* Avondale Coll., Auckland, Auckland Univ. *Career:* school teacher, librarian, other casual employment 1954–75; Robert Burns Fellow Univ. of Otago 1964; Writing Fellow, Vic. Univ. of Wellington 1989; Katherine Mansfield Memorial Fellow, Menton, France 1992. *Publications include:* Plumb 1978, Meg 1981, Sole Survivor 1983, Collected Stories 1986, Prowlers 1987, The Burning Boy 1990, Going West 1992, Crime Story 1994, Loving Ways 1996, Live Bodies 1998, Ellie and the Shadow Man 2001, The Scornful Moon 2004; juvenile fiction includes: Under the Mountain 1979, The O Trilogy 1982–85, The Fat Man 1994; also scripts for film and TV. *Honours:* Hon. DLitt (Vic.) 1987,

(Auckland) 2004; NZ Fiction Award 1976, 1979, 1982, 1991, 1993, NZ Book of the Year Award (Wattle Award) 1979, 1993, James Tait Black Memorial Prize 1979, NZ Children's Book of the Year Award 1986, 1995, Prime Minister's Prize 2004. *Address:* 41 Chelmsford Street, Ngaio, Wellington, New Zealand.

GEE, Shirley; British dramatist; b. 25 April 1932, London, England; m. Donald Gee 1965, two s. *Education:* Webber-Douglas Acad. of Music and Drama. *Career:* mem. Society of Authors; Writers Guild. *Publications:* Stones, 1974; Moonshine, 1977; Typhoid Mary, 1979; Bedrock, 1982; Never in My Lifetime, 1983; Flights, 1984; Long Live the Babe, 1985; Ask for the Moon, 1986; Against the Wind, 1988; Warrior, 1989. Other: Stage adaptations, including The Forsyte Saga (co-adapter); Children's poems, stories and songs. *Honours:* Radio Times Drama Bursary Award, 1974; Pye Award, 1979; Jury's Special Commendation, Prix Italia, 1979; Giles Cooper Awards, 1979, 1983; Sony Award, 1983; Samuel Beckett Award, 1984; Susan Smith Blackburn Prize, 1985.

GEHLHOFF-CLAES, Astrid Veronica, PhD; German writer; b. 6 Jan. 1928, Leverkusen; d. of Heinrich Claes and Wilma Claes; m. Joachim Gehlhoff 1957; two d. *Education:* Univ. of Cologne. *Career:* writer 1956–; Founder-Chair. Org. for writers working with prisoners 1975–88; Deutsche Literaturfonds Scholarship 1985; Guest, Villa Massimo 1991, 1992. *Publications include:* poetry: Der Mannequin 1956, Meine Stimme mein Schiff 1962, Gegen Abend ein Orangenbaum 1983, Nachruf auf einen Papagei 1989; play: Didos Tod 1964; short stories: Erdbeereis 1980; novel: Abschied von der Macht 1987, Juselu der Erinnerung 2002; publisher: Else Lasker-Schüler: Briefe an Karl Kraus 1959, 1960, Bis die Tür aufbricht: Literatur hinter Gittern (anthology) 1982, Einen Baum umarmen: Briefwechsel mit Felix Kamphausen 1976–91; trans. to German of books by Henry James; literary science: Der lyrische Sprachstil 2003. *Honours:* Bundesverdienstkreuz, First Class 1986, Verdienststorden des Landes Nordrhein-Westfalen 1990; Förderungspreis zum Gerhart-Hauptmann-Preis, Freie Volksbühne Berlin 1962, Förderungspreis zum Immermann-Preis, Düsseldorf 1965, Früde Drasbe Gabe, Düsseldorf 2003. *Address:* Rheinallee 133, 40545 Düsseldorf, Germany. *Telephone:* (211) 555925.

GEIER, Joan Austin, BS; American poet and writer; b. 6 March 1934, New York, NY; m. Walter Geier 1956; two s. one d. *Education:* Hunter College, CUNY. *Career:* mem. Brooklyn Poetry Circle, Poetry Soc. of America. *Publications:* Garbage Can Cat, 1976; Mother of Tribes, 1987; A Formal Feeling Comes, 1994. Contributions: Good Housekeeping; Christian Science Monitor; New York Newsday; Catholic Digest; Poetry Society of America Quarterly; SPSM&H; A Formal Feeling Comes; The Lyric; Poetpourri; Negative Capability; Hiram Poetry Review. *Honours:* Poetry Awards, World Order of Narrative Poets, 1980, 1987, 1990, 1992; Gustav Davidson Award, Poetry Society of America, 1982; John Masefield Award, World Order of Narrative Poets, 1983; Amelia Special Award for Haiku, 1985. *Address:* 556 H 102 Main Street, Roosevelt Island, NY 10044, USA.

GEIMAN, Leonid Mikhailovich, DrTechSci; Russian scientific publisher; b. 12 Aug. 1934, Moscow. *Education:* Moscow Ore Inst. *Career:* researcher ore industry research Orgs; Head of Div. Publishers' Sovietskaya Encyclopaedia 1963–88; Prof. Moscow Ore Inst.; researcher All-Union Inst. of Foreign Geology; f. Ind. Encyclopaedic Ed. House (ETA); Pres. Encyclopaedic Creative Asscn; mem. Russian Acad. of Natural Sciences 1992, Academician-Sec. Dept of Encyclopaedia. *Publications:* Russian Encyclopaedia of Banks 1995, Russian Nat. Electronic Encyclopaedia 1995, Encyclopaedia of Moscow Streets 1996, Encyclopaedia America 1997. *Address:* Russian Academy of Natural Sciences, Varshavskoye shosse 8, 113105 Moscow, Russia (office). *Telephone:* (495) 954-26-11 (office).

GEISMAR, Ludwig Leo, MA, PhD; American academic (retd) and writer; b. 25 Feb. 1921, Mannheim, Germany; m. Shirley Ann Cooperman 1948; three d. *Education:* Univ. of Minnesota, Hebrew Univ., Jerusalem. *Career:* coordinator of Social Research, Ministry of Social Welfare, Israel, 1954–56; Research Dir, Family Centred Project, St Paul, Minnesota, USA, 1956–59; Assoc. Prof., 1959–62, Prof., Social Work and Sociology, Dir, Social Work Research Center, Grad. School of Social Work and Dept of Sociology, 1963–91, Rutgers Univ. *Publications:* Understanding the Multi-Problem Family: A Conceptual Analysis and Exploration in Early Identification (with M. A. LaSorte) 1964, The Forgotten Neighborhood: Site of an Early Skirmish in the War on Poverty (with J. Krisberg) 1967, Preventive Intervention in Social Work 1969, Family and Community Functioning 1971, Early Supports for Family Life 1972, 555 Families: A Social Psychological Study of Young Families in Transition 1973, Families in an Urban Mold (with S. Geismar) 1979, A Quarter Century of Social Work Education (ed. with M. Dinerman) 1984, Family and Delinquency: Resocializing the Young Offender (with K. Wood) 1986, Families at Risk (with K. Wood) 1989, The Family Functioning Scale: A Guide to Research and Practice (with M. Camasso) 1993, In the Shadow of the Holocaust 2005. *Honours:* Presidential Citation, Rutgers Univ. 1990. *Address:* 1050 George Street, Suite 9L, New Brunswick, NJ 08901, USA.

GELBART, Larry; American playwright and scriptwriter; b. 25 Feb. 1928, Chicago, Ill.; s. of Harry Gelbart and Frieda Gelbart; m. Pat Marshall 1956; three s. one d. *Career:* prin. writer, sometime dir and co-producer (first four seasons) M*A*S*H*; other television shows including Caesar's Hour, United States, The Bob Hope Show, The Danny Kaye Show; scriptwriter for various radio shows; Dir A Funny Thing Happened on the Way to the Forum, Chichester Festival Theatre, UK 1986; mem. Writers Guild of America,

Authors League, Motion Picture Acad. of Arts and Sciences, Directors Guild of America, PEN Int. *Plays:* My LA (revue), The Conquering Hero (musical), A Funny Thing Happened on the Way to the Forum (musical), Jump, Mastergate, Sly Fox, City of Angels (musical), Power Failure. *Films:* Notorious Landlady 1962, The Thrill of It All 1963, The Wrong Box 1966, Oh, God 1977, Movie Movie 1978, Neighbors 1981, Tootsie 1982, Blame it on Rio 1984, Barbarians at the Gate 1994, Weapons of Mass Distraction 1997, Bedazzled 2000, C-Scam (also dir) 2000. *Television includes:* Your Show of Shows 1950, Caesar's Hour 1954, The Danny Kaye Show 1963, The Marty Feldman Comedy Machine 1971, M*A*S*H (also developer) 1972, United States 1980, Mastergate 1992, Barbarians at the Gate 1993, Weapons of Mass Distraction 1997, And Starring Pancho Villa as Himself 2003. *Publication:* Laughing Matters 1998. *Honours:* Hon. DLitt (Union Coll.) 1986, Hon. LHD (Hofstra) 1999; Tony Award for co-authoring A Funny Thing Happened on the Way to the Forum, Writers' Guild of America Awards for Oh, God, Movie Movie, Tootsie, 3 M*A*S*H* episodes, and for And Starring Pancho Villa as Himself 2003, Peabody Awards for M*A*S*H*, The Danny Kaye Show, Emmy Awards for M*A*S*H* and V.I.P., Edgar Allan Poe Award for Oh, God, Los Angeles Film Critics', New York Film Critics' and Nat. Soc. of Film Critics' Awards for Best Screenplay for Tootsie, Golden Rose, Montreux for writing/producing The Marty Feldman Comedy Machine, AMA citation for distinguished services 2001; other awards and distinctions. *Address:* 807 North Alpine Drive, Beverly Hills, CA 90210-2901, USA.

GELLIS, Roberta Leah, (Max Daniels, Priscilla Hamilton, Leah Jacobs), BA, MS; American author; b. 27 Sept. 1927, New York, NY; m. Charles Gellis 1947, one s. *Education:* Hunter College, CUNY, Brooklyn Polytechnic Institute. *Publications:* Knight's Honor, 1964; Bond of Blood, 1965; The Dragon and the Rose, 1977; The Sword and the Swan, 1977; The Space Guardian (as Max Daniels), 1978; The Roselynde Chronicles series: Roselynde, 1978, Alinor, 1978, Joanna, 1979, Gilliane, 1980, Rhiannon, 1982, Sybelle, 1983; Offworld (as Max Daniels), 1979; The Love Token (as Priscilla Hamilton), 1979; The Royal Dynasty series: Siren Song, 1980, Winter Song, 1982, Fire Song, 1984; A Silver Mirror, 1989; The Napoleonic Era series: The English Heiress, 1980, The Cornish Heiress, 1981, The Kent Heiress, 1982, Fortune's Bride, 1983, A Woman's Estate, 1984; The Tales of Jernaeve series: Tapestry of Dreams, 1985, Fires of Winter, 1986, Irish Magic, 1995, Shimmering Splendor, 1995, Enchanted Fire, 1996, Irish Magic II, 1997; Dazzling Brightness, 1994.

GELMAN, Aleksandr Isaakovich; Russian playwright and scriptwriter; b. 25 Oct. 1933, Moldavia; m. Tatyana Pavlovna Kaletskaya; two s. *Education:* Kishinev Univ. *Career:* mem. CPSU 1956–90; worked in factories 1956–67; corresp. for daily papers 1967–71; wrote scripts for series of documentary films 1971–74; work with Moscow Art Theatre 1975–; People's Deputy of the USSR 1989–91. *Film scripts include:* Night Shift 1971, Consider me Grown Up 1974, Xenia, Fyodor's Favourite Wife 1974 (all with T. Kaletskaya), Prize 1975, Clumsy Man 1979, We, The Undersigned 1981, Zinulya 1984. *Theatre work includes:* A Man with Connections, The Bonus, The Bench, We, the Undersigned, Misha's Party (jtly.), Pretender 1999, Zinulya, Back, Connection. *Television documentary:* Gorbachev: After Empire 2001. *Publication:* Book of Plays 1985. *Honours:* USSR State Prize 1976. *Address:* Tverskoy blvd 3, Apt. 12, 103104 Moscow, Russia. *Telephone:* (495) 202-68-59. *E-mail:* idcg@cityline.ru (home).

GELMAN, Juan; Argentine poet and writer; b. 1930, Buenos Aires. *Career:* Ed. Panorama 1969, Crisis 1973; Dir of literary supplement to La Opinión 1971; bd mem. of newspaper, Noticias 1974; correspondent Página 12; political exile in Europe 1976–89. *Publications:* Violín y otras cuestiones 1956, El juego en que andamos 1959, Velorio del solo 1961, Gotán 1956–1962 1962, Cólera Buey 1965, Los poemas de Sidney West 1969, Fábulas 1971, Relaciones 1973, Hechos 1974–1978 1978, Comentarios 1978–1979, Notas 1979, Citas 1979, Carta Abierta 1980, Si dulcemente 1980, Bajo la lluvia ajena 1980, Hacia el Sur 1982, Com/posiciones 1983–1984 1986, Eso 1983–1984, Dibaxu 1983–1985, La junta luz: Oratorio a las madres de Plaza de Mayo 1985, Anunciaciones 1988, Interrupciones I 1988, Interrupciones II 1988, Carta a mi madre 1989, Salarios del impío 1984–1992 1993, La abierta oscuridad 1993, Incompletamente 1997, Debí decir te amo 1997, Ni el flaco perdón de Diós/Hijos de desaparecidos (with Mara La Madrid) 1997, Prosa de prensa 1997, Nueva prosa de prensa 1999, Tantear la noche 2000; contrib. to numerous anthologies. *Honours:* Premio Nacional de Poesía 1997. *Address:* c/o University of California Press, 2120 Berkeley Way, Berkeley, CA 94704-1012, USA. *E-mail:* askucp@ucpress.edu (office). *Website:* www.juangelman.org.

GEMS, Iris Pamela (Pam); British playwright; b. Bransgore, Dorset; d. of the late Jim Price and Elsie Mabel Annetts; m. Keith Leopold Gems 1949; two s. two d. *Education:* Brockenhurst Grammar School, Univ. of Manchester. *Career:* career playwright; mem. Dramatists' Guild (USA), Writers' Guild. *Plays:* Betty's Wonderful Christmas 1974, Dusa, Fish, Stas and Vi 1976, Queen Christina 1977, Piaf 1978, Franz into April 1978, The Treat 1979, Pasionaria 1981, Aunt Mary 1983, Camille 1985, The Danton Affair 1986, The Blue Angel 1991, Deborah's Daughter 1994, Stanley 1995 (Best Play, Evening Standard Awards 1996, Best Play, Olivier Awards 1997), Marlene 1996, The Snow Palace 1998, Nelson 2005, Mrs Pat 2006. *Adaptations:* Uncle Vanya 1981, A Doll's House 1983, The Cherry Orchard 1984, Ghosts 1992, The Seagull 1995, Yerma 2003, The Lady from the Sea 2003, The Little Mermaid 2004. *Novels:* Mrs Frampton 1989, Bon Voyage, Mrs Frampton 1990. *Literary*

Agent: c/o Jenny Casarotto, National House, 60–66 Wardour Street, London, W1V 4ND, England. *Telephone:* (20) 7287-4450. *Fax:* (20) 7287-9128.

GEN, Getsu; Japanese novelist; b. (Gen Minehide), 10 Feb. 1965, Osaka. *Publications:* novels: Ikyo no otoshigo (Born Out of Wedlock in a Foreign Land) 1998, Oppai (Breasts) 1998, Kage no sumika (A Dwelling in the Shade) (Akutagawa Prize) 1999.

GENET, Jacqueline Hélène Juliette Valentine, DèsL; French academic; *Professor Emerita, University of Caen;* b. 24 Feb. 1932, Evreux; d. of Jean Veyssié and Hélène Veyssié (née Delarue); m. Jean Genet 1961; two s. *Education:* Ecole Normale Supérieure de Sèvres, Univ. of Oxford, UK and Univ. of Paris-Sorbonne. *Career:* secondary school teacher 1957–66; Lecturer, later Sr Lecturer Univ. of Limoges 1966–74; Sr Lecturer Univ. of Caen 1974–77, Prof. 1977–92, Prof. Emer. 1992–, Pres. of Univ. 1983–88; Pres. Soc. des Anglicistes de l'Enseignement Supérieur 1990–92; fmr Vice-Pres. Int. Asscn for the Study of Anglo-Irish Literature. *Publications:* W. B. Yeats: les fondements et l'évolution de la création poétique: Essai de psychologie littéraire 1976, La poétique de W. B. Yeats 1990, Le Théâtre de W. B. Yeats 1995; numerous works of criticism, articles and translations. *Honours:* Chevalier de l'Ordre nat. du Mérite; Commdr des Palmes Académiques; Dr hc (Nat. Univ. of Ireland) 1990, (Würzburg) 1995. *Address:* University of Caen, Esplanade de la Paix, 14032 Caen (office); 13 rue de Bretteville, 14000 Caen, France (home). *Telephone:* (2) 31-85-21-78 (home). *E-mail:* jacqueline.genet2@ wanadoo.fr (home).

GENOVESE, Eugene Dominick, BA, MA, PhD; American academic and writer; b. 19 May 1930, New York, NY; m. Elizabeth Ann Fox 1969. *Education:* Brooklyn Coll., CUNY and Columbia Univ. *Career:* Asst Prof., Polytechnical Inst., Brooklyn 1958–63; Assoc. Prof., Rutgers Univ. 1963–67; Prof. of History 1967–69, Social Science Research Fellow 1968–69, Sir George Williams Univ., Montréal; Visiting Prof., Columbia Univ. 1967, Yale Univ. 1969; Prof. of History 1969–90, Distinguished Prof. of Arts and Sciences 1985–90, Univ. of Rochester; Pitt Prof. of American History and Institutions, Univ. of Cambridge, England 1976–77; Sunderland Fellow and Visiting Prof. of Law, Univ. of Michigan 1979; Visiting Mellon Prof., Tulane Univ. 1986; Distinguished Scholar-in-Residence, Univ. Center, GA 1990–95; Fellow, American Acad. of Arts and Sciences; mem. Historical Soc. (pres.), Nat. Asscn of Scholars. *Publications:* The Political Economy of Slavery 1965, The World the Slaveholders Made 1969, In Red and Black 1971, Roll, Jordan, Roll 1974, From Rebellion to Revolution 1979, Fruits of Merchant Capital (with Elizabeth Fox-Genovese) 1983, The Slaveholder's Dilemma 1991, The Southern Tradition 1994, The Southern Front 1995, A Consuming Fire 1998, The Mind of the Master Class (with Elizabeth Fox-Genovese) 2005; contrib. to scholarly journals. *Honours:* Richard Watson Gilder Fellow, Columbia Univ. 1959, Center for Advanced Study in the Behavioral Sciences Fellow, Stanford, CA 1972–73, Nat. Humanities Center Fellow, Research Triangle Park, North California 1984–85, Mellon Fellow 1987–88, Guggenheim Fellowship 1987–88, Bancroft Prize 1974. *Address:* 1487 Sheridan Walk NE, Atlanta, GA 30324, USA.

GENTLE, Mary Rosalyn, (Roxanne Morgan), BA, MA; British writer; b. 29 March 1956, Sussex, England. *Publications:* A Hawk in Silver, 1977; Golden Witchbreed, 1983; Ancient Light, 1987; Scholars and Soldiers, 1989; Rats and Gargoyles, 1990; The Architecture of Desire, 1991; Grunts!, 1992; Left to His Own Devices, 1994. Co-Editor: The Weerde Book 1, 1992; Villains!, 1992; The Weerde Book 2, The Book of the Ancients, 1993; A Secret History: The Book of Ash #1, 1999; Carthage Ascendant: The Book of Ash #2, 2000; The Wild Machines, The Book of Ash #2, 2000; Lost Burgundy, The Book of Ash #4, 2000; Ash: A Secret History, 2000; 1610: A Sundial in a Grave, 2003. As Roxanne Morgan: Dares, 1995; Bets, 1997; A Game of Masks, 1999; Degrees of Desire 2001, Ilario: The Lion's Eye 2006; contrib. to reviews. *Honours:* BSFA Award for Best Novel 2000, Sidewise Award for Alternative History, Best Long Fiction Award 2000. *Address:* 29 Sish Lane, Stevenage, Herts, England.

GEORGE, (Susan) Elizabeth, MS; American author; b. 26 Feb. 1949, Warren, OH; d. of Robert and Anne George; m. 1st Ira Toibin 1971 (divorced 1995); m. 2nd Thomas McCabe 2002. *Education:* Foothill Community Coll., Univ. of California and California State Univ. *Career:* teacher, El Toro High School, Calif. 1975–87, Coastline Community Coll., Fountainvalley, Calif. 1988–92; has lectured at Irvine Valley Coll., Irvine, Calif. 1989, Univ. of Calif. Extension 1990, Edinboro Univ. Summer School at Exeter Coll., Oxford, UK 1993, Univ. of British Columbia, Canada 1993, Univ. of Oklahoma 1995. *Television:* The Inspector Lynley Mysteries (BBC Productions). *Publications:* A Great Deliverance (Anthony Award, Bouchercon XXI 1989, Agatha Award, Malice Domestic 1989, Le Grand Prix de Literature Policière, Mystery Writers of France 1990) 1988, Payment in Blood 1989, Well-Schooled in Murder (MIMI Award 1991) 1990, Sisters in Crime, Vol. II – The Evidence Exposed 1990, A Suitable Vengeance 1991, For the Sake of Elena 1992, Missing Joseph 1993, A Novel by Any Other Name 1994, Playing for the Ashes 1994, In the Presence of the Enemy 1996, Women on the Case (ed.) 1996, Deception on His Mind 1998, In Pursuit of the Proper Sinner 1999, A Traitor to Memory 2001, I, Richard 2002, Crime From the Mind of a Woman (ed.) 2002, A Place of Hiding 2003, Write Away 2004, A Moment on the Edge (ed.) 2004, With No One as Witness 2005. *Honours:* Hon. DHumLitt (Calif. State Univ.); numerous honours and awards including the establishment of The Elizabeth George Collection at Boston Univ. 1989, One of Forty Graduates Who Have Made a Difference, Univ. of California, Riverside 1994, Visions and Visionaries, Honoring Six

Graduates from California State Univ., Fullerton. *Literary Agent:* Deborah Schneider, 250 W 57th Street, New York, NY 10107, USA. *Address:* 4111 Shorebreak Drive, Huntington Beach, CA 92649, USA (home). *Website:* www .elizabethgeorgeonline.com.

GEORGE, François, (Mathurin Maugarlonne); French writer and philosopher; b. 1947, Sceaux. *Career:* mem. editorial bd, Les Temps Modernes 1977–; founder mem., Asscn des amis d'Arsène Lupin. *Publications include:* Autopsie de Dieu 1965, Prof à T. 1974, Deux études sur Sartre 1976, La Loi et le phénomène 1978, Souvenirs de la maison Marx 1980, Staline à Paris 1982, Histoire personnelle de la France 1983, Alceste vous salue bien 1988, Plan de la nuit, De Bonaparte et de l'exception gaulliste, Arsène Lupin, gentilhomme-philosopheur (with André Comte-Sponville) 1996, Traité de l'ombre 2000, Un Philosophe dans la résistance 2001, À la rencontre des disparus 2004, Le Concept d'existence: deux études sur Sartre 2005, Caverne cosmos 2006. *Address:* c/o Éditions Grasset, 61 rue des Saints-Pères, 75006 Paris, France. *E-mail:* dfanelli@grasset.fr.

GEORGE, Jean Craighead, BA; American author and illustrator; b. 21 July 1919, Washington, DC; m. John L. George 1944 (divorced 1963); two s. one d. *Education:* Pennsylvania State University. *Career:* Reporter, Washington Post, 1943–46; Roving Ed., Reader's Digest, 1965–84. *Publications:* My Side of the Mountain 1959, Summer of the Falcon 1962, The Thirteen Moons 1967–69, Julie of the Wolves 1972, Going to the Sun 1976, Wounded Wolf 1978, The American Walk Book 1978, River Rats 1979, The Grizzly Bear with the Golden Ears 1982, The Cry of the Crow 1982, Journey Inward 1982, Talking Earth 1983, How to Talk to Your Animals 1985, Water Sky 1987, One Day in the Woods 1988, as musical 1989, Shark Beneath the Reef 1989, On the Far Side of the Mountain 1990, One Day in a Tropical Rain Forest 1990, Missing 'Gator of Gumbo Limbo 1992, The Fire Bug Connection 1993, Dear Rebecca Winter is Here 1993, The First Thanksgiving 1993, Julie 1994, Animals Who Have Won Our Hearts 1994, The Tarantula in My Purse 1996, Look to the North 1997, Julie's Wolf Pack 1997, Arctic Son 1998, Cliff Hanger 1999, Snow Bear 2002, Charlie's Raven 2004, Luck: the Story of Sandhill Crane 2006. *Honours:* Newbery Honor Book 1960, Newbery Medal 1973, Roger Baras Award 2007. *Address:* 20 William Street, Chappaqua, NY 10514, USA.

GEORGE, Jonathan (see Burke, John Frederick)

GEORGE, Kathleen Elizabeth, BA, MA, MFA, PhD; American academic, dramatist and writer; b. 7 July 1943, Johnstown, PA; m. Hilary Thomas Masters 1994. *Education:* University of Pittsburgh. *Career:* Asst Prof., Carlow College, 1968–76; Asst Prof., 1976–81, Assoc. Prof., 1981–2001, Prof., 2001–, University of Pittsburgh. *Publications:* Rhythm in Drama, 1980; Playwriting: The First Workshop, 1994; The Man in the Buick and Other Stories, 1999; Taken (novel), 2001; various short fiction; contrib. to reviews and journals. *Honours:* Virginia Center for the Arts Fellowships, 1980–83; Pennsylvania Arts Council Grants, 1982, 1987; MacDowell Colony Fellowships, 1996, 2002; Mary Anderson Center Fellowship, 1996. *E-mail:* georgeke@pitt.edu. *Website:* www.kathleengeorge.net.

GERDES, Eckhard, BA, MA, MFA; American novelist, playwright and educator; b. 17 Nov. 1959, Atlanta, GA; m. Persis Alisa Wilhelm 1988, three s. *Education:* University of Dubuque, IA, Roosevelt University, Chicago, School of the Art Institute of Chicago. *Career:* Ed., Journal of Experimental Fiction, 1994–; Instructor, Macon State College, 1998–. *Publications:* Projections, 1986; Truly Fine Citizen, 1989; Ring in a River, 1994. Contributions: Rampike; Oyez Review; Coe Review; Tomorrow Magazine; Planet Roc; Strong Coffee; No Magazine; Random Weirdness. *Honours:* Richard Pike Bissell Creative Writing Awards, 1987, 1988.

GERGELY, Ágnes, MA, PhD; Hungarian poet, novelist and translator; b. 1933, Endröd. *Education:* ELTE Univ. of Liberal Arts, Budapest. *Career:* formerly secondary school teacher, radio prod., ed. of publishing house, features ed. Nagyvilág (literary magazine); Hon. Fellow Int. Writing Program, Univ. of Iowa 1973–74; Lecturer in English, ELTE Univ. of Liberal Arts, Budapest 1992–2003. *Publications include:* novels: Tolmács (trans. as The Interpreter) 1973, A chicagói változat (trans. as The Chicago Version) 1976, Stációk (trans. as Stages Along the Way) 1983, Örizetlenek (trans. as The Unguarded) 2000; poetry: Requiem for a Sunbird: Forty Poems 1997. *Honours:* Attila József Prize 1977, 1987, Déry Prize 1985, 1996, Milán Füst Prize 1994, Getz Corporation Lifetime Achievement Award, USA 1996, Kossuth Prize 2000. *Address:* c/o Hungarian Cultural Centre, 10 Maiden Lane, Covent Garden, London, WC2E 7NA, England.

GERHARDT, Renata; German publisher and translator; b. 14 April 1926, Berlin; m. Rainer M. Gerhardt 1948 (died 1954); two s. *Education:* Univs of Freiburg and Heidelberg. *Career:* Co-Founder, Publ. Verlag der Fragmente, Freiburg and Breisgau –1954; Co-Ed Fragmente Int. Revue für Moderne Dichtung –1954; Founder Gerhardt Verlag, Berlin 1962, publr of Surrealist art books and literature; trans. into German of modern and avant-garde writers, including Ezra Pound, Gertrude Stein, Henry Miller, Alfred Jarry, Antonin Artaud, Vladimir Nabokov, etc. *Address:* c/o Jenaerstrasse 7, 10717 Berlin, Germany.

GERMAIN, Sylvie; French writer; b. 1948, Châteauroux. *Education:* Sorbonne, Paris. *Publications:* novels: Le Livre des nuits 1985, Nuit d'Ambre 1987, Jours de colère 1989, Opéra muet 1989, L'Enfant Méduse 1991, La Pleurante des rues de Prague 1992, Immensités 1993, Eclats de sel 1996,

L'Encre du poulpe 1998, Tobie des marais 1998, La Chanson des mal-aimants 2002, Magnus (Prix Goncourt des Lycéens) 2005; essays: Les Echos du silence 1996, Céphalophores 1996, Patience et songe de lumière: Vermeer 1996, Bohuslav Reyneck à Petrov: un nomade en sa demeure 1998, Etty Hillesum 1999, Mourir un peu 2000, La Grande nuit de Toussaint, Le Temps qu'il fait 2000, Cracovie à vol d'oiseau 2000, Célébration de la Paternité 2001, J'ai envie de rompre le silence (with René Vouland and Gérard Vouland) 2001, Les Personnages 2004. *Address:* c/o Dedalus Ltd, Langford Lodge, St Judith's Lane, Sawtry, Cambridgeshire PE28 5XE, England.

GEROVA, Darina Dimitrova; Bulgarian writer and journalist; b. 2 June 1934, Sofia; d. of Dimitar Guerov and Nevena Guerova; m. Vladimir Grancharov 1962 (died 1989); two s. *Education:* Univ. of Sofia. *Career:* ed. and journalist, Trud, Zhenata dnes (Women Today), Mladeg, Narodna Cultura, Septemvri etc.; freelance 2002–. *Publications include:* novels: Noon Rain 1967, Dusty Sun 1969, Hut on the Top 1972, Hello Sun! 1976, Post Festum 1981, Eve From the Third Floor 1982 (film adaptation 1987), We Have Sinned, O Lord! 1987, Icons For Non-Believers 1990, The Pain of Woman 1995, A Date at the Seaside 2004; numerous articles, reviews, essays and short stories on educ., youth, nat. culture and status of women. *Honours:* awards from Union of Bulgarian Journalists 1968, 1987, SS Cyril and Methodius Medal (First Grade) 1983. *Address:* 1618 Sofia, Buxton bl. 19 vh. E, Bulgaria (home). *Telephone:* (2) 856-18-69 (home).

GERRARD, Nicci, (Nicci French); British writer; m. Sean French 1990; two s. two d. *Career:* also writes with Sean French, under joint pseudonym of Nicci French. *Publications:* Soham: a Story of Our Times 2004, Solace 2005; as Nicci French: The Memory Game 1997, The Safe House 1998, Killing Me Softly 1999, Beneath the Skin 2000, The Red Room 2001, Land of the Living 2003, Secret Smile 2004, Things We Knew Were True 2004, Catch Me When I Fall 2005, Losing You 2007. *Literary Agent:* PFD, Drury House, 34–43 Russell Street, London, WC2B 5HA, England. *Address:* The Old Rectory, Elmsett, Ipswich IP7 6NA, England (home). *E-mail:* seanicci@dircon.co.uk.

GERRISH, Brian Albert, BA, MA, STM, PhD; British/American theologian and writer; *John Nuveen Professor Emeritus, University of Chicago*; b. 14 Aug. 1931, London, England; m. 1st; one s. one d.; m. 2nd Dawn Ann De Vries 1990; one d. *Education:* Queens' Coll., Cambridge, Union Theological Seminary, New York, Columbia Univ. *Career:* Asst Pastor West End Presbyterian Church NY 1956–58; tutor philosophy of Religion Union Theological Seminary NY 1957–58; Instructor McCormick Theological Seminary Chicago 1958–59, Asst Prof. 1959–63, Assoc. Prof. 1963–65; Assoc. Prof. 1965–68, Prof. 1968–85, John Nuveen Prof. 1985–96, John Nuveen Prof. Emer. 1996–, Divinity School, Univ. of Chicago; Co-Ed., Journal of Religion 1972–85; Distinguished Service Prof. of Theology, Union Theological Seminary, Virginia 1996–2002; Fellow American Acad. of Arts and Sciences. *Publications:* Grace and Reason: A Study in the Theology of Luther 1962, Tradition and the Modern World: Reformed Theology in the Nineteenth Century 1978, The Old Protestantism and the New: Essays on the Reformation Heritage 1982, A Prince of the Church: Schleiermacher and the Beginnings of Modern Theology 1984, Grace and Gratitude: The Eucharistic Theology of John Calvin 1993, Continuing the Reformation: Essays on Modern Religious Thought 1993, Saving and Secular Faith: An Invitation to Systematic Theology 1999, The Pilgrim Road: Sermons on Christian Life 2000; editor: The Faith of Christendom: A Source Book of Creeds and Confessions 1963, Reformers in Profile 1967, Reformatio Perennis: Essays on Calvin and the Reformation in Honor of Ford Lewis Battles 1981, Reformed Theology for the Third Christian Millennium: The 2001 Sprunt Lectures 2003. *Honours:* Dr hc (Univ. of St Andrews, Scotland) 1984; Guggenheim Fellowship, 1970. *Address:* 9142 Sycamore Hill Place, Mechanicsville, VA 23116, USA (home). *Telephone:* (804) 550-1377 (home).

GERSOVITZ, Sarah Valerie, MA, RCA; Canadian artist and playwright; b. Montréal, PQ; d. of Solomon and Eva Gamer; m. Benjamin Gersovitz 1944; two s. one d. *Education:* Macdonald Coll. School for Teachers, Québec, PQ and Concordia Univ., Montréal, PQ. *Career:* fmr teacher of Art and Art History; Art Critic Arts-Atlantic 1984–; work rep. in perm. collections including Library of Congress, Washington, DC and New York Public Library, USA, Nat. Gallery of S Australia, The Israel Museum, Jerusalem, Instituto Culturel Peruano, Lima, Univ. of Kaiserslautern, Germany, Montréal Museum of Fine Arts, The House of Humour and Satire, Gabrovo, Bulgaria; public and private collections in England, France, Brazil, Venezuela, Hungary, Poland, Italy USA, China and widely in Canada; fmr mem. Council RCA; mem. Dramatists Guild. *Exhibitions include:* solo: Univ. of Kaiserslautern, Germany, and Instituto Culturel Peruano, Lima; 75 int. biennials in Canada, USA, Venezuela, Colombia, Brazil, Peru, UK, Norway, Germany, Switzerland, France, Spain, Italy, Yugoslavia, Czech Repub., Hungary, Bulgaria, Hong Kong, Repub. of China (Taiwan), Australia, Repub. of Korea, Poland, Chile. *Plays include:* A Portrait of Portia, The Picasso Affair (First Prize, Nat. Playwriting Competition 1982), The Artist and Food for Thought, The Studio, Eh, Harry? (First Prize, Jacksonville Univ. 1988), The Winding Staircase (First Prize Country Playhouse Playwriting Competition, Houston, TX 1985), Person-to-Person, Nighty-Night, The Panel, Survey Show, Desjardin's Garden, The Black Ceiling, Patchwork Quilt, Box Camera, Ceremony, Reservation for Dinner, Lullaby, The Classical Hour, The Fine Art of Dealing Fine Art, and others. *Publications:* Portrait of Portia 1989; contrib. articles to Ceramics, Art & Perception and others. *Honours:* numerous awards include Nat. Gallery of S Australia Purchase Award, First Prize Int. Jury, 9th Int. Biennale, Gabrovo, Bulgaria 1989, First Prize Concours Graphique, l'Université de Sherbrooke, First Prize and Gold Medal, Seagram Fine Arts Exhbn, Graphic Art Prize, Winnipeg Show Biennial, Anaconda Award (twice), Canadian Painter-Etchers and Engravers, Purchase of corpus of graphic works (316 prints) by Bibliothèque Nat. de Québec. *Address:* 4360 Montrose Avenue, Westmount, PQ H3Y 2B1, Canada. *Telephone:* (514) 933-5048. *Fax:* (514) 933-5048. *E-mail:* b.sv.gersovitz@sympatico.ca; gersovitz@aei.ca.

GERSTLER, Amy, BA; American poet and writer; b. 24 Oct. 1956, San Diego, CA. *Education:* Pitzer College. *Publications:* Poetry: Yonder, 1981; Christy's Alpine Inn, 1982; White Marriage/Recovery, 1984; Early Heavens, 1984; The True Bride, 1986; Bitter Angel, 1990; Nerve Storm, 1993; Crown of Weeds, 1997; Medicine, 2000. Fiction: Martine's Mouth, 1985; Primitive Man, 1987. Other: Past Lives (with Alexis Smith), 1989. Contributions: Magazines. *Honours:* National Book Critics Circle Award, 1991.

GERVAIS, Charles Henry Martin, BA, MA; Canadian poet, writer and editor; b. 20 Oct. 1946, Windsor, ON; m. Donna Wright 1968, two s. one d. *Education:* University of Guelph, University of Windsor. *Career:* staff, Toronto Globe and Mail, 1966, Canadian Press, Toronto, 1967; Reporter, Daily Commercial News, Toronto, 1967, Chatham Daily News, 1972–73; Teacher of Creative Writing, St Clair College, Windsor, 1969–71; Publisher, Black Moss Press, Windsor, 1969–; Ed., Sunday Standard, Windsor, 1972; General News Reporter, 1973–74, 1976–81, Bureau Chief, 1974–76, Religion Ed., 1979–80, Book Ed., 1980–, Entertainment Writer, 1990–, Windsor Star. *Publications:* Poetry: Sister Saint Anne, 1968; Something, 1969; Other Marriage Vows, 1969; A Sympathy Orchestra, 1970; Bittersweet, 1972; Poems for American Daughters, 1976; The Believable Body, 1979; Up Country Lines, 1979; Silence Comes with Lake Voices, 1980; Into a Blue Morning: Selected Poems, 1982; Public Fantasy: The Maggie T. Poems, 1983; Letters From the Equator, 1986; Autobiographies, 1989; Playing God: New Poems, 1994. Other: The Rumrunners: A Prohibition Scrapbook, 1980; Voices Like Thunder, 1984; The Border Police: One Hundred and Twenty-Five Years of Policing in Windsor, 1992; Seeds in the Wilderness: Profiles of World Religious Leaders, 1994; From America Sent: Letters to Henry Miller, 1995. Editor: The Writing Life: Historical and Critical Views of the Tish Movement, 1976. Children's Books: How Bruises Lost His Secret, 1975; Doctor Troyer and the Secret in the Moonstone, 1976; If I Had a Birthday Everyday, 1983. *Honours:* Western Ontario Newspaper Awards, 1983, 1984, 1987.

GERVAIS, Ricky; British writer and comedian; b. 25 June 1961, Reading, Berks., England; partner Jane Fallon. *Education:* Ashmead School, Univ. of London. *Career:* mem. pop duo Seona Dancing 1983–84; entertainments officer, Univ. of London; Man. pop band Suede; Music Adviser, TV drama This Life (Island World/BBC 2) 1996–97. *Plays:* Animals 2002, Politics 2004. *Television:* The 11 O'Clock Show (TalkBack/Channel 4) 1999–2000, Bruiser (BBC 2) 2000, Meet Ricky Gervais (TalkBack/Channel 4) 2000, The Office (BBC 2) 2001–03, Extras (BBC 2) 2005. *Radio:* BBC Radio 1, XFM London. *Films include:* Dog Eat Dog 2001, Valiant (voice) 2005, For Your Consideration 2006, Night at the Museum 2006. *Publications:* The Office: Scripts Series 1 2002, The Office: Scripts Series 2 2003, Flanimals (juvenile) 2004, More Flanimals 2005, Flanimals of the Deep (British Book Award for Children's Book of the Year 2007) 2006. *Honours:* BAFTA Awards, including Best Comedy Performance 2007, British Comedy Awards, Golden Globes (USA), Hon. Rose d'Or Award, Lucerne 2006. *Address:* c/o Faber and Faber Ltd, 3 Queen Square, London, WC1N 3AU, England.

GERY, John Roy Octavius, MA; American academic and poet; b. 2 June 1953, Reading, PA; m. Biljana D. Obradović; one s. *Education:* Princeton University, University of Chicago, Stanford University. *Career:* Lecturer, Stanford University and San Jose State University 1977–79; Instructor 1979–84, Asst Prof. 1984–88, Assoc. Prof. 1988–95, Prof. of English 1995–2000, Research Prof. of English 2000–, University of New Orleans; Founding Dir, Ezra Pound Center for Literature, Brunnenburg, Italy 1990–; Visiting Prof., University of Iowa 1991–92; mem. Acad. of American Poets, Assoc. Writing Programs, MLA, Poets and Writers. *Publications:* Charlemagne: A Song of Gestures 1983, The Burning of New Orleans 1988, Three Poems 1989, The Enemies of Leisure 1995, Nuclear Annihilation and Contemporary American Poetry 1996, For the House of Torkom (co-trans.) 1999, American Ghost: Selected Poems 1999, Davenport's Version 2003, A Gallery of Ghosts 2005; contribs to reviews and journals. *Honours:* Deep South Writers Poetry Award 1987, Charles William Duke Long Poem Award 1987, Wesleyan Writers' Conference Poetry Fellowship 1989, National Endowment for the Arts Fellowship 1992–93, Critics' Choice Award for Poetry 1996, European Award Circle Franz Kafka 2000, Louisiana Artist Fellowship 2002, Summer Poet-in-Residence, Bucknell Univ. 2001, 2003. *Address:* c/o Department of English, University of New Orleans, New Orleans, LA 70148-2315, USA.

GEVE, Thomas, BSc; Israeli engineer and writer; b. 1929, Germany; m. 1963; one s. two d. *Publications:* Youth in Chains 1958, Guns and Barbed Wire 1987, There Are No Children Here 1997, Aufbrüche 2000. *Address:* PO Box 4727, Haifa, Israel.

GEVIRTZ, Susan, BA, MA, PhD; American poet and writer; b. 27 Oct. 1955, Los Angeles, CA; one d. *Education:* Evergreen State Coll., St John's Graduate Inst., Santa Fe, NM, Univ. of California at Santa Cruz. *Career:* Teaching Asst, Univ. of California at Santa Cruz 1983–87; teacher-poet, California Poets in the Schools, San Francisco 1984–86; teacher, Aegean Coll. of Fine Arts, Paros, Greece 1985; Assoc. Ed., HOW(ever) journal 1985–90; instructor, Univ. of San

Francisco 1988–89, California Coll. of Arts and Crafts, Oakland 1989–91; Asst Prof., Hutchins School of Liberal Studies, Sonoma State Univ., Rohnert Park, CA 1989–98; Prof., MFA in Poetry Programs, Univ. of San Francisco and San Francisco State Univ. 2000–; Prof., MA in Visual Criticism Program, California Coll. of the Arts 2002–; Prof. Hellenic Int. School of the Arts, Paros, Greece; Organiser (with Greek poet Siarita Korka) Paros Symposium of US and Greek poets, translators and scholars; currently collaborating with British sound artist Robin Rimbard aka Scanner. *Publications:* poetry: Korean and Milkhouse 1991, Domino: Point of Entry 1992, Linen minus 1992, Taken Place 1993, Prosthesis: Caesarea 1994, Black Box Cutaway 1998, Spelt (with Myung Mi Kim) 2000, Hourglass Transcripts 2001; other: Feminist Poetics: A Consideration of the 'Female' Construction of Language (assoc. ed.) 1984, Narrative's Journey: The Fiction and Film Writing of Dorothy Richardson 1995; contribs to anthologies, journals and magazines. *Honours:* awards, grants and fellowships.

GEYER, Georgie Anne, BSc, BA; American journalist; *Syndicated Columnist, Universal Press;* b. 2 April 1935, Chicago, IL; d. of Robert George Geyer and Georgie Hazel Geyer. *Education:* Northwestern Univ., IL and Univ. of Vienna. *Career:* reporter, Southtown Economist, Chicago 1958; Society Reporter, Chicago Daily News 1959–60, Gen. Assignment Reporter 1960–64, Latin America Corresp. 1964–67, roving Foreign Corresp., columnist 1967–75; Syndicated Columnist, Los Angeles Times Syndicate 1975–80; columnist, Universal Press Syndicate 1980–; Lyle M. Spencer Prof. of Journalism, Syracuse Univ., NY 1976; int. lecture tours on American journalism sponsored by Int. Communication Agency, Nigeria, Somalia, Tanzania, Zambia 1979, Indonesia, Philippines 1981, Belgium, Iceland, Norway, Portugal 1982; regular TV and radio appearances; Sr Fellow Annenberg Washington Program in Communications Policy Studies 1992–; Fellow Soc. of Professional Journalists 1992–. *Publications:* The New Latins 1970, The New 100 Years War 1972, The Young Russians 1976, Buying the Night Flight (autobiog.) 1983, Guerilla Prince: The Untold Story of Fidel Castro 1991, Waiting for Winter to End: An Extraordinary Journey Through Soviet Central Asia 1994, Americans No More: The Death of Citizenship 1996, Tunisia: a Journey Through a Country That Works 2002, When Cats Reigned Like Kings 2004. *Honours:* 21 hon. degrees (Northwestern, Loyola, Univ. of S Carolina, and others); numerous awards include American Newspaper Guild First Prize 1962, Overseas Press Club Award for Best Writing on Latin America 1967, Weintal Prize Citation Georgetown Univ. 1984, Chicago Foundation for Literature Award 1984, Alumni Award, Northwestern Univ. 1991, Retired Intelligence Officers Award 2000, Soc. of Professional Journalists Hall of Fame 2001, Chicago Headline Club Lifetime Achievement Award 2003, Woman Extraordinaire Award Int. Women Assocs 2004. *Address:* The Plaza, 800 25th Street NW, Washington, DC 20037, USA. *Telephone:* (202) 333-9176 (office). *Fax:* (202) 333-3198 (office). *E-mail:* gigi_geyer@juno.com (office). *Website:* www.uexpress.com (office).

GHELLAB, Abdelkarim, BA; Moroccan writer; *Editor-in-Chief, H'izb Al-Istiqlal Independence Party;* b. 1919. *Education:* Al-Qarawiyyin Univ. of Fes, Cairo Univ. *Career:* worked in several govt depts, including Foreign Affairs and Education; Ed.-in-Chief H'izb Al-Istiqlal (Independence Party); Ed. A'alam newspaper; sr founding mem. Union des Ecrivains du Maroc. *Publications include:* novels: Saba'at 'abwab (Seven Doors) 1965, Dafanna Al-Mad'i (We Buried the Past) 1968, Lm'aallam Ali (Master Ali) 1971, Wa 'ada Azzawraqu 'ila Annaba'i (The Boat Returned to the Source) 1988; non-fiction: Maa'rakatuna Al-A'arabiya fi Muwajahati Al-'istia'mar (Our Arab Struggle Against Colonialism) 1967, Maa'a Al-'adab wa Al-'udaba-' (On Literature and Literary Figures) 1974, A'alam Shaa'ir Al-H'amra-' (The World of the Poet of the Red Town – Marrakech) 1981, Tarikh Al-H'araka Al-Wataniya bilmaghrib (A History of the Nationalist Movement in Morocco) 1987, Fi Al-Fikr Assiyasi (On Political Thought) 1992. *Address:* L'Union des Ecrivains du Maroc, 5 rue Ab Bakr Seddik, Rabat, Morocco. *Website:* www.unecma.net.

GHEORGHE, Ion; Romanian poet; b. 16 Aug. 1935, Florica, Buzău. *Education:* Bucharest Univ. *Career:* Ed. Luceafărul magazine 1963–; worked in Ministry of Culture 1992; cultural attaché, Romanian Embassy in China 1994–96. *Publications:* Pâine şi sare 1957, Căile pământului 1960, Ţara rândunelelor 1963, Cariatida 1964, Nopţi cu lună pe Oceanul Atlantic: Scrisori esenţiale 1966, Zoosophia 1967, Vine iarba 1968, Cavalerul trac 1969, Mai mult ca plânsul: Icoane pe sticlă 1970, Megalitice 1972, Avatara 1972, Poeme 1972, Cultul Zburătorului: Opiniile autorului despre lumea miturilor autohtone 1974, Noimele 1976, Dacia Feniks 1978, Proba logosului 1979, Cenuşile 1980, Joaca jocului 1984, Şi mai joaca jocului 1985, Condica în versuri 1987, Zalmoksiile 1988, Muzaios 2001, Elegii politice 2002, Cogaioanele: Munţii Marilor pontifi 2004. *E-mail:* ion-gheorghe@as.ro. *Website:* www.ion-gheorghe.as.ro.

GHEORGHIU, Mihnea, PhD, DLitt; Romanian academic, poet, writer and actor; b. 5 May 1919, Bucharest; s. of Dumitru Gheorghiu and Alexandrina Gheorghiu; m. Anda Boldur 1953; one d. *Education:* Fratii Buzesti High School, Craiova, Univ. of Bucharest and studies in France, Italy and UK, School of Artillery Officers, Craiova. *Career:* Chief Ed. Scînteia Tineretului (newspaper) 1944–46; Lecturer and Assoc. Prof. of English Language, Acad. of Econ. Studies, Bucharest 1946–48, Prof. 1948–50; Prof. of Theatralogy and Filmology, Inst. of Theatre and Film Art, Bucharest 1954–69; Founder and Ed.-in-Chief Secolul 20 (monthly int. literary review) 1961–63; Ed.-in-Chief Romanian-American Review; Chair. of Bd Social Future (sociology and political sciences bi-monthly), Studies in the History of Art 1975–; Pres. Nat. Film Council 1963–65; Vice-Pres. Nat. Cttee for Culture and Art 1965–68; Pres. Inst. for Cultural Relations 1968–72, Acad. of Social and Political Sciences 1972–89, Romanian Filmmakers' Union 1990–; Corresp. mem. Romanian Acad. 1974, mem. 1996, Pres. Section for Arts, Architecture and Audiovisual 1992–; Adviser UNESCO European Centre for Higher Educ.; mem. Club of Rome, Soc. Européenne de Culture, Venice, Acad. Mondiale de Prospective Sociale, Geneva, New York Acad. of Sciences, Int. Shakespeare Asscn 1964–2000, Nat. Acad. of History of Caracas, Int. Asscn of Film and TV Authors. *Film screenplays and scripts:* Porto Franco 1962, Tudor 1963–64, Zodia Feciorei 1967, Pădurea pierdută 1992, Cantemir & Muşchetarul român (Prize of Cineasts' Union of Romania) 1974, Hyperion 1975, Tănase Scatiu 1976, Burebista 1980. *Plays:* Tudor din Vladimiri (Tudor of Vladimiri), Istorii dramatice (Dramatic Histories), Capul (The Head), Zodia Taurului (Taurus' Sign), Patetica '77 (Pathetica '77), Fierul si aurul (Iron and Gold). *Radio:* has written more than 20 plays. *Publications:* poetry: Anna-Mad 1941, Ultimul peisaj al orasului cenusiu (Last Landscape of the Grey Town 1946, Balade (Ballads) 1956, Ultimul peisaj (The Last Landscape) 1974; other: Orientations in World Literature 1957, Doua ambasade (Two Embassies) 1958, Scenes of Shakespeare's Life 1958, Dionysos 1969, Letters from the Neighbourhood 1971, Scenes of Public Life 1972, Five Worlds as Spectacle (collection of plays) 1980, Tobacco Flowers (essays) 1984, Enigma in Fleet Street (novel) 1988, The Two Roses (collection of tales) 1992; translations from Shakespeare, Walt Whitman, Burns, Gabriel García Márquez, etc. *Honours:* Hon. Citizen of New Orleans; Ordre des Arts et des Lettres (France), Italian Order of Merit, Grosse Verdienstkreuz mit Stern (FRG), Order of Orange-Nassau (Netherlands); Nat. State Prize, Special Prize, Int. Film Festivals of Barcelona, Buenos Aires and Cork 1964, 1966, I. L. Caragiale Prize, Romanian Acad. 1972, Prize of Writers' Union of Romania 1975, Erasmus Medal. *Address:* Mendeleev Street 28-30, Sector 1, 70169 Bucharest (office); Dionisie Lupu 74, Bucharest, Romania (home). *Telephone:* 6504969 (home); 6505741 (office). *Fax:* 3111246 (office).

GHEZALI, Salima; Algerian newspaper editor; *Editor-in-Chief, La Nation;* b. 1958; m. (divorced); two c. *Career:* fmr schoolteacher, Mitidja Hills; Ed.-in-Chief La Nation weekly newspaper 1994–96, 2001–, newspaper suspended by Algerian authorities 1996–2001; f. Women of Europe and North Africa Asscn, Asscn for Women's Emancipation 1989; f. Nyssa magazine. *Honours:* Int. Press Club Award 1996, Sakharov Human Rights Prize 1997, Olof Palme Prize 1997. *Address:* La Nation, 33 rue Larbi Ben M'hidi, Algiers, Algeria.

GHOSE, Zulfikar, BA; British academic, poet and writer; *Professor of English, University of Texas at Austin;* b. 13 March 1935, Sialkot, Pakistan. *Education:* Keele Univ. *Career:* Prof. of English, Univ. of Texas at Austin 1969–. *Publications:* poetry: The Loss of India 1964, Jets from Orange 1967, The Violent West 1972, A Memory of Asia 1984, Selected Poems 1991; fiction: The Contradictions 1966, The Murder of Aziz Khan 1967, The Incredible Brazilian the Native 1972, The Beautiful Empire 1975, Crump's Terms 1975, A Different World 1978, Hulme's Investigations into the Bogan Script 1981, A New History of Torments 1982, Don Bueno 1983, Figures of Enchantment 1986, The Triple Mirror of the Self 1992; criticism: Hamlet, Prufrock and Language 1978, The Fiction of Reality 1983, The Art of Creating Fiction 1991, Shakespeare's Mortal Knowledge 1993, Veronica and the Góngora Passion 1998; autobiography: Confessions of a Native-Alien 1965. *Address:* c/o Department of English, University of Texas at Austin, Austin, TX 78712, USA. *E-mail:* zulfji@gmail.com.

GHOSH, Amitav, BA, MA, DPhil; Indian writer and academic; *Visiting Professor, Department of English and American Literature and Language, Harvard University;* b. 1956, Kolkata; m. Deborah Baker. *Education:* St Stephen's Coll., Delhi Univ., Institut Bourguiba des Langues Vivantes, Tunis and Univ. of Oxford. *Career:* Visiting Fellow Centre for Social Sciences, Trivandrum, Kerala 1982–83; Research Assoc. Dept of Sociology, Delhi Univ. 1983–87, Lecturer Dept of Sociology 1987; Visiting Prof. Depts of Literature and Anthropology, Univ. of Virginia, Charlottesville 1988; Visiting Prof. South Asia Centre, Columbia Univ. 1989; Visiting Prof. Dept of Anthropology, Univ. of Pennsylvania 1989; Fellow Centre for Studies in Social Science, Kolkata 1990–92; Adjunct Prof. Dept of Anthropology, Columbia Univ. 1993, Visiting Prof. 1994–97; Distinguished Visiting Prof. American Univ. in Cairo 1994; fiction workshop Sarah Lawrence Coll., New York 1996; Distinguished Prof. Dept of Comparative Literature, Queens Coll., CUNY 1999–2003; Visiting Prof., Dept of English and American Literature and Language, Harvard Univ. 2004–. *Publications:* The Circle of Reason (Prix Médicis Étranger 1990) 1986, The Shadow Lines (Sahitya Akademi Award 1990) 1988, In an Antique Land (non-fiction) 1992, The Calcutta Chromosome (Arthur C. Clark Award 1997) 1996, Dancing in Cambodia and At Large in Burma (essays) 1998, Countdown 1999, The Glass Palace (Frankfurt International e-Book Awards Grand Prize for Fiction 2001) 2000, The Hungry Tide (Hutch Crossword Book Prize 2005) 2004, Sea of Poppies (2008); contrib. articles in Ethnology, Granta, The New Republic, New York Times, Public Culture, Subaltern Studies, Letra Internacional, Cultural Anthropology, Observer Magazine, Wilson Quarterly, The New Yorker, Civil Lines, American Journal of Archaeology, Kenyon Review, Desh. *Honours:* Ananda Puraskar 1990, Best American Essays award 1995, Pushcart Prize 1999. *Address:* Department of English and American Literature and Language, Harvard University, Barker Center, 12 Quincy Street, Cambridge, MA 02138, USA (home). *Telephone:* (617) 495-4029 (home). *Fax:* (617) 496-8737 (office). *E-mail:* aghosh@fas.harvard.edu (office); amitav@

amitavghosh.com. *Website:* www.fas.harvard.edu/~english (office); www.amitavghosh.com.

GIBBON, Gary, BA; British journalist; *Political Editor, Channel 4 News*; b. 15 March 1965, s. of Robert and Elizabeth Gibbon; m. Laura Pulay 1993; two s. *Education:* Balliol Coll., Oxford. *Career:* fmr journalist BBC; joined Channel 4 News 1990, Political Prod. 1992–94, Political Correspondent 1994–2005, Political Ed. 2005–. *Address:* Channel 4 News, ITN, 200 Gray's Inn Road, London, WC1X 8XZ, England. *Telephone:* (20) 7430-4990. *Website:* www.channel4.com/news/.

GIBBONS, Kaye; American writer; b. 1960, Nash County, NC; m. (divorced); three d. *Education:* North Carolina State University, University of North Carolina at Chapel Hill. *Publications:* Ellen Foster, 1987; A Virtuous Woman, 1989; A Cure for Dreams, 1991; Charms for the Easy Life, 1993; Sights Unseen, 1995; On the Occasion of My Last Afternoon, 1998. *Honours:* Sue Kaufman Prize for First Fiction, American Acad. and Institute of Arts and Letters, 1988; Citation, Ernest Hemingway Foundation, 1988; National Endowment for the Arts Fellowship, 1989; Nelson Algren Heartland Award for Fiction, Chicago Tribune, 1991; PEN/Revson Foundation Fellowship, 1991.

GIBBONS, (William) Reginald (Jr), AB, MA, PhD; American academic, poet, writer and translator; *Professor of English, Northwestern University*; b. 7 Jan. 1947, Houston, TX; m. Cornelia Maude Spelman 1983; one step-s. one step-d. *Education:* Princeton Univ., Stanford Univ. *Career:* Lecturer, Livingston Coll., Rutgers Univ. 1975–76, Princeton Univ. 1976–80, Columbia Univ. 1980–81; Ed., TriQuarterly magazine 1981–97; Prof. of English, Northwestern Univ. 1981–; Core Faculty, MFA Program for Writers, Warren Wilson Coll. 1989–; Fulbright Fellowship, Spain 1971–72; Guggenheim Fellowship 1984; Nat. Endowment for the Arts Fellowship 1984–85; Illinois Arts Council Fellowship 1987; mem. Associated Writing Programs, The Guild Complex (co-founder), PEN American Center, Poetry Soc. of America, Texas Inst. of Letters. *Publications:* Roofs Voices Roads (poems) 1979, The Ruined Motel (poems) 1981, Criticism in the University (ed. with Gerald Graff) 1985, The Writer in Our World (ed.) 1986, Saints (poems) 1986, Writers from South Africa (ed.) 1988, William Goyen: A Study of the Short Fiction 1991, Thomas McGrath: Life and the Poem (ed. with Terrence Des Pres) 1991, Maybe It Was So (poems) 1991, Five Pears or Peaches (short stories) 1991, New Writings from Mexico (ed. and principal trans.) 1992, Sweetbitter (novel) 1994, Sparrow: New and Selected Poems 1997, Homage to Longshot O'Leary (poems) 1999, Selected Poems of Luis Cernuda (trans.) 2000, Euripides' Bakkhai (trans. with Charles Segal) 2001, It's Time (poems) 2002, Sophokles' Antigone (trans. with Charles Segal) 2003, In the Warhouse (poems) 2004, Fern-Texts (poems) 2005; contrib. to many journals, reviews, quarterlies and magazines. *Honours:* co-winner Denver Quarterly Trans. Award 1977, Texas Inst. of Letters Short Story Award 1986, Poetry Soc. of America John Masefield Memorial Award 1991, Friends of the Chicago Public Library Carl Sandburg Award 1992, Anisfield-Wolf Book Award 1995, Texas Inst. of Letters Jesse Jones Award 1995, Pushcart Prize 1997, Shenandoah magazine Thomas H. Carter Prize 1998, Balcones Poetry Prize 1998, Folger Shakespeare Library O. B. Hardison Jr Poetry Prize 2004. *Address:* Department of English, 215 University Hall, Northwestern University, Evanston, IL 60208, USA. *Telephone:* (847) 491-7294 (office). *Fax:* (847) 467-1545 (office). *E-mail:* rgibbons@northwestern.edu (office).

GIBSON, Graeme, CM, BA; Canadian writer; b. 9 Aug. 1934, London, ON; m. Margaret Atwood; two s. one d. *Education:* Univ. of Waterloo, Univ. of Edinburgh, Univ. of Western Ontario. *Career:* mem. Int. PEN (Canadian Centre, pres. 1987–89), Writers' Union of Canada (chair. 1974–75). *Publications:* Five Legs 1969, Communion 1971, Eleven Canadian Novelists 1973, Perpetual Motion 1982, Gentleman Death 1993, A Bedside Book of Birds: An Avian Miscellany 2005. *Honours:* Toronto Arts Award 1990, Harbourfront Festival Prize 1993. *Address:* c/o Random House of Canada Ltd, One Toronto Street, Unit 300, Toronto, ON M5C 2V6, Canada.

GIBSON, Ian, BA; Irish historian and writer; b. 1939, Dublin. *Education:* Trinity Coll., Dublin. *Career:* Lecturer in Spanish, Queen's Univ., Belfast; Reader in Modern Spanish Literature, Univ. of London. *Publications:* La represión nacionalista de Granada en 1936 y la muerte de Federico García Lorca 1971, The Death of Lorca 1975, The English Vice: Beating, Sex and Shame in Victorian England and After 1979, The Assassination of Federico García Lorca 1983, Federico García Lorca: A Life 1989, Fire in the Blood 1992, Lorca's Granada: A Practical Guide 1992, Salvador Dalí: The Early Years (with others) 1995, The Shameful Life of Salvador Dalí 1997, Vida, Pasión y Muerte de Federico García Lorca 1998, Dalí-Lorca: La pasión que no pudo ser 1999, The Erotomaniac: The Secret Life of Henry Spencer Ashbee 2002, Viento del sur (novel) 2002, Yo, Rubén Darío: Memorias póstumas de un Rey de la Poesía (novel) 2002, Cela, el hombre que quiso ganar 2003, Dalí joven, Dalí genial 2004; contrib. to numerous magazines and newspapers. *Honours:* Duff Cooper Memorial Prize, James Tait Black Memorial Prize, Premio Así Fue, Univ. of Barcelona. *E-mail:* iangibson@arrakis.es.

GIBSON, (George) Morgan, BA, MA, PhD; American academic, poet, critic and writer; b. 6 June 1929, Cleveland, OH; s. of George Miles Gibson, Jr and Mary Elizabeth Gibson (née Leeper); m. 1st Barbara Gibson 1950 (divorced 1972); two d.; m. 2nd Keiko Matsui Gibson 1978; one s. *Education:* Oberlin Coll., Univ. of Iowa. *Career:* Asst, then Assoc. Prof. of English, Univ. of Wisconsin at Milwaukee, 1961–72; Chair. Grad. Faculty, Goddard Coll., Vt 1972–75, Osaka Univ., Japan 1975–79; Visiting Prof., Michigan State Univ.

1979, Univ. of Illinois 1982, Knox Coll. 1989–91; Prof., Chukyo Univ., Japan 1987–89, Japan Women's Univ., Tokyo 1993–96, Kanda Univ. of Int. Studies 1997–2000; Lecturer, Pennsylvania State Univ. 1991–93. *Plays:* Madam CIA, Strongroom. *Publications:* Stones Glow Like Lovers' Eyes 1970, Crystal Sunlake 1971, Kenneth Rexroth 1972, Dark Summer 1977, Wakeup 1978, Speaking of Light 1979, Kokoro: Heart-Mind 1979, The Great Brook Book 1981, Revolutionary Rexroth: Poet of East-West Wisdom 1986, and online 2000, Among Buddhas in Japan 1988, Winter Pilgrim 1993; editor: several books and journals; contribs to anthologies, books, journals and reviews. *Honours:* several awards and grants. *Address:* 3-17-604 Sakashita-cho, Isogo-ku, Yokohama -shi 235-0003, Japan. *E-mail:* nonzenpoet@mac.com (home). *Website:* homepage.mac.com/chrisgib/Family/Menu35.html (home).

GIBSON, Rex; South African journalist; b. 11 Aug. 1931, Salisbury; s. of Arthur David Gibson and Mildred Joyce Adam; three d. *Education:* King Edward VII School, Johannesburg. *Career:* articled clerk 1948–52; entered journalism 1952, joined Rand Daily Mail 1959, Chief Sub-Ed. 1962, Arts Ed. 1969, Asst Ed. then Chief Asst Ed. 1969–72, Deputy Ed. 1973–76, Ed. 1982–85; Founding Ed. Mining News 1967; Ed. The Northern Reporter (first local suburban newspaper) 1968–69; Ed. The Sunday Express 1976–82; Deputy Ed. The Star, Johannesburg 1985–93; Deputy Man. Dir Sussens Mann Communications 1993–; Bursar Imperial Relations Trust 1960. *Honours:* Atlas World Review Joint Int. Ed. of the Year Award 1979, Pringle Award for Journalism 1979.

GIBSON, Walter Samuel, BFA, MA, PhD; American academic and writer; *Andrew W. Mellon Professor Emeritus of the Humanities, Case Western Reserve University*; b. 31 March 1932, Columbus, OH. *Education:* Ohio State Univ., Harvard Univ. *Career:* Asst Prof., Case Western Reserve Univ. 1966–71, Assoc. Prof. 1971–78, Acting Chair. 1970–71, Chair. 1971–79, Dept of Art, Andrew W. Mellon Prof. of the Humanities 1978–97, Andrew W. Mellon Prof. Emer. of the Humanities 1997–; Murphy Lecturer, Univ. of Kansas and the Nelson-Atkins Museum of Art 1988; Clark Visiting Prof. of Art History, Williams Coll. 1989, 1992; mem. American Asscn of Netherlandic Studies Coll. Art Asscn, Historians of Netherlandish Art, Midwest Art History Soc., Renaissance Soc. of America, Soc. for Emblem Studies. *Publications:* Hieronymus Bosch 1973, The Paintings of Cornelis Engebrechtsz 1977, Bruegel 1977, Hieronymus Bosch: An Annotated Bibliography 1983, 'Mirror of the Earth': The World Landscape in Sixteenth-Century Flemish Painting 1989, Pieter Bruegel the Elder: Two Studies 1991, Pleasant Places: The Rustic Landscape from Bruegel to Ruisdael 2000, Peter Bruegel and the Art of Laughter 2006; contribs to scholarly books and journals. *Honours:* Fulbright Scholarships 1960–61, 1984, Guggenheim Fellowship 1978–79, Fellow-in-Residence, Netherlands Inst. for Advanced Study, Wassenaar 1995–96. *Address:* 938 Mason Hill Road N, VT 05261-9767, USA. *Telephone:* (802) 823-5861. *Fax:* (802) 823-0287.

GIBSON, William; American dramatist, writer and poet; b. 13 Nov. 1914, New York, NY; m. 1st (divorced); m. 2nd Margaret Brenman 1940, two s. *Education:* CUNY. *Career:* mem. Authors League of America; Dramatists Guild; PEN. *Publications:* Plays (with dates of production and publication): I Lay in Zion, 1943, 1947; A Cry of Players, 1948, 1969; The Ruby, 1955; The Miracle Worker, 1957, 1957; Two for the Seesaw, 1958, 1960; Dinny and the Witches, 1959, 1960; Golden Boy (with Clifford Odets), 1964, 1965; John and Abigail, 1969, 1972; The Body and the Wheel, 1974, 1975; The Butterfingers Angel, Mary and Joseph, Herod the Nut, and the Slaughter of 12 Hit Carols in a Pear Tree, 1974, 1975; Golda, 1977, 1977; Goodly Creatures, 1980, 1986; Monday After the Miracle, 1982, 1983; Handy Dandy, 1984, 1986; Raggedy Ann: The Musical Adventure, 1985, 1986. Novel: The Cobweb, 1954. Poetry: Winter Crook, 1948; A Mass for the Dead, 1968. Criticism: Shakespeare's Game, 1978. Contributions: Magazines. *Honours:* Harriet Monroe Memorial Prize for Poetry, 1945; Sylvania Award, 1957.

GIBSON, William Ford, BA; American writer; b. 17 March 1948, Conway, SC; m. Deborah Thompson 1972, one s. one d. *Education:* University of British Columbia. *Publications:* Neuromancer, 1984; Count Zero, 1986; Burning Chrome (short stories with John Shirley, Bruce Sterling, and Michael Swanwick), 1986; Mona Lisa Overdrive, 1988; The Difference Engine (with Bruce Sterling), 1990; Agrippa: A Book of the Dead (with Dennis Ashbaugh and Keven Begos Jr), 1992; Virtual Light, 1993; Pattern Recognition, 2002. Other: Dream Jumbo (performance art text), 1989; Johnny Mnemonic (screenplay), 1995. Contributions: anthologies and journals. *Honours:* Ditmar Award, Australian National Science Fiction Foundation, 1984; Hugo Award, World Science Fiction Society, 1984; Nebula Award, SFWA, 1984; Porgie Award, West Coast Review of Books, 1984.

GIDDENS, Baron (Life Peer), cr. 2004; **Anthony Giddens,** PhD; British sociologist; *Chairman and Director, Polity Press Limited*; b. 18 Jan. 1938; m. Jane Ellwood 1963; two d. *Education:* Minchenden School, Southgate, Univ. of Hull, LSE, Univ. of Cambridge. *Career:* Lecturer in Sociology, Univ. of Leicester 1961–70; Visiting Asst Prof., Simon Fraser Univ., Vancouver 1967–68, Univ. of Calif., LA 1968–69; Lecturer in Sociology and Fellow King's Coll., Cambridge 1970–84, Reader in Sociology 1984–86, Prof. of Sociology 1986–96; Dir LSE 1997–2003; Chair. and Dir Polity Press Ltd 1985–; Dir Blackwell-Polity Ltd 1985–; Chair. and Dir Centre for Social Research 1989–; BBC Reith Lecturer 1999; numerous visiting professorships; Founder of 'The Third Way'; Hon. Fellow LSE 2004; mem. Russian Acad. of Sciences. *Publications:* Capitalism and Modern Social Theory 1971, Politics and

Sociology in the Thought of Max Weber 1972, Emile Durkheim: selected writings (ed. and trans.) 1972, The Class Structure of the Advanced Societies 1973, New Rules of Sociological Method 1976, Positivism and Sociology (ed.) 1973, Elites and Power in British Society (with P. H. Stanworth) 1974, Studies in Social and Political Theory 1977, Emile Durkheim 1978, Central Problems in Social Theory 1979, A Contemporary Critique of Historical Materialism 1981, Sociology: a brief but critical introduction 1982, Classes, Conflict and Power (with D. Held) 1982, Classes and the Division of Labour (with G. G. N. Mackenzie) 1982, Profiles and Critiques in Social Theory 1983, The Constitution of Society: outline of the theory of structuration 1984, The Nation-State and Violence 1985, Durkheim on Politics and the State 1986, Social Theory and Modern Sociology 1987, Social Theory Today (with Jon Turner) 1988, Sociology 1988, The Consequences of Modernity 1990, Modernity and Self-Identity 1991, Human Societies 1992, The Transformation of Intimacy 1992, Beyond Left and Right 1994, Reflexive Modernisation (with Ulrich Beck and Scott Lash) 1994, Politics, Sociology and Social Theory 1995, In Defence of Sociology 1996, Conversations with Anthony Giddens: making sense of modernity (with Christopher Pierson) 1998, The Third Way: the renewal of social democracy 1998, Runaway World: how globalisation is reshaping our lives 1999, The Third Way and its Critics 2000, On the Edge: living with global capitalism (ed., with Will Hutton) 2000, The Global Third Way Debate 2001, The Progressive Manifesto 2003; contrib. articles, review articles and book reviews to professional journals and newspapers. *Honours:* Nat. Order of the Southern Cross (Brazil), Grand Cross, Order of the Infante Dom Henrique (Portugal); Hon. DLitt (Salford), (Hull), (Open Univ.), (South Bank); Dr hc (Vesalius Coll., Vrije Univ. Brussels); Prince of Asturias Award (Spain) 2002. *Address:* Polity Press, 65 Bridge Street, Cambridge CB2 1UR, England (office).

GIESBERT, Franz-Olivier; French journalist and writer; *Editor, Le Point;* b. 18 Jan. 1949, Wilmington, Del., USA; s. of Frederick Giesbert and Marie Allain; m. 1st Christine Fontaine (divorced); two s. one d.; m. 2nd Natalie Freund 2000; one s., one d. *Education:* Centre de Formation des Journalistes. *Career:* journalist at Le Nouvel Observateur 1971, Sr Corresp. in Washington 1980, Political Ed. 1981, Ed.-in-Chief 1985–88; Ed.-in-Chief Le Figaro 1988–2000, Figaro Magazine 1997–2000, mem. Editorial Bd Le Figaro 1993–2000, Figaro Magazine 1997–2000; Ed. Le Point 2000–; Dir/presenter 'le Gai savoir' TV programme, Paris Première cable channel 1997–2001, Dir Culture et Dépendances France 3 TV channel 2001–; mem. jury Prix Théophraste Renaudot 1998–, Prix Louis Hachette, Prix Aujourd'hui; mem. Conseil Admin Musée du Louvre Paris 2000. *Publications:* François Mitterrand ou la tentation de l'Histoire (essay) 1977, Monsieur Adrien (novel) 1982, Jacques Chirac (biog.) 1987, Le Président 1990, L'Affreux (Grand Prix du Roman de l' Acad. Française) 1992, La Fin d'une Époque 1993, La Souille (William the Conqueror and Interallie Prize), Le Vieil homme et la Mort 1996, François Mitterrand, une vie 1996, Le Sieur Dieu (Prix Jean d'Heurs de Nice Baie des Anges) 1998, Mort d'un berger 2002, L'Abatteur 2003, La Tragédie du président: scènes de la vie politique 2006. *Honours:* Aujourd'hui Best Essay Prize 1975, Prix Gutenberg 1987, Prix Pierre de Monaco 1997, Prix Richelieu 1999, Prix Itheme for Best Talk Show 1999. *Address:* Le Point, 74 avenue du Maine, 75682 Paris Cedex, France. *Telephone:* 1-44-10-10-10 (office). *Fax:* 1-44-10-12-49 (office). *E-mail:* fogiesbert@lepoint.tm.fr (office).

GIFFORD, Barry Colby; American writer; b. 18 Oct. 1946, Chicago, IL; m. Mary Lou Nelson 1970; one s. one d. *Education:* Univ. of Missouri, Univ. of Cambridge. *Publications:* Jack's Book (co-author, biog.) 1978, Port Tropique 1980, Landscape with Traveler 1980, The Neighborhood of Baseball 1981, The Devil Thumbs a Ride 1988, Ghosts No Horse Can Carry 1989, Wild at Heart 1990, Sailor's Holiday 1991, New Mysteries of Paris 1991, A Good Man to Know 1992, Night People 1992, Arise and Walk 1994, Hotel Room Trilogy 1995, Baby Cat-Face 1995, The Phantom Father 1997, Lost Highway (co-author) 1997, Flaubert at Key West 1997, Perdita Durango 1997, The Sinaloa Story 1998, Bordertown 1998, The Wild Life of Sailor & Lula 1998, My Last Martini 1999, Southern Nights 1999, Wyoming 2000, Replies to Wang Wei 2001, American Falls 2002, The Rooster Trapped in the Reptile Room: A Barry Gifford Reader 2003, Brando Rides Alone 2003, Do the Blind Dream? 2004, The Stars Above Veracruz 2006; contrib. to Punch, Esquire, Rolling Stone. *Honours:* American Library Asscn Notable Book Awards 1978, 1988, NEA Fellowship 1982, Maxwell Perkins Award 1983, PEN Syndicated Fiction Award 1987, Premio Brancati, Italy 1993, Christopher Isherwood Foundation Prize for Fiction 2006. *Literary Agent:* Curtis Brown Ltd, 10 Astor Place, New York, NY 10003, USA. *Website:* www.barrygifford.com.

GIGGAL, Kenneth, (Henry Marlin, Angus Ross); British writer; b. 19 March 1927, Dewsbury, Yorkshire, England. *Career:* mem. Savage Club, Arms and Armour Society. *Publications:* The Manchester Thing, 1970; The Huddersfield Job, 1971; The London Assignment, 1972; The Dunfermline Affair, 1973; The Bradford Business, 1974; The Amsterdam Diversion, 1974; The Leeds Fiasco, 1975; The Edinburgh Exercise, 1975; The Ampurias Exchange, 1976; The Aberdeen Conundrum, 1977; The Congleton Lark, 1979; The Hamburg Switch, 1980; A Bad April, 1980; The Menwith Tangle, 1982; The Darlington Jaunt, 1983; The Luxembourg Run, 1985; Doom Indigo, 1986; The Tyneside Ultimatum, 1988; Classic Sailing Ships, 1988; The Greenham Plot, 1989; The Leipzig Manuscript, 1990; The Last One, 1992; John Worsley's War, 1992. Other: Television scripts and films. Contributions: many magazines, national and international. *Honours:* Truth Prize for Fiction 1954.

GIGUERE, Diane Liliane; Canadian writer; b. 6 Dec. 1937, Montréal, QC. *Education:* Collège Marie de France, Conservatory of Dramatic Arts. *Career:* mem. Writers' Union, Québec, Asscn of French-Speaking Writers at Home and Overseas. *Publications:* Le Temps des Jeux 1961, L'Eau est Profonde 1965, Dans les Ailes du vent 1976, L'Abandon 1993, Un Dieu fantôme 2001, Chronique d'un temps Fixe 2005. *Honours:* Prix du Cercle du Livre de France 1961, Guggenheim Fellowship 1969, France Québec Prize 1977. *Address:* 60 rue William Paul 304, Ile des Soeurs, QC H3E 1N5, Canada. *E-mail:* cali@info.internet.net (home).

GIKANDI, Simon; Ugandan writer. *Career:* Robert Haydon Prof. of English Language and Literature, Univ. of Michigan, USA. *Publications include:* non-fiction: Reading the African Novel 1987, Reading Chinua Achebe: Language and Ideology in Fiction 1991, Writing in Limbo: Modernism and Caribbean Literature 1992, Maps of Englishness: Writing Identity in the Culture of Colonialism 1997, Cambridge Studies in African and Caribbean Literature: Ngugi wa Thiong'o 2000, The Cambridge History of African and Caribbean Literature (with F. Abiola Irele) 2004; editor: Uganda's Katakiro in England (Exploring Travel) by Ham Mukasa 1998, Death and the King's Horsemen by Wole Soyinka 2002, Encyclopedia of African Literature 2002. *Honours:* Fellow of John Simon Guggenheim Memorial Foundation. *Literary Agent:* c/o Cambridge University Press, The Edinburgh Building, Shaftesbury Road, Cambridge, CB2 2RU, England. *Telephone:* (1223) 312393. *Fax:* (1223) 315052. *Website:* www.cup.cam.ac.uk.

GIL, David Georg, BA, MSW, DSW; American academic and writer; *Professor of Social Policy, Brandeis University;* b. (Georg Engel), 16 March 1924, Vienna, Austria; s. of Oscar Engel and Helene Engel Weiss; m. Eva Breslauer 1947; two s. *Education:* certificate in psychotherapy with children, Israeli Soc. for Child Psychiatry, diploma in social work, School of Social Work, Hebrew Univ., Jerusalem, Israel and Univ. of Pennsylvania. *Career:* agricultural work in Sweden and Palestine 1939–43; social work practice and research in Palestine, Israel and USA 1943–64; Prof. of Social Policy in Heller School for Social Policy and Management, Brandeis Univ. 1964–; mem. Nat. Asscn of Social Workers, American Orthopsychiatric Asscn, Asscn of Humanist Sociology. *Publications:* Violence Against Children 1970, Unravelling Social Policy 1973, The Challenge of Social Equality 1976, Beyond the Jungle 1979, Child Abuse and Violence (ed.) 1979, Toward Social and Economic Justice (co-ed. with Eva Gil) 1985, The Future of Work (co-ed. with Eva Gil) 1985, Confronting Injustice and Oppression 1998; contrib. of more than 50 articles to professional journals, book chapters, book reviews. *Honours:* Brandeis Univ. Heller School Leadership in Human Services 1999, Nat. Asscn of Social Workers Massachusetts Social Worker of the Year 2000, Council on Social Work Educ. Presidential Award 2006. *Address:* Heller School for Social Policy and Management, Brandeis University, Waltham, MA 02454-9110, USA (office). *Telephone:* (781) 736-3827 (office). *Fax:* (781) 736-3306 (office). *E-mail:* gil@brandeis.edu (office).

GILB, Dagoberto, BA, MA; American writer; b. 31 July 1950, Los Angeles, CA; m. Rebeca Santos 1978; two s. *Education:* Univ. of California at Santa Barbara. *Career:* fmr construction worker, carpenter; visiting writer, Univ. of Texas 1988–89, Univ. of Arizona 1992–93, Univ. of Wyoming 1994; teacher, MFA programme at Southwest Texas State Univ., San Marcos, TX; mem. Texas Inst. of Letters, PEN. *Publications:* Winners on the Pass Line 1985, The Magic of Blood (PEN/Hemingway Award 1994) 1993, The Last Known Residence of Mickey Acuña 1994, Woodcuts of Women (short stories) 2001, Gritos: Essays 2003; contrib. essays and fiction to periodicals, including The New Yorker, Harper's, The Best American Essays, Threepenny Review. *Honours:* James D. Phelan Award, Dobie Paisano Fellowship, Nat. Endowment for the Arts Fellowship 1992, Whiting Writers' Award 1993, Texas Inst. of Letters Best Book of Fiction Award 1993, Ernest Hemingway Foundation Award 1994, Guggenheim Fellowship 1995. *Address:* c/o Department of English, Southwest Texas State University, 601 University Drive, San Marcos, TX 78666, USA.

GILBERT, Bentley Brinkerhoff, AB, MA, PhD, FRHistS; American writer; b. 5 April 1924, Mansfield, OH. *Education:* Miami Univ., Oxford, OH, Univ. of Cincinnati and Univ. of Wisconsin. *Career:* faculty mem., Univ. of Cincinnati, Colorado Coll. 1955–67; faculty mem., Univ. of Illinois at Chicago 1967–70, Prof. of History 1967–; Ed., Journal of British Studies 1978–83; mem. North American Conference on British Studies. *Publications:* The Evolution of National Insurance in Great Britain: The Origins of the Welfare State 1966, Britain Since 1918 1967, British Social Policy 1970, David Lloyd George: A Political Life, Vol. I The Architect of Change 1863–1912 1987, Vol. II The Organiser of Victory 1912–1916 1992, Britain 1914–1945: The Aftermath of Power 1996; contrib. to reference works and professional journals. *Honours:* Guggenheim Fellowship 1973–74, Soc. of Midland Authors Biography Prize 1993, various grants. *Address:* c/o Department of History, University of Illinois at Chicago, Chicago, IL 60607; 681 South Homer Road, Mansfield, OH 44906-3363, USA (home).

GILBERT, Daniel T., BA, PhD; American psychologist and writer; *Harvard College Professor, Harvard University;* b. 1957. *Education:* Univ. of Colorado at Denver, Princeton Univ. *Career:* Asst Prof., Univ. of Texas at Austin 1985–90, Assoc. Prof. 1990–95, Prof. 1995–96; Prof., Harvard Univ. 1996–2005, Harvard Coll. Prof. 2005–(10); gave Edward E. Jones Memorial Lectures, Princeton Univ. 2003; Ford Visiting Prof. of Behavioral Science, Univ. of Chicago School of Business 2003; gave Forry and Micken Lecture,

Amherst Coll. 2005; Nat. Science Foundation Predoctoral Fellow 1981–84; Princeton Univ. Porter Ogden Jacobus Fellowship 1984–85; Univ. of Texas at Austin Raymond Dickson Centennial Endowed Teaching Fellowship 1987–88; Fellow Center for Advanced Study in the Behavioral Sciences 1991–92, Soc. for Personality and Social Psychology 1996, American Psychological Asscn 1997, Soc. of Experimental Social Psychology 1993, American Philosophical Soc. 1999, American Psychological Soc. 2003; John Simon Guggenheim Memorial Foundation Fellowship 1999. *Publications include:* The Handbook of Social Psychology (co-ed., fourth edition) 1998, The Selected Works of Edward E. Jones (ed.) 2003, Stumbling on Happiness (Royal Society Prize for Science Books 2007) 2006; contrib. science fiction stories to magazines; numerous articles to scientific journals. *Honours:* Univ. of Colorado at Denver Outstanding Graduate Award 1981, Univ. of Colorado at Denver Nell G. Fahrion Award for Excellence in Psychology 1981, Princeton Univ. Merit Prizes 1981, 1982, 1983, Univ. of Texas at Austin Pres.'s Assocs Teaching Excellence Award 1990–91, Nat. Inst. of Mental Health Research Scientist Development Award 1991–96, American Psychological Asscn Distinguished Scientific Award for an Early Career Contribution to Psychology 1992, James McKeen Cattell Award 1999, Harvard Univ. Phi Beta Kappa Teaching Prize 1999. *Address:* Department of Psychology, Harvard University, Cambridge, MA 02138, USA (office). *Telephone:* (617) 495-3892 (office). *E-mail:* gilbert@wjh.harvard.edu (office). *Website:* www.wjh.harvard.edu/~dtg/gilbert.htm (office).

GILBERT, David, MA; British retail executive; *Managing Director, Waterstone's Booksellers Ltd;* b. 1954; m.; two c. *Education:* Univ. of E Anglia, Sussex Univ. *Career:* Product Man./Buyer Boots 1975–81; Product Man., Marketing Man. Dixons 1981–87, Marketing Dir 1987–91, Group Marketing Dir Dixons and Currys 1991–93, Group Operations Dir 1993–95, Man. Dir Currys 1995–2000, apptd to Group Bd Dixons PLC 1997, COO 2000–04; Man. Dir Waterstone's Booksellers 2004–. *Address:* Waterstone's Booksellers Ltd, Capital Court, Capital Interchange Way, Brentford, Middlesex TW8 0EX, England.

GILBERT, Harriett Sarah, Dip; British writer; b. 25 Aug. 1948, London, England. *Education:* Rose Bruford College of Speech and Drama. *Career:* Co-Books Ed., City Limits magazine, 1981–83; Deputy Literary Ed., 1983–86, Literary Ed., 1986–88, New Statesman; Presenter, Meridian Books Programme, BBC World Service Radio, 1991–; Lecturer in Journalism, City University, London, 1992–; mem. Writers Guild of Great Britain. *Publications:* I Know Where I've Been, 1972; Hotels with Empty Rooms, 1973; An Offence Against the Persons, 1974; Tide Race, 1977; Running Away, 1979; The Riding Mistress, 1983; A Women's History of Sex, 1987; The Sexual Imagination (ed.), 1993. Contributions: Time Out; City Limits; New Statesman; Guardian; BBC; Australian Broadcasting Corporation; Washington Post; BBC World Service Radio.

GILBERT, Jack, BA, MA; American poet and writer; b. 17 Feb. 1925, Pittsburgh, PA. *Education:* University of Pittsburgh, San Francisco State University. *Career:* University of California at Berkeley, 1958–59, San Francisco State University, 1962–63, 1965–67, 1971, Syracuse University, 1982–83, University of San Francisco, 1985; Prof., Kyoto University, Tokyo, 1974–75; Chair, Creative Writing, University of Alabama, Tuscaloosa, 1986. *Publications:* Poetry: Views of Jeopardy, 1962; Monolithos, 1982; The Great Fires: Poems, 1982–1992, 1994. Contributions: various reviews, journals, and periodicals. *Honours:* Yale Younger Poet Award, 1962; Guggenheim Fellowship, 1964; National Endowment for the Arts Award, 1974; First Prize, American Poetry Review, 1983; Stanley Kunitz Prize, 1983; Lannan Award, 1995.

GILBERT, John Raphael, BA; British writer; b. 8 April 1926, London, England; m.; three s. *Education:* Columbia Univ., King's Coll., London. *Publications:* Modern World Book of Animals, 1947; Cats, Cats, Cats, 1961; Famous Jewish Lives, 1970; Myths of Ancient Rome, 1970; Pirates and Buccaneers, 1971; Highwaymen and Outlaws, 1971; Charting the Vast Pacific, 1971; National Costumes of the World, 1972; World of Wildlife, 1972–74; Miracles of Nature, 1975; Knights of the Crusades, 1978; Vikings, 1978; Prehistoric Man, 1978; Leonardo da Vinci, 1978; La Scala, 1979; Dinosaurs Discovered, 1980; Macdonald Guide to Trees, 1983; Macdonald Encyclopedia of House Plants, 1986; Theory and Use of Colour, 1986; Macdonald Encyclopedia of Roses, 1987; Gardens of Britain, 1987; Macdonald Encyclopedia of Butterflies and Moths, 1988; Trekking in the USA, 1989; Macdonald Encyclopedia of Orchids, 1989; Macdonald Encyclopedia of Bulbs, 1989; Trekking in Europe, 1990; Macdonald Encyclopedia of Herbs and Spices, 1990; Macdonald Encyclopedia of Bonsai, 1990; Macdonald Encyclopedia of Amphibians and Reptiles, 1990; Macdonald Encyclopedia of Saltwater Fishes, 1992; Decorating Chinese Porcelain, 1994.

GILBERT, Sir Martin John, Kt, CBE, MA, DLitt, FRSL; British historian and academic; *Fellow, Merton College, Oxford;* b. 25 Oct. 1936, s. of Peter and Miriam Gilbert; m. 1st Helen Robinson 1963; one d.; m. 2nd Susan Sacher; two s.; m. 3rd Esther Poznansky. *Education:* Highgate School and Magdalen Coll., Oxford. *Career:* Sr Research Fellow, St Antony's Coll., Oxford 1960–62, Fellow, Merton Coll., Oxford 1962–; Visiting Prof. Univ. of S Carolina 1965, Tel Aviv 1979, Hebrew Univ. of Jerusalem 1980–; official biographer of Sir Winston Churchill 1968–; Gov., Hebrew Univ. of Jerusalem 1978–; Non-Governmental Rep. UN Commn. on Human Rights, Geneva 1987, 1988; mem. Prime Minister's del. to Israel, Gaza and Jordan 1995, to USA 1995; has lectured on historical subjects throughout Europe and USA; adviser to BBC and ITV for various documentaries; script designer and co-author, Genocide (Acad. Award for best documentary feature film) 1981; presenter History Channel 1996–; Recent History Corresp. Sunday Times 1967. *Publications:* The Appeasers (with R. Gott) 1963, Britain and Germany between the Wars 1964, The European Powers 1900–1945 1965, Plough My Own Furrow: The Life of Lord Allen of Hurtwood 1965, Servant of India: A Study of Imperial Rule 1905–1910 1966, The Roots of Appeasement 1966, Recent History Atlas 1860–1960 1966, Winston Churchill 1966, British History Atlas 1968, American History Atlas 1968, Jewish History Atlas 1969, First World War Atlas 1970, Winston S. Churchill, Vol. III, 1914–16 1971, companion vol. 1973, Russian History Atlas 1972, Sir Horace Rumbold: Portrait of a Diplomat 1973, Churchill: a photographic portrait 1974, The Arab-Israeli Conflict: its history in maps 1974, Winston S. Churchill, Vol. IV, 1917–22 1975, companion vol. 1977, The Jews in Arab Lands: their history in maps 1975, Winston S. Churchill, Vol. V, 1922–39, 1976, companion Vols 1980, 1981, 1982, The Jews of Russia: Illustrated History Atlas 1976, Jerusalem Illustrated History Atlas 1977, Exile and Return: The Emergence of Jewish Statehood 1978, Children's Illustrated Bible Atlas 1979, Final Journey, the Fate of the Jews of Nazi Europe 1979, Auschwitz and the Allies 1981, Atlas of the Holocaust 1982, Winston S. Churchill, Vol. VI, 1939–41 1983, The Jews of Hope: A Study of the Crisis of Soviet Jewry 1984, Jerusalem: Rebirth of a City 1985, Shcharansky: Hero of our Time 1986, Winston S. Churchill, Vol. VII, 1941–45 1986, The Holocaust, The Jewish Tragedy 1986, Winston Churchill, Vol. VIII 1945–65 1988, Second World War 1989, Churchill, A Life 1991, The Churchill War Papers: At the Admiralty (ed.), Atlas of British Charities 1993, In Search of Churchill: A Historian's Journey 1994, The First World War: A Complete History 1994, The Churchill War Papers: 'Never Surrender' (ed.) 1995, The Day the War Ended 1995, Jerusalem in the 20th Century 1996, The Boys, Triumph over Adversity 1996, A History of the World in the Twentieth Century (Vol. I 1900–1933) 1997, (Vol. II 1933–1951) 1998, (Vol. III 1952–1999) 1999, Holocaust Journey: Travelling in Search of the Past 1997, Israel, A History 1998, Winston Churchill and Emery Reeves; Correspondence 1998, Never Again: A History of the Holocaust 1999, The Jewish Century 2001, History of the Twentieth Century 2001, The Churchill War Papers: '1941, the Ever-Widening War' (ed.) 2001, Letters to Auntie Fori: 5,000 Years of Jewish History and Faith 2002, The Righteous: the Unsung Heroes of the Holocaust 2002, D-Day 2004, Churchill at War: His "Finest Hour" in Photographs, Churchill and America 2005, Kristallnacht: Prelude to Destruction 2006, Somme: The Heroism and Horror of War 2006, Will of the People: Churchill and Parliamentary Democracy 2006, Churchill and the Jews 2007. *Honours:* Hon. Fellow Univ. of Wales, Lampeter 1997; Hon. DLitt (Westminster Coll., Fulton, Mo.) 1981. *Address:* Merton College, Oxford OX1 4JD, England.

GILBERT, Robert Andrew, BA; British antiquarian bookseller, editor and writer; b. 6 Oct. 1942, Bristol, England; m. Patricia Kathleen Linnell 1970; three s. two d. *Education:* Univ. of Bristol. *Career:* Ed. Ars Quatuor Coronatorum 1994–2001; mem. Soc. of Authors. *Publications:* The Golden Dawn: Twilight of the Magicians 1983, A. E. Waite: A Bibliography 1983, The Golden Dawn Companion 1986, A. E. Waite: Magician of Many Parts 1987, The Treasure of Montsegur (with W. N. Birks) 1987, Elements of Mysticism 1991, World Freemasonry: An Illustrated History 1992, Freemasonry: A Celebration of the Craft (with J. M. Hamill) 1992, Casting the First Stone 1993, The Golden Dawn Scrapbook 1997; editor: The Oxford Book of English Ghost Stories (with M. A. Cox) 1986, Victorian Ghost Stories: An Oxford Anthology (with M. A. Cox) 1991, The Rise of Victorian Spiritualism (series ed.) 2000, The House of the Hidden Light 2003; contrib. to Ars Quatuor Coronatorum, Avallaunius, Christian Parapsychologist, Dictionary of Gnosis and Western Esotericism, Gnosis, Hermetic Journal, Cauda Pavonis, Yeats Annual, Dictionary of National Biography, Dictionary of Nineteenth Century British Scientists. *Address:* 215 Clevedon Road, Tickenham, Clevedon, BS21 6RX, England. *E-mail:* sacregis42@hotmail.com.

GILBERT, Virginia, BA, MFA, PhD; American academic, poet, writer and photographer; b. 19 Dec. 1946, Elgin, IL. *Education:* Iowa Wesleyan Coll., Univ. of Iowa, Univ. of Nebraska-Lincoln. *Career:* Peace Corps, Repub. of Korea 1971–73; Admin., the Writers' Community, Acad. of American Poets 1976; ESL instructor, Iran 1976–79; Instructor, Coll. of Lake County, IL 1979; teaching asst, Univ. of Nebraska 1984–87; Asst Prof. of English and Creative Writing, Alabama A & M Univ. 1980–92, Assoc. Prof. 1992–2001, Prof. 2001–07 (retd); mem. Associated Writing Programs, MLA, Peace Corps Volunteer Asscn, Peace Corps Volunteer Readers and Writers Asscn, Poetry Soc. of America, Poets and Writers. *Photography:* photographs in numerous exhbns. *Publications:* To Keep at Bay the Hounds 1985, The Earth Above 1993, That Other Brightness 1996, Greatest Hits 2004; contrib. to anthologies, including Ordinary and Sacred as Blood, Claiming the Spirit Within: A Source Book of Women's Poetry; contrib. to journals, reviews and quarterlies. *Honours:* NEA Fellowship 1976–77, Best Pictures of the Year Huntsville Photographic Soc. 1980–81, 1984, Special Merit Award Kodak Int. Newspaper Snapshot Awards 1986, Best Nebraska Entrant Seventh Annual Cornhusker Int. Exhbn of Photography 1987, second prize Hackney Literary Awards 1990, first place Sakura Festival Haiku Contest 1992, Fulbright Fellow to China 1992, Lecturer for the Alabama Humanities Foundation's Speaker's Bureau 1997–98, first place Alabama State Poetry Soc. Poetry Slam 1998, Alabama Poet of the Year 2001. *Telephone:* (256) 464-9130 (home). *E-mail:* VGpoet@aol.com (home).

GILCHRIST, Ellen Louise, BA, PhD; American writer and poet; *Andrew W. Mellon Fellow in the Humanities, Tulane University*; b. 20 Feb. 1935, Vicksburg, MS; d. of William Garth and Aurora Gilchrist; three s. *Education:* Millsaps Coll., MS and Univ. of Arkansas. *Career:* freelance writer and journalist; commentator Nat. Public Radio news, Washington 1984–85; fmr writer-in-residence, MA programme Univ. of Arkansas, Fayetteville; Andrew W. Mellon Fellow in the Humanities, Tulane Univ., New Orleans 2005–; mem. Authors' Guild, Authors' League of America; Nat. Educ. Asscn grant 1979, NEA grant in fiction 1979. *Publications:* The Land Surveyor's Daughter (poems) 1979, In the Land of Dreamy Dreams (short stories) 1981, The Annunciation (novel) 1983, Victory Over Japan: A Book of Stories (American Book Award) 1984, Drunk With Love (short stories) 1986, Riding Out the Tropical Depression (poems) 1986, Falling Through Space: The Journals of Ellen Gilchrist 1987, The Anna Papers (novel) 1988, Light Can be Both Wave and Particle: A Book of Stories 1989, I Cannot Get You Close Enough (three novellas) 1990, Net of Jewels (novel) 1992, Starcarbon: A Meditation on Love (Mississippi Acad. of Arts and Science Fiction Award 1994) 1992, Anabasis: A Journey to the Interior 1994, An Age of Miracles (short stories) 1995, The Courts of Love 1997, Rhoda: A Life in Stories 1995, Sarah Conley 1997, Collected Stories 2001, The Cabal and Other Stories 2002, I, Rhoda Manning, Go Hunting with my Daddy and Other Stories 2002; contrib. to many journals and periodicals. *Honours:* four hon. doctorates; Poetry Award Mississippi Arts Festival 1968, Univ. of Arkansas Poetry Award 1976, New York Quarterly Craft in Poetry Award 1978, Pushcart Prizes 1979–80, 1983, Prairie Schooner Fiction Award 1981, Mississippi Acad. of Arts and Science Fiction Award 1982, 1985, Saxifrage Award 1983, Univ. of Arkansas J. William Fulbright Prize 1985, Mississippi Inst. of Arts and Letters Literary Award 1985, Univ. of N Carolina, Chapel Hill Thomas Wolfe Award 2004. *Address:* 834 Eastwood Drive, Fayetteville, AR 72701, USA.

GILES, Frank Thomas Robertson, MA; British journalist (retd) and writer; b. 31 July 1919, London, England; m. Lady Katharine Sackville 1946; one s. two d. *Education:* Wellington Coll., Brasenose Coll., Oxford. *Career:* Asst Correspondent Paris Bureau, The Times newspaper 1947–50, Chief Correspondent Rome Bureau 1950–53, and Paris Bureau 1953–61, Foreign Ed. 1961–77, Deputy Ed. 1967–81, Ed. 1981–83; Dir, The Times Newspapers 1981–85. *Publications:* A Prince of Journalists: The Life and Times of Henri de Blowitz 1962, Sundry Times (autobiog.) 1986, Forty Years On (ed.) 1990, The Locust Years: History of the Fourth French Republic (Franco-British Soc. Prize) 1991, Corfu: The Garden Isle (ed.) 1994, Napoleon Bonaparte, England's Prisoner 2001; contrib. to books, newspapers and periodicals, including the Dictionary of National Biography. *Address:* 42 Blomfield Road, London, W9 2PF, England.

GILES, Molly; American academic and writer; b. 12 March 1942, California; m. 1st Daniel Giles 1961 (divorced 1974); m. 2nd Richard King 1976 (divorced); three c. *Education:* University of California at Berkeley, 1960–61; BA, 1978, MA, 1980, San Francisco State University. *Career:* Lecturer in Creative Writing, San Francisco State University, 1980–99; Assoc. Prof. of Creative Writing, University of Arkansas, Fayetteville, 1999–. *Publications:* Rough Translations, 1985; Creek Walk and Other Stories, 1996; Iron Shoes, 2000. Contributions: periodicals. *Honours:* Flannery O'Connor Award for Short Fiction, 1986; National Book Critics Circle Citation for Excellence in Book Reviewing, 1991; Small Press Best Fiction/Short Story Award, 1998. *Address:* c/o Department of English, University of Arkansas, Fayetteville, AR 72701, USA.

GILL, Anton; British writer; b. 22 Oct. 1948, Essex, England; m. Nicola Susan Browne 1982. *Education:* Clare College, Cambridge. *Publications:* The Journey Back From Hell; Berlin to Bucharest; City of the Horizon; City of Dreams; A Dance Between Flames; City of the Dead; An Honourable Defeat; The Devil's Mariner, 1997; Peggy Guggenheim: The Life of an Art Addict, 2001; The Great Escape, 2002; The Egyptians: The Kingdom of the Pharaohs Brought to Life, 2003, Empire's Children 2007. *Honours:* H. H. Wingate Award. *Address:* c/o Mark Lucas, L.A.W., Elsinore House, 77 Fulham Road, London, W6 8JA, England.

GILL, David Lawrence William, BA, PGCE; British poet and writer; b. 3 July 1934, Chislehurst, Kent; m. Irene Henry 1958; two s. one d. *Education:* Univ. Coll., London, Univ. of Birmingham, London External. *Career:* teacher, Bedales 1960–62, Nyakasura School, Uganda 1962–64, Magdalene Coll. School, Oxford 1965–71; Lecturer, Newland Park Coll. of Educ., later incorporated into Bucks Coll. of Higher Educ. 1971–79, Sr Lecturer 1979–87; EFL in Lisbon 1987–88, in Tokyo 1988–89; own micro-school with Irene Gill: Oxford Residential English 1992–2004. *Publications:* Men Without Evenings 1966, The Pagoda and Other Poems 1969, In the Eye of the Storm 1975, The Upkeep of the Castle 1978, Karel Klimsa (by Ondra Lysohorsky, trans.) 1984, One Potato, Two Potato (with Dorothy Clancy) 1985, Legends, Please 1986, The White Raven 1989, The New Hesperides 1991, The Cemetery of Pleasures 2003, A Little Collateral Damage 2003, Carp in the Wind 2004; contrib. to many journals, reviews and magazines. *Address:* 38 Yarnells Hill, Botley, Oxford, OX2 9BE, England. *Telephone:* (1865) 242719 (home). *E-mail:* irenedavidgill@btinternet.com (home).

GILL, Stephen Matthew, BA, MA; British poet, writer and editor; b. 25 June 1932, Sialkot, Pakistan; m. Sarala Gill 1970, one s. two d. *Education:* Punjab Univ., Meerut Coll., Agra Univ., India Univ. of Ottawa, Canada, Univ. of Oxford. *Career:* Ed. Canadian World Federalist 1971–73, 1977–79, Writer's Lifeline 1982–; Pres. Vesta Publications Ltd 1974–90; mem. Christian Cultural Asscn of South Asians (Vice-Pres.), International Acad. of Poets (Fellow), PEN International, World Acad. of Arts and Culture, World Federalists of Canada, Amnesty International, Writers Union of Canada. *Publications:* Poetry: Reflections and Wounds 1978, Moans and Waves 1989, The Dove of Peace 1989, The Flowers of Thirst 1991, Songs for Harmony 1992, Flashes 1994, Aman Di Ghuggi 1994, Divergent Shades 1995, Shrine 1999; fiction: Life's Vagaries (short stories) 1974, Why 1976, The Loyalist City 1979, Immigrants 1982; non-fiction: Six Symbolist Plays of Yeats 1974, Discovery of Bangladesh 1975, Scientific Romances of H. G. Wells 1975, English Grammar for Beginners 1977, Political Convictions of G. B. Shaw 1980, Sketches of India 1980; editor: various anthologies; contrib. to more than 250 publs. *Honours:* Hon. DLitt (World Univ.) 1986; World Acad. of Arts and Culture 1990, Int. Eminent Poet, Int. Poets Acad., Chennai 1991, Pegasus Int. Poetry for Peace Award, Poetry in the Arts, Austin, Tex., USA 1991, Laureate Man of Letters, United Poets Laureate International 1992, Poet of Peace Award, Pakistan Asscn, Orleans, Ont. 1995, Mawaheb Culture Friendship Medal, Mawaheb Magazine 1997, Sahir Award of Honour 1999. *Address:* PO Box 32, Cornwall, ON K6H 5R9, Canada. *E-mail:* stefgill@hotmail.com.

GILLIES, Valerie, MA, MLitt; British poet and writer; *The Edinburgh Makar*; b. 4 June 1948, Edmonton, AB, Canada; m. William Gillies 1972; one s. two d. *Education:* Univ. of Edinburgh, Univ. of Mysore, India. *Career:* writer-in-residence, Duncan of Jordanstone Coll. of Art, Dundee 1988–90, Univ. of Edinburgh 1995–98; Sr Hosp. Arts Worker, Artlink 1994–2002; Creative Writing Fellow, Univ. of Edinburgh 2002–05; The Edinburgh Makar (poet laureate) 2005–(08); Fellow Soc. of Authors, Scotland. *Achievements:* landmark poem inscriptions for sculptures, Source of the Tweed 1998, Galloway Forest Park 2001, Coldstream 2001, Leaderfoot 2001, city of Edinburgh 2007. *Publications:* Trio: New Poets from Edinburgh 1971, Each Bright Eye: Selected Poems 1977, Bed of Stone 1984, Leopardi: A Scottish Quair 1987, Tweed Journey 1989, The Chanter's Tune 1990, The Jordanstone Folio 1990, The Ringing Rock 1995, Men and Beasts 2000, The Lightning Tree 2002; contributions: Radio, television, reviews, and journals. *Honours:* Scottish Arts Council Bursary 1976, and Book Award 1996, Eric Gregory Award 1976, Creative Scotland Award 2005. *Address:* 67 Braid Avenue, Edinburgh, EH10 6ED, Scotland (home). *Telephone:* (131) 447-2876 (home). *E-mail:* valeriegillies@hotmail.com (home).

GILLON, Adam, MA, PhD; American academic, writer, film-maker and poet; b. 17 July 1921, Poland; m. Isabella Zamojre 1946, one s. (deceased) one d. *Education:* Hebrew Univ. of Jerusalem, Columbia Univ., New York. *Career:* Prof. of English, Acadia Univ., NS 1957–62, Univ. of Haifa, 1979–84; Prof. of English and Comparative Literature, State Univ. of New York at New Paltz 1962–81, Prof. Emeritus 1981–; Founder and Pres. Joseph Conrad Soc. of America; Founding Ed. Joseph Conrad Today; mem. Haiku Soc. of America, MLA, Polish Inst. of Arts and Sciences. *Film:* The Bet – A Film by Adam Gillon (writer, dir and producer) 1993–96. *Publications:* poetry: Selected Poems and Translations 1962, In the Manner of Haiku: Seven Aspects of Man 1967, Daily New and Old: Poems in the Manner of Haiku 1971, Strange Mutations in the Manner of Haiku 1973, Summer Morn... Winter Weather: Poems 'Twixt Haiku and Senryu 1975, The Withered Leaf: A Medley of Haiku and Senryu 1982; fiction: A Cup of Fury 1962, Jared 1986; non-fiction: The Eternal Solitary: A Study of Joseph Conrad 1960, Joseph Conrad: Commemorative Essays (ed.) 1975, Conrad and Shakespeare and Other Essays 1976, Joseph Conrad 1982, Joseph Conrad: Comparative Essays 1994; other: trans., radio plays, and screenplays; contribs to journals, reviews, and periodicals. *Honours:* Alfred Jurzykowski Foundation Award 1967, Joseph Fels Foundation Award 1970, Nat. Endowment for the Humanities Grant 1985, Gold Award, Worldfest Int. Film Festival 1993, Adam Gillon Book Award for Conrad Criticism, Joseph Conrad Soc. of America 2004. *Address:* Lake Illyria, 490 Route 299 W, New Paltz, NY 12561, USA (home). *Telephone:* (845) 255-0616 (home). *E-mail:* conradfilm@aol.com (home).

GILMAN (BUTTERS), Dorothy; American author and children's writer; b. 25 June 1923, New Brunswick, NJ; m. Edgar A. Butters 1945 (divorced) 1965, two s. *Education:* Pennsylvania Acad. of Fine Arts, University of Pennsylvania and Art Students League. *Career:* mem. Authors' Guild. *Publications:* fiction: The Unexpected Mrs Pollifax, 1966, in the UK as Mrs Pollifax, Spy, 1971; Uncertain Voyage, 1967; The Amazing Mrs Pollifax, 1970; The Elusive Mrs Pollifax, 1971; A Palm for Mrs Pollifax, 1973; A Nun in the Closet, 1975, in the UK as A Nun in the Cupboard, 1976; The Clairvoyant Countess, 1975; Mrs Pollifax on Safari, 1977; A New Kind of Country, 1978; The Tightrope Walker, 1979; Mrs Pollifax on the China Station, 1983; The Maze in the Heart of the Castle, 1983; Mrs Pollifax and the Hong Kong Buddha, 1985; Mrs Pollifax and the Golden Triangle, 1988; Incident at Badamya, 1989; Mrs Pollifax and the Whirling Dervish, 1990; Mrs Pollifax and the Second Thief, 1993; Mrs Pollifax Pursued, 1995. Children's Fiction: Enchanted Caravan, 1949; Carnival Gypsy, 1950; Ragamuffin Alley, 1951; The Calico Year, 1953; Four-Party Line, 1954; Papa Dolphin's Table, 1955; Girl in Buckskin, 1956; Heartbreak Street, 1958; Witch's Silver, 1959; Masquerade, 1961; Ten Leagues to Boston Town, 1962; The Bells of Freedom, 1963. Contributions: Magazines. *Honours:* Catholic Book Award 1975.

GILMAN, George G. (see Harknett, Terry)

GILMAN, Rebecca; American playwright; b. Trussville, AL. *Plays:* My Sin and Nothing More 1997, The Land of Little Horses 1998, The Glory of Living

1999, Spinning into Butter 2000, Boy Gets Girl 2000, Blue Surge 2002, The Sweetest Swing in Baseball 2004. *Honours:* London Evening Standard Award for Most Promising Playwright 1999, American Theatre Critics' Asscn Osborn Award. *Address:* c/o Faber and Faber Ltd, 3 Queen Square, London, WC1N 3AU, England. *Telephone:* (20) 7465-0045. *Fax:* (20) 7465-0034. *Website:* www.faber.co.uk.

GILMAN, Sander Lawrence, BA, PhD; American academic and writer; b. 21 Feb. 1944, Buffalo, NY; m. Marina von Eckardt 1969. *Education:* Tulane University, University of Munich, Free University of Berlin. *Career:* Prof. of German Language and Literature; Prof. of Psychiatry. *Publications:* Nietzchean Parody, 1976; The Face of Madness: Hugh W. Diamond and the Origin of Psychiatric Photography, 1976; Bertold Brecht's Berlin, 1976; Seeing the Insane, 1981; Sexuality: An Illustrated History, 1989; The Jew's Body, 1991; Freud, Race and Gender, 1993; The Case of Sigmund Freud: Medicine and Identity at Fin de Siècle, 1994; Re-emerging Jewish Culture in Today's Germany, 1994; Franz Kafka, The Jewish Patient, 1995; Jews in Today's German Culture, 1995; Fat Boys: A Slim Book 2004; also scholarly edns of German texts and monographs. *Address:* c/o Department of Modern Languages, Cornell University, 203 Merrill Hall, Ithaca, NY 14853-0001, USA.

GILMOUR, David, BA, FRSL; British writer; b. 14 Nov. 1952, London, England; m. Sarah Anne Bradstock 1975, one s. three d. *Education:* Balliol Coll., Oxford. *Career:* Deputy Ed. and Contributing Ed., Middle East International, London 1978–85; Research Fellow, St Antony's Coll., Oxford 1996–97. *Publications:* Dispossessed: The Ordeal of the Palestinians 1980, Lebanon: The Fractured Country 1983, The Transformation of Spain: From Franco to the Constitutional Monarchy 1985, The Last Leopard: A Life of Giuseppe di Lampedusa (Scottish Arts Council Spring Book Award 1988, Marsh Biography Award 1989) 1988, The Hungry Generations 1991, Cities of Spain 1992, Curzon 1994, The Long Recessional: The Imperial Life of Rudyard Kipling 2001, The Ruling Caste: Imperial Lives in the Victorian Raj 2005, The Last Leopard 2007; contrib. to periodicals, including New York Review of Books, the Spectator, Financial Times. *Honours:* Duff Cooper Prize 1994, Elizabeth Longford Prize for Historical Biography 2003. *Literary Agent:* Aitken Alexander Associates Ltd, 18–21 Cavaye Place, London, SW10 9PT, England. *Telephone:* (20) 7373-8672. *Fax:* (20) 7373-6002. *E-mail:* reception@aitkenalexander.co.uk. *Website:* www.aitkenalexander.co.uk. *Address:* 27 Ann Street, Edinburgh, EH4 1TL, Scotland (home).

GILROY, Frank Daniel, BA; American dramatist, screenwriter, writer, producer and director; b. 13 Oct. 1925, New York, NY; m. Ruth Dorothy Gaydos 1954; three s. *Education:* Dartmouth College, Yale School of Drama. *Career:* mem. Dirs Guild of America; Dramatists Guild, pres., 1969–71; Writers Guild of America. *Publications:* Fiction: Private, 1970; Little Ego (with Ruth Gilroy), 1970; Little Ego (with Ruth Gilroy), 1970; From Noon Till Three, 1973. Non-Fiction: I Wake Up Screening: Everything You Need to Know About Making Independent Films Including a Thousand Reasons Not To, 1993. Other: Plays: Who'll Save the Plowboy?, 1957; The Subject was Roses, 1962; That Summer, That Fall, 1967; The Only Game in Town, 1968; The Next Contestant, 1978; Last Licks, 1979; Real to Reel, 1987; Match Point, 1990; A Way with Words, 1991; Give the Bishop My Faint Regards, 1992; Any Given Day, 1993. Films: The Fastest Gun Alive (with Russell House), 1956; Gallant Hours (with Beirne Lay Jr), 1960; Desperate Characters, 1970; From Noon till Three, 1977; Once in Paris, 1978; The Gig, 1985; The Luckiest Man in the World, 1989. *Honours:* Obie Award, 1962; Outer Circle Award, 1964; Drama Critics Circle Award, 1964; New York Theatre Club Award, 1964–65; Tony Award, 1965; Pulitzer Prize for Drama, 1965; Best Screenplay Award, Berlin Film Festival, 1970. *Address:* c/o Dramatists Guild, 1501 Broadway, New York, NY 10036, USA.

GINZBURG, Carlo; Italian historian and academic; b. 1939, Turin; m. 1st (divorced); m. 2nd Luisa Ciammitti; two d. *Education:* Scuola Normale Superiore, Pisa, Warburg Institute, London. *Career:* Prof. of Modern History, University of Bologna, 1970–; several visiting fellowships. *Publications:* I benandanti: Stregoneria e culti agrari tra Cinquecento e Seicento, 1966, English trans. as The Night Battles: Witchcraft and Agrarian Cults in the Sixteenth and Seventeenth Centuries, 1983; Il nicodemismo: Simulazione e dissimulazione religiosa nell'Europa del '500, 1970; Giochi di pazienza: Un seminario sul Beneficio di Cristo (with Adriano Prosperi), 1975; Il formaggio e i vermi: Il cosmo di un mugnaio del '500, 1976, English trans. as The Cheese and the Worms: The Cosmos of a Sixteenth-Century Miller, 1980; Indagini su Piero: Il Battesimo, il Ciclo di Arezzo, la Flagellazione di Urbino, 1981, English trans. as Clues, Myths, and the Historical Method, 1989; Storia notturna: Una decifrazione del sabba, 1989, English trans. as Ecstacies: Deciphering the Witches' Sabbath, 1991; Il giudice e lo storico: Considerazioni in margine al processo sofri, 1991; Il registro: Carcere politico di Civitavecchia (ed. with Aldo Natoli and Vittorio Foa), 1994. *Honours:* Citta di Montesilvano, 1989. *Address:* c/o Departimento di Storia, Universita degli Studi, Piazza San Giovanni in Monte 2, 40124 Bologna, Italy.

GIOIA, (Michael) Dana, MA, MBA; American writer and poet; *Chairman, National Endowment for the Arts*; b. 24 Dec. 1950, Los Angeles; m. Mary Hiecke 1980; three s. (one deceased). *Education:* Stanford and Harvard Univs. *Career:* fmr Visiting Writer, Colorado Coll., Johns Hopkins Univ., Wesleyan Univ.; Chair. Nat. Endowment for the Arts 2003–; mem. Bd and Vice-Pres. Poetry Soc. of America; mem. Wesleyan Univ. Writers' Conf.; regular contrib. to various journals, reviews and periodicals including San Francisco magazine (classical music critic). *Publications include:* The Ceremony and Other Stories 1984, Daily Horoscope 1986, Mottetti: Poems of Love (trans.) 1990, The Gods of Winter 1991, Can Poetry Matter? 1992, An Introduction to Poetry 1994, The Madness of Hercules (trans.) 1995, Interrogations at Noon (American Book Award 2002) 2001, Nosferatu (opera libretto with Alva Henderson) 2001, The Barrier of a Common Language (essays) 2003, Twentieth-century American Poetry 2004, Twentieth-century American Poetics 2004, 100 Great Poets of the English Language 2005; also ed. of several works of literary criticism. *Honours:* Esquire Best of New Generation Award 1984, Frederick Bock Prize for Poetry 1985. *Address:* National Endowment for the Arts, 1100 Pennsylvania Avenue, NW, Washington, DC 20506 (office); 7190 Faught Road, Santa Rosa, CA 95403, USA (office). *Telephone:* (202) 682-5414 (office). *Fax:* (202) 682-5639 (office). *Website:* www.nea.gov (office).

GIOSEFFI, Daniela, BA, MFA; Italian/Greek/Polish/American poet, novelist, literary critic, editor and teacher; b. 12 Feb. 1941, Orange, NJ, USA; m. 1st Richard J. Kearney 1965 (divorced 1982); one d.; m. 2nd Dr Lionel B. Luttinger 1986. *Education:* Montclair State College, Catholic University of America. *Career:* fmr actress and dancer; Prof. of World Literature and Intercultural Communication (retd); mem. editorial bd VIA, magazine of literature and culture at Purdue Univ.; Pres. Skylands Writers' Asscn Inc.; Ed www.PoetsUSA.com; Ed.-in-Chief Electronic Magazine of Literature; Ed. literary websites: njpoets.com, italianamericanwriters.com, gioseffi.com; mem. PEN, Acad. of American Poets, Nat. Book Critics' Circle, Poetry Soc. of America, Poets' House, New York. *Radio broadcast:* interview and poetry reading on Library of Congress radio show 'The Poet and the Poem' (Nat. Public Radio) 2006. *Theatre:* Care of the Body, The Sea Hag in the Cave of Sleep, The Birth Dance of Earth, The Brooklyn Bridge Poetry Walk. *Publications:* The Great American Belly Dance (novel) 1977, Eggs in the Lake (poems) 1979, Earth Dancing: Mother Nature's Oldest Rite 1980, Women on War 1990, On Prejudice: A Global Perspective 1993, Words, Wounds and Flowers 1995, Dust Disappears by Carilda Oliver Labra (trans.) 1995, In Bed With the Exotic Enemy: Stories and Novella 1997, Going On (poems) 2000, Symbiosis (poems) 2002, New & Selected Poems: Blood Autumn 2006; verse inscribed in marble on wall of Penn Station, NYC 2002; contrib. to Nation, Chelsea, Ambit, Poetry Review, Modern Poetry Studies, Anteus, The Paris Review, American Book Review, The Hungry Mind Review, Prairie Schooner, Independent publishers, Poetry East, The Cortland Review, Big City Lit, Mississippi Review, Pif magazine, Poet Lore, Rain Taxi, Chelsea Review, Rattupallax.com. *Honours:* New York State Council for the Arts Award Grants in Poetry 1972, 1977, American Book Award 1990, PEN American Centre Short Fiction Award 1990, World Peace Award 1993, American Asscn of Educators lifetime achievement award in education and creative writing 2003. *Address:* 57 Montague Street, 8G, Brooklyn Heights, New York, NY 11201, USA. *Telephone:* (718) 643-3837 (office); (347) 683-9462 (home). *E-mail:* daniela@garden.net (home). *Website:* www.gioseffi.com; www.poetsUSA.com.

GIOVANNI, Nikki, BA; American poet and academic; *University Distinguished Professor and Gloria D. Smith Professor of Black Studies, Virginia Polytechnic Institute and State University*; b. 7 June 1943, Knoxville, Tenn.; d. of Jones Giovanni and Yolande Watson; one s. *Education:* Fisk Univ. and Univ. of Pennsylvania. *Career:* Asst Prof. of Black Studies, City Coll. of New York 1968; Assoc. Prof. of English, Rutgers Univ. 1968–72; Prof. of Creative Writing, Coll. Mt. St Joseph on the Ohio 1985; Univ. Distinguished Prof. and Gloria D. Smith Prof. of Black Studies, Va Polytechnic Inst. and State Univ. Blacksburg 1987–; founder, Nixtom Ltd 1970; Visiting Prof. Ohio State Univ. 1984; recordings and TV appearances. *Publications:* Black Feeling, Black Talk 1968, Black Judgement 1968, Re: Creation 1970, Poem of Angela Yvonne Davis 1970, Spin A Soft Black Song 1971, Gemini 1971, My House 1972, A Dialogue: James Baldwin and Nikki Giovanni 1973, Ego Tripping and Other Poems for Young Readers 1973, A Poetic Equation: Conversations Between Nikki Giovanni and Margaret Walker 1974, The Women and the Men 1975, Cotton Candy on a Rainy Day 1978, Vacationtime 1980, Those Who Ride the Night Winds 1983, Sacred Cows . . . and other Edibles 1988, Conversations with Nikki Giovanni 1992, Racism 101 1994, Grand Mothers 1994, Blues: For All the Changes 1999, Quilting the Black-Eyed Pea: Poems and Not-Quite Poems 2002. *Honours:* recipient of numerous awards and hon. degrees. *Address:* Department of English, PO Box 0112, Virginia Polytechnic Institute and State University, Blacksburg, VA 24063, USA (office). *Telephone:* (540) 231-9453 (office). *Website:* athena.english.vt.edu (office).

GIRARD, Keith; American editor; *Ed.-in-Chief, Billboard magazine*. *Career:* fmr reporter, The Washington Post; Ed. Daily Record and Investment News; Ed.-in-Chief, Billboard magazine 2003–. *Address:* Billboard, VNU eMedia Inc., 770 Broadway, Sixth Floor, New York, NY 10003, USA. *Website:* www.billboard.com.

GIRARD, René Noël, PhD; French/American academic and writer; *Professor Emeritus, Stanford University*; b. 25 Dec. 1923, Avignon; s. of Joseph Girard and Thérèse Fabre; m. Martha Virginia McCullough 1951; two s. one d. *Education:* Lycée d'Avignon, Ecole des Chartes and Indiana Univ. *Career:* Instructor of French, Indiana Univ. 1947–51, Duke Univ. 1952–53; Asst Prof. Bryn Mawr Coll. 1953–57; Assoc. Prof. The Johns Hopkins Univ. 1957–61, Prof. 1961–68, Chair. Romance Languages 1965–68, James M. Beall Prof. of French and Humanities 1976–80; Prof. Inst. d'études françaises Bryn Mawr, Avignon 1961–68, Dir 1969; Distinguished Faculty Prof. of Arts and Letters, State Univ. of New York at Buffalo 1971–76; Andrew B. Hammond Prof. of

French Language, Literature and Civilization, Stanford Univ. 1981–95, Courtesy Prof. of Religious Studies and Comparative Literature 1986–95, Dir Program of Interdisciplinary Research, Dept of French and Italian 1987–95, Prof. Emer. 1995–; mem. Center for Int. Security and Arms Control, 1990–95; Fellow American Acad. of Arts and Sciences 1979–, Guggenheim Fellow 1960, 1967; elected mem. Acad. française 2005. *Publications include:* Mensonge romantique et vérité romanesque 1961, Dostoïevski: du double à l'unité 1963, La violence et le sacré 1972, Des choses cachées depuis la fondation du monde 1978, Le bouc émissaire 1982, La route antique des hommes pervers 1985, The Girard Reader 1996, Shakespeare: Les feux de l'envie 1990, A Theatre of Envy. William Shakespeare 1991, Quand ces choses commenceront 1994, Je vois Satan tomber comme l'éclair 1999, (in English) 2001, Celui par qui le scandale arrive 2001, La voix méconnue du réel 2002, Les Origines de la Culture 2004. *Honours:* mem. Acad. Française 2005; Hon. DLit (Vrije Univ.) 1985, Hon. DTheol (Innsbruck) 1988, (St Mary's Seminary, Baltimore) 2003, (Montreal) 2004, (London) 2005, Hon. DLit (Padua) 2001; Chevalier, Ordre Nat. de la Légion d'honneur 1984, Officier, Ordre des Arts et Lettres 1984; Acad. Française Prize 1973, Grand Prix de Philosophie 1996; Prix Médicis-Essai 1990, Premio Nonino (Percoto, Udine, Italy) 1998, Dr Leopold Lucas Prize, Tübingen 2006.

GISCOMBE, C. S., BA, MFA; American poet, writer and academic; b. 30 Nov. 1950, Dayton, OH; m. Katharine Wright 1975, one d. *Education:* SUNY at Albany, Cornell University. *Career:* Faculty, Syracuse University, 1977, Cornell University, 1980–89; Prof. of English, Illinois State University, 1989–98, Pennsylvania State University, 1998–; mem. Poets and Writers. *Publications:* poetry: Postcards, 1977; Here, 1994; Giscombe Road, 1998; Two sections from 'Practical Geography: Five Poems', 2000; Inland, 2001. Other: Intro and Out of Dislocation, 2000. Contributions: periodicals. *Honours:* Creative Artists Public Service Fellowship, 1981–82; National Endowment for the Arts Fellowship, 1986–87; New York Foundation for the Arts Fellowship, 1988; Carl Sandburg Award for Poetry, 1998.

GIVNER, Joan Mary, BA, MA, PhD; British academic (retd) and writer; b. 5 Sept. 1936, Manchester, England; m. David Givner 1965, two d. *Education:* University of London, Washington University, St Louis. *Career:* Prof. of English, University of Regina, 1965–95; Ed., Wascana Review, 1984–92; mem. Saskatchewan Writers' Guild. *Publications:* Katherine Anne Porter: A Life, 1982; Tentacles of Unreason, 1985; Katherine Anne Porter: Conversations (ed.), 1987; Unfortunate Incidents, 1988; Mazo de la Roche: The Hidden Life, 1989; Scenes from Provincial Life, 1991; The Self-Portrait of a Literary Biographer, 1993; In the Garden of Henry James, 1996. *E-mail:* dgivner@attglobal.net. *Website:* uregina.ca/~givnerj.

GJESSING, Ketil; Norwegian poet and writer; b. 18 Feb. 1934, Oslo. *Education:* Univ. of Oslo. *Career:* teacher, Atlantic Coll. (now United World Coll. of the Atlantic) 1965–66; dramaturg at the Radio Drama Dept, Norwegian Broadcasting Corp. 1966–99; adviser, Klassisk Musikkmagasion 2001; mem. Norwegian Authors' Asscn, Norwegian Authors' Centre, Norwegian Translators' Asscn. *Publications:* 10 collections of poetry, including Dans på roser og glass (Dance on Roses and Glass) 1996; contrib. to Aftenposten (newspaper), Vinduet, Samtiden (magazines) and others. *Honours:* Gyldendals Pris 1983, Språklig Samlings Litteraturpris 1996. *Address:* Dannevigsvn 12, 0463 Oslo, Norway (home). *Telephone:* (22) 382351 (home).

GLADWELL, Malcolm, BA; Canadian (b. British) writer; b. 1963, England. *Education:* Univ. of Toronto. *Career:* grew up in Canada; science writer, The Washington Post, later New York bureau chief 1987–96; staff writer, The New Yorker 1996–. *Publications:* The Tipping Point: How Little Things can Make a Big Difference 2000, Blink: The Power of Thinking Without Thinking 2005. *Address:* c/o The New Yorker, 4 Times Square, New York, NY 10036-6592, USA. *E-mail:* malcolm@gladwell.com. *Website:* www.gladwell.com.

GLAISTER, Lesley Gillian, MA, FRSL; British writer; b. 4 Oct. 1956, Wellinborough, Northamptonshire, England; three s. *Education:* Univ. of Sheffield. *Publications:* novels: Honour Thy Father, Trick or Treat, Digging to Australia, Limestone and Clay 1993, Partial Eclipse 1994, The Private Parts of Women 1996, Easy Peasy 1997, Sheer Blue Bliss 1999, Now You See Me 2001, As Far As You Can Go 2004, Nina Todd Has Gone 2007; plays: Bird Calls (Crucible Theatre, Sheffield) 2003. *Honours:* Somerset Maugham Award, Betty Trask Award, Yorkshire Author of the Year Award 1993. *Address:* 16 Kirkland Street, Peebles, EH45 8EV, Scotland.

GLANVILLE, Brian Lester; British writer and journalist; b. 24 Sept. 1931, London; s. of James A. Glanville and Florence Manches; m. Elizabeth De Boer 1959; two s. two d. *Education:* Charterhouse. *Career:* first sports columnist and football corresp. Sunday Times 1958–92; sports columnist, The People 1992–96, football writer, The Times 1996–98, Sunday Times 1998–; literary adviser, Bodley Head 1958–62. *Plays for radio:* The Rise of Gerry Logan, The Diary, I Could Have Been King, A Visit to the Villa. *Television:* original writer of That Was The Week That Was 1962; wrote BBC documentary European Centre Forward (winner Berlin Prize) 1963. *Publications:* novels: Along the Arno 1956, The Bankrupts 1958, Diamond 1962, The Rise of Gerry Logan 1963, A Second Home 1965, A Roman Marriage 1966, The Artist Type 1967, The Olympian 1969, A Cry of Crickets 1970, The Comic 1974, The Dying of the Light 1976, The Catacomb 1988, Dictators 2001; sport: Champions of Europe 1991, Story of the World Cup 1993, The Arsenal Stadium History 2006; short stories: A Bad Streak 1961, The Director's Wife 1963, The King of Hackney Marshes 1965, The Thing He Loves 1985, Love Is Not Love; plays: A Visit to

the Villa 1981, Underneath the Arches (musical, co-author) 1981, The Diary (radio play) 1986, Football Memories (autobiog.) 1999. *Honours:* Silver Bear Award, Berlin Film Festival, for European Centre Forward (BBC TV documentary) 1963. *Address:* 160 Holland Park Avenue, London, W11 4UH, England. *Telephone:* (20) 7603-6908 (home). *Fax:* (20) 7603-6908 (home).

GLEN, Duncan Munro; British academic, poet, writer, editor and publisher; *Professor Emeritus, Nottingham Trent University;* b. 11 Jan. 1933, Cambuslang, Lanarkshire; m. Margaret Eadie 1957; one s. one d. *Education:* Edinburgh Coll. of Art. *Career:* Lecturer to Principal Lecturer, Cen. Lancashire Univ., 1965–78; Prof. and Head of Dept of Visual Communication, Nottingham Trent Univ. 1972–87, Prof. Emer. 1987–; Ed. Akros 1965–83, Scottish Poetry Library Newsletter 1988–2007, Zed 2 O 1991–; Fellow, Chartered Soc. of Designers. *Publications:* Hugh MacDiarmid and the Scottish Renaissance 1964, Selected Essays of Hugh MacDiarmid (ed.) 1969, In Appearances: A Sequence of Poems 1971, The Individual and the Twentieth Century Scottish Literary Tradition 1971, Buits and Wellies: A Sequence of Poems 1976, Gaitherings (poems) 1977, Realities (poems) 1980, The Turn of the Earth: A Sequence of Poems 1985, The Autobiography of a Poet 1986, Tales to Be Told 1987, European Poetry in Scotland (ed.) 1990, Selected Poems 1965–90 1991, The Poetry of the Scots 1991, Hugh MacDiarmid: Out of Langhoom and Into the World 1992, Echoes: Frae Classical and Italian Poetry 1992, The Bright Writers' Guides to Scottish Culture 1995, A Nation in a Parish: A New Historical Prospect of Scotland 1995, Splendid Lanarkshire 1997, Selected New Poems 1987–1996 1998, Illustrious Fife 1998, A New History of Cambuslang 1998, Selected Scottish and Other Essays 1999, Scottish Literature: A New History from 1299 to 1999 1999, Printing Type Designs: A New History from Gutenburg to 2000 2001, Ravenscraig Castle 2001, Winter: A Poem, and Other Verses by James Thomson (ed.) 2002, Historic Fife Murders 2002, Robert Louis Stevenson and the Covenanters on the Bass Rock and 'The Tale of Tod Lapraik' 2002, Ruined Rural Fife Churches 2002, A Photographic Celebration at the Ruins of Bighty Farm 2002, The Ruins of Newark Castle, St Monans, Autumn 2002 2003, Crossing Schools of Art: An Illustrated Historical Memoir 2003, Stevenson's Scotland (ed.) 2003, Poets and Paintings: Reinterpretations, An Essay 2004, Kircaldy: A New Illustrated History 2004, In Search of Serif Books 2006, Small Press Publishers of Scotland 2006, Collected Poems 1965–2005 2006; contribs to numerous journals and magazines. *Honours:* Dr hc (Paisley) 2000; Special Award for Services to Scottish Literature, Scottish Arts Council 1975, Howard Sergeant Poetry Award 1993. *Address:* 33 Lady Nairn Avenue, Kirkcaldy, Fife, KY1 2AW, Scotland.

GLENDINNING, Hon. Victoria, CBE, MA, FRSL; British author and journalist; b. 23 April 1937, Sheffield; d. of Baron Seebohm of Hertford and Lady Seebohm (née Hurst); m. 1st O. N. V. Glendinning 1959 (divorced 1981); four s.; m. 2nd Terence de Vere White 1981 (died 1994); m. 3rd Kevin O'Sullivan 1996. *Education:* St Mary's School, Wantage, Millfield School, Somerville Coll., Oxford and Univ. of Southampton. *Career:* part-time teaching 1960–69; part-time psychiatric social work 1970–73; Editorial Asst Times Literary Supplement 1974–78; Pres. English Centre of PEN 2001; Vice-Pres. Royal Soc. of Literature 2000. *Publications:* A Suppressed Cry 1969, Elizabeth Bowen: Portrait of a Writer 1977, Edith Sitwell: A Unicorn Among Lions 1981, Vita: A Biography of V. Sackville-West 1983, Rebecca West: A Life 1987, The Grown-Ups (novel) 1989, Hertfordshire 1989, Trollope 1992, Electricity (novel) 1995, Sons and Mothers (co-ed.) 1996, Jonathan Swift 1998, Flight (novel) 2001, Leonard Woolf (biog.) 2006; articles in newspapers and journals. *Honours:* Hon. DLitt (Southampton Univ.) 1994; Dr hc (Ulster) 1995; Hon. LittD (Dublin Univ.) 1995; Hon. DUniv (York) 2000.

GLENDOWER, Rose (see Harris, Marion Rose)

GLICKMAN, James A., BA, MFA; American educator and writer; b. 29 Dec. 1948, Davenport, IA; m. Elissa Deborah Gelfand 1982; one s. *Education:* University of Iowa Writers' Workshop. *Career:* Instructor, University of Arizona Law School, Tucson, 1972; English Teacher, Community College of Rhode Island, Lincoln, 1972–; Faculty Mem., Radcliffe Seminars, Cambridge, Massachusetts, 1985–88. *Publications:* Sounding the Waters, 1996; The Crossing Point, 1999. Contributions: Short stories to periodicals including Kansas Quarterly; Redbook; Ladies Home Journal; Worcester Review. *Literary Agent:* Aaron Priest Literary Agency, 708 Third Avenue, 23rd Floor, New York, NY 10017-4103, USA. *Address:* 51 McGilpin Road, Sturbridge, MA 01566-1230, USA.

GLIORI, Debi; British children's writer and illustrator; b. Glasgow; five c. *Education:* Edinburgh Coll. of Art. *Publications:* writer and illustrator: New Big Sister 1991, New Big House 1992, When I'm Big 1992, My Little Brother 1992, A Lion at Bedtime 1993, Mr Bear Babysits 1994, The Snowchild 1994, Mr Bear's Picnic 1995, Little Bear and the Wish Fish 1995, Mr Bear Says (series) 1995–, The Snow Lambs 1995, Princess and the Pirate King 1996, Mr Bear to the Rescue 1996, Hello, Baby Bear 1998, Mr Bear's New Baby 1998, Give him my Heart 1998, No Matter What 1999, Mr Bear's Holiday (Scottish Arts Council Children's Book Award) 2000, Flora's Blanket 2001, Pure Dead Magic 2001, Polar Bolero 2001, Where, Oh Where, is Baby Bear? 2001, Pure Dead Wicked 2002, Tickly Under There 2002, Can I Have a Hug? 2002, Flora's Flowers 2002, Debi Gliori's Bedtime Stories 2002, Penguin Post 2002, Flora's Surprise 2003, Little Owl's Swim 2003, Little Fox's Picnic 2003, Hush, Little Chick 2003, Wake Up, Little Rabbit! 2003, Pure Dead Brilliant 2003, Deep Trouble 2004, Where Did That Baby Come From? 2004, Deep Water 2005,

Pure Dead Trouble 2005, Deep Fear 2006, Pure Dead Batty 2006; illustrator of books by other authors, including: The Oxford A.B.C. Picture Dictionary 1990, Dulcie Dando (Sue Stops) 1990, Margery Mo (Margaret Donaldson) 1991, The Incredible Shrinking Hippo (Stephanie Baudet) 1991, Lizzie and her Puppy (David Martin) 1993, Amazing Alphabets (Lisa Bruce) 1993, A Present for Big Pig (Kate Simpson) 1994, How the Reindeer Got Their Antlers (G. McCaughrean) 1995, Clever Counting: Combinatorics 1997, What Can I Give Him? (Christina Georgina Rossetti) 1998, Tell Me Something Happy Before I Go to Sleep (Joyce Dunbar) 1998, The Very Small (Joyce Dunbar) 2000, Tell Me What it's Like to be Big (Joyce Dunbar) 2001, This is the Star (Joyce Dunbar) 2002, Always and Forever (Alan Durant) 2003; poetry: Noisy Poems 1997, DK Book of Nursery Rhymes (ed.) 2000. *Address:* c/o Bloomsbury Publishing PLC, 36 Soho Square, London, W1D 3QY, England (office). *E-mail:* csm@bloomsbury.com (office).

GLISSANT, Édouard, DPhil; French academic, writer, dramatist and poet; b. 21 Sept. 1928, Sainte-Marie, Martinique. *Education:* Sorbonne, Université de Paris, Musée de l'homme, Paris. *Career:* Instructor in Philosophy, Lycée des Jeunes Filles, Fort-de-France, Martinique, 1965; Founder, 1967, Dir, 1967–78, Institut Martiniquais d'Etudes, Fort-de-France; Co-Founder, ACOMA Review, 1970; Ed., UNESCO, Paris, France, 1981–88; Distinguished Prof. and Dir of Center for French and Francophone Studies, Louisiana State University, Baton Rouge, USA, 1988–. *Publications:* Poetry: Un champ d'îles, 1953; La terre inquiète, 1954; Les Indes: Poèmes de l'une et l'autre terre, 1955; Le sel noir, 1959; Le sang rivé, 1960; Poèmes, 1963; Boises, 1979; Pays rêvé, pays réel, 1985; Fastes, 1992. Non-Fiction: Soleil de la conscience, 1956; L'intention poétique, 1969; Le discours antillais, 1981, English trans. as Caribbean Discourse: Selected Essays, 1989; Poétique de la relation, 1990. Fiction: La Lézarde, 1958; Le quatrième siècle, 1964; Malemort, 1975; La case du commandeur, 1981; Mahagony, 1987; Tout-monde, 1993. Play: Monsieur Toussaint, 1961, revised version, 1978. *Honours:* Ordre des Francophones d'Amérique, Québec; Prix Rénaudot, 1958; Prix Charles Veillon, 1965; Award, 12th Putterbaugh Conference, Norman, Oklahoma, 1989; Hon. LittD, York University, 1989; Roger Callois International Prize, 1991.

GLOAG, Julian, BA, MA, FRSL; British novelist; b. 2 July 1930, London; one s. one d. *Education:* Magdalene Coll., Cambridge. *Career:* mem. Authors Guild. *Television screenplays:* Only Yesterday 1986, The Dark Room 1988. *Publications:* Our Mother's House 1963, A Sentence of Life 1966, Maundy 1969, A Woman of Character 1973, Sleeping Dogs Lie 1980, Lost and Found 1981, Blood for Blood 1985, Only Yesterday 1986, Love as a Foreign Language 1991, Le passeur de la nuit 1996, Chambre d'ombre 1996. *Address:* c/o Michelle Lapautre, 6 rue Jean Carriès, 75007 Paris (office); 36 rue Gabrielle, 75018 Paris, France (home).

GLOCER, Thomas (Tom) Henry, BA, JD; American lawyer and business executive; *CEO, Thomson-Reuters;* b. 8 Oct. 1959, NY; s. of Walter Glocer and Ursula Glocer (née Goodman); m. Maarit Leso 1988; one s. one d. *Education:* Columbia Univ., Yale Univ. Law School. *Career:* mergers and acquisitions lawyer, Davis Polk and Wardwell, New York, Paris and Tokyo 1985–93; joined Reuters 1993, mem. Legal Dept Gen. Counsel, Reuters America Inc., New York 1993–96, Exec. Vice-Pres., Reuters America Inc. and CEO Reuters Latin America 1996–98, CEO Reuters business in the Americas 1998–2001, Reuters Inc. 2000–01, CEO Reuters Group (Thomson-Reuters following merger with Thomson 2007) PLC 2001–; Dir New York City Investment Fund 1999–2003, Instinet Corpn 2000–; mem. Advisory Bd Singapore Monetary Authority 2001–; mem. Corp. Council, Whitney Museum of American Art 2000–. *Publications:* author of computer software, including Coney Island: A Game of Discovery (co-author) 1983. *Honours:* New York Hall of Science Award 2000, John Jay Alumni Award 2001. *Address:* Thomson-Reuters, Reuters Building, Canary Wharf, London, E14 5EP, England (office). *Telephone:* (20) 7250-1122 (office). *Fax:* (20) 7542-4064 (office). *Website:* www.reuters.com (office).

GLOVER, Douglas Herschel, BA, MLitt, MFA; Canadian writer and editor; *Faculty Member, Vermont College;* b. 14 Nov. 1948, Simcoe, Ont.; s. of Murray Glover and Jean Ross; divorced; two s. *Education:* York Univ., Univ. of Edinburgh, UK, Univ. of Iowa, USA. *Career:* various writer-in-residencies; Lecturer, Skidmore Coll. 1992, 1993; Visiting Prof., Colgate Univ. 1995; Visiting Prof., State Univ. of NY, Albany 1996–98, 2000–01; Visiting Prof., Skidmore Coll. 1998–2000; Faculty mem. MFA in Writing Program, Vermont Coll. 1994–; McGee Prof. of Writing, Davidson Coll. 2005; Ed. Coming Attractions 1991–95, Best Canadian Stories 1996–2006; mem. Writers' Union of Canada. *Publications:* The Mad River 1981, Precious 1984, Dog Attempts to Drown Man in Saskatoon 1985, The South Will Rise at Noon 1988, A Guide to Animal Behaviour 1991, Coming Attractions (co-ed., five vols) 1991–95, The Life and Times of Captain N 1993, The Journey Prize Anthology (ed.) 1994, Best Canadian Stories (ed.) 1996, 1997, 2000–03, Notes from a Prodigal Son 1999, Sixteen Categories of Desire 2000, Elle 2003, Bad News of the Heart 2003, The Enamoured Knight 2004; contrib. to numerous journals and magazines. *Honours:* Canadian Fiction Magazine Contrib.'s Prize 1985, Literary Press Group Writers' Choice Award 1986, Nat. Magazine Award for Fiction 1990, Gov.-Gen.'s Award for Fiction 2003. *Literary Agent:* c/o Anne McDermid & Associates Ltd, 83 Willcocks Street, Toronto, ON M5S 1C9, Canada. *Telephone:* (416) 324-8845. *Fax:* (416) 324-8870. *E-mail:* info@mcdermidagency.com. *Website:* www.mcdermidagency.com.

GLOVER, Jane Alison, CBE, MA, DPhil, FRCM; British conductor; *Music Director, Music of the Baroque, Chicago;* b. 13 May 1949, d. of the late Robert Finlay Glover and Jean Muir. *Education:* Monmouth School for Girls and St Hugh's Coll., Oxford. *Career:* Jr Research Fellow St Hugh's Coll. 1973–75, Lecturer in Music 1976–84, Sr Research Fellow 1982–84; Lecturer St Anne's Coll., Oxford 1976–80, Pembroke Coll. 1979–84; mem. Oxford Univ. Faculty of Music 1979–; professional conducting debut at Wexford Festival 1975; operas and concerts for BBC, Glyndebourne 1982–, Royal Opera House 1988–, Covent Garden, English Nat. Opera 1989–, London Symphony Orchestra, London Philharmonic Orchestra, Royal Philharmonic Orchestra, Philharmonia, Royal Scottish Orchestra, English Chamber Orchestra, Royal Danish Opera, Glimmerglass Opera, New York 1994–, Australian Opera 1996– and many orchestras in Europe and USA; Prin. Conductor London Choral Soc. 1983–2000; Artistic Dir London Mozart Players 1984–91; Prin. Conductor Huddersfield Choral Soc. 1989–96; Music Dir Music of the Baroque, Chicago 2002–; mem. BBC Cen. Music Advisory Cttee 1981–85, Music Advisory Cttee Arts Council 1986–88; Gov. RAM 1985–90, BBC 1990–95. *Television:* documentaries and series and presentation, especially Orchestra 1983, Mozart 1985. *Radio:* talks and series including Opera House 1995, Musical Dynasties 2000. *Publications:* Cavalli 1978, Mozart's Women: His Family, His Friends, His Music 2005; contribs to The New Monteverdi Companion 1986, Monteverdi 'Orfeo' Handbook 1986; articles in numerous journals. *Honours:* Hon. DMus (Exeter) 1986, (CNAA) 1991, (London) 1992, (City Univ.) 1995, (Glasgow) 1996; Hon. DLitt (Loughborough) 1988, (Bradford) 1992; Dr hc (Open Univ.) 1988, (Brunel) 1997. *Literary Agent:* c/o Askonas Holt Ltd., Lonsdale Chambers, 27 Chancery Lane, London, WC2A 1PF, England. *Telephone:* (20) 7400-1700. *Fax:* (20) 7400-1799. *E-mail:* info@askonasholt.co.uk. *Website:* www.askonasholt.co.uk; www.baroque.org.

GLOVER, Judith; British author; b. 31 March 1943, Wolverhampton, England; two d. *Education:* Wolverhampton High School for Girls, Aston Polytechnic. *Publications:* Drink Your Own Garden (non-fiction), 1979; The Sussex Quartet: The Stallion Man, 1982, Sisters and Brothers, 1984, To Everything a Season, 1986; Birds in a Gilded Cage, 1987; The Imagination of the Heart, 1989; Tiger Lilies, 1991; Mirabelle, 1992; Minerva Lane, 1994; Pride of Place, 1995, Sussex Place-Names 1997. *Address:* c/o Artellus Ltd, 30 Dorset House, Gloucester Place, London, NW1 5AD, England.

GŁOWACKI, Janusz; Polish writer, playwright and screenwriter; b. 13 Sept. 1938, Poznań; m.; one d. *Education:* Warsaw Univ. *Career:* columnist in Kultura weekly 1964–81; lecturer in many colls and univs in USA including Bennington, Yale, Cornell, Columbia; playwright in residence New York Shakespeare Festival 1984 and Mark Taper Forum, LA 1989; Fellow in Writing, Univ. of Iowa 1977, 1982; Hon. mem. Univ. of Iowa 1977, 1982; Nat. Endowment for the Arts Fellowship 1988, Master of Arts Atlantic Center for the Arts 1991; mem. American and Polish PEN Club 1984–, Polish Film Union. *Publications:* short stories: Nowy taniec la-ba-da 1970, Paradis 1973, Polowanie na muchy 1974, My Sweet Raskolnikov 1977, Opowiadania wybrane 1978, Skrzek. Coraz trudniej kochać 1980, Rose Café 1997; novels: Moc truchleje 1981, Ostani cieć 2001; screenplays: Rejs 1970, Psychodrama (with Marek Piwowski) 1971, Polowanie na muchy 1971, Trzeba zabić tę miłość 1974, No Smoking Section (co-author) 1987, Hairdo (Tony Cox Screenwriting Award, Nantucket Film Festival, USA 1999) 1999; plays: Cudzołóstwo ukarane 1971, Mecz 1977, Obciach 1977, Kopciuch (Cinders) (Premio Molière, Argentina 1986) 1981, Fortinbras Gets Drunk 1986, Hunting Cockroaches (1st Prize, American Theatre Critics Asscn 1986, Joseph Kesselring Award 1987, Hollywood Drama League Critics' Award 1987) 1986, Antigone in New York (Le Balladine Award for the Best Play of 1997 in theatres of up to 250 seats) 1993, Ścieki, Skrzeki, karaluchy (selected works) 1996, Czwarta siostra (Grand Prize, Int. Theatre Festival, Dubrovnik 2001) 2000. *Honours:* Joseph Kesserling Award 1987, Drama League of New York Playwrighting Award 1987, Guggenheim Award 1988, Alfred Jurzykowski Foundation Award 1997. *Address:* ul. Bednarska 7 m. 4, 00-310 Warsaw, Poland; 845 West End Avenue Apt 4B, New York, NY 10025, USA. *Website:* www.januszglowacki.com.

GLÜCK, Louise Elisabeth; American poet, writer and academic; *Parish Senior Lecturer in English, Williams College;* b. 22 April 1943, New York, NY; d. of Daniel and Beatrice (née Grosby) Glück; m. 1st Charles Hertz (divorced); one s.; m. 2nd John Dranow 1977 (divorced 1996). *Education:* Sarah Lawrence Coll., Bronxville, New York and Columbia Univ., New York. *Career:* artist-in-residence, Goddard Coll., Plainfield, VT 1971–72, faculty mem. 1973–74; poet-in-residence, Univ. of North Carolina at Greensboro 1973; Visiting Prof. Univ. of Iowa 1976–77; Elliston Prof. of Poetry Univ. of Cincinnati, OH 1978; Visiting Prof. Columbia Univ. 1979; Holloway Lecturer Univ. of California at Berkeley 1982; faculty mem., bd mem., MFA Writing Program at Warren Wilson Coll., Swannoa, NC 1980–84; Visiting Prof. Univ. of California at Davis 1983; Scott Prof. of Poetry, Williams Coll., MA 1983, part-time Sr Lecturer in English 1984–97, Parish Sr. Lecturer in English 1997–; Regents Prof. of Poetry Univ. of California at Los Angeles 1985–88; Baccalaureate Speaker Williams Coll. 1993; Poet Laureate of Vermont 1994; visiting mem. faculty Harvard Univ., MA 1995; Hurst Prof. Brandeis Univ. 1996; Special Consultant in Poetry at Library of Congress, Washington, DC 1999–2000; Poet Laureate of the USA 2003–04; Fellow, American Acad. of Arts and Sciences; mem. PEN, American Acad. and Institute of Arts and Letters, Acad. of American Poets (bd of chancellors 1999–). *Publications:* poetry: Firstborn 1968, The House on the Marshland 1975, The Garden 1976, Descending

Figure 1980, The Triumph of Achilles 1985, Ararat 1990, The Wild Iris (Pulitzer Prize for Poetry 1993) 1992, Proofs and Theories: Essays on Poetry 1994, The First Four Books of Poems 1995, Meadowlands 1996, Vita Nova 1999, The Seven Ages 2001, October 2004, Averno 2007; contrib. to many anthologies and periodicals. *Honours:* Rockefeller Foundation Grant 1968–69, Nat. Educ. Asscn grants 1969–70, 1979–80, 1988–89, National Endowment for the Arts Fellowships 1969–70, 1979–80, 1988–89, Vermont Council for the Arts Grant 1978–79; Hon. LLD (Williams Coll.) 1993, (Skidmore Coll.) 1995, (Middlebury Coll.) 1996; Acad. of American Poets Prize 1967, Eunice Tietjens Memorial Prize 1971, Guggenheim Foundation Grant 1975–76, 1987–88, American Acad. and Inst. of Arts and Letters Literary Award 1981, Nat. Book Critics' Circle Award for poetry 1985, Poetry Soc. of America Melville Cane Award 1986, Wellesley Coll. Sara Teasdale Memorial Prize 1986, Bobbitt Natil Prize, Library of Congress 1992, William Carlos Williams Award 1993, PEN/Martha Albrand Award 1995, New Yorker Magazine Award in Poetry 1999, English Speaking Union Ambassador Award 1999, Bollingen Prize 2001. *Literary Agent:* Steven Barclay Agency, 12 Western Avenue, Petaluma, CA 94952, USA. *Telephone:* (707) 773-0654. *Fax:* (707) 778-1868. *Website:* www.barclayagency.com. *Address:* Department of English, Stetson Hall, Office D11, Williams College, Williamstown, MA 01267 (office); 14 Ellsworth Park, Cambridge, MA 02139, USA. *Telephone:* (413) 597-2559 (office). *Website:* www.williams.edu/English (office); www.artstomp.com/gluck/.

GLUCKSMANN, André; French philosopher and essayist; b. 1937, Boulogne-Billancourt. *Education:* Lyon, Ecole Normale Supérieure de Saint Cloud. *Career:* researcher Centre National de la Recherche Scientifique (CNRS). *Publications:* non-fiction: Le Discours de la guerre 1967, La Cuisinière et le Mangeur d'hommes 1975, Maîtres penseurs 1977, Etat, le marxisme et les camps de concentration 1979, La Force du vertige 1983, La Fêlure du monde: éthique et sida 1994, Dostoïevski à Manhattan 2002, Ouest contre ouest 2003, Le Discours de la haine 2004; contrib. articles to numerous publications, including Wall Street Journal, Le Monde. *Address:* c/o Editions Plon, 76 rue Bonaparte, 75006 Paris, France.

GLYNN, Ian Michael, MD, PhD, FRCP, FRS; British scientist and academic; *Professor Emeritus of Physiology, University of Cambridge*; b. 3 June 1928, London; s. of Hyman and Charlotte Glynn; m. Muriel Franklin 1958; one s. two d. *Education:* City of London School, Trinity Coll. Cambridge, Univ. Coll. Hosp. London. *Career:* House Physician, Cen. Middlesex Hosp. 1952–53; Nat. Service RAF Medical Branch 1956–57; MRC Scholar Physiological Lab. Cambridge 1956, Fellow, Trinity Coll. 1955–, demonstrator in Physiology 1958–63, Lecturer 1963–70, Reader 1970–75, Prof. of Membrane Physiology 1975–86, Prof. of Physiology 1986–95, Prof. Emer. 1995–, Vice-Master Trinity Coll. 1980–86; Visiting Prof., Yale Univ. 1969; mem. British MRC 1976–80, Council of Royal Soc. 1979–81, 1991–92, Agric. Research Council 1981–86; Chair. Editorial Bd Journal of Physiology 1968–70; Hon. foreign mem. American Acad. of Arts and Sciences 1984, American Physiological Soc. *Publications:* The Sodium Pump (with J. C. Ellory) 1985; An Anatomy of Thought: the Origin and Machinery of the Mind 1999; The Life and Death of Smallpox (with Jenifer Glynn) 2004; papers in scientific journals. *Honours:* Hon. MD (Univ. of Aarhus) 1988. *Address:* Trinity College, Cambridge, CB2 1TQ, England (office). *Telephone:* (1223) 353079 (office). *E-mail:* img10@cam.ac.uk (office).

GODBER, John Harry, BEd, MA, PhD, DLitt; British playwright, film and theatre director and actor; *Professor of Contemporary Theatre, Liverpool Hope University*; b. 18 May 1956, Hemsworth, W Yorks.; s. of Harry Godber and Dorothy Godber; m. Jane Thornton; two d. *Education:* Minsthorpe High, Bretton Hall Coll., Wakefield, Univ. of Leeds. *Career:* fmr Head of Drama, Minsthorpe High; Artistic Dir Hull Truck Theatre Co. 1984–; currently Prof. of Contemporary Theatre, Liverpool Hope Univ. Coll. *Plays:* 49 stage plays, including Happy Jack 1982, September in the Rain 1983, Up 'n' Under (Laurence Olivier Comedy of the Year Award 1984) 1984, Bouncers (seven Los Angeles Critics' Awards 1986) 1985, Blood, Sweat and Tears 1986, Shakers, Teechers 1987, Salt of the Earth 1988, On the Piste 1990, Happy Families 1991, April in Paris 1992, The Office Party, Passion Killers 1994, Lucky Sods 1995, Dracula 1995, Gym and Tonic 1996, Weekend Breaks 1997, It Started with a Kiss 1997, Unleashed 1998, Perfect Pitch, Thick as a Brick (music by John Pattison) 1999, Big Trouble in Little Bedroom 1999, Seasons in the Sun 2000, On a Night Like This 2000, This House 2001, Departures, Moby Dick, Men of the World, Reunion, Roast Beef and Yorkshire Pudding; also radio plays and TV programmes. *Film:* Up 'n' Under (writer and dir) 1998. *Television:* The Ritz (BBC 2 series), The Continental (BBC Christmas Special), My Kingdom for a Horse (BBC film) 1991, Chalkface (BBC series) 1991, Bloomin' Marvellous (BBC comedy series) 1997, Thunder Road (BBC 4 film), Oddsquad (BBC); has also written numerous episodes of Brookside, Crown Court and Grange Hill. *Honours:* honorary lecturer at Bretton Hall College; Hon. DLitt (Hull) 1988, (Lincoln) 1997; Sunday Times Playwright Award 1981, Joseph Jefferson Award, Chicago 1988, Fringe First Winner (five times), BAFTA Awards for Best Schools Drama and for Best Original Drama 2005. *Literary Agent:* c/o Alan Brodie, ABR, 6th Floor, Fairgate House, 78 New Oxford Street, London, WC1A 1HB. *Telephone:* (20) 7079-7990. *Fax:* (20) 7079-7991. *Website:* www.alanbrodie.com. *Address:* 12 Station Road, North Ferriby, HU14 3DQ, England (home). *Telephone:* (1482) 633854 (home). *E-mail:* johnhgodber@hotmail.com (home). *Website:* www.johngodber.co.uk (office).

GODBOUT, Jacques, BA, MA; Canadian author, poet and filmmaker; b. 27 Nov. 1933, Montréal, QC; m. Ghislaine Reiher 1954, two c. *Education:* Univ. of Montréal. *Career:* Lecturer, 1969, Writer-in-Residence, 1991–92, University of Montréal; Visiting Lecturer, University of California at Berkeley, 1985. *Publications:* Fiction: L'aquarium, 1962; Le couteau sur la table, 1965, English trans. as Knife on the Table, 1968; Salut Galarneau!, 1967, English trans. as Hail Galarneau!, 1970; D'Amour, PQ, 1972; L'île au dragon, 1976, English trans. as Dragon Island, 1979; Les tetes a Papineau, 1981; Une histoire americaine, 1986, English trans. as an American Story, 1988; Le temps des Galarneau, 1993. Poetry: Carton-pate, 1956; Les pavés secs, 1958; La chair est un commencement, 1959; C'est la chaude loi des hommes, 1960; La grande muraille de Chine (with J. R. Colombo), 1969. Essays: Le réformiste, 1975; Le murmure marchand, 1984; L'écran du bonheur, 1990; Journal: Ecrivain de province, 1991. Other: many films. *Honours:* Prix France-Canada, 1962; Prix de l'Académie Française, 1965; Governor-General's Award for Fiction, 1968; various film prizes.

GODFREY, (William) Dave, BA, MFA, PhD; Canadian novelist; b. 9 Aug. 1938, Winnipeg, MB; m. Ellen Swartz 1963; two s. one d. *Education:* University of Iowa, Stanford University, University of Chicago. *Career:* General Ed., Canadian Writers Series, McClelland and Stewart, 1968–72; Co-Founding Ed., News Press, Toronto, 1969–73; Ed., Press Porcepic, Erin, Ontario, 1972–; Vice-Pres., Inter Provincial Asscn for Telematcis and Telidon, 1982–. *Publications:* The New Ancestors, 1970; Short Stories: Death Goes Better with Coca Cola, 1967; New Canadian Writing, 1968, 1969; Dark Must Yield, 1978. *Honours:* University of Western Ontario Pres.'s Medal, 1965; Canada Council Award, 1969; Governor-General's Award, 1971.

GODFREY, Paul; British playwright and director; b. 16 Sept. 1960, Exeter, Devon, England. *Publications:* Inventing a New Colour, 1988; A Bucket of Eels, 1989; Once in a While the Odd Thing Happens, 1990; The Panic, 1991; The Blue Ball, 1993; The Modern Husband, 1994; The Candidate, 1995; The Invisible Woman, 1996; Catalogue of Misunderstanding, 1997; Collected Plays, Vol. One, 1998; Tiananmen Square, 1999; The Oldest Play, 2000; Linda, 2000; The Best Sex of my Life (screenplay), 2003. *Literary Agent:* AP Watt Ltd, 20 John Street, London, WC1N 2DR, England.

GODINE, David R., MA, EdM; American publisher; b. 4 Sept. 1944, Cambridge, Mass; s. of Morton R. Godine and Bernice Beckwith; m. Sara Sangree Eisenman 1988; one s. one d. *Education:* Dartmouth Coll., Harvard Univ. *Career:* f. David R. Godine Publishers Inc., Publisher and Pres. 1969–; mem. Bds Massachusetts Historical Soc., Massachusetts Horticultural Soc.; Fellow, Pierpoint Morgan Library. *Publication:* Renaissance Books of Science 1970. *Honours:* Dwiggins Award 1984. *Address:* David R. Godine Publishers Inc., 9 Hamilton Place, Boston, MA 02108 (office); 196 School Street, Milton, MA 02186, USA (home). *Telephone:* (617) 451-9600 (office). *Fax:* (617) 350-0250 (office). *E-mail:* info@godine.com (office). *Website:* www.godine.com (office).

GODLEE, Fiona N., MD; British editor, writer and publisher; *Editor, British Medical Journal*; m. ..; two c. *Career:* Asst Ed., British Medical Journal (BMJ) from 1990; Editorial Dir, establishing open-access online publisher BioMed Central, Current Science Group 2000–03; Head of Knowledge div. BMJ Publishing Group 2003–04, Ed., British Medical Journal 2004–; fmr Pres. World Asscn of Medical Eds; Chair., Cttee on Publication Ethics (COPE) 2004–05; Harkness Fellow, Harvard Univ. 1994; mem. Royal Coll. of Physicians. *Address:* BMJ Publishing Group Ltd, BMA House, Tavistock Square, London, WC1H 9JR, England. *Website:* www.bmjpg.com; www.publicationethics.org.uk.

GODWIN, Gail Kathleen, PhD; American writer; b. 18 June 1937, Birmingham, Ala; d. of Mose Godwin and Kathleen Krahenbuhl; m. 1st Douglas Kennedy 1960 (divorced 1961); m. 2nd Ian Marshall 1965 (divorced 1966). *Education:* Peace Jr Coll. Raleigh, NC and Univs of NC and Iowa. *Career:* news reporter, Miami Herald 1959–60; reporter, consultant, US Travel Service, London 1961–65; Editorial Asst Saturday Evening Post 1966; Fellow, Center for Advanced Study, Univ. of Ill. Urbana 1971–72; lecturer, Iowa Writers' Workshop 1972–73, Vassar Coll. 1977, Columbia Univ. Writing Program 1978, 1981; American specialist, USIS 1976; Guggenheim Fellow 1975–76; librettist for various productions; mem. PEN, Authors' Guild, Authors' League, Nat. Book Critics' Circle; American Acad. and Inst. of Arts and Letters Literature Award 1981. *Publications:* novels including: The Perfectionists 1970, Glass People 1972, The Odd Woman 1974, Violet Clay 1978, A Mother and Two Daughters 1982, The Finishing School 1985, A Southern Family 1987, Father Melancholy's Daughter 1991, The Good Husband 1994, Evensong 1998, Evenings At Five 2003, Queen of the Underworld 2005; non-fiction: Heart 2001; The Making of A Writer: Journals (ed.) 1961–63; also short stories, uncollected stories, novellas and librettos. *Honours:* other awards and distinctions. *Address:* PO Box 946, Woodstock, NY 12498-0946, USA.

GODWIN, Parke; American novelist; b. 28 Jan. 1929, New York, NY. *Education:* American Univ. *Publications:* The Masters of Solitude (co-author), 1978; Firelord, 1980; Wintermind (co-author), 1982; A Memory of Lions, 1983; A Cold Blue Light (co-author), 1983; Beloved Exile, 1984; The Fire When It Comes, 1984; The Last Rainbow, 1985; A Truce with Time (A Love Story with Occasional Ghosts), 1988; Invitation to Camelot: An Arthurian Anthology of Short Stories (ed.), 1988; Waiting for the Galactic Bus, 1988; The Snake Oil Wars: or, Scheherazade Ginsberg Strikes Again, 1989; Sherwood, 1991; Robin and the King, 1993; Limbo Search, 1995; The Tower of Beowulf, 1995; Lord of Sunset, 1998. As Kate Hawks: The Lovers, 1999; Watch by Moonlight, 2001,

The Night You Could Hear Forever 2007. *Honours:* World Fantasy Award 1982. *Address:* 736 Auburn Ravine Terrace, No. 535, Auburn, CA 95603, USA.

GODWIN, Rebecca Thompson, BA, MA; American writer; b. 9 July 1950, Charleston, SC; m. 1st; two d.; m. 2nd Deane Bogardus 1988. *Education:* Coastal Carolina College, Middlebury College. *Career:* teacher, Bennington Writing Workshops, 1995; Wildacres Writing Workshops, 1996; mem. Associated Writing Programs. *Publications:* Private Parts, 1992; Keeper of the House, 1994. Contributions: South Carolina Review; Paris Review; Iris; Crescent Review; First Magazine. *Honours:* Winner, S. C. Fiction Project, 1988; National Endowment for the Arts Grant, 1994–95. *Address:* PO Box 211, Poestenkill, NY 12140, USA.

GOEDICKE, Patricia, BA, MA; American academic and poet; *Professor Emerita, University of Montana*; b. (Patricia Ann McKenna), 21 June 1931, Boston, Mass; m. 1st Victor Goedicke 1956; m. 2nd Leonard Wallace Robinson 1971. *Education:* Middlebury Coll., Ohio Univ. *Career:* Lecturer in English, Ohio Univ. 1963–68, Hunter Coll., CUNY 1969–71; Assoc. Prof. of Creative Writing, Instituto Allende 1972–79; Visiting Writer-in-Residence, Kalamazoo Coll. 1977; Guest Faculty, Writing Programme, Sarah Lawrence Coll. 1980; Visiting Poet-in-Residence, Univ. of Montana 1981–83, Assoc. Prof. 1983–90, Prof. of Creative Writing 1990–2004, Prof. Emer. 2004–; mem. Acad. of American Poets, Associated Writing Programs, Poetry Soc. of America. *Publications:* Between Oceans 1968, For the Four Corners 1976, The Trail That Turns on Itself 1978, The Dog That Was Barking Yesterday 1980, Crossing the Same River 1980, The King of Childhood 1984, The Wind of Our Going 1985, Listen Love 1986, The Tongues We Speak: New and Selected Poems 1989, Paul Bunyan's Bearskin 1992, Invisible Horses 1996, As Earth Begins to End 2000. Contributions: Reviews, journals, and periodicals. *Honours:* Nat. Endowment for the Arts Fellowship 1976, Duncan Frazier Prize 1976, William Carlos Williams Prize 1977, Pushcart Prize 1977–78, Hon. Mention, Arvon Int. Poetry Competition 1987, Calvin Kizer Poetry Prize 1987, Hon. Award, Memphis State Review 1988, Research Grant 1989, Distinguished Scholar 1991, Univ. of Montana, Residency, Rockefeller Center, Bellaggio, Italy 1993, Distinguished Alumna, Ohio Univ. 2002, Ohioana Poetry Award 2002, Chad Walsh Poetry Prize 2002, H. G. Merriam Award for Distinguished Contribs to Montana Literature 2003, Start Award 2003. *Address:* 310 McLeod Avenue, Missoula, MT 59801, USA (home). *Telephone:* (406) 549-0343 (home). *E-mail:* goedicke@bresnan.net (home).

GOERKE, Natasza; Polish short story writer and poet; b. 1960, Poznań. *Education:* Mickiewicz Univ., Poznań, Jagiellonian Univ., Kraków. *Publications:* Fractale, 1994; Ksiega Pasztetów, 1997; Pozegnania plazmy, 1999; various collections published in trans. in German and English. Contributions: The Eagle and the Crow (anthology), 1996; numerous magazines. *Honours:* Czas Kultury Prize 1993, Akademie Schloss Solitude six-month stipendium, Stuttgart 1995.

GOFF, Martyn, CBE, FIAL, FRSA, FRSL; British author; *Chairman, Advisory Committee and Administrator, Man Booker Prize*; b. 7 June 1923, s. of Jacob Goff and Janey Goff. *Education:* Clifton Coll. *Career:* served in RAF 1941–46; worked in film 1946–48; book seller 1948–70; established Booker Prize (later Man Booker Prize) 1969, Admin. 1970–, Chair. Advisory Cttee Man Booker Prize 2002–; CEO, Book Trust 1970–88, Vice-Pres. 2000– (Deputy Chair. 1991–92, 1996–97, Chair. 1992–96); Fiction Reviewer, Daily Telegraph 1975–88, Non-fiction Reviewer 1988–; Dir and Exec. Chair. Sotheran Ltd antiquarian bookseller 1988–; mem. Arts Council Literature Panel 1973–81, British Nat. Bibliography Research Fund 1976–88, British Library Advisory Council 1977–82, PEN Exec. Cttee 1978–, Exec. Cttee Greater London Arts Council 1982–88, Library and Information Services Council 1984–86; mem. Bd British Theatre Asscn 1983–85; Chair. Paternosters '73 Library Advisory Council 1972–74, New Fiction Soc. 1975–88, School Bookshop Asscn 1977–, Soc. of Bookmen 1982–84 (Pres. 1997–), 1890s Soc. 1990–99, Nat. Life Story Collections 1996–2004, Poetry Book Soc. 1996–99 (mem. Bd 1992–99), Wingate Scholarships 1988–2004, H. H. Wingate Foundation 1998–, Books for Keeps; Vice-Pres. Royal Overseas League 1996–; Dir Nat. Book League, Battersea Arts Centre 1992–97 (Trustee 1981–85); Trustee Cadmean Trust 1981–99, Nat. Literary Trust 1993–2004. *Publications:* fiction: The Plaster Fabric 1957, A Season With Mammon 1958, A Sort of Peace 1960, The Youngest Director 1961, Red on the Door 1962, The Flint Inheritance 1965, Indecent Assault 1967, The Liberation of Rupert Bannister 1978, Tar and Cement 1988; non-fiction: A Short Guide to Long Play 1957, A Further Guide to Long Play 1958, LP Collecting 1960, Why Conform? 1968, Victorian and Edwardian Surrey 1972, Record Choice 1974, Royal Pavilion 1976, Organising Book Exhibitions 1982, Publishing 1988, Prize Writing: An Original Collection of Writings by Past Winners to Celebrate 21 Years of the Booker Prize (ed.) 1989. *Honours:* Hon. DLitt (Oxford Brookes); The Bookseller Services to Bookselling Award 2001. *Address:* Henry Sotheran Ltd, 2 Sackville Street, London, W1S 3DP (office); 95 Sisters Avenue, London, SW11 5SW, England (home). *Telephone:* (20) 7734-1150 (office); (20) 7228-8164 (home). *Fax:* (20) 7434-2019 (office); (20) 7738-9893 (home).

GOLD, Herbert, BA, MA, LèsL; American author; b. 9 March 1924, Cleveland, OH; m. 1st Edith Zubrin 1948 (divorced 1956); two d.; m. 2nd Melissa Dilworth 1968 (divorced 1975); two s. one d. *Education:* Columbia Univ., Sorbonne, Univ. of Paris. *Career:* Lecturer, Western Reserve University, 1951–53; Faculty, Wayne State University, 1954–56; Visiting Prof., Cornell University, 1958, University of California at Berkeley, 1963, 1968, Harvard University, 1964, Stanford University, 1967; Mcguffey Lecturer in English, Ohio University, 1971; Regents Prof., 1973, Visiting Prof., 1974–79, 1985, University of California at Davis. *Publications:* fiction: Birth of a Hero, 1951; The Prospect Before Us, 1954; The Man Who Was Not With It, 1956; 15 x 3 (short stories with R. V. Cassill and James B. Hall), 1957; The Optimist, 1959; Therefore Be Bold, 1960; Love and Like (short stories), 1960; Salt, 1963; Father: A Novel in the Form of a Memoir, 1967; The Great American Jackpot, 1969; Biafra Goodbye, 1970; The Magic Will: Stories and Essays of a Decade, 1971; My Last Two Thousand Years, 1972; Swiftie the Magician, 1974; Waiting for Cordelia, 1977; Slave Trade, 1979; He/She, 1980; Family: A Novel in the Form of a Memoir, 1981; True Love, 1982; Mister White Eyes, 1984; Stories of Misbegotten Love, 1985; A Girl of Forty, 1986; Lovers and Cohorts: Twenty Seven Stories, 1986; Dreaming, 1988; She Took My Arm as if She Loved Me, 1997; Daughter Mine, 2000. Non-Fiction: The Age of Happy Problems, 1962; A Walk on the West Side: California on the Brink, 1981; Travels in San Francisco, 1990; Best Nightmare on Earth: A Life In Haiti, 1991; Bohemia: Where Art, Angst, Love and Strong Coffee Meet, 1993. Contributions: various periodicals. *Honours:* Guggenheim Fellowship 1957, Ohioana Book Award 1957, National Institute of Arts and Letters grant 1958, Longview Foundation Award 1959, California Literature Medal 1968, Commonwealth Club Award for Best Novel, San Francisco 1982, Sherwood Anderson Prize for Fiction 1989; Hon. LHD (Baruch Coll., CUNY) 1988.

GOLDBARTH, Albert, BA, MFA; American poet, writer and academic; b. 31 Jan. 1948, Chicago, IL. *Education:* Univ. of Illinois, Univ. of Iowa, Univ. of Utah. *Career:* Instructor, Elgin Community Coll., IL 1971–72, Central YMCA Community Coll., Chicago 1971–73, Univ. of Utah 1973–74; Asst Prof., Cornell Univ. 1974–76; Visiting Prof., Syracuse Univ. 1976; Asst Prof. of Creative Writing, Univ. of Texas at Austin from 1977; currently Adele Davis Distinguished Prof. of Humanities in the Dept of English, Wichita State Univ. *Publications:* poetry: Under Cover 1973, Coprolites 1973, Opticks: A Poem in Seven Sections 1974, January 31 1974, Keeping 1975, A Year of Happy 1976, Comings Back: A Sequence of Poems 1976, Curve: Overlapping Narratives 1977, Different Flashes 1979, Eurekas 1980, Ink Blood Semen 1980, The Smuggler's Handbook 1980, Faith 1981, Who Gathered and Whispered Behind Me 1981, Goldbarth's Book of Occult Phenomena 1982, Original Light: New and Selected Poems 1973–1983 1983, Albert's Horoscope Almanac 1986, Arts and Sciences 1986, Popular Culture 1989, Delft: An Essay Poem 1990, Heaven and Earth: A Cosmology 1991, Across the Layers: Poems Old and New 1993, The Gods 1993; fiction: Marriage and Other Science Fiction 1994; essays: A Sympathy of Souls 1990, Great Topics of the World: Essays 1994; editor: Every Pleasure: The 'Seneca Review' Long Poem Anthology 1979. *Honours:* Theodore Roethke Prize 1972, Ark River Review Prizes 1973, 1975, NEA grants 1974, 1979, Guggenheim Fellowship 1983. *Address:* c/o English Department, Box 14, Wichita State University, Wichita, KS 67260-0014, USA (office).

GOLDBERG, Barbara June, MA, MEd, MFA; American writer, poet and editor; *Senior Speechwriter, AARP*; b. 26 April 1943, Wilmington, DE; m. 1st J. Peter Kiers 1963 (divorced 1970); m. 2nd Charles Goldberg 1971 (divorced 1990), two s. *Education:* Mt Holyoke College, Yeshiva Univ., Columbia Univ., American Univ. *Career:* Man. speechwriters, AARP (fmrly American Asscn of Retired Persons) 1998–2004, Sr Speechwriter 2004–; Dir Editorial Board, The Word Works publrs 1987–99; Dir Editorial Services American Speech-Language-Hearing Asscn 1988–98; Exec. Ed., Poet Lore 1990–98; mem. Poetry Soc. of America; individual mem. Associated Writing Programs. *Publications:* Berta Broad Foot and Pepin the Short: A Merovingian Romance 1985, Cautionary Tales (Camden Award) 1990, Marvelous Pursuits (Violet Reed Hass Award) 1995, The Royal Baker's Daughter (Felix Pollak Poetry Prize) 2008; three books of poems in Hebrew translation including Night Watch; translations: The Stones Remember: Native Israeli Poetry 1996, After the First Rain: Israeli Poems on War and Peace 1998, The Fire Stays in Red: Poems of Ronny Someck (trans. with Moshe Dor) 2001; editor: The First Yes: Poems on Communication 1996; contribs to American Poetry Review, American Scholar, Gettysburg Review, Paris Review, Poetry, Virginia Quarterly. *Honours:* two Nat. Endowment for the Arts Fellowships, four Maryland State Art Council Fellowships for poetry, Armand G. Erpf Award Columbia Univ.'s Trans. Center, Witter Bynner Foundation Award, Violet Reed Haas Poetry Award, Felix Pollak Poetry Prize. *Address:* 6703 Fairfax Road, Chevy Chase, MD 20815, USA. *E-mail:* bjgoldberg@comcast.net.

GOLDEN, Arthur, MA; American writer; b. 1957, Chattanooga, Tenn.; m.; two c. *Education:* Harvard Coll., Columbia Univ., Boston Univ. *Career:* magazine journalist, Tokyo 1980–82; tutor in literature and creative writing, Boston Univ.; mem. advisory council, Grub Street, Inc. *Publications:* Memoirs of a Geisha 1997. *Literary Agent:* Leigh Feldman, Darhansoff, Verrill & Feldman Literary Agents, 236 W 26th Street, Suite 802, New York, NY 10001, USA. *Telephone:* (917) 305-1300. *Fax:* (917) 305-1400.

GOLDEN, Mark, MA, PhD; Canadian academic and writer; *Professor of Classics, University of Winnipeg*; b. 6 Aug. 1948, Winnipeg, Man.; m. Monica Becker 1985; one s. *Education:* Univ. Coll., Toronto, Univ. of Toronto. *Career:* Lecturer, later Asst Prof., Univ. of British Columbia 1980–82; Asst Prof., later Prof. of Classics, Univ. of Winnipeg 1982–; Nat. Humanities Center Fellow, Research Triangle Park, NC 1987–88; Visiting Research Fellow, Univ. of New England, Armidale, NSW, Australia 1992; Visiting Fellow, Clare Hall, Cambridge, UK 1995; Center for Hellenic Studies Summer Scholar, Washington, DC 1996. *Publications:* Children and Childhood in Classical

Athens 1990, Inventing Ancient Culture: Historicism, Periodization and the Ancient World (co-ed. with Peter Toohey) 1997, Sport and Society in Ancient Greece 1998, Sex and Difference in Ancient Greece and Rome (co-ed. with Peter Toohey) 2003, Sport in the Ancient World from A to Z 2004; contrib. to scholarly books and journals. *Honours:* Rogers Award for Excellence in Research and Scholarship, Univ. of Winnipeg 1998, Ioannides Memorial Lecturer, Univ. of Western Ontario 1999, Fordyce Mitchel Memorial Lecturer, Univ. of Missouri, Columbia 2000, Stubbs Lecturer, Univ. Coll., Toronto 2004, Edson Memorial Lecturer, Univ. of Wisconsin, Madison 2005. *Address:* Department of Classics, University of Winnipeg, Winnipeg, Man. R3B 2E9, Canada (office). *E-mail:* m.golden@uwinnipeg.ca (office).

GOLDIN, Barbara Diamond, BA; American writer and teacher; b. 4 Oct. 1946, New York, NY; m. Alan Goldin 1968 (divorced 1990); one s. one d. *Education:* University of Chicago, Boston University, Western Washington University. *Publications:* Just Enough Is Plenty: A Hanukkah Tale, 1988; The World's Birthday: A Story About Rosh Hashanah, 1990; The Family Book of Midrash: Fifty-two Stories from the Sages, 1990; Cakes and Miracles: A Purim Tale, 1991; Fire!: The Beginnings of the Labor Movement, 1992; The Magician's Visit: A Passover Tale, 1993; The Passover Journey: A Seder Companion, 1994; Red Means Good Fortune: A Story of San Francisco's China Town, 1994; Night Lights: A Sukkot Story, 1994; Bat Mitzvah: A Jewish Girl's Coming of Age, 1995; Creating Angels: Stories of Tzedakah, 1996; Coyote and the Fire Stick: A Pacific Northwest Indian Tale, 1996; While the Candles Burn: Eight Stories for Hanukkah, 1996; The Girl Who Lived with the Bears, 1997. Contributions: various publications. *Honours:* National Jewish Book Award, 1989; Sydney Taylor Book Award, 1991, and Body-of-Work Award, 1997; Asscn of Jewish Libraries Award, 1992; American Library Asscn Notable Book Citation, 1995.

GOLDMAN, Paul Henry Joseph, BA; British art historian; *Associate Fellow, Institute of English Studies, University of London;* b. 3 April 1950, London; m. Corinna Maroulis 1987. *Education:* Univ. of London, Postgraduate Diploma in Art Gallery and Museum Studies, Univ. of Manchester, Diploma, Museums Asscn in Art. *Career:* Asst Keeper, Dept of Prints and Drawings, British Museum, London, 1974–97; Founder and Cttee mem. Imaginative Book Illustration Soc.; mem. RSA, Soc. of Authors; Fellow, Museums Asscn; Assoc. Fellow, Inst. of English Studies, Univ. of London; Trustee, Cartoon Art Trust. *Publications:* Sporting Life: An Anthology of British Sporting Prints 1983, Looking at Prints, Drawings and Watercolours 1988, Victorian Illustrated Books 1850–1870: The Heyday of Wood-Engraving 1994, Victorian Illustration: The Pre-Raphaelites, the Idyllic School and the High Victorians 1996 (revised 2004), Retrospective Adventures, Forrest Reid, Author and Collector (ed. with Brian Taylor) 1998, John Everett Millais: Illustrator and Narrator 2004, Beyond Decoration – The Illustrations of John Everett Millais 2005; contribs to journals, reviews, and quarterlies. *Honours:* Hon. Prof., School of English, Communication and Philosophy, Univ. of Cardiff. *Address:* Meadow View, East Orchard, Shaftesbury, Dorset SP7 0LG, England (home).

GOLDMAN, William, MA; American author and screenwriter; b. 12 Aug. 1931, Chicago, Ill.; s. of M. Clarence Goldman and Marion Weil; m. Ilene Jones 1961; two d. *Education:* Oberlin Coll. and Columbia Univ. *Publications:* novels: The Temple of Gold 1957, Your Turn to Curtsy, My Turn to Bow 1958, Soldier in the Rain 1960, Boys and Girls Together 1964, The Thing of It Is 1967, No Way to Treat a Lady (under pseudonym Harry Longbaugh), Father's Day 1971, The Princess Bride 1973, Marathon Man 1974, Wigger 1974, Magic 1976, Tinsel 1979, Control 1982, The Silent Gondoliers 1983, The Color of Light 1984; play: Blood, Sweat and Stanley Poole 1961 (with James Goldman); musical comedy: A Family Affair (with James Goldman and John Kander) 1962; non-fiction: Adventures in the Screen Trade 1983, Hype and Glory 1990; Four Screenplays 1995, Five Screenplays 1997, Which Lie Did I Tell? 2000; screenplays: Harper 1966, Butch Cassidy and the Sundance Kid 1969, The Princess Bride 1973, Marathon Man 1976, All the President's Men 1976, A Bridge Too Far 1977, Magic 1978, Heat 1985, Brothers 1987, Year of the Comet 1992, Memoirs of an Invisible Man 1992, Chaplin 1992, Indecent Proposal 1993, Maverick 1994, The Ghost and the Darkness 1996, Absolute Power 1997, Hearts in Atlantis 2001, Dreamcatcher 2003. *Honours:* Acad. Award for best original screenplay for Butch Cassidy and the Sundance Kid 1970, Acad. Award for best screenplay adaptation 1977, Laurel Award for Lifetime Achievement in Screenwriting 1983. *Literary Agent:* William Morris, 151 El Camino Drive, Beverly Hills, CA 90212-1804, USA.

GOLDMARK, Peter Carl, Jr, BA; American newspaper executive; b. 2 Dec. 1940, New York; s. of Peter Carl Goldmark and Frances Charlotte Trainer; m. Aliette Marie Misson 1964; three d. *Education:* Harvard Univ. *Career:* worked for US Office of Econ. Opportunity, Washington; fmr teacher of history Putney School, Vt; employed in Budget Office, City of New York for four years, later Asst Budget Dir Program Planning and Analysis then Exec. Asst to the Mayor 1971; Sec. Human Services, Commonwealth of Mass. 1972–75; Dir of Budget, NY State 1975–77; Exec. Dir Port Authority of NY and NJ 1977–85; joined Times Mirror Co., Los Angeles 1985, fmr Sr Vice-Pres. Eastern Newspapers Div.; Pres. Rockefeller Foundation 1988–97; Chair. and CEO Int. Herald Tribune 1998–2003; mem. Bd of Dirs Financial Accounting Foundation, Lend Lease Corpn, Whitehead Inst. for Biomedical Research. *Address:* c/o International Herald Tribune, 6 bis rue des Graviers, 92521 Neuilly Cédex, France (office).

GOLDSMITH, Howard, (Ward Smith, Dayle Courtney), BA, MA; American author and editor; b. 24 Aug. 1945, New York, NY. *Education:* CUNY, Univ. of Michigan. *Career:* Editorial Consultant, Mountain View Center for Environmental Educ., Univ. of Colorado 1970–85; Senior Ed., Santillana Publishing Co. 1980–85; mem. Poets and Writers, SFWA, Soc. of Children's Book Writers and Illustrators. *Publications:* The Whispering Sea 1976, What Makes a Grumble Smile? 1977, The Shadow and Other Strange Tales 1977, Terror by Night 1977, Spine-Chillers 1978, Sooner Round the Corner 1979, Invasion: 2200 A.D. 1979, Toto the Timid Turtle 1980, The Ivy Plot 1981, Three-Ring Inferno 1982, Plaf Le Paresseux 1982, Ninon, Miss Vison 1982, Toufou Le Hibou 1982, Fourtou Le Kangourou 1982, The Tooth Chicken 1982, Mireille l'Abeille 1982, Little Dog Lost 1983, Stormy Day Together 1983, The Sinister Circle 1983, Shadow of Fear 1983, Treasure Hunt 1983, The Square 1983, The Circle 1983, The Contest 1983, Welcome, Makoto! 1983, Helpful Julio 1984, The Secret of Success 1984, Pedro's Puzzling Birthday 1984, Rosa's Prank 1984, A Day of Fun 1984, The Rectangle 1984, Kirby the Kangaroo 1985, Ollie the Owl 1985, The Twiddle Twins' Haunted House 1985, Young Ghosts 1985, Von Geistern Besessen 1987, The Further Adventures of Batman 1989, Visions of Fantasy 1989, The Pig and the Witch 1990, Mind-Stalkers 1990, Spooky Stories 1990, Little Quack and Baby Duckling 1991, The Proust Syndrome 1992, The President's Train 1991, The Future Light of the World 1993, Evil Tales of Evil Things 1991, The Twiddle Twins' Music Box Mystery 1996, The Gooey Chewy Contest 1996, The Twiddle Twins' Amusement Park Mystery 1997, McGraw-Hill Science Through Stories Series 1998, The Twiddle Twins' Single Footprint Mystery 1999, The Tooth Fairy Mystery 1999, Danger Zone 1999, Strike up the Band 2000, Thomas Edison to the Rescue 2003, Mark Twain at Work 2003, John F. Kennedy and the Stormy Sea 2005; contribs to periodicals, journals, magazines, reviews and newspapers. *Honours:* US Public Health Service Fellowship 1965, Rackham Predoctoral Fellowship, Univ. of Michigan 1966, Phi Sigma Science Award 1966. *Address:* 41-07 Bowne Street, Suite 6B, Flushing, NY 11355-5629, USA.

GOLDSTEIN, Laurence Alan, BA, PhD; American academic, writer, poet and editor; *Professor of English, University of Michigan;* b. 5 Jan. 1943, Los Angeles, CA; m. Nancy Jo Copeland 1968; two s. *Education:* Univ. of California, Los Angeles, Brown Univ. *Career:* instructor, Brown Univ. 1968–70; Asst Prof., Univ. of Michigan 1970–78, Assoc. Prof. 1978–85, Prof. of English 1985–; Ed. Michigan Quarterly Review 1977–. *Publications:* Ruins and Empire: The Evolution of a Theme in Augustan and Romantic Literature 1977, Altamira 1978, The Automobile and American Culture (ed. with David L. Lewis) 1983, The Flying Machine and Modern Literature 1986, The Three Gardens 1987, Writers and Their Craft: Short Stories and Essays on the Narrative (ed. with Nicholas Delbanco) 1991, Seasonal Performances: A Michigan Quarterly Review Reader (ed.) 1991, The Female Body: Figures, Styles, Speculations (ed.) 1992, The American Poet at the Movies: A Critical History 1994, The Male Body: Features, Destinies, Exposures (ed.) 1994, Cold Reading 1995, The Movies: Texts, Receptions, Exposures (ed. with Ira Konigsberg) 1996, Robert Hayden: Essays on the Poetry (ed. with Robert Chrisman) 2001, A Room in California 2005, Writing Ann Arbor: A Literary Anthology 2005; contribs to books, anthologies, reviews and journals. *Honours:* Distinguished Service Award, Univ. of Michigan 1977, Univ. of Michigan Press Book Award 1995. *Address:* Department of English, University of Michigan, Ann Arbor, MI 48109, USA (office). *E-mail:* lgoldste@umich.edu (office).

GOLDSTEIN, Rebecca Newberger, BA, PhD; American writer; b. 23 Feb. 1950, White Plains, NY; m. Sheldon Goldstein 1969; two d. *Education:* Princeton Univ. and Barnard Coll., Columbia Univ. *Career:* Asst Prof. of Philosophy, Barnard Coll. 1976–86; Visiting Prof. of Philosophy Honours Programme, Rutgers Univ. 1988–90; Prof. of Creative Writing MFA Programme, Columbia Univ. 1993–96; Scholar-in-Residence, Brandeis Univ. 1999–2000; Visiting Prof. of Philosophy, Trinity Coll., Hartford, CT 2001–06; Nat. Science Foundation Fellowship Award for philosophy of science 1972–75; Whiting Foundation Fellowship Award in Philosophy 1975–76; American Council for Learned Societies Fellowship 1984; John D. and Catherine T. MacArthur Foundation Fellowship 1996–2001; Bogliasco Foundation Fellow 1998; Fellow American Acad. of Arts and Sciences 2005; Guggenheim Fellowship 2006–07; Radcliffe Fellow, Radcliffe Inst. for Advanced Study, Harvard Univ. 2006–07. *Publications:* fiction: The Mind-Body Problem (Feminista journal 100 Great 20th Century Works of Fiction by Women 2000) 1983, The Late-Summer Passion of a Woman of Mind 1989, The Dark Sister (Whiting Foundation Writer's Award 1994) 1993, Strange Attractors: Stories (Nat. Jewish Book Honor Award 1994) 1993, Mazel (Nat. Jewish Book Award 1995, Univ. of Hartford Edward Lewis Wallant Award 1996) 1995, Properties of Light: A Novel of Love, Betrayal and Quantum Physics (Massachusetts Book Award Honors in Fiction 2001) 2000; contrib. short stories to journals, including Commentary, New Traditions, Prairie Schooner, Tikkun; non-fiction: Incompleteness: The Proof and Paradox of Kurt Gödel 2005, Betraying Spinoza: The Renegade Jew Who Gave us Modernity 2006; contrib. essays and reviews to newspapers, journals and magazines, including Black Clock, Commentary, Nature, NEST, New York Review of Books, New York Times, New York Times Book Review, Seed, Shma, Tikkun. *Honours:* Dr hc (Spertus Inst., Chicago, IL) 2000; Barnard Coll. Montague Prize for excellence in philosophy 1972, Prairie Schooner Award for Best Short Story of 1997. *Website:* www.trincoll.edu/~rgoldste.

GOLDSTEIN, Robert Justin, BA, MA, PhD; American academic and writer; *Research Associate, University of Michigan, Ann Arbor*; b. 28 March 1947, Albany, NY. *Education:* Univ. of Illinois, Univ. of Chicago. *Career:* Research and Admin. Asst, Univ. of Illinois 1972–73; Lecturer, San Diego State Univ. 1974–76; Asst Prof., Assoc. Prof., Full Prof., Oakland Univ., Rochester, MI 1976–2005; Research Assoc., Univ. of Michigan, Ann Arbor 2003–. *Publications:* Political Repression in Modern America 1978, Political Repression in Nineteenth Century Europe 1983, Political Censorship of the Press and the Arts in Nineteenth Century Europe 1989, Censorship of Political Caricature in Nineteenth Century France 1989, Saving 'Old Glory': The History of the American Flag Desecration Controversy 1995, Burning the Flag: The Great 1989–90 American Flag Desecration Controversy 1996, Desecrating the American Flag: Key Documents from the Controversy from the Civil War to 1995 1996, Flag Burning and Free Speech: The Case of Texas v. Johnson 2000, The War for the Public Mind: Political Censorship in Nineteenth-Century Europe 2000, Political Censorship: 'The New York Times' Twentieth Century in Review 2001. *Telephone:* (734) 996-8031 (USA) (office). *E-mail:* goldstei@oakland.edu (office).

GOLDSWORTHY, Peter, BMed, BSurg; Australian poet and writer; b. 12 Oct. 1951, Minlaton, SA; m. Helen Louise Wharldall 1972, one s. two d. *Education:* University of Adelaide. *Publications:* Number Three Friendly Street: Poetry Reader (co-ed.), 1979; Readings from Ecclesiastes, 1982; This Goes With This, 1988; Maestro (novel), 1989; This Goes With That: Poems 1974–2001, 2001. *Honours:* Commonwealth Poetry Prize, 1982; South Australia Poetry Award, 1988.

GOLDSWORTHY, Vesna, MA, PhD; Serbian/British radio broadcaster and writer; *Reader in English Literature and Creative Writing, University of Kingston*; b. (Vesna Bjelogrlic), 1 July 1961, Belgrade. *Education:* Univs of Belgrade and London. *Career:* emigrated to London 1980s; fmrly worked at BBC, reading the news for Serbian section of the World Service; also teacher, Univ. of London and St Lawrence Univ., New York, USA; currently Reader in English Literature and Creative Writing, Univ. of Kingston, runs Centre for Suburban Studies. *Publications:* Inventing Ruritania: The Imperialism of the Imagination 1998, Chernobyl Strawberries (memoir) 2005; contrib. of articles and chapters to Cambridge Guide to Women's Writing in English 1999, Representing Lives: Women and Autobiography 1999, Routledge International Encyclopedia of Women's Studies 2000, London Review of Books. *Address:* Department of English, University of Kingston, Penrhyn Road, Kingston-upon-Thames, Surrey, KT1 2EE, England (office). *Telephone:* (20) 8547-2000 (office). *Fax:* (20) 8547-7388 (office). *E-mail:* v.goldsworthy@kingston.ac.uk (office). *Website:* www.kingston.ac.uk (office); www.chernobylstrawberries.com (home).

GOLEMBIOVSKY, Igor Nestorovich; Russian journalist; *Founder and Editor, Noviye Izvestiya*; b. 7 Sept. 1935, Samtredia, Georgia; m.; one s. *Education:* Tbilisi State Univ. *Career:* journalist activities since 1958; with Izvestia 1966–, Deputy Ed. of Div., Special Corresp., Deputy Exec. Sec., Exec. Sec., First Deputy Ed.-in-Chief 1988–91, Ed.-in-Chief 1991–97; Founder and Ed. Noviye Izvestiya 1997–. *Publications:* author of articles on key problems of social and political life. *Address:* Noviye Izvestiya, Dolgorukovskaya str. 19/8, 103006 Moscow, Russia. *Telephone:* (495) 795-31-57. *Fax:* (495) 795-31-38.

GOLLANCZ, Livia Ruth, ARCM; British musician (French horn) and publishing executive; b. 25 May 1920, d. of Victor Gollancz and Ruth Lowy. *Education:* St Paul's Girls' School and Royal Coll. of Music, London. *Career:* French horn player, London Symphony Orchestra 1940–43, Hallé Orchestra 1943–45, Scottish Orchestra 1945–46, BBC Scottish Orchestra 1946–47, Royal Opera House, Covent Garden, London 1947, Sadler's Wells, London 1950–53; Editorial Asst, Typographer Victor Gollancz Ltd, Publrs, London 1953, Dir 1954–90, Governing Dir, Jt Man. Dir 1965–85, Chair. 1983–89, Consultant 1990–93. *Publication:* Victor Gollancz, Reminiscences of Affection (ed.) 1968. *Address:* 26 Cholmeley Crescent, London, N6 5HA, England.

GÖLLNER, Theodor, PhD; German musicologist; *Director, Commission of Music History, Bavarian Academy of Sciences*; b. 25 Nov. 1929, Bielefeld; s. of Friedrich Göllner and Paula Brinkmann; m. Marie Louise Martinez 1959; one s. one d. *Education:* Univs of Heidelberg and Munich. *Career:* Lecturer, Univ. of Munich 1958–62, Asst Prof., Assoc. Prof. 1962–67; Prof., Univ. of Calif. Santa Barbara 1967–73; Prof., Chair. Inst. of Musicology, Univ. of Munich 1973–97; mem., Dir Comm. of Music History, Bavarian Acad. of Sciences 1982–; mem. European Acad. of Sciences and Arts 1991–. *Publications:* Formen früher Mehrstimmigkeit 1961, Die mehrstimmigen liturgischen Lesungen 1969, Die Sieben Worte am Kreuz 1986, Et incarnatus est in Bachs h-moll-Messe und Beethovens Missa solemnis 1996, Die Tactuslehre in den deutschen Orgelquellen des 15. Jahrhunderts 2003, (ed.) Münchner Veröffentlichungen zur Musikgeschichte 1977–2006, Münchner Editionen zur Musikgeschichte 1979–97, Die psalmodische Tradition bei Monteverdi und Schütz 2006. *Address:* Institute of Musicology, University of Munich, Geschwister-Scholl-Platz 1, 80539 Munich (office); Bahnweg 9, 82229 Seefeld, Germany (home). *Telephone:* (1089) 21802364 (office). *E-mail:* TheodorGoellner@aol.com (home).

GOMERY, Douglas, BS, MA, PhD; American academic and writer; *Resident Scholar, Library of American Broadcasting, University of Maryland*; b. 5 April 1945, New York, NY; m. Marilyn Moon 1973. *Education:* Lehigh Univ., Univ. of Wisconsin at Madison. *Career:* Instructor to Assoc. Prof., Univ. of Wisconsin at Milwaukee 1974–81; Visiting Prof., Univ. of Wisconsin at Madison 1977, Northwestern Univ. 1981, Univ. of Iowa 1982, Univ. of Utrecht 1990, 1992; Assoc. Prof., Univ. of Maryland 1981–86, Prof., Dept of Radio-TV-Film 1987–92, then Coll. of Journalism 1992–, currently Resident Scholar, Library of American Broadcasting; Sr Researcher, Woodrow Wilson Center for Int. Scholars, Washington, DC 1988–92. *Publications:* High Sierra: Screenplay and Analysis 1979, Film History: Theory and Practice (with Robert C. Allen) 1985, The Hollywood Studio System 1986, The Will Hays Papers 1987, American Media (with Philip Cook and Lawrence W. Lichty) 1989, The Art of Moving Shadows (with Annette Michelson and Patrick Loughney) 1989, Movie History: A Survey 1991, Shared Pleasures 1992, The Future of News (with Philip Cook and Lawrence W. Lichty) 1992, A Media Studies Primer (with Michael Cornfield and Lawrence W. Lichty) 1997, Media in America (ed.) 1998, Who Owns the Media? (Picard Prize) 2000, The Coming of Sound 2004; contribs to books and scholarly journals. *Honours:* Jeffrey Weiss Literary Prize, Theatre Historical Soc. 1988, Prize, Theatre Library Assen 1992. *Address:* Library of American Broadcasting, University of Maryland, MD 20742 (office); 4817 Drummond Avenue, Chevy Chase, MD 20815, USA (home). *Telephone:* (301) 405-9160 (office); (301) 951-4385 (home). *E-mail:* dgomery@umd.edu (office).

GOMEZ, Jewelle Lydia, BA, MS; American writer and poet; b. 11 Sept. 1948, Boston, MA. *Education:* Northeastern University, Columbia Graduate School of Journalism. *Career:* Assoc., 1984–91, Dir of Literature, 1991–93, New York State Council on the Arts; Adjunct Prof., New College of California, 1994, Menlo College, CA, 1994; Writer-in-Residence, California Arts Council, 1995–96; mem. American Center of Poets and Writers; PEN. *Publications:* The Gilda Stories, 1991; Forty-Three Septembers, 1993; Oral Tradition, 1995. Contributions: various publications.

GÖNCZ, Árpád, LLD; Hungarian fmr head of state and writer; b. 10 Feb. 1922, Budapest; s. of Lajos Göncz and Ilona Heimann; m. Mária Zsuzsanna Göntér 1946; two s. two d. *Education:* Pázmány Péter University of Arts and Sciences, Budapest. *Career:* employed as banking clerk with Nat. Land Credit Inst.; joined Ind. Smallholders, Landworkers and Bourgeois Party; leading positions in Ind. Youth Org.; Ed.-in-Chief Generation (weekly); sentenced in 1957 to life imprisonment as defendant in political Bibó trial; released under amnesty 1963; then freelance writer and literary translator, especially of English works; Pres. Hungarian Writers Federation 1989–90, Hon. Pres. 1990–; founding mem. Free Initiatives Network, Free Democratic Fed., Historic Justice Cttee; mem. of Parl. 1990; Acting Pres. of Hungary May–Aug. 1990, Pres. of Hungary 1990–2000. *Publications include:* Men of God (novel) 1974, Encounters (short stories) 1980, Homecoming and Other Stories (short stories) 1991, Hungarian Medea (play), Balance (play), Iron Bars (play), A Pessimistic Comedy (play), Persephone (play), political essays; translated more than 100 works, mostly by British and American authors, including James Baldwin, Edgar Lawrence Doctorow, William Faulkner, William Golding, Ernest Hemingway, William Styron, Susan Sontag, John Updike, Edith Wharton and others. *Honours:* Hon. KCMG 1991; Dr hc (Butler) 1990, (Connecticut) 1991, (Oxford) 1995, (Sorbonne) 1996, (Bologna) 1997; Attila József Prize 1983, Wheatland Prize 1989, Premio Meditteraneo 1991, George Washington Prize 2000, Pro Humanitate Award 2001, Polish Business Oscar Award 2002. *Address:* Office of the Former President, 1055 Budapest, Kossuth tér 4, Hungary (office). *Telephone:* (1) 441-3550 (office). *Fax:* (1) 441-3552 (office).

GONZÁLEZ, Ángel; Spanish poet; b. 1925, Oviedo. *Career:* Prof., Univ. of New Mexico, Albuquerque 1972–90; mem. Spanish Royal Acad. 1996–; winner of several literary prizes including Premio Príncipe de Asturias 1985. *Publications include:* Áspero mundo (Harsh World), Prosemas y menos, Palabra sobre palabra (Word upon Word). *Address:* c/o Spanish Royal Academy, Calle Felipe IV 4, 28014 Madrid, Spain.

GONZÁLEZ, Justo Luis, MA, PhD, DDL; American theologian, writer and editor; b. 9 Aug. 1937, Havana, Cuba; m. 1st Erlantina Ramos 1959 (divorced 1972); one d.; m. 2nd Catherine Gunsalus 1973. *Education:* University of Havana, Seminario Evangélico de Teología, Matanzas, Yale University, University of Strasbourg, Seminario Evangélico de Puerto Rico. *Career:* Prof. of Historical Theology, Seminario Evangélico de Puerto Rico, 1961–69; Research Fellow, Yale University, 1968; Asst Prof. of World Christianity, 1969–71, Assoc. Prof., 1971–77, Emory University; Visiting Prof. of Theology, Interdenominational Theological Center, 1977–88; Ed., Apuntes, 1980–2000; Adjunct Prof. of Theology, Columbia Theological Seminary, 1988–91; mem. United Methodist Church; many ecumenical commissions and task forces. *Publications:* The Development of Christianity in the Latin Caribbean, 1969; A History of Christian Thought, Vol. I, From the Beginnings to the Council of Chalcedon, 1970, Vol. II, From Saint Augustine to the Eve of the Reformation, 1971, Vol. III, From the Reformation to the Present, 1979; Their Souls Did Magnify the Lord: Studies on Biblical Women (with Catherine Gunsalus González), 1977; Rejoice in Your Saviour: A Study for Lent-Easter (with Catherine Gunsalus González), 1979; Liberation Preaching: The Pulpit and the Oppressed (with Catherine Gunsalus González), 1980; In Accord: Let Us Worship (with Catherine Gonsalus González), 1981; The Story of Christianity, Vol. I, Early and Medieval Christianity, 1984, Vol. II, From the Reformation to the Present, 1985; Paul: His Impact on Christianity (with Catherine Gunsalus González), 1987; The Crusades: Piety Misguided, 1988; Monasticism: Patterns of Piety, 1988; The Theological Education of Hispanics, 1988; Christian Thought Revisited: Three Types of Theology, 1989; A Faith More Precious Than Gold: A Study of 1 Peter (with Catherine Gunsalus González), 1989;

Faith and Wealth: A History of Early Christian Ideas on the Origin, Significance, and Use of Money, 1990; Mañana: Christian Theology from a Hispanic Perspective, 1990; Each in Our Own Tongue: A History of Hispanic Methodism (ed.), 1991; Voces: Voices from the Hispanic Church (ed.), 1992; Out of Every Tribe and Nation: Christian Theology at the Ethnic Roundtable, 1992; The Liberating Pulpit (with Catherine Gunsalus González), 1994; Journey Through the Bible, Vol. 11, Luke, 1994, Vol. 13, Acts of the Apostles, 1995; When Christ Lives in Us, 1995; Santa Biblia: The Bible Through Hispanic Eyes, 1996; Church History: An Essential Guide, 1996; Revelation (with Catherine Gunsalus González), 1997; For the Healing of the Nations: The Book of Revelation in an Age of Cultural Conflict, 1999; Mark's Message for the New Millennium, 2000; Acts: The Gospel of the Spirit, 2001; The Changing Shape of Church History, 2003. Other: many books in Spanish. Contributions: numerous books, reference works, journals, periodicals, etc. *Address:* 336 S Columbia Drive, Decatur, GA 30030, USA.

GONZÁLEZ, Ray, MFA; American writer, poet, editor and essayist; b. El Paso, TX. *Education:* Univ. of Texas at El Paso, Southwest Texas State Univ. *Career:* Literary Dir, Guadaloupe Cultural Arts Centre, San Antonio; Poetry Ed., Bloomsbury Review for over 20 years; Ed., Guadaloupe Review; founder, Luna poetry journal 1998. *Publications include:* poetry: The Heat of Arrivals 1996, Cabato Sentora 1999, Memory Fever 1999, Turtle Pictures 2000; essays: The Underground Heart: Essays from Hidden Landscapes 2002; short story collections: Circling the Tortilla Dragon 2002; editor: Touching the Fire: 15 Poets of the Latino Renaissance 1998; contributor to Best American Poetry 1999–2000, The Pushcart Prize: Best of the Small Presses 2000, The Norton Anthology of Nature Writing. *Honours:* Illinois Arts Council Fellowship in Poetry 1998; Amercian Book Award for Excellence in Editing 1993, Josephine Miles Book Award for Excellence in Literature 1997, Minnesota Book Award for Poetry 2001. *Address:* c/o Curbstone Press, 321 Jackson Street, Willimantic, CT 06226-1738, USA. *E-mail:* info@curbstone.org. *Website:* www.curbstone.org.

GONZÁLEZ GALLEGO, Rubén David; Russian writer; b. 20 Sept. 1968, Moscow; s. of David Rafael González Oviedo and Aurora Gallego Rodríguez. *Career:* emigrated to Prague, Czech Repub. 2001; lived in Madrid, Spain 2002–05; now resident in Germany. *Publications:* Byeloye na chernom (trans. as White on Black) (Booker-Open Russia Prize) 2003. *Address:* c/o Alfaguara de Novela, Torrelaguna 60, 28043, Madrid, Spain. *Telephone:* (91) 7449060. *Fax:* (91) 7449224. *E-mail:* info@tea-at-5.com (office). *Website:* www.tea-at-5.com (office); www.alfaguara.santillana.es.

GOOCH, John, BA, PhD; British academic and writer; b. 25 Aug. 1945, Weston Favell, England; m. Catharine Ann Staley 1967, one s. one d. *Education:* King's College, London. *Career:* Asst Lecturer in History, 1966–67, Asst Lecturer in War Studies, 1969, King's College, University of London; Lecturer in History, 1969–81, Senior Lecturer, 1981–84, Reader in History, 1984–88, Prof. of History, 1988–92, University of Lancaster; Ed., Journal of Strategic Studies, 1978–; Secretary of the Navy Senior Research Fellow, US Naval War College, 1985–86; Visiting Prof. of Military and Naval History, Yale University, 1988; Prof. of International History, University of Leeds, 1992–; mem. Army Records Society, chair. of the council, 1983–; FRHistS, vice-pres., 1990–94. *Publications:* The Plans of War: The General Staff and British Military Strategy c.1900–1916; Armies in Europe, 1980; The Prospect of War: Studies in British Defence Policy 1847–1942, 1981; Politicians and Defence: Studies in the Formulation of British Defence Policy 1847–1970, 1981; Strategy and the Social Sciences, 1981; Military Deception and Strategic Surprise, 1982; Soldati e Borghesi nell' Europa Moderna, 1982; Army, State and Society in Italy 1870–1915, 1989; Decisive Campaigns of the Second World War, 1989; Military Misfortunes: The Anatomy of Failure in War (with Eliot A Cohen), 1990; Airpower: Theory and Practice, 1995. Contributions: scholarly journals. *Honours:* Premio Internazionale di Cultura, Città di Anghiari, 1983; Knight, Royal Military Order of Vila Viçosa, Portugal, 1991. *Address:* School of History, University of Leeds, Leeds LS2 9JT, England. *Telephone:* (113) 343-3585. *E-mail:* j.gooch@leeds.ac.uk.

GOOCH, Stanley Alfred, BA, DipEd, BSc; British writer; b. 13 June 1932, London, England; m. Ruth Senior 1961. *Education:* King's College, London, Institute of Education, London, Birkbeck College, London. *Publications:* Four Years On, 1966; Total Man, 1972; Personality and Evolution, 1973; The Neanderthal Question, 1977; The Paranormal, 1978; Guardians of the Ancient Wisdom, 1979; The Double Helix of the Mind, 1980; The Secret Life of Humans, 1981; Creatures from Inner Space, 1984; The Child with Asthma, 1986; Cities of Dreams, 1989. Contributions: New Scientist; New Society; British Journal of Psychology; British Journal of Social and Clinical Psychology; British Journal of Educational Psychology; International Journal of Human Development. *Honours:* Royal Literary Fund Awards, 1984, 1987, 1994.

GOODALL, Dame Jane, DBE, PhD; British ethologist; *Founder, Jane Goodall Institute;* b. 3 April 1934, London; d. of Mortimer Herbert Morris-Goodall and Vanne Morris-Goodall (née Joseph); m. 1st Hugo Van Lawick 1964 (divorced 1974); one s.; m. 2nd M. Derek Bryceson 1975 (died 1980). *Education:* Uplands School, Univ. of Cambridge. *Career:* Sec. Univ. of Oxford; Asst Ed. Documentary Film Studio; Asst Sec. to Louis Leakey, worked in Olduvai Gorge, then moved to Gombe Stream Game Reserve (now Gombe Nat. Park), camp became Gombe Stream Research Centre 1964; Scientific Dir Gombe Wildlife Research Inst. 1967–; founder and mem. Bd of Dirs Jane Goodall Inst. for Wildlife Research 1977–; Visiting Prof., Stanford Univ., Calif. 1971–75; A. D. White Prof.-at-Large, Cornell Univ., NY 1996–2002; mem. Advisory Panel World Summit on Sustainable Devt 2002; visiting lecturer, numerous univs; speaker on conservation issues, appearing on numerous TV shows including: 20/20, Nightline, Good Morning America. *Film:* Jane Goodall's Wild Chimpanzees 2002. *Publications:* In the Shadow of Man 1971, Chimpanzees of Gombe: Patterns of Behavior 1986, The Chimpanzee Family Book 1989, Through a Window 1990, Visions of Caliban 1993, Jane Goodall: With Love 1994, Dr. White 1999, 40 Years at Gombe 1999, Brutal Kinship 1999, Reason for Hope 1999, Africa in My Blood: An Autobiography in Letters 2000, Beyond Innocence: An Autobiography in Letters, the Later Years 2001, Performance and Evolution in the Age of Darwin 2002, Ten Trusts: What We Must Do to Care for the Animals We Love 2002, Harvest for Hope 2005; for children: Grub: the Bush Baby, Chimpanzees I Love: Saving Their World and Ours 2001, My Life with the Chimpanzees. *Honours:* Légion d'honneur 2006; Hon. Visiting Prof. in Zoology, Dar es Salaam Univ. 1973–; Hon. Foreign mem. American Acad. of Arts and Sciences; hon. doctorates from numerous univs, including: Utrecht Univ., Netherlands, Ludwig-Maximilians Univ., Munich, Univ. of Stirling, UK, Providence Univ., Taiwan, Univ. of Guelph and Ryerson Univ., Canada, Buffalo Univ., Tufts Univ. and other univs in USA; Franklin Burr Award, Nat. Geographic Soc. 1963–64, Conservation Award, New York Zoological Soc. 1974, Albert Schweitzer Award, Int. Women's Inst. 1987, Nat. Geographic Soc. Centennial Award 1988, Kyoto Prize 1990, Hubbard Medal for Exploration, Nat. Geographic Soc. 1995, Medal of Mt Kilimanjaro 1996, John Hay Award, Orion Soc. 1998, Gandhi/King Peace Award 2001, UN Messenger of Peace 2002–, Benjamin Frinklin Medal 2003, Prince of Asturias Award 2003, Time European Heroes, UNESCO Gold Medal 2006. *Address:* c/o The Jane Goodall Institute for Wildlife Research, Education and Conservation, 4245 North Fairfax Drive, #600, Arlington, VA 22203, USA (office). *Telephone:* (703) 682 9220 (office). *Fax:* (703) 682 9312 (office). *Website:* www.janegoodall.org (office).

GOODHEART, Eugene, MA, PhD; American academic and writer; *Edytha Macy Gross Professor of Humanities Emeritus, Brandeis University;* b. 26 June 1931, New York, NY; m. Joan Bamberger; one s. one d. *Education:* Columbia Coll., Univ. of Virginia, Sorbonne Univ., Paris, Columbia Univ. *Career:* Instructor, Bard Coll. 1958–60, Asst Prof. 1960–62; Asst Prof., Univ. of Chicago 1962–66; Assoc. Prof., Mount Holyoke Coll. 1966–67; Assoc. Prof., MIT 1967–70, Prof. 1970–74; Visiting Prof., Wellesley Coll. 1968; Prof., Boston Univ. 1974–83; Edytha Macy Gross Prof. of Humanities Emer., Brandeis Univ. 1983–, also Dir, Center for the Humanities 1986–; Adjunct Prof. of English, Columbia Univ. 1986; Corresponding Ed., Partisan Review, 1978–; mem. PEN. *Publications:* The Utopian Vision of D. H. Lawrence, 1963; The Cult of the Ego: The Self in Modern Literature, 1968; Culture and the Radical Conscience, 1978; The Failure of Criticism, 1978; The Skeptic Disposition in Contemporary Criticism, 1984; Pieces of Resistance, 1987; Desire and Its Discontents, 1991; The Reign of Ideology, 1996; Does Literary Studies Have a Future?, 1999; Confessions of a Secular Jew, 2001; Novel Practices: Classic Modern Fiction 2004. Contributions: journals and periodicals. *Honours:* Fulbright Scholarship, Paris, 1956–57; ACLS Fellowship, 1965–66; Guggenheim Felowship, 1970–71; Nat. Endowment for the Humanities Senior Fellowship, 1981; Nat. Humanities Center Fellow, 1987–88; Rockefeller Foundation Fellowship, Bellagio, Italy, 1989. *Address:* c/o Department of English, Brandeis University, Waltham, MA 02254, USA (office). *Telephone:* (781) 736-2160 (office). *Fax:* (781) 736-2179 (office). *E-mail:* goodhear@brandeis.edu (office).

GOODISON, Lorna Gaye; Jamaican poet, painter and writer; b. 1 Aug. 1947, Kingston; one d. *Education:* art schools in Kingston and New York, USA. *Career:* teacher of Creative Writing, USA and Canada; has participated in literary festivals in New York, London and Erlangen. *Publications:* poetry: Poems 1974, Tamarind Season 1980, I Am Becoming My Mother 1986, Heartease 1988, Selected Poems 1992, To Us All Flowers Are Roses 1995; short stories: Baby Mother and the King of Swords 1989. *Honours:* Institute of Jamaica Centenary Prize 1981, Commonwealth Poetry Prize 1986. *Address:* 8 Marley Close, Kingston 6, Jamaica.

GOODMAN, Elinor Mary; British political broadcaster and journalist; b. 11 Oct. 1946, d. of Edward Weston Goodman and Pamela Longbottom; m. Derek John Scott 1985. *Education:* pvt. schools and secretarial coll. *Career:* Consumer Affairs Corresp. Financial Times newspaper 1971–78, Political Corresp. 1978–82; Political Corresp. Channel Four News (TV) 1982–88, Political Ed. 1988–2005. *Address:* Martinscote, Oare, Marlborough, Wilts. SN8 4JA, England.

GOODMAN, Jonathan; British author, poet, publisher and editor; b. 17 Jan. 1931, London, England. *Career:* Theatre Dir and Television Prod., various companies, United Kingdom, 1951–64; Dir, Anmbar Publications Ltd, London, 1967–; Gen. Ed., Celebrated Trials Series, David & Charles (Publishers) Ltd, Newton Abbott, Devon, 1972–. *Publications:* Martinee Idylls (poems), 1954; Instead of Murder (novel), 1961; Criminal Tendencies (novel), 1964; Hello Cruel World Goodbye (novel), 1964; The Killing of Julia Wallace, 1969; Bloody Versicles, 1971; Posts-Mortem, 1971; Trial of Ian Brady and Myra Hindley (ed.), 1973; Trial of Ian Ruth Ellis (ed.), 1975; The Burning of Evelyn Foster, 1977; The Last Sentence (novel), 1978; The Stabbing of George Harry Storrs, 1982; Pleasure of Murder, 1983; Railway Murders, 1984; Who-He, 1984; Seaside Murders, 1985; The Crippen File (ed.) 1985; The Underworld (with I. Will), 1985; Christmas Murders (ed.) 1986; The Moors Murders,

1986; Acts of Murder, 1986; Murder in High Places, 1986; The Slaying of Joseph Bowne Elwell, 1987.

GOODWEATHER, Hartley (see King, Thomas Hunt)

GOODWIN, Doris Helen Kearns, BA, PhD; American historian; b. 4 Jan. 1943, Rockville Centre, NY; m. Richard Goodwin 1973, three s. *Education:* Colby College, Harvard University. *Career:* Research Assoc., US Dept of Health, Education, and Welfare, 1966; Special Asst, US Dept of Labor, 1967, and to Pres. Lyndon B. Johnson, 1968; Asst Prof., 1969–71, Asst Dir, Institute of Politics, 1971, Assoc. Prof. of Government, 1972, Harvard University; Special Consultant to Pres. Lyndon B. Johnson, 1969–73; mem. Amnerican Political Science Asscn; Council on Foreign Relations; Group for Applied Psychoanalysis; Signet Society; Women Involved. *Publications:* Lyndon Johnson and the American Dream, 1976; The Fitzgeralds and the Kennedys: An American Saga, 1987; No Ordinary Time: Franklin and Eleanor Roosevelt: The Home Front in World War II, 1994; Wait Till Next Year: A Memoir, 1997; Every Four Years: Presidential Campaigns and the Media Since 1896, 2003; Team of Rivals 2005. Contributions: books and television. *Honours:* Fulbright Fellow, 1966; White House Fellow, 1967; Pulitzer Prize for History, 1995.

GOONERATNE, Malini Yasmine, AO, PhD, DLitt; Australian academic, writer and poet; *Professor Emerita, Macquarie University;* b. 22 Dec. 1935, Colombo, Sri Lanka; d. of S.J.F. Dias and Esther Mary (née Ramkeesoon) Bandaranaike; m. Brendon Gooneratne 1962; one s. one d. *Education:* Bishop's Coll. (Colombo), Univs of Ceylon and Cambridge (UK). *Career:* Lecturer in English Ceylon Univ. 1965–72; Sr Lecturer in English Macquarie Univ., NSW, Australia 1972, Assoc. Prof. 1979, Dir Postcolonial Literature and Language Research Centre 1988–93, Chair. of English Literature 1991–99, Prof. Emer. 1999–; Nat. Co-ordinator Commonwealth Visiting Fellowship 1989; Resident Fellow Literary Criterion Centre, India 1990; Visiting Prof. Edith Cowan Univ., WA 1991, Univ. of Michigan, USA 1991; Patron Jane Austen Soc. of Australia 1990; Vice-Pres. FILLM 1990–; mem. Australian Fed. of Univ. Women, Australian Soc. of Authors. *Publications include:* English Literature in Ceylon 1815–1878 1968, Jane Austen 1970, Word, Bird, Motif (poems) 1971, The Lizard's Cry and Other Poems 1972, Alexander Pope 1976, Diverse Inheritance: a Personal Perspective on Commonwealth Literature 1980, 6,000 Feet Death Dive: Poems 1981, Relative Merits: the Bandaranaike Family of Sri Lanka 1986, A Change of Skies 1991, Celebrations and Departures: Poems 1991, The Pleasures of Conquest 1995, This Inscrutable Englishman: Sir John D'Oyly, Baronet (1774–1824) (with B. Gooneratne) 1999, Masterpiece and Other Stories 2002, Celebrating Sri Lankan Women's English Writing 2002. *Honours:* Marjorie Barnard Literary Award for Fiction 1992, Raja Rao Award 2001. *Address:* Macquarie University, Department of English, College of Humanities, North Ryde, NSW 2109, Australia (office). *Telephone:* (2) 9876-2111 (office). *Fax:* (2) 9876-8698 (office). *E-mail:* yasmine@humanities.mq.edu.au (office). *Website:* www.nla.gov.au/ms/findaids/9094.html (office).

GOOS, Maria; Dutch playwright, screenwriter and director; b. 1956, Breda; m. Peter Blok; two d. *Education:* Acad. of Dramatic Art, Maastricht. *Career:* director with theatre companies; Artistic Man., De Kompaan theatre group. *Screenplays include:* Familie 2001, Cloaca 2003. *Television screenplays:* De Keizerin van België 1990, Oog in oog (series) 1990, Klokhuis 1991, Hartslag 1991, Pleidooi (series) 1991–94, Oud geld (series) 1995–97, Familie 1999, Icarus 1999, Ver van huis 2000, De Aanklacht 2000, Leef! 2002, Lieve Mensen (also dir) 2003. *Plays:* writer and director: En toen Mamma 1982, Blessuretijd 1983, Tussen Zussen 1983, Een avond in Extase 1984, De Keizerin van België 1985, Helden 1986, De Kuba Walda's 1998, Nu Even Niet 2001, Smoeder (also actress) 2004; writer only: Alles is liefde 1988, Eeuwig Jong 1988, Draaikonten 1997, Krambamboelie 1999, Familie 1999, Cloaca 2002, Nu Even Well 2003; director only: In het uiterste geval by Paul Binnerts 1987. *Honours:* Acad. Award Nederland for Best Series 1998–99, for Best TV Drama 2004, Lira Script Award 2001, Golden Gate Award 2002, Publieksprijs en de speciale juryprijs 2003. *Address:* Kik Productions, Postbus 13120, 3507 Utrecht LC, Netherlands (office). *E-mail:* info@kikproductions.nl (office). *Website:* www.mariagoos.nl.

GORALIK, Linor, BSc; Russian writer and journalist; b. 1975, Dnepropetrovsk, Ukraine. *Education:* Beer-Sheva Univ. *Career:* lived in Israel 1989–2000; worked as a computer programmer, IT man. and lecturer before becoming a full-time writer; Culture Ed. and columnist, Grani.ru online magazine; freelance contrib. to The Russian Journal, XXL, Elle, Paradox. *Publications:* novels: Nyet (The Net, with Sergei Kuznetsov) 2004, Polovina Neba (Half of the Sky, with Stanislav Lvovsky) 2004; non-fiction: Nedetskaya Yeda (Not Baby Food) 2005, The Hollow Woman: Barbie's World Inside and Outside 2006. *Honours:* Triumph Prize for best young poet 2003. *E-mail:* linor@russ.ru. *Website:* litera.ru/slova/linor.

GORDIMER, Nadine, FRSL; South African writer; b. 20 Nov. 1923, Springs; d. of Isidore Gordimer and Nan Myers; m. 2nd Reinhold Cassirer 1954 (died); one s. one d. *Education:* convent school. *Career:* mem. African Nat. Congress 1990–; Vice-Pres. International PEN; Goodwill Amb. UNDP; mem. Congress of S African Writers; mem. jury Man Booker Int. Prize 2007. *Publications:* The Soft Voice of the Serpent (stories), The Lying Days (novel) 1953, Six Feet of the Country (stories) 1956, A World of Strangers (novel) 1958, Friday's Footprint (stories) 1960, Occasion for Loving (novel) 1963, Not For Publication (stories) 1965, The Late Bourgeois World (novel) 1966, South African Writing Today (co-ed.) 1967, A Guest of Honour (novel) 1970, Livingstone's Companions (stories) 1972, The Black Interpreters (literary criticism) 1973, The Conservationist (novel) 1974, Selected Stories 1975, Some Monday for Sure (stories) 1976, Burger's Daughter 1979, A Soldier's Embrace (stories) 1980, July's People (novel) 1981, Something Out There (novella) 1984, A Sport of Nature (novel) 1987, The Essential Gesture (essays) 1988, My Son's Story (novel) 1990, Jump (short stories) 1991, Crimes of Conscience (short stories) 1991, None to Accompany Me (novel) 1994, Writing and Being (lectures) 1995, The House Gun 1997, Living in Hope and History: Notes on our Century (essays) 1999, The Pickup 2001, Loot and Other Stories 2003, Telling Tales (ed. and contrib.) 2004, Get A Life 2005, Beethoven was One-Sixteenth Black 2007. *Honours:* Hon. Fellow, American Acad. of Arts and Letters, American Acad. of Arts and Sciences; Hon. Mem. American Inst. of Arts and Letters; Commdr, Ordre des Arts et des Lettres 1987; Charles Eliot Norton Lecturer in Literature, Harvard Univ. 1994; Dr hc (Cambridge) 1992, (Oxford) 1994; WHSmith Literary Award 1961, Thomas Pringle Award (English Acad. of SA) 1969, James Tait Black Memorial Prize 1971, Booker Prize (co-winner) 1974, Grand Aigle d'Or Prize (France) 1975, CNA Literary Award (S Africa) 1974, 1979, 1981, 1991, Scottish Arts Council Neil M. Gunn Fellowship 1981, Modern Language Asscn Award (USA) 1981, Premio Malaparte (Italy) 1985, Nelly Sachs Prize (Germany) 1985, Bennett Award (USA) 1987, Benson Medal (Royal Soc. of Literature) 1990, Nobel Prize for Literature 1991, Primo Levi Award 2002, Mary McCarthy Award 2003, Bavarian State Premier's Hon. Award (part of the Corine Int. Book Prize), Grinzane Cavour Prize 2007. *Literary Agent:* c/o AP Watt Ltd, 20 John Street, London, WC1N 2DR, England. *Telephone:* (20) 7405-6774. *Fax:* (20) 7831-2154. *E-mail:* apw@apwatt.co.uk. *Website:* www.apwatt.co.uk.

GORDON, Donald Ramsay, BA, MA; Canadian writer; *Editor, Long Ridge Writers' Group;* b. 14 Sept. 1929, Toronto, ON; m. Helen E. Currie 1952, three s. *Education:* Queen's University, Kingston, University of Toronto, LSE, England. *Career:* writer, Filing Ed., The Canadian Press, Toronto, Montréal, Edmonton, 1955; Asst Ed., The Financial Post, Toronto, 1955–57; European Correspondent, Canadian Broadcasting Corporation, London, 1957–63; Asst Prof., Assoc. Prof., Political Science, University of Calgary, Alberta, 1963–66, University of Waterloo, Ontario, 1966–75; Self-employed Writer, Consultant, 1975–81; Chief Writer, The Image Corporation, Waterloo, 1983–92; Instructor, Conestoga College, Kitchener, Ontario, 1991–, Long Ridge Writers' Group, West Redding, CT, USA, 1992–. *Publications:* International Institute of Education 1963, Language, Logic and the Mass Media, 1966; The New Literacy, 1971; The Media, 1972; Fineswine, 1984; The Rock Candy Bandits, 1984; S.P.E.E.D., 1984; The Prosperian Papers, 1989; The Choice, 1990; The Sex Shoppe, 1991, The Rock Candy Bandits 2003, Moustapha's Mischief 2003. *Honours:* Ford Foundation Fellowship 1954, Canada Council Research Fellowship 1969, Ontario Arts Council Award 1999. *Address:* 134 Iroquois Place, Waterloo, Ont. N2L 2S5, Canada. *E-mail:* proseking@msn.com (home). *Website:* rockcandybandits.com (home).

GORDON, Graeme, BA, DEJF; British writer; b. 21 June 1966, Epsom, England. *Education:* University of Sussex, University of Strasbourg, III. *Career:* mem. Writers' Guild of Great Britain. *Publications:* Fiction: Bayswater Bodycount, 1995; Barking Mad. *Address:* c/o Serpent's Tail, 3A Exmouth House, Pine Street, London EC1R 0JH, England.

GORDON, Jaimy, BA, MA, DA; American academic and writer; b. 4 July 1944, Baltimore, MD; m. Peter Blickle 1988. *Education:* Antioch Coll., Brown Univ. *Career:* Writer-in-Residence, Rhode Island State Council on the Arts, 1975–77; Dir, Creative Writing Program, Stephens College, Columbia, MO, 1980–81; Asst Prof., 1981–87, Assoc. Prof., 1987–92, Prof. of English, 1992–, Western Michigan University, Kalamazoo. *Publications:* Shamp of the City-Solo, 1974; The Bend, the Lip, the Kid (narrative poem), 1978; Circumspections from an Equestrian Statue, 1979; Maria Beig: Lost Weddings (trans. with Peter Blickle), 1990; She Drove Without Stopping, 1990; Bogeywoman, 1999. Contributions: Magazines. *Honours:* National Endowment for the Arts Fellowships, 1979, 1991; American Acad. and Institute of Arts and Letters Award, 1991.

GORDON, John William; British writer; b. 19 Nov. 1925, Jarrow-on-Tyne, England; m. Sylvia Young 1954; one s. one d. *Career:* mem. Soc. of Authors. *Publications:* The Giant Under the Snow, 1968; The House on the Brink, 1970; The Ghost on the Hill, 1976; The Waterfall Box, 1978; The Spitfire Grave, 1979; The Edge of the World, 1983; Catch Your Death, 1984; The Quelling Eye, 1986; The Grasshopper, 1987; Ride the Wind, 1989; Secret Corridor, 1990; Blood Brothers, 1991; Ordinary Seaman (autobiog.), 1992; The Burning Baby, 1992; Gilray's Ghost, 1995; The Flesh Eater, 1998; The Midwinter Watch, 1998; Skinners, 1999; The Ghosts of Blacklode, 2002. *Address:* 99 George Borrow Road, Norwich, Norfolk NR4 7HU, England.

GORDON, Lois, BA, MA, PhD; American academic and writer; b. Englewood, NJ; m. Alan Lee Gordon 1961; one s. *Education:* Univ. of Michigan, Univ. of Wisconsin. *Career:* Lecturer in English, City Coll., CUNY 1964–66; Asst Prof. of English, Univ. of Missouri, Kansas City 1966–68; Asst Prof., Fairleigh Dickinson Univ. 1968–71, Assoc. Prof. 1971–75, Prof. of English 1975–, Chair. Dept of English and Comparative Literature 1982–90; Visiting Exchange Prof., Rutgers Univ. 1994; mem. Acad. of American Poets, Authors' Guild, Harold Pinter Soc., Int. League for Human Rights, MLA, PEN, Samuel Beckett Soc. *Publications:* Stratagems to Uncover Nakedness: The Dramas of Harold Pinter 1969, Donald Barthelme 1981, Robert Coover: The Universal Fictionmaking Process 1983, American Chronicle: Six Decades in American

Life, 1920–1980 1987, American Chronicle: Seven Decades in American Life, 1920–1990 1990, Harold Pinter Casebook 1990, The Columbia Chronicle of American Life, 1910–1992 1995, The Columbia World of Quotations 1996, The World of Samuel Beckett, 1906–1946 1996, American Chronicle: Year by Year Through the Twentieth Century 1999, Pinter at 70 2001, Reading Godot 2002, Nancy Cunard: Heiress, Muse, Political Idealist 2007; contrib. to journals, reviews and newspapers. *Address:* c/o Yale University Press, 47 Bedford Square, London, WC1B 3DP, England (office).

GORDON, Lyndall Felicity, BA, PhD, FRSL; South African biographer and academic; *Senior Research Fellow, St Hilda's College, Oxford*; b. 4 Nov. 1941, Cape Town, South Africa; m. Siamon Gordon 1963; two d. *Education:* Univ. of Cape Town, Columbia Univ., New York, USA. *Career:* Asst Prof. of English, Columbia Univ. 1975–76; Lecturer in English, Jesus Coll., Oxford 1977–84; Tutor in English 1984–95, Sr Research Fellow 1995–, St Hilda's Coll., Oxford. *Publications:* Eliot's Early Years 1977, Virginia Woolf: A Writer's Life 1984, Eliot's New Life 1988, Shared Lives 1992, Charlotte Brontë: A Passionate Life 1994, A Private Life of Henry James: Two Women and His Art 1998, T. S. Eliot: An Imperfect Life 1998, Vindication: A Life of Mary Wollstonecraft 2006. *Honours:* Rose Mary Crawshay Prize British Acad. 1978, James Tait Black Memorial Prize 1985, Southern Arts Prize 1989, Cheltenham Festival Prize 1994. *Address:* St Hilda's College, Oxford, OX4 1DY, England (office).

GORDON, Mary Catherine, BA, MA; American writer; b. 8 Dec. 1949, Far Rockaway, Long Island, NY; m. 1st James Brian 1974 (divorced); m. 2nd Arthur Cash 1979; one s. one d. *Education:* Barnard Coll., Syracuse Univ. *Career:* teacher of English, Dutchess Community Coll., Poughkeepsie, NY 1974–78, Amherst Coll., MA 1979; Millicent C. McIntosh Prof. of English, Barnard Coll. 1988–; Guggenheim Fellowship 1993. *Publications:* Final Payments 1978, The Company of Women 1980, Men and Angels 1985, Temporary Shelter (short stories) 1987, The Other Side 1989, Good Boys and Dead Girls (essays) 1992, The Rest of Life: Three Novellas 1993, The Shadow Man: A Daughter's Search for her Father (memoir) 1996, Spending: A Utopian Divertimento 1998, Seeing Through Places: Reflections on Geography and Identity 2000, Joan of Arc 2000, Pearl 2005, The Stories of Mary Gordon (short stories) 2006, Circling My Mother (memoir) 2007. *Honours:* Janet Heidinger Kafka Prize 1979, 1981, Lila Acheson Wallace-Readers' Digest Writers' Award 1992, O. Henry Award 1997, The Story Prize 2007. *Address:* 15 Claremont Avenue, New York, NY 10027, USA.

GÓREC-ROSINSKI, Jan, MJ; Polish poet, writer, essayist and journalist; b. 6 Jan. 1920, Króglik; m. Maria Barbara Dobrzalska-Górec 1938; three s. *Education:* Nicolai Copernici Univ., Torun. *Career:* journalist, Polish radio, 1957–58; Ed., Fakty, 1989–, Metafora (literary magazine), 1989–; mem. Union of Polish Writers in Warsaw. *Publications:* Jamark arlekinów, 1963; Ucieczka z Wiezy Babel, 1964; Bluznierstwo garncarza, 1965; Zaprzeszle horyzonty, 1968; Molitwa za dobrinu, 1968; Czas odnajdywania, 1970; Zywa galaz, 1971; W kamieniu, 1973; Poezje wybrane, 1976; Ulica Sokratesa, 1978; Eroica, 1980; Sen Syzyfa, 1982; Wzejscie slonc, 1985; Departures, 1985; Czyje bedzie królestwo, 1987; Kredowy Bóg, 1987; Czlowiek Podzielony, 1988; Czarnopis, poezje wybrane, 1989; Siedem wieczerników, 1990; Krzyczec beda kamienie, 1991; Czarna perla, 1992; Sloneczny splot, 1993; Demony, 1994; Przechodzien róz, 1995; Rajska jablon, 1995; Przychodzacy: sacrum et profanum, 1997; Mesjasz zbuntowany: dramat mityczny, 2001. Contributions: many publications. *Honours:* Council Award, Bydgoszcz People's Province, 1968; Workers' Publishing Co-operative Award, 1979; Klemens Janicki Award, 1986; International Poetic November Award, 1987; Prof. T. Kotarbinski Prize, 1989; Pres. of Bydgoszcz Artistic Award, 2000; Commander's Order and Star from Pres. of Poland, 2002.

GORES, Joseph Nicholas, MA; American writer, novelist and screenwriter; b. 25 Dec. 1931, Rochester, MN; m. Dori Corfitzen 1976, one s. one d. *Education:* University of Notre Dame, Stanford University. *Career:* Story Ed., B. L. Stryker Mystery Movie Series, ABC-TV, 1988–89; mem. MWA, pres., 1986; International Asscn of Crime Writers; CWA; Private Eye Writers of America. *Publications:* A Time of Predators, 1969; Marine Salvage (non-fiction), 1971; Dead Skip, 1972; Final Notice, 1973; Interface, 1974; Hammett, 1975; Gone, No Forwarding, 1978; Come Morning, 1986; Wolf Time, 1989; Mostly Murder (short stories), 1992; 32 Cadillacs, 1992; Dead Man, 1993; Menaced Assassin, 1994; Contract Null and Void, 1996; Cases, 1998; Speak of the Devil (short stories), 1999; Stakeout on Page Street (short stories), 2000; Cons, Scams and Grifts, 2001, Glass Tiger (novel) 2006; contrib. to numerous magazines and anthologies; eight film scripts; television drama. *Honours:* Best First Novel, 1969, Best Short Story, 1969, Edgar, Best Episodic TV Drama, 1975, MWA; Falcon, Maltese Falcon Society of Japan, 1986. *Address:* PO Box 446, Fairfax, CA 94978, USA. *Telephone:* (415) 454-3462. *Fax:* (415) 454-3143.

GÖRGEY, Gábor; Hungarian poet, novelist and playwright. *Career:* Minister of Cultural Heritage for Hungary. *Publications:* Lilla-Cápák Nyugalom 1976, Légifolyosó 1977, Találkozás egy fél kutyával 1980, Egy vacsora anatómiája 1981, A fél kutya másik fele 1983, Munkavilágítás 1984, A diva bosszúja 1988, Meteoropata nemzet 1989, Mindig újabb kuty ák jönnek 1991, Waterloo kellos közepén 1994. *Address:* c/o Hungarian Cultural Centre, 10 Maiden Lane, Covent Garden, London, WC2E 7NA, England.

GOSAIBI, Ghazi al-, PhD; Saudi Arabian diplomatist, politician and writer; *Minister of Labour*; b. 2 March 1940, al-Hasa; s. of Abdul Rahman Algosaibi and Fatma Algosaibi; m. Sigrid Presser 1968; three s. one d. *Education:* Univs of Cairo, Southern Calif. and London. *Career:* Asst Prof. King Saud Univ., Riyadh 1965, then Prof. and Head of Political Science and Dean of Faculty of Commerce; Dir Saudi Railways 1974; Minister of Industry and Electricity 1975, of Health 1982; Amb. to Bahrain 1984, to UK (also accred to Ireland) 1992–2002; fmrly Minister of Agric. and Water, Minister of Water and Electricity; currently Minister of Labour. *Publications include:* prose: Yes, (Saudi) Minister! A Life in Administration, Seven, An Apartment Called Freedom, The Dilemma of Development, The Gulf Crisis: An Attempt to Understand, Arabian Essays, Dansko, A Revolution in the Sunnah; 18 collections of poetry. *Address:* Ministry of Labour, Omar bin al-Khatab St, Riyadh 11157, Saudi Arabia (office). *Telephone:* (1) 477-8888 (office). *Fax:* (1) 478-9175 (office). *Website:* www.mol.gov.sa (office).

GOSLING(-HARE), Paula Louise, (Ainslie Skinner, Holly Baxter), BA; American writer; b. 12 Oct. 1939, Michigan; m. 1st Christopher Gosling 1968 (divorced 1978); two d.; m. 2nd John Hare 1982. *Education:* Wayne State Univ. *Career:* mem. CWA, chair., 1982; Society of Authors. *Publications:* A Running Duck, 1976; Zero Trap, 1978; The Woman in Red, 1979; Losers Blues, 1980; Minds Eye (as Ainslie Skinner), 1980; Monkey Puzzle, 1982; The Wychford Murders, 1983; Hoodwink, 1985; Backlash, 1987; Death Penalties, 1990; The Body in Blackwater Bay, 1992; A Few Dying Words, 1994; The Dead of Winter, 1995; Death and Shadows, 1999; Underneath Every Stone, 2000; Richochet, 2002, Tears of the Dragon 2004. *Honours:* Gold Dagger, CWA; Arts Achievement Award, Wayne State Univ. *Literary Agent:* Greene & Heaton Ltd, 37 Goldhawk Road, London, W12 8QQ, England.

GOSSETT, Philip, BA, MFA, PhD; American musicologist, academic and writer; *Robert W. Reneker Distinguished Service Professor, University of Chicago*; b. 27 Sept. 1941, New York, NY; m. Suzanne S. Gossett 1963; two s. *Education:* Amherst Coll., Columbia Univ., Princeton Univ. *Career:* Asst Prof., Univ. of Chicago 1968–73, Assoc. Prof. 1973–77, Prof. 1977–84, Chair Dept of Music 1978–84, 1989, Robert W. Reneker Distinguished Service Prof. 1984–, Dean Division of Humanities 1989–99; Visiting Assoc. Prof., Columbia Univ. 1975; Direttore dell'edizione, Edizione critica delle Opere di Gioachino Rossini 1978–; Meadows Visiting Prof., Southern Methodist Univ. 1980; Gen. Ed., Works of Giuseppe Verdi 1981–; Assoc. Prof., Universitá degli Studi, Parma 1983, and Rome 1994; Visiting Prof., Univ. of Paris 1988; Five-Coll. Visiting Prof. 1989; Gauss Seminars, Princeton Univ. 1991; 'Consulenza musicologica', Verdi Festival, Parma 2000–; Hambro Visiting Prof. of Opera Studies, Univ. of Oxford 2001; Visiting Scholar, Phi Beta Kappa 2002–03; Fellow American Acad. of Arts and Sciences 1989; Woodrow Wilson Fellowship 1963–64; Fulbright Scholar, Paris 1965–66; Martha Baird Rockefeller Fellowship 1967–68; Guggenheim Fellowship 1971–72; Nat. Endowment for the Humanities Sr Fellowship 1982–83; mem. American Inst. of Verdi Studies, American Musicological Soc. (Pres. 1994–96), Int. Musicological Soc., Società Italiana di Musicologia, Soc. for Textual Scholarship (Pres. 1993–95). *Publications:* The Operas of Rossini: Problems of Textual Criticism in Nineteenth-Century Opera (two vols) 1970, Treatise on Harmony, by Jean-Philippe Rameau (trans. and ed.) 1971, The Tragic Finale of Tancredi 1977, Early Romantic Opera (ed. with Charles Rosen) 1978–83, Le Sinfonie di Rossini 1981, Rossini Tancredi (critical edn) 1983, Italian Opera 1810–1840 (ed., 25 vols) 1984–92, 'Anna Bolena' and the Maturity of Gaetano Donizetti 1985, Il barbiere di Siviglia 1992, Rossini Ermione (with P. Brauner) 1995, Don Pasquale 1999, Semiranide (with A. Zedda) 2001, Divas and Scholars: Performing Italian Opera 2006; contrib. to reference works, scholarly books and professional journals. *Honours:* Hon. DHL (Amherst Coll. .) 1993; hon. mem. Accademia Filarmonica di Bologna 1992, Accademico Onorario Accademia di Santa Cecilia Rome 2003; Visiting Scholar, Phi Beta Kappa 2002–03; American Musicological Soc. Alfred Einstein Award 1969, Medaglio d'Oro prima classe, Italy 1985, American Acad. of Composers, Authors and Publishers Deems Taylor Award 1986, Mellon Distinguished Achievement Award 2004; Grand Ufficiale dell'Ordine al Merito 1997, Cavaliere di Gran Croce 1998, Order of Rio Branca, Brazil 1998, Socio Straniero, Ateneo Veneto 2001. *Address:* c/o Department of Music, University of Chicago, 1010 E 59th Street, Chicago, IL 60637, USA (office); 5810 S. Harper Avenue, Chicago, IL 60637 (home). *Telephone:* (773) 834-4181 (office); (773) 955-3738 (home). *Fax:* (773) 955-0247 (home). *E-mail:* phgs@uchicago.edu (office).

GÖTHE, (Lars) Staffan; Swedish playwright, actor and director; *Professor, University of Lund*; b. 20 Dec. 1944, Luleå; s. of the late Thorsten Göthe and of Margit Grape-Göthe; m. Kristin Byström 1969; one s. *Education:* Acad. of Performing Arts, Gothenburg. *Career:* actor and playwright, regional theatre of Växjö 1971, Folkteatern, Gothenburg 1974; Headmaster Acad. of Performing Arts, Malmö 1976; actor, Folkteatern, Gävleborg 1983; Dir The RTC Co. 1986–95; actor and playwright, Royal Dramatic Theatre, Stockholm 1995–2003; Prof. of Theatre Acad., Univ. of Lund 2003–. *Plays:* En natt i februari 1972, Den gråtande polisen 1980, La strada dell'amore 1986, En uppstoppad hund 1986, Den perfekta Kyssen 1990, Arma Irma 1991, Boogie Woogie 1992, Blått Hus Med Röda Kinder 1995, Ruben Pottas Eländiga Salonger 1996, Ett Lysande Elände 1999, Temperance 2000, Byta Trottoar 2001, Stjärnan Över Lappland 2005. *Publication:* Lysande Eländen (complete works) 2004. *Honours:* Royal Medal Litteris et Artibus, Award of Royal Swedish Acad. 2005. *Address:* Vindragarvägen 8, 117 50 Stockholm, Sweden (home). *Telephone:* (8) 668-38-18 (office).

GOTO, Hiromi, BA; Japanese writer; b. 31 Dec. 1966, Chiba-ken; two c. *Education:* Univ. of Calgary. *Career:* writer-in-residence Emily Carr Inst. of Art, Design and Media 2003–04; mem. Writers' Union of Canada (co-chair.

racial minority cttee 1995–97). *Publications:* Chorus of Mushrooms (Commonwealth Writers Prize Best First Book (Canada-Caribbean Region) 1995, co-winner Canada-Japan Book Award 1995) 1994, The Water of Possibility 2001, The Kappa Child (James Tiptree Jr Memorial Award) 2001. *Address:* c/o Emily Carr Institute of Art & Design & Media, 1399 Johnston Street, Granville Island, Vancouver, BC V6H 3R9, Canada. *E-mail:* hiromi_goto@ shaw.ca.

GOTTLIEB, Robert Adams, BA; American editor and critic; b. 29 April 1931, New York; s. of Charles Gottlieb and Martha (née Kean) Gottlieb; m. 1st Muriel Higgins 1952; m. 2nd Maria Tucci 1969; two s. one d. *Education:* Columbia Coll. and Cambridge Univ. *Career:* employee Simon and Schuster 1955–65, Ed.-in-Chief 1965–68; Ed.-in-Chief Alfred A. Knopf 1968–87, Pres. 1973–87; Ed.-in-Chief The New Yorker 1987–92; now dance and book critic for New York Observer, New York Times, The New Yorker and New York Review of Books. *Publications:* Reading Jazz 1996, Reading Lyrics (co-author) 2000, George Balanchine – The Ballet Maker 2004. *Address:* 237 East 48th Street, New York, NY 10017, USA.

GOULD, Alan David, BA, DipEd; British poet and novelist; b. 22 March 1949, London; m. Anne Langridge 1984; two s. *Education:* ANU, Canberra, Australia. *Career:* Creative Fellow, ANU 1978; Writer-in-Residence, Geelong Coll. 1978, 1980, 1982, 1985, Australian Defence Forces Acad. 1986, Lincoln Humberside Arts Centre 1988; mem. Literature Bd of the Australia Council 2002–06. *Publications:* poetry: Icelandic Solitaries 1978, Astral Sea 1981, The Pausing of the Hours 1984, The Twofold Place 1986, Years Found in Likeness 1988, Former Light (selected poems) 1992, Momentum 1992, Mermaid 1996, Dalliance and Scorn 1999, A Fold in the Light 2001, The Past Completes Me, Selected Poems 1973–2003; fiction: The Man Who Stayed Below 1984, The Enduring Disguises 1988, To The Burning City 1991, Close Ups 1994, The Tazyrik Year 1998, The Schoonermaster's Dance 2000; essays: The Totem Ship 1996; contrib. to various Australian publications. *Honours:* New South Wales Premier's Prize for Poetry 1981, Prizes for Fiction 1985, 1992, Philip Hodgins Memorial Medal 1999, Royal Blind Society Audio Book of the Year 1999, Co-winner Courier-Mail Book of the Year 2001, Co-winner A.C.T. Book of the Year 2001. *Address:* 6 Mulga Street, O'Connor, ACT 2602, Australia. *E-mail:* tazyrik@hotmail.com.au (home).

GOULDEN, Joseph C., (Henry S. A. Becket); American writer; b. 23 May 1934, Marshall, Texas,; m. 1st, two s.; m. 2nd Leslie Cantrell Smith 1979. *Education:* Univ. of Texas, 1952–56. *Career:* staff writer, Dallas Morning News, Philadelphia Inquirer, 1958–68. *Publications:* The Curtis Caper, 1965; Monopoly, 1968; Truth is the First Casualty, 1969; The Money Givers, 1971; The Superlawyers, 1972; Meany: The Unchallenged Strong Man of American Labor, 1972; The Benchwarmers, 1974; Mencken's Last Campaign (ed.), 1976; The Best Years, 1976; The Million Dollar Lawyers, 1978; Korea: The Untold Story of the War, 1982; Myth-Informed (with Paul Dickson), 1983; The News Manipulators (with Reed Irvine and Cliff Kincaid), 1983; Jerry Wurf: Labor's Last Angry Man, 1982; The Death Merchant, 1984; There Are Alligators in Our Sewers (with Paul Dickson), 1984; Dictionary of Espionage (as Henry S. A. Becket), 1987; Fit to Print: A. M. Rosenthal and His Times, 1988, The Money Lawyers 2006. Contributions: over 200 articles to magazines. *Honours:* Nat. Magazine Award 1976. *Address:* 1534 29th Street NW, Washington, DC 20007, USA. *E-mail:* josephg894@aol.com.

GOVIER, Katherine Mary, MA; Canadian writer; b. 4 July 1948, Edmonton, AB; d. of George Wheeler and Doris Eda Govier; m. John Allen Honderich 1981; one s. one d. *Education:* Univ. of Alberta and York Univ. (ON). *Career:* Writing first published 1972; fiction and non-fiction published by major British and Canadian magazines 1973–81; Lecturer in English Ryerson Polytech Inst., Toronto, ON 1973–74; Contrib., Ed. Toronto Life magazine 1975–77; Visiting Lecturer Creative Writing Programme, York Univ. 1982–86; Research Fellow Univ. of Leeds, UK 1986; Chair. Writers' Devt Trust 1990–91; mem. PEN Canada (Vice-Pres. 1996–97), Writers' Union of Canada; Nat. Magazine Award 1979; Foundation for the Advancement of Canadian Letters Authors' Award 1979. *Publications:* Going Through the Motions 1981, Random Descent (3rd edn) 1987; Short stories: Fables of Brunswick Avenue 1985, Before and After (2nd edn) 1994; Novels: Between Men 1987, Hearts of Flame 1991, The Immaculate Conception Photography Gallery 1994, Angel Walk 1996, Creation 2003; Short stories included in Oxford Book of Canadian Short Stories, Canadian Short Stories (ed R. Weaver) 1985, More Stories by Canadian Women (ed R. Sullivan) 1987, Oxford Book of Canadian Short Stories (ed M. Atwood and R. Weaver) 1995. *Address:* c/o Elaine Markson Agency, 44 Greenwich Ave, New York, NY 10011, USA (Agent); 54 Farnham Ave, Toronto, ON M4V 1H4, Canada (home).

GOW, Michael; Australian playwright and writer; b. 14 Feb. 1955, Sydney. *Plays:* Away 1986, Furious 1991, Sweet Phoebe 1994, Live Acts on Stage. *Publications:* fiction: The Kid 1983, The Astronaut's Wife 1984, On Top of the World 1986, Europe 1987, 1841 1988, All Stops Out (juvenile) 1991. *Literary Agent:* RGM Associates, PO Box 128, Surry Hills, NSW 2010, Australia. *Telephone:* (2) 9281-3911. *Fax:* (2) 9281-4705. *E-mail:* info@rgm.com.au. *Website:* www.rgm.com.au.

GOWDY, Barbara Louise, CM; Canadian novelist and short story writer; b. 25 June 1950, Windsor, ON. *Education:* York Univ. *Career:* mem. PEN Canada, Writer's Union of Canada. *Publications:* Through the Green Valley (novel) 1988, Falling Angels (novel) 1989, We So Seldom Look on Love (short stories) 1992, Mister Sandman (novel) 1995, The White Bone (novel) 1998, The

Romantic (novel) 2003, Helpless (novel) 2007; contrib. to Best American Short Stories, The New Oxford Book of Canadian Short Stories, The Penguin Anthology of Stories by Canadian Women. *Honours:* Marian Engel Award. *Literary Agent:* Westwood Creative Artists, 94 Harbord Street, Toronto, ON M5S 1G6, Canada.

GOWERS, Andrew, MA; British journalist; *Head of Corporate Communications, Lehman Brothers;* b. 19 Oct. 1957, Reading, Berks.; s. of Michael Gowers and Anne Gowers; m. Finola Gowers (née Clarke); one s. one d. *Education:* Trinity School, Croydon and Univ. of Cambridge. *Career:* grad. trainee, Reuters 1980, Brussels Corresp. 1981, Zurich Corresp. 1982, joined Foreign Desk, Financial Times (FT), London 1983, Agric. Corresp. 1984, Commodities Ed. 1985, Middle East Ed. 1987, Foreign Ed. 1992, Deputy Ed. 1994, Acting Ed. 1997, Ed. FT Deutschland (German Language Business Paper) 1999, Ed. FT 2001–05; columnist Evening Standard, Sunday Times 2005–06; Leader Gowers' Review of Intellectual Property for UK Government 2005–06; Head of Corporate Communications Lehman Brothers 2006–. *Publication:* Arafat, The Biography (co-author) 1991. *Address:* 17 Gilkes Crescent, Dulwich, London, SE21 7BP, England (home). *Telephone:* (20) 8299-6761 (home). *Fax:* (20) 8299-3102 (home). *E-mail:* andrewgowers@btinternet.com (home).

GOYTISOLO, Juan; Spanish writer; b. 5 Jan. 1931, Barcelona; m. Monique Lange 1978 (died 1996). *Education:* Univs of Barcelona and Madrid. *Career:* emigrated to France 1957; reporter, Cuba 1965; assoc. with Gallimard Publishing Co.; Visiting Prof. at various univs in USA. *Writing for television:* Alquibla (TVE series). *Publications:* fiction: Juegos de manos (trans. as The Young Assassins) 1954, Duelo en el Paraíso (trans. as Children of Chaos) 1955, El circo (El mañana efímero trilogy vol. one) 1957, Fiestas (El mañana efímero trilogy vol. two) 1958, La resaca (El mañana efímero trilogy vol. three) 1958, La isla 1961, La chanca 1962, Señas de identidad (trans. as Marks of Identity) 1966, Reivindicación del conde don Julián (trans. as Count Julian) 1970, Juan sin tierra (trans. as John the Landless) 1975, Colera de Aquines 1979, Makbara 1980, Paisajes después de la batalla (trans. as Landscapes After the Battle) 1982, Las virtudes del pájaro solitario (trans. as The Virtues of the Solitary Bird) 1988, La cuarentena (trans. as Quarantine) 1991, La saga de los Marx (trans. as The Marx Family Saga) 1993, Campos de Níjar 1993, Las semanas del jardín (trans. as The Garden of Secrets) 1997, Carajicomedia (trans. as A Cock-Eyed Comedy) 2000, Telón de boca 2003; non-fiction: Crónicas Sarracinas (essays, trans. as Saracen Chronicles) 1982, Coto vedado (autobiog., trans. as Forbidden Territory) 1985, En los reinos de Taifa (autobiog., trans. as Realms of Strife) 1986, Cuaderno de Sarajevo (Premio francés Méditerranée) 1994, Reconocimiento (Gran Premio Proartes de Narrativa Iberoamericana) 1997, Pájaro que ensucia su propio nido (essays) 2001, Cinema Eden: Essays from the Muslim Mediterranean 2004, El Lucernario. La pasión crítica de Manuel Azaña 2004; short stories, travel narratives, literary criticism, essays. *Honours:* Premio Europalia de la Comunidad Europea 1985, Premio Nelly-Sachs, Dortmund 1993, Premio Octavio Paz de Poesía y Ensayo, Mexico 2002, Premio Juan Rulfo 2004. *Address:* c/o Sickle Moon Books, Eland Publishing Ltd, Third Floor, 61 Exmouth Market, London, EC1R 4QL, England. *E-mail:* jgoytiso@sauce.pntic .mec.es.

GRACE, Patricia Frances; New Zealand (Maori) writer; b. 1937, Wellington; m., seven c. *Education:* St Mary's College, Wellington Teachers College. *Career:* Teacher, Primary and Secondary Schools, King Country, Northland and Porirua; Writing Fellow, Victoria University, Wellington, 1985. *Publications:* Mutuwhenua: The Moon Sleeps, 1978; Potiki, 1986; Cousins, 1992; Baby No-Eyes, 1998. Short Stories: Waiariki, 1975; The Dream Sleepers and Other Stories, 1980; Electric City and Other Stories, 1980; Selected Stories, 1991; The Sky People, 1994; Collected Stories, 1994; Baby No-Eyes, 1998, Dogside Story (novel) 2001, Tu (novel) 2004; other: several books for children. *Honours:* Hon. HLD (Victoria Univ.) 1989; New Zealand Fiction Award 1987, Kiriyama Pacific Rim Prize for Literature 2001. *Address:* c/o Pearson Education New Zealand Ltd, Private Bag 102908, NSMC, Auckland, New Zealand.

GRAEME, Roderic (see Jeffries, Roderic Graeme)

GRAFF, Henry Franklin, BSS, MA, PhD; American academic and writer; *Professor of History Emeritus, Columbia University;* b. 11 Aug. 1921, New York, NY; m. Edith Krantz 1946; two d. *Education:* City College, CUNY, Columbia University. *Career:* Fellow in History, 1941–42, Tutor in History, 1946, City College, CUNY; Lecturer, 1946–47, Instructor to Assoc. Prof., 1946–61, Chair., Dept of History, 1961–64, Prof. of History, 1961–91, Prof. Emeritus, 1991–, Columbia University; Lecturer, Vassar College, 1953, Yale School of Medicine, 1993; Presidential appointee, National Historical Publications Commission, 1965–71, Pres. John F. Kennedy Assassination Records Review Board, 1993–98; Senior Fellow, Freedom Foundation Media Studies Center, New York City, 1991–92; Dean's Distinguished Lecturer in the Humanities, Columbia University College of Physicians and Surgeons, 1992; mem. American Historical Asscn; Authors' Guild; Council on Foreign Relations; Organization of American Historians; PEN; Society of American Historians; Corresponding mem., Massachusetts Historical Society. *Publications:* Bluejackets with Perry in Japan 1952, The Modern Researcher (with Jacques Barzun) 1962, American Themes (with Clifford Lord) 1963, Thomas Jefferson 1968, American Imperialism and the Philippine Insurrection 1969, The Tuesday Cabinet: Deliberation and Decision on Peace and War under Lyndon B. Johnson 1970, The Call of Freedom (with Paul J. Bohannan) 1978,

The Promise of Democracy 1978, This Great Nation 1983, The Presidents: A Reference History 1984, America: The Glorious Republic 1985, Grover Cleveland 2002; contrib. to scholarly journals and to general periodicals. *Honours:* Townsend Harris Medal City College CUNY 1966; Mark Van Doren Award 1981, Great Teacher Award 1982, Columbia University; Kidger Award New England History Teachers Asscn 1990; Presidential Medal George Washington University 1997; James Madison Award American Library Asscn 1999; Lifetime Achievement Award Westchester Community College Foundation 2000. *Address:* 47 Andrea Lane, Scarsdale, NY 10583, USA. *E-mail:* prehist@aol.com.

GRAFTON, Anthony Thomas, BA, MA, PhD; American historian, academic and writer; b. 21 May 1950, New Haven, CT; m. Louise Ehrlich 1972; one s. one d. *Education:* University of Chicago. *Career:* Instructor in History, Cornell University, 1974–75; Asst Prof., 1975, Assoc. Prof., 1976–85, Prof., 1985–88, Andrew Mellon Prof. of History, 1988–93, Dodge Prof. of History, 1993–2000, Henry Putnam University Prof., 2000–, Princeton University; Exhibit Curator, New York Public Library, New York, 1992; Meyer Schapiro Lecturer, Columbia University, 1996–96; mem. Renaissance Society of America; American Philosophical Society. *Publications:* Joseph Scaliger: A Bibliography, 1852–1982 (ed. with H. J. de Jonge), 1982; Joseph Scaliger: A Study in the History of Classical Scholarship, Vol. 1, Textual Criticism and Exegesis, 1983, Vol. 2, Historical Chronology, 1993; From Humanism to the Humanities: Education and the Liberal Arts in Fifteenth- and Sixteenth-Century Europe (with Lisa Jardine), 1986; Forgers and Critics: Creativity and Duplicity in Western Scholarship, 1990; The Transmission of Culture in Early Modern Europe (with Ann Blair), 1990; Defenders of the Text: The Traditions of Scholarship in an Age of Science, 1450–1800, 1991; New Worlds, Ancient Texts: The Power of Tradition and the Shock of Discovery (with April Shelford and Nancy Siraisi), 1992; The Foundations of Early Modern Europe, 1460–1559 (with Eugene F. Rice), 1994; The Footnote: A Curious History, 1997; Cardano's Cosmos: The Worlds and Works of a Renaissance Astrologer, 1999; Natural Particulars: Nature and the Disciplines in Renaissance Europe (ed. with Nancy Siraisi), 1999; Leon Battista Alberti: Master Builder of the Italian Renaissance, 2000; Bring Out Your Dead: The Past as Revelation, 2001. Contributions: periodicals including: Proceedings of the American Philosophical Society; History and Theory; Journal of the Warburg and Courtauld Institutes; Journal of Roman Studies. *Honours:* Danforth Fellow, 1971–75; Grant-in-Aid, ACLS, 1977; Rollins Bicentennial Professorship, Princeton University, 1978; Guggenheim Fellow, 1988–89; Fairchild Fellow, California Technical Institute, 1988–89; Prize for History, Los Angeles Times, 1993; Behrmann Fellow, Princeton University, 1994–95; Bainton Prize, Sixteenth-Century Studies Conference, 1999; Marron Prize, American Historical Asscn, 2000. *Address:* c/o Department of History, Dickinson Hall, Princeton University, Princeton, NJ 08544, USA.

GRAFTON, Sue, BA; American writer; b. 24 April 1940, Louisville, Ky; d. of C.W. Grafton and Vivian Harnsberger; m. 3rd Steven F. Humphrey; one s. two d. from previous marriages. *Education:* Univ. of Louisville, Ky. *Career:* worked as admissions clerk, cashier and clinic sec., St John's Hosp., Santa Monica, CA; receptionist, later medical educ. sec., Cottage Hosp., Santa Barbara, CA. *Television:* has written numerous films for TV, including Walking Through the Fire (Christopher Award) 1979, Sex and the Single Parent, Mark, I Love You, Nurse; also adaptations of Caribbean Mystery and Sparkling Cyanide by Agatha Christie. *Publications:* Keziah Dane 1967, The Lolly-Madonna War 1969, A is for Alibi 1982, B is for Burglar 1985, C is for Corpse 1986, D is for Deadbeat 1987, E is for Evidence 1988, F is for Fugitive 1989, G is for Gumshoe 1990, H is for Homicide 1991, I is for Innocent 1992, J is for Judgement 1993, K is for Killer 1994, L is for Lawless 1995, M is for Malice 1996, N is for Noose 1998, O is for Outlaw 1999, P is for Peril 2001, Q is for Quarry 2003, R is for Ricochet 2004, S is for Silence (RIO Award of Excellence 2007) 2006, T is for Trespass 2007; Killer in the Family (jt author with S. Humphrey), Love on the Run (jt author with S. Humphrey). *Address:* PO Box 41447, Santa Barbara, CA 93140, USA (office). *Website:* www.suegrafton.com (office).

GRAHAM, Charles S. (see Tubb, Edwin Charles)

GRAHAM, Donald Edward, BA; American newspaper publisher; *Chairman and CEO, The Washington Post Company*; b. 22 April 1945, Baltimore, Md; s. of late Philip L. Graham and of Katharine Meyer Graham; m. Mary L. Wissler 1967; one s. three d. *Education:* Harvard Univ. *Career:* joined the Washington Post 1971, Asst Man. Ed./Sports 1974–75, Asst Gen. Man. 1975–76, Exec. Vice-Pres. and Gen. Man. 1976–79, Publr 1979–; Pres., CEO The Washington Post Co. 1991–93, Chair., CEO 1993–; fmrly reporter and writer for Newsweek. *Address:* The Washington Post, 1150 15th Street, NW, Washington, DC 20071, USA (office). *Telephone:* (202) 334-7138 (office). *Fax:* (202) 334-4536 (office). *Website:* www.washpostco.com (office).

GRAHAM, Henry; British academic and poet; b. 1 Dec. 1930, Liverpool. *Education:* Liverpool Coll. of Art. *Career:* Lecturer in Art History, Liverpool Polytechnic 1968–90; Poetry Ed. Ambit, London 1969–. *Publications:* Good Luck to You Kafka/You'll Need It Boss 1969, Soup City Zoo 1969, Passport to Earth 1971, Poker in Paradise Lost 1977, Europe After Rain 1981, Bomb 1985, The Very Fragrant Death of Paul Gauguin 1987, Jardin Gobe Avions 1991, The Eye of the Beholder 1997, Bar Room Ballads 1999, Kafka in Liverpool 2002; contribs to Ambit, Transatlantic Review, Prism International Review, Evergreen Review; numerous anthologies world-wide. *Honours:* Arts Council Literature Awards 1969, 1971, 1975, Royal Literary Fund Awards 2003–07. *Address:* Flat 5, 23 Marmion Road, Liverpool, L17 8TT, England (home). *Telephone:* (151) 726-0741 (home).

GRAHAM, James (see Patterson, Harry)

GRAHAM, Jorie, BFA, MFA; American poet and academic; *Boylston Professor of Rhetoric and Oratory, Harvard University*; b. 9 May 1951, New York, NY; m. James Galvin. *Education:* New York Univ. and Univ. of Iowa. *Career:* Poetry Ed. Crazy Horse 1978–81, The Colorado Review 1990–; Contributing Ed., Boston Review, Conjunctions, Denver Quarterly; Asst Prof. Murray State Univ., KY 1978–79, Humboldt State Univ., Arcata, CA 1979–81; Instructor Columbia Univ. 1981–83; staff mem. Writers' Workshop and Prof. of English, Univ. of Iowa 1983–1998; Chancellor Acad. of American Poets 1997–; Boylston Prof. of Rhetoric and Oratory in the Dept of English and American Literature and Language, Harvard Univ. 1998–. *Publications:* Hybrids of Plants and of Ghosts 1980, Erosion 1983, The End of Beauty 1987, The Best American Poetry (ed. with David Lehman) 1990, Region of Unlikeness 1991, Materialism 1993, The Dream of the Unified Field (Pulitzer Prize in Poetry 1996) 1995, Errancy 1997, Swarm 1999, Never 2002, Overlord 2004. *Honours:* American Acad. of Poets Award 1977, Poetry Northwest Young Poets Prize 1980, Pushcart Prizes 1980, 1982, Ingram Merrill Foundation grant 1981, Great Lakes Colleges Asscn Award 1981, American Poetry Review Prize 1982, Bunting Fellow Radcliffe Inst. 1982, Guggenheim Fellowship 1983–84, John D. and Catherine T. MacArthur Foundation Fellowship 1990,. *Address:* Department of English, Harvard University, 12 Quincy Street, Cambridge, MA 02138, USA (office). *Telephone:* (617) 495-1189 (office). *Fax:* (617) 496-8737 (office). *E-mail:* graham2@fas.harvard.edu (office). *Website:* www.fas.harvard.edu/~english (office).

GRAHAM, Robert (Bob) Donald; Australian writer and illustrator; b. 20 Oct. 1942, Sydney; m. Carolyn Smith 1968; one s. one d. *Education:* Julian Ashton School of Fine Art, Sydney. *Career:* mem. Australian Soc. of Authors, British Soc. of Authors. *Publications:* Pete and Roland 1981, Here Comes John 1983, Here Comes Theo 1983, Pearl's Place 1983, Libby, Oscar and Me 1984, Bath Time for John 1985, First There Was Frances 1985, Where is Sarah? 1985, The Wild 1986, The Adventures of Charlotte and Henry 1987, Crusher is Coming! 1987, The Red Woollen Blanket 1987, Has Anyone Here Seen William? 1988, Bringing Home the New Baby 1989, Grandad's Magic 1989, Greetings from Sandy Beach 1990, Rose Meets Mr Wintergarten 1992, Brand New Baby 1992, Spirit of Hope 1993, Zoltan the Magnificent 1994, Queenie the Bantam 1997, Buffy 1999, Max (Smarties Prize Gold Medal for Picture Book) 2000, Charlotte and Henry 2000, Let's Get a Pup (Early Childhood CBC Picture Book of the Year 2002, Boston Globe Horn picture book award 2002) 2001, Jethro Byrde 2002, Tales From the Waterhole 2004, Oscar's Half Birthday 2005, Dimity Dumpty 2006. *Honours:* Australian Picture Book of the Year 1988, 1991, 1993, 2002, Highly Commended, Kate Greenaway Medals 1997, Winner (Kate Greenaway) 2002, Smarties Gold Medal 2000, Boston Globe Horn Picture Book Award 2002. *Address:* c/o Walker Books Ltd, 87 Vauxhall Walk, London, SE11 5HJ, England. *Telephone:* (20) 7793-0909. *Website:* www.walkerbooks.co.uk.

GRAHAM, Sonia (see Sinclair, Sonia Elizabeth)

GRAINVILLE, Patrick; French novelist; b. 1 June 1947, Villers-sur-mer; s. of Jacques and Suzanne (née Laquerre) Grainville; m. Françoise Lutgen 1971. *Education:* Lycée Deauville, Sorbonne. *Career:* teacher, Lycée de Sartrouville 1975–96; mem. CNRS literature section 1975. *Publications:* La toison 1972, La lisière 1973, L'abîme 1974, Les flamboyants 1976, La Diane rousse 1978, Le dernier viking 1980, Les fortresses noires 1982, La caverne céleste 1984, Le paradis des orages 1986, L'atelier du peintre 1988, L'orgie, La neige 1990, Colère 1992, Mathieu (jtly.) 1993, Les anges et les faucons 1994, Le lien 1996, Le tyran éternel 1998, Le tour de la fin du monde, Une femme me cache 2000. *Honours:* Prix Goncourt for Les flamboyants 1976; Officier, Ordre nat. du Mérite, Ordre des Arts et des lettres. *Address:* c/o Editions du Seuil, 27 rue Jacob, 75261 Paris cedex 06, France.

GRAN, Peter; American academic and writer; b. 14 Dec. 1941, Jersey City, NJ; m. Judith Abbott 1966. *Education:* BA, Yale University, 1964; MA, 1965, PhD, 1974, University of Chicago. *Career:* Core Faculty, Friends World College, 1974–75; Visiting Asst Prof. of History, University of California, Los Angeles, 1975–77, University of Texas, Austin, 1977–79; Asst, Assoc., Full Prof. of History, Temple University, 1979–. *Publications:* Islamic Roots of Capitalism: Egypt, 1760–1840, 1979, revised edn as Al-Judhur al-Islamiyah li-l-ra'smaliya: Misr 1760–1840, 1992; Beyond Eurocentrism: A New View of Modern World History, 1996. Contributions: books and journals. *Honours:* National Endowment for the Humanities Award, American Research Center in Egypt, 1992; Senior Fulbright Fellow, Cairo, 1994. *Address:* Department of History, Temple University, 951 Gladfelter Hall, Philadelphia, PA 19122, USA. *E-mail:* pgran@astrs.temple.edu.

GRANADOS, Paul (see Kent, Arthur William Charles)

GRANDES HERNÁNDEZ, Almudena; Spanish writer; b. 7 May 1960, Madrid. *Education:* Universidad Complutense. *Publications:* Las edades de Lulú (novel) (Premio Sonrisa Vertical) 1989, Te llamaré Viernes (novel) 1991, Malena es un nombre de tango (novel) 1994, Modelos de mujer (short stories) 1996, Atlas de geografía humana (novel) 1998, Los aires difíciles (novel) 2002, Mercado de Barceló (stories and articles) 2003, Castillos de cartón (novel) 2004, Estaciones de paso (short stories) 2005, El corazón helado (novel) 2007.

Honours: Premio Rossone d'Oro, Italy 1997. *Address:* c/o Tusquets Editores SA, Cesare Cantù, 8.08023 Barcelona, Spain (office). *Website:* www .almudenagrandes.com.

GRANDOWER, Elissa (see Waugh, Hillary Baldwin)

GRANGÉ, Jean-Christophe; French writer; b. 1961, Paris. *Career:* fmr independent journalist, established own news agency. *Publications:* Le Vol des cigognes (trans. as Flight of the Storks) 1994, Les Rivières pourpres (trans. as Blood-Red Rivers) 1997, Le Concile de pierre (trans. as The Stone Council) 2000, L'Empire des loups (trans. as Empire of the Wolves) 2003. *Address:* c/o Éditions Albin Michel, 22 rue Huyghens, 75014 Paris, France. *Website:* www.jc-grange.com.

GRANGE, Peter (see Nicole, Christopher Robin)

GRANN, Phyllis, BA; American publisher and editor; b. 2 Sept. 1937, London, UK; d. of Solomon Grann and Louisa (Bois-Smith) Eitingon; m. Victor Grann 1962; two s. one d. *Education:* Barnard Coll. *Career:* Sec., Doubleday Publrs., New York 1958–60; Ed., William Morrow Inc., New York 1960–62, David McKay Co., New York 1962–70, Simon & Schuster Inc., New York 1970; Vice-Pres. Simon & Schuster Inc. 1976; Pres., Publr G. P. Putnam's & Sons, New York 1976–86; Pres. Putnam Publishing Group Inc. (now Penguin Putnam Inc.), New York 1986–96, CEO 1987–96, Chair. 1997–2001; Vice-Chair. Random House, Inc. 2001–02. *Address:* c/o Random House, Inc., 201 East 50th Street, New York, NY 10014, USA (office).

GRANT, Anne Underwood, AB; American writer; b. 24 Feb. 1946, Savannah, Ga; m. Maxwell Berry Grant, Jr (divorced); one s. one d. *Education:* University of North Carolina at Chapel Hill, Warren Wilson College. *Career:* Community Assoc., N Carolina Arts Council, Raleigh early 1970s; Communications Dir Good Will Publishers, Gastonia, NC early 1980s; Pres. Underwood Grant Advertising, Charlotte, NC 1980s–mid-1990s; Pres. Tarra-diddle Players 1990s; mem. Bd Dirs MWA 1997–99, Pres. Southeast Chapter 1997–99; Chair. Southern Mystery Gathering 1999. *Publications:* Multiple Listing 1998, Smoke Screen 1998, Cuttings 1999, Voices in the Sand 2000. *Address:* 587 George Chastain Road, Horse Shoe, NC 28742, USA. *E-mail:* annieug@sprynet.com.

GRANT, Charles, BA; American writer; b. 12 Sept. 1942, Newark, NJ. *Education:* Trinity College, Hartford, CT. *Publications:* The Shadow of Alpha, 1976; The Curse, 1976; The Hour of the Oxrum Dead, 1977; Writing and Selling Science Fiction (ed.), 1977; The Ravens of the Moon, 1978; The Sound of Midnight, 1978; Shadows (ed., nine vols) 1978–86; Nightmares (ed.), 1979; The Last Call of Mourning, 1979; Legion, 1979; Tales from the Nightside, 1981; Glow of Candles and Other Stories, 1981; Nightmare Seasons, 1982; Night Songs, 1984; The Tea Party, 1985; The Pet, 1986; The Orchards, 1987; Something Stirs, 1992.

GRANT, John, (Jonathan Gash, Graham Gaunt), BM, BS; British physician and writer; b. 30 Sept. 1933, Bolton, Lancashire, England; m. Pamela Richard 1955, three d. *Education:* University of London. *Career:* GP, London 1958–59; Pathologist London and Essex 1959–62; Clinical Pathologist, Hannover and Berlin 1962–65; Lecturer in Clinical Pathology and Head of the Pathology Division, University of Hong Kong 1965–68; Microbiologist, Hong Kong and London 1968–71; Head Bacteriology Unit, School of Hygiene and Tropical Medicine, University of London 1971–88; mem. International College of Surgeons, fellow; Royal Society of Tropical Medicine, fellow; MRCS 1958; LRCP 1958. *Publications:* As Jonathan Gash: The Judas Pair 1977; Gold by Gemini 1978; The Grail Tree 1979; Spend Game 1981; The Vatican Rip 1981; The Sleepers of Erin 1983; Firefly Gadroom 1984; The Gondola Scam 1984; Pearlhanger 1985; The Tartan Ringers 1986; Moonspender 1987; Jade Woman 1989; The Very Last Gambado 1990; The Great California Game 1991; The Lies of Fair Ladies 1992; Paid and Loving Eyes 1993; The Sin Within Her Smile 1994; The Grace of Older Women 1995; The Possessions of a Lady 1996; The Rich and the Profane 1998; A Rag, a Bone, and a Hank of Hair 2000; Bone Dancing 2002, Finding Davey 2005. As Graham Gaunt: The Incomer 1982. *Honours:* CWA Award 1977. *Address:* Silver Willows, Chapel Lane, West Bergholt, Colchester, Essex C06 3EF, England.

GRANT, John (see Barnett, Paul Le Page)

GRANT, Linda, MA; British journalist and writer; b. 15 Feb. 1951, Liverpool, England. *Education:* Univ. of York, MacMaster Univ., Hamilton, ON, Canada, Simon Fraser Univ., Vancouver, Canada. *Career:* journalist 1985–; fmr columnist, Jewish Chronicle; feature writer, Guardian 1995–2000; chair. of judges, Jewish Quarterly Prize 1998; gave George Orwell Memorial Lecture, Sheffield Univ. 2000; mem., advisory panel of the MA in Creative Writing, Middlesex Univ.; mem. Soc. of Authors (man. cttee). *Publications:* fiction: The Cast Iron Shore (David Higham First Novel Award) 1996, When I Lived in Modern Times (Orange Prize for Fiction) 2000, Still Here 2002, Suppose a City 2005; non-fiction: Sexing the Millennium: A Political History of the Sexual Revolution 1993, Remind Me Who I Am Again (MIND/Allen Lane Book of the Year, Age Concern Book of the Year) 1998, The People on the Street: A Writer's View of Israel 2006; contrib. essays in collections. *Literary Agent:* c/o Derek Johns, AP Watt Ltd, 20 John Street, London, WC1N 2DR, England. *Address:* c/o Virago Press, Brettenham House, Lancaster Place, London, WC2E 7EN, England. *Website:* www.lindagrant.co.uk.

GRANT, Nicholas (see Nicole, Christopher Robin)

GRANT, Roderick; British author; b. 16 Jan. 1941, Forres, Morayshire, Scotland. *Publications:* Adventure in My Veins 1968, Seek Out the Guilty 1969, Where No Angels Dwell 1969, Gorbals Doctor 1970, The Dark Horizon (with Alexander Highlands) 1971, The Lone Voyage of Betty Mouat 1973, The Stalking of Adrian Lawford 1974, The Clutch of Caution 1975, The 51st Highland Division at War 1976, Strathalder: A Highland Estate 1978, A Savage Freedom 1978, The Great Canal 1978, A Private Vendetta 1978, But Not in Anger: The RAF in the Transport Role (with Christopher Cole) 1979, Clap Hands for the Singing Molecatcher: Scenes from a Scottish Childhood 1989, On the Rim of Time 2000, Wild Bird in My Open Hand 2001. *Address:* c/o Lightning Source UK Ltd, 6 Precedent Drive, Rooksley, Milton Keynes, Bucks., MK13 8PR, England. *Telephone:* (1908) 443555. *Fax:* (1908) 443594. *E-mail:* enquiries@lightningsource.co.uk.

GRASS, Günter Wilhelm; German writer, poet and artist; b. 16 Oct. 1927, Danzig (now Gdańsk, Poland); m. 1st Anna Schwarz 1954 (divorced 1978); three s. one d.; m. 2nd Ute Grunert 1979. *Education:* Conradinum, Danzig, Kunstakademie, Düsseldorf, Höchschule für Bildende Künste, Berlin. *Career:* served in Luftwaffe 1944–45; adviser to Städtischen Bühnen Frankfurt am Main 1967–70; mem. Akad. der Künste, Berlin (pres. 1983–86), American Acad. of Arts and Sciences; mem. Social Democratic Party (resgnd Dec. 1992). *Plays:* Beritten, hin und zurück 1954, Hochwasser 1954, Die bösen Köche 1957, Noch Zehn Minuten bis Buffalo 1957, Onkel, Onkel 1958, Zweiunddreissig Zähne 1959, Die Plebejer proben den Aufstand 1965, Davor 1968, Die Vogelscheuchen (ballet) 1970. *Publications:* Die Vorzüge der Windhühner (poems, prose and drawings) 1955, Die Blechtrommel (novel, trans. as The Tin Drum) (Award for Best Foreign Novel, France 1962) 1959, Gleisdreieck (poems and drawings) 1960, Katz und Maus (novella, trans. as Cat and Mouse) 1961, Hundejahre (novel, trans. as Dog Years) 1963, Ausgefragt (poems and drawings) 1967, Über das Selbstverständliche 1968, Örtlich betäubt (novel) 1969, Aus dem Tagebuch einer Schnecke 1972, Dokumente zur politischen Wirkung 1972, Mariazuehren (poems and drawings) 1973, Die Bürger und seine Stimme 1974, Der Butt (novel, trans. as The Flounder) 1976, Denkzettel 1978, Das Treffen in Telgte (novel, trans. as The Meeting in Telgte) 1979, Kopfgeburten oder Die Deutschen sterben aus (novel, trans. as Headbirths, or the Germans are Dying Out) 1980, Aufsätze zur Literatur 1980, Zeichnen und Schreiben Band I 1982, Widerstand lernen-Politische Gegenreden 1980–83 1984 Band II 1984, On Writing and Politics 1967–83 1985, Die Rättin (novel) 1986, Züngezeigen 1987, Werkansgabe (10 vols) 1987, Die Gedichte 1955–1986 1988, Deutscher Lastenausgleich: Wider das dumpfe Einheitsgebot 1990, Two States—One Nation? 1990, Vier Jahrzehnte: Ein Werkstattbericht (drawings and notes) 1991, Unkenrufe (novel, trans. as The Call of the Toad) 1992, Rede vom Verlust: Über den Niedergang der politischen Kultur im geiinten Deutschland 1992, Der Ruf der Kröte (novel) 1992, Studienausgabe (12 vols) 1994, Ein weites Feld (trans. as Too Far Afield) 1995, Fundsachen für Nichtleser (poems) 1997, Auf ein anderes Blatt 1999, Vom Abenteuer der Aufklärung (jtly) 1999, Mein Jahrhundert (trans. as My Century) 1999, Nie wieder schweigen 2000, Fünf Jahrzehnte 2001, Im Krebsgang (novel, trans. as Crabwalk) 2002, Telling Tales (contrib. to charity anthology) 2004, Letzte Tänze (watercolours and drawings) 2003, Beim Häuten der Zwiebel (trans as Peeling the Onion, autobiog.) 2006. *Honours:* Dr hc (Kenyon Coll.) 1965, (Harvard) 1976, Lyric Prize, Süddeutscher Rundfunk 1955, Group 47 Prize 1959, Literary Prize, Asscn of German Critics 1960, Georg-Büchner Prize 1965, Theodor-Heuss Prize 1969, Int. Feltrinelli Prize 1982, Karel Čapek Prize 1994, Sonning Arts Prize (Denmark) 1996, Thomas Mann Prize 1996, Hermann Kestan Medal 1995, Nobel Prize for Literature 1999, Premio Príncipe de Asturias 1999. *Address:* Glockengiesserstrasse 21, 23552 Lübeck, Germany.

GRAU, Shirley Ann, BA; American writer; b. 8 July 1929, New Orleans, LA; m. James Feibleman 1955, two s. two d. *Education:* Tulane University. *Publications:* The Black Prince 1955, The Hard Blue Sky 1958, The House on Coliseum Street 1961, The Keepers of the House 1964, The Condor Passes 1971, The Wind Shifting West 1973, Evidence of Love 1977, Nine Women 1985, Roadwalkers 1994; contribs to New Yorker, Saturday Evening Post, etc. *Honours:* Pulitzer Prize for Fiction 1965. *Address:* c/o JCA, 174 Sullivan Street, New York, NY, 10012, USA. *E-mail:* s.grau@worldnet.att.net.

GRAVER, Elizabeth, BA, MFA; American writer and academic; *Professor of English and Creative Writing, Boston College;* b. 2 July 1964, Los Angeles, Calif.; d. of Lawrence and Suzanne Graver; m. James Pingeor; two d. *Education:* Wesleyan Univ., Washington Univ. *Career:* Visiting Prof. of English and Creative Writing, Boston Coll. 1993–95, Asst Prof. of Creative Writing and English 1995–99, Assoc. Prof. 1999–2005, Full Prof. 2005–. *Publications:* Have You Seen Me? (story collection) 1991; novels: Unravelling 1997, The Honey Thief 1999, Awake 2004; contribs to Best American Short Stories, Story, Southern Review, Antaeus, Southwest Review, O. Henry Prize Stories, Ploughshares, Best American Essays, Pushcart Prize Anthology, other journals and anthologies. *Honours:* Fulbright Fellowship, Guggenheim Fellowship, Drue Heinz Literature Prize, Nat. Endowment for the Arts Fellowship, Best American Short Stories 1991 and 2001, Prize Stories, The O. Henry Awards 1994, 1996, 2001, Best American Esssays 1998, Cohen Prize for the Short Story 2001, Pushcart Prize 2001. *Literary Agent:* c/o Richard Parks, The Richard Parks Agency, Box 693, Salem, NY 12865, USA. *Telephone:* (518) 853-9466. *E-mail:* rp@richardparksagency.com. *Website:* www .richardparksagency.com. *Address:* Carney Hall, English Department, Boston

College, Chestnut Hill, MA 02167, USA (office). *Telephone:* (617) 552-4154 (office). *E-mail:* graver@bc.edu (office).

GRAVER, Lawrence Stanley, BA, PhD; American academic; b. 6 Dec. 1931, New York, NY; m. Suzanne Levy Graver 1960, two d. *Education:* City College, CUNY, University of California, Berkeley. *Career:* Asst Prof., University of California, Los Angeles, 1961–64; Assoc. Prof., 1964–71, Prof., 1971–, Williams College; mem. MLA. *Publications:* Conrad's Short Fiction, 1968; Carson McCullers, 1969; Mastering the Film, 1974; Beckett: The Critical Heritage, 1979; Beckett: Waiting for Godot, 1989; An Obsession with Anne Frank: Meyer Levin and The Diary, 1995. Contributions: New York Times Book Review: Saturday Review: New Republic: New Leader; 19th Century Fiction.

GRAVES, Keller (see Rogers, Evelyn)

GRAVES, Richard Perceval, MA; British author; b. 21 Dec. 1945, Brighton, Sussex; two s. one d. *Education:* St John's Coll., Oxford. *Career:* Arnold Lodge School 1968; Harrow School 1969; Holme Grange School 1969–71; Ellesmere College 1971–73; mem. Housman Soc., Powys Soc. (Chair. 2001–05), Soc. of Authors. *Publications:* Lawrence of Arabia and His World 1976, A.E. Housman: The Scholar-Poet 1979, The Brothers Powys 1983, Robert Graves: The Assault Heroic 1986, Robert Graves: The Years with Laura Riding 1990, Richard Hughes 1994, Robert Graves and The White Goddess 1995, Changing Perceptions: The Poets of the Great War 2005. *Honours:* Hawthornden Fellowship 1999. *Literary Agent:* c/o The Sayle Literary Agency, 86 King's Parade, Cambridge, CB2 1SJ, England. *Address:* 7 Lilymead Avenue, Bristol, BS4 2BY, England (home). *Telephone:* (117) 972-4835 (home). *E-mail:* author@richardgraves.org (home). *Website:* www.richardgraves.org (home).

GRAVES, Roy Neil, MA, DA; American academic, poet and writer; *Professor of English, University of Tennessee at Martin;* b. 2 Feb. 1939, Medina, Tenn.; m. Sue Lain Hunt 1965 (divorced 1982); one s. two d. *Education:* Princeton Univ., Duke Univ., Univ. of Mississippi. *Career:* Asst Prof. of English, Lynchburg Branch, Univ. of Virginia 1965–67; Asst Prof. 1967–68, Assoc. Prof. of English 1968–69, Central Virginia Community College, Lynchburg; Asst Prof., Univ. of Tennessee at Martin 1969–77, Assoc. Prof. 1977–82, Prof. of English 1982–. *Publications:* River Region Monographs: Reports on People and Popular Culture (ed.) 1975, 'Medina' and Other Poems 1976, Hugh John Massey of the Royal Hall: The Lost Master Poet of Fourteenth-Century England and the Lost Runes 1977, Out of Tennessee: Poems, with an Introduction 1977, The Runic 'Beowulf' and Other Lost Anglo-Saxon Poems, Reconstructed and Annotated 1979, Shakespeare's Lost Sonnets: The 154 Runic Poems Reconstructed and Introduced 1979, Somewhere on the Interstate (poems) 1987, Shakespeare's Sonnets Upside Down 1995, Always at Home Here: Poems and Insights from Six Tennessee Poets (edited by Ernest Lee) 1997, web publ. of Shakespeare's Lost Sonnets 2003; contribs to reference works and scholarly journals, poems in anthologies and periodicals. *Honours:* Nat. Endowment for the Humanities Grant 1975, Cunningham Teacher/Scholar Award, Univ. of Tennessee at Martin 1997, First Place, Southern Poets over 50 Competition, Kennesaw State Univ. 2002. *Address:* Department of English, University of Tennessee at Martin, Martin, TN 38238, USA (office). *Telephone:* (731) 881-7301 (office). *Fax:* (731) 881-7276 (office). *E-mail:* ngraves@utm.edu (office). *Website:* www.utm.edu/~ngraves (home); www.utm.edu/staff/ngraves/shakespeare.

GRAY, Alasdair James; British writer and painter; b. 28 Dec. 1934, Glasgow; s. of Alexander Gray and Amy Fleming; m. 1st Inge Sørensen (divorced); one s.; m. 2nd Morag McAlpine 1991. *Education:* Glasgow School of Art. *Career:* art teacher, Glasgow and Lanarkshire 1958–62; scene painter, Pavilion and Citizens' theatres 1962–63; freelance writer and painter 1963–76; artist recorder, People's Palace Local History Museum, Glasgow 1976–77; Writer-in-Residence, Glasgow Univ. 1977–79; freelance writer and painter 1979–2001; Prof. of Creative Writing, Univ. of Glasgow 2001–2003; painter of mural decorations in Oran Mor Leisure Centre, Glasgow, 2003–; works in collections of People's Palace Local History Museum, Glasgow, Collin's Gallery, Strathclyde Univ., Hunterian Museum, Univ. of Glasgow; mural paintings in Palace Rigg Nature Reserve Exhibition Centre, New Cumbernauld, Abbot's House Local History Museum, Dunfermline, The Ubiquitous Chip Restaurant, Glasgow; mem. Soc. of Authors, Scottish Artists Union. *Exhibitions include:* Retrospective, Collins Gallery Glasgow 1974; Retrospective, Glasgow, Edinburgh and Aberdeen Art Galleries 1987–88. *Radio plays include:* Quiet People 1968, The Trial of Thomas Muir 1970, Dialogue 1971, Homeward Bound 1973, The Loss of the Golden Silence 1973, McGrothy and Ludmilla 1993, Working Legs 1998. *Television plays include:* The Fall of Kelvin Walker 1967, The Man Who Knew about Electricity 1973, The Story of a Recluse 1987. *Works include:* has designed and illustrated several books including Shoestring Gourmet 1986, Songs of Scotland 1997. *Publications include:* The Comedy of the White Dog (short story) 1979, Lanark: A Life in Four Books (novel) 1981, Unlikely Stories Mostly 1982, Janine (novel) 1984, The Fall of Kelvin Walker (novel) 1985, Lean Tales (co-writer) 1985, Five Scottish Artists (catalogue) 1986, Saltire Self-Portrait 4 (autobiographical sketch) 1988, Old Negatives (four verse sequences) 1989, Something Leather (novel) 1990, McGrotty and Ludmilla (novel) 1990, Poor Things (novel) 1992, Why Scots Should Rule Scotland (polemic) 1992, Ten Tales Tall and True (Short Stories) 1993, A History Maker (novel) 1994, Mavis Belfrage (novel) 1996, Working Legs (play) 1997, The Book of Prefaces 2000, Sixteen Occasional Poems 2000, A Study in Classic Scottish Writing 2001, The

Ends of Our Tethers: 13 Sorry Stories 2003, How We Should Rule Ourselves (polemic, with Adam Tomkins) 2005. *Honours:* Saltire Soc. Award 1981, Times Literary Supplement Award 1983, Whitbread and Guardian Awards 1992. *Literary Agent:* c/o Zoe Waldie, 20 Powis Mews, London, W11 1JN, England. *Address:* 2 Marchmont Terrace, Glasgow, G12 9LT, Scotland. *Telephone:* (141) 339-0093. *Website:* www.alasdairgray.co.uk.

GRAY, Angela (see Daniels, Dorothy)

GRAY, Caroline (see Nicole, Christopher Robin)

GRAY, Douglas, MA, FBA; British/New Zealand academic; *Professor Emeritus, Lady Margaret Hall;* b. 17 Feb. 1930, Melbourne, Australia; s. of Emmerson Gray and Daisy Gray; m. Judith Claire Campbell 1959; one s. *Education:* Wellington Coll. NZ, Victoria Univ. of Wellington, Merton Coll., Oxford. *Career:* Asst Lecturer, Vic. Univ. of Wellington 1952–54, Lecturer in English, Pembroke and Lincoln Colls Oxford 1956–61, Fellow in English, Pembroke Coll. 1961–80, J. R. R. Tolkien Prof. of English Literature and Language and Fellow of Lady Margaret Hall, Oxford 1980–97, Prof. Emer. 1997–, Hon. Fellow, Lady Margaret Hall 1997–. *Publications:* Themes and Images in the Medieval English Lyric 1972, A Selection of Religious Lyrics 1974, Robert Henryson 1979, Oxford Book of Late Medieval Verse and Prose 1985 (ed.), J. A. W. Bennett, Middle English Literature 1986 (ed.); From Anglo-Saxon to Early Middle English 1994 (jt ed.); Selected Poems of Robert Henryson and William Dunbar (ed.) 1998; Oxford Companion to Chaucer 2003 (ed.). *Honours:* Hon. LittD (Victoria Univ. of Wellington) 1995. *Address:* 31 Nethercote Road, Tackley, Oxford, OX5 3AW, England (home). *Telephone:* (1869) 331319 (home).

GRAY, Dulcie Winifred Catherine, CBE, FRSA, FLS; British actress, playwright and author; b. (Dulcie Savage-Bailey), 20 Nov. 1920, Kuala Lumpur, Federated Malay States (now Malaysia); d. of the late Arnold Savage-Bailey and Kate Edith Clulow Gray; m. Michael Denison (deceased) 1939. *Education:* England and Malaya. *Career:* has worked in theatre and films since 1939; repertory includes Aberdeen, Edin., Glasgow, Harrogate; debut as Sorrel in Hay Fever 1939. *Theatre includes:* The Little Foxes, Midsummer Night's Dream 1942, Brighton Rock, Landslide 1943, Lady from Edinburgh 1945, Dear Ruth, Wind is 90 1946, Queen Elizabeth Slept Here 1949, Sweet Peril 1952, We Must Kill Toni, The Diary of a Nobody 1954, Love Affair (also writer) 1956, Double Cross 1958, Let Them Eat Cake 1959, Candida 1960, Heartbreak House 1961, Where Angels Fear to Tread 1963, An Ideal Husband 1965, Happy Family 1967, Number 10 1967, Out of the Question 1968, Three 1970, The Wild Duck 1970, Ghosts 1972, At the End of the Day 1973, Time and the Conways (tour) 1977, A Murder is Announced 1977, Lloyd George Knew my Father (tour) 1980, A Coat of Varnish 1982, School for Scandal (British Council 50th Anniversary European Tour) 1983, The Living Room 1987, The Best of Friends (tour) 1990, 1991, The Importance of Being Earnest (tour) 1991, Tartuffe 1991–92, Two of a Kind (tour) 1995, The Ladykillers (tour) 1999, Les Liaisons Dangereuses (tour) 2000, The Lady Vanishes (tour) 2001. *Films include:* They Were Sisters 1944, Wanted for Murder 1945, A Man about the House 1946, Mine Own Executioner 1947, The Glass Mountain 1948, There Was a Young Lady 1953, A Man Could Get Killed 1965, The Black Crow 1994. *Radio includes:* Front Line Family (BBC serial) 1941; numerous plays. *Television includes:* Howards' Way (series) 1985–90, several plays. *Publications:* Murder on the Stairs, Murder in Melbourne, Baby Face, Epitaph for a Dead Actor, Murder on a Saturday, Murder in Mind, The Devil Wore Scarlet, No Quarter for a Star, The Murder of Love, Died in the Red, The Actor and His World (with Michael Denison), Death in Denims, Butterflies on my Mind (Times Educational Supplement Sr Information Book Prize 1978), Dark Calypso, The Glanville Women, Anna Starr, Mirror Image, Looking Forward, Looking Back (autobiog.), J. B. Priestly (biog.). *Honours:* Queen's Silver Jubilee Medal 1977. *Address:* Shardeloes, Missenden Road, Amersham, Bucks., HP7 0RL, England (home). *Telephone:* (1494) 725555 (home).

GRAY, Francine du Plessix, BA; American author; b. 25 Sept. 1930, Warsaw, Poland; d. of Bertrant du Plessix and Tatiana Yakovleva du Plessix; m. Cleve Gray 1957; two s. *Education:* Bryn Mawr Coll., Black Mountain Coll., Barnard Coll. *Career:* reporter, United Press International, New York City, 1952–54; Asst Ed., Realites Magazine, Paris, 1954–55; Book Ed., Art in America, New York City, 1962–64; Visiting Prof., CUNY 1975, Yale Univ. 1981, Columbia Univ. 1983, Princeton Univ., Brown Univ., Vassar Coll.; Ferris Prof., Princeton Univ. 1986; Annenberg Fellow, Brown Univ. 1997; Gladys Krieble Delmas Chair, Vassar Coll. 2001; mem. American Acad. of Arts and Letters, American Acad. of Arts and Sciences. *Publications:* Divine Disobedience: Profiles in Catholic Radicalism 1970, Hawaii: The Sugar-Coated Fortress 1972, Lovers and Tyrants 1976, World Without End 1981, October Blood 1985, Adam and Eve and the City 1987, Soviet Women: Walking the Tightrope 1991, Rage and Fire: A Life of Louise Colet 1994, At Home with the Marquis de Sade: A Life 1998, Simone Weil 2001, Them: A Memoir of Parents 2005. *Honours:* Officier, Ordre des Arts et des Lettres; Putnam Creative Writing Award, Barnard Coll. 1952, Nat. Book Critics' Circle Award 2006. *Literary Agent:* Janklow-Nesbitt Literary Agency, 445 Park Avenue, New York, 10022, USA. *Telephone:* (212) 355-1724. *Address:* c/o The Penguin Press, 375 Hudson Street, New York, NY 10024, USA.

GRAY, John; British philosopher, academic and writer. *Career:* staff, Inst. of Economic Affairs (UK), Cato Inst., Inst. for Humane Studies, The Liberty Fund, Social Philosophy and Policy Center (all USA); Prof. of Politics, Univ. of

Oxford; currently Prof. of European Thought, LSE. *Publications include:* non-fiction: Hayek on LIberty 1984, Liberalism 1986, Voltaire 1998, False Dawn: The Delusions of Global Capitalism 1998, Two Faces of Liberalism 2000, Straw Dogs: Thoughts on Humans and Other Animals 2003, Al Qaeda and What it Means to be Modern 2003, Heresies: Against Progress and Other Illusions 2004, Black Mass 2007; editor: On Liberty and other essays by John Stuart Mill 1998; contrib. to The Guardian, TLS, Granta (Granta 77: What We Think of America), Journal of Ethics, Demos. *Honours:* Fellow, Jesus Coll., Oxford. *Address:* c/o London School of Economics and Political Science, Houghton Street, London, WC2A 2AE, England. *Telephone:* (20) 7955-7905. *E-mail:* j.gray@lse.ac.uk. *Website:* www.lse.ac.uk.

GRAY, Simon James Holliday, (Hamish Reade), CBE, MA; British writer, playwright and teacher; b. 21 Oct. 1936, Hayling Island; s. of Dr James Davidson Gray and Barbara Cecelia Mary Holliday; m. 1st Beryl Mary Kevern 1965 (divorced); one s. one d.; m. 2nd Victoria Katherine Rothschild 1997. *Education:* Westminster School, Dalhousie Univ., Halifax, NS, Canada and Trinity Coll., Cambridge. *Career:* Supervisor in English, Univ. of BC, Canada 1960–63, Sr Instructor 1963–64; Lecturer in English, Queen Mary Coll., Univ. of London 1965–84; Co-Dir The Common Pursuit, Promenade Theatre, New York 1986; Dir Phoenix Theatre 1988. *Plays:* Wise Child 1968, Sleeping Dog 1968, Dutch Uncle 1969, The Idiot 1971, Spoiled 1971, Butley (Evening Standard Award) 1971, Otherwise Engaged (Best Play, New York Drama Critics' Circle, Evening Standard Award) 1975, Plaintiffs and Defendants 1975, Two Sundays 1975, Dog Days 1976, Molly 1977, The Rear Column 1978, Close of Play 1979, Quartermaine's Terms 1981, Tartuffe 1982, Chapter 17 1982, Common Pursuit 1984, Melon 1987, The Holy Terror and Tartuffe 1990, Hidden Laughter 1990, Cell Mates 1994, Simply Disconnected 1996, Life Support 1997, Just the Three of Us 1997, The Late Middle Classes 1999, Japes 2001, Little Nell 2006. *Radio plays:* The Rector's Daughter (adaptation) 1992, Suffer the Little Children 1993, With a Nod and a Bow 1993, Cell Mates 1995. *Television:* After Pilkington 1987, Old Flames 1990, They Never Slept 1991, Running Late 1992, Unnatural Pursuits (Emmy Award, New York 1993) 1992, Femme Fatale 1993. *Film:* A Month in the Country 1997. *Publications:* novels: Colmain 1963, Simple People 1965, Little Portia 1967, A Comeback for Stark 1968, Breaking Hearts 1997; non-fiction: An Unnatural Pursuit and Other Pieces 1985, How's That for Telling 'Em, Fat Lady (memoirs) 1988, Fat Chance 1995, Enter a Fox (memoirs) 2001, The Smoking Diaries (memoirs) 2004, The Year of the Jouncer 2006. *Honours:* Hon. Fellow, Queen Mary Coll., Univ. of London; several drama awards in UK and USA. *Literary Agent:* Judy Daish Associates, 2 St Charles Place, London, W10 6EG, England. *Telephone:* (20) 8964-8811. *Fax:* (20) 8964-8966.

GRAY, Stephen; South African novelist, poet and editor; b. 1941, Cape Town. *Education:* Univ. of Cape Town, Univ. of Cambridge, UK and Univ. of Iowa, USA. *Career:* Prof. of English, Rand Afrikaans Univ., Johannesburg –1992. *Play:* Schreiner: A One-Woman Play 1983. *Publications:* fiction: Visible People 1977, Caltrop's Desire 1980, Time of Our Darkness 1988, Born of Man 1989, War Child 1994, My Serial Killer and Other Stories 2005; poetry: It's About Time 1974, Hottentot Venus and Other Poems 1979, Love Poems: Hate Poems 1982, Apollo Café and Other Poems 1982–89 1989, Season of Violence 1992, Selected Poems 1960–92 1994, Gabriel's Exhibition 1998; non-fiction: Southern African Literature: An Introduction 1979, John Ross: The True Story 1987, Human Interest and Other Pieces 1993, Accident of Birth: An Autobiography 1993, Freelancers and Literary Biography in South Africa 1999, Life Sentence: A Biography of Herman Charles Bosman 2005, Indaba: Interviews with African Writers 2005; editor: C. Louis Leipoldt's Stormwrack 1980, Modern South African Stories 1981, Modern South African Poetry 1984, The Penguin Book of Southern African Stories 1985, The Penguin Book of Southern African Verse 1988, South Africa Plays: New South African Drama 1994, The Natal Papers of 'John Ross' 1996. *Address:* c/o Human & Rousseau, POB 5050, Cape Town 8000, South Africa (office). *E-mail:* humanhk@humanrousseau.com (office).

GRAYLING, Anthony C., MA, DPhil, FRSA; British philosopher and author; *Professor of Philosophy, Birkbeck College, London*; b. 3 April 1949; m. Katie Hickman; three c. *Education:* Univ. of Oxford. *Career:* Coll. Lecturer 1985–91, Sr Research Fellow 1991–97, St Anne's Coll., Oxford; Lecturer, Inst. of Philosophy, Chinese Acad. of Social Sciences 1984; Dir Sino-British Summer School in Philosophy, Beijing 1988, 1993; Contributing Ed., Philosophical Annual of Chinese Acad. of Social Sciences; Visiting Prof., Univ. of Tokyo 1997; Lecturer, Univs of Chiba, Nagoya and Hokkaido, Japan and Lublin Univ., Poland 1993; Reader in Philosophy, Birkbeck Coll., London, Prof. of Philosophy 2003–; Jan Hus Visiting Fellow, Inst. of Philosophy, Czech Acad. of Sciences 1994, 1996; Supernumerary Fellow, St Anne's Coll., Oxford 1997; mem. Aristotelian Soc. (Hon. Sec. 1993–2001), Fellow, World Econ. Forum 2001. *Play:* On Religion (with Mick Gordon), London 2006–07. *Radio:* current affairs and arts broadcasting. *Publications:* An Introduction to Philosophical Logic 1982, The Refutation of Scepticism 1985, Berkeley: The Central Arguments 1986, Wittgenstein 1988, William Hazlitt 1989, China: A Literary Companion (with Susan Whitfield) 1994, Philosophy: A Guide Through the Subject (ed.) 1995, Russell 1996, Philosophy: Further Through the Subject 1998, Moral Values 1998, The Quarrel of the Age: The Life and Times of William Hazlitt 2001, Wittgenstein: A Very Short Introduction 2001, The Meaning of Things 2002, Russell: A Very Short Introduction 2002, The Reason of Things: Applying Philosophy to Life 2003, Meditations for the Humanist: Ethics for a Secular Age 2002, Life, Sex and Ideas: The Good Life Without God

2003, What is Good?: The Search for the Best Way to Live 2003, The Mystery of Things 2004, The Heart of Things: Applying Philosophy to the 21st Century 2005, Among the Dead Cities: Was the Allied Bombing of Civilians in WWII a Necessity or a Crime? 2006, The Form of Things 2006, Against All Gods 2007, The Choice of Hercules 2007, Towards the Light 2007. *Literary Agent:* c/o Felicity Bryan, 2 North Parade, Banbury Road, Oxford, OX2 6LX. *Telephone:* (1865) 513816. *E-mail:* cc@felicitybryan.com. *Website:* www.felicitybryan.com. *Address:* School of Philosophy, Birkbeck College, Malet Street, London, WC1E 7HX, England (office). *Telephone:* (20) 7631-6383 (office). *Fax:* (20) 7631-6564 (office). *E-mail:* a.grayling@bbk.ac.uk (office); mail@acgrayling.com. *Website:* www.bbk.ac.uk/phil (office); www.acgrayling.com.

GREACEN, Robert; Irish poet and writer; b. 1920, Derry, Northern Ireland. *Education:* Methodist Coll., Belfast and Trinity Coll., Dublin. *Career:* fmrly worked at United Nations Asscn, London; fmr lecturer in adult education; fmr Poetry Consultant Winthrop Univ., South Carolina; cttee mem. Irish Writers' Union; elected mem. Aosdána. *Publications:* poetry: The Bird 1941, One Recent Evening 1944, On the Barricades: Poems 1944, The Undying Day 1948, Faber Book of Contemporary Poetry (ed. with Valentin Iremonger) 1949, A Garland for Captain Fox 1975, I, Brother Stephen 1978, Young Mr Gibbon 1979, A Bright Mask 1985, Carnival at the River 1990, Collected Poems 1944–1994 (Irish Times Award for Literature 1995) 1995, Protestant Without a Horse 1997, Ecstasy 1999, Captain Fox – A Life 2000, Lunch at the Ivy 2002, Selected and New Poems 2006; non-fiction: The Art of Noel Coward 1953, The world of C. P. Snow 1962, Even Without Irene (autobiog.) 1969, Brief Encounters: Literary Dublin and Belfast in the 1940's 1991, The Only Emperor 1992, The Sash My Father Wore (autobiog.) 1997, Rooted in Ulster (essays) 2001; contrib. numerous articles and book reviews to magazines and newspapers. *Honours:* Arts Council of Northern Ireland bursaries 1971, 1984. *Address:* c/o Aosdána – The Arts Council, 70 Merrion Square, Dublin 2, Ireland. *E-mail:* aosdana@artscouncil.ie.

GREAVES, Richard Lee, BA, MA, PhD, FRHistS; American academic and writer; b. 11 Sept. 1938, Glendale, CA; m. Judith Rae Dieker 1959; two d. *Education:* Bethel Coll., Berkeley Baptist Divinity School, Univ. of London, Univ. of Missouri. *Career:* Assoc. Prof. of History, Florida Memorial Coll. 1964–65; Asst Prof. of History, William Woods Coll. 1965–66, Eastern Washington State Coll. 1966–69; Assoc. Prof. of Humanities, Michigan State Univ. 1969–72; Prof. of History 1972–89, Robert O. Lawton Distinguished Prof. of History 1989–, Florida State Univ.; mem. American Historical Asscn, American Philosophical Soc., American Soc. of Church History (pres. 1991), Baptist Historical Soc., Historians of Early Modern Europe, Int. John Bunyan Soc. (pres. 1992–95). *Publications:* The Puritan Revolution and Educational Thought: Background for Reform 1969, John Bunyan 1969, An Annotated Bibliography of John Bunyan Studies 1972, Elizabeth I: Queen of England (ed.) 1974, The Miscellaneous Works of John Bunyan (ed.), Vol. 2 1976, Vol. 8 1979, Vol. 9 1981, Vol. 11 1985, Theology and Revolution in the Scottish Reformation: Studies in the Thought of John Knox 1980, Society and Religion in Elizabethan England 1981, John Bunyan: A Reference Guide (ed. with James Forrest) 1982, Biographical Dictionary of British Radicals in the Seventeenth Century (ed. with Robert Zaller, three vols) 1982, 1983, 1984, Saints and Rebels: Seven Nonconformists in Stuart England 1985, Triumph Over Silence: Women in Protestant History (ed.) 1985, Deliver Us From Evil: The Radical Underground in Britain, 1660–1663 1986, Civilizations of the World: The Human Adventure (with Robert Zaller, Philip Cannistrano and Rhoads Murphey) 1990, Enemies Under His Feet: Radicals and Nonconformists in Britain, 1664–1677 1990, Civilization in the West (with Robert Zaller and Jennifer Roberts) 1992, Secrets of the Kingdom: British Radicals from the Popish Plot to the Revolution of 1688–89 1992, John Bunyan and English Nonconformity 1992, God's Other Children: Protestant Nonconformists and the Emergence of Denominational Churches in Ireland, 1660–1700 1997, Dublin's Merchant-Quaker: Anthony Sharp and the Community of Friends, 1643–1707 1998, Glimpses of Glory: John Bunyan and English Dissent 2002; contrib. to scholarly books and journals. *Honours:* Nat. Endowment for the Humanities grants 1967, 1980, Walter D. Love Memorial Prize, Conference on British Studies 1970, Andrew W. Mellon Fellow 1977, ACLS Fellow 1977, 1983, 1987, American Philosophical Soc. Fellow 1993, Albert C. Outler Prize, American Soc. of Church History 1996, Rockefeller Foundation Fellow, Bellagio Center, Italy 1998, Guggenheim Fellowship 2000. *Address:* Department of History, Florida State University, Tallahassee, FL 32306-2200, USA. *Website:* mailer.fsu.edu/~rgreaves.

GREELEY, Andrew Moran, AB, STB, STL, MA, PhD; American academic and writer; b. 5 Feb. 1928, Oak Park, IL. *Education:* St Mary of the Lake Seminary, Univ. of Chicago. *Career:* Ordained, Roman Catholic Priest, 1954; Asst Pastor, Church of Christ the King, Chicago, 1954–64; Sr Study Dir, 1961–68, Program Dir for Higher Education, 1968–70, Dir of Center for the Study of American Pluralism, 1971–85, Research Assoc., 1985–, Prof. of Social Science, 1991–, Univ. of Chicago; Prof. of Sociology, Univ. of Arizona at Tucson, 1978–; mem. American Catholic Sociological Soc., American Sociological Asscn, Religious Research Asscn, Soc. for the Scientific Study of Religion. *Publications include:* non-fiction: The Catholic Experience: An Interpretation of the History of American Catholicism 1967, Uncertain Trumpet: The Priest in Modern America 1968, What Do We Believe?: The Stance of Religion in America (with Martin E. Marty and Stuart E. Rosenberg) 1968, Life for a Wanderer: A New Look at Christian Spirituality 1969, Come Blow Your Mind with Me (essays) 1971, The Jesus Myth 1971, What a Modern

Catholic Believes about God 1971, The Denominational Society: A Sociological Approach to Religion in America,1972, The Sinai Myth 1972, The Devil, You Say! Man and His Personal Devils and Angels 1974, The Sociology of the Paranormal: A Reconnaissance 1975, Death and Beyond 1976, The Great Mysteries: An Essential Catechism 1976, The Mary Myth: On the Femininity of God 1977, The Best of Times, The Worst of Times (with J. N. Kotre) 1978, Religion: A Secular Theory 1982, Confessions of a Parish Priest: An Autobiography 1986, God in Popular Culture 1989, Myths of Religion 1989, Complaints Against God 1989, Andrew Greeley (autobiog.) 1990, The Bible and Us: A Priest and a Rabbi Read Scripture Together (with Jacob Neusner) 1990, Faithful Attraction: Discovering Intimacy, Love and Fidelity in American Marriage 1991, Love Affair: A Prayer Journal 1992, The Sense of Love 1992, I Hope You're Listening God 1997, Furthermore (autobiog.) 1999, The Catholic Revolution 2004, Priests: A Calling in Crisis 2004, The Making of the Pope 2005; fiction: Nora Maeve and Sebi 1976, The Magic Cup: An Irish Legend 1979, The Cardinal Sins 1981, Ascent into Hell 1984, God Game 1986, All About Women 1989, Fall from Grace 1993, Star Bright: A Christmas Story 1997, The Bishop at Sea 1997, A Midwinter's Tale 1998, The Bishop and the Three Kings 1998, Irish Mist 1999, Younger Than Springtime 1999, The Bishop and the Missing L Train 2000, A Christmas Wedding 2000, Irish Love 2001, The Bishop and the Beggar Girl of St Germain 2001, September Song 2001, Irish Stew 2002, The Bishop in the West Wing 2002, Second Spring 2003, The Bishop Goes to University 2003, Emerald Magic 2004, Priestly Sins 2004, The Golden Years 2004, Irish Cream 2005, Irish Crystal 2006. *Honours:* C. Albert Kobb Award, National Catholic Education Asscn, 1977; Mark Twain Award, Society for the Study of Midwestern Literature, 1987; several hon. doctorates. *Address:* 1155 E 60th Street, Chicago, IL 60637, USA. *Telephone:* (773) 256-6281 (office). *Fax:* (773) 753-7866 (office). *E-mail:* wilk-roberta@norc.org (office). *Website:* www.agreeley.com.

GREEN, Brian (see Card, Orson Scott)

GREEN, Dan, BA; American book publishing executive; b. 28 Sept. 1935, Passaic, NJ; s. of Harold Green and Bessie Roslow; m. Jane Oliphant 1959; two s. *Education:* Syracuse Univ., NY. *Career:* Publicity Dir Dover Press 1957–58; Station WNAC-TV 1958–59; Bobbs-Merrill Co. 1959–62; Simon & Schuster Inc. 1962–85, Assoc. Publr 1976–80, Vice-Pres., Publr 1980–84; Pres. Trade Publishing Group 1984–85; Founder, Publr, Kenan Press 1979–80; CEO Grove Press and Weidenfeld & Nicolson, New York 1985–89; Pres. Kenan Books, New York 1989–, Pom Literary Agency 1989. *Address:* Pom Inc., 611 Broadway, New York, NY 10012 (office); Kenan Books, 611 Broadway, New York, NY 10012, USA. *Telephone:* (212) 673-3835 (office). *Fax:* (212) 673-4653 (office). *E-mail:* pom-inc@att.net (office).

GREEN, Debbie Tucker; British playwright. *Career:* fmr stage man. *Plays:* Born Bad 2003, Dirty Butterfly 2003. *Address:* c/o Nick Hern Books Ltd, The Glasshouse, 49a Goldhawk Road, London, W12 8QP, England. *Telephone:* (20) 8749-4953. *Fax:* (20) 8735-0250. *Website:* www.nickhernbooks.co.uk.

GREEN, Hannah (see Greenberg, Joanne)

GREEN, Jonathon, BA; British writer and broadcaster; b. 20 April 1948, Kidderminster, Worcestershire, England; two s. *Education:* Brasenose Coll., Oxford. *Publications:* Book of Rock Quotes I 1977, Famous Last Words 1979, The Book of Sports Quotes (with D. Atyeo) 1979, Directory of Infamy 1980, Don't Quote Me: The Other Famous Last Words (with D. Atyeo) 1981, The Book of Royal Quotes (with D. Atyeo) 1981, Book of Political Quotes 1982, Book of Rock Quotes II 1982, Contemporary Dictionary of Quotations 1982, What a Way to Go 1983, Newspeak: A Dictionary of Jargon 1983, revised edn as The Dictionary of Jargon 1987, The Dictionary of Contemporary Slang 1984, The Cynics' Lexicon 1984, Sweet Nothings: A Book of Love Quotes 1985, Consuming Passions: A Book of Food Quotes 1985, It Takes All Sports: Sporting Anecdotes (with D. Atyeo) 1986, The Slang Thesaurus 1986, The A to Z of Nuclear Jargon 1986, Says You: A Twentieth-Century Quotation Finder 1988, Day in the Life: Voices from the English Underground, 1961–71 1988, The Bloomsbury Good Word Guide 1988, The Encyclopedia of Censorship 1990, Them: Voices from the Immigrant Community in Contemporary Britain 1990, The Dictionary of Political Language 1991, Neologisms: A Dictionary of Contemporary Coinage 1991, It: The State of Sex Today 1992, All Dressed Up: The Sixties and the Counter-Culture 1998, Cassell Dictionary of Slang 1998, Cannabis: The Story of the Weed that Rocked the World 2005. *Literary Agent:* Lucas Alexander Whitey, Elsinore House, 77 Fulham Palace Road, London, W6 8JA, England. *Address:* 117 Ashmore Road, London, W9 3DA, England (home).

GREEN, Martin Burgess, BA, DipEd, MA, PhD; British academic and writer; b. 21 Sept. 1927, London, England; m. Carol Elizabeth Hurd 1967, one s. two d. *Education:* St John's College, Cambridge, King's College, London, Sorbonne, Univ. of Paris, University of Michigan. *Career:* Instructor, Wellesley College, Massachussetts, USA, 1957–61; Lecturer, Birmingham University, England, 1965–68; Prof. of English, Tufts University, Medford, Massachusetts, 1968–. *Publications:* Mirror for Anglo-Saxons, 1960; Reappraisals, 1965; Science and the Shabby Curate of Poetry, 1965; Yeats's Blessings on von Hugel, 1968; Cities of Light and Sons of the Morning, 1972; The von Richthofen Sisters, 1974; Children of the Sun, 1975; The Earth Again Redeemed (novel), 1976; Transatlantic Patterns, 1977; The Challenge of the Mahatmas, 1978; Dreams of Adventure, Deeds of Empire, 1980; The Old English Elegies, 1983; Tolstoy and Gandhi, 1983; The Great American Adventure, 1984; Montains of Truth, 1986; The Triumph of Pierrot (with J. Swan), 1986.

GREEN, Rose Basile, FRSA, MA, PhD; American poet and writer; b. 19 Dec. 1914, New Rochelle, NY; d. of Salvatore Basile and Caroline Basile; m. Raymond S. Green 1942; one s. one d. *Education:* Coll. of New Rochelle, Columbia Univ., New York and Univ. of Pennsylvania. *Career:* teacher, Torrington High School, Conn. 1936–42; writer, researcher, Cavalcade of America, NBC 1940–42; Assoc. Prof. of English and Registrar Univ. of Tampa 1942–43; Special Lecturer in English, Temple Univ. 1953–57; Prof. of English, Cabrini Coll. 1957–70; Exec. Dir American Inst. of Italian Studies; Vice-Pres. and Dir Nat. Italian-American Foundation; Chair. Nat. Advisory Council for Ethnic Heritage Studies; mem. American Acad. of Political and Social Sciences, Acad. of American Poets, American Studies Asscn, Ethnic Studies Asscn, American Asscn of Univ. Women. *Publications:* Cabrinian Philosophy of Education 1967, Lauding the American Dream 1980, The Life of Mother Frances Xavier Cabrini 1984, The Pennsylvania People 1984, Challenger Countdown 1988, Five Hundred Years of America 1492–1992 1992, The Distaff Side: Great Women of American History 1995; poetry: To Reason Why 1972, Primo Vino 1974, 76 for Philadelphia 1975, Woman, The Second Coming 1977, Century Four 1981, Songs of Ourselves 1983; criticism: The Italian-American Novel: A Document of the Interaction of Two Cultures 1974. *Honours:* Cavalier of the Repub. of Italy; Hon. LHD (Gwynedd-Mercy Coll.) 1979, (Cabrini Coll.) 1982; Daughters of the American Revolution Nat. Bicentennial Award for Poetry 1976; Nat. Amita Award for Literature 1976. *Address:* 308 Manor Road, Lafayette Hill, PA 19444-1741, USA.

GREEN, Sharon, BA; American writer; b. 6 July 1942, New York, NY; m. (divorced); three s. *Education:* New York University. *Career:* mem. SFWA. *Publications:* The Crystals of Mida, 1982; The Warrior Within, 1982; The Warrior Enchained, 1983; An Oath to Mida, 1983; Chosen of Mida, 1984; The Warrior Rearmed, 1984; Mind Guest, 1984; Gateway to Xanadu, 1985; The Will of the Gods, 1985; To Battle the Gods, 1986; The Warrior Challenged, 1986; Rebel Prince, 1986; The Far Side of Forever, 1987; The Warrior Victorious, 1987; Lady Blade, Lord Fighter, 1987; Mists of the Ages, 1988; Hellhound Magic, 1989; Dawn Song, 1990; Haunted House, 1990; Silver Princess, Golden Knight, 1993; The Hidden Realms, 1993; Werewolfmoon, 1993; Fantasy Man, 1993; Flame of Fury, 1993; Dark Mirror, Dark Dreams, 1994; Silken Dreams, 1994; Enchanting, 1994; Wind Whispers, Shadow Shouts, 1995. Contributions: anthologies and magazines. *Website:* www.sharongreen.net.

GREEN, Simon Richard, BA, MA; British writer; b. 25 Aug. 1955, Bradford-on-Avon, Wiltshire, England. *Education:* Thames Polytechnic, Leicester Univ. *Publications:* Hawk and Fisher (aka No Haven for the Guilty) 1990, Winner Takes All (aka Devil Takes the Hindmost) 1991, The God Killer 1991, Blue Moon Rising 1991, Robin Hood: Prince of Thieves 1991, Guard Against Dishonour 1991, Wolf in the Fold (aka Vengeance from a Lonely Man) 1991, Mistworld 1992, Ghostworld 1993, Blood and Honour 1993, Down Among the Dead Men 1993, Shadows Fall 1994, Hellworld 1995, Deathstalker 1995, Deathstalker Rebellion 1996, Deathstalker War 1997, Deathstalker Honour 1998, Deathstalker Destiny 1999, Beyond the Blue Moon 2000, Drinking Midnight Wine 2001, The Man with The Golden Torc 2007. *Address:* 40 St Laurence Road, Bradford-on-Avon, Wiltshire BA15 1JQ, England.

GREEN, Terence Michael, BA, BEd, MA; Canadian writer and poet; b. 2 Feb. 1947, Toronto, ON; m. Merle Casci 1994, two s. *Education:* University of Toronto, University College, Dublin. *Career:* English teacher, East York Collegiate Institute, Toronto, 1968; juror for Philip K. Dick Award, 1995; mem. SFWA; Writers' Union of Canada; Crime Writers of Canada. *Publications:* The Woman Who is the Midnight Wind (short stories), 1987; Barking Dogs (novel), 1988; Children of the Rainbow (novel), 1992; Shadow of Ashland (novel), 1996; Blue Limbo (novel), 1997. Contributions: anthologies including Northern Stars; Northern Frights; Ark of Ice; Dark Visions; Conversations with Robertson Davies; Tesseracts; The Writer's Voice 2; Aurora: The New Canadian Writing; Short stories, articles, interviews, reviews and poetry in periodicals including Globe and Mail; Books in Canada; Quarry; Magazine of Fantasy and Science Fiction; Isaac Asimov's SF Magazine; Twilight Zone; Unearth; Thrust; SF Review; SF Chronicle; Poetry Toronto; Leisure Ways. *Honours:* Canada Council Grants; Ontario Art Council Grants; Participant, Harborfront Festival of Authors. *Address:* c/o Tor/Forge, 175 Fifth Avenue, New York, NY 10010, USA.

GREEN, Timothy Seton, BA; British writer; b. 29 May 1936, Beccles; m. Maureen Snowball 1959; one d. *Education:* Christ's Coll., Cambridge, Univ. of Western Ontario, Canada. *Career:* London Corresp., Horizon 1959–62, American Heritage 1959–62, Life, 1962–64; Ed. Illustrated London News 1964–66. *Publications:* The World of God 1968, The Smugglers 1969, Restless Spirit, UK edn as The Adventurers 1970, The Universal Eye 1972, World of Gold Today 1973, How to Buy Gold 1975, The Smuggling Business 1977, The World of Diamonds 1981, The New World of Gold 1982, The Prospect for Gold 1987, The World of Gold 1993, The Good Water Guide 1994, New Frontiers in Diamonds: The Mining Revolution 1996, The Gold Companion 1997, The Millennium in Gold 1999, The Millennium in Silver 1999, The Ages of Gold 2007. *Address:* 8 Ponsonby Place, London, SW1P 4PT, England (home).

GREENBERG, Alvin David, BA, MA, PhD; American academic, poet and writer; b. 10 May 1932, Cincinnati, OH; m. 1st; two s. one d.; m. 2nd Janet Holmes 1993. *Education:* University of Cincinnati, University of Washington. *Career:* Faculty, University of Kentucky, 1963–65; Prof. of English, 1965–2002, Prof. Emer. 2002–, Chair, Dept of English, 1988–93, Macalester

College; Fulbright Lecturer, University of Kerala, India, 1966–67; Ed., Minnesota Review, 1967–71. *Publications:* Poetry: The Metaphysical Giraffe, 1968; The House of the Would-Be Gardener, 1972; Dark Lands, 1973; Metaform, 1975; In/Direction, 1978; And Yet, 1981; Heavy Wings, 1988; Why We Live with Animals, 1990. Fiction: The Small Waves, 1965; Going Nowhere, 1971; The Invention of the West, 1976. Short Stories: The Discovery of America and Other Tales of Terror, 1980; Delta q, 1983; The Man in the Cardboard Mask, 1985; How the Dead Live, 1998. Play: A Wall, 1971. Opera Libretti: Horspfal, 1969; The Jealous Cellist, 1979; Apollonia's Circus, 1994. Contributions: many reviews, journals, and quarterlies. *Honours:* National Endowment for the Arts Fellowships, 1972, 1992; Bush Foundation Artist Fellowships, 1976, 1981; Associated Writing Programs Short Fiction Award, 1982; Nimrod/Pablo Neruda Prize in Poetry, 1988; Loft-McKnight Poetry Award, 1991, and Distinction in Poetry Award, 1994; Chelsea Award for Poetry, 1994; Minnesota State Arts Board Fellowship, 1996. *Address:* Department of English, Macalester College, 1600 Grand Avenue, St Paul, MN 55105, USA.

GREENBERG, Joanne, (Hannah Green), BA; American writer and teacher; b. 24 Sept. 1932, New York, NY; m. Albert Greenberg 1955; two s. *Education:* American Univ. *Career:* mem. Authors' Guild, PEN, Colorado Authors' League, Nat. Asscn of the Deaf. *Publications:* The King's Persons, 1963; I Never Promised You a Rose Garden, 1964; The Monday Voices, 1965; Summering: A Book of Short Stories, 1966; In This Sign, 1970; Rites of Passage, 1972; Founder's Praise, 1976; High Crimes and Misdemeanors, 1979; A Season of Delight, 1981; The Far Side of Victory, 1983; Simple Gifts, 1986; Age of Consent, 1987; Of Such Small Differences, 1988; With the Snow Queen (short stories), 1991; No Reck'ning Made, 1993; Where the Road Goes, 1998. Contributions: articles, reviews, short stories to numerous periodicals. *Honours:* Harry and Ethel Daroff Memorial Fiction Award, 1963; William and Janice Epstein Fiction Award, 1964; Marcus L. Kenner Award, 1971; Christopher Book Award, 1971; Freida Fromm Reichman Memorial Award, 1971; Rocky Mountain Women's Institute Award, 1983; Denver Public Library Bookplate Award, 1990; Colorado Author of the Year.

GREENBERG, Martin, BA; American academic (retd), writer and translator; b. 3 Feb. 1918, Norfolk, VA; m. Paula Fox 1962, one s. *Education:* University of Michigan. *Career:* Ed. Schocken Books 1946–49, Commentary magazine 1953–60; Lecturer New School for Social Research, New York City 1961–67; Asst Prof. to Prof. of English C. W. Post College 1963–88; mem. Acad. of American Poets. *Publications:* The Terror of Art: Kafka and Modern Literature 1968, The Hamlet Vocation of Coleridge and Wordsworth 1986; translator: The Diaries of Franz Kafka 1914–23, The Marquise of O and Other Stories 1960, Five Plays (von Kleist) 1988, Faust, Part One 1992, Faust, Part Two 1996. *Honours:* Literature Award American Acad. and Institute of Arts and Letters 1989, Harold Morton Landon Trans. Award 1989. *Address:* 306 Clinton Street, New York, NY 11201, USA.

GREENBLATT, Stephen J., PhD; American academic; *Cogan University Professor of the Humanities, Harvard University*; b. 7 Nov. 1943, Cambridge, MA; s. of Harry Greenblatt and Mollie Brown; three s.; m. Ramie Targoff 1998. *Education:* Yale Univ., Pembroke Coll., Cambridge. *Career:* Asst Prof. of English, Univ. of Calif., Berkeley 1969–74, Assoc. Prof. 1974–79, Prof. of English 1979–97; Prof. of English, Harvard Univ. 1997–, Cogan Univ. Prof. of the Humanities 2000–; numerous visiting professorships; Fellow, American Acad. of Arts and Sciences, Wissenschaftskolleg zu Berlin; mem. Int. Asscn of Univ. Profs of English, MLA, Renaissance Soc. of America. *Publications:* Three Modern Satirists: Waugh, Orwell and Huxley 1965, Sir Walter Raleigh: The Renaissance Man and his Roles 1970, Renaissance Self-Fashioning: From More to Shakespeare 1980, Allegory and Representation (ed.) 1981, Power of Forms 1982, Representing the English Renaissance 1988, Shakespearean Negotiations: The Circulation of Social Energy in Renaissance England 1988, Learning to Curse: Essays in Early Modern Culture 1990, Marvelous Possessions: The Wonder of the New World 1991, Redrawing the Boundaries of Literary Study in English 1992, New World Encounters 1992, The Norton Shakespeare (ed.) 1997, The Norton Anthology of English Literature (ed.) 2000, Practising New Historicism 2000, Hamlet in Purgatory 2001, Will in the World: How Shakespeare Became Shakespeare 2004; contribs to scholarly journals. *Honours:* Guggenheim Fellow 1975, 1983; Porter Prize 1969, British Council Prize 1982, James Russell Lowell Prize 1989, Distinguished Teaching Award, Erasmus Inst. Prize 2001, Mellon Distinguished Humanist award 2002. *Address:* Department of English, Harvard University, Cambridge, MA 02138, USA (office). *Telephone:* (617) 495-2101 (office). *E-mail:* greenbl@fas.harvard.edu (office).

GREENE, Alvin Carl, BA; American academic, historian and writer; b. 4 Nov. 1923, Abilene, TX; m. 1st Betty Jo Dozier 1950; three s. one d.; m. 2nd Judy Dalton 1990. *Education:* Phillips University, Kansas State College, Abilene Christian College, Hardin-Simmons University, University of Texas at Austin. *Career:* Co-Dir, Centre for Texas Studies, University of North Texas; mem. Texas Institute of Letters, pres., 1969–71, fellow 1981–; Writers Guild of America, West; PEN International. *Publications:* A Personal Country, 1969; The Santa Claus Bank Robbery, 1972; The Last Captive, 1972; Dallas: The Deciding Years, 1972; The Highland Park Woman, 1984; Taking Heart, 1990. Contributions: Atlantic; McCalls; Southwestern History Quarterly; New York Times Book Review. *Honours:* National Conference of Christians and Jews, 1964; Dobie-Paisano Fellow, 1968; Fellow, Texas State History Asscn, 1990. *Address:* 4359 Shirley Drive, Dallas, TX 75229, USA.

GREENE, Brian R., PhD; American physicist and academic; *Professor of Physics and Mathematics, Columbia University*. *Education:* Harvard Univ., Univ. of Oxford. *Career:* post-doctoral fellow, Harvard Univ. 1987–90; Asst Prof. Cornell Univ. 1990, Assoc. Prof. 1995, later Prof.; currrently Prof. of Physics and Mathematics, Columbia Univ.; Dir Theoretical Advanced Study Inst. 1996; has lectured in more than 20 countries; mem. Editorial Bd Physical Review D, Advance in Theoretical and Mathematical Physics. *Television:* The Theory of Everything 2003. *Publications:* journal papers: Duality in Calabi-Yau Moduli Space (with M. R. Plesser) 1990, Calabi-Yau Moduli Space, Mirror Manifolds and Spacetime Topology Change in String Theory (with P. S. Aspinwall and D. R. Morrison) 1994, Black Hole Condensation and the Unification of String Vacua (with D. R. Morrison and A. Strominger) 1995, Orbifold Resolution by D-Branes (with M. R. Douglas and D. R. Morrison) 1997, D-Brane Topology Changing Transitions 1998; books: The Elegant Universe (Aventis Prize for Science Books 2000) 1999, The Fabric of the Cosmos: Space, Time and the Texture of Reality 2004. *Address:* Faculty of Science, Columbia University, New York, NY 10032, USA (office). *Telephone:* (212) 854-3349 (office). *E-mail:* greene@phys.columbia.edu. *Website:* www.phys.columbia.edu/faculty/greene.htm.

GREENE, Constance Clarke; American writer; b. 27 Oct. 1924, New York, NY; m. Philip M. Greene 1946, two s. three d. *Education:* Skidmore College. *Publications:* A Girl Called Al, 1969; Leo the Lioness, 1970; The Good-Luck Bogie Hat, 1971; Unmaking of Rabbit, 1972; Isabelle the Itch, 1973; The Ears of Louis, 1974; I Know You, Al, 1975; Beat the Turtle Drum, 1976; Getting Nowhere, 1977; I and Sproggy, 1978; Your Old Pal, Al, 1979; Dotty's Suitcase, 1980; Double-Dare O'Toole, 1981; Al(exandra) the Great, 1982; Ask Anybody, 1983; Isabelle Shows Her Stuff, 1984; Star Shine, 1985; Other Plans, 1985; The Love Letters of J. Timothy Owen, 1986; Just Plain Al, 1986; Isabelle and Little Orphan Frannie, 1988; Monday I Love You, 1988; Al's Blind Date, 1989; Funny You Should Ask, 1992; Odds on Oliver, 1992. Contributions: Magazines and newspapers. *Honours:* American Library Asscn Notable Books, 1970, 1977, 1987.

GREENE, Douglas G., BA, MA, PhD; American editor, historian and educator; b. 24 Sept. 1944, Middletown, CT, USA; m. Sandra Virginia Stangland 1966; one s. one d. *Education:* University of Southern Florida, University of Chicago. *Career:* Instructor in History, University of Montana, Missoula, 1970–71; Prof. of History, 1971–83, Dir, Institute for Humanities, 1983–, Old Dominion University, Norfolk, Virginia; Publisher, Crippen and Landru Books, 1994–; mem. MWA. *Publications:* Bibliographia Oziana: A Concise Bibliographical Checklist of the Oz Books by L. Frank Baum and His Successors (co-author), 1976; W. W. Denslow (co-author), 1976; Diaries of the Popish Plot: Being the Diaries of Israel Tonge, Sir Robert Southwell, John Joyne, Edmund Warcup, and Thomas Dangerfield, and Including Titus Oates's 'A True Narrative of the Horrid Plot' (1679) (compiler, author of introduction), 1977; The Meditations of Lady Elizabeth Delaval: Written between 1661 and 1671 (ed., author of introduction), 1978; John Dickson Carr, The Door to Doom, and Other Detections (ed., author of introduction), 1980; John Dickson Carr, The Dead Sleep Lightly (ed., author of introduction), 1983; Ruth Plumly Thompson, The Wizard of Way-Up and Other Wonders (co-ed.), 1985; Death Locked In: An Anthology of Locked Room Stories (co-ed.), 1987; The Collected Short Fiction of Ngaio March (ed., author of introduction), 1989; John Dickson Carr, Fell and Foul Play (ed., author of introduction), 1991; John Dickson Carr, Merrivale, March, and Murder (ed., author of introduction), 1991; John Dickson Carr: The Man Who Explained Miracles, 1995; Detection by Gaslight: Fourteen Victorian Detective Stories (ed., author of introduction), 1997. *Literary Agent:* Phyllis Westberg, Harold Ober Assocs, 425 Madison Avenue, New York, NY 10017, USA. *Address:* 627 New Hampshire Avenue, Norfolk, VA 23508-2132, USA. *E-mail:* Crippenl@pilot.infi.net.

GREENE, Graham Carleton, CBE, MA; British publisher; b. 10 June 1936, Berlin, Germany; s. of Sir Hugh Carleton Greene and Helga Mary Connolly; m. 1st Judith Margaret Gordon Walker 1957 (divorced); m. 2nd Sally Georgina Horton 1976; one s.; also one step-s. one step-d. *Education:* Eton Coll. and Univ. Coll., Oxford. *Career:* Dir Jonathan Cape Ltd 1962–90, Man. Dir 1966–88; Dir Chatto, Virago, Bodley Head and Jonathan Cape Ltd 1969–88, Chair. 1970–88; Dir Book Reps (NZ) Ltd 1971–88, CVBC Services 1972–88, Australasian Publishing Co. Ltd (Chair. 1978–88) 1969–88, Guinness Peat Group PLC 1973–87, Triad Paperbacks 1975–88, Greene King PLC 1979–, Statesman and Nation Publishing Co. (Chair. 1981–85) 1980–85, Statesman Publishing Co. Ltd (Chair. 1981–85) 1980–85, Random House Inc. 1987–88, Jupiter Int. Investment Trust PLC 1989–2001, Henry Sotheran Ltd 1990–, Ed Victor Ltd 1991–, Rosemary Sandberg Ltd 1991–2002, Libra KFT (Budapest) 1991–, London Merchant Securities PLC 1996– (Chair. 2000–); Chair. Random House UK Ltd 1988–90, British Museum Devt Trust 1986–93 (Vice-Chair. 1993–2004), British Museum Publications (now British Museum Co.) Ltd 1998–2002 (Chair. 1988–96), Museums and Galleries Comm. 1991–96, Vice Pres. 1997–; Chair. Nation Pty Co. Ltd 1981–87, New Society 1984–86, Great Britain–China Centre (Chair. 1986–1997); Dir Garsington Opera Ltd 1996–; mem. Bd of British Council 1977–88, mem. Council of Publishers Asscn (Pres. 1977–79) 1969–88; Trustee, British Museum 1978–2002 (Chair. 1996–2002), Open Coll. of the Arts 1990–97; Int. Cttee of Int. Publishers Asscn 1977–88, Groupe des Editeurs de Livres de la CEE 1977–86 (Pres. 1984–86). *Honours:* Chevalier, Ordre des Arts et Lettres; Hon. DLitt (Keele Univ.) 2002, Hon. DCL (Univ. E Anglia) 2002, Hon. DLitt (Buckingham) 2004. *Address:* 6 Bayley Street, Bedford Square, London,

WC1B 3HE, England. *Telephone:* (20) 7304-4101. *Fax:* (20) 7304-4102 (office). *E-mail:* grahamc.greene@virgin.net (office).

GREENE, Jonathan Edward, BA; American poet, writer, editor, publisher and book designer; *Publisher, Gnomon Press;* b. 19 April 1943, New York, NY; m. 1st Alice-Anne Kingston 1963 (divorced); one d.; m. 2nd Dobree Adams 1974. *Education:* Bard Coll. *Publications:* The Reckoning 1966, Instance 1968, The Lapidary 1969, A 17th Century Garner 1969, An Unspoken Complaint 1970, The Poor in Church, by Arthur Rimbaud (trans) 1973, Scaling the Walls 1974, Glossary of the Everyday 1974, Peripatetics 1978, Jonathan Williams: A 50th Birthday Celebration (ed.) 1979, Once a Kingdom Again 1979, Quiet Goods 1980, Idylls 1983, Small Change for the Long Haul 1984, Trickster Tales 1985, Les Chambres des Poètes 1990, The Man Came to Haul Stone 1995, Of Moment 1998, Inventions of Necessity: Selected Poems 1998, Incidents of Travel in Japan 1999, A Little Ink in the Paper Sea 2001, Book of Correspondences 2002, Watching Dewdrops Fall 2003, Hummingbird's Water Trough 2003, Fault Lines 2004, On the Banks of Monks Pond: The Thomas Merton/Jonathan Greene Correspondence 2004, The Death of A Kentucky Coffee-Tree & Other Poems 2006, Gists, Orts, Shards: A Commonplace Book 2006, Hut Poems 2007; contribs to anthologies, reviews, quarterlies, and journals. *Honours:* Nat. Endowment for the Arts Fellowships 1969, 1978, Southern Fed. of State Arts Agencies Fellowship 1977, Kentucky Arts Council Fellowship 2003. *Address:* PO Box 475, Frankfort, KY 40602-0475, USA. *Telephone:* (502) 223-1858. *Fax:* (502) 223-1858. *E-mail:* jgnomon@aol.com (home). *Website:* www.southernartistry.org.

GREENFIELD OF OTMOOR, Baroness (Life Peer), cr. 2001, of Otmoor in the County of Oxfordshire; **Susan Adele Greenfield,** CBE, DPhil; British pharmacologist; *Professor in Synaptic Pharmacology, University of Oxford;* b. 1 Oct. 1950, d. of Reginald Myer Greenfield and Doris Margaret Winifred Greenfield; m. Peter William Atkins 1991. *Education:* Godolphin and Latymer School for Girls, St Hilda's Coll., Oxford. *Career:* MRC Training Fellow Univ. Lab. of Physiology, Oxford 1977–81; fmrly with Coll. de France, Paris; MRC-INSERM French Exchange Fellow 1979–80; Jr Research Fellow Green Coll., Oxford 1981–84, lecturer in Synaptic Pharmacology 1985–96, Prof. in Synaptic Pharmacology 1996–, Gresham Prof. of Physic Gresham Coll. 1995–; Dir Royal Inst. 1998–; Visiting Fellow Inst. of Neuroscience La Jolla, USA 1995; Sr Research Fellow Lincoln Coll. Oxford; Hon. Fellow St Hilda's Coll. Oxford, Royal Coll. of Physicians 2000; Visiting Distinguished Scholar Queen's Univ., Belfast 1996; Trustee Science Museum 2003. *Radio appearances include:* Start the Week, Any Questions and other discussion programmes; presenter of Turn On, Turn Off series on drugs and the brain, Today Programme. *Television appearances include:* Dimbleby Lecture 1999, author and presenter of Brain Story 'Landmark' (series of programmes on the brain) 2000, Big Ideas in Science, Channel 5 (UK). *Publications include:* numerous articles in learned journals; Mindwaves (co-ed. with C. B. Blakemore) 1987, Journey to the Centres of the Brain (with G. Ferry) 1994, Journey to the Centres of the Mind 1995, The Human Mind Explained (ed.) 1996, The Human Brain: A Guided Tour 1997; Brainpower (ed.) 2000, Brain Story 2000, Private Life of the Brain 2000, Tomorrow's People: How 21st Century Technology is Changing the Way We Think and Feel 2003. *Honours:* awarded 21 Hon. DSc degrees 1997–2002; Woman of Distinction, Jewish Care 1998, Michael Faraday Medal, Royal Soc. 1998, 2000, Légion d'Honneur2003. *Address:* Department of Pharmacology, Mansfield Road, Oxford, OX1 3QT (office). *Telephone:* (1865) 271628 (office). *Fax:* (1865) 271853 (office). *E-mail:* susan.greenfield@pharm.ox.ac.uk (office).

GREENLAND, Colin, MA, DPhil; British writer; b. 17 May 1954, Dover, Kent, England. *Education:* Pembroke Coll., Oxford. *Career:* Writer-in-Residence, North East London Polytechnic 1980–82; mem. Science Fiction Foundation, Science Fiction Writers' Conf., Milford, BSFA (Council mem.). *Publications:* The Entropy Exhibition 1983; Daybreak on a Different Mountain 1984, Magnetic Storm (with Roger and Martyn Dean) 1984, Interzone: The First Anthology (co-ed.) 1985, The Freelance Writer's Handbook (with Paul Kerton) 1986, The Hour of the Thin Ox 1987, Storm Warnings (co-ed.) 1987, Other Voices 1988, Take Back Plenty 1990, Michael Moorcock: Death is No Obstacle 1992, Harm's Way 1993, Seasons of Plenty 1995, The Plenty Principle 1997, Mother of Plenty 1998, Spiritfeather 2000, Finding Helen 2002; contribs to numerous anthologies and periodicals. *Honours:* Eaton Award for Science Fiction Criticism 1985, Arthur C. Clarke Award 1992, BSFA Award 1992, Eastercon Award 1992, Guest of Honour, Evolution, Nat. Science Fiction Easter Convention 1996. *Literary Agent:* c/o Maggie Noach Literary Agency, 22 Dorville Crescent, London, W6 0HJ, England. *E-mail:* colin.greenland@ntlworld.com (home).

GREENLAW, Lavinia, BA, MA, FRSL; British poet; *Senior Lecturer in Creative Writing, Goldsmiths College, London;* b. 30 July 1962, London, England. *Education:* Kingston Polytechnic, London Coll. of Printing, Courtauld Inst. *Career:* British Council Fellow in Writing, Amherst Coll., Mass, USA 1995; Writer-in-Residence, Science Museum, London 1995, Wellington Coll. 1996, Mishcon de Reya solicitors 1997–98, Aldeburgh Poetry Festival 1998, Aldeburgh Festival 2003, Calouste Gulbenkian/Royal Soc. of Medicine 2005; Fellow in Writing, Sevenoaks School 1997; Reader-in-Residence, Royal Festival Hall 2000; Sr Lecturer in Creative Writing, Goldsmiths Coll., Univ. of London 2002–. *Music:* Hamelin (libretto for Ian Wilson/Schleswig-Holsteinisches Landestheater) 2003, Slow Passage, Low Prospect (song cycle for Richard Baker/Aldeburgh Festival) 2004, Minsk (libretto for Ian Wilson/Feldkirch Festival) 2005, Written on a Train (song

cycle for Richard Baker/Borlotti-Buitoni Trust) 2006. *Radio:* drama: The Blood of Strangers (adaptation) 2002, Remembering Mum 2003, Night and Day: Virginia Woolf (adaptation) 2003, The Kamikaze Handbook 2004, The Innocence of Radium 2004; documentaries include Essex Rag, The Red in My Mind: Emily Dickinson, The Year's Four Corners, A Drink of Glass, The Land of Giving In. *Publications:* poetry: The Cost of Getting Lost in Space (pamphlet) 1991, Love from a Foreign City (pamphlet) 1992, Night Photograph 1993, A World Where News Travelled Slowly (Forward Prize for Best Poem of the Year 1997) 1997, Thoughts of a Night Sea (with photographs by Garry Fabian Miller) 2002, Minsk 2003, Signs and Humours: The Poetry of Medicine (ed.) 2007; prose: Mary George of Allnorthover (novel) (Prix du Premier Roman 2003) 2001, An Irresponsible Age (novel) 2006; other: The Importance of Music to Girls (memoir) 2007; contribs to TLS, London Review of Books, New Yorker, Paris Review, Poetry Review, Verse, New Statesman, The Observer, The Telegraph, The Guardian, The Financial Times, American Poet. *Honours:* Eric Gregory Award 1990, Arts Council of England Writers Award 1995, Wingate Scholarship 1998, NESTA Fellowship 2000, Spycher-Leuk Literaturpreis (Switzerland) 2002, Cholmondeley Award 2003, Prix du Premier Roman (France) 2003, Soc. of Authors Travelling Scholarship 2005. *Literary Agent:* c/o Derek Johns, AP Watt, 20 John Street, London, WC1N 2DR, England. *Telephone:* (20) 7405-6774. *Fax:* (20) 7831-2154. *E-mail:* djohns@apwatt.co.uk. *Website:* www.apwatt.co.uk; www.laviniagreenlaw.co.uk.

GREENLEAF, Stephen Howell, BA, JD; American writer; b. 17 July 1942, Washington, DC; m. Ann Garrison 1968, one s. *Education:* Carleton College, University of California at Berkeley, University of Iowa. *Career:* admitted to the Bar, California, 1968, Iowa, 1977; Instructor in Writing, University of Washington Extension, 1993–96, Iowa Summer Writing Festival, 1995–2000. *Publications:* Grave Error, 1979; Death Bed, 1980; Child Proof, 1981; State's Evidence, 1982; Fatal Obsession, 1983; The Ditto List, 1985; Beyond Blame, 1986; Toll Call, 1987; Impact, 1989; Book Case, 1991; Blood Type, 1992; Southern Cross, 1993; False Conception, 1994; Flesh Wounds, 1996; Past Tense, 1997; Strawberry Sunday, 1999; Ellipsis, 2000. *Honours:* Maltese Falcon Award, Japan 1993.

GREER, Bonnie, American writer, playwright and critic; b. 1948, Chicago, IL. *Education:* studied with David Mamet and Elia Kazan in New York. *Career:* theatre critic, Time Out, London; Gov., London Int. Film School; bd mem., Royal Opera House; judge for Orange Prize; regular contributor to radio, including Night Waves (BBC Radio 3), Front Row (BBC Radio 4) and television, including Booker Prize (Channel 4), Late Review and Newsnight Review (BBC2); Arts Council Playwright-in-Residence, Soho Theatre, Black Theatre Co-operative; Arts Council England Playwright-in-Residence, Pascal Theatre Co., London. *Plays:* Mundo Negra 1993, God Likes No Ugly. *Publications:* Hanging by her Teeth 1995, Ways into Shakespeare 1996, Riding the 903 2003. *Honours:* Verity Bargate Award for Best New Play. *Literary Agent:* Sheil Land Associates Ltd, 43 Doughty Street, London, WC1N 2LF, England. *Telephone:* (20) 7405-9351. *Fax:* (20) 7831-2127. *E-mail:* info@sheilland.co.uk.

GREER, Germaine, PhD; Australian feminist, author and broadcaster; b. 29 Jan. 1939, Melbourne; d. of Eric Reginald Greer and Margaret May (Lafrank) Greer. *Education:* Star of the Sea Convent, Vic., Melbourne and Sydney Univs and Cambridge Univ., England. *Career:* Sr Tutor in English, Sydney Univ. 1963–64; Asst Lecturer then Lecturer in English, Warwick Univ. 1967–72, Prof. of English and Comparative Studies 1998–2003; lecturer throughout N America with American Program Bureau 1973–78, to raise funds for Tulsa Bursary and Fellowship Scheme 1980–83; Visiting Prof., Grad. Faculty of Modern Letters, Univ. of Tulsa 1979, Prof. of Modern Letters 1980–83, Founder-Dir of Tulsa Centre for the Study of Women's Literature, Founder-Ed. Tulsa Studies in Women's Literature 1981; Dir Stump Cross Books 1988–; Special Lecturer and Unofficial Fellow, Newnham Coll., Cambridge 1989–98; broadcaster/journalist/columnist/reviewer 1972–; Jr Govt Scholarship 1952, Diocesan Scholarship 1956, Sr Govt Scholarship 1956, Teacher's Coll. Studentship 1956, Commonwealth Scholarship 1964; numerous television appearances and public talks including discussion with Norman Mailer (q.v.) in The Theatre of Ideas, New York. *Film appearance:* Rabbit Fever 2006. *Television:* The Late Review, Celebrity Big Brother. *Publications:* The Female Eunuch 1969, The Obstacle Race: The Fortunes of Women Painters and Their Work 1979, Sex and Destiny: The Politics of Human Fertility 1984, Shakespeare (co-ed.) 1986, The Madwoman's Underclothes (selected journalism 1964–85) 1986, Kissing the Rod: An Anthology of 17th Century Women's Verse (co-ed.) 1988, Daddy, We Hardly Knew You 1989 (J. R. Ackerly Prize and Premio Internazionale Mondello), The Uncollected Verse of Aphra Behn (ed.) 1989, The Change: Women, Ageing and the Menopause 1991, The Collected Works of Katherine Philips, the Matchless Orinda, Vol. III: The Translations (co-ed.) 1993, Slip-Shod Sybils: Recognition, Rejection and The Woman Poet 1995, The Surviving Works of Anne Wharton (co-ed.) 1997, The Whole Woman 1999, John Wilmot, Earl of Rochester 1999, 101 Poems by 101 Women (ed.) 2001, The Boy 2003, Poems for Gardeners (ed.) 2003, Whitefella Jump Up The Shortest Way to Nationhood 2004, Shakespeare's Wife 2007; articles for Listener, Spectator, Esquire, Harper's Magazine, Playboy, Private Eye and other journals. *Honours:* Dr hc (Univ. of Griffith, Australia) 1996, (Univ. of York, Toronto) 1999, (UMIST) 2000; hon. degrees (Melbourne) 2003, (Essex) 2003, (Anglia Polytechnic) 2003; Australian Living Treasure Nat. Trust Award Centenary Medal 2003. *Literary Agent:* Aitken Alexander

Associates Ltd, 18–21 Cavaye Place, London, SW10 9PT, England. *Telephone:* (20) 7373-8672. *Fax:* (20) 7373-6002. *E-mail:* reception@aitkenalexander.co.uk. *Website:* www.aitkenalexander.co.uk.

GRÉGOIRE, Marie (Menie); French journalist and writer; b. 15 Aug. 1919, Cholet; d. of Maurice Laurentin and Marie Laurentin (née Jactel); m. Roger Grégoire 1943 (deceased); three d. *Education:* Univ. de Paris (Sorbonne), Ecole des Hautes Etudes and Inst. d'Art et d'Archéologie, Paris. *Career:* psychoanalyst; speaker for the Alliance française in Finland, Italy, Sweden, USA 1950–; journalist with various newspapers and periodicals including Le Monde and Esprit; Editorial Writer Marie-Claire; presented two daily women's radio programmes on Radio-Télé Luxembourg (RTL) 1967–81, columnist 1981–86, Ed. 1980–86; presented Avec le temps (TV) 1984; columnist, France-Soir 1986–99; mem. Conseil supérieur de l'information sexuelle, de la régulation des naissances et de l'éducation familiale 1974–, various nat. comms. *Publications:* Le métier de femme 1964, Femmes (two vols) 1966, La belle Arsène, Passeport du couple 1967, Les cris de la vie 1971, Ménie Grégoire raconte... 1972, Telle que je suis 1976, Des passions et des rêves 1981, Tournelune 1983, Sagesse et folie des Français 1986, Nous aurons le temps de vivre 1987, La France et ses immigrés 1988, La Dame du Puy du Fou 1990, Le petit roi du Poitou 1992, La magicienne 1993, Le Bien aimé 1996, Les dames de la Loire 2001–03, Comme une lame de fond (100,000 lettres qui disent le mal-être des corps et des coeurs) 2007. *Honours:* Officier de la Légion d'honneur 1990. *Address:* 3 rue Chapon, 75003 Paris, France (home). *Telephone:* (1) 42-77-53-81 (home). *Fax:* (1) 40-27-08-95 (home).

GREGOR-DELLIN, Martin; German writer, poet, dramatist and editor; b. 3 June 1926, Naumberg; m. Annemarie Dellin 1951, one d. *Education:* University of Leipzig. *Career:* writer, Ed., Halle, 1951–58, Munich, 1962–66; Writer for Radio, Frankfurt am Main, 1961–62; Freelance Novelist, Ed., Biographer, Poet, 1966–; mem. German Acad. for Language and Literature; Bavarian Acad. for Fine Arts; Asscn of German Writers; PEN. *Publications:* Jakob Haferglanz (novel), 1956; Der Man mit der Stoppuhr (poems), 1957; Der Nullpunkte (novel), 1959; Der Kandelaber (novel), 1962; Einer (novel), 1965; Aufbruch ins Ungewisse, 1968; Richard Wagner, Die Revolution als Oper, 1973; Das Riesenrad Erzählungen, 1976; Im Zeitalter Kafkas, 1979; Richard Wagner: Sein Leben, sein Werk, sein Jahrhundert, 1980, in English trans. as Richard Wagner: His Life, His Work, His Century, 1983; Schlabrendorf, oder, Die Republik, 1982; Richard Wagner: Eine Biographie in Bildern, 1982; Luther: Eine Annäherung, 1983; Richard Wagner: Leben, Werk, Wirkung, 1983; Heinrich Schütz: Sein Leben, sein Werk, Seine Zeit, 1984; Was ist grösse?: Sieben Deutsche und ein deutsches Problem, 1985; Italienisches Traumbuch, 1986. Editor: Anthologies and various other books. Other: several radio plays. Contributions: essays and poetry to numerous anthologies. *Honours:* Förderpreis, Andreas-Gryphius Preis, 1963; Ostdeutscher Schrifttimuspreis, 1963; Stereo Radio Play Prize, 1967; Munich Literary Prize, 1971; Die Goldene Feder, Critics Prize, 1972; Grand Prix de la Critique Musicale Française, 1982; Fernseh-Kulturpreis, Eduard-Rhein-Stiftung, 1984; Cross of Merit, First Class, Federal Republic of Germany.

GREGORY, Philippa, PhD; British writer; b. 9 Jan. 1954, Kenya; m.; two c. *Education:* Sussex Univ., Edinburgh Univ. *Career:* trained as a journalist and was apprenticed at The News, Portsmouth; worked for BBC Radio for two years; has taught at Univ. of Durham, Open Univ., Teesside Polytechnic; f. The Gardens for Gambia charity; Fellow Kingston Univ. *Publications:* novels: Wideacre 1987, The Favoured Child 1989, Meridon 1990, The Wise Woman 1992, A Respectable Trade 1992, Fallen Skies 1993, Mrs Hartley and the Growth Centre 1995, Perfectly Correct 1996, The Little House 1997, Earthly Joys 1998, The Virgin Earth 1999, Midlife Mischief 1998, Zelda's Cut 2000, The Other Boleyn Girl (also adapted for TV) (Parker Romantic Novel of the Year) 2002, The Queen's Fool 2003, The Virgin's Lover 2004, The Constant Princess 2005, The Boleyn Inheritance 2006; contrib. short stories, features and reviews to newspapers and magazines. *Website:* www.philippagregory.com.

GREGORY, Richard Langton, CBE, DSc, FRS, FRSE, FInstP; British academic and writer; *Professor Emeritus of Neuropsychology and Senior Research Fellow, University of Bristol;* b. 24 July 1923, London; m. 1st Margaret Hope Pattison Muir 1953 (divorced 1966); one s. one d.; m. 2nd Freja Mary Balchin (divorced 1976). *Education:* Downing Coll., Cambridge and Univ. of Bristol. *Career:* researcher, MRC Applied Psychology Research Unit, Cambridge 1950–53; Univ. Demonstrator, later Lecturer, Dept of Psychology, Univ. of Cambridge 1953–67; Fellow, Corpus Christi Coll., Cambridge 1962–67; Prof. of Bionics, Univ. of Edinburgh 1967–70; Prof. of Neuropsychology and Dir of the Brain and Perception Lab., Univ. of Bristol 1970–88, Prof. Emer. and Sr Research Fellow 1988–; Founder-Ed. Journal of Perception 1972–; Founder and Chair. of the Trustees 1983–91, Pres. 1991–, Exploratory Hands-on Science Centre; mem. Royal Inst. *Publications:* Recovery from Early Blindness (with Jean Wallace) 1963, Eye and Brain 1966 (5th edn 1997), The Intelligent Eye 1970, Illusion in Nature and Art (co-ed.) 1973, Concepts and Mechanisms of Perception 1974, Mind in Science 1981, Odd Perceptions (essays) 1986, The Oxford Companion to the Mind (ed.) 1987 (2nd edn 2004), Evolution of the Eye and Visual System (co-ed.), Vol. II of Vision and Visual Dysfunction 1991, Even Odder Perceptions (essays) 1994, The Artful Eye 1995, Mirrors in Mind 1996; contrib. to scientific journals. *Honours:* Hon. Fellow, Corpus Christi Coll., Cambridge; several hon. doctorates; Royal Soc. Michael Faraday Medal 1993, Royal Soc. Medawar Prize Lecture 2001, Spectacle Makers' Co. Lord Crook Medal 1996, Hughlings Jackson Gold Medal, Royal Soc. of Medicine 1999, BNA Award 2005, Newton Medal 2006. *Address:* Department of Experimental Psychology, University of Bristol, 12A Priory Road, Clifton, Bristol, BS8 1TU (office); 23 Royal York Crescent, Clifton, Bristol, BS8 4JX, England (home). *Telephone:* (117) 928-8461 (office); (117) 973-9701 (home). *Fax:* (117) 928-8461 (office); (117) 973-9701 (home). *E-mail:* richard.gregory@bris.ac.uk (office). *Website:* www.richardgregory.org (office).

GREIG, Andrew; British poet and writer; b. 1951, Bannockburn, Scotland; m. Lesley Glaister. *Education:* Univ. of Edinburgh. *Publications:* poetry: Men on Ice 1977, Surviving Passages 1982, A Flame in Your Heart (with Kathleen Jamie) 1986, The Order of the Day 1990, Western Swing 1994, Into You 2000; novels: Electric Brae 1992, The Return of John Macnab 1996, When They Lay Bare 1999, That Summer 2000, The Clouds Above 2002, In Another Light 2004; non-fiction: Summit Fever 1985, Kingdoms of Experience 1986, Preferred Lies: A Journey to the Heart of Scottish Golf 2006. *Literary Agent:* c/o Capel and Land, 29 Wardour Street, London, W1V 3HB, England.

GREIG, David; Scottish playwright. *Plays:* Maggie and the Cat, Savage Reminiscence, Stalinland (Citizens Stalls, Glasgow) 1993, Europe (Traverse Theatre, Edinburgh) 1994, One Way Street (Traverse Theatre, Edinburgh) 1995, Airport (Traverse Theatre, Edinburgh) 1996, The Architect (Traverse Theatre, Edinburgh) 1996, Caledonia Dreaming (Traverse Theatre, Edinburgh) 1997, Local (Tramway, Glasgow) 1998, Timeless (Donmar Warehouse, London) 1998, Mainstream (McRobert, Stirling) 1999, The Cosmonaut's Last Message to the Woman he Once Loved in the Former Soviet Union (Lyric Studio, London) 1999, Danny 306 + Me (4 Ever) (Traverse Theatre, Edinburgh) 1999, The Speculator (Traverse Theatre, Edinburgh) 1999, Candide 2000 (adaptation, Old Fruitmarket, Glasgow) 2000, The Greeks (translation, Tramway, Glasgow) 2000, Victoria (The Pit, London) 2000, Casanova (Tron, Glasgow) 2001, Dr Korczak's Example (Shawlands Academy) 2001, Outlying Islands (Traverse Theatre, Edinburgh) 2002, Caligula (translation, Donmar Warehouse, London) 2003, San Diego (Royal Lyceum, Edinburgh Festival) 2003, Suspect Culture (Tron Theatre, Glasgow) 2003, 8000m (Glasgow, Tramway) 2004, When The Bulbul Stopped Singing (adaptation, Traverse Theatre, Edinburgh) 2004, Pyrenees (Menier Chocolate Factory, London) 2005, The American Pilot (Other Place, Stratford-upon-Avon) 2005. *Literary Agent:* Casarotto Ramsay and Associates Ltd, National House, 60–65 Wardour Street, London, W1V 3HP, England. *Telephone:* (20) 7287-4450. *Fax:* (20) 7287-9128. *E-mail:* agents@casarotto.co.uk. *Website:* www.casarotto.co.uk.

GREIG, Geordie Carron, MA, FRSA; British journalist; *Editor, Tatler;* b. 16 Dec. 1960, London; s. of Sir Carron Greig and Monica Greig (née Stourton); m. Kathryn Elizabeth Terry 1995; one s. two d. *Education:* Eton Coll. and St Peter's Coll., Oxford. *Career:* reporter, South East London and Kentish Mercury 1981–83, Daily Mail 1984–85, Today 1985–87; reporter, The Sunday Times 1987–89, Arts Corresp. 1989–91, New York Corresp. 1991–95, Literary Ed. 1995–99; Ed. of Tatler 1999–. *Publication:* Louis and the Prince 1999. *Address:* Tatler, Condé Nast Publications Ltd, Vogue House, Hanover Square, London, W1S 1JU, England (office). *Telephone:* (20) 7499-9080 (office). *Fax:* (20) 7493-1641 (office).

GREILSAMER, Laurent, LèsL; French journalist; *Editor Le Monde;* b. 2 Feb. 1953, Neuilly; s. of Marcel Greilsamer and Francine Alice Greilsamer; m. Claire Méheut 1979; three s. *Education:* Ecole Supérieure de Journalisme, Lille. *Career:* Le Figaro 1974–76, Quotidien de Paris 1976; ed. Le Monde 1977–84, sr reporter 1984–94, 1994–2005, Ed. 2005–. *Publications:* Interpol, le siège de soupçon 1986, Un certain Monsieur Paul, L'affaire Touvier 1989, Hubert Beuve-Méry 1990, Enquête sur l'affaire du sang contaminé 1990, Les juges parlent 1992, Interpol, Policiers sans frontières 1997, Le Prince foudroyé, la vie de Nicholas de Staël 1998, Où vont les juges? 2002, L'Eclair au front, la vie de René Char 2004. *Honours:* Prix des lectrices d'Elle 1999, Grand Prix de la Critique 2004. *Address:* c/o Le Monde, 80 Boulevard Blanqui, 75013 Paris, France. *Telephone:* 1-57-28-26-05 (office). *Fax:* 1-57-28-21-22 (office). *E-mail:* greilsamer@lemonde.fr (office).

GRENNAN, Eamon, MA, PhD; Irish/American academic and poet; *Professor of English, Vassar College;* b. 13 Nov. 1941, Dublin, Ireland; one s. two d. *Education:* Univ. Coll., Dublin, Harvard Univ. *Career:* Lecturer in English, Univ. Coll., Dublin 1966–67; Asst Prof., Lehman Coll., CUNY 1971–74; Asst Prof., Vassar Coll. 1974–83, Assoc. Prof. 1983–89, Prof. 1989–. *Publications:* Wildly for Days 1983, What Light There Is 1987, Twelve Poems 1988, What Light There Is and Other Poems 1989, As If It Matters 1991, So It Goes 1995, Selected Poems of Giacomo Leopardi (trans.) 1995, 1997, Relations: New and Selected Poems 1998, Facing the Music: Irish Poetry in the 20th Century 1999, Still Life with Waterfall 2001, The quick of It 2004, Oedipus at Colonus (trans. with Rachel Kitzinger) 2004; contribs to anthologies and periodicals. *Honours:* Nat. Endowment for the Humanities Grant 1986, Nat. Endowment for the Arts Grant 1991, Guggenheim Fellowship 1995, Lenore Mrshall Poetry Prize 2003. *Address:* Department of English, Vassar College, Poughkeepsie, NY 12604, USA (office). *Telephone:* (845) 437-5655 (office). *Fax:* (845) 437-7578 (office). *E-mail:* grennan@vassar.edu (office).

GRENVILLE, John Ashley Soames, BA, PhD; British historian and academic; *Professor Emeritus, Institute of German Studies, University of Birmingham;* b. 11 Jan. 1928, Berlin, Germany; m. 1st Betty Anne Rosenberg 1960 (died 1974); three s.; m. 2nd Patricia Carnie 1975; one d. one step-d. *Education:* Birkbeck Coll., London, LSE, Yale Univ., Univ. of London. *Career:*

Postgraduate Scholar, Univ. of London 1951–53; Asst Lecturer to Lecturer, Nottingham Univ. 1953–64, Reader in Modern History 1964–65; Commonwealth Fund Fellow 1958–59; Postdoctoral Fellow, Yale Univ. 1960–63; Prof. of Int. History, Leeds Univ. 1965–69; Ed., Fontana History of War and Society 1969–78, Leo Baeck Year Book 1992–; Prof. of Modern History, Univ. of Birmingham 1969–94, Prof. Emer. Inst. of German Studies 1994–; mem. exec. bd Leo Baeck Inst. *Publications:* The Coming of the Europeans (with J. G. Fuller) 1962, Lord Salisbury and Foreign Policy 1964, Politics, Strategy and American Diplomacy: Studies in Foreign Policy 1873–1917 (with G. B. Young) 1966, The Major International Treaties 1914–1973: A History and Guide 1974, (two-vol. edn) 1987, 2000, Europe Reshaped 1848–1878 1975, Nazi Germany 1976, World History of the Twentieth Century, Vol. I 1900–1945 1980, Collins World History of the Twentieth Century 1994, A History of the World from the 20th to the 21st Century 2005; films with N. Pronay: The Munich Crisis 1968, The End of Illusion: From Munich to Dunkirk 1970; contrib. to scholarly journals. *Honours:* Int. Congress of Historians Award for Distinguished Service to Bibliography 2005. *Address:* c/o School of History, University of Birmingham, Birmingham, B15 2TT, England (office). *Fax:* (121) 323-3278 (home). *E-mail:* johngrenville@btinternet.com (home).

GRENVILLE, Kate, BA, MA, DCA; Australian writer; b. 14 Oct. 1950, Sydney; d. of Kenneth Grenville Gee and Nance Russell; m. Bruce Petty 1986; one s. one d. *Education:* Univ. of Tech., Sydney, Univ. of Colorado at Boulder, USA, Univ. of Sydney. *Career:* ed. of documentary films, Film Australia 1971–76; freelance journalist, London and Paris 1977–80; Sub-Ed. Subtitling Unit, Multicultural TV, Sydney 1982–85; reviewer; journalist; writer-in-residence at univs and Nat. Film School, Sydney 1986–; Sr Fellowship, Australia Council Bicentennial Comm. *Publications:* Bearded Ladies 1984, Lilian's Story 1985, Dreamhouse 1986, Joan Makes History 1988, The Writing Book 1990, Making Stories 1992, Dark Places 1995, The Idea of Perfection (Orange Prize 2001) 1999, Writing From Start to Finish 2001, The Secret River (Commonwealth's Prize 2006) 2005. *Honours:* Vogel/Australian Award 1985, Victorian Premier's Literary Award 1995. *Literary Agent:* Barbara Mobbs Agency, PO Box 126 Edgecliff, NSW 2027, Australia. *Website:* www.users.bigpond.com/kgreville.

GRENZ, Stanley J.; American academic and theologian; *Pioneer McDonald Professor of Theology, Carey Theological College;* b. 7 Jan. 1950, Alpena, MI, USA; m. Edna Sturhahn; one s. one d. *Education:* BA, University of Colorado, 1973; MDiv, Denver Conservative Baptist Seminary, 1976; DTheol magna cum laude, University of Munich, 1980. *Career:* Pioneer McDonald Prof. of Baptist Heritage, Theology and Ethics, Carey Theological College, Vancouver, 1990–2002; Affiliate Prof., Northern Baptist Theological Seminary, Lombard, IL, 1996–99; Distinguished Prof. of Theology, Baylor University, Waco, TX, 2002–03; Pioneer McDonald Prof. of Theology, Carey Theological Coll., Vancouver, BC, 2003–; mem. Baptist World Alliance; Canadian Evangelical Theological Society, Exec. Committee, 1996–2000; American Acad. of Religion, Regional Pres., 1986–87; National Assen of Baptist Profs of Religion, Pres., 1989–90. *Publications:* Isaac Backus: Puritan and Baptist, 1983; The Baptist Congregation, 1985; Prayer: The Cry for the Kingdom, 1988; Reason for Hope: The Systematic Theology of Wolfhart Pannenberg, 1990; AIDS: Ministry in the Midst of an Epidemic (co-author), 1990; Sexual Ethics: A Biblical Perspective, 1990; Twentieth-Century Theology: God and the World in a Transitional Age (co-author), 1992; Revisioning Evangelical Theology, 1993; Theology for the Community of God, 1994; Betrayal of Trust: Sexual Misconduct in the Pastorate (co-author), 1995; Women and the Church: A Biblical Theology of Women in Ministry (co-author), 1995; A Primer on Postmodernism, 1996; Created for Community: Connecting Christian Belief with Christian Living, 1996; Who Needs Theology?: An Invitation to the Study of God (co-author), 1996; The Moral Quest: Foundations for Christian Ethics, 1997; What Christians Really Believe. . . and Why, 1998; Welcoming But Not Affirming: An Evangelical Response to Homosexuality, 1998; Pocket Dictionary of Theological Terms (co-author), 1999; Renewing the Center: Evangelical Theology in a Post-theological Era, 2000; Beyond Foundationalism: Shaping Theology in a Postmodern Context (co-author), 2001; The Social God and the Relational Self: A Trinitarian Theology of the Imago Dei, 2001, Rediscovering the Trinune God: The Trinity in Contemporary Theology 2004. *Honours:* Fulbright Scholar in Germany, 1987–88; Christianity Today Book Awards, 1992, 1993, 1998, 1999, 2000; Theological Scholarship, Research Award, Assen of Theological Schools in the United States and Canada, 1993; First Place, Christian Writing Awards, Faith Today and Evangelical Fellowship of Canada, 1995, 1997; Henry Luce III Fellow in Theology, 1999–2000. *Address:* Carey Theological College, 5920 Iona Drive, Vancouver, BC V6T 1J6, Canada. *E-mail:* sgrenz@stanleyjgrenz.com. *Website:* www.stanleyj.grenz.com.

GRESHNEVIKOV, Anatoly Nikolaevich; Russian journalist and writer; *Deputy Chairman, State Duma Committee for Environment;* b. 29 Aug. 1956, Borisoglebsky Dist, Yaroslavl region; two c. *Education:* Leningrad State Univ. *Career:* head correspondence dept Novoye Vremya newspaper, Borisoglebsk; elected to Yaroslavl Regional Soviet and RSFSR Congress of People's Deputies 1990; mem. RSFSR Supreme Soviet and Cttee on Ecological Issues and Rational Use of Natural Resources; State Duma Deputy 1993–; mem. Russian Way faction 1993–95, Narodvlastiye (Sovereignty of the People) parl. group 1995–99; stood as ind. 2003, now mem. Rodina (Motherland) faction (mem. Political Council); mem. Cttee for Environment 1993–95, Secr. 1995–99, Deputy Chair. 1999–; mem. Russian Writers' Union, Russian Creative Union

of Cultural Workers. *Publications include:* Sound Ecosystem – Healthy Society, The President Doesn't Hear the Ecologists; 'The Era of Environmental Apocalypse' series: The Caspian in the Nets of Poachers, Sticks and Staves for Scenic Forests, The Call of Arctic, Sale: Beavers, Tigers, Falcons, Land Is Being Lost, Fighting Dolphins and Ring Dogs, Dangerous Climate. *Honours:* Order of the Holy and Righteous Prince Daniil of Moscow (Rank III), Russian Orthodox Church; prizes from USSR Journalists' Union, Selskaya Zhizn newspaper 1989, Selskaya Nov and Novy Mir magazines, 850th Anniversary of Moscow Medal, 300th Anniversary of St Petersburg Medal. *Address:* c/o State Duma of the Federal Assembly of the Russian Federation, Okhotny ryad 1, 103265 Moscow, Russia. *Telephone:* (495) 2923759.

GREY, Amelia (see Skinner, Gloria Dale)

GREY, Anthony Keith, OBE; British writer, broadcaster and publisher; *Founder and Chairman, The Tagman Press;* b. 5 July 1938, Norwich, Norfolk; m. Shirley McGuinn 1970; two d. *Career:* journalist, Eastern Daily Press 1960–64; Foreign Correspondent, Reuters, East Berlin and Prague 1965–67, Beijing 1967–69; est. imprint, The Tagman Press, Norfolk, UK 1998; mem. PEN International, Royal Inst. of Int. Affairs, Soc. of Authors, Groucho Club. *Publications:* Hostage in Peking 1970, A Man Alone 1971, Some Put Their Trust in Chariots 1973, Crosswords from Peking 1975, The Bulgarian Exclusive 1976, Himself (radio play) 1976, The Chinese Assassin 1978, Saigon 1982, The Prime Minister was a Spy 1983, Peking 1988, The Naked Angels 1990, The Bangkok Secret 1990, Tokyo Bay 1996, Hostage in Peking Plus 2004, What is the Universe In? 2004; other: BBC World Service radio documentary series, UFO's: Fact, Fiction or Fantasy 1997. *Honours:* UK Journalist of the Year 1970. *Literary Agent:* PFD, Drury House, 34–43 Russell Street, London, WC2B 5HA, England. *Address:* The Tagman Press, Lovemore House, 5 Caley Close, Sweet Briar Estate, Norwich, NR3 2BU, England (office). *Telephone:* (845) 644-4186 (office). *Fax:* (845) 644-4187 (office). *E-mail:* editorial@tagman-press.com (office). *Website:* www.tagman-press.com (office).

GREY, Charles (see Tubb, Edwin Charles)

GREY, Marina, (Marina Chiappe); French writer and historian; b. 5 March 1919, Ekaterinodar, Russia; d. of Gen. Anton Denikine; m. 1st Jean Boudet 1941; one s.; m. 2nd Jacques Lassaigne 1948; m. 3rd Jean-François Chiappe 1961. *Education:* schools in Malakoff, Chartres and Sèvres. *Career:* emigrated from Russia to France 1926; journalist working on French radio and TV 1944–65; writer of novels and historical books 1965–. *Publications include:* Les Armées blanches 1968, La Saga de l'exil (three vols) 1979, 1980, 1984, Hébert, le père Duchesne agent royaliste (Acad. de Paris Prix Eugène Colas) 1983, Mon père, le général Denikine 1985, Enquête sur la mort de Louis XVII 1989, Les Romanov 1991, Le Baron de Batz, le d'Artagnan de la révolution 1991, Qui a tué Raspoutine. *Honours:* literary prizes from Soc. des gens de lettres 1973, Acad. française 1979, 1983, Ville de Paris 1984. *Address:* 10 rue de Fontenay, 78000 Versailles, France. *Telephone:* (1) 39-50-55-45.

GRIBBIN, John R., MSc, PhD; British astrophysicist and writer; b. 1946; m. Mary Gribbin; two s. *Education:* Sussex Univ., Univ. of Cambridge. *Career:* Ed., Nature magazine 1970–75; science journalist, The Times; Visiting Fellow in Astronomy, Univ. of Sussex. *Publications include:* fiction: Brother Esau 1982, Double Planet 1988, Father to the Man 1989, Ragnarok 1991, Reunion 1991, Innervisions 1993; non-fiction: The Jupiter Effect 1974, Forecasts, Famines and Freezes 1976, Timewarps 1979, Our Changing Universe 1977, The Death of the Sun 1980, The Monkey Puzzle 1983, Spacewarps 1984, In Search of Schrodinger's Cat 1984, Amateur Astronomer 1985, In Search of the Double Helix 1985, The Hole in the Sky 1988, The Omega Point 1988, Winds of Change 1989, Cosmic Coincidence 1989, Hothouse Earth 1990, Blinded by the Light 1991, The Matter Myth 1992, In Search of the Big Bang 1992, Being Human 1993, In the Beginning 1993, Einstein: a Life in Science (with Michael White) 1994, In Search of the Edge of Time 1995, Companion to the Cosmos 1996, Schrodinger's Kittens and the Search for Reality 1996, Fire on Earth (with Mary Gribbin) 1996, Mendel in 90 Minutes (with Mary Gribbin) 1997, Richard Feynman: A Life in Science (with Michael White) 1998, Almost Everyone's Guide to Science 1999, Q is for Quantum 1999, The Search for Superstrings, Symmetry and the Theory of Everything 2000, The Case of the Missing Neutrinos 2000, Darwin: A Life in Science (with Michael White) 2000, The Birth of Time 2000, Stardust (with Mary Gribbin) 2001, Space: Our Final Frontier 2001, Science: A History 1534–2001 2002, Ice Age: How a Change of Climate Made Us Human (with Mary Gribbin) 2003, Stephen Hawking: A Life in Science (with Michael White) 2003, Deep Simplicity: Chaos, Complexity and the Emergence of Life 2004, The Men who Measured the Universe 2004, Fitzroy: The Remarkable Story of Darwin's Captain and the Invention of the Weather Forecast (with Mary Gribbin) 2004, The Fellowship: the Story of a Revolution 2005, The Universe: A Biography 2007; contrib. to New Destinies VII 1988, What's the Big Idea? Chaos and Uncertainty 1999, The Science of Philip Pullman's 'His Dark Materials' 2003, numerous journals, magazines and newspapers. *Honours:* Annual Award of the Gravity Research Foundation. *Literary Agent:* Bruce Hunter, David Higham Associates, 5–8 Lower Street, Golden Square, London, W1F 9HA, England. *Telephone:* (20) 7434-5900. *Fax:* (20) 7437-1072. *Website:* www.biols.susx.ac.uk/home/John_Gribbin/.

GRICHKOVETS, Evguéni; Russian playwright; b. 1966, Kémérovo, Siberia. *Publications:* plays incl. Zima. *Honours:* Moscow Festival Innovation Prize 2000.

GRIDBAN, Volsted (see Tubb, Edwin Charles)

GRIFFIN, Jasper, MA, FBA; British classical scholar; b. 29 May 1937, London; s. of Frederick William Griffin and Constance Irene Cordwell; m. Miriam Tamara Dressler 1960; three d. *Education:* Balliol Coll., Oxford. *Career:* Jackson Fellow, Harvard Univ. 1960–61; Dyson Research Fellow, Balliol Coll., Oxford 1961–63, Fellow and Tutor in Classics 1963–, Univ. Reader 1989–, Prof. of Classical Literature 1992–; Public Orator 1992–; T. S. Eliot Memorial Lectures, Univ. of Kent 1984. *Publications:* Homer on Life and Death 1980, Snobs 1982, Latin Poets and Roman Life 1985, The Mirror of Myth 1985, Virgil 1986; Ed. The Oxford History of the Classical World 1986, Homer: The Odyssey 1987, The Iliad: Book Nine 1995; articles and reviews. *Address:* Balliol College, Oxford, England. *Telephone:* (1865) 277782.

GRIFFIN, Keith Broadwell, DPhil, FAAS; British academic and writer; b. 6 Nov. 1938, Colón, Panama; m. Dixie Beth Griffin 1956; two d. *Education:* Williams Coll., Williamstown, Mass, USA, Univ. of Oxford. *Career:* Fellow and Tutor in Econs, Magdalen Coll., Oxford 1965–76, Pres., 1979–88; Cecil and Ida Green Visiting Prof., Univ. of British Columbia 1986; Distinguished Prof. of Econs 1988–2004, Chair. Dept of Econs 1988–93, Univ. of California at Riverside. *Publications:* The Green Revolution: An Economic Analysis, 1972; The Political Economy of Agrarian Change, 1974; Land Concentration and Rural Poverty, 1976; International Inequality and National Poverty, 1978; The Transition to Egalitarian Development (with Jeffrey James), 1981; Growth and Equality in Rural China (with Ashwani Saith), 1981; World Hunger and the World Economy, 1987; Alternative Strategies for Economic Development, 1989; Implementing a Human Development Strategy (with Terry McKinley), 1994; Studies in Globalization and Economic Transitions, 1996; Economic Reform in Vietnam (ed.), 1998; Studies in Development Strategy and Systemic Transformation, 2000; Poverty Reduction in Mongolia (ed.), 2003. Contributions: scholarly books and journals. *Honours:* Hon. Fellow, Magdalen Coll., Oxford 1988; Hon. DLitt (Williams Coll.) 1980. *Address:* c/o Department of Economics, University of California at Riverside, Riverside, CA 92521, USA (office). *E-mail:* griffin@mail.ucr.edu (office); keithdixiegriffin@sbcglobal.net (home).

GRIFFITH, Patricia Browning, BA; American novelist and dramatist; *Associate Professor, The George Washington University;* b. 9 Nov. 1935, Fort Worth, TX; m. William Byron Griffith 1960; one d. *Education:* Baylor Univ. *Career:* Assoc. Adjunct Prof., The George Washington Univ.; Pres. PEN/Faulkner Foundation Award for Fiction 1995–99, Co-Chair. PEN/Faulkner Foundation 2005–07. *Publications:* fiction: The Future is Not What it Used to Be 1970, Tennessee Blue 1981, The World Around Midnight 1991, Supporting the Sky 1996; plays: Outside Waco 1984, Safety 1987, Risky Games 1992; contribs to anthologies and periodicals. *Honours:* NEA grant 1978, American Library Asscn Notable Book 1992. *Address:* Department of English, Rome Hall, The George Washington University, Washington, DC 20052 (office); 1215 Geranium Street NW, Washington, DC 20012, USA (home). *Telephone:* (202) 994-2135 (office); (202) 829-7780 (home).

GRIFFITHS, Helen, (Helen Santos); British writer; b. 8 May 1939, London, England. *Publications:* Horse in the Clouds, 1957; Wild and Free, 1958; Moonlight, 1959; Africano, 1960; The Wild Heart, 1962; The Greyhound, 1963; Wild Horse of Santander, 1965; Dark Swallows, 1965; Leon, 1966; Stallion of the Sands, 1967; Moshie Cat, 1968; Patch, 1969; Federico, 1970; Russian Blue, 1973; Just a Dog, 1974; Witch Fear, 1975; Pablo, 1976; Kershaw Dogs, 1978; The Last Summer, 1979; Blackface Stallion, 1980; Dancing Horses, 1981; Hari's Pigeon, 1982; Rafa's Dog, 1983; Jesus, As Told By Mark, 1983; Dog at the Window, 1984. As Helen Santos: Caleb's Lamb, 1984; If Only, 1987; Pepe's Dog, 1996. *Honours:* highly commended, Carnegie Medal Award 1966, Silver Pencil Award for Best Children's Book, Netherlands 1978. *Address:* 9 Ashley Terrace, Bath, Avon BA1 3DP, England. *E-mail:* helensantos@lineone.net.

GRIFFITHS, Jay; British writer; b. Manchester. *Education:* Univ. of Oxford. *Publications:* non-fiction: Pip Pip: A Sideways Look at Time (Discover Award for Non-Fiction, USA 2003) 1999, Wild: An Elemental Journey 2007; fiction: Anarchipelago 2007. *Literary Agent:* David Godwin Associates, 55 Monmouth Street, London, WC2H 9DG, England. *Telephone:* (20) 7240-9992. *Fax:* (20) 7395-6110.

GRIFFITHS, Paul Anthony, BA, MSc; British music critic and writer; b. 24 Nov. 1947, Bridgend, Glamorgan, Wales. *Education:* Lincoln Coll., Oxford. *Career:* music critic for various journals 1971–; Area Ed. 20th Century Music, New Grove Dictionary of Music and Musicians 1973–76; music critic, The Times 1982–92, New Yorker 1992–96, New York Times 1997–; compiled Mozart pasticcio The Jewel Box for Opera North 1991, Purcell pasticcio Aeneas in Hell 1995. *Publications:* A Concise History of Modern Music 1978, Boulez 1978, A Guide to Electronic Music 1979, Cage 1981, Peter Maxwell Davies 1982, The String Quartet 1983, György Ligeti 1983, Bartók 1984, Olivier Messiaen 1985, New Sounds, New Personalities: British Composers of the 1980s 1985, An Encyclopedia of 20th Century Music 1986, Myself and Marco Polo (novel) 1987, The Life of Sir Tristram (novel) 1991, The Jewel Box (opera libretto) 1991, Stravinsky 1992, Modern Music and After 1995, libretti for Tan Dun's opera, Marco Polo 1996, libretti for Elliott Carter's opera, What Next? 1999, The Sea on Fire 2004, A Concise History of Western Music 2006. *Address:* c/o Cambridge University Press, The Edinburgh Building, Shaftesbury Road, Cambridge, CB2 2RU, England.

GRIFFITHS, Trevor, BA; British playwright; b. 4 April 1935, Manchester; s. of Ernest Griffiths and Anne Connor; m. 1st Janice Elaine Stansfield 1961 (died 1977); one s. two d.; m. 2nd Gillian Cliff 1992. *Education:* Manchester Univ. *Career:* taught English language and literature 1957–65; Educ. Officer, BBC 1965–72; Dir Saint Oscar 1990, The Gulf Between Us 1992, Who Shall be Happy...? 1995, Food for Ravens 1997. *Film scripts:* Reds (with Warren Beatty, WGA Award 1981) 1981, Fatherland 1986. *Plays include:* Occupations 1972, The Party 1974, Comedians 1976, Oi for England 1981, Real Dreams 1984, The Gulf Between Us 1992, Thatcher's Children 1993, Who Shall Be Happy 1994. *TV includes:* All Good Men 1974, Through the Night 1976, Country 1981, Sons and Lovers 1982, The Last Place on Earth 1985, Hope in the Year, Two 1994, Food for Ravens 1997 (Royal TV Soc. Best Regional Programme 1998, Gwyn A. Williams Special Award, BAFTA Wales 1998). *Publications:* Occupations, Sam Sam 1972, The Party 1974, Comedians 1976, All Good Men, Absolute Beginners, Through the Night, Such Impossibilities, Thermidor and Apricots 1977, Deeds (co-author), The Cherry Orchard (trans.) 1978, Country 1981, Oi for England, Sons and Lovers (TV version) 1982, Judgement Over the Dead 1986, Fatherland, Real Dreams 1987, Collected Plays for TV 1988, Piano 1990, The Gulf Between Us 1992, Hope in the Year Two, Thatcher's Children 1994, Plays One (Collected Stage Plays) 1996, Food for Ravens 1998, These Are The Times 2005, Theatre Plays One 2007, Theatre Plays Two 2007. *Honours:* Writer's Award, British Acad. of Film and TV Artists 1981. *Address:* c/o Peters Fraser & Dunlop, Drury House, 34-43 Russell Street, London, WC2B 5HA, England. *Telephone:* (20) 7344-1000. *Fax:* (20) 7836-9539.

GRIMWOOD, Jon Courtenay; British writer and journalist; b. Valetta, Malta; m. 1st (divorced); one s.; m. 2nd. *Career:* fmr ed. and publisher; journalist, contrib. to newspapers and magazines, including Guardian, Independent, Esquire, Maxim, SFX, Focus, Manga Mania. *Publications:* novels: neoAddix 1997, Lucifer's Dragon 1998, reMix 1999, redRobe 2000, Pashazade (Arabesk series vol. I) 2001, Effendi (Arabesk series vol. II) 2002, Felaheen (Arabesk series vol. III) (BSFA Award for Best Novel) 2003, Stamping Butterflies 2004, End of the World Blues 2006; other: Mrs T's Bedside Book 1985, Royal Family Bedside Book 1986, Photohistory of the 20th Century 1986, Election Bedside Book 1987, Bug (short story) 1999. *Address:* c/o Gollancz, Wellington House, 125 Strand, London, WC2R 0BB, England. *E-mail:* jon@hardcopy.demon.co.uk. *Website:* website: www.j-cg.co.uk.

GRISEZ, Germain, MA, PhL, PhD; American academic; *Most Reverend Harry J. Flynn Professor of Christian Ethics, Mount Saint Mary's University;* b. 30 Sept. 1929, University Heights, Ohio; m. Jeannette Selby 1951 (deceased); four c. *Education:* John Carroll Univ., Univ. Heights, Ohio, Dominican Coll. of St Thomas Aquinas, River Forest, Ill. and Univ. of Chicago. *Career:* Asst Prof. to Prof., Georgetown Univ. Washington, DC 1957–72; part-time Lecturer in Medieval Philosophy, Univ. of Virginia, Charlottesville 1961–62; Special Asst to HE Cardinal O'Boyle, Archbishop of Washington 1968–69; consultant (part-time) Archdiocese of Washington 1969–72; Prof. of Philosophy, Campion Coll. Univ. of Regina, Canada 1972–79; Most Rev. Harry J. Flynn Prof. of Christian Ethics, Mount St Mary's Univ., Emmitsburg, Md 1979–; mem. Catholic Theol. Soc. of America, American Catholic Philosophical Asscn. *Publications:* Contraception and the Natural Law 1964, Abortion: The Myths, the Realities and the Arguments 1970, Beyond the New Morality (with Russell Shaw) 1974, Free Choice (with others) 1976, Life and Death with Liberty Justice (with Joseph M. Boyle Jr) 1979, The Way of the Lord Jesus, Vol. I, Christian Moral Principles (with others) 1983, Vol. II, Living a Christian Life (with others) 1993, Vol. III, Difficult Moral Questions (with others) 1997, Nuclear Deterrence, Morality and Realism (with J. Finnis and Joseph M. Boyle) 1987, Fulfilment in Christ (with Russell Shaw) 1991, Personal Vocation: God Calls Everyone by Name (with Russell Shaw) 2003, God: A Philosophical Preface to Faith 2005; numerous articles in learned journals. *Honours:* Pro ecclesia et pontifice medal 1972; Cardinal Wright Award for service to the Church 1983 and other awards. *Address:* Mount Saint Mary's University, 16300 Old Emmitsburg Road, Emmitsburg, MD 21727-7799, USA (office). *Telephone:* (301) 447-5771 (office). *E-mail:* grisez@msmary.edu (office). *Website:* www.msmary.edu (office).

GRISHAM, John, BS, JD; American writer and lawyer; b. 8 Feb. 1955, Jonesboro, AR; m. Renée Jones; one s. one d. *Education:* Mississippi State Univ., Univ. of Mississippi, law school. *Career:* called to the Bar, Miss. 1981; attorney in Southaven, Miss. 1981–90; mem. Miss. House of Representatives 1984–90. *Film screenplay:* The Gingerbread Man 1998. *Publications:* A Time to Kill 1989, The Firm 1991, The Pelican Brief 1992, The Client 1993, The Chamber 1994, The Rainmaker 1995, The Runaway Jury 1996, The Partner 1997, The Street Lawyer 1998, The Testament 1999, The Brethren 2000, A Painted House 2001, Skipping Christmas 2001, The Summons 2002, The King of Torts 2003, Bleachers 2003, The Last Juror 2004, The Broker 2005, The Innocent Man (non-fiction) 2006. *Honours:* Lifetime Achievement Award, British Book Awards 2007. *Address:* c/o Doubleday & Co. Inc., 1540 Broadway, New York, NY 10036, USA. *Website:* www.jgrisham.com.

GROENEWOLD, Sabine, DPhil; German publishing executive; b. 18 Oct. 1940, Hamburg; m. Kurt Groenewold. *Education:* Univs of Hamburg, Tübingen and Salamanca, Spain. *Career:* Asst Prof., later Assoc. Prof., Univs of New York, Hamburg, Kassel and Berlin 1969–88; Publr and Ed. Europäische Verlagsanstalt, Rotbuch Verlag, Hamburg 1989–; Founder Sabine Groenewold Verlage KG. *Publications:* numerous articles on Spanish and Latin-American literature 1972–. *Address:* Sabine Groenewold Verlage

KG, Bei den Muhren 70, 20457 Hamburg, Germany (office). *Telephone:* (40) 4501940 (office). *Fax:* (40) 45019450 (office). *E-mail:* info@sabine-groenewold-verlage.de (office). *Website:* www.sabine-groenewold-verlage.de (office).

GROSS, Claudia; German novelist; b. 26 July 1956, Arolsen, Hesse. *Publications include:* Scholarium 2002. *Address:* c/o The Toby Press, PO Box 8531, New Milford, CT 06776-8531, USA. *Website:* www.tobypress.com.

GROSS, John Jacob, MA; British writer, editor and publisher; b. 12 March 1935, London; s. of late Abraham and Muriel Gross; m. Miriam May 1965 (divorced 1988); one s. one d. *Education:* City of London School, Wadham Coll., Oxford and Princeton Univ. *Career:* Ed. with Victor Gollancz Ltd 1956–58; lecturer, Queen Mary Coll., Univ. of London 1959–62, Hon. Fellow 1988; Fellow of King's Coll., Cambridge 1962–65; Asst Ed. Encounter 1963–65; Literary Ed. New Statesman 1972–73; Ed. Times Literary Supplement 1974–81; Literary Ed. Spectator 1983; journalist, New York Times 1983–88; theatre critic Sunday Telegraph 1989–2005; Dir Times Newspapers Holdings Ltd (fmrly Times Newspapers Ltd) 1982; editorial consultant The Weidenfeld Publishing Group 1982; a Trustee Nat. Portrait Gallery 1977–84; Fellow Queen Mary Coll. 1987. *Publications:* Dickens and the Twentieth Century (ed. with Gabriel Pearson) 1962, John P. Marquand 1963, The Rise and Fall of the Man of Letters: Aspects of English Literary Life since 1800 1969, James Joyce 1970, Rudyard Kipling: The Man, His Work and His World (ed.) 1972, The Oxford Book of Aphorisms (ed.) 1983, The Oxford Book of Essays (ed.) 1991, Shylock 1992, The Modern Movement (ed.) 1992, The Oxford Book of Comic Verse (ed.) 1994, The New Oxford Book of English Prose (ed.) 1998, A Double Thread: Growing Up English and Jewish in London 2001, The New Oxford Book of Literary Anecdotes (ed.) 2006. *Honours:* Hon. DHL (Adelphi Univ.) 1995; Duff Cooper Memorial Prize 1969. *Address:* 74 Princess Court, Queensway, London, W2 4RE, England (home).

GROSS, Philip John, BA; British writer, poet and creative writing teacher; b. 27 Feb. 1952, Delabole, England. *Education:* Univ. of Sussex, Polytechnic of North London. *Career:* numerous residencies and teaching posts. *Stage productions:* Rising Star (play) 1996, Snail Dreaming (opera, with composer Glyn Evans) 1997, Dancing the Knife (dance drama, with Medea Mahdavi) 2002. *Publications:* for children: Manifold Manor 1989, The Song of Gail and Fludd 1991, The All-Nite Café (Signal Award for Children's Poetry 1994) 1993, Plex 1994, The Wind Gate 1995, Scratch City (poems) 1996, Transformer 1996, Psylicon Beach 1998, Facetaker 1999, Going for Stone 2002, Marginaliens 2003, The Lastling 2003, The Storm Garden 2006; poetry: Familiars 1983, The Ice Factory 1984, Cat's Whisker 1987, The Air Mines of Mistila (with Sylvia Kantaris) 1988, The Son of the Duke of Nowhere 1991, I.D. 1994, A Cast of Stones 1996, The Wasting Game 1998, Changes of Address: Poems 1980–98 2001, Mappa Mundi 2003, The Egg of Zero 2006. *Honours:* Eric Gregory Award 1981, Arts Council Bursary for Writing for Young People 1990. *E-mail:* contact@philipgross.co.uk. *Website:* www.philipgross.co.uk.

GROSSER, Alfred, DèsSc; French academic, writer and journalist; b. 1 Feb. 1925, Frankfurt; s. of the late Paul Grosser and Lily Grosser (née Rosenthal); m. Anne-Marie Jourcin 1959; four s. *Education:* Univs of Aix en Provence and Paris. *Career:* Asst Dir UNESCO Office in Germany 1950–51; Asst Prof. Univ. of Paris 1951–55; lecturer, later Prof. Inst. d'études politiques 1954, Prof. Emer. 1992; Dir Studies and Research, Fondation nat. des Sciences politiques 1956–92; with Ecole des hautes études commerciales 1961–66, 1986–88, with Ecole Polytechnique 1974–95; Political Columnist La Croix 1955–65, 1984–, Le Monde 1965–94, Ouest-France 1973–, L'Expansion 1979–89; Pres. Centre d'information et de recherche sur l'Allemagne contemporaine 1982–, Eurocréation 1986–92 (Hon. Pres. 1992–); mem. Bd L'Express 1998–2003. *Publications:* L'Allemagne de l'Occident 1953, La démocratie de Bonn 1958, Hitler, la presse et la naissance d'une dictature 1959, La Quatrième Republique et sa politique extérieure 1961, La politique extérieure de la Ve République 1965, Au nom de quoi? Fondements d'une morale politique 1969, L'Allemagne de notre temps 1970, L'explication politique 1972, les Occidentaux: Les pays d'Europe et les Etats Unis depuis la guerre 1978, Le sel de la terre. Pour l'engagement moral 1981, Affaires extérieures: la politique de la France 1944–84, 1984 (updated 1989), L'Allemagne en Occident 1985, Mit Deutschen streiten 1987, Vernunft und Gewalt. Die französische Revolution und das deutsche Grundgesetz heute 1989, Le crime et la mémoire 1989 (revised 1991), Mein Deutschland 1993, Was ich denke 1995, Les identités difficiles 1996, Une Vie de Français (memoirs) 1997, Deutschland in Europa 1998, Les fruits de leur arbre: regard athée sur les Chrétiens 2001, L'Allemagne de Berlin 2002, La France, semblable et differente 2005. *Honours:* Grosses Verdienstkreuz mit Stern 1995 und Schulterband 2003; Grand Officier Légion d'Honneur 2001; Dr hc (Aston, Birmingham, UK) 2001, (European Univ. of Humanities, Minsk, Belarus) 2001; Peace Prize, Union of German Publrs 1975; Grand Prix, Acad. des Sciences Morales et Politiques 1998. *Address:* 8 rue Dupleix, 75015 Paris, France (home). *Telephone:* 1-43-06-41-82 (home). *Fax:* 1-40-65-00-76 (home). *E-mail:* grosser.alfred@wanadoo.fr (home).

GROSSKURTH, Phyllis, BA, MA, PhD; Canadian academic and writer; b. 16 March 1924, Toronto, ON; m. 1st Robert A. Grosskurth; two s. one d.; m. 2nd Mavor Moore 1968 (divorced 1980); m. 3rd Robert McMullan 1986. *Education:* Univ. of Toronto, Univ. of Ottawa, Univ. of London. *Career:* Lecturer, Carleton Univ., 1964–65; Prof. of English, 1965–87, Faculty, Humanities and Psychoanalysis Programme, 1987–95, Univ. of Toronto; mem. PEN. *Publications:* John Addington Symonds: A Biography, 1964; Notes on Browning's Works, 1967; Leslie Stephen, 1968; Gabrielle Roy, 1969; Havelock Ellis: A Biography, 1980; The Memoirs of John Addington Symonds (ed.), 1984; Melanie Klein: Her World and Her Work, 1986; Margaret Mead: A Life of Controversy, 1988; The Secret Ring: Freud's Inner Circle and the Politics of Psychoanalysis, 1991; Byron: The Flawed Angel, 1997. Contributions: periodicals. *Honours:* Hon. DSL (Trinity Coll., Univ. of Toronto) 1992, Dr hc (St Mary's Univ., Halifax) 2002; Gov.-Gen.'s Award for Non-Fiction, 1965; Univ. of British Columbia Award for Biography, 1965; Guggenheim Fellowships, 1977–78, 1983; Rockefeller Foundation Fellowship, 1982; Canada Council Arts Award, 1989–90; Social Science and Humanities Research Grant, 1982–92. *Address:* 147 Spruce Street, Toronto, ON M5A 26J, Canada.

GROSSMAN, David, BA; Israeli writer; b. 25 Jan. 1954, Jerusalem; m. Michal Grossman; two s. (one deceased) one d. *Education:* Hebrew Univ., Jerusalem. *Publications:* Hiyukh ha-gedi (trans. as The Smile of the Lamb) 1983, 'Ayen 'erekh–ahavah (trans. as See Under: Love) 1986, Ha-Zeman ha-tsahov (non-fiction, trans. as The Yellow Wind) 1987, Gan Riki: Mahazeh bi-shete ma'arakhot (play, trans. as Rikki's Kindergarten) 1988, Sefer hakikduk hapnimi (trans. as The Book of Intimate Grammar) 1991, Hanochachim hanifkadim (non-fiction, trans. as Sleeping on a Wire: Conversations with Palestinians in Israel) 1992, The Zigzag Kid (in trans.) (Premio Mondelo, Premio Grinzane), Duel (in trans.), Be My Knife (in trans.) 2002, Someone to Run With (in trans.) 2003, Death as a Way of Life: Dispatches from Jerusalem (non-fiction, in trans.) 2003, Her Body Knows (novel, in trans.), Lovers and Strangers (novel, in trans.) 2005, Lion's Honey: The Myth of Samson; also short stories, children's books, contribs to periodicals. *Honours:* Chevalier, Ordre des Artes et Lettres; Children's Literature Prize, Ministry of Educ. 1983, Prime Minister's Hebrew Literature Prize 1984, Israeli Publishers' Asscn Prize for Best Novel 1985, Vallombrosa Prize (Italy) 1989, Nelly Sachs Prize (Germany) 1992, Prix Eliette von Karajan (Austria), Premio Grinzane (Italy), Premio Mondelo (Italy), Vittorio de Sica Prize (Italy), Marsh Award for Children's Literature in Translation (UK), Juliet Club Prize (Italy), Buxtehuder Bulle (Germany), Sapir Prize (Israel), Italian Critics Prize (Italy), Nelly Sachs Prize (Germany), Mane Sperber Prize (Austria), Bernstein Prize (Israel), Bialik Prize (Israel). *Literary Agent:* c/o Managing Editor, The Deborah Harris Agency, 9 Yael Street, Jerusalem 93502, Israel. *Telephone:* (2) 6722145; (2) 6722143. *Fax:* (2) 6725797. *E-mail:* iaustern@netvision.net.il.

GROULT, Benoîte Marie Rose, LèsL; French writer and journalist; b. 31 Jan. 1920, Paris; d. of André Groult and Nicole Groult (née Poiret); m. 1st Pierre Heuyer 1944 (died 1945); m. 2nd Georges de Caunes 1946; two d.; m. 3rd Paul Guimard 1951; one d. *Education:* Univ. of Paris-Sorbonne. *Career:* fmr teacher of Latin; journalist on Elle and Marie-Claire magazines; co-f. (with Claude Servan-Schreiber) F Magazine 1978; currently writer and freelance journalist; Pres. Comm. pour la Féminisation des noms de métiers 1985–; mem. Jury Prix Fémina 1979–. *Publications include:* La part des choses (Prix de l' Acad. de Bretagne) 1972, Ainsi soit-elle 1975, Le féminisme au masculin 1977, Les vaissaux du cœur (English title Salt on our Skin 1992, translated also to German) 1989, Olympe de Gouges (biog.), Pauline Roland (biog.), Histoire d'une evasion (autobiog.) 1998; With sister (Flora Groult): Journal à quatre mains (English title Double-Handed Diary) 1958, Le féminin pluriel (English title Feminine Plural) 1961, Il était deux fois, La touche étoile 2006. *Honours:* Officière de la Légion d'Honneur 1995; Commandeuse de l'Ordre Nat. du Mérite; Prix Bretagne 1975. *Address:* 54 rue de Bourgogne, 75007 Paris; 3 rue de la Croix, 83400 Hyères, France (home). *Telephone:* (1) 47-05-33-30 (office); (4) 94-65-19-53 (home). *Fax:* (4) 94-65-81-95.

GRUFFYDD, Peter, BA; British writer, poet, translator and actor; b. 12 April 1935, Liverpool, England; m. 1st; one s. one d.; m. 2nd Susan Soar 1974; two s. *Education:* Univ. of Wales, Bangor. *Career:* mem. Equity, PEN Int. (founder-mem. Welsh Branch 1993), Welsh Union of Writers, Yr Academi Gymraeg. *Publications:* Triad, 1963; Welsh Voices, 1967; Poems, 1969; The Lilting House, 1970; Poems, 1972; The Shivering Seed, 1972; On Censorship, 1985; Environmental Teletex, 1989; Damned Braces, 1993. Contributions: anthologies and periodicals. *Honours:* Eric Gregory Trust, 1963; Second Prize, Young Poets Competition, Welsh Arts Council, 1969; First Prizes, 1984, 1994, Third Prizes, 1986, 1991, 1993, Aberystwyth Open Poetry Competitions; Duncan Lawrie Prize, Arvon-Observer International Poetry Competition, 1993. *Address:* 21 Beech Road, Norton, Stourbridge, West Midlands DY8 2AS, England.

GRUMBACH, Doris Isaac, AB, MA; American author, critic and academic (retd); b. 12 July 1918, New York, NY; m. Leonard Grumbach 1941 (divorced 1972); four d. *Education:* Washington Square College, Cornell University. *Career:* Assoc. Ed., Architectural Forum, 1942–43; Teacher of English, Albany Acad. for Girls, New York, 1952–55; Instructor, 1955–58, Asst Prof., 1958–60, Assoc. Prof., 1960–69, Prof. of English, 1969–73, College of Saint Rose, Albany; Visiting University Fellow, Empire State College, 1972–73; Literary Ed., New Republic, 1973–75; Adjunct Prof. of English, University of Maryland, 1974–75; Prof. of American Literature, American University, Washington, DC, 1975–85; Columnist and reviewer for various publications, radio, and television; mem. PEN. *Publications:* The Spoil of the Flowers, 1962; The Short Throat, the Tender Mouth, 1964; The Company She Kept (biog. of Mary McCarthy), 1967; Chamber Music, 1979; The Missing Person, 1981; The Ladies, 1984; The Magician's Girl, 1987; Coming Into the End Zone, 1992; Extra Innings: A Memoir, 1993; Fifty Days of Solitude, 1994; The Book of Knowledge: A Novel, 1995; The Presence of Absence, 1998; The Pleasure of Their Company, 2000. Contributions: books and periodicals.

GRÜNBAUM, Adolf, BA, MS, PhD; American academic and writer; *Chairman, Center for Philosophy of Science;* b. 15 May 1923, Cologne, Germany; m. Thelma Braverman 1949; one d. *Education:* Wesleyan and Yale Univs. *Career:* Faculty, Lehigh Univ. 1950–55, Prof. of Philosophy 1955–56, Selfridge Prof. of Philosophy 1956–60; Visiting Research Prof., Minnesota Center for the Philosophy of Science 1956, 1959; Andrew Mellon Prof. of Philosophy of Science, Univ. of Pittsburgh 1960–, Dir 1960–78, later Chair. Center for Philosophy of Science, Research Prof. of Psychiatry 1979–, Research Prof., Dept of History and Philosophy of Science 2007–; Werner Heisenberg Lecturer, Bavarian Acad. of Sciences 1985; Gifford Lecturer, Univ. of St Andrews 1985; Visiting Mellon Prof., Calif. Inst. of Tech. 1990; Leibniz Lecturer, Univ. of Hannover 2003; Pres. Div. of Logic, Methodology and Philosophy of Science, Int. Union for History and Philosophy of Science 2004–05, Union Pres. 2006–07; mem. American Acad. of Arts and Sciences, American Philosophical Asscn (Pres. Educational Div. 1982–83), Acad. Internationale de Philosophie des Sciences, Philosophy of Science Asscn (Pres. 1965–67, 1968–70), AAAS (Vice-Pres. 1963). *Publications:* Philosophical Problems of Space and Time 1963 (also Russian edn), Modern Science and Zeno's Paradoxes, second edn 1968, Geometry and Chronometry in Philosophical Perspective 1968, The Foundations of Psychoanalysis: A Philosophical Critique 1984 (also several foreign language edns), Psicoanalisi: Obiezioni e Risposte 1988; Validation in the Clinical Theory of Psychoanalysis 1993, La Psychanalyse à l'Épreuve 1993; more than 380 contribs to books and scholarly journals. *Honours:* Dr hc (Konstanz, Germany) 1995; J. Walker Tomb Prize, Princeton Univ. 1958, Alumni Honour Citation, Wesleyan Univ. 1959, Festschriften published in his honour 1983, 1993, 2006, Sr US Scientist Prize, Alexander von Humboldt Foundation 1985, Fregene Prize for Science, Italian Parliament 1989, Master Scholar and Prof. Award, Univ. of Pittsburgh 1989, Wilbur Lucius Cross Medal, Yale Univ. 1990, Laureate International Acad. of Humanism. *Address:* 7141 Roycrest Place, Pittsburgh, PA 15208-2737, USA (home). *Telephone:* (412) 624-5738 (office); (412) 241-7036 (home). *Fax:* (412) 648-1068 (office); (412) 371-6692 (home). *E-mail:* grunbaum@pitt .edu (office). *Website:* www.pitt.edu (office).

GRÜNBEIN, Durs; German poet and writer; b. 9 Oct. 1962, Dresden; m.; one d. *Publications:* Grauzone morgens (poems) 1988, Schädelbasislektion (poems) 1991, Den teuren Toten (poems) 1994, Falten und Fallen (poems) (Peter-Huchel-Preis 1995) 1994, Galilei vermißt Dantes Hölle und bleibt an den Maßen hängen (essays) 1996, Nach den Satiren (poems) 1999, Das erste Jahr (essays) 2001, Erklärte Nacht (poems) 2002, Warum schriftlos leben (essays) 2003, Vom Schnee oder Descartes in Deutschland (poem) 2003, Der Misanthrop auf Capri (poems) 2005, Porzellan (poems) 2005, Antike Dispositionen (essays) 2005. *Honours:* Nicolaus-Born-Preis 1993, Georg-Büchner-Preis, Darmstadt 1995, Literaturpreis der Stadt Marburg 2000, Premio Nonino, Salzburg 2000, Friedrich-Nietzsche-Literaturpreis des Landes Sachsen-Anhalt 2004, Hölderlin-Preis der Stadt Bad Homburg 2005, Berliner Literaturpreis der Preußischen Seehandlung 2006. *Address:* c/o Suhrkamp Verlag, Postfach 101945, 60019 Frankfurt am Main, Germany. *E-mail:* geschaftsleitung@suhrkamp.de.

GRUNBERG, Arnon; Dutch writer; b. 1971, Amsterdam. *Education:* Vossius Gymnasium. *Publications:* Blauwe Maandagen (novel, trans. as Blue Mondays) (Anton Wachter-prijs) 1994, Figuranten 1997, De troost van de slapstick (essays) 1998, Het veertiende kippetje 1998, Liefde is business 1999, Fantoompijn (novel, trans. as Phantom Pain) (AKO-Literatuurprijs) 2000, Amuse-Bouche (short stories, in trans.) 2008. *Address:* c/o Nijgh & Van Ditmar, Singel 262, Amsterdam, Netherlands. *E-mail:* info@grunberg.nl. *Website:* www.grunberg.nl.

GRUNENBERG, Nina; German journalist; b. 7 Oct. 1936, Dresden; d. of Valentin and Dorothea Grunenberg; m. Reimar Lüst. *Career:* Corresp. Die Zeit newspaper, Chief Reporter 1995–2001. *Publications:* Journalisten, Reportagen-Sammlung 1967, Schweden-Report (jtly) 1973, Japan-Report (jtly) 1981, Reise ins andere Deutschland (jtly) 1986, Die Chefs 1990, Wo die Macht Spielt 2000. *Honours:* Theodor-Wolff-Preis 1973, Quandt-Medienpreis 1990. *Address:* Bellevue 49, 2000 Hamburg 60, Germany.

GRUSA, Jiří, PhD; Czech writer, poet, politician and diplomatist; *President, International PEN;* b. 10 April 1938, Pardubice, East Bohemia; m. *Education:* Charles Univ., Prague. *Career:* worked for periodicals Tvář, Sešity and Nové knihy; banned from publishing 1968; arrested 1974 after distributing 19 copies of his novel The Questionnaire, but released after two months; citizenship revoked 1981; lived in West Germany 1982–90; Amb. to Germany 1991–97, to Austria 1998–2004; Minister of Educ. 1997–98; Dir Diplomatic Acad., Vienna, Austria 2005–; Pres. Int. PEN 2004–; mem. Deutsche Akademie für Sprache und Dichtung, Freie Akademie der Künste, Hamburg, European Acad. for Sciences and the Arts. *Publications:* poems: Torna (The Satchel) 1962, Svetla lhuta (The Light Period) 1964, Cviceni muceni (Learning – Suffering) 1969, Modlitba k Janince (Prayer to Janinka) 1972, Hodina nadeje (The Hour Named Hope, anthology) 1978, Mimner oder Das Tier der Trauer (Mimner or the Animal of Mourning) 1986, Babylonwald 1990, Wandersteine 1994; novels: Damsky gambit (Queen's Gambit) 1974, Dotaznik (The Questionnaire) 1975, Dr Kokeš mistr Panny 1983, Grusas Wacht am Rhein aneb Putovni ghetto 2004; non-fiction: Franz Kafka aus Prag 1983, Prag – einst Stadt der Tschechen, Deutschen und Juden (Prague, Once the City of Czechs, Germans and Jews, co-ed.) 1993, Gebrauchsanweisung für Tschechien (Blueprint for Czechia) 1999, Glücklich Heimatlos (Homeless and Happy) 2002, Umeni starnout (The Art of Aging) 2004, Die Macht der

Mächtigen oder Die Macht der Machtlosen (The Might of the Mighty or the Might of the Mightless, with Vaclav Havel) 2006; essays: Česko – How to Use It; trans. of works of Kafka, Nestroy, Schiller, Rilke. *Honours:* Grosses Verdienstkreuz mit Stern (Germany) 2006, Silbernes Ehrenkreuz (Austria) 2005, Silbernes Komturkreuz mit dem Stern des Ehrenzeichens für Verdienste um das Bundesland Niederösterreich 2004, Grosses goldenes Ehrenzeichen am Bande (Germany) 2004; Jiri-Kolar Prize 1976, Egon Hostovsky Prize 1978, Andreas Gryphius Prize 1996, Internationaler Brücke Prize zu Görlitz 1998, Inter Nationes Culture Prize 1998, Goethe Medal 1999, Jaroslav Seifert Prize 2002. *Address:* Diplomatic Academy of Vienna, Favoritenstrasse 15a, 1040 Vienna, Austria (office). *Telephone:* (1) 5057272 (office). *Fax:* (1) 5042265 (office). *E-mail:* info@da-vienna.ac.at (office).

GRUSHIN, Olga; American (b. Russian) writer; b. 1971, Moscow; m.; one s. *Education:* Pushkin Museum of Fine Arts, Moscow State Univ., Emory Univ., Atlanta. *Career:* fmr personal interpreter for Pres. Jimmy Carter, translator at the World Bank, law firm research analyst, Washington, DC; Ed., Dumbarton Oaks Research Library and Collection, Harvard Univ. 1996–2001; full-time writer 2001–. *Publications:* novel: The Dream Life of Sukhanov 2006; short stories: Spiders Did It (in Happy) 1998, The Stamp Fever (in Green Mountains Review) 1998, At Thirteen Minutes to Three (in artisan: a journal of craft) 1999, The Night before Christmas (in Art Times) 2000, And the Third Glass (in Confrontation) 2001, The Last Offering (in Artful Dodge) 2002, Seven Variations of the Theme of Untied Shoelaces (in The Massachusetts Review) 2002, The Daughter of Kadmos (in Partisan Review) 2002; also essays and reviews in The New York Times, Vogue (UK), Michigan Quarterly Review. *Address:* c/o Penguin Publicity, 375 Hudson Street, New York, NY 10014, USA (office). *E-mail:* olga@olgagrushin.com. *Website:* www.olgagrushin.com.

GRYZUNOV, Sergey Petrovich; Russian journalist; b. 23 July 1949, Kuybyshev; m.; one s. *Education:* Moscow State Univ., Acad. of Public Sciences, Cen. Communist Party Cttee. *Career:* fmr ed. Novosti, then reviewer, then Deputy Head of Bureau, Yugoslavia; Deputy Chair. Cttee on Press April–Sept. 1994, Chair. 1994–95; mem. Pres. Yeltsin's Election Campaign March 1996; Vice-Pres. ICN Pharmaceutical Corpn 1998–2000; Vice-Pres. Moscow News Publrs 2000–. *Address:* Moscow News, Tverskaya str. 16/2, 103829 Moscow, Russia (office). *Telephone:* (495) 200-20-10 (office).

GSTEIGER, Fredy, MBS; Swiss journalist and editor; *Editor-in-Chief, Die Weltwoche;* b. 1962, Berne. *Education:* Univ. of St. Gallen, Switzerland, Univ. of Lyons, France and Univ. of Québec, Canada. *Career:* fmr. Econ. Journalist, Der Bunde, Berne; Foreign Ed. St. Galler Tagblatt 1988–89; Middle East Ed., Die Zeit, Hamburg, Germany 1989–93, Paris Corresp. 1993–97; Ed.-in-Chief Die Weltwoche, Zürich 1997–. *Address:* Die Weltwoche, Förrlibuckstrasse 10, 8021 Zürich, Switzerland (office). *Telephone:* (1) 4487311 (office). *Fax:* (1) 4487127 (office). *E-mail:* redaktion@weltowoche.ch (office). *Website:* www .weltwoche.ch (office).

GU, Hua; Chinese novelist; b. (Luo Hongyu), 20 June 1942, Jiahe County, Hunan. *Education:* Chenzhou Agricultural School, Coll. for Young Writers. *Career:* research worker, Chenzhou Agricultural Research Inst. 1961–75; mem. writing staff, Chenzhou Song and Dance Ensemble 1975–79; mem. Writers' Asscn of Hunan Prov. 1981–87; Hon. Fellow Univ. of Iowa, Int. Writing Program 1987–. *Publications include:* A Log Cabin Overgrown with Creepers, A Small Town Called Hibiscus, The Prison for the Scholars, Virgin Widows, Pagoda Ridge. *Address:* Chenzhou Association of Literary and Art Workers, Chenzhou, People's Republic of China.

GUARDIA DE ALFARO, Gloria, MA; Panamanian writer and journalist; b. 12 March 1940, San Cristóbal, Venezuela; d. of Carlos A. Guardia-Jaén and Olga Zeledón de Guardia; m. Ricardo A. Alfaro-Arosemena 1968; one d. *Education:* Colegio de las Esclavas del Sagrado Corazón (Panamá), Roycemore School for Girls (Evanston, IL), Vassar Coll. (NY), Columbia Univ. (NY, USA) and Univ. Complutense de Madrid (Spain). *Career:* began writing 1961; journalist Agencia Latinoamericana 1975–90; Columnist on La Prensa, Panamá 1980–83, El Panamá-América 1990; mem. Panamanian Acad. of Letters 1985, Librarian and mem. Bd of Dirs 1990; apptd mem. Editorial Bd Panorama Católico 1988, Editora Mariano Arosemena 1990; Hon. mem. Real Academia Española 1989; Hon. Scholarship Vassar Coll. 1958–1963; numerous awards including Honor al Mérito (Soc. of Spanish and Latin-American Writers) 1961, Premio Nacional Ricardo Miró 1966, Cen. American Book Award 1976. *Publications include:* Novels: El último juego 1977, Libertad En Llamas 2001; Short stories: Otra vez Bach 1983, Cartas Apocrifas 1990, Hora Santa 1996; Essays: Estudios sobre el pensamiento poético de Pablo Antonio Cuadra 1971, La búsqueda del rostro 1983; Editor: Palabras preliminares, Obras completas de María Olimpia de Obaldía 1976; numerous monographs. *Address:* CP 101830, Zona 10, Santa Fe de Bogotá; Calle 87, 1A –84, Santa Fe de Bogotá, Colombia (home). *Telephone:* (1) 256-1540 (home). *Fax:* (1) 218-4236.

GUARE, John, AB, MFA; American dramatist; b. 5 Feb. 1938, New York, NY; m. Adele Chatfield-Taylor 1981. *Education:* Georgetown Univ., Yale Univ. *Career:* co-founder, Eugene O'Neill Theater Center, Waterford, CT, 1965; resident playwright, New York Shakespeare Festival, 1976; Seminar-in-Writing Fellow, 1977–78, Adjunct Prof., 1978–81, Yale University; Co-Ed., Lincoln Center New Theatre Review, 1977–; Visiting Artist, Harvard University, 1990–91; Fellow, Juilliard School, 1993–94; mem. American Acad. of Arts and Letters; Dramatists Guild. *Publications:* Plays: Theatre

Girl, 1959; The Toadstool Boy, 1960; The Golden Cherub, 1962; Did You Write My Name in the Snow?, 1962; To Wally Pantoni, We Leave a Credenza, 1964; The Loveliest Afternoon of the Year, 1966; Something I'll Tell You Tuesday, 1966; Muzeeka, 1967; Cop-Out, 1968; A Play by Brecht, 1969; Home Fires, 1969; Kissing Sweet, 1969; The House of Blue Leaves, 1971, as a musical, 1986; Two Gentlemen of Verona, 1971; A Day for Surprises, 1971; Un Pape a New York, 1972; Marco Polo Sings a Solo, 1973; Optimism, or the Adventures of Candide, 1973; Rich and Famous, 1974; Landscape of the Body, 1977; Take a Dream, 1978; Bosoms and Neglect, 1979; In Fireworks Lie Secret Codes, 1981; Lydie Breeze, 1982; Gardenia, 1982; Stay a While, 1984; Women and Water, 1984; Gluttony, 1985; The Talking Dog, 1985; Moon Over Miami, 1989, revised version as Moon Under Miami, 1995; Six Degrees of Separation, 1990; Four Baboons Adoring the Sun, 1992; Chuck Close, 1995; The War Against the Kitchen Sink (vol. of plays), 1996. *Honours:* Obie Awards, 1968, 1971, 1990; New York Drama Critics Circle Awards, 1969, 1971, 1972, 1990; Drama Desk Awards, 1972; Tony Awards, 1972, 1986; Joseph Jefferson Award, 1977; Award of Merit, American Acad. of Arts and Letters, 1981; Los Angeles Film Critics Award, 1981; National Society of Film Critics Circle Award, 1981; New York Film Critics Award, 1981; Venice Film Festival Grand Prize, 1981; Olivier Best Play Award, 1993; New York State Governor's Award, 1996.

GUARNIERI, Patrizia, MA, PhD; Italian historian and academic; *Professor of History, Faculty of Psychology, University of Florence*; b. 16 June 1954, Florence; one s. one d. *Education:* University of Florence, University of Urbino, Fulbright Visiting Scholar, Harvard University, Mass. *Career:* Lecturer University of Florence, 1978–81, Stanford University Programme in Italy, 1982–93; Prof., History of Science, University of Trieste, 1988–91; Prof. of History, Univ. of Florence 2004–; Man. Ed. Medicina & Storia; mem. European Asscn of the History of Psychiatry, SISSCO. *Publications:* Introduzione a James, 1985; Individualita' Difformi, 1986; L'Ammazzabambini, 1988, English edn as A Case of Child Murder, 1992; Between Soma and Psyche, 1988; Theatre and Laboratory, 1988; The Psyche in Trance, 1990; Carta Penna e Psiche, 1990; La Storia della Psichiatria, 1991; Per Una Storia delle Scienze del Bambino, 1996; Dangerous Girls, Family Secrets and Incest Law in Italy, 1998, Children and Health in Europe 1750–2000 (ed.) 2004; contrib. to Kos, Physis, Nuncius, Belfagor, Medicina & Storia. *Honours:* CNR-NATO Fellow Wellcome Centre of the History of Medicine 1983; Jean Monnet Fellow European Univ. Inst., Fiesole 1989. *Address:* Via S. Niccolo 89a, 50125 Florence, Italy. *E-mail:* pguarnieri@unifi.it (office).

GUCCIONE, Robert (Bob) Charles Joseph Edward Sabatini; American publisher; b. 17 Dec. 1930, Brooklyn; s. of Anthony Guccione and Nina Guccione; m. Kathy Keeton 1988; five c. from previous m. *Career:* artist 1948–55, 1992–; fmr cartoonist and greetings card designer; Man. London American; founder Penthouse Media Group, Inc and publr Penthouse Magazine, 1965–; also Publr Forum, Variations, Penthouse Letters, Omni, Saturday Review, Four Wheeler, Longevity, Girls of Penthouse, Compute, Open Wheel, Stock Car Racing, Superstock and Drag, Hot Talk; Chair. CEO Gen. Media Inc. (now Penthouse Media Group Inc) 1988–2004; producer of film Caligula 1979; exec. producer, TV show Omni: The New Frontier, Omni: Visions of Tomorrow. *Address:* c/o Penthouse Media Group, Inc, 2 Penn Plaza, New York, NY 10121, USA (office).

GUERIN, Orla, MA; Irish journalist; *Middle East Correspondent, BBC Television*; b. May 1966. *Education:* Coll. of Commerce, Dublin, Univ. Coll. Dublin. *Career:* newscaster, presenter and Foreign Corresp. with Irish State TV, RTE, Dublin 1990–94; joined BBC TV as news corresp. 1995, Southern Europe Corresp. covering the Balkans and conflict in the Basque country, among other stories 1996–2000, Middle East Corresp. 2001–. *Honours:* Hon. DUniv (Essex) 2002; The Jacobs Award for Broadcasters (Ireland) 1992, London Press Club Broadcaster of the Year Award 2002, News and Factual Award, Women in Film and Television (UK) 2003. *Address:* c/o Ten O'Clock News, BBC Television Centre, Wood Lane, London, W12 7RJ, England (office).

GUEST, Henry (Harry) Bayly, BA, DèsSc; British poet and writer; b. 6 Oct. 1932, Glamorganshire, Wales; m. Lynn Doremus Dunbar 1963; one s. one d. *Education:* Trinity Hall, Cambridge, Sorbonne, Univ. of Paris. *Career:* Lecturer, Yokohama Nat. Univ. 1966–72; Head of Modern Languages, Exeter School 1972–91; Teacher of Japanese, Exeter Univ. 1979–95; mem. Poetry Soc., General Council 1972–76; Hawthornden Fellow 1993. *Publications:* Arrangements 1968, The Cutting-Room 1970, Post-War Japanese Poetry (ed. and trans.) 1972, A House Against the Night 1976, Days 1978, The Distance, the Shadows 1981, Lost and Found 1983, The Emperor of Outer Space (radio play) 1983, Lost Pictures 1991, Coming to Terms 1994, Traveller's Literary Companion to Japan 1994, So Far 1998, The Artist on the Artist 2000, A Puzzling Harvest 2002, Time After Time 2005; contribs to reviews, quarter-lies, and journals. *Honours:* Hon. Research Fellow, Univ. of Exeter 1994–; Hon. DLitt (Plymouth) 1998. *Address:* 1 Alexandra Terrace, Exeter, Devon, EX4 6SY, England (home). *Telephone:* (1392) 257142 (home).

GUIGNABODET, Liliane (Lily), LèsL; French writer; b. 26 March 1939, Paris; d. of Moïse and Olympia N. Graciani; m. Jean Guignabodet 1961; one s. two d. *Education:* primary school in Sofia (Bulgaria), Lycée Jules Ferry, Paris, Sorbonne and Univ. of London. *Career:* Prof. of French, San José, USA 1961–62; Prof. of Arts and Culture, Ecole Technique d'IBM France 1966–69; author 1977–; mem. PEN Club Français, Asscn des Ecrivains Croyants, Société des Gens de Lettres, Acad. Européenne des Sciences, des Arts et des

Lettres, Acad. Valentin, Jury du Prix de Journalisme de l' Asscn Franco-Bulgare. *Publications:* L'écume du silence 1977, Le bracelet indien 1980, Natalia 1983, Le livre du vent 1984, Dessislava 1986, Car les hommes sont meilleurs que leur vie 1991, Un sentiment inconnu 1998. *Honours:* Prix George Sand 1977, Grand Prix du Roman, Acad. Française 1983, Grand prix du Roman, Ville de Cannes 1991. *Address:* 55 rue Caulaincourt, 75018 Paris; 16 chemin du Clos d'Agasse, 06650 Le Rouret, France. *Telephone:* 1-46-06-09-86. *Fax:* 1-46-06-09-86. *E-mail:* lguignabodet@club-internet.fr.

GUILLOU, Jan; Swedish writer and journalist; b. 17 Jan. 1944, Södertälje. *Television series:* Talismanen (with Henning Mankell) 2001. *Publications:* fiction: Om kriget kommer 1971, Det stora avslöjandet 1974, Ondskan (Prix France Culture 1990) 1981, Coq Rouge: berättelsen on en Svensk spion 1986, Den demokratiske terroristen 1987, I nationens intresse (Bästa svenska kriminalroman 1988) 1988, Fiendens fiende 1989, Den hedervärde mördaren 1990, Gudarnas Berg 1990, Vendetta 1991, Ingen mans land 1992, Den enda segern 1993, I hennes majestäts tjänst 1994, En medborgare höjd över varje misstanke 1995, Hamlon: en skiss till en möjlig fortsättning 1995, Vägen till Jerusalem 1998, Tempelriddaren 1999, Riket vid vägens slut 2000, Arvet efter Arn 2001, I Arns fotspår 2002, Tjuvarnas marknad 2004, Madame Terror 2006; non-fiction: Handbok för rättslösa 1975, Journalistik 1976, Irak – det Nya Arabien 1977, Artister 1979, Reporter 1979, Berättelser från det Nya Riket 1982, Justitiemord 1983, Nya berättelser 1984, Åsikter 1990, Stora machoboken 1990, Grabbarnas stora presentbok 1991, On jakt och jägare: från fagerhult till sibirien 1996, Svenskarna, invandrarna och svartskallarna: mitt livs viktigaste reportage 1996, Antirasistiskt lexikon 1997, Häxornas försvarare 2002, Kolumnisten 2005. *Honours:* Stora Journalistpriset 1984, Aftonbladets TV Pris 1984, SKTF Pris-årets Författare 1998, Årets Bok-Månadens boks litterära pris 2000. *E-mail:* jan.guillou@aftonbladet.se.

GUISEWITE, Cathy Lee, BA; American cartoonist; b. 5 Sept. 1950, Dayton, OH; d. of William Lee and Anne Guisewite; m. Chris Wilkinson; one step-s. one d. *Education:* Univ. of Michigan, Ann Arbor. *Career:* worked as advertising writer for five years; cr. Cathy comic strip syndicated in around 500 newspapers 1976–; TV specials featuring cartoon characters (Emmy Award 1987). *Publications include:* The Cathy Chronicles 1978 (republished as What's a Nice Single Girl Doing with a Double Bed?! and, I Think I'm Having a Relationship with a Blueberry Pie! 1981), Motherly Advice from Cathy's Mom 1987, A Hand to Hold, an Opinion to Reject 1987, My Granddaughter Has Fleas 1989, $14 in the Bank and a $200 Face in My Purse 1990, Reflections (A Fifteenth Anniversary Collection) 1991, Only Love Can Break a Heart, but a Shoe Sale Can Come Close 1992, Revelations from a 45-Pound Purse 1993, Abs of Steel, Buns of Cinnamon 1997, I'd Scream Except I Look so Fabulous 1999, Shoes: Chocolate for the Feet 2000; collections of daily cartoon strips. *Honours:* several hon. degrees; numerous awards including Outstanding Communicator of the Year Award, Los Angeles Advertising Women 1982, named one of America's 25 Most Influential Women 1984, 1986, Reuben Award, Nat. Cartoonists Soc. 1993. *Address:* c/o Universal Press Syndicate, 4520 Main Street, Suite 700, Kansas City, MO 64111-7701, USA. *Website:* www.ucomics.com/cathy.

GULZAR; Indian film-maker, poet and lyricist; b. (Sampooran Singh), 18 Aug. 1936, Deena, Jhelum Dist (now in Pakistan). *Career:* came to Delhi following partition; started as poet and was associated with Progressive Writers Asscn; joined Bimal Roy Productions in 1961; first break as lyricist came when he wrote Mora Gora Ang Lai Lae for Bimal Roy's Bandini 1963; began writing for films for dirs Hrishikesh Mukherjee and Asit Sen; turned filmmaker with first film Mere Apne 1971; began partnership with Sanjeev Kumar. *Films directed:* Shriman Satyawadi (Asst Dir) 1960, Kabuliwala (Chief Asst Dir) 1961, Bandini (Asst Dir) 1963, Mere Apne 1971, Parichay 1972, Koshish 1972, Achanak 1973, Mausam (Nat. Award for Best Dir, Filmfare The Best Dir Award) 1975, Khushboo 1975, Aandhi (Storm) 1975, Kitaab (also Producer) 1977, Kinara (also Producer) 1977, Meera 1979, Sahira 1980, Namkeen 1982, Angoor 1982, Suniye 1984, Aika 1984, Ek Akar 1985, Ijaazat (Guest) 1987, Ghalib (TV) 1988, Libaas 1988, Lekin… (But…) 1990, Ustad Amjad Ali Khan 1990, Pandit Bhimsen Joshi 1992, Maachis 1996, Hu Tu Tu 1999. *Film roles in:* Jallianwalla Bagh 1979, Grihapravesh (The Housewarming) (as himself) 1979, Wajood (guest appearance as himself) 1998, Chachi 420 (uncredited cameo appearance during end credits) 1998. *Film dialogue or scripts:* Sangharsh 1968, Aashirwad (The Blessing) 1968, Khamoshi 1969, Anand 1970, Guddi (Darling Child) 1971, Mere Apne 1971, Koshish (Nat. Award for Best Screenplay) 1972, Bawarchi 1972, Namak Haraam (The Ungrateful) 1973, Achanak 1973, Mausam 1975, Khushboo 1975, Chupke Chupke 1975, Aandhi (Storm) 1975, Palkon Ki Chhaon Mein 1977, Meera 1979, Grihapravesh (The Housewarming) 1979, Khubsoorat (Beautiful) 1980, Basera 1981, Namkeen 1982, Angoor 1982, Masoom (Innocent) 1983, New Delhi Times 1986, Ek Pal (A Moment) 1986, Ijaazat (Guest) 1987, Mirza Ghalib (TV) 1988, Lekin… (But…) 1990, Rudaal (The Mourner) 1993, Maachis 1996, Chachi 420 1998, Hu Tu Tu 1999, Saathiya 2002. *Film song lyrics:* Swami Vivekananda 1955, Shriman Satyawadi 1960, Kabuliwala 1961, Prem Patra (Love Letter) 1962, Bandini 1963, Purnima 1965, Sannata 1966, Biwi Aur Makan 1966, Do Dooni Char 1968, Aashirwad (The Blessing) 1968, Rahgir 1969, Khamoshi 1969, Anand 1970, Guddi (Darling Child) 1971, Anubhav (Experience) 1971, Seema 1971, Mere Apne 1971, Parichay 1972, Koshish 1972, Doosri Seeta 1974, Chor Machaye Shor 1974, Mausam 1975, Khushboo 1975, Aandhi (Storm) 1975, Shaque 1976, Palkon Ki Chhaon Mein 1977, Kinara 1977, Gharaonda (The Nest) 1977, Ghar

(Home) 1978, Meetha (Sweet and Sour) 1978, Devata 1978, Gol Maal (Hanky Panky) 1979, Ratnadeep (The Jewelled Lamp) 1979, Grihapravesh (The Housewarming) 1979, Sitara 1980, Thodisi Bewafaii 1980, Swayamvar 1980, Khubsoorat (Beautiful India) 1980, Garam 1981, Basera 1981, Namkeen 1982, Angoor 1982, Sadma 1983, Masoom (Innocent) 1983, Ghulami 1985, Jeeva 1986, Ek Pal (A Moment) 1986, Ijaazat (Guest) (Nat. Award for Best Lyricist) 1987, Libaas 1988, Lekin... (But...) 1990, Maya Memsaab (Maya: The Enchanting Illusion) 1992, Rudaali (The Mourner) 1993, Mammo 1994, Daayraa (The Square Circle, USA) 1996, Maachis 1996, Aastha (Aastha in the Prison of Spring) 1997, Satya 1998, Dil Se... (From the Heart, USA) 1998, Chachi 420 1998, Hu Tu Tu 1999, Khoobsurat 1999, Fiza 2000, Aks 2001, Asoka (Ashoka the Great, USA) 2001, Filhaal... 2002, Leela 2002, Lal Salaam (Red Salute) 2002, Dil Vil Pyar Vyar 2002, Makdee (The Web of the Witch) 2002, Saathiya 2002, Chupke Se 2003, Pinjar (The Cage) 2003, Jaan-E-Mann 2006. *Publications:* books on poetry, Dhuaan (book of short stories, Sahitya Acad. Award 2003), twelve books for children, including Ekta (Nat. Council for Educ. Research and Training Award 1989). *Honours:* Padmabhushan, Govt of India 2004; five Nat. Awards, 17 Filmfare Awards, including seven for Best Lyricist, Filmfare Lifetime Achievement Award 2002.

GUNESEKERA, Romesh; Sri Lankan writer and poet; b. 1954, Colombo; m. Helen; two d. *Publications:* Monkfish Moon (short stories) 1992, Reef (novel) 1994, The Sandglass (novel) 1998, Heaven's Edge (novel) 2002, The Match (novel) 2006. *Honours:* New York Times Notable Book of the Year 1993, Yorkshire Post Best First Work Award 1994, Premio Mondello 1997, Ranjana, Sri Lanka 2005. *Literary Agent:* c/o Bill Hamilton, A. M. Heath & Co. Ltd, 79 St Martin's Lane, London, WC2N 4RE, England. *Telephone:* (20) 7836-4271. *Fax:* (20) 7497-2561. *Website:* www.romeshgunesekera.com.

GUNNARS, Kristjana, MA; Icelandic writer, poet, translator and academic; b. 19 March 1948, Reykjavík; d. of Gunnar Bodvarsson and Tove Christensen Bodvarsson; one c. *Education:* Oregon State Univ., USA and Univ. of Regina, Sask., Canada. *Career:* family moved to Oregon 1964; Asst Ed. Iceland Review, Iceland 1980–81; freelance writer, translator and ed. 1981–; Writer-in-Residence, Regina Public Library, Canada 1988–89, Univ. of Alberta, Edmonton, Canada 1989–90, Assoc. Prof. of English 1991, Prof. of Creative Writing 1991–2004; Lecturer, Okanagan Coll., BC, Canada 1990–91; Visiting Prof., Univ. of Trier, Germany 1992, Oslo, Norway 1998; mem. PEN, Writers' Union of Canada, League of Canadian Poets, Composers', Authors' and Publishers' Asscn of Canada, Alliance of Canadian Cinema, TV and Radio Artists. *Publications:* Settlement Poems I and II 1980, 1981, One-Eyed Moon Maps 1981, Wake-Pick Poems 1982, Stephan G. Stephansson, In Retrospect (trans.) 1982, The Axe's Edge 1983, The Night Workers of Ragnarök 1985, The Papers of Dorothy Livesay (co-author) 1985, Crossing the River: Essays in Honor of Margaret Laurence (ed.) 1988, Stephan G. Stephansson, Selected Prose and Poetry (trans.) 1988, The Prowler 1989, Carnival of Longing 1989, Zero Hour 1991, Unexpected Fictions, New Icelandic Canadian Writing (ed.), The Guest House and Other Stories 1992, The Substance of Forgetting 1992, The Rose Garden: Reading Marcel Proust 1993, Exiles Among You 1996, Night Train to Nykøbing 1996, When Chestnut Trees Blossom 2002, Silence of the Country 2002. *Address:* c/o Department of English, University of Alberta, Edmonton, Alberta, T6G 2E2, Canada.

GUNSTON, Bill, (William Tudor Gunston), OBE, FRAeS; British author and editor; b. 1 March 1927, London; m. Margaret Anne 1964; two d. *Education:* Univ. Coll., Durham, City Univ., London. *Career:* pilot, RAF 1946–48; editorial staff, Flight 1951–55, Tech. Ed. 1955–64; Tech. Ed., Science Journal 1964–70; team mem. Jane's All the World's Aircraft 1969–; freelance author 1970–; Dir So Few Ltd; Ed. Jane's Aero-Engines 1995–. *Publications:* more than 370 books, including The Development of Piston Aero Engines 1999, Modern Fighting Helicopters 1999, Aerospace Dictionary 1999, The Illustrated History of McDonnell Douglas Aircraft 2000, Hamlyn History of Military Aviation 2000, Soviet X-planes 2000, The Encyclopedia of Modern Warplanes 2001, Aviation Year by Year 2001, Rolls-Royce Aero Engines 2001, Aviation: The First 100 Years 2002, The Development of Jet and Turbine Aero Engines 2002, Flight Path (biog.) 2002, Night Fighters 2003, Cambridge Aerospace Dictionary 2004, Encyclopaedia of World Aircraft Constructors 2005; contribs to 188 periodicals, 18 partworks, 75 video scripts. *Address:* High Beech, Kingsley Green, Haslemere, Surrey, GU27 3LL, England (home). *Telephone:* (1428) 644282 (home). *Fax:* (1428) 644282 (home). *E-mail:* bill.gunston@tiscali.co.uk (home).

GUO, Xiaolu, MA; Chinese novelist, film director and screenwriter; b. 1973, Zhejiang Province; single. *Education:* Beijing Film Acad., Nat. Film and TV School, London. *Career:* moved to UK 2002. *Film and television:* Far and Near (documentary) (ICA/Becks Futures Prize) 2003, The Concrete Revolution (documentary) 2004, How Is Your Fish Today? (Grand Jury Prize, Creteil Int. Women's Film Festival, France 2007) 2006; as scriptwriter: Love in the Internet Age 1999, House 1999, A Boat in the Sea (TV series) 2000, Knowledge Can Change Your Fate (film series) 1998. *Publications:* novels: 20 Fragments of Fenfang's Youth (in Chinese) 2000, Village of Stone (in Chinese) 2004, A Concise Chinese-English Dictionary for Lovers (in English) 2007; essay collections (in Chinese): Flying in my Dreams 2000, Movie Map 2001, Notes on Movie Theory 2002; single essays: Cinema and Adam's Rib 1999, A Chinese Writer's Journey to the West 2003, Blasing the Past in China 2003, Flashback of a Not-so-far-from home 2003, East Beast, West Beauty 2004; poems (in Chinese): Love and Middle Class Life 2001, Medicine 2002, Kew Garden 2002, Dear 2003, Scenery 2003, Notes 2004, Blindness 2004; other: Who is My Mother's Boyfriend (collected film scripts) 1999. *Literary Agent:* Toby Eady Associates Ltd, Third Floor, 9 Orme Court, London, W2 4RL, England. *Telephone:* (20) 7792-0092. *Fax:* (20) 7792-0879. *Website:* www.tobyeadyassociates.co.uk. *E-mail:* xiaolu@guoxiaolu.com. *Website:* www.guoxiaolu.com.

GUPPY, Stephen Anthony, BA, MA; Canadian writer, poet and teacher; b. 10 Feb. 1951, Nanaimo, BC; m. Nelinda Kazenbroot 1986, one s. one d. *Education:* University of Victoria. *Career:* teacher, School District No. 69, Qualicum, BC, 1982–85; Instructor of English and Creative Writing, Malaspina University College, Nanaimo, 1986–. *Publications:* Ghostcatcher (poems), 1979; Rainshadow: Stories from Vancouver Island (anthology, co-ed.), 1982; Another Sad Day at the Edge of the Empire (short stories), 1985; Blind Date with the Angel (poems), 1998. Contributions: Short stories to anthologies including: Best Canadian Short Stories; The Journey Prize Anthology. *Honours:* Second Prize, Scottish International Open Poetry Competition, 1997. *Address:* 2184 Michigan Way, Nanaimo, BC V9R 5S5, Canada. *E-mail:* guppy@mala.bc.can.

GUPTA, Tanika, BA; British playwright and screenwriter; b. 1 Dec. 1963, London; d. of the late Tapan Kumar Gupta and of Gairika Gupta; m.; three d. *Education:* Univ. of Oxford. *Career:* began her writing career in 1991 when she was a finalist in BBC Young Playwrights' Festival with 'Asha' (45-minute radio play); Writer-in-Residence, Soho Theatre 1996–98; Pearson Writer-in-Residence, Royal Nat. Theatre 2000–01; currently writing for BBC Asian Network's new soap, Silver Street and under comms with Birmingham Rep, Bolton Octagon and Nat. Youth Theatres. *Plays include:* Skeleton 1997, The Good Woman of Szechuan (trans.), Voices in the Wind, The Waiting Room (John Whiting Award 2000) 2000, Sanctuary 2002, Inside Out 2002, Fragile Land 2003, Hobson's Choice by Harold Brighouse (adaptation) 2003, The Country Wife 2004, Gladiator Games (Sheffield Crucible/Stratford East), Sugar Mummies (Royal Court, London) 2006, Catch (Group Play, Royal Court) 2006. *Radio:* Asha 1991, Badal and His Bike (Radio 5) 1993, Pankhiraj, The Bounty Hunter 1997, Ananda Sananda 1997, The Whispering Tree (Prix ex Aequeo Bratislava 1998), The Queen's Retreat 1999, Muse of Fusion 1999, The Book of Secrets (adaptation of novel by M. G. Vassanji) 1999, Betrayal – The Secret, The Trial of William Davidson, Stowaway 2001, ten-part adaptation of Arundhati Roy's The God of Small Things (Women's Hour, Radio 4) 2004, The Parting (Radio 4) 2004; for BBC World Service and Radio 3: The Eternal Bubble, Voices On The Wind, Red Oleanders (adaptation of play by Rabindranath Tagore), A Second Chance 2003, Chitra (Amnesty International Media Award) 2005; regular contrib. to Westway. *Television:* Flight (BBC 2, Fipa D'argent Prize 1997, EMMA Award for Best TV Production 1998) 1995; pilot scripts for A Suitable Boy (Enigma/Channel 4/Cinema Verity), The Fiancee, The Rhythm of Raz and Bideshi 1995 (all award-winning short films); series: EastEnders (BBC 1), The Bill (Thames/ITV), Crossroads, Grange Hill and London Bridge; adaptation of J. M. Coetzee's The Lives of Animals (60-minute film for BBC 4) 2002; episodes of All About Me (sit-com for Celador), Banglatown Banquet (BBC 2) (Prix Europa Special Commendation) 2006. *Publications:* all her stage plays; Rebecca and the Neighbours (short story included in Asian Women Writers' Collective Anthology, Flaming Spirits). *Honours:* Asian Woman of Achievement (Arts and Culture) 2003. *Literary Agent:* The Agency (London) Ltd, 24 Pottery Lane, Holland Park, London, W11 4LZ, England. *Telephone:* (20) 7727-1346. *Fax:* (20) 7727-9037. *E-mail:* info@theagency.co.uk. *Website:* www.theagency.co.uk.

GURGANUS, Allan, BA, MFA; American writer and artist; b. 11 June 1947, Rocky Mount, NC. *Education:* Monterey Language School, Radioman and Cryptography School, University of Pennsylvania, Pennsylvania Acad. of Fine Arts, Harvard University, Sarah Lawrence College, University of Iowa Writers' Workshop, Stanford University. *Career:* Prof. of Fiction Writing, 1972–74, Writer's Workshop, 1989–90, University of Iowa: Prof. of Fiction Writing, Stanford University, 1974–76, Duke University, 1976–78, Sarah Lawrence College, 1978–86; artist; mem. American Acad. of Arts and Sciences 2004, American Acad. of Arts and Letters 2007. *Publications:* Oldest Living Confederate Widow Tells All, 1989; White People: Stories and Novellas, 1991; Practical Heart, 1993; Plays Well With Others, 1997; The Practical Heart: Four Novellas, 2001. Contributions: periodicals. *Honours:* Fellowship of Southern Writers 2004, John Simon Guggenheim Fellow 2006; National Endowment for the Arts Grants, 1976–77, 1987–88; Ingram Merrill Grant, 1986; Sue Kaufman Prize for First Fiction, American Acad. and Institute of Arts and Letters, 1990; Books Across the Sea Ambassador Book Award, English-Speaking Union of the United States, 1990; Los Angeles Times Book Prize, 1991. *Address:* c/o Amanda Urban, International Creative Management, 40 W 57th Street, New York, NY 10019, USA.

GURLEY BROWN, Helen; American writer and editor; *Editor-in-Chief, Cosmopolitan International Editions;* b. 18 Feb. 1922, Green Forest, Ark.; d. of Ira M. and Cleo (Sisco) Gurley; m. David Brown 1959. *Education:* Texas State Coll. for Women, Woodbury Coll. *Career:* Exec. Sec. Music Corpn of America 1942–45, William Morris Agency 1945–47; Copywriter Foote, Cone & Belding advertising agency, Los Angeles 1948–58; advertisement writer and account exec. Kenyon & Eckhard advertising agency, Hollywood 1958–62; Ed.-in-Chief Cosmopolitan magazine 1965–97, Editorial Dir Cosmopolitan Int. Edns 1972–, Ed.-in-Chief 1997–; mem. Authors' League of America, American Soc. of Magazine Eds, AFTRA; establishment of Helen Gurley Brown Research Professorship at Northwestern Univ. 1986. *Publications:* Sex and the Single Girl 1962, Sex and the Office 1965, Outrageous Opinions 1967, Helen Gurley

Brown's Single Girl's Cook Book 1969, Sex and the New Single Girl 1970, Having It All 1982, The Late Show: A Semiwild but Practical Survival Guide for Women over 50 1993, The Writer's Rules: The Power of Positive Prose 1998, I'm Wild Again: Snippets from My Life and a Few Brazen Thoughts 2000, Dear Pussycat: Personal Correspondence of Helen Gurley Brown 2004. *Honours:* Hon. LLD (Woodbury) 1987; Hon. DLitt (Long Island) 1993; Francis Holm Achievement Award 1956–59, Univ. of S. Calif. School of Journalism 1971, Special Award for Editorial Leadership of American Newspaper Woman's Club 1972, Distinguished Achievement Award in Journalism, Stanford Univ. 1977, New York Women in Communications Inc. Award 1985, Publrs.' Hall of Fame 1988, Henry Johnson Fisher Award, Magazine Publrs of America 1995. *Address:* Cosmopolitan, 959 8th Avenue, New York, NY 10019 (office); 1 West 81st Street, New York, NY 10024, USA (home). *Telephone:* (212) 649-3555 (office). *Fax:* (212) 649-3529 (office).

GURNAH, Abdulrazak; Tanzanian novelist, literary critic and editor; *Lecturer in English Literature, University of Kent;* b. 1948, Zanzibar. *Career:* currently Lecturer in English Literature, Univ. of Kent and Contributing Ed. journal, Wasafiri. *Publications:* Memory of Departure 1987, Pilgrim's Way 1988, Dottie 1990, Essays on African Writing: A Re-Evaluation (ed.) 1993, Paradise 1994, Essays on African Writing: Contemporary Literature (ed.) 1995, Admiring Silence 1996, By the Sea 2001, Desertion 2005; numerous works for radio; contrib. to Wole Soyinka: An Appraisal 1994, Modernism and Empire 1998, Essays and Criticism 2000, New Writing 9. *Address:* c/o School of English, Rutherford College, University of Kent, Canterbury, Kent CT2 7NX, England. *E-mail:* A.S.Gurnah@ukc.ac.uk. *Website:* www.wasafiri.org.

GURNEY, Albert Ramsdell, MFA; American playwright; b. 1 Nov. 1930, Buffalo, NY; s. of Albert R. Gurney and Marion Gurney (née Spaulding); m. Mary F. Goodyear 1957; two s. two d. *Education:* Williams Coll., Yale School of Drama. *Career:* joined MIT, Faculty of Humanities 1960–96, Prof. 1970–96. *Publications include:* plays: The Dining Room, The Cocktail Hour, Love Letters, Later Life, A Cheever Evening, Sylvia, Overtime; Let's Do It!, The Guest Lecturer, Labor Day, Far East, Ancestral Voices 1999, Human Events 2000, Buffalo Gal 2001, The Fourth Wall 2002, Big Bill 2004, Mrs Farnsworth 2004; novels: The Gospel According to Joe, Entertaining Strangers, The Snow Ball; opera libretto: Stawberry Fields 1999. *Honours:* Hon. DDL (Buffalo State Univ., Williams Coll.); Drama Desk Award 1971, American Acad. of Arts and Letters Award 1987, Lucille Lortel Award 1992, William Inge Award 2000. *Address:* 40 Wellers Bridge Road, Roxbury, CT 06783-1616, USA (home). *Telephone:* (860) 354-3692 (home). *Fax:* (860) 354-3692 (home). *E-mail:* a.r .gurney@worldnet.att.net (home).

GURR, Andrew John, BA, MA, PhD; British/New Zealand academic and writer; *Professor Emeritus, University of Reading;* b. 23 Dec. 1936, Leicester, England; m. Elizabeth Gordon 1961; three s. *Education:* Univ. of Auckland, New Zealand, Univ. of Cambridge. *Career:* Lecturer, Leeds University, 1962; Prof., University of Nairobi, 1969; University of Reading, 1976–; mem. International Shakespeare Asscn; Asscn of Commonwealth Literature and Language Studies; Society for Theatre Research; Malone Society. *Publications:* The Shakespeare Stage 1574–1642 1970, Writers in Exile 1982, Katherine Mansfield 1982, Playgoing in Shakespeare's London 1987, Studying Shakespeare 1988, Rebuilding Shakespeare's Globe 1989, The Shakespearian Playing Companies 1996, The Shakespeare Company 1594–1642 2004; editor: Plays of Shakespeare and Beaumont and Fletcher; contrib. to scholarly journals and periodicals. *Honours:* Hon. DLitt (Auckland Univ.) 2004. *Address:* c/o Department of English, University of Reading, PO Box 218, Reading, Berkshire RG6 2AA, England.

GURR, David, BSc; Canadian writer; b. 5 Feb. 1936, London, England; m. Judith Deverell 1958 (divorced 1991); two s. one d. *Education:* Canadian Naval College, University of Victoria, BC. *Career:* Career Officer, Royal Canadian Navy 1954–70; house designer and builder 1972–81; mem. Crime Writers of Canada, Writers' Guild of America, Writers' Union of Canada. *Publications:* Troika 1979, A Woman Called Scylla 1981, An American Spy Story 1984, The Action of the Tiger 1984, On the Endangered List 1985, The Ring Master 1987, The Voice of the Crane 1989, Arcadia West: The Novel 1994, The Charlatan 2000.

GUSEV, Pavel Nikolayevich; Russian journalist; *Editor-in-Chief, Moskovsky Komsomolets;* b. 4 April 1949, Moscow; s. of Nikolai Gusev and Alla Guseva; m. Eugenia Efimova; two d. *Education:* Moscow Inst. of Geological Survey, Maxim Gorky Inst. of Literature. *Career:* Komsomol work 1975–; First Sec. Komsomol Cttee of Krasnaya Presnya Region of Moscow 1975–80; Exec. Cen. Komsomol Cttee 1980–83; Ed.-in-Chief. Moskovsky Komsomolets (newspaper) 1983–; Minister Govt of Moscow, Head Dept of Information and Mass Media Jan.–Oct. 1992; press adviser to Mayor of Moscow 1992–95. *Plays:* I Love You, Constance (Moscow Gogol Theatre) 1993, Cardinal's Coat (Maly Theatre) 2002. *Address:* Moskovsky Komsomolets, 1905 Goda Str. 7, 123995 Moscow, Russia. *Telephone:* (495) 259-50-36 (office). *Fax:* (495) 259-46-39 (office). *E-mail:* letters@mk.ru (office). *Website:* www.mk.ru (office).

GUSMAN, Mikhail Solomonovich; Russian journalist; *First Deputy Director-General, ITAR-TASS Agency;* b. 23 Jan. 1950, Baku, Azerbaijan; m.; one s. *Education:* Baku Higher CPSU School, Azerbaijan Inst. of Foreign Languages. *Career:* Deputy Chair. Cttee of Youth Orgs, Azerbaijan 1973–86; Head of Information Dept, then Head of Press Centre, USSR Cttee of Youth Orgs 1986–91; Head Gen. Admin. of Information Co-operation INFOMOL 1991–95; Vice-Pres. Int. Analytic Press Agency ANKOM-TASS 1995–98; Head

Chief Dept of Int. Co-operation, Public Contacts and Special Projects ITAR-TASS 1998–99, Deputy Dir-Gen., First Deputy Dir-Gen. 1999–; Co-Founder World Congress of Russian Press 1999; Exec. Dir World Asscn of Russian Press. *Honours:* Diploma of the USSR Supreme Soviet, numerous medals. *Address:* ITAR-TASS Agency, Tverskoy blvd 10-12, 103009 Moscow, Russia (office). *Telephone:* (495) 290-59-89 (office).

GUSTAFSSON, Lars Erik Einar, DPhil; Swedish writer, philosopher and academic; *Jamail Distinguished Professor Emeritus in the Plan II Program, University of Texas;* b. 17 May 1936, Västerås; s. of Einar Gustafsson and Margaretha Carlsson; m. 1st Madeleine Gustafsson 1962; m. 2nd Dena Alexandra Chasnoff 1982; two s. two d.; m. 3rd Agneta Blomqvist 2005. *Education:* Uppsala Univ. *Career:* Editor-in-Chief, Bonniers Litterära Magasin 1966–72; Research Fellow, Bielefeld Inst. of Advanced Studies 1980–81; Adjunct Prof., Univ. of Texas 1983–, Jamail Distinguished Prof. in the Plan II Program 1995, now Prof. Emer.; Aby Warburg Foundation Prof., Hamburg 1997; mem. Akad. der Wissenschaften und der Literatur, Mainz, Akad. der Künste, Berlin, Royal Swedish Acad. of Eng, Bayerische Akad. der schönen Künste, Munich; Fellow Berlin Inst. of Advanced Studies 2004–05. *Exhibitionsinclude:* Galleri Händer, Stockholm 1989, 1991, Galerie am Savignyplatz, Berlin 2001, 2003. *Television:* 18th Century Pessimism (Swedish TV2), The Philosophers (syndicated). *Plays:* Celebration at Night, Zürich, Frankfurt, Berlin 1979. *Publications:* The Death of a Beekeeper 1978, Language and Lies 1978, Stories of Happy People 1981, Bernard Foy's Third Castle 1986, The Silence of the World before Bach (poems) 1988, Fyra Poeter 1988, Problemformuleringsprivilegiet 1989, Det sällsamma djuret från norr 1989, The Afternoon of a Tiler 1991, Historien med Hunden 1993, The Tail of the Dog 1997, Windy 1999, A Time in Xanadu 2003,. *Honours:* Officier des Arts et des Lettres; Kommendör des Bundesverdienstzeichens, Literis et Artibus; Prix Charles Veillon, Heinrich Steffen Preis, Övralidspriset, Bellman Prize of Swedish Acad.; John Simon Guggenheim Memorial Fellow of Poetry 1993. *Address:* University of Texas, Waggener Hall, Room 413, Department of Philosophy, Austin, TX 78712 (office); PMB 317, 3112 Windsor Road, Austin, TX 78703, USA. *Telephone:* (512) 471-5632 (office). *E-mail:* lars.gustafsson@ ownit.nu (office). *Website:* www.utexas.edu/depts/german/faculty/gustafsson .html (office).

GUTCHEON, Beth Richardson, BA; American writer; b. 18 March 1945, Sewickley, PA; m. Jeffrey Gutcheon 1968, one s. *Education:* Radcliffe Coll. *Publications:* fiction: The New Girls, 1979; Still Missing, 1981; Domestic Pleasures, 1991; Saying Grace, 1995; Five Fortunes, 1998; More Than You Know, 2000. Non-Fiction: The Perfect Patchwork Primer, 1973; Abortion: A Woman's Guide, 1973; The Quilt Design Workbook (with Jeffrey Gutcheon), 1975. Film Scripts: The Children of Theatre Street, 1977; Without a Trace, 1983; The Good Fight, 1992. Contributions: periodicals.

GUTERSON, David, BA, MFA; American author; b. 4 May 1956, Seattle; s. of Murray Guterson and Shirley (née Zak) Guterson; m. Robin Ann Radwick 1979; three s. one d. *Education:* Univ. of Washington, Brown Univ. *Career:* high school English teacher Bainbridge Island, Washington 1984–94; contrib. sports journalism for Sports Illustrated and Harper's, fmr Contributing Ed. Harper's. *Publications:* The Country Ahead of Us, The Country Behind (short stories) 1989, Family Matters: Why Home Schooling Makes Sense 1992, Snow Falling on Cedars (PEN/Faulkner Award for Ficition, Barnes & Noble Discovery Award, Pacific NW Booksellers Award 1995) 1994, East of the Mountains 1998, Our Lady of the Forest 2003. *Literary Agent:* Georges Borchardt Inc., 136 East 57th Street, New York, NY 10020, USA.

GUTHRIE, Alan (see Tubb, Edwin Charles)

GUTIÉRREZ, Pedro Juan; Cuban novelist, poet, painter and journalist; b. 1950, Matanzas. *Education:* Universidad de la Habana. *Career:* fmrly diverse range of employment, including ice-cream seller, soldier, sugar cane cutter, and many others; fmrly journalist, Bohemia journal, Havana; currently writer and painter. *Publications:* short story collections: Trilogía sucia de La Habana (Dirty Havana Trilogy: Anclado en tierra de nadie, Nada que hacer, Sabor a mí), Melancolía de los leones; novels: El rey de la Habana, Animal tropical, El insaciable hombre araña (trans. as The Insatiable Spiderman), Carne de perro, Nuestro GG en La Habana, El nido de la serpiente: memorias del hijo del heladero; poetry: Espléndidos peces plateados, Fuego contra los herejes, Yo y una lujuriosa negra vieja, Lulu la perdida y otros poemas de John Snake. *Honours:* Premio Alfonso García-Ramos (Spain) 2000, Premio Narrativa Sur del Mundo (Italy) 2003. *Address:* Apdo Postal 6239, 10600 Havana, Cuba. *Website:* www.pedrojuangutierrez.com.

GUTIONTOV, Pavel Semenovich; Russian journalist; b. 23 Jan. 1953. *Education:* Moscow State Univ. *Career:* mem. of staff Moskovski Komsomolets 1970–75; fmr corresp. Komsomolskaya Pravda, then Head of Div. 1975–85; special corresp. Sovetskaya Rossiya 1985–87; political observer Izvestia; Co-Chair. Liberal Journalists Club –1997; Chair. Cttee for Defence of Freedom of Speech and Journalists' Rights; Sec. Russian Journalists' Union. *Publications:* Games in the Fresh Air of Stagnation 1990, Fate of Drummers 1997 and numerous articles. *Honours:* winner of numerous professional prizes. *Address:* Russian Journalists' Union, Zubovsky blvd 4, 119021 Moscow, Russia (office). *Telephone:* (495) 201-23-95 (office).

GUTTERIDGE, Donald George, BA; Canadian poet, writer and academic; *Professor Emeritus, University of Western Ontario;* b. 30 Sept. 1937, Sarnia, Ont.; m. Anne Barnett 1961; one s. one d. *Education:* Chatham Coll. Inst.,

Ont., Univ. of Western Ontario, London. *Career:* Asst Prof., Univ. of Western Ontario 1968–75, Assoc. Prof. 1975–77, Prof. of English Methods 1977–93, Prof. Emer. 1993–. *Publications:* poetry: Riel – A Poem for Voices 1968, The Village Within 1970, Death at Quebec and Other Poems 1972, Saying Grace: An Elegy 1972, Coppermine: The Quest for North 1973, Borderlands 1975, Tecumseh 1976, A True History of Lambton County 1977, God's Geography 1982, The Exiled Heart: Selected Narratives 1986, Love in the Wintertime 1982, Flute Music in the Cello's Belly 1997, Bloodlines 2001; fiction: Bus-Ride 1974, All in Good Time 1980, St Vitus Dance 1986, Shaman's Ground 1988, How the World Began 1991, Summer's Idyll 1993, Winter's Descent 1996, Bewilderment 2001, Turncoat 2003, Solemn Vows 2003, Something More Miraculous 2004. *Honours:* Pres.'s Medal, Univ. of Western Ontario 1971, Canada Council Travel Grant 1973. *Address:* 114 Victoria Street, London, Ont. N6A 2B5, Canada. *Telephone:* (519) 434-5843. *E-mail:* dongutteridge@rogers.com.

GUTTMAN, Robert, MA; American journalist; *Editor-in-Chief, Transatlantic magazine, Center for Transatlantic Relations. Education:* Indiana Univ., American Univ., Washington, DC. *Career:* fmr int. economist, US Dept of Commerce; fmr press sec., White House; writer/researcher for presidential cands 1968, 1972 and 1976; Ed.-in-Chief, Pres. and Publr Political Profiles Inc. 1979–89; fmr Adjunct Prof. of Political Communications, George Washington Univ.; fmr Adjunct Prof. of American Politics and Communications, American Univ.; Head of Publs, EC Office, Washington DC and Ed.-in-Chief, Europe magazine 1989–2003; founder and Ed.-in-Chief Transatlantic magazine 2003–; Sr Fellow, Center for Transatlantic Relations, Johns Hopkins Univ. 2004–; fmr presenter, radio current affairs programme. *Address:* Center for Transatlantic Relations, 1717 Massachusetts Avenue, NW, Suite 525, Washington, DC 20036, USA (office). *Telephone:* (202) 663-5880 (office). *Fax:* (202) 663-5879 (office). *E-mail:* rguttman@jhu.edu (office). *Website:* transatlantic.sais-jhu.edu (office).

GUY, John, PhD; British writer and historian; b. 1949, Australia; m. Julia Fox. *Education:* Univ. of Cambridge. *Career:* Research Fellow, Selwyn Coll. 1970; writer and reviewer, The Sunday Times, The Guardian, The Economist, Times Literary Supplement, BBC History Magazine, History Today; Fellow, Clare Coll., Cambridge. *Television:* presenter Timewatch: The King's Servant (BBC 2) 2001, Renaissance Secrets (four-part series, BBC 2); contrib. to Meet the Ancestors (BBC 2), Time Team (Channel 4), Royal Deaths and Diseases (Channel 4). *Publications:* non-fiction: The Cardinal's Court: The Impact of Thomas Wolsey in Star Chamber 1977, The Public Career of Sir Thomas More 1980, Law and Social Change in British History 1984, The Court of Star Chamber and its Records to the Reign of Elizabeth I 1985, Christopher St German on Chancery and Statute 1985, Reassessing the Henrician Age (with Alistair Fox) 1986, The Complete Works of St Thomas More, Vol. X: The Debellation of Salem and Bizance (co-ed.) 1987, Tudor England 1990, The Tudors and Stuarts (with John Morrill) 1992, The Reign of Elizabeth I: Court and Culture in the Last Decade 1995, The Tudor Monarchy 1997, Cardinal Wolsey 1998, Politics, Law and Counsel in Tudor and Early-Stuart England 2000, Thomas More 2000, The Tudors: A Very Short Introduction 2000, My Heart is My Own: The Life of Mary, Queen of Scots (Whitbread Biography Award 2004) 2004; contrib. to The Oxford History of Britain 1988, The Oxford Illustrated History of Britain 1992, The Oxford Illustrated History of Tudor and Stuart Britain 2000, The Short Oxford History of the British Isles: The Sixteenth Century 1485–1603 2001. *Honours:* Hon. Prof., Univ. of St Andrews 2003; Yorke Prize 1976, Marsh Biography Award 2005. *Literary Agent:* c/o Robinson Literary Agency, Block A511, The Jam Factory, 27 Green Walk, London, SE1 4TT, England. *Website:* www.johnguy.co.uk.

GUY, Rosa Cuthbert; American writer; b. 9 Jan. 1928, Trinidad. *Career:* Writer-in-Residence, Michigan Technical University; mem. Harlem Writers Guild (pres.), PEN. *Publications:* The Friends, 1973; Ruby, 1976; Edith Jackson, 1978; The Disappearance, 1979; A Measure of Time, 1983; New Guys Around the Block, 1983; Pee Wee and Big Dog, 1984; I Heard a Bird Sing, 1986; Music of Summer, 1992; My Love My Love, 1996. Play: Once on This Island (adaptation of My Love My Love), 1990. Contributions: New York Times Sunday Magazine; Red Book; Cosmopolitan. *Honours:* The Other Award, England, New York Times Best of the Best. *Address:* 20 W 72nd Street, New York, NY 10023, USA.

GWYNN, Robert Samuel, BA, MA, MFA; American academic, writer, poet and editor; b. 13 May 1948, Leaksville, NC; m. 1st Faye La Prade 1969 (divorced 1977); m. 2nd Donna Kay Skaggs Simon 1977; one s. *Education:* Davidson College, University of Arkansas. *Career:* Instructor in English, Southwest Texas State University, San Marcos, 1973–76; University Prof. of English, Lamar University, Beaumont, TX, 1976–; many poetry readings throughout the USA; mem. Associated Writing Programs; Poetry Society of America; Conference of College Teachers of English; South Central MLA; Texas Asscn of Creative Writing Teachers; Texas Institute of Letters. *Publications:* Bearing and Distance (poems), 1977; The Narcissiad (poems), 1981; The Drive-In, 1986; Dictionary of Literary Biography, Second Series, Vol. 105: American Poets Since World War II (ed., contributor), 1991; Drama: A HarperCollins Pocket Anthology (ed.), 1993; Fiction: A HarperCollins Pocket Anthology (ed.), 1993; Poetry: A HarperCollins Pocket Anthology (ed.), 1993; The Area Code of God (poems), 1994; The Advocates of Poetry: A Reader of American Poet-Critics of the Modern Era, 1996; No Word of Farewell (poems), 1996; Fiction: A Longman Pocket Anthology (ed., contributor), 1997. Contributions: anthologies including: Texas Poets in Concert: A Quartet; Rebel Angels: Twenty-Five Poets of the New Formation; The Store of Joys; More than 70 articles, poems and reviews to periodicals including: Sparrow; Tar River Poetry; Sewanee Review; Hudson Review; Poetry Northwest; Texas Monthly. *E-mail:* rsgwynn@mail.com.

H

HAAVIKKO, Paavo Juhani; Finnish writer and publisher; b. 25 Jan. 1931, Helsinki; s. of Heikki Adrian Haavikko and Rauha Pyykönen; m. 1st Marja-Liisa Vartio (née Sairanen) 1955 (died 1966); one s. one d.; m. 2nd Ritva Rainio (née Hanhineva) 1971. *Career:* worked in real estate concurrently with career as writer 1951–67; mem Bd, Finnish Writers' Asscn 1962–66; mem. State Cttee for Literature 1966–67; mem. Bd of Yhtyneet Kuvalehdet magazine co. and Suuri Suomalainen Kirjakerho (Great Finnish Book Club) 1969; Literary Dir Otava Publishing Co. 1967–83; Publr Arthouse Publishing Group 1983–. *Publications:* Tiet etäisyyksiin 1951, Tuuliöinä 1953, Synnyinmaa 1955, Lehdet lehtiä 1958, Talvipalatsi 1959, Runot 1962, Puut, kaikki heidän vihreytensä 1966, Neljätoista hallitsijaa 1970, Puhua vastata opettaa 1972, Runoja matkalta salmen ylitse 1973, Kaksikymmentä ja yksi 1974, Kaksiky m mentä ja yksi 1974, Runot 1949–1974 1975, Runoelmat 1975, Viiniä, Kirjoitusta 1976, Toukokuu, ikuinen 1988 (poems); Poésie 1965, Jahre 1967, Geschichte 1967, Selected Poems 1968, The Superintendent 1973, Le palais d'hiver 1976 (translations); Münchhausen, Nuket 1960, Ylilääkäri 1968, Sulka 1973, Harald Pitkäikäinen 1974 (plays); Ratsumies 1974 (libretto); Yksityisiä Asioita 1960, Toinen taivas ja maa 1961, Vuodet 1962, Lasi Claudius Civiliksen salaliittolaisten pöydällä 1964 (prose); Kansakuninan linja 1977, Yritys omaksikuvaksi 1987, Kansakunnan linja 1990, Vuosien aurinkoiset varjot (memoirs), Prospero (memoirs) 1967–1995, Lamavuodesta 91 kriisivuoden 92 kautta katastrofivuoteen 93 1992, Talvipalatsi : yhdeksän runoa 1993, Puiden ylivertaisuudesta 1993, Tulevaisuudesta 1996, Gedichte! Gedichte 1997. *Honours:* Academician hc; six state prizes for literature; Neustadt Int. Prize for Literature 1984, Nordic Prize of Swedish Acad.; Pro Finlandia Medal; Nossack-Akademiepreise, Akademie der Wissenschaften und der Literatur, Mainz. *Address:* Art House Oy, Bulevardi 19C, 00120 Helsinki, Finland. *Telephone:* (9) 6932727. *Fax:* (9) 6949028.

HABERMAS, Jürgen, DPhil; German academic and writer; *Professor Emeritus of Philosophy, University of Frankfurt;* b. 18 June 1929, Düsseldorf; m. Ute Habermas-Wesselhoeft 1955; one s. two d. *Education:* Univs of Bonn and Göttingen. *Career:* Research Asst, Inst. für Soziale Forschung, Frankfurt 1956; Prof. of Philosophy, Univ. of Heidelberg 1961, of Philosophy and Sociology, Univ. of Frankfurt 1964; Dir Max Planck Inst., Starnberg, Munich 1971; Prof. of Philosophy, Univ. of Frankfurt 1983–94, Prof. Emer. 1994–; mem. Academia Europaea; Foreign mem. American Acad. of Arts and Sciences 1984, British Acad. of Science 1994. *Publications:* Strukturwandel der Öffentlichkeit 1962, Theorie und Praxis 1963, Erkenntnis und Interesse 1968, Legitimationsprobleme im Spätkapitalismus 1973, Theorie des kommunikativen Handelns 1981, Moralbewusstsein und Kommunikatives Handeln 1983, Der Philosophische Diskurs ober Moderne 1985, Eine Art Schadensabwicklüng 1987, Nachmetaphysisches Denken 1988, Nachholende Revolution 1990, Texte und Kontexte 1991, Erläuterungen zur Diskursetnik 1991, Faktizität und Geltung 1992, Vergangenheit als Zukunft 1993, Die Normalität einer Berliner Republik 1995, Die Einbeziehung des Anderen 1996, Vom sinnlichen Eindruck zum symbolischen Ausdruck 1997, Die postnationale Konstellation 1998, Wahrheit und Rechtfertigung 1999, Zeit und Übergänge 2001, Kommunikatives Handeln und Detranszendentalisierte Vernuft 2001, Die Zukunft der Menschlichen Natur 2001, Zeitdiagnosen 2003, Der gespaltene Westen 2004. *Honours:* Hon. DD (New School for Social Research) 1984; hon. degrees from Hebrew Univ. (Jerusalem), Univs of Hamburg, Buenos Aires, Evanston (Northwestern), Utrecht, Athens, Bologna, Paris, Tel-Aviv, Cambridge, Harvard; Hegel Prize 1972, Sigmund Freud Prize 1976, Adorno Prize 1980, Geschwister Scholl Prize 1985, Leibniz Prize 1986, Sonning Prize 1987, Jaspers Prize 1997, Culture Prize of the State of Hesse 1999, Friedenspreis des deutschen Buchhandels 2001, Prince of Asturias Award for Social Science 2003, Kyoto Prize for Philosophy 2004. *Address:* Department of Philosophy, University of Frankfurt, Grüneburgplatz 1, 60629 Frankfurt am Main (office); Ringstrasse 8B, 82319 Starnberg, Germany. *Telephone:* (8151) 13537 (home). *Fax:* (8151) 13537 (home).

HABGOOD, Baron (Life Peer), cr. 1995, of Calverton in the County of Buckinghamshire; **Rt Rev. and Rt Hon. John Stapylton Habgood,** PC, DD, MA, PhD; British ecclesiastic (retd); b. 23 June 1927, Stony Stratford; s. of Arthur Henry Habgood and Verre Chetwynd-Stapylton; m. Rosalie Mary Anne Boston 1961; two s. two d. *Education:* Eton Coll., King's Coll. Cambridge Univ. and Cuddesdon Coll., Oxford. *Career:* Demonstrator in Pharmacology, Univ. of Cambridge 1950–53; Fellow, King's Coll. Cambridge 1952–55, Hon. Fellow 1984; Curate, St Mary Abbott's Church, Kensington 1954–56; Vice-Prin. Westcott House, Cambridge 1956–62; Rector, St John's Church, Jedburgh, Scotland 1962–67; Prin. Queen's Coll., Birmingham 1967–73; Bishop of Durham 1973–83; Archbishop of York 1983–95; Pres. (UK) Council on Christian Approaches to Defence and Disarmament 1976–95; Chair. World Council of Churches' Int. Hearing on Nuclear Weapons 1981; mem. Council for Science and Society 1975–90, Council for Arms Control 1981–95; Moderator of Church and Soc. Sub-Unit, World Council of Churches 1983–90; Chair. UK Xenotransplantation Interim Regulatory Authority 1997–2003. *Publications:* Religion and Science 1964, A Working Faith 1980, Church and Nation in a Secular Age 1983, Confessions of a Conservative Liberal 1988, Making Sense 1993, Faith and Uncertainty 1997, Being a Person 1998, Varieties of Unbelief 2000, The Concept of Nature 2002. *Honours:* Hon. DD (Durham) 1975, (Cambridge) 1984, (Aberdeen) 1988, (Huron) 1990, (Hull) 1991, (Oxford) 1996,

(Manchester) 1996, (London) 2005; Hon. DUniv (York) 1996; Hon. DHL (York, Pa) 1995; Bampton Lecturer, Univ. of Oxford 1999, Gifford Lecturer, Univ. of Aberdeen 2000. *Address:* 18 The Mount, Malton, N Yorks., YO17 7ND, England (home). *E-mail:* js.habgood@btinternet.com (home).

HABIB, Randa, MA; Jordanian journalist; *Director and Head, Agence France Presse, Jordan;* b. 16 Jan. 1952, Beirut, Lebanon; d. of Farid Habib; m. Adnan Gharaybeh 1973; one s. one d. *Education:* French Lycée, Rio de Janeiro and Univ. of Beirut. *Career:* corresp., Agence France Presse (AFP) 1980, Dir and Head AFP Office, Amman 1987–; corresp., Radio Monte Carlo 1988–, Jordan Times, also for several int. publs and TV; Chair. Foreign Press Club, Jordan. *Honours:* Chevalier Ordre nat. du Mérite 2001; Médaille du Travail (France) 2000. *Address:* Agence France Presse, Jebel Amman, 2nd Circle, PO Box 3340, Amman 11181, Jordan (office). *Telephone:* (6) 4642976 (office). *Fax:* (6) 4654680 (office). *E-mail:* randa.habib@afp.com (office).

HABILA, Helon; Nigerian writer and academic; *Faculty Member, Graduate Creative Writing Program, Department of English, George Mason University;* b. 1967, Kaltungo, Gombe State; m.; one d. *Education:* Univ. of Jos. *Career:* Lecturer in English and Literature, Fed. Polytechnic, Bauchi 1997–99; fmr contrib. to Hints magazine, Lagos; fmr Arts Ed. Vanguard newspaper, Lagos; African Writing Fellow Univ. of E Anglia, UK 2002–04; Chinua Achebe Fellow of Africana Global Studies, Bard Coll., New York 2005–06; faculty mem. Dept of English, Grad. Creative Writing Program, George Mason Univ. 2007–; Contributing Ed. Virginia Quarterly Review. *Publications:* Mai Kaltungo (biog.) 1997, Prison Stories (short stories) 2000, Waiting for an Angel 2002 (Commonwealth Prize for Best First Book, African Region, 2003), Measuring Time 2007; co-ed. New Writing 14 (British Council Anthology), Miracles, Dreams, and Jazz; short stories and poems in anthologies. *Honours:* first prize MUSON Festival Poetry Competition (for poem Another Age) 2000, Caine Prize for African Writing, UK (for short story Love Poems) 2001. *Address:* 117 Science and Technology Bldg, George Mason University, Fairfax, VA 22030 (office); Graduate Creative Writing Program, 4400 University Drive, MSN 3E4, Fairfax, VA 22030, USA (office). *Telephone:* (703) 993-1180 (office). *E-mail:* hhabila@gmu.edu (office). *Website:* creativewriting.gmu.edu (office).

HACHETTE, Jean-Louis, LenD; French publisher; b. 30 June 1925, Paris; s. of Louis and Blanche (née Darbou) Hachette; m. Y. de Bouillé 1954; one s. two d. *Education:* Collège Stanislas, Paris and Faculté de Droit, Paris. *Career:* joined Librairie Hachette (f. by great-grandfather in 1826) 1946 (now Hachette Livre); entire career spent with Librairie Hachette, Admin. Dir 1971–; Pres. Librairie Générale Française 1954–. *Address:* Librairie Générale Française, 43 quai de Grenelle, 75905 Paris, Cédex 15, France. *Website:* www.hachette.com.

HACKER, Katharina; German writer; b. 1967, Frankfurt. *Education:* Freiburg Univ., Hebrew Univ., Jerusalem. *Publications include:* Morpheus (novel) 1998, Der Bademeister (novel, trans. as The Lifeguard) 2000. *Address:* c/o The Toby Press, PO Box 8531, New Milford, CT 06776-8531, USA. *Website:* www.tobypress.com.

HACKER, Marilyn, BA; American poet, writer, critic, editor and teacher; b. 27 Nov. 1942, New York, NY; one d. *Education:* New York Univ. *Career:* Ed., Quark: A Quarterly of Speculative Fiction 1969–71, The Kenyon Review 1990–94; Jenny McKean Moore Chair in Writing, George Washington Univ. 1976–77; mem. Editorial Collective, The Little Magazine 1977–80, Ed.-in-Chief 1979; teacher School of General Studies, Columbia Univ. 1979–81; Visiting Artist, Fine Arts Work Center, Provincetown, MA 1981; Visiting Prof., Univ. of Idaho 1982; Ed.-in-Chief, Thirteenth Moon: A Feminist Literary Magazine 1982–86; writer-in-residence, SUNY at Albany 1988, Columbia Univ. 1988; George Elliston Poet-in-Residence, Univ. of Cincinnati 1988; Distinguished Writer-in-Residence, American Univ., Washington, DC 1989; Visiting Prof. of Creative Writing, SUNY at Binghamton 1990, Univ. of Utah 1995, Barnard Coll. 1995, Princeton Univ. 1997; Fannie Hurst Poet-in-Residence, Brandeis Univ. 1996; Prof. of English, City Coll. of New York 1999–; Prof. of French, CUNY Graduate Center 2003–. *Publications:* Presentation Piece 1974, Separations 1976, Taking Notice 1980, Assumptions 1985, Love, Death and the Changing of the Seasons 1986, The Hang-Glider's Daughter: New and Selected Poems 1990, Going Back to the River 1990, Selected Poems: 1965–1990 1994, Winter Numbers 1994, Edge (trans. of poems by Claire Malroux) 1996, Squares and Courtyards 2000, A Long-Gone Sun (trans. of poems by Claire Malroux) 2000, Here There Was Once a Country (trans. of poems by Vénus Khoury-Ghata) 2001, She Says (trans. of poems by Vénus Khoury-Ghata) 2003, Desesperato 2003, Birds and Bison (trans. of poems by Claire Malroux) 2004, Poetry to Heal Your Blues (ed.) 2006, Essays on Departure: New and Selected Poems 1980–2005 2006; contrib. to numerous anthologies and other publications. *Honours:* NEA grants 1973–74, 1985–86, 1995, Nat. Book Award in Poetry 1975, Guggenheim Fellowship 1980–81, Ingram Merrill Foundation grant 1984–85, Poetry Soc. of America Robert F. Winner Awards 1987, 1989, Poetry Soc. of America John Masefield Memorial Award 1994, Lambda Literary Awards 1991, 1995, Acad. of American Poets Lenore Marshall Award 1995, American Acad. of Arts and Letters Poets' Prize 1995, American Acad. of Arts and Letters Award in

Literature 2004. *Address:* 33 rue de Turenne, 75003 Paris, France; 230 W 105th Street, New York, NY 10025, USA.

HACKER, Peter Michael Stephen, BA, MA, DPhil; British philosopher, librarian and writer; *Fellow, St John's College, Oxford*; b. 15 July 1939, London, England; m. Sylvia Imhoff 1963; two s. one d. *Education:* Queen's Coll., Oxford, St Antony's Coll., Oxford. *Career:* Jr Research Fellow, Balliol Coll., Oxford 1965–66; Fellow and Tutor in Philosophy, St John's Coll., Oxford 1966–, Librarian 1986–; Visiting Prof., Swarthmore Coll., USA 1973, 1986, Univ. of Michigan, Ann Arbor, USA 1974, Queen's Univ., Kingston, Ont., Canada 1985. *Publications:* Insight and Illusion: Wittgenstein and the Metaphysics of Experience 1972, second edn as Insight and Illusion: Themes in the Philosophy of Wittgenstein 1986, Law, Morality and Society: Essays in Honour of H. L. A. Hart (co-ed. and contrib.) 1977, Wittgenstein: Understanding and Meaning (with G. P. Baker) 1980, much revised 2nd edn 2004, Frege: Logical Excavations (with G. P. Baker) 1984, Language, Sense and Nonsense: A Critical Investigation into Modern Theories of Language (with G. P. Baker) 1984, Scepticism, Rules and Language (with G. P. Baker) 1984, Wittgenstein: Rules, Grammar and Necessity (with G. P. Baker) 1985, Appearance and Reality: A Philosophical Investigation into Perception and Perceptual Qualities 1987, The Renaissance of Gravure: The Art of S. W. Hayter (ed. and contributor) 1988, Wittgenstein: Meaning and Mind 1990, Gravure and Grace: The Engravings of Roger Vieillard (ed. and contributor) 1993, Wittgenstein: Mind and Will 1996, Wittgenstein's Place in Twentieth Century Analytic Philosophy 1996, Wittgenstein on Human Nature 1997, Wittgenstein: Connections and Controversies 2001, Philosophical Foundations of Neuroscience (with M. R. Bennett) 2003; contrib. to reference works, scholarly books and professional journals. *Honours:* British Acad. Research Reader 1985–87, Leverhulme Sr Research Fellow 1991–94. *Address:* St John's College, Oxford, OX1 3JP, England (office).

HADAS, Rachel, BA, MA, PhD; American academic, poet and writer; *Board of Governors Professor of English, Rutgers University*; b. 8 Nov. 1948, New York, NY; m. 1st Stavros Kondilis 1970 (divorced) 1978; m. 2nd George Edwards 1978; one s. *Education:* Radcliffe Coll., Johns Hopkins Univ., Princeton Univ. *Career:* Asst Prof., Rutgers Univ. 1982–87, Assoc. Prof. 1987–92, Prof. of English 1992–2000, Bd of Govs Prof. of English 2000–; Adjunct Prof., Columbia Univ., New York 1992–93; Visiting Prof., Princeton Univ. 1995, 1996; Fellow, American Acad. of Arts and Sciences; mem. Modern Greek Studies Asscn, Modern Language Asscn, PEN, Poetry Soc. of America. *Publications:* Starting From Troy 1975, Slow Transparency 1983, A Son from Sleep 1987, Pass It On 1989, Living in Time 1990, Unending Dialogue 1991, Mirrors of Astonishment 1992, Other Worlds Than This 1994, The Empty Bed 1995, The Double Legacy 1995, Halfway Down the Hall (New and Selected Poems) 1998, Merrill Cavafy, Poems and Dreams 2000, Indelible 2001, Laws 2004, The River of Forgetfulness 2006; contribs to various periodicals. *Honours:* Ingram Merrill Foundation Fellowship 1976–77, Guggenheim Fellowship 1988–89, American Acad. and Inst. of Arts and Letters Award 1990, O. B. Hardison Award 2000, Scholars and Writers, New York Public Library 2000–01. *Address:* 838 West End Avenue, #3A, New York, NY 10025 (home); Department of English, Faculty of Arts and Sciences-Newark, 360 Dr Martin Luther King Jr Blvd, 520 Hill Hall, Newark, NJ 07102-1801, USA (office). *Telephone:* (212) 666-4482 (home); (973) 353-5279 ext. 520 (office). *Fax:* (212) 666-5533 (home); (973) 353-1450 (office). *E-mail:* rhadas@andromeda.rutgers.edu (office).

HADDAD, Joumana; Lebanese journalist, poet and translator; b. 1970, Beirut. *Career:* arts journalist, an-Nahar newspaper 1997–, now Chief Ed. of the cultural pages. *Publications:* poetry collections: The Time of a Dream 1995, Invitation to a Secret Dinner 1998, Abyss 2000, I Haven't Sinned Enough (anthology) 2004, The Return of Lilith 2004; translations of poetry; contrib. to literary magazines, including Alhucema (Spain), Fornix (Peru), Hojas Sueltas (Colombia), Kalimat (Australia), Europe (France), Supérieur inconnu (France). *Honours:* Arab Press Prize, Dubai 2006. *E-mail:* contact@joumanahaddad.com. *Website:* www.joumanahaddad.com.

HADDON, Mark, MA; British writer and illustrator; b. 1962, Northampton; m. Sos Eltis; one s. *Education:* Merton Coll., Oxford, Edinburgh Univ. *Career:* positions at Mencap and other charity orgs; illustrator and cartoonist; painter; television work. *Screenwriting:* Microsoap (Royal Television Soc. Best Children's Drama), episodes of Starstreet, Fungus and the Bogeyman (adaptation). *Publications:* fiction: Gilbert's Gobstopper 1988, A Narrow Escape for Princess Sharon 1989, Toni and the Tomato Soup 1989, Agent Z Meets the Masked Crusader 1993, Gridzbi Spudvetch! 1993, In the Garden 1994, On Holiday (aka On Vacation) 1994, At Home 1994, At Playgroup 1994, Titch Johnson 1994, Agent Z Goes Wild 1994, Agent Z and the Penguin from Mars 1995, Real Porky Philips 1995, The Sea of Tranquillity 1996, Secret Agent Handbook 1999, Ocean Star Express 2001, Agent Z and the Killer Bananas 2001, The Ice Bear's Cave 2002, The Curious Incident of the Dog in the Night Time (Booktrust Teenage Prize 2003, Guardian Children's Fiction Prize 2003, South Bank Show Best Book Prize 2004, Whitbread Best Novel and Book of the Year 2004, Commonwealth Writers Prize for best first book 2004, Soc. of Authors McKitterick Prize 2004, WHSmith Children's Book of the Year 2004, Waterstone's Literary Fiction award 2004) 2003, A Spot of Bother 2006; poetry: The Talking Horse and the Sad Girl and the Village Under the Sea 2005. *Address:* c/o Jonathan Cape Ltd, 20 Vauxhall Bridge Road, London, SW1V 2SA, England. *Telephone:* (20) 7840-8400.

HADLOW, Janice; British broadcasting executive; *Controller, BBC Four*. *Career:* production trainee, BBC 1986, later producer on Radio 4, Ed. Late Show, Deputy Head music and arts dept, Jt Head of history dept –1999; Head of History, Arts and Religion, Channel 4 1999, later Head of Specialist Factual Group, Channel 4 –2004; Controller, BBC Four 2004–. *Publication:* The Nunnery: The Six Daughters of George III (with Martin Davidson) 2004. *Address:* BBC Four, BBC Television Centre, Wood Lane, London, W12 7RJ, England. *Website:* www.bbc.co.uk/bbcfour.

HAGÈGE, Claude, LèsL, TH; Tunisian linguist and writer; b. Carthage. *Career:* teacher Lycée Carnot, Tunis 1959–61, Lycées Victor Duruy et Saint-Louis, Paris 1963–66; Prof. of Linguistics Univ. of Poitiers 1963–66; Chief of Confs Univ. of Paris XII Val-de-Marne 1971–74, Univ. of Paris IV 1976–78, Univ. of Paris III 1977–78; Dir of Linguistic Studies Ecole Pratique des Hautes Etudes 1977; teacher Collège de France 1982–. *Publications:* La Structure des langues 1982, L'Homme de paroles 1985, Le Français et les siècles 1987, Le Souffle de la langue 1992, L'Enfant aux deux langues 1996, Le Français, histoire d'un combat 1996, Halte à la mort des langues 2001, Les Destins du français 2005. *Honours:* Officier, Ordre des Palmes académiques 1995, Chevalier, Ordre des Arts et des Lettres 1995, Officier, Légion d'honneur 2005; Prix Volney de l' Acad. des Inscriptions et Belles-Lettres 1981, Grand Prix de l'Essai de la Soc. des Gens de Lettres 1986, Grand Prix de l' Acad. Française 1986, CNRS Médaille d'or 1995, Prix du Mot d'or des langues 2003. *Address:* Collège de France, 11 place Marcelin Berthelot, 75231 Paris Cédex 05, France (office). *Telephone:* 1-44-27-17-03 (office). *Fax:* 1-44-27-13-29 (home). *E-mail:* claude.hagege@college-de-france.fr (office); claude-hagege@wanadoo.fr (home). *Website:* claude.hagege.wanadoo.fr (home).

HAGGER, Nicholas Osborne, MA; British poet, verse dramatist, lecturer, writer and philosopher and cultural historian; b. 22 May 1939, London, England; m. 1st Caroline Virginia Mary Nixon 1961; one d.; m. 2nd Madeline Ann Johnson 1974; two s. *Education:* Worcester Coll., Oxford. *Career:* Lecturer in English, Univ. of Baghdad 1961–62; Prof. of English Literature, Tokyo Univ. of Education and Keio Univ., Tokyo 1963–67, Tokyo Univ. 1964–65; Lecturer in English, Univ. of Libya, Tripoli 1968–70; freelance feature writer for The Times 1970–72; mem. Soc. of Authors. *Publications:* The Fire and the Stones: A Grand Unified Theory of World History and Religion 1991, Selected Poems: A Metaphysical's Way of Fire 1991, The Universe and the Light: A New View of the Universe and Reality 1993, A White Radiance: The Collected Poems 1958–93 1994, A Mystic Way: A Spiritual Autobiography 1994, Awakening to the Light: Diaries, Vol. 1 1958–67 1994, A Spade Fresh with Mud: Collected Stories, Vol. 1 1995, The Warlords: From D-Day to Berlin, A Verse Drama 1995, A Smell of Leaves and Summer: Collected Stories, Vol. 2 1995, Overlord, The Triumph of Light 1944–1945: An Epic Poem, Books 1–2 1995, Books 3–6 1996, Books 7–9, 10–12 1997, The One and the Many 1999, Wheeling Bats and a Harvest Moon: Collected Stories, Vol. 3 1999, Prince Tudor, A Verse Drama 1999, The Warm Glow of the Monastery Courtyard: Collected Stories, Vol. 4 1999, The Syndicate: The Story of the Coming World Government 2004, The Secret History of the West: The Influence of Secret Organisations on Western History from the Renaissance to the 20th Century 2005, Classical Odes: Poems on England, Europe and a Global Theme, and of Everyday Life in the One 2006, The Light of Civilization 2006, Overlord (one-vol. edn) 2006, Collected Poems 1958–2005 2006, Collected Verse Plays 2007, Collected Short Stories 2007, The Secret Founding of America 2007, The Rise and Fall of Civilizations 2007, The Last Tourist in Iran 2007, Universalism 2008. *E-mail:* info@nicholashagger.co.uk. *Website:* www.nicholashagger.co.uk.

HAHN (GARCES), Oscar Arturo, MA, PhD; American poet, writer and academic; b. 5 July 1938, Iquique, Chile; m. Nancy Jorquera 1971; one d. *Education:* University of Chile, University of Iowa, University of Maryland at College Park. *Career:* Prof. of Hispanic Literature, University of Chile, 1965–73; Instructor, University of Maryland at College Park, 1974–77; Asst Prof., 1977–79, Assoc. Prof. of Spanish-American Literature, 1979–, University of Iowa; mem. Instituto Internacional de Literatura Iberoamericana; MLA of America. *Publications:* Esta rosa negra (poems), 1961; Agua final (poems), 1967; Arte de morir (poems), 1977, English trans. as The Art of Dying, 1987; El cuento fantástico hispanoamericano en el siglo XIX, 1978; Mal de amor, 1981, English trans. as Love Breaks, 1991; Imagenes nucleares, 1983; Texto sobre texto, 1984; Tratado de sortilegios, 1992; Antología poética, 1993; Antología virtual, 1996; ¿Qué hacia yo el once de septiembre de 1973? (with Matias Rivas and Roberto Merino), 1997; Antología retroactiva, 1998; Versos robados/Stolen Verses and Other Poems, 2000. Contributions: Literary journals. *Honours:* Premio Alerce, 1961; Poetry Award, University of Chile, 1966; Hon. Fellow, International Writing Program, 1972. *Address:* c/o Department of Spanish, University of Iowa, Iowa City, IA 52240, USA.

HAHN, Susan; American poet, playwright and editor; b. 11 Nov. 1947, Chicago, IL; m. Frederic L. Hahn 1967; one s. *Career:* staff 1980–, Ed. 1997–, TriQuarterly literary magazine; Co-Founder/Co-Ed., TriQuarterly Books 1988–. *Publications:* Harriet Rubin's Mother's Wooden Hand 1991, Incontinence 1993, Melancholia et cetera 1995, Confession 1997, Holiday 2001, Mother in Summer 2002, Golf (play) 2005, Self/Pity 2005, The Scarlet Ibis 2007; contrib. to many reviews, quarterlies and journals. *Honours:* Illinois Arts Council Literary Awards, 1985, 1990, 1996, 1997; Society of Midland Authors Award for Poetry, 1994; Pushcart Prizes for Poetry, 2000, 2003; George Kent Prize, Poetry magazine, 2000; Guggenheim Fellowship, 2003. *Address:* 1377 Scott Avenue, Winnetka, IL 60093, USA.

HAHN, Ulla, DPhil; German writer; b. 30 April 1946, Brachthausen, Sauerland. *Education:* Univs of Cologne and Hamburg. *Career:* Lecturer, Univs of Hamburg, Bremen, Oldenburg 1975–80; Radio Ed., Bremen 1979–91; freelance writer 1992–. *Publications include:* Herz über Kopf 1981, Spielende 1983, Freudenfeuer 1985, Unerhörte Nähe 1988, Ein Mann im Haus 1991, Galileo und zwei Frauen 1997, Das Verborgene Wort 2003. *Honours:* Leonce und Lena Award 1981, Hölderlin Award 1985, Roswitha von Sandersheim Medal 1986, Medal of FRG . *Address:* DVA, Neckarstrasse 121, Postfach 106012, 7000 Stuttgart 1 (Publr); Breitenfelderstrasse 86, 2000 Hamburg 20, Germany (home). *Telephone:* (40) 485495 (home).

HAIBLUM, Isidore, BA; American writer; b. 23 May 1935, New York, NY. *Education:* City College, CUNY. *Publications:* The Tsaddik of the Seven Wonders, 1971; The Return, 1973; Transfer to Yesterday, 1973; The Wilk Are Among Us, 1975; Interworld, 1977; Outerworld, 1979; Nightmare Express, 1979; Faster Than a Speeding Bullet: An Informal History of Radio's Golden Age (with Stuart Silver), 1980; The Mutants Are Coming, 1984; The Identity Plunderers, 1984; The Hand of Gantz, 1985; Murder in Yiddish, 1988; Bad Neighbors, 1990; Out of Sync, 1990; Specterworld, 1991; Crystalword, 1992. Contributions: periodicals.

HAIGH, Christopher, BA, PhD, FRHistS; British academic and writer; b. 28 Aug. 1944, Birkenhead, England; two d. *Education:* University of Cambridge, Victoria University of Manchester. *Career:* Lecturer in History, Victoria University of Manchester, 1969–79; Lecturer in Modern History, Christ Church, Oxford, 1979–. *Publications:* The Last Days of the Lancashire Monasteries, 1969; Reformation and Resistance in Tudor Lancashire, 1975; The Cambridge Historical Encyclopaedia of Great Britain and Ireland, 1984; The Reign of Elizabeth l, 1985; The English Reformation Revised, 1987; Elizabeth l: A Profile in Power, 1988; English Reformations: Religion, Politics and Society Under the Tudors, 1993.

HAILEY, Elizabeth Forsythe, BA; American writer and dramatist; b. 31 Aug. 1938, Dallas, Texas; m. Oliver Daffan Hailey 1960 (died 1993); two d. *Education:* Sorbonne, Univ. of Paris, Hollins Coll., Va. *Career:* mem. Authors League of America, PEN USA. *Publications:* Fiction: A Woman of Independent Means 1978, Life Sentences 1982, Joanna's Husband and David's Wife 1986, Home Free 1991; plays: A Woman of Independent Means 1984, Joanna's Husband and David's Wife 1989; contribs to books and periodicals. *Honours:* Silver Medal for Best First Novel, Commonwealth Club of California 1978, Los Angeles Drama Critics Award 1983. *Address:* 11747 Canton Place, Studio City, CA 91604, USA.

HAINES, John Meade; American poet, writer and teacher; b. 29 June 1924, Norfolk, VA; m. 1st Jo Ella Hussey 1960; m. 2nd Jane McWhorter 1970 (divorced 1974); m. 3rd Leslie Sennett 1978 (divorced); four c. *Education:* National Art School, Washington, DC, American University, Hans Hoffman School of Fine Art, New York, University of Washington. *Career:* Poet-in-Residence, University of Alaska, 1972–73; Visiting Prof. in English, University of Washington, 1974; Visiting Lecturer in English, University of Montana, 1974; Writer-in-Residence, Sheldon Jackson College, 1982–83, Ucross Foundation, 1987, Montalvo Center for the Arts, 1988, Djerassi Foundation, 1988; Visiting Lecturer, University of California at Santa Cruz, 1986, Wordsworth Conference, Grasmere, England, 1996; Visiting Writer, The Loft Mentor Series, 1987, George Washington University, 1991–92; Visiting Prof., Ohio University, 1989–90; Elliston Fellow in Poetry, University of Cincinnati, 1992; Chair in Creative Arts, Austin Peay State University, Clarksville, Tennessee, 1993; mem. Acad. of American Poets; Alaska Conservation Society; Natural Resources Defense Council; PEN American Center; Poetry Society of America; Sierra Club; Wilderness Society. *Publications:* Poetry: Winter News, 1966; Suite for the Pied Piper, 1968; The Legend of Paper Plates, 1970; The Mirror, 1970; The Stone Harp, 1971; Twenty Poems, 1971; Leaves and Ashes, 1975; In Five Years, 1976; Cicada, 1977; In a Dusty Light, 1977; The Sun on Your Shoulder, 1977; News From the Glacier: Selected Poems, 1960–80, 1982; New Poems: 1980–1988, 1990; Rain Country, 1990; The Owl in the Mask of a Dreamer, 1993. Non-Fiction: Minus Thirty-One and the Wind Blowing: Nine Reflections About Living on the Land (with others), 1980; Living Off the Country: Essays on Poetry and Place, 1981; Other Days, 1982; Of Traps and Snares, 1982; Stories We Listened To, 1986; You and I and the World, 1988; The Stars, the Snow, the Fire, 1989; Fables and Distances: New and Selected Essays, 1996; A Guide to the Four-Chambered Heart, 1996. Contributions: periodicals. *Honours:* Guggenheim Fellowships, 1965–66, 1984–85; National Endowment for the Arts Grant, 1967–68; Amy Lowell Scholarship, 1976–77; Governor's Award for lifetime contributions to the arts in Alaska, 1982; Hon. LD, University of Alaska, 1983; Ingram Merrill Foundation Grant, 1987; Lenore Marshall Nation Award, 1991; Literary Award, American Acad. of Arts and Letters, 1995.

HAINING, Peter Alexander, (Peter Alex, Jim Black, Richard De'ath, William Patrick, Richard Peters, Richard Peyton, Sean Richards); British writer; b. 2 April 1940, Enfield, Middlesex, England; m., three c. *Career:* fmr Publishing Dir, New English Library, London; mem. PEN Int. *Publications:* Tune in for Fear 1985, Supernatural Sleuths 1986, Tales of Dungeons and Dragons 1986, Poltergeist 1987, Irish Tales of Terror 1988, The Mummy 1988, The Scarecrow: Fact and Fable 1988, Bob Hope: Thanks for the Memory 1989, The Day War Broke Out 1989, Hook, Line and Laughter 1989, The Legend of Garbo 1990, The Legend That is Buddy Holly 1990, Spitfire Summer 1990, The English Highwayman 1991, Sinister Gambits 1991, Great Irish Stories of the Supernatural 1992, The Supernatural Coast 1992, The Television Detectives Omnibus 1992, The Armchair Detectives 1993, Great Irish Detective Stories 1993, The MG Log 1993, Masters of the Macabre 1993, Tombstone Humour 1993, The Complete Maigret 1994, London After Midnight 1995, Murder at the Races 1995, Agatha Christie's Poirot 1996, Murder on the Railways 1996, The Wizards of Odd 1997, The Un-Dead: The Legend of Bram Stoker and Dracula 1997, Great Irish Humorous Stories 1998, Sweeney Todd: The Real Story of the Demon Barber of Fleet Street 1998, Invasion: Earth 1998, The Nine Lives of Doctor Who 1999, The Classic Era of American Pulp Magazines 2000, The Wizard's Den 2001, The Classic Era of Crime Fiction 2002, The Jail That Went to Sea 2003, The Mystery of Rommel's Gold 2004, Where the Eagle Landed 2004, A Slip of the Pen 2004, The Chianti Raiders 2005, The Banzai Hunters 2007, The Jail That Went to Sea 1007, The Mystery of Rommel's Gold 2007, Where the Eagle Landed 2007. *Honours:* British Fantasy Award for Lifetime Achievement 2001. *Address:* Peyton House, Boxford, Suffolk, England (office).

HAKIM, Seymour (Sy), AB, MA; American poet, writer, artist and educator; b. 23 Jan. 1933, New York, NY; m. Odetta Roverso 1970. *Education:* Eastern New Mexico University, New York University. *Career:* Consultant Ed., Poet Gallery Press, New York, 1970; Ed., Overseas Teacher, 1977; mem. Asscn of Poets and Writers; National Photo Instructors' Asscn; Italo-Brittanica Asscn. *Publications:* The Sacred Family, 1970; Manhattan Goodbye (poems), 1970; Under Moon, 1971; Museum of the Mind, 1971; Wine Theorem, 1972; Substituting Memories, 1976; Iris Elegy, 1979; Balancing Act, 1981; Birth of a Poet, 1985; Eleanor, Goodbye, 1988; Michaelangelo's Call, 1999. Other: Exhibits with accomanying writings: 1970, 1973, 1982–83, 1985. Contribitions: Overseas Educator; California State Poetry Quarterly; American Writing; Dan River Anthology; Its On My Wall; Older Eyes; Art Exhibition and Reading, New York, 1999; Life Shards, 2000; Artwork/readings NYC, 2000.

HAKOSHIMA, Shinichi; Japanese newspaper executive. *Career:* joined Asahi Shimbun Co. (newspaper publr) 1962, posts included Chief of Econ. News section, Man. Ed. Tokyo Head Office, Exec. Man. Dir 1994, Pres. and CEO 1999–2005; Dir NSK (Japanese Newspaper Publrs and Eds Asscn) 1999–, Chair. 2003–. *Address:* c/o Asahi Shimbun Co., 5-3-2 Tsukuyi, Chuo-ku, Tokyo 104-8011, Japan (office). *Telephone:* (3) 3345-0131 (office). *Fax:* (3) 3345-0358 (office). *Website:* www.asahi.com (office).

HALAM, Ann (see Jones, Gwyneth)

HALDEMAN, Joe William, BS, MFA; American novelist; b. 9 June 1943, Oklahoma City, OK; m. Mary Gay Potter 1965. *Education:* Univs of Maryland and Iowa. *Career:* Assoc. Prof., Writing Programme, MIT 1983–; mem. SFWA, Authors' Guild, Poets and Writers, Nat. Space Inst., Writers' Guild. *Publications:* War Year 1972, Cosmic Laughter (ed.) 1974, The Forever War 1975, Mindbridge 1976, Planet of Judgement 1977, All My Sins Remembered 1977, Study War No More (ed.) 1977, Infinite Dreams 1978, World Without End 1979, Worlds 1981, There is No Darkness (co-author) 1983, Worlds Apart 1983, Nebula Awards 17 (ed.) 1983, Dealing in Futures 1985, Body Armour 2000 (co-ed.) 1986, Tool of the Trade 1987, Supertanks (co-ed.) 1987, Starfighters (co-ed.) 1988, The Long Habit of Living 1989, The Hemingway Hoax 1990, Worlds Enough and Time 1992, 1968, 1995, None So Blind 1996, Forever Peace 1997, Saul's Death and Other Poems 1997, Forever Free 1999, The Coming 2000, Guardian 2002, Camouflage 2004, Old Twentieth 2005, War Stories 2005, A Separate War 2006. *Honours:* Purple Heart, US Army 1969; Nebula Awards 1975, 1990, 1993, 1998, 2005, Hugo Awards 1976, 1977, 1991, 1995, 1998, Rhysling Awards 1984, 1990, 2001, World Fantasy Award 1993, John Campbell Award 1998, Tiptree Award 2004, SESFA Awards 2003, 2004. *Address:* 5412 NW 14th Avenue, Gainesville, FL 32605, USA. *Website:* www.earthlink.net/~haldeman.

HALIM, Huri (see Offen, Yehuda)

HALL, Angus; British author and editor; b. 24 March 1932, Newcastle upon Tyne, England. *Career:* Ed., IPC Publishers, London, 1971–, BPC Publishers, London, 1972–. *Publications:* London in Smoky Region, 1962; High-Bouncing Lover, 1966; Live Like a Hero, 1967; Comeuppance of Arthur Hearne, 1967; Qualtrough, 1968; Late Boy Wonder, 1969; Devilday, 1970; To Play the Devil, 1971; Scars of Dracula, 1971; Long Way to Fall, 1971; On the Run, 1974; Signs of Things to Come: A History of Divination, 1975; Monsters and Mythic Beasts, 1976; Strange Cults, 1977; The Rigoletto Murder, 1978; Self-Destruct, 1985.

HALL, Donald Andrew, BA, BLitt, LHD, DLitt; American poet, writer and academic; *Poet Laureate;* b. 20 Sept. 1928, New Haven, CT; s. of Donald A. Hall and Lucy (née Wells) Hall; m. 1st Kirby Thompson 1952 (divorced 1969); one s. one d.; m. 2nd Jane Kenyon 1972 (died 1995). *Education:* Harvard Univ., Univ. of Oxford, Stanford Univ. *Career:* Jr Fellow Harvard Univ. 1954–57; Asst Prof. Univ. of Michigan 1957–61, Assoc. Prof. 1961–66, Prof. of English 1966–75; Poetry Ed. Paris Review 1953–62; Consultant Harper & Row 1964–81; Poet Laureate of the USA 2006–; Guggenheim Fellow 1963, 1972; mem. Authors' Guild, American Acad. of Arts and Letters. *Publications:* poetry: Poems 1952, Exile 1952, To the Loud Wind and Other Poems 1955, Exiles and Marriages 1955, The Dark Houses 1958, A Roof of Tiger Lilies 1964, The Alligator Bride: Poems New and Selected 1969, The Yellow Room: Love Poems 1971, A Blue Wing Tilts at the Edge of the Sea: Selected Poems 1964–1974 1975, The Town of Hill 1975, Kicking the Leaves 1978, The Toy

Bone 1979, The Twelve Seasons 1983, Brief Lives 1983, Great Day at the Cows' House 1984, The Happy Man 1986, The One Day: A Poem in Three Parts (Nat. Book Circle Critic's Award 1989) 1988, Old and New Poems 1990, The One Day and Poems (1947–1990) 1991, The Museum of Clear Ideas 1993, Lucy's Christmas 1994, I Am the Dog, I Am the Cat 1994, Lucy's Summer 1995, The Old Life 1996, Without: Poems 1998, The Painted Bed 2000, White Apples and the Taste of Stone: Selected Poems 1946–2006 2006; short stories: The Ideal Bakery 1987, Willow Temple 2002; prose: Henry Moore: The Life and Work of a Great Sculptor 1966, Marianne Moore: The Cage and the Animal 1970, The Gentleman's Alphabet Book 1972, Writing Well 1973, Goatfoot Milktongue Twinbird: Interviews, Essays and Notes on Poetry 1970–76 1978, The Weather for Poetry: Essays, Reviews and Notes on Poetry 1977–81 1982, Poetry and Ambition: Essays 1982–1988 1988, Here at Eagle Pond 1990, Their Ancient Glittering Eyes 1992, Life Work 1993, Death to Death of Poetry 1994, Principal Products of Portugal 1995, Breakfast Served Any Time All Day 2003, The Best Day The Worst Day (biog.) 2005; editor: Harvard Advanced Anthology (with L. Simpson and R. Pack) 1950, The New Poets of England and America (with R. Pack) 1957, Second Selection 1962, A Poetry Sampler 1962, Contemporary American Poetry (with W. Taylor) 1962, Poetry in English (with S. Spender) 1963, A Concise Encyclopaedia of English and American Poets and Poetry 1963, Faber Book of Modern Verse 1966, The Modern Stylists 1968, A Choice of Whitman's Verse 1968, Man and Boy 1968, Anthology of American Poetry 1969, Pleasures of Poetry (with D. Emblen) 1971, A Writer's Reader 1976, Remembering Poets: Reminiscences and Opinions: Dylan Thomas, Robert Frost, T. S. Eliot, Ezra Pound 1978, To Read Literature 1981, To Read Poetry 1982, Oxford Book of American Literary Anecdotes 1981, Claims for Poetry 1982, Oxford Book of Children's Verse in America 1985, To Read Fiction 1987, Anecdotes of Modern Art (with Pat Corrigan Wykes) 1990. *Honours:* Univ. of Oxford Newdigate Prize for Poetry 1952, Acad. of American Poets Lamont Poetry Selection 1955, Edna St Vincent Millay Memorial Prize 1956, Longview Foundation Award 1960, Sarah Josepha Hale Award 1983, Leonore Marshal Award 1987, Los Angeles Times Book Award 1989, Poetry Soc. of America Robert Frost Silver Medal 1991, New Hampshire Writers and Publishers Project Lifetime Achievement Award 1992, New England Booksellers Asscn Award 1993, Ruth Lilly Prize 1994.

HALL, James Byron, BA, MA, PhD; American writer, poet and academic; b. 21 July 1918, Midland, OH; m. Elizabeth Cushman 1946, one s. four d. *Education:* Miami Univ., Oxford, OH, Univ. of Hawaii, Univ. of Iowa, Kenyon Coll. *Career:* writer-in-residence, Miami Univ., Oxford, OH 1948–49, Univ. of North Carolina at Greensville 1954, Univ. of British Columbia 1955, Univ. of Colorado 1963; Instructor, Cornell Univ. 1952–54; Asst Prof., Univ. of Oregon 1954–57, Assoc. Prof. 1958–60, Prof. of English 1960–65; Prof. of English and Dir Writing Center, Univ. of California at Irvine 1965–68; Provost, Univ. of California at Santa Cruz 1968–75, Provost Emeritus 1983–88; mem. Associated Writing Programs (pres. 1965–66), American Asscn of Univ. Profs, Nat. Writers' Union, Oregon Book Awards (trustee 1992–2001). *Publications:* fiction: Not by the Door, 1954; Racers to the Sun, 1960; Mayo Sergeant, 1968. Short Story Collections: 15 x 3 (with Herbert Gold and R. V. Cassill), 1957; Us He Devours, 1964; The Short Hall, 1980; I Like It Better Now, 1992. Poetry: The Hunt Within, 1973; Bereavements (collected and selected poems), 1991. Non-Fiction: Perspectives on William Everson (co-ed.), 1992; Art and Craft of the Short Story, 1995; The Extreme Stories +3; contrib. to anthologies and other publications. *Honours:* Octave Thanet Prize, 1950; Rockefeller Foundation Grant, 1955; Oregon Poetry Prize, 1958; Emily Clark Balch Fiction Prize, 1967; Chapelbrook Award, 1967; James B. Hall Gallery named in his honour, University of California Regents, 1985; James B. Hall Traveling Fellowship founded in his honour, University of California at Santa Cruz, 1985. *Address:* c/o Castle Peak Editions, PO Box 277, Murphy, OR 97533, USA (office).

HALL, Jane Anna; American writer, poet and artist; b. 4 April 1959, New London, Conn. *Education:* Barbizon School, Westbrook High School. *Career:* Founder-ed. Poetry in Your Mailbox Newsletter 1989–; mem. Romance Writers of America, Connecticut Poetry Soc. *Art works:* exhibited at 23 solo shows. *Compositions:* ten songs including lyrics (non-classical). *Publications:* Cedar and Lace 1986, Satin and Pinstripe 1987, Fireworks and Diamonds 1988, Stars and Daffodils 1989, Sunrises and Stonewalls 1990, Mountains and Meadows 1991, Moonlight and Water Lilies 1992, Sunset and Beaches 1993, Under Par Recipes 1994, New and Selected Poems 1986–1994 1994, Poems for Children 1986–1995 1995, Butterflies and Roses 1996, Hummingbirds and Hibiscus 1997, Swans and Azaleas 1998, Damselflies and Peonies 1999, Egrets and Cattails 2000, Doves and Rhododendron 2001, Bluebirds and Mountain Laurel 2002, The Full Moon Looks Like (juvenile) 2002, Beach Poems Vol. I 2002, Spring Poems Vol. I 2003, Summer Poems Vol. I 2003, Autumn Poems Vol. I 2003, Winter Poems Vol. I 2003, Cardinals and Maples 2003, Wedding Poems Vol. I 2004, Sandpipers and Driftwood 2004, Emeralds and Gardenias 2005, Dragonflies and Pearls 2006, Rubies and Iris 2007; contrib. to several publs. *Honours:* second prizes, Connecticut Poetry Soc. Contest 1983, 1986, various certificates. *Address:* PO Box 629, Westbrook, CT 06498, USA.

HALL, Oakley Maxwell, (Jason Manor), BA, MFA; American author; b. 1 July 1920, San Diego, CA; m. Barbara Erdinger 1945, one s. three d. *Education:* University of California, Berkeley, University of Iowa. *Career:* Dir, Programs in Writing, University of California, Irvine, 1969–89, Squaw Valley Community of Writers, 1969–. *Publications:* So Many Doors, 1950; Corpus of Joe Bailey, 1953; Mardios Beach, 1955; Warlock, 1958; The Downhill Racers, 1962; The Pleasure Garden, 1962; A Game for Eagles, 1970; Report from Beau Harbor, 1971; The Adelita, 1975; The Badlands, 1978; Lullaby, 1982; The Children of the Sun, 1983; The Coming of the Kid, 1985; Apaches, 1986; The Art and Craft of Novel Writing, 1989. *Honours:* Commonwealth Club of California Silver Medal, 1954; Western Writers of America Golden Spur Award, 1984; Cowboy Hall of Fame Wrangler Award, 1989.

HALL, Sir Peter Geoffrey, Kt, MA, PhD, FBA; British geographer and academic; *Bartlett Professor of Planning and Regeneration, Bartlett School of Planning, University College London*; b. 19 March 1932, London; s. of Arthur Vickers and Bertha (née Keefe) Hall; m. 1st Carla M. Wartenberg 1962 (dissolved 1967); m. 2nd Magdalena Mróz 1967. *Education:* Blackpool Grammar School and St Catharine's Coll., Cambridge. *Career:* Asst Lecturer, Birkbeck Coll., Univ. of London 1956–60, Lecturer 1960–65; Reader in Geography with special reference to planning, LSE 1966–67; Prof. of Geography, Univ. of Reading 1968–89, Prof. Emer. 1989–; Prof. of City and Regional Planning, Univ. of Calif. (Berkeley) 1980–92, Prof. Emer. 1993–, Dir Inst. of Urban and Regional Devt 1989–92; Special Adviser to Sec. of State for the Environment 1991–94; Bartlett Prof. of Planning and Regeneration, Bartlett School of Planning, Univ. Coll., London 1992–; mem. South East Econ. Planning Council 1966–79, Social Science Research Council 1974–80; mem. Academia Europea. *Publications:* The Industries of London 1962, London 2000 1963, Labour's New Frontiers 1964, Land Values (ed.) 1965, The World Cities 1966, Von Thünen's Isolated State (ed.) 1966, Theory and Practice of Regional Planning 1970, The Containment of Urban England 1973, Planning and Urban Growth 1973, Urban and Regional Planning 1974, Europe 2000 1977, Growth Centres in the European System 1980, Great Planning Disasters 1980, The Inner City in Context (ed.) 1981, Silicon Landscapes (ed.) 1985, Can Rail Save the City? 1985, High-Tech America 1986, Western Sunrise 1987, Cities of Tomorrow 1988, The Carrier Wave 1988, London 2001 1989, The Rise of the Gunbelt 1992, Technopoles of the World 1993, Sociable Cities 1998, Cities in Civilization 1998, Urban Future 21 2000, Working Capital 2002, The Polycentric Metropolis 2006. *Honours:* Hon. Fellow, St Catherine's Coll., Cambridge 1988; nine hon. degrees; Gill Memorial Prize, Royal Geographical Soc. 1968, Adolphe Bentinck Prize 1979, Founder's Medal, Royal Geographical Soc. 1988, Prix Vautrin Lud 2001, Gold Medal, Royal Town Planning Inst. 2003, Deputy Prime Minister's Lifetime Achievement Award 2005, Balzan Int. Prize 2005. *Address:* 12 Queens Road, London, W5 2SA (home); Institute of Community Studies, 18 Victoria Park Square, London, E2 9PF (office); Bartlett School of Planning, University College London, Wates House, 22 Gordon Street, London, WC1H 0QB, England. *Telephone:* (20) 8997-3717 (home); (20) 8810-8723 (office). *Fax:* (20) 7679-7502 (office). *E-mail:* p.hall@ucl.ac.uk (office).

HALL, Sir Peter Reginald Frederick, Kt, CBE, MA; British theatre director and film director; b. 22 Nov. 1930, Bury St Edmunds, Suffolk; s. of late Reginald Hall and Grace Hall; m. 1st Leslie Caron 1956 (divorced 1965); one s. one d.; m. 2nd Jacqueline Taylor 1965 (divorced 1981); one s. one d.; m. 3rd Maria Ewing 1982 (divorced 1989); one d.; m. 4th Nicola Frei 1990; one d. *Education:* Perse School and St Catharine's Coll., Cambridge. *Career:* produced and acted in over 20 plays at Cambridge; first professional production The Letter, Windsor 1953; produced in repertory at Windsor, Worthing and Oxford Playhouse; two Shakespearean productions for Arts Council; Artistic Dir Elizabethan Theatre Co. 1953; Asst Dir London Arts Theatre 1954, Dir 1955–57; formed own producing co., Int. Playwright's Theatre 1957; Man. Dir Royal Shakespeare Co., Stratford-upon-Avon and Aldwych Theatre, London 1960–68 (resgnd), Assoc. Dir –1973; mem. Arts Council 1969–73; Co-Dir, Nat. Theatre (now Royal Nat. Theatre) with Lord Olivier April-Nov. 1973, Dir 1973–88; f. Peter Hall Co. 1988; Artistic Dir Glyndebourne 1984–90; Artistic Dir The Old Vic 1997; Wortham Chair in Performing Arts, Houston Univ., Tex. 1999; Chancellor Kingston Univ. 2000–; Dir Kingston Theatre 2003–; Assoc. Prof. of Drama, Warwick Univ. 1964–67; mem. Bd Playhouse Theatre 1990–91; acted in The Pedestrian (film) 1973. *Productions:* Blood Wedding, The Immoralist, The Lesson, South, Mourning Becomes Electra, Waiting for Godot, Burnt Flowerbed, Waltz of the Toreadors, Camino Real, Gigi, Wrong Side of the Park, Love's Labours Lost, Cymbeline, Twelfth Night, A Midsummer Night's Dream, Coriolanus, Two Gentlemen of Verona, Troilus and Cressida, Ondine, Romeo and Juliet, The Wars of the Roses (London Theatre Critics' Award for Best Dir 1963), Becket, The Collection, Cat on a Hot Tin Roof, The Rope Dancers (on Broadway), The Moon and Sixpence (opera, Sadler's Wells), Henry VI (parts 1, 2 and 3), Richard III, Richard II, Henry IV (parts 1 and 2), Henry V, Eh?, The Homecoming (London Theatre Critics' Award for Best Dir 1965, Antoinette Perry Award for Best Dir 1966), Moses and Aaron (opera, Covent Garden), Hamlet (London Theatre Critics' Award for Best Dir 1965), The Government Inspector, The Magic Flute (opera), Staircase, Work is a Four Letter Word (film) 1968, Macbeth, Midsummer Night's Dream (film) 1969, Three into Two Won't Go (film) 1969, A Delicate Balance, Dutch Uncle, Landscape and Silence, Perfect Friday (film) 1971, The Battle of Shrivings, La Calisto (opera, Glyndebourne Festival) 1970, The Knot Garden (opera, Covent Garden) 1970, Eugene Onegin (opera, Covent Garden) 1971, Old Times 1971, Tristan and Isolde (opera, Covent Garden) 1971, All Over 1972, Il Ritorno d'Ulisse (opera, Glyndebourne Festival) 1972, Alte Zeiten (Burgtheater, Vienna) 1972, Via Galactica (musical, Broadway) 1972, The Homecoming (film) 1973, Marriage of Figaro (opera, Glyndebourne) 1973, The Tempest 1973, Landscape (film) 1974, Akenfield (film) 1974, Happy Days 1974, John Gabriel Borkman 1974, No Man's Land 1975, Judgement 1975, Hamlet 1975, Tamburlaine the Great 1976, Don Giovanni (opera, Glyndebourne Festival) 1977, Volpone (Nat.

Theatre) 1977, Bedroom Farce (Nat. Theatre) 1977, The Country Wife (Nat. Theatre) 1977, The Cherry Orchard (Nat. Theatre) 1978, Macbeth (Nat. Theatre) 1978, Betrayal (Nat. Theatre) 1978, Così Fan Tutte (opera, Glyndebourne) 1978, Fidelio (opera, Glyndebourne) 1979, Amadeus (Nat. Theatre) 1979, Betrayal (New York) 1980, Othello (Nat. Theatre) 1980, Amadeus (New York) (Tony Award for Best Dir 1981) 1980, Family Voices (Nat. Theatre) 1981, The Oresteia (Nat. Theatre) 1981, A Midsummer Night's Dream (opera, Glyndebourne) 1981, The Importance of Being Earnest (Nat. Theatre) 1982, Other Places (Nat. Theatre) 1982, The Ring (operas, Bayreuth Festival) 1983, Jean Seberg (musical, Nat. Theatre) 1983, L'Incoronazione di Poppea (opera, Glyndebourne) 1984, Animal Farm (Nat. Theatre) 1984, Coriolanus (Nat. Theatre) 1984, Yonadab (Nat. Theatre) 1985, Carmen (opera, Glyndebourne) 1985, (Metropolitan Opera) 1986, Albert Herring (opera, Glyndebourne) 1985, The Petition (New York and Nat. Theatre) 1986, Simon Boccanegra (opera, Glyndebourne) 1986, Salome (opera, Los Angeles) 1986, Coming in to Land (Nat. Theatre) 1986, Antony and Cleopatra (Nat. Theatre) 1987, Entertaining Strangers (Nat. Theatre) 1987, La Traviata (Glyndebourne) 1987, Falstaff (Glyndebourne) 1988, Salome (Covent Garden) 1988, Cymbeline (Nat. Theatre) 1988, The Winter's Tale (Nat. Theatre) 1988, The Tempest 1988, Orpheus Descending 1988, Salome (opera, Chicago) 1988, Albert Herring 1989, Merchant of Venice 1989, She's Been Away (TV) 1989, New Year (opera, Houston and Glyndebourne) 1989, The Wild Duck 1990, Born Again (musical) 1990, The Homecoming 1990, Orpheus Descending (film) 1990, Twelfth Night 1991, The Rose Tattoo 1991, Tartuffe 1991, The Camomile Lawn (TV) 1991, The Magic Flute 1992, Four Baboons Adoring the Sun (New York) 1992, Siena Red 1992, All's Well That Ends Well (RSC) 1992, The Gift of the Gorgon (RSC) 1992, The Magic Flute (LA) 1993, Separate Tables 1993, Lysistrata 1993, She Stoops to Conquer 1993, Piaf (musical) 1993, An Absolute Turkey (Le Dindon) 1994, On Approval 1994, Hamlet 1994, Jacob (TV) 1994, Never Talk to Strangers (film) 1995, Julius Caesar (RSC) 1995, The Master Builder 1995, The Final Passage (TV) 1996, Mind Millie for Me 1996, The Oedipus Plays (Nat. Theatre at Epidaurus and Nat. Theatre) 1996, A School for Wives 1995, A Streetcar Named Desire 1997, The Seagull 1997, Waste 1997, Waiting for Godot 1997, 1998, King Lear 1997, The Misanthrope 1998, Major Barbara 1998, Simon Boccanegra (Glyndebourne) 1998, Filumena 1998, Amadeus 1998, Kafka's Dick 1998, Measure for Measure (LA) 1999, A Midsummer Night's Dream (LA) 1999, Lenny (Queens Theatre) 1999, Amadeus (LA, NY) 1999, Cuckoos 2000, Tantalus (Denver, Colo) 2000, Japes 2000, Romeo and Juliet (LA) 2001, Japes 2001, Troilus and Cressida (NY) 2001, Tantalus 2001, A Midsummer Night's Dream (Glyndebourne) 2001, Otello (Glyndebourne) 2001, Japes (Theatre Royal) 2001, The Royal Family (Theatre Royal) 2001, Lady Windermere's Fan (Theatre Royal) 2002, The Bacchai (Olivier Theatre) 2002, Design for Living (Theatre Royal, Bath) 2003, Betrayal (Theatre Royal, Bath) 2003, The Fight for Barbara (Theatre Royal, Bath) 2003, As You Like It (Theatre Royal, Bath) 2003, Cuckoos (Theatre Royal, Bath) 2003, The Marriage of Figaro (Lyric Opera of Chicago) 2003, Happy Days (Arts Theatre, London) 2003, Man and Superman (Theatre Royal, Bath) 2004, Galileo's Daughter (Theatre Royal, Bath) 2004. *Publications:* The Wars of the Roses 1970, Shakespeare's three Henry VI plays and Richard III (adapted with John Barton), John Gabriel Borkman (English version with Inga-Stina Ewbank) 1975, Peter Hall's Diaries: The Story of a Dramatic Battle 1983, Animal Farm: a stage adaptation 1986, The Wild Duck 1990, Making an Exhibition of Myself (autobiog.) 1993, An Absolute Turkey (new trans. of Feydeau's Le Dindon, with Nicki Frei) 1994, The Master Builder (with Inga-Stina Ewbank) 1995, Mind Millie for Me (new trans. of Feydeau's Occupe-toi d'Amélie, with Nicki Frei), The Necessary Theatre 1999, Exposed by the Mask 2000, Shakespeare's Advice to the Players 2003. *Honours:* Hon. Fellow St Catharine's Coll. Cambridge 1964; Chevalier, Ordre des Arts et des Lettres 1965; Dr hc (York) 1966, (Reading) 1973, (Liverpool) 1974, (Leicester) 1977, (Essex) 1993, (Cambridge) 2003; Hon. DSocSc (Birmingham) 1989; Hamburg Univ. Shakespeare Prize 1967, Evening Standard Special Award 1979, Evening Standard Award for Outstanding Achievement in Opera 1981, Evening Standard Best Dir Award for The Oresteia 1981, Evening Standard Best Dir Award for Antony and Cleopatra 1987, South Bank Show Lifetime Achievement Award 1998, Olivier Special Award for Lifetime Achievement 1999, New York Shakespeare Soc. Medal 2003. *Address:* 48 Lamont Road, London, SW10 0HX, England. *E-mail:* phpetard@aol.com (office).

HALL, Philip David; British journalist; b. 8 Jan. 1955, s. of Norman Philip Hall and Olive Jean Hall; m. Marina Thomson 1997; two c. *Education:* Beal Grammar School, Ilford. *Career:* reporter, Dagenham Post 1974–77, Ilford Recorder 1977–80; Sub-Ed. Newham Recorder 1980–84, Weekend Magazine 1984–85; reporter, The People 1985–86, Chief Reporter 1986–89, News Ed. 1989–92; News Ed. Sunday Express 1992–93; Asst Ed. (Features) News of the World 1993–94, Deputy Ed. 1994–95, Ed. 1995–2000; with Max Clifford Assocs 2000–01; Ed.-in-Chief Hello! 2001–02; founder and Chair. Phil Hall Assocs. (public relations) 2004–; mem. Press Complaints Comm. 1998–2000, 2002–. *Address:* Phil Hall Associates, 19 Cato Street, London, W1H 5HR, England (office). *Telephone:* (20) 7535-3350 (office). *E-mail:* info@philhallassociates.com (office). *Website:* www.philhallassociates.com (office).

HALL, Rodney, AM; Australian writer, musician and actor; b. 18 Nov. 1935, s. of D. E. Hall; m. Maureen McPhail 1962; three d. *Education:* City of Bath School for Boys, UK, Brisbane Boys' Coll., Univ. of Queensland. *Career:* leader Baroque Music Group; published over 500 poems in Australia, UK, USA, USSR, Philippines, France, India, several published books of poetry and novels; Creative Arts Fellow ANU 1968, Literary Bd Fellow 1974–80, tutor, New England Univ. Summer School of Music 1967–71, 1977–80; Lecturer, Dept of Foreign Affairs; Recorder, Canberra School of Music 1979–83; Chair. Australia Council 1991–94. *Publications:* Selected Poems 1975, Just Relations 1982, Kisses of the Enemy 1987, Captivity Captive 1988, The Second Bridegroom 1991, The Grisly Wife 1994, The Island in the Mind 1996. *Honours:* Miles Franklin Award 1994. *Address:* c/o Dawn Devery, Australia Council, PO Box 788, Strawberry Hill, NSW 2012, Australia.

HALL, Roger Leighton, BA, MA, DipEd, QSO; British dramatist; b. 17 Jan. 1939, Woodford, Wells, Essex, England; m. Dianne Sturm 1968; one s. one d. *Education:* Victoria Univ., Wellington, New Zealand. *Career:* emigrated to New Zealand 1958; Robert Burns Fellow, Otago Univ. 1977, 1978; Fullbright Visiting Lecturer, Georgetown Univ., DC 2000; mem. PEN New Zealand; Scriptwriters Guild; Arts Foundation of New Zealand, gov. *Publications:* Plays: Glide Time, 1976; Middle Age Spread, 1977; State of the Play, 1978; Prisoners of Mother England, 1979; The Rose, 1981; Hot Water, 1982; Fifty-Fifty, 1982; Multiple Choice, 1984; Dream of Sussex Downs, 1986; The Hansard Show, 1986; The Share Club, 1987; After the Crash, 1988; Conjugal Rites, 1990; By Degrees, 1993; Market Forces, 1995; Social Climbers, 1995; C'mon Black, 1996; The Book Club, 1999; You Gotta Be Joking, 1999; Take a Chance on Me, 2001; A Way of Life, 2001; Spreading Out 2004. Other: Musicals with Philip Norman and A. K. Grant; many plays for radio, television, and children. *Honours:* Hon. DLitt (Victoria Univ.) 1996; Fulbright Travel Award 1982, Turnovsky Award, Outstanding Contribution to the Arts 1987, CNZM 2003. *Address:* c/o Playmarket, PO Box 9767, Wellington, New Zealand. *E-mail:* roger.h@xtra.co.nz.

HALL, Sarah, MLitt; British writer and poet; b. 1974, Cumbria. *Education:* Univ. of Wales, Aberystwyth, St Andrews Univ. *Career:* tutor in creative writing, St Andrews Univ.; emigrated to North Carolina, USA. *Publications:* Haweswater (Betty Trask Award, Commonwealth First Novel Prize 2003) 2002, The Electric Michelangelo 2004, The Carhullan Army 2007. *Address:* c/o Faber and Faber, 3 Queen Square, London, WC1N 3AU, England. *Telephone:* (20) 7465-0045. *Fax:* (20) 7465-0034. *Website:* www.faber.co.uk.

HALLIBURTON, David Garland, BA, MA, PhD; American academic and writer; b. 24 Sept. 1933, San Bernardino, CA; m. 1960, three c. *Education:* University of California-Riverside. *Career:* Asst Prof. of English, 1966–72, Assoc. Prof. of English, Comparative Literature, Modern Thought and Literature, 1972–80, University of California-Riverside, Riverside; Prof. of English, Stanford University, Stanford, CA, 1980–; mem. MLA. *Publications:* Edgar Allan Poe: A Phenomenological View, 1973; Poetic Thinking: An Approach to Heidegger, 1982; The Color of the Sky: A Study of Stephen Crane, 1989; The Fateful Discourse of Worldly Things, 1997. Contributions: periodicals including: Modern Fiction Studies; Papers in Language and Literatures; Studies in Romanticism. *Honours:* Grant, American Philosophical Society, 1970; Fellow, ACLS, 1971–72.

HALLIDAY, Mark, PhD; American poet and academic; b. 1949. *Education:* Brandeis Univ. *Career:* teacher, Wellesley Coll., Univ. of Pennsylvania, West Michigan Univ., Indiana Univ.; teacher of creative writing, Ohio Univ. 1996–. *Publications:* poetry: Little Star 1987, Tasket Street 1992, Selfwolf 1999; non-fiction: The Sighted Singer (with Allen Grossman) 1991, Stevens and the Interpersonal 1991; contrib. to Slate magazine (online). *Honours:* Juniper Prize. *Address:* English Department, 360 Ellis Hall, Ohio University, Athens, OH 45701, USA. *Telephone:* (740) 593-2838. *Fax:* (740) 593-2818. *E-mail:* English.Department@ohio.edu.

HALLIGAN, Marion, BA, DipEd; Australian writer; b. 16 April 1940, Newcastle, NSW; m. Graham James Halligan 1963 (died 1998); one s. one d. *Education:* University of Newcastle. *Career:* several writer-in-residencies; Chair. Word Festival Canberra 1987–93; Chair. Literature Board, Australia Council, 1992–95; mem. Australian Society of Authors; Australian Symposium of Gastronomy. *Publications:* Self Possession, 1987; The Living Hothouse, 1988; The Hanged Man in the Garden, 1989; Spider Cup, 1990; Eat My Words (essays), 1990; Lovers' Knots: A Hundred-Year Novel, 1992; The Worry Box, 1993; Wishbone, 1994; Cockles of the Heart (essays), 1996; Out of the Picture, 1996; Collected Stories, 1997; Those Women Who Go to Hotels (co-author), 1997; The Midwife's Daughters (children's), 1997; The Golden Dress (novel), 1998; The Fog Garden (novel), 2001; The Point (novel), 2003, The Taste of Memory (autobiog.) 2004; contrib. to anthologies and periodicals. *Honours:* Australian Literature Board Grants 1981, 1987, Braille Book of the Year Award 1989, Steele Rudd Award 1991, Age Book of the Year Award 1992, Australian Capital Territory Book of the Year Award, 1993, 2004, 3M Talking Book of the Year Award 1993, Nita B. Kibble Award 1993. *Address:* 6 Caldwell Street, Hackett, ACT 2602, Australia. *Telephone:* (2) 62497120 (office). *E-mail:* wishbone@webone.com.au (office).

HALPERN, Daniel, MFA; American editor and writer; *Editorial Director, The Ecco Press*; b. 11 Sept. 1945, Syracuse, NY; s. of Irving Halpern and Rosemary Halpern; m. Jeanne Carter 1982; one d. *Education:* California State Univ. and Columbia Univ., New York. *Career:* Ed.-in-Chief, The Ecco Press (Antaeus) 1970–; Adjunct Prof., Columbia Univ. 1975–; Dir Nat. Poetry Series 1978–; Visiting Prof., Princeton Univ. 1975–76, 1987–88; Nat. Endowment for the Arts Fellowship 1974, 1975, 1987; Robert Frost Fellowship, CAPS; Guggenheim Fellow 1988. *Publications:* poetry: Travelling on Credit 1972, Street Fire 1975, Life Among Others 1978, Seasonal Rights 1982, Tango 1987, Halpern's Guide to the Essential Restaurants of Italy 1990, Foreign Neon

1991, Selected Poems 1994, Antaeus 1970 1996, Something Shining 1998; ed. several anthologies. *Honours:* numerous awards including Carey Thomas Award for Creative Publishing. *Address:* The Ecco Press, 100 West Broad Street, Hopewell, NJ 08525, USA. *Telephone:* (609) 466-4748 (office).

HALSEY, Alan, BA; British bookseller and poet; b. 22 Sept. 1949, Croydon, Surrey, England. *Career:* mem. Thomas Lovell Beddoes Soc., David Jones Soc. *Publications:* Yearspace 1979, Another Loop in Our Days 1980, Present State 1981, Perspectives on the Reach 1981, The Book of Coming Forth in Official Secrecy 1981, Auto Dada Cafe 1987, A Book of Changes 1988, Five Years Out 1989, Reasonable Distance 1992, The Text of Shelley's Death 1995, A Robin Hood Book 1996, Fit to Print (with Karen McCormack) 1998, Days of '49 (with Gavin Selerie) 1999, Wittgenstein's Devil: Selected Writings, 1978–98 2000, Sonatas and Preliminary Sketches 2000, Dante's Barber Shop 2001, Lives of the Poets: A Preliminary Count (with Martin Corless-Smith) 2002, Death's Jest Book, by Thomas Lovell Beddoes (ed.) 2003, In Addition: Seventeen Lives of the Poets (trans.) 2004, The Epigrams & Fragments of Mercurialis the Younger 2004, Marginalien 2005; contrib. to Critical Quarterly, Conjunctions, North Dakota Quarterly, Writing, Ninth Decade, Poetica, South West Review, Poetry Wales, Poesie Europe, O Ars, Figs, Interstate, Prospice, Reality Studios, Fragmente, Screens and Tasted Parallels, Avec, Purge, Grille, Acumen, Shearsman, Oasis, New American Writing, Agenda, Colorado Review, Talisman, PN Review, Resurgence, West Coast Line, The Gig, Boxkite, The Paper, Chicago Review, Envelope, Ecorché, Fence, Kiosk, New Arcadians Journal, Queen Street Quarterly. *Address:* 40 Crescent Road, Nether Edge, Sheffield, S7 1HN, England. *E-mail:* alan@nethedge.demon.co .uk (office). *Website:* www.westhousebooks.co.uk (office).

HAMAD, Turki-al; Saudi Arabian writer and academic; b. 1952, Jordan. *Education:* univs in USA. *Career:* moved to Saudi Arabia as a child; taught political science, Riyadh –1995; full-time writer 1995–. *Publications:* Atyaf al-aziqah al-mahjurah trilogy: Adama, Shumaisi, Karadib. *Address:* c/o Saqi Books, 26 Westbourne Grove, London, W2 5RH, England. *Website:* www .saqibooks.com.

HAMBRICK-STOWE, Charles Edwin, BA, MDiv, MA, PhD; American writer; b. 4 Feb. 1948, Worcester, MA; m. Elizabeth Anne Hambrick-Stowe 1971, two s. one d. *Education:* Hamilton College, Pacific School of Religion, Boston University Graduate School. *Career:* Religion Columnist, Evening Sun Newspaper, Carrol County, MD, 1982–85; mem. American Historical Asscn; American Society of Church History; American Acad. of Religion. *Publications:* Massachusetts Militia Companies and the Officers of the Lexington Alarm, 1976; Practice of Piety: Puritan Devotional Disciplines in 17th Century New England, 1982; Early New England Meditative Poetry: Anne Bradstreet and Edward Taylor, 1988; Theology and Identity: Traditions, Movements and Issues in the United Church of Christ, 1990; Charles G. Finney and The Spirit of American Evangelicalism, 1996; Living Theological Heritage: Colonial and Early National Beginnings, 1998. Contributions: Reference works, books and journals. *Honours:* Jamestown Prize for Early American History 1980.

HAMBURGER, Anne Ellen; British poet, writer, actress and teacher; b. (Anne Beresford), 10 Sept. 1928, Redhill, Surrey, England; m. Michael Hamburger 1951; one s. two d. *Education:* Central School of Dramatic Art, London. *Career:* actress, various repertory companies,1946–48, BBC Radio 1960–74; teacher; General Council, Poetry Soc. 1976–78; cttee mem., Aldeburgh Poetry Festival 1989, adviser on agenda, Editorial Bd 1993–96. *Publications:* poetry: Walking Without Moving, 1967; The Lair, 1968; The Courtship, 1972; Footsteps on Snow, 1972; The Curving Shore, 1975; Songs a Thracian Taught Me, 1980; The Songs of Almut, 1980; The Sele of the Morning, 1988; Charm with Stones (Lyrik im Hölderlinturm), 1993; Landscape With Figures, 1994; Selected and New Poems, 1997; No Place for Cowards, 1998; Hearing Things, 2002; Collected Poems 2006. Other: Struck by Apollo (radio play, with Michael Hamburger), 1965; The Villa (radio short story), 1968; Alexandros Poems of Vera Lungu (trans.), 1974; Duet for Three Voices (dramatized poems for Anglia TV), 1982; Snapshots from an Album, 1884–1895, 1992. Contributions: periodicals. *Address:* Marsh Acres, Middleton, Saxmundham, Suffolk IP17 3NH, England (office). *Telephone:* (1728) 648247 (home).

HAMBURGER, Philip Paul, BA, MS; American writer; b. 2 July 1914, Wheeling, WV; m. 1st Edith Iglauer 1942; m. 2nd Anna Walling Matson 1968, two s. *Education:* Johns Hopkins University, Columbia University. *Career:* staff writer, The New Yorker, 1939–; mem. Authors League of America; PEN USA; Board of Dirs, Authors League Fund; National Press Club, Washington; Century Asscn; Fellow, American Acad. of Arts and Sciences. *Publications:* The Oblong Blur and Other Odysseys, 1949; J. P. Marquand, Esquire, 1952; Mayor Watching and Other Pleasures, 1958; Our Man Stanley, 1963; An American Notebook, 1965; Curious World, A New Yorker at Large, 1987; Friends Talking in the Night, 1999; Matters of State – A Political Excursion, 2000. Contributions: The New Yorker. *Honours:* New York Public Library Literary Lion Award, 1986; George Polk Career Award, 1994; Columbia Journalism Alumni Award, 1997. *Address:* c/o The New Yorker, 4 Times Square, New York, NY 10036, USA.

HAMDARD, Peer Syed Sufaid Shah; Pakistani journalist; *Chief Editor, Daily Wabdat. Career:* started career as journalist with Anjam newspaper 1960, has also worked for Bang-i-Haram and Shabbaz; founding Ed. Alwahdat newspaper; currently Ed. Daily Wabdat; Chair. Frontier Eds Council; Vice-Pres. CPNE. *Honours:* Tamgha-i-Imtiaz 1998 President's Award for Pride of

Performance 2005. *Address:* Daily Wabdat, 20 Islamia Club Building, Khyber Bazar, Peshawar, Pakistan (office).

HAMED, Abdul Samay; Afghan writer, editor and poet; *Editor, Telaya magazine;* b. 1967, Badakhshan province. *Education:* trained as a physician. *Career:* helped start ten publications in Afghanistan until forced into exile by the Taliban regime 1998; returned to Afghanistan 2002; f. Asscn for the Defence of Afghan Writers' Rights 2002; f., writer and Ed. Telaya magazine 2002–; Dir Mediothek media centre. *Publications include:* Mountains of our Minds (with Bob McKerrow) 2004; poetry: Daaman-e Dosheeza-e Daryaacha, Hazaar-o Duomeen Shab, Dar Aakher-e Bayaanya-e Dood, Hendwaanah. *Honours:* Cttee to Protect Journalists Int. Press Freedom Award 2003. *Address:* c/o Hamid Zazai, Co-ordinator Mediothek Community Centers, Chahar-ye Qala-ye Fatullah Khan, Next to Medina Bazar, Kabul, Afghanistan. *Telephone:* (70) 284497. *E-mail:* samay_hamed1@hotmail.com.

HAMELIN, Claude, BPed, BSc, MSc, PhD; Canadian poet, writer and scientist; b. 25 Aug. 1943, Montréal, QC; m. Renée Artinian 1970, one s. one d. *Publications:* poetry: Fables des quatre-temps, 1990; Lueurs froides, 1991; Nef des fous, 1992; Néant bleu/Nada azul/Blue Nothingness, 1994; novel: Roman d'un quartier, 1993. Contributions: anthologies and journals.

HAMILL, (William) Pete; American journalist and writer; b. 24 June 1934, New York, NY; m. 1st Ramona Negron 1962 (divorced 1970); two d.; m. 2nd Fukiko Aoki 1987. *Education:* Pratt Inst., Mexico City Coll. *Career:* reporter, later columnist, 1960–74, 1988–93, New York Post; Contributing Ed. Saturday Evening Post 1963–64; Contributor, Village Voice and New York Magazine 1974–; Columnist, New York Daily News 1975–79, 1982–84, Esquire Magazine 1989–91; Ed. Mexico City News 1986–87; mem. Writers Guild of America. *Publications:* fiction: A Killing for Christ 1968, The Gift 1973, Flesh and Blood 1977, Dirty Laundry 1978, Deadly Piece 1979, The Guns of Heaven 1983, Loving Women 1990, Tokyo Sketches 1992, Snow in August 1997, Forever 2002, North River 2007; non-fiction: Irrational Ravings 1971, The Invisible City: A New York Sketchbook 1980, A Drinking Life: A Memoir 1994, Tools as Art: The Hechinger Collection 1995, Piecework 1996, News is a Verb 1998, Why Sinatra Matters 1998, Diego Rivera 1999, Subway Series Reader 2000, Downtown: My Manhattan 2004; screenplays: Doc 1971, Badge 373 1973, Liberty 1986, Neon Empire 1987; Contribs to many periodicals. *Honours:* Meyer Berger Award, Columbia School of Journalism 1962, Newspaper Reporters Asscn Award 1962, 25 Year Achievement Award, Society of Silurians 1989; Peter Kihss Award 1992. *Address:* c/o Esther Newberg, International Creative Management, 40 West 57th Street, New York, NY 10019, USA (office). *Telephone:* (212) 556-5600 (office). *E-mail:* hamill@petehamill.com (home). *Website:* www.petehamill.com (home).

HAMILL, Sam Patrick; American poet, publisher, editor and translator; b. 9 May 1943, California; m. 1st Nancy Larsen 1964 (divorced); one d.; m. 2nd Tree Swenson 1973 (divorced); m. 3rd Gray Foster. *Education:* Los Angeles Valley College, University of California at Santa Barbara. *Career:* Co-Founder, Copper Canyon Press, 1972–; Writer-in-Residence, Reed College, University of Alaska, South Utah State University, South Oregon College, Austin College, Trinity College, 1974–, Dept of Correction, Washington, Alaska, California, 1976–88; Columnist, Port Townsend Leader, 1990–93; mem. PEN American Center; Poetry Society of America; Acad. of American Poets. *Publications:* poetry: Heroes of the Teton Mythos, 1973; Petroglypics, 1975; Uintah Blue, 1975; The Calling Across Forever, 1976; The Book of Elegaic Geography, 1978; Triada, 1978; Animae, 1980; Fatal Pleasure, 1984; The Nootka Rose, 1987; Passport, 1988; A Dragon in the Clouds, 1989; Mandala, 1991; Destination Zero: Poems 1970–1995, 1995; essays: At Home in the World, 1980; Basho's Ghost, 1989; A Poet's Work: The Other Side of Poetry, 1990; editor or co-editor of anthologies, selected poems, collections, including: Endless River: Li Po and Tu Fu: A Friendship in Poetry, 1993; Love Poems from the Japanese, 1994; Twenty-Five Years of Poetry from Copper Canyon Press, 1996. Trans. or co-trans. of Chinese, Estonian, Latin, Japanese and ancient Greek works. Contributions: poetry, essays and trans to numerous anthologies and literary magazines. *Honours:* College Ed.'s Award, Best College Journal, Co-ordinating Council of Literary Magazines, 1972; Washington Gov.'s Arts Awards to Copper Canyon Press, 1975, 1990; National Endowment for the Arts Fellowship, 1980; Pacific Northwest Booksellers' Award, 1980; Guggenheim Fellowship, 1983; Pushcart Prizes, 1989, 1996; Lila Wallace-Reader's Digest Writing Fellowship, 1992–93.

HAMILTON, Carol Jean Barber, BS, MA; American writer, poet and educator; b. 23 Aug. 1935, Enid, Okla; m. (divorced); two s. one d. *Education:* Phillips Univ., Univ. of Cen. Oklahoma. *Career:* Prof. of English, Rose State Coll.; Prof. in Creative Studies, Univ. of Cen. Oklahoma; Poet Laureate of Oklahoma 1995–97; mem. Poetry Soc. of Oklahoma, Individual Artists of Oklahoma, Mid Oklahoma Writers, American Acad. of Poetry, Soc. of Children's Book Writers and Illustrators, Authors' Guild. *Publications:* juvenile: The Dawn Seekers 1987, Legends of Poland 1993, The Mystery of Black Mesa 1995, I'm Not From Neptune 2003; poetry: Daring the Wind 1988, Once the Dust 1992, Breaking Bread, Breaking Silence, Legerdemain, Gold: Greatest Hits, I, People of the Llano, Vanishing Point; contrib. to Christian Science Monitor, Commonweal, New York Quarterly, Christian Century, Arizona Quarterly, Hawaii Review, Midwest Quarterly Review, Oklahoma Today, Kansas Quarterly, Arkansas Review, New Orleans Review, Southern Poetry Review, Chariton Review, Windsor Review, Baltimore Review, Nimrod, Sojourners, Wisconsin Review, Southwester in American Literature,

International Poetry Review. *Honours:* Oklahoma Book Award for Poetry 1992, Byline Literary Award for poetry 1994, for short story 1987, Pegasus Award 1995, Chiron Review Chapbook Award 2000, David Ray Poetry Award 2000, Warren Keith Lewis Poetry Award 2002. *Address:* 9608 Sonata Court, Midwest City, OK 73130, USA (home). *Telephone:* (405) 732-4336 (home). *E-mail:* hamiltoncj@earthlink.net (home). *Website:* www.carolhamilton.org (home).

HAMILTON, Jane, BA; American writer; b. 1957, Oak Park, IL; m. Robert Willard 1982, two c. *Education:* Carleton College, Northfield, MN. *Publications:* The Book of Ruth, UK edn as The Frogs Are Still Singing, 1989; A Map of the World, 1994; The Short History of a Prince, 1998; Disobedience, 2000. *Honours:* Ernest Hemingway Foundation Award, PEN American Center, 1989.

HAMILTON, John Maxwell, BA, MS, PhD; American academic and writer; *Dean and Professor, Manship School of Mass Communication;* b. 28 March 1947, Evanston, Ill.; m. Regina Frances Nalewajek 1975; one s. *Education:* Marquette Univ., Univ. of New Hampshire, Boston Univ., George Washington Univ. *Career:* reporter, Milwaukee Journal 1967–69; journalist, Washington, DC 1973–75; foreign corresp., Latin America 1976–78; Special Asst and Asst Admin., Agency for Int. Devt, Washington, DC 1978–81; Staff Assoc., Foreign Affairs Sub-cttee on Int. Econ. Policy and Trade, US House of Reps, Washington, DC 1981–82; Chief US Foreign Policy Corresp., Int. Reporting Information Systems, Washington, DC 1982–83; Dir Main Street America and the Third World, Washington, DC 1985–87; Sr Counsellor, World Bank, Washington, DC 1983–85, 1987–92; commentator, Market Place Public Radio 1990–2003; Dean and Prof., Manship School of Mass Communication 1992–; Hopkins Breazeale Foundation Prof., Louisiana State Univ. at Baton Rouge 1998; Dir Treas. Int. Center for Journalists 1989–; mem. Bd Dirs Lamar Advertising; Fellow, Shorenstein Center, Kennedy School, Harvard 2002; mem. Asscn of Schools of Journalism and Mass Communication, Soc. of Professional Journalists, Council on Foreign Relations 2004–. *Publications:* Main Street America and the Third World 1986, Edgar Snow: A Biography 1988, Entangling Alliances: How the Third World Shapes Our Lives 1990, Hold the Press: The Inside Story on Newspapers (with George Krimsky) 1996, Casanova Was a Book Lover: And Other Naked Facts and Provocative Curiosities About Reading, Writing and Publishing 2000; contrib. to books, scholarly journals and general periodicals and newspapers. *Honours:* many grants, Los Angeles Times Critic's Choice 1988, Sigma Delta Chi-Kappa Tau Alpha Research Award 1988, Marquette Univ. By-line Award 1993, Second Place, Green Eyeshade Awards 1999, 2000, Freedom Forum Journalism Admin. of the Year 2003. *Address:* c/o Office of the Dean, Manship School of Mass Communication, Louisiana State University, Baton Rouge, LA 70803-0001 (office); 3 Hidden Oak Lane, Baton Rouge, LA 70810, USA (home). *Telephone:* (225) 819-8510 (home). *Fax:* (225) 578-2125 (office). *E-mail:* jhamilt@lsu.edu.

HAMILTON, Peter F.; British writer; b. 1960, Rutland, England. *Publications:* Mindstar Rising (Greg Mandel series) 1993, A Quantum Murder (Greg Mandel series) 1994, The Nano Flower (Greg Mandel series) 1995, The Reality Dysfunction (book one, Night's Dawn trilogy) 1996, The Neutronium Alchemist (book two, Night's Dawn trilogy) 1997, Escape Route (novella) 1997, The Web: Lightstorm (juvenile) 1998, A Second Chance at Eden (short stories) 1998, The Naked God (book three, Night's Dawn trilogy) 1999, The Confederation Handbook 2000, Futures 2001, Fallen Dragon 2001, Watching Trees Grow 2002, Misspent Youth 2002, Pandora's Star 2004, Judas Unchained 2005, The Dreaming Void 2007; contrib. short stories to magazines, including Fear, Interzone, and to anthologies, including In Dreams, New Worlds. *Address:* c/o Pan Macmillan, 20 New Wharf Road, London, N1 9RR, England.

HAMILTON, Priscilla (see Gellis, Roberta Leah)

HAMILTON-PATERSON, James, BA; British writer and poet; b. 6 Nov. 1941, London, England. *Education:* Windlesham House, Sussex, Bickley Hall, Kent, King's School, Canterbury, Exeter Coll., Oxford, King's Coll., London. *Career:* teacher in Hertfordshire –1961, in Tripoli, Libya 1966; orderly, St Stephen's Hospital, London 1966–68; staff, New Statesman 1969–74; features ed., Nova magazine 1974–75; science columnist, Das Magazin, Zurich 2000–02; Die Weltwocher 2002–; currently resides in the Philippines and Tuscany, Italy. *Publications:* poetry: Option Three 1974, Dutch Alps 1984; novels: Playing with Water 1987, Gerontius (Whitbread First Novel Award) 1989, The Bell-Boy (aka That Time in Malomba) 1990, Griefwork 1993, Ghosts of Manila 1994, Loving Monsters 2001, Cooking with Fernet Branca 2004, Amazing Disgrace 2006; short story collections: The View from Mount Dog 1986, The Music 1995; juvenile: Flight Underground 1969, The House in the Waves 1970, Hostage! 1980; non-fiction: Very Personal War: The Story of Cornelius Hawkridge 1971, Mummies: Death and Life in Ancient Egypt (with Carol Andrews) 1978, Seven-Tenths 1992, The Great Deep: The Sea and Its Thresholds 1993, America's Boy: A Century of Colonialism in the Philippines 1998, Three Miles Down 1998. *Honours:* Oxford Newdigate Prize 1964. *Address:* c/o Faber and Faber Ltd, 3 Queen Square, London, WC1N 3AU, England.

HAMLYN, David Walter, BA, MA; British philosopher, academic and writer; *Professor Emeritus of Philosophy, Birkbeck College, London;* b. 1 Oct. 1924, Plymouth, England; m. Eileen Carlyle Litt 1949; one s. one d. *Education:* Exeter Coll., Oxford. *Career:* Research Fellow, Corpus Christi Coll., Oxford,

1950–53; Lecturer, Jesus Coll., Oxford 1953–54; Lecturer, Birkbeck Coll., Univ. of London 1954–63, Reader 1963–64, Prof. of Philosophy and Head of Dept of Philosophy 1964–88, Head of Dept of Classics 1981–86, Vice-Master 1983–88, Fellow 1988, Prof. Emer. of Philosophy 1988–; Ed. Mind 1972–84; Consulting Ed., Journal of Medical Ethics, 1981–90; mem. Aristotelian Soc. (Pres. 1977–78), Univ. of London Senate 1981–87, National Cttee for Philosophy 1986–92 (Hon. Vice-Pres. 1992–2003), Royal Inst. of Philosophy (mem. Council 1968–, mem. Exec. Cttee 1971–97, Vice-Chair. 1991–95). *Publications:* The Psychology of Perception 1957, Sensation and Perception 1961, Aristotle's De Anima, Books II–III 1968, The Theory of Knowledge 1970, Experience and the Growth of Understanding 1978, Schopenhauer 1980, Perception, Learning and the Self 1983, Metaphysics 1984, History of Western Philosophy 1987, In and Out of the Black Box 1990, Being a Philosopher 1992, Understanding Perception 1996; contribs to books and professional journals. *Address:* 38 Smithy Knoll Road, Hope Valley, Calver, Derbyshire, S32 3XW, England. *Telephone:* (1433) 631326.

HAMMAD, Suheir; Palestinian/American poet and political activist; b. 25 Oct. 1973, Amman, Jordan. *Career:* emigrated with family to USA aged five; frequent readings and radio appearances. *Performance:* Russell Simmons Presents Def Poetry Jam on Broadway (original cast mem. and writer) (TONY Award for Special Theatrical Event) 2003. *Plays:* Blood Trinity (New York Hip Hop Theater Festival) 2002, ReOrientalism (libretto, commissioned by Center for Cultural Exchange) 2003, Half A Lifetime (producer, documentary). *Publications:* Born Palestinian, Born Black 1996, Drops of This Story 1996; contrib. to anthologies and periodicals, including The Amsterdam News, Black Renaissance/Renaissance Noire, Brilliant Corners, Clique, Drum Voices Revue, Essence, Long Shot, Atlanta Review, Bomb, Brooklyn Bridge, Fierce, Stress Hip-Hop Magazine, Quarterly Black Review of Books, Color Lines, Spheric, The Olive Tree Review, The Hunter Envoy, Meridians, Signs, 33 Things Every Girl Should Know About Women's History. *Honours:* Hunter Coll. Audre Lorde Writing Award 1995, 2000, Morris Center for Healing Poetry Award 1996, New York Mills Artist Residency 1998, Van Lier Fellowship 1999, Asian/Pacific/American Studies Inst. at NYU Emerging Artist Award 2001. *E-mail:* suheir@suheirhammad.com. *Website:* www.suheirhammad.com.

HAMMARSTRÖM, Stina Margareta, MA; Swedish editor and fmr publishing executive; b. 21 Feb. 1945, Stockholm; d. of Sven Hammarström and Karin Hammarström; m. Gösta Åberg 1979; one d. *Career:* Ed. Bokförlaget Prisma AB (Publrs), Stockholm 1970–79; Publr Hammarström & Åberg Bokförlag AB 1979–90; apptd Ed. AB Rabén & Sjögren Bokförlag, Stockholm 1990; now freelance ed. *Address:* Föreningsvägen 33, 12047 Enskede Gård, Sweden (home). *Telephone:* (8) 918894 (office). *E-mail:* stina.hammarstrom@telia.com (office).

HAMMER, David Lindley, BA, JD; American advocate and writer; b. 6 June 1929, Newton, Ia; s. of Neal Paul Hammer and Agnes Marilyn Hammer (née Reece); m. Audrey Lowe 1953; one s. two d. *Education:* Grinnell Coll., Univ. of Iowa Law School. *Career:* served in US Army 1951–53; called to the Bar of Iowa 1956, US Dist Court (Northern Dist) Iowa 1959, US Dist Court (Southern Dist) Iowa 1969, US Supreme Court 1977, US Court Appeals (8th Circuit) 1996; Partner, Hammer Simon & Jensen, Galena, Ill. and Iowa; mem. Grievance Comm., Iowa Supreme Court 1973–85, Advisory Rules Cttee 1986–92; mem. Bd Dirs Linwood Cemetery Asscn 1973– (Pres. 1983–84), Dubuque Museum of Art 1998–2001 (Hon. Dir), Finley Hosp. (also Past Pres. and Hon. Dir), Finley Foundation 1988–95; Past Campaign Chair. and Past Pres. United Way; fmr mem. Bd Dirs Carnegie Stout Public Library; Fellow, American Coll. of Trial Lawyers; mem. ABA, Young Lawyers Iowa (Past Pres.), Iowa Defense Counsel Asscn (Pres. 1991–92, Del. to Defense Research Inst. 1992–93), Asscn of Defense Trial Attorneys (mem. Exec. Council 1983–86, Past Chair. Iowa Chapter), Iowa State Bar Asscn (Past Chair. Continuing Legal Educ. Cttee), Iowa Acad. of Trial Lawyers, Dubuque Co. Bar Asscn (Past Pres.), Baker Street Irregulars; Republican. *Publications:* Poems From the Ledge 1980, The Game is Afoot 1983, For the Sake of the Game 1986, The 22nd Man 1989, To Play the Game 1990, Skewed Sherlock 1992, The Worth of the Game 1992, The Quest 1993, My Dear Watson 1994, The Before Breakfast Pipe 1995, A Dangerous Game 1997, The Vital Essence 1999, A Talent for Murder 2000, Yonder in the Gaslight 2000, Straight Up With a Twist 2001, You Heard What Jesse Said 2002, Heaven Will Protect My Working Girl 2004, College Fairest of My Dreams 2004, Cases of Identity 2006; contrib. to American Journal of Philately, Baker Street Journal, Sherlock Holmes Journal. *Address:* Hammer, Simon & Jensen, 770 Main Street, The Steele Centre, Dubuque, IA 52001-6820 (office); Laurel Cottage, 720 Laurel Park Road, Dubuque, IA 52003, USA (home). *Telephone:* (563) 583-4010 (office); 583-3730 (home). *Fax:* (563) 583-3402 (office). *E-mail:* dhammer@hammerlawoffices.com (office).

HAMMES, Gordon G., PhD; American biochemist, academic and fmr university vice-chancellor; *University Distinguished Service Professor of Biochemistry, Medical Center, Duke University;* b. 10 Aug. 1934, Fond du Lac, Wis.; s. of Jacob Hammes and Betty (Sadoff) Hammes; m. Judith Ellen Frank 1959; one s. two d. *Education:* Princeton Univ. and Univ. of Wisconsin. *Career:* Postdoctoral Fellow, Max Planck Inst. für physikalische Chemie, Göttingen, FRG 1959–60; instructor, subsequently Assoc. Prof., MIT, Cambridge, Mass. 1960–65; Prof., Cornell Univ. 1965–88, Chair. Dept of Chem. 1970–75, Horace White Prof. of Chem. and Biochemistry 1975–88, Dir Biotechnology Program 1983–88; Prof., Univ. of Calif., Santa Barbara

1988–91, Vice-Chancellor for Academic Affairs 1988–91; Prof., Duke Univ., Durham, NC 1991–, Vice-Chancellor Duke Univ. Medical Center 1991–98, Univ. Distinguished Service Prof. of Biochemistry 1996–; mem. Physiological Chem. Study Section, Physical Biochemistry Study Section, Training Grant Cttee, NIH; mem. Bd of Counsellors, Nat. Cancer Inst. 1976–80, Advisory Council, Chem. Dept, Princeton 1970–75, Polytechnic Inst., New York 1977–78, Boston Univ. 1977–85; mem. Nat. Research Council, US Nat. Comm. for Biochemistry 1989–95; mem. ACS, American Soc. of Biochemistry and Molecular Biology (Pres. 1994–95), NAS, American Acad. of Arts and Sciences; Ed. Biochemistry 1992–2003. *Publications:* Principles of Chemical Kinetics, Enzyme Catalysis and Regulation, Chemical Kinetics: Principles and Selected Topics (with I. Amdur), Thermodynamics and Kinetics for the Biological Sciences 2000, Spectroscopy for the Biological Sciences 2005, Physical Chemistry for the Biological Sciences 2007; numerous learned articles. *Honours:* ACS Award in Biological Chem. 1967, William C. Rose Award, American Soc. of Biochemistry and Molecular Biology 2002. *Address:* 11 Staley Place, Durham, NC 27705 (home); Department of Biochemistry, Duke University, Box 3711, Medical Center, Durham, NC 27710, USA (office). *Telephone:* (919) 684-8848 (office). *Fax:* (919) 684-9709 (office). *E-mail:* hamme001@mc.duke.edu (office). *Website:* www.mc.duke.edu/index3.htm (office).

HAMMICK, Georgina; British writer and poet; b. 24 May 1939, Hampshire, England; m. 1961; one s. two d. *Education:* Académie Julian, Paris, Salisbury Art School. *Career:* mem. Writers' Guild. *Publications:* A Poetry Quintet (poems) 1976, People for Lunch 1987, Spoilt (short stories) 1992, The Virago Book of Love and Loss (ed.) 1992, The Arizona Game 1996; contrib. to journals and periodicals. *Literary Agent:* The Sayle Literary Agency, Bickerton House, 25–27 Bickerton Road, London, N19 5JT, England. *Telephone:* (20) 7263-8681. *Fax:* (20) 7561-0529. *Address:* Bridgewalk House, Brixton, Deverill, Warminster, Wiltshire BA12 7EJ, England.

HAMMOND, Jane (see Poland, Dorothy Elizabeth Hayward)

HAMPSHIRE, Susan, OBE; British actress and writer; b. 12 May 1942, d. of the late George Kenneth Hampshire and June Hampshire; m. 1st Pierre Granier-Deferre 1967 (divorced 1974); one s. (one d. deceased); m. 2nd Sir Eddie Kulukundis 1981. *Education:* Hampshire School, Knightsbridge. *Stage roles include:* Expresso Bongo 1958, Follow that Girl 1960, Fairy Tales of New York 1961, Marion Dangerfield in Ginger Man 1963, Kate Hardcastle in She Stoops to Conquer 1966, On Approval 1966, Mary in The Sleeping Prince 1968, Nora in A Doll's House 1972, Katharina in The Taming of the Shrew 1974, Peter in Peter Pan 1974, Jeannette in Romeo and Jeannette 1975, Rosalind in As You Like It 1975, Miss Julie 1975, Elizabeth in The Circle 1976, Ann Whitefield in Man and Superman 1977, Siri Von Essen in Tribades 1978, Victorine in An Audience Called Edouard 1978, Irene in The Crucifer of Blood 1979, Ruth Carson in Night and Day 1979, Elizabeth in The Revolt 1980, Stella Drury in House Guest 1981, Elvira in Blithe Spirit 1986, Marie Stopes in Married Love, The Countess in A Little Night Music 1989, Mrs Anna in The King and I 1990, Gertie in Noel and Gertie 1991, The Countess of Marshwood in Relative Values 1993, Suzanna Andler in Suzanna Andler, Alicia Christie in Black Chiffon 1995–96, Sheila Carter in Relatively Speaking 2000–01, Felicity Marshwood in Relative Values 2002, Miss Shepherd in The Lady in the Van 2004–05, The Fairy Godmother in Cinderella, Wimbledon 2005–06, The Bargain 2007. *Television roles:* Andromeda in The Andromeda Breakthrough (series) 1962, Katy (series) 1962, Fleur Forsyte in The Forsyte Saga (mini-series) 1967, Becky Sharp in Vanity Fair (mini-series) 1967, Sarah Churchill, Duchess of Marlborough, in The First Churchills (mini-series) 1969, Baffled! 1973, Dr. Jekyll and Mr. Hyde 1973, Glencora Palliser in The Pallisers 1974, The Story of David 1976, Kill Two Birds 1976, Lady Melford in Dick Turpin 1981, Madeline Neroni in The Barchester Chronicles (mini-series) 1982, Martha in Leaving 1984, Martha in Leaving II 1985, Going to Pot 1985, Don't Tell Father (series) 1992, Esme Harkness in The Grand 1996–98, Miss Catto in Coming Home 1998–99, Miss Catto in Nancherrow 1999, Molly in Monarch of the Glen 1999–2005, Lucilla Drake in Sparkling Cyanide 2003. *Films include:* The Woman in the Hall 1947, Idle on Parade (uncredited) 1959, Upstairs and Downstairs 1959, Expresso Bongo (uncredited) 1960, The Long Shadow 1961, During One Night 1961, The Three Lives of Thomasina 1964, Night Must Fall 1964, Wonderful Life 1964, Paris in August 1965, The Fighting Prince of Donegal 1966, Monte Carlo or Bust 1969, Malpertuis 1971, A Time for Loving 1971, Rogan, David Copperfield, Living Free 1972, Neither the Sea Nor the Sand 1972, Le fils 1973, Peccato mortale (aka Roses and Green Peppers) 1973, Bang! 1977. *Publications:* Susan's Story (autobiographical account of dyslexia) 1981, The Maternal Instinct, Lucy Jane at the Ballet 1985, Lucy Jane on Television 1989, Trouble Free Gardening 1989, Every Letter Counts 1990, Lucy Jane and the Dancing Competition 1991, Easy Gardening 1991, Lucy Jane and the Russian Ballet 1993, Rosie's First Ballet Lesson 1997. *Honours:* Hon. DLitt (City Univ., London) 1984, (St Andrews) 1986, (Exeter) 2001; Hon. DArts (Pine Manor Coll., Boston, USA) 1994; Dr hc (Kingston) 1994; Emmy Award, Best Actress for The Forsyte Saga 1970, for The First Churchills 1971, for Vanity Fair 1973, E. Poe Prize du Film Fantastique, Best Actress for Malpertius 1972. *Address:* c/o Chatto & Linnit Ltd, 123A King's Road, London, SW3 4PL, England. *Telephone:* (20) 7352-7722. *Fax:* (20) 7352-3450.

HAMPSON, Norman, MA, DUniv; British historian and academic; b. 8 April 1922, Leyland, Lancs.; s. of Frank Hampson and Elizabeth Jane Hampson (née Fazackerley); m. Jacqueline Gardin 1948; two d. *Education:* Manchester Grammar School and Univ. Coll. Oxford. *Career:* war service in RN and Free French Navy 1941–45; Lecturer and Sr Lecturer in French History, Univ. of Manchester 1948–67; Prof. of Modern History, Univ. of Newcastle-upon-Tyne 1967–74; Prof. of History, Univ. of York 1974–89. *Publications:* La Marine de l'An II 1959, A Social History of the French Revolution 1963, The Enlightenment 1968, The Life and Opinions of Maximilien Robespierre 1974, Danton 1978, Will and Circumstance: Montesquieu, Rousseau and the French Revolution 1983, Prelude to Terror 1988, Saint-Just 1991, The Perfidy of Albion 1998, Not Really What You'd Call a War 2001. *Honours:* Hon. DLitt (Edin.) 1989. *Address:* 305 Hull Road, York, YO10 3LU, England (home). *Telephone:* (1904) 412661 (home).

HAMPTON, Angeline Agnes, (A. A. Kelly), BA, LèsL, DèsL; British writer; b. 28 Feb. 1924, London, England; m. George Hughan Hampton 1944, one s. three d. *Education:* University of London, University of Geneva, Switzerland. *Career:* mem. International Asscn for the Study of Anglo-Irish Literature; Society of Authors; PEN International. *Publications:* Liam O'Flaherty the Storyteller, 1976; Mary Lavin: Quiet Rebel, 1980; Joseph Campbell, 1879–1944, Poet and Nationalist, 1988; The Pillars of the House (ed.), 1987; Wandering Women, 1994; The Letters of Liam O'Flaherty (ed.), 1996. Contributions: English Studies; Comparative Education; Eire, Ireland; Hibernia; Linen Hall Review; Geneva News and International Report; Christian. *Honours:* British Acad. grant 1987.

HAMPTON, Christopher James, CBE, MA, FRSL; British playwright; b. 26 Jan. 1946, Fayal, the Azores, Portugal; s. of Bernard Patrick and Dorothy Patience (née Herrington) Hampton; m. Laura Margaret de Holesch 1971; two d. *Education:* Lancing Coll., New Coll., Oxford. *Career:* wrote first play When Did You Last See My Mother? 1964; Resident Dramatist, Royal Court Theatre 1968–70; freelance writer 1970–. *Plays:* When Did You Last See My Mother? 1967, Total Eclipse 1969, The Philanthropist 1970, Savages 1973, Treats 1976, Able's Will (TV) 1978, Tales from Hollywood 1983, Les Liaisons Dangereuses 1985, White Chameleon 1991, Alice's Adventures Underground 1994, The Talking Cure 2002. *Translations include:* Marya (Babel) 1967, Uncle Vanya, Hedda Gabler 1970, A Doll's House 1971 (film 1974), Don Juan 1972, Tales from the Vienna Woods 1977 (film 1979), Don Juan Comes Back from the War 1978, The Wild Duck 1980, Ghosts 1983, Tartuffe 1984, Faith, Hope and Charity 1989, Art 1996, An Enemy of the People 1997, The Unexpected Man 1998, Conversations After a Burial 2000, Life × Three 2001, Three Sisters 2003. *Directed:* (films) Carrington 1995, The Secret Agent 1996, Imagining Argentina 2003. *Opera libretto:* Waiting for the Barbarians (music by Philip Glass) 2005. *Publications:* When Did You Last See My Mother? 1967, Total Eclipse 1969 (film 1995), The Philanthropist 1970, Savages 1973, Treats 1976, Able's Will (TV) 1978, The History Man (TV adaptation of novel by Malcolm Bradbury) 1981, The Portage to San Cristobal of A.H. (play adaptation of novel by George Steiner) 1983, Tales from Hollywood 1983, The Honorary Consul (film adaptation of a novel by Graham Greene) 1983, Les Liaisons Dangereuses (adaptation of a novel by Laclos) 1985, Hotel du Lac (TV adaptation of a novel by Anita Brookner q.v.) 1986, The Good Father (film adaptation of a novel by Peter Prince) 1986, Wolf at the Door (film) 1986, Dangerous Liaisons (film) 1988, The Ginger Tree (adaptation of novel by Oswald Wynd, TV) 1989, White Chameleon 1991, Sunset Boulevard (book and lyrics with Don Black) 1993, Alice's Adventures Underground (with Martha Clarke) 1994, Carrington (film) 1995, Mary Reilly (film) 1996, The Secret Agent (film) 1996, Nostromo (screenplay) 1997, The Quiet American (film) 2002, Collected Screenplays 2002, The Talking Cure 2002. *Honours:* Officier, Ordre des Arts et des Lettres 1998; Evening Standard Award for Best Comedy 1970, 1983, for Best Play 1986, Plays and Players London Critics' Award for Best Play 1970, 1973, 1985; Los Angeles Drama Critics' Circle Award 1974, Laurence Olivier Award for Best Play 1986, New York Drama Critics' Circle Award for Best Foreign Play 1987, Prix Italia 1988, Writers' Guild of America Screenplay Award 1989, Academy Award for Best Adapted Screenplay 1989, BAFTA Award for Best Screenplay 1990, Special Jury Award, Cannes Film Festival 1995, Tony Awards for Best Original Score (lyrics) and Best Book of a Musical 1995, Scott Moncrieff Prize 1997. *Address:* 2 Kensington Park Gardens, London, W11, England. *Telephone:* (20) 7229-2188. *Fax:* (20) 7229-7644 (office).

HAN, Ung-bin; North Korean writer. *Publications:* Hopes for Good Fortune, Second Thoughts 2002; contrib. short fiction to Chosôn munhak magazine. *Address:* c/o Ministry of Culture, Pyongyang, Democratic People's Republic of Korea.

HAN SUYIN, MB, BS, LRCP, MRCS; British author and medical practitioner; b. 12 Sept. 1916, Xinyang, China; d. of Y. T. Chow (née Zhou) and M. Denis; m. 1st Gen. P. H. Tang 1938 (died 1947); m. 2nd L. F. Comber 1952 (divorced 1968); m. 3rd Col Vincent Ruthnaswamy 1971; two adopted d. *Education:* Yenching Univ., Peking, China, Univ. of Brussels, Belgium, Royal Free Hospital, Univ. of London. *Career:* in London 1945–49; employed Queen Mary Hospital, Hong Kong 1948–52, Johore Bahru Hospital, Malaya 1952–55; pvt. medical practice 1955–64; Lecturer in Contemporary Asian Literature, Nanyang Univ., Singapore 1958–60; Hon. Prof., Univ. of Alberta and six Chinese univs. *Publications:* Destination Chungking 1942, A Many-Splendoured Thing 1952, . . .And the Rain My Drink 1956, The Mountain is Young 1958, Cast but One Shadow 1962, Winter Love 1962, The Four Faces 1963, The Crippled Tree 1965, A Mortal Flower 1966, China in the Year 2001 1967, Birdless Summer 1968, Morning Deluge – Mao Tse-tung and the Chinese Revolution 1972, Wind in the Tower 1976, Lhasa, the Open City 1977,

My House has Two Doors 1980, Phoenix Harvest 1980, Till Morning Comes 1982, The Enchantress (novel) 1985, A Share of Loving 1987, Tigers and Butterflies 1990, Fleur de Soleil, Les Yeux de Demain, La Peinture Chinoise, Chine Insolite, Wind in My Sleeve (autobiog.) 1992, Eldest Son: Zhou Enlai and the making of Modern China (1898–1976) 1994; three photography books. *Address:* c/o Jonathan Cape, 32 Bedford Square, London, WC1, England. *Address:* 37 Montoie, Lausanne 1007, Switzerland.

HANBURY-TENISON, (Airling) Robin, OBE, MA, FLS, FRGS, DL; British explorer, conservationist, writer, broadcaster and farmer; b. 7 May 1936, London, England; m. 1st Marika Hopkinson (died 1982); one d. one s.; m. 2nd Louella Edwards (née Williams) 1983; one s. two step s. *Education:* Eton Coll., Windsor, Magdalen Coll., Oxford. *Career:* has been on over 30 expeditions worldwide; Chief Exec. British Field Sports Soc., now Countryside Alliance 1995–98; mem. Royal Geographical Soc. (RGS) (Council mem. 1968–82, 1995–, Vice-Pres. 1982–86), Survival International (Pres. 1969–), Soc. of Authors; Trustee, Ecological Foundation 1988–2005; Patron, Cornwall Heritage Trust. *Television films:* The Last Great Journey on Earth 1969, Trans-Africa Hovercraft Expedition 1970, A Time for Survival 1972, Mysteries of the Green Mountain 1978, Antiques at Home 1984, White Horse over France 1985, Great Wall of China 1987, Odyssey (series presenter) 1988, Collectors' Lot 1998, The Lost World of Mulu 1999, Reflections in the Sand 2000, Testament 20 00. *Publications:* The Rough and the Smooth 1969, A Question of Survival for the Indians of Brazil 1973, A Pattern of Peoples: A Journey Among the Tribes of the Outer Indonesian Islands 1975, Mulu: The Rain Forest 1980, The Aborigines of the Amazon Rain Forest: The Yanomami 1982, Worlds Apart (autobiog.) 1984, White Horses Over France 1985, A Ride Along the Great Wall 1987, Fragile Eden: A Ride Through New Zealand 1989, Spanish Pilgrimage: A Canter to St James 1990, The Oxford Book of Exploration 1993, Worlds Within 2005; children's books: Jake's Escape 1996, Jake's Treasure, Jake's Safari 1998; contrib. to The Times, Telegraph, Express, New Scientist, Field, Traveller, Spectator, Literary Review and Frontiers Column, Geographical Magazine 1995–98. *Honours:* Dr hc (Univ. of Mons-Hainaut) 1991; RGS Gold Medal 1979, Krug Award for Excellence 1980, Thomas Cook Travel Book Award 1984, Mungo Park Medal RSGS 2001. *Address:* Cabilla Manor, Cardinham, Bodmin, Cornwall, PL30 4DW, England (office). *Telephone:* (1208) 821224 (office). *Fax:* (1208) 821267 (office). *E-mail:* robin@cabilla.co.uk (office). *Website:* www.cabilla.co.uk (office); www.robinsbooks.co.uk.

HANCOCK, Geoffrey White, BFA, MFA; Canadian writer and literary journalist; b. 14 April 1946, New Westminster, NB; m. Gay Allison 1983, one d. *Education:* University of British Columbia. *Career:* Ed.-in-Chief, Canadian Fiction Magazine, 1975; Consulting Ed., Canadian Author and Bookman, 1978; Fiction Ed., Cross-Canada Writers Quarterly, 1980; Literary Consultant, CBC Radio, 1980; mem. Periodical Writers of Canada. *Publications:* Magic Realism, 1980; Illusion: Fables, Fantasies and Metafictions, 1983; Metavisions, 1983; Shoes and Shit: Stories for Pedestrians, 1984; Moving Off the Map: From Story to Fiction, 1986; Invisible Fictions: Contemporary Stories from Quebec, 1987; Canadian Writers at Work: Interviews, 1987; Singularities, 1990; Fast Travelling, 1995. Contributions: Toronto Star; Writer's Quarterly; Canadian Author and Bookman; Books In Canada; Canadian Forum. *Honours:* Fiona Mee Award for Literary Journalism, 1979.

HANDKE, Peter; Austrian writer, dramatist and poet; b. 6 Dec. 1942, Griffen-Altenmarkt; one d. *Education:* Univ. of Graz. *Publications:* Die Hornissen (novel) 1963, Begrüßung des Aufsichtsrats 1963, Sprechstücke 1964, Der Hausierer (novel) 1965, Kaspar (trans. as Kaspar and Other Plays) 1967, Das Mündel will Vormund sein 1968, Die Innenwelt der Außenwelt der Innenwelt (trans. as The Innerworld of the Outerworld of the Innerworld) 1968, Die Angst des Tormanns beim Elfmeter (trans. as The Goalie's Anxiety at the Penalty Kick) 1969, Wind und Meer 1970, Chronik der laufenden Ereignisse 1970, Der Ritt über den Bodensee 1970, Der kurze Brief zum langen Abschied (trans. as Short Letter, Long Farewell) 1971, Wunschloses Unglück (trans. as A Sorrow Beyond Dreams) 1972, Ich bin ein Bewohner des Elfenbeinturms 1972, Die Unvernünftigen sterben aus 1973, Als das Wünschen noch geholfen hat (trans. as Nonsense and Happiness) 1974, Die Stunde der wahren Empfindung (trans. as A Moment of True Feeling) 1974, Die linkshändige Frau (trans. as The Left-Handed Woman) 1976, Das Gewicht der Welt: Ein Journal 1977, Langsame Heimkehr 1979, Das Ende des Flanierens 1980, Die Lehre der Sainte-Victoire 1980, Kindergeschichte 1981, Über die Dörfer 1981, Die Geschichte des Bleistifts 1982, Phantasien der Wiederholung 1983, Der Chinese des Schmerzes 1983, Die Wiederholung 1986, Die Abwesenheit (trans. as Absence) 1987, Nachmittag eines Schriftstellers 1987, Das Spiel vom Fragen oder Die Reise zum sonoren Land 1989, Versuch über die Müdigkeit 1989, Versuch über die Jukebox 1990, Versuch über den geglückten Tag: Ein Wintertagtraum 1990, Die Stunde da wir nichts voneinander wußten 1991, Langsam im Schatten: Gesammelte Verzettelungen 1980–92 1992, Mein Jahre in der Niemandsbucht 1994, Noch einmal für Thukydides 1995, Zurüstungen für die Unsterblichkeit 1995, Eine winterliche Reise zu den Flüssen Donau, Save, Morawa und Drina oder Gerechtigkeit für Serbien (trans. as A Journey to the Rivers: Justice for Serbia) 1996, In einer dunklen Nacht ging ich aus meinem stillen Haus (novel) 1997, Lucie im Wald mit den Dingsda 1999, Die Fahrt im Einbaum oder Das Stück zum Film vom Krieg 1999, Unter Tränen fragend. Nachträgliche Aufzeichnungen von zwei Jugoslawien-Durchquerungen im Krieg, März und April 1999 2000, Der Bildverlust oder Durch die Sierra des Gredos (novel) 2002, Mündliches und Schriftliches. Zu Büchern, Bildern und Filmen 1992–2002 2002, Untertagblues 2003, Don Juan (erzählt von ihm selbst) (Siegfried Unseld Preis) 2004, Spuren der Verirrten 2006, Kali 2007. *Honours:* Gerhart Hauptmann Prize 1967, Peter Rosegger Literary Prize 1972, Schiller Prize, Mannheim 1972, Büchner Prize 1973, Prix Georges Sadoul 1978, Kafka Prize 1979, Salzburg Literary Prize 1986, Great Austrian (state) Prize 1987, Bremen Literary Prize, Hamburg 1991, Franz Grillparzer Prize, Hamburg 1991, Goethe Inst. Drama Prize, Munich 1993, Prize of Honour of the Schiller Memorial Prize 1995. *Address:* c/o Suhrkamp Verlag, Postfach 101945, 60019 Frankfurt am Main, Germany. *Website:* www.suhrkamp.de.

HANDLER, Daniel, (Lemony Snicket); American writer; b. 28 Feb. 1970, San Francisco, CA; m. Lisa Brown; one s. *Education:* Lowel High School, San Francisco and Wesleyan Univ. *Film screenplays:* Rick 2003, Lemony Snicket's A Series of Unfortunate Events 2004, Kill the Poor 2006. *Publications:* fiction: A Series of Unfortunate Events, Vol. 1: The Bad Beginning 1999, Vol. 2: The Reptile Room 1999, Vol. 3: The Wide Window 1999, Vol. 4: The Miserable Mill 2000, Vol. 5: The Austere Academy 2000, Vol. 6: The Ersatz Elevator 2001, Vol. 7: The Vile Village 2001, Vol. 8: The Hostile Hospital 2001, Vol. 9: The Carnivorous Carnival 2002, Vol. 10: The Slippery Slope 2003, Vol. 11: The Grim Grotto 2004, Vol. 12: The Penultimate Peril (Quill Book Award for Children's Chapter Book/Middle Grade 2006) 2004, Vol. 13: The End 2006; non-fiction: The Unauthorised Autobiography 2002, various other series tie-in books; adult novels: The Basic Eight 1999, Watch Your Mouth 2000, Adverbs 2006. *Address:* c/o Harper Collins Children's Books, 1350 Avenue of the Americas, New York, NY 10019, USA (office). *E-mail:* lsnicket@harpercollins.com. *Website:* www.lemonysnicket.com.

HANDLIN, Oscar, PhD, LLD, LHD, DHL, LittD; American historian and academic; b. 29 Sept. 1915, Brooklyn; s. of Joseph Handlin and Ida Handlin (née Yanowitz); m. 1st Mary Flug 1937; one s. two d.; m. 2nd Lilian Bombach 1977. *Education:* Univs of Harvard, Michigan, Seton Hall, Lowell and Cincinatti. *Career:* History Instructor, Brooklyn Coll. 1936–38, Harvard Univ. 1939–44; Asst Prof., Harvard Univ. 1944–48, Assoc. Prof. 1948–54, Prof. of History 1954–, Dir Cen. for Study of Liberty in America 1958–66, Winthrop Prof. of History 1962–65, Charles Warren Prof. of History 1965–72, Dir Charles Warren Cen. for Studies in American History 1965–72, Carl H. Pforzheimer Univ. Prof. 1972–84, Dir Univ. Library 1979–83, Carl M. Loeb Prof. 1984–86; Harmsworth Prof., Univ. of Oxford 1972–73; Vice-Chair. US Bd Foreign Scholarships 1962–65, Chair. 1965–66; Trustee New York Public Library 1973–; Brandeis Univ. Fellow 1965–; Fellow, American Acad. of Arts and Sciences 1983, American Philosophical Soc. 1996. *Publications:* Boston's Immigrants 1941, Commonwealth 1947, This was America 1949, The Uprooted, The American People in the Twentieth Century 1954, Adventure in Freedom 1954, Chance or Destiny 1955, Race and Nationality in American Life 1956, Readings in American History, Al Smith and his America 1958, Immigration as a Factor in American History 1959, The Newcomers – Negroes and Puerto Ricans in a Changing Metropolis 1959, American Principles and Issues 1961, The Dimensions of Liberty 1961, The Americans 1963, Fire-Bell in the Night 1964, Children of the Uprooted 1966, Popular Sources of Political Authority 1967, History of the United States 1967, America, a History 1968, The American College and American Culture 1970, Statue of Liberty 1971, Facing Life–Youth and the Family in American History 1971, A Pictorial History of Immigration 1972, The Wealth of the American People 1975, Truth in History 1979, Abraham Lincoln and the Union 1980, The Distortion of America 1981, Liberty and Power 1986, Liberty in Expansion 1989, Liberty in Peril 1991, Liberty and Equality 1994, From the Outer World 1997; ed. several publs. *Honours:* History Prize, Union League Club 1934, J.H. Dunning Prize, American History Asscn 1941, Award of Honour, Brooklyn Coll., 1945, Pulitzer Prize for History 1952, Guggenheim Fellow 1954, Christopher Award 1958, Robert H. Lord Award 1972. *Address:* Widener 783, Cambridge, MA 02138 (office); 18 Agassiz Street, Cambridge, MA 02140, USA (home). *Telephone:* (617) 495-7931 (office); (617) 661-3145 (home). *E-mail:* ohandlin@fas.harvard.edu (office); lilioscar@aol.com (home).

HANKIN, Elizabeth Rosemary; British writer and journalist; b. (Elizabeth Gill), 16 Oct. 1950, Newcastle upon Tyne, England; m. Richard Hankin 1973 (divorced 1988) one d. *Education:* Emma Willard School. *Publications:* fiction: The Singing Winds, 1995; Far from My Father's House, 1995; Under a Cloud-Soft Sky, 1996; The Road to Berry Edge, 1997. *Address:* 6 Watling Way, Lanchester, Durham, DH7 0HN, England.

HANLEY, Clifford Henry Calvin; British writer and dramatist; b. 28 Oct. 1922, Glasgow, Scotland; m. Anna Clark 1948, one s. two d. *Education:* Eastbank Acad., Glasgow. *Career:* Prof. of Creative Writing, York Univ., Toronto 1979; mem. Ours Club, Glasgow (pres.), PEN (Scottish pres. 1975). *Publications:* Dancing in the Streets, 1958; The Taste of Too Much, 1960; Nothing But the Best, 1964; Prissy, 1978; The Scots, 1980; Another Street Another Dance, 1983. Plays: The Durable Element, 1961; Oh For an Island, 1966; Dick McWhittie, 1967; Jack O'The Cudgel, 1969; Oh Glorious Jubilee, 1970; The Clyde Moralities, 1972. Contributions: numerous articles in magazines and journals. *Honours:* Acad. Award for Best Foreign Documentary 1960.

HANNAH, Barry, BA, MA, MFA; American author; b. 23 April 1942, Meridian, MI; m. (divorced); three s. *Education:* Mississippi College, Clinton, University of Arkansas. *Career:* Teacher, Clemson University, 1967–73, University of Alabama, Tuscaloosa, 1975–80; Writer-in-Residence, Middlebury College,

Vermont, 1974–75, University of Iowa, 1981, University of Mississippi, University, 1982, 1984–85, University of Montana, Missoula, 1982–83. *Publications:* Geronimo Rex, 1972; Nightwatchmen, 1973; Airships, 1978; Ray, 1981; Two Stories, 1982; Black Butterfly, 1982; Power and Light, 1983; The Tennis Handsome, 1983; Captain Maximus, 1985; Hey Jack!, 1987; Boomerang, 1989; Never Die, 1991; Bats Out of Hell, 1993. Contributions: Magazines. *Honours:* Bellaman Foundation Award, 1970; Atherton Fellowship, Bread Loaf Writers Conference, 1971; Arnold Gingrich Award, Esquire Magazine, 1978; American Acad. of Arts and Letters Award, 1978.

HANNAH, Sophie, MA; British poet and writer; b. 1971, Manchester; m. Dr Deiniol Jones; one d. one s. *Education:* Univ. of Manchester. *Career:* Fellow Commoner, Trinity Coll., Cambridge; Fellow, Wolfson Coll., Oxford; tutor, Writing School, Manchester Metropolitan Univ. *Publications:* poetry: Early Bird Blues 1993, Second Helping of Your Heart 1994, Hero and the Girl Next Door 1995, Hotels Like House (Arts Council Writers' Award) 1996, Leaving and Leaving You 1999, First of the Last Chances 2003, Selected Poems 2006; fiction: Carrot the Goldfish 1992, Gripless 1999, Cordial and Corrosive 2000, The Superpower of Love 2001, Little Face 2006, Hurting Distance 2007; trans.: The Book about Moomin, Mymble and Little My 2001, Who Will Comfort Toffle 2003; contrib. to The Box Room 2001, Hyphen: An Anthology of Short Stories by Poets 2003, Leeds Stories 2 2004. *Honours:* Eric Gregory Award 1995. *Address:* c/o Carcanet Press, Fourth Floor, Alliance House, Cross Street, Manchester, M2 7AP, England (office). *Website:* www.sophiehannah.com.

HANSEN, Erik Fosnes; Norwegian novelist; b. 6 June 1965, New York, USA; m. *Publications:* Falketårnet 1985, Salme ved reisens slutt (novel, Psalm at Journey's End) 1990, Beretninger om beskyttelse (novel) 1998, Underveis. Et portrett av Prinsesse Märtha Louise (non-fiction) 2001; contrib. articles in numerous magazines and newspapers. *Honours:* Riksmålsprisen 1998, Bokhandlerprisen 1998, NRK P2-lytternes pris 1999. *Address:* c/o Secker & Warburg, Random House, 20 Vauxhall Bridge Road, London SW1V 2SA, England.

HANSEN, Ron, BA, MFA; American writer; b. 8 Dec. 1947, Omaha, NE. *Education:* Creighton University, University of Iowa, Stanford University. *Career:* fmr Prof. of English, Cornell University. *Publications:* The Desperadoes, 1979; The Assassination of Jesse James by the Coward Robert Ford, 1983; The Shadowmaker, 1986; You Don't Know What Love Is, 1987; Nebraska Stories, 1989; Mariette in Ecstacy: A Novel, 1992; Atticus, 1996; Hitler's Niece, 1999; Isn't it Romantic?, An Entertainment, 2003.

HANSON, William Stewart, PhD, FSA, FSA Scot; British archaeologist and writer; *Professor of Roman Archaeology, University of Glasgow*; b. 22 Jan. 1950, Doncaster, Yorks.; m. Lesley Macinnes; one d. *Education:* Univ. of Manchester. *Career:* Sr Lecturer in Archaeology, Univ. of Glasgow 1990–2000, Prof. of Roman Archaeology 2000–. *Publications:* Rome's North-West Frontier: The Antonine Wall (co-author) 1983, Agricola and the Conquest of the North 1987, Scottish Archaeology: New Perceptions (co-ed.) 1991, Roman Dacia: The Making of a Provincial Society (co-ed.) 2004, Elginhaugh: A Flavian Fort and its Annexe 2007, A Roman Frontier Fort in Scotland: The First Century Fort at Elginhaugh 2007; contrib. to major academic archaeological and antiquarian journals and collected works. *Address:* Department of Archaeology, University of Glasgow, The Gregory Building, Lilybank Gardens, Glasgow, G12 8QQ, Scotland (office). *Telephone:* (141) 330-4915 (office). *Fax:* (141) 330-3544 (office). *E-mail:* w.hanson@archaeology.gla.ac.uk (office). *Website:* www.gla.ac.uk/archaeology/staff/wsh/index.html (office).

HAO, Tran Manh; Vietnamese poet, writer and critic; b. 21 July 1949, Nam Dinh Province. *Education:* Gorky Inst. of Literature, Moscow, Russia. *Career:* mem. Viet Nam Writers' Union. *Publications include:* poetry: Truong Son cua be (trans. as Baby's Truong Son) 1974, Giai Phong (trans. as Liberation) 1974, Tieng chim go cua (trans. as The Sound of the Bird Knocking at the Door) 1976, Van Nghe Giai Phong (trans. as Liberation and Arts) 1976, Hoa vua di vua no (trans. as The Flowers are Walking and Blooming at the Same Time) 1981, Mat troi trong long dat (trans. as The Underground Sun) 1981, Ba cap nui va mot hon nui le (trans. as Three Pairs of Mountains and One Standing-Alone Mountain) 1981, Tu chiec o troi cua me (trans. as From Mother's Heavenly Umbrella) 1987, Cuoc chien tranh khon nguoi (trans. as The Endless War) 1988, Minh anh trong mot the gioi (trans. as One You in One World) 1991, Dat nuoc hinh tia chop (trans. as Lightning-Shaped Country) 1994, Chuon chuon can ron (trans. as Dragonfly Biting the Navel) 1995, Tho tu tuyet (trans. as Four-Line Poems) 1995, Tho luc bat Tran Manh Hao (trans. as Tran Manh Hao's Six-Eight-Word-Metre Poetry) 2001; novels: Chia khoa cua moi nguoi (trans. as Everybody's Key) 1987, Trang mat (trans. as Honeymoon) 1989, Ly than (trans. as Separated) 1989, Sinh ra de yeu nhau (trans. as Born to Love Each Other) 1989; juvenile short stories: Cay trong vuon (trans. as Trees in the Garden) 1980, Chu heo dat (trans. as The Earthen Pig) 1981; criticism: Tho phan tho (trans. as Poetry against Poetry) 1995, Phe binh phan phe binh (trans. as Criticism against Criticism) 1996. *Honours:* Nat. Poetry Award for Children's Literature 1995, Nat. Poetry Awards 1996, 1999. *Address:* c/o Thanh Nien, 5 Ly Thuong Kiet, Hanoi, Viet Nam. *Website:* www.thanhnien.com.vn.

HARADA, Masako, (Satoko Kizaki); Japanese writer; b. 14 Nov. 1939, Changchung, China; m. Hiroshi Harada 1962, two d. *Education:* Tokyo Women's Univ. Junior Coll. *Publications:* Rasoku 1982, Umi-to Rosoku 1985, Aogiri (trans. as The Phoenix Tree and Other Stories) 1985, Shizumeru tera (trans. as The Sunken Temple) 1987, Nami-Half-way 1988, Sanzoku-no-Haka 1989, Kagami-no-Tani 1990, Toki-no-Shizuku 1991, Atonaki-Niwa-ni 1991, Shiawase no chiisana tobira 1994. *Honours:* Akutagawa Prize 1985.

HARBISON, Peter, MA, DPhil, MRIA, FSA; Irish archaeologist, art historian and editor; *Honorary Academic Editor, Royal Irish Academy*; b. 14 Jan. 1939, Dublin; s. of Dr James Austin Harbison and Sheelagh Harbison (née McSherry); m. Edelgard Soergel 1969; three s. *Education:* St Gerard's School, Bray, Glenstal, Univ. Coll. Dublin and Univs of Marburg, Kiel and Freiburg. *Career:* awarded travelling scholarship by German Archaeological Inst. 1965; archaeological officer, Irish Tourist Bd 1966–84, editorial publicity officer 1984–86, Ed. Ireland of the Welcomes (magazine) 1986–95; Sec. Friends of the Nat. Collections of Ireland 1971–76; mem. Council, Royal Irish Acad. 1981–84, 1993–96, 1998–2001, 2004–, Vice-Pres. 1992–93, 2006–07, Hon. Academic Ed. 1997–; Prof. of Archaeology, Royal Hibernian Acad. of Arts; Chair. Nat. Monuments Advisory Council 1986–90, Dublin Cemeteries Cttee 1986–89, 1996–2002, Bunratty Castle Ownership and Furniture Trusts 2004–; Vice-Pres. for Leinster, Royal Soc. of Antiquities of Ireland 2005–07; Guest Prof., Univ. of Vienna summer 2004; Corresp. mem. German Archaeological Inst. *Publications:* Guide to National Monuments of Ireland 1970, The Archaeology of Ireland 1976, Irish Art and Architecture (co-author) 1978, Pre-Christian Ireland (Archaeological Book of the Year Award 1988) 1988, Pilgrimage in Ireland 1991, Beranger's Views of Ireland 1991, The High Crosses of Ireland 1992, Irish High Crosses 1994, Ancient Ireland (with Jacqueline O'Brien) 1996, Ancient Irish Monuments 1997, Beranger's Antique Buildings of Ireland, L'Art Médiéval en Irlande 1998, Spectacular Ireland 1999, The Golden Age of Irish Art 1999, The Crucifixion in Irish Art 2000, Cooper's Ireland 2000, Our Treasure of Antiquities 2002, Treasures of the Boyne Valley 2003, Ireland's Treasures 2004, Beranger's Rambles in Ireland 2004, A Thousand Years of Church Heritage in East Galway 2005; articles in books and journals. *Honours:* Hon. mem. Royal Hibernian Acad. of Arts 1998; Hon. Fellow, Trinity Coll., Dublin 2000; Hon. mem. Royal Inst. of Architects of Ireland. *Address:* 5 St Damian's, Loughshinny, Skerries, Co. Dublin (home); Royal Irish Academy, 19 Dawson Street, Dublin 2, Republic of Ireland (office). *Telephone:* (1) 8490940 (home); (1) 6762570 (office). *Fax:* (1) 6762346 (office). *E-mail:* p.harbison@ria.ie (office). *Website:* www.ria.ie (office).

HARCOURT, Geoffrey Colin, AO, PhD, LittD, FASSA; Australian academic; *Emeritus Fellow, Jesus College and Reader Emeritus in the History of Economic Theory, University of Cambridge*; b. 27 June 1931, Melbourne; s. of Kenneth and Marjorie Harcourt (née Gans); m. Joan Bartrop 1955; two s. two d. *Education:* Univ. of Melbourne and Univ. of Cambridge, UK. *Career:* Lecturer in Econs, Univ. of Adelaide 1958–62, Sr Lecturer 1962–65, Reader 1965–67, Prof. (Personal Chair) 1967–85, Prof. Emer. 1988–; Lecturer in Econs and Politics, Univ. of Cambridge 1964–66, 1982–90, Reader in the History of Econ. Theory 1990–98, Reader Emer. 1998–, Dir of Studies in Economics and Fellow of Trinity Hall, Cambridge 1964–66, Fellow and Lecturer in Econs, Jesus Coll., Cambridge 1982–98, Fellow Emer. 1998–, Pres. 1988–92; Leverhulme Exchange Fellow Keio Univ., Tokyo 1969–70; Visiting Fellow, Clare Hall, Cambridge 1972–73; Visiting Prof., Univ. of Toronto, Canada 1977, 1980, Univ. of Melbourne 2002; Visiting Fellow, ANU 1997; Pres. Economic Soc. of Australia and New Zealand 1974–77; mem. Council Royal Econ. Soc. 1990–95, Life mem. 1998–; Distinguished Fellow, Econ. Soc. of Australia 1996, History of Econs Soc., USA 2004; Academician Acad. of Learned Socs for the Social Sciences (AcSS) 2003; Fellow Acad. of the Social Sciences in Australia 1971 (exec. cttee mem. 1974–77). *Publications:* Economic Activity (with P. H. Karmel and R. H. Wallace) 1967, Readings in the Concept and Measurement of Income (ed., with R. H. Parker) 1969 (2nd edn with R. H. Parker and G. Whittington) 1986, Capital and Growth, Selected Readings (ed., with N. F. Laing) 1971, Some Cambridge Controversies in the Theory of Capital 1972, The Microeconomic Foundations of Macroeconomics (ed.) 1977, The Social Science Imperialists, Selected Essays (edited by Prue Kerr) 1982, Keynes and his Contemporaries (ed.) 1985, Controversies in Political Economy, Selected Essays of G. C. Harcourt (edited by Omar Hamouda) 1986, International Monetary Problems and Supply-Side Economics: Essays in Honour of Lorie Tarshis (edited with Jon S. Cohen) 1986, On Political Economists and Modern Political Economy, Selected Essays of G. C. Harcourt (ed. by Claudio Sardoni) 1992, Post-Keynesian Essays in Biography: Portraits of Twentieth Century Political Economists 1993, The Dynamics of the Wealth of Nations. Growth, Distribution and Structural Change: Essays in Honour of Luigi Pasinetti (edited with Mauro Baranzini) 1993, Income and Employment in Theory and Practice. Essays in Memory of Athanasios Asimakopulos (ed. with Alessandro Roncaglia and Robin Rowley) 1994, Capitalism, Socialism and Post-Keynesianism. Selected Essays of G. C. Harcourt 1995, A 'Second Edition' of The General Theory (two vols, co-ed. with P. A. Riach) 1997, 50 Years a Keynesian and Other Essays 2001, Selected Essays on Economic Policy 2001, L'Economie rebelle de Joan Robinson (ed.) 2001, Joan Robinson: Critical Assessments of Leading Economists (five vols, ed. with Prue Kerr) 2002, Editing Economics: Essays in Honour of Mark Perlman (co-ed.) 2002, Capital Theory (3 Vols, ed. with Christopher Bliss and Avi Cohen) 2005, The Structure of Post-Keynesian Economics: The Core Contributions of the Pioneers 2006. *Honours:* Hon. Fellow, Queen's Coll., Melbourne 1998, Sugden Fellow 2002; Hon. Prof., Univ. of NSW 1997, 1999; Hon. mem. European Soc. for the History of Economic Thought 2004; Hon. LittD (De Montfort Univ.) 1997; Hon. DCom (Melbourne) 2003; Hon. Dr rer. pol (Fribourg) 2003; Wellington Burnham Lecturer, Tufts Univ., Medford, Mass 1975, Edward

Shann Memorial Lecturer, Univ. of Western Australia 1975, Newcastle Lecturer in Political Economy, Univ. of Newcastle 1977, Acad. Lecturer, Acad. of the Social Sciences in Australia 1978, G. L. Wood Memorial Lecturer, Univ. of Melbourne 1982, John Curtin Memorial Lecturer, ANU 1982, Special Lecturer in Econs, Univ. of Manchester 1984, Lecturer, Nobel Conf. XXII, Gustavus Adolphus Coll., Minn. 1986, Laws Lecturer, Univ. of Tennessee at Knoxville 1991, Donald Horne Lecturer 1992, Sir Halford Cook Lecturer, Queen's Coll., Univ. of Melbourne, Kingsley Martin Memorial Lecturer, Cambridge 1996, Colin Clark Memorial Lecturer, Brisbane 1997, Bernard Hesketh Lecturer, Univ. of Minn., Kansas City 2006. *Address:* 43 New Square, Cambridge, CB1 1EZ (home); Jesus College, Cambridge, CB5 8BL, England (office). *Telephone:* (1223) 760353 (office). *E-mail:* fellows-secretary@jesus.cam .ac.uk (office); GCH3@cam.ac.uk (home).

HARDEN, Blaine Charles, BA, MA; American journalist and author; *National Correspondent covering American West, The Washington Post;* b. 4 April 1952, Moses Lake, WA; m. Jessica Kowal; one s. one d. *Education:* Gonzaga Univ., Syracuse Univ. *Career:* Africa Corresp., Washington Post 1985–89, East European Corresp. 1989–93, reporter 1995–97, Nat. Corresp. covering American West, Seattle 2003–; Nat. Corresp. New York Times 1997–2002. *Publications:* Africa: Dispatches From a Fragile Continent 1990, A River Lost: The Life and Death of Columbia 1996; contribs to Washington Post, New York Times Magazine, Smithsonian Magazine, Discovery Magazine. *Honours:* Livingston Award for Young Journalists 1986, Martha Albrand Citation for First Book of Non-Fiction, PEN 1991, Ernie Pyle Award for Human Interest Reporting 1993. *Address:* c/o Washington Post, 1150 15th Street NW, Washington, DC 20071, USA (office). *Telephone:* (206) 328-3224 (office). *E-mail:* hardenb@washpost.com (office).

HARDING, James, BA, PhD, PGCE, FRSL; English writer; b. 1929. *Education:* Univ. of Bristol, Sorbonne, Paris, Univ. of London. *Career:* Sr Lecturer in French, Univ. of Greenwich 1966–94. *Publications:* Saint-Saëns and His Circle, 1965; The Duke of Wellington, 1968; Sacha Guitry, 1968; Massenet, 1970; Rossini, 1971; The Ox on the Roof, 1972; Lord Chesterfield's Letters to his Son, 1973; Gounod, 1974; Lost Illusions: Paul Léautaud and His World, 1974; Erik Satie, 1975; The Astonishing Adventure of General Boulanger, 1976; Poulenc: My Friends and Myself (trans.), 1978; Folies de Paris: The Rise and Fall of French Operetta, 1979; Offenbach, 1980; Maurice Chevalier, 1982; Jacques Tati: Frame by Frame, 1984; James Agate, 1986; Ivor Novello, 1987; The Rocky Horror Show Book, 1987; Cochran, 1988; Gerald du Maurier, 1989; George Robey and the Music Hall, 1991; Emlyn Williams, A Life, 1993; P. Ramlee, Bright Star, 2002. *Address:* 100 Ridgmount Gardens, Torrington Place, London WC1E 7AZ, England.

HARDWICK, Elizabeth, MA; American author; b. 27 July 1916, Lexington, Ky; d. of Eugene Allen Hardwick and Mary (née Ramsey) Hardwick; m. Robert Lowell 1949 (divorced 1972); one d. *Education:* Kentucky Univ., Columbia Univ. *Career:* Assoc. Prof. Barnard Coll.; Guggenheim Fellow 1947; mem. American Acad., Inst. of Arts and Letters (Gold Medal for Criticism 1993), American Acad. of Arts and Sciences; Founder, Advisory Ed. New York Review of Books. *Publications:* (novels) The Ghostly Lover 1945, The Simple Truth 1955, Sleepless Nights 1979; (essays) A View of My Own 1962, Seduction and Betrayal 1974, Bartleby in Manhattan 1983, Sight Readings 1998; Herman Melville, A Life 2000; Ed. The Selected Letters of William James 1960; contribs to New Yorker. *Honours:* Dr hc (Smith Coll., Kenyon Coll., Skidmore Coll., Bard Coll.); George Jean Nathan Award 1966. *Address:* 15 W 67th Street, New York, NY 10023, USA (home).

HARDWICK, Mollie, FRSA; British writer; b. 1916, Manchester; d. of Joseph Greenhalgh and Anne Frances Atkinson; m. Michael John Drinkrow Hardwick 1961 (died 1991); one s. *Education:* Manchester High School for Girls. *Career:* announcer, BBC Radio, Northern Region 1940–45, Drama Dept 1946–62; freelance writer 1963–. *Publications include:* Stories from Dickens 1968, Emma, Lady Hamilton 1969, Mrs Dizzy 1972, Upstairs Downstairs: Sarah's Story 1973, The Years of Change 1974, The War to End Wars 1975, Mrs Bridges' Story 1975, Alice in Wonderland (play) 1975, The World of Upstairs Downstairs 1976, Beauty's Daughter (Elizabeth Goudge Award) 1976, The Duchess of Duke Street: The Way Up 1976, The Golden Years 1976, The World Keeps Turning 1977, Charlie is my Darling 1977, The Atkinson Heritage 1978, Thomas and Sarah 1978, Thomas and Sarah: Two for a Spin 1979, Lovers Meeting 1980, Juliet Bravo 2 1980, Monday's Child 1981, Calling Juliet Bravo: New Arrivals 1981, I Remember Love 1982, The Shakespeare Girl 1983, By the Sword Divided 1983, The Merrymaid 1984, Girl with a Crystal Dove 1985, Malice Domestic 1986, Parson's Pleasure 1987, Uneaseful Death 1988, Blood Royal 1988, The Bandersnatch 1989, Perish in July 1989, The Dreaming Damozel 1990, Come Away Death 1997; numerous publs with Michael Hardwick, plays and scripts for radio and TV and contribs to journals.

HARDY, Barbara Gladys, BA, MA, FRSL, FBA; British academic and writer; b. 27 June 1924, England; m. Ernest Dawson Hardy (deceased); two d. *Education:* Univ. Coll. London. *Career:* Prof. of English, Royal Holloway Coll., London 1965–70; Prof. of English Literature, Birkbeck Coll., London 1970–89, Prof. Emerita 1989–; mem. Dickens Soc. (Pres. 1987–88), Thomas Hardy Soc. (Vice-Pres. 1991–), Welsh Acad.; Fellow Royal Holloway Coll., London, Univ. of Wales, Swansea. *Publications:* The Novels of George Eliot: A Study in Form 1959, The Appropriate Form: An Essay on the Novel 1964, Middlemarch: Critical Appoaches to the Novel (ed.) 1967, Charles Dickens: The Later Novels 1968, Critical Essays on George Elliot (ed.) 1970, The

Exposure of Luxury: Radical Themes in Thackeray 1970, Tellers and Listeners: The Narrative Imagination 1975, A Reading of Jane Austen 1975, The Advantage of Lyric: Essays on Feeling in Poetry 1977, Particularities: Readings in George Eliot 1982, Forms of Feeling in Victorian Fiction 1985, Narrators and Novelists: Collected Essays 1987, Swansea Girl 1993, London Lovers (novel) 1996, Henry James: The Later Writing 1996, Shakespeare's Storytellers 1997, Dylan Thomas: An Original Language 2000, Thomas Hardy: Imagining Imagination 2000, Severn Bridge: New and Collected Poems 2001, George Eliot: A Critic's Biography 2006, The Yellow Carpet: New and Collected Poems 2006. *Honours:* Hon. mem. MCA 1973, Hon. DUniv (Open Univ.) 1982, Hon. Fellow Birkbeck Coll., London 1991, Hon. Prof. of English, Univ. of Wales, Swansea 1991,; hon. degrees; Rose Mary Cranshaw Prize 1962, Sagittarius Prize 1997. *Address:* School of English and Humanities, Birkbeck College, Malet Street, London WC1E 7HX (office); Flat G, 88 Philbeach Gardens, London SW5 9EU, England (home). *Telephone:* (20) 370-2601 (home).

HARDY, Frank; Australian novelist; b. 21 March 1917, Southern Cross, Vic. *Career:* Pres., Realist Writers Group, Melbourne, Sydney, 1954–74; Co-Founder, Australian Society of Authors, Sydney, 1968–74; Pres., Carringbush Writers, Melbourne, 1980–83. *Publications:* The Four Legged Lottery, 1958; Power Without Glory, 1962; The Outcasts of Follgarah, 1971; Who Shot George Kirkland?, 1981; Warrant of Distress, 1983; The Obsession of Oscar Oswald, 1983. Short Stories: The Loser Now Will be Later to Win, 1985; Hardy's People, 1986. Plays: Black Diamonds, 1956; The Ringbolter, 1964; Who Was Harry Larse?, 1985; Faces in the Street: An Epic Drama, 1990. *Address:* 9/76 Elizabeth Bay Road, Elizabeth Bay, NSW 2011, Australia.

HARDY, Jules, MA, PhD; British novelist; b. Bristol. *Career:* publishing, teaching. *Publications:* novels: Altered Land 2001, Mister Candid 2003, Blue Earth 2005. *Honours:* WH Smith Fresh Talent Award. *Literary Agent:* c/o Ed Victor Ltd, 6 Bayley Street, Bedford Square, London, WC1B 3HB, England.

HARE, Sir David, Kt, MA, FRSL; British playwright and theatre director; b. 5 June 1947, Hastings, Sussex; s. of Clifford Theodore Rippon Hare and Agnes Cockburn Gilmour; m. 1st Margaret Matheson 1970 (divorced 1980); two s. one d.; m. 2nd Nicole Farhi 1992. *Education:* Lancing Coll., Jesus Coll., Cambridge. *Career:* Literary Man. and Resident Dramatist, Royal Court 1969–71; Resident Dramatist, Nottingham Playhouse 1973; f. Portable Theatre 1968, Joint Stock Theatre Group 1975, Greenpoint Films 1983; Assoc. Dir Nat. Theatre 1984–88, 1989–; UK/US Bicentennial Fellowship 1978; Hon. Fellow Jesus Coll. Cambridge 2001. *Plays:* Slag, Hampstead 1970, Royal Court 1971, New York Shakespeare Festival (NYSF) 1971, The Great Exhibition, Hampstead 1972, Brassneck (with Howard Brenton q.v.), Nottingham Playhouse 1973 (also Dir), Knuckle, Comedy Theatre 1974, Fanshen, Inst. of Contemporary Arts 1975, Hampstead 1975, Nat. Theatre 1992, Teeth 'n' Smiles, Royal Court 1975 (also Dir), Wyndhams 1976 (also Dir), Plenty, Nat. Theatre 1978 (also Dir), NYSF and Broadway 1982 (also Dir), Albery 1999, A Map of the World, Nat. Theatre 1983 (also Dir) NYSF 1985 (also Dir), Pravda: A Fleet Street Comedy (with Howard Brenton), Nat. Theatre 1985 (also Dir), The Bay at Nice, Nat. Theatre 1986 (also Dir), The Secret Rapture, Nat. Theatre 1988, NYSF and Broadway 1989 (also Dir), Racing Demon, Nat. Theatre 1990, 1993, Broadway 1995, Murmuring Judges, Nat. Theatre 1992, 1993, The Absence of War, Nat. Theatre 1993, Skylight, Nat. Theatre 1995, Wyndhams and Broadway 1996, Vaudeville 1997, Amy's View, Nat. Theatre 1997, Aldwych 1998, Broadway 1999, The Judas Kiss, Almeida and Broadway 1998 (Dir on radio only), Via Dolorosa, Royal Court 1998 (also acted), Almeida and Broadway 1999 (also acted), My Zinc Bed, Royal Court 2000 (also Dir), The Breath of Life, Theatre Royal, Haymarket 2002, The Permanent Way, Nat. Theatre 2003, Stuff Happens, Nat. Theatre 2004, The Vertical Hour (Music Box Theatre, Broadway) 2006. *Plays adapted:* The Rules of the Game, Nat. Theatre 1971, Almeida 1992, The Life of Galileo, Almeida 1994, Mother Courage and Her Children, Nat. Theatre 1995, Ivanov, Almeida and Broadway 1997 (Dir on radio only), The Blue Room, Donmar and Broadway 1998, Theatre Royal 2000, Platonov, Almeida 2001, The House of Bernarda Alba, Lorca 2005. *Plays directed:* Christie in Love, Portable Theatre 1969, Fruit, Portable Theatre 1970, Blowjob, Portable Theatre 1971, England's Ireland, Portable Theatre 1972 (co-Dir), The Provoked Wife, Palace, Watford 1973, The Pleasure Principle, Theatre Upstairs 1973, The Party, Nat. Theatre 1974, Weapons of Happiness, Nat. Theatre 1976, Devil's Island, Joint Stock 1977, Total Eclipse, Lyric 1981, King Lear, Nat. Theatre 1986, The Designated Mourner, Nat. Theatre 1996, Heartbreak House, Almeida 1997. *TV screenplays:* Man Above Men (BBC) 1973, Licking Hitler (BBC) 1978 (also Dir), Dreams of Leaving (BBC) 1979 (also Dir), Saigon: Year of the Cat (Thames) 1983 (also assoc. producer), Heading Home (BBC) 1991 (also Dir), The Absence of War (BBC) 1995. *Film screenplays:* Wetherby 1985 (also Dir), Plenty 1985, Paris by Night 1989 (also Dir), Strapless 1990 (also Dir), Damage 1992, The Secret Rapture 1993 (also assoc. producer), Via Dolorosa 2000 (also actor), The Hours (adaptation of Michael Cunningham's novel) 2001, Lee Miller 2003, The Corrections (adaptation of Jonathan Franzen's novel) 2005. *Film directed:* The Designated Mourner 1996 (also produced). *Opera libretto:* The Knife, New York Shakespeare Festival 1988 (also Dir). *Publications:* Writing Lefthanded 1991, Asking Around 1993, Acting Up: A Diary 1999, Obedience, Struggle and Revolt (collection of speeches) 2005. *Honours:* Evening Standard Drama Award 1970, John Llewelyn Rhys Prize 1974, BAFTA Best Play of the Year 1978, New York Critics' Circle Awards 1983, 1990, 1997, 1999, Golden Bear Award for Best

Film 1985, Evening Standard Drama Award for Best Play 1985, Plays and Players Best Play Awards 1985, 1988, 1990, City Limits Best Play 1985, Drama Magazine Awards Best Play 1988, Laurence Olivier Best Play of the Year 1990, 1996, Time Out Award 1990, Dramalogue Award 1992, Time Out Award for Outstanding Theatrical Achievement 1998, Outer Critics' Circle Award 1999, Drama League Award 1999, Drama Desk Award 1999, Joan Cullman Award 1999; Officier, Ordre des Arts et des Lettres 1997. *Literary Agent:* Casarotto Ramsay Ltd, 60–66 Wardour Street, London, W1V 3HP, England.

HARGITAI, Peter; American/Hungarian writer; b. 28 Jan. 1947, Budapest, Hungary; m. Dianne Kress, 24 July 1967, one s. one d. *Education:* MFA, University of Massachusetts, 1988. *Career:* Lecturer in English, University of Miami, 1980–85, University of Massachusetts, 1987–88; Prof. and Writing Specialist, Florida International University, 1990–; mem. PEN International; Literary Network, New York. *Publications:* Forum: Ten Poets of the Western Reserve, 1976; Perched on Nothings Branch, 1986; Magyar Tales, 1989; Budapest to Bellevue, 1989; Budapesttöl New Yorkig és tovább..., 1991; Fodois Budget Zion, 1991; The Traveler, 1994; Attila: A Barbarian's Bedtime Story, 1994. Contributions: North Atlantic Review; Colorado Quarterly; Nimrod; College English; California Quarterly; Spirit; Prairie Schooner; Poetry East; Cornfield Review; Blue Unicorn. *Honours:* Acad. of American Poets Trans. Award, 1988; Fulbright Grant, 1988; Florida Arts Council Fellowship, 1990; Fust Milan Award, Hungarian Acad. of Sciences, 1994. *E-mail:* hargitai@fiu.edu. *Website:* www.freewebs.com/hargitai.

HARGRAVE, Leonie (see Disch, Thomas Michael)

HARING, Firth (see Fabend, Firth Haring)

HARJO, Joy, BA, MFA; American poet, musician, lyricist, writer and screenwriter and photographer; *Joseph M. Russo Professor of Creative Writing, University of New Mexico*; b. 9 May 1951, Tulsa, OK; d. of Allen W. Foster, Jr and Wynema Jewell Baker; one s. one d. *Education:* Inst. of American-Indian Arts, Univ. of New Mexico, Univ. of Iowa. *Career:* Instructor, Inst. of American-Indian Arts 1978–79, 1983–84, Santa Fe Community Coll. 1983–84; Lecturer, Arizona State Univ. 1980–81; Asst Prof., Univ. of Colorado at Boulder 1985–88; Assoc. Prof., Univ. of Arizona at Tucson 1988–90; Prof., Univ. of New Mexico 1991–97, Joseph M. Russo Prof. of Creative Writing 2005–; Prof., UCLA 2001–; numerous tours and festival appearances; Nat. Endowment for the Arts Creative Writing Fellowships 1978, 1992; Arizona Comm. on the Arts Poetry Fellowship 1989; Woodrow Wilson Fellowship 1993; Witter Bynner Poetry Fellowship 1994; mem. PEN (Advisory Bd), Nat. Council of the Arts. *Screenplay:* A Thousand Roads (signature film of the National Museum of the American Indian). *Compositions:* Letter From The End of The 20th Century, The Musician Who Became A Bear. *Recordings:* Letter From The End of The 20th Century, Eagle Song (video) 2002, Native Joy 2003, Native Joy for Real 2004, She Had Some Horses 2006. *Publications:* The Last Song 1975, What Moon Drove Me To This? 1980, She Had Some Horses 1983, Secrets From the Center of the World (with Stephen Strom) 1989, In Mad Love and War 1990, Fishing 1992, The Woman Who Fell From the Sky 1994, Reinventing the Enemy's Language 1997, A Map to the Next World 2000, The Good Luck Cat 2000, How We Became Human 2002; contrib. to many anthologies, magazines and recordings. *Honours:* Dr hc (Benedictine Coll.) 1992; Pushcart Prize in Poetry 1987, in Poetry Anthology 1990, American-Indian Distinguished Achievement in the Arts Award 1990, Before Columbus Foundation American Book Award 1991, New York Univ. Delmore Schwartz Memorial Award 1991, Mountains and Plains Booksellers Award for Best Book of Poetry 1991, Poetry Soc. of America William Carlos Williams Award 1991, Native Writers Circle of the Americas Lifetime Achievement Award 1995, Oklahoma Book Arts Awards 1995, State of New Mexico Gov.'s Award for Excellence in the Arts 1997, Lila Wallace-Reader's Digest Writers Award 1998–2000. *Literary Agent:* Mekko Productions Inc., 1140 D Alewa Drive, Honolulu, HI 96817, USA. *Telephone:* (808) 595-8198. *E-mail:* mekkopoet@earthlink.net; nativesax@yahoo.com. *Website:* www.joyharjo.com.

HARKNETT, Terry, (Frank Chandler, David Ford, George G. Gilman, William M. James, Charles R. Pike, James Russell, William Terry); British writer; b. 14 Dec. 1936, Rainham, Essex, England. *Career:* Ed., Newspaper Features Ltd, 1958–61; Reporter and Features Ed., National Newsagent, 1961–72. *Publications:* (as George G. Gilman): Edge series: The Godforsaken, 1982; Arapaho Revenge, 1983; The Blind Side, 1983; House of the Range, 1983; Edge Meets Steele No. 3 Double Action, 1984; The Moving Cage, 1984; School for Slaughter, 1985; Revenge Ride, 1985; Shadow of the Gallows, 1985; A Time for Killing, 1986; Brutal Border, 1986; Hitting Paydirt, 1986; Backshort, 1987; Uneasy Riders, 1987. Adam Steele series: Canyon of Death, 1985; High Stakes, 1985; Rough Justice, 1985; The Sunset Ride, 1986; The Killing Strain, 1986; The Big Gunfight, 1987; The Hunted, 1987; Code of the West, 1987. The Undertaker series: Three Graves to a Showdown, 1982; Back from the Dead, 1982; Death in the Desert, 1982. As William Terry: Red Sun (novelization of screenplay), 1972. As Frank Chandler: A Fistful of Dollars (novelization of screenplay), 1972. As Charles R. Pike: Jubal Cade series: The Killing Trail, 1974; Double Cross, 1974; The Hungary Gun, 1975. As William M. James: Apache series: The First Death, 1974; Duel to the Death, 1974; Fort Treachery, 1975. As Terry Harknett: The Caribbean, 1972. As James Russell: The Balearic Islands, 1972. As David Ford: Cyprus, 1973. *Address:* Spring Acre, Springhead Road, Uplyme, Lyme Regis, Dorset DT7 3RS, England.

HARLAN, Louis Rudolph, BA, MA, PhD; American academic and historian; b. 13 July 1922, West Point, MS; m. Sadie Morton 1947; two s. *Education:* Emory Univ., Vanderbilt Univ., Johns Hopkins Univ. *Career:* Asst to Assoc. Prof., East Texas State Coll. 1950–59; Assoc. Prof. to Prof., Univ. of Cincinnati 1959–66; Prof. of History, Univ. of Maryland, Coll. Park 1966–84, Distinguished Prof. of History 1984–92, Prof. Emeritus 1992–; Fellow Soc. of American Historians; mem. American Historical Asscn (pres. 1989), Asscn for the Study of Afro-American Life and History, Nat. Historical Publications and Records Commission, Organization of American Historians (pres. 1989–90). *Publications:* Separate and Unequal 1958, The Booker T. Washington Papers (ed., 14 vols) 1972–89, Booker T. Washington: Vol. I The Making of a Black Leader 1972, Vol. II The Wizard of Tuskegee 1983, Booker T. Washington in Perspective 1988, All at Sea 1996; contrib. to periodicals. *Honours:* Bancroft Prizes 1973, 1984, Guggenheim Fellowship 1975, Pulitzer Prize in Biography 1984, Albert J. Beveridge Award 1984, Julian P. Boyd Award 1989, Nat. Historical Publications and Records Commission Award 1991. *Address:* 160 Kendal Drive, Cottage 1022, Lexington, VA 24450, USA (home).

HARLE, Elizabeth (see Roberts, Irene)

HARLEMAN, Ann, BA, MFA, PhD; American writer and educator; b. 28 Oct. 1945, Youngstown, OH; m. Bruce A. Rosenberg 1981, one d. *Education:* Rutgers Univ., Princeton Univ., Brown Univ. *Career:* Asst Prof. of English, Rutgers Univ. 1973–74; Asst Prof., Univ. of Washington 1974–79, Assoc. Prof. of English 1979–84; Visiting Prof. of Rhetoric, MIT 1984–86; Visiting Scholar, Program in American Civilization, Brown Univ. 1986–; Cole Distinguished Prof. of English, Wheaton Coll. 1992; Prof. of English, Rhode Island School of Design 1994–; mem. MLA (chair. of gen. linguistics exec. cttee), Poets and Writers, PEN American Center. *Publications:* fiction: Happiness 1994, Bitter Lake 1996, Thoreau's Laundry 2007; contrib. short stories to Alaska Quarterly Review, American Fiction, Boston Review, Chicago Tribune, Glimmer Train, Good Housekeeping, Green Mountains Review, Greensboro Review, Hotel Amerika, Madison Review, Ms, Nebraska Review, New England Review, The Ohio Review, Oxford Magazine, Ploughshares, Primavera, Southwest Review, Shenandoah, Story, Toyon Virginia Quarterly Review, Witness; contrib. poems to Apalachee Quarterly, Ascent, Greensboro Review, High Plains Literary Review, Kansas Quarterly, Southern Review, Yankee; non-fiction: Graphic Representation of Models in Linguistic Theory 1976; contrib. articles to journals and books. *Honours:* Guggenheim Fellowship 1976, Fulbright Fellowship 1980, MacDowell Colony Fellow 1988, Nat. Endowment for the Humanities Fellowship 1989, Rhode Island State Council on the Arts Fellowship 1990, 1997, PEN Syndicated Fiction Award 1991, Iowa Short Fiction Prize 1993, Sr Fellow ACLS 1993, Bogliasco Foundation Fellowship 1998. *Literary Agent:* Gail Hochman, Brandt & Hochman Literary Agency, 1501 Broadway, 23rd Floor, New York, NY 10036, USA. *Telephone:* 212-840-5760. *E-mail:* Ann_Harleman@Brown.edu. *Website:* www.annharleman.com.

HARMAN, Gilbert Helms, BA, PhD; American academic and writer; *Professor of Philosophy, Princeton University*; b. 26 May 1938, E Orange, NJ; s. of William H. Harman, Jr and Marguerite Page; m. Lucy Newman 1970; two d. *Education:* Swarthmore Coll. and Harvard Univ. *Career:* faculty mem. Dept of Philosophy, Princeton Univ. 1963–, Prof. of Philosophy 1971–, Co-Dir Cognitive Science Lab. 1986–2000; Fellow, Cognitive Science Soc. 2003; mem. American Philosophical Asscn, Philosophy of Science Asscn, Soc. for Philosophy and Psychology, American Psychological Soc., Linguistic Soc. of America, American Acad. of Arts and Sciences 2005. *Publications:* Semantics of Natural Language (co-ed. with Donald Davidson) 1971, Thought 1973, On Noam Chomsky (ed.) 1974, The Logic of Grammar (ed. with Donald Davidson) 1975, The Nature of Morality: An Introduction to Ethics 1977, Change in View: Principles of Reasoning 1986, Skepticism and the Definition of Knowledge 1990, Conceptions of the Human Mind (ed.) 1993, Moral Relativism and Moral Objectivity (with Judith Jarvis Thomson) 1996, Reasoning, Meaning and Mind 1999, Explaining Values and other Essays in Moral Philosophy 2000; contrib. to scholarly journals. *Honours:* Jean Nicod Prize 2005. *Address:* Department of Philosophy, Princeton University, Princeton, NJ 08544-1006 (office); 106 Broadmead Street, Princeton, NJ 08540, USA (home). *Telephone:* (609) 258-4301. *Fax:* (609) 258-1502. *E-mail:* harman@princeton.edu (office). *Website:* www.princeton.edu/~harman.

HARMON, Maurice, BA, HDE, MA, AM PhD; Irish academic, poet, writer and editor; *Professor Emeritus, University College Dublin*; b. 21 June 1930, Dublin. *Education:* Univ. Coll., Dublin, Harvard Univ., USA. *Career:* Lecturer in English, Univ. Coll. Dublin 1964–76, Assoc. Prof. of Anglo-Irish Literature and Drama 1976–90, Prof. Emer. 1990–; Ed. University Review 1964–68, Irish University Review 1970–86, Poetry Ireland Review 2000–01. *Publications:* Seán O'Faoláin: A Critical Introduction 1966, Modern Irish Literature 1800–1967: A Reader's Guide 1967, Fenians and Fenianism: Centenary Papers (ed.) 1968, The Celtic Master: Contributions to the First James Joyce Symposium 1969, Romeo and Juliet, by Shakespeare (ed.) 1970, J. M. Synge Centenary Papers 1971 (ed.) 1971, King Richard II, by Shakespeare (ed.) 1971, Coriolanus, by Shakespeare (ed.) 1972, The Poetry of Thomas Kinsella 1974, The Irish Novel in Our Time (ed. with Patrick Rafroidi) 1976, Select Bibliography for the Study of Anglo-Irish Literature and Its Backgrounds 1976, Richard Murphy: Poet of Two Traditions (ed.) 1978, Irish Poetry After Yeats: Seven Poets (ed.) 1979, Image and Illusion: Anglo-Irish Literature and Its Contexts (ed.) 1979, A Short History of Anglo-Irish Literature From Its Origins to the Present (with Roger McHugh) 1982, The Irish Writer and the

City (ed.) 1985, James Joyce: The Centennial Symposium (with Morris Beja et al) 1986, Austin Clarke: A Critical Introduction 1989, The Book of Precedence (poems) 1994, Seán O'Faoláin: A Life 1994, A Stillness at Kiawah (poems) 1996, No Author Better Served: The Correspondence of Samuel Beckett and Alan Schneider 1998, The Last Regatta (poems) 2000, Tales of Death (poems) 2001, The Colloquy of the Old Men (trans.) 2001, The Dolmen Press: A Celebration 2001, The Doll with Two Backs and Other Poems 2004, Selected Essays 2006. *Address:* 20 Sycamore Road, Mount Merrion, Blackrock, Co. Dublin, Ireland (home).

HARPER, Michael Steven, BA, MA; American academic and poet; b. 18 March 1938, New York, NY; m.; three c. *Education:* California State Univ. at Los Angeles, Univ. of Iowa Writers' Workshop, Brown Univ. *Career:* Visiting Prof., Lewis and Clark Coll. 1968–69, Reed Coll. 1968–69, Harvard Univ. 1974–77, Yale Univ. 1976; Prof. of English, Brown Univ. 1970–; Benedict Distinguished Prof., Carleton Coll. 1979; Elliston Poet and Distinguished Prof., Univ. of Cincinnati 1979; Nat. Endowment for the Humanities Prof., Colgate Univ. 1985; Distinguished Minority Prof., Univ. of Delaware 1988, Macalester Coll. 1989; first Poet Laureate of the State of Rhode Island 1988–93; Phi Beta Kappa Visiting Scholar 1991; Berg Distinguished Visiting Prof., New York Univ. 1992; mem. American Acad. of Arts and Sciences. *Publications:* Dear John, Dear Coltrane 1970, History is Your Own Heartbeat 1971, History as Apple Tree 1972, Song: I Want a Witness 1972, Debridement 1973, Nightmare Begins Responsibility 1975, Images of Kin 1977, Chant of Saints (co-ed.) 1979, Healing Song for the Inner Ear 1985, Songlines: Mosaics 1991, Every Shut Eye Ain't Asleep (co-ed.) 1994, Honorable Amendments 1995, Collected Poems 1996, Family Sequences 1998, Songlines in Michaeltree 1999, Selected Poems 2002, Sweet Homeland (with Rebecca Bella Wangh) 2002, Use Trouble 2005, I Do Believe in People: Remembrances of W. Warren Harper (1915–2004); audio: Double Take (with Paul Austerlitz, bass clarinet) 2004, Our Book of Trane (with Paul Austerlitz, bass clarinet) 2004; contribs to Carleton Miscellany, Obsidian, The Vintage Anthology of African American Poetry 1750–2000. *Honours:* Hon. DLitt (Trinity Coll., CT, Coe Coll., IN, Notre Dame Coll., NH, Kenyon Coll., OH, Rhode Island Coll.); Black Acad. of Arts and Letters Award 1972, Nat. Inst. of Arts and Letters grants 1975, 1976, 1985, Guggenheim Fellowship 1976, Poetry Soc. of America Melville Cane Award 1978, Rhode Island Council of the Arts Governor's Poetry Award 1987, United Negro Coll. Fund Robert Hayden Memorial Poetry Award 1990, New York Public Library Literary Lion 1992, George Kent Poetry Award 1996, Claiborne Pell Award 1997. *Address:* Brown University, Box 1923, Providence, RI 02912-1923, USA (office). *Telephone:* (401) 863-2705 (office). *Fax:* (401) 863-2290 (office). *E-mail:* michael_harper@brown.edu.

HARPER, Stephen Dennis; British journalist and writer; b. 15 Sept. 1924, Newport, Monmouthshire, Wales. *Career:* mem. Society of Authors. *Publications:* Fiction: A Necessary End, 1975; Mirror Image, 1976; Live Till Tomorrow, 1977; White Christmas in Saigon, 1990. Non-Fiction: Last Sunset, 1978; Miracle of Deliverance, 1985; Capturing Enigma, 1999; Imperial War Museum Book of Modern Warfare (contributor), 2002. *Address:* Green Dene Lodge, Green Dene, East Horsley, Surrey KT24 5RG, England. *E-mail:* stephen@greendene.freeserve.co.uk.

HARRIES, Owen; British editor, fmr government official and academic; *Senior Fellow, Centre for Independent Studies;* b. Wales. *Education:* Univs of Wales and Oxford. *Career:* taught for 20 years Univ. of Sydney, NSW; apptd Sr Adviser to shadow Foreign Affairs Minister, Australia 1974, subsequently Dir of Policy Planning, Dept of Foreign Affairs; Sr Adviser to Prime Minister; Amb. to UNESCO 1982–83; Visiting Fellow, Heritage Foundation USA 1983–85; founder and Ed.-in-Chief The National Interest (journal) Washington DC 1985–2001; currently Sr Fellow Centre for Independent Studies, Australia; Sr Assoc. Center for Strategic and Int. Studies USA. *Publications include:* Liberty and Politics (ed.) 1976, Australia and the Third World (ed.) 1979, America's Purpose (ed.) 1991. *Address:* Centre for Independent Studies, POB 92, St Leonards, NSW 1590, Australia (office). *Telephone:* (2) 9438-4377 (office). *Fax:* (2) 9439-7310 (office). *E-mail:* cis@cis.org.au (office). *Website:* www.cis.org.au (office).

HARRIES, Rt Rev. Richard Douglas, DD, FKC, FRSL; British ecclesiastic; b. 2 June 1936, s. of Brig. W. D. J. Harries and G. M. B. Harries; m. Josephine Bottomley 1963; one s. one d. *Education:* Wellington Coll., Royal Mil. Acad, Sandhurst, Selwyn Coll, Cambridge, Cuddesdon Coll., Oxford. *Career:* Lt, Royal Corps of Signals 1955–58; Curate, Hampstead Parish Church 1963–69; Chaplain, Westfield Coll. 1966–69; Lecturer, Wells Theological Coll. 1969–72; Warden, Salisbury and Wells Theological Coll. 1971–72; Vicar, All Saints, Fulham, London 1972–81; Dean, King's Coll., London 1981–87; Bishop of Oxford 1987–2006; Vice-Chair. Council of Christian Action 1979–87, Council for Arms Control 1982–87; Chair. Southwark Ordination Course 1982–87, Shalom, End Loans to South Africa (ELSTA) 1982–87, Christian Evidence Soc.; Chair. Church of England Bd of Social Responsibility 1996–2001; Consultant to the Archbishops on Jewish-Christian Relations 1986–92; Chair. Council of Christians and Jews 1993–2001, House of Lords select Cttee on Stem Cell Research 2001–02; Visiting Prof., Liverpool Hope Coll. 2002; mem. Home Office Advisory Cttee for Reform of Law on Sexual Offences 1981–85, Bd Christian Aid 1994–2001, Royal Comm. on Lords Reform 1999–, Nuffield Council of Bioethics 2002–, Human Fertilisation and Embryology Authority 2003–. *Publications:* Prayers of Hope 1975, Turning to Prayer 1978, Prayers of Grief and Glory 1979, Being a Christian 1981, Should Christians Support Guerrillas? 1982, The Authority of Divine Love 1983, Praying Round the

Clock 1983, Seasons of the Spirit (co-ed.) 1984, Prayer and the Pursuit of Happiness 1985, Reinhold Niebuhr and the Issues of Our Time (ed.) 1986, Morning has Broken 1985, Christianity and War in a Nuclear Age 1986, C. S. Lewis: The Man and his God 1987, Christ is Risen 1988, Is There a Gospel for the Rich? 1992, Art and the Beauty of God 1993, The Value of Business and its Values (co-author) 1993, The Real God 1994, Questioning Faith 1995, A Gallery of Reflections 1995, In the Gladness of Today 2000, Christianity: Two Thousand Years (co-ed.) 2000, God Outside the Box: Why Spiritual People Object to Christianity 2002, After the Evil: Christianity and Judaism in the Shadow of the Holocaust 2003, The Passionate Act 2004, Praying the Eucharist 2004, The Passion in Art 2005; contrib. to several books; numerous articles. *Honours:* Hon. Fellow, Selwyn Coll., Cambridge; Hon. Fellow, Acad. of Medical Sciences 2004; Hon. DD (London) 1996; Hon. DUniv (Oxford Brookes) 2001; Sir Sigmund Steinberg Award 1989. *Address:* c/o Diocesan Church House, North Hinksey Lane, Oxford, OX2 0NB, England. *Telephone:* (1865) 208222.

HARRIS, Jana, BS, MA; American writer, poet and teacher; b. 21 Sept. 1947, San Francisco, CA; m. Mark Allen Bothwell. *Education:* Univ. of Oregon, San Francisco State Univ. *Career:* Instructor in Creative Writing, New York Univ. 1980, Univ. of Washington 1986–, Pacific Lutheran Univ. 1988; founder and Ed. of cyberspace poetry journal, Switched-on Gutenberg; mem. Associated Writing Programs, PEN, Poetry Soc. of America, Nat. Book Critics Circle. *Publications:* This House That Rocks with Every Truck on the Road 1976, Pin Money 1977, The Clackamas 1980, Alaska (novel) 1980, Who's That Pushy Bitch? 1981, Running Scared 1981, Manhattan as a Second Language 1982, The Sourlands: Poems by Jana Harris 1989, Oh How Can I Keep on Singing: Voices of Pioneer Women (poems) (Washington State Governor's Writers Award) 1993, The Dust of Everyday Life (poems) (Andres Berger Award) 1998, The Pearl of Ruby City (novel) 1998, We Never Speak of It: Idaho-Wyoming Poems 1889 2003; contrib. to periodicals. *Honours:* Berkeley Civic Arts Commemoration Grant 1974, Washington State Arts Council Fellowship 1993, Pushcart Prize for Poetry 2001, Prairie Schooner Reader's Choice Award 2004. *Address:* 32814 120th Street SE, Sultan, WA 98294, USA (office). *Telephone:* (360) 793-1848 (office). *E-mail:* jnh@u.washington.edu (office). *Website:* www.janaharris.net; www.switched-ongutenberg.org.

HARRIS, Jane; British writer and scriptwriter; b. Belfast, Northern Ireland; m. Tom Shankland. *Education:* Univ. of East Anglia. *Career:* fmr writer-in-residence, Durham Prison. *Film scripts include:* Bait 1999, Going Down 2000. *Publications:* The Observations (novel) 2006; contrib. short stories to anthologies and magazines. *Honours:* Arts Council England Writer's Award 2000. *Address:* c/o Faber and Faber Ltd, 3 Queen Square, London, WC1N 3AU, England (office).

HARRIS, Joanne; British writer; b. 1964, Yorks., England; m. Kevin; one d. *Education:* Saint Catharine's Coll., Cambridge. *Career:* fmr French teacher, Leeds Grammar School for 15 years. *Publications:* The Evil Seed 1989, Sleep, Pale Sister 1993, Chocolat 1999, Blackberry Wine 2000, Five Quarters of the Orange 2001, Coastliners 2002, The French Kitchen: A Cookbook, Holy Fools 2003, Jigs & Reels (short stories) 2004, Gentlemen & Players 2005, Runemarks (juvenile) 2006, The Lollipop Shoes 2007. *Honours:* Hon. DLitt (Huddersfield) 2003, (Sheffield) 2004. *Address:* c/o Transworld Publishers, 61–63 Uxbridge Road, London, W5 5SA, England. *Website:* www.joanne-harris.co.uk.

HARRIS, Jocelyn Margaret, MA, PhD; New Zealand academic and writer; b. 10 Sept. 1939, Dunedin; one s. one d. *Education:* University of Otago, University of London. *Career:* Personal Chair., Dept of English, University of Otago; mem. Australian and South Pacific 18th Century Society. *Publications:* Samuel Richardson: Sir Charles Grandison (ed.), 1972; Samuel Richardson, 1989; Jane Austen's Art of Memory, 1989; Samuel Richardson's Published Commentary on Clarissa, 1747–1765, Vol. I (ed. with Tom Keymer). Contributions: scholarly journals.

HARRIS, Marion Rose, (Rose Glendower, Rosie Harris, Marion Rose, Rose Young, Rosie Young); British writer; b. 12 July 1925, Cardiff, S Wales; m. Kenneth Mackenzie Harris 1943; two s. one d. *Career:* Ed./Owner Regional Feature Service 1964–74; Editorial Controller, W. Foulsham and Co. Ltd 1974–82; mem. Soc. of Authors, Romantic Novelists Asscn, Welsh Acad. *Publications:* as Marion Harris: Captain of Her Heart 1976, Just a Handsome Stranger 1983, The Queen's Windsor 1985, Soldiers' Wives 1986, Officers' Ladies 1987, Nesta 1988, Heart of the Dragon 1988, Amelda: Heart of the Dragon Vol. II, The Old Dragon 1989, Sighing for the Moon (also as Rose Glendower) 1991; as Rose Young: To Love and Love Again 1993, Secret of Abbey Place 1999, Love Can Conquer 1999; as Rosie Harris: Turn of the Tide 2002, Troubled Waters 2002, Patsy of Paradise Place 2003, One Step Forward 2003, Looking for Love 2003, Pins and Needles 2004, Winnie of the Waterfront 2004, At Sixes and Sevens 2005, The Cobbler's Kids 2005, Sunshine and Showers 2005, Megan of Merseyside 2006, The Power of Dreams 2006, A Mother's Love 2006, Sing For Your Supper 2007, Waiting for Love 2007. *Address:* Walpole Cottage, Long Drive, Burnham, Slough, SL1 8AJ, England (office). *Telephone:* (1628) 605717 (office). *E-mail:* marionharris@btinternet.com (office); rosiebooks@btinternet.com (office).

HARRIS, Randy Allen, BA, MA, MSc, MS, PhD; Canadian academic and writer; b. 6 Sept. 1956, Kitimat, BC; m. Indira Naidoo-Harris 1984. *Education:* Queen's Univ., Dalhousie Univ., Univ. of Alberta, Rensselaer Polytechnic Inst. *Publications:* Acoustic Dimensions of Functor Comprehension in Broca's

Aphasia 1988, Linguistics Wars 1993, Landmark Essays in Rhetoric of Science 1997, Voice Interaction Design 2005, Rhetoric and Incommensurability 2005; contrib. to College English, Perspectives on Science, Rhetoric Review, Historiographia Linguistica, Rhetoric Society Quarterly, Neuropsychologia. *Honours:* Heritage Scholar, Rensselaer Scholar, Killam Scholar, Killam Fellow. *Address:* Department of English, University of Waterloo, Waterloo, ON N2L 3G1, Canada (office).

HARRIS, Robert Dennis, FRSL; British journalist and writer; b. 7 March 1957, Nottingham; s. of late Dennis Harris and Audrey Harris; m. Gill Hornby 1988; two s. two d. *Education:* Univ. of Cambridge. *Career:* Pres. Cambridge Union; Dir and reporter, BBC 1978–86; Political Ed. Observer 1987–89; columnist Sunday Times 1989–92, 1996–97. *Publications:* non-fiction: A Higher Form of Killing (with Jeremy Paxman) 1982, Gotcha! 1983, The Making of Neil Kinnock 1984, Selling Hitler 1987, Good and Faithful Servant 1990; novels: Fatherland 1992, Enigma 1995 (film 2001), Archangel 1998, Pompeii 2003, Imperium 2006. *Address:* Old Vicarage, Kintbury, Berkshire RG17 9TR, England.

HARRIS, Rosemary Jeanne; British writer; b. 20 Feb. 1923, London, England; d. of the late Sir Arthur Harris and Barbara Daisy Harris (née Kyrle Money). *Education:* privately and Chelsea School of Art, Courtauld Inst. *Career:* children's book reviewer, The Times, London 1970–73; mem. Soc. of Authors (fmr chair. children's writers group). *Publications:* The Summer-House 1956, Voyage to Cythera 1958, Venus with Sparrows 1961, All My Enemies 1967, The Nice Girl's Story (aka Nor Evil Dreams) 1968, The Moon in the Cloud 1968, A Wicked Pack of Cards 1969, The Shadow on the Sun 1970, The Seal-Singing 1971, The Child in the Bamboo Grove 1972, The Bright and Morning Star 1972, The King's White Elephant 1973, The Double Snare 1974, The Lotus and the Grail: Legends from East to West (aka Sea Magic and Other Stories of Enchantment) 1974, The Flying Ship 1975, The Little Dog of Fo 1976, Three Candles for the Dark 1976, I Want to Be a Fish 1977, A Quest for Orion 1978, Beauty and the Beast (folklore) 1979, Green Finger House 1980, Tower of the Stars 1980, The Enchanted Horse 1981, Janni's Stork 1981, Zed 1982, Summers of the Wild Rose 1987, Love and the Merry-Go-Round 1988, Ticket to Freedom 1991, The Wildcat Strike 1995, The Haunting of Joey M'basa 1996. *Honours:* Library Asscn Carnegie Medal 1967.

HARRIS, Ruth Elwin; British writer; b. 22 June 1935, Bristol, England; m. Christopher J. L. Bowes 1964, two s. one d. *Education:* Bristol, England. *Career:* mem. Society of Authors. *Publications:* The Quantocks Quartet: The Silent Shore, 1986; The Beckoning Hills, 1987; The Dividing Sea, 1989; Billie: The Nevill Letters 1914–1916, 1991; Beyond the Orchid House, 1994.

HARRIS, Thomas; American writer; b. 1940, Jackson, TN; s. of William Thomas Harris, Jr and Polly Harris; m. (divorced); one d. *Education:* Baylor Univ., TX. *Career:* worked on newsdesk Waco News-Tribune; mem. staff Associated Press, New York City 1968–74. *Publications:* Black Sunday 1975, Red Dragon 1981, The Silence of the Lambs (Bram Stoker Best Novel Award) 1988, Hannibal 1999, Hannibal Rising 2006. *Address:* c/o Arrow, Random House, 20 Vauxhall Bridge Road, London, SW1V 2SA, England. *Website:* www.thomasharris.com.

HARRIS, (Theodore) Wilson; Guyanese poet and novelist; b. 24 March 1921, New Amsterdam; m. 1st Cecily Carew 1945; m. 2nd Margaret Whitaker 1959. *Education:* Queen's Coll., Georgetown. *Career:* Visiting Lecturer, SUNY at Buffalo 1970; writer-in-residence, Univ. of the West Indies, Jamaica, Scarborough Coll., Univ. of Toronto 1970, Univ. of Newcastle, NSW 1979; Commonwealth Fellow in Caribbean Literature, Leeds Univ. 1971; Visiting Prof., Univ. of Texas, Austin 1972, 1981–82, Univ. of Mysore 1978, Yale Univ. 1979; Regents Lecturer, Univ. of California, Santa Cruz 1983. *Publications:* poetry: Fetish 1951, The Well and the Land 1952, Eternity to Season 1954; fiction: The Guyana Quartet 1960–63, Tumatumari 1968, Black Marsden 1972, Companions of the Day and Night 1975, Da Silva's Cultivated Wilderness 1977, Genesis of the Clowns 1977, The Tree of the Sun 1978, The Angel at the Gate 1982, The Carnival Trilogy 1985–90, Resurrection at Sorrow Hill 1993, The Dark Jester 2001, The Mask of the Beggar 2003, The Ghost of Memory 2006; short stories. *Address:* c/o Faber and Faber Ltd, 3 Queen Square, London, WC1N 3AU, England.

HARRIS, Zinnie, BA, MA; British playwright; b. (Zinnie Shaw), 23 Dec. 1972, Oxford; d. of Dr Mark Shaw and Francesca Shaw; m. John Harris 1995; two s. *Education:* Univs of Oxford and Hull. *Plays:* By Many Wounds 1998, Further Than the Furthest Thing 2000, Nightingale and Chase 2001, Midwinter 2004, Solstice 2005, Julie 2006. *Television scripts:* Born with Two Mothers (Windfall films/Channel 4) 2005, Spooks (Kudos/BBC 1 Episode 5, Series 5) 2006. *Publications:* By Many Wounds 1998, Further Than the Furthest Thing 2000, Nightingale and Chase 2001, Midwinter 2004, Solstice 2005. *Honours:* Peggy Ramsay New Writing Award, John Whiting Award, Arts Foundation Fellowship Award, Pearson Bursary Scheme. *Literary Agent:* c/o Mel Kenyon, Casarotto Ramsay & Associates Ltd, Waverley House, 7–12 Noel Street, London, W1F 8GO, England. *Telephone:* (20) 7287-4450. *Fax:* (20) 7287-9128. *E-mail:* mel@casarotto.uk.com. *Website:* www.casarotto.uk.com.

HARRISON, Sir Brian Howard, Kt, MA, DPhil, FRHistS, FBA; British historian and academic; *Professor Emeritus of Modern British History, Corpus Christi College, Oxford;* b. 9 July 1937, s. of Howard Harrison and Mary Elizabeth Savill; m. Anne Victoria Greggain 1967. *Education:* Merchant Taylors' School, Northwood and St John's Coll., Oxford. *Career:* Nat. Service,

2nd Lt Malta Signal Squadron 1956–58; Sr Scholar, St Antony's Coll., Oxford 1961–64; Jr Research Fellow, Nuffield Coll., Oxford 1964–67; Fellow and Tutor in Modern History and Politics, Corpus Christi Coll., Oxford 1967–2000, Sr Tutor 1984–86, 1988–90, Univ. Reader in Modern British History 1990–2000, Vice-Pres. 1992, 1993, 1996–98, Prof. of Modern British History 1996– (now Prof. Emeritus); Ed. Oxford Dictionary of Nat. Biography 2000–04; Visiting Prof., Univ. of Michigan at Ann Arbor 1970–71, Harvard Univ. 1973–74; Visiting Fellow, Melbourne Univ. 1975, ANU 1995; Emeritus Fellow Corpus Christi Coll., Oxford 2004–. *Publications include:* Drink and the Victorians 1971, Separate Spheres: the Opposition to Women's Suffrage in Britain 1978, Robert Lowery: Radical and Chartist (ed. with Patricia Hollis) 1979, Peaceable Kingdom: Stability and Change in Modern Britain 1982, A Hundred Years Ago: Britain in the 1880s in Words and Photographs (with Colin Ford) 1983, Prudent Revolutionaries: Portraits of British Feminists Between the Wars 1987, The History of the University of Oxford, vol. 8: The Twentieth Century (ed.) 1994, Corpuscles: a History of Corpus Christi College, Oxford in the Twentieth Century, Written by its Members (ed) 1994, The Transformation of British Politics 1860–1995 1996, Civil Histories: essays presented to Sir Keith Thomas (co-ed. and contrib.) 2000, Oxford Dictionary of National Biography (ed.) 2004. *Address:* c/o Corpus Christi College, Merton Street, Oxford, OX1 4JF, England.

HARRISON, Elizabeth Fancourt; British author; b. 12 Jan. 1921, Watford, Hertfordshire, England. *Career:* mem. Society of Authors, Romantic Novelists' Asscn. *Publications:* Coffee at Dobree's, 1965; The Physicians, 1966; The Ravelston Affair, 1967; Corridors of Healing, 1968; Emergency Call, 1970; Accident Call, 1971; Ambulance Call, 1972; Surgeon's Call, 1973; On Call, 1974; Hospital Call, 1975; Dangerous Call, 1976; To Mend a Heart, 1977; Young Dr Goddard, 1978; A Doctor Called Caroline, 1979; A Surgeon Called Amanda, 1982; A Surgeon's Life, 1983; Marrying a Doctor, 1984; Surgeon's Affair, 1985; A Surgeon at St Mark's, 1986; The Surgeon She Married, 1988; The Faithful Type, 1993; The Senior Partner's Daughter, 1994; Made for Each Other, 1995.

HARRISON, James (Jim) Thomas, BA, MA; American writer and poet; b. 11 Dec. 1937, Grayling, Mich.; s. of Winfield Sprague Harrison and Norma Olivia Harrison (née Wahlgren); m. Linda May King 1960; two d. *Education:* Michigan State Univ. *Career:* Asst Prof. of English, SUNY at Stony Brook 1965–66. *Film screenplays:* Cold Feet (with Tom McGuane) 1989, Revenge (with Jeffrey Fishkin) 1990, Wolf (with Wesley Strick) 1994. *Publications:* fiction: Wolf: A False Memoir 1971, A Good Day to Die 1973, Farmer 1976, Legends of the Fall 1979, Warlock 1981, Sundog 1984, Dalva 1988, The Woman Lit by Fireflies 1990, Sunset Limited 1990, Julip 1994, The Road Home 1998, The Beast God Forgot to Invent 2000, True North 2004, The Summer He Didn't Die 2005, Returning to Earth 2007; poetry: Plain Song 1965, Locations 1968, Walking 1969, Outlyer and Ghazals 1971, Letters to Yesinin 1973, Returning to Earth 1977, New and Selected Poems, 1961–81 1982, The Theory and Practice of Rivers 1986, After Ikkyu and Other Poems 1996, The Shape of the Journey 1998, Braided Creek: A Conversation in Poetry 2003, Livingston Suite 2005, Saving Daylight 2006; non-fiction: Just Before Dark 1991, The Raw and the Cooked: Adventures of a Roving Gourmand 2001. *Honours:* NEA grant 1967–69, Guggenheim Fellowship 1968–69.

HARRISON, Sarah, BA; British author; b. 7 Aug. 1946, Exeter, England. *Education:* University of London. *Career:* Journalist, IPC Magazines, London, 1967–71; freelance novelist/writer 1971–. *Publications:* fiction: Flowers of the Field, 1980; A Flower That's Free, 1984; Hot Breath, 1985; An Imperfect Lady, 1987; Cold Feet, 1989; Foreign Parts, 1991; The Forests of the Night, 1992; Be An Angel, 1993; Both Your Houses, 1995; Life After Lunch, 1996; Flowers Won't Fax, 1997; That Was Then, 1998; Heaven's On Hold, 1999; The Grass Memorial, 2002; The Dreaming Stones, 2002; A Dangerous Thing, 2003, The Nightingale's Nest 2006; The Divided Heart, 2003, Swan Music 2004; children's fiction: In Granny's Garden, 1980; Lark Rise series: Laura and Edmond, 1986; Laura and Old Lumber, 1986; Laura and the Lady, 1986; Laura and the Squire, 1986; non-fiction: How to Write a Blockbuster, 1995. *Literary Agent:* c/ Sheila Crowley, AP Watt Ltd, 20 John Street, London WC1N 2DR, England. *Telephone:* (1462) 742056. *Fax:* (1462) 742549. *E-mail:* novel.sarah@virgin.net. *Website:* www.sarah-harrison.net.

HARRISON, Sue Ann, BA; American novelist; b. (Sue Ann McHaney), 29 Aug. 1950, Lansing, MI; m. Neil Douglas Harrison 1969; one s. two d. (one deceased). *Career:* mem. Soc. of Midland Authors. *Publications:* Mother Earth, Father Sky 1990, My Sister the Moon 1992, Brother Wind 1994, Sisu 1997, Song of the River 1997, Cry of the Wind 1998, Call Down the Stars 2001. *Address:* 23382 S Rocky Point Road, Pickford, MI 49774, USA (home). *E-mail:* sue@sueharrison.com (office). *Website:* www.sueharrison.com (office).

HARRISON, Tony; British poet and dramatist; b. 30 April 1937, Leeds; s. of Harry Ashton Harrison and Florence (née Wilkinson) Horner. *Education:* Leeds Grammar School and Univ. of Leeds. *Writing for television and film:* Yan Tan Tethera 1983, The Big H 1984, 'V' 1987, Loving Memory 1987, The Blasphemers' Banquet 1989, Black Daisies for the Bride 1993, A Maybe Day in Kazakhstan 1994, The Shadow of Hiroshima 1995, Prometheus 1998, Crossings 2002. *Plays:* Aikin Mata (with J. Simmons) 1965, The Misanthrope (version of Molière's play) 1973, Phaedra Britannica (version of Racine's Phèdre) 1975, The Passion 1977, Bow Down 1977, The Bartered Bride (libretto) 1978, The Oresteia (trans.) 1981, The Mysteries 1985, The Trackers of Oxyrhynchus 1990, The Common Chorus 1992, Square Rounds 1992, Poetry or Bust 1993, The Kaisers of Carnuntum 1995, The Labourers of Herakles 1995, The Prince's Play 1996, Fire and Poetry 1999. *Publications include:* poetry: Earthworks 1964, Newcastle is Peru 1969, The Loiners 1970, Poems of Palladas of Alexandria (ed. and trans.) 1973, From the School of Eloquence and Other Poems 1978, Continuous 1981, A Kumquat for John Keats 1981, US Martial 1981, Selected Poems 1984, Fire-Gap 1985, 'V' 1985, Dramatic Verse, 1973–1985 1985, 'V' and Other Poems 1990, A Cold Coming: Gulf War Poems 1991, The Gaze of the Gorgon and other poems 1992, The Shadow of Hiroshima and other film/poems 1995, Permanently Bard 1995, Laureate's Block and other poems 2000, Under the CLock 2005; collections of plays: Plays 1 1985, Theatre Works 1973–1985 1986, Plays 2 2002, Plays 3 1996, Plays 4 2002, Plays 5 2004, Hecuba 2005. *Honours:* Cholmondeley Award for Poetry, Geoffrey Faber Memorial Award, European Poetry Translation Prize, Whitbread Poetry Prize 1993, Mental Health Award 1994, Prix Italia 1994, Northern Rock Foundation Writers' Award 2004. *Address:* c/o Gordon Dickerson, 2 Crescent Grove, London, SW4 7AH.

HARRISON, William Neal, BA, MA; American writer and academic; *University Professor Emeritus, University of Arkansas*; b. 29 Oct. 1933, Dallas, TX; m. Merlee Kimsey 1957; two s. one d. *Education:* Texas Christian Univ., Vanderbilt Univ., Univ. of Iowa. *Career:* Faculty, Dept of English, Univ. of Arkansas at Fayetteville 1964–99. *Publications:* The Theologian 1965, In a Wild Sanctuary 1969, Lessons in Paradise 1971, Roller Ball Murder and Other Stories 1974, Africana 1977, Savannah Blue 1981, Burton and Speke 1982, Three Hunters 1989, The Buddha in Malibu: New and Selected Stories 1998, The Blood Latitudes 1999, Texas Heat: Stories 2005; other: screenplays; contribs to anthologies and periodicals. *Honours:* Guggenheim Fellowship 1973–74, Nat. Endowment for the Arts Grant 1977, Christopher Award 1979. *Address:* 350 Sequoyah Drive, Fayetteville, AR 72701 (home); Department of English, University of Arkansas at Fayetteville, Fayetteville, AR 72701, USA (office). *E-mail:* billmerlee@earthlink.net (home).

HARRISS, Gerald Leslie, MA, DPhil, FBA; British historian and university teacher; b. 22 May 1925, London; s. of W.L. Harriss and M.J.O. Harriss; m. Margaret Anne Sidaway 1959; two s. three d. *Education:* Chigwell School, Essex, Magdalen Coll., Oxford. *Career:* war service in RNVR 1944–46; Univ. of Oxford 1946–53; Lecturer, Univ. of Durham 1953–65, Reader 1965–67; Fellow and Tutor in History, Magdalen Coll., Oxford 1967–92, Fellow Emer. 1992–, Reader in Modern History, Univ. of Oxford 1990–92. *Publications:* King, Parliament and Public Finance in Medieval England 1975, Henry V: the Practice of Kingship (ed.) 1985, Cardinal Beaufort 1988, K.B. McFarlane, Letters to Friends (ed.) 1997, Shaping the Nation: England 1360–1461 2005. *Address:* Fairings, 2 Queen Street, Yetminster, Sherborne, Dorset, DT9 6LL, England (home).

HARROWER, David; British playwright; b. 1967. *Plays:* Knives in Hens 1995, Kill the Old, Torture their Young 1998, Begin Again 1999, Presence 2001, The Chysalids 2001, Ivanov, by Anton Chekhov (adaptation) 2002, The Girl on the Sofa, by Jon Fosse (adaptation) 2002, Dark Earth 2003, Tales from the Vienna Woods 2003, Purple, by Jon Fosse (adaptation) 2003, Blackbird (King's Theatre, Edinburgh; Best New Play, Laurence Olivier Awards 2007) 2005. *Publications:* Six Characters Looking for an Author (ed.) 2001. *Literary Agent:* Casarotto Ramsay & Associates Ltd, National House, 60–65 Wardour Street, London, W1V 3HP, England. *Telephone:* (20) 7287-4450. *Fax:* (20) 7287-9128. *E-mail:* agents@casarotto.co.uk. *Website:* www.casarotto.co.uk.

HARRS, (Margaret) Norma; Northern Irish writer; b. 15 Sept. 1935; m. Leonard Michael Harrs; two s. *Career:* mem. Writers' Union of Canada, Playwrights' Union of Canada (treasurer 1997–99). *Publications:* A Certain State of Mind 1980, Love Minus One & Other Stories 1994, Where Dreams Have Gone 1997, Sonya (play), The 40th Birthday Party (play), Essential Conflict (play); contrib. to anthologies, including Ladies Start Your Engines 1997, Elements of English 1999; contrib. to journals, including Pittsburgh Review, Kairos, Antigonish Review, Room of One's Own. *Honours:* Ontario Literary Grant 1988, Canada Council Travel Grant 1997. *Address:* 171 Fifth Line, Fraserville, South Monaghan, ON K0L 1V0, Canada. *E-mail:* norharrs@nexicom.net. *Website:* www.normaharrs.com.

HARSENT, David, FRSL; British poet; b. 9 Dec. 1942, Devonshire, England; m. 1st (divorced); two s. one d.; m. 2nd; one d. *Career:* fiction and poetry reviewer, Times Literary Supplement (twelve years); poetry reviewer, The Spectator (four years); poetry and TV reviewer, The New Review (three years); theatre critic, The New Statesman (two years). *Publications:* novel: From an Inland Sea 1985; poetry: Tonight's Lover 1968, A Violent Country 1969, Ashridge 1970, After Dark 1973, Truce 1973, Dreams of the Dead 1977, Mister Punch 1984, Selected Poems 1989, Storybook Hero 1992, News From the Front 1993, The Sorrow of Sarajevo (trans. of poems by Goran Simic) 1996, The Potted Priest 1997, Sprinting from the Graveyard (trans. of poems by Goran Simic) 1997, Playback 1997, A Bird's Idea of Flight 1998, Marriage 2002, Legion (Forward Prize for Best Collection) 2005, New Selected Poems 2007; as editor: New Poetry 7 1981, Poetry Book Society Supplement 1983, Savremena Britanska Poezija 1988, Another Round at the Pillars, a festschrift for Ian Hamilton 1999, Raising the Iron 2003; contrib. to Poetry Introduction 1 1968; libretto: Serenade the Silkie (music by Julian Grant) 1989, Gawain (for Harrison Birtwistle's opera) 1991, The Woman and the Hare (music by Harrison Birtwistle) 1998, When She Died (opera for TV, music by Jonathan Dove) 2002, The Ring Dance of the Nazarene (music by Harrison Birtwistle)

2004, The Minotaur (music by Harrison Birtwistle) 2008. *Honours:* Eric Gregory Award 1967, Cheltenham Festival Prize 1968, Arts Council Bursaries 1969, 1984, Geoffrey Faber Memorial Prize 1978, Soc. of Authors Travel Fellowship 1989; appointed Distinguished Writing Fellow, Hallam Univ., Sheffield 2005. *Literary Agent:* Jonathan Clowes Literary Agency, 10 Iron Bridge House, Bridge Approach, London, NW1 8BD, England.

HART, Anrea (see Freemantle, Brian Harry)

HART, Ellen, BA; American writer; b. 10 Aug. 1949, Minneapolis, MN; two d. *Education:* Ambassador Univ. *Career:* mem. Sisters in Crime. *Publications:* Hallowed Murder, 1989; Vital Lies, 1991; Stage Fright, 1992; A Killing Cure, 1993; The Little Piggy Went to Murder, 1994; A Small Sacrifice, 1994; Faint Praise, 1995; For Every Evil, 1995; Robber's Wine, 1996; The Oldest Sin, 1996; Murder in the Air, 1997; Wicked Games, 1998. *Honours:* Lambda Literary Award 1994, 1996, Minnesota Book Award 1995, 1996.

HART, Josephine; Irish writer; b. Mullingar, Co. Westmeath; m. Maurice Saatchi; two s. *Career:* Founder Gallery Poets, London; Producer various plays in West End, London, including Lorca's The House of Bernarda Alba (Evening Standard Award), Noel Coward's The Vortex and Iris Murdoch's The Black Prince; Presenter Books by My Bedside, Thames TV; mem. judging panel Irish Times–Aer Lingus Int. Fiction Prize 1992. *Publications:* novels: Damage 1991, Sin 1996, Oblivion 1997, The Stillest Day 1998, The Reconstructionist 2001; anthology: Catching Life By the Throat: How to Read Poetry and Why (ed) 2006. *Address:* c/o Random House, 20 Vauxhall Bridge Road, London, SW1V 2SA, England. *Website:* www.josephinehart.com.

HART, Kevin, BA, PhD, FAHA; Australian academic and poet; *Notre Dame Professor of Philosophy and Literature, University of Notre Dame*; b. 5 July 1954, London, England; s. of James Henry Hart and Rosina Mary Wootton; m. Rita Judith Hart; two d. *Education:* Australian Nat. Univ., Stanford Univ., USA and Univ. of Melbourne. *Career:* Lecturer in English, Univ. of Melbourne 1986–87; Lecturer to Sr Lecturer in Literary Studies, Deakin Univ., Victoria 1987–91; Assoc. Prof., Monash Univ. 1991–95, Prof. of English 1995–2002; Foundation Prof. of Australian and New Zealand Studies, Georgetown Univ., Washington, DC, USA 1996–97; Visiting Prof., Villanova Univ., USA 2001; Prof. of English, Univ. of Notre Dame, Ind., USA 2002–04, Notre Dame Prof. of Philosophy and Literature, Dept of Philosophy 2004–, Fellow, Nanovic Inst.; mem. and Vice-Pres. Johnson Soc. of Australia. *Publications:* Nebuchadnezzar, 1976, The Departure 1978, The Lines of the Hand: Poems 1976–79, Your Shadow 1984, The Trespass of the Sign 1989, Peniel 1990, The Buried Harbour (trans.) 1990, A D. Hope 1992, The Oxford Book of Australian Religious Verse (ed.) 1994, New and Selected Poems 1995, Dark Angel 1996, Samuel Johnson and the Culture of Property 1999, Wicked Heat 1999, Flame Tree: Selected Poems 2002, The Impossible 2003, Postmodernism 2004 The Dark Gaze: Maurice Blanchot and the Sacred 2004, The Power of Contestation (with Geoffrey Hartman) 2004, Derrida and Religion (with Yvonne Sherwood) 2004, The Experience of God (with Barbara Wall) 2005, Counter-Experiences: Reading Jean-Luc Marion 2007; contribs to Arena Journal, The Critical Review, Boxkite, Heat, Verse. *Honours:* Australian Literature Bd Fellowship 1977, NSW Premier's Award 1985, Victorian Premier's Award for Poetry 1985, Grace Levin Awards for Poetry 1991, 1995, Christopher Brennan Award for Poetry 1999. *Address:* Department of Philosophy, 100 Malloy Hall, University of Notre Dame, Notre Dame, IN 46556-4619, USA (office). *Telephone:* (574) 631-4579 (office). *E-mail:* khart2@nd.edu (office).

HART, Veronica (see Kelleher, Victor)

HART-DAVIS, Duff, BA; British writer; b. 3 June 1936, London, England. *Education:* Univ. of Oxford. *Career:* feature writer 1972–76, Literary Ed. 1976–77, Asst Ed. 1977–78, Sunday Telegraph; Country Columnist, The Independent 1986–2001. *Publications:* The Megacull 1968, The Gold of St Matthew (aka The Gold Trackers) 1968, Spider in the Morning 1972, Ascension: The Story of a South Atlantic Island 1972, Peter Fleming (biog.) 1974, Monarchs of the Glen 1978, The Heights of Rimring 1980, Fighter Pilot (with C. Strong) 1981, Level Five 1982, Fire Falcon 1984, The Man-Eater of Jassapur 1985, Hitler's Games 1986, Armada 1988, The House the Berrys Built 1990, Horses of War 1991, Country Matters 1991, Wildings: The Secret Garden of Eileen Soper 1992, Further Country Matters 1993, When the Country Went to Town 1997, Raoul Millais 1998, Fauna Britannica 2002, Audubon's Elephant 2003, Honorary Tiger 2005, Pavilions of Splendour (ed.) 2005, King's Counsellor: Abdication and War: The Diaries of Sir Alan 'Tommy' Lascelles (ed.) 2006. *Address:* Owlpen Farm, Uley, Dursley, Gloucestershire GL11 5BZ, England (home). *Telephone:* (1453) 860239 (home).

HARTCUP, Adeline, MA; British writer; b. 26 April 1918, Isle of Wight, England; m. John Hartcup 1950; two s. *Education:* Univ. of Oxford. *Career:* editorial staff mem., Times Educational Supplement; Hon. Press Officer, Kent Voluntary Service Council. *Publications:* Angelica, 1954; Morning Faces, 1963; Below Stairs in the Great Country Houses, 1980; Children of the Great Country Houses, 1982; Love and Marriage in the Great Country Houses, 1984; Spello: Life Today in Ancient Umbria, 1985. Contributions: Times Educational Supplement; Harper's & Queen; Times Higher Educational Supplement. *Address:* 8F Compton Road, London, N1 2PA, England (home). *Telephone:* (20) 7226-1924 (home).

HARTILL, Rosemary Jane, BA; British writer and broadcaster; *Member, Youth Justice Board for England and Wales*; b. 11 Aug. 1949, Oswestry, Shropshire. *Education:* Univ. of Bristol. *Career:* BBC Religious Affairs

Corresp. 1982–88, Presenter BBC World Service Meridian Books Programme 1990–92, 1994; ind. broadcaster 1989–; mem. Youth Justice Bd for England and Wales 2004–; mem. Bd Shared Interest 1996–2005, Critical Investment and Reward Service 1997–2001, Nat. Probation Service, Northumbria 2001–07, Strategic Health Authority, Northumberland, Tyne and Wear 2002–05, Northumbria Courts 2004–07. *Publications:* Emily Brontë: Poems (ed.) 1973, Wild Animals 1976, In Perspective 1988, Writers Revealed 1989, Were You There? 1995, Visionary Women: Florence Nightingale (ed.) 1996; contribs to various periodicals. *Honours:* Hon. DLitt (Hull) 1995, (Bristol) 2000; Sandford St Martin Trust Personal Award 1994. *Address:* Old Post Office, 24 Eglingham Village, Alnwick, Northumberland NE66 2TX, England (home).

HARTLAND, Michael (see James, Michael Leonard)

HARTLEY, Aidan; writer; b. 1965. *Education:* Univ. of Oxford, Univ. of London. *Career:* grew up in Africa; foreign correspondent, Reuters, then freelance 1996–. *Publications:* The Zanzibar Chest: A Memoir of Love and War 2003. *Literary Agent:* c/o Grove/Atlantic, 841 Broadway, Fourth Floor, New York, NY 10003, USA. *Telephone:* (212) 614-7874. *Fax:* (212) 614-7886. *E-mail:* dseager@groveatlantic.com. *E-mail:* info@thezanzibarchest.com. *Website:* www.thezanzibarchest.com.

HÄRTLING, Peter; German writer and journalist; b. 13 Nov. 1933, Chemnitz; s. of Rudolf Härtling and Erika Härtling (née Häntzschel); m. Mechthild Maier 1959; two s. two d. *Education:* Gymnasium (Nürtingen/ Neckar). *Career:* childhood spent in Saxony, Czechoslovakia and Württemberg; journalist 1953–; Literary Ed. Deutsche Zeitung und Wirtschaftszeitung, Stuttgart and Cologne; Ed. of magazine Der Monat 1962–70, also Copublisher; Ed. and Man. Dir S. Fischer Verlag, Frankfurt 1968–74, Ed. Die Väter; mem. PEN, Akad. der Wissenschaften und der Literatur Mainz, Akad. der Künste Berlin, Deutsche Akad. für Sprache und Dichtung Darmstadt. *Publications:* Yamins Stationen (poetry) 1955, In Zeilen zuhaus (essays) 1957, Palmström grüsst Anna Blume (essays) 1961, Spielgeist-Spiegelgeist (poetry) 1962, Niembsch oder Der Stillstand (novel) 1964, Janek (novel) 1966, Das Familienfest (novel) 1969, Gilles (play) 1970, Ein Abend, Eine Nacht, Ein Morgen (novel) 1971, Neue Gedichte 1972, Zwettl – Nachprüfung einer Erinnerung (novel) 1973, Eine Frau (novel) 1974, Hölderlin (novel) 1976, Anreden (poetry) 1977, Hubert oder Die Rückkehr nach Casablanca (novel) 1978, Nachgetragene Liebe (novel) 1980, Die dreifache Maria 1982, Vorwarnung 1983, Sätze von Liebe 1983, Das Windrad (novel) 1983, Ich rufe die Wörter zusammen 1984, Der spanische Soldat oder Finden under Erfinden 1984, Felix Guttmann (novel) 1985, Waiblingers Augen (novel) 1987, Die Mösinger Pappel 1987, Waiblingers Augen 1987, Der Wanderer (novel) 1988, Briefe von drinnen und draußen (poetry) 1989, Herzwand (novel) 1990, Brüder under Schwestern: Tagebuch eines Synodalen 1991, Schubert (novel) 1992, Božena (novel) 1994, Schumanns Schatten (novel) 1996, Grosse, Kleine Schwester (novel) 1998, Hoffmann oder Die vielfältige Liebe (novel) 2001, Leben lernen (autobiog.) 2004, Die Lebenslinie (autobiog.) 2005. *Honours:* Hon. Prof. 1996; Hon. DPhil 2001; Dr hc (Giessen) 2002; Literaturpreis des Deutschen Kritikerverbandes 1964, Literaturpreis des Kulturkreises der Deutschen Industrie 1965, Literarischer Förderungspreis des Landes Niedersachsen 1965, Prix du meilleur livre étranger, Paris 1966, Gerhart Hauptmann Preis 1971, Deutscher Jugendbuchpreis 1976, Stadtschreiber von Bergen-Enkheim 1978–79, Hölderlin-Preis 1987, Lion-Feuchtwanger-Preis 1992, Stadtschreiber von Mainz 1995, Leuschner-Medaille des Landes Hessen 1996, Grosses Bundesverdienstkreuz 1996, Eichendorff-Preis 1999, Deutsche Jugendbuchpreis 2001, Deutscher Bücherpreis 2002. *Address:* Finkenweg 1, 64546 Mörfelden-Walldorf, Germany. *Telephone:* (6105) 6109 (office). *Fax:* (6105) 74687 (office). *E-mail:* peter@haertling.de (office). *Website:* www.haertling.de (office).

HARTMAN, Geoffrey H., BA, PhD; American fmr academic and writer; b. 11 Aug. 1929, Frankfurt am Main, Germany; m. Renee Gross 1956; one s. one d. *Education:* Queens College, CUNY, Yale Univ. *Career:* Fulbright Fellow Univ. of Dijon 1951–52; Faculty Yale Univ. 1955–62; Assoc. Prof. Univ. of Iowa 1962–64, Prof. of English 1964–65; Prof. of English and Comparative Literature Cornell Univ. 1965–67; Karl Young Prof. Yale Univ. 1974–94, Sterling Prof. 1994–97; Gauss Seminarist Princeton Univ. 1968; Dir School of Theory and Criticism, Dartmouth College 1982–87; Assoc. Fellow Center for Research in Philosophy and Literature, Univ. of Warwick 1993; Fellow Woodrow Wilson International Center 1995; mem. American Acad. of Arts and Sciences, MLA. *Publications:* The Unmediated Vision 1954, André Malraux 1960, Wordsworth's Poetry 1964, Beyond Formalism 1970, The Fate of Reading 1975, Akiba's Children 1978, Criticism in the Wilderness 1980, Saving the Text 1981, Easy Pieces 1985, The Unremarkable Wordsworth 1987, Minor Prophecies 1991, A Critic's Journey 1999, Scars of the Spirit 2003; editor: Romanticism: Vistas, Instances, Continuities 1973, Psychoanalysis and the Question of the Text 1978, Shakespeare and the Question of Theory 1985, Bitburg in Moral and Political Perspective 1986, Midrash and Literature 1986, Holocaust Remembrance: The Shapes of Memory 1993. Monographs: The Longest Shadow: In the Aftermath of the Holocaust 1996, The Fateful Question of Culture 1997 (ACLA Renee Wellek Prize 1997), A Critic's Journey 1999, Scars of the Spirit: The Struggle Against Inauthenticity 2002. *Honours:* Guggenheim Fellowships 1969, 1986; Hon. LHD (Queens College, CUNY) 1990, (Hebrew Union Coll., Cincinnatti) 2003; Keats-Shelley Asscn Distinguished Scholar Award 1997; Tanner Lectures, 1999; Haskins Lecturer, 2000. *Address:* 260 Everit Street, New Haven, CT 06511, USA.

HARTMAN, Jan, BA; Swedish dramatist and writer; b. 23 May 1938, Stockholm. *Education:* Phillips Andover Acad., Harvard Coll., USA. *Career:* Resident Playwright, Theatre of The Living Arts, Philadelphia, Pa, USA 1964–65, Theatre at St Clements, New York 1977–78; Founder-Dir Playwrights' Theatre Project Circle in the Square 1967–69, Eleventh Hour Productions 1977; Adjunct Prof. of Dramatic Writing and Shakespeare, New York Univ. 1981–93; Visiting Prof., Syracuse Univ. 1985–94; mem. PEN, Writers' Guild of America, Eugene O'Neill Memorial Theatre Foundation, Dramatists' Guild, BAFTA, Foreign Press Asscn, UK. *Publications:* fiction: Joshua, Envy, The Wail 1998; plays: (for film, TV and radio) Into Exile (BBC Radio) 1999–2000, The Protégé (BBC Radio) 2000, The Albanian Women (Westdeutsche Randfunk), Mother Teresa – In the Name of God's Poor, The Next War, Genealogy of Evil, The Great Wallendas, Second Sight, Song of Myself, Kepler's Room, Abelard and Heloise, Flight 981, The American War Crimes Trial, Fragment of a Last Judgement, Freeman! Freeman!, The Legend of Daniel Boone; contribs to Dramatists Guild Quarterly, The Observer, New York Times, Our Generation. *Honours:* Guggenheim Fellowship for Playwriting, two Emmy Awards, two Christopher Awards, Writers' Guild of America Award; numerous grants. *Address:* 5 Tatlintown, Wareside, Herts., SG12 7RP, England. *E-mail:* jhartman_uk@yahoo.co.uk.

HARTNETT, David William, BA, MA, DPhil; British writer, poet and editor; b. 4 Sept. 1952, London, England; m. Margaret R. N. Thomas 1976, one s. one d. *Education:* University of Oxford. *Career:* Co-Ed., Poetry Durham magazine; Dir, Contributing Ed., Leviathan Publishing Ltd, Leviathan Quarterly. *Publications:* poetry: A Signalled Love, 1985; House of Moon, 1988; Dark Ages, 1992; At the Wood's Edge, 1997. Fiction: Black Milk, 1994; Brother to Dragons, 1998. Contributions: TLS. *Honours:* TLS/Cheltenham Festival Poetry Competition, 1989.

HARTNETT, Sonya, BA; Australian writer; b. 23 March 1968, Melbourne, Vic. *Education:* Royal Melbourne Inst. of Technology. *Career:* mem. St Martin's Theatre, Melbourne (bd mem.). *Publications:* Trouble All the Way 1984, Sparkle and Nightflower 1986, The Glass House 1990, Wilful Blue 1994, Sleeping Dogs 1995, The Devil Latch 1996, Black Foxes 1996, Princes 1997, Thursday's Child 2002, What the Birds See 2003, Stripes of the Sidestep Wolf 2004, Surrender 2005, The Silver Donkey 2006. *Honours:* Int. Books for Youth Prize 1996, Children's Book Council of Australia Honor Book 1996, Guardian Children's Fiction Prize 2002. *Address:* c/o Penguin Books, PO Box 257, Ringwood, Vic. 3134, Australia.

HARTUNG, Harald; German poet, academic and critic; *Professor, Technische Universität Berlin;* b. 29 Oct. 1932, Herne; s. of Richard Hartung and Wanda Hartung; m. Freia Schnackenburg 1979; two s. *Career:* secondary school teacher 1960–66; Prof., Pädagogische Hochschule Berlin 1971–80, Tech. Univ. Berlin 1980–; mem. Akad. der Künste, Berlin, PEN. *Publications:* Experimentelle Literatur und Konkrete Poesie 1975, Das Gewöhnliche Licht 1976, Augenzeit 1978, Deutsche Lyrik seit 1965 1985, Traum im Deutschen Museum 1986, Luftfracht 1991, Jahre mit Windrad 1996, Masken und Stimmen 1996, Jahrhundertgedächtnis.Deutsche Lyrik im 20.Jahrhundert 1998, Langsamer träumen, Gedichte (2002. *Honours:* Kunstpreis Berlin, Drostepreis 1987, Premio Antico Fattore 1999. *Address:* Technische Universität Berlin, Str. des 17 Juni 135, 10623 Berlin (office); Rüdesheimer Platz 4, 14197 Berlin, Germany. *Telephone:* (30) 314-0 (office). *Fax:* (30) 314-23222 (office). *Website:* www.tu-berlin.de (office).

HARUF, (Alan) Kent, BA, MFA; American writer; b. 24 Feb. 1943, Pueblo, CO; m. 1st Virginia Koon (divorced); m. 2nd Cathy Dempsey; three d. *Education:* Nebraska Wesleyan Univ., Univ. of Iowa. *Career:* Asst Prof., Nebraska Wesleyan Univ. 1986–91; Assoc. Prof., Southern Illinois Univ. 1991–2000. *Publications:* The Tie That Binds 1984, Where You Once Belonged 1991, Plainsong 1999, Eventide 2005; contrib. to anthologies and periodicals. *Honours:* Whiting Writer's Award 1986, Maria Thomas Award 1991, Mt Plains Booksellers Award 2000, Alex Award 2000. *Address:* c/o Southern Illinois University, Retired Employees Dept, 4503 Carbondale, IL 62901, USA.

HARVEY, Anne Berenice, LGSM, AGSM; British actress, writer, poet, editor and broadcaster; b. 27 April 1933, London, England; m. Alan Harvey 1957, one s. one d. *Education:* Guildhall School of Music and Drama, London. *Career:* lectures, talks, readings at literary festivals, galleries; platform programmes, broadcasting; Dir, Guildhall Players, Perranporth, Cornwall 1954–59; Fellow Soc. of Teachers of Speech & Drama 2004; mem. Poetry Society, Friends of the Dymock Poets, Eighteen Nineties Society, Imaginative Book Illustration Society, Walter de la Mare Society (founder mem.), Wilfred Owen Society, John Masefield Society, Children's Books History Soc.; Edward Thomas Fellowship, Charlotte Mary Yonge Fellowship; executor Eleanor Farjeon estate. *Radio:* as writer and presenter: A Life Kept Always Young: The Life of Eleanor Farjeon (BBC Radio 4), A Writer's Life: The Life of Noel Streatfeild (BBC Radio 4), Adlestrop Revisited (BBC Radio 4), Kings and Queens (BBC Radio 4); various Radio 2 Arts Programmes (BBC Radio 2). *Publications:* A Present for Nellie, 1981; Poets in Hand, 1985; Of Caterpillars, Cats and Cattle, 1987; In Time of War: War Poetry, 1987; Something I Remember (selected poetry of Eleanor Farjeon), 1987; A Picnic of Poetry, 1988; The Language of Love, 1989; Six of the Best, 1989; Faces in the Crowd, 1990; Headlines from the Jungle (with Virginia McKenna), 1990; Occasions, 1990; Flora's Red Socks, 1991; Shades of Green, 1991; Elected Friends (poems for and about Edward Thomas), 1991; He Said, She Said, They Said (conversation poems, ed.), 1993; Solo Audition: Speeches for Young Actors, 1993; Criminal Records: Poetry of Crime (ed.), 1994; Methuen Book of Duologues, 1995; Starlight, Starbright: Poems of Night, 1995; Swings and Shadows: Poems of Times Past and Present, 1996; Words Aloud, two vols (ed.), 1998; Eleanor Farjeon, The Last Four Years (ed.); Blackbird Has Spoken: Selected Poems of Eleanor Farjeon (ed.), 1999; Eleanor Farjeon, Come Christmas (ed.), 2000; Adlestrop Revisited (ed.), 2000; When Christmas Comes (anthology, ed.), 2002, Party Pieces (anthology; ed.) 2005. Series Editor: Poetry Originals, 1992–95. Contributions: radio, journals, and magazines. Honours: Signal Poetry Award 1992. Address: 37 St Stephen's Road, Ealing, London, W13 8HJ, England (home). Telephone: (20) 8997-6443 (home). Fax: (20) 8997-6314 (home). E-mail: harvey.anne@tiscali.co.uk (home).

HARVEY, Brett; American writer and critic; b. 28 April 1936, New York, NY; one s. one d. Education: Northwestern Univ. Career: Drama and Literature Dir, WBAI-FM, 1971–74; Publicity and Promotion Dir, The Feminist Press, Old Westbury, NY, 1974–80; Exec. Dir American Soc. of Journalists & Authors 2000–. Publications: My Prairie Year, 1986; Immigrant Girl, 1987; Cassie's Journey, My Prairie Christmas, 1990; The Fifties: A Women's Oral History, 1993. Contributions: Village Voice; New York Times Book Review; Psychology Today; Voice Literary Supplement; Mirabella; Mother Jones; Mademoiselle. Address: 305 Eighth Avenue, Brooklyn, NY 11215, USA.

HARVEY, Caroline (see Trollope, Joanna)

HARVEY, Jack (see Rankin, Ian James)

HARVEY, John Barton, MA; British writer and poet; b. 21 Dec. 1938, London; three c. Education: Goldsmiths Coll., London, Hatfield Polytechnic, Univ. of Nottingham. Career: teacher of English in secondary schools 1965–75; part-time Lecturer in Film and Literature, Univ. of Nottingham 1980–86; fmrly tutor on residential writing courses, Arvon Foundation; teacher, Squaw Valley Community of Writers Fiction Workshop, Northern California 1995; Man. Slow Dancer Press 1977–99, Ed. Slow Dancer magazine –1993. Radio: Wasted Years 1995, Cutting Edge 1996, Slow Burn 1997, Cheryl 2001; adaptations of works by A.S. Byatt, Richard Ford, Bobbie Ann Mason, Jayne Anne Phillips, Paul Scott and Graham Greene (including The End of the Affair, winner of Silver Sony Radio Drama Award 1998. Television: Lonely Hearts (New York Festivals bronze medal for Screenplay for Best TV Drama Series 1992) 1991, Rough Treatment 1992, Hard Cases (series, Central TV); adaptations of Arnold Bennett works Anna of the Five Towns, Sophia and Constance. Publications: novels: Avenging Angel (as Thom Ryder) 1975, Angel Alone (as Thom Ryder) 1975, Kill Hitler! (as Jon Barton) 1976, Amphetamines and Pearls 1976, The Geranium Kiss 1976, River of Blood (as John J. McLaglen) 1976, Forest of Death (as Jon Barton) 1977, Lightning Strikes (as Jon Barton) 1977, The Raiders (as L. J. Coburn) 1977, Evil Breed (as J. B. Dancer) 1977, Black Blood (as Jon Hart) 1977, High Slaughter (as Jon Hart) 1977, Triangle of Death (as Jon Hart) 1977, Guerilla Attack (as Jon Hart) 1977, Shadow of Vultures (as John J. McLaglen) 1977, Death in Gold (as John J. McLaglen) 1977, Junkyard Angel 1977, Neon Madman 1977, Cross-Draw (as John J. McLaglen) 1978, Death Raid (as Jon Hart) 1978, Judgement Day (as J. B. Dancer) 1978, Bloody Shiloh (as L. J. Coburn) 1978, Blood Rising (as William M. James) 1979, Cannons in the Rain (as J. D. Sandon) 1979, Border Affair (as J. D. Sandon) 1979, The Hanged Man (as J. B. Dancer) 1979, Vigilante! (as John J. McLaglen) 1979, Frame 1979, Blood Money (as William S. Brady) 1979, Killing Time (as William S. Brady) 1980, Blood Kin (as William S. Brady) 1980, Cherokee Outlet (as John B. Harvey) 1980, Blood Trail (as John B. Harvey) 1980, Tago (as John B. Harvey) 1980, The Silver Lie (as John B. Harvey) 1980, Sun Dance (as John J. McLaglen) 1980, Billy the Kid (as John J. McLaglen) 1980, Till Death. . . (as John J. McLaglen) 1980, Blood Brother (as William M. James) 1980, Mazatlan (as J. D. Sandon) 1980, Death Dragon (as William M. James) 1981, Wheels of Thunder (as J. D. Sandon) 1981, Blind 1981, Blood on the Border (as John B. Harvey) 1981, Ride the Wide Country (as John B. Harvey) 1981, Desperadoes (as William S. Brady) 1981, Dead Man's Hand (as William S. Brady) 1981, Whiplash (as William S. Brady) 1981, Sierra Gold (as William S. Brady) 1982, Death and Jack Shade (as William S. Brady) 1982, Endgame (as James Mann) 1982, Arkansas Breakout (as John B. Harvey) 1982, John Wesley Hardin (as John B. Harvey) 1982, Dying Ways (as John J. McLaglen) 1982, Hearts of Gold (as John J. McLaglen) 1982, Durango (as J. D. Sandon) 1982, Death Ride (as William M. James) 1983, The Hanging (as William M. James) 1983, Border War (as William S. Brady) 1983, Killer! (as William S. Brady) 1983, War-Party (as William S. Brady) 1983, Wild Blood (as John J. McLaglen) 1983, California Bloodlines (as John B. Harvey) 1983, The Skinning Place (aka The Fatal Frontier) (as John B. Harvey) 1983, Dancer Draws a Wild Card (as Terry Lennox) 1985, Lonely Hearts 1989, Rough Treatment 1990, Cutting Edge 1991, Off Minor 1992, Wasted Years 1993, Cold Light (Grand Prix du Roman Noir Etranger du Cognac 2000) 1994, Living Proof 1995, Easy Meat 1996, Still Water 1997, Last Rites (Sherlock Award Winner for Best British Detective 1999) 1998, In a True Light 2001, Flesh and Blood (CWA Silver Dagger for Fiction 2004) 2004, Ash and Bone 2005, Darkness and Light 2006, Gone to Ground 2007; juvenile: What About It, Sharon? 1979, Reel Love 1982, Sundae Date 1983, What Game Are You Playing? 1983, Footwork 1984, Wild Love 1986, Last Summer 1986, Kidnap! 1987, Daylight Robbery! 1987, Hot Property! 1987, Terror Trap! 1988, Downeast to Danger 1988, Runner! Beaver 1988; poetry: Provence (chapbook) 1978, The Old Postcard Trick (chapbook) 1985, Neil Sedaka Lied (chapbook) 1987, The Downeast Poems (chapbook) 1989, Sometime Other Than Now (with Sue Dymoke) (chapbook) 1989,

Territory (chapbook) 1992, Ghosts of a Chance 1992, Bluer Than This 1998. Honours: CWA Cartier Diamond Dagger 2007. Literary Agent: Lutyens & Rubinstein, 231 Westbourne Park Road, London, W11 1EB, England. Telephone: (20) 7792-4855. Website: www.mellotone.co.uk.

HARVEY, John Robert, BA, MA, PhD; British academic and writer; University Reader in Literature and Visual Culture, Emmanuel College; b. 25 July 1942, Bishops Stortford, Hertfordshire, England; m. Julietta Chloe Papadopoulou 1968, one d. Education: Univ. of Cambridge. Career: Vice-Master, Emmanuel Coll., Cambridge 2002–04, currently Univ. Reader in Literature and Visual Culture; Ed., Cambridge Quarterly 1978–86. Publications: non-fiction: Victorian Novelists and Their Illustrators 1970, Men in Black 1995; fiction: The Plate Shop 1979, Coup d'Etat 1985, The Legend of Captain Space 1990; contrib. to London Review of Books, Sunday Times, Sunday Telegraph, Listener, Encounter, Cambridge Quarterly, Essays in Criticism, Royal Academy Magazine, Textual Practice, Fashion Theory. Honours: David Higham Prize 1979. Address: Emmanuel College, St Andrew's Street, Cambridge, CB2 3AP, England (office). E-mail: jrh49@cam.ac.uk (office).

HARVEY, Steven, BA, MA, PhD; American academic, writer and poet; b. 9 June 1949, Dodge City, KS; m. Barbara Hupfer 1971, two s. two d. Education: Wake Forest University, Johns Hopkins University, Middlebury College, University of Virginia. Career: Prof. of English, Young Harris College, GA, 1976–; Instructor in Writing, John C. Campbell Folk School, 1995–; mem. Associated Writing Programs. Publications: Powerlines (poems), 1976; A Geometry of Lilies (non-fiction), 1993; Lost in Translation (non-fiction), 1997; In a Dark Wood: Personal Essays by Men on Middle Age, 1997; Bound for Shady Grove (non-fiction), 2000. Contributions: periodicals. Honours: MacDowell Colony Fellowship, 1994. Address: PO Box 356, Young Harris, GA 30582, USA. E-mail: sharvey@yhc.edu.

HARVOR, Erica Elisabeth Arendt, MA; Canadian writer; b. 26 June 1936, Saint John, NB; d. of Kjeld Deichmann and Erica Matthiesen; m. Stig Harvor 1957 (divorced 1977); two s. Education: Saint John High School and Concordia Univ. Career: Tutor Concordia Univ. 1986–87, currently Writer-in-Residence; Course Dir and Part-time Lecturer in Creative Writing, Div. of the Humanities, York Univ. (Toronto) 1987–93; mem. Canadian juries; reader and tutor in field; First Prize CBC's New Canadian Writing Series 1965, Ottawa Short Story Competition 1970, The League of Canadian Poets' Nat. Poetry Prize 1989, 1991; The Malahat Long Poem Prize 1990; Confed. Poets' Prize 1991, 1992. Publications: Women and Children 1973 (re-issued as Our Lady of All The Distances 1991), If Only We Could Drive Like This Forever 1988, Fortress of Chairs (poems) 1992, Let Me Be The One 1996, Excessive Joy Injures the Heart 2002; works featured in journals, magazines and anthologies. Address: c/o The Writers' Union of Canada, 24 Ryerson Avenue, Toronto, ON M5T 2P3, Canada.

HARWOOD, Lee, BA; British poet, writer and translator; b. 6 June 1939, Leicester, England; m. (divorced); two s. one d. Education: Queen Mary Coll., London. Career: mem. Nat. Poetry Secretariat (chair. 1974–76), Poetry Soc., London (chair. 1976–77). Publications: Title Illegible 1965, The Man with Blue Eyes 1966, The White Room 1968, The Beautiful Atlas 1969, Landscapes 1969, The Sinking Colony 1970, Penguin Modern Poets 19 (with John Ashbery and Tom Raworth) 1971, The First Poem 1971, New Year 1971, Captain Harwood's Log of Stern Statements and Stout Sayings 1973, Freighters 1975, HMS Little Fox 1975, Boston-Brighton 1977, Old Bosham Bird Watch and Other Stories 1977, Wish You Were Here (with A. Lopez) 1979, All the Wrong Notes 1981, Faded Ribbons 1982, Wine Tales (with Richard Caddel) 1984, Crossing the Frozen River: Selected Poems 1988, Monster Masks 1985, Dream Quilt (short stories) 1985, Rope Boy to the Rescue 1988, The Empty Hill: Memories and Praises of Paul Evans 1945–1991 (ed. with Peter Bailey) 1992, In the Mists: Mountain Poems 1993, Morning Light 1998, Evening Star 2004, Collected Poems 1964–2004 2004; trans. of works by Tristan Tzara; contrib. to journals, reviews and magazines. Honours: Poetry Foundation Award, New York 1966, Alice Hunt Bartlett Prize, Poetry Soc., London 1976.

HARWOOD, Ronald, CBE, FRSL; British author and playwright; b. (Ronald Horwitz), 9 Nov. 1934, Cape Town, South Africa; s. of the late Isaac Horwitz and Isobel Pepper; m. Natasha Riehle 1959; one s. two d. Education: Sea Point Boys' High School, Cape Town and Royal Acad. of Dramatic Art. Career: actor 1953–60; author 1960–; Artistic Dir Cheltenham Festival of Literature 1975; presenter, Kaleidoscope, BBC Radio 1973, Read All About It, BBC TV 1978–79, All The World's A Stage, BBC TV; Chair. Writers' Guild of GB 1969; Visitor in Theatre, Balliol Coll. Oxford 1986; Pres. PEN (England) 1989–93, Int. PEN 1993–97; Gov. Cen. School of Speech and Drama; author of numerous TV plays and screenplays; mem. Council Royal Soc. of Literature 1998–2001, chair. 2001–04; Trustee Booker Foundation 2002. TV plays include: The Barber of Stamford Hill 1960, Private Potter (with Casper Wrede) 1961, The Guests 1972, Breakthrough at Reykjavik 1987, Countdown to War 1989. Screenplays include: A High Wind in Jamaica 1965, One Day in the Life of Ivan Denisovich 1971, Evita Perón 1981, The Dresser 1983, Mandela 1987, The Browning Version 1994, Cry, Beloved Country 1995, Taking Sides 2002, The Pianist 2002 (Acad. Award for Best Adapted Screenplay 2003), The Statement, Being Julia. Plays include: Country Matters 1969, The Good Companions (musical libretto) 1974, The Ordeal of Gilbert Pinfold 1977, A Family 1978, The Dresser 1980, After the Lions 1982, Tramway Road 1984, The Deliberate Death of a Polish Priest 1985,

Interpreters 1985, J. J. Farr 1987, Ivanov (from Chekhov) 1989, Another Time 1989, Reflected Glory 1992, Poison Pen 1994, Taking Sides 1995, The Handyman 1996, Equally Divided 1998, Quartet 1999, Mahler's Conversion 2002. *Publications include:* fiction: All the Same Shadows 1961, The Guilt Merchants 1963, The Girl in Melanie Klein 1969, Articles of Faith 1973, The Genoa Ferry 1976, César and Augusta 1978, Home 1993; non-fiction: Sir Donald Wolfit, CBE: His Life and Work in the Unfashionable Theatre (biog.) 1971; editor: A Night at the Theatre 1983, The Ages of Gielfud 1984, Dear Alec: Guinness at Seventy-Five 1989, The Faber Book of the Theatre 1994; vols of essays and short stories. *Honours:* Chevalier des Arts et Lettres 1996; Hon. DLitt (Keele) 2002; New Standard Drama Award 1981, Drama Critics Award 1981, Molière Award for Best Play, Paris 1993. *Literary Agent:* Judy Daish Associates, 2 St Charles Place, London, W10 6EG, England. *Telephone:* (020) 8964-8811.

HASHMI, (Aurangzeb) Alamgir, MA, DLit; Pakistani academic, poet, writer, editor and broadcaster; b. 15 Nov. 1951, Lahore. *Education:* Univ. of Louisville, Univ. of Punjab. *Career:* Instructor in English, Govt Coll., Lahore 1971–73; Lecturer Forman Christian Coll., Lahore 1973–74, Univ. of Berne, Univ. of Basel 1982; Davidson Int. Visiting Scholar Univ. of N Carolina 1974–75; Lecturer in English Univ. of Louisville 1975–78, Univ. of Zürich and Volkshochschule, Zürich 1980–85; Asst Prof. of English Univ. of Bahawalpur, Pakistan 1979–80; Lecturer in English, Univ. of Basel, Univ. of Bern 1982; Prof. of English and Commonwealth Literature Univ. of Geneva, Univ. of Fribourg 1985; Assoc. Prof. of English Int. Islamic Univ., Islamabad 1985–86; Research Prof. of English, American and Comparative Literature, Quaid-i-Azam Univ., Islamabad 1986–2000; Prof. of English and Head of Dept of English, Univ. of Azad Jammu and Kashmir, Muzaffarabad 1986–87; Prof. and Ed., PIDE, Islamabad 1988–; Course Dir, Foreign Service Acad., Islamabad 1988–; Prof. of English and Comparative Literature Pakistan Futuristics Inst., Islamabad 1990, Univ. of Iceland 2000; Founder and Chair. Standing Int. Cttee on English in S Asia; founder and Chair. Townsend Poetry Prize Cttee; judge Commonwealth Literature Prize, nat. literature prizes, Pakistan Acad. of Letters 1998–; jury mem. Neustadt Int. Prize for Literature; Ed., Advisory Ed., Editorial Adviser and referee for numerous int. scholarly and literary journals and book series; thesis supervisor and external examiner for many univs worldwide; broadcaster, scriptwriter, ed. Radio Pakistan and Pakistan TV 1968–; adviser Nat. Book Council of Pakistan 1989–95, Nat. Book Foundation 1993–; Fellow Int. Centre for Asian Studies, Int. PEN; Rockefeller Foundation Fellow 1994; mem. Council Asscn for Commonwealth Studies; mem. Poetry Soc., Associated Writing Programs, Asscn for Asian Studies, New York Acad. of Sciences Council on Nat. Literatures, Asscn for Commonwealth Literature and Language Studies, Int. Asscn of Univ. Profs of English, Modern Language Asscn of America. *Publications:* poetry: The Oath and Amen: Love Poems 1976, America is a Punjabi Word 1979, An Old Chair 1979, My Second in Kentucky 1981, This Time in Lahore 1983, Neither This Time/ Nor That Place 1984, Inland and Other Poems 1988, The Poems of Alamgir Hashmi 1992, Sun and Moon and Other Poems 1992, Others to Sport with Amaryllis in the Shade 1992, A Choice of Hashmi's Verse 1997, The Ramazan Libation: Selected Poems 2003; other: Pakistani Literature (two vols; ed., second edn as Pakistani Literature: The Contemporary English Writers) 1978, Ezra Pound 1983, Commonwealth Literature 1983, The Worlds of Muslim Imagination (ed.) 1986, The Commonwealth, Comparative Literature and the World 1988, Pakistani Short Stories in English (ed.) 1992, Postindependence Voices in South Asian Writings (co-ed.) 2001; contrib. to many books, journals and periodicals. *Honours:* Hon. DLitt (Centre Universitaire de Luxembourg) 1984, (San Francisco State Univ.) 1984; First Prize, All Pakistan Creative Writing Contest 1972, Patras Bokhari Award, Pakistan Acad. of Letters 1985, Roberto Celli Memorial Award 1994; numerous other academic and literary distinctions, prizes and citations from different countries. *Address:* 1542 Service Road West, G-11/2, Islamabad, Pakistan. *E-mail:* alamgirhashmi@yahoo.co.uk.

HASLAM, Gerald William, MA, PhD; American writer and academic; *Professor Emeritus of English, Sonoma State University*; b. 18 March 1937, Bakersfield, CA; m. Janice E. Pettichord 1961; three s. two d. *Education:* San Francisco State Coll., Washington State Univ., Union Grad. School. *Career:* Instructor in English, San Francisco State Coll. 1966–67; Prof. of English, Sonoma State Univ. 1967–97, Prof. Emer. 1997–; contributing writer, West (Los Angeles Times magazine) 2006–; Pres. Western Literature Asscn 1984; mem. Bd Dirs California Studies Asscn, Bd Trustees Yosemite Asscn. *Publications:* fiction: Okies: Selected Stories 1973, Masks: A Novel 1976, The Wages of Sin: Stories 1980, Hawk Flights: Visions of the West: Short Stories 1983, Snapshots: Glimpses of the Other California: Selected Stories 1985, The Man Who Cultivated Fire and Other Stories 1987, That Constant Coyote: California Stories 1990, Condor Dreams and Other Fictions 1994, The Great Tejon Club Jubilee: Stories 1995, Manuel and the Madman (with Janice E. Haslam) 2000, Straight White Male 2000; other: Forgotten Pages of American Literature (ed.) 1970, The Language of the Oilfields: Examination of an Industrial Argot 1972, Western Writings (ed.) 1974, Afro-American Oral Literature (ed.) 1974, California Heartland: Writing from the Great Central Valley (co-ed. with James D. Houston) 1978, Voices of a Place: The Great Central Valley 1986, A Literary History of the American West (co-ed. with J. Golden Taylor) 1987, Baiting the Hook 1990, Coming of Age in California: Personal Essays 1990, The Other California: The Great Central Valley in Life and Letters 1990, Many Californias: Literature from the Golden State (ed.) 1992, Out of the Slush Pile (with Stephen Glasser) 1993, The Horned Toad 1995, Where Coyotes Howl and Wind Blows Free: Growing Up in the West (co-ed. with Alexandra Russell) 1995, Workin' Man Blues: Country Music in California (with Alexandra Russell and Richard Chon) 1999, Straight White Male 2000, Haslam's Valley 2005. *Honours:* California Arts Council Fellowship 1989, Josephine Miles Award, PEN 1990, Bay Area Book Reviewers' Award 1993, Benjamin Franklin Award, Publishers' Marketing Asscn 1993, Commonwealth Club Medal 1994, Award of Merit, Asscn for State and Local Historians 1994, Distinguished Achievement Award, Western Literature Asscn 1999, Laureate, San Francisco Public Library 1998, Ralph J. Gleason Award 2000, Carey McWilliams Award 2000, Western States Book Award for Fiction 2000, Certificate for Citation, Asscn for State and Local History 2001, Sequoia: Giant of the Valley Award 2003, Certificate of Commendation Calif. Arts Council, Delbert and Edith Wyler Award, Western Literature Asscn 2005. *Address:* PO Box 969, Penngrove, CA 94951, USA. *Telephone:* (707) 792-2944 (office). *Fax:* (707) 792-2944 (office). *E-mail:* ghaslam@sonic.net (office). *Website:* www.geraldhaslam.com (office).

HASLUCK, Nicholas Paul, AM; Australian writer and poet; b. 17 Oct. 1942, Canberra, ACT. *Education:* University of Western Australia, University of Oxford. *Career:* barrister, solicitor, Supreme Court of Western Australia, 1968; Deputy Chair., Australia Council, 1978–82; Chair., Literature Board, 1998–2001. *Publications:* Fiction: Quarantine 1978, The Blue Guitar 1980, The Hand that Feeds You: A Satiric Nightmare 1982, The Bellarmine Jug 1984, The Country without Music 1990, The Blosseville File 1992, Offcuts From a Legal Literary Life 1993, A Grain of Truth 1994, Our Man K 1999, The Legal Labyrinth 2003. Stories: The Hat on the Letter O and Other Stories, 1978. Poetry: Anchor and Other Poems, 1976; On the Edge, 1980; Chinese Journey, 1985. *Honours:* Age Book of the Year Award 1984. *Address:* 14 Reserve Street, Claremont, WA 6010, Australia.

HASS, Robert Louis, BA, MA, PhD; American poet, writer, translator, editor and academic; b. 1 March 1941, San Francisco, CA; m. Earlene Joan Leif 1962 (divorced 1986); two s. one d. *Education:* St Mary's Coll. of California, Stanford Univ. *Career:* Asst Prof., SUNY at Buffalo 1967–71; Prof. of English, St Mary's Coll. of California 1971–89, Univ. of California, Berkeley 1989–; Visiting Lecturer, Univ. of Virginia 1974, Goddard Coll. 1976, Columbia Univ. 1982, Univ. of California, Berkeley 1983; poet-in-residence, The Frost Place, Franconia, NH 1978; Poet Laureate of the USA 1995–97. *Publications:* Poetry: Field Guide, 1973; Winter Morning in Charlottesville, 1977; Praise, 1979; The Apple Tree at Olema, 1989; Human Wishes, 1989; Sun under Wood, 1996. Other: Twentieth Century Pleasures: Prose on Poetry, 1984; Into the Garden – A Wedding Anthology: Poetry and Prose on Love and Marriage, 1993. Translations: Czesław Miłosz's The Separate Notebooks (with Robert Pinsky), 1983; Czesław Miłosz's Unattainable Earth (with Czesław Miłosz), 1986; Czesław Miłosz's Collected Poems, 1931–1987 (with Louis Iribane and Peter Scott), 1988. Editor: Rock and Hawk: A Selection of Shorter Poems by Robinson Jeffers, 1987; The Pushcart Prize Xll (with Bill Henderson and Jorie Graham), 1987; Tomaz Salamun: Selected Poems (with Charles Simic), 1988; Selected Poems of Tomas Tranströmer, 1954–1986 (with others), 1989; The Essential Haiku: Versions of Basho, Buson and Issa, 1994. Contributions: anthologies and other publications. *Honours:* Woodrow Wilson Fellowship, 1963–64; Danforth Fellowship, 1963–67; Yale Series of Younger Poets Award, Yale University Press, 1972; US-Great Britain Bicentennial Exchange Fellow in the Arts, 1976–77; William Carlos Williams Award, 1979; National Book Critics Circle Award, 1984; Award of Merit, American Acad. of Arts and Letters, 1984; John D. and Catherine T. MacArthur Foundation Grant, 1984. *Literary Agent:* Steven Barclay Agency, 12 Western Avenue, Petaluma, CA 94952, USA. *Telephone:* (707) 773-0654. *Fax:* (707) 778-1868. *Website:* www.barclayagency.com. *Address:* PO Box 807, Inverness, CA 94937, USA.

HASSNER, Pierre; French writer and academic; b. 31 Jan. 1933, Bucharest, Romania. *Education:* École Normale Supérieure. *Career:* Lecturer in Int. Relations and History of Political Thought, Institut d'Études Politiques, Paris, European Center of John Hopkins Univ. Bologna; Emeritus Research Dir, Center for Int. Studies and Research (CERI), Paris. *Publications:* La violence et la paix (trans. as Violence and Peace: From the Atomic Bomb to Ethnic Cleansing) 1995, La terreur et l'empire: La violence et la paix II 2003, Washington et le monde: Dilemmes d'une superpuissance (with Justin Vaisse) 2003, Guerre et Sociétés: Etats et violence aprés la guerre froide (ed. with Roland Marchal) 2003; contrib. articles to Revue de Synthèse, Critique Internationale, Commentaire, The Natinoal Interst, Cahiers de Chaillot, Esprit, Europe Unbound, Le Débat, Politique Internationale. *Honours:* Prix Tocqueville 2003. *Address:* Center for International Studies and Research—Sciences Po, 56 rue Jacob, 75006 Paris, France. *Telephone:* 1 58 71 70 00. *Fax:* 1 58 71 70 90. *E-mail:* hassner@ceri-sciences-po.org. *Website:* www.ceri-sciences-po.org.

HASTINGS, Graham (see Jeffries, Roderic Graeme)

HASTINGS, March (see Levinson, Leonard)

HASTINGS, Sir Max Macdonald, Kt, FRSL, FRHistS; British writer and broadcaster; b. 28 Dec. 1945, London; s. of Macdonald Hastings and Anne Scott-James (Lady Lancaster); m. 1st Patricia Edmondson 1972 (divorced 1994); one s. (and one s. deceased) one d.; m. 2nd Penelope Grade 1999. *Education:* Charterhouse and Univ. Coll., Oxford. *Career:* reporter, London Evening Standard 1965–67, 1968–70; Fellow, US World Press Inst. 1967–68; reporter, current affairs, BBC Television 1970–73; freelance journalist, broadcaster and author 1973–; columnist, Evening Standard 1979–85, Daily

Express 1981–83, Sunday Times 1985–86; Ed. Daily Telegraph 1986–95, Dir 1989–95, Ed.-in-Chief 1990–95; Ed. Evening Standard 1996–2002; Dir Evening Standard Ltd 1996–2002; columnist Daily Mail 2002–, Guardian 2004–; book reviewer Sunday Times 2006–; mem. Press Complaints Comm. 1990–92; Trustee Liddell Hart Archive, King's Coll. London 1988–2004, Nat. Portrait Gallery 1995–2004; Pres. Council for the Protection of Rural England 2002–. *Television:* documentaries: Ping-Pong in Peking 1971, The War About Peace 1983, Alarums and Excursions 1984, Cold Comfort Farm 1985, The War in Korea (series) 1988, We Are All Green Now 1990, Spies (in series Cold War) 1998, Churchill and His Generals (series) 2003. *Publications:* America 1968: The Fire, The Time 1968, Ulster 1969, The Struggle for Civil Rights in Northern Ireland 1970, Montrose: The King's Champion 1977, Yoni: Hero of Entebbe 1979, Bomber Command 1979, The Battle of Britain (with Lee Deighton) 1980, Das Reich 1981, Battle for the Falklands (with Simon Jenkins) 1983, Overlord: D-Day and the Battle for Normandy 1984, Victory in Europe 1985, The Oxford Book of Military Anecdotes (ed.) 1985, The Korean War 1987, Outside Days 1989, Scattered Shots 1999, Going to the Wars 2000, Editor (memoir) 2002, Armageddon: The Battle for Germany 1944–45 2004, Warriors: Extraordinary Tales from the Battlefields 2005, Country Fair 2005, Nemesis: The Battle for Japan 1944–45 2007. *Honours:* Hon. Fellow, King's Coll. London 2004; Hon. DLitt (Leicester) 1992; Journalist of the Year 1982, Reporter of the Year 1982, Somerset Maugham Prize for Non-fiction 1979, Ed. of the Year 1988. *Literary Agent:* c/o PFD, Drury House, 34–43 Russell Street, London, WC2B 5HA, England. *Telephone:* (20) 7344-1000. *Website:* www.pfd .co.uk.

HASTINGS, Michael Gerald; British playwright; b. 2 Sept. 1938, London, England; m. 1st; two s. one d.; m. 2nd Victoria Hardie 1975. *Plays:* Don't Destroy Me 1956, Yes and After 1957, The World's Baby 1960, Blue as his Eyes the Tin Helmet He Wore 1962, For the West (Congo) 1964, Lee Harvey Oswald: A Far Mean Streak of Indepence Brought on by Negleck 1966, The Silence of Saint-Just 1970, Gloo Joo 1977, For the West (Uganda) 1978, Full Frontal 1979, Carnival War 1982, Tom and Viv 1984, The Emperor (with Jonathan Miller) 1986, A Dream of People 1991, Unfinished Business 1994, Calico 2004, Man and Boy: Dada 2004, Love Counts 2006. *Libretti:* Man and Boy: Dada (music by Michael Nyman) 2004, Love Counts (music by Michael Nyman) 2006. *Films:* The Nightcomers 1972, Tom and Viv 1993. *Television:* The Search for the Nile 1970, Murder Rap 1988. *Publications:* plays: Three Plays (Don't Destroy Me, Yes and After, and The World's Baby) 1966, The Silence of Saint-Just 1970, Tom and Viv 1985, Three Political Plays (The Silence of Lee Harvey Oswald, For the West, and The Emperor) 1990, A Dream of People 1992, Unfinished Business and Other Plays 1994; fiction: The Game 1957, The Frauds 1960, Tussy is Me: A Romance 1970, The Nightcomers 1972, And in the Forest the Indians 1975, Bart's Mornings and Other Tales from Modern Brazil 1975; translations: La Nona, by Roberto Cossa, Seven Characters in Search of an Author, by Luigi Pirandello; poetry: Love Me Lambeth and Other Poems 1961; non-fiction: The Handsomest Young Man in England: Rupert Brooke 1967, Sir Richard Burton: A Biography 1978. *Honours:* Arts Council Award 1956, Emmy Award 1972, Writers' Guild Award 1972, Somerset Maugham Award 1972, Evening Standard Award for Comedy of the Year 1978. *Address:* 2 Helix Gardens, Brixton Hill, London, SW2, England.

HASTINGS, Lady Selina, MA; British writer; b. 5 March 1945, Oxford. *Education:* St Hugh's Coll., Oxford. *Career:* books page, Daily Telegraph 1968–82; Literary Ed., Harper's & Queen 1986–94. *Publications:* biographies: Nancy Mitford 1985, Evelyn Waugh 1994, Rosamond Lehmann: A Life 2002; children's books; contrib. to newspapers and periodicals. *Honours:* Marsh Biography Award 1993–96. *Address:* Rogers, Coleridge & White Ltd, 20 Powis Mews, London, W11 1JN, England (office).

HASWELL, Chetwynd John Drake, (George Foster, Jock Haswell); British fmr soldier and writer; b. 18 July 1919, Penn, Buckinghamshire, England; m. Charlotte Annette Petter 1947; two s. one d. *Education:* Winchester College, Royal Military College, Sandhurst. *Career:* soldier 1939–60; author Service Intelligence, Intelligence Centre, Ashford 1966–84; Regimental Historian for the Queen's Regiment. *Publications:* as George Foster: Indian File, 1960; Soldier on Loan, 1961. as Jock Haswell: The Queen's Royal Regiment, 1967; The First Respectable Spy, 1969; James II, Soldier and Sailor, 1972; British Military Intelligence, 1973; Citizen Armies, 1973; The British Army, 1975; The Ardent Queen, Margaret of Anjou, 1976; The Battle for Empire, 1976; Spies and Spymasters, 1977; The Intelligence and Deception of the D-Day Landings, 1979; The Tangled Web, 1985; The Queen's Regiment, 1986; Spies and Spying, 1986. *Address:* The Grey House, Lyminge, Folkestone, Kent CT18 8ED, England (home). *Telephone:* (1303) 862232 (home).

HATCHER, Robin Lee; American novelist; b. 10 May 1951, Payette, ID; m. Jerrold W. Neu 1989, two d. *Education:* gen. high school diploma. *Career:* mem. Romance Writers of America, pres., 1992–94; The Authors' Guild. *Publications:* Stormy Surrender, 1984; Heart's Landing, 1984; Thorn of Love, 1985; Passion's Gamble, 1986; Heart Storm, 1986; Pirate's Lady, 1987; Gemfire, 1988; The Wager, 1989; Dream Tide, 1990; Promised Sunrise, 1990; Promise Me Spring, 1991; Rugged Splendor, 1991; The Hawk and the Heather, 1992; Devlin's Promise, 1992; Midnight Rose, 1992; A Frontier Christmas, 1992; The Magic, 1993; Where the Heart Is, 1993; Forever, Rose, 1994; Remember When, 1994; Liberty Blue, 1995; Chances Are, 1996; Kiss me Katie, 1996; Dear Lady, 1997; Patterns of Love, 1998; In His Arms, 1998; The Forgiving Hour, 1999; Hometown Girl; Taking Care of the Twins; Whispers

from Yesterday; Daddy Claus, 1999; The Shepherd's Voice, 2000; The Story Jar, 2001; Ribbon of Years, 2001; Firstborn, 2002. Contributions: various publications. *Honours:* Emma Merritt Award, 1998; Heart of Romance Readers Choice Award, 1996; RITA Awards, 1999, 2001; Christy Award for Excellence in Christian Fiction, 2000; RWA Lifetime Achievement Award, 2001.

HATOUM, Milton, MA; Brazilian academic, poet, writer and translator; *Professor of French Literature, University of Amazonas Manaus;* b. 19 Aug. 1952, Manaus. *Education:* State University of São Paulo, Sorbonne, University of Paris. *Career:* Prof. of French Literature, University of Amazonas Manaus 1983–. *Publications:* Um rio entre ruinas (poems) 1978, Relato de um Certo Oriente (novel) 1989, Dois Irmãos (novel) 2000; trans. into Portuguese include: La Croisade des enfants by Marcel Schwob, Trois Contes by Gustave Flaubert, Representations of the Intellectual by Edward Said; contrib. to periodicals. *Honours:* Jabuti Award 2000. *Address:* Rua Dr Veiga Filho, 83/131, 012229-001, São Paulo, SP, Brazil. *E-mail:* mhatoum@uol.com .br.

HATTENDORF, John Brewster, AB, AM, DPhil, FRHistS; American academic and writer; b. 22 Dec. 1941, Hinsdale, IL; m. Berit Sundell 1978, three d. *Education:* Kenyon Coll., Brown Univ., Univ. of Oxford. *Career:* serving Officer, US Navy, 1964–73; Prof. of Military History, National University of Singapore, 1981–83; Ernest J. King Prof. of Maritime History, US Naval War College, 1984–; mem. Navy Records Society; Hakluyt Society; Academie du Var; Royal Swedish Acad. of Naval Science; Society for Nautical Research. *Publications:* The Writings of Stephen B. Luce, 1975; On His Majesty's Service, 1983; Sailors and Scholars, 1984; A Bibliography of the Works of A. T. Mahan, 1986; England in the War of the Spanish Succession, 1987; Maritime Strategy and the Balance of Power, 1989; The Limitations of Military Power, 1990; Mahan on Naval Strategy, 1990; Mahan is Not Enough, 1993; British Naval Documents (co-ed.), 1993; Ubi Sumnus: The State of Maritime and Naval History, 1994; Doing Naval History, 1995; Sea of Words (with Dean King), 1995; Maritime History: The Age of Discovery, 1996; Maritime History: The Eighteenth Century, 1996. Contributions: Naval War College Review; International History Review.

HATTERSLEY, Baron (Life Peer), cr. 1997, of Sparkbrook in the County of West Midlands; **Roy Sydney George Hattersley,** PC, BSc (Econ.); British politician and writer; b. 28 Dec. 1932, s. of the late Frederick Roy Hattersley and Enid Hattersley (née Brackenbury); m. Molly Loughran 1956. *Education:* Sheffield City Grammar School, Univ. of Hull. *Career:* Journalist and Health Service exec. 1956–64; mem. Sheffield City Council 1957–65; MP for Sparkbrook Div. of Birmingham 1964–97; Parl. Pvt. Sec. to Minister of Pensions and Nat. Insurance 1964–67; Dir Campaign for European Political Community 1965; Jt Parl. Sec. Dept of Employment and Productivity 1967–69; Minister of Defence for Admin 1969–70; Opposition Spokesman for Defence 1970–72, for Educ. 1972–74, for the Environment 1979–80, for Home Affairs 1980–83, on Treasury and Econ. Affairs 1983–87, on Home Affairs 1987–92; Minister of State for Foreign and Commonwealth Affairs 1974–76; Sec. of State for Prices and Consumer Protection 1976–79; Deputy Leader of the Labour Party 1983–92; Pres. Local Govt Group for Europe 1998–; Public Affairs Consultant IBM 1971, 1972; Columnist Punch, The Guardian, The Listener 1979–82; Visiting Fellow, Inst. of Politics, Univ. of Harvard 1971, 1972, Nuffield Coll., Oxford 1984–; Labour. *Publications:* Nelson – A Biography 1974, Goodbye to Yorkshire – A Collection of Essays 1976, Politics Apart – A Collection of Essays 1982, Press Gang 1983, A Yorkshire Boyhood 1983, Choose Freedom: The Future for Democratic Socialism 1987, Economic Priorities for a Labour Government 1987, The Maker's Mark (novel) 1990, In That Quiet Earth (novel) 1991, Skylark's Song (novel) 1994, Between Ourselves (novel) 1994, Who Goes Home? 1995, Fifty Years On 1997, Buster's Diaries: As Told to Roy Hattersley 1998, Blood and Fire: The Story of William and Catherine Booth and their Salvation Army 1999, A Brand from the Burning: The Life of John Wesley 2002, The Edwardians 2004, Borrowed Time: The Story of Britain Between the Wars 2007; contrib. to newspapers and journals. *Honours:* Hon. LLD (Hull) 1985; Dr hc (Aston) 1997. *Address:* 59 St Martin's Lane, London, WC2N 4JS (office); House of Lords, Westminster, London, SW1A 0PW, England. *Telephone:* (20) 7836-3533 (office). *Fax:* (20) 7836-3531 (office). *E-mail:* roy.hattersley@ukgateway.net (office).

HAUG, Frigga, DPhil; German sociologist and publisher; b. 28 Nov. 1937, Mülheim/Ruhr; d. of Heinz and Melanie Langenberger; m. 1st Mr Laudan 1959 (divorced 1965); one d.; m. 2nd Wolfgang Fritz Haug 1965. *Education:* Mädchengymnasium Mülheim/Ruhr and Free Univ. of Berlin. *Career:* nurse; social worker 1957–58; interpreter; Ed. and Publr Das Argument (social sciences journal) 1968–; Lecturer Univs of Copenhagen, Berlin, Marburg (Germany) 1971–; Distinguished Prof. Univs of Sydney, Australia 1985, Innsbruck, Austria 1988, Klagenfurt 1992, Ontario Inst. for Studies in Educ., Toronto 1992, Duke Univ., Durham, NC 1997; Prof. Hamburger Universität für Wirtschaft und Politik 1978–2001; Ed. Ariadne women's crime series 1988–1997; research into women's studies and labour; mem. women's editorial bd 1981–. *Publications include:* Kritik der Rollentheorie 1974, Gesellschaftliche Produktion und Erziehung 1977, Development of Work 1978, Education for Femininity 1980, Subjekt Frau 1985, Contradictions in Automated Labour 1987, Sexualisierung des Körpers 1988, (English 1987, 2000), Kitchen and State 1988, Erinnerungsarbeit 1990, Die andere Angst 1991, Beyond Female Masochism 1993, Hat die Leistung ein Geschlecht? 1993, Sündiger Genuß?, Filmerfahrungen von Frauen 1995, Frauen-Politiken

1996, Lustmolche und Köderfrauen 1997, Vorlesungen zur Einführung in die Erinnerungsarbeit 1999 (English 2002), Lernverhältnisse. Selbstbewegungen und Selbstblockierungen 2003; approx. 100 articles in ten languages. *Address:* c/o Argument-Verlag, Eppendorfer Weg 95, 20259 Hamburg (office); Wittumhalde 5, 73732 Esslingen/N, Germany (home). *Telephone:* (711) 882-48-59 (home). *Fax:* (711) 88-48-63 (home). *E-mail:* FriggaHaug@aol.com (home). *Website:* www.friggahaug.inkrit.de (office).

HAUGAARD, Erik Christian; Danish writer; b. 13 April 1923, Copenhagen; m. 1st Myra Seld 1949 (died 1981); one s. one d.; m. 2nd Masako Taira 1986 (died 1996). *Career:* mem. Authors' Guild, Soc. of Authors, British PEN, Danish Authors' Union. *Publications:* The Little Fishes 1967, Orphas of the Wind 1969, The Untold Tale 1972, Hans Christian Andersen's Fairy Tales (trans.) 1973, Chase Me Catch Nobody 1980, Leif the Unlucky 1982, The Samurai's Tale 1984, Princess Horrid 1990, The Boy and the Samurai 1991, The Death of Mr Angel 1992, Under the Black Flag 1993, The Revenge of the Forty-Seven Samurai 1995. *Honours:* Herald Tribune Award, Boston Globe-Horn Book Award, Jane Addams Award, Danish Cultural Ministry Award, Phoenix Award. *Literary Agent:* Dorothy Markinko Mcintosh and Otis, 353 Lexington Avenue, New York, NY 10016, USA. *Address:* Toad Hall, Ballydehob, West Cork, Ireland (home).

HAUGEN, Paal-Helge; Norwegian poet, writer and dramatist; b. 26 April 1945, Valle. *Education:* Univ. of Oslo. *Career:* freelance writer; Chair. Norwegian State Film Production Board 1980–85, Bd of Literary Advisers, Asscn of Norwegian Authors 1984–88; Advisor, Norwegian Council of Culture 1992–2000. *Publications include:* Anne (novel) 1968, Stone Fences 1986, Meditasjonar over Georges de la Tour (poems) 1990, Sone O (poems) 1992, Wintering with the Light 1995, Poesi: Collected Poems 1965–1995 1995; other: plays for stage, radio and TV, six opera libretti, including The Maid of Norway 2000, A. – a shadow opera 2001 (CD 2003), The Green Knight 2004; contribs to professional journals. *Honours:* Dobloug Prize 1986, Richard Wilbur Prize, USA 1986, Norwegian Literary Critics Prize 1990, Norwegian National Brage Prize 1992, Grieg Prize for texts set to music 2001. *Literary Agent:* c/o J. W. Cappelen AS, PO Box 350, 1010, Oslo, Norway. *Address:* Skrefjellv 5, 4645 Nodeland, Norway (home). *E-mail:* phaugen@online.no (home).

HAUPTMAN, William Thornton, BFA, MFA; American dramatist and writer; b. 26 Nov. 1942, Wichita Falls, TX; m. 1st Barbara Barbat 1968 (divorced 1977); one d.; m. 2nd Marjorie Endreich 1985, one s. *Education:* University of Texas at Austin, Yale University School of Drama. *Publications:* plays: Hear, 1977; Domino Courts/Comanche Cafe, 1977; Big River (with Roger Miller), 1986; Gillette, 1989. Television Drama: A House Divided (series), 1981. Fiction: Good Rockin' Tonight and Other Stories, 1988; The Storm Season, 1992. *Honours:* National Endowment for the Arts Grant, 1977; Boston Theatre Critics Circle Award, 1984; Tony Award, 1985; Drama-Lounge Award, 1986; Jesse Jones Award, Texas Institute of Letters, 1989.

HAVEL, Václav; Czech fmr head of state, playwright and writer; b. 5 Oct. 1936, Prague; s. of Václav M. Havel and Božena Havel (née Vavrečková); m. 1st Olga Šplíchalová 1964 (died 1996); m. 2nd Dagmar Veškrnová 1997. *Education:* Acad. of Arts, Drama Dept, Prague. *Career:* worked as freelance; fmr spokesman for Charter 77 human rights movement, received a sentence of 14 months in 1977, suspended for three years, for "subversive" and "antistate" activities, under house arrest 1978–79; mem. Cttee for the Defence of the Unjustly Prosecuted (VONS), convicted and sentenced to 4½ years' imprisonment for sedition 1979, released March 1983, arrested Jan. 1989 and sentenced to nine months' imprisonment for incitement and obstruction Feb. 1989; sentence reduced to eight months and charge changed to misdemeanour March 1989; released May 1989; f. Civic Forum 1989; Pres. of Czechoslovakia 1989–92, Pres. of Czech Repub. 1993–2003; C-in-C of Armed Forces 1989–92; Chair. Prague Heritage Fund 1993–; mem. jury Int. Prize Awarding Body for Human Rights 1994–; mem. Acad. des Sciences Morales et Politiques. *Plays include:* Garden Party 1963, Memorandum 1965, The Increased Difficulty of Concentration 1968, The Conspirators 1971, The Beggar's Opera 1972, Audience 1975, Vernissage 1975, The Mountain Resort 1976, Protest 1978, The Mistake 1983, Largo Desolato 1984, Temptation 1985, Redevelopment 1987, Tomorrow! 1988. *Publications include:* Letters to Olga (in Czech, as Dopisy Olge) 1983, Disturbing the Peace (in Czech, as Dálkový výslech) 1986, (English) 1990, Václav Havel or Living in Truth (essays, in English) 1986, Open Letters: Selected Writings 1965–1990 (in English) 1991, Selected Plays by Václav Havel (in English) 1992, Summer Meditations (in Czech, as Ledric piemidánt) 1991, (English) 1992, Plays (in Czech, as Hry) 1991, Toward a Civil Society 1994, The Art of the Impossible (speeches) 1997, In Various Directions (in Czech, as Do různých stran) 1999, Spisy (seven vols) 1999. *Honours:* Hon. mem. Acad. of Sciences and Arts, Salzburg; Hon. Citizen of Vrtislav 2001;Grand Cross, Order of the Legion of Honour 1990, Order of White Eagle, Poland 1993, Golden Hon. Order of Freedom, Slovenia 1993, Chain of Order of Isabel of Castille, Spain 1995, Hon. KCB, UK 1996, Grand Cross Order with Chain (Lithuania) 1999, Federal Cross for Merit, Berlin 2000; numerous hon. degrees including Dr hc (York Univ., Toronto, Le Mirail Univ., Toulouse) 1982, (Columbia Univ., New York, Hebrew Univ., Jerusalem, Frantisek Palacky Univ., Olomouc, Charles Univ., Prague, Comenius Univ., Bratislava) 1990, (Free Univ. of Brussels, St Gallen Univ.) 1991, (Bar Ilan Univ., Israel, Kiev Univ., Ukraine, Jordan Univ., Oxford) 1997, (Glasgow) 1998, (Manitoba, St Thomas Univ., USA) 1999, (Bilkent Univ., Turkey) 2000; Austrian State Prize for European Literature 1968, Jan Palach Prize 1982, (JAMU, Brno) 2001, Erasmus Prize 1986, Olof Palme Prize 1989, German

Book Trade Peace Prize 1989, Simón Bolívar Prize 1990, Malaparte Prize 1990, UNESCO Prize for the Teaching of Human Rights 1990, Chalemagne Prize 1991, Sonning Cultural Prize 1991, Athinai Prize (Onassis Foundation) 1993, Theodor Heuss Prize 1993, Indira Gandhi Prize 1994, European Cultural Soc. Award 1993, Philadelphia Liberty Medal 1994, Premi Internacional Catalunya 1995, TGM Prize (Canada) 1997, Medal of Danish Acad. 1997, European Statesman Prize (USA), 1997, Husajn bin Ali Distinction (Jordan) 1997, J. W. Fulbright Prize for Int. Understanding (USA) 1997, Le Prix Spécial Europe, European Theatre Council 1997, Cino del Duca Prize (France), Prince of Asturias Prize (Spain) 1997, Charles Univ. Medal 1998, Open Soc. Prize, Budapest Univ., Gazeta Wyborcza Prize (Poland), St Vojtěch Prize (Slovakia) 1999, Citizen Prize, Berlin 2000, Evelyn Burkey's Prize, Author's Guild of America 2000, Elie Wiesel Prize 2000. *Address:* Dělostřelecká 1, 160 00 Prague 6, Czech Republic. *Telephone:* (2) 2437-1111. *Fax:* (2) 2437-3300. *E-mail:* vaclav.havel@volny.cz (office).

HAVIARAS, Stratis, MFA; Greek writer and fmr librarian; b. 28 June 1935, Nea Kios, Argos; s. of Christos Haviaras and Georgia Hadzikyriakos; m. 1st Gail Flynn 1967 (divorced 1973); m. 2nd Heather Cole 1990; one d. *Education:* Goddard Coll. *Career:* fmr construction worker; lived in USA 1959–61; went to USA following colonels' coup in Greece 1967, obtaining position at Harvard Univ. Library; Curator, Poetry Room, Harvard Univ. Library 1974–2000; Founder and Ed. Harvard Review 1992–2000, Founding Ed. Emer. 2000–; Faculty mem., Harvard Univ. Summer School; Admin. and Instructor, writing and translation workshops, Athens; mem. PEN (New England), Signet, Soc. Imaginaire, Hellenic Authors' Soc. *Publications:* four vols of Greek poetry 1963, 1965, 1967, 1972, Crossing the River Twice (poems in English) 1976, Millennial Afterlives 2000; fiction: When the Tree Sings 1979, The Heroic Age 1984; other: The Canon by C. P. Cavafy (trans.) 2004, Seamus Heaney: a Celebration (ed.) 1996; contrib. to newspapers and magazines. *Honours:* Nat. Book Critics' Circle Awards. *Address:* 19 Clinton Street, Cambridge, MA 02139, USA; 136 Em. Benaki Street, 11473 Athens, Greece. *Telephone:* (617) 354-4724.

HAWASS, Zahi, PhD; Egyptian archaeologist and Egyptologist; *Secretary-General of the Supreme Council of Antiquities;* b. 28 May 1947, Damietta. *Education:* Alexandria Univ., Cairo Univ., Univ. of Pennsylvania, USA. *Career:* Inspector of Antiquities of Middle Egypt, Tuna El-Gebel and Mallawi 1969, Italian Expedition, Sikh Abada, Minia 1969, Edfu-Esna, Egypt 1969, Pa Yale Expedition at Abydos 1969, Western Delta at Alexandria 1970, Embaba, Giza 1972–74, Abu Simbel 1973–74, Pennsylvania Expedition, Malkata, Luxor 1974, Giza Pyramids (for Boston Museum of Fine Arts) 1974–75; First Inspector of Antiquities, Embaba and Bahariya Oasis 1974–79, Chief Inspector 1980, Gen. Dir 1987–98; Gen. Dir Saqqara and Bahariya Oasis 1987–98; apptd Archaeological Site Man. Memphis 1991; Under-Sec. of State for Giza Monuments 1998–2002; Sec.-Gen. of the Supreme Council of Antiquities 2002–; Dir of numerous excavations, conservation projects and discoveries including tombs of the pyramid builders at Giza and the Valley of the Golden Mummies in Bahariya; numerous consultancy roles; mem. Bd Egyptian Nat. Museum 1996–; Trustee Egyptian Nat. Museum; Sound and Light Co. 1990; mem. German Archaeological Inst. 1991–, Russian Acad. of Natural Sciences 2001–; Explorer-in-Residence Nat. Geographic 2001; mem. of numerous cttees. *Television:* numerous appearances in documentaries and features on Egypt including BBC, CNN, Discovery Channel, History Channel, National Geographic, The Learing Channel. *Publications:* Valley of the Golden Mummies 2000, Silent Images: Women in Pharaonic Egypt 2000, Secrets from the Sand 2003, Hidden Treasures of Ancient Egypt 2004, The Curse of the Pharaohs (children's book), Tutankhamun and the Golden Age of the Pharaohs 2005, Mountains of the Pharaohs 2006, The Great Book of Ancient Egypt: In the Realm of the Pharaohs 2006, The Royal Tombs of Egypt 2006; numerous papers on Egyptology and archaeology. *Honours:* Hon. PhD (American Univ., Cairo) 2005; Grantee Mellon Fellowship, Univ. of Pennsylvania, Presidential Medal 1988, Golden Plate Award, American Acad. of Achievement 2000, Distinguished Scholar of the Year Asscn of Egyptian-American Scholars 2000, Silver Medal Russian Acad. of Natural Sciences 2001, Achievement Award Mansoura Univ. 2002, named one of Five Distinguished Egyptians Egyptological Soc. of Spain 2002, Paestum Archaeology Award 2006, one of Time magazine's Top 100 Most Influential People of the Year 2005, Emmy Award Nat. Acad. of Television Arts & Sciences 2006. *Address:* 3 El Adel Abow Bakr Street, Zamalek, Cairo (office); 42 Aden Street, Mohandiseen, Cairo, Egypt (home). *Telephone:* (202) 736-5645 (office). *Fax:* (202) 735-7239 (office). *E-mail:* pyramiza2004@yahoo.com (office). *Website:* www.guardians.net/hawass (office).

HAWKING, Stephen William, CH, CBE, BA, PhD, FRS; British academic and writer; *Lucasian Professor of Applied Mathematics, University of Cambridge;* b. 8 Jan. 1942, Oxford, England; s. of Dr F. Hawking and Mrs E. I. Hawking; m. 1st Jane Wilde 1965 (divorced); two s. one d.; m. 2nd Elaine Mason 1995. *Education:* St Albans School, Univ. Coll., Oxford, Trinity Hall, Cambridge. *Career:* Research Fellow, Gonville and Caius Coll., Cambridge 1965–69, Fellow for Distinction in Science 1969–; Research Asst, Inst. of Astronomy, Cambridge 1972–73; Research Asst, Dept of Applied Math. and Theoretical Physics, Univ. of Cambridge 1973–75, Reader in Gravitational Physics 1975–77, Prof. 1977–79, Lucasian Prof. of Applied Math. 1979–; mem. Inst. of Theoretical Astronomy, Cambridge 1968–72; mem. Papal Acad. of Science 1986; Foreign mem. American Acad. Arts and Sciences 1984. *Publications:* The Large Scale Structure of Spacetime (with G. F. R. Ellis) 1973, General

Relativity: An Einstein Centenary Survey (ed. with W. Israel) 1979, Is the End in Sight for Theoretical Physics?: An Inaugural Lecture 1980, Superspace and Supergravity: Proceedings of the Nuffield Workshop (ed. with M. Rocek) 1981, The Very Early Universe: Proceedings of the Nuffield Workshop (co-ed.) 1983, 300 Years of Gravitation (with W. Israel) 1987, A Brief History of Time: From the Big Bang to Black Holes 1988, Hawking on the Big Bang and Black Holes 1992, Black Holes and Baby Universes and Other Essays 1993, The Cambridge Lectures: Life Works 1995, The Nature of Space and Time (with Roger Penrose) 1996, The Universe in a Nutshell (Aventis Prize 2002) 2001, The Theory of Everything: The Origin and Fate of the Universe 2002, The Future of Spacetime (co-ed.) 2002, On the Shoulders of Giants 2002, A Briefer History of Time (with Leonard Mlodinow) 2005; also individual lectures, contrib. to scholarly books and journals. *Honours:* several hon. degrees; Hon. Fellow, Univ. Coll., Oxford 1977, Trinity Hall, Cambridge 1984; Eddington Medal 1975, Pontifical Acad. of Sciences Pius XI Gold Medal 1975, Cambridge Philosophical Soc. William Hopkins Prize 1976, Wolf Foundation Prize for Physics 1988, Inst. of Physics Maxwell Medal 1976, Royal Soc. Hughes Medal 1976, Albert Einstein Award 1978, Royal Astronomical Soc. Gold Medal 1985, Inst. of Physics Paul Dirac Medal and Prize 1987, Sunday Times Special Award for Literature 1989, Britannica Award 1989, RSA Albert Medal 1999, Royal Soc. Copley Medal 2006. *Address:* Department of Applied Mathematics and Theoretical Physics, Silver Street, Cambridge, CB3 9EW, England (office). *Telephone:* (1223) 337843 (office). *Website:* www.damtp.cam.ac.uk (office); www.hawking.org.uk.

HAWLICEK, Hilde; Austrian politician; *President, International Institute for Children's Literature and Reading Research;* b. 14 April 1942, Vienna. *Career:* mem. Nationalrat (Parl.) 1976–87, 1990–95, 1996; Minister of Educ., the Arts and Sport 1987–90; mem. European Parl. (Vice-Pres. PSE) 1995–99, Vice-Pres. Cttee on Culture, Youth, Educ. and the Media, mem. Del. for Relations with the Maghreb Countries and the Arab Maghreb Union; Pres. Int. Inst. for Children's Literature and Reading Research. *Address:* Mayerhofgasse 6, 1040 Vienna, Austria. *Telephone:* (1) 50503-59. *Fax:* (1) 50503-5917. *E-mail:* office@jugendliteratur.net (office). *Website:* www.jugendliteratur.net (office).

HAWTHORNE, Susan, DipEd, BA, MA; Australian academic, publisher, poet and writer; b. 30 Nov. 1951, Wagga Wagga, NSW. *Education:* Melbourne Teachers College, La Trobe University, University of Melbourne. *Career:* Tutor, Koori Teacher Education Programme, Deakin University, 1986; Ed. and Commissioning Ed., Penguin Books, Australia, 1987–91; Publisher, Spinifex Press, 1991–; Lecturer, Dept of Communication and Language Studies, Victoria University of Technology, 1995–; mem. Australian Society of Authors; Fellowship of Australian Authors; PEN International; Victoria Writers Centre. *Publications:* Difference (ed.), 1985; Moments of Desire, 1989; The Exploring Frangipani, 1990; Angels of Power, 1991; The Falling Woman, 1992; The Language in My Tongue: Four New Poets, 1993; The Spinifex Quiz Book, 1993; Australia for Women (co-ed.), 1994; Car Maintenance, Explosives and Love (co-ed.), 1997; CyberFeminism (co-ed.), 1999; Bird, 1999. Contributions: journals, reviews, and periodicals.

HAYDEN, Dolores, BA, MArch; American architect, academic and writer; b. 15 March 1945, New York, NY; m. Peter Marris 1975; one d. *Education:* Mount Holyoke Coll., Girton Coll., Cambridge, Harvard Grad. School of Design. *Career:* Lecturer, Univ. of California, Berkeley 1973; Assoc. Prof., MIT 1973–79; Prof., UCLA 1979–91, Yale Univ. 1991–; mem. American Studies Asscn, Org. of American Historians. *Publications:* Seven American Utopias 1976, The Grand Domestic Revolution 1981, Redesigning the American Dream 1984, The Power of Place: Urban Landscapes as Public History 1995, Playing House 1998, Line Dance 2001, Building Suburbia 2003, A Field Guide to Sprawl 2004, American Yard 2004; contribs to numerous journals. *Honours:* Nat. Endowment for the Humanities Fellowship 1976, Nat. Endowment for the Arts Fellowship 1980, Guggenheim Fellowship 1981, Rockefeller Foundation Fellowship 1981, ACLS-Ford Foundation Fellowship 1988, Assn of American Publrs' Award 1995. *Address:* School of Architecture, Yale University, PO Box 208242, 180 York Street, New Haven, CT 06520, USA (office). *Telephone:* (203) 432-2288 (office). *Fax:* (203) 432-7175 (office). *E-mail:* dolores.hayden@yale.edu (office). *Website:* www.architecture.yale.edu (office); www.doloreshayden.com.

HAYES, Charles Langley (see Holmes, Bryan John)

HAYMAN, David, BA, PhD; American academic, writer and editor; b. 7 Jan. 1927, New York, NY; m. Loni Goldschmidt 1951, two d. *Education:* New York University, University of Paris. *Career:* Instructor, 1955–57, Asst Prof., 1957–58, Assoc. Prof. of English, 1958–65, University of Texas; Prof. of English and Comparative Literature, University of Iowa, 1965–73; Prof. of Comparative Literature, 1973–96, Eujire-Bascon Prof. in the Humanities, 1990–96, Prof. Emeritus, 1997–, University of Wisconsin, Madison. *Publications:* Joyce et Mallarmé, 1956; A First-Draft Version of Finnegans Wake, 1963; Configuration Critique de James Joyce (ed.), 1965; Ulysses: The Mechanics of Meaning, 1970; Form in Fiction (with Eric Rabkin), 1974; Ulysses: Critical Essays (with Clive Hart), 1974; The James Joyce Archive (ed.), 1978; Philippe Sollers: Writing and the Experience of Limits (ed. and co-trans.), 1980; Re-forming the Narrative, 1987; The Wake in Transit, 1990; Probes: Genetic Studies in Joyce (with Sam Slote), 1994; James Joyce: Epiphanias (ed.), 1996. Contributions: many scholarly books and journals. *Honours:* Guggenheim Fellowship, 1958–59; National Endowment for the

Humanities Fellowship, 1979–80; Harry Levin Prize, American Comparative Literature Asscn, 1989.

HAYMAN, Ronald, BA, MA; British writer; b. 4 May 1932, Bournemouth, Dorset; m. (divorced); two d. *Education:* Trinity Hall, Cambridge. *Career:* mem. Soc. of Authors. *Plays:* Playing the Wife, Chichester Festival Theatre 1995. *Publications:* Harold Pinter 1968, Samuel Beckett 1968, John Osborne 1968, John Arden 1968, Robert Bolt 1969, John Whiting 1969, Collected Plays of John Whiting (ed.), two vols 1969, Techniques of Acting 1969, The Art of the Dramatist and Other Pieces, by John Whiting (ed.) 1970, Arthur Miller 1970, Tolstoy 1970, Arnold Wesker 1970, John Gielgud 1971, Edward Albee 1971, Eugène Ionesco 1972, Playback 1973, The Set-Up 1974, Playback 2 1974, The First Thrust 1975, The German Theatre (ed.) 1975, How to Read a Play 1977, The Novel Today 1967–75 1976, My Cambridge (ed.) 1977, Tom Stoppard 1977, Artaud and After 1977, De Sade 1978, Theatre and Anti-Theatre 1979, British Theatre Since 1955: A Reassessment 1979, Nietzsche: A Critical Life 1980, K: A Biography of Kafka 1981, Brecht: A Biography 1983, Fassbinder: Film Maker 1984, Brecht: The Plays 1984, Günter Grass 1985, Secrets: Boyhood in a Jewish Hotel 1932–54 1985, Writing Against: A Biography of Sartre 1986, Proust: A Biography 1990, The Death and Life of Sylvia Plath 1991, Tennessee Williams: Everyone Else Is an Audience 1994, Thomas Mann 1995, Hitler and Geli 1997, Nietzsche's Voices 1997, A Life of Jung 1999. *Address:* The Penthouse, Highpoint, London, N6 4AZ, England (home).

HAYS, Robert Glenn, MS, PhD; American journalism educator and writer; b. 23 May 1935, Carmi, Ill.; m. Mary Elizabeth Corley 1957; two s. *Education:* Southern Illinois Univ. *Career:* reporter, Granite City Press-Record 1961–63; public relations writer, Southern Illinois Univ. 1963–66, Alumni Ed. 1966–71; Asst Scientist, Illinois Board of Natural Resources and Conservation 1971–73; Journalism Faculty, Sam Houston State Univ. 1974–75, Univ. of Illinois 1975–86, 1987–; Chair. Dept of Mass Communications, Southeast Missouri Univ. 1986–87; Founding mem. Research Soc. of American Periodicals; mem. Asscn for Educ. in Journalism and Mass Communications, Illinois Press Asscn, Investigative Reporters and Eds, Missouri Press Asscn, Soc. of Professional Journalists, American Civil Liberties Union (Chapter Steering Cttee 1991–93), Nat. Org. for Women. *Publications:* G-2: Intelligence for Patton 1971 (new edn 1999), Country Ed 1974, State Science in Illinois 1980, Early Stories From the Land 1995, A Race at Bay: New York Times Editorials on the 'Indian Problem' 1860–1900 1997; contrib. to periodicals and journals. *Honours:* Int. ACE Award of Excellence 1993, 1994, Univ. of Illinois Acad. of Teaching Excellence Award 1996. *Address:* 2314 Glenoak Drive, Champaign, IL 61821, USA (home). *E-mail:* r-hays1@uiuc.edu (office).

HAYTHE, Justin, BA, MFA; British screenwriter and writer; *Associate Editor, Fence magazine;* b. 1973, London. *Education:* Middlebury Coll., VT, Sarah Lawrence. *Career:* Assoc. Ed. Fence magazine. *Publications:* The Fabulous Wardrobe of Mrs Pat Campbell (short story) 2003, The Honeymoon (novel) 2004, The Clearing (screenplay) 2004. *Literary Agent:* Elaine Markson Litreary Agency, 44 Greenwich Avenue, New York, NY 10011, USA.

HAZEN, Robert Miller, PhD; American geophysicist, musician and writer; *Clarence Robinson Professor of Earth Science, George Mason University;* b. 1 Nov. 1948, Rockville Centre, NY; m. Margaret Hindle 1969; one s. one d. *Education:* Massachusetts Inst. of Tech. and Harvard Univ. *Career:* NATO Fellow, Univ. of Cambridge, UK 1975–76; Research Scientist, Geophysical Lab., Carnegie Inst., Washington, DC 1976–; Clarence Robinson Prof. of Earth Science, George Mason Univ.; trumpeter with many orchestras; mem. ACS, American Geophysical Union, History of Science Soc., Int. Guild of Trumpeters; Mineralogical Soc. of America. *Publications:* Comparative Crystal Chemistry 1982, Poetry of Geology 1982, Music Men 1987, The Breakthrough 1988, Science Matters 1990, Keepers of the Flame 1991, The New Alchemist 1993, The Sciences 1995, Why Aren't Black Holes Black? 1997, The Diamond Makers 1999, Physics Matters 2003, Genesis: The Scientific Quest for Life's Origin 2005; contrib. to many scientific journals and to periodicals. *Honours:* Mineralogical Soc. of America Award 1981, Ipatief Prize 1984, ASCAP-Deems Taylor Award 1988, Educ. Press Asscn Award 1992, Elizabeth Wood Science Writing Award 1998. *Address:* Geophysical Laboratory, Carnegie Institution, 5251 Broad Branch Road NW, Washington, DC 20015, USA (office). *Telephone:* (202) 478-8962 (office). *E-mail:* r.hazen@gl.ciw.edu (office). *Website:* www.gl.ciw.edu (office).

HAZLETON, Lesley, BA, MA; American/British writer; b. 20 Sept. 1945, Reading, England. *Education:* Manchester University, Hebrew University of Jerusalem. *Career:* mem. PEN American Center. *Publications:* Israeli Women 1978, Where Mountains Roar 1980, In Defence of Depression 1984, Jerusalem, Jerusalem 1986, England, Bloody England 1989, Confessions of a Fast Woman 1992, Everything Women Always Wanted to Know About Cars 1995, Driving to Detroit 1998, Mary 2004, Jezebel 2007, Karbala 2008; contrib. to many periodicals and magazines. *Address:* Watkins Loomis Agency Inc., 133 E 35th Street, Suite 1, New York, NY 10016, USA (office).

HAZO, Samuel John, BA, MA, PhD; American academic, writer and poet; *President and Director, International Poetry Forum;* b. 19 July 1928, Pittsburgh, PA. *Education:* University of Notre Dame, Duquesne University, University of Pittsburgh. *Career:* faculty mem., Duquesne University 1955–65, Dean College of Arts and Sciences 1961–66, Prof. of English 1965–; Pres. and Dir, International Poetry Forum 1966–; State Poet, Commonwealth of Pennsylvania 1993–2003. *Publications:* Discovery and Other Poems 1959, The Quiet Wars 1962, Hart Crane: An Introduction and

Interpretation (revised edn as Smithereened Apart: A Critique of Hart Crane) 1963, The Christian Intellectual Studies in the Relation of Catholicism to the Human Sciences (ed.) 1963, A Selection of Contemporary Religious Poetry (ed.) 1963, Listen With the Eye 1964, My Sons in God: Selected and New Poems 1965, Blood Rights 1968, The Blood of Adonis (with Ali Ahmed Said) 1971, Twelve Poems (with George Nama) 1972, Seascript: A Mediterranean Logbook 1972, Once for the Last Bandit: New and Previous Poems 1972, Quartered 1974, Inscripts 1975, The Very Fall of the Sun 1978, To Paris 1981, The Wanton Summer Air 1982, Thank a Bored Angel 1983, The Feast of Icarus 1984, The Color of Reluctance 1986, The Pittsburgh That Starts Within You 1986, Silence Spoken Here 1988, Stills 1989, The Rest is Prose 1989, Lebanon 1990, Picks 1990, The Past Won't Stay Behind You 1993, The Pages of Day and Night 1995, The Holy Surprise of Right Now 1996, As They Sail 1999, Spying for God 1999, Mano a Mano: The Life of Manolete 2001, Just Once 2002, A Flight to Elsewhere 2005, The Power of Less 2005. *Honours:* Maurice English Poetry Award 2003, Griffin Award for Writing Univ. of Notre Dame 2005. *Address:* 785 Somerville Drive, Pittsburgh, PA 15243 (home); International Poetry Forum, 3333 Fifth Avenue, Pittsburgh, PA 15213, USA (office). *Telephone:* (412) 621-9893 (office). *Fax:* (412) 621-9898 (office). *E-mail:* ipf1@earthlink.net (office). *Website:* www.thepoetryforum.org (office).

HAZZARD, Shirley, FRSL; Australian/American writer; b. 30 Jan. 1931, Sydney, Australia; d. of Reginald Hazzard and Catherine Hazzard; m. Francis Steegmuller 1963 (died 1994). *Education:* Queenwood School, Sydney. *Career:* Special Operations Intelligence, Hong Kong 1947–48; UK High Commr's Office, Wellington, NZ 1949–50; UN, New York (Gen. Service Category) 1952–61; novelist and writer of short stories and contrib. to The New Yorker 1960–; Guggenheim Fellow 1974; mem. American Acad. of Arts and Letters, American Acad. of Arts and Sciences. *Publications:* short stories: Cliffs of Fall 1963; novels: The Evening of the Holiday 1966, People in Glass Houses 1967, The Bay of Noon 1970, The Transit of Venus (Nat. Critics Circle Award for Fiction 1981) 1980, The Great Fire (Nat. Book Award for Fiction) 2003, Australia (Miles Franklin Prize 2004) 2004; non-fiction: Defeat of an Ideal: A Study of the Self-destruction of the United Nations 1973, Countenance of Truth: The United Nations and the Waldheim Case 1990, Greene on Capri (memoir) 2000. *Honours:* Hon. Citizen of Capri 2000; American Acad. of Arts and Letters Award in Literature 1966, First Prize, O. Henry Short Story Awards 1976, Nat. Book Critics Award for Fiction, USA 1981, Boyer Lecturer, Australia 1984, 1988, Clifton Fadiman Medal for Literature 2001, Nat. Book Award for Fiction 2003, William Dean Howells Medal, American Acad. of Arts and Letters 2005.

HEADLEY, John Miles, MA, PhD; American historian and academic; b. 23 Oct. 1929, New York, NY, USA. *Education:* Princeton abd Yale Univs. *Career:* Instructor, Univ. of Massachusetts, Amherst 1959–61; Instructor to Asst Prof., Univ. of British Columbia, Vancouver 1962–64; Asst Prof., Univ. of North Carolina at Chapel Hill 1964–66, Assoc. Prof. 1966–69, Prof. 1969–2003, Prof. Emer. 2003–. *Publications:* Luther's View of Church History 1963, Medieval and Renaissance Studies, Vol. III (ed.) 1968, Responsio ad Lutherum, Complete Works of St Thomas More, Vol. V (ed.) 1969, The Emperor and his Chancellor: A Study of the Imperial Chancellery under Gattinara 1983, San Carlo Borromeo: Catholic Reform and Ecclesiastical Politics in the Second Half of the Sixteenth Century (ed. and contributor) 1988, The Oxford Encyclopedia of the Reformation (assoc. ed.) 1996, Tommaso Campanella and the Transformation of the World 1997, Empire, Church and World: The Quest for Universal Order 1997, Confessionalization in Europe 1555–1700 (ed. and contrib.); contrib. to various scholarly books and journals. *Honours:* Guggenheim Fellowship 1974, Institute for Arts and Humanities Fellowship 1989. *Address:* Department of History, University of North Carolina at Chapel Hill, Chapel Hill, NC 27599-3195, USA (office).

HEALD, Timothy Villiers, (David Lancaster), MA, FRSL; British journalist and writer; b. 28 Jan. 1944, Dorset, England; m. 1st Alison Martina Leslie 1968 (divorced), two s. two d.; m. 2nd Penelope Byrne 1999. *Education:* Balliol Coll., Oxford. *Career:* reporter Sunday Times 1965–67; Feature Ed. Town magazine 1967; Feature Writer Daily Express 1967–72; Assoc. Ed. Weekend Magazine, Toronto 1977–78; columnist Observer 1990; Visiting Fellow Jane Franklin Hall 1997, 1999, Univ. Tutor in Creative Writing 1999, 2000, Univ. of Tasmania; writer-in-residence Univ. of South Australia 2001; mem. CWA (chair. 1987–88), PEN, Soc. of Authors. *Publications:* It's a Dog's Life 1971, Unbecoming Habits 1973, Blue Book Will Out 1974, Deadline 1975, Let Sleeping Dogs Die 1976, The Making of Space 1976, John Steed: An Authorized Biography 1977, Just Desserts 1977, H.R.H.: The Man Who Will be King (with M. Mohs) 1977, Murder at Moose Jaw 1981, Caroline R 1981, Masterstroke 1982, Networks 1983, Class Distinctions 1984, Red Herrings 1985, The Character of Cricket 1986, Brought to Book 1988, The Newest London Spy (ed.) 1988, Business Unusual 1989, By Appointments: 150 Years of the Royal Warrant 1989, A Classic English Crime (ed.) 1990, My Lord's (ed.) 1990, The Duke: A Portrait of Prince Philip 1991, Honorable Estates 1992, Barbara Cartland: A Life of Love 1994, Denis: The Authorized Biography of the Incomparable Compton 1994, Brian Johnston: The Authorized Biography 1995, A Classic Christmas Crime (ed.) 1995, Beating Retreat: Hong Kong Under the Last Governor 1997, Stop Press 1998, A Peerage for Trade 2001, Village Cricket 2004, Death and the Visiting Fellow 2004, Death and the D'Urbervilles 2005, Princess Margaret 2007; contrib. to newspapers and periodicals. *Address:* 66 The Esplanade, Fowey, Cornwall PL23 1JA, England.

Telephone: (1726) 832781. *Fax:* (1726) 833246. *E-mail:* tim@timheald.com. *Website:* www.timheald.com.

HEALEY, Baron (Life Peer), cr. 1992, of Riddlesden in the County of West Yorkshire; **Denis Winston Healey,** PC, CH, MBE, FRSL; British politician; b. 30 Aug. 1917, Mottingham; s. of William Healey; m. Edna May Edmunds 1945; one s. two d. *Education:* Bradford Grammar School and Balliol Coll., Oxford. *Career:* Maj., Royal Engineers 1945; Sec. Labour Party Int. Dept 1945–52; MP 1952–92; Sec. of State for Defence 1964–70; Chancellor of the Exchequer 1974–79; Opposition Spokesman for Treasury and Econ. Affairs 1979–80, for Foreign and Commonwealth Affairs 1980–87; Chair. Interim Ministerial Cttee of IMF 1977–79; Deputy Leader of Labour Party 1980–83; Pres. Birkbeck Coll. London 1993–99. *Publications:* The Curtain Falls 1951, New Fabian Essays 1952, Neutralism 1955, Fabian International Essays 1956, A Neutral Belt in Europe 1958, NATO and American Security 1959, The Race Against the H Bomb 1960, Labour Britain and the World 1963, Healey's Eye (photographs) 1980, Labour and a World Society 1985, Beyond Nuclear Deterrence 1986, The Time of My Life (autobiog.) 1989, When Shrimps Learn to Whistle (collection of essays) 1990, My Secret Planet 1992, Denis Healey's Yorkshire Dales 1995, Healey's World (photographs) 2002. *Honours:* Hon. Fellow, Balliol Coll. Oxford 1980; Freeman of Leeds 1991; Grand Cross of Order of Merit, FRG 1979; Hon. DLitt (Bradford) 1983; Hon. LLD, (Sussex) 1989, (Leeds) 1991. *Address:* House of Lords, Westminster, London, SW1A 0PW (office). *Telephone:* (20) 7219-3546 (office).

HEALEY, Robin Michael, BA, MA; British historian and biographer; *Co-Editor, ALS Journal*; b. 16 Feb. 1952, London; s. of Lt Commdr T. B. Healey and Vera Healey (née Paulson). *Education:* Univ. of Birmingham. *Career:* Documentation Officer, Tamworth Castle and Cambridge Museum of Archaeology and Anthropology 1977–79; Museum Asst, Saffron Walden Museum 1983–84; Research Asst, History of Parliament 1985–92; Ed. Hertfordshire Soc. Jubilee Yearbook 1986; Visiting Research Fellow, Univ. of Manchester 1997–2003; Ed. Lewisletter 2001–; Co-Ed. ALS Journal 2006–; mem. Charles Lamb Soc. (Exec. 1987–), Alliance of Literary Socs (press officer 1997–2005), Wyndham Lewis Soc. *Publications:* Hertfordshire: A Shell Guide 1982, Diary of George Mushet (1805–13) 1982, Grigson at Eighty 1985, A History of Barley School 1995, My Rebellious and Imperfect Eye: Observing Geoffrey Grigson 2002; contrib. to Biographical Dictionary of Modern British Radicals 1984, Domesday Book 1985, Secret Britain 1986, Dictionary of Literary Biography 1991, Encyclopaedia of Romanticism 1992, Consumer Magazines of the British Isles 1993, Postwar Literatures in English 1998–, I Remember When I Was Young 2003, Oxford Dictionary of National Biography 2004, Country Life, Hertfordshire Countryside, Guardian, Literary Review, Private Eye, Book and Magazine Collector, Independent, TLS, Art Newspaper, Mensa Magazine, Charles Lamb Bulletin, Cobbett's New Political Register, Rare Book Review, Lancet, Wyndham Lewis Annual, British Medical Association Journal. *Honours:* First Prize, Birmingham Post Poetry Contest 1974; various research awards. *Address:* 80 Hall Lane, Great Chishill, Royston, Herts., SG8 8SH, England. *Telephone:* (1763) 837058. *E-mail:* robinheal@aol.com (office).

HEALY, Jeremiah, (Terry Devane); American novelist. *Education:* Rutgers Coll., Harvard Law School. *Career:* Prof., New England School of Law, 18 years; mem. Private Eye Writers of America (fmr pres.) Shamus Awards (fmr chair.), Int. Asscn of Crime Writers (pres. 2000–). *Publications:* as Jeremiah Healy: Blunt Darts 1984, The Staked Goat 1986, So Like Sleep 1987, Swan Dive 1988, Yesterday's News 1989, Right to Die 1991, Shallow Graves 1992, Foursome 1993, Act of God 1994, Rescue 1995, Invasion of Privacy 1996, The Only Good Lawyer 1998, The Stalking of Sheilah Quinn 1998, The Concise Cuddy (short stories) 1998, Spiral 1999, Turnabout 2001, Cuddy Plus One (short stories) 2003; as Terry Devane: Uncommon Justice 2001, Juror Number Eleven 2002, A Stain Upon the Robe 2003; contrib. shorts stories to collections, including Irreconcilable Differences, Blonde & Blue: Classic Private Eyes, Mom, Apple Pie, and Murder. *Honours:* Shamus Award 1986. *Literary Agent:* Sandy Balzo, Balzo Communications, 750 E Briar Ridge Drive, Brookfield, WI 53045, USA. *Telephone:* (262) 784-2591. *Fax:* (262) 784-3468. *E-mail:* balzocom@aol.com. *Address:* c/o Penguin Putnam, 375 Hudson Street, New York, NY 10014, USA. *E-mail:* jeremiah_healy@yahoo.com. *Website:* www.jeremiahhealy.com.

HEANEY, Seamus, CLit; Irish poet and author; *Ralph Waldo Emerson Poet in Residence, Harvard University*; b. 13 April 1939, Northern Ireland; s. of Patrick Heaney and Margaret Heaney (née McCann); m. Marie Devlin 1965; two s. one d. *Education:* St Columb's Coll., Londonderry, Queen's Univ., Belfast. *Career:* Lecturer, St Joseph's Coll. of Educ., Belfast 1963–66, Queen's Univ., Belfast 1966–72; freelance writer 1972–75, Lecturer, Carysfort Coll. 1975–81, Sr Visiting Lecturer, Harvard Univ. 1982–84, Boylston Prof. of Rhetoric and Oratory 1985–97, Ralph Waldo Emerson Poet in Residence 1998–; Prof. of Poetry, Univ. of Oxford 1989–94. *Poems:* Eleven Poems 1965, Death of a Naturalist 1966, Door into the Dark 1969, Wintering Out 1972, North 1975, Field Work 1979, Selected Poems 1965–1975 1980, Station Island 1984, The Haw Lantern 1987, New Selected Poems 1966–1987 1990, Seeing Things 1991, The Spirit Level 1996 (Whitbread Book of the Year Award 1997), Opened Ground: Poems 1966–96 1998 (Irish Times Literary Award 1999), Beowulf: A New Verse Translation 1999, Electric Light 2001, The Testament of Cresseid (a retelling of Robert Henryson's poem) 2005, District and Circle (T.S. Eliot Prize for Poetry) 2006. *Prose:* Preoccupations: Selected Prose 1968–1978 1980, The Government of the Tongue 1988, The Place of Writing

1990, The Redress of Poetry (lectures) 1995, Finders Keepers: Selected Prose 1971–2001 2002, The Midnight Verdict 2002. *Anthology:* The School Bag 1997 (co-ed. with Ted Hughes). *Plays:* The Cure at Troy 1991, The Burial at Thebes (Abbey Theatre, Dublin) 2004. *Translations:* Sweeney Astray 1984, Sweeney's Flight 1992, Laments, by Jan Kochanowski (with Stanislaw Baranczak); Beowulf: a New Verse Translation (Whitbread Book of the Year 1999) 1999. *Honours:* Hon. DLitt (Oxford) 1997, (Birmingham) 2000; Commdr des Arts et Lettres; WH Smith Prize 1975, Bennet Award 1982, Sunday Times Award for Excellence in Writing 1988, Lannan Literary Award 1990, Nobel Prize for Literature 1996. *Literary Agent:* Steven Barclay Agency, 12 Western Avenue, Petaluma, CA 94952, USA. *Telephone:* (707) 773-0654. *Fax:* (707) 778-1868. *Website:* www.barclayagency.com. *Address:* c/o Faber and Faber, 3 Queen Square, London, WC1N 3AU, England. *Telephone:* (20) 7465-0045. *Fax:* (20) 7465-0034.

HEARON, Shelby, BA; American novelist; b. 18 Jan. 1931, Marion, KY; m. 1st Robert Hearon Jr 1953 (divorced 1976); one s. one d.; m. 2nd Billy Joe Lucas 1981 (divorced 1995); m. 3rd William Halpern 1995. *Education:* University of Texas at Austin. *Career:* Visiting Lecturer, University of Texas at Austin, 1978–80; Visiting Assoc. Prof., University of Houston, 1981, Clark University, 1985, University of California at Irvine, 1987; Visiting Prof., University of Illinois at Chicago, 1993, Colgate University, 1993, University of Massachusetts at Amherst, 1994–96, Middlebury College, 1996–98; mem. Associated Writing Programs; Authors' Guild; Authors League; PEN American Centre; Poets and Writers; Texas Institute of Letters. *Publications:* Armadillo in the Grass, 1968; The Second Dune, 1973; Hannah's House, 1975; Now and Another Time, 1976; A Prince of a Fellow, 1978; Painted Dresses, 1981; Afternoon of a Faun, 1983; Group Therapy, 1984; A Small Town, 1985; Five Hundred Scorpions, 1987; Owning Jolene, 1989; Hug Dancing, 1991; Life Estates, 1994; Footprints, 1996; Ella in Bloom, 2001, Year of the Dog 2007; other: Best Friends for Life (based on Life Estates), CBS-TV, 1998. Contributions: Magazines. *Honours:* Guggenheim Fellowship in Fiction, 1982; National Endowment for the Arts Fellowship in Fiction, 1983; Ingram Merrill Foundation Grant, 1987; American Acad. of Arts and Letters Literature Award, 1990. *Address:* 246 S Union Street, Burlington, VT 05401, USA (home). *Telephone:* (502) 660-4349 (home).

HEAT-MOON, William Least, (William Lewis Trogdon), BA, MA, PhD; American writer; b. 27 Aug. 1939, Kansas City, MO; m. 1st Lezlie (divorced 1978); m. 2nd Linda. *Education:* University of Missouri at Columbia. *Career:* Teacher of English, Stephens College, Columbia, MO, 1965–68, 1972, 1978; Lecturer, School oif Journalism, University of Missouri, 1984–87. *Publications:* Blue Highways: A Journey into America, 1982; PrairyErth (a deep map), 1991; River Horse, 1999. Contributions: newspapers and magazines. *Honours:* New York Times Notable Book Citations, 1983, 1991; Books-Across-the-Sea Award, 1984; Christopher Award, 1984; American Library Asscn Best Non-Fiction Work, 1991.

HEATER, Derek Benjamin, BA, PGCE; British writer; b. 28 Nov. 1931, Sydenham, England; one s. one d. *Education:* Univ. Coll. London, Inst. of Education, Univ. of London. *Career:* Ed. Teaching Politics 1973–79; Co-Ed. (with Bernard Crick) Political Realities Series 1974–93; mem. Politics Asscn, co-f., 1969; Council for Education in World Citizenship, hon. life mem. *Publications:* Political Ideas in the Modern World 1960, Order and Rebellion 1964, World Affairs (with Gwyneth Owen) 1972, Contemporary Political Ideas 1974, Britain and the Outside World 1976, Essays in Political Education (with Bernard Crick) 1977, World Studies 1980, Our World This Century 1982, Peace Through Education 1984, Reform and Revolution 1987, Refugees 1988, Case Studies in Twentieth-Century World History 1988, Citizenship: The Civic Ideal in World History, Politics and Education 1990, The Idea of European Unity 1992, The Remarkable History of Rottingdean 1993, Introduction to International Politics (with G. R. Berridge) 1993, Foundations of Citizenship (with Dawn Oliver) 1994, National Self-Determination 1994, World Citizenship and Government 1996, The Theory of Nationhood: A Platonic Symposium 1998, History of Sutton Grammar School: Keeping Faith 1899–1999 1999, What is Citizenship? 1999, World Citizenship: Cosmopolitan Thinking and Its Opponents 2002, A History of Education for Citizenship 2003, A Brief History of Citizenship 2004, Citizenship in Britain 2006, The Dying Man's Clues 2006; contrib. to reference works, scholarly journals. *Honours:* Children's Book of the Year Award for Refugees 1988, Fellow Politics Asscn 1994. *Address:* 3 The Rotyngs, Rottingdean, Brighton, BN2 7DX, England (home). *Telephone:* (1273) 307890 (home).

HEATH, Chris; British journalist and writer. *Career:* journalist, Jamming! 1984–85, Smash Hits 1984–89, The Guardian, The Face, The Daily Telegraph, The Sunday Telegraph, Empire, Rolling Stone, GQ; fmr Contributing Ed., Details magazine; official biographer, Pet Shop Boys, Robbie Williams. *Publications:* Pet Shop Boys, Literally 1990, Pet Shop Boys Vs America 1993, Feel: Robbie Williams 2004. *Address:* c/o Ebury Press, Random House UK Ltd, Random House, 20 Vauxhall Bridge Road, London, SW1V 2SA, England (office).

HEATH, Roy Aubrey Kelvin, BA; Guyanese writer and dramatist; b. 13 Aug. 1926, Georgetown, British Guiana; m. Aemilia Oberli; three c. *Education:* University of London. *Career:* teacher, London, 1959–; called to the Bar, Lincoln's Inn, 1964. *Publications:* Fiction: A Man Come Home, 1974; The Murderer, 1978; From the Heat of Day, 1979; One Generation, 1980; Genetha, 1981; Kwaku, or, The Man Who Could Not Keep His Mouth Shut,

1982; Orealla, 1984; The Shadow Bridge, 1988. Non-Fiction: Art and History, 1983; Shadows Round the Moon (memoirs), 1990. Play: Inez Combray, 1972. *Honours:* Drama Award, Theatre Guild of Guyana, 1971; Fiction Prize, The Guardian, London, 1978; Guyana Award for Literature, 1989. *Address:* c/o Harper/Collins, 77 Fulham Palace Road, London W6 8J, England.

HEATHCOTT, Mary (see Keegan, Mary Constance)

HEBALD, Carol, BA, MFA; American writer; b. 6 July 1934, New York, NY. *Education:* University of Iowa, City College, CUNY. *Career:* mem. PEN American Centre; Authors' Guild of America. *Publications:* Three Blind Mice, 1989; Clara Kleinschmidt, 1989; Martha (play), 1991; The Heart Too Long Suppressed, 2001. Contributions: Antioch Review; Kansas Quarterly; Texas Quarterly; Massachusetts Review; The Humanist; New Letters; Confrontation; North American Review; New York Tribune; PEN International. *Address:* 425 Madison Avenue, Suite 1001, New York, NY 10017, USA.

HECKLER, Jonellen, BA; American writer and poet; b. 28 Oct. 1943, Pittsburgh, PA; m. Lou Heckler 1968, one s. *Education:* University of Pittsburgh. *Career:* mem. Authors' Guild. *Publications:* Safekeeping, 1983; A Fragile Peace, 1986; White Lies, 1989; Circumstances Unknown, 1993; Final Tour, 1994. Contributions: numerous poems and short stories in Ladies Home Journal Magazine, 1975–83.

HEDIN, Mary Ann, BS, MA; American writer and poet; b. 3 Aug. 1929, Minneapolis, MN; m. Roger Willard Hedin, three s. one d. *Education:* University of Minnesota, University of California. *Career:* Fellow, Yaddo, 1974; Writer-in-Residence, Robinson Jeffers Town House Foundation, 1984–85; mem. Authors' Guild; PEN; American Poetry Society. *Publications:* Fly Away Home, 1980; Direction, 1983. Contributions: anthologies and journals. *Honours:* John H. McGinnis Memorial Award, 1979; Iowa School of Letters Award for Short Fiction, 1979.

HEDRICK, Joan Doran; American academic and writer; b. 1 May 1944, Baltimore, MD; m. Travis K. Hedrick 1967; two d. *Education:* AB, Vassar College, 1966; PhD, Brown University, 1974. *Career:* Prof. of History, Trinity College, Hartford, CT; mem. American Studies Asscn; MLA. *Publications:* Solitary Comrade: Jack London and His Work, 1982; Harriet Beecher Stowe: A Life, 1994; The Oxford Harriet Beecher Stowe Reader, 1999. *Honours:* Pulitzer Prize in Biography, 1995. *Address:* c/o Department of History, Trinity College, Hartford, CT 06106, USA.

HEFFER, Simon James, MA; British journalist and writer; *Associate Editor, Daily Telegraph*; b. 18 July 1960, Chelmsford, Essex; s. of the late James Heffer and of Joyce Mary Clements; m. Diana Caroline Cleef 1987; two s. *Education:* King Edward VI School, Chelmsford and Corpus Christi Coll., Cambridge. *Career:* medical journalist 1983–85; freelance journalist 1985–86; Leader Writer Daily Telegraph 1986–91, Deputy Political Corresp. 1987–88, political sketch writer 1988–91, political columnist 1990–91, Deputy Ed. 1994–96; Deputy Ed. The Spectator 1991–94; columnist Evening Standard 1991–93, Daily Mail 1993–94, 1995–; Assoc. Ed. Daily Telegraph 2005–. *Publications:* A Tory Seer (Jt Ed. with C. Moore) 1989, A Century of County Cricket (Ed.) 1990, Moral Desperado: A Life of Thomas Carlyle 1995, Power and Place: The Political Consequences of King Edward VII 1998, Like the Roman: The Life of Enoch Powell 1998, Nor Shall My Sword; the Reinvention of England 1999, Vaughan Williams 2000, The Great British Speeches 2007. *Honours:* Charles Douglas-Home Prize 1993. *Address:* The Daily Telegraph, 1 Canada Square, London, E14 5DT, England (office). *Telephone:* (20) 7538-5000 (office). *Fax:* (20) 7538-7610 (office). *E-mail:* simon.heffer@telegraph.co.uk (office). *Website:* www.telegraph.co.uk (office).

HEFFERNAN, Thomas Patrick Carroll, AB, MA, PhD; American/Irish academic, writer and poet; *Professor of American Studies, Kagoshima Kenritsu Daigaku;* b. 19 Aug. 1939, Hyannis, MA; s. of Thomas Hugh Carroll Heffernan and Mary Elizabeth Sullivan Heffernan; m. Nancy E. Iler 1972 (divorced 1977). *Education:* Boston College, University of Manchester, England, Universita per Stranieri, Perugia, Italy, Sophia University, Tokyo. *Career:* Poet in Schools, North Carolina Dept of Public Instruction, Raleigh 1973–77; Visiting Artist, Poetry, North Carolina Dept of Community Colleges 1977–81, South Carolina Arts Commission 1981–82; Co-Ed., The Plover (Chidori), bilingual haiku journal, Japan 1989–92; Prof. of English, Kagoshima Prefectural University, Japan; mem. MLA; Japan English Literary Society; Japan American Literary Society, Renaissance Inst. (Tokyo), Japan Asscn of Language Teachers, Haiku Soc. of America. *Plays:* as actor: principal role in Solitaire, Double Solitaire, Harry Roat in Wait Until Dark; as mem. of Central Piedmont Repertory Co.: The Doctor in Something's Afoot, The Wizard in The Wizard of Oz. *Publications:* Mobiles 1973, A Poem is a Smile You Can Hear (ed.) 1976, A Narrative of Jeremy Bentham 1978, The Liam Poems 1981, City Renewing Itself 1983, Art and Emblem: Early Seventeenth Century English Poetry of Devotion 1991, Gathering in Ireland 1996, White Edge, Curling Wave 2002, Christmas Gifts in South Japan and Other Haiku Essays 2003; contribs to anthologies and other publications. *Honours:* National Endowment for the Arts Fellowship 1977, Gordon Barber Memorial Award 1979, Portfolio Award 1983, Roanoke Chowan Prize 1982. *Address:* Kagoshima Prefectural University, 1-52-1 Shimo-Ishiki-cho, Kagoshima-shi, 890-0005, Japan. *Telephone:* (99) 220-1111 (office); (99) 258-7502 (home). *Fax:* (99) 220-1115 (office). *E-mail:* heffern@k-kentan.ac.jp (office); thomasheffernan@yahoo.com (home).

HEFFRON, Doris, BA, MA; Canadian writer; b. 18 Oct. 1944, Noranda, QC; m. 1st William Newton-Smith 1968 (divorced); two d.; m. 2nd D. L. Gauer 1980. *Education:* Queen's University, Kingston, ON. *Career:* Tutor, University of Oxford, 1970–80, The Open University, 1975–78, University of Malaysia, 1978; Writer-in-Residence, Wainfleet Public Library, 1989–90; mem. Authors Society; PEN; Writers Union of Canada. *Publications:* A Nice Fire and Some Moonpennies, 1971; Crusty Crossed, 1976; Rain and I, 1982; A Shark in the House, 1996, City Wolves 2005; contrib. to various publications. *Honours:* Canada Council Arts Grant, 1974. *Address:* Little Creek Wolf Range, RR No. 1 Clarksburg, ON N0H 1J0, Canada. *Website:* www3.sympatico .ca/dheffron.

HEFNER, Hugh Marston, BS; American publisher; *Chairman Emeritus, Playboy Enterprises, Inc.*; b. 9 April 1926, Chicago, Ill.; s. of Glenn L. Hefner and Grace Hefner (née Swanson); m. 1st Mildred Williams 1949 (divorced 1959); one s. one d.; m. 2nd Kimberley Conrad 1989 (divorced); two s. *Education:* Univ. of Illinois. *Career:* Ed.-in-Chief Playboy Magazine 1953–, Oui Magazine 1972–81; Chair. Emer. Playboy Enterprises 1988–; Pres. Playboy Club Int. Inc. 1959–86. *Honours:* Int. Press Directory Int. Publisher Award 1997. *Address:* Playboy Enterprises Inc., 680 North Lake Shore Drive, Chicago, IL 60611, USA (office). *Telephone:* (312) 751-8000 (office). *Fax:* (312) 751-2818 (office). *Website:* www.playboyenterprises.com (home).

HEGARTY, Frances, (Frances Fyfield), BA, LLB; British writer and lawyer; b. 1949. *Education:* Univ. of Newcastle upon Tyne. *Career:* part-time lawyer 1987–2000; novelist 1987–; Helen West book series televised 1995–2001. *Publications include:* as Frances Fyfield: A Question of Guilt 1988, Deep Sleep (Silver Dagger Award) 1991, A Clear Conscience (Grand Prix de Littérature Policière 1998) 1994, Without Consent 1996, Blind Date 1998, Staring at the Light 1999, Undercurrents 2000, Helen West Omnibus 2001, The Nature of the Beast 2001, Seeking Sanctuary 2003, Looking Down 2004, Safer Than Houses 2005 The Art of Drowning 2006; as Frances Hegarty: The Playroom 1991, Half Light 1992, Let's Dance 1995. *Literary Agent:* Rogers Coleridge White, 20 Powis Mews, London, W11 1JN, England.

HEGI, Ursula Johanna, BA, MA; German writer, poet and critic; *Professor of English, Eastern Washington University*; b. 23 May 1946, Büderich; two s. *Education:* Univ. of New Hampshire. *Career:* Instructor, Univ. of New Hampshire 1980–84; book critic, Los Angeles Times, New York Times, Washington Post 1982–; Asst Prof., Eastern Washington Univ. 1984–89, Assoc. Prof. 1989–95, Prof. of English 1995–; visiting writer various univs; mem. Associated Writing Programs, Nat. Book Critics Circle (mem. bd of dirs 1992–94). *Publications:* fiction: Intrusions 1981, Unearned Pleasures and Other Stories 1988, Floating in My Mother's Palm 1990, Stones from the River 1994, Salt Dancers 1995, The Vision of Emma Blau 1999, Hotel of the Saints (short stories) 2001, Sacred Time 2004; non-fiction: Tearing the Silence: On Being German in America 1997; contrib. to anthologies, newspapers, journals and magazines. *Honours:* Indiana Fiction Award 1988, National Endowment for the Arts Fellowship 1990, New York Times Best Books Selections 1990, 1994, Pacific Northwest Booksellers Asscn Award 1991, Governor's Writers Awards 1991, 1994. *Address:* c/o Department of English, Eastern Washington University, Cheney, WA 99004, USA.

HEIDSIECK, Bernard; French performance poet; b. 1928, Paris. *Education:* Istituto Politico. *Career:* co-creator sound poetry 1950s, action poems 1960s; fmr co-Dir Banque Française du Commerce Extérieur, Paris; fmr Pres. Commission Poésie du Centre Nat. du Livre. *Recordings:* Poèmes Partition D2 and D3Z 1973, Partition V 1973, Trois Biopsies + Un Passe-Partout 1970, P Puissance B 1983, Canal Street 1986. *Publications:* poetry: Sitôt dit 1955, B2B3 1967, Portraits-Pétales 1973, D2 + D3Z 1973, Partition V 1973, Encoconnage 1975, Foules 1975, Dis-moi ton utopie 1975, Poésie action/ Poésie sonore 1955–75 1976, Participation à Tanger I 1978, Participation à Tanger II 1979, Poésie sonore et caves romaines suivi de Poème-Partition D4P 1984, Derviche/Le Robert 1988, Poème-Partition A 1992, Poème-Partition R 1994, Poème-Partition N 1995, Coléoptères and Co (with P. A. Gette) 1997, Poème-Partition T 1998, Vaduz 1999, Poème-Partition Q 1999, Respirations et brèves rencontres 2000, Nous étions bien peu en... 2001, Partition V 2001, Canal Street 2001, Poème-Partition F 2001, Le Carrefour de la chaussée d'Antin 2001, Notes convergentes 2001, La Poinçonneuse 2002, Ça ne sera pas long 2003, Lettre à Brion 2004, Démocratie II 2004. *Honours:* Grand Prix Nat. de Poésie 1991. *Address:* c/o Editions Al Dante, 10 rue Nicolas Appert, 75011 Paris, France.

HEIGERT, Hans A., DPhil; German journalist; b. 21 March 1925, Mainz; m. Hildegard Straub 1951; three s. two d. *Education:* Ludwigburg High School, Univs. of Stuttgart, Heidelberg and Oklahoma. *Career:* served with army 1943–45 before resuming education; worked as a journalist in newspapers, radio and TV from 1950, becoming Chief Ed., Süddeutsche Zeitung 1970–85; mem. Presidium Goethe Inst., Munich 1984–93 (Pres. 1989–93). *Publications:* Stätten der Jugend 1958, Sehnsucht nach der Nation 1966, Deutschlands falsche Träume 1968. *Honours:* winner of Theodor Heuss Preis 1969; Bayerischer Verdienstorden 1974, Bundesverdienstkreuz 1979, Bayerische Verfassuncpmedaille. *Address:* 82110 Germering Oberbayern, Eichenstrasse 12, Germany. *Telephone:* (89) 847676.

HEIGHTON, Steven, MA; Canadian author and academic; b. Toronto. *Education:* Silverthorn Coll. Inst., Queen's Univ. *Career:* Ed. Quarry magazine 1988–94; Writer-in-Residence, Concordia Univ. 2002–03; Jack McLelland Writer-in-Residence, Massey Coll., Univ. of Toronto 2004; participating author American Movements II course, Univ. of New Orleans 2006; instructor Summer Literature Seminars, Herzen Univ., Russia 2007. *Publications include:* Stalin's Carnival (poetry) 1989, Foreign Ghosts (travelogue/poetry) 1989, Flight Paths of the Emperor (stories) 1992, Théâtre de revenants (French translation of Flight Paths of the Emperor) 1994, The Ecstasy of Skeptics (poetry) 1994, On earth as it is (stories) 1995, The Admen Move on Lhasa: Writing and Culture in a Virtual World (essays) 1997, La rose de l'érèbe (French translation of On Earth As It Is) 1998, The Shadow Boxer (novel) 2000, The Address Book (poetry) 2004, Afterlands (novel) 2006; poetry, fiction and critical articles in nat. and int. periodicals and anthologies 1984–. *Honours:* Gerald Lampert Award for Best First Book of Poetry 1990, Air Canada Award 1990, Gold Medal for Fiction, Nat. Magazine Awards 1992, Petra Kenney Award 2002, Gold Medal for Poetry Nat. Magazine Awards 2004. *Literary Agent:* Anne McDermid Agency, 83 Willcocks Street, Toronto, ON M5S 1C9, Canada. *E-mail:* anne@mcdermidagency.com; sheighton@kos .net (office). *Website:* www.mcdermidagency.com; www.stevenheighton.com.

HEIKAL, Mohamed Hassanein; Egyptian journalist; b. 1923; m.; three s. *Career:* reporter, The Egyptian Gazette 1943, Akher Sa'a magazine 1945; Ed. Al-Akhbar daily newspaper 1956–57; Ed. Al-Ahram 1957, Chair. Bd Dirs 1961–74; mem. Central Cttee Socialist Union 1968; Minister of Information and Foreign Affairs 1970; arrested Sept. 1981, released Nov. 1981. *Publications:* Nahnou wa America 1967, Nasser: The Cairo Documents 1972, The Road to Ramadan 1975, Sphinx and Commissar 1979, The Return of the Ayatollah 1981, Autumn of Fury 1983, Cutting the Lion's Tail 1986, Suez Through Egyptian Eyes 1986, Boiling Point 1988, (The) Explosion 1990, Illusions of Triumph 1992, Arms and Politics 1993, Secret Channels 1996. *Address:* c/o HarperCollins Publishers, 77–85 Fulham Palace Road, Hammersmith, London, W6 8JB, England.

HEIM, Scott, BA, MA, MFA; American writer and poet; b. 26 Sept. 1966, Hutchinson, KS. *Education:* University of Kansas, Columbia University. *Publications:* Saved from Drowning: Poems, 1993; Mysterious Skin (novel), 1995; In Awe (novel), 1997. *Honours:* William Herbert Carruth Award for Poetry, 1991; Edna Osborne Whitcomb Fiction Prize, 1991.

HEIN, Christoph; German novelist and playwright; b. 8 April 1944, Heinzendorf, Schlesien. *Education:* Gymnasium Berlin, Univ. of Leipzig, Humboldt Univ., Berlin. *Career:* dramatist and playwright, Volksbühne Berlin 1971–79; author 1979–. *Plays:* Schlötel oder Was solls 1974, Cromwell 1980, Lassalle fragt Herrn Herbert nach Sonja 1981, Die wahre Geschichte des Ah Q 1983, Passage 1987, Die Ritter der Tafelrunde 1989, Randow 1994, Bruch 1998, Himmel auf Erden 1998, In Acht und Bann 1998, Mutters Tag 2000, Noach (opera) 2001, Zur Geschichte des menschlichen Herzens 2002. *Publications:* fiction: Einladung zum Lever Bourgeois (stories) 1980, Nachfahrt und früher Morgen (juvenile) 1980, Der fremde Freund (novel) 1982, Horns Ende (novel) 1985, Das Wildpferd unterm Kachelofen (juvenile) 1985, Der Tangospieler (novel) 1989, Die Vergewaltigung (stories) 1991, Matzeln 1991, Das Napoleonspiel (novel) 1993, Exekution eines Kalbes und andere Erzählungen 1994, Von allem Anfang an (novel) 1997, Willenbrock (novel) 2000, Mama ist gegangen (juvenile) 2003, Landnahme 2004, In seiner frühen Kindheit ein Garten (novel) 2005; non-fiction: Die wahre Geschichte des Ah Q (plays/essays) 1984, Schlötel oder Was solls (essays) 1986, Öffentlich arbeiten. Essays und Gespräche 1987, Die fünfte Grundrechenart. Aufsätze und Reden 1986–1989 1990, Als Kind habe ich Stalin gesehen (essays/speeches) 1990, Die Mauern von Jerichow 1996. *Honours:* Chevalier, Ordre des Arts et des Lettres; Heinrich Mann-Preis der Akad. der Künste Berlin 1982, (westdeutscher) Kritikerpreis für Literatur Berlin 1983, Literaturpreis Hamburg 1985, Lessing Prize 1989, Stefan Andres Prize, Schweich 1989, Erich Fried Prize, Vienna 1990, Ludwig Mülheims Prize 1992, Berliner Literaturpreis der Stiftung Preussische Seehandlung 1992, Norddt. Literaturpreis 1998, Peter-Weiss-Preis 1998, Solothurner Literaturpreis 2000, Premio Grinzane Cavour Turin 2002, State Prize for European Literature Austria 2002, Schiller-Gedächtnispreis 2004, Ver.di-Literaturpreis 2004. *Address:* c/o Suhrkamp-Verlag, Postfach 10 19 45, 60019 Frankfurt am Main, Germany.

HEINSEN, Geerd; German journalist; *Editor, Orpheus.* *Career:* Ed., Orpheus Oper International magazine. *Address:* Orpheus, Ritterstraße 11, 10969 Berlin, Germany. *Telephone:* (30) 6 14 68 40. *Fax:* (30) 6 14 68 65. *E-mail:* info@orpheusoper.de. *Website:* www.orpheusoper.de.

HEJDA, Zbyněk; Czech poet and translator; b. 2 Feb. 1930, Hradci Králové. *Education:* Charles Univ., Prague. *Career:* historian 1953–58; mem. Prague City Council 1958–68; ed. in a publishing house, lost his job after signing Charter 77 document calling for improved human rights 1977; various part-time positions –1989; full-time writer 1989–; taught medical ethics Charles Univ. 1990s; fmr Ed. Tvář literary journal; Co-Ed. Střední Evropa (Central Europe) 1985–. *Publications include:* Všechna slast 1964, Blízkosti smrti 1978, Lady Felthamová 1979, Tři básně 1987, Pobyt v sanatoriu 1993, Nikoho tam nepotkám 1994, Básně 1996, Překlady 1998, Valse mélancolique; trans. of works by Emily Dickenson, Georg Trakl, Gottfried Benn. *Honours:* Jaroslav Seifert Prize 1996. *Address:* c/o Ministry of Culture, Maltéské nám. 471/1, 118 11 Prague 1, Czech Republic.

HEJINIAN, Lyn, BA; American poet and writer; b. 17 May 1941, Alameda, CA; m. 1st John P. Hejinian 1961 (divorced 1972); one s. one d.; m. 2nd Larry Ochs 1977. *Education:* Harvard Univ. *Career:* founder-Ed., Tuumba Press, 1976–84; Co-Founder and Co-Ed., Atelos; Prof., Dept of English, University of California at Berkeley; mem. Fellow, Acad. of American Poets. *Publications:* A

Great Adventure, 1972; A Thought is the Bride of What Thinking, 1976; A Mask of Motion, 1977; Gesualdo, 1978; Writing is an Aid to Memory, 1978; My Life, 1980; The Guard, 1984; Redo, 1984; Individuals, 1988; Leningrad: American Writers in the Soviet Union (with Michael Davidson, Ron Silliman, and Barrett Watten), 1991; The Hunt, 1991, revised edn as Oxota: A Short Russian Novel, 1991; The Cell, 1992; The Cold of Poetry, 1994; Two Stein Talks, 1995; Guide, Grammar, Watch and the Thirty Nights, 1996; The Little Book of a Thousand Eyes, 1996; Wicker (with Jack Collom), 1996; The Traveler and the Hill (with Emilie Clark), 1998; Sight, 1999; Sunflower (with Jack Collom), 2000; Chartings, 2000; Happily, 2000; The Beginner, 2000; The Language of Enquiry, 2000; A Border Comedy, 2001; Slowly, 2002. Contributions: journals.

HELD, Michael J., MA; American publisher; *Director, Division of Scholarly Journals and Professional Periodicals, American Academy of Pediatrics.* *Career:* fmr Pres. Council of Science Edn; fmr Exec. Dir Rockefeller Univ. Press; currently Dir Div. of Scholarly Journals and Professional Periodicals, American Acad. of Pediatrics. *Address:* American Academy of Pediatrics, 141 Northwest Point Blvd, Elk Grove Village, IL 60007, USA (office). *Telephone:* (847) 434-7899 (office). *Fax:* (847) 434-8899 (office). *E-mail:* mheld@aap.org (office). *Website:* www.aap.org (office).

HELGADÓTTIR, Guðrun; Icelandic politician and writer; b. 7 Sept. 1935, Hafnarfjördur; d. of Helgi Guðlangsson and Ingigerður Eyjólfsdóttir; two s. two d. *Education:* Reykjavík Grammar School and Univ. *Career:* worked as sec. at Reykjavík Grammar School 1957–70; Head of Dept, Nat. Social Security Inst. 1973–80; mem. Reykjavík City Council 1978–82; elected mem. Althingi (Parl., People's Alliance) 1979, Speaker (first woman) 1988–91; Pres. United Alliance 1988; writes fiction for 7–13 year olds; her children's play Óvitar (Infants) opened at National Theatre of Iceland in 1979 and has also been staged in the Faeroes and in Norway. *Publications include:* for children: Jón Oddur og Jón Bjarni (Jón Oddur and Jón Bjarni) 1974, Ástarsaga úr fjöllunum (A Giant Love Story) 1981, Undan Illgresinu (From Beneath the Weeds) (The Nordic Prize for Children's Books) 1992, Ekkert að þakka (The Pleasure's Mine) 1995, Englajól (The Angels' Christmas Tree) 1997, Dagbladet; several illustrated books for young children with illustrations by known artists as well as a TV play and a novel for adults. *Honours:* numerous awards including Thorbjörn Egner Fund Prize, IBBY Iceland Award. *Address:* Túngata 43, 101 Reykjavík, Iceland (home). *Telephone:* (1) 23124 (home).

HELLENGA, Robert, BA, PhD; American teacher and writer; b. 5 Aug. 1941; m. Virginia Killion 1963; three d. *Education:* Univ. of Michigan, Queen's Univ., Belfast, Northern Ireland, Princeton Univ. *Career:* Knox Coll. 1968–; mem. Soc. of Midland Authors, Illinois Arts Alliance. *Publications:* fiction: The Sixteen Pleasures 1994, The Fall of a Sparrow 1998, Blues Lessons 2002, Philosophy Made Simple 2006; contribs to Iowa Review, Chicago Review, California Quarterly, Columbia, Ascent, Farmer's Market, Chicago Tribune Magazine, TriQuarterly, Crazyhorse, Mississippi Valley Review, Black Warrior Review, New York Times Magazine, The Gettysburg Review. *Honours:* several fellowships and grants, Illinois Arts Council Artist's Literary Award, 1985, PEN Syndicated Fiction Award 1988, Soc. of Midland Authors Award for Fiction 1995, Knox Coll. Faculty Achievement Award 1997–98. *Literary Agent:* c/o Henry Dunow, Dunow Carlson Lerner Literary Agency, 27 W 20th Street, Suite 1107, New York, NY 10011, USA. *Telephone:* (212) 645-7606. *E-mail:* henry@dclagency.com; henry@dunowcarlson.com. *Website:* www.dunowcarlson.com. *Address:* 343 N Prairie Street, Galesburg, IL 61401, USA (home). *Telephone:* (309) 343-8957 (home). *E-mail:* rhelleng@knox.edu (home). *Website:* www.roberthellenga.com (home).

HELLER, Agnes, MA, PhD; Hungarian academic and writer; b. 12 May 1929, Budapest; m. 1st Istvan Hermann 1949, one d.; m. 2nd Ferenc Feher 1963, one s. *Education:* University of Budapest, Hungarian Acad. of Sciences. *Career:* Reader in Sociology, La Trobe University, Bundoora, Vic., Australia; Prof. of Philosophy, New School for Social Research, New York, 1985–; mem. Société Européenne. *Publications:* Renaissance Man, 1978; A Theory of History, 1981; Hungary 1956 Revisited: The Message of a Revolution – A Quarter-Century After (co-author), 1983; Dictatorship Over Needs (co-author), 1983; Lukacs Reappraised, 1983, UK edn as Lukacs Revalued, 1983; The Power of Shame: A Rational Perspective, 1985; Reconstructing Aesthetics: Writings of the Budapest School (co-ed.), 1986; Doomsday or Deterrence?: On the Antinuclear Issue (co-author), 1986; Eastern Left, Western Left: Totalitarianism, Freedom and Democracy (co-author), 1987; Beyond Justice, 1987; The Postmodern Political Condition (co-author), 1988; General Ethics, 1988; A Philosophy of Morals, 1990; Can Modernity Survive?, 1990; From Yalta to Glasnost: The Dismantling of Stalin's Empire (co-author), 1991; The Grandeur and Twilight of Radical Universalism (co-author), 1991; A Philosophy of History in Fragments, 1993; The Limits to Natural Law and the Paradox of Evil, 1993; An Ethics of Personality, 1995. Contributions: Academic journals. *Honours:* Lessing Prize, Hamburg 1991. *Address:* Gutenberg ter 4, u.4, Budapest 1088, Hungary. *E-mail:* aheller@emc.elte.hu.

HELLER, (Franz) André; Austrian poet, writer, singer and theatre producer; b. 22 March 1947, Vienna. *Career:* actor 1965–67; co-founder, Ö3 radio station 1967; recording artist 1968–83; dir. TV documentaries 1978–. *Publications include:* short story collections: Die Ernte der Schlaflosigkeit in Wien 1976, Auf und davon: Erzähites, Schlamassel, Als ich ein Hund war; novel: Schättentaucher; poetry: Sitzt ana und glaubt er is zwa (with Helmut Qualtinger); picture books: Jagmandir: Traum und Wiklichkeit, Die Zauber-

gärten des André Heller. *Address:* c/o Verlagsgruppe Random House, Neumarkter str. 28, 81673 Munich, Germany; Artevent, Singerstr. 8, 1010 Vienna, Austria. *E-mail:* contact@andreheller.com. *Website:* www.andreheller .com.

HELLER, Michael, BS, MA; American poet, writer and teacher; b. 11 May 1937, New York, NY; m. 1st Doris Whytal 1962 (divorced 1978); m. 2nd Jane Augustine 1979; one s. *Education:* Rensselaer Polytechnic Institute, New York Univ. *Career:* Faculty, 1967, Acting Dir, 1986–87, Academic Co-ordinator, 1987–91, American Language Institute, New York Univ.; Poet and Teacher, New York State Poets in the Schools, 1970–; mem. American Acad. of Poets; MLA; New York State Poets in Public Service; PEN; Poetry Society of America; Poets and Writers; Poets House. *Publications:* Two Poems, 1970; Accidental Center, 1972; Figures of Speaking, 1977; Knowledge, 1979; Marble Snows, Origin, 1979; Conviction's Net of Branches: Essays on the Objectivist Poets and Poetry, 1985; Marginalia in a Desperate Hand, 1986; In the Builded Place, 1990; Carl Rakosi: Man and Poet (ed.), 1993; Wordflow: New and Selected Poems, 1997; Living Root: A Memoir, 2000; Exigent Futures: New and Selected Poems, 2003. Contributions: anthologies, reference books, journals. *Honours:* Coffey Poetry Prize, New School for Social Research, 1964; Poetry in Public Places Award, 1975; New York State Creative Artists Public Service Fellowship in Poetry, 1975–76; National Endowment for the Humanities Grant, 1979; Di Castagnola Award, Poetry Society of America, 1980; Outstanding Writer Citations, Pushcart Press, 1983, 1984, 1992; New York Fellowship in the Arts, 1989; Fund for Poetry Award 2003. *Address:* 346 E 18th Street, New York, NY 10003, USA.

HELLER, Zoë, BA; British novelist and journalist; b. 1965, London; one d. *Education:* St Anne's Coll., Oxford, Columbia Univ., New York, USA. *Career:* worked as feature writer, critic and columnist for several newspapers, including Independent on Sunday, Sunday Times, Daily Telegraph 1993–; lives in New York. *Publications:* Everything You Know 1999, What Was She Thinking? – Notes on a Scandal 2003; contrib. to Harper's Bazaar, The Independent, City Limits, Granta, Vogue, Vanity Fair, The New Yorker, The New Republic. *Honours:* British Press Awards Columnist of the Year 2002. *Address:* c/o Fig Tree, 80 Strand, London, WC2R 0RL, England.

HELLIER, Trudy; Australian playwright, filmmaker and actress. *Education:* RMIT Univ., Melbourne. *Television appearances:* MDA, Welcher & Welcher, Marshall Law, Frontline, Round the Twist, Sea Change, The Games, Guinevere Jones, Blue Heelers, Halifax fp. *Plays as writer:* Trapped 1996, Blind Faith 2001, The Family Trust (co-writer). *Screenplays:* Break and Enter 1997, Trapped 2002, Dog Daze. *Honours:* Australian Film Inst. Award 1999. *Literary Agent:* c/o RGM Associates, PO Box 128, Surry Hills, NSW 2010, Australia. *Telephone:* (2) 9281-3911. *Fax:* (2) 9281-4705. *E-mail:* info@rgm .com.au. *Website:* www.rgm.com.au.

HELPRIN, Mark, AB, AM; American writer; b. 28 June 1947, New York, NY; m. Lisa Kennedy 1980; two d. *Education:* Harvard Univ., Magdalen Coll., Oxford. *Career:* fmrly served in the British Merchant Navy, Israeli infantry, Israeli Air Force; contributing ed., The Wall Street Journal; speechwriter for Senator Robert J. Dole 1996; mem. Council on Foreign Relations; Sr Fellow The Claremont Inst.; Fellow American Acad. in Rome; fmr Guggenheim Fellow. *Publications:* A Dove of the East and Other Stories 1975, Refiner's Fire: The Life and Adventures of Marshall Pearl, a Foundling 1977, Ellis Island and Other Stories 1981, Winter's Tale 1983, Best American Short Stories (ed. with Shannon Ravenel) 1988, Swan Lake 1989, A Soldier of the Great War 1991, Memoir from Antproof Case 1995, A City in Winter (novella) (World Fantasy Best Novella Award 1997) 1996, The Veil of Snows 1997, The Pacific and Other Stories 2005, Freddy and Fredericka 2005; contrib. to The New Yorker, The Atlantic Monthly, The New Criterion, National Review, The American Heritage, The Wall Street Journal, The New York Times. *Honours:* American Acad. and Institute of Arts and Letters Prix de Rome 1982, Nat. Jewish Book Award 1982. *Address:* c/o The Claremont Institute, 937 W Foothill Boulevard, Suite E, Claremont, CA 91711, USA.

HELWIG, David Gordon, MA; Canadian writer; b. 5 April 1938, Toronto; s. of William Helwig and Ivy Helwig; m. Nancy Keeling 1959; two d. *Education:* Univ. of Toronto and Univ. of Liverpool, UK. *Career:* Lecturer, then Asst Prof., Queen's Univ., Kingston, Ont. 1962–74, also Asst Prof. 1976–80; literary man. CBC 1974–76. *Radio plays:* many radio dramas for CBC. *Publications:* collections of poetry and novels, including Figures in a Landscape 1968, The Time of Her Life, This Human Day 2000, The Year One 2004. *Honours:* CBC Poetry Award 1983, Atlantic Poetry Award 2004. *Address:* Belfast, PEI C0A 1A0, Canada. *Telephone:* (902) 659-2942. *E-mail:* jgdh@pei.sympatico.ca. *Website:* www.davidhelwig.com.

HELY-HUTCHINSON, Timothy Mark, MA; British publisher; *Group Chief Executive, Hodder Headline Ltd;* b. 26 Oct. 1953, London; s. of Earl of Donoughmore and Countess of Donoughmore (née Parsons). *Education:* Eton Coll. and Univ. of Oxford. *Career:* Man. Dir Macdonald & Co. (Publrs) Ltd 1982–86, Headline Book Publishing PLC 1986–93; Group Chief Exec. Hodder Headline Ltd 1993–; Dir W. H. Smith PLC 1999–, Chair. W. H. Smith News Ltd 2002–04; Group Chief Exec. Hachette Livre UK Ltd 2004–. *Honours:* Venturer of the Year (British Venture Capital Asscn) 1990, Publr of the Year (British Book Awards) 1992. *Address:* Hodder Headline Ltd, 338 Euston Road, London, NW1 3BH (office). *Telephone:* (20) 7873-6011 (office). *Fax:* (20) 7873-6012 (office). *Website:* www.hodderheadline.co.uk (office).

HELYAR, Jane Penelope Josephine, (Josephine Poole); British writer; b. 12 Feb. 1933, London; m. 1st T. R. Poole 1956; m. 2nd V. J. H. Helyar 1975; one s. five d. *Television scripts:* The Harbourer 1975, Touch and Go (for children) 1977, The Sabbatical 1981, The Breakdown 1981, Miss Constantine 1981, Ring a Ring a Rosie 1983, With Love, Belinda 1983, The Wit to Woo 1983, Fox 1984, Buzzard 1984, Dartmoor Pony 1984. *Publications:* A Dream in the House 1961, Moon Eyes 1965, The Lilywhite Boys 1967, Catch as Catch Can 1969, Yokeham 1970, Billy Buck 1972, Touch and Go 1976, When Fishes Flew 1978, Hannah Chance 1980, Diamond Jack 1983, The Country Diary Companion (to accompany Central TV series) 1983, Three for Luck 1985, Wildlife Tales 1986, The Loving Ghosts 1988, Angel 1989, This is Me Speaking 1990, Snow White (picture book) 1991, Paul Loves Amy Loves Christo 1992, Scared to Death 1994, Pinocchio (re-written) 1994, Deadly Inheritance 1995, The Water Babies (re-written) 1996, Hero 1997, Jack and the Beanstalk (picture book) 1997, Joan of Arc (picture book) 1998, Run Rabbit 1999, Fair Game 2000, Scorched 2003, Anne Frank (picture book) 2005. *Literary Agent:* c/o Celia Catchpole, 56 Gilpin Avenue, East Sheen, London, SW14 8QY. *E-mail:* celiacatchpole@yahoo.co.uk. *Address:* Poundisford Lodge, Poundisford, Taunton, Somerset TA3 7AE, England (home).

HEMLEY, Robin, BA, MFA; American academic and writer; b. 28 May 1958, New York, NY; m. Beverly Bertling Hemley 1987, two d. *Education:* Indiana University, University of Iowa. *Career:* Assoc. Prof. of English, University of North Carolina at Charlotte, 1986–94; Asst Prof. of English, Western Washington University, Bellingham, 1994–. *Publications:* The Mouse Town, 1987; All You Can Eat, 1988; The Last Studebaker, 1992; Turning Life Into Fiction, 1994.

HEMMING, John Henry, CMG, MA, DLitt, FSA; British/Canadian writer and publisher; *Chairman, Hemming Group Ltd*; b. 5 Jan. 1935, Vancouver, BC; s. of H. Harold Hemming, OBE, MC and Alice L. Hemming, OBE; m. Sukie Babington-Smith 1979; one s. one d. *Education:* Eton Coll., UK, McGill Univ. and Univ. of Oxford, UK. *Career:* Dir and Sec. Royal Geographical Soc. 1975–96; Jt Chair. Hemming Group Ltd 1976–; Chair. Brintex Ltd, Newman Books Ltd; explorations in Peru and Brazil 1960, 1961, 1971, 1972, 1986–88, led Maracá Rainforest Project, Brazil (largest ever Amazon research programme by a European country) 1987–88. *Publications:* The Conquest of the Incas 1970, Tribes of the Amazon Basin in Brazil (with others) 1973, Red Gold: The Conquest of the Brazilian Indians 1978, The Search for El Dorado 1978, Machu Picchu 1982, Monuments of the Incas 1983, Change in the Amazon Basin (two vols) (ed.) 1985, Amazon Frontier: The Defeat of the Brazilian Indians 1987, Maracá 1988, Roraima, Brazil's Northernmost Frontier 1990, The Rainforest Edge (ed.) 1993, Royal Geographical Society Illustrated (ed.) 1997, The Golden Age of Discovery 1998, Die If You Must: Brazilian Indians in the Twentieth Century 2003. *Honours:* Hon. Fellow, Magdalen Coll. Oxford 2004; Hon. DLitt (Warwick) 1989, (Stirling) 1991; Commander, Order of Southern Cross (Brazil) 1998; Pitman Literary Prize 1970, Christopher Award (USA) 1971, Founder's Medal, Royal Geographical Soc. 1989, Bradford Washburn Medal, Boston Museum of Science 1989, Mungo Park Medal, Royal Scottish Geographical Soc. 1988; Orden al Mérito (Peru), Special Award, Instituto Nacional de Cultura (Peru) 1996, Citation of Merit, Explorers' Club (New York) 1997. *Address:* 10 Edwardes Square, London, W8 6HE (home); Hemming Group Ltd, 32 Vauxhall Bridge Road, London, SW1V 2SS, England (office). *Telephone:* (20) 7602-6697 (home); (20) 7973-6634 (office). *Fax:* (20) 7233-5049 (office). *E-mail:* j.hemming@hgluk.com (office). *Website:* www.hgluk.com (office).

HEMON, Aleksandar; American writer and journalist; b. 1965, Sarajevo. *Career:* fmr Cultural Ed. Dani magazine, Sarajevo; emigrated to Chicago, USA 1992. *Publications:* fiction: The Question of Bruno (Los Angeles Times Book Review book of the year) 2000, Nowhere Man (novel) 2003, Pretext 7: Cut That Fence (ed.) 2003. *Address:* c/o Picador USA, 175 Fifth Avenue, New York, NY 10010, USA.

HEN, Józef, (Korab), Polish writer and playwright; b. 8 Nov. 1923, Warsaw; s. of Roman Cukier and Ewa Cukier; m. Irena Hen 1946; one s. one d. *Career:* self-educated; Lecturer, Sorbonne, France 1993 and Univ. of Warsaw 1995–96; mem. Acad. des Sciences, Belles Lettres et des Beaux Arts, Bordeaux, France; mem. Polish PEN Club. *Film screenplays include:* Krzyż walecznych (Cross of Valour) 1959, Kwiecień (April) 1961, Nikt nie woła (Nobody's Calling) 1961, Bokser i śmierć (The Boxer and Death), Prawo i pięść (Law and the Fist) and Don Gabriel. *Screenplays for TV serials:* Życie Kamila Kuranta (The Life of Kamil Kurant) 1983, Crimen and Królewskie Sny (Royal Dreams) 1987. *Theatre plays:* Ja, Michał z Montaigne (I, Michel de Montaigne) 1984, Justyn! Justyn!, Popołudnie kochanków (Lovers' Afternoon) 1994. *Publications include:* Skromny chłopiec w haremie (A Modest Boy in a Harem) 1957, Kwiecień (April) 1960 (Book of the Year 1961), Teatr Heroda (Herod's Theatre) 1966, Twarz pokerzysty (Pokerface) 1970, Oko Dajana (Dayan's Eye, as Korab) 1972, Yokohama 1973, Crimen 1975, Bokser i śmierć (The Boxer and Death) 1975, Ja, Michał z Montaigne (I, Michel de Montaigne) 1978, Milczące między nami (Silent between Us) 1985, Nie boję się bezsennych nocy (I'm Not Afraid of Sleepless Nights), 3 books 1987, 1992, 2001, Królenskie sny (Royal Dreams) 1989, Nikt nie woła (Nobody's Calling) 1990, Nowolipie 1991, Odejście Afrodyty (Aphrodite's Departure) 1995, Najpiękniejsze lata (The Most Beautiful Years) 1996, Niebo naszych ojcow (Sky of Our Fathers 1997, Błazen – wielki mąż (Jester – The Great Man) (ZAiKS Book of the Year Award 1999) 1998, Mójprzyjaciel Król (My Friend the King) (Booker's Club Book of the Year Award 2005) 2003, Księga Gniewu i Miłości (A Book of Anger and

Love) 2006. *Address:* Al. Ujazdowskie 8 m. 2, 00-478 Warsaw, Poland (home). *Telephone:* (22) 629-19-03 (home).

HENDERSON, Neil Keir, MA; British poet and writer; b. 7 March 1956, Glasgow, Scotland. *Education:* Univ. of Glasgow. *Publications:* Maldehyde's Discomfiture, or A Lady Churned 1997, Fish-Worshipping – As We Know It 2001, An English Summer in Scotland and Other Unlikely Events 2005; contrib. to anthologies, including Mystery of the City 1997, Loveable Warts: A Defence of Self-Indulgence, Chapman 87 1997, Red Candle Treasury 1998, Mightier Than the Sword: The Punch-Up of the Poses, Chapman 91 1998, Haggis: The Thinking Man's Buttock, Chapman 98 2001, Labyrinths 6 (showcased) 2002, Electric Sheep 2004, Spiders and Flies 2005. *Address:* 46 Revoch Drive, Knightswood, Glasgow, G13 4SB, Scotland.

HENDRY, Diana Lois, MLitt; British poet and writer; b. 2 Oct. 1941, Meols, Wirral; d. of Leslie McLonomy and Amelia McLonomy; m. George Hendry (divorced 1981); one s. one d. *Education:* W Kirby Grammar School for Girls, Wirral and Univ. of Bristol. *Career:* Reporter and Feature Writer for Western Mail, Cardiff 1960–65; freelance journalist 1965–80; teacher (part-time) Clifton Coll. 1987–90; Tutor in Literature (part-time), Open Univ. 1987–92; Bristol Polytechnic 1987–93; Tutor in Creative Writing, Univ. of Bristol 1995–; fmr Writer-in-Residence Fairfield Grammar School and Dumfries & Galloway Royal Infirmary 1997–98. *Publications include:* Midnight Pirate 1984, Fiona Finds Her Tongue 1985, Double Vision 1989, The Not-Anywhere House 1989, The Rainbow Watchers 1989, The Carey Street Cat 1989, A Camel Called April 1990, A Moment for Joe 1990, Christmas in Exeter Street 1991, Wonderful Robert and Sweetie Pie Nell 1990, Kid Kibble 1991, Harvey Angell (Whitbread Literary Award, Children's Novel Section) 1991, The Thing-in-a-Box 1992, Back Soon 1993, Why Father Christmas Was Late for Hartlepool 1993, Dog Dottington 1995, Happy Old Birthday, Owl 1995, The Thing-on-two-Legs 1995, Making Blue 1995, Strange Goings-on 1995, The Awesome Bird 1995, Flower Street Friends 1995, Harvey Angell and the Ghost Child (Scottish Arts Council Award) 1997, Fiona Says 1998, Minders 1998, The Very Noisy Night 2000, The Very Busy Day 2001, The Very Snowy Christmas 2005, Catch a Gran 2006; has published four collections of poems, Making Blue, Borderers, Twelve Lilts: Psalms and Responses and Sparks! (with Tom Pow). *Honours:* Third Prize Peterloo Poetry Competition 1991, Second Prize 1993; First Prize Honsman Soc. Poetry Competition 1996. *Address:* c/o Mariscat Press, Hamish Whyte, 3 Mariscat Road, Glasgow, G41 4ND, Scotland.

HENLEY, Elizabeth (Beth) Becker, BFA, PhD; American playwright and actress; b. 8 May 1952, Jackson, MS; d. of Charles and Lydy Henley. *Education:* Southern Methodist Univ., Univ. of Illinois. *Film screenplays:* Nobody's Fool 1986, Crimes of the Heart 1986, Miss Firecracker 1989, Signatures 1990, Revelers 1994, Impossible Marriage 1998. *Publications:* plays: Crimes of the Heart 1981, The Wake of Jamey Foster 1982, Am I Blue 1982, The Miss Firecracker Contest 1984, The Lucky Spot 1987, The Debutante Ball 1988, Abundance 1990, Signatures 1990, Beth Henley: Monologues for Women 1992, Control Freaks 1993, Revelers 1994, Collected Plays: Volume I, 1980–1989 2000, Collected Plays: Volume II, 1990–1999 2000, Family Week 2000. *Honours:* Pulitzer Prize for Drama 1981, NY Drama Critics Circle Best Play Award 1981, George Oppenheimer/Newsday Playwriting Award 1980–81.

HENNESSY, Helen (see Vendler, Helen Hennessy)

HENNESSY, Peter John, BA, PhD (Cantab), FRHS, FRSA; British academic and writer; *Attlee Professor of Contemporary History, Queen Mary, University of London*; b. 28 March 1947, London, England; m. Enid Mary Candler 1969; two d. *Education:* St John's Coll., Cambridge, LSE, Harvard Univ., USA. *Career:* Sr Fellow 1984–85, Visiting Fellow 1986–91, Policy Studies Inst.; columnist, New Statesman 1986–87, The Independent 1987–91; co-founder and Co-Dir 1986–89, mem. of the bd 1989–98, Inst. of Contemporary British History; Visiting Fellow, Univ. of Reading 1988–94, Royal Inst. of Public Administration 1989–92, Univ. of Nottingham 1989–95; Visiting Prof. of Govt, Univ. of Strathclyde 1989–; Pnr, Intellectual R&D 1990–; Prof. of Contemporary History, Queen Mary, Univ. of London 1992–, now Attlee Prof. of Contemporary History; Gresham Prof. of Rhetoric, Gresham Coll., London 1994–97; Chair., Kennedy Memorial Trust 1995–2000; vice-pres., Royal Historical Soc. 1996–; mem. Johnian Soc. (pres. 1995). *Publications:* States of Emergency (with Keith Jeffery) 1983, Sources Close to the Prime Minister (with Michael Cockerell and David Walker) 1984, What the Papers Never Said 1985, Cabinet 1986, Whitehall 1989, Never Again: Britain 1945–51 1992, The Hidden Wiring: Unearthing the British Constitution 1995, Muddling Through: Power, Politics and the Quality of Government in Postwar Britain 1996, The Prime Minister: The Office and its Holders Since 1945 2001, The Secret State: Whitehall and the Cold War 1945–70 2002, Having It So Good: Britain in the Fifties 2006; contrib. to scholarly books and journals, to radio and television. *Honours:* Dr hc (Univ. of West of England) 1995, (Univ. of Westminster) 1996, (Kingston Univ.) 1998; Duff Cooper Prize 1993, NCR Book Award for Non-Fiction 1994.

HENNING JOCELYN, Ann Margareta Maria, (Countess of Roden), BA; Swedish writer, dramatist, translator and broadcaster; b. 5 Aug. 1948, Göteborg; m. Earl of Roden 1986; one s. *Education:* University of Lund. *Career:* Artistic Dir, Connemara Theatre Co; mem. Irish Playwrights' and Scriptwriters' Guild; Irish Writers' Union. *Publications:* Modern Astrology, 1983; The Connemare Whirlwind Trilogy, 1990–94; Keylines, 2000. Plays:

Smile, 1972; Baptism of Fire, 1997; The Alternative, 1998. Contributions: Swedish and Irish radio and television. *E-mail:* roden@ireland.com. *Website:* www.keylines2000.com.

HENRY, Stuart Dennis, BA, PhD; British academic, writer and editor; b. 18 Oct. 1949, London, England; m. Lee Doric 1988. *Education:* University of Kent. *Career:* Research Sociologist, University of London, 1975–78; Research Fellow, Middlesex University, 1978–79; Senior Lecturer, Nottingham Trent University, 1979–83; Asst Prof., Old Dominion University, Norfolk, Virginia, 1984–87; Prof., Eastern Michigan University, 1987–98; Co-Ed., Critical Criminologist 1997; Prof. of Sociology and Chair. of Dept of Sociology, Valparaiso University, 1998; mem. American Sociological Asscn; American Society of Criminology. *Publications:* Self-help and Health: Mutual Aid for Modern Problems (with D. Robinson), 1977; The Hidden Economy: The Context and Control of Borderline Crime, 1978; Private Justice: Toward Integrated Theorizing in the Sociology of Law, 1983; Making Markets: An Interdisciplinary Perspective on Economic Exchange (with R. Cantor and S. Rayner), 1992; The Deviance Process (with E. H. Pfuhl), third edn, 1993; Criminological Theory (with W. Einstadter), 1995; Constitutive Criminology: Beyond Postmodernism (with D. Milovanovic), 1996; Essential Criminology (with M. Lanier), 1998. Editor: Informal Institutions: Alternative Networks in the Corporate State, 1981; The Informal Economy (with L. Ferman and M. Hoyman), 1987; Degrees of Deviance: Student Accounts of their Deviant Behavior, 1989; Work Beyond Employment in Advanced Capitalist Countries: Classic and Contemporary Perspectives on the Informal Economy (with L. Ferman and L. Berndt), 2 vols, 1993; Social Control: Aspects of Non-State Justice, 1994; Employee Dismissal: Justice at Work, 1994; Inside Jobs: A Realistic Guide to Criminal Justice Careers for College Graduates, 1994; The Criminology Theory Reader (with W. Einstadter), 1998; The Criminology Theory Reader, 1998. Contributions: scholarly books and journals. *Address:* 5700 Cass Avenue, Wayne State University, Detroit MI 48202, USA. *E-mail:* ah2195@wayne.edu.

HENSHER, Philip Michael, BA, PhD, FRSL; British writer; b. 20 Feb. 1965, London, England. *Education:* Lady Margaret Hall, Oxford, Jesus Coll., Cambridge. *Career:* clerk House of Commons 1990–96; chief book reviewer Spectator 1994–; art critic Mail on Sunday 1996–; columnist The Independent; mem. RSL (mem. of council 2000–). *Publications:* Other Lulus 1994, Kitchen Venom 1996, Pleasured 1998, The Bedroom of the Mister's Wife (short stories) 1999, The Mulberry Empire 2002, The Fit 2004; other: libretto for opera Powder her Face, by Thomas Adès. *Honours:* Somerset Maugham Award 1996. *Literary Agent:* AP Watt Ltd, 20 John Street, London, WC1N 2DR, England. *Address:* 83A Tennyson Street, London, SW8 3TH, England.

HEPBURN, Ronald William, MA, PhD; British academic (retd) and writer; b. 16 March 1927, Aberdeen, Scotland; m. Agnes Forbes Anderson 1953; two s. one d. *Education:* Univ. of Aberdeen. *Career:* Asst 1952–55, Lecturer 1955–60, Dept of Moral Philosophy, Univ. of Aberdeen; Visiting Assoc. Prof., New York Univ. 1959–60; Prof. of Philosophy, Univ. of Nottingham 1960–64; Prof. of Philosophy 1964–75, Prof. of Moral Philosophy 1975–96, Univ. of Edinburgh; Stanton Lecturer in the Philosophy of Religion, Univ. of Cambridge 1965–68. *Publications:* Metaphysical Beliefs (jtly) 1957, Christianity and Paradox: Critical Studies in Twentieth-Century Theology 1958, Wonder and Other Essays: Eight Studies in Aesthetics and Neighbouring Fields 1984, The Reach of the Aesthetic 2001; contrib. to scholarly books and journals. *Address:* 8 Albert Terrace, Edinburgh, EH10 5EA, Scotland (home). *Telephone:* (131) 447-3831 (home). *E-mail:* ronaldhepburn@aol.com (home).

HERALD, Kathleen (see Peyton, Kathleen Wendy)

HERBERT, Brian Patrick, BA; American writer; b. 29 June 1947, Seattle, WA; s. of Frank Herbert. *Education:* Univ. of California at Berkeley. *Career:* mem. L-5 Soc., Nat. Writers' Club, SFWA, Horror Writers Asscn. *Publications:* Classic Comebacks 1981, Incredible Insurance Claims 1982, Sidney's Comet 1983, The Garbage Chronicles 1984, Sudanna, Sudanna 1985, Man of Two Worlds (with Frank Herbert) 1986, Prisoners of Arionn 1987, The Notebooks of Frank Herbert's Dune (ed.) 1988, Memorymakers (with Marie Landis) 1991, The Race for God 1990, Never as it Seems (ed.) 1992, Songs of Muad' Dib (ed.) 1992, Blood on the Sun (with Marie Landis) 1996, House Atreides (with Kevin J. Anderson) 1999, A Whisper of Caladan Seas (with Kevin J. Anderson) 1999, House Harkonnen (with Kevin J. Anderson) 2001, The Road to Dune (with Kevin J. Anderson) 2005, Hunters of Dune (with Kevin J. Anderson) 2006; contrib. short stories in various anthologies and other publications. *Address:* PO Box 10164, Bainbridge Island, WA 98110, USA. *Website:* www.dunenovels.com.

HERBERT, James John; English writer; b. 8 April 1943, London; s. of Herbert Herbert and Catherine Herbert (née Riley). *Education:* St Aloysius Coll., Highgate, Hornsey Coll. of Art. *Career:* Art Dir Group Head Charles Barker Advertising. *Films:* The Rats 1982, The Survivor 1986, Fluke 1995, Haunted 1995. *Publications:* The Rats 1974, The Fog 1975, The Survivor 1976, Fluke 1977, The Spear 1978, Lair 1979, The Dark 1980, The Jonah 1981, Shrine 1983, Domain 1984, Moon 1985, The Magic Cottage 1986, Sepulchre 1987, Haunted 1988, Creed 1990, Portent 1992, James Herbert: By Horror Haunted 1992, James Herbert's Dark Places 1993, The City 1994, The Ghosts of Sleath 1994, '48 1996, Others 1999, Once... 2001, Devil in the Dark: Biography 2003, Nobody True 2003, The Secret of Crickley Hall 2006. *Address:* David Higham Associates, 5–8 Lower John Street, Golden Square, London, W1F 9HA, England (office). *Website:* www.jamesherbert.net (home).

HERDMAN, John Macmillan, BA, MA, PhD; British writer; b. 20 July 1941, Edinburgh, Scotland; m. 1st Dolina Maclennan 1983 (divorced); m. 2nd Mary Ellen Watson 2002. *Education:* Magdalene Coll., Cambridge. *Career:* Creative Writing Fellow, Edinburgh Univ. 1977–79; William Soutar Fellow, Perth 1990–91. *Publications:* Descent 1968, A Truth Lover 1973, Memoirs of My Aunt Minnie/Clapperton 1974, Pagan's Pilgrimage 1978, Stories Short and Tall 1979, Voice Without Restraint: Bob Dylan's Lyrics 1982, Three Novellas 1987, The Double in Nineteenth-Century Fiction 1990, Imelda and Other Stories 1993, Ghostwriting 1996, Cruising (play) 1997, Poets, Pubs, Polls and Pillarboxes 1999, Four Tales 2000, The Sinister Cabaret 2001, Triptych 2004, My Wife's Lovers 2007. *Honours:* Scottish Arts Council Book Awards 1978, 1993. *Address:* Roselea, Bridge of Tilt, Pitlochry, Perthshire PH18 5SX, Scotland. *Website:* www.johnherdman.co.uk.

HERMANN, Judith; German writer; b. 1970, Berlin. *Publications:* Sommerhaus Spaeter (short stories) 1999, Nothing But Ghosts (short stories, in trans.) 2004. *Address:* c/o Flamingo, HarperCollins Publishers Ltd, 77–85 Fulham Palace Road, London, W6 8JB, England.

HERMARY-VIEILLE, Catherine; French writer; b. 8 Oct. 1943, Paris; d. of Jacques and Jacqueline (née Dubois) Hermary; m. Jean Vieille 1962; one s. one d. *Education:* Coll. Ste Marie de Passy (Paris and Noisy), Ecole Nat des Langues Orientales (Paris), Univ. of Paris VIII–Vincennes à St-Denis, Manhattanville Coll. (NY, USA). *Career:* Asst Embassy of Cyprus, Paris 1968–69; began career as writer 1981; Reporter for various newspapers; mem. PEN-Club, Islam-Occident, Asscn des Ecrivains de Langue Française; Prix Georges Dufau de l' Acad. Française; Officier des Arts et des Lettres, Chevalier de la Légion d'honneur. *Publications:* Le grand vizir de la nuit (Prix Fémina) 1981, L'épiphanie des dieux (Prix Ulysse) 1982, La marquise des ombres 1984, L'infidèle (Prix Radio-Télé Luxembourg—RTL) 1986, Romy 1988, Le rivage des adieux 1989, Le jardin des Henderson 1990, Un amour fou (Prix des Maisons de la Presse) 1991, La piste des turquoises 1992, La pointe aux tortues 1994, Lola 1994, L'Initié 1996, L'Ange Noir 1998 (Prix Littéraire du Quartier Latin), Les Dames de Brières 1999, L'Etang du Diable 2000, La fille du Feu 2000, La Crépuscule des Rois (La Rose d'Anjou, Les Reines de Coeur, Les Lionnes d'Angleterre). *Address:* Shelton Mill, 371 Shelton Mill Road, Charlottesville, VA 22903, USA. *E-mail:* catherinehv@yahoo.com.

HERNDON, Nancy Ruth, MA; American writer; b. (Nancy Fairbanks), 29 May 1934, St Louis, MO; m. William C. Herndon 1956; two s. *Education:* Rice Univ. *Career:* Lecturer in English, Rice Univ. 1956–58, New York Univ. 1959–61, Univ. of Mississippi 1963–64, Florida Atlantic Univ. 1966, Univ. of Texas at El Paso 1976–81; mem. Sisters in Crime, Now, Planned Parenthood; Smithsonian Assoc. *Publications:* Wanton Angel 1989, Widow's Fire 1990, Virgin Fire 1991, Bride Fire 1992, The Fourth Gift 1993, Reluctant Lovers 1993, Elusive Lovers 1994, Acid Bath 1995, Widows' Watch 1995, Lethal Statues 1996, Hunting Game 1996, Time Bombs 1997, C.O.P. Out 1998, Casanova Crimes 1999, Crime Brulee 2001, Truffled Feathers 2001, Death à l'orange 2002, Chocolate Quake 2003, The Perils of Paella 2004, Holy Guacamole 2004, Mozzarella Most Murders 2005, Three-Course Murder 2006, Bon Bon Voyage 2006. *Honours:* Fellowship, Rice Univ. 1956–58, New York Univ. 1959–61, El Paso Writers Hall of Fame 1997. *Address:* 6504 Pino Drive, El Paso, TX 79912, USA (home). *Telephone:* (915) 581-6178 (office). *E-mail:* nherndon@elp.rr.com (home). *Website:* nancyfairbanks.com (home).

HERRA, Maurice (see Asselineau, Roger Maurice)

HERRALDE, Jorge; Spanish publisher; *Publisher, Editorial Anagrama;* b. Barcelona. *Career:* Founder and Publr Editorial Anagrama 1969–. *Publications:* Opiniones mohicanas (collection of articles) 2000, Flashes sobre escritores y otros textos editoriales 2003, El Observatorio editorial 2004, Para Roberto Bolaño 2005, Por orden alfabético. Escritores, editores, amigos 2006. *Honours:* Hon. OBE (UK) 2005; Commdr, Ordre des Arts et des Lettres 2006; Premio Nacional a la mejor labor editorial cultural de España 1994, Premio Tarda d'Argento al mejor editor europeo 1999, Premio Clarín 2000, Feria Int. del Libro de Guadalajara: Homenaje al mérito editorial 2002, Creu de Sant Jordi 2000, Premio Nazionale per la Traduzione Italia 2003, Premio Grinzane 2005. *Address:* Editorial Anagrama SA, Pedró de la Creu 58, 08034 Barcelona, Spain (office). *E-mail:* anagrama@anagrama-ed.es (office). *Website:* www.anagrama-ed.es (office).

HERRERA, Juan Felipe; American poet and writer; b. 27 Dec. 1948, Fowler, CA. *Career:* Assoc. Prof. of Chicano and Latin American Studies, California State Univ., Fresno. *Publications include:* poetry: Facegames 1987, Akrilika 1989, Love After the Riots 1996, Night Train to Tuxlta, Mayan Drifter: Chicano Poet in the Lowlands of America 1997, Laughing Out Loud I Fly: Poems in Spanish and English 1998; novels: Crashboomlove: A Novel in Verse 1999; juvenile: The Upside Down Boy 2000, Calling the Doves 2001. *Address:* c/o Curbstone Press, 321 Jackson Street, Willimantic, CT 06226-1738, USA. *Website:* www.curbstone.org.

HERSH, Burton David, BA; American author and biographer; b. 18 Sept. 1933, Chicago, IL; m. Ellen Eiseman 1957, one s. one d. *Education:* Harvard College. *Career:* mem. Authors' Guild; American Society of Journalists and Authors; PEN. *Publications:* The Ski People, 1968; The Education of Edward Kennedy, 1972; The Mellon Family, 1978; The Old Boys, 1992; The Shadow Pres., 1997. Contributions: many magazines. *Honours:* Fulbright Scholar 1955–56, Book Find Selection 1972, Book-of-the-Month Club 1978.

HERSH, Seymour Myron, BA; American journalist and writer; b. 8 April 1937, Chicago, IL; m. Elizabeth Sarah Klein 1964; two s. one d. *Education:* Univ. of Chicago. *Career:* Chicago City News Bureau 1959; corresp. United Press International 1962–63, Associated Press 1963–67, The New Yorker 1992–; mem. of staff New York Times 1972–79; nat. corresp. Atlantic Monthly 1983–86. *Publications:* Chemical and Biological Warfare: America's Hidden Arsenal 1968, My Lai 4: A Report on the Massacre and Its Aftermath 1970, Cover-Up: The Army's Secret Investigation of the Massacre at My Lai 1972, The Price of Power: Kissinger in the Nixon White House 1983, The Target is Destroyed: What Really Happened to Flight 007 and What America Knew About It 1986, The Samson Option: Israel's Nuclear Arsenal and America's Foreign Policy 1991, The Dark Side of Camelot 1997, Against All Enemies: Gulf War Syndrome: The War Between America's Ailing Veterans and Their Government 1999, Chain of Command: The Road from 9/11 to Abu Ghraib 2004; contribs to various magazines. *Honours:* Pulitzer Prize for Int. Reporting 1970, George Polk Memorial Awards 1970, 1973, 1974, 1981, Scripps-Howard Public Service Award 1973, Sidney Hillman Award 1974, John Peter Zenger Freedom of the Press Award 1975, Los Angeles Times Book Prize 1983, Nat. Book Critics Circle Award 1983, Investigative Reporters and Editors Prizes 1983, 1992, Nat. Magazine Award 2004. *Address:* 1211 Connecticut Avenue NW, Suite 320, Washington, DC 20036, USA.

HERTMANS, Stefan, MA; Belgian novelist and poet; b. 31 March 1951, Ghent. *Education:* Univ. of Ghent. *Career:* Prof., Acad. of Fine Arts, Ghent 1991–; organizer, Studium Generale High School, Ghent 2002–. *Plays:* Kopnaad, Mind the Gap, Dood van Empedokles (Death of Empedokles), Tyranny of Time. *Publications:* Ruimte (translated as Space) 1981, Melksteen 1986, Zoutsneeuw 1987, Gestolde wolken 1987, Bezoekingen Gedichten 1988, Oorverdovende Steen: Essays over literatuur 1988, Steden: Verhalen onderweg 1988, Sneeuwdoosjes 1989, De grenzen van woestijnen Verhalen 1989, Kopnaad: Eentekstvoor vier stemmen 1992, Muziek voor de overtocht: Gedichten 1994, Naar Merelbeke 1994, Francescos paradox: Gedichten 1995, Fugas en pimpelmezen: Over actualiteit, kunst en Kritiek 1995, Annunciaties 1997, Het bedenkelijke 1999, Goya als hond 1999, Mind the Gap 2000, Intercities: Topographics 2001, Als op de eerste dag (translated as Like the First Day) 2001, Harder Dan Sneeuw 2004, Kaneelvinfers 2005; contrib. to Modern Poetry in Translation 1997, short story in Review of Contemporary Fiction 1994, The Literary Review 1997, Chelsea 1999, Grand Street 70, Against Nature 2002. *Honours:* Multatuli Prize 1988, State Prize for Poetry 1995. *E-mail:* stefan@stefanhertmans.be (home). *Address:* De Bezige Bij, PO Box 75184, 1070 AD, Amsterdam, The Netherlands (office). *Website:* www .debezigebij.nl (office); www.hogent.be/studiumgenerale (office); www .stefanhertmans.be (home).

HERTZ, Noreena, BA, PhD, MBA; British economist, academic and writer; *Distinguished Fellow and Associate Director, Centre for International Business and Management, Judge Institute of Management Studies, University of Cambridge*; b. 24 Sept. 1967, London; single. *Education:* Univ. Coll. London, Univ. of Cambridge, UK, Wharton School of the Univ. of Pennsylvania. *Career:* attended business school in USA; helped establish first Leningrad (now St Petersburg) stock exchange 1991; Int. Finance Corpn adviser to Russian Govt on econ. reforms 1992; fmr head of research team working on prospects for regional econ. co-operation in the Middle East; currently Distinguished Fellow and Assoc. Dir, Centre for Int. Business and Man., Judge Inst. of Man. Studies, Univ. of Cambridge, UK; Belle van Zuylen Chair of Global Political Economy, Utrecht Univ. April–Sept. 2005; attended World Econ. Forum 2002; regular commentator on TV and radio. *Television includes:* documentary film of her book The Silent Takeover (Channel 4) 2001. *Publications include:* Russian Business in the Wake of Reform (doctoral thesis) 1996, The Silent Takeover: Global Capitalism and the Death of Democracy 2001, IOU: The Debt Threat and Why We Must Defuse It 2004; contribs to New Statesman, the Observer, the Guardian and the Washington Post. *Address:* Centre for International Business and Management, Judge Institute of Management, Trumpington Street, Cambridge, CB2 1AG (office); c/o Fourth Estate Ltd, 77–85 Fulham Palace Road, London, W6 8JB, England. *Telephone:* (20) 7724-0829 (office). *Fax:* (20) 7724-1726 (office). *E-mail:* noreenah@yahoo.com (office). *Website:* www.jims.cam.ac.uk (office).

HERVEY, Evelyn (see Keating, Henry Reymond Fitzwalter)

HERZBERG, Judith; Dutch poet, playwright and scriptwriter; b. 4 Nov. 1934, Amsterdam. *Education:* Montessori Lyceum. *Career:* teacher at film schools in Netherlands and Israel. *Film scripts:* scriptwriter: Charlotte, Leedvermaak, Qui Vive. *Publications:* Slow Boat 1964, Meadow Grass 1968, Flies 1970, Grazing Light 1971, 27 Love Songs 1973, Botshol 1980, Remains of the Day 1984, Twenty Poems 1984, But What: Selected Poems 1988, The Way 1992, What She Meant to Paint 1998, Small Catch 1999, Do You Know What Else I Never Know 2002, Sometimes Often 2004; plays: Near Archangel 1971, It Is Not a Dog 1973, That Day May Dawn 1974, Lea's Wedding 1982, The Fall of Icarus 1983, And/Or 1984, The Little Mermaid 1986, Scratch 1989, Lulu (adaptation of Wedekind) 1989, A Good Head 1991, Rijgdraad 1995, The Nothing-factory 1997, Wie Is Van Wie 1999, Simon 2002; children's book: Laika 2004; other: texts for the stage and film 1972–88, trans including The Trojan Women (Euripides), Ghosts (Ibsen), screenplays and TV plays. *Honours:* Jan Campert Prize 1980, Bayerische Filpreis 1980, Joost van der Vandel Prize 1984, Charlotte Koehler Prize 1988, Cestoda Prize 1988, Netherlands-Vlaamse Drama Prize 1989, Constantijn Huyens Prize 1995,

P.C. Hooft Prize for Poetry 1997. *Address:* c/o De Harmonie, PO Box 3547, 1001 AH Amsterdam, The Netherlands.

HESSAYON, David Gerald, OBE, BSc, PhD; British writer; b. 13 Feb. 1928, Manchester, England; m. Joan Parker Gray 1951; two d. *Education:* Univs of Leeds and Manchester. *Career:* mem. Soc. of Authors. *Publications:* The House Plant Expert 1980, The Armchair Book of the Garden 1983, The Tree and Shrub Expert 1983, The Flower Expert 1984, The Indoor Plant Spotter 1985, The Garden Expert 1986, The Home Expert 1987, The Fruit Expert 1990, Be Your Own Greenhouse Expert 1990, The New House Plant Expert 1991, The Garden DIY Expert 1992, The Rock and Water Garden Expert 1993, The Flowering Shrub Expert 1994, The Greenhouse Expert 1994, The Flower Arranging Expert 1994, The Container Expert 1995, The Bulb Expert 1995, The Easy-Care Gardening Expert 1996, The New Bedding Plant Expert 1996, The New Rose Expert 1996, The New Vegetable and Herb Expert 1997, The New Lawn Expert 1997, The Evergreen Expert 1998, The New Flower Expert 1999, The Pocket Flower Expert 2001, The Pocket Garden Troubles Expert 2001, The Pocket Tree and Shrub Expert 2001, The Pocket House Plant Expert 2002, The Pocket Vegetable Expert 2002, The Garden Revival Expert 2004, The House Plant Expert Book 2 2005, The Pest and Weed Expert 2007. *Honours:* Nat. British Book Awards Lifetime Achievement Trophy 1992, Royal Horticultural Soc. Gold Veitch Memorial Medal 1992, Gardening Book of the Year Award 1993, Roy Hay Memorial Award 1998, Garden Writer's Guild Lifetime Achievement Award 2005. *Address:* c/o Expert, 61–63 Uxbridge Road, London, W5 5SA, England. *Website:* www .booksattransworld.co.uk/expertGarden/home.htm.

HETHERINGTON, Norriss Swigart, BA, MA, PhD; American academic and writer; b. 30 Jan. 1942, Berkeley, CA; m. Edith Wiley White 1966, one s. one d. *Education:* University of California, Berkeley, Indiana University. *Career:* Lecturer in Physics and Astronomy, Agnes Scott College, Decatur, GA, 1967–68; Asst Prof. of Mathematics and Science, York University, Toronto, Ontario, 1970–72; Administrative Specialist, National Aeronautics and Space Aministration, 1972; Asst Prof. of History, University of Kansas, 1972–76; Asst Prof. of Science, Technology and Society, Razi University, Sanandaj, Iran, 1976–77; Visiting Scholar, University of Cambridge, 1977–78; Research Assoc., Office for History of Science and Technology, University of Calfornia, Berkeley, 1978–; Assoc. Prof. of the History of Science, University of Oklahoma at Norman, 1981; Dir, Institute for the History of Astronomy, 1988–. *Publications:* Ancient Astronomy and Civilization, 1987; Science and Objectivity: Episodes in the History of Astronomy, 1988; The Edwin Hubble Papers, 1990; Encyclopedia of Cosmology, 1993; Cosmology: Historical, Literary, Philosophical, Religious and Scientific Perspectives, 1993; Hubble's Cosmology: A Guided Study of Selected Texts, 1996. *Honours:* Goddard Historical Essay Award 1974.

HETTICH, Michael, BA, MA, PhD; American academic and writer; b. 25 Sept. 1953, New York, NY; m. Colleen Ahern 1980; one s. one d. *Education:* Hobart Coll., Univ. of Denver, Univ. of Miami. *Publications:* Lathe, 1987; White Birds, 1989; A Small Boat, 1990; Immaculate Bright Rooms, 1994; Many Simple Things, 1997; Sleeping With The Light On; The Point of Touching. Contributions: Poetry East; Witness; Literary Review; Miami Herald; Salt Hills Journal. *Honours:* State of Florida Artist Fellowship. *Address:* 561 NE 95th St, Miami Shores, FL 33138, USA.

HEWETT, Dorothy Coade, AM, BA, MA; Australian poet, writer and dramatist; b. 21 May 1923, Perth, WA. *Education:* University of Western Australia. *Publications:* Bobbin Up (novel), 1959; What About the People? (poems with Merv Lilly), 1962; The Australians Have a Word for It (short stories), 1964; Windmill Country (poems), 1968; The Hidden Journey (poems), 1969; The Chapel Perilous, or The Perilous Adventures of Sally Bonner, 1971; Sandgropers: A Western Australian Anthology, 1973; Rapunzel in Suburbia (poems), 1975; Miss Hewett's Shenanigans, 1975; Greenhouse (poems), 1979; The Man from Mukinupin (play), 1979; Susannah's Dreaming (play), 1981; The Golden Oldies (play), 1981; Selected Poems, 1990; Wild Card (autobiog.), 1990.

HEYEN, William Helmuth, MA, PhD; American academic, poet and writer; *Professor Emeritus of English, State University of New York (SUNY)*; b. 1 Nov. 1940, New York, NY; m. Hannelore Greiner 1962; one s. one d. *Education:* SUNY at Brockport, Ohio Univ. *Career:* Asst Prof. to Prof. of English and Poet-in-Residence, SUNY at Brockport 1967–2000; Sr Fulbright Lecturer in American Literature, Germany 1971–72; Visiting Creative Writer, Univ. of Wisconsin at Milwaukee 1980; Visiting Writer, Hofstra Univ. 1981, 1983, Southampton Coll. 1984, 1985; Visiting Prof. of English, Univ. of Hawaii 1985; Workshop Leader, Chautauqua Inst. 1993, 1996, 2000, 2004. *Publications:* Depth of Field 1970, Noise in the Trees: Poems and a Memoir 1974, American Poets in 1976 (ed.) 1976, The Swastika Poems 1977, Long Island Light: Poems and a Memoir 1979, The City Parables 1980, Lord Dragonfly: Five Sequences 1981, Erika: Poems of the Holocaust 1984, The Generation of 2000: Contemporary American Poets (ed.) 1984, Vic Holyfield and the Class of 1957: A Romance 1986, The Chestnut Rain: A Poem 1986, Brockport, New York: Beginning with 'And' 1988, Falling From Heaven (co-author) 1991, Pterodactyl Rose: Poems of Ecology 1991, Ribbons: The Gulf War 1991, The Host: Selected Poems 1965–1990 1994, With Me Far Away: A Memoir 1994, Crazy Horse in Stillness: Poems 1996, Pig Notes and Dumb Music: Prose on Poetry 1998, Diana, Charles and the Queen: Poems 1998, September 11, 2001: American Writers Respond 2002, The Hummingbird Corporation: Stories

2002, The Rope: Poems 2004, Shoah Train: Poems 2004, Home: Autobiographies, Etc. 2005, Titanic & Icebert: Early Essays & Reviews 2006, The Confessions of Doc Williams & Other Poems 2006; contribs to many books, chapbooks, journals and magazines. *Honours:* Borestone Mountain Poetry Prize 1965, National Endowment for the Arts Fellowships 1973–74, 1984–85, American Library Asscn Notable American Book 1974, Ontario Review Poetry Prize 1977, Guggenheim Fellowship 1977–78, Eunice Tietjens Memorial Award 1978, Witter Bynner Prize for Poetry 1982, New York Foundation for the Arts Poetry Fellowship 1984–85, Lillian Fairchild Award 1996, Small Press Book Award for Poetry 1997, Andrew Eiseman Award 2004. *Address:* 142 Frazier Street, Brockport, NY 14420, USA (home). *Telephone:* (585) 395-5831 (office). *E-mail:* wheyen@rochester.rr.com (home).

HIAASEN, Carl Andrew; American novelist and journalist; *Columnist, Miami Herald;* b. 12 March 1953, Plantation, Fort Lauderdale, FL; s. of Odel Hiaasen and Patricia Hiaasen; m. 1st Connie Lyford 1970 (divorced 1996); one s.; m. 2nd Fenia Clizer 1999; one s. one step-s. *Education:* Emory Univ., Univ. of Florida. *Career:* reporter Cocoa Today, Florida 1974–76; reporter Miami Herald 1976–79, investigative reporter 1979–85, weekly columnist 1985–. *Publications:* fiction: Trap Line (with William Montalbano) 1981, Powder Burn (with William Montalbano) 1981, A Death in China (with William Montalbano) 1986, Tourist Season 1986, Double Whammy 1987, Skin Tight 1989, Native Tongue 1991, Strip Tease 1993, Stormy Weather 1993, Lucky You 1997, Sick Puppy 2000, Basket Case 2002, Hoot (Newbery Award 2003) 2002, Skinny Dip 2004, Flush (juvenile) 2005, Nature Girl 2007; non-fiction: Team Rodent: How Disney Devours the World 1998. *Honours:* Damon Runyon Award for services to journalism 2003. *Literary Agent:* The Lavin Agency, 77 Peter Street, Fourth Floor, Toronto, ON M5V 2G4, Canada. *E-mail:* tgagnon@ thelavinagency.com. *Website:* www.thelavinagency.com; www.carlhiaasen .com.

HIATT, Fred, BA; American journalist; b. 1955, Washington. *Career:* City Hall reporter, Atlanta Journal-Constitution 1979–80; reporter, The Washington Star 1981; Va Reporter, The Washington Post 1981–83, Pentagon Reporter 1983–86, NE Asia Co-Bureau Chief 1987–90, Moscow Co-Bureau Chief 1991–95, Ed. editorial page 1996–. *Publications:* The Secret Sun 1992 (novel), If I Were Queen of the World 1997 (children's book), Baby Talk 1999. *Address:* The Washington Post, 1150 15th Street, NW, Washington, DC 20071, USA (office). *Website:* www.washingtonpost.com (office).

HIBBERT, Christopher, MC, MA, FRSL; British writer; b. 5 March 1924, Enderby, Leicestershire; s. of the late Canon H. V. Hibbert; m. Susan Piggford 1948; two s. one d. *Education:* Radley Coll., Oriel Coll., Oxford. *Career:* served in Second World War, Capt. London Irish Rifles (twice wounded) 1943–45; partner, firm of land agents and auctioneers 1949–58. *Publications:* The Road to Tyburn 1957, King Mob 1958, Wolfe at Quebec 1959, The Destruction of Lord Raglan 1961, Corunna 1961, Benito Mussolini 1962, The Battle of Arnhem 1962, The Roots of Evil 1963, The Court at Windsor 1964, Agincourt 1964, The Wheatley Diary (ed.) 1964, Garibaldi and his Enemies 1965, The Making of Charles Dickens 1967, Waterloo: Napoleon's Last Campaign (ed.) 1967, An American in Regency England: The Journal of Louis Simond (ed.) 1968, Charles I 1968, The Grand Tour 1969, London: Biography of a City 1969, The Search for King Arthur 1970, Anzio: The Bid for Rome 1970, The Dragon Wakes: China and the West 1793–1911 1970, The Personal History of Samuel Johnson 1971, George IV, Vol. I: Prince of Wales 1762–1811 1972, Vol. II: Regent and King 1812–1830 1973, The Rise and Fall of the House of Medici 1974, Edward VII: A Portrait 1976, The Great Mutiny: India 1857 1978, The French Revolution 1980, Africa Explored: Europeans in the Dark Continent 1796–1889 1982, The London Encyclopaedia (ed.) 1983, Queen Victoria in her Letters and Journals 1984, Rome: Biography of a City 1985, Cities and Civilizations 1985, The English: A Social History 1986, Venice: Biography of a City 1988, The Encyclopaedia of Oxford (ed.) 1988, The Virgin Queen: The Personal History of Elizabeth I 1990, Redcoats and Rebels: The War for America 1770–1781 1990, Captain Gronow: His Reminiscences of Regency and Victorian Life (ed.) 1991, Cavaliers and Roundheads: The English at War 1642–1649 1993, Florence: Biography of a City 1993, Nelson: A Personal History 1994, A Soldier of the 71st 1996, Wellington: A Personal History 1997, No Ordinary Place: Radley College and the Public School System 1847–1997 1997, George III: A Personal History 1998, Queen Victoria: A Personal History 2000, The Marlboroughs: John and Sarah Churchill 1650–1744 2001, Napoleon: Wives and Women 2002, Disraeli: A Personal History 2004. *Honours:* Hon. DLitt (Leicester) 1996; Heinemann Award for Literature 1962, McColvin Medal Library Asscn 1989. *Literary Agent:* David Higham Associates, 5–8 Lower John Street, Golden Square, London, W1F 9HA. *Address:* 6 Albion Place, West Street, Henley-on-Thames, Oxfordshire, RG9 2DT, England. *Telephone:* (1491) 575235.

HICK, John Harwood, PhD, DPhil, DLitt; British academic; *Danforth Professor Emeritus of the Philosophy of Religion, Claremont Graduate University;* b. 20 Jan. 1922, Scarborough, Yorks.; s. of Mark Day Hick and Mary Aileen Hirst; m. Joan Hazel Bowers 1953 (died 1996); three s. (one deceased) one d. *Education:* Bootham School, York, Univs of Edinburgh and Oxford, Westminster Theological Coll., Cambridge. *Career:* Minister, Belford Presbyterian Church, Northumberland 1953–56; Asst Prof. of Philosophy, Cornell Univ., USA 1956–59; Stuart Prof. of Christian Philosophy, Princeton Theological Seminary, USA 1959–64; Lecturer in Divinity, Univ. of Cambridge 1964–67; H. G. Wood Prof. of Theology, Univ. of Birmingham 1967–80, now Prof. Emer., Fellow, Inst. for Advanced Research in Arts and Social

Sciences; Danforth Prof. of Philosophy of Religion, Claremont Grad. Univ., Calif., USA 1980–92; Prof. Emer. 1992–, Chair., Dept of Religion, Dir Blaisdell Programs in World Religions and Cultures 1983–92; Gifford Lecturer, Univ. of Edinburgh 1986–87; Guggenheim Fellow 1963–64, 1986–87; SA Cook Bye-Fellow, Gonville and Caius Coll., Cambridge 1963–64; Vice-Pres. World Congress of Faiths, British Soc. for the Philosophy of Religion. *Publications include:* Faith and Knowledge, Evil and the God of Love, God and the Universe of Faiths, Death and Eternal Life, Arguments for the Existence of God, Problems of Religious Pluralism, God Has Many Names, Philosophy of Religion, The Second Christianity, An Interpretation of Religion, Disputed Questions in Theology and the Philosophy of Religion, The Metaphor of God Incarnate, The Rainbow of Faiths, The Fifth Dimension, John Hick: An Autobiography; Ed.: The Myth of God Incarnate, The Many-Faced Argument, The Myth of Christian Uniqueness, The Existence of God, Truth and Dialogue, Christianity and Other Religions, Faith and the Philosophers. *Honours:* Hon. Prof., Univ. of Wales; Hon. TheolDr (Uppsala) 1977; Hon. DD (Glasgow) 2002; Grawemeyer Award in Religion 1991. *Address:* 144 Oak Tree Lane, Selly Oak, Birmingham, B29 6HU, England. *Telephone:* (121) 689-4803. *E-mail:* j.h.hick@bham.ac.uk (home). *Website:* www.johnhick.org.uk (home).

HICKEY, Christine Dwyer; Irish novelist and writer; b. Dublin. *Career:* Hon. Sec. Irish PEN. *Film screenplay:* No Better Man (adapted from short story). *Publications:* novels: The Dancer 1995, The Gambler 1996, The Gatemaker 2000, Tatty 2004. *Honours:* winner Listowel Writers' Week short-story competition (twice), winner Observer/Penguin short-story competition. *Address:* c/o New Island, 2 Brookside, Dundrum Road, Dublin 14, Ireland.

HICKOK, Gloria Vando (see Vando (Hickok), Gloria)

HICKSON, Jill Lesley Norton, MBA; Australian literary agent and business executive; b. 28 Sept. 1948, d. of Staveley Fredrick Norton Hickson and Jean Halse Rogers; m. Neville K. Wran 1976; one d. *Education:* Univ. of Sydney and Australian Grad. School of Man. *Career:* programmer/announcer 2MBS FM 1975–76; Int. Relations Man. Quantas Airways 1976–81; Literary Agent and Man. Dir Hickson Assocs Pty Ltd 1983–99; consultant Curtis Brown Australia Pty Ltd 1999–; mem. Bd Dirs Ansett NZ, NSW Conservatorium of Music 1984–89, Sydney Opera House Trust 1985–89, Sydney Symphony Orchestra 1986; mem. Australian Inst. of Int. Affairs, Australian Soc. of Authors, Australian Writers' Guild, Grad. Man. Soc.; Patron Fellowship of Australian Writers, United Music Teachers' Asscn of NSW, 2MBS FM Music Foundation, Domestic Animal Birth Control Soc.; mem. Cttee State Library NSW Foundation, Art Gallery NSW Foundation. *Honours:* Cecil Hall Prize, Australian Inst. of Man. 1972, Schroder Darling Finance Prize, Inst. of Dirs Prize. *Address:* PO Box 271, Woollahra, NSW 2025, Australia.

HIGGINBOTHAM, (Prieur) Jay, BA; American archivist and writer; *Director Emeritus, Mobile Municipal Archives;* b. 16 July 1937, Pascagoula, MS; m. Alice Louisa Martin 1970; two s. one d. *Education:* Univ. of Mississippi, Hunter College, CUNY, American Univ., Washington, DC. *Career:* Head, Local History Dept, Mobile Public Library 1973–83; Dir Mobile Municipal Archives 1983–2001, Dir Emer. 2001–; mem. and Chair. Mobile Assembly of Sages and Savants, 1983–2001. *Publications:* The Mobile Indians 1966, The World Around 1966, Family Biographies 1967, The Pascagoula Indians 1967, Pascagoula: Singing River City 1968, Mobile: City by the Bay 1968, The Journal of Sauvole 1969, Fort Maurepas: The Birth of Louisiana 1969, re-published 1998, Brother Holyfield 1972, A Voyage to Dauphin Island 1974, Old Mobile: Fort Louis de la Louisiane 1702–1711 1977, Fast Train Russia 1983, Autumn in Petrishchevo 1986, Discovering Russia 1989, Mauvila 1990, Kazula (play) 1991, Man, Nature and the Infinite 1998, Alma 2002, Narrow is the Way 2004, One Man in the Universe 2005; contrib. to Library Journal, The Humanist, Harvard International Review, Soviet Literature, Louisiana History, Encyclopaedia Britannica. *Honours:* General L. Kemper Williams Prize, Louisiana Historical Asscn 1977, Award of Merit, Mississippi Historical Soc. 1978, Alabama Library Asscn, Non-Fiction Award 1978, Gilbert Chinard Prize 1978, Elizabeth Gould Award 1981, Alabama Humanitarian Award 1999. *Address:* 60 N Monterey Street, Mobile, AL 36604, USA. *Telephone:* (251) 208-7735 (office); (251) 471-5276 (home). *Fax:* (251) 208-7428 (office).

HIGGINS, Aidan; Irish writer; b. 3 March 1927, Celbridge, County Kildare. *Education:* Clongowes Wood Coll., County Kildare. *Publications:* Stories Felo De Se 1960, Langrishe, Go Down (James Tait Black Memorial Prize 1967) 1966, Balcony of Europe 1972, Scenes from a Receding Past 1977, Bornholm Night Ferry 1983, Helsingor Station and Other Departures 1989, Ronda Gorge and Other Precipices: Travel Writings 1959–90, Lions of The Grunewald (novel) 1993, Donkey's Years (Memories of a Life as Story Told) 1995, Secker, Flotsam & Jetsam (collected stories) 1997, Dog Days 1998, A Bestiary 2004. *Honours:* British Arts Council grant, Irish Acad. of Letters Award 1970, American Ireland Fund 1977. *Address:* c/o Dalkey Archive Press, ISU Campus 8905, Normal, IL 61790-8905, USA.

HIGGINS, Jack (see Patterson, Harry)

HIGGINS, Rita Ann; Irish poet and playwright; b. 1955, Galway. *Career:* writer-in-residence, Galway County 1987, National Univ. of Ireland, Galway 1994–95, Offaly County Council 1998–99; Green Honors Prof., Texas Christian Univ., USA 2000. *Plays:* Face Licker Come Home 1991, God of the Hatch Man 1992, Colie Lally Doesn't Live in a Bucket 1993, Down All the Roundabouts 1999. *Publications:* poetry: Goddess on the Mervue Bus 1986,

Witch in the Bushes 1988, Goddess and Witch 1990, Philomena's Revenge 1992, Higher Purchase 1996, Sunny Side Plucked: New and Selected Poems 1996, An Awful Racket 2001; editor: Out the Clara Road: The Offaly Anthology 1999. *Honours:* Peadar O'Donnell Award 1989. *Address:* c/o Bloodaxe Books Ltd, Highgreen, Tarset, Northumberland NE48 1RP, England. *Website:* www .bloodaxebooks.com.

HIGH, Peter Brown, BA, MA, PhD; American academic and writer; *Professor of Film and Literature, Nagoya University;* b. 6 Sept. 1944, New York, NY; m. 1972; one s. *Education:* American Univ., California State Univ., Nagoya Univ. *Career:* columnist, Asahi Shimbun, Japanese Language 1987–92; Prof. of Film and Literature, Nagoya Univ. 1987–. *Publications:* An Outline of American Literature, 1985; Read All About It, 1986; A Journalist Looks at Popular Culture, 1991; The Imperial Screen: Japanese Cinema and the 15-Year War, 1995; A History of Cinema, 1997; Assorted language textbooks in the ESL field. Contributions: journals. *Honours:* Soc. for Media and Cinema Studies Katherine Kovacs Best Book of 2004. *Address:* c/o Department of Film and Literature, Nagoya University, Furo-cho, Chikusa-ku, Nagoya 464-8601; 43 Meidai Shukusha, Kogawa-cho, Chikusa-ku, Nagoya, Japan. *E-mail:* peterbhigh2004@yahoo.com (home).

HIGHAM, Charles; British writer; b. 18 Feb. 1931, London, England. *Career:* film critic, Nation, Sydney 1961–63; Literary Ed., The Bulletin, Sydney 1963–68; Hollywood feature writer, New York Times 1971–80; Visiting Regents' Prof., Univ. of California at Santa Cruz 1990. *Publications:* The Earthbound and Other Poems, 1959; Noonday Country: Poems 1954–1865, 1966; The Celluloid Muse: Hollywood Directors Speak (ed. with J. Greenberg), 1969; Hollywood in the Forties (ed. with J. Greenberg), 1969; The Films of Orson Welles, 1970; The Voyage to Brindisi and Other Poems 1966–1969, 1970; Ziegfeld, 1972; Cecil B. DeMille, 1973; The Art of the American Film, 1900–1971, 1973; Ava, 1974; Kate: The Life of Katharine Hepburn, 1975; Warner Brothers, 1975; Charles Laughton: An Intimate Biography, 1976; Marlene: The Life of Marlene Dietrich, 1977; Errol Flynn: The Untold Story, 1980; Star Maker: The Autobiography of Hal B. Wallis, 1980; Bette: The Life of Bette Davis, 1981; Trading with the Enemy: An Exposae of the Nazi-American Money Plot 1933–1949, 1983; Princess Merle (with Roy Moseley), 1983; Sisters: The Story of Olivia de Haviland and Joan Fontaine, 1984; Audrey: The Life of Audrey Hepburn, 1984; American Swastika, 1985; Orson Welles: The Rise and Fall of an American Genius, 1986; Palace: My Life in the Royal Family of Monaco (with Baron C. de Massy), 1986; Brando: The Unauthorized Biography, 1987; Wallis: The Secret Lives of the Duchess of Windsor, 1988; Cary Grant: The Lonely Heart (with Roy Moseley), 1989; Elizabeth and Philip: The Untold Story of the Queen of England and Her Prince (with Roy Moseley), 1991; Rose: The Life of Rose Fitzgerald Kennedy, 1994; The Civilization of Angkor, 2001; Murder in Hollywood 2005, Dark Lady 2006; contrib. to newspapers, reviews and magazines. *Address:* John Hawkins and Sons, 71 W 23rd Street, New York, NY 100010, USA.

HIGHAM, Robin (David Stewart); American academic, writer and editor; b. 20 June 1925, London, England; m. Barbara Davies 1950; one s. three d. (two deceased). *Education:* AB, 1950, PhD, 1957, Harvard University; MA, Claremont Graduate School, CA, 1953. *Career:* Instructor, University of Massachusetts, 1954–57; Asst Prof., University of North Carolina at Chapel Hill, 1957–63; Assoc. Prof., 1963–66, Prof. of History, 1966–98, Kansas State University; Ed., 1968–88, Ed. Emeritus 1989–98, Military Affairs; Ed., 1970–88, Ed. Emeritus, 1989–98, Aerospace Historian; Founder-Pres., Sunflower University Press, 1977–; Ed. and Co-Publisher, Journal of the West, 1977–1998; mem. International Commission of Military History. *Publications:* Britain's Imperial Air Routes, 1918–39, 1960; The British Rigid Airship, 1908–31, 1961; Armed Forces in Peacetime: Britain, 1918–39, 1963; The Military Intellectuals in Britain, 1918–39, 1966; A Short History of Warfare (with David H. Zook), 1966; Air Power: A Concise History, 1973; The Compleat Academic, 1975; A Brief Guide to Scholarly Editing (with Mary Cisper and Guy Dresser), 1982; Diary of a Disaster: British Aid to Greece, 1940–41, 1986; The Bases of Air Strategy 1915–1945, 1998; editor: various books, including: Civil Wars in the Twentieth Century, 1972; A Guide to the Sources of British Military History, 1971; A Guide to the Sources of US Military History, 1975; The Rise of the Wheat State: A History of Kansas Agriculture (with George E. Ham), 1986; Russian Aviation and Air Power (with John T. Greenwood and Von Handesty), 1998; A Military History of Tsarist Russia (with Frederick W. Kagan), 2001; A Military History of the Soviet Union (with Frederick W. Kagan), 2001; A Military History of China (with David Graff), 2001, Why Air Forces Fail (with Stephen J. Harris) 2005; contrib. to reference works, scholarly books, and professional journals. *Honours:* Social Science Research Council National Security Policy Research Fellow, 1960–61; Victor Gondos Award, 1983, Samuel Eliot Morison Award, 1986, American Military Institute; Kansas Governor's Aviation Honor Award, 2000. *Address:* 2961 Nevada Street, Manhattan, KS 66502, USA (home). *Telephone:* (385) 539-3668 (home). *E-mail:* marolync@flinthills.com (office).

HIGHLAND, Monica (see See, Carolyn)

HIGSON, Philip John Willoughby-, BA, MA, PhD, PGCE, FRHistS, FRSA, FSA; British poet, translator, editor, historian and art historian and playwright; b. 21 Feb. 1933, Newcastle-under-Lyme, Staffs., England. *Education:* Univs of Liverpool and Keele. *Career:* Lecturer, then Sr Lecturer in History, Univ. Coll., Chester (now Univ. of Chester) 1972–89, Visiting Lecturer 1989–90; Chair., Pres. and Anthology Ed. Chester Poets 1974–92; Pres. The Baudelaire Soc., Chester and Paris 1992–; mem. Soc. of Authors. *Publications:* The Riposte and Other Poems 1971, Sonnets to My Goddess 1983, Maurice Rollinat's Les Névroses: Selected English Versions (trans.) 1986, A Warning to Europe: The Testimony of Limouse (co-author) 1992, The Complete Poems of Baudelaire with Selected Illustrations by Limouse (ed. and principal trans.) 1992, Limouse Nudes 1994, Sonnets to My Goddess in This Life and the Next (two-part sequence) (David St John Thomas Poetry Publication Prize 1996) 1995, Childhood in Wartime Keele: Poems of Reminiscence 1995, Poems on the Dee 1997, Inner City Love-Revolt: Footage from a Fifties Affair 2000, A Poet's Pilgrimage: The Shaping of a Creative Life 2000, Sonnets to My Goddess in This Life and the Next: The Prize-Winning Volume Expanded 2002, The Jewelled Nude: A Play About Baudelaire and Queen Pomaré 2002, Poems of Sauce and Satire: A Humorous Selection 2002, Maurice Rollinat: A Hundred Poems from Les Névroses 2003, Ut Pictura Poesis: Pictorial Poems 2004, Manichaean Contrasts (poems) 2004, Souvenir of a Triple Launch: play, translations, sonnets 2004, D'Annunzio: Selected poems translated and introduced 2005, Baudelaire and Limouse: Their Ennobling Mission for Art 2006; contrib. of historical articles to Oxford Dictionary of National Biography and to journals, including Antiquaries Journal, Genealogists' Magazine, Coat of Arms, Northern History, Transactions of the Historic Society of Lancashire and Cheshire, and of the Lancashire and Cheshire Antiquarian Society; poems to The Picador Book of Erotic Verse 1978, Rhyme Revival 1982, Poet's England: Staffordshire 1987, Red Candle Treasury 1998, and to journals, including Critical Quarterly, Chester Poets Anthologies, Collegian, Candelabrum, The Eclectic Muse, Mandrake Poetry Review, Cadmium Blue Literary Journal, Lexikon, Rebirth, Solar Flame, Romantic Renaissance, Rubies in the Darkness, Quantum Leap, The Poet Tree, A Bard Hair Day, Metverse Muse, Bulletin de la Société 'Les Amis de Maurice Rollinat'. *Honours:* First Prize for an Established Poet, The Eclectic Muse, Vancouver 1990, prizewinner, Lexikon Poetry Competition 1996, First Prize, Rubies in the Darkness Poetry Competition 2003. *Address:* 1 Westlands Avenue, Newcastle-under-Lyme, Staffs. ST5 2PU, England.

HIJUELOS, Oscar, BA, MA; American writer; b. 24 Aug. 1951, New York, NY. *Education:* City Coll., CUNY. *Publications:* Our House in the Last World 1983, The Mambo Kings Play Songs of Love 1989, The Fourteen Sisters of Emilio Montez O'Brien 1993, Mr Ive's Christmas 1995, Empress of the Splendid Season 1999, A Simple Habana Melody (From When the World Was Good) 2002. *Honours:* Pushcart Press Outstanding Writer 1978, Bread Loaf Writers' Conference Scholarship 1980, Ingram Merrill Foundation Grant 1983, Nat. Endowment for the Arts Fellowship 1985, American Acad. in Rome Fellowship 1985, Pulitzer Prize in Fiction 1990. *Literary Agent:* Harriet Wasserman Literary Agency, E 36th Street, New York, NY 10016, USA.

HILDEBIDLE, John, BA, MA, PhD; American poet, writer and academic; b. 2 Feb. 1946, Hartford, CT; m. Nichola Gilsdorf 1978, one s. one d. *Education:* Harvard University. *Career:* Lecturer in English and American Literature, 1980–83, Mem., Extension Faculty, 1981–, Harvard University; Asst Prof. of Literature, MIT, 1983–; mem. MLA of America; National Council of Teachers of English; Thoreau Society. *Publications:* Poetry: The Old Chore, 1981; One Sleep, One Waking, 1994; Defining Absence, 1999. Other: Modernism Reconsidered (ed. with Robert J. Kiely), 1983; Thoreau: A Naturalist's Liberty, 1983; Stubbornness: A Field Guide, 1986; Five Irish Writers: The Errand of Keeping Alive, 1989; A Sense of Place; Poetry from Ireland (with Dorys Crow Grover and Michael D. Riley), 1995. Contributions: anthologies and periodicals. *Honours:* Book Award, San Francisco Poetry Center, 1982; Katherine Anne Porter Prize, Tulsa Arts and Humanities Council, 1984; Anniversary Award for Poetry, Associated Writing Programs, 1984; John Gardner Short Fiction Prize, 1987.

HILL, Anthony Robert; Australian writer and journalist; b. 24 May 1942, Melbourne, Vic.; m. Gillian Mann 1965; one d. *Career:* mem. Australian Soc. of Authors. *Publications:* The Bunburyists 1985, Antique Furniture in Australia 1985, Birdsong 1988, The Burnt Stick 1994, Spindrift 1996, The Grandfather Clock 1996, Growing Up and Other Stories 1999, Soldier Boy 2001, Forbidden 2002, Young Digger 2002, The Shadow Dog 2003, Animal Heroes 2005, River Boy 2006, Harriet 2006, Lucy's Cat and the Rainbow Birds 2007. *Honours:* Children's Book Council of Australia Honour Book 1995, 2002, NSW Premier's Award 2002. *Address:* PO Box 7085, Yarralumla, ACT 2600, Australia. *Telephone:* (612) 6281-1358.

HILL, Eric; British children's writer and illustrator; b. 7 Sept. 1927, London; m. Gillian Hill; one s. one d. *Career:* fmrly served with the RAF; drew cartoons for Illustrated and Lilliput magazines; worked in advertising and graphic design agencies before becoming a freelance art dir and illustrator; creator of Spot series of children's books 1980–. *Publications include:* Spot series: Where's Spot?, Spot's First Walk, Puppy Love, Spot's Birthday Party, Spot Tells the Time, Sweet Dreams, Spot!, Spot at the Fair, Spot Goes to the Farm, Spot's Baby Sister, Time for Bed, Spot, Spot's New Game, Spot and his Grandma, Spot's Tummy Ache, Spot's Garden, Spot's Camping Trip; other titles: The Park 1982, Help Your Child to Read series (including Poorly Pig, Bad Bear, Fast Frog, Double Ducks, Silly Sheep), Up There 1982, At Home 1982, My Pets 1982, Opposites 1983, Good Morning Baby Bear 1984, Eric Hill's Crazy Mix or Match 1984, My Day at Home 1998, My Animal Friends 2002. *Address:* c/o Ladybird Books, 80 Strand, London, WC2R 0RL, England (office). *E-mail:* ladybird@penguin.co.uk.

HILL, Geoffrey William, MA, FRSL; British poet and academic; *University Professor of Literature and Religion, Boston University*; b. 18 June 1932, s. of William George Hill and Hilda Beatrice Hill (née Hands); m. 1st Nancy Whittaker 1956 (divorced 1983); three s. one d.; m. 2nd Alice Goodman 1987; one d. *Education:* County High School, Bromsgrove and Keble Coll., Oxford. *Career:* mem. academic staff, Univ. of Leeds 1954–80, Prof. of English Literature 1976–80; Univ. Lecturer in English and Fellow, Emmanuel Coll., Cambridge 1981–88; Univ. Prof. of Literature and Religion, Boston Univ. 1988–; Co-Dir Editorial Inst., Boston Univ. 1998–2004; Churchill Fellow, Univ. of Bristol 1980; Clark Lecturer, Trinity Coll., Cambridge 1986; Tanner Lecturer, Brasenose Coll., Oxford 2000; Assoc. Fellow, Centre for Research in Philosophy and Literature, Univ. of Warwick 2003; Empson Lecturer, Univ. of Cambridge 2005; Fellow, American Acad. of Arts and Sciences 1996. *Publications:* poetry: Poems 1952, For the Unfallen (Gregory Award 1961) 1959, Preghiere 1964, King Log (Hawthornden Prize 1969, Geoffrey Faber Memorial Prize 1970) 1968, Mercian Hymns (Alice Hunt Bartlett Award) 1971, Somewhere is Such a Kingdom: Poems 1952–71 1975, Tenebrae (Duff Cooper Memorial Prize 1979) 1978, The Mystery of the Charity of Charles Péguy 1983, Collected Poems 1985, New and Collected Poems 1952–1992 1994, Canaan 1996, The Triumph of Love 1998, Speech! Speech! 2000, The Orchards of Syon 2002, Scenes from Comus 2005, Without Title 2006, Selected Poems 2006; poetic drama: Henrik Ibsen's Brand: a version for the English stage 1978 (produced at Nat. Theatre, London 1978); criticism: The Lords of Limit: essays on literature and ideas 1984, The Enemy's Country 1991, Style and Faith 2003. *Honours:* Hon. Fellow, Keble Coll., Oxford 1981, Emmanuel Coll., Cambridge 1990; Hon. DLitt (Leeds) 1988; Whitbread Award 1971, RSL Award (W. H. Heinemann Bequest) 1971, Loines Award, American Acad. and Inst. of Arts and Letters 1983, Ingram Merrill Foundation Award in Literature 1985, Kahn Award 1998, T. S. Eliot Prize, Ingersoll Foundation 2000. *Address:* University Professors, Boston University, 745 Commonwealth Avenue, Boston, MA 02215, USA. *Telephone:* (617) 358-1773 (office). *Fax:* (617) 353-6917 (office). *E-mail:* editinst@bu.edu (office). *Website:* www.bu.edu/editinst (office).

HILL, Jane Bowers, BA, MA, PhD; American academic, editor, writer and poet; *Professor and Chairman, University of West Georgia*; b. 17 Oct. 1950, Seneca, SC; m. Robert W. Hill 1980; one d. *Education:* Clemson Univ., Univ. of Illinois. *Career:* Assoc. Ed. Peachtree Publrs 1986–88; Sr Ed. Longstreet Press 1988–91; Dir Kennesaw Summer Writers' Workshop 1988–92; Asst Prof., Univ. of West Georgia 1992–; mem. Modern Language Asscn. *Publications:* An American Christmas: A Sampler of Contemporary Stories and Poems (ed.) 1986, Our Mutual Room: Modern Literary Portraits of the Opposite Sex (ed.) 1987, Songs: New Voices in Fiction (ed.) 1990, Cobb County: At the Heart of Change (ed.) 1991, Gail Godwin 1992; contrib. to numerous stories, poems, essays and reviews. *Honours:* Frank O'Connor Prize for Fiction 1989, Syvenna Foundation Fellow 1991, Monticello Fellowship for Female Writers 1992. *Address:* University of West Georgia, 1601 Maple Street, Carrollton, GA 30118 (office); 1419 Arden Drive, Marietta, GA 30008, USA (home). *Telephone:* (678) 839-6512 (office). *Fax:* (678) 839-4849 (office). *E-mail:* jhill@westga.edu (office); janehill@mindspring.com (home). *Website:* www.westga.edu/~jhill (office).

HILL, John (see Koontz, Dean Ray)

HILL, John Spencer, BA, MA, PhD; Canadian academic and writer; b. 22 Oct. 1943, Brantford, ON; m. 1966; two s. one d. *Education:* Queen's University, University of Toronto, Canada. *Career:* Asst Prof. of English, Royal Military College of Canada, 1967–69, 1972–73; Lecturer, University of Western Australia, 1973–79; Prof. of English Literature, University of Ottawa, 1979–. *Publications:* Imaginations in Coleridge, 1978; John Milton: Poet, Priest and Prophet, 1979; The Last Castrato (novel), 1995; Ghirlandaio's Daughter (novel), 1996; Infinity, Faith and Time, 1997. Contributions: scholarly journals. *Honours:* Critics' Choice Award, San Francisco Review of Books, 1995; Arthur Ellis Award, Crime Writers of Canada, 1996.

HILL, Justin, BA, MA; British novelist; b. 1971, Freeport, Grand Bahama. *Education:* St Peter's School, York, Univs of Durham and Lancaster. *Career:* fmrly worked for an aid agency in Shanxi, People's Repub. of China, as a teacher in Eritrea. *Theatre:* appearance in Macbeth, Galway Town Hall Theatre 2003. *Publications:* A Bend in the Yellow River 1997, The Drink and Dream Teahouse (Geoffrey Faber Memorial Prize 2002) 2001, Ciao Asmara 2002, Passing Under Heaven (Soc. of Authors Somerset Maugham Award 2005) 2004; reviews for The Guardian and TLS. *Honours:* Third XiaoXiang Friendship Award, Hunan Province (China), Betty Trask Award 2000, ranked by the Independent on Sunday amongst Top 20 Young British Writers 2001. *Address:* c/o Little Brown, Brettenham House, Lancaster Place, London, WC2E 7EN, England. *E-mail:* hi@justinhillauthor.com (office). *Website:* www.justinhillauthor.com (office).

HILL, Pamela, (Sharon Fiske), BSc, DA; British writer; b. 26 Nov. 1920, Nairobi, Kenya. *Education:* Glasgow School of Art, Univ. of Glasgow. *Career:* mem. RSL, Society of Authors. *Publications:* Flaming Janet, 1954; The Devil of Aske, 1972; The Malvie Inheritance, 1973; Homage to a Rose, 1979; Fire Opal, 1980; This Rough Beginning, 1981; My Lady Glamis, 1981; Summer Cypress, 1981; The House of Cray, 1982; The Governess, 1985; Venables, 1988; The Sutburys, 1987; The Brocken, 1991; The Sword and the Flame, 1991; Mercer, 1992; The Silver Runaways, 1992; O Madcap Duchess, 1993; The Parson's Children, 1993; The Man from the North, 1994; Journey Beyond

Innocence, 1994; The Charmed Descent, 1995; The Inadvisable Marriages, 1995; Saints' Names for Confirmation, 1995; Alice the Palace, 1996; Murder in Store, 1996; Widow's Veil, 1997. Contributions: periodicals.

HILL, Peter; British journalist and newspaper editor; *Editor, Daily Express.* *Career:* Ed. Daily Star 1998–2003, Daily Express 2003–; mem. Press Complaints Commission 2003–. *Honours:* Editor of the Year, What the Papers Say Awards 2002. *Address:* Daily Express, 10 Lower Thames Street, London, EC3R 6EN, England (office).

HILL, Reginald Charles, (Dick Morland, Patrick Ruell, Charles Underhill), BA; British novelist and playwright; b. 3 April 1936, West Hartlepool, Co. Durham, England. *Education:* St Catherine's Coll., Oxford. *Publications:* A Clubbable Woman 1970, An Advancement of Learning 1971, Fell of Dark 1971, A Fairly Dangerous Thing 1972, An Affair of Honour (play) 1972, Ruling Passion 1973, A Very Good Hater 1974, An April Shroud 1975, Another Death in Venice 1976, A Pinch of Snuff 1978, The Spy's Wife 1980, A Killing Kindness 1980, Who Guards the Prince 1982, Traitor's Blood 1983, Dead Heads 1983, Exit Lines 1984, No Man's Land 1985, Child's Play 1987, The Collaborators 1987, There Are No Ghosts in the Soviet Union (short stories) 1987, Underworld 1988, Pascoe's Ghost (short stories) 1989, Bones and Silence 1990, One Small Step 1990, Recalled to Life 1992, Pictures of Perfection 1994, Blood Sympathy 1994, The Wood Beyond 1995, Born Guilty 1995, Asking for the Moon 1996, Killing the Lawyers 1997, On Beulah Height 1998, Singing the Sadness 1999, Arms and the Women 2000, Beyond the Bone 2000, Dialogues of the Dead 2001, Death's Jest-Book 2002, Good Morning, Midnight 2003, The Stranger House 2005, The Death of Dalziel 2007, The Roar of the Butterflies 2007; as Dick Morland: Heart Clock 1973, Albion! Albion! 1974; as Patrick Ruell: The Castle of Demon 1971, Red Christmas 1972, Death Takes the Low Road 1974, Urn Burial 1975, The Long Kill 1986, Death of a Dormouse 1987, Dream of Darkness 1989, The Only Game 1991; as Charles Underhill: Captain Fantom 1978, The Forging of Fantom 1979. *Honours:* Gold Dagger Award 1990, Diamond Dagger Award 1995. *Literary Agent:* AP Watt Ltd, 20 John Street, London, WC1N 2DR, England.

HILL, Roberta, (Roberta Hill Whiteman), BA, MFA, PhD; American poet and academic; *Associate Professor of English and American Indian Studies, University of Wisconsin at Madison*; b. 1947; three c. *Education:* Univs of Wisconsin, Montana and Minnesota. *Career:* has taught at Oneida and Rosebud Native American reservations, Univ. of Wisconsin at Eau Claire, and Poet-in-the-Schools programmes in Minnesota, Arizona, Oklahoma; currently Assoc. Prof. of English and American Indian Studies, Univ. of Wisconsin at Madison; mem. Oneida Nation of Wisconsin; mem. Advisory Bd Wicazo Sa Review. *Publications:* poetry: Star Quilt 1984, Philadelphia Flowers 1996; contribs to The Southern Review, Northwest Review, American Poetry Review, The Nation. *Honours:* NEA grant, Lila Wallace Reader's Digest Fund Award, Univ. of Wisconsin Chancellor's Award. *Address:* Department of English, University of Wisconsin, 7187 Helen C. White Hall, 600 N Park Street, Madison, WI 53706, USA (office). *E-mail:* rhwhitm@wisc.edu. *Website:* www.wisc.edu/english.

HILL, Susan Elizabeth, BA, FRSL; British writer and playwright; b. 5 Feb. 1942, d. of the late R. H. Hill and Doris Hill; m. Prof. Stanley W. Wells 1975; two d. (and one d. deceased). *Education:* grammar schools in Scarborough and Coventry and King's Coll. London. *Career:* literary critic, various journals 1963–; numerous plays for BBC 1970–; Fellow, King's Coll. London 1978; presenter, Bookshelf, BBC Radio 1986–87; Founder and Publr Long Barn Books 1996–. *Publications:* The Enclosure 1961, Do Me a Favour 1963, Gentleman and Ladies 1969, A Change for the Better 1969, I'm the King of the Castle 1970, The Albatross 1971, Strange Meeting 1971, The Bird of the Night 1972, A Bit of Singing and Dancing 1973, In the Springtime of the Year 1974, The Cold Country and Other Plays for Radio 1975, The Ramshackle Company (play) 1981, The Magic Apple Tree 1982, The Woman in Black 1983 (stage version 1989), One Night at a Time (for children) 1984, Through the Kitchen Window 1984, Through the Garden Gate 1986, Mother's Magic (for children) 1986, The Lighting of the Lamps 1987, Lanterns Across the Snow 1987, Shakespeare Country 1987, The Spirit of the Cotswolds 1988, Can it be True? (for children) 1988, Family (autobiog.) 1989, Susie's Shoes (for children) 1989, Stories from Codling Village (for children) 1990, I've Forgotten Edward (for children) 1990, I Won't Go There Again (for children) 1990, Pirate Poll (for children) 1991, The Glass Angels 1991, Beware! Beware! 1993, King of Kings 1993, Reflections from a Garden (with Rory Stuart) 1995, Contemporary Women's Short Stories 1995 (Ed., with Rory Stuart), Listening to the Orchestra (short stories) 1996, The Second Penguin Book of Women's Short Stories 1997, The Service of Clouds 1998, The Boy Who Taught the Beekeeper to Read and Other Stories 2003, The Various Haunts of Men 2004, The Pure in Heart 2005, The Risk of Darkness 2006. *Address:* Longmoor Farmhouse, Ebrington, Chipping Campden, Glos., GL55 6NW, England. *Telephone:* (1386) 593352. *Fax:* (1386) 593443.

HILL, Tobias, BA; British writer, poet, editor and music critic; b. 30 March 1970, London, England. *Education:* Sussex Univ. *Career:* teacher, Apex School, Anjo, Aichi, Japan 1993–94; music critic, Telegraph on Sunday 1994–; Poetry Ed., Richmond Review 1995–96; Books Ed., Don't Tell It magazine 1995–96. *Publications:* Year of the Dog (poems) 1995, Midnight in the City (poems) 1996, Skin (short stories) 1997, Zoo (poems) 1998, Underground (novel) 1999, The Love of Stones (novel) 2002, The Cryptographer (novel) 2003, Nocturne in Chrome & Sunset Yellow 2006; contrib. to Observer, Times,

Telegraph. *Honours:* Poetry Book Society Recommendation 1996, University of Cambridge Harper-Wood Studentship for Literature 1996, Eric Gregory Award, National Poetry Foundation 1996, PEN-Macmillan Award for Fiction 1997, Ian St James Award 1997. *Address:* c/o Salt Publishing Ltd, PO Box 937, Great Wilbraham, Cambridge, CB1 5JX, England.

HILLERMAN, Tony, BA, MA; American academic and writer; b. 27 May 1925; m. Mary Unzner 1948; three s. three d. *Education:* Oklahoma State Univ., Univ. of Oklahoma, Univ. of New Mexico. *Career:* reporter, Borger News Herald, TX 1948; City Ed., Morning Press-Constitution, Lawton, OK 1948–50; political reporter, Oklahoma City 1950–52, Bureau Man., Santa Fe 1952–54, United Press International; political reporter and Exec. Ed., New Mexican, Santa Fe 1954–63; Assoc. Prof. 1965–66, Prof. of Journalism 1966–85, Prof. Emeritus 1985–, Univ. of New Mexico. *Publications:* fiction: The Blessing Way 1970, The Fly on the Wall 1971, Dance Hall of the Dead 1973, Listening Woman 1977, The People of Darkness 1978, The Dark Wind 1981, Ghostway 1984, A Thief of Time 1985, Skinwalkers 1986, The Joe Leaphorn Mysteries (collection) 1989, Talking God 1989, Coyote Waits 1990, Best of the West: An Anthology of Classic Writing from the American West (ed.) 1991, The Jim Chee Mysteries (collection) 1992, Sacred Clowns 1993, Finding Moon 1994, The Fallen Man 1996, The First Eagle 1998, Hunting Badger 1999, The Wailing Wind 2002, The Shape Shifter 2006; non-fiction: The Spell of New Mexico (ed.) 1984, Indian Country: America's Sacred Land 1987, Hillerman Country: A Journey Through the Southwest with Tony Hillerman 1991, Talking Mysteries: A Conversation with Tony Hillerman (with Ernie Bulow) 1991, New Mexico, Rio Grande and Other Essays 1992, Seldom Disappointed: A Memoir 2001; contrib. to The Oxford Book of the American Detective Story 1996, The Best American Mystery Stories of the Century 2000, and to magazines. *Honours:* MWA Edgar Allan Poe Award 1974. *Address:* c/o HarperCollins Publishers, 10 East 53rd Street, New York, NY 10022, USA. *Website:* tonyhillermanbooks.com.

HILLES, Robert Edward, BA, MSc; Canadian poet, writer and academic; b. 13 Nov. 1951, Kenora, ON; m. Rebecca Susan Knight 1980; two c. *Education:* University of Calgary. *Career:* Prof. of Computer Programming, 1983–, Senior Prof., 1994–, DeVry Institute of Technology, Calgary, AB; mem. League of Canadian Poets; Writers' Union of Canada; Writers' Guild of Alberta. *Publications:* Look the Lovely Animal Speaks, 1980; The Surprise Element, 1982; An Angel in the Works, 1983; Outlasting the Landscape, 1989; Finding the Lights On, 1991; A Breath at a Time, 1992; Cantos From a Small Room, 1993; Raising of Voices, 1993; Near Morning, 1995; Kissing the Smoke, 1996; Nothing Vanishes, 1996; Breathing Distance, 1997. Contributions: anthologies and periodicals. *Honours:* Gov.-Gen.'s Literary Award for Poetry, 1994; Best Novel Award, Writers' Guild of Alberta, 1994. *Address:* Booming Ground, UBC Creative Writing, Buch E-462, 1866 Main Mall, Vancouver, BC V6T 1Z1, Canada.

HILLIER, Bevis, FRSA; British writer and editor; b. 28 March 1940, s. of the late Jack Ronald Hillier and of Mary Louise Palmer. *Education:* Reigate Grammar School and Magdalen Coll., Oxford. *Career:* Editorial Staff, The Times 1963–68, Antiques Corresp. 1970–84, Deputy Literary Ed. 1981–84; Ed. British Museum Soc. Bulletin 1968–70; Guest Curator, Minn. Inst. of Arts 1971; Ed. The Connoisseur 1973–76; Assoc. Ed., Los Angeles Times 1984–88; Ed. Sotheby's Preview 1990–93. *Publications:* Master Potters of the Industrial Revolution: The Turners of Lane End 1965, Pottery and Porcelain 1700–1914 1968, Art Deco of the 1920s and the 1930s 1968, Posters 1969, Cartoons and Caricatures 1970, The World of Art Deco 1971, 100 Years of Posters 1972, Austerity-Binge 1975, The New Antiques 1977, Greetings from Christmas Past 1982, The Style of the Century 1900–1980 1983, John Betjeman: A Life in Pictures 1984, Young Betjeman 1988, Early English Porcelain 1992, Art Deco Style, A Tonic to the Nation: The Festival of Britain (co-ed.) 1951 1976, Betjeman: The Bonus of Laughter 2004. *Literary Agent:* The Maggie Noach Literary Agency, 21 Redan Street, London, W14 0AB, England.

HILLIS, Rick, BEd, MFA; Canadian writer, poet and teacher; b. 3 Feb. 1956, Nipawin, SK; m. Patricia Appelgren 1988, one s. one d. *Education:* University of Victoria, University of Saskatchewan, Concordia University, University of Iowa, Stanford University. *Career:* Stegner Fellow, 1988–90, Jones Lecturer, 1990–92, Stanford University; Lecturer, California State University at Hayward, 1990; Chesterfield Film Writer's Fellowship, 1991–92; Visiting Asst Prof. of English, Reed College, 1992–96. *Publications:* The Blue Machines of Night (poems), 1988; Coming Attractions (co-author), 1988; Canadian Brash (co-author), 1990; Limbo Stories, 1990. Contributions: anthologies and periodicals. *Honours:* Canada Council grants 1985, 1987, 1989; Drue Heinz Literature Prize, 1990.

HILSUM, Lindsey, BA; British journalist; *International Editor, Channel Four News (UK);* b. 3 Aug. 1958, d. of Cyril Hilsum and Betty Hilsum. *Education:* Univ. of Exeter. *Career:* joined Oxfam working in Guatemala and Haiti 1979; began journalism career freelance reporting from Mexico and the Caribbean 1980; worked for three years as Information Officer for UNICEF, Nairobi; covered events in E Africa for BBC and The Guardian newspaper 1986–89; Sr Producer BBC World Service 1990–93, reported from Rwanda, Middle East, Mexico, S Africa, S Pacific; Diplomatic Corresp. Channel Four News 1996–, currently also Int. Ed.; regular contrib. to New Statesman, Granta, Observer, Times Literary Supplement. *Honours:* Amnesty Int. Press Award 1997, TV News Award 2004, Royal Television Soc. Specialist Journalist of the Year 2003, Emmy Award for coverage of fall of Saddam Hussein (jtly)

2004, Royal Television Soc. TV Journalist of the Year Award 2005, James Cameron Award 2005, Women in Film and Television Award 2005. *Address:* Channel Four News, ITN, 200 Grays Inn Road, London, WC1X 8XZ, England (office). *Fax:* (20) 7430-4667 (office). *E-mail:* news@channel4.com (office). *Website:* www.channel4.com/news (office).

HILTON, Suzanne McLean, BA; American writer; b. 3 Sept. 1922, Pittsburgh, PA; m. Warren Mitchell Hilton 1946, one s. one d. *Education:* Beaver Coll. (now Arcadia Univ.). *Career:* Ed., Bulletin of Old York Road Historical Society, 1976–92, Bulletin of Historical Society of Montgomery County, 1987–89; Assoc. Ed., Montgomery County History, 1983; now retd; mem. Society of Children's Book Writers and Illustrators; Philadelphia Children's Reading Round Table. *Publications:* How Do They Get Rid of It?, 1970; How Do They Cope with It?, 1970; Beat It, Burn It and Drown It, 1974; Who Do You Think You Are?, 1976; Yesterday's People, 1976; Here Today and Gone Tomorrow, 1978; Faster than a Horse: Moving West with Engine Power, 1983; Montgomery County: The Second Hundred Years, 1983; The World of Young Tom Jefferson, 1986; The World of Young George Washington, 1986; The World of Young Herbert Hoover, 1987; The World of Young Andrew Jackson, 1988; A Capital Capitol City, 1991; Miners, Merchants and Maids, 1995. Contributions: Historical journals. *Honours:* Legion of Honour, Chapel of the Four Chaplains, 1978; Award for Excellence in Non-Fiction, Drexel University, 1979; Golden Spur, Western Writers of America, 1980; Gold Disc, Beaver College (now Arcadia Univ.) 1981. *Address:* 3320 108th Street NW, Gig Harbour, WA 98332, USA.

HILTON, Tessa; British newspaper editor; b. 18 Feb. 1951, d. of Michael Hilton and Phyllis Hilton; m. Graham Ball 1976; two s. one d. *Education:* St Mary's School, Gerrards Cross. *Career:* journalist, Sunday Mirror 1970–78, Ed. 1994; freelance writer 1978–85; Ed. Mother magazine 1985–87; Exec. Today 1987–91; Ed. Femail, Daily Mail 1991–94; Asst Ed. Sun 1994; Deputy Ed. Express then Ed. Express on Sunday magazine 1996–99; Ed.-at-Large Woman & Home; mem. judging panel, Penguin/Orange Reading Group Prize 2003, UKPG Award for Regional Newspaper of the Year and Free Newspaper of the Year 2004. *Publication:* The Great Ormond Street Book of Child Health 1990, The Great Ormond Street New Baby And Child Care Book: The Essential Guide for Parents of Children Aged 0–5 (co-author) 1997. *Address:* c/o IPC Media Limited, King's Reach Tower, Stamford Street, London, SE1 9LS, England.

HIMMELFARB, Gertrude, PhD, FBA, FRHistS; American historian, academic and writer; *Professor Emerita, City University of New York;* b. 8 Aug. 1922, New York, NY; d. of Max Himmelfarb and Bertha (Lerner) Himmelfarb; m. Irving Kristol 1942; one s. one d. *Education:* Brooklyn Coll., CUNY, Univ. of Chicago, Girton Coll., Cambridge. *Career:* Distinguished Prof. of History, Graduate School, City Univ. New York 1965–88, Prof. Emer. 1988–; Fellow, American Philosophical Soc., American Acad. of Arts and Sciences, Royal Historical Soc., etc.; many public and professional appts.; Guggenheim Fellow 1955–56, 1957–58; Nat. Endowment for the Humanities Fellowship 1968–69, American Council of Learned Socs. Fellowship 1972–73, Woodrow Wilson Int. Center Fellowship 1976–77, Rockefeller Foundation, Humanities Fellowship 1980–81, and other fellowships. *Publications:* Lord Acton: A Study in Conscience and Politics 1952, Darwin and the Darwinian Revolution 1959, Victorian Minds 1968, On Liberty and Liberalism: The Case of John Stuart Mill 1975, The Idea of Poverty 1984, Marriage and Morals Among the Victorians 1986, The New History and the Old 1987, Poverty and Compassion: The Moral Imagination of the Late Victorians 1991, On Looking Into the Abyss: Untimely Thoughts on Culture and Society 1994, The De-Moralization of Society From Victorian Virtues to Modern Values 1995, One Nation, Two Cultures 1999, The Road to Modernity: The British, French and American Enlightenments 2004. *Honours:* numerous hon. degrees including Hon. DHumLitt (Boston) 1987, (Yale) 1990; Hon. DLitt (Smith Coll.) 1977; Rockefeller Foundation Award 1962–63. *Address:* 2510 Virginia Avenue, NW, Washington, DC 20637, USA.

HINDE, Thomas (see Chitty, Sir Thomas Wiles)

HINE, (William) Daryl; Canadian/American poet, writer and translator; b. 24 Feb. 1936, Burnaby, BC, Canada. *Education:* McGill University, 1954–58; MA, 1965, PhD, 1967, University of Chicago. *Career:* Asst Prof. of English, University of Chicago, 1967–69; Ed., Poetry magazine, Chicago, 1968–78. *Publications:* Poetry: Five Poems 1954; The Carnal and the Crane, 1957; The Devil's Picture Book, 1960; Heroics, 1961; The Wooden Horse, 1965; Minutes, 1968; Resident Alien, 1975; In and Out: A Confessional Poem, 1975; Daylight Saving, 1978; Selected Poems, 1980; Academic Festival Overtures, 1985; Arrondissements, 1988; Postscripts, 1992. Novel: The Prince of Darkness and Co, 1961. Other: Polish Subtitles: Impressions from a Journey, 1962; The 'Poetry' Anthology 1912–1977 (ed. with Joseph Parisi), 1978. Translator: The Homeric Hymns and the Battle of the Frogs and the Mice, 1972; Theocritus: Idylls and Epigrams, 1982; Ovid's Heroines: A Verse Translation of the Heroides, 1991; Hesiod's Works, 2000; Puerilities from the Greek Anthology, 2001. *Honours:* Canada Foundation-Rockefeller Fellowship, 1958; Canada Council Grants, 1959, 1979; Ingram Merrill Foundation Grants, 1962, 1963, 1983; Guggenheim Fellowship, 1980; American Acad. of Arts and Letters Award, 1982; John D. and Catherine T. MacArthur Foundation Fellowship, 1986, Harold Morton Landon Translation Award 2005. *Address:* 2740 Ridge Avenue, Evanston, IL 60201, USA.

HINES, Donald Merrill, BS, MAT, PhD; American writer and teacher; b. 23 Jan. 1931, St Paul, MN; m. Linda Marie Arnold 1961, three s. *Education:* Lewis and Clark Coll., Portland, OR, Reed Coll., Portland, OR, Indiana Univ. *Career:* faculty, Washington State University, 1968–77, King Saud University, Abha, Saudi Arabia, 1982–90, Blue Mountain Community College, Pendleton, Oregon, 1990–91; mem. American Folklore Society. *Publications:* Cultural History of the Inland Pacific Northwest Frontier, 1976; Tales of the Okanogans, 1976; Tales of the Nez Perce, 1984; The Forgotten Tribes: Oral Tales of the Tenino and Adjacent Mid-Columbia River Indian Nations, 1991; Ghost Voices: Yakima Indian Myths, Legends, Humor and Hunting Stories, 1992; Celilo Tales: Wasco Myths, Legends, Tales of Magic and the Marvelous, 1996. Contributions: journals. *Honours:* Ford Foundation Fellowship, 1965; Third Prize, Chicago Folklore Contest, University of Chicago, 1970.

HINOJOSA-SMITH, Rolando; American writer and academic; *Garwood Professor, University of Texas at Austin*; b. 21 Jan. 1929, Mercedes, TX, USA; one s. two d. *Education:* BS, University of Texas at Austin, 1953; MA, New Mexico Highlands University, Las Vegas, 1963; PhD, University of Illinois, 1969. *Career:* Asst Prof., Trinity University, San Antonio, 1968–70; Assoc. Prof., 1970–74, Dean, College of Arts and Sciences, 1974–76, Vice-Pres. for Academic Affairs, 1976–77, Texas A and I University, Kingsville; Chair, Dept of Chicano Studies, 1977–80, Prof., 1980–81, University of Minnesota; Prof., University of Texas at Austin 1981–, Garwood Prof. 1985–; mem. MLA; PEN; Salado Institute. *Publications:* Estampas del valle y otras obras, 1972, English trans as Sketches of the Valley and Other Works, 1980, The Valley, 1983; Klail City y sus alrededores, 1976, English trans. as Klail City, 1987; Korean Love Songs from Klail City Death Trip, 1978; Claros varones de Belken, 1981, English trans. as Fair Gentlemen of Belken County, 1987; Mi querido Rafa, 1981, English trans. as Dear Rafe, 1985; Rites and Witnesses, 1982; Partners in Crime, 1985; Los amigos de Becky, 1990, English trans. as Becky and Her Friends, 1990; The Useless Servants, 1993; Ask a Policeman, 1998. Contributions: anthologies, reviews, journals, and periodicals. *Honours:* Quinto Sol Literary Award for Best Novel, 1972; Casa de las Américas Award for Best Novel, 1976; Southwest Studies on Latin America Award for Best Writing in the Humanities, 1981; University of Illinois College of Liberal Arts Award, 1987, and Alumni Achievement Award, 1998; Lon C. Tinkle Award, Texas Institute of Letters, 1998. *Address:* c/o Dept of English, PAR 108, University of Texas at Austin, Austin, TX 78712 (office); 3111 Parker Lane #178, Austin, TX 78741, USA (home). *Telephone:* (512) 471-4991 (office); (512) 445-7379 (home). *Fax:* (512) 471-4909. *E-mail:* rorro@mail.utexas.edu (office).

HINSON, Edward Glenn; American academic and writer; b. 27 July 1931, St Louis, MO; m. Martha Anne Burks 1956; one s. one d. *Education:* BA, Washington University, St Louis, 1954; BD, 1957, ThD, 1962, Southern Baptist Theological Seminary, Louisville; DPhil, University of Oxford, 1973. *Career:* Prof., Southern Baptist Theological Seminary, 1959–92, Wake Forest University, 1982–84; Visiting Prof., St John's University, Collegeville, Minnesota, 1983, Catholic University of America, 1987, University of Notre Dame, 1989; Prof. of Spirituality and John F. Loftis Prof. of Church History, Baptist Theological Seminary, Richmond, Virginia, 1992–; mem. American Society of Church History; Asscn Internationale des Patristique; International Thomas Merton Society; National Asscn of Baptist Profs of Religion, pres., 1993–94; North American Patristics Society; Societas Liturgica. *Publications:* The Church: Design for Survival, 1967; Seekers after Mature Faith, 1968; A Serious Call to a Contemplative Life-Style, 1974; Soul Liberty, 1975; The Early Church Fathers, 1978; The Reaffirmation of Prayer, 1979; A History of Baptists in Arkansas, 1980; The Evangelization of the Roman Empire, 1981; Are Southern Baptists Evangelicals?, 1983; Religious Liberty, 1991; Spirituality in Ecumenical Perspective, 1993; The Church Triumphant: A History of Christianity up to 1300, 1995; The Early Church, 1996; Love at the Heart of Things: A Biography of Douglas V. Steere, 1998. Contributions: Festschriften, reference works, and journals. *Honours:* American Asscn of Theological Schools Fellowship, 1966–67; Prof. of the Year, Southern Baptist Theological Fellowship, 1975–76; Johannes Quasten Medal, Catholic University of America; Cuthbert Allen Award, Ecumenical Institute of Belmont Abbey/Wake Forest University, 1992. *Address:* 3400 Brook Road, Richmond, VA 23227, USA.

HINTON, Peter; Canadian playwright and director; *Artistic Director, National Arts Centre English Theatre*. *Career:* has held numerous posts in Canadian theatre, including Assoc. Artistic Dir Theatre Passe Muraille and Canadian Stage Co., Toronto, Artistic Dir Playwrights Theatre Centre, Vancouver, Dramaturg-in-Residence Playwrights' Workshop, Montréal, Artistic Assoc. Stratford Festival; Artistic Dir Nat. Arts Centre English Theatre 2005–; has taught at Ryerson Theatre School and Nat. Theatre School of Canada. *Plays:* Façade, Urban Voodoo (with Jim Millan), The Swanne trilogy: George III: The Death of Cupid 2002, Princess Charlotte: The Acts of Venus 2003, Queen Victoria: The Seduction of Nemesis 2004. *Libretti:* (with Peter Hannan): The Diana Cantata, 120 Songs for the Marquis de Sade (Alcan Performing Arts Award 2002). *Plays directed include:* Scary Stories by Gordon Armstrong (Jessie Richardson Award for Directing 1995), Hush and the Crimson Veil by Allen Cole, Serpent Kills by Blake Brooker, Possible Worlds by John Mighton, Geometry in Venice by Michael McKenzie, Burning Vision by Marie Clements, Frida K by Gloria Montero, Girls! Girls! Girls! by Greg MacArthur. *Publications:* essays in Theatrum, The Canadian Theatre Review, Between the Lines: a collection of interviews and articles on Dramaturgy in Canada. *E-mail:* phinton@nac-cna.ca (office). *Website:* www.nac-cna.ca/en/theatre/ (office).

HINTON, Susan Eloise (S. E.); American writer; b. 1948, Tulsa, OK; m. David Inhofe 1970; one s. *Career:* writer of teenage fiction and films. *Film appearances:* Tex. 1982, The Outsiders 1983. *Screenplay:* Rumble Fish (jtly). *Publications:* The Outsiders (Chicago Tribune Book, World Spring Festival Honour Book 1967, Media and Methods Maxi Award 1975, Massachusetts Children's Book Award 1979) 1967, That Was Then, This is Now (Chicago Tribune Book, World Spring Festival Honour Book 1971, Massachusetts Children's Book Award 1978) 1971, Rumble Fish (Land of Enchantment Award New Mexico Library Asscn 1982) 1975, Tex. (Sue Hefly Award 1983) 1979, Taming the Star Runner 1988, Big David, Little David 1994, The Puppy Sister 1997, Hawkes Harbor 2005, Some of Tim's Stories 2007. *Honours:* Golden Archer Award 1983, Author Award American Library Asscn Young Adult Services Div/School Library Journal 1988. *Address:* Press Relations, Delacorte Press, 1540 Broadway Suite Bd, New York, NY 10036, USA (office).

HIPPOLYTE, Kendel; Saint Lucia poet; b. 1952, Castries; m. Jane King. *Career:* co-founder Lighthouse Theatre Co. 1984; fmr research and publs officer, Folk Research Centre; taught at St Mary's Coll. and Sir Arthur Lewis Community Coll. *Publications:* poetry: Island in the Sun, Side Two... 1980, Bearings 1986, The Labyrinth 1991, Night Vision 2006; contrib. poems to anthologies, including The Penguin Book of Caribbean Verse in English 1986, The Heinemann Book of Caribbean Poetry 1992, Wheel and Come Again 1998, Crossing Water 1999; editor: A Collection of Essays by St Lucian Writers (co-ed.) 1980, Nine St Lucian Poets (ed.) 1988. *Address:* c/o Peepal Tree Press, 17 King's Avenue, Leeds, LS6 1QS, England.

HIRANO, Keiichiro; Japanese writer; b. 22 June 1975, Kamagori, Aichi Pref. *Education:* studied law, Kyoto Univ. *Publications:* novels: Nisshoku (Eclipse) (Akutagawa Prize 1999) 1998, Ichigetsu Monogatari (A One Month Story) 1999, Soso (The Funeral) 2002; short stories: Takasegawa 2003, Shitatariochiru tokei-tachi no hamon (The Ripples of Dripping Clocks) 2005. *E-mail:* web@k-hirano.com. *Website:* www.k-hirano.com.

HIRSCH, Edward Mark, BA, PhD; American poet and writer; *President, Guggenheim Foundation*; b. 20 Jan. 1950, Chicago, IL; m. Janet Landay 1977; one s. *Education:* Grinnell College, University of Pennsylvania. *Career:* teacher, Poetry in the Schools Program, New York and Pennsylvania, 1976–78; Asst Prof., 1978–82, Assoc. Prof. of English, 1982–85, Wayne State University; Assoc. Prof., 1985–88, Prof. of English, 1988–2002, University of Houston; Pres. Guggenheim Foundation 2002–; mem. Authors' Guild; MLA; PEN; Poetry Society of America; Texas Institute of Letters. *Publications:* For the Sleepwalkers, 1981; Wild Gratitude, 1986; The Night Parade, 1989; Earthly Measures, 1994; Transforming Vision (ed.), 1994; On Love, 1998; How to Read a Poem and Fall in Love with Poetry, 1999; Responsive Reading, 1999, Lay Back in Darkness 2003; contrib. to many anthologies, books, journals and periodicals. *Honours:* Awards, 1975–77, Peter I B. Lavan Younger Poets Award, 1983, Acad. of American Poets; Ingram Merrill Foundation Award, 1978; ACLS Fellow, 1981; National Endowment for the Arts Fellowship, 1982; Delmore Schwartz Memorial Poetry Award, New York University, 1985; Guggenheim Fellowship, 1986–87; Texas Institute of Letters Award in Poetry, 1987; National Book Critics Circle Award, 1987; Rome Prize, American Acad. and Institute of Arts and Letters, 1988; Robert and Hazel Ferguson Memorial Award for Poetry, Friends of Chicago Literature, 1990; Lila Wallace-Reader's Digest Writing Fellow, 1993; Woodrow Wilson Fellow, 1994, 1995; Lyndhurst Prize, 1994–96, MacArthur Fellowships 1998–2002. *Address:* 315 W 98th Street, Apt 5B, New York, NY 10025-5556, USA. *Telephone:* (212) 687-4470 (office). *E-mail:* eh@gf.org (office).

HIRSCHMAN, Jack, BA, AM, PhD; American poet and translator; b. 13 Dec. 1933, New York, NY; m. Ruth Epstein 1954; one s. one d. *Education:* City Coll. CUNY, Indiana Univ. *Career:* editorial team of journal Left Curve 1983–, correspondent for The People's Tribune. *Publications:* poetry: Fragments, 1952; A Correspondence of Americans, 1960; Two, 1963; Interchange, 1964; Kline Sky, 1965; YOD, 1966; London Seen Directly, 1967; Wasn't Like This in the Woodcut, 1967; William Blake, 1967; A Word in Your Season (with Asa Benveniste), 1967; Ltd Interchangeable in Eternity: Poems of Jackruthdavidcelia Hirschman, 1967; Jerusalem, 1968; Aleph, Benoni and Zaddik, 1968; Jerusalem Ltd, 1968; Shekinah, 1969; Broadside Golem, 1969; Black Alephs: Poems 1960–68, 1969; NHR, 1970; Scintilla, 1970; Soledeth, 1971; DT, 1971; The Burning of Los Angeles, 1971; HNYC, 1971; Les Vidanges, 1972; The R of the Ari's Raziel, 1972; Adamnan, 1972; K'wai Sing: The Origin of the Dragon, 1973; Cantillations, 1973; Aur Sea, 1974; Djackson, 1974; Cockroach Street, 1975; The Cool Boyetz Cycle, 1975; Kashtaniyah Segodnyah, 1976; Lyripol, 1976; The Arcanes of Le Comte de St Germain, 1977; The Proletarian Arcane, 1978; The Jonestown Arcane, 1979; The Caliostro Arcane, 1981; The David Arcane, 1982; Class Questions, 1982; Kallatumba, 1984; The Necessary Is, 1984; The Bottom Line, 1988; Sunsong, 1988; The Tirana Arcane, 1991; The Satin Arcane, 1991; Endless Threshold, 1992; The Back of a Spoon, 1992; The Heartbeat Arcane, 1993; The Xibalba Arcane, 1994, The Arcane on a Stick 1995, The Graffiti Arcane 1995, Culture and Struggle 1995, The Green Chakra Arcane 1996, L'Arcano di Pasolini 1996, L'Arcano di Shupsl 1996, 36 1996, The Grit Arcane 1997, The Open Gate 1998, I Knew I Had a Brother 1999, The Archaic Now Arcane 2000, In the Crazy Hotel of My Last 2000, The Murder of Giordano Bruno 2001, The Lotus Bikini Arcane 2002, Front Lines 2002, Fists on Fire 2003, I Was Born Murdered 2004, Arcanes 2004, Wanted

You to Know It 2004. Editor: Hip Pocket Poems 1960–01, Artaud Anthology, 1965, Amerus Anthology 1978, Frammis 1979, Would You Wear My Eyes: A Tribute to Bob Kaufman, 1989, Partisans 1995, 500,000 Azaleas: The Selected Poems of Efrain Huerta 2001, Open Gate: An Anthology of Haitian Creole Poetry 2001, Art on the Line 2002. Translator: over 50 vols, 1970–2004. *Address:* PO Box 26517, San Francisco, CA 94126; 354 Columbus Avenue # 454, San Francisco, CA 94133, USA (home). *Telephone:* (415) 421-6776 (home). *E-mail:* aggiefalk@hotmail.com (home).

HIRSHFIELD, Jane, AB; American poet, writer, editor and lecturer; b. 24 Feb. 1953, New York, NY. *Education:* Princeton Univ. *Career:* California Poet in the Schools 1980–85; faculty, various writers' conferences 1984–; Artist-in-Residence, Djerassi Foundation 1987–90; Lecturer, Univ. of San Francisco 1991–; Visiting Poet-in-Residence, Univ. of Alaska, Fairbanks 1993; Adjunct Prof., Northern Michigan Univ. 1994; Assoc. Faculty, Bennington Coll. 1995; Visiting Assoc. Prof., Univ. of California at Berkeley 1995; Core Faculty, Bennington Coll., MFA Writing Seminars 1999–; Elliston Visiting Poet, Univ. of Cincinnati 2000; Fellow Lindisfarne Asscn 1995–; mem. Associated Writing Programs, Authors' Guild, Djerassi Resident Artist Program (bd mem. 1996–), PEN American Center. *Publications:* Alaya (poems) 1982, Of Gravity and Angels (poems) 1988, The Ink Dark Moon: Poems by Ono no Komachi and Izumi Shikibu (trans. with Aratani) 1988, The October Palace (poems) 1994, Women in Praise of the Sacred: 43 Centuries of Spiritual Poetry by Women (ed.) 1994, The Lives of the Heart (poems) 1997, Nine Gates: Entering the Mind of Poetry (essays) 1997, Given Sugar, Given Salt (poems) 2001, Mirabai: Ecstatic Poems (trans. with Bly) 2004, After (poems) 2006; contrib. to many anthologies, journals and reviews. *Honours:* Yaddo Fellowships 1983, 1985, 1987, 1989, 1992, 1996, 2002, Guggenheim Fellowship 1985, San Francisco Foundation Joseph Henry Jackson Award 1986, Columbia Univ. Trans. Center Award 1987, Poetry Soc. of America Awards 1987, 1988, Pushcart Prize 1988, Commonwealth Club of California Poetry Medals 1988, 1994, Dewar's Young Artists Recognition Award in Poetry 1990, MacDowell Colony Fellowship 1994, Bay Area Book Reviewers Awards 1994, 2001, Poetry Center Book Award 1995, Rockefeller Foundation Fellowship at Bellagio Study Center, Italy 1995. *Literary Agent:* Steven Barclay Agency, 12 Western Avenue, Petaluma, CA 94952, USA. *Telephone:* (707) 773-0654. *Fax:* (707) 778-1868. *Website:* www.barclayagency.com. *Address:* c/o Michael Katz, 367 Molino Avenue, Mill Valley, CA 94941, USA.

HIRSI ALI, Ayaan; Dutch/Somali politician; b. 13 Nov. 1967, Mogadishu. *Education:* Univ. of Leiden. *Career:* emigrated from Somalia to Netherlands 1992; trans. 1995–2001; staff mem. Wiardi Beckman Stichting 2001–02; mem. Partij van de Arbeid (PvdA) (Labour Party) 2001–02, Volkspartij voor Vrijheid en Democratie (VVD) (People's Party for Freedom and Democracy) 2002–; MP 2003–; mem. Parl. Comms for Children and Welfare, Foreign Affairs and Devt, Integration, and Internal Affairs 2003–. *Publications:* De Zoontjesfabriek (The Son Factory) 2002, The Caged Virgin (essays) 2006, Infidel (autobiog.) 2007. *Address:* c/o VVD Algemeen Secretariat, Postbus 30836, 2500 GV The Hague, The Netherlands (office). *E-mail:* A.HirsiAli@tk.parlement.nl.

HISLOP, Ian David, BA; British editor, writer and broadcaster; *Editor, Private Eye magazine;* b. 13 July 1960, s. of the late David Atholl Hislop and of Helen Hislop; m. Victoria Hamson 1988; one s. one d. *Education:* Ardingly Coll. and Magdalen Coll., Oxford. *Career:* joined Private Eye (satirical magazine) 1981, Deputy Ed. 1985–86, Ed. 1986–; Columnist The Listener magazine 1985–89, The Sunday Telegraph 1996–; TV critic The Spectator magazine 1994–96. *Radio:* The News Quiz (BBC Radio 4) 1985–90, Fourth Column 1992–95, Lent Talk 1994, Gush (scriptwriter, with Nick Newman) 1994, Words on Words 1999, The Hislop Vote 2000, A Revolution in 5 Acts 2001, The Patron Saints 2002, A Brief History of Tax (BBC Radio 4) 2003, The Choir Invisible (BBC Radio 4) 2003, Blue Birds over the White Cliffs of Dover (BBC Radio 4) 2004, Are We Being Offensive Enough (BBC Radio 4) 2004. *TV scriptwriting:* Spitting Image 1984–89, The Stone Age (with Nick Newman) 1989, Briefcase Encounter 1990, The Case of the Missing 1991, He Died a Death 1991, Harry Enfield's Television Programme 1990–92, Harry Enfield and Chums 1994–97, Mangez Merveillac 1994, Dead on Time 1995, Gobble 1996, Sermon from St. Albion's, Granada 1998, Confessions of a Murderer 1999, My Dad is the Prime Minister 2003. *TV performer:* Have I Got News for You (BBC) 1990–. *TV presenter:* Canterbury Tales, Channel 4 1996, School Rules, Channel 4 1997, Pennies from Bevan, Channel 4 1998, Great Railway Journeys (BBC) 1999, Who Do You Think You Are? (BBC 2) 2004, Not Forgotten (Channel 4) 2005. *Publications:* various Private Eye collections 1985–, contribs to newspapers and magazines on books, current affairs, arts and entertainment. *Honours:* BAFTA Award for Have I Got News for You 1991, Editors' Editor, British Soc. of Magazine Eds 1991, Magazine of the Year, What the Papers Say 1991, Editor of the Year, British Soc. of Magazine Eds 1998, Award for Political Satire, Channel 4 Political Awards 2004. *Address:* Private Eye, 6 Carlisle Street, London, W1V 5RG, England (office). *Telephone:* (20) 7437-4017 (office). *Website:* www.private-eye.co.uk (office).

HITCHCOCK, Hugh Wiley, BA, MMus, PhD; American musicologist, writer and editor; b. 28 Sept. 1923, Detroit, MI. *Education:* Dartmouth Coll., Univ. of Michigan. *Career:* faculty mem. Univ. of Michigan 1947–61; Prof. of Music, Hunter Coll., CUNY 1961–71; Ed., Prentice-Hall History of Music Series 1965–, Earlier American Music 1972–98, Recent Researches in American Music 1976–94; mem. Exec. Cttee and Area Ed. for the Americas, The New Grove Dictionary of Music and Musicians 1980; Co-Ed. The New Grove Dictionary of American Music 1986; Prof. of Music, Brooklyn Coll., CUNY

1971–80, Distinguished Prof. of Music 1980–93, Founder-Dir Inst. for Studies in American Music 1971–93; J. Paul Getty Center for Art History and the Humanities Scholar 1985–86; mem. American Musicological Soc. (Pres. 1991–92, Hon. mem. 1994–), Charles Ives Soc. (Pres. 1973–93), Music Library Asscn (Pres. 1966–68). *Publications:* Music in the United States: A Historical Introduction 1969, Charles Ives Centennial Festival-Conference 1974, Ives 1977, An Ives Celebration: Papers and Panels of the Charles Ives Centennial Festival-Conference (ed. with Vivian Perlis) 1977, The Phonograph and Our Musical Life 1980, The Music of Ainsworth's Psalter 1612 (with L. Inserra) 1981, The Works of Marc-Antoine Charpentier: Catalogue Raisonné 1982, Ives: A Survey of the Music 1983, Marc-Antoine Charpentier 1990, critical edn of Charles Ives, 129 Songs 2004; contrib. to scholarly books and professional journals. *Honours:* Hon. mem. American Musicological Soc. 1994; Chevalier, Ordre des Arts et Lettres 1995; Fulbright Sr Research Fellowships 1954–55, 1968–69, Guggenheim Fellowship 1968–69, Nat. Endowment for the Humanities grant 1982–83; Inducted into American Classical Music Hall of Fame 1999, Soc. for American Music lifetime achievement award 2003. *Address:* 1192 Park Avenue, No. 10-E, New York, NY 10128, USA (home). *Telephone:* (917) 492-1131 (home). *Fax:* (212) 369-0146 (home). *E-mail:* hwhitchcock@aol.com (home).

HITCHENS, Christopher Eric, BA; British/American journalist and writer; b. 13 April 1949, Portsmouth, England; m. 1st Eleni Meleagrou 1981; one s. one d.; m. 2nd Carol Blue 1991; one d. *Education:* Balliol Coll., Oxford. *Career:* social science correspondent, THES 1971–73; writer and Asst Ed. 1973–81, columnist and Washington correspondent 1982–, New Statesman; columnist, The Nation 1982–2002, Vanity Fair 1982–, also columnist Slate; contributor, London Review of Books 1989–; Mellon Prof. of English, Univ. of Pittsburgh 1997. *Publications:* Karl Marx and the Paris Commune 1971, James Callaghan 1976, Hostage to History: Cyprus From the Ottomans to Kissinger 1984, Imperial Spoils: The Curious Case of the Elgin Marbles 1986, Prepared for the Worst: Selected Essays 1989, Blood, Class and Nostalgia: Anglo-American Ironies 1990, For the Sake of Argument: Selected Essays 1993, When the Borders Bleed: The Struggle of the Kurds 1994, The Missionary Position: Mother Teresa in Theory and Practice 1995, No One Left to Lie to 1999, Letters to a Young Contrarian 2001, Orwell's Victory 2001, Love, Poverty and War: Journeys and Essays 2005, Thomas Paine's Rights of Man: A Biography 2006, God is Not Great: How Religion Poisons Everything 2007. *Address:* c/o Slate, 1800 M Street, NW, Suite 330, Washington, DC 20036, USA. *Telephone:* (202) 261-1310. *E-mail:* dcoffice@slate.com. *Website:* www.slate.com.

HJÖRNE, Lars Goran; Swedish newspaper editor and publisher; b. 20 Oct. 1929, Gothenburg; s. of the late Harry Hjörne; m. Lena Hjörne (née Smith); one s. one d. *Career:* Chief Ed. Göteborgs-Posten 1969–89, Chair. 1969–95, Hon. Chair. 1995–; Hon. British Consul-Gen. in Gothenburg 1991–98. *Honours:* Hon. OBE. *Address:* Polhemsplatsen 5, 405 02 Gothenburg (office); Stora Vägen 43, 260 43 Arild, Sweden (home). *Telephone:* (31) 62-40-00 (office); (42) 34-68-03 (home).

HJÖRNE, Peter Lars; Swedish newspaper editor and publisher; *Editor-in-Chief, Göteborgs-Posten;* b. 7 Sept. 1952, Gothenburg; s. of Lars Hjörne and Anne Gyllenhammar; m. 2nd Karin Linnea Tufvesson Hjörne 1995; five d. *Education:* Göteborgs Högre Samskola and Univ. of Gothenburg. *Career:* Man. Trainee John Deere Co., USA 1978–79; Exec. Asst Göteborgs-Posten 1979–82, Deputy Man. Dir 1983–85, Man. Dir 1985–93, Publisher and Ed.-in-Chief 1993–. *Address:* Göteborgs-Posten, Polhemsplatsen 5, 405 02 Gothenburg, Sweden (office). *Telephone:* 31-62-40-00 (office). *Fax:* 31-15-76-92. *E-mail:* peter.hjorne@gp.se (office). *Website:* www.gp.se (office).

HOAGLAND, Edward, AB; American author; b. 21 Dec. 1932, New York; s. of Warren Eugene Hoagland and Helen Kelley Morley; m. 1st Amy J. Ferrara 1960 (divorced 1964); m. 2nd Marion Magid 1968 (died 1993); one d. *Education:* Harvard Univ. *Career:* faculty mem. New School for Social Research, New York 1963–64, Rutgers Univ. 1966, Sarah Lawrence Coll., Bronxville, New York 1967, 1971, City Univ. 1967, 1968, Univ. of Iowa 1978, 1982, Columbia Univ. 1980, 1981, Brown Univ. 1988, Bennington Coll., Bennington, Vt 1987–2005, Univ. of Calif. at Davis 1990, 1992, Beloit Coll., Wis. 1995; Gen. Ed. Penguin Nature Library 1985–2004; Houghton Mifflin Literary Fellow 1954; American Acad. of Arts and Letters Travelling Fellow 1964; Guggenheim Fellow 1964, 1975; mem. American Acad. of Arts and Letters. *Publications:* Cat Man 1956, The Circle Home 1960, The Peacock's Tail 1965, Notes from the Century Before: A Journal from British Columbia 1969, The Courage of Turtles 1971, Walking the Dead Diamond River 1973, The Moose on the Wall: Field Notes from the Vermont Wilderness 1974, Red Wolves and Black Bears 1976, African Calliope: A Journey to the Sudan 1979, The Edward Hoagland Reader 1979, The Tugman's Passage 1982, City Tales 1986, Seven Rivers West 1986, Heart's Desire 1988, The Final Fate of the Alligators 1992, Balancing Acts 1992, Tigers and Ice 1999, Compass Points 2001, Hoagland on Nature 2003; numerous essays and short stories. *Honours:* Longview Foundation Award 1961, Prix de Rome 1964, O. Henry Award 1971, Brandeis Univ. Citation in Literature 1972, New York State Council on Arts Award 1972, Nat. Book Critics' Circle Award 1980, American Acad. of Arts and Letters Harold D. Vursell Memorial Award 1981, Nat. Endowment for the Arts Award 1982, NY Public Library Literary Lion Award 1988, Nat. Magazine Award 1989, Lannan Foundation Literary Award 1993, Boston Public Library Literary Lights Award 1995. *Address:* PO Box 51, Barton, VT 05822, USA (home).

HOBAN, Russell Conwell, FRSL; American writer; b. 4 Feb. 1925, Lansdale, PA; s. of Abram Hoban and Jenny Hoban (née Dimmerman); m. 1st Lillian Aberman 1944 (divorced 1975, died 1998); one s. three d.; m. 2nd Gundula Ahl 1975; three s. *Education:* Lansdale High School and Philadelphia Museum School of Industrial Art. *Career:* served US Infantry, Italy 1943–45; gen. illustrator Wexton co., New York 1950–51; TV Art Dir Batten, Barton, Durstine & Osborne (BBDO) Advertising, New York 1951–56; freelance illustrator 1956–65; copywriter, Doyle Dane Bernbach, New York 1965–67; novelist and author of children's books 1967–; mem. PEN, Soc. of Authors. *Writing for theatre:* The Carrier Frequency (Impact Theatre Co-operative) 1984, Riddley Walker (Manchester Royal Exchange Theatre Co.) 1986, The Second Mrs Kong (opera libretto, premiere Glyndebourne) 1994. *Radio play:* Perfect and Endless Circles 1995. *Publications:* adult fiction: The Lion of Boaz-Jachin and Jachin-Boaz 1973, Kleinzeit 1974, Turtle Diary 1975, Riddley Walker (John W. Campbell Memorial Award and Australian Science Fiction Achievement Award 1983) 1980, Pilgermann 1983, The Medusa Frequency 1987, Angelica's Grotto 1991, The Moment under the Moment (stories, essays and libretto) 1992, Fremder 1996, The Trokeville Way 1996, Mr Rinyo-Clacton's Offer 1998, Amaryllis Night and Day 2001, The Bat Tattoo 2002, Her Name Was Lola 2003, Come Dance with Me 2005, Linger Awhile 2006; juvenile fiction includes: Bedtime for Frances 1960, Baby Sister for Frances 1964, The Mouse and his Child 1967, Best Friends for Frances 1969, The Pedalling Man 1970, The Sea-thing Child 1972, How Tom Beat Captain Najork and his Hired Sportsmen (Whitbread Prize for children's book) 1974, Dinner at Alberta's 1975, A Near Thing for Captain Najork 1975, The Twenty-Elephant Restaurant 1978, Ace Dragon 1980, The Marzipan Pig 1986, The Rain Door 1986, Ponders 1988, Bread and Jam for Frances 1993, Birthday for Frances 1994, The Trokeville Way 1996, Trouble on Thunder Mountain 1999, Jim's Lion 2001; poetry: The Last of the Wallendas 1997; contrib. essays and articles to Granta, The Fiction Magazine. *Honours:* Ditmar Award 1983. *Literary Agent:* David Higham Associates Ltd, 5–8 Lower John Street, Golden Square, London, W1R 4HA, England. *Telephone:* (20) 7437-7888 (office). *Fax:* (20) 7437-1072 (office). *E-mail:* noctys@globalnet.co.uk (home).

HOBB, Robin (see Ogden, Margaret Astrid Lindholm)

HOBSBAWM, Eric John Ernest, CH, MA, PhD, FBA; British academic (retd) and university administrator; *President, Birkbeck College, London*; b. 9 June 1917, Alexandria; s. of Leopold Percy Hobsbawm and Nelly Gruen; m. Marlene Schwarz 1962; one s. one d. *Education:* in Vienna, Berlin, London and Univ. of Cambridge. *Career:* Lecturer, Birkbeck Coll. 1947–59, Reader 1959–70, Prof. of Econ. and Social History 1970–82, Prof. Emer. 1982–, currently Pres.; Fellow, King's Coll., Cambridge 1949–55, Hon. Fellow 1973–; Andrew D. White Prof.-at-Large, Cornell Univ. 1976–82; Prof., New School for Social Research, New York 1984–97. *Publications:* Primitive Rebels 1959, The Age of Revolution 1962, Labouring Men 1964, Industry and Empire 1968, Captain Swing 1969, Bandits 1969, Revolutionaries 1973, The Age of Capital 1975; Ed. Storia del Marxismo (five vols) 1978–82, Worlds of Labour 1984, The Age of Empire 1875–1914 1987, Politics for a Rational Left: Political Writing 1989, Nations and Nationalism since 1780 1990, Echoes of the Marseillaise 1990, The Jazz Scene 1992, The Age of Extremes 1914–1991 1994, On History (essays) 1997, Uncommon People: Resistance, Rebellion and Jazz 1998, On the Edge of the New Century 2000, Interesting Times 2002, Globalisation, Democracy and Terrorism 2007. *Honours:* Hon. Foreign mem. American Acad. of Arts and Sciences, Hungarian Acad. of Sciences, Accad. delle Scienze, Turin; Chevalier des Palmes académiques, Order of the Southern Cross (Brazil) 1996; Dr hc (Stockholm) 1970, (Chicago) 1976, (East Anglia) 1982, (New School) 1982, (Bard Coll.) 1985, (York Univ., Canada) 1986, (Pisa) 1987, (London) 1993, (Essex) 1996, (Columbia Univ.) 1997, (Buenos Aires, Univ. of ARCIS, Santiago, Chile) 1998, (Univ. de la República, Montevideo, Uruguay) 1999, (Turin) 2000, (Oxford) 2001, (Pennsylvania) 2002, (Thessaloniki) 2004, (The Japan Acad.). *Address:* Birkbeck College, University of London, Malet Street, Bloomsbury, London, WC1E 7HX, England (office). *Telephone:* (20) 7631-6000 (office). *Fax:* (20) 7631-6270 (office). *Website:* www.bbk.ac.uk (office).

HOBSON, Charlotte; British writer; b. 23 Aug. 1970, Salisbury, Wilts.; d. of Anthony Hobson and Tanya Hobson (née Vinogradoff); m. Philip Marsden 1999; one s. one d. *Education:* Univ. of Edinburgh. *Publications:* Black Earth City: A Year in the Heart of Russia 2001; contrib. to Virgin Soil 2001, Granta 64: The Wild East, Poor People 2003, Petersburg Perspectives 2003. *Honours:* Somerset Maugham Award 2002. *Literary Agent:* c/o AP Watt Ltd, 20 John Street, London, WC1N 2DR, England. *Telephone:* (20) 7405-6774. *Fax:* (20) 7831-2154. *E-mail:* apw@apwatt.co.uk. *Website:* www.apwatt.co.uk. *Telephone:* (1326) 270273 (home).

HOBSON, Fred Colby, Jr, MA, PhD; American academic and writer; *Lineberger Professor in the Humanities, University of North Carolina*; b. 23 April 1943, Winston-Salem, NC; m. 1967 (divorced); one d. *Education:* Univ. of North Carolina, Duke Univ. *Career:* Prof. of English, Univ. of Alabama 1972–86; Prof. of English and Co-Ed., Southern Review, Louisiana State Univ. 1986–89; Prof. of English, Lineberger Prof. in the Humanities and Co-Ed., Southern Literary Journal, Univ. of North Carolina at Chapel Hill 1989–. *Publications:* Serpent in Eden: H. L. Mencken and the South 1974, Literature at the Barricades: The American Writer in the 1930s (co-ed.) 1983, Tell About the South: The Southern Rage to Explain 1984, South-Watching: Selected Essays of Gerald W. Johnson (ed.) 1984, The Southern Writer in the Post-Modern World 1990, Mencken: A Life 1994, Thirty-Five Years of Newspaper

Work by H. L. Mencken (co-ed.) 1994, The Literature of the American South: A Norton Anthology (co-ed.) 1998, But Now I See: The Southern White Racial Conversion Narrative 1999, South to the Future: An American Region in the Twenty-First Century (ed.) 2002, Faulkner's Absalom, Absalom!: An Oxford Casebook (ed.) 2003, The Silencing of Emily Mullen and Other Essays 2005, Off the Rim: Basketball and Other Religions in a Carolina Childhood 2006; contributions: Virginia Quarterly Review, Sewanee Review, Atlantic Monthly, Kenyon Review, New York Times Book Review, American Literature, TLS. *Honours:* Lillian Smith Award, 1984; Jules F. Landry Awards, 1984, 1999. *Address:* 110 Hunters Ridge Road, Chapel Hill, NC 27517 (home); Department of English, University of North Carolina at Chapel Hill, NC 27599-3520, USA. *Telephone:* (919) 942-0417 (home); (919) 962-4005 (office). *E-mail:* fhobson@email.unc.edu.

HOCH, Edward Dentinger; American writer; b. 22 Feb. 1930, Rochester, NY; s. of Earl G. Hoch and Alice D. Hoch; m. Patricia McMahon 1957. *Education:* Univ. of Rochester. *Career:* mem. Authors' Guild, CWA, MWA (Pres. 1982–83), Science Fiction Writers of America. *Publications:* The Shattered Raven 1969, The Transvection Machine 1971, The Judges of Hades and Other Simon Ark Stories 1971, The Spy and the Thief 1971, City of Brass and Other Simon Ark Stories 1971, The Fellowship of the Hand 1973, The Frankenstein Factory 1975, The Thefts of Nick Velvet 1978, The Quests of Simon Ark 1984, Leopold's Way 1985, The Night My Friend 1991, Diagnosis Impossible: The Problems of Dr. Sam Hawthorne 1996, The Ripper of Storyville and Other Ben Snow Tales 1997, The Velvet Touch 2000, The Old Spies Club 2001, The Night People 2001, The Iron Angel 2003, More Things Impossible: The Second Casebook of Dr. Sam Hawthorne 2006; contrib. to Ellery Queen's Mystery Magazine. *Honours:* MWA Edgar Allan Poe Award 1967, MWA Grand Master 2001, Boucheron Awards 1998, 2001, Lifetime Achievement Award 2001. *Address:* 2941 Lake Avenue, Rochester, NY 14612, USA (home). *Telephone:* (585) 865-1179 (office). *Fax:* (585) 663-5057 (office). *E-mail:* edhoch@frontiernet.net (office).

HOCHHUTH, Rolf; Swiss playwright; b. 1 April 1931; m.; three s. *Career:* fmr publisher's reader; Resident Municipal Playwright, Basel 1963; mem. PEN of FRG. *Publications:* plays: The Representative 1962, The Employer 1965, The Soldiers 1966, Anatomy of Revolution 1969, The Guerillas 1970, The Midwife 1972, Lysistrata and the NATO 1973, A German Love Story (novel) 1980, Judith 1984, The Immaculate Conception 1989. *Address:* PO Box 661, 4002 Basel, Switzerland.

HOCHSCHILD, Adam, AB; American author and journalist; b. 5 Oct. 1942, New York, NY; s. of Harold Hochschild and Mary Hochschild (née Marquand); m. Arlie Russell 1965; two s. *Education:* Harvard Univ. *Career:* reporter, San Francisco Chronicle 1965–66; ed. and writer, Ramparts Magazine 1966–68, 1973–74; Co-founder, ed., writer, Mother Jones Magazine 1974–81, 1986–87; commentator, nat. public radio 1982–83, public interest radio 1987–88; Regents Lecturer, Univ. of California at Santa Cruz 1987; Lecturer, Grad. School of Journalism, Univ. of California at Berkeley 1992–; Fulbright Lecturer, India 1997–98; mem. PEN, Nat. Writers' Union, Nat. Book Critics' Circle. *Publications:* Half the Way Home: A Memoir of Father and Son 1986, The Mirror at Midnight: A South African Journey 1990, The Unquiet Ghost: Russians Remember Stalin 1994, Finding the Trapdoor: Essays, Portraits, Travels 1997, King Leopold's Ghost: A Story of Greed, Terror and Heroism in Colonial Africa 1998, Bury the Chains: Prophets and Rebels in the Fight to Free an Empire's Slaves 2005; contrib. to New Yorker, Harper's, New York Times, Los Angeles Times, Washington Post, Progressive, Village Voice, Granta, New York Review of Books, Mother Jones. *Honours:* World Affairs Council Thomas Storke Award 1987, Overseas Press Club of America Madeleine Dane Ross Award 1995, Soc. of American Travel Writers Lowell Thomas Award 1995, PEN/Spielvogel-Diamonstein Award for the Art of the Essay 1998, California Book Awards Gold Medals 1999, 2006, J. Anthony Lukas Prize 1999, Lionel Gelber Prizes, Canada 1999, 2006, Duff Cooper Prize, UK 2000, Soc. of Professional Journalists Award for best magazine article 2000, Los Angeles Times Book Prize 2006, PEN USA Literary Award 2006. *Literary Agent:* Georges Borchardt Inc., Literary Agent, 136 E 57th Street, New York, NY 10022, USA. *Telephone:* (212) 753-5785. *Fax:* (212) 838-6518. *E-mail:* Georges@gbagency.com. *Address:* 84 Seward Street, San Francisco, CA 94114, USA (home).

HOCKING, Mary Eunice, FRSL; British writer; b. 8 April 1921, London. *Career:* local govt officer 1946–70; mem. Soc. of Authors. *Publications:* The Winter City 1961, Visitors to the Crescent 1962, The Sparrow 1964, The Young Spaniard 1965, Ask No Question 1967, A Time of War 1968, Checkmate 1969, The Hopeful Traveller 1970, The Climbing Frame 1971, Family Circle 1972, Daniel Come to Judgement 1974, The Bright Day 1975, The Mind Has Mountains 1976, Look, Stranger! 1978, He Who Plays the King 1980, March House 1981, Good Daughters 1984, Indifferent Heroes 1985, Welcome Strangers 1986, An Irrelevant Woman 1987, A Particular Place 1989, Letters from Constance 1991, The Very Dead of Winter 1993, The Meeting Place 1996. *Address:* 3 Church Row, Lewes, Sussex, England (home).

HODAČOVÁ, Helena, PhD; Czech writer; b. 16 Sept. 1916, Jičín; d. of O. Homoláč; m. François Svoboda 1939; one s. one d. (deceased). *Education:* Charles Univ., Prague and Univ. of Paris (Sorbonne). *Career:* writer of poetry since age of 15; Publicist, Lidové Noviny; first books part of Czechoslovak Avant-Garde movt, later publs deal with problems of everyday life. *Publications:* L'Harpe éolienne 1943, Ciel blanc – terre noire 1964, La Vie du peintre O. Homoláč, Demi-temps vertigineux, Les Oiseaux s'envolent: biographie d'une librettiste du compositeur Smetana, The Chinese 1996. *Address:* Pod lipkami 4, 150 00 Prague 5, Czech Republic. *Telephone:* (2) 523436.

HODGE, Jane Aiken, BA, AM; British author; b. 4 Dec. 1917, Watertown, MA, USA; m. Alan Hodge 1948 (died 1979); two d. *Education:* Somerville Coll., Oxford, Radcliffe Coll. *Career:* mem. Soc. of Authors, Liberal Democratic Party. *Publications:* fiction: Maulever Hall 1964, The Adventurers 1965, Watch the Wall, My Darling 1966, Here Comes a Candle 1967, The Winding Stair 1968, Marry in Haste 1970, Greek Wedding 1970, Savannah Purchase 1971, Strangers in Company 1973, Shadow of a Lady 1974, One Way to Venice 1975, Rebel Heiress 1975, Runaway Bride 1976, Judas Flowering 1976, Red Sky at Night: Lover's Delight? 1978, Last Act 1979, Wide is the Water 1981, The Lost Garden 1981, Secret Island 1985, Polonaise 1987, First Night 1989, Leading Lady 1990, Windover 1992, Escapade 1993, Whispering 1995, Bride of Dreams 1996, Unsafe Hands 1997, Susan in America 1998, Caterina 1999, A Death in Two Parts 2000, Deathline 2003; non-fiction: The Double Life of Jane Austen 1972, The Private World of Georgette Heyer 1984, Passion and Principle: The Loves and Lives of Regency Women 1996; contrib. to newspapers and journals. *Address:* 23 Eastport Lane, Lewes, East Sussex, BN7 1TL, England.

HODGE, Roger D., MA; American editor; *Editor, Harper's Magazine;* b. 12 Aug. 1967, Del Rio, TX; m. Deborah A. Hodge; two c. *Education:* Univ. of the South, Sewanee, TN and New School for Social Research, New York. *Career:* joined Harper's Magazine, New York as intern 1996, readings section 1997, Ed. readings section 1999–2003, Sr Ed. and author Harper's Weekly Review 2000–04, organized redesign of Harpers.org 2003, Deputy Ed. 2004–06, Ed. 2006–. *Address:* Harper's Magazine, 666 Broadway, 11th Floor, New York, NY 10012, USA. *E-mail:* letters@harpers.org. *Website:* www.harpers.org/RogerDHodge.html.

HODGINS, Jack Stanley, BEd, FRSC; Canadian novelist and teacher; b. 3 Oct. 1938, Vancouver Island, BC; m. Dianne Child 1960, two s. one d. *Education:* Univ. of British Columbia. *Career:* mem. PEN, Writers' Union of Canada. *Publications:* Spit Delaney's Island, 1976; The Invention of the World, 1977; The Resurrection of Joseph Bourne, 1979; The Honorary Patron, 1987; Innocent Cities, 1990; Over Forty in Broken Hill, 1992; A Passion for Narrative, 1993; The Macken Charm, 1995; Broken Ground, 1998. *Honours:* Gibson First Novel Award 1978, Gov.-Gen.'s Award for Fiction 1980, Canada-Australia Literature Prize 1986, Commonwealth Literature Prize 1988, British Columbia Book Prizes Ethel Wilson Award 1999; Hon. DLitt (Univ. of British Columbia) 1995, (Malaspina Univ.) 1998.

HODROVÁ, Daniela, MA, PhDr, DrSc; Czech writer and literary theorist; b. 5 July 1946, Prague; d. of Zdeněk Hodr; m. 1st Karel Milota 1985 (died 2002); m. 2nd Jaroslav Skopek 2004 (died 2005). *Education:* Charles Univ., Prague. *Career:* mem. Literary Theory Dept, Inst. of Czech and World Literature, Prague 1974–. *Publications include:* Hledání románu 1989, Podobojí 1991, Visite Privée—Prague 1991, Kukly (Cocoons) 1991, Trýznivé město (The Suffering City, trilogy of novels) 1991–92, Roman zasvěcení (Novel of Initiation) 1994, Místa s tajemstulm (Mysterious Places) 1994, Perunův den (Perun's Day) 1994, Ztracené děti (Lost Children) 1997, . . .na okraji chaosu. . . (On the Edge of Chaos) 2001, Komedie (Comedy) 2003. *Address:* Lucemburská 1, 130 00 Prague 3, Czech Republic.

HOE, Susanna Leonie, BA; British historian; b. 14 April 1945, Southampton; m. Derek Roebuck 1981. *Education:* London School of Econs, Univ. of Papua, New Guinea. *Career:* campaign co-ordinator, British Section, Amnesty International 1977–80; Tutor, Dept of Anthropology and Sociology, Univ. of Papua New Guinea 1985–86; TEFL teacher, Women's Centre, Hong Kong 1991–97. *Publications:* Lady in the Chamber (novel) 1971, God Save the Tsar (novel) 1978, The Man Who Gave his Company Away (biog.) 1978, The Private Life of Old Hong Kong (history) 1991, Chinese Footprints (history) 1996, Stories for Eva (reader for learning English) 1997, The Taking of Hong Kong (history, with Derek Roebuck) 1999, Women at the Siege, Peking 1900 (history) 2000, At Home in Paradise (travel, autobiog.) 2003, Madeira: Women, History, Books and Places 2004, Crete: Women, History, Books and Places 2005; contrib. to Times (Papua New Guinea), Liverpool Post, Women's Feature Service. *Honours:* Hon. Research Fellow, Centre of Asian Studies, Univ. of Hong Kong; Rangi Hiroa Pacific History Prize 1984. *Address:* 20A Plantation Road, Oxford, OX2 6JD, England. *Telephone:* (1865) 513681. *Fax:* (1865) 554199. *E-mail:* susanna@Lhoe.fsnet.co.uk. *Website:* www.holobooks .co.uk.

HØEG, Peter; Danish writer; b. 1957, Copenhagen; m.; two d. *Education:* Univ. of Copenhagen. *Career:* worked as sailor, ballet dancer, athlete and actor before becoming full-time writer; f. Lolwe Foundation 1996. *Publications:* The History of Danish Dreams 1988, Tales of the Night (short stories) 1990, Miss Smilla's Feeling for Snow 1992 (film 1997), Borderliners 1994, The Woman and the Ape 1996. *Address:* c/o Lolwe Foundation, Gothersgade 135, Copenhagen K 1123, Denmark. *Telephone:* 33-16-19-02. *Fax:* 33-16-19-02.

HOFFMAN, Adina; American writer; b. 1967, Mississippi; m. Peter Cole. *Career:* Visiting Prof., Wesleyan Univ., Middlebury Coll.; editorial bd mem., Ibis Editions; film critic for American Prospect, Jerusalem Post. *Publications:* House of Windows: Portraits from a Jerusalem Neighbourhood 2000; contrib. to The Washington Post, TLS, Boston Globe, New York Newsday, Tin House,

Co-Exist Magazine, The Forward, BBC World Service. *Address:* c/o Ibis Editions, PO Box 8074, German Colony, Jerusalem, Israel. *E-mail:* ibis@netvision.net.il. *Website:* www.ibiseditions.com.

HOFFMAN, Alice, MA; American writer and screenwriter; b. 16 March 1952, New York, NY; m. Tom Martin; two s. *Education:* Adelphi Univ., Stanford Univ. *Screenplays:* Independence Day 1983, Practical Magic 1998, The River King 2005. *Publications:* novels: Property Of 1977, The Drowning Season 1979, Angel Landing 1980, White Horses 1982, Fortune's Daughter 1985, Illumination Night 1987, At Risk 1988, Seventh Heaven 1990, Turtle Moon 1992, Second Nature 1994, Practical Magic 1996, Here on Earth 1997, Local Girls 1999, Aquamarine 2001, The River King 2001, Blue Diary 2001, The Probable Future 2003, Blackbird House 2004, The Ice Queen 2005, Skylight Confessions 2007; teenage and children's ficton: Horsefly, Fireflies, Aquamarine 2001, Indigo 2002, Water Tales 2003, Green Angel 2003, Moondog 2004, The Foretelling 2006; contrib. to Redbook, American Review, Playgirl magazine. *Address:* c/o Penguin Putnam, 375 Hudson Street, New York, NY 10014, USA (office). *Website:* www.alicehoffman.com (office).

HOFFMAN, Daniel Gerard, MA, PhD; American academic, poet and writer; b. 3 April 1923, New York, NY; m. Elizabeth McFarland 1948; two c. *Education:* Columbia Univ. *Career:* Visiting Prof., Univ. of Dijon, France 1956–57; Asst Prof., Swarthmore Coll., PA 1957–60, Assoc. Prof. 1960–65, Prof. of English 1965–66; Elliston Lecturer, Univ. of Cincinnati 1964; Lecturer, Int. School of Yeats Studies, Sligo, Ireland, 1965; Prof. of English, Univ. of Pennsylvania 1966–83, Poet-in-Residence 1978–, Felix E. Schelling Prof. of English 1983–93, Prof. Emer. 1993–; Consultant in Poetry, Library of Congress, Washington, DC 1973–74, Hon. Consultant in American Letters, 1974–77; Poet-in-Residence, Cathedral of St John the Divine, New York City, 1988–99; Visiting Prof. of English, King's Coll., London, 1991–92; mem. Acad. of American Poets (Chancellor 1973–97, Chancellor Emer. 1997–). *Oratorio:* libretto for Brotherly Love (music by Ezra Laderman) 2000. *Publications:* poetry: An Armada of Thirty Whales, 1954; A Little Geste and Other Poems, 1960; The City of Satisfactions, 1963; Striking the Stones, 1968; Broken Laws, 1970; Corgi Modern Poets in Focus 4 (with others), 1971; The Center of Attention, 1974; Able Was I Ere I Saw Elba: Selected Poems 1954–1974, 1977; Brotherly Love, 1981; Hang-Gliding from Helicon: New and Selected Poems 1948–1988, 1988; Middens of the Tribe 1995, Darkening Water 2002, Beyond Silence: Selected Shorter Poems 1948–2003 2003, Makes You Stop and Think: Sonnets 2005; other: The Poetry of Stephen Crane 1957, Form and Fable in American Fiction 1961, Barbarous Knowledge: Myth in the Poetry of Yeats, Graves and Muir 1967, Poe Poe Poe Poe Poe Poe Poe 1972, Faulkner's Country Matters: Folklore and Fable in Yoknapatawpha 1989, Words to Create a World: Interviews, Essays and Reviews of Contemporary Poetry 1993, Zone of the Interior: A Memoir 1942–1947; editor: several books. *Honours:* American Acad. of Arts and Letters Grant, 1967; Ingram Merrill Foundation Grant, 1971; Nat. Endowment for the Humanities Fellowship, 1975–76; Guggenheim Fellowship, 1983; Hon. DHL (Swarthmore Coll.) 2005; Yale Series of Younger Poets Award, 1954; Ansley Prize, 1957; ACLS Fellowships, 1961–62, 1966–67; Columbia Univ. Medal for Excellence, 1964; Hungarian PEN Medal, 1980; Hazlett Memorial Award, 1984; Paterson Poetry Prize, 1989, Aiken Taylor Award for Modern American Poetry 2003, Rense Poetry Prize 2005. *Address:* 502 Cedar Lane, Swarthmore, PA 19081 (home); c/o Department of English, University of Pennsylvania, Philadelphia, PA 19104, USA. *Telephone:* (610) 544-4438 (home).

HOFFMAN, Eva Alfreda, PhD; Polish/American writer; b. 1 July 1945, Kraków, Poland. *Education:* Harvard Univ. *Career:* Ed. Week in Review, Arts and Leisure, New York Times 1981–87, The New York Times Book Review 1987–90; fmr Prof. of Literature and Creative Writing, Columbia Univ., Univ. of Minnesota, Tufts Univ.; Visiting Prof., Dept of the Humanities, MIT; broadcasts on BBC Radio 3; mem. PEN, New York Univ. Inst. for the Humanities. *Publications:* Lost in Translation: A Life in a New Language 1989, Exit Into History: A Journey Through the New Eastern Europe 1993, Shtetl: A History of a Small Town and an Extinguished World 1997, The Secret: A Fable for Our Time 2001, After Such Knowledge: Where Memory of the Holocaust Ends and History Begins 2004; contrib. to newspapers and periodicals. *Honours:* American Acad. of Arts and Letters Award 1990, Whiting Award 1992, Guggenheim Fellowship 1993, Prix Italia. *Literary Agent:* Georges Borchardt, 136 E 57th Street, New York, NY 10022, USA; Gill Coleridge, Rogers, Coleridge & White Ltd, 20 Powis Mews, London, W11 1JN, England.

HOFFMAN, Mary Margaret Lassiter, BA, MA; British writer and journalist; b. 20 April 1945, Eastleigh, Hampshire, England; m. Stephen James Barber 1972; three d. *Education:* Newnham College, Cambridge; University College London. *Career:* Ed. Armadillo children's book review magazine online 1999–; mem. Soc. of Authors. *Publications:* 85 children's books, including: Amazing Grace, 1991; Henry's Baby, 1993; Grace and Family, 1995; Song of the Earth, 1995; An Angel Just Like Me, 1997; Sun, Moon and Stars, 1998; Three Wise Women, 1999; Starring Grace, 2000; Stravaganza: City of Masks, 2002; Lines in the Sand (ed.), 2003; Stravaganza: City of Stars, 2003; Encore, Grace!, 2003; Bravo, Grace! 2005, Stravaganza: City of Flowers 2005, The Falconer's Knot 2007, Princess Grace 2007; contrib. to Daily Telegraph, Guardian, Independent, Sunday Times, Specialist Children's Book Press. *Honours:* Waldenbooks Best Children's Book Honor Award, 1991; Primary English Award, 1995; Hon. Fellow, Library Asscn, 1998. *Literary Agent:* Rogers, Coleridge & White Ltd, 20 Powis Mews, London, W11 1JN, England.

Website: www.maryhoffmann.co.uk; www.stravaganza.co.uk; www.armadillomagazine.com.

HOFFMAN, William, BA; American writer; b. 12 April 1939, New York, NY. *Education:* City Coll., CUNY. *Career:* mem. American Society of Composers, Authors, and Publishers; Dramatists Guild; PEN; Writers Guild of America. *Publications:* As Is, 1985; The Ghosts of Versailles (libretto for opera by John Corigliano), 1991. Editor: New American Plays 2, 3, 4, 1968, 1970, 1971; Gay Plays, 1977. Contributions: journals and magazines. *Honours:* Drama Desk Award, 1985; Obie, 1985; International Classical Music Award, 1991; Emmy, 1992; WGA Award, 1992; Erwin Piscator Award, 1994.

HOFFMANN, Donald; American architectural critic and historian; b. 24 June 1933, Springfield, Ill.; m. Theresa McGrath 1958; four s. one d. *Education:* Univs of Chicago and Kansas City. *Career:* gen. assignment reporter, Kansas City Star 1956–65, Art Critic 1965–90; Asst Ed. Journal of the Society of Architectural Historians 1970–72; Life mem. Art Inst. of Chicago. *Publications:* The Meanings of Architecture: Buildings and Writings by John Wellborn Root (ed.) 1967, The Architecture of John Wellborn Root 1973, Frank Lloyd Wright's Fallingwater 1978, Frank Lloyd Wright's Robie House 1984, Frank Lloyd Wright: Architecture and Nature 1986, Frank Lloyd Wright's Hollyhock House 1992, Understanding Frank Lloyd Wright's Architecture 1995, Frank Lloyd Wright's Dana House 1996, Frank Lloyd Wright, Louis Sullivan and the Skyscraper 1998, Frank Lloyd Wright's House on Kentuck Knob, 2000, Mark Twain in Paradise: His Voyages to Bermuda 2006. *Honours:* Nat. Endowment for the Humanities Fellowship 1970–71, Nat. Endowment for the Arts Fellowship 1974, Graham Foundation Grant 1981. *Address:* 6441 Holmes Street, Kansas City, MO 64131-1110, USA. *Telephone:* (816) 333-0355. *E-mail:* donhoff@homerelay.net.

HOFFMANN, Roald, PhD; American chemist and academic; *Frank H. T. Rhodes Professor of Humane Letters, Cornell University*; b. 18 July 1937, Złoczów, Poland; s. of Hillel Safran and Clara Rosen, step-s. of Paul Hoffmann; m. Eva Börjesson 1960; one s. one d. *Education:* Columbia and Harvard Univs. *Career:* Jr Fellow, Soc. of Fellows, Harvard Univ. 1962–65; Assoc. Prof. of Chem., Cornell Univ. 1965–68, Prof. 1968–74, John A. Newman Prof. of Physical Science 1974–96, Frank M. Rhodes Prof. of Humane Letters 1996–; mem. American Acad. of Arts and Sciences, NAS, American Philosophical Soc.; Foreign mem. Royal Soc., Indian Nat. Acad. of Sciences, Royal Swedish Acad. of Sciences; mem. USSR (now Russian) Acad. of Sciences, Societas Scientarum Fennica 1986. *Play:* Oxygen (with Carl Djerassi). *Publications:* Conservation of Orbital Symmetry 1969, The Metamict State 1987, Solids and Surfaces 1988, Gaps and Verges 1990, Chemistry Imagined (co-author)1993, The Same and Not the Same 1995, Old Wine, New Flasks (co-author) 1997, Memory Effects 1999, Soliton 2002, Catalísta (Spanish) 2002. *Honours:* Hon. DTech (Royal Inst. of Technology, Stockholm) 1977; Hon. DSc (Yale) 1980, (Columbia) 1982, (Hartford) 1982, (City Univ. of New York) 1983, (Puerto Rico) 1983, (Uruguay) 1984, (La Plata) 1984, (Colgate) 1985, (State Univ. of New York at Binghamton) 1985, (Ben Gurion Univ. of Negev) 1989, (Lehigh) 1989, (Carleton) 1989, (Md) 1990, (Ariz.) 1991, (Bar-Ilan Univ.) 1991, (Central Fla) 1991, (Athens) 1991, (Thessaloniki) 1991, (St Petersburg) 1991, (Barcelona) 1992, (Northwestern Univ.) 1996, (The Technion) 1996, (Durham) 2000; ACS Award 1969, Fresenius Award 1969, Harrison Howe Award 1969, Annual Award of Int. Acad. of Quantum Molecular Sciences 1970, Arthur C. Cope Award, ACS 1973, Linus Pauling Award 1974, Nichols Medal 1980, shared Nobel Prize for Chemistry 1981, Inorganic Chemistry Award, ACS 1982, Nat. Medal of Science 1984, Nat. Acad. of Sciences Award, in Chemical Sciences 1986, Priestley Medal 1990. *Address:* Department of Chemistry and Chemical Biology, 222A Baker Laboratory, Cornell University, Ithaca, NY 14853-1301, USA (office). *Telephone:* (607) 255-3419 (office). *Fax:* (607) 255-5707 (office). *E-mail:* rh34@cornell.edu (office). *Website:* www.chem.cornell.edu (office).

HOFMANN, Michael, BA; German/British poet, dramatist and translator; b. 25 Aug. 1957, Freiburg, Germany. *Education:* Magdalene College, Cambridge. *Career:* Visiting Assoc. Prof., Creative Writing Dept, University of Michigan, Ann Arbor, 1994; Visiting Distinguished Lecturer, University of Florida, Gainesville, 1994–; 2nd Craig-Kade Writer in Residence Rutgers Univ. 2003; Visiting Assoc. Prof. Barnard Coll. and New School Univ. 2005. *Publications:* Nights in the Iron Hotel 1983, Acrimony 1986, K.S. in Lakeland: New and Selected Poems 1990, Corona, Corona 1993, After Ovid: New Metamorphoses (co-ed. with James Lasdun) 1994, Penguin Modern Poets 13 1998, Approximately Nowhere 1999, Behind the Lines 2002, Faber Book of Twentieth Century German Poems (ed.) 2005; plays: The Double Bass (adaptation of a play by Patrick Suskind) 1987, The Good Person of Sichuan (adaptation of a play by Brecht) 1989, Mother Courage (adaptation of a play by Brecht) 2006; other: trans; contrib. to The London Review of Books, TLS, Guardian, Poetry (Chicago). *Honours:* Cholmondeley Award, 1984; Geoffrey Faber Memorial Prize, 1988; Schlegel Tieck Prizes, 1988, 1992; Arts Council Writers Bursary, 1997–98; PEN/Book of the Month Club Trans. Prize, 1999; Helen and Kurt Wolff Prize, 2000, Oxford Weidenfeld Trans. Prize 2004. *Address:* c/o Faber and Faber, 3 Queen Square, London WC1N 3AU, England.

HOFSTADTER, Douglas Richard, MS, PhD; American academic and writer; *Distinguished Professor, College of Arts and Sciences Professor of Cognitive Science and of Computer Science, and Director, Center for Research on Concepts and Cognition, Indiana University, Bloomington*; b. 15 Feb. 1945, New York, NY; m. Carol Ann Brush 1985 (died 1993); one s. one d. *Education:* Stanford Univ., Univ. of Oregon. *Career:* Visiting Scholar, Stanford Univ. 1975–77, 1980–81, 1997; Asst Prof. of Computer Science, Indiana Univ. 1977–80, Assoc. Prof. of Computer Science 1980–83, Distinguished Prof., Coll. of Arts and Sciences Prof. of Cognitive Science and Computer Science, Prof. of Comparative Literature, Philosophy, Psychology and the History and Philosophy of Science, also Dir Center for Research on Concepts and Cognition 1988–; Visiting Scientist, MIT, 1983–84, Istituto per la Ricerca Scientifica e Technologica, Povo, Trento, 1993–94; Walgreen Prof. for the Study of Human Understanding and Prof. of Psychology and Cognitive Science, Univ. of Michigan, 1984–88; mem. American Assсn for Artificial Intelligence, Cttee for the Scientific Investigation of Claims of the Paranormal, Cognitive Science Soc., Golden Key Nat. Honor Soc. *Music:* compositions for piano. *Exhibitions:* The Nature of Whirly Art, Univ. of Calgary Art Museum 1991, For the Love of Line and Pattern: Studies Inspired by Alphabets and Music, Henry Radford Hope School of Fine Arts Gallery, Indiana Univ. 1998, and The Cooper Union's Great Hall Gallery, New York 1999, Wexner Gallery, Ohio State Univ., Columbus 1999, Ambigrammi e Creativita, Kaiser Arts Gallery, Genoa 2003. *Publications:* Gödel, Escher, Bach: An Eternal Golden Braid 1979, The Mind's I: Fantasies and Reflections on Self and Soul (co-ed. with Daniel C. Dennett) 1981, Metamagical Themas: Questing for the Essence of Mind and Pattern 1985, Ambigrammi: Un microcosmo ideale per lo studio della creativita 1987, Fluid Concepts and Creative Analogies: Computer Models of the Fundamental Mechanisms of Thought 1995, Rhapsody on a Theme by Clément Marot 1996, Le Ton beau de Marot: In Praise of the Music of Language 1997, Eugene Onegin: A Novel in Verse, by Alexander Sergeevich Pushkin, A Novel Versification by Douglas Hofstadter 1999, I Am a Strange Loop 2007; contribs to scholarly books and journals. *Honours:* Pulitzer Prize for General Non-Fiction 1980, American Book Award 1980, Guggenheim Fellowship 1980–81, Sr Fellow, Michigan Soc. of Fellows 1985, Arts and Sciences Alumni Fellows Award, Univ. of Oregon 1997. *Address:* Center for Research on Concepts and Cognition, Indiana University, 510 N Fess Street, Bloomington, IN 47408-3288, USA (office). *Telephone:* (812) 855-6965 (office). *Fax:* (812) 855-6966 (office). *E-mail:* dughof@indiana.edu (office). *Website:* www.cogsci.indiana.edu (office).

HOGAN, Desmond, BA, MA; Irish writer and teacher; b. 10 Dec. 1950, Ballinasloe. *Education:* University College, Dublin. *Career:* Strode Fellow, University of Alabama 1989. *Publications:* novels: The Ikon Maker 1976, The Leaves on Grey 1980, A Curious Street 1984, A New Shirt 1984, Farewell to Prague 1995; other: A Short Walk to the Sea (play) 1976, A Link with the River (short stories) 1989, The Edge of the City (travel writing) 1993, Lark's Eggs: New and Selected Stories 2005. *Honours:* John Llewellyn Memorial Prize, 1980; Irish Post Award, 1985; Deutscher Akademischer Austauschdienst Fellowship, Berlin, 1991. *Address:* The Lilliput Press, 62–63 Sitric Road, Arbour Hill, Dublin 7, Ireland. *E-mail:* info@lilliputpress.ie.

HOGAN, James Patrick; British writer; b. 27 June 1941, London, England; m. 1st Iris Crossley 1961 (divorced 1977); three d.; m. 2nd Lynda Shirley Dockerty (divorced 1980); m. 3rd Jackie Price 1983; three s. *Education:* Royal Aircraft Establishment Technical Coll., Reading Technical Coll. *Publications:* Inherit the Stars, 1977; The Genesis Machine, 1978; The Gentle Giants of Ganymede, 1978; The Two Faces of Tomorrow, 1979; Thrice Upon a Time, 1980; Giants' Star, 1981; Voyage from Yesteryear, 1982; Code of the Lifemaker, 1983; The Proteus Operation, 1985; Minds, Machines and Evolution (short stories), 1986; Endgame Enigma, 1987; The Mirror Maze, 1989; The Infinity Gambit, 1991; The Multiplex Man, 1992; Entoverse, 1992; Realtime Interrupt, 1995; The Immortality Option, 1995; Paths to Otherwhere, 1996; Bug Park, 1997; Mind Matters, 1998. Contributions: anthologies and magazines.

HOGAN, Kathleen (Kay) Margaret; Irish/American writer; b. 13 Feb. 1935, New York, NY; m. James P. Hogan, four s. one d. *Education:* high school. *Career:* started writing 1985. *Publications:* The El Train, 1882; The Silent Men, 1984; Widow Women, 1985; Little Green Girl, 1986; Of Saints and Other Things, 1992; The Women Wore Black, 1993, Roses 1994, Across the Clothesline 1997, The Letter 1995, Tulips in Ottawa 2004. Contributions: Descant; Long Pond Review; Journal of Irish Literature; North Country Anthology; Catholic Girls Anthology; Glens Falls Review, Bless Me Father Anthology, Saratoga Anthology. *Honours:* Parnassus Award Coll. for Creative Writing 1997, Best Short Story of the Year Catholic Magazine Competition. *Address:* 154 East Avenue, Saratoga Springs, NY 12866, USA.

HOGAN, Linda, MA; American poet, novelist and academic; *Professor of English, University of Colorado*; b. 16 July 1947, Denver, CO; d. of Charles Henderson and Cleo Henderson; m. Pat Hogan (divorced); two d. *Education:* Univ. of Colorado at Boulder. *Career:* descended from Oklahoma Chickasaw tribe; Assoc., Rocky Mountain Women's Inst., Univ. of Denver 1979–80; Poet-in-the-Schools, Colorado and Oklahoma 1980–84; Asst Prof., Tribes Program, Colorado Coll. 1982–84; Assoc. Prof. of American and American Indian Studies, Univ. of Minnesota 1984–89; Prof. of English, Univ. of Colorado at Boulder 1989–. *Publications:* poetry: Calling Myself Home 1979, Eclipse 1983, Seeing Through the Sun 1985, Savings 1988, The Book of Medicines 1993; fiction: A Piece of Moon (play) 1981, That Horse 1985, The Stories We Hold Secret: Tales of Women's Spiritual Development (ed. with Carol Bruchac and Judith McDaniel) 1986, Mean Spirit 1990, Solar Storms 1995, Power 1998; non-fiction: Dwellings: A Spiritual History of the Natural World 1995, Intimate Nature: The Bond Between Women and Animals 1998, Woman Who Watches Over the World: A Native Memoir 2001. *Honours:* Guggenheim

Fellowship; Lannan Award for Poetry; Nat. Endowment for the Arts Grant; American Book Award 1986, Oklahoma Book Award for Fiction 1990, Colorado Book Awards 1994, 1997, Wordcraft Circle Writer of the Year 2002; mem. Authors' Guild, Nat. American Studies Program, Nat. Council of Teachers of English, PEN West, Writers Guild. *Address:* c/o Department of English, University of Colorado, Boulder, CO 80302, USA.

HOGAN, Robert Goode, BA, MA, PhD; American academic and writer; b. 29 May 1930, Boonville, MO; m. 1st Betty Mathews 1950 (divorced 1978); two s. three d.; m. 2nd Mary Rose Callaghan 1979. *Education:* Univ. of Missouri. *Career:* publisher, Proscenium Press 1964–; Prof. of English, University of Delaware 1970–; Ed., Journal of Irish Literature 1972–, George Spelvin's Theatre Book 1978–85. *Publications:* Experiments of Sean O'Casey, 1960; Feathers from the Green Crow, 1962; Drama: The Major Genres (ed. with S. Molin), 1962; Arthur Miller, 1964; Independence of Elmer Rice, 1965; Joseph Holloway's Abbey Theatre (ed. with M. J. O'Neill), 1967; The Plain Style (with H. Bogart), 1967; After the Irish Renaissance, 1967; Seven Irish Plays (ed.), 1967; Joseph Holloway's Irish Theatre (ed. with M. J. O'Neill), 3 vols, 1968–70; Dion Boucicault, 1969; The Fan Club, 1969; Betty and the Beast, 1969; Lost Plays of the Irish Renaissance (with J. Kilroy), 1970; Crows of Mephistopheles (ed.), 1970; Towards a National Theatre (ed.), 1970; Eimar O'Duffy, 1972; Mervyn Wall, 1972; Conor Cruise O'Brien (with E. Young-Bruehl), 1974; A History of the Modern Irish Drama, Vol. 1, The Irish Literary Theatre (with J. Kilroy), 1975, Vol. II, Laying the Foundation (with J. Kilroy), 1976, Vol. III, The Abbey Theatre 1905–09 (with J. Kilroy), 1978, Vol. IV, The Rise of the Realists, 1910–1915 (with R. Burnham and D. P. Poteet), 1979, Vol. V, The Art of the Amateur 1916–1920 (with R. Burnham), 1984, Vol. VI, The Years of O'Casey (with R. Burnham), 1992; The Dictionary of Irish Literature (ed.), 1979; Since O'Casey, 1983; The Plays of Frances Sheridan (ed. with J. C. Beasley), 1984; Guarini's The Faithful Shepherd (trans. by Thomas Sheridan, ed. and completed with E. Nickerson), 1990; Murder at the Abbey (with J. Douglas), 1993. *Address:* c/o Proscenium Press, University of Delaware Library, 181 S College Avenue, Newark, DE 19717-5267, USA.

HOGE, James F., Jr, BA, MA; American academic and editor; *Peter G. Peterson Chair and Editor, Foreign Affairs, Council on Foreign Relations.* *Education:* Yale Univ., Univ. of Chicago, Harvard Univ. *Career:* fmr Ed.-in-Chief Chicago Sun-Times newspaper, then Publr and Pres. NY Daily News; fmr Dir Council on Foreign Relations, now Peter G. Peterson Chair and Ed., Foreign Affairs (journal) 1992–; Congressional Fellow, American Political Science Asscn 1962; Fellow John F. Kennedy School of Govt Harvard Univ. 1991; Sr Fellow Freedom Forum Media Studies Columbia Univ. 1992; Dir Foundation for Civil Society, Human Rights Watch; mem. Bd of Dirs Int. Center for Journalists (ICFJ) 1992–; mem. American Council on Germany; Chair. Program Cttee American Ditchley Foundation. *Television:* The Threat of Terrorism (documentary writer and narrator). *Publications include:* The American Encounter: The United States and the Making of the Modern World (co-ed.) 1997, How Did This Happen? Terrorism and the New War (co-ed.) 2001; numerous articles, reviews and chapters in journals, newspapers and books. *Honours:* Hon. degree (Columbia Coll.) 1985; Public Service Award, Univ. of Chicago 1973, Award for Contributions to Journalism The Better Govt Asscn of Chicago 1975, Public Service Award The Citizens Cttee for NY City 1985, 6 Pulitzer Prizes (to Chicago Sun Times while Ed. and Publr), Pulitzer Prize (to New York Daily News while Publr). *Address:* Foreign Affairs, 58 East 68th Street, New York, NY 10021-5987, USA (office). *Telephone:* (212) 434-9504 (office). *Fax:* (212) 434-9849 (office). *E-mail:* jhoge@cfr.org (office). *Website:* www.foreignaffairs.org (office).

HOGGARD, James Martin, BA, MA; American academic, poet, writer and translator; *Perkins-Prothro Distinguished Professor of English, Midwestern State University;* b. 21 June 1941, Wichita Falls, Tex.; m. Lynn Taylor Hoggard 1976; one s. one d. *Education:* Southern Methodist Univ., Univ. of Kansas. *Career:* teaching asst, Univ. of Kansas 1963–65; Instructor then Prof. of English, Midwestern State Univ. 1966–2000, Perkins-Prothro Distinguished Prof. of English 2000–; Guest Prof., Instituto Allende, San Miguel de Allende, Mexico, 1977, 1978, Univ. of Mosul, Iraq 1990; Exchange Prof., Instituto Tecnologico de Estudias Superiores de Monterrey, Chihuahua, Mexico 1993; mem. American Literary Trans Asscn, American Studies Asscn of Texas, PEN, Conf. of Coll. Teachers of English, Texas Inst. of Letters (Pres. 1994–98). *Publications:* poetry: Eyesigns: Poems on Letters and Numbers 1977, The Shaper Poems 1983, Two Gulls, One Hawk 1983, Breaking an Indelicate Statue 1986, Medea in Taos 2000, Rain in a Sunlit Sky 2000, Wearing the River: New Poems 2005; fiction: Trotter Ross 1981, Rev. 1999, Riding the Wind and Other Tales 1997, Patterns of Illusion: Stories and a Novella 2002; non-fiction: Elevator Man 1983; contribs to anthologies, reviews, quarterlies, journals and magazines. *Honours:* Soeurette Diehl Fraser Award, Stanley Walker Award, Brazos Bookstore (Houston) Short Story Award, NEA Creative Writing Fellowship; grants and citations. *Address:* Department of English, Midwestern State University, Wichita Falls, TX 76308, USA (office). *Telephone:* (940) 397-4123 (office); (940) 761-5908 (home). *Fax:* (940) 397-4931 (office). *E-mail:* james.hoggard@mwsu.edu (office); jhoggard@sw.rr.com (home).

HOGGART, Richard, MA, DLitt; British sociologist, writer and academic (retd); b. 24 Sept. 1918, Leeds; s. of Tom Longfellow Hoggart and Adeline Emma Hoggart (née Long); m. Mary Holt France 1942; two s. one d. *Education:* Cockburn Grammar School and Univ. of Leeds. *Career:* RA 1940–46; Staff Tutor and Sr Staff Tutor, Univ. Coll. of Hull and Univ. of Hull 1946–59; Sr Lecturer in English, Univ. of Leicester 1959–62; Visiting Prof., Univ. of Rochester, NY 1956–57; Prof. of English, Univ. of Birmingham 1962–73; Pres. British Asscn of fmr UN Civil Servants 1978–86; Chair. European Museum of the Year Award Cttee 1977–, Broadcasting Research Unit 1980–90; mem. Albemarle Cttee on Youth Services 1958–60, Youth Service Devt Council 1960–62, Pilkington Cttee on Broadcasting 1960–62; Gov. Birmingham Repertory Theatre 1963–70; Dir Centre for Contemporary Cultural Studies 1964–73; mem. BBC Gen. Advisory Council 1959–60, 1964–70, Arts Council of GB 1976–81, Culture Advisory Cttee of UK Nat. Comm. to UNESCO 1966–70, Communications Advisory Cttee of UK Nat. Comm. to UNESCO 1977–79, Wilton Park Academic Council 1983–; Chair. Arts Council Drama Panel 1977–80, Vice-Chair. Arts Council 1980–81, Chair. Advisory Council for Adult and Continuing Educ. 1977–83, The Statesman and Nation Publishing Co. Ltd 1978–81; Gov. Royal Shakespeare Theatre 1966–88; Asst Dir-Gen. for Social Sciences, Humanities and Culture UNESCO 1970–75; Warden of Goldsmiths' Coll., London 1976–84; Chair. Book Trust 1995–97; Pres. Nat. Book Cttee 1997–. *Publications:* Auden 1951, The Uses of Literacy 1957, W. H. Auden – A Selection 1961, Teaching Literature 1963, The Critical Moment 1964, How and Why Do We Learn 1965, Technology and Society 1966, Essays in Literature and Culture 1969, Speaking to Each Other 1970, Only Connect (Reith Lectures) 1972, An Idea and Its Servants 1978, An English Temper 1982, The Future of Broadcasting (ed. with Janet Morgan) 1978, An Idea of Europe (with Douglas Johnson) 1987, A Local Habitation (autobiog.) 1988, Liberty and Legislation (ed.) 1989, A Sort of Clowning 1990, An Imagined Life 1992, Townscape with Figures 1994, The Way We Live Now 1995, First and Last Things 1999, Hoggart en France 1999, Between Two Worlds 2001, Everyday Language and Everyday Life 2003, Mass Media in a Mass Society: Myth and Reality 2004, Promises to Keep: Thoughts in Old Age 2005. *Honours:* Hon. Visiting Prof., Univ. of E Anglia 1985–, Univ. of Surrey 1985–; Hon. Fellow, Sheffield City Polytechnic 1983, Goldsmiths' Coll. 1987, Ruskin Coll. Oxford 1994; Hon. DUniv (Open Univ.) 1972, (Surrey) 1981; Hon. DèsSc (Bordeaux) 1974, (Paris) 1987; Hon. LLD (CNAA) 1982, (York Univ., Toronto) 1988; Hon. LittD (E Anglia) 1986, (Metropolitan Univ. of London) 2003; Hon. DLitt (Leicester), (Hull) 1988, (Keele) 1995, (Metropolitan Univ. of Leeds) 1995, (Westminster) 1996, (Sheffield) 1999, (London) 2000; Hon. EdD (E London) 1998; BBC Reith Lecturer 1971. *Literary Agent:* Curtis Brown Ltd, Haymarket House, 28–29 Haymarket, London, SW1Y 4SP, England. *Telephone:* (20) 7393-4400. *Fax:* (20) 7393-4401. *E-mail:* info@curtisbrown.co.uk. *Website:* www.curtisbrown.co.uk.

HOGWOOD, Christopher Jarvis Haley, CBE, MA, FRSA; British musician, conductor, musicologist and keyboard player, writer, editor and broadcaster; b. 10 Sept. 1941, Nottingham; s. of Haley Evelyn and Marion Constance Hogwood (née Higgott). *Education:* Univ. of Cambridge, Charles Univ., Prague, Czechoslovakia. *Career:* keyboard continuo, Acad. of St Martin-in-the-Fields 1965–76, keyboard soloist 1970–76, Consultant Musicologist 1971–76; founder-mem. Early Music Consort of London 1965–76; writer and presenter, The Young Idea (BBC Radio) 1972–82; founder and Dir Acad. of Ancient Music 1973–2006, Emer. Dir 2006–; mem. Faculty of Music, Univ. of Cambridge 1975–; Artistic Dir King's Lynn Festival 1976–80; Dir Handel and Haydn Soc., Boston, USA 1986–2001, Conductor Laureate 2001–; Dir of Music, St Paul Chamber Orchestra, Minn., USA 1987–92, Prin. Guest Conductor 1992–98; Visiting Artist, Harvard Univ. 1988–89, Tutor, Mather House 1991–93; Artistic Adviser, Australian Chamber Orchestra 1989–93; Artistic Dir Summer Mozart Festival, Nat. Symphony Orchestra, USA 1993–2001; Assoc. Dir Beethoven Acad., Antwerp 1998–2002; Prin. Guest Conductor, Kammerorchester Basel, Switzerland 2000–; Kayden Visiting Artist, Learning from Performers Programme, Harvard Univ. 2001; Prin. Guest Conductor, Orquesta Ciudad de Granada 2001–04; Int. Prof. of Early Music Performance, RAM, London 1992–; Visiting Prof., Dept of Music, King's Coll., London 1992–96; Series Ed. Music for London Entertainment 1983–97; mem. Editorial Cttee C.P.E. Bach Edn (Md) 1986–98, Chair. Advisory Bd C.P.E. Bach Complete Works 1999–; mem. Editorial Bd Early Music (Oxford Univ. Press) 1993–97, Early Music Performers, Peacock Press 2002, Bd Eds Bohuslav Martinu Foundation 2003–, Advisory Panel, Eighteenth-Century Music, Cambridge Univ. Press 2003; Pres. Early Music Wales 1996–, Nat. Early Music Asscn (NEMA) 2000, The Handel Inst. 2000–, Orchestra Sinfonica di Milano Giuseppi Verdi 2003–. *Publications:* Music at Court 1977, The Trio Sonata 1979, Haydn's Visits to England 1980, Music in Eighteenth Century England (co-author) 1983, Handel 1984, Holmes' Life of Mozart (ed.) 1991, The Keyboard in Baroque Europe (ed.) 2003; many edns of musical scores; contribs to The New Grove Dictionary of Music and Musicians 1980 and 2001; numerous recordings. *Honours:* Hon. Prof. of Music, Univ. of Keele 1986–90, Univ. of Cambridge 2002–; Hon. Fellow, Jesus Coll., Cambridge 1989, Pembroke Coll., Cambridge 1992; Hon. mem. Royal Acad. of Music 1995; Freeman Worshipful Co. of Musicians 1989; Hon. DMus (Keele) 1991; Winner, Yorkshire Post Music Book Award 1984, Walter Willson Cobbett Medal (Worshipful Co. of Musicians) 1986, UCLA Award for Artistic Excellence 1996, Scotland on Sunday Music Prize, Edin. Int. Festival 1996, Distinguished Musician Award (Inc. Soc. of Musicians) 1997, Martinu Medal (Bohuslav Martinu Foundation) Prague 1999; Handel & Haydn Soc. Fellowship named 'The Christopher Hogwood Historically Informed Performance Fellowship' 2001, Regione Liguria per il suo contributo all'arte e alla filogia della musica 2003. *Address:* 10 Brookside, Cambridge, CB2 1JE, England. *Telephone:* (1223) 363975. *Fax:* (1223) 327377. *E-mail:* office@hogwood.org (office). *Website:* www.hogwood.org (office).

HOLBROOK, David Kenneth, MA; British author and poet; b. 9 Jan. 1923, Norwich; m. Morgot Holbrook 1949; two s. two d. *Education:* Downing Coll., Cambridge. *Career:* Fellow, King's Coll., Cambridge 1961–65, Sr Leverhulme Research Fellow 1965, Leverhulme Research Fellow Emer. 1988–90; Writer-in-Residence Dartington Hall 1972–73; Fellow and Dir of English Studies, Downing Coll. 1981–88, Fellow Emer. 1988; mem. English Asscn (Founding Fellow 2000), Soc. of Authors. *Publications:* English for Maturity 1961, Imaginings 1961, Against the Cruel Frost 1963, English for the Rejected 1964, The Secret Places 1964, Flesh Wounds 1966, Children's Writing 1967, The Exploring Word 1967, Object Relations 1967, Old World New World 1969, English in Australia Now 1972, Chance of a Lifetime 1978, A Play of Passion 1978, English for Meaning 1980, Selected Poems 1980, Nothing Larger than Life 1987, The Novel and Authenticity 1987, A Little Athens 1990, Edith Wharton and the Unsatisfactory Man 1991, Jennifer 1991, The Gold in Father's Heart 1992, Where D. H. Lawrence Was Wrong About Women 1992, Creativity and Popular Culture 1994, Even If They Fail 1994, Tolstoy, Women and Death 1996, Wuthering Heights: A Drama of Being 1997, Getting it Wrong with Uncle Tom 1998, Bringing Everything Home (poems) 1999, A Study of George MacDonald and the Image of Woman 2000, Lewis Carroll: Nonsense Against Sorrow 2001, Going Off the Rails 2003, English in a University Education 2006; contrib. to numerous professional journals. *Honours:* Festschrift 1996. *Address:* 1 Tennis Court Terrace, Cambridge, CB2 1QX, England. *E-mail:* dkh1000@cam.ac.uk (office).

HOLDEN, Anne Jacqueline, QSO, JP, LLB, MA; New Zealand writer and lawyer; b. 11 May 1928, Whakatane; d. of Harold A. Dare and Mildred Dare; m. Henry Curran Holden 1954; two s. two d. *Education:* Auckland Girls' Grammar School, Hamilton High School, Univ. of Auckland, Victoria Univ. of Wellington, Auckland Coll. of Educ. *Career:* teacher of English and art history 1951–86; barrister and solicitor 1989–; case-worker, Wellington Community Law Centre 1990–; part-time Lecturer in Law, Wellington Polytechnic 1990; mem. Indecent Publications Tribunal 1991. *Film:* The Bedroom Window 1987. *Play:* Going Up, Mr Martin? 1965. *Publications:* novels: Rata 1965, The Empty Hills 1967, Death After School 1968, The Witnesses 1971, The Girl on the Beach 1973, No Trains at the Bay 1976. *Address:* 72 Amritsar Street, Khandallah, Wellington 4, New Zealand. *Telephone:* (4) 479-2621.

HOLDEN, Anthony Ivan, MA; British journalist and writer; b. 22 May 1947, Southport, England; m. 1st Amanda Warren 1971 (divorced 1988); m. 2nd Cynthia Blake 1990. *Education:* Merton Coll., Oxford. *Career:* correspondent, Sunday Times 1973–77; columnist (Atticus) 1977–79, Chief US correspondent 1979–81, The Observer; Features Ed. and Asst Ed., The Times 1981–82; freelance journalist and author, broadcaster on radio and television. *Publications:* Agememnon of Aeschylus 1969, The Greek Anthology 1973, The St Albans Poisoner 1974, Charles, Prince of Wales 1979, Their Royal Highnesses 1981, Of Presidents, Prime Ministers and Princes 1984, The Queen Mother 1985, Charles 1988, Olivier 1988, Big Deal 1990, The Last Paragraph (ed.) 1990, A Princely Marriage 1991, The Oscars 1993, The Tarnished Crown 1993, Tchaikovsky 1995, Diana: A Life, A Legacy 1997, Charles at Fifty 1998, William Shakespeare 2000, The Wit in the Dungeon 2005, The Man Who Wrote Mozart 2006, Bigger Deal: A Year on the New Poker Circuit 2007. *Honours:* British Press Award for Columnist of the Year 1977, Fellow, Center for Scholars and Writers, New York Public Library 1999–2000. *Literary Agent:* Rogers, Coleridge & White Ltd, 20 Powis Mews, London, W11 1JN, England.

HOLDEN, Joan, BA, MA; American dramatist; b. 18 Jan. 1939, Berkeley, CA; m. 1st Arthur Holden 1958 (divorced); m. 2nd Daniel Chumley 1968, three d. *Education:* Reed College, Portland, OR, University of California at Berkeley. *Career:* Ed., Pacific News Service, 1973–75; Instructor in Playwriting, University of California at Davis, 1975, 1977, 1979, 1983, 1985, 1987. *Publications:* Americans, or, Last Tango in Huahuatenango (with Daniel Chumley), 1981; Factwindo Meets the Moral Majority (with others), 1981; Factwindo vs Armaggedonman, 1982; Steeltown, 1984; Spain/36, 1986; The Mozangola Caper (with others), 1986; Seeing Double, 1989; Back to Normal, 1990; Offshore, 1993. *Honours:* Obie Awards, 1973, 1990; Rockefeller Foundation Grant, 1985; Edward G. Robbins Playwriting Award, 1992.

HOLDSTOCK, Robert, (Robert Black, Ken Blake, Chris Carlsen, Robert Faulcon, Richard Kirk), BSc, MSc; British writer; b. 2 Aug. 1948, Hythe, Kent, England. *Education:* Univ. Coll. of North Wales, London School of Hygiene and Tropical Medicine. *Publications:* non-fiction: Alien Landscapes (with Malcolm Edwards) 1979, Tour of the Universe: The Journey of a Lifetime (with Malcolm Edwards) 1980, Magician: The Lost Journals of the Magus Geoffrey Carlyle (with Malcolm Edwards) 1982, Realms of Fantasy (with Malcolm Edwards) 1983, Lost Realms (with Malcolm Edwards) 1985; fiction: Eye Among the Blind 1976, Earthwind 1977, Necromancer 1978, Stars of Albion (co-ed.) 1979, Where Time Winds Blow 1981, In the Valley of the Statues (short stories) 1982, The Emerald Forest (film novel) 1985, The Fetch 1991, Ancient Echoes 1996; Mythago Wood series: Mythago Wood (British Science Fiction Award for best SF Novel 1985, World Fantasy Award for Best Novel 1985, Grand Prix de l'Imaginaire 2003) 1984, Lavondyss (British Science Fiction Award for best SF Novel 1989) 1988, The Bone Forest (short stories) 1991, The Hollowing 1993, Merlin's Wood 1994, Gate of Ivory, Gate of Horn 1997; Merlin Codex series: Celtika 2001, The Iron Grail (Czech Acad. Science Fiction, Fantasy and Horror Award for Best Novel 2002) 2002, The Broken Kings 2007; numerous short stories; as Robert Black: Legend of the Werewolf (film novel) 1976, The Satanists (film novel) 1977; as Ken Blake: Cry Wolf 1981, Operation Susie 1982, The Untouchables 1982, You'll be All Right 1982; as Chris Carlsen: Shadow of the Wolf 1977, The Bull Chief 1977, The Horned Warrior 1979; as Robert Faulcon: The Stalking 1983, The Talisman 1983, The Ghost Dance 1983, The Shrine 1984, The Hexing 1984, The Labyrinth 1987; as Richard Kirk: Raven Series: Vol. 1: Swordsmistress of Chaos (with Angus Wells) 1978, Vol. 2: A Time of Ghosts 1978, Vol. 4: Lords of the Shadows 1979. *Honours:* British Science Fiction Awards for Short Fiction 1982, (jtly) 1994, World Fantasy Award for Best Novella (jtly) 1992, Prix d'Imaginales 2004. *Address:* c/o Gollancz, Orion House, 5 Upper Saint Martin's Lane, London, WC2H 9EA, England. *Website:* www.robertholdstock.com.

HOLLAND, Cecelia Anastasia, BA; American writer; b. 31 Dec. 1943, Henderson, NV. *Education:* Pennsylvania State University, Connecticut College. *Publications:* The Firedrake, 1966; Rakosy, 1967; Kings in Winter, 1968; Until the Sun Falls, 1969; Ghost on the Steppe, 1969; The King's Road, 1970; Cold Iron, 1970; Antichrist, 1970; Wonder of the World, 1970; The Earl, 1971; The Death of Attila, 1973; The Great Maria, 1975; Floating Worlds, 1976; Two Ravens, 1977; The Earl, 1979; Home Ground, 1981; The Sea Beggars, 1982; The Belt of Gold, 1984; Pillar of the Sky, 1985; The Bear Flag, 1992; Jerusalem, 1996; The Soul Thief, 2002. *Honours:* Guggenheim Fellowship 1981–82. *Address:* c/o Alfred A. Knopf, 1745 Broadway, Suite B1, New York, NY 10019-4305, USA.

HOLLAND, Norman Norwood, BS, LLB, PhD; American scholar and writer; *Marston-Milbauer Eminent Scholar, University of Florida at Gainesville*; b. 19 Sept. 1927, New York, NY; m. Jane Kelley 1954; one s. one d. *Education:* Massachusetts Inst. of Tech., Harvard Univ. *Career:* Instructor to Assoc. Prof., MIT 1955–66; McNulty Prof. of English, SUNY at Buffalo 1966–83; Assoc. Prof., Univ. of Paris 1971–72, 1985; Marston-Milbauer Eminent Scholar, Univ. of Florida at Gainesville 1983–; mem. American Acad. of Psychoanalysis, Boston Psychoanalytic Soc.; Fellow, American Council of Learned Socs 1974–75. *Publications:* The First Modern Comedies 1959, The Shakespearean Imagination 1964, Psychoanalysis and Shakespeare 1966, The Dynamics of Literary Response 1968, Poems in Persons: An Introduction to the Psychoanalysis of Literature 1973, 5 Readers Reading 1975, Laughing: A Psychology of Humor 1982, The I 1985, The Brain of Robert Frost: A Cognitive Approach to Literature 1988, Holland's Guide to Psychoanalytic Psychology and Literature-and-Psychology 1990, The Critical I 1992, Death in a Delphi Seminar 1995, Meeting Movies 2006. *Honours:* Guggenheim Fellowship 1979–80. *Address:* Department of English, University of Florida at Gainesville, Gainesville, FL 32611, USA (office).

HOLLAND, Tom, BA, MA; British writer; b. 5 Jan. 1968, Oxford; s. of Martin Holland and Jans Holland; m. Sadie; two d. *Education:* Univ. of Cambridge. *Career:* previously worked in radio. *Publications:* Attis 1995, Lord of the Dead: The Secret History of Byron 1995, The Vampyre: Being the True Pilgrimage of George Gordon, Sixth Lord Byron 1995, Supping with Panthers 1996, Supping with Vampyres 1996, Deliver Us from Evil 1997, Importance of Being Frank 1997, Sleeper in the Sands 1998, The Bonehunter 2001, Rubicon: The Last Years of the Roman Republic (Hessel-Tiltman Prize 2004) 2003, Persian Fire: The First World Empire, Battle for the West 2005. *Address:* c/o Little, Brown & Co., Time Warner Book Group, Brettenham House, Lancaster Place, London, WC2E 7EN, England.

HOLLANDER, John, PhD; American poet and academic; *Sterling Professor Emeritus of English, Yale University*; b. 28 Oct. 1929, New York; s. of Franklin Hollander and Muriel Hollander (née Kornfeld); m. 1st Anne Loesser 1953 (divorced 1977); two d.; 2nd Natalie Charkow 1981. *Education:* Columbia, Harvard and Indiana Univs. *Career:* Lecturer in English, Connecticut Coll. 1957–59; Instructor in English, Yale Univ. 1959–61, Asst Prof. of English 1961–64, Assoc. Prof. 1964–66, Prof. 1977–85, A. Bartlett Giamatti Prof. 1986–95, Sterling Prof. of English 1995–2002, Sterling Prof. Emer. 2002–; Prof. of English, Hunter Coll., New York 1966–77; Christian Gauss Seminarian, Princeton Univ. 1962; Visiting Prof., School of Letters and Linguistic Inst., Indiana Univ. 1964; Visiting Prof., Seminar in American Studies, Salzburg, Austria 1965; Clark Lecturer, Trinity Coll., Cambridge 2000; editorial assoc. for Poetry Partisan Review 1959–65; mem. Poetry Bd Wesleyan Univ. Press 1959–62; mem. Editorial Bd Raritan 1981–; Chancellor Acad. of American Poets 1981–, MacArthur Fellow 1990–95; Fellow, American Acad. of Arts and Sciences, Ezra Stiles Coll., Yale Univ. 1961–64, Nat. Endowment for Humanities 1973–, Silliman Coll. 1977–; Overseas Fellow, Churchill Coll., Univ. of Cambridge 1967–68; mem. American Acad. of Arts and Letters (Sec. 2000–03), Asscn of Literary Scholars and Critics (Pres. 2000). *Publications include:* A Crackling of Thorns 1958, The Untuning of the Sky 1961, Movie-Going and Other Poems 1962, Visions from the Ramble 1965, Types of Shape 1969 (enlarged edn) 1991, The Night Mirror 1971, Town and Country Matters 1972, Selected Poems 1972, The Head of the Bed 1974, Tales Told of the Fathers 1975, Vision and Resonance 1975, Reflections on Espionage 1976, 1999, Spectral Emanations 1978, In Place 1978, Blue Wine 1979, The Figure of Echo 1981, Rhyme's Reason 1981 (enlarged edn) 1989, Powers of Thirteen 1983, In Time and Place 1986, Harp Lake 1988, Some Fugitives Take Cover 1988, Melodious Guile 1988, William Bailey 1991, Tesserae 1993, Selected Poetry 1993, The Gazer's Spirit 1995, The Work of Poetry 1997, The Poetry of Everyday Life 1998, Figurehead and Other Poems 1999, Picture Window 2003; contributor of numerous poems and articles to journals; ed. and contributing ed. of numerous books including: Poems of Ben Jonson 1961, The Wind and the Rain 1961, Jiggery-Pokery 1966, Poems of Our

Moment 1968, Modern Poetry: Essays in Criticism 1968, American Short Stories Since 1945 1968, The Oxford Anthology of English Literature (with Frank Kermode q.v.), 1973, For I. A. Richards: Essays in his Honor 1973, Literature as Experience (with Irving Howe and David Bromwich) 1979, The Essential Rossetti 1990, American Poetry: the Nineteenth Century 1993, Animal Poems (ed.) 1994, Garden Poems (ed.) 1996, Marriage Poems (ed.) 1997, Frost (ed.) 1997, Committed to Memory (ed.) 1999, Figurehead and Other Poems 1999, War Poems (ed.) 1999, Selected Poetry 1999, Sonnets (ed.) 2000, A Gallery of Poems 2001, American Wits (ed.) 2003, Selected Poems of Emma Lazarus 2005, Poems Haunted and Bewitched 2005; contributing ed. Harper's magazine 1969–71. *Honours:* Hon. DLitt (Marietta Coll.) 1982; Hon. DHL (Indiana) 1990, (CUNY Grad. Center) 2001, (New School Univ.) 2003; Hon. DFA (Maine Coll. of Art) 1993; Nat. Inst. of Arts and Letters Award 1963, Levinson Prize 1964, Washington Monthly Prize 1976, Guggenheim Fellow 1979–80, Bollingen Prize 1983, Ambassador Book Award English Speaking Union 1994, Governor's Arts Award for Poetry, State of Connecticut 1997, Robert Penn Warren–Cleanth Brooks Award 1998, Poet Laureate State of Connecticut 2006–. *Address:* Department of English, Yale University, PO Box 208302, New Haven, CT 06520, USA (office). *Telephone:* (203) 432-4566 (office). *Fax:* (203) 387-3497 (office). *E-mail:* john.hollander@yale.edu (office). *Website:* www.yale.edu/english (office).

HOLLANDER, Paul, BA, MA, PhD; American academic and writer; *Professor Emeritus, University of Massachusetts Amherst;* b. 3 Oct. 1932, Budapest, Hungary; m. Mina Harrison 1977; one d. *Education:* London School of Econs, UK, Univ. of Illinois, Princeton Univ. *Career:* Asst Prof., Russian Research Center, Harvard Univ. 1963–68, Research Fellow and Assoc. 1963–; Assoc. Prof., Univ. of Massachusetts at Amherst 1968–73, Prof. of Sociology 1973–2000, Prof. Emer. 2000–; Scholar-in-Residence, Rockefeller Study and Conf. Center, Bellagio, Italy 1984; Visiting Scholar, Hoover Inst. 1985, 1986, 1993; mem. Nat. Asscn of Scholars. *Publications:* American and Soviet Society: A Reader in Comparative Sociology and Perception (ed.) 1969, Soviet and American Society: A Comparison 1973, Political Pilgrims: Travels of Western Intellectuals to the Soviet Union, China and Cuba 1928–1978 1981, The Many Faces of Socialism 1983, The Survival of the Adversary Culture 1988, Decline and Discontent: Communism and the West Today 1992, Anti-Americans: Critiques at Home and Abroad 1965–1990 1992, Anti-Americanism: Irrational and Rational 1995, Political Will and Personal Belief: The Decline and Fall of Soviet Communism 1999, Discontents: Postmodern and Postcommunist 2002, Understanding Anti-Americanism: Its Origins and Impact at Home and Abroad (ed.) 2004, From the Gulag to the Killing Fields (ed.) 2006, The End of Commitment: Revolutionaries, Intellectuals and Political Morality 2006; contrib. to scholarly and general publs. *Honours:* Guggenheim Fellowship 1974–75, Peter Shaw Award, Nat. Asscn of Scholars 2002. *Address:* 35 Vernon Street, Northampton, MA 01060, USA (home). *Telephone:* (413) 586-5546 (home). *Fax:* (413) 584-4591 (home). *E-mail:* Hollander@soc.umass.edu (home); hollanderaz@yahoo.com (home).

HOLLERAN, Andrew; American author; b. 1942. *Education:* Harvard Univ., Univ. of Iowa. *Publications:* Dancer from the Dance, 1978; Nights in Aruba, 1983; Ground Zero, 1988; The Beauty of Men, 1996; In September, the Light Changes, 1999. Contributions: anthologies and periodicals.

HOLLINGHURST, Alan James, BA, MLitt, FRSL; British writer; b. 26 May 1954, Stroud, Gloucestershire; s. of the late James Kenneth Hollinghurst and of Elizabeth Lilian Hollinghurst (née Keevil). *Education:* Canford School, Dorset and Magdalen Coll., Oxford. *Career:* Asst Ed. Times Literary Supplement 1982–84, Deputy Ed. 1985–90, Poetry Ed. 1991–95; Visiting Prof. Univ. of Houston 1998; Old Dominion Fellow Princeton Univ. 2004. *Publications:* Confidential Chats with Boys (poems) 1982, The Swimming-Pool Library (novel) (Somerset Maugham Award 1989, American Acad. of Arts and Letters E. M. Forster Award 1989) 1988, Bajazet, by Racine (trans.) 1991, The Folding Star (novel) (James Tait Black Memorial Prize) 1994, New Writing 4 (ed. with A. S. Byatt) 1995, The Spell (novel) 1998, Three Novels, by Ronald Firbank (ed.) 2000, A. E. Housman: Poems Selected by Alan Hollinghurst (ed.) 2001, The Line of Beauty (novel) (Man Booker Prize for Fiction) 2004. *Literary Agent:* Antony Harwood Ltd, 103 Walton Street, Oxford, OX2 6EB, England.

HOLLINGSHEAD, Gregory Albert Frank, BA, MA, PhD; Canadian academic and writer; b. 25 Feb. 1947, Toronto, ON; m. Rosa Spricer, one s. *Education:* University of Toronto, University of London. *Career:* Asst Prof., 1975–81, Assoc. Prof., 1981–93, Prof. of English University of Alberta 1993–2005; Dir of Writing Programs Banff Centre 1999–; mem. PEN Canada, Writers Guild of Alberta, Writers' Union of Canada. *Publications:* Famous Players, 1982; White Buick, 1992; Spin Dry, 1992; The Roaring Girl, 1995; The Healer, 1998, Bedlam 2004. *Honours:* Georges Bugnet Awards for Excellence in the Novel, 1993, 1999; Howard O'Hagan Award for Excellence in Short Fiction 1993, 1996; Gov.-Gen.'s Award for Fiction, 1995; Writers' Trust Rogers Fiction Prize, 1999. *Address:* c/o Department of English, University of Alberta, Edmonton, AB T6G 2E5, Canada. *Website:* www.greg.hollingshead.com (home).

HOLLINGWORTH, Clare, OBE; British journalist; b. 10 Oct. 1911, d. of John Albert Hollingworth and Daisy Gertrude Hollingworth; m. 1st Vyvyan Derring Vandeleur Robinson 1936 (divorced 1951); m. 2nd Geoffrey Spence Hoare 1952 (died 1966). *Education:* Girls' Collegiate School, Leicester, Grammar School, Ashby-de-la-Zouch, School of Slavonic Studies, Univ. of London. *Career:* mem. staff League of Nations Union 1935–38; worked in Poland for Lord Mayor's Fund for Refugees from Czechoslovakia 1939; Corresp. for Daily Telegraph Poland, Turkey, Cairo (covered Desert Campaigns, troubles in Persia and Iraq, Civil War in Greece and events in Palestine) 1941–50, for Manchester Guardian (covered Algerian War and trouble spots including Egypt, Aden and Viet Nam), based in Paris 1950–63; Guardian Defence Corresp. 1963–67; foreign trouble-shooter for Daily Telegraph (covering war in Viet Nam) 1967–73, Corresp. in China 1973–76, Defence Corresp. 1976–81; Far Eastern Corresp. in Hong Kong for Sunday Telegraph 1981–; Research Assoc. (fmrly Visiting Scholar), Centre for Asian Studies, Univ. of Hong Kong 1981–. *Publications:* Poland's Three Weeks War 1940, There's A German Just Behind Me 1945, The Arabs and the West 1951, Mao and the Men Against Him 1984, Front Line 1990. *Honours:* Hon. DLitt (Leicester) 1993; Granada Journalist of the Year Award and Hannan Swaffer Award 1963; James Cameron Award for Journalism 1994. *Address:* 302 Ridley House, 2 Upper Albert Road, Hong Kong Special Administrative Region, People's Republic of China. *Telephone:* 2868-1838 (Hong Kong).

HOLLIS, Matthew; British poet and editor; b. 1971, Norwich. *Career:* Asst Ed., Oxford Univ. Press 1998–2001; Ed., Faber and Faber Ltd 2002–. *Publications:* poetry: The Boy on the Edge of Happiness (pamphlet) 1996, Ground Water 2004; co-editor: Strong Words 2000, 101 Poems Against War 2003. *Honours:* Eric Gregory Award 1999. *Address:* c/o Faber and Faber Ltd, 3 Queen Square, London, WC1N 3AU, England. *Website:* www.faber.co.uk; www.matthewhollis.com.

HOLLO, Anselm; Finnish/American academic, poet, writer, translator and editor; *Professor of Poetry, Poetics and Translation, Naropa University, Boulder;* b. 12 April 1934, Helsinki, Finland; m. Jane Dalrymple-Hollo. *Education:* University of Helsinki, University of Tübingen. *Career:* Visiting Prof. SUNY at Buffalo 1967, University of Iowa 1968–73, Bowling Green State University, Ohio 1971–73, Hobart and William Smith Colleges, Geneva, New York 1973–75, Southwest Minnesota State College, Marshall 1977–78; Distinguished Visiting Poet Michigan State University 1974; Assoc. Prof. of Literature and Creative Writing University of Maryland 1975–77; Margaret Bannister Distinguished Writer-in-Residence Sweet Briar College 1978–81; Poet-in-Residence 1981, Visiting Lecturer 1985–89, Kerouac School of Poetics, Boulder; Visiting Lecturer in Poetics New College of California, San Francisco 1981–82; Book Reviewer Baltimore Sun 1983–85; Distinguished Visiting Prof. of Poetry University of Colorado at Boulder 1985; Contributing Ed. The New Censorship 1989–; Assoc. Prof. of Poetry Poetics and Trans. Naropa University, Boulder 1989–. *Publications:* poetry: Sojourner Microcosms: New and Selected Poems 1959–77, 1978, Finite Continued 1981, Pick Up the House: New and Selected Poems 1986, Outlying Districts: New Poems 1990, Near Miss Haiku 1990, Blue Ceiling 1992, High Beam: 12 Poems 1993, West is Left on the Map 1993, Survival Dancing 1995, Corvus: New Poems 1995, Hills Like Purple Pachyderms 1997, AHOE: And How on Earth 1997, Rue Wilson Monday 2000, Notes on the Possibilities and Attractions of Existence: New and Selected Poems 1965–2000 2001; prose: Caws and Causeries: Around Poetry and Poets 1999. *Honours:* Yaddo Residency Fellowship 1978, National Endowment for the Arts Fellowship in Poetry 1979, PEN/American-Scandinavian Foundation Award for Poetry in Trans. 1980, American-Scandinavian Foundation Award for Poetry in Trans. 1989, Fund for Poetry Award for Contributions to Contemporary Poetry 1989, 1991, Stein Award in Innovative American Poetry 1996, Grez-sur-Loing Foundation Fellowship 1998, Baltic Centre for Writers and Trans Residency Fellowship 2002, San Francisco Poetry Center Award 2002, Acad. of American Poets Harold Norton Landon Poetry Trans. Prize 2004. *Address:* 3336 14th Street, Boulder, CO 80304, USA.

HOLLOWAY, Robin Greville, PhD, DMus; British composer, writer and academic; *Professor of Musical Composition;* b. 19 Oct. 1943, Leamington Spa; s. of Robert Charles Holloway and Pamela Mary Holloway (née Jacob). *Education:* St Paul's Cathedral Choir School, King's Coll. School, Wimbledon, King's Coll., Cambridge and New Coll., Oxford. *Career:* Lecturer in Music, Univ. of Cambridge 1975–, Reader in Musical Composition 1999–, Prof. 2001–; Fellow, Gonville and Caius Coll., Cambridge 1969–. *Compositions include:* Garden Music Op. 1 1962, First Concerto for Orchestra 1969, Scenes from Schumann Op. 13 1970, Evening with Angels Op. 17 1972, Domination of Black Op. 23 1973, Clarissa (opera) Op. 30 1976, Second Concerto for Orchestra Op. 40 1979, Brand (dramatic ballad) Op. 48 1981, Women in War Op. 51 1982, Seascape and Harvest Op. 55 1983, Viola Concerto Op. 56 1984, Peer Gynt 1985, Hymn to the Senses for chorus 1990, Serenade for strings 1990, Double Concerto Op. 68, The Spacious Firmament for chorus and orchestra Op. 69, Violin Concerto Op. 70 1990, Boys and Girls Come Out To Play (opera) 1991, Winter Music for sextet 1993, Frost at Midnight Op. 78, Third Concerto for Orchestra Op. 80 1994, Clarinet Concerto Op. 82 1996, Peer Gynt Op. 84 1984–97, Scenes from Antwerp Op. 85 1997, Gilded Goldberg for two pianos 1999, Symphony 1999, Missa Caiensis 2001, Cello Sonata 2001, Spring Music Op. 96 2002, String Quartet No. 1 2003, String Quartet No. 2 2004. *Recordings:* Sea Surface Full of Clouds chamber cantata, Romanza for violin and small orchestra Op. 31, 2nd Concerto for Orchestra Op. 40, Horn Concerto Op. 43, Violin Concerto Op. 70, Third Concerto for orchestra, Fantasy Pieces Op. 16, Serenade in DC Op. 41, Gilded Goldberg Op. 86, Missa Caiensis, Organ Fantasy, Woefully Arrayed. *Publications:* Wagner and Debussy 1978, On Music: Essays and Diversions 1963–2003 2004; numerous articles and reviews. *Address:* Gonville and Caius College, Cambridge, CB2 1TA (office); Finella, Queen's Road, Cambridge, CB3 9AH,

England (home). *Telephone:* (1223) 335424. *E-mail:* rgh1000@cam.ac.uk (home). *Website:* www.rhessays.co.uk (home).

HOLME OF CHELTENHAM, Baron (Life Peer), cr. 1990, of Cheltenham in the County of Gloucestershire; **Richard Gordon Holme,** CBE, PC, MA; British politician, publisher and business executive; b. 27 May 1936, London; s. of Jack Richard Holme and Edna Holme (née Eggleton); m. Kay Powell 1958; two s. two d. *Education:* Royal Masonic School, St John's Coll. Oxford, Harvard Business School, USA. *Career:* served in 10th Gurkha Rifles in Malaya 1954–56; Marketing Man., Unilever 1959–64; Dir Penguin Books 1964–66; Chair. BPC Publishing 1966–70; Pres. CRM Books, Calif., USA 1970–74; Dir Nat. Cttee for Electoral Reform 1976–84; Chair. Constitutional Reform Centre 1985, Threadneedle Publishing Group 1988–, Hollis Directories 1989–98, Prima Europe 1992–1995, Brasseys Ltd 1996–98; Pres. Liberal Party 1980–81; Liberal Democrat Parl. Spokesman on NI, House of Lords 1992–99; Chair. Broadcasting Standards Comm. 1999–2000; Chair. of Govs English Coll., Prague; Chair. Hansard Soc. for Parl. Govt 2000–; Dir Rio Tinto PLC 1995–98; Chancellor Univ. of Greenwich 1998–; Vice-Chair. LEAD Int. 2003–; Chair. Advisory Bd British-American Project 2000–. *Publications:* No Dole for the Young 1975, A Democracy Which Works 1978, The People's Kingdom (jt ed.) 1987, 1688–1988: Time for a New Constitution 1988. *Address:* House of Lords, London, SW1A 0PW, England. *Telephone:* (20) 7753-2454.

HOLMES, Bryan John, (Charles Langley Hayes, Ethan Wall, Jack Darby, Sean Kennedy), BA; British lecturer (retd) and writer; b. 18 May 1939, Birmingham; m. 1962; two s. *Education:* Univs of Keele and Birmingham. *Publications:* The Avenging Four 1978, Hazard 1979, Blood, Sweat and Gold 1980, Gunfall 1980, A Noose for Yanqui 1981, Shard 1982, Bad Times at Backwheel 1982, Guns of the Reaper 1983, On the Spin of a Dollar 1983, Another Day, Another Dollar 1984, Dark Rider 1987, I Rode with Wyatt 1989, Dollars for the Reaper 1990, A Legend Called Shatterhand 1990, Loco 1991, Shatterhand and the People 1992, The Last Days of Billy Patch 1992, Blood on the Reaper 1992, All Trails Lead to Dodge 1993, Montana Hit 1993, A Coffin for the Young 1994, Comes the Reaper 1995, Utah Hit 1995, Dakota Hit 1995, Viva Reaper 1996, The Shard Brand 1996, High Plains Death 1997, Smoking Star 1997, Crowfeeders 1999, North of the Bravo 2000, Bradford's Pocket Crossword Dictionary 2001, Bradford's Guide to Solving Crosswords 2002, Jake's Women 2002, Solving Cryptic Crosswords 2003, Bloomsbury's Pocket Crossword Dictionary 2003, Rio Grande Shoot-Out 2004, Trail of the Reaper 2004, The Expediter 2004, Three Graves to Fargo 2004, Trouble in Tucson 2005, Wyoming Hit 2005, Shotgun 2005, Black's Pocket Crossword Dictionary (2nd edn) 2005; contrib. to professional and academic journals. *Address:* c/o Robert Hale Ltd, Clerkenwell Green, London, EC1R 0HT, England.

HOLMES, Charlotte Amalie; American academic and writer; b. 26 April 1956, Georgia; m. James Brasfield 1983; one s. *Education:* BA, Louisiana State University, 1977; MFA, Columbia University, 1980. *Career:* Editorial Asst, Paris Review, 1979–80; Assoc. and Managing Ed., Ecco Press, 1980–82; Instructor, Western Carolina University, 1984–87; Asst Prof., 1987–93, Assoc. Prof., 1993–, Pennsylvania State University; mem. Associated Writing Programs. *Publications:* Gifts and Other Stories, 1994. Contributions: periodicals. *Honours:* Stegner Fellowship, Stanford University, 1982; North Carolina Arts Council Grant, 1986; Pennsylvania Council on the Arts Fellowships, 1988, 1993; Bread Loaf Writer's Conference National Arts Club Scholarship, 1990; Poets and Writers Award, 1993; DH Lawrence Fellowship, 2000. *Literary Agent:* Neil Olson, Donadio and Olson. *Address:* c/o Department of English, Pennsylvania State University, University Park, PA 16802, USA.

HOLMES, Diana, MA, DPhil; British academic, writer and editor; *Professor of French, University of Leeds*; b. 28 Jan. 1949, Preston, Lancs.; m. Nicolas W. Cheesewright, 18 June 1983; one s. one d. *Education:* Univ. of Sussex, La Nouvelle Sorbonne Université de Paris III. *Career:* Lecturer in French, Wolverhampton Polytechnic 1975–80, Sr Lecturer in French 1984–90, Prin. Lecturer in French 1990; Part-time Lecturer in French, N London Polytechnic 1981–84; Lecturer, Keele Univ. 1992–94, Sr Lecturer 1994–95, Prof. of French and Head of French Studies 1995–99; Prof. of French, Univ. of Leeds 1999–2003; Visiting Scholar, Centre for Gender Studies, Univ. of British Columbia, Canada 2006; Ed. Modern and Contemporary France 1996–2003; Co-organiser Women in French. *Publications:* Colette 1991, French Women's Writing 1848–1994 1996, Truffaut (co-author) 1998, French Film Directors series (co-ed. and contrib.) 1998, Rachilde – Gender, Decadence and the Woman Writer 2002; contrib. to books and periodicals, including French Studies, L'Esprit Créateur; articles on women writers and on cinema. *Honours:* Chevalier des Palmes académiques 1998. *Address:* 151 Compton Road, Wolverhampton, West Midlands, WV3 9JT, England (home). *Telephone:* (113) 343-3469 (office). *E-mail:* d.holmes@leeds.ac.uk (office).

HOLMES, George Arthur, PhD, FRHistS, FBA; British historian; *Chichele Professor of Medieval History Emeritus, University of Oxford*; b. 22 April 1927, Aberystwyth, Wales; s. of the late John Holmes and Margaret Holmes; m. Evelyn Anne Klein 1953; two s. (one deceased), two d. *Education:* Ardwyn County School, Aberystwyth, Univ. Coll. Aberystwyth and St John's Coll. Cambridge. *Career:* Fellow, St John's Coll. Cambridge 1951–54; Tutor, St Catherine's Coll. Oxford 1954–62, Fellow and Tutor 1962–89, Vice-Master 1969–71, Emer. Fellow 1990–; Chichele Prof. of Medieval History and Fellow, All Souls Coll., Oxford 1989–94, Emer. Fellow 1994–; Visiting Prof., Harvard Univ. Center for Italian Renaissance Studies, Florence 1995–; mem. Inst. for Advanced Study, Princeton, NJ, USA 1967–68; Chair. Victoria County History

Cttee, Inst. of Historical Research 1979–89; Jt Ed. English Historical Review 1974–81; Del., Oxford Univ. Press 1982–92; Fellow Emer., Leverhulme Trust 1996–98. *Publications:* The Estates of the Higher Nobility in Fourteenth-Century England 1957, The Later Middle Ages 1962, The Florentine Enlightenment 1400–1450 1969, Europe: Hierarchy and Revolt 1320–1450 1975, The Good Parliament 1975, Dante 1980, Florence, Rome and the Origins of the Renaissance 1986, The Oxford Illustrated History of Medieval Europe (ed.) 1988, The First Age of the Western City 1300–1500 1990, Art and Politics in Renaissance Italy (ed.) 1993, Renaissance 1996, The Oxford Illustrated History of Italy (ed.) 1997. *Honours:* Serena Medal for Italian Studies, British Acad. 1993. *Address:* Highmoor House, Primrose Lane, Weald, Bampton, Oxon., OX18 2HY, England (home). *Telephone:* (1993) 850408 (home).

HOLMES, John (see Souster, (Holmes) Raymond)

HOLMES, Leslie Templeman, BA, MA, PhD; British academic and writer; b. 5 Oct. 1948, London, England; m. Susan Mary Bleasby 1971 (divorced 1989). *Education:* Hull University, Essex University. *Career:* Prof. of Political Science, University of Melbourne. *Publications:* The Policy Progress in Communist States, 1981; The Withering Away of the State? (ed.), 1981; Politics in the Communist World, 1986; The End of Communist Power, 1993; Post-Communism, 1997; Europe: Rethinking the Boundaries (co-ed.), 1998; Citizenship and Identity in Europe (co-ed.), 1999. *Honours:* Fellow, Acad. of the Social Sciences in Australia 1995. *E-mail:* leslieth@unimelb.edu.au.

HOLMES, Richard Gordon Heath, OBE, MA, FBA, FRSL; British writer and poet; *Professor of Biographical Studies, University of East Anglia*; b. 5 Nov. 1945, London; s. of Dennis Patrick Holmes and Pamela Mavis Gordon; pnr Rose Tremain. *Education:* Downside School, Churchill Coll., Cambridge. *Career:* literacy features writer, The Times 1967–92; Visiting Fellow, Trinity Coll., Cambridge 2000; Prof. of Biographical Studies, Univ. of E Anglia 2001–. *Radio:* BBC Radio: Inside the Tower 1977, To the Tempest Given 1992, The Nightwalking (Sony Award) 1995, Clouded Hills 1999, Runaway Lives 2000, The Frankenstein Project 2002. *Publications:* Thomas Chatterton: The Case Re-Opened 1970, One for Sorrows (poems) 1970, Shelley: The Pursuit 1974, Shelley on Love (ed.) 1980, Coleridge 1982, Nerval: The Chimeras (with Peter Jay) 1985, Footsteps: Adventures of a Romantic Biographer 1985, Mary Wollstonecraft and William Godwin (ed.) 1987, Kipling: Something Myself (ed. with Robert Hampson) 1987, Coleridge: Early Visions 1989, Dr Johnson and Mr Savage 1993, Coleridge: Selected Poems (ed.) 1996, The Romantic Poets and Their Circle 1997, Coleridge: Darker Reflections 1998, Sidetracks: Explorations of a Romantic Biographer 2000, Classic Biographies (series) 2004–, Insights: The Romantic Poets and Their Circle 2005. *Honours:* Hon. DLitt (E Anglia) 2000, (Tavistock Inst.) 2001; Somerset Maugham Award 1977, James Tait Black Memorial Prize 1994, Whitbread Book of the Year Prize 1989, Duff Cooper Prize 1998. *Address:* c/o HarperCollins, 77 Fulham Palace Road, London, W6 8JB, England.

HOLROYD, Sir Michael de Courcy Fraser, Kt, FRHistS, CLit; British writer; *President, Royal Society of Literature*; b. 27 Aug. 1935, London; s. of Basil Holroyd and Ulla Holroyd (née Hall); m. Margaret Drabble 1982. *Education:* Eton Coll. *Career:* Chair. Soc. of Authors 1973–74, Nat. Book League 1976–78; Pres. English Centre of PEN 1985–88; Chair. Strachey Trust 1990–95, Public Lending Right Advisory Cttee 1997–2000, Royal Soc. of Literature 1998–2001 (Pres. 2003–); Vice-Pres. Royal Literary Fund 1997–; mem. Arts Council (Chair. Literature Panel) 1992–95; Gov. Shaw Festival Theatre, Niagara-on-the-Lake 1993–; Trustee Laser Foundation 2001–03. *Publications:* Hugh Kingsmill: A Critical Biography 1964, Lytton Strachey: A Critical Biography 1967–68 (new edn 1994), A Dog's Life (novel) 1969, The Best of Hugh Kingsmill (ed) 1970, Lytton Strachey by Himself: A Self-Portrait (ed) 1971, Unreceived Opinions (essays) 1973, Augustus John 1974–75 (new edn 1996), The Art of Augustus John (with Malcolm Easton) 1974, The Genius of Shaw (ed) 1979, The Shorter Strachey (ed with Paul Levy) 1980, William Gerhardie's God's Fifth Column (ed with Robert Skidelsky) 1981, Essays by Diverse Hands (ed) Vol. XLII 1982, Peterley Harveset: The Private Diary of David Peterley (ed) 1985, Bernard Shaw: Vol. 1: The Search for Love 1988, Vol. II: The Pursuit of Power 1989, Vol. III: The Lure of Fantasy 1991, Vol. IV: The Last Laugh 1992, Vol. V: The Shaw Companion 1992, Bernard Shaw 1997 (one-vol. biog.), Basil Street Blues 1999, Works on Paper: The Craft of Biography and Autobiography 2002, Mosaic: Portraits in Fragments 2004. *Honours:* Hon. DLitt (Ulster) 1992, (Sheffield, Warwick) 1993, (East Anglia) 1994, (LSE) 1998; Saxton Memorial Fellowship 1964, Bollingen Fellowship 1966, Winston Churchill Fellowship 1971, Irish Life Arts Award 1988, Meilleur Livre Etranger 1995, Heywood Hill Prize 2001, David Cohen Prize for Literature 2005. *Literary Agent:* A. P. Watt Ltd, 20 John Street, London, WC1N 2DL, England. *Telephone:* (20) 7405-6774. *Fax:* (20) 7831-2154. *E-mail:* apw@apwat.co.uk. *Website:* www.apwatt.co.uk. *Telephone:* (20) 7405-6774 (home). *Fax:* (20) 7831-2154 (home).

HOLT, Anne; Norwegian writer; b. 16 Nov. 1958, Larvik. *Career:* fmr lawyer, journalist, TV news ed. *Publications:* Blind Gudinne 1993, Salige er de som tørster 1994, Demonens død 1995, Mea culpa 1997, Løvens gap 1997, I hjertet av VM 1998, Død joker 1999, Bernhard Pinkertons store oppdrag 1999, Uten ekko 2000, Det som er mitt 2001, Sannheten bortenfor 2003, Det som aldri skjer 2004, Presidentens valg 2006. *E-mail:* webmaster@anne-holt.com. *Website:* www.anne-holt.com.

HOLT, George (see Tubb, Edwin Charles)

HOLT, Hazel, BA; British writer; b. 3 Sept. 1928, Birmingham, England; m. Geoffrey Louis Holt 1951, one s. *Education:* Newnham College, Cambridge. *Career:* Ed., International African Institute, London, 1950–74; Reviewer, Feature Writer, Stage and Television Today, London, 1975–80; Writer, 1989–. *Publications:* A Very Private Eye: An Autobiography in Diaries and Letters (co-ed. and annotator), 1984; Barbara Pym, Civil to Strangers and Other Writings (ed.), 1988; Mrs Malory Investigates, 1989; Gone Away, 1989; The Cruellest Month, 1991; A Lot to Ask: A Life of Barbara Pym, 1991; Mrs Malory and the Festival Murders, 1993, also as Uncertain Death; Mrs Malory: Detective in Residence, 1994; The Shortest Journey, 1994; Mrs Malory Wonders Why, 1995; Superfluous Death, 1995; Mrs Malory: Death of a Dean, 1996; Mrs Malory and the Only Good Lawyer, 1997; Dead and Buried, 1998; Fatal Legacy, 1999; Lilies that Fester, 2000; Delay of Execution, 2001; Leonora, 2002; Death in Practice, 2003. *Address:* Tivington Knowle, Nr Minehead, Somerset TA24 8SX, England.

HOLT, Samuel (see Westlake, Donald Edwin)

HOMBERGER, Eric Ross, BA, MA, PhD; American academic and writer; b. 30 May 1942, Philadelphia, Pennsylvania; m. Judy Jones 1967, two s. one d. *Education:* University of California at Berkeley, University of Chicago, University of Cambridge. *Career:* Temporary Lecturer in American Literature, University of Exeter, 1969–70; Lecturer, 1970–88, Reader in American Literature, 1988–, University of East Anglia; Visiting Faculty, University of Minnesota, 1977–78; Visiting Prof. of American Literature, University of New Hampshire, 1991–92; mem. British Asscn for American Studies. *Publications:* The Cambridge Mind: Ninety Years of the 'Cambridge Review', 1879–1969 (ed. with William Janeway and Simon Schama), 1970; Ezra Pound: The Critical Heritage (ed.), 1972; The Art of the Real: Poetry in England and America since 1939, 1977; The Second World War in Fiction (ed. with Holger Klein and John Flower), 1984; John le Carre, 1986; American Writers and Radical Politics, 1900–1939: Equivocal Commitments, 1987; The Troubled Face of Biography (ed. with John Charmley), 1987; John Reed, 1990; John Reed and the Russian Revolution: Uncollected Articles, Letters and Speeches in Russia, 1917–1920 (ed. with John Biggart), 1992; The Historical Atlas of New York City, 1994; Scenes from the Life of a City: Corruption and Conscience in Old New York, 1994; The Penguin Historical Atlas of North America, 1995; New York City, 2002; Mrs Astor's New York: Money and Social Power in a Gilded Age, 2002. Contributions: periodicals. *Honours:* Leverhulme Fellowship, 1978–79; Gilder Lehrman Institute Fellowship in American History, 1999. *E-mail:* e.homberger@uea.ac.uk.

HOME, Stewart Ramsay, (Harry Bates, Monty Cantsin, Karen Eliot); British writer; b. 24 March 1962, Merton, S London; s. of Julia Callan-Thompson. *Career:* mem. Soc. of Authors. *Exhibitions:* Humanity In Ruins, Central Space, London 1988; Vermeer II, workfortheeyetodo London 1996, Hallucination Generation: High Modernism in a Tripped Out World, Arnolfini, Bristol 2006; numerous group shows. *Films:* Eclipse & Re-Emergence of the Oedipus Complex 2004, Screams in Favour of De Sade 2002; numerous others, mainly shorts screened at specialist art cinemas and art events (not on commercial release). *Publications:* Assault on Culture 1988, Pure Mania 1989, Defiant Pose 1991, No Pity 1993, Red London 1994, Neoism, Plagiarism & Praxis 1995, Cranked Up Really High 1995, Slow Death 1996, Come Before Christ & Murder Love 1997, Blow Job 1997, Cunt 1999, Confusion Incorporated: A Collection of Lies, Hoaxes and Hidden Truths 1999, Whips and Furs: My Life as a Bon Vivant Gambler and Love Rat 2000, 69 Things to Be Done with a Dead Princess 2002, Down and Out in Shoreditch and Hoxton 2004, Tainted Love 2005; Memphis Underground 2007; contrib. to Guardian, Big Issue, Independent, Art Monthly, Edinburgh Review, New Art Examiner, Konkret. *Honours:* Arts Council of England Writers' Award 2001. *Literary Agent:* Antony Harwood. *Address:* BM Senior, London, WC1N 3XX, England. *Website:* stewarthomesociety.org.

HOMEL, David; American/Canadian writer, journalist and translator; b. 1952, Chicago, Ill.; two s. *Education:* Univ. of Toronto, Indiana Univ. *Career:* Tutor in Translation, Concordia Univ., Toronto. *Screenplays:* Great North, Todo Incluido. *Publications:* fiction: Electrical Storms 1988, Rat Palms (Canadian Book and Periodical Marketers, Paperback of the Year 1993) 1992, Sonya and Jack (Prix Millepages for Best Foreign Literary Fiction, France) 1995, Get on Top 1999, The Speaking Cure (Hugh McLennan Prize for Fiction, Jewish Public Library Prize for Fiction 2004) 2003; non-fiction: Mapping Literature: The Art and Politics of Literary Translation 1988; contrib. to The Gazette, La Press. *Honours:* Gov.-Gen.'s Award for Translation 1995, 2001, QWF Prize for Translation 2003. *Literary Agent:* Anne McDermid & Associates Ltd, 92 Willcocks Street, Toronto, Ont. M5S 1C8, Canada. *E-mail:* dhomel@alcor.concordia.ca.

HOMES, A. M.; American writer; b. 1961, Washington, DC. *Films:* Wanted 1994, The Safety of Objects 2001, Freunde (aka The Whiz Kids) 2001, Jack (TV teleplay) 2004. *Publications:* Jack (Deutscher Jugendliteraturpreis) 1989, The Safety of Objects 1990, In a Country of Mothers 1993, The End of Alice 1995, Appendix A 1995, Music for Torching 1999, Things You Should Know (short stories) 2002, Los Angeles 2002, This Book Will Save Your Life (novel) 2006, The Mistress's Daughter 2007; contrib. to Vanity Fair, Art Forum, The New York Times, The New Yorker, Granta. *Honours:* fellowships from The Center for Scholars and Writers, New York Public Library, Guggenheim Foundation, NEA and New York Foundation for the Arts; Benjamin Franklin Award 2000.

Address: Wylie Agency, 250 West 37th Street, New York, NY 10107, USA (office).

HONAN, Park, MA, PhD, FRSL; American biographer, writer and editor; *Professor Emeritus, University of Leeds;* b. 17 Sept. 1928, Utica, NY. *Education:* Univ. of Chicago, Univ. of London, UK. *Career:* Prof. of English and American Literature, Univ. of Leeds 1984–93, Prof. Emer. 1993–. *Publications:* Browning's Characters: A Study in Poetic Technique 1961, Shelley (ed.) 1963, Bulwer Lytton's Falkland (ed.) 1967, The Complete Works of Robert Browning (co-ed., nine vols) 1969–, The Book, The Ring and The Poet: A Biography of Robert Browning (co-author) 1975, Matthew Arnold: A Life 1981, Jane Austen: Her Life 1987, The Beats: An Anthology of 'Beat' Writing (ed.) 1987, Authors' Lives: On Literary Biography and the Arts of Language 1990, Shakespeare: A Life 1998, Christopher Marlowe: Poet & Spy 2005. *Honours:* British Acad. Awards, Leverhulme Award, Huntington Library Fellowship, Folger Shakespeare Library Fellowship 1991. *Address:* School of English, University of Leeds, Leeds, LS2 9JT, England (office).

HONAN, William Holmes, BA, MA; American journalist and writer; b. 11 May 1930, New York, NY; m. Nancy Burton 1975, two s. one d. *Education:* Oberlin College, University of Virginia. *Career:* Ed., The Villager, New York, 1957–60; Asst Ed., New Yorker Magazine, 1960–64, New York Times Magazine, 1969–70; Assoc. Ed., Newsweek, New York City, 1969; Travel Ed., 1970–72, 1973–74, Arts and Leisure Ed., 1974–82, Culture Ed., 1982–88, Chief Cultural Correspondent, 1988–93, National Higher Education Correspondent, 1993–2000, General Assignment, 2000–, New York Times; Managing Ed., Saturday Review, 1972–73. *Publications:* Greenwich Village Guide, 1959; Ted Kennedy: Profile of a Survivor, 1972; Bywater: The Man Who Invented the Pacific War, 1990; Visions of Infamy: The Untold Story of How Journalist Hector C. Bywater Devised the Plans that Led to Pearl Harbour, 1991; Fire When Ready, Gridley! – Great Naval Stories from Manila Bay to Vietnam (ed.), 1992; Treasure Hunt: A New York Times Reporter Tracks the Quedlinburg Treasures, 1997; Zingers (a play), 2002. Contributions: periodicals.

HONE, Joseph; British writer and broadcaster; b. 25 Feb. 1937, London; m. Jacqueline Mary Yeend 1963; one s. one d. *Education:* Kilkenny Coll., Sandford Park School, Dublin; St Columba's Coll., Dublin. *Career:* mem. Upton House Cricket Club. *Publications:* The Flowers of the Forest 1982, Children of the Country 1986, Duck Soup in the Black Sea 1988, Summer Hill 1990, Firesong 1997; Contributions: periodicals. *Literary Agent:* Aitken Alexander Associates Ltd, 18–21 Cavaye Place, London, SW10 9PT, England. *Telephone:* (20) 7373-8672. *Fax:* (20) 7373-6002. *E-mail:* reception@aitkenalexander.co.uk. *Website:* www.aitkenalexander.co.uk.

HONEYMAN, Brenda (see Clarke, Brenda Margaret Lilian)

HONGO, Garrett, BA, MFA; American poet, writer and academic; *Distinguished Professor of Poetry, University of Oregon;* b. 1951, Volcano, HI; m.; two s. *Education:* Pomona Coll., Univ. of Michigan and Univ. of California at Irvine. *Career:* founder and Dir Asian Exclusion Act theatre group, Seattle 1975–77; Dir of Creative Writing Program, Univ. of Oregon 1989–93, currently Distinguished Prof. of Poetry. *Publications:* poetry: Yellow Light 1982, The River of Heaven (Acad. of American Poets Lamont Prize) 1988, The Open Boat: Poems from Asian America (ed.) 1992; non-fiction: Volcano: A Memoir of Hawaii (Oregon Book Award) 1995, Under Western Eyes: Personal Essays from Asian America (ed.); contribs to American Poetry Review, Antaeus, Field, Georgia Review, New England Review, Ploughshares, Parnassus, New York Times, Los Angeles Times, Hawaii Herald, The New Yorker. *Address:* Creative Writing Program, 5243 University of Oregon, Eugene, OR 97403-5243, USA (office). *E-mail:* crwrweb@darkwing.uoregon.edu (office).

HONIG, Edwin, MA; American academic and poet; *Professor Emeritus, Brown University;* b. 3 Sept. 1919, New York; s. of Abraham David Honig and Jane Freundlich; m. 1st Charlotte Gilchrist 1940 (died 1963); m. 2nd Margot S. Dennes 1963 (divorced 1978); two s. *Education:* Univ. of Wisconsin. *Career:* Instructor in English Purdue Univ. 1942–43, New York Univ. and Ill. Inst. Tech. 1946–47, Univ. of NM 1947–48, Claremont Coll. 1949, Harvard Univ. 1949–52, Briggs-Copeland Asst Prof. of English, Harvard 1952–57; mem. Faculty Brown Univ. 1957, Prof. of English 1960–82, of Comparative Literature 1962–82, Chair. Dept of English 1967, Prof. Emer. 1983–; Visiting Prof. Univ. of Calif., Davis 1964–65; Mellon Prof. Boston Univ. 1977; Dir Copper Beech Press; Guggenheim Fellow 1948, 1962; Amy Lowell Travelling Poetry Fellow 1968. *Publications:* (poems) The Moral Circus 1955, The Gazebos 1960, Survivals 1964, Spring Journal 1968, Four Springs 1972, Shake a Spear With Me, John Berryman 1974, At Sixes 1974, The Affinities of Orpheus 1976, Selected Poems (1955–1976) 1979, Interrupted Praise 1983, Gifts of Light 1983, God Talk 1992, The Imminence of Love: Poems 1962–92 1993; (plays) The Widow 1953, The Phantom Lady 1964, Life is a Dream, Calisto and Melibea (play/libretto) 1972, Ends of the World and Other Plays 1983, Calderón: Six Plays 1993; (selected prose of Fernando Pessoa) Always Astonished 1988; (criticism) García Lorca 1944, Dark Conceit: The Making of Allegory 1959, Calderón and the Seizures of Honor 1972, The Poet's Other Voice 1985; (stories) Foibles and Fables of an Abstract Man 1979; (anthologies) (with Oscar Williams): The Mentor Book of Major American Poets 1961, The Major Metaphysical Poets 1968; Spenser 1968; also translations of works by García Lorca, Calderón de la Barca, Fernando Pessoa, Miguel Hernández and Lope de Vega; produced opera Calisto and Melibea 1979, play Life is a Dream

1988, The Phantom Lady; A Glass of Green Tea With Honig 1993. *Honours:* Golden Rose Award New England Poetry Club 1961, Poetry Prize, Saturday Review 1956, Nat. Inst. of Arts and Letters Award 1966, NEA Award (in poetry) 1980, (in transl.) 1983, Columbia Univ. Translation Center Nat. Award 1985; Kt of St James of the Sword, Portugal 1987, Kt of Queen Isabel, Spain 1996. *Address:* Brown University, Box 1852, Providence, RI 02912 (office); 229 Medway Street, Apt. 305, Providence, RI 02906, USA (home). *Telephone:* (401) 831-1027. *Website:* www.brown.edu/Departments/English/Writing (office).

HONORÉ, Christophe; French writer, critic and film director; b. 10 April 1970, Carhaix, Finistère. *Education:* Université de Rennes. *Plays:* Les Débutantes 1998, Le Pire du troupeau 2001. *Films:* Les Filles ne savent pas nager (writer) 2000, Nous deux (writer, dir) 2001, 17 fois Cécile Cassard (writer, dir) 2002, Tout contre Léo (writer, dir) 2002, Novo (writer) 2002, Ma mère (writer, dir) 2004, Le Clan (writer) 2004, Dans Paris (writer, dir) 2006. *Publications:* novels: L'Infamille 1997, La Douceur 1999, Scarborough 2002, Le Livre pour enfants 2005; juvenile novels: Tout contre Léo 1995, C'est plus fort que moi 1996, Je joue très bien tout seul 1997, L'Affaire p'tit Marcel 1997, Zéro de lecture 1998, Une toute petite histoire d'amour 1998, Je ne suis pas une fille à papa 1998, Les Nuits où personne ne dort 1999, Mon cœur Bouleversé 1999, Bretonneries 1999, M'aimer 2003, Torse nu 2005, Noël, c'est couic! 2005, Viens 2006. *Literary Agent:* c/o Jean-François Gabard, ZELIG, 57 rue Réaumur, 75002 Paris, France. *Telephone:* 1 44-78-81-10. *Fax:* 1 44-78-07-65. *E-mail:* zelig@zelig-fr.com. *Website:* www.zelig-fr.com; christophehonore.free.fr.

HOOD, Daniel, BA; American writer and editor; b. 3 Nov. 1967, New Rochelle, NY. *Education:* Georgetown University. *Career:* Art Dir, IMP, publishers, New York City, 1989–94; Desktop Man., Wall Street Journal Europe, Brussels, Belgium, 1994–96; Managing Ed., Faulkner and Gray, publishers, New York City, 1996–2000; Business Ed., Daily News Express, New York, 2000–01; mem. SFWA. *Publications:* Fantasy Fiction: Fanuilh, 1994; Wizard's Heir, 1996; Beggar's Banquet, 1997; Scales of Justice, 1998; King's Cure, 2000. *Literary Agent:* Donald Maass Literary Agency, 157 W 57th Street, Suite 1003, New York, NY 10019, USA. *Address:* 315 E 92nd Street, No. 2E, New York, NY 10128, USA. *E-mail:* danhood@earthlink.net.com.

HOOKER, Jeremy Peter, BA, MA; British lecturer, poet and writer; *Reader in English Literature, Professor, University of Glamorgan*; b. 23 March 1941, Warsash, Hampshire, England. *Education:* University of Southampton. *Career:* Arts Council Creative Writing Fellow, Winchester School of Art, 1981–83; fmr Lecturer in English, Bath College of Higher Education, and Netherlands and USA; currently Reader in English Literature, Prof. Univ. of Glamorgan; mem. Fellow, Academi Gymreig, 2000; Richard Jefferies Society, pres., 1999. *Publications:* The Elements, 1972; Soliloquies of a Chalk Giant, 1974; Solent Shore: New Poems, 1978; Landscape of the Daylight Moon, 1978; Englishman's Road, 1980; Itchen Water, 1982; Poetry of Place, 1982; A View from the Source: Selected Poems, 1982; Master of the Leaping Figures, 1987; The Presence of the Past, 1987; In Praise of Windmills, 1990; Their Silence a Language (with Lee Grandjean), 1994; Writers in a Landscape, 1996; Our Lady of Europe, 1997; Groundwork (with Lee Grandjean), 1998. Contributions: Reviews and journals. *Honours:* Eric Gregory Award, 1969; Welsh Arts Council Literature Prize, 1975. *Address:* Old School House, 7 Sunnyside, Frome, Somerset BA11 1LD, England.

HOOKS, Bell, MA, PhD; American critic, writer, cultural theorist and activist; b. (Gloria Jean Watkins), 25 Sept. 1952, Hopkinsville, KY. *Education:* Crispus Attucks High School, Hopkinsville, Stanford Univ., Univ. of Wisconsin, Univ. of California at Santa Cruz. *Career:* English Prof. and Sr Lecturer in Ethnic Studies, Univ. of Southern California; lead numerous courses at Univ. of California and San Fransisco State Univ. 1980s; tutor in African and Afro-American Studies, Yale Univ. 1985; Assoc. Prof. of Women's Studies and American Literature, Oberlin Coll., OH 1988; Distinguished Prof. of English, City Coll., New York 1994; f. Hambone magazine. *Publications include:* poetry: And There We Wept (chapbook) 1978, The Woman's Mourning Song 1993; non-fiction: Ain't I a Woman: Black Women and Feminism 1981, Feminist Theory from Margin to Center 1984, Talking Back: Thinking Feminist, Thinking Black 1989, Yearning: Race, Gender and Cultural Politics 1990, Breaking Bread: Insurgent Black Intellectual Life (with Cornel West) 1991, Black Looks: Race and Representation 1992, Sisters of the Yam: Black Women and Self-recovery 1993, Teaching to Transgress: Education as the Practice of Freedom 1994, Outlaw Culture: Resisting Representations 1994, Art on my Mind: Visual Politics 1995, Killing Rage: Ending Racism 1995, Bone Black: Memories of Girlhood 1996, Reel to Real: Race, Sex and Class at the Movies 1996, Seduction and Surrender 1997, Wounds of Passion: A Writing Life 1997, Remembered Rapture: The Writer at Work 1999, Feminism is for Everybody: Passionate Politics 2000, Where We Stand: Class Matters 2000, Salvation: Black People and Love 2001, All About Love 2001, Communion: The Female Search for Love 2002, Rock my Soul: Black People and Self-Esteem 2002, Teaching Community: A Pedagogy of Hope 2003, We Real Cool: Black Men and Masculinity 2003, The Will to Change 2004; juvenile: Happy to be Nappy (with Christopher Raschka) 1999, Be Boy Buzz 2002, Homemade Love 2002; contrib. to numerous journals. *Honours:* Lila Wallace-Reader's Digest Fund Writer's Award 1994. *Address:* c/o The City College of New York, 138th Street and Convent Avenue, New York, NY 10031, USA.

HOOVER, Paul Andrew, BA, MA; American poet, writer, editor and educator; *Professor of Creative Writing, San Francisco State University*; b. 30 April 1946, Harrisonburg, Va; m. Maxine Chernoff 197; two s. one d. *Education:* Manchester Coll., Univ. of Illinois. *Career:* Ed. OINK! 1971–85; Founder-mem. 1974, mem. Bd Dirs 1974–87, Pres. 1975–78, The Poetry Center of Chicago at School of the Art Inst.; Poet-in-Residence, Columbia Coll. 1974–2003; Co-Founder and Ed. New American Writing 1986–; Fellow, Simon's Rock of Bard Coll. 1988–; Visiting Prof. in Creative Writing, San Francisco State Univ. 2003–06, Prof. of Creative Writing 2006–; mem. Associated Writing Programs, Co-ordinating Council of Literary Magazines, Modern Language Asscn of America. *Publications:* poetry: Hairpin Turns 1973, The Monocle Thugs 1977, Letter to Einstein Beginning Dear Albert 1979, Somebody Talks a Lot 1983, Nervous Songs 1986, Idea 1987, The Novel: A Poem 1990, Viridian 1997, Totem and Shadow: New and Selected Poems 1999, Rehearsal in Black 2001, Winter (Mirror) 2002; other: Saigon, Illinois (novel) 1988, Postmodern American Poetry: A Norton Anthology (ed.) 1993, Fables of Representation (essays) 2004, Poems in Spanish 2005, Edge and Fold 2006; contrib. to numerous anthologies, reviews, quarterlies and journals. *Honours:* Nat. Endowment for the Arts Poetry Fellowship 1980, Illinois Arts Council Artist's Fellowships 1983, 1984, 1986, General Electric Foundation Award for Younger Writers 1984, Carl Sandburg Award, Friends of the Chicago Public Library 1987, Gwendolyn Brooks Poet Laureate Award 1988, Shifting Foundation Grants 1990, 1991, Gertrude Stein Award in Innovative American Poetry 1994–95, Winner, Contemporary Poetry Series Competition, University of Georgia 1997, San Francisco Literary Laureate Award, Friends of the San Francisco Public Library 2000, Jerome J. Shestack Prize, American Poetry Review 2003. *Address:* 369 Molino Avenue, Mill Valley, CA 94941, USA (home). *Telephone:* (415) 338-3157 (office). *Fax:* (415) 384-0364. *E-mail:* viridian@hotmail.com (office). *Website:* www.newamericanwriting.com (office); www.paulhooverpoetry.blosspot.com (home).

HOPE, Christopher David Tully, MA, FRSL; South African writer; b. 26 Feb. 1944, Johannesburg; s. of Dudley Mitford Hope and Kathleen Mary Hope; m. Eleanor Marilyn Margaret Klein; two s. *Education:* Natal Univ., Univ. of the Witwatersrand. *Career:* mem. Soc. of Authors. *Publications:* A Separate Development 1981, Private Parts 1982, The King, the Cat and the Fiddle (with Yehudi Menuhin) 1983, Kruger's Alp (Whitbread Prize for Fiction 1985) 1984, The Dragon Wore Pink 1985, The Hottentot Room 1986, Black Swan 1987, White Boy Running 1988, My Chocolate Redeemer 1989, Moscow! Moscow! 1990, Serenity House 1992, The Love Songs of Nathan J. Swirsky 1993, Darkest England 1996; poetry: Cape Drives 1974, In the Country of the Black Pig 1981, Englishman 1985, Me, the Moon and Elvis Presley 1997, Signs of the Heart 1999, Heaven Forbid 2002, Brothers Under the Skin 2003, My Mother's Lovers 2006; contrib. to TLS, London Magazine, Les Temps Modernes. *Honours:* Cholmondeley Award 1972, David Higham Award 1981, Int. PEN Award 1983, Whitbread Award 1986, CNA Literary Award (S Africa) 1989. *Literary Agent:* Rogers, Coleridge & White Ltd, 20 Powis Mews, London, W11 1JN, England. *Telephone:* (20) 7221-3717. *Fax:* (20) 7229-9084.

HOPE, Ronald Sidney, CBE, BA, MA, DPhil; British writer; b. 4 April 1921, London; m. Marion Whittaker 1947; one s. one d. *Education:* New Coll., Oxford. *Career:* Fellow, Brasenose Coll., Oxford 1945–47, Dir Seafarers' Educ. Service, London 1947–76; Dir The Marine Soc. 1976–86. *Publications:* Spare Time at Sea 1954, Economic Geography 1956, Dick Small in the Half Deck, Ships 1958, The British Shipping Industry 1959, The Shoregoer's Guide to World Ports 1963, Seamen and the Sea 1965, Introduction to the Merchant Navy 1965, Retirement from the Sea 1967, In Cabined Ships at Sea 1969, Twenty Singing Seamen 1979, The Seamen's World 1982, A New History of British Shipping 1990, Poor Jack: The Perilous History of the Merchant Seaman, 2001. *Address:* 2 Park Place, Dollar, FK14 7AA, England. *Telephone:* (1259) 742045.

HOPE-SIMPSON, Jacynth Ann, (Helen Dudley), MA, DipEd; British writer; b. 10 Nov. 1930, Birmingham, England. *Education:* University of Lausanne, University of Oxford. *Publications:* The Stranger in the Train, 1960; The Bishop of Kenelminster, 1961; The Man Who Came Back, 1962; The Bishop's Picture, 1962; The Unravished Bridge, 1963; The Witch's Cave, 1964; The Hamish Hamilton Book of Myths and Legends, 1965; The Hamish Hamilton Book of Witches, 1966; Escape to the Castle, 1967; The Unknown Island, 1968; They Sailed from Plymouth, 1970; Elizabeth I, 1971; Tales in School, 1971; The Gunner's Boy, 1973; Save Tarranmoor!, 1974; Always on the Move, 1975; The Hijacked Hovercraft, 1975; Black Madonna, 1976; Vote for Victoria, 1976; The Making of the Machine Age, 1978; The Hooded Falcon, 1979; Island of Perfumes, 1985; Cottage Dreams, 1986.

HOPKINS, Antony, CBE, FRCM; British composer, writer and broadcaster (retd); b. 21 March 1921, London; s. of the late Hugh Reynolds and Marjorie Reynolds; m. Alison Purves 1947 (died 1991). *Education:* Berkhamsted School and Royal Coll. of Music with Cyril Smith. *Career:* fmr Lecturer, Royal Coll. of Music 15 years; Dir Intimate Opera Co. 1952–64; composed incidental music for theatre (Old Vic, Stratford-upon-Avon), radio and cinema. *Radio:* presenter of series, Talking About Music (BBC) 1954–92. *Compositions include:* operas: Lady Rohesia, Three's Company, Hands Across the Sky, Dr Musikus, Ten o'clock Call, The Man from Tuscany; ballet music: Etude, Café des Sports; others: Psalm 42, Magnificat and Nunc Dimittis for girls' choir), A Time for Growing, Early One Morning, Partita for solo violin, John and the Magic Music Man for narrator and orchestra (Grand Prix Besançon Film

Festival) 1976, songs, recorder pieces, three piano sonatas; incidental music, including Oedipus, The Love of Four Colonels, Cast a Dark Shadow, Pickwick Papers, Billy Budd, Decameron Nights. *Publications:* Talking about Symphonies 1961, Talking about Concertos 1964, Music All Around Me 1967, Music Face to Face 1971, Talking about Sonatas 1971, Downbeat Guide 1977, Understanding Music 1979, The Nine Symphonies of Beethoven 1980, Songs for Swinging Golfers 1981, Sounds of Music 1982, Beating Time (autobiog.) 1982, Pathway to Music 1983, The Concertgoer's Companion Vol. I 1984, Vol. II 1986, The Seven Concertos of Beethoven 1996; contrib. to numerous books. *Honours:* Hon. FRAM; Hon. Fellow, Robinson Coll. Cambridge 1980; Hon. DUniv (Stirling) 1980; Hon. Dr of Arts (Bedford) Italia Prizes for composition 1952, 1957, City of Tokyo Medal for services to music 1973, Royal Coll. of Music Chappell Gold Medal 1943, Royal Coll. of Music Cobbett Prize. *Address:* Woodyard Cottage, Ashridge, Berkhamsted, Herts., HP4 1PS, England (home). *Telephone:* (1442) 842257 (home).

HOPKINSON, Simon; Australian playwright, director and writer. *Career:* Artistic Dir, Australian Theatre for Young People, New England Theatre Co., Darwin Theatre Group; fmr resident dramatist and Assoc. Dir, Melbourne Theatre Co.; founder, Theatre-in-Education Co., Australia; specialist consultant for children's television, Australian Broadcasting Authority. *Theatre includes:* Lipstick Dreams, Wedding Games, Happy Families. *Television includes:* Bananas in Pyjamas (co-creator, writer) 1991 (also subsequent stage shows), Driven Crazy, Chuck Finn, Fast Tracks, Gloria's House, Petals. *Films include:* The Magic Pudding. *Publications (on CD-ROM):* Oz – The Magical Adventure 2000, Bananas in Pyjamas: It's Fun Time, It's Party Time. *Literary Agent:* RGM Associates, PO Box 128, Surry Hills, NSW 2010, Australia. *Telephone:* (2) 9281 3911. *Fax:* (2) 9281 4705. *E-mail:* info@rgm.com.au. *Website:* www.rgm.com.au.

HOPKIRK, Joyce, FRSA; British journalist and editor (retd); b. 2 March, Newcastle upon Tyne; d. of Walter Nicholson and Veronica Nicholson (née Keelan); m. 1st Peter Hopkirk 1962; one d.; m. 2nd William James Lear 1974; one s. *Education:* La Sagesse Convent and Middle St Secondary School (Newcastle upon Tyne). *Career:* reporter, Gateshead Post 1955; Founder-Ed. Majorcan News 1959; reporter, Daily Sketch 1960; Royal Reporter, Daily Express 1961; Ed. Fashion magazine 1967; Women's Ed. Sun newspaper 1967; Launch Ed. Cosmopolitan magazine 1971–72; Asst Ed. Daily Mirror 1973–78, Asst Ed. Sunday Mirror 1985; Women's Ed. Sunday Times 1982; Editorial Dir Elle magazine 1984; Ed.-in-Chief She magazine 1986–89; currently freelance journalist; Dir Editors Unlimited 1990–; Co-Chair. PPA Awards 1998–; mem. Competition Comm. 1999–2001, 2001–06. *Video cassette:* Successful Slimming 1978. *Publications:* Successful Slimming 1976, Successful Slimming Cookbook 1978, Splash (co-author) 1995, Best of Enemies 1996, Double Trouble 1997, Unfinished Business 1998, Relative Strangers 1999, The Affair 2000; six novels published as Val Hopkirk. *Honours:* Ed. of the Year 1972, Women's Magazines Ed. of the Year 1988. *Address:* Gadespring, 109 Piccotts End, Hemel Hempstead, Herts., HP1 3AT, England. *Telephone:* (1442) 245608.

HORNBY, Nick; British journalist and novelist; b. 1957, London, England. *Publications:* Contemporary American Fiction (essays) 1992, Fever Pitch (memoir) 1992, (screenplay) 1997, My Favourite Year: A Collection of New Football Writing (ed.) 1993, High Fidelity (novel) 1995, Speaking With the Angel (ed.) 2000, About a Boy (novel) 2000, How to be Good (novel) 2001, 31 Songs (non-fiction) 2003, A Long Way Down 2005, The Complete Polysyllabic Spree (collected columns) 2006; contrib. to Sunday Times, TLS, Literary Review, New York Times, New Yorker, the Believer. *Honours:* William Hill Sports Book of the Year Award 1992, Writers' Guild Best Fiction Book Award 1995, American Acad. of Arts and Letters E. M. Forster Award 1999, WHSmith Fiction Award 2002, London Award 2003. *Literary Agent:* PFD, Drury House, 34–43 Russell Street, London, WC2B 5HA, England.

HORNE, Sir Alistair Allan, Kt, MA; British writer, journalist and lecturer; b. 9 Nov. 1925, London, England; m. 1st Renira Margaret Hawkins; three d.; m. 2nd The Hon. Mrs Sheelin Eccles 1987. *Education:* Jesus Coll., Cambridge. *Career:* foreign correspondent, Daily Telegraph 1952–55; official biographer for Prime Minister Harold Macmillan 1979; mem. Soc. of Authors, RSL. *Publications:* Back into Power 1955, The Land is Bright 1958, Canada and the Canadians 1961, The Fall of Paris 1870–1871 1965, To Lose a Battle: France 1940 1969, Death of a Generation 1970, The Paris Commune 1971, Small Earthquake in Chile 1972, Napoleon, Master of Europe 1805–1807 1979, The French Army and Politics 1870–1970 1984, Macmillan, Vol. I 1894–1956 1985, Vol. II 1957–1986 1989, A Bundle from Britain 1993, The Lonely Leader: Monty 1944–45 1994, How Far from Austerlitz: Napoleon 1805–1815 1996, Telling Lives (ed.) 2000, Seven Ages of Paris: Portrait of a City 2002, The Age of Napoleon 2004, Friend or Foe: An Anglo-Saxon History of France 2004; contrib. to various periodicals. *Honours:* Hawthornden Prize 1963, Yorkshire Post Book of Year Prize 1978, Wolfson Literary Award 1978, Enid Macleod Prize 1985; Chevalier, Légion d'honneur 1993. *Literary Agent:* The Wylie Agency, 4–8 Rodney Street, London, N1 9JH, England. *Address:* The Old Vicarage, Turville, Nr Henley on Thames, Oxfordshire RG9 6QU, England.

HOROVITZ, Michael, OBE, BA, MA; British writer, poet, editor and publisher; *Editor and Publisher, New Departures International Review;* b. 4 April 1935, Frankfurt am Main, Germany. *Education:* Brasenose Coll., Oxford. *Career:* Ed. and Publisher, New Departures International Review 1959–; founder, co-ordinator, and torchbearer, Poetry Olympics Festivals 1980–. *Publications:* Europa (trans.) 1961, Alan Davie 1963, Declaration 1963,

Strangers: Poems 1965, Poetry for the People: An Essay in Bop Prosody 1966, Bank Holiday: A New Testament for the Love Generation 1967, Children of Albion (ed.) 1969, The Wolverhampton Wanderer: An Epic of Football, Fate and Fun 1970, Love Poems 1971, A Contemplation 1978, Growing Up: Selected Poems and Pictures 1951–1979 1979, The Egghead Republic (trans.) 1983, A Celebration of and for Frances Horovitz 1984, Midsummer Morning Jog Log 1986, Bop Paintings, Collages and Drawings 1989, Grandchildren of Albion (ed.) 1992, Wordsounds and Sightlines: New and Selected Poems 1994, Grandchildren of Albion Live (ed.) 1996, The POW! Anthology 1996, The POP! Anthology 2000, The POM! Anthology 2001, Jeff Nuttall's Wake 2004, A New Waste Land: Timeship Earth at Nillennium 2004. *Address:* c/o New Departures International Review, PO Box 9819, London, W11 2GQ, England.

HOROWITZ, Anthony; British writer and screenwriter; b. 5 April 1955, London; m. Jill Green; two s. *Education:* Orley Farm School London, Rugby School, Univ. of York. *Writing for television:* Dramarama, Boon, Robin of Sherwood, Poirot, The Gift (adaptation), Murder Most Horrid, The Last Englishman, Chiller, Crime Traveller, Midsomer Murders, Murder in Mind (also creator), Menace, Foyle's War (also creator). *Film screenplay:* The Gathering 2002. *Play:* Mindgame 2000. *Publications:* The Sinister Secret of Frederick K. Bower 1979, Misha, the Magician and the Mysterious Amulet 1981, Devil's Door Bell 1983, Enter Frederick K. Bower 1985, Night of the Scorpion 1985, The Myths and Mythology 1985, Robin the Hooded Man (with Richard Carpenter) 1986, The Silver Citadel 1986, Public Enemy #2 1987, Adventurer 1987, Crossbow: The Adventures of William Tell 1987, The Falcon's Malteser 1987, Groosham Grange 1988, Just Ask for Diamond 1989, Day of the Dragon 1989, Groosham Grange II: The Unholy Grail 1991, South by South East 1991, The Puffin Book of Horror Stories (ed.) 1994, Granny 1994, The Switch 1996, Death Walks Tonight: Horrifying Stories 1996, The Devil and his Boy 1998, Horowitz Horror 1999, More Horowitz Horror 2000, Stormbreaker 2000, Point Blank 2001, Skeleton Key 2002, Eagle Strike 2003, Alex Rider 2003, I Know What You Did Last Wednesday 2003, Return to Groosham Grange 2003, The Blurred Man 2003, Scorpia 2004, Three of Diamonds 2004, The Killing Joke 2004, Ark Angel: Alex Rider Book 6 (British Book Awards Red House Children's Book of the Year 2006) 2005, The Power of Five: Raven's Gate 2005, The Power of Five: Evil Star 2006. *Address:* c/o Orchard Books, The Watts Publishing Group, 96 Leonard Street, London, EC2A 4XD, England. *Website:* www.orchardbooks.co.uk.

HOROWITZ, Irving Louis, BSS, MA, PhD; American academic, writer, editor and publisher; *Hannah Arendt Distinguished Professor of Social and Political Theory, Rutgers University;* b. 25 Sept. 1929, New York, NY; m. 1st Ruth Lenore Horowitz 1950 (divorced 1964); two s.; m. 2nd Mary Curtis Horowitz 1979. *Education:* City Coll., CUNY, Columbia Univ. and Univ. of Buenos Aires. *Career:* Assoc. Prof. Univ. of Buenos Aires 1955–58; Postgraduate Fellow Brandeis Univ. 1958–59; Asst Prof. Bard Coll. 1960; Chair Dept of Sociology, Hobart and William Smith Colls 1960–63; Ed.-in-Chief Transaction Soc. 1962–94; Assoc. Prof. to Prof. of Sociology, Washington Univ., St Louis 1963–69; Pres. Transaction Books 1966–94; Chair Dept of Sociology, Livingston Coll., Rutgers Univ. 1969–73; Prof. of Sociology Grad. Faculty, Rutgers Univ. 1969–, Hannah Arendt Distinguished Prof. of Social and Political Theory 1979–; Bacardi Chair of Cuban Studies Miami Univ., 1992–93; Editorial Chair. and Pres. Emer. Transaction/USA and Transaction/UK; Bd Chair. ILH Foundation for Social Policy 1998–2004; mem. American Acad. of Arts and Sciences, American Asscn of Univ. Profs, American Political Science Asscn (APSA), Authors' Guild, Council on Foreign Relations, Int. Soc. of Political Psychology (founder), Nat. Asscn of Scholars. *Publications:* Idea of War and Peace in Contemporary Philosophy 1957, Philosophy, Science and the Sociology of Knowledge 1960, Radicalism and the Revolt Against Reason: The Social Theories of Georges Sorel 1962, The War Game: Studies of the New Civilian Militarists 1963, Professing Sociology: The Life Cycle of a Social Science 1963, Revolution in Brazil: Politics and Society in a Developing Nation 1964, The Rise and Fall of Project Camelot 1967, Three Worlds of Development: The Theory and Practice of International Stratification 1967, Latin American Radicalism: A Documentary Report on Nationalist and Left Movements 1969, Sociological Self-Images 1969, The Knowledge Factory: Masses in Latin America 1970, Cuban Communism 1970, Foundations of Political Sociology 1972, Social Science and Public Policy in the United States 1975, Ideology and Utopia in the United States 1977, Dialogues on American Politics 1979, Taking Lives: Genocide and State Power 1979, Beyond Empire and Revolution 1982, C. Wright Mills: An American Utopian 1983, Winners and Losers 1985, Communicating Ideas 1987, Daydreams and Nightmares: Reflections of a Harlem Childhood 1990, The Decomposition of Sociology 1993, Behemoth: Main Currents in the History and Theory of Political Sociology 1999, Searching for the Soul of American Foreign Policy: The Cuban Embargo and the National Interest 2000, Tributes: An Informal History of Social Science in the Twentieth Century 2004; contribs to professional journals. *Honours:* APSA Harold D. Lasswell Award, Festschrift 1994, Nat. Jewish Book Award in Biography/Autobiography, Inter-Univ. Armed Forces Soc. Lifetime Service Award, Laissez-Faire Soc. Civil Liberties Award. *Address:* Transaction Publishers, Rutgers University, Piscataway, NJ 08854 (office); 1247 State Road, Route 206, Blanwenberg Road-Rocky Hill Intersection, Princeton, NJ 08540, USA (home). *Telephone:* (732) 445-2280 (office); (609) 921-1479 (home). *Fax:* (732) 445-3138 (office); (609) 921-7225 (home). *E-mail:* ihorowtiz@transactionpub.com (office). *Website:* www .transactionpub.com (office).

HORROCKS, Paul John; British editor; *Editor, Manchester Evening News;* b. 19 Dec. 1953, s. of Joe Horrocks and Eunice Horrocks; m. Linda Jean Walton 1976; two s. one d. one step-d. *Education:* Bolton School. *Career:* reporter, Daily Mail 1974–75; reporter, Manchester Evening News 1975–80, Crime Corresp. 1980–87, News Ed. 1987–91, Asst Ed. 1991–95, Deputy Ed. 1995–97, Ed. 1997–; Pres. UK Soc. of Editors; mem. Organizing Cttee, Commonwealth Games, Manchester 2002; Vice-Pres. Community Foundation for Greater Manchester; Patron Francis House Children's Hospice; mem. Bd New Children's Hosp.; Trustee Tatton Trust. *Address:* Manchester Evening News, 1 Scott Place, Manchester, M3 3RN, England (office). *Telephone:* (161) 2112465 (office). *Fax:* (161) 2112030 (office). *Website:* www .manchesteronline.co.uk (office).

HORTON, Richard C., FRCP; British physician; *Editor, The Lancet. Career:* Visting Prof., London School of Hygiene and Tropical Medicine; Ed., publisher, The Lancet; bd mem. Council of Science Editors 1994–. *Publications:* non-fiction: Preventing Coronary Artery Disease (with Martin Kendall) 1997, How to Publish in Biomedicine 1997, Second Opinion: Doctors and Diseases 2003, Health Wars: On the Global Front Lines of Modern Medicine 2003, MMR: Science and Fiction 2004; contrib. to New York Review of Books, London Review of Books, The Lancet, journals. *Address:* The Lancet, 32 Jamestown Road, London, NW1 7BY, England (office). *Telephone:* (20) 7424-4910 (office). *Fax:* (20) 7424-4911 (office). *E-mail:* richard.horton@lancet.com (office).

HORWITZ, Allan Kolski; South African writer and performance poet. *Career:* f. and co-ordinator, Botsotso Publishing, mem. editorial board, Botsotso Magazine; f., Botsotso Jesters performance poetry group. *Publications:* Call from the Free State (poems) 1979, Un/Common Ground (fiction) 2003; contribs to Unity In Flight short story anthology 2001, Donga, The Literate Gymnast, LitNet. *Address:* Botsotso, Box 23910, Joubert Park 2044. *Telephone:* (011) 487-2112. *E-mail:* botsotso@artslink.co.za. *Website:* www .botsotso.org.za. *Address:* Postnet Suite 136, Private Bag X2600, Houghton, South Africa.

HORWOOD, Harold Andrew; Canadian author; b. 2 Nov. 1923, St John's, NF; m. Cornelia Lindsmith 1973, one s. one d. *Education:* Prince of Wales College, St John's, NF. *Career:* mem., House of Assembly, NF, Liberal Party, 1949–51; Columnist, Evening Telegram, St John's, NF, 1952–58; Writer-in-Residence, University of Western Ontario, 1976–77, University of Waterloo, 1980–82; mem. Writers' Union of Canada (chair. 1980–81). *Publications:* Tomorrow Will be Sunday (novel), 1966; The Foxes of Beachy Cove, 1967; Newfoundland, 1969; White Eskimo: A Novel of Labrador, 1972; Beyond the Road: Portraits and Visions of Newfoundlands, 1976; Bartlett: The Great Canadian Explorer, 1977; The Colonial Dream 1497/1760, 1978; Only the Gods Speak (short stories), 1979; Tales of the Labrador Indians, 1981; A History of Canada, 1984; Pirates and Outlaws of Canada 1610–1932 (with E. Butts), 1984; A History of the Newfoundland Ranger Force, 1986; Corner Brook: A Social History of a Paper Town, 1986; Historic Newfoundland (with John de Visser), 1986; Remembering Summer (novel), 1987; Dancing on the Shore, 1987; Bandits and Privateers: Canada in the Age of Gunpowder (with E. Butts), 1987; Joey: The Life and Political Times of Joey Smallwood, 1989; The Magic Ground, 1996; A Walk in the Dream Time: Growing Up in Old St John's, 1997; Evening Light (novel), 1998; Among the Lions, a Lamb in the Literary Jungle, 2000; Cycle of the Sun (poetry), 2003. Contributions: numerous journals and magazines. *Honours:* Best Scientific Book of the Year, 1967; Canada Council Senior Arts Award, 1975; Mem. of the Order of Canada, 1980.

HORWOOD, William; British novelist; b. 1944, Oxford, England; m. 1st; m. 2nd; m. 3rd; six c. *Education:* Sir Roger Manwood's School, Sandwich, Univ. of Bristol. *Career:* frmly worked at trade magazine Campaign, feature ed. Daily Mail –1978. *Publications:* Duncton Wood 1980, The Stonor Eagles 1982, Callanish 1984, Skallagrigg 1987, Duncton Quest 1988, Duncton Found 1989, Duncton Tales 1991, The Book of Silence 1992, Duncton Rising 1993, Duncton Stone 1993, The Willows in Winter 1993, Toad Triumphant 1995, Journeys to the Heartland 1995, The Willows and Beyond 1996, Seekers at the Wulfrock 1997, Mole Gets Lost 1997, Flying into Danger 1997, Toad in Trouble 1997, Willows at Christmas 1998, The Boy With No Shoes (autobiog.) 2004. *Address:* c/o Hodder Headline, 338 Euston Road, London, NW1 3BH, England.

HOSKING, Geoffrey Alan, PhD, FBA, FRHistS; British historian and academic; *Professor of Russian History, University College London;* b. 28 April 1942, Troon, Ayrshire; s. of Stuart Hosking and Jean Smillie; m. Anne Lloyd Hirst 1970; two d. *Education:* Maidstone Grammar School, Moscow State Univ., Kings Coll., Cambridge, St Antony's Coll., Oxford. *Career:* Lecturer in Govt, Univ. of Essex 1966–71, Lecturer in History 1972–76, Sr Lecturer and Reader in History 1976–84; Prof. of Russian History, School of Slavonic Studies, Univ. of London 1984–99, 2004–, Leverhulme Research Prof. 1999–2004; Deputy Dir School of Slavonic and East European Studies, Univ. of London 1996–98; Visiting Prof. in Political Science Univ. of Wisocnsin-Madison, USA 1971–72, Slavisches Institut, Univ. of Cologne, Germany 1980–81; mem. Booker Prize Jury for Russian Fiction 1993. *Publications:* The Russian Constitutional Experiment 1973, Beyond Socialist Realism 1980, The First Socialist Society: A History of the Soviet Union from Within 1985, The Awakening of the Soviet Union 1990, The Road to Post-Communism: Independent Political Movements in the Soviet Union 1985–91 (with J. Aves and P. Duncan) 1992, Russia: People and Empire (1552–1917)

1997, Myths and Nationhood (ed. with George Schöpflin) 1997, Russian Nationalism Past and Present (ed. with Robert Service) 1998, Reinterpreting Russia (ed. with Robert Service) 1999, Russia and the Russians: A History from Rus to Russian Federation 2001, Rulers and Victims: The Russians in the Soviet Union 2006. *Honours:* Dr hc (Russian Acad. of Sciences) 2000; LA Times History Book Prize 1986, BBC Reith Lecturer 1988, US Ind. Publrs History Book Prize 2001. *Address:* School of Slavonic and East European Studies, University College London, Gower Street, London, WC1E 6BT (office); 18 Camden Mews, London, NW1 9DA, England (home). *Telephone:* (20) 76792-8815 (office). *E-mail:* g.hosking@ucl.ac.uk (office).

HOSPITAL, Janette Turner, (Alex Juniper), MA; Australian writer and academic; *Professor and Distinguished Writer-in-Residence, University of South Carolina;* b. 12 Nov. 1942, Melbourne; d. of Adrian Charles Turner and Elsie Turner; m. Clifford Hospital 1965; one s. one d. *Education:* Univ. of Queensland, and Queen's Univ., Canada. *Career:* high school teacher, Queensland 1963–66; librarian, Harvard Univ. 1967–71; Lecturer in English, St Lawrence Coll., Kingston, Ont., in maximum and medium-security fed. penitentiaries for men 1971–82; professional writer 1982–; Writer-in-Residence and lecturer Writing Program, MIT 1985–86, 1987, 1989, Writer-in-Residence Univ. of Ottawa, Canada 1987, Univ. of Sydney, Australia 1989, Queen's Univ. at Herstmonceux Castle, UK 1994; Adjunct Prof. of English, La Trobe Univ., Melbourne 1990–93; Visiting Fellow and Writer-in-Residence Univ. of E Anglia, UK 1996; O'Connor Chair. in Literature, Colgate Univ., Hamilton, NY 1999; Dickey Prof. and Distinguished Writer-in-Residence, Univ. of S Carolina 1999–. *Publications:* The Ivory Swing (Seal First Novel Award) 1982, The Tiger in the Tiger Pit 1983, Borderline 1985, Charades 1988, The Last Magician 1992, Oyster 1996, Due Preparations for the Plague 2003; short story collections: Dislocations (Fellowship of Australian Writers Fiction Award 1988) 1986, Isobars 1990, Collected Stories 1995, North of Nowhere, South of Loss 2003; as Alex Juniper: A Very Proper Death 1991; numerous articles. *Honours:* Dr hc Griffith Univ. (Queensland) 1995; Hon. DLitt (Univ. of Queensland) 2003; several awards for novels and short stories; Gold Medal, Nat. Magazine Awards (Canada) 1991 (for travel writing), First Prize, Magazine Fiction, Foundation for the Advancement of Canadian Letters 1982. *Address:* Department of English, University of South Carolina, Welsh Humanities Office Building, Room 504, Columbia, SC 29208, USA (office); c/o Barbara Mobbs, PO Box 126, Edgecliff, Sydney, NSW 2027, Australia; c/o Mic Cheetham, 11–12 Dover Street, London, W1X 3PH, England. *Telephone:* (803) 777-2186 (office). *E-mail:* hospitjt@gwm.sc.edu (office). *Website:* www.cla.sc.edu/ENGL (office).

HOSSEINI, Khaled; Afghan writer and physician; b. 1965, Kabul; m.; one s. one d. *Education:* Santa Clara Univ., UC San Diego School of Medicine. *Career:* moved to Paris, France aged 11, to San Jose, CA, USA in 1980; physician 1996–. *Publications:* The Kite Runner (novel) 2004, A Thousand Splendid Suns 2007. *Literary Agent:* Judy Lubershane Agency, 2151 Massachusetts Avenue, Lexington, MA 02421, USA. *Telephone:* (781) 274-0717. *Fax:* (781) 274-0671. *E-mail:* jlubershane@rcn.com. *Address:* c/o Riverhead Books, 375 Hudson Street, New York, NY 10014, USA. *Website:* www .khaledhosseini.com.

HOTCHNER, Aaron Edward, LLB; American author and dramatist; b. 28 June 1920, St Louis, MO. *Education:* Washington University, St Louis. *Career:* mem. Authors League; Dramatists Guild; PEN. *Films:* Adventures of a Young Man, King of the Hill. *Television:* Man Who Lived at the Ritz, For Whom Bell Tolls, The Killers, Looking for Miracles. *Publications:* The Dangerous American, 1958; The White House (play), 1964; Papa Hemingway: A Personal Memoir, 1966; The Hemingway Hero (play), 1967; Treasure, 1970; Do You Take This Man? (play), 1970; King of the Hill, 1972; Looking for Miracles, 1974; Doris Day: Her Own Story, 1976; Sophia: Living and Loving, 1979; Sweet Prince (play), 1980; The Man Who Lived at the Ritz, 1982; Choice People, 1984; Hemingway and His World, 1988; Welcome to the Club (musical), 1989; Blown Away, 1990; Louisiana Purchase, 1996; Exactly Like You (musical), 1998; After the Storm, 2001; The Day I Fired Alan Ladd and Other World War Two Adventures, 2002, Shameless Exploitation in Pursuit of the Common Good 2003, They All Come to Elaine's 2004, Dear Papa, Dear Hotch 2005, The World of Nick Adams (concert with music) 2002, 2003; contrib. to magazines. *Honours:* Hon. DHL, Washington University, 1992; Distinguished Alumni Award, Washington University Law School, 1992. *Address:* 14 Hillandale Road, Westport, CT 06880, USA (home). *Telephone:* (203) 726-5686 (home). *E-mail:* ahotchner@newmansown.com (home).

HOUELLEBECQ, Michel, DipAgr; French novelist and poet; b. 26 Feb. 1958, Réunion; m. 1st 1980 (divorced); one s.; m. 2nd Marie-Pierre Gauthier 1998. *Career:* first works (poetry) published in Nouvelle Revue de Paris 1985. *Publications include:* Contre le monde, contre la vie 1991, Rester vivant 1991, La poursuite de bonheur (Prix Tristan Tzara) 1992, Extension du domaine à la lutte 1994, Le sens du combat (Prix de Flore) 1996, Interventions, Les Particules élémentaires (Prix Novembre), Renaissance 1999, Lanzarote 2000, Plateforme (Impac Prize) 2002, La Possibilité d'une île (trans. as The Possibility of An Island) 2005, HP Lovecraft: Against the World, Against Life 2006. *Honours:* Grand Prix Nat. des Lettres Jeune Talent 1998. *Address:* Editions Fayard, 13 rue du Montparnasse, 75006 Paris, France.

HOUGH, (Helen) Charlotte, (Charlotte Ackroyd); British writer and artist; b. 24 May 1924, Hants.; d. of Henry Woodyatt and Helen Johnson; m. 1st Richard Hough 1941 (divorced 1973); four d.; m. 2nd Louis Ackroyd 1997.

Education: Frensham Heights. *Career:* WRNS in World War II; writer and illustrator for children; mem. CWA, PEN, Soc. of Authors. *Publications:* Jim Tiger 1956, Morton's Pony 1957, The Hampshire Pig 1958, The Story of Mr Pinks 1958, The Animal Game 1959, The Homemakers 1959, The Trackers 1960, Algernon 1962, Three Little Funny Ones 1962, The Owl in the Barn 1964, More Funny Ones 1965, Red Biddy 1966, Anna and Minnie 1967, Sir Frog 1968, My Aunt's Alphabet 1969, A Bad Child's Book of Moral Verse 1970, The Bassington Murder (adult novel) 1980. *Literary Agent:* c/o Curtis Brown Ltd, 28–29 Haymarket, London, SW1Y 4SP, England. *Telephone:* (20) 7393-4400. *Fax:* (20) 7393-4401. *E-mail:* info@curtisbrown.co.uk. *Website:* www.curtisbrown.co.uk. *Address:* 1A Ivor Street, London, NW1 9PL, England (home). *Telephone:* (20) 7267-8915 (home).

HOUGHTON, Eric; British teacher and author; b. 4 Jan. 1930, West Yorks.; s. of Alfred William Houghton and Mary Elizabeth Houghton (née Meffer); m. Cecile Wolffe 1954; one s. one d. *Education:* Sheffield City Coll. of Educ. *Career:* mem. Soc. of Authors, Children's Writers' Group. *Publications:* The White Wall 1961, Summer Silver 1963, They Marched with Spartacus 1963, Boy Beyond the Mist 1966, A Giant Can Do Anything 1975, The Mouse and the Magician 1976, The Remarkable Feat of King Caboodle 1978, Steps Out of Time 1979, Gates of Glass 1987, Walter's Wand 1989, The Magic Cheese 1991, The Backwards Watch 1991, Vincent the Invisible 1993, Rosie and the Robbers 1997, The Crooked Apple Tree 1999. *Honours:* American Jr Book Award 1964. *Address:* The Crest, 42 Collier Road, Hastings, East Sussex, TN34 3JR, England.

HOUSSI, Majid al-; Tunisian writer, poet and academic; *Professor and Chair of French, Università Ca' Foscari, Venice*; b. 1941. *Education:* Padua Univ. *Career:* moved to Italy 1962; fmr Lecturer in French Inst. des Langues et Littératures Romanes Padua Univ.; apptd Prof. and Chair of French Language, Faculté d'Economie, Ancona Polytechnic Univ. 1990, Dir Inst. des Langues 1990–99, Dir Centre Inter-Deptl des Services Linguistiques; currently Prof. and Chair of French Univ. Ca' Foscari, Venice. *Publications:* Je voudrais ésotériquement te conter 1972, Imagivresse (Prix Univ. di Padova) 1973, Iris-Ifriqiya 1981, Ahméta-O 1981, Pour une histoire du théâtre tunisien 1982, L'Espace scriptural de Tahar Ben Jelloun 1983, Maghreb: panorama letterario 1991, Albert Camus, un effet spatial algérien 1992, Le Verger des poursuites 1992, Albert Camus, le désir de Méditerranée 1993, L'Image du Maghreb dans les lettres françaises du XIXème siècle 1994, Préface et choix des textes à la Vie errante de Guy de Maupassant 1995, Regards sur la littérature tunisienne (co-author) 1997, La Cité méditerranéenne 1997, Pour une nouvelle pédagogie du français 1998, Des voix dans la traversée (Prix Comar 2000) 1999, Salammbô, le désir de perfection 1999, Regards sur la littérature marocaine de langue française (co-author) 2000, Les Arabismes dans la langue française: du moyen âge à nos jours 2001, Le Français pour les étudiants en sciences économiques 2001, Le Regard du coeur 2002; contrib. numerous articles to journals and chapters in books. *Honours:* Grand Officier au Mérite Educatif de la République Tunisienne. *Address:* c/o Università Ca' Foscari, Dorsoduro 3246, 30123 Venice, Italy.

HOUSTON, James D., BA, MA; American writer; b. 10 Nov. 1933, San Francisco, Calif.; m. Jeanne Toyo Wakatsuki 1957; one s. two d. *Education:* San Jose State Coll., Stanford Univ. *Career:* Lecturer in English, Stanford Univ. 1967–68; Lecturer in Writing, Univ. of California at Santa Cruz 1969–88, Visiting Prof. in Literature 1989–93; Writer-in-Residence, Villa Montalvo, Saratoga, Calif. 1980, 1992, Centrum Foundation, Port Townsend, Washington 1992; Distinguished Visiting Writer, Univ. of Hawaii 1983; Allen T. Gilliland Chair in Telecommunications, San Jose State Univ. 1985, Lurie Chair and Distinguished Visiting Prof. of Creative Writing 2006; Visiting Writer, Univ. of Michigan 1985, Univ. of Oregon 1994, George Mason Univ., Fairfax 1999; Writer-in-Residence, Deutsche Bundesbank, Frankfurt 2002; mem. PEN Center West. *Films:* Farewell to Manzanar (with Jean Wakatsuki Houston and John Korty) 1976, Li'a: The Legacy of a Hawaiian Man 1988, Listen to the Forest 1991, The Hawaiian Way: The Art and Family Tradition of Slack Key 1993, Words, Earth and Aloha: The Sources of Hawaiian Music 1995. *Publications:* fiction: Between Battles 1968, Gig 1969, A Native Son of the Golden West 1971, Continental Drift 1978, Gasoline: The Automotive Adventures of Charlie Bates (short stories) 1980, Love Life 1987, The Last Paradise 1998, Snow Mountain Passage 2001, Bird of Another Heaven 2007; non-fiction: Farewell to Manzanar (with Jeanne Wakatsuki Houston) 1973, Open Field (with John R. Brodie) 1974, Three Songs for My Father 1974, Californians: Searching for the Golden State 1982, One Can Think About Life After the Fish is in the Canoe, and Other Coastal Sketches 1985, The Men in My Life, and Other More or Less True Recollections of Kinship 1987, In the Ring of Fire: A Pacific Basin Journey 1997, Hawaiian Son: The Life and Music of Eddie Kamae 2004; editor: The Literature of California Vol. 1 (with Jack Hicks, Maxine Hong Kingston and Al Young) 2000; contrib. to various anthologies. *Honours:* Wallace Stegner Writing Fellow, Stanford Univ. 1966–67, Joseph Henry Jackson Award 1967, Humanitas Prize 1976, Nat. Endowment for the Arts grants 1976–77, Research Fellow, East-West Center, Honolulu 1984, American Book Award 1983, Hawaii Int. Film Festival Special Award 1989, Rockefeller Foundation Writer's Residency, Bellagio, Italy 1995, American Book Award 1999, Distinguished Achievement Award, Western Literature Asscn 1999, Carey McWilliams Award 2000, Commonwealth Club Californiana Silver Medal 2001. *Address:* 2-1130 East Cliff Drive, Santa Cruz, CA 95062, USA. *Website:* www.jamesdhouston.com.

HOUSTON, R. B. (see Rae, Hugh Crauford)

HOVANNISIAN, Richard G.; American academic and writer; b. 9 Nov. 1932, Tulare, CA; m. Vartiter Kotcholosian 1957; four c. *Education:* BA in History, 1954, MA in History, 1958, University of California at Berkeley; Certificate in Armenian, Collège Armènien, Beirut, 1956; PhD in History, University of California at Los Angeles, 1966. *Career:* Lecturer, 1962–69, Prof. of Armenian and Near Eastern History, 1969–, Assoc. Dir, G. E. von Grunebaum Center of Near Eastern Studies, 1979–95, University of California at Los Angeles; Assoc. Prof. of History, St Mary's College, Los Angeles, 1965–69; Chair., Modern Armenian History, Armenian Educational Foundation, 1987–; Guest Lecturer; Consultant; mem. American Asscn for the Advancement of Slavic Studies; American Historical Asscn; Armenian Acad. of Science; Middle East Studies Asscn, fellow; National Asscn of Armenian Studies; Oral History Asscn; Society for Armenian Studies, founder-pres., 1974–75, 1990–92. *Publications:* Armenia on the Road to Independence, 1967; The Republic of Armenia, Vol. I, 1971, Vol. II, 1982, Vols III–IV, 1996; The Armenian Holocaust, 1980; The Armenian Genocide in Perspective, 1986; The Armenian Genocide: History, Politics, Ethics, 1992; The Armenian People from Ancient to Modern Times, Vol. I, The Dynastic Periods: From Antiquity to the Fourteenth Century, Vol. II, Foreign Dominion to Statehood: The Fifteenth to Twentieth Century, 1997. Co-Author: Transcaucasia: Nationalism and Social Change, 1983; Le Crime de Silence: Le Gènocide des Armèniens, 1984; Toward the Understanding and Prevention of Genocide, 1984; A Crime of Silence, 1985; Genocide: A Critical Bibliographic Review, 1988; Embracing the Other: Philosophical, Psychological, and Historical Perspectives on Altruism, 1992; Diasporas in World Politics, 1993; Genocide and Human Rights, 1993; Genocide: Conceptual and Historical Dimensions, 1994; The Legacy of History in Russia and the New States of Eurasia, 1994. Contributions: many professional journals and to periodicals. *Honours:* Humanities Institute Fellow, 1972; Guggenheim Fellowship, 1974–75; National Endowment for the Humanities Grant, 1981–82; California Council for the Humanities Grant, 1985–86; numerous awards, citations, and recognitions. *Address:* 101 Groverton Place, Los Angeles, CA 90077, USA.

HOVE, Chenjerai, BA; Zimbabwean journalist and writer; b. 9 Feb. 1956, Zvishavane; s. of R. Muza Hove and Jessie Muza Hove; m. Thecla Hove 1978; three s. two d. *Education:* Gweru Teacher's Coll. *Career:* high school teacher 1978–81; Ed. Mambo Press, Gweru 1981; Sr Ed. Zimbabwe Publishing house, Harare 1985; Ed. Cultural Features, Interpress Service 1988; Writer-in-Residence, Univ. of Zimbabwe 1991–94; Visiting Prof. Lewis and Clark Coll., Oregon, USA 1995; full-time writer 1999–; in exile in France 2002–. *Publications:* Swimming in Floods of Tears (co-author) 1983, Red Hills of Home 1985, Bones (Zimbabwe Book Publishers Literary Award 1988, Noma Award for Publishing in Africa 1989) 1988, Shadows 1991, Guardians of the Soil 1996, Ancestors 1996, Shebeen Tales: Messages from Harare 1997, Rainbows in the Dust 1998. *Honours:* Democracy and Freedom of Speech in Africa Prize, Berlin 2001. *Address:* c/o Édition Actes Sud, BP 38, 13633 Arles Cedex, France (office).

HOWARD, Anthony Michell, CBE, MA; British journalist; b. 12 Feb. 1934, London; s. of the late Canon W. G. Howard and Janet Howard (née Rymer); m. Carol Anne Gaynor 1965. *Education:* Westminster School and Christ Church, Oxford. *Career:* on editorial staff Manchester Guardian 1959–61; Political Corresp. New Statesman 1961–64; Whitehall Corresp. Sunday Times 1965; Washington Corresp. Observer 1966–69; Asst Ed. New Statesman 1970–72, Ed. 1972–78; Ed. The Listener 1979–81; Deputy Ed. The Observer 1981–88; Presenter Face the Press, Channel Four 1982–85; Presenter, reporter BBC TV 1989–92; Obituaries Ed., The Times 1993–99, weekly columnist 1999–2005; Harkness Fellow, USA 1960. *Publications:* The Making of the Prime Minister (with Richard West) 1965; ed. The Crossman Diaries 1964–70, 1979, Rab: The Life of R. A. Butler 1987, Crossman: The Pursuit of Power 1990; ed. The Times Lives Remembered 1993, Basil Hume: The Monk Cardinal 2005. *Honours:* Hon. Student, Christ Church, Oxford 2003; Hon. LLD (Nottingham) 2001, Hon. DLitt (Leicester) 2003; Gerald Barry Award, What the Papers Say 1998. *Address:* 11 Campden House Court, 42 Gloucester Walk, London, W8 4HU; Dinham Lodge, Ludlow, Shropshire, SY8 1EH, England. *Telephone:* (20) 7937-7313 (London); (1584) 878457 (Shropshire).

HOWARD, Clark, (Rich Howard); American author; b. 1934. *Career:* as Rich Howard: boxing columnist (On the Strip) The Ring magazine 1968–70; mem. MWA. *Publications:* The Arm 1967, A Movement Toward Eden 1969, The Doomsday Squad 1970, The Killings 1973, Last Contract 1973, Summit Kill 1975, Mark the Sparrow 1975, The Hunters 1976, The Last Great Death Stunt 1976, Six Against the Rock 1977, The Wardens 1979, Zebra: The True Account of the 179 Days of Terror in San Francisco 1979, UK edn as The Zebra Killings 1980, American Saturday 1981, Brothers in Blood 1983, Dirt Rich 1986, Hard City 1990, Love's Blood 1993, City Blood 1994, Crowded Lives and Other Stories of Desperation and Danger 2000, Challenge the Widow-Maker and Other Stories of People in Peril 2000. *Honours:* Edgar Allan Poe Award 1980, Ellery Queen Awards 1985, 1986, 1988, 1990, 1999, Derringer Award 2003. *Address:* Box 1527, Palm Springs, CA 92263, USA. *E-mail:* rchoward440@cs.com (home).

HOWARD, Deborah Janet, MA, PhD, FRSE; British academic and writer; *Professor of Architectural History, University of Cambridge*; b. 26 Feb. 1946, London; m. Malcolm S. Longair 1975; one s. one d. *Education:* Newnham Coll., Cambridge and Univ. of London. *Career:* Prof. of Architectural History, Univ. of Cambridge; Fellow, St John's Coll., Cambridge; Fellow, Soc. of Antiquaries of Scotland, Soc. of Antiquaries. *Publications:* Jacopo Sansovino: Architecture and Patronage in Renaissance Venice 1975, The Architectural History of Venice 1980 (revised and enlarged edn 2002), Scottish Architecture from the Reformation to the Restoration 1560–1660 1995, La Scuola Grande della Misericordia di Venezia (with G. Fabbri and S. Mason) 1999, Venice and the East: The Impact on the Islamic World on Venetian Architecture 1100–1500 2000; contribs to professional journals. *Honours:* Hon. Fellow, Royal Incorporation of Architects of Scotland. *Address:* St John's College, Cambridge, CB2 1TP, England (office). *Telephone:* (1223) 339360 (office). *Fax:* (1223) 332960 (office).

HOWARD, Elizabeth Jane, CBE, FRSL; British writer; b. 26 March 1923, London, England; d. of David Liddon and Katharine M. Howard; m. 1st Peter M. Scott 1942; one d.; m. 2nd James Douglas-Henry 1959; m. 3rd Kingsley Amis 1965 (divorced 1983, deceased). *Education:* at home and at London Mask Theatre School. *Career:* BBC TV modelling 1939–46; Sec. Inland Waterways Asscn 1947; then professional writer, including plays for TV; Hon. Artistic Dir Cheltenham Literary Festival 1962; Artistic Co-Dir Salisbury Festival of Arts 1973; mem. Authors Lending and Copyright Soc. *Film scripts:* Getting It Right 1985, The Attachment 1986, The Very Edge. *Television:* Our Glorious Dead, Sight Unseen, Skittles, adaptations of After Julius (three plays for TV), Something in Disguise (six plays) 1982. *Publications:* The Beautiful Visit 1950, The Long View 1956, The Sea Change 1959, After Julius 1965, Something in Disguise 1969, Odd Girl Out 1972, Mr Wrong 1975, A Companion for Lovers (ed.) 1978, Getting it Right (Yorkshire Post Novel of the Year) 1982, Howard and Maschler on Food: Cooking for Occasions (co-author) 1987, The Light Years (The Cazalet Chronicle Vol. One) 1990, Green Shades (gardening anthology) 1991, Marking Time (The Cazalet Chronicle Vol. Two) 1991, Confusion (The Cazalet Chronicle Vol. Three) 1993, Casting Off (The Cazalet Chronicle Vol. Four) 1995, Falling 1999, Slipstream (autobiog.) 2002; contrib. to The Times, Sunday Times, Telegraph, Encounter, Vogue, Harpers & Queen. *Honours:* John Llewellyn Rhys Memorial Prize 1950, Yorkshire Post Prize 1982. *Literary Agent:* Jonathan Clowes Ltd, 10 Iron Bridge House, Bridge Approach, London, NW1 8BD, England. *Telephone:* (20) 7722-7674. *Fax:* (20) 7722-7677. *Address:* c/o Pan MacMillan Ltd, 20 New Wharf Road, London, N1 9RR, England.

HOWARD, Ellen, BA; American writer; b. 8 May 1943, New Bern, NC; m. Charles Howard Jr 1975, four d. *Education:* University of Oregon, Portland State University. *Career:* mem. Authors' Guild; Society of Children's Book Writers and Illustrators. *Publications:* Circle of Giving, 1984; When Daylight Comes, 1985; Gillyflower, 1986; Edith Herself, 1987; Her Own Song, 1988; Sister, 1990; The Chickenhouse House, 1991; The Cellar, 1992; The Tower Room, 1993; The Big Seed, 1993; Murphy and Kate, 1995; The Log Cabin Quilt, 1996; A Different Kind of Courage, 1996. *Honours:* Golden Kite Honor Book, 1984; Christopher Award, 1997.

HOWARD, Lynette Desley (see Stevens, Lynsey)

HOWARD, Maureen, BA; American lecturer and writer; b. 28 June 1930, Bridgeport, CT; m. 1st Daniel F. Howard 1954 (divorced 1967); one d.; m. 2nd David J. Gordon 1968 (divorced); m. 3rd Mark Probst 1981. *Education:* Smith Coll. *Career:* Lecturer, New School for Social Research, New York 1967–68, 1970–71, 1974–, Univ. of California at Santa Barbara 1968–69, Amherst Coll., Brooklyn Coll., CUNY, Columbia Univ. *Publications:* fiction: Not a Word About Nightingales 1961, Bridgeport Bus 1966, Before My Time 1975, Grace Abounding 1982, Expensive Habits 1986, Natural History 1992, A Lover's Almanac 1998, Big as Life: Three Tales for Spring 2001, The Silver Screen 2004; non-fiction: Facts of Life (autobiog.) 1978; editor: Seven American Women Writers of the Twentieth Century 1977, Contemporary American Essays 1984. *Honours:* Guggenheim Fellowship 1967–68, Radcliffe Inst. Fellow 1967–68, Nat. Book Critics Circle Award 1980, Ingram Merrill Foundation Fellow 1988, New York Public Library Literary Lion 1993. *Address:* c/o Viking Publicity, 375 Hudson Street, New York, NY 10014, USA.

HOWARD, Sir Michael Eliot, Kt, CH, CBE, MC, MA, DLitt, FBA, FRHistS; British historian; *Regius Professor Emeritus of Modern History, University of Oxford*; b. 29 Nov. 1922, London; s. of the late Geoffrey Eliot Howard and of Edith Howard (née Edinger). *Education:* Wellington Coll., Christ Church, Oxford. *Career:* served in army 1942–45; Asst Lecturer, Lecturer in History, King's Coll., London 1947–53; Lecturer, Reader in War Studies, Univ. of London 1953–63; Prof. of War Studies, Univ. of London 1963–68; Fellow in Higher Defence Studies, All Souls Coll., Oxford 1968–77; Chichele Prof. of the History of War, Univ. of Oxford 1977–80; Regius Prof. of Modern History, Univ. of Oxford 1980–89, Prof. Emer. 1989–; Robert A. Lovett Prof. of Mil. and Naval History, Yale Univ. 1989–93; Leverhulme Lecturer 1996; Lee Kuan Yew Distinguished Visitor, Nat. Univ. of Singapore 1996; Founder and Pres. Emer. Int. Inst. for Strategic Studies; mem. The Literary Soc. (Pres. –2004); Foreign mem. American Acad. of Arts and Sciences. *Publications:* The Coldstream Guards 1920–1946 (with John Sparrow) 1951, Disengagement in Europe 1958, Wellingtonian Studies 1959, The Franco-German War 1961, The Theory and Practice of War 1965, The Mediterranean Strategy in the Second World War 1967, Studies in War and Peace 1970, Grand Strategy, Vol. IV (in UK History of Second World War) 1972, The Continental Commitment 1973, War in European History 1976, Clausewitz on War (trans. with Peter Paret) 1976, War and the Liberal Conscience 1978, Restraints on War (ed.) 1979, The Causes of Wars 1983, Clausewitz 1983, Strategic Deception: British Intelligence in the Second World War 1990, The Lessons of History (essays) 1991, The Oxford History of the Twentieth Century (co-ed. with W. R. Louis) 1998, The Invention of Peace 2000, The First World War 2001. *Honours:* Hon. Fellow, Oriel Coll., Oxford 1990; Hon. Student Christ Church 1990; Order of Merit; Hon. LittD (Leeds) 1979; Hon. DLitt (London) 1988; Duff Cooper Memorial Prize 1961, Wolfson Foundation History Award 1972, NATO Atlantic Award 1989, Chesney Memorial Gold Medal, Royal United Services Inst., Samule Eliot Morrison Prize, Soc. for Mil. History 1992, Paul Nitze Award, Center for Naval Analysis 1994, Political Book Prize, Friedrich Ebert Stiftung 2002. *Address:* The Old Farm, Eastbury, Hungerford, Berks., RG17 7JN, England (home). *Telephone:* (1488) 71387. *Fax:* (1488) 71387.

HOWARD, Philip Nicholas Charles, MA, FRSL; British editor, journaliist and writer; *Leader Writer and Columnist, The Times*; b. 2 Nov. 1933, London, England; m. Myrtle Janet Mary Houldsworth 1959; two s. one d. *Education:* Trinity College, Oxford. *Career:* Staff, Glasgow Herald, 1959–64; Staff, 1964–, Literary Ed., 1978–92, Leader Writer and Columnist, 1992–, The Times; London Ed., Verbatim, 1977–; mem. Classical Asscn, pres., 2002; Friends of Classics, founder-patron; Horatian Society; Literary Society; Society of Bookmen. *Publications:* The Black Watch, 1968; The Royal Palaces, 1970; London's River, 1975; New Words for Old, 1977; The British Monarchy, 1977; Weasel Words, 1978; Words Fail Me, 1980; A Word in Your Ear, 1983; The State of the Language: English Observed, 1984; The Times Bicentenary Stamp Book (co-author), 1985; We Thundered Out: 200 Years of the Times, 1785–1985, 1985; Winged Words, 1988; Word-Watching, 1988; London: The Evolution of a Great City (co-author), 1989; A Word in Time, 1990; The Times Bedside Book (ed.), 1991; Reading a Poem, 1992. *Address:* The Times, 1 Pennington Street, London E1 (office); Flat 1, 47 Ladbroke Grove, London W11 3AR, England (home). *Telephone:* (20) 7782-7175 (office). *Fax:* (20) 7782-5229 (home). *E-mail:* philipnchoward@compuserve.com.

HOWARD, Richard Joseph, BA, MA; American poet, critic, editor and translator; b. 13 Oct. 1929, Cleveland, OH. *Education:* Columbia Univ., Sorbonne, Univ. of Paris. *Career:* Lexicographer, World Publishing Co, 1954–58; Poetry Ed., New American Review, New Republic, Paris Review, Shenandoah, Western Humanities Review; Rhodes Prof. of Comparative Literature, Univ. of Cincinnati. *Publications:* Poetry: Quantities, 1962; The Damages, 1967; Untitled Subjects, 1969; Findings, 1971; Two-Part Inventions, 1974; Fellow Feelings, 1976; Misgivings, 1979; Lining Up, 1984; Quantities/Damages, 1984; No Traveller, 1989; Like Most Revelations: New Poems, 1994; Trappings, 1999; Talking Cures, 2002. Criticism: Alone with America: Essays on the Art of Poetry in the United States Since 1950, 1969; Passengers Must Not Ride on Fenders, 1974. Editor: Preferences: Fifty-One American Poets Choose Poems from Their Own Work and from the Past, 1974; The War in Algeria, 1975, The Silent Treatment 2006. Translator: numerous books, from French. Contributions: Magazines and journals. *Honours:* Guggenheim Fellowship, 1966–67; Harriet Monroe Memorial Prize, 1969; Pulitzer Prize in Poetry, 1970; Levinson Prize, 1973; Cleveland Arts Prize, 1974; American Acad. and Institute of Arts and Letters Medal for Poetry, 1980; American Book Award for Trans., 1983; PEN American Center Medal for Trans., 1986; France-American Foundation Award for Trans., 1987; National Endowment for the Arts Fellowship, 1987; MacArthur Fellowship, 1996. *Address:* c/o Turtle Point Press, 233 Broadway, Room 946, New York, NY 10279, USA.

HOWARD, Roger, MA; British dramatist, poet, author and lecturer; *Founder-Director, Theatre Underground*; b. 19 June 1938, Warwick, England; m. Anne Mary Zemaitis 1960; one s. *Education:* RADA, London, Univ. of Bristol, Univ. of Essex. *Career:* Teacher Nankai Univ., Tientsin, People's Republic of China 1965–67; Lecturer Univ. of Beijing 1972–74; Fellow in Creative Writing Univ. of York 1976–78; Writing Fellow Univ. of East Anglia 1979; Lecturer 1979–93, Founder-Dir Theatre Underground 1979–, Lecturer in Literature 1979–93, Ed. New Plays series 1980–, Senior Lecturer in Literature 1993–2003, Univ. of Essex. *Publications:* A Phantastic Satire (novel) 1960, From the Life of a Patient (novel) 1961, To the People (poems) 1966, Praise Songs (poems) 1966, The Technique of the Struggle Meeting 1968, The Use of Wall Newspapers 1968, New Short Plays I 1968, Fin's Doubts 1968, Episodes from the Fighting in the East 1971, The Hooligan's Handbook 1971, Slaughter Night and Other Plays 1971, Method for Revolutionary Writing 1972, Culture and Agitation: Theatre Documents (ed.) 1972, Contemporary Chinese Theatre 1977, Mao Tse-tung and the Chinese People 1978, The Society of Poets 1979, A Break in Berlin 1980, The Siege 1981, Partisans 1983, Ancient Rivers 1984, The Speechifier 1984, Contradictory Theatres 1985, Senile Poems 1988, The Tragedy of Mao and Other Plays 1989, Britannia and Other Plays 1990, Selected Poems 1966–96 1997, Three War Plays 2004; contrib. to anthologies, newspapers and journals. *Address:* c/o Theatre Underground, Department of Literature, University of Essex, Wivenhoe Park, Colchester, Essex CO4 3SQ, England.

HOWATCH, Susan, LLB; British writer; b. 14 July 1940, Leatherhead, Surrey; d. of G. S. Sturt; m. Joseph Howatch 1964 (separated 1975); one d. *Education:* Sutton High School, King's Coll., London. *Career:* emigrated to USA 1964, lived in Ireland 1976–80, returned to UK 1980; first book published 1965; Fellow, King's Coll. London 1999–; f. Starbridge Lectureship in Theology and Natural Science Univ. of Cambridge 1992; mem. Soc. of Authors. *Publications:* novels: The Dark Shore 1965, The Waiting Sands 1966, Call in the Night 1967, The Shrouded Walls 1968, April's Grave 1969, The Devil on Lammas Night 1970, Penmarric 1971, Cashelmara 1974, The Rich are Different 1977, Sins of the Fathers 1980, The Wheel of Fortune 1984, Glittering Images 1987, Glamorous Powers 1988, Ultimate Prizes 1989,

Scandalous Risks 1991, Mystical Paths 1992, Absolute Truths 1994, A Question of Integrity (US title: The Wonder Worker) 1997, The High Flyer 1999, The Heartbreaker 2003. *Honours:* Winifred Mary Stanford Memorial Prize 1991. *Literary Agent:* Aitken Alexander Associates Ltd, 18–21 Cavaye Place, London, SW10 9PT, England. *Telephone:* (20) 7373-8672. *Fax:* (20) 7373-6002. *E-mail:* reception@aitkenalexander.co.uk (office). *Website:* www .aitkenalexander.co.uk.

HOWE, Fanny; American academic, author, poet and dramatist; b. 15 Oct. 1940, Buffalo, NY; one s. two d. *Education:* Stanford University. *Career:* Lecturer, Tufts University, 1968–71, Emerson College, 1974, Columbia University Extension and School of the Arts, 1975–78, Yale University, 1976, Harvard University Extension, 1977, MIT, 1978–87; Prof. of Writing and American Literature, University of California at San Diego, 1987–; Assoc. Dir, Study Center, University College London, 1993–95; Distinguished Visiting Writer-in-Residence, Mills College, 1996–97. *Publications:* Fiction: Forty Whacks, 1969; First Marriage, 1975; Bronte Wilde, 1976; Holy Smoke, 1979; The White Slave, 1980; In the Middle of Nowhere, 1984; Taking Care, 1985; The Lives of a Spirit, 1986; The Deep North, 1988; Famous Questions, 1989; Saving History, 1992; Nod, 1998. Young Adult Fiction: The Blue Hills, 1981; Yeah, But, 1982; Radio City, 1983; The Race of the Radical, 1985. Poetry: Eggs, 1980; The Amerindian Coastline Poem, 1976; Poem from a Single Pallet, 1980; Alsace Lorraine, 1982; For Erato, 1984; Introduction to the World, 1985; Robeson Street, 1985; The Vineyard, 1988; The Quietist, 1992; The End, 1992; O'Clock, 1995; One Crossed Out, 1997; Q, 1998. Contributions: many anthologies, reviews, quarterlies, journals, and magazines. *Honours:* MacDowell Colony Fellowships, 1965, 1990; National Endowment for the Arts Fellowships in Fiction, 1969, and in Poetry, 1991; Bunting Institute Fellowship, 1974; St Botolph Award for Fiction, 1976; Writer's Choice Award for Fiction, 1984; Village Voice Award for Fiction, 1988; California Council on the Arts Award for Poetry, 1993; Lenore Marshall Poetry Prize, Acad. of American Poets, 2001.

HOWE, Susan, BFA; American poet and academic; b. 10 June 1937. *Education:* Museum of Fine Arts, Boston. *Career:* Butler Fellow in English, 1988, Prof. of English, 1991–, SUNY at Buffalo; Visiting Scholar and Prof. of English, Temple University, Philadelphia, 1990, 1991; Visiting Poet and Leo Block Prof., University of Denver, 1993–94; Visiting Brittingham Scholar, University of Wisconsin at Madison, 1994; Visiting Poet, University of Arizona, 1994; Visiting Prof., Stanford University, 1998; mem. Acad. of American Poets, board of chancellors, 2000–; American Acad. of Arts and Sciences. *Publications:* Poetry: Hinge Picture, 1974; The Western Borders, 1976; Secret History of the Dividing Line, 1978; Cabbage Gardens, 1979; The Liberties, 1980; Pythagorean Silence, 1982; Defenestration of Prague, 1983; Articulation of Sound Forms in Time, 1987; A Bibliography of the King's Book, or Eikon Basilike, 1989; The Europe of Trusts: Selected Poems, 1990; Singularities, 1990; The Nonconformist's Memorial, 1993; Frame Structures: Early Poems 1974–1979, 1996; Pierce-Arrow, 1999; Bad-Hangings, 2000. Other: My Emily Dickinson, 1985; Incloser, 1990; The Birthmark: Unsettling the Wilderness in American Literary History, 1993. *Honours:* Before Columbus Foundation American Book Awards, 1980, 1986; New York State Council of the Arts Residency, 1986; Pushcart Prize, 1987; New York City Fund for Poetry Grant, 1988; Roy Harvey Pearce Award, 1996; Guggenheim Fellowship, 1996–97; Distinguished Fellow, Stanford Humanities Centre, 1998; Hon. degrees, National Univ. of Ireland, 2000, St Joseph Coll., Hartford, CT, 2003; State of New York Distinguished Prof., 2002.

HOWE, Tina, BA; American playwright; b. 1937, New York; d. of Quincy and Mary (née Post) Howe; m. Norman Levy 1961; one s. one d. *Education:* Sarah Lawrence Coll. (Bronxville, NY) and Columbia and Chicago Teacher Training Colls. *Career:* Adjunct Prof., Goldberg Dept of Dramatic Writing, New York Univ. 1983–; Visiting Prof., Hunter Coll. Dept of Theatre 1990–; mem. Council Dramatists' Guild; Guggenheim Fellow 1990. *Plays include:* Closing Time 1959, The Nest 1969, Birth and After Birth 1973, Museum 1976, The Art of Dining 1979, Appearances (unpublished) 1982, Painting Churches 1983, Coastal Disturbances 1986, Approaching Zanzibar 1989, One Shoe Off 1989, Swimming 1991, Teeth 1991, Birth and After Birth 1995, Pride's Crossing (New York Drama Critics Circle Award for Best Play 1998) 1997, Divine Fallacy 1999, Rembrant's Gift 2002, Such Small Hands 2003,. *Honours:* Dr hc (Bowdoin Coll) 1988; Obie for Distinguished Playwriting 1983; Outer Critics Circle Award 1983; Tony nomination for Best Play 1987; American Acad. of Arts and Letters Award in Literature 1993. *Address:* Hunter College Department of Theatre, North Building 522, New York, NY 10021; Goldberg Department of Dramatic Writing, New York University, 721 Broadway, 7th Floor, New York, NY 10003; c/o ICM, 825 8th Avenue, New York, NY 10019, USA. *Telephone:* (212) 998-1940 (NYU); (212) 556-5600 (ICM). *E-mail:* theater@icmtalent.com. *Website:* www.hunter.cuny.edu/theatre; www.hunter .cuny.edu/theatre/grad.shtml.

HOWELL, Anthony; British poet, writer and editor; b. 20 April 1945, London, England. *Education:* Leighton Park School, Royal Ballet School, London. *Career:* Lecturer, Grenoble Univ., Cardiff School of Art; Ed., Softly, Loudly Books, London, Grey Suit. *Publications:* poetry: Inside the Castle 1969, Femina Deserta 1971, Oslo: A Tantric Ode 1975, The Mekon 1976, Notions of a Mirror: Poems Previously Uncollected 1964–82 1983, Winter's Not Gone 1984, Why I May Never See the Walls of China 1986, Howell's Law 1990, Near Cavalry: Selected Poems of Nick Lafitte (ed.) 1992, Dancers in Daylight 2003; fiction: In the Company of Others 1986, First Time in Japan

1995. *Honours:* Welsh Arts Council Bursary 1989. *E-mail:* anthony@ther00m .wanadoo.co.uk. *Website:* www.anthonyhowell.org.

HOWELLS, Coral Ann, MA, PhD; British/Australian academic and writer; *Professor of English and Canadian Literature, University of Reading;* b. 22 Oct. 1939, Maryborough, Qld, Australia; m. Robin Jonathan Howells 1963; two d. *Education:* Univ. of Queensland and Univ. of London. *Career:* Prof. of English and Canadian Literature, Univ. of Reading 1996–; mem. British Asscn for Canadian Studies, Pres. 1992–94; Assoc. Ed. Int. Journal for Canadian Studies, 1998–; mem. Council, Foundation for Canadian Studies in the UK 1998–, Canadian Memorial Scholarship Academic Selection Cttee 1999–. *Publications:* Love, Mystery and Misery: Feeling in Gothic Fiction 1978, Private and Fictional Words: Canadian Women Novelists of the 1970s and 80s 1987, Jean Rhys 1991, Margaret Atwood 1996, Alice Munro 1998, Contemporary Canadian Women's Fiction: Refiguring Identities 2003, Cambridge Companion to Margaret Atwood (ed.) 2006; contribs to many academic journals. *Honours:* Margaret Atwood Soc. Best Book Award 1997. *Address:* School of English and American Literature, University of Reading, Whiteknights, Reading, RG6 6AA, Berks., England (office). *Telephone:* (118) 378-7001 (office). *Fax:* (118) 378-6561 (office). *E-mail:* c.a.howells@reading.ac.uk (office). *Website:* www.rdg.ac.uk/english (office).

HOYLAND, Michael David; British academic (retd), author and poet; b. 1 April 1925, Nagpur, India; m. Marette Nicol Fraser 1948, two s. two d. *Career:* school teacher 1951–63; Lecturer, Kesteven College of Education 1963–65, Sr Lecturer in Art 1963–80; mem. Stamford Writers Group; PEN; Welland Valley Art Society; East Anglian Potters Asscn. *Publications:* Introduction Three, 1967; Art for Children, 1970; Variations: An Integrated Approach to Art, 1975; A Love Affair with War, 1981; The Bright Way In, 1984; Dominus-Domina (play); Poems in journals and a collection; 6 Short Stories. Contributions: Reviewing for Ore; Jade.

HOYLE, Peter, BA; British writer and fmr librarian; b. 25 Oct. 1939, Accrington, Lancs.; m. Barbara Croop; one s. one d. *Education:* Univ. of Liverpool. *Radio:* stories broadcast on BBC Radio 3 and Radio 4's Morning Story. *Publications:* The Man in the Iron Mask 1984, Brantwood 1986, Missing Man 2002; contrib. to Stand, PN Review, New Stories 1, New Statesman. *Honours:* North West Arts Bursary 1984. *Address:* 19 Hexham Avenue, Bolton, Lancs., BL1 5PP, England (home). *Telephone:* (1204) 847147 (home).

HOYLE, Trevor; British writer; b. Rochdale, England; m. 1962; one s. one d. *Career:* mem. Soc. of Authors. *Radio:* drama: GIGO 1990, Conflagration 1991, Randle's Scandals 1992, Haunted Hospital 2006. *Television:* Whatever Happened to the Heroes (Granada). *Publications:* The Relatively Constant Copywriters 1972, The Adulterer 1972, Rule of Night 1975, Rock Fix 1977, Seeking the Mythical Future 1977, Through the Eye of Time 1977, The Gods Look Down 1978, The Man Who Travelled on Motorways 1979, Earth Cult 1979, The Stigma 1980, Bullet Train 1980, The Last Gasp 1983, Vail 1984, K.I.D.S. 1988, Blind Needle 1994, Mirrorman 1999, Rule of Night (reissue) 2003, (Italian edition) 2006. Other: several film and television adaptations and radio dramas; contribs to periodicals, Oxford Good Fiction Guide 2001. *Honours:* Radio Times Drama Award 1991, British Winner, Transatlantic Review Story Competition. *Literary Agent:* Tanja Howarth Literary Agency, 19 New Row, London, WC2N 4LA, England.

HUANG, Yongyu; Chinese artist and poet; b. 1924, Fenghuang Co., Hunan Prov. *Career:* best known for his satirical picture of an owl with its left eye closed, produced during the 'Gang of Four' era; Vice-Chair. Chinese Artists' Asscn 1985–; mem. Nationalities Cttee 7th CPPCC. *Honours:* Commendatore (Italy) 1986. *Address:* Central Academy of Fine Arts, Beijing, People's Republic of China.

HÜBSCHER, Angelika; German writer; b. 4 April 1912, Busbach, nr Bayreuth; d. of Ferdinand Maria Knote and Margarete Bernewitz; m. Arthur Hübscher 1950; two step-d. one s. (died 1982). *Education:* privately, Humanistisches Gymnasium, Bayreuth and Univ. of Heidelberg. *Career:* sacked from Ministry of Foreign Affairs, Berlin by Gestapo 1940; interpreter for Heidelberg Police Dept after 1945; reader for Stahberg Verlag (publrs); Hon. mem. Bd Dirs Schopenhauer Gesellschaft –1992; Pres. Int. Women's Club 1986–87; f. Cultura '87 1987; f. Schopenhauer Foundation 1988. *Publications:* editor: Casanova: Histoire de ma vie, Schopenhauer (Zurich edn); Schopenhauer und Frankfurt (catalogue and exhbn) 1994; writer, ed. many books on Schopenhauer. *Honours:* Chevalier des Palmes académiques 1967, Bundesverdienstkreuz 1977, Ehrenbrief des Landes Hessen 1976. *Address:* Beethovenstrasse 48, 60325 Frankfurt/Main 1, Germany. *Telephone:* (69) 745219.

HUCKER, Hazel Zoë, JP, BSc (Econ); British economics teacher and novelist; b. 7 Aug. 1937, London; m. Michael Hucker 1961, two s. (one deceased) one d. *Education:* LSE. *Career:* mem. Soc. of Authors. *Publications:* The Aftermath of Oliver 1993, La Herencia del Recuerdo 1994, A Dangerous Happiness 1994, Cousin Susannah 1995, Trials of Friendship 1996, The Real Claudia Charles 1998, Changing Status 2000. *Literary Agent:* MBA Literary Agents Ltd, 62 Grafton Way, London, W1T 5DW, England. *Address:* 11 Waterhouse Close, Twyford, Winchester, Hampshire SO21 1PN (home). *Telephone:* (1962) 712796 (home).

HUDDLE, David, BA, MA, MFA; American academic, writer and poet; b. 11 July 1942, Ivanhoe, VA; m. Lindsey M. Huddle; two d. *Education:* University of Virginia, Hollins College, Columbia University. *Career:* Faculty, Warren Wilson College, 1981–85; Prof. of English, University of Vermont, 1982–; Ed., New England Review, 1993–94. *Publications:* A Dream With No Stump Roots In It, 1975; Paper Boy, 1979; Only the Little Bone, 1986; Stopping by Home, 1988; The High Spirits, 1992; The Writing Habit: Essays on Writing, 1992; The Nature of Yearning, 1992; Intimates, 1993; Tenormen, 1995; Summer Lake: New and Selected Poems, 1999; The Story of a Million Years, 1999; Not: A Trio – A Novella and Two Stories, 2000; La Tour Dreams of the Wolf Girl, 2002, Grayscale (poems) 2004. Contributions: Esquire; Harper's; New York Times Book Review; Kentucky Poetry Review; Texas Quarterly; Poetry; Shenandoah; American Poetry Review. *Honours:* Hon. Doctorate of Humanities, Shenandoah College and Conservatory, Virginia, 1989; Bread Loaf School of English Commencement Speaker, 1989; Robert Frost Prof. of American Literature, 1991. *Address:* Department of English, University of Vermont, Burlington, VT 05405, USA.

HUDGINS, Andrew Leon, Jr, BA, MA, MFA; American academic, poet and writer; b. 22 April 1951, Killeen, TX. *Education:* Huntingdon College, University of Alabama, Syracuse University, University of Iowa. *Career:* Adjunct Instructor, Auburn University, 1978–81; Teaching-Writing Fellow, University of Iowa, 1981–83; Lecturer, Baylor University, 1984–85; Prof. of English, University of Cincinnati, 1985–; mem. Texas Institute of Letters. *Publications:* Poetry: Saints and Strangers, 1985; After the Lost War: A Narrative, 1988; The Never-Ending: New Poems, 1991; The Glass Hammer: A Southern Childhood, 1994; Babylon in a Jar, 1998. Non-Fiction: The Glass Anvil (essays), 1997. Contributions: numerous journals. *Honours:* Wallace Stegner Fellow in Poetry, Stanford University, 1983–84; Yaddo Fellowships, 1983, 1985, 1987, 1988, 1991; Acad. of American Poets Award, 1984; MacDowell Colony Fellowship, 1986; National Endowment for the Arts Fellowships, 1986, 1992; Ingram Merrill Foundation Grant, 1987; Poets' Prize, 1988; Witter Bynner Award, American Acad. and Institute of Arts and Letters, 1988; Alfred Hodder Fellow, Princeton University, 1989–90; Poetry Award, Texas Institute of Letters, 1991; Ohioana Poetry Award, 1997. *Address:* Ohio State University, Department of English, 164 Denney Hall, 164 West 17th Avenue, Columbus, OH 43210, USA. *E-mail:* hudgins.6@osu.edu.

HUDSON, Christopher; British writer; b. 29 Sept. 1946, England; m. Kirsty McLeod 1978; one s. *Education:* Jesus Coll., Cambridge. *Career:* ed., Faber and Faber 1968; Literary Ed. The Spectator 1971, The Standard 1981; Editorial Page Ed. The Daily Telegraph 1992, 1994. *Publications:* Overlord 1975, The Final Act 1980, Insider Out 1982, The Killing Fields 1984, Colombo Heat 1986, Playing in the Sand 1989, Spring Street Summer 1993. *Address:* Little Dane, Biddenden, Kent TN27 8JT, England (home).

HUDSON, Helen (see Lane, Helen)

HUDSON, Jeffrey (see Crichton, (John) Michael)

HUELLE, Paweł; Polish writer and journalist; b. 10 Sept. 1957, Gdańsk. *Education:* Gdańsk Univ. *Career:* Dir Polish Television Centre, Gdańsk 1994–99; columnist for Gazety Wyborczej; teacher of literature, philosophy and history. *Publications:* Weiser Dawidek (trans. as Who was David Weiser?) 1987, Opowiadania na czas przeprowadzki (trans. as Stories for a Time of Relocation) 1991, Wiersze (poems) 1994, Pierwsza miłość i inne opowiadania (trans. as First Love and Other Stories) 1996, Inne Historie (Different Stories) 1999, Mercedes-Benz. Z listów do Hrabala (trans. as Mercedes Benz) 2001, Byłem samotny i szczęśliwy 2002, Hans Castorp w Sopocie. Zaginiony rozdział z 'Czarodziejskiej Góry' (trans. as Castorp) 2004. *Address:* c/o Gazety Wyborczej, ul. Czerska 8/10, 00-732 Warsaw, Poland.

HUFANA, Alejandrino, AB, MA, MS; Philippine editor, writer, poet and dramatist; b. 22 Oct. 1926, San Fernando. *Education:* University of the Philippines, University of California at Berkeley, Columbia University. *Career:* Co-Founding Ed., Signatures Magazine, 1955, Comment Magazine, 1956–67; Co-Founding Ed., 1967–68, Literary Ed., 1987–, Heritage Magazine; Dir, Cultural Center of the Philippines Library, 1970–85; Prof., 1975, Dir, Creative Writing Center, 1981–85, University of the Philippines. *Publications:* 13 Kalisud, 1955; Man in the Moon, 1956; Sickle Season, 1948–58, 1959; Poro Point, 1955–60, 1961; Curtain Raisers: First Five Plays, 1964; A Philippine Cultural Miscellany, 1970; The Wife of Lot and Other New Poems, 1971; Notes on Poetry, 1973; Sieg Heil, 1975; Philippine Writing, 1977; Shining On, 1985; Dumanon, 1994; No Facetious Claim: Notes on Writers and Writing, 1995; Enuegs, 1999; Survivor, 1999; Kaputt, 1999. *Address:* c/o Heritage Magazine, 20218 Tajauta Avenue, Carson, CA 90746, USA.

HUGGAN, Jean Isabel, BA; Canadian writer; b. 21 Sept. 1943, Kitchener, Ont.; d. of Cecil Ronald Howey and Catherine Innes Howey; m. Bob Huggan 1970; one d. *Education:* Univ. of Western Ontario. *Career:* Editorial Asst, Macmillan Publishing Co. 1965–66; teacher 1968–72; reporter, photographer and columnist, The Belleville Intelligencer 1973–76; teacher of creative writing, Univ. of Ottawa 1985–87. *Publications include:* First Impressions 1980, Best Canadian Stories (contrib) 1983, The Elizabeth Stories 1984, 1987, Stories by Canadian Women (Vol. II) 1987, New American Short Stories 1988, Soho Square 1990, The Time of Your Life (contrib) 1992, You Never Know 1993, Unbecoming Daughters of the Empire 1993, Gates of Paradise II (contrib) 1994, Serpent à Plumes 1994, The Seasons of Women 1996, When We Were Young 1997, Altre Terre 1997, Penguin Anthology of Stories by Canadian Women 1999, Dropped Threads 2000. *Honours:* First Prize for film script Nat. Film Bd contest for women writers 1977, Joe Savago Award—

New Voice of 1987 (Quality Paperback Book Club) 1987, Alan Swallow Literary Award 1987.

HUGHES, Frieda, BA; British/American poet, artist and children's author; *Poetry Columnist, The Times;* b. 1960, England; d. of Ted Hughes and Sylvia Plath; m. Laszlo Lukacs. *Education:* St Martin's School of Art, London. *Career:* poetry columnist The Times 2006–. *Exhibitions:* numerous solo, joint and group exhibitions as painter 1989–. *Artistic achievement:* project of 45 poems and 45 paintings, one for every year of her life to 2005. *Publications:* poetry: Wooroloo 1999, Stonepicker 2001, Waxworks 2002; juvenile fiction: Getting Rid of Aunt Edna (short stories) 1986, The Meal a Mile Long, Waldorf and the Sleeping Granny, The Thing in the Sink, Rent a Friend, The Tall Story, Three Scary Stories, Forty-Five (poems) 2007. *Literary Agent:* c/o Ros Edwards, Edwards Fuglewicz, 49 Great Ormond Street, London WC1N 3HZ. *Telephone:* (20) 7405-6725. *Fax:* (20) 7405-6725. *E-mail:* ros@efla.co.uk. *Address:* c/o Bloodaxe Books Ltd, Highgreen, Tarset, Northumberland NE48 1RP, England. *Website:* www.friedahughes.com (home).

HUGHES, Glyn; British author and poet; b. 25 May 1935, Middlewich, Cheshire, England; one s. *Education:* Regional College of Art, Manchester. *Career:* teacher, Lancashire and Yorkshire 1956–72; Arts Council Fellow, Bishop Grosseteste College, Lincoln 1979–81; Southern Arts Writer-in-Residence, Farnborough 1982–84; Arts Council Writer-in-Residence, D. H. Lawrence Centenary Festival 1985. *Publications:* fiction: Where I Used to Play on the Green 1982, The Hawthorn Goddess 1984, The Rape of the Rose 1987, The Antique Collector 1990, Roth 1992, Brontë 1996; autobiography: Millstone Grit 1975, Fair Prospects 1976; poetry: Neighbours 1970, Rest the Poor Struggler 1972, Best of Neighbours 1979; play: Mary Hepton's Heaven 1984; plays for BBC Radio 4: Pursuit 1999, Mr Lowry's Loves 2001, Glorious John 2002, When Twilight Falls 2004; and several plays for BBC school broadcasts on radio and television. *Honours:* Welsh Arts Council Poets Prize 1970, Guardian Fiction Prize 1982, David Higham Fiction Prize 1982. *Literary Agent:* Mic Cheetham Agency, 11–12 Dover Street, London W1X 3PH, England. *Address:* Mors House, 1 Mill Bank Rd, Mill Bank, Sowerby Bridge, West Yorkshire HX6 3DY, England (home). *E-mail:* glyn.millbank@virgin.net. *Website:* www.glynhughes.co.uk.

HUGHES, Gwyneth, BA; American poet, playwright and short story writer; b. 10 May 1929, Berkeley, CA; m. Henri Lasry 1951; two s. one d. *Education:* Univ. of California, Berkeley. *Career:* mem. Society of Authors, UK, Dramatists' Guild, USA. *Publications:* Augmented Seventh (poems), After Gladys Adams (short stories), Henry's Navy Blue Hair (short stories), Escapements (plays in verse); contrib. to numerous journals and magazines. *Address:* c/o Lasry, 106 blvd Diderot, 75012 Paris, France. *E-mail:* gwyneth.hughes@wanadoo.fr.

HUGHES, Ian (see Paterson, Alistair Ian)

HUGHES, John Lawrence, BA; American publisher; b. 13 March 1925, New York; s. of John C. Hughes and Margaret Kelly; m. Rose M. Pitman 1947; three s. one d. *Education:* Yale Univ. *Career:* reporter, Nassau Review Star, Rockville Centre, Long Island, NY 1949; Asst Sr Ed., Pocket Books, Inc. New York 1949–59; Vice-Pres. Washington Square Press 1958; Sr Ed., Vice-Pres., Dir William Morrow & Co. 1960–65; Pres. and CEO 1965–85; Pres. The Hearst Trade Book Group 1985–87, Chair., CEO 1988–90, Ed.-at-Large, Group Adviser 1990–; Consultant, Ed.-at-Large HarperCollins Publrs., NY 1999–; Trustee, Yale Univ. Press, Pierpont Morgan Library, Library of America, Acad. of American Poets; mem. Bd Asscn of American Publishers 1986–90 (Chair. 1988–90); mem. Bd Nat. Book Awards 1982–94 (Chair. 1988–89). *Honours:* mem. Publrs Hall of Fame 1989. *Address:* HarperCollins Publishers, 10 East 53rd Street, New York, NY 10022-5299 (office); PO Box 430, Southport, CT 06490, USA (home). *Telephone:* (212) 207-7569 (office); (203) 259-8957 (home). *Fax:* (212) 207-7506 (office); (203) 259-8142 (home). *E-mail:* larry.hughes@harpercollins.com (office). *Website:* www.harpercollins.com (office).

HUGHES, John W.; American film producer, screenwriter and director; b. 18 Feb. 1950, Lansing, Mich.; m. Nancy Ludwig; two s. *Education:* Univ. of Arizona. *Career:* copywriter and Creative Dir Leo Burnett Co.; Ed. Nat. Lampoon magazine which led to writing screenplay of Nat. Lampoon's Class Reunion; founder and Pres. Hughes Entertainment 1985–. *Films:* National Lampoon's Class Reunion (screenplay) 1982, National Lampoon's Vacation (screenplay) 1983, Mr. Mom (screenplay) 1983, Nate and Hayes (screenplay) 1983, Sixteen Candles (screenplay and dir) 1984, National Lampoon's European Vacation (screenplay) 1985, Weird Science (screenplay and dir) 1985, The Breakfast Club (screenplay, dir and producer) 1985, Ferris Bueller's Day Off (screenplay, dir and producer) 1986, Pretty in Pink (screenplay and producer) 1986, Some Kind of Wonderful (screenplay and producer) 1987, Planes, Trains and Automobiles (screenplay, dir and producer) 1987, The Great Outdoors (screenplay and producer) 1988, She's Having a Baby (screenplay, dir and producer) 1988, National Lampoon's Christmas Vacation (screenplay and producer) 1989, Uncle Buck (screenplay, dir and producer) 1989, Home Alone (screenplay and producer) 1990, Career Opportunities (screenplay and producer) 1990, Dutch (screenplay and producer) 1991, Curly Sue (screenplay, dir and producer) 1991, Only the Lonely (co-producer) 1991, Beethoven (screenplay, as Edmond Dantès) 1992, Home Alone 2: Lost in New York (screenplay and producer) 1992, Dennis the Menace (screenplay and producer) 1993, Baby's Day Out (screenplay and producer) 1994, Miracle on 34th Street (screenplay and producer) 1994, 101 Dalmatians (screenplay)

1996, Home Alone 1997, Reach the Rock 1998, New Port South 1999, 102 Dalmatians 2000, Just Visiting 2001. *Honours:* Commitment to Chicago Award 1990, NATO/ShoWest Producer of the Year 1990. *Literary Agent:* Jacob Bloom, Bloom and Dekom, 150 South Rodeo Drive, Beverly Hills, CA 90212; Hughes Entertainment, 10201 West Pico Boulevard, Los Angeles, CA 90064, USA.

HUGHES, Linda Jean, BA; Canadian newspaper publisher; *President and Publisher, The Edmonton Journal;* b. 27 Sept. 1950, d. of Edward Rees and Madge Preston; m. George Ward 1978; one s. one d. *Education:* Univs of Victoria and Toronto. *Career:* Reporter on Victoria Times 1972–73, Head Legislature Bureau 1974–76; City Hall Reporter, Copy Ed. on The Edmonton Journal 1976–77, Editorial Writer 1978–80, Head Legislature Bureau, Asst City Ed. 1980, City Ed. 1981–84, Asst Man. Ed. 1984–87, Ed. 1987–91, Publr and Pres. 1992–; Southam News Services, Ottawa 1979; Southam Fellow Univ. of Toronto 1977–78. *Honours:* Hon. DLitt (Athabasca) 1997, Hon. DIur (Univ. of Alberta) 2003, Grant MacEwan Community Coll. Hon. Diploma in Journalism and Distinguished Citizen Award (Grant MacEwan Community Coll.) 1999, Distinguished Alumni Award, Univ. of Vic. 2000 Jr Achievement Alberta Business Hall of Fame 2004. *Address:* The Edmonton Journal, POB 2421, Edmonton, Alberta, T5J 2S6, Canada (office). *Telephone:* (780) 429-5129 (office). *Fax:* (780) 429-5536 (office). *Website:* www.edmontonjournal.com.

HUGHES, Richard Edward, BA, MEd; American writer, poet and teacher; b. 31 Oct. 1950, Los Angeles, CA; m. Dalcy Beatriz Camacho 1989, one c. *Education:* California State University, University of Hawaii. *Career:* Prof. of English as a Second Language, American Samoa Community College, Pago Pago, 1984–86; Instructor in English, Cambria English Institute, Los Angeles, 1986–88; Freelance Writer, 1988–; mem. PEN; Poets and Writers. *Publications:* Isla Grande (novel), 1994; Legends of the Heart (novel), 1997. Contributions: poems to magazines and anthologies. *Honours:* Henri Coulette Award for Poetry, Acad. of American Poets, 1981.

HUGHES, Robert Studley Forrest, AO; Australian art critic and writer; b. 28 July 1938, Sydney, NSW; m. Victoria Whistler 1981; one s. *Education:* Saint Ignatius Coll., Sydney and Univ. of Sydney. *Career:* staff, Time magazine, New York 1970–; writer and narrator of art documentaries, BBC-TV, London 1974–. *Publications:* The Art of Australia 1966, Heaven and Hell in Western Art 1970, The Fatal Shore 1987, Nothing if Not Critical 1990, Frank Auerbach 1990, Barcelona 1992, Culture of Complaint 1993, American Visions: The Epic History of Art in America 1997, Goya (biog.) 2003, Things I Didn't Know (memoir) 2006; contrib. to various publications. *Honours:* College Art Asscn of America Frank Jewett Mather Awards 1982, 1985, Duff Cooper Prize 1987, WHSmith Literary Award 1987, first prize Olimpiada Cultural, Spain 1992. *Address:* c/o Time Magazine, Time-Life Building, Rockefeller Center, New York, NY 10020, USA.

HUGHES, Shirley, OBE, FRSL; British writer and illustrator; b. 16 July 1927, Hoylake, Wirral; d. of Thomas James Hughes and Kathleen Hughes (née Dowling); m John Sebastian Papendrek Vulliamy 1952; two s. one d. *Education:* West Kirby High School for Girls, Liverpool Art School and Ruskin School of Drawing and Fine Art, Oxford. *Career:* freelance writer and illustrator; lecturer in field; Advisory Cttee Public Lending Rights Registrar 1984–88; Library and Information Services Council 1989–92; mem. Soc. of Authors (man. cttee 1983–86). *Publications:* Lucy & Tom Series: Lucy & Tom's Day, Lucy & Tom's Christmas, Lucy & Tom at the Seaside, Lucy & Tom Go To School, Lucy & Tom's abc, Lucy & Tom's 123 1960–87; Dogger, The Trouble with Jack 1970, Sally's Secret 1973, Helpers, It's Too Frightening for Me 1977, Moving Molly 1978, Up and Up 1979, Here Comes Charlie Moon, Charlie Moon and the Big Bonanza Bust Up 1982, Alfie Gets in First, Alfie's Fee, Alfie Gives a Hand 1983, An Evening at Alfie's 1984, The Nursery Collection (six vols) 1985–86, Chips and Jessie 1985, Another Helping of Chips 1986, The Big Alfie and Annie Rose Story Book 1988, Out and About 1988, Angel Mae 1989, The Big Concrete Lorry 1989, The Snow Lady 1990, Wheels 1991, The Big Alfie Out of Doors Story Book 1992, Stories by Firelight 1993, Giving, Bouncing, Chatting, Hiding 1994, Rhymes for Annie Rose 1995, Enchantment in the Garden 1996, Alfie and the Birthday Surprise 1997, The Lion and the Unicorn 1998, Mother and Child Treasury (ed.) 1998, Abel's Moon 1999, Alfie's Numbers 1999, The Shirley Hughes Collection 2000, Alfie Weather 2001, Annie Rose is My Little Sister 2002, A Life Drawing: Recollections of an Illustrator (autobiog.) 2002, Ella's Big Chance: A Fairy Tale Retold (Kate Greenaway Medal) 2003, Olly and Me 2004, Alfie Wins a Prize 2004, A Brush With the Past 1900–1950: The Years That Changed Our Lives 2005, Alfie's World – A Celebration 2006. *Honours:* Hon. DLitt (East Anglia) 2004, (Liverpool) 2004; Children's Rights Award 1976, Kate Greenaway Medal 1978, Silver Pencil Award, Netherlands 1980, Eleanor Farjeon Award 1984; Hon. Fellow Library Asscn 1997, Hon. Fellow Liverpool John Moores Univ. 2003. *Address:* c/o Random House Children's Books, 61–63 Uxbridge Road, London, W5 5SA, England (office).

HULME, Keri; New Zealand novelist; b. 9 March 1947, Christchurch, NZ. *Education:* Canterbury Univ., Christchurch. *Career:* worked as tobacco picker, fish and chip cook, TV dir and woollen mill worker and studied law, before becoming full-time writer 1972; Writer-in-Residence Otago Univ. 1978, Univ. of Canterbury, Christchurch 1985. *Publications:* The Bone People 1984, The Windeater 1987, Homeplaces 1989, Strands (poems) 1992, Bait 1996. *Honours:* awarded New Zealand Book of the Year Award 1984, Mobil Pegasus Prize 1984, Booker McConnell Prize for Fiction, UK 1985. *Address:* c/o Hodder

& Stoughton Ltd, 338 Euston Road, London, NW1 3BH, England; PO Box 1, Whataroa, South Westland, Aotearoa, New Zealand.

HULSE, Michael William, MA; British poet, writer, translator, editor and publisher; b. 12 June 1955, Stoke-on-Trent, Staffordshire, England. *Education:* University of St Andrews. *Career:* Lecturer, University of Erlangen-Nuremberg, 1977–79, Catholic University of Eichstätt, 1981–83; Part-time Lecturer, University of Cologne, 1985–95; Trans., Deutsche Welle TV, Cologne, 1986–2000; Assoc. Ed., Littlewood Arc, Todmorden, 1992–98; Visiting Lecturer, University of Zürich, 1994; Founder-Editorial Dir, Leviathon publishing house, Amsterdam, 2000–; mem. Poetry Society; Society of Authors. *Publications:* poetry: Monochrome Blood 1980, Dole Queue 1981, Knowing and Forgetting 1981, Propaganda 1985, Eating Strawberries in the Necropolis 1991, Monteverdi's Photographs 1995; other: The New Poetry (with David Kennedy and David Morley) 1993; numerous trans.; contrib. to anthologies. *Honours:* First Prize, National Poetry Competition, 1978; Second Prize, TLS/Cheltenham Literature Festival Poetry Competition, 1987; First Prizes, Bridport Poetry Competition, 1988, 1994; Hawthornden Castle Fellowship, 1991. *Address:* c/o Bloodaxe Books Ltd, Highgreen, Tarset, Northumberland NE48 1RP, England.

HUMAYDANE-YOUNES, Imane; Lebanese writer, journalist and sociologist; b. 1956, Ayn Enoub. *Publications:* novels: Ville à vif (title translated) 1997, B Mithil… Mithil Beirut 2007. *Address:* c/o Editions Verticales, 33 rue Saint-andré-des-arts, 75006 Paris, France (office).

HUMPHREYS, Emyr Owen, FRSL; British author and poet; b. 15 April 1919, Clwyd, Wales; m. Elinor Myfanwy 1946; three s. one d. *Education:* Univ. Coll., Aberystwyth and Univ. Coll., Bangor. *Publications:* The Little Kingdom 1946, The Voice of a Stranger 1949, A Change of Heart 1951, Hear and Forgive 1952, A Man's Estate 1955, The Italian Wife 1957, A Toy Epic 1958, The Gift 1963, Outside the House of Baal 1965, Natives 1968, Ancestor Worship 1970, National Winner 1971, Flesh and Blood 1974, Landscapes 1976, The Best of Friends 1978, The Kingdom of Bran 1979, The Anchor Tree 1980, Pwyll a Riannon 1980, Miscellany Two 1981, The Taliesin Tradition 1983, Salt of the Earth 1985, An Absolute Hero 1986, Open Secrets 1988, The Triple Net 1988, Bonds of Attachment 1990, Outside Time 1991, Unconditional Surrender 1996, The Gift of a Daughter 1998, Collected Poems 1999, Dal Pen Rheswm 1999, Ghosts and Strangers 2001, Conversations and Reflections 2002, Old People Are a Problem 2003, The Shop 2005. *Honours:* Hon. Prof. of English, Univ. Coll. of N Wales, Bangor; Hon. DLitt (Univ. of Wales) 1990, (Univ. of Glamorgan) 2005, Somerset Maugham Award 1953, Hawthornden Prize 1959, Soc. of Authors Travel Award 1978, Welsh Arts Council Prize 1983, Welsh Book of the Year 1992, 1999, Cymmrodorion Medal 2003. *Address:* Llinon, Penyberth, Llanfairpwll, Ynys Môn, Gwynedd, LL61 5YT, Wales (home). *Telephone:* (1248) 714540 (home). *E-mail:* ehumphreys@llinon.fsnet.co.uk (home).

HUMPHREYS, Josephine, AB, MA; American novelist; b. 2 Feb. 1945, Charleston, SC; m. Thomas A. Hutcheson 1968, two s. *Education:* Duke University, Yale University. *Publications:* Dreams of Sleep, 1984; Rich in Love, 1987; The Fireman's Fair, 1991; Nowhere Else on Earth, 2000. Contributions: newspapers and periodicals. *Honours:* PEN, Ernest Hemingway Foundation, 1985; Guggenheim Fellowship, 1985; Lyndhurst Prize, 1986.

HUMPHRIES, (John) Barry, AO, CBE; Australian entertainer and author; b. 17 Feb. 1934, s. of J.A.E. Humphries and L.A. Brown; m. 1st Rosalind Tong 1959; two d.; m. 2nd Diane Millstead; two s.; m. 3rd Lizzie Spender 1990. *Education:* Melbourne Grammar and Univ. of Melbourne. *Career:* repertory seasons at Union Theatre, Melbourne 1953–54, Phillip Street Revue Theatre, Sydney 1956, Demon Barber Lyric, Hammersmith 1959, Oliver, New Theatre 1960; one-man shows (author and performer): A Nice Night's Entertainment 1962, Excuse I 1965, Just a Show 1968, A Load of Olde Stuffe 1971, At Least You Can Say That You've Seen It 1974, Housewife Superstar 1976, Isn't It Pathetic at His Age 1979, A Night with Dame Edna 1979, An Evening's Intercourse with Barry Humphries 1981–82, Tears Before Bedtime 1986, Back with a Vengeance, London 1987–88, Look at Me When I'm Talking to You 1993–94, Edna: The Spectacle 1998, Dame Edna: The Royal Tour, San Francisco 1998, Remember You're Out 1999; numerous plays, films and broadcasts; best-known for his comic characterizations of Dame Edna Everage, Sir Les Patterson and Sandy Stone; Pres. Frans de Boewer Soc. (Belgium); Vice-Pres. Betjeman Soc. 2001–. *Publications:* Bizarre 1964, Innocent Austral Verse 1968, The Wonderful World of Barry McKenzie (with Nicholas Garland) 1970, Bazza Holds his Own (with Nicholas Garland) 1972, Dame Edna's Coffee Table Book 1976, Les Patterson's Australia 1979, Treasury of Australian Kitsch 1980, A Nice Night's Entertainment 1981, Dame Edna's Bedside Companion 1982, The Traveller's Tool 1985, The Complete Barry McKenzie 1988, My Gorgeous Life: The Autobiography of Dame Edna Everage 1989, The Life and Death of Sandy Stone 1991, More Please: An Autobiography 1992, Women in the Background (novel) 1996, My Life As Me (autobiog.). *Honours:* Dr hc (Melbourne Univ., Griffith Univ.); Hon. LLD (Melbourne) 2003; J.R. Ackerley Prize, Golden Rose of Montreux, Outer Critics Circle Award. *Address:* c/o Janet Linden, PBJ Management, 7 Soho Street, London, W1D 3DQ, England. *Telephone:* (20) 7287-1112. *Fax:* (20) 7287-1191. *E-mail:* general@pbjmgt.co.uk. *Website:* www.pbjmgt.co.uk.

HUMPHRY, Derek John; American/British journalist, author, broadcaster and publisher; *President, Euthanasia Research and Guidance Organization;*

b. 29 April 1930, Bath, England. *Education:* municipal schools, UK. *Career:* Messenger Boy, Yorkshire Post, London 1945–46; Cub Reporter, Evening World, Bristol 1946–51; Jr Reporter, Evening News, Manchester 1951–55; Reporter, Daily Mail 1955–61; Deputy Ed. The Luton News 1961–63; Ed. Havering Recorder 1963–67, World Federation of Right-To-Die Societies Newsletter 1980; Hemlock Quarterly 1983–92, Euthanasia Review 1986–88, World Right to Die Newsletter 1992–94; Home Affairs Corresp., The Sunday Times 1966–78; Special Writer, Los Angeles Times 1978–79; Pres. Norris Lane Press, Oregon USA; Founder Hemlock Soc., USA 1980, Exec. Dir 1980–92; Founder Euthanasia Research and Guidance Org. 1993, Pres. 1993–; Dir World Fed. of Right-To-Die Socs 1980–, The Final Exit Network 2003–; contrib. to Is This The Day? (theatre), Good Bye, My Love (drama). *Publications:* Because They're Black 1971, Police Power and Black People 1972, Passports and Politics 1974, The Cricket Conspiracy 1976, False Messiah 1977, Jean's Way 1978, Let Me Die Before I Wake 1982, The Right to Die!: Understanding Euthanasia 1986, Final Exit 1991 (also English, Italian and Spanish edns), Dying with Dignity 1992, Lawful Exit 1993, Freedom to Die 1998, The Good Euthanasia Guide 2003–. *Honours:* Martin Luther King Memorial Prize 1972, Socrates Award 1997, Saba Medal for contrib. to the World Right-to-Die Movement 2000. *Address:* 24829 Norris Lane, Junction City, OR 97448-9559, USA (home). *Telephone:* (541) 999-1873 (home). *Fax:* (541) 998-1873 (home). *E-mail:* ergo@finalexit.org (office); derekhumphry@starband.net (home). *Website:* www.finalexit.org/dhumphry (office); www.assistedsuicide.org (home).

HUNEBELLE, Danielle; French journalist, writer and television producer; b. 10 May 1922, Paris; d. of André Weill and Germaine Weill (née Cordon); two d. *Education:* Lycées Racine and Molière, Paris and Univ. of Paris-Sorbonne. *Career:* actress 1945–48; journalist 1948–; war corresp. in Greece 1948; worked in army information office in Indochina 1951; Special Envoy for Le Monde newspaper 1951; Sr Reporter for Réalités magazine 1952–72; TV Producer, made documentaries about Ho Chi Minh and Henry Kissinger and produced Jeux de Société series and docu-dramas; Founder Société des Publications Danielle Hunebelle 1973, Publr in French and English of La Lettre Int. de Danielle Hunebelle; now retd. *Publications include:* Philippine, Les plumes du paon, Rien que les hommes, Dear Henry. *Honours:* Chevalier de la Légion d'honneur, des Arts et Lettres. *Address:* Elia, 06190 Cap Martin, France. *Telephone:* (4) 93-57-77-47. *E-mail:* a.hunebelle@laposte.net (home).

HUNT, Gill (see Tubb, Edwin Charles)

HUNTINGTON, Samuel Phillips, MA, PhD; American academic and writer; *Albert J. Weatherhead III University Professor, Harvard University*; b. 18 April 1927, New York, NY; s. of Richard Huntington and Dorothy S. Phillips; m. Nancy Alice Arkelyan 1957; two s. *Education:* Harvard and Yale Univs and Univ. of Chicago. *Career:* Instructor in Govt, Harvard Univ. 1950–53, Asst Prof. 1953–58; Asst Dir Inst. of War and Peace Studies, Columbia Univ. 1958–59, Assoc. Dir 1959–62, Assoc. Prof. of Govt 1959–62; Prof. of Govt, Harvard Univ. 1962–67, Frank G. Thomson Prof. of Govt 1967–81, Clarence Dillon Prof. of Int. Affairs 1981–82, Eaton Prof. of Science of Govt 1982–95, Albert J. Weatherhead III Univ. Prof. 1995–, Chair. Harvard Acad. for Int. and Area Studies 1996–2004; Co-Ed. Foreign Policy Quarterly 1970–77; Dir John M. Olin Inst. for Strategic Studies 1989–99; Co-ordinator of Security Planning for Nat. Security Council, White House, Washington, DC 1977–78; Fellow, Center for Advanced Study of Behavioral Sciences, Stanford Univ. 1969–70; Visiting Fellow, All Souls Coll. Oxford, UK 1973; Fellow, Woodrow Wilson Int. Center for Scholars, Washington, DC 1983–84; Fellow, American Acad. of Arts and Sciences; Sr Research Assoc. IISS, London 1990; mem. American Political Science Asscn (Pres. 1986–87), Council on Foreign Relations, Int. Political Science Asscn; many other academic and professional appointments. *Publications:* The Soldier and the State: The Theory and Politics of Civil-Military Relations 1957, The Common Defense: Strategic Programs in National Politics 1961, Changing Patterns of Military Politics (co-ed.) 1962, Political Power: USA/USSR (co-author) 1964, Political Order in Changing Societies 1968, Authoritarian Politics in Modern Society: The Dynamics of Established One-Party Systems (co-ed.) 1970, The Crisis of Democracy (co-author) 1975, No Easy Choice: Political Participation in Developing Countries (with J. M. Nelson) 1976, American Politics: The Promise of Disharmony 1981, The Strategic Imperative: New Policies for American Security 1982, Living with Nuclear Weapons (co-author) 1983, Global Dilemmas (co-ed.) 1985, Reorganizing America's Defense (co-ed.) 1985, Understanding Political Development (co-ed.) 1987, The Third Wave: Democratization in the Late Twentieth Century 1991, The Clash of Civilizations and the Remaking of the World Order 1996, Culture Matters: How Values Shape Human Progress 2000, Who Are We?: The Challenges to America's National Identity 2004; contrib. scholarly articles to books, monographs. *Honours:* Silver Pen Award 1960, Guggenheim Fellow 1972–73, Grawemayer World Order Award 1992. *Address:* WCFIA, Harvard University, Room 112, 1727 Cambridge Street, Cambridge, MA 02138, USA (office). *Telephone:* (617) 495-4432 (office). *Fax:* (617) 384-9259 (office). *E-mail:* bbaiter@wcfia.harvard.edu (office). *Website:* www.wcfia.harvard.edu (office).

HUONG, Duong Thu; Vietnamese writer and screenwriter; b. 3 Jan. 1947, Thai Binh Prov.; m. 1968 (divorced 1981); one s. one d. *Education:* Ecole de Théorie Professionnelle, Ministry of Culture and Ecole de Formation Littéraire Nguyen Du. *Career:* volunteer, Cultural Activities, Binh Tri Thien 1968–77; film studio work, North Viet Nam 1977–; first female combatant/war corresp. at front when China attacked Vietnam in 1979; mem. Exec. Cttee Asscn des Cinéastes 1989; books banned in Viet Nam; expelled from Vietnamese CP 1989, imprisoned without trial for speech advocating political reform April 1991, accused by Vietnamese Govt of collaborating with 'reactionary organizations' and smuggling 'secret documents' out of the country; recognized by PEN Writers' Club, Anmesty International, and other human rights orgs as a political prisoner; her arrest and imprisonment sparked int. protest; released from prison 1991. *Publications in translation:* Beyond Illusions 1987 (trans. 2002), Paradise of the Blind 1988 (trans. 1991), Fragments of a Life 1989, Novel Without a Name (trans. 1995), Memories of a Pure Spring (trans. 2000), No Man's Land 2005; four scripts, one children's novel, ten collections of stories. *Honours:* first prize Concours de récit 1979, Gold Medal, two Silver Medals Vietnamese Film Festivals for feature films scripted. *Address:* Association des Cinéastes Vietnamiens, 51 rue de Tran hung Dao, Hanoi, Viet Nam; c/o Editions des Femmes, 6 rue de Mézières, 75006 Paris, France.

HURD OF WESTWELL, Baron (Life Peer), cr. 1997, of Westwell in the County of Oxfordshire; **Douglas Richard Hurd,** CH, CBE, PC; British politician, diplomatist, banker and author; *Deputy Chairman, Coutts Bank*; b. 8 March 1930, Marlborough; s. of the late Baron Hurd and Stephanie Corner; m. 1st Tatiana Elizabeth Michelle Eyre 1960 (divorced 1982); three s.; m. 2nd Judy Smart 1982; one s. one d. *Education:* Eton Coll., Trinity Coll., Cambridge. *Career:* joined diplomatic service 1952; served in Beijing 1954–56, UK Mission to UN 1956–60, Pvt. Sec. to Perm. Under-Sec. of State, Foreign Office 1960–63, in British Embassy, Rome 1963–66; joined Conservative Research Dept 1966, Head of Foreign Affairs Section 1968; Private Sec. to Leader of the Opposition 1968–70, Political Sec. to the Prime Minister 1970–74; MP for Mid-Oxon 1974–83, for Witney 1983–97; Opposition Spokesman on European Affairs 1976–79, Minister of State, FCO 1979–83, Home Office 1983–84; Sec. of State for NI 1984–85; Home Sec. 1985–89; Sec. of State for Foreign and Commonwealth Affairs 1989–95; mem. Royal Comm. for Lords Reforms 1999–; Deputy Chair. NatWest Markets 1995–98; Dir NatWest Group 1995–99; Chair. British Invisibles 1997–2000; Deputy Chair. Coutts and Co. 1998–; cand. for Conservative Leadership 1990; Chair. Prison Reform Trust 1997–2001; Chair. Booker Prize Cttee 1998; Sr Adviser to Hawkpoint Partners Ltd 1999–; Chair. Council for Effective Dispute Resolution (CEDR) 2001–04; High Steward Westminster Abbey 2000–; Jt Pres. Royal Inst. Int. Affairs 2002–. *Publications:* The Arrow War 1967, Send Him Victorious (with Andrew Osmond) 1968, The Smile on the Face of the Tiger 1969, Scotch on the Rocks 1971, Truth Game 1972, Vote to Kill 1975, An End to Promises 1979, War Without Frontiers (with Andrew Osmond) 1982, Palace of Enchantments (with Stephen Lamport) 1985, The Last Day of Summer 1992, The Search for Peace 1997, The Shape of Ice 1998, Ten Minutes to Turn the Devil (short stories) 1999, Image in the Water 2001, Memoirs 2003. *Honours:* Spectator Award for Parliamentarian of the Year 1990. *Address:* House of Lords, Westminster, London, SW1A 0PW, England. *Telephone:* (20) 7665-4538 (office); (20) 7219-3000. *Fax:* (20) 7665-4694 (office).

HURST, Frances (see Mayhar, Ardath)

HUSSAIN, Fahmida, PhD; Pakistani writer, literary critic and academic; *Director, Shah Abdul Latif Bhitai Chair, University of Karachi. Education:* Univ. of Sindh and Univ. of Karachi. *Career:* teacher in Sindhi Dept, Univ. of Karachi for over 20 years, currently Dir Shah Abdul Latif Bhitai Chair; mem. Co-ordination Council for Promotion of Shah Abdul Latif Bhitai Studies; mem. of jury, Kamal-i-Fun literary award 2003. *Publications:* Shah Abdul Latif Bhitai Jee Shairee Ma Aurt Jo Roop (Pakistan Acad. of Letters Book of the Year), Adabi Tanqeed Fun Aeen Tareekh 1996, numerous articles in journals and magazines. *Honours:* President's Award for Pride of Performance 2005. *Address:* Department of Sindhi, University of Karachi, Karachi, Pakistan (office). *E-mail:* saleem@sindhi.ku.edu.pk. *Website:* www.uok.edu.pk.

HUSSEIN, Aamer, BA, FRSL; British (b. Pakistani) writer, academic and literary critic; *Lecturer in English, University of Southampton*; b. 8 April 1955, Karachi, Pakistan; s. of The Nawab Ahmed Husain and Begum Sabiha (née Malik). *Education:* School of Oriental and African Studies, Univ. of London. *Career:* moved to London, England aged 15; researcher on films for MIP and TV documentaries 1981–87; first fiction and reviews published in arts journals Artrage and Bazaar 1986–; Visiting Lecturer at various univs, including Postcolonial Writing Fellow, Univ. of Southampton 2000; Royal Literary Fund Writing Fellow, Imperial Coll., London 2003–06; Lecturer, Inst. of English Studies, Univ. of London 2004–; Lecturer in English, Univ. of Southampton 2006–; Contrib. Ed. Wasafiri literary journal. *Publications:* short story collections: Mirror to the Sun 1993, This Other Salt 1999, Hoops of Fire: Fifty Years of Fiction by Pakistani Women (co-ed.) 2000, Cactus Town and Other Stories 2002, Turquoise 2002, Insomnia 2007; contrib. to The Independent, TLS, New Statesman. *Address:* c/o Saqi Books, 26 Westbourne Grove, London, W2 5RH, England. *E-mail:* aamerhussein@btinternet.com (home).

HUSTON, Nancy Louise, BA; Canadian writer; b. 16 Sept. 1953, Calgary, AB; m. Tzvetan Todorov 1981; one s. one d. *Education:* Sarah Lawrence Coll., École des Hautes Études. *Career:* writer-in-residence, American Univ., Paris 1989; facilitator, South African Writers Workshop 1994; Visiting Prof., Harvard Univ. 1994. *Publications:* Désirs et réalités: textes choisis (essay) 1978–94, Jouer au papa et à l'amant (essay) 1979, Dire et interdire: éléments de jurologie (essay) 1980, Les Variations Goldberg (novel, trans. as The Goldberg Variations) 1981, Mosaïque de la pornographie (essay) 1982, À l'amour comme à la guerre (non-fiction) 1984, Histoire d'Omaya (novel, trans. as The Story of Omaya) 1985, Lettres parisiennes (non-fiction) 1986, Trois fois septembre (novel) 1989, Journal de la création (essay) 1990, Véra veut la vérité (juvenile) 1992, Dora demande des détails (juvenile) 1993, Cantique des plaines (novel, trans. as Plainsong) (Prix Canada-Suisse 1995) 1993, La Virevolte (novel) 1994, Tombeau de Romain Gary (essay) 1995, Pour un patriotisme de l'ambiguïté (essay) 1995, Instrument des ténèbres (novel, trans. as Instrument of Darkness) (Prix Goncourt des Lycéens 1996, Prix du Livre Inter 1997) 1996, L'Empreinte de l'ange (novel, trans. as The Mark of the Angel) (Grand prix des lectrices de Elle 1999) 1998, Les Souliers d'or (juvenile) 1998, Prodige: polyphonie (novel) 1999, Nord Perdu (essay) 1999, Limbes (essay) 2000, Dolce agonia (novel) 2001, Une adoration (novel) 2003, Professeurs de désespoir (essay) 2004, Lignes de faille (Prix Femina, Prix France Télévisions) 2006. *Honours:* Prix Binet Sangle de l'Académie Française 1980, Prix Contrepoint 1981, Prix du Gouverneur-Général 1993, Prix Louis Hémon 1995. *Address:* c/o Actes Sud, 18 rue Séguier, 75006 Paris, France.

HUSTVEDT, Siri, PhD; American poet and writer; b. 19 Feb. 1955, Northfield, Minn.; d. of the late Lloyd Hustvedt and of Ester Vegan Hustvedt; m. Paul Auster 1981; one d. *Education:* Columbia Univ. *Career:* worked as ed. and trans. *Publications:* Reading to You (poems) 1982, The Blindfold (novel) 1990, The Enchantment of Lily Dahl (novel) 1996, Yonder: Essays 1998, What I Loved (novel, Prix des Libraires de Québec) 2003, Mysteries of the Rectangle (essays) 2005, A Plea for Eros (essays) 2006; contrib. to Paris Review. *Literary Agent:* c/o ICM International Creative Management, 40 West 57th Street, New York, NY 10019, USA; c/o ICM International Creative Management, 4–6 Soho Square, London, W1D 3PZ, England. *Telephone:* (212) 556-5764 (USA); (20) 7432-0800 (UK). *Fax:* (212) 556-5624 (USA); (20) 7432-0808 (UK).

HUTCHEON, Linda Ann Marie, FRSC, MA, PhD; Canadian academic and writer; *Distinguished University Professor, University of Toronto;* b. 24 Aug. 1947, Toronto, ON; m. Michael Alexander Hutcheon 1970. *Education:* Univ. of Toronto and Cornell Univ., USA. *Career:* Asst, Assoc. and Full Prof. of English, McMaster Univ. 1976–88; Prof. of English and Comparative Literature, Univ. of Toronto 1988–96, Distinguished Univ. Prof. 1996–; mem. Modern Language Asscn of America, American Acad. of Arts and Sciences. *Publications:* Narcissistic Narrative 1980, Formalism and the Freudian Aesthetic 1984, A Theory of Parody 1985, A Poetics of Postmodernism 1988, The Canadian Postmodern 1988, The Politics of Postmodernism 1989, Splitting Images 1991, Irony's Edge 1995, Opera: Desire, Disease, Death (with Michael Hutcheon) 1996, Bodily Charm: Living Opera (with Michael Hutcheon), 2000, Opera: The Art of Dying (with Michael Hutcheon), 2004. Editor: Other Solitudes 1990, Double-Talking 1992, Likely Stories 1992, A Postmodern Reader 1993, Rethinking Literary History: A Forum on Theory 2002; contribs to Diacritics, Textual Practice, Cultural Critique and other journals. *Honours:* Hon. LLD 1995, Hon. DLitt 1999, 2005; Killam Prize 2005. *Address:* Department of English, University of Toronto, Toronto, ON M5S 3K1, Canada (office). *Telephone:* (416) 978-6616 (office). *Fax:* (416) 978-2836 (office). *E-mail:* l.hist@utoronto.ca (office).

HUTCHINSON, Gregory Owen, BA, MA, DPhil; British writer; *Professor Greek and Latin Languages and Literature, Oxford University;* b. 5 Dec. 1957, London, England; m. Yvonne Downing 1979, one d. *Education:* Balliol and Christ Church Colleges, Oxford. *Publications:* Aeschylus, Septem Contra Thebas (ed.), 1985; Hellenistic Poetry, 1988; Latin Literature from Seneca to Juvenal: A Critical Study, 1993; Cicero's Correspondence: A Literary Study, 1998; Greek Lyric Poetry: A Commentary on Selected Larger Pieces, 2001. *Address:* Exeter College, Oxford, OX1 3DP, England (office).

HUTTERLI, Kurt; Canadian/Swiss writer, poet and artist; b. 18 Aug. 1944, Bern, Switzerland; m. Marianne Büchler 1966; one s. one d. *Education:* Secondary School Teacher Diploma Univ. of Bern 1966. *Career:* mem. PEN Switzerland, Autorinnen und Autoren der Schweiz, Berner Schriftsteller-Verein. *Publications:* Aber 1972, Herzgrün 1974, Felsengleich 1976, Die Faltsche 1977, Das Matterköpfen 1978, Ein Hausmann 1980, Finnlandisiert 1982, Überlebenslust 1984, Elchspur 1986, Baccalà 1989, Gaunerblut 1990, Mir kommt kein Tier ins Haus 1991, Stachelflieder 1991, Katzensprung 1993, Die sanfte Piratin 1994, Im Fischbauch 1998, Hotel Goldtown 2000, Der Clown im Mond 2000, Arche Titanic 2000, Der Rocky Mountain King 2003, Das Centovalli Brautgeschenk 2004, Omleto 2004, Wie es euch nicht gefällt 2006; contrib. to Der Bund, Stuttgarter Zeitung, Drehpunkt, Einspruch. *Honours:* Poetry Prize City of Bern 1971, Book Prizes City of Bern 1972, 1978, Theatre Awards 1976, 1982, 1987. *Address:* RR2, S53/C9, Oliver, BC V0H 1T0, Canada.

HUTTON, Ronald Edmund, MA, DPhil; British historian; b. 19 Dec. 1953, Ootacamund, India; m. Lisa Radulovic 1988 (divorced 2003). *Education:* Univ. of Cambridge. *Career:* Prof. of History Bristol University 1996–; mem. Royal Historical Society; Folklore Society; Fellow, Society of Antiquaries. *Publications:* The Royalist War Effort 1981, The Restoration 1985, Charles II 1989, The British Republic 1990, The Pagan Religions of the Ancient British Isles 1991, The Rise and Fall of Merry England 1994, The Stations of the Sun 1996, The Triumph of the Moon: A History of Modern Pagan Witchcraft 1999, Shamans 2001, Witches, Druids and King Arthur: Studies in Paganism, Myth and Magic 2003, Debates in Stuart History 2004; contrib. to journals. *Honours:* Benjamin Franklin Prize 1993. *Address:* 13 Woodland Road, Bristol BS8 1TB, England.

HUTTON, Will Nicholas, MBA; British writer and broadcaster; *Chief Executive, Work Foundation;* b. 21 May 1950, London; s. of the late William Hutton and Dorothy Haynes; m. Jane Atkinson 1978; one s. two d. *Education:* Chislehurst and Sidcup Grammar School, Univ. of Bristol and Institut Européen d' Admin des Affaires (INSEAD), Fontainebleau, France. *Career:* with Phillips & Drew (stockbrokers) 1971–77; Sr Producer Current Affairs, BBC Radio 4 1978–81; Dir and Producer The Money Programme, BBC 2 1981–83; Econs Corresp. Newsnight, BBC 2 1983–88; Ed. European Business Channel 1988–90; Econs Ed. The Guardian 1990–95, Asst Ed. 1995–96; Ed. The Observer 1996–98, Ed.-in-Chief 1998–2000; Chief Exec. The Work Foundation (fmrly The Industrial Soc. –2002) 2000–; Gov. LSE 2000–. *Publications:* The Revolution That Never Was: An Assessment of Keynesian Economics 1986, The State We're In 1994, The State to Come 1997, The Stakeholding Society 1998, The World We're In 2002, The Writing on the Wall: China and the West in the 21st Century 2007. *Honours:* Hon. DLitt (Kingston) 1995, (De Montfort) 1996; Political Journalist of the Year, What the Papers Say 1993. *Address:* The Work Foundation, Peter Runge House, 3 Carlton Terrace, London, SW1Y 5DG (office); 34 Elms Avenue, London, N10 2JP, England (home). *Telephone:* (20) 7004-7103 (office). *Fax:* (20) 7004-7111 (office). *E-mail:* sholden@theworkfoundation.com (office). *Website:* www.theworkfoundation.com (office).

HWANG, David Henry, BA; American dramatist and screenwriter; b. 11 Aug. 1957, Los Angeles, CA; m. 1st Ophelia Chong 1985; m. 2nd Kathryn Layng 1993; one s. *Education:* Stanford Univ., Yale Drama School. *Career:* dramaturg, Asian American Theatre Centre, San Francisco 1987–; mem. Dramatists' Guild (bd of dirs 1988–). *Plays:* FOB 1980, The Dance and the Railroad 1981, Family Devotions 1981, Sound and Beauty 1983, The Sound of a Voice 1984, As the Crow Flies 1986, Rich Relations 1986, M Butterfly 1988, Bondage 1992, Face Value 1993, Trying to Find Chinatown 1996, Golden Child 1996. *Screenplays:* M Butterfly 1993, Golden Gate 1993. *Other works:* 1000 Airplanes on the Roof (musical) 1988, Forbidden Nights (TV play) 1990, The Voyage (libretto) 1992, Elton John and Tim Rice's Aida (co-librettist, Broadway) 2000, Flower Drum Song (revised libretto, Broadway) 2002, The Fly (opera libretto). *Honours:* Drama-Logue Awards 1980, 1986, Obie Award 1981, Rockefeller Foundation Fellowship 1983, Guggenheim Fellowship 1984, Nat. Endowment for the Arts Fellowship 1987, Tony Award for Best Play 1988, Outer Critics Circle Award for Best Broadway Play 1988, John Gassner Award 1988. *Literary Agent:* Writers and Artists Agency, 19 W 44th Street, Suite 1410, New York, NY 10036, USA.

HWANG, Sok-yong; North Korean novelist; b. 1943, Zhanchung, Manchuria, China. *Career:* drafted into Korean army, fought in Viet Nam war 1966–69; fmr labourer and political activist in S Korea; took part in cultural exchange with N Korea 1989; went into voluntary exile in Germany and USA, imprisoned on his return to Seoul 1993, pardoned 1998. *Publications:* The Pagoda (short story) (Chosun Ilbo New Year Prize) 1970, The Chronicle of a Man Named Han (novel) 1970, The Road to Sampo (short stories) 1974, Chang Kil-san (serialised novel) 1974–84, The Shadow of Arms (novel) 1985, The Old Garden (novel) (Danjae Award, Yi San Literary Award) 2000, The Guest (novel) 2001. *Honours:* Manhae Grand Prize for Literature 2004. *Address:* c/o Seven Stories Press, 140 Watts Street, New York, NY 10013, USA. *E-mail:* info@sevenstories.com.

HYDE, Lewis, BA, MA; American academic, author, poet, editor and translator; b. 16 Oct. 1945, Boston, MA; m. Patricia Auster Vigderman 1981; one step-s. *Education:* University of Minnesota, University of Iowa. *Career:* Instructor in Literature, University of Iowa, 1969–71; Lecturer in Expository Writing, 1983–85, Briggs-Copeland Asst Prof. of English, 1985–89, Dir, Creative Writing Programme, 1988–89, Harvard University; Henry R. Luce Prof. of Art and Politics, 1989–2001, Richard L. Thomas Prof. of Creative Writing, 2001–, Kenyon College. *Publications:* Twenty Poems of Vicente Aleixandre (ed. and trans. with Robert Bly), 1977; A Longing for the Light: Selected Poems of Vicente Aleixandre (ed. and trans. with others), 1979; World Alone, by Vicente Aleixandre (trans. with David Unger), 1982; The Gift: Imagination and the Erotic Life of Property, 1983; On the Work of Allen Ginsberg (ed.), 1984; Alcohol and Poetry: John Berryman and the Booze Talking, 1986; This Error is the Sign of Love (poems), 1988; Trickster Makes This World: Mischief, Myth, and Art, 1998; Selected Essays of Henry D. Thoreau (ed. and annotator), 2002. Contributions: numerous journals, quarterlies, reviews. *Honours:* Acad. of American Poets Prize, 1966; National Endowment for the Arts Creative Writing Fellowships, 1977, 1982, 1987; Columbia University Trans. Center Award, 1979; National Endowment for the Humanities Fellowship for Independent Study and Research, 1979; Massachusetts Council on the Arts and Humanities Fellowship In Poetry, 1980; MacDowell Colony Fellowships, 1989, 1991, 1996, 1999, 2000; Scholar-in-Residence, Rockefeller Study and Conference Center, Bellagio, Italy, 1991; John D. and Catherine T. MacArthur Foundation Fellowship, 1991–96; Getty Scholar, 1993–94; Hon. DFA, San Francisco Art Institute, 1997; Osher Fellow, 1998.

HYLAND, Paul, BSc; British poet and travel writer; b. 15 Sept. 1947, Poole, Dorset. *Education:* Univ. of Bristol. *Career:* mem. Soc. of Authors, Poetry Soc., PEN, The Magic Circle, Int. Brotherhood of Magicians. *Publications:* Purbeck: The Ingrained Island 1978, Wight: Biography of an Island 1984, The Black Heart 1988, Indian Balm 1994, Backwards Out of the Big World 1996, Discover Dorset: Isle of Purbeck 1998, Ralegh's Last Journey 2003; poetry: Poems of Z 1982, The Stubborn Forest 1984, Getting into Poetry 1992, Kicking

Sawdust 1995, Art of the Impossible 2004. *Honours:* Eric Gregory Award 1976, Alice Hunt Bartlett Award 1985, Authors' Foundation 1995. *Literary Agent:* c/o David Higham Associates Ltd, 5–8 Lower John Street, Golden Square, London, W1F 9HA, England. *Telephone:* (20) 7434-5900. *Fax:* (20) 7437-1072. *E-mail:* dha@davidhigham.co.uk. *Website:* www.davidhigham.co.uk. *E-mail:* write@paul-hyland.co.uk.

HYMAN, Harold Melvin, BA, MA, PhD; American academic and author; b. 24 July 1924, New York, NY; m. Ferne Beverly Handelsman 1946, two s. one d. *Education:* University of California at Los Angeles, Columbia University. *Career:* Asst Prof., Earlham College, 1952–55; Visiting Asst Prof., 1955–56, Prof., 1963–68, University of California at Los Angeles; Assoc. Prof., Arizona State University, Tempe, 1956–57; Prof. of History, University of Illinois, 1963–68; William P. Hobby Prof. of History, 1968–96, Prof. Emeritus, 1997–, Rice University; Graduate Faculty in Political Science, University of Tokyo, 1973; Faculty of Law, Keio University, 1973; Adjunct Prof. of Legal History, Bates College of Law, University of Houston, 1977, and of American Legal History, School of Law, University of Texas, 1986; Meyer Visiting Distinguished Prof. of Legal History, School of Law, New York University, 1982–83; mem. American Historical Asscn, American Society of Legal History (pres. 1994–95), Organization of American Historians, Southern Historical Asscn. *Publications:* Era of the Oath: Northern Loyalty Tests During the Civil War and Reconstruction, 1954; To Try Men's Souls: Loyalty Tests in American History, 1959; Stanton: The Life and Times of Lincoln's Secretary of War (with Benjamin P. Thomas), 1962; Soldiers and Spruce: The Loyal Legion of Loggers and Lumbermen, the Army's Labor Union of World War I, 1963; A More Perfect Union: The Impact of the Civil War and Reconstruction on the Constitution, 1973; Union and Confidence: The 1860s, 1976; Equal Justice Under Law: Constitutional History, 1835–1875 (with William Wiecek), 1982; Quiet Past and Stormy Present?: War Powers in American History, 1986; American Singularity: The 1787 Northwest Ordinance, the 1862 Homestead-Morrill Acts, and the 1944 G.I. Bill, 1986; Oleander Odyssey: The Kempners of Galveston, 1870–1980, 1990; The Reconstruction Justice of Salmon P. Chase: In Re Turner and Texas v White, 1997; Craftsmanship and Character: A History of the Vinson & Elkins Law Firm of Houston, 1917–1990s, 1998. Editor: several books. Contributions: scholarly journals. *Honours:* Albert J. Beveridge Award, American Historical Asscn, 1952; Coral H. Tullis Memorial Prize, Texas A & M University Press, 1990; T. R. Fehrenbach Book Award, Texas Historical Commission, 1990; Ottis Lock Endowment Award, East Texas Historical Asscn, 1991.

HYMAN, Timothy; British painter and writer on art; b. 17 April 1946, Hove; s. of Alan Hyman and Noreen Gypson; m. Judith Ravenscroft 1982. *Education:* Charterhouse and Slade School of Fine Art. *Career:* Curator Narrative Paintings at Arnolfini and ICA Galleries, etc. 1979–80; public collections include Arts Council, Bristol City Art Gallery, Museum of London, Contemporary Art Soc., British Museum, Govt Art Collection, Los Angeles Co. Museum; Visiting Prof. at Baroda, India, two British Council lecture tours 1981–83; Artist in Residence at Lincoln Cathedral 1983–84, Sandown Racecourse 1992; Purchaser for Arts Council Collection 1985; selector, John Moores Prize 1995; Lead curator Stanley Spencer retrospective exhbn, Tate Gallery, London 2001–; Co-curator British Vision, Museum of Fine Arts, Ghent 2007. *Exhibitions:* started to exhibit at Blond 1980, solo exhbns 1981, 1983 and 1985; Austin/Desmond (solo exhbn 1990, 2000, 2003, 2006), Castlefield Gallery, Manchester 1993, Gallery Chemould, Bombay 1994, Gallery M, Flowers East 1994; group exhbns at Royal Acad., Hayward Gallery, Whitechapel Art Gallery, Nat. Portrait Gallery, Museum of London. *Publications:* Hodgkin 1975, Kitaj 1977, Beckmann 1978, Balthus 1980, Narrative Paintings 1979, English Romanesque 1984, Kiff 1986, Domenico Tiepolo 1987, Bhupen Khakhar (monograph) 1998, Bonnard (monograph) 1998, Carnivalesque (catalogue) 2000, Stanley Spencer (catalogue) 2001, Sienese Painting (monograph) 2003; numerous articles on contemporary figurative painting in London Magazine, Artscribe, Times Literary Supplement 1975–. *Honours:* Leverhulme Award 1992, Rootstein Hopkins Foundation Award 1995, Wingate Award 1998, Medaglio Beato Angelico, Florence 2005. *Address:* 62 Myddelton Square, London, EC1, England. *Telephone:* (20) 7837-1933.

HYNES, Samuel, DFC, PhD, FRSL; American academic and writer; *Professor Emeritus, Department of English, Princeton University;* b. 29 Aug. 1924, Chicago; s. of Samuel Lynn and Margaret (Turner) Hynes; m. Elizabeth Igleheart 1944; two d. *Education:* Univ. of Minnesota, Columbia Univ. *Career:* served in USMCR 1943–46, 1952–53; mem. faculty, Swarthmore Coll. 1949–68, Prof. of English Literature 1965–68; Prof. of English, Northwestern Univ., Evanston, Ill. 1968–76; Prof. of English, Princeton Univ. 1976–90, Woodrow Wilson Prof. of Literature 1978–90, Prof. Emer. 1990–; Fulbright Fellow 1953–54; Guggenheim Fellow 1959–60, 1981–82; Bollingen Fellow 1964–65; American Council of Learned Socs Fellow 1969, 1985–86; Nat. Endowment for Humanities Sr Fellow 1973–74, 1977–78. *Publications:* The Pattern of Hardy's Poetry (Explicator Award 1962), William Golding 1964, The Edwardian Turn of Mind 1968, Edwardian Occasions 1972, The Auden Generation 1976, Flights of Passage: Reflections of a World War Two Aviator 1988; Ed.: Further Speculations by T. E. Hulme 1955, The Author's Craft and Other Critical Writings of Arnold Bennett 1968, Romance and Realism 1979, Complete Poetical Works of Thomas Hardy, Vol. I 1982, Vol. II 1984, Vol. III 1985, Vols IV, V 1995, Thomas Hardy 1984, A War Imagined: The First World War and English Culture 1990, Complete Short Fiction of Joseph Conrad (Vol. I–III) 1992, (Vol. IV) 1993, The Soldiers' Tale 1997 (Robert F. Kennedy Book Award 1998), The Growing Seasons: An American Boyhood Before the War 2003. *Honours:* American Acad. of Arts and Letters Award in Literature 2004. *Address:* 130 Moore Street, Princeton, NJ 08540; Department of English, 22 McCosh Hall, Princeton University, Princeton, NJ 08544-1006, USA (office). *Website:* web.princeton.edu/sites/english/new_web/index.htm (office).

I

IBBOTSON, Eva; Austrian writer; b. 1925, Vienna; m. Alan Ibbotson; four c. *Education:* Univ. of London, Univ. of Cambridge. *Publications include:* juvenile: The Great Ghost Rescue 1975, Which Witch 1979, Magic Flutes 1982, A Countess Below Stars 1983, The Worm and the Toffee-Nosed Princess 1983, Glove Shop in Vienna and other stories 1984, A Company of Swans 1985, The Haunting of Hiram C. Hopgood 1987, Madensky Square 1988, Not Just a Witch 1989, The Morning Gift 1993, Native: The Beauty and the Wonder 1994, The Secret of Platform 13 1995, Dial-A-Ghost 1996, A Song for Summer 1997, Island of the Aunts 2000, Monster Mission 2001, Journey to the River Sea 2001, The Emperor's Horse 2004, The Star of the Kazan 2004, The Haunting of Granite Falls 2005, The Secret Countess 2007. *Address:* c/o Puffin Books, Penguin Books UK, 80 Strand, London, WC2R 0LR, England. *E-mail:* puffin@ penguin.co.uk. *Website:* www.puffin.co.uk.

IBRAGIMBEKOV, Maksud Mamed Ibragim ogli; Azerbaijani/Russian writer, scriptwriter and playwright; b. 1935, Baku; s. of Mamed Ibragim Ibragimbekov and Fatima Alekper-kyzy Meshadibekova; m. Anna Yuryebna Ibragimbekova (née Gerulaitis); one s. *Education:* Baku Polytech. Inst., High Scenario and Directoral Courses, Moscow. *Career:* Supt Aztyazhpromstroi 1960–62; freelance scriptwriter, theatre dir 1964–; mem. USSR Union of Writers 1965–; mem. Azerbaijan Parl. 1985–(2005); Pres. PEN Club, Azerbaijan 1991–; Chair. Nobility Ass. of Azerbaijan. *Films:* Latest Night of Childhood, Djabish-muallim, Who is Going to Travel to Truskavets?, Latest Interview. *Plays:* Mesozoic Story (Moscow Maly Theatre) 1975, Death of All the Good (Leningrad Theatre of Young Spectator) 1978, Men for Young Woman (Dramatic Theatre) 1992, The Oil Boom is Smiling on Everyone 2002. *Television:* Gold Voyage 1993, The History with Happy End 1998. *Publications:* Who is Going to Travel to Truskavets?, There Was Never a Better Brother, Let Him Stay With Us; novels and prose in magazines and separate editions. *Honours:* Order of Labour Red Banner 1981, Order of Glory of Azerbaijan Repub. 1995; State Prize of Azerbaijan Repub. 1975, People's Writer of Azerbaijan 1998. *Address:* 28 Boyuk Qala str., 370004 Baku (office); 38 Kutkashenli str., 370006 Baku, Azerbaijan (home). *Telephone:* (12) 4929843 (office); (12) 4975300 (home). *Fax:* (12) 4928459 (office). *E-mail:* maksud@planet-az.com (office); Maksud@azeurotel.com (home).

IBRAHIM, Sonallah; Egyptian writer; b. 1937, Cairo; m. 1975; one step-d. *Education:* Cairo Univ. *Career:* fmr journalist; Visiting Assoc. Prof. Dept of Near Eastern Studies, Univ. of California at Berkeley 1999. *Publications:* Tilka al-Raiha (The Smell of It) 1966, Star of August 1974, The Committee 1981, Beirut Beirut 1984, Zaat 1992, Sharaf (Best Egyptian Novel 1998) 1997, Warda 2000, Amrikanli 2004. *Honours:* Eweiss Prize 1994, Galeb Halasa Prize 1995, Ibn Rush Prize 2004. *Address:* Ali Fahmi Kamel St 2, 11351 Heliopolis, Cairo, Egypt (home); c/o Syracuse University Press, 621 Skytop Road, Suite 110, Syracuse, NY 13244-5290, USA (office). *Telephone:* (202) 633-2301 (home). *E-mail:* selorfaly@hotmail.com (home).

IDLE, Eric, BA; British writer, lyricist and actor; b. 29 March 1943, South Shields, Tyne and Wear, England; m. 1st Lynn Ashley (divorced); one s.; m. 2nd Tania Kosevich; one d. *Education:* Royal School, Wolverhampton and Pembroke Coll., Cambridge. *Films:* Albert Carter, Q.O.S.O. (writer) 1968, And Now for Something Completely Different (actor, writer) 1971, Monty Python and the Holy Grail (actor, writer, exec. prod.) 1975, Life of Brian (actor, writer) 1979, The Meaning of Life (actor, writer) 1983, Yellowbeard (actor) 1983, European Vacation (actor) 1985, The Transformers: The Movie (voice) 1986, The Adventures of Baron Munchausen (actor) 1988, Nuns on the Run (actor) 1990, Missing Pieces (actor) 1991, Too Much Sun (actor) 1991, Mom and Dad Save the World (actor) 1992, Splitting Heirs (actor, writer, exec. prod.) 1993, Casper (actor) 1995, The Wind in the Willows (actor) 1996, Quest for Camelot (voice) 1998, Rudolph the Red-Nosed Reindeer: The Movie (voice) 1998, The Secret of NIMH 2: Timmy to the Rescue (voice) 1998, Pirates: 3D Show (actor, writer) 1999, Journey into Your Imagination (actor) 1999, Hercules: Zero to Hero (voice) 1999, South Park: Bigger Longer & Uncut (voice) 1999, Dudley Do-Right (actor) 1999, Brightness (actor) 2000, 102 Dalmatians (voice) 2000, Pinocchio (voice) 2002, Hollywood Homicide (actor) 2003, Ella Enchanted (actor) 2004, The Nutcracker and the Mouseking (voice) 2004, Delgo (voice) 2007, Shrek the Third 2007. *Television:* Alice in Wonderland (actor) 1966, The Frost Report (series, writer) 1966, No, That's Me Over Here! (series, writer) 1967, At Last the 1948 Show (series, actor) 1967, Do Not Adjust Your Set (series, actor and writer) 1967–69, Simply Sheila (writer) 1968, According to Dora (series, writer) 1968, We Have Ways of Making You Laugh (series, actor and writer) 1968, Broaden Your Mind (series, writer) 1968, Hark at Barker (series, writer) 1969, Monty Python's Flying Circus (four series, actor and writer) 1969–74, Euroshow 71 (actor) 1971, The Two Ronnies (series, writer) 1971, The Ronnie Barker Yearbook (writer) 1971, Ronnie Corbett in Bed (writer) 1971, Monty Python's Fliegender Zirkus (actor, writer) 1972, Christmas Box (writer) 1974, Commander Badman (writer) 1974, Rutland Weekend Television (series, actor and writer) 1975, The Rutles (actor, writer, dir) 1978, The Mikado (film, actor) 1987, Nearly Departed (series, actor) 1989, Around the World in 80 Days (series, actor) 1989, Mickey Mouse Works (series, voice) 1999, Suddenly Susan (series, actor) 1999–2000, House of Mouse (series, voice) 2001, The Scream Team (film, actor) 2002, Rutles 2: Can't Buy Me Lunch (writer, dir) 2002, Christmas Vacation 2: Cousin Eddie's

Island Adventure (film, actor) 2003, The Simpsons (voice) 2003–07, Super Robot Monkey Team Hyperforce Gol (voice) 2004–05. *Stage productions:* I'm Just Wild About Harry (actor, Edinburgh Festival) 1963, Monty Python Live at the Hollywood Bowl (actor, writer) 1982, The Mikado (actor, ENO) 1987, (actor, Houston Opera House) 1989, Monty Python's Spamalot (writer, The Shubert Theatre, Broadway) 2005. *Compositions:* songs for Monty Python's Flying Circus series 1969, Always Look on the Bright Side of Life.. (for Life of Brian film) 1979, Bruces' Philosophers Song (for Monty Python Live at the Hollywood Bowl) 1982, Sit On My Face (for Monty Python Live at the Hollywood Bowl) 1982, songs for The Meaning of Life film 1983, The Adventures of Baron Munchausen (song, for film) 1988, One Foot in the Grave (TV series theme song) 1990, That's Death (song for video game, Discworld II: Missing Presumed...!?) 1996, songs for Monty Python's Spamalot stage production 2005. *Publications include:* Hello Sailor 1975, The Rutland Dirty Weekend Book 1976, Pass the Butler 1982, Monty Python's Flying Circus: Just the Words (co-author, two vols) 1989, The Fairly Incomplete and Rather Badly Illustrated Monty Python Song Book (co-author) 1994, The Quite Remarkable Adventures of the Owl and the Pussycat (co-author) 1996, The Road to Mars 1998, The "Pythons" Autobiography by the "Pythons" (co-author) 2003, The Greedy Bastard Diary: A Comic Tour of America 2005. *Address:* c/o HarperEntertainment, 10 E 53rd Street, New York, NY 10022, USA.

IERONIM, Ioana; Romanian poet, translator and diplomatist; *Programme Director, Fulbright Exchange, Bucharest;* b. 1947, Transylvania. *Education:* Univ. of Bucharest. *Career:* fmr ed. and trans. for various scientific and encyclopedic publs; apptd Cultural Counsellor, Romanian Embassy in the USA; currently Programme Dir Fulbright Exchange, Bucharest. *Publications:* poetry: The Curtain 1983, Monday Mornings 1987, Poems 1986, The Fool's Triumph 1992, The Triumph of the Water Witch (co-trans.) 2000, Munci, zile, alunecari de teren: Poeme/proze 1970–2000 2001. *Address:* c/o Fulbright Commission, Ing. Costinescu Street, Nr.2 Sector 1, Bucharest, Romania.

IGGERS, Georg Gerson, BA, AM, PhD; German/American historian; *Distinguished Professor Emeritus, State University of New York at Buffalo;* b. 7 Dec. 1926, Hamburg, Germany; m. Wilma Abeles 1948, three s. *Education:* Univ. of Richmond Virginia, Univ. of Chicago, New School for Social Research, New York. *Career:* Instructor Univ. of Akron 1948–50; Assoc. Prof. Philander Smith Coll. 1950–56; Visiting Prof. Univ. of Arkansas 1956–57, 1964, Univ. of Rochester, New York 1970–71, Univ. of Leipzig 1992; Assoc. Prof. Dillard Univ., New Orleans 1957–63; Visiting Assoc. Prof. Tulane Univ. 1957–60, 1962–63; Assoc. Prof. Roosevelt Univ., Chicago 1963–65; Prof. SUNY at Buffalo 1965–78, Distinguished Prof. 1978–97, Distinguished Prof. Emer. 1997–; Visiting Scholar Technische Hochschule, Darmstadt 1991, Forschungsschwerpunkt Zeithistorische Studien, Potsdam 1993, 1998, Univ. of Århus, Denmark 1998, Univ. of New England, Australia 1999, Univ. of Vienna 2002; Fellow Int. Inst. of Cultural Studies, Vienna 2000; mem. Int. Commission for the History and Theory of Historiography (pres. 1995–2000). *Publications:* Cult of Authority: Political Philosophy of the Saint Simonians 1958, German Conception of History 1968, Leopold von Ranke: The Theory and Practice of History (co-ed.) 1973, New Directions in European Historiography 1975, International Handbook of Historical Studies (co-ed.) 1979, Social History of Politics (ed.) 1985, Aufklärung und Geschichte (co-ed.) 1986, Leopold von Ranke and the Shaping of the Historical Discipline (co-ed.) 1990, Marxist Historiography in Transition: Historical Writings in East Germany in the 1980s (ed.) 1991, Geschichtswissenschaft 20. Jahrhundert 1993, Historiography in the Twentieth Century: From Scientific Objectivity to the Postmodern Challenge 1997, Zwei Seiten der Geschichte (autobiog. with Wilma Iggers) 2002, Turning Points in Historiography (co-ed.) 2002; contrib. to scholarly journals. *Honours:* foreign mem. Acad. of Sciences of German Democratic Republic 1990–92; Alexander von Humboldt Foundation Research Prize 1995–96; Hon. PhD (Univ. of Richmond) 2001, (Darnstadt Tech. Univ.) 2006. *Address:* Department of History, State University of New York at Buffalo, Buffalo, NY 14260, USA (office).

IGGULDEN, John (Jack) Manners; Australian writer and industrialist; b. 12 Feb. 1917, Brighton, Vic.; m. Helen Carroll Schapper; one s. (deceased) two d. *Career:* man., family-owned manufacturing companies 1940–59; writer 1959–70; businessman 1970–; part-time writer 1980–; currently Chair., Planet Lighting, Lucinda Glassworks, Bellingen, NSW. *Publications:* Breakthrough 1960, The Storms of Summer 1960, The Clouded Sky 1964, Dark Stranger 1965, Summer's Tales 3 1966, Manual of Standard Procedures, Gliding Federation of Australia 1964, Gliding Instructor's Handbook 1968, The Promised Land Papers Vol. 1: The Revolution of the Good 1986, Vol. 2: How Things Are Wrong and How to Fix Them 1988, Vol. 3: The Modification of Freedom 1993, Silent Lies 1997, Good World 1998, The Good World Reader 2004; memoir series: Second Son 2005, Equal Partners 2005, The Blue Skies 2006, The Dark Clouds 2006, Late Starter 2007. *Address:* 'Evandale', Promised Land, Bellingen, NSW 2454, Australia.

IGLORIA, Luisa A., PhD; Philippine poet and essayist; *Associate Professor of English, Old Dominion University;* b. (Ma. Luisa B. Aguilar-Cariño), 1961, Baguio City. *Education:* UP Baguio, Ateneo de Manila Univ., Univ. of Ill. at Chicago, USA. *Career:* Fulbright Fellow Univ. of Ill. at Chicago; currently

Assoc. Prof. Dept of English, Old Dominion Univ.; mem. Asscn of Writers and Writing Programs, Philippine Literary Arts Council. *Publications include:* poetry: Cordillera Tales (Nat. Book Award for Poetry 1991) 1990, Cartography: A Collection of Poetry on Baguio (Nat. Book Award 1993) 1992, Encanto 1994, In the Garden of the Three Islands 1995, Blood Sacrifice (Nat. Book Award for Poetry 1998) 1997, Songs for the Beginning of the Millennium 1999, Not Home, But Here: Writing from the Filipino Diaspora (ed) 2003; prose: Wedding Night (special mention The Pushcart Prize Anthology: Best of the Small Presses) 2003, The Birdcage Maker (poem, Fugue) (first prize Fugue Award Competition in Poetry) 2004, Trill & Mordent (Second Prize, Editions Prize for Poetry, WordTech Editions 2004) 2005; contrib. to numerous anthologies, journals and periodicals, including Poetry East, Crab Orchard Review, The Missouri Review, Smartish Pace, New Letters, Our Own Voice electronic literary journal for Philippine people in the diaspora www.oovrag.com. *Honours:* Virginia Comm. for the Arts Fiction Fellowship/Independent Artist Award 2001, first prize Fugue Literary Journal Award Competition in Poetry 2004, 11 Palanca Awards for Literature, Palanca Hall of Fame Distinction. *Address:* Creative Writing Program and Department of English, 200 Batten Arts and Letters, Old Dominion University, Hampton Boulevard, Norfolk, VA 23529, USA. *Telephone:* (757) 683-3929 (office). *Fax:* (757) 683-3241 (office). *E-mail:* ligloria@odu.edu (office). *Website:* al.odu.edu/english/faculty/ligloria.shtml (office); www.lib.odu.edu/litfest/27th (office); www.luisaigloria.com (home).

IGNATENKO, Vitaly Nikitich; Russian journalist; b. 19 April 1941, Sochi; m. Svetlana Ignatenko; one s. *Education:* Moscow Univ. *Career:* corresp., Deputy Ed.-in-Chief Komsomolskaya Pravda 1963–75; Deputy Dir-Gen. TASS (USSR Telegraph Agency) 1975–78; Deputy Head of Int. Information Section, CPSU Cen. Cttee 1978–86; Ed.-in-Chief Novoe Vremya 1986–90; Asst to fmr Pres. Gorbachev, Head of Press Service 1990–91; Dir-Gen. Agency ITAR-TASS 1991–; Deputy Chair. Council of Ministers 1995–97; Pres., Chair. of Bd Russian Public TV (ORT) 1998–; Pres. World Asscn of Russian Press; mem. Int. Acad. of Information Science, Russian Fed. Comm. on UNESCO Affairs, Union of Russian Journalists, Union of Russian Cinematographers. *Publications:* several books and more than 30 film scripts. *Honours:* Order of the Friendship of Peoples (twice) 1996, Order of Merit to the Fatherland 1999; Lenin Prize 1978, Prize of USSR Journalists' Union 1975. *Address:* ITAR-TASS, Tverskoy blvd 10, 125993 Moscow, Russia (office). *Telephone:* (495) 629-79-25 (office). *Fax:* (495) 203-31-80 (office).

IGNATIEFF, Michael, BA, MA, PhD; Canadian writer, historian, academic and politician; b. 12 May 1947, Toronto, Ont.; m. 1st Susan Barrowclough 1977; one s. one d.; m. 2nd Zsuzsanna Zsohar. *Education:* Univ. of Toronto, Harvard Univ., Univ. of Cambridge. *Career:* reporter, Globe and Mail, Toronto 1966–67; teaching Fellow, Harvard Univ. 1971–74; Asst Prof., Univ. of British Columbia, Vancouver 1976–78; Sr Research Fellow, King's Coll., Cambridge 1978–84; Visiting Prof., École des Hautes Études, Paris 1985; editorial columnist, The Observer, London 1990–93; correspondent for BBC, Observer, New Yorker 1984–2000; mem., Int. Comm. on Sovereignty and Intervention; Carr Prof. of Human Rights Practice Harvard Univ. 2000–05, Dir Carr Center for Human Rights Policy, John F. Kennedy School of Govt 2001–05; Chancellor Jackman Visiting Prof. in Human Rights Policy, Univ. of Toronto 2005; MP (Liberal) for Etobicoke-Lakeshore Jan. 2006–, assoc. critic for Human Resources and Skills Devt in Official Opposition Shadow Cabinet 2006; announced campaign for leadership of Liberal party March 2006. *Television:* host Thinking Aloud (BBC) 1986–, Voices (Channel Four) 1986, The Late Show (BBC 2) 1989–. *Publications:* A Just Measure of Pain: The Penitentiary in the Industrial Revolution 1978, Wealth and Virtue: The Shaping of Classical Political Economy in the Scottish Enlightenment (ed. with Istvan Hont) 1983, The Needs of Strangers: An Essay on the Philosophy of Human Needs 1984, The Russian Album: A Family Memoir (RSL W. H. Heinemann Award, UK, Governor-General Award, Canada 1988) 1987, Asya 1991, Scar Tissue (novel) 1993, Blood and Belonging: Journeys into the New Nationalism 1993, Isaiah Berlin: A Life 1998, The Warrior's Honor: Ethnic War and the Modern Conscience 1998, Virtual War: Kosovo and Beyond 2000, The Rights Revolution (Massey Lectures 2000) 2001, Human Rights as Politics and Idolatry (Tanner Lectures) 2001, Charlie Johnson in the Flames 2003, The Lesser Evil: Political Ethics in an Age of Terror 2004, After Paradise 2005; contrib. to New York Times, New Yorker, New York Review of Books. *Honours:* Hon. doctorate (Bishop's Univ.) 1995; Lionel Gelber Award 1994. *Address:* Etobicoke Constituency Office, 656 The Queensway, Toronto, ON M8Y 1K7, Canada (office). *Telephone:* (416) 251-5510 (office). *Fax:* (416) 251-2845 (office). *Website:* www.michaelignatieffmp.ca (office).

IGNATIUS, David; American journalist and editor; b. 1950, Cambridge, Mass.; m. Eve Ignatius; three d. *Education:* Harvard Univ. and King's Coll. Cambridge, UK. *Career:* Ed. The Washington Monthly magazine 1975; reporter The Wall Street Journal 1976–86, assignments included Steelworkers Corresp., Pittsburgh, Senate Corresp., Washington DC, Middle East Corresp., Chief Diplomatic Corresp.; Ed. Sunday Outlook, The Washington Post 1986–90, Foreign Ed. 1990–93, apptd Asst Managing Business Ed. 1993, then Assoc. Ed.; Exec. Ed. International Herald Tribune 2000–03; mem. Washington Post Writer's Group 2003–; contrib. to The New York Times Magazine, The Atlantic Monthly, Foreign Affairs and The New Republic. *Publications include:* Agents of Innocence 1987, SIRO 1991, The Bank of Fear 1994, A Firing Offense 1997, The Sun King 1999. *Honours:* Frank Knox Fellow, Harvard–Oxford Univs 1973–75; Edward Weintal Prize for Diplo-

matic Reporting 1985, Gerald Loeb Award for Commentary 2000. *Address:* Washington Post Writers Group, 1150 15th Sreet, NW Washington, DC 20071, USA (office). *Telephone:* (202) 334-6375 (office). *Fax:* (202) 334-5669 (office). *E-mail:* writersgrp@washpost.com (office). *Website:* www.postwritersgroup.com (office).

IHIMAERA-SMILER, Witi, BA; New Zealand (Maori) author; b. 7 Feb. 1944, Gisborne, New Zealand. *Education:* Univ. of Auckland, Victoria Univ. *Career:* fmr diplomat, New Zealand Ministry of Foreign Affairs 1973–89; faculty mem., Univ. of Auckland 1990–, now Prof. and Distinguished Creative Fellow in Maori Literature. *Publications:* Pounamu, Pounamy 1972, Tangi 1973, Whanau 1974, Maori 1975, The New Net Goes Fishing 1977, Into the World of Light 1980, The Matriarch 1986, The Whale Rider 1987, Dear Miss Mansfield 1989. *Honours:* Distinguished Companion of the New Zealand Order of Merit 2005. *Address:* Arts 1 Building, 5 Room 517, University of Auckland, 14a Symonds Street, Auckland 1142, New Zealand (office). *E-mail:* w.ihimaera@auckland.ac.nz (office).

IJUIN, Shizuka; Japanese novelist; b. 9 Feb. 1950, Yamaguchi Pref.; m. 1st Natsume Masako; m. 2nd Shino Hiroko. *Education:* Rikkyo Univ. *Career:* fmr freelance dir of TV commercials. *Films:* scriptwriter on adaptions of his own novels, Chibusa 1993, Kikansha sensei 2004. *Publications:* novels: Chibusa (Breasts) (Yoshikawa Eiji Prize for New Writers) 1991, Kaikyo (The Strait) 1991, Ukezuki (The Crescent Moon) (Naoki Prize) 1992, Toge no koe 1992, Hakushu 1992, Ukezuki 1992, Kikansha sensei 1994, Kinou Sukecchi (Yesterday Sketch) 1999, Goro-goro (Rolling Away) (Yoshikawa Prize for Literature) 2002. *E-mail:* info@ijuin-shizuka.com. *Website:* www.ijuin-shizuka.com.

IKEDA, Daisaku; Japanese Buddhist philosopher and author; *President, Soka Gakkai International;* b. 2 Jan. 1928, Tokyo; s. of Nenokichi Ikeda and Ichi Ikeda; m. Kaneko Shiraki 1952; two s. *Education:* Fuji Coll. *Career:* Pres. Soka Gakkai 1960–79, Hon. Pres. 1979–; Pres. Soka Gakkai Int. 1975–; Founder Soka Univ., Soka Univ. of America, Soka Women's Coll., Tokyo, Kansai Soka Schools, Soka Kindergartens (Japan, Hong Kong, Singapore, Malaysia and Brazil), Makiguchi Foundation for Educ., Inst. of Oriental Philosophy, Boston Research Center for the 21st Century, Toda Inst. for Global Peace and Policy Research, Tokyo, Shizuoka Fuji Art Museum, Min-On Concert Asscn, Victor Hugo House of Literature and Komeito Party; mem. Advisory Bd World Centers of Compassion for Children Int., Ireland 2004–; Poet Laureate, World Acad. of Arts and Culture, USA 1981–; Foreign mem. Brazilian Acad. of Letters 1993–. *Exhibition:* Dialogue with Nature (photographic exhbn shown in many countries 1988–). *Publications:* The Human Revolution Vols I–VI 1972–99, The Living Buddha 1976, Choose Life (with A. Toynbee) 1976, Buddhism: The First Millennium 1977, Songs From My Heart 1978, Glass Children and Other Essays 1979, La Nuit Appelle L'Aurore (with R. Huyghe) 1980, A Lasting Peace Vols I–II 1981, 1987, Life: An Enigma, a Precious Jewel 1982, Before It Is Too Late (with A. Peccei) 1984, Buddhism and Cosmos 1985, The Flower of Chinese Buddhism 1986, Human Values in a Changing World (with B. Wilson) 1987, Unlocking the Mysteries of Birth and Death 1988, 2003, The Snow Country Prince 1990, A Lifelong Quest for Peace (with L. Pauling) 1992, Choose Peace (with J. Galtung) 1995, A New Humanism: The University Addresses of Daisaku Ikeda 1996, The Wisdom of the Lotus Sutra, Vols I–VI (in Japanese) 1996–2000, Ikeda-Jin Yong Dialogue (in Japanese) 1998, The New Human Revolution, Vols I–XV (in Japanese) 1998–2006, The Way of Youth 2000, For the Sake of Peace 2000, Soka Education 2001, Diálogo sobre José Martí (with C. Vitier) 2001, The World is Yours to Change 2002, Choose Hope (with D. Krieger) 2002, Alborada del Pacífico (with P. Aylwin) 2002, On Being Human (with R. Simard and G. Bourgeault) 2002, Global Civilization: A Buddhist–Islamic Dialogue (with M. Tehranian) 2003, Fighting for Peace 2004, Planetary Citizenship (with H. Henderson) 2004, One by One 2004, Moral Lessons of the Twentieth Century (with M. Gorbachev) 2005, Revolutions: To Green the Environment, To Grow the Human Heart (with M. S. Swaminathan) 2005, A Quest for Global Peace (with J. Rothblat) 2006, and other writings on Buddhism, civilization, life and peace. *Honours:* Hon. Prof., Nat. Univ. of San Marcos 1981, Peking Univ. 1984 and others; Hon. Senator, European Acad. of Sciences and Arts 1997–; Hon. Adviser World Fed. of UN Asscns (WFUNA) 1999–; Hon. mem., The Club of Rome 1996–, Inst. of Oriental Studies of Russian Acad. of Sciences 1996–, and others; Order of the Sun of Peru with Grand Cross 1984, Grand Cross, Order of Merit in May (Argentina) 1990, Nat. Order of Southern Cross (Brazil) 1990, Kt Grand Cross of the Most Noble Order of the Crown (Thailand) 1991, Hon. Cross of Science and the Arts (Austria) 1992, Kt Grand Cross of Rizal (Philippines) 1996, Order of Lomonosov (Russia) 2005 and others; Dr hc (Moscow State Univ.) 1975, (Sofia) 1981, (Buenos Aires) 1990, (Univ. of the Philippines) 1991, (Ankara) 1992, (Fed. Univ. of Rio de Janeiro) 1993, (Glasgow) 1994, (Hong Kong) 1996, (Havana) 1996, (Univ. of Ghana) 1996, (Cheju Nat. Univ.) 1999, (Delhi) 1999, (Queens Coll. City Univ. of NY) 2000, (Univ. of Sydney) 2000, (Morehouse Coll.) 2002 and others; UN Peace Award 1983, Kenya Oral Literature Award 1986, UNHCR Humanitarian Award 1989, Rosa Parks Humanitarian Award (USA) 1993, Simon Wiesenthal Center Int. Tolerance Award (USA) 1993, Tagore Peace Award, The Asiatic Soc. (India) 1997 and others. *Address:* 32 Shinano-machi, Shinjuku-ku, Tokyo 160-8583, Japan (office). *Telephone:* (3) 5360-9831 (office). *Fax:* (3) 5360-9885 (office). *E-mail:* sgipr@sgi.gr.jp (office). *Website:* www.sgi.org (office).

IKSTENA, Nora, BA; Latvian writer; b. 1969, Rīga. *Education:* Univ. of Latvia. *Career:* Guest Ed. Review of Contemporary Fiction (special issue on new Latvian fiction), USA 1995–97; columnist Diena newspaper; Pres. Latvian Centre for Literature. *Publications:* novels: Dzīves svinēšana (trans. as A Celebration of Life) 1998, Jaunavas mācība (trans. as The Education of the Virgin) 2001; short stories: Nieki un izpriecas (trans. as Trifles and Amusements) 1995, Maldīgas romances (trans. as Misleading Romances) 1997; non-fiction: Pānākšana: Grāmata par Annu Rūmani Keninu (biog., trans. as The Homecoming) 1993, Brīnumainā kārtā (trans. as But Then, Miraculously...) 1999, Vija Vētra: Deja un dvēsele (trans. as Vija Vētra: The Dance and the Soul) 2001; contrib. to reviews, journals and anthologies. *Honours:* Hans Christian Andersen Amb. for 2005 bicentenary (Denmark); Ministry of Culture Award for achievements in literature 1998. *Address:* c/o Atena Publishers Ltd, Blaumana iela 16/18-2a, 1011 Rīga, Latvia. *Telephone:* 6728-3973. *Fax:* 6728-2375. *E-mail:* atena@atena.lv.

IMPEY, Rosemary (Rose) June; British writer; b. 7 June 1947, Northwich, Cheshire, England; two d. *Education:* teacher's certificate. *Publications:* Who's a Clever Girl, Then 1985, The Baked Bean Queen 1986, The Girls Gang 1986, Desperate for a Dog 1988, The Flat Man 1988, Letter to Father Christmas 1988, Instant Sisters 1989, Joe's Cafe 1990, Revenge of the Rabbit 1990, First Class 1992, Trouble with the Tucker Twins 1992, Orchard Book of Fairytales 1992, Animal Crackers 1993, Sir Billy Bear and Other Friends 1996, Potbelly and the Haunted House 1996, Fireballs from Hell 1996, Sleepover Club 1997, Feather Pillows 1997. *Address:* c/o Egmont, 239 Kensington High Street, London, W8 6SA, England. *E-mail:* info@egmont.co.uk.

INDRIÐASON, Arnaldur, BA; Icelandic journalist, film critic, historian and writer; b. 8 Jan. 1961, Reykjavík; m.; three c. *Education:* Univ. of Iceland. *Career:* journalist Morgunbladid newspaper 1981–82, film critic 1986–2001; freelance scriptwriter 1982–86. *Publications:* novels: Synir duftsins (trans. as Sons of Earth) 1997, Dauðarósir (Silent Kill) 1998, Napóleonsskjölin (Operation Napoleon) 1999, Mýrin (trans. as Jar City) (Skandinaviska Kriminalselskapet Glass Key 2002) 2000, Leyndardómar Reykjavíkur2000 (The Reykjavik 2000 Mystery) 2000, Grafarþögn (trans. as Silence of the Grave) (Skandinaviska Kriminalselskapet Glass Key 2003, CWA Gold Dagger 2005) 2001, Röddin (The Voice) (The Martin Beck Award for Translation, Sweden 2005) 2002, Betty (Betty) 2003, Kleifarvatn (The Draining Lake) 2004, Vetrarborgin (Winter City) 2005. *Address:* c/o Harvill Press, Random House, 20 Vauxhall Bridge Road, London, SW1V 2SA, England.

INGALLS, Rachel Holmes, BA; American author; b. 13 May 1940, Boston, MA. *Education:* Radcliffe College. *Career:* mem. American Acad. and Institute of Arts and Letters, fellow. *Publications:* Theft, 1970; The Man Who Was Left Behind, 1974; Mediterranean Cruise, 1973; Mrs Caliban, 1982; Binstead's Safari, 1983; I See a Long Journey, 1985; The Pearlkillers, 1986; The End of the Tragedy, 1987; Something to Write Home About, 1990; Black Diamond, 1992; Be My Guest, 1992; Days Like Today, 2001. *Honours:* First Novel Award, Author's Club, England, 1971; British Book Marketing Council Best Book Award, 1986.

INGHAM, Daniel (see Lambot, Isobel Mary)

INGHAM, Kenneth, OBE, MC, DPhil; British writer; *Professor Emeritus, University of Bristol*; b. 9 Aug. 1921, Harden, England; m. Elizabeth Mary Southall 1949; one s. one d. *Education:* Keble Coll., Oxford. *Career:* Lecturer, Makerere Coll., Uganda 1950–56, Prof. 1956–62; Dir of Studies, Royal Mil. Acad., Sandhurst 1962–67; Prof. of History, Univ. of Bristol 1967–84, Head Dept of History 1970–84, part-time Prof. of History 1984–86, Prof. Emer. 1986–; mem. Royal African Soc., Royal Historical Soc. *Publications:* Reformers in India 1956, The Making of Modern Uganda 1958, A History of East Africa 1962, The Kingdom of Toro in Uganda 1975, Jan Christian Smuts: The Conscience of a South African 1986, Politics in Modern Africa 1990, Obote: A Political Biography 1994; contrib. to reference books and professional journals. *Address:* The Woodlands, 94 West Town Lane, Bristol, BS4 5DZ, England (home). *Telephone:* (117) 977-6588 (home).

INGLE, Stephen James, BA, DipEd, MA, PhD; British writer and academic; *Professor of Politics, University of Stirling*; b. 6 Nov. 1940, Ripon, Yorkshire, England; s. of James Ingle and Violet Grace Ingle (née Stephenson); m. Margaret Anne Farmer 1964; two s. one d. *Education:* Univ. of Sheffield, Victoria Univ., NZ. *Career:* Lecturer, then Sr Lecturer, Dept of Politics, Univ. of Hull –1991; Prof. of Politics, Univ. of Stirling 1991–, Head, Dept of Politics 1991–2002; Visiting Research Fellow, Victoria Univ., NZ 1993; mem. Political Studies Asscn. *Publications:* Socialist Thought in Imaginative Literature 1979, Parliament and Health Policy 1981, British Party System 1989, George Orwell: A Political Life 1993, Narratives of British Socialism 2002; contrib. to many publs in the fields of politics and literature. *Honours:* Commonwealth Scholar 1964–67, Erasmus Scholar 1989. *Address:* Department of Politics, University of Stirling, Stirling, FK9 4LA, Scotland (office). *Telephone:* (1786) 467593 (office). *Fax:* (1786) 466266 (office). *E-mail:* s.j.ingle@stir.ac.uk (office). *Website:* www.politics.stir.ac.uk (office).

INGRAMS, Richard Reid; British journalist; *Editor, The Oldie*; b. 19 Aug. 1937, London; s. of Leonard St Clair and Victoria (née Reid) Ingrams; m. Mary Morgan 1962 (divorced 1993); two s. (one deceased) one d. *Education:* Shrewsbury School, Univ. Coll., Oxford. *Career:* co-founder Private Eye 1962, Ed. 1963–86, Chair. 1974–; founder and Ed. The Oldie 1992–; TV critic The Spectator 1976–84; columnist The Observer 1988–90, 1992–. *Publications:* Private Eye on London (with Christopher Booker and William Rushton) 1962, Private Eye's Romantic England 1963, Mrs Wilson's Diary (with John Wells) 1965, Mrs Wilson's Second Diary 1966, The Tale of Driver Grope 1968, The Bible for Motorists (with Barry Fantoni) 1970, The Life and Times of Private Eye (ed.) 1971, Harris in Wonderland (as Philip Reid with Andrew Osmond) 1973, Cobbett's Country Book (ed.) 1974, Beachcomber: the works of J. B. Morton (ed.) 1974, The Best of Private Eye 1974, God's Apology 1977, Goldenballs 1979, Romney Marsh (with Fay Godwin) 1980, Dear Bill: The Collected Letters of Denis Thatcher (with John Wells) 1980, The Other Half 1981, Piper's Places (with John Piper) 1983, Dr Johnson by Mrs Thrale (ed.) 1984, Down the Hatch (with John Wells) 1985, Just the One (with John Wells) 1986, John Stewart Collis: A Memoir 1986, The Best of Dear Bill (with John Wells) 1986, Mud in Your Eye (with John Wells) 1987, The Eye Spy Look-alike Book (ed.) 1988, The Ridgeway 1988, You Might As Well Be Dead 1988, England: An Anthology 1989, No. 10 1989, On and On... Further Letters of Denis Thatcher (with John Wells) 1990, The Oldie Annual (ed.) 1993, The Oldie Annual II (ed.) 1994, Malcolm Muggeridge (ed.) 1995, I Once Met (ed.) 1996, The Oldie Annual III (ed.) 1997, Jesus: Authors Take Sides (anthology) 1999, The Oldie Annual IV (ed.) 1999, The Life and Adventures of William Cobbett (biog.) 2005. *Address:* c/o The Oldie, 45–46 Poland Street, London, W1V 4AU, England. *Telephone:* (20) 7734-2225. *Fax:* (20) 7734-2226.

INKSTER, Tim; Canadian poet, printer, designer and publisher; b. 26 Sept. 1949, Toronto, ON; m. Elke Inkster. *Education:* University of Toronto. *Career:* designer, printer, Press Porcepic, Erin, Ontario, 1971–74; Co-owner, The Porcupine's Quill, Erin, 1974–; mem. League of Canadian Poets; American Institute of Graphic Arts; Society of Graphic Designers of Canada. *Publications:* poetry: For Elke, 1971; The Topolobampo Poems and Other Memories, 1972; Mrs Grundy, 1983; The Coach House Press, 1974; The Crown Prince Waits for a Train, 1976; Blue Angel, 1981; Other: Letters, Riddles and Miscellany, 1976; The Porcupine's Quill Reader (co-ed.), 1997; Autobiographic films: Print Shop, 1976; Tin Inkster: Colours of a Poet, 1976. *Address:* 68 Main Street, Erin, ON N0B 1T0, Canada.

INNAURATO, Albert Francis, BA, BFA, MFA; American playwright, writer and stage director; b. 2 June 1947, Philadelphia, PA. *Education:* Temple University, California Institute of the Arts, Yale University. *Career:* Playwright-in-Residence, Public Theatre, New York City, 1977, Circle Repertory Theatre, New York City, 1979, Playwright's Horizons, New York City, 1983; Adjunct Prof., Columbia University, Princeton University, 1987–89; Instructor, Yale School of Drama, 1993; mem. Dramatists Guild; Writers Guild of America. *Publications:* Plays: Earthworms, 1974; Gemini, 1977; The Transfiguration of Bennon Blimpie, 1977; Verna the USO Girl, 1980; Gus and Al, 1988; Magda and Callas, 1988. Other: Coming of Age in Soho, 1985. Contributions: newspapers and journals. *Honours:* Guggenheim Fellowship, 1976; Rockefeller Foundation Grant, 1977; Obie Awards, 1977, 1978; Emmy Award, 1981; National Endowment for the Arts Grants, 1986, 1989; Drama League Award, 1987.

INNES, Brian, BSc, MRSC; British writer and publisher (retd); b. 4 May 1928, Croydon, Surrey, England; m. 1st Felicity McNair Wilson 1956; m. 2nd Eunice Lynch 1971; three s. *Education:* King's Coll. London. *Career:* Asst Ed. Chemical Age 1953–55; Assoc. Ed. The British Printer 1955–60; Art Dir Hamlyn Group 1960–62; Dir Temperance Seven Ltd 1961–; Proprietor Brian Innes Agency 1964–66, Immediate Books 1966–70, FOT Library 1970–; Creative Dir and Deputy Chair. Orbis Publishing Ltd 1970–86; Editorial Dir Mirror Publishing 1986–88; numerous recordings, films, radio and television broadcasts; many photographs published; mem. Arts Club, Chartered Soc. of Designers, RSA, Inst. of Paper, Printing and Publishing, CWA, British Actors' Equity, RSL, Royal Soc. of Chemistry. *Publications:* Book of Pirates 1966, Book of Spies 1967, Book of Revolutions 1967, Book of Outlaws 1968, Flight 1970, Saga of the Railways 1972, Horoscopes 1976, The Tarot 1977, Book of Change 1979, The Red Baron Lives 1981, Red Red Baron 1983, The Havana Cigar 1983, Crooks and Conmen 1993, Catalogue of Ghost Sightings 1996, The History of Torture 1998, Death and The Afterlife 1999, Dreams 1999, Bodies of Evidence 2000, A Long Way from Pasadena 2001, Snapshots of the Sixties 2002, United Kingdom 2002, Myths of Ancient Rome 2002, Profile of a Criminal Mind 2003, The Body in Question 2005; contrib. to Man, Myth & Magic, Take Off, Real Life Crimes, Fire Power, The Story of Scotland, Discover Scotland, Marshall Cavendish Encyclopaedia of Science. *Honours:* Royal Variety Command Performance 1961. *Address:* 21 Southwick Mews, London, W2 1JG, England (office); Les Forges de Montgaillard, 11330 Montgaillard, France (home). *Telephone:* (4) 68-45-09-43 (home). *Fax:* (4) 68-45-09-43 (home). *E-mail:* binnes1@compuserve.com.

INNESS-BROWN, Elizabeth Ann, MFA; American writer, editor and educator; *Professor of English, St Michael's College, Colchester*; b. 1 May 1954, Rochester, NY; m. Keith Calvert Monley 1987; one s. *Education:* St Lawrence Univ., Columbia Univ. *Career:* Asst Prof. of English, Univ. of Southern Mississippi, Hattiesburg 1979–84, Acting Dir Center for Writers' Grad. Program in Creative Writing 1983, Assoc. Prof. of English 1985–86; Ed. English News 1980–84, 1985–86, Mississippi Review 1983; Contributing Ed., Pushcart Prize 1983–, Boulevard 1985–; Visiting Writer, St Lawrence Univ., Canton, NY 1984–85, Purdue Univ., West Lafayette, Ind. 1987, Univ. of Hartford, Hartford, Conn. 1987–88; English Lecturer, St Michael's Coll., Colchester, Vt 1988–90, Dir Writing Center 1988–, Asst Prof. 1990–94, Assoc. Prof. of English 1994–2001, Prof. of English 2001–; Adjunct and Field Faculty, Vermont Coll. 1988–90. *Publications:* Satin Palms 1981, Here 1994, Burning Marguerite (novel) 2002; contrib. to anthologies and periodicals. *Honours:*

Youth Foundation Fellowship 1977, research grant, Univ. of Southern Mississippi 1980, listed as outstanding writer, Pushcart Prize 1980, 1981, 1989, 1992, Associated Writing Programs Award in Short Fiction 1981, St Lawrence Univ. Award for Short Fiction 1982, Millay Council for the Arts Fellow 1982, Nat. Endowment for the Arts grant 1982, Pushcart Prize 1982, Yaddo Fellow 1982. *Literary Agent:* c/o Emma Parry, Fletcher & Parry, 121 E 17th Street, New York, NY 10003, USA. *Address:* St Michael's College, Colchester, VT 05439, USA. *E-mail:* einness-brown@smcvt.edu (office).

INOUE, Hisashi; Japanese playwright and novelist; *President, Japan P.E.N. Club;* b. 1934, Yamagata Pref. *Education:* Sofia Univ. *Career:* during univ. studies worked part-time for a theatre in Asakusa; began writing radio and TV scripts, including educational programmes and children's drama late 1950s; writer Hyokkori hyotan-jima (The Floating Island Gourd), NHK TV 1964–69; est. name as playwright and novelist early 1970s; played important role in so-called parody boom of 1970s; writer of lectures, essays and commentaries on the production of rice; Pres. Japan P.E.N. Club 2003–. *Publications:* Tegusari Shinju (The Love Suicide in Manacles) 1972, Kirikirijin (The Kirikirians) 1981, The Face of Jizo, The Great Doctor Yabuhara 1990. *Honours:* several major theatre and literary prizes including Naoki Prize, People of Cultural Merit Award, Govt of Japan 2004. *Website:* www.japanpen.or.jp.

INUKAI, Tomoko, BA; Japanese journalist and writer; b. 18 April 1931, Tokyo; d. of Mototake and Katsuko Hatano; m. Yasuhiko Inukai 1953 (divorced 1978); one s. one d. *Education:* Univs of Gakushin and Illinois (USA). *Career:* Journalist Far E. Bureau, Chicago Daily News 1957–60; published first book 1968; mem. Cttee Social Policy Council, Econ. Planning Agency 1988, Cttee Tokyo Metropolitan Marine Park 1990; solo art exhibition Tokyo 1992; Del. to Jt Japan Inst. for Social and Econ. Affairs and Swiss Inst. of Int. Studies Japan Symposium, Zurich, Switzerland 1979. *Publications include:* How to Avoid Housekeeping: to be free from the house 1968, Men and Women: new relationships 1982, Suspicious Circuit 1986, Japan Rediscovering Kabuki 1989. *Address:* 25-19 Kamiyama-cho, Shibuya-ku, Tokyo 150, Japan. *Telephone:* (3) 469-4691. *Fax:* (3) 460-3040.

IOANNIDOU-ADAMIDOU, Irena; Cypriot writer and translator; b. 5 Feb. 1939, Famagusta; d. of the late Cleanthis Ioannides and of Anastasia Ioannides (née Galanou); m. Panos Adamides 1961; two d. *Education:* Brillantmont International Coll., Acad. of Music, Lausanne, Switzerland and Univ. of Vienna, Austria. *Career:* writer since the age of 16; collaboration with Cyprus Broadcasting Corpn and numerous other TV and radio stations and theatres 1962–; mem. Public Relations Cttee, Cyprus PEN 1980–86; mem. Nat. Soc. of Greek Writers, Soc. of Greek Playwrights, Soc. of Greek Literary Translators. *Publications include:* novels: Hommes, chemins et destin 1959, Maria Cristina 1960, Symphonie Héroïque 1961, Dans les bras de la mer 1962, Mme Rime 1963, Mattinata 1964, Nous vivrons 1981, Un ciel comme le nôtre 1981; Plays: Le parfum 1968, Le suicide 1970, La vengeance 1975, Visite 1977, Conflit 1978, Le cerf-volant 1980, Le champ 1982, Délit prémédité 1983, Post mortem 1986, Lutte secrète 1987, Syméos 1989, Le conseil conjugal (First Prize, Cyprus Radio) 1990, The Suspects (winner VII Third World International Playwright Competition 1994), The Robbery; short stories: Syméos (Pan-Hellenic Prize, Athens) 1986, La Fille de Théodore 1991, Student Short Story International (12); has translated works from French, English, Spanish, etc by writers including Alfred de Musset, Molière, Boris Vian, Romain Rolland, Diego Fabbri, Strindberg, Natalia Ginzburg, Arthur Miller. *Honours:* numerous awards and prizes. *Address:* 92 Makenios III Avenue, Nicosia, Cyprus. *Telephone:* (2) 376899.

IOANNOU, Susan, BA, MA; Canadian writer and poet; *Director, Wordwrights Canada;* b. 4 Oct. 1944, Toronto, ON; m. Lazaros Ioannou 1967; one s. one d. *Education:* Univ. of Toronto. *Career:* Managing Ed. Coiffure du Canada 1979–80; Assoc. Ed. Cross-Canada Writers' Magazine 1980–89; Poetry Ed. Arts Scarborough Newsletter 1980–85; Poetry Instructor, Toronto Board of Educ. 1982–94, Univ. of Toronto 1989–90; Dir Wordwrights Canada 1985–; mem. League of Canadian Poets, Writers' Union of Canada, Arts and Letters Club of Toronto, Canadian Poetry Asscn. *Publications:* Spare Words 1984, Motherpoems 1985, The Crafted Poem 1985, Familiar Faces, Private Griefs 1986, Ten Ways to Tighten Your Prose 1988, Writing Reader-Friendly Poems 1989, Clarity Between Clouds 1991, Read-Aloud Poems: For Students from Elementary through Senior High School 1993, Polly's Punctuation Primer 1994, Where the Light Waits 1996, A Real Farm Girl 1998, A Magical Clockwork: The Art of Writing the Poem 2000, Coming Home 2004. *Honours:* Arts Scarborough Poetry Award 1987, Media Club of Canada Memorial Award 1990, Okanagan Short Story Award 1997. *Address:* Wordwrights Canada, PO Box 456, Station O, Toronto, ON M4A 2P1, Canada (office).

IPARRAGUIRRE, Sylvia; Argentine novelist; b. 4 July 1947, Junín, Buenos Aires; m. Abelardo Castillo 1976. *Career:* Prof. of Modern Literature, Instituto de Literatura Hispanoamericana de la Facultad de Filosofía y Letras, Universidad de Buenos Aires 1986–; co-founder of literary journal El Ornitorrinco. *Publications:* En el invierno de las ciudades (short stories) (Premio Municipal de Literatura) 1988, Probables lluvias por la noche (short stories) 1993, El Parque (novel) 1996, Tierra del Fuego: una biografía del fin del mundo (novel) (Sor Juana Inés de la Cruz Prize) 2000; contrib. short stories and essays to newspapers and literary journals, including El Escarabajo de Oro, Clarín, Página\12, ETC, Contexto, Puro Cuento, Tramas, Cuadernos Hispanoamericanos, and short stories to numerous anthologies. *Address:* c/o Curbstone Press, 321 Jackson Street, Willimantic, CT 06226-1738, USA. *E-mail:* info@curbstone.org. *Website:* www.curbstone.org.

IRBY, Kenneth Lee, BA, MA, MLS, PhD; American writer, poet and teacher; b. 18 Nov. 1936, Bowie, TX. *Education:* University of Kansas, Harvard University, University of California. *Career:* Assoc. Prof. of English, University of Kansas, Lawrence. *Publications:* The Roadrunner Poem, 1964; Kansas-New Mexico, 1965; Movements/Sequences, 1965; The Flower of Having Passed Through Paradise in a Dream, 1968; Relation, 1970; To Max Douglas, 1971; Archipelago, 1976; Catalpa, 1977; Orexis, 1981; Riding the Dog, 1982; A Set, 1983; Call Steps, 1992; Antiphonal and Fall to Fall, 1994. Contributions: anthologies and magazines.

IRELAND, David Neil, AM; Australian novelist; b. 24 Aug. 1927, Lakemba, NSW. *Education:* state schools in NSW. *Publications:* Image in the Clay (play) 1962, The Chantic Bird 1968, The Unknown Industrial Prisoner 1971, The Flesheaters 1972, Burn 1974, The Glass Canoe 1976, The Wild Colonial Boy (short story) 1979, A Woman of the Future 1979, City of Women 1981, Archimedes and the Eagle 1984, Bloodfather 1987, The Chosen 1997. *Honours:* Adelaide Advertiser Award 1966, Age Book of the Year Award 1980. *Address:* c/o Penguin Group (Australia), 250 Camberwell Road, Camberwell, Vic. 3124, Australia.

IRELAND, Kevin Mark, OBE; New Zealand writer and poet; b. 18 July 1933, Auckland; m. Phoebe Caroline Dalwood; two s. *Career:* Writer-in-Residence, Canterbury Univ. 1986; Sargeson Fellow, Auckland Univ. 1987, Literary Fellow 1989; mem. NZSA (PEN) (Nat. Pres. PEN 1990–92); Vice-Chair. Sargeson Trust 2005; Vice-Pres. North Shore Cricket Club 2000; Patron Torpedo Bay Indoor Bowling Club 2000. *Publications:* poetry: Face to Face 1964, Educating the Body 1967, A Letter From Amsterdam 1972, Orchids, Hummingbirds and Other Poems 1974, Poems 1974, A Grammar of Dreams 1975, Literary Cartoons 1978, The Dangers of Art: Poems 1975–80 1980, Practice Night in the Drill Hall 1984, The Year of the Comet 1986, Selected Poems 1987, Tiberius at the Beehive 1990, Skinning a Fish 1994, Anzac Day: Selected Poems 1997, Fourteen Reasons for Writing 2001, Walking the Land 2003; other: Sleeping with the Angels (short stories) 1995, Blowing My Top (novel) 1996, The Man Who Never Lived (novel) 1997, Under the Bridge and Over the Moon (memoir) 1998, The Craymore Affair (novel) 2000, Backwards to Forwards (memoir) 2002, Getting Away With It (novel) 2004, On Getting Old (essays) 2005, How to Catch a Fish (essays) 2005. *Honours:* Hon. DLitt 2000; NZ Nat. Book Award for Poetry 1979, Commemorative Medal 1990, Montana Award for History and Biography 1999, NZ Prime Minister's Award for Literary Achievement (Poetry) 2004. *Address:* 3A Everest Street, Devonport, Auckland 9, New Zealand. *E-mail:* kireland@xtra.co.nz (home).

IRVING, Clifford Michael, (John Luckless), BA; American writer and screenwriter; b. 5 Nov. 1930, New York, NY. *Education:* Cornell University. *Publications:* On a Darkling Plain, 1956; The Losers, 1957; The Valley, 1962; The 38th Floor, 1965; Spy, 1969; The Battle of Jerusalem, 1970; Fake, 1970; Global Village Idiot, 1973; Project Octavio, 1978; The Death Freak, 1979; The Hoax, 1981; Tom Mix and Pancho Villa, 1982; The Sleeping Spy, 1983; The Angel of Zin, 1984; Daddy's Girl, 1988; Trial, 1990; Final Argument, 1993.

IRVING, Janet Turnbull, MA; Canadian literary agent; b. 16 April 1954, Toronto; d. of Donald Gibson and Joan Heloise Turnbull; m. John Irving 1987; one s. *Education:* Univ. of Toronto. *Career:* Ed. Authors' Marketing Services Ltd 1979; Ed. Doubleday Canada Ltd 1980, Man. Ed. 1981; Vice-Pres., Publr and Dir Seal Books 1984–87; Pres. The Turnbull Agency 1987–, Curtis Brown Canada Ltd 1989–99; Ed. Bantam Canada Inc.; Founding-Pres. The Canadian Business Task Force on Literacy; Co-founder (with her husband) and Chair. Bd of Trustees Maple Street School (ind. primary school), Vt. *Address:* c/o Board of Trustees, Maple Street School, 322 Maple Street, Manchester Centre, VT 05255, USA. *Telephone:* (802) 362-7137. *Fax:* (802) 362-3492. *E-mail:* maplests@sover.net. *Website:* www.maplestreetschool.com.

IRVING, John Winslow, BA, MFA; American writer; b. 2 March 1942, Exeter, NH; s. of Colin F. N. Irving and Frances Winslow; m. 1st Shyla Leary 1964 (divorced 1981); two s.; m. 2nd Janet Turnbull 1987; one s. *Education:* Univs of Pittsburgh, Vienna, New Hampshire and Iowa. *Career:* Asst Prof. of English, Mt. Holyoke Coll. 1967–72, 1975–78; writer-in-residence, Univ. of Iowa 1972–75; with Bread Loaf Writers' Conf. 1976; Rockefeller Foundation grantee 1971–72; Nat. Endowment for Arts Fellow 1974–75, Guggenheim Fellow 1976–77; mem. American Acad. of Arts and Letters 2001. *Publications:* novels: Setting Free the Bears 1969, The Water-Method Man 1972, The 158-Pound Marriage 1974, The World According to Garp 1978, The Hotel New Hampshire 1981, The Cider House Rules 1985, screenplay (Acad. Award for the best adapted screenplay 2000) 1999, A Prayer for Owen Meany 1989, A Son of the Circus 1994, A Widow for One Year 1998, The Fourth Hand 2001, Until I Find You 2005; non-fiction: An Introduction to Great Expectations 1986, Trying to Save Piggy Sneed (memoirs, short stories and essays) 1996, An Introduction to A Christmas Carol 1996, My Movie Business (memoir) 1999; contrib. to New York Times Book Review, New Yorker, Rolling Stone, Esquire, Playboy. *Honours:* Nat. Book Award 1980, O. Henry Award 1981. *Literary Agent:* Turnbull Agency, PO Box 757, Dorset, VT 05251, USA.

ISAACS, Anne, BA, MS; American writer; b. 2 March 1949, Buffalo, NY; one s. two d. *Education:* University of Michigan, SUNY at Buffalo. *Career:* numerous positions in environmental education 1975–90. *Publications:* Swamp Angel, 1994, (broadcast adaptation, 1995); Treehouse Tales, 1997; Cat up a Tree,

1998; Torn Thread, 2000. *Honours:* Ralph Caldecott Honor Book, American Library Assen Notable Books Selection, New York Times Best Illustrated Books Citation, School Library Journal Best Books, Publishers Weekly Best Books, Honor Book, Boston Globe-Horn Book, Children's Book of the Year List, Child Study Children's Book Committee, National Council of Teachers of English Notable Trade Book in Language Arts.

ISAACS, Susan; American novelist and screenwriter; b. 7 Dec. 1943, New York, NY; m. 1968, one s. one d. *Education:* Queens College, CUNY. *Career:* mem. Authors' Guild; International Assen of Crime Writers; MWA; National Book Critics Circle; PEN; Poets and Writers, Chair. of the Board; Creative Coalition; American Society of Journalists and Authors. *Publications:* Compromising Positions, 1978; Close Relations, 1980; Almost Paradise, 1984; Shining Through, 1988; Magic Hour, 1991; After All These Years, 1993; Lily White, 1996; Red, White and Blue, 1998; Brave Dames and Wimpettes: What Women are really doing on Page and Screen, 1999; Long Time No See, 2001. Contributions: newspapers and magazines. *Honours:* Hon. Doctor of Letters, Dowling College, 1988; Hon. Doctor of Humane Letters, Queens College, CUNY, 1996; Barnes & Noble Writers for Writers Award, 1996; John Steinbeck Award, 1999.

ISEGAWA, Moses; Dutch writer; b. 1963, Kampala, Uganda. *Career:* resettled in Netherlands 1990. *Publications:* Abyssinian Chronicles (in trans.) 1999, Slangenkuil (trans. as Snakepit) 1999, Twee chimpansees (trans. as Two Chimpanzees, non-fiction) 2001. *Address:* c/o Picador, 20 New Wharf Road, London, N1 9RR, England.

ISHIGURO, Kazuo, OBE, MA, DLitt, FRSL; British writer; b. 8 Nov. 1954, Nagasaki, Japan; s. of Shizuo Ishiguro and Shizuko Ishiguro; m. Lorna Anne Macdougall 1986; one d. *Education:* Woking Grammar School, Univs of Kent and East Anglia. *Career:* fmr community worker, Renfrew; writer 1980–. *Publications include:* A Pale View of Hills (RSL Winifred Holtby Prize 1983) 1982, A Profile of Arthur J. Mason (TV play) 1985, An Artist of the Floating World (Whitbread Book of the Year, Fiction Prize 1986) 1986, The Gourmet (TV play) 1987, The Remains of the Day (Booker Prize 1989) 1989, The Unconsoled (Cheltenham Prize 1995) 1995, When We Were Orphans (novel) 2000, The Saddest Music in the World (screenplay, co-author) 2003, Never Let Me Go (novel) 2005, White Countess (screenplay) 2005. *Honours:* Hon. DLit (Kent) 1990, (East Anglia) 1995, (St Andrews) 2003; Chevalier, Ordre des Arts et Lettres 1998; Premio Scanno 1995, Premio Mantova 1998. *Literary Agent:* Rogers, Coleridge and White Ltd, 20 Powis Mews, London, W11 1JN, England. *Telephone:* (20) 7221-3717. *Fax:* (20) 7229-9084.

ISKANDER, Fazil Abdulovich; Russian/Abkhaz writer; b. 6 March 1929, Sukhumi, Georgian SSR; m.; one s. one d. *Education:* Maxim Gorky Inst. of Literature, Moscow. *Career:* first works Publ 1952; USSR People's Deputy 1989–91; Pres. Assen of Authors and Publrs against Piracy; Head, World of Culture Assen; Vice-Pres. Russian Acad. of Arts; Academician of RAN, Natural Sciences Dept, Bayerische Akad. der Khönen Künste. *Films include:* Time of Lucky Finds, Crime Kings 1986, A Little Giant of Big Sex, A Night with Stalin. *Plays:* Djamchuch – A Son of a Deer 1986, A Greeting from Zürüpa (The One Who Thinks About Russia) 1999. *Publications include:* Green Rain 1960, Youth of the Sea 1964, Goatibex Constellation 1966, Forbidden Fruit 1966 (English trans. 1972), Summer Forest 1969, Time of Lucky Finds 1970, Tree of Childhood and Other Stories 1970, Sandro from Chegem 1978, Metropol (co-ed.) 1979, Small Giant of the Big Sex 1979, Rabbits and Boa Constrictors 198, The Path (poems) 1987, School Waltz or the Energy of Shame 1990, Poets and Tsars 1991, Man and His Surroundings 1992, Pshada 1993, Sofichka 1996, The One Who Thinks About Russia and the American 1997, Poet 1998, The Swallow's Nest 2000 and other stories. *Honours:* Dr hc (Norwich Univ., USA); Malaparti Prize (Italy) 1985, USSR State Prize 1989, State Prize of Russia 1993, A. Sakharov Prize, A. Pushkin Prize (Germany) 1994, Moscow-Penne Prize (Italy) 1996, Triumph Prize (Russia) 1998. *Address:* Leningradski prosp. 26, korp. 2, Apt. 67, 125040 Moscow, Russia. *Telephone:* (495) 973-94-53 (office); (495) 212-73-60. *Fax:* (495) 973-94-53 (office).

ISLAM, Mazhar ul; Pakistani writer and folklorist; *Director, Lok Virsa.* *Education:* Punjab Univ., Lahore. *Career:* writer of short stories, novels and works on folklore studies; Dir, Lok Virsa (Nat. Inst. of Folk and Traditional Heritage). *Publications:* short stories: Baton ki Barish mein Bheegti Larki, Gurya ki Aankh say Shehrko Daykho, Ghoron kay Shehr mein Akela Aadmi, Bolian, Khat mein post ki Huye Dophr, Aye Khuda; novel: Mohabbat Murda Phoolon ki symphony; non-fiction: Folklore ki Pahli Kitab, Lok Punjab. *Honours:* President's Award for Pride of Performance 2005. *Address:* Lok Virsa, POB 1184, Shakarparian, Islamabad 81, Pakistan (office).

ISLER, Alan David, BA, MA, PhD; American academic; b. (writer), 12 Sept. 1934, London, England. *Education:* Hunter Coll., CUNY, Columbia Univ. *Career:* Asst Prof. of English, Huron Coll., Univ. of Western Ontario, Canada 1965–67; Assoc. Prof. of English, Queens Coll., CUNY 1967–95; Visiting Lecturer, Univ. of Tel-Aviv 1971–72; mem. Renaissance Soc. of America. *Publications:* novels: The Prince of West End Ave 1994, Kraven Images 1996, Clerical Errors 2001, The Living Proof 2005; short story collections: The Bacon Fancier: four tales 1997, Op.Non.Cit 1997; contrib. to periodicals, including Univ. of Toronto Quarterly. *Honours:* Nat. Jewish Book Award 1994. *Address:* c/o Department of English, Queens College, City University of New York, Flushing, NY 11367, USA.

ISRAEL, Jonathan Irvine, DPhil, FBA; British academic and writer; b. 22 Jan. 1946, London, England; m. Jenny Tatjana Winckel 1985, one s. one d. *Education:* Queens' College, Cambridge, St Antony's College, Oxford. *Career:* Lecturer, University of Hull, 1972–74; Lecturer, 1974–81, Reader, 1981–84, Prof. of Dutch History and Institutions, 1985–, University College London. *Publications:* Race, Class and Politics in Colonial Mexico, 1975; The Dutch Republic and the Hispanic World, 1982; European Jewry in the Age of Mercantilism, 1550–1750, 1985; Dutch Primacy in World Trade, 1585–1740, 1989; Empires and Entrepots: The Dutch, the Spanish Monarchy and the Jews, 1585–1713, 1990; The Anglo-Dutch Movement: Essays on the Glorious Revolution and its World Impact (ed.), 1991; The Dutch Republic, 1995; Conflict of Empires: Spain, the Low Countries and the Struggle for World Supremacy, 1585–1713, 1997; Radical Enlightenment, 2001. Contributions: scholarly books and journals.

ITANI, Frances, CM, RN, BA, MA; Canadian novelist and poet; b. Belleville, Ont. *Education:* Univs of Alberta and New Brunswick, McGill Univ., Montréal Gen. Hosp. School of Nursing. *Career:* nursing, then teaching and writer-in-residence positions at Univ. of Ottawa, Trent Univ., The Banff Centre, Nepean Public Library; full-time writer. *Publications:* poetry: No Other Lodgings 1978, Rentee Bay 1983, A Season of Mourning 1988; juvenile: Linger by the Sea 1979; short story collections: Pack Ice 1989, Truth or Lies 1989, Man Without Face 1994, Leaning, Leaning Over Water 1998, Poached Egg on Toast 2004; novel: Deafening 2003. *Honours:* Canadian Fiction Magazine Best Short Story 1987, Ottawa-Carleton Book Award for Fiction 1995, 2005, first prize CBC/Tilden Literary Award for Fiction 1995, 1996, Drummer-General's Award for Fiction 2004, Commonwealth Writers Prize (Caribbean and Canada Region) for Best Book 2004, Grant MacEwan Coll. Book of the Year 2004–05, CAA Jubilee Award for Best Book (Short Stories) 2005. *Address:* c/o WCA, 94 Harbord Street, Toronto, ON M5S 1G6, Canada (office). *Telephone:* (416) 964-3302 (office). *Fax:* (416) 975-9209 (office).

IVĂNESCU, Mircea; Romanian poet and translator; b. 26 March 1931, Bucharest. *Education:* Univ. of Bucharest. *Career:* fmr Ed. World Literature Press; has translated works by F. Scott Fitzgerald and William Faulkner, and James Joyce's Ulysses. *Publications:* poetry: Versuri 1968, Poesii 1970, Alte versuri 1972, Alte poeme 1973, Poeme 1973, Amintiri 1973, Alte poesii 1976, Poesii nouă 1982, Poeme nouă 1983, Alte poeme nouă 1986, Versuri vechi 1988, Poeme vechi, nouă 1989, Versuri 1996, Poezii 1997, Poesii vechi şi nouă 1999; contrib. poems to anthologies and journals, including Square Lake, Harvard Review. *Address:* c/o Minerva Editura, 46–56 Bd. Metalurgiei, sector 4, OP 82, CP 92, Bucharest 041833, Romania.

IVANJI, Ivan; Serbian writer and translator; b. 24 Jan. 1929, Zrenjanin, Yugoslavia (now in Serbia). *Career:* deported to Auschwitz and Buchenwald 1944; worked as building technician, teacher, and in journalism, publishing, theatre and diplomatic service; embassy-counsellor Yugoslav Embassy, Bonn 1974–78; interpreter for Josip Broz Tito, including at KSZE founding conf., Helsinki 1975, summit of Communist and Workers Parties, East Berlin 1976, summit of bloc-free states, Havana 1979; writes in German and Serbian; Sec.-Gen. Yugoslav Writers' Assen 1982–88. *Publications include:* Die Tänzerin und der Krieg (novel) 2002, Das Kinderfräulein (novel) 1998, Der Aschenmensch von Buchenwald (novel) 1999; short stories, essays, plays, poems and trans. *Address:* c/o Picus Verlag, Friedrich-Schmidt-Platz 4, 1080 Vienna, Austria.

IVANOVA, Natal'ya Borisovna, PhD; Russian editor and literary critic; *Deputy Editor-in-Chief, Znamya;* b. 17 May 1945; m. 3rd Alexandr Rybakov (deceased); one d. *Education:* Moscow State Univ. *Career:* journalist, Znamya (monthly) 1972–86, Deputy Ed.-in-Chief 1991–; journalist, Druzhba Narodov; mem. Exec. Cttee European Forum, Moscow; mem. Aprel'lit movt, Moscow Assen, Russian Fed. Writers' Union, PEN Centre, Commonwealth of Writers' Unions 1992–, European Cultural Centre, Geneva, Switzerland. *Publications include:* The Prose of Jurij Grifonov 1984, Laugh Against Terror, or Fazil 1990, Nowstalgia 2002, Pasternak and Others 2003; Co-ordinator Caucasus in Search of the Future project 2000. *Honours:* literary awards from Literaturnaja Gazeta, Druzba Narodov and Znamya. *Address:* Znamya, ul Bolshaja Sadovaja, 2/46, 123001 Moscow (office); Prospect Mira 49–86, 129110 Moscow, Russia (home). *Telephone:* (495) 299-39-60 (office); (495) 593-03-54 (home). *Fax:* (495) 299-52-83 (office). *E-mail:* ivanova@znamlit.ru (office). *Website:* magazines.russ.ru/znamia (office).

IVASHKIN, Alexander Vasilevich, MMus, PhD, DMus; British/New Zealand cellist, conductor, writer and critic; *Professor of Music and Director of the Centre for Russian Music, University of London;* b. 17 Sept. 1948, Blagoveshchensk, Russia; m. Natalia Mikhailovna Pavlutskaya 1969. *Education:* Gnessin Special Music School, Russian Acad. of Music, Moscow, Russian Art History Inst. *Career:* solo cellist, Bolshoi Theatre Orchestra, Moscow 1971–91; mem. Bd Dirs Bolshoi Opera Co. 1987–91; solo recitals and appearances with orchestras, chamber music concerts, recording in over 30 countries in Europe, Russia, USA, Australia, Japan and NZ; Artistic Dir Bolshoi Soloists 1978–91; Prof. of Cello, Univ. of Canterbury, NZ 1991–99; Artistic Dir Adam Int. Cello Festival/Competition 1995–; Prof. of Music and Dir Centre for Russian Music, Univ. of London 1999–. *Recordings include:* Shostakovich, Cello Concertos Nos 1 and 2 1998; Schnittke, Complete Cello Music 1998–2002; Schumann, Gretchaninov, Cello Concertos 1999–2000; Prokofiev, Complete Cello Music 1996–2002; Tcherepnin, Complete Cello Music 2000; Roslavets, Complete Cello Music 2001; Rachmaninov, Complete

Cello Music 2003; Kancheli: Cello Concertos 2002–05. *Publications:* Krzysztof Penderecki 1983, Charles Ives and 20th Century Music 1991, Conversation with A. Schnittke 1994, Alfred Schnittke 1996, Rostrospective (on M. Rostropovich) 1997, A. Schnittke Reader 2002. *Literary Agent:* Salpeter Artists Management, 28 Cheverton Road, London, N19 3AY, England; Ivy Artists, Postbus 592, 1200 AN Hilversum, Netherlands. *Telephone:* (20) 7919-7646. *Fax:* (20) 7919-7247. *E-mail:* salpeter@ukonline.co.uk. *Address:* Music Department, Goldsmiths College, University of London, London, SE14 6NW, England (office). *E-mail:* a.ivashkin@gold.ac.uk (office).

IVIMY, May (see Badman, May Edith)

IWAI, Katsuhito, BA, PhD; Japanese economist and writer; *Professor of Economics, University of Tokyo;* b. 2 March 1947, Tokyo. *Education:* Univ. of Tokyo, Massachusetts Inst. of Tech., USA. *Career:* Asst Prof. of Econs, Yale Univ. 1973–79, Sr Research Assoc., Cowles Foundation for Research in Econs 1979–81; Assoc. Prof. of Econs, Univ. of Tokyo 1981–89, Prof. of Econs 1989–, Dean Grad. School of Econs 2001–03; Visiting Assoc. Prof. of Int. Affairs, Princeton Univ., USA 1988–89; Visiting Prof., Univ. of Pennsylvania 1988–89; Visiting Fellow, Dipartimento di Economia Politica, Università di Siena, Italy 1997; mem. Science Council of Japan 2005–. *Publications:* in English: Disequilibrium Dynamics: A Theoretical Analysis of Inflation and Unemployment (Grand Prix of Nikkei Econ. Books Cultural Award 1982) 1981; in Japanese: Venice no Shonin no Shihon Ron (Capitalism According to the Merchant of Venice) 1985, Fukinkou Dougaku no Riron (Theory of Disequilibrium Dynamics) 1987, Kahei Ron (Money) (Suntory Academic Award) 1993, Gendai no Keizai Riron (Modern Economic Theory, co-ed.) 1994, Shihonshugi wo Kataru (Talks on Capitalism) 1994, 21 Seiki no Shihonshugi Ron (On 21st Century Capitalism) 2000, Kaisha ha Korekara Dounaru no ka (What Will Become of the Corporation?) (Kobayashi Hideo Award 2003, Shûkan Daiyamondo Best Economics Book of the Year) 2003, Kaisha ha Dareno Mono ka (To Whom Does the Corporation Belong) 2005, Shihonshugi kara Shiminshugi he (From Capitalism to Civil Society) 2006, others; contrib. of numerous articles to newspapers and academic journals. *Address:* Faculty of Economics, University of Tokyo, 7-3-1 Hongo, Bunkyo-ku, Tokyo 113-0033, Japan (office). *E-mail:* iwai@e.u-tokyo.ac.jp (office). *Website:* www.iwai-k.com.

IYAYI, Festus, PhD; Nigerian novelist; b. 29 Sept. 1947, Ibadan. *Education:* Annunciation Catholic College, Kiev Institute of Economics, University of Bradford, Yorkshire. *Career:* Lecturer, University of Benin. *Publications:* Violence, 1979; The Contract, 1982; Heroes, 1986; Awaiting Court Martial, 1996. *Honours:* Asscn of Nigerian Authors Prize, 1987; Commonwealth Writers Prize, 1988; Pius Okigbo Africa Prize for Literature, 1996; Nigerian Author of the Year, 1996.

IZRAELEWICZ, Erik, DEcon; French journalist; *Editor-in-Chief, Les Echos;* b. 6 Feb. 1954, Strasbourg. *Education:* Haute Ecole de Commerce, Centre de Formation des Journalistes and Univ. de Paris I. *Career:* journalist, L'Expansion 1981–85; Banking Finance Ed. Le Monde 1986–88, Head of Econ. Service 1989–92, Deputy Ed.-in-Chief 1992–94, New York Corresp. 1993–94, Econs Reporter, Europe 1994–95, leader writer 1994, Ed.-in-Chief 1996; currently Ed.-in-Chief Les Echos. *Address:* Les Echos, 46 rue de la Boétie, 75381 Paris, Cedex 08, France.

J

JACCOTTET, Philippe; Swiss poet and writer; b. 30 June 1925, Moudon. *Education:* University of Lausanne. *Publications:* Poetry: Requiem, 1947; L'Effraie et autres poésies, 1953; L'ignorant: Poèmes 1952–56. Airs: Poèmes 1961–64; Poésie 1946–67; Leçons, 1969; Chants d'en bas, 1974; Breathings, 1974; Pensées sous les nuages, 1983; Selected Poems, 1987; Cahier de verdure, 1990; Libretto, 1990. Other: Through the Orchard, 1975; Des Histoires de passage: Prose 1948–78; Autres Journées, 1987; Trans. of works by Robert Musil, Thomas Mann, Leopardi, Homer and Hölderlin. *Honours:* Larbaud Prize 1978. *Address:* c/o Editions Gallimard, 5 rue Sebastien-Bottin, 75007 Paris, France.

JACK, Ian; British writer and journalist; *Editor, Granta magazine. Career:* journalist, Scotland 1960s; variously reporter, feature writer, Foreign Corresp., Sunday Times 1970–86; co-f. Independent on Sunday 1989, Ed. 1991–95; Ed. Granta magazine 1995–. *Publications include:* Before the Oil Ran Out 1987, The Crash that Stopped Britain 2001; various Granta anthologies. *Honours:* Journalist of the Year 1986, Editor of the Year 1992. *Address:* Granta, 2–3 Hanover Yard, Noel Road, London, N1 8BE, England (office). *Telephone:* (20) 7704-9776 (office). *Fax:* (20) 7704-0474 (office). *E-mail:* ijack@granta.com (office). *Website:* www.granta.com (office).

JACK, Ian (Robert James), MA, DPhil, FBA; British academic, writer and editor; *Professor of English Literature Emeritus, University of Cambridge;* b. 5 Dec. 1923, Edinburgh, Scotland; m. 1st Jane Henderson MacDonald 1948 (divorced); two s. one d.; m. 2nd Margaret Elizabeth Crone 1972; one s. *Education:* George Watson's Coll., Univ. of Edinburgh, Merton Coll., Oxford. *Career:* Lecturer in English Literature 1950–55, Sr Research Fellow 1955–61, Brasenose Coll., Oxford; Visiting Prof., Univ. of Alexandria 1960, Univ. of Chicago 1968–69, Univ. of California at Berkeley 1968–69, Univ. of British Columbia 1975, Univ. of Virginia 1980–81, Tsuda Coll., Tokyo 1981, New York Univ. 1989; Lecturer in English Literature 1961–73, Reader in English Poetry 1973–76, Prof. of English Literature 1976–89, Prof. Emeritus 1989–, Univ. of Cambridge; Fellow 1961–89, Librarian 1965–75, Fellow Emeritus 1989–, Pembroke Coll., Cambridge; de Carle Lecturer, Univ. of Otago 1964; Warton Lecturer in English Poetry, British Acad. 1967; mem. Brontë Soc. (vice-pres. 1973–), Browning Soc. (pres. 1980–83), Charles Lamb Soc. (pres. 1970–80), Johnson Soc., Lichfield (pres. 1986–87). *Publications:* Augustan Satire 1952, English Literature 1815–1832, Vol. X of The Oxford History of English Literature 1963, Keats and the Mirror of Art 1967, Browning's Major Poetry 1973, The Poet and his Audience 1984; editor: Brontë novels (Clarendon edn, seven vols) 1969–72, The Poetical Works of Browning 1983, Vols I–V 1983–95; contrib. to scholarly books and professional journals. *Honours:* Leverhulme Emeritus Fellow 1990–91, Hon. Fellow, Merton Coll., Oxford 1997. *Address:* Highfield House, High Street, Fen Ditton, Cambridgeshire CB5 8ST, England.

JACK, Ronald Dyce Sadler, MA, DLitt, PhD, FRSE; British academic and writer; *Professor Emeritus, University of Edinburgh;* b. 3 April 1941, Ayr, Scotland; s. of the late Muirice Jack; m. Kirsty Nicolson 1967; two d. *Education:* Univ. of Glasgow, Univ. of Edinburgh. *Career:* Lecturer, Univ. of Edinburgh 1965–78, Reader 1978–87, Prof. 1987–2004, Prof. Emer. 2004–; Visiting Prof., Univ. of Virginia 1973–74, Univ. of Strathclyde 1993; Distinguished Visiting Prof., Univ. of Connecticut 1998; W. Ormiston Roy Fellow, Univ. of S Carolina 2003; Fellow, English Asscn 2000; mem. Medieval Acad. of America, Scottish Text Soc. *Publications:* Scottish Prose 1550–1700 1972, The Italian Influence on Scottish Literature 1972, A Choice of Scottish Verse 1560–1660 1978, The Art of Robert Burns (co-author) 1982, Sir Thomas Urquhart (co-author) 1984, Alexander Montgomerie 1985, Scottish Literature's Debt to Italy 1986, The History of Scottish Literature, Vol. I 1988, Patterns of Divine Comedy 1989, The Road to the Never Land 1991, Of Lion and Unicorn 1993, The Poems of William Dunbar 1997, Mercat Anthology of Early Scottish Literature 1997, Oxford Dictionary of National Biography (asst ed.) 2004, Scotland in Europe (ed.) 2005; contrib. to Review of English Studies, Modern Language Review, Comparative Literature, Studies in Scottish Literature. *Honours:* Robert Bruce Award 1986. *Address:* University of Edinburgh, David Hume Tower, George Square, Edinburgh, EH8 9JX (office); 54 Buckstone Road, Edinburgh, EH10 6HN, Scotland (home). *Telephone:* (131) 445-3498 (home). *E-mail:* r.d.s.jack@ed.ac.uk (office); RDSJack@aol.com (home).

JACKMAN, Brian; British journalist and writer; b. 25 April 1935, Epsom, Surrey, England; m. 1st 1964 (divorced 1992); one d.; m. 2nd 1993. *Education:* grammar school. *Career:* staff, Sunday Times 1970–90; Contributing Ed., Condé Nast Traveller; mem. RGS, Fauna and Flora Preservation Soc.; patron Tusk Trust. *Publications:* We Learned to Ski 1974, Dorset Coast Path 1977, The Marsh Lions 1982, The Countryside in Winter 1986, My Serengeti Years 1987, Roaring at the Dawn 1996, The Big Cat Diary 1996, Touching the Wild 2003; contrib. to Sunday Times, The Times, Daily Telegraph, Daily Mail, Country Living, Country Life, BBC Wildlife. *Honours:* TTG Travel Writer of the Year 1982, Wildscreen Award 1982. *Address:* Spick Hatch, West Milton, Nr Bridport, Dorset DT6 3SH, England (home). *E-mail:* brian@spickhatck.freeserve.co.uk.

JACKMAN, Stuart Brooke; British clergyman, editor and writer; b. 22 June 1922, Manchester, England. *Career:* Congregational Minister, Barnstaple,

Devon, 1948–52, Pretoria, 1952–55, Caterham, Surrey, 1955–61, Auckland, 1961–65, Upminster, Essex, 1965–67, Oxford, Surrey, 1969–; Ed., Council for World Mission, 1967–71, Oxted, Surrey, 1969–81, Melbourne, Cambridgeshire, 1981–87. *Publications:* Portrait in Two Colours, 1948; But They Won't Lie Down, 1954; The Numbered Days, 1954; Angels Unawares, 1956; One Finger for God, 1957; The Waters of Dinyanti, 1959; The Daybreak Boys, 1961; The Desirable Property, 1966; The Davidson Affair, 1966; The Golden Orphans, 1968; Guns Covered with Flowers, 1973; Slingshot, 1975; The Burning Men, 1976; Operation Catcher, 1980; A Game of Soldiers, 1981; The Davidson File, 1981; Death Wish, 1998. *Literary Agent:* Curtis Brown Ltd, Haymarket House, 28–29 Haymarket, London, SW1Y 4SP, England. *Telephone:* (20) 7393-4400. *Fax:* (20) 7393-4401. *E-mail:* info@curtisbrown.co.uk. *Website:* www.curtisbrown.co.uk.

JACKOWSKA, Nicki, ANEADip, BA, MA; British poet, novelist, writer and teacher; b. 6 Aug. 1942, Brighton, Sussex, England; m. Andrzej Jackowski 1970 (divorced); one d. *Education:* University of Sussex. *Career:* founder and tutor, Brighton Writing School; Writer-in-Residence at various venues; Readings; Radio and television appearances; mem. Poetry Society. *Publications:* The House That Manda Built, 1981; Doctor Marbles and Marianne, 1982; Earthwalks, 1982; Letters to Superman, 1984; Gates to the City, 1985; The Road to Orc, 1985; The Islanders, 1987; News from the Brighton Front, 1993; Write for Life, 1997; Lighting a Slow Fuse, New and Selected Poems, 1998. Contributions: various publications. *Honours:* winner Stroud Festival Poetry Competition, 1972; Continental Bursary, South East Arts, 1978; C. Day-Lewis Fellowship, 1982; Arts Council Writer's Fellowship, 1984–85; Arts Council of England Writer's Bursary, 1994.

JACKSON, Belle (see Carr, Margaret)

JACKSON, E. F. (see Tubb, Edwin Charles)

JACKSON, Everatt (see Muggeson, Margaret Elizabeth)

JACKSON, Jane (see Pollard, Jane)

JACKSON, Kenneth Terry, BA, MA, PhD; American academic and writer; *Barzun Professor of History and Social Sciences, Columbia University;* b. 27 July 1939, Memphis, TN; m. Barbara Ann Bruce 1962; two s. (one deceased). *Education:* Univ. of Memphis, Univ. of Chicago. *Career:* Asst Prof. 1968–71, Assoc. Prof. 1971–76, Prof. 1976–87, Mellon Prof. 1987–90, Barzun Prof. of History and Social Sciences 1990–, Chair., Dept of History 1994–97, Columbia Univ.; Visiting Prof., Princeton Univ. 1973–74, George Washington Univ. 1982–83, Univ. of California at Los Angeles 1986–87; Chair., Bradley Commission on History in the Schools 1987–90, Nat. Council for History Education 1990–92; Woodrow Wilson Foundation Fellow 1961–62, Nat. Endowment for the Humanities Sr Fellow 1979–80; Guggenheim Fellowship 1983–84; mem. American Historical Asscn, Urban Society Asscn (pres. 1994–), Soc. of American Historians (pres. 1998–2000), Organization of American Historians (pres. 2000–01), New York Historical Soc. (pres. and CEO 2001–04). *Publications:* The Ku Klux Klan in the City 1915–1930 1967, American Vistas (ed. with L. Dinnerstein, two vols) 1971, Cities in American History (ed. with S. K. Schultz) 1972, Atlas of American History 1978, Columbia History of Urban Life (general ed.) 1980–, Crabgrass Frontier: The Suburbanization of the United States 1985, Silent Cities: The Evolution of the American Cemetery (with Camilo Verqara) 1989, Dictionary of American Biography (ed.-in-chief) 1991–95, Scribner's Encyclopedia of American Lives (ed.-in-chief) 1995–2005; Encyclopaedia of New York City 1995, Empire City: New York Through the Centuries 2001; contribs to scholarly books and professional journals. *Honours:* four hon. doctorates; Bancroft Prize 1986, Francis Parkman Prize 1986, Columbia Univ. Mark Van Doren Great Teaching Award 1989, Univ. of Memphis Outstanding Alumni Award 1989, New York State Scholar of the Year 2001, Columbia Univ. Nicholas Murray Butler Medal. *Address:* c/o Department of History, 603 Fayerweather Hall, Columbia University, New York, NY 10027, USA (office). *Telephone:* (212) 854-2555 (office); (914) 666-5721 (home). *Fax:* (212) 932-0602 (office); (914) 666-4310 (home). *E-mail:* ktj1@columbia.edu (office).

JACKSON, Richard Paul, BA, MA, PhD; American writer, poet, academic and editor; *UC Foundation Professor of English, University of Tennessee, Chattanooga;* b. 17 Nov. 1946, Lawrence, Mass; s. of Richard Jackson and Mary Jackson; m. Theresa Harvey 1999; one d. *Education:* Merrimack Coll., Middlebury Coll., Yale Univ. *Career:* UC Foundation Prof. of English, Univ. of Tennessee, Chattanooga; Faculty, Vermont Coll., MFA 1988–; Dir Meacham Writing Workshops; Univ. of Tennessee, Chattanooga; Faculty, Vermont Coll., MFA 1988–; Journal Ed. Poetry Miscellany; readings in Israel, Czech Repub., Hungary, UK, Romania, Serbia, Slovenia, Bosnia, Switzerland, and throughout USA; mem. PEN, Associated Writing Programs. *Publications:* Part of the Story 1983, Acts of Mind 1983, Worlds Apart 1987, Dismantling Time in Contemporary Poetry 1989, Alive All Day 1993, Heart's Bridge 1999, Heartwall 2000, Half Lives 2001, Unauthorized Autobiography: New and Selected Poems 2004; contrib. to Georgia Review, Antioch Review, North American Review, New England Review. *Honours:* Order of Freedom (Slovenia); Nat. Endowment for the Humanities Fellowship 1980, Nat. Endowment for the Arts Fellowship 1985, Fulbright Exchange Fellowships

1986, 1987, Agee Prize 1989, CSU Poetry Award 1992, Juniper Prize 2000, five Pushcart Prizes, Guggenheim Fellowship, Witter-Bynner Fellowship, Teaching Awards from Univ. of Tennessee, Chattanooga and Vermont Coll. *Address:* 3413 Alta Vista Drive, Chattanooga, TN 37411, USA (home). *Telephone:* (423) 624-7279 (office). *E-mail:* svobodni@aol.com (office). *Website:* members .authorsguild.net/svobodni.

JACKSON, Robert Louis; American academic, writer and editor; b. 10 Nov. 1923, New York, NY; m. Elizabeth Mann Gillette 1951; two d. *Education:* BA, Cornell University, 1944; MA, 1949, Certificate, Russian Institute, 1949, Columbia University; PhD, University of California at Berkeley, 1956. *Career:* Instructor, 1954–58, Asst Prof., 1958–67, Prof. of Russian Literature, 1967–91, B. E. Bensinger Prof. of Slavic Languages and Literatures, 1991–, Yale University; mem. North American Dostoevsky Society, pres., 1971–77; International Dostoevsky Society, pres., 1977–83; North American Chekhov Society, founder and pres., 1988–; Vyacheslav Ivanov Convivium, founder and pres., 1981–. *Publications:* Dostoevsky's Underground Man in Russian Literature, 1958; Dostoevsky's Quest for Form: A Study of His Philosophy of Art, 1966; The Art of Dostoevsky, 1981; Dialogues with Dostoevsky: The Overwhelming Questions, 1993. Editor: Chekhov: Collected Critical Essays, 1967; Crime and Punishment: Collected Critical Essays, 1974; Dostoevsky: Collected Critical Essays, 1984; Reading Chekhov's Text, 1993. Contributions: Professional journals. *Honours:* Distinguished Scholarly Career Award, 1993, Prize for Outstanding Work in the field of Slavic Languages and Literature, 1994, American Asscn of Teachers of Slavic and East European Languages; Hon. Doctorate, Moscow State University, 1994. *Address:* c/o Dept of Slavic Languages and Literatures, Yale University, PO Box 208236, New Haven, CT 06520, USA.

JACOBS, Barbara, BA, PGCE; British journalist and writer; b. 6 Feb. 1945, St Helens, England; m. Mark Jacobs 1968, divorced, one s. *Education:* Leicester University. *Career:* freelance journalist 1978–. *Publications:* Ridby Graham, 1982; Two Times Two, 1984; The Fire Proof Hero, 1986; Desperadoes, 1987; Listen to My Heartbeat, 1988; Stick, 1988; Goodbye My Love, 1989; Just How Far, 1989; Loves a Pain, 1990; Not Really Working, 1990. Contributions: periodicals.

JACOBS, Leah (see Gellis, Roberta Leah)

JACOBS, Steve; South African writer; b. 1955, Port Elizabeth, S Africa. *Education:* Univ. of Cape Town. *Career:* sub-ed. and web producer, The Sydney Morning Herald, The Sun-Herald, Sydney, Australia. *Publications:* Light in a Stark Age (short stories) 1984, Diary of an Exile (two novellas) 1986, Under the Lion (novel) 1993, The Enemy Within (novel) 1995. *Address:* c/o African Writers Series, Heinemann Educational Publishers, Halley Court, Jordan Hill, Oxford, OX2 8EJ, England.

JACOBSON, Dan, BA, FRSL; British (b. South African) writer; *Professor Emeritus of English, University College London*; b. 7 March 1929, Johannesburg; s. of Hyman Michael and Liebe Jacobson (née Melamed); m. Margaret Pye 1954; two s. one d. *Education:* Boys' High School, Kimberly, Univ. of Witwatersrand, S Africa. *Career:* worked in business and journalism in SA, settled in England 1955; Fellow in Creative Writing, Stanford Univ., Calif. 1956–57; Prof. of English, Syracuse Univ., New York 1965–66; Visiting Fellow, State Univ. of NY 1971, Humanities Research Centre, ANU, Canberra 1981; Lecturer, Univ. Coll. London 1975–79, Reader in English, Univ. of London 1979–87, Prof. of English, Univ. Coll. London 1988–94, Prof. Emer. 1995–, Fellow 2005–. *Publications:* fiction: The Trap 1955, A Dance in the Sun 1956, The Price of Diamonds 1957, The Evidence of Love 1960, The Beginners 1965, The Rape of Tamar 1970, The Wonder-Worker 1973, Inklings (short stories) 1973, The Confessions of Josef Baisz 1977, Her Story 1987, Hidden in the Heart 1991, The God-Fearer 1992, All For Love 2005; non-fiction: The Story of the Stories (criticism) 1982, Time and Time Again (autobiog.) 1985, Adult Pleasures (criticism) 1988, The Electronic Elephant (travel) 1994, Heshel's Kingdom (travel) 1998, A Mouthful of Glass (trans.) 2000, Ian Hamilton in Conversation with Dan Jacobson (interview) 2002. *Honours:* Hon. DLitt (Witwatersrand) 1997; John Llewelyn Rhys Award 1958, W. Somerset Maugham Award 1961, Jewish Chronicle Award 1971, H. H. Wingate Award 1978, J. R. Ackerley Award for Autobiography 1986, Mary Eleanor Smith Poetry Prize 1992. *Address:* c/o A.M. Heath & Co., 79 St Martin's Lane, London, WC2N 4RE, England (office). *Telephone:* (20) 7836-4271 (office).

JACOBSON, Howard, BA, MA; British novelist and critic; b. 25 Aug. 1942, Manchester, England; m. 1st Rosalin Sadler 1978 (divorced 2004); one s.; m. 2nd Jenny De Yong 2005. *Education:* Downing Coll., Cambridge. *Career:* Lecturer, Univ. of Sydney 1965–68; Supervisor, Selwyn Coll., Cambridge 1969–72; Sr Lecturer, Wolverhampton Polytechnic 1974–80; TV critic, The Sunday Correspondent 1989–90; columnist, The Independent 1998–; occasional reviewer, The Sunday Times. *Television:* writer, presenter: Yo, Mrs Askew! (BBC 2) 1991, Roots Schmoots (Channel 4) 1993, Sorry, Judas (Channel 4) 1993, Seriously Funny: An Argument for Comedy (Channel 4) 1997, Howard Jacobson Takes on the Turner (Channel 4) 2000, Why the Novel Matters (South Bank Show special, LWT) 2002. *Publications:* Shakespeare's Magnanimity: Four Tragic Heroes, Their Friends and Families 1978, Coming From Behind 1983, Peeping Tom 1984, Redback 1986, In the Land of Oz 1987, The Very Model of a Man 1992, Roots Schmoots 1993, Seeing With the Eye: The Peter Fuller Memorial Lecture 1993, Seriously Funny 1997, No More Mister Nice Guy 1998, The Mighty Walzer 1999, Who's Sorry Now 2002, The Making of Henry 2004, Kalooki Nights 2006. *Honours:* Jewish Quarterly and

Wingate Prize 2000, Bollinger Everyman Wodehouse Prize 2000. *Literary Agent:* c/o Curtis Brown Ltd, 28–29 Haymarket, London, SW1Y 4SP, England. *Telephone:* (20) 7393-4400. *Fax:* (20) 7393-4401. *E-mail:* info@curtisbrown.co .uk. *Website:* www.curtisbrown.co.uk.

JACOBUS, Lee A., BA, MA, PhD; American academic and writer; b. 20 Aug. 1935, Orange, NJ; m. Joanna Jacobus 1958, two c. *Education:* Brown University, Claremont Graduate University. *Career:* Faculty, Western Connecticut State University, 1960–68; Asst Prof., 1968–71, Assoc. Prof., 1971–76, Prof. of English, 1976–, University of Connecticut; Visiting Prof., Brown University, 1981; Visiting Fellow, Yale University, 1983, 1996. *Publications:* Improving College Reading, 1967; Issues and Responses, 1968; Developing College Reading, 1970; Humanities Through the Arts (with F. David Martin), 1974; John Cleveland: A Critical Study, 1975; Sudden Apprehension: Aspects of Knowledge in Paradise Lost, 1976; The Paragraph and Essay Book, 1977; The Sentence Book, 1980; Humanities: The Evolution of Values, 1986; Writing as Thinking, 1989; Shakespeare and the Dialectic of Certainty, 1993; Substance, Style and Strategy, 1998. Editor: Aesthetics and the Arts, 1968; 17 From Everywhere: Short Stories from Around the World, 1971; Poems in Context (William T. Moynihan), 1974; Longman Anthology of American Drama, 1982; The Bedford Introduction to Drama, third edn, 1997; A World of Ideas, fourth edn, 1994; Teaching Literature: An Introduction to Critical Reading, 1996. Contributions: scholarly books, journals, and other publications.

JACOBUS, Mary, BA, MA, DPhil; British academic and writer; *Director, Centre for Research in the Arts, Social Sciences and Humanities*; b. 4 May 1944, Cheltenham, Gloucestershire, England. *Education:* Univ. of Oxford. *Career:* Lecturer, Dept of English, Manchester Univ. 1970–71; Fellow, Tutor in English, Lady Margaret Hall, Oxford 1971–80; Lecturer in English, Univ. of Oxford 1971–80; Assoc. Prof. 1980–82, Prof. 1982–, John Wendell Anderson Prof. of English 1989–2000, Cornell Univ., Ithaca, NY; Grace 2 Prof. of English, Univ. of Cambridge 2000–; Dir, Centre of Research in the Arts, Social Sciences and Humanities (CRASSH) 2006–; Fellow, Churchill Coll., Cambridge; mem. MLA. *Publications:* Tradition and Experiment in Wordsworth's Lyrical Ballads (1798) 1976, Women Writing and Women about Women (ed.) 1979, Reading Women 1986, Romanticism, Writing, and Sexual Difference: Essays on The Prelude 1989, Body/Politics: Women and the Discourses of Science (co-ed.) 1989, First Things: The Maternal Imaginary 1995, Psychoanalysis and the Scene of Reading 1999, The Poetics of Psychoanalysis: In the Wake of Klein 2005; contrib. to numerous magazines and journals. *Honours:* Guggenheim Fellowship 1988–89, Nat. Endowment for the Humanities Award 2000–01, Hon. Fellow Lady Margaret Hall, Oxford 2000–. *Address:* Faculty of English, Univ. of Cambridge, Cambridge, CB3 9DP, England (office). *Telephone:* (1223) 335070 (office). *E-mail:* mlj25@cam.ac.uk (office). *Website:* www.english.cam.ac.uk (office); www.crassh.cam.ac.uk (office).

JACOBY, Hildegard (Hilla); German writer and photographer; b. 20 April 1922, Berlin; d. of Heinrich Gerberding and Else Gerberding (née Klein); m. Max-Moshe Jacoby. *Education:* Oberlyzeum Weissensee, Berlin. *Career:* actress, dir children's theatre and artistic producer 1945–; lecturer, writer, photographer for illustrated books (with Max-Moshe Jacoby) 1973–; exhbns of photographs in Berlin and London 1990. *Publications include:* Shalom 1978, The Land of Israel 1978, Sweden 1978, Hallelujah Jerusalem 1980, New York 1981, The Last Hours with Jesus 1982, The Jews, God's People 1983, I am with you 1985, Who Saves Tina? (for children) 1985, Do Not fear 1985, I Am With You 1985, The Ten Commandments – That We May Live 1987, Israel, the Miracle 1988, Walking With Jesus in the Holy Land 1989, Mit Jesus unterwegs 1990, Nächstes Jahr in Jerusalem 1995, The Land of the Bible 1997, A Camera Trip through the Holy Land 1999; also children's books. *Honours:* two Kodak Photo Book Prizes (with Max-Moshe Jacoby) 1978, 1981. *Address:* Spessartstrasse 15, 14197 Berlin, Germany (home). *Telephone:* (30) 8211815 (home). *Fax:* (30) 8211815 (home).

JACOBY, Russell, BA, MA, PhD; American historian and writer; b. 23 April 1945, New York, NY; m. Naomi Glauberman, one s. one d. *Education:* University of Chicago, University of Wisconsin at Madison, University of Rochester, École Pratique des Hautes Études, Paris. *Career:* Lecturer in Social Science, Boston University, 1974–75; Scholar-in-Residence, Brandeis University, 1975–76; Lecturer in History, 1976–79, Visiting Assoc. Prof. of History, 1992–, University of California at Los Angeles; Visiting Asst Prof. of History, University of California at Irvine, 1979–80; Visiting Assoc. Prof. of Humanities, Simon Fraser University, 1983–84; Visiting Scholar-Assoc. Prof., Longergan University College-Liberal Arts College, Concordia University, 1985–86; Visiting Senior Lecturer, University of California at San Diego, 1986–87; Visiting Assoc. Prof. of History, University of California at Riverside, 1988–90. *Publications:* Social Amnesia: A Critique of Conformist Psychology from Adler to Laing, 1975; Dialectic of Defeat: Contours of Western Marxism, 1981; The Repression of Psychoanalysis: Otto Fenichel and the Political Freudians, 1983; The Last Intellectuals: American Culture in the Age of Academe, 1987; Dogmatic Wisdom: How the Culture Wars Divert Education and Distract America, 1994; The Bell Curve Debate: History, Documents, Opinions (ed. with Naomi Glauberman), 1995; The End of Utopia: Politics and Culture in an Age of Apathy, 1999. Contributions: anthologies, reviews, quarterlies and journals. *Honours:* National Endowment for the Humanities Fellowship, 1976; Mellon Postdoctoral Fellowship, 1976–77; Guggenheim Fellowship, 1980–81.

JACQUEMARD, Simonne; French novelist, poet and essayist; b. 6 May 1924, Paris; d. of André and Andrée (Raimondi) Jacquemard; m. 2nd Jacques Brosse 1955. *Education:* Inst. Saint-Pierre, Univ. of Paris. *Career:* teacher of music; collaborator, Laffont-Bompiani Dictionaries; contributor to Figaro Littéraire, La Table Ronde; travelled in USSR, Egypt, Greece, Italy, N Africa and Spain. *Dance:* Sacred dances of India; flamenco dance shows 1982–2000. *Publications:* Les fascinés 1951, Sable 1952, La leçon des ténèbres 1954, Planant sur les airs 1960, Compagnons insolites 1961, Le veilleur de nuit 1962 (Prix Renaudot 1962), L'orangerie 1963, Les derniers rapaces 1965, Dérive au zénith 1965, Exploration d'un corps 1965, Navigation vers les îles 1967, A l'état sauvage 1967, L'éruption du Krakatoa 1969, La thessalienne 1973, Des roses pour mes chevreuils 1974, Le mariage berbère 1975, Danse de l'orée 1979, Le funambule 1981, Lalla Zahra 1983, La fête en éclats 1985, Les belles échappées 1987, L'huître dans la perle 1993, Le Jardin d'Hérodote 1995, L'Éphèbe couronné de lierre 1995, La Gloire d'Ishwara 1996, Vers l'estuaire ébloui 1996, Trois mystiques grecs 1997, Orphée ou l'initiation mystique (jtly) 1998, L'Oiseau 1963, 1998 (Prix Jacques Lacroix, l'Académie française 1999), Héraclite d'Ephèse 2003, Rituels 2004, Pythagore et l'Harmonie des Sphères 2004. *Honours:* Prix Renaudot 1962, Grand prix Thyde-Monnier 1984; Officier Ordre des Arts et des Lettres 1993, Chevalier Légion d'honneur 1999. *Address:* Le Verdier, 24620 Sireuil, France.

JACQUES, Paula; French author and broadcaster; b. 8 May 1949, Cairo; d. of Jacques Abadi and Esther Sasson; m. (divorced 1970). *Career:* worked as comedienne in Africa; joined Radio France Internationale as reporter, worked on Après-midi de France-Culture, L'Oreille en coin 1975–90; presenter Nuits-noires France-Inter radio 1997–, Cosmopolitaine 2000–; sometime writer F Magazine; mem. jury Prix Femina 1996–, Prix des Cinq Continents. *Play:* Zanouba. *Publications:* Lumière de l'oeil 1980, Un baiser froid comme la lune 1983, L'Heritage de Tante Carlotta 1987, Deborah et les anges dissipés (Prix Femina 1991), La Déscente au Paradis (Prix Nice Baie des Anges) 1995, Les femmes avec leur amour 1997, Gilda Stambouli souffre et se plaint... (Prix Europe 1) 2001, Rachel-Rose et l'officier arabe (Prix des Sables d'Olonne) 2006. *Address:* France-Inter, 116 avenue du Président Kennedy, 75220 Paris cédex 16, France.

JAFFE, Harold; American writer and academic. *Career:* Prof. of Creative Writing and Literature, San Diego State Univ.; Ed.-in-Chief, Fiction Int. *Publications:* Mourning Crazy Horse 1982, Dos Indios 1983, Beasts 1986, Madonna and Other Spectacles 1988, Eros Anti-Eros 1990, Straight Razor 1995, Othello Blues 1996, Sex for the Millennium 1999, False Positive 2002, 15 Serial Killers 2003. *Honours:* two Nat. Endowment of the Arts grants, California Arts Council grant, Rockefeller Fellowship, NY CAPS grant, two Fulbright grants. *Address:* c/o Curbstone Press, 321 Jackson Street, Willimantic, CT 06226-1738, USA. *E-mail:* info@curbstone.org. *Website:* www.curbstone.org.

JAFFREY, Madhur, CBE; Indian actress and cookery writer; b. 13 Aug. 1937, Delhi; m. 1st Saeed Jaffrey (divorced 1965); three c.; m. 2nd Sanford Allen 1969. *Education:* Univ. of Delhi and Royal Acad. of Dramatic Art (London). *Career:* Has appeared in numerous radio and TV plays and acted on Broadway (New York) and in several films; writes on Indian cookery for the New York Times and other journals; currently living in the UK. *Films include:* Shakespeare Wallah (Best Actress Award, Berlin Film Festival, Germany), Guru, Autobiography of a Princess, Heat and Dust, Assam Garden. *Play:* Medea. *TV appearances include:* Madhur Jaffrey's Indian Cookery (series), Firm Friends 1992. *Publications:* Invitation to Indian Cooking (latest edn) 1987, Madhur Jaffrey's Cook Book: Food for Family and Friends 1989, Far Eastern Cookery 1989, Days of the Banyan Tree 1990, Eastern Vegetarian Cooking (latest edn) 1990, A Taste of India (latest edn) 1991, Illustrated Indian Cooking, Climbing the Mango Trees: A Memoir of a Childhood in India 2005.

JAHR-STILCKEN, Angelika; German publishing executive; *Publisher, Editor-in-Chief and Journalist Member, Executive Board, Gruner + Jahr AG;* b. 26 Oct. 1941; m. Rudolf Stilcken 1977; one s. one d. *Education:* Univs of Hamburg and Munich. *Career:* began as trainee journalist at Die Welt; spent time in USA at McCall's, Glamour, Vogue and Time Magazine; began career in Germany as Deputy Ed.-in-Chief at es, Petra, Schöner Wohnen 1969, later Ed.-in-Chief; launched Essen und Trinker 1972, Schöner Essen 1985; Ed.-in-Chief Häuser; helped develop concept of Schöner Wohnen Decoration 1989; Gen. Man. Living publishing group 1994–, publishing Flora Garten 1996–, Living at Home 2000–, Essen und Trinken für Jeden Tag 2003–; mem. Supervisory Bd Nestlé Deutschland AG 1996–; Publr, Ed.-in-Chief and Journalist mem. Exec. Bd Gruner + Jahr AG 2000–. *Address:* Gruner + Jahr AG & Co. KG, Druck- und Verlagshaus, Am Baumwall 11, Postfach 110011, 20459 Hamburg, Germany (office). *Telephone:* (40) 37032700 (office). *Fax:* (40) 37035851 (office). *E-mail:* Jahr.Angelika@guj.de (office). *Website:* www.guj.de (office).

JAKES, John William, AB, MA; American writer; b. 31 March 1932, Chicago, IL; m. Rachel Ann Payne 1951; one s. three d. *Education:* DePauw Univ., Ohio State Univ. *Career:* Research Fellow, Univ. of South Carolina 1989; mem. Authors' Guild, Authors' League of America, Dramatists' Guild, PEN, Western Writers of America, Century Asscn. *Publications:* Brak the Barbarian 1968, Brak the Barbarian Versus the Sorceress 1969, Brak Versus the Mark of the Demons 1969, Six Gun Planet 1970, On Wheels 1973, The Bastard 1974, The Rebels 1975, The Seekers 1975, The Titans 1976, The Furies 1976, The Best of John Jakes 1977, The Warriors 1977, Brak: When the Idols Walked 1978, The Lawless 1978, The Americans 1980, Fortunes of Brak 1980, North and South 1982, Love and War 1984, Heaven and Hell 1988, California Gold 1989, The Best Western Stories of John Jakes 1991, Homeland 1993, New Trails (co-ed.) 1994, American Dreams 1998, On Secret Service 2000, Charleston 2002, Savannah (or A Gift for Mr Lincoln) 2004; contrib. to magazines. *Honours:* Hon. LLD (Wright State Univ.) 1976, Hon. LittD (DePauw Univ.) 1977, Hon. LDH (Winthrop Coll.) 1985, (Univ. of South Carolina) 1993, Hon. DH (Ohio State Univ.) 1996; Porgie Award 1977, Ohioana Book Award 1978, Ohio State Univ. Distinguished Alumni Award 1995, Cowboy Hall of Fame Western Heritage Literature Award 1995, Ohio State Univ. Alumni Asscn Professional Achievement Award 1997, South Carolina Humanities Asscn Career Achievement Award 1998, Univ. of South Carolina Thomas Cooper Library Soc. Medal 2002. *Address:* c/o Rembar and Curtis, 19 W 44th Street, New York, NY 10036, USA (office). *E-mail:* jjfiction@aol.com (office). *Website:* www.johnjakes.com.

JAMES, Canute W., BA; Jamaican journalist; b. St Ann. *Education:* Manchester School, Mandeville, Univ. of W Indies (UWI). *Career:* sub-ed. The Gleaner; radio reporter, reporter and news reader for BBC, London, UK 1971–73; Head Current Affairs Programming, Jamaica Broadcasting Corpn 1973; Sr Reporter Jamaica Daily News 1973–76, Ed. 1976–80; journalist Financial Times 1980–; contribs. to The Journal of Commerce, Time, The Miami Herald and others. *Honours:* Cabot Prize 1995.

JAMES, Clive Vivian Leopold; Australian writer, broadcaster, journalist and poet; b. 7 Oct. 1939, Kogarah, NSW; s. of Albert A. James and Minora M. Darke. *Education:* Sydney Technical High School, Sydney Univ. and Pembroke Coll. Cambridge. *Career:* Asst Ed. Morning Herald, Sydney 1961; Pres. of Footlights at Cambridge, UK; television critic, The Observer 1972–82, feature writer 1972–; Dir Watchmaker Productions 1994–; as lyricist for Pete Atkin, record albums include: Beware of the Beautiful Stranger, Driving Through Mythical America, A King at Nightfall, The Road of Silk, Secret Drinker, Live Libel, The Master of the Revels; also songbook, A First Folio (with Pete Atkin). *Television series include:* Cinema, Up Sunday, So It Goes, A Question of Sex, Saturday Night People, Clive James on Television, The Late Clive James, The Late Show with Clive James, Saturday Night Clive, Fame in the 20th Century, Sunday Night Clive, The Clive James Show, Clive James on Safari; numerous TV documentaries including Clive James meets Katharine Hepburn 1986, Clive James meets Jane Fonda, Clive James meets Mel Gibson 1998, Clive James meets the Supermodels 1998, Postcard series 1989–. *Publications:* non-fiction: The Metropolitan Critic 1974, The Fate of Felicity Fark in the Land of the Media 1975, Peregrine Prykke's Pilgrimage through the London Literary World 1976, Britannia Bright's Bewilderment in the Wilderness of Westminster 1976, Visions Before Midnight 1977, At the Pillars of Hercules 1979, First Reactions 1980, The Crystal Bucket 1981, Charles Charming's Challenges on the Pathway to the Throne 1981, From the Land of Shadows 1982, Glued to the Box 1982, Flying Visits 1984, Snakecharmers in Texas 1988, The Dreaming Swimmer 1992, Clive James on Television 1993, Fame 1993, The Speaker in Ground Zero 1999, Even as we Speak (essays) 2000, Reliable Essays 2001, The Meaning of Recognition: New Essays 2001–2005 2005, North Face of Soho 2006, Alone in the Café 2007; novels: Brilliant Creatures 1983, The Remake 1987, The Silver Castle 1996; autobiography: Unreliable Memoirs 1980, Falling Towards England: Unreliable Memoirs Vol. II 1985, Unreliable Memoirs Vol. III 1990, May Week was in June 1990, Brrm! Brrm! or The Man from Japan or Perfume at Anchorage 1991, Fame in the 20th Century 1993, The Metropolitan Critic 1993, North Face of Soho: Unreliable Memoirs Vol. IV; poetry: Fanmail 1977, Poem of the Year 1983, Other Passports: Poems 1958–85 1986, The Book of My Enemy: Collected Verse 1958–2003 2004, Cultural Amnesia 2007; contribs to numerous publs including Commentary, Encounter, Listener, London Review of Books, Nation, New Review, New Statesman, New York Review of Books, New Yorker, TLS. *Address:* PFD, Drury House, 34–43 Russell Street, London, WC2B 5HA, England (office). *Telephone:* (20) 7344-1000 (office).

JAMES, Dana (see Pollard, Jane)

JAMES, Erica; British novelist; b. 1960, Hampshire; two s. *Publications:* novels: A Breath of Fresh Air 1996, Time for a Change 1997, Airs and Graces 1997, A Sense of Belonging 1998, Act of Faith 1999, The Holiday 2000, Precious Time 2001, Hidden Talents 2002, Paradise House 2003, Love and Devotion 2004, Gardens of Delight (Romantic Novelists' Asscn Romantic Novel of the Year 2006) 2005. *Address:* c/o Orion Publishing Group, Orion House, 5 Upper St Martin's Lane, London, WC2H 9EA, England. *E-mail:* publicity.enquiries@orionbooks.co.uk.

JAMES, Michael Leonard, MA, FRSA; British government official, writer and broadcaster; b. 7 Feb. 1941, Cornwall; s. of the late Leonard James and Marjorie James; m. Jill Tarján 1975; two d. *Education:* Christ's Coll., Cambridge. *Career:* entered govt service (GCHQ) 1963; Pvt. Sec. to Rt Hon. Jennie Lee, Minister for the Arts 1966–68; DES 1968–71; Planning Unit of Rt Hon Margaret Thatcher, Sec. of State for Educ. and Science 1971–73, Asst Sec. 1973; Deputy Chief Scientific Officer 1974; served in London, Milan, Paris 1973–78; Dir, IAEA Vienna 1978–83; Adviser, Int. Relations to Comm. of the European Union, Brussels 1983–85; a Chair. Civil Service Selection Bds 1983–93; Chair. The Hartland Press Ltd 1985–2001, Wade Hartland Films Ltd 1991–2000; Gov. East Devon Coll. of Further Educ., Tiverton 1985–91, Colyton Grammar School 1985–90, Sidmouth Community Coll. 1988–2004,

Chair. Bd of Govs 1998–2001; Chair. Gen. Medical Council Professional Conduct Cttee 2000–06; mem. Immigration Appeal Tribunal 1987–2005, Devon and Cornwall Rent Assessment Panel 1990–, Asylum and Immigration Tribunal 2005–; feature writer and book reviewer, The Times (thriller critic 1989–90, travel corresp. 1993–), Daily Telegraph (thriller critic 1993–2000), Sunday Times, Guardian. *TV and radio include:* Seven Steps to Treason (BBC Radio 4) 1990, Sonja's Report (ITV documentary) 1990, Masterspy: interviews with KGB defector Oleg Gordievsky (BBC Radio 4) 1991. *Publications:* Internationalization to Prevent the Spread of Nuclear Weapons (co-author) 1980; novels as Michael Hartland: Down Among the Dead Men 1983, Seven Steps to Treason (South West Arts Literary Award) 1985, The Third Betrayal 1986, Frontier of Fear 1989, The Year of the Scorpion 1991, The Verdict of Us All (short stories) (jtly) 2006; other: Masters of Crime – Lionel Davidson and Dick Francis 2006; novel as Ruth Carrington: Dead Fish 1998. *Honours:* Hon. Fellow, Univ. of Exeter 1985–. *Address:* Cotte Barton, Branscombe, Devon EX12 3BH, England.

JAMES OF HOLLAND PARK, Baroness (Life Peer), cr. 1991, of Southwold in the County of Suffolk; **Phyllis Dorothy (P. D.) James,** OBE, JP, FRSL, FRSA; British author; b. 3 Aug. 1920, Oxford, England; d. of Sidney Victor James and Dorothy Amelia Hone; m. Ernest Connor Bantry White 1941 (deceased 1964); two d. *Education:* Cambridge Girls' High School. *Career:* Admin., Nat. Health Service 1949–68; Prin., Home Office 1968; Police Dept 1968–72; Criminal Policy Dept 1972–79; JP, Willesden 1979–82, Inner London 1984; Chair. Soc. of Authors 1984–86, Pres. 1997–; mem. of BBC General Advisory Council 1987–88, Gov. of BBC 1988–93; Assoc. Fellow Downing Coll., Cambridge 1986; mem. Bd of British Council 1988–93, Arts Council; Chair. Arts Council Literary Advisory Panel 1988–92; mem. Detection Club; mem. Church of England Liturgical Comm. 1991–; Hon. Fellow, St Hilda's Coll., Oxford 1996, Downing Coll., Cambridge 2000, Girton Coll., Cambridge 2000. *Publications:* Cover Her Face 1962, A Mind to Murder 1963, Unnatural Causes 1967, Shroud for a Nightingale 1971, The Maul and the Pear Tree (with T. A. Critchley) 1971, An Unsuitable Job for a Woman 1972, The Black Tower 1975, Death of an Expert Witness 1977, Innocent Blood 1980, The Skull Beneath the Skin 1982, A Taste for Death 1986, Devices and Desires 1989, The Children of Men 1992, Original Sin 1994, A Certain Justice 1997, Time To Be in Earnest 1999, Death in Holy Orders 2001, The Murder Room 2003, The Lighthouse 2005. *Honours:* Hon. DLitt (Buckingham) 1992, (Herts.) 1994, (Glasgow) 1995, (Durham) 1998, (Portsmouth) 1999; Hon. LitD (London) 1993; Dr hc (Essex) 1996;; Grand Master Award of the Mystery Writers of America 1999. *Literary Agent:* Greene & Heaton Ltd, 37A Goldhawk Road, London, W12 8QQ, England.

JAMES, Russell; British writer; b. 5 Oct. 1942, Gillingham, Kent, England; m. Jill Redfern 1978; two d. one s. *Publications:* Underground 1989, Daylight 1990, Payback 1991, Slaughter Music 1995, Count Me Out 1996, Oh, No, Not My Baby: A Noir Mystery 1999, Painting in the Dark 2000, Pick Any Title 2002, The Annex 2002, No One Gets Hurt 2003, The English Sextet 2006, The Great Detectives 2007; contrib. to periodicals. *Address:* c/o Jane Conway-Gordon, 1 Old Compton Street, London, W1V 5PH, England. *Website:* www .russelljames.co.uk.

JAMES, William M. (see Harknett, Terry)

JAMIE, Kathleen, MA; Scottish poet and writer; b. 13 May 1962, Johnston, Renfrewshire; m. Phil Butler; two c. *Education:* Currie High School, Univ. of Edinburgh. *Career:* part-time Lecturer in Creative Writing, Univ. of St Andrews 1999–. *Publications:* poetry: Black Spiders 1982, The Way We Live 1987, The Queen of Sheba 1994, Mr & Mrs Scotland are Dead: Selected Poems 1980–94 1994, Jizzen 1999, The Tree House (Forward Prize 2004, Scottish Arts Council Book of the Year 2005) 2004, Findings 2005; non-fiction: The Golden Peak: Travels in Northern Pakistan 1992, The Autonomous Region: Poems and Photographs from Tibet (with Sean Mayne Smith) 1993, Among Muslims: Meetings at the Frontiers of Pakistan 2002, Findings (essays) 2005. *Honours:* Eric Gregory Award 1981, Scottish Arts Council Book Award 1982, 1988, Somerset Maugham Award 1995, Forward Poetry Prize 1996, Geoffrey Faber Memorial Prize 1996, 2000, Scottish Arts Council Creative Scotland Award 2001. *Literary Agent:* Peter Straus, Rogers, Coleridge and White, 20 Powis Mews, London, W11 1JN, England. *E-mail:* peters@rcwlitagency.co.uk. *Address:* The School of English, Castle House, The Poetry House, University of St Andrews, St Andrews, Fife KY16 9AL, Scotland.

JAMIESON, Kathleen Hall, BA, MA, PhD; American academic and writer; b. 24 Nov. 1946, Minneapolis, MN; m. Robert Jamieson, 1968, two s. *Education:* Marquette University, University of Wisconsin. *Career:* Prof. of Communications, University of Maryland, 1971–86, University of Texas at Austin, 1986–89; Prof. of Communications, 1989–, Dir, Annenberg School of Communications, 1993–, University of Pennsylvania, Philadelphia; Assoc. Ed., several journals; Television news appearances as Political Analyst. *Publications:* Debating Crime Control (co-author), 1967; A Critical Anthology of Public Speeches (compiler), 1978; Form and Genre: Shaping Rhetorical Action (co-ed.), 1978; Age Stereotyping and Television (ed.), 1978; Televised Advertising and the Elderly, 1978; The Interplay of Influence: Mass Media and Their Publics in News, Advertising, and Politics (co-author), 1982; Packaging the Presidency: A History and Criticism of Presidential Campaign Advertising, 1984; Eloquence in an Electronic Age: The Transformation of Political Speechmaking, 1988; Presidential Debates: The Challenge of Creating an Informed Electorate (co-author), 1988; Deeds Done in Words:

Presidential Rhetoric and the Genres of Governance (co-author), 1990; Dirty Politics: Deception, Distraction, and Democracy, 1992; 1-800-President: The Report of the Twentieth Century Fund Task Force on Television and the Campaign of 1992 (co-author), 1993; Beyond the Double Bind: Women and Leadership, 1995; Spiral of Cynicism: The Press and the Public Good, 1996. Contributions: periodicals and professional journals. *Honours:* numerous fellowships, grants and teaching, research and academic awards; Golden Anniversary Book Award, 1984, Winans-Wichelns Book Award, 1989, Speech Communication Asscn.

JANÉS, Clara, LicenFil, MA; Spanish poet, writer and translator; b. 6 Nov. 1940, Barcelona; d. of the late Josep Janés. *Education:* Pamplona Univ. and Sorbonne, Univ. of Paris. *Publications:* Isla del suicidio (poems), Las estrellas vencidas (poems) 1964, La noche de Abel Micheli (novel) 1965, Desintegración (novel) 1969, La vida callada de Federico Monpou (biog.) (Premio Ciudad de Barcelona de Ensayo 1972) 1972, Tentativa de encuentro y tentativa de olvido (short story) (Premio Café Gijón 1972) 1972, Límite humano (poems) 1973, Aprender a envejecer (essay) 1973, En busca de Cordelia y Poemas rumanos (poems) 1975, Cartas a Adriana (novel) 1976, Antología personal 1959–1979 (poems) 1979, Libro de alienaciones (poems) 1980, Sendas de Rumanía (novel) 1981, Eros (poems) 1981, Pureza canelo (biog.) 1981, Vivir (poems) (Premio Ciudad de Barcelona de Poesía 1983) 1983, Kampa: poesía, música y voz (poems) 1986, Las primeras poetisas en lengua castellana (poems) 1986, Fósiles (poems) 1987, Federico Mompou: vida, textos y documentos (essay) 1987, Lapidario (poems) 1988, Creciente fértil (poems) 1989, Los caballos del sueño (novel) 1989, Jardín y laberinto (biog.) 1990, Esbozos (poems) 1990, El hombre de Adén (novel) 1991, Emblemas (poems) 1991, Espejismos (novel) 1991, Las palabras de la tribu: escritura y habla (essay) 1993, Rosas de fuego (poems) 1996, Cirlot, el no mundo y la poesía imaginal (essay) 1996, Diván del ópalo de fuego (poems) 1996, Espejos de agua (short stories) 1997, La indetenible quietud (poems) 1998, El libro de los pájaros (poems) 1999, Arcángel de sombra (poems) (Premio Ciudad de Melilla 1998) 2000, Los secretos del bosque (Premio de Poesía Gil de Biedma 2002) 2001, Paralajes (poems) 2002; contrib. numerous short stories to anthologies; translations, particularly of Czech poetry, also French, English, and Persian and Turkish verse. *Honours:* Premio Nacional de Traducción 1997. *Address:* c/o Ediciones Bassarai, Apdo No. 1630-01080, Vitoria-Gasteiz, Spain.

JANES, J(oseph) Robert, BASc, MEng; Canadian writer; b. 23 May 1935, Toronto, ON; m. Gracia Joyce Lind 1958; two s. two d. *Education:* Univ. of Toronto. *Career:* qualified as mining engineer and geologist; worked in industry and research, then as teacher and univ. lecturer –1970; full-time writer 1970–; mem. Crime Writers of the United Kingdom, Historical Novel Soc. (UK), Int. Asscn of Crime Writers (N American Branch). *Publications:* juvenile fiction: The Tree-Fort War 1976, Theft of Gold 1980, Danger on the River 1982, Spies for Dinner 1984, Murder in the Market 1985; adult fiction: The Toy Shop 1981, The Watcher 1982, The Third Story 1983, The Hiding Place 1984, The Alice Factor 1991, Mayhem (St Cyr/Kohler series) 1992, Carousel (St Cyr/Kohler series) 1992, Kaleidoscope (St Cyr/Kohler series) 1993, Salamander (St Cyr/Kohler series) 1994, Mannequin (St Cyr/Kohler series) 1994, Dollmaker (St Cyr/Kohler series) 1995, Stonekiller (St Cyr/Kohler series) 1995, Sandman (St Cyr/Kohler series) 1996, Gypsy (St Cyr/Kohler series) 1997, Madrigal 1999, Beekeeper 2001, Flykiller 2002; non-fiction: Holt Geophoto Resource Kits 1972, Rocks, Minerals and Fossils 1973, Earth Science 1974, Geology and New Global Tectonics 1976, Searching for Structure (co-author) 1977, Teachers' Guide: Searching for Structure (co-author) 1977, The Great Canadian Outback 1978, Airphoto Interpretation and the Canadian Landscape (with J. D. Mollard) 1984; contrib. to Toronto Star, Toronto Globe and Mail, The Canadian, Winnipeg Free Press, Canadian Children's Annual. *Honours:* Canadian Institute of Mining and Metallurgy Thesis Award 1958, grants from J. P. Bicknell Foundation 1975, Canada Council 1977, Ontario Arts Council 1981, Canada Council travel grant 2002. *Literary Agent:* Acacia House, 62 Chestnut Avenue, Brantford, Toronto, ON N3T 4C2, Canada. *Address:* PO Box 1590, Niagara-on-the-Lake, ON L0S 1J0, Canada. *Website:* www.jrobertjanes.com.

JÁNOSHÁZY, György, LLB; Romanian writer and editor; b. 20 June 1922, Cluj; m. Annamária Biluska 1980; one s. *Education:* Bolyai Univ., Cluj, Acad. of Dramatic Arts, Tg Mures, Bolyai Univ. *Career:* journalist 1945–48; art sec., stage man. Hungarian Opera, Cluj 1949–59; Ed. Korunk monthly 1958–63, Igaz Szó monthly 1963–90, Deputy Gen. Ed. 1969–; mem. Writers' Union of Romania, Tg Mures Asscn (sec. 1981–90), Hungarian Writers' Union. *Publications:* Lepkék szekrényben (trans. as Butterflies in a Glass Case) 1994, Innen semerre (trans. as From Here in No Direction) 1995, Böllérek miséje (trans. as Butchers' Mass) 1999, Úszó sziget (trans. as Floating Island) 2002, Bagolytükör (trans. as Owe Mirror) 2003, Vízöntő (trans. as Watercarrier) 2005; numerous translations, essays on literature and the arts; contrib. to anthologies, reviews and journals. *Honours:* Order of Labour 1968, Gold Merit Cross (Hungary) 1997; Tg Mures Writers' Asscn Prize 1974, Cultural Merit Medal 1981, Lató Prize 1992, 1999, Szentgyörgyi Albert Soc. Prize 1995, Writers' Union of Romania Prize 2000, Hungarian Journalists' Asscn Golden Feather, Romania 2002, Hungarian Writers' Union Arany János Prize 2003. *Address:* Str Parangului 24/9, 540369 Tg Mures, Romania (home). *Telephone:* (365) 407697 (home). *E-mail:* janoshazy@rdslink.ro (home).

JANOWITZ, Tama, MA; American writer; b. 12 April 1957, San Francisco, Calif.; d. of Frederick Janowitz and Phyllis Janowitz (née Winer). *Education:*

Lexington High School, Barnard Coll., Hollins Coll., Roanoke and Yale School of Drama. *Career:* fmr model; Asst Art Dir Kenyon and Eckhardt advertising agency 1977; Alfred Hodder Fellow, Princeton Univ. 1988–89. *Publications:* short stories: Slaves of New York (also screenplay) 1986, Sunpoisoning; novels: American Dad 1981, A Cannibal in Manhattan 1987, The Male Cross-dresser Support Group, By the Shores of Gitchee Gumee 1996, A Certain Age 2000, Peyton Amberg 2003; non-fiction: Area Code 212 – New York Days, New York Nights 2002; for children: Hear That? (illustrated by Tracy Dockery) 2001; contribs to Vogue, Elle, New York Times Sunday Magazine. *Honours:* Hon. MFA (Columbia) 1985. *Address:* 92 Horatio Street, Suite 5E, New York, NY 10014, USA (home).

JANSSON, Jan-Magnus, PhD; Finnish academic and publisher; b. 24 Jan. 1922, Helsinki; s. of Carl Gösta and Anna-Lisa Jansson (née Kuhlefelt); m. 1st Kerstin Edgren 1948 (divorced 1970); m. 2nd Marita Hausen 1970 (divorced 1975); m. 3rd Siv Dahlin 1976; two d. *Education:* Helsinki Univ. *Career:* Prof. of Political Science, Helsinki Univ. 1954–74; Minister of Trade and Industry 1973–74; Ed.-in-Chief Hufvudstadsbladet 1974–87; Chair. Bd Finnish Inst. of Foreign Affairs 1959–85; Chair. Paasikivi Soc. 1964–66, 1975–85, Swedish People's Party in Finland 1966–73, Parl. Defence Comms. 1970–71, 1975–76, 1980–81, mem. Governmental Comms. for Constitutional Reform 1983–90; mem. Bd Int. Political Science Assoc. 1958–61; Chancellor Åbo Akad. (Swedish Univ. of Finland) 1985–90; mem. Regia Societas Humaniorum Litterarum, Lund. *Publications:* Hans Kelsens statsteori 1950, Frihet och jämlikhet 1952, Politikens teori 1969, Idé och verklighet i politiken 1972, Ledare 1981, Från splittring till samverkan: parlamentarismen i Finland 1992, Tidiga Möten (memoirs) 1996, Från Regeringsformen till Grundlagen 2000; and two collections of poetry. *Honours:* Commdr Order of the White Rose of Finland, Commdr Grand Cross of the Order of the Lion of Finland, Cross of Liberty; Hon. LLD (Helsinki) 1990. *Address:* Mannerheimvägen 42 B 27, 00260 Helsinki 26, Finland (home). *Telephone:* (9) 493424 (home). *Fax:* (9) 493424 (home).

JARDINE, Lisa Anne, CBE, BA, MA, PhD, FRHistS, FRSA; British historian; *Professor of Renaissance Studies, Queen Mary, University of London;* b. 12 April 1944; m. 1st Nicholas Jardine 1969 (divorced 1979); one s. one d.; m. 2nd John Robert Hare 1982; one s. *Education:* Cheltenham Ladies' Coll., Newnham Coll., Cambridge, Univ. of Essex. *Career:* Resident Fellow Warburg Inst., Univ. of London 1971–74; Lecturer in Renaissance Literature Univ. of Essex 1974; Resident Fellow Cornell Univ. 1974–75; Resident Fellow Girton Coll., Cambridge 1974–75, Fellow King's Coll. 1975–76, Fellow Jesus Coll. 1976–89, Lecturer in English Univ. of Cambridge 1976–89, Reader in Renaissance English 1989; Davis Center Fellow Princeton Univ. 1987–88; Prof. of Renaissance Studies Queen Mary, Univ. of London 1989–; mem. Arts and Humanities Research Council (AHRC—fmrly Arts and Humanities Research Bd) 2002– (Chair. working party on public understanding of the arts and humanities 2002, Dir Research Centre for Editing Lives and Letters 2002–, Chair. Museums and Collections Cttee 2004–); Trustee Victoria & Albert Museum 2003– (chair. collections cttee 2004–, mem. Bethnal Green Museum Cttee 2004–), United Westminster Schools Foundation; Chair. of Governors Westminster City School 1999–. *Television and radio:* presenter Night Waves (BBC Radio 3) 1992–96, regular appearances on TV and radio programmes. *Publications:* Francis Bacon: Discovery and the Art of Discourse 1974, Still Harping on Daughters: Women and Drama in the Age of Shakespeare 1983, From Humanism to the Humanities (with Anthony Grafton) 1986, What's Left?: Women in Culture and the Labour Movement (with Julia Swindells) 1989, Erasmus: Man of Letters 1993, Reading Shakespeare Historically 1996, Wordly Goods: A New History of the Renaissance 1996, Erasmus: The Education of a Christian Prince (ed.) 1997, Hostage to Fortune: The Troubled Life of Francis Bacon (with Alan Stewart) 1998, Ingenious Pursuits: Building the Scientific Revolution 1999, Francis Bacon: The New Organon and Other Writings (ed. with M. Silverthorne) 1999, Global Interests: Renaissance Art Between East and West (with Jerry Brotton) 2000, On a Grander Scale: The Outstanding Career of Sir Christopher Wren 2002, Living History (series ed. with Amanda Foreman) 2002–, The Curious Life of Robert Hooke: The Man Who Measured London (biog.) 2003, London's Leonardo (ed. with J. Bennett, M. Cooper and M. Hunter) 2003, The Awful End of Prince William the Silent: The First Assassination of a Head of State with a Hand-Gun 2005. *Honours:* Hon. Fellow King's Coll., Cambridge 1995; Dr hc (Sheffield Hallam Univ.). *Address:* AHRC Centre for Editing Lives and Letters, Arts Research Centre, Queen Mary, Mile End Road, London, E1 4NS, England (office). *E-mail:* l.a.jardine@qmul.ac.uk.

JARMAN, Douglas, BA, PhD; British lecturer and writer; b. 21 Nov. 1942, Dewsbury, Yorkshire, England; m. Angela Elizabeth Brown 1970; two d. *Education:* Hull Univ., Durham Univ., Liverpool Univ. *Career:* Lecturer in Music, Univ. of Leeds 1970–71; Lecturer 1974–86, Principal Lecturer 1986, Academic Studies, Royal Northern Coll. of Music, Manchester; Artistic Dir, Young Musicians' Chamber Music Festival; Chair., Psappha; mem. advisory bd, Music Analysis. *Recording:* Talk, Lulu, The Historical Background (recording of The Complete Lulu). *Publications:* The Music of Alban Berg 1979, Kurt Weill 1982, Wozzeck 1989, The Berg Companion 1989, Alban Berg, Lulu 1991, Expressionism Reassessed 1993, Alban Berg: Violin Concerto (critical edn) 1998, Hans Werner Henze at the RNCM (vols 1–3) 1999, The Twentieth Century String Quartet 2002, Alban Berg: Chamber Concerto (critical edn) 2004; contrib. to Perspectives of New Music, Musical Quarterly, Musical Times, Music Review, Journal of Royal Musical Association, News-

letter of International Alban Berg Society, Alban Berg Studien vol. 2. *Honours:* Hon. Fellow, Royal Northern Coll. of Music 1986; Hon. Prof. of Music, Univ. of Manchester 2002. *Address:* 1 Birch Villas, Birchcliffe Road, Hebden Bridge, HX7 8DA, England.

JARMAN, Mark Foster, BA, MFA; American academic and poet; b. 5 June 1952, Mt Sterling, KY; m. Amy Kane Jarman 1974, two d. *Education:* University of California at Santa Cruz, University of Iowa. *Career:* Teacher and Writing Fellow, University of Iowa, 1974–76; Instructor, Indiana State University, Evansville, 1976–78; Visiting Lecturer, University of California at Irvine, 1979–80; Asst Prof., Murray State University, KY, 1980–83; Asst Prof., 1983–86, Assoc. Prof., 1986–92, Prof. of English, 1992–, Vanderbilt University; mem. Associated Writing Programs; MLA; Poetry Society of America; Poets Prize Committee. *Publications:* Poetry: North Sea, 1978; The Rote Walker, 1981; Far and Away, 1985; The Black Riviera, 1990; Iris, 1992; Questions for Ecclesiastes, 1997; Unholy Sonnets, 2000; To the Green Man, 2004. Other: The Reaper Essays (with Robert McDowell), 1996; Rebel Angels: 25 Poets of the New Formalism (ed. with David Mason), 1996; The Secret of Poetry, 2001; Body and Soul: Essays on Poetry, 2002. Contributions: journals, periodicals, and magazines. *Honours:* Joseph Henry Jackson Award, 1974; Acad. of American Poets Prize, 1975; National Endowment for the Arts Grants, 1977, 1983, 1992; Robert Frost Fellowship, Bread Loaf Writers' Conference, 1985; Guggenheim Fellowship, 1991–92; Lenore Marshall Poetry Prize, 1998.

JARMUSCH, Jim; American film director and screenwriter; b. 22 Jan. 1953, Akron, OH. *Education:* Medill School of Journalism, Northwestern Univ., Evanston, Ill., Colombia Coll., SC. *Career:* teaching asst to Nicholas Ray at New York Univ. Graduate Film School 1976–79; has worked on several films as sound recordist, cameraman and actor. *Films:* Permanent Vacation (writer, dir) 1980, You Are Not I (writer) 1981, The New World (dir) 1982, Stranger Than Paradise (writer, dir) (Camera d'Or Award, Cannes Film Festival 1984) 1983, Down By Law (writer, dir) 1986, Coffee and Cigarettes (short film, writer and dir) 1986, Mystery Train (writer, dir) 1989, Coffee and Cigarettes II (short film, writer and dir) 1989, Night on Earth (writer, dir) 1992, Coffee and Cigarettes III (short film, writer and dir) 1993, Dead Man (writer, dir) 1995, Year of the Horse (dir) 1997, Ghost Dog: The Way of the Samurai (writer, dir) 1999, Ten Minutes Older: The Trumpet (writer, dir) 2002, Coffee and Cigarettes (writer, dir) 2003, Broken Flowers 2005. *Music videos directed include:* The Lady Don't Mind (Talking Heads) 1986, Sightsee MC! (Big Audio Dynamite) 1987, It's Alright With Me (Tom Waits) 1991, I Don't Wanna Grow Up (Tom Waits) 1992, Dead Man Theme (Neil Young) 1995, Big Time (Neil Young and Crazy Horse) 1996. *Literary Agent:* c/o Bart Walker, Creative Artists Agency LLC, 162 5th Avenue, 6th Floor, New York, NY 10010, USA. *Telephone:* (212) 277-9000.

JARRAR, Nada Awar; Lebanese/Australian novelist; b. Australia; m. Bassem; one d. *Career:* has lived in the USA, Australia, France and UK; returned to Lebanon 2001. *Publications:* novels: Somewhere, Home (Commonwealth Best First Book Award) 2004, Dreams of Water 2007; contrib. to newspapers and anthologies. *Address:* c/o Vintage, 20 Vauxhall Bridge Road, London, SW1V 2SA, England (office). *E-mail:* vintageeditorial@randomhouse.co.uk (office).

JARVIS, Sharon, BFA; American literary agent, publisher, editor and writer; b. 1 Oct. 1943, New York, NY. *Education:* Hunter College, CUNY. *Career:* Copy Ed., Ace Books, 1969; Asst Managing Ed., Popular Library, 1971; Ed., Ballantine Books, 1972, Doubleday and Co, 1975; Senior Ed., Playboy Books, 1978; mem. International Fortean Organization; The Holistic Consortium; American Booksellers Asscn; Artists for Art. *Publications:* The Alien Trace (with K. Buckley), 1984; Time Twister, 1984; Inside Outer Space, 1985; True Tales of the Unknown, 1985; True Tales of the Unknown: The Uninvited, 1989; True Tales of the Unknown: Beyond Reality, 1991; Dead Zones, 1992; Dark Zones, 1992; Pitching Your Project, 1999; The Cosmic Countdown, 2003.

JASINSKA-JEDROSZ, Elzbieta; Polish musicologist; b. 11 Jan. 1949, Katowice; m. Janusz Jedrosz 1970; one s. *Education:* Warsaw Univ. *Career:* engaged in bibliographic documentation of Polish musical works and in other tasks at Archive of 20th Century Polish Composers, Polish Composers Archive, Warsaw Univ. Library Music Collection 1973–; mem. Polish Composers' Union, Karol Szymanowski Music Asscn, Zakopane, Polish Librarians' Asscn, Asscn of Polish Musicians. *Publications:* Music and Polish Musicians in French 1925–1950 1977, Karol Szymanowski 1882–1937 1983, The Manuscripts of Karol Szymanowski's Musical Works (catalogue) 1983, Karol Szymanowski in the Polish Collections (guide-book, co-author) 1989, Karol Szymanowski: Writer-Poet-Thinker 1997, The Manuscripts of the Young Poland's Composers (catalogue) 1997, Collection of the 20th Century Polish Composers' Archives 1999, Four Seasons: Selected Poetry 2004; contrib. to Muzyka 1981, Ruch Muzyczny 1980, 1981, 1983, 1988–89, 1998–99, 2002–05, Pagine 1989, Przeglad Biblioteczny 1989, 2002, Polski Rocznik Muzykologiczny 2004. *Honours:* hons for popularization of Karol Szymanowski's compositions 1998. *Address:* Biblioteka Uniwersyteka w Warszawie, ul. Dobra 56/66, 00312 Warsaw (office); u. Janinówka 11 m 122, 03562 Warsaw, Poland (home). *Telephone:* (22) 5525746 (office); (22) 6791952 (home). *Fax:* (22) 5525659 (office). *E-mail:* e.m.jasinska@uw.edu.pl (office). *Website:* www.buw.uw.edu.pl (office).

JASPER, David, MA, DD, PhD; British academic, ecclesiastic and writer; *Professor of Literature and Theology, University of Glasgow;* b. 1 Aug. 1951,

Stockton on Tees, England; m. Alison Elizabeth Collins 1976; three d. *Education:* Jesus Coll., Cambridge, St Stephen's House, Oxford, Keble Coll., Oxford, Hatfield Coll., Durham. *Career:* Dir Centre for the Study of Literature and Theology, Univ. of Durham 1986–91; Dir Centre for the Study of Literature and Theology, Univ. of Glasgow 1991–, Prof. of Literature and Theology 1998–; Ed. Literature and Theology; Gen. Ed. Macmillan series Studies in Religion and Culture; Ida Cornelia Beam Distinguished Visiting Prof., Univ. of Iowa 2002–03; Dana Fellow, Emory Univ., Atlanta, Ga 1991; Fellow and Dir Soc. for Arts, Religion and Culture 2000; mem. European Soc. for Literature and Religion (Sec.), American Acad. of Religion, MLA. *Publications:* Coleridge as Poet and Religious Thinker 1985, The New Testament and the Literary Imagination 1987, The Study of Literature and Religion 1989, Rhetoric Power and Community 1992, Reading in the Canon of Scripture 1995, The Sacred and Secular Canon in Romanticism 1999, The Sacred Desert 2004, A Short Introduction to Hermeneutics 2004. *Honours:* Hon. Fellow, Research Foundation, Univ. of Durham 1991. *Address:* Netherwood, 124 Old Manse Road, Wishaw, Lanarkshire, ML2 0EP, Scotland. *Telephone:* (141) 330-4405 (office); (1698) 373286 (home). *Fax:* (141) 330-4943 (office). *E-mail:* D.Joseph@arts.gla.ac.uk (office). *Website:* www.religions.divinity.gla.ac.uk (office).

JAY, Sir Antony Rupert, CVO, BA, MA, FRSA; British writer and producer; b. 20 April 1930, London, England; m. Rosemary Jill Watkins 1957, two s. two d. *Education:* Magdalene Coll., Cambridge. *Career:* staff mem., BBC 1955–64; Chair., Video Arts Ltd 1972–89; writer (with Jonathan Lynn), Yes, Minister and Yes, Prime Minister (BBC TV series) 1980–88. *Publications:* Management and Machiavelli 1967, To England With Love (with David Frost) 1967, Effective Presentation 1970, Corporation Man 1972, The Householder's Guide to Community Defence Against Bureaucratic Aggression 1972, Yes, Minister (with Jonathan Lynn, three vols) 1981–83, The Complete Yes, Minister (with Jonathan Lynn) 1984, Yes, Prime Minister (with Jonathan Lynn, two vols) 1986–87, The Complete Yes, Prime Minister (with Jonathan Lynn) 1989, Elizabeth R 1992, Oxford Dictionary of Political Quotations (ed.) 1996, How to Beat Sir Humphrey 1997. *Honours:* Hon. MA (Sheffield Univ.) 1987, Hon. Dr of Business Admin. (Int. Management Centre, Buckingham) 1988; Companion, Inst. of Management 1992. *Address:* c/o Oxford University Press, Great Clarendon Street, Oxford, OX2 6DP, England (office).

JAY, Martin Evan, BA, PhD; American writer and academic; *Sidney Hellman Ehrman Professor, University of California, Berkeley;* b. 4 May 1944, New York, NY; m. Catherine Gallagher 1974; two d. *Education:* Union Coll., Harvard Univ. *Career:* Asst Prof., Univ. of California, Berkeley 1971–76, Assoc. Prof. 1976–82, Prof. of History 1982–, Sidney Hellman Ehrman Prof. 1997–; mem. American Historical Asscn, Soc. for Exile Studies. *Publications:* The Dialectical Imagination: A History of the Frankfurt School and the Institute of Social Research, 1923–1950 1973, Adorno 1984, Marxism and Totality 1984, Permanent Exiles 1985, Fin de Siècle Socialism 1989, Downcast Eyes 1993, Force Fields 1993, Cultural Semantics 1997–98, Refractions of Violence 2003, Songs of Experience 2004; contrib. to Salmagundi. *Honours:* American Acad. of Arts and Sciences Herbert Baxter Adams Award 1996, Aby Warburg Stiftung Wissenschaftspreis, Hamburg 2003. *Address:* 718 Contra Costa Avenue, Berkeley, CA 94707, USA.

JEAL, Tim, MA; British writer; b. 27 Jan. 1945, London, England; m. Joyce Timewell 1969; three d. *Education:* Christ Church, Oxford. *Career:* mem. Soc. of Authors. *Publications:* For Love of Money 1967, Somewhere Beyond Reproach 1969, Livingstone 1973, Cushing's Crusade 1974, Until the Colours Fade 1976, A Marriage of Convenience 1979, Baden-Powell 1989, The Missionary's Wife 1997, Deep Water 2000, Swimming with my Father 2004, Stanley: The Impossible Life of Africa's Greatest Explorer 2007. *Honours:* Llewelyn Rhys Memorial Prize (jtly) 1974, Writers' Guild Laurel Award. *Address:* c/o Faber and Faber Ltd, 3 Queen Square, London, WC1N 3AU, England (office).

JEAMBAR, Denis; French journalist; *CEO, Editions du Seuil. Career:* mem. staff, Paris-Match 1970–73; Le Point 1973–95 (Ed. 1993–95); Ed. Radio station Europe 1 1995–96; Ed.-in-Chief weekly L'Express 1996–2006; CEO Editions du Seuil 2006–. *Publications:* Sur la route de Flagstaff 1980, George Gershwin 1982, Le PC dans la maison 1984, Dieu s'amuse 1985, Eloge de la trahison (with Yves Roucaute) 1988, Le Poisson pourrit par la tête (with José Frèches) 1992, Le Self-service électoral (with Jean-Marc Lech) 1993, Le Jour ou la girafe s'est assise 1994, La Grande Lessive: anarchie et corruption (with Jean-Marc Lech) 1995, L'Inconnu de Goa 1996, Questions de France 1996, Un Secret d'état 1997, Les Dictateurs à penser et autres donneurs de leçons 2004, Accusé Chirac, levez vous! 2005, Le Défi du monde avec Claude Allègre 2006, Nos enfants nous haïront (with Jacqueline Rémy) 2006. *Address:* Editions du Seuil, 27 rue Jacob, 75006 Paris, France (office).

JEFFERSON, Alan Rigby; British writer; b. 20 March 1921, Ashtead, Surrey, England; m. 1st, one s.; m. 2nd two s. one d.; m. 3rd Antonia Dora Raeburn 1976; two s.; three s. one d. (from previous m.). *Education:* Rydal School, Colwyn Bay, Old Vic Theatre School. *Career:* administrator, London Symphony Orchestra 1968–69; Visiting Prof. of Vocal Interpretation, Guildhall School of Music and Drama, London 1968–74; Man., BBC Concert Orchestra, London 1969–73; Ed., The Monthly Guide to Recorded Music 1980–82; mem. Royal Soc. of Musicians, Soc. of Authors. *Publications:* The Operas of Richard Strauss in Great Britain 1910–1963 1964, The Lieder of Richard Strauss 1971, Delius (Master Musicians series) 1972, The Life of Richard Strauss 1973, Inside the Orchestra 1974, Strauss (Master Musicians series) 1975, Discography of Richard Strauss' Operas 1975, The Glory of Opera 1976, Strauss (Short Biographies series) 1978, Sir Thomas Beecham 1979, The Complete Gilbert and Sullivan Opera Guide 1984, Der Rosenkavalier 1986, Lotte Lehmann, A Centenary Biography 1988, Elisabeth Schwarzkopf (biog.) 1996, An Introduction to Classical Music (CD-ROM) 1996; contrib. to periodicals, including Blätter Internationale Richard Strauss Gesellschaft (Vienna), Classical Express.

JEFFREYS, Diarmuid; British writer, journalist and television producer; m. *Career:* producer of current affairs and documentary programs for the BBC, Channel 4 and other television channels. *Publications:* The Bureau: Inside the Modern FBI 1995, Aspirin: The Remarkable Story of a Wonder Drug 2004. *Address:* c/o Bloomsbury Publishing Plc, 38 Soho Square, London, W1D 3HB, England.

JEFFRIES, Roderic Graeme, (Peter Alding, Jeffrey Ashford, Hastings Draper, Roderic Graeme, Graham Hastings); British writer; b. 21 Oct. 1926, London, England; m. Rosemary Powys Woodhouse 1958; one s. one d. *Education:* Univ. of Southampton. *Career:* served at sea 1943–49; barrister-at-law, Gray's Inn 1953. *Publications:* Evidence of the Accused 1961, Exhibit No. Thirteen 1962, Police and Detection 1962, The Benefits of Death 1963, An Embarrassing Death 1964, Dead Against the Lawyers 1965, Police Dog 1965, Death in the Coverts 1966, A Deadly Marriage 1967, Police Car 1967, A Traitor's Crime 1968, River Patrol 1969, Dead Man's Bluff 1970, Police Patrol Boat 1971, Traffic 1972, Mistakenly in Mallorca 1974, Two Faced Death 1976, The Riddle in the Parchment 1976, The Boy Who Knew Too Much 1977, Troubled Deaths 1977, Murder Begets Murder 1978, Eighteen Desperate Hours 1979, The Missing Man 1980, Just Desserts 1980, Unseemly End 1981, Voyager into Danger 1981, Peril at Sea 1983, Deadly Petard 1983, Three and One Make Five 1984, Layers of Deceit 1985, Sunken Danger 1985, Meeting Trouble 1986, Almost Murder 1986, Relatively Dangerous 1987, The Man Who Couldn't Be 1987, Death Trick 1988, Dead Clever 1989, Too Clever by Half 1990, A Fatal Fleece 1991, Murder's Long Memory 1992, Murder Confounded 1993, Death Takes Time 1994, An Arcadian Death 1995, An Artistic Way to Go 1996, A Maze of Murders 1997, The Ambiguity of Murder 1999, An Enigmatic Disappearance 2000, Definitely Deceased 2001, Seeing is Deceiving 2002, An Intriguing Murder 2002, An Air of Murder 2003, A Sunny Disappearance 2005, Murder Delayed 2006, Murder Needs Imagination 2007; as Peter Alding: The C.I.D. Room 1967, Circle of Danger 1968, Murder Among Thieves 1969, Guilt Without Proof 1971, Despite the Evidence 1971, Call Back to Crime 1972, Field of Fire 1973, The Murder Line 1974, Six Days to Death 1975, Murder Is Suspected 1978, Ransom Town 1979, A Man Condemned 1981, Betrayed by Death 1982, One Man's Justice 1983; as Jeffrey Ashford: Counsel for the Defence 1960, Investigations are Proceeding 1961, The Burden of Proof 1962, Will Anyone Who Saw the Accident. . . 1963, Enquiries Are Continuing 1964, The Hands of Innocence 1965, Consider the Evidence 1966, Hit and Run 1966, Forget What You Saw 1967, Grand Prix Monaco 1968, Prisoner at the Bar 1969, Grand Prix Germany 1970, To Protect the Guilty 1970, Bent Copper 1971, Grand Prix United States 1971, A Man Will Be Kidnapped Tomorrow 1972, Grand Prix Britain 1973, The Double Run 1973, Dick Knox at Le Mans 1974, The Color of Violence 1974, Three Layers of Guilt 1975, Slow Down the World 1976, Hostage to Death 1977, The Anger of Fear 1978, A Recipe for Murder 1979, The Loss of the Culion 1981, Guilt with Honour 1982, A Sense of Loyalty 1983, Presumption of Guilt 1984, An Ideal Crime 1985, A Question of Principle 1986, A Crime Remembered 1987, The Honourable Detective 1988, A Conflict of Interests 1989, An Illegal Solution 1990, Deadly Reunion 1991, Twisted Justice 1992, Judgement Deferred 1993, The Bitter Bite 1994, The Price of Failure 1995, Loyal Disloyalty 1996, A Web of Circumstances 1997, The Cost of Innocence 1998, An Honest Betrayal 1999, Murder Will Out 2000, Looking-glass Justice 2001, A Truthful Injustice 2002, Fair Exchange is Robbery 2003, Evidentially Guilty 2004, Deadly Corruption 2005; as Hastings Draper: Wiggery Pokery 1956, Wigged and Gowned 1958, Brief Help 1961; as Roderic Graeme: Brandy Ahoy! 1951, Concerning Blackshirt 1952, Where's Brandy? 1953, Blackshirt Wins the Trick 1953, Blackshirt Passes By 1953, Salute to Blackshirt 1954, Brandy Goes a Cruising 1954, The Amazing Mr Blackshirt 1955, Blackshirt Meets the Lady 1956, Paging Blackshirt 1957, Blackshirt Helps Himself 1958, Double for Blackshirt 1958, Blackshirt Sets the Pace 1959, Blackshirt Sees it Through 1960, Blackshirt Finds Trouble 1961, Blackshirt Takes the Trail 1962, Blackshirt on the Spot 1963, Call for Blackshirt 1963, Blackshirt Saves the Day 1964, Danger for Blackshirt 1965, Blackshirt at Large 1966, Blackshirt in Peril 1967, Blackshirt Stirs Things Up 1969, as Graham Hastings: Twice Checked 1959, Deadly Game 1961. *Address:* Apdo 5, Ca Na Paiaia, 07460 Pollensa, Mallorca, Spain.

JELINEK, Elfriede; Austrian writer, dramatist and poet; b. 20 Oct. 1946, Mürzzuschlag, Styria; m. Gottfried Hüngsberg. *Education:* Vienna Conservatory, Albertsgymnasium, Vienna and Univ. of Vienna. *Career:* mem. Graz Writers' Assen. *Screenplays:* Die Ausgesperrten (TV) 1982, Malina (from novel by Ingeborg Bachmann) 1991. *Plays include:* Raststätte, Wolken. Heim, Das Werk, Totenauberg: ein Stück, Ein Sportstück, Das Lebewohl, In den Alpen. *Radio:* numerous pieces for radio, including wenn die sonne sinkt ist für manche schon büroschluss (radio play) 1974. *Publications:* Lisas Schatten (poems) 1967, wir sind lockvögel baby! (novel) 1970, Michael: ein Jugendbuch für die Infantilgesellschaft (novel) 1972, Die Liebhaberinnen (novel, trans. as Women as Lovers) 1975, bukolit (novel) 1979, Die Ausgesperrten (novel, trans.

as Wonderful, Wonderful Times) 1980, ende: gedichte von 1966–1968 1980, Die endlose Unschuldigkeit (essays) 1980, Was geschah, nachdem Nora ihren Mann verlassen hatte oder Stützen der Gesellschaft 1980, Die Klavierspielerin (novel, trans. as The Piano Teacher) 1983, Burgtheater 1984, Clara S 1984, Oh Wildnis, oh Schutz vor ihr (non-fiction) 1985, Krankeit oder moderne Frauen 1987, Lust (novel) 1989, Wolken. Heim 1990, Die Kinder der Toten (novel) 1995, Macht nichts: eine kleine Trilogie des Todes 1999, Gier: ein Unterhaltungsroman 2000, Der Tod und das Mädchen I–V: Prinzessinnendramen 2003, Greed (novel) 2006; translations of other writers' works, including Thomas Pynchon, Georges Feydeau, Eugène Labiche, Christopher Marlowe; film scripts and an opera libretto. *Honours:* The Young Austrian Culture Week Poetry and Prose Prize 1969, Austrian Univ. Students' Poetry Prize 1969, Austrian State Literature Stipendium 1972, City of Stadt Bad Gandersheim Roswitha Memorial Medal 1978, West German Interior Ministry Prize for Film Writing 1979, West German Ministry of Education and Art Appreciation Prize 1983, City of Cologne Heinrich Böll Prize 1986, Province of Styria Literature Prize 1987, City of Vienna Literature Appreciation Prize 1989, City of Aachen Walter Hasenclever Prize 1994, City of Bochum Peter Weiss Prize 1994, Rudolf Alexander Schroder Foundation Bremen Prize for Literature 1996, Georg Büchner Prize 1998, Berlin Theatre Prize 2002, City of Düsseldorf Heinrich Heine Prize 2002, Mülheim and der Ruhr Festival of Theatre Dramatist of the Year 2002, 2004, Else Lasker Schüler Prize, Mainz 2003, Lessing Critics' Prize, Wolfenbüttel 2004, Stig Dagerman Prize, Älvkarleby 2004, The Blind War Veterans' Radio Theatre Prize, Berlin 2004, Nobel Prize for Literature 2004. *Address:* Jupiterweg 40, 1140 Vienna, Austria. *Website:* www.elfriedejelinek.com.

JELINEK, Henriette; French writer; b. 1923. *Career:* fmr teacher; full-time writer 1968–. *Film screenplays:* L'Adolescente 1978, Premier voyage 1980. *Publications:* novels: La Vache multicolore 1963, Le Gentil Liseron 1963, La Route du whisky 1964, Portrait d'un séducteur 1965, La Marche du fou 1967, La Vie de famille 1969, Les Bêtes n'aiment pas l'amour des hommes 1972, Dans la nuit des deux mondes 1975, Ann Lee rachète les âmes 1978, L'Adolescente 1979, Le Porteur de Dieu 1979, Madame le Président de la République française 1981, Une goutte de poison 1987, Le Destin de Iouri Voronine (Grand Prix du roman de l'Académie française) 2005; contrib. articles to Le Monde, Le Matin de Paris. *Address:* c/o Editions de Fallois, 22 rue La Boetie, 75008 Paris, France.

JELLICOE, (Patricia) Ann, OBE; British playwright and director; b. 15 July 1927, Middlesborough, Yorkshire, England; m. 1st C. Knight-Clarke 1950 (divorced 1961); m. 2nd Roger Mayne 1962; one s. one d. *Education:* Polam Hall, Darlington, Queen Margaret's, York and Cen. School of Speech and Drama, London. *Career:* actress, stage man., and dir 1947–51; founder and Dir Cockpit Theatre 1952–54; teacher, Cen. School of Speech and Drama 1954–56; Literary Man. Royal Court Theatre 1973–75; founder and Dir Colway Theatre Trust 1979–85, Pres. 1986; Pres. Dorchester Community Plays Asscn 1997. *Plays:* The Sport of My Mad Mother 1958, The Knack 1961, Shelley, or The Idealist 1965, The Rising Generation 1967, The Giveaway 1969, You'll Never Guess! 1973, Clever Elsie, Smiling John, Silent Peter 1974, A Good Thing or a Bad Thing 1974, Flora and the Bandits 1976, The Reckoning 1978, The Bargain 1979, The Tide 1980, The Western Women 1984, Mark og Mønt 1988, Under the God 1989, Changing Places; translations: Rosmersholm 1960, The Lady From the Sea 1961, The Seagull (jtly) 1963, Der Freischütz 1964. *Publications:* non-fiction: Some Unconscious Influences in the Theatre 1967, Shell Guide to Devon (with Roger Mayne) 1975, Community Plays: How to Put Them On 1987. *Address:* Colway Manor, Lyme Regis, Dorset DT7 3HD, England.

JEN, Gish; Chinese/American writer; b. 1955, Long Island, NY; d. of Norman and Agnes Jen; m. David O'Connor; two c. *Education:* Harvard Univ. *Publications:* novels: In the American Society 1986, Typical American 1991, Mona in the Promised Land 1996, The Love Wife 2004; short stories: Who's Irish? 1999; contrib. to Best American Short Stories 1988, Best American Short Stories of the Century, Ploughshares, The New Yorker, Atlantic Monthly, The New Republic, Los Angeles Times, New York Times. *Honours:* Lannan Award for Fiction, American Acad. of Arts and Letters Strauss Living Award. *Literary Agent:* c/o Maxine Groffsky, Maxine Groffsky Literary Agency, 852 Broadway, Suite 708, New York, NY 10003, USA.

JENCKS, Charles Alexander, MA, PhD; American architectural historian and designer; b. 1939, Baltimore, Md; m. Maggie Keswick (deceased); three s. one d. *Education:* Harvard Univ., Univ. of London, UK. *Career:* studied under Siegfried Giedon and Reyner Banham; with Architectural Asscn 1968–88; Lecturer, UCLA 1974–; has lectured at over forty univs including Univs of Peking, Shanghai, Paris, Tokyo, Milan, Venice, Frankfurt, Montréal, Oslo, Warsaw, Barcelona, Lisbon, Zurich, Vienna, Edinburgh, Columbia, Princeton, Yale and Harvard; producer of furniture designs for Sawaya & Moroni, Milan 1986–; currently Ed. Consultant Architectural Design and Ed. Academy Editions, London; contrib. to Sunday Times Magazine, Times Literary Supplement, The Observer, The Independent (all UK); mem. Selection Cttee Venice Biennale 1980; Juror for Phoenix City Hall 1985; Curator Wight Art Centre, LA and Berlin 1987; mem. RSA, London, Acad. Forum of Royal Acad., London. *Furniture designs include:* 'Architecture in Silver': Tea and Coffee Service, Alessi, Italy 1983, Symbolic Furniture exhbn, Aram Designs, London 1985; other furniture and drawings collected by museums in Japan and Victoria & Albert Museum, London. *Architectural works include:* Garagia Rotunda, Truro, MA 1976–77, The Elemental House (with Buzz Yudell), LA,

The Thematic House (with Terry Farrell), London 1979–84, The Garden of Six Senses 1998, The Garden of Cosmic Speculation, Scotland 2001, Landform Veda, Scottish Gallery of Modern Art, Edinburgh 2002, Portello Park, Milan 2003. *Television includes:* two feature films written for BBC on Le Corbusier and Frank Lloyd Wright. *Publications include:* Meaning in Architecture (co-ed.) 1969, Architecture 2000: Predictions and Methods 1971, Adhocism (co-author) 1972, Modern Movements in Architecture 1973, Le Corbusier and the Tragic View of Architecture 1974, The Language of Post-Modern Architecture 1977, The Daydream Houses of Los Angeles 1978, Bizarre Architecture 1979, Late-Modern Architecture 1980, Signs, Symbols and Architecture (co-author) 1980, Skyscrapers-Skycities 1980, Architecture Today 1982, Kings of Infinite Space 1983, Towards a Symbolic Architecture 1985, What is Post-Modernism? 1987, Post-Modernism – The New Classicism in Art and Architecture 1987, The Prince, The Architects and New Wave Monarchy 1988, The New Moderns 1990, The Post-Modern Reader (ed.) 1992, The Architecture of the Jumping Universe 1995, Theories and Manifestos of Contemporary Architecture 1997, New Science – New Architecture? 1997, The Chinese Garden (with Maggie Keswick), Le Corbusier and the Architecture of Continual Revolution 2000, The New Paradigm in Architecture 2002, The Garden of Cosmic Speculation 2003. *Honours:* Fulbright Scholarship (Univ. of London) 1965–67, NARA Gold Medal for Architecture 1992. *Address:* c/o Royal Academy Forum, Royal Academy of Arts, Burlington House, Piccadilly, London, W1J 0BD, England (office).

JENKINS, Alan; British poet and writer; *Deputy Editor, The Times Literary Supplement;* b. 1955, Kingston, Surrey, England. *Education:* Univ. of Sussex. *Career:* Poetry and Fiction Ed., later Deputy Ed., TLS 1981–; poetry critic Observer, then Independent on Sunday 1985–90; taught creative writing, Bread Loaf, Princeton, Arvon Foundation, Poetry Soc.; currently teacher, American Univ., Paris. *Publications:* In the Hot-House 1988, Greenheart 1990, Harm 1994, The Drift 2000, Little Black Book 2003, A Shorter Life 2005; contrib. to London Review of Books, numerous newspapers, journals. *Honours:* Eric Gregory Award for poetry 1981, Forward Prize for Best Collection 1994. *Address:* The Times Literary Supplement, Admiral House, 66–68 East Smithfield, London, E1W 9BX, England.

JENKINS, Catherine Anne May, BA, MA; Canadian writer and poet; b. 18 Feb. 1962, Hamilton, Ont. *Education:* Trent Univ., Peterborough, Ont. *Career:* mem. The Writers' Union of Canada, Editors' Asscn of Canada. *Publications:* Submerge (chapbook) 1997, Written in the Skin (anthology, contrib.) 1998, Blood, Love and Boomerangs (poems) 1999, Swimming in the Ocean (novel) 2002, In Our Own Words: A Generation Defining Itself (anthology, contrib.) 2005; contrib. to Descant, Pottersfield Portfolio, Lichen, Rampike, Queen Street Quarterly, Room of One's Own, Blood and Aphorisms, Carleton Arts Review, Quill and Quire, The Toronto Star, The Globe and Mail, Dream Catcher, Magma Poetry Magazine, Poetry Croydon, Books in Canada, Canadian Bookseller. *E-mail:* solidus@sympatico.ca (home). *Website:* www.catherinejenkins.com.

JENKINS, Sir Simon David, Kt, BA; British journalist; b. 10 June 1943, Birmingham; s. of Daniel Jenkins; m. Gayle Hunnicutt 1978; one s. one step-s. *Education:* Mill Hill School, St John's Coll., Oxford. *Career:* worked for Country Life Magazine 1965; News Ed. Times Educ. Supplement 1966–68; Leader-Writer, Columnist, Features Ed. Evening Standard 1968–74; Insight Editor, Sunday Times 1974–76; Ed. Evening Standard 1977–78; Political Ed. The Economist 1979–86; columnist Sunday Times 1986–90, The Spectator 1992–95, The Times 1992–; Ed. The Times 1990–92; Dir Faber and Faber (Publr) Ltd 1981–90; mem. Bd, Old Vic Co. 1979–81; Part-time mem. British Rail Bd 1979–90, London Regional Transport Bd 1984–86; founder and Dir Railway Heritage Trust 1985–90; Gov. Museum of London 1984–87, Bryanston School 1986–94; Dir The Municipal Journal 1980–90; Deputy Chair. Historic Bldgs and Monuments Comm. 1985–90, English Heritage; Trustee World Monuments Funds 1995–; mem. South Bank Bd 1985–90; mem. Millennium Comm. 1994–2000; Chair. Comm. for Local Democracy 1993–95, Bldg Books Trust 1994–, Booker Prize Judges 2000; mem. Human Fertilization and Embryology Authority 2001–. *Publications:* A City at Risk 1971, Landlords to London 1975, Newspapers: The Power and the Money 1979, The Companion Guide to Outer London 1981, Images of Hampstead 1982, The Battle for the Falklands 1983, With Respect, Ambassador 1985, The Market for Glory 1986, The Selling of Mary Davies and other writings 1993, Against the Grain 1994, Accountable to None: The Tory Nationalization of Britain 1995, England's Thousand Best Churches 1999, England's Thousand Best Houses 2003, Big Bang Localism 2004, Thatcher and Sons 2006. *Honours:* Hon. DLitt (Univ. of London, City Univ.); Edgar Wallace Prize 1997, Rio Tinto David Watt Memorial Prize 1998; Journalist of the Year, Granada Awards 1988, Columnist of the Year 1993. *Address:* c/o The Times, 1 Pennington Street, London, E98 1TT, England.

JENKINS, Terence Andrew, BA, PhD, FRHistS; British historian, writer and editor; b. 30 May 1958, England. *Education:* Univ. of East Anglia, Norwich and Univ. of Cambridge. *Career:* British Acad. Postdoctoral Fellow, Univ. of Cambridge 1987–90; Lecturer, Univ. of East Anglia 1990–91, 1992–93, 1995–96, Univ. of Exeter 1991–92, Univ. of Bristol 1996–97; Sr Research Officer, History of Parliament, London 1998–. *Publications:* Gladstone, Whiggery and the Liberal Party, 1874–1886 (Univ. of Cambridge Prince Consort Prize for History) 1988, The Parliamentary Diaries of Sir John Trelawny (ed.), Vol. 1 1858–1865 1990, Vol. 2 1868–1873 1994, The Liberal Ascendency, 1830–1886 1994, Disraeli and Victorian Conservatism 1996,

Parliament, Party and Politics in Victorian Britain 1996, Sir Robert Peel 1999, Britain: A Short History 2001; contrib. to periodicals, including Historical Journal, English Historical Review, History Today, Parliamentary History, BBC History magazine. *Address:* History of Parliament, 18 Bloomsbury Square, London, WC1A 2NS, England (office). *E-mail:* tjenkins@histparl.ac.uk (office). *Website:* www.histparl.ac.uk (office).

JENS, Walter, (Walter Freiburger, Momos), DPhil; German critic, philologist and novelist; *Honorary President, Akademie der Künste Berlin-Brandenburg*; b. 8 March 1923, Hamburg; s. of Walter and Anna (Martens) Jens; m. Inge Puttfarcken 1951; two s. *Education:* Hamburg and Freiburg im Breisgau Univs. *Career:* Asst Univs. of Hamburg and Tübingen 1945–49; Dozent Univ. of Tübingen 1949–56, Prof. of Classical Philology and Rhetoric 1956–88; Prof. Emer. 1988–; Visiting Prof. Univ. of Stockholm 1964, Univ. of Vienna 1984; Dir Seminar für Allgemeine Rhetorik (Tübingen) 1967–; mem. Gruppe 47 1950, German PEN 1961– (Pres. 1976–82, Hon. Pres. 1982–), Berliner Akad. der Künste 1961–, Deutsche Akad. für Sprache und Dichtung 1962–, Deutsche Akad. der Darstellenden Künste (Frankfurt) 1964–, Freie Akad. der Künste (Hamburg) 1964; Pres. Akad. der Künste Berlin-Brandenburg 1989–97, Hon. Pres. 1997–. *Publications include:* Nein–Die Welt der Angeklagten (novel) 1950, Der Blinde (novel) 1951, Vergessene Gesichter (novel) 1952, Der Mann, der nicht alt werden wollte (novel) 1955, Die Stichomythie in der frühen griechischen Tragödie 1955, Hofmannsthal und die Griechen 1955, Das Testament des Odysseus (novel) 1957, Statt einer Literaturgeschichte (Essays on Modern Literature) 1957, Moderne Literatur—moderne Wirklichkeit (essay) 1958, Die Götter sind sterblich (Diary of a Journey to Greece) 1959, Deutsche Literatur der Gegenwart 1961, Zueignungen 1962, Herr Meister (Dialogue on a Novel) 1963, Euripides-Büchner 1964, Von deutscher Rede 1969, Die Verschwörung (TV play) 1970, Am Anfang der Stall, am Ende der Galgen 1973, Fernsehen-Themen und Tabus 1973, Der tödliche Schlag (TV play) 1974, Der Prozess Judas (novel) 1975, Der Ausbruch (libretto) 1975, Republikanische Reden 1976, Eine deutsche Universität, 500 Jahre Tübinger Gelehrtenrepublik 1977, Zur Antike 1979, Die Orestie des Aischylos 1979, Warum ich Christ bin (Ed.) 1979, Ort der Handlung ist Deutschland (essays) 1979, Die kleine grosse Stadt Tübingen 1981, Der Untergang (drama) 1982, In letzter Stunde (Ed.) 1982, Aufruf zum Frieden 1983, In Sachen Lessing 1983, Kanzel und Katheder 1984, Momos am Bildschirm 1984, Dichtung und Religion (with H. Küng) 1985, Roccos Erzählung 1985, Die Friedensfrau 1986, Theologie und Literatur 1986, Das A und das O–die Offenbarung der Johannes 1987, Deutsche Lebensläufe 1987, Feldzüge eines Republikaners 1988, Juden und Christen in Deutschland 1988, Reden 1989, Schreibschule 1991, Die sieben letzten Worte am Kreuz 1992, Die Friedensfrau 1992, Mythen der Dichter 1993, Am Anfang das Wort 1993, Menschenwürdig sterben 1995, Macht der Erinnerung 1997, Aus gegebenem Anlass 1998, Wer am besten red't ist der reinste Mensch 2000, Der Römerbrief 2000, 'Der Teufel lebt nicht mehr, mein Herr': Erdachte Monologe – imaginäre Gespräche 2001, Pathos und Präzision, Texte zur Theologie 2002, Frau Thomas Mann: Das Leben der Katharina Pringsheim (with I. Jens) 2003; Kabias Hütter: Das ausserordeutliche heben der Hedwig Pringsheim (with I. Jens) 2005. *Honours:* Hon. DPhil; Prix Amis de la Liberté 1951, Schleussner Schüller Prize 1956, Kulturpreis der deutschen Industrie 1959, Lessing Prize 1968, DAG Prize 1976, Heinrich-Heine Prize 1981, Adolf-Grimme 1984, Theodor-Heuss Prize, (with I. Jens) 1988, Alternativer Büchnerpreis 1989, Hermann-Sinsheimer Prize 1989, Österreichischer Staatspreis für Kulturpublizistik 1990, Frankfurter Poetik-Vorlesungen 1992; Tübinger Universitätsmedaille 1979, Österreichisches Verdienstzeichen 1993, Bruno-Snell-Plakette (Univ. of Hamburg) 1997, Ernst-Reuter-Plakette 1998, Deutscher Predigtpreis 2002, Corine Int. Buchpreis (with I. Jens) 2003. *Address:* Sonnenstrasse 5, 72076 Tübingen, Germany. *Fax:* (7071) 600693.

JENSEN, Liz, FRSL; British novelist; b. Oxfordshire; two s. *Career:* fmr journalist in the Far East and France, BBC journalist and producer, sculptor. *Publications:* novels: Egg Dancing 1995, Ark Baby 1998, The Paper Eater 2000, War Crimes for the Home 2002, The Ninth Life of Louis Drax 2004, My Dirty Little Book of Stolen Time 2006. *Address:* c/o Bloomsbury Publishing, 38 Soho Square, London, W1D 3HB, England. *Website:* www.lizjensen.com.

JENSEN, Ruby Jean; American author; b. 1 March 1930; m. Vaughn Jensen, one d. *Publications:* The House That Samuel Built, 1974; The Seventh All Hallows Eve, 1974; Dark Angel, 1978; Hear the Children Cry, 1981; Such a Good Baby, 1982; Mama, 1983; Home Sweet Home, 1985; Annabelle, 1987; Chain Letter, 1987; House of Illusions, 1988; Jump Rope, 1988; Death Stone, 1989; Baby Dolly, 1991; Celia, 1991; The Reckoning, 1992; The Living Exile, 1993; The Haunting, 1994.

JERSILD, Per Christian; Swedish writer; b. 1935, Katrineholm; m. Ulla Flyxe 1960; two s. *Education:* Karolinska Institute. *Career:* Staff, Institute of Social Medicine, Stockholm, 1963–66; Stockholm Civil Service Welfare Dept; social psychiatrist, Huddinge hospital, 1974–78; Asst Prof. of Social and Preventive Medicine and medical adviser, National Govt Administration Board; writer, 1977–. *Publications:* Räknelära (short stories), 1960; Till Varmare Länder, 1961; Ledig Lördag, 1963; Calvinols Resa Genom Världen, 1965; Pyton (with Lars Ardelius), 1966; Prins Valiant Ock Konsum, 1966; Till Varmare Länder, 1967; Obs! Sammanträde Pågår, 1967; Sammanträde Pågor (TV play), 1967; Grisjakten, 1968; Fänrik Duva, 1969; Vi Ses I Song My, 1970; Drömpojken: En Paranoid Historia (Recovery in Schizophrenia), 1970; Uppror Bland Marsinen, 1972; Stumpen, 1973; Djurdoktorn (The Animal Doctor), 1973; Den Elektriska Kaninen, 1974; Barnens Ö (Children's Island), 1976; Moskvafeber, 1977; Babels Hus (House of Babel), 1978; Gycklarnas Hamlet. Och Monologerna Balans Och En Rolig Halvtimme, 1980; En Levande Själ (A Living Soul), 1980; Professionella Bekännelser, 1981; Efter Floden (After the Flood), 1982; Lit De Parade, 1983; Den Femtionde Frälsaren, 1984; Geniernas Återkomst, 1987; Svarta Villan, 1987; Ryktet Smittar: En Monolog An Aids, 1988; Ett Ensamt Öra, 1989; Fem Hjärtan In En Tändsticsask, 1989; Humpty-Dumpty's Fall, En Livsåskådsningsbok, 1990; Alice Och Nisse I Lustiga Huset, 1991; Holgerssons, 1991; Röda Hund, 1991; Hymir, 1993; En Gammal Kärlek, 1995; En Gammal Kylskåp Och Enförkyld Hund, 1995; Sena Sagor, 1998; Darwins Ofullbordade: Om Människans Biologiska Natur, 1999; Ljusets Drottning, 2000; Hundra Fristående Kolumner I Dagens Nyheter, 2002. Contributions: Dagens Nyheter; FIB/Kulturfront. *Honours:* Swedish Society for Promotion of Literature grand prize, 1981; De Nio prize, 1998. *Address:* c/o University of Nebraska Press, 233 N Eighth Street, Lincoln, NE 68588-0255, USA.

JESIH, Boris, PhD; Slovenian artist and poet; b. 8 Aug. 1943, Škofja Loka; s. of Svetoslav and Kristina Jesih; m. Bojana Žokalj 1970 (divorced 1981); one s. one d. *Education:* Acad. of Fine Arts, Ljubljana, Berlin. *Career:* works appear in numerous collections; has published several books of poetry; Ed.-in-Chief Razprave in Gradivo, Inst. of Ethnic Studies, Ljubljana. *Exhibitions include:* 37th Biennale, Venice 1978, Premio le Arti 1971, 11–15th Biennale of Graphic Arts, Ljubljana 1975–83, 6–10th Biennale of Graphic Art, Cracow 1976–84, Premio Biella 1976, British Print Biennale, Bradford 1980, 1982, 1984, Die Kunst vom Stein, Vienna 1985. *Publications include:* The Apple Tree and the Grafts 1979. *Honours:* 10 nat. and 10 int. awards. *Address:* Department of Fine Arts Education, University of Ljubljana, Kardeljeva Ploscad 16, 1000 Ljubljana (office). *Telephone:* (1) 589-22-00 (office). *Fax:* (1) 589-22-33 (office). *Website:* www.pef.uni-lj.si/index_en.html (office).

JESSUP, Frances, BA; British novelist, poet and playwright; b. 29 July 1936, England; m. Clive Turner 1960 (divorced 1996); one s. three d. *Education:* King's Coll. London. *Career:* organiser, Theatre Writing, Haslemere, UNA 1992; Programme Sec., Wey Poets 2000; organiser, Healthy Planet Poems, Electric Theatre 2001, 2006; Signing the Charter, Haslemere UNA Branch Theatre; mem. UNA SC Exec., PEN, MEND 2004–. *Television:* Unusual Afternoon (BBC2 TV 30 minute theatre) 1972. *Publications:* The Fifth Child's Conception 1970, Deutsch Penguin 1972, The Car: A Fable for Voices 1999, Three Short Plays; contrib. to anthologies and magazines, including Hard Lines 3, Acumen, The Lantern, Weyfarers, Manifold, New Poems 6, Earth Love, Savoir Faire. *Honours:* Moor Park Coll. First Prize for Fiction and Poetry 1972, UNA Trust Award for Peace Play Festival 1988, Univ. of Surrey Arts Cttee Literary Festival Award 1991, Nuffield Theatre Theatre Writing Bursary 1993, Arvon Foundation Award 1999, Skyros Poetry Award 2005. *Address:* 20 Heath Road, Haslemere, GU27 3QN, England. *E-mail:* francesjess@clara.co.uk.

JETER, K. W., BA, MA; American novelist; b. 1950, Los Angeles, CA; m. Geri Jeter. *Education:* San Francisco State University. *Publications:* Seeklight, 1975; The Dreamfields, 1976; Morlock Night, 1979; Soul Eater, 1983; Dr Adder, 1984; The Glass Hammer, 1985; Night Vision, 1985; Death Arms, 1987; Infernal Devices: A Mad Victorian Fantasy, 1987; Mantis, 1987; Dark Seeker, 1987; Farewell Horizontal, 1989; In the Land of the Dead, 1989; The Night Man, 1990; Madlands, 1991; Wolf Flow, 1992; Dark Horizon: Alien Nation, 1993; Warped: Star Trek, Deep Space Nine, 1995; Blade Runner 2: The Edge of Human, 1995; Blade Runner: Replicant Night, 1996. *Literary Agent:* c/o Russ Galen, Scovil, Chichak, Galen Literary Agency, 381 Park Avenue Soutoh, Suite 1020, New York, NY 10016, USA. *Telephone:* (212) 679-8686. *Fax:* (212) 679-6710. *E-mail:* russellgalen@scglit.com. *Website:* www.kwjeter.com.

JHA, Raj Kamal; Indian writer and journalist; *Executive Editor, Indian Express, New Delhi*; b. 1966, Kolkata. *Education:* Indian Inst. of Technology, Kharagpur, Univ. of Southern California, USA. *Career:* journalist, The Statesman, India Today; Deputy Ed., currently Exec. Ed., Indian Express, New Delhi. *Publications:* novels: The Blue Bedspread 1999, If You are Afraid of Heights 2003, Fireproof 2007. *Address:* c/o The Indian Express Group, C-6, Qutab Institutional Area, New Delhi 110 016, India. *E-mail:* editor@expressindia.com. *Website:* www.expressindia.com.

JHABVALA, Ruth Prawer, CBE, MA; British/American author and screenwriter; b. 7 May 1927, Cologne, Germany; d. of Marcus Prawer and Eleonora Cohn; sister of Siegbert Salomon Prawer (q.v.); m. C. S. H. Jhabvala 1951; three d. *Education:* Hendon Co. School and London Univ. *Career:* born in Germany of Polish parentage; refugee to England 1939; lived in India 1951–75, in USA 1975–; Neill Gunn Int. Fellowship 1979. *Film screenplays:* Shakespeare-Wallah 1965, The Guru 1969, Bombay Talkie 1970, Autobiography of a Princess 1975, Roseland 1977, Hullabaloo over Georgie and Bonnie's Pictures (TV) 1978, The Europeans 1979, Jane Austen in Manhattan 1980, Quartet 1981, The Courtesans of Bombay (TV) 1983, The Bostonians 1984, A Room with a View 1986, Madame Sousatzka 1988, Mr & Mrs Bridge 1989, Howards End 1992, The Remains of the Day 1993, Jefferson in Paris 1995, Surviving Picasso 1996, A Soldier's Daughter Never Cries 1998, The Golden Bowl 2000, Le Divorce 2003. *Publications:* novels: To Whom She Will 1955, Nature of Passion 1956, Esmond in India 1958, The Householder (also screenplay) 1960, Get Ready for Battle 1962, A Backward Place 1962, A New Dominion 1971, Heat and Dust (also screenplay) 1975, In Search of Love and Beauty 1983, Three Continents 1987, Poet and Dancer 1993, Shards of

Memory 1995, My Nine Lives 2004; short story collections: A Stronger Climate 1968, An Experience of India 1970, How I Became a Holy Mother 1976, Out of India: Selected Stories 1986, East into Upper East 1998. *Honours:* Booker Award for best novel 1975, MacArthur Foundation Award 1984, Acad. Award for Best Screenplay 1986, 1992. *Address:* 400 East 52nd Street, New York, NY 10022, USA.

JIANG, Rong; Chinese novelist. *Career:* writes under a pseudonym; prof. of political economy at a univ. in Beijing; fmrly lived on the Inner Mongolian steppe 1967–78. *Publication:* Lang Tuteng (novel, trans. as The Wolf Totem) 2004. *Address:* Penguin Chinese Division, c/o Penguin Group Australia, PO Box 701, Hawthorn, Australia.

JIANG, Zilong; Chinese writer; *Vice-Chairman, Chinese Writers' Association*; b. 2 June 1941, Cang Xian, Hebei; s. of Jiang Junsan and Wei Huanzhang; m. Zhang Qinglian 1968; one s. one d. *Career:* worker Tianjin Heavy Machinery Plant 1958; navy conscript 1960–65; Vice-Chair. Chinese Writers' Asscn 1996–. *Publications:* A New Station Master 1965, One Day for the Chief of the Bureau of Electromechanics 1976, Manager Qiao Assumes Office 1979, Developer 1980, Diary of a Plant Secretary 1980, All the Colours of the Rainbow 1983, Yan-Zhao Dirge 1985, Serpent Deity 1986, Jiang Zilong Works Collection (eight vols) 1996, Human Vigour 2000, Ren Qi 2000, Empty Hole 2001. *Honours:* Nat. Short Story Prize 1979. *Address:* No. 7 Dali Road, Heping District, Tianjin (home); Tianjin Writers' Association, Tianjin, People's Republic of China. *Telephone:* (22) 23304153 (office); (22) 23306250 (home). *Fax:* (22) 23304159 (office); (22) 23306250 (home). *E-mail:* jzltj@hotmail.com (home).

JIANG AN DAO (see Parkin, Andrew Terence Leonard)

JILES, Paulette, BA; American poet and writer; b. 1943, Salem, MO. *Education:* University of Missouri. *Career:* Teacher, David Thompson University, Nelson, BC, 1984–85; Writer-in-Residence, Phillips Acad., Andover, Massachusetts, 1987–; mem. Writers' Union of Canada. *Publications:* poetry: Waterloo Express, 1973; Celestial Navigation, 1983; The Jesse James Poems, 1987; Flying Lessons: Selected Poems, 1995; prose: Sitting in the Club Car Drinking Rum & Karma-Kola, 1986; The Late Great Human Roadshow, 1986; Blackwater, 1988; Song to the Rising Sun, 1989; Cousins, 1991; North Spirit, 1995; Enemy Women, 2001. *Honours:* Governor-General's Award, 1984; Gerald Lampert Award, 1984; Pat Lowther Award, 1984; ACTRA Award for Best Original Drama, 1989.

JIN, Ha, BA, MA, PhD; Chinese writer, poet and academic; *Professor, Department of English, Boston University*; b. (Jin Xuefei), 21 Feb. 1956, Jinzhou; m. Lisah Bian 1982; one c. *Education:* Heilongjian Univ., Harbin, Shangdong Univ., Jinan, Brandeis Univ. *Career:* faculty mem. Dept of English, Emory Univ. 1993–2002, Boston Univ. 2002–; wrote libretto for opera (with Tan Dun), The First Emperor (Metropolitan Opera, New York) 2006. *Publications:* fiction: Ocean of Words: Army Stories 1996, Under the Red Flag 1997, In the Pond 1998, Waiting 1999, The Bridegroom (short stories) 2000, The Crazed 2002, War Trash (novel) 2004; poetry: Between Silences 1990, Facing Shadows 1996, Wreckage 2001. *Honours:* PEN/Hemingway Award 1997, Flannery O'Connor Award 1997, Nat. Book Award 1999, PEN/Faulkner Award 2000, Asian American Literary Award 2001. *Address:* c/o Department of English, Boston University, 236 Bay State Road, Boston, MA 02215, USA (office). *Telephone:* (617) 353-2506 (office). *Fax:* (617) 353-3653 (office). *E-mail:* xjin@bu.edu (office). *Website:* www.bu.edu/english (office).

JIN, Yong; Chinese writer, journalist and newspaper publisher; b. (Louis Cha Liang Yong), 1923, Haining, Zhejiang Prov. *Education:* Dongwu Law School. *Career:* writer, Ta Kung Pao newspaper, Shanghai, later Hong Kong; later became film reviewer and screenwriter; first martial arts novel serialised in Xin Wan Bao newspaper, Hong Kong 1955; f. newspaper Ming Bao Daily, Hong Kong; ceased writing novels in 1972. *Publications:* (titles translated) Legend of the Book and the Sword, The Sword Stained With Royal Blood (Vol. I Crimson Saber Saga), Fox Volant of the Snowy Mountain, The Young Flying Fox, Legend of the Condor Heroes (Vol. I Condor trilogy), Return of the Condor Heroes (Vol. II Condor trilogy), Heavenly Sword Dragon Saber (Vol. III Condor trilogy), Demi Gods Semi Devils, Way of the Heroes, Requiem of Ling Sing, The Proud Smiling Wanderer, The Duke of Mount Deer (Vol. II Crimson Saber Saga). *Address:* c/o The Chinese University Press, The Chinese University of Hong Kong, Sha Tin, N.T., Hong Kong (office). *Website:* www.chineseupress.com (office).

JOENSUU, Matti Yrjänä; Finnish novelist; b. 31 Oct. 1948, Helsinki. *Career:* policeman; writer 1976–. *Publications include:* Harjunpää ja pyromaani 1978, Harjunpää ja poliisin poika 1983, Harjunpää och kalla döden 1983, Harjunpää ja rakkauden lait 1985, Harjunpää ja kiusantekijät 1986, Harjunpää ja heimolaiset 1987, Harjunpää ja rakkauden nälkä 1993, Harjunpää ja pahan pappi 2003. *Address:* c/o Arcadia Books Ltd, 15–16 Nassau Street, London, W1W 7AB, England.

JOFFE, Josef, PhD; German journalist, editor and international relations scholar; *Publisher-Editor, Die Zeit*; b. 15 March 1944; m. Dr Christine Joffe; two d. *Education:* Harvard Univ., USA. *Career:* Foreign and Editorial Page Dir Suddeutsche Zeitung 1985–2000; Publr-Ed. Die Zeit newspaper 2000–; Professorial Lecturer, Johns Hopkins Univ. 1982–84; Adjunct Prof. of Political Science, Stanford Univ. 2004–, Fellow, Inst. for Int. Studies and Hoover Inst., Stanford 2004–; Visiting Prof. of Govt, Harvard Univ. 1999–2000; Visiting Lecturer, Princeton Univ., Dartmouth Univ.; Founding Bd mem. The

National Interest 1995–2005; Assoc., Olin Inst. for Strategic Studies, Harvard Univ.; mem. Editorial Bd International Security, Prospect. *Publications include:* The Limited Partnership: Europe, the United States and the Burdens of Alliance 1987, The Great Powers 1998, Überpower: The Imperial Temptation of America 2006; numerous articles in scholarly journals and chapters in books. *Honours:* Order of Merit, Germany 1998; hon. degree (Swarthmore) 2002, (Lewis and Clark Coll.) 2005; Theodor-Wolff-Prize in Journalism (Germany), Ludwig Börne Prize in Essays/Literature (Germany). *Address:* Die Zeit, Speersort 1, 20095 Hamburg, Germany (office). *Telephone:* (40) 328-00 (office). *Fax:* (40) 3280-596 (office). *E-mail:* gentsch@zeit.de (office). *Website:* www.zeit.de (office).

JOHANSEN, Hanna; Swiss (b. German) writer; b. (Hanna Margarete Meyer), 17 June 1939, Bremen, Germany; m. Adolf Muschg 1967–90; two s. *Education:* Univs of Marburg and Göttingen and Ithaca Univ., NY, USA. *Career:* writer of novels and children's stories 1978–. *Publications include:* novels: Die Stehende Uhr 1978, Trocadero 1980, Die Analphabetin 1982, Zurück nach Orambi 1986, Ein Mann vor der Tür 1988, Kurnovelle 1994, Ein Maulwurf kommt immer allein 1994, Universalgeschichte der Monogamie 1997, Halbe Tage, ganze Jahre 1998, Sei doch mal still! 2001, Lena 2004; short stories: Über den Wunsch, sich Wohlzufühlen 1985, Die Schöne am Unteren Bildrand 1990, Dinosaurier gibt es nicht 1992, Über den Himmel 1993, Die Hühneroper (jtly) 2004; five children's books 1983–89, Henrietta and the Golden Eggs 2002, Omps! – ein Dinosaurier zu viel 2003; other: Der Füsch, München (with Rotraut Susanne Berner) 1995, Die Hexe zieht den Schlafsack enger (with Käthi Bhend) 1995, Bist du schon wach? (with Rotraut Susanne Berner) 1998, Vom Hühnchen, das goldene Eier legen wollte (with Käthi Bhend) 1998, Maus, die Maus, liest ein langes Buch (with Klaus Zumbühl) 2000, Maus, die Maus, liest und liest (with Klaus Zumbühl) 2000. *Honours:* Ehrengabe des Kantons Zürich 1980, Marie-Louise Kaschnitz Prize 1986, Conrad Ferdinand Meyer Prize 1987, Swiss Youth Book Prize 1990, Schiller Prize 1991, 2002, Children's Book Prize Nordrhein-Westphalia 1991, Austrian Children's and Youth's Book Prize 1993, Literature Prize, Kärnten beim Ingeborg-Bachmann-Wettbewerb, Klagenfurt 1993, Phantastik Prize, Wetzlar 1993, Solothurner Literature Prize 2003. *Address:* Vorbühlstrasse 7, 8802 Kilchberg, Switzerland (home).

JOHANSSON-BACKE, Karl Erik, BEd; Swedish teacher (retd), writer, dramatist and poet; b. 24 Nov. 1914, Stockholm; m. Kerstin Gunhild Bergquist 1943, one s. three d. *Career:* mem. Swedish Authors' Federation. *Publications:* fiction: A Pole in the River 1950, Daybreak 1954, The Mountain of Temptation 1983, The Tree and the Bread 1987, King of the Mountains 1993; poetry: Lust and Flame 1981. *Honours:* many literary awards 1961–93; hon. mem. Swedish Playwrights' Federation.

JOHN, Katherine (see Watkins, Karen Christna)

JOHNSON, Alison Findlay, BPhil, MA; British author; b. 19 Nov. 1947, Stafford, England; m. Andrew J. D. Johnson 1973, one d. *Education:* Aberdeen University, University of Oxford. *Publications:* A House by the Shore, 1986; Scarista Style, 1987; Children of Disobedience, 1989; Islands in the Sound, 1989; The Wicked Generation, 1992. Contributions: West Highland Press; The Times.

JOHNSON, (Alexander) Boris (de Pfeffel); British politician and journalist; b. 19 June 1964, New York, NY, USA; s. of Stanley Patrick Johnson and Charlotte Fawcett; m. 1st Allegra Mostyn-Owen; m. 2nd Marina Wheeler 1993; two s. two d. *Education:* Eton Coll. and Balliol Coll., Oxford. *Career:* journalist with The Times 1987–88; EC Corresp., The Daily Telegraph 1989–94, Asst Ed. and Chief Political Columnist 1994–99, currently columnist; Ed. The Spectator 1999–2005; MP (Conservative) for Henley 2001–; Vice-Chair. Conservative Party 2003–04; Shadow Minister for the Arts 2004; Shadow Minister for Higher Educ. 2005–. *Television:* The Dream of Rome (BBC2) 2006. *Publications:* Friends, Voters, Countrymen 2001, Seventy-Two Virgins (novel) 2004, The Dream of Rome 2006, The British 2007, Life in the Fast Lane: The Johnson Guide to Cars 2007. *Honours:* What the Papers Say Award for Columnist of the Year 2006. *Address:* House of Commons, London, SW1A 0AA (office); Constituency Office, 8 Gorwell. Watlington, OX49 5QE, England (office). *Telephone:* (20) 7219-8192 (office). *Fax:* (20) 7219-1885 (office). *E-mail:* johnsonb@parliament.uk (office). *Website:* www.boris-johnson.com (office).

JOHNSON, Charles Richard, BS, MA, PhD; American author and academic; *Professor, Department of English, University of Washington, Seattle*; b. 23 April 1948, Evanston, Ill.; m. Joan New 1970; one s. one d. *Education:* Southern Illinois Univ., State Univ. of NY, Stoneybrook. *Career:* fmr cartoonist and filmmaker; Lecturer, Univ. of Washington, Seattle 1975–79, Assoc. Prof. of English 1979–82, Prof. 1982–; Co.-Dir Twin Tigers (martial arts studio). *Publications include:* novels: Faith and the Good Thing 1974, Oxherding Tale 1982, Middle Passage 1990; The Sorcerer's Apprentice (short stories); Being and Race: Black Writing Since 1970 1988, The Middle Passage 1990, All This and Moonlight 1990, In Search of a Voice (with Ron Chernow) 1991; Black Humor, Half-Past Nation Time (drawings); Booker, Charlie Smith and the Fritter Tree (broadcast plays); numerous reviews, essays and short stories. *Honours:* recipient of US Nat. Book Award for Middle Passage 1990. *Address:* University of Washington, Department of English, Engl. G N-30, Seattle, WA 98105 (office); c/o Atheneum Publishers, Macmillan Publishing Company, 866 3rd Avenue, New York, NY 10022, USA. *Telephone:* (206) 543-4233 (office). *Website:* depts.washington.edu/engl (office).

JOHNSON, Colin; Australian novelist; b. 23 July 1939, Beverley, WA. *Career:* Lecturer, University of Queensland, St Lucia. *Publications:* Wild Cat Falling, 1965; Long Live Sandawara, 1979; Before the Invasion: Aboriginal Life to 1788, 1980; Doctor Wooreddy's Prescription for Enduring the End of the World, 1983; Doin' Wildcat, 1988; Dalwurra: The Black Bittern, 1988; Writing from the Fringe, 1990. *Honours:* Wieckhard Prize, 1979; Western Australia Literary Award, 1989.

JOHNSON, David Charles, MA, PhD; British composer, music historian, writer and music publisher; b. 27 Oct. 1942, Edinburgh, Scotland; one s. *Education:* Univs of Aberdeen and Cambridge. *Career:* organized recitals for Edinburgh Festival 1975, 1985, 1986, 1988; cellist, McGibbon Ensemble 1980–96; Tutor in Musical History, Univ. of Edinburgh 1988–94; f. self-publishing co., David Johnson Music Edns 1990; mem. PRS, MCPS. *Compositions:* five operas, Piobaireached for solo recorder, God, Man and the Animals (recorded by Alison Wells, soprano, and instrumental ensemble 2001, Metier, England), Piano Trio, Sonata for cello and piano, Seven MacDiarmid Songs for soprano, trumpet and piano, 12 Preludes and Fugues for piano (recorded by Ian Hobson 1998, Zephyr, USA), three suites for solo cello; other songs, chamber and orchestral music. *Recordings:* The Art of Robert Burns (recorded by The Musicians of Edinburgh, Scotstown, USA) 2003, More Art of Robert Burns 2005. *Publications:* Music and Society in Lowland Scotland 1972, Ten Georgian Glees for Four Voices (ed.) 1981, Scottish Fiddle Music in the 18th Century 1984, The Scots Cello Book 1990, Stepping Northward 1990, Scots on the Fiddle 1991, Chamber Music of 18th Century Scotland 2000, John Mahon Clarinet Concerto (ed.) 2006, Earl of Kelly Quartet in B Flat (ed.) 2007; contrib. to The New Grove Dictionary of Music and Musicians 1981, 2001. *Address:* 8 Shandon Crescent, Edinburgh, EH11 1QE, Scotland. *Telephone:* (131) 337-4621 (office). *E-mail:* david@djmusiceditions.freeserve.co.uk (office).

JOHNSON, Denis; American writer and poet; b. 1949, Munich, Germany. *Publications:* Poetry: The Man Among the Seals, 1969; Inner Weather, 1976; The Incognito Lounge and Other Poems, 1982; The Veil, 1987; The Throne of the Third Heaven of the Nations Millennium General Assembly: Poems Collected and New, 1995. Other: Angels, 1983; Fiskadoro, 1985; The Stars at Noon, 1986; Resuscitation of a Hanged Man, 1991; Jesus' Son, 1993; Already Dead: A Californian Gothic, 1997; The Name of the World, 2000; Seek: Reports from the Edges of America & Beyond, 2001. *Honours:* Whiting Writers' Award, 1986; American Acad. of Arts and Letters Literature Award, 1993; several grants.

JOHNSON, Diane Lain, AA, BA, MA, PhD; American writer; b. 28 April 1934, Moline, IL; m. 1st B. Lamar Johnson Jr 1953; four c.; m. 2nd John Frederick Murray 1969. *Education:* Stephens College, University of Utah, University of California at Los Angeles. *Career:* Asst Prof. to Prof. of English, University of California at Davis 1968–87; mem. International PEN, Writers' Guild of America. *Publications:* Fair Game 1965, Loving Hands at Home 1968, Burning 1971, Lesser Lives: The True History of the First Mrs Meredith 1972, The Shadow Knows 1975, Lying Low 1978, Terrorists and Novelists 1982, Dashiell Hammett: A Life 1983, Persian Nights 1987, Health and Happiness 1990, Natural Opium: Some Travelers' Tales 1993, Le Divorce 1997, Le Mariage 2000, L'Affaire 2003; contrib. to newspapers, periodicals and magazines. *Honours:* Guggenheim Fellowship, 1977–78; Rosenthal Award, 1979, Harold and Mildred Strauss Living Stipend, 1988–92, American Acad. of Arts and Letters; Los Angeles Times Medal, 1994. *Address:* 24 Edith Street, San Francisco, CA 94133, USA.

JOHNSON, Elizabeth Ann, BA, MA, PhD; American theologian and writer; *Distinguished Professor of Theology, Fordham University;* b. 6 Dec. 1941, New York, NY. *Education:* Brentwood Coll., Manhattan Coll., Catholic Univ. of America. *Career:* Prof. of Theology, Catholic Univ. of America 1981–91; Distinguished Prof. of Theology, Fordham Univ. 1991–; mem. Catholic Theological Soc. of America (pres. 1996–97), American Acad. of Religion, Coll. Theology Soc., American Theological Soc. (pres. 2006–07). *Publications:* Consider Jesus: Waves of Renewal in Christology 1990, She Who Is: The Mystery of God in Feminist Theological Discourse 1992, Women, Earth, and Creator Spirit 1993, Friends of God and Prophets: A Feminist Theological Reading of the Communion of Saints 1998, The Church Women Want 2002, Truly Our Sister: A Theology of Mary in the Communion of Saints 2003, Dangerous Memories: A Mosaic of Mary in Scripture 2004; contrib. to scholarly books and journals. *Honours:* Dr hc (St Mary's Coll.) 1992, (Maryknoll School of Theology) 1994, (Chicago Theological Union) 1997, (Siena Coll.) 1998, (Coll. of New Rochelle) 2004, (Villanova Univ.) 2005, (St Joseph's Coll., CT) 2006, Hon. DHumLitt (Le Moyne Coll., Syracuse, NY) 1999, (St Joseph Coll., Brooklyn, NY) 2001, Hon. Dr of Pedagogy (Manhattan Coll., Riverdale, NY) 2002, Hon. DD (Jesuit School of Theology, Berkeley, CA) 2003; Univ. of Louisville Grawemeyer Award in Religion, Crossroad Women's Studies Award 1992. *Address:* Department of Theology, Fordham University, Bronx, New York, NY 10458, USA (office). *Telephone:* (718) 817-3247 (office). *Fax:* (718) 817-5787 (office). *E-mail:* ejohnson@fordham.edu (office).

JOHNSON, George Laclede, BA, MA; American writer; b. 20 Jan. 1952, Fayetteville, AR. *Education:* Univ. of New Mexico, Albuquerque and American Univ., Washington, DC. *Career:* reporter, The Albuquerque Journal 1975–77; special assignment reporter, The Minneapolis Star 1979–82; staff ed., The Week in Review, The New York Times 1986–94; writer, The New York Times 1995–. *Publications:* Architects of Fear: Conspiracy Theories and Paranoia in American Politics (PEN Los Angeles Center Special Achievement in Nonfiction) 1984, Machinery of the Mind: Inside the New Science of Artificial Intelligence 1986, In the Palaces of Memory: How We Build the Worlds Inside Our Heads 1991, Fire in the Mind: Science, Faith and the Search for Order 1995, Strange Beauty: Murray Gell-Mann and the Revolution in 20th-Century Physics 1999, A Shortcut Through Time: The Path to the Quantum Computer 2003, Miss Leavitt's Stars: The Untold Story of the Woman Who Discovered How to Measure the Universe 2005; contrib. to journals and newspapers, including Atlantic Monthly, New York Times, Scientific American, Slate, Time, Wired. *Honours:* Alicia Patterson Journalism Fellow 1984, New York Times Publr's Award 1991, AAAS Science Journalism Award 1999, Templeton-Cambridge Journalism Fellowships in Science and Religion, Cambridge, UK 2005. *Literary Agent:* c/o Ms Esther Newberg, International Creative Management, 40 West 57th Street, New York, NY 10019, USA. *Telephone:* (212) 556-5622. *Fax:* (212) 556-5624. *E-mail:* johnson@santafe.edu (office). *Website:* sciwrite.org/glj; santafereview.com.

JOHNSON, Haynes Bonner, BJ, MS; American journalist, academic and writer; b. 9 July 1931, New York, NY; m. Julia Ann Erwin 1954 (divorced); two s. three d. *Education:* University of Missouri, University of Wisconsin. *Career:* reporter, Wilmington News-Journal, DE, 1956–57; Reporter to Special Assignments Correspondent, Washington Star, 1957–69; Commentator, Washington Week in Review, 1967–94, The News Hour with Jim Lehrer, 1994–, PBS TV; National Correspondent, 1969–73, Asst Managing Ed., 1973–77, Columnist, 1977–94, Washington Post; Ferris Prof. of Journalism and Public Affairs, Princeton University, 1975–78; Guest Scholar, Brookings Institution, 1987–91; Regents Lecturer, University of California at Berkeley, 1992; Prof. of Political Commentary and Journalism, George Washington University, 1994–96; Prof. of Journalism, University of Maryland at College Park, 1998–; mem. National Acad. of Public Administration. *Publications:* Dusk at the Mountain, 1963; The Bay of Pigs, 1964; Fulbright: The Dissenter (with Bernard M. Gwertzman), 1968; Army in Anguish (with George C. Wilson), 1972; Lyndon (with Richard Harwood), 1973; The Fall of a President (ed.), 1974; The Working White House, 1975; In the Absence of Power, 1980; The Landing (with Howard Simons), 1986; Sleepwalking Through History, 1991; Divided We Fall, 1994; The System (with David S. Broder), 1996; The Best of Times: America in the Clinton Years, 2001. *Honours:* Pulitzer Prize for National Reporting, 1966; Hon. Doctorates, Wheeling Jesuit University, 1997, University of Missouri, 1999. *Address:* Philip Merrill College of Journalism, University of Maryland, 1117 Journalism Building, MD 20742-7111, USA. *Telephone:* (301) 405-2408 (office). *E-mail:* hjohnson@jmail.umd.edu (office).

JOHNSON, Hugh Eric Allan, OBE, MA; British writer, editor and broadcaster; b. 10 March 1939, London; s. of the late Guy F. Johnson CBE and Grace Kittel; m. Judith Eve Grinling 1965; one s. two d. *Education:* Rugby School, King's Coll., Cambridge. *Career:* feature writer, Condé Nast Magazines 1960–63; Ed. Wine and Food Magazine 1963–65; Wine Corresp. Sunday Times 1965–67, Travel Ed. 1967; Ed. Queen Magazine 1968–70; Wine Ed. Gourmet Magazine 1971–72; Wine Ed. Cuisine Magazine (New York) 1983–84; Chair. Winestar Productions Ltd 1984–, The Hugh Johnson Collection Ltd, The Movie Business; Pres. Sunday Times Wine Club 1973–, Circle of Wine Writers 1997–; founder mem. Tree Council 1974, founder The Plantsman (quarterly) 1979; Dir Château Latour 1986–2001; Editorial Consultant The Garden (Royal Horticultural Soc. Journal) 1975–2005, columnist, Tradescant's Diary 1975–; Sec. Wine and Food Soc. 1962–63; Gardening Corresp. New York Times 1986–87. *Television includes:* Wine – A User's Guide (series) 1986, Vintage – A History of Wine (series) 1989, Return Voyage 1992. *Publications:* Wine 1966, Frank Schoonmaker's Encyclopaedia of Wine (Ed. of English edn) 1967, The World Atlas of Wine 1971, The International Book of Trees 1973, The California Wine Book (with Bob Thompson) 1976, Understanding Wine (Sainsbury Guide) 1976, Hugh Johnson's Pocket Wine Book (annually since 1977), The Principles of Gardening 1979, revised edn with new title, Hugh Johnson's Gardening Companion 1996, Hugh Johnson's Wine Companion 1983, How to Handle a Wine (video) 1984; Hugh Johnson's Cellar Book 1986, The Atlas of German Wines 1986, How to Enjoy Your Wine 1985, The Wine Atlas of France (with Hubrecht Duijker) 1987, The Story of Wine 1989, The Art and Science of Wine (with James Halliday) 1992, Hugh Johnson on Gardening: The Best of Tradescant's Diary 1993, Tuscany and Its Wines 2000, Hugh Johnson's Wine Country 2005, Wine: A Life Uncorked 2005. *Honours:* Hon. Chair. 'Wine Japan' 1989–93; Hon. Pres. Int. Wine and Food Soc.; Fellow Commoner King's Coll. Cambridge 2001; Hon. Freeman of the Vintner's Co. 2003; Chevalier, Ordre nat. du Mérite 2003; Dr hc (Essex) 1998; André Simon Prize 1967, 1989, Glenfiddich Award 1972, 1984, 1989, Marqués de Cáceres Award 1984, Wines and Vines Trophy 1982, Grand Prix de la Communication de la Vigne et du Vin 1992, 1993, Decanter Magazine Man of the Year 1995, Von Rumor Award, Gastronomische Akad., Germany 1998, Gold Veitch Memorial Medal, Royal Horticultural Soc. 2000. *Address:* 73 St James's Street, London, SW1A 1PH; Saling Hall, Great Saling, Essex, CM7 5DT, England. *Telephone:* (1371) 850243.

JOHNSON, Linton Kwesi, BA; British poet and writer; b. 24 Aug. 1952, Chapeltown, Jamaica. *Education:* Goldsmiths Coll., London. *Career:* family emigrated to London 1963; involved in Black Panther movement, London; wrote for NME and Melody Maker in 1970s and 1980s; regular TV/radio apppearances as an authority on reggae; C. Day-Lewis Fellowship 1977, Assoc. Fellow, Warwick Univ. 1985; founder LKJ Records and LKJ Music

Publishers; trustee, George Padmore Inst. *Recordings include:* Dread Beat An' Blood, Forces of Victory, More Time, LKJ Live in Paris. *Publications:* Voices of the Living and the Dead 1974, Dread Beat an' Blood 1975, Inglan is a Bitch 1980, Tings an' Times: Selected Poems 1991, Mi Revalueshanary Fren: Selected Poems 2002; contrib. to recordings, television. *Honours:* Hon. Fellow, Wolverhampton Polytechnic 1987, Goldsmiths Coll., London 2002; Hon. Visiting Prof., Middlesex Univ. 2004; Italian literary awards 1990, 1998, Silver Musgrave Medal Inst. of Jamaica 2005. *Address:* PO Box 623, Herne Hill, London, SE24 OLS, England (office). *Telephone:* (20) 7738-7647 (office). *Fax:* (20) 7738-7647 (office). *E-mail:* info@lkjrecords.com (office). *Website:* www.lkjrecords.com (office).

JOHNSON, Nora, BA; American author; b. 31 Jan. 1933, Los Angeles, CA; m. 1st Leonard Siwek 1955; m. 2nd John A. Milici 1965, two s. two d. *Education:* Smith College. *Career:* mem. Authors' Guild; PEN. *Publications:* The World of Henry Orient, 1958; A Step Beyond Innocence, 1961; Love Letter in the Dead Letter Office, 1966; Flashback, 1979; You Can Go Home Again, 1982; The Two of Us, 1984; Tender Offer, 1985; Uncharted Places, 1988; Perfect Together, 1991. Contributions: newspapers and magazines. *Honours:* McCall's Short Story Prize, 1962; O. Henry Award Story, 1982; New York Times Best Book Citations, 1982, 1984.

JOHNSON, Paul Bede, BA; British journalist, historian and broadcaster; b. 2 Nov. 1928, Barton; s. of William Aloysius and Anne Johnson; m. Marigold Hunt 1957; three s. one d. *Education:* Stonyhurst and Magdalen Coll., Oxford. *Career:* Asst Exec. Ed. Réalités, Paris 1952–55; Asst Ed. New Statesman 1955–60, Deputy Ed. 1960–64, Ed. 1965–70, Dir 1965; DeWitt Wallace Prof. of Communications, American Enterprise Inst., Washington, DC 1980; mem. Royal Comm. on the Press 1974–77, Cable Authority 1984–90; freelance writer. *Publications:* The Offshore Islanders 1972, Elizabeth I: a Study in Power and Intellect 1974, Pope John XXIII 1975, A History of Christianity 1976, Enemies of Society 1977, The National Trust Book of British Castles 1978, The Civilization of Ancient Egypt 1978, Civilizations of the Holy Land 1979, British Cathedrals 1980, Ireland: Land of Troubles 1980, The Recovery of Freedom 1980, Pope John Paul II and the Catholic Restoration 1982, Modern Times 1983 (revised 1991), History of the Modern World: From 1917 to the 1980s 1984, The Pick of Paul Johnson 1985, Saving and Spending 1986, The Oxford Book of Political Anecdotes (ed.) 1986, The History of the Jews 1987, Intellectuals 1988, The Birth of the Modern: World Society 1815–1830 1991, Wake Up Britain! 1994, The Quest for God 1996, To Hell with Picasso and other essays 1996, A History of the American People 1997, The Renaissance 2000, Napoleon 2002, Art: A New History 2003, The Vanished Landscape: A 1930s Childhood in the Potteries 2004, Creators: From Chaucer to Walt Disney 2006. *Honours:* Book of the Year Prize, Yorkshire Post 1975, Francis Boyer Award for Services to Public Policy 1979, King Award for Excellence (Literature) 1980, Pilkington Literary Award 2003, Presidential Medal of Freedom, USA 2006. *Address:* 29 Newton Road, London, W2 5JR; The Coach House, Over Stowey, nr Bridgwater, Somerset TA5 1HA, England. *Telephone:* (20) 7229-3859 (London); (1278) 732393 (Somerset). *Fax:* (20) 7792-1676 (London).

JOHNSON, (John) Stephen, MA, DPhil; British writer; b. 3 June 1947, Mansfield, England. *Education:* Univ. of Oxford. *Publications:* The Roman Fort of the Saxon Shore 1976, Later Roman Britain 1980, Late Roman Fortifications 1983, Hadrian's Wall 1989, Rome and its Empire 1989. *Address:* 49 Branksome Road, Norwich, NR4 6SW, England.

JOHNSON, Susan Ruth, BA; Australian writer; b. 30 Dec. 1956, Brisbane; d. of John Joseph Johnson and Barbara Ruth Johnson (née Bell); m. 1st John Patrick Burdett 1989 (divorced 1991); m. 2nd Leslie William Webb 1994; one s. *Education:* Clayfield Coll., Brisbane and Univ. of Queensland. *Career:* journalist, The Courier-Mail 1975, The Australian Women's Weekly 1977–78, The Sun-Herald 1980–81, The Sydney Morning Herald 1981–82, The National Times 1982–84; full-time writer 1984–; resident Keesing Studio, Cité Int. des Arts, Paris (awarded by Literature Bd, Australia Council) –1992; Ed. Saturday Extra, in The Age 1999–2001; mem. Australian Soc. of Authors; several fellowships awarded by Australia Council 1986–92. *Publications:* fiction: Latitudes: New Writing from the North (ed. with Mary Roberts) 1986, Message from Chaos 1987, Flying Lessons 1990, A Big Life 1993, WomenLoveSex (ed., short stories) 1996, Hungry Ghosts 1996; non-fiction: A Better Woman (memoir) 1999, The Broken Book (biog.) 2005. *Address:* Margaret Connolly and Associates, POB 48, Paddington, NSW 2021, Australia (office). *E-mail:* sjreaders@hotmail.com (office). *Website:* www.abetterwoman.net (office).

JOHNSON, Terry, BA; British dramatist and screenwriter; b. 20 Dec. 1955, England. *Education:* Univ. of Birmingham. *Plays:* Insignificance 1982, Cries from the Mammal House 1984, Unsuitable for Adults 1985, Tuesday's Child (with Kate Lock) 1987, Imagine Drowning 1991, Hysteria 1993, Dead Funny 1994, Cleo, Camping, Emmanuelle and Dick 1998, The London Cuckolds 1998, Hitchcock Blonde 2003, Piano/Forte 2006. *Film screenplays:* Insignificance 1985, Absolute Beginners (with others) 1986, Killing Time 1985, Way Upstream 1987. *Television screenplays:* Time Trouble 1985, Tuesday's Child (with Kate Lock) 1985, Way Upstream 1987, 99-1 (with others) 1994, Blood and Water 1995, The Bite 1996, Cor Blimey! 2000, Not Only But Also 2004. *Honours:* Evening Standard Drama Award 1983. *Literary Agent:* Curtis Brown Ltd, Haymarket House, 28–29 Haymarket, London, SW1Y 4SP,

England. *Telephone:* (20) 7393-4400. *Fax:* (20) 7393-4401. *E-mail:* info@curtisbrown.co.uk. *Website:* www.curtisbrown.co.uk.

JOHNSON, William Stacy, AB, JD, MDiv, PhD; American theologian and lawyer; b. 13 July 1956, Pinehurst, NJ. *Education:* Davidson College, Wake Forest University, Union Theological Seminary, Harvard University. *Career:* Assoc. Prof. of Theology, Austin Presbyterian Theological Seminary, Austin, Texas, 1992–; Attorney-at-Law; mem. Karl Barth Society of North America; American Acad. of Religion; American Asscn for the Advancement of Science. *Publications:* Theology, History, and Culture (ed.), 1996; The Mystery of God: Karl Barth and the Postmodern Foundations of Theology, 1997. *Address:* Austin Presbyterian Theological Seminary, 100 E 27th St, Austin, TX 78705, USA. *E-mail:* wsjnson@ix.netcom.com.

JOHNSON-DAVIES, Denys; Canadian translator and writer; b. 1922, Vancouver. *Education:* Univ. of Cambridge. *Career:* fmrly worked for the BBC Arabic Service, teacher at Fouad al-Awwal Univ., Cairo; Arabic–English translator. *Publications include:* Memories in Translation (memoir) 2006; editor: Arabic Short Stories, The Mountain of Green Tea (with Yahya al-Tahir 'Abd Allah), The Island of Animals (with Khemir Sabiha), The Anchor Book of Modern Arabic Fiction 2006; translations: Short Stories, by Mahmoud Teymour 1947, The Tree Climber, by Tawfiq al-Hakim, Bandarshah, by al-Tayyib Salih, Houses Behind the Trees, by Mohamed el-Bisatie, The Slave's Dream and Other Stories, by Nabil Naoum Gorgy, Blood Feud and Other Stories, by Yusuf Sharouni and Yusuf Sharuni, Season of Migration to the North, by Tayeb Salih, The Time and the Place, and Other Stories, by Naguib Mahfouz, Arabian Nights and Days, by Naguib Mahfouz and Najib Mahfuz, The Wiles of Men and Other Stories, by Salwa Bakr, The Journey of Ibn Fattouma, by Naguib Mahfouz and Najib Mahfuz, Echoes of an Autobiography, by Naguib Mahfouz and Nadine Gordimer. *Address:* c/o Anchor Publicity, 1745 Broadway, 20th Floor, New York, NY 10019, USA (office).

JOHNSTON, George Benson, BA, MA; Canadian poet and translator; b. 7 Oct. 1913, Hamilton, ON; m. Jeanne McRae 1944; three s. three d. *Education:* University of Toronto. *Career:* Faculty, Dept of English, Mount Allison University, Sackville, New Brunswick, 1947–49, Carleton College, later University, Ottawa, 1949–79. *Publications:* poetry: The Cruising Auk, 1959; Home Free, 1966; Happy Enough: Poems 1935–1972, 1972; Between, 1976; Taking a Grip, 1979; Auk Redivivus: Selected Poems, 1981; Ask Again, 1984; Endeared by Dark: The Collected Poems, 1990; What is to Come: Selected and New Poems, 1996. Prose: Carl: Portrait of a Painter, 1986. Translator: Over 10 vols, 1963–94. *Honours:* hon. doctorates.

JOHNSTON, Jennifer; Irish writer; b. 12 Jan. 1930, Dublin; d. of Denis Johnston and Shelah Richards; m. 1st Ian Smyth; two s. two d.; m. 2nd David Gilliland. *Education:* Park House School, Dublin, Trinity Coll., Dublin. *Plays:* The Desert Lullaby, Moonlight and Music; several radio and TV programmes. *Publications:* How Many Miles to Babylon?, The Old Jest, The Christmas Tree, The Invisible Worm 1991, The Illusionist 1995, Two Moons, The Railway Station Man 1986, Shadows on Our Skin, The Gingerbread Woman, The Porch 1986, The Invisible Man 1986, The Desert Lullaby 1996, This is Not a Novel 2003, Grace and Truth 2005. *Honours:* Hon. Fellow Trinity Coll., Dublin; Hon. DLitt (New Univ. of Ulster, Queen's Univ., Belfast, Trinity Coll., Dublin, Nat. Univ. of Ireland); Whitbread Prize 1980, Giles Cooper Award 1989, Premio Giuseppe Acerbi 2003. *Address:* Brook Hall, Culmore Road, Derry, BT48 8JE, Northern Ireland (home). *Telephone:* (28) 7135-1297 (home).

JOHNSTON, Julia Ann; Canadian writer; b. 21 Jan. 1941, Smith Falls, ON; m. Basil W. Johnston 1963, four d. *Education:* University of Toronto, Trent University. *Career:* mem. Canadian Society of Children's Authors; Writers' Union of Canada. *Publications:* There's Going to be a Frost 1979, Don't Give Up the Ghosts 1981, Tasting the Alternative 1982, After 30 Years of Law, Ken Starvis Sculpts New Career 1990, Hero of Lesser Causes 1992, The Interiors of Pots 1992, Adam and Eve and Pinch Me 1994, The Only Outcast 1998, Love Ya Like A Sister (Ed.) by Katie Ouniour, In Spite of Killer Bees 2001. *Honours:* Hon. DLitt (Trent) 1996; Governor-General's Literary Award 1992, School Library Best Book 1993, Joan Fassler Memorial Award 1994, Ruth Schwartz Young Adult Book Award 1995, Canadian Library Asscn Young Adult Book Award 1995, Vicky Metcalf Award for body of work inspirational to youth 2003. *Address:* 463 Hunter Street W, Peterborough, ON K9H 2M7, Canada.

JOHNSTON, Kenneth Richard, BA, MA, PhD; American academic and writer; *Ruth N. Halls Chair of English, Indiana University;* b. 20 April 1938, Marquette, MI; m. 1st Elizabeth Louise Adolphson (divorced); two s. one d.; m. 2nd Ilinca Marina Zarifopol (deceased); one s. *Education:* Augustana College, Univ. of Chicago, Yale Univ. *Career:* Instructor in English, Augustana College 1962–63; Asst Prof., Indiana Univ. 1966–70, Assoc. Prof. 1970–75, Prof. of English 1975–2002, Ruth N. Halls Chair of English 2002–; Sr Fulbright Lecturer, Univ. of Bucharest 1974–75; Cox Family Distinguished Scholar, Univ. of Colorado 2003; mem. British Asscn for Romantic Studies, MLA, North American Soc. for the Study of Romanticism, Wordsworth-Coleridge Asscn. *Publications:* The Rhetoric of Conflict (ed.) 1969, Wordsworth and 'The Recluse' 1984, Wordsworth and Romanticism (with Gene W. Ruoff) 1987, The Age of William Wordsworth: Critical Essays on the Romantic Tradition (ed. with Gene W. Ruoff) 1988, Romantic Revolutions: Criticism and Theory (ed. with Karen Hanson) 1990, The Hidden Wordsworth: Poet, Lover, Rebel, Spy 1998; contrib. to scholarly books and journals. *Honours:* Hon. Fellow Inst. for Advanced Study in the Humanities, Univ. of Edinburgh 1998; Guggenheim Fellowship, Nat. Endowment for the Humanities Fellowships, Fulbright

Fellow, UK 2005–06, Mellon Emer. Fellow 2006–07. *Address:* c/o Department of English, Indiana University, Bloomington, IN 47405, USA (office). *E-mail:* johnstonk@indiana.edu (office).

JOHNSTON, Ronald John, MA, PhD, FBA; British geographer and academic; *Professor of Geography, University of Bristol;* b. 30 March 1941, Swindon; s. of Henry Louis Johnston and Phyllis Joyce (née Liddiard) Johnston; m. Rita Brennan 1963; one s. one d. *Education:* The Commonweal Co. Secondary Grammar School, Swindon, Univ. of Manchester, Monash Univ. *Career:* Teaching Fellow, then lecturer, Dept of Geography, Monash Univ., Australia 1964–66; lecturer then Reader, Dept of Geography, Univ. of Canterbury, NZ 1967–74; Prof. of Geography, Univ. of Sheffield 1974–92, Pro-Vice-Chancellor for Academic Affairs 1989–92; Vice-Chancellor Univ. of Essex 1992–95; Prof. of Geography, Univ. of Bristol 1995–; Co-Ed. Environment and Planning 1979–2005, Progress in Human Geography 1979–2007; mem. Acad. of Learned Socs for the Social Sciences; Fellow, British Acad. *Publications:* author or co-author of more than 50 books, including Geography and Geographers, Philosophy and Human Geography, City and Society, The Geography of English Politics, A Nation Dividing?, Bell-ringing: the English Art of Change-Ringing, An Atlas of Bells; Ed. or Co-Ed. of more than 20 books, including Geography and the Urban Environment (six vols), The Dictionary of Human Geography; author or co-author of more than 700 articles in academic journals. *Honours:* Hon. DUniv (Essex) 1996; Hon. LLD (Monash, Australia) 1999; Hon. DLitt (Sheffield) 2002; Hon. DLH (Bath) 2005; Murchison Award, Royal Geographical Soc. (RGS) 1984, Victoria Medal (RGS) 1990, Hons Award for Distinguished Contribs, Asscn of American Geographers 1991, Prix Vautrin Lud 1999. *Address:* School of Geographical Sciences, University of Bristol, Bristol, BS8 1SS, England (office). *Telephone:* (117) 928-9116 (office). *Fax:* (117) 928-7878 (office). *E-mail:* r.johnston@bris.ac.uk (office). *Website:* www.bris.ac.uk/geog (office).

JOHNSTON, William; Irish writer, academic and priest; b. 30 July 1925, Belfast, Northern Ireland; s. of William Johnston and Winifred Clearkin. *Education:* Sophia Univ., Tokyo, Japan. *Career:* ordained a Jesuit Roman Catholic priest 1957; Prof. of Theology, Sophia University, Tokyo, 1960–90. *Publications:* The Mysticism of the Cloud of Unknowing, 1967; S. Endo: Silence (trans.), 1969; The Still Point: On Zen and Christian Mysticism, 1970; Christian Zen, 1971; The Cloud of Unknowing and the Book of Privy Counselling (ed.), 1973; Silent Music, 1974; The Inner Eye of Love, 1978; The Mirror Mind, 1981; T. Nagai, The Bells of Nagasaki (trans.), 1984; The Wounded Stag, 1985; Being in Love: The Practice of Christian Prayer, 1988; Letters to Contemplatives, 1991; Mystical Theology, 1995; Arise My Love.: Mysticism for a New Era, 2000, Mystical Journey (autobiog.). *Address:* c/o S. J. House, 7 Kioi-Cho, Chiyoda-ku, Tokyo 102, Japan (home).

JÓKAI, Anna, BA; Hungarian writer; b. 24 Nov. 1932, Budapest; d. of Gyula Jókai and Anna Jókai (née Lukács); m. 3rd Sándor Kapocsi 1983; one s. one d. *Education:* Univ. Eötvös Loránd, Budapest. *Career:* accountant 1951–61; teacher 1961–76; freelance writer 1976–; Pres. Hungarian Writers' Asscn 1990–93. *Publications include:* 4447 1968, Tartozik és követel (Debit and Credit, novel) 1970, Napok (Days, novel) 1972, A reimsi angyal (The Angel from Reims, short-stories) 1975, Jákob lajtorjája (Jacob's Ladder, novel) 1982, A feladat (The Task, novel) 1985, Az együttlét (The Being Together, novel) 1987, Szegény Sudár Anna (Poor Anna Sudár, novel) 1989, Ne féljetek (Fear Not, novel) (Book of the Year Prize 1998), Virágvasárnap alkonyán (Sunset of Flower-Sunday, poems) 2004, Majd (The Future, short stories) 2005, Breviarium 2005. *Honours:* Jòzsef Attila Prize 1971, Int. Pietrczak Pax Literary Prize, Poland 1980, Kossuth Prize 1994, Hungarian Heredity Prize 1998, The Book of the Year Prize 1998, Centre for European Times Prize 1999, Hungarian Art Prize 2000, Arany János Grand-Prize 2004, Prima Primissima Prize 2004, Stephanus Prize 2006. *Address:* Vas Gereben u. 211, 1194 Budapest, Hungary (home). *Telephone:* (1) 357-2411 (home). *Fax:* (1) 357-2411 (home).

JOLLY, James; British writer. *Education:* Univ. of Bristol, Univ. of Reading. *Career:* producer, Record Review (BBC Radio 3); Asst Ed. Gramophone –1989, Ed. 1990–2005, Ed.-in-Chief 2006–; co-presenter The Classical Collection (BBC Radio 3) 2007. *Publications as editor:* The Greatest Classical Recordings of All Time 1995, The Gramophone Opera 75: The 75 Best Opera Recordings of All Time 1997, The Gramophone Opera Good CD Guide 1998, The Gramophone Classical 2001 Good CD Guide (co-ed.) 2002. *Address:* Gramophone, Haymarket Magazines Ltd, PO Box 568, Haywards Heath, Sussex RH16 3XQ, England (office). *Website:* www.gramophone.co.uk.

JONAS, Manfred, BS, AM, PhD; American historian and academic; *John Bigelow Professor Emeritus of History, Union College;* b. 9 April 1927, Mannheim, Germany; m. Nancy Jane Greene 1952; two s. two d. *Education:* City Coll., CUNY, Harvard Univ. *Career:* Visiting Prof. for North American History, Free Univ. of Berlin, 1959–62; Asst Prof. to Prof. of History, Union Coll., Schenectady, NY 1963–81, Washington Irving Prof. in Modern Literary and Historical Studies 1981–86, John Bigelow Prof. of History 1986–96, Emer. 1996–; Dr Otto Salgo Visiting Prof. of American Studies, Eötvös Lorand Univ., Budapest, Hungary 1983–84. *Publications:* Die Unabhängigkeitserklärung der Vereingten Staaten 1964, Isolationism in America 1935–1941 1966, American Foreign Relations in the 20th Century 1967, Roosevelt and Churchill: Their Secret Wartime Correspondence 1975, New Opportunities in the New Nation 1982, The United States and Germany: A Diplomatic History 1984; contribs to Diplomatic History, The Historian, Mid-America,

American Studies, Maryland Historical Magazine, Essex County Historical Collections, Jahrbuch für Amerikastudien. *Address:* Department of History, Union College, Schenectady, NY 12308, USA (office). *E-mail:* jonasm@union .edu (office).

JONES, Alun Arthur Gwynne (see Chalfont)

JONES, Alys, BA; Welsh writer; b. 15 Sept. 1944, Newborough, Anglesey, North Wales; m. Robin Jones 1973; one s. one d. *Education:* Univ. Coll., Bangor, North Wales. *Career:* teacher in Welsh, Maesteg Comprehensive School 1966–67, Machynlleth Secondary School, Powys 1967–70, Ysgol Dyffryn Conwy, Llanrwst 1970–74, Ysgol Glan Clwyd, Llanelwy 1974–75. *Publications:* Ysbrydion y Môr, 1982; Storiau Non, 1982; Storiau Huw a'i Ffrindiau, 1987; Dirgelwch Neuadd Henffordd, 1987; Mac Pync, 1987; Storiau Cornel y Cae, 1988; Yr Ysbryd Arian, 1989; Y Gadwyn, 1989; Jetsam, 1991; Straeon Cornel y Stryd, 1994; Cuthbert Caradog, 1998; Pwtyn Escapes, 1998; Pwtyn ar Goll, 2001; Clymau Ddoe, 2001; Pwtyn and Pwtan go to School, 2001; Pwytn and Pwtan Meet, 2002. Contributions: CIP; Heno Heno (short story anthology), 1990; group reading booklet, Isle of Anglesey County Council, 2000. *Address:* Llys Alaw, 18 Ystad Eryri, Bethel, Caernarfon, Gwynedd, North Wales.

JONES, Robert (Bobi) Maynard, BA, MA, PhD, DLitt, FBA; British academic and writer; *Professor Emeritus, University of Wales, Aberystwyth;* b. 20 May 1929, Cardiff, Wales; m. Anne Elizabeth James 1952; one s. one d. *Education:* Univ. of Wales, Cardiff. *Career:* Lecturer, Trinity Coll., Carmarthen 1956–58; Lecturer, Univ. of Wales, Aberystwyth 1959–67, Sr Lecturer to Reader 1967–79, Prof. of Welsh and Dept 1980–89, Prof. Emer. 1989–; Chair. Yr Academi Gymreig 1975–79. *Publications:* Y Gân Gyntaf 1956, Nid yw Dŵr Yn Plygu 1958, Rhwng Taf A Thaf 1960, Allor Wydn 1971, Tafod Y Llenor 1974, Llên Cymru A Chrefydd 1977, Seiliau Beirniadaeth 1984–85, Hunllef Arthur 1986, Llenyddiaeth Gymraeg 1902–1936 1987, Selected Poems 1987, Casgliad o Gerddi 1989, Crio Chwerthin 1990, Cyfriniaeth Gymraeg 1994, Canu Arnaf 1994, 1995, Ysbryd Y Cwlwm 1998, Ynghylch Tawelwch 1998, Tair Rhamant Arthuraidd 1998, O'r Bedd i'r Crud 2000, Mawl a'i Gyfeillion 2000, Mawl a Gelynion ei Elynion 2002, Ôl Troed 2003, Beirniadaeth Gyfansawdd 2003, Rhy Iach 2004, Y Fadarchen Hudol 2005, Meddwl y Gynghanedd 2005. *Honours:* Welsh Arts Council Prizes 1956, 1959, 1971, 1987, 1990, 1998. *Address:* Tandderwen, Ffordd Llanbadarn, Aberystwyth, SY23 1HB, Wales (home). *Telephone:* (1970) 626603 (home). *Fax:* (1970) 626603 (home).

JONES, Brian; British poet and writer; b. 1938, London, England. *Publications:* Poems, 1966; A Family Album, 1968; Interior, 1969; The Mantis Hand and Other Poems, 1970; For Mad Mary, 1974; The Spitfire on the Northern Line, 1975; The Island Normal, 1980; The Children of Separation, 1985; Freedom John, 1990. *Honours:* Cholmondeley Award, 1967; Eric Gregory Award, 1968.

JONES, Charlotte; British playwright and writer; m. Paul Bazely. *Education:* Balliol Coll., Oxford. *Career:* fmr actress. *Plays:* Airswimming (Battersea Arts Centre, London) 1997, In Flame (Bush Theatre, London) 1999, Martha, Josie and the Chinese Elvis (Octagon, Bolton) 1999, Humble Boy (Royal Nat. Theatre, London) 2001, The Dark (Donmar Warehouse, London) 2004, The Woman in White (The Book) 2004, The Lightening Play (Almeida Theatre) 2006. *Radio:* for BBC Radio 4: The Sound of Solitary Waves, Mary Something Takes the Veil, Future Perfect, A Seer of Sorts, Sea Symphony for Piano and Child 2001, Blue Air Love and Flowers. *Television:* Bessie and the Bell (Carlton) 2000, Mother's Ruin (Carlton) 2001. *Film:* Dogstar 2000. *Publications:* In Flame 2001, Martha, Josie and the Chinese Elvis 1999, Humble Boy 2001, The Woman in White (book to musical, based on Wilkie Collins' novel) 2004. *Honours:* Manchester Evening News Best Play Award 1999, Pearson TV Best Play Award 1999, Critics' Circle Award for Most Promising Playwright 2000, Susan Smith Blackburn Award 2001, Critics' Circle Best New Play Award 2002, People's Choice Best New Play Award 2002. *Literary Agent:* PFD, Drury House, 34–43 Russell Street, London, WC2B 5HA, England.

JONES, Christopher Dennis, BA; American playwright; b. 13 Dec. 1949, New York; m. Gwendoline Shirley Rose 1979. *Education:* University of Pittsburgh. *Career:* Resident Playwright, Carnaby Street Theatre, London, 1975–76, New Hope Theatre, London, 1977–78; mem. Writer's Guild of Great Britain. *Publications:* Plays: Passing Strangers, 1975; Nasty Corners, 1977; New Signals, 1978; In Flight Reunion, 1979; Sterile Landscape, 1982; Ralph Bird's River Race, 1985; Dying Hairless With a Rash, 1985; Bitter Chalice, 1987; Begging the Ring, 1989; Burning Youth, 1989. Contributions: Country Life; Arts Review.

JONES, Diana Wynne, BA; British writer; b. 16 Aug. 1934, London, England; m. John A. Burrow 1956; three s. *Education:* St Anne's Coll., Oxford. *Career:* writer of books for children, young adults and adults 1973–; mem. Soc. of Authors, BSFA. *Film:* Howl's Moving Castle (animated film directed by Hayao Miyazaki) 2004. *Publications:* Changeover 1970, Wilkin's Tooth 1973, The Ogre Downstairs 1974, Cart and Cwidder (Dalemark quartet book one) 1975, Dogsbody 1975, Eight Days of Luke 1975, Power of Three 1976, Drowned Ammet (Dalemark quartet book two) 1977, Charmed Life (Chrestomanci series) (Guardian Award for Children's Books 1978) 1977, Who Got Rid of Angus Flint? 1978, The Spellcoats (Dalemark quartet book three) 1979, The Four Grannies 1980, The Magicians of Caprona (Chrestomanci series) 1980, The Homeward Bounders 1981, The Time of the Ghost 1981,

Witch Week (Chrestomanci series) 1982, Archer's Goon 1984, Warlock at the Wheel and Other Stories 1984, The Skiver's Guide 1984, Fire and Hemlock 1985, Howl's Moving Castle 1986, A Tale of Time City 1987, The Lives of Christopher Chant (Chrestomanci series) 1988, Chair Person 1989, Hidden Turnings (ed.) 1989, Wild Robert 1989, Castle in the Air 1990, Black Maria 1991, Yes Dear 1992, A Sudden Wild Magic 1992, The Crown of Dalemark (Dalemark quartet book four) 1993, Stopping for a Spell: Three Fantasies 1993, Hexwood 1993, Fantasy Stories (ed.) 1994, Everard's Ride 1995, The Time of the Ghost 1996, A Tough Guide to Fantasyland 1996, Minor Arcana 1996, Deep Secret 1997, Dark Lord of Derkholm 1998, Year of the Griffin 2000, Mixed Magics (Chrestomanci series) 2000, The Merlin Conspiracy 2003, Aunt Maria 2003, Unexpected Magic: Collected Stories 2004, Stealer of Souls 2004, Conrad's Fate (Chrestomanci series) 2005, The Pinhoe Egg 2006. *Honours:* Hon. DLitt (Univ. of Bristol) 2006; Boston Globe/Horn Honour Book 1986, Mythopoeic Fantasy Awards 1995, 1999, Karl Edward Wagner Fantasy Award 1999, Phoenix Award 2006. *Literary Agent:* c/o Laura Cecil, 17 Alwyne Villas, London, N1 2HG, England. *Address:* c/o HarperCollins Publishers, 77–85 Fulham Palace Road, Hammersmith, London, W6 8JB, England (office). *Website:* www.dianawynnejones.com.

JONES, Douglas Gordon, MA; Canadian poet and retd academic; b. 1 Jan. 1929, Bancroft, ON. *Education:* Queen's Univ., Kingston, ON. *Career:* Prof., Univ. of Sherbrooke, Québec 1963–94. *Publications:* poetry: Frost on the Sun 1957, The Sun is Axeman 1961, Phrases from Orpheus 1967, Under the Thunder the Flowers Light Up the Earth 1977, A Throw of Particles: Selected and New Poems 1983, Balthazar and Other Poems 1988, The Floating Garden 1995, Wild Asterisks in Cloud 1997, Grounding Sight 1999; other: Butterfly on Rock: A Study of Themes and Images in Canadian Literature 1970. *Honours:* Hon. DLitt (Guelph Univ.) 1982; Univ. of Western Ontario Pres.'s Medal 1976, Gov.-Gen.'s Award for Poetry 1977, and for Translation 1993. *Address:* 120 Houghton Street, North Hatley, QC J0B 2C0, Canada (home). *Telephone:* (819) 842-2404 (home). *Fax:* (819) 842-1106 (home). *E-mail:* dgjones@abacom .com (home).

JONES, Dylan; British journalist; *Editor-in-Chief, GQ magazine;* m. *Career:* Ed., Arena 1989–92; fmrly Ed. i-D magazine, Group Ed. Wagadon (publisher of Arena, The Face, etc.), Sr Ed. The Sunday Times, The Observer, Ed.-at-Large The Sunday Times Magazine; has also worked for The Independent and The Guardian; currently Editor-in-Chief, GQ; Chair. British Soc. of Magazine Editors. *Publications include:* Jim Morrison: Dark Star 1991, Sex, Power and Travel: 10 Years of Arena (ed. and contrib.) 1996, Meaty, Beaty, Big and Bouncy: Classic Rock and Pop Writing from Elvis to Oasis 1996, Ultra Lounge: The Lexicon of Easy Listening 1997, iPod, Therefore I Am 2005. *Honours:* four Magazine Editor of the Year awards 1993. *Address:* GQ, Vogue House, Hanover Square, London, W1S 1JU, England. *Website:* www.gq-magazine.co .uk.

JONES, Edward P.; American writer; b. Washington, DC. *Education:* Holy Cross Coll., Univ. of Virginia. *Publications:* Lost in the City (short stories) 1992, The Known World (novel) (Pulitzer Prize for Fiction 2004, Int. IMPAC Dublin Literary Award 2005) 2003, All Aunt Hagar's Children 2006. *Honours:* PEN/Hemingway Award 1993, Nat. Book Critics' Circle Award for Fiction, Lannan Foundation grant. *Address:* c/o HarperCollins Publishers Inc., 10 East 53rd Street, New York, NY 10022, USA (office). *Website:* www .harpercollins.com.

JONES, Evan Lloyd, BA, MA; Australian poet, writer and photographer; b. 20 Nov. 1931, Preston, Vic.; m. 1st Judith Anne Dale 1954; one s.; m. 2nd Margot Sanguinetti 1966; three d. *Education:* Univ. of Melbourne, Stanford Univ., USA. *Publications:* poetry: Inside the Whale 1960, Understandings 1967, Recognitions 1978, Left at the Post 1984, Alone at Last! (CD); prose: Kenneth Mackenzie 1969, The Poems of Kenneth Mackenzie (ed. with Geoffrey Little) 1972; contrib. of innumerable essays and reviews in venues ranging from learned journals to newspapers, on topics ranging from literature to physics. *Address:* PO Box 122, Carlton North, Vic. 3054 (office); 104 Garton Street, Carlton North, Vic. 3054, Australia (home). *Telephone:* (3) 9380-6664 (home). *Fax:* (3) 9388-1283 (home). *E-mail:* jonesel@ihug.com.au (home).

JONES, Frederick Malcolm Anthony, MA, PhD; British academic, writer and poet; *Senior Lecturer, School of Archaeology, Classics and Egyptology, University of Liverpool;* b. 14 Feb. 1955, Middx, England; two s. *Education:* Univs of Newcastle upon Tyne, Leeds and St Andrews. *Career:* Asst Lecturer, Univ. of Cape Town, SA 1982–86; Teacher of Classics, Cobham Hall, Kent 1987–89; Lecturer in Classics and Ancient History, Univ. of Liverpool 1989–96, Sr Lecturer in Classics, School of Archaeology, Classics and Egyptology 1996–; mem. Cambridge Philological Soc., Soc. for the Promotion of Roman Studies. *Publications:* Congreve's Balsamic Elixir 1995, Nominum Ratio 1996; contribs to journals, reviews and periodicals. *Honours:* one of ten jt winners, Northern Poetry Competition 1991, Felicia Hemans Prize for Lyrical Poetry 1991. *Address:* School of Archaeology, Classics and Egyptology, University of Liverpool, Room 2.08, 12 Abercromby Square, Liverpool, L69 3BX, England (office). *Telephone:* (151) 794-2347 (office). *Fax:* (151) 794-2442 (office). *E-mail:* fjones@liv.ac.uk (office). *Website:* www.liv.ac.uk/sace/ organisation/people/jones.htm (office); www.jonesprints.co.uk (home).

JONES, Gwyneth, (Ann Halam); British writer and critic; b. 14 Feb. 1952, Manchester; m.; one s. *Education:* Univ. of Sussex. *Publications:* novels: Divine Endurance 1984, Escape Plans 1986, The Hidden Ones 1988, Kairos 1988, White Queen 1991, Flowerdust 1993, North Wind 1994, Seven Tales and a Fable 1995, Phoenix Cafe 1997, Bold as Love 2001, Castles Made of Sand 2002, Midnight Lamp 2003, Band of Gypsys 2004, Life 2004, Rainbow Bridge 2006; criticism: Deconstructing The Starships – Science Fiction and Reality 1999; juvenile: The Haunting of Jessica Raven 1997, Don't Open Your Eyes 2000; other: Identifying the Object – A Collection of Short Stories 1993; as Ann Halam: novels: Ally Ally Aster 1981, The Alder Tree 1982, King Death's Garden 1986, The Daymaker 1987, Transformations 1988, The Skybreaker 1990, Dinosaur Junction 1991, The Haunting of Jessica Raven 1993, The Fear Man 1995, The Powerhouse – A Horror Story 1997, Crying in the Dark 1998, The N.I.M.R.O.D. Conspiracy 1999, Don't Open Your Eyes 2000, The Shadow on the Stairs 2000, Dr Franklin's Island 2001, Taylor Five 2002, Finders Keepers 2004, Siberia 2005, The Visitor 2006, Snakehead 2007; contrib. to Wild Hearts in Uniform, in Fictions (ed Darko Suvin) 2005. *Honours:* two World Fantasy Awards, BFSA Short Story Award, Tiptree Award 1992, Arthur C. Clarke Award 2001; as Ann Halam: Children of the Night Award 1995, W Sussex Book Award 2001. *Literary Agent:* c/o David Higham Associates, 5–8 Lower John Street, Golden Square, London, W1F 9HA, England. *Telephone:* (20) 7434-5900. *Fax:* (20) 7437-1072. *E-mail:* dha@ davidhigham.co.uk. *Website:* www.davidhigham.co.uk. *E-mail:* gwyneth .jones@ntlworld.com (home). *Website:* www.boldaslove.co.uk; homepage .ntlworld.com/gwynethann (home).

JONES, Ivor Wynne; British journalist, author and lecturer; b. 28 March 1927, Liverpool, England; m. Marion-Jeannette Wrighton 1958, one s. one d. *Education:* Caernarfon Grammar School and BBC Engineering Training School. *Career:* co-founder of broadcasting in Cyprus; Ed. Caernarvon and Denbigh Herald 1953; Columnist 1955–, Welsh Political Correspondent 1969–92, Chief Welsh Correspondent 1980–92, Liverpool Daily Post; Research Ed. Llechwedd Slate Caverns, Blaenau Ffestiniog 1972–; mem. Yr Academi Gymreig (Welsh Acad.), Royal Historical Soc., Lewis Carroll Soc., UK, Lewis Carroll Soc. of North America, Lewis Carroll Soc. of Japan. *Publications:* Money for All 1969, Arian I Bawb 1969, Betws-y-coed, The Mountain Resort 1972, Shipwrecks of North Wales 1973, Betws-y-coed and the Conway Valley 1974, Llandudno, Queen of the Welsh Resorts 1975, America's Secret War in Welsh Waters 1976, Luftwaffe Over Clwyd 1977, U-Boat Rendezvous at Llandudno 1978, Minstrels and Miners 1986, Wales and Israel 1988, Baden-Powell, The Welsh Dimension 1992, The Order of St John in Wales 1993, Colwyn Bay: A Brief History 1995, Gold, Frankenstein and Manure 1997, BFBS Cyprus 1948–98 1998, Alice's Welsh Wonderland 1999, Wilder Wales 2001, Llandudno Queen of Welsh Resorts 2002, Victorian Slate Mining 2003, The Cairo Eisteddfod 2003, Money Galore 2003; contrib. to various historical journals. *Honours:* European Architectural Year Book Design Award 1975. *Address:* Pegasus, Llandudno Road, Penrhyn Bay, Llandudno, LL30 3HN, Wales (home).

JONES, J. Farragut (see Levinson, Leonard)

JONES, Joanna (see Burke, John Frederick)

JONES, J(on) Sydney, BA; American writer and teacher; b. 6 April 1948, Britton, SD. *Education:* Williamette University, University of Oregon, University of Vienna, Austria. *Career:* Journalist, 1971–76; Instructor, English as a Second Language and Writing, 1977–; mem. American Society of Journalists and Authors; Authors' Guild. *Publications:* Bike and Hike: Sixty Tours around Great Britain and Ireland, 1977; Vienna Inside-Out: Sixteen Walking Tours, 1979; Hitler in Vienna, 1983; Tramping in Europe: A Walking Guide, 1984; Viennawalks, 1985; Time of the Wolf, 1990; The Hero Game, 1992; Frankie, 1997. Contributions: articles to over 100 newspapers in the USA and Europe. *Literary Agent:* Evan Marshall, 6 Tristam Place, Pine Brook, NJ 07058, USA. *E-mail:* sjones@cats.ucsc.edu.

JONES, Julia; British writer and dramatist; b. 27 March 1923, Liverpool, England; m. Edmund Bennett 1950, one s. one d. *Education:* RADA, London. *Career:* mem. Dramatist Club, Writers' Guild of Great Britain. *Publications:* The Navigators,1986; over 50 plays for stage, film, radio and television. *Honours:* Prague Television Festival First Prize for Drama 1970.

JONES, (Everett) Le Roi Imamu Baraka; American poet and dramatist; b. 7 Oct. 1934, Newark, NJ; s. of Coyette L. Jones and Anna Lois (Russ) Jones; m. 1st Hettie R. Cohen 1958 (divorced 1965); two step-d.; m. 2nd Sylvia Robinson (Bibi Amina Baraka) 1966; five c.; one step-c. *Education:* Howard Univ., New School and Columbia Univ. *Career:* served with USAF; taught poetry at New School Social Research, drama at Columbia Univ., literature at Univ. of Buffalo; Visiting Prof., San Francisco State Univ.; began publishing 1958; founded Black Arts Repertory Theater School, Harlem 1964, Spirit House, Newark 1966; Whitney Fellowship 1963, Guggenheim Fellowship 1965; Fellow, Yoruba Acad. 1965; Visiting Lecturer, Afro-American Studies, Yale Univ. 1977–78; Asst Prof. of African Studies State Univ. of New York 1980–83, Assoc. Prof. 1983–85, Prof. 1985–; mem. Int. Co-ordinating Cttee of Congress of African Peoples; mem. Black Acad. of Arts and Letters. *Publications include:* Preface to a Twenty Volume Suicide Note 1961, Dante 1962, Blues People 1963, The Dead Lecturer 1963, Dutchman 1964, The Moderns 1964, The System of Dante's Hell 1965, Home 1965, Jello 1965, Experimental Death Unit 1965, The Baptism–The Toilet 1966, Black Mass 1966, Mad Heart 1967, Slave Ship 1967, Black Music 1967, Tales 1968, Great Goodness of Life 1968, Black Magic, Four Black Revolutionary Plays 1969, Black Art 1969, In Our Terribleness 1970, Junkies are Full of Shhh ..., Bloodrites 1970, Raise 1971, It's Nation Time 1971, Kawaida Studies 1972, Spirit Reach 1972, Afrikan

Revolution 1973, Hard Facts: Excerpts 1975, Spring Song 1979, AM/TRAK 1979, In the Tradition: For Black Arthur Blythe 1980, Reggae or Not! Poems 1982, The Autobiography of Le Roi Jones/Amiri Baraka 1984, Thornton Dial: Images of the Tiger 1993, Shy's, Wise, Y's: The Griot's Tale 1994; several film scripts; ed. Hard Facts 1976. *Address:* c/o State University of New York, Department of African Studies, Stony Brook, NY 11794, USA.

JONES, Madison Percy, BA, MA; American writer and academic (retd); b. 21 March 1925, Nashville, TN; m. Shailah McEvilley 1951, three s. two d. *Education:* Vanderbilt Univ., Univ. of Florida. *Career:* Instructor, Miami Univ. of Ohio 1953–54, Univ. of Tennessee 1955–56; Prof. of English and Writer-in-Residence, Auburn Univ. 1956–87; mem. Alabama Acad. of Distinguished Authors, Fellowship of Southern Writers. *Publications:* The Innocent 1957, Forest of the Night 1960, A Buried Land 1963, An Exile 1967, A Cry of Absence 1971, Passage Through Gehenna 1978, Season of the Stranger 1983, Last Things 1989, To the Winds 1996, Nashville 1864: The Dying of the Light 1997, Herod's Wife 2003; contrib. to journals and magazines. *Honours:* Sewanee Review Writing Fellowship 1954–55, Rockefeller Foundation Fellowship 1968, Alabama Library Asscn Book Award 1968, Guggenheim Fellowship 1973–74, Sewanee Review Lytle Annual Short Story Prize 1994, Ingersol Foundation T. S. Eliot Award 1998, US Civil War Center Michael Shaara Award 1998, Alabama Arts Foundation Harper Lee Award 1999. *Address:* 800 Kuderna Acres, Auburn, AL 36830, USA.

JONES, Malcolm Vince, BA, PhD; British academic and writer; *Professor Emeritus of Slavonic Studies, University of Nottingham;* b. 7 Jan. 1940, Stoke-sub-Hamdon, England; m. Jennifer Rosemary Durrant 1963; one s. one d. *Education:* Univ. of Nottingham. *Career:* Prof. Emer. of Slavonic Studies, Univ. of Nottingham; mem. British Asscn for Slavonic and East European Studies (Vice-Pres. 1988–91), British Univs' Asscn of Slavists (Pres. 1986–88), Int. Dostoyevsky Soc. (Pres. 1995–98). *Publications:* Dostoyevsky: The Novel of Discord 1976, New Essays on Tolstoy (ed.) 1978, New Essays on Dostoyevsky (ed. with Garth M. Terry) 1983, Dostoyevsky After Bakhin 1990, The Cambridge Companion to the Classic Russian Novel (ed. with Robin Feuer Miller) 1998, Dostoevsky and the Dynamics of Religious Experience 2005; contribs to scholarly journals. *Address:* Department of Russian and Slavonic Studies, University of Nottingham, University Park, Nottingham, NG7 2RD, England (office).

JONES, Marie, OBE; Northern Irish playwright and actress; b. 1951, Belfast; three c. *Career:* co-founder, writer-in-residence, Charabanc Theatre Co. 1983–90; co-founder, Double Joint Theatre Co. 1991. *Film appearances include:* In the Name of the Father, Best, Rebel Heart. *Plays:* Lay Up Your Ends 1983, Oul' Delf and False Teeth 1984, Now You're Talking 1985, Gold on the Streets 1986, Girls in the Big Picture 1987, Somewhere over the Balcony 1988, Under Napoleon's Nose 1988, The Hamster Wheel 1990, Weddings Wee'ins and Wakes 1990, The Government Inspector (adaptation of Gogol) 1994, A Night in November 1994, Ethel Workman is Innocent 1995, Women on the Verge of HRT 1996, A Night to Remember 1998, Stones in his Pockets 1999, The Blind Fiddler 2000, A Very Weird Manner 2003, The Blood of the Lamb 2007. *Writing for television:* Tribes 1990, The Hamster Wheel 1991, Fighting the Shadows 1992, Wingnut and the Sprog 1994. *Honours:* Hon. DLitt (Queen's Belfast, Ulster); Evening Standard Award for Best West End Comedy, John Hewitt Award, Olivier Award, Irish Times Theatre Award, Glasgow Mayfest Award. *Telephone:* (20) 7393-4400. *E-mail:* ben@curtisbrown.co.uk.

JONES, Mervyn; British writer; b. 27 Feb. 1922, London, England. *Education:* New York University. *Career:* Asst Ed., 1955–60, Drama Critic, 1958–66, Tribune; Asst Ed., New Statesman, London, 1966–68. *Publications:* No Time to Be Young, 1952; The New Town, 1953; The Last Barricade, 1953; Helen Blake, 1955; Guilty Men (with Michael Foot), 1957; Suez and Cyprus, 1957; On the Last Day, 1958; Potbank, 1961; Big Two (aka The Antagonists), 1962; Two Ears of Corn: Oxfam in Action (aka In Famine's Shadow: A Private War on Hunger), 1965; A Set of Wives, 1965; John and Mary, 1966; A Survivor, 1968; Joseph, 1970; Mr Armitage Isn't Back Yet, 1971; Life on the Dole, 1972; Holding On (aka Twilight of the Day), 1973; The Revolving Door, 1973; Lord Richard's Passion, 1974; Strangers, 1974; K. S. Karol: The Second Chinese Revolution (trans.), 1974; The Pursuit of Happiness, 1975; The Oil Rush (with Fay Godwin), 1976; Scenes from Bourgeois Life, 1976; Nobody's Fault, 1977; Today the Struggle, 1978; The Beautiful Words, 1979; A Short Time to Live, 1980; Two Women and Their Men, 1982; Joanna's Luck, 1985; Coming Home, 1986; Chances, 1987; That Year in Paris, 1988; A Radical Life, 1991; Michael Foot, 1994.

JONES, Michael Frederick; British journalist; b. 3 July 1937, Gloucester; s. of the late Glyn F. Jones and Elizabeth Coopey; m. Sheila Dawes 1959; three s. *Education:* Crypt Grammar School, Gloucester. *Career:* reporter on prov. newspapers 1956–64; Financial Times 1964–65; Daily Telegraph 1965–67; Business News Asst Ed. The Times 1967–70; Man. Ed. The Asian, Hong Kong 1971; News Ed. Sunday Times 1972, Political Corresp. 1975, Political Ed. 1984, Assoc. Ed. 1990–95, Assoc. Ed. (Politics) 1995–2002; Chair. Parl. Press Gallery, House of Commons 1989–91; Media Adviser, Memorial to the Women of World War II, London 2004–05; Visiting Fellow, Goldsmith's Coll., Univ. of London 2000–02. *Publication:* Betty Boothroyd: The Autobiography (collaborated) 2001. *Address:* 115 Cliffords Inn, Fetter Lane, London, EC4A 1BX, England (home). *Telephone:* (20) 7430-0443 (home). *E-mail:* micjon1937@hotmail.com (home).

JONES, Richard Andrew, III, BA, MA, MFA; British academic, poet, writer and editor; *Professor of English, DePaul University;* b. 8 Aug. 1953, London, England. *Education:* Univ. of Virginia, Vermont Coll. *Career:* Production Ed., CBS Books 1978–80; Ed., Poetry East 1979–, Scandinavian Review 1982–83; Adjunct Faculty, Piedmont Coll. 1981–82; Dir of Publications, American-Scandinavian Foundation 1982–83; Lecturer, Univ. of Virginia 1982–86; Teaching Fellow, Vermont Coll. 1985–87; Asst Prof., Ripon Coll. 1986–87; Prof. of English, DePaul Univ. 1987–; Illinois Artists Fellowship 1990–91; mem. Co-ordinating Council of Literary Magazines, Poetry Soc. of America. *Publications:* Windows and Walls 1982, Of Solitude and Silence: Writings on Robert Bly (ed., with Kate Daniels) 1982, Poetry and Politics (ed.) 1984, Innocent Things 1985, The Inward Eye: The Photographs of Ed Roseberry (ed., with S. Margulies) 1986, Walk On 1986, Country of Air 1986, Sonnets 1990, At Last We Enter Paradise 1991, A Perfect Time 1994, The Abandoned Garden 1997, 48 Questions 1998, The Last Believer in Words (ed.) 1998, The Stone It Lives On 1999, The Blessing: New and Selected Poems 2000; contrib. to numerous publications. *Honours:* Swedish Writers' Union Excellence Prize 1982, Co-ordinating Council of Literary Magazines Eds' Award 1985, and Citation of Special Commendation 1988, Council for Wisconsin Writers Posner Award for Best Book of Poetry 1986, Illinois Arts Council Awards 1991, 1995, 1996, 1997, 2000, 2002, Soc. of Midland Authors Award for Best Book of Poetry 2000, Via Sapentia Lifetime Achievement Award 2000. *Address:* c/o Department of English, DePaul University, 802 W Belden Avenue, Chicago, IL 60614, USA.

JONES, Rodney, BA, MFA; American poet and writer; b. 11 Feb. 1950, Hartselle, AL; m. 1st Virginia Kremza 1972 (divorced 1979); m. 2nd Gloria Nixon de Zepeda 1981, two c. *Education:* University of Alabama, University of North Carolina at Greensboro. *Career:* mem. Associated Writing Programs, MLA. *Publications:* Going Ahead, Looking Back, 1977; The Story They Told Us of Light, 1980; The Unborn, 1985; Transparent Gestures, 1989; Apocalyptic Narrative and Other Poems, 1993. Contributions: periodicals. *Honours:* Lavan Younger Poets Award, Acad. of American Poets, 1986; Younger Writers Award, General Electric Foundation, 1986; Jean Stein Prize, American Acad. and Institute of Arts and Letters, 1989; National Book Critics Circle Award, 1989.

JONES, Russell Celyn, MA; British novelist and critic; *Professor of Creative Writing, Birkbeck College, London;* b. 1955, Swansea, Wales; one s. two d. *Education:* Univ. of London and Iowa Univ., USA. *Career:* Lecturer in Creative Writing, Univ. of East Anglia, Univ. of Warwick, Western Cape Univ., South Africa; Prof. in Creative Writing, Birkbeck Coll., London 2003–; book reviewer, The Times; mem. Judging Panel, John Llewellyn Rhys Prize 1998, Booker Prize 2002: Dir Soc. of Authors. *Publications:* novels: Soldiers and Innocents 1990, Small Times 1992, An Interference of Light 1995, The Eros Hunter 1998, Surface Tension 2001, Ten Seconds from the Sun 2005; short fiction in anthologies: Time Out Book of New York Stories 1997, The Ex-Files 1998, Time Out Book of London Short Stories 2000, Summer Magic 2003; non-fiction: Dylan Thomas's Wales, The Atlas of Literature (ed. Malcolm Bradbury) 1996, Standards in Creative Writing Teaching, The Creative Writing Coursebook 2001. *Honours:* Fellowships at Iowa Univ., USA, Univ. of E Anglia; David Higham Prize for Best First Novel 1990, Welsh Arts Council Fiction Award 1991, Soc. of Authors Award 1996. *Literary Agent:* c/o AP Watt Ltd, 20 John Street, London, WC1N 2DR, England. *Telephone:* (20) 7405-6774. *Fax:* (20) 7831-2154. *E-mail:* apw@apwatt.co.uk. *Website:* www.apwatt.co.uk. *Address:* School of English and Humanities, Birkbeck, University of London, Malet Street, London, WC1E 7HX, England (office). *Telephone:* (20) 7679-1063 (office). *E-mail:* r.jones@bbk.ac.uk (office).

JONES, Sally Roberts, BA, ALA; British author and publisher; b. 30 Nov. 1935, London, England. *Education:* University College of North Wales, North-Western Polytechnic. *Career:* Senior Asst, Reference Library, London Borough of Havering, 1964–67; Reference Librarian, Borough of Port Talbot, Wales, 1967–70; Publisher, Alun Books, 1977–; Royal Literary Fund Fellow, University of Wales, Swansea, 1999–2001, Assoc. Fellow, 2002–02; mem. Port Talbot Historical Society. *Publications:* Turning Away, 1969; Elen and the Goblin, 1977; The Forgotten Country, 1977; Books of Welsh Interest, 1977; Allen Raine, 1979; Relative Values, 1985; The History of Port Talbot, 1991; Pendarvis, 1992. *Honours:* Welsh Arts Council Literature Prize 1970. *Address:* 3 Crown Street, Port Talbot, SA13 1BG, Wales.

JONES, J. Steve, PhD; British geneticist and writer; *Professor of Genetics, University College London;* b. 24 March 1944, Aberystwyth, Wales. *Education:* Wirral Grammar School, studied in Edinburgh and Chicago. *Career:* currently Prof. of Genetics, Univ. Coll. London; UCL representative to London Regional Science Centre; Pres. Galton Inst.; several visiting professorships, including Harvard Univ., Univ. of Chicago, Univ. of California at Davis, Univ. of Botswana, Fourah Bay Coll., Sierra Leone and Flinders Univ., Adelaide. *Radio and television includes:* gave Reith Lectures on 'The Language of the Genes' 1991, Blue Skies (BBC Radio 3), In the Blood (six-part TV series on human genetics) 1996. *Publications:* Genetics for Beginners (with B. van Loon) 1991, The Cambridge Encyclopedia of Human Evolution (ed. with R. D. Martin, D. Pilbeam) 1992, The Language of the Genes (Rhone-Poulenc Book Prize, Yorkshire Post First Book Prize 1994) 1993, In The Blood 1995, Almost like a Whale: The Origin of Species Updated (aka Darwin's Ghost) 1999, Y: The Descent of Men 2002, The Single Helix: A Turn Around the World of Science 2005; also around 100 scientific papers in a variety of journals and contrib. column, View from the Lab, to The Daily Telegraph. *Honours:* Royal

Soc. Faraday Medal for public understanding of science 1997, BP Natural World Book Prize 1999, 2000, Inst. of Biology Charter Medal 2002. *Address:* Department of Biology, University College London, Gower Street, London, WC1E 6BT, England (office). *E-mail:* j.s.jones@ucl.ac.uk (office). *Website:* www.ucl.ac.uk/biology/academic-staff/jones/jones.htm (office).

JONG, Erica Mann, MA; American writer and poet; b. 26 March 1942, New York; d. of Seymour Mann and Eda (Mirsky) Mann; m. 1st Michael Worthman 1963 (divorced 1965); m. 2nd Allan Jong 1966 (divorced 1975); m. 3rd Jonathan Fast 1977 (divorced 1983); one d.; m. 4th Kenneth David Burrows 1989. *Education:* Barnard Coll. and Columbia Univ., New York. *Career:* mem. Faculty, English Dept City Univ. of New York 1964–65, 1969–70; Overseas Div. Univ. of Md 1967–69; mem. Literature Panel, NY State Council on Arts 1972–74; mem. Faculty Salzburg Seminar, Salzburg, Austria 1993; Hon. Fellow (Welsh Coll. of Music and Drama) 1994. *Publications:* poetry: Fruits and Vegetables 1971, Half-Lives 1973, Loveroot 1975, At the Edge of the Body 1979, Ordinary Miracles 1983, Becoming Light: Poems New and Selected 1991; novels: Fear of Flying 1973, How to Save Your Own Life 1977, Fanny: Being the True History of Fanny Hackabout-Jones 1980, Parachutes and Kisses 1984, Serenissima: A Novel of Venice (aka Shylock's Daughter: A Novel of Love in Venice) 1987, Any Woman's Blues 1990, Inventing Memory: A Novel of Mothers and Daughters 1997, Sappho's Leap 2004; non-fiction: Witches 1981, Megan's Book of Divorce (for children) 1984, The Devil at Large: Erica Jong on Henry Miller 1993, Fear of Fifty: A Midlife Memoir 1994, Composer Zipless: Songs of Abandon from the Erotic Poetry of Erica Jong 1995, What Do Women Want? Bread. Roses. Sex. Power. 1998. *Honours:* New York State Council on the Arts Grants 1971, Nat. Endowment of the Arts grant 1973; Acad. of American Poets Prize 1971, Poetry magazine Bess Hokin Prize 1971, Poetry Soc. of America Alice Faye di Castagnola Award 1972, Deuville Film Festival Prix Littéraire 1997. *Literary Agent:* c/o K. D. Burrows, Erica Jong Productions, 425 Park Avenue, New York, NY 10022-3506, USA. *Telephone:* (212) 980-6922. *Fax:* (212) 421-5279. *E-mail:* erica@ericajong.com. *Website:* www.ericajong.com (office).

JOOLZ (see Denby, Joolz)

JORDAN, Leonard (see Levinson, Leonard)

JORDAN, Neil Patrick, BA; Irish writer and film director; b. 25 Feb. 1950, Sligo; three s. two d. *Education:* St Paul's Coll. Raheny, Dublin and Univ. Coll. Dublin. *Career:* co-f. Irish Writers' Co-operative, Dublin 1974. *Films directed:* Angel 1982, Company of Wolves 1984, Mona Lisa 1986, High Spirits 1988, We're No Angels 1989, The Miracle 1990, The Crying Game 1992, Interview with the Vampire 1994, Michael Collins (Golden Lion, Venice 1996) 1995, The Butcher Boy 1997, In Dreams 1999, The End of the Affair 1999, Not I 2000, The Good Thief 2002, Breakfast on Pluto (Best Dir, Best Writer, Irish Film and Television Awards 2007) 2005. *Publications:* Night in Tunisia and Other Stories (Guardian Fiction Award 1979) 1976, The Past 1979, The Dream of a Beast 1983, Sunrise with Sea Monster 1994, Nightlines 1995, Shade (novel) 2004. *Honours:* Dr hc (Univ. Coll. Dublin) 2005; London Film Critics' Circle Award 1984, London Evening Standard Most Promising Newcomer Award 1982, Los Angeles Film Critics' Circle Award 1992, NY Film Critics' Circle Award 1992, Writers Guild of America Award 1992, BAFTA Awards 1992, 2000, Golden Lion, Venice Film Festival 1996, Silver Bear, Berlin Film Festival 1997. *Literary Agent:* Jenne Casarotto Co. Ltd, National House, 60–66 Wardour Street, London, WIV 3HP, England. *Address:* 2 Martello Terrace, Bray, Co. Wicklow, Ireland.

JOSE, Francisco Sionil; Philippine writer, social activist and publisher; b. 3 Dec. 1924, Rosales; m. Teresita 1949. *Education:* Univ. of Santo Tomas. *Career:* fmr journalist and ed. The Commonwealth, United States Information Service, The Manila Times Sunday Magazine, Progress, Comment, Manila; Man. Ed. The Asia Magazine, Hong Kong 1961–62; Information Officer The Colombo Plan, Sri Lanka 1962–64; correspondent The Economist 1968–69; f. of publishing house, Solidaridad 1965–, journal Solidarity 1966–, Chair. Solidarity Foundation 1987–; fmr Lecturer Univ. of The Philippines, Manila, De La Salle Univ., Manila, Far Eastern Univ., Manila, Univ. of Santo Tomas, Univ. of Calif. at Berkeley, USA; writer-in-residence Nat. Univ. of Singapore 1987, Stanford Univ., USA 2005; founder and nat. sec. PEN (Philippines branch). *Publications:* novels: Rosales Saga: The Pretenders 1962, Tree 1978, My Brother, My Executioner 1979, Two Filipino Women 1981, Mass 1982, Po-on (Dusk) 1984, Ermita 1988, Gagamba 1991, Three Filipino Women 1992, Viajero 1993, Sin 1994, Sins 1996, Ben Singkol 2002; short story collections: The God Stealer and Other Stories 1968, Waywaya, Eleven Filipino Short Stories 1980, Platinum, Ten Filipino Stories 1983, Olvidon and Other Short Stories 1988, Puppy Love 1999, The Molave and the Orchid 2004; poetry: Questions 1988; non-fiction: In Search of the Word: Selected Essays of F. Sionil Jose, We Filipinos: Our Moral Malaise, Our Moral Heritage 1999; editor: Equinox I 1965, Asian PEN Anthology 1966, A Filipino Agenda for the 21st Century 1987. *Honours:* Order of Sacred Treasure, Japan 2001; Hon. PhD (Univ. of the Philippines, Manila) 1992, (De La Salle Univ., Manila) 1995, (Far Eastern Univ., Manila) 2000; three Nat. Press Club Annual Journalism Awards, three first prizes Palanca Annual Award for the English Short Story, City of Manila Award for Literature 1979, Cultural Centre of the Philippines Novel Award 1979, Literature Award (Gawad para sa Sining) 1989, Ramon Magsaysay Award for Journalism, Literature and Creative Communication Arts 1980, Tawid Award for Literature 1980, Palanca Annual Award for the English Novel 1981, National Artist for Literature, The Philippines 2001,

Pablo Neruda Award, Chile 2004. *Address:* Solidariad Publishing House, 531 Padre Faura, Ermita, Manila, The Philippines (office). *Telephone:* (2) 523-0870 (office). *Fax:* (2) 525-5038 (office). *E-mail:* soli@skyinet.net (office).

JOSEPH, Ammu, BA, BSc; Indian journalist. *Education:* Women's Christian Coll., Chennai, Syracuse Univ., New York, USA. *Career:* fmr Asst Ed. Eve's Weekly; fmr Magazine Ed. The India Post; Visiting Lecturer in Journalism, Sophia Coll. Polytechnic 1995–; columnist for The Hindu's Young World 1996–; Editorial Consultant for Voices for Change quarterly; freelance writer for various publs. *Publications include:* Whose News? The Media and Women's Issues (co-author and co-editor) 1994, Women in Journalism: Making News 2000, Terror, Counter-Terror: Women Speak Out (co-editor) 2003. *Address:* c/o The Media Foundation, 11c Dewan Shree, 30 Ferozshah Rd, New Delhi 11002, India (office).

JOSEPH, Jenny, BA, FRSL; British writer, poet and lecturer; b. 7 May 1932, Birmingham, England; m. C. A. Coles 1961 (died 1985); one s. two d. *Education:* St Hilda's Coll., Oxford. *Career:* mem. council Nat. Poetry Soc. of Great Britain 1975–78. *Publications:* The Unlooked-for Season 1960, "Warning" 1961, Boots 1966, Rose in the Afternoon 1974, The Thinking Heart 1978, Beyond Descartes 1983, Persephone 1986, The Inland Sea 1989, Beached Boats 1991, Selected Poems 1992, Ghosts and Other Company 1995, Extended Smiles 1997, Warning 1997, All the Things I See (poems for children) 2000, Led by the Nose: a garden of smells 2002, Extreme of Things 2006; contrib. to anthologies and magazines. *Honours:* Eric Gregory Award 1962, Cholmondeley Award 1974, Arts Council of Great Britain Award 1975, James Tait Black Memorial Prize for Fiction 1986, Soc. of Authors Travelling Scholarship 1995, Forward Prize 1995. *Literary Agent:* c/o Johnson & Alcock Ltd, Clerkenwell House, 45–47 Clerkenwell Green, London, EC1R 0HT, England. *Address:* 17 Windmill Road, Minchinhampton, Gloucestershire GL6 9DX, England.

JOSEPH, Lawrence, BA, JD, MA; American poet, essayist, critic and academic; b. 10 March 1948, Detroit, MI; m. 1976. *Education:* University of Michigan, University of Cambridge. *Career:* Law Clerk, Michigan Supreme Court, Justice G. Mennen Williams; Litigator, Shearman Sterling, New York City; Creative Writing Prof., Princeton University, NJ; Prof. of Law, St John's University School of Law, Jamaica, New York, 1987–; mem. PEN American Centre; Poetry Society of America; Poets House; National Writers Voice. *Publications:* Shouting at No One, 1983; Curriculum Vitae, 1988; Before Our Eyes, 1993; Lawyerland: What Lawyers Talk about When They Talk about Law, 1997. Contributions: Paris Review; Nation; Village Voice; Partisan Review; Poetry; Boulevard; Kenyon Review. *Honours:* Hopwood Award for Poetry, 1970; Agnes Lynch Starrett Poetry Prize, 1982; National Endowment for the Arts Poetry Award, 1984; Fellowship, University of Cambridge.

JOSIPOVICI, Gabriel David, BA, FRSL, FBA; British writer, dramatist and academic; b. 8 Oct. 1940, Nice, France. *Education:* St Edmund Hall, Oxford. *Publications:* fiction: The Inventory 1968, Words 1971, Mobius the Stripper 1974, The Present 1975, Migrations 1977, The Air We Breathe 1981, Contre-Jour 1986, In the Fertile Land 1987, The Big Glass 1990, In a Hotel Garden 1993, Moo Pak 1994, Now 1997, Goldberg: Variations 2002, Everything Passes 2006; essays: The World and the Book 1971, The Lessons of Modernism 1977, The Book of God: A Response to the Bible 1988, Text and Voice 1992, Touch 1996, On Trust 1998, A Life 2001, The Singer on the Shore 2005; plays: Dreams of Mrs Frazer 1973, AG 1976, Vergil Dying 1977, Mr Vee 1991; contrib. to Encounter, New York Review of Books, London Review of Books, TLS. *Honours:* Lord Northcliffe Lectures, Univ. of London 1981; Lord Weidenfeld Visiting Prof. of Comparative Literature, Univ. of Oxford 1996–97. *Literary Agent:* Johnson & Alcock Ltd, Clerkenwell House, 45–47 Clerkenwell Green, London, EC1R 0HT, England. *Address:* 60 Prince Edwards Road, Lewes, Sussex BN7 1BH, England.

JOUANNEAU, Joël; French writer and director; b. 1946, Celle, Loir-et-Cher. *Career:* f. amateur theatre collective, Grand Luxe 1970–; journalist Révolution early 1980s; Assoc. Artist Théâtre de Sartrouville 1989–, Co-Dir 1999–2003; teacher, École du Théâtre Nat. de Strasbourg 1992–2000, Conservatoire d'art dramatique, Paris 2000–. *Plays directed include:* La Dédicace (Théâtre Gérard Phillipe) 1984, L'Hypothèse (Festival d'Avignon) (also film) 1987, Minetti (also film) 1988, Les Enfants Tanner (also film) 1990, En attendant Godot 1991, Au coeur des ténèbres 1992, Le Rayon vert 1994, Compagnie 1995, Fin de partie 1995, L'Idiot 1995, Les Reines 1997, Coriolanus (Théâtre de l'Athénée, Paris) 1998, Juste la fin du monde (Théâtre Vidy Lausanne) 1999, Oh! les beaux jours 2001, Les Trois jours de la queue du dragon (opera for children) 2001, Madame on meurt ici! (Théâtre Vidy Lausanne) 2002, J'étais dans ma maison et j'attendais que la pluie vienne (Théâtre du peuple, Bussang) 2004, Kaddish pour l'enfant qui ne naîtra pas (with Jean-Quentin Châtelain) (Théâtre ouvert de Lucien et Micheline Attoun, Paris) 2004, Embrasser les ombres (Théâtre du Vieux-Colombier – Comédie Française) 2004. *Plays written include:* Nuit d'orage sur Gaza 1985, Le Bourrichon (Prix du Syndicat de la critique dramatique et musicale 1989) 1987, Kiki l'Indien 1987, Mamie Ouate en Papouasie (co-writer) 1990, Gauche Uppercut (Prix de la Critique de la SACD) 1991, Le Marin perdue en mer 1992, Le Condor 1994, Opus Allegria 147 (Prix du Syndicat de la Critique 1996) 1993, Dernier Rayon 1998, La Main bleue, Les Dingues de Knoxville 1999, L'Inconsolé 2001, Yeul le jeune 2001, L'Adoptée 2003, L'Ebloui 2004. *Films:* as director: L'Hypothèse (Prix spécial du jury du Festival de Riccione, Italy) 1987, Simon Tanner 1993, Endspiel 1996, Les Amants 2005. *Address:* 26 rue des Danes, 56290 Port-Louis, France. *E-mail:* joeljouanneau@wanadoo.fr.

JOYCE, Graham, BEd, MA, PhD; British writer; b. 22 Oct. 1954, Keresley, Coventry, England; m. Suzanne Lucy Johnsen 1988; one d. one s. *Education:* Univ. of Leicester. *Career:* mem. Soc. of Authors. *Publications:* Dreamside 1991, Dark Sister 1992, House of Lost Dreams 1993, Requiem 1995, The Tooth Fairy 1996, Spiderbite (juvenile) 1997, The Stormwatcher 1998, Indigo 1999, Leningrad Nights (short stories) 2000, Smoking Poppy 2001, The Facts of Life 2003, The Limits of Enchantment 2005, TWOC 2005. *Honours:* Derleth Awards 1993, 1996, 1997, 1999, World Fantasy Award 2004, Grand Prix de l'Imaginaire 2004. *Literary Agent:* c/o Luigi Bonomi, Luigi Bonomi Associates, 91 Great Russell Street, London, WC1B 3BS, England. *E-mail:* graham@grahamjoyce.net. *Website:* www.grahamjoyce.net.

JUDD, Alan, (Holly Budd), FRSL; British writer; b. 1946, Kent, England. *Education:* Univ. of Oxford. *Career:* army, Foreign Office; motoring correspondent, The Spectator. *Publications:* as Alan Judd: A Breed of Heroes 1981, Short of Glory 1984, The Noonday Devil 1987, Tango 1989, Ford Madox Ford 1990, The Devil's Own Work 1991, First World War Poets (with David Crane) 1997, The Quest for 'C': Sir Mansfield Cumming and the Founding of the British Secret Service 1999, Legacy 2001, The Kaiser's Last Kiss 2003, Dancing with Eva 2007; as Holly Budd: The Office Life Little Instruction Book 1996; contrib. to newpapers and magazines. *Honours:* RSL Award 1982, W. H. Heinemann Literature Award 1990, Guardian Fiction Award 1991. *Literary Agent:* David Higham Associates, 5–8 Lower John Street, Golden Square, London, W1F 9HA, England.

JUDD, Denis Onan, BA, PGCE, PhD, FRHistS; British historian and writer; b. 28 Oct. 1938, Byfield, Northants., England; m. Dorothy Woolf 1964; three s. one d. *Education:* Univs of Oxford and London. *Career:* awarded professorship 1990. *Publications:* Balfour and the British Empire 1968, The Boer War 1977, 2002, Radical Joe: Joseph Chamberlain 1977, Prince Philip 1981, Lord Reading 1982, Alison Uttley 1986, Jawaharlal Nehru 1993, Empire: The British Imperial Experience 1996, The Lion and the Tiger: The Rise and Fall of the British Raj 2004; other: two books for children; other history books and biographies; contrib. to History Today, History, Journal of Imperial and Commonwealth History, Literary Review, Daily Telegraph, New Statesman, International Herald Tribune, Independent, BBC History Magazine, Mail on Sunday. *Address:* 20 Mount Pleasant Road, London, NW10 3EL, England. *E-mail:* denisjudd@ntlworld.com.

JUDSON, John, BA, MFA; American educator, editor, writer and poet; b. 9 Sept. 1930, Stratford, CT. *Education:* Colby College, University of Maine, University of Iowa. *Career:* Ed., Juniper Press, Northeast/Juniper Books, literary magazine and chapbook series, 1961–; Prof. of English, University of Wisconsin, La Crosse, 1965–93. *Publications:* Two From Where It Snows (co-author), 1963; Surreal Songs, 1968; Within Seasons, 1970; Voyages to the Inland Sea, six vols, 1971–76; Finding Worlds in Winter; West of Burnam South of Troy, 1973; Ash Is the Candle's Wick, 1974; Roots from the Onion's Dark, 1978; A Purple Tale, 1978; North of Athens, 1980; Letters to Jirac II, 1980; Reasons Why I Am Not Perfect, 1982; The Carrabassett Sweet William Was My River, 1982; Suite for Drury Pond, 1989; Muse(sic), 1992; The Inardo Poems, 1996.

JUDT, Tony, BA, PhD, FRHistS; British historian and academic; *Erich Maria Remarque Professor in European Studies, New York University*; b. 1948, London, England. *Education:* King's Coll., Cambridge and Ecole Normale Supérieure, Paris. *Career:* fmrly taught at Univs of Cambridge, Oxford and Berkeley; Prof. of History, now Erich Maria Remarque Prof. in European Studies, New York Univ.; founder and Dir Remarque Inst., New York Univ. 1995–; Fellow American Acad. of Arts and Sciences; Guggenheim Fellow 1989. *Publications:* La Reconstruction du parti Socialiste 1921–1926 1976, Socialism in Provence 1871–1914: A Study in the Origins of the Modern French Left 1979, Marxism and the French Left: Essays on Labour and Politics in France 1830–1981 1986, Resistance and Revolution in Mediterranean Europe 1939–1948 1989, Past Imperfect: French Intellectuals 1944–1956 1992, A Grand Illusion? An Essay on Europe 1996, The Burden of Responsibility: Blum, Camus, Aron and the French Twentieth Century 1998, The Politics of Retribution in Europe: World War Two and its Aftermath (ed.) 2000, Postwar: A History of Europe Since 1945 2005; contrib. to The New Republic, The New York Review of Books, The New York Times, TLS and other journals. *Address:* Faculty of Arts and Science, New York University, King Juan Carlos I of Spain Center, 53 Washington Square South, 302, New York, NY 10012, USA (office).

JUERGENSMEYER, Mark Karl, BA, MDiv, MA, PhD; American academic and writer; *Director, Orfalea Center of Global and International Studies*; b. 13 Nov. 1940, Carlinville, IL; m. Sucheng Chan 1969. *Education:* University of Illinois at Urbana-Champaign, Columbia University, Union Theological Seminary, New York, University of California at Berkeley. *Career:* Lecturer, 1971–72, Dir, Religious Studies Program, 1977–89, University of California at Berkeley; Lecturer, 1973–74, Assoc. Prof., 1974–84, Prof., 1984–89, Dir, Comparative Religion Program, 1984–89, Graduate Theological Union, Berkeley; Distinguished Visiting Prof., University of California at Santa Cruz, 1988; Dean, Asian and Pacific Studies, and Prof. of Religion and Political Science, University of Hawaii, 1989–93; Prof. of Sociology, 1993–, Dir, Orfalea Center of Global and International Studies, 1995–, University of California at Santa Barbara; Chair, Pacific Rim Research Program, University of California System, 1994–97; Halle Distinguished Visiting Prof. of Global Learning, Emory University, 2002. *Publications:* Sikh Studies: Comparative Perspectives on a Changing Tradition (co-ed.), 1979; Religion as Social Vision: The Movement Against Untouchability in 20th-Century Punjab, 1982; Fighting with Gandhi, 1984, revised edn as Gandhi's Way: A Handbook of Conflict Resolution, 2002; Songs of the Saints of India (co-trans.), 1988; Imagining India: Essays on Indian History by Ainslie Embres (ed.), 1989; Teaching the Introductory Course in Religious Studies (ed.), 1991; A Bibliographic Guide to the Comparative Study of Ethics (co-ed.), 1991; Radhasoami Reality: The Logic of a Modern Faith, 1991; Violence and the Sacred in the Modern World (ed.), 1992; The New Cold War?: Religious Nationalism Confronts the Secular State, 1993; Terror in the Mind of God: The Global Rise of Religious Violence, 2000. *Contributions:* Reference works, scholarly books and professional journals. *Honours:* International Fellow, Columbia University, 1963–65; Indo-American Fellowship, India, 1978; American Institute of Indian Studies Senior Research Grants, 1979, 1983, 1985, 1986; Fellow, Woodrow Wilson International Center for Scholars, Washington, DC, 1986; Guggenheim Fellowship, 1988–90; Fellow, United States Institute of Peace, 1989–91; Fellow, ACLS, 1996. *Address:* c/o Global and International Studies, 3042 Humanities and Social Sciences Bldg, University of California at Santa Barbara, Santa Barbara, CA 93106, USA.

JULY, Serge; French journalist; b. 27 Dec. 1942, Paris; one s. *Career:* journalist Clarté 1961–63; Vice-Pres. Nat. Union of Students 1965–66; French teacher Coll. Sainte-Barbe, Paris 1966–68; Asst Leader Gauche prolétarienne 1969–72 (disbanded by the Govt); co-f. newspaper, Libération 1973, Chief Ed. 1973–2006, Publishing Dir 1981, Man. Dir 1981–2006; Reporter Europe 1983; mem. Club de la presse Europe 1976–. *Publications:* Vers la guerre civile (with Alain Geismar and Erlyne Morane) 1969, Dis maman, c'est quoi l'avant-guerre? 1980, Les Années Mitterrand 1986, La Drôle d'Année 1987, Le Salon des artistes 1989, La Diagonale du Golfe 1991, Entre quatre z'yeux (with Alain Juppé).

JUNGER, Sebastian, BA; American author and journalist; b. 1962, Belmont, MA. *Education:* Wesleyan Univ., CT. *Career:* climber and arborist 1989–96; foreign reporter 1996–; author 1997–. *Publications:* novels: The Perfect Storm 1997, Fire 2001, A Death in Belmont 2006; contrib. to Outside, City Paper, American Heritage, Men's Journal, Vanity Fair. *Honours:* Nat. Magazine Award, SAIS-Novartis Award, New England PEN Award 2007. *Address:* c/o Fourth Estate, HarperCollins Publishers Ltd, 77–85 Fulham Palace Road, London, W6 8JB, England (office).

JUNGK, Peter Stephan, American/Austrian writer; b. 19 Dec. 1952, Santa Monica, Calif; s. of Robert Jungk; m Lillian Birnbaum; one d. *Education:* Univ. of California at Los Angeles and American Film Inst. *Films:* documentary films for German TV. *Publications:* Stechpalmenwald 1978, Rundgang 1981, Franz Werfel: A Life in Prague, Vienna, and Hollywood 1990, Shabbat: A Rite of Passage in Jerusalem, A Life Torn by History: Franz Werfel 1890–1945 1990, Tigor 1991, Die Unruhe der Stella Federspiel 1996, Die Erbschaft 1999, Der König von Amerika 2001, The Snowflake Constant 2002, The Perfect American 2004, Die Reise über den Hudson 2005. *Address:* c/o Faber and Faber Ltd, 3 Queen Square, London, WC1N 3AU, England; 9B rue Michel Chasles, 75012 Paris, France (home). *Fax:* 1-43-45-48-99 (office). *E-mail:* peterjungk@gmail.com (home).

JUNKINS, Donald Arthur, BA, STB, STM, AM, PhD; American poet, writer and academic; b. 19 Dec. 1931, Saugus, MA; m. 1st; two s. one d.; m. 2nd Kaimei Zheng 1993; one step-s. *Education:* University of Massachusetts, Boston University. *Career:* Instructor, 1961–62, Asst Prof., 1962–63, Emerson College, Boston; Asst Prof., Chico State College, CA, 1963–66; Asst Prof., 1966–69, Assoc. Prof., 1969–74, Dir, Master of Fine Arts Program in English, 1970–78, 1989–90, Prof. of English, 1974–95, Prof. Emeritus, 1995–, University of Massachusetts, Amherst; mem. PEN; Hemingway Society; Fitzgerald Society. *Publications:* The Sunfish and the Partridge, 1965; The Graves of Scotland Parish, 1969; Walden, One Hundred Years After Thoreau, 1969; And Sandpipers She Said, 1970; The Contemporary World Poets (ed.), 1976; The Uncle Harry Poems and Other Maine Reminiscences, 1977; Crossing By Ferry: Poems New and Selected, 1978; The Agamenticus Poems, 1984; Playing for Keeps: Poems, 1978–1988, 1989; Andromache, by Euripides (trans.), 1998; Journey to the Corrida, 1998; Lines from Bimini Waters, 1998. Contributions: Longman Anthology of American Poetry: Colonial to Contemporary; reviews, journals and magazines. *Honours:* Bread Loaf Writers Conference Poetry Scholarship, 1959; Jennie Tane Award for Poetry, 1968; John Masefield Memorial Award, 1973; National Endowment for the Arts Fellowships, 1974, 1979.

JUST, Ward Swift; American writer; b. 5 Sept. 1935, Michigan City, IN. *Education:* Lake Forest Acad., IL, Cranbrook School, Michigan, Trinity Coll., Hartford, CT. *Career:* reporter, Waukegan News-Sun, IL 1957–59; reporter 1962–63, correspondent 1963–65, Newsweek magazine; correspondent, Washington Post 1965–70; Berlin Prize Fellowship 1998. *Publications:* To What End: Report from Vietnam 1968, A Soldier of the Revolution 1970, Military Men 1970, The Congressmen Who Loved Flaubert and Other Washington Stories 1973, Stringer 1974, Nicholson at Large 1975, A Family Trust 1978, Honor, Power, Riches, Fame and the Love of Women 1979, In the City of Fear 1982, The American Blues 1984, The American Ambassador 1987, Jack Gance 1989, Twenty-One Selected Stories 1990, The Translator 1991, Ambition and Love 1994, Echo House 1997, A Dangerous Friend 1999, Lowell Limpett 2001, The Weather in Berlin 2002, An Unfinished Season 2004, Forgetfulness 2006; contrib. to anthologies and periodicals. *Honours:* O. Henry Awards 1985, 1986. *Address:* Vineyard Haven, MA 02568, USA.

JUTEAU, Monique, MA; Canadian poet and writer; b. 8 Jan. 1949, Montréal, QC; d. of Aldéo Juteau and Jeanne Tranquil. *Career:* mem. Soc. des Écrivains de la Mauricie, Union des écrivaines et des écrivains québécois. *Publications:* poetry: La Lune Aussi 1975, Regard Calligraphes 1986, Trop Plein D'Angles 1990, Des jours de chemins perdus et retrouvés 1997; fiction: En Moins de Deux 1990, L'Emporte-Clé 1994, La Fin des Terres 2001, Une histoire pour chaque jour de la semaine 2003, Le voyage a dit 2005; contrib. to various publs.

Honours: Prix Gerald-Godin 1998, Prix Félix-Antoine-Savard 2001, Télé-Québec Prix Daring 2002, Second Prize, Radio-Canada Grands Prix Littéraires 2002, Télé-Québec Amb. 2003, Prix du Conseil des Arts et des Lettres à la Création artistique, Région Centre-du-Québec. *Address:* 19200 Forest, Bécancour, QC G9H 1P9, Canada. *Telephone:* (819) 233-2983 (home). *E-mail:* monique.juteau@uqtr.ca (office). *Website:* www.litterature.org/ile32000.asp?numero=265.

K

KAAVERI (see Kannan, Lakshmi)

KABAKOV, Alexander Abramovich; Russian writer and journalist; *Departmental Editor, Commersant Publishing;* b. 22 Oct. 1943, Novosibirsk; m.; one d. *Education:* Dniepropetrovsk Univ. *Career:* engineer space rocket production co. 1965–70; journalist Gudok 1972–88; columnist, then Deputy Ed.-in-Chief Moscow News 1988–97; special corresp. Commersant Publishing 1997–2000, Departmental Ed. 2000–; columnist New Media Publishing Group 2002–; first literary publ. 1975. *Publications:* Cheap Novel 1982, Cafe Yunost 1984, Oil, Comma, Canvas 1986, Approach of Kristapovich (triology) 1985, Obviously False Fabrications (collection of short stories) 1989, No Return 1989, Story-Teller 1991, Imposter 1992, The Last Hero (novel) 1995, Selected Prose 1997, One Day from the Life of a Fool 1998, The Arrival Hall 1999, Youth Café 2000, The Journey of an Extrapolator 2000, The Tardy Visitor 2001, Qualified as Escape 2001, Survivor 2003. *Honours:* Moscow Journalists' Union Prize 1989, Best Pens of Russia Award 1999, Short Story of the Year Award 1999. *Address:* New Media Publishing Group, Pyatnitzkaya str. 55, Moscow, Russia (office). *Telephone:* (495) 411-63-90 (office); (495) 994-83-45 (home); (495) 101-77-24.

KACEM, Abdelaziz; Tunisian essayist; b. 1933. *Career:* taught at Sorbonne, Univ. of Paris. *Publications:* Le Frontal 1983, Culture Arabe/ Culture Française: La Parenté Reniée 2002, Le voile est-il islamique? 2004; contrib. to Bulletin du Centre Culturel Arabe, La Gazette de la Presse Francophone. *Honours:* Hon. Curator, Bibliothèque de Tunis' Grand Prix de l'Académie Française 1998. *Address:* c/o Editions Harmattan, 5–7 rue de l'Ecole Polytechnique, Paris 75005, France.

KADARÉ, Ismail; Albanian writer; b. 28 Jan. 1936, Gjirokastër; s. of Halit Kadaré; m. Elena Gushi 1963; two d. *Education:* Univ. of Tirana and Gorky Inst., Moscow. *Career:* full-time writer since 1963; works translated into more than 30 languages; sought political asylum in Paris 1990; mem. Albanian Acad.; corresponding, then Assoc. Foreign mem. Acad. des sciences morales et politiques; mem. Acad. of Arts, Berlin, Acad. Mallarmé. *Plays:* Mauvaise saison pour Olymp. *Publications:* fiction: Gjenerali i ushtërisë së vdekur (trans. as The General of the Dead Army) 1963, Kështjella (trans. as The Castle) 1970, Kronikë në gur (trans. as Chronicle in Stone) 1971, The Great Winter (novel, in trans.) 1973, Ura më tri harque (trans. as The Three-Arched Bridge) 1978, The Twilight (in trans.) 1978, The Niche of Shame (in trans.) 1978, Kush e solli doruntinen (trans. as Who Brought Back Doruntine?) 1980, Prilli i thyer (trans. as Broken April) 1980, Nëpunësi I pallatit të ëndrrave (trans. as The Palace of Dreams) 1980, Nje dosje per Homerin (trans. as The H Dossier) 1980, Koncert në fund të dimrit (trans. as The Concert) 1985, Eschyle or The Eternal Loser (in trans.) 1988, Albanian Spring (in trans.) 1991, Le Monstre (in trans.) 1991, Piramida (trans. as The Pyramid) 1992, La Grande muraille 1993, Le Firman aveugle 1993, Clair de Lune 1993, L'Ombre 1994, L'Aigle 1996, Spiritus 1996, Oeuvres 1993–97 (12 vols) 1997, Temps barbares, de l'Albanie au Kosovo 1999, Il a fallu ce deuil pour se retrouver 2000, Froides fleurs d'avril (trans. as Spring Flowers, Spring Frost) 2000, L'envol du migrateur 2001, Vie, jeu et mort de Lul Mazrek 2002, La fille d'Agamemnon 2003, Le successeur 2003; six vols of poetry 1954–80, criticism, essays. *Honours:* Dr hc (Grenoble III) 1992, (St Etienne) 1997; Prix Mondial Cino del Duca 1992, Int. Booker Prize 2005. *Address:* c/o Librairie Arthème Fayard, 75 rue des Saints Pères, 75006 Paris (office); 63 blvd Saint-Michel, 75005 Paris, France (home). *Telephone:* (1) 43-29-16-20 (home).

KADMON, Jean Ball Kosloff, BA; American/Israeli poet, novelist and painter; b. 1 Aug. 1922, Denver, CO; m. 1945, two s. *Education:* University of Alberta, University of Chicago. *Career:* anthropologist, International Centre for Community Development, Haifa, Israel, 1964–65; Sociologist, Jewish Agency, Israel, 1966–68; mem. Israel Asscn of Writers in English; Voices Israel Poetry Asscn. *Publications:* Moshav Segev, 1972; Clais and Clock, 1988; Peering Out, 1996; MacKenzie Breakup, 1997, High Grandeur (poem) 2005, Commentary (poem) 2005, Lyric (poem) 2005, Solar Heater (poem) 2005, Guru (poem) 2005, Bus Voyage Station (novel) 2005, Summer Madness (novel) 2005, Shadows of the Oleander (novel) 2006. *Honours:* Second Prize, New Zealand International Writers Workshop, 1981; First prize, Ruben Rose International Poetry Contest, 2001. *Address:* 12 Zerubavel Street, Jerusalem 93504, Israel. *Telephone:* (2) 6733048. *E-mail:* kadmonj@yahoo.com.

KADOHATA, Cynthia Lynn; American writer; b. 7 Feb. 1956, Chicago, IL; m. 1992. *Education:* Los Angeles City College, University of South Carolina, University of Pittsburgh, Columbia University. *Publications:* The Floating World, 1989; In the Heart of the Valley of Love, 1992. Contributions: newspapers and magazines. *Honours:* National Endowment for the Arts grant 1991, Whiting Writers Award 1991.

KAGAN, Andrew Aaron, BA, MA, PhD; American art historian, art adviser and writer; b. 22 Sept. 1947, St Louis, MO; m. Jayne Wilner 1987. *Education:* Washington Univ., Harvard Univ. *Career:* Advisory Ed., Arts Magazine, 1975–89; Critic of Art, Music, Architecture, St Louis Globe Democrat, 1978–81; mem. Wednesday Night Society, founder, dir. *Publications:* Paul Klee/Art and Music, 1983; Rothko, 1987; Trova, 1988; Marc Chagall, 1989; Paul Klee at the Guggenheim, 1993; Absolute Art, 1995. Contributions: McMillan Dictionary of Art; Arts Magazine; Burlington Magazine; Others.

Honours: Harvard Prize Fellowship, 1970–77; Kingsbury Fellowship, 1977–78; Goldman Prize, 1985.

KAGAN, Donald, MA, PhD; American academic and writer; *Professor of Classics and History, Yale University;* b. 1 May 1932, Kurshan, Lithuania; m. Myrna Dabrusky 1955; two s. *Education:* Brooklyn College, CUNY, Brown University, Ohio State University. *Career:* part-time Instructor in History, Capital University, Columbus, Ohio 1957–58; Instructor in History, Pennsylvania State University 1959–60; Asst Prof. of Histor, Cornell University 1960–63, Assoc. Prof. of History 1964–66, Prof. of History 1967–69; Prof. of History and Classics Yale University 1969–, Chair. 1972–75, Acting Chair. 1986–87, Dept of Classics, Master, Timothy Dwight College 1976–78, Richard M. Colgate Prof. of History and Classics 1979–90, Dean, Yale College 1989–92, Bass Prof. of History and Western Civilization 1991–95, Hillhouse Prof. of History and Classics 1995–2002, Sterling Prof. of Classics and History 2002–; Fellow, Center for Advanced Study in the Behavioural Sciences, Stanford, CA 1992–93; Guest Scholar, Woodrow Wilson International Center for Scholars 1996; Jefferson Lecturer Nat. Endowment for the Humanities 2005. *Publications:* The Decline and Fall of the Roman Empire in the West (ed.) 1962, third edn as The End of the Roman Empire, Decline or Transformation? 1992, The Great Dialogue: A History of Greek Political Thought From Homer to Polybius 1965, Readings in Greek Political Thought (ed.) 1965, Problems in Ancient History (ed.), two vols 1966, Great Issues in Western Civilization (ed. with L. P. Williams and Brian Tierney), two vols 1967, The Outbreak of the Peloponnesian War 1969, Hellenic History, by Botsford and Robinson, revised edn 1969, The Archidamian War 1974, The Western Heritage (with Steven Ozment and Frank M. Turner) 1979, The Peace of Nicias and the Sicilian Expedition 1981, The Heritage of World Civilizations (with Albert Craig, William Graham, Steven Ozment and Frank M. Turner) 1986, The Fall of the Athenian Empire 1987, Pericles of Athens and the Birth of Democracy 1990, On the Origins of War and Preservation of Peace 1995, While America Sleeps (with Frederick W. Kagan) 2000, The Peloponnesian War 2003; contribs to scholarly books and professional journals, and to general periodicals. *Honours:* Hon. doctorates (New Haven) 1988, (Adelphi) 1990, (Dallas) 2001; Fulbright Fellowship 1958–59, Center for Hellenic Studies Fellowship, Washington, DC 1966–67, Nat. Endowment for the Humanities Senior Fellowship 1971–72Sidney Hook Memorial Award, National Asscn of Scholars 1994: Harwood Byrnes '08/Richard B. Sewall Teaching Prize, Yale College 1998, National Humanities Medal 2002. *Address:* 37 Woodstock Road, Hamden, CT 06517, USA.

KAGAN, Robert, BA, MA; American writer and journalist; b. 28 Sept. 1958, Athens, Greece; m. Victoria Nuland; one s. one d. *Education:* Yale Coll., Harvard Univ. *Career:* foreign policy adviser to Congressman Jack Kemp 1983; policy planning staff at US State Dept and principal speechwriter to Sec. of State George P. Schultz 1984–88; Sr Assoc. at the Carnegie Endowment for International Peace 1997–, Dir, US Leadership Project; mem., Council on Foreign Relations. *Publications:* non-fiction: A Twilight Struggle - American Power and Nicaragua (1977–1990) 1996, Present Dangers - Crisis and Opportunity in American Foreign and Defense Policy (ed. with William Kristol) 2000, Of Paradise and Power - America and Europe in the New World Order 2003, Dangerous Nation: America and the World 1600–1900 2006; contrib. journalism to Foreign Affairs, Foreign Policy Commentary, New York Times, New Republic, Wall Street Journal, National Interest, Policy Review, Weekly Standard (contrib. ed.); columnist, The Washington Post. *Address:* c/o Carnegie Endowment for International Peace, 1779 Massachusetts Avenue NW, Washington, DC 20036, USA. *Telephone:* (202) 483-7600. *Fax:* (202) 483-1840. *E-mail:* info@ceip.org. *Website:* www.ceip.org.

KAHN, James, BA, MD; American physician and writer; b. 30 Dec. 1947, Chicago, IL. *Education:* University of Chicago. *Career:* resident, Los Angeles County Hospital, 1976–77; University of California at Los Angeles, 1978–79; Physician, Emergency Room, Rancho Encino Hospital, Los Angeles, 1978–. *Publications:* Diagnosis Murder 1978, Nerves in Patterns (with Jerome McGann) 1978, World Enough and Time 1982, Time's Dark Laughter 1982, Poltergeist 1982, Return of the Jedi 1983, Indiana Jones and the Temple of Doom 1984, Goonies 1985, Timefall 1986, Poltergeist II 1986, Melrose Place (writer-producer) 1995–1999, Star Trek: Vogayer (writer-producer) 2001–02. *Address:* c/o Danielle Egan-Miller, 410 S Michigan Avenue, Suite 460, Chicago, IL 60605, USA.

KAHN, Sy; American academic, writer and poet; b. 15 Sept. 1924, New York, NY; m. Janet Baker; one s. *Education:* BA, Univ. of Pennsylvania, 1948; MA, Univ. of Connecticut, 1951; PhD, Univ. of Wisconsin, 1957. *Career:* Asst Prof., Beloit College, 1955–60, Univ. of South Florida, 1960–63; Prof. of English and Humanities, Raymond College, 1963–68; Prof. of Drama and English, 1968–86, Chair., Dept of Drama, 1970–81, Prof. Emeritus, 1986–, Univ. of the Pacific; Fulbright Prof. of American Literature, Univ. of Salonika, Greece, 1958–59, Univ. of Warsaw, 1966–67, Univ. of Vienna, 1970–71, Univ. of Porto, Portugal, 1985–86; Guest Prof. Univ. of Wales, Swansea 1987, 1996, Justis Liebig Univ. Giessen, Germany 1987; mem. MLA. *Publications:* Our Separate Darkness, 1963; Triptych, 1964; The Fight is With Phantoms, 1966; A Later Sun, 1966; Another Time, 1968; Interculture (ed.) 1975, Facing Mirrors, 1981; Devour the Fire: Selected Poems of Harry Crosby (ed.), 1984; Between Tedium and Terror: A Soldier's World War II Diary, 1993. Contributions: various anthologies, journals, reviews and quarterlies. *Honours:* Gardner Writing Awards, University of Wisconsin, 1954, 1955; Crosby Writing Fellowships, 1962, 1963; Borestone Poetry Award, 1964; Promethean Lamp Prize, 1966; Grand Prize in Poetry, University of the Pacific, 1985, Port Townsend Angel of the Arts Award 2003. *Address:* 1212 Holcomb Street, Port Townsend, WA 98368, USA.

KAKU, Michio, BS, PhD; American theoretical physicist, writer and academic; *Henry Semat Professor in Theoretical Physics, City College, CUNY;* b. 24 Jan. 1947. *Education:* Harvard Univ., Univ. of California Berkeley Radiation Laboratory. *Career:* Lecturer, Princeton Univ. 1973; fmr Visiting Prof., Inst. for Advanced Study, Princeton Univ., and New York Univ.; co-founder of string field theory; currently Henry Semat Prof. in Theoretical Physics, City Coll., CUNY. *Radio:* Explorations in Science (weekly programme on WBAI). *Television:* Making Time (BBC, four-part series) 2006, numerous appearances and contributions to documentaries. *Publications:* Nuclear Power: Both Sides (with Jennifer Trainer) 1982, To Win a Nuclear War: The Pentagon's Secret War Plans (with Daniel Axelrod) 1986, Beyond Einstein: The Cosmic Quest for the Theory of the Universe 1987, Introduction to Superstrings and M-Theory 1988, Strings, Conformal Fields and M-Theory 1991, Quantum Field Theory: A Modern Introduction 1993, Hyperspace: A Scientific Odyssey Through Parallel Universes, Time Warps and the Tenth Dimension 1994, Visions: How Science Will Revolutionize the 21st Century 1997, Einstein's Cosmos: How Albert Einstein's Vision Transformed Our Understading of Space and Time 2004, Parallel Worlds: A Journey Through Creation, Higher Dimensions and the Future of the Cosmos 2004; contrib. numerous articles to journals and magazines, including Astronomy, Discover, BBC Focus Magazine (UK), Cosmos (Australia), New Scientist (UK), Time, Wall Street Journal. *Address:* Department of Physics, City College of New York, Marshak Science Building J-419, 160 Convent Avenue, New York, NY 10031, USA. *E-mail:* kaku@sci.ccny.cuny.edu; mkaku@aol.com. *Website:* www.mkaku.org.

KALB, Jonathan, BA, MFA, DFA; American theatre critic and academic; b. 30 Oct. 1959, Englewood, NJ; m. Julie Heffernan 1988; two s. *Education:* Wesleyan Univ., Yale School of Drama. *Career:* Theatre Critic, The Village Voice, 1987–97; Asst Prof. of Performance Studies, 1990–92, Asst Prof. of Theatre, 1992–95, Assoc. Prof. of Theatre, 1996–2002, Prof. of Theatre, 2003–, Hunter College, CUNY; Chief Theatre Critic, New York Press, 1997–2001; mem. MLA; PEN American Centre. *Publications:* Beckett in Performance, 1989; Free Admissions: Collected Theater Writings, 1993; The Theater of Heiner Müller, 1998; Play by Play: Theater Essays and Reviews 1993–2002, 2003. Contributions: newspapers and journals. *Honours:* Fulbright Hays Grant, 1988–89; T. C. G. Jerome Fellowship, 1989–90; George Jean Nathan Award for Dramatic Criticism, 1990–91.

KALECHOFSKY, Roberta, BA, MA, PhD; American writer and publisher; b. 11 May 1931, New York, NY; m. Robert Kalechofsky 1953, two s. *Education:* Brooklyn College, CUNY, New York University. *Career:* Literary Ed., Branching Out, Canada, 1973–74; Contributing Ed., Margins, 1974–77, On the Issues, 1987–94; charter mem. National Writers Union; mem. Authors' Guild. *Publications:* Stephen's Passion, 1975; La Hoya, 1976; Orestes in Progress, 1976; Solomon's Wisdom, 1978; Rejected Essays and Other Matters, 1980; The 6th Day of Creation, 1986; Bodmin 1349, 1988; Haggadah for the Liberated Lamb, 1988; Autobiography of a Revolutionary: Essays on Animals and Human Rights, 1991; Justice, My Brother, 1993; Haggadah for the Vegetarian Family, 1993; K'tia: A Savior of the Jewish People, 1995; A Boy, a Chicken and the Lion of Judah: How Ari Became a Vegetarian (children's book), 1995; Vegetarian Judaism: A Guide for Everyone, 1998. Contributions: Confrontation; Works; Ball State University Forum; Western Humanities Review; Rocky Mountain Review; Between the Species; So'western; Response; Reconstructionist. *Honours:* National Endowment for the Arts Fellowship, 1962; Hon. Mem., Israel Bibliophile Society, 1982; Literary Fellowship in Fiction, Massachusetts Council on the Arts, 1987.

KALETSKY, Anatole, MA; British journalist; *Associate Editor and Economic Commentator, The Times (UK);* b. 1 June 1952, Moscow, Russia; s. of Jacob Kaletsky and Esther Kaletsky; m. Fiona Murphy 1985; two s. one d. *Education:* Melbourne High School, Australia, Westminster City School and King's Coll., Cambridge, UK and Harvard Univ., USA. *Career:* Hon. Sr Scholar King's Coll., Cambridge 1973–74; Kennedy Scholar, Harvard Univ. 1974–76; financial writer, The Economist 1976–79; leader writer, Financial Times 1979–81, Washington Corresp. 1981–83, Int. Econs Corresp. 1984–86, Chief New York Bureau 1986–90, Moscow Assignment 1990; Econs Ed. The Times 1990–96, Assoc. Ed. and econ. commentator 1992–; Dir Kaletsky Econ. Consulting 1997–; mem. Advisory Bd UK Know-How Fund for E Europe and fmr Soviet Union 1991–; Royal Econs Soc. 1999–. *Publications:* The Costs of Default 1985, In the Shadow of Debt 1992. *Honours:* Specialist Writer of the Year, British Press Awards 1980, 1992, Press Awards Commentator of the Year 1995, What the Papers Say 1996, Financial Journalist of the Year, Wincott Foundation Award 1997. *Address:* The Times, 1 Pennington Street, London, E1 9XY, England (office). *Telephone:* (20) 7782-5000 (office). *Fax:* (20) 7782-5046 (office). *Website:* www.timesonline.co.uk (office).

KAMANDA, Kama Sywor, DipHumLit, BJ, BA, LèsL; Democratic Republic of the Congo writer, poet, novelist, playwright and lecturer; b. 11 Nov. 1952, Luebo; s. of the late Malaba Kamenga and Kony Ngalula. *Education:* Journalism School, Kinshasa, Univ. of Kinshasa, Univ. of Liège, Belgium.

Career: lecturer at various univs, schools, etc.; literary critic for several newspapers; mem. French Soc. of Men of Letters, Conseil International d'Etudes Francophones, Belgian Soc. of Authors, Composers and Editors (SABAM), Maison de la poésie (MAPI), Dakar, Senegal. *Publications:* Les Résignations 1986, Éclipse d'étoiles 1987, Les Contes du griot Vol. 1 1988, Vol. 2: La Nuit des griots 1992, Vol. 3: Les Contes des veillées africaines 1998, La Somme du néant 1989, L'Exil des songes 1992, Les Myriades des temps vécus 1992, Les Vents de l'épreuve 1993, Lointaines sont les rives du destin 1994, Quand dans l'âme les mers s'agitent 1994, L'Étreinte des mots 1995, Chants de brumes 1997, Oeuvre Poétique 1999, Les Contes du crépuscule 2000, Le Sang des solitudes 2002, Contes 2003, La Traversée des mirages 2006, La Joueuse du kora 2006. *Honours:* Académie Française Paul Verlaine Award 1987, Académie Française Théophile Gautier Award 1993, Louise Labé Award 1990, Black Africa Asscn of French-Speaking Writers Award 1991, Acad. Inst. of Paris Special Poetry Award 1992, Silver Jasmine for Poetic Originality 1992, Gen. Council Agen Special Prize for French-Speaking Countries 1992, Greek Poets and Writers Asscn Melina Mercouri Award 1999, Int. Poets Acad. India Poet of the Millennium Award 2000, Joal Fadiouth hon. citation, Senegal 2000, Int. Soc. of Greek Writers Poetry Award 2002, Int. Council for French Studies Maurice-Cagnon Exceptional Contribution Honor Certificate 2005, World Acad. of Letters Master Diploma for Specialty Honors in Writing, USA 2006, United Cultural Convention Int. Peace Prize, USA 2006. *Address:* 18 Am Moul, 7418 Buschdorf, Luxembourg (office). *Telephone:* (352) 26610948 (office). *Fax:* (352) 26610948 (office). *E-mail:* kamanda@pt.lu. *Website:* www.kamanda.net.

KAMATH, M. V., BSc; Indian journalist and broadcasting executive; *Chairman, Prasar Bharati (Broadcasting Corporation of India);* b. 1921, Udupi. *Career:* upon graduation from univ. worked for five years as chemist; changed careers and became reporter, then special adviser, then Ed. Free Press Journal, Mumbai 1946–54; Foreign Corresp. Times of India reporting from Germany and France, Ed. Sunday Times 1967–69, US Corresp. Times of India, Washington DC 1969–78; Ed. Illustrated Weekly 1978–81; columnist in numerous newspapers and magazines 1981–; mem. Bd of Dirs Prasar Bharati (Broadcasting Corpn of India) 2002, Chair. 2003–. *Publications:* over 40 books including The United States and India 1776–1976 1976, Philosophy of Death and Dying 1978, The Other Face of India 1988, A Banking Odyssey: The Canara Bank Story 1991, Ganesh Vasudeo Mavalankar 1992, Management Kurien-Style: The Story of the White Revolution, Points and Lines, Charat RAM: A Biography 1994, Journalist's Handbook 1995, Gandhi's Coolie: Life and Times of Ramkrishna Bajaj 1995, Professional Journalism 1996, Some of Us are Lucky 1996, Milkman from Anand: The story of Verghese Kurien 1996, Sai Baba of Shirdi: A Unique Saint (jtly) 2005. *Honours:* Padma Bhushan 2004. *Address:* Prasar Bharati, Doordarshan Bhavan, Copernicus Marg, New Delhi 110001 (office); Kalyanpur House, 3rd Road, Near Railway Station, Kar, Mumbai, India (home). *Telephone:* (22) 26483418 (home). *Website:* www.ddindia.com (office).

KAMINER, Wladimir; German writer, journalist and DJ; b. 1967, Moscow, USSR; m.; two c. *Career:* moved to Germany 1990; DJ, Russian Disco, Berlin. *Publications:* Russendisko (short stories) 2000, Frische Goldjungs (ed.) 2001, Schönhauser Allee 2001, Militärmusik 2001, Die Reise nach Trulala 2002, Helden des Alltags (with Helmut Höge) 2002, Dschungelbuch 2003, Ich mache mit Sorgen, Mama 2004, Karaoke 2005, Küche totalitas 2006; contrib. to FAZ, taz and the Frankfurter Rundschau. *Address:* c/o Random House UK Ltd, Random House, 20 Vauxhall Bridge Road, London, SW1V 2SA, England. *Website:* www.russendisko.de.

KAMINSKY, Stuart Melvin, BS, MA, PhD; American academic and writer; b. 29 Sept. 1934, Chicago, IL. *Education:* University of Illinois, Northwestern University. *Career:* Dir of Public Relations and Asst to the Vice-Pres. for Public Affairs, University of Chicago, 1969–72; Faculty, later Prof. of Radio, Television, and Film, Northwestern University, 1972–. *Publications:* Non-Fiction: Don Siegal: Director, 1973; Clint Eastwood, 1974; American Film Genres: Approaches to a Critical Theory of Popular Film, 1974; Ingmar Bergman: Essays in Criticism (ed. with Joseph Hill), 1975; John Huston: Maker of Magic, 1978; Basic Filmmaking (with Dana Hodgdon), 1981; American Television Genres (with Jeffrey Mahan), 1984. Fiction: Bullet for a Star, 1977; Murder on the Yellow Brick Road, 1978; You Bet Your Life, 1979; The Howard Hughes Affair, 1979; Never Cross a Vampire, 1980; Death of a Dissident, 1981; High Midnight, 1981; Catch a Falling Clown, 1981; He Done Her Wrong, 1983; When the Dark Man Calls, 1983; Black Knight on Red Square, 1983; Down for the Count, 1985; Red Chameleon, 1985; Exercise in Terror, 1985; Smart Moves, 1987; A Fine Red Rain, 1987; Lieberman's Day, 1994; Vengeance, 1999; Murder on the Trans-Siberian Express, 2001; Retribution, 2001.

KAMPFNER, John; British writer and journalist; *Editor, New Statesman.* *Career:* fmr foreign corresp. with Reuters and Daily Telegraph; Chief Political Corresp. Financial Times mid-1990s; fmr political commentator Today programme (BBC Radio 4); Political Ed. New Statesman 2002–05, Ed. 2005–; regular appearances on radio and TV. *Television documentary films:* (all for BBC) Israel Undercover 2002, The Ugly War: Children of Vengeance (Foreign Press Asscn Award for Film of the Year and Journalist of the Year) 2002, War Spin 2003, Robin Cook: The Lost Leader (profile) 2003, Clare Short: The Conscientious Objector (profile) 2003, Who Runs Britain (series) 2004. *Publications:* Inside Yeltsin's Russia: Corruption, Conflict, Capitalism 1995, Robin Cook: The Life and Times of Tony Blair's Most Awkward Minister 1999,

Blair's Wars 2003, Dangerous Liaisons: Blair, Britain and the Failure of Europe 2007; contrib. to The Herald, The Observer, The Independent, The Guardian, Daily Express, The Times, Sunday Times, Daily Mail, Financial Times, Los Angeles Times, Daily Telegraph, Evening Standard,. *Honours:* British Soc. of Magazine Eds. Ed. of the Year Award for Current Affairs Magazines 2006. *Literary Agent:* Knight Ayton Management, 114 St Martin's Lane, London, WC2N 4BE, England. *Telephone:* (20) 7836-5333. *Fax:* (20) 7836-8333. *E-mail:* info@knightayton.co.uk. *Website:* www.knightayton.co.uk. *Address:* New Statesman, Third Floor, 52 Grosvenor Gardens, London, SW1W 0AU, England (office). *Telephone:* (20) 7881-5676 (office). *Fax:* (20) 7259-0181 (office). *E-mail:* info@newstatesman.co.uk (office); john@jkampfner.net (home). *Website:* www.newstatesman.com (office); www.jkampfner.net (home).

KAN, Sergei; American academic and writer; b. 31 March 1953, Moscow, Russia; m. Alla Glazman 1976; one d. *Education:* Moscow State University, 1970–73; BA, Boston University, 1976; MA, 1978, PhD, 1982, University of Chicago. *Career:* Lecturer, Sheldon Jackson College, Sitka, AK, 1979–80, University of Massachusetts, Boston, 1982–83; Part-time Asst Prof., Northeastern University, 1981–83; Asst Prof., University of Michigan, 1983–89; Asst Prof., 1989–92, Assoc. Prof. of Anthropology and of Native American Studies, 1992–98, Prof. of Anthropology and Native American Studies, 1998–, Dartmouth College; mem. Alaska Anthropological Asscn; American Assn for the Advancement of Slavic Studies; American Ethnological Society; American Society for Ethnohistory; International Arctic Social Science Assn. *Publications:* Symbolic Immortality: The Tlingit Potlatch of the Nineteenth Century, 1989; Memory Eternal: Tlingit Culture and Russian Orthodox Christianity Through Two Centuries, 1999. Contributions: books and scholarly journals. *Honours:* Robert F. Heizer Prize, American Society for Ethnohistory, 1987; American Book Award, Before Columbus Foundation, 1990; ACLS Fellowship, 1993–94; National Endowment for the Humanities Fellowships, 1993–94, 1999–2000. *Address:* 18 Wellington Circle, Lebanon, NH 03766, USA.

KANDEL, Michael, PhD; American editor and writer; b. 24 Dec. 1941, Baltimore, MD. *Education:* Indiana Univ. *Career:* Asst Ed., MLA; Consultant Science Fiction Ed., Harcourt; Trans. of Stanislaw Lem; mem. PEN Club; SFWA. *Publications:* Strange Invasion, 1989; In Between Dragons, 1991; Captain Jack Zodiac, 1993; Panda Ray, 1996. *Address:* Modern Language Association, 26 Broadway, Third Floor, New York, NY 10004-1789, USA. *E-mail:* mkandel@mla.org.

KANE, Cheikh Hamidou; Senegalese novelist; b. 1928, Mataru, Senegal. *Education:* Univ. of Paris, Ecole Nationale de la France d'Outre-Mer. *Career:* frmly Dir, Dept of Economic Planning and Development, Governor, Thies Region, Commissioner of Planning; worked for UNICEF. *Publications:* L'Aventure Ambiguë (Ambiguous Adventure), 1961; Les Gardiens du Temple, 1995. *Honours:* Grand Prix Litteraire de l'Afrique Noir, 1962.

KANE, Paul, BA, MA, MPhil, PhD; American poet, critic and academic; b. 23 March 1950, Cobleskill, NY; m. Christine Reynolds 1980. *Education:* Yale University, University of Melbourne. *Career:* Instructor, Briarcliff College, 1975–77; Assoc., Institute for World Order, 1982; Dir of Admissions and Instructor, Wooster School, 1982–84; Part-time Instructor, Yale University, 1988–90; Prof. of English, Vassar College, 1990–; mem. Acad. of American Poets; PEN; Poetry Society of America. *Publications:* The Farther Shore, 1989; A Hudson Landscape (with William Cliff), 1993; Ralph Waldo Emerson: Collected Poems and Translations, 1994; Poetry of the American Renaissance, 1995; Australian Poetry: Romanticism and Negativity, 1996; Emerson: Essays and Poems, 1996; Drowned Lands, 2000. Contributions: articles, poems, and reviews in New Republic; Paris Review; Poetry; Sewanee Review; Partisan Review; Raritan; Antipodes; The New Criterion. *Honours:* Fulbright Scholar, 1984–85; National Endowment for the Humanities Grant, 1998; Guggenheim Fellowship, 1999.

KANEHARA, Hitomi; Japanese novelist; b. 1983, Tokyo. *Publications:* Hebi ni Piasu (trans. as Snakes and Earrings) (Akutagawa Prize (jtly) 2004) 2003, Ash Baby 2004, Amebic 2005; contrib. to Subaru magazine. *Address:* Azusa Takagi, c/o Shueisha Inc, 3-13-1 Jinbocho, Chiyoda-ku, Tokyo 101-8050 (office); 3-28-12 Bubaicho, Fuchushi, Tokyo 183-0033, Japan (home). *Telephone:* (3) 3230-6092 (office). *Fax:* (3) 3221-1387 (office). *E-mail:* takagi-bungei@shueisha.co.up (office).

KANENGONI, Alexander; Zimbabwean author; b. 1951, Chivhu. *Education:* Saint Paul's Teacher Training College, Univ. of Zimbabwe. *Career:* Project Officer, Ministry of Education and Culture 1983; Head of Research Services, Zimbabwe Broadcasting Corpn 1988–. *Publications:* Vicious Circle (novel) 1983, When the Rainbird Cries (novel) 1988, Effortless Tears (short stories) 1993, Echoing Silences (novel) 1998. *Honours:* Zimbabwe Book Publishers' Literary Awards 1994.

KANIGEL, Robert, BS; American writer and academic; *Professor of Science Writing, Massachusetts Institute of Technology*; b. 28 May 1946, New York, NY; m. 1st Judith Schiff Pearl 1981 (divorced); one s.; m. 2nd Sarah Merrow. *Education:* Rensselaer Polytechnic Inst., Troy, NY. *Career:* freelance writer 1970–; instructor, Johns Hopkins Univ. School of Continuing Studies 1985–91; Visiting Prof. of English, Univ. of Baltimore, and Sr Fellow, Inst. of Publications Design 1991–99; Prof. of Science Writing 1999–, Dir, Graduate Program in Science Writing 2001–, MIT; mem. Authors' Guild, American Soc.

of Journalists and Authors. *Publications:* Apprentice to Genius: The Making of a Scientific Dynasty 1986, The Man Who Knew Infinity: A Life of the Genius Ramanujan 1991, The One Best Way: Frederick Winslow Taylor and the Enigma of Efficency 1997, Vintage Reading: From Plato to Bradbury, a Personal Tour of Some of the World's Best Books 1998, High Season: How One French Riviera Town Has Seduced Traders for Two Thousand Years 2002, Faux Real: An Alchemy of Leather (2007); contrib. to New York Times Magazine, The Sciences, Health, Psychology Today, Science 85, Johns Hopkins Magazine, Washington Post, Civilization. *Honours:* Grady-Stack Award 1989, Alfred P. Sloan Foundation grant 1991, 2005, Elizabeth Eisenstein Prize 1994, American Soc. of Journalists and Authors Author of the Year 1998. *Address:* 14N-420, Massachusetts Institute of Technology, 77 Massachusetts Avenue, Cambridge, MA 02139, USA (office). *Telephone:* (617) 253-0087 (office). *E-mail:* kanigel@mit.edu (office).

KANN, Mark E., BA, MA, PhD; American academic and writer; b. 24 Feb. 1947, Chicago, IL; m. Kathy Michael 1969, one s. *Education:* University of Wisconsin, Madison. *Career:* Asst Prof., 1975–81, Assoc. Prof., 1981–88, Prof. of Political Science, 1988–, University of Southern California at Los Angeles. *Publications:* Thinking About Politics: Two Political Sciences, 1980; The American Left: Failures and Fortunes, 1983; Middle Class Radicals in Santa Monica, 1986; On the Man in Question: Gender and Civic Virtue in America, 1991; A Republic of Men: The American Founders, Gendered Language, and Political Patriachy 1998, The Gendering of American Politics 1999, Punishment, Prisons, and Patriarchy: Liberty and Power in the Early National American Republic 2005; contrib. to numerous newspapers, journals and magazines. *Honours:* various research and teaching awards. *Address:* Department of Political Science, University of Southern California, Los Angeles, CA 90089, USA.

KANN, Peter Robert; American publisher, business executive and journalist; *Chairman, Dow Jones & Company, Inc.*; b. 13 Dec. 1942, New York; s. of Robert Kann and Marie Breuer; m. 1st Francesca Mayer 1969 (died 1983); m. 2nd Karen House 1984; one s. three d. *Education:* Harvard Univ. *Career:* with The Wall Street Journal 1964–; journalist, New York 1964–67, Viet Nam 1967–68, Hong Kong 1968–75, Publr and Ed. Asian Edn 1976–79, Assoc. Publr 1979–88; Exec. Vice-Pres. Dow Jones & Co. 1986, Pres. int. and magazine groups 1986–89, mem. Bd of Dirs 1987; Publr and Editorial Dir The Wall Street Journal 1989–2002; Pres. Dow Jones & Co. New York 1989–91, Chair. 1991–, CEO 1991–2006; Chair. Bd Far Eastern Econ. Review 1987–89; Trustee Asia Soc. 1989–94, Inst. for Advanced Study, Princeton 1990–, Aspen Inst. 1994–; mem. Pulitzer Prize Bd 1987–96. *Honours:* Pulitzer Prize for int. reporting 1972. *Address:* Dow Jones & Company, 1 World Financial Center, 200 Liberty Street, New York, NY 10281, USA (office). *Telephone:* (212) 416-2000 (office). *Fax:* (212) 416-4348 (office). *Website:* www.dj.com (office).

KANNAN, Lakshmi, (Kaaveri), MA, PhD; Indian writer and poet; b. 13 Aug. 1947, Mysore; m. L. V. Kannan (deceased); two s. *Career:* participant Int. Writing Program, Iowa Univ. USA; writer-in-residence on Charles Wallace Trust Fellowship, Univ. of Kent at Canterbury, UK 1993; Fellow, Indian Inst. of Advanced Study, Shimla, India; scholar-in-residence, American Studies Research Centre, Hyderabad; Bharat Soka Gakkai, Indian chapter Soka Gakkai Int.; f. mem., governing body, Poetry Soc. of India, New Delhi; mem., India Int. Centre, Delhi; Group Chief, Bharat Soka Gakkai. *Publications include:* poems: Impressions 1974, The Glow and the Grey 1976, Exiled Gods 1985, Unquiet Waters 2005; fiction: Rhythms (short stories) 1986, Parijata (short stories) 1992, India Gate (short stories) 1993, Going Home (novel) 1998; other works in Tamil and in Hindi trans. *Honours:* Hon. Fellow in Writing Univ. of Iowa, USA, Ilakkiya Chintani Award for best short story in Tamil, Chennai, Katha Award for Best Translation, New Delhi. *Address:* B-XI/8193, Vasant Kunj, New Delhi 110 070, India. *Telephone:* (11) 26897793. *E-mail:* lakshmi_kaaveri@yahoo.com; kannan01lakshmi@sify.com.

KANT, Hermann Paul Karl, BA; German writer; b. 14 June 1926, Hamburg; m. Marion Meyer 1982; two s. two d. *Education:* Univ. of Berlin. *Career:* mem. PEN Centre, Germany, Writers' Assn (pres. 1979–89). *Publications:* Ein bisschen Südsee 1962, Die Aula 1965, In Stockholm 1971, Eine Übertretung 1971, Das Impressum 1972, Der Aufenthalt 1977, Der dritte Nagel 1980, Zu den Unterlagen 1981, Bronzezeit 1986, Die Summe 1988, Abspann (memoir) 1991, Kormoran 1992, Escape 1994, Okarina 2002, Kino 2005. *Honours:* Hon. DrPhil (Greifswald) 1980; Heinrich Heine Prize 1962, Heinrich Mann Prize 1967, Nat. Prizes 1973, 1977, Goethe Prize 1985. *Address:* Prälank-Dorf 4, 17235 Neustrelitz, Germany (home). *Telephone:* (3981) 202975 (home). *E-mail:* HMYRONK@aol.com (home).

KANTARIS, Sylvia, CertEd, MA, PhD; British poet, writer and teacher; b. 9 Jan. 1936, Grindleford, Derbyshire, England; m. Emmanuel Kantaris 1958; one s. one d. *Education:* Sorbonne, Univ. of Paris, Univ. of Bristol, Univ. of Queensland, Australia. *Career:* school teacher, Bristol 1957–58, London 1958–62; Tutor, Univ. of Queensland 1963–66, Open Univ., England 1974–84; Extra-Mural Lecturer, Univ. of Exeter 1974–; Writer in the Community, Cornwall 1986–87; mem. Poetry Soc. of GB, South West Arts (literature panel 1983–87, literary consultant 1974–). *Publications:* Time and Motion 1975, Stocking Up 1981, The Tenth Muse 1983, News From the Front (with D. M. Thomas) 1983, The Sea at the Door 1985, The Air Mines of Mistila (with Philip Gross) 1988, Dirty Washing: New and Selected Poems 1989, Lad's Love 1993; contribs to many anthologies, newspapers and magazines and numerous academic and literary essays and reviews published in UK, USA, France and

Australia. *Honours:* Hon. DLitt (Exeter) 1989; Nat. Poetry Competition Award 1982, Major Arts Council Literature Award 1991, Soc. of Authors Award 1992. *Address:* 14 Osborne Parc, Helston, Cornwall, TR13 8PB, England. *Telephone:* (1326) 574578. *E-mail:* sylvia@kantaris.com. *Website:* www.kantaris.com/sylvia.

KANTOR, Peter, MA; Hungarian poet and editor; b. 5 Nov. 1949, Budapest. *Education:* Budapest ELTE Univ. *Career:* Literary Ed. Kortars magazine 1984–86; Poetry Ed. Élet és Irodalom magazine 1997–2000; mem. Writers' Asscn, International PEN. *Publications:* Kavics 1976, Halmadar 1981, Sebbel Lobbal 1982, Gradicsok 1985, Hogy no az eg 1988, Naplo, 1987–89 1991, Font lomb, lent avar 1994, Mentafü (selected poems) 1994, Bucsu és Megérkezés 1997, Lóstaféta 2002, Kétszáz lépcsö föl és le 2005; contrib. to various publications. *Honours:* George Soros Fellowship 1988–89, Wessely Laszlo Award 1990, Dery Tibor Award 1991, Fulbright Fellowship 1991–92, Fust Milan Award 1992, József Attila Award 1994, George Soros Award 1999, Vas István Award 2004. *Address:* Stollar Bela u 3/a, Budapest 1055, Hungary. *E-mail:* peterkantor@freemail.hu.

KANTŮRKOVÁ, Eva; Czech writer; b. 11 May 1930, Prague; d. of Jiří Síla and Dobromila Sílová; m. 1st Mr Štern 1949; m. 2nd Mr Kantůrek; two s. *Education:* Charles Univ., Prague. *Career:* writer 1964–, unable to publish works in Czechoslovakia 1970–89; imprisoned by Czechoslovak authorities because of book which was printed abroad 1981–82; mem. Czech Parl. 1990–92; mem. Czech Centrum PEN Club, Asscn of Czech Writers; numerous novels, short stories, essays, plays and screenplays. *Screenplays include:* Funeral Ceremony (Second Prize, Film Festival, Montréal, Canada) 1990, My Friends in the Black House (TV) (First and Second Prizes, Cannes Film Festival). *Honours:* Tom Stoppard Prize 1985, Jan Palach Prize 1989, Egon Hostovsky Prize 1998. *Address:* Xaveriova 13, 150 00 Prague 5, Czech Republic. *Telephone:* (2) 5156-4382.

KAPLAN, Harold, BA, MA; American academic and writer; b. 3 Jan. 1916, Chicago, IL; m. Isabelle M. Ollier 1962; one s. two d. *Education:* Univ. of Chicago. *Career:* Instructor of English, Rutgers Univ. 1946–49; Prof. of English, Bennington Coll. 1950–72; Prof. of English, Northwestern Univ. 1972–86, Prof. Emeritus 1986–; Visiting Prof. in American Literature in France, Italy, Israel; Chair. Studies in American Culture 1972–74. *Publications:* The Passive Voice 1966, Democratic Humanism and American Literature 1972, Power and Order 1981, Conscience and Memory: Meditations in a Museum of the Holocaust 1994, Poetry, Politics and Culture 2006. *Honours:* Fulbright Lecturer 1967, 1981, Rockefeller Foundation Humanities Fellowship 1982. *Address:* 219 Meadowbrook Drive, Bennington, VT 05201, USA (home). *Telephone:* (802) 442-7148 (home). *Fax:* (802) 442-7148 (home). *E-mail:* harkap@sover.net (home).

KAPLAN, Justin, BS; American biographer and editor; b. 5 Sept. 1925, New York, NY; m. Anne F. Bernays 1954, three d. *Education:* Harvard University. *Career:* Senior Ed., Simon & Schuster Inc, New York City, 1954–59; Lecturer in English, Harvard University, 1969, 1973, 1976, 1978; Writer-in-Residence, Emerson College, Boston, 1977–78; Visiting Lecturer, Griffith University, Brisbane, Australia, 1983; Jenks Prof. of Contemporary Letters, College of the Holy Cross, Worcester, Massachusetts, 1992–95; mem. American Acad. of Arts and Letters; American Acad. of Arts and Sciences, fellow; Society of American Historians, fellow. *Publications:* Mr Clemens and Mark Twain, 1966; Lincoln Steffens: A Biography, 1974; Mark Twain and His World, 1974; Walt Whitman: A Life, 1980; The Language of Names (with Anne Bernays), 1997; Back Then (with Anne Bernays), 2002. Editor: Dialogues of Plato, 1948; With Malice Toward Women, 1949; The Pocket Aristotle, 1956; The Gilded Age, 1964; Great Short Works of Mark Twain, 1967; Mark Twain: A Profile, 1967; Walt Whitman: Complete Poetry and Collected Prose, 1982; The Harper American Literature, 1987; Best American Essays, 1990. General Editor: Bartlett's Familiar Quotations, 17th edn, 2002. Contributions: newspapers, journals and magazines. *Honours:* Pulitzer Prize for Biography, 1967; National Book Award, 1967; Guggenheim Fellowship, 1975–76; American Book Award, 1981; Hon. DHL, Marlboro College, 1984; Bellagio Study and Conference Center Residency, 1990.

KAPLAN, Morton A., BS, PhD; American political scientist, academic, writer, editor and publisher; *Professor Emeritus, University of Chicago;* b. 9 May 1921, Philadelphia, Pa; m. Azie Mortimer 1967. *Education:* Temple Univ., Columbia Univ. *Career:* Fellow 1952–53, Research Assoc. 1958–62, Center of Int. Studies, Princeton, NJ; Asst Prof., Haverford Coll. 1953–54; Fellow, Center for Advanced Study in the Behavioral Sciences, Stanford, Calif. 1955–56; Asst Prof., Univ. of Chicago 1956–61, Assoc. Prof. 1961–65, Prof. of Political Science 1965–89, Distinguished Service Prof. 1989–91, Prof. Emer. 1991–; Visiting Assoc. Prof., Yale Univ. 1961–62; mem. staff, Hudson Inst. 1961–78, Consultant 1978–80; Dir Center for Strategic and Foreign Policy Studies 1976–85; Ed. and Publr The World and I 1985–2004; mem. American Political Science Asscn. *Publications:* System and Process in International Politics 1957, Some Problems in the Strategic Analysis of International Politics 1959, The Communist Coup in Czechoslovakia (co-author) 1960, The Political Foundations of International Law (with N. de B. Katzenbach) 1961, Macropolitics: Essays on the Philosophy and Science of Politics 1969, On Historical and Political Knowing: An Enquiry into Some Problems of Universal Law and Human Freedom 1971, On Freedom and Human Dignity: The Importance of the Sacred in Politics 1973, The Rationale for NATO: Past and Present 1973, Alienation and Identification 1976, Justice, Human Nature

and Political Obligation 1976, Towards Professionalism in International Theory: Macrosystem Analysis 1979, Science, Language and the Human Condition 1984, The Soviet Union and the Challenge of the Future (co-ed.), four vols 1988–89, Morality and Religion (co-ed.) 1992, Law in a Democratic Society 1993, The World of 2044: Technological Development and the Future of Society (co-ed.) 1994, Character and Identity: Philosophical Foundations of Political and Sociological Perspectives (ed. and co-author) 1998, Character and Identity: Sociological Foundations of Literary and Historical Perspectives 2000; contrib. to many books and professional journals. *Address:* 5446 S Ridgewood Court, Chicago, IL 60615, USA.

KAPLAN, Robert D., BA; American writer; b. 23 June 1952, New York, NY; m. Maria Cabral; one s. *Education:* Univ. of Connecticut. *Publications:* Surrender or Starve: The Wars Behind the Famine 1988, Soldiers of God: With the Mujahidin in Afghanistan 1990, Balkan Ghosts: A Journey Through History 1993, The Arabists: The Romance of an American Elite 1993, The Ends of the Earth: A Journey at the Dawn of the Twenty-First Century 1996, An Empire Wilderness: Travels Into America's Future 1998, The Coming Anarchy: Shattering the Dreams of the Post Cold War 2000, Eastward to Tartary: Travels in the Balkans, the Middle East, and the Caucasus 2000, Mediterranean Winter 2005; contrib. to periodicals. *Literary Agent:* c/o Bill Hamilton, AM Heath & Co. Ltd, 6 Warwick Court, Holborn, London, WC1R 5DJ, England. *Telephone:* (20) 7242-2811. *Fax:* (20) 7242-2711.

KAPLINSKI, Jaan; Estonian poet, writer and translator (retd); b. 22 Jan. 1941, Tartu (Dorpat); s. of Jerzy Kaplinski and Nora Raudsepp; m. Tüa Toomet 1969; one s. one d.; three s. one d. with Tüa Toomet. *Education:* Univ. of Tartu. *Career:* mem. Estonian parliament 1992–95; Lecturer in History of Western Civilization Univ. of Tartu; columnist at various Estonian and Scandinavian newspapers; has written around 900 poems, 20 stories and some plays; mem. Universal Acad. of Cultures, Estonian Writers' Union, European Acad. of Poetry. *Publications include:* poetry: Ma vaatasin päikese aknasse 1976, Uute kivide kasvamine 1977, The New Heaven & Earth of Jaan Kaplinski 1981, Raske on kergeks saada 1982, Tule tagasi helmemänd 1984, Õhtu toob tagasi kõik 1985, Käoraamat: Luulet 1956–80 1986, The Wandering Border 1987, The Same Sea in Us All 1990, Sjunger näktergalen än i Dorpat?: En brevväxling 1990, I Am The Spring in Tartu and other poems in English 1991, Non-Existent Frontier 1995, Võimaluste võimalikkus 1997, Öölinnud, öömötted yölintuja, yöajatuksia: Luuletusi 1995–97 1998, Evening Brings Everything Back 2004. *Honours:* IV Class Order of Nat. Coat of Arms 1997, Chevalier, Légion d'honneur 2000, Order of the Lion of Finland 2003. *Address:* Nisu 33–9, 50407 Tartu, Estonia (home); c/o Bloodaxe Books Ltd, Highgreen, Tarset, Northumberland NE48 1RP, England (office). *Telephone:* 645-9489 (home). *E-mail:* jaan@kaplinski.com (home). *Website:* www.jaan.kaplinski .com (home).

KAPUTIKIAN, Silva; Armenian poet and writer; b. 1919, Yerevan; m. Hovaness Shiraz. *Education:* Yerevan State Univ., Gorky Inst. of Literature, Moscow. *Career:* works include poetry, essays, children's literature and travel writing; political activist and human rights campaigner; mem. Armenian Writers' Union. *Publications:* poetry: Oreri het (With the Days) 1945, On the Shores of the Ganges 1947, Im harazatnere (My Intimates) 1953, Srtabats zruits (Candid Conversation) 1955, Bari yert (Bon Voyage) 1957, Mtorumner chanaparhi kesin (Midway Reflections) 1961, Yot kayaranner (Seven Stations) 1966, Im eje My Page 1968, Depi khorke leran (Toward the Mountain's Depths) 1972, Lilit 1981, Dzmer e galis (Winter is Arriving) 1983; children's books: Pokrik Ara, akanj ara (Little Ara, Listen) 1950, Mer Lalike, sirunike (Our Pretty Lalik) 1955, Tane, bakum, poghotsum (At Home, in the Yard, in the Street) 1953, Mi tarov el metsatsank (Older by One More Year) 1958, Menk ognum enk mairikin (We're Helping Mother) 1961, Tsaghkanots (Flower Garden) 1984, Partez (Garden) 2002. *Honours:* hon. mem. Yerevan Nat. Acad. of Sciences.

KARAHASAN, Dževad; Bosnia and Herzegovina writer and dramatist; b. 1953, Duvno, Yugoslavia. *Education:* Univ. of Sarajevo. *Career:* worked at Zenica theatre 1976–78; Ed., Odjek magazine, Sarajevo 1979–86; Prof. of Drama, Univ. of Sarajevo 1986–93; Visiting Prof., Univ. of Salzburg, Austria 1994–95, Univ. of Innsbruck, Austria 1995–97, Univ. of Göttingen, Germany 1995–97; Stadtschreiber Graz, Austria 1997–2003; Univ. Prof. Sarajevo. *Plays:* Al-Mukoffo, Klagenfurt/Salzburg 1994, Der entrückte Engel – Soricem auteo, Salzburg 1995, Das Konsert der Vögel – Koncert ptico, Vienna 1997, Snow and Death 2002. *Publications:* novels: Istočui Diwau 1989, Schajrijar's Ring 1994, Sara und Serafina 1999, The Nocturnal Council 2003; non-fiction: Sarajevo: Exodus of a City 1994, Knjiga vrtova (trans. as The Book of Gardens) 2001. *Honours:* Leipzig European Understanding Literary Award, Charles Veillon Prize for Essay, France 1995, Bruno Kreisky Prize for Politics Book of the Year, Austria 1995, Int. Prize for Dialogue 1997, Ileroler Prize 1999. *Address:* c/o Antibarbarus, Nova Ves 4, Hrvatska, Zagreb (office); Insel Verlag, Lindenstrasse 29–35, 60325 Frankfurt am Main, Germany (office); Augusta Brauna 1, 71000 Sarajevo, Bosnia Herzegovina (home). *Telephone:* (69) 75601731 (Germany) (office); 33445899 (B:H) (home). *Fax:* (69) 75601750 (Germany) (office). *E-mail:* landes@suhrkamp.de (office); dragana.tomasevic@ gmx.at (home). *Website:* www.suhrkamp.de (office).

KARBO, Karen Lee, BA, MA; American writer; b. 1956, Detroit, MI; m. 1st (divorced); m. 2nd Kelley Baker 1988. *Education:* University of Southern California at Los Angeles. *Publications:* Trespassers Welcome Here, 1989; The

Diamond Lane, 1991; Motherhood Made a Man Out of Me, 2000; Generation Ex: Tales from the Second Wives Club, 2001. Contributions: periodicals.

KARIM, Fawzi, BA; Iraqi/British poet, writer and painter; b. 1 July 1945, Baghdad; m. 1980; two s. *Education:* Coll. of Arts, Baghdad. *Career:* Ed.-in-Chief and Publr Al-laza Al-Shiria quarterly, London; freelance writer; mem. Poetry Soc., England, Union of Iraqi Writers. *Publications:* poetry: Where Things Begin 1969, I Raise My Hand in Protest 1973, Madness of Stone 1977, Stumbling of a Bird 1985, We Do Not Inherit the Earth 1988, Schemes of Adam 1991, Pestilential Continents 1995 (French trans. Continent de douleurs 2003, Swedish trans. Epidemiemas Kontinent 2005), Selected Poems, 1968–1995 1995, Cairo 1995, Collected Poems (two vols) 2000, The Foundling Years 2003, Selected Poems 2004, The Last Gypsies 2005, The Night of Abil Alaa 2007; prose: From Exile to Awareness 1972, City of Copper 1995, The Emperor's Clothes, on Poetry 2000, The Musical Virtues 2002, Return to Gardenia 2004, Diary of the End of a Nightmare 2005, Breakdown of the Generation of the Sixties, Dangers of Intellectual Passions 2006; reviews of classical music and English poetry in Asharq Alawsat Arabic newspaper, London 1980s–. *E-mail:* fawzi46@hotmail.com (home).

KARKARIA, Bachi; Indian editor; *Consulting Editor, The Times of India;* m.; two s. *Education:* Loreto Coll., Calcutta, Calcutta Univ. *Career:* began career at Illustrated Weekly of India 1969; Asst Ed. The Statesman, Calcutta (first woman) 1980; Group Editorial Director, Mid Day Multimedia Ltd 2000–02; Ed. Sunday Times of India 1998–2000, Resident Ed. The Times of India 2003, in charge of Delhi section, then Nat. Metro Ed., now Consulting Ed. and columnist; mem. Int. Women's Media Foundation; mem. Bd World Editors' Forum 2002–, India AIDS Initiative of Bill and Melinda Gates Foundation; Jefferson Fellow, East West Center, Honolulu; mem. Professional Women's Advisory Bd, American Biographical Inst. *Publications include:* Dare to Dream: The Life of M.S. Oberoi 2007. *Honours:* Media India Award (for human interest stories) 1992, Mary Morgan-Hewitt Award for Lifetime Achievement 1994. *Address:* The Times of India, 7 Bahadur Shah Zafar Marg, New Delhi 110 002, India (office). *Telephone:* (11) 23492049 (office). *Fax:* (11) 23351606 (office). *Website:* www.timesofindia.com (office).

KARLIN, Wayne Stephen, BA, MA; American writer, teacher and editor; *Professor of Languages and Literature, College of Southern Maryland;* b. 13 June 1945, Los Angeles, Calif.; m. Ohnmar Thein 1977; one s. *Education:* American Coll., Jerusalem, Goddard Coll., Vt. *Career:* Pres., Co-Ed. First Casualty Press 1972–73; Prof. of Languages and Literature, Coll. of Southern Maryland 1984–; Visiting Writer, William Joiner Center for the Study of War and Social Consequences, Univ. of Massachusetts, Boston 1989–93; Dir of Fiction, Literary Festival, St Mary's Coll. 1994–2002; Ed. Curbstone Press Vietnamese Writers series 1996–; mem. Associated Writing Programs. *Film:* scriptwriter, Song of the Stork 2002. *Radio:* producer, writer, Shared Weight series (NPR) 2006. *Publications:* Crossover 1984, Lost Armies 1988, The Extras 1989, US 1993, Rumors and Stones: A Journey 1996, Prisoners (Paterson Prize for Fiction 1999) 1998, The Wished-for Country 2002, War Movies 2005; contrib. to anthologies and periodicals. *Honours:* Air Medal, Combat Aircrew Insignia; Maryland State Arts Council Fellowship in Fiction and Individual Artist Award 1988, 1991, 1993, 2001, Nat. Endowment for the Arts Fellowship 1993, 2003, Critics' Choice Award 1995–96, Paterson Prize in Fiction 1999. *Literary Agent:* c/o Harold Ober Associates, 425 Madison Avenue, New York, NY 10017, USA. *Address:* PO Box 239, St Mary's City, MD 20686 (home); c/o Curbstone Press, 321 Jackson Street, Willimantic, CT 06226-1738, USA. *Telephone:* (240) 725-5451 (office). *E-mail:* waynek@csmd .edu (office).

KARNAD, Girish, MA; Indian playwright, film-maker and actor; b. 19 May 1938, Matheran; s. of Raghunath Karnad and Krishnabai Karnad; m. Saraswarthy Ganapathy 1980; one s. one d. *Education:* Karnatak Coll., Dharwad and Univ. of Oxford. *Career:* Rhodes Scholar, Oxford 1960–63; Pres. Oxford Union Soc. 1963; Asst Man. Oxford Univ. Press, Madras 1963–69; Man. 1969–70; Homi Bhabha Fellow 1970–72; Dir Film & TV Inst. of India, Pune 1974, 1975; Visiting Prof. and Fulbright Scholar-in-Residence Univ. of Chicago 1987–88; Indian Co-Chair., Media Cttee, Indo-US Subcomm. 1984–93; Chair. Sangeet Natak Akademi (Nat. Acad. of Performing Arts) 1988–93; Dir The Nehru Centre, London 2000; Fellow Sangeet Natak Acad. 1994. *Plays:* Yayati 1961, Tughlaq 1964, Hayavadana 1971, Anjumallige 1976, Nagamandala 1988, Taledanda 1990, Agni Mattu Male 1995, Tipu Sultan Kanda Kanasu 2000, Bali 2002. *Films:* Vamsha Vriksha 1971, Kaadu 1973, Tabbaliyu Neenade Magane 1977, Ondanondu Kaaladalli 1978, Utsav 1984, Cheluvi 1992, Kanooru Heggadithi 1999, Iqbal (as actor) 2005. *Radio:* Ma Nishada 1986, The Dreams of Tipu Sultan 1997. *TV:* Antaraal 1996, Swarajnama 1997, Kanooru Ki Thakurani 1999, wrote and presented The Bhagavad Gita for BBC Two 2002. *Honours:* Hon. DLitt (Univ. of Karnataka) 1994; several awards for film work; Padma Bhushan 1992, Bharatiya Jnanapith Award 1999, Sahitya Acad. Award 1994. *Address:* The Nehru Centre, 8 South Audley Street, London, W1K 1HF, England (office); 697, 15th Cross, JP Nagar Phase II, Bangalore 560 078, India (home). *Telephone:* (20) 7491-3567, (20) 7493-2019 (office); (80) 659 0463 (Bangalore); (20) 7355-2069 (home). *Fax:* (20) 7409-3360 (office); (80) 659-0019 (Bangalore). *E-mail:* gkarnad38@aol.com (home); nerhucentre@aol.com (office). *Website:* www .nehrucentre.org.

KARNOW, Stanley, BA; American journalist and writer; b. 4 Feb. 1925, New York, NY; m. 1st Claude Sarraute 1948 (divorced 1955); m. 2nd Annette Kline 1959; two s. one d. *Education:* Harvard Univ., Univ. of Paris. *Career:* correspondent, Time magazine, Paris 1950–57; Bureau Chief, North Africa 1958–59, Hong Kong 1959–62; Time-Life; special correspondent, Observer, London 1961–65; Time Inc 1962–63; NBC News 1973–75; Far East correspondent, Saturday Evening Post 1963–65; Far East correspondent 1965–71, diplomatic correspondent 1971–72, Washington Post; Assoc. Ed., New Republic 1973–75; columnist, King Features 1975–88, Le Point, Paris 1976–83, Newsweek International 1977–81; Ed., International Writers Service 1976–86; Chief Correspondent, Viet Nam: A Television History (series, PBS) 1983; Chief Correspondent and narrator, The US and the Philippines: In Our Image (series, PBS) 1989; mem. Asia Soc., Council on Foreign Relations, PEN American Centre, Soc. of American Historians. *Publications:* Southeast Asia 1963, Mao and China: From Revolution to Revolution 1972, Vietnam: A History 1983, In Our Image: America's Empire in the Philippines 1989, Asian Americans in Transition (co-author) 1992, Paris in the Fifties 1997; contrib. to books, newspapers, journals and magazines. *Honours:* Neiman Fellow 1957–58, East Asian Research Center Fellow 1970–71, Peabody Award 1984, Pulitzer Prize in History 1990. *Address:* 10850 Spring Knowlls Drive, Rockville, MD 20854, USA. *Telephone:* (301) 299-3116 (home). *Fax:* (301) 299-4834 (home). *E-mail:* karnow@erols .com (home).

KAROL, Alexander (see Kent, Arthur William Charles)

KARPOV, Vladimir Vasilyevich; Russian author and editor; b. 28 July 1922, Orenburg; s. of Vasiliy Karpov and Lydia Karpov; m. Evgenia Vasilievna Karpov 1956; one s. two d. *Education:* Military Acad., Moscow and Gorky Literary Inst. *Career:* arrested 1941, sent to camp, released to join a penal Bn, subsequently distinguishing himself in mil. reconnaissance work; mem. CPSU 1943–91; started publishing (novels, stories, essays) 1948–; Deputy Ed. of Oktyabr 1974–77; Sec. of Presidium of USSR Union of Writers 1981–86, First Sec. 1986–91; Chief Ed. of Novy mir 1981–86; Deputy to the Presidium of the USSR Supreme Soviet 1984–89; mem. CPSU Cen. Cttee 1988–90, USSR People's Deputy 1989–91; mem. Acad. of Mil. Sciences. *Publications:* The Marshal's Baton 1970, Take Them Alive 1975, The Regimental Commander 1982–84, The Eternal Struggle 1987, Marshal Zhukov, (Vol. I) 1989, (Vol. II) 1992, (Vol. III) 1995, Selected Works (3 Vols), The Destiny of a Scout (novel) 1999, The Executed Marshals 2000. *Honours:* Hon. DLitt (Strathclyde Univ.); State Prize 1986, Hero of Soviet Union 1944. *Address:* Kutozovsky prosp. 26, Apt. 94, Moscow, Russia. *Telephone:* (495) 249-26-12. *Fax:* (495) 200-02-93.

KASHU'A, Said; Israeli writer and journalist; b. Tira. *Education:* Israel Arts and Sciences Acad. High School, Jerusalem. *Publications include:* short stories: Dancing Arabs 2002. *Honours:* Fellow, John Simon Guggenheim Memorial Foundation. *Address:* c/o Grove Press, 841 Broadway, New York, NY 10003-4793, USA.

KASISCHKE, Laura, BA, MFA; American poet, writer and teacher; b. 5 Dec. 1961, Lake Charles, LA; m. William Abernethy 1994, one s. *Education:* University of Michigan, Columbia University. *Career:* Instructor in Writing, South Plains College, Levelland, Texas, 1987–88; Visiting Lecturer in Creative Writing and Literature, Eastern Michigan University, 1989–90; Instructor in Creative Writing and Literature, Washtenaw Community College, Ann Arbor, 1990–; Assoc. Prof., University of Nevada, Las Vegas, 1994–95. *Publications:* Poetry: Brides, Wives, and Widows, 1990; Wild Brides, 1992; Housekeeping in a Dream, 1995. Fiction: Suspicious River, 1996; The Life Before Her Eyes, 2001. Contributions: numerous periodicals. *Honours:* Michael Gutterman Poetry Award, 1983; Marjorie Rapaport Poetry Award, 1986; Michigan Council for the Arts Individual Artist Grant, 1990; Ragdale Foundation Fellowships, 1990–92; Elmer Holmes Bobst Award for Emerging Writers, 1991; Bread Loaf Fellow in Poetry, 1992; MacDowell Colony Fellow, 1992; Creative Artists Award, Arts Foundation of Michigan, 1993; Alice Fay DiCastagnola Award, 1993; Pushcart Prize, 1993; Barbara Deming Memorial Award, 1994; National Endowment for the Arts Fellowship, 1994; Poets & Writers Exchange Fellowship, 1994.

KASSABOVA, Kapka, BA, MA; Bulgarian poet, novelist and journalist; b. 1973, Sofia. *Education:* Univ. of Otago, Dunedin, Victoria Univ. of Wellington, New Zealand. *Career:* teacher of English, Marseilles, France 1998. *Publications:* poetry: All Roads Lead to the Sea 1997, Dismemberment 1998, Someone Else's Life 2003; novels: Reconnaissance 1999, Love in the Land of Midas 2000; travel writing: Globetrotter's Guide to Dheli, Jaipur and Agra 2002; contrib. to Critic, NZ Listener. *Honours:* Buddie Finlay Sargeson Fellowship 1999; New Zealand Soc. of Authors Jessie McKay Award for the Best First Book of Poetry, Commonwealth Writers' Prize for Best First Book in the SE Asia-Pacific Region 2000, Cathay Pacific NZ Travel Writer of the Year Award 2002. *Address:* c/o Bloodaxe Books Ltd, Highgreen, Tarset, Northumberland NE48 1RP, England. *Website:* www.bloodaxebooks.com.

KASSEM, Louise (Lou) Sutton Morrell; American writer; b. 10 Nov. 1931, Elizabethton, TN; m. Shakeep Kassem 1951; four d. *Education:* East Tennessee State Univ., Univ. of Virginia, Vassar Coll. *Career:* mem. Soc. of Children's Book Writers, Writers in Virginia, Appalachian Writers, Nat. League of American Pen Women, Authors' Guild. *Publications:* Dance of Death 1984, Middle School Blues 1986, Listen for Rachel 1986, Secret Wishes 1989, A Summer for Secrets 1989, A Haunting in Williamsburg 1990, The Treasures of Witch Hat Mountain 1992, Odd One Out 1994, The Druid Curse 1994, The Innkeeper's Daughter 1996, Sneeze on Monday 1997; contrib. to

Alan Review, Signal, Chicken Soup for Kids' Souls, Chicken Soup for Pre-Teen Souls, The Writer, North Carolina Educ. Asscn. *Honours:* American Library Asscn Notable Book in Social Studies 1986, Virginia State Reading Assn Best Book for Young Readers. *Address:* 715 Burruss Drive NW, Blacksburg, VA 24060, USA. *Telephone:* (540) 552-2241. *E-mail:* lmk1931@aol.com.

KATTAN, Naïm, OC, FRSC; Canadian writer; b. 26 Aug. 1928, Baghdad, Iraq; s. of the late Nessim and Hela Kattan; m. Gaetane Laniel 1961; one s. *Education:* Univ. of Baghdad and Sorbonne, Paris. *Career:* newspaper corresp. in Near East and Europe, broadcaster throughout Europe; emigrated to Canada 1954; Int. Politics Ed. for Nouveau Journal 1961–62; fmr teacher at Laval Univ.; fmr Sec. Cercle Juif de langue française de Montreal; freelance journalist and broadcaster; Prof., Univ. of Québec, Montreal; Assoc. Dir Canada Council; mem. Académie Canadienne-Française; Pres. Royal Soc. of Canada. *Publications:* (novels) Adieu Babylone 1975, Les Fruits arrachés 1981, La Fiancée promise 1983, La Fortune du passager 1989, La Célébration 1997, L'Anniversaire 2000; (essays) Le Réel et le théâtral 1970, Ecrivains des Amériques, Tomes I–III, Le Repos et l'Oubli 1987, Le Père 1990, Farida 1991, La Reconciliation 1992, A. M. Klein 1994, La Distraction 1994, Culture: Alibi ou liberté 1996, Idoles et images 1996, Figures bibliques 1997, L'Amour reconnu 1999, Le Silence des adieux 1999, Le gardien de mon frère 2003, La Parole et le lieu 2004, Les Villes de naissance, L'Ecrivain migrant, Farewell Babylon: Coming of Age in Jewish Baghdad 2007; also numerous short stories and criticisms. *Honours:* Chevalier Légion d'honneur; Officier des Arts et Lettres de France; Chevalier Ordre nat. du Québec; Dr. hc (Middlebury Coll.). *Address:* 2463 rue Sainte Famille No. 2114, Montreal, PQ, H2X 2K7, Canada. *Telephone:* (514) 499-2836. *Fax:* (514) 499-9954. *E-mail:* kattan.naim@uqom.

KATZ, Hilda; American poet and artist; b. 2 June 1909, Bronx, NY; d. of Max Katz and Lina Katz (née Schwartz). *Education:* Nat. Acad. of Design. *Career:* special collections include US Nat. Museum 1965, Univ. of Maine 1965, Library of Congress 1965–71, Metropolitan Museum of Art 1965–66, 1980, Nat. Gallery of Art 1966, Nat. Collection of Fine Arts 1966–71, Nat. Air and Space Museum 1970, New York Public Library 1971, 1978, US Museum of History and Tech. 1972, Naval Museum 1972, Smithsonian Inst. 1979, Israel Nat. Museum, Jerusalem 1980–81, Jewish Heritage, New York 1989, Jewish Nat. and Univ. Library, Israel 1990; works in perm. collections including Fogg Museum, Colorado Springs Fine Arts Center, Newark Public Library, Addison Gallery of American Art, Safed Museum, Israel, Musée Nat. d'Art Contemporain, Paris, France, Yad Vashem Memorial Archives, Israel; commemorative poetry at New York State Museum of Art. *Solo exhibitions include:* Bowdoin Coll. Art Museum 1951, California State Library 1953, Jewish Museum 1956, Ball State Teachers' Coll. 1957, Miami Beach Art Center, Richmond Art Asscn 1959, State Museum of Albany 1989, Jewish Theological Seminary of America 1989. *Publications include:* (as Hilda Weber) Anthologies: The Bloom 1984–85, 1987, Perfume and Fragrance 1988, 1989, Lightning and Rainbows 1989, 1990. *Address:* 915 West End Avenue, Apt 5D, New York, NY 10025, USA.

KATZ, Steve, BA, MA; American writer, poet, screenwriter and academic; *Professor of English, University of Colorado at Boulder*; b. 14 May 1935, New York, NY; m. Patricia Bell 1956 (divorced); three s. *Education:* Cornell Univ., Univ. of Oregon. *Career:* English Language Inst., Lecce, Italy 1960; overseas faculty, Univ. of Maryland, Lecce, Italy 1961–62; Asst Prof. of English, Cornell Univ. 1962–67; Lecturer in Fiction, Univ. of Iowa 1969–70; Writer-in-Residence, Brooklyn Coll., CUNY 1970–71, Co-Dir Projects in Innovative Fiction 1971–73, Adjunct Asst Prof., Queens Coll., CUNY 1973–75; Assoc. Prof. of English, Univ. of Notre Dame 1976–78; Assoc. Prof. of English, Univ. . of Colorado at Boulder 1978–82, Prof. of English 1982–; mem. Authors' League of America, PEN International, Writers' Guild. *Publications:* fiction: The Lestriad 1962, The Exaggerations of Peter Prince 1968, Posh 1971, Saw 1972, Moving Parts 1977, Wier and Pouce 1984, Florry of Washington Heights 1987, Swanny's Ways 1995, Antonello's Lion 2005, Kisssss: A Miscellany 2007; short story collections: Creamy and Delicious: Eat my Words (in Other Words) 1970, Stolen Stories 1985, 43 Fictions 1991; poetry: The Weight of Antony 1964, Cheyenne River Wild Track 1973, Journalism 1990; screenplay: Grassland 1974. *Honours:* PEN Grant 1972, Creative Artists Public Service grant 1976, Nat. Educational Assn grants 1976, 1982, GCAH Book of the Year 1991, America Award in Fiction 1995. *Address:* 669 Washington Street, No. 602, Denver, CO 80203, USA. *E-mail:* elbonoz@earthlink.net (home).

KAUFMAN, Alan, BA; American writer, poet and editor; b. 12 Jan. 1952, New York, NY. *Education:* City College, CUNY, Columbia University. *Career:* founder-Ed. Jewish Arts Quarterly 1974–75, Davka: Jewish Cultural Revolution 1996–97, TATTOOJEW.COM 1998–2001; Ed.-in-Chief Jewish Frontier 1987–88; American Ed. Tel Aviv Review 1989; freelance feature writer for Los Angeles Times, San Francisco Chronicle, Partisan Review, San Francisco Examiner, Salon.com, etc. *Exhibition:* Acrylic Paintings (exhibited with David Newman and Tim Wicks, San Francisco) 2003, 2004. *Publications:* The New Generation: Fiction for Our Time from America's Writing Programs (ed.) 1987; Who Are We? (poems) 1997; The Outlaw Bible of American Poetry (ed.) 1999, 2004; Jew Boy: A Memoir 2000, Matches (novel) 2005; contrib. to anthologies and periodicals. *Honours:* Firecracker Alternative Book Award 2000. *Literary Agent:* c/o William Clark Associates, 154 Christopher Street, Suite 3C, New York, NY 10014, USA. *Telephone:* (212) 675-2784. *Fax:* (646) 349-1658. *E-mail:* wmclark@wmclark.com.

KAUFMAN, Charles (Charlie) Stewart; American screenwriter; b. Nov. 1958, W Hartford, Conn.; m. Denise Kaufman. *Education:* Boston Univ., NY Univ. *Career:* worked in newspaper circulation dept, The Star Tribune, Minneapolis, Minn. 1986–90; contrib. to National Lampoon, LA 1991; began scriptwriting 1991; cr. short films shown on Late Night with David Letterman TV show 1990s; writer 30 episodes for TV shows 1991–96; Producer Misery Loves Company (TV series) 1995. *Screenplays include:* films: Being John Malkovich 1999, Human Nature 2001, Adaptation (Best Screenplay, Broadcast Film Critics Assn, Chicago Film Critics Assn, Nat. Bd of Review, Toronto Film Critics Assn) 2002, Confessions of a Dangerous Mind 2002, Eternal Sunshine of the Spotless Mind (Nat. Bd of Review Best Original Screenplay Award 2004, BAFTA Award 2005, Writers' Guild of America Award for best original screenplay 2005, Acad. Award for Best Original Screenplay 2005) 2004; TV: Get A Life 1991–92, The Edge 1992–93, The Trouble with Larry 1993, Ned and Stacey 1996–97, The Dana Carvey Show 1996. *Literary Agent:* United Talent Agency, 9560 Wilshire Boulevard, Fifth Floor, Beverly Hills, CA 90212, USA.

KAUFMAN, Sir Gerald Bernard, Kt, PC, MA, MP; British politician; b. 21 June 1930, s. of Louis Kaufman and Jane Kaufman. *Education:* Leeds Grammar School and Queen's Coll., Oxford. *Career:* Asst Gen. Sec. Fabian Soc. 1954–55; political staff, Daily Mirror 1955–64; Political Corresp., New Statesman 1964–65; Parl. Press Liaison, Labour Party 1965–70; MP for Manchester, Ardwick 1970–83, for Manchester, Gorton 1983–; Under-Sec. of State for the Environment 1974–75; Minister of State, Dept of Industry 1975–79; mem. Parl. Cttee of Labour Party 1980–92; Opposition Spokesman for Home Affairs 1983–87; Shadow Foreign Sec. 1987–92; Chair. House of Commons Nat. Heritage Select Cttee 1992–97, Culture, Media and Sport Select Cttee 1997–2005; mem. Labour Party Nat. Exec. Cttee 1991–92; mem. Royal Comm. on House of Lords Reform 1999; Chair. Booker Prize Judges 1999. *Publications:* How to Live under Labour (co-author) 1964, To Build the Promised Land 1973, How to Be a Minister 1980 (revised edn 1997), Renewal: Labour's Britain in the 1980s 1983, My Life in the Silver Screen 1985, Inside the Promised Land 1986, Meet Me in St Louis 1994. *Honours:* Hillai-e-Pakistan 1999. *Address:* House of Commons, Westminster, London, SW1A 0AA (office); 87 Charlbert Court, Eamont Street, London, NW8, England (home). *Telephone:* (20) 7219-5145 (office). *Fax:* (20) 7219-6825 (office).

KAUFMANN, Myron S., AB; American novelist; b. 27 Aug. 1921, Boston, MA; m. Paula Goldberg 1960 (divorced 1980); one s. two d. *Education:* Harvard Univ. *Publications:* fiction: Remember Me To God 1957, Thy Daughter's Nakedness 1968, The Love of Elspeth Baker 1982. *Address:* Apt 104, 59 Pond Street, Sharon, MA 02067, USA (home). *Telephone:* (781) 784-6419 (home).

KAUFMANN, Thomas DaCosta, BA, MA, MPhil, PhD; American academic and writer; b. 7 May 1948, New York, NY; m. Virginia Burns Roehrig 1974 (divorced 1998); one d. *Education:* Yale University, Warburg Institute, London and Harvard University. *Career:* Asst Prof., 1977–83, Assoc. Prof., 1983–89, Prof. of Art History, 1989–, Princeton University; Visiting professorships and curatorships; mem. College Art Assn of America; Renaissance Society of America; Verband Deutscher Kunsthistorien. *Publications:* Variations on the Imperial Theme, 1978; Drawings From the Holy Roman Empire 1540–1650, 1982; L'Ecole de Prague, 1985; Art and Architecture in Central Europe 1550–1620, 1985; The School of Prague: Painting at the Court of Rudolf II, 1988; Central European Drawings 1680–1800, 1989; The Mastery of Nature, 1993; Court, Cloister and City, 1995. Contributions: books and professional journals. *Honours:* Marshall-Allison Fellow, 1970; David E. Finley Fellow, National Gallery of Art, Washington, DC, 1974–77; ACLS Award, 1977–78, and Fellowship, 1982; Senior Fellow, Alexander von Humboldt Stiftung, Berlin and Munich, 1985–86, 1989–90; Guggenheim Fellowship, 1993–94; Herzog August Bibliothek Fellow, Wolfenbüttel, 1994.

KAUR, Prabhjot (see Prabhjot Kaur)

KAVALER, Lucy Estrin, BA; American writer; b. 29 Aug. 1930, New York, NY; m. 1948; one s. one d. *Education:* Oberlin College, OH; Fellowship, Advanced Science Writing, Columbia University Graduate School. *Publications:* Private World of High Society, 1960; Mushrooms, Molds and Miracles, 1965; The Astors, 1966; Freezing Point, 1970; Noise the New Menace, 1975; A Matter of Degree, 1981; The Secret Lives of the Edmonts, 1989; Heroes and Lovers, 1995. Contributions: Smithsonian; Natural History; McCall's; Reader's Digest; Redbook; Primary Cardiology; Woman's Day (encyclopaedia); Skin Cancer Foundation Journal; Memories; Female Patient. *E-mail:* lucykavaler@lucykavaler.com. *Website:* www.lucykavaler.com.

KAVALER, Rebecca, AB; American writer; b. 26 July 1930, Atlanta, GA; m. Frederic Kavaler 1955; two s. *Education:* University of Georgia. *Career:* mem. PEN. *Publications:* Further Adventures of Brunhild, 1978; Doubting Castle, 1984; Tigers in the Woods, 1986; A Little More Than Kin, 2002. Contributions: anthologies and magazines. *Honours:* short stories included in Best of Nimrod, 1957–69; Best American Short Stories, 1972; Award for Short Fiction, Associated Writing Programs, 1978; National Endowment for the Arts Fellowships, 1979, 1985. *Address:* 425 Riverside Drive, New York, NY 10025, USA. *E-mail:* rkavaler@msn.com.

KAVANAGH, Dan (see Barnes, Julian Patrick)

KAVANAGH, Patrick Joseph, MA, FRSL; British poet, writer and editor; b. 6 Jan. 1931, Worthing, Sussex, England; m. 1st Sally Philipps 1956 (died 1958); m. 2nd Catherine Ward 1965; two s. *Education:* Merton Coll., Oxford. *Career:* columnist, The Spectator 1983–96, TLS 1996–2002. *Publications:* poetry: One and One 1960, On the Way to the Depot 1967, About Time 1970, Edward Thomas in Heaven 1974, Life Before Death 1979, Selected Poems 1982, Presences: New and Selected Poems 1987, An Enchantment 1991, Collected Poems 1992, Something About 2004; fiction: A Song and Dance 1968, A Happy Man 1972, People and Weather 1978, Scarf Jack: The Irish Captain 1978, Rebel for Good 1980, Only By Mistake 1980; non-fiction: The Perfect Stranger 1966, People and Places 1988, Finding Connections 1990, Voices in Ireland: A Traveller's Literary Companion 1994, A Kind of Journal 2003, Selected Prose 2003; editor: The Collected Poems of Ivor Gurney 1982, The Oxford Book of Short Poems (with James Michie) 1985, The Bodley Head G. K. Chesterton 1985, Selected Poems of Ivor Gurney 1990, A Book of Consolations 1992. *Honours:* Richard Hillary Prize 1966, Guardian Fiction Prize 1968, Cholmondeley Poetry Prize 1993. *Literary Agent:* c/o PFD, Drury House, 34–43 Russell Street, London, WC2B 5HA, England.

KAVANAUGH, Cynthia (see Daniels, Dorothy)

KAWADA, Junzo; Japanese anthropologist and writer; *Professor of Cultural Anthropology, Hiroshima City University;* b. 1934, Tokyo. *Education:* Tokyo Univ. *Career:* Prof. of Cultural Anthropology, Hiroshima City Univ.; mem. Universal Acad. of Cultures, Inst. for the Study of the Languages and Cultures of Asia and Africa, Tokyo; Assoc. Ed. Anthropological Science. *Publications:* non-fiction: Kotoba kotoba kotoba: Moji to Nihongo o kangaeru (Words, Native and Imported: Orthography and the Japanese Language), Koe (Voices) 1988, Nishi no kaze, minami no kaze (West Wind, South Wind) 1992, Oto-Kotoba-Ningen (Sound-Word-Man) (with Toru Takemitsu) 1992, Genese et Dynamique de la Royaute: Les Mosi Merdinoaux 2002; translations: Claude Lévi-Strauss: L'anthropologie face aux problèmes du monde moderne (jtly); contrib. numerous articles to scholarly journals, including Dialogue Among Civilisations Vol. II, Annales: Histoire, Sciences Sociales, Revue Gabonaise des Sciences de l'Homme. *Honours:* Koizumi Fumio Prize 2001. *Address:* Faculty of International Studies, Hiroshima City University, 3-4-1 Ozuka-Higashi, Asa-Minami-Ku, Hiroshima 731-3194, Japan (office). *E-mail:* j-kawada@intl .hiroshima-cu.ac.jp (office).

KAWAMOTO, Koji; Japanese author and critic. *Career:* Pres., International Comparative Literary Asscn (ICLA); Vice-Pres., Oternae Univ.; teaches literature at the Univ. of Tokyo. *Publications:* non-fiction: The Poetics of Japanese Verse - Imagery, Structure and Meter 1999. *Address:* c/o Paola Mildonian, Letterature Comparate, Dipartim. di Studi Anglo-Americani e Ibero-Americani, Universitè Ca' Foscari-Venezia, Ca' Garzoni, S. Marco 3417, 30124, Venice, Italy.

KAY, Guy Gavriel, BA, LLB; Canadian writer; b. 7 Nov. 1954, Weyburn, SK; m. Laura Beth Cohen 1984; two s. *Education:* Univ. of Manitoba, Univ. of Toronto. *Career:* prin. writer and Assoc. Prod., The Scales of Justice (CBC Radio drama) 1981–90; mem. Asscn of Canadian Radio and TV Artists, Law Soc. of Upper Canada. *Publications:* The Summer Tree 1984, The Darkest Road 1986, The Wandering Fire 1986, Tigana 1990, A Song for Arbonne 1992, The Lions of Al-Rassan 1995, The Last Light of the Sun 2004, Ysabel 2007; contrib. to journals. *Honours:* Aurora Prizes 1986, 1990. *Literary Agent:* Curtis Brown Ltd, Haymarket House, 28–29 Haymarket, London, SW1Y 4SP, England. *Telephone:* (20) 7393-4400. *Fax:* (20) 7393-4401. *E-mail:* info@ curtisbrown.co.uk. *Website:* www.curtisbrown.co.uk.

KAY, Jackie, MBE, BA, PhD; British writer and poet; b. 9 Nov. 1961, Glasgow; d. of John and Helen Kay; pnr Carol Ann Duffy; one s. *Education:* Stirling Univ., Scotland. *Career:* Literature Touring Co-ordinator Arts Council 1991–93; mem. Poetry Soc., Writers' Guild. *Publications:* poetry: The Adoption Papers (Eric Gregory Award, Saltire and Forward Prizes) 1991, Other Lovers (Somerset Maugham Award) 1993, Off Colour 1998, New and Selected Poems 2003, Life Mask 2005; juvenile: Two's Company 1992, Three Has Gone 1994, The Frog Who Dreamed She Was an Opera Singer 1998, Strawgirl 2002; other: Outlines Bessie Smith (biog.) 1997, Trumpet (Guardian Fiction Prize, Scottish Arts Council Book Award) 1998, Why Don't You Stop Talking (short stories) 2003, Wish I Was Here (short stories) 2006; also several TV documentaries; contribs to Poetry Review, Spare Rib, Conditions, Poetry Wales, Chapman, Rialto, Poetry Matters, London Poetry Newsletter, City Limits. *Honours:* British Book Award for Writer of the Year 2007. *Address:* 62 Kirkton Road, London, N15 5EY; c/o Picador Books, Macmillan Publishers, 25 Eccleston Place London, SW1W 9NF, England.

KAYE, Geraldine Hughesdon, BSc; British writer; b. 14 Jan. 1925, Watford, Herts, England; m. 1948 (divorced 1975); one s. two d. *Education:* LSE. *Career:* mem. PEN, West Country Writers, Society of Authors. *Publications:* Comfort Herself, 1985; A Breath of Fresh Air, 1986; Summer in Small Street, 1989; Someone Else's Baby, 1990; A Piece of Cake, 1991; Snowgirl, 1991; Stone Boy, 1991; Hands Off My Sister, 1993; Night at the Zoo, 1995; Forests of the Night, 1995; Late in the Day, 1997; The Dragon Upstairs, 1997; My Second Best Friend, 1998; Between Us (adult novel), 1998. *Honours:* The Other Award 1986.

KAYE, Marvin Nathan, BA, MA; American writer; b. 10 March 1938, Philadelphia, PA; m. Saralee Bransdorf 1963, one d. *Education:* Pennsylvania State University, University of Denver. *Career:* Senior Ed., Harcourt Brace Jovanovich; Artistic Dir, Open Book Theatre Company 1975–; Adjunct Prof. of Creative Writing, New York University, 1975–; Seminar Dir, Smithsonian Institution, Washington, DC, 1998–; mem. several professional organizations. *Publications:* The Histrionic Holmes, 1971; A Lively Game of Death, 1972; A Toy is Born, 1973; The Stein and Day Handbook of Magic, 1973; The Grand Ole Opry Murders, 1974; The Handbook of Mental Magic, 1974; Bullets for Macbeth, 1976; The Incredible Umbrella, 1977; Catalog of Magic, 1977; My Son the Druggist, 1977; The Laurel and Hardy Murders, 1977; My Brother the Druggist, 1979; The Amorous Umbrella, 1981; The Possession of Immanuel Wolf, 1981; The Soap Opera Slaughters, 1982; Ghosts of Night and Morning, 1985; Fantastique, 1993. With Parke Godwin: The Masters of Solitude, 1978; Wintermind, 1982; A Cold Blue Light, 1983. Editor: Fiends and Creatures, 1975; Brother Theodore's Chamber of Horrors, 1975; Ghosts, 1981; Masterpieces of Terror and the Supernatural, 1985; Ghosts of Night and Morning, 1987; Devils and Demons, 1987; Weird Tales, the Magazine That Never Dies, 1988; Witches and Warlocks, 1989; 13 Plays of Ghosts and the Supernatural, 1990; Haunted America, 1991; Lovers and Other Monsters, 1991; Sweet Revenge, 1992; Masterpieces of Terror and the Unknown, 1993; Frantic Comedy, 1993; The Game is Afoot, 1994; Angels of Darkness, 1995; Readers Theatre: How to Stage It, 1995; The Resurrected Holmes, 1996; Page to Stage, 1996; The Best of Weird Tales, 1923, 1997; The Confidential Casebook of Sherlock Holmes, 1998; Don't Open This Book, 1998. Contributions: Amazing; Fantastic; Galileo; Family Digest; Columnist, Science Fiction Chronicle.

KAYSEN, Susanna; American writer; b. 11 Nov. 1948, Cambridge, MA. *Publications:* Asa, as I Knew Him 1987, Far Afield 1990, Girl, Interrupted 1993, The Camera My Mother Gave Me 2001. *Address:* c/o Jonathan Matson, Harold Matson Company Inc., 276 Fifth Avenue, New York, NY 10001, USA.

KAZANTSEV, Aleksei Nikolayevich; Russian playwright, actor and director; b. 11 Dec. 1945, Moscow; s. of Prof. of Moscow State Univ.; m. Natalya Vyacheslavovna Somova; one s. *Education:* Moscow State Univ., Drama Studio of Cen. Theatre for Children, Studio School of Moscow Art Theatre. *Career:* Founder and Artistic Dir (with M. Roshchin) Dramaturg magazine 1992; Founder and Dir Center of Drama and Staging 1998. *Plays include:* Anton and Others 1975, Old House 1976, And The Silver Thread Will Break 1979, Great Buddha, Help Them! 1986, Yevgenya's Dreams 1990, This That World 1992, Running Strangers 1996, Brothers and Lisa 1998, Kremlin, Come to Me! 2001; *Stage productions include:* Strawberry Field, Nest of a Wood-Grouse, Riga Drama Theatre, If I Stay Alive, Moscow Mossoviet Theatre, Death of Tarelkin, Center of Drama and Staging (Stanislavsky Prize, Chaika Prize, Prize of Moscow). *Address:* Palikha str. 7-9, korp. 2, Apt 54, 127055 Moscow, Russia (home). *Telephone:* (495) 972-65-85 (home). *Fax:* (495) 972-65-85 (home). *E-mail:* Kazantsev-Center@mail.ru (office).

KAZANTZIS, Judith; British poet and novelist; b. 14 Aug. 1940, Oxford, England; m. 2nd Irving Weinman; one d. one s. (from previous marriage). *Education:* Univ. of Oxford. *Career:* Royal Literary Fund Fellow, Univ. of Sussex 2005–06; judge of several poetry prize competitions; mem. Soc. of Authors, English PEN, Palestine Solidarity Campaign, Nicaragua Solidarity Campaign, Campaign for Nuclear Disarmament. *Publications:* poetry: Minefield 1977, The Wicked Queen 1980, Touch Papers (co-author) 1982, Let's Pretend 1984, Flame Tree 1988, A Poem for Guatemala (pamphlet) 1988, The Rabbit Magician Plate 1992, Selected Poems 1977–92 1995, Swimming Through the Grand Hotel 1997, The Odysseus Papers: Fictions on the Odyssey of Homer 1999, In Cyclop's Cave (trans. of book IX of The Odyssey) 2002, Just After Midnight 2004; prose: Of Love and Terror (novel) 2002; contribs to anthologies and periodicals. *E-mail:* j.kazantzis@telco4u.com. *Website:* www .writersartists.net.

KEANE, Fergal Patrick, OBE; Irish journalist and broadcaster; b. 6 Jan. 1961, s. of the late Eamon Brendan Keane and of Mary Hasset; m. Anne Frances Flaherty 1986; one s. *Education:* Terenure Coll., Dublin and Presentation Coll., Cork. *Career:* trainee reporter Limerick Leader 1979–82; reporter Irish Press Group, Dublin 1982–84, Radio Telefis Eireann, Belfast 1986–89 (Dublin 1984–86); Northern Ireland Corresp. BBC Radio 1989–91, South Africa Corresp. 1991–94, Asia Corresp. 1994–97, Special Corresp. 1997–; presenter Fergal Keane's Forgotten Britain (BBC) 2000. *Publications:* Irish Politics Now 1987, The Bondage of Fear 1994, Season of Blood: A Rwandan Journey 1995, Letter to Daniel 1996, Letters Home 1999, A Stranger's Eye 2000, There will be Sunlight Later: A Memoir of War 2004, All of These People (memoir) 2005. *Honours:* Hon. DLitt (Strathclyde) 2001, (Staffs.) 2002; James Cameron Prize 1996, Bayeux Prize for war reporting 1999; Reporter of the Year Sony Silver Award 1992 and Sony Gold Award 1993, Int. Reporter of the Year 1993, Amnesty Int. Press Awards, RTS Journalist of the Year 1994, BAFTA Award 1997. *Address:* c/o BBC Television Centre, Wood Lane, London, W12 7RJ, England.

KEARNEY, Martha Catherine; British journalist; *Presenter, The World at One, BBC Radio 4;* b. 8 Oct. 1957, d. of Hugh Kearney and Catherine Kearney; m. Christopher Thomas Shaw 2001. *Education:* Brighton and Hove High School, George Watson's Ladies' Coll., Edinburgh and St Anne's Coll., Oxford. *Career:* worked for LBC/IRN Radio 1980–87, as reporter AM breakfast show, presenter AM and Nightline phone-in, lobby correspondent for IRN; worked on A Week in Politics (Channel 4) 1987–88; worked for BBC from 1988, reporter On the Record (BBC 1) 1988–94, Panorama 1993, presenter Woman's Hour (BBC Radio 4) 1999–, reporter Newsnight 1994–2000, Political Ed. Newsnight 2000–07, presenter The World at One (BBC Radio 4) 2007–.

Honours: TRIC Radio Presenter of the Year 2003, House Magazine Political Commentator of the Year 2005. *Address:* BBC TV Centre, Wood Lane, London, W12 7RJ, England. *E-mail:* martha.kearney@bbc.co.uk. *Website:* www.bbc.co .uk.

KEARNS, Marguerite, (Marguerite Culp), BA; American writer; b. 17 Feb. 1943, Norristown, PA. *Education:* Beaver College, Glenside, PA, Temple University, Philadelphia. *Career:* mem. National Writers' Union, PEN. *Publications:* Freedom Deferred (online) 2002, Big Brother 2002, For Love's Sake Only 2002; contrib. to newspapers and journals. *Honours:* New York State Bar Asscn Award in Journalism 1974.

KEATING, Henry Reymond Fitzwalter, (Evelyn Hervey), FRSL; British writer; b. 31 Oct. 1926, St Leonards-on-Sea, Sussex; s. of John Hervey Keating and Muriel Keating; m. Sheila Mary Mitchell 1953; three s. one d. *Education:* Merchant Taylors' School, Trinity Coll., Dublin. *Career:* journalist 1952–59; Chair. Crime Writers Asscn 1970–71, Soc. of Authors 1983, 1984; Pres. The Detection Club 1985–2001. *Publications:* Death and the Visiting Firemen 1959, Zen There Was Murder 1960, A Rush on the Ultimate 1961, The Dog It Was That Died 1962, Death of a Fat God 1963, The Perfect Murder 1964, Is Skin Deep, Is Fatal 1965, Inspector Ghote's Good Crusade 1966, Inspector Ghote Caught in Meshes 1967, Inspector Ghote Hunts the Peacock 1968, Inspector Ghote Plays a Joker 1969, Inspector Ghote Breaks an Egg 1970, Inspector Ghote Goes by Train 1971, The Strong Man 1971, Inspector Ghote Trusts the Heart 1972, Bats Fly Up for Inspector Ghote 1974, The Underside 1974, A Remarkable Case of Burglary 1975, Murder Must Appetize 1976, Filmi, Filmi Inspector Ghote 1976, Agatha Christie: First Lady of Crime (ed) 1977, A Long Walk to Wimbledon 1978, Inspector Ghote Draws a Line 1979, Sherlock Holmes, the Man and his World 1979, The Murder of the Maharajah 1980, Go West, Inspector Ghote 1981, The Lucky Alphonse 1982, The Sheriff of Bombay 1983, Under a Monsoon Cloud 1984, Mrs Craggs, Crimes Cleaned Up 1985, Writing Crime Fiction 1986, The Body in the Billiard Room 1987, Dead on Time 1988, Inspector Ghote, His Life and Crimes 1989, The Iciest Sin 1990, Cheating Death 1992, The Rich Detective 1993, Doing Wrong 1994, The Good Detective 1995, Asking Questions 1996, In Kensington Gardens Once 1997, The Soft Detective 1997, Bribery, Corruption Also 1999, Jack, the Lady Killer 1999, The Hard Detective 2000, Breaking and Entering 2000, A Detective in Love 2001, A Detective Under Fire 2002, The Dreaming Detective 2003, A Detective at Death's Door 2004, One Man and His Bomb 2006, Rules, Regs and Rotten Eggs 2007. *Honours:* Gold Dagger Award 1964, 1980, Diamond Dagger Award 1996. *Address:* 35 Northumberland Place, London, W2 5AS, England. *Telephone:* (20) 7229-1100.

KEAY, John Stanley Melville, BA; British writer and broadcaster; b. 18 Sept. 1941, Devon, England; m. Julia Keay; four c. *Education:* Ampleforth Coll., York, Magdalen Coll., Oxford. *Publications:* Into India 1973, When Men and Mountains Meet 1977, The Gilgit Game 1979, India Discovered 1981, Eccentric Travellers 1982, Highland Drove 1984, Explorers Extraordinary 1985, The Royal Geographical Society's History of World Exploration 1991, The Honourable Company 1991, Collins Encyclopaedia of Scotland (with Julia Keay) 1994, Indonesia: From Sabang to Merauke 1995, The Explorers of the Western Himalayas 1996, Last Post: Empire's End 1997, India: A History 2000, The Great Arc 2000, Sowing the Wind: The Seeds of Conflict in the Middle East 2003, Mad About the Mekong: Exploration and Empire in South East Asia 2005, The Spice Route 2005. *Address:* Succoth, Dalmally, Argyll, Scotland.

KEE, Robert, CBE, MA; British journalist, writer and broadcaster; b. 5 Oct. 1919, Calcutta, India; s. of late Robert and Dorothy F. Kee; m. 1st Janetta Woolley 1948 (divorced 1950); one d.; m. 2nd Cynthia Judah 1960 (divorced 1989); one s. (and one s. deceased) one d.; m. 3rd Catherine M. Trevelyan 1990. *Education:* Rottingdean School, Stowe School and Magdalen Coll., Oxford. *Career:* journalist, Picture Post 1948–51; picture ed. Who 1952; foreign corresp. Observer 1956–57, Sunday Times 1957–58; literary ed. Spectator 1957; TV reporter Panorama, BBC 1958–62; TV Reporters Int., This Week, Faces of Communism (four parts, also for Channel 13, USA) ITV 1962–78; Ireland: a TV history (13 parts, also for Channel 13, USA), Panorama, BBC 1979–82; TVam 1982–83, Presenter 7 Days (Channel 4), ITV 1984–88; numerous BBC radio broadcasts 1946–97. *Publications:* A Crowd Is Not Company 1947, The Impossible Shore 1949, A Sign of the Times 1955, Broadstrop in Season 1959, Refugee World 1960, The Green Flag 1972, Ireland: A History 1980, The World We Left Behind 1984, The World We Fought For 1985, Trial and Error 1986, Munich: The Eleventh Hour 1988, The Picture Post Album 1989, The Laurel and the Ivy: Parnell and Irish Nationalism 1993. *Honours:* BAFTA Richard Dimbleby Award 1976. *Address:* c/o Rogers, Coleridge and White, 20 Powis Mews, London, W11 1JN, England. *Telephone:* (20) 7221-3717.

KEEBLE, Neil Howard, BA, DPhil, DLitt, FRSE, FEA, FRHistS, FRSA; British academic, writer and editor; *Deputy Principal, University of Stirling;* b. 7 Aug. 1944, London, England; m. Jenny Bowers 1968; two s. one d. *Education:* Univs of Lampeter, Oxford and Stirling. *Career:* Lecturer in English, Univ. of Århus 1969–74; Lecturer, Univ. of Stirling 1974–88, Reader in English 1988–95, Prof. of English 1995–, Deputy Prin. 2001–; Fellow, English Asscn 2000. *Publications:* Richard Baxter: Puritan Man of Letters 1982, The Literary Culture of Nonconformity 1987, Calendar of the Correspondence of Richard Baxter (co-author) 1991, The Restoration: England in the 1660s 2002; ed.: The Autobiography of Richard Baxter 1974, The Pilgrim's Progress 1984, John

Bunyan: Conventicle and Parnassus 1988, The Cultural Identity of Seventeenth-Century Woman 1994, Lucy Hutchinson, Memoirs of the Life of Colonel Hutchinson 1995, The Cambridge Companion to Writing of the English Revolution 2001, Daniel Defoe, Memoirs of the Church of Scotland 2002, John Bunyan: Reading Dissenting Writing 2002, Andrew Marvell, Remarks Upon a Late Disingenuous Discourse 2003; numerous articles on cultural history 1500–1700 in academic journals. *Honours:* Hon. Fellow, Univ. of Wales, Lampeter 2000. *Address:* Deputy Principal's Office, University of Stirling, Stirling, FK9 4LA, Scotland (office). *Telephone:* (1786) 467013 (office). *E-mail:* n.h.keeble@stir.ac.uk.

KEEFFE, Barrie Colin; British dramatist, novelist, director and university tutor; *Tutor, City University London;* b. 31 Oct. 1945, London; s. of the late Edward Thomas Keeffe and Constance Beatrice Keeffe (née Marsh); m. 1st Sarah Dee (Truman) 1969 (divorced 1975); m. 2nd Verity Eileen Bargate 1981 (died 1981); two step-s.; m. 3rd Julia Lindsay 1983 (divorced 1991). *Education:* East Ham Grammar School. *Career:* fmrly actor with Nat. Youth Theatre, journalist; has written plays for theatre, TV and radio; fmrly resident writer Shaw Theatre, London, RSC; assoc. writer Theatre Royal, Stratford East, also mem. Bd; Assoc. Soho Theatre Co.; Writers' Mentor, Nat. Theatre 1999–2002; tutor, City Univ., London 2001–; Bye-Fellow, Christ's Coll., Cambridge 2003–04; UN Amb., 50th Anniversary Year 1995; mem. Soc. des auteurs et compositeurs dramatiques. *Theatre plays include:* Only a Game 1973, A Sight of Glory 1975, Scribes 1975, Here Comes the Sun 1976, Gimme Shelter 1977, A Mad World My Masters 1977, Barbarians 1977, Frozen Assets 1978, Sus 1979, Heaven Scent 1979, Bastard Angel 1980, She's So Modern 1980, Black Lear 1980, Chorus Girls 1981, Better Times 1985, King of England 1988, My Girl 1989, Not Fade Away 1990, Wild Justice 1990, I Only Want to Be With You 1995, Shadows on The Sun 2001. *Plays directed include:* A Certain Vincent, A Gentle Spirit, Talking of Chekov (Amsterdam and London), My Girl (London and Bombay), The Gary Oldman Fan Club (London). *Film:* The Long Good Friday (screenplay). *Television plays include:* Substitute 1972, Not Quite Cricket 1977, Gotcha 1977, Nipper 1977, Champions 1978, Hanging Around 1978, Waterloo Sunset 1979, No Excuses (series) 1983, King 1984. *Radio plays include:* Good Old Uncle Jack 1975, Pigeon Skyline 1975, Self- Portrait 1977, Paradise 1990, On the Eve of the Millennium 1999, Tales 2000, Feng Shui and Me 2000, The Five of Us 2002. *Publications:* novels: Gadabout 1969, No Excuses 1983; screenplay: The Long Good Friday 1998; Barrie Keeffe Plays I 2001. *Honours:* French Critics' Prix Révélation 1978, Thames TV Playwright Award 1979, Giles Cooper Award Best Radio Plays, Mystery Writers of America Edgar Allan Poe Award 1982. *Address:* 110 Annandale Road, London, SE10 0JZ, England. *E-mail:* barriekeeffe@aol.com (office).

KEEGAN, Sir John, Kt, OBE; British military historian and journalist; b. 15 May 1934, London; s. of Francis Joseph Keegan and Eileen Mary Bridgman; m. Susanne Keegan; two s. two d. *Education:* privately and Balliol Coll. Oxford. *Career:* awarded travel grant to study American Civil War in USA; writer of political reports for US Embassy, London, 1957–59; lecturer, Sr lecturer War Studies Dept Royal Mil. Acad. Sandhurst 1959–86; war correspondent for The Atlantic Monthly Telegraph, Beirut 1984; Defence Ed., Daily Telegraph 1986–; Delmas Prof. of History, Vassar Coll. 1997–98; contributing ed. US News and World Report 1986–; Dir E Somerset NHS Trust 1991–97; Commr Commonwealth War Graves Comm. 2000–; Trustee Heritage Lottery Fund 1994–2000; BBC Reith Lecturer 1998. *Publications include:* The Face of Battle 1976, The Nature of War 1981, Six Armies in Normandy: From D-Day to the Liberation of Paris 1982, Zones of Conflict: An Atlas of Future Wars 1986, Soldiers: A History of Men in Battle 1986, The Mask of Command 1987, Who's Who in Military History (with A. Wheatcroft) 1987, The Price of Admiralty: The Evolution of Naval Warfare 1989, The Second World War 1990, Churchill's Generals (ed.) 1991, A History of Warfare 1993, Warpaths: travels of a military historian in North America 1995, Who's Who in World War 2 1995, The Battle for History: Re-fighting World War II 1995, Warpaths 1996, The First World War 1998, The Penguin Book of War 1999; ed. and co-ed. of several mil. reference works. *Honours:* Hon. Fellow Balliol Coll. Oxford; Hon. LLD (New Brunswick) 1997; Hon. LittD (Queen's Univ. Belfast) 2000; Hon. DLitt (Bath) 2001; Samuel Eliot Morrison Prize US Soc. for Mil. History 1996. *Address:* The Manor House, Kilmington, nr Warminster, Wilts., BA12 6RD, England. *Telephone:* (1985) 844856.

KEEGAN, Mary Constance, (Mary Heathcott, Mary Raymond); British author; b. 30 Sept. 1914, Manchester, England. *Career:* editorial positions, London Evening News, 1934–40, Straits Times and Singapore Free Press, 1940–42, MOI All-India Radio, 1944, Time and Tide, 1945, John Herling's Labor Letter, 1951–54. *Publications:* As Mary Keegan, Mary Heathcott or Mary Raymond: If Today Be Sweet, 1956; Island of the Heart, 1957; Love Be Wary, 1958; Her Part of the House, 1960; Hide My Heart, 1961; Thief of My Heart, 1962; Never Doubt Me, 1963; Shadow of a Star, 1963; Take-Over, 1965; Girl in a Mask, 1965; The Divided House, 1966; The Long Journey Home, 1967; I Have Three Sons, 1968; That Summer, 1970; Surety for a Stranger, 1971; The Pimpernel Project, 1972; The Silver Girl, 1973; Villa of Flowers, 1976; April Promise, 1980; Grandma Tyson's Legacy, 1982.

KEEGAN, William James; British journalist and writer; *Associate Editor, The Observer.* b. 3 July 1938, London, England; m. 1st Tessa Ashton 1967 (divorced 1982); two s. two d.; m. 2nd Hilary Stonefrost 1992; one s. two d. *Career:* Economics Ed. 1977, Assoc. Ed. 1983–, The Observer; Visiting Prof. of Journalism, Sheffield University 1989–; mem. Dept of Applied Economics, Cambridge, advisory board 1988–93. *Publications:* Consulting Father Wintergreen (novel) 1974, A Real Killing (novel) 1976, Who Runs the Economy? 1979, Mrs Thatcher's Economic Experiment 1984, Britain Without Oil 1985, Mr Lawson's Gamble 1989, The Spectre of Capitalism 1992, 2066 and All That 2000, The Prudence of Mr Gordon Brown 2003; contrib. to The Tablet; Frequent Broadcaster. *Honours:* hon. doctorates. *Address:* 76 Lofting Road, London, N1 1JB, England.

KEELEY, Edmund Leroy, BA, DPhil; American academic, writer and translator; *Charles Barnwell Strant Professor of English Emeritus, Princeton University;* b. 5 Feb. 1928, Damascus, Syria; m. Mary Stathatos-Kyris 1951. *Education:* Princeton Univ., Univ. of Oxford. *Career:* instructor, Brown Univ. 1952–53; Fulbright Lecturer, Univ. of Thessaloniki 1953–54, 1986; instructor 1954–57, Asst Prof. 1957–63, Assoc. Prof. 1963–70, Prof. of English and Creative Writing 1970–92, Charles Branwell Straut Class of 1923 Prof. of English 1992–94, Prof. Emeritus 1994–, Princeton Univ.; Visiting Lecturer, Univ. of Iowa 1962–63, Univ. of the Aegean 1988; writer-in-residence, Knox Coll. 1963; Visiting Prof., New School for Social Research, New York 1980, Columbia Univ. 1981, King's Coll. London 1996; Fulbright Lecturer 1985, and Research Fellow 1987, Univ. of Athens; Sr Assoc. mem., St Antony's Coll., Oxford 1996; mem. American Acad. of Arts and Sciences, Acad. of Athens, American Literary Trans Asscn, Authors' Guild, Modern Greek Studies Asscn (pres. 1969–73, 1982–84), PEN American Center (pres. 1991–93), Poetry Soc. of America. *Publications:* fiction: The Libation 1958, The Gold-Hatted Lover 1961, The Impostor 1970, Voyage to a Dark Island 1972, A Wilderness Called Peace 1985, School for Pagan Lovers 1993, Some Wine for Remembrance 2001; non-fiction: Cavafy's Alexandria 1976, Modern Greek Poetry: Voice and Myth 1982, The Salonika Bay Murder: Cold War Politics and the Polk Affair 1989, Albanian Journal: The Road to Elbasan 1996, George Seferis and Edmund Keeley: Correspondence, 1951–1971 1997, Inventing Paradise: The Greek Journey, 1937–1947 1999, On Translation: Reflections and Conversations 2000, Borderlines: A Memoir 2005; translator: Six Poets of Modern Greece (with Philip Sherrard) 1960, Vassilis Vassilikos: The Plant, the Well, the Angel (with Mary Keeley) 1964, George Seferis: Collected Poems (with Philip Sherrard) 1967, Odysseus Elytis: The Axion Esti (with George Savidis) 1974, C. P. Cavafy: Collected Poems (with Philip Sherrard and George Savidis) 1975, Angelos Sikelianos: Selected Poems (with Philip Sherrard) 1979, Odysseus Elytis: Selected Poems (with Philip Sherrard) 1981, Yannis Ritsos: Repetitions, Testimonies, Parentheses 1991, A Greek Quintet (with Philip Sherrard) 1992, A Century of Greek Poetry (ed. with Peter Bien, Peter Constantine, Karen Van Dyck) 2004; contrib. to books and journals. *Honours:* Dr hc (Univ. of Athens) 1994, Hon. DHumLitt (Richard Stockton Coll. of New Jersey) 2006; American Acad. of Arts and Letters Rome Prize Fellow 1959–60, American Acad. of Arts and Letters Award in Literature 1999, Guggenheim Fellowships 1959–60, 1973, Columbia Univ. Trans. Center –PEN Award 1975, Harold Morton Landon Trans. Award 1980, Nat. Endowment for the Arts Fellowships 1981, 1988–89, Bellagio Study Center Rockefeller Foundation Scholar, Italy 1982, 1989, Research Fellow Virginia Center for the Creative Arts 1983, 1984, 1986, 1990, Pushcart Prize Anthology 1984, First European Prize for Trans. of Poetry 1987, PEN-Ralph Manheim Medal for Trans. 2000, London Hellenic Soc. Criticos Prize 2000, The Yale Review Prize 2003, Gennadius Library Trustees' Annual Award 2003, Hellenic Public Radio Phidippides Award 2004; Commander, Order of the Phoenix (Greece) 2001. *Address:* 140 Littlebrook Road, Princeton, NJ, USA.

KEEN, Geraldine (see Norman, Geraldine Lucia)

KEEN, Suzanne Parker, AB, AM, PhD; American academic and poet; *Thomas H. Broadus Professor, Washington and Lee University, Lexington;* b. 10 April 1963, Bethlehem, PA; m. Francis MacDonnell 1992. *Education:* Brown Univ., Harvard Univ. *Career:* Asst Prof. of English, Yale Univ. 1990–95; Assoc. Prof., Washington and Lee Univ., Lexington, VA 1995–2001, Prof. 2001–05, Thomas H. Broadus Prof. 2005–; mem. MLA, Soc. for the Study of Narrative Literature, North American Victorian Socs Asscn, Thomas Hardy Asscn. *Publications:* Victorian Renovations of the Novel: Narrative Annexes and the Boundaries of Representation 1998, Romances of the Archive in Contemporary British Fiction 2001, Narrative Form 2003, Empathy and the Novel 2007, Milk Glass Mermaid 2007; contrib. to anthologies, reviews and journals. *Honours:* Brown Univ. Kim Ann Arstark Poetry Prize 1985, Acad. of American Poets Prize 1987, Virginia Commission for the Arts Individual Artist Fellowship 1998, Nat. Endowment for the Humanities Fellowship 1999. *Address:* c/o Department of English, Washington and Lee University, Lexington, VA 24450, USA.

KEENAN, Brian, BA, MA, PhD; Northern Irish writer; b. 28 Sept. 1950, Belfast, Northern Ireland; m. Audrey Doyle 1993; two s. *Education:* Ulster Univ., Queen's Univ., Belfast. *Career:* Instructor in English, American Univ., Beirut, Lebanon 1985–86; Writer-in-Residence, Trinity Coll., Dublin 1993–94. *Publications:* An Evil Cradling: The Five-Year Ordeal of a Hostage 1992, Blind Fight (screenplay) 1995, Between Extremes 1999, Turlough 2000, Four Quarters of Light 2004. *Honours:* Time/Life International PEN Award 1992, Ewart Biggs Award 1992, Irish Times Award 1992, Christopher Award, New York 1993. *Address:* c/o Elaine Steel, 110 Gloucester Aveneu, London, NW1 8JA, England (office). *Telephone:* (20) 8348-0918 (office). *Fax:* (20) 8341-9807 (office). *E-mail:* ecmsteel@aol.com (office).

KEENE, Dennis, BA, MA, DPhil; British academic (retd), poet, writer and translator; b. 10 July 1934, London, England; m. Keiko Kurose 1962; one d. *Education:* Univ. of Oxford. *Career:* Asst Lecturer in English Literature, Univ.

of Malaya 1958–60; Lecturer in English Language and Literature, Kyoto Univ. 1961–63; Invited Prof. of English Literature, Haile Selassie I Univ., Ethiopia 1964–65; Lecturer in English Literature, Kyushu Univ. 1965–69; Asst Prof. 1970–76, Prof. of English Literature 1976–81, 1984–93, Japan Women's Univ. *Publications:* poetry: Surviving 1980, Universe and Other Poems 1984; prose: Problems in English 1969, Yokomitsu Riichi, Modernist 1980, Wasurerareta Kuni, Nippon 1995; editor: Selected Poems of Henry Howard, Earl of Surrey 1985; translator: Grass For My Pillow (novel by Saiichi Maruya) 2002, over 10 books of Japanese poems, novels and short stories 1974–2002. *Honours:* Independent Foreign Fiction Special Award 1990, Noma Trans. Prize 1992. *Address:* 77 Staunton Road, Headington, Oxford, OX3 7TL, England (home). *Telephone:* (1865) 768483 (home). *Fax:* (1865) 768483 (home).

KEENE, Donald, BA, MA, PhD, DLitt; American academic, writer and translator; *Shincho Professor Emeritus of Japanese, Columbia University;* b. 18 June 1922, New York, NY. *Education:* Columbia Univ., Univ. of Cambridge. *Career:* Lecturer, Univ. of Cambridge 1948–53; guest Ed., Asahi Shimbun, Tokyo, Japan; Prof., Columbia Univ. 1953–1992, Shincho Prof. Emeritus of Japanese 1992–; mem. Japan Soc., New York (dir 1979–82), American Acad. of Arts and Letters, Japan Acad. (foreign mem.). *Publications:* The Battles of Coxinga 1951, The Japanese Discovery of Europe 1952, Japanese Literature: An Introduction for Western Readers 1953, Living Japan 1957, Bunraku, the Puppet Theater of Japan 1965, No: The Classical Theatre of Japan 1966, Landscapes and Portraits 1971, Some Japanese Portraits 1978, World Within Walls 1978, Meeting with Japan 1978, Travels in Japan 1981, Dawn to the West 1984, Travellers of a Hundred Ages 1990, Seeds in the Heart 1993, On Familiar Terms 1994, Modern Japanese Diaries 1995, Emperor of Japan 2002, Yoshimasa and the Silver Pavilion 2003, A Frog in the Well 2006; editor: Anthology of Japanese Literature 1955, Modern Japanese Literature 1956, Sources of Japanese Tradition 1958, Twenty Plays of the No Theater 1970; translator: The Setting Sun 1956, Five Modern No Plays 1957, No Longer Human 1958, Major Plays of Chikamatsu 1961, The Old Woman, the Wife and the Archer 1961, After the Banquet 1965, Essays in Idleness 1967, Madame de Sade 1967, Friends 1969, The Man Who Turned into a Stick 1972, Three Plays of Kobo Abe 1993, The Narrow Road to Oku 1997, The Tale of the Bamboo Cutter 1998, The Breaking Jewel 2003. *Honours:* Hon. DLitt (Tohoku) 1997, (Waseda) 1998, (Tokyo Univ. of Foreign Languages) 1999, (Keiwa) 2000, (Kyoto Sangyō) 2002. *Address:* 407 Kent Hall, Columbia University, New York, NY 10027 (home); 445 Riverside Drive, New York, NY 10027, USA (home). *Telephone:* (212) 222-1449 (home). *Fax:* (212) 222-1449 (home). *E-mail:* dk8@columbia.edu (home).

KEHLMANN, Daniel, PhD; German/Austrian novelist; b. 13 Jan. 1975, Munich, Germany; s. of Michael Kehlmann. *Career:* moved to Vienna 1981; Guest Lecturer in Poetics, Johannes Gutenberg Univ., Mainz 2001, FH Wiesbaden 2005–06; writer-in-residence, New York Univ. 'Deutsches Haus' 2006, Univ. of Göttingen 2006–07; mem. Mainzer Akademie der Wissenschaften und der Literatur. *Publications:* Beerholms Vorstellung (novel) (Förderpreis des Kulturkreises der deutschen Wirtschaft) 1997, Unter der Sonne (short stories) 1998, Mahlers Zeit (novel) 1999, Der fernste Ort (novel) 2001, Ich und Kaminski (novel) 2003, Die Vermessung der Welt (novel, trans. as Measuring the World) (Heimito von Doderer Prize) 2005, Wo ist Carlos Montúfar? (essays) 2005; contrib. to Süddeutsche Zeitung, Frankfurter Rundschau, Frankfurter Allgemeine Zeitung, Literaturen. *Honours:* Candide Award 2005. *Address:* c/o Quercus Publishing, 21 Bloomsbury Square, London, WC1A 2NS, England (office).

KEILLOR, Garrison Edward, BA; American writer and broadcaster; b. (Gary Edward Keillor), 7 Aug. 1942, Anoka, MN; s. of John P. Keillor and Grace R. (Denham) Keillor; m. 1st Mary Guntzel (divorced 1976, died 1998); one s.; m. 2nd Ulla Skaerved (divorced); m. 3rd Jenny Lind Nilsson; one d. *Education:* Anoka High School and Univ. of Minn. *Career:* journalist 1962–63; radio announcer and presenter 1969–73; cr. and host A Prairie Home Companion radio show 1974–87, 1993–; host American Radio Co. 1989–93; staff writer The New Yorker 1987–92. *Film:* A Prairie Home Companion 2006. *Publications:* Happy to Be Here 1982, Lake Wobegon Days (Grammy Award for best non-musical recording 1987) 1985, Leaving Home 1987, We Are Still Married: Stories and Letters 1989, WLT: A Radio Romance 1991, Wobegon Boy The Book of Guys 1993, Cat, You Better Come Home (children's book) 1995, The Old Man Who Loved Cheese 1996, The Sandy Bottom Orchestra 1996, Wobegon Boy 1997, ME by Jimmy (Big Boy) Valente as told to Garrison Keillor 1999, Lake Wobegon Summer 1956 2001, Love Me 2004; contrib. to newspapers and magazines. *Honours:* George Foster Peabody Award 1980, Ace Award for best musical host (A Prairie Home Companion) 1988, Best Music and Entertainment Host Awards 1988, 1989, American Acad. and Institute of Arts and Letters Medal 1990, Music Broadcast Communications Radio Hall of Fame 1994, Nat. Humanities Medal 1999. *Address:* A Prairie Home Companion, Minnesota Public Radio, 45 Seventh Street E, St Paul, MN 55101, USA (office). *Website:* prairiehome.publicradio.org (office).

KEIN, Sybil, BS, MA, PhD; American academic, poet, dramatist and musician; b. 29 Sept. 1939, New Orleans, LA; m. Felix Provost 1960 (divorced 1969); one s. two d. *Education:* Xavier University, Aspen School of Arts, Louisiana State University, University of Michigan, 1975. *Career:* Instructor, 1972–75, Asst Prof., 1975–78, Assoc. Prof., 1979–88, Prof. of English, 1988–, University of Michigan at Flint. *Publications:* Bessie, Bojangles and Me, 1975; Visions from the Rainbow, 1979; Gombo People: Poésies Créoles de la Nouvelle Orleans,

1981; Delta Dancer, 1984; An American South, 1997. Contributions: anthologies and journals. *Honours:* several teaching awards; Creative Artist Awards for Poetry, Michigan Council for the Arts, 1981, 1984, 1989; Chercheur Associé, Centre d'Etudes Afro-Americaines, Université de la Sorbonne Nouvelle, 1990. *E-mail:* sybkein@aol.com.

KEITH, William John, BA, MA, PhD, FRSC; Canadian fmr academic, literary critic and poet; b. 9 May 1934, London, England; m. Hiroko Teresa Sato 1965. *Education:* Jesus Coll., Cambridge, Univ. of Toronto. *Career:* Lecturer, 1961–62, Asst Prof., 1962–66, McMaster University; Assoc. Prof., 1966–71, Prof. of English, 1971–95, Prof. Emeritus, 1995–, University of Toronto; Ed., University of Toronto Quarterly, 1976–85; mem. Richard Jefferies Society, hon. pres., 1974–91. *Publications:* Richard Jefferies: A Critical Study, 1965; Charles G. D. Roberts, 1969; The Rural Tradition, 1974; Charles G. D. Roberts: Selected Poetry and Critical Prose (ed.), 1974; The Poetry of Nature, 1980; The Arts in Canada: The Last Fifty Years (co-ed.), 1980; Epic Fiction: The Art of Rudy Wiebe, 1981; A Voice in the Land: Essays by and About Rudy Wiebe (ed.), 1981; Canadian Literature in English, 1985 (revised and expanded edn, 2 vols 2007); Regions of the Imagination, 1988; Introducing The Edible Woman, 1989; A Sense of Style: Studies in the Art of Fiction in English-Speaking Canada, 1989; An Independent Stance: Essays on English-Canadian Criticism and Fiction, 1991; Echoes in Silence (poems), 1992; Literary Images of Ontario, 1992; The Jefferies Canon, 1995; In the Beginning and Other Poems, 1999; Canadian Odyssey: A Reading of Hugh Hood's The New Age/Le nouveau siècle, 2002. Contributions: journals. *Address:* University College, University of Toronto, Toronto, ON M5S 3H7, Canada (office).

KELEK, Necla; German (b. Turkish) sociologist and writer; b. 1957, Istanbul, Turkey. *Publications:* Islam im Alltag 2002, Die verlorenen Söhne (Lost Sons), Die fremde Braut (The Foreign Bride) (Geschwister-Scholl-Preis) 2005. *Address:* c/o Verlag Kiepenheuer & Witsch GmbH & Co. KG, Rondorfer Str. 5, Cologne 50968, Germany. *E-mail:* verlag@kiwi-koeln.de.

KELLEHER, Victor, (Veronica Hart), BA, DipEd, MA, DLitt; Australian writer; b. 19 July 1939, London, England; m. Alison Lyle 1962, one s. one d. *Education:* University of Natal, University of St Andrews, University of the Witwatersrand, University of South Africa. *Career:* Jr Lecturer in English, University of the Witwatersrand, 1969; Lecturer, 1970–71, Senior Lecturer in English, 1972–73, University of South Africa, Pretoria; Lecturer in English, Massey University, Palmerston North, New Zealand, 1973–76; Lecturer, 1976–79, Senior Lecturer, 1980–83, Assoc. Prof. of English, 1984–87, University of New England, Armidale, Australia; mem. Australian Society of Authors. *Publications:* Voices from the River, 1979; Forbidden Paths of Thual, 1979; The Hunting of Shadroth, 1981; Master of the Grove, 1982; Africa and After, 1983; The Beast of Heaven, 1983 Papio, 1983; The Green Piper, 1984; Taronga, 1986; The Makers, 1987; Em's Story, 1988; Baily's Bones, 1988; The Red King, 1989; Wintering, 1990; Brother Night, 1990; Del-Del, 1991; To the Dark Tower, 1992; Micky Darlin, 1992; Where the Whales Sing, 1994; Parkland, 1994; Double God (as Veronica Hart), 1994; The House that Jack Built (as Veronica Hart), 1994; Earthsong, 1995; Storyman, 1996; Fire Dancer, 1996; Slow Burn, 1997; Into the Dark, 1999; The Ivory Trail, 1999. Contributions: anthologies and magazines.

KELLENBERGER, James, PhD; American academic and writer; *Professor of Philosophy, California State University at Northridge*; b. 4 May 1938, San Francisco, Calif.; m. Anne Dunn 1981, one s. one d. *Education:* San Jose State Univ., Univ. of California at Berkeley, Univ. of Oregon. *Career:* Lecturer in Logic, Cameroon Coll. of Arts and Science 1962–64; Asst Prof., California State Univ. at Northridge 1967–71, Assoc. Prof. 1971–75, Prof. of Philosophy 1975–; Visiting Prof., Albion Coll., Michigan 1971–72; Adjunct Prof. of Religion, Claremont Grad. School 1991; mem. American Philosophical Asscn, Soc. of Christian Philosophers. *Publications:* Religious Discovery, Faith and Knowledge 1972, The Cognitivity of Religion: Three Perspectives 1985, God-Relationships With and Without God 1989, Inter-Religious Models and Criteria (ed.) 1993, Relationship Morality 1995, Kierkegaard and Nietzsche: Faith and Eternal Acceptance 1997, Moral Relativism, Moral Diversity, and Human Relationships 2001; contrib. to scholarly books, reviews, quarterlies and journals. *Address:* Department of Philosophy, California State University at Northridge, 18111 Nordhoff Street, Northridge, CA 91330, USA (office). *E-mail:* james.kellenberger@csun.edu (office).

KELLER, Bill, BA; American newspaper editor; *Executive Editor, The New York Times*; b. 18 Jan. 1949; m. Emma Gilbey; one s. two d. *Education:* Pomona Coll., Wharton School Univ. of PA. *Career:* reporter The Portland Oregonian 1970–79, Congressional Quarterly Weekly Report, Washington, DC 1980–82, The Dallas Times Herald 1982–84; domestic corresp. The New York Times 1984–86, Russian Corresp. and Bureau Chief, Moscow 1986–91, Bureau Chief, Johannesburg, SA 1992–95, Foreign Ed., NY 1995–97, Man. Ed. 1997–2001, Op-Ed. Columnist and Sr Writer 2001–03, Exec. Ed. July 2003–; Trustee Pomona Coll. *Honours:* Pulitzer Prize for coverage of the USSR 1989. *Address:* The New York Times, 229 West 43rd Street, New York, NY 10036, USA (office). *Telephone:* (212) 556-1234 (office). *E-mail:* executive-editor@nytimes.com (office). *Website:* www.nytimes.com (office).

KELLER, Evelyn Fox, PhD; American historian and academic; *Professor of History and Philosophy of Science, Massachusetts Institute of Technology*; b. 20 March 1936, New York; m. Joseph B. Keller 1964 (divorced); one s. one d. *Education:* Radcliffe Coll., Brandeis and Harvard Univs. *Career:* Asst Research Scientist, New York Univ. 1963–66, Assoc. Prof. 1970–72; Assoc. Prof., State Univ. of New York, Purchase 1972–82; Prof. of Math. and Humanities, Northwestern Univ. 1982–88; Prof. Univ. of Calif., Berkeley 1988–92; Prof. of History and Philosophy of Science, MIT 1992–; mem. Inst. of Advanced Studies, Princeton 1987–88; Visiting Fellow, later Scholar, MIT 1979–84, Visiting Prof. 1985–86; Pres. West Coast History of Science Soc. 1990–91; MacArthur Fellow 1992–97; Guggenheim Fellowship 2000–01; Moore Scholar, Cal. Inst. Tech. 2002; Winton Chair, Univ. of Minnesota 2002–05; Dibner Fellow 2003; Radcliffe Inst. Fellow 2005; Rothschild Lecturer, Harvard Univ. 2005; Plenary Speaker, International History of Science Congress, Beijing, 2005. *Publications include:* A Feeling for the Organism 1983, Reflections on Gender and Science 1985, Secrets of Life, Secrets of Death 1992, Keywords in Evolutionary Biology (ed.) 1994, Refiguring Life 1995, Feminism and Science (co-author) 1996, The Century of the Gene 2000, Making Sense of Life 2002. *Honours:* Dr hc (Mount Holyoke Coll.) 1991, (Univ. of Amsterdam) 1993, (Simmons Coll.) 1995, (Rensslaer Polytechnic Inst.) 1995, (Tech. Univ. of Luleå, Sweden) 1996, (New School Univ.) 2000, (Allegheny Coll.) 2000, (Wesleyan Univ.) 2001, (Dartmouth Coll.) 2007; numerous awards including Mina Shaughnessey Award 1981–82, Radcliffe Graduate Soc. Medal 1985, Macarthur Foundation Award 1992–97, Medal of the Italian Senate 2001, Chaire Blaise Pascal 2005–07. *Address:* Massachusetts Institute of Technology, E51-171, 77 Massachusetts Avenue, Cambridge, MA 02139, USA (office). *Telephone:* (617) 253-8722 (office). *Fax:* (617) 253-8118 (office). *E-mail:* efkeller@mit.edu (office). *Website:* web.mit.edu.sts (office).

KELLERMAN, Jonathan Seth, AB, AM, PhD; American writer, clinical child psychologist and academic; *Clinical Professor of Pediatrics, Keck School of Medicine, University of Southern California*; b. 9 Aug. 1949, New York, NY; m. Faye Kellerman; one s. three d. *Education:* Univ. of California at Los Angeles, Univ. of Southern California at Los Angeles. *Career:* freelance illustrator 1966–72, Dir Psychsocial Program 1976–81, staff psychologist 1975–81, Children's Hospital of Los Angeles; Clinical Assoc. Prof., Univ. of Southern California School of Medicine, Los Angeles 1979–, now Clinical Prof. of Pediatrics; Head Jonathan Kellerman PhD and Assocs, Los Angeles 1981–88. *Publications:* fiction: When the Bough Breaks 1985, Blood Test 1986, Over the Edge 1987, The Butcher's Theatre 1988, Silent Partner 1989, Time Bomb 1990, Private Eyes 1992, Devil's Waltz 1993, Bad Love 1994, Daddy, Daddy Can You Touch the Sky? 1994, Self-Defense 1995, The Web 1996, Survival of the Fittest 1997, Billy Straight 1999, Monster 2000, On Death 2000, Flesh and Blood 2001, The Murder Book 2002, The Conspiracy Club 2003, Therapy 2004, Twisted 2004, Rage 2005, Gone 2006, Capital Crimes (with Faye Kellerman) 2006; non-fiction: Psychological Aspects of Childhood Cancer 1980, Helping the Fearful Child: A Parents' Guide to Everyday Problem Anxieties 1981. *Honours:* MWA Edgar Allen Poe Award 1985, Anthony Boucher Award 1986. *Address:* Department of Pediatrics, Keck School of Medicine, MS 71, 4650 Sunset Boulevard, Los Angeles, CA 90027, USA (office). *Telephone:* (323) 669-2303 (office). *Fax:* (323) 953-8566 (office). *Website:* www.usc.edu/schools/medicine/departments/pediatrics (office); www.jonathankellerman.com.

KELLEY, Kitty, BA; American writer; b. 4 April 1942, Spokane, Wash.; m. Michael Edgley (divorced). *Education:* Univ. of Washington. *Career:* worked for four years as press asst to US Senator Eugene McCarthy; editorial asst, Washington Post 1969–71; freelance journalist and writer of biogs 1971–; currently developing TV show The Kitty Kelley Show. *Publications:* The Glamour Spas 1973, Jackie Oh! 1978, Elizabeth Taylor: The Last Star 1981, His Way: The Unauthorized Biography of Frank Sinatra 1986, Nancy Reagan: The Unauthorized Biography 1991, The Royals 2001, The Family: The Real Story of the Bush Dynasty 2004; contribs to magazines and newspapers, including New York Times, The Washington Post, Wall Street Journal, Newsweek, People, Ladies Home Journal, McCall's, Los Angeles Times, Chicago Tribune. *Honours:* Outstanding Author Award, American Soc. of Journalists and Authors 1987, Philip M. Stern Award. *Address:* c/o Doubleday, 1745 Broadway, New York, NY 10019, USA.

KELLEY, Leo Patrick, BA; American author; b. 10 Sept. 1928, Wilkes Barre, PA. *Education:* New School for Social Research, New York. *Publications:* The Counterfeits, 1967; Odyssey to Earthdeath, 1968; Time Rogue, 1970; The Coins of Murph, 1971; Brother John, 1971; Mindmix, 1972; Time: 110100, 1972, UK edn as The Man From Maybe, 1974; Themes in Science Fiction: A Journey Into Wonder (ed.), 1972; The Supernatural in Fiction (ed.), 1973; Deadlocked (novel), 1973; The Earth Tripper, 1973; Fantasy: The Literature of the Marvellous (ed.), 1974. Science fiction novels for children: The Time Trap, 1977; Backward in Time, 1979; Death Sentence, 1979; Earth Two, 1979; Prison Satellite, 1979; Sunworld, 1979; Worlds Apart, 1979; Dead Moon, 1979; King of the Stars, 1979; On the Red World, 1979; Night of Fire and Blood, 1979; Where No Star Shines, 1979; Vacation in Space, 1979; Star Gold, 1979; Goodbye to Earth, 1979. Western novels: Luke Sutton series, 9 vols, 1981–90; Cimarron series, 20 vols, 1983–86; Morgan, 1986; A Man Named Dundee, 1988; Thunder Gods Gold, 1988.

KELLMAN, Steven G., BA, MA, PhD; American literary critic and academic; *Professor of Comparative Literature, University of Texas, San Antonio*; b. 15 Nov. 1947, Brooklyn, NY. *Education:* State Univ. of NY at Binghamton, Univ. of California, Berkeley. *Career:* Ed.-in-Chief Occident 1969–70; Asst Prof., Bemidji State Univ., Minnesota 1972–73; Lecturer, Univ. of Tel-Aviv, Israel 1973–75; Visiting Lecturer, Univ. of California, Irvine 1975–76; Asst Prof., Univ. of Texas, San Antonio 1976–80, Assoc. Prof. 1980–85, Prof. 1985–, Ashbel Smith Prof. of Comparative Literature 1995–2000; Fulbright Sr

Lecturer, USSR 1980; Visiting Assoc. Prof., Univ. of California, Berkeley 1982; Literary Scene Ed. USA Today; Partners of the Americas Lecturer, Peru 1988, 1995; Nat. Endowment for the Humanities Summer Seminar, Natal, SA 1996; John E. Sawyer Fellow, Longfellow Inst., Harvard Univ. 1997; Fulbright Distinguished Chair, Bulgaria 2000; mem. Nat. Book Critics' Circle (mem. Bd Dirs 1996–2002). *Publications:* The Self-Begetting Novel 1980, Approaches to Teaching Camus's The Plague (ed.) 1985, Loving Reading: Erotics of the Text 1985, The Modern American Novel 1991, The Plague: Fiction and Resistance 1993, Perspectives on Raging Bull 1994, Into The Tunnel (co-ed.) 1998, Leslie Fiedler and American Culture (co-ed.) 1999, The Translingual Imagination 2000, UnderWords: Perspectives on Don DeLillo's Underworld (co-ed.) 2002, Switching Languages: Translingual Writers Reflect on Their Craft (ed.) 2003, Redemption: The Life of Henry Roth 2005; contrib. to Chicago Tribune, San Antonio Light, Nation, Georgia Review, Newsweek, Modern Fiction Studies, Midstream, New York Times Book Review, Washington Post Book World, Gettysburg Review, The American Scholar, Atlantic Monthly, Forward, Atlanta Journal and Constitution, San Francisco Chronicle, Texas Observer, Film Critic, San Antonio Current. *Honours:* H.L. Mencken Award 1986, Fulbright travel grant, People's Repub. of China 1995, inducted into Texas Inst. of Letters 2005, Arts and Letters Award San Antonio Public Library Foundation 2005, New York Soc. Library Award for Biog. 2006 First Place, Art Criticism, Asscn of Alternative Newsweeklies 2006. *Address:* 302 Fawn Drive, San Antonio, TX 78231, USA (office). *Telephone:* (210) 458-5216 (office). *Fax:* (210) 458-5366 (office). *E-mail:* kellman@lonestar.utsa.edu (office).

KELLOGG, Marjorie Bradley; American academic and writer; b. 30 Aug. 1946, Cambridge, MA. *Education:* BA, summa cum laude, Vassar College, 1967; University of California at Los Angeles, 1967–68. *Career:* Scenic Designer, on and off Broadway, regional theatres and films, 1970–; Visiting Prof., Princeton University, 1983–84, 1985–86; Resident Designer, Alliance Theater, 1992–94; Adjunct Prof., Columbia University, 1993–95; Assoc. Prof. of Design, Colgate University, 1995–; mem. Science Fiction Writers of America; United Scenic Artists. *Publications:* A Rumor of Angels, 1983; Lear's Daughters, two vols, 1986; The Book of Earth, 1995; The Book of Water, 1997. *Honours:* several awards for design. *Address:* RD 1, PO Box 62-A, Sidney Center, NY 13839, USA. *E-mail:* mkellogg@wpe.com.

KELLS, Susannah (see Cornwell, Bernard)

KELLY, A. A. (see Hampton, Angeline Agnes)

KELLY, Cathy; Irish writer; b. Belfast. *Career:* fmr journalist, Dublin. *Publications include:* Woman to Woman 1997, She's the One 1998, Never Too Late 1999, Someone Like You (Parker Romantic Novel of the Year) 2000, What She Wants 2001, Just Between Us 2002, Best of Friends 2003, Always and Forever 2005, Past Secrets 2006. *Address:* c/o HarperCollins (author mail), Ophelia House, Fulham Palace Road, London, W6, England. *Website:* www.cathy-kelly.com.

KELLY, Christopher Paul, MA; British novelist and producer; b. 24 April 1940, Cuddington, Cheshire, England; m. Vivien Ann Day 1962; one s. one d. *Education:* Clare Coll., Cambridge. *Career:* mem. Writer's Guild. *Television as producer:* Soldier, Soldier (two series, ITV), Kavanagh QC (five series, ITV), Monsignor Renard (series, ITV), Without Motive (series). *Publications:* The War of Covent Garden 1989, The Forest of the Night 1991, Taking Leave 1995, A Suit of Lights 2000. *Literary Agent:* c/o Broo Doherty, Wade and Doherty Literary Agency, 33 Cormorant Lodge, Thomas More Street, London, E1W 1AU, England. *Telephone:* (20) 7488-4177 (office). *E-mail:* xtopherkelly@aol.com (home).

KELLY, Jim; American journalist; *Managing Editor, Time Inc.;* b. 15 Dec. 1953, Brooklyn, New York; m. Lisa Henricksson; one s. *Education:* Princeton Univ. *Career:* joined Time magazine 1977, as writer Nation section, Foreign Ed. early 1990s, Deputy Man. Ed. 1996–2000, Man. Ed. 2001–06, Man. Ed. Time Inc. 2006–; Ed. Corporate Welfare series 1998, Visions 21 series 1999–2000. *Address:* Time Inc., Time-Life Building, Rockefeller Center, 1271 Avenue of the Americas, New York, NY 10020-1393, USA (office). *Telephone:* (212) 522-1212 (office). *Fax:* (212) 522-0323 (office). *Website:* www.time.com (office).

KELLY, Milton Terrence, BA, BEd; Canadian writer, poet and dramatist; b. 30 Nov. 1946, Toronto, ON. *Education:* York University, University of Toronto. *Career:* Reporter, Moose Jaw Times Harald, 1974–75; Columnist, Globe and Mail, 1979–80; Teacher of Creative Writing, York University, 1987–92, 1995; Writer-in-Residence, North York Public Library, 1992, Metropolitan Toronto Reference Library, 1993; mem. International PEN; Writers' Union of Canada. *Publications:* Fiction: I Do Remember the Fall, 1978; The More Loving One, 1980; The Ruined Season, 1982; A Dream Like Mine, 1987; Breath Dances Between Them, 1990; Out of the Whirlwind, 1995; Save Me, Joe Louis, 1998. Poetry: Country You Can't Walk In, 1979; Country You Can't Walk In and Other Poems, 1984. Other: The Green Dolphin (play), 1982; Wildfire: The Legend of Tom Longboat (screenplay), 1983. Contributions: many anthologies, reviews, quarterlies, and journals. *Honours:* Canada Council Grants; Ontario Arts Council Grants; Toronto Arts Council Award for Poetry, 1986; Governor-General's Award for Fiction, 1987; Award for Journalism, 1995. *Address:* 60 Kendal, Toronto, ON M5R 1L9, Canada.

KELLY, Robert, AB; American academic, poet and writer; b. 24 Sept. 1935, New York, NY. *Education:* City College, CUNY, Columbia University. *Career:* Ed., Chelsea Review, 1957–60, Matter magazine and Matter publishing,

1964–, Los 1, 1977; Lecturer, Wagner College, 1960–61; Founding Ed. (with George Economou), Trobar magazine, 1960–64, Trobar Books, 1962–65; Instructor, 1961–64, Asst Prof., 1964–69, Assoc. Prof., 1969–74, Prof. of English, 1974–86, Dir, Writing Programme, 1980–93, Asher B. Edelman Prof. of Literature, 1986–, Bard College; Asst Prof., SUNY at Buffalo, 1964; Visiting Lecturer, Tufts University, 1966–67; Poet-in-Residence, California Institute of Technology, Pasadena, 1971–72, University of Kansas, 1975, Dickinson College, 1976. *Publications:* Poetry: Armed Descent, 1961; Her Body Against Time, 1963; Round Dances, 1964; Tabula, 1964; Entasy, 1964; Matter/Fact/Sheet/1, 1964; Matter/Fact/Sheet/2, 1964; Lunes, 1964; Lectiones, 1965; Words in Service, 1966; Weeks, 1966; Songs XXIV, 1967; Twenty Poems, 1967; Devotions, 1967; Axon Dendron Tree, 1967; Crooked Bridge Love Society, 1967; A Joining: A Sequence for H D, 1967; Alpha, 1968; Finding the Measure, 1968; From the Common Shore, Book 5, 1968; Songs I–XXX, 1969; Sonnets, 1969; We Are the Arbiters of Beast Desire, 1969; A California Journal, 1969; The Common Shore, Books I–V: A Long Poem About America in Time, 1969; Kali Yuga, 1971; Flesh: Dream: Book, 1971; Ralegh, 1972; The Pastorals, 1972; Reading Her Notes, 1972; The Tears of Edmund Burke, 1973; Whaler Frigate Clippership, 1973; The Bill of Particulars, 1973; The Belt, 1974; The Loom, 1975; Sixteen Odes, 1976; The Lady of, 1977; The Convections, 1978; The Book of Persephone, 1978; The Cruise of the Pnyx, 1979; Kill the Messenger Who Brings the Bad News, 1979; Sentence, 1980; The Alchemist to Mercury, 1981; Spiritual Exercises, 1981; Mulberry Women, 1982; Under Words, 1983; Thor's Thrush, 1984; Not This Island Music, 1987; The Flowers of Unceasing Coincidence, 1988; Oahu, 1988; A Strange Market, 1992; Mont Blanc, 1994. Fiction: The Scorpions, 1967; Cities, 1971; Wheres, 1978; A Transparent Tree: Ten Fictions, 1985; Doctor of Silence, 1988; Cat Scratch Fever: Fictions, 1990; Queen of Terrors: Fictions, 1994. Other: A Controversy of Poets: An Anthology of Contemporary American Poetry (ed. with Paris Leary), 1965; Statement, 1968; In Time, 1971; Sulphur, 1972; A Line of Sight, 1974. *Honours:* Los Angeles Times Book Prize, 1980; American Acad. of Arts and Letters Award, 1986.

KELMAN, James; British writer; b. 9 June 1946, Glasgow; m. Marie Connors; two d. *Education:* Greenfield Public School, Govan. *Plays:* Hardie and Baird, The Last Days 1991, One, Two – Hey (R and B musical, toured 1994). *Radio:* The Art of the Big Bass Drum (play, BBC Radio 3) 1998. *Publications include:* novels: The Bus Conductor Hines 1984, A Chancer 1985, A Disaffection (James Tait Black Memorial Prize) 1989, How Late It Was, How Late (Booker Prize) 1994, Translated Accounts 2001, You Have to be Careful in the Land of the Free 2004; short stories: An Old Pub Near the Angel 1973, Short Tales from the Nightshift 1978, Not Not While the Giro 1983, Lean Tales 1985, Greyhound for Breakfast (Cheltenham Prize) 1987, The Burn (short stories, Scottish Arts Council Book Award) 1991, Busted Scotch 1997, The Good Times (Scottish Writer of the Year Award) 1998; plays: The Busker 1985, In the Night 1988; other: And the Judges Said (essays) 2002. *Honours:* Spirit of Scotland Award. *Literary Agent:* Rodgers, Coleridge and White Ltd, 20 Powis Mews, London, W11 1JN, England. *Telephone:* (20) 7240-3444.

KELMAN, Judith Ann, BS, MA, MS; American writer; b. 21 Oct. 1945, New York, NY; m. Edward Michael Kelman 1970, two s. *Education:* Cornell University, New York University, Southern Connecticut State College. *Career:* mem. American Society of Journalists and Authors; MWA; Authors' Guild. *Publications:* Prime Evil, 1986; Where Shadows Fall, 1988; While Angels Sleep, 1990; Hush Little Darlings, 1991; Someone's Watching, 1992; The House on the Hill, 1993; If I Should Die, 1994; One Last Kiss, 1995; More Than You Know, 1996; Fly Away Home, 1997. Contributions: anthologies and periodicals. *Address:* 60 Thornwood Road, Stamford, CT 06903, USA. *E-mail:* jkelman@jkelman.com.

KELNER, Simon; British newspaper editor; *Editor-in-Chief, The Independent;* b. 9 Dec. 1957, Manchester. *Education:* Bury Grammar School, Preston Polytechnic. *Career:* Trainee Reporter, Neath Guardian 1976–79; Sports Reporter, Extel 1979–80; Sports Ed., Kent Evening Post 1980–83; Asst Sports Ed., The Observer 1983–86; Deputy Sports Ed., The Independent 1986–89; Sports Ed., Sunday Corresp. 1989–90; Sports Ed., The Observer 1990–91, Ed. 1991–93; Sports Ed., The Independent on Sunday 1993–95, Night Ed., The Independent 1995, Features Ed. 1995–96; Ed. Night and Day Magazine, Mail on Sunday 1996–98; Ed.-in-Chief, The Independent 1998–; Patron The Journalism Soc. 2004–. *Publications:* To Jerusalem and Back 1996. *Honours:* Hon. Fellowship, Univ. of Cen. Lancashire; Ed. of the Year, What the Papers Say Awards 1999, 2003, Newspaper Ed. of the Year, What the Papers Say Awards 2004, Edgar Wallace Award 2000, 2004, Newspaper of the Year, British Press Awards 2004, GQ Editor of the Year 2004, Media Achiever of the Year, Campaign Media Awards 2004, Marketeer of the Year, Marketing Week Effectiveness Awards 2004. *Address:* The Independent, Independent House, 191 Marsh Wall, London, E14 9RS, England (office). *Telephone:* (20) 7005-2000 (office). *Fax:* (20) 7005-2022 (office). *E-mail:* s.kelner@independent.co.uk (office). *Website:* www.independent.co.uk (office).

KELSALL, Malcolm Miles, BA, BLitt, MA; British academic, writer and editor; *Professor Emeritus of English, University of Cardiff;* b. 27 Feb. 1938, London, England; m. Mary Emily Ives 1961. *Education:* Univ. of Oxford. *Career:* Asst Lecturer, Univ. of Exeter 1963–64; Lecturer, Univ. of Reading 1964–75; Prof. of English, Univ. of Cardiff 1975–2003, Prof. Emer. 2003–. *Publications:* Christopher Marlowe 1981, Studying Drama 1985, Byron's Politics 1987, Encyclopedia of Literature and Criticism (ed.) 1990, The Great

Good Place: The Country House and English Literature 1992, Jefferson and the Iconography of Romanticism 1999, Literary Representations of the Irish Country House 2003; editor of several plays; contrib. to scholarly journals. *Honours:* Elma Dangerfield Prize 1991;British Acad. Warton Lecturer 1992, Marchand Lecturer 2005.

KELTON, Elmer Stephen, (Lee McElroy), BA; American novelist and agricultural journalist; b. 29 April 1926, Andrews, Tex.; m. Anna Lipp 1947; two s. one d. *Education:* Univ. of Texas. *Career:* mem. Western Writers of America (Pres. 1963–64), Texas Inst. of Letters. *Publications:* The Day the Cowboys Quit 1971, The Time It Never Rained 1973, The Good Old Boys 1978, The Wolf and the Buffalo 1980, Stand Proud 1984, The Man Who Rode Midnight 1987, Honor at Daybreak 1991, Slaughter 1992, The Far Canyon 1994, The Pumpkin Rollers 1996, Cloudy in the West 1997, The Smiling Country 1998, The Buckskin Line 1999, Badger Boy 2001, The Way of the Coyote 2001, Ranger's Trail 2002, Texas Vendetta 2003, Jericho's Road 2004, Six Bits a Day 2005; contrib. to numerous articles to magazines and newspapers. *Honours:* seven Western Writers of America Spur Awards, four Nat. Cowboy Hall of Fame Western Heritage Awards, Texas Inst. of Letters Tinkle-McCombs Achievement Award, Western Literature Asscn Lifetime Achievement Award, Larry McMurtry Lone Star Lifetime Achievement Award. *Address:* 2460 Oxford, San Angelo, TX 76904, USA.

KEMAL, Yaşar; Turkish writer and journalist; b. 1923, Adana; m. 1st Thilda Serrero 1952 (deceased); one s.; m. 2nd Ayse Semiha Baban 2002. *Career:* self-educated; mem. Académie Universelle des Cultures, Paris. *Publications:* (in English) Memed, My Hawk 1961, The Wind from the Plain 1963, Anatolian Tales 1968, They Burn the Thistles 1973, Iron Earth, Copper Sky 1974, The Legend of Ararat 1975, The Legend of the Thousand Bulls 1976, The Undying Grass 1977, The Lords of Akchasaz (Part I), Murder in the Ironsmiths' Market 1979, The Saga of a Seagull 1981, The Sea-Crossed Fisherman 1985, The Birds Have Also Gone 1987, To Crush the Serpent 1991, Salman the Solitary 1997, The Story of an Island Vols I–IV 1998; novels, short stories, plays and essays in Turkish. *Honours:* Dr hc (Strasbourg) 1991, (Akdeniz Univ., Antalya) 1991, (Mediterranean Univ.) 1992, (Free Univ., Berlin) 1998; Prix Mondial Cino del Duca 1982, VIII Premi Internacional Catalunya, Barcelona 1996, Peace Prize of German Book Trade 1997, Prix Nonino, Percoto, Italy 1997, Stig Dagerman Prize, Sweden 1997, Norwegian Authors Union Prize 1997, Prix Ecureuil de littérature étrangère, Bordeaux 1998; Hellman-Hammett Award, New York 1996; Commdr, Légion d'honneur 1984. *Address:* P.K. 14, Basinköy, Istanbul, Turkey.

KEMP, Rev. Anthony Eric, LTCL, FTCL, CertEd, DipEd, MA, DPhil, FRSA; British priest, music educator, chartered psychologist and counsellor; *Curate, All Saints Church, Wokingham;* b. 2 Jan. 1934, Tanga, Tanzania; m. Valerie Francis 1964; one s. one d. *Education:* Coll. of St Mark and St John, Trinity Coll. of Music, Univ. of London, Univ. of Sussex. *Career:* Lecturer in Music 1964, Sr Lecturer 1967, Brighton Coll. of Education; Principal Lecturer and Head of Music, Coll. of St Mark and St John 1972; Lecturer 1973, Sr Lecturer 1987, Prof. 1996, Emeritus Prof. 1999–, Univ. of Reading; Sr Research Fellow Univ. of Surrey, Roehampton 1999; Visiting Prof., Sibelius Acad., Helsinki 1995–2003; Curate, All Saints Church, Wokingham; mem. Incorporated Soc. of Musicians, Int. Soc. for Music Education (chair. of research commission 1988–90), Music Education Council (chair. 1989–92). *Publications:* Fun to Make Music 1975, Considering the Mind's Ear 1984, Research in Music Education, Festschrift for Arnold Bentley 1988, Some Approaches to Research in Music Education 1992, The Musical Temperament: Psychology and Personality of Musicians 1996; contrib. to Psychology of Music 1981, 1982, 1999, International Journal of Music Education 1984, 1986, 1988, Council for Research in Music Education Bulletin 1985, 1987, British Journal of Music Education 1987, 1990, Quarterly Journal of Music Teaching and Learning 1995, Musical Performance: An International Journal 2000, New Grove Dictionary of Music and Musicians 2001. *Honours:* Hon. MusDoc (Sibelius Acad., Helsinki) 2003; Hon. Fellow, London Coll. of Music 1983, British Psychological Soc. 1997; Univ. of Hong Kong Raysen Huang Fellowship 1989, Univ. of British Columbia Distinguished Scholars Fellowship 1990. *Address:* 18 Blagrove Lane, Wokingham, Berkshire RG41 4BA, England (home). *Telephone:* (118) 978-2756 (home). *Fax:* (118) 978-2756 (home). *E-mail:* a.e.kemp@bt.internet.com.

KEMP, Martin John, MA, DLitt, FBA, FRSA, FRSE; British art historian and academic; *Professor, Department of History of Art, University of Oxford;* b. 5 March 1942, Windsor; s. of Frederick Maurice Kemp and Violet Anne (née Tull) Kemp; m. Jill Lightfoot 1966 (divorced 2003); one s. one d. *Education:* Windsor Grammar School, Downing Coll., Cambridge and Courtauld Inst. of Art, London. *Career:* Lecturer in History of Western Art, Dalhousie Univ., NS, Canada 1965–66; Lecturer in History of Fine Art, Univ. of Glasgow 1966–81; Prof. of Fine Arts, Univ. of St Andrew's 1981–90; Prof. of History, Royal Scottish Acad. 1985–; Prof. of History and Theory of Art, Univ. of St Andrew's 1990–95; Prof. of History of Art, Univ. of Oxford 1995–, now Head of Dept, Fellow Trinity Coll. Oxford 1995–; Provost St Leonard's Coll., Univ. of St Andrew's 1991–95; mem. Inst. for Advanced Study, Princeton, NJ, USA 1984–85; Slade Prof., Univ. of Cambridge 1987–88; Benjamin Sonenberg Visiting Prof., Inst. of Fine Arts, New York Univ. 1988; Wiley Visiting Prof., Univ. of N Carolina, Chapel Hill 1993; British Acad. Wolfson Research Prof. 1993–98; Trustee Nat. Galleries of Scotland 1982–87, Vic. and Albert Museum, London 1986–89, British Museum 1995–, Ashmolean Museum 1995–; Pres. Leonardo da Vinci Soc. 1988–97; Chair. Asscn of Art Historians

1989–92; mem. Exec. Scottish Museums Council 1990–95; Dir and Chair. Graeme Murray Gallery 1990–92; Dir Wallace Kemp/Artakt 2001; mem. Bd Interalia 1992–, Bd Museum Training Inst. 1993–98, Council British Soc. for the History of Science 1994–97; mem. Visual Arts Advisory Panel, Arts Council of England 1996–; Visiting mem., Getty Center, Los Angeles 2002; Mellon Sr Fellow, Canadian Centre for Architecture, Montreal 2004; Fellow, Royal Soc. of Sciences, Uppsala 1995. *Publications:* Leonardo da Vinci: The Marvellous Works of Nature and Man 1981, Leonardo da Vinci (co-author) 1989, Leonardo on Painting (co-author) 1989, The Science of Art: Optical Themes in Western Art from Brunelleschi to Seurat 1990, Behind the Picture: Art and Evidence in the Italian Renaissance 1997, Immagine e Verità 1999, The Oxford History of Western Art (ed.) 2000, Spectacular Bodies (with Marina Wallace) 2000, Visualizations The Nature Book of Science and Art 2001, Leonardo 2004, Leonardo da Vinci: Experience, Experiment and Design 2006, Seen/Unseen 2006, The Human Animal 2007. *Honours:* Hon. mem. American Acad. of Arts and Sciences 1996–, Hon. Fellow, Downing Coll. 1999; Hon. DLitt (Heriot Watt Univ.) 1995; Mitchell Prize 1981; Armand Hammer Prize for Leonardo Studies 1992; Pres.'s Prize, Italian Asscn of America 1992. *Address:* Department of History of Art, Centre for Visual Studies, Second Floor, Littlegate House, St Ebbes, Oxford, OX1 1PT (office); Trinity College, Oxford, OX1 3BH. *Telephone:* (1865) 286830 (office). *Fax:* (1865) 286831 (office). *E-mail:* martin.kemp@trinity.ox.ac.uk (office). *Website:* www.hoa.ox.ac.uk (office).

KEMP, Patricia (Penny), (Penny Chalmers), BA, MEd; Canadian writer and poet; *Series Editor, Pendas Productions;* b. 4 Aug. 1944, Strathroy, Ont.; d of Jim Kemp and Anne Kemp; m. Gavin Stairs; two c. *Education:* Univ. of Western Ontario, Univ. of Toronto. *Career:* has taught creative writing and sounding in Canadian schools, from kindergarten to univ. since 1966; as sound poet and playwright, performs in arts festivals around the world, giving readings and workshops; various writer-in-residencies; one of four poets discussed in Poets, Poetry and New Media: Attending to the Teaching and Learning of Poetry (faculty.uoit.ca/hughes/research.htm); Publr Pendas Productions; Series Ed. Pendas Poets Series; Asscn of Canadian Studies speaker in Brazil, India; mem. League of Canadian Poets, Playwrights' Guild of Canada, Writers' Union. *Music:* several of her series of Sound Operas were produced for Artword Theatre in Toronto and in London, Ont., Aeolian Hall's Summer Music Festival 2005, 2006, Sound Opera ANIMUS performed at The Aeolian Performing Arts Centre, Trance Dance Form was launched and performed at the Aeolian 2006, at Summer Soirée's Opening Night; mytown.ca/poemforpeace includes video of her Poem for Peace in Many Voices (and many of the 101 trans. of the poem; video shows one of the Poem for Peace performances in London). *Publications:* 25 books of poetry and plays as well as 10 CDs of Sound Opera and Sound Poetry, including Bearing Down 1972, Binding Twine 1984, Some Talk Magic 1986, Eidolons 1990, Throo 1990, The Universe is One Poem 1990, What the Ear Hears Last 1994, Four Women 1999, Vocal Braidings 2001, Sarasvati Scapes 2002, Poem for Peace in Two Voices 2003, C'Loud 2004, Gathering Voice 2004. *Honours:* Canada Council Arts grants 1979–80, 1981–82, 1991–92, 1994, 1999, 2001, Ontario's Grad. Scholarship 1987–88, videopoem won Vancouver Videopoem Festival's Voice Award, proclaimed a foremother of Canadian poetry by The League of Poets. *Address:* Pendas Productions, 525 Canterbury Road, London, ON N6G 2N5, Canada (office). *E-mail:* pendas@pennkemp.ca (office). *Website:* www.mytown.ca/pennkemp (office); www.mytown.ca/pennletters; pennkemp.ca.

KEMSKE, Floyd, BA, MA; American writer; b. 11 March 1947, Wilmington, DE; m. Alice Geraldine Morse 1968. *Education:* University of Delaware, Michigan State University. *Career:* mem. National Writers' Union. *Publications:* Lifetime Employment, 1992; The Virtual Boss, 1993; Human Resources, 1995; The Third Lion, 1997; Jigsaw Puzzles: Hole in One, 1997; Unbridled Fear, 1997; Cooking Commando, 1997; Purrfect Medicine, 1998; Murder on the Hindenburg, 1999; Labor Day, 2000.

KENDALL, Carol Seeger, AB; American writer; b. 13 Sept. 1917, Bucyrus, OH; m. Paul Murray Kendall 1939; two d. *Education:* Ohio Univ. *Career:* mem. Authors' League of America, Authors' Guild. *Publications:* The Black Seven 1946, The Baby Snatcher 1952, The Other Side of the Tunnel 1956, The Gammage Cup 1959, as The Minnipins 1960, The Big Splash 1960, The Whisper of Glocken 1965, Sweet and Sour Tales from China, retold by Carol Kendall and Yao-Wen Li 1978, The Firelings 1981, Haunting Tales from Japan 1985, The Wedding of the Rat Family 1988. *Honours:* Ohioana Award 1960, Newbery Honour Book 1960, American Library Asscn Notable Book 1960, Parents Choice Award 1982, Mythopoeic Soc. Aslan Award 1983. *Address:* 1501 Inverness Drive, Apt 201, Lawrence, KS 66047, USA (home). *Telephone:* (785) 842-4440.

KENEALLY, Thomas Michael, AO, FRSL; Australian writer; b. 7 Oct. 1935, Sydney; s. of Edmund Thomas and Elsie Margaret Keneally; m. Judith Mary Martin 1965; two d. *Education:* St Patrick's Coll., Strathfield, NSW. *Career:* Lecturer in Drama, Univ. of New England, Armidale, NSW 1968–70; Visiting Prof. Univ. of Calif., Irvine 1985, Prof. Dept of English and Comparative Literature 1991–95; Berg Prof. Dept of English, New York Univ. 1988; Pres. Nat. Book Council of Australia –1987; Chair. Australian Soc. of Authors 1987–90, Pres. 1990–; mem. Literary Arts Bd 1985–; mem. Australia-China Council; mem. American Acad. of Arts and Sciences; Founding Chair. Australian Republican Movt 1991–93. *Publications:* The Place at Whitton 1964, The Fear 1965, Bring Larks and Heroes 1967, Three Cheers for the Paraclete 1968, The Survivor 1969, A Dutiful Daughter 1970, The Chant of

Jimmie Blacksmith 1972, Blood Red, Sister Rose 1974, Gossip from the Forest 1975, Moses and the Lawgiver 1975, Season in Purgatory 1976, A Victim of the Aurora 1977, Ned Kelly and the City of Bees 1978, Passenger 1978, Confederates 1979, Schindler's Ark (Booker Prize 1982) 1982, Outback 1983, The Cut-Rate Kingdom 1984, A Family Madness 1985, Australia: Beyond the Dreamtime (contrib.) 1987, The Playmaker 1987, Towards Asmara 1989, Flying Hero Class 1991, Now and in Time to Be: Ireland and the Irish 1992, Woman of the Inner Sea 1992, The Place Where Souls Are Born: A Journey into the American Southwest 1992, Jacko: The Great Intruder 1993, The Utility Player – The Story of Des Hassler (non-fiction) 1993, Our Republic (non-fiction) 1993, A River Town 1995, Homebush Boy: A Memoir 1995, The Great Shame: And the Triumph of the Irish in the English-Speaking World 1998, Bettany's Book 2000, An American Scoundrel: The Life of the Notorious Civil War General Dan Sickles (non-fiction) 2002, An Angel in Australia 2002, Abraham Lincoln (biog.) 2003, The Office of Innocence 2003, The Tyrant's Novel 2004, The Commonwealth of Thieves: The Story of the Founding of Australia (non-fiction) 2006, The Widow and Her Hero 2007. *Honours:* Hon. DLit (Univ. of Queensland), (Nat. Univ. of Ireland) 1994; Hon. DLitt (Fairleigh Dickenson Univ., USA) 1996, (Rollins Coll., USA) 1996; Royal Soc. of Literature Prize, Los Angeles Times Fiction Prize 1983. *Literary Agent:* Curtis Brown (Australia) Pty Ltd, PO Box 19, Paddington, NSW 2021, Australia.

KENNEDY, Adrienne Lita, BS; American dramatist; b. 13 Sept. 1931, Pittsburgh, PA; m. Joseph C. Kennedy 1953 (divorced 1966); two s. *Education:* Ohio State University, Columbia University, New School for Social Research, American Theatre Wing, Circle in the Square Theatre School, New York. *Career:* Playwright, Actors Studio, New York City, 1962–65; Lecturer, Yale University, 1972–74; Princeton University, 1977; CBS Fellow, School of Drama, New York City, 1973; Visiting Assoc. Prof., Brown University, 1979–80; Distinguished Lecturer, University of California, Berkeley, 1980, 1986; Visiting Lecturer, 1990, 1991, Visiting Prof., 1997–2000, Harvard University; mem. PEN. *Publications:* Plays: Funnyhouse of a Negro, 1964; Cities in Bezique, 1965; A Rat's Mass, 1966; A Lesson in Dead Language, 1966; The Lennon Plays, 1968; Sun, 1969; An Evening With Dead Essex, 1972; A Movie Star Has to Star in Black and White, 1976; In One Act, 1988; Deadly Triplets, 1990; She Talks to Beethoven, 1990; Ohio State Murders, 1992; The Alexander Plays, 1992; Sleep Deprivation Chamber: A Theatre Piece (with Adam Kennedy), 1996; Adrienne Kennedy Reader, 2001. Other: People Who Led to My Plays, 1987; Letter to My Students, 1992. Contributions: anthologies. *Honours:* Obie Awards, 1964, 1996; Guggenheim Fellowship, 1968; Rockefeller Foundation Fellowships, 1968, 1974; National Endowment for the Arts Fellowships, 1973, 1993; Manhattan Borough Pres.'s Award, 1988; American Acad. of Arts and Letters Award, 1994; Lila Wallace-Reader's Digest Award, 1994; Pierre Lecomte du Novy Award, Lincoln Center for the Performing Arts, New York, 1994.

KENNEDY, Alison Louise (A. L.), BA; British writer; b. 22 Oct. 1965, Dundee, Scotland. *Education:* Warwick Univ. *Career:* community arts worker for Clydebank & District 1988–89; writer-in-residence, Hamilton & East Kilbride Social Work Dept 1989–91, for Project Ability, Arts & Special Needs 1989–95, Copenhagen Univ. 1995; book reviewer for The Scotsman, Glasgow Herald, BBC, STV, The Telegraph 1990–; Ed. New Writing Scotland 1993–95; part-time Lecturer St Andrews Univ. 2002–; columnist The Guardian; stand-up comedian 2005–. *Films:* Stella Does Tricks (writer) 1997. *Television:* Ghostdancing (BBC TV drama/documentary, writer and presenter) 1995, Dice (series I and II, with John Burnside, Canadian TV). *Radio:* Born a Fox (BBC Radio 4 drama) 2002, Like an Angel (BBC Radio 4 drama) 2004. *Plays:* The Audition (Fringe First Award) 1993, Delicate (performance piece for Motion-house dance co.) 1995, True (performance project for Fierce Productions and Tramway Theatre) 1998. *Publications:* Night Geometry and the Garscadden Trains 1991, Looking for the Possible Dance 1993, Now That You're Back 1994, So I Am Glad 1995, Tea and Biscuits 1996, Original Bliss 1997, The Life and Death of Colonel Blimp 1997, Everything You Need 1999, On Bullfighting 1999, Indelible Acts 2002, Paradise 2004, Day 2007. *Honours:* DSc hc; Somerset Maugham Award, Encore Award, Saltire Scottish Book of the Year, SAC Book Award, Best of Young British Novelists (twice). *Literary Agent:* Antony Harwood Ltd, 103 Walton Street, Oxford, OX2 6EB, England. *Telephone:* (1865) 559615. *Fax:* (1865) 554173. *Website:* www.a-l-kennedy.co .uk.

KENNEDY, David Michael, BA, MA, PhD; American academic and writer; *Donald J. McLachlan Professor of History, Stanford University;* b. 22 July 1941, Seattle, WA; m. Judith Ann Osborne 1970; two s. one d. *Education:* Stanford Univ., Yale Univ. *Career:* Asst Prof. 1967–72, Assoc. Prof. 1972–80, Prof. 1980–, William Robertson Coe Prof. of History and American Studies 1988–93, Chair, Dept of History 1990–94, Donald J. McLachlan Prof. of History 1993–, Stanford Univ.; Harmsworth Prof. of American History, Univ. of Oxford 1995–96; Ed., The Oxford History of the United States 1999–; Fellow, American Acad. of Arts and Sciences, American Philosophical Soc. *Publications:* Birth Control in America: The Career of Margaret Sanger 1970, Social Thought in America and Europe (ed. with Paul A. Robinson) 1970, Progressivism: The Critical Issues (ed.) 1971, The American People in the Depression 1973, The American People in the Age of Kennedy 1973, The American Pageant: A History of the Republic (with Thomas A. Bailey and Lizabeth Cohen, sixth to 13th edns) 1979–2005, Over Here: The First World War and American Society 1980 (revd 2004), The American Spirit: United States History as Seen by Contemporaries (ed. with Thomas A. Bailey, fifth to 11th edns) 1983–2005, Power and Responsibility: Case Studies in American Leadership (ed. with Michael Parrish) 1986, Freedom from Fear: The American People in Depression and War, 1929–1945 1999; contrib. to reference works, scholarly books, learned journals, periodicals, etc. *Honours:* Guggenheim Fellowship 1975–76, Center for Advanced Study in the Behavioural Sciences Fellowship 1986–87, Stanford Humanities Center Fellowship 1989–90, Hon. DLitt (LaTrobe Univ.) 2001; John Gilmary Shea Prize 1970, Bancroft Prize 1971, Ambassador's Book Award, English-Speaking Union 2000, Francis Parkman Prize, Soc. of American Historians 2000, Pulitzer Prize in History 2000. *Address:* c/o Department of History, Stanford University, Stanford, CA 94305, USA. *Telephone:* (650) 723-0351. *Fax:* (650) 725-0597. *E-mail:* dmk@stanford.edu. *Website:* history.stanford .edu/faculty/dkennedy.

KENNEDY, Donald, MA, PhD; American academic and editor; b. 18 Aug. 1931, New York; s. of William D. and Barbara (Bean) Kennedy; m. 1st Barbara J. Dewey 1953; two d.; m. 2nd Robin Beth Wiseman 1987; two step-s. *Education:* Harvard Univ. *Career:* Asst Prof. Syracuse Univ. 1956–59, Assoc. Prof. 1959–60; Asst Prof. Stanford Univ. 1960–62, Assoc. Prof. 1962–65, Prof. 1965–77, Chair. Dept of Biological Sciences 1965–72, Benjamin Crocker Prof. of Human Biology 1974–77, Vice-Pres. and Provost 1979–80, Pres. 1980–92, Pres. Emer. and Bing Prof. of Environmental Science 1992–; Sr Consultant, Office of Science and Tech. Policy, Exec. Office of the Pres. 1976–77; Commr of Food and Drug Admin. 1977–79; Ed.-in-Chief Science 2000–; Fellow, American Acad. of Arts and Sciences; mem. NAS. *Publications:* The Biology of Organisms (with W. M. Telfer) 1965, Academic Duty 1997; over 60 articles in scientific journals. *Honours:* Hon. DSc (Columbia Univ., Williams Coll., Michigan, Rochester, Ariz., Whitman Coll., Coll. of William and Mary); Dinkelspiel Award 1976. *Address:* Stanford University, Institute for International Studies, Encina Hall 401, Stanford, CA 94305 (office); 532 Channing Avenue, #302, Palo Alto, CA 94301, USA (home). *E-mail:* kennedyd@stanford .edu (office).

KENNEDY, Geraldine; Irish journalist; *Editor, The Irish Times;* b. 7 Sept. 1951, Tramore, Co. Waterford; d. of James Kennedy and Nora McGrath; m. David J. Hegarty; two d. *Education:* Convent S.H.M., Ferrybank, Waterford. *Career:* Political Corresp. The Sunday Tribune 1980–82, The Sunday Press 1982–87; mem. Dáil Éireann (Irish Parl.) 1987–89; Public Affairs Corresp. The Irish Times 1990–93, Political Corresp. 1993–99, Political Ed. 1999–2002, Duty Ed. 2000–02, Ed. 2002–, Dir Irish Times Ltd 2002–. *Honours:* Dr hc (Queen's Univ., Belfast) Journalist of the Year 1994. *Address:* The Irish Times, POB 74, 24–28 Tara Street, Dublin 2, Ireland (office). *Telephone:* (1) 6758000 (office). *Fax:* (1) 6758035 (office). *E-mail:* editor@irish-times.ie (office). *Website:* www.ireland.com (office).

KENNEDY OF THE SHAWS, Baroness (Life Peer) cr. 1997, of Cathcart in the City of Glasgow; **Helena Ann Kennedy,** QC, FRSA; British lawyer; b. 12 May 1950, Glasgow; d. of Joshua Kennedy and Mary Jones; partner (Roger) Iain Mitchell 1978–84; one s.; m. Dr Iain L. Hutchison 1986; one s. one d. *Education:* Holyrood Secondary School, Glasgow and Council of Legal Educ. *Career:* called to the Bar, Gray's Inn 1972; mem. Bar Council 1990–93; mem. CIBA Comm. into Child Sexual Abuse 1981–83; mem. Bd City Limits Magazine 1982–84, New Statesman 1990–96, Counsel Magazine 1990–93; mem. Council, Howard League for Penal Reform 1989–, Chair. Comm. of Inquiry into Violence in Penal Insts for Young People (report 1995); Commr BAFTA inquiry into future of BBC 1990, Hamlyn Nat. Comm. on Educ. 1991–; Visiting lecturer, British Postgrad. Medical Fed. 1991–; Adviser, Mannheim Inst. on Criminology, LSE 1992–; Leader of inquiry into health, environmental and safety aspects of Atomic Weapons Establishment, Aldermaston (report 1994); Chancellor, Oxford Brookes Univ. 1994–2001; Chair. British Council 1998–, Human Genetics Comm. 2000–; author of official report (Learning Works) for Further Educ. Funding Council on widening participation in further educ. 1997; Pres. School of Oriental and African Studies, London Univ. 2002–; mem. Advisory Bd, Int. Centre for Prison Studies 1998; Chair. London Int. Festival of Theatre, Standing Cttee for Youth Justice 1992–97; Chair. Charter 88 1992–97; Pres. London Marriage Guidance Council, Birth Control Campaign, Nat. Children's Bureau, Hillcroft Coll.; Vice-Pres. Haldane Soc., Nat. Ass. of Women; mem. British Council's Law Advisory Cttee Advisory Bd for Study of Women and Gender, Warwick Univ., Int. Bar Asscn's Task Force on Terrorism; presenter of various programmes on radio and TV and creator of BBC drama series Blind Justice 1988; Patron, Liberty; mem. Acad. de Cultures Internationales. *Publications:* The Bar on Trial (jtly) 1978, Child Abuse within the Family (jtly) 1984, Balancing Acts (jtly) 1989, Eve was Framed 1992, Just Law: the Changing Face of Justice and Why it Matters to Us All 2004; articles on legal matters, civil liberties and women. *Honours:* Hon. Fellow Inst. of Advanced Legal Studies, Univ. of London 1997; Hon. mem. Council, Nat. Soc. for Prevention of Cruelty to Children; 18 hon. LLD s from British and Irish Univs; Women's Network Award 1992, UK Woman of Europe Award 1995; Campaigning and Influencing Award, Nat. Fed. of Women's Insts 1996, Times Newspaper Lifetime Achievement Award in the Law (jtly) 1997; Spectator Magazine's Parl. Campaigner of the Year 2000. *Address:* House of Lords, London, SW1A 0PW, England (office). *Telephone:* (20) 7219-5353 (office); (1708) 379482 (home). *Fax:* (200 7219-5979 (office); (1708) 379482 (home). *E-mail:* info@ helenakennedy.co.uk (home). *Website:* www.parliament.uk (office); www .helenakennedy.co.uk (home).

KENNEDY, James C., BBA; American publishing and media executive; *Chairman and CEO, Cox Enterprises Inc.*; b. 1947, Honolulu; m. *Education:* Univ. of Denver. *Career:* with Atlanta Newspapers 1976–79; Pres. Grand Junction Newspapers 1979–80; Publr Grand Junction Daily Sentinel 1980–85; Vice-Pres. newspaper Div. Cox Enterprises Inc. 1985–86, Exec. Vice-Pres., Pres. 1986–87, COO, Chair. 1987–; Chair., CEO Cox Enterprises Inc. 1988–. *Cycling achievements:* past Masters Nat., Pan American and World Champion in 3000 meter pursuit; served as capt. of four-man team that won Race Across AMerica (RAAM) 1992, setting world record. *Address:* Cox Enterprises Inc., PO Box 105357, Atlanta, GA 30348 (office); 1601 W Peachtree Street NE, Atlanta, GA 30309, USA (home). *Telephone:* (678) 645-0000 (office). *Fax:* (678) 645-1079 (office). *Website:* www.coxenterprises.com (office).

KENNEDY, Sir Ludovic Henry Coverley, Kt, MA, FRSL; Scottish broadcaster and writer; b. 3 Nov. 1919, Edinburgh; s. of late Capt. E. C. Kennedy, RN and of Rosalind Kennedy; m. Moira Shearer King 1950 (died 2006; one s. three d. *Education:* Eton Coll., Christ Church, Oxford. *Career:* served in RN 1939–46 (attained rank of Lt); Pvt. Sec. and ADC to Gov. of Newfoundland 1943–44; Librarian, Ashridge (Adult Educ.) Coll. 1949; Ed., feature, First Reading (BBC Third Programme) 1953–54; Lecturer for British Council, Sweden, Finland, Denmark 1955, Belgium, Luxembourg 1956; contested Rochdale by-election 1958, gen. election 1959 as Liberal candidate; Pres. Nat. League of Young Liberals 1959–61, mem. Liberal Party Council 1965–67; TV and radio: introduced Profile, ATV 1955–56; newscaster, ITV 1956–58; introducer On Stage, Associated Rediffusion 1957, This Week, Associated Rediffusion 1958–59; Chair. BBC features: Your Verdict 1962, Your Witness 1967–70; commentator BBC's Panorama 1960–63, Television Reports Int. (also producer) 1963–64; introducer BBC's Time Out 1964–65, World at One 1965–66; presenter Liberal Party's Gen. Election TV Broadcasts 1966, The Middle Years, ABC 1967, The Nature of Prejudice, ATV 1968, Face The Press, Tyne-Tees 1968–69, 1970–72, Against the Tide, Yorkshire TV 1969, Living and Growing, Grampian TV 1969–70, 24 Hours, BBC 1969–72, Ad Lib, BBC 1970–72, Midweek, BBC 1973–75, Newsday, BBC 1975–76, Tonight, BBC 1976–80, A Life with Crime BBC 1979, presenter Lord Mountbatten Remembers 1980, Change of Direction 1980, Did You See? BBC 1980–88, Great Railway Journeys of the World BBC 1980, Chair. Indelible Evidence BBC 1987, 1990, A Gift of the Gab BBC 1989, Portrait BBC 1989; mem. Council Navy Records Soc. 1957–70; Pres. Sir Walter Scott Club, Edin. 1968–69; Chair. Royal Lyceum Theatre Co. of Edin. 1977–84; Chair. Judges, NCR Book Award 1990–91; Pres. Voluntary Euthanasia Soc. 1995–; FRSA 1974–76; Voltaire Memorial Lecturer 1985. *Films include:* The Sleeping Ballerina, The Singers and the Songs, Scapa Flow, Battleship Bismarck, Life and Death of the Scharnhorst, U-Boat War, Target Tirpitz, The Rise of the Red Navy, Lord Haw-Haw, Who Killed the Lindbergh Baby?, Elizabeth: The First Thirty Years, A Life of Richard Dimbleby, Happy Birthday, dear Ma'am, Murder in Belgravia: The Lucan Affair, Princess to Queen. *Publications:* Sub-Lieutenant 1942, Nelson's Band of Brothers 1951, One Man's Meat 1953, Murder Story 1956, Ten Rillington Place 1961, The Trial of Stephen Ward 1964, Very Lovely People 1969, Pursuit: the Chase and Sinking of the Bismarck 1974, A Presumption of Innocence: the Amazing Case of Patrick Meehan 1975, The Portland Spy Case 1978, Wicked Beyond Belief: The Luton Post Office Murder Case 1980, Menace: The Life and Death of the Tirpitz 1979, The Airman and the Carpenter: The Lindbergh Case and the Framing of Richard Hauptmann 1985, On My Way to the Club (autobiog.) 1989, Euthanasia: The Good Death 1990, Truth to Tell (collected writings) 1991, In Bed with an Elephant: A Journey through Scotland's Past and Present 1995, All in the Mind: A Farewell to God 1999; Gen. Ed. The British at War 1973–77; Ed. A Book of Railway Journeys 1980, A Book of Sea Journeys 1981, A Book of Air Journeys 1982, 36 Murders and Two Immoral Earnings 2002. *Honours:* Hon. DL (Strathclyde) 1985, (Southampton) 1993; Dr hc (Edin.) 1990, (Stirling) 1991; Richard Dimbleby Award (BAFTA) 1989, Bar Council Special Award 1992; Cross First Class, Order of Merit (Fed. Repub. of Germany). *Address:* c/o Rogers, Coleridge and White, 20 Powis Mews, London, W11 1JN, England (office).

KENNEDY, (George) Michael (Sinclair), CBE, MA, CRNCM, FIJ; British journalist and music critic; b. 19 Feb. 1926, Chorlton-cum-Hardy, Manchester; s. of Hew G. Kennedy and Marian F. Kennedy; m. 1st Eslyn Durdle 1947 (died 1999); m. 2nd Joyce Bourne, 10 Oct. 1999. *Education:* Berkhamsted School. *Career:* staff music critic, The Daily Telegraph 1941–50, Northern Music Critic 1950–60, Northern Ed. 1960–86, Jt Chief Music Critic 1986–89; Chief Music Critic, The Sunday Telegraph 1989–2005; Gov. Royal Northern Coll. of Music. *Publications:* The Hallé Tradition: A Century of Music 1960, The Works of Ralph Vaughan Williams 1964, Portrait of Elgar 1968, Elgar: Orchestral Music 1969, Portrait of Manchester 1970, History of the Royal Manchester College of Music 1971, Barbirolli: Conductor Laureate 1971, Mahler 1974, The Autobiography of Charles Hallé, with Correspondence and Diaries (ed.) 1976, Richard Strauss 1976, Britten 1980, Concise Oxford Dictionary of Music (ed.) 1980, The Hallé 1858–1983 1983, Strauss: Tone Poems 1984, Oxford Dictionary of Music (ed.) 1985, Adrian Boult 1987, Portrait of Walton 1989, Music Enriches All: The First 21 Years of the Royal Northern College of Music, Manchester 1994, Richard Strauss: Man, Musician, Enigma (French critics prize for musical biog. 2003) 1999, The Life of Elgar 2004, Buxton: an English Festival 2004; contrib. to newspapers and magazines, including Gramophone, Listener, Musical Times, Music and Letters, The Sunday Telegraph, BBC Music Magazine. *Honours:* Hon. mem.

Royal Manchester Coll. of Music 1971, Hon. mem. Royal Philharmonic Soc. 2006; Hon. MA (Manchester) 1975; Hon. MusD (Manchester) 2003. *Address:* The Bungalow, 62 Edilom Road, Manchester, M8 4HZ, England (home). *Telephone:* (161) 740-4528 (home). *E-mail:* majkennedy@bungalow62.fsnet.co .uk.

KENNEDY, Moorhead, AB, JD; American foundation administrator and writer; b. 5 Nov. 1930, New York, NY; m. Louisa Livingston 1955, four s. *Education:* Princeton University, Harvard University, National War College. *Career:* Foreign Service Officer, 1961–69, 1975–78, Dir, Office of Investment Affairs, 1971–74, US Dept of State; Exec. Dir, Cathedral Peace Institute, New York City, 1981–83, Council for International Understanding, New York City, 1983–90; Pres., Moorhead Kennedy Institute, New York City, 1990–97; mem. American Foreign Service Asscn; Americans for Middle East Understanding; International Advisory Committee, International Centre, New York. *Publications:* The Ayatollah in the Cathedral, 1986; Terrorism: The New Warfare, 1988; Hostage Crisis, 1989; Death of a Dissident, 1990; Fire in the Forest, 1990; Metalfabriken, 1993; Grocery Store, 1993; Nat-Tel, 1995; The Moral Authority of Government, 2000. Contributions: books and professional journals. *Honours:* Medal for Valor, US Dept of State, 1981; Gold Medal, National Institute of Social Sciences, 1991; many hon. doctorates.

KENNEDY, Pagan, MA; American writer and teacher; b. 7 Sept. 1962, Washington, DC. *Education:* Wesleyan, Conn. and Johns Hopkins Univs, Md. *Career:* Publr Pagan's Head magazine 1988–93; columnist, Village Voice 1990–93; Adjunct Instructor, Boston Coll. 1995–; contribs to The Nation, Spin, Seventeen, Interview, etc. *Publications:* Elvis's Bathroom (short stories) 1989, Stripping and Other Stories 1994, 'Zine 1995, Spinsters (novel) 1996, The Exes (novel) 1998; non-fiction: Platforms: A Microwaved Cultural Chronicle of the 1970s 1994, Pagan Kennedy's Living: A Handbook for Maturing Hipsters 1997, Black Livingstone: A True Tale of Adventure in the Nineteenth-Century Congo 2002, The First Man-Made Man 2007. *Honours:* Nat. Endowment for the Arts Award 1993. *Address:* c/o High Risk Books, 180 Varick Street, New York, NY 10014, USA. *E-mail:* pagan@user1.channel1.com.

KENNEDY, Paul Michael, CBE, MA, DPhil, FRHistS, FBA; British historian and academic; *J. Richardson Dilworth Professor of History and Director, International Security Studies, Yale University*; b. 17 June 1945, Wallsend; s. of John Patrick Kennedy and Margaret (née Hennessy) Kennedy; m. 1st Catherine Urwin 1967 (died 1998); three s.; m. 2nd Cynthia Farrar 2001. *Education:* St Cuthbert's Grammar School, Newcastle-upon-Tyne, Univ. of Newcastle and Oxford Univ. *Career:* Research Asst to Sir Basil Liddell Hart 1966–70; Lecturer, Reader and Prof., Univ. of E Anglia 1970–83; J. Richardson Dilworth Prof. of History, Yale Univ. 1983–, Dir Int. Security Studies 1988–; Visiting Fellow Inst. for Advanced Study, Princeton 1978–79; Fellow, Alexander von Humboldt Foundation, American Philosophical Soc., American Acad. of Arts and Sciences. *Publications:* The Samoan Tangle 1974, The Rise and Fall of British Naval Mastery 1976, The Rise of the Anglo-German Antagonism 1980, The Realities Behind Diplomacy 1981, Strategy and Diplomacy 1983, The Rise and Fall of the Great Powers 1988, Grand Strategy in War and Peace 1991, Preparing for the Twenty-First Century 1993, Pivotal States: A New Framework for US Policy in the Developing World (ed.) 1998, The Parliament of Man: The United Nations and the Quest for World Government 2006. *Honours:* Hon. DHL (New Haven, Alfred, Long Island, Connecticut); Hon. DLitt (Newcastle, East Anglia); Hon. LLD (Ohio); Hon. MA (Yale, Union, Quinnipiac); Dr hc (Leuven). *Address:* Department of History, Yale Univ., PO Box 208353, New Haven, CT 06520-8353, USA (office). *Telephone:* (203) 432-6242 (office). *Fax:* (203) 432-6250 (office). *E-mail:* paul.kennedy@yale.edu (office). *Website:* www.yale.edu/iss (office).

KENNEDY, Thomas Eugene, BA, MFA, PhD; American writer, editor, translator and teacher; *Core Faculty in Fiction and Creative Nonfiction, MFA Program, Fairleigh Dickinson University*; b. 9 March 1944, New York, NY; s. of the late George Ryan Kennedy and Ethel May Paris; m. Monique M. Brun 1974 (divorced 1997); one s. one d.; partner, Alice Maud Guldbrandsen. *Education:* Fordham Univ., New York, Vermont Coll., Norwich Univ., Copenhagen Univ., Denmark. *Career:* Guest Ed. Nordic Section Frank magazine 1987; European Ed. Rohwedder 1988–89; International Ed. Cimarron Review, 1989–99, Potpourri, 1993–2000; Contributing Ed. Pushcart Prize 1990–; Advisory Ed. Short Story 1990–95, Literary Review 1996–; mem. Editorial Bd International Quarterly 1994, Absinthe 2002–; Int. Ed. Story Quarterly 2000–; Co-Ed. Best New Writing 2007–; mem. panel, Thomas E. Kennedy: A Lifetime in Literature, US Asscn of Writers & Writing Programs, Atlanta, Ga 2007. *Music:* song lyrics recorded on record album Hammer, San Francisco/Atlantic label 1970. *Film:* Thomas E. Kennedy: Copenhagen Quartet (documentary) 2004. *Publications:* Andre Dubus: A Study 1988, Crossing Borders (novel) 1990, The American Short Story Today 1991, Robert Coover: A Study 1992, Index, American Award Stories 1993, A Weather of the Eye (novel) 1996, Unreal City (short stories) 1996, New Danish Fiction (ed.) 1995, The Book of Angels (novel) 1997, Drive, Dive, Dance and Fight (short stories) 1997, New Irish Writing (ed.) 1997, Stories and Sources (ed.) 1998, Poems and Sources (ed.) 2000, Realism and Other Illusions (essays) 2002, Kerrigan's Copenhagen, A Love Story (novel) 2002, The Secret Life of the Writer (co-ed.) 2002, Bluett's Blue Hours (novel) 2003, Greene's Summer (novel) 2004, Danish Fall (novel) 2005, The Literary Traveler (essays) 2005, A Passion in the Desert (novel) 2007, Cast Upon the Day (stories) 2007; other: The Literary Traveler (online column) 2001–, Writers on the Job (online column) 2004–. *Honours:* Angoff Award 1988, Pushcart Prize 1990, O. Henry

Prize 1994, Gulf Coast Short Story Prize 2002, Frank Expatriate Writing Award 2002, Prize, The European Story Competition 2005, Copenhagen Poetry Day Grass Prize 2006. *Address:* Strandboulevarden 118, 2100 Copenhagen, Denmark (home). *Telephone:* 35424290 (office); 20322963 (home). *E-mail:* tek@adslhome.dk (office). *Website:* www.thomasekennedy.com; www.copenhagenquartet.com.

KENNEDY, William Joseph, BA; American author and academic; *Professor of Creative Writing and Director, New York State Writers' Institute, University at Albany, State University of New York*; b. 16 Jan. 1928, Albany, New York; s. of William J. Kennedy and Mary E. McDonald; m. Ana Segarra 1957; one s. two d. *Education:* Siena Coll., New York. *Career:* Asst Sports Ed., columnist, Glens Falls Post Star, New York 1949–50; reporter, Albany Times-Union, New York 1952–56, special writer 1963–70; Asst Man. Ed., columnist, P.R. World Journal, San Juan 1956; reporter, Miami Herald 1957; corresp. Time-Life Publs, Puerto Rico 1957–59; reporter, Knight Newspapers 1957–59; Founding Man. Ed. San Juan Star 1959–61; lecturer, State Univ. of New York, Albany 1974–82, Prof. of English 1983–; Visiting Prof. Cornell Univ. 1982–83; Exec. Dir and founder, NY State Writers' Inst. 1983–; Nat. Endowment for Arts Fellow 1981, MacArthur Foundation Fellow 1983. *Publications include:* The Ink Truck 1969, Legs 1975, Billy Phelan's Greatest Game 1978, Ironweed 1983, O Albany! (non-fiction) 1983, Charlie Malarkey and the Belly Button Machine (children's book) 1986, Quinn's Book 1988, Very Old Bones 1992, Riding the Yellow Trolley Car 1993, Charlie Malarkey and the Singing Moose (children's book) 1994, The Flaming Corsage 1996, Grand View (play) 1996, Roscoe 2002; film scripts, The Cotton Club 1984, Ironweed 1987; also short stories, articles in professional journals. *Honours:* several hon. degrees; Gov. of New York Arts Award 1984, Creative Arts Award, Brandeis Univ. 1986; Pulitzer Prize and Nat. Book Critics Circle Award 1984 for Ironweed. *Address:* New York State Writers Institute, New Library, LE 320, University at Albany, State University of New York, Albany, NY 12222 (office); Department of English, University at Albany, State University of New York, Humanities 333, 1400 Washington Avenue, Albany, NY 12222, USA. *Telephone:* (518) 442-5620 (office). *Fax:* (518) 442-5621 (office). *E-mail:* writers@uamail.albany.edu (office). *Website:* www.albany.edu/writers-inst (office); www.albany.edu/english (office).

KENNEDY, X. J. (Joseph Charles), BSc, MA; American poet and writer; b. 21 Aug. 1929, Dover, NJ; m. Dorothy Mintzlaff 1962; four s. one d. *Education:* Seton Hall Univ., Columbia Univ. and Sorbonne Univ. of Paris. *Career:* Teaching Fellow 1956–60, Instructor 1960–62, Univ. of Michigan; Poetry Ed., The Paris Review 1961–64; Lecturer, Women's Coll. of the Univ. of North Carolina 1962–63; Asst Prof. to Prof., Tufts Univ. 1963–79; full-time writer 1979–; mem. Authors' Guild, John Barton Wolgamot Soc., MLA, PEN. *Publications:* Nude Descending a Staircase (Acad. of American Poets Lamont Award 1961) 1961, An Introduction to Poetry (with Dana Gioia) 1968, The Bedford Reader 1982, Cross-Ties: Selected Poems (Los Angeles Times Book Award 1985) 1985, Dark Horses: New Poems 1992, The Lords of Misrule: Poems 1992–2002 (Poets' Prize 2004) 2003; contrib. to newspapers and journals. *Honours:* Dr hc (Lawrence Univ.), (Adelphi Univ.), (Westfield State Coll.); Univ. of the South and The Sewanee Review Aiken-Taylor Award for Modern American Poetry, Guggenheim Fellowship, Nat. Arts Council Fellowship, American Acad. and Inst. of Arts and Letters Michael Braude Award, Shelley Memorial Award, New England Poetry Club Golden Rose, Nat. Council of Teachers of English Award for Excellence in Children's Poetry 2000. *Address:* c/o Johns Hopkins University Press, 2715 North Charles Street, Baltimore, MD 21218-4363, USA. *Website:* www.xjanddorothymkennedy.com.

KENNELL, Nigel M., BA, MA, PhD; Canadian classicist; b. 29 Nov. 1955, London, England; m. Stefanie Adelaide Hillert Suszko 1985. *Education:* University of British Columbia, University of Toronto, American School of Classical Studies, Athens, Greece. *Career:* Lecturer in Classics, Brock University, St Catherine's, Ontario, Canada, 1985–86; Asst Prof., 1986–92, Assoc. Prof. of Classics, 1992–, Memorial University, St John's University, NF; Research Asst, Institute for Advanced Study, Princeton, NJ, 1992–93; Research Assoc., Collège de France, Paris, 1993; mem. Archeological Institute of America; Classical Asscn of Canada; Society for the Promotion of Hellenic Studies; Canadian Academic Centre in Athens; Asscn of Ancient Historians; American School of Classical Studies Alumni Asscn. *Publications:* The Gymnasium of Virtue, 1996. Contributions: American Journal of Archaeology; American Journal of Philology; Epigraphica Anatolica; Hesperia; Phoenix; Zeitschrift für Papyrologie und Epigraphik. *Honours:* Choice Outstanding Academic Book 1996. *Address:* c/o College Year in Athens, PO Box 390890, Cambridge, MA 02139, USA. *E-mail:* info@cyathens.org.

KENNELLY, (Timothy) Brendan, MA, PhD, DLitt; Irish academic, poet, writer and dramatist; *Professor of Modern Literature, Trinity College, Dublin*; b. 17 April 1936, Ballylongford, County Kerry. *Education:* Trinity Coll., Dublin, Leeds Univ., England. *Career:* Prof. of Modern Literature and Sr Fellow, Trinity Coll., Dublin 1973–2005, now Prof. Emer., (Fellow 1967–2005, now Emer.). *Publications:* poetry: Cast a Cold Eye (with Rudi Holzapfel) 1959, The Rain, The Moon (with Rudi Holzapfel) 1961, The Dark About Our Loves (with Rudi Holzapfel) 1962, Green Townlands: Poems (with Rudi Holzapfel) 1963, Let Fall No Burning Leaf 1963, My Dark Fathers 1964, Up and At It 1965, Collection One: Getting Up Early 1966, Good Souls to Survive 1967, Dream of a Black Fox 1968, Selected Poems 1969, A Drinking Cup: Poems from the Irish 1970, Bread 1971, Love Cry 1972, Salvation, the Stranger 1972, The Voices 1973, Shelley in Dublin 1974, A Kind of Trust 1975, New and Selected Poems 1976, Islandman 1977, The Visitor 1978, A Girl: 22 Songs 1978, A Small Light 1979, In Spite of the Wise 1979, The Boats Are Home 1980, The House That Jack Didn't Build 1982, Cromwell: A Poem 1983, Moloney Up and At It 1984, Selected Poems 1985, Mary: From the Irish 1987, Love of Ireland: Poems From the Irish 1989, A Time for Voices: Selected Poems 1960–1990 1990, The Book of Judas: A Poem 1991, Breathing Spaces: Early Poems 1992, Poetry My Arse 1995, The Man Made of Rain 1998, The Singing Tree 1998, Begin 1999, Glimpses 2001, The Little Book of Judas 2002, Martial Art 2003, Familiar Strangers: New and Selected Poems 1960–2004, Now 2006; fiction: The Crooked Cross 1963, The Florentines 1967; plays: Medea 1991, The Trojan Women 1993, Antigone 1996, Blood Wedding 1996, When Then Is Now: Three Greek Plays 2006; criticism: Journey into Joy: Selected Prose 1994; other prose: Real Ireland 1984, Ireland Past and Present (ed.) 1985; contrib. poems to anthologies, including The Penguin Book of Irish Verse 1970, Landmarks of Irish Drama 1988, Joycechoyce: The Poems in Verse and Prose of James Joyce (with A. Norman Jeffares) 1992, Irish Prose Writings: Swift to the Literary Renaissance (with Terence Brown) 1992, Between Innocence and Peace: Favourite Poems of Ireland 1993, Dublines (with Katie Donovan) 1994, Ireland's Women: Writings Past and Present (with Katie Donovan and A. Norman Jeffares) 1994. *Honours:* AE Monorial Prize for Poetry 1967, Critics' Special Harveys Award 1988, American Ireland Funds Literary Award 1999. *Address:* c/o School of English, Trinity College, Dublin 2, Ireland. *Telephone:* (1) 896-1111.

KENNELLY, Laura B., BA, MA, PhD; American writer and poet; *Editor, Grasslands Review*; b. 28 July 1941, Denton, TX; m. 1st Kevin Kennelly 1961 (divorced 1996); m. 2nd Robert Mayerovitch 1996; four s. one d. two step-d. *Education:* Univ. of North Texas. *Career:* Adjunct Prof., Univ. of North Texas 1976–94, Texas Woman's Univ. 1995; Ed., Grasslands Review 1989–; Assoc. Ed., Bach: Journal of the Riemenschneider Bach Inst., Baldwin-Wallace Coll.; music reviewer, WCLV radio; mem. Texas Asscn of Creative Writing Teachers (pres. 1993–95). *Publications:* The Passage of Mrs Jung (chapbook) 1990, A Certain Attitude 1995; contrib. to San Jose Studies, Studies in Contemporary Satire, Exquisite Corpse, New Mexico Humanities Review, Australian Journal of Communication. *Honours:* first place North Central Texas Coll. Poetry Contest 1988, first place Univ. of North Texas Centennial Poem Award 1990. *Address:* PO Box 626, Berea, OH 44017, USA. *E-mail:* LKennell@bw.edu.

KENNET, (2nd Baron) cr. 1935, of the Dene; **Wayland Young,** MA, FRIBA; British writer and politician; b. 2 Aug. 1923, London; s. of Edward Hilton Young (Lord Kennet) and Kathleen Bruce; m. Elizabeth Ann Adams 1948; one s. five d. *Education:* Stowe School, Trinity Coll., Cambridge, Univ. for Foreigners, Perugia. *Career:* Royal Navy 1942–45; Foreign Office 1946–47, 1949–51; Corresp. for Observer newspaper in Italy 1953–55; mem. Parl. Assemblies Council of Europe and Western European Union 1962–65; Chair. British Cttee for International Co-operation Year 1965; Parl. Sec. Ministry of Housing and Local Govt 1966–70; Chair. Int. Parl. Confs on the Environment 1971–78; Chair. Advisory Cttee on Oil Pollution of the Sea 1970–74; Chair. Council for the Protection of Rural England 1971–72; Opposition Spokesman on Foreign Affairs and Science Policy, House of Lords 1971–74; Dir Europe Plus Thirty Project 1974–75; mem. European Parl. 1978–79; Chief Whip SDP, House of Lords 1981–83, SDP Spokesman on Foreign Affairs and Defence 1981–90; Vice-Chair. Parl. Office of Science and Tech. 1989–93; Vice-Pres. Parl. and Scientific Cttee 1989–98; rejoined Labour Party 1990; Pres. Architecture Club 1984–94; mem. North Atlantic Ass. 1997–2000. *Publications:* The Italian Left 1949, Old London Churches (with Elizabeth Young) 1956, The Montesi Scandal 1957, Strategy for Survival 1959, The Profumo Affair 1963, Eros Denied 1965, Preservation 1972, The Futures of Europe 1976, London's Churches (with Elizabeth Young) 1986, Northern Lazio: An Unknown Italy (with Elizabeth Young) 1990; Ed. Disarmament and Arms Control 1963–65, The Rebirth of Britain 1982, Parliaments and Screening 1994; Novels: The Deadweight 1952, Now or Never 1953, Still Alive Tomorrow 1958. *Address:* 100 Bayswater Road, London, W2 3HJ, England (home). *E-mail:* lizyoung@gn.apc.org (office).

KENNEY, Catherine, , MA, PhD; American writer, academic and arts administrator; *Director of Development, Apple Tree Theatre*; b. 3 Oct. 1948, Memphis, Tennessee, USA; d. of J. D. and Norma Kirby McPhee; one s. *Education:* Siena Coll., Loyola Univ., Chicago. *Career:* fmr Chair. and Prof. of English, Mundelein Coll., Loyola Univ.; fmr Exec. Dir, Irish American Heritage Center, Chicago; Dir of Devt, Apple Tree Theatre, Highland Park, IL 2005–; mem., Faculty of the American Man. Asscn. *Publications:* Thurber's Anatomy of Confusion, 1984; The Remarkable Case of Dorothy L. Sayers, 1990; Dorothy L. (play), 1993. Contributions: books, scholarly journals and newspapers. *Honours:* American Asscn of University Women Grant 1983. *Address:* 228 Stanley Avenue, Park Ridge, IL 60068, USA. *Telephone:* (847) 207-4004 (office). *E-mail:* proudfootproductions@sbcglobal.net. *Website:* www.appletreetheatre.com.

KENNY, Adele, BA, MS; American poet, writer, editor and consultant; *Poetry Editor, Tiferet Journal of Spiritual Literature*; b. 28 Nov. 1948, Perth Amboy, NJ. *Education:* Kean Univ., Coll. of New Rochelle. *Career:* Artist-in-Residence, Middlesex Co. Arts Council 1979–80; Poetry Ed. New Jersey ArtForm 1981–83, Tiferet Journal of Spiritual Literature; Assoc. Ed. Muse-Pie Press 1988–; Dir Carriage House Poetry Reading Series 1998–; Cultural Arts Dir Kuran Arts Center 1999–; Instructor, Stamler Police Acad. 1998–;

mem. Haiku Soc. of America (Pres. 1987–88, 1990), Poetry Soc. of America, Poets and Writers Inc. *Exhibition:* Jailhouse Revival, NJ Inst. of Tech. 2006. *Publications:* An Archeology of Ruins 1982, Illegal Entries 1984, The Roses Open 1984, Between Hail Marys 1986, Migrating Geese 1987, The Crystal Keepers Handbook 1988, Counseling Gifted, Creative and Talented Youth Through the Arts 1989, Castles and Dragons 1990, Questi Momenti 1990, Starship Earth 1990, We Become By Being 1994, Staffordshire Spaniels 1997, At the Edge of the Woods 1997, Staffordshire Animals 1998, Photographic Cases: Victorian Design Sources 2001, Chosen Ghosts 2001, Staffordshire Figures: History in Earthenware 1740–1900 2004; contrib. to periodicals. *Honours:* Writer's Digest Award 1981, New Jersey State Council on the Arts Fellowships 1982, 1987, Merit Book Awards 1983, 1986, 1987, 1991, Henderson Award 1984, Roselip Award 1988, Haiku Quarterly Award 1989, Allen Ginsberg Poetry Award 1993, Women of Excellence Award 1999. *Address:* 207 Coriell Avenue, Fanwood, NJ 07023, USA (office). *Telephone:* (908) 889-7223 (office). *E-mail:* yorkshirehouse@worldnet.att.net (office). *Website:* home.att.net/~yorkshirehouse (office).

KENNY, Sir Anthony John Patrick, Kt, DPhil, FBA; British philosopher and university teacher; *President, Royal Institute of Philosophy*; b. 16 March 1931, Liverpool; s. of John Kenny and Margaret Kenny (née Jones); m. Nancy Caroline Gayley 1966; two s. *Education:* Gregorian Univ., Rome, Italy, St Benet's Hall, Oxford. *Career:* ordained Catholic priest, Rome 1955; curate, Liverpool 1959–63; returned to lay state 1963; Asst Lecturer, Univ. of Liverpool 1961–63; Lecturer in Philosophy, Exeter and Trinity Colls, Oxford 1963–64; Tutor in Philosophy, Balliol Coll., Oxford 1964, Fellow 1964–78, Sr Tutor 1971–72, 1976–77, Master 1978–89; Warden Rhodes House 1989–99; Professorial Fellow, St John's Coll., Oxford 1989–99; Pro-Vice-Chancellor, Univ. of Oxford 1984–99, Pro-Vice Chancellor for Devt 1999–2001; Wilde Lecturer in Natural and Comparative Religion, Oxford 1969–72; Jt Gifford Lecturer, Univ. of Edinburgh 1972–73; Stanton Lecturer, Univ. of Cambridge 1980–83; Speaker's Lecturer in Biblical Studies, Univ. of Oxford 1980–83; Visiting Prof., Stanford and Rockefeller Univs and Univs of Chicago, Washington, Michigan and Cornell; Vice-Pres. British Acad. 1986–88, Pres. 1989–93; Chair. Bd British Library 1993–96 (mem. Bd 1991–96); Pres. Royal Inst. of Philosophy 2005–; Del. and mem. of Finance Cttee, Oxford Univ. Press 1986–93; Ed. The Oxford Magazine 1972–73; mem. Royal Norwegian Acad. 1993–, American Philosophical Soc. 1994–, American Acad. of Arts and Sciences 2003–. *Publications:* Action, Emotion and Will 1963, Responsa Alumnorum of English College, Rome (two vols) 1963, Descartes 1968, The Five Ways 1969, Wittgenstein 1973, The Anatomy of the Soul 1974, Will, Freedom and Power 1975, Aristotelian Ethics 1978, Freewill and Responsibility 1978, The God of the Philosophers 1979, Aristotle's Theory of the Will 1979, Aquinas 1980, The Computation of Style 1982, Faith and Reason 1983, Thomas More 1983, The Legacy of Wittgenstein 1984, A Path from Rome 1985, The Logic of Deterrence 1985, The Ivory Tower 1985, Wyclif – Past Master 1985, Wyclif's De Universalibus 1985, Rationalism, Empiricism and Idealism 1986, Wyclif in His Times 1986, The Road to Hillsborough 1986, Reason and Religion (essays) 1987, The Heritage of Wisdom 1987, God and Two Poets 1988, The Metaphysics of Mind 1989, Mountains 1991, What is Faith? 1992, Aristotle on the Perfect Life 1992, Aquinas on Mind 1992, The Oxford Illustrated History of Western Philosophy (ed.) 1994, Frege 1995, A Life in Oxford 1997, A Brief History of Western Philosophy 1998, Essays on the Aristotelian Tradition 2001, Aquinas on Being 2002, The Unknown God 2003, A New History of Western Philosophy (one vol.) 2003, A New History of Western Philosophy Vol. 1: Ancient Philosophy 2004, Vol. 2: Medieval Philosophy 2005, Arthur Hugh Clough: A Poet's Life 2005, What I Believe 2006, Life, Liberty and the Pursuit of Utility (with C. Kenny) 2006, The Rise of Modern Philosophy 2006. *Honours:* Hon. Bencher, Lincoln's Inn 1999; Hon. DLitt (Bristol) 1982, (Denison Univ.) 1986, (Liverpool) 1988, (Glasgow) 1990, (Lafayette) 1990, (Trinity Coll., Dublin) 1992, (Hull) 1993, (Belfast) 1994; Hon. DCL (Oxford) 1987; Hon. DLit (London) 2002; Aquinas Medal 1996. *Address:* St John's College, Oxford, OX1 3JP, England (office). *Telephone:* (1865) 764174 (home). *E-mail:* ajpk@f2s.com (home).

KENNY, Maurice, PhD; American (Mohawk) poet and writer; *Associate Visiting Professor and Writer in Residence, State University of New York, Potsdam*; b. 1929, Watertown, NY. *Education:* Butler Univ., St Lawrence Univ. and New York Univ. *Career:* founder and fmr Ed. Contact II literary magazine; fmr Ed. and Publisher Strawberry Press; fmr Poetry Ed. Adirondac Magazine; Visiting Prof. Univ. of Oklahoma at Norman, En'owkin Center at Univ. of Victoria, Paul Smith's Coll.; currently Assoc. Visiting Prof. and writer-in-residence State Univ. of New York (SUNY) at Potsdam; numerous appointments as writer-in-residence, including American Indian Community House, New York, Oneida Indian Nation, Wisconsin, Univ. of California at Berkeley, Columbia Univ., St Lawrence Univ., Gettysburg Coll., North Country Community Coll., Syracuse Community Writers, SUNY at Fredonia, Silver Bay Asscn; served on panels, including New York Foundation for the Arts, North Carolina Arts Council, New York State Council on the Arts, Educational Testing Service Arts Recognition and Talent Search; fmr mem. bd of dirs Co-ordinating Council of Literary Magazines, New York Foundation for the Arts, WSLU-FM radio station; currently Art Dir Blue Moon Cafe, Saranac Lake. *Radio:* Dug-Out (New American Radio) 1990. *Television:* Reno Hill... Little Big Horn (NBC), Poems, Poets and the Song (CBS). *Publications:* poetry: Dead Letters Sent 1958, I Am the Sun 1976, North: Poems of Home 1977, Dancing Back Strong the Nations 1979, Rivers 1979, Only as Far as Brooklyn 1979, Kneading the Blood 1981, Boston Tea Party 1982, The Smell of

Slaughter 1982, Blackroabe 1983, The Mama Poems (American Book Award) 1984, Between Two Rivers: Selected Poems 1956–84 1985, Prayer for Philip Deer in the Sierras 1987, Wounds Beneath the Flesh: Fifteen Native American Poets (ed.) 1987, Humans and/or Not So Humans 1988, Greyhounding This America 1989, The Short and Long of It 1990, Last Mourning in Brooklyn 1991, Tekonwatonti: Molly Brant 1992, On Second Thought: A Compilation (poems and essays) 1995, In the Time of the Present 2000, Carving Hawk: New and Selected Poems 1953–2000 2002; contrib. poems to numerous anthologies; short stories: Rain and Other Fictions 1985, Stories for a Winter's Night 1999, Tortured Skins and Other Fictions 2000; non-fiction: Backward to Forward (essays) 1997; contrib. to Trends, Calaloo, World Literature Today, American Indian Quarterly, Blue Cloud Quarterly, Wicazo Sa Review, Saturday Review, New York Times. *Honours:* Dr hc (St Lawrence Univ.); Wordcraft Circle of Native Writers Elder Recognition Award 2000, Nat. Public Radio Award for Broadcasting. *Address:* SUNY Potsdam, 44 Pierrepont Avenue, Potsdam, NY 13676-2294 (office); Apt 4, 49 Pierrepont Avenue, Potsdam, NY 13676-2120, USA (home). *Telephone:* (315) 267-2950 (office); (315) 268-1607 (home). *E-mail:* kennymf@potsdam.edu (office).

KENRICK, Tony; Australian author; b. 23 Aug. 1935, Sydney, NSW. *Career:* Advertising Copywriter, Sydney, Toronto, San Francisco, New York, London, 1953–72. *Publications:* The Only Good Body's a Dead One, 1970; A Tough One to Lose, 1972; Two for the Price of One, 1974; Stealing Lillian, 1975; The Seven Day Soldiers, 1976; The Chicago Girl, 1976; Two Lucky People, 1978; The Nighttime Guy, 1979; The 81st Site, 1980; Blast, 1983; Faraday's Flowers, 1985; China White, 1986; Neon Tough, 1988; Glitterbug, 1991; Round Trip, 1996.

KENT, Alexander (see Reeman, Douglas Edward)

KENT, Arthur William Charles, (James Bradwell, M. DuBois, Paul Granados, Alexander Karol, Alex Stamper, Brett Vane); British author; b. 31 Jan. 1925, London, England. *Education:* City Literary Institute, London. *Career:* journalist, News Chronicle, London 1943–46, Australian Daily Mirror 1947–53, Beaverbook Newspapers, UK 1957–69, BBC, London 1970–71. *Publications:* Sunny (as Bret Vane), 1953; Gardenia (as Bret Vane), 1953; Broadway Contraband (as Paul Granados), 1954; El Tafile (as M. DuBois), 1954; Légion Étrangere (as M. DuBois), 1954; March and Die (as M. DuBois), 1954; Revolt at Zaluig (as Alex Stamper), 1954; Inclining to Crime, 1957; Special Edition Murder, 1957; Kansas Fast Gun, 1958; Stairway to Murder, 1958; Wake Up Screaming, 1958; The Camp on Blood Island (with G. Thomas), 1958; Last Action, 1959; Broken Doll, 1961; Action of the Tiger, 1961; The Weak and the Strong, 1962; The Counterfeiters, 1962; Long Horn, Long Grass, 1964; Black Sunday, 1965; Plant Poppies on My Grave, 1966; Red Red Red, 1966; Fall of Singapore (with I Simon), 1970; The Mean City (as James Bradwell), 1971; A Life in the Wind (with Z. de Tyras), 1971; Sword of Vengeance (as Alexander Karol), 1973; Dark Lady (as Alexander Karol), 1974; The King's Witchfinder (as Alexander Karol), 1975; Maverick Squadron, 1975; The Nowhere War, 1975.

KENT, Helen (see Polley, Judith Anne)

KENT, Jeffrey (Jeff) John William, BSc (Econ), PGCE; English musician (keyboards, percussion), singer, writer and lecturer; b. 28 July 1951, Stoke-on-Trent; m. Rosalind Ann Downs 1987. *Education:* Univ. of London, Crewe Coll. of Higher Educ. *Career:* freelance writer and ed. 1972–; lecturer in Humanities, various Staffordshire colls 1974–; performing musician 1975–; Dragon Fair 1984; Open Air Concert, Chamberlain Square, Birmingham 1984; Guest speaker 1986–; lecturer in writing and publishing, Stoke on Trent Coll. 1994–; Green Party Conf. Concert 1987; Artists for the Planet Concert 1989; appearance on BBC Midlands TV, launching album 1992; Only One World tour 2000. *Recordings include:* albums: Tales from the Land of the Afterglow Part 1, Part 2 1984, Port Vale Forever 1992, Only One World 2000. *Publications:* The Rise and Fall of Rock 1983, Principles of Open Learning 1987, Routes to Change: A Collection of Essays for Green Education (co-author) 1988, The Last Poet: The Story of Eric Burdon 1989, Back to Where We Once Belonged! 1989, The Valiants' Years: The Story of Port Vale 1990, Port Vale Tales 1991, Port Vale Forever 1992, 100 Walks in Staffordshire (co-author) 1992, The Port Vale Record 1879–1993 1993, Port Vale Personalities 1996, The Mercia Manifesto: A Blueprint for the Future inspired by the Past 1997, Port Vale Grass Roots 1997, The Potteries Derbies 1998, A Draft Constitution for Mercia 2001, The Mysterious Double Sunset 2001, The Constitution of Mercia 2003; contributions to Alsager Chronicle, Education Now, Eric Burdon Connection Newsletter, First Hearing, Hard Graft, NATFHE Journal, The Sentinel, TAG-mag, etc. *Address:* Cherry Tree House, 8 Nelson Crescent, Cotes Heath, via Stafford, ST21 6ST, England (office). *Telephone:* (1782) 791673 (office). *E-mail:* witan@mail.com (office).

KENYON, Bruce Guy, (Meredith Leigh); American writer; b. 16 Aug. 1929, Cadillac, Michigan, USA; m. Marian Long 1950 (divorced 1954). *Career:* mem. Authors' Guild; Authors League. *Publications:* Rose White, Rose Red, 1983; The Forrester Inheritance, 1985; Fair Game, 1986; A Marriage of Inconvenience, 1986; Wild Rose, 1986; The Counterfeit Lady, 1987; An Elegant Education, 1987; A Lady of Qualities, 1987; Return to Cheyne Spa, 1988; A Certain Reputation, 1990. Contributions: periodicals.

KENYON, Michael, MA; British writer; b. 26 June 1931, Huddersfield, Yorkshire, England; three d. *Education:* Wadham Coll., Oxford. *Career:* mem. Detection Club. *Publications:* May You Die in Ireland 1965, The 100,000

Welcomes 1970, Mr Big 1973, The Rapist 1976, A Healthy Way to Die 1986, Peckover Holds the Baby 1988, Kill the Butler! 1991, Peckover Joins the Choir 1992, A French Affair 1992, Peckover and the Bog Man 1994; contrib. 40 articles to Gourmet Magazine. *Address:* 164 Halsey Street, Southampton, NY 11968, USA.

KEOGH, Dermot Francis, BA, MA, PhD; Irish academic and historian; *Head of Department of Modern History, University College, Cork*; b. 12 May 1945, Dublin; m. Ann 1973; two s. two d. *Education:* Univ. Coll., Dublin, European Univ. Inst., Florence. *Career:* Lecturer in History Univ. Coll., Cork 1970–, Jean Monnet Prof. of Modern Integration 1990–, Acting Head Dept of Modern History 1999–2000, Head 2003–; Visiting Prof. Dept of History Colby Coll., USA 1998; Jean Monnet Fellow Dept of History and Civilisation European Univ. Inst. Florence, Italy 2001–02; Fulbright Prof. Boston Coll. Social Welfare Research Inst. Boston, USA summer 2002; mem. Archives Advisory Group Dept of Justice 2006; mem. Royal Irish Acad. 2002. *Publications:* The Vatican, the Bishops and Irish Politics 1919–1939, 1985; The Rise of the Irish Working Class 1890–1914, 1983; Ireland and Europe 1919–1989, 1989; Church and Politics in Latin America, 1990; Ireland, 1922–1993, 1993; Jews in Twentieth Century Ireland, 1998, Documents on Irish Foreign Policy, Vols I-IV; contrib. to academic journals and national press. *Honours:* Fellow, Woodrow Wilson Centre for Scholars, Washington, DC, 1988; James S. Donnelly Sr Prize American Conf. for Irish Studies. *Address:* Dept of Modern History, University College, Cork, Ireland. *Telephone:* (21) 4902687 (office). *Fax:* (21) 4273369 (office). *E-mail:* d.keogh@ucc.ie (office). *Website:* www.ucc.ie/academic/history/ (office).

KEOHANE, Robert Owen, BA, MA, PhD; American political scientist and academic; *Professor of International Affairs, Woodrow Wilson School, Princeton University*; b. 3 Oct. 1941, Chicago, Ill.; s. of Robert Emmet Keohane and Marie Irene Keohane (née Pieters); m. Nannerl Overholser 1970; three s. one d. *Education:* Shimer Coll., Illinois, Harvard Univ. *Career:* Fellow Harvard Univ., Woodrow Wilson School of Public and Int. Affairs, Princeton Univ. 1961–62; mem. Woodrow Wilson Award Cttee 1982, Chair. Nominating Cttee 1990–91, Chair. Minority Identification Project 1990–92; Instructor, then Assoc. Prof. Swathmore Coll. 1965–73; Assoc. Prof., then Prof. Stanford Univ. 1973–81; Ed. Int. Org. 1974–80, mem. Bd Eds 1968–77, 1982–88, 1992–97, 1998–, Chair. 1986–87; Prof. Brandeis Univ. 1981–85; Pres. Int. Studies Asscn 1988–89, Chair. Nominations Cttee 1985; Prof., then Stanfield Prof. of Int. Peace, Harvard Univ. 1985–96, Chair. Dept of Govt 1988–92; James B. Duke Prof. of Political Science, Duke Univ. –2004; Prof. of Int. Affairs, Woodrow Wilson School, Princeton Univ. 2004–; Sherill Lecturer, Yale Univ. Law School 1996; Pres. American Political Science Asscn 1999–2000; mem. NAS 2005; Fellow, American Acad. of Arts and Sciences1983–, Center for Advanced Study in Behavioral Sciences 1977–78, 1987–88, 2004–05; Frank Kenan Fellow, Nat. Endowment for the Humanities 1995–96; Bell. *Publications include:* After Hegemony: Cooperation and Discord in the World Political Economy 1984, Neorealism and Its Critics 1986, International Institutions and State Power: Essays in International Relations Theory 1989; (as co-ed.): Transnational Relations and World Politics 1972, The New European Community: Decision-Making and Institutional Change 1991, Ideas and Foreign Policy 1993, From Local Commons to Global Interdependence 1994, Institutions for Environmental Aid: Pitfalls and Promises 1996, Internationalization and Domestic Politics 1996, Imperfect Unions: Security Institutions Across Time and Space 1999, Exploration and Contestation in the Study of World Politics 1998, Legalization and World Politics 2000; (as co-author): Power and Interdependence: World Politics in Transition 1977, Institutions for the Earth: Sources of Effective International Environmental Protection 1993, After the Cold War: State Strategies and International Institutions in Europe, 1989–91 1993, Designing Social Inquiry: Scientific Inference in Qualitative Research 1994. *Honours:* Research Fellow German Marshall Fund 1977–78; Fellow Council on Foreign Relations 1967–69, Guggenheim Foundation 1992–93; Sr Foreign Policy Fellow Social Science Research Council 1986–88; Bellagio Resident Fellow 1993; Hon. PhD (Univ. of Aarhus, Denmark) 1988; Grawemeyer Award for Ideas Improving World Order 1989, First Mentorship Award, Soc. for Women in Int. Political Economy 1997, Skytte Prize, Johan Skytte Foundation, Uppsala, Sweden 2005. *Address:* Woodrow Wilson School, 408 Robertson Hall, Princeton University, Princeton, NJ 08544-1013, USA (office). *Telephone:* (609) 258-1856 (office). *Fax:* (609) 258-0019 (office). *E-mail:* rkeohane@princeton.edu (office). *Website:* www.wws.princeton.edu/rkeohane (office).

KEPEL, Gilles; French sociologist and writer. *Career:* Prof. of the Middle East, Institut d'Études Politiques, Paris. *Publications:* non-fiction: Muslim Extremism in Egypt: The Prophet and Pharaoh 1985, The Revenge of God: Resurgence of Islam, Christianity and Judaism in the Modern World 1993, Allah in the West: Islamic Movements in America and Europe 1997, Jihad: The Trail of Political Islam 2002, Bad Moon Rising: A Chronicle of the Middle East Today 2003, The War for Muslim Minds: Islam and the West 2004. *Honours:* Tel-Aviv Prize for Literature 1990, Newman Prize 2003. *Address:* Institut d'Études Politiques de Paris, 2002 - 27 rue Saint-Guillaume, 75337 Paris Cédex 07, France.

KERBER, Linda Kaufman, AB, MA, PhD; American academic and writer; *May Brodbeck Professor of Liberal Arts and Professor of History, University of Iowa*; b. 23 Jan. 1940, New York, NY; m. Richard Kerber 1960; two s. *Education:* Barnard College, New York University, Columbia University. *Career:* Lecturer, 1963–67, Asst Prof., 1968, Stern College for Women, Yeshiva University; Asst Prof., San Jose State College, 1969–70; Visiting Asst Prof., Stanford University, 1970–71; Assoc. Prof. Univ. of Iowa 1971–75, Prof. of History 1975–, May Brodbeck Prof. of Liberal Arts 1985–; Visiting Prof. University of Chicago 1991–92; Harmsworth Prof. of American History Oxford Univ. 2006–07; mem. American Acad. of Arts and Sciences, American Antiquarian Society, American Studies Asscn (pres. 1988), Organization of American Historians (pres. 1997), Society of American Historians, PEN American Center, American Historical Asscn (pres. 2006). *Publications:* Federalists in Dissent: Imagery and Ideology in Jeffersonian America, 1970; Women of the Republic: Intellect and Ideology in Revolutionary America, 1980; Women's America: Refocusing the Past (co-ed.), 1982; The Impact of Women on American Education, 1983; History Will Do It No Justice: Women's Lives in Revolutionary America, 1987; US History as Women's History: New Feminist Essays (co-ed.), 1995; Toward an Intellectual History of Women: Essays, 1997; No Constitutional Right to Be Ladies: Women and the Obligations of Citizenship, 1998. Contributions: Professional journals. *Honours:* National Endowment for the Humanities Fellowships, 1976, 1983–84, 1994; National Humanities Center Fellowship, 1990–91; Guggenheim Fellowship, 1990–91. *Address:* c/o Department of History, University of Iowa, Iowa City, IA 52242, USA (home). *Telephone:* (319) 335-2302 (office).

KERET, Etgar; Israeli writer, screenwriter and actor; *Lecturer Department of Film and Television, Tel-Aviv University*; b. 1967, Tel-Aviv. *Career:* currently Lecturer, Dept of Film and Television, Tel-Aviv Univ.; also columnist for a Jerusalem weekly newspaper and draws a comic strip for a Tel-Aviv newspaper. *Film screenplays:* Devek Metoraf 1994, Ha-Chavera Shel Korbi 1994, Breaking the Pig (voice) 1998, Mashehu Totali 2000, A Buck's Worth 2005, Wristcutters: A Love Story 2006, Three Towers 2006. *Films as actor:* Malka Lev Adom (Skin Deep, also dir) 1996, Clara Hakedosha 1996, Mashehu Totali 2000, Meduzot (also dir, Caméra d'Or, Cannes Film Festival 2007) 2007. *Television screenplays:* Ha-Hamishia Hakamerit 1994, Aball'e 2001, Eretz Nehederet (series) 2003. *Publications include:* short stories: Pipelines 1992, Gaza Blues (with Samir el-Youssef) 2004, The Nimrod Flip-Out 2005, The Bus Driver Who Wanted to be God 2005, Missing Kinssinger 2007; also four graphic novels. *Address:* c/o Department of Film and Television, Tel-Aviv University, POB 39040, Tel-Aviv 69978, Israel.

KERMAN, Joseph Wilfred, BA, PhD; American musicologist, writer, critic and editor; b. 3 April 1924, London, England; m. Vivian Shaviro 1945; two s. one d. *Education:* New York Univ., Princeton Univ. *Career:* Dir of Graduate Studies, Westminster Choir Coll., Princeton 1949–51; Asst Prof. 1951–56, Assoc. Prof. 1956–60, Prof. of Music 1960–71, 1974–94, Chair., Dept of Music 1960–63, 1991–93, Univ. of California at Berkeley; Heather Prof. of Music, Univ. of Oxford 1971–74; Fellow, Wadham Coll., Oxford 1972–74; founder/Co-Ed., 19th Century Music 1977–89; Ed. California Studies in 19th Century Music 1980–; Charles Eliot Norton Prof. of Poetry, Harvard Univ. 1997–98; Fellow, American Acad. of Arts and Sciences 1973, American Philosophical Soc. 2001. *Publications:* Opera as Drama 1956, The Elizabethan Madrigal: A Comparative Study 1962, Beethoven Quartets 1967, A History of Art and Music (with Horst W. Janson and Dora Jane Janson) 1968, Listen (with Vivian Kerman) 1972, Beethoven Studies (ed. with Alan Tyson) 1973, The Masses and Motets of William Byrd 1981, The New Grove Beethoven (with Alan Tyson) 1983, Contemplating Music: Challenges to Musicology 1985, Music at the Turn of the Century (ed.) 1990, Write All These Down: Essays on Music 1994, Concerto Conversations 1999, The Art of Fugue: Bach Fugues for Keyboard 1715–1750 2005; contrib. to scholarly journals, including New York Review of Books. *Honours:* Guggenheim Fellowship 1960, Fulbright Fellowship 1966; National Inst. and American Acad. of Arts and Letters Award 1956, Hon. Fellow, Royal Acad. of Music, London 1972, hon. mem. American Musicological Soc. 1995. *Address:* Music Department, University of California, Berkeley, CA 94720 (office); 107 Southampton Avenue, Berkeley, CA 94707, USA (home).

KERMODE, Sir (John) Frank, Kt, MA, FBA, FRSL; British writer and academic; b. 29 Nov. 1919, Douglas, Isle of Man; s. of John Pritchard Kermode and Doris Kennedy; m. Maureen Eccles 1947 (divorced); one s. one d. *Education:* Univ. of Liverpool. *Career:* John Edward Taylor Prof., Univ. of Manchester 1958–65; Winterstoke Prof., Univ. of Bristol 1965–67; Lord Northcliffe Prof., Univ. Coll., London 1967–74; King Edward VII Prof., Univ. of Cambridge 1974–82; Julian Clarence Levi Prof., Humanities Dept, Univ. of Columbia, New York 1983, 1985; Charles Eliot Norton Prof. of Poetry, Harvard Univ. 1977–78; Foreign mem. American Acad. of Arts and Sciences, Accad. dei Lincei, Rome 2002. *Publications:* Romantic Image 1957, Wallace Stevens 1960, The Sense of an Ending 1967, Lawrence 1973, The Classic 1975, The Genesis of Secrecy 1979, The Art of Telling 1983, Forms of Attention 1985, History and Value 1988, The Literary Guide to the Bible (ed. with Robert Alter) 1989, An Appetite for Poetry 1989, Poetry, Narrative, History 1989, The Uses of Error 1991, The Oxford Book of Letters (with Anita Kermode) 1995, Not Entitled: A Memoir 1995, Shakespeare's Language 2000, Pleasing Myself 2001, Pieces of My Mind 2003, The Age of Shakespeare 2004, Pleasure and Change 2004. *Honours:* Hon. mem. American Acad. of Arts and Letters 1999–; Officier, Ordre des Arts et des Sciences; Hon. DHL (Chicago); Hon. DLitt (Liverpool) 1981, (Amsterdam), (Yale) 1995, (Wesleyan) 1997, (London) 1997, (Columbia) 2002, (Harvard) 2004. *Address:* 9 The Oast House, Grange Road, Cambridge, CB3 9AP, England. *Telephone:* (1223) 357931. *E-mail:* frankkermode@lineone.net (home).

KERN, E. R. (see Kerner, Fred)

KERN, Gregory (see Tubb, Edwin Charles)

KERNAGHAN, Eileen Shirley; Canadian writer; b. 6 Jan. 1939, Enderby, BC; m. Patrick Walter Kernaghan 1959, two s. one d. *Education:* University of British Columbia. *Career:* mem. Burnaby Writers Society; Federation of British Columbian Writers; Writers Union of Canada. *Publications:* The Upper Left-Hand Corner: A Writer's Guide for the Northwest (co-author), 1975; Journey to Aprilioth, 1980; Songs for the Drowned Lands, 1983; Sarsen Witch, 1988; Walking After Midnight, 1991. Contributions: journals and periodicals. *Honours:* Silver Porgy Award, West Coast Review of Books, 1981; Canadian Science Fiction and Fantasy Award, 1985.

KERNER, Fred, (F. R. Eady, Frohm Fredericks, Frederika Frohm, E. R. Kern, Frederick Kerr, D. F. Renrick, M. N. Thaler), BA; Canadian journalist, author and publisher (retd); b. 15 Feb. 1921, Montreal, QC; s. of Samuel Kerner and Vera Goldman; m. Sally Dee Stouten 1959; two s. one d. *Education:* Sir George Williams Univ. (Concordia Univ.), Montreal. *Career:* fmr Publr Publishing Projects, Inc.; mem. WIPO, Acad. of Canadian Writers, European Acad. of Arts, Sciences and Humanities, Org. of Canadian Authors and Publrs, Canadian Authors' Asscn, Periodical Writers' Asscn of Canada, Canadian Writers' Foundation, Asscn of American Publrs, Mystery Writers of America, Writers' Union of Canada, Authors' Guild, Authors' League of America, International PEN, Nat. Speakers' Asscn, American Acad. of Politics and Social Sciences. *Publications:* Eat, Think and Be Slender (with L. Kotkin) 1954, The Magic Power of Your Mind (with W. Germain) 1956, Ten Days to a Successful Memory (with J. Brothers) 1957, Stress and Your Heart 1961, Don't Count Calories (as Frederick Kerr) 1962, Secrets of Your Supraconscious (with W. Germain) 1965, What's Best for Your Child and You (with D. Goodman) 1966, Buy High, Sell Higher (with J. Reid) 1966, It's Fun to Fondue (as M. N. Thaler) 1968, Nadia (with I. Grumeza) 1977, Careers in Writing 1985, Mad About Fondue 1986, Prospering Through the Coming Depression (with A. Willman) 1988, Home Emergency Handbook and First Aid Guide 1990, Fabulous Fondues 2000; editor: Love is a Man's Affair 1958, Treasury of Lincoln Quotations 1965, The Canadian Writers' Guide (various edns), Selling Your Short Fiction 1992; contrib. to many books, magazines and journals. *Honours:* American Heritage Foundation Award 1952, Allen Sangster Award 1982, Air Canada Award 1982, Canadian Book Publrs' Council Award 1984, Int. Mercury Award 1990; Queen's Silver Jubilee Medal 1977. *Address:* 1405–1555 Finch Avenue E, Willowdale, ON M2J 4X9, Canada (office). *Telephone:* (416) 493-3111 (office). *Fax:* (416) 493-3111 (office). *E-mail:* fkerner@pubproj.com (office).

KERR, Carole (see Carr, Margaret)

KERR, David; British writer and academic; *Associate Professor of English, University of Botswana;* b. 1942, Carlisle, Cumbria. *Career:* f. and dir of theatre companies in UK, Malawi, Zambia and Botswana; Assoc. Prof. of English, Univ. of Botswana. *Publications:* non-fiction: African Popular Theatre 1996; poetry: Tangled Tongues 2003. *Address:* c/o Flambard Press, Stable Cottage, East Fourstones, Hexham, Northumberland NE47 5DX, England. *Telephone:* (1434) 674360. *Fax:* (1434) 674178. *Website:* www.flambardpress.co.uk.

KERR, (Anne) Judith; British children's writer and illustrator; b. 14 June 1923, Berlin, Germany; m. Nigel Kneale; one s. *Career:* sec., Red Cross, London, England 1941–45; teacher and textile designer 1948–53; script ed., scriptwriter, BBC TV, London 1953–58. *Publications:* The Tiger Who Came to Tea 1968, Mog the Forgetful Cat 1970, When Hitler Stole Pink Rabbit 1971, When Willy Went to the Wedding 1972, The Other Way Round (aka Bombs on Aunt Dainty) 1975, Mog's Christmas 1976, A Small Person Far Away 1978, Mog and the Baby 1980, Mog in the Dark 1983, Mog and Me 1984, Mog's Family of Cats 1985, Mog's Amazing Birthday Caper 1986, Mog and Bunny 1988, Mog and Barnaby 1990, How Mrs Monkey Missed the Ark 1992, The Adventures of Mog 1993, Mog on Fox Night 1993, Mog in the Garden 1994, Mog's Kittens 1994, Mog and the Vee Ee Tee 1996, The Big Mog Book 1997, Birdie Halleluyah 1998, Mog's Bad Thing 2000, The Other Goose 2001, Goodbye Mog 2002, Goose in a Hole 2005. *Honours:* Officer's Cross of the Order of Merit, Federal Repub. of Germany 2007. *Address:* c/o Harper Collins Publishers, 77–85 Fulham Palace Road, London, W6 8JB, England (office).

KERR, Katharine; American novelist; b. 3 Oct. 1944, Cleveland, OH; m. Howard Kerr 1973. *Education:* Stanford Univ. *Publications:* Daggerspell 1986, Darkspell 1987, The Bristling Wood (aka Dawnspell: The Bristling Wood) 1989, The Dragon Revenant (aka Dragonspell: The Southern Sea) 1990, Polar City Blues 1991, A Time of Exile: A Novel of the Westlands 1991, A Time of Omens: A Novel of the Westlands 1992, Resurrection 1992, Days of Blood and Fire: A Novel of the Westlands (aka A Time of War: Days of Blood and Fire) 1993, Days of Air and Darkness: A Novel of the Westlands (aka A Time of Justice: Days of Air and Darkness) 1994, Freeze Frames (co-author) 1995, Snare 2003; contrib. to anthologies. *Literary Agent:* Larsen-Pomada Literary Agency, 1029 Jones Street (between California and Pine Streets), San Francisco, CA 94109, USA. *E-mail:* larsenpoma@aol.com. *Website:* www.deverry.com.

KERR, Philip Ballantyne, LLM; British writer; b. 22 Feb. 1956, Edinburgh, Scotland; s. of William Kerr and Ann Brodie; m. Jane Thynne 1991; two s. one d. *Education:* Northampton Grammar School and Birmingham Univ. *Career:* film critic, New Statesman. *Play:* Bluesbreakers 2002. *Publications:* adult fiction: March Violets 1989, The Pale Criminal 1990, The Penguin Book of Lies (ed.) 1990, A German Requiem 1991, A Philosophical Investigation 1992, The Penguin Book of Fights, Feuds, and Heartfelt Hatreds: An Anthology of Antipathy (ed.) 1992, Dead Meat 1993, Gridiron (aka The Grid) 1993, Esau 1996, A Five-Year Plan 1997, The Second Angel 1998, The Shot 1999, Dark Matter 2002, The One from the Other 2007; juvenile fiction (as P.B. Kerr): Children of the Lamp: The Akhenaten Adventure 2004, Children of the Lamp: The Blue Djinn of Babylon 2005. *Honours:* Prix de Romans L'Aventures, Deutsches Krimi Prize. *Literary Agent:* A. P. Watt Literary Agents, 20 John Street, London, WC1N 2DR, England. *Telephone:* (20) 7405-6774. *Fax:* (20) 7430-1952. *Website:* www.apwatt.co.uk. *E-mail:* pbk@pbkerr.com. *Website:* www.pbkerr.com.

KERSHAW, Sir Ian, BA, DPhil, FBA, FRHistS; British academic and writer; b. 29 April 1943, Oldham, England; m. Dame Janet Elizabeth Murray Gammie 1966; two s. *Education:* Univ. of Liverpool, Merton Coll., Oxford. *Career:* Asst Lecturer in Medieval History, Univ. of Manchester 1968–70, Lecturer 1970–74, Lecturer in Modern History 1974–79, Sr Lecturer 1979–87, Reader Elect 1987; Visiting Prof. of Contemporary History, Ruhr-Univ., Bochum, Germany 1983–84; Prof. of Modern History, Univ. of Nottingham 1987–89, Univ. of Sheffield 1989–; Fellow, Alexander von Humboldt-Stiftung 1976, Wissenschaftskolleg zu Berlin 1989–90. *Television:* consultant to historical series on BBC 2, ZDF, Spiegel TV 1994–. *Publications:* Rentals and Ministers' Accounts of Bolton Priory, 1473–1539 (ed.) 1969, Bolton Priory: The Economy of a Northern Monastery 1973, Der Hitler-Mythos: Volksmeinung und Propaganda im Dritten Reich 1980, Popular Opinion and Political Dissent in the Third Reich: Bavaria, 1933–1945 1983, The Nazi Dictatorship: Problems and Perspectives of Interpretation 1985, Weimar: Why Did German Democracy Fail? (ed.) 1990, Hitler: A Profile in Power 1991, Stalinism and Nazism (co-ed. with M. Lewin) 1997, Hitler 1889–1936: Hubris 1998, Hitler 1936–1945: Nemesis 2000, The Bolton Priory Compotus 1286–1325 (co-ed. with D. Smith) 2001, Making Friends with Hitler: Lord Londonderry and Britain's Road to War (Soc. of Authors Elizabeth Longford Prize for Historical Biog. 2005) 2004, Fateful Choices 2007; contrib. to scholarly journals. *Honours:* Bundesverdienstkreuz (Germany) 1994; Hon. Fellow, Merton Coll. Oxford 2006; Dr hc (Manchester) 2004, (Stirling) 2004; Wolfson Literary Award 2000, Bruno Kreisky Prize (Austria) 2000, British Acad. Book Prize 2001. *Address:* Room C7, Department of History, University of Sheffield, 387 Glossop Road, Sheffield, Yorks., S10 2TN, England (office). *Telephone:* (114) 222-2550 (office). *Fax:* (114) 278-8304 (office). *E-mail:* b.eaton@sheffield.ac.uk (office). *Website:* www.shef.ac.uk/history/staff/ian_kershaw.html (office).

KERTÉSZ, Imre; Hungarian writer and translator; b. 9 Nov. 1929, Budapest; m. 2nd Magda Kertész. *Career:* deported to Auschwitz, then Buchenwald during World War II 1944; worked for newspaper Világosság, Budapest 1948–51 (dismissed when it adopted CP line); mil. service 1951–53; ind. writer and trans. of German authors such as Nietzsche, Schnitzler, Freud, Roth, Wittgenstein and Canetti 1953–; has also written musicals for the theatre; his works have been translated into German, Spanish, French, English, Czech, Russian, Swedish and Hebrew. *Publications include:* Sorstalanság (trans. as Fatelessness) (Jewish Quarterly Wingate Literary Prize 2006) (made into film 2005) 1975, A nyomkeresö (The Pathfinder) 1977, A kudarc (Fiasco) 1988, Kaddis a meg nem születetett gyermekért (Kaddish for a Child not Born 1997) 1990, Az angol labogó (The English Flag) 1991, Gályanapló (Galley Diary) 1992, A Holocaust mint kultúra (The Holocaust as Culture) 1993, Jegyzökönyv 1993, Valaki más: a változás kró'nikája (I, Another: Chronicle of a Metamorphosis) 1997, A gondolatnyi csend, amig kivégzöoztag újratölt (Moment of Silence while the Execution Squad Reloads) 1998, A száműzött nyelv (The Exiled Language) 2001, Felszámolás: regény (Liquidation) 2003. *Honours:* Brandenburg Literary Prize 1995, Leipzig Book Prize for European Understanding 1997, WELT-Literaturpreis 2000, Ehrenpreis der Robert-Bosch-Stiftung 2001, Hans-Sahl-Preis 2002, Nobel Prize in Literature 2002. *Address:* c/o Magvetö Press, Balassi B.U. 7, 1055 Budapest, Hungary (office); c/o Northwestern University Press, 625 Colfax Street, Evanston, IL 60208-4210, USA (office).

KERTZER, David I., PhD; American historian, anthropologist, writer and academic; *Dupee University Professor of Social Science, Brown University;* b. 20 Feb. 1948, New York City; m. Susan; one d., one s. *Education:* Brown Univ., Brandeis Univ. *Career:* Asst Prof. of Anthropology, Bowdoin Coll. 1973–79, Assoc. Prof. 1979–84, Prof. 1984–89, William R. Kenan, Jr Prof. 1989–92, Chair. Dept of Sociology and Anthropology 1979–81, 1984–86, 1987–88, 1992; Paul Dupee, Jr Univ. Prof. of Social Science, Brown Univ. 1992–, also Prof. of Anthropology 1992–, of History 1992–2001, of Italian Studies 2001–; Fulbright Sr Lecturer, Univ. of Catania 1978; Professore a contratto, Univ. of Bologna 1987; Visiting Fellow Trinity Coll., Cambridge, UK 1991; Visiting Scholar, Posthumous Inst. and Univ. of Amsterdam 1994; Visiting Dir of Studies, Ecole des Hautes Etudes en Sciences Sociales, Paris 1994; Prof. of Educ., American Acad. of Rome 1999; Fulbright Chair, Univ. of Bologna 2000; Visiting Prof., Ecole Normale Superieure, Paris 2002; guest lecturer at over 40 univs world-wide; Co-Founder and Co-Ed. Journal of Modern Italian Studies 1994–; Ed. Book Series: New Perspectives in Anthropological and Social Demography 1996–; Pres. Soc. for the Anthropology of Europe 1994–96; mem. Editorial Bd Social Science History 1987–96, 2001–04, Journal of Family History 1990–, Continuity and Change 1996–2000, Int. Studies Review 1998–2002; mem. Jury Lynton History Prize 2000–01; mem. Exec. Bd American Anthropological Asscn 1995–96, NIH Population Review Cttee 1996–99, Nat. Research Council Cttee on Population 1999–, German Marshall

Fund Advisory Bd 2000–02; Vice-Pres. Social Science History Asscn 2005–06; Fellow American Acad. of Arts and Sciences 2005–. *Publications include:* Comrades and Christians: Religion and Political Struggle in Communist Italy 1980, Famiglia Contadina e Urbanizzazione 1981, Family Life in Central Italy 1880–1910: Sharecropping, Wage Labour and Coresidence (Marraro Prize, Soc. for Italian Historical Studies 1985) 1984, Ritual, Politics and Power 1988, Family, Political Economy and Demographic Change (Marraro 1990) 1989, Sacrificed for Honor: Italian Infant Abandonment and the Politics of Reproductive Control 1993, Politics and Symbols: The Italian Communist Party and the Fall of Communism, 1996, The Kidnapping of Edgardo Mortara (Nat. Jewish Book Award 1997, Best Book of the Year, Publishers Weekly, Toronto Globe and Mail 1997; stage version 'Edgard Mine' by Alfred Uhry premiered 2002) 1997, The Popes Against the Jews (UK edn The Unholy War 2002) 2001, Prisoner of the Vatican 2004; contrib. to numerous nat. and state newspapers, contrib., ed. or co-ed. of numerous books, author of over 60 journal articles and 50 academic papers. *Honours:* Fellowship Center for Advances Studies, Stanford 1982, Guggenheim Fellowship 1986, Nat. Endowment for the Humanities Fellowship 1995, Rockefeller Foundation Fellowship, Bellagio, Italy 2000. *Address:* Department of Anthropology, Box 1921, Brown University, Providence, RI 02912, USA (office). *Telephone:* (401) 863-3251 (office). *Fax:* (401) 863-7588 (office). *E-mail:* David_Kertzer@Brown .edu (office). *Website:* www.davidkertzer.com (office).

KESSLER, Jascha Frederick, BA, MA, PhD LittD; American academic, poet, writer, dramatist and critic; b. 27 Nov. 1929, New York, NY; m. 1950; two s. one d. *Education:* Univ. of Heights Coll. of New York Univ., Univ. of Michigan. *Career:* Faculty, Univ. of Michigan 1951–54, New York Univ. 1954–55, Hunter Coll., CUNY 1955–56, Hamilton Coll. 1957–61; Prof. of English and Modern Literature, Univ. of California at Los Angeles 1961–1992, Prof. Emer. 1992–; Arts Commr City of Santa Monica, CA 1990–96; mem. Asscn of Literary Scholars and Critics, ASCAP. *Publications:* poetry: Whatever Love Declares 1969, After the Armies Have Passed 1970, In Memory of the Future 1976, revised edn as Collected Poems 2000; fiction: An Egyptian Bondage (short stories) 1967, Death Comes for the Behaviorist (novellas) 1983, Classical Illusions (short stories) 1985, Transmigrations: 18 Mythologems 1985, Siren Songs and Classical Illusions (short stories) 1992, Rapid Transit 1948: An Unsentimental Education (novel) 2000; plays: Selected Plays 1998, Christmas Carols and Other Plays 2000; other: The Anniversary (opera libretto), numerous translations of poetry collections and fairy tales, including Traveling Light (Finnish Literary Translation Centre Award 2001). *Honours:* Nat. Endowment for the Arts Fellowship 1974, Rockefeller Foundation Fellowship 1979, Hungarian PEN Club Memorial Medal 1979, Translation Center George Soros Foundation Prize 1989, California Arts Council Fellowship 1993–94, many translation prizes. *Address:* c/o Department of English, University of California at Los Angeles, Los Angeles, CA 90095-1530 (office); 218 16th Street, Santa Monica, CA 90402–2216, USA (home). *Fax:* (310) 393-067 (office); (530)684-5120 (home). *E-mail:* jkessler@ucla.edu (office); urim1@ verizon.net (home). *Website:* www.jaschakessler.com.

KESSLER, Lauren Jeanne; American writer and academic; b. 4 April 1951, New York, NY; m. Thomas Hager 1984; two s. one d. *Education:* BS, Northwestern University, 1971; MS, University of Oregon, 1975; PhD, University of Washington, 1980. *Career:* Dir, Graduate Program in Literary Nonfiction, School of Journalism and Communications, University of Oregon. *Publications:* The Dissident Press: Alternative Journalism in American History, 1984; When Worlds Collide, 1984; Aging Well, 1987; Mastering the Message, 1989; After All These Years: Sixties Ideals in a Different World, 1990; The Search, 1991; Stubborn Twig: A Japanese Family in America, 1993; Full Court Press, 1997; Happy Bottom Riding Club: The Life and Times of Pancho Barnes, 2000, Clever Girl: Elizabeth Bentley, the Spy Who Ushered in the McCarthy Era 2003. Contributions: scholarly journals. *Honours:* Excellence in Periodical Writing Award, Council for the Advancement of Secondary Education, 1987; Frances Fuller Victor Award for Literary Non-Fiction, 1994. *Address:* c/o School of Journalism and Communication, University of Oregon, Eugene, OR 97403, USA. *Website:* laurenkessler.uoregon.edu.

KEYES, Daniel, BA, MA; American author; b. 9 Aug. 1927, New York, NY; m. Aurea Georgina Vazquez 1952, two d. *Career:* Lecturer, Wayne State University 1962–66; Prof., English, Ohio University from 1966. *Publications:* Flowers for Algernon, 1966, filmed as Charly; The Touch, 1968; The Fifth Sally, 1980; The Minds of Billy Milligan (non-fiction), 1986; Daniel Keyes Short Stories, 1993; Daniel Keyes Reader, 1994; The Milligan Wars, 1995.

KHADER, Hassan; Palestinian writer, translator and editor; *Managing Editor, al-Karmel;* b. 1953, Gaza. *Education:* univ. in Cairo. *Career:* fmr Ed. literary journal of the Palestinian Liberation Org.; currently Man. Ed. al-Karmel literary magazine; Asst Prof. an-Najah Nat. Univ.; Dir of Creative Writing, Ministry of Culture. *Publications:* non-fiction: Time and Hostages: Theories of Literary Criticism, Memoirs of Exile, Splinters of Reality and Glass (essays) 2002; contrib. to al-Ahram weekly. *E-mail:* editor@alkarmel.org (office). *Website:* www.alkarmel.org.

KHADRA, Yasmina; Algerian writer; b. 1956; m. *Education:* cadet school. *Career:* armed forces –2000; female pseudonym of Mohammed Moulessehoul. *Publications include:* fiction: Houria 1984, La Fille du pont 1985, El Kahira 1986, De l'autre côté de la ville 1988, Le Privilège du phénix 1989, Le Dingue au bistouri 1990, La Foire des Enfoirés 1993, Les Agneaux du seigneur (trans. as In the Name of God) 1998, Morituri 1997, Double blanc (trans. as Double

Blank) 1998, L'Automne aux chimères 1998, A quoi rêvent les loups (trans. as Wolf Dreams) 1999, L'Imposture des mots 2002, Les Hirondelles de Kaboul (trans. as The Swallows of Kabul) 2002, Cousine K 2003, La Part du mort 2004, L'Attentat (trans. as The Attack) 2005; non-fiction: L'Écrivain (autobiog.) 2001. *Address:* c/o Vintage, 20 Vauxhall Bridge Road, London, SW1V 2SA, England.

KHAKETLA, Masechele; Lesotho teacher and writer. *Education:* Morija Training Coll. and Univ. of Fort Hare. *Career:* Co-Founder and Propr Iketsetseng Primary School; teacher, Basutholand High School; High Court Assessor. *Publications include:* Mosali eo o'nehileng Eena, Mahlopha a senya, Ka u Lotha, Khotosoaneng, Selibelo sa Nkhono, Pelo ea monna, Ho isa Lefung, Mosiuoa Masilo, Mantsopa, Molamu oa kotjana. *Honours:* Hon. DLitt (Nat. Univ.) 1983. *Address:* PO Box 65, Maseru 100, Lesotho. *Telephone:* 313877.

KHALIFA, Sahar, BA, MA, PhD; Palestinian writer and feminist; b. 1941, Nablus; m. 1959 (divorced); two d. *Education:* Rosary Coll. and Bir Zeit Univ., Chapel -Hill Univ., NC and Iowa Univs, USA. *Career:* began writing 1967–; moved to USA to study; returned to Nablus 1988; f. Women's Affairs Center, Nablus, Gaza City 1991, Amman 1994. *Publications include:* novels (in trans.): We Are Not Your Slave Girls Anymore 1974, Wild Thorns 1975, The Sunflower 1980, Memoirs of an Unrealistic Woman 1986, The Door of the Courtyard 1990, The Inheritance 1997. *Honours:* Fulbright scholarship 1980. *Address:* c/o Saqi Books, 26 Westbourne Grove, London, W2 5RH, England. *Website:* www.saqibooks.com.

KHAN, Haseena Moin, MA; Pakistani screenwriter; b. 20 Nov. 1938, Kanpur, India; d. of the late Moinuddin Khan and Aziz Fatima. *Education:* Univ. of Karachi, Harvard Univ., Boston Coll. *Career:* began writing stories and plays in coll.; playwright, Pakistan TV Corpn 1971–; headmistress of a girls' high school; has written numerous plays and TV serials. *Television serials:* Shahzori 1972, Kiran Kahani 1973, Zer Zabar Pesh 1974, Uncle Urfi 1975, Roomi 1976, Parchaiyan 1977, Dhund 1978, Ankahi 1979, Tanhaiyan 1981, Dhoop Kinaray 1983, Aahat 1987, Tansen 1991, Pal Do Pal, Aik Umeed 2001, Storplus, Door Door Shaw. *TV plays include:* Sangsar, Gurya Ralta, Paani Pe Likha tha, Chup Darya, Despardis, Aanso Dua, Aik Naye Mod Por, Shayed Ke Bahor Aye, Kuchto Kaha Hata. *Films:* Henna for Rajkapoor. *Publications:* Pulsarat ka Safar (novel); short stories and articles in English and Urdu newspapers. *Honours:* awards include TV Writer Award, Awami Award, Civil Award, Governor Award, Pride of Performance Nat. Award 1988, Nigar Award, Johns Hopkins Univ. Award 1992. *Address:* A 190, Block I, N Nazimabad, Karachi, Pakistan (home). *Telephone:* (21) 6638563 (home).

KHANFAR, Wadah; Jordanian journalist; *Director-General, Al-Jazeera Satellite Network. Career:* joined Al-Jazeera 1999, fmr corresp. Africa Bureau, New Delhi corresp. on war in Afghanistan 2002, Baghdad Bureau Chief 2003, Man. Dir Al-Jazeera 2003–06, Dir-Gen. Al-Jazeera Satellite Network 2006–. *Address:* Al-Jazeera Satellite Network, POB 23123, Doha, Qatar (office). *Telephone:* 4890881 (office). *Fax:* 4885333 (office). *Website:* english.aljazeera .net (office).

KHANG, Ma Van; Vietnamese writer; b. (Dinh Trong Doan), 1 Dec. 1936, Kim Lien, nr Hanoi. *Education:* Hanoi Pedagogical Univ. *Career:* fmr headmaster in Lao Cai Province; Deputy Ed.-in-Chief, Lao Cai newspaper; Ed.-in-Chief, Labor Publishing House 1976; Ed.-in-Chief, Foreign Literary Review section, Exec. Cttee mem. 1995–2000, Viet Nam Writers' Asscn. *Publications in translation:* novels: The French Silver Coin 1979, Summer Rain 1982, The Athlete in his Arena 1982, Border Area 1983, Young Moon 1984, The Garden in the Season of Falling Leaves 1986, The Lonely Orphan 1989, A Marriage Without Certificate 1989, Bi, The Wandering Dog 1992, Against the Flood 1999; short story collections: A Beautiful Day 1986, Ripe Fruits in Autumn 1988, The Strong Breeze 1992, Moonlight on the Small Yard 1995, Suburb 1996, The Classical Circle 1997, Lotus Marsh 1997, A Windy Afternoon 1998. *Honours:* Viet Nam Writers' Asscn Best Novel 1986, Best Short Story Collection 1995, ASEAN Literary Prize 1998. *Address:* c/o Curbstone Press, 321 Jackson Street, Willimantic, CT 06226-1738, USA. *E-mail:* info@curbstone.org. *Website:* www.curbstone.org.

KHARRAT, Edwar al-, LLB; Egyptian author; b. 16 March 1926, Alexandria; s. of Kolta Faltas Youssef al-Kharrat; m. 1958; two s. *Education:* Alexandria Univ. *Career:* storehouse asst, Royal Navy Victualling Dept, Alexandria 1944–46; clerk, Nat. Bank of Egypt 1946–48; clerk, Nat. Insurance Co. 1950–55; Dir of Tech. Affairs Afro-Asian People's Solidarity Org. 1959–67, Asst Sec.-Gen. 1967–73, Pres. 1967–; mem. Afro-Asian Writers' Asscn (Asst Sec.-Gen. 1967–72), Egyptian Writers' Union, Egyptian PEN; trans. and broadcaster for Egyptian Broadcasting Service; Assoc. Sr mem. St Antony's Coll., Oxford 1979; Ed. The Lotus, Afro-Asian Writings. *Publications include:* short stories: High Walls 1959, Hours of Pride 1972 (State Prize), Suffocations of Love and Mornings 1983; novels: Rama and the Dragon 1979, The Railway Station 1985, The Other Time 1985, Saffron Dust 1986, The Ribs of Desert 1987, Girls of Alexandria 1990, Creations of Flying Desires 1990, Waves of the Nights 1991, Stones of Bobello 1992, Penetrations of Love and Perdition 1993, My Alexandria 1994, Ripples of Salt Dreams 1994, Fire of Phantasies 1995, Soaring Edifices 1997, Certitude of Thirst 1997, Throes of Facts and Folly 1998, Boulders of Heaven 2000, Path of Eagle; poetry: Cry of the Unicorn 1998, Seven Clouds 2000; literary criticism: Transgeneric Writing 1994, The New Sensibility 1994, From Silence to Rebellion 1994, Hymn to Density 1995, Beyond Reality 1998, Voices of Modernity in Fiction 1999, Modernist Poetry in Egypt 2000, Fiction and Modernity 2003, The Fiction Scene 2003. *Honours:*

Franco-Arab Friendship Prize 1991, Ali Al Owais Award (for fiction) 1996, Cavifis Prize 1998, State Merit Award 2000. *Address:* 45 Ahmad Hishmat Street, Zamalek, Cairo, Egypt. *Telephone:* (2) 7366367. *Fax:* (2)7366367.

KHATCHADOURIAN, Haig, BA, MA, PhD; American academic, writer and poet; b. 22 July 1925, Old City, Jerusalem, Palestine; m. Arpiné Yaghlian 1950, two s. one d. *Education:* American University of Beirut, Lebanon, Duke University, USA. *Career:* American University of Beirut, Lebanon, 1948–49, 1951–67; Andrew Mellon Postdoctoral Fellow Univ. of Pittsburgh 1963–64; Prof. of Philosophy, University of Southern California at Los Angeles, 1968–69; Prof. of Philosophy, 1969–94, Emeritus Prof., 1994–, University of Wisconsin at Milwaukee; Liberal Arts Fellow in Philosophy and Law Harvard Law School 1982–83; mem. Fellow, Royal Society for the Encouragement of Arts, Manufacture and Commerce; Foreign Mem., Armenian Acad. of Philosophy; Founding Mem., International Acad. of Philosophy. *Publications:* The Coherence Theory of Truth: A Critical Evaluation, 1961; Traffic with Time (co-author, poems), 1963; A Critical Study in Method, 1967; The Concept of Art, 1971; Shadows of Time (poems), 1983; Music, Film and Art, 1985; Philosophy of Language and Logical Theory: Collected Papers, 1996; The Morality of Terrorism, 1998; Community and Communitarianism, 1999; The Quest for Peace Between Israel and the Palestinians, 2000. Contributions: numerous professional and literary journals including Armenian Mind. *Address:* Department of Philosophy, University of Wisconsin, Milwaukee, WI 53201, USA.

KHATIBI, Abdelkébir; Moroccan novelist and critic; *Director, Institut Universitaire de la Recherche Scientifique;* b. 1938. *Career:* currently Dir, Institut Universitaire de la Recherche Scientifique. *Play:* Le Prophète voilé 1979. *Publications include:* non-fiction: La Mémoire tatouée: autobiographie d'un décolonisé 1971, La Blessure du nom propre 1974, L'Art calligraphique Arabe (trans. as The Splendour of Islamic Calligraphy) 1976, Le Lutteur de classe à la manière taoiste 1977, Le Livre du sang 1979, De la mille et troisième nuit 1980, Maghreb pluriel 1983, Amour bilingue 1983, Dédicace à l'année qui vient 1986, Figures de l'étranger dans la littérature française 1987, Par-dessus l'épaule 1988, Paradoxes du sionisme 1990, Penser le Maghreb 1993, L'Alternance et les partis politiques au Maroc 1999; essay: Le Roman Maghrébin 1979; novel: Un été à Stockholm 1990. *Address:* c/o Institut Universitaire de la Recherche Scientifique, 52 Charii Omar Ibn Khattab, BP 8027, 10102 Agdal-Rabat, Morocco.

KHELLADI, Aissa; Algerian novelist, journalist, playwright and poet; *Director, Algérie Littérature/Action;* b. 1953. *Education:* Université d'Alger. *Career:* co-founder Nouvel Hebdo 1990, Hebdo Libéré 1991; fmr journalist, Ruptures weekly publ.; exiled in France 1994; co-founder and Dir Algérie Littérature/Action literary journal 1996–. *Play:* Le Paradis des fausses espérances 1999. *Publications:* novels: Peurs et mensonges 1996, Rose d'abîme 1998, Spoliation 1998; non-fiction: Algérie: les islamistes face au pouvoir 1992; contrib. to Les Temps modernes. *Address:* Algérie Littérature/Action, c/o Marsa Editions, 103 Boulevard MacDonald, Paris 75019, France (office). *E-mail:* algerie.litterature@free.fr (office). *Website:* www.algerie-litterature.com.

KHERDIAN, David, BS; American author and poet; b. 17 Dec. 1931, Racine, WI; m. 1st Kato Rozeboom 1968 (divorced 1970); m. 2nd Nonny Hogrogian 1971. *Education:* University of Wisconsin. *Career:* Founder-Ed., Giligia Press, 1966–72, Press at Butterworth Creek, 1987–88, Fork Roads: Journal of Ethnic American Literature, 1995–96; Rare Book Consultant, 1968–69, Lecturer, 1969–70, Fresno State College; Poet-in-the-Schools, State of New Hampshire, 1971; Dir, Two Rivers Press, 1978–86; Founder, Ed., Stopinder: A Gurdjieff Journal for our Time, 2000; mem. PEN. *Publications:* On the Death of My Father and Other Poems, 1970; Homage to Adana, 1970; Looking Over Hills, 1972; The Nonny Poems, 1974; Any Day of Your Life, 1975; Country Cat, City Cat, 1978; I Remember Root River, 1978; The Road from Home: The Story of an Armenian Girl, 1979; The Farm, 1979; It Started With Old Man Bean, 1980; Finding Home, 1981; Taking the Soundings on Third Avenue, 1981; The Farm Book Two, 1981; Beyond Two Rivers, 1981; The Song of the Walnut Grove, 1982; Place of Birth, 1983; Right Now, 1983; The Mystery of the Diamond in the Wood, 1983; Root River Run, 1984; The Animal, 1984; Threads of Light: The Farm Poems Books III and IV, 1985; Bridger: The Story of a Mountain Man, 1987; Poems to an Essence Friend, 1987; A Song for Uncle Harry, 1989; The Cat's Midsummer Jamboree, 1990; The Dividing River/The Meeting Shore, 1990; On a Spaceship with Beelzebub: By a Grandson of Gurdjieff, 1990; The Great Fishing Contest, 1991; Junas's Journey, 1993; Asking the River, 1993; By Myself, 1993; Friends: A Memoir, 1993; My Racine, 1994; Lullaby for Emily, 1995. Editor: several books. Other: various times. Honours: Jane Addams Peace Award, 1980; Banta Award, 1980; Boston Globe/Horn Book Award, 1980; Lewis Carroll Shelf Award, 1980; Newbery Honor Book Award, 1980; Friends of American Writers Award, 1982.

KHOURI, Callie; American screenwriter and film director; b. 27 Nov. 1957, San Antonio, TX. *Films:* Thelma & Louise (screenwriter, prod.) (Acad. Award 1992) 1991, Something to Talk About (screenwriter) 1995, Divine Secrets of the Ya-Ya Sisterhood (screenwriter, dir) 2002, Hollis & Rae (screenwriter, prod., dir) 2006. *Literary Agent:* c/o International Creative Management, 8942 Wilshire Blvd, Beverly Hills, CA 90048, USA. *Telephone:* (310) 550-4000. *E-mail:* film@icmtalent.com. *Website:* www.icmtalent.com.

KHOURY, Elias; Lebanese novelist and literary critic; b. 1948, Ashrafiyyeh, nr Beirut. *Education:* studied in Beirut and Paris, France. *Career:* PLO

Research Centre 1973–79; Publisher of journal, Su'un filastiniya (Palestinian Affairs) 1976–79; Ed. culture section of journal, As-Safir –1991, culture section of daily newspaper, an-Nahar 1992–; Dir Masrah Beyrut theatre 1993–98; fmr Prof. Columbia Univ., Lebanese Univ., American Univ. of Beirut, and Lebanese American Univ.; Global Distinguished Prof. of Middle Eastern and Islamic Studies 2004–05. *Publications:* An 'ilaqat al-da'irah (novel) 1975, Al-Jabal al-Saghir (novel) 1977, Dirasat fi naqd al-shi'r (criticism) 1979, Abwab al-Madinah (novel) 1981, Al-wujuh al-baida' (novel) 1981, Al-dhakira wa'l-mafquda (criticism) 1982, Al-mubtada' wa'l-khabar (short stories) 1984, Tajribat al-ba'th 'an ufq (criticism) 1984, Zaman al-ihtilal (criticism) 1985, Rahlat Gandhi al-Saghir (novel) 1989, Mamlakat al-Ghuraba (novel) 1993, Majma' al-Asrar (novel) 1994, Bab al-Shams (novel) (Palestine Prize 1998) 1998, Ra'ihat al-Sabun (novel) 2000, Yalo (novel) 2002. *Honours:* Lettre Ulysses Award 2005. *Address:* c/o An-Nahar, Immeuble an-Nahar, place des Martyrs, Marfa', Beirut 2014 5401, Lebanon.

KHOURY-GHATA, Vénus; Lebanese/French novelist and poet; b. 1937, Bsherre; m. 1st (divorced); three c.; m. 2nd Jean Ghata (died 1981); one d. *Education:* Etude de Lettres, Liban. *Career:* fmr journalist; moved to France 1973; fmr contributor and translator, Europe magazine; Pres. Prix des Cinq Continents, Prix Yvon Goll, Prix France Liban; mem. selection cttee, Prix Mallarmé, Prix Max-Pol-Fouchet, Prix Max-Jacob; frequent radio broadcaster. *Publications:* poetry: (first collection) 1966, Les Ombres et leurs cris (Prix Guillaume-Apollinaire) 1980, Monologue du mort (Prix Mallarmé) 1987, Fable pour un peuple d'argile (Grand Prix de la Société des gens de lettres) 1992, Anthologie person-elle 1997, Elle dit 1999, Here There Was Once a Country (anthology in trans.) 2001, La Compassion des pierres 2001, She Says (trans.) 2003; novels: Vacarme pour une lune morte 1983, Bayarmine 1990, Mortemaison 1992, La maitresse du notable (Liberaturpreis) 1992, La Maestra 1994, Les Fiancées du Cap Ténès 1995, Une maison au bord des larmes 1998, Privilège des morts 2001, La Compassion des pierres 2001, Le Moine, l'ottoman et la femme du grand argentier 2003; contrib. in trans. to Ambit, Banipal: a Journal of Modern Arab Literature, Columbia, Field, Contemporary Poetry and Poetics, Gobshite Quarterly, Jacket, Luna, The Manhattan Review, Metre, The New Yorker, Poetry, Shenandoah, Verse, Poetry London. *Honours:* Prix Supervielle 1997; Chevalier, Légion d'honneur 2000. *Address:* 16 avenue Raphael, 75016 Paris, France. *Telephone:* 1-45-04-06-37.

KHRISTOV, Boris Kirilov; Bulgarian poet and writer; b. 1945, Krapets, Pernik. *Education:* Univ. of Tŭrnovo. *Career:* worked as a teacher, journalist and editor; work was frequently banned by govt –1989. *Publications:* poetry: Vecheren trompet (Evening Trumpet) 1977, Chesten krŭst (Cross My Heart) 1982, Dumi i grafiti (Words and Graffiti) 1991, Dumi vŭrkhu drugi dumi (Words on Words) 1991, Cherni bukvi vŭrkhu cheren list (Black Letters on a Black Page) 1997; prose: Izpitanieto: Spomeni za protsesa i sudbata na Traicho Kostov i negovata grupa 1995.

KHUE, Le Minh; Vietnamese writer and editor. *Career:* war correspondent, Tien Phong (Vanguard), Giaia Phong (Liberation); Chief Fiction Ed., Vietnam Writers' Asscn. *Publications:* The Stars, The Earth, The River 1997; as co-editor: The Other Side of Heaven: Post-War Fiction by Vietnamese and American Writers 1995. *Address:* c/o Vietnam Writers' Association, Nguyen Dinh Chieu Str., Hanoi, Viet Nam. *E-mail:* nhavan.bdn@fpt.vn.

KHWAJA, Waqas Ahmad, BA, LLB, MA, PhD; Pakistani academic, lawyer, writer, poet and editor; b. 14 Oct. 1952, Lahore; m. Maryam Khurshid 1978; four c. *Education:* Government College, Lahore, Emory University. *Career:* Visiting Prof., Quaid-e-Azam Law College, 1988–91, Punjab Law College, 1988–92; Visiting Faculty, Lahore College for Arts and Sciences, 1989–90, Punjab University, 1990–91; Asst Prof. of English, Agnes Scott College, 1995–; mem. MLA of America; Writers Group, Lahore, Founder, 1984, convener and gen. ed., 1984–92. *Publications:* Cactus: An Anthology of Recent Pakistani Literature (ed. and trans.), 1984; Six Geese from a Tomb at Medum (poems), 1987; Mornings in the Wilderness (ed. and trans.), 1988; Writers and Landscapes (prose and poems), 1991; Miriam's Lament and Other Poems, 1992; Short Stories from Pakistan (ed. and trans.), 1992. Contributions: newspapers and magazines. *Honours:* Ansley Miller Scholar, Emory University, 1981; International Writing Fellowship, US Information Agency and University of Iowa, 1988; Hon. Fellow, University of Iowa, 1988; Commemorative Medal, Islamic Philosophic Society, Lahore, 1991. *Address:* Agnes Scott College, 141 East College Avenue, Decatur, GA 30030, USA (office). *E-mail:* wkhwaja@agnesscott.edu (office).

KIAROSTAMI, Abbas, BA; Iranian film director, producer, writer and photographer; b. 22 June 1940, Tehran; m. (divorced); two s. *Education:* Tehran Coll. of Fine Arts. *Career:* worked as designer and illustrator (commercials, film credit titles and children's books); involved in establishment of film making Dept at Inst. for Intellectual Devt of Children and Young Adults (Kanoon); ind. film maker from early 1990s; has made over 20 films, including shorts, educational films, documentaries. *Exhibitions include:* Forest Without Leaves (installation, V&A, London) 2005, Trees in Snow (photographs, V&A, London) 2005. *Films directed:* Nan va koucheh (Bread and Alley, short) (debut production of Kanoon film Dept) 1970, Zangu-e tafrih (Breaktime) 1972, Tajrobeh (The Experience) 1973, Mossafer (The Traveller) 1974, Man ham mitoumam (So Can I, short) 1975, Do rah-e hal baraye yek massaleh (Two Solutions for One Problem, short) 1975, Lebasi bara-ye arusi (A Wedding Suit) 1976, Rang-ha (Colours, short) 1976, Bozorgdasht-e mo'allem (Tribute to the Teachers, documentary) 1977, Az oghat-e faraghat-e khod chegouneh estefadeh konim: Rang-zanie (How to Make Use of Leisure Time: Painting, short) 1977, Gozarech (The Report) 1977, Rah-e hal (Solution, short) 1978, Ghazieh-e shekl-e aval, ghazieh-e shekl-e douuom (First Case, Second Case) 1979, Dandan-dard (Toothache, short) 1979, Beh tartib ya bedoun-e tartib (Orderly or Disorderly, short) 1981, Hamsorayan (The Chorus, short) 1982, Hamshahri (Fellow Citizen) 1983, Avali-ha (First-Graders, documentary) 1984, Khaneh-je doost kojast? (Where Is the Friend's House?, first film of the 'Koker trilogy') 1987, Mashq-e shab (Homework, documentary) 1989, Namay-eh nazdik (Close-Up, documentary) 1990, Zendegi va digar hich (And Life Goes On. . ., second film of the 'Koker trilogy') (aka Va zendegi edemah darad—Life and Nothing More) (Cannes Film Festival Rossellini Prize) 1991, Zir-e darakhtan-e zeyton (Through the Olive Trees, final film of the 'Koker trilogy') 1994, Tavalod-e noor (Plus Dinner for One, short) 1996, Ta'am-e gilas (The Taste of Cherry) (Cannes Film Festival Palme d'Or) 1997, Bad mara khahad bourd (The Wind Will Carry Us) (Venice Film Festival Grand Jury Prize) 1999, ABC Africa (documentary) 2001, Ta'ziyeh 2002, 10 (also writer) 2002, Five (also writer) 2003, Ten Minutes Older (short) 2003, 10 on Ten (also writer) 2004, Tickets (with others, also writer) 2004. *Film screenplays*: The Key 1987, The Journey 1995, Badkonak-e sefid (The White Balloon) (Cannes Film Festival Caméra d'Or) 1995, Istgah-e matrouk (The Deserted Station) 2002, Talaye sorgh (Crimson Gold) 2003. *Publications*: Walking with the Wind: Poems 2001. *Honours*: more than 50 int. prizes including special prize of the Pasolini Foundation 1995, UNESCO Fellini Medal 1997. *Address*: c/o Zeitgeist Films Ltd, 247 Center Street, Second Floor, New York, NY 10013, USA.

KIBEDI VARGA, Aron, PhD; Dutch/Hungarian academic and poet; *Professor of French Literature, Vrije Universiteit, Amsterdam*; b. 4 Feb. 1930, Szeged, Hungary; m. 1st T. Spreij 1954; m. 2nd K. Agh 1964; m. 3rd S. Bertho 1991; four s. one d. *Education*: Univs of Amsterdam, Leiden, Sorbonne. *Career*: Lecturer in French Literature, Vrije Universiteit, Amsterdam 1954–66, Prof. of French Literature 1971–; Prof. of French Literature, Univ. of Amsterdam 1966–71; Visiting Prof. Iowa Univ. 1971, Yale Univ. 1975, Princeton Univ. 1980, Rabat Univ. 1985, Coll. de France 1992; mem. Cttee Int. Soc. for the History of Rhetoric 1979–83; Pres. Int. Asscn Word and Image Studies 1987–93; mem. Royal Netherlands Acad. of Sciences 1981–; mem. Hungarian Acad. of Sciences 1990–. *Publications*: criticism: Les Constantes du Poème 1963, Rhétorique et Littérature 1970, Théorie de la Littérature (ed.) 1981, Discours récit, image 1989, Les Poétiques du classicisme (ed.) 1990, Le Classicisme 1998, Szavak, világok 1998, Noé könyvei 1999, Amszterdami krónika 2000, És felébred aminek neve van 2002, A jelen 2003; poetry (in Hungarian): Kint és Bent 1963, Téged 1975, Szépen 1991, Hántani, fosztani 2000, Oldás 2004. *Honours*: Dr hc (Pécs) 1994. *Address*: Department of French, Vrije Universiteit, Amsterdam, Netherlands (office). *Telephone*: (20) 4446456 (office). *Fax*: (20) 4446500 (office).

KIBERD, Declan, MRIA; Irish literary critic and educator; b. 24 May 1951, Dublin. *Education*: Trinity Coll., Dublin, Univ. of Oxford, UK. *Career*: Lecturer in English and Prof. of Anglo-Irish Literature and Drama, Univ. Coll., Dublin. *Publications*: Synge and the Irish Language 1979, Men and Feminism in Modern Literature 1985, Omnium Gatherum – Essays for Richard Ellmann (co-ed.) 1989, An Crann Faoi Bhlath-The Flowering Tree – Contemporary Irish Poems with Verse Translations (co-ed.) 1991, The Student's Annotated Ulysses (ed.) 1992, Idir Dhá Chúltur 1993, Inventing Ireland – The Literature of the Modern Nation 1996, Irish Classics 2000, The Irish Writer and the World 2005. *Honours*: Irish Times Literature Prize 1997, American Cttee of Irish Studies Award 1997, 2001, Truman Capote Award for Literary Criticism 2002. *Address*: J203, Department of English, University College, Belfield, Dublin 4, Ireland (office). *Telephone*: (1) 7168348 (office).

KIBIROV, Timur Yuryevich; Russian poet; b. (Zapoyev), 15 Feb. 1955, Shepetovka, Ukraine; m. Yelena Ivanovna Borisova; one d. *Education*: Krupskaya Moscow Regional Pedagogical Inst. *Career*: jr researcher All-Union Research Inst. of Arts 1981–93; ed. Tsikady (Publr) 1993–; first poems published in Yunost and Continent 1989. *Publications*: collections of poetry: Calendar 1990, Verses about Love 1993; Sentiments 1994; verses in leading literary journals. *Honours*: Pushkin Prize (Germany) 1993, Prize of Druzhba Narodov (magazine) 1993. *Address*: Ostrovityanova str. 34, korp. 1, Apt. 289, Moscow, Russia (home). *Telephone*: (495) 420-6175 (home).

KIDDER, Tracy, AB, MFA; American writer; b. 12 Nov. 1945, New York, NY; m. Frances T. Toland 1971; one s. one d. *Education*: Harvard Univ., Univ. of Iowa. *Career*: fmr army officer; Contributing Ed., Atlantic Monthly 1982–. *Publications*: The Road to Yuba City: A Journey into the Juan Corona Murders 1974, The Soul of a New Machine 1981, House 1985, Among Schoolchildren 1989, Old Friends 1993, Home Town 1999, Mountains Beyond Mountains 2003, My Detachment (memoir) 2005. *Honours*: Atlantic Monthly Atlantic First Award 1978, Sidney Hillman Foundation Prize 1978, Pulitzer Prize in General Non-Fiction 1982, American Book Award 1982, Ambassador Book Award 1990, Robert F. Kennedy Award 1990, New England Book Award 1994. *Address*: c/o Random House Inc., 1745 Broadway, New York, NY 10019, USA.

KIDMAN, Dame Fiona Judith, DNZM, OBE; New Zealand writer; b. 26 March 1940, Hawera; d. of Hugh Eric Eakin and Flora Cameron Eakin (née Small); m. Ian Kidman 1960; one s. one d. *Education*: small rural schools in the north of NZ. *Career*: Founding Sec./Organizer NZ Book Council 1972–75;

Sec. NZ Centre, PEN 1972–76, Pres. 1981–83; Pres. NZ Book Council 1992–95, Pres. of Honour 1997–; f. Writers in Schools, Words on Wheels (touring writing co.), Writers Visiting Prisons, Randell Cottage Writers Trust. *Publications*: A Breed of Women 1979, Mandarin Summer 1981, Mrs. Dixon and Friend (short stories) 1982, Paddy's Puzzle 1983, The Book of Secrets 1986, Unsuitable Friends (short stories) 1988, True Stars 1990, Wakeful Nights (poems selected and new) 1991, The Foreign Woman (short stories) 1994, Palm Prints (autobiog. essays) 1995, Ricochet Baby 1996, The House Within 1997, The Best of Fiona Kidman's Short Stories 1998, New Zealand Love Stories; An Oxford Anthology (ed.) 1999, A Needle in the Heart (short stories) 2002, Songs from the Violet Café (novel) 2003; The Best New Zealand Fiction (ed.) 2004. *Honours*: many literary prizes including NZ Book Awards (fiction category), Queen Elizabeth II Arts Council Award for Achievement, Victoria Univ. Writers' Fellow; NZ Scholarship in Letters; A. W. Reed Award for Lifetime Achievement 2001. *Address*: 28 Rakau Road, Hataitai, Wellington, New Zealand. *Fax*: (4) 386-1895. *E-mail*: fiona@fionakidman.co.nz (home).

KIERAN, Sheila Harriet; Canadian writer and consultant; b. 4 May 1930, Toronto, Ont.; d. of Seymour Ginzler and Ida Ginzler (née Schulman); m. 1951 (divorced 1968); four s. two d. (and one d. deceased). *Education*: Columbia Univ., USA and Univ. of Toronto. *Career*: Dir Public Participation, Royal Comm. on Violence in the Communications Industry 1975–77; Sr Policy Adviser Ministry of the Environment 1985–87; Speech-writer to several govt ministers 1987–90; writer of govt reports; Sr Editorial Adviser to Gov.-Gen. of Canada; Ed. Royal Comm. on the Future of the Toronto Waterfront and other govt reports and documents; numerous articles for TV, radio and journals. *Publications include*: The Non-Deductible Woman: A Handbook for Working Wives and Mothers 1970, The Chatelaine Guide to Marriage (contrib.) 1974, The Family Matters: Two Centuries of Family Law and Life in Ontario 1986. *Address*: 66 Badgerow Avenue, Toronto, Ontario, M4M 1V4, Canada.

KILALEA, Rory; Zimbabwean short story writer and film producer. *Career*: Prod., own co. Rory Kilalea Films, producer of films and numerous advertisements. *Films produced*: A Dry White Season (also man.) 1989, Jit 1990. *Publications*: Whine of a Dog (short story in The New Writer) 1998, Zimbabwe Boy (short story in Asylum 98 and Other Stories) 2001. *Address*: Rory Kilalea Films, 7 Everett Close, Avondale, Harare, Zimbabwe.

KILGUS, Martin A., MA, PhD; German journalist; *Editor, SWR Public Radio, Television & Internet*; b. 15 March 1963, Stuttgart; s. of Alfred Kilgus and Charlotte-Pauline Hofmann. *Education*: Wirtemberg-Gymnasium, Stuttgart, Univ. of Stuttgart and The American Univ., Washington, DC, USA. *Career*: traineeship, NBC Radio; joined Dept for Ethnic Broadcasting, SDR Radio & TV, Stuttgart 1989; worked as ed. for migrants' audio broadcasts; 1991; now Ed. with SWR (fmrly SDR) Radio, TV & Internet; Chair. Int. Educ. Information Exchange (IEIE e.V.), Stuttgart 1996–; Vice-Chair. German Asscn for the UN BW; special field of research and activity include Digital Audio Broadcasting (DAB) and multi-lingual broadcasts. *Honours*: Caritas Prize for Journalism. *Address*: SWR Public Radio, TV & Internet, Neckarstrasse 230, 70190 Stuttgart, Germany (office). *Telephone*: (711) 9292648 (office). *Fax*: (711) 929182648 (office). *E-mail*: martin.kilgus@swr.de (office). *Website*: www.swr.de/international (office).

KILLDEER, John (see Mayhar, Ardath)

KILLOUGH, (Karen) Lee; American writer; b. 5 May 1942, Syracuse, KS. *Career*: mem. SFWA, MWA, Sisters In Crime. *Publications*: A Voice Out of Ramah, 1979; The Doppelganger Gambit, 1979; The Monitor, the Miners, and the Shree, 1980; Aventine, 1981; Deadly Silents, 1982; Liberty's World, 1985; Spider Play, 1986; Blood Hunt, 1987; The Leopard's Daughter, 1987; Bloodlinks, 1988; Dragon's Teeth, 1990; Bloodwalk, 1997; Bridling Chaos, 1998; Blood Games, 2001; Wilding Nights, 2002. *Address*: PO Box 1167, Manhattan, KS 66505, USA. *E-mail*: klkillo@flinthills.com.

KILROY, Thomas, BA, MA, FRSL; Irish writer, dramatist and academic; b. 23 Sept. 1934, Callan; m. 1st; three s.; m. 2nd Julia Lowell Carlson 1981; one d. *Education*: University College, Dublin. *Career*: Emeritus Prof. of Modern English, NUI Galway, 2002; mem. Irish Acad. of Letters 1973. *Publications*: Death and Resurrection of Mr Roche (play), 1968; The Oneill (play), 1969; The Big Chapel (novel), 1971; Talbots' Box (play), 1977; The Seagull (play adaptation), 1981; Double Cross (play), 1986; Ghosts, 1989; The Madame McAdam Travelling Theatre (play), 1990; Gold in the Streets (television), 1993; Six Characters in Search of An Author (adaptation), 1996; The Secret Fall of Constance Wilde (play), 1997: My Scandalous Life, 2001; The Shape of Metal (play), 2003, Henry (play) 2005; Contributions: Radio, television, journals, and magazines. *Honours*: Guardian Fiction Prize, 1971; Heinemann Award for Literature, 1971; Irish Acad. of Letters Prize, 1972; American-Irish Foundation Award for Literature, 1974. *Address*: c/o Aosdána, The Arts Council, 70 Merrion Square, Dublin 2, Ireland. *E-mail*: aosdana@artscouncil.ie.

KILWORTH, Garry Douglas, (Garry Douglas), BA; British writer; b. 5 July 1941, York, England; m. Annette Jill Bailey 1962, one s. one d. *Career*: mem. PEN, Crimean War Soc. *Publications*: In Solitary, 1977; The Night of Kadar, 1979; Split Second, 1979; Theatre of Timesmiths, 1984; Songbirds of Pain, 1984; Witchwater Country, 1986; Spiral Winds, 1987; The Wizard of Woodworld, 1987; Abandonati, 1988; Hunter's Moon, 1989; In the Hollow of the Deep-Sea Wave, 1989; The Foxes of First Dark, 1990; Standing on

Samshan, 1992; Angel, 1993; In The Country of Tattooed Men, 1993; Hogfoot Right And Bird-Hands, 1993; Archangel, 1994; A Midsummer's Nightmare, 1996; The Roof of Voyaging, 1996; The Princely Flower, 1997; Land-of-Mists, 1998; Thunder Oak, 1998; Windjammer Run, 1998; Castle Storm, 1998; Shadow-Hawk, 1999; The Devil's Own, 2001; The Winter Soldiers, 2002, Attica 2006; as Garry Douglas: Highlander 1986, The Street 1988; other: anthologies; contrib. to magazines and newspapers. *Honours:* Gollancz Short Story Award, Sunday Times, 1974; Carnegie Medal Commendation, Librarian Asscn, 1991; Lancashire Children's Book of the Year Award, 1995. *Address:* Wychwater, The Chase, Ashington, Essex, England.

KIM, Hong-ik; North Korean writer. *Career:* lives in Seoul, Republic of Korea. *Publications:* He's Alive (in trans.). *Address:* c/o Korean PEN Centre, Room 1105, Oseong B/D, 13-5 Youido-dong, Yongdungpo-ku, Seoul, 150-010, Republic of Korea.

KIM, Ji-woon; South Korean filmmaker and screenwriter; b. 6 July 1964, Seoul. *Films:* Choyonghan kajok (The Quiet Family, writer, dir) 1998, Banchikwang (The Foul King, writer, dir) 2000, Coming Out (writer, dir) 2001, Saam gaang (Three, segment 'Memories', dir, writer) 2002, Janghwa, Hongryeon (A Tale of Two Sisters, writer, dir) 2003, Dalkomhan insaeng (A Bittersweet Life, writer, dir) 2005.

KIM, Suji Kwock, BA, MFA; American writer and academic. *Education:* Yale Coll., Univ. of Iowa, Seoul Nat. Univ. and Yonsei Univ., S Korea, Stanford Univ., Calif. *Career:* fmr Asst Prof. of English, Drew Univ., Madison, NJ; wrote texts for choral works by Mayako Kubo, Tokyo Philharmonic Chorus, premiered 2007. *Play:* Private Property (co-author). *Publications:* Notes from the Divided Country 2003; Ed.: anthology of American poetry for the Nat. Endowment for the Arts and the US Embassy in Austria; contrib. to New York Times, Washington Post, Los Angeles Times, SLATE, Nat. Public Radio, The Nation, The New Republic, The New Statesman, Paris Review, American Religious Poems (ed. Harold Bloom), American War Poetry (ed. Lorrie Goldensohn), Poetry, Yale Review, Harvard Review, Salmagundi, Three-penny Review, Ploughshares, Southwest Review. *Honours:* Fulbright Fellowship, Wallace Stegner Fellowship, Nat. Endowment for the Arts Fellowship, Fine Arts Work Center Fellowship, grants from: New York Foundation for the Arts, California Arts Council, San Francisco Arts Comm., Washington State Artist Trust, Korea Foundation, and Blakemore Foundation for Asian Studies; Whiting Writers' Award, Walt Whitman Award, Acad. of American Poets 2002, The Nation/Discovery Award, Bay Area Book Reviewers' Award. *Address:* c/o National Endowment for the Arts, Literature Division, 1100 Pennsylvania Avenue, NW, #722, Washington, DC 20004-2501, USA. *Telephone:* (202) 682-5551. *E-mail:* SujiKwockKim@gmail.com (office).

KINCAID, Jamaica; Antigua and Barbuda writer; b. (Elaine Potter Richardson), 25 May 1949, St John's; d. of Annie Richardson; m. Allen Shawn; one s. one d. *Career:* staff writer The New Yorker 1976; teaches at Harvard Univ.; lives in Vt, USA; mem. American Acad. of Arts and Letters. *Publications include:* At the Bottom of the River (short stories; American Acad. and Inst. of Arts and Letters Morton Dauwen Zabel Award) 1983, Annie John (novel) 1985, A Small Place (non-fiction) 1988, Lucy (novel) 1990, The Autobiography of My Mother 1995, My Brother 1997, My Favorite Plant 1998, Poetics of Place (with Lynn Geesaman) 1998, My Garden (non-fiction) 1999, Talk Stories 2001, Mr Potter 2002, Among Flowers: A Walk in the Himalaya 2005. *Honours:* numerous hon. degrees; Morton Dauwen Zabel Award American Acad. and Inst. of Arts and Letters 1983, Lila Wallace-Reader's Digest Fund Annual Writer's Award 1992. *Address:* c/o Farrar Straus & Giroux, 19 Union Square West, New York, NY 10003, USA.

KING, (David) Clive; British novelist; b. 28 April 1924, Richmond, Surrey, England; m. 1st Jane Tuke 1948; one s. one d.; m. 2nd Penny Timmins 1974; one d. *Education:* Downing Coll. *Career:* mem. Soc. of Authors. *Publications:* The Town That Went South, 1959; Stig of the Dump, 1963; The Twenty-Two Letters, 1966; The Night the Water Came, 1973; Snakes and Snakes, 1975; Me and My Million, 1976; Ninny's Boat, 1980; The Sound of Propellers, 1986; The Seashore People, 1987; seven other books. *Honours:* Boston Globe-Horn Book Award, Honour Book 1980. *Address:* Pond Cottage, Low Road, Thurlton, Norwich NR14 6PZ, England.

KING, Cynthia; American writer; b. 27 Aug. 1925, New York, NY; m. Jonathan King 1944 (died 1997); three s. *Education:* Bryn Mawr Coll., Univ. of Chicago, New York Univ. Writers' Workshop. *Career:* Assoc. Ed., Hillman Periodicals 1945–50; Managing Ed., Fawcett Publications 1950–55; mem. Authors' Guild, Poets and Writers, Detroit Working Writers (pres. 1979–81). *Publications:* In the Morning of Time 1970, The Year of Mr Nobody 1978, Beggars and Choosers 1980, Sailing Home 1982; contrib. book reviews to New York Times Book Review, Detroit News, Houston Chronicle, LA Daily News, short fiction to Good Housekeeping, Texas Stories & Poems, Quartet. *Honours:* Michigan Council for the Arts grant 1986, Detroit Women Writers Spring Readings Award 2002. *Address:* 228 River Street, Bethel, VT 05032, USA. *E-mail:* tonibking@adelphia.net.

KING, Daren, BA; British screenwriter, novelist, journalist and illustrator; b. 8 March 1974, Herts. *Education:* Bath Spa Univ. *Publications:* Boxy an Star 1999, Jim Giraffe 2004, Tom Boler 2005, Smally's Party (illustrated) 2005, Mouse Noses on Toast (juvenile) (Nestlé Children's Book Prize) 2006; contrib. of short stories to Arena magazine, and to books, All Hail the New Puritans, Piece of Flesh, New Writing 13. *Honours:* Arena Magazine Creative Man of the Year 2005. *Literary Agent:* c/o Conville & Walsh Ltd, 2 Ganton Street, London, W1F 7QL, England. *E-mail:* hello@darenking.co.uk. *Website:* www .darenking.co.uk.

KING, Sir David Anthony, Kt, PhD, ScD, FRS, FRSC, FInstP; British academic and research scientist; *Government Chief Scientific Adviser;* b. 12 Aug. 1939, Durban, South Africa; s. of Arnold King and Patricia Vardy; m. Jane Lichtenstein 1983; three s. one d. *Education:* St John's Coll., Johannesburg, Univ. of Witwatersrand, Johannesburg, Imperial Coll. London. *Career:* Lecturer in Chemical Physics, Univ. of E Anglia, Norwich 1966–74; Brunner Prof. of Physical Chemistry, Univ. of Liverpool 1974–88, Head Dept of Inorganic, Physical and Industrial Chem. 1983–88; 1920 Prof. of Physical Chem., Dept of Chem., Cambridge Univ. 1988–, Head Dept of Chem. 1993–2000; Fellow St John's Coll. 1988–95; Master of Downing Coll. 1995–2000; Chief Scientific Adviser to UK Govt 2000–; Head, Office of Science and Tech. 2000–; Ed. Chemical Physics Letters 1990–2001; Pres. Asscn of Univ. Teachers 1976–77; Chair. British Vacuum Council 1982–85; mem. Comité de Direction, Centre Cinétique et Physique, Nancy 1974–81, Research Awards Advisory Cttee Leverhulme Trust 1980–91 (Chair. 1995–2001), Direction Cttee (Beirat) Fritz Haber Inst., Berlin 1981–93; Chair. European Science Foundation Programme 'Gas–Surface Interactions' 1991–96, Kettle's Yard Gallery, Cambridge 1989–2001; Shell Scholar 1963–66; Assoc. Fellow Third World Acad. of Sciences 2000; Fellow Queen's Coll. 2001–; Foreign mem. American Acad. of Arts and Sciences 2002. *Publications:* The Chemical Physics of Solid Surfaces and Heterogeneous Catalysis (seven vols) (co-ed. with D.P. Woodruff) 1980–94; over 450 original publs in the scientific literature. *Honours:* Hon. Fellow Indian Acad. of Sciences, Downing Coll., Univ. of Cardiff 2001; Hon. DSc (Liverpool) 2001, (E Anglia) 2001, (Stockholm) 2003, (Genoa) 2002, (Leicester) 2002, Cardiff (2002), (Witwatersrand) 2003, (St Andrews) 2003, (York) 2004; Royal Soc. of Chem. Awards, Surface Chem. 1978, Tilden Lecturer 1988, Medal for Research, British Vacuum Council 1991, Liverside Lectureship and Medal 1997–98, Royal Soc. Rumford Medal 2003. *Address:* Office of Science and Technology, 1 Victoria Street, London, SW1H 0ET (office); Department of Chemistry, University of Cambridge, Lensfield Road, Cambridge, CB2 1EN (office); 20 Glisson Road, Cambridge, CB1 2EW, England (home). *Telephone:* (20) 7215-3820 (London) (office); (1223) 336338 (Cambridge) (office); (1223) 315629 (home). *Fax:* (20) 7215-0314 (London) (office); (1223) 762829 (Cambridge) (office). *E-mail:* mpst.king@dti .gsi.gov.uk (office). *Website:* www.ost.gov.uk (office).

KING, Francis Henry, (Frank Cauldwell), CBE, OBE, MA, FRSL; British writer; b. 4 March 1923, Adelboden, Switzerland; s. of the late Eustace Arthur Cecil King and Faith Mina Read. *Education:* Shrewsbury School and Balliol Coll., Oxford. *Career:* served in British Council 1948–62, Regional Dir, Kyoto, Japan 1958–62; theatre critic Sunday Telegraph 1978–88; Pres. English PEN 1978–86, Int. PEN 1986–89, Vice-Pres. Int. PEN 1989–. *Publications:* novels: To the Dark Tower 1946, Never Again 1947, The Dividing Stream 1951, The Widow 1957, The Man on the Rock 1957, The Custom House 1961, The Last of the Pleasure Gardens 1965, The Waves Behind the Boat 1967, A Domestic Animal 1970, Flights 1973, A Game of Patience 1974, The Needle 1975, Danny Hill 1977, The Action 1978, Act of Darkness 1983, Voices in an Empty Room 1984, Frozen Music (novella) 1987, The Woman Who Was God 1988, Punishments 1989, The Ant Colony 1991, Secret Lives 1991, The One and Only 1994, Ash on an Old Man's Sleeve 1996, Dead Letters 1997, Prodigies 2001, The Nick of Time 2003; short stories: So Hurt and Humiliated 1959, The Japanese Umbrella 1964, The Brighton Belle 1968, Hard Feelings 1976, Indirect Method 1980, One is a Wanderer 1985, A Hand at the Shutter 1996, The Sunlight on the Garden 2006; biog.: E. M. Forster and His World 1978, My Sister and Myself: The Diaries of J. R. Ackerley 1982; travel: Florence 1982, Florence: A Literary Companion 1991, Yesterday Came Suddenly (autobiog.) 1993. *Honours:* Somerset Maugham Prize 1952, Katherine Mansfield Short Story Prize 1965, Yorkshire Post Prize 1984. *Address:* 19 Gordon Place, London, W8 4JE, England (home). *Telephone:* (20) 7937-5715 (home). *E-mail:* fhk@dircon.co.uk (home).

KING, Janey (see Thomas, Rosie)

KING, Larry L.; American playwright, author and actor; b. 1 Jan. 1929, Putnam, TX; m. Barbara S. Blaine, two s. three d. *Education:* Texas Technical University, Harvard University, Duke University. *Career:* Visiting Ferris Prof. of Journalism and Political Science, Princeton University, 1973–74; Poet Laureate (life), Monahans (Texas) Sandhills Literary Society, 1977–. *Publications:* Plays: The Kingfish, 1979; The Best Little Whorehouse in Texas, 1978; Christmas: 1933, 1986; The Night Hank Williams Died, 1988; The Golden Shadows Old West Museum, 1989; The Best Little Whorehouse Goes Public, 1994; The Dead Presidents' Club, 1996. Other: The One-Eyed Man (novel), 1966; ...And Other Dirty Stories, 1968; Confessions of a White Racist, 1971; The Old Man and Lesser Mortals, 1974; Of Outlaws, Whores, Conmen, Politicians and Other Artists, 1980; Warning: Writer at Work, 1985; None But a Blockhead, 1986; Because of Lozo Brown, 1988. Contributions: Harper's; Atlantic Monthly; Life; New Republic; Texas Monthly; Texas Observer; New York; Playboy; Parade; Esquire; Saturday Evening Post; National Geographic.

KING, Laurie R., (Leigh Richards), BA, MA; American writer; b. 19 Sept. 1952, Oakland, CA; m. Noel Q. King 1977; one s. one d. *Education:* Univ. of California, Santa Cruz, Graduate Theological Union, Berkeley. *Career:* mem. MWA, Sisters in Crime, Int. Asscn of Crime Writers, CWA. *Publications:* A

Grave Talent 1993, The Beekeeper's Apprentice 1994, To Play the Fool 1995, A Monstrous Regiment of Women 1995, With Child 1996, A Letter of Mary 1997, The Moor 1998, A Darker Place 1999, O Jerusalem 1999, Night Work 2000, Folly 2001, Justice Hall 2002, Keeping Watch 2003, The Game 2004, Califia's Daughters (as Leigh Richards) 2004, Locked Rooms 2005, The Art of Detection 2006. *Honours:* Dr hc (Church Divinity School of the Pacific) 1997; Edgar Award for Best First Novel 1993, Creasey Award for Best First Novel 1995, Nero Wolfe Award for Best Novel 1996, Macavity Award 2002. *Address:* PO Box 1152, Freedom, CA 95019, USA. *Website:* www.laurierking.com.

KING, Paul (see Drackett, Philip Arthur)

KING, Philip (see Levinson, Leonard)

KING, Stephen Edwin, (Richard Bachman), BS; American writer and screenwriter; b. 21 Sept. 1947, Portland, ME; s. of Donald King and Nellie R. (née Pillsbury) King; m. Tabitha J. Spruce 1971; two s. one d. *Education:* Univ. of Maine. *Career:* teacher of English, Hampden Acad., ME 1971–73; writer-in-residence, Univ. of Maine at Orono 1978–79; mem. Authors' Guild of America, Screen Artists' Guild, Screen Writers of America, Writers' Guild. *Television:* Kingdom Hospital. *Publications:* novels: Carrie 1974, Salem's Lot 1975, The Shining 1976, The Stand 1978, The Dead Zone 1979, Firestarter 1980, Cujo 1981, Different Seasons 1982, The Dark Tower I: The Gunslinger 1982, Christine 1983, Pet Cemetery 1983, The Talisman (with Peter Straub) 1984, It 1986, The Eyes of the Dragon 1987, Misery 1987, The Dark Tower II: The Drawing of the Three 1987, Tommyknockers 1987, The Dark Half 1989, The Dark Tower III: The Waste Lands 1991, Needful Things 1991, Gerald's Game 1992, Dolores Claiborne 1992, Insomnia 1994, Rose Madder 1995, Desperation 1996, The Green Mile (serial novel) 1996, The Dark Tower IV: Wizard and Glass 1997, Bag of Bones 1997, The Girl Who Loved Tom Gordon 1999, Hearts in Atlantis 1999, Riding the Bullet 2000, The Plant (serial novel) 2000, Dreamcatcher 2001, Black House (with Peter Straub) 2001, From a Buick 8 2002, The Dark Tower V: Wolves of the Calla 2003, The Dark Tower VI: Song of Susannah 2004, The Dark Tower VII: The Dark Tower 2004, The Colorado Kid 2005, Cell 2006, Lisey's Story 2006; other: Night Shift (short stories) 1978, Danse Macabre (non-fiction) 1980, Different Seasons (short stories) 1982, Creepshow (comic book) 1982, Cycle of the Werewolf (illustrated novel) 1984, Skeleton Crew (short stories) 1985, Four Past Midnight (short stories) 1990, Nightmares and Dreamscapes (short stories) 1993, Head Down (story) 1993, Six Stories (short stories) 1997, Storm of the Century (screenplay) 1999, On Writing: A Memoir of the Craft (revised edn as Secret Windows) 2000, Everything's Eventual: 14 Dark Tales (short stories) 2002, Faithful (non-fiction, with Stewart O'Nan) 2005, numerous short stories, screenplays and television plays; as Richard Bachman: Rage 1977, The Long Walk 1979, Roadwork 1981, The Running Man 1982, Thinner 1984, The Regulators 1996, Blaze 2007. *Honours:* Medal for Distinguished Contribution to American Letters, Nat. Book Foundation 2003. *Address:* 49 Florida Avenue, Bangor, ME 04401, USA (office). *Website:* www.stephenking.com (office).

KING, Thomas Hunt, (Hartley Goodweather), CM, MA, PhD; American/Canadian academic, writer and photographer; *Professor of English, University of Guelph*; b. 24 April 1943, Sacramento, Calif.; m. Kristine Adams 1970 (divorced 1980); one s.; partner, Helen Hoy 1984; one s. one d. *Education:* Chico State Univ., Univ. of Utah. *Career:* Dir Native Studies, Univ. of Utah 1971–73, Co-ordinator History of the Indians of the Americas Program 1977–79; Assoc. Dean Student Services, Humboldt State Univ. 1973–77; Asst Prof. of Native Studies, Univ. of Lethbridge 1978–89, Chair Native Studies 1985–87; Assoc. Prof. of American Studies/Native Studies, Univ. of Minnesota 1989–95, Chair Native Studies 1991–93; Assoc. Prof. of English, Univ. of Guelph 1995–2003, Prof. of English 2003–. *Film:* Medicine River 1993. *Radio:* Dead Dog Cafe Comedy Hour (CBC Radio) 1996–2003. *Publications:* The Native in Literature: Canadian and Comparative Perspectives (ed. with Helen Hoy and Cheryl Calver) 1987, An Anthology of Short Fiction by Native Writers in Canada (ed.) 1988, All My Relations: An Anthology of Contemporary Canadian Native Fiction (ed.) 1990, Medicine River 1990, A Coyote Columbus Story 1992, Green Grass, Running Water 1993, One Good Story, That One 1993, Coyote Sings to the Moon 1998, Truth and Bright Water 1999, Dreadful Water Shows Up (as Hartley Goodweather) 2002, The Truth about Stories 2003, Coyote's New Suit 2004, A Short History of Indians in Canada, 2005, The Red Power Murders (as Hartley Goodweather) 2006; other: films and radio and television drama; contribs to reference works, books, anthologies, reviews, quarterlies and journals. *Honours:* Writers' Guild of Alberta Best Novel Award 1991, Oakland PEN Josephine Miles Award 1991, Canadian Authors Award for Fiction 1994, Aboriginal Radio Award 2000, American Library Asscn Notable Book Citation 2001, Nat. Aboriginal Achievement Award 2003, Ontario Trillium Book Award 2004, Western Literature Asscn Distinguished Achievement Award 2004. *Address:* 7 Ardmay Crescent, Guelph, ON N1E 4L4, Canada (home).

KING-ARIBISALA, Karen; Nigerian writer; b. Guyana; m.; one s. *Career:* sr lecturer, Dept of English, Univ. of Lagos. *Publications:* Our Wife and Other Stories (short stories) (Commonwealth Writers Prize Best First Book, Africa Region) 1990, Kicking Tongues 1998. *Address:* c/o African Writers Series, Heinemann Educational Publishers, Halley Ctour, Jordan Hill, Oxford OX2 8EJ, England.

KING-HELE, Desmond George, MA, FRS; British writer and scientist; b. 3 Nov. 1927, Seaford, Sussex; s. of late S. G. King-Hele and Mrs B. King-Hele; m. Marie Newman 1954 (separated 1992); two d. *Education:* Epsom Coll. and Trinity Coll., Cambridge. *Career:* Royal Aircraft Establishment, Farnborough 1948–88 (research on earth's gravity field and upper atmosphere by analysis of satellite orbits), Deputy Chief Scientific Officer, Space Dept 1968–88; mem. Int. Acad. of Astronautics 1961–; Chair. British Nat. Cttee for the History of Science, Medicine and Tech. 1985–89, History of Science Grants Cttee 1990–93; Ed. Notes and Records of the Royal Soc. 1989–96; Bakerian Lecturer, Royal Soc. 1974, Wilkins Lecturer, Royal Soc. 1997. *Radio:* dramas: A Mind of Universal Sympathy 1973, The Lunaticks 1978. *Publications:* Shelley: His Thought and Work 1960, Satellites and Scientific Research 1960, Erasmus Darwin 1963, Theory of Satellite Orbits in an Atmosphere 1964, Observing Earth Satellites 1966, Essential Writings of Erasmus Darwin 1968, The End of the Twentieth Century? 1970, Poems and Trixies 1972, Doctor of Revolution 1977, Letters of Erasmus Darwin 1981, Animal Spirits 1983, The R.A.E. Table of Earth Satellites 1957–1989, 1990, Erasmus Darwin and the Romantic Poets 1986, Satellite Orbits in an Atmosphere 1987, A Tapestry of Orbits 1992, John Herschel 1992, Erasmus Darwin: A Life of Unequalled Achievement 1999, Antic and Romantic 2000, Charles Darwin's The Life of Erasmus Darwin 2002, The Collected Letters of Erasmus Darwin 2006; more than 300 scientific or literary papers in various learned journals. *Honours:* Hon. DSc (Univ. of Aston) 1979, Hon. DUniv (Univ. of Surrey) 1986; Soc. of Authors' Medical History Prize 1999; Eddington Medal, Royal Astronomical Soc. 1971, Chree Medal, Inst. of Physics 1971, Nordberg Medal, Int. Cttee on Space Research 1990. *Address:* 7 Hilltops Court, 65 North Lane, Buriton, Hants., GU31 5RS, England (home). *Telephone:* (1730) 261646 (home).

KING-SMITH, Dick, BEd; British writer; b. 27 March 1922, Bitton, Gloucestershire, England. *Education:* Univ. of Bristol. *Career:* fmr soldier, farmer, travelling salesman, shoe factory operative, teacher and TV presenter. *Publications include:* The Fox Busters 1978, Daggie Dogfoot, The Mouse Butcher, Magnus Powermouse, The Queen's Nose, The Sheep-Pig (Guardian Fiction Award 1984), Noah's Brother, Yob, E.S.P., Friends and Brothers, Dodos are Forever, Sophie's Snail, The Trouble with Edward, Martin's Mice, The Water Horse, Paddy's Pot of Gold, Alpha Beasts, The Hodgeheg, Ace: The Very Important Pig, Harry's Mad, The Invisible Dog, The Merman, A Mouse Called Wolf, Mysterious Miss Slade, Smasher, Spider Sparrow, The Stray, Three Terrible Trins, Harriet the Hare (Children's Book Award 1995), Dick King-Smith's Animal Friends, All Pigs are Beautiful, I Love Guinea Pigs, Blessu, Clever Duck, All Because of Jack, The Crown-starver, Charlie Muffin's Miracle Mouse, Funny Frank, The Roundhill, Titus Rules!, Binnie Bone, The Golden Goose, Lady Lollypop, Aristotle, Chewing the Cud (autobiog.) 2001, Jungle Jingles (poems) 2002. *Honours:* Hon. MLitt (Univ. of Bristol), Hon. MA (Univ. of Bath); Children's Author of the Year 1992. *Address:* c/o Puffin Publicity, 80 Strand, London, WC2R 0RL, England.

KINGDON, Robert McCune, AB, MA, PhD; American historian, academic and writer; b. 29 Dec. 1927, Chicago, Ill. *Education:* Oberlin Coll., OH, Columbia Univ., New York, Univ. of Geneva, Swiatzerland. *Career:* Instructor to Asst Prof., Univ. of Massachusetts 1952–57; Visiting Instructor, Amherst Coll. 1953–54; Asst Prof. to Prof. of History, Univ. of Iowa 1957–65; Visiting Prof., Stanford Univ. 1964, 1980; Prof. of History, Univ. of Wisconsin, Madison 1965–, Hilldale Prof. of History 1988–98; Ed. Sixteenth Century Journal 1973–97; mem. Inst. for Research in the Humanities 1974–, Dir 1975–87; mem. American Soc. of Reformation Research (Pres. 1971), Int. Fed. of Socs and Insts for the Study of the Renaissance, Renaissance Soc. of America (mem. Exec. Bd 1972–92), American Soc. of Church History (Pres. 1980). *Publications:* Geneva and the Coming of the Wars of Religion in France 1555–1563 1956, Registres de la Compagnie des Pasteurs de Genévè au Temps de Calvin (co-ed. with J.-F. Bergier) (two vols) 1962, 1964, William Cecil: Execution of Justice in England (ed.) 1965, William Allen: A True, Sincere and Modest Defence of English Catholics (ed.) 1965, Geneva and the Consolidation of the French Protestant Movement 1564–1572 1967, Calvin and Calvinism: Sources of Democracy (co-ed. with R. D. Linder) 1970, Theodore de Béze: Du Droit des magistrats (ed.) 1971, Transition and Revolution: Problems and Issues of European Renaissance and Reformation History (ed.) 1974, The Political Thought of Peter Martyr Vermigli 1980, Church and Society in Reformation Europe 1985, Myths About the St Bartholomew's Day Massacres 1572–1576 1988, A Bibliography of the Works of Peter Martyr Vermigli (co-ed. with J. P. Donnelly) 1990, Adultery and Divorce in Calvin's Geneva 1995, Registres du Consistoire de Genève au temps de Calvin (co-ed.), Vol. I 1996, Vol. II 2001, Vol. III 2004; contrib. to scholarly journals. *Address:* 4 Rosewood Circle, Madison, WI 53711, USA. *E-mail:* rkingdon@wiscmail.wisc.edu (office).

KINGSOLVER, Barbara, MS; American writer; b. 8 April 1955, Annapolis, Md; m. Steven Hopp; two d. *Education:* DePauw Univ., Indiana, Univ. of Arizona. *Career:* scientific writer, Office of Arid Land Studies, Univ. of Ariz. 1981–85; freelance journalist 1985–87, novelist 1987–; book reviewer NY Times 1988–, LA Times 1989–, San Francisco Chronicle, The Nation, The Progressive, The Washington Post, Women's Review of Books, and others; Woodrow Wilson Foundation/Llia Wallace Fellowship 1992; established The Bellwether Prize for Fiction: In Support of a Literature of Social Change 1997. *Publications:* The Bean Trees (Enoch Pratt Library Youth-to-Youth Books Award) 1988, Holding the Line 1989, Homeland and Other Stories 1989, Animal Dreams (Edward Abbey Award for Ecofiction, PEN/USA West Fiction Award) 1990, Another America 1992, Pigs in Heaven (Mountains and Plains Booksellers Award for Fiction, Los Angeles Times Fiction Prize) 1993, High Tide in Tucson 1995, The Poisonwood Bible (Village Voice Best Books 1998, New York Times Top Ten Books 1998, Los Angeles Times Best Books for 1998,

Independence Publisher Brilliance Audio 1999, Booksense Prize 1999, Nat. Book Award (SA) 2000) 1998, Prodigal Summer 2000, Small Wonder 2002, Last Stand 2002, Animal, Vegetable, Miracle: Our Year of Seasonal Eating 2007. *Honours:* Hon. LittD (DePauw) 1994; Nat. Writers Union Andrea Egan Award 1998, Arizona Civil Liberties Union Award 1998, Nat. Humanities Medal 2000, Best American Science and Nature Writing 2001, Gov.'s Nat. Award in the Arts, Kentucky 2002, John P. McGovern Award for the Family 2002, Physicians for Social Responsibility Nat. Award 2002. *Address:* PO Box 160, Meadowview, VA 24361 (office); c/o Harper Collins, 10 East 53rd Street, New York, NY 10022, USA.

KINGSTON, Maxine Hong, BA; American author and academic; *Professor Emerita, Department of English, University of California, Berkeley;* b. 27 Oct. 1940, Stockton, Calif.; d. of Tom Kingston and Ying Lan Hong (née Chew); m. Earll Kingston 1962; one s. *Education:* Univ. of California, Berkeley. *Career:* taught English, Sunset High School, Hayward, Calif. 1965–66, Kahuku High School, Hawaii 1967, Kahaluu Drop-In School 1968, Kailua High School 1969, Honolulu Business Coll. 1969, Mid-Pacific Inst., Honolulu 1970–77; Prof. of English, Visiting Writer, Univ. of Hawaii, Honolulu 1977; Thelma McCandless Distinguished Prof., Eastern Mich. Univ., Ypsilanti 1986; Chancellor's Distinguished Prof., Univ. of California, Berkeley 1990–, now Prof. Emer. *Publications:* The Woman Warrior: Memoirs of a Girlhood Among Ghosts 1976 (Nat. Book Critics Circle Award for non-fiction), China Men 1981 (Nat. Book Award), Hawaii One Summer 1987 (Ka Palapola Po'okela Award 1999), Through The Black Curtain 1988, Tripmaster Monkey – His Fake Books 1989 (PEN USA West Award in Fiction), The Literature of California (ed.) 2001, To Be The Poet 2002; The Fifth Book of Peace 2002, Veterans of War, Veterans of Peace (ed.) 2006; short stories, articles and poems. *Honours:* Mademoiselle Magazine Award 1977, Anisfield-Wolf Book Award 1978, Stockton (Calif.) Arts Comm. Award 1981, Hawaii Award for Literature 1982, NEA Writing Fellow 1980, Guggenheim Fellow 1981, named Living Treasure of Hawaii 1980, American Acad. and Inst. Award in Literature 1990, Nat. Humanities Medal 1997, Fred Cody Lifetime Achievement Award 1998, John Dos Passos Prize 1998, Ka Palapola Po'okela Award 1999, Commonwealth Club Silver Medal 2001, California State Library Gold Medal 2002, Spirituality and Health Book Award, KPFA Peace Award 2005, Red Hen Press Lifetime Achievement Award 2006. *Address:* Department of English, University of California, 413 Wheeler Hall, Berkeley, CA 94720, USA (office). *Telephone:* (510) 643-5127 (office). *E-mail:* yinglan@berkeley.edu (office). *Website:* english .berkeley.edu (office).

KINGTON, Miles Beresford, BA; British writer and journalist; b. 13 May 1941, Downpatrick, Northern Ireland; m. 1st Sarah Paine 1964 (divorced 1987); one s. one d.; m. 2nd Caroline Maynard 1987; one s. *Education:* Trinity Coll., Oxford. *Career:* double bass player Instant Sunshine (cabaret group) 1975–95; jazz reviewer 1965, staff The Times 1967–73, literary ed. 1973–80, columnist 1980–87; columnist, The Independent 1987–. *Publications:* The World of Alphonse Allais (revised edn as A Wolf in Frog's Clothing) 1977, four Franglais books 1979–82, Moreover, Too... 1985, Welcome to Kington 1985, The Franglais Lieutenant's Woman 1986, Steaming Through Britain 1990, Anthology of Jazz (ed.) 1992, Someone Like Me: Tales from a Borrowed Childhood (autobiog.) 2005. *Address:* c/o The Independent, Independent House, 191 Marsh Wall, London, E14 9RS (office); Lower Hayes, Limpley Stoke, Bath, BA2 7FR, England (home). *Telephone:* (1225) 722262 (home).

KINLOCH, David, MA; DPhil; British academic, poet and editor; *Reader in English, University of Strathclyde;* b. 21 Nov. 1959, Glasgow, Scotland. *Education:* University of Glasgow, Balliol College, Oxford. *Career:* Junior Research Fellow St Anne's College, Oxford 1985–87; Research Fellow University of Wales 1987–89; Lecturer University of Salford 1989–90; Lecturer University of Strathclyde 1990–94, Senior Lecturer 1994–2006, Reader in English 2006–; Ed., Southfields Magazine; Founder/Co-Ed., Verse Poetry Magazine. *Publications:* Other Tongues (co-author) 1990, Dustie-Fute 1992, Paris-Forfar 1994, Un Tour d'Ecosse 2001, In My Father's House 2005; contrib. reviews, journals and magazines. *Honours:* Robert Louis Stevenson Memorial Fellowship 2004, Scotish Arts Council Writer's Bursary 2006. *Address:* c/o Department of English Studies, University of Strathclyde, Glasgow, Scotland.

KINNELL, Galway, MA; American writer and academic; *Erich Maria Remarque Professor in Creative Writing, New York University;* b. 1 Feb. 1927, Providence, RI; s. of James S. Kinnell and Elizabeth Mills; m. 1st Inés Delgado de Torres 1965; (divorced) one s. two d.; m. 2nd Barbara K. Bristol 1997. *Education:* Princeton Univ. and Univ. of Rochester. *Career:* Guggenheim Fellow 1963–64, 1974–75; MacArthur Fellow 1984; Dir Writing Programme New York Univ. 1981–84, Samuel F. B. Morse Prof. of Arts and Sciences 1985–92, Erich Maria Remarque Prof. of Creative Writing 1992–; named Vt State Poet 1989–93; mem. Nat. Inst., Acad. of Arts and Letters. *Publications:* poetry: What a Kingdom it Was 1960, Flower Herding on Mount Monadnock 1963, Body Rags 1966, The Book of Nightmares 1971, The Avenue Bearing the Initial of Christ into the New World 1974, Mortal Acts, Mortal Words 1980, Selected Poems 1982, The Past 1985, Imperfect Thirst 1994; novel: Black Light 1966; children's story: How the Alligator Missed Breakfast 1982; trans.: The Poems of François Villon 1965, On the Motion and Immobility of Douve by Yves Bonnefoy 1968, The Lackawanna Elegy by Yvan Goll 1970, The Essential Rilke; interviews: Walking Down the Stairs 1977. *Honours:* Award of Nat. Inst. of Arts and Letters 1962, Cecil Hemley Poetry Prize 1969, Medal of Merit 1975, Pulitzer Prize 1983, Nat. Book Award

1983, Frost Medal 2001. *Address:* 1218 Town Road 16, Sheffield, VT 05866 (home); Department of English, New York University, 19 University Place, New York, NY 10003, USA (office). *Website:* www.nyu.edu/gsas/dept/english (office).

KINNEY, Arthur Frederick, MA, PhD; American academic, writer and editor; b. 5 Sept. 1933, Cortland, NY. *Education:* Syracuse Univ., Columbia Univ., Univ. of Michigan. *Career:* Instructor Yale University 1963–66; Asst Prof. 1966–69, Assoc. Prof. 1969–73, Prof. 1973–85, Thomas W. Copeland Prof. of Literary History 1985– University of Massachusetts at Amherst; Founder-Ed. English Literary Renaissance journal 1971–; Adjunct Prof. Clark University 1973–, New York University 1992–; Dir Massachusetts Center for Renaissance Studies 1996–; mem. MLA; Renaissance English Text Society, pres. 1985–; Renaissance Society of America; Shakespeare Asscn of America, trustee 1995–98; Sixteenth-Century Studies Conference Asscn. *Radio recordings:* Renaissance Reflections (CD of broadcasts on NPR Morning Edition, WFCR). *Publications:* On Seven Shakespearean Tragedies 1968, On Seven Shakespearean Comedies 1968, Rogues, Vagabonds, and Sturdy Beggars 1973, Elizabethan Backgrounds 1974, Faulkner's Narrative Poetics: Style As Vision 1978, William Faulkner: The Compson Family (ed.) 1982, Flannery O'Connor's Library: Resources of Being 1985, William Faulkner's The Sartoris Family (ed.) 1985, Poetics & Praxis, Understanding and Imagination: The Collected Essays of O.B. Hardison (ed.) 1986, Essential Articles for the Study of Sir Philip Sidney 1986, Humanist Poetics 1986, John Skelton: Priest as Poet 1987, Renaissance Historicism 1987, Continental Humanist Poetics 1989, William Faulkner: The McCaslin Family (ed.) 1990, Dorothy Parker's The Coast of Illyria (ed.) 1990, Classical, Renaissance, and Postmodern Acts of the Imagination: Essays in Honor of O. B. Hardison Jr (ed.) 1994, William Faulkner: The Sutpen Family (ed.) 1996, Go Down, Moses: The Miscegenation of Time 1997, Dorothy Parker Revisited 1998, Shakespeare, Text and Theatre (ed.) 1999, Renaissance Drama: An Anthology of Plays and Performances Edited from Manuscript and Early Quartos (ed.) 1999, The Cambridge Companion to English Literature 1500–1600 2000, Tudor England: An Encyclopaedia 2000, Blackwell Companion to Renaissance Drama (ed.) 2001, Lies Like Truth: Shakespeare, Macbeth and the Cultural Moment 2001, New Essays on Hamlet 2001, Shakespeare by Stages 2003, Shakespeare's Webs: Networks of Meaning in Renaissance Drama 2004, Shakespeare and Cognition 2006, Challenging Humanism: Essays in Honor of Dominic Baker-Smith 2006; contributions to scholarly books and professional journals. *Honours:* Senior Huntington Library Fellow 1973–74, 1978, 1983, Senior National Endowment for the Humanities Fellow 1973–74, 1987–88, Senior Folger Shakespeare Library Fellow 1974, 1990, 1992, Fulbright Fellow, Christ Church, Oxford 1977–78, Chancellor's Medal, University of Massachusetts at Amherst 1985, Outstanding Teacher Award 1990, Paul Oskar Kristeller Lifetime Achievement Award 2006. *Address:* Center for Renaissance Studies, POB 2300, Amherst, MA 01004, USA (office). *Telephone:* (413) 577-3600 (office). *Fax:* (413) 577-3605 (office).

KINNEY, Harrison Burton, BA, MA; American writer; b. 16 Aug. 1921, Mars Hill, ME; m. Doris Getsinger 1952; one s. three d. *Education:* Washington and Lee Univ., Columbia Univ. *Career:* mem. Authors' Guild. *Publications:* The Lonesome Bear 1949, The Last Supper of Leonardo da Vinci by Lumen Martin Winter 1953, Has Anybody Seen My Father? 1960, The Kangaroo in the Attic 1960, James Thurber: His Life and Times 1993, The Thurber Letters: The Wit, Wisdom and Surprising Life of James Thurber 2003; contrib. to periodicals. *E-mail:* hkinney@inwriting.org. *Website:* www.harrisonkinney.com.

KINSELLA, John; Australian poet, writer, editor and publisher; *Editor, Salt;* b. 1963, Perth, WA. *Education:* Univ. of Western Australia. *Career:* writer-in-residence Churchill Coll., Cambridge 1997; Ed. Salt literary journal; Publisher, Ed. Folio (Salt) Publishing; Richard L. Thomas Prof. of Creative Writing, Kenyon Coll., USA 2001, then Prof. of English; fmr Adjunct Prof., Edith Cowan University, Western Australia, and Principal of the Landscape and Language Centre; Fellow Churchill Coll., Cambridge. *Publications:* poetry: The Frozen Sea 1983, Night Parrots 1989, The Book of Two Faces 1989, Poems 1991, Ultramarine (with Anthony Lawrence) 1992, Eschatologies 1991, Full Fathom Five 1993, Syzygy 1993, Erratum/Frame(d) 1995, Intensities of Blue (with Tracy Ryan) 1995, The Silo: A Pastoral Symphony 1995, The Radnoti Poems 1996, The Undertow: New and Selected Poems 1996, Lightning Tree 1996, Graphology (ed.) 1997, Poems: 1980–1994 1997, voice-overs (with Susan Schultz) 1997, The Hunt 1998, Kangaroo Virus (with Ron Sims) 1998, Sheep Dip 1998, Pine (with Keston Sutherland) 1998, alterity: poems without tom raworth 1998, The Benefaction (ed.) 1999, Fenland Pastorals 1999, Visitants 1999, Counter-Pastorals 1999, Wheatlands 2000, Zone 2000, Zoo (with Coral Hull) 2000, The Hierarchy of Sheep 2001, Speed Factory (with Bernard Cohen, McKenzie Wark and Terri-ann White) 2002, Rivers (with Peter Porter and Sean O'Brien) 2002, Lightning Tree 2003, Peripheral Light: New and Selected Poems (Western Australian Premier's Book Award for Poetry 2004) 2003, Doppler Effect 2004, Auto 2001, Outside the Panopticon 2002, Four Australian Poets (with others) 2003, The New Arcadia 2005; prose: Genre (novel) 1997, Grappling Eros (short stories) 1998, Crop Circles (play in verse) 1998, Paydirt (play), The Wasps (play), From Poetry to Politics and Back Again 2000, Divinations: Four Plays 2003, Peter Porter in Conversation with John Kinsella (with Peter Porter) 2003. *Honours:* Western Australia Premier's Award for Poetry 1993, Harri Jones Memorial Prize for Poetry, Adelaide Festival John Bray Poetry Award 1996, Sr Fellowships Literature Bd of the Australia Council, Young Australian

Creative Fellowship, Grace Leven Poetry Prize, The Age Poetry Book of the Year. *Address:* Salt Publishing Ltd, PO Box 937, Great Wilbraham, Cambridge, CB1 5JX, England. *Website:* www.johnkinsella.org.

KINSELLA, Thomas; Irish poet; b. 4 May 1928, Dublin; s. of John Paul and Agnes Casserly Kinsella; m. Eleanor Walsh 1955; one s. two d. *Career:* Irish Civil Service 1946–65, resgnd as Asst Prin. Officer, Dept of Finance 1965; Artist-in-Residence, Southern Ill. Univ. 1965–67, Prof. of English 1967–70; Prof. of English, Temple Univ., Philadelphia 1970–90; Dir Dolmen Press Ltd, Cuala Press Ltd, Dublin; founded Peppercanister (pvt. publishing enterprise), Dublin 1972; mem. Irish Acad. of Letters 1965–, American Acad. of Arts and Sciences 2000–; Guggenheim Fellowship 1968–69, 1971–72. *Publications:* Poems 1956, Another September (poems) 1958, Downstream (poems) 1962, Nightwalker and Other Poems 1966, Notes from the Land of the Dead (poems) 1972, Butcher's Dozen 1972, New Poems 1973, Selected Poems 1956–1968 1973, Song of the Night and Other Poems 1978, The Messenger (poem) 1978, Fifteen Dead (poems) 1979, One and Other Poems 1979, Poems 1956–1973, Peppercanister Poems 1972–1978 1979; Songs of the Psyche (poems) 1985, Her Vertical Smile (poem) 1985, St Catherine's Clock (poem) 1987, Out of Ireland (poems) 1987, Blood and Family (collected poems from 1978) 1988, Poems from Centre City 1990, Personal Places (poems) 1990, One Fond Embrace (poem) 1990, Madonna and other Poems 1991, Open Court (poem) 1991, Butcher's Dozen (anniversary reissue) 1992, From Centre City (collected poems from 1990) 1994, The Dual Tradition: an Essay on Poetry and Politics in Ireland 1995, Collected Poems 1956–94, The Pen Shop (poem) 1997, The Familiar (poems) 1999, Godhead (poems) 1999, Citizen of the World (poems) 2001, Littlebody (poem) 2001, Marginal Economy (poems) 2006, Readings in Poetry (essays) 2006, A Dublin Documentary (poems) 2006; The Táin (trans.) 1969; Selected Poems of Austin Clarke 1976; co-ed. Poems of the Dispossessed 1600–1900 (with 100 translations from the Irish) 1981; Ed.: Ireland's Musical Heritage; Sean O'Riada's Radio Talks on Irish Traditional Music 1981, The New Oxford Book of Irish Verse (including all new trans from the Irish) 1986. *Honours:* Hon. DLitt (Nat. Univ. of Ireland) 1985; Hon. Sr Fellow, School of English, Univ. Coll. Dublin 2003; Guinness Poetry Award 1958, Irish Arts Council Triennial Book Award 1960, Denis Devlin Memorial Award 1966, 1969, 1992, First European Poetry Award 2001.

KINSELLA, William Patrick, BA, MFA; Canadian writer and poet; b. 25 May 1935, Edmonton, Alberta; s. of John M. Kinsella and Olive M. Elliot; m. 1st Myrna Salls 1957; m. 2nd Mildred Heming 1965; m. 3rd Ann Knight 1978; m. 4th Barbara L. Turner 1999, three d. *Education:* Eastwood High School, Edmonton and Univs of Victoria and Iowa. *Career:* recipient Houghton Mifflin Literary Fellowship 1982. *Publications:* stories: Dance Me Outside 1977, Scars 1978, Shoeless Joe Jackson Comes to Iowa 1980, Born Indian 1981, The Moccasin Telegraph 1983, The Thrill of the Grass 1984, The Alligator Report 1985, The Fencepost Chronicles 1986, Five Stories 1987, Red Wolf, Red Wolf 1987, The Further Adventures of Slugger McBatt (reissued as Go the Distance 1995) 1988, The Miss Hobbema Pageant 1989, Dixon Cornbelt League 1993, Brother Frank's Gospel Hour 1994, The Secret of the Northern Lights 1998, The Silas Stories 1998, Japanese Baseball 2000; novels: Shoeless Joe 1982, The Iowa Baseball Confederacy 1986, Box Socials 1991, The Winter Helen Dropped By 1995, If Wishes Were Horses 1996, Magic Time 1998; other works: The Ballad of the Public Trustee 1982, The Rainbow Warehouse (poetry, with Ann Knight) 1989, Two Spirits Soar: The Art of Allen Sapp 1990, Even at this Distance (poetry, with Ann Knight) 1993. *Honours:* Books in Canada First Novel Award 1982; Canadian Authors' Asscn Award for Fiction 1982; Writers Guild Alberta Award for Fiction 1982, 1983; Vancouver Award for Writing 1987; Stephen Leacock Award for Humour 1987; Canadian Booksellers Asscn Author of the Year 1987. *Address:* 9442 Nowell, Chilliwack, BC, V2P 4X7, Canada (office); PO Box 3067 Sumas, WA 98295, USA.

KINSLEY, Michael, BA, JD; American journalist; b. 9 March 1951, Detroit, Mich.; m. Patty Stonesifer. *Education:* Cranbrook Kingswood School, Mich., Harvard Univ., Magdalen Coll., Oxford, UK and George Washington Univ. *Career:* journalist, The New Republic (magazine), Ed. 1978–95, writing 'TRB from Washington' column; editorial posts at Washington Monthly, Harper's, The Economist; Co-host Crossfire TV program (CNN) 1989–95; Founding Ed. Slate online magazine 1995–2002, columnist 2002–04; Editorial and Opinion Ed. Los Angeles Times 2004–05; columnist Time magazine 2006–; fmr columnist Wall Street Journal, The Times (London), Washington Post; contrib. to New Yorker, Reader's Digest, Condé Nast Traveler, Vanity Fair; American Ed. Guardian Unlimited (London) 2006. *Honours:* Columbia Journalism Review Editor of the Year 1999. *Address:* Time, Inc., 1271 Avenue of the Americas, New York, NY 10020, USA. *Telephone:* (212) 522-1212. *Fax:* (212) 522-0602. *Website:* www.time.com.

KINZIE, Mary, BA, MA, PhD; American poet, critic and academic; *Professor of English, Northwestern University. Education:* Northwestern Univ., Free Univ. of Berlin, Johns Hopkins Univ. *Career:* Exec. Ed., TriQuarterly magazine 1975–78; instructor 1975–78, Lecturer 1978–85, Assoc. Prof. 1985–90, Martin J. and Patricia Koldyke Outstanding Teaching Prof. 1990–92, Prof. of English 1990–, Dir of Creative Writing Program 1979–, Northwestern Univ.; Sr Fellowship, Nat. Humanities Center 2005–06; mem. PEN, Poetry Soc. of America, Soc. of Midland Authors. *Publications:* poetry: The Threshold of the Year 1982, Summers of Vietnam 1990, Masked Women 1990, Autumn Eros and Other Poems 1991, Ghost Ship 1996, Drift 2003; non-fiction: The Cure of Poetry in an Age of Prose: Moral Essays on the Poet's Calling 1993, The Judge is Fury: Dislocation and Form in Poetry 1994, A

Poet's Guide to Poetry 2000, A Poet's Prose: Selected Writings of Louise Bogan 2005; contrib. to various books, anthologies, reviews, quarterlies, journals and magazines. *Honours:* Illinois Arts Council Awards 1977, 1978, 1980, 1982, 1984, 1988, 1990, 1993, and Artist grant 1983, DeWitt Wallace Fellow MacDowell Colony 1979, Devins Award for a First Vol. of Verse 1982, Guggenheim Fellowship 1986, Southwest Review Elizabeth Matchett Stover Memorial Award in Poetry 1987, Poetry Soc. of America Celia B. Wagner Award 1988, Pres.'s Fund for the Humanities Research grant 1990–91. *Address:* c/o College of Arts and Sciences, Department of English, Northwestern University, University Hall 215, Evanston, IL 60208-2240, USA.

KIRALY, Sherwood; American writer and editor; b. 23 Oct. 1949, Chicago, IL; m. 1st; one s. one d.; m. 2nd Patti J. Reynolds 1987. *Education:* Knox College. *Publications:* California Rush, 1990; Diminished Capacity, 1995; Big Babies, 1996. Contributions: newspapers and television.

KIRANOVA, Evgenia, LLB; Bulgarian journalist and magazine editor; *President, Women's Union for Dignity and Equality;* b. 23 Jan. 1929, Sofia; m. 1st Dencho Denchev 1948 (divorced 1967); one s. one d.; m. 2nd Ivan Delchev 1973. *Education:* Univ. of Sofia. *Career:* Sec. World Democratic Fed. of Women 1954–57; Deputy Ed. Bulgarian-Soviet Friendship 1957–66; Head Foreign Dept Bulgarian Writers' Union 1966–67; Ed. Pogled (Review) 1968–72; Foreign Commentator Bulgarian Radio and TV 1972–73; World Peace Council Sec., Helsinki 1973–82; Sec-Gen., Vice-Pres. Int. Cttee of Solidarity with Cyprus 1975; Political Observer and Deputy Gen. Dir Sofia Press Agency 1985–90; Ed-in-Chief Nie Jhenite women's magazine 1990; Founder, Pres. Women's Union for Dignity and Equality; Vice-Pres. Bulgarian section Int. Women's Fed. of Business and Professional Women. *Publications:* Well Known and Beloved 1960, Legal Defence of Motherhood 1965, Cyprus Drama, Women in the Contemporary World, Fight for Peace, Suomi, The River Run Back (ed.), Our Tzvetana (ed.). *Address:* 1712 Sofia, J. K. Mladost 3, bl 316, vh A, Bulgaria. *Telephone:* (2) 8814022. *E-mail:* jenyk@cablebg.net.

KIRINO, Natsuo; Japanese novelist; b. 1951, Kanazawa; m.; one c. *Publications include:* Kao ni Furikakaru Ame (Edogawa Ranpo Prize 1993) 1993, Tenshi ni Misuterareta Yoru 1994, Fire Ball Blues 1995, Mizu no Nemuri Hai no Yume 1995, Out (Mystery Writers of Japan Award) 1997, Yawarakana hohu (Soft Cheeks) (Naoki Prize) 1999, Kogen 2000, Fire Ball Blues 2 2001, Gyokuran 2001, Dark 2002, Real World 2003, Grotesque (Izumi Kyoka Literary Award) 2003, Zangyakuki (What Remains) 2004, I'm Sorry, Mama 2004, Tamamoe! 2005, Boken no Kuni 2005, Grotesque 2007; short story collections: Sabiru Kokor 1997, Diorama 1998, Rose Gaden 2000, Ambos Mundos 2005. *Address:* c/o International Creative Management Inc., 40 West 57th Street, New York NY 10019, USA (office). *Telephone:* (212) 556-5665 (office). *Fax:* (212) 556-5665 (office). *Website:* www.icmtalent.com/flash.html (office).

KIRK, Pauline Marguerite, MA; British writer and poet; b. 14 April 1942, Birmingham, England; m. Peter Kirk 1964; one s. one d. *Education:* Nottingham University, Sheffield University, Monash University, Bretton Hall College, Leeds University. *Career:* Teacher, Methodist Ladies College, 1965–66; Teaching Fellow, Monash University, 1965–69; Tutor-Counsellor, Asst Senior Counsellor, Open University, 1971–88; Senior Officer, Leeds Dept of Social Service, 1988–95; Partner, Fighting Cock Press, 1996–; mem. Aireings, Partner, Fighting Cock Press, 1997–; Pennine Poets; Society of Authors. *Publications:* Fiction: Waters of Time, 1988; The Keepers, 1996. Poetry: Scorpion Days, 1982; Red Marl and Brick, 1985; Rights of Way, 1990; Travelling Solo, 1995; Return to Dreamtime, 1996; No Cure in Tears, 1997; Owlstone, 2002. Criticism: Brian Merrikin Hill: Poet and Mentor, 1999. Editor: A Survivor Myself: Experiences of Child Abuse, 1994; Local history booklets for Leeds City Council; Poetry Collections: Dunegrass, Brakken City, 1997; Chernobyl's Cloud, Natural Light, Kingfisher Days, 1998; The Imaginator, 2000; Imaginary Gates, 2001; Patterns in the Dark (second edn), 2001; Webbed Skylights of Tall Oaks (with Clare Chapman), 2002. Contributions: anthologies and other publications. *Honours:* Yorkshire and Humberside Arts New Beginnings Award, 1994. *Address:* 45 Middlethorpe Drive, York YO24 1NA, England.

KIRK, Richard (see Holdstock, Robert)

KIRKPATRICK, Clayton, AB; American newspaper editor; b. 8 Jan. 1915, Waterman, Ill.; s. of Clayton Matteson Kirkpatrick and Mable Rose Swift; m. Thelma Marie De Mott 1943 (died 1998); two s. two d. *Education:* Univ. of Ill. *Career:* reporter, City News Bureau, Chicago 1938; mem. staff, Chicago Tribune 1938–, Day City Ed. 1958–61, City Ed. 1961–63, Asst Man. Ed. 1963–65, Man. Ed. 1965–67, Exec. Ed. 1967–69, Ed. 1969–79; Vice-Pres. Chicago Tribune Co. 1967–77, Exec. Vice-Pres. 1977–79, Pres. 1979–81, Chair. 1981; Del. to 19th Gen. Conf., UNESCO, Nairobi 1976. *Honours:* Bronze Star Medal for service in World War II; Elijah Parish Lovejoy Award, Colby Coll. 1978; William Allen White Award, Univ. of Kansas 1977; Fourth Estate Award, Nat. Press Club 1979. *Address:* 471 Stagecoach Run, Glen Ellyn, IL 60137, USA (home).

KIRKPATRICK, Sidney Dale, BA, MFA; American writer and filmmaker; b. 4 Oct. 1955, New York, NY; m. 1983; two s. *Education:* Hampshire Coll., Amherst, New York Univ. *Career:* Reader, Huntington Library 1992; mem. PEN Center West, Bd of Dirs 1991–92. *Film:* My Father the President (Dir; Winner, American Film Festival 1982). *Television:* The Indomitable Teddy Roosevelt (NBC, Assoc. Producer) 1985. *Publications:* A Cast of Killers 1986,

Turning the Tide 1991, Lords of Sipan 1992 Edgar Cayce, an American Prophet 2000 The Revenge of Thomas Eakins 2006; contribs to Los Angeles Times, American Film. *Address:* c/o Jonklow and Nesbit, 445 Park Avenue, New York, NY 10022, USA. *E-mail:* sdk3rd@earthlink.net (office).

KIRKUP, James Harold, BA, FRSL; British writer; b. 23 April 1918, South Shields; s. of James Harold Kirkup and Mary Johnson. *Education:* Durham Univ. *Career:* Gregory Fellow in Poetry, Leeds Univ. 1950–52; Visiting Poet, Bath Acad. of Art 1953–56; travelling lectureship from Swedish Ministry of Education 1956–57; Prof. of English Language and Literature, Salamanca (Spain) 1957–58; Prof. of English Literature, Tohoku Univ. 1959–61; Visiting Prof. of English Literature, Japan Women's Univ., Tokyo 1964–69; Visiting Prof. and Poet in Residence, Amherst Coll. Mass. 1968–69; Prof. of English Literature, Univ. of Nagoya, Japan 1969–72; Morton Visiting Prof. in Int. Literature, Ohio Univ. 1975–76; Playwright in Residence, Sherman Theatre, Univ. Coll., Cardiff 1976–77; Prof. of English Literature, Kyoto Univ. of Foreign Studies 1977–89; Tutor, Arvon Foundation 1979; obituarist for The Independent and The Guardian newspapers 1994–; Literary Ed. Orient-West Magazine, Tokyo 1963–65; founder Pres. The British Haiku Soc. 1991–96; Literary Adviser Ko Haiku Magazine, Nagoya, Japan; trans. of poetry on www.brindin.com and Yale Univ. Beineke Library of Rare Books & Manuscripts. *Music:* libretto for An Actor's Revenge (music by Minoru Miki) 1975. *Plays:* trans. The Prince of Homburg (Kleist), Don Carlos (Schiller), The Physicists (Friedrich Dürrenmatt), The True Mystery of the Nativity, The True Mystery of the Passion. *Radio:* Poetry Please (BBC Radio). *Publications:* The Cosmic Shape 1947, The Drowned Sailor 1948, The Creation 1950, The Submerged Village 1951, A Correct Compassion 1952, A Spring Journey 1954, Upon This Rock, The Dark Child, The Triumph of Harmony 1955, The True Mystery of the Nativity, Ancestral Voices, The Radiance of the King 1956, The Descent into the Cave, The Only Child (autobiography) 1957, The Peach Garden, Two Pigeons Flying High (TV plays), Sorrows, Passions and Alarms (autobiography) 1960, The True Mystery of the Passion, The Prodigal Son (poems) 1956–60, These Horned Islands (travel) 1962, The Love of Others (novel) 1962, Tropic Temper (travel) 1963, Refusal to Conform, Last and First Poems 1963, The Heavenly Mandate 1964, Japan Industrial, Vols I and II 1964–65, Tokyo (travel) 1966, Bangkok (travel) 1967, Paper Windows 1967, Michael Kohlhaas 1967, Filipinescas (travel) 1968, One Man's Russia (travel) 1968, Streets of Asia (travel) 1969, Hong Kong (travel) 1969, White Shadows, Black Shadows: Poems of Peace and War 1969, The Body Servant: Poems of Exile 1971, Japan Behind the Fan 1970, Streets of Asia 1969, Pier Gynt 1970, Insect Summer (novel) 1971, A Bewick Bestiary 1971, Transmental Vibrations 1972, Brand (Ibsen) 1972, The Magic Drum (play for children) 1972, (story for children) 1973, Peer Gynt 1973, The Winter Moon, Selected Poems of Takagi Kyozo, Cyrano de Bergerac 1974, Play Strindberg 1974, The Conformer 1975, Don Carlos 1975, Heaven, Hell and Hara-Kiri 1975, Background to English Literature 1975, An English Traveller in Japan 1975, Frank the Fifth, Portrait of a Planet 1976, Scenes from Sesshu 1977, Modern Japanese Poetry (anthology) 1978, Dengoban Messages: One-line Poems, Zen Contemplations, Enlightenment 1979, Cold Mountain Poems, The Guardian of the Word, Aspects of Europe, Countries and Customs, British Traditions and Superstitions 1980, James Kirkup's Tales from Shakespeare 1969–84, Scenes from Sutcliffe 1981, The British Lady and Gentleman, I am Count Dracula 1981, Ecce Homo 1981, To The Unknown God 1982, The Bush Toads 1982, Folktales Japanesque 1982, To the Ancestral North (poems for autobiog.) 1983, The Glory that was Greece 1984, The Sense of the Visit 1984, Hearn in my Heart 1984; An Actor's Revenge (opera) 1979, Friends in Arms, Shunkinsho 1980, No More Hiroshimas 1982, 1995, 2004, The Damask Drum (opera) 1984, Trends and Traditions 1985, Dictionary of Body Language 1985, English with a Smile 1986, Fellow Feelings (poems) 1986, Portraits and Souvenirs 1987, The Mystery and Magic of Symbols 1987, The Cry of the Owl: Native American Folktales and Legends 1987, I of All People, Scenes from American Life, I Remember America, Everyday English Superstitions 1988, The Best of Britain 1989, Everyday English Proverbs 1989, Gaijin on the Ginza 1992, A Poet Could Not But Be Gay 1992, Throwback (Poems) 1992, First Fireworks (Poems) 1992, Me All Over: Memoirs of a Misfit (autobiog.) 1993, Queens Have Died Young and Fair (novel) 1993, Strange Attractors (poems) 1994, Blue Bamboo (Haiku) 1994, Words or Contemplation (poems) 1993, Noems, Koans & A Navel Display 1995, A Certain State of Mind 1995, Blindsight (trans. Hervé Guibert) 1995, Paradise (trans. Hervé Guibert) 1996, Collected Longer Poems 1996, Selected Shorter Poems 1996, Counting to 9,999 1996, Look at it This Way! (Poems for young people) 1995, A Child of the Tyne (autobiography) 1996, A Book of Tanka 1996, The Patient Obituarist: New Poems 1996, Burning Giraffes: Modern Japanese Poets 1996, Broad Daylight: Poems East and West 1996, Figures in a Setting 1996, Utsusemi (tanka) 1996, Two Classic German Dramas: Kleist's Prince of Homburg and Schiller's Don Carlos 1997, The Nativity and the Passion: Two Mystery Plays 1997, How to Cook Women: Selected Poetry and Prose by Takagi Kyozo 1997, He Dreamed He Was a Butterfly 1998, Pikadon: An Epic 1998, Tanka Tales 1998, One-Man Band: Poems Without Words 1999, Tokonoma (haiku and tanka, with woodcuts by Naoko Matsubara), Tankalphabet 2001, A Tiger in Your Tanka 2001, In Thickets of Memory: Tanka by Saito Fumi (trans.), 2002, Pages from the Seasons: Tanka by Fumiko Miura 2002, Shields Sketches 2002, An Island in the Sky: Poems for Andorra 2003, The Best Way to Travel: from the Works of Zhuangzi 2004, Myself as an Anatomical Love-Making Chart, and Other Poems, by Takahashi Mutsuo (trans.) 2005, We of Zipangu: Poems by Takahashi Mutsuo (trans., with Tamaki Mutsuo) 2006; A Pilgrimage in Hell:

Poems by Iwan Gilkin 2007, The Authentic Touch: New Poems 2007; numerous poems, plays and essays and trans. from French, German, Japanese, Italian and Norwegian; contrib. poems to Japanese haiku and tanka magazines Ko and Tanka Journal, and obituaries to The Independent. *Honours:* Atlantic Award in Literature (Rockefeller Foundation) 1959, Japan Festival Foundation Award for A Book of Tanka 1997, Scott-Moncrieff Prize for Translation 1997. *Address:* Atic D, Edifici Les Bons, Avinguda de Rouillac 7, Encamp, AD200, Andorra (home). *Telephone:* (376) 831065 (home). *Fax:* (376) 831065 (home).

KIRSCH, Jonathan, BA, JD; American novelist, writer, reviewer and attorney; b. 19 Dec. 1949, Los Angeles, CA; m. Ann Benjamin 1970, one s. one d. *Education:* University of California, Santa Cruz, Loyola University School of Law. *Career:* book reviewer, Los Angeles Times Book Review 1968–; Ed., California magazine, formerly New West 1977–83; correspondent, Newsweek 1979–80; Attorney, Kirsch and Mitchell, Los Angeles 1988–. *Publications:* Bad Moon Rising (novel), 1977; Lovers in a Winter Circle (novel), 1978; Kirsch's Handbook of Publishing Law: For Authors, Publishers, Editors, and Agents, 1995; The Harlot by the Side of the Road: Forbidden Tales of the Bible, 1997; Moses: A Life, 1998. Contributions: More than 1,000 articles and book reviews to newspapers and magazines. *Literary Agent:* Laurie Fox, Linda Chester Literary Agency, Rockefeller Center, 630 Fifth Ave, New York, NY 10111, USA. *Address:* Kirsch and Mitchell, 2029 Century Park E, Suite 2750, Los Angeles, CA 90067, USA. *E-mail:* ursus@aol.com.

KIRSCH, Sarah, DipA; German author and poet; b. 16 April 1935, Limlingerode; m. Rainer Kirsch 1958 (divorced 1968); one s. *Education:* University of Halle, Johannes R. Becher Institute, Leipzig. *Publications:* Landaufenthalt, 1967; Die Vögel signen im Regen am Schönsten, 1968; Zaubersprüche, 1973; Es war der merkwürdigste Sommer, 1974; Musik auf dem Wasser, 1977; Rückenwind, 1977; Drachensteigen, 1979; Sieben Häute: Ausgewählte Gedichte 1962–79, 1979; La Pagerie, 1980; Erdreich, 1982; Katzenleben, 1984; Hundert Gedichte, 1985; Landwege: Eine Auswahl 1980–85, 1985; Irrstern, 1986; Allerlei-Rauh, 1988; Schneewärme, 1989; Die Flut, 1990; Spreu, 1991; Schwingrasen, 1991; Sic! natur!, 1992; Erlkönigs Tochter, 1992; Das simple Leben, 1994; Winternachtigall, 1995; Ich Crusoe, 1995; Nachtsonnen, 1995; Bodenlos, 1996. *Honours:* Petrarca Prize, 1976; Austrian State Prize for Literature, 1981; Austrian Critics Prize, 1981; Gandersheim Literary Prize, 1983; Hölderlin Prize, Bad Homburg, 1984; Art Prize, Schleswig-Holstein, 1987; Author-in-Residence, City of Mainz, 1988; Heinrich-Heine-Gesellschaft Award, Düsseldorf, 1992; Peter Huchel Prize, 1993; Konrad Adenauer Foundation Literature Prize, 1993; Büchner Prize, 1996.

KISSINGER, Henry Alfred, MA, PhD; American academic, international consultant and fmr government official; *Chairman, Kissinger McLarty Associates;* b. 27 May 1923, Fuerth, Germany; s. of Louis Kissinger and Paula Stern; m. 1st Anne Fleisher 1949 (divorced 1964); one s. one d.; m. 2nd Nancy Maginnes 1974. *Education:* George Washington High School, Harvard Coll., Harvard Univ. *Career:* went to USA 1938; naturalized US Citizen 1943; US Army 1943–46; Dir Study Group on Nuclear Weapons and Foreign Policy, Council of Foreign Relations 1955–56; Dir Special Studies Project, Rockefeller Brothers Fund 1956–58; Consultant, Weapons System Evaluation Group, Joint Chiefs of Staff 1956–60, Nat. Security Council 1961–63, US Arms Control and Disarmament Agency 1961–69, Dept of State 1965–68 and to various other bodies; Faculty mem. Harvard Univ. 1954–69; Dept of Govt and Center for Int. Affairs; faculty Harvard Univ. Center for Int. Affairs 1960–69; Dir Harvard Int. Seminar 1951–69, Harvard Defense Studies Program 1958–69, Asst to Pres. of USA for Nat. Security Affairs 1969–75; Sec. of State 1973–77; prominent in American negotiations for the Viet Nam settlement of Jan. 1973 and in the negotiations for a Middle East ceasefire 1973, 1974; Trustee, Center for Strategic and Int. Studies 1977–; Chair. Kissinger Assocs Inc. (since 1999 Kissinger McLarty Assocs Inc.) 1982–; mem. Pres.'s Foreign Intelligence Advisory Bd 1984–90; Chair. Nat. Bipartisan Comm. on Cen. America 1983–84; fmr Chair. US Comm. investigating Sept. 11 attacks; Counsellor to J. P. Morgan Chase Bank and mem. of its Int. Advisory Council; Hon. Gov. Foreign Policy Asscn; Sr Fellow, Aspen Inst., syndicated columnist LA Times 1984–; Adviser to Bd of Dirs American Express, Forstmann Little & Co., Dir Emer. Freeport McMoran Copper and Gold Inc., Conti Group Cos Ltd, The TCW Group, US Olympic Cttee, Int. Rescue Cttee; Chair. American Int. Group, Int. Advisory Bd; mem. Exec. Cttee Trilateral Comm.; Chair. Eisenhower Exchange Fellowships; Chancellor The Coll. of William and Mary; Hon. Chair. World Cup USA 1994. *Publications:* Nuclear Weapons and Foreign Policy 1956, A World Restored: Castlereagh, Metternich and the Restoration of Peace 1812–22 1957, The Necessity for Choice: Prospects of American Foreign Policy 1961, The Troubled Partnership: A Reappraisal of the Atlantic Alliance 1965, American Foreign Policy (3 essays) 1969, White House Years 1979, For the Record 1981, Years of Upheaval 1982, Observations: Selected Speeches and Essays 1982–84 1985, Diplomacy 1994, Years of Renewal 1999, Does America Need a Foreign Policy? 2001, Ending the Vietnam War 2003, Crisis 2003; and numerous articles on US foreign policy, international affairs and diplomatic history. *Honours:* Woodrow Wilson Book Prize 1958, American Inst. for Public Service Award 1973, Nobel Peace Prize 1973, American Legion Distinguished Service Medal 1974, Wateler Peace Prize 1974, Presidential Medal of Freedom 1977, Medal of Liberty 1986, Hon. KCMG 1995, and many other awards and prizes. *Address:* 350 Park Avenue, New York, NY 10022; Suite 400, 1800 K Street, NW, Washington, DC 20006,

USA. *Telephone:* (212) 759-7919 (NY); (202) 822-8182 (DC). *Website:* www
.kmaglobal.com.

KITAMURA, So; Japanese playwright; b. 5 July 1952, Ohtsu-shi; m. Konomi
Kitamura; one d. *Career:* Leader Project Navi 1986–. *Publications:* plays
include: Hogiuta, So-Ko Gingatetsudo no yoru. Novels include: Kaijin
nijumenso den (Shincho sha), Seido no majin (Shincho sha), Kenji (Kadokawa). *Honours:* awards include Kishida Gikyoku-sho 1984, Kinoleuni-ya
engeki-sho 1989. *Address:* Project Navi, 11–13 Imaike-Minami, Chikusa-ku,
Nagoya-shi, Aichi 464, Japan. *Telephone:* (52) 731-2867.

KITANO, Takeshi; Japanese film director, actor, comedian and screenwriter; b. 18 Jan. 1947, Tokyo. *Education:* Meiji Univ. *Films:* Makoto-chan
(actor) 1980, Danpu wataridori (actor) 1981, Manon (actor) 1981, Sukkari...
sono ki de! (actor) 1981, Merry Christmas, Mr. Lawrence (actor) 1983, Jukkai
no mosquito (actor) 1983, Kanashii kibun de joke (actor) 1985, Yasha (actor)
1985, Komikku zasshi nanka iranai! (actor) 1986, Anego (actor) 1988, Sono
otoko, kyobo ni tsuki (writer, director, actor) 1989, Hoshi tsugu mono (actor)
1990, 3-4x jugatsu (writer, director, actor) 1990, Ano natsu, ichiban shizukana
umi (writer, director) 1991, Sakana kara daiokishin! (actor) 1992, Erotikkuna
kankei (actor) 1992, Sonatine (writer, director, actor) 1993, Kyôso tanjô
(writer, actor) 1993, Minnâ-yatteruka! (writer, director, actor) 1995, Johnny
Mnemonic (actor) 1995, Gonin (actor) 1995, Kidzu ritan (writer, director)
1996, Hana-bi (writer, director, actor) (Venice Film Festival Golden Lion)
1997, Tokyo Eyes (actor) 1998, Kikujiro no natsu (writer, director, actor) 1999,
Gohatto (actor) 1999, Brother (writer, director, actor) 2000, Batoru rowaiaru
(Battle Royale) (actor) 2000, Dolls (writer, director) 2002, Asakusa Kid
(writer) 2002, Battle Royale II (actor) 2003, Zatôichi (writer, director, actor)
(Venice Film Festival Silver Lion) 2003, Izô: Kaosu mataha fujôri no kijin
(actor) 2004, Chi to hone 2004, Takeshis' 2005, Gegege no Kitano 2007.
Address: Office Kitano Inc., Tokyo, Japan. *E-mail:* office@office-kitano.co.jp.
Website: www.office-kitano.co.jp.

KITCHEN, Martin, BA, PhD, FRHistS, FRSC; British academic and writer; b. 21
Dec. 1936, Nottingham, England. *Education:* Magdalen Coll., Oxford and
Univ. of London. *Career:* faculty mem. 1966–76, Prof. of History 1976–, Simon
Fraser Univ., Burnaby, BC. *Publications:* The German Officer Corps
1890–1914 1968, A Military History of Germany 1975, The Silent Dictator-
ship: The Politics of the German High Command Under Hindenburg and
Ludendorff 1976, Fascism 1976, The Political Economy of Germany
1815–1914 1978, The Coming of Austrian Fascism 1980, Germany in the
Age of Total War 1981, British Policy Towards the Soviet Union During the
Second World War 1986, Europe Between the Wars 1988, The Origins of the
Cold War in Comparative Perspective: American, British and Canadian
Relations with the Soviet Union, 1941–48 1988, Nazi Germany at War 1994,
The British Empire and Commonwealth: A Short History 1996, The
Cambridge Illustrated History of Germany 1996, Kasper Hauser 2001, The
German Offensives of 1918 2001, Nazi Germany: A Critical Introduction 2004,
A History of Modern Germany 1800–2000 2006; contribs to professional
journals. *Honours:* American Military Acad. Moncado Prize 1978. *Address:* c/o
Department of History, Simon Fraser University, Burnaby, BC V5A 1S6
(office); 24B, 6128 Patterson Avenue, Burnaby, BC V5H 4P3, Canada (home).
Telephone: (604) 291-3521 (office); (604) 433-0119 (home). *Fax:* (604) 291-5837
(office); (604) 433-0119 (home). *E-mail:* kitchen@sfu.ca (office).

KITSIKIS, Dimitri, MA, PhD, FRSC; Canadian/French/Greek poet, historian
and academic; *Professor Emeritus, Department of History, University of
Ottawa;* b. 2 June 1935, Athens; s. of the late Nikolas Kitsikis and Beata
Petychakis; m. 1st Anne Hubbard 1955 (divorced 1973); one s. one d.; m. 2nd
Ada Nikolaros 1975; one s. one d. *Education:* American Coll. Athens, Ecole des
Roches, Normandy, Lycée Lakanal and Lycée Carnot, Paris and Sorbonne,
Paris. *Career:* Research Assoc. Grad. Inst. of Int. Studies, Geneva 1960–62,
Centre for Int. Relations, Nat. Foundation of Political Science, Paris 1962–65,
Nat. Centre for Scientific Research, Paris 1965–70; Assoc. Prof. of History of
Int. Relations, Univ. of Ottawa 1970–83, Prof. 1983–96, Emer. Prof. 1996–; Sr
Research Scholar, Nat. Centre of Social Research, Athens 1972–74; founder,
Ed. Intermediate Region (journal) 1996–; adviser to govts of Greece and
Turkey; numerous visiting professorships and other appts; f. Dimitri Kitsikis
Public Foundation and Library, Athens 2006. *Publications include:* Propa-
ganda and Pressure in International Politics 1963, The Role of the Experts at
the Paris Peace Conference of 1919 1972, A Comparative History of Greece
and Turkey in the 20th Century 1978, History of the Greek-Turkish Area
1981, The Ottoman Empire 1985, The Third Ideology and Orthodoxy 1990,
The Old Calendarists 1995, Turkish-Greek Empire 1996, The Byzantine
Model of Government 2001, Bektashism and Alevism 2006, A Comparative
History of Greece and China 2007; co-author of 33 other books; six vols of
poetry, two vols of poetry and painting; over 100 scholarly articles. *Honours:*
First Prize in Poetry, Abdi Ipekçi Peace and Friendship Prize 1992. *Address:*
Department of History, University of Ottawa, ON K1N 6N5, Canada (office);
29 Travlantoni, Zographou, Athens 15772, Greece (home); 2104 Benjamin
Avenue, Ottawa, ON K2A 1P4, Canada (home). *Telephone:* (613) 562-5735
(Ottawa) (office); (613) 834-4634 (Ottawa) (home); (210) 777-6937 (Athens).
Fax: (613) 562-5995 (Ottawa) (office). *E-mail:* dimitri.kitsikis@uottawa.ca
(office); dkitsiki@rogers.com (home). *Website:* ca.geocities.com/dimitri
-kitsikis@rogers.com (office).

KITTREDGE, William Alfred, (Owen Rountree), BS, MFA; American
academic and writer; *Professor Emeritus of English, University of Montana;*
b. 14 Aug. 1932, Portland, OR; one s. one d. *Education:* Oregon State Univ.,
Univ. of Iowa. *Career:* Prof. Emeritus of English, Univ. of Montana.
Publications: The Van Gogh Field 1977, We Are Not In This Together 1982,
Owning It All 1984, Hole in the Sky 1992, Who Owns the West? 1996, Portable
Western Reader (ed.) 1998, Balancing Water 2000, The Nature of Generosity
2000, Southwestern Homelands 2002, The Best Short Stories of William
Kittredge 2002, The Willow Field 2006; contrib. to Time, Newsweek, New
York Times, Wall Street Journal, Esquire, Outside, Paris Review. *Honours:*
NEH Charles Frankel Award 1994, Los Angeles Times Lifetime Achievement
Kirsch Award 2007. *Literary Agent:* Amanda Urban, ICM, 40 W 57th Street,
New York, NY, USA. *Address:* 143 S Fifth Street E, Missoula, MT 59801, USA.

KIZAKI, Satoko (see Harada, Masako)

KIZER, Carolyn Ashley, BA; American writer; b. 10 Dec. 1925, Spokane,
Wash.; d. of Benjamin and M. (née Ashley) Kizer; m. 1st Stimson Bullitt 1948
(divorced); two d. one s.; m. 2nd John Woodbridge 1975. *Education:* Sarah
Lawrence Coll., Columbia Univ., New York and Univ. of Washington. *Career:*
Writer-in-Residence, Ohio Univ. 1974, Center Coll., Ky 1979, E Washington
Univ. 1980, Bucknell Univ. 1982, State Univ. of New York 1982; Prof. of
Poetry, Univ. of Maryland 1976–77, Univ. of Cincinatti 1981, Univ. of
Louisville 1982, Columbia Univ. 1982, Stanford Univ. 1986; Sr Fellow,
Princeton Univ. 1986; Visiting Prof., Univ. of Arizona 1989, 1990, Univ. of
California, Davis 1991; Cole Royalty Chair., Univ. of Alabama 1995; mem.
PEN, Poetry Soc. of America, Acad. of American Poets, Amnesty Int.
Publications include: The Ungrateful Garden 1961, Knock Upon Silence
1965, Midnight Was My Cry 1971, Mermaids in the Basement: Poems for
Women 1984, Yin: New Poems (Pulitzer Prize for Poetry 1985) 1984, The
Nearness of You (Theodore Roethke Prize 1988) 1987, The Essential Clare (ed)
1993, On Poems and Poets 1994, Picking and Choosing: Prose on Prose 1995,
100 Great Poems by Women (ed) 1995, Cool, Calm and Collected 2003.
Honours: Hon. DLitt (Whitman Coll.) 1986, (St Andrew's) 1989, (Mills) 1990;
American Acad. and Inst. of Arts and Letters Award 1985, Gov.'s Award, State
of Washington 1965, 1985, 1995, 1998, Theodore Roethke Memorial Poetry
Award 1988, Frost Medal, John Masefield Memorial Award. *Address:* 19772
8th Street East, Sonoma, CA 95476, USA.

KLAM, Matthew; American writer; b. 1964. *Education:* Univ. of New
Hampshire, Hollins Coll., Va. *Career:* teacher of creative writing, St Albans
School, American Univ., Stockholm Univ., Sweden. *Publications:* Sam the Cat
and other stories 2000; contrib. to The New Yorker, Harpers, Allure, USA
Weekend, Nerve, The Washington Post Magazine, New York Times Magazine.
Honours: Robert Bingham/PEN Award, Nat. Endowment for the Arts grant,
Whiting Writer's Award, O'Henry Award. *Address:* c/o Random House Inc.,
1745 Broadway, New York, NY 10019, USA. *E-mail:* MattKlam@gmail.com
(home). *Website:* www.matthewklam.com.

KLAPPERT, Peter, BA, MA, MFA; American academic, poet and writer; b. 14
Nov. 1942, Rockville Center, NY. *Education:* Cornell Univ., Univ. of Iowa.
Career: Instructor, Rollins College, 1968–71; Briggs-Copeland Lecturer,
Harvard University, 1971–74; Visiting Lecturer, New College, 1972; Writer-
in-Residence, 1976–77, Asst Prof., 1977–78, College of William and Mary; Asst
Prof., 1978–81, Prof., 1981–91, Prof., 1991–, Dir, MFA Degree Program in Poetry, 1995–98,
George Mason University; mem. Acad. of American Poets; Associated Writing
Programs; Assboth of Literary Scholars and Critics; PEN; Poetry Society of
America; Writers' Center, Bethesda, MD. *Publications:* On a Beach in
Southern Connecticut, 1966; Lugging Vegetables to Nantucket, 1971; Circular
Stairs, Distress in the Mirrors, 1975; Non Sequitur O'Connor, 1977; The Idiot
Princess of the Last Dynasty, 1984; '52 Pick-Up: Scenes From the Conspiracy,
A Documentary, 1984; Chokecherries: New and Selected Poems 1966–1999,
2000. Contributions: many anthologies, books, journals, and magazines.
Honours: Yale Series of Younger Poets Prize, 1970; Yaddo Resident Fellow-
ships, 1972, 1973, 1975, 1981; MacDowell Colony Resident Fellowships, 1973,
1975; National Endowment for the Arts Fellowships, 1973, 1979; Lucille
Medwick Award, Poetry Society of America, 1977; Virginia Center for the
Creative Arts Resident Fellowships, 1978, 1979, 1981, 1983, 1984, 1987, 1993,
1995; Millay Colony for the Arts Resident Fellowship, 1981; Ingram Merrill
Foundation Grant, 1983; Klappert-Ai Poetry Award established in his honour
by Gwendolyn Brooks, George Mason University, 1987; Poet-Scholar,
American Library Asscn-National Endowment for the Humanities Voices
and Visions Project, 1988. *Address:* 2003 Klingle Rd NW, Washington, DC
20010, USA. *E-mail:* petermail@earthlink.net.

KLASS, Perri Elizabeth, AB, MD; American writer and pediatrician; b. 29
April 1958, Trinidad; two s. one d. *Education:* Radcliffe College, Harvard
University, Harvard Medical School. *Career:* mem. PEN New England, exec.
board; American Acad. of Pediatrics; American Medical Women's Asscn;
Massachusetts Medical Society; Tilling Society. *Publications:* Recombinations
(novel), 1985; I Am Having An Adventure (short stories), 1986; A Not Entirely
Benign Procedure (essays), 1987; Other Women's Children (novel), 1990; Baby
Doctor (essays), 1992. Contributions: New York Times Magazine; Massachu-
setts Medicine; Discover; Vogue, Glamour; Esquire; Boston Globe Magazine;
Mademoiselle; TriQuarterly; North American Review. *Honours:* O. Henry
Awards, 1983, 1984, 1991, 1992, 1995; Honors Award, New England chapter,
American Medical Writers Asscn, 1995. *Address:* Reach Out and Read
National Center, 56 Roland Street, Suite 100D, Boston, MA 02129-1243, USA.
E-mail: info@reachoutandread.org.

KLEIN, Étienne, DèsSc, PhD; French physicist and writer; *Physicist, Commissariat à l'énergie atomique;* b. 1958, Paris. *Education:* Ecole centrale, Univ. de Paris VII. *Career:* physicist CEA 1983–, Dir Sciences de la Matière, teacher Ecole Centrale; worked in Proton Accelerator Study Group CERN 1992–93. *Publications:* Conversations avec le Sphinx: Les paradoxes en physique 1991, Regards sur la matière: des quanta et des choses 1993, Le Temps et sa flèche (with Michel Spiro) 1994, Prédiction et probabilité 1998, La Quête de l'unité (with Marc Lachièze-Rey) 2000, L'Atome au pied du mur et autres nouvelles 2000, L'Unité de la physique 2000, Le Temps existe-t-il? 2002, Les Tactiques de Chronos 2003, La Science nous menace-t-elle? 2003, Quand la science a dit c'est bizarre! 2003, Petit voyage dans le monde des quantas (Prix Jean Rostand) 2004, Il était sept fois la Révolution: Albert Einstein et les autres... 2005, Les Atomes de l'univers 2005. *Honours:* Prix Jean Pessin 1997, Prix Grammaticakis-Neumann 2000, Prix Jean Rostand 2004. *Address:* c/o CEA/Saclay (Essonne), 91191 Gif-sur-Yvette Cédex, France. *Telephone:* 1-69-08-74-12 (office); 1-45-65-09-24 (home). *E-mail:* klein@dsmdir.cea.fr (office). *Website:* www.cea.fr.

KLEIN, Joseph (Joe), AB; American journalist and writer; b. 7 Sept. 1946, New York; m. Janet Eklund 1967 (divorced 1975); two s. *Education:* University of Pennsylvania. *Career:* reporter, Beverly/Peabody Times, Beverly, Massachusetts, 1969–72, WGBH-TV, Boston, 1972; News Ed., Real Paper, Boston, 1972–74; Assoc. Ed., 1974–78, Washington Bureau Chief, 1976, Rolling Stone Magazine; Senior Ed., 1992–96, Contributing Ed., 1996–, Newsweek Magazine; Columnist, New Yorker Magazine, 1996–. *Publications:* Woody Guthrie: A Life, 1980; Payback: Five Marines After Vietnam, 1984; Primary Colors: A Novel of Politics (published anonymously), 1996; The Running Mate, 2000; The Natural (non-fiction), 2001. Contributions: newspapers and magazines. *Honours:* Robert Kennedy Journalism Award 1973, Washington Monthly Journalism Award 1989, National Headliner Award 1994; Hon. DLitt (Franklin and Marshall Coll., Lancaster, PA) 1990.

KLEIN, Naomi; Canadian writer, journalist and social critic; b. 1970, Montréal. *Career:* syndicated columnist for The Globe and Mail, Canada and The Guardian, UK; contrib. to numerous publs including The Nation, The Guardian, New Statesman, Newsweek International, New York Times, Village Voice and Ms. Magazine; campaigner on issues of devt econs, corp. accountability and consumer affairs; has travelled throughout N America, Asia, Latin America and Europe giving lectures and workshops on corp. branding and econ. globalization 1996–; frequent media commentator; guest lecturer at Harvard Univ., Yale Univ., McGill Univ. and New York Univ. *Publication:* No Logo: Taking Aim at the Brand Bullies (translated into 22 languages) 2000, The Shock Doctrine: The Rise of Disaster Capitalism 2007. *Honours:* Canadian Nat. Business Book Award 2001, Le Prix Médiations, France 2001, Ms. Magazine's Women of the Year Award 2001. *Address:* c/o Random House of Canada Ltd., 1 Toronto Street, Unit 300, Toronto, Ont., M5C 2V6, Canada (office). *E-mail:* admin@nologo.org (office). *Website:* www.nologo.org (office).

KLEIN, Richard; American writer; b. 1941, USA. *Publications:* Cigarettes are Sublime, 1993; Eat Fat, 1996; Pop Surrealism (non-fiction, with Dominique Nahas), 1998; Jewelry Talks, 2001.

KLEIN, Robin; Australian writer; b. 28 Feb. 1936, Kempsey, NSW; d. of Lesley Macquarie and Mary (née Cleaver) McMaugh; m. Karl Klein 1956 (divorced 1980); two s. two d. *Education:* Newcastle Girls' High School, NSW. *Career:* has written numerous children's books. *Publications include:* The Giraffe in Pepperell Street 1978, Honoured Guest 1979, Thing (Jr Book of the Year, Children's Book Council of Australia 1983) 1982, Sprung! 1982, Junk Castle 1983, Penny Pollard's Diary 1983, Oodoolay 1983, Hating Alison Ashley (Special Award, W Australian Young Readers' Book Award, Winner Sr Category, KOALA Awards 1987) 1984, Thalia the Failure 1984, Thingnapped 1984, Brock and the Dragon 1984, Penny Pollard's Letters 1984, Ratbags and Rascals 1984, People Might Hear You 1984, Seeing Things 1984, Hating Alison Ashley 1985, Battlers 1985, Halfway Across the Country and Turn Left 1985, The Enemies 1985, Annabel's Ghost 1985, Snakes and Ladders 1985, Boss of the Pool 1986, The Princess Who Hated It 1986, Games 1986, Penny Pollard in Print 1986, Halfway Across the Galaxy and Turn Left 1986, The Lonely Hearts Club 1987, Robin Klein's Crookbook 1987, Get Lost 1987, The Last Pirate 1987, Christmas 1987, I Shot an Arrow 1987, Birk the Berserker 1987, Stanley's Smile 1988, Annabel's Party 1988, Irritating Irma 1988, The Kidnapping of Clarissa Montgomery 1988, Jane's Mansion 1988, Laurie Loved Me Best 1988, Penny Pollard's Passport 1988, Dear Robin 1988, Against the Odds 1989, The Ghost in Abigail Terrace 1989, Came Back to Show You I Could Fly (Human Rights Award for Literature 1989, Australian Children's Book of the Year Award, Older Readers 1990, named a White Raven Book at Bologna Children's Book Fair 1990) (filmed as Say A Little Prayer 1993) 1989, Penny Pollard's Guide to Modern Manners 1989, Tearaways 1990, Boris And Borsch (Honour Book, Australian Children's Book Council Awards 1991) 1990, The Listmaker 1990 (South Australian Festival Award for Literature 1990), All in the Blue Unclouded Weather 1991, Dresses of Red and Gold 1992, Seeing Things 1993, Turn Right for Zyrgow 1994, The Sky in Silver Lace 1995. *Honours:* Dr hc (Univ. of Newcastle) 2004; Dromkeen Medal 1991. *Address:* c/o Curtis Brown Australia, PO Box 19 Paddington, NSW 2021, Australia.

KLEIN, Theodore Eibon Donald, AB, MFA; American writer and editor; b. 15 July 1947, New York, NY. *Education:* Brown University, Columbia University. *Career:* Ed.-in-Chief, Brown Daily Herald, 1968, Twilight Zone magazine, 1981–85, Crime Beat magazine, 1991–93; mem. Arthur Machen Society. *Publications:* The Ceremonies (novel), 1984; Dark Gods (story collection), 1985. Contributions: New York Times; New York Daily News; Washington Post Book World; Film column, Night Cry Magazine; Writer's Digest. *Honours:* British Fantasy Society Award for Best Novel 1985, World Fantasy Award for Best Novella 1986.

KLEIN, Zachary; American writer; b. 6 July 1948, New Brunswick, NJ; two s. *Education:* Hillel Acad., Jewish Educational Centre, Mirrer Yeshia and University of Wisconsin. *Publications:* Still Among the Living, 1990; Two Way Toll, 1991; No Saving Grace, 1994. *Honours:* Notable Book of 1990, New York Times; Ed.'s Choice, Drood Review.

KLEINZAHLER, August; American poet and writer; b. 10 Dec. 1949, Jersey City, NJ. *Education:* Univ. of Wisconsin, Madison, Univ. of Victoria. *Career:* Visiting Holloway Lecturer, Univ. of California, Berkeley 1987; Visiting Writer on Grad. Programs, Brown Univ. 1996, Univ. of Iowa 1997, Univ. of Texas 1999, 2006, Stanford Univ. 2000; mem. Poetry Soc. of America. *Publications:* A Calendar of Airs 1978, News and Weather: Seven Canadian Poets (ed.) 1982, Storm Over Hackensack 1985, On Johnny's Time 1988, Earthquake Weather 1989, Red Sauce, Whiskey and Snow 1995, Live from the Hong Kong Nile Club: Poems, 1975–1990 2000, The Strange Hours Travelers Keep (Griffin Int. Poetry Prize) 2004, Cutty, One Rock (prose) 2004; contrib. to newspapers and magazines. *Honours:* Gen. Electric Award for Younger Writers 1983, Bay Area Book Reviewers Award 1985, Guggenheim Fellowship 1989, Lila Wallace-Reader's Digest Writers' Awards 1991–94, Award in Literature American Acad. of Arts and Letters 1997, Commonwealth Club of Calif. Gold Medal for Poetry 2004, Griffin Int. Poetry Prize 2004.

KLIKOVAC, Igor; Bosnia and Herzegovina poet and editor; b. 16 May 1970. *Education:* University of Sarajevo. *Career:* Ed., Literary Review, Sarajevo, 1991–92; Ed., Stone Soup Magazine, London, 1995–. *Publications:* Last Days of Peking (poems), 1996. Contributions: Literary Review; Echo; Bridge; Transitions; Stone Soup; New Iowa Review. *Address:* 37 Chesterfield Road, London W4 3HQ, England.

KLÍMA, Ivan, MA; Czech author and dramatist; b. 14 Sept. 1931, Prague; s. of Vilém and Marta Klíma; m. Helena Malá-Klímová 1958; one s. one d. *Education:* Charles Univ., Prague. *Career:* Ed. Československy spisovatel (publishing house) 1958–63; Ed. Literárni noviny 1963–67, Literárni Listy 1968, Listy 1968–69; Visiting Prof. Univ. of Mich. Ann Arbor 1969–70, Univ. of Calif. at Berkeley 1998; freelance author publishing abroad 1970–89; columnist Lidove Noviny newspaper; mem. Council, Czech Writers 1989–; Ed.'s Council, Lidové noviny 1996–97; Exec. Pres. Czech PEN Centre 1990–93, Deputy Pres. 1993–. *Publications:* Ship Named Hope 1968, A Summer Affair 1972, My Merry Mornings (short stories) 1979, My First Loves (short stories) 1985, Love and Garbage 1987, Judge on Trial 1987, My Golden Trades (short stories) 1992, The Island of Dead Kings 1992, The Spirit of Prague (essays, jtly) 1994, Waiting for the Dark, Waiting for the Light 1996, The Ultimate Intimacy (novel) 1997, No Saints or Angels 1999, Between Security and Insecurity: Prospects for Tomorrow 2000, Lovers for a Day: New and Collected Stories on Love 2000, Karel Capek: Life and Work 2002, The Premier and the Angel (in Czech) 2004; plays: The Castle 1964, The Master 1967, The Sweetshop Myriam 1968, President and the Angel, Klara and Two Men 1968, Bridegroom for Marcela 1968, The Games 1975, Kafka and Felice 1986; contribs to magazines. *Honours:* Hostovský Award, New York 1985, George Theiner Prize (UK) 1993, Franz Kafka Prize 2002, Medal for Outstanding Service to the Czech Repub. 2002. *Address:* České Centrum Mezinárodního, PEN Klubu, ul. 28, října 9, 11000 Prague 1 (office); Na Dubině 5, 14700 Prague 4, Czech Republic (home). *Telephone:* (2) 24221926 (office).

KLINKOWITZ, Jerome, BA, MA, PhD; American writer and academic; *Professor of English, University of Northern Iowa;* b. 24 Dec. 1943, Milwaukee, WI; m. 1st Elaine Plaszynski 1966; m. 2nd Julie Huffman 1978; one s. one d. *Education:* Marquette Univ., Univ. of Wisconsin. *Career:* Asst Prof., Northern Illinois Univ. 1969–72; Assoc. Prof. 1972–75, Prof. of English 1975–, Univ. Distinguished Scholar 1985–, Univ. of Northern Iowa; Fellow, Univ. of Wisconsin 1968–69; mem. PEN American Center, MLA, Authors Guild, Eighth Air Force Historical Soc. *Publications:* Literary Disruptions 1975, The Life of Fiction 1977, The American 1960s 1980, The Practice of Fiction in America 1980, Kurt Vonnegut 1982, Peter Handke and the Postmodern Transformation 1983, The Self Apparent Word 1984, Literary Subversions 1985, The New American Novel of Manners 1986, Rosenberg/Barthes/Hassan: The Postmodern Habit of Thought 1988, Short Season and Other Stories 1988, Their Finest Hours: Narratives of the RAF and Luftwaffe in World War II 1989, Slaughterhouse-Five: Reinventing the Novel and the World 1990, Listen: Gerry Mulligan/An Aural Narrative in Jazz 1991, Donald Barthelme: An Exhibition 1991, Writing Baseball 1991, Structuring the Void 1992, Basepaths 1995, Yanks Over Europe 1996, Here at Ogallala State U. 1997, Keeping Literary Company 1998, Vonnegut in Fact 1998, Owning a Piece of the Minors 1999, With the Tigers Over China 1999, You've Got To Be Carefully Taught: Relearning and Relearning Literature 2001, The Vonnegut Effect 2004, Pacific Skies 2004, The Enchanted Quest of Dana and Ginger Lamb 2005; contrib. over 250 essays to Partisan Review, New Republic, Nation, American Literature; short stories to North American Review, Chicago Tribune, San Francisco Chronicle. *Honours:* PEN Syndicated Fiction Prizes 1984, 1985. *Address:* Department of English, University of Northern

Iowa, Cedar Falls, IA 50614-0502, USA. *Telephone:* (319) 273-2571 (office). *Fax:* (319) 273-5807 (office).

KLJUSEV, Nikola, DEconSc; Macedonian politician, economist and poet; b. 2 Oct. 1927, Stip; s. of Emanuel Kljusev and Lenka Kljusev; m. 1956; one s. one d. *Education:* Belgrade Univ. *Career:* Asst Researcher Inst. for Industrial Scientific Research, Skopje 1953–60; Sr Researcher Inst. of Econs, Skopje 1960–67; Prof. Skopje Univ. 1968–91; mem. Macedonian Acad. of Arts and Sciences; Ed.-in-Chief, Economic Interview 1971–78, Dean Faculty of Econs Skopje Univ.; Prime Minister of Macedonia 1991–92; researcher 1992–98; Minister of Defence 1998–99; Pres. Council VMRO-DPMNE independent; Head, Centre for Strategic Research. *Publications:* economics titles: Period of Activization of Investment 1963, Criteria and Methods for Evaluation of Economic Efficiency of Investments 1965, Usage of Productive Capacity in Industry 1967, Policy and Economics of Investment in Companies 1968, Efficiency of Investment in Macedonian Industry 1969, Selected Problems of Theory and Policy of Economic Development 1978, Theory and Policy of Economic Development 1979, Investments (Theory, Economics, Policy) 1980, Macedonian Economy in Transition 2002; poetry: Stone Island 1994, Antithesis 1994, The Power of the Word 1994, Ode to the Word 1995, Non-germinated Seed 1996, I am Sending Out Sunny Rays 2006; Selected Works (six vols) 2001; essays: trilogy: I Faith and Delusion, II Unslept Nights, III Visions 1997–2000, Dictionary of the Heart 2001; fiction: Lenman (novel) 2005. *Honours:* Golden Wreath Award, 13 Nov. Prize, 11 Oktomvri Award for life's work. *Address:* Dimitar Mirasciev 19, Skopje, Macedonia. *Telephone:* (2) 3235400 (office); (2) 773003 (home). *Fax:* (2) 3235541 (office). *E-mail:* nkljusev@manu.edu.mk (office). *Website:* www.manu.edu.mk (office).

KLUBACK, William, AB, AM, PhD; American writer and academic; b. 6 Nov. 1927, New York, NY. *Education:* George Washington University, Columbia University, Hebrew University, Jerusalem. *Publications:* Paul Valéry, 6 vols, 1987–97; Juan Ramon Jiménez, 1995; Benjamin Fondane, 1996; Emil Cioran, 1997; Léopold Sédar Senghor, 1997. Contributions: Midstream; Shofar; Archives de Philosophie.

KLUGE, Paul Frederick, BA, MA, PhD; American writer; *Writer-in-Residence, Kenyon College*; b. 24 Jan. 1942, Berkeley Heights, NJ; m. Pamela Hollie 1977. *Education:* Kenyon Coll., Univ. of Chicago. *Career:* Visiting Prof. 1987–97, writer-in-residence 1997–, Kenyon Coll. *Publications:* The Day That I Die 1976, Eddie and the Cruisers 1980, Season for War 1984, MacArthur's Ghost 1987, The Edge of Paradise: America in Micronesia 1991, Alma Mater: A College Homecoming 1993, Biggest Elvis 1996, Final Exam 2005; contrib. to periodicals. *Honours:* Fulbright Fellowship Univ. of Bucharest, Romania 2006. *Address:* c/o Department of English, Kenyon College, Gambler, OH 43022, USA. *Telephone:* (740) 427-5407 (office). *E-mail:* klugef@kenyon.edu (office). *Website:* www.pfkluge.com (office).

KLUGER, Steve; American writer and dramatist; b. 24 June 1952, Baltimore, MD. *Education:* University of Southern California. *Publications:* Changing Pitches, 1984; Lawyers Say the Darndest Things, 1990; Last Days of Summer, 1998. Stage Plays: Cafe 50s, 1988–89; James Dean Slept Here, 1989; Pilots of the Purple Twilight, 1989; Jukebox Saturday Night, 1990; Yank: World War II From The Guys Who Brought You Victory, 1990; Bullpen, 1990; Bye Bye Brooklyn, 1997. Films: Once Upon a Crime, 1992; Yankee Doodle Boys, 1996; Bye Bye Brooklyn, 1997; Almost Like Being in Love, 1997. Contributions: Chicago Tribune; Los Angeles Times; Sports Illustrated; Inside Sports; Diversion; Playboy; Science Digest.

KNAAK, Richard Allen, BA; American author; b. 28 May 1961, Chicago, IL. *Education:* University of Illinois. *Career:* mem. SFWA. *Publications:* The Legend of Huma, 1988; Firedrake, 1989; Ice Dragon, 1989; Kaz the Minotaur, 1990; Wolfhelm, 1990; Shadow Steed, 1990; The Shrouded Realm, 1991; Children of the Drake, 1991; Dragon Tome, 1992; The Crystal Dragon, 1993; King of the Grey, 1993; The Dragon Crown, 1994; Frostwing, 1995.

KNEALE, Matthew Nicholas Kerr, BA; British writer; b. 24 Nov. 1960, London, England; m. Shannon Russell 2000. *Education:* Magdalen Coll., Oxford. *Publications:* Whore Banquets 1987, Inside Rose's Kingdom 1989, Sweet Thames 1992, English Passengers 2000, Small Crimes in an Age of Abundance 2005, When We Were Romans 2007. *Honours:* Somerset Maugham Award 1988, John Llewellyn Rhys Prize 1993, Whitbread Book of the Year 2000, Prix Relay du roman d'évasion 2002. *Literary Agent:* Rogers, Coleridge & White Ltd, 20 Powis Mews, London, W11 1JN, England.

KNECHT, Robert Jean, MA, DLitt, FRHistS; British academic and writer; *Professor of French History Emeritus, University of Birmingham*; b. 20 Sept. 1926, London, England; m. 1st Sonia Hodge 1956 (died 1984); m. 2nd Maureen White 1986. *Education:* Univ. of London. *Career:* Asst Lecturer 1956–59, Lecturer 1959–68, Sr Lecturer in Modern History 1969–78, Reader 1978–85, Prof. of French History 1985–92, Prof. Emeritus and Hon. Sr Research Fellow 1992–, Univ. of Birmingham; Dir d'études associe, École des Hautes Études en Sciences Sociales, Paris 1994; mem. Société de l'Histoire de France, Soc. for Renaissance Studies (chair. 1989–92), Soc. for the Study of French History (co-founder 1987, chair. 1995–98). *Publications:* The Voyage of Sir Nicholas Carewe to the Emperor Charles V in the Year 1529 (ed.) 1959, Francis I and Absolute Monarchy 1969, Renaissance and Reformation 1969, The Fronde 1975, Francis I 1982, revised edn as Renaissance Warrior and Patron: The Reign of Francis I 1994, French Renaissance Monarchy: Francis I and Henry II 1984, The French Wars of Religion 1559–1598 1989, Richelieu 1991, The

Rise and Fall of Renaissance France 1996, Catherine de'Medici 1998, Un Prince de la Renaissance: François 1er et son royaume 1998, The French Civil Wars 2000, The French Religious Wars 2002, Catherine de Médicis: pouvoir royal, amour maternel 2003, The Valois Kings of France 1328–1589 2004; contrib. to reference works, scholarly books and professional journals. *Honours:* Chevalier, Ordre des Palmes Académiques. *Address:* 79 Reddings Road, Moseley, Birmingham, B13 8LP, England. *Telephone:* (121) 449-1916 (home).

KNIGHT, Andrew Stephen Bower; British editor and newspaper executive; *Director, News Corporation*; b. 1 Nov. 1939, s. of M. W. B. Knight and S. E. F. Knight; m. 1st Victoria Catherine Brittain 1966 (divorced); one s.; m. 2nd Begum Sabiha Rumani Malik 1975 (divorced 1991); two d.; m. 3rd Marita Georgina Phillips Crawley 2006. *Career:* Ed. The Economist 1974–86; Chief Exec. Daily Telegraph 1986–89, Ed.-in-Chief 1987–89; Chair. News Int. PLC 1990–94; Chair. Ballet Rambert 1984–87; Chair. Times Newspaper Holdings 1990–94; Dir News Corpn 1991–, Rothschild Investment Trust CP 1996–; Chair. Shipston Home Nursing 1996–; Chair. Jerwood Charity 2003–; mem. Advisory Bd Center for Econ. Policy Research, Stanford Univ., USA 1981–; Gov. mem. Council of Man. Ditchley Foundation 1982–; now farms in Warwicks. and Dannevirke, NZ. *Address:* Compton Scorpion Manor, Shipston-on-Stour, Warwickshire, CV36 4PJ, England (home).

KNIGHT, Arthur Winfield, AA, BA, MA; American academic (retd), writer, poet and film critic; b. 29 Dec. 1937, San Francisco, CA; m. Kit Duell 1976; one d. *Education:* Santa Rosa Junior Coll., San Francisco State Univ. *Career:* Prof. of English California Univ. of Pennsylvania 1966–93; film critic Russian River News, Guerneville, CA 1991–92, Anderson Valley Advertiser, Boonville, CA 1992–2006, Potpourri, Prairie Village, KS 1993–95; part-time Prof. Univ. of San Francisco 1995–2000, Univ. of Calif. at Davis 2004–05; ran writing workshop Western Nevada Community Coll., Yerington Sept. 2006; mem. Western Writers of America. *Publications:* A Marriage of Poets (with Kit Knight) 1984, King of the Beatniks 1986, The Beat Vision (co-ed.) 1987, Wanted! 1988, Basically Tender 1991, Cowboy Poems (aka Outlaws, Lawmen and Bad Women) 1993, Tell Me An Erotic Story 1993, The Darkness Starts Up Where You Stand 1996, The Secret Life of Jesse James 1996, The Cruelest Month 1997, Johnnie D. (novel) 2000, Blue Skies Falling (novel) 2001, James Dean's Diaries (novel) 2005; contrib. to reviews, quarterlies and journals. *Honours:* first place Joycean Lively Arts Guild Poetry Competition 1982. *Literary Agent:* c/o Nat Sobel, Sobel Weber Associates Inc, 146 E 19th Street, New York, NY 10003-2404, USA. *Address:* 303 Sherry Way, Yerington, NV 89447, USA (home). *Telephone:* (775) 463-4773 (home).

KNIGHT, Bernard, CBE, MB, BCh, MD, MRCP, FRCPath; British academic and writer; *Professor Emeritus of Forensic Pathology, University of Wales*; b. 3 May 1931, Cardiff, Wales. *Education:* Univ. of Wales, Gray's Inn. *Career:* Lecturer in Forensic Medicine, Univ. of London 1959–62; Medical Ed. Medicine, Science and the Law 1960–63; Lecturer, Coll. of Medicine, Univ. of Wales 1962–65, Sr Lecturer 1965–76, Reader to Prof. and Consultant in Forensic Pathology 1976–96, Prof. Emer. 1996–; Sr Lecturer in Forensic Pathology, Univ. of Newcastle 1965–68; Man. Ed. 1992–96, Pathology Ed. 1980–92, Forensic Science International; writer of fiction, non-fiction, biography, radio and TV scripts 1963–; mem. Crime Writers Asscn (CWA), The Medieval Murderers' Promotion Group. *Publications:* fiction: The Lately Deceased 1963, Thread of Evidence 1965, Mistress Murder 1968, Policeman's Progress 1969, Tiger at Bay 1970, Murder, Suicide or Accident 1971, Deg Y Dragwyddoldeb 1972, The Sanctuary Seeker 1998, The Poisoned Chalice 1998, Crowner's Quest 1998, The Awful Secret 1999, The Tinner's Corpse 2000, The Grim Reaper 2001, Fear in the Forest 2003, Brennan 2003, The Witch Hunter 2004, Figure of Hate 2005, The Tainted Relic (jtly) 2005, The Elixir of Death 2006, The Sword of Shame (jtly) 2006; non-fiction: Legal Aspects of Medical Practice 1972, Discovering the Human Body 1980, Forensic Radiology 1981, Lawyer's Guide to Forensic Medicine 1982, Sudden Death in Infancy 1983, Post-Modern Technicians Handbook 1984, Pocket Guide to Forensic Medicine 1985, Simpson's Forensic Medicine (10th edn) 1991, (11th edn) 1996, Forensic Pathology 1991, The Estimation of the Time Since Death (ed.) 1995; contrib. to Red Herrings (CWA monthly bulletin). *Honours:* Hon. DSc 1996, Hon. LLD 1998, Hon. DM 2000, Hon. PhD 2001; CWA Leo Harris Award 2005. *Address:* 26 Millwood, Cardiff, CF14 0TL, Wales (home). *Telephone:* (29) 2075-2798 (home). *E-mail:* knight@whodunnit.freeserve.co .uk (home). *Website:* mysite.freeserve.com/bernard_knight (home).

KNIGHT, David Marcus, MA, DPhil; British academic and writer; *Professor Emeritus of History and Philosophy of Science, University of Durham*; b. 30 Nov. 1936, Exeter, England; s. of Rev. Marcus Knight, subsequently Dean of Exeter, and Claire Hewett; m. Sarah Prideaux 1962; two s. four d. *Education:* Univ. of Oxford. *Career:* Lecturer, Univ. of Durham 1964–75, Sr Lecturer 1975–88, Reader 1988–91, Prof. of History and Philosophy of Science 1991–, now Prof. Emer.; Gen. Ed. Cambridge Science Biographies 1996–; mem. British Asscn, British Soc. for the History of Science (Pres. 1995–96), Royal Inst. *Publications:* Atoms and Elements: A Study of Theories of Matter in England in the 19th Century 1967, Natural Science Books in English 1600–1900 1972, Sources for the History of Science 1660–1914 1975, The Nature of Science: The History of Science in Western Culture since 1600 1977, Zoological Illustration: An Essay Towards a History of Printed Zoological Pictures 1977, The Transcendental Part of Chemistry 1978, Ordering the World: A History of Classifying Man 1981, The Age of Science: The Scientific World View in the 19th Century 1986, A Companion to the Physical Sciences

1989, Ideas in Chemistry: A History of the Science 1992, Humphry Davy: Science and Power 1992, Science in the Romantic Era 1998, The Making of the Chemist 1789–1914 1998, Science and Spirituality: The Volatile Connection 2003, Public Understanding of Science: A History of Communicating Scientific Ideas 2006; contrib. to scholarly books and journals. *Honours:* Templeton Foundation Award for teaching science and religion courses 1998, ACS Edelstein Award for history of chem. 2003. *Address:* Department of Philosophy, University of Durham, 50 Old Elvet, Durham, DH1 3HN, England (office). *Telephone:* (191) 334-6550 (office). *Fax:* (191) 334-6551 (office). *E-mail:* d.m.knight@durham.ac.uk (office). *Website:* www.durham.ac.uk/philosophy (office).

KNIGHT, Gareth (see Wilby, Basil Leslie)

KNIGHT, Kathleen (Kit), BA; Ukrainian writer and poet; b. 21 Sept. 1952, North Kingston, RI, USA; m. Arthur Winfield Knight 1976, one d. *Education:* Calif. University of Pennsylvania. *Career:* Co-Ed., Unspeakable Visions of the Individual, 1976–88; poet and columnist, Russian River News, Guerneville, Calif. 1988–92; poet/columnist, film critic, Russian River Times, Monte Rio, Calif. 1997–99; reviewer, Citizen's Echo, Calif. 2000–; film critic City Times, Gold River News, Citrus Heights, Calif. 2002–05; guest columnist Sr Spectrum, Sacramento, Calif. 2006–. *Publications:* A Marriage of Poets (with Arthur Winfield Knight) 1984, Women of Wanted Men 1994, The Greatest Kisser in the Northern Hemisphere (poems) 2004; contrib. to periodicals. *Honours:* Perry Award for Best Achievement in Poetry 1994.

KNIGHT, Steven, BA; British screenwriter and playwright; b. 5 Aug. 1959. *Education:* Univ. Coll., London. *Career:* writer and producer, Capital Radio 1983–87; writer for TV 1990–; now screenwriter. *Play:* The President of An Empty Room (Nat. Theatre, London) 2005. *Film screenplays:* Gypsy Woman 2001, Dirty Pretty Things (Variety Ten Screenwriters to Watch Award 2002, British Ind. Film Awards Best British Screenplay 2003, Edgar Award for Best Motion Picture Screenplay, Best Cinema South Bank Show Awards 2003, London Film Critics' Circle Best British Screenwriter Award 2003, Evening Standard British Film Award for Best Film, Humanitas Award 2004) 2002, Amazing Grace 2006. *Television writing includes:* Carrott's Commercial Breakdown (series) 1989, Canned Carrott (series) 1990, The Detectives (series, also dir) 1993, Who Wants To Be A Millionaire (series co-creator) 1998, All About Me (series, also creator) 2002. *Publications:* The Movie House (WHSmith Fresh Talent Award) 1993, Alphabet City 1995, Out of the Blue 1997. *Literary Agent:* c/o Natasha Galloway, PFD, Drury House, 34–43 Russell Street, London, WC2B 5HA, England. *Telephone:* (20) 7344-1000. *Fax:* (20) 7836-9543. *Website:* www.pfd.co.uk.

KNIGHT, William Edwards, BA, MA; American writer and publisher; b. 1 Feb. 1922, Tarrytown, NY; m. Ruth L. Lee 1946, two s. *Education:* Yale College, US Army Air Force, Yale University, Industrial College of the Armed Forces, State Dept Senior Seminar in Foreign Policy. *Career:* B-24 Co-Pilot, 1944–45; Foreign Service Officer, US Dept of State, 1946–75; Pres. and CEO, Araluen Press, 1982–; mem. Yale Club; Washington Independent Writers; Diplomatic and Consular Officers Retired; American Foreign Service Asscn; Army/Navy Country Club; Randolph Mountain Club. *Publications:* The Tiger Game, 1986; The Bamboo Game, 1993; Footprints in the Sand (light verse), 1995; Letter to the Twenty-Second Century: An American Family's Odyssey, 1998; The Devil's End Game, 2002. Contributions: journals.

KNIGHTLEY, Phillip George, AO; Australian journalist and writer; b. 23 Jan. 1929, Sydney, NSW; m. Yvonne Fernandes 1964; one s. two d. *Education:* Canterbury Boys' High School, Sydney. *Career:* reporter, Northern Star, Lismore 1948–49, Herald, Melbourne 1952–54; reporter, Daily Mirror, Sydney 1954–56, Foreign Corresp. 1956–60; Ed. Imprint, Mumbai 1960–62; Special Corresp., Sunday Times 1965–85; Visiting Prof. of Journalism, Univ. of Lincoln; mem. Soc. of Authors, Royal Overseas League, The Queen's Club. *Publications:* Philby: The Spy Who Betrayed a Generation (with Bruce Page and David Leitch) 1968, The Games (with Hugh Atkinson) 1968, The Secret Lives of Lawrence of Arabia (with Colin Simpson) 1969, The First Casualty: The War Correspondent as Hero Propagandist and Myth-Maker, Crimea to Vietnam 1975, Lawrence of Arabia 1976, The Death of Venice (with Stephen Fay) 1976, Suffer the Children (ed.) 1979, The Vestey Affair 1981, The Second Oldest Profession: The Spy as Bureaucrat, Patriot, Fantasist, and Whore 1986, An Affair of State: The Profumo Case and the Framing of Stephen Ward (with Caroline Kennedy) 1987, Philby: KGB Masterspy 1988, A Hack's Progress 1997, Australia: A Biography of a Nation 2000. *Honours:* Hon. Doctor of Arts (City Univ., Sydney Univ.); Overseas Press Club of America Award for Best Book on Foreign Affairs 1975, British Journalist of the Year Awards 1980, 1988. *Literary Agent:* c/o The Sayle Literary Agency, 8B Kings Parade, Cambridge, CB2 1SJ, England. *Telephone:* (1223) 303035. *Fax:* (1223) 301638. *Address:* 4 Northumberland Place, London W2 5BS, England (home). *Telephone:* (20) 7229-2179 (office). *Fax:* (20) 7229-9113 (office). *E-mail:* phillipgk@aol.com (home).

KNOPF, Alfred, Jr, AB; American publisher (retd); b. 17 June 1918, New York; s. of Alfred A. Knopf and Blanche Wolf; m. Alice Laine 1952; one s. two d. *Education:* Union Coll. *Career:* began career with Alfred A. Knopf Co. 1945–58; left to co-found Atheneum Publishers 1959, Chair. 1964–88; fmr Vice-Chair. Scribner Book Cos; fmr Sr Vice-Pres. Macmillan Publishing Co. *Address:* 530 East 72nd Street, Apartment 18F, New York, NY 10021, USA (home).

KNOPP, Lisa, BA, MA, PhD; American academic, writer and poet; b. 4 Sept. 1956, Burlington, IA; m. Colin Ramsay 1990 (divorced 1996); one s. one d. *Education:* Iowa Wesleyan College, Western Illinois University, University of Nebraska, Lincoln. *Career:* Teaching Asst, 1988–93, Lecturer, 1994–95, University of Nebraska, Lincoln; Asst Prof., Southern Illinois University, 1995; mem. Associated Writing Programs; Asscn for the Study of Literature and the Environment; Western Literature Asscn. *Publications:* Field of Vision (essays), 1996. Contributions: anthologies, newspapers and periodicals. *Honours:* Frank Vogel Scholar in Non-Fiction, Bread Loaf Writers Conference, 1992; Second Place, Society of Midland Authors, 1996.

KNOTT, William (Bill) Cecil, AA, BA, MA; American writer; b. 7 Aug. 1927, Boston, MA. *Education:* Boston University, SUNY at Oswego. *Career:* served US Air Force 1946–47; teacher, high schools in Connecticut, W Virginia, New Jersey and New York 1951–67; Prof. of English, SUNY at Potsdam 1967–82; mem. Western Writers of America (pres. 1980–81). *Publications:* Circus Catch 1963, Scatback 1964, Long Pass 1966, Night Pursuit 1966, Junk Pitcher 1967, Lefty's Long Throw 1967, High Fly to Center 1972, Fullback Fury 1974, The Craft of Fiction 1974, Taste of Vengeance 1975, Lyncher's Moon 1980, Longarm and the Railroaders 1980, Longarm on the Yellowstone 1980, The Golden Mountain 1980, Mission Code: King's Pawn 1981, The Trailsman Series (15 vols) 1984–86, The Golden Hawk Series (nine vols) 1986–88, Red Skies Over Wyoming 1986, The Texan 1987, Longarm and the Outlaws of Skull Canyon 1990, Longarm and the Tattooed Lady 1990. *Address:* c/o Western Writers of America, 209 E Iowa, Cheyenne, WY 82009, USA.

KNOX, Elizabeth, BA; New Zealand novelist; b. 15 Feb. 1959, Wellington; m. Fergus Barrowman 1989; one s. *Education:* Victoria University, Wellington. *Career:* Writer-in-Residence Victoria Univ. of Wellington 1997. *Publications:* After Z Hour 1987, Paremata 1989, Treasure 1992, Pomare 1994, Glamour and the Sea 1996, Tawa 1998, The Vintner's Luck 1998, Black Oxen 2000, The High Jump: A New Zealand Childhood 2000, Billie's Kiss 2001, Daylight 2003; essays: Origins, Authority and Imaginary Games 1988, Afraid 1991, Take As Prescribed 1991, The Receding Lion: A Vulgar Manifesto 1992, Going to the Gym 1992, Privacy: the Art of Julia Morison 1993, Heat 1993, Where We Stopped 1995, Reuben Avenue 1996, On Being Picked Up 2000, Getting Over It 1998, On the Am Track 2000, Assemble in Bunny Street 1999, A Stilled Cascade 1999, Beverages 2000, Provenance 2000, Starling 2002, The Love School 2003, Patience 2003, Hands and Hooves 2004; other: The Dig (short film script), 1994. *Honours:* Officer of the New Zealand Order of Merit; ICI Bursary 1988, PEN Award 1988, PEN Fellowship 1991, QEII Arts Council Scholarship in Letters 1993, New Zealand Book Council Lecture Award 1998, Katherine Mansfield Memorial Fellowship 1999, Deutz Medal for Fiction 1999, Arts Foundation of NZ Laureate Award 2000, Tasmania Pacific Region Prize 2001. *Literary Agent:* AP Watt Ltd, 20 John Street, London, WC1N 2DR, England. *Address:* PO Box 11-806, Wellington, New Zealand.

KNOX-JOHNSTON, Sir Robin, CBE, MA, RD, FRIN; British master mariner and author; b. 17 March 1939, Putney, London, England; m. 1962 (died 2003); one d. *Career:* mem. Younger Brother, Trinity House; Honourable Company of Master Mariners; Royal Institute of Navigation; National Maritime Museum, Cornwall. *Publications:* A World of My Own, 1969; Sailing, 1974; Twilight of Sail, 1978; Last But Not Least, 1978; Seamanship, 1986; The BOC Challenge 1986–87, 1987; The Cape of Good Hope, 1989; The History of Yachting, 1990; The Columbus Venture, 1991; Sea Ice Rock (with Chris Bonington), 1992; Cape Horn, 1994; Beyond Jules Verne, 1995. Contributions: Yachting World; Cruising World; Guardian. *Honours:* Hon. DTech (Nottingham Trent Univ.) 1993. *Literary Agent:* Curtis Brown Ltd, Haymarket House, 28–29 Haymarket, London, SW1Y 4SP, England. *Telephone:* (20) 7393-4400. *Fax:* (20) 7393-4401. *E-mail:* info@curtisbrown.co.uk. *Website:* www.curtisbrown.co.uk. *Address:* St Francis Cottage, Torbryan, Newton Abbot, Devon TQ12 5UR, England (home).

KNUDSEN, Lisbeth; Danish newspaper editor and executive manager; b. 7 June 1953, Copenhagen. *Career:* Political Ed. Berlingske Tidende 1975–84, Business Ed. 1984–88, Sunday Ed. 1988–89, Ed. 1989–90; Ed.-in-Chief and Exec. Man. Apressen/Det Friktuelt 1990–98; Man. Dir Danish Broadcasting Corpn 1998–. *Address:* DR & DR TV, TV-Byen, 2860 Soborg, Denmark. *E-mail:* dr@dr.dk.

KNUDSON, Rozanne R.; American writer; b. 1 June 1932, Washington, DC. *Education:* BA, Brigham Young University, 1954; MA, University of Georgia, 1958; PhD, Stanford University, 1967. *Publications:* Selected Objectives in the English Language Arts (with Arnold Lazarus) 1967, Sports Poems (ed. with P. K. Ebert) 1971, Zanballer 1972, Jesus Song 1973, You Are the Rain 1974, Fox Running 1974, Zanbanger 1977, Zanboomer 1978, Weight Training for the Young Athlete (with F. Colombo) 1978, Starbodies (with F. Colombo) 1978, Rinehart Lifts 1980, Just Another Love Story 1982, Speed 1982, Muscles 1982, Punch 1982, Zan Hagen's Marathon 1984, Babe Didrikson 1985, Frankenstein's 10 K 1987, Martina Navratilova 1986, Rinehart Shouts 1986, Julie Brown 1987, American Sports Poems (ed. with May Swenson) 1987, The Love Poems of May Swenson (ed. and selector) 1992, 2004, The Wonderful Pen of May Swenson 1993, The Complete Poems to Solve (ed. and selector) 1993, Nature (ed. and selector) 1994, May Out West (ed. and selector) 1994, May Swenson: A Poet's Life in Photos 1996. *Address:* 73 Blvd, Sea Cliff, NY 11579, USA (home). *Telephone:* (516) 244-1704 (home). *E-mail:* cberglie@netscape.net (home).

KOCH, Christopher John, BA, DLitt; Australian author; b. 16 July 1932, Hobart, Tasmania; m. Irene Vilnonis 1960, one s. *Education:* University of Tasmania. *Publications:* The Boys in the Island, 1958; Across the Sea Wall, 1965; The Doubleman, 1965; The Year of Living Dangerously, 1978; Crossing the Gap (essays), 1987; Highways to War, 1995; Out of Ireland, 1999. *Honours:* National Book Council Award for Australian Literature, 1979; Miles Franklin Prize, 1985, 1996; AO, 1995. *Address:* c/o 16 Winton Street, Warrawee, Sydney, NSW 2074, Australia.

KOCH, Joanne Barbara, (Joanna Z. Adams), BA, MA, PhD; American writer and dramatist; *Associate Professor of English, National-Louis University, Chicago;* b. 28 March 1941, Chicago, IL; m. Lewis Z. Koch 1964; one s. two d. *Education:* Cornell Univ., Columbia Univ., Southern Illinois Univ. *Career:* syndicated columnist, with Lewis Z. Koch, for Newspaper Enterprise Asscn 1971–75; Dir of Graduate Writing Program, Assoc. Prof. of English, National-Louis Univ., Chicago; Guest Lecturer on Women's Studies and Screenwriting, Northwestern Univ., Columbia Coll., Chicago; mem. Dramatists' Guild, Soc. of Midland Authors, Women in Film, Women in Theatre. *Plays:* Haymarket: Footnote to a Bombing (Piscator Foundation-SIU Int. Playwriting Award) 1985, Teeth (Illinois Arts Council grant) 1988, Hearts in the Wood (musical, with James Lucas) (Illinois Arts Council Playwriting Fellowship) 1992, Saul Bellow's Stories on Stage: A Silver Dish and The Old System (adaptations, with Sarah Cohen) (Streisand Festival Award) 1993, Nesting Dolls (PBS Broadcast, SIU Best New Play Award) 1994, Sophie, Totie & Belle (with Sarah Cohen) 1995, Safe Harbor 1999, A Leading Woman (Driehaus Foundation grant) 2002, Henrietta Szold: Woman of Valor (with Sarah Cohen) (Brandeis Univ. Hadassah Inst. Research grant) 2002, Courage Like a Wild Horse 2004, American Klezmer (musical, with Sarah Cohen, Owen Kalt, Ilya Levinson) 2004, Soul Sisters (with Sarah Cohen) 2005. *Publications:* The Marriage Savers (with Lewis Z. Koch) 1976, Readings in Psychology Today (contributor) 1978, Children: development through adolescence (with Allison Clarke-Stewart) 1983, Marriage and Family (with Diane Levande, Lewis Z. Koch) 1983, Child Psychology (with Clarke-Stewart) 1985, Good Parents for Hard Times (with Linda Freeman) 1991, Shared Stages: the Drama of Blacks and Jews (co-ed.) 2005; novels, as Joanna Z. Adams: Makeovers 1987, Rushes 1988, Intimate Connections 1989. *Honours:* Family Service Asscn award for writing 1974, American Psychoanalytic Asscn/Harris Media Award for Psychology Today article 1978. *Address:* 343 Dodge Avenue, Evanston, IL 60202, USA. *Telephone:* (847) 864-5357. *Fax:* (847) 864-2312. *E-mail:* jkoch@nl .edu.

KOEGLER, Hans Herbert, MA, PhD; German academic and writer; *Associate Professor of Philosophy and Graduate Studies Coordinator, University of North Florida;* b. 13 Jan. 1960, Darmstadt. *Education:* Johann Wolfgang von Goethe Univ., Frankfurt am Main. *Career:* Dissertation Fellow, German Fellowship Foundation, 1987–91; Research Fellow, Visiting Scholar, Northwestern Univ., New School for Social Research, Univ. of California at Berkeley, 1989–90; Asst Prof., Univ. of Illinois at Urbana-Champaign, 1991–97; Asst Prof., 1997–99, Assoc. Prof. of Philosophy Univ. of North Florida 1999–; Visiting Prof. Univ. of Boston, USA 1997, Charles Univ., Prague, Czech Repub. 2003, Alpe Adria Univ., Klagenfurt 2004. *Publications:* Die Macht des Dialogs: Kritische Hermeneutik nach Gadamer, 1992; Michel Foucault: Ein antihumanistischer Aufklarer, 1994, 2004; The Power of Dialogue: Critical Hermeneutics After Gadamer and Foucault, 1996, 1999; Empathy and Agency: The Problem of Understanding in the Human Sciences, 2000; contrib. to journals, reviews, periodicals and magazines. *Address:* c/o Department of Philosophy, University of North Florida, 4567 St Johns Bluff Road S, Jacksonville, FL 32224-2645, USA.

KOELB, Clayton, BA, MA, PhD; American academic and writer; *Guy B. Johnson Professor and Chairman, Department of Germanic Languages, University of North Carolina, Chapel Hill;* b. 12 Nov. 1942, New York, NY; m. 1st Susan J. Noakes 1979; one s. one d.; m. 2nd Janice Koelb (née Hewlett) 1999. *Education:* Harvard Univ. *Career:* Asst Prof., Assoc. Prof., Prof. of German and Comparative Literature, Univ. of Chicago 1969–91, Chair. Dept of Germanic Languages 1978–82; Visiting Prof., Purdue Univ. 1984–85, Princeton Univ. 1985–86; Visiting Eugene Falk Prof., Univ. of N Carolina, Chapel Hill 1990, Guy B. Johnson Prof. 1991–, Chair. Dept of Germanic Languages 1997–; mem. Modern Language Asscn of America, Int. Asscn for Philosophy and Literature, Semiotics Soc. of America, Kafka Soc. of America, Asscn of Literary Scholars and Critics, German Studies Asscn, American Asscn of Teachers of German. *Publications:* The Incredulous Reader 1984, Thomas Mann's Goethe and Tolstoy 1984, The Current in Criticism 1987, Inventions of Reading 1988, The Comparative Perspective on Literature 1988, Kafka's Rhetoric 1989, Nietzsche as Postmodernist 1990, Thomas Mann's Death in Venice: A Critical Edition 1994, Legendary Figures 1998, Camden House History of German Literature: The 19th Century 2005, A Franx Kafka Encyclopedia 2005; contribs to professional journals. *Honours:* Germanistic Soc. of America Fellow 1964–65, Woodrow Wilson Foundation Fellow 1965, Danforth Foundation Fellow 1965–69, Susan Anthony Potter Prize, Harvard Univ. 1970, Guggenheim Fellowship 1993–94. *Address:* University of North Carolina, 414 Dey Hall, Chapel Hill, NC 27599, USA (office). *Telephone:* (919) 962-0470 (office). *E-mail:* ckoelb@email.unc.edu (office). *Website:* www.unc .edu/depts/german/personnel/koelb-p.html (office).

KOESTENBAUM, Wayne, BA, MA, PhD; American academic, poet, writer and critic; *Distinguished Professor of English, City University of New York;* b. 20 Sept. 1958, San Jose, CA. *Education:* Harvard Coll., Johns Hopkins Univ.,

Princeton Univ. *Career:* Assoc. Prof. of English, Yale Univ. 1988–97; Co-Ed., The Yale Journal of Criticism 1991–96; Prof. of English, CUNY 1997–, now Distinguished Prof.; Whiting Fellowship in the Humanities 1987–88; Yale Univ. Morse Fellowship 1990–91. *Publications:* Double Talk: The Erotics of Male Literary Collaboration 1989, Ode to Anna Moffo and Other Poems 1990, The Queen's Throat: Opera, Homosexuality, and the Mystery of Desire 1993, Rhapsodies of a Repeat Offender 1994, Jackie Under My Skin: Interpreting an Icon 1995, The Milk of Inquiry 1999, Cleavage: Essays on Sex, Stars and Aesthetics 2000, Andy Warhol 2001, Model Homes 2004, Moira Orfei in Aigues-Mortes 2004, Best-Selling Jewish Porn Films 2006; other: Jackie O (libretto for the opera by Michael Daugherty) 1997; contribs to anthologies, books, newspapers, reviews, quarterlies and journals. *Honours:* Twentieth Century Literature Prize in Literary Criticism 1988, co-winner Discovery/The Nation Poetry Contest 1989, New York Times Book Review Notable Book 1993, Whiting Writer's Award 1994. *Address:* c/o English Program, Graduate School and University Center, City University of New York, 365 Fifth Avenue, New York, NY 10016, USA.

KOGAN, Norman, BA, PhD; American academic (retd) and writer; b. 15 June 1919, Chicago, IL; m. Meryl Reich 1946; two s. *Education:* Univ. of Chicago. *Career:* Faculty 1949–88, Dir, Center for Italian Studies 1967–76, Univ. of Connecticut; Visiting Prof., Univ. of Rome 1973, 1979, 1987; Pres., Conference Group on Italian Politics 1975–77; Chair., Southern Europe Commission, Council for the Int. Exchange of Scholars 1976–80; mem. Soc. for Italian Historical Studies (exec. sec., treas. 1966–76), Connecticut State Chapter of the Fulbright Asscn (pres. 1990–95). *Publications:* Italy and the Allies 1956, The Government of Italy 1962, The Politics of Italian Foreign Policy 1963, A Political History of Postwar Italy 1966, Storia Politica dell' Italia Repubblicana 1982, A Political History of Italy: The Postwar Years 1983; contrib. to Yale Law Journal, Il Ponte, Western Political Quarterly, Journal of Politics, Comparative Politics, Indiana Law Journal. *Honours:* Knight, Order of Merit of the Italian Republic 1971; Career Achievement Award, Italian Studies 2003.

KOGAWA, Joy Nozomi, CM; Canadian writer; b. 6 June 1935, Vancouver, BC; d. of the late Gordon Goichi and Lois Masui (née Yao) Nakayama; one s. one d. *Education:* R. I. Baker School, Alberta and Univ. of Alberta. *Career:* writer, Prime Minister's Office 1974–76; Writer-in-Residence, Univ. of Ottawa 1978–; Dir Canadian Civil Liberties Asscn; mem. Writers' Union of Canada, PEN Int.; Fellow Ryerson Polytechnical Univ. 1991; fmr Pres. Toronto Dollar Community Projects, Inc. *Publications:* poetry: The Splintered Moon 1967, A Choice of Dreams 1974, Jericho Road 1977, Woman in the Woods 1985, A Song of Lilith 2000, A Garden of Anchors 2003; novels: Obasan (Books in Canada First Novel Award 1981, Canadian Authors' Asscn Book of the Year Award 1982, Notable Book, American Library Asscn 1982, American Book Award, Before Columbus Foundation 1983, Periodical Distributors of Canada and Foundation for the Advancement of Canadian Letters Award for Paperback Fiction 1983) 1981; children's fiction: Naomi's Road 1986; novels: Itsuka 1992, The Rain Ascends 1995, Emily Kato 2005. *Honours:* Hon. LLD (Lethbridge) 1991, (Simon Fraser) 1993, (Queen's) 2003, (Windsor) 2003; Hon. DLitt (Guelph) 1992, (British Columbia) 2001; Hon. DD (Knox Coll., Toronto) 1999; Urban Alliance Race Relations Award 1994, Grace MacInnis Visiting Scholar Award 1995, Asscn of Asian-American Studies Lifetime Achievement Award 2001, Nat. Asscn of Japanese Canadians Nat. Award 2001. *Address:* #1418, 25 The Esplanade, Toronto, Ontario, M5E 1W5 (home); #308, 1050 Jervis Street, Vancouver, BC, V6E 2C1, Canada (home). *Telephone:* (416) 363-9130 (Toronto) (home); (604) 687-3554 (Vancouver) (home). *Fax:* (416) 363-9130 (Toronto) (home); (604) 687-3554 (Vancouver) (home). *E-mail:* joy.kogawa@ rogers.ca (home).

KOHOUT, Pavel; Czech novelist, playwright and poet; b. 20 July 1928, Prague; m. 1st Alena Vránová; m. 2nd Anna Kohoutová; m. 3rd Jelena Mašínová 1970; one s. one d. *Career:* fmr mem. Communist Party of Czechoslovakia, subsequently reformist, then dissident; co-author Charter 77 human rights manifesto; expelled to Austria; playwright Divadlo na Vinohradech theatre 1963–66; ed. of periodicals; worked at Assoc. Centre for Economics and Politics (CEP), Prague; mem. Deutsche Akademie für Sprache und Schöpfung. *Plays:* Poor Murderer (Ethel Barrymore Theater, New York, USA) 1976, Fool's Mate (New End Theatre, Hampstead, London, UK) 1990, Fire in the Basement (Traverse Theatre, Edinburgh, UK) 1998. *Publications:* Taková láska (Such a Love) 1958, Dvanáct: Dvanáct obrazu ze zivota dvanácti mladých hercu (Divadlo) 1963, Z deníku kontrarevolucionáře (From the Diary of a Counterrevolutionary) 1968, Pat aneb Hra králů (Stalemate or the Game of Kings 1978, Atest (Testimonial) 1979, Katyne 1980, The Hangwoman 1981, Kde je zakopán pes (Where the Dog is Buried, memoirs) 1987, Ecce Constantia 1990, I Am Snowing: The Confessions of a Woman of Prague 1994, The Widow Killer 1998; contrib. to numerous anthologies and literary and political periodicals. *Honours:* Grosser Staatspreis für Europäische Literatur, Austria.

KOHUT, Thomas August, MA, PhD; American academic and writer; b. 11 March 1950, Chicago, IL; m. Susan Neeld Kohut 1975; one s. one d. *Education:* Oberlin Coll., Univ. of Minnesota, Cincinnati Psychoanalytic Inst. *Career:* Asst Clinical Prof. of Psychiatry, Univ. of Cincinnati 1982–84; Asst Prof., Williams Coll. 1984–90, Assoc. Prof. 1990–95, Sue and Edgar Wachenheim III Prof. of History 1995–, Dean of the Faculty 2000–, Acting Provost 2003; Guest Prof., Univ. of Munich 1988, Univ. of Siegen 1991–92, 1995–96; mem. American Historical Asscn, German Studies Asscn; mem. Bd of Trustees, Austen Riggs Center, Stockbridge, MA. *Publications:* Wilhelm II and the

Germans: A Study in Leadership 1991; contribs to scholarly books, journals and anthologies. *Honours:* Deutscher Akademischer Austauschdienst Grant 1978–79, Int. Research and Exchanges Board Grant 1979, Fulbright Scholarship 1987–88, Köhler Foundation Grant 1996. *Address:* c/o Department of History, Williams College, Williamstown, MA 01267, USA. *Telephone:* (413) 597-4351 (office). *E-mail:* thomas.a.kohut@williams.edu (office).

KOŁAKOWSKI, Leszek, DPhil, FBA; Polish/British academic (retd); b. 23 Oct. 1927, Radom; s. of Jerzy Kołakowski and Lucyna (née Pietrusiewicz) Kołakowska; m. Tamara Dynenson 1949; one d. *Education:* Łódź and Warsaw Univs. *Career:* Asst (logic), Łódź Univ. 1947–49; Asst Warsaw Univ. 1950–54, Chair. Section of History of Philosophy 1959–68 (expelled by govt for political reasons); Visiting Prof. McGill Univ., Montréal 1968–69; Prof. Univ. of Calif., Berkeley 1969–70; Sr Research Fellow, All Souls Coll., Oxford Univ. 1970–1995, Fellow Emer.; Prof. Yale Univ. 1975, Univ. of Chicago 1981–94; mem. American Acad. of Arts and Sciences, British Acad., Bayerische Akad. der Künste, Institut Int. de Philosophie, Acad. Europaea, Acad. Universelle des Cultures, Polish Acad. of Sciences; mem. PEN Club, Polish Philosophical Soc., Polish Writers Asscn, Philosophical Soc., Oxford. *Publications include:* Individual and Infinity (in Polish) 1958, Marxism and Beyond 1968, Chrétiens sans église 1968, Positivist Philosophy 1970, Conversations with the Deveil 1972, Positivist Philosophy 1972, Die Gegenwärtigkeit des Mythos 1973, Husserl and the Search for Certitude 1975, Leben trotz Geschichte 1977, Main Currents of Marxism 1976–78 (three vols), Religion If There Is No God 1982, Bergson 1985, Metaphysical Horror 1988, Modernity on Endless Trial 1990, God Owes Us Nothing 1994, Freedom, Fame, Lying and Betrayal 1999, My Correct Views on Everything (in Polish) 1999, Mini-Lectures on Maxi-Issues (three vols in Polish, trans in various languages), In Praise of Inconsistency (three vols in Polish), What the Greek Philosophers Ask us About (in Polish, Vol. 1), The Eyes of Spinoza 2004; several fairy tales, dramas and Biblical stories. *Honours:* Hon. Fellow All Souls Coll., Oxford; Dr hc (Bard Coll., New York, Reed Coll., Portland, USA, State Univ. of New York, Adelphi Univ., New York, Łódź, Gdańsk, Sczecin, Wroclaw); Alfred Jurzykowski Award 1969, Friedenpreis des deutschen Buchhandels 1977, Prix Européen d'Essai Zurich 1980, Prix d'Erasme and McArthur Foundation Prize 1983, Jefferson Award 1986, Prix Tocqueville 1994, Bloch Prize 1995, White Eagle Order 1997, Premio Nonino 1998, John W. Kluge Prize 2003. *Address:* 77 Hamilton Road, Oxford, OX2 7QA, England.

KOLBE, Uwe; German poet, writer and translator; b. 17 Oct. 1957, Berlin; three s. *Education:* Johannes R. Becher Inst., Leipzig. *Career:* early work published in Sinn und Form and Mitteldeutsche Verlag journals; Co-Ed. Mikado literary journal 1982–87; Visiting Lecturer Univ. of Austin, Texas and Univ. of Vienna; Dir Studio of Literature and Theatre, Tübingen Univ. 1997–2004; poet-in-residence Oberlin Coll., Ohio 2007. *Publications:* poetry: Hineingeboren (Born Into) 1980, Abschiede und andere Liebesgedichte (Farewells and Other Love Poems) 1983, Bornholm II 1986, Nicht wirklich platonisch (Not Really Platonic) 1994, Die Situation 1994, Vineta 1998, Die Farben des Wassers (The Colour of Water) 2001, Sailor's Home (co-author) 2005; essays: Vaterlandkanal. Ein Fahrtenbuch (Fatherland-Channel: A Logbook) 1990, Renegatentermine: 30 Versuche, die eigene Erfahrung zu behaupten (Renegate's Appointments: 30 Attempts at Asserting One's Own Experience) 1998; novel: Thrakische Spiele 2005. *Honours:* City of Berlin (West) Arts Award 1987, Friedrich Hölderlin Award, Bad Homburg 1987, Henschel Translation Award 1988, Nicolas-Born Prize, Munich 1988, Berlin Literature Award 1992, Friedrich Hölderlin Award, Tübingen 1993, Literaturhaeuser Award 2006.

KOLLER, James, BA; American writer, poet and artist; b. 30 May 1936, Oak Park, IL; m. (divorced); two s. four d. *Education:* North Central Coll., Naperville, IL. *Publications:* poetry: Two Hands 1965, Brainard and Washington Street Poems 1965, The Dogs and Other Dark Woods 1966, Some Cows 1966, I Went To See My True Love 1967, California Poems 1971, Bureau Creek 1975, Poems for the Blue Sky 1976, Messages-Botschaften 1977, Andiamo 1978, O Didn't He Ramble-O ware er nicht unhergezogen 1981, Back River 1981, One Day at a Time 1981, Great Things Are Happening-Grossartoge Dige passieren 1984, Give the Dog a Bone 1986, Graffiti Lyriques (with Franco Beltrametti), graphics and texts 1987, Openings 1987, Fortune 1987, Roses Love Sunshine 1989, This Is What He Said (graphics and texts) 1991, In the Wolf's Mouth, Poems 1972–88 1995, The Bone Show 1996, Travaux de Voirie 1997, Iron Bells 1999, After Days of Rain 1999, Close to the Ground 2000, Looking for his Horses 2003, Crows Talk to Him 2003, Hungry Wolf 2004, Ashes & Embers 2004, Snows Gone By 2004; other: Messages 1972, Working Notes 1960–82 1985, Gebt dem alten Hund'nen Knochen (Essays, Gedichte and Prosa 1959–85) 1986, The Natural Order (essay and graphics) 1990, Like It Was (selected poems, prose and fiction) 2000, Un Reading di Poesie 2002; fiction: If You Don't Like Me You Can Leave Me Alone 1974, Shannon Who Was Lost Before 1975, The Possible Movie (with Franco Beltrametti) 1997. *Address:* PO Box 629, Brunswick, ME 04011, USA.

KOLM, Ronald Akerson, (Rank Cologne), BA; American writer, editor and publisher; *Manager, Coliseum Bookstore, New York City*; b. 21 May 1947, Pittsburgh, PA; m. Donna Sterling 1984; two s. *Education:* Albright Coll. *Publications:* Plastic Factory 1989, Welcome to the Barbecue 1990, Suburban Ambush 1991, Rank Cologne 1991, The Unbearables (ed.) 1995, Crimes of the Beats (ed.) 1998, Help Yourself! (ed.) 2002, Neo Phobe 2006, Up is Up, But So is Down 2006. *Honours:* papers in the Fales Collection, New York Univ. Library, also archived in Ohio State Univ.; currently Man. Coliseum Bookstore, New York City. *Address:* 30–73 47th Street, Long Island City, NY 11103, USA (home).

KOLYADA, Nikolai Vladimirovich; Russian actor, writer and playwright; b. 4 Dec. 1957, Presnogorkovka, Kustanai region, Kazakhstan. *Education:* Sverdlovsk Higher School of Theatre Arts. *Career:* actor Sverdlovsk Drama theatre 1972–77; mem. USSR Writers' Union 1989–; teacher Yekaterinburg Inst. of Theatre Arts 1998–; Ed.-in-Chief Ural Journal 1999–. *Plays:* Forfeits, Our Unsociable Sea or A Fool's Vessels, Barakb Lashkaldak, Parents' Day, Slingshot, Chicken, Polonaise, Mannequin, A Tale About the Dead Tsarina, Persian Lilac; *Theatre:* Chicken Blindness. *Publications:* Plays for Beloved Theatre 1994. *Honours:* Sverdlovsk Komsomol Cttee Prize 1978, Teatralnaya Zhizn (magazine) Prize 1988, Schloss Solitude Academy Award, Stuttgart, Germany 1992. *Address:* Ural Journal, Malysheva str. 24, 620219 GSP 352, Yekaterinburg, Russia. *Telephone:* (3432) 759754. *Fax:* (3432) 769741. *E-mail:* editor@mail.ur/ru. *Website:* www.koljada.uralinfo.ru/.

KOMRIJ, Gerrit; Dutch poet, novelist, essayist and playwright; b. 30 March 1944, Winterswijk. *Education:* Univ. of Amsterdam. *Career:* fmr Ed., literary magazine Maatstaf; founder of the Poetry Club and poetry magazine Awater; Ed. the Sandwich series of poetry anthologies; he has written under the pseudonyms Gerrit Andriesse, Joris Paridon, Mr Pennewip and Griet Rijmrok; Dichter des Vaderlands (Dutch Poet Laureate) 2000–04 (resigned post early). *Publications:* Maagdenburgse halve bollen 1968, Alle vlees is als gras of Het knekelhuis op de dodenakker (Poetry Prize of Amsterdam 1970) 1969, Ik heb Goddank twee goede longen 1971, Tutti-frutti 1972, Daar is het gat van de deur 1974, Fabeldieren 1975, Horen, zien en zwijgen. Vreugdetranen over de treurbuis 1977, Capriccio 1978, Dood aan de grutters 1978, Heremijntijd, exercities en ketelmuziek 1978, Papieren tijgers (Busken Huet Prize 1979) 1978, De Nederlandse poëzie van de negentiende en twintigste eeuw in duizend en enige gedichten 1979, De stankbel van de Nieuwezijds 1979, Het schip De Wanhoop 1979, Averechts 1980, Verwoest Arcadië 1980, De os op de klokketoren (Herman Gorter Prize 1982) 1981, Onherstelbaar verbeterd 1981, De phoenix spreekt 1982, Gesloten circuit 1982, Het chemisch huwelijk 1982, De paleizen van het geheugen 1983, Dit helse moeras 1983, Het boze oog 1983, Alles onecht 1984, Schrijfrecept 1984, De gelukkige schizo 1985, Verzonken boeken 1986, Lof der simpelheid 1988, Humeuren en temperamenten 1989, De pagode 1990, Over de bergen 1990, Met het bloed dat drukinkt heet 1991, Over de noodzaak van tuinieren 1991, De ondergang van het regenwoud 1993, Dubbelster 1993, Intimiteiten 1993, Alle gedichten tot gisteren 1994, De Nederlandse poëzie van de twaalfde tot en met de zestiende eeuw in duizend en enige bladzijden 1994, De buitenkant 1995, Een zakenlunch in Sintra en andere Portugese verhalen 1996, In liefde bloeyende: de Nederlandse poëzie van de 12de tot de 20ste eeuw in tien gedichten: een voorproefje 1996, Kijken is bekeken worden 1996, Niet te geloven 1997, Pek en zwavel 1997, In liefde bloeyende: de Nederlandse poëzie van de twaalfde tot en met de twintigste eeuw in honderd en enige gedichten (Gouden Uil prize 1999) 1998, Lood en hagel 1998, De Afrikaanse poëzie in duizend en enige gedichten 1999, De Afrikaanse poëzie: 10 gedichten en een lexicon 1999, 52 sonnetten bij het verglijden van de eeuw 2000, Poëzie is geluk 2000, De klopgeest 2001, Hutten en paleizen 2001, Luchtspiegelingen 2001, Trou moet blycken, of Opnieuw in liefde bloeyende: de Nederlandse poëzie van de twaalfde tot en met de eenentwintigste eeuw in honderd en enige gedichten 2001, Vreemd pakhuis 2001, Vreemde melodieën 2001; contrib. to Vrij Nederland magazine, NRC Handelsblad newspaper. *Honours:* hon. doctorate (Univ. of Leiden) 2000; Cestoda Prize 1975, Kluwer-prijs 1983, P. C. Hooft-prijs 1993. *Literary Agent:* Bas Pauw, Singel 464, 1017 Amsterdam, Netherlands. *Telephone:* (20) 620 62 61. *Fax:* (20) 620 71 79. *E-mail:* b.pauw@nlpvf.nl.

KOMUNYAKAA, Yusef, BA, MA, MFA; American academic and poet; b. 29 April 1947, Bogalusa, LA; m. Mandy Sayer, 1985. *Education:* Univ. of Colorado, Colorado State Univ., Univ. of California at Irvine. *Career:* Correspondent, then Ed. military newspaper, The Southern Cross; fmrly taught poetry, New Orleans schools, and creative writing, Univ. of New Orleans; Visiting Prof., Indiana Univ. at Bloomington 1985, Assoc. Prof. of Afro-American Studies 1987–96; Prof. of Creative Writing, Princeton Univ. 1997–, now Prof. of the Council of the Humanities and Creative Writing Program; mem. Bd of Chancellors, Acad. of American Poets 1999–; many poetry readings. *Publications:* poetry: Dedications and Other Darkhorses 1977, Lost in the Bonewheel Factory 1979, Copacetic 1984, I Apologize for the Eyes in My Head (San Francisco Poetry Center Award 1986) 1986, Toys in a Field 1987, Dien Cai Dau (Dark Room Poetry Prize 1988) 1988, February in Sydney 1989, Magic City 1992, Neon Vernacular: New and Selected Poems 1977–1989 (Université de Rennes William Faulkner Prize 1994, Pulitzer Prize in Poetry 1994, Kingsley Tufts Poetry Award 1994) 1993, Thieves of Paradise (Southern Literary Asscn Hanes Poetry Prize 1997, Poetry Magazine Levinson Prize 1998, Poetry Soc. of America Shelley Memorial Award) 1998, Talking Dirty to the Gods 2000, Pleasure Dome: New and Collected Poems 1975–1999 2001, Scandalize My Name 2002, Taboo: Wishbone Trilogy Part One 2004; prose: The Jazz Poetry Anthology (ed. with J. A. Sascha Feinstein) 1991, The Insomnia of Fire, by Nguyen Quang Thieu (trans., with Martha Collins) 1995, The Second Set: The Jazz Poetry Anthology Vol. 2 (ed. with J. A. Sascha Feinstein) 1996, Blue Notes: Essays, Interviews and Commentaries 2000. *Honours:* two NEA Creative Writing Fellowships 1981, 1987, Thomas Forcade Award, Union League Civic Arts and Poetry Prize, Chicago 1998, Ruth Lilly Poetry Prize 2001. *Address:* Creative Writing Program, 185 Nassau Street, Princeton University, Princeton, NJ 08544, USA (office). *E-mail:* .

KÖNIG, Hans; German writer; b. 30 Sept. 1925, Erlangen; m. 1949; one s. *Career:* mem. Verband Fränkischer Schriftsteller; Pegnesischer Blumenorden. *Publications:* Der Pelzermärtl kummt, 1977; Woss wissd denn ihr, 1981; Anekdoten Erzählungen Originale aus Erlangen, 1981–84; Burschen, Knoten und Philister – Erlanger Studentenleben von 1843–1983, 1984; Erlangen vorwiegend heiter – ein unterhaltsamer Streifzug dürch die Stadt und ihre Geschichte, 1988; Wie es Lem so is, 1994. Contributions: anthologies, journals and periodicals. *Honours:* Verdienstmedaille und Verdienstkreuz der Bundesrepublik Deutschland, 1985–91; Kultureller Ehrenbrief der Stadt Erlangen, 1989; Ehrenkrenz des Pegnesischen Blumenordens, 1995; Frankenwurtel, 1999.

KONRÁD, György; Hungarian novelist and essayist; b. 2 April 1933, Berettyóújfalu, nr Debrecen; s. of József Konrád and Róza Klein; m. Judit Lakner; three s. two d. *Education:* Debrecen Reform Coll., Madách Gymnasium, Budapest, Eötvös Loránd Univ., Budapest. *Career:* teacher at general gymnasium in Csepel; Ed. Életképek 1956; social worker, Budapest 7th Dist Council 1959–65; Ed. Magyar Helikon 1960–66; urban sociologist on staff of City Planning Research Inst. 1965–73; full-time writer 1973–; Pres. Akad. der Künste Berlin-Brandenburg 1997; Visiting Prof. of Comparative Literature, Colorado Springs Coll. 1988; Corresp. mem. Bayerische Akad., Munich; fmr Pres. Int. PEN. *Publications include:* novels: A látogató (The Case Worker) 1969, A városlapító (The City Builder) 1977, A cinkos (The Loser) 1982, Kerti mulatság (Feast in the Garden) (Vol. 1 of trilogy Agenda) 1989, Kóóra (Stone Dial) (Vol. 2 of Agenda) 1995; essays: Új lakótelepek szociológiai problémái 1969, Az értelmiség utja az osztályhatalomhoz (The Intellectuals on the Road to Class Power) 1978, Az autonómia kisértése (The Temptation of Autonomy) 1980, Antipolitics 1986, Esszék 91–93 (Essays 1991–93) 1993, The Melancholy of Rebirth 1995, Várakozás (Expectation) 1995, Áramló leltár 1996, Láthatatlan hang (The Invisible Voice: Meditations on Jewish Themes) 2000. *Honours:* Herder Prize, Vienna-Hamburg 1984, Charles Veillon European Essay, Zürich 1985, Fredfonden Peace Foundation, Copenhagen 1986, Fed. Critics' Prize for Novel of the Year (FRG) 1986, Maecenas Prize 1989, Manès-Sperber Prize 1990, Kossuth Prize, Friedens-Preis des Deutschen Buchhandels 1991, Karlspreis zu Aachen 2001; numerous scholarships. *Address:* Torockó utca 3, 1026 Budapest, Hungary. *Telephone:* (1) 560-425.

KOONTZ, Dean Ray, (David Axton, Brian Coffey, Deanna Dwyer, K. R. Dwyer, John Hill, Leigh Nichols, Anthony North, Richard Paige, Owen West), BS; American writer; b. 9 July 1945, Everett, Pa; s. of Raymond Koontz and Florence Logue; m. Gerda Ann Cerra 1966. *Education:* Shippensburg Univ. *Career:* fmr teacher of English; freelance author 1969–; work includes novels, short stories, science fiction/fantasy, social commentary/phenomena and journalism. *Publications:* (under various names) Star Quest 1968, The Fall of the Dream Machine 1969, Fear That Man 1969, Anti-Man 1970, Beastchild 1970, Dark of the Woods 1970, The Dark Symphony 1970, Hell's Gate 1970, The Crimson Witch 1971, A Darkness in My Soul 1972, The Flesh in the Furnace 1972, Starblood 1972, Time Thieves 1972, Warlock 1972, A Werewolf Among Us 1973, Hanging On 1973, The Haunted Earth 1973, Demon Seed 1973, Strike Deep 1974, After the Last Race 1974, Nightmare Journey 1975, The Long Sleep 1975, Night Chills 1976, The Voice of the Night 1980, Whispers 1980, The Funhouse 1980, The Eyes of Darkness 1981, The Mask 1981, House of Thunder 1982, Phantoms 1983, Darkness Comes 1984, Twilight 1984, The Door to December 1985, Strangers 1986, Shadow Fires 1987, Watchers 1987, Twilight Eyes 1987, Oddkins 1988, Servants of Twilight 1988, Lightning 1988, Midnight 1989, The Bad Place 1990, Cold Fire 1991, Hideaway 1992, Dragon Tears 1992, Winter Moon 1993, The House of Thunder 1993, Dark Rivers of the Heart 1994, Mr Murder 1994, Fun House 1994, Strange Highways 1994, Icebound 1995, Intensity 1995, The Key to Midnight 1995, Ticktock 1996, Santa's Twin 1996, Sole Survivor 1996, Fear Nothing 1997, Seize the Night 1998, False Memory 1999, From the Corner of his Eye 2001, One Door Away From Heaven 2001, By the Light of the Moon 2002, The Face 2003, Odd Thomas 2003, Life Expectancy 2004, Frankenstein 2: City of Night (with Ed Gorman) 2004, Forever Odd 2005, The Husband 2006, Brother Odd 2006, The Good Guy 2007. *Honours:* Hon. DLitt (Shippensburg) 1989. *Address:* POB 9529, Newport Beach, CA 92658, USA.

KOOSER, Theodore (Ted), BS, MA; American poet and writer; b. 25 April 1939, Ames, Ia; m. 1st Diana Tresslar 1962 (divorced 1969); one s.; m. 2nd Kathleen Rutledge 1977. *Education:* Ia State Univ., Univ. of Neb. *Career:* underwriter, Bankers Life Neb. 1965–73; part-time instructor in creative writing 1970–, sr underwriter, Lincoln Benefit Life 1973–84, Vice-Pres. 1984–98; currently Visiting Prof., Univ. of Neb., Lincoln; Ed. and Publr, Windflower Press; Poet Laureate of the USA 2004–06. *Publications:* Official Entry Blank 1969, Grass County 1971, Twenty Poems 1973, A Local Habitation and a Name 1974, Shooting a Farmhouse: So This is Nebraska 1975, Not Coming to be Barked At 1976, Voyages to the Inland Sea (with Harley Elliott) 1976, Hatcher 1978, Old Marriage and New 1978, Cottonwood County (with William Kloefkorn) 1979, Windflower Home Almanac of Poetry (ed.) 1980, Sure Signs: New and Selected Poems (Soc. of Midland Authors Poetry Prize) 1980, One World at a Time 1985, The Blizzard Voices 1986, As Far as I Can See: Contemporary Writers of the Middle Plains (ed.) 1989, Etudes 1992, Weather Central 1994, A Book of Things 1995, A Decade of Ted Kooser Valentines 1996, Riding with Colonel Carter 1999, Winter Morning Walks: 100 Postcards to Jim Harrison (Nebraska Book Award for poetry 2001) 2000, Braided Creek: A Conversation in Poetry (with Jim Harrison) 2003, Local Wonders: Seasons in the Bohemian Alps (Friends of American Writers Chicago Award, ForeWord Magazine Gold Award for Autobiography, Nebraska Book Award for Nonfiction 2003) 2002, Delights and Shadows (Pulitzer Prize for Poetry 2005) 2004, The Poetry Home Repair Manual 2004, Flying at Night: Poems 1965–1985 2005; contrib. to The American Poetry Review, Antioch Review, Cream City Review, The Hudson Review, Kansas Quarterly, The Kenyon Review, Midwest Quarterly, The New Yorker, Poetry Northwest, Poetry, Prairie Schooner, Shenandoah, Tailwind. *Honours:* John H. Vreeland Award for Creative Writing 1964, Prairier Schooner Prizes in Poetry 1976, 1978, NEA Literary Fellowships 1976, 1984, Columbia Magazine Stanley Kunitz Poetry Prize 1984, Governor's Arts Award 1988, Mayor's Arts Award 1989, Poetry Northwest Richard Hugo Prize 1994, Nebraska Arts Council Merit Award 2000, Pushcart Prize, James Boatwright Prize. *Address:* 1820 Branched Oak Road, Garland, NE 68360-9303 (home); c/o Department of English, 202 Andrews Hall, PO Box 880333, Lincoln, NE 68588-0333, USA (office). *E-mail:* TKOOSER2@unl.edu.

KOPIT, Arthur, AB; American dramatist and screenwriter; b. 10 May 1937, New York, NY; m. Leslie Ann Garis; two s. one d. *Education:* Harvard University. *Career:* Fellow, 1974–75, Playwright-in-Residence, 1975–76, Wesleyan University; CBS Fellow, 1976–77, Adjunct Prof. of Playwriting, 1977–80, Yale University; Adjunct Prof. of Playwriting, City College, CUNY, 1981–; mem. Dramatists Guild; Hasty Pudding Society; PEN; Signet Society; Writers Guild of America. *Publications:* Plays: Questioning of Nick, 1957; Gemini, 1957; Don Juan in Texas, 1957; On the Runway of Life You Never Know What's Coming Off Next, 1957; Across the River and Into the Jungle, 1958; Sing to Me Through Open Windows, 1959; To Dwell in a Place of Strangers, 1959; Aubade, 1959; Oh Dad, Poor Dad, Mamma's Hung You in the Closet and I'm Fellin' So Sad, 1960; Asylum, or What the Gentlemen Are Up To, and As For the Ladies, 1963; Mhil'daim, 1963; Chamber Music, 1965; Sing to Me Through Open Windows, 1965; The Day the Whores Came Out to Play Tennis, 1965; Indians, 1968; What's Happened to the Thorne's House, 1972; The Conquest of Everest, 1973; The Hero, 1973; Louisiana Territory, or Lewis and Clark Lost and Found, 1975; Secrets of the Rice, 1976; Wings, 1978; End of the World, 1984; Road to Nirvana, 1991. Contributions: Films and television. *Honours:* Vernon Rice Award, 1960; Outer Critics Circle Award, 1960; Guggenheim Fellowship, 1967; Rockefeller Foundation Grant, 1968; American Institute of Arts and Letters Award, 1971; National Endowment for the Humanities Grant, 1974; Prix Italia, 1978; Tony Award, 1982.

KOPS, Bernard; British poet, writer and dramatist; b. 28 Nov. 1926, London; m. Erica Gordon 1956; four c. *Career:* Lecturer, Spiro Inst. 1985–86, Surrey Educ. Authority, Ealing Educ. Authority, Inner London Educ. Authority, Arts Educational School/Acting Co. 1989–90, City Literary Inst. 1990–93. *Publications:* poetry: Poems 1955, Poems and Songs 1958, Anemone for Antigone 1959, Erica, I Want to Read You Something 1967, For the Record 1971, Barricades in West Hampstead 1988, Grandchildren and Other Poems 2000; other: Awake for Mourning 1958, Motorbike 1962, Autobiography, The World is a Wedding 1963, Yes From No Man's Land 1965, By the Waters of Whitechapel 1970, The Passionate Past of Gloria Gaye 1971, Settle Down Simon Katz 1973, Partners 1975, On Margate Sands 1978; 32 plays, including The Hamlet of Stepney Green 1958, Goodbye World 1959, Change for the Angel 1960, Stray Cats and Empty Bottles 1961, Enter Solly Gold 1962, The Boy Who Wouldn't Play Jesus 1965, More Out Than In 1980, Ezra 1981, Simon at Midnight 1982, Some of These Days 1990, Sophie: Last of the Red Hot Mamas 1990, Playing Sinatra 1991, Androcles and the Lion 1992, Dreams of Anne Frank 1992, Who Shall I Be Tomorrow? 1992, Call in the Night 1995, Green Rabbi 1997, Cafe Zeitgeist 1998, Collected Plays (three vols) 1998, 2000, 2002, Shalom Bomb 2000, Returning We Hear the Larks 2004, I Am Isaac Babel 2005, The Opening 2005, Knocking on Heaven's Door 2005–06. *Honours:* Arts Council Bursaries 1957, 1979, 1985, and Awards 1991, 2003, C. Day-Lewis Fellowship 1981–83, London Fringe Award 1993, Writer's Guild of GB Best Radio Play Awards 1995, 1996. *Literary Agent:* c/o Emily Hayward, Sheil Land Associates, 52 Doughty Street, London, WC1N 2LS, England. *Telephone:* (20) 7405-9351. *Fax:* (20) 7831-2127. *E-mail:* ehayward@sheilland.co.uk. *Address:* 41B Canfield Gardens, London, NW6 3JL, England (home). *Telephone:* (20) 7624-2940 (home); (20) 7624-2840 (home). *E-mail:* bernardkops@tiscali.co.uk (home).

KORDA, Michael Vincent, BA; American publishing executive; *Editor-in-Chief, Simon & Schuster Inc.*; b. 8 Oct. 1933, London, England; s. of Vincent Korda and Gertrude (née Musgrove) Korda; m. Carolyn Keese 1958; one s. *Education:* Magdalen Coll., Oxford, UK. *Career:* served RAF 1952–54; joined Simon and Schuster, New York 1958–, firstly as Ed., then Sr Ed., Man. Ed., Exec. Ed., now Sr Vice-Pres. and Ed.-in-Chief; mem. Nat. Soc. of Film Critics, American Horse Shows Assn. *Publications:* Male Chauvinism: How It Works 1973, Power: How to Get It, How to Use It 1975, Success! 1977, Charmed Lives 1979, Worldly Goods 1982, The Fortune 1989, Man to Man: Surviving Prostate Cancer 1997, Another Life, 2000, Country Matters 2002, Horse People 2003, Ulysses S. Grant: The Unlikely Hero 2004. *Address:* Simon and Schuster, 1230 Avenue of the Americas, New York, NY 10020, USA. *Telephone:* (212) 698-7000. *Fax:* (212) 698-7099. *Website:* www.simonsays.com.

KORG, Jacob, MA, PhD; American academic and writer; *Professor of English Emeritus, University of Washington, Seattle*; b. 21 Nov. 1922, New York, NY. *Education:* City Coll., CUNY, Columbia Univ., New York. *Career:* Bard Coll. 1948–50; City Coll., CUNY 1950–55; Asst and later Assoc. Prof., Univ. of Washington, Seattle 1955–65, Prof. of English 1965–91, Prof. Emer. 1991–;

mem. Int. Asscn of Univ. Profs of English, Modern Language Asscn, Asscn of Literary Scholars and Critics. *Publications:* Westward to Oregon (co-ed. with S. F. Anderson) 1958, Thought in Prose (co-ed. with R. S. Beal) 1958, An Introduction to Poetry 1959, London in Dickens's Day (ed.) 1960, The Complete Reader (co-ed. with R. S. Beal) 1961, George Gissing's Commonplace Book (ed.) 1962, George Gissing: A Critical Biography 1963, Dylan Thomas 1965, The Force of Few Words 1966, Twentieth Century Interpretations of Bleak House (ed.) 1968, The Poetry of Robert Browning (ed.) 1971, George Gissing: Thyrza (ed.) 1974, George Gissing: The Unclassed (ed.) 1978, Language in Modern Literature 1979, Browning and Italy 1983, Ritual and Experiment in Modern Poetry 1995, Winter Love: Ezra Pound and H. D. 2003; contribs to professional journals. *Address:* Department of English, University of Washington, 900 University Street, Apt 14–0, Seattle WA 98101, USA (office). *Telephone:* (206) 525-2276 (office). *E-mail:* korg@u.washington.edu (office).

KORMONDY, Edward John, BA, MS, PhD; American academic and writer; b. 10 June 1926, Beacon, NY. *Education:* Tusculum Coll., Univ. of Michigan. *Career:* Instructor in Zoology and Curator of Insects, Museum of Zoology, Univ. of Michigan 1955–57; Asst Prof. to Prof. of Biology, Oberlin Coll. 1957–68; Dir Comm. on Undergraduate Educ. in the Biological Sciences and the Office of Biological Educ., American Inst. of Biological Sciences 1968–71; mem. Faculty, Evergreen State Coll., Olympia, Wash. 1971–79, Interim Acting Dean 1972–73, Vice-Pres. and Provost 1973–78; Sr Professional Assoc., NSF 1979; Provost and Prof. of Biology, Univ. of Southern Maine, Portland 1979–82; Vice-Pres. for Academic Affairs and Prof. of Biology, California State Univ., Los Angeles 1982–86; Sr Vice-Pres. Univ. of Hawaii 1991–93, Chancellor and Prof. of Biology, Univ. of Hawaii at Hilo and at West Oahu 1986–93; Pres. Univ. of West Los Angeles 1995–97; Special Asst to the Pres., Pacific Oaks Coll. 2000–05. *Publications:* Introduction to Genetics 1964, Readings in Ecology (ed.) 1965, Readings in General Biology (ed., two vols) 1966, Concepts of Ecology 1969, Population and Food (ed. with R. Leisner) 1971, Pollution (co-ed. with R. Leisner) 1971, Ecology (co-ed. with R. Leisner) 1971, Environmental Education: Academia's Response (with J. Aldrich) 1972, General Biology: The Natural History and Integrity of Organisms (with others) 1977, Handbook of Contemporary Developments in World Ecology (with F. McCormick) 1981, Environmental Sciences: The Way the World Works (with B. Nebel) 1981, Biology (with B. Essenfield) 1984, International Handbook of Pollution Control 1989, Environmental Education: Academia's Response (with P. Corcoran) 1997, Fundamentals of Human Ecology (with D. Brown) 1998, University of Hawaii-Hilo: A College in the Making (with F. Inouye) 2001; contrib. to professional journals. *Honours:* Hon. DSc (Tusculum Coll.) 1997. *Address:* 1388 Lucile Avenue, Los Angeles, CA 90026-1520, USA (home). *Telephone:* (323) 666-6372 (home). *Fax:* (323) 666-1258 (home). *E-mail:* ekor@aol.com (home).

KORNFELD, Robert Jonathan, BA; American dramatist, writer and poet; b. 3 March 1919, Newtonville, MA; m. Celia Seiferth 1945; one s. *Education:* Harvard Univ., Columbia Univ., Tulane Univ., New York Univ., New School for Social Research, Circle-in-the-Square School of Theatre, Playwrights' Horizons Theatre School and Laboratory. *Career:* visiting artist, American Acad., Rome 1996; playwright-in-residence, Univ. of Wisconsin 1998; mem. Authors' League, Dramatists' Guild, Nat. Arts Club, New York Drama League, PEN, Theater for the New City (bd mem. 2002), Bronx County Democratic Cttee, Times Square Playwrights. *Plays written:* A Dream Within a Dream (opera libretto) 1987, Ligeia (opera libretto) 1987, Music For Saint Nicholas 1992, Hot Wind From the South 1995, The Hanged Man 1996. *Plays produced:* Hot Wind From the South 1995, The Hanged Man 1996, Father New Orleans 1997, The Queen of Carnival 1997, The Art of Love 1998, The Celestials 1998, Passage in Purgatory, Shanghai, China 2000, The Gates of Hell 2002. *Publications:* non-fiction: Great Southern Mansions 1977, Landmarks of the Bronx (jtly) 1990; fiction and poetry; contrib. to various publications. *Honours:* numerous awards and prizes. *Address:* The Withers Cottage, 5286 Sycamore Avenue, Riverdale, NY 10471, USA (home). *Telephone:* (718) 549-6643 (home). *E-mail:* rojokosr@aol.com (home).

KOROTYCH, Vitaliy Alekseyevich; Russian/Ukrainian writer and poet; *Editor, Boulevard magazine*; b. 26 May 1936, Kiev; s. of Aleksey Korotych and Zoa Korotych; m. Zinaida Korotych 1958; two s. *Education:* Kiev Medical Inst. *Career:* physician 1959–66; Ed. Ukrainian literary journal Ranok 1966–77; Ed.-in-Chief Vsesvit magazine 1978–86; Ed.-in-Chief Ogonyok weekly magazine 1986–91; Sec. of Ukrainian Writers' Union 1966–69; mem. USSR Writers' Union 1981–90; USSR People's Deputy 1989–91; Prof. Boston Univ., USA 1991–98, returned to Moscow; ed. Boulevard magazine and others 1998–. *Publications include:* Golden Hands 1961, The Smell of Heaven 1962, Cornflower Street 1963, O Canada! 1966, Poetry 1967, Metronome (novel) 1982, The Face of Enmity (novel) 1984, Memory, Bread and Love 1986, Le Visage de la haine (travel essays) 1988, Glasnost and Perestroika 1990, The Waiting Room (memoirs, Vol. I) 1991, On My Behalf (memoirs, Vol. II) 2000, Selected Poems 2005, Selected Essays 2005; many translations from English into Ukrainian and other Slavonic languages. *Honours:* several Russian, Ukrainian, Polish and Bulgarian decorations and medals including two USSR State Prizes, A. Tolstoy Prize 1982, Int. Julius Fuchik Prize 1984, Wiental Prize, Georgetown Univ. (USA) 1987, Int. Ed. of the year, W P Revue (USA) 1989. *Address:* Trifonovskaya str. 11, Apt. 256, 127018 Moscow, Russia (home). *Telephone:* (495) 689-03-84 (home). *Fax:* (495) 689-03-84 (home). *E-mail:* ziter@telecont.ru (home).

KORZENIK, Diana, BA, EdD; American academic, writer and artist; *Professor Emerita, Massachusetts College of Art, Boston*; b. 15 March 1941, New York, NY. *Education:* Oberlin Coll., Vassar Coll., Columbia Univ., Harvard Univ. Grad. School of Educ. *Career:* Prof. Emer., Massachusetts Coll. of Art, Boston; Founder, first Pres. and Bd mem. Friends of Longfellow House; mem. Advisory Bd Teen Voices magazine; mem. American Antiquarian Soc., Massachusetts Historical Soc. *Art exhibitions include:* Writers' Room of Boston 2003. *Publications:* Art and Cognition (co-ed. with Leondar & Perkins) 1977, Drawn to Art 1986, Art Making and Education (with Maurice Brown) 1993, The Cultivation of American Artists (co-ed. with Sloat and Barnhill) 1997, Objects of American Art Education (LEAB Award American Library Asscn) 2004; contrib. to professional journals and to magazines. *Honours:* Woodrow Wilson Fellow 1962, Boston Globe L.L. Winship Literary Award 1986, Nat. Art Educ. Asscn Lowenfeld Award 1998. *Address:* 7 Norman Road, Newton Highlands, MA 02461, USA. *Telephone:* (617) 965-9338. *E-mail:* dkorzenik@comcast.net (home).

KORZHAVIN, Naum; Russian author and poet; b. (Mandel Emmanuel Moiseyevich Korzhavin), 14 Oct. 1925, Kiev. *Education:* Karaganda Mining Inst. and Gorky Inst. of Literature, Moscow 1959. *Career:* first publication 1941; exiled to West (USA) 1974; revisited Moscow 1989; citizenship and membership of Writers' Union restored 1990. *Publications include:* The Years 1963, Where Are You? 1964, Bread, Children in Auschwitz, Autumn in Karaganda, Verse 1981, Selected Verse 1983, Interlacements 1987, Letter to Moscow 1991, The Time is Given 1992, To Myself 1998; contributor to émigré dissident journal Kontinent. *Address:* 28c Colborne Road, Apt 2, Brighton, MA 02135, USA.

KOSICE, Gyula; Argentine artist and poet; b. 26 April 1924, Košice, Czechoslovakia (now Slovakia); s. of Joseph F. Kosice and Eta Kosice (née Berger); m. Haydée Itaovit 1947; two d. *Education:* Acad. of Arts, Buenos Aires. *Career:* co-f. Arturo magazine 1944, Concrete Art Invention 1945; f. Madí Art Movement 1946, f., Ed. Universal Madí Art magazine 1947; first use of neon gas in art 1946; introduction of water as essential component of his work 1948; creator Hydrospatial City (concept) 1948–; works include sculptures, hydrospatial courses, hydromurals; works in museums and pvt. collections in Argentina, Latin America, USA, Europe and Asia. *Exhibitions:* over 35 solo and 600 jt exhbns including Madí Art Exhbn Salon des Réalités Nouvelles, Paris 1948, 50-year retrospective Museum of Fine Arts, Buenos Aires 1991, Homenaje a Kosice, Museo Arte Moderno Buenos Aires 1994, anthology exhbn (120 works) Centro Recoleta, Buenos Aires 1999–, Digital Works Centro Recoleta, Buenos Aires 2003. *Publications:* Invención 1945, Madí Manifesto 1946, Golse-Se (poems) 1952, Peso y Medida de Alberto Hidalgo 1953, Antología Madí 1955, Geocultura de la Europa de Hoy 1959, Poème hydraulique 1960, Arte Hidrocinético 1968, La Ciudad Hidroespacial 1972, Arte y Arquitectura del Agua 1974, Arte Madí 1982, Obra Poética 1984, Entrevisiones 1984, Teoría sobre el Arte 1987, Arte y Filosofía Porvenirista 1996, Madí grafias 2001. *Honours:* Best Art Book, Asscn of Art Critics for Arte Madi 1982, Ordre des Arts et des Lettres 1989, Premio Trayectoria en el Arte, Nat. Arts Foundation 1994, Ciudadano Ilustre de la Ciudad de Buenos Aires 1997, Homenaje por Trayectoria de 62 Amős, Centro Recoleta 2003. *Address:* Humahuaca 4662, Buenos Aires (office); República de la India 3135 6° A, 1425 Buenos Aires, Argentina (home). *Telephone:* (1) 867-1240 (office); (1) 801-8615 (home). *Fax:* (1) 807-0115 (home). *E-mail:* gyula@kosice.com.ar (home). *Website:* www.kosice.com.ar (office).

KOSTASH, Myrna Ann, BA, MA; Canadian writer; b. 2 Sept. 1944, Edmonton. *Education:* Univ. of Alberta, Univ. of Toronto. *Career:* writer-in-residence The Loft, Minneapolis USA 1993, Regina Public Library 1996–97, Saskatoon Public Library 2002–03, Univ. of Alberta 2003–04; documentary writer/researcher Canadian Broadcasting Corpn; mem. Writers' Union of Canada (chair. 1993–94), Writers' Guild of Alberta (pres. 1989–90), Canadian Conference of the Arts (bd of govs 1996–), PEN Canada, Parkland Inst. (bd 2001–). *Publications:* All of Baba's Children 1977, Long Way From Home 1980, No Kidding 1988, Bloodlines 1993, The Doomed Bridgeroom: A Memoir 1998, The Next Canada: In Search of the Future Nation 2000, Reading the River: A Traveller's Companion to the North Saskatchewan River 2005; contrib. to Saturday Night, Canadian Forum, Brick, Border Crossings, Canadian Geographic, Prairie Fire, Journal of Canadian Studies, Signs, mostovi, Literature na swiece; radio documentaries. *Honours:* Queen's Jubilee Medal; Canada Council Senior Artist Grants, Nat. Magazine Silver Prize. *Address:* 110, 11716 – 100 Avenue, Edmonton, AB T5K 2G3, Canada (home). *E-mail:* kostashm@yahoo.ca (office). *Website:* www.writersunion.ca (office).

KOSTELANETZ, Richard Cory, AB, MA; American writer, poet, critic, artist and composer; b. 14 May 1940, New York, NY. *Education:* Brown Univ., King's Coll., London, Columbia Univ., Morley Coll., London, New School for Social Research, New York. *Career:* Literary Dir, Future Press, New York 1976–; sole proprietor, Archae Editions, New York 1978–; contributing ed. to various journals; guest lecturer and reader at many colls and univs; numerous exhibitions as an artist; Master Artist Pollock-Krasner Foundation 2001, Atlantic Center for the Arts, New Smyrna Beach, Fla 2002; Woodrow Wilson Fellowship 1962–63; Fulbright Fellowship 1964–65; Pulitzer Fellowship 1965–66; Guggenheim Fellowship 1967; Fellow New Asscn of Sephardic/ Mizrahi Artists and Writers Int. 2000–02; mem. American PEN, American Soc. of Composers, Authors and Publishers, Int. Asscn of Art Critics. *Publications include:* poetry: Visual Language 1970, I Articulations/Short Fictions 1974, Portraits From Memory 1975, Numbers: Poems and Stories

1976, Rain Rains Rain 1976, Illuminations 1977, Numbers Two 1977, Richard Kostelanetz 1980, Turfs/Arenas/Fields/Pitches 1980, Arenas/Fields/Pitches/Turfs 1982, Fields/Pitches/Turfs/Arenas 1990, Solos, Duets, Trios, and Choruses 1991, Wordworks: Poems Selected and New 1993, Paritions 1993, Repartitions 1994, More Wordworks 2004; fiction: In the Beginning (novel) 1971, Constructs (five vols) 1975–91, One Night Stood (novel) 1977, Tabula Rasa: A Constructivist Novel 1978, Exhaustive Parallel Intervals (novel) 1979, Fifty Untitled Constructivist Fictions 1991, 3-Element Stories 1998, Kaddish and Other Short Pieces 2004; non-fiction: Recyclings: A Literary Autobiography (two vols) 1974, 1984, The End of Intelligent Writing: Literary Politics in America 1974, Metamorphosis in the Arts 1980, The Old Poetries and the New 1981, The Grants-Fix: Publicly Funded Literary Granting in America 1987, The Old Fictions and the New 1987, On Innovative Music(ian)s 1989, Unfinished Business: An Intellectual Nonhistory 1990, The New Poetries and Some Old 1991, Published Encomia 1967–91 1991, On Innovative Art(ist)s 1992, A Dictionary of the Avant-Gardes 1993, On Innovative Performance(s) 1994, Fillmore East: 25 Years After: Recollections of Rock Theatre 1995, An ABC of Contemporary Reading 1995, Crimes of Culture 1995, Radio Writings 1995, John Cage (Ex)plain(ed) 1996, Thirty Years of Critical Engagement with John Cage 1996, One Million Words of Booknotes 1958–1993 1996, Political Essays 1999, Three Canadian Geniuses 2001, SoHo: The Rise and Fall of an Artists' Colony 2003, Dis/sections 2003, Thirty-Five Years of Visible Writing, 2004, Autobiographies at 60 2004, Autobiographies at 50 2006; plays: Collected Performance Texts 1998; editor of many books; films, videotapes, radio scripts, recordings; contribs to many anthologies, numerous poems, articles, essays, reviews in journals and other publications. *Honours:* Nat. Endowment for the Arts grants 1976, 1978–79, 1981–82, 1985 (twice), 1986, 1990–91, American Institute of Graphic Arts One of Best Books award 1976, Pushcart Prize 1977, Deutscher Akademischer Austauschdienst Stipend, Berlin 1981–83, American Soc. of Composers, Authors and Publishers Awards 1983–91, 1992–2004. *Address:* PO Box 444, Prince Street Station, New York, NY 10012-0008; PO Box 454, Rockaway Beach, NY 11693, USA. *Website:* www.richardkostelanetz.com.

KOSTENKO, Lina Vasilievna; Ukrainian poet; b. 19 March 1930, Rzhischevo, Kiev Region. *Education:* Kiev Pedagogical Inst. and Maxim Gorky Inst. of Literature, Moscow. *Publications:* Rays of the Earth 1957, Sails 1958, Wanderings of the Heart 1961, On the Shores of the Eternal River 1977, Inimitability 1980, Marusya Churay (novel in verse) 1979–82, The Integral of the Cosmos, The Scythian Odyssey 1981, Snow in Florence, A Duma About the Non-Azov Brothers, The Garden of Unmelting Sculptures 1987, Selected Works 1989, Berestechko (historical poem) 2000, Landscapes of Memory: The Selected Later Poetry of Lina Kostenko 2002; children's verse: The Lilac King; numerous publs in literary magazines. *Honours:* Taras Shevchenko Prize 1987. *Address:* Chkalova str. 52, Apt 8, 252054 Kiev, Ukraine (home). *Telephone:* (44) 224-70-38 (home).

KOTKER, (Mary) Zane, (Maggie Strong); American writer; b. 2 Jan. 1934, Waterbury, CT; m. Norman Kotker 1965; one s. one d. *Education:* MA, Columbia University 1959–60. *Publications:* novels: Bodies in Motion 1972, A Certain Man 1976, White Rising 1981, Mainstay (as Maggie Strong) 1988, Try to Remember 1997. *Honours:* National Endowment for the Arts Grant 1972.

KOTZWINKLE, William; American writer; b. 22 Nov. 1938, Scranton, Pennsylvania; m. Elizabeth Gundy 1970. *Education:* Rider College; Pennsylvania State University. *Publications:* Elephant Bangs Train, 1971; Hermes 3000, 1971; The Fat Man, 1974; Night-Book, 1974; Swimmer in the Secret Sea, 1975; Doctor Rat, 1976; Fata Morgana, 1977; Herr Nightingale and the Satin Woman, 1978; Jack in the Box, 1980; Christmas at Fontaine's, 1982; E.T., the Extra-Terrestrial: A Novel, 1982; Superman III, 1983; Queen of Swords, 1983; E.T., the Book of the Green Planet: A New Novel, 1985; Seduction in Berlin, 1985; Jewell of the Moon, 1985; The Exile, 1987; The Midnight Examiner, 1989; Hot Jazz Trio, 1989; The Game of Thirty, 1994. Other: many children's books. *Honours:* National Magazine Awards for Fiction, 1972, 1975; O. Henry Prize, 1975; World Fantasy Award for Best Novel, 1977; North Dakota Children's Choice Award, 1983, and Buckeye Award, 1984.

KOUDIL, Hafsa Zinai; Algerian writer, film-maker and actress; b. 1951. *Career:* living in Tunisia; campaigns for the rights of women and against the Islamicization of Algeria. *Films:* Le démon au féminin (writer and dir) 1994, Viva Laldjérie (actress) 2004. *Publications include:* La Fin d'un rêve (autobiog.) 1984, Le Passé décomposé 1993, Le Mariage de jouissance (screenplay).

KOUMI, Margaret (Maggie); British journalist; b. 15 July 1942, d. of the late Yiasoumis Koumi and Melexidia Paraskeva; m. Ramon Sola 1980. *Education:* Buckingham Gate, London. *Career:* sec. Thomas Cook 1957–60; sub-ed., feature and fiction writer Visual Features Ltd 1960–66; sub-ed. TV World 1966–67; Production Ed. 19 Magazine 1967–69, Ed. 1969–86, concurrently Ed. Hair Magazine; Man. Ed. Practical Parenting, Practical Health, Practical Hair and Beauty 1986–87; Jt Ed. Hello! 1988–93, Ed. 1993–2001, Consultant Ed. 2001–. *Publication:* Beauty Care 1981, Claridges – Within The Image 2004. *Honours:* Jt Ed. of the Year Award 1991. *E-mail:* anniebowman@hellomagazine.com (office).

KOURVETARIS, George A., BS, MA, PhD; American/Greek academic, writer and editor; *Professor of Sociology, Northern Illinois University, DeKalb and Editor of the Journal of Political and Military Sociology*; b. 21 Nov. 1933, Eleochorion, Arcadia, Greece; m. 1st Toula Savas 1966 (divorced 1987); two s. one d.; m. 2nd Vassia Dumas Siapkaris 1998. *Education:* Teacher's Coll., Tripolis, Greece, Loyola Univ., Chicago, USA, Roosevelt Univ., Chicago, Northwestern Univ., Evanston, IL. *Career:* Asst Prof., Chicago City Coll. 1967; Fellow and Lecturer, Northwestern Univ. 1967–68; Asst Prof. 1969–73, Assoc. Prof. 1973–78, Prof. of Sociology 1978–, Northern Illinois Univ., DeKalb; Founder-Ed., The Journal of Political and Military Sociology 1973–; founder video/DVD production co. The Paideia Projects-NFP 2003–; mem. American Sociological Asscn, European Community Studies Asscn, Modern Greek Studies Asscn, Southeast European Asscn. *Recordings:* series on the Golden Age of Pericles (Paideia Projects, production of video/DVD). *Publications:* First and Second Generation Greeks in Chicago: An Inquiry Into Their Stratification and Mobility Patterns 1971, Social Origins and Political Orientations of Officer Corps in a World Perspective (co-author) 1973, World Perspectives in the Sociology of the Military (co-ed.) 1977, Political Sociology: Readings in Research and Theory (co-ed.) 1980, Society and Politics: An Overview and Reappraisal of Political Sociology (co-author) 1980, A Profile of Modern Greece: In Search of Identity (co-author) 1987, Social Thought 1994, The Impact of European Integration: Political, Sociological, and Economic Changes (co-ed.) 1996, Political Sociology: Structure and Process 1997, Studies on Greek Americans 1997, Studies in Modern Greek Society and Politics 1999, The New Balkans: Disintegration and Reconstruction (co-ed.) 2002; poetry: Nostalgias Kai Xenitias 1992, Stohasmoi (Conjectures) 2004; contrib. to various scholarly books, journals and encyclopaedias, over 70 articles and over 35 book reviews; several poems in Greek and English in journals and newspapers. *Honours:* various academic grants and awards, Greek American Community Services Heritage Award, Chicago 1987, Hellenic Council on Education Recognition Award, Chicago 1991, Recognition Award for the Silver Anniversary of the Founding of the Journal of Political and Military Sociology 1998, American Sociological Asscn Award for 30 Years of Distinguished Publication (for The Journal of Political and Military Sociology) 2002, Pan Arcadian Fed. of America Award 2004. *Address:* 109 Andresen Court, DeKalb, IL 60115, USA. *Telephone:* (815) 753-6433 (office); (815) 758-4088 (home). *Fax:* (815) 753-6302 (office). *E-mail:* ykourvet@niu.edu.

KOZER, José, BA, MA, PhD; Cuban/American academic, poet and writer; b. 28 March 1940, Havana, Cuba; m. Guadalupe Kozer 1974; two d. *Education:* Univ. of Havana, New York Univ., Queens Coll., CUNY. *Career:* Prof. of Spanish Literature and Language, Queens Coll., CUNY 1960–97; fmr Co-Ed. Enlace magazine, New York. *Publications:* poetry (14 chapbooks, 29 books include): Padres y otras profesiones 1972, Por la libre 1973, Este judío de números y letras 1975, Y así tomaron posesión en las ciudades 1978, La rueca de los semblantes 1980, Jarrón de las abreviaturas 1980, Antología breve 1981, The Ark Upon the Number 1982, Bajo este cien 1983, La garza sin sombras 1985, Díptico de la restitucion 1986, El carillón de los muertos 1987, Carece de causa 1988, Prójimos/Intimates 1990, De donde oscilan los seres en sus proporciones 1990, Una índole 1993, Trazas del lirondo 1993, A Caná 1995, Et mutabile 1995, Los paréntesis 1995, La maquinaria ilimitada 1996, AAA1144 1997, Réplicas 1997, Dípticos 1998, Farándula 1999, Al traste 1999, No buscan reflejarse: Antología poética (1972–1980) 2001, Rupestres 2001, Rosa cúbica 2002, Anima 2002, Madame Chu & Outros Poemas 2002, Un caso llamado FK 2002, Ogi No Mato 2005, Y Del Esparto la Invariabilidad 2005, Stet 2005; prose: Mezcla para dos tiempos, Una huella destartalada; anthology: Medusario Muestra de Poesia Latinoamericana (co-ed. with Roberto Echavarren, Jacobo Sefamí) 1996; contrib. to numerous poetry magazines, literary journals and newspapers in N and S America, Spain. *Honours:* Gulbenkin Prize, Portugal 1967, CINTAS Foundation Award 1973, Julio Tovar Poetry Prize 1974, CUNY/PSC Foundation Award 1991. *Address:* 500 Three Islands Blvd, Apt 1209, Hallandale, FL 33009, USA. *E-mail:* josekozer@aol.com (home).

KOZHOKIN, Mikhail Mikhailovich, CandHist; Russian journalist; b. 23 Feb. 1962, Moscow. *Education:* Moscow State Univ. *Career:* Jr researcher, researcher, Sr researcher Inst. of USA and Canada, USSR (now Russian) Acad. of Sciences 1988–92, Sr researcher Cen. of Econ. and Political Studies, worked with G. Yavlinsky 1992–93; Head Information Dept ONEXIM bank 1993–96; Deputy Chair. Exec. Cttee 1996–; Asst to First Deputy Chair. of Russian Govt, mem. Govt Comm. on Econ. Reform 1997–; Dir Holding Co. Interros on work with mass media and public relations; Chair. Bd of Dirs Izvestia (newspaper) 1997–98, Ed.-in-Chief 1998–2003 (resgnd). *Address:* c/o Izvestia, Tverskaya str. 18, korp. 1, 127994 Moscow, Russia (office).

KOZIOŁ-PRZYBYLAK, Urszula, BA; Polish writer and poet; b. 20 June 1931, Rakówka; d. of Hipolit Kozioł and Czestawa Kozioł (née Kargol); m. Feliks Przybylak 1960. *Education:* Univ. of Wrocław. *Career:* high school teacher 1954–71; Literary Ed. Poglądy (Opinions) 1956; Literary Ed. Odra 1971–. *Publications include:* poetry: Gumowe klocki (Rubber Blocks) 1957, W rytmie korzeni (In the Rhythm of the Roots) 1963, Smuga i promień (A Trace and a Ray) 1965, Lista obecności (Attendance Record) 1967, W rytmie słońca (In the Rhythm of the Sun) 1974, Wybór wierszy (Select Poetry) 1976, Poezje wybrane (second edn) 1986, Žalnik (Laments) 1989, Postoje słowa (Stations of Words) 1995, Wielka Pauza (A Great Pause) 1996, W płynnym stanie 1998, Stany nieoczywistośći 1999, Supliki 2005; prose: Osobnego sny i przypowieści 1997; novels: Postoje pamięci (Stations of Memory, third edn) 1964–2004, Ptaki dla myśli (Birds for Thought, second edn) 1971; short stories: Z poczekalni (From the Waiting Room) 1978, Osobnego sny i przypowieści (The Dreams and Parables of the Separate One) 1978, Noli me tangere 1984; : Król malowany (The Painted King) 1978, Trzy Światy (Three Worlds) 1981, Podwórkowcy (Yard Kids) 1982, Spartolino 1982, Psujony (Spoilers) 1982, Zbieg z Bobony (Escapee from Bobona) 1983, Dziwna podróż Bączka do Gryslandii (Strange Voyage of Bug to Grysland) 1984, Magiczne imię (A Magic Name) 1985, O stołku (About a Chair) 1987, Zgaga 1990. *Honours:* Kommandeur-Kreuz zum Orden der Wiedergelurf Polens 1997; Dr hc (Wrocław) 2003; Autumnal Encounters Festival of Gdańsk Literary Prize 1963, Polish Students' Asscn Władysław Broniewski Prize 1964, Literary Prize of Wrocław 1965, Kościelski Foundation of Geneva Prize 1969, Polish Ministry of Culture Literary Prize 1971, Kultur Preis Schlesien, Hanover 1998, PEN-Club Award 1998, Joseph von Eichendorff Prize, Wangen, Germany 2002. *Address:* Komandorska 37/6, 53-342 Wrocław, Poland (home). *Telephone:* (71) 3435516 (office); (71) 3673853 (home). *Fax:* (71) 3435516 (office). *E-mail:* odra@odra.net.pl (office). *Website:* www.odra.net.pl.

KOZOL, Jonathan, BA; American writer; b. 5 Sept. 1936, Boston; s. of Dr Harry L. Kozol and Ruth Massell Kozol. *Education:* Harvard Coll. and Magdalen Coll., Oxford, UK. *Career:* Rhodes Scholar 1958; teacher in Boston area 1964–72; lecturer at numerous univs 1973–2006; Guggenheim Fellow 1972, 1984; Field Foundation Fellow 1973, 1974; Rockefeller Fellow 1978, Sr Fellow 1983. *Publications:* Death At An Early Age 1967, Free Schools 1972, The Night Is Dark 1975, Children of the Revolution 1978, On Being a Teacher 1979, Prisoners of Silence 1980, Illiterate America 1985, Rachel and Her Children: Homeless Families in America 1988, Savage Inequalities: Children in America's Schools 1991, Amazing Grace 1995, Ordinary Resurrections 2000, The Shame of the Nation: The Restoration of Apartheid Schooling in America 2005. *Honours:* Nat. Book Award 1968, Robert F. Kennedy Book Award 1989, New England Book Award 1992, Anisfield-Wolf Book Award 1996, Nation Magazine Book Award 2005. *Address:* PO Box 145, Byfield, MA 01922, USA. *Telephone:* 465-9325 (office). *Fax:* 462-8557 (office); (978) 462-8557 (home). *E-mail:* jonathankozol@gmail.com.

KRALL, Hanna; Polish journalist and writer; b. 20 May 1937, Warsaw; m. Jerzy Szperkowicz; one d. *Education:* Univ. of Warsaw. *Career:* reporter, Życie Warszawy 1955–66, Polityka 1966–, corresp. in Moscow 1966–69; corresp., Tygodnik Powszechny, Gazeta Wyborcza; freelance writer early 1980s–. *Publications include:* Na wschód od Arbatu (East of the Arbat) 1972, Zdążyć przed Panem Bogiem (Shielding the Flame) 1977, Sześć odcieni bieli (Six Shades of White) 1978, Sublokatorka (The Sub-tenant) 1985, Hipnoza (Hypnosis) 1989, Trudności ze wstawaniem (Difficulties Getting Up) 1990, Taniec na cudzym weselu (Dance at a Stranger's Wedding) 1993, Co się stało z naszą bajką (What's Happened to Our Fairy Tale) 1994, Dowody na istnienie (Proofs of Existence) 1996, Tam już nie ma żadnej rzeki (There is No River There Anymore) 1998, To ty jesteś Daniel (So You Are Daniel) 2001 (books translated into over 10 languages). *Honours:* Prize of Minister of Culture and Art 1989, J. Shocken Literary Prize (Germany), Solidarity Cultural Prize 1995, Kulture Foundation Award 1999, Leipzig Book Fair Award 2000. *Address:* Stowarzyszenie Pisarzy Polskich, ul. Krakowskie Przedmieście 87/89, 00-079 Warsaw, Poland (office).

KRAMER, Aaron, BA, MA, PhD; American academic, author, poet and translator; b. 13 Dec. 1921, New York, NY; m. Katherine Kolodny 1942, two d. *Education:* Brooklyn College, CUNY, New York University. *Career:* Instructor, 1961–63, Asst Prof., 1963–66, Adelphi University; Lecturer, Queens College, CUNY, 1966–68; Assoc. Prof., 1966–70, Prof. of English, 1970–91, Prof. Emeritus, 1991–, Dowling College, Oakdale, New York; mem. American Society of Composers, Authors and Publishers; Asscn for Poetry Therapy; Edna St Vincent Millay Society; e. e. cummings Society; International Acad. of Poets; PEN; Walt Whitman Birthplace Asscn, exec. board, 1969–85. *Publications:* The Glass Mountain, 1946; Poetry and Prose of Heine, 1948; Denmark Vesey, 1952; The Tinderbox, 1954; Serenade, 1957; Tune of the Calliope, 1958; Moses, 1962; Rumshinsky's Hat, 1964; Rilke: Visions of Christ, 1967; The Prophetic Tradition in American Poetry, 1968; Poetry Therapy (co-author), 1969; Melville's Poetry, 1972; On the Way to Palermo, 1973; Poetry the Healer (co-author), 1973; The Emperor of Atlantis, 1975; O Golden Land, 1976; Death Takes a Holiday, 1979; Carousel Parkway, 1980; The Burning Bush, 1983; In the Suburbs, 1986; A Century of Yiddish Poetry, 1989; Indigo, 1991; Life Guidance Through Literature (co-author), 1991; Dora Teitelboim: Selected Poems (ed. and trans.), 1995. Contributions: professional journals. *Honours:* Hart Crane Memorial Award, 1969; Eugene O'Neill Theatre Center Prize, 1983; National Endowment for the Humanities Grant, 1993; Festschrift published in his honour, 1995.

KRAMER, Dale Vernon; American academic and writer; b. 13 July 1936, Mitchell, SD; m. Cheris Gamble Kramarae 1960; two c. *Education:* BS, South Dakota State University, 1958; MA, 1960, PhD, 1963, Case Western Reserve University. *Career:* Instructor, 1962–63, Asst Prof., 1963–65, Ohio University; Asst Prof., 1965–67, Assoc. Prof., 1967–71, Prof. of English, 1971–96, Acting Head, Dept of English, 1982, 1986–87, Assoc. Dean, College of Arts and Sciences, 1992–95, University of Illinois; Assoc. Mem., Center for Advanced Study, Urbana, IL, 1971; Assoc. Vice-Provost, University of Oregon, 1990; mem. Asscn of American University Profs; Asscn for Documentary Editing; MLA; Society for Textual Scholarship; Victorian Periodicals Society. *Publications:* Charles Robert Maturin, 1973; Thomas Hardy: The Forms of Tragedy, 1975; Critical Approaches to the Fiction of Thomas Hardy (ed.), 1979; Thomas Hardy: The Woodlanders (ed.), 1981; Thomas Hardy: The Mayor of Casterbridge (ed.), 1987; Critical Essays on Thomas Hardy: The Novels (ed.), 1990; Thomas Hardy: Tess of the d'Urbervilles, 1991; The Cambridge Companion to

Thomas Hardy, 1999. Contributions: Professional journals. *Honours:* American Philosophical Society Grants, 1969, 1986; National Endowment for the Humanities Grant, 1986; Boydston Prize, Asscn for Documentary Editing, 1997. *Address:* c/o Dept of English, University of Illinois at Urbana-Champaign, Urbana, IL 61801, USA.

KRAMER, Larry D., BA; American writer; b. 25 June 1935, Bridgeport, Conn. *Education:* Yale Univ. *Career:* Production Exec. Columbia Pictures Corpn, London 1961–65; Asst to Pres. United Artists, New York; producer-screenwriter, Women in Love 1970; co-founder, Gay Men's Health Crisis Inc., New York 1981; founder, ACT UP-AIDS Coalition to Unleash Power, New York 1988. *Publications:* Faggots 1978, The Normal Heart (play) 1985, Just Say No 1988, The Furniture of Home 1989, The Destiny of Me 1993, The People Themselves: Popular Constitutionalism and Judicial Review 2005.

KRAMER, Lawrence Eliot, BA, MPhil, PhD; American academic, writer and editor; b. 21 Aug. 1946, Philadelphia, PA; m. Nancy S. Leonard 1973. *Education:* University of Pennsylvania, Yale University. *Career:* Asst Prof. of English, University of Pennsylvania, 1972–78; Asst Prof., 1978–81, Assoc. Prof., 1981–87, Prof. of English and Comparative Literature, 1987–95, Prof. of English and Music, 1995–, Fordham University; Co-Ed., 19th Century Music; Visiting Prof., Yale University, 1994, Columbia University, 2001; mem. American Musicological Society; Society for Music Theory. *Publications:* Music and Poetry: The Nineteenth Century and After, 1985; Music as Cultural Practice, 1800–1900, 1990; Classical Music and Postmodern Knowledge, 1995; After the Lovedeath: Sexual Violence and the Making of Culture, 1997; Franz Schubert: Sexuality, Subjectivity, Song, 1998; Walt Whitman and Modern Music: War, Desire, and the Trials of Nationhood (ed.), 2000; Musical Meaning: Toward a Critical History, 2001, Opera and Modern Culture: Wagner and Strauss 2004. Contributions: scholarly books and journals. *Address:* 791 Slate Quarry Road, Rhinebeck, NY 12572, USA.

KRAMER, Dame Leonie Judith, AC, DBE, DPhil, FAHA, FACE; Australian academic; *Professor Emerita of Australian Literature, University of Sydney*; b. 1 Oct. 1924, d. of the late A.L. Gibson and G. Gibson; m. Harold Kramer 1952 (deceased); two d. *Education:* Presbyterian Ladies Coll., Melbourne and Univs of Melbourne and Oxford. *Career:* Tutor, St Hugh's, Coll., Oxford 1949–52; Assoc. Prof. Univ. of NSW 1963–68; Prof. of Australian Literature, Univ. of Sydney, 1968–89, Prof. Emer. 1989–; Deputy Chancellor, Univ. of Sydney 1988–91, Chancellor 1991–2001; Vice-Pres. Australian Asscn for Teaching of English 1967–70; Vice-Pres. Australian Soc. of Authors 1969–71; mem. Nat. Literature Bd of Review 1970–73; mem. Council, Nat. Library of Australia 1975–81; Pres., then Vice-Pres. Australian Council for Educ. Standards 1973–; mem. Univs Comm. 1974–86; Commr Australian Broadcasting Comm. (ABC) 1977–81, Chair. 1982–83, Dir Australia and NZ Banking Group 1983–94, Western Mining Corpn 1984–96, Quadrant Magazine Co. Ltd 1986–99 (Chair. 1988–99); mem. Council Nat. Roads and Motorists' Asscn 1984–95, Council Foundation for Young Australians 1989–2000, Asia Soc. 1991–2000; Nat. Pres. Australia-Britain Soc. 1984–93, Order of Australia Asscn 2001–04; mem. Council ANU 1984–87; mem. Bd of Studies, NSW Dept. of Educ. 1990–2001; Chair. Bd of Dirs Nat. Inst. of Dramatic Art (NIDA) 1987–91, Deputy Chair. 1991–95; Sr Fellow Inst. of Public Affairs (IPA) 1988–96; Commr Electricity Comm. (NSW) 1988–95; mem. World Book Encyclopaedia Advisory Bd 1989–99, Int. Advisory Cttee Encyclopaedia Britannica 1991–99, NSW Council of Australian Inst. of Co. Dirs 1992–2001; Chair. Operation Rainbow Australia Ltd 1996–2003; mem. Governing Council Old Testament House, Canberra 1998–2001; Gov. Medical Benefits Fund 2005–. *Publications include:* (as L. J. Gibson) Henry Handel Richardson and Some of Her Sources 1954; (as Leonie Kramer): Australian Poetry 1961 (ed.) 1962, Companion to Australia Felix 1962, Myself When Laura 1966, A Guide to Language and Literature (with Robert D. Eagleson) 1977, A. D. Hope 1979, The Oxford History of Australian Literature (ed.) 1981, The Oxford Anthology of Australian Literature (ed. with Adrian Mitchell) 1985, My Country: Australian Poetry and Short Stories – Two Hundred Years (two vols) 1985, James McAuley: Poetry, Essays etc. (ed.) 1988, David Campbell: Collected Poems (ed.) 1989, Collected Poems of James McAuley 1995. *Honours:* Hon. Fellow, St Hugh's Coll. Oxford 1994, St Andrew's Coll., Univ. of Sydney, Janet Clarke Hall, Univ. of Melbourne 2005; Hon. DLitt (Tasmania), 1977 (Queensland) 1991, (NSW) 1992; Hon. LLD (Melbourne) 1983, (ANU) 1984; Hon. MA (Sydney) 1989; Hon. Prof. Dept of English (Sydney) 2002; Britannica Award 1986. *Address:* A20–John Woolley, Room S365, University of Sydney, Sydney NSW 2006 (office); 12 Vaucluse Road, Vaucluse, NSW 2030 Australia (home). *Telephone:* (2) 93514164 (office). *Fax:* (2) 93514773 (office). *E-mail:* L.Kramer@staff.unisyd.edu.au (office).

KRAMER, Lotte Karoline; British poet and painter; b. 22 Oct. 1923, Mainz, Germany; m. Frederic Kramer 1943; one s. *Education:* studied art and history of art. *Career:* mem. Decorative and Fine Arts Soc., PEN, Peterborough Museum Soc., Poetry Soc., Ver Poets, Writers in Schools. *Publications:* Scrolls 1979, Ice Break 1980, Family Arrivals 1981, A Lifelong House 1983, The Shoemaker's Wife 1987, The Desecration of Trees 1994, Earthquake and Other Poems 1994, Selected and New Poems 1980–1997, The Phantom Lane 2000, Heimweh/Homesick 1999, Poem on London Underground Trains 2003, Black Over Red 2005; contrib. to anthologies, newspapers, reviews, quarterlies and journals. *Honours:* Second Prize, York Poetry Competition 1972, Eastern Arts Board Bursary 1999, Second Prize, Manchester Cathedral Poetry Competition 2002. *Address:* 4 Apsley Way, Longthorpe, Peterborough, PE3 9NE, England (home). *Telephone:* (1733) 264378 (home).

KRANTZ, Judith, BA; American author; b. 9 Jan. 1928, New York City; d. of Jack David Tarcher and Mary Brager; m. Stephen Krantz 1954; two s. *Education:* Wellesley Coll. *Career:* contrib. to Good Housekeeping 1948–54, McCalls 1954–59, Ladies Home Journal 1959–71; contributing ed. Cosmopolitan 1971–79. *Publications:* Scruples 1978, Princess Daisy 1980, Mistral's Daughter 1982, I'll Take Manhattan 1986, Till We Meet Again 1988, Dazzle 1990, Scruples Two 1992, Lovers 1994, Spring Collection 1996, The Jewels of Teresa Kant 1998, Sex & Shopping: Confessions of a Nice Jewish Girl 2000. *Literary Agent:* c/o Esther Newberg, International Creative Management Inc. (ICM), 40 West 57th Street, New York, NY 10019, USA. *Telephone:* (212) 556-5600 (office). *Website:* www.icmtalent.com (office).

KRAPF, Norbert, MA, PhD; American academic and writer; *Emeritus Professor of English, Long Island University;* b. 14 Nov. 1943, Jasper, IN; m. 1970; one s. one d. *Education:* St Joseph's Coll., Ind., Univ. of Notre Dame. *Career:* Faculty 1970–84, Prof. of English 1984–95, Prof. Emer. 1995–, Long Island Univ.; Fulbright Prof. of American Poetry, Univ. of Freiburg 1980–81, Univ. of Erlangen, Nuremburg 1989–90. *Publications:* Arriving on Paumanok 1979, Lines Drawn from Durer 1981, Circus Songs 1983, A Dream of Plum Blossoms 1985, Under Open Sky: Poets on William Cullen Bryant (ed.) 1986, Beneath the Cherry Sapling: Legends from Franconia (ed. and trans.) 1988, Shadows on the Sundial: Selected Early Poems of Rainer Maria Rilke (ed. and trans.) 1990, Somewhere in Southern Indiana: Poems of Midwestern Origins 1993, Finding the Grain: Pioneer Journals and Letters from Dubois County, IN 1996, Blue-eyed Grass: Poems of Germany 1997: Bittersweet Along the Expressway: Poems of Long Island 2000, The Country I Come From: Poems 2002, Looking for God's Country: Poems 2005; contribs to professional journals. *Honours: Poetry Soc. of America Lucille Medwick Memorial Award 1999. Address:* c/o Department of English, Long Island University, Brookville, NY 11548 (office); 356 Miami Street, Indianapolis, IN 46204, USA (home). *Telephone:* (317) 636-0943 (home). *E-mail:* nkrapf@indy.rr.net (home). *Website:* www.krapfpoetry.com.

KRATT, Mary, BA, MA; American writer and poet; b. 7 June 1936, Beckley, WV; m. Emil F. Kratt 1959; one s. two d. *Education:* Agnes Scott Coll., Univ. of N Carolina at Charlotte. *Career:* mem. N Carolina Writers' Conf. (Chair. 1991–92), N Carolina Writers' Network (Bd mem.), Poets and Writers. *Publications:* Southern Is 1985, Legacy: The Myers Park Story 1986, The Imaginative Spirit: Literary Heritage of Charlotte and Mecklenburg County 1988, A Little Charlotte Scrapbook 1990, A Bird in the House 1991, The Only Thing I Fear is a Cow and a Drunken Man (poems and prose) 1991, Charlotte: Spirit of the New South 1992, On the Steep Side (poems) 1993, Small Potatoes (poems) 1999, Valley (poems) 2000, Remembering Charlotte: Postcards from a New South City 1905–50 2000, New South Women 2001; contrib. to newspapers, reviews and magazines. *Honours:* Lyricist Prize 1982, Oscar Arnold Young Award for Best Original Poetry Book by a North Carolinian 1983, N Carolina Poetry Soc. Sidney Lanier Award 1985, St Andrews Writer and Community Award 1994, Agnes Scott Coll. Distinguished Alumnae Writer Award 1994, MacDowell Colony residency 1996, Brockman Poetry Book Award 2000. *Address:* 3328 Providence Plantation Lane, Charlotte, NC 28270, USA.

KRAUSS, Nicole; American poet and writer; b. 1974, New York, NY; m. Jonathan Safran Foer. *Education:* Stanford Univ., Univ. of Oxford, Courtauld Inst., London. *Publications:* Future Emergencies (short story, in Esquire), Man Walks into a Room (novel) 2003, The Future Dictionary of America (with Dave Eggers and Jonathan Safran Foer) 2004, The History of Love (novel) 2005; contrib. poems to publs, including Ploughshares, Doubletake, PN Review, and fiction to The New Yorker, Esquire, Best American Short Stories. *Address:* c/o Random House, 1745 Broadway, New York, NY 10019, USA.

KRAUSSER, Helmut; German novelist; b. 1964, Esslinger. *Education:* Univ. of Munich. *Career:* fmrly nightwatchman, pop singer, radio announcer, journalist. *Publications:* novels: Thanatos: Das schwarze Buch 1986, Könige über dem Ozean 1989, Fette Welt (Fat World) 1992, Der grosse Bagarozy (trans. as The Great Bagarozy) 1997, Schweine und Elefanten 1999. *Address:* c/o Dedalus Ltd, Langford Lodge, St Judith's Lane, Sawtry, Cambridgeshire PE28 5XE, England. *E-mail:* info@dedalusbooks.com. *Website:* www.dedalusbooks.com.

KRAUTHAMMER, Charles, MD; American psychiatrist and journalist; b. 13 March 1950, New York; s. of Shulim Krauthammer and Thea Krauthammer; m. Robyn Trethewey; one s. *Education:* McGill Univ., Balliol Coll. Oxford and Harvard Univs, Medical School. *Career:* Resident in Psychiatry, Mass. Gen. Hosp. Boston 1975–78; Scientific Adviser, Dept of Health and Human Services, Washington, DC 1978–80; speech writer to Vice-Pres. Walter Mondale, Washington, DC 1980–81; Sr Ed. The New Republic, Washington, DC 1981–88; essayist, Time Magazine 1983–; syndicated columnist, The Washington Post 1984–; mem. Bd of Advisers, The Nat. Interest, Public Interest; mem. President's Council on Bioethics 2002–. *Publications:* Cutting Edges 1985; contribs. to psychiatric journals. *Honours:* Nat. Magazine Award (for essays), American Soc. of Magazine Eds 1984, First Amendment Award, People for the American Way 1985, Pulitzer Prize (for commentary) 1987. *Address:* c/o The Washington Post Writers Group, 1150 15th Street, NW, Washington, DC 20071, USA. *Website:* www.washingtonpost.com.

KRAUZER, Steven Mark, (Terry Nelson Bonner), BA, MA; American writer; b. 9 June 1948, Jersey City, NJ; m. Dorri T. Karasek 1992; two d. *Education:* Yale University, University of New Hampshire. *Career:* mem. Writers Guild of America West; Authors' Guild; Authors League; MWA. *Publications:* The Cord Series, 1982–86; The Executioner Series, 1982–83; Blaze, 1983; The Diggers, 1983; The Dennison's War Series, 1984–86; Framework, 1989; Brainstorm, 1991; Rojak's Rule, 1992. Anthologies: Great Action Stories, 1977; The Great American Detective, 1978; Stories into Film, 1979; Triquarterly 48: Western Stories, 1980. Contributions: Magazines.

KRAWIEC, Richard, BS, MA; American writer; b. 9 May 1952, Brockton, MA; m. Mary Sturrock 1983, two s. *Education:* Suffolk University, University of New Hampshire. *Career:* mem. Associated Writing Programs; Authors' Guild; Poets and Writers. *Publications:* Time Sharing, 1986; Cardinal: A Contemporary Anthology from North Carolina (ed.), 1986; Faith in What?, 1996; And Fools of God, 2000. Contributions: newspapers and magazines. *Honours:* National Endowment for the Arts Fellowship, 1992; North Carolina Arts Council Fellowship, 1999.

KREMP, Herbert, DPhil; German journalist; b. 12 Aug. 1928, Munich; s. of Johann and Elisabeth Kremp; m. Brigitte Steffal 1956; two d. (one deceased). *Education:* Munich Univ. *Career:* reporter, Frankfurter Neue Presse 1956–57; Political Ed. Rheinische Post 1957–59; Dir Political Dept, Der Tag, Berlin 1959–61; Bonn Corresp. Rheinische Post 1961–63; Ed.-in-Chief, Rheinische Post 1963–68; Ed.-in-Chief, Die Welt 1969–77, Co-Ed. 1981–, Co-Publr 1984–87, Chief Corresp. in Beijing 1977–81, Ed.-in-Chief 1981–85, apptd Chief Corresp. in Brussels 1987, Co-Ed., Springer Group newspapers 1984–87, currently commentator, Die Welt, Berliner Morgenpost, Welt am Sonntag, Bild, B.Z. Berlin, Hamburger Abendblatt. *Publications:* Am Ufer der Rubikon: Eine politische Anthropologie, Die Bambusbrücke: Ein asiatisches Tagebuch 1979, Wir brauchen unsere Geschichte 1988. *Honours:* Konrad Adenauer Prize 1984, Bundesverdienstkreuz 1988. *Address:* c/o Die Welt, Kochstrasse 50, 10969 Berlin, Germany.

KRESS, Nancy, BS, MS, MA; American teacher and writer; b. 20 Jan. 1948, Buffalo, NY; m. 1st Michael Kress (divorced); two s.; m. 2nd Mark P. Donnelly 1988. *Education:* SUNY at Plattsburgh, SUNY at Brockport. *Career:* elementary school teacher, Penn Yan 1970–73; Adjunct Instructor, SUNY at Brockport 1980–; sr copywriter, Stanton and Hucko, Rochester 1984–; mem. SFWA. *Publications:* The Prince of Morning Bells, 1981; The Golden Grove, 1984; The White Pipes, 1985; Trinity and Other Stories, 1985; An Alien Light, 1988; Brain Rose, 1990; Maximum Light, 1998. Contributions: anthologies and periodicals. *Honours:* SFWA Nebula Award 1985.

KRIEGER, Murray, MA, PhD; American academic and writer; b. 27 Nov. 1923, Newark, NJ; m. Joan Alice Stone 1947; one s. one d. *Education:* Rutgers Univ., Univ. of Chicago, Ohio State Univ. *Career:* Prof. of English and Dir of the Program in Criticism, Univ. of California at Irvine 1966–85; Prof. of English, Univ. of California at Los Angeles 1972–83; Univ. Prof. 1974–94, Co-Dir 1975–77, Dir 1977–81, School of Criticism and Theory, Hon. Sr Fellow 1981–, Dir Humanities Research Inst. 1987–89, Univ. Research Prof. 1994–, Univ. of California; Fellow American Acad. of Arts and Sciences; mem. Acad. of Literary Studies, Int. Asscn of Univ. Profs of English, MLA. *Publications:* The Problems of Aesthetics (ed. with Eliseo Vivas) 1953, The New Apologists for Poetry 1956, The Tragic Vision: Variations on a Theme in Literary Interpretation 1960, A Window to Criticism: Shakespeare's Sonnets and Modern Poetics 1964, Northrop Frye in Modern Criticism (ed.) 1966, The Play and Place of Criticism 1967, The Classic Vision: The Retreat from Extremity in Modern Literature 1971, Theory of Criticism: A Tradition and its System 1976, Directions for Criticism: Structuralism and Its Alternatives (ed. with L. S. Dembo) 1977, Poetic Presence and Illusion: Essays in Critical History and Theory 1979, Arts on the Level: The Fall of the Elite Object 1981, The Aims of Representation: Subject/Text/History (ed.) 1987, Words about Words about Words: Theory, Criticism and the Literary Text 1988, A Reopening of Closure: Organicism Against Itself 1989, Ekphrasis: The Illusion of the Natural Sign 1992, The Ideological Imperative: Repression and Resistance in Recent American Theory 1993, The Institution of Theory 1994. *Honours:* several Research Fellowships; Humboldt Foundation Research Prize, Federal Republic of Germany, 1986–87; Medal, University of California at Irvine, 1990. *Address:* c/o University of California Humanities Research Institute, 307 Administration Building, Irvine, CA 92697-3350, USA.

KRIPKE, Saul Aaron, BA, LHD; American philosopher and academic; *Professor Emeritus of Philosophy, Princeton University;* b. 13 Nov. 1940, Bay Shore, New York; s. of Myer Samuel Kripke and Dorothy Kripke; m. Margaret P. Gilbert 1976. *Education:* Harvard Univ. *Career:* Soc. of Fellows, Harvard Univ. 1963–66, concurrently Lecturer with rank of Asst Prof., Princeton Univ. 1964–66; Lecturer, Harvard Univ. 1966–68; Assoc. Prof., Rockefeller Univ. 1968–72, Prof. 1972–76; McCath Prof. of Philosophy, Princeton Univ. 1978–98, now Emer.; Fellow, American Acad. of Arts and Sciences; Corresp. Fellow, British Acad.; Fulbright Fellow 1962–63; Guggenheim Fellow 1968–69, 1977–78; Visiting Fellow, All Souls Coll., Oxford, UK 1977–78, 1989–90; Visiting Prof. The Hebrew Univ. 1998–; other visiting professorships etc. *Publications:* Naming and Necessity 1980, Wittgenstein on Rules and Private Language 1982; numerous papers in professional journals and anthologies. *Honours:* Hon. DHumLitt (Univ. of Neb. at Omaha) 1977, (Johns Hopkins Univ.) 1997, (Univ. of Haifa) 1998. *Address:* Department of Philosophy, Princeton University, Princeton, NJ 08544-1006, USA.

KRIST, Gary Michael, AB; American writer; b. 23 May 1957, New Jersey; m. Elizabeth Cheng 1983; one d. *Education:* Princeton Univ., Fulbright Scholar at Universität Konstanz. *Career:* mem. PEN, Nat. Book Critics' Circle.

Publications: The Garden State (short stories) 1988, Bone by Bone (short stories) 1994, Bad Chemistry (novel) 1998, Chaos Theory (novel) 1999, Extravagance (novel) 2002, The White Cascade (non-fiction); contribs to New York Times Book Review, Wall Street Journal, Salon Internet, Washington Post, Hudson Review, New Republic. *Honours:* Sue Kaufman Prize, American Acad. of Arts and Letters 1989, Stephen Crane Award 2000. *E-mail:* eric@janklow.com*E-mail:* gary@garykrist.com (home). *Website:* www.garykrist.com.

KRISTEVA, Julia, DèsL; French psychoanalyst and writer; b. 24 June 1941, Silven, Bulgaria; m. Philippe Sollers 1967; one s. *Education:* Univ. of Sofia and Ecole des Hautes Etudes en Sciences Sociales, Paris, Univ. of Paris VII. *Career:* researcher in linguistics and French literature Lab. of Social Anthropology, Ecole des Hautes Etudes en Sciences Sociales 1967–73; Prof. Univ. of Paris VII 1973–99, Prof. classe exceptionelle 1999–; Chargé de mission auprès du Pres. for the handicapped; Visiting Prof. Columbia Univ., NY 1974, Univ. of Toronto 1992; psychoanalyst and writer; mem. editorial bd Telquel 1970–82; mem. Soc. psychanalytique de Paris, American Acad. of Arts and Sciences, Inst. Universitaire de France, British Acad., Acad. universelle des cultures. *Publications include:* Séméiotike: Recherches pour une sémanalyse 1969, Le Texte du roman, approche sémiologique d'une structure discursive transformationnelle 1970, La Révolution du langage poétique: l'avant-garde à la fin du XIXème siècle, Lautréamont et Mallarmé 1974, Des chinoises 1974, Polylogue 1977, Folle Vérité (with Jean Michel Ribettes) 1979, Pouvoirs de l'horreur: Essai sur l'abjection 1980, Le Langage, cet inconnu 1981, Histoires d'amour 1985, Au commencement était l'amour 1985, Soleil noir, dépression et mélancolie 1987, Etrangers à nous-mêmes (Prix Henri Hertz 1989) 1988, Les Samouraïs 1990, Lettre ouverte à Harlem Désir 1990, Le Vieil homme et les loups 1991, Les Nouvelles maladies de l'âme 1993, Le Temps sensible: Proust et l'expérience littéraire (essay) 1994, Possessions 1996, Sens et non-sens de la révolte 1996, La Révolte intime 1997, L'Avenir d'une révolte 1998, Le Génie féminin, Vol. 1: Hannah Arendt 1999, Vol. 2: Melanie Klein 2000, Colette 2002, Meurtre à Byzance 2004, La Haine et le Pardon: Pouvoirs et limites de la psychanalyse III 2005. *Honours:* Chevalier, Ordre des Arts et des Lettres 1987, Chevalier, Légion d'honneur 1997, Officier, Ordre Nat. du Mérite 2004; Dr hc (Western Ont., Canada) 1995, (Victoria, Toronto) 1997, (Harvard) 1999, (Univ. Libre de Belgique) 2000, (Bayreuth) 2000, (Toronto) 2000, (Sofia) 2002, (New School, NY) 2003; Prix Henri Hertz Chancellerie des Universités de Paris 1989, Holbeg Prize, Norway 2004, Grande Médaille de Vermeil de la Mairie de Paris 2005. *Address:* Université de Paris VII, 2 place Jussieu, 75005 Paris, France (office). *Telephone:* 1-44-27-63-71 (office). *E-mail:* kristeva@paris7.jussieu.fr (office). *Website:* julia-kristeva.com (office).

KRISTOF, Agota; Swiss (b. Hungarian) writer; b. 30 Oct. 1935, Csikvánd; d. of Kristof Kálmán and Antonia Turchányi; m. 1st Jean Béri 1954; m. 2nd Jean-Pierre Baillod 1963; two d. one s. *Education:* Szombathely (Hungary). *Career:* writer since age of 14; left Hungary 1956; began writing plays in French 1970; factory worker 1983–88; first book published 1986; full-time writer 1988–; Prix Européen ADELF 1986; Prix France-Inter 1992. *Publications:* Un rat qui passe, La fille de l'arpenteur, L'expiation, Le grand cahier 1986, La preuve 1988, Le troisième mensonge 1991, Hier 1995. *Address:* c/o 13 rue de Vieux-Châtel, 2000 Neuchâtel, Switzerland.

KRISTOL, Irving; American editor, writer and academic; *Co-Editor, The Public Interest*; b. 22 Jan. 1920, New York, NY; m. Gertrude Himmelfarb 1942; one s. one d. *Education:* City College, CUNY. *Career:* Managing Ed., Commentary Magazine, 1947–52; Co-Founder and Co-Ed., Encounter magazine, 1953–58; Ed., The Reporter magazine, 1959–60; Exec. Vice-Pres., Basic Books Inc, 1961–69; Co-Ed., The Public Interest magazine, 1965–; Faculty, New York University, 1969–88; John M. Olin Senior Fellow, American Enterprise Institute, 1987–; mem. American Acad. of Arts and Sciences, fellow; Council on Foreign Relations. *Publications:* On the Democratic Idea in America, 1972; Two Cheers for Capitalism, 1978; Reflections of a Neoconservative, 1983; Neoconservatism: The Autobiography of an Idea, 1995. Editor: Encounters (with Stephen Spender and Melvin Lasky), 1963; Confrontation: The Student Rebellion and the University (with Daniel Bell), 1969; Capitalism Today, 1971; The American Commonwealth (with Nathan Glazer), 1976; The Americans (with Paul Weaver), 1976; The Crisis in Economic Theory, 1981; Third World Instability (with others), 1985. Contributions: various publications. *Address:* The Public Interest, 1112 16th Street NW, Suite 140, Washington, DC 20036, USA (office).

KROETSCH, Robert, BA, MA, PhD, FRSC; Canadian academic, writer and poet; b. 26 June 1927, Heisler, AB. *Education:* Univ. of Alberta, Middlebury Coll., VT, McGill Univ. and Univ. of Iowa. *Career:* purser on Mackenzie River boats 1948–50; Dir of Information and Education, US Air Force, Goose Bay, Labrador 1951–54; Asst Prof. of English, SUNY at Binghamton 1961–65, Assoc. Prof. of English 1965–68, Prof. of English 1968–78; founder and Co-Ed., Boundary 2: A Journal of Postmodern Literature 1972–78; Prof. of English, Univ. of Manitoba 1978–85, Distinguished Prof. from 1985. *Publications:* novels: But We Are Exiles 1965, The Words of My Roaring 1966, The Studhorse Man (Governor-General's Award for Fiction 1969) 1969, Gone Indian 1973, Badlands 1975, What the Crow Said 1978, Alibi 1983, The Puppeteer 1992; poetry: The Stone Hammer Poems: 1960–75 1975, Seed Catalogue 1977, The Sad Phoenician 1979, Field Notes: 1–8, A Continuing Poem 1981, Advice to My Friends 1985, Excerpts from the Real World: A Prose Poem in Ten Parts 1986, Completed Field Notes 1989; non-fiction: Alberta 1968, The Crow Journals 1980, Letters to Salonika 1983, Essays: Robert Kroetsch (criticism) 1983, The Lovely Treachery of Words: Essays Selected and New 1989, A Likely Story: The Writing Life (autobiog.) 1995, The Hornbooks of Rita K. 2001. *Honours:* Fellow Univ. of Iowa 1960–61, Fellow Bread Loaf Writers' Conference 1966, Killam Award 1986–88. *Address:* c/o Department of English, University of Manitoba, 625 Fletcher Argue Building, 28 Trueman Walk, Winnipeg, MB R3T 5V5, Canada.

KROKER, Arthur W., BA, MS, PhD; Canadian academic, writer and editor; b. 27 Aug. 1945, Winnipeg, MB; m. Marilouise DiRusso, 9 Aug. 1975, one c. *Education:* University of Windsor, Purdue University, McMaster University. *Career:* Asst Prof., 1975–80, Dir, Canadian Studies, 1979–80, Assoc. Prof. of Political Science, 1980–81, University of Winnipeg; Founding Ed., Canadian Journal of Political and Social Theory, 1975–93, renamed CTHEORY: Theory, Technology, and Culture, 1993–; Assoc. Prof., 1981–87, Prof. of Political Science, 1987–, Concordia University, Montréal; Guest Lecturer, colleges, universities, art museums; mem. Canadian Political Science Asscn; Canadian Communication Asscn; Asscn for Canadian Studies; Conference for the Study of Political Thought. *Publications:* Technology and the Canadian Mind: Innis, McLuhan and Grant, 1984; Panic Encyclopedia: The Definitive Guide to the Postmodern Scene, 1989; The Possessed Individual: Technology and the French Postmodern, 1992; Spasm: Virtual Reality, Android Music, and Electric Flesh, 1993; Data Trash: The Theory of the Virtual Class (co-author), 1994; Hacking the Future: Stories for the Flesh-Eating 90s (co-author), 1996; Digital Delirium (co-ed.), 1997. Contributions: anthologies; Articles and reviews to periodicals. *Honours:* Grants, Social Sciences and Humanities Research Council of Canada; Invited Distinguished Fellow, Society of the Humanities, Cornell University, 1999. *Address:* University of Victoria, Department of Political Science, PO Box 1700 STN CSC, Victoria, BC V8W 2Y2, Canada.

KRONENFELD, Judy Zahler, BA, MA, PhD; American poet and writer; *Lecturer, Creative Writing Department, University of California, Riverside*; b. 17 July 1943, New York, NY; d. of Samuel Zahler and Stella Jupiter Zahler; m. David Brian Kronenfeld 1964; one s. one d. *Education:* Smith Coll., Univ. of Oxford UK, Stanford Univ. *Career:* Visiting Scholar, Univ. of California, Riverside 1977–78, 1981–83, Instructor 1978, Visiting Asst Prof., English Dept 1980–81, 1988–89, Lecturer, Creative Writing Dept 1984–; Lecturer, Univ. of California, Irvine 1972–73, 1978–79, 1984, 1985–86, Visiting Assoc. Prof., English and Comparative Literature 1987; Asst Prof., Purdue Univ. 1976–77. *Publications:* Shadow of Wings (poems) 1991, King Lear and the Naked Truth: Rethinking the Language of Religion and Resistance 1998, Disappeared Down Dark Wells and Still Falling (poems) 2000, Ghost Nurseries 2005; contrib. of articles in scholarly books and journals, poems in anthologies, reviews, quarterlies and magazines. *Honours:* Award for the Best Undergraduate Thesis in English, Smith Coll. 1964, Leverhulme Trust Fund Fellowship 1968–69, Squaw Valley Community of Writers Scholarship 1983, Non-Senate Academic Distinguished Researcher Award, Univ. of California at Riverside 1996–97, Co-Winner first Annual Poetry Contest, The dA Center for the Arts, Pomona, Calif. 2002. *Address:* 3314 Celeste Drive, Riverside, CA 92507, USA.

KROSS, Jaan; Estonian writer and translator; b. 19 Feb. 1920, Tallinn; s. of Jaan Kross and Pauline Kross (née Uhlberg); m. 3rd Ellen Niit-Kross 1958; two s. two d. (one from previous m.). *Education:* Tartu Univ. *Career:* involved in nat. resistance under the Nazi occupation 1943–44; arrested by Nazis Sept. 1944; Lecturer Tartu Univ. 1945–46; arrested by Soviet authorities in 1946 and imprisoned in Intalager (Gulag), Komi Autonomous Repub. 1946–50; deported to Krasnoyarsk region 1950–54; fully exonerated 1960; Sec. Estonian Writers' Union 1976–81, Deputy Chair. 1981–; published prose and poetry 1970–; mem. Riigikogu (Estonian Parl.) 1992–93. *Publications:* Kolme katku vahel (Between Three Plagues) 1970, Keisri hull (trans. as The Czar's Madman) 1978, Professor Martensi ärasõit (trans. as Professor Martens' Departure) 1984, Wikmani poisid (The Wikman Boys) 1988, Väljakaevamised (Excavations) 1990, Vandenõu (trans. as The Conspiracy and Other Stories) 1995, Mesmeri ring (Mesmer's Circle) 1995, Paigallend (trans. as Treading Air) 1998, Tahtamaa (Tahtamaa) 2001, Kallid kaasteelised (Dear Fellow-travellers) 2003, Omaeluloolisus ja alltekst (Autobiographism and Subtext) 2003. *Honours:* Dr hc (Tartu Univ.) 1989, (Helsinki Univ.) 1990; Prix du Meilleur Livre Etranger 1989, Amnesty Int. Golden Flame Prize for Literature 1990, Baltic Ass. Literature Prize 1999. *Address:* Harju Street 1, Apt. 6, 10146 Tallinn, Estonia (home). *Telephone:* (2) 441-697 (home).

KRÜGER, Manfred Paul, DPhil; German writer, academic and editor; *Lecturer, Institute for Spiritual Science and Arts, Nuremberg and Fachhochschule Ottersberg*; b. 23 Feb. 1938, Köslin; s. of Paul Krüger and Hildegard Krüger; m. Christine Petersen 1962; three s. four d. *Education:* Oberrealschule Ansbach, Heidelberg Univ., Tübingen Univ. *Career:* Asst Prof., Erlangen Univ. 1966–73; Lecturer Inst. for Spiritual Science and Arts, Nuremberg 1972–; Lecturer Fachhochschule Ottersberg 1980–; Co-Ed. of the weekly Goetheanum 1984–96. *Publications:* Gérard de Nerval 1966, Wandlungen des Tragischen 1973, Nora Ruhtenberg 1976, Bilder und Gegenbilder 1978, Wortspuren 1980, Denkbilder 1981, Literatur und Geschichte 1982, Mondland 1982, Nah ist er 1983, Meditation 1983, Rosenroman 1985, Meditation und Karma 1988, Anthroposophie und Kunst 1988, Ästhetik der Freiheit 1992, Ichgeburt 1996, Das Ich und seine Masken 1997, Die Verklärung auf dem Berge 2003. *Address:* Rieterstrasse 20, 90419 Nuremberg, Germany. *Telephone:* (911) 338678.

KRUGMAN, Paul Robin, PhD; American economist and academic; *Professor of Economics and International Affairs, Princeton University*; b. 28 Feb. 1953, Albany, New York; s. of David Krugman and Anita Krugman; m. Robin Leslie Bergman 1983. *Education:* Yale Univ., Massachusetts Inst. of Tech. *Career:* Asst Prof., Yale Univ. 1977–79; Asst Prof. MIT 1979–80, Assoc. Prof. 1980–82, Prof. 1983–2000; Sr Staff Economist, Council of Econ. Advisers 1982–83; Columnist, New York Times 1999–; Prof. of Econs and Int. Affairs, Princeton Univ. 2000–. *Publications:* Market Structure and Foreign Trade (with E. Helpman) 1985, International Economics, Theory and Policy (with M. Obsfeld) 1988, The Age of Diminished Expectations 1990, Rethinking International Trade 1990, Geography and Trade 1991, Currencies and Crises 1992, Peddling Prosperity 1994, The Great Unravelling: From Boom to Bust in Three Short Years 2003. *Honours:* John Bates Clark Medal 1991. *Address:* Department of Economics, 414 Robertson Hall, Princeton University, Princeton, NJ 08544, USA. *E-mail:* pkrugman@princeton.edu (office). *Website:* www.econ.princeton.edu (office).

KRUKOWSKI, Lucian Wladyslaw, BA, BFA, MS, PhD; American academic, artist and writer; *Professor Emeritus of Philosophy, Washington University, St Louis*; b. 22 Nov. 1929, New York, NY; m. Marilyn Denmark 1955; one d. *Education:* Brooklyn Coll., CUNY, Yale Univ., Pratt Inst., Washington Univ., St Louis. *Career:* Faculty, Pratt Inst. 1955–69; Dean School of Fine Arts 1969–77, Prof. of Philosophy 1977–96, Chair Dept of Philosophy 1986–89, Prof. Emeritus of Philosophy 1996–, Washington Univ., St Louis; mem. American Philosophical Asscn, Soc. for Aesthetics. *Art Exhibitions:* one-person shows in New York and St Louis, paintings in museums and pvt. collections. *Publications:* Art and Concept 1987, Aesthetic Legacies 1992; anthologies, including The Arts, Society, and Literature 1984, The Reasons of Art 1985, Cultural Literacy and Arts Education 1990, Ethics and Architecture 1990, The Future of Art 1990, Schopenhauer, Philosophy and the Arts 1996; contrib. to professional journals. *Address:* 6003 Kingsbury, St Louis, MO 63112, USA. *Telephone:* (314) 863-5094 (home). *E-mail:* lkruko@hotmail.com (home).

KRUPAT, Arnold, BA, MA, PhD; American academic, writer and editor; b. 22 Oct. 1941, New York, NY; one s. one d. *Education:* New York Univ., Columbia Univ. *Career:* Prof., Sarah Lawrence Coll. *Publications:* For Those Who Come After, 1985; I Tell You Now (ed. with Brian Swann), 1987; Recovering the Word (ed. with Brian Swann), 1987; The Voice in the Margin, 1989; Ethnocriticism: Ethnography, History, Literature, 1992; New Voices: Essays on Native American Literature (ed.), 1993; Native American Autobiography (ed.), 1993; The Turn to the Native: Studies in Culture and Criticism, 1996; Everything Matters: Autobiographical Essays by Native American Writers (ed. with Brian Swann), 1997; Red Matters: Native American Studies, 2002. Contributions: numerous critical journals. *Address:* Sarah Lawrence College, Bronxville, NY 10708, USA.

KRUZHKOV, Grigory; Russian poet, children's writer and translator; b. 1945. *Education:* Tomsk Univ., Siberia and post-graduate studies in physics at Serpukhov nr Moscow. *Career:* translator of English language poetry, including collections by W. B. Yeats, John Donne, John Keats, Robert Frost, Lewis Carroll; Visiting Lecturer Columbia Univ., USA 2001; jury mem. British Council Russia Poetry Translation Competition 2006; mem. PEN Russia. *Publications include:* The Book of Nonsense, Nostalgia for Obelisks: Literary Dreams; juvenile: Guillaum the Gnome and the Moon Kitten, The Rainy Island, Where Things Came From 1995, Big Ben Tales (compiler and trans.) (Int. Bd on Books for the Young Diploma 1996); contrib. to Amerika: Contemporary Russian Writers on the US 2004, Glas: New Russian Writing. *Honours:* State Prize for Literature (translation) 2006. *E-mail:* ftm@litagent .ru. *Website:* www.litagent.ru.

KUBAISI, Tarrad al-; Iraqi journalist; b. 1937, Hit; m. Widdad Al-Jourani 1962; one s. two d. *Education:* Coll. of Literature, Univ. of Baghdad. *Career:* Ed.-in-Chief, Al-Mawsu'a Al-Sagira (small encyclopaedia) 1976–77; Ed.-in-Chief, Al-Aqlam (magazine) 1978–81; Al-Maurid (magazine) 1984–87, 1989–90; Man. and Ed.-in-Chief, Afaq Arabia (magazine) 1991; Press Office and Iraq Cultural Centre, London 1982–84; Press Attaché, Morocco 1988–89; later Chair. Cultural Affairs Office. *Publications:* Introductions in Sumerian Sufi-African Poetry 1971, The New Iraqi Poetry 1972, The Stony Forest Trees 1975, The Forest and Seasons 1979, Al-Munzalat Book (Vol. I) 1992, (Vol. II) 1995, The Artistic Construction in Epic Literature 1994. *Address:* c/o PO Box 4032, Adhamiya, Baghdad, Iraq. *Telephone:* 4436044 (office); 5544746 (home).

KUCBELOVÁ, Katarína, MA; Slovak poet and screenwriter; b. 1979, Banská Bystrica. *Education:* Acad. of Dramatic Art, Bratislava. *Career:* works as a script ed.; has written scripts for two short films, also writes poetry, prose and film reviews. *Publications:* poetry: Duály (Duals); contrib. to anthologies, including A Fine Line: New Poetry from Eastern and Central Europe 2004. *Address:* c/o Literarne Informacne Centrum, Nam. SNP 12, Bratislava 812 24, Slovakia. *E-mail:* lic@litcentrum.sk.

KULTERMANN, Udo, PhD; American academic and writer; *Professor Emeritus of Architecture, Washington University, St Louis*; b. 14 Oct. 1927, Stettin, Germany. *Education:* Univ. of Greifswald, Univ. of Münster. *Career:* Dir City Art Museum, Leverkusen 1959–64; study tour, Nigeria, Ghana, Senegal, Morocco 1962; lecture, First Int. Congress for African Culture, Harare, Zimbabwe (fmrly Salisbury, Rhodesia) 1962; Prof. of Architecture 1967–94, Prof. Emer. 1994–, Washington Univ., St Louis; Int. Corresp., MIMAR, Singapore/London 1981–92; mem. Nat. Faculty of Humanities, Arts, and Sciences, Atlanta 1986–; Corresp. mem. Croatian Acad. of Sciences and Arts, Zagreb 1997–. *Publications:* Architecture of Today 1958, Hans und Wassili Luckhardt: Bauten und Projekte 1958, Dynamische Architektur 1959, New Japanese Architecture 1960, Junge deutsche Bildhauer 1963, Der Schlüssel zur Architektur von heute 1963, New Architecture in Africa 1963, New Architecture in the World 1965, Geschichte der Kunstgeschichte: Der Weg einer Wissenschaft 1966, Architektur der Gegenwart 1967, The New Sculpture 1967, Gabriel Grupello 1968, The New Painting 1969, New Directions in African Architecture 1969, Kenzo Tange: Architecture and Urban Design 1970, Modern Architecture in Color (with Werner Hofmann) 1970, Art and Life: The Function of Intermedia 1970, New Realism 1972, Ernest Trova 1977, Die Architektur im 20. Jahrhundert 1977, I Contemporanei: Storia della scultura nel mondo 1979, Architecture in the Seventies 1980, Architekten der Dritten Welt 1980, Contemporary Architecture in Eastern Europe 1985, Kleine Geschichte der Kunsttheorie 1987, Visible Cities-Invisible Cities: Urban Symbolism and Historical Continuity 1988, Art and Reality: From Fiedler to Derrida: Ten Approaches 1991, Architecture in the 20th Century 1993, Die Maxentius Basilika: Ein Schlüsselwerk Spätantiker Architektur 1996, Architektur der Welt (ed.) 1996–, St James Modern Masterpieces: The Best of Art, Architecture, Photography and Design Since 1945 (ed.) 1998, Contemporary Architecture in the Arab States: Renaissance of a Region 1999, Architecture in South and Central Africa in World Architecture: A Critical Mosaic 1900–2000 (ed.) 2000, Thirty Years After: The Future of the Past 2002, Architecture and Revolution – The Visions of Boullée and Ledoux 2003; contrib. to books, encyclopedias and periodicals. *Honours:* Dr hc (Acad. of Art, Tallinn) 2004; Distinguished Faculty Award Washington Univ., St Louis 1985. *Address:* 300 Mercer Street, Apt 17B, New York, NY 10003, USA. *E-mail:* ukulter@rcn.com (home).

KUMIN, Maxine Winokur, MA; American writer and poet; b. 6 June 1925, Philadelphia; d. of Peter Winokur and Doll Simon; m. Victor M. Kumin 1946; one s. two d. *Education:* Radcliffe Coll. *Career:* consultant in poetry, Library of Congress 1981–82; Fellow, Acad. of American Poets, Chancellor 1995–; Visiting Prof. MIT 1984, Univ. of Miami 1995, Pitzer Coll. 1996; McGee Prof. of Writing, Davidson Coll. 1997; Writer-in-Residence Fla Int. Univ. 1998; Poet Laureate, State of New Hampshire 1989; Nat. Endowment for the Arts Grant 1966, Nat. Council on the Arts Fellowship 1967, Acad. of American Poets Fellowship 1985; mem. Poetry Soc. of America, PEN America, Authors' Guild, Writers' Union. *Publications:* poetry: Halfway 1961, The Privilege 1965, The Nightmare Factory 1970, Up Country: Poems of New England, New and Selected 1972, House, Bridge, Fountain, Gate 1975, The Retrieval System 1978, Our Ground Time Here Will Be Brief 1982, Closing the Ring 1984, The Long Approach 1985, Nurture 1989, Looking for Luck 1992, Connecting the Dots 1996, Selected Poems 1960–1990 1997, The Long Marriage 2001, Bringing Together: Uncollected Early Poems 2003; fiction: Through Dooms of Love 1965, The Passions of Uxport 1968, The Abduction 1971, The Designated Heir 1974, Why Can't We Live Together Like Civilised Human Beings? 1982; other: In Deep: Country Essays 1987, To Make a Prairie: Essays on Poets, Poetry, and Country Living 1989, Women, Animals, and Vegetables: Essays and Stories 1994, Quit Monks or Die! 1999, Inside the Halo and Beyond (memoir) 2000, Always Beginning (essays) 2000; also short stories, children's books and poetry contribs. to nat. magazines. *Honours:* various hon. doctorates; Lowell Mason Palmer Award 1960, William Marion Reedy Award 1968, Eunice Tietjens Memorial Prize 1972, Pulitzer Prize for Poetry 1973, American Acad. of Arts and Letters Award 1980, Poetry magazine Levinson Award 1987, American Acad. and Inst. of Arts Award 1989, Sarah Josepha Hale Award 1992, The Poet's Prize 1994, Aiken Taylor Poetry Prize 1995, Harvard Grad. School of Arts and Sciences Centennial Award 1996, Ruth Lilly Poetry Prize 1999. *Literary Agent:* Scott Waxman Agency Inc., 1650 Broadway, Suite 1011, New York, NY 10019, USA.

KUMMINGS, Donald D., BA, MA, PhD; American academic, poet and writer; *Professor of English, University of Wisconsin, Parkside*; b. 28 July 1940, Lafayette, IN; m. 1st (divorced) 1978; m. 2nd 1987; two s. *Education:* Purdue Univ., Indiana Univ. *Career:* teaching asst Purdue Univ. 1963–64; instructor, Adrian Coll., Michigan 1964–66; Assoc. Instructor, Indiana Univ. 1966–70; Asst Prof. 1970–75, Chair Dept of English 1974–76, 1991–94, Assoc. Prof. 1975–85, Prof. of English 1985–, Univ. of Wisconsin, Parkside; Book Review Ed., The Mickle Street Review 1983–90. *Publications:* Walt Whitman, 1940–1975: A Reference Guide 1982, The Open Road Trip: Poems 1989, Approaches to Teaching Whitman's Leaves of Grass 1990, The Walt Whitman Encyclopedia (ed. with J. R. LeMaster) 1998, A Companion to Walt Whitman 2006; contrib. to anthologies, reviews, quarterlies and journals. *Honours:* Acad. of American Poets Prize 1969, Council for Wisconsin Writers Posner Poetry Prize 1990, Carnegie Foundation for the Advancement of Teaching Wisconsin Prof. of the Year 1997. *Address:* c/o Department of English, University of Wisconsin, Parkside, Kenosha, WI 53141, USA (office). *Fax:* (262) 595-2271 (office). *E-mail:* kumming@uwp.edu (office).

KUNDERA, Milan; Czech/French novelist; b. 1 April 1929, Brno; s. of Dr Ludvik Kundera and Milada Kunderová-Janosikova; m. Věra Hrabánková 1967. *Education:* Film Faculty, Acad. of Music and Dramatic Arts, Prague. *Career:* Asst, later Asst Prof., Film Faculty, Acad. of Music and Dramatic Arts, Prague 1958–69; Prof., Univ. of Rennes 1975–80; Prof. Ecole des hautes études en sciences sociales, Paris 1980–; mem. Union of Czechoslovak Writers 1963–69; mem. Editorial Bd Literární noviny 1963–67, 1968. *Publications:* drama: Jacques and his mother, an homage to Diderot 1971–81; short stories:

Laughable Loves (Czechoslovak Writers' Publishing House Prize) 1970; novels: The Joke (Union of Czechoslovak Writers' Prize 1968) 1967, Life is Elsewhere (Prix Médicis) 1973, La Valse aux adieux (The Farewell Waltz) (Premio letterario Mondello 1978) 1976, Livre du rire et de l'oubli (The Book of Laughter and Forgetting) 1979, The Unbearable Lightness of Being (Los Angeles Times Prize) 1984, Immortality (The Independent Prize, UK 1991) 1989, Slowness 1995, L'Identità (Identity) 1997, La Ignorancia (Ignorance) 2000; essays: The Art of the Novel 1987, Les Testaments trahis (Aujourd'hui Prize, France 1993) 1993, The Curtain 2005. Honours: Dr hc (Michigan) 1983; Commonwealth Award 1981, Prix Europa-Littérature 1982, Jerusalem Prize 1985, Prix de la critique de l' Acad. Française 1987, Nelly Sachs Preis 1987, Österreichische Staatspreis für Europäische Literatur 1988, Jaroslav-Seifert Prize (Czech Repub.) 1994, Medal of Merit (Czech Repub.) 1995, J. G. Herder Prize (Austria) 2000, Grand Prize Acad. Française (for novels Slowness, Identity and Ignorance) 2001. Website: www.faber.co.uk.

KUNERT, Günter; German writer; b. 6 March 1929, Berlin; s. of Adolf Kunert and Edith Warschauer; m. Marianne Todten 1951. Career: Visiting Assoc. Prof., Univ. of Tex. at Austin 1972; Writer-in-Residence, Univ. of Warwick 1975; mem. Akad. der Künste (Hamburg and Mannheim), Akad. für Sprache und Dichtung, Darmstadt; Pres. PEN Centre of German-speaking Writers Abroad. Film: Abschied and others. Play: The Time Machine (based on the novel by H. G. Wells). TV screenplays include: King Arthur 1990, An Obituary of the Wall 1991, Endstation: Harembar 1991 and 13 others. Radio: 10 radio plays. Publications: 60 volumes of poetry, prose, satire, essays, novels, short stories and lectures. Honours: Bundesverdienstkreuz (First Class); Dr hc (Allegheny Coll., Penn.) 1988, (Torino) Heinrich Mann Prize, Akad. der Künste (E Berlin) 1962, Becher Prize for Poetry 1973, Heinrich Heine Prize (City of Düsseldorf) 1985, Hölderlin Prize 1991, E.R. Curtius Prize 1991, Georg-Trakl-Preis (Austria). Address: Schulstrasse 7, 25560 Kaisborstel, Germany. Telephone: (4892) 1414. Fax: (4892) 8403.

KÜNG, Dinah Lee; American journalist and author; b. Detroit, MI; m.; three c. Career: reporter, Washington Post, National Public Radio, International Herald Tribune, The Economist; Hong Kong bureau chief, Business Week; mem. Council on Foreign Relations, PEN Int., Overseas Press Club, Foreign Correspondents Club of Hong Kong. Publications: novels: Left in the Care of 1998, A Visit from Voltaire 2003. Honours: Overseas Press Club Award for Best Human Rights Coverage 1992. Address: c/o Peter Halban Publishers Ltd, 22 Golden Square, London, W1F 9JW, England. Telephone: (20) 7437-9300. Fax: (20) 7437-9512. E-mail: books@halbanpublishers.com. Website: www .halbanpublishers.com.

KÜNG, Hans, DTheol; Swiss theologian and academic; President, Foundation for a Global Ethic; b. 19 March 1928, Sursee, Lucerne. Education: Gregorian Univ., Rome, Italy, Inst. Catholique and Univ. of the Sorbonne, Paris, France. Career: ordained priest 1954; mem. practical ministry, Lucerne Cathedral 1957–59; Scientific Asst for Dogmatic Catholic Theol., Univ. of Münster Westfalen 1959–60; Prof. of Fundamental Theology, Univ. of Tübingen 1960–63; Prof. of Dogmatic and Ecumenical Theology and Dir, Inst. Ecumenical Research 1963–80, Prof. of Ecumenical Theology, Dir Inst. of Ecumenical Research (under direct responsibility of Pres. and Senate Univ. of Tübingen) 1980–96, Prof. Emer. 1996–; Guest Prof., Univ. of Chicago 1981, of Mich. 1983, of Toronto 1985, of Rice Univ., Houston 1987; numerous guest lectures at univs worldwide; mem. PEN; Pres. Foundation Global Ethic, Germany 1995–, Switzerland 1997–; Co-Pres. World Conf. on Religion and Peace, New York; Founding mem. Int. Review of Theology, Concilium. Publications: The Council: Reform and Reunion 1961, That the World May Believe 1963, The Council in Action 1963, Justification: The Doctrine of Karl Barth and a Catholic Reflection 1964, (with new introductory chapter and response of Karl Barth) 1981, Structures of the Church 1964, (with new preface) 1982, Freedom Today 1966, The Church 1967, Truthfulness 1968, Menschwerdung Gottes 1970, Infallible? – An Inquiry 1971, Why Priests? 1972, Fehlbar? – Eine Bilanz 1973, On being a Christian 1976, Signposts for the Future 1978, The Christian Challenge 1979, Freud and the Problem of God 1979, Does God Exist? 1980, The Church – Maintained in Truth 1980, Eternal Life? 1984, Christianity and the World Religions: Paths to Dialogue with Islam, Hinduism and Buddhism (with others) 1986, The Incarnation of God 1986, Church and Change: The Irish Experience 1986, Why I am still a Christian 1987, Theology for the Third Millennium: An Ecumenical View 1988, Christianity and Chinese Religions (with Julia Ching) 1989, Paradigm Change in Theology: A Symposium for the future 1989, Reforming the Church Today 1990, Global Responsibility: In Search of a New World Ethic 1991, Judaism 1992, Credo: The Apostles' Creed Explained for Today 1993, Great Christian Thinkers 1994, Christianity 1995, A Dignified Dying: a plea for personal responsibility (with Walter Jens) 1995, Yes to a Global Ethic (ed.) 1996, A Global Ethic for Global Politics and Economics 1997, Breaking Through (with others) 1998, The Catholic Church: A Short History 2001, Women in Christianity 2001, Tracing the Way: Spiritual Dimensions of the World Religions 2002, My Struggle for Freedom (memoirs) 2003, Islam: Past, Present and Future 2006; ed. Journal of Ecumenical Studies, Revue Internationale de Théologie Concilium, Theological Meditations, Ökumenische Theologie. Honours: Hon. Citizen City of Syracuse, Italy 2002, Tübingen, Germany 2002, Mozart Hon. Chair, European Acad. of Yuste, Spain 2004; Grosses Bundesverdienstkreuz mit Stern 2003; numerous hon. doctorates including Hon. DD (Univ. of Wales) 1998, (Florida Int. Univ.) 2002, (Ecumenical Theological Seminary, Detroit) 2003, Hon. LHD (Ramapo Coll.,

NY) 1999, (Hebrew Union Coll., Cincinnati) 2000, Hon. DPhil (Univ. of Genova) 2004; Ludwig-Thoma Medal 1975, Oskar Pfister Award, American Psychiatric Asscn 1986, Karl Barth Prize, Evangelische Kirche der Union, Berlin 1992, Hirt Prize, Zürich 1993, Prize for Zivilcourage Zürich 1995, Univ. of Tübingen 1996, Theodor Heuss Prize, Stuttgart 1998, Interfaith Gold Medallion of the Int. Council of Christians and Jews 1998, Martin Luther Towns Prize 1999, Ernst-Robert-Curtius Literary Award Bonn 2001, Göttingen Peace Award 2002, Juliet Hollister Award of the Temple of Understanding 2004, Niwano Peace Prize 2005. Address: Waldhäuserstrasse 23, 72076 Tübingen, Germany. Telephone: 62646. Fax: 610140. E-mail: office@weltehos .org (office).

KUNKEL, Thor; German novelist and theatre director; b. 1963, Frankfurt. Education: studied in Frankfurt, San Francisco. Career: moved to London, worked in the media; apptd Creative Head of an int. advertising agency, Netherlands 1992; freelance writer, playwright and dir 1996–. Publications: The Black Light Terranium 2000, Ein Brief an Hanny Porter 2001, Final Stage 2004, bin Shoppen 2006. Honours: Ernst-Willner Award, Literaturstipendium der Preuβ Seehandlung. Literary Agent: Bakker, Friedbergstr. 12, 14057 Berlin-Charlottenburg, Germany. Telephone: (49) 69 2560 0358 (office). E-mail: thor@thorkunkel.de (office). Website: www.thorkunkel.de.

KUNSTLER, James Howard, BS; American writer; b. 19 Oct. 1948, New York, NY; m. 1996. Education: Brockport State Coll. Publications: The Wampanaki Tales 1979, A Clown in the Moonlight 1981, The Life of Byron Jaynes 1983, An Embarrassment of Riches 1985, Blood Solstice 1986, The Halloween Ball 1987, The Geography of Nowhere 1993, Home From Nowhere 1996, The City in Mind: Notes on the Urban Condition 2002, The Long Emergency 2005; contrib. to Atlantic Monthly, New York Times Sunday Magazine. Honours: Humanities Prize 1995. Address: c/o Atlantic Books, Ormond House, 26–27 Boswell Street, London, WC1N 3JZ, England.

KUNZE, Reiner; German writer; b. 16 Aug. 1933, Oelsnitz/Erzgeb.; s. of Ernst Kunze and Martha Kunze (née Friedrich); m. Dr Elisabeth Mifka 1961; one s. one d. Education: Univ. of Leipzig. Career: mem. Bavarian Acad. of Fine Arts, Acad. of Arts, West Berlin 1975–92, German Acad. for Languages and Literature, Darmstadt, Free Acad. of Arts Mannheim, Sächsische Akad. der Künste, Dresden. Photography: solo exhibitions in Berlin, Düsseldorf, Frankfurt, Offenbach, Würzburg and other cities in Germany and Austria. Publications: Sensible Wege 1969, Der Löwe Leopold 1970, Zimmerlautstärke 1972, Brief mit blauem Siegel 1973, Die wunderbaren Jahre 1976, Auf eigene Hoffnung 1981, Eines jeden einziges Leben 1986, Das weisse Gedicht 1989, Deckname 'Lyrik' 1990, Wohin der Schlaf sich schlafen legt 1991, Mensch ohne Macht 1991, Am Sonnenhang 1993, Wo Freiheit ist... 1994, Steine und Lieder 1996, Der Dichter Jan Skácel 1996, Bindewort 'deutsch' 1997, Ein Tag auf dieser Erde 1998, Die Aura der Wörter 2002, Der Kuss der Koi 2002, Wo wir zu Hause das salz haben 2003, Die Chausseen der Dichter (with Mireille Gansel) 2004, Bleibt nur die eigne stirn 2005. Honours: Hon. mem. Collegium Europaeum Jenense of Friedrich-Schiller-Universität Jena; Dr hc; numerous awards and prizes including Literary Prize of Bavarian Acad. of Fine Arts 1973, Georg Trakl Prize (Austria) 1977, Andreas Gryphius Prize 1977, Georg Büchner Prize 1977, Bavarian Film Prize 1979, Eichendorff Literature Prize 1984, Weilheimer Literaturpreis 1997, Europapreis für Poesie, Serbia 1998, Friedrich Hölderlin-Preis 1999; Hans Sahl Prize 2001; Bayerischer Verdienstorden 1988, Grosses Verdienstkreuz der BRD 1993; Bayerischer Maximiliansorden für Wissenschaft und Kunst 2001, Kunstpreis zur Deutschtschechischen Verständigung 2002, Ján Smrek Preis 2003, STAB Preis 2004, Übersetzer Preis 'Premia Bohemica' 2004. Address: Am Sonnenhang 19, 94130 Obernzell, Germany.

KUNZIG, Robert; American science journalist. Career: Contributing Ed., Discover magazine. Publications: The Restless Sea 1999, Mapping the Deep (Aventis Prize 2001) 2000. Honours: American Asscn for the Advancement of Science Westinghouse Science Journalism Award, American Geophysical Union Walter Sullivan Award for Excellence in Science Journalism. Address: Discover Magazine, 90 Fifth Avenue, New York, NY 10011, USA. E-mail: editorial@discover.com. Website: www.discover.com.

KUNZRU, Hari Mohan Nath, BA, MA; British writer and journalist; b. 1969, Woodford Green, Essex, England; s. of Krishna Mohan Nath Kunzru and Hilary Ann David. Education: Wadham Coll., Oxford and Warwick Univ. Career: fmr journalist, Music Ed. Wallpaper magazine, Assoc. Ed. Wired magazine, Contrib. Ed. Mute magazine. Publications: novels: The Impressionist (Observer Young Travel Writer of the Year 1999, Betty Trask Prize 2002) 2002, Transmission 2004, My Revolutions 2007; other: short stories, journalism; contrib. to Wired, London Review of Books, Guardian, Observer, New York Times, Daily Telegraph, BBC Midnight Review. Honours: Somerset Maugham Award 2003, John Llewellyn Rhys Prize 2003, Granta Best of Young British Novelists 2003, Lire 50 Écrivains Pour Demain 2005, British Book Award for Decibel Writer of the Year 2005. Literary Agent: Curtis Brown, Haymarket House, 28–29 Haymarket, London, SW1 4SP, England. Telephone: (20) 7396-6600. Website: www.harikunzru.com.

KUPPNER, Frank; British writer and poet; b. 1951, Glasgow, Scotland. Education: Univ. of Glasgow. Publications: fiction: Ridiculous! Disgusting! 1989, A Very Quiet Street 1989, A Concussed History of Scotland 1990, Something Very Like Murder 1994; poetry: A Bad Day for the Sung Dynasty 1984, The Intelligent Observation of Naked Women 1987, Everything is

Strange 1994, A God's Breakfast 2004. *Address:* c/o Carcanet Press, Fourth Floor, Alliance House, Cross Street, Manchester, M2 7AP, England.

KÜR, Pinar, DèsL; Turkish writer, screenwriter and academic; b. 15 April 1943, Bursa; d. of Behram Kür and Halide Ismet Kür (née Zerluhan); m. Can Kolukisaoğlu 1964 (divorced 1979); one s. *Education:* Forest Hills High School and Queens Coll., New York and Univs of the Bosphorus, Istanbul and Paris (Sorbonne). *Career:* writer, State Theatre of Ankara 1971–73; apptd Lecturer in English, Istanbul Univ. 1979; Lecturer in Literature, Istanbul Bilgi Universifesi 1996. *Films:* Bir kadin, bir hayat 1985, Asılacak Kadan (A Woman to Hang) 1986, Yarin, Yarin (Tomorrow, Tomorrow) 1987. *Publications include:* novels: Yarin, Yarin (Tomorrow, Tomorrow) 1976, Küçük Oyuncu (Petty Player) 1977, Asılacak Kadan (A Woman to Hang) 1979, Bitmeyen Aşk (Unending Love) 1986, Bir Cinayet Romanı (A Crime Novel) 1989, Sonuncu Sonbahar (The Last Fall); short stories: Bir Deli Ağaç (A Tormented Tree) 1981, Akışi Olmayan Sular (Still Waters, Sait Faik Award 1984) 1983; numerous magazine and newspaper articles and translations into Turkish. *Honours:* Sait Faik Award 1984. *Address:* Turna Sokak 7/3, Elmadağ, 80230 Istanbul, Turkey. *Telephone:* (1) 2415148. *E-mail:* kurpinar@hotmail.com (home).

KURAHASHI, Yumiko; Japanese writer; b. 1935, Shikoku. *Education:* Meiji Univ., Univ. of Iowa, USA. *Career:* began writing experimental Japanese fiction 1960–; pioneered post-War Japanese fantasy literature; technique ranges from parodies of classical literature to gothic erotica, ghost stories, futuristic science and avant-garde works; first short story Parutai (The Party) won Meiji Univ. Intramural Fiction Competition 1960. *Publications:* Parutai (The Party) 1961, Kai no naka (Inside the Shell), Hebi (Snake), Kon'yaku (The Engagement), Baajinia (Vriginia) 1968, Sumiyakisuto Q no bōken (The Adventure of Sumiyakist Q) 1989, Yume no ukihashi (Bridge of Dreams) 1971, Han higeki (Anti-tragedies) 1972, Shiro no naka no shiro (A Castle within a Castle), Shunposhion (Symposium), Kōkan (Fraternity), Amanonkoku ōkanki (The Record of the Journey to the Amanon Empire), Otona no tame no zankoku dōwa (Cruel Fairy Tales for Adults) 1984, Creepy Little Stories 1985, The Woman with the Flying Head and Other Stories 1997. *Honours:* Women's Literary Prize, Tamura Toshiko Prize, Izumi Kyoka Prize, and others; Fulbright Scholar, Univ. of Iowa 1966.

KUREISHI, Hanif, BA; British writer and dramatist; b. 5 Dec. 1954, Bromley; m. Tracey Scoffield; three c. *Education:* King's Coll., London. *Career:* worked as typist at Riverside Studios; Writer-in-Residence, Royal Court Theatre, London 1981, 1985–86. *Stage plays:* Soaking the Heat 1976, The Mother Country (Thames TV Playwright Award) 1980, The King and Me 1980, Outskirts (RSC) 1981, Cinders (after the play by Janusz Glowacki) 1981, Borderline (Royal Court) 1981, Artists and Admirers (after a play by Ostrovsky, with David Leveaux) 1981, Birds of Passage (Hampstead Theatre) 1983, Mother Courage (adaptation of a play by Brecht, RSC) 1984, Sleep With Me (Nat. Theatre) 1999, When the Night Begins (Hampstead Theatre) 2004. *Screenplays:* My Beautiful Laundrette (Evening Standard Best Film Award 1986, New York Critics' Best Screenplay Award 1987) 1986, Sammy and Rosie Get Laid 1988, London Kills Me (also directed) 1991, My Son The Fanatic 1997, The Mother 2002. *Television:* The Buddha of Suburbia (BBC) 1993. *Publications:* fiction: The Buddha of Suburbia (Whitbread Award for Best First Novel) 1990, The Black Album 1995, Love in a Blue Time (short stories) 1997, Intimacy 1998, Midnight All Day (short stories) 1999, Gabriel's Gift 2000, The Body 2002, Telling Tales (contrib. to charity anthology) 2004; non-fiction: The Rainbow Sign (autobiog.) 1986, Eight Arms to Hold You (essay) 1991, Dreaming and Scheming: Reflections on Writing and Politics (essays) 2002, My Ear at his Heart (autobiog.) (Prix France Culture littérature étrangère, France 2005) 2004, The Word and The Bomb (essays) 2005; ed.: The Faber Book of Pop (co-ed.) 1995; stories in Granta, Harpers (USA), London Review of Books and The Atlantic; regular contrib. to New Statesman and Society. *Honours:* Chevalier, Ordre des Arts et Lettres 2002; George Devine Award 1981. *Literary Agent:* c/o Rogers, Coleridge & White Ltd, 20 Powis Mews, London, W11 1JN, England.

KURKOV, Andrey; Ukrainian author and screenwriter; b. 1961, St Petersburg, USSR. *Education:* Foreign Language Inst., Kiev. *Career:* fmr journalist, film cameraman. *Publications:* novels in trans.: A Matter of Death and Life 1996, Death and the Penguin 1996, The Case of the General's Thumb 2003, Penguin Lost 2003; other: four children's books, various screenplays. *Address:* c/o The Harvill Press, Random House, 20 Vauxhall Bridge Road, London, SW1V 2SA, England. *Website:* www.randomhouse.co.uk.

KURTZ, Katherine Irene, BS, MA; American writer; b. 18 Oct. 1944, Coral Gables, FL; m. Scott Roderick MacMillan 1983; one s. *Education:* Univ. of Miami, Univ. of California, Los Angeles. *Career:* mem. Authors' Guild, Science Fiction and Fantasy Writers of America, Inc. *Publications:* Deryni Rising 1970, Deryni Checkmate 1972, High Deryni 1973, Camber of Culdi 1976, Saint Camber 1978, Camber the Heretic 1981, Lammas Night 1983, The Bishop's Heir 1984, The King's Justice 1985, The Quest for Saint Camber 1986, The Legacy of Lehr 1986, The Deryni Archives 1986, The Harrowing of Gwynedd 1989, Deryni Magic: A Grimoire 1990, King Javan's Year 1992, The Bastard Prince 1994, Two Crowns for America 1996, King Kelson's Bride 2000, St Patrick's Gargoyle 2001, In the King's Service 2003, Childe Morgan 2006; with Deborah Turner Harris: The Adept 1991, Lodge of the Lynx 1992, The Templar Treasure 1993, Dagger Magic 1994, Death of an Adept 1996, The Temple and the Stone 1998, The Temple and the Crown 2001; with Robert Reginald: Codex Derynianus 1998; editor: Tales of the Knights Templar 1995, On Crusade 1998, Deryni Tales 2002, Crusade of Fire 2002; various short stories. *Honours:* Edmund Hamilton Memorial Award 1977, Balrog Award 1982. *Address:* 1417 North Augusta Street, Staunton, VA 24401, USA. *E-mail:* kkurtz@iol.ie (home). *Website:* www.deryni.net.

KURUMATANI, Chokitsu; Japanese novelist; b. 1 July 1945, Himeji City, Hyogo Pref. *Education:* Keio Univ. *Career:* fmrly worked in advertising and publishing cos and as a cook's helper. *Publications:* novels: Shiotsubo no saji (The Salt Bowl Spoon) (Mishima Yukio Prize) 1992, Hyoryubutsu (Drifting Object) (Hirabayashi Taiko Award) 1995, Akame Shijuuyataki Shinju Misui (Naoki Sanjugo Award), Musashimaru, Han jidaiteki dokumushi 2004, Hibari no su o sagashita hi 2005. *Address:* c/o Kodansha International, Otowa YK Building, 1-17-14 Otowa, Bunkyo-ku, Tokyo 112-8652, Japan. *E-mail:* sales@kodansha-intl.co.jp.

KURZMAN, Dan, BA; American writer; b. 27 March 1929, San Francisco, CA; m. Florence Knopf. *Education:* University of California at Berkeley, Sorbonne, University of Paris. *Career:* Correspondent, International News Service, 1948, NBC, Middle East, 1950–53, Washington Post, 1962–69; Feature Writer, Marshall Plan Information Office, Paris, 1948–49; Bureau Chief, McGraw Hill World News Service, Tokyo, 1954–59; Contributor, Washington Star, 1975–80, Independent News Alliance, 1979–84, San Francisco Chronicle, 1991–92. *Publications:* Kishi and Japan: The Search for the Sun, 1960; Subversion of the Innocents, 1963; Santo Domingo: Revolt of the Damned, 1965; Genesis 1948: The First Arab-Israeli War, 1970; The Race for Rome, 1975; The Bravest Battle: The Twenty-Eight Days of the Warsaw Ghetto Uprising, 1976; Miracle of November: Madrid's Epic Stand 1936, 1980; Ben-Gurion: Prophet of Fire, 1983; Day of the Bomb: Countdown to Hiroshima, 1985; A Killing Wind: Inside Union Carbide and the Bhopal Catastrophe, 1987; Fatal Voyage: The Sinking of the USS Indianapolis, 1990; Left to Die: The Tragedy of the USS Juneau, 1994; Blood and Water: Sabotaging Hitler's Bomb, 1995; Soldier of Peace: The Life of Yitzhak Rabin, 1922–1995, 1998; Disaster: The Great San Francisco Earthquake and Fire of 1906, 2001. Contributions: New York Times Op-Ed Page, 1988–; Washington Post, book reviewer, 1988–; Los Angeles Times, book reviewer, 1988–.

KURZWEIL, Raymond (Ray) C., BS; American computer scientist and business executive; *Chairman and CEO, Kurzweil Technologies*; b. 12 Feb. 1948, Queens, NY; m. Sonya R. Kurzweil. *Education:* Massachusetts Inst. of Tech. *Career:* aspired to become an inventor from age of five; built and programmed his own computer to compose original melodies aged 15; founder and fmr CEO Kurzweil Computer Products, Inc. 1974–80, Kurzweil Music Systems, Inc. 1982–90, Kurzweil Applied Intelligence, Inc. 1982–97, Kurzweil Educational Systems, Inc. 1996; Chair. Strategy and Tech. Cttee Bd Dirs, Wang Laboratories, Inc. 1993–98; Founder, Chair. and CEO Kurzweil Technologies, Inc. 1995–, FAT KAT, Inc. 1999–, Kurzweil Cyber Art Technologies, Inc. 2000–; Founder, Pres. and CEO Medical Learning Co., Inc. and FamilyPractice.com 1997; Founder, CEO and Ed.-in-Chief www.KurzweilAI.net 2001–; Co-Founder, Chair. and Co-CEO Ray & Terry's Longevity Products, Inc. 2003; mem. Bd Dirs Medical Manager Corpn 1997–2000, Inforte 1999–, United Therapeutics 2002–; Chair. and Founder The Kurzweil Foundation; Chair. Robots and Beyond: The Age of Intelligent Machines (exhbn on Artificial Intelligence presented at eight leading science museums) 1987–90; Dir Massachusetts Computer Software Council; fmr Dir Boston Computer Soc.; Incorporator, Boston Museum of Science; mem. MIT Corpn Visiting Cttee, MIT School of Humanities, MIT School of Music, Bd of Overseers, New England Conservatory of Music; fmr mem. Tech. Advisory Cttee, Nat. Center on Adult Literacy, Univ. of Pennsylvania; wrote 'The Futurecast' (monthly column in Library Journal 1991–93); developed first computerized Four-Way Analysis of Variance (statistical program) 1964, first computer-based Expert System for College Selection 1967, first Text-to-Speech speech synthesis 1975, first CCD Flatbed Scanner 1975, first Print-to-Speech Reading Machine for the Blind (Kurzweil Reading Machine) 1976, first Omni-Font (any-type font) Optical Character Recognition (now Xerox Text-Bridge) 1976, first Computer Music Keyboard capable of accurately reproducing sounds of the grand piano and other orchestral instruments (Kurzweil 250) 1984, first Knowledge Base System for Creating Medical Reports (Kurzweil VoiceMED) 1985, first commercially marketed Large Vocabulary Speech Recognition (Kurzweil Voice Report) 1987, first Speech Recognition Dictation System for Windows (Kurzweil Voice for Windows) 1994, first Continuous Speech Natural Language Command and Control Software (Kurzweil VoiceCommands) 1997, first Print-to-Speech Reading System for Persons with Reading Disabilities that Reads from a Displayed Image of the Page (Kurzweil 3000), first Virtual Performing and Recording Artist (Ramona) to perform in front of a live audience with a live band 2001, first 'host/hostess' Avatar on the Web to combine lifelike photo-realistic, moving and speaking facial image with a conversational engine 2001. *Film:* The Age of Intelligent Machines (The Chris Plaque, Columbus Int. Film Festival 1987, Creative Excellence Award, US Industrial Film and Video Festival 1987, Gold Medal – Science Educ., Int. Film and TV Festival of New York 1987, CINE Golden Eagle Award 1987, Tech. Culture Award, Int. Festival of Scientific Films, Belgrade 1988, Prize of the President of the Festival, Int. Film Festival of Czechoslovakia 1988) 1987. *Publications:* The Age of Intelligent Machines (MIT Press Best Seller 1991, Silicon Valley Best Seller 1991, Most Outstanding Computer Science Book of 1990 Award, Asscn of American Publishers 1991) 1990, The 10% Solution for a Healthy Life (Regional Best Seller

1993) 1993, The Age of Spiritual Machines, When Computers Exceed Human Intelligence (Nat. and Regional Best Sellers 1999, 2000, Literary Lights Prize, Boston Public Library 1999) 1999, Are We Spiritual Machines, Ray Kurzweil versus the Critics of Strong AI 2002, Fantastic Voyage: Live Long Enough to Live Forever (co-author) 2004, The Singularity is Near, When Humans Transcend Biology 2005. *Honours:* Hon. Chair. for Innovation, White House Conf. on Small Business 1986; Hon. DHumLitt (Hofstra Univ.) 1982, (Misericordia Coll.) 1989, (Landmark Coll.) 2002, Worcester Polytechnic Inst. 2005; Hon. DMus (Berklee Coll. of Music) 1987; Hon. DSc (Northeastern Univ.) 1988, (Rensselaer Polytechnic Inst.) 1988, (New Jersey Inst. of Tech.) 1990, (City Univ. of New York) 1991, (Dominican Coll.) 1993; Hon. DEng (Merrimack Coll.) 1989; Dr hc in Science and Humanities (Michigan State Univ.) 2000; First Prize, Int. Science Fair in Electronics and Communications 1965, Mass's Gov.'s Award 1977, Grace Murray Hopper Award, Asscn for Computing Machinery (ACM) 1978, Nat. Award, Johns Hopkins Univ. 1981, admitted to Computer Industry Hall of Fame 1982, Pres.'s Computer Science Award 1982, Francis Joseph Campbell Award, American Library Asscn 1983, Best of the New Generation Award, Esquire Magazine 1984, Distinguished Inventor Award, Intellectual Property Owners 1986, The White House Award for Entrepreneurial Excellence 1986, Inventor of the Year Award, awarded by MIT, Boston Museum of Science and Boston Patent Law Asscn 1988, MIT Founders Award 1989, Engineer of the Year Award, Design News magazine 1990, Louis Braille Award, Associated Services for the Blind 1991, Massachusetts Quincentennial Award for Innovation and Discovery 1992, ACM Fellow Award 1993, Gordon Winston Award, Canadian Nat. Inst. for the Blind 1994, Dickson Prize, Carnegie Mellon Univ. 1994, Access Prize, American Foundation for the Blind 1995, Software Industry Achievement Award, Massachusetts Software Council 1996, Pres.'s Award, Asscn on Higher Educ. and Disability 1997, Stevie Wonder/SAP Vision Award for Product of the Year (for the Kurzweil 1000) 1998, Nat. Medal of Tech. 1999, Lemelson-MIT Prize 2000, Second Annual American Composers' Orchestra Award for the Advancement of New Music in America 2001, inducted into Nat. Inventors' Hall of Fame, US Patent Office 2002. *Address:* Kurzweil Technologies, Inc., PMB 193 733, Turnpike Street, North Andover, MA 01845 (office); Kurzweil Technologies, Inc., 15 Walnut Street, Wellesley Hills, MA 02481, USA (office). *Telephone:* (718) 263-0000 (office). *Fax:* (718) 263-9999 (office). *E-mail:* raymond@kurzweiltech.com (office). *Website:* www.KurzweilTech.com (office); www.KurzweilAI.net (office).

KUSHNER, Aleksandr Semyonovich; Russian poet; b. 14 Sept. 1936, Leningrad; s. of Semyon Semyonovich Kushner and Asya Aleksandrovna Kushner; m. Elena Vsevolodavna Nevzglyadova 1981; one s. *Education:* Leningrad Pedagogical Inst. *Career:* lecturer in literature 1959–69. *Publications include:* First Impression 1962, Night Watch 1966, Omens 1969, Letter 1974, Direct Speech 1975, Voice 1978, Canvas 1981, The Tavrichesky Garden 1984, Daydreams 1986, Poems 1986 (Selected Poems), The Hedgerow 1988, A Night Melody 1991, Apollo in the Snow (selected essays on Russian literature of the nineteenth and twentieth centuries and personal memoirs) 1991, Apollo in the Snow (selected poems trans. into English) 1991, On the Gloomy Star (State Prize 1995) 1995, Selected Poetry 1997, The Fifth Element 1999, The Bush 2002, Cold Month of May 2005, Selected Poems 2005, Apollo in the Grass (essays on poetry) 2005, In the New Century 2006; essays in literary journals. *Honours:* Northern Palmira Award 1995, Russian Fed. State Award 1995, German Pushkin Award, Alfred Toepter Foundation 1999, Russian Fed. Alexander Pushkin Award 2001, Nat. 'The Poet' Award 2005. *Address:* Kaluzhsky pereulok No. 9, Apt 48, 193015 St Petersburg, Russia (home). *Telephone:* (812) 577-32-56 (home). *E-mail:* kushner@mail.lanck.net (home).

KUSHNER, Tony, BA, MFA; American playwright; b. 16 July 1956, New York, NY. *Education:* Columbia Univ., New York Univ. *Career:* Playwright-in-Residence, Juilliard School, New York 1990–92. *Publications:* Yes, Yes, No, No 1985, Actors on Acting 1986, Stella 1987, A Bright Room Called Day 1987, Hydriotaphia 1987, The Illusion 1988, The Persistence of Prejudice 1989, Widows (with Ariel Dorfman) 1991, Angels in America: A Gay Fantasia on National Themes, Part One: Millennium Approaches (Pulitzer Prize 1993) 1991, Part Two: Perestroika 1992, Slavs! 1994, Holocaust and the Liberal Imagination 1994, Thinking About the Longstanding Problems of Virtue and Happiness 1995, Homebody/Kabul 2001, Caroline, or Change (Best New Musical, Laurence Olivier Awards 2007) 2006. *Honours:* Tony Award 1993, 1994, Critics' Circle Award, London Evening Standard Award. *Literary Agent:* Steven Barclay Agency, 12 Western Avenue, Petaluma, CA 94952, USA. *Telephone:* (707) 773-0654. *Fax:* (707) 778-1868. *Website:* www.barclayagency.com.

KUSKIN, Karla Seidman, (Nicholas J. Charles); American children's writer and illustrator; b. 17 July 1932, New York, NY; m. 1st Charles M. Kuskin 1955 (divorced 1987); one s. one d.; m. 2nd William L. Bell 1989. *Education:* Antioch College 1950–53, BFA, Yale University 1955. *Career:* Illustrator for several publishers; Conductor of poetry and writing workshops. *Publications:* Roar and More 1956, James and the Rain 1957, In the Middle of the Trees 1958, The Animals and the Ark 1958, Just Like Everyone Else 1959, Which Horse is William? 1959, Square As a House 1960, The Bear Who Saw the Spring 1961, All Sizes of Noises 1962, Alexander Soames: His Poems 1962, How Do You Get From Here to There? 1962, ABCDEFGHIJKLMNOPQRSTUVWXYZ 1963, The Rose on My Cake 1964, Sand and Snow 1965, Jane Anne June Spoon and Her Very Adventurous Search for the Moon 1966, The Walk the Mouse Girls Took 1967, Watson, the Smartest Dog in the USA 1968, In the Flaky Frosty Morning 1969, Any Me I Want To Be: Poems 1972, What Did You Bring Me? 1973, Near the Window Tree: Poems and Notes 1975, A Boy Had a Mother Who Brought Him a Hat 1976, A Space Story 1978, Herbert Hated Being Small 1979, Dogs and Dragons, Trees and Dreams: A Collection of Poems 1980, Night Again 1981, The Philharmonic Gets Dressed 1982, Something Sleeping in the Hall 1985, The Dallas Titans Get Ready for Bed 1986, Jerusalem, Shining Still 1987, Soap Soup, 1992, A Great Miracle Happened Here: A Chanukah Story 1993, Patchwork Island 1994, City Dog 1994, City Noise 1994, Paul 1994, James and the Rain 1995, Thoughts, Pictures and Words (autobiog. for children) 1995, The Upstairs Cat 1997, The Sky is Always in the Sky (poems) 1998, I Am Me 2000, The Animals and the Ark 2002, Moon Have You Met My Mother (poetry collection) 2003, Roar and More 2004, Under My Hood I've Got a Hat 2005, So, What's It Like to be a Cat? 2005 contrib. to magazines and periodicals. *Honours:* Book Show Awards, American Institute of Graphic Arts 1955–60, Children's Book Award, International Reading Asscn 1976, Children's Book Council Showcase Selections 1976–77, National Council of Teachers of English Award for Poetry 1979, Children's Science Book Award, New York Acad. of Sciences 1980, American Library Asscn Awards 1980, 1982, 1993, School Library Journal Best Book 1987, John S. Burrough Science Award 1992, Bank Street Coll. of Educ. Lifetime Achievement Award 2004. *Address:* 96 Joralemon Street, New York, NY 11201; 16631 Mariner Drive NE, Bainbridge Island, WA 98110, USA.

KÜTHEN, Hans-Werner, MA, PhD; German musicologist; b. 26 Aug. 1938, Cologne; m. Annette Magdalena Leinen; one s. *Education:* Bonn Univ., studied in Bologna. *Career:* Ed., Beethoven Archives; mem. Gesellschaft für Musikforschung, VG Musikedition; Patron of the Verein Beethoven-Haus Bonn. *Publications:* On Beethoven: Essay, Kammermusik mit Bläsern 1969, Article Beethoven Herder, Das Grosse Lexikon der Musik 1978, Complete edition, Henle, München: Ouverturen und Wellingtons Sieg 1974, Critical Report, separately 1991, Klavierkonzerte I (nos 1–3) 1984, Klavierkonzerte II (nos 4–5) 1996, Klavierkonzerte III (Wo0 4, Wo0 6, op. 61a) 2004, each with Critical Report; contrib. to int. professional publications, including Beethoven yearbooks, congress reports, scholarly periodicals; journal contribs include: International Congress of the Gesellschaft für Musikforschung, Freiburg i.Br, 1993: Gradus ad partituram; Erscheinungsbild und Funktionen der Solostimme in Beethovens Klavierkonzerten, Congress Report, 1999; Gradus ad Partituram: Appearance and Essence in the Solo Part of Beethoven's Piano Concertos, Beethoven Forum Vol. 9 No. 2, Urbana-Champaign, Ill. 2002; Ein unbekanntes Notierungsblatt Beethovens aus der Entstehungszeit der Mondscheinsonate, Prague, 1996; Rediscovery and reconstruction of an authentic version of Beethoven's Fourth Piano Concerto for pianoforte and 5 strings, see Beethoven Journal Vol. 13 No. 1, San José, 1998 and Bonner Beethoven-Studien Vol. 1, Bonn 1999; On Viadana: Article V in Herder-Lex, 1982, id in Lexikon für Theologie und Kirche, Herder, 2000; Co-Editor, Beethoven im Herzen Europas. Leben und Nachleben in den Böhmischen Ländern, 2000; Ed., Beethoven und die Rezeption der Alten Musik, Report of the Int. Symposium, Bonn 2000, Die hohe Schule der Überlieferung, Bonn 2002; A Lost Sonority: Beethoven's imitation of the Aeolian Harp, Arietta Vol. 4, London 2004; Wer schrieb den Endtext des Violinkonzerts op. 61 von Beethoven? Franz Alexander Pössinger als letze Instanz für den Komponisten, Bonner Beethoven-Studien Vol. 4, Bonn 2005; Coriolanus Overture, conducting score with Preface, Wiesbaden 2005. *Address:* Am Hofgarten 7, 53113 Bonn, Germany.

KUTTNER, Paul; American publicity director (retd) and writer; b. 20 Sept. 1922, Berlin, Germany; m. Ursula Timmermann 1963 (divorced 1970); one s. *Education:* Bryanston Coll., Dorset, UK. *Career:* child actor in films of Fritz Lang, G. W. Pabst, and Gerhard Lamprecht, Germany 1930–31; US Publicity Dir, Guinness Book of World Records 1964–89; Publicity Dir, Sterling Publishing Co. Inc. 1989–98. *Films include:* M 1931, Kammeradschaft, Emil und die Detektive; appeared in documentaries including The Kindertransport: My Knees Were Jumping 1991, Into the Arms of Strangers 2000, Die Rote Kapelle 2003. *Publications:* The Man Who Lost Everything 1976, Condemned 1983, Absolute Proof 1984, The Iron Virgin 1985, History's Trickiest Questions 1990, Arts & Entertainment's Trickiest Questions 1993, Science's Trickiest Questions 1994, The Holocaust: Hoax or History? – The Book of Answers to Those Who Would Deny the Holocaust 1997, An Endless Struggle: Reminiscences and Reflections (autobiog.) 2007; several translations of books; contrib. to Der Weg, London Week. *Address:* 37 26 87th Street, Apt 5C, Jackson Heights, NY 11372, USA (home). *Telephone:* (718) 446-2179 (home).

KWEI-ARMAH, Kwame; British actor, playwright and singer; b. (Ian Roberts), 1967, London; three c. *Education:* Barbara Speake Stage School. *Career:* writer-in-residence, Bristol Old Vic 1999–01; currently writer on attachment to the Nat. Theatre Studio; took part in Celebrity Fame Acad. (BBC) 2003. *Plays as writer:* Big Nose (adaptation of Rostand's Cyrano De Bergerac, Belgrade Theatre, Coventry) 1999, Blues Brother Soul Sister (musical, Bristol Old Vic) 2000, A Bitter Herb (Peggy Ramsey Bursary, Bristol Old Vic) 2001, Hold On (Durham Theatre Royal) 2002, Elmina's Kitchen (Royal Nat. Theatre, Charles Wintour Award for Most Promising Playwright, Evening Standard Theatre Awards 2004) 2003, Fix Up (Royal Nat. Theatre) 2004. *Plays as actor:* Mozart and Salieri (Crucible, Sheffield). *Films:* Cutthroat Island 1995. *Television:* Between The Lines 1994, Casualty 1999–2004, Holby City 2000, Pride 2004. *Recordings:* album: Kwame 2003. *Honours:* Evening Standard Charles Wintour Award for Most Promising Playwright 2003.

Literary Agent: c/o A & C Black Publishing Ltd., 38 Soho Square, London, W1D 3HB, England. *Telephone:* (20) 7758-0200. *Fax:* (20) 7758-0222. *Website:* www.acblack.com. *Address:* 19c Beaconsfield Road, London, N1 3AA, England.

KYLE, Duncan (see Broxholme, John Franklin)

KYLE, Susan Eloise Spaeth, (Diana Blayne, Diana Palmer), BA; American author; b. 12 Dec. 1946, Cuthbert, GA; m. James Edward Kyle 1972, one s. *Education:* Piedmont Coll. *Career:* mem. Authors' Guild. *Publications:* Heather's Song, 1982; Diamond Spur, 1988; Amelia, 1993; Nora, 1994; All That Glitters, 1995; many other books. Contributions: journals and magazines.

L

LA PLANTE, Lynda; British television dramatist and novelist; *Chairman, La Plante Productions Ltd;* b. 15 March 1946, Formby; m. Richard La Plante (divorced). *Education:* Royal Coll. of Dramatic Art. *Career:* fmr actress; appeared in The Gentle Touch, Out, Minder; founder and Chair. La Plante Productions 1994–. *Television includes:* Prime Suspect 1991, 1993, 1995, Civvies, Framed, Seekers, Widows (series), Comics (two-part drama) 1993, Cold Shoulder 2 1996, Cold Blood, Bella Mafia 1997, Trial and Retribution 1997–, Killer Net 1998, Mind Games 2000, The Warden 2001, Framed 2002, Widows (mini-series) 2002, The Commander 2003. *Publications include:* The Widows 1983, The Widows II 1985, The Talisman 1987, Bella Mafia 1991, Framed 1992, Civvies 1992, Prime Suspect 1992, Seekers 1993, Entwined 1993, Prime Suspect 2 1993, Lifeboat 1994, Cold Shoulder 1994, Prime Suspect 3 1994, She's Out 1995, The Governor 1996, Cold Blood 1996, Trial and Retribution 1997, Cold Heart 1998, Trial and Retribution 2 1998, Trial and Retribution 3 1999, Trial and Retribution 4 2000, Sleeping Cruelty 2000, Trial and Retribution 5 2002, Trial and Retribution 6 2002, Royal Flush 2002, Like a Charm (short stories) 2004, Above Suspicion (novel) 2004, The Red Dahlia 2006. *Address:* La Plante Productions Ltd, Paramount House, 162–170 Wardour Street, London, W1F 8ZX, England (office). *Telephone:* (20) 7734-6767. *Fax:* (20) 7734-7878. *Website:* www.laplanteproductions.com.

LA TOURETTE, Jacqueline, (Sabrina Grant); American writer; b. (Jacqueline Gibeson), 5 May 1926, Denver, CO. *Education:* San Jose State Coll. *Publications:* The Joseph Stone, 1971; A Matter of Sixpence, 1972; The Madonna Creek Witch, 1973; The Previous Lady, 1974; The Pompeii Scroll, 1975; Shadows in Umbria, 1979; The Wild Harp, 1981; Patarran, 1983; The House on Octavia Street, 1984; The Incense Tree, 1986.

LAABI, Abdellatif; Moroccan poet, novelist, essayist and translator; b. 1942, Fès; m. Jocelyne Laabi 1964; three c. *Education:* Rabat Univ. *Career:* French teacher at coll. in Rabat; founder Souffles literary journal 1966–72 (publ. banned); founder Atlantes Publishing Co. and Association de Recherche Culturelle; imprisoned for 'crimes of opinion', Kénitra 1973–80; exiled in France 1985–; mem. Académie Mallarmé. *Plays:* Exercices de tolérance, Le juge de l'ombre. *Publications:* poetry: Le Règne de barbarie 1980, Histoire des sept crucifiés de l'espoir 1980, Sous le bâillon le poème 1981, Discours sur la colline arabe 1985, L'Ecorché vif 1986, Tous les déchirements 1990, L'Etreinte du monde 1993, Le Spleen de Casablanca 1996, Fragments d'une genèse oubliée 1998, Poèmes périssables 2000, Petit musée portatif 2002, L'Automne promet 2003, Les Fruits du corps 2003, Ruses de vivant 2004, Ecris la vie 2005, Oeuvre poétique 2006; novels: L'Oeil et la nuit 1969, Le Chemin des ordalies 1982, Les Rides du lion 1989, Le Fond de la jarre 2002; non-fiction: La Parole confisquée 1982, La Brûlure des interrogations 1985, Un Continent humain 1997, L'Ecriture au tournant 2000, Rimbaud et Shéhérazade 2000, Les Rêves sont têtus 2001, Chroniques de la citadelle d'exil 2005, Pourquoi cours-tu après la goutte d'eau? 2006; juvenile: L'Orange bleue 1995; translator: La Poésie palestinienne contemporaine (anthology, co-ed. and trans.) 1990, La Poésie marocaine de l'indépendance à nos jours (anthology, ed. and trans.) 2005, poetry by Aïcha Arnaout, Qassim Haddad, Mohammed Bennis, Saadi Youssef, Faraj Bayrakdar, Abdallah Zrika, Ghassan Kanafani, Mohamed al-Maghout, Hassan Hamdane, Mahmoud Darwich, Samih al-Qassim, Abdelwahab al-Bayati, Hanna Mina, Abdallah Zrika. *Honours:* Prix de l'amitié franco-arabe 1979, Prix de la liberté PEN Club français 1980, African Literature Asscn Fonlon Nichols Prize 1999, Wallonie-Bruxelles poetry prize 1999, Prix de poésie Alain Bosquet 2006. *Address:* 8 rue de Mesly, 94000 Créteil, France (home). *Telephone:* 1-48-99-26-40 (home). *E-mail:* jalaabi@free.fr (home). *Website:* www.laabi.net (home).

LABERGE, Andrée, PhD; Canadian novelist; b. 1953, Québec City. *Career:* doctor of epidemiology, also trained and worked as a social worker; combines writing with career as public health researcher. *Publications:* Les Oiseaux de verre 2000, L'Aguayo 2001, La Rivière du loup (Gov.-Gen.'s Literary Award) 2006. *Address:* c/o XYZ Publishing, 1781 Saint Hubert Street, Montréal, QC H2L 3Z1, Canada (office). *E-mail:* info@xyzedit.qc.ca (office).

LABERGE, Marie; Canadian dramatist, author, poet and editor; b. 29 Nov. 1950, Québec. *Education:* Université Laval, Conservatoire d'art dramatique de Québec. *Career:* Pres., Centre d'essai des auteurs dramatiques, 1987–89; Theatre Ed., Editions du Boréal, 1991–. *Publications:* Avec l'hiver qui s'en vient, 1981; Ils étaient venus pour..., 1981; C'était avant la guerre à l'Anse à Gilles, 1981, English trans. as Before the War, Down at l'Anse à Gilles, 1986; Jocelyne Trudelle trouvée morte dans ses larmes, 1983; Deux tangos pour toute une vie, 1985; L'homme gris, 1986, English trans. as Night, 1988; Le Night Cap Bar, 1987; Oublier, 1987, English trans. as Forgetting, 1988; Aurélie, ma soeur, 1988, English trans. as Aurélie, My Sister, 1989; Le Blanc, 1989; Juillet, 1989; Quelques adieux, 1992; Pierre, ou, La consolation, 1992; Annabelle, 1996; Le gout du bonheur, 2000. *Contributions:* Film, radio, television and various publications. *Honours:* Gov.-Gen.'s Award for Drama, 1982; Chevalier, Ordre des Arts et des Lettres, 1989; Prix des Lectrices de Elle-Québec, 1992.

LABIN, Suzanne, LèsSc; French writer and journalist; b. 6 May 1913, Paris; m. Edouard Labin 1935. *Education:* Univ. of Paris (Sorbonne). *Career:* Articles published world-wide; conf. and lecture tours world-wide; human rights activist; Pres. Freedom League; Sec. Société des Gens de Lettres; Dr hc (London); Prix de la Liberté; Grand Officier de l'Ordre du Mérite Européen; Prix Henri Malherbe, Asscn des Ecrivains Combattants. *Publications include:* Stalin the Terrible 1950, The Anthill 1959, Techniques of Soviet Propaganda 1960, Fifty Years USSR/USA 1962, Sellout in Vietnam 1964, Promise and Reality 1967, Hippies, Drugs, Promiscuity 1970, Le monde des drogués 1975, La violence politique 1978, Israël: le crime de vivre 1981, Les colombes rouges 1985, Les états térroristes, La guerre des lâches 1987, Vivre en dollars et votez en roubles 1988, Les pièges de Gorbatchev 1990, Des menteurs masochistes vous trompent: Voulez vous savoir pourquoi? 1992, Les Indignations selectives de la gauche: Anti-colonialistes, anti racistes, anti sexistes selectifs 1993, L'Etonnante Suzanne Labin: son coeur, sa lutte, son message 1995. *Address:* 3 rue Thiers, 75116 Paris, France. *Telephone:* (1) 45-53-74-09.

LaBUTE, Neil; American playwright and film writer and director; b. 19 March 1963, Detroit, Mich.; m.; two c. *Education:* Brigham Young Univ., Univ. of Kan., New York Univ. *Films include:* In the Company of Men (writer, dir) (Sundance Film Festival Filmmakers' Trophy, Soc. of Tex. Film Critics Best Original Screenplay Award, New York Film Critics' Circle Best First Film) 1997, Your Friends and Neighbors (writer, dir) 1998, Tumble (writer) 2000, Nurse Betty (dir) 2000, Possession (screenplay writer, dir) 2002, The Shape of Things (writer, dir) 2003, The Wicker Man 2006. *Theatre productions include:* Woyzeck, Dracula, Sangguinarians & Sycophants, Ravages, Rounder, Lepers, Filthy Talk For Troubled Times, In the Company of Men (Asscn for Mormon Letters Award for Drama 1993) 1992, Bash: Latterday Plays 2000, The Shape of Things 2001, The Distance From Here (Almeida, London) 2002, The Mercy Seat 2002, Merge 2003, Wrecks (Everyman Palace, Cork) 2005, This is How it Goes (New York, and Donmar Warehouse London) 2005, Some Girl(s) 2005. *Television includes:* Bash: Latter-Day Plays 2001. *Publications include:* In the Company of Men 1998, Your Friends and Neighbors 1999, Bash: Latterday Plays 2000, The Shape of Things 2001, The Distance from Here 2003, The Mercy Seat 2003, Seconds of Pleasure (short stories) 2004. *Literary Agent:* William Morris Agency, One William Morris Place, Beverly Hills, CA 90212, USA. *Telephone:* (310) 859-4000 (office). *Fax:* (310) 859-4462 (office). *Website:* www.wma.com (office).

LACEY, Robert, BA, DipEd, MA; British writer; b. 3 Jan. 1944, Guildford, Surrey, England. *Education:* Selwyn Coll., Cambridge. *Career:* Asst Ed., Sunday Times Magazine 1969–73; Ed., Look! pages, Sunday Times 1973–74; Co-Ed., Co-Publisher Cover magazine 1999–2000. *Publications:* The French Revolution (two vols) 1968, The Rise of Napoleon 1969, The Peninsular War 1969, 1812: The Retreat From Moscow 1969, Robert, Earl of Essex: An Elizabethan Icarus 1971, The Life and Times of Henry Vlll 1972, The Queens of the North Atlantic 1973, Sir Walter Raleigh 1973, Sir Francis Drake and the Golden Hinde 1975, Heritage of Britain (ed., contrib.) 1975, Majesty: Elizabeth II and the House of Windsor 1977, The Kingdom: Arabia and the House of Saud 1981, Princess 1982, Aristocrats 1983, Ford: The Men and the Machine 1986, God Bless Her: Her Majesty Queen Elizabeth the Queen Mother 1987, Little Man: Meyer Lansky and the Gangster Life 1991, Grace 1994, Sotheby's: Bidding for Class 1998, The Year 1000 (with Danny Danziger) 1999, Royal: Her Majesty Queen Elizabeth II 2002, Great Tales from English History: Cheddar Man to the Peasants' Revolt 2003, From Chaucer to the Glorious Revolution 2004, Battle of the Boyne to DNA 2006. *Address:* c/o Curtis Brown, 28/29 Haymarket, London, SW1Y 4SP, England.

LACKEY, Mercedes, BS; American writer; b. 24 June 1950, Chicago, IL; m. 1st Anthony Lackey 1972 (divorced); m. 2nd Larry Dixon 1990. *Education:* Purdue University. *Career:* mem. SFWA. *Publications:* Arrow's Flight, 1987; Arrows of the Queen, 1987; Arrow's Fall, 1988; Oathbound, 1988; Magic's Pawn, 1989; Oathbreakers, 1989; Reap the Whirlwind (with C. J. Cherryh), 1989; Children of the Night, 1990; Knight of Ghosts and Shadows (with Ellen Guon), 1990; Magic's Price, 1990; Magic's Promise, 1990; By the Sword, 1991; The Elvenbane (with Andre Norton), 1991; Jinx High, 1991; Winds of Fate, 1991; Born to Run (with Larry Dixon), 1992; Castle of Deception (with Joshua Sherman), 1992; The Lark and the Wren, 1992; The Last Herald Mage, 1992; Summoned to Tourney (with Ellen Guon), 1992; The Ship Who Searched (with Anne McCaffrey), 1992; Wheels of Fire (with Mark Shepherd), 1992; Winds of Change, 1992; Wing Commander: Freedom Flight (with Ellen Guon), 1992; Burning Water, 1993; Fortress of Frost and Fire (with Ru Emerson), 1993; If I Pay Thee Not in Gold (with Piers Anthony), 1993; Prison of Souls (with Mark Shepherd), 1993; Rediscovery: A Novel of Darkover (with Marion Zimmer Bradley), 1993; The Robin and the Kestrel, 1993; When the Bough Breaks (with Holly Lisle), 1993; Winds of Fury, 1993; The Black Gryphon (with Larry Dixon), 1994; A Cast of Corbies (with Joshua Sherman), 1994; Chrome Circle (with Larry Dixon), 1994; Sacred Ground, 1994; Storm Warning, 1994; The Eagle and the Nightingales, 1995; Elvenblood (with Andre Norton), 1995; The Fire Rose, 1995; Storm Rising, 1995; Tiger Burning Bright (with Andre Norton and Marion Zimmer Bradley), 1995; The White Gryphon (with Larry Dixon), 1995; Firebird, 1996; Lammas Night, 1996; The Silver Gryphon (with Larry Dixon), 1996; Storm Breaking, 1996; Four and Twenty Blackbirds, 1997; Owlflight (with Larry Dixon), 1997; Owlsight (with Larry Dixon), 1998; The Black Swan, 1999; The Chrome Bone (with Larry Dixon), 1999; Owlknight (with Larry Dixon), 1999; The River's Gift, 1999; Werehunter,

1999; Brightly Burning, 2000; Beyond the World's End, 2001; The Serpent's Shadow, 2001. Contributions: many anthologies and periodicals.

LACOUTURE, Jean Marie-Gérard, DenSoc; French writer; b. 9 June 1921, Bordeaux; s. of Antoine-Joseph Lacouture and Anne-Marie Servantie; m. Simone Grésillon; one d. *Career:* journalist 1946–72; Press Attaché, Résidence-Générale of France, Morocco 1947–49; Diplomatic Ed. Combat 1950–51; reporter, Le Monde 1951–72; corresp., France-Soir, Egypt 1954–56; Research Fellow, Harvard Univ. 1966; Dir of Collections, Editions du Seuil 1962–80. *Publications include:* Cinq Hommes et la France 1961, De Gaulle 1965, Le Vietnam entre deux paix 1965, Hô Chi Minh 1967, Nasser 1971, André Malraux, une vie dans le siècle 1973, Un sang d'encre 1974, Léon Blum 1977, Survive le peuple cambodgien! 1978, Signes du Taureau 1979, François Mauriac (two vols) 1980, Pierre Mendès France 1981, Le Piéton de Bordeaux 1981, Profils perdus 1983, De Gaulle (three vols) 1984–86, Algérie: la guerre est finie 1985, Champollion: Une vie de lumières 1989, Enquête sur l'auteur 1989, Jésuites (two vols) 1991–92, Voyous et gentlemen: une histoire du rugby 1993, le Désempire (jtly) 1993, Une adolescence du siècle 1994, Mes héros et nos monstres 1995, Montaigne à cheval 1996, Histoire de France en cent tableaux 1997, Mitterrand (two vols) 1998, Greta Garbo: la dame aux caméras 1999, Stendhal – Le bonheur vagabond 2004; several works in collaboration with Simonne Lacouture and others. *Honours:* Officer, Légion d'honneur, Commdr des Arts et Lettres; Prix Sola Cabiati de la Ville de Paris 1996. *Address:* 37 quai des Grands Augustins, 75006 Paris, France.

LADJALI, Cécile, DLit; French writer and teacher; b. 1971, Lausanne. *Education:* Sorbonne, Univ. of Paris. *Career:* student teacher, Institut universitaire de formation des maîtres, Créteil; now French teacher, Lycée Évariste-Gallois, Noisy-le-Grand. *Publications:* Murmures (poems) 2001, Tohu-Bohu (tragic play) 2002, Les Souffleurs (novel) 2002, Éloge de la transmission: le maître et l'élève (non-fiction, with George Steiner) 2003, La Chapelle Ajax (novel) 2005. *Address:* c/o Actes Sud, 18 rue Séguier, 75006 Paris, France. *E-mail:* accueil.paris@actes-sud.fr.

LAFERRIÈRE, Dany; Canadian (b. Haitian) writer; b. 17 April 1953, Port-au-Prince, Haiti. *Career:* journalist for Petit Samedi Soir and Radio Haïti; went into exile 1976, moving to Montréal, Canada, where worked as journalist, TV presenter for Télévision Quatre Saisons network; now lives in Miami, USA; writes in French. *Films:* Voodoo Taxi (writer) 1991, Vite, je n'ai pas que cela à faire (writer), Le Violon rouge (actor) 1998, Le Goût des jeunes filles (adaptation of novel) 2004, Comment conquérir l'Amérique en une nuit (writer, dir) 2004, Vers le sud (writer) 2005. *Publications include:* Comment faire l'amour avec un nègre sans se fatiguer (novel, trans. as How to Make Love to a Negro Without Getting Tired) 1985, Éroshima (novel, trans. as Eroshima) 1987, L'Odeur du café (trans. as An Aroma of Coffee) (Prix Carbet de la Caraïbe) 1991, Le Goût des jeunes filles (novel, trans. as Dining with the Dictator) (Prix Edgar-l'Espérance) 1992, Cette grenade dans la main du jeune nègre est-elle une arme ou un fruit? (novel, trans. as Why Must a Black Writer Write About Sex?) (Prix RFO du Livre 2002) 1993, Chronique de la dérive douce (poems, trans. as A Drifting Year) 1994, Pays sans chapeau (novel, trans. as Down Among the Dead Men) 1996, La Chair du maître 1997, Le Charme des après-midi sans fin (novel) 1997, Dans l'oeil du cyclone 1999, Le Cri des oiseaux foux (novel) (Marguerite Yourcenar Prize 2001) 2000, Je suis fatigué 2000, Les Annees 80 dans ma vieille Ford 2005, Vers le sud 2006, J'écris comme je vis 2006, Je suis fou de Vava (juvenile) (Governor-General's Literary Award) 2006. *Address:* c/o Éditions Grasset, 61 rue des Saints-Pères, 75006 Paris, France.

LAFFIN, John Alfred Charles, MA, DLitt; Australian author, journalist and lecturer; b. 21 Sept. 1922, Sydney, NSW; m. Hazelle Stonham 1943 (died 1997); one s. two d. *Career:* Battlefield Archaeologist; Adviser/Consultant, War, Military History and Islam; Founder, John Laffin Australian Battlefield Museum, 1988; mem. Society of Authors, UK; Australian Society of Authors; Pres., Families and Friends of the First A I F. *Publications:* Return to Glory, 1953; Digger: Story of the Australian Soldier, 1959; Codes and Ciphers, 1964; Anzacs at War, 1965; Jackboot: Story of the German Soldier, 1965; The Hunger to Come, 1966; Women in Battle, 1967; Devil's Goad, 1970; Americans in Battle, 1972; The Arab Mind, 1974; Dagger of Islam, 1979; Damn the Dardanelles!, 1980; Fight for the Falklands, 1982; The PLO Connections, 1982; Australian Army at War 1899–1975, 1982; The Man the Nazis Couldn't Catch, 1984; On the Western Front, 1985; Know the Middle East, 1985; Brassey's Battles, 1986; War Annual 1, 1986; War Annual 2, 1987; Battlefield Archaeology, 1987; War Annual 3, 1987; Western Front, 1916–17: The Price of Honour, 1988; Western Front, 1917–18: The Cost of Victory, 1988; Holy War – Islam Fights, 1988; War Annual 4, 1988; British Butchers and Bunglers of World War I, 1989; War Annual 5, 1991; The Western Front Illustrated, 1991; Dictionary of Africa Since 1960, 1991; Guidebook to Australian Battlefields of France and Flanders 1916–18, 1992; Digging up the Diggers, War, 1993; Panorama of the Western Front, 1993; A Western Front Companion, 1994; Forever Forward, 1994; War Annual 6, 1994; Aussie Guide to Britain, 1995; Hitler Warned Us, 1995; War Annual 7, 1995; Brassey's Book of Espionage 1996; War Annual 8, 1997; British VCs of World War II, 1997; The Spirit and the Source (poems), 1997; Gallipoli, 1999; The Somme, 1999; Raiders: Great Exploits of the Second World War, 1999; The Battle of Hamel: Australians' Finest Victory, 1999; Combat Surgeons, 1999; A Kind of Immortality (autobiog.), Vol. 1, 2000. Contributions: newspapers, magazines and journals.

LAFFONT, Robert Raoul, LenD; French publishing executive; b. 30 Nov. 1916, Marseille; s. of Raymond Laffont and Nathalie Périer; m. Hélène Furterer 1987; three s. two d. (from previous marriages). *Education:* Lycée Pérrier, Marseille and Ecole des Hautes Etudes Commerciales, Paris. *Career:* Lt 94th Regt of Artillery, Montagne; f. Editions Robert Laffont, Marseille 1941, transferred to Paris 1945, Pres. 1959–86; Fondateur du Pont-Royal. *Publication:* Robert Laffont, éditeur 1974, Léger étonnement avant le saut 1995. *Honours:* Chevalier, Légion d'Honneur, Officier, Ordre Nat. du Mérite. *Address:* Editions Robert Laffont, 24 avenue Marceau, 75008 Paris (office); 11 rue Pierre Nicole, Paris 75005, France (home). *Telephone:* 43-29-12-33 (office); 43-26-02-41 (home).

LAGZDINS, Viktors, DipEd; Latvian writer; b. 28 Aug. 1926, Rīga; s. of Oto Lagzdins and Adele Freiberga; m. Dzidra Reita 1952; one d. *Education:* Pedagogic School, Liepaja, Riga Pedagogic Inst. *Career:* teacher 1947–58; journalist, Liepaja newspaper 1958–63; Riga magazine 1963–87; mem. Writers' Union of Latvia (chair. of the prose section 1979–80). *Publications include:* Parbaude (trans. as The Test) 1959, Indianu Virsaitis Drossirdigais Kikakis 1963, Kedes Loks 1972, Nakts Mezazos (trans. as A Night at Elk Farm) 1976, Zili Zala (trans. as The Blue and the Green) 1986, Nulles gada odiseja (trans. as Year Zero Odyssey, WWII) 2006. *Honours:* IBA Award of Excellence (UK) 2006. *Address:* Agenskalna iela 22-48, Rīga 1046, Latvia (home). *Telephone:* 6762-4242 (home).

LAHIRI, Jhumpa, BA, MA, PhD; British/American novelist and teacher; b. 1967, London, England; m.; one s. *Education:* Barnard Coll. and Boston Univ. *Career:* fmr tutor in Creative Writing, Boston Univ., Rhode Island School of Design. *Publications:* novels: Interpreter of Maladies (Pulitzer Prize for Fiction 2000) 1999, The Namesake 2003; short story contrib. to The New Yorker 1998. *Honours:* PEN/Hemingway Award, the New Yorker Debut of the Year award, an American Academy of Arts and Letters Addison Metcalf Award, Guggenheim Fellowship 2002. *Address:* c/o Houghton Mifflin Co., 222 Berkeley Street, Boston, MA 02116, USA.

LAI, Jimmy; Hong Kong business executive, journalist and publisher. *Career:* Propr Giordano (retail clothing chain) 1980–, Chair. 1980–94; Publr Next Magazine 1990–, Apple Daily 1995–. *Address:* Apple Daily, 6/F Garment Centre, 576–586 Castle Peak Road, Cheung Sha Wan; Next Magazine, Westlands Centre, 10/F, 20 Westlands Road, Quarry Bay, Hong Kong, Special Administrative Region, People's Republic of China. *Telephone:* 29908685 (Apple Daily); 28119686 (Next Magazine). *Fax:* 23708908 (Apple Daily); 28113862 (Next Magazine).

LAI, Larissa, BA; Canadian writer and poet; b. 13 Sept. 1967, La Jolla, CA, USA. *Education:* University of British Columbia. *Career:* Asst Curator, Yellow Peril: Reconsidered, 1990; Co-ordinator, Saw Video Co-op, 1991; Television and Video Assoc., Banff Centre for the Arts, 1994; Ed., Front Magazine, 1994–95; Gallery Animateur, Vancouver Art Gallery, 1996–97; Writer-in-Residence, University of Calgary, 1997–98; mem. Writers Union of Canada; Asian Canadian Writers Workshop. *Publications:* fiction: New Reeboks, 1994; The Home Body, 1994; Water, and Other Measures of Distance, 1996; The Voice of the Blind Concubine, 1996; The Peacock Hen, 1996. Poetry: The Birdwoman, 1990; Lullabye for the Insect Catcher, 1990; Eighty Years Bathing, 1991; Where, 1991; Trap I, 1991; Trap II, 1991; Bone China, 1991; Nora, 1991; Glory, 1991; Arrangements, 1991; Shade, 1991; Nostalgia, 1992; Calling Home, 1992; The Escape, 1992; Tell: Longing and Belonging, 1994. *Honours:* Astraea Foundation Emerging Writers Award, 1995.

LAIRD, Elizabeth Mary Risk, BA, MLitt; British writer; b. 21 Oct. 1943, Wellington, New Zealand; m. David Buchanan McDowall 1975; two s. *Education:* Bristol Univ., Edinburgh Univ. *Publications:* Red Sky in the Morning 1988, Arcadia 1990, Kiss the Dust 1991, Hiding Out 1993, Secret Friends 1996, Jay 1997, The Wild Things Series 1999–2000, Jake's Tower 2001, The Garbage King 2003, A Little Piece of Ground 2003, Paradise End 2004, Oranges in No Man's Land 2006. *Honours:* Children's Book Award 1992, Glass Globe Award Dutch Royal Geographical Soc. 1992, Smarties Young Judges Award 1994, Lancashire Book Award 1997. *Address:* 31 Cambrian Road, Richmond, Surrey TW10 6JQ, England. *Website:* www.elizabethlaird.co.uk.

LAIRD, Nick; Northern Irish writer, lawyer, poet and critic; b. 1975, Cookstown, Co. Tyrone; m. Zadie Smith 2004. *Education:* Univ. of Cambridge. *Career:* writer Times Literary Supplement; fmr Visiting Fellow Harvard Univ. *Publications:* Firmhand the Queried 2004, The Last Saturday in Ulster 2004, To A Fault (poems) 2004, Utterly Monkey (novel) (Soc. of Authors Betty Trask Prize 2006) 2005; contrib. poems to various journals in UK and USA, including London Review of Books, TLS, New Writing 11. *Honours:* Quiller-Couch Award for Creative Writing, Eric Gregory Award 2004, Rooney Prize for Irish Literature 2005, Irish Chair of Poetry Prize 2005, Aldeburgh First Collection Award 2005. *Address:* c/o Faber and Faber Ltd, 3 Queen Square, London, WC1N 3AU, England.

LAKE, David John, BA, MA, DipEd, PhD; Australian academic and writer; b. 26 March 1929, Bangalore, India; m. Marguerite Ivy Ferris 1964; one d. three step-c. *Education:* Trinity College, Cambridge, University of Wales, Bangor, University of Queensland, Australia. *Publications:* Hornpipes and Funerals (poems) 1973, The Canon of Thomas Middleton's Plays 1975, Walkers on the Sky 1976, The Right Hand of Dextra 1977, The Wildings of Westron 1977, The Gods of Xuma 1978, The Man who Loved Morlocks 1981, The Changelings of

Chaan 1985; editor: H.G.Wells, The Invisible Man, The First Men in the Moon; contrib. to Extrapolation, Science Fiction Studies, Foundation, Notes and Queries, Explicator, Ring Bearer, Wellsian. *Honours:* Ditmar Awards for Best Australian Science Fiction Novel 1977, 1982, and for Short Fiction 1999. *Address:* 7 Eighth Avenue, St Lucia, Qld 4067, Australia. *E-mail:* djlake@ optusnet.com.au.

LAKO, Natasha; Albanian politician and writer; b. 13 May 1948, Korça; m. Sjevlan Shanaj 1970; one s. one d. *Education:* Univ. of Tirana. *Career:* teacher 1966–68; journalist 1968–71; scriptwriter 1976–88; freelance writer 1989–91; worked for New Albania Film Studios, Tirana; mem. Parl. (Kuvendi Popullor—Democratic Party) 1991. *Films include:* Nusja dhe shtetërrethimi (script supervisor) 1978, Ballë për ballë (script supervisor and line producer) 1979, Mësonjëtorja 1979, Partizani i vogël Velo 1980, Rruga e lirisë 1982, Një emër midis njerzëve 1983, Fjalë pa fund 1986, Një vitë i gjatë 1987, Muri i gjallë 1989, Lule të kuqe, lule të zeza (aka Black Flowers) 2003. *Television includes:* Koha nuk pret 1984, Fletë të bardha 1990. *Publications include:* poetry: Marsi brenda nesh (March within us) 1972, E para fjalë e botë (The World's First Word) 1979, Këmisha e pranverës (The Spring Shirt) 1984, Yllësia e fjalëve (Constellation of Words) (Migjeni Prize 1986) 1986, Natyrë e qetë (Quiet Nature) 1990, Thesi me pëllumba (The Bag of Doves) 1995; novel: Stinët e jetës (The Seasons of Life) 1977; poems translated into German and Dutch. *Honours:* Film Festival Prize for Screenplays 1980. *Telephone:* (42) 23502. *Fax:* (42) 22540.

LAKSHMI, C. S. (see Ambai)

LAL, Deepak Kumar, MA, BPhil; British academic; *James S. Coleman Professor of International Development Studies, Department of Economics, UCLA;* b. 3 Jan. 1940, Lahore, India; s. of the late Nand Lal and of Shanti Devi; m. Barbara Ballis 1971; one s. one d. *Education:* Doon School, Dehra Dun, St Stephen's Coll., Delhi, India, Jesus Coll., Oxford. *Career:* Indian Foreign Service 1963–65; Lecturer, Christ Church, Oxford 1966–68; Research Fellow, Nuffield Coll., Oxford 1968–70; Lecturer, Univ. Coll. London 1970–79, Reader 1979–84, Prof. of Political Economy, Univ. of London 1984–93, Prof. Emer. 1993–; James S. Coleman Prof. of Int. Devt Studies, UCLA 1991–; Consultant, Indian Planning Comm. 1973–74; Research Admin., World Bank, Washington, DC 1983–87; Dir Trade Policy Unit, Centre for Policy Studies 1993–96, Trade and Devt Unit, Inst. of Econ. Affairs 1997–2002; consultancy assignments ILO, UNCTAD, OECD, IBRD Ministry of Planning, Sri Lanka, Repub. of Korea 1970–. *Publications:* Wells and Welfare 1972, Methods of Project Analysis 1974, Appraising Foreign Investment in Developing Countries 1975, Unemployment and Wage Inflation in Industrial Economies 1977, Men or Machines 1978, Prices for Planning 1980, The Poverty of "Development Eonomics" 1983, Labour and Poverty in Kenya (with P. Collier) 1986, Stagflation, Savings and the State (co-ed. with M. Wolf) 1986, The Hindu Equilibrium (two vols) 1988, 1989, Public Policy and Economic Development (co-ed. with M. Scott) 1990, Development Economics (four vols) (ed.) 1991, The Repressed Economy 1993, Against Dirigisme 1994, The Political Economy of Poverty, Equity and Growth (with H. Myint) 1996, Unintended Consequences 1998, Unfinished Business 1999, Trade, Development and Political Economy (co-ed. with R. Snape) 2001, In Praise of Emires 2004, The Hindu Equilibrium 2005, Reviving the Invisible Hand: The Case for Classical Liberalism in the 21st Century 2006. *Address:* Department of Economics, 8369 Bunche Hall, UCLA, Box 951477, Los Angeles, CA 90095-1477, USA (office); A30 Nizamuddin West, New Delhi 110013, India; 2 Erskine Hill, London, NW11 6HB, England. *Telephone:* (310) 825-4521 (office); (310) 206-2382 (office); 462 9465 (New Delhi); (20) 8458-3713 (London). *Fax:* (310) 825-9528 (office). *Website:* econweb.sscnet.ucla.edu (office).

LAM, Vincent; Canadian writer and physician; b. 5 Sept. 1974, London, ON; m. Margarita Lam; one s. *Education:* Univ. of Toronto. *Career:* emergency room physician Toronto East General Hospital. *Publications:* Bloodletting and Miraculous Cures (short stories) (Scotiabank Giller Prize for Excellence in English-language Canadian Fiction, Royal Conservatory of Music Cecilia Zhang Award) 2006, The Flu Pandemic and You (non-fiction, with Colin Lee) 2006, A Quiet Snow (short story) 2007, Cholon, Near Forgotten (novel) 2007; contrib. fiction to Carve and non-fiction to the Globe and Mail, National Post, Toronto Star, Toronto Life Magazine, University of Toronto Medical Journal. *Honours:* Young Writer's Development Trust short story competition award. *Literary Agent:* Anne McDermid & Associates, 83 Willcocks Street, Toronto, ON M5S 1C9, Canada. *Telephone:* (416) 324-8845. *Fax:* (416) 324-8870. *E-mail:* info@mcdermidagency.com. *E-mail:* contact2007@vincentlam.ca. *Website:* www.vincentlam.ca.

LAMB, Andrew Martin, MA, FIA; British writer on music and writer on cricket; b. 23 Sept. 1942, Oldham, Lancashire, England; m. Wendy Ann Davies 1970; one s. two d. *Education:* Corpus Christi Coll., Oxford. *Career:* life mem. Lancashire County Cricket Club. *Publications:* Jerome Kern in Edwardian London 1985, Ganzl's Book of the Musical Theatre (with Kurt Ganzl) 1988, Skaters' Waltz: The Story of the Waldteufels 1995, An Offenbach Family Album 1997, Shirley House to Trinity School 1999, 150 Years of Popular Musical Theatre 2000, Leslie Stuart: Composer of Florodora 2002, Fragson: the Triumphs and the Tragedy (with Julian Myerscough) 2004; editor: The Moulin Rouge 1990, Light Music from Austria 1992, Leslie Stuart: My Bohemian Life 2003; contrib. to The New Grove Dictionary of Music and Musicians, The New Grove Dictionary of American Music, The New Grove Dictionary of Opera, Gramophone, Musical Times, Classic CD, American Music, Music and Letters, Wisden Cricket Monthly, Cricketer, Listener, Notes. *Address:* 12 Fullers Wood, Croydon, CR0 8HZ, England (home). *Telephone:* (20) 8777-5114 (home). *E-mail:* andrew@light-music.net (home). *Website:* www.light-music.net.

LAMB, Christina, MA; British journalist; b. 15 May 1965, London; d. of Kenneth Ernest Edward and Anne Doreen Lamb. *Education:* Nonsuch High School (Surrey) and Univ. Coll. (Oxford). *Career:* News Reporter Cen. TV 1987–88; Financial Times Corresp. in Afghanistan and Pakistan 1988–89, in Brazil 1990; London Times War Corresp.; Young Journalist of the Year 1988. *Publication:* Waiting for Allah 1991, The Africa House 2000, The Sewing Circles of Herat 2003, Tea with Pinochet 2007. *Address:* c/o Author Mail, Penguin Books, 80 Strand, London, WC2R 0RL, England.

LAMBDIN, Dewey Whitley, II, BS; American writer; b. 21 Jan. 1945, San Diego, CA; m. 1st Melinda Alice Phillips 1971; m. 2nd Julie Dawn Pascoe 1984. *Education:* Montana State Univ. *Career:* mem. Sisters in Crime. *Publications:* The King's Coat, 1989; The French Admiral, 1990; King's Commission, 1991; King's Privateer, 1992; The Gun Ketch, 1993; For King and Country, 1994; HMS Cockerel, 1995; King's Commander, 1997. *Contributions:* newspapers and periodicals. *Honours:* Theme Vault, University of Tennessee 1963.

LAMBERT, Angela Maria, BA; British writer and journalist; b. 14 April 1940, Beckenham, Kent, England; m. Martin Lambert 1962 (divorced 1966); one s. two d. *Education:* St Hilda's Coll., Oxford. *Career:* publishing 1961–62; journalism 1962–63; politics 1964–67; newspaper journalism 1967–72; television reporter 1972–88; newspaper feature writer and columnist, The Independent 1988–95, Daily Mail 1995–2000, The Sunday Telegraph 2001–03; mem. English PEN (exec. cttee 1991–96). *Publications:* non-fiction: Unquiet Souls 1984, 1939: The Last Season of Peace 1989, The Lost Life of Eva Braun 2006; fiction: Love Among the Single Classes 1986, No Talking after Lights 1989, A Rather English Marriage 1991, The Constant Mistress 1994, Kiss and Kin 1997, Golden Lads and Girls 1998, The Property of Rain 2001; several contribs to other publications 1965–. *Honours:* Romantic Novel of the Year 1988. *Literary Agent:* c/o Caradoc King, AP Watt Ltd, 20 John Street, London, WC1N 2DR, England. *Telephone:* (20) 7244-9762 (office).

LAMBERT, Derek William, (Richard Falkirk); British journalist and author; b. 10 Oct. 1929, London, England. *Career:* journalist, Devon, Norfolk, Yorkshire and national newspapers 1950–68. *Publications:* Fiction: For Infamous Conduct, 1970; Grans Slam, 1971; The Great Land, 1977; The Lottery, 1983. Mystery Fiction: Angels in the Snow, 1969; The Kites of War, 1970; The Red House, 1972; The Yermakov Transfer, 1974; Touch the Lion's Paw, 1975; The Saint Peter's Plot, 1978; The Memory Man, 1979; I, Said the Spy, 1980; Trance, 1981; The Red Dove, 1982; The Judas Code, 1983; The Golden Express, 1984; The Man Who Was Saturday, 1985; Chase, 1987; Triad, 1988. Mystery Novels as Richard Falkirk: The Chill Factor, 1971; The Twisted Wire, 1971; Blackstone, 1972; Beau Blackstone, 1973; Blackstone's Fancy, 1973; Blackstone and the Scourge of Europe, 1974; Blackstone Underground, 1976; Blackstone on Broadway, 1977. Other: The Sheltered Days: Growing Up in the War, 1965; Don't Quote Me – But, 1979; And I Quote, 1980; Unquote, 1981; Just Like the Blitz: A Reporter's Notebook, 1987; The Night and the City, 1989; The Gate of the Sun, 1990.

LAMBERT, Richard Peter, BA; British journalist and organization official; *Director-General, Confederation of British Industry (CBI);* b. 23 Sept. 1944, s. of Peter Lambert and Mary Lambert; m. Harriet Murray-Browne 1973; one s. one d. *Education:* Fettes Coll. and Balliol Coll. Oxford. *Career:* mem. staff, Financial Times 1966–2001, Lex Column 1972, Financial Ed. 1978, New York Corresp. 1982, Deputy Ed. 1983, Ed. Financial Times 1991–2001; lecturer and contrib. to The Times 2001–; external mem. Bank of England Monetary Policy Cttee (MPC) 2003–06; Dir-Gen. Confederation of British Industry (CBI), London 2006–; Dir (non-exec.) London Int. Financial Futures Exchange (LIFFE), AXA Investment Mans, Int. Rescue Cttee UK; Chair. Visiting Arts; Gov. Royal Shakespeare Co.; UK Chair. Franco-British Colloque; mem. UK – India Round Table; mem. Int. Advisory Bd, British-American Business Inc. *Honours:* Hon. DLitt (City Univ. London) 2000; Princess of Wales Amb. Award 2001, World Leadership Forum Business Journalist Decade of Excellence Award 2001. *Address:* CBI, Centre Point, 103 New Oxford Street, London, WC1A 1DU, England (office). *Telephone:* (20) 7395-8001 (office). *Website:* www .cbi.org.uk (office).

LAMBOT, Isobel Mary, (Daniel Ingham, Mary Turner), BA, PGCE; British novelist; b. 21 July 1926, Birmingham, England; m. Maurice Edouard Lambot 1959 (deceased). *Education:* Liverpool University, Birmingham University. *Career:* Tutor in Creative Writing, Lichfield Evening Institute, 1973–80; mem. CWA; Society of Authors; Writers' Guild of Great Britain; MWA. *Publications:* As Isobel Lambot: Taste of Murder, 1966; Deadly Return, 1966; Shroud of Canvas, 1967; Dangerous Refuge, 1967; Danger Merchant, 1968; The Queen Dies First, 1968; Killer's Laughter, 1968; Let the Witness Die, 1969; Point of Death, 1969; Watcher on the Shore, 1971; Come Back and Die, 1972; Grip of Fear, 1974; The Identity Trap, 1978; Past Tense, 1979; Rooney's Gold, 1984; Still Waters Run Deadly, 1987; Blood Ties, 1987; Bloody Festival, 1991; The Flower of Violence, 1992; The Craft of Writing Crime Novels, 1992. As Daniel Ingham: Contract for Death, 1972. As Mary Turner: The Justice Hunt, 1975; So Bright a Lady, 1977; Runaway Lady, 1980. *Contributions:* Women's journals.

LAMBRAKIS, Christos D.; Greek newspaper proprietor and journalist; b. 24 Feb. 1934, s. of the late Dimitrios Ch. Lambrakis. *Education:* LSE. *Career:* Publr and Ed. weekly Tachydromos (Courier) 1955–, now Chair.; succeeded father as propr of dailies To Vima (Tribune), Ta Nea (News) and the weeklies Economicos Tachydromos (Economic Courier) 1957, Omada (The Team) 1958; Publr monthly Epoches 1963; Pres. Greek Section, Int. Press Inst.; imprisoned (Folegandros Prison Island) Nov. 1967; Chair. Lambrakis Research Foundation. *Address:* c/o Lambrakis Press SA, Michalakopoulou str., 80, 115 28 Athens, Greece. *Telephone:* (21) 3657000. *Fax:* (21) 3686445. *E-mail:* info@in .gr. *Website:* www.dol.gr.

LAMBRON, Marc; French journalist and writer; b. 4 Feb. 1957, Lyon; s. of Paul Lambron and Jacqueline Lambron (née Denis); m. Sophie Missoffe 1983; one s. two d. *Education:* Ecole normale supérieure, Institut d'etudes politiques, Ecole nationale d' admin. *Career:* columnist, Point 1986–, Madame Figaro; mem. Conseil d'Etat 1985–. *Publications:* L'Impromptu de Madrid 1988, La nuit des masques 1990, Carnet de bal 1992, L'oeil du silence 1993, 1941 1997, Etrangers dans la nuit 2001, Carnet de bal II 2003, Les Menteurs 2004, Une saison sur la terre 2006. *Honours:* Chevalier, Ordre des Arts et des Lettres, Chevalier, Légion d'honneur 2004; Prix des Deux Magots 1989, Prix Colette 1991, Prix Fémina 1993. *Address:* 17 rue Lagrange, 75005 Paris, France. *Telephone:* 1-40-51-02-12. *Fax:* 1-46-33-43-18.

LAMM, Donald Stephen, BA; American publisher; *Literary Agent, Carlisle & Company;* b. 31 May 1931, New York; s. of Lawrence W. Lamm and Aleen A. Lassner; m. Jean S. Nicol 1958; two s. one d. *Education:* Fieldston School, Yale Univ. and Univs of Oxford, UK. *Career:* Counter-intelligence Corps, US Army 1953–55; joined W. W. Norton & Co. Inc. 1956, college rep. 1956–59, Ed. 1959–2000, Dir 1964–2000, Vice-Pres. 1968–76, Chair. 1984–2000; Pres. Yale Univ. Press 1984–2000; currently Literary Agent, Carlisle & Co.; mem. Editorial Bd The American Scholar; Regents Lecturer, Univ. of Calif., Berkeley 1997–99; mem. Advisory Council Inst. of Early American History and Culture 1979–82; mem. Council on Foreign Relations 1978–; mem. Council, Woodrow Wilson Center, Int. Advisory Bd, Logos; Guest Fellow, Yale Univ. 1980, 1985; Trustee, The Roper Center 1984–; Fellow, Branford Coll. Yale Univ. 1985–2000, Center for Advanced Study in Behavioral Sciences 1998–99; Guest Fellow Woodrow Wilson Center 1996; Pres. Bd of Govs Yale Univ. 1986–; Ida H. Beam Distinguished Visiting Prof. Univ. of Iowa 1987–88; mem. American Acad. of Arts and Sciences (first book publisher elected in AAAS history); Vice-Pres. Phi Beta Kappa Soc. 2003–; Trustee Univ. of Calif. Press. *Publications:* Economics and the Common Reader 1989, Beyond Literacy 1990, Book Publishing in the United States Today 1997, Perception, Cognition and Language 2000. *Address:* Carlisle & Co., 24 East 64th Street, New York, NY 10021 (office); 741 Calle Picacho, Santa Fe, NM 87301, USA (home).

LAMMING, George Eric; Barbadian novelist; b. 8 June 1927, Carrington Village. *Career:* Writer-in-Residence, University of the West Indies, Jamaica 1967–68. *Publications:* In the Castle of My Skin, 1953; The Emigrants, 1955; Of Age and Innocence, 1958; Water with Berries, 1971; Natives of My Person, 1972. Short Stories: David's Walk, 1948; A Wedding in Spring, 1960; Birthday Weather, 1966; Birds of a Feather, 1970. *Honours:* Guggenheim Fellowship, 1954; Maugham Award, 1957; Canada Council Fellowship, 1962; DLitt, University of the West Indies, 1980.

LAMMON, Martin, BA, MA, PhD; American academic and poet; b. 19 June 1958, Wilmington, OH; m. Frances Elizabeth Davis 1996. *Education:* Wittenberg University, Ohio University. *Career:* Visiting Instructor in English, Juniata College, Huntingdon, Pennsylvania, 1988–91; Asst Prof., then Assoc. Prof. of English, Fairmont State College, West Virginia, 1991–97; Co-Founder and Co-Ed., Kestrel: A Journal of Literature and Art, 1992–97; Prof. of English and Fuller E. Callaway Endowed Flannery O'Connor Chair in Creative Writing, Georgia College and State University, Milledgeville, 1997–; mem. Associated Writing Programs. *Publications:* Written in Water, Written in Stone: Twenty Years of Poets on Poetry (ed.), 1996; News From Where I Live: Poems, 1998. Contributions: periodicals. *Honours:* Fellow, West Virginia Commission on the Arts, 1994; Arkansas Poetry Award, University of Arkansas Press, 1997; Neruda Prize for Poetry, Nimrod International Journal, 1997. *Address:* 103 Cambridge Drive S, Milledgeville, GA 31061-9047, USA. *E-mail:* mlammon@mail.gac.peachnet.edu.

LAMONT-BROWN, Raymond, MA, JP; British writer and broadcaster; b. 20 Sept. 1939, Horsforth; m. 2nd Dr Elizabeth Moira McGregor 1985. *Career:* Managing Ed., Writers Monthly 1984–86; mem., Soc. of Authors, Scotland, Rotary Int. (Pres. St Andrews Branch 1984–85); Fellow, Soc. of Antiquaries of Scotland. *Publications include:* Discovering Fife 1988, The Life and Times of Berwick-upon-Tweed 1988, The Life and Times of St Andrews 1989, Royal Murder Mysteries 1990, Scottish Epitaphs 1990, Scottish Superstitions 1990, Scottish Witchcraft 1994, Scottish Folklore 1996, St Andrews 1996, Kamikaze: Japan's Suicide Samurai 1997, Scotland of One Hundred Years Ago 1998, Kempeitai: Japan's Dreaded Military Police 1998, Edward VII's Last Loves 1998, Tutor to the Dragon Emperor 1999, John Brown: Queen Victoria's Highland Servant 2000, Royal Poxes and Potions 2001, Ships from Hell 2002, Fife in History and Legend 2003, Villages of Fife 2003, Humphry Davy 2004, Andrew Carnegie 2005, St Andrews: City by the Northern Sea 2006; contrib. to magazines and newspapers, TV and radio scripts. *Address:* 11 Seabourne Gardens, Broughty Ferry, Dundee, DD5 2RT, Scotland.

LAMPITT, Dinah, (Deryn Lake); British author; b. 6 March 1937, Essex, England; m. L. F. Lampitt 1959 (deceased); one s. one d. *Education:* Regent Street Polytechnic, London. *Career:* mem. Society of Authors; CWA. *Publications:* Sutton Place, 1983; The Silver Swan, 1984; Fortune's Soldier, 1985; To Sleep No More, 1987; Pour the Dark Wine, 1989; The King's Women, 1992; As Shadows Haunting, 1993; Banishment, 1994; Death in the Dark Walk, 1995; Death at the Beggar's Opera, 1996; Death at the Devil's Tavern, 1997; Death on the Romney Marsh, 1998. Serials: The Moonlit Door; The Gemini Syndrome; The Staircase; The Anklets; The Wardrobe, Death in the Peerless Pool 1999, Death at Apothecaries Halll 2000, Death in the West Wind 2001, Death at St James's Palace 2002, Death in the Valley of Shadows 2003, Death in the Setting Sun 2005, Death and the Cornish Fiddler 2006, The Governor's Ladies 2006; contrib. numerous short stories to women's magazines. *Literary Agent:* c/o Vanessa Holt Ltd, 59 Crescent Road, Leigh-on-Sea, Essex S59 2PF, England. *Telephone:* (1702) 473787. *E-mail:* info@vanessaholt.eclipse.co.uk. *Website:* www.derynlake.com (home).

LAMPLUGH, Lois Violet, BA; British writer; b. 9 June 1921, Barnstaple, Devon, England; m. Lawrence Carlile Davis 1955; one s. one d. *Education:* Open University. *Career:* Editorial Staff, Jonathan Cape Publishers, 1946–56; mem. West Country Writers' Asscn. *Publications:* The Pigeongram Puzzle, 1955; Nine Bright Shiners, 1955; Vagabond's Castle, 1957; Rockets in the Dunes, 1958; Sixpenny Runner, 1960; Midsummer Mountains, 1961; Rifle House Friends, 1965; Linhay on Hunter's Hill, 1966; Fur Princess and Fir Prince, 1969; Mandog, 1972; Sean's Leap, 1979; Winter Donkey, 1980; Falcon's Tor, 1984; Barnstaple: Town on the Taw, 1983; History of Ilfracombe, 1984; Minehead and Dunster, 1987; A Shadowed Man: Henry Williamson, 1990; Take Off From Chivenor, 1990; Sandrabbit, 1991; Lundy: Island Without Equal, 1993; A Book of Georgeham and the North West Corner of Devon, 1995; Ilfracombe in Old Photographs, 1996; Two Rivers Meeting, 1998; Four Centuries of Devon Dialect, forthcoming. Contributions: Western Morning News.

LAN, David Mark, BA, BSc, PhD; British writer, dramatist, artistic director and social anthropologist; *Artistic Director, Young Vic Theatre, London;* b. 1 June 1952, Cape Town, South Africa. *Education:* Univ. of Cape Town and LSE, England. *Career:* academic researcher 1979–84; Writer-in-Residence, Royal Court Theatre 1995–97; Artistic Dir Young Vic Theatre 2000–. *Plays:* Painting a Wall 1974, Bird Child 1974, Homage to Been Soup 1975, Paradise 1975, The Winter Dancers 1977, Not in Norwich 1977, Red Earth 1978, Sergeant Ola and his Followers 1979, Flight 1986, A Mouthful of Birds (with Caryl Churchill) 1986, Desire 1990, The Ends of the Earth 1996; adaptations: Ghetto 1989, Hippolytos 1991, Ion 1993, The She Wolf 1996, Uncle Vanya 1998, The Cherry Orchard 2000. *Plays directed include:* for Young Vic: Julius Caesar 2000, A Raisin in the Sun 2001 (Lyric Hammersmith and UK tour 2005), Doctor Faustus 2002, The Daughter-in-Law 2002, The Skin of Our Teeth 2004, The Soliders' Fortune 2007; other: Pericles (Nat. Theatre Studio), The Glass Menagerie (Watford) 1998, As You Like It (Wyndhams) 2005. *Radio play:* Charley Tango 1995. *Television:* The Sunday Judge (film) 1985, The Crossing (film) 1988, Welcome Home Comrades (film) 1990, Dark City (film) 1990, Artist Unknown (writer, dir) 1996, Royal Court Diaries (writer, dir) 1997. *Publications:* Guns and Rain, Guerrillas and Spirit Mediums in Zimbabwe 1985. *Honours:* John Whiting Award 1977, George Orwell Memorial Award 1983, Zürich Int. Television Prize 1990, Olivier Award 2004. *Literary Agent:* c/o Judy Daish Associates, 2 St Charles Mews, London, W10 6EG, England.

LANCASTER, David (see Heald, Timothy Villiers)

LANCASTER-BROWN, Peter; Australian author; b. 13 April 1927, Cue, WA; m. Johanne Nyrerod 1953, one s. *Education:* studied astronomy, surveying, mining engineering and civil engineering. *Career:* mem. Society of Authors. *Publications:* Twelve Came Back, 1957; Call of the Outback, 1970; What Star is That?, 1971; Astronomy in Colour, 1972; Australia's Coast of Coral and Pearl, 1972; Comets, Meteorites, and Men, 1973; Megaliths, Myths, and Men, 1976; Planet Earth in Colour, 1976; Megaliths and Masterminds, 1979; Fjord of Silent Men, 1983; Astronomy, 1984; Halley and His Comet, 1985; Halley's Comet and the Principia, 1986; Skywatch, 1993. Contributions: Blackwood's Nature; New Scientist; Sky and Telescope.

LANCHESTER, John; British novelist and journalist; b. 1962, Hamburg, Germany; m. Miranda Carter; two s. *Education:* football writer, obituary writer, book ed., restaurant critic; editorial bd, London Review of Books. *Publications:* The Debt to Pleasure 1996, Mr Phillips 2000, Fragrant Harbour 2002, Family Romance: A Memoir 2007; contrib. to Granta, New York Times Book Review, New York Times Magazine, The New Yorker. *Honours:* Whitbread First Novel Award, Hawthornden Prize. *Address:* c/o London Review of Books, 28 Little Russell Street, London, WC1A 2HN, England.

LANDES, David S., PhD; American economist and academic; *Professor Emeritus, Department of Economics, Harvard University;* b. 29 April 1924, New York; s. of Harry Landes and Sylvia Landes; m. Sonia Tarnopol 1943; one s. two d. *Education:* City Coll., New York, Harvard Univ. *Career:* Jr Fellow, Soc. of Fellows, Harvard Univ. 1950–53; Asst Prof. of Econs, Columbia Univ., New York 1952–55, Assoc. Prof. 1955–58; Fellow, Center for Advanced Study in Behavioral Sciences, Stanford, Calif. 1957–58; Prof. of History and Econs, Univ. of Calif., Berkeley 1958–64; Prof. of History, Harvard Univ. 1964–72, LeRoy B. Williams Prof. of History and Political Science 1972–75, Robert Walton Goelet Prof. of French History 1975–81, Prof. of Econs 1977–98,

Coolidge Prof. of History 1981, now Prof. Emer.; Chair. Faculty Cttee on Social Studies 1981; Pres. Council on Research in Econ. History 1963–66; Dir Center for Middle Eastern Studies, Harvard Univ. 1966–68; Acting Dir Center for West European Studies, Harvard Univ. 1969–70; Pres. Econ. History Asscn 1976–77; Ellen McArthur Lecturer, Univ. of Cambridge 1964; Visiting Prof., Univ. of Paris IV 1972–73, Univ. of Zürich and Eidgenössische Technisch Hochschule, Zürich 1978; Richards Lectures, Univ. of Va 1978, Janeway Lectures, Princeton Univ. 1983; mem. Bd of Eds, various journals of history; Fellow, NAS, American Acad. of Arts and Sciences, American Philosophical Soc., British Acad., Royal Historical Soc.; Overseas Fellow, Churchill Coll., Cambridge 1968–69; Visiting Fellow, All Souls, Oxford 1985; mem. American Historical Asscn, Econ. History Asscn (also Trustee), Econ. History Soc., Soc. for French Historical Studies, Soc. d'Histoire Moderne and others; Assoc. mem. Fondation Royaumont pour le Progrès des Sciences de l'Homme. *Publications:* Bankers and Pashas 1958, The Unbound Prometheus 1968, Revolution in Time: Clocks and the Making of the Modern World 1983, The Wealth and Poverty of Nations: Why Some Are So Rich and Some So Poor 1998, Dynasties: Fortune & Misfortune in the World's Greatest Family Businesses 2007, and other books and articles on econ. and social history. *Honours:* Dr hc (Lille) 1973. *Address:* 24 Highland Street, Cambridge, MA 02138, USA (home). *Telephone:* (617) 354-6308 (office); (617) 354-6308 (home). *Fax:* (617) 354-5335 (home). *E-mail:* soniatl@aol.com (home). *Website:* www .economics.harvard.edu (office).

LANDESMAN, Jay Irving; American writer, dramatist, producer and publisher; b. 15 July 1919, St Louis, MO; m. Frances Deitsch 1950; two s. *Education:* Univ. of Missouri, Rice Inst., Houston. *Career:* mem. American Federation of Television and Radio Artists, Dramatists' Guild. *Film:* Anxiety (prod.). *Publications:* The Nervous Set (novel) 1954, as a musical 1959, A Walk on the Wild Side (musical) 1960, Molly Darling (musical) 1963, The Babies (play) 1969, Bad Nipple (novel) 1970, Rebel Without Applause (memoir) 1987, Small Day Tomorrow (screenplay) 1990, Jaywalking (memoir) 1992. *Address:* 8 Duncan Terrace, London, N1 8BZ, England (office). *Telephone:* (20) 7837-7290 (office). *Fax:* (20) 7833-1925 (office). *E-mail:* jay@landesman.freeserve.co .uk (office).

LANDIS, J(ames) D(avid), BA; American publisher and writer; b. 30 June 1942, Springfield, MA; m. 1st Patricia Lawrence Straus 1964 (divorced); one d.; m. 2nd Denise Evelyn Tillar 1982; two s. *Education:* Yale Coll. *Career:* Asst Ed., Abelard Schuman 1966–67; Ed. to Sr Ed. 1967–80, Sr Vice-Pres. 1985–91, Publisher and Ed.-in-Chief 1988–91, William Morrow & Co.; Editorial Dir, Sr Vice-Pres. and Publisher, Quill Trade paperbacks 1980–85; mem. PEN. *Publications:* The Sisters Impossible 1979, Love's Detective 1984, Daddy's Girl 1984, Joey and the Girls 1987, The Band Never Dances 1989, Looks Aren't Everything 1990, Lying in Bed (American Acad. of Arts and Letters Morton Dauwen Zabel Award for Fiction 1996) 1995, Longing 2001, Artist of the Beautiful 2005. *Honours:* Roger Klein Award for Editing 1973, Advocate Humanitarian Award 1977. *Address:* c/o Random House, 1745 Broadway, New York, NY 10019, USA.

LANDIS, Jill Marie, BA; American writer and teacher; b. 8 Nov. 1948, Clinton, IN; m. Sephen Landis 1971. *Education:* California State University, Long Beach. *Career:* Teacher, various writing workshops and seminars; mem. Romance Writers of America; Novelists Inc; Authors' Guild. *Publications:* Sunflower, 1988; Wildflower, 1989; Rose, 1990; Jade, 1991; Come Spring, 1992; Past Promises, 1993; Until Tomorrow, 1994; After All, 1995; Last Chance, 1995; Day Dreamer, 1996; Just Once, 1997; Glass Beach, 1998. Contributions: anthologies, including: Loving Hearts, 1992; Sweet Hearts, 1993; Three Mothers and a Cradle, 1995; Heartbreak Ranch, 1997; Summer Love, 1997.

LANDON, Howard Chandler Robbins, BMus; American writer, musicologist and academic; *John Bird Professor of Music, University College Cardiff*; b. 6 March 1926, Boston, MA; s. of William G. Landon and Dorothea LeB. Robbins; m. 1st Christa Landon; m. 2nd Else Radant 1977. *Education:* Lenox School, Mass., Swarthmore Coll. and Boston Univ. *Career:* corresp. The Times 1958–61; Hon. Professorial Fellow, Univ. Coll. Cardiff 1971–78, John Bird Prof. of Music 1978–; Prof. of the Humanities, Middlebury Coll., Vt 1980–83. *Publications:* The Symphonies of Joseph Haydn 1955, The Mozart Companion (ed. with Donald Mitchell) 1956, The Collected Correspondence and London Notebooks of Joseph Haydn 1959, Essays on the Viennese Classical Style: Gluck, Haydn, Mozart, Beethoven 1970, Beethoven: A Documentary Study 1970, Joseph Haydn: Chronicle and Works (five vols) 1976–80, Haydn: A Documentary Study 1981, Mozart & the Masons 1983, Handel and his World 1984, 1791: Mozart's Last Year 1987, Haydn: his Life and Music (with D. Jones) 1988, Mozart: The Golden Years 1989, The Mozart Compendium (ed.) 1990, Mozart and Vienna 1991, Five Centuries of Music in Venice (with John Julius Norwich) 1991, Vivaldi: Voice of the Baroque 1992, Une Journée particulière de Mozart 1993, The Mozart Essays 1995, Horns in High C (memoirs) 1999. *Honours:* Verdienstkreuz für Kunst und Wissenschaft (Austria); Hon. DMus (Boston) 1969, (Belfast) 1974, (Bristol) 1982, (Toulouse) 1991; Siemens Prize (Germany) 1992. *Address:* Château de Foncoussières, 81800 Rabastens (Tarn), France (home). *Telephone:* 5-63-40-61-45 (home). *Fax:* 5-63-40-62-61 (home). *E-mail:* foncous@aol.com (home).

LANE, Helen, (Helen Hudson), BA, MA, PhD; American writer; b. 31 Jan. 1920, New York, NY; m. Robert Lane 1944; two s. *Education:* Bryn Mawr Coll., Columbia Univ. *Career:* mem. Authors' Guild, Authors' League, American

PEN. *Publications:* Tell the Time to None 1966, Meyer Meyer 1967, The Listener 1968, Farnsbee South 1971, Criminal Trespass 1986, A Temporary Residence 1987, Dinner at Six: Voices from the Soup Kitchen 2002; contrib. to Antioch Review, Sewannee Review, Virginia Quarterly, Northwest Review, Mademoiselle, Quarterly Review of Literature, Red Book, Ellery Queen, Mid-Stream, Best American Short Stories, O. Henry Prize Stories, Ploughshares, Mediterranean Review. *Honours:* Virginia Quarterly Prize Story 1963. *Address:* 200 Leeden Hill Drive, No. 600B, Hamden, CT 06517, USA (home). *E-mail:* helen.lane@5net.net (home).

LANE, Millicent Elizabeth Travis, BA, MA, PhD; Canadian poet and writer; b. (Millicent Elizabeth Travis) 23 Sept. 1934, San Antonio, TX, USA; m. Lauriat Lane 1957; one s. one d. *Education:* Vassar Coll., Cornell Univ. *Career:* assistantships, Cornell Univ., Univ. of New Brunswick; poetry reviewer, Fiddlehead Magazine; mem. League of Canadian Poets (life mem. 2003–), Writers' Federation of New Brunswick. *Publications:* Five Poets: Cornell 1960, An Inch or So of Garden 1969, Poems 1969–72 1973, Homecomings 1977, Divinations and Shorter Poems, 1973–78 1980, Walking Under the Nebulae 1981, Reckonings: Poems 1979–83 1988, Solid Things: Poems New and Selected 1993, Temporary Shelter 1993, Night Physics 1994, Keeping Afloat 2001, Touch Earth 2004; contrib. to reviews, quarterlies and journals. *Honours:* Hon. Research Assoc., Univ. of New Brunswick, Pat Lowther Prize, League of Canadian Poets 1980, Atlantic Poetry Prize 2002, Alden Nowlan Prize for Literary Excellence 2003. *Address:* 807 Windsor Street, Fredericton, NB E3B 4G7, Canada.

LANE, Nick, BSc, PhD; British writer and academic; m. Ana Hidalgo; one s. *Education:* Imperial Coll., London and Royal Free Hospital Medical School, London. *Career:* Scientific Officer, MRC Clinical Research Centre, Northwick Park Hospital 1988–91; medical writer, Oxford Clinical Communications 1995–96; sr writer and prod., Medi Cine Int. 1996–99, Strategic Dir, Adelphi Medi Cine 1999–2002; science writer and freelance communications consultant 2002–. *Publications:* Monitoring of mitochondrial NADH levels by surface fluorometry as an indication of ischaemia during hepatic and renal transplantation (chapter in Oxygen Transport to Tissue Vol. XVII, with others) 1996, Oxygen: The Molecule that Made the World 2002, Life in the Frozen State (chapter: The Future of Cryobiology; also co-ed.) 2004, Power, Sex, Suicide: Mitochondria and the Meaning of Life 2005, Mitochondria: Key to Complexity (chapter in Origins of Mitochondria and Hydrogenosomes) 2006; contrib. to journals, including Biochemical Pharmacology, Biochemical Society Transactions, Biologist, British Medical Journal, Journal of the Royal Society of Medicine, Journal of Theoretical Biology, Kidney International, The Lancet, New Scientist, The Sciences, Scientific American, Transplantation. *Honours:* Hon. Sr Research Fellow, Univ. Coll. London 1997–; Daily Telegraph Young Science Writer of the Year Award 1993, New Scientist Millennial Science Essay Competition prize winner 1994. *Website:* pages .britishlibrary.net/nick.lane/.

LANE, Patrick; Canadian writer and poet; b. 26 March 1939, Nelson, BC; four s., one d. *Education:* University of British Columbia. *Career:* Ed., Very Stone House, Publishers, Vancouver, 1966–72; Writer-in-Residence, University of Manitoba, Winnepeg, 1978–79, University of Ottawa, 1980, University of Alberta, Edmonton, 1981–82, Saskatoon Public Library, 1982–83, Concordia University, 1985, Globe Theatre Co, Regina, Saskatchewan, 1985–; mem. League of Canadian Poets; Writer's Union of Canada; PEN, Canada. *Publications:* Letters From the Savage Mind, 1966; For Rita: In Asylum, 1969; Calgary City Jail, 1969; Separations, 1969; Sunflower Seeds, 1969; On the Street, 1970; Mountain Oysters, 1971; Hiway 401 Rhapsody, 1972; The Sun Has Begun to Eat the Mountain, 1972; Passing into Storm, 1973; Beware the Months of Fire, 1974; Certs, 1974; Unborn Things: South American Poems, 1975; For Riel in That Gawdam Prison, 1975; Albino Pheasants, 1977; If, 1977; Poems, New and Selected, 1978; No Longer Two People (with Lorna Uher), 1979; The Measure, 1980; Old Mother, 1982; Woman in the Dust, 1983; A Linen Crow, a Caftan Magpie, 1985; Milford and Me, 1989; Winter, 1990; Mortal Remains, 1992; Too Spare, Too Fierce, 1995; Selected Poems, 1978–1997, 1997; The Bare Plum of Winter Rain, 2000. Contributions: Most major Canadian magazines, American and English journals. *Honours:* Governor-General's Award for Poetry, 1979; Canadian Authors' Asscn Award, 1985; British Columbia Book Award, 1997.

LANE, Roumelia; British writer; b. 31 Dec. 1927, Bradford, West Yorkshire, England; m. Gavin Green 1949, one s. one d. *Career:* mem. Society of Authors of Great Britain, Writers Guild of Great Britain, Writers Guild of America (East and West). *Publications:* Sea of Zanj; Rose of the Desert; Cafe Mimosa; Harbour of Deceit; Desert Haven; Bamboo Wedding; Night of the Beguine; The Chasm; The Nawindi Flier. Television and film scripts: Stardust; The Chasm; Tender Saboteur; Chantico; Turn of the Tide; Gilligan's Last Gamble; Where Are the Clowns?; Death From the Past. Contributions: various journals and magazines. *Address:* Casa Mimosa, Santa Eugenia, Majorca, Beleares, Spain.

LANG, King (see Tubb, Edwin Charles)

LANG(-DILLENBURGER), Elmy; German writer and painter; b. 13 Aug. 1921, Pirmasens; d. of Hermann and Else (née Haber) Lang; one s. *Education:* Munich, Göttingen, Paris and Salzburg (Austria). *Career:* fmr foreign Corresp.; currently freelance writer and journalist; stories have appeared in newspapers, magazines and anthologies; mem. Die Kogge (writers' asscn), European Authors Asscn, Asscn Européenne François Mauriac, Regensburg

Int. *Publications include:* novels: Frühstück auf französisch, Der Rabenwald 1985, Ich – Vincent van Gogh 1990, Bis der Adler stürzt 1997, Nele und der Arnikadoktor 2003, Ohne Liebe läuft nichts 2005, Ansichten eines Hundes 2005; poetry: Mitternachtsspritzer 1970, Ping-pong Pinguin (also English), Blick ins Paradies 1978, 1980, Das Wort 1980, Limericks 1984, Stufen zum Selbst 1986, Lebenszeichen 1988, Der Schäfer von Madrid, Verdammt geliebtes Leben, Vie maudite bien aimée 1993, Hieroglyphen des Lebens 1999, Lebensboot 2006; short stories: Paradies mit Streifen 1994; plays: Die Bodenguckkinder (Ground Looking Children), Er Sprach Immer von Tauben, Die Puppe Darf Nicht Mehr Tanzen 2002; also children's books. *Honours:* Diploma di Merito dell' Univ. delle Arti, Salsomaggiore (Italy) 1982; Landgrafenmedaille der Stadt Pirmasens 1986; Gran Premio d'Europa La Musa dell'Arte 1990; ELK-Feder 1991. *Address:* Strobelallee 62, 66953 Pirmasens, Germany (home). *Telephone:* (6331) 41425 (home). *Fax:* (6331) 41425 (home).

LANGE, Hartmut; German author and dramatist; b. 31 March 1937, Berlin; s. of Johanna Lange and Karl Lange; m. Ulrike Ritter 1971. *Education:* Babelsberg Film School. *Career:* playwright at Deutsches Theater, Berlin 1961–65; freelance writer, W Berlin 1965–. *Publications:* Die Selbstverbrennung 1982, Deutsche Empfindungen 1983, Die Waldsteinsonate 1984, Das Konzert 1986, Die Ermüdung 1988, Vom Werden der Vernunft 1988, Gesammelte Theaterstücke (Collected Plays) 1988, Die Wattwanderung 1990, Die Reise nach Triest 1991, Die Stechpalme 1993, Schnitzlers Würgeengel 1995, Der Herr im Café 1996, Italienische Novellen 1998, Eine andere Form des Glücks 1999, Die Bildungsreise 2000, Das Streichquartett 2001, Irrtum als Erkenntnis 2002, Leptis Magna 2003, Der Wanderer 2005. *Honours:* Gerhart-Hauptmann-Preis 1968, Literatur Preis der Adenauer Stiftung 1998, Ehrengabe der Schiller-Stiftung von 1859 2000, Stalo Svevo Preis 2003, Preis der Literatur Novol 2004. *Address:* Hohenzollerndamm 197, 10717 Berlin, Germany; 06010 Niccone, Perugia, Italy.

LANGE, John (see Crichton, (John) Michael)

LANGE, Mechthild, MA; German journalist; b. Hamburg. *Education:* In Hamburg, Berlin, Munich and Geneva (Switzerland). *Career:* Freelance journalist; Dramatic Adviser Deutsches Schauspielhaus, Hamburg 1986–89; mem. editorial staff, producer NDR-Fernsehen TV 1972–; has written numerous theatre reviews for Frankfurter Rundschau nat newspaper; Adolf-Grimme Preis 1972. *Publication:* Regie im Theater (jtly) 1989. *Address:* NDR-Fernsehen, Red Kunst, Literatur Theater, Gazellenkamp, 2 Hamburg, Germany (office); Isestr 134, 20149 Hamburg, Germany (home). *Telephone:* (40) 415465225 (office); (40) 4603738 (home). *Fax:* (40) 41565470 (office).

LANGER, Lawrence Lee; American academic and writer; b. 20 June 1929, New York, NY; m. Sondra Weinstein 1951; one s. one d. *Education:* BA, City College, CUNY, 1951; MA, 1952, PhD, 1961, Harvard University. *Career:* Instructor, 1956–61, Asst Prof., 1961–66, Assoc. Prof., 1966–72, Prof., 1972–76, Alumnae Chair Prof., 1976–92, Prof. Emeritus, 1992–, Simmons College; mem. PEN. *Publications:* The Holocaust and the Literary Imagination, 1975; The Age of Artocity: Death in Modern Literature, 1978; Versions of Survival: The Holocaust and the Human Spirit, 1982; Holocaust Testimonies: The Ruins of Memory, 1991; Admitting the Holocaust: Collected Essays, 1994; Art from the Ashes: A Holocaust Anthology, 1994. Contributions: journals. *Honours:* National Book Critics Circle Award 1991. *Address:* 249 Adams Avenue, West Newton, MA 02165, USA.

LANGFORD, Gary Raymond, BA, MA, DipEd; New Zealand writer, dramatist, poet and academic; b. 21 Aug. 1947, Christchuch; one d. *Education:* University of Canterbury, Christchurch Secondary Teachers College. *Career:* Senior Lecturer in Creative Writing, University of Western Sydney, 1986; Writer-in-Residence, University of Canterbury, 1989. *Publications:* over 20 books, including novels and poetry. Other: Plays and scripts for stage, radio, and television. Contributions: anthologies and other publications. *Honours:* Australia Council Young Writers Fellowship, 1976; Alan Marshall Award, 1983.

LANGFORD GINIBI, Ruby, (Ginibi (Black Swan); Australian (aboriginal) writer and poet; b. 26 Jan. 1934, Box Ridge Mission, Coraki, NSW; m. (divorced); four s. five d. (three deceased). *Education:* Casino High School, NSW. *Career:* mem. Australian Soc. of Authors. *Publications:* Don't Take your Love to Town 1988, Real Deadly 1992, My Bundjalung People 1994, Haunted by the Past 1998, All my Mob, Only Gammoa, Koori Voices, Language and Legends of the Bundjalung Tribes and Nation; contrib. to Women's Weekly, HQ, Sun Herald, Meanjin, Best of Independent (monthly) 1990, A to Z Authorship by Ken Methold, Aboriginal English 1996, Australian Literary Studies, Canonozities by Southerlys 1997. *Honours:* Human Rights Literature 1988, Hon. Fellowship 1995. *Literary Agent:* Level 7, 61 Marlborough Street, Surry Hills NSW 2010, Australia. *Telephone:* (2) 9319-7199. *E-mail:* info@cameronsmanagement.com.au. *Website:* members.dodo.com.au/~ginibi (home).

LANGLAND, Joseph Thomas; American academic and writer; b. 16 Feb. 1917, Spring Grove, Minnesota; m. Judith Gail Wood 1943; two s. one d. *Education:* AA, Santa Ana College, 1936; BA, 1940, MA, 1941, Graduate Studies, 1946–48, University of Iowa; Harvard University, Columbia University, 1953–54. *Career:* Instructor, Dana College, 1941–42, University of Iowa, 1946–48; Asst, then Assoc. Prof., University of Wyoming, 1948–49; Assoc. Prof. to Prof., 1959–80, Prof. Emeritus, 1980–, University of Massachusetts. *Publications:* A Dream of Love, 1986; Twelve Poems, 1991;

Selected Poems, 1992. Contributions: Reviews, quarterlies, journals, and magazines. *Honours:* Ford Foundation Faculty Fellowship; Amy Lowell Poetry Fellowship; New England Living Legend; Chancellor's Prize. *Address:* 18 Morgan Circle, Amherst, MA 01002, USA.

LANGSLET, Lars Roar, MA; Norwegian writer; b. 5 March 1936, Nesbyen; s. of Knut Langslet and Alma Langslet. *Education:* Univ. of Oslo. *Career:* Assoc. Prof. 1969–89; MP 1969–89; Minister of Culture and Science 1981–86; writer Aftenposten newspaper 1990–97; Ed. Ordet 1997–; State Scholarship 1997–99; Pres. of Norwegian Acad. for Language and Literature 1995–. *Publications:* Karl Marx 1963, Conservatism 1965, (biogs of) John Lyng 1989, King Olav V 1995, St Olav 1995, King Christian IV 1997, King Christian VIII 1998–99, Ludvig Holberg 2001. *Honours:* Commdr Order of St Olav, Dannebrog, Order of Gregory the Great, etc. *Address:* Norske Akademi for Sprog og Litteratur, Inkognitogt, 24, 0256 Oslo 2 (office); Rosenborggt. 5, 0356 Oslo, Norway. *Telephone:* 22-46-34-12. *Fax:* 22-55-37-43. *E-mail:* lars.roar.langslet@netcom.no (office).

LANGTON, Jane Gillson, BA, MA; American writer; b. 30 Dec. 1922, Boston, Mass; m. William Langton 1943 (died 1997); three s. *Education:* Wellesley Coll., Univ. of Michigan, Radcliffe Coll. *Publications:* The Transcendental Murder 1964, Dark Nantucket Noon 1975, The Memorial Hall Murder 1978, Natural Enemy 1982, Emily Dickinson is Dead 1984, Good and Dead 1986, Murder at the Gardner 1988, The Dante Game 1991, God in Concord 1992, Divine Inspiration 1993, The Shortest Day 1995, Dead as a Dodo 1996, The Face on the Wall 1998, The Thief of Venice 1999, Murder at Monticello 2001, The Escher Twist 2002, The Deserter, Murder at Gettysburg 2003, Steeple Chase 2005; juvenile: Her Majesty, Grace Jones 1961, Diamond in the Window 1962, The Swing in the Summerhouse 1967, The Astonishing Stereoscope 1971, The Boyhood of Grace Jones 1972, Paper Chains 1977, The Fledgling 1980, The Fragile Flag 1984, The Time Bike 2000, The Mysterious Circus 2005. *Honours:* Newbery Honor Book 1981, Nero Wolfe Award 1984, Boucheron Lifetime Achievement Award 2000. *Address:* 9 Baker Farm Road, Lincoln, MA 01773, USA (home). *Telephone:* (781) 259-9148 (home). *E-mail:* janelangton@earthlink.net. *Website:* www.janelangton.com.

LANSDALE, Joe Richard; American writer; b. 28 Oct. 1951, Gladwater, TX; m. 1st Cassie Ellis 1970 (divorced 1972); m. 2nd Karen Ann Morton 1973; one s. one d. *Education:* Tyler Junior Coll., Univ. of Texas at Austin, Stephen F. Austin State Univ. *Career:* mem. Horror Writers of America (vice-pres. 1987–88), Western Writers of America (treas. 1987). *Television writing:* four episodes Batman: The Animated Series (Critters (with Steve Gerber), Read My Lips, Showdown, Perchance to Dream), one episode Superman: The Animated Series (Identity Crisis). *Publications:* Act of Love (novel) 1980, The Nightrunners (novel) 1983, Texas Night Riders (novel, as Ray Slater) 1983, Dead in the West (novel) 1986, Magic Wagon (novel) 1986, The Drive-In (novel) 1988, The Best of the West (anthology ed.) 1989, By Bizarre Hands (short stories) 1989, Cold in July (novel) 1989, The Drive-In 2 (novel) 1989, New Frontier (anthology ed.) 1989, Razored Saddles (anthology, ed. with Pat Lo Brutto) 1989, Savage Season (novel) 1990, Batman: Captured by the Engines (novel) 1991, On the Far Side of the Cadillac Desert with Dead Folks 1991, Stories by Mama Lansdale's Youngest Boy (short stories, aka Best Sellers Guaranteed) 1991, The Steel Valentine 1991, Batman in Terror on the High Skies (juvenile novel) 1992, Dark at Heart (anthology, ed. with Karen Lansdale) 1992, Steppin' Out, Summer '68 1992, Tight Little Stitches on a Dead Man's Back 1992, Drive-By (with Andrew H. Vachss) 1993, Jonah Hex: Two-Gun Mojo (five-issue comic series) 1993, Lone Ranger and Tonto (four-issue comic series) 1993, Dead in the West (two-issue comic series, with Neil Barrett Jr) 1993, Electric Gumbo (short stories) 1994, Mucho Mojo (novel) 1994, Weird Business (anthology, ed. with Richard Klaw) 1994, The West That Was (non-fiction, ed. with Thomas W. Knowles) 1994, Wild West Show (non-fiction, ed. with Thomas W. Knowles) 1994, Writer of the Purple Rage (short stories) 1994, My Dead Dog Bobby (short story) 1995, Tarzan: The Lost Adventure (novel, with Edgar Rice Burroughs) 1995, Two-Bear Mambo (novel) 1995, Blood and Shadows (four-issue comic series) 1996, Fist Full of Stories (and Articles) 1996, Supergirl Annual #2 (comic book, with Neil Barrett) 1996, Weird War Tales #2 (short story) 1996, Atomic Chili (novel) 1997, Bad Chili (novel) 1997, The Good, the Bad & the Indifferent (short stories) 1997, The Boar (novel) 1998, Gangland #4 (comic book, with Rick Klaw) 1998, Private Eye Action As You Like It (short stories, with Lewis Shiner) 1998, Rumble Tumble (novel) 1998, Freezer Burn (novel) 1999, Something Lumber This Way Comes (juvenile novel) 1999, Waltz of Shadows (novel) 1999, The Bottoms 2000, Zeppelins West 2000, Captains Outrageous 2001, Sunset and Sawdust 2005, A Fine Dark Line 2006. *Address:* 199 Country Road 508, Nacogdoches, TX 75961, USA. *Website:* www.joerlansdale.com.

LANTRY, Mike (see Tubb, Edwin Charles)

LAPHAM, Lewis H., BA; American writer and editor; *Editor Emeritus, Harper's Magazine;* b. 8 Jan. 1935, San Francisco; m.; three c. *Education:* Yale Univ., Univ. of Cambridge, UK. *Career:* reporter San Francisco Examiner newspaper 1957–59, New York Herald Tribune 1960–62; Ed. Harper's Magazine 1976–81, 1983–2005, Ed. Emer. and columnist 2005–; syndicated newspaper columnist 1981–87; univ. lecturer; appearances on American and British TV, broadcasts on nat. public radio. *Publications:* Fortune's Child (essays) 1980, Money and Class in America 1988, Imperial Masquerade 1990, Hotel America: Scenes in the Lobby of the Fin-de-Siècle 1995, Waiting for the

Barbarians 1997, The Agony of Mammon 1999, Lapham's Rules of Influence 1999, Theater of War 2002, 30 Satires 2003, Gag Rule 2004; contrib. 'Notebook' monthly essay Harper's Magazine; also contrib. to Commentary, Nat. Review, Yale Literary Magazine, Elle, Fortune, Forbes, American Spectator, Vanity Fair, Parade, Channels, Maclean's, London Observer, New York Times, Wall Street Journal. *Honours:* Nat. Magazine Award for Essays 1995, Thomas Paine Journalism Award 2002. *Address:* c/o Harper's Magazine, 666 Broadway, New York, NY 10012, USA (office). *E-mail:* ann@harpers.org (office). *Website:* www.harpers.org.

LAPID, Haim; Israeli writer and critic; b. 1967, nr Tel-Aviv. *Education:* Tel-Aviv Univ. *Career:* served in the Israeli army as paratrooper; fmrly taught Social and Behavioural Psychology; Lecturer on Negotiation Theory, organizational consultant for hi-tech industries. *Publications include:* novels: Reshimotav Ha-Nistarot (trans. as The Secret Notes of my Deputy) 1983, Breznitz 1992, Pesha Ha-Ketivah (trans. as The Crime of Writing) 1998, Ha-Mehila (trans. as The Burrow) 2002; short story collections: Meshicha Negdit (trans. as Opposite Attraction) 1995; non-fiction: Ahavot Rishonot (trans. as First Loves) 1993. *Address:* c/o The Toby Press, PO Box 8531, New Milford, CT 06776-8531, USA. *Website:* www.tobypress.com.

LAPIERRE, Dominique; French journalist, writer and philanthropist; b. 30 July 1931, Châtelaillon, Charente-Maritime; s. of Jean Lapierre and Luce Lapierre (née Andreotti); m. 2nd Dominique Conchon 1980; one d. (by first m.). *Education:* Lycée Condorcet, Paris and LaFayette Univ., Easton, USA. *Career:* Ed. Paris Match Magazine 1954–67; founder and Pres. Action Aid for Lepers' Children of Calcutta. *Publications:* Un dollar les mille kilomètres 1949, Honeymoon around the World 1953, En liberté sur les routes d'U.R.S.S. 1957, Russie portes ouvertes 1957, Les Caïds de New York 1958, Chessman m'a dit 1960, The City of Joy 1985, Beyond Love 1991, A Thousand Suns 1998, Five Past Midnight in Bhopal 2002, It Was Once the USSR 2006; with Larry Collins: Is Paris Burning? 1964, ...Or I'll Dress You In Mourning 1967, O Jerusalem 1971, Freedom at Midnight 1975, The Fifth Horseman 1980, Is New York Burning? 2004. *Honours:* Citizen of Honour of the City of Calcutta; Chevalier Légion d'Honneur 2000; Commdr Confrérie du Tastevin 1990; Grand Cross of the Order of Social Solidarity (Spain) 2002; Dr hc (Lafayette Univ.) 1982; Christopher Book Award 1986, 2002, Gold Medal of Calcutta, Int. Rainbow Prize, UN 2000, Vatican Prize for Peace 2000, Gold Medal of the City of Milan 2006. *Address:* 37 Rue Charles-Laffitte, 92200 Neuilly; Les Bignoles, Val de Rian, 83350 Ramatuelle, France. *Telephone:* 1-46-37-34-34 (Neuilly); 4-94-97-17-31 (Ramatuelle). *Fax:* 4-94-97-38-05. *E-mail:* D.Lapierre@wanadoo.fr (home). *Website:* cityofjoyaid.org (office).

LAPINE, James Elliot, BA, MFA; American dramatist and film and stage director; b. 10 Jan. 1949, Mansfield, OH; m. Sarah Marshall Kernochan 1985, one d. *Education:* Franklin and Marshall College, California Institute of the Arts. *Career:* Dir of several plays and films; Lecturer on drama; mem. Dramatists Guild. *Publications:* Photographs, 1977; Table Settings, 1980; Twelve Dreams, 1983; Sunday in the Park with George, 1984; Into the Woods, 1987; Falsettoland, 1990; Luck, Pluck and Virtue, 1993; Passion, 1994. *Honours:* Obie Award, 1977; George Oppenheimer/Newsday Award, 1983; Pulitzer Prize for Drama, 1984; New York Critic's Circle Awards, 1984, 1988; Tony Awards, 1988, 1992, 1994.

LAPPÉ, Frances Moore, BA; American lecturer and writer; *Co-Founder, Small Planet Institute*; b. 10 Feb. 1944, Pendleton, Ore.; d. of John Moore and Ina Moore; m. 1st Marc Lappé 1967 (divorced 1977, died 2005); one s. one d.; m. 2nd J. Baird Callicott 1985 (divorced 1991); m. 3rd Paul Martin DuBois 1991 (divorced 1999, died 2005). *Education:* Earlham Coll., Ind. *Career:* Co-Founder and mem. staff, Inst. for Food and Devt Policy, San Francisco, Calif. 1975–90; Co-Founder and Co-Dir Centre for Living Democracy, Brattleboro, VT 1990, Small Planet Inst., Cambridge, Mass; adviser to Simple Living, Project Censored, Fairness and Accuracy in Reporting, Earthsave, Union of Concerned Scientists. *Publications include:* Diet for a Small Planet 1971, Now We Can Speak 1982, What To Do After You Turn Off the TV: Fresh Ideas for Enjoying Family Time 1985, What Can We Do? 1980, Aid as Obstacle 1980, Nicaragua: What Difference Could a Revolution Make?, Mozambique and Tanzania: Asking the Big Questions (co-author) 1980, Food and Farming in the New Nicaragua 1982, World Hunger: Ten Myths 1982, World Hunger: Twelve Myths (co-author) 1986, Casting New Molds: First Steps Toward Worker Control in a Mozambique Factory (co-author) 1980, Food First: Beyond the Myth of Scarcity (co-author) 1977, Betraying the National Interest (co-author) 1987, Rediscovering America's Values 1989, Taking Population Seriously (co-author) 1990, The Quickening of America: Rebuilding Our Nation, Remaking Our Lives 1994, Hope's Edge – The Next Diet for a Small Planet (co-author) (Nautilus Award 2003) 2002, You Have the Power – Choosing Courage in a Culture of Fear 2004, Democracy's Edge 2005; co-author of chapter in Feeding The Future – From Fat to Famine: How to Solve the World's Food Crises 2004; contribs to The New York Times, Los Angeles Times, Readers' Digest, Christian Century, Chemistry, Le Monde Diplomatique, National Civic Review, Tikkun, Harper's. *Honours:* 17 hon. doctorates, including Hon. PhD (St Mary's Coll.) 1983, (Lewis and Clark Coll.) 1983, (Macalester Coll.) 1986, (Hamline Univ.) 1987, (Earlham Coll.) 1989, (Kenyon Coll.) 1989, (Univ. of Michigan) 1990, (Nazareth Coll.) 1990, (Niagara Coll.) 1993, (Allegheny Coll.); named to Nutrition Hall of Fame, Center for Scientific and Public Interest 1981, Mademoiselle Magazine Award 1977, World Hunger Media Award 1982, Henry George Award, Right Livelihood Award (Sweden) 1987, inducted into Natural Health Magazine's Hall of Fame 2000, Rachel Carson Award, Nat. Nutritional Foods Asscn 2003. *Address:* The Small Planet Institute, 25 Mt Auburn Street, Suite 203, Cambridge, MA 02138 (office). *Telephone:* (617) 441-6300 (ext. 115) (office). *Fax:* (617) 441-6307 (office). *E-mail:* info@smallplanetinstitute.org (office). *Website:* www.smallplanetinstitute.org (office).

LAPPING, Brian Michael, CBE, BA; British television producer and journalist; *Chairman, Brook Lapping Productions*; b. 13 Sept. 1937, London, England; s. of Max Lapping and Doris Lapping; m. Anne Shirley Lucas Lapping CBE; three d. *Education:* Pembroke Coll., Cambridge. *Career:* reporter, Daily Mirror, London 1959–61; reporter and Deputy Commonwealth Corresp., The Guardian, London 1961–67; Ed. Venture, Fabian Soc. monthly journal 1965–69; feature writer, Financial Times, London 1967–68; Deputy Ed. New Society, London 1968–70; TV producer, Granada Television Ltd 1970–88;; Chief Exec. Brian Lapping Assocs 1988–; Chair. Brook Lapping Productions 2003–, Teachers' TV 2003–. *Television productions:* Exec. Producer: World in Action 1976–78, The State of the Nation 1978–80, End of Empire 1980–85, Countdown to War 1989, Hypotheticals (three programmes annually for BBC 2), The Second Russian Revolution (eight programmes for BBC 2) 1991, Question Time (weekly for BBC 1) 1991–94, The Washington Version (for BBC 2) 1992, Watergate (for BBC 2) 1994, Fall of the Wall (for BBC 2) 1994, The Death of Yugoslavia 1995, The 50 Years War: Israel and the Arabs 1998, Hostage 1999, Endgame in Ireland 2002, Tackling Terror 2002, The Fall of Milosevic 2003, Elusive Peace, Israel and the Arabs 2005. *Publications:* More Power to the People (co-ed.) 1968, The Labour Government 1964–70 1970, The State of the Nation: Parliament (ed.) 1973, The State of the Nation: The Bounds of Freedom 1980, End of Empire 1985, Apartheid: A History 1986. *Honours:* three Broadcasting Press Guild Awards, four Royal Television Soc. Awards, three Emmy, Peabody, DuPont batons, three Golden Gate Awards, four New York TV Festival Awards, 12 int. awards 1995. *Address:* Brook Lapping Productions, 6 Angler's Lane, London, NW5 3DG (office); 61 Eton Avenue, London, NW3, England (home). *Telephone:* (20) 7428-3117 (office); (20) 7586-1047 (home). *E-mail:* bmlapping@aol.com (home). *Website:* www.teachers.tv (office).

LAPTEV, Ivan Dmitrievich, DPhilSc; Russian editor and journalist; b. 15 Oct. 1934, Sladkoye, Omsk Dist; m. Tatyana Kareva 1966; one d. *Education:* Siberian Road Transport Inst., Acad. of Social Sciences. *Career:* worked for CPSU Cen. Cttee; mem. CPSU 1960–91; worked at Omsk River Port 1952–60; teacher 1960–61; instructor, Soviet Army Sports Club 1961–64, literary collaborator and special corresp. Sovietskaya Rossiya 1964–67; Consultant for Kommunist (later named Free Thought) 1967–73; work with CPSU Cen. Cttee 1973–78; Section Ed. Pravda 1978–82, Deputy Ed. 1982–84; Chief Ed. Izvestiya 1984–90; mem. USSR Supreme Soviet 1989–91; People's Deputy of the USSR 1989–91; Chair. Council of Union 1990–91; Gen. Man. Izvestiya Publrs 1991–94; Deputy Chair. Fed. Press Cttee 1994–95, Chair. 1995–99; Head of Sector Professional Acad. of State Service to Russian Presidency 1995–; mem. Int. Acad. of Information 1993; Pres. Asscn of Chief Eds and Publrs 1993–. *Publications:* Ecological Problems 1978, The World of People in the World of Nature 1986; over 100 scientific articles on ecological problems. *Address:* Academy of State Service, Vernadskogo prosp. 84, 117606 Moscow, Russia. *Telephone:* (495) 436-99-07.

LAQUEUR, Walter; American historian, academic, editor and political commentator; *Academic Director, Center for Strategic and International Studies*; b. 26 May 1921, Breslau, Germany (now Wrocław, Poland); s. of Fritz Laqueur and Else Berliner; m. 1st Barbara Koch 1941 (deceased); m. 2nd C. S. Wichmann; two d. *Career:* Ed. Survey 1955–65; Dir Inst. of Contemporary History and Wiener Library, London 1964–91; Founding Ed. Journal of Contemporary History 1965–; Prof. of History Brandeis Univ. 1967–72; Prof. of History, Tel-Aviv Univ. 1970–87; Prof. of Govt Georgetown Univ. 1977–90; Chair. Int. Research Council, Center for Strategic and Int. Studies, Washington DC 1973–2001, currently Academic Dir; Ed. Washington Papers 1973–2001, Washington Quarterly 1978–2001; Visiting Prof. of History, Harvard Univ. 1977; Rockefeller Fellow, Guggenheim Fellow. *Publications:* Young Germany 1962, The Road to War 1967 1968, Europe Since Hitler 1970, A History of Zionism 1972, Confrontation 1974, Weimar 1974, Guerrilla 1976, Terrorism 1977, A Continent Astray: Europe 1970–78 1979, The Missing Years (novel) 1980, The Terrible Secret 1981, Farewell to Europe (novel) 1981, Germany Today 1985, A World of Secrets 1985, Breaking the Silence 1986, The Age of Terrorism 1987, The Long Road to Freedom 1989, Stalin 1990, Thursday's Child has Far to Go (autobiog.) 1993, Black Hundred 1993, The Dream That Failed 1994, Fascism 1997, Generation Exodus 2001, Yale Encyclopedia of the Holocaust (Ed.) 2001, No End to War 2003. *Honours:* several hon. degrees. *Address:* Center for Strategic and International Studies, 1800 K Street, NW, Suite 400, Washington, DC 20006, USA (office); c/o Journal of Contemporary History, 4 Devonshire Street, London, W1N 2BH, England. *Telephone:* (202) 887-0217 (office). *Fax:* (202) 775-3199 (office). *E-mail:* wlaqueur@csis.org (office); walter@laqueur.net (home). *Website:* www.csis.org (office).

LARA BOSCH, José Manuel; Spanish media executive; *President, Grupo Planeta*; s. of the late José Manuel Lara Hernández and María Teresa Bosch Carbonell; m.; four c. *Career:* CEO Grupo Planeta (owns TV and radio stations, publishing imprints, chain of bookshops, newspapers and real estate firms) 1998–2003, Pres. 2003–; Pres. Antena 3, Quiero TV, UTECA; Chair. Inst. of Family Businesses 2001–, Fundación José Manuel Lara; fmr Vice-Pres. Círculo de Economía; mem. admin. council of Fira de Barcelona. *Address:*

Grupo Planeta SA, Edifici Planeta, Diagonal 662–664, 08034 Barcelona, Spain (office). *Telephone:* (93) 4929899 (office). *Fax:* (93) 4928562 (office). *E-mail:* direccion@planeta.es (office).

LARMELA, Kaisa, MA; Finnish magazine editor; b. 28 Nov. 1943, Turku; d. of Kaarlo and Sirkku Honka; m. Harri Larmela 1965; one d. one s. *Education:* Helsinki Univ. *Career:* journalist 1964–, Ed. 1976–; Ed-in-Chief et-lehti 1989. *Publications:* contrib. numerous articles to magazines 1994–. *Honours:* Finnish Asscn of Magazine Eds-in-Chief Julius-Journalist-Prize 1993. *Address:* et-lehti, Höy Läämötie 1, POB 100, 00040 Helsinki, Finland. *Telephone:* (0) 1205475. *Fax:* (0) 1205428. *E-mail:* kaisi.larmela@helsinkimedia.fi.

LARSEN, Eric Everett, BA, MA, PhD; American writer; b. 29 Nov. 1941, Northfield, MN; m. Anne Schnare 1965; two d. *Education:* Carleton Coll. and Univ. of Iowa. *Career:* Prof. of English, John Jay Coll. of Criminal Justice, CUNY 1971–2006, Prof. Emer. 2006–; mem. Nat. Asscn of Scholars, Asscn of Literary Scholars and Critics, Nat. Book Critics Circle. *Publications:* fiction: An American Memory 1988, I Am Zoe Handke 1992; non-fiction: A Nation Gone Blind: America in an Age of Simplification and Deceit 2006;contrib. to Harper's, New Republic, Nation, Los Angeles Times Book Review; North American Review, New England Review. *Honours:* Chicago Tribune Heartland Prize 1988. *Address:* 250 West 99th Street, 8A, New York, NY 10025, USA (office). *Telephone:* (212) 866-7425 (office). *E-mail:* ericlarsen@ericlarsen.net (office). *Website:* www.ericlarsen.net.

LARSEN, Jeanne Louise, BA, MA, PhD; American academic, writer, poet and translator; b. 9 Aug. 1950, Washington, DC; m. Thomas Hugh Mesner 1977; one step-s. one step-d. *Education:* Oberlin College, Hollins College, Nagasaki University, University of Iowa. *Career:* Lecturer, Tunghai University, 1972–74; Asst Prof., 1975, 1980–86, Assoc. Prof., 1986–92, Prof. of English, 1992–98, Hollins College; Prof. of English, Hollins University, 1998–; mem. Asscn for Asian Studies; Authors' Guild; International Asscn for the Fantastic in the Arts; PEN; Poets and Writers. *Publications:* Fiction: Silk Road, 1989; Bronze Mirror, 1991; Manchu Palaces, 1996. Poetry: James Cook in Search of Terra Incognita: A Book of Poems, 1979. Other: Brocade River Poems: Selected Works of the Tang Dynasty Courtesan Xue Tao (trans. and ed.), 1987; Engendering the Word: Feminist Essays in Psychosexual Poetics (ed. with others), 1989. Contributions: scholarly books, anthologies, learned journals and periodicals. *Honours:* First Selection, Associated Writing Programs' Annual Poetry Book Competition, 1979; Resident Fellowships, Virginia Center for the Creative Arts, 1982, 1986, 1987, 1989, 1990, 1995; John Gardner Fellowship in Fiction, Bread Loaf Writers' Conference, 1990; William L. Crawford Award for Year's Best New Novelist, International Asscn for the Fantastic in the Arts, 1990; National Endowment for the Arts Fellowship in Trans., 1995.

LARSSON, Åsa; Swedish crime writer; b. 1966, Kiruna; m.; two c. *Education:* studied in Uppsala. *Career:* fmr tax lawyer; full-time writer. *Publications:* (titles in translation) The Savage Altar (aka Sun Storm) (Award for Best First Crime Novel, Sweden) 2006, The Blood Spilt 2007. *Address:* c/o Penguin Books, 80 Strand, London, WC2R 0RL, England (office).

LARUE, Monique, BPh, MA, DèsL; Canadian writer and teacher; b. 1948, Montréal, QC. *Education:* Univ. of Montréal, Sorbonne, Univ. of Paris. *Career:* teacher Dept of French, Collège Edouard Montpetit, Montréal 1974–; mem. Académie des Lettres du Québec. *Publications:* La cohorte fictive 1979, Les faux fuyants 1982, Copies conformes (trans. as True Copies) 1989, Promenades littéraires dans Montréal (with Jean-Francois Chassay) 1989, La démarche du crabe 1995, La Gloire de cassiodore 2002. *Honours:* Grand Prix du livre de Montréal 1990, Prix du Journal de Montréal 1996, Prix du roman du Gouverneur Général du Canada 2002. *Address:* c/o Union des écrivaines et des écrivains québécois, La Maison des écrivains, 3492 avenue Laval, Montréal, QC H2X 3C8, Canada.

LASICA, Milan, AM; Slovak actor, dramatist and scriptwriter; b. 3 Feb. 1940, Zvolen; s. of Vojtech Lasica and Edita Šmáliková; m. Magdalena Vašáryová; two d. *Education:* Univ. of Musical Arts, Bratislava. *Career:* dramatist Slovak TV 1964–67; actor with theatres Divadlo na Korze 1967–71, Divaldo Večerní Brno 1971–72, Nová scéna 1972–89; f. Štúdio S-Bratislava 1989, Dir 1989–; co-operation as actor, dramatist and scriptwriter with Slovak and Czech TV, radio and theatres Semafor, Divadlo bez zábradlí and Labyrint. *Films include:* Sladké hry minulého léta (TV) 1969, Srdečný pozdrav ze zeměkoule (also screenwriter) 1982, Tři veteráni (Three Veterans) 1983, Vážení přátelé 1989, Tajomstvo alchymistu Storitza 1991, Vystrel na Bonaparta (TV) 1992, O psíckovi a macicke 1993, Mimozemšťané, Saturnin 1994, Výchova dívek v Čechách (Bringing Up Girls in Bohemia) 1997, Pasti, pasti, pasticky (Traps) 1998, Hanele 1999. *Films directed include:* Úlet (TV) 2002. *Plays include:* Cyrano, Don Juan, Mrtvé duše. *Honours:* TV Prize Monte Carlo Festival. *Address:* Stúdio Lasica-Satinský, Nám 1 Mája 5, Bratislava, Slovakia (office). *Telephone:* (2) 5292-1584 (office). *Fax:* (2) 5292-5082 (office).

LASKOWSKI, Jacek Andrzej, MagPhil; British dramatist and translator; *Literature Officer, Arts Council England, East Midlands;* b. 4 June 1946, Edinburgh, Scotland; m. Anne Grant Howieson 1978; two d. *Education:* Jagiellonian Univ., Kraków, Poland. *Career:* Literary Man., Haymarket Theatre, Leicester, 1984–87; mem. Soc. of Authors, (Vice-Chair., Broadcasting Cttee 1983–83), Writers' Guild of Great Britain; Literature Officer, Arts Council England, East Midlands. *Publications:* plays produced: Dreams to

Damnation, BBC Radio 3, 1977; Pawn Takes Pawn, BBC Radio 4, 1978; The Secret Agent, BBC Radio 4, 1980; Nostromo, BBC Radio 4, 1985; Phoney Physician (after Molière), 1986; Orestes/Electra (with Nancy Meckler), 1987; Wiseguy Scapino (after Molière), 1993. *Address:* 52 Holme Road, West Bridgfond, Nottingham NG2 5AD, England (home). *E-mail:* jalaskowski@tiscali.co.uk (home); jacek.laskowski@artscouncil.org.uk (office).

LATHAM, Alison Mary, BMus; British editor and writer; b. (Alison Mary Goodall), 13 July 1948, Southsea; m. Richard Latham; three s. *Education:* The Maynard School, Exeter, Birmingham Univ. *Career:* Sr Copy Ed., The New Grove Dictionary of Music and Musicians 1971–77; Asst Ed., The Grove Concise Dictionary of Music 1986–88; Co-Ed., The Musical Times 1977–88; Publications Ed., Royal Opera House, Covent Garden 1989–2000; Ed., Edinburgh Festival programmes 2003–; mem. Royal Soc. of Arts, Royal Musical Asscn, Soc. of Authors, Critics Circle. *Publications:* The Cambridge Music Guide (with Stanley Sadie) 1985, Verdi in Performance (ed. with Roger Parker) 2001, The Oxford Companion to Music (ed.) 2002, Sing Ariel: Essays and Thoughts for Alexander Goehr's Seventieth Birthday (ed.) 2003, The Oxford Dictionary of Musical Terms 2004, The Oxford Dictionary of Musical Works 2004. *Address:* c/o Joanna Harris, Oxford University Press, Walton Street, Oxford, OX2 6DP, England (office). *Telephone:* (1865) 556767 (office). *Fax:* (1865) 354635 (office). *E-mail:* joanna.harris@oup.com (office). *Website:* www.oup.com (office).

LATYNINA, Yuliya Leonidovna; Russian journalist and writer; b. 16 June 1966, Moscow; d. of Alla Latynina and Leonid Latynin. *Education:* studied medieval Europe. *Career:* presenter of TV current affairs programme Yest Mneniye, TVS; writer Novaya Gazeta newspaper –2003; currently journalist, Izvestiya newspaper; writer of crime novels. *Publications include:* Sto polei (A Hundred Fields), Delo o lazorevom pisme, Delo o propavshem boge, Kolduny i ministry, Insaider, Klearh i Gerakleya, Povest o blagonravnom myatezhnike,Povest o Zolotom Gosudare, Propovednik, Stag Hunting. *Honours:* awards for best business journalism. *Address:* c/o Novaya Gazeta, 10100 Moscow, Petapovskii per. 3, Russia (office). *Telephone:* (495) 921-5739 (office). *Fax:* (495) 923-6888 (office). *Website:* www.latynina.by.ru (office).

LAU, Evelyn Yee-Fun; Canadian writer; b. 2 July 1971, Vancouver. *Career:* Published poems and short stories in magazines from the age of 12; Air Canada Award for Most Promising Writer Under 30; Vantage Women of Originality Award 1999. *Publications include:* Runaway: Diary of a Street Kid (autobiog., adapted for TV as The Diary of Evelyn Lau) 1989, You Are Not Who You Claim (Milton Acorn People's Poetry Award) 1990, Oedipal Dreams 1992, Fresh Girls & Other Stories 1993, Other Women 1995, Choose Me (short stories) 1999.

LAURENS, André Antoine; French journalist; *Vice-President and Director-General, L'Indépendant;* b. 7 Dec. 1934, Montpellier (Hérault); s. of André Laurens and Mme Laurens (née Raymonde Balle). *Education:* Lycée de Montpellier. *Career:* journalist, L'Eclaireur Meridional (fortnightly), Montpellier 1953–54, Agence centrale de Presse, Paris 1958–62; mem. political staff, Le Monde 1963–69, Asst to head of political Dept 1969–82; Dir Le Monde 1982–84, Chief writer 1986–, Ombudsman 1994–; Vice-Pres. Soc. des Rédacteurs; Vice-Pres. and Dir-Gen. L'Indépendant 2000–. *Publications:* Les nouveaux communistes 1972, D'une France à l'autre 1974, Le Métier politique ou la conquête du pouvoir 1980. *Address:* L'Independant, Mas de la Garrigue, 2 avenue Alfred Sauvy, BP 105, 66605 Rivesaltes (office); 58 rue de la Roquette, Paris 75011 (home); 1 Espace Mediterraneé, Perpignan 66605 , France (home). *Telephone:* 4-68-64-88-88 (office). *Fax:* 4-68-64-88-49 (office). *Website:* www.lindependant.com (office).

LAURENS, Joanna, BA; British playwright; b. 1978. *Education:* Queen's Univ., Belfast. *Career:* writer on attachment at the Nat. Theatre, London; currently writer-in-residence, RSC. *Plays:* The Three Birds (Critics' Circle Most Promising Playwright Award, Time Out Award for Most Outstanding New Talent) 2000, Five Gold Rings (Almeida, London) 2003, Poor Beck (RSC) 2004. *Literary Agent:* PFD, Drury House, 34–43 Russell Street, London, WC2B 5HA, England.

LAURENTS, Arthur, BA; American playwright; b. 14 July 1917, New York; s. of Irving Laurents and Ada Robbins. *Education:* Cornell Univ. *Career:* radio scriptwriter 1939–40; mem. Screenwriters Guild, Acad. Motion Picture Arts and Sciences; Dir La Cage aux Folles (Tony Award) 1983, Sydney (Best Dir Award) 1985, London 1986, Birds of Paradise 1987; screenwriter, co-producer film The Turning Point 1977; writer and Dir of several Broadway plays including The Enclave 1973, Gypsy 1974, 1989; mem. Acad. of Motion Picture Arts and Sciences, Authors League, Dramatists Guild, PEN, Screenwriters Guild, Theatre Hall of Fame. *Publications:* novels: The Way We Were 1972, The Turning Point 1977; memoir: Original Story By 2000; screenplays: The Snake Pit 1948, Rope 1948, Caught 1948, Anna Lucasta 1949, Anastasia 1956, Bonjour Tristesse 1958, The Way We Were 1972, The Turning Point (Writers Guild of America Award, Screenwriters' Guild Award and Golden Globe Award) 1978; plays: Home of the Brave (American Acad. of Arts and Letters Award) 1946, The Bird Cage 1950, The Time of the Cuckoo 1952, A Clearing in the Woods 1956, Invitation to a March 1960, The Enclave 1973, Scream 1978, Jolson Sings Again 1995, The Radical Mystique 1995, My Good Name 1997, Big Potato 2000, Venecia (also dir) 2001, Claude Lazlo 2001, The Vibrator 2002, Closing Bell 2002, Attacks on the Heart 2003, Two Lives 2003, Collected Plays 2004; musical plays: West Side Story 1957, Gypsy 1959, Anyone Can Whistle 1964, Do I Hear a Waltz? 1964, Hallelulah Baby 1967, Nick and Nora

1991. *Honours:* Tony Award 1967, 1984, Drama Desk Award 1974, William Inge Festival Award 2004. *Literary Agent:* William Morris Agency, 1325 Avenue of the Americas, New York, NY 10019, USA.

LAURIE, (James) Hugh Callum, OBE; British actor and writer; b. 11 June 1959, s. of the late (William George) Ranald (Mundell) Laurie; m. Jo Laurie 1989; two s. one d. *Education:* Eton Coll., Univ. of Cambridge. *Career:* fmr Pres. Footlights, Univ. of Cambridge. *Television appearances:* Santa's Last Christmas, Alfresco (series, also writer) 1983, The Crystal Cube (also writer) 1983, Mrs Capper's Birthday 1985, Saturday Live (writer) 1986, A Bit of Fry and Laurie (series, also writer) 1986–91, The Laughing Prisoner (also writer) 1987, Blackadder the Third (series) 1987, Up Line 1987, Blackadder: The Cavalier Years 1988, Les Girls (series) 1988, Blackadder's Christmas Carol 1988, Blackadder Goes Forth (series) 1989, Hysteria 2! 1989, Jeeves and Wooster (series) 1990–92, Treasure Island (series) 1993, All or Nothing at All 1993, Look at the State We're In! (series, also dir) 1995, The Adventures of Mole 1995, The Best of Tracey Takes On... 1996, The Place of Lions 1997, Blackadder Back & Forth 1999, Little Grey Rabbit (series) 2000, Preston Pig (series) 2000, Life with Judy Garland: My and My Shadows 2001, Second Star to the Left 2001, Spooks (series) 2002, Stuart Little (series) 2003, Fortysomething (series, also dir) 2003, The Young Visiters [sic] 2003, House (Golden Globe Award for Best Performance in a Drama TV Series 2006, Golden Globe Award for Best Actor in a Drama TV Series 2007, Screen Actors' Guild Award for Outstanding Performance by a Male Actor in a Drama Series 2007) 2004–. *Films:* Plenty 1985, Strapless 1989, Peter's Friends 1992, A Pin for the Butterfly 1994, Sense and Sensibility 1995, 101 Dalmatians 1996, The Snow Queen's Revenge 1996, The Borrowers 1997, Spice World 1997, The Ugly Duckling 1997, The Man in the Iron Mask 1998, Cousin Bette 1998, Stuart Little 1999, Carnivale 2000, Maybe Baby 2000, Lounge Act 2000, The Piano Tuner 2001, Chica de Río 2001, Stuart Little 2 2002, Flight of the Phoenix 2004. *Publications:* Fry and Laurie 4 (with Stephen Fry) 1994, The Gun Seller 1996. *Address:* c/o Christian Hodell, Hamilton Hodell Ltd, Ground Floor, 24 Hanway Street, London, W1T 1UH, England. *Telephone:* (20) 7636-1221.

LAURO, Shirley, BS, MS; American actress, playwright and teacher; b. (Shirley Shapiro), 18 Nov. 1933, Des Moines, IA; m. 1st Norton Mezvinsky (divorced); m. 2nd Louis Paul Lauro 1973. *Education:* Northwestern Univ., Univ. of Wisconsin at Madison. *Career:* actress on stage and in films and television; Instructor, City College, CUNY, 1967–71, Yeshiva University, 1971–76, Manhattan Community College, 1978, Marymount Manhattan College, 1978–79; Literary Consultant, 1975–80, Resident Playwright, 1976–, Ensemble Studio Theatre, New York City; Resident Playwright, Alley Theatre, Houston, 1987; Adjunct Prof. of Playwrighting, Tisch School of the Arts, New York University, 1989–; mem. Authors' Guild; Authors League; Dramatists Guild; League of Professional Theatre Women; PEN; Writers' Guild of America. *Publications:* The Edge, 1965; The Contest, 1975; Margaret and Kit, 1979; In the Garden of Eden, 1982; Sunday Go to Meetin', 1986; Pearls on the Moon, 1987; A Piece of My Heart, 1992; A Moment in Time, 1994; The Last Trial of Clarence Darrow, 1997; Railing it Uptown, 1997. Contributions: periodicals.

LAUZANNE, Bernard, LèsL; French journalist; b. 22 June 1916, Paris; s. of Gaston Lauzanne and Sylvia Scarognino; m. Lucie Gambini 1949; two d. *Education:* Lycée Condorcet and Univ. of Paris. *Career:* war service and prisoner of war in Germany 1939–45; joined Radiodiffusion Française (RTF) and worked on programme 'Paris vous parle' 1945–59; Chief Sub-Ed., Le Monde 1945–59, News Ed. 1959–69, Asst Ed. 1969–74, Ed. 1974–78, Man. Ed. 1978–83; Directeur de Collection Éditions Denoël 1983–; Pres. France-Japan Asscn, Comité d'histoire de la radiodiffusion 1991–; Lauréat de l' Acad. française 1987; Chevalier, Légion d'honneur, Croix de guerre, Commdr of Sacred Treasure, Japan. *Address:* Éditions Denoël, 9 rue du Cherche-Midi, 75278 Paris Cedex 06 (office); 5 rue Jean-Bart, 75006 Paris, France (home). *Telephone:* 1-42-84-01-74.

LAVEN, Mary; British academic and writer. *Career:* Lecturer in History, Univ. of Cambridge; Fellow, Jesus Coll., Cambridge. *Publications:* Virgins of Venice: Enclosed Lives and Broken Vows in the Renaissance Convent 2002. *Honours:* Mail on Sunday/John Llewellyn Rhys Prize. *Address:* c/o Jesus College, Cambridge, CB5 8BL, England.

LAVENTHOL, David, MA; American publisher; b. 15 July 1933, Philadelphia; s. of Jesse Laventhol and Clare Horwald; m. Esther Coons 1958; one s. one d. *Education:* Yale Univ. and Univ. of Minnesota. *Career:* reporter, later News Ed., St Petersburg Times 1957–63; City Ed. New York Herald Tribune 1963–66; Asst Man. Ed. The Washington Post 1966–69; Assoc. Ed. Newsday 1969, Exec. Ed. 1969–70, Ed. 1970–78, Publr and CEO 1978–86, Chair. 1986–87; Group Vice-Pres. Times Mirror 1981–86, Sr Vice-Pres. 1986, Pres. 1987–93; CEO and Publr LA Times 1989–93; Ed.-at-Large Times Mirror Co., LA 1994–98, Consultant Ed. 1998–99; Ed. and Publr Columbia Journalism Review 1999–2003; Chair. Pulitzer Prize Bd 1988–89; Vice-Chair. Int. Press Inst. 1985–92, Chair. 1992–95; Chair. Museum of Contemporary Art, LA 1993–97, Cttee to Protect Journalists –2005; Dir Newspaper Advertising Bureau, American Press Inst. 1988–, LA Times Washington Post/News Service, Times Mirror Foundation, United Negro Coll. Fund; mem. Bd Dirs Assoc. Press 1993–96, Columbia Journalism School 1995–, Nat. Parkinson Foundation 1995–, Saratoga Performing Arts Center 1993–96; mem. American Soc. of Newspaper Eds Writing Awards Bd, American Newspaper Publr Asscn, Century Asscn, Council on Foreign Relations. *Address:* c/o Columbia Journalism Review, Columbia University, 2950 Broadway, New York, NY 10027, USA (office).

LAVERS, Norman, BA, MA, PhD; American teacher and writer; b. 21 April 1935, Berkeley, CA; m. Cheryl Dicks 1967, one s. *Education:* San Francisco State Univ., Univ. of Iowa. *Publications:* Mark Harris (criticism) 1978; Selected Short Stories, 1979; Jerzy Kosinski (criticism) 1982; The Northwest Passage (novel), 1984; Pop Culture Into Art: The Novels of Manuel Puig (criticism), 1988; Growing up in Berkeley with the Bomb (autobiog.), 1998. Contributions: Ed., Arkansas Review; Contributing Ed., Bird Watcher's Digest. *Honours:* National Endowment for the Arts Fellowships, 1982, 1991; Ed.'s Choice Award, 1986; Hohenberg Award, 1986; O. Henry Award, 1987; Pushcart Award, 1992; William Peden Prize, 1992; Porter Fund Award, 1995.

LAVERY, Bryony; British playwright; b. 1947, Dewsbury. *Career:* Tutor-Lecturer on MA playwriting course, Birmingham Univ. 1989–92; Artistic Dir, various theatre seasons and festivals. *Plays:* Of All Living (London) 1967, Days at Court (London) 1968, Warbeck (London) 1969, Germany Calling (with Peter Leabourne, London) 1976, I was too Young at the Time to Understand Why my Mother was Crying (London) 1976, Sharing (London) 1976, The Catering Service (Edinburgh Festival) 1976, Snakes (London) 1977, Bag (Young Vic Theatre) 1977, Grandmother's Footsteps (King's Head Theatre, London) 1977, Floorshow (cabaret with Caryl Churchill, Monstrous Regiment, London) 1977, Helen and her Friends (London) 1978, Missing (Sheffield Crucible) 1979, Sugar and Spice (Ipswich, Suffolk) 1979, The Wild Bunch (Women's Theatre Group, London) 1979, Time Gentlemen Please (London) 1979, Unemployment: An Occupational Hazard (London) 1979, Gentlemen Prefer Blondes (adaptation, London) 1980, Hot Time (Common Stock Theatre Tour) (Pink Paper Play of the Year 1991) 1980, The Family Album (London) 1980, The Joker (London) 1980, Zulu (with Patrick Barlow, ICA, London) 1981, Female Trouble (cabaret, Theatrespace, London) 1981, More Female Trouble (Drill Hall, London) 1982, For Maggie, Betty and Ida (Drill Hall, London) 1982, Götterdämmerung (adaptation, Nat. Theatre of Brent) 1982, The Black Hole of Calcutta (Drill Hall, London) 1982, Calamity (Tricycle Theatre, London) 1983, The Zulu Hut Club (London) 1984, Origin of the Species (Birmingham Repertory Theatre) 1984, Over and Out (on tour) 1985, Witchcraze (BAC, London) 1985, Getting Through (musical, on tour) 1985, Sore Points (London) 1986, Mummy (with Sally Owen and L. Ortolja, Drill Hall, London) 1987, Madagascar (London) 1987, The Headless Body (London) 1987, The Dragon Wakes (London) 1988, Frozen (Birmingham Repertory Theatre) (TMA Best New Play, Eileen Anderson Central TV Award for Best Play) 1998, The Two Marias (Theatre Centre, London) 1988, Puppet States (Riverside Studios, London) 1988, The Drury Lane Ghost (with Nona Sheppard, London) 1989, Wicked (Oval House Theatre, London) 1990, Her Aching Heart (Oval House Theatre, London) 1990, Kitchen Matters (Royal Court, London) 1990, Flight (Perspectives Theatre, Denmark) 1991, The Way to Cook a Wolf (BAC Studio, London) 1993, Nothing Compares to You (Birmingham Repertory Theatre) 1995, Down Among the Mini-Beasts (Polka, London) 1996, Ophelia 1996, Goliath (Newcastle Playhouse) 1997, More Light (Royal Nat. Theatre) 1997, Shot Through the Heart (Ludlow Castle) 2000, Illyria (ACT, San Francisco) 2000, A Wedding Story (Birmingham Repertory Theatre) 2000, Behind the Scenes at the Museum (adaptation, Theatre Royal, York) 2000, The Magic Toyshop (Wolsey, Ipswich) 2001, Cherished Disappointments in Love (trans., Soho Theatre, London) 2001, Precious Bane (Pentabus) 2003, Thyestes (Furies) (RSC) 2003, Discontented Winter (Old Rep, Birmingham) 2004, A Dolls House (adaptation, Birmingham Repertory Theatre) 2004, Last Easter (Lucille Lortel Theatre, New York) 2004, Dracula (adaptation, Birmingham Rep.) 2005, Smoke (New Vic Theatre) 2006, Discontented Winter: House Remix (Royal Nat. Theatre, London) 2005. *Radio plays:* Laying Ghosts 1992, Wuthering Heights (adaptation) 1994, My Cousin Rachel (adaptation) 1994, Twelve Days of Christmas 1994, Velma and Therese 1996, No Joan of Arc 1997, The Smell of Him 1998, A High Wind in Jamaica (adaptation) 2000, Requiem 2000, Lady Audley's Secret (adaptation) 2000, Wise Children (adaptation) 2003. *Television and film:* Revolting Women (for BBC2), Buy (for Channel 4) 2000, Restless Farewell 2003, Goodbye? 2003. *Honours:* Hon. DArts (De Montfort Univ.). *Literary Agent:* PFD, Drury House, 34–43 Russell Street, London, WC2B 5HA, England. *Telephone:* (20) 7344-1000. *Fax:* (20) 7836-9539. *E-mail:* postmaster@pfd.co.uk. *Website:* www.pfd.co.uk.

LAVIN, S. R., BA, MA; American poet and writer; b. 2 April 1945, Springfield, MA; two s. four d. *Education:* AIC, Trinity Coll. *Career:* poet-in-residence, Clark Univ., Worcester, MA 1972; Prof. of English, Castleton State Coll., Vermont 1987–99; Priest of the Order of Melchizedek. *Songs:* published with Peer Corpn 1972–78. *Publications:* poetry: The Stonecutters at War with the Cliff Dwellers 1972, Cambodian Spring 1973, Let Myself Shine 1979; fiction: Metacomet; translation: I and You, by Martin Buber; contrib. to Cold Drill, Hiram, I.P.R., Mandrake, Stand, Vermont Literary Magazine, Chinese Poetry International. *Honours:* Leonardo da Vinci Award for Poetry, Firenze, Italy 1976. *Address:* c/o Parchment Press, 52 S River Street, Coxsackie, NY 12051, USA (office). *Telephone:* (202) 577-3641 (office). *E-mail:* srlavin@hotmail.com (office).

LAW, Michael, (Michael Kreuzenau), BA; British dramatist, writer and translator; b. 17 April 1925, Kerman, Iran; m. Dorothea V. Schön 1954; four s.; m. Elizabeth Yarnold 2005. *Education:* Univ. of Cambridge. *Career:* Lecturer in Education, Univ. of Leeds 1969–83; mem. Soc. of Authors, Writers' Guild. *Plays:* Two or Three Ghosts 1997, A Companion for Claire (premiered

Questors Theatre, Ealing 1993) 1997, Helen of Rhodes 1997, Aquarium (premiered Mercury Theatre, Colchester 1980) 1997, The Magic Man 1997, A Guest for the Sabbath 1997, Have-You-Any-Idea-What-Time-It-Is! 1998, Just Us (premiered Questors Theatre, Ealing 1993) 1998, The Nurses' Tale 1998, The Wench is Dead 1998, Come and Get Me! 1998, Looking After Molly (premiered Questors Theatre, Ealing 1999) 1999, As Time Goes By 2004, The Sci Fi Man 2004, The Dissonance Quartet 2006, The Serving-Maid's Story 2006. *Publications:* The Vienna Opera House (trans.) 1955, Caricature from Leonardo to Picasso (trans.) 1957, Seven German Readers for Schools 1960–75, How to Read German (textbook) 1963; 13 published plays 1997–2004; contrib. to numerous educational journals. *Honours:* numerous drama prizes, including First and Second Prizes, London Writers' Competition, AJ Gooding Award, Understanding Play Competition). *Address:* 101 Bittacy Rise, Mill Hill, London, NW7 2HJ, England (home). *Telephone:* (20) 8371-1541 (office). *E-mail:* michael.law9@btinternet.com (office).

LAWRENCE, Clifford Hugh, MA, DPhil, FRHistS; British academic and writer; *Professor of Medieval History Emeritus, University of London*; b. 28 Dec. 1921, London, England; m. Helen Maud Curran 1953; one s. five d. *Education:* Univ. of Oxford. *Career:* Asst Lecturer, Bedford Coll., London 1951, Lecturer 1953–63, Reader in Medieval History 1963–70; External Examiner, Univ. of Newcastle upon Tyne 1972–74, Univ. of Bristol 1975–77, Univ. of Reading 1977–79; Prof. of Medieval History 1970–87, Prof. Emeritus 1987–, Univ. of London; mem. Soc. of Antiquaries. *Publications:* St Edmund of Abingdon: A Study in Hagiography and History 1960, The English Church and the Papacy in the Middle Ages 1965, The University in State and Church (Vol. 1 of The History of the University of Oxford) 1984, Medieval Monasticism: Forms of Religious Life in Western Europe in the Middle Ages 1984, The Friars: The Impact of the Early Mendicant Movement on Western Society 1994, The Life of St Edmund, by Matthew Paris (trans.) 1996, The Letters of Adam Marsh (ed. and trans.) 2006; contrib. to reference works, scholarly books and journals. *Address:* 11 Durham Road, London, SW20 0QH, England (home). *Telephone:* (20) 8964-3820 (home).

LAWRENCE, Karen Ann, BA, MA; Canadian writer; b. 5 Feb. 1951, Windsor, Ont.; m. Robert Gabhart 1982; one s. *Education:* Univs of Windsor and Alberta. *Career:* mem. Writers' Union of Canada, Asscn of Canadian Radio and Television Artists. *Publications:* Nekuia: The Inanna Poems 1980, The Life of Helen Alone (also screenplay) 1986, Springs of Living Water 1990. *Honours:* WHSmith/Books in Canada First Novel Award 1987, PEN Los Angeles Center Best First Novel Award 1987. *Address:* 2153 Pine Street, San Diego, CA 92103, USA. *E-mail:* karenannlawrence@cox.net (home).

LAWRENCE, Louise; British novelist; b. 5 June 1943, Surrey, England; m. Graham Mace 1987, one s. two d. *Publications:* Andra, 1971; Power of Stars, 1972; Wyndcliffe, 1974; Sing and Scatter Daisies, 1977; Star Lord, 1978; Cat Call, 1980; Earth Witch, 1981; Calling B for Butterfly, 1982; Dram Road, 1983; Children of the Dust, 1985; Moonwind, 1986; Warriors of Taan, 1986; Extinction is Forever, 1990; Ben-Harran's Castle, 1992; The Disinherited, 1994.

LAWRENCE, P. (see Tubb, Edwin Charles)

LAWS, Stephen; British writer and local council administrator; b. 13 July 1952, Newcastle upon Tyne, England; m. Lyn Hunter 1980 (divorced 1989); one d. *Education:* College of Arts and Technology. *Career:* County and Borough Council administrative positions; Senior Committee Administrator for Central Administration, Newcastle City Council, Newcastle upon Tyne, 1982–; mem. British Fantasy Society; National Asscn of Local Government Officers. *Publications:* Ghost Train, 1985; Spectre, 1985; The Wyrm, 1987; The Frighteners, 1990; Darkfall, 1992; Voyages into Darkness (co-author), 1993; Macabre, 1994; Annabel Says, 1997. Contributions: articles and short stories to periodicals. *Honours:* Three Sunday Sun Awards, for short stories; Radio Newcastle Award, for short story. *Address:* c/o Publicity Director, Souvenir Press Ltd, 43 Great Russell Street, London, WC1B 3PA, England.

LAWSON, Chet (see Tubb, Edwin Charles)

LAWSON, Hon. Dominic Ralph Campden, BA, FRSA; British journalist and editor; b. 17 Dec. 1956, London; s. of Nigel Lawson, now Lord Lawson of Blaby and the late Lady (Vanessa) Ayer; m. 1st Jane Fiona Wastell Whytehead 1982 (divorced 1991); m. 2nd Hon. Rosamond Monckton 1991; two d. *Education:* Westminster School, Christchurch, Oxford. *Career:* mem. staff World Tonight and The Financial World Tonight, BBC 1979–81; mem. staff Financial Times (Energy Corresp. and Lex column) 1981–87; Deputy Ed. The Spectator 1987–90, Ed. 1990–95; Ed. The Sunday Telegraph 1995–2005; columnist, Sunday Corresp. 1990, The Financial Times 1991–94, Daily Telegraph 1994–95. *Publications:* Korchnoi, Kasparov 1983, Britain in the Eighties (jtly) 1989; ed. The Spectator Annual 1992, 1993, 1994, The Inner Game 1993. *Honours:* Harold Wincott Prize for Financial Journalism, Ed. of the Year, Soc. of Magazine Eds. 1990.

LAWSON, Nigella Lucy, BA; British journalist, food writer and broadcaster; b. 6 Jan. 1960, d. of Baron Nigel Lawson of Blaby and Vanessa Salmon; m. 1st John Diamond 1992 (died 2001); two c.; m. 2nd Charles Saatchi 2003. *Education:* Univ. of Oxford. *Career:* began writing restaurant column, The Spectator 1985; fmr Deputy Literary Ed. The Sunday Times; journalist or columnist for numerous publs including Evening Standard, The Guardian, The Daily Telegraph, The Observer, The Times Magazine, Vogue, Gourmet magazine (USA), Bon Appetit (USA). *Television includes:* Nigel Slater's Real

Food (UK Channel 4) 1998, Nigella Bites (Channel 4) 2000–01, Forever Summer (Channel 4) 2002, Nigella (ITV 1) 2005. *Publications:* How to Eat: The Pleasures and Principles of Good Food 1998, How To Be A Domestic Goddess: Baking and the Art of Comfort Cooking 2000, Nigella Bites 2001, Forever Summer 2002, Feast: Food that Celebrates Life 2004. *Honours:* Illustrated Book of the Year, British Book Awards 1998, Author of the Year, British Book Awards 2000, Cookery Book of the Year, Guild Food Writers 2001, Gold Ladle for Best TV Food Show, World Food Media Awards 2001, Lifestyle Book of the Year, WH Smith Book Awards 2002. *Address:* Pabulum Productions Limited, 11 Conway Street, London W1T 6BL, England (office). *Website:* www.nigella.com (office).

LAWSON, Philip (see Bishop, Michael Lawson)

LAWSON, Sarah Anne, MA, PhD; American/British writer, poet and translator; b. 4 Nov. 1943, Indianapolis, Ind.; m. Alastair Pettigrew 1969 (deceased 1992). *Education:* Indiana Univ., Univ. of Pennsylvania, Univ. of Glasgow. *Career:* mem. English PEN, Poetry Soc., RSL, Soc. of Authors, Translators' Asscn. *Publications:* poetry: Dutch Interiors 1985, Down Where the Willow is Washing her Hair 1995, Below the Surface 1996, Twelve Scenes of Malta 2000, Friends in the Country 2004, All the Tea in China 2006; translations: The Treasure of the City of Ladies, by Christine de Pisan 1985, A Foothold in Florida, by René de Laudonnière 1992, The Girls' Consent, by Leandro Fernández de Moratín 1998, Jacques Prévert, Selected Poems 2002, All My Friends are Crazy, by Sera Anstadt 2006; other: A Fado for My Mother 1996; contrib. to anthologies, including New Writers and Writing 16 1979, Poetry Introduction 6 1986, reviews, quarterlies and journals. *Honours:* C. Day-Lewis Fellowship 1979–80, Hawthornden Fellowship 2005. *Address:* 186 Albyn Road, London, SE8 4JQ, England (home).

LAYARD, Baron (Life Peer), cr. 2000, of Highgate in the London Borough of Haringey; **Peter Richard Grenville Layard,** BA, MSc; British economist and academic; *Co-Director, Centre for Economic Performance, London School of Economics*; b. 15 March 1934, Welwyn Garden City; s. of John Willoughby Layard and Doris Layard; m. Molly Meacher 1991. *Education:* Univ. of Cambridge, London School of Econs. *Career:* school teacher, London Co. Council 1959–61; Sr Research Officer, Robbins Cttee on Higher Educ. 1961–64; Deputy Dir Higher Educ. Research Unit, LSE 1964–74, Lecturer, LSE 1968–75, Reader 1975–80, Prof. of Econs 1980–99, Co-Dir Centre for Econ. Performance 1990–, Head, Centre for Labour Econ. 1974–90; Consultant, Centre for European Policy Studies, Brussels 1982–86; mem. Univ. Grants Cttee 1985–89; Chair. Employment Inst. 1987–92; Co-Chair., World Economy Group of the World Inst. for Devt Econs Research 1989–93; Econ. Adviser to Russian Govt 1991–97; Fellow Econometric Soc. *Publications:* Cost Benefit Analysis 1973, Causes of Poverty (with D. Piachaud and M. Stewart) 1978, Microeconomic Theory (with A. A. Walters) 1978, More Jobs, Less Inflation 1982, The Causes of Unemployment (Co-Ed. with C. Greenhalgh and A. Oswald) 1984, The Rise in Unemployment (Co-Ed. with C. Bean and S. Nickell) 1986, How to Beat Unemployment 1986, Handbook of Labor Economics (Co-Ed. with Orley C. Ashenfelter) 1987, The Performance of the British Economy (jtly) 1988, Unemployment: Macroeconomic Performance and the Labour Market (jtly) 1991, East-West Migration: the alternatives (jtly) 1992, Post-Communist Reform: Pain and Progress 1993 (jtly), Macroeconomics: a Text for Russia 1994, The Coming Russian Boom 1996 (jtly), What Labour Can Do 1997, Tackling Unemployment 1999, Tackling Inequality 1999, What the Future Holds (Co-Ed. with R. Cooper), Happiness: Lessons from a New Science 2005. *Address:* Centre for Economic Performance, London School of Economics, Houghton Street, London, WC2A 2AE (office); 45 Cholmeley Park, London, N6 5EL, England (home). *Telephone:* (20) 7955-7281 (office). *Fax:* (20) 7955-7595 (office). *E-mail:* r.layard@lse.ac.uk (office). *Website:* cep.lse.ac.uk/layard (office).

LAZARUS, Arnold Leslie, BA, BS, MA, PhD; American writer and poet; b. 20 Feb. 1914, Revere, MA; m. Keo Felker 1938, two s. two d. *Education:* University of Michigan, Middlesex Medical School, University of California, Los Angeles. *Career:* mem. Acad. of American Poets; American Society for Theatre Research; Comparative Literature Asscn; MLA; Poetry Society of America. *Publications:* Entertainments and Valedictions, 1970; Harbrace Adventures in Literature (ed. with R. Lowell and E. Hardwick), 1970; Modern English (ed. with others), 1970; A Suit of Four, 1973; The Indiana Experience, 1977; Beyond Graustark (with Victor H. Jones), 1981; Glossary of Literature and Composition (ed. with H. Wendell Smith), 1983; Best of George Ade (ed.), 1985; Some Light: New and Selected Verse, 1988; A George Jean Nathan Reader (ed.), 1990. Contributions: numerous periodicals. *Honours:* Ford Foundation Fellow, 1954; Kemper McComb Award, 1976.

LAZARUS, Henry (see Slavitt, David Rytman)

LAZENBY, John Francis, MA; British academic and writer; *Professor Emeritus of Ancient History, University of Newcastle upon Tyne*; b. 14 April 1934, Tiruchirapalli, Tamil Nadu, India; m. Elizabeth Mary Leithead 1967; one s. one d. *Education:* Keble Coll., Oxford, Magdalen Coll., Oxford. *Career:* Lecturer in Ancient History, King's Coll., Newcastle upon Tyne, Univ. of Durham 1959–62; Lecturer 1962–71; Sr Lecturer 1971–79, Reader 1979–94, Prof. 1994–99, of Ancient History, Prof. Emeritus 1999–, Univ. of Newcastle upon Tyne. *Publications:* The Catalogue of the Ships in Homer's Iliad 1970, Hannibal's War 1978, The Spartan Army 1985, The Defence of Greece 490–479 BC 1993, The First Punic War 1996, The Peloponnesian War 2004; contrib. to scholarly journals. *Address:* 15 Rectory Terrace, Gosforth,

Newcastle upon Tyne, NE3 1YB, England (home). *Telephone:* (191) 2858000 (home). *Fax:* (191) 2858000 (home).

Le CARRÉ, John (see Cornwell, David John Moore)

Le CLÉZIO, Jean Marie Gustave; French/British writer; b. 13 April 1940, Nice; s. of Raoul Le Clézio and Simone Le Clézio; m. 1st Rosalie Piquemal 1961; one d.; m. 2nd Jemia Jean 1975. *Education:* Lycée and Univ. de Nice. *Career:* travelled in Nigeria 1948, England (studied at Bristol and London Univs), USA 1965. *Publications:* Le procès-verbal (The Interrogation) 1963, La fièvre (Fever) (short stories) 1965, Le procès 1965, Le déluge 1966, L'extase matérielle (essay) 1967, Terra amata (novel) 1967, Le livre des fuites 1969, La guerre 1970, Haï 1971, Conversations 1971, Les géants 1973, Mydriase 1973, Voyages de l'autre côté 1975, Les prophéties du Chylam Balam 1976, Mondo et autres histoires, L'inconnu sur la terre 1978, Désert 1980, Trois villes saintes 1980, La ronde et autres faits divers 1982, Journal du chercheur d'or 1985, Voyage à Rodrigues 1986, Le rêve mexicain (essay) 1988, Printemps et autres saisons 1989, Sirandanes, Suivi de Petit lexique de la langue créole et des oiseaux (jtly) 1990, Onitsha 1991, Etoile errante 1992, Diego et Frida 1993, La Quarantaine 1995, Le Poisson d'or 1997, La Fête chantée 1997, Hasard et Angoli Mala 1999, Coeur brûlé et autres romances 2000. *Honours:* Chevalier des Arts et Lettres, Légion d'honneur; Prix Renaudot 1963, Grand Prix Paul Morand (Acad. française) 1980, Grand Prix Jean Giono 1997, Prix Prince de Monaco 1998. *Address:* c/o Editions Gallimard, 5 rue Sébastien-Bottin, 75007 Paris, France.

LE COZ, Martine; French novelist; b. Sept. 1955. *Publications include:* Gilles de Raiz ou La confession imaginaire 1989, Léo, la nuit 1997, Le chagrin du zèbre 1998, Le nègre et la Méduse 1999, La beauté, Céleste (Prix Renaudot) 2001. *Address:* c/o Editions du Rocher, 6 place St-Sulpice, 75279 Paris Cedex 06, France (office).

LE GENDRE, Bertrand; French journalist; b. 25 Feb. 1948, Neuilly-sur-Seine; s. of Bernard Le Gendre and Catherine Chassaing de Borredon; m. 1st Jacqueline de Linares 1987 (divorced 1995); one s.; m. 2nd Nadia du Luc-Baccouche 1995; one s. *Education:* Collège Sainte-Croix-de-Neuilly, Univ. of Paris X, Institut d'études politiques, Paris, Institut des hautes études de défense nationale. *Career:* joined Le Monde as journalist 1974, in charge of judicial desk 1983, Reporter 1987, Ed.-in-Chief 1993–2000; Visiting Assoc. Prof., Univ. de Paris II 2000–; Sub-Ed. Gallimard 1986–89. *Honours:* Prix de la Fondation Mumm pour la presse écrite 1986. *Address:* Le Monde, 80 Boulevard Auguste-Blanqui, 75707 Paris Cedex 13 (office); 16 rue de la Glacière, 75013 Paris, France (home). *Telephone:* 1-57-28-26-14 (office). *E-mail:* legendre@lemonde.fr (office).

LE GOFF, Jacques Louis; French historian and academic; b. 1 Jan. 1924, Toulon; s. of Jean Le Goff and Germaine Ansaldi; m. Anna Dunin-Wasowicz 1962; one s. one d. *Education:* Lycées, Toulon, Marseilles and Louis-le-Grand, Paris, Ecole normale supérieure, Paris. *Career:* history teacher 1950; Fellow of Lincoln Coll., Oxford 1951–52; mem. Ecole française de Rome 1953–54; Asst at Univ. of Lille 1954–59; Prof., then Dir of Studies, 6th Section, Ecole des hautes études (EHE) 1960–72, Pres. Ecole des hautes études en sciences sociales (fmr 6th Section of EHE) 1972–77; mem. Comité nat. de la recherche scientifique 1962–70, Comité des travaux historiques 1972, Conseil supérieur de la Recherche 1985–87; Co-Dir reviews Annales-Economies, sociétés, civilisations and Ethnologie Française 1972; Pres. commission scientifique Ecole Nationale du Patrimoine; mem. Acad. Culturelles des Cultures 1990. *Publications:* Marchands et banquiers du Moyen Age 1956, Les Intellectuels au Moyen Age 1957, Le Moyen Age 1962, La Civilisation de l'occident médiéval 1964, Pour un autre Moyen Age (trans. as Time, Work and Culture in the Middle Ages) 1978, La Naissance du purgatoire 1981, L'Apogée de la chrétienté 1982, L'Imaginaire médiéval (trans. as The Medieval Imagination) 1985, La Bourse et la vie 1986, Histoire de la France religeuse (co-author) 1988, L'Homme médiéval (trans. as Medieval Callings) 1989, L'Etat et les pouvoirs 1989, St Louis 1996, Une Vie pour l'histoire 1996, L'Europe racontée aux jeunes 1996, Un Autre Moyen Age 1999, Saint François d'Assise 1999, Dictionnaire raisonné de l'Occident médiéval 1999, La Vieille Europe et la nôtre 2000, Le Moyen Age en images 2001, A la recherche du Moyen Age 2002, Dieu au Moyen Age 2003, Héros du Moyen Age: le Saint et le Roi 2004, Vu long Moyen Age 2004, Héros et Merveilles du Moyen Age 2004, Le Moyen Age expliqué aux enfants 2006. *Honours:* Grand Prix Nat. 1987, Gold Medal, CNRS 1991, Grand Prix Gobert 1996, Grand Prix d'Histoire 1997, Prix d'Histoire Heineken 2004, Prix Dan David 2007. *Address:* c/o Ecole des Hautes, Etudes en Sciences Sociales, 54 Boulevard Raspail, 75006 Paris (office); 5 rue de Thionville, 75019 Paris, France (home).

LE GUIN, Ursula Kroeber, BA, MA; American writer and poet; b. 21 Oct. 1929, Berkeley, CA; d. of Alfred L. Kroeber and Theodora K. Kroeber; m. Charles A. Le Guin 1953; one s. two d. *Education:* Radcliffe Coll., Columbia Univ. *Career:* taught French, Mercer Univ., Univ. of Ida 1954–56; teacher, resident writer or visiting lecturer at numerous univs, including Bennington Coll., Portland State Univ., Pacific Univ., Reading Univ., Univ. of Calif. at San Diego, Indiana Writers' Conf., Kenyon Coll., Clarion West Writers' Workshop, First Australian Workshop in Speculative Fiction, etc. 1971–; Mellon Prof. Tulane Univ. 1986; mem. Science Fiction Research Asscn, Authors' League, Writers' Guild W, PEN; Fellow Columbia Univ. 1952, Fulbright Fellow 1953; Arbuthnot Lecturer, American Library Asscn 2004. *Films:* King Dog (screenplay) 1985. *Television:* The Lathe of Heaven. *Publications:* fiction: Rocannon's World 1966, Planet of Exile 1966, City of Illusion 1967, A Wizard of Earthsea (Earthsea series) (Boston Globe-Horn Award) 1968, The Left Hand of Darkness (Nebula Award, Hugo Award) 1969, The Tombs of Atuan (Earthsea series) (Newbery Silver Medal 1972) 1970, The Lathe of Heaven (Locus Award 1973) 1971, The Farthest Shore (Earthsea series) (Nat. Book Award) 1972, The Dispossessed: An Ambiguous Utopia (Hugo Award, Nebula Award) 1974, The Wind's Twelve Quarters (short stories) 1975, The Word for World is Forest 1976, Very Far Away from Anywhere Else 1976, Orsinian Tales (short stories) 1976, Malafrena 1979, The Beginning Place 1980, The Compass Rose (short stories) (Locus Award 1984) 1982, The Eye of the Heron 1983, Always Coming Home (Kafka Award 1986) 1985, Buffalo Gals (short stories) (Hugo Award 1988, Int. Fantasy Award 1988) 1987, Tehanu (Earthsea series) (Nebula Award) 1990, Searoad (short stories) (H. L. Davis Award 1992) 1991, A Fisherman of the Inland Sea (short stories) 1994, Four Ways to Forgiveness (short stories) (Locus Award) 1995, Unlocking the Air (short stories) 1996, The Telling (Locus Award, Endeavor Award) 2000, Tales from Earthsea (Earthsea series) (Locus Award, Endeavor Award) 2001, The Other Wind (Earthsea series) 2001, The Birthday of the World (short stories) 2002, Changing Planes (short stories) 2003, Kalpa Imperial (translation) 2003, Gifts 2004, Voices 2006, Powers 2007; juvenile fiction: Leese Webster 1979, Cobbler's Rune 1983, Solomon Leviathan 1988, Catwings 1988, A Visit from Dr Katz 1988, Fire and Stone 1989, Catwings Return 1989, Fish Soup 1992, A Ride on the Red Mare's Back 1992, Wonderful Alexander and the Catwings 1994, Jane on her Own 1999, Tom Mouse 2002, Gifts 2004; poetry: Wild Angels 1974, Walking in Cornwall (chapbook) 1976, Tillai and Tylissos (chapbook, with Theodora Kroeber) 1979, Hard Words 1981, In the Red Zone (chapbook, with Henk Pander) 1983, Wild Oats and Fireweed 1988, No Boats (chapbook) 1992, Blue Moon over Thurman Street (with Roger Dorband) 1993, Going out with Peacocks 1994, Sixty Odd 1999, Selected Poems of Gabriela Mistral (translation) 2003, Incredible Good Fortune 2006; non-fiction: Dancing at the Edge of the World (criticism) 1989, The Language of the Night (criticism) 1992, A Winter Solstice Ritual for the Pacific Northwest (chapbook, with Vonda N. McIntyre) 1991, Findings (chapbook) 1992, The Art of Bunditsu (chapbook) 1993, Lao Tzu: Tao Te Ching: A Book About the Way and the Power of the Way (trans.) 1997, The Twins, The Dream/Las Gemelas, El Sueño (trans. with Diana Bellessi) 1997, Steering the Craft (criticism) 1998, The Wave in the Mind (criticism) 2004; contrib. to periodicals, including New Yorker, Omni, Redbook, Fantasy and Science Fiction, Fantastic, Amazing, Playboy, Playgirl, Tri-Quarterly, Kenyon Review, Calyx, Milkweed, Mr Cogito, Seattle Review, NW Review, Open Places, Backbone, Orion, Parabola, Paradoxa, Yale Review, Antaeus Foundation, SF Studies, Critical Inquiry. *Honours:* Hon. DLitt (Bucknell Univ., Lawrence Univ.); Hon. DHumLitt (Lewis and Clark Coll., Occidental Coll., Emory Univ., Univ. of Ore., Western Ore. State, Kenyon, Portland State); Hugo Awards 1973, 1975, Jupiter Awards 1975, 1976, Nebula Awards 1975, 1990, 1996, Gandalf Award 1979, Lewis Carroll Shelf Award 1979, Prix Lectures-Jeunesse 1987, American Acad. and Inst. of Arts and Letters Harold Vursell Award 1991, Pushcart Prize 1991, Hubbub annual poetry award 1995, Asimov's Reader's award 1995, Theodore Sturgeon Award 1995, James Tiptree Jr Retrospective Award 1995, 1996, 1997, Locus Award 1995, 1996, 2002, Bumbershoot Arts Award, Seattle, WA 1998, LA Times Robert Kirsch Lifetime Achievement Award 2000, Pacific NW Booksellers' Asscn Lifetime Achievement Award 2001, Willamette Writers' Lifetime Achievement Award 2002, PEN/Malamud Award for Short Fiction 2002, SFWA Grand Master Nebula Award for lifetime achievement 2003, YALSA Margaret A. Edwards Award 2004, PEN/USA Award for Children's Literature 2005. *Address:* Virginia Kidd Agency, PO Box 278, Milford, PA 18337 (office); c/o Bill Contardi, William Morris Agency, 1350 Avenue of the Americas, New York, NY 10019, USA (office). *Website:* www .ursulakleguin.com.

LE MAR, Angie; British writer and performer. *Education:* Univ. of Cambridge. *Television:* The Real McCoy (BBC2), Get Up Stand Up (Channel 4). *Radio:* The Ladies' Room (Choice FM London). *Plays:* Funny Black Women on the Edge (writer, dir and performer) 2003, Live at the Palladium (performer) 2003, Sisters Under the Skin (writer) 2004. *Honours:* BECA Best Stand-Up Female 2000, BECA Most Original Material 2001, Men & Women of Merit 2002, European Federation of Black Women (EFBWO) in Business 2002. *Address:* c/o Choice FM Radio, 291–299 Borough High Street, London, SE1 1JG, England. *Website:* www.angielemar.com.

LE PLASTRIER, Robert (see Warner, Francis)

LEACH, Penelope, PhD, CPsychol; British psychologist and writer; *President, National Childminding Association;* b. 19 Nov. 1937, d. of the late Nigel Marlin Balchin and Elisabeth Balchin; m. Gerald Leach 1963; one s. one d. *Education:* The Perse School, Cambridge, Newnham Coll., Cambridge and London School of Econs. *Career:* mem. staff, Home Office 1960–61; Lecturer in Psychology, LSE 1965–67; Research Officer and Research Fellow, MRC 1967–76; Medical Ed. Penguin Books 1970–78; Research Consultant, Int. Centre for Child Studies 1984–90; Founder and Dir Lifetime Productions (childcare videos) 1985–87; Founder and Parent Educ. Co-ordinator End Physical Punishment for Children 1989–; Commr Comm. on Social Justice 1993–95; Vice-Pres. Pre-School Playgroups Asscn 1977, Health Visitors Asscn 1982–98; Pres. Child Devt Soc. 1992–93 (Chair. 1993–95), Nat. Childminding Asscn 1999–; Prin. Investigator and Dir Families Children and Childcare Study; mem. Voluntary Licensing Authority on In-vitro Fertilisation 1985–89, Advisory Council American Inst. for Child, Adolescent and Family Studies 1993–. *Publications include:* Babyhood 1974, Baby and Child 1977, 1989, Who

Cares? 1979, The Parents' A–Z 1984; The First Six Months 1987, The Babypack 1990, Children First 1994, Your Baby and Child: New Version For a New Generation 1997. *Honours:* Hon. Fellow, British Psychological Soc. 1988, Dept of Mental Health, Bristol 1988; Hon. Sr Research Fellow, Leopold Muller Univ. Dept of Child and Family Mental Health, Royal Free and Univ. Coll. Medical School 1998–2002, Tavistock Centre 2000–, Univ. of Oxford 2002–; Hon. DEd . *Address:* National Childminding Association, Royal Court, 81 Tweedy Road, Bromley, Kent BR1 1TG, England (office). *Telephone:* (0845) 880-0044 (office). *E-mail:* info@ncma.org.uk (office). *Website:* www.ncma.org .uk (office).

LEAKEY, Richard Erskine Frere, FRAI; Kenyan palaeontologist and conservationist; b. 19 Dec. 1944, Nairobi; s. of the late Louis Leakey and Mary Leakey; m. Meave Gillian Epps 1970; three d. *Education:* the Duke of York School, Nairobi. *Career:* trapper of primates for research 1961–65; co-leader of research expeditions to Lake Natron 1963–64, Omo River 1967; Dir Root & Leakey Safaris (tour co.) 1965–68; archaeological excavation, Lake Baringo 1966; Admin. Dir Nat. Museums of Kenya 1968–74, Dir and Chief Exec. 1974–89; research in Nakali/Suguta Valley 1978; leader of research projects, Koobi Fora 1979–81, W Turkana 1981–82, 1984–89, Buluk 1983; Dir Wildlife Conservation and Man. Dept 1989–90; Dir Kenya Wildlife Service 1990–94, 1998–99; Man. Dir Richard Leakey & Assocs Ltd 1994–98; nominated MP Nat. Ass. –1999; Perm. Sec., Sec. to the Cabinet, Head of the Public Service, Office of the Pres., Rep. of Kenya 1999–2001; numerous hon. positions including Chair. Wildlife Clubs of Kenya 1969–80 (Trustee 1980–), Foundation for Research into the Origins of Man (USA) 1971–85, Kenya Nat. Cttee of the United World Colls 1982–, E African Wildlife Soc. 1984–89, SAIDIA 1989–; Chair. Bd of Trustees, Nat. Museums of Kenya 1989–94; Co-Founder, Gen.-Sec. Safina Party 1995–98; Life Trustee L. S. B. Leakey Foundation; Trustee Nat. Fund for Disabled in Kenya 1980–95, Agricultural Research Foundation, Kenya 1986–; has given more than 750 public and scholarly Lectures. *Television documentaries:* Bones of Contention, Survival Anglia 1975, The Making of Mankind, BBC 1981, Earth Journal (presenter), NBC 1992. *Publications:* numerous articles on finds in the field of palaeontology in scientific journals, including Nature, Journal of World History, Science, American Journal of Physical Anthropology, etc.; contrib. to General History of Africa (Vol. I), Perspective on Human Evolution and Fossil Vertebrates of Africa; Origins (book, with R. Lewin) 1977, People of the Lake: Man, His Origins, Nature and Future (book, with R. Lewin) 1978, The Making of Mankind 1981, Human Origins 1982, One Life 1983, Origins Reconsidered (with R. Lewin) 1992, Origins of Humankind (with R. Lewin) 1995, The Sixth Extinction (with R. Lewin) 1995, Wildlife Wars (with V. Morrell) 2001. *Honours:* Foreign Hon. mem. American Acad. of Arts and Sciences 1998; Order of the Burning Spear, Kenya 1993; nine hon. degrees; numerous awards and honours including James Smithsonian Medal, USA 1990, Gold Medal, Royal Geographical Soc., UK 1990, World Ecology Medal, Int. Centre for Tropical Ecology, USA 1997. *Address:* PO Box 24926, Nairobi, Kenya (home). *Telephone:* (2) 710949 (office). *Fax:* (2) 710955 (office). *E-mail:* leakey@ wananchi.com (home).

LEALE, B(arry) C(avendish); British poet; b. 1 Sept. 1930, Ashford, Middlesex, England; s. of Charles Frederick Leale and Winifred May Leale (née Burrows). *Education:* Municipal Coll., Southend-on-Sea. *Publications:* Under a Glass Sky 1975, Preludes 1977, Leviathan and Other Poems 1984, The Colours of Ancient Dreams 1984; contrib. to anthologies and periodicals. *Address:* Flat 38, Davey's Court, 33 Bedfordbury, London, WC2N 4BW, England (home).

LEAPMAN, Michael Henry; British writer and journalist; b. 24 April 1938, London; m. Olga Mason 1965; one s. *Career:* journalist, The Times, 1969–81; mem. RSA, Soc. of Authors, Nat. Union of Journalists. *Publications:* One Man and His Plot 1976, Yankee Doodles 1982, Companion Guide to New York 1983, Barefaced Cheek 1983, Treachery 1984, The Last Days of the Beeb 1986, Kinnock 1987, The Book of London (ed.) 1989, London's River 1991, Treacherous Estate 1992, Eyewitness Guide to London 1993, Master Race (with Catrine Clay) 1995, Witnesses to War 1998, The Ingenious Mr Fairchild 2000, The World for a Shilling 2001, Inigo: The Troubled Life of Inigo Jones, Architect of the English Renaissance 2003; contribs to numerous magazines and journals. *Honours:* Campaigning Journalist of the Year, British Press Award 1968, Thomas Cook Travel Book Award, Best Guide Book of 1983, Garden Writers Guild Award 1995, Times Education Supplement Sr Book Award 1999. *Literary Agent:* Felicity Bryan, 2A North Parade, Oxford, OX2 6PE, England. *Address:* 13 Aldebert Terrace, London, SW8 1BH, England. *E-mail:* mhleapman@msn.com (home).

LEAR, Peter (see Lovesey, Peter)

LEASOR, (Thomas) James, (Andrew Macallan), BA, MA, FRSA; British writer; b. 20 Dec. 1923, Erith, Kent, England; m. Joan Margaret Bevan 1951; three s. *Education:* City of London School and Oriel Coll., Oxford. *Career:* served with British Army, India, Burma, Malaya 1942–46; feature writer and foreign correspondent, Daily Express, London 1948–55; editorial adviser, Newnes and Pearson, later IPC, publishing 1955–69; Dir, Elm Tree Books 1970–73. *Publications:* novels include: The One That Got Away (also film), Passport to Oblivion (filmed as Where the Spies Are), Passport to Peril, Boarding Party (filmed as The Sea Wolves), Michaels in Africa (also TV serial), Who Killed Sir Harry Oakes (also TV series as Murder in Paradise); also non-

fiction books. *Honours:* Order of St John. *Address:* Swallowcliffe Manor, Salisbury, Wiltshire SP3 5PB, England.

LEAVITT, David, BA; American writer; b. 23 June 1961, Pittsburgh, PA. *Education:* Yale Univ. *Career:* Prof. of English, Univ. of Florida 2000–; mem. PEN, Authors' Guild. *Publications:* Family Dancing 1984, The Lost Language of Cranes 1986, Equal Affections 1989, A Place I've Never Been 1990, While England Sleeps 1993, The Penguin Book of Gay Short Stories (ed. with Mark Mitchell) 1994, Arkansas 1997, The Page Turner 1998, Martin Bauman 2000, Florence: A Delicate Case 2002, The Body of Jonah Boyd 2004, The Stories of David Leavitt 2005, The Man Who Knew Too Much: Alan Turing and the Invention of the Computer 2006; contrib. to periodicals. *Honours:* O. Henry Award 1984, Nat. Endowment for the Arts grant 1985, Guggenheim Fellowship 1990, New York Public Library Literary Lion 1995. *Literary Agent:* The Wylie Agency, 250 W 57th Street, Suite 2114, New York, NY 10107, USA.

LEBOW, Jeanne, AB, MA, PhD; American writer, poet, teacher and photographer; b. 29 Jan. 1951, Richmond, VA; m. 1st Howard Lebow 1975 (divorced 1981); m. 2nd Steve Shepard 1985. *Education:* College of William and Mary, Hollins College, University of Southern Mississippi. *Career:* Instructor, Memphis State University, 1982–84; Teaching Asst, University of Southern Mississippi, 1984–87; Fulbright Lecturer in American Studies, University of Ouagadougou, Burkina Faso, 1987–88; Asst Prof., Northeast Missouri State University, 1988–92; Freelance Nature Columnist, 1991–; Adjunct Prof., 1992–93, 1994–95, Visiting Prof., 1993–94, University of Southern Mississippi. *Publications:* The Outlaw James Copeland and the Champion-Belted Empress (poems), 1991. Contributions: anthologies, books, reviews, and journals. *Honours:* National Award, Georgia State Poetry Society, 1983; Mississippi Humanities Council Grants, 1994, 1995. *Address:* PO Box 1295, Gautier, MS 39553, USA. *E-mail:* shepart@datasync.com.

LEBRECHT, Norman; British writer; b. 11 July 1948, London, England; m. Elbie Spivack 1977; three d. *Education:* Bar Ilan Univ., Israel. *Career:* radio and television producer 1969–78; writer 1978–; Asst Ed., Evening Standard, London 2002–; mem. Soc. of Authors. *Publications:* Discord 1982, Hush! Handel's in a Passion 1985, The Book of Musical Anecdotes 1985, Mahler Remembered 1987, The Book of Musical Days 1987, The Maestro Myth 1991, Music in London 1991, The Companion to Twentieth-Century Music 1992, When the Music Stops 1996, Who Killed Classical Music? 1997, Covent Garden: Dispatches from the English Culture War, 1945–2000 2000, The Song of Names (Whitbread First Novel Award) 2002, Maestros, Masterpieces and Madness: The Secret Life and Shameful Death of the Classical Record Industry 2007. *Literary Agent:* Curtis Brown Ltd, Haymarket House, 28–29 Haymarket, London, SW1Y 4SP, England. *Telephone:* (20) 7393-4400. *Fax:* (20) 7393-4401. *E-mail:* info@curtisbrown.co.uk. *Website:* www.curtisbrown .co.uk. *Address:* 3 Bolton Road, London, NW8 0RJ, England (home).

LEBRUN HOLMES, Sandra; Australian writer, film-maker and researcher; b. 24 April 1924, Bulcoomatta Station, NSW; m. Cecil William Holmes 1956; two s. one d. *Education:* Sydney Univ. *Career:* mem. Australian Soc. of Authors, Film Directors' Guild. *Recordings:* Sound of Melanesia 1954, Land of the Morning Star: Songs and Music of Arnhem Land 1962, Hunter of the Black 1989. *Publications:* Yirawala: Artist and Man 1972, Yirawala: Painter of the Dreaming 1992, Faces in the Sun (autobiog.) 1999; contrib. to various publications. *Address:* Box 439 PO, Potts Pt, NSW 2011, Australia. *Telephone:* 93604194 (office).

LEDERMAN, Leon M., PhD; American physicist and academic; *Pritzker Professor of Science, Department of Biology, Chemistry and Physical Sciences, Illinois Institute of Technology;* b. 15 July 1922, New York City; s. of the late Morris Lederman; m. 1st Florence Gordon; two d. one s.; m. 2nd Ellen Lederman. *Education:* City Coll. of New York, Columbia Univ., New York. *Career:* entered US Army 1943, rank of 2nd Lt Signal Corps 1946; grad. research involved building a Wilson Cloud Chamber for Cyclotron Project, Columbia Univ. 1948–51, Asst Prof. of Physics 1951–58, Prof. of Physics 1958–79; organised g-2 experiment, CERN 1958; Dir Nevis Labs 1961–78; Dir Fermi Nat. Accelerator Laboratory 1979–89, Dir Emer. 1989–; Prof. of Physics, Univ. of Chicago 1989–; currently Pritzker Prof. of Science, Illinois Inst. of Tech.; apptd Science Adviser to Gov. of Illinois 1989; Pres. American Asscn for the Advancement of Science 1991–; Resident Scholar IMSA Great Minds Program 1998; Founding mem. High Energy Physics Advisory Panel, Int. Cttee on Future Accelerators; Co-Founder and mem. Bd Trustees Illinois Math. and Science Acad.; mem. American, Finnish and Argentine Nat. Acads of Science; serves on 13 bds of dirs of museums, schools, science orgs and govt agencies; recipient of fellowships from Ford, Guggenheim, Ernest Kepton Adams and Nat. Science Foundations. *Publications include:* Nuclear and Particle Physics (with J. Weneser) 1969, From Quarks to the Cosmos: Tools of Discovery (with David N. Schramm) 1989, Portraits of Great American Scientists 2001, Symmetry and the Beautiful Universe (with Christopher T. Hill) 2004; numerous scientific articles. *Honours:* Hon. DSc (City Coll. of New York, Univ. of Chicago, Illinois Inst. of Tech., Northern Illinois Univ., Lake Forest Coll., Carnegie Mellon Univ., Univ. of Pisa, Univ. of Guanajuarto); Nat. Medal of Science 1965, Elliot Cresson Medal, Franklin Inst. 1976, Wolf Prize for Physics 1982, Nobel Prize for Physics 1988, Enrico Fermi Prize. *Address:* Illinois Institute of Technology, LS 106, 3300 South Federal Street, Chicago, IL 60616-3793 (office); Fermilab, PO Box 500, Batavia, IL 60510-0500, USA (office). *Telephone:* (312) 567-8920 (office); (630) 840-3000 (Fermilab) (office). *Fax:* (630) 840-4343 (Fermilab) (office). *E-mail:* lederman@iit.edu (office);

lederman@fnal.gov (office). *Website:* www.iit.edu (office); www.fnal.gov (office).

LEE, Chang-rae, BA, MFA; American novelist; b. 29 July 1965, Seoul, Republic of Korea; m. Michelle Branca 1993. *Education:* Phillips Exeter, Yale Univ., Univ. of Oregon. *Career:* moved to USA 1968; Asst Prof., Univ. of Oregon; Prof. and Dir, MFA program, Hunter Coll., CUNY. *Publications:* Native Speaker 1995 (PEN/Hemingway Award for First Fiction), A Gesture Life 1999 (screenplay 2000), Aloft 2004; contribs to The New York Times Magazine. *Honours:* American Book Award, Before Columbus Foundation 1995, American Library Asscn Notable Book of the Year Award 1995, Barnes & Noble Discover Great New Writers Award 1995, one of New Yorker magazine's best fiction writers under 40. *Address:* c/o Creative Writing Program, Hunter College, City University of New York, 695 Park Avenue, New York, NY 10021, USA.

LEE, (William) David, BA, PhD; American poet and academic; b. 13 Aug. 1944, Matador, TX; m. Jan M. Lee 1971; one s. one d. *Education:* Colorado State University, Idaho State University, University of Utah. *Career:* Prof. of English, 1971–, Chair, 1973–82, Acting Chair, 1984–85, Dept of English, Head, 1987, Dept of Language and Literature, Southern Utah University; Poetry Ed., Weber Studies, 1986–; John Neihardt Distinguished Lectureships, State of Nebraska, 1990, 1996; First Poet Laureate, State of Utah, 1997; mem. National Foundation for Advancement of the Arts, board of dirs, 1996–; Western States Foundation; Writers at Work, board of advisers, 1993–. *Publications:* The Porcine Legacy, 1978; Driving and Drinking, 1979; Shadow Weaver, 1984; The Porcine Canticles, 1984; Paragonah Canyon, Autumn, 1990; Day's Work, 1990; My Town, 1995; Covenants, 1996; The Fish, 1997; The Wayburne Pig, 1998; A Legacy of Shadows: Poems 1979–1999, 1999. Contributions: many anthologies, reviews, quarterlies, journals, and magazines. *Honours:* National Endowment for the Arts Fellowship, 1985; First Place, Poetry, Creative Writing Competition, 1988, Publication Prize, 1989, Utah Arts Council; Outstanding Utah Writer, Utah Endowment for the Humanities and National Council of Teachers of English, 1990; Governor's Award for Lifetime Achievement, Utah, 1994; Western States Book Award, 1995; Mountain and Plain Booksellers Award, 1995; Gov.'s Award in the Humanities, 2001; Bronze Minuteman Award for Lifetime Service to State and Nation, 2000, Ward Roylance Award 2005.

LEE, Dennis Beynon, CM, BA, MA; Canadian poet and writer; b. 31 Aug. 1939, Toronto, ON; m. 1st; one s. one d.; m. 2nd Susan Perly 1985. *Education:* University of Toronto. *Career:* Lecturer, University of Toronto, 1963–67; Ed., House of Anasi Press, 1967–72; Consulting Ed., Macmillan of Canada, 1972–78; Poetry Ed., McClelland and Stewart, 1981–84; mem. PEN, Canada; Writers' Union of Canada. *Publications:* Poetry: Kingdom of Absence, 1967; Civil Elegies, 1972; The Gods, 1979; The Difficulty of Living on Other Planets, 1998; Riffs, 1993; Nightwatch: New and Selected Poems, 1968–96, 1996. Children's Poetry: Wiggle to the Laundromat, 1970; Alligator Pie, 1974; Nicholas Knock, 1974; Garbage Delight, 1977; Jelly Belly, 1983; Lizzy's Lion, 1984; The Ice Cream Store, 1991. Non-Fiction: Savage Fields, 1977. Contributions: journals and magazines. *Honours:* Governor-General's Award for Poetry 1972.

LEE, Hamilton, BS, MA, DEd; Chinese/American academic, poet and writer; b. 10 Oct. 1921, Zhouxian, Shandong, China; m. Jean C. Chang 1945; one s. three d. *Education:* Beijing Normal University, University of Minnesota, Wayne State University, Detroit. *Career:* teacher of English, High Schools, Taiwan, 1948–56; Research Assoc., Wayne State University, Detroit, 1958–64; Visiting Prof. of Chinese Literature, Seton Hall University, summer, 1964; Asst Prof., Moorhead State University, 1964–65; Visiting Scholar, Harvard University, 1965 and Summer 1966; Assoc. Prof., University of Wisconsin at La Crosse, 1965–66; Prof., 1966–84, Prof. Emeritus, 1984–, East Stroudsburg University, Pennsylvania; Visiting Fellow, Princeton University, 1976–78; mem. Acad. of American Poets; distinguished mem., mem. of advisory panel, International Society of Poets; Poetry Society of America; Pennsylvania Poetry Society; World Literary Acad., fellow; World Future Society. *Publications:* Readings in Instructional Technology, 1970; Relection (poems), 1989; Revelation (poems), 1991. Contributions: numerous anthologies, journals, and literary magazines. *Honours:* many poetry contest awards; Ed.'s Choice, National Library of Poetry, 1994.

LEE, Harper; American writer; b. (Nelle Harper Lee), 28 April 1926, Monroeville, Ala; d. of Amasa Coleman and Frances Finch Cunningham Lee. *Education:* Huntingdon Coll., Univ. of Ala and Univ. of Oxford, UK. *Career:* began career as airline reservation clerk, Eastern Airlines and BOAC (NY) 1950s; writing debut 1960; mem. Nat. Council of Arts 1966–71. *Publications:* fiction: To Kill A Mockingbird (Pulitzer Prize for Fiction 1961, Best Sellers' Paperback of the Year Award 1962) 1960; essays: Love: In Other Words (essay in Vogue) 1961, Christmas to Me (essay in McCalls) 1961, When Children Discover America (essay in McCalls) 1965, High Romance and Adventure (essay, part of Ala History and Heritage Festival) 1983; contribs to numerous magazines. *Honours:* Hon. DHumLitt (Spring Coll., Ala) 1997; Alabama Library Asscn Award 1961, Nat. Conference of Christians and Jews Brotherhood Award 1961, Los Angeles Public Library Literary Award 2005. *Address:* c/o J.B. Lippincott Co., 227 East Washington Square, Philadelphia, PA 19106, USA.

LEE, Hermione, MA, MPhil, FRSL, FBA, CBE; British academic, writer and broadcaster; *Goldsmiths' Professor of English Literature, University of Oxford*; b. 29 Feb. 1948, Winchester; d. of Dr Benjamin Lee and Josephine Lee; m. John Barnard 1991. *Education:* Univ. of Oxford. *Career:* Instructor, Coll. of William and Mary, Williamsburg, Va 1970–71; Lecturer, Dept of English, Univ. of Liverpool 1971–77; Lecturer Dept of English, Univ. of York 1977–87, Sr Lecturer 1987–90, Reader 1990–93, Prof. 1993–98; Goldsmiths' Chair of English Literature and Fellow New Coll., Oxford 1998–; presenter of Book Four on Channel Four TV (UK) 1982–86; Chair. judges Man Booker Prize for Fiction 2006; Fellow, Royal Soc. of Literature; Mel and Lois Tukman Fellow, Dorothy and Lewis B. Cullman Center for Scholars and Writers, NY Public Library 2004–05; Foreign Hon. mem., American Acad. of Arts and Sciences. *Publications:* The Novels of Virginia Woolf 1977, Elizabeth Bowen 1981 (2nd. ed. 1999), Philip Roth 1982, The Secret Self I 1985 and II 1987, The Mulberry Tree: Writings of Elizabeth Bowen 1986, Willa Cather: A Life Saved Up 1989, Virginia Woolf 1996, Virginia Woolf: Moments of Being (Ed.) 2002, Body Parts: Essays on Life-Writing 2005, Virginia Woolf's Nose 2005, Edith Wharton (biog.) 2007. *Honours:* Hon. Fellow St Hilda's Coll. Oxford 1998, St Cross Coll. Oxford 1998; Hon. DLitt (Liverpool) 2002, (York) 2007. *Address:* New College, Oxford, OX1 3BN, England (office). *Telephone:* (1865) 279482 (office). *E-mail:* hermione.lee@new.ox.ac.uk (office).

LEE, John Darrell; American writer and fmr academic; b. 12 March 1931, Indiahoma, Oklahoma. *Education:* BA, Texas Technological College, 1952; MSJ, West Virginia University, 1965. *Career:* Former Prof. of Journalism. *Publications:* Caught in the Act, 1968; Diplomatic Persuaders, 1968; Assignation in Algeria, 1971; The Ninth Man, 1976; The Thirteenth Hour, 1978; Lago, 1980; Stalag Texas, 1990. *Literary Agent:* Don Congdon Associates Inc, 156 Fifth Avenue, Suite 625, New York, NY 10010, USA.

LEE, Kuei-shien; Taiwanese poet, essayist, translator, chemical engineer and patent agent; b. 19 June 1937, Taipei; m. Wang Huei-uei 1965; one s. one d. *Education:* Taipei Inst. of Technology, European Language Center, Ministry of Education. *Career:* mem. Int. Acad. of Poets (founder-fellow), Li Poetry Soc., Rilke Gesellschaft, Taiwan PEN (pres. 1995). *Publications:* (in Chinese): poetry: 14 works 1963–2001; essays: 20 works 1971–2002; translator: 25 works 1969–2001; contrib. to anthologies and other publications. *Honours:* Hon. PhD in chemical engineering (Marquis Giuseppe Scicluna Int. Univ. Foundation) 1985; Albert Einstein Int. Acad. Foundation Alfred Nobel Medal for Peace 1991, Li Poetry Soc. Poetic Creation Award 1994, Sec.-Gen. Asian Poets Conference 1995, Best World Poet of the Year 1997, 1998, Poet of the Millennium Award 2000, New Millennium Michael Madhusudan Award 2002, Taiwan Premier Culture Award 2002. *Address:* Room 705, Asia Enterprise Center, No. 142 Minchuan E Road, Sec 3, Taipei 105, Taiwan.

LEE, Lance Wilds, BA, MFA; American dramatist, poet, writer and editor; b. 25 Aug. 1942, New York, NY; s. of the late David Levy and of Lucile Levy (née Wilds); m. Jeanne Barbara Hutchings 1962; two d. *Education:* Boston Univ., Brandeis Univ., Yale School of Drama. *Career:* Lecturer, Univ. of Bridgeport 1967–68; Asst Prof., UCLA 1971–73; California State Univ. at Northridge 1981–; Instructor, Southern Connecticut State Coll. 1968; Sr Lecturer, then Asst Prof., Univ. of Southern California, Los Angeles 1968–71; mem. Acad. of American Poets, Poetry Soc. of America, PEN. *Publications:* Fox, Hound and Huntress (play) 1973, Time's Up (play) 1979, The Understructure of Screenwriting (with Ben Brady) 1988, Wrestling with The Angel (poems) 1990, A Poetics for Screenwriters 2001, Second Chances (novel) 2001, Time's Up and Other Plays 2001, Becoming Human (poems) 2001; with others: On the Waterfront 2003, The Death and Life of Drama 2005, Human/Nature 2006; contribs to reviews, quarterlies, journals, and periodicals, in England and USA. *Honours:* Arts of the Theatre Foundation Fellowship 1967, Univ. of Southern California Research and Publication Grants 1970, 1971, Rockefeller Foundation Grant, Office for Advanced Drama Research 1971, Theatre Devt Fund Grant 1976, Nat. Endowment for the Arts Fellowship 1976, Squaw Valley Scholarships in Poetry 1982, 1983, Port Townsend Writers Conf. Scholarship in Poetry 1985. *Literary Agent:* Reece Halsey Agency, 8733 Sunset Boulevard, Los Angeles, CA 90069, USA. *Telephone:* (310) 652-7595.

LEE, Li-Young; American poet; b. 19 Aug. 1957, Jakarta, Indonesia; m. Donna Lee 1978; two c. *Education:* Univ. of Pittsburgh, Univ. of Arizona, SUNY at Brockport. *Publications:* Rose 1986, The City in Which I Love You 1990, The Winged Seed: A Remembrance 1995, Book of My Nights 2001. *Honours:* New York Univ. Delmore Schwartz Memorial Poetry Award 1986, Ludwig Vogelstein Foundation Fellowship 1987, Mrs Giles Whiting Foundation Writer's Award 1988, Acad. of American Poets Lamont Poetry Selection 1990. *Address:* c/o BOA Editions Ltd, 260 East Avenue, Rochester, NY 14604, USA. *E-mail:* info@boaeditions.org.

LEE, Stewart Graham, BA; British writer, comedian and director; b. 5 April 1968, Solihull, West Midlands. *Education:* Univ. of Oxford. *Career:* writer-performer, The Oxford Revue 1987–89; solo stand-up work 1989–; writer-performer with Richard Herring in double act Lee & Herring 1991–99; rock music critic, The Sunday Times 1995–. *Radio:* On The Hour (writer, BBC Radio 4) 1991–92, Lionel Nimrod's Inexplicable World (BBC Radio 4) 1992–93, Lee & Herring's Fist Of Fun (BBC Radio 1) 1993, Lee & Herring (BBC Radio 1) 1994–95, patron and regular presenter for Resonance FM London 2002–. *Television:* Fist Of Fun (BBC2) 1995–96, Harry Hill (script ed., Avalon TV/Channel 4) 1997–2000, This Morning with Richard Not Judy (BBC2) 1998–99, Attention Scum (writer and dir, BBC2) 2000. *Theatre:* Jerry Springer – The Opera (co-writer and dir) 2002, Stewart Lee: '90s Comedian (Soho Theatre)

2005, writer-performer for Edinburgh Festival shows, including Cluub Zarathustra, Pea Green Boat, King Dong Vs Moby Dick. *Publications:* Lee & Herring's Fist Of Fun (with Richard Herring) 1995, The Perfect Fool 2001; contrib. to Vox, Q, The Guardian. *Honours:* Writers' Guild Award 1992, Sony Gold Award 1992, Evening Standard Theatre Awards 2003, Critics Circle Theatre Awards 2003. *Literary Agent:* Avalon Management, 4a Exmoor Street, London, W10 6BD, England. *Telephone:* (20) 7598-8000. *Website:* www .stewartlee.co.uk.

LEE, Tanith; British writer and playwright; b. 19 Sept. 1947, London; d. of Bernard Lee and Hylda Lee; m. John Kaiine 1992. *Education:* Prendergast Grammar School. *Television and radio writing:* two episodes of Blake's Seven (BBC TV), several radio plays. *Publications:* The Betrothed (short stories) 1968, The Dragon Hoard (juvenile) 1971, Princess Hynchatti and Some Other Surprises (juvenile) 1972, Animal Castle (juvenile) 1972, Companions on the Road (juvenile) 1975, The Birthgrave 1975, Don't Bite the Sun 1976, The Storm Lord 1976, The Winter Players (juvenile) 1976, East of Midnight (juvenile) 1977, Drinking Sapphire Wine 1977, Volkhavaar 1977, Vazkor, Son of Vazkor 1978, Quest for the White Witch 1978, Night's Master 1978, The Castle of Dark (juvenile) 1978, Shon the Taken (juvenile) 1979, Death's Master 1979, Electric Forest 1979, Sabella (aka The Blood Stone) 1980, Kill the Dead 1980, Day by Night 1980, Delusion's Master 1981, The Silver Metal Lover 1982, Cyrion (short stories) 1982, Prince on a White Horse (juvenile) 1982, Sung in Shadow 1983, Anackire 1983, Red as Blood, or Tales from the Sisters Grimmer 1983, The Dragon Hoard 1984, The Beautiful Biting Machine (short stories) 1984, Tamastara, or the Indian Nights (short stories) 1984, Days of Grass 1985, The Gorgon and Other Beastly Tales 1985, Dreams of Dark and Light 1986, Women as Demons: The Male Perception of Women Through Space and Time 1989, Blood of Roses 1990, Black Unicorn 1995, The Book of the Mad 1998, The Book of the Dead 1998, White as Snow 2000, East of Midnight 2001, Queen of the Wolves 2001, Faces Under Water 2002, Wolf Wing 2002, Piratica (juvenile) 2004, Fatal Woman (short stories) 2004, Thirty-Four (novel) 2004, Death of the Day 2004, Cast a Bright Shadow (book I of Lionwolf trilogy) 2004. *Honours:* August Derleth Award 1985, World Fantasy Award. *Address:* c/o Pan Macmillan, 20 New Wharf Road, London, N1 9RR, England. *Website:* www.tanithlee.com.

LEE, Warner (see Battin, B. W.)

LEE, Wayne C., (Lee Sheldon); American writer; b. 2 July 1917, Lamar, NE. *Career:* mem. Western Writers of America (pres. 1970–71), Nebraska Writers' Guild (pres. 1974–76). *Publications:* Prairie Vengeance, 1954; Broken Wheel Ranch, 1956; Slugging Backstop, 1957; His Brother's Guns, 1958; Killer's Range, 1958; Bat Masterson, 1960; Gun Brand, 1961; Blood on the Prairie, 1962; Thunder in the Backfield, 1962; Stranger in Stirrup, 1962; The Gun Tamer, 1963; Devil Wire, 1963; The Hostile Land, 1964; Gun in His Hand, 1964; Warpath West, 1965; Fast Gun, 1965; Brand of a Man, 1966; Mystery of Scorpion Creek, 1966; Trail of the Skulls, 1966; Showdown at Julesburg Station, 1967; Return to Gunpoint, 1967; Only the Brave, 1967; Doomed Planet (as Lee Sheldon), 1967; Sudden Guns, 1968; Trouble at Flying H, 1969; Stage to Lonesome Butte, 1969; Showdown at Sunrise, 1971; The Buffalo Hunters, 1972; Suicide Trail, 1972; Wind Over Rimfire, 1973; Son of a Gunman, 1973; Scotty Philip: The Man Who Saved the Buffalo (non-fiction), 1975; Law of the Prairie, 1975; Die Hard, 1975; Law of the Lawless, 1977; Skirmish at Fort Phil Kearney, 1977; Gun Country, 1978; Petticoat Wagon Train, 1978; The Violent Man, 1978; Ghost of a Gunfighter, 1980; McQuaid's Gun, 1980; Trails of the Smoky Hill (non-fiction), 1980; Shadow of the Gun, 1981; Guns at Genesis, 1981; Putnam's Ranch War, 1982; Barbed Wire War, 1983; The Violent Trail, 1984; White Butte Guns, 1984; War at Nugget Creek, 1985; Massacre Creek, 1985; The Waiting Gun, 1986; Hawks of Autumn, 1986; Wild Towns of Nebraska (non-fiction), 1988; Arikaree War Cry, 1992; Bad Men and Bad Towns (non-fiction), 1993; Deadly Days in Kansas (non-fiction), 1997. *Address:* PO Box 906, Imperial, NE 69033, USA.

LEECH, Geoffrey Neil, BA, MA, DLitt, PhD, FBA; British academic and writer; *Professor Emeritus of Linguistics and English Language, University of Lancaster;* b. 16 Jan. 1936, Gloucester, England; m. Frances Anne Berman 1961; one s. one d. *Education:* Univ. Coll., London, Univ. of Lancaster. *Career:* Asst Lecturer, Univ. Coll. London 1962–64, Lecturer 1965–69; Reader, Univ. of Lancaster 1969–74, Prof. of Linguistics and English Language 1974–1996, Research Prof. in English Linguistics 1996–2002, Prof. Emer. of Linguistics and English Language 2002–; Visiting Prof., Brown Univ., USA 1972, Kobe Univ., Japan 1984, Kyoto Univ., Japan 1991, Meikai Univ., Japan 1999; mem. Academia Europaea, Det Norske Videnskaps-Akademi. *Publications:* English in Advertising 1966, A Linguistic Guide to English Poetry 1969, Towards a Semantic Description of English 1969, Meaning and the English Verb 1971, A Grammar of Contemporary English (with R. Quirk, S. Greenbaum and J. Svartvik) 1972, Semantics 1974, A Communicative Grammar of English (with J. Svartvik) 1975, Explorations in Semantics and Pragmatics 1980, Style in Fiction (with Michael H. Short) 1981, English Grammar for Today (with R. Hoogenraad and M. Deuchar) 1982, Principles of Pragmatics 1983, A Comprehensive Grammar of the English Language (with R. Quirk, S. Greenbaum and J. Svartvik) 1985, Computers in English Language Teaching and Research (co-ed. with C. N. Candlin) 1986, The Computational Analysis of English (co-ed. with R. Garside and G. Sampson) 1987, An A–Z of English Grammar and Usage 1989, Introducing English Grammar 1992, Statistically-driven Computer Grammars in English (co-ed. with E. Black and R. Garside) 1993, Spoken English on Computer (co-ed. with G. Myers and J. Thomas)

1995, Corpus Annotation (co-ed. with R. Garside and T. McEnery) 1997, Longman Grammar of Spoken and Written English (with D. Biber, S. Johansson, S. Conrad and E. Finegan) 1999, Word Frequency in Written and Spoken English (with P. Rayson and A. Wilson) 2001, Longman Student Grammar of Spoken and Written English (with D. Biber and S. Conrad) 2002, A Glossary of English Grammar 2006, English: One Tongue, Many Voices (with Jan Svartvik) 2006; contrib. to A Review of English Literature, International Journal of Corpus Linguistics, Language Learning, Lingua, New Society, Linguistics, Dutch Quarterly Review of Anglo-American Letters, TLS, Prose Studies, The Rising Generation, Transactions of the Philological Society, English Language and Linguistics, International Journal of Pragmatics, Journal of Foreign Language Teaching, ICAME Journal. *Honours:* Hon. FilDr (Univ. of Lund) 1987; Hon. DLitt (Univ. of Wolverhampton) 2002; Harkness Fellowship 1964–65. *Address:* Department of Linguistics and English Language, University of Lancaster, Lancaster, LA1 4YT, England (office). *Telephone:* (1524) 593036 (office). *Fax:* (1524) 843085 (office). *Website:* www.ling.lancs.ac.uk/staff/geoff/geoff.htm (office).

LEEDOM-ACKERMAN, Joanne, MA; American writer; b. 7 Feb. 1947, Dallas, TX; m. Peter Ackerman 1972; two s. *Education:* Principia Coll. ., Johns Hopkins Univ., Brown Univ. *Career:* mem. Int. PEN (Vice-Pres., Writers in Prison Cttee 1993–97, Int. Sec. 2004–). *Publications:* No Marble Angels 1985, The Dark Path to the River 1988, Women for All Seasons (ed.) 1989; contrib. to anthologies, newspapers and magazines. *Fax:* (202) 965-9869 (home). *E-mail:* jlajoanne@aol.com (home).

LEESON, Robert Arthur, BA; British journalist and writer; b. 31 March 1928, Barnton, Cheshire; m. Gunvor Hagen 1954; one s. one d. *Education:* Univ. of London. *Career:* Literary Ed., Morning Star, London 1960–80; mem. Int. Bd of Books for Young People, British Section (Treas. 1972–91), Writers' Guild of Great Britain (Chair. 1985–86). *Publications:* Third Class Genie 1975, Silver's Revenge 1978, Travelling Brothers 1979, It's My Life 1980, Candy for King 1983, Reading and Righting 1985, Slambash Wangs of a Compo Gormer 1987, Coming Home 1991, Zarnia Experiment 1–6 1993, Robin Hood 1994, Red, White and Blue 1996, Liar 1999, The Song of Arthur 2000, My Sister Shahrazad 2001, Onda Wind Rider 2003, Partners in Crime 2003; contrib. to newspapers and journals. *Honours:* Eleanor Farjeon Award for Services to Children and Literature 1985. *Address:* 18 McKenzie Road, Broxbourne, Hertfordshire EN10 7JH, England.

LEFFLAND, Ella Julia, BA; American writer; b. 25 Nov. 1931, Martinez, CA. *Education:* San Jose State College. *Publications:* Mrs Munck, 1970; Love out of Season, 1974; Last Courtesies, 1979; Rumors of Peace, 1980; The Knight, Death and the Devil, 1990. *Contributions:* New Yorker; Harper's; Atlantic Monthly; Mademoiselle; New York Magazine; New York Times. *Honours:* Gold Medals for Fiction, 1974, 1979, Silver Medal, 1991, Commonwealth Club of California; O. Henry First Prize, 1977; Bay Area Book Reviewers Award for Fiction, 1990.

LEGGATT, Alexander Maxwell, BA, MA, PhD, FRSC; Canadian academic and writer; *Professor Emeritus of English, University College, Toronto;* b. 18 Aug. 1940, Oakville, ON; m. Anna Thomas 1964; four d. *Education:* Univ. of Toronto, Shakespeare Inst., Stratford-on-Avon (affiliated with Univ. of Birmingham). *Career:* Lecturer 1965–67, Asst Prof. 1967–71, Assoc. Prof. 1971–75, Prof. of English 1975–2006, Univ. Coll., Univ. of Toronto, Prof. Emer. 2006–; Assoc. Ed., Modern Drama 1972–75; Editorial Bd, English Studies in Canada 1984–91, Univ. of Toronto Quarterly 1996–2006, Studies in Theatre and Performance 1999–2006, Renaissance and Reformation 2000–06; mem. Amnesty Int., Anglican Church of Canada (lay reader 1979–), Int. Asscn of Univ. Profs of English, Int. Shakespeare Asscn (exec. cttee 1987–96), PEN Canada, Arts and Letters Club of Toronto. *Publications:* Citizen Comedy in the Age of Shakespeare 1973, Shakespeare's Comedy of Love 1974, Ben Jonson: His Vision and his Art 1981, English Drama: Shakespeare to the Restoration 1988, Shakespeare's Political Drama 1988, Harvester-Twayne New Critical Introductions to Shakespeare: King Lear 1988, Coriolanus: An Annotated Bibliography (co-author) 1989, Craft and Tradition: Essays in Honour of William Blissett (co-ed.) 1990, Shakespeare in Performance: King Lear 1991, Jacobean Public Theatre 1992, English Stage Comedy 1490–1990 1998, Introduction to English Renaissance Comedy 1999, Cambridge Companion to Shakespearean Comedy (ed.) 2002, Approaches to Teaching English Renaissance Drama (co-ed.) 2002, Shakespeare's Tragedies 2005, William Shakespeare's Macbeth: A Sourcebook (ed.) 2005; contrib. to many scholarly journals. *Honours:* Guggenheim Fellowship 1985–86, Killam Research Fellowship 1995, Univ. of Toronto Outstanding Teaching Award 1995, Univ. of Toronto Alumni Awards of Excellence Faculty Award 1998, Chancellor Jackman Research Fellowship in the Humanities 2004. *Address:* 2593 St Clair Avenue East, Toronto, ON M4B 1MZ, Canada (home). *Telephone:* (416) 755-2325 (home). *Fax:* (416) 755-3036 (home).

LEGRAS, Anny, (Anny Duperey); French actress and writer; b. 28 June 1947, Rouen; d. of Lucien Legras and Ginette Legras; fmr pnr Bernard Giraudeau; one s. one d. *Education:* Conservatoire d'Art Dramatique, Rouen and Paris. *Career:* numerous appearances on stage, in films and on TV. *Plays include:* La guerre de Troie n'aura pas lieu (Prix Gérard Philipe, Best Foreign Theatre Actress, Canada) 1975–78, Attention fragile (co-adaptor) 1978–80, Duo pour une soliste 1984, Le secret 1987, Le plaisir de rompre, Le pain de ménage 1990, Quand elle dansait 1994, Un mari idéal 1995; Sarah 2003–04. *Films include:* Stavisky 1973, Un éléphant ça trompe énormément 1976, Psy

1981, Le grand pardon 1982, Mille milliards de dollars 1982, Meurtres à domicile 1982, Les compères 1983, La triche 1984. *Television includes:* Un château au soleil (Sept d'or for Best Actress) 1988, La face de l'ogre (also dir) 1988, Une famille formidable (Sept d'or for Best Actress) 1992, Charlemagne 1994, La vocation d'Adrienne 1997, Chère Marianne 1999; Le voyage de la grande Duchesse 2002, Familles formidables 2002, Une vie en retour 2005, Forailles formidables 2005, Le otre: Oscar et la dorae rose 2005–06. *Publications:* L'Admiroir (Acad. française Prix Alice Barthou) 1976, Le Nez de Mazarin 1986, Le Voile noir 1992, Je vous écris… 1993, Les chats de hasard 1999, Allons voir plus loin, veux-tu 2002, Une Soirée 2005. *Honours:* Chevalier, Légion d'honneur; Prix Dussane 1984. *Address:* c/o Danielle Gain, Cinéart, 36 rue de Ponthieu, 75008 Paris, France (office). *Telephone:* 1-56-69-33-00 (office).

LEHANE, Dennis; American novelist; b. 1966, Dorchester, Boston, MA. *Publications:* A Drink Before the War 1994, Darkness Take My Hand 1996, Sacred 1997, Gone Baby Gone 1998, Prayers for Rain 1999, Mystic River 2001, Shutter Island 2003, Coronado 2006. *Honours:* Anthony Award, Barry Award for Best Novel, Massachusetts Book Award in Fiction. *Address:* c/o Bantam, 61–63 Uxbridge Road, London, W5 5SA, England. *Website:* www .dennislehanebooks.com.

LEHMAN, David Cary, BA, MA, PhD; American writer, poet and editor; b. 11 June 1948, New York, NY; m. Stefanie Green 1978, one s. *Education:* Columbia University, University of Cambridge. *Career:* Instructor, Brooklyn College, CUNY, 1975–76; Asst Prof., Hamilton College, Clinton, New York, 1976–80; Fellow, Society for the Humanities, Cornell University, 1980–81; Lecturer, Wells College, Aurora, New York, 1981–82; Book Critic and Writer, Newsweek, 1983–89; Series Ed., The Best American Poetry, 1988–, Poets on Poetry, 1994–; Editorial Adviser in Poetry, W. W. Norton & Co, 1990–93. *Publications:* Some Nerve, 1973; Day One, 1979; Beyond Amazement: New Essays on John Ashbery (ed.), 1980; James Merrill: Essays in Criticism (ed.), 1983; An Alternative to Speech, 1986; Ecstatic Occasions, Expedient Forms: 65 Leading Contemporary Poets Select and Comment on Their Poems (ed.), 1987; Twenty Questions, 1988; The Perfect Murder: A Study in Detection, 1989; Operation Memory, 1990; The Line Forms Here, 1992; Signs of the Times: Deconstruction and the Fall of Paul de Man, 1992; The Best American Poetry (ed. with Charles Simic), 1992; The Best American Poetry (ed. with Louise Glück), 1993; The Big Question, 1995; Valentine Place, 1996, The Oxford Book of American Poetry (ed.) 2006. Contributions: anthologies, newspapers, reviews and journals. *Honours:* Acad. of American Poets Prize, 1974; Ingram Merrill Foundation Grants, 1976, 1982, 1984; National Endowment for the Humanities Grant, 1979; National Endowment for the Arts Fellowship, 1987; American Acad. of Arts and Letters Fellowship, 1990; Lila Wallace-Reader's Digest Fund Writers Award, 1991–94.

LEHRER, Keith Edward, BA, AM, PhD; American philosopher, academic, writer and artist; *Regents Professor of Philosophy, University of Arizona*; b. 10 Jan. 1936, Minneapolis, Minn.; m.; two s. *Education:* Univ. of Minnesota, Brown Univ. *Career:* Instructor and Asst Prof., Wayne State Univ. 1960–63; Asst Prof. to Prof., Univ. of Rochester 1963–73; Visiting Assoc. Prof., Univ. of Calgary, Canada 1966; Prof., Univ. of Arizona 1974–90, Regents Prof. of Philosophy 1990–; Assoc., CREA, École Polytechnique, Paris 1993–94; Visiting Fellow, Univ. of London 1996, ANU 1997; mem. American Philosophical Asscn (Pres. 1989, Chair. Nat. Bd of Officers) 1992–95), Council for Philosophical Studies, Institut Int. de Philosophie, Paris and Lund; Fellow, AAAS. *Exhibitions:* Univ. of Graz Library 2005, Univ. of Santa Clara Library 2005. *Publications:* Philosophical Problems and Arguments: An Introduction (with James Cornman) 1968, Knowledge 1978, Rational Consensus in Science and Society: A Philosophical and Mathematical Study (with Carl Wagner) 1981, Thomas Reid 1989, Metamind 1990, Theory of Knowledge 1990, 2000, Self-Trust: A Study of Reason, Knowledge and Autonomy 1997; ed. several books; contrib. to numerous books and journals. *Honours:* Hon. Prof., Karl-Franzens-Univ., Graz 1985–; Dr hc (Graz) 1997; Hon. Mem. Vereinigung für Wissenschaftliche Grundlagen-forschung, Austria; ACLS Fellowship 1973–74, Nat. Endowment for the Humanities Fellowship 1980, Guggenheim Fellowship 1983–84, Brown Univ. Citation for Distinguished Achievement 1988. *Address:* 65 Sierra Vista Drive, Tucson, AZ 85719, USA (home). *E-mail:* lehrer@email.arizona.edu (office). *Website:* web.arizona.edu/~phil/faculty/klehrer.htm (office).

LEICHUK, Alan; American writer and teacher; b. 15 Sept. 1938, New York, NY; m. Barbara 1981; two s. *Education:* BA, Brooklyn College, CUNY, 1960; MA, 1963, PhD, 1965, Stanford University. *Career:* Brandeis University, 1966–81; Amherst College, 1982–84; Dartmouth College, 1985–; Visiting Writer, Prof., Haifa University, 1986–87, CUNY, 1993; Visiting Writer, University of Rome II, 1996; Salgo Prof. in American Literature, ELTE University, Budapest, 1999–2000. *Publications:* Fiction: American Mischief, 1973; Shrinking, 1978; Miriam in Her Forties, 1985; Brooklyn Roy, 1990; Playing the Game, 1995. For Young Adults: On Home Ground, 1987; Eight Great Hebrew Short Novels (co-ed.), 1982. Contributions: New York Times Book Review; New Republic; Dissent; Atlantic Monthly; New York Review of Books. *Honours:* Guggenheim Fellowship, 1976–77; Fulbright Award, 1986–87. *Address:* c/o Georges Borchardt, 136 E 57th Street, New York, NY 10022, USA.

LEIGH, Danny; British writer and critic; b. 1972; m. *Career:* fmr musician; journalist, writing about music and film (contrib. to Sight and Sound, The

Guardian). *Publications:* novels: The Greatest Gift 2004, The Monsters of Gramercy Park 2005. *Address:* c/o Faber and Faber Ltd, 3 Queen Square, London, WC1N 3AU, England .

LEIGH, Meredith (see Kenyon, Bruce Guy)

LEIGH, Mike, OBE; British dramatist and film and theatre director; b. 20 Feb. 1943, Salford, Lancs.; s. of the late A. A. Leigh and the late P. P. Leigh (née Cousin); m. Alison Steadman 1973 (divorced 2001); two s. *Education:* Royal Acad. of Dramatic Art, Camberwell School of Arts and Crafts, Cen. School of Art and Design, London Film School. *Career:* Chair. Govs London Film School 2001–. *Plays:* The Box Play 1965, My Parents Have Gone to Carlisle, The Last Crusade of the Five Little Nuns 1966, Nenaa 1967, Individual Fruit Pies, Down Here and Up There, Big Basil 1968, Epilogue, Glum Victoria and the Lad with Specs 1969, Bleak Moments 1970, A Rancid Pong 1971, Wholesome Glory, The Jaws of Death, Dick Whittington and His Cat 1973, Babies Grow Old, The Silent Majority 1974, Abigail's Party 1977 (also TV play), Ecstasy 1979, Goose-Pimples (London Evening Standard and London Drama Critics' Choice Best Comedy Awards 1981) 1981, Smelling A Rat 1988, Greek Tragedy 1989 (in Australia), 1990 (in UK), It's a Great Big Shame! 1993, Two Thousand Years (Cottlesloe Theatre, London) 2005. *Television films:* A Mug's Game 1972, Hard Labour 1973, The Permissive Society, The Birth of the 2001 F.A. Cup Final Goalie, Old Chums, Probation, A Light Snack, Afternoon 1975, Nuts in May, Knock for Knock 1976, The Kiss of Death 1977, Abigail's Party 1977, Who's Who 1978, Grown-Ups 1980, Home Sweet Home 1981, Meantime 1983, Four Days in July 1984, The Short and Curlies 1987. *Feature films:* Bleak Moments (Golden Leopard, Locarno Film Festival, Golden Hugo, Chicago Film Festival 1972) 1971, High Hopes (Int. Critics' Prize, Venice Film Festival 1989, London Evening Standard Peter Sellers Best Comedy Film Award 1990) 1989, Life is Sweet 1991, Naked (Best Dir Cannes Film Festival 1993) 1993, Secrets and Lies (winner Palme d'Or) 1996, (Alexander Korda Award, BAFTA 1997), Career Girls 1997, Topsy-Turvy 1999 (London Evening Standard Best Film 1999, Los Angeles Film Critics' Circle Best Film 1999, New York Film Critics' Circle Best Film 1999), All or Nothing 2002, Vera Drake (Best British Ind. Film, Best Dir, British Ind. Film Awards, Best Film, Evening Standard British Film Awards 2005, David Lean Award for Achievement in Direction, BAFTA Awards 2005) 2004. *Radio play:* Too Much of a Good Thing 1979. *Publications:* Abigail's Party and Goose-Pimples 1982, Ecstasy and Smelling a Rat 1989, Naked and other Screenplays 1995, Secrets and Lies 1997, Career Girls 1997, Topsy-Turvy 1999, All or Nothing 2002. *Honours:* Officier des Arts et des Lettres; Hon. MA (Salford) 1991, (Northampton) 2000; Hon. DLitt (Staffs.) 2000, (Essex) 2002. *Address:* c/o Peters, Fraser & Dunlop, Drury House, 34–43 Russell Street, London, WC2B 5HA, England. *Telephone:* (20) 7344-1000.

LEITH, Linda, BA, PhD; Canadian writer and editor; b. 13 Dec. 1949, Belfast, Northern Ireland; m. András Barnabás Göllner 1974, three s. *Education:* McGill University, Queen Mary College, London. *Publications:* Telling Differences: New English Fiction From Quebec (anthology), 1989; Introducing Hugh MacLennan's 'Two Solitudes' (essay), 1990; Birds of Passage (novel), 1993; The Tragedy Queen (novel), 1995. Contributions: many magazines and journals. *Address:* c/o Blue Metropolis Foundation, 661 Rose-de-Lima, Montreal Quebec H4C 2L7, Canada. *E-mail:* lindaleith@videotron.ca. *Website:* www.lindaleith.com.

LEITHAUSER, Brad, BA, JD; American poet, writer and academic; *Emily Dickinson Senior Lecturer in the Humanities, Mount Holyoke College*; b. 27 Feb. 1953, Detroit, MI; m. Mary Jo Salter 1980, one d. *Education:* Harvard Univ. *Career:* Research Fellow, Kyoto Comparative Law Center, 1980–83; Visiting Writer, Amherst Coll., 1984–85; Lecturer, Mount Holyoke Coll. 1987–, currently Emily Dickinson Sr Lecturer in the Humanities. *Publications:* Poetry: Hundreds of Fireflies, 1982; A Seaside Mountain: Eight Poems from Japan, 1985; Cats of the Temple, 1986; Between Leaps: Poems 1972–1985, 1987; The Mail from Anywhere: Poems, 1990. The Odd Last Thing She Did 1998, Lettered Creatures 2005, Curves and Angels 2006; Fiction: The Line of Ladies, 1975; Equal Distance, 1985; Hence, 1989; Seaward, 1993, A Few Corrections 2001, Darlington's Fall 2002; Non-Fiction: Penchants & Places: Essays and Criticism, 1995. Editor: The Norton Book of Ghost Stories, 1994; No Other Book, 1999. *Honours:* Order of the Falcon (Iceland) 2005; Harvard Univ.-Acad. of American Poets Prizes, 1973, 1975; Harvard Univ. McKim Garrison Prizes, 1974, 1975; Amy Lowell Traveling Scholarship, 1981–82; Guggenheim Fellowship, 1982–83; Lavan Younger Poets Award, 1983; John D. and Catherine T. MacArthur Foundation Fellowship, 1983–87; 2004 Meribeth E. Cameron Faculty Award for Scholarship, Mount Holyoke Coll. 2004. *Address:* 8 Park Street, 24, South Hadley, MA 01075, USA. *Telephone:* (413) 538-2808. *E-mail:* bleithau@mtholyoke.edu. *Website:* www.mtholyoke.edu/acad/engl/profiles/leithauser.shtml.

LELAND, Christopher Towne, BA, MA, PhD; American writer and academic; b. 17 Oct. 1951, Tulsa, Oklahoma. *Education:* Pomona College, University of California at San Diego. *Career:* Prof. of English, Wayne State University, 1990–; mem. Poets and Writers; MLA. *Publications:* Mean Time, 1982; The Last Happy Men: The Generation of 1922, Fiction and the Argentine Reality, 1986; Mrs Randall, 1987; The Book of Marvels, 1990; The Prof. of Aesthetics, 1994; Letting Loose, 1996; The Art of Compelling Fiction, 1998. Contributions: Principal Translator, Open Door by Luise Valenzvela 1988. *Honours:* Fellow, Massachusetts Artists Foundation, 1985. *Address:* c/o Dept of English, Wayne State University, Detroit, MI 48202, USA.

LELCHUK, Alan, BA, MA, PhD; American writer; *Professor of Literature and Writing, Dartmouth College*; b. 15 Sept. 1938, New York, NY; m. Barbara Kreiger 1979; two s. *Education:* Brooklyn Coll., Stanford Univ. *Career:* Brandeis Univ. 1966–81; Assoc. Ed. Modern Occasions 1980–82; Amherst Coll. 1982–84; Prof. of Literature and Writing, Dartmouth Coll. 1985–; Fulbright Writer-in-Residence, Haifa Univ., Israel 1986–87; Visiting Writer, City Coll., CUNY 1991; Ed., Publr Steerforth Press, South Royalton, Vt 1993–; Salgo Prof. of American Literature and Writing, ELTE Univ., Budapest, Hungary 1999–2000; Fulbright Prof., Int. Univ. of Moscow 2003–04; Fulbright Sr Specialist Prof., Moscow State Univ. 2005; mem. PEN, Authors' Guild. *Publications:* American Mischief 1973, Miriam at Thirty-Four 1974, Shrinking: The Beginning of My Own Ending 1978, 8 Great Hebrew Short Novels (co-ed.) 1983, Miriam in her Forties 1985, On Home Ground 1987, Brooklyn Boy 1989, Playing the Game 1995, Ziff: A Life? 2003; contrib. to New York Times Book Review, Sewanee Review, Atlantic, New Republic, Dissent, New York Review of Books. *Honours:* Guggenheim Fellowship 1976–77, Mishkenot Sha'Ananim Resident Fellow 1976–77, Fulbright Awards 1986–87, (Russia) 2003–04, Manuscript Collection Mugar Memorial Library, Boston Univ. *Address:* RFD 2, Canaan, NH 03741 (office); 176 Fethwood Farms Road, Canaan, NH 03741, USA (home). *Telephone:* (603) 523-4241 (home). *E-mail:* alan.lelchuk@dartmouth.edu (office).

LELYVELD, Joseph Salem; American journalist; b. 5 April 1937, Cincinnati; s. of Arthur Joseph Lelyveld and Toby Bookholz; m. Carolyn Fox 1958; two d. *Education:* Columbia Univ., New York. *Career:* reporter, Ed. New York Times 1963–, Foreign Corresp. Johannesburg, New Delhi, Hong Kong, London 1965–86, columnist, staff writer 1977, 1984–85, Foreign Ed. 1987–89, Deputy Man. Ed. 1989–90, Man. Ed. 1990–94, Exec. Ed. 1994–2001, Interim Exec. Ed. 2003. *Publication:* Move Your Shadow (Pulitzer Prize) 1985, Omaha Blues: A Memory Loop 2005. *Honours:* George Polk Memorial Award 1972, 1984. *Address:* c/o New York Times, 229 W 43rd Street, New York, NY 10036, USA.

LEMASTER, Jimmie Ray, BS, MA, PhD; American academic, poet, writer and editor; *Professor of English and Director of American Studies, Baylor University*; b. 29 March 1934, Pike County, OH; m. Wanda May Ohnesorge 1966; one s. two d. *Education:* Defiance Coll., Bowling Green State Univ., OH. *Career:* Faculty, Defiance Coll. 1962–77; Prof. of English and Dir of American Studies, Baylor Univ. 1977–; Assoc. Ed. 1988–90, Ed. 1992–96, JASAT (Journal of the American Studies Asscn of Texas); mem. American Studies Asscn, Conference of Coll. Teachers of English, Jesse Stuart Foundation (bd of dirs 1989–99), Mark Twain Circle of America, MLA. *Publications:* poetry: The Heart is a Gypsy 1967, Children of Adam 1971, Weeds and Wildflowers 1975, First Person, Second 1983, Purple Bamboo 1986, Journey to Beijing 1992, Journeys Around China 2004; other: Jesse Stuart: A Reference Guide 1979, Jesse Stuart: Kentucky's Chronicler-Poet 1980, The New Mark Twain Handbook (with E. Hudson Long) 1985; editor: Poets of the Midwest 1966, The World of Jesse Stuart: Selected Poems 1975, Jesse Stuart: Essays on His Work (with Mary Washington Clarke) 1977, Jesse Stuart: Selected Criticism 1978, Jesse Stuart on Education 1992, The Mark Twain Encyclopedia (with James D. Wilson) 1993, Walt Whitman: An Encyclopedia (with Donald D. Kummings) 1998, China Teacher: An Intimate Journal 2005. *Honours:* Hon. DLitt (Defiance Coll.) 1988; South and West Inc Publishers Award 1970, Ohio Poet of the Year 1976, American Library Asscn Outstanding Reference Source Citation 1993. *Telephone:* (254) 910-2910 (USA) (office); (254) 772-9829 (USA) (home). *E-mail:* j.r.lemaster@baylor.edu.

LENKIEWICZ, Rebecca; British playwright and actress; b. 1969, Plymouth. *Education:* Central School of Speech and Drama, London, Kent Univ. *Plays as actress:* Tales from Ovid, Bollocks, A Midsummer Night's Dream, Flight, Half Moon, King Lear, Twelfth Night, Two Gentlemen of Verona, Soho. *Television as actress:* State of Play, Casualty, Doctors, Down to Earth, The Inspector Lynley Mysteries. *Film as actress:* Wonderland 1999. *Plays as writer:* Soho 2000, The Night Season (Critics Circle Theatre Award for Most Promising Playwright 2005) 2004, Shoreditch Madonna (Soho Theatre, London) 2005. *Radio as writer:* Fighting for Words (BBC Radio 4) 2004. *Honours:* Fringe First, Edinburgh Festival 2000, Critics' Circle award for most promising playwright 2004. *Literary Agent:* c/o Georgina Ruffhead, David Higham Associates, 5–8 Lower John Street, Golden Square, London, W1F 9HA, England. *Telephone:* (20) 7434-5900. *Fax:* (20) 7437-1072. *E-mail:* dha@davidhigham.co.uk. *Website:* www.davidhigham.co.uk.

LENTRICCHIA, Frank, BA, MA, PhD; American academic and writer; b. 23 May 1940, Utica, NY; m. 1st Karen Young 1967 (divorced 1973); two c.; m. 2nd Melissa Christensen 1973 (divorced 1992); m. 3rd Johanna McAuliffe 1994; one c. *Education:* Utica Coll. of Syracuse Univ., Duke Univ. *Career:* Asst Prof., Univ. of California at Los Angeles 1966–68; Asst Prof. 1968–70, Assoc. Prof. 1970–76, Prof. 1976–82, Univ. of California at Irvine; Autrey Prof. of Humanities, Rice Univ. 1982–84; Gilbert Prof. of Literature, Duke Univ. 1984–; mem. MLA, PEN. *Publications:* The Gaiety of Language: An Essay on the Radical Poetics of W. B. Yeats and Wallace Stevens 1968, Robert Frost: Modern Poetics and the Landscapes of Self 1975, Robert Frost: A Bibliography, 1913–1974 (ed. with Melissa Christensen Lentricchia) 1976, After the New Criticism 1980, Criticism and Social Change 1983, Ariel and the Police 1988, Critical Terms for Literary Study 1990, New Essays on White Noise 1991, Introducing Don DeLillo 1991, The Edge of Night: A Confession 1994, Modernist Quartet 1994, Johnny Critelli and The Knifemen: Two Novels 1996, The Music of the Inferno: A Novel 1999, Lucchesi and The Whale 2001, Dissent from the Homeland (with Stanley Hauerwas) 2002, Close Reading: The Reader (with Andrew DuBois) 2003, Modernist Lyric in the Culture of Capital (with Andrew DuBois) 2003, Crimes of Art and Terror (with Jody McAuliffe) 2003; contrib. to professional journals. *Address:* c/o Program in Literature, Duke University, Durham, NC 27708, USA (office). *Telephone:* (919) 684-6172 (office); (919) 401-3645 (home). *Fax:* (919) 401-3645 (home). *E-mail:* frll@duke.edu (office).

LENZ, Siegfried; German writer; b. 17 March 1926, Lyck, East Prussia; m. Liselotte Lenz. *Education:* High School, Samter and Univ. of Hamburg. *Career:* Cultural Ed. Die Welt 1949–51; freelance writer 1952–. *Publications:* include novels: Es waren Habichte in der Luft 1951, Duell mit dem Schatten 1953, Der Mann im Strom 1957, 1958, Brot und Spiele 1959, Stadtgespräche 1963, Deutschstunde 1968, Das Vorbild 1973, Heimatmuseum 1978, Der Verlust 1981, Ein Kriegsende 1984, Die Auflehnung 1994; stories: So zärtlich war Suleyken 1955, Jäger des Spotts 1958, Das Feuerschiff 1960, Der Spielverderber 1965, Einstein überquert die Elbe bei Hamburg 1975; plays: Zeit der Schuldlosen 1961, Das Gesicht 1963, Haussuchung (radio plays) 1967. *Honours:* Gerhart Hauptmann Prize 1961, Bremer Literaturpreis 1962, German Freemasons' Literary Prize 1970, Kulturpreis, Goslar 1978, Bayern Literary Prize 1995, Goethe Prize 1999; Hon. Citizen of Hamburg 2001–. *Address:* Preusserstrasse 4, 22605 Hamburg, Germany. *Telephone:* 880-83-09.

LEONARD, Elmore, PhB; American novelist and screenwriter; b. 11 Oct. 1925, New Orleans; s. of Elmore John and Flora Amelia Leonard (née Rivé); m. 1st Beverly Claire Cline 1949 (divorced 1977); three s. two d.; m. 2nd Joan Leanne Lancaster 1979 (died 1993); m. 3rd Christine Kent 1993. *Education:* Univ. of Detroit. *Career:* mem. Writers' Guild of America, Authors' Guild, MWA, Western Writers of America, PEN. *Publications:* novels: The Bounty Hunters 1953, The Law at Randado 1954, Escape from Five Shadows 1956, Last Stand at Saber River 1959, Hombre 1961, The Big Bounce 1969, The Moonshine War 1969, Valdez is Coming 1970, Forty Lashes Less One 1972, Mr Majestyk 1974, Fifty-Two Pickup 1974, Swag 1976, Unknown Man # 89 1977, The Hunted 1977, The Switch 1978, Gold Coast 1979, Gun Sights 1979, City Primeval 1980, Split Images 1981, Cat Chaser 1982, Stick 1983, La Brava 1983, Glitz 1985, Bandits 1986, Touch 1987, Freaky Deaky 1988, Killshot 1989, Get Shorty 1990, Maximum Bob 1991, Rum Punch 1992, Pronto 1993, Riding the Rap 1995, Out of Sight 1996, Jackie Brown 1997, Cuba Libre (also film screenplay) 1998, Be Cool (also film screenplay) 1999, Pagan Babies 2000, Tishomingo Blues 2002, When the Women Come Out to Dance 2002, A Coyote's in the House (juvenile) 2004, Mr Paradise 2004, The Hot Kid 2006; short story collections: Dutch Treat 1985, Double Dutch Treat 1986, The Tonto Woman and Other Stories 1998, The Complete Western Stories 2006. *Honours:* Hon. DLitt (Florida Atlantic Univ.) 1995, (Univ. of Detroit Mercy) 1997; MWA Edgar Allan Poe Award 1984, MWA Grand Master Award 1992, Mich. Foundation for the Arts Award for Literature 1985, Cartier Diamond Dagger Award 2006. *Address:* c/o Michael Siegel, 9150 Wilshire Blvd, Suite 350, Beverly Hills, CA 90212, USA. *Website:* www.elmoreleonard.com.

LEONARD, Hugh, (John Keyes Byrne); Irish playwright; b. (John Joseph Byrne), 9 Nov. 1926, Dublin; m. Paule Jacquet 1955 (died 2000); one d. *Education:* Presentation Coll., Dún Laoghaire. *Career:* worked as civil servant 1945–49; Script Ed. Granada TV, England 1961–63; Literary Ed., Abbey Theatre, Dublin 1976–77; Programme Dir, Dublin Theatre Festival 1978–. *Stage plays include:* The Big Birthday 1957, A Leap in the Dark 1957, Madigan's Lock 1958, A Walk on the Water 1960, The Passion of Peter Ginty 1961, Stephen D 1962, The Poker Session 1963, Dublin 1 1963, The Saints Go Cycling In 1965, Mick and Mick 1966, The Quick and the Dead 1967, The Au Pair Man 1968, The Barracks 1969, The Patrick Pearse Motel 1971, Da 1973, Thieves 1973, Summer 1974, Times of Wolves and Tigers 1974, Irishmen 1975, Time Was 1976, A Life 1977, Moving Days 1981, The Mask of Moriarty 1984, Moving 1991, Senna for Sonny 1994, The Lily Lally Show 1994, Chamber Music (2 plays) 1994, Magic 1997, Love in the Title 1998. *Writing for television includes:* Silent Song 1967, Nicholas Nickleby 1977, London Belongs to Me 1977, The Last Campaign 1978, The Ring and the Rose 1978, Strumpet City 1979, The Little World of Don Camillo 1980, Kill 1982, Good Behaviour 1982, O'Neill 1983, Beyond the Pale 1984, The Irish RM 1985, A Life 1986, Troubles 1987, Parnell and the Englishwoman 1988, A Wild People 2001. *Films:* Herself Surprised 1977, Da 1984, Widows' Peak 1984, Troubles 1984, Banjaxed 1995. *Adaptations:* Great Expectations 1995, A Tale of Two Cities 1996. *Publications:* Home Before Night (autobiog.) 1979, Out After Dark (autobiog.) 1988, Parnell and the Englishwoman 1989, I, Orla! 1990, Rover and other Cats (a memoir) 1992, The Off-Shore Island (novel) 1993, The Mogs (for children) 1995, Magic 1997, Fillums (novel) 2003. *Honours:* Hon. DHL (RI); Hon. DLitt (Trinity Coll. Dublin); Writers' Guild Award 1966, Tony Award, Critics Circle Award, Drama Desk Award, Outer Critics Award 1978. *Address:* 6 Rossaun, Pilot View, Dalkey, Co. Dublin, Ireland. *Telephone:* (1) 280-9590. *E-mail:* panache@indigo.ie (office).

LEONARD, Mark; British research institute director; *Founding Director, Foreign Policy Centre*. *Career:* worked on policy and strategy devt for several nat. govts, int. governmental assocs and cos; Dir of European Programme, Demos –1998; Founding Dir. Foreign Policy Centre (FPC) 1998–. *Publications include:* research reports: Rebranding Britain, Network Europe 1998, The Future Shape of Europe 2000, Public Diplomacy (co-author) 2000, Public Diplomacy in the Middle East, Re-Ordering the World: The Long-Term Implications of September 11 (collection of essays), What Does China Think? 2007; 24 articles, including Rebranding Europe; Why Europe Will Run the

21st Century 2004. *Address:* Foreign Policy Centre, The Mezzanine, Elizabeth House, 39 York Road, London, SE1 7NQ, England (office). *Telephone:* (20) 7401-5350 (office). *Fax:* (20) 7401-5351 (office). *E-mail:* info@fpc.org.uk (office). *Website:* www.fpc.org.uk (office).

LEONARD, Richard (Dick) Lawrence, MA; British journalist, editor, broadcaster and writer; *Senior Research Associate, Foreign Policy Centre*; b. 12 Dec. 1930, Ealing, Middlesex, England; m. Irene Heidelberger 1963; one s. one d. *Education:* Inst. of Education, London and Essex Univ. *Career:* Sr Research Fellow, Essex Univ. 1968–70; MP Labour Party, Romford 1970–74; Asst Ed., The Economist 1974–85; Visiting Prof., Free Univ. of Brussels 1988–96; Brussels and European Union Correspondent, The Observer 1989–96; Sr Adviser, Center for European Policy Studies 1994–2000; Sr Research Assoc., Foreign Policy Centre 2004–; mem. Fabian Soc. (chair. 1977–78), Reform Club. *Publications:* Elections in Britain 1968, The Backbencher and Parliament (co-ed.) 1972, Paying for Party Politics 1975, The Socialist Agenda (co-ed.) 1981, World Atlas of Elections (co-author) 1986, Pocket Guide to the EEC 1988, Elections in Britain Today 1991, The Economist Guide to the European Community (10th edn as The Economist Guide to the European Union) 2005, Replacing the Lords 1995, Eminent Europeans (co-author) 1996, Crosland and New Labour (ed.) 1998, The Pro-European Reader (co-ed.) 2001, A Century of Premiers: Salisbury to Blair 2004, 19th Century Premiers: Pitt to Rosebery 2007; contrib. to newspapers and periodicals worldwide. *Address:* 32 rue des Bégonias, 1170 Brussels, Belgium.

LEONARD, Tom, MA; British writer and poet; *Professor of Creative Writing, University of Glasgow*; b. 22 Aug. 1944, Glasgow, Scotland; m. Sonya Maria O'Brien 1971; two s. *Education:* Univ. of Glasgow. *Career:* Writer-in-Residence, Renfrew Dist Libraries 1986–89, Univ. of Glasgow/Univ. of Strathclyde 1991–92, Bell Coll. of Tech. 1993–94; Prof. of Creative Writing, Univ. of Glasgow 2001–. *Publications:* Intimate Voices (Writing 1965–83) 1984, Situations Theoretical and Contemporary 1986, Radical Renfrew (ed.) 1990, Nora's Place 1990, Places of the Mind: The Life and Work of James Thomson 'BV' 1993, Reports From the Present 1995, access to the silence: poems and posters 1984–2004 2004, Being a Human Being 2006. *Honours:* Jt Winner, Saltire Scottish Book of the Year Award 1984. *Address:* 56 Eldon Street, Glasgow, G3 6NJ, Scotland (home). *E-mail:* mail@tomleonard.co.uk (office). *Website:* www.tomleonard.co.uk.

LEONG, Russell Charles, (Wallace Lin), BA, MFA; American writer, poet and editor; *Adjunct Full Professor of English, University of California at Los Angeles*; b. 7 Sept. 1950, San Francisco, CA. *Education:* San Francisco State Coll., Nat. Taiwan Univ., Univ. of California at Los Angeles. *Career:* Adjunct Full Prof. of English, Dept of English, and Ed. Amerasia Journal, Asian American Studies Center, Univ. of California at Los Angeles. *Publications:* fiction: Phoenix Eyes and Other Stories (American Book Award 2001) 2000; poetry: The Country of Dreams and Dust (PEN Josephine Miles Literature Award) 1993; non-fiction: A History Reclaimed: An Annotated Bibliography of Chinese Language Materials on the Chinese of America (ed. with Jean Pang Yip) 1986, Frontiers of Asian American Studies: Writing, Research, and Criticism (ed. with G. Nomura, R. Endo and S. Sumida) 1989, Moving the Image: Independent Asian Pacific American Media Arts 1970–1990 (ed.) 1991, Los Angeles—Struggle toward Multiethnic Community: Asian America, African America, and Latino Perspectives (ed. with Edward T. Chang) 1995, Asian American Sexuality: Dimensions of the Gay and Lesbian Experience 1996; contrib. to anthologies and periodicals. *Address:* c/o Asian American Studies Center, 3230 Campbell Hall, University of California at Los Angeles, Los Angeles, CA 90095-1546, USA. *E-mail:* rleong@ucla.edu.

LEONTYEV, Mikhail Vladimirovich; Russian journalist; b. 12 Oct. 1958, Moscow; m.; two c. *Education:* Moscow Plekhanov Inst. of Nat. Econs. *Career:* political reviewer Kommersant (newspaper) 1987–90; on staff newspaper Atmoda (Riga) and Experimental Creative Cen. in Moscow 1989–91; Ed. Div. of Politics Nezavisimaya Gazeta (newspaper) 1990–92; First Deputy Ed.-in-Chief Business MN (daily) 1992–93; First Deputy Ed.-in-Chief Segodnya (newspaper) 1993–97; political reviewer TV-Cen. Channel 1997–98, ORT Channel 1999–; Ed.-in-Chief journal Fas 2000–. *Address:* Obshchestvennoye Rossiyskoe Televideniye (ORT), Akademika Koroleva str. 12, 127000 Moscow, Russia (office). *Telephone:* (495) 217 94-72 (office); (495) 217-94-73 (office).

LEOTTA, Guido; Italian writer, poet, publisher and musician; b. 2 May 1957, Faenza; one s. *Career:* Pres., Tratti/Mobydick Cultural Co-operative and Publishing House, 1987; Author and Co-ordinator, Tratti Folk Festival, 1989–2007; plays saxophone and flute with blues-jazz quintet Faxtet. *Recordings:* CDs and audio books: Villes Visions (with French poet Sylviane Dupuis), Blue Notebook (with Flemish poet Willem M. Roggeman) 2007. *Publications:* Sacsaphone (collected novels), 1981; Anatre (short stories), 1989; Il Bambino Ulisse (children's stories), 1995; Passo Narrabile (novel), 1997; Leviatamo (poems), 1999; Doppio Diesis (novel), 2000, Inverni Dispari (poems) 2001, Il Silenzio del Trombone (short stories) 2003, Il Tempo è un Cerchio infinito epaziente (novel) 2007; contrib. to anthologies and magazines. *Honours:* Premio Leonforte for Children's Stories, 1991; Laoghaire Poetry Prize, Ireland, 1994; Premio Selezione Bancarellino, 1996. *Address:* Via San Michele 3, 48018 Faenza, Italy. *Telephone:* (546) 681819. *E-mail:* tratti@fastwebnet.it.

LEPSCHY, Anna Laura, BLitt, MA; Italian academic and writer; *Professor of Italian, University College, London*; b. 30 Nov. 1933, Turin, Italy; m. 1962.

Education: Somerville Coll., Oxford. *Career:* Prof. of Italian, Univ. Coll., London; Hon. Research Fellow, Univ. of Cambridge; mem. Pirandello Soc. (pres. 1988–92), Soc. for Italian Studies (chair. 1988–95), Asscn for the Study of Modern Italy, Associazione Internazionale di Lingua e Letteratura Italiana (vice-pres. 1998–). *Publications:* Viaggio in Terrasanta 1480 1966, The Italian Language Today (co-author) 1977, Tintoretto Observed 1983, Narrativa e Teatro fra due Secoli 1984, Varietà linguistiche e pluralità di codici nel Rinascimento 1996, Davanti a Tintoretto 1998, L'amanuense analfabeta e altri saggi (co-author) 1999; contrib. to Italian Studies, Romance Studies, Studi Francesi, Studi sul Boccaccio, Studi Novecenteschi, Yearbook of the Pirandello Society, Modern Languages Notes, Lettere Italiane. *Honours:* Hon. Fellow Somerville Coll., Oxford; Ufficiale al Merito della Repubblica Italiana 1994, Commendatore della Repubblica Italiana 2003. *Address:* Department of Italian, University College, Gower Street, London, WC1E 6BT, England. *Telephone:* (20) 7679-7784 (office). *E-mail:* a.lepschy@ucl.ac.uk.

LERMAN, Rhoda, BA; American writer; b. 18 Jan. 1936, Far Rockaway, NY; m. Robert Lerman 1957, one s. two d. *Education:* University of Miami. *Career:* National Endowment for the Arts Distinguished Prof. of Creative Writing, Hartwick College, Oneonta, New York, 1985; Visiting Prof. of Creative Writing, 1988, 1990, Chair in English Literature, 1990, SUNY at Buffalo. *Publications:* Call Me Ishtar, 1973; Girl That He Marries, 1976; Eleanor, a Novel, 1979; Book of the Night, 1984; God's Ear, 1989; Animal Acts, 1994.

LERNER, Laurence David, MA, FRSL; British retd academic, writer and poet; b. 12 Dec. 1925, Cape Town, South Africa; m. Natalie Winch 1948; four s. *Education:* Univ. of Cape Town, Pembroke Coll. ., Cambridge. *Career:* Lecturer, Univ. Coll. of the Gold Coast, 1949–53, Queen's Univ., 1953–62; Lecturer to Prof., Univ. of Sussex, 1962–84; Kenan Prof., Vanderbilt Univ., Nashville, Tennessee, 1985–95; several visiting professorships. *Publications:* Poems, 1955; Domestic Interior and Other Poems, 1959; The Directions of Memory: Poems 1958–63, 1964; Selves, 1969; A.R.T.H.U.R.: The Life and Opinions of a Digital Computer, 1974; The Man I Killed, 1980; A.R.T.H.U.R. and M.A.R.T.H.A., or, The Loves of the Computer, 1980; Chapter and Verse: Bible Poems, 1984; Selected Poems, 1984; Rembrandt's Mirror, 1987. Fiction: The Englishmen, 1959; A Free Man, 1968; My Grandfather's Grandfather, 1985. Play: The Experiment, 1980. Non-Fiction: The Truest Poetry, 1960; The Truthtellers: Jane Austen, George Eliot, Lawrence, 1967; The Uses of Nostalgia, 1973; An Introduction to English Poetry, 1975; Love and Marriage: Literature in its Social Context, 1979; The Frontiers of Literature, 1988; Angels and Absences, 1997; Philip Larkin, 1997; Wandering Prof., 1999. Contributions: newspapers, reviews, journals, and magazines. *Honours:* South-East Arts Literature Prize, 1979. *Address:* Abinger, 1-B Gundreda Road, Lewes, East Sussex BN7 1PT, England.

LERNER, Rabbi Michael Phillip, AB, MA, PhD; American writer; b. 7 Feb. 1943, Newark, NJ. *Education:* Columbia Univ., Univ. of California at Berkeley. *Career:* Rabbi of Beyt Tikkun synagogue; founder Ed., TIKKUN magazine 1986–. *Publications:* Surplus Powerlessness 1986, Jewish Renewal 1994, Blacks and Jews 1995, The Politics of Meaning 1995, Spirit Matters: Global Healing and the Wisdom of the Soul 2000, Best Contemporary Jewish Writing (ed.) 2001, Healing Israel/Palestine 2003, The Geneva Accord and Other Strategies for Middle East Peace 2004, The Left Hand of God: Taking Our Country Back from the Relligious Right 2006; contrib. to newspapers and magazines. *Honours:* PEN Award 2001. *Address:* c/o Tikkun Magazine, 2342 Shattuck Avenue, #1200, Berkeley, CA 94704, USA. *E-mail:* RabbiLerner@tikkun.org. *Website:* www.tikkun.org.

LERNER, Robert Earl, BA, MA, PhD; American academic and writer; *Peter B. Ritzma Professor in the Humanities, Northwestern University*; b. 8 Feb. 1940, New York, NY; m. Erdmut Krumnack 1963; two d. *Education:* Univ. of Chicago, Princeton Univ. and Univ. of Münster. *Career:* Instructor, Princeton Univ. 1963–64; Asst Prof., Western Reserve Univ. 1964–67; Asst Prof., Northwestern Univ. 1967–71, Assoc. Prof. 1971–76, Prof. 1976–, Peter B. Ritzma Prof. in the Humanities 1993–; Fellow, Woodrow Wilson Center for Scholars 1996–97. *Publications:* The Age of Adversity: The Fourteenth Century 1968, The Heresy of the Free Spirit in the Later Middle Ages 1972, Western Civilizations (co-author, ninth–12th edns) 1980–98, World Civilizations (co-author, sixth–ninth edns) 1982–97, The Powers of Prophecy: The Cedar of Lebanon Vision from the Mongol Onslaught to the Dawn of the Enlightenment 1983, Weissagungen über die Päpste (with Robert Moynihan) 1985, Johannes de Rupescissa, Liber secretorum eventuum: Edition critique, traduction et introduction historique (with C. Morerod-Fattebert) 1994, Propaganda Miniata: Le origini delle profezie papali 'Ascende Calve' (with Orit Schwartz) 1994, Neue Richtungen in der hoch – und spätmittelalterlichen Bibelexegese (ed.) 1995, The Feast of Saint Abraham 2000; contrib. to professional journals, Times Literary Supplement. *Honours:* Fulbright Sr Fellowship 1967–68, Nat. Endowment for the Humanities research grant 1972–73, American Acad. in Rome Fellowship 1983–84, Guggenheim Fellowship 1984–85, Rockefeller Foundation Study Center Residency, Bellagio, Italy 1989, Historisches Kolleg, Munich, Forschungspreis 1992, Stipendiat 1992–93, Max-Planck-Gesellschaft Prize for Int. Co-operation 1998. *Address:* Department of History, Northwestern University, Evanston, IL 60208, USA (office).

LEROI, Armand Marie, BSc, PhD; Dutch evolutionary biologist; *Reader in Evolutionary Developmental Biology, Imperial College London*; b. 16 July 1964, Wellington, New Zealand. *Education:* Dalhousie Univ., Halifax,

Canada, Univ. of California at Irvine, USA. *Career:* postdoctoral work at the Albert Einstein Coll. of Medicine, New York; Lecturer Imperial Coll. London 1996–2001, Reader in Evolutionary Developmental Biology 2001–. *Television:* Mutants (three-part series, Channel 4) 2004. *Publications:* Mutants: On the Form, Varieties and Errors of the Human Body (Guardian First Book Award 2004) 2003; contrib. to London Review of Books; numerous research papers. *Address:* Department of Biological Sciences, Silwood Park Campus, Imperial College London, Ascot, Berkshire SL5 7PY, England (office). *E-mail:* a.leroi@imperial.ac.uk (office). *Website:* www.armandleroi.com.

LEROY, Gilles; French writer; b. 28 Dec. 1958, Bagneux. *Publications:* Habibi (novel) 1987, Maman est morte 1990, Les Derniers seront les premiers (short stories) 1991, Madame X (novel) 1992, Les Jardins publics (novel) 1994, Les Maîtres du monde (novel) 1996, Machines à sous (novel) 1998, Soleil noir (novel) 2000, L'amant russe (novel) 2002, Grandir (novel) 2004, Le Jour des fleurs (play) 2004, Champsecret (novel) 2005. *Honours:* Chevalier des Arts et des Lettres; Prix de la Nouvelle, Nanterre 1992, Prix Valery-Larbaud 1999, Prix Millepages 2004, Prix du roman de Cabourg 2004. *Address:* c/o Mercure de France SA, Subsidiary of Editions Gallimard, 26 rue de Conde, 75006 Paris (office); Le Bois Spert, Boissy-les-Perche 28340, France (home). *Telephone:* (2) 37-37-60-38 (home). *E-mail:* gil.leroy@gmail.com (home).

LESCHAK, Peter, BA; American writer and fireman; b. 11 May 1951, Chisholm, MN; m. Pamela Cope May 1974. *Education:* Ambassador Coll., TX. *Career:* Contributing Ed., Twin Cities magazine 1984–86, Minnesota Monthly 1984–89; mem. Authors' Guild. *Publications:* Letters from Side Lake 1987, The Bear Guardian 1990, Bumming with the Furies 1993, Seeing the Raven 1994, Hellroaring 1994, The Snow Lotus 1996, Rogues and Toads 1999, Trials by Wildfire 2000, Ghosts of the Fireground 2002. *Honours:* Minnesota Book Award 1991. *Address:* PO Box 51, Side Lake, MN 55781, USA. *E-mail:* pleschak@cpinternet.com.

LESOURNE, Jacques François; French newspaper editor and academic; *President, Futuribles International*; b. 26 Dec. 1928, La Rochelle; s. of André Lesourne and Simone Lesourne (née Guille); m. Odile Melin, 1961; one s. two d. *Education:* Lycée Montaigne, Bordeaux, École Polytechnique, École Nationale Supérieure des Mines de Paris. *Career:* Head Econ. Service of French Collieries 1954–57; Dir Gen., later Pres. METRA Int. and SEMA 1958–75; Prof. of Econs École des Mines de Saint-Étienne 1958–61; Prof. of Industrial Econs École Nationale Supérieure de la Statistique 1960–63; Pres. Asscn Française d'Informatique et de Recherche Operationnelle 1966–67; mem. Council Int. Inst. of Applied Systems Analysis, Vienna 1973–79, Inst. of Man. Science 1976–79; Prof. Conservatoire Nat. des Arts et Métiers 1974–; Dir Projet Interfuturs OECD 1976–79; Dir of Studies, Inst. Auguste Comte 1979–81; Pres. Comm. on Employment and Social Relations of 8th Plan 1979–81; mem. Comm. du Bilan 1981, Council European Econ. Asscn 1984–89; Pres. Asscn Française de Science Économique 1981–83, Int. Federation of Operational Research Socs 1986–89; Dir and Man. Ed. Le Monde 1991–94; Pres. Futuribles Int. 1993–, Centre for Study and Research on Qualifications 1996–; Bd mem. Acad. des Technologies. *Publications:* Economic Technique and Industrial Management 1958, Du bon usage de l'étude économique dans l'entreprise 1966, Les systèmes du destin 1976, L'entreprise et ses futurs 1985, Éducation et société, L'après-Communisme, de l'Atlantique à l'Oural 1990, The Economics of Order and Disorder 1991, Vérités et mensonges sur le chômage 1995, Le Modèle français: Grandeur et Décadence 1998, Un Homme de notre Siècle 2000, Ces Avenirs qui n'ont pas eu lieu 2001, Leçons de Microéconomie évolutionniste (with A. Orléan and B. Wallises) 2002, Democratie: Marché et Gouvernance, Quels Avenirs? 2004, Evolutionary Microeconomics (with André Orléan and Bernard Walliser) 2006. *Honours:* Officier, Légion d'honneur, Commdr, Ordre nat. du Mérite, Officier des Palmes Académiques. *Address:* 52 rue de Vaugirard, 75006 Paris, France (home). *Telephone:* 1-43-25-66-05 (home). *Fax:* 1-56-24-47-98. *E-mail:* jolesourne@wanadoo.fr. *Website:* www.futuribles.com (office).

LESSARD, Suzannah, BA; American writer; b. 12 Jan. 1944, Islip, NY; one s. *Education:* Columbia School of General Studies. *Career:* Ed., Contributor, Washington Monthly, 1969–73; Staff Writer, New Yorker, 1975–95; mem. PEN. *Publications:* The Architect of Desire: Beauty and Danger in the Stanford White Family. *Honours:* Whiting Award, 1995; Woodrow Wilson International Center for Scholars Fellow, 2001–02; Jenny Moore Writer's Fellowship, George Washington University, 2002–03. *Address:* c/o The Dial Press, 1540 Broadway, New York, NY 10036, USA.

LESSER, Milton (see Marlowe, Stephen)

LESSER, Rika, BA, MFA; American poet, translator and educator; b. 21 July 1953, Brooklyn, NY. *Education:* Yale Univ., Conn., Univ. of Göteborg, Sweden, Columbia Univ., New York. *Career:* Visiting Lecturer, Yale Univ. 1976, 1978, 1987–88, Baruch Coll., CUNY 1979; poetry workshop instructor, Young Men's and Young Women's Hebrew Asscn, New York 1982–85, 2002–; Jenny McKean Moore Visiting Lecturer in English, George Washington Univ. 1985–86; Master Artist-in-Residence, Atlantic Center for the Arts, New Smyrna Beach, Fla 1998; Adjunct Assoc. Prof. of Tans., Columbia Univ. 1998, 2005; featured poet, Geraldine R. Dodge Poetry Festival 2000; poetry workshop instructor, 92nd Street Y, New York 2002; Guest Lecturer, Literary Trans., Grad. Writing Program, New School Univ. 2003–06; mem. Acad. of American Poets, American PEN, ASCAP, Associated Writing Programs, Poets and Writers, Authors' Guild. *Publications:* poetry: Etruscan Things 1983, All We Need of Hell 1995, Growing Back: Poems 1972–1992, 1997; trans. 11 books 1975–96. *Honours:* Ingram Merrill Foundation Award 1978–79, Harold Morton Landon Trans. Prize for Poetry, Acad. of American Poets 1982, Batchelder Award 1990, American-Scandinavian Foundation Trans. Prize 1992, 2002, George Bogin Memorial Award, Poetry Soc. of America 1992, Swedish Writers' Foundation Award 1995, Swedish Acad. Poetry Trans. Prize 1996, Fulbright-Hays Sr Scholar Award, English Dept, Stockholm Univ. 1999, Nat. Endowment for the Arts Fellowship 2001, grants from Barbro Osher Pro Suecia Foundation and American-Scandinvian Foundation 2006. *Address:* 133 Henry Street, Apt 5, New York, NY 11201, USA (home). *Telephone:* (718) 852-1163 (office). *E-mail:* rika.lesser.mc.74@aya.yale.edu (office).

LESSING, Doris May, CH, CLit; British writer; b. 22 Oct. 1919, Kermanshah, Persia; d. of Alfred Cook Tayler and Emily Maude Tayler (née McVeagh); m. 1st F. A. C. Wisdom 1939–43; m. 2nd Gottfried Anton Nicolai Lessing 1944 (divorced 1949; two s. (one deceased) one d. *Education:* Roman Catholic Convent and Girls' High School, Salisbury, Southern Rhodesia. *Career:* Assoc. mem. American Acad. of Arts and Letters 1974; Nat. Inst. of Arts and Letters (USA) 1974; mem. Inst. for Cultural Research 1974; Pres. Book Trust 1996–. *Publications:* novels: The Grass is Singing 1950, Children of Violence (Martha Quest 1952, A Proper Marriage 1954, A Ripple from the Storm 1965, The Four-Gated City 1969), Retreat to Innocence 1956, The Golden Notebook (Prix Médicis for French trans., Carnet d'Or 1976) 1962, Landlocked 1965, Briefing for a Descent into Hell 1971, The Summer Before the Dark 1973, The Memoirs of a Survivor 1974, Canopus in Argos series (Re: Colonised Planet 5, Shikasta 1979, The Marriages between Zones Three, Four and Five 1980, The Sirian Experiments 1981, The Making of the Representative for Planet 8 1982, The Sentimental Agents in the Volyen Empire 1983), The Diary of a Good Neighbour (as Jane Somers) 1983, If the Old Could (as Jane Somers) 1984, The Diaries of Jane Somers 1984, The Good Terrorist 1985 (WHSmith Literary Award 1986, Palermo Prize and Premio Internazionale Mondello 1987), The Fifth Child 1988, Love, Again 1996, Playing the Game 1996, Mara and Dann: an Adventure 1999, Ben, in the World 2000, The Old Age of El Magnifico 2000, The Sweetest Dream 2001, The Story of General Dann and Mara's Daughter, Griot and the Snow Dog 2005, The Cleft 2007; short stories: Collected African Stories: Vol. 1, This Was the Old Chief's Country 1951, Vol. 2, The Sun Between Their Feet 1973, Five 1953, The Habit of Loving 1957, A Man and Two Women 1963, African Stories 1964, Winter in July 1966, The Black Madonna 1966, The Story of a Non-Marrying Man and Other Stories 1972, A Sunrise on the Veld 1975, A Mild Attack of the Locusts 1977, Collected Stories: Vol. 1, To Room Nineteen 1978, Vol. 2, The Temptation of Jack Orkney 1978, London Observed: Stories and Sketches 1992, The Grandmothers 2003; non-fiction includes: Going Home 1957 (revised edn 1968), In Pursuit of the English 1960, Particularly Cats 1967, Particularly Cats and More Cats 1989, African Laughter: Four Visits to Zimbabwe 1992, Under My Skin: Volume One of My Autobiography to 1949 (Los Angeles Times Book Prize 1995, James Tait Memorial Prize 1995) 1994, Walking in the Shade: Volume Two of My Autobiography 1949–62 1997, Time Bites 2004; plays: Each His Own Wilderness 1958, Play with a Tiger 1962, The Singing Door 1973; other: Fourteen Poems 1959, A Small Personal Voice 1974, Doris Lessing Reader 1990. *Honours:* Hon. Fellow, MLA (US) 1974, Companion of Honour 1999; D.Fellow in Literature (East Anglia) 1991; Hon. DLitt (Princeton) 1989, Durham (1990), (Warwick) 1994, (Bard Coll. New York State) 1994, (Harvard) 1995, (Oxford) 1996; Somerset Maugham Award 1954, Soc. of Authors 1954–, Austrian State Prize for European Literature 1981, Shakespeare Prize, Hamburg 1982, Grinzane Cavour Award, Italy 1989, Woman of the Year, Norway 1995, Premio Internacional Cataluña, Spain 1999, David Cohen Literary Prize 2001, Príncipe de Asturias Prize, Spain 2001, PEN Award 2002. *Address:* c/o Jonathan Clowes Ltd, 10 Iron Bridge House, Bridge Approach, London, NW1 8BD, England. *Telephone:* (20) 7722-7624 (office). *Fax:* (20) 7794-0985 (home). *E-mail:* jonathanclowes@aol.com.

LESTARI, Dewi, (Dee); Indonesian novelist and singer; b. 20 Jan. 1976. *Education:* grad. of political and social sciences. *Career:* f. singing trio RSD (Rida, Sita, Dewi); f. Truedee Books to publish her first novel 2001–. *Publication:* Supernova (novel) 2001, Supernova 2.1: Akar 2003.

LETHEM, Jonathan Allen; American writer and editor; b. 19 Feb. 1964, New York, NY. *Education:* High School for Music and Art, New York; Bennington Coll., Vermont. *Publications:* Gun, with Occasional Music (novel) 1994, Amnesia Moon (novel) 1995, The Wall of the Sky, The Wall of the Eye (short stories) 1996, As She Climbed Across the Table (novel) 1997, Girl in Landscape (novel) 1998, Motherless Brooklyn (novel) 1999, This Shape We're In (novel) 2000, The Vintage Book of America (ed.) 2000, Da Capo Best Music Writing (ed. with Paul Bresnick) 2002, The Fortress of Solitude (novel) 2003, Men and Cartoons (short stories) 2004, The Disappointment Artist 2005, You Don't Love Me Yet (novel) 2007. *Honours:* CWA Silver Dagger Award, The Salon Book Award, Nat. Book Critics' Circle Award.

LETTE, Kathy; Australian author and playwright; b. 11 Nov. 1958, Sydney; d. of Mervyn Lette and Val Lette; m. Geoffrey Robertson (q.v.) 1990; one s. one d. *Career:* fmr columnist, Sydney and NY; fmr satirical news writer and presenter Willasee Show, Channel 9; fmr TV sitcom writer Columbia Pictures, LA; fmr guest presenter This Morning with Richard and Judy, ITV; writer-in-residence, The Savoy, London 2003. *Plays include:* Wet Dreams 1985, Perfect Mismatch 1985, Grommits 1986, I'm So Happy For You, I Really Am 1991. *Films:* Puberty Blues 1982, Mad Cow 2001. *Publications:* Puberty Blues (with G. Carey) 1979, Hit and Ms 1984, Girls' Night Out 1987, The Llama Parlour 1991, Foetal Attraction 1993, Mad Cows 1996, She Done Him Wrong (essays),

The Constant Sinner by Mae West (introduction) 1995, Altar Ego 1998, Nip 'n Tuck 2001, Dead Sexy 2003, How to Kill Your Husband 2005, A Stitch in Time 2005; contribs to Sydney Morning Herald, The Bulletin, Cleo Magazine. *Honours:* Australian Literature Board Grant 1982. *Address:* c/o Pan Macmillan, 25 Eccleston Place, London, SW1W 9NF (office); c/o Ed Victor, 6 Bayley Street, London, WC1B 3HB, England. *Telephone:* (20) 7304-4100 (office). *Fax:* (20) 7304-4111 (office). *E-mail:* kathy.lette@virgin.net (office). *Website:* www.kathylette.com (office).

LEUTENEGGER, Gertrud; Swiss writer; b. 7 Dec. 1948, Schwyz; m. M. von Wartburg 1989; one d. *Education:* Schauspielakademie (Zurich). *Publications include:* Vorabend 1975, Ninive 1977, Lebewohl, Gute Reise 1980, Gouverneur 1981, Komm ins Schiff 1983, Kontinent 1985, Das verlorene Monument 1985, Meduse 1988, Acheron 1994, Sphärenklang 1999, Pomona 2004, Gleich nach dem Gotthard kommt der Mailänder Dom 2006. *Honours:* Ingeborg Bachmann Critics' Prize 1978, Drostepreis 1979. *Address:* Scheideggstrasse 85, 8038 Zurich, Switzerland.

LEVEL, Brigitte Marie Adélaïde, (Anne Acoluthe), DèsL; French writer; b. 31 Oct. 1918, Paris; d. of Maurice Level and Jacqueline Level (née Ancey de Curnieu); m. Christian Léon-Dufour 1941 (died 1983); four s. (two deceased) four d. (one deceased). *Education:* Cours du Colisée, Paris and Univ. of Paris (Sorbonne). *Career:* Prof., Univ. of Paris 1959–85; participant in numerous confs since retirement 1985; Producer Radio-Courtoisie 1988–; Pres. Acad. of Still Life Art 1994; Pres. French Poets Soc. 1985; Vice-Pres. Défense de la langue française, Hon. Vice-Pres. 2005– (Pres. Cercle Paul-Valéry). *Publications include:* as Anne Acoluthe, Geneviève Minne, Zoé Zou: poetry: La girafe dépeignée, L'oiseau bonheur, L'arche de Zoé, Le temps des guitares 1990, Le Zoo de Zoulou 1994; prose: Le caveau 1729–1939, Guillaume Apollinaire, André Level: lettres 1976, Masques 1990, Le poète et l'oiseau 1991, Le poète à la pêche, La bestiaire de Lais, Fables et fabulettes. *Honours:* Officier des Palmes Académiques 1971, Officier du Mérite Agricole 1981, Officier Ordre des Arts et des Lettres 1986, Chevalier Ordre nat. du mérite 1989; numerous other awards including Prix Acad. française, Prix Acad. des Jeux floraux (églantine), Grand Prix Pascal Bonetti 1988, Grand Prix des Poètes français 1996, Prix Daudet 1998 and Médaille de Vermeil de la Ville de Paris. *Address:* 22 rue Legendre, 75017 Paris, France. *Telephone:* (1) 46-22-71-25.

LEVENSON, Christopher; Canadian poet, editor, translator and educator; b. 13 Feb. 1934, London, England. *Education:* University of Cambridge; University of Bristol; MA, University of Iowa, 1970. *Career:* Teacher, University of Münster, 1958–61, Carleton University, Ottawa, 1968–99; Ed.-in-Chief, ARC magazine, 1978–88; Founder-Dir, ARC Reading Series, Ottawa, 1981–91; Series Ed., Harbinger Poetry Series, 1995–99; Poetry Ed., Literary Review of Canada, 1997; mem. League of Canadian Poets. *Publications:* Poetry: In Transit, 1959; Cairns, 1969; Stills, 1972; Into the Open, 1977; The Journey Back, 1978; Arriving at Night, 1986; The Return, 1986; Half Truths, 1990; Duplicities: New and Selected Poems, 1993; The Bridge, 2000; Belvédère (trans.), 2002. Other: Seeking Heart's Solace (trans.), 1981; Light of the World (trans.), 1982; Reconcilable Differences: The Changing Face of Poetry by Canadian Men Since 1970 (ed.), 1994. Other: Requiem 53 (contributed texts to requiem for 50th anniversary of Dutch floods of 1953), 2003. Contributions: various anthologies, reviews, quarterlies, and journals. *Honours:* Eric Gregory Award, 1960; Archibald Lampman Award, 1987. *Address:* 333 St Andrew Street, Ottawa, ON K1N 5G9, Canada. *E-mail:* clevenson@rogers.com.

LEVER, Sir (Tresham) Christopher Arthur Lindsay, Bt , MA, FRGS, FLS; British naturalist and writer; b. 9 Jan. 1932, London; s. of Sir Tresham Lever, Bt and Frances Yowart; m. 1st 1970; m. 2nd Linda Weightman McDowell Goulden 1975. *Education:* Eton, Trinity Coll., Cambridge. *Career:* fmrly stockbroker, accountant, co. dir 1954–64; Fellow WWF UK 2005–; consultant, trustee and council mem. various conservation and animal welfare organizations. *Publications:* Goldsmiths and Silversmiths of England 1975, The Naturalised Animals of the British Isles 1977, Naturalised Mammals of the World 1985, Naturalised Birds of the World 1987, The Mandarin Duck 1990, They Dined on Eland: The Story of the Acclimatisation Societies 1992, Naturalised Animals: The Ecology of Successfully Introduced Species 1994, Naturalised Fishes of the World 1996, The Cane Toad: The History and Ecology of a Successful Colonist 2001, Naturalised Reptiles and Amphibians of the World 2003; contrib. to many books, professional journals and general publications. *Honours:* Hon. life mem., Brontë Soc. 1988, Hon. life Pres. Tusk Trust 2004–. *Address:* Newell House, Winkfield, Berkshire SL4 4SE, England. *Telephone:* (1344) 882604. *Fax:* (1344) 891744.

LÉVESQUE, Anne-Michèle, BS; Canadian writer; b. 29 May 1939, Val d'Or, QC; m. (deceased); two d. *Education:* Univ. of Montréal, Outremont Business Coll. *Career:* mem. Regroupement des Écrivains de l'Abitibi-TemisCamingue, Union des écrivaines et des écrivains québécois, Conseil de la Culture de l'Abitibi-Térniscamingue, Aventuriers de la Plume, Cercle des Écrivains. *Publications:* Persil Frisé 1992, A La Recherche d'un Salaud 1995, Fleurs de Corail 1995, La Maison du Puits Sacré 1997, Quartiers divers 1997, Meurtres à la sauce tomate 1999, Rapt 2000, Abitibissimo 2000, Fleur Invitait au Troisième 2001, La Revanche des Dieux 2002, Rumeurs et Marées 2002, AZ-3 (poems) Vol. I 2003, Vol. II 2004; contrib. to Lumière d'Encre, Arcade magazines. *Honours:* First Prize, Concours Littéraire 1991, Arthur Ellis Award for Best Mystery Novel in French (Canada) 2002. *Address:* 184 Williston Street, Val d'Or, QC J9P 4S7, Canada (office). *Telephone:* (819) 825-

4190 (office). *E-mail:* corail@cablevision.qc.ca. *Website:* www.cablevision.qc.ca/aml.

LEVEY, Sir Michael Vincent, Kt, LVO, FBA, FRSL; British art historian; b. 8 June 1927, London; s. of the late O. L. H. Levey and Gladys Mary Milestone; m. Brigid Brophy 1954 (died 1995); one d. *Education:* Oratory School and Exeter Coll., Oxford. *Career:* officer, British Army 1945–48; Asst Keeper Nat. Gallery 1951–66, Deputy Keeper 1966–68, Keeper 1968–73, Deputy Dir 1970–73, Dir 1973–86; Slade Prof. of Art Cambridge Univ. and Fellow of King's Coll. Cambridge 1963–64; Slade Prof. of Art, Oxford Univ. 1994–95; fmr Chair. Nat. Dirs Conf.; Foreign mem. Ateneo Veneto, Italy. *Publications:* Edited Nat. Gallery Catalogues: 18th Cent. Italian Schools 1956, The German School 1959, Painting in XVIIIth Century Venice 1959; From Giotto to Cézanne 1962, Later Italian Pictures in the Royal Collection 1964, Dürer 1964, A Room-to-room Guide to the National Gallery 1964, Rococo to Revolution 1966, Fifty Works of English and American Literature We Could do Without (with Brigid Brophy and Charles Osborne) 1967, Bronzino 1967, Early Renaissance 1967 (awarded Hawthornden Prize 1968), A History of Western Art 1968, Holbein's Christina of Denmark, Duchess of Milan 1968, 17th and 18th Cent. Italian Schools (Nat. Gallery Catalogue) 1971, Painting at Court 1971, The Life and Death of Mozart 1971, Art and Architecture in 18th Cent. France (co-author) 1972, High Renaissance 1975, The World of Ottoman Art 1976, The Case of Walter Pater 1978, Sir Thomas Lawrence (Exhbn catalogue) 1979, The Painter Depicted (Neurath Lecture) 1982, Tempting Fate (fiction) 1982, An Affair on the Appian Way (fiction) 1984, Giambattista Tiepolo 1986 (Banister Fletcher Prize), The National Gallery Collection 1987, Men At Work (fiction) 1989, The Soul of the Eye (anthology) 1990, Painting and Sculpture in France 1700–1789 1993, Florence: A Portrait 1996, The Chapel is on Fire (memoir) 2000, The Burlington Magazine (anthology) 2003, Sir Thomas Lawrence 2005. *Honours:* Hon. Fellow, Exeter Coll., Oxford; Hon. LittD (Manchester). *Address:* 36 Little Lane, Louth, Lincs. LN11 9DU, England.

LEVI, Arrigo, PhD; Italian journalist and political writer; b. 17 July 1926, Modena; s. of Enzo Levi and Ida Levi (née Donati); m. Carmela Lenci 1952; one d. *Education:* Univs of Buenos Aires and Bologna. *Career:* refugee in Argentina 1942–46; Negev Brigade, Israeli Army 1948–49; BBC European Services 1951–53; London Corresp. Gazzetta del Popolo and Corriere d'Informazione 1952–59; Moscow Corresp. Corriere della Sera 1960–62; news anchorman on Italian State Television 1966–68; special corresp. La Stampa 1969–73, Ed. in Chief 1973–78, Special Corresp. 1978–; columnist on int. affairs, The Times 1979–83; Leader Writer, Corriere della Sera 1988–. *Publications:* Il potere in Russia 1965, Journey among the Economists 1972. *Honours:* Premio Trento 1987, Premio Luigi Barzini 1995, Premio Ischia Internazionale di Giornalismo 2001. *Address:* c/o Piazza S. Carlo 206, 10121 Turin, Italy.

LÉVI-STRAUSS, Claude; French anthropologist, academic and writer; *Honorary Professor, Collège de France;* b. 28 Nov. 1908, Brussels, Belgium; s. of Raymond Lévi-Strauss and Emma Lévy; m. 1st Dina Dreyfus 1932; m. 2nd Rose Marie Ullmo 1946, one s.; m. 3rd Monique Roman 1954; one s. *Education:* Lycée Janson de Sailly, Paris and Univ. de Paris à la Sorbonne. *Career:* Prof. Univ. of São Paulo, Brazil 1935–39; Visiting Prof. New School for Social Research, New York 1942–45; Cultural Counsellor, French Embassy to USA 1946–47; Assoc. Dir Musée de l'Homme, Paris 1949–50; Dir of Studies, Ecole Pratique des Hautes Etudes, Paris 1950–74; Prof. Collège de France 1959–82, Hon. Prof. 1983–; mem. Acad. Française; Foreign mem. Royal Acad. of the Netherlands, Norwegian Acad. of Sciences and Letters, American Acad. of Arts and Sciences, American Acad. and Inst. of Arts and Letters, British Acad.; Foreign Assoc. US NAS. *Publications:* La vie familiale et sociale des indiens Nambikwara 1948, Les structures élémentaires de la parenté 1949, Tristes tropiques 1955, Anthropologie structurale 1958, Le totémisme aujourd'hui 1962, La pensée sauvage 1962, Le cru et le cuit 1964, Du miel aux cendres 1967, L'origine des manières de table 1968, L'homme nu 1971, Anthropologie structurale deux 1973, La voie des masques 1975, 1979, Le regard éloigné 1983, Paroles données 1984, La potière jalouse 1985, De près et de loin (with Didier Eribon) 1988, Histoire de Lynx 1991, Regarder, écouter, lire 1993, Saudades do Brasil 1994. *Honours:* Hon. mem. Royal Anthropological Inst., American Philosophical Soc. and London School of Oriental and African Studies; Grand-Croix, Légion d'Honneur, Commdr Ordre Nat. du Mérite, des Palmes académiques, des Arts et des Lettres; Dr hc (Brussels, Harvard, Yale, Chicago, Columbia, Oxford, Stirling, Zaire, Mexico, Uppsala, Johns Hopkins, Montréal, Québec, Visva-Bharati Univ., India); Prix Paul Pelliot 1949; Huxley Memorial Medal 1965, Viking Fund Gold Medal 1966, Gold Medal CNRS 1967; Erasmus Prize 1973, Aby M. Warburg Prize 1996, Int. Prize, Catalunya 2002. *Address:* Laboratoire d'Anthropologie Sociale, Collège de France, 52 rue du Cardinal Lemoine, 75005 Paris (office); 2 rue des Marronniers, 75016 Paris, France (home). *Telephone:* 1-44-27-17-31 (office); 1-42-88-34-71 (home). *Fax:* 1-44-27-17-66 (office). *E-mail:* eva-kempinski@collège-de-france.fr (office). *Website:* www.ehess.fr/centres/las (office).

LEVIN, Gabriel; French/Israeli/American poet, translator and editor; b. 13 Dec. 1948, France. *Career:* mem. Editorial Bd Ibis Editions, Jerusalem. *Publications include:* poetry: Sleepers of Beulah 1992, Ostraca 1999; prose: Hezekiah's Tunnel 1997, Pleasant if Somewhat Rude Views 2005; translations: Poems from the Diwan, by Yehuda Halevi 2002, The Little Bookseller Oustaz Ali, by Ahmed Rassim 1997, Never Mind, by Taha Muhammad Ali 2000; editor: Found in Translation: A Hundred Years of Modern Hebrew

Poetry 1999; contrib. to Times Literary Supplement, American Poetry Review, American Book Review, Boston Review, Parnassus, PN Review. *Address:* c/o Ibis Editions, PO Box 8074, German Colony, Jerusalem, Israel. *E-mail:* ibis@netvision.net.il. *Website:* www.ibiseditions.com.

LEVIN, Gerald Manuel, BA, LLB; American fmr media executive; *Presiding Director, Moonview Sanctuary*; b. 6 May 1939, Philadelphia; s. of David Levin and Pauline Schantzer; m. 1st Carol S. Needlemam 1959 (divorced 1970), two s. (one s. deceased), one d.; m. 2nd Barbara Riley 1970, one s. one d.; m. 3rd Laurie Perlman 2005. *Education:* Haverford Coll. and Univ. of Pa. *Career:* Assoc. Simpson, Thatcher & Bartlett, New York 1963–67; Gen. Man., COO Devt and Resources Corpn New York 1967–71; Rep. Int. Basic Economy Corpn Tehran 1971–72; Vice-Pres. Programming, Home Box Office, New York 1972–73, Pres., CEO 1973–76, Chair., CEO 1976–79; Group Vice-Pres. (Video), Time Inc. New York 1979–84, Exec. Vice-Pres. 1984–88, Vice-Chair., Dir 1988–90; Vice-Chair., Dir Time-Warner Inc. 1990–92, Jt CEO 1992–93, CEO and Chair. 1992–2001, CEO AOL Time Warner (created after merger of Time Warner and American Online 2000) 2001–02 (retd); currently Presiding Dir Moonview Sanctuary (spiritual healing firm); Dir NY Stock Exchange; Treas. NY Philharmonic Orchestra; mem. Bd of Dirs Living Memorial to the Holocaust (Museum of Jewish Heritage). *Honours:* Hon. LLD (Texas Coll.) 1985, (Middlebury Coll.) 1994, Hon. LHD (Univ. of Denver) 1995; Media Person of the Year Award, Cannes Lions Int. Advertising Festival 2001. *Address:* Moonview Sanctuary, POB 1518, Santa Monica, CA 90406, USA. *Telephone:* (866) 601-0601. *E-mail:* glevin@moonviewsanctuary.com. *Website:* www.moonviewsanctuary.com.

LEVIN, Ira, AB; American writer and dramatist; b. 27 Aug. 1929, New York, NY; s. of Charles Levin and Beatrice Levin (née Schlansky); m. 1st Gabrielle Aronsohn 1960 (divorced 1968); three s.; m. 2nd Phyllis Finkel 1979 (divorced 1982). *Education:* Horace Mann School, Drake Univ., Iowa, New York Univ. *Career:* US Army 1953–55, wrote training films for the troops and a service comedy No Time for Sergeants (film version released 1958); mem. Authors' Guild, Authors' League of America, ASCAP, Dramatists Guild (mem. Council 1980–). *Plays:* No Time for Sergeants 1956, Interlock 1958, Critic's Choice 1960, General Seeger 1962, Drat! The Cat! 1965, Dr Cook's Garden 1967, Veronica's Room 1973, Deathtrap 1978, Break a Leg 1981, Cantorial 1982, Footsteps 2003. *Television:* Lights Out (series, episode 'Leda's Portrait') 1951, General Electric Theater (series, episode 'The Devil You Say') 1953, The United States Steel Hour (series, episodes 'No Time for Sergeants', 'The Notebook Warrior') 1953. *Publications:* A Kiss Before Dying 1953, Rosemary's Baby 1967, This Perfect Day 1970, The Stepford Wives 1972, The Boys from Brazil 1976, Sliver 1991, Son of Rosemary 1997. *Honours:* MWA Edgar Allan Poe Awards 1953, 1980, MWA Grand Master Award 2003. *Literary Agent:* Harold Ober Associates, 425 Madison Avenue, New York, NY 10017, USA.

LEVINE, Ellen; American magazine editor; *Editorial Director, Hearst Magazines*; b. 19 Feb. 1943, d. of Eugene Jack and Jean Jacobson; m. Richard U. Levine 1964; two s. *Education:* Wellesley Coll. *Career:* reporter The Record, Hackensack, NJ 1964–70; Ed. Cosmopolitan, New York 1976–82; Ed-in-Chief Cosmopolitan Living 1980–81, Woman's Day 1982–91, Redbook 1991–94, Good Housekeeping 1994–2006, Editorial Dir Hearst Magazines 2006–; mem. Bd of Dirs New York Restoration Project, Gaylord Entertainment and Finlay Enterprises, Inc., Lifetime Television; mem Bd of Advisors New York Women in Communications; fmr Dir NJ Bell, Knight Commr Attorney-Gen's Comm. on Pornography 1985–86; mem. Exec. Cttee Sen. Bill Bradley 1984. *Publications:* Planning Your Wedding, Waiting for Baby, Rooms That Grow With Your Child. *Honours:* New York Women in Communications Inc. Matrix Award 1989, Birmingham Southern Coll. Honor Award 1991, Leadership in Media Award, American Legacy Foundation 2003, WISER Award, Heinz Family Philanthropies 2003, Wind Beneath My Wings Leadership Award, New York Restoration Project 2003. *Address:* The Hearst Corporation, 959 8th Avenue, New York, NY 10019, USA (office). *Telephone:* (212) 649-2000 (office). *Fax:* (212) 649-2108 (office). *Website:* www.hearst.com/magazines (office).

LEVINE, Paul, BA, JD; American writer and lawyer; b. 9 Jan. 1948, Williamsport, PA; m. Alice Holmstrom 1975 (divorced 1992); one s. one d. *Education:* Pennsylvania State Univ., Univ. of Miami. *Career:* admitted to the Bar, State of Florida, 1973, US Supreme Court, 1977, District of Columbia, 1978, Commonwealth of Pennsylvania, 1989; Attorney and/or Partner, various law firms, 1973–91; mem. American Bar Asscn; American Trial Lawyers Asscn; Authors' Guild. *Publications:* What's Your Verdict?, 1980; To Speak for the Dead, 1990; Night Vision, 1992; False Dawn, 1994; Mortal Sin, 1994; Slashback, 1995; Fool Me Twice, 1996.

LEVINE, Philip, BA, AM, MFA; American poet, writer and retd academic; b. 10 Jan. 1928, Detroit, MI; m. Frances Artley 1954; three s. *Education:* Wayne State Univ., Univ. of Iowa, studied with John Berryman. *Career:* Instructor 1958–69, Prof. of English 1969–92, California State Univ. at Fresno; Elliston Prof. of Poetry, Univ. of Cincinnati 1976; poet-in-residence, Nat. Univ. of Australia, Canberra 1978; Visiting Prof. of Poetry, Columbia Univ. 1978, 1981, 1984, New York Univ. 1984, 1991, Brown Univ. 1985; Chair. Literature Panel, Nat. Endowment for the Arts 1985; various poetry readings; NEA grants 1969, 1976, 1981, 1987; Guggenheim Fellowships 1974, 1981; mem. American Acad. of Arts and Letters, Acad. of American Poets (chancellor 2000–). *Publications:* poetry: On the Edge 1961, Silent in America: Vivas for Those Who Failed 1965, Not This Pig 1968, 5 Detroits 1970, Thistles: A Poem of Sequence 1970, Pili's Wall 1971, Red Dust 1971, They Feed, They Lion 1972,

1933 1974, New Season 1975, On the Edge and Over: Poems Old, Lost, and New 1976, The Names of the Lost 1976, 7 Years from Somewhere 1979, Ashes: Poems New and Old 1979, One for the Rose 1981, Selected Poems 1984, Sweet Will 1985, A Walk with Tom Jefferson 1988, New Selected Poems 1991, What Work Is 1991, The Simple Truth: Poems 1994, The Mercy 1995, Breath 2004; non-fiction: Don't Ask (interviews) 1979, Earth, Stars, and Writers (with others, lectures) 1992, The Bread of Time: Toward an Autobiography 1994; contrib. to many anthologies and reviews. *Honours:* San Francisco Foundation Joseph Henry Jackson Award 1961, Frank O'Hara Prizes 1973, 1974, American Acad. of Arts and Letters Award of Merit 1974, Levinson Prize 1974, Univ. of Chicago Harriet Monroe Memorial Prize for Poetry 1976, Leonore Marshall Award for Best American Book of Poems 1976, American Book Award for Poetry 1979, Nat. Book Critics Circle Prize 1979, American Library Asscn Notable Book Award 1979, New England Poetry Soc. Golden Rose Award 1985, Ruth Lilly Award 1987, New York Univ. Elmer Holmes Bobst Award 1990, Nat. Book Award for Poetry 1991, Commonwealth Club of California Silver Medal in Poetry 1992, 2000, Pulitzer Prize in Poetry 1995. *Address:* 4549 N Van Ness Blvd, Fresno, CA 93704, USA.

LEVINE, Stuart George, (Esteban O'Brien Córdoba), PhD; American academic, writer and musician; *Professor Emeritus, University of Kansas*; b. 25 May 1932, New York, NY; m. Susan Fleming Matthews 1963; two s. one d. *Education:* Harvard and Brown Univs. *Career:* Instructor, Univ. of Kansas 1958–61, Asst Prof. 1961–65, Assoc. Prof. 1965–69, Chair. Dept of American Studies 1965–70, Prof. 1969–92, Prof. Emer. 1992–; Visiting Prof., Kansas State Univ. 1964, Univ. of Missouri at Kansas City 1966, 1974, California State Univ. at Los Angeles 1969, 1971; Fulbright Distinguished Lecturer, Naples, Italy 1995; Fulbright Professorships, Argentina, Mexico, Costa Rica, Chile; Guest Professorship, Univ. of the West Indies, Mona; Founder-Ed. American Studies 1959–90; many engagements as a professional French horn player. *Achievements:* several one-man shows of his paintings. *Television:* Portfolio (writer and host, weekly music programme). *Publications:* Materials for Technical Writing 1963, The American Indian Today (with Nancy O. Lurie) 1968, Edgar Poe, Seer and Craftsman 1972, The Short Fiction of Edgar Allan Poe: An Annotated Edition (with Susan F. Levine) 1976, The Monday-Wednesday-Friday Girl and Other Stories 1994, Eureka: Edgar Allan Poe (with Susan F. Levine) 2004, Poe's Critical Theory: The Major Documents (ed. with Susan F. Levine) 2007; contribs to various scholarly reviews, quarterlies and journals. *Honours:* Anisfield-Wolf Award in Race Relations 1968, Theodore Blegen Award 1975, Citation for 30-year editorship of American Studies 1989, Gross Award for Short Fiction 1994. *Address:* Department of English, University of Kansas, Lawrence, KS 66045 (office); 1644 University Drive, Lawrence, KS 66044, USA (home). *Telephone:* (785) 864-4520 (office); (785) 842-0356 (home).

LEVINSON, Jerrold, BS, PhD; American academic and writer; *Professor, University of Maryland at College Park*; b. 11 July 1948, New York, NY; m. Karla Hoff 1985 (divorced 2004); one d. *Education:* MIT, Univ. of Michigan. *Career:* Asst Prof., SUNY at Albany 1974–75; Asst Prof. 1976–81, Assoc. Prof. 1981–91, Prof. 1991–, Univ. of Maryland at College Park; Visiting Prof., Univ. of London 1991, Johns Hopkins Univ. 1993, Univ. of Rennes 1998, Columbia Univ. 2000; mem. American Soc. for Aesthetics (pres. 2001–03). *Publications:* Music, Art, and Metaphysics 1990, The Pleasures of Aesthetics 1996, Music in the Moment 1998, Aesthetics and Ethics (ed.) 1998, Oxford Handbook of Aesthetics (ed.) 2002, Contemplating Art 2006. *Honours:* Nat. Endowment for the Humanities Fellowship 1980. *Address:* 4209 Underwood Street, University Park, MD 20782, USA. *E-mail:* jl32@umail.umd.edu.

LEVINSON, Leonard, (Nicholas Brady, Clay Dawson, Josh Edwards, J. Farragut Jones, Leonard Jordan, Philip King, John Mackie, Bruno Rossi, Cynthia Wilkerson), BA; American writer; b. 1935, New Bedford, MA. *Education:* Michigan State Univ. *Career:* other pseudonyms include Michael Bodren, Frank Burleson, Lee Chang, Glen Chase, Richard Hale Curtis, Gordon Davis, Richard Gallagher, March Hastings, Robert Novak, Philip Rawls, Jonathon Scofield, Jonathon Trask. *Publications:* as Bruno Rossi: Worst Way To Die 1974, Headcrusher 1974; as Nicholas Brady: Shark Fighter 1975; as Leonard Jordan: Operation Perfida 1975, Without Mercy 1981; as Cynthia Wilkerson: Sweeter Than Candy 1978, The Fast Life 1979; as Philip King: Hydra Conspiracy 1979; as Gordon Davis: The Battle of the Bulge 1981; as John Mackie: Hit the Beach 1983, Nightmare Alley 1985; as Clay Dawson: Gold Town 1989; as J. Farragut Jones: 40 Fathoms Down 1990; as Josh Edwards: Searcher 1990, Warpath 1991. *Literary Agent:* Lowenstein-Yost Associates Inc, Suite 601, 121 W 27th Street, New York NY 10001, USA. *Telephone:* (212) 206-1630. *Fax:* (212) 727-0280.

LEVY, Andrea, BA; British writer; b. 7 March 1956, London; d. of Amy and Winston Levy; m. Bill Mayblin; two step-d. *Education:* Highbury Hill High School, London and Middlesex Polytechnic. *Career:* fmr graphic designer. *Publications:* Every Light in the House Burnin' 1994, Never Far from Nowhere 1996, Fruit of the Lemon 1999, Small Island (Orange Prize 2004, Whitbread Novel of the Year and Whitbread Prize 2005, Commonwealth Writers Prize 2005, Orange Prize for Fiction tenth anniversary award 2005) 2004. *Honours:* Dr hc (Middlesex) Arts Council Award 1998. *Literary Agent:* David Grossman Literary Agency, 118B Holland Park Avenue, London, W11 4VA, England. *Telephone:* (20) 7221-2770. *Fax:* (20) 7221-1445. *Address:* c/o Review Press, Hodder Headline, 338 Euston Road, London, NW1, England.

LÉVY, Bernard-Henri; French writer and philosopher; b. 5 Nov. 1948, Beni-Saf, Algeria; s. of André Lévy and Ginette Lévy; m. 1st Sylvie Bouscasse 1980; one s. one d.; m. 2nd Arielle Sonnery 1993. *Education:* Ecole Normale Supérieure (rue d'Ulm), Paris. *Career:* War Corresp. for Combat 1971–72; Lecturer in Epistemology, Univ. of Strasbourg, in Philosophy, Ecole Normale Supérieure 1973; mem. François Mitterrand's Group of Experts 1973–76; joined Editions Grasset as Ed. 'nouvelle philosophie' series 1973; Ed. Idées section, Quotidien de Paris; Contrib. to Nouvel Observateur and Temps Modernes 1974; co-founder Action Int. contre la Faim 1980, Radio Free Kabul 1981, SOS Racisme; f. and Dir Règle du jeu 1990–; Pres. Supervisory Council Sept-Arte 1993–; seconded by French Govt to Kabul, Afghanistan 2002. *Film directed:* Le Jour la Nuit 1997. *Publications:* Bangladesh: Nationalisme dans la révolution 1973, Les Indes rouges 1973, La barbarie à visage humain 1977 (Prix d'honneur 1977), Le testament de Dieu 1979, L'idéologie française 1981, Questions de principe 1983, Le diable en tête (Prix Médicis) 1984, Impressions d'Asie 1985, Questions de principe II 1986, Eloge des intellectuels 1987, Les derniers jours de Charles Baudelaire (Prix Interallié) 1988, Questions de principe III 1990, Frank Stella: Les années 80 1990, Les bronzes de César 1991, Les aventures de la liberté 1991, Piet Mondrian 1992, Piero Della Francesca 1992, Le jugement dernier (play) 1992, Questions de principe IV 1992, Les hommes et les femmes (jtly) 1993, Un jour dans la mort de Sarajevo (screenplay, jtly) 1993, Bosna! (screenplay, jtly) 1994, La pureté dangereuse 1995, Questions de principe V 1995, Le lys et la cendre 1996, Comédie 1997, The Rules of the Game 1998 (revised edn What Good Are Intellectuals?: 44 Writers Share Their Thoughts 2000), Le siècle de Sartre 2000, Réflexion sur la guerre, Le mal et la fin de l'histoire 2001, Mémoire vive 2001, Qui a tué Daniel Pearl? 2003, American Vertigo 2006. *Address:* c/o Editions Grasset et Fasquelle, 61 rue des Saint-Pères, 75006 Paris, France. *Telephone:* 1-44-39-22-00. *Fax:* 1-42-22-64-18.

LEVY, Marc; French writer; b. 16 Oct. 1961, Boulogne Billancourt. *Education:* Université Paris-Dauphine. *Career:* worked for the Red Cross 1979–85. *Publications:* Et si c'était vrai... 2000, Où es-tu? 2001, Sept jours pour une éternité... 2003, La Prochaine fois 2004, Vous revoir 2005, Mes amis Mes amours 2006. *Literary Agent:* Susanna Lea Associates, 28 rue Bonaparte, 75006 Paris, France. *Telephone:* 1-53-10-28-40. *Fax:* 1-53-10-28-49. *E-mail:* postmaster@susannalea.com. *Website:* www.susannalea.com; www.marclevy.info.

LEVY, Peter B., BA, MA, PhD; American historian; b. 11 May 1956, Burlingame, CA; m. Diane Krejsa 1984, one s. one d. *Education:* University of California, Berkeley, Columbia University. *Career:* Visiting Assisitant Prof. of History, Rutgers University, Newark Campus, NJ, 1986–88; Assoc. Prof. of History, York College, Pennsylvania, 1989–; mem. American Historical Assocn; Organization of American Historians. *Publications:* Let Freedom Ring: A Documentary History of the Modern Civil Rights Movement (co-ed.), 1992; The New Left and Labor in the 1960s, 1994; Encyclopedia of the Reagan-Bush Years, 1996; The Civil Rights Movement, 1998; America in the Sixties: Right, Left, and Center, 1999. *Address:* 1214 Temfield Road, Towson, MD 21286, USA. *E-mail:* plevy@ycp.edu.

LEWIN, Hugh; South African writer; b. 1939, Eastern Transvaal. *Career:* joined African Resistance Movement 1964; imprisoned 1965–72; on release, moved to London, later Zimbabwe; returned to South Africa 1990; fmr Dir, Inst. for the Advancement of Journalism; mem. Truth Commission Human Rights Violations Cttee; currently a media trainer. *Publications include:* Bandiet: Seven Years in a South African Jail 1974, Jafta 1989, The Picture That Came Alive 1993, Bandiet Out of Jail 2001. *Honours:* Olive Schreiner Prize 2001–02. *Address:* c/o Random House Inc, 1745 Broadway, New York, NY 10019, USA. *Website:* www.randomhouse.com.

LEWIN, Michael Zinn, AB; British/American writer and dramatist; b. 21 July 1942, Cambridge, MA; one s. one d. *Education:* Harvard Univ., Churchill Coll., Cambridge. *Career:* Co-Ed., CWA Annual Anthology 1992–94; mem. Detection Club, CWA, Authors' Guild. *Radio plays:* The Loss Factor, The Way We Die Now, The Enemies Within, Arrest is as Good as a Change, Rainey Shines, Ask the Right Question, Missing Woman, Cross Rems Of, Rough Cider (adapted from Peter Lovesey novel), Keystone (adapted from Peter Lovesey novel), The Silent Salesman, Who Killed Gnutley Almond?, Place of Safety, The Interests of the Child, Jingle. *Plays:* Deadlock (for Dr Fosters Travelling Theatre) 1990, Who Killed Frankie Almond? 1995, Whooodunnit? 1998. *Publications:* novels: Ask the Right Question 1971, The Way we Die Now 1973, The Enemies Within 1974, Night Cover 1976, The Next Man (novelization of film) 1976, The Silent Salesman 1978, Outside In 1980, Missing Woman 1981, Hard Line (Falcon Award for Best Foreign Novel of the Year, Japan 1987) 1982, Out of Season (aka Out of Time) 1984, Late Payments 1986, And Baby Will Fall (aka Child Proof) 1988, Called by a Panther (Raymond Chandler Soc. of Germany Marlowe Award for Best PI Novel 1992) 1991, Underdog 1993, Family Business 1995, Cutting Loose 1999, Family Planning 1999, Eye-Opener 2004; short story collections: Telling Tales 1994, Rover's Tales 1998, The Reluctant Detective and Other Stories 2001; non-fiction: How to Beat College Tests: A Guide to Ease the Burden of Useless Courses 1970; contrib. numerous short stories to magazines and anthologies. *Honours:* Mid-America Mystery Conference Mystery Masters Award 1994. *Address:* Garden Flat, 15 Bladud Buildings, Bath, BA1 5LS, England. *Website:* www.michaelzlewin.com.

LEWIN, Roger A., BA, MD; American psychiatrist, teacher, writer and poet; b. 22 Jan. 1946, Cleveland, OH; m. 1st Julia Vandivort 1977 (died 1988); one d.; m. 2nd Joan Lilienthal 1990. *Education:* Harvard Univ., Wright State Univ. *Career:* resident, Sheppard and Enoch Pratt Hosp., Towson, Md 1981–85, psychiatrist 1985–91, teacher and supervisor 1991–; pvt. practice of psychiatry 1981–. *Publications:* Losing and Fusing (co-author) 1992, Compassion 1996, New Wrinkles (poems) 1996, Creative Collaboration in Psychotherapy 1997, Spring Fed Pond 2003. *Honours:* Ford Foundation Grant 1965, Ginsburg Fellow Group for the Advancement of Psychiatry 1981–85. *Address:* 504 Club Lane, Towson, MD 21286, USA. *E-mail:* oaktree@comcast.net (home).

LEWING, Anthony Charles, (Mark Bannerman); British writer; b. 12 July 1933, Colchester, England; m. Françoise Faury 1966; one s. one d. *Education:* King's Coll. School, Wimbledon. *Career:* Royal Army Ordnance Corps 1951–53, Royal Army Pay Corps 1958–89; civil service 1989–95. *Publications:* Grand Valley Feud 1995, The Beckoning Noose 1996, Escape to Purgatory 1996, The Early Lynching 1997, Renegade Rose 1997, Ride into Destiny 1997, Goose Pimples 1997, Man Without a Yesterday 1998, Trail to Redemption 1998, Bridges to Cross (as Rowena Carter) 1998, Short Story World 1999, Comanchero Rendezvous 1999, The Cornish Woman 1999, Frank Riddle – Frontiersman 1999, Pinkerton Man 2000, Galvanized Yankee 2001, Rail-roaded 2001, Lust to Kill 2003, Blind Trail 2004, Bender's Boot 2004, The Frontiersman 2004, Hog-Tied Hero 2005, Fury at Troon's Ferry 2005, Legacy of Head 2005, Gunsmoke at Adobe Walls 2006; contrib. over 300 short stories in magazines, newspapers and anthologies. *Address:* Greenmantle, Horseshoe Lane, Ash Vale, Surrey, GU12 5LJ, England. *Telephone:* (1252) 679779. *E-mail:* anthony.lewing@ntlworld.com.

LEWIS, Anthony, AB; American journalist and academic; b. 27 March 1927, New York, NY; m. 1st Linda Rannells 1951 (divorced); one s. two d.; m. 2nd Margaret H. Marshall 1984. *Education:* Harvard Univ. *Career:* deskman, Sunday Dept 1948–52, reporter, Washington Bureau 1955–64, Chief London Bureau 1965–72, editorial columnist 1969–2001, New York Times; reporter, Washington Daily News 1952–55; Lecturer on Law, Harvard Univ. 1974–89; James Madison Visiting Prof., Columbia Univ. 1983–; mem. American Acad. of Arts and Sciences. *Publications:* Gideon's Trumpet 1964, Portrait of a Decade: The Second American Revolution 1964, Make No Law: The Sullivan Case and the First Amendment 1991, Written into History: Pulitzer Prize Reporting of the Twentieth Century from the New York Times (ed.) 2001; contrib. to professional journals. *Honours:* Hon. DLitt (Adelphi Univ.) 1964, (Rutgers Univ.) 1973, (Williams Coll.) 1978, (Clark Univ.) 1982, Hon. LLD (Syracuse Univ.) 1979, (Colby Coll.) 1983, (Northeastern Univ.) 1987; Heywood Broun Award 1955, Pulitzer Prizes for Nat. Reporting 1955, 1963, Nieman Fellow 1956–57, MWA Best Fact-Crime Book Award 1964, Presidential Citizen's Medal 2001. *Address:* 1010 Memorial Drive, Cambridge, MA 02138, USA. *Telephone:* (617) 354-2229 (office); (617) 876-3641 (home). *Fax:* (617) 354-2458 (office); (617) 876-3641 (home).

LEWIS, Arnold, MA, PhD; American architectural historian, art historian and academic; b. 13 Jan. 1930, New Castle, Pa; m. Beth Irwin 1958; two s. one d. *Education:* Allegheny Coll., Univ. of Wisconsin, Univ. of Bonn and Univ. of Munich, Germany. *Career:* Wells Coll., Aurora, New York 1962–64; Coll. of Wooster, OH 1964–96; mem. Coll. Art Asscn, Soc. of Architectural Historians (Dir 1979–82). *Publications:* American Victorian Architecture 1975, Wooster in 1876 1976, American Country Houses of the Gilded Age 1983, American Interiors of the Gilded Age (with James Turner and Steven McQuillin) 1987, An Early Encounter with Tomorrow: Europeans, Chicago's Loop, and the World's Columbian Exposition 1997; contrib. to Journal of the Society of Architectural Historians. *Honours:* Founder's Award, Journal of the Society of Architectural Historians 1974, Western Reserve Book Award, Soc. of Architectural Historians 1977, Barzun Prize in Cultural History, American Philosophical Soc. 1998. *Address:* Department of Art, College of Wooster, Wooster, OH 44691, USA (office). *Telephone:* (330) 264-3515 (home). *E-mail:* alewis@wooster.edu (office); lewisda@earthlink.net (home).

LEWIS, Bernard, PhD, FBA, FRHistS; American writer and academic; *Cleveland E. Dodge Professor Emeritus of Near Eastern Studies, Princeton University;* b. 31 May 1916, London, England; m. Ruth Hélène Oppenhejm 1947 (divorced 1974); one s. one d. *Education:* Univs of London and Paris. *Career:* Lecturer in Islamic History, School of Oriental Studies, Univ. of London 1938; served in RAC and Intelligence Corps 1940–41; attached to Foreign Office 1941–45; Prof. of History of the Near and Middle East, Univ. of London 1949–74; Cleveland E. Dodge Prof. of Near Eastern Studies, Princeton Univ. 1974–86, Prof. Emer. 1986–; Dir Annenberg Research Inst., Philadelphia 1986–90; Visiting Prof. of History, Univ. of Calif. at LA 1955–56, Columbia Univ. 1960, Ind. Univ. 1963, Princeton Univ. 1964, Univ. of Calif. at Berkeley 1965, Coll. de France 1980, École des Hautes Études en Sciences Sociales, Paris 1983, 1988, Univ. of Chicago 1985; Visiting mem. Inst. for Advanced Study, Princeton Univ. 1969, mem. 1974–86; A. D. White Prof.-at-Large, Cornell Univ. 1984–90; mem. Bd of Dirs Institut für die Wissenschaften von Menschen, Vienna 1988; Jefferson Lecturer in the Humanities, US Nat. Endowment for the Humanities 1990; Tanner Lecturer, Brasenose Coll., Oxford 1990; Henry M. Jackson Memorial Lecturer (Seattle) 1992; mem. British Acad., American Philosophical Soc. 1973, American Acad. of Arts and Sciences 1983; American Oriental Soc., Corresp. mem. Inst. d'Egypte, Cairo 1969–, Inst. de France 1994–; Fellow, Univ. Coll., London 1976. *Publications:* The Origins of Ismā'ilism: A Study of the Historical Background of the

Fatimid Caliphate 1940, Turkey Today 1940, British Contributions to Arabic Studies 1941, Handbook of Diplomatic and Political Arabic 1947, Land of Enchanters (ed.) 1948, The Arabs in History 1950, Notes and Documents from the Turkish Archives: A Contribution to the History of the Jews in the Ottoman Empire 1952, Encyclopedia of Islam (co-ed.) 1956–86, The Emergence of Modern Turkey 1961, The Kingly Crown 1961, Historians of the Middle East (co-ed. with P. M. Holt) 1962, Istanbul and the Civilization of the Ottoman Empire 1963, The Middle East and the West 1964, The Assassins: A Radical Sect in Islam 1967, The Cambridge History of Islam (ed. with P. M. Holt and Ann K. S. Lambton, two vols) 1970, Race and Colour in Islam 1971, Islam in History: Ideas, Men and Events in the Middle East 1973, Islamic Civilization (ed.) 1974, Islam from the Prophet Muhammad to the Capture of Constantinople (ed. and trans., two vols) 1974, History: Remembered, Recovered, Invented 1975, Studies in Classical and Ottoman Islam: Seventh to Sixteenth Centuries 1976, The World of Islam: Faith, People, Culture (ed.) 1976, Population and Revenue in the Towns of Palestine in the Sixteenth Century (with Amnon Cohen) 1978, The Muslim Discovery of Europe 1982, Christians and Jews in the Ottoman Empire (two vols) 1982, The Jews of Islam 1984, Semites and Anti-Semites: An Inquiry into Conflict and Prejudice 1986, As Others See Us (co-ed.) 1986, The Political Language of Islam 1988, Race and Slavery in the Middle East: A Historical Enquiry 1990, Islam and the West 1993, The Shaping of the Modern Middle East 1994, Cultures in Conflict: Christians, Muslims and Jews in the Age of Discovery 1995, The Middle East: Two Thousand Years of History from the Rise of Christianity to the Present Day 1995, The Future of the Middle East 1997, The Multiple Identities of the Middle East 1998, A Middle East Mosaic: Fragments of Life, Letters and History 2000, Music of a Distant Drum, Classical Arabic, Persian, Turkish and Hebrew Poems 2001, What Went Wrong? Western Impact and Middle Eastern Response 2002, The Crisis of Islam: Holy War and Unholy Terror 2003, From Babel to Dragomans: Interpreting the Middle East 2004; numerous contribs to professional journals. *Honours:* Hon. mem. Turkish Historical Soc., Société Asiatique, Paris, Atatürk Acad. of History, Language and Culture, Ankara, Turkish Acad. of Sciences; Hon. Fellow SOAS, London 1986; 15 hon. doctorates including (Hebrew Univ., Jerusalem) 1974, (Tel-Aviv) 1979, (State Univ. of NY Binghamton, Univ. of Penn., Hebrew Union Coll., Cincinnati) 1987, (Univ. of Haifa, Yeshiva Univ., New York) 1991, (Bar-Ilan Univ.) 1992, (Brandeis) 1993, (Ben-Gurion, Ankara) 1996; Citation of Honour, Turkish Ministry of Culture 1973, Harvey Prize, Technion-Israel Inst. of Tech. 1978, Educ. Award for Outstanding Achievement in Promotion of American-Turkish Studies 1985, Atatürk Peace Prize 1998. *Address:* c/o Department of Near Eastern Studies, 110 Jones Hall, Princeton University, Princeton, NJ 08544, USA. *Telephone:* (609) 258-4280.

LEWIS, Charles (see Dixon, Roger)

LEWIS, David Levering, BA, MA, PhD; American academic and writer; *Julius Silver University Professor and Professor of History, New York University*; b. 25 May 1936, Little Rock, AR; m. 1st Sharon Siskind 1966 (divorced 1988); two s. one d.; m. 2nd Ruth Ann Stewart 1994; one d. *Education:* Fisk Univ., Columbia Univ., LSE. *Career:* Lecturer, Univ. of Ghana 1963–64, Howard Univ., Washington, DC 1964–65; Asst Prof., Univ. of Notre Dame 1965–66; Assoc. Prof., Morgan State Coll., Baltimore 1966–70, Federal City Coll., Washington, DC 1970–74; Prof. of History, Univ. of the District of Columbia 1974–80, Univ. of California at San Diego, La Jolla 1981–85; Martin Luther King Jr Prof. of History, Rutgers Univ. 1985–2003; Julius Silver Univ. Prof. and Prof. of History, New York Univ. 2003–; mem. African Studies Asscn, American Asscn of Univ. Profs, American Historical Asscn, Authors' Guild, Organization of American Historians, Soc. for French Historical Studies, Southern Historical Asscn, American Acad. of Arts and Sciences, American Philosophical Soc. *Publications:* Martin Luther King: A Critical Biography 1971, Prisoners of Honor: The Dreyfus Affair 1973, District of Columbia: A Bicentennial History 1977, When Harlem Was in Vogue: The Politics of the Arts in the Twenties and the Thirties 1981, Harlem Renaissance: Art of Black America (with others) 1987, The Race to Fashoda: European Colonialism and African Resistance in the Scramble for Africa 1988, W. E. B. Du Bois: Biography of a Race, 1868–1919 1994, The Portable Harlem Renaissance Reader (ed.) 1994, W. E. B. Du Bois: A Reader (ed.) 1995, W. E. B. Du Bois: The Fight for Equality and the American Century 2001. *Honours:* American Philosophical Soc. grant 1967, Social Science Research Council grant 1971, Nat. Endowment for the Humanities grant 1975, Woodrow Wilson Int. Center for Scholars Fellow 1977–78, Guggenheim Fellowship 1986, Bancroft Prize 1994, Ralph Waldo Emerson Prize 1994, Pulitzer Prizes for Biography 1994, 2001, Francis Parkman Prize 1994, Fellow John D. and Catherine T. MacArthur Foundation 1999. *Address:* c/o Department of History, Van Dyck Hall, Rutgers University, New Brunswick, NJ 08903 (office); 784 Columbus Avenue, Apt 100, New York, NY 10025, USA (home). *Fax:* (845) 758-0215 (home). *E-mail:* david.levering.lewis@nyu.edu (office); dleveringlewis@msn.com (home).

LEWIS, Desmond Francis, BA; British poet and writer; b. 18 Jan. 1948, Colchester, Essex, England; m. Denise Jean Woolgar 1970; one s. one d. *Education:* Lancaster University. *Publications:* contrib. hundreds of prose poems and stories to various UK and US publications.

LEWIS, Gwyneth, MA, DPhil, FRSL; British poet and writer; b. 1959, Cardiff, Wales; m. Leighton. *Education:* Girton Coll., Cambridge, Univ. of Harvard, USA, Columbia Univ., USA, Balliol Coll., Oxford. *Career:* fmr freelance journalist in New York, USA and documentary prod. and dir, BBC Wales;

composed the bilingual inscription on the front of Cardiff's Wales Millennium Centre, opened in 2004; Nat. Poet of Wales 2005–06. *Publications:* Redflight/Barcud (libretto), Llwybrau bywyd (poems) 1977, Ar y groesfford (poems) 1978, Sonedau Redsa a Cherddi Eraill 1990, Parables and Faxes (poems) (Aldeburgh Poetry Festival Prize) 1995, Cyfrif Un ac Un yn Dri (poems) 1996, Zero Gravity (poems) 1998, Y Llofrudd Iaith (poems) (Welsh Arts Council Book of the Year) 2000, Sunbathing in the Rain: A Cheerful Book About Depression (non-fiction) 2002, Keeping Mum (poems) 2003, The Most Beautiful Man from the Sea (oratorio) 2005, Two in a Boat: A Marital Voyage 2005, Tair mewn Un (poems) 2005, Chaotic Angels (poems) 2005, Dolffin (libretto) 2006. *Honours:* Hon. Fellow, Univ. of Cardiff 2005; Harkness Fellow 1982, Eric Gregory Award 1987, Nat. Endowment for Science, Technology and the Arts Fellowship 2002, Wellcome Trust Sciart Award. *Literary Agent:* c/o Zoe Waldie, Rogers, Coleridge & White Literary Agency, 20 Powis Mews, London, W11 1JN, England. *Telephone:* (20) 7221-3717. *Fax:* (20) 7229-9084. *Website:* www.rcwlitagency.co.uk. *Telephone:* (20) 7792-3485 (office). *E-mail:* gl@gwynethlewis.com (office). *Website:* www.gwynethlewis.com (office).

LEWIS, Jeremy Morley, MA, FRSL; British writer; b. 15 March 1942, Salisbury, Wiltshire; m. Petra Lewis 1968, two d. *Education:* Trinity Coll., Dublin and Sussex Univ. *Career:* Ed., Andre Deutsch Ltd 1969–70, OUP 1977–79; Literary Agent, AP Watt Ltd 1970–76; Dir, Chatto and Windus 1979–89; Deputy Ed., London Magazine 1991–94; Editorial Consultant, Peters, Fraser & Dunlop Group Ltd 1994–2002; Commissioning Ed., The Oldie 1997–; Consultant Ed., Literary Review 2004–; mem. R. S. Surtees Soc. (Sec.). *Publications:* Playing for Time 1987, Chatto Book of Office Life 1992, Kindred Spirits 1995, Cyril Connolly: A Life 1997, Tobias Smollett 2003, Penguin Special: The Life and Times of Allen Lane 2005. *Literary Agent:* Aitken Alexander Associates Ltd, 18–21 Cavaye Place, London, SW10 9PT, England. *Telephone:* (20) 7373-8672. *Fax:* (20) 7373-6002. *E-mail:* reception@aitkenalexander.co.uk. *Website:* www.aitkenalexander.co.uk. *Address:* c/o The Oldie, 65 Newman Street, London, W1T 3EG, England.

LEWIS, Mervyn (see Frewer, Glyn Mervyn Louis)

LEWIS, Russell T., BA, JD; American newspaper executive; b. 1948. *Education:* State Univ. of New York at Stony Brook, Brooklyn Law School. *Career:* joined New York Times as a copy boy, while attending coll. 1966; litigation assoc. Cahill, Gordon and Reindel 1973; staff attorney New York Times legal dept 1977; Pres., Gen. Man. The New York Times, New York 1993–97, Pres., CEO 1997–2004 (retd). *Honours:* Acad. of Man. Distinguished Exec. of the Year 2002, American Lung Asscn of NY Life & Breath Award 2002, Nat. Human Relations Award, American Jewish Cttee 2003. *Address:* c/o The New York Times, 229 West 43rd Street, New York, NY 10036, USA (office).

LEWIS, Anthony (Tony) Robert, CBE, DL, MA; British sports commentator, journalist, writer and fmr cricketer; *Director, Welsh National Opera*; b. 6 July 1938, Swansea, Wales; s. of Wilfrid Lewis and Florence Lewis (née Flower); m. Joan Pritchard 1962; two d. *Education:* Neath Grammar School, Christ's Coll. Cambridge. *Career:* right-hand batsman; teams: Glamorgan, Cambridge Univ.; double blue and debut at int. level; led Glamorgan to their second Co. Championship title 1969; played in nine Tests (eight as Capt.) scoring 457 runs (average 32.64); 20,495 first-class runs (average 32.4) including 30 hundreds; retd 1974; became cricket commentator and journalist; Pres. Marylebone Cricket Club (MCC) 1998–2000, secured admission of women into MCC Club, Trustee 2002–; fmr Chair. Glamorgan Co. Cricket Club (CCC), Pres. 1987–93, 2003–; Chair. Welsh Tourist Bd 1992–2000; led successful Welsh campaign to host 2010 Ryder Cup; Chair. (non-exec.) World Snooker Ltd 2003–; Dir Welsh Nat. Opera 2003–. *Publications:* A Summer of Cricket 1976, Playing Days 1985, Double Century 1987, Cricket in Many Lands 1991, MCC Masterclass 1994, Taking Fresh Guard 2003. *Honours:* Hon. Fellow, St David's Univ. Coll., Lampeter 1993, Univ. of Glamorgan 1995, Univ. of Wales, Swansea 1996, Univ. of Cardiff 1999. *Address:* Castellau, Near Llantrisant, Mid Glamorgan CF72 8LP, Wales (home); c/o Angie Bainbridge Management, 3 New Cottages, The Holt, Washington, West Sussex, RH20 4AW, England (office). *Telephone:* (1903) 8933748 (office). *Fax:* (1903) 891320 (office). *E-mail:* angie.bainbridge@btopenworld.com (office).

LEWIS, Warn B., Jr, BA, MA, PhD; American academic and writer; b. 8 May 1938, Minneapolis, Minnesota; m. Erika Cornehl 1961, three d. *Education:* Amherst College, University of Minnesota at Twin Cities, University of Pennsylvania. *Career:* Asst Prof. of German, University of Iowa, Iowa City, 1968–71; Asst Prof., 1971–73, Assoc. Prof. of German, 1973–99, Prof. of German, 1999–, University of Georgia, Athens; mem. International Brecht Society; Modern Language Asscn of America; German Studies Asscn; Society for Exile Studies; Eugene O'Neill Society; Northeast MLA, Chair., German-American Literary Relations, 1985–86, 1989–90; South Atlantic MLA. *Publications:* Poetry and Exile: An Annotated Bibliography of the Works and Criticism of Paul Zech, 1975; Eugene O'Neill: The German Reception of America's First Dramatist, 1984; German and International Perspectives on the Spanish Civil War: The Aesthetics of Partisanship (contributor), 1992; Paul Zech's The Bird in Langfoot's Belfry (ed.), 1993; The Ironic Dissident: Frank Wedekind in the View of His Critics, 1997. *Contributions:* Comparative Literature Studies; Modern Language Studies; German Quarterly; German Life and Letters; Modern Drama. *Honours:* Fellow, Alexander von Humboldt Foundation, 1979–80. *Address:* 490 S Milledge Avenue, Athens, GA 30605, USA. *E-mail:* wlewis@arches.uga.edu.

LEWIS, William (Bill) Edward; British poet, writer, editor, artist and storyteller and mythographer; b. 1 Aug. 1953, Maidstone, Kent; m. Ann Frances Morris 1981. *Career:* Writer-in-Residence, Brighton Festival 1985; Creative Writing Tutor, HM Prison, Maidstone 1984–86; teacher (mythology courses), Kent Children's Univ. and Adult Educ. 1994–2003; Guest Lecturer on Myth, Univ. of Eastern Connecticut, Univ. of Rhode Island, USA; Founder-mem. Medway Poets, Stuckist Group. *Exhibitions include:* photography: Fire in the Dust, The Brook Chatham 1990, Faces from Turtle Island, Medway Festival 1993; paintings: Stuck! Stuck! Stuck!, Gallery 108, London 1999, The First Art Show of the New Millennium, Salon des Arts, London 2000, The Resignation of Sir Nicholas Serota, Gallery 108, London, The Real Turner Prize Show, The Pure Gallery, London 2000, Vote Stuckist, Artbank and The Fridge Gallery, London 2001, Stuck up North, Newcastle Arts Centre, The Stuckists, Musée d'Adzac, Paris 2001 and 2005, Punk Victorian, Walker Gallery, Liverpool 2004. *Recordings:* Blackberry Ghosts 1994, The Medway Poets Album 1998, Collected Poems Vol. 1 2005, Collected Prose Vol. 1 2005. *Illustrations:* The Winter Solstice by John Matthews, The Green Man by John Matthews. *Publications:* Poems 1975–83 1983, Night Clinic 1984, Communion 1986, Rage Without Anger 1987, Skyclad Christ 1992, Paradigm Shift (ed.) 1992, Coyote Cosmos (short stories) 1994, Translation Women 1996, Industry of Letters, The Book of North Kent Writers (co-ed.) 1996, The Wine of Connecting (poems) 1996, Intellect of the Heart (poems) 1997, Shattered English: Complete North Kent Poems 1998, Leaving the Autoroute (short stories) 1999, Beauty is the Beast (poems) 2000, Blackberry Ghosts: Collected Poems 1975–2003 2003, The Book of Misplaced but Imperishable Names (prose) 2003, The Medway Scene (co-ed. and contrib.), The Arts in Medway Vols I and II (co-ed. and contrib.) 2004; contrib. to Best Horror and Fantasy 1997, 1998, The Green Man 2003, Jungewelt, numerous anthologies, reviews and journals. *Address:* The Medway Delta Press, PO Box 479, Chatham, Kent, ME4 5WX, England (office). *E-mail:* medwaydeltapress@yahoo.co.uk (office). *Website:* www.medwaydeltapress.com (office). *Telephone:* (1634) 827308 (home).

LEWIS-SMITH, Anne Elizabeth, (Emily Devereaux, A. McCormick, Quilla Slade); British poet, writer, editor and publisher; b. 14 April 1925, London, England; m. Peter Lewis-Smith 1944; one s. two d. *Career:* Asst Ed. 1967–83, Ed. 1983–91, Envoi; Ed., Aerostat 1973–78, British Asscn of Friends of Museums Yearbook 1985–91; Publisher, Envoi Poets Publications 1986–; mem. PEN. *Publications:* Seventh Bridge 1963, The Beginning 1964, Flesh and Flowers 1967, Dandelion Flavour 1971, Dinas Head 1980, Places and Passions 1986, In the Dawn 1987, Circling Sound 1996, Feathers, Fancies and Feelings 2000, Off Duty! 2006, Every Seventh Wave 2006; contrib. to newspapers and magazines. *Honours:* Tissadier Diploma for Services to Int. Aviation, Debbie Warley Award for Services to Int. Aviation, Dorothy Tutin Award for Services to Poetry. *Address:* Pen Ffordd, Newport, Pembrokeshire SA42 0QT, Wales.

LEWYCKA, Marina, DPhil; British writer; *Lecturer in Media Studies, Sheffield Hallam University*; b. Kiel, Germany; m.; one d. *Education:* Keele, York, Leeds, Sheffield Hallam Univs. *Career:* b. of Ukrainian parents in refugee camp in Germany at the end of World War II; moved to England 1950s; currently Lecturer in Media Studies Sheffield Hallam Univ. *Publications:* A Short History of Tractors in Ukrainian (novel) (Bollinger Everyman Wodehouse Prize for comic fiction 2005, Saga Award for Wit 2005, British Book Awards Waterstones Newcomer of the Year 2006) 2005, Two Caravans 2007. *Literary Agent:* c/o Bill Hamilton, A. M. Heath & Company Ltd, 6 Warwick Court, Holborn, London, WC1R 5DJ, England. *Telephone:* (20) 7242-2811. *Fax:* (20) 7242-2711. *Website:* www.amheath.com. *Address:* c/o School of Cultural Studies, Sheffield Hallam University, Psalter Lane Campus, Sheffield, S11 8UZ, England.

LEY, Alice Chetwynd, DipSoc; British novelist and teacher; b. 12 Oct. 1913, Halifax, Yorkshire, England; m. Kenneth James Ley 1945, two s. *Education:* Univ. of London. *Career:* Tutor in Creative Writing, Harrow Coll. of Further Education 1962–84, Lecturer in Sociology and Social History 1968–71; mem. Jane Austen Soc., Romantic Novelists' Asscn (chair. 1971–73, hon. life mem. 1987–), Soc. of Women Writers and Journalists. *Publications:* The Jewelled Snuff Box 1959, The Guinea Stamp (aka The Courting of Joanna) 1961, Master of Liversedge (aka The Master and the Maiden) 1966, The Clandestine Betrothal 1967, The Toast of the Town 1969, A Season at Brighton 1971, Tenant of Chesdene Manor (aka Beloved Diana) 1974, An Advantageous Marriage 1977, The Sentimental Spy 1977, A Regency Scandal 1979, A Conformable Wife 1981, A Reputation Dies 1982, The Intrepid Miss Haydon 1983, A Fatal Assignation 1987, Masquerade of Vengeance 1989. *Honours:* Gilchrist Award 1962.

LEYS, Simon (see Ryckmans, Pierre)

LEYTON, Sophie (see Walsh, Sheila)

L'HEUREUX, John Clarke, AB, LPhil, LTheol, MA; American academic and writer; b. 26 Oct. 1934, South Hadley, MA; m. Joan Ann Polston 1971. *Education:* Weston College, Boston College, Woodstock College, Harvard University. *Career:* Writer-in-Residence, Georgetown University, 1964–65, Regis College, 1968–69; Ordained Roman Catholic Priest, 1966, laicized, 1971; Staff Ed., 1968–69, Contributing Ed., 1969–83, The Atlantic; Visiting Prof., Hamline University, 1971, Tufts College, 1971–72; Visiting Asst Prof., Harvard University, 1973; Asst Prof., 1973–79, Dir, Creative Writing Programme, 1976–89, Assoc. Prof., 1979–81, Prof., 1981–, Lane Prof. of the

Humanities, 1985–90, Stanford University. *Publications:* Quick as Dandelions, 1964; Rubrics for a Revolution, 1967; Picnic in Babylon, 1967; One Eye and a Measuring Rod, 1968; No Place for Hiding, 1971; Tight White Collar, 1972; The Clang Birds, 1972; Family Affairs, 1974; Jessica Fayer, 1976; Desires, 1981; A Woman Run Mad, 1988; Comedians, 1990; An Honorable Profession, 1991; The Shrine at Altamira, 1992; The Handmaid of Desire, 1996; Having Everything, 1999; The Miracle, 2002.

LHOMEAU, Franck; French editor and publisher; *Founder Director, Editions Joseph K*; b. 1955, Nantes. *Education:* Univ. de Paris VIII. *Career:* co-f. Le Temps Singulier publishing house –1982; f. Editions Joseph K 1994–; created Temps noir review 1998–. *Publications:* Marcel Proust à la recherche d'un éditeur (with Alain Coelho) 1988, Dictionnaire des littératures policières 2003. *Address:* c/o Editions Joseph K, 21 rue Geoffrey Drouet, 44000 Nantes, France.

LI, Bihua; Taiwanese novelist and screenwriter. *Publications:* Her Pao chu yen hua 1983, The Last Princess of Manchuria 1992, Farewell my Concubine (also co-writer of screenplay) 1993. *Address:* c/o HarperCollins Publishing, 10 E 53rd Street, New York, NY 10022, USA. *Website:* www.harpercollins.com.

LI, Renchen; Chinese journalist; b. Oct. 1941, Changyi County, Shandong Prov. *Education:* Fudan Univ. *Career:* mem. CCP 1975–; Features and Photos Service, Comm. for Cultural Relations with Foreign Countries 1964–66; Ed. Huizhou Bao, Anhui Prov., Ed. People's Daily and Deputy Dir Commentary Dept People's Daily 1983–86; Deputy Ed.-in-Chief, Renmin Ribao (People's Daily) 1986–; writes under pen name Chen Ping. *Address:* Renmin Ribao, 2 Jin Tai Xi Lu, Choo Yong Men Nai, Beijing 100733, People's Republic of China. *Telephone:* (1) 65092121. *Fax:* (1) 65091982.

LI, Xiao; Chinese writer; b. 1950, Shanghai; s. of Ba Jin. *Education:* Fudan Univ. *Publications:* novels: Tianqiao (The Overpass) 1989, Zuihou de wancan (The Last Supper) 1993, Yao a yao yao dao waipo qiao 1995, Sishi er li (A Man is Established at Forty) 1996; over 20 short stories published. *Address:* c/o Ministry of Culture, 10 Chaoyangmen Bei Jie, Dongcheng Qu, Beijing 100020, People's Republic of China.

LIBBY, Ronald Theodore, BA, MA, PhD; American academic and writer; *Professor of Political Science, University of North Florida*; b. 20 Nov. 1941, Los Angeles, Calif.; two d. *Education:* Washington State Univ., Pullman, Univ. of Washington, Seattle. *Career:* Lecturer, Univ. of Botswana, Lesotho, and Swaziland 1973–75, Malawi 1975–76, Zambia 1976–79; Visiting Asst Prof., Univ. of Notre Dame 1981–83; Sr Lecturer, Univ. of the West Indies, Jamaica 1983–85, Victoria Univ. of Wellington, NZ 1987–89; Visiting Assoc. Prof., Northwestern Univ. 1985–86; Sr Research Fellow, ANU 1986–87; Prof. and Chair. Dept of Political Science, Southwest State Univ., Marshall, Minn. 1989–96, Saint Joseph's Univ., Phila 1996–2000; Prof. of Political Science, Univ. of N Florida, Jacksonville 2000–. *Publications:* Towards an Africanized US Policy for Southern Africa 1980, The Politics of Economic Power in Southern Africa 1987, Hawke's Law: The Politics of Mining and Aboriginal Land Rights in Australia 1989, Protecting Markets: US Policy and the World Grain Trade 1992, Eco-Wars: Political Campaigns and Social Movements 1999, Treating Doctors as Drug Dealers 2005; contrib. to scholarly books and journals. *Honours:* grants, Visiting Research Scholar, Univ. of California at Irvine 1972, Choice magazine Outstanding Academic Book 1990. *Address:* Department of Political Science and Public Administration, University of North Florida, 4567 St Johns Bluff Road, South Jacksonville, FL 32224-2645 (office); 117 Turtle Bay Lane, Ponte Verde Beach, FL 32082, USA (home). *Telephone:* (904) 620-1927 (office); (904) 808-4612 (home). *Fax:* (904) 620-2979 (office); (904) 824-5913 (home). *E-mail:* rlibby@unf.edu (office); rtl2129@aol.com (home). *Website:* www.unf.edu/~rlibby (office).

LIBERAKI, Margarita; Greek novelist and dramatist; b. 1919, Athens; d. of Themistuclis and Sapho Liberaki; m. Georges Karapanos 1941 (divorced); one d. *Education:* Athens Univ. *Career:* lives in Paris and Greece, writes in Greek and French; plays performed at Festival d'Avignon, Festival of Athens, Nat. Theatre, Athens. *Publications:* The Trees 1947, The Straw Hats 1950, Trois étés 1950, The Other Alexander 1952, The Mystery 1976; plays: Kandaules' Wife 1955, The Danaids 1956, L'autre Alexandre 1957, Le saint prince 1959, La lune a faim 1961, Sparagmos 1965, Le bain de mer 1967, Erotica 1970, Zoe 1985; film scripts: Magic City 1953, Phaedra 1961, Three Summers (TV series) 1996, Diaspora 1999. *Address:* 7 rue de L'Eperon, 75006 Paris, France; 2 Strat. Sindesmou, 106 73 Athens, Greece. *Telephone:* 1-46-33-05-92 (Paris).

LICHTENSTEIN, Nelson, PhD; American historian; b. 15 Nov. 1944, Frederick, MD; m. Eileen Boris 1979, one s. *Education:* University of California at Berkeley. *Career:* Asst Prof., Assoc. Prof., Catholic University of America, 1981–89; Prof., University of Virginia, 1989–; mem. American Historical Asscn; Organization of American Historians. *Publications:* Political Profiles: The Kennedy Years (ed.), 1976; Political Profiles: The Johnson Years (ed.), 1976; Labor's War at Home: The CIO in World War II, 1982; On the Line: Essays in the History of Auto Work (co-ed.), 1989; Major Problems in the History of American Workers: Documents and Essays (ed.), 1991; Industrial Democracy in America: The Ambiguous Promise (co-ed.), 1993; The Most Dangerous Man in Detroit: Walter Reuther and the Fate of American Labor, 1995; The United States, 1940–2000, 2000.

LICKONA, Thomas Edward, BA, MA, PhD; American developmental psychologist, academic and writer; b. 4 April 1943, Poughkeepsie, NY; m. Judith Barker 1966, two s. *Education:* Siena College, Ohio University, SUNY at Albany. *Career:* Instructor, SUNY at Albany, 1968–70; Asst Prof., 1970–75, Assoc. Prof., 1975–82, Prof. of Education, 1982–, SUNY at Cortland; Visiting Prof., Harvard University, 1978–79, Boston University, 1979–80; numerous radio and television talk show appearances; mem. Asscn for Moral Education; Character Counts Coalition, advisory board; Character Education Partnership, board of dirs; Medical Institute for Sexual Health, advisory board. *Publications:* Open Education: Increasing Alternatives for Teachers and Children (ed. with Jessie Adams, Ruth Nickse, and David Young), 1973; Moral Development and Behavior: Theory, Research, and Social Issues (ed.), 1976; Raising Good Children: Helping Your Child Through the Stages of Moral Development, 1983; Educating for Character: How Our Schools Can Teach Respect and Responsibility, 1991; Sex, Love and You (with Judith Lickona and William Boudreau), 1994. Contributions: journals and magazines. *Honours:* Distinguished Alumni Award, SUNY at Albany; Christopher Award, 1992.

LIDDLE, Peter Hammond, BA, PGCE, MLitt, PhD, FRHistS; British historian, writer and archivist; *Director, The Second World War Experience Centre, Leeds*; b. 26 Dec. 1934, Sunderland, England. *Education:* Univ. of Sheffield, Univ. of Nottingham, Loughborough Coll. of Physical Education, Univ. of Newcastle, Univ. of Leeds. *Career:* History Teacher, Havelock School, Sunderland 1957; Head, History Dept, Gateacre Comprehensive School, Liverpool 1958–67; Lecturer, Notre Dame Coll. of Educ. 1967; Lecturer in History, Sunderland Polytechnic 1967–70, Sr Lecturer 1970–88; Keeper of the Liddle Collection, Univ. of Leeds 1988–99; Dir, The Second World War Experience Centre, Leeds 1999–; mem. British Audio Visual Trust, British Military History Comm. *Publications:* Men of Gallipoli 1976, World War One: Personal Experience Material for Use in Schools 1977, Testimony of War 1914–18 1979, The Sailor's War 1914–18 1985, Gallipoli: Pens, Pencils and Cameras at War 1985, 1916: Aspects of Conflict 1985, Home Fires and Foreign Fields 1985, The Airman's War 1914–18 1987, The Soldier's War 1914–18 1988, Voices of War 1988, The Battle of the Somme 1992, The Worst Ordeal: Britons at Home and Abroad 1914–18 1994, Facing Armageddon: The First World War Experienced (co-ed. and contributor) 1996, Passchendaele in Perspective: The Third Battle of Ypres (ed. and contributor) 1997, At the Eleventh Hour (co-ed. and contributor) 1998, For Five Shillings a Day (co-ed. and contributor) 2000, The Great World War, 1914–45 (co-ed. and contributor), two vols 2000–01, D Day: By Those Who Were There 2004; contrib. to journals and books; Founder and Ed. of following journals: The Poppy and the Owl 1988–99, Everyone's War 1999–. *Honours:* MLitt Univ. of Newcastle 1975, PhD Univ. of Leeds 1997; Distinguished Lecturer Sam Houston State Univ., Huntsville, TX 2003. *Address:* The Second World War Experience Centre, 5 Feast Field, Horsforth, Leeds LS18 4TJ (office); Prospect House, 39 Leeds Rd, Rawdon, Leeds LS19 6NW, England (home). *Telephone:* (113) 2584993 (office); (113) 2505829 (home). *Fax:* (113) 2582557 (office). *E-mail:* enquiries@war-experience.org (office); peterhliddle@yahoo.co.uk (home). *Website:* www.war-experience.org (office).

LIDDY, James, (Daniel Reeves), BA, MA; Irish academic, poet and writer; *Professor of English, University of Wisconsin at Milwaukee*; b. 1 July 1934, Dublin. *Education:* Nat. Univ. of Ireland, Barrister-at-Law King's Inns, Dublin. *Career:* Visiting Lecturer, San Francisco State Coll. 1967–68; Visiting Asst Prof., SUNY at Binghamton 1969, Univ. of Wisconsin at Parkside 1972–73; Visiting Lecturer, Lewis and Clark Coll., Portland, OR 1970, Univ. Coll., Galway 1973–74; Asst Prof., Denison Univ., OH 1970–71; Lecturer, Delgado Community Coll., New Orleans 1975; Visiting Asst Prof. 1976, Lecturer and poet-in-residence 1976–80, Asst Prof. 1981–82, Assoc. Prof. 1982–88, Prof. of English 1988–, Univ. of Wisconsin at Milwaukee; mem. Aosdána, Irish Acad. of Arts and Letters. *Publications:* poetry: In a Blue Smoke 1964, Blue Mountain 1968, A Life of Stephen Dedalus 1968, A Munster Song of Love and War 1969, Orpheus in the Ice Cream Parlour 1975, Corca Bascin 1977, Comyn's Lay 1979, Moon and Starr Moments 1982, At the Grave of Father Sweetman 1984, A White Thought in a White Shade 1987, In the Slovak Bowling Alley 1990, Art is Not for Grownups 1990, Trees Warmer Than Green: Notes Towards a Video of Avondale House 1991, Collected Poems 1994, Epitaphery 1997, Gold Set Dancing 2000, I Only Know That I Love Strength in My Friends and Enemies 2003, The Doctor's House (autobiog.) 2005; other: Esau My Kingdom for a Drink 1962 Patrick Kavanagh: An Introduction to His Work 1971, Baudelaire's Bar Flowers (trans.) 1975, You Can't Jog for Jesus: Jack Kerouac as a Religious Writer 1985, Young Men Go Walking (novella) 1986, The Doctor's House, an autobiography 2004; contribs to books and journals. *Honours:* Univ. of Wisconsin at Parkside Teaching Award 1973, Council of Wisconsin Writers Prize for Poetry 1995. *Address:* c/o Department of English and Comparative Literature, University of Wisconsin at Milwaukee, PO Box 413, Milwaukee, WI 53201, USA. *Telephone:* (414) 229-5441 (office); (414) 962-6165 (home). *E-mail:* liddy@uwm.edu (office).

LIDSTONE, John Barrie Joseph, FCIM; British writer and business executive; b. 21 July 1929; m. Primrose Vivien 1957; one d. *Education:* Univ. of Manchester, RAF Education Officers' Course. *Career:* nat. service, RAF 1947–48; English Master, Repton 1949–52; Shell-Mex and BP and Assoc. cos 1952–62; Deputy Man. Dir Vicon Agricultural Machinery Ltd 1962–63; Dir and Gen. Man. Marketing Selections Ltd 1969–72; Dir Marketing Improvements Group plc 1968–93, Dir and Gen. Man. 1972–74, Deputy Man. Dir 1974–88, Deputy Chair. 1988–89, Dir (non-exec.) 1989–93; mem. Chemical and Allied Products Industrial Training Bd 1975–79, Nat. Inter-Active Video Centre 1988–90; Dartnell lecture tours, USA 1978–82; mem. UK Management Consultancies Asscn 1978–88 (Chair. 1986–87); Ed. Lidstorian 1985–88; mem. Nat. Exec. Cttee Chartered Inst. of Marketing 1985–90; Dir (non-exec.) Kalamazoo plc 1986–91, North Hampshire Trust Co. Ltd 1986–93, St Nicholas' School Fleet Educational Trust Ltd 1982–90, 1995–96; Sr Visiting Lecturer, Univ. of Surrey 1990–98; gave expert evidence to House of Commons Public Admin Select Cttee on reform of honours system 2004 (included in report, A Matter of Honour: Reforming the Honours System); mem. Court of Assts, Guild of Man. Consultants 1993; Marketing Ed. Pharm Times 1994–; mem. BAFTA; Fellow, Inst. of Man. Consultants, Inst. of Man. *Films:* film and video technical adviser and scriptwriter for The Persuaders 1975, Negotiating Profitable Sales 1979, Training Salesmen on the Job 1981, Marketing for Managers 1985, Marketing Today 1985, Reaching Agreement and Interviewing 1987. *Publications:* Training Salesmen on the Job 1975, Recruiting and Selecting Successful Salesmen 1976, Negotiating Profitable Sales 1977, Motivating Your Sales Force 1978, Making Effective Presentations 1985, The Sales Presentation (co-author) 1985, Profitable Selling 1986, Marketing Planning for the Pharmaceutical Industry 1987, Manual of Sales Negotiation 1991, Manual of Marketing for University of Surrey 1991, Beyond the Pay Packet 1992, Face the Press 1992, Presentation and Media Planning for the Pharmaceutical Industry 2003; contrib. chapters to The Best of Dilemma and Decision 1985, Marketing in the Service Industries 1985, Marketing Handbook (third edn) 1989, Gower Book of Management Skills (second edn) 1992, The Director's Manual 1992, The Marketing Book (third edn) 1994, Ivanhoe Guide to Management Consultants 1994, International Encyclopedia of Business and Management 1988, The Reform of the Honours System (Churchill Lecture) 1998; contrib. articles to The Times, Sunday Times, Daily Telegraph, Sunday Telegraph, Financial Times, Observer, Long Range Planning, International Management, Management Today, Marketing, Marketing Week. *Honours:* Freeman of City of London, Liveryman Worshipful Co. of Marketers; US Industrial Film Festival Award for Creative Excellence 1982.

LIEBER, Robert James, BA, PhD; American writer; *Professor of Government and International Affairs, Georgetown University*; b. Chicago, Ill. *Education:* Univ. of Wisconsin, Univ. of Chicago, Harvard Univ. *Career:* Asst Prof., Univ. of California, Davis 1968–72, Assoc. Prof. 1972–77, Chair. Dept of Political Science 1975–76, 1977–80, Prof. 1977–81; Visiting Prof., Fudan Univ., Shanghai, People's Repub. of China 1988; Postdoctoral Fellow, St Antony's Coll., Oxford, UK 1969–70; Research Assoc., Center for Int. Affairs, Harvard Univ. 1974–75; Fellow, Woodrow Wilson Int. Center for Scholars, Washington, DC 1980–81, 1999–2000; Prof. of Govt and Int. Affairs, Georgetown Univ., Washington, DC 1982–, Chair. Dept of Govt 1990–96, Acting Chair. Dept of Psychology 1997–99; mem. American Political Science Asscn, Council on Foreign Relations. *Publications:* British Politics and European Unity: Parties, Elites, and Pressure Groups 1970, Theory and World Politics 1972, Contemporary Politics: Europe (co-author) 1976, Oil and the Middle East War 1976, Eagle Entangled: US Foreign Policy in a Complex World (co-ed. and contrib.) 1979, Will Europe Fight for Oil? (ed.) 1983, Eagle Defiant: US Foreign Policy in the 1980s (co-ed. and contrib.) 1983, The Oil Decade: Conflict and Cooperation in the West 1986, Eagle Resurgent?: The Reagan Era in American Foreign Policy (co-ed. and contrib.) 1987, Eagle in a New World: American Grand Strategy in the Post-Cold War Era (co-ed. and contrib.) 1992, Eagle Adrift: American Foreign Policy at the End of the Century (ed. and contrib.) 1997, No Common Power: Understanding International Relations (fourth edn) 2001, Eagle Rules? Foreign Policy and American Primacy in the 21st Century (ed. and contrib.) 2002, The American Era: Power and Strategy for the 21st Century (Book of the Year Award (Bronze) in Political Science, Fore Word magazine 2005) 2005, (ed.) 2007; contrib. to scholarly books, professional journals and gen. periodicals. *Honours:* William Jennings Bryan Prize for Best Undergraduate Essay on a Political Subject, Univ. of Wisconsin, Council on Foreign Relations Int. Affairs Fellowship 1973–74, Guggenheim Fellowship 1973–74, Rockefeller Int. Relations Fellowship 1978–79, Ford Foundation grant 1981, Public Policy Scholar, Woodrow Wilson Int. Center for Scholars 1999–2000, 21st Annual Jerome Nemer Lecturer, The Casden Inst., Univ. of Southern California 2001. *Address:* Department of Government, Georgetown University, Washington, DC 20057-1034, USA (office). *Telephone:* (202) 687-5920 (office). *E-mail:* lieberr@georgetown.edu (office). *Website:* explore.georgetown.edu/people/lieberr/?Action=View&PageTemplateID=95.

LIEBERMAN, Herbert Henry, AM; American novelist, playwright and ; b. 22 Sept. 1933, New Rochelle, NY; m. Judith Barsky 1963; one d. *Education:* City College, CUNY, Columbia Univ. *Career:* mem. Mystery Writers of America, Int. Asscn of Crime Writers. *Plays:* Matty and the Moron and Madonna, Tigers in Red Weather. *Publications:* The Adventures of Dolphin Green, 1967; Crawlspace, 1971; The Eighth Square, 1973; Brilliant Kids, 1975; City of the Dead, 1976; The Climate of Hell, 1978; Nightcall from a Distant Time Zone, 1982; Night Bloom, 1984; The Green Train, 1986; Shadow Dancers, 1989; Sandman Sleep, 1993; The Girl with the Botticelli Eyes, 1996; The Concierge 1998; The Vagabond of Holmby Park, 2003. *Honours:* First Prize for Playwriting, Univ. of Chicago, 1963; Guggenheim Fellowship, 1964; Grand Prix de Littérature Policière, Paris, 1978. *Address:* c/o Georges Borchardt, 136 East 57th Street, New York, NY 10022, USA. *Telephone:* (212) 753-5785 (office).

LIEBERMAN, Laurence, BA, MA; American academic, poet, writer and editor; *Professor of English and Creative Writing, University of Illinois at Urbana-Champaign*; b. 16 Feb. 1935, Detroit, Mich.; m. Bernice Braun 1956;

one s. two d. *Education:* Univ. of Michigan, Univ. of California. *Career:* Assoc. Prof. of English, Coll. of the Virgin Islands 1964–68; Assoc. Prof. of English, Univ. of Illinois at Urbana-Champaign 1968–70, Prof. of English and Creative Writing 1970–; Poetry Ed., Univ. of Illinois Press 1971–; mem. Acad. of American Poets, Associated Writing Programs, Poetry Soc. of America. *Publications:* The Unblinding (poems) 1968, The Achievement of James Dickey 1968, The Osprey Suicides (poems) 1973, Unassigned Frequencies: American Poetry in Review 1964–77 1977, God's Measurements 1980, Eros at the World Kite Pageant: Poems 1979–83 1983, The Mural of Wakeful Sleep (poems) 1985, The Creole Mephistopheles (poems) 1990, New and Selected Poems: 1962–92 1993, The St Kitts Monkey Feuds (poem) 1995, Beyond the Muse of Memory: Essays on Contemporary American Poets 1995, Dark Songs: Slave House and Synagogue 1996, Compass of the Dying (poems) 1998, The Regatta in the Skies: Selected Long Poems 1999, Flight from the Mother Stone 2000, Hour of the Mango Black Moon 2004; contribs to anthologies, reviews, journals and magazines. *Honours:* Yaddo Foundation Fellowship 1964, Illinois Arts Council Fellowship 1981, Nat. Endowment for the Arts Fellowship 1986–87, Jerome J. Shestack Poetry Prize, American Poetry Review 1986–87. *Address:* 1304 Eliot Drive, Urbana Urbana, IL 61801, USA. *Telephone:* (217) 333-2390 (office). *Fax:* (217) 333-4321 (office).

LIEBERMANN, Berta R.; Austrian poet; b. 16 March 1921, Glashütten; m. Albert Liebermann 1967. *Publications include:* Heimweh, Planet der Glücklichkeit, Traumnetz der silberner Spinne, Spätlicht, Verwehte Spuren, Rückruf der Vergangenheit, Roter Oleander, Urlaute der Schöpfung, Urwind der Frühe, Verstreute Blüten III, Gespräche mit einem Engel; contribs to newspapers on the arts. *Honours:* Hon. DLitt (Albert Einstein Acad., Mo., USA); *Salsomaggiore Award 1982, Albert Einstein Medal (USA) 1990. Address:* Kieferbachstraße 6, 83088 Kiefersfelden, Germany. *Telephone:* (8033) 8104.

LIEBERTHAL, Kenneth Guy, BA, MA, PhD; American academic and writer; *Professor Political Science, University of Michigan*; b. 9 Sept. 1943, Asheville, NC; m. Jane Lindsay, 15 June 1968, two s. *Education:* Dartmouth College, Columbia University. *Career:* Instructor, 1972, Asst Prof., 1972–75, Assoc. Prof., 1976–82, Prof., 1982–83, Political Science Dept, Swarthmore College; Visiting Prof., 1983, Prof., 1983–, Political Science Dept, William Davidson Prof. of Business Administration, University of Michigan Business School, 1995–, Arthur F. Thurnau Prof. of Political Science, 1995–, University of Michigan, Ann Arbor; Special Asst to the Pres. and Senior Dir for Asia, National Security Council, White House, 1998–2000; Sr Fellow The Brookings Inst.; mem. Advisory Bd Nat. Bureau of Asian Research, The Pyle Center, Research Center on Contemporary China (Beijing Univ.), Center for China in the World Economy (Tsinghua Univ.), Stonebridge Int.; mem. Editorial Board, China Economic Review, China Quarterly, Journal of Contemporary China, Asia Policy, China: An International Journal, Journal of International Business Education. *Publications:* Policy Making in China: Leaders, Structures and Processes (with Michel Oksenberg), 1988; Research Guide to Central Party and Government Meetings in China 1949–86 (with Bruce Dixon), 1989; Perspectives on Modern China: Four Anniversaries (co-ed.), 1991; Bureaucracy, Politics and Policy Making in Post-Mao China (co-ed.), 1991; Governing China, 1995. Contributions: Foreign Affairs, China Quarterly, Harvard Business Review; Book reviews to American Political Science Review; China Economic Review; China Quarterly. *Honours:* Bailey Morris-Eck Lecturer, Salzburg, Austria 2006, Rosenfield Lecturer, Grinnell Coll. 2007; McKenzie Prize Harvard Business Review 1998, Distinguished Faculty Achievement Award Univ. of Michigan 2004. *Address:* 701 Tappan Street, Room D3224, Ann Arbor, MI 48104-1234, USA (office). *Telephone:* (734) 764-6120 (office). *Fax:* (734) 936-0279 (office). *E-mail:* kliebert@umich.edu (office). *Website:* www.umich.edu (office).

LIEBESCHUETZ, John Hugo Wolfgang Gideon, BA, PhD; British academic (retd) and writer; b. 22 June 1927, Hamburg, Germany; m. Margaret Rosa Taylor 1955; one s. three d. *Education:* Univ. of London. *Career:* Prof. and Head of Dept of Classical and Archaeological Studies, Univ. of Nottingham, 1979–92. *Publications:* Antioch, 1972; Continuity and Change in Roman Religion, 1979; Barbarians and Bishops, 1992; From Diocletian to the Arab Conquest, 1992; Decline and Fall of the Roman City, 2001, Ambrose of Milan: Political Letters and Speeches, 2005. *Honours:* Fellow, British Acad., 1992–; Corresponding Fellow, German Archaeological Inst., 1994–; Fellow, Univ. Coll. London, 1997; Fellow, Soc. of Antiquaries; mem. Princeton Inst. of Advanced Studies 1993. *Address:* 1 Clare Valley, The Park, Nottingham NG7 1BU, England. *E-mail:* wolf@liebeschuetz5472.fsnet.co.uk.

LIEBLER, Michael Lynn, BA, MA; American lecturer and poet; b. 24 Aug. 1953, Detroit, MI; m. Pamela Mary Liebler 1976; one s. one d. *Education:* Oakland University, Rochester, MI. *Career:* part-time Instructor, Henry Ford Community College, 1980–86; Lecturer, 1981–92, Senior Lecturer, 1992–, Wayne State University; Detroit Dir, National Writers' Voice Project, 1995–; Arts and Humanities Dir, YMCA of Metro Detroit; mem. American Asscn of University Profs; Associated Writing Programs; MLA; National Council of Teachers of English; National Writers Voice Project; National Writers Corp Program; Poetry Resource Center of Michigan, pres., 1987–93; Popular Culture Asscn. *Publications:* Measuring Darkness, 1980; Breaking the Voodoo: Selected Poems, 1990; Deliver Me, 1991; Stripping the Adult Century Bare, 1995; Brooding the Heartlands, 1998. Contributions: Rattle; Exquisite Corpse; Cottonwood Review; Relix Magazine; Christian Science Monitor; Detroit Sunday Journal; Review of Contemporary Fiction; American Book Review. *Address:* PO Box 120, Roseville, MI 48066, USA.

LIEHU, Rakel Maria; Finnish poet and writer; b. 3 Sept. 1939, Nivala. *Career:* newspaper columnist and translator. *Publications include:* Kubisseja (poems, trans. as Cubisms) 1992, Murehtimatta! Smaragdinen (poems, trans. as Grieve Not! Emerald) 1993, Readymade (poems) 1995, Skorpionin sydän (poems, trans. as Scorpion's Heart) 1997, Helene (novel) 2003; also trans. of German and Swedish poetry; contrib. to Zeitschrift für Literatur, Kunst und Zeitkritik. *Honours:* Asscn of Authors Prize 1992. *Address:* c/o Penumbra Press, POB 940, Manotick, ON K4M 1A8, Canada (office).

LIFSHIN, Lyn Diane, BA, MA; American poet and teacher; b. 12 July 1944, Burlington, VT. *Education:* Syracuse University, University of Vermont. *Career:* Instructor, SUNY at Cobleskill, 1968, 1970; Writing Consultant, New York State Mental Health Dept, Albany, 1969, Empire State College of SUNY at Saratoga Springs, 1973; Poet-in-Residence, Mansfield State College, Pennsylvania, 1974, University of Rochester, New York, 1986, Antioch's Writers' Conference, Ohio, 1987. *Publications:* Poetry: Over 75 collections, including: Upstate Madonna: Poems, 1970–74, 1975; Shaker House Poems, 1976; Some Madonna Poems, 1976; Leaning South, 1977; Madonna Who Shifts for Herself, 1983; Kiss the Skin Off, 1985; Many Madonnas, 1988; The Doctor Poems, 1990; Apple Blossoms, 1993; Blue Tattoo, 1995; The Mad Girl Drives in a Daze, 1995, Barbie Poems, Marilyn Monroe. Editor: Tangled Vines: A Collection of Mother and Daughter Poems, 1978; Ariadne's Thread: A Collection of Contemporary Women's Journals, 1982; Unsealed Lips, 1988; other: In Mirrors, Upstate: An Unfinished Story, The Daughter I Don't Have, Cold Comfort (Paterson Review Award) 1997, Before It's Light (Paterson Review Award) 2000, The Licorice Daughter: My Year With Ruffian 2006, Another Woman Looks Like Me 2007. Contributions: many books and numerous other publications, including journals. *Honours:* Hart Crane Award; Bread Loaf Scholarship; Yaddo Fellowships, 1970, 1971, 1975, 1979, 1980; MacDowell Fellowship, 1973; Millay Colony Fellowships, 1975, 1979; Jack Kerouac Award, 1984; Centennial Review Poetry Prize, 1985; Madeline Sadin Award, New York Quarterly, 1986; Footwork Award, 1987; Esterscefler Award, 1987. *Address:* 2142 Appletree Lane, Niskayuna, NY 12309, USA. *Website:* www.lynlifshin.com.

LIFTON, Robert Jay, MD; American psychiatrist, academic and writer; *Lecturer in Psychiatry, Cambridge Health Alliance/Harvard Medical School*; b. 16 May 1926, New York, NY; m. Betty Kirschner 1952; two d. *Education:* Cornell Univ., New York Medical Coll. *Career:* intern, Jewish Hosp. of Brooklyn, New York 1948–49; Resident, State Univ. Medical Center, VA Program, Northport and Brooklyn, NY 1949–51; Resident Fellow, Washington School of Psychiatry, Hong Kong and Washington, DC 1954–55; Research Assoc. in Psychiatry, Harvard Medical School 1955–61; Foundation's Fund for Research Assoc. Prof. of Psychiatry 1961–67; Prof. of Psychiatry, Yale Univ. School of Medicine, New Haven, Conn. 1967–85; Distinguished Prof. of Psychiatry and Psychology and Dir Center on Violence and Human Survival, John Jay Coll. of Criminal Justice, Grad. School and Univ. Center, and Mount Sinai School of Medicine, CUNY 1985–2003; Lecturer in Psychiatry, Cambridge Health Alliance/Harvard Medical School 2003–; several guest lectureships; mem. American Psychiatric Asscn, Asscn of Asian Studies, Fed. of American Scientists, Soc. for Psychological Study of Social Issues; Fellow, American Acad. of Arts and Sciences 1970. *Publications:* Thought Reform and the Psychology of Totalism: A Study of Brainwashing in China 1961, The Woman in America (ed.) 1965, America and the Asian Revolutions (ed.) 1966, Revolutionary Immorality: Mao Tse-Tung and the Chinese Cultural Revolution 1968, Death in Life: Survivors of Hiroshima 1969, History and Human Survival 1970, Boundaries: Psychological Man in Revolution 1970, Crimes of War (co-ed. with R. A. Falk and G. Kolko) 1971, Home from the War: Vietnam Veterans–Neither Victims Nor Executioners 1973, Living and Dying (with Eric Olson) 1974, Explorations in Psychohistory: The Wellfleet Papers (co-ed. with E. Olson) 1975, The Life of the Self 1976, Six Lives, Six Deaths: Portraits from Modern Japan (with Shuichi Kato and Michael Reich) 1979, The Broken Connection: On Death and the Continuity of Life 1979, Indefensible Weapons: The Political and Psychological Case Against Nuclearism (with Richard A. Falk) 1982, Last Aid: Medical Dimensions of Nuclear War (co-ed. with E. Chivian, S. Chivian and J. E. Mack) 1982, In a Dark Time: Images for Survival (co-ed. with N. Humphrey) 1984, The Nazi Doctors: Medical Killing and Psychology of Genocide 1986, The Future of Immortality and Other Essays for a Nuclear Age 1987, The Genocidal Mentality: Nazi Holocaust and Nuclear Threat (with Eric Markusen) 1990, The Protean Self: Human Resilience in an Age of Fragmentation 1993, Hiroshima in America: Fifty Years of Denial 1995, Destroying the World to Save It: Aum Shinrikyo, Apocalyptic Violence and the New Global Terrorism 1999, Who Owns Death?: Capital Punishment, the American Conscience and the End of Executions (with Greg Mitchell) 2000, Beyond Invisible Walls: The Psychological Legacy of Soviet Trauma (co-ed. with J. D. Lindy) 2001, Superpower Syndrome: America's Apocalyptic Confrontation with the World 2003, Crimes of War: Iraq (co-ed. with R. Falk and I. Gendzier) 2006; contrib. to professional journals. *Honours:* various hon. degrees, Hon. DHumLitt or Hon. DSc, including those from Lawrence Univ., Appleton, Wis. 1971, New York Medical Coll. 1977, Univ. of Vermont 1984, Universität-Munchen, Munich, Germany 1989, State Univ. of NY Coll. at New Paltz 1991, Saybrook Inst. Grad. School and Research Center, San Francisco, Calif. 1995, Colgate Univ., Hamilton, NY 1999; Nat. Book Award in the Sciences 1969, Van Wyck Brooks Award 1969, Hiroshima Gold Medal 1975,

Gandhi Peace Award 1984, Bertrand Russell Soc. Award 1985, Holocaust Memorial Award 1986, Nat. Jewish Book Award 1987, Los Angeles Times Book Prize for History 1987, Lisl and Leo Eitinger Award, Oslo 1988, American Orthopsychiatrists Asscn Max A. Hayman Award 1992, Psychiatric Inst. Nat. Living Treasure Award 1994, Outstanding Achievement Award, Armenian-American Soc. for Studies on Stress and Genocide 1996, Pioneer Award, Int. Soc. for Traumatic Stress Studies 1985, Boston Public Library Literary Lights Award 2006. *Address:* Department of Psychiatry, 1493 Cambridge Street, Cambridge, MA 02139, USA (office).

LIGHTMAN, Alan Paige, AB, PhD; American physicist, writer and academic; *Adjunct Professor of Humanities, Creative Writing, Physics, Massachusetts Institute of Technology*; b. 28 Nov. 1948, Memphis, TN; m. Jean Greenblatt 1976; two d. *Education:* Princeton Univ., California Inst. of Technology. *Career:* Postdoctoral Fellow Cornell Univ. 1974–76; Asst Prof. Harvard Univ. 1976–79; staff scientist Smithsonian Astrophysical Observatory, Cambridge 1979–88; Prof. of Science and Writing MIT 1988–2002, John E. Burchard Chair 1995–2001, f. Grad. Program in Science Writing 2001, Adjunct Prof. of Humanities, Creative Writing, Physics 2002–; Fellow American Acad. of Arts and Sciences; Fellow American Physical Soc.; mem. American Astronomical Soc. *Publications:* fiction: Einstein's Dreams 1993, Good Benito 1994, The Diagnosis 2000, Reunion 2003; non-fiction: Problem Book in Relativity and Gravitation 1974, Radiative Process in Astrophysics (with George B. Rybicki) 1976, Time Travel and Papa Joe's Pipe 1984, A Modern Day Yankee in a Connecticut Court and Other Essays on Science 1986, Origins: The Lives and Worlds of Modern Cosmologists (with Roberta Brawer) 1990, Ancient Light: Our Changing View of the Universe (adapted from Origins) 1991, Great Ideas in Physics 1992, Time for the Stars: Astronomy in the 1990s 1992, The World is Too Much with Me: Finding Private Space in the Wired World 1992, Dance for Two: Selected Essays 1996, A Sense of the Mysterious: Science and the Human Spirit 2005; editor: Revealing the Universe: Prediction and Proof in Astronomy (with James Cornell) 1982, The Best American Essays 2000; contrib. to professional journals and literary magazines. *Honours:* Asscn of American Publishers Most Outstanding Science Book in the Physical Sciences Award 1990, Boston Globe Winship Book Prize 1993, American Inst. of Physics Andrew Gemant Award 1996, Nat. Public Radio Book of the Month 1998, Distinguished Alumnus Award Calif. Inst. of Tech. 2003. *Address:* Massachusetts Institute of Technology, Room 14E-303, 77 Massachusetts Avenue, Cambridge, MA 02139, USA. *Telephone:* (617) 253-2308. *Website:* web.mit.edu/humanistic/www/faculty/lightman.html.

LIKHANOV, Albert Anatolyevich; Russian writer, journalist and human rights activist; *President, International Association of Children's Funds*; b. 13 Sept. 1935, Kirov; m. Liliya Alexandrovna; one c. *Education:* Urals Gorky State Univ., Yekaterinburg. *Career:* Contrib. Kirovskaya Pravda newspaper 1958–61; Ed. Komsomolskoye Plemya 1961–64; Corresp. for Western Siberia Komsomolskaya Pravda, Novosibirsk 1964–66; various posts central cttee of Komsomol (Young Communists' League) 1966; Exec. Sec. Smena magazine 1967–75, Ed.-in-Chief 1975–88; Chair. All-Union Creative Youth Council 1979; Pres. Asscn of Literary and Artistic Figures for Children and Youth, Union of Soviet Socs for Friendship and Cultural Relations with Foreign Countries 1982–87; Chair. Lenin Soviet Children's Fund 1987; Dir Research Inst. of Childhood 1989–; People's Deputy of the USSR 1989–92, mem. USSR Supreme Soviet; founder Dom Children's Fund; founder Bozhiy Mir, Ditna Chelovecheskoye and Putevodnaya Zvezda journals; Chair. Russian Children's Fund 1991–; Pres. Int. Asscn of Children's Funds 1992–. *Publications include:* Semeinye Obstoyatelstva (trilogy, trans. as Family Circumstances) 1974, selected works (two vols) 1976, essays (four vols) 1986–87, Russkiye Malchiki (trans. as Russian Boys) 1995, Mushskaya Shkola (trans. as Boys' School) 1995, essays (six vols) 2000, Nikto (trans. as Nobody) 2000, Slomannaya Kukla (trans. as A Broken Doll) 2002. *Honours:* Order of the Red Banner of Labour, Order of the Badge of Honour, Russian Orthodox Church Order of the Holy and Righteous Prince Daniil of Moscow, Russian Orthodox Church Order of Sergiy of Radonezh, Order for Service to the Fatherland (Rank IV), Russian Orthodox Church Order of St Innokentiy 2002; Russian State Prize, Lenin Komsomol Prize, Ostrovsky Prize, Polevoy Prize, Int. Korchak Prize, Int. Gorky Prize, Victor Hugo Prize (France), Tolstoy Int. Gold Medal 1995. *Address:* c/o International Association of Children's Funds, Russian Children's Fund, Armyansky per. 11/2a, 101963 Moscow, Russia. *Telephone:* (495) 9258200. *Fax:* (495) 2002276.

LILIENTHAL, Alfred Morton, BA, LLD; American author, historian, attorney and academic; b. 25 Dec. 1913, New York, NY. *Education:* Cornell University, Columbia University School of Law. *Career:* Ed., Middle East Perspective, 1968–85; mem. University Club; Cornell Club; National Press Club; Capital Hill Club. *Publications:* What Price Israel?, 1953; There Goes the Middle East, 1958; The Other Side of the Coin, 1965; The Zionist Connection I, 1978; The Zionist Connection II, 1982. Contributions: numerous journals. *Honours:* National Press Club Book Honours 1982.

LILLINGTON, Kenneth James; British author, dramatist and academic (retd); b. 7 Sept. 1916, London, England. *Education:* St Dunstan's Coll., Wandsworth Training Coll. *Career:* fmr Lecturer in English Literature, Brooklands Technical Coll., Weybridge, Surrey. *Publications:* The Devil's Grandson, 1954; Soapy and the Pharoah's Curse, 1957; Conjuror's Alibi, 1960; The Secret Arrow, 1960; Blue Murder, 1960; A Man Called Hughes, 1962; My Proud Beauty, 1963; First (and Second) Book of Classroom Plays, 1967–68; Fourth (and Seventh) Windmill Book of One-Act Plays, 1967–72; Cantaloup Crescent, 1970; Olaf and the Ogre, 1972; Nine Lives (ed.), 1977; For Better for Worse, 1979; Young Map of Morning, 1979; What Beckoning Ghost, 1983; Selkie, 1985; Full Moon, 1986. *Address:* c/o Faber and Faber Ltd, 3 Queen Square, London, WC1N 3AU, England (office).

LIM, Catherine, PhD; Singaporean writer; one s. one d. *Education:* Regional English Language Centre. *Career:* writer, first book published 1978. *Publications include:* Little Ironies: Stories of Singapore 1978, Or Else: The Lightning God and Other Stories 1980, The Serpent's Tooth 1982, The Shadow of a Dream: Love Stories of Singapore 1987, Love's Lonely Impulses 1992, Deadline for Love & Other Stories 1992, The Best of Catherine Lim 1993, The Woman's Book of Superlatives 1993, Meet Me on the Queen Elizabeth II 1993, The Bondmaid 1997, The Teardrop Story Woman 1998, Following the Wrong God Home 2002, The Song of Silver Frond 2003. *Address:* 5 Upper St Martin's Lane, London, WC2H 9EA, England.

LIM, Shirley Geok-lin, MA, PhD; Malaysian/American academic, author and poet; *Professor of English, University of California at Santa Barbara*; b. 27 Dec. 1944, Malacca, Malaysia; m. Dr Charles Bazerman 1972; one s. *Education:* Univ. of Malaya, Brandeis Univ. *Career:* Lecturer and Teaching Asst, Univ. of Malaya 1967–69; Teaching Fellow, Queens College, CUNY 1972–73; Asst Prof., Hostos Community College, CUNY 1973–76; Lecturer, Universiti Sains, Penang, Malaysia 1974; Assoc. Prof., SUNY at Westchester 1976–90; Writer-in-Residence, Univ. of Singapore 1985, East West Center, Honolulu 1988; Prof. of Asian American Studies 1990–93, Prof. of English and Women's Studies 1993–, Univ. of California at Santa Barbara (UCSB); Fulbright Distinguished Lecturer, Nanyang Technological Univ. 1996; Chair, Prof. of English, Univ. of Hong Kong 1999–2001; mem. American Studies; Asscn for Asian American Studies; Asscn for Commonwealth Languages and Literatures; MLA; Multi-Ethnic Literatures of the United States; National Women's Studies Asscn. *Publications:* Crossing the Peninsula and Other Poems 1980, Another Country and Other Stories 1982, No Man's Grove and Other Poems 1985, Modern Secrets: New and Selected Poems 1989, Nationalism and Literature: Literature in English from the Philippines and Singapore 1993, Monsoon History: Selected Poems 1994, Writing Southeast/Asia in English: Against the Grain 1994, Life's Mysteries: The Best of Shirley Lim 1995, Among the White Moon Faces: An Asian-American Memoir of Homelands 1996, Two Dreams: Short Stories 1997, What the Fortune Teller Didn't Say 1998, Joss and Gold 2001; editor: The Forbidden Stitch: An Asian American Women's Anthology 1989, Approaches to Teaching Kingston's The Woman Warrior 1991, Reading the Literatures of Asian America 1992, One World of Literature 1993, Transnational Asia Pacific 1999, Asian American Literature: An Anthology 2000, Tilting the Continent 2000, Power, Race and Gender in Academe 2000, Moving Poetry 2001; contribs to anthologies, books, reviews, quarterlies and journals. *Honours:* numerous grants and fellowships, Fulbright Scholarship 1969–72, Commonwealth Poetry Prize 1980, American Book Awards 1990, 1997; J. T. Stewart Award 1999; Distinguished Lecturer, Univ. of Western Australia 1999; UCSB Research Lecturer Award 2002; Salzburg American Studies Lecturer 2003. *Address:* c/o English Department, University of California at Santa Barbara, Santa Barbara, CA 93106, USA. *Telephone:* (805) 893-8584 (office). *Fax:* (805) 893-4622. *E-mail:* slim@english.ucsb.edu (office).

LIM, Suchen Christine; Malaysian teacher, writer and dramatist; b. 15 July 1948; two s. *Education:* National University of Singapore. *Publications:* Ricebowl, 1984; The Amah: A Portrait in Black and White (play), 1986; Gift From the Gods, 1990; Fistful of Colours, 1993; A Bit of Earth, 2000. Contributions: anthologies and journals. *Honours:* Shell Short Play Award, National University of Singapore, 1986; Singapore Literature Prize, 1992; Fulbright Award, 1996. *E-mail:* suchenchristinelim@hotmail.com.

LIMA, Robert, BA, MA, PhD; American academic, writer, poet, dramatist and translator and editor; *Fellow Emeritus, Institute for the Arts and Humanistic Studies, Pennsylvania State University*; b. 7 Nov. 1935, Havana, Cuba; s. of Robert F. Lima and Juanita Millares; m. Sally Murphy 1964; two s. two d. *Education:* Villanova Univ., New York Univ. *Career:* Lecturer, Hunter Coll., CUNY 1962–65; Asst Prof., Pennsylvania State Univ. 1965–69, Assoc. Prof. 1969–73, Prof. of Spanish and Comparative Literature 1973–2002, Fellow Emer. 2002–; Sr Fulbright Scholar and Visiting Prof., Pontifica Universidad Católica del Peru 1976–77; poet-in-residence Universidad de San Marcos, Peru 1976–77; Visiting Scholar and Lecturer Univ. of Yaunde, Cameroon 1986; USIA Lecturer in Peru, Cameroon, Equatorial Guinea; mem. Poetry Soc. of America, Int. PEN, American Center; Fellow Emeritus, Inst. for the Arts and Humanistic Studies; Academician, Academia Norteamericana de la Lengua Española; corresponding mem., Real Academia Española. *Plays:* Episode in Sicily (premiered at UNESCO Int. Drama Festival, PA) 1959, The Lesson 1960, The Inmates of St Mary Egyptian (premiered at Pennsylvania State Univ., also performed at Edinburgh Fringe Festival) 1980. *Publications:* Reader's Encyclopedia of American Literature (co-ed., revised edn) 1962, The Theatre of García Lorca 1963, Borges the Labyrinth Maker (ed. and trans.) 1965, Ramón del Valle-Inclán 1972, An Annotated Bibliography of Ramón del Valle-Inclán 1972, Dos ensayos sobre teatro español de los veinte (co-author) 1984, Valle-Inclán: The Theatre of his Life 1988, Savage Acts: Four Plays (ed. and trans.) 1993, Borges and the Esoteric (ed. and contrib.) 1993, Valle-Inclán: El teatro de su vida 1995, Dark Prisms: Occultism in Hispanic Drama 1995, Homenaje a/Tribute to Martha T. Halsey (co-ed. and contrib.) 1995, Ramón del Valle-Inclán, An Annotated Bibliography, Vol. I: The Works 1999, The Alchemical Art of Leonora Carrington, Special Issue of Cauda Pavonis,

Studies in Hermeticism (ed. and contrib.) 2001, The Dramatic World of Valle-Inclán 2003, Stages of Evil: Occultism in Western Theater and Drama 2005; poetry: Fathoms 1981, The Olde Ground 1985, Mayaland 1992, Sardinia/Sardegna 2001, Tracking the Minotaur 2003; contrib. to many books, reference works, anthologies, newspapers, reviews, quarterlies and journals. *Honours:* Kt Commdr, Order of Queen Isabel of Spain 2003; Fellowships, Villanova Univ. Coll. of Arts and Sciences Distinguished Alumnus Medal 1999, Enxebre Orden da Vieira 2002. *Address:* c/o Department of Spanish, Italian, and Portuguese, Pennsylvania State University, 211 Burrowes Building, University Park, PA 16802, USA. *Fax:* (814) 863-7944 (office). *E-mail:* rxl2@psu.edu (office). *Website:* www.personal.psu.edu/rxl2.

LIMONOV, Eduard; Russian writer and poet; b. (Eduard Veniaminovich Savenko), 22 Feb. 1943, Dzerzhinsk, Gorky Dist; m. 1st Yelena Limonova Shchapova 1971 (divorced); m. 2nd Natalia Medvedeva (divorced). *Career:* first wrote poetry at age of 15; in Kharkov 1965–67, moved to Moscow in 1967, worked as a tailor; left USSR 1974; settled in NY 1975; moved to Paris 1982; participant in Russian nationalist movt 1990–; returned to Russia 1991; Chair. Nat. Radical Party 1992–93; Chair. Nat. Bolshevik Party 1994–; arrested on terrorism and conspiracy charges 2001, sentenced by Saratov Oblast Court to four years' imprisonment for illegal acquisition and possession of arms April 2003, released June 2003; f. Russia without Putin movement Jan. 2004. *Publications include:* verse and prose in Kontinent, Ekho, Kovcheg, Apollon –1977 (in trans. in England, USA, Austria and Switzerland), It's Me – Eddie (novel) 1979, Russian (Russkoye) (verse) 1979, Diary of a Failure 1982, Teenager Savenko: Memoir of a Russian Punk 1983, The Young Scoundrel (memoir) 1986, The Death of Contemporary Heroes 1993, The Murder of the Sentry 1993, Selected Works (3 vols) 1999, The Exile (with Mark Ames and Matt Taibbi) 2000, My Political Biography; articles in Russian Communist and Nationalist newspapers 1989–.

LIN, Wallace (see Leong, Russell Charles)

LIN, Yanni; Hong Kong writer. *Publications include:* Ming yue 1985, Song jun he chu 1989, Qing chun zhi zang 1990, Wei wo er sheng 1990, Xue si gu ren ren si xue 1991.

LINACRE, Sir (John) Gordon Seymour, Kt, CBE, AFC, DFM, CCMI; British newspaper executive; b. 23 Sept. 1920, Sheffield; s. of John J. Linacre and Beatrice B. Linacre; m. Irene A. Gordon 1943; two d. *Education:* Firth Park Grammar School, Sheffield. *Career:* served RAF, rank of Squadron Leader 1939–46; journalistic appointments Sheffield Telegraph/Star 1937–47; Kemsley News Service 1947–50; Deputy Ed. Newcastle Journal 1950–56, Newcastle Evening Chronicle 1956–57; Ed. Sheffield Star 1958–61; Asst Gen. Man. Sheffield Newspapers Ltd 1961–63; Exec. Dir Thomson Regional Newspapers Ltd, London 1963–65; Man. Dir Yorkshire Post Newspapers Ltd 1965–83, Deputy Chair. 1981–83, Chair. 1983–90, Pres. 1990–; Dir United Newspapers PLC 1969–91, Deputy Chair. 1981–91, Chief Exec. 1983–88; Deputy Chair. Express Newspapers PLC 1985–88; also fmr Chair. United Provincial Newspapers Ltd, Sheffield Newspapers Ltd, Lancashire Evening Post Ltd, Northampton Mercury Co. Ltd, East Yorkshire Printers Ltd etc.; Dir Yorkshire TV 1969–90; Chair. Leeds Univ. Foundation 1989–2000; Chair. Chameleon TV Ltd 1994–; Chair. Opera North Ltd 1978–98, Pres. 1998–; many other professional and public appointments. *Honours:* Commendatore, Ordine al Merito della Repubblica Italiana 1973, Grand Ufficiale 1987; Kt Order of the White Rose, Finland 1987; Hon. LLD (Leeds) 1991. *Address:* White Windows, Staircase Lane, Bramhope, Leeds, LS16 9JD, England. *Telephone:* (113) 284-2751.

LINCOLN, Bruce Kenneth, BA, PhD; American academic and writer; *Caroline E. Haskell Professor of the History of Religions, University of Chicago;* b. 5 March 1948, Philadelphia, PA; m. Louise Gibson Hassett 1971; two d. *Education:* Haverford Coll., Univ. of Chicago. *Career:* Asst Prof. of Humanities, Religious Studies and South Asian Studies, Univ. of Minnesota 1976–79, Assoc. Prof. 1979–84, Prof. and Chair, Religious Studies Programme 1979–86, Prof. of Comparative Studies in Discourse and Society 1986–93; Visiting Prof., Università degli Studi di Siena, Italy, 1984–85, Univ. of Uppsala, Sweden 1985, Novosibirsk State Pedagogical Inst., Russia 1991, Univ. of Copenhagen, Denmark 1998, Collège de France, 2003; Prof. of the History of Religions, Anthropology, Classics and Middle Eastern Studies, Univ. of Chicago 1993–2000, Caroline E. Haskell Prof. of the History of Religions 2000–. *Publications:* Priests, Warriors, and Cattle: A Study in the Ecology of Religions, 1981; Emerging from the Chrysalis: Studies in Rituals of Women's Initiation, 1981; Religion, Rebellion, Revolution: An Interdisciplinary and Crosscultural Collection of Essays (ed.), 1985; Myth, Cosmos, and Society: Indo-European Themes of Creation and Destruction, 1986; Discourse and the Construction of Society: Comparative Studies of Myth, Ritual, and Classification, 1989; Death, War, and Sacrifice: Studies in Ideology and Practice, 1991; Authority: Construction and Corrosion, 1994; Theorizing Myth: Narrative, Ideology and Scholarship, 1999; Holy Terrors: Thinking about Religion after September 11, 2002. Contributions: Professional journals. *Honours:* ACLS Grant, 1979; Rockefeller Foundation Grant, 1981; Best New Book in History of Religion Citation, ACLS, 1981; Guggenheim Fellowship, 1982–83; National Endowment for the Humanities Grant, 1986; Outstanding Academic Book Citation, Choice, 1989; Scholar of the Coll., Univ. of Minnesota, 1990–93; Excellence in the Study of Religion (Analytical-Descriptive Studies), American Acad. of Religion, 2000; Gordon J. Laing Prize, Univ. of Chicago Press, 2003. *Address:* Swift Hall, 1025 East 58th Street, University of Chicago, Chicago IL 60637, USA (office). *Telephone:* (773) 703-5083 (office). *E-mail:* blincoln@uchicago.edu (office).

LINDBERG, Tod, BA; American writer and journalist; *Editor, Policy Review;* b. 1960, Syracuse, NY; m. Tina Linberg: two d. *Education:* Univ. of Chicago. *Career:* fmr Exec. Ed. National Interest, Man. Ed. Public Interest; Deputy Man. Ed. Insight Magazine –1991; Ed. Editorial Page, The Washington Times 1991–98, weekly columnist 1996–; Ed. Policy Review, Washington, DC 1999–; fmr Media Fellow and Lecturer on Politics, Hoover Inst., Stanford Univ., currently Research Fellow; contribs to Commentary, Nat. Review, Wall St Journal, USA Today, Los Angeles Times; mem. Bd of Educ., Chicago 1978–81; mem. Bd of Visitors, Inst. on Political Journalism, Georgetown Univ.; mem. Council on Foreign Relations; media appearances on public affairs TV programmes including Evening Exchange, Nightline, Dateline, Hardball and Crossfire. *Honours:* Associated Press Best Editorial Award 1997. *Address:* Policy Review, 21 Dupont Circle, NW, Suite 310, Washington, DC 20036, USA (office). *Telephone:* (202) 466-6730 (office). *Fax:* (202) 466-6733 (office). *E-mail:* polrev@hoover.stanford.edu (office). *Website:* www.policyreview.org (office).

LINDBLOM, Charles Edward, BA, PhD; American academic and writer; b. 21 March 1917, Turlock, Calif.; m. Rose K. Winther 1942 (died 2002); two s. one d. *Education:* Stanford Univ., Calif., Univ. of Chicago. *Career:* instructor, Univ. of Minnesota 1939–46; Asst Prof. to Prof., Yale Univ. 1946–; Pres. American Political Science Asscn. *Publications:* Unions and Capitalism 1949, Politics, Economics and Welfare 1953, The Intelligence of Democracy 1965, The Policy Making Process 1968, Politics and Markets 1977, Usable Knowledge 1979, Democracy and the Market System 1988, Inquiry and Change 1990, The Market System 2001; contrib. to professional journals. *Address:* 3940 Old Santa Fe Trail, Santa Fe, NM 87505, USA (home). *Telephone:* (505) 820-2353 (home).

LINDE, Nancy, BA, MA; American academic, writer and poet; b. 21 Dec. 1949, New York, NY; m. Stephan A. Khinoy 1980 (divorced 1990). *Education:* CUNY. *Career:* Lecturer, College of Staten Island, CUNY, 1978–85, 1988–; Mem., Board of Dirs, Woodstock Writers Worskhop, 1980–; mem. American Aikido Federation. *Publications:* Arabesque (screenplay) 1969, The Orange Cat Bistro (novel) 1996; contrib. poems to periodicals. *Honours:* CUNY Poetry Prize 1970.

LINDEMAN, Jack; American academic, poet and writer; b. 31 Dec. 1924, Philadelphia, Pa. *Education:* West Chester State Coll., Pa, Univ. of Pennsylvania, Univ. of Mississippi, Villanova Univ. *Career:* Ed. Whetstone 1955–61; Faculty, Lincoln Univ., Pa 1963–64, Temple Univ. 1964–65; Faculty, Kutztown Univ., Pa 1969–85, Prof. Emer. 1985–; Poetry Ed. Time Capsule 1981–83; mem. Poets and Writers. *Publications:* Twenty-One Poems, The Conflict of Convictions, Appleseed Hollow 2001, As If 2005; contrib. to anthologies, quarterlies, reviews, journals and magazines, including Apocalypse, Bellowing Ark, Beloit Poetry Journal, Blueline, Blue Unicorn, Bryant Literary Review, California Poetry Quarterly, California Quarterly, Christian Science Monitor, Colorado Quarterly, Commonweal, Dickinson Review, Eureka Literary Magazine, Harper's Bazaar, High Plains Review, Hollins Critic, International Poetry Review, Kansas Quarterly, Massachusetts Review, Nation, New World Writing, Oregon East, Poetry, Prairie Schooner, Red Hawk Review, Rocky Mountain Review, Slant, South Carolina Review, Southern Poetry Review, Southwest Review, Calapooya, Chiron Review, Poetry Motel, The Poet's Page, San Fernando Poetry Journal, Southwest Review, White Pelican Review. *Honours:* Achievement Award For Outstanding Achievement, A Peace of Mind Poetry: Expedition 2003–04. *Address:* 133 South Franklin Street, Fleetwood, PA 19522-1810, USA. *Telephone:* (610) 944-9554. *Fax:* (610) 944-9554. *E-mail:* jklnfltwpt@enter.net.

LINDEY, Christine, BA; art historian; b. 26 Aug. 1947, France. *Education:* Courtauld Institute, London. *Publications:* Superrealist Painting and Sculpture, 1980; 20th Century Painting: Bonnard to Rothko, 1981; Art in the Cold War, 1990.

LINDHOLM, Megan (see Ogden, Margaret Astrid Lindholm)

LINDNER, Carl Martin, BS, MA, PhD; American academic and poet; *Professor of English, University of Wisconsin at Parkside;* b. 31 Aug. 1940, New York, NY; one s. one d. *Education:* City College, CUNY, Univ. of Wisconsin at Madison. *Career:* Asst Prof. 1969–74, Assoc. Prof. 1974–87, Prof. of English 1987–, Univ. of Wisconsin at Parkside. *Publications:* Vampire 1977, The Only Game 1981, Shooting Baskets in a Dark Gymnasium 1984, Angling into Light 2001, Eat and Remember 2001; contrib. reviews to journals and periodicals. *Honours:* Wisconsin Arts Board Creative Writing Fellowship for Poetry, 1981; Stella C. Gray Teaching Excellence Awards, 1990–91, 2000–01; University of Wisconsin at Parkside Award for Excellence in Research and Creative Activity, 1996. *Address:* c/o Department of English, University of Wisconsin at Parkside, PO Box 2000, Wood Road, Kenosha, WI 53141, USA.

LINDOP, Grevel Charles Garrett, MA, BLitt, PhD; British academic, poet, writer and editor; b. 6 Oct. 1948, Liverpool, England; m. Amanda Therese Marian Cox 1981; one s. two d. *Education:* Liverpool Coll., Wadham and Wolfson Colls, Oxford, Univ. of Manchester. *Career:* Lecturer, Univ. of Manchester 1971–84, Sr Lecturer 1984–93, Reader in English Literature 1993–96, Prof. of Romantic and Early Victorian Studies 1996–2001; Dir Temenos Acad. and Ed. Temenos Acad. Review 2000–03; Fellow, Temenos Acad., Wordsworth Trust. *Publications:* poetry: Against the Sea 1970, Fools' Paradise 1977, Moon's Palette 1984, Tourists 1987, A Prismatic Toy 1991,

Selected Poems 2000, Touching the Earth: Books I–IV 2001, Playing With Fire 2006; prose: British Poetry Since 1960 (with Michael Schmidt) 1971, The Opium-Eater: A Life of Thomas De Quincey 1981, A Literary Guide to the Lake District 1993, The Path and the Palace: Reflections on the Nature of Poetry 1996; editor: Selected Poems, by Thomas Chatterton 1971, Confessions of an English Opium-Eater and Other Writings, by Thomas De Quincey 1985, The White Goddess, by Robert Graves 1997, The Works of Thomas De Quincey, 21 vols 2000–2003; contrib. to Poetry Nation Review, TLS, Stand, Poetry London. *Honours:* Lake District Book of the Year Award 1993, Poetry London Prize 2005. *Address:* 216 Oswald Road, Chorton-cum-Hardy, Manchester, M21 9GW, England (home). *E-mail:* gcglindop@aol.com (home). *Website:* www.grevel.co.uk.

LINDQVIST, Sven, PhD; Swedish writer; b. 1932, Stockholm; m. Agneta Stark 1986; one s. one d. *Education:* Stockholm Univ. *Publications include:* China in Crisis 1965, The Myth of Wu Tao-tzu 1967, The Shadow: Latin America Faces the Seventies 1972, Dig Where You Stand: How to Research a Job 1978, Land and Power in South America 1979, Exterminate All the Brutes 1996, The Skull Measurer's Mistake 1997, Desert Divers 2000, A History of Bombing 2001, Bench Press 2003, Terra Nullius 2007. *Honours:* Dr hc (Uppsala Univ.), hon. professorship from Swedish government. *Address:* c/o Granta Books, 2–3 Hanover Yard, Noel Road, London, N1 8BE, England (office); Bellman 15, 11847 Stockholm, Sweden (home). *Fax:* (8) 643 1942 (home). *E-mail:* mail@svenlindqvist.net. *Website:* www.svenlindqvist.net.

LINDSAY, (John) Maurice, CBE, TD; Scottish poet, writer and editor; b. 21 July 1918, Glasgow; m. 1946; one s. three d. *Education:* Glasgow Acad., Scottish Nat. Acad. of Music. *Career:* Programme Controller, Border TV 1959–62, Chief Interviewer 1962–67; Dir, The Scottish Civic Trust 1967–83; Ed., Scottish Review 1975–85; Pres., Asscn for Scottish Literary Studies 1982–83; Hon. Sec.-Gen., Europa Nostra 1983–90; mem. Asscn of Scottish Literary Studies. *Publications:* The Advancing Day 1940, Predicament 1942, No Crown for Laughter 1943, The Enemies of Love: Poems 1941–45 1946, Selected Poems 1947, At the Wood's Edge 1950, Ode for St Andrew's Night and Other Poems 1951, The Exiled Heart: Poems 1941–56 1957, Snow Warning and Other Poems 1962, One Later Day and Other Poems 1964, This Business of Living 1971, Comings and Goings 1971, Selected Poems 1942–72 1973, The Run from Life: More Poems 1942–72 1975, Walking Without an Overcoat: Poems 1972–76 1977, Collected Poems (two vols) 1979, 1993, A Net to Catch the Wind and Other Poems 1981, The French Mosquitoe's Woman and Other Diversions 1985, Requiem for a Sexual Athlete and Other Poems and Diversions 1988, The Scottish Dog (with Joyce Lindsay) 1989, Collected Poems 1940–1990 1990, The Theatre and Opera Lover's Quotation Book (with Joyce Lindsay) 1993, News of the World: Last Poems 1995, Speaking Likenesses 1997, The Burns Quotation Book (with Joyce Lindsay) 1999, Worlds Apart (poems) 2000, Glasgow: Fabric of a City 2001, Looking Up Where Heaven Isn't 2005, The Edinburgh Book of the 20th Century (with Lesley Duncan) 2005; edns of poetry, plays, etc. *Honours:* Hon. DLitt (Glasgow) 1982; Hon. Fellow Royal Incorporation of Architects in Scotland, Hon. Gov. The Glasgow Acad. 2003. *Address:* Park House, 104 Dumbarton Road, Bowling, G60 5BB, Scotland.

LINDSEY, David L., BA; American writer and editor; b. 6 Nov. 1944, Kingsville, Texas; m. Joyce Lindsey. *Education:* University of North Texas. *Career:* freelance ed. 1972–80; founder, Heidelberg Publishers; Acquisitions Ed. for the Humanities, University of Texas Press. *Publications:* Mysteries: Black Gold, Red Death, 1983; A Cold Mind, 1983; Heat from Another Sun, 1984; Spiral, 1986; In the Lake of the Moon, 1988; Mercy, 1990; Body of Truth, 1992; An Absence of Light, 1994; Requiem for a Glass Heart, 1996; The Color of Night, 1999; Animosity, 2001. *Honours:* Bochumer Krimi Archiv Award, Best Suspense Novel of the Year, Germany, 1992. *Literary Agent:* Aaron Priest Literary Agency, 708 Third Avenue, 23rd Floor, New York, NY 10017, USA. *E-mail:* dlindsey1@austin.rr.com.

LINE, David (see Davidson, Lionel)

LINETT, Deena, DEd; American academic and writer; b. 30 Aug. 1938, Boston, MA; two s. one d. *Education:* Rutgers Univ. *Career:* Prof. of English, Montclair State University; Fellowship, Centre for Writers and Translators, Gotland, Sweden 2004–; mem. PEN American Center, Poets and Writers, Acad. of American Poets, Poetry Society of America. *Publications:* On Common Ground, 1983; The Translator's Wife, 1986; Rare Earths: Poems, 2001. Contributions: journals. *Honours:* Yaddo Fellowships, 1981, 1985; PEN-Syndicated Fiction Project, 1990; Residency, Hawthornden Castle International Retreats for Writers, 1996, 2001. *Address:* c/o Department of English, Montclair State University, Upper Montclair, NJ 07043, USA. *Telephone:* (973) 655-7320 (office). *Fax:* (973) 746-2236 (home).

LINGARD, Joan Amelia, DipEd, MBE; British author; b. 8 April 1932, Edinburgh, Scotland; three d. *Education:* Moray House Training College, Edinburgh. *Career:* mem. Society of Authors in Scotland (chair. 1982–86); Hon. Vice-Pres., Scottish PEN; Dir, Edinburgh Book Festival. *Publications:* children's books: The Twelfth Day of July, 1970; Frying as Usual, 1971; Across the Barricades, 1972; Into Exile, 1973; The Clearance, 1974; A Proper Place, 1975; The Resettling, 1975; Hostages to Fortune, 1976; The Pilgrimage, 1976; The Reunion, 1977; The Gooseberry, 1978; The File on Fraulein Berg, 1980; Strangers in the House, 1981; The Winter Visitor, 1983; The Freedom Machine, 1986; The Guilty Party, 1987; Rags and Riches, 1988; Tug of War, 1989; Glad Rags, 1990; Between Two Worlds, 1991; Hands Off Our School!,

1992; Night Fires, 1993; Lizzie's Leaving, 1995; Dark Shadows, 1998; A Secret Place, 1998; Tom and the Tree House, 1998; The Egg Thieves, 1999; River Eyes, 2000; Natasha's Will, 2000; Me and My Shadow, 2001; Tortoise Trouble, 2002; Tell the Moon to Come Out, 2003; fiction: Liam's Daughter, 1963; The Prevailing Wind, 1964; The Tide Comes In, 1966; The Headmaster, 1967; A Sort of Freedom, 1968; The Lord on Our Side, 1970; The Second Flowering of Emily Mountjoy, 1979; Greenyards, 1981; Sisters by Rite, 1984; Reasonable Doubts, 1986; The Women's House, 1989; After Colette, 1993; Lizzie's Leaving, 1995; Dreams of Love and Modest Glory, 1995; The Kiss 2002, Encarnita's Journey 2005, After You've Gone 2007. *Honours:* Scottish Arts Council Bursary, 1967–68; Preis der Leseratten ZDF, Germany, 1986; Buxtehuder Bulle, Germany, 1987; Scottish Arts Council Award, 1994. *Literary Agent:* David Higham Associates, 5–8 Lower John Street, Golden Square, London, W1F 9HA, England.

LINGEMAN, Richard Roberts, BA; American editor and writer; b. 2 Jan. 1931, Crawfordsville, IN; m. Anthea Judy Nicholson 1965; one d. *Education:* Haverford Coll., Yale Law School, Columbia Univ. Graduate School. *Career:* Exec. Ed., Monocle magazine 1960–69; Sr Ed., The Nation 1978–; Assoc. Ed. and columnist, The New York Times Book Review 1969–78; mem. Authors' Guild, Nat. Book Critics Circle, New York Historical Soc., PEN, Soc. of American Historians. *Publications:* Drugs from A to Z 1969, Don't You Know There's a War On? The American Home Front 1941–1945 1971, Small Town America: A Narrative History 1620–Present 1980, Theodore Dreiser: At the Gates of the City, 1871–1907 1986, Theodore Dreiser: An American Journey, 1908–1945 1990, Sinclair Lewis: Rebel from Main Street 2002, Double Lives: American Writers' Friendships 2006. *Honours:* Chicago Sun-Times Book of the Year Award 1990. *Address:* c/o The Nation, 33 Irving Place, New York, NY 10003, USA (office).

LINKLATER, Magnus Duncan, BA; British journalist, broadcaster and writer; b. 21 Feb. 1942, Orkney, Scotland; m. Veronica Lyle 1967; two s. one d. *Education:* Univ. of Freiburg; Sorbonne, Univ. of Paris; Trinity Hall, Cambridge. *Career:* Reporter, Daily Express, Manchester, 1965–66, London Evening Standard, 1966–67; Editorial positions, Evening Standard, 1967–69, Sunday Times, 1969–72, 1975–83, Sunday Times Colour Magazine, 1972–75; Managing Ed., News, The Observer, 1983–86; Ed., London Daily News, 1987, The Scotsman, 1988–94; Columnist, The Times, 1994–; Broadcaster, Radio Scotland, 1994–; Chair., Scottish Arts Council, 1996–. *Publications:* Hoax: The Inside Story of the Howard Hughes/Clifford Irving Affair (with Stephen Fay and Lewis Chester), 1972; Jeremy Thorpe: A Secret Life (with Lewis Chester and David May), 1979; Massacre: The Story of Glencoe, 1982; The Falklands War (with others), 1982; The Fourth Reich: Klaus Barbie and the Neo-Fascist Connection (with Isabel Hilton and Neal Ascherson), 1984; Not With Honour: Inside Story of the Westland Scandal (with David Leigh), 1986; For King and Conscience: The Life of John Graham of Claverhouse, Viscount Dundee (with Christian Hesketh), 1989; Anatomy of Scotland (co-ed.), 1992; Highland Wilderness (with Colin Prior), 1993; People in a Landscape, 1997. *Honours:* Hon. DArts, Napier University, 1994; Hon. LLD, University of Aberdeen, 1997; Hon. DLitt, Glasgow University, 2001; Fellow, Royal Society of Edinburgh. *Address:* 5 Drummond Place, Edinburgh EH3 6PH, Scotland. *E-mail:* magnus.linklater@blueyonder.co.uk.

LINNEY, Romulus, AB, MFA; American dramatist and writer; b. 21 Sept. 1930, Philadelphia, PA; m. 1st Ann Leggett Sims 1963 (divorced 1966); one d.; m. 2nd Jane Andrews 1967; one d. *Education:* Oberlin College, Yale School of Drama, New School for Social Research, New York. *Career:* Visiting Assoc. Prof. of Dramatic Arts, University of North Carolina at Chapel Hill, 1961; Dir of Fine Arts, North Carolina State College, Raleigh, 1962–64; Faculty, Manhattan School of Music, New York City, 1964–72; Visiting Prof., Columbia University, 1972–74, Connecticut College, 1979, University of Pennsylvania, 1979–86, Princeton University, 1982–85; mem. Actor's Equity Asscn; Authors' Guild; Authors League of America; Dirs Guild; PEN. *Publications:* Plays: The Sorrows of Frederick, 1966; Democracy and Esther, 1973; The Love Suicide at Schofield Barracks, 1973; Holy Ghosts, 1977; Old Man Joseph and His Family, 1978; El Hermano, 1981; The Captivity of Pixie Shedman, 1981; Childe Byron, 1981; F.M., 1984; The Death of King Philip, 1984; Sand Mountain, 1985; A Woman Without a Name, 1986; Pops, 1987; Heathen Valley, 1990; Three Poets, 1990; Unchanging Love, 1990; Juliet–Yancey–April Snow, 1990; Spain, 1993. Fiction: Heathen Valley, 1962; Slowly, by Thy Hand Unfurled, 1965; Jesus Tales, 1980. *Honours:* National Endowment for the Arts Grant, 1974; Guggenheim Fellowship, 1980; Obie Awards, 1980, 1990; Mishma Prize, 1981; American Acad. and Institute of Arts and Letters Award, 1984; Rockefeller Foundation Fellowship, 1986.

LINSCOTT, Gillian; British journalist and writer; b. 27 Sept. 1944, Windsor, England; m. Tony Geraghty 1988. *Education:* Somerville Coll., Oxford. *Career:* mem. Soc. of Authors, Crime Writers' Asscn (CWA). *Publications:* A Healthy Body 1984, Murder Makes Tracks 1985, Knightfall 1986, A Whiff of Sulphur 1987, Unknown Hand 1988, Murder, I Presume 1990, Sister Beneath the Sheet 1991, Hanging on the Wire 1992, Stage Fright 1993, Widow's Peak 1994, Crown Witness 1995, Dead Man's Music 1996, Dance on Blood 1998, Absent Friends 1999, The Perfect Daughter 2000, Dead Man Riding 2002, The Garden 2002, Blood on the Wood 2003. *Honours:* CWA Ellis Peters Historical Dagger 2000, Herodotus Award, Historical Mystery Appreciation Soc. *Address:* Wood View, Hope Under Dinmore, Leominster, Herefords., HR6 0PP, England.

LIPMAN, Elinor, AB; American writer; b. 16 Oct. 1950, Lowell, MA; m. Robert M. Austin 1975, one s. *Education:* Simmons College, Boston. *Career:* Lecturer, Smith College, 1997–; mem. Authors' Guild. *Publications:* Into Love and Out Again (short stories), 1987; Then She Found Me, 1990; The Way Men Act, 1992; Isabel's Bed, 1995; The Inn at Lake Devine, 1999; The Ladies' Man, 1999; The Dearly Departed, 2001; The Pursuit of Alice Thrift, 2003, My Latest Grievance 2005. Contributions: Yankee; Playgirl; Ascent; Ladies Home Journal; Cosmopolitan; Self; New England; Living; Redstart; Wigwag. *Honours:* Distinguished Story Citations, Best American Short Stories, 1984, 1985. *Address:* 67 Winterberry Lane, Northampton, MA 01060, USA.

LIPPY, Charles Howard, MA, MDiv, PhD; American academic, writer and editor; *LeRoy A. Martin Distinguished Professor of Religious Studies, University of Tennessee at Chattanooga*; b. 2 Dec. 1943, Binghamton, NY. *Education:* Dickinson Coll., Union Theological Seminary, Princeton Univ. *Career:* Asst Prof., Oberlin Coll. 1972–74, West Virginia Wesleyan Coll. 1975–76; Visiting Assoc. Prof., Miami Univ. 1974–75; Asst Prof., Clemson Univ. 1976–80, Assoc. Prof. 1980–85, Prof. of History and Religion 1985–88, Prof. of Religion 1988–94; Visiting Scholar, Univ. of North Carolina at Chapel Hill 1984; Visiting Prof. of Religion, Emory Univ. 1990–91, Visiting Research Scholar 2000–01; LeRoy A. Martin Distinguished Prof. of Religion Studies, Univ. of Tennessee at Chattanooga 1994–; mem. American Acad. of Religion, American Catholic Historical Asscn, American Soc. of Church History, American Studies Asscn, Organization of American Historians, Soc. for the Scientific Study of Religion, South Carolina Acad. of Religion (pres. 1981–82), United Methodist Historical Soc. *Publications:* Seasonable Revolutionary: The Mind of Charles Chauncy 1981, A Bibliography of Religion in the South 1985, Religious Periodicals of the United States: Academic and Scholarly Journals (ed.) 1986, Encyclopedia of the American Religious Experience (ed. with Peter W. Williams, three vols) 1988, Twentieth-Century Shapers of American Popular Religion (ed.) 1989, The Christadelphians in North America 1989, Christianity Comes to the Americas, 1492–1776 (with Robert Choquette and Stafford Poole) 1992, Religion in South Carolina (ed.) 1993, Being Religious, American Style: A History of Popular Religiosity in the United States 1994, Popular Religious Magazines of the United States (ed. with P. Mark Fackler) 1995, Modern American Popular Religion: A Critical Assessment and Annotated Bibliography 1996, The Evangelicals: A Historical, Thematic and Biographical Guide (with Robert H. Krapohl) 1999, Pluralism Comes of Age: American Religion in the Twentieth Century 2000, Where Rivers Run and Mountains Rise (ed. with John L. Topolewski and Nancy Topolewski) 2002, Do Real Men Pray? 2005, Encyclopedia of Religion in the South (ed. with Samuel S. Hill) 2005; contrib. to reference works, scholarly books and journals. *Honours:* several grants, Outstanding Academic Book Citations, Choice 1987, 1989, 2001, American Library Asscn Outstanding Reference Work Citation 1988. *Address:* 711 Hurricane Creek Road, Chattanooga, TN 37421, USA. *Telephone:* (423) 425-4340 (office); (423) 892-0355 (home). *Fax:* (423) 425-4153 (office). *E-mail:* charles-lippy@utc.edu (office).

LIPSEY, David Lawrence; British journalist and writer; b. 21 April 1948, Cheltenham, Gloucestershire, England; m. Margaret Robson 1982, one d. *Education:* Magdalen Coll., Oxford. *Career:* Research Asst, General and Municipal Workers' Union, 1970–72; Special Adviser to Anthony Crossland, MP, 1972–77; Staff, Prime Minister, 1977–79; Journalist, 1979–80, Ed., 1986–88, New Society; Political Staff, 1980–82, Economics Ed., 1982–86, The Sunday Times; Co-Founder and Deputy Ed., The Sunday Correspondent, 1988–90; Assoc. Ed., The Times, 1990–92; Journalist, 1992–, Political Ed., 1994–, The Economist; mem. Fabian Society, chair., 1981–82. *Publications:* Labour and Land, 1972; The Socialist Agenda: Crosland's Legacy (ed. with Dick Leonard), 1981; Making Government Work, 1982; The Name of the Rose, 1992.

LIPSKA, Ewa; Polish poet; b. 8 Oct. 1945, Kraków. *Education:* Acad. of Fine Arts, Kraków. *Career:* Co-Ed. Pismo 1981–83; mem. editorial Bd Dekada Literacka 1990–92; First Sec. Polish Embassy, Vienna 1991–95, Adviser 1995–97; Deputy Dir Polish Inst., Vienna 1991–95, Dir 1995–97; mem. Asscn of Polish Writers, Polish and Austrian PEN Club. *Publications include:* Wiersze (Poems) 1967, Drugi zbiór wierszy (Second Vol. of Poems) 1970, Trzeci zbiór wierszy (Third Vol. of Poems) 1972, Czwarty zbiór wierszy (Fourth Vol. of Poems) 1974, Piaty zbiór wierszy (Fifth Vol. of Poems) 1978, Zywa smierc (Living Death) 1979, Dom Spokojnej Mlodosci (House of the Quiet Youth) 1979, Nie o smierc tutaj chodzi, lecz o bialy kordonek 1982, Utwory wybrane (Selected Poems) 1986, Przechowalnia ciemnosci 1985, Strefa ograniczonego postoju 1990, Wakacje Mizantropa (Misantrope's Holidays) 1993, Stypendysci czasu 1994, Wspólnicy zielonego wiatraczka 1996, Ludzie dla poczatkujacych (People for Beginners) 1997, Zycie zastepcze (Substitute Life) (Polish-German edition 1998), Godziny poza godzinami (After-hours Hours) 1999, Biale truskawki (White Strawberries) 2000, Sklepy zoologiczne (Pet Shops) 2001, Uwaga stopien 2002; selections of poems translated include Versei (Hungary) 1979, Vernisaz (Czechoslovakia) 1979, Such Times (Canada) 1981, Huis voor een vredige jeugd 1982, Auf den Dächern der Mausoleen (Germany) 1983, En misantrops ferie (Denmark) 1990, Meine Zeit. Mein Leib. Mein Leben (Austria) 1990, Poet? Criminal? Madman? (UK) 1991, Wakancitie na mizantropa (Bulgaria) 1994, Zon (Sweden) 1997, Stipiendisti Wremiena (Yugoslavia) 1998, Mennesker for Begyndere (Denmark) 1999, Mesohu me vdekjen (Albania) 2000, Menseen voor beginners (Netherlands) 2000, Sedemnast cervenych vevericiek (Slovakia) 2001, Selection of Poems (Israel) 2001, Fresas Blancas (Spain) 2001, Pet Shops (UK) 2002, Uwaga 2002, Ja 2003. *Honours:* Koscielscy Foundation Award (Switzerland) 1973, Robert Graves PEN Club Award 1979, Ind. Foundation of Supporting of Polish Culture—Polcul Foundation Award 1990, PEN Club Award 1992, Alfred Jurzykowski Foundation Award (USA) 1993, City of Kraków Award 1995, Andrzej Bursa Award 1997, Literary Laurel 2002. *Address:* ul. Zbrojów 10 m. 13, 30-042 Kraków, Poland (home). *Website:* ewa_lipska@hotmail.com (home).

LIPSKEROV, Dmitry; Russian writer and playwright. *Career:* co-f., Debut Prize 2001. *Publications:* Gotlib's Space; The Forty Years of Chanchzhoe (novel), 2001; Relatives (novel), 2001. *Address:* c/o EKSMO Publishing House, Klari Tsetkin ul., d.18/5, Moscow 127299, Russia. *E-mail:* info@eksmo.ru.

LISLE, Holly; American writer; b. Oct. 1960, Salem, OH. *Education:* Richmond Community College. *Career:* mem. SFWA. *Publications:* Arhel series: Fire in the Mist, 1992, Bones of the Past, 1993, Mind of the Magic, 1995. Minerva Wakes, 1993; When the Bough Breaks (co-author), 1993; The Rose Sea (co-author), 1994; Mall, Mayhem and Magic, 1995; Glenraven (co-author), 1996. Devil's Point series: Sympathy for the Devil, 1996, The Devil and Dan Cooley (co-author), 1996, Hell on High (co-author), 1997; Hunting the Corrigan's Blood, 1997. Bard's Tale series: Thunder of the Captains (co-author), 1996, Wrath of the Princes (co-author), 1997, Curse of the Black Heron, in press; Glenraven: In the Shadow of the Rift (co-author), in press. Contributions: Short stories to anthologies including Women of War; The Enchanter Reborn; Chicks in Chainmail. *Honours:* Compton Crook Award for Best First Novel, 1993. *Literary Agent:* Scovil, Chichak, Galen Literary Agency, 381 Park Avenue S, Suite 1020, New York, NY 10016, USA.

LISNYANSKAYA, Inna Lvovna; Russian writer and poet; b. 24 June 1928, Baku; m. Semen I. Lipkin (died 2003); one d. *Career:* began writing poetry at age 10; first works published 1948; poems published in Moscow literary journal Novyi mir (New World) and Iunost (Youth) 1957–; in internal exile 1979–89, following contribs to literary almanac Metropole; resgnd from Union of Writers 1980 (membership restored 1989). *Publications include:* This Happened to Me 1957, Faithfulness 1958, Not Simply Love 1963, At First Hand 1966, Grape Light 1978, Rains and Mirrors 1983, Verse 1970–83, 1984, On the Edge of Sleep 1984, The Circle 1985, Airy Layer 1990, Poetry 1991, The Music of Akhmatova's 'Poem without a Hero' 1991, After Everything 1994, The Lonely Gift 1995, The Box with a Triple Bottom (Study on Akhmatova's Poem Without the Hero) 1995, Selected Poetry 2000; contribs to literary journals including Novyi mir, Oktiabr, Znamia. *Address:* Usievicha Street 8, Apt 16, 125315 Moscow, Russia. *Telephone:* (495) 155-75-98.

LISTER, Gwen, BA; Namibian journalist; *Editor, The Namibian*; b. 5 Dec. 1953, East London, S Africa; one s. one d. *Education:* Univ. of Cape Town. *Career:* began career as journalist with Windhoek Advertiser 1975; Co-Founder (with Hannes Smith) Windhoek Observer 1978, Political Ed. 1978–84 (S African authorities banned newspaper during coverage of independence talks 1984, ban defeated, resgnd because of accusations by newspaper sr staff 1984); Founder The Namibian newspaper 1985, Ed. 1985– (copies confiscated by authorities, advertising boycott by business community, office bldg burned down 1988, prohibition of govt advertising in newspaper 2001); Co-founder Media Inst. of Southern Africa, fmr Chair. Governing Council and mem. Trust Funds Bd; mem. UNESCO Press Freedom Council, African Advisory Bd Int. Women's Media Foundation, Advisory Bd Int. Consortium of Investigative Journalists. *Honours:* Inter Press Service Int. Journalism Award 1988, S African Soc. of Journalists Pringle Prize for Journalism 1988, Cttee to Protect Journalists Int. Journalism Award 1991, Nieman Fellowship, Harvard Univ. 1995–96, Media Inst. of S Africa Press Freedom Award 1997, named Int. Press Inst. Press Freedom Hero 2000, Int. Women's Media Foundation Courage in Journalism Award 2004. *Address:* The Namibian, POB 20783, 42 John Meinert Street, Windhoek (office). *Telephone:* (61) 279600/3 (office). *Fax:* (61) 279602 (office). *E-mail:* gwen@namibian.com.na (office). *Website:* www.namibian.com.na (office).

LISTER, Richard Percival, BSc, FRSL; British author, poet and painter; b. 23 Nov. 1914, Nottingham; m. Ione Mary Wynniatt-Husey 1985. *Education:* Manchester Univ. *Career:* author, painter, poet since 1949. *Publications:* fiction: The Way Backwards 1950, The Oyster and the Torpedo 1951, Rebecca Redfern 1953, The Rhyme and the Reason 1963, The Questing Beast 1965, One Short Summer 1974; poetry: The Idle Demon 1958, The Albatross 1986; travel: A Journey in Lapland 1965, Turkey Observed 1967, Glimpses of a Planet 1997; biography: The Secret History of Genghis Khan 1969, Marco Polo's Travels 1976, The Travels of Herodotus 1979; short story collections: Nine Legends 1991, Two Northern Stories 1996; contrib. to Punch, New Yorker, Atlantic Monthly. *Address:* Flat 11, 42 St James Gardens, London, W11 4RQ, England (home). *Telephone:* (20) 7371-3856 (home).

LITT, Toby; British writer; b. 1968, Ampthill, Bedfordshire, England. *Education:* Worcester Coll., Oxford, Univ. of East Anglia. *Career:* lived in Prague 1990–93; mem. English PEN. *Publications:* Adventures in Capitalism (short stories) 1996, Beatniks (novel) 1997, Corpsing (novel) 2000, Deadkidsongs (novel) 2001, Exhibitionism (short stories) 2002, Finding Myself (novel) 2003, Ghost Story 2004, Hospital 2007; contrib. to anthologies, including Class Work 1995, Neonlit 1998, Fortune Hotel 1998, Girlboy 1999, New Writing 8 1999, All Hail the New Puritans 2000, The Mammoth Book of Best New Erotica 2000, New English Book of Internet Stories 2000, Time Out Book of London Stories 2 2000, New Writing 9 2000; contrib. to The Idler, The Erotic Review, Interzone, Ambit, Concrete, Passport, The Guardian, Big Issue, Modern Painters, Art Quarterly. *Honours:* Curtis Brown Fellowship 1995.

Literary Agent: The Marsh Agency, 11 Dover Street, London, W1S 4LJ, England. *Telephone:* (20) 7399-2800. *Fax:* (20) 7399-2801. *Website:* www .marsh-agency.co.uk. *Address:* c/o Hamish Hamilton, Penguin Books Ltd, 80 Strand, London, WC2R 0RL, England. *Website:* www.tobylitt.com.

LITTELL, Jonathan; American/French novelist; b. 10 Oct. 1967, New York, USA; s. of Robert Littell; m.; two c. *Education:* Yale Univ. *Career:* spent most of childhood in France; worked for int. humanitarian organization, Action Against Hunger 1994–2001, head of mission in Chechnya. *Publications:* fiction: Bad Voltage 1989, Les Bienveillantes (Prix Goncourt, Grand Prix du Roman de l'Académie française) 2006; non-fiction: The Security Organs of the Russian Federation – A Brief History 1991–2005 2006. *Address:* c/o Editions Gallimard, 5 rue Sébastien-Bottin, 75328 Paris, France (office).

LITTELL, Robert; American writer; b. 1935, New York, NY. *Career:* journalist Newsweek 1964; writer of Cold War espionage fiction. *Publications include:* Read America First 1968, If Israel Lost the War (with Richard Z. Cheznoff and Edward Klein) 1969, The Czech Black Book 1969, The Defection of A. J. Lewinter 1973, Sweet Reason 1974, The October Circle 1976, Mother Russia 1978, The Debriefing 1979, The Amateur 1981, The Sisters 1985, The Revolutionist 1988, The Once and Future Spy 1990, An Agent in Place 1991, The Visiting Professor 1994, Walking Back the Cat 1996, For the Future of Israel (with Shimon Peres) 1998, The Company 2002, Legends: A Novel of Dissimulation 2005, Vicious Circles 2007. *Address:* c/o Overlook/Penguin Publicity, 375 Hudson Street, New York, NY 10014, USA (office).

LITTLE, Charles Eugene, BA; American writer; *Director, American Land Publishing Project;* b. 1 March 1931, Los Angeles, CA; m. Ila Dawson. *Education:* Wesleyan Univ. *Career:* began career as Advertising Exec., Foote, Cone & Belding, New York; Editorial Dir, Open Space Action Magazine, 1968–69; Ed.-in-Chief, American Land Forum, 1980–86; full-time writer 1986–; Books Ed., Wilderness Magazine, 1987–97; Consulting Ed., Johns Hopkins Univ. Press, 1989–97; Dir, American Land Publishing Project 2000–; Adjunct Faculty mem., Geography Dept, Univ. of New Mexico 2001–. *Publications:* Challenge of the Land, 1969; Space for Survival (with J. G. Mitchell), 1971; A Town is Saved... (with photos by M. Mort), 1973; The American Cropland Crisis (with W. Fletcher), 1980; Green Fields Forever, 1987; Louis Bromfield at Malabar (ed.), 1988; Greenways for America, 1990; Hope for the Land, 1992; Discover America: The Smithsonian Book of the National Parks, 1995; The Dying of the Trees, 1995; An Appalachian Tragedy 1998; Encyclopedia of Environmental Studies 2001; Sacred Landsof Indian America 2001. Contributions: Magazines and journals. *Address:* 33 Calle del Norte, Placitas, NM 87043, USA.

LITVINOFF, Emanuel; British writer and dramatist; b. 30 June 1915, London, England. *Career:* Dir, Contemporary Jewish Library, London, 1958–88; Founder, Jews in Eastern Europe, journal, London. *Publications:* Conscripts: A Symphonic Declaration, 1941; The Untried Soldier, 1942; A Crown for Cain, 1948; The Lost Europeans, 1959; The Man Next Door, 1968; Journey Through a Small Planet, 1972; Notes for a Survivor, 1973; A Death Out of Season, 1974; Soviet Anti-Semitism: The Paris Trial (ed.), 1974; Blood on the Snow, 1975; The Face of Terror, 1978; The Penguin Book of Jewish Short Stories (ed.), 1979; Falls the Shadow, 1983.

LIU, Shahe; Chinese poet; b. 11 Nov. 1931, Chengdu, Sichuan Prov.; m. 1st 1966; one s. one d.; m. 2nd 1992. *Education:* Sichuan Univ. *Career:* mem. editorial staff The Stars (poetry magazine) –1957 and 1979–; satirical poem Verses of Plants (1957) led to condemnation as 'bourgeois rightist'; in labour camp during Cultural Revolution 1966–77, rehabilitated 1979. *Publications include:* Night on the Farm 1956, Farewell to Mars 1957, Liu Shahe Poetic Works 1982, Travelling Trace 1983, Farewell to my Home 1983, Sing Alone 1989, Selected Poems of Seven Chinese Poets 1993, Random Notes by Liu Shahe 1995, River of Quicksand (poetry) 1995, River of Quicksand (short texts) 2001. *Address:* 30 Dacisi Road, Chengdu City, Sichuan Province, People's Republic of China. *Telephone:* (28) 6781738 (home).

LIU, Timothy, BA, MA; American poet, writer and academic; *Associate Professor of English, William Paterson University;* b. 2 Oct. 1965, San Jose, Calif.; s. of Ching C. Liu and Lida Liu; partner, Christopher Arabadjis. *Education:* Brigham Young Univ., Univ. of Houston. *Career:* Asst Prof., Cornell Coll. 1994–98, William Paterson Univ., 1998–; Holloway Lecturer, Univ. of California 1997; Distinguished Visiting Writer, Univ. of N Carolina, Wilmington 2001; Core Faculty mem. Bennington Coll. 2005–; mem. Associated Writing Programs, PEN American Center. *Publications:* A Zipper of Haze 1988, Vox Angelica 1992, Burnt Offerings 1995, Say Goodnight 1998, Word of Mouth: An Anthology of Gay American Poets 2000, Hard Evidence 2001, Of Thee I Sing 2004, For Dust Thou Art 2005; contribs to reviews, quarterlies and journals. *Honours:* Norma Farber First Book Award, Poetry Soc. of America 1992, John Ciardi Fellowship, Bread Loaf Writers' Conf. 1993, Holloway Lecturer, Univ. of California, Berkeley 1997, Judge's Choice Award, Bumbershoot Festival 1998, Open Book Beyond Margins Award, PEN America Center 2000, Book of the Year Award, Publishers' Weekly 2004. *Address:* Department of English, William Paterson University, 300 Pompton Road, Wayne, NJ 07470, USA (office). *Telephone:* (973) 720-3567 (office). *Fax:* (973) 720-2189 (office). *E-mail:* liut@wpunj.edu (office).

LIU, Xinwu; Chinese writer; b. 4 June 1942, Chengdu, Sichuan Prov.; s. of Liu Tianyan and Wang Yuntao; m. Lu Xiaoge 1970; one s. *Education:* Beijing Teachers' Coll. *Career:* school teacher 1961–76; with Beijing Publishing House

1976–80; lived in Beijing 1950–; Ed.-in-Chief People's Literature 1987–89; professional writer 1980–; mem. Standing Cttee, China All Nation Youth Fed. –1992; mem. Council, Chinese Writers' Asscn. *Publications:* short stories: Class Counsellor (Nationwide Short Story Prize) 1977, The Position of Love 1978, I Love Every Piece of Green Leaves (Nationwide Short Story Prize) 1979, Black Walls 1982, A Scanning over the May 19th Accident 1985; novels: Ruyi (As You Wish) 1980, Overpass 1981, Drum Tower (Mao Dun Literature Prize) 1984; Liu Xinwu Collected Works (eight vols) 1993. *Address:* 8 Building No. 1404, Anding Menwai Dongheyan, Beijing 100011, People's Republic of China. *Telephone:* 4213965 (home).

LIVELY, Penelope Margaret, OBE, CBE, FRSL; British writer; b. 17 March 1933, Cairo, Egypt; d. of Roger Low and Vera Greer; m. Jack Lively 1957; one s. one d. *Education:* St Anne's Coll. Oxford. *Career:* mem. Bd British Library 1993–99, Bd British Council 1998–; mem. Soc. of authors, PEN. *Publications:* juvenile fiction: Astercote 1970, The Whispering Knights 1971, The Wild Hunt of Hagworthy 1971, The Driftway 1972, Going Back 1973, The Ghost of Thomas Kempe (Carnegie Medal) 1973, The House in Norham Gardens 1974, Boy Without a Name 1975, Fanny's Sister 1976, The Stained Glass Window 1976, A Stitch in Time (Whitbread Award) 1976, Fanny and the Monsters 1978, The Voyage of QV66 1978, Fanny and the Battle of Potter's Piece 1980, The Revenge of Samuel Stokes 1981, Uninvited Ghosts and Other Stories 1984, Dragon Trouble, Debbie and the Little Devil 1984, A House Inside Out 1987, The Cat, the Crow and the Banyan Tree 1994, Heatwave 1996, Beyond the Blue Mountains: Stories 1997, Spiderweb 1998, In Search of a Homeland: The Story of the Aeneid 2001; fiction: The Road to Lichfield 1977, Nothing Missing but the Samovar and Other Stories (Southern Arts Literature Prize) 1978, Treasures of Time (Nat. Book Award) 1979, Judgement Day 1980, Next to Nature, Art 1982, Perfect Happiness 1983, Corruption and Other Stories 1984, According to Mark 1984, Moon Tiger (Booker-McConnell Prize) 1986, Pack of Cards: Stories 1978–86 1986, Passing On 1989, City of the Mind 1991, Cleopatra's Sister 1993, The Photograph 2003; non-fiction: The Presence of the Past: An Introduction to Landscape History 1976, Oleander, Jacaranda (autobiog.) 1994, A House Unlocked (memoir) 2001, Making It Up 2005, Consequences 2007; television and radio scripts; contrib. to numerous journals and magazines. *Honours:* Hon. Fellow Swansea Univ. 2002; Hon. DLitt (Tufts Univ.) 1993, (Warwick) 1998. *Literary Agent:* David Higham Associates, 5–8 Lower John Street, Golden Square, London, W1F 4HA, England. *Telephone:* (20) 7434-5900. *Fax:* (20) 7437-1072.

LIVINGS, Henry; British writer and playwright; b. 20 Sept. 1929, Prestwich, Lancashire, England. *Education:* Liverpool University. *Publications:* Stop it Whoever You Are, 1961; Nil Caborundum, 1963; Kelly's Eye and Other Plays, 1965; Eh?, 1965; The Little Mrs Foster Show, 1967; Good Grief!, 1968; Honour and Offer, 1969; The Ffinest Ffamily in the Land, 1970; Pongo Plays 1–6, 1971; The Jockey Drives Late Nights, 1972; Six More Pongo Plays, 1974; Jonah, 1975; That the Medals and the Baton Be Put in View: The Story of a Village Band 1875–1975, 1975; Cinderella, 1976; Pennine Tales, 1983; Flying Eggs and Things: More Pennine Tales, 1986; The Rough Side of the Boards, 1994.

LJUNGGREN, Olof, LLB; Swedish publisher and business executive; b. 5 Jan. 1933, Eskilstuna; s. of Lars Ljunggren and Elisabeth Ljunggren; m. 1st Lena Carlsöö; m. 2nd Margreth Bäcklund; three s. *Education:* Univ. of Stockholm. *Career:* Sec. Tidningarnas Arbetsgivareförening (Swedish Newspaper Employers' Asscn) 1959–62, Pres. and CEO 1962–66; Deputy Pres. and CEO Allers Förlag AB 1967–72, Pres. and CEO 1972–74; Pres. and CEO Svenska Dagbladet 1974–78; Pres. and CEO Svenska Arbetsgivareföreningen (Swedish Employers' Confed.) 1978–89; Chair. of Bd Askild & Kärnekull Förlag AB 1971–74, Nord Artel AB 1971–78, Centralförbundet Folk och Försvar (Vice-Chair. 1978–83) 1983–86, Richard Hägglöf Fondkommission AB 1984–87, Svenska Dagbladet 1989–91, Liber AB 1990–98 (Vice-Chair. 1998–), Intentia AB 1994–, AMF 1995–, AFA 1995–2001, Addum AB 1996–99, Consolis AB Oy 1997–; mem. Bd, SPP 1978–93, Investor 1989–92, Providentia 1989–92, Alfa Laval 1989–92, Trygg Hansa 1990–95, and numerous other bds. *Honours:* Kt Commdr Order of the White Rose of Finland 1982, The King's Medal of the 12th Dimension with the Ribbon of the Order of the Seraphim 1987, Kommendörskorset av Den Kgl. Norske Fortjenstorden; Hon. MD. *Address:* Skeppargatan 7, 114 52 Stockholm, Sweden. *Telephone:* (707) 472346 (office); (8) 6678785 (home). *Fax:* (8) 6678785 (home). *E-mail:* olof.ljunggren2@ comhem.se (home).

LLEWELLYN, Sam, BA, MA; British author; b. 2 Aug. 1948, Isles of Scilly; m. Karen Wallace 1975, two s. *Education:* St Catherine's College, Oxford. *Career:* Ed., Picador, 1973–76; Senior Ed., McClelland and Stewart, 1976–79; Pres., Publisher, Arch Books, 1982–; Captain, SY Lucille, 1993–; mem. Society of Authors; CPRE; British Acad.; Cruising Asscn. *Publications:* Hell Bay, 1980; The Worst Journey in the Midlands, 1983; Dead Reckoning, 1987; Blood Orange, 1988; Death Roll, 1989; Pig in the Middle, 1989; Deadeye, 1990; Blood Knot, 1991; Riptide, 1992; Clawhammer, 1993; Maelstrom, 1994; The Rope School, 1994; The Magic Boathouse, 1994; The Iron Hotel, 1996; Storm Force from Navarone, 1996; The Polecat Cafe, 1998; The Shadow in the Sands, 1998; Thunderbolt from Navarone, 1998; The Sea Garden, 2000; Wonderdog, 2000; The Malpas Legacy, 2001; Little Darlings 2004; Nelson 2004; Bad,Bad Darlings 2005; Emperor Smith, The Man Who Built Scilly 2005; The Return of Otaki Eric 2005. Contributions: The Times, The Telegraph. *Honours:* Premio di Letteratura per l'Infanzia 1992. *Literary Agent:* Araminbe Whiting Law, 14 Vernon Street, London, W14 0RJ, England. *Fax:* (20) 7471-7900 (office). *Website:* www.samllewellyn.com.

LLOYD, Sir Geoffrey Ernest Richard, Kt, PhD, FBA; British academic; *Emeritus Professor of Ancient Philosophy and Science, University of Cambridge*; b. 25 Jan. 1933, London; s. of William Ernest Lloyd and Olive Irene Neville Lloyd; m. Janet Elizabeth Lloyd 1956; three s. *Education:* Charterhouse and King's Coll. Cambridge. *Career:* Asst Lecturer in Classics, Cambridge Univ. 1965–67, Lecturer 1967–74, Reader in Ancient Philosophy and Science 1974–83, Prof. 1983–2000, Emer. Prof. 2000–; Master, Darwin Coll., Cambridge 1989–2000, Hon. Fellow 2000–; Fellow King's Coll. 1957–89, Hon. Fellow 1990–; A. D. White Prof.-at-Large, Cornell Univ. 1990–96; Chair. East Asian History of Science Trust 1992–2002; mem. Japan Soc. for the Promotion of Science, Int. Acad. of the History of Science; Zhu Kezhen Visiting Prof., Inst. for the History of Natural Science, Beijing 2002. *Publications:* Polarity and Analogy 1966, Aristotle, the Growth and Structure of his Thought 1968, Early Greek Science: Thales to Aristotle 1970, Greek Science after Aristotle 1973, Hippocratic Writings (ed.) 1978, Aristotle on Mind and the Senses (ed., with G. E. L. Owen) 1978, Magic, Reason and Experience 1979, Science, Folklore and Ideology 1983, Science and Morality in Greco-Roman Antiquity 1985, The Revolutions of Wisdom 1987, Demystifying Mentalities 1990, Methods and Problems in Greek Science 1991, Adversaries and Authorities 1996, Aristotelian Explorations 1996, Greek Thought (ed.) 2000, The Ambitions of Curiosity 2002, The Way and the Word (with N. Sivin) 2002, In the Grip of Disease, Studies in the Greek Imagination 2003, Ancient Worlds, Modern Reflections 2004, The Delusions of Invulnerability 2005, Principles and Practices in Ancient Greek and Chinese Science 2006. *Honours:* Foreign Hon. mem. American Acad. of Arts and Sciences 1995; Hon. LittD (Athens) 2003; Sarton Medal 1987. *Address:* 2 Prospect Row, Cambridge, CB1 1DU, England (home). *Telephone:* (1223) 355970 (home). *E-mail:* gel20@hermes.cam.ac.uk (office).

LLOYD, John Nicol Fortune, MA; British journalist; *Editor, Financial Times Magazine*; b. 15 April 1946, s. of Christopher Lloyd and Joan A. Fortune; m. 1st Judith Ferguson 1974 (divorced 1979); m. 2nd Marcia Levy 1983 (divorced 1997); one s. *Education:* Waid Comprehensive School and Univ. of Edinburgh. *Career:* Ed. Time Out 1972–73; reporter, London Programme 1974–76; Producer, Weekend World 1976–77; industrial reporter, labour corresp., industrial and labour ed., Financial Times 1977–86; Ed. New Statesman 1986–87, Assoc. Ed. 1996–2003; with Financial Times 1987– (Moscow Corresp. 1991–95), now Editor Financial Times Magazine; freelance journalist 1996–; Dir East-West Trust, New York 1997–, Foreign Policy Centre 1999–. *Publications:* The Politics of Industrial Change (with Ian Benson) 1982, The Miners' Strike: Loss without Limit (with Martin Adeney) 1986, In Search of Work (with Charles Leadbeater) 1987, Counterblasts (contrib.) 1989, Rebirth of a Nation: an Anatomy of Russia 1998, Re-engaging Russia 2000, The Protest Ethic 2001, What the Media are Doing to Our Politics 2004, The Republic of Entertainment 2005. *Honours:* Journalist of the Year, Granada Awards 1984, Specialist Writer of the Year, IPC Awards 1985; Rio Tinto David Watt Memorial Prize 1997. *Address:* Financial Times, One Southwark Bridge, London, SE1 9HL, England (office). *Telephone:* (20) 7873-3000 (office). *Website:* www.ft.com.

LLOYD, Kathleen Annie, (Kathleen Conlon, Kate North), BA; British writer; b. 4 Jan. 1943, Southport; m. Frank Lloyd 1962 (divorced); one s. *Education:* King's Coll., Univ. of Durham. *Career:* mem. Soc. of Authors. *Publications:* Apollo's Summer Look 1968, Tomorrow's Fortune 1971, My Father's House 1972, A Twisted Skein 1975, A Move in the Game 1979, A Forgotten Season 1980, Consequences 1981, The Best of Friends 1984, Face Values 1985, Distant Relations 1989, Unfinished Business 1990; as Kate North: Land of My Dreams 1997, Gollancz 1997; contribs to Atlantic Review, Cosmopolitan, Woman's Journal, Woman, Woman's Own. *Address:* 26A Brighton Road, Birkdale, Southport, PR8 4DD, England.

LLOYD, Trevor Owen, MA, DPhil; Canadian/British academic and writer; *Emeritus Professor of History, University of Toronto*; b. 30 July 1934, London, England. *Education:* Merton Coll., Oxford, Nuffield Coll. Oxford. *Career:* Lecturer Dept of History, Univ. of Toronto 1959–63, Asst Prof. 1963–67, Assoc. Prof. 1967–73, Prof. 1973–97, Emeritus Prof. 1997–; mem. William Morris Soc., Victorian Studies Asscn of Ontario, Royal Historical Soc. *Publications:* Canada in World Affairs 1957–59 1968, The General Election of 1880 1968, Suffragettes International 1971, The Growth of Parliamentary Democracy in Britain 1973, Empire, Welfare State, Europe: English History 1906–1992 (revised edn as Empire, Welfare State, Europe: The United Kingdom 1906–2001) 1993, The British Empire 1558–1995 1996, Empire: The History of the British Empire 2001; contrib. to various journals. *Honours:* Guggenheim Fellowship 1978–79. *Address:* Department of History, University of Toronto, Toronto, M5S 3G3 (office); 15 McMurrich Street, Apt 502, Toronto, M5R 3M6, Canada (home). *Telephone:* (416) 978-4810 (office); (416) 960-5556 (home).

LLOYD-JONES, Sir (Peter) Hugh (Jefferd), Kt, MA, FBA; British classical scholar; *Regius Professor of Greek Emeritus, University of Oxford*; b. 21 Sept. 1922, St Peter Port, Guernsey; s. of Brevet-Major W. Lloyd-Jones, DSO and Norah Leila Jefferd; m. 1st Frances Elisabeth Hedley 1953 (divorced 1981); two s. one d.; m. 2nd Mary R. Lefkowitz 1982. *Education:* Lycée Français du Royaume-Uni (London), Westminster School and Christ Church, Oxford. *Career:* served in Indian Intelligence Corps 1942–46; Fellow, Jesus Coll. Cambridge 1948–54; Fellow and E.P. Warren Praelector in Classics, Corpus Christi Coll. Oxford 1954–60, Regius Prof. of Greek and Student of Christ Church 1960–89, Prof. Emer. 1989–; J. H. Gray Lecturer, Cambridge 1961; Visiting Prof. Yale Univ. 1964–65, 1967–68; Sather Prof. of Classical Literature, Univ. of Calif. at Berkeley 1969–70; Alexander White Visiting Prof. Univ. of Chicago 1972; Visiting Prof., Harvard Univ. 1976–77; mem. British Acad., Acad. of Athens; Corresp. mem. American Acad. of Arts and Sciences, Nordrhein-Westfälische Akad. der Wissenschaften, Accad. di Archeologia, Lettere e belle Arti di Napoli, Bayerische Akad. der Wissenschaften, American Philosophical Soc. *Publications:* Appendix to Aeschylus (Loeb Classical Library) 1957, Menandri Dyscolus (Oxford Classical Texts) 1960; The Justice of Zeus 1971, (ed.) Maurice Bowra: a Celebration 1974, Females of the Species 1975, Myths of the Zodiac 1978, Mythical Beasts 1980, Blood for the Ghosts 1982, Classical Survivals 1982, Supplementum Hellenisticum (with P. J. Parsons) 1983, Supplementum Supplementi 2005; translated Paul Maas, Greek Metre 1962, Aeschylus Agamemnon, The Libation-Bearers and The Eumenides 1970, Sophoclea (with N. G. Wilson) 1990, Academic Papers (2 Vols) 1990, Vol. III 2005, Sophoclis Fabulae (with N. G. Wilson) 1990, Greek in a Cold Climate 1991, Sophocles (Loeb Classical Library, 3 Vols) 1994–96, Sophocles: Second Thoughts (with N. G. Wilson) 1997; edited The Greeks 1962, Tacitus 1964; articles and reviews in periodicals. *Honours:* Hon. DHumLitt (Chicago) 1970; Hon. DPhil (Tel Aviv) 1984; Hon. PhD (Thessaloniki) 1999, (Göttingen) 2002; Chancellor's Prize for Latin Prose, Ireland and Craven Scholarships 1947. *Address:* 15 West Riding, Wellesley, MA 02482, USA. *Telephone:* (781) 237-2212. *Fax:* (781) 237-2246. *E-mail:* mlefkowitz@wellesley.educ (home).

LLYWELYN, Robin, BA; Welsh writer; b. 24 Nov. 1958, Bangor. *Education:* Univ. Coll. Wales, Aberystwyth. *Publications:* Seren Wen ar Gefndir Gwyn (trans. as White Star) (Nat. Eisteddfod Prose Medal) 1992, O'r harbwr gwag i'r cefnfor gwyn (trans. as From Empty Harbour to White Ocean) 1994, Y Dwr Mawr Llwyd (short stories, trans. as The Big Grey Water) 1996, Y Filltir Sgwar 1996, Gwartheg ar y Drafforddd 1999, Gwr y Plas 2000, Y Syrcas 2004, Un Diwrnod yn yr Eisteddfod 2004. *Honours:* Welsh Arts Council Book of the Year 1993, BBC Wales Writer of the Year Award 1994, Daniel Owen Memorial Prize. *Address:* c/o Parthian Books, The Old Surgery, Napier Street, Cardigan, SA43 1ED, Wales. *E-mail:* robin@swyddfa.co.uk. *Website:* www.llywelyn.com.

LO LIYONG, Taban, BA, MFA; Ugandan novelist, poet and essayist; b. 1939, Kajokaji, Sudan. *Education:* Nat. Teachers' Coll., Kampala, Uganda, Howard Univ., Washington, DC and Univ. of Iowa, USA. *Career:* taught at univs in Kenya, Tanzania, Papua New Guinea, Sudan, Japan and Australia; currently Prof. of Literature, Univ. of Venda, South Africa. *Publications:* poetry: Frantz Fanon's Uneven Ribs: With Poems More and More 1971, Another Nigger Dead 1972, Ballads of Underdevelopment: Poems and Thoughts 1974, To Still a Passion 1977, The Cows of Shambat 1992, Carrying Knowledge up a Palm Tree 1997, Homage to Onyame 1998; prose: Fixions 1969, Eating Chiefs: Lwo Culture from Lolwe to Malkal 1970, Uniformed Man: Essays 1977, Thirteen Offensives Against our Enemies: Essays 1977, Meditations 1978, Images of Women in Folktales and Short Stories of Africa, Another Last Word 1990. *Address:* University of Venda, Private bag X5050, Thohoyandou 0950, Northern Province, South Africa.

LOADES, David Michael, MA, PhD, DLitt, FRHistS; British academic (retd) and writer; b. 19 Jan. 1934, Cambridge; m. Judith Anne Atkins 1987. *Education:* Emmanuel Coll., Cambridge. *Career:* Lecturer in Political Science, Univ. of St Andrews 1961–63; Lecturer in History, Univ. of Durham 1963–70; Sr Lecturer 1970–77, Reader 1977–80, Prof. of History 1980–96, Univ. College of North Wales, Bangor; Dir, British Acad. John Foxe Project 1993; fellow Soc. of Antiquaries of London. *Publications:* Two Tudor Conspiracies 1965, The Oxford Martyrs 1970, The Reign of Mary Tudor 1979, The Tudor Court 1986, Mary Tudor: A Life 1989, The Tudor Navy 1992, John Dudley: Duke of Northumberland 1996, Tudor Government 1997, England's Maritime Empire 2000, Elizabeth: The Golden Reign of Gloriana 2003, Elizabeth I 2003, Intrigue and Reason: The Tudor Court 1547–1558 2004; Ed.: The Papers of George Wyatt 1968, The End of Strife 1984, Faith and Identity 1990, John Foxe and the English Reformation 1997, John Foxe: An Historical Perspective 1999, The Anthony Roll of Henry VIII (with C. S. Knighton) 2000, Letters from the Mary Rose (with C. S. Knighton) 2002, The Chronicles of the Tudor Queens 2002, John Foxe: at Home and Abroad 2004, Henry VIII: Court, Church and Conflict 2007; contrib. to journals. *Address:* The Cottage, Priory Lane, Burford, Oxon. OX18 4SG, England.

LOBO, Tatiana; Chilean writer; b. 1939, Puerto Montt. *Publications:* novels: Asalto al paraíso (trans. as Assault on Paradise) 1993, Calypso 1996; short stories: Tiempo de Claveles 1989; non-fiction: Entre Dios y el Diablo: Mujeres de la colonia: crónicas 1993, Negros y Blancos: Todo Mezclado (with Mauricio Meléndez) 1997. *Address:* c/o Curbstone Press, 321 Jackson Street, Willimantic, CT 06226-1738, USA. *E-mail:* info@curbstone.org. *Website:* www.curbstone.org.

LOBO ANTUNES, António, MD; Portuguese novelist; b. 1 Sept. 1942, Lisbon; s. of João Alfredo Lobo Antunes and Maria Margarida Almeida Lima; three d. *Education:* higher educ. in Portugal. *Career:* fmr doctor and psychiatrist; now full-time writer (his experience of the Portuguese colonial war in Africa being a major influence). *Publications include:* twenty-six novels. *Honours:* French Culture Prize 1996, 1997, Prix du Meilleur Livre Etranger, Rosália de Castro Prize 1999, European Literature Prize of Austria 2000, Latin Union Int. Prize 2003, Jerusalem Prize 2003, Camões Prize 2007. *Address:* Avenida Afonso III 23, 3°c, 1900 Lisbon, Portugal. *Telephone:* 8155566.

LOCHHEAD, Douglas Grant, MA, BLS, FRSC; Canadian poet, writer and academic; *Professor Emeritus of Canadian Studies, Mount Allison University, Sackville*; b. 25 March 1922, Guelph, ON; m. Jean St Clair 1949 (deceased); two d. *Education:* McGill Univ., Univ. of Toronto. *Career:* Librarian Victoria Coll., BC 1951–52, Cornell Univ., Ithaca, New York 1952–53, Dalhousie Univ., Halifax, NS 1953–60, York Univ., Toronto 1960–63; Librarian and Fellow, Massey Coll. 1963–75; Prof. of English, Univ. Coll., Univ. of Toronto 1963–75; Davidson Prof. of Canadian Studies and Dir of the Centre for Canadian Studies 1975–87, Prof. Emer. 1987–, Mount Allison Univ., Sackville, NB; Visiting Prof., Univ. of Edinburgh 1983–84; mem. League of Canadian Poets; life mem., Bibliographical Soc. of Canada. *Publications:* The Heart is Fire 1959, It is all Around 1960, Millwood Road Poems 1970, The Full Furnace: Collected Poems 1975, A & E 1980, Battle Sequence 1980, High Marsh Road 1980, The Panic Field 1984, Tiger in the Skull: New and Selected Poems 1959–85 1986, Dykelands 1989, Upper Cape Poems 1989, Black Festival: A Long Poem 1991, Homage to Henry Alline & Other Poems 1992, Breakfast at Mel's and Other Poems of Love and Places 1997, All Things Do Continue (poems) 1997, Cape Enragé: Poems on a Raised Beach 2000, Weathers: New and Selected Poems 2002, Orkney: October Diary 2002: Midgic: A Place, A Poem 2003, La Strada di Tantramar, versi per un diario 2004; contrib. to various publications. *Honours:* Hon. DLitt (St Mary's) 1987, (New Brunswick) 2006, Hon. LLD (Dalhousie) 1987; Golden Dog Award 1974, NB Govt Award in English Literature 2001, Poet Laureate of Sackville, NB 2003, Carlo Betochi Int. Poetry Prize, Florence, Italy 2005. *Address:* 9 Quarry Lane, Sackville, NB E4L 4G3, Canada (office). *Telephone:* (506) 536-1189 (home).

LOCHHEAD, Liz; British poet, playwright, screenwriter and teacher; b. 26 Dec. 1947, Motherwell. *Career:* fmr art school teacher, Glasgow and Bristol; Lecturer, Univ. of Glasgow. *Television includes:* Damages (BBC). *Publications include:* poetry: Memo for Spring 1972, The Grimm Sisters 1981, Dreaming of Frankenstein and Collected Poems 1984, True Confessions and True Clichés 1985, Bagpipe Muzak 1991, Cuba/Dog House (with Gina Moxley) 2000; plays: Blood and Ice 1982, Silver Service 1984, Dracula (adaptation) 1989, Mary Queen of Scots Got Her Head Chopped Off 1989, Molière's Tartuffe (Scots trans. in rhyming couplets), Perfect Days 1998, Medea (adaptation) 2000, Misery Guts (adaptation) 2002; screenplay: Now and Then 1972; anthology contribs: Penguin Modern Poets Vols 3 and 4, Shouting It Out 1995. *Honours:* BBC Scotland Prize 1971, Scottish Arts Council Award 1972. *Address:* c/o Nick Hern Books Ltd, The Glasshouse, 49A Goldhawk Road, London, W12 8QP, England (office).

LOCKE, Hubert Gaylord, BA, BD, MA; American academic and writer; *Professor of Public Service, University of Washington, Seattle*; b. 30 April 1934, Detroit, MI; two d. *Education:* Wayne State Univ., Univ. of Chicago, Univ. of Michigan. *Career:* Asst Dir 1957–62, Dir 1967–70, Office of Religious Affairs, Adjunct Asst Prof. of Urban Education 1970–72, Wayne State Univ.; Assoc. Prof. of Urban Studies and Dean of the Coll. of Public Affairs and Community Service, Univ. of Nebraska 1972–75; Prof. 1976–, Assoc. Dean Coll. of Arts and Sciences 1976–77, Vice-Provost for Academic Affairs 1977–82, Dean Graduate School of Public Affairs 1982–87, John and Marguerite Corbally Prof. of Public Service 1996–, Univ. of Washington, Seattle; mem. bd of dirs, Nat. Council on Crime and Delinquency, Seattle Symphony; mem. Comm. on Judicial Conduct, State of Washington. *Publications:* The Detroit Riot of 1967 1969, The Care and Feeding of White Liberals 1970, The German Church Struggle and the Holocaust (ed. with Franklin H. Littell) 1974, The Church Confronts the Nazis (ed.) 1984, Exile in the Fatherland: The Prison Letters of Martin Niemöller (ed.) 1986, The Barmen Confession: Papers from the Seattle Assembly (ed.) 1986, The Black Antisemitism Controversy: Views of Black Protestants (ed.) 1992, Learning from History 2000, Searching for God in God-Forsaken Times and Places 2003; contrib. to books and professional journals. *Honours:* Hon. Dr of Divinity (Payne Theological Seminary) 1968, (Chicago Theological Seminary) 1971, Hon. DHumLitt (Univ. of Akron) 1971, (Univ. of Nebraska) 1992, (Univ. of Bridgeport) 1997; Michigan Bar Asscn Liberty Bell Award 1967, Wayne State Univ. Distinguished Alumni Award 1979. *Address:* c/o 2801 First Avenue 609, Seattle, WA 98121, USA. *Telephone:* (206) 379-0863 (home).

LOCKE, Ralph Paul, MA, PhD; American musicologist, teacher and writer; *Professor of Musicology, Eastman School of Music, University of Rochester*; b. 9 March 1949, Boston, MA; m. Lona M. Farhi 1979; two d. *Education:* Harvard Univ., Univ. of Chicago. *Career:* Faculty, Eastman School of Music, Univ. of Rochester, NY 1975–, Sr Ed. Eastman Studies in Music; mem. Editorial Bd Univ. of Rochester Press, Journal of Musicological Research, Ad Parnassum, Verdi Forum; mem. American Musicological Soc., Int. Musicological Soc., Soc. for American Music. *Publications:* Music, Musicians, and the Saint-Simonians 1986, Cultivating Music in America: Women Patrons and Activists Since 1860 1997; contribs to reference books and professional journals. *Honours:* Best Article Citation, Music Library Asscn 1980, Galler Dissertation Prize 1981, ASCAP-Deems Taylor Awards 1992, 1996, 1999, 2003, H. Colin Slim Award for article on Aida, American Musicological Soc. 2006. *Address:* Department of Musicology, Eastman School of Music, 26 Gibbs Street, Rochester, NY 14604, USA (office). *Telephone:* (585) 274-1455 (office).

LOCKE, Robert Howard, (Clayton Bess), BA, MA, MS; American librarian, playwright and author; b. 30 Dec. 1944, Vallejo, CA. *Education:* California State University, Chico, San Francisco State University, Simmons College, Boston. *Plays:* The Dolly; Play; Rose Jewel and Harmony; On Daddy's Birthday; Murder and Edna Redrum; Premiere. *Publications:* as Clayton Bess: Story for a Black Night, 1982; The Truth About the Moon, 1984; Big Man and the Burn-Out, 1985; Tracks, 1986; The Mayday Rampage, 1993. *Honours:* Best First Novel, Commonwealth Club of California, 1982; Best Book for Young Adults, American Library Asscn, 1987.

LOCKERBIE, D(onald) Bruce, AB, MA; American scholar and writer; *Chairman, Paideia Inc.*; b. 25 Aug. 1935, Capreol, ON, Canada. *Education:* New York University. *Career:* Scholar-in-Residence, Stony Brook School, New York, 1957–91; Visiting Consultant at American Schools in Asia and Africa, 1974; Visiting Lecturer/Consultant to American universities; Chair. Paideia, Inc. 1984–. *Publications:* Billy Sunday, 1965; Patriarchs and Prophets, 1969; Hawthorne, 1970; Melville, 1970; Twain, 1970; Major American Authors, 1970; Success in Writing (with L. Westdahl), 1970; Purposeful Writing, 1972; The Way They Should Go, 1972; The Liberating Word, 1974; The Cosmic Center: The Apostles' Creed, 1977; A Man under Orders: Lt Gen William K. Harrison, 1979; Who Educates Your Child?, 1980; The Timeless Moment, 1980; Asking Questions, 1980; Fatherlove, 1981; In Peril on the Sea, 1984; The Christian, the Arts and Truth, 1985; Thinking and Acting Like a Christian, 1989; Take Heart (with L. Lockerbie), 1990; College: Getting In and Staying In (with D. Fonseca), 1990; A Passion for Learning, 1994; From Candy Sales to Committed Donors, 1996; Dismissing God, 1998, A Christian Paideia 2005. *Honours:* Hon. DHL (Eastern Coll.) 1985, (Taylor Univ.) 1993. *Address:* PO Box 26, Stony Brook, NY 11790, USA.

LOCKLEY, John, MA, MB BChir; British doctor and writer; b. 10 Feb. 1948, Sale, Cheshire; m. Mavis June Watt 1972; two s. one d. *Education:* Gonville and Caius Coll., Cambridge. *Career:* House Surgeon, Royal London Hospital 1972; Vocational Training Course for General Practice, Colchester 1973; General Practitioner, Ampthill, Bedfordshire, England 1976–; Ed., Torus 2000; Fellow Soc. of Medical Writers; mem. Soc. of Authors. *Publications:* The Complete BBC Computer User Handbook 1988, Acorn to PC: Changing from DFS and ADFS to DOS 1990, A Practical Workbook for the Depressed Christian 1991, Headaches – A Comprehensive Guide to Relieving Headaches and Migraine 1993, After the Fire 1994, After the Fire II – A Still Small Voice 1996, After the Fire III – Chronicles 1998; contrib. many articles to General Practitioner, Daily Telegraph, Daily Mail and Guardian, Doctor Magazine. *Honours:* Medeconomics GP Writer of the Year 1989. *Address:* 107 Flitwick Road, Ampthill, Bedfordshire MK45 2NT, England. *Telephone:* (1525) 631395 (office). *E-mail:* john.lockley@gmail.com.

LOCKLIN, Gerald, BA, MA, PhD; American author, poet, dramatist, literary critic and academic; *Professor Emeritus of English, California State University of Long Beach*; b. 17 Feb. 1941, Rochester, NY. *Education:* St John Fisher College, University of Arizona. *Career:* Instructor in English, California State College at Los Angeles, 1964–65; Asst Prof. to Prof. of English, California State University at Long Beach, 1965–; mem. Associated Writing Programs; e. e. cummings Society; Hemingway Society; PEN; Western Literature Asscn. *Publications:* Sunset Beach, 1967; The Toad Poems, 1970; Poop and Other Poems, 1973; Toad's Europe, 1973; Locked In, 1973; Son of Poop, 1974; Tarzan and Shane Meet the Toad (with others), 1975; The Chase: A Novel, 1976; The Criminal Mentality, 1976; The Four-Day Week and Other Stories, 1977; Pronouncing Borges, 1977; A Weekend on Canada, 1979; The Cure: A Novel for Speed Readers, 1979; Two Summer Sequences, 1979; Two Weeks on Mr Stanford's Farm, 1980; The Last of Toad, 1980; Two for the Seesaw and One for the Road, 1980; Scenes from a Second Adolescence, 1981; A Clear and Present Danger to Society, 1981; By Land, Sea, and Air, 1982; Why Turn a Perfectly Good Toad into a Prince?, 1983; Fear and Paternity in the Pauma Valley, 1984; The Ensenada Poems (with Ray Zepada), 1984; The Case of the Missing Blue Volkswagen, 1984; The Phantom of the Johnny Carson Show, 1984; We Lose L.A. (with Ray Zepeda), 1985; The English Mini-Tour, 1987; Gringo and Other Poems, 1987; Gerald Haslam, 1987; A Constituency of Dunces, 1988; Children of a Lesser Demagogue, 1988; On the Rack, 1988; Lost and found, 1989; The Treasure of the Sierra Faulkner, 1989; The Gold Rush and Other Stories, 1989; The Rochester Trip, 1990; The Conference, 1990; The Illegitimate Son of Mr Madman, 1991; The Firebird Poems, 1992; A New Geography of Poets (ed. with Edward Field and Charles Stetler), 1992; The Old Mongoose and Other Poems, 1994; Big Man on Canvas, 1994; The Cabo Conference, 1995; Charles Bukowski: A Sure Bet, 1996; The Pittsburgh Poems, 1996; The Macao/Hong Kong Trip, 1996; The Hospital Poems, 1998; Two Novellas (with Donna Hilbert), 1998; Down and Out: A Novel for Adults, 1999; Hemingway Colloquium: The Poet Goes to Cuba, 1999; Candy Bars, 2000; A Simpler Time, a Simpler Place: Three Mid-Century Stories, 2000; The Iceberg Theory, 2000; Four Jazz Women, 2000; Art and Life, 2000; The Sixth Jazz Chapbook, 2001; Familiarities, 2001; The Life Force Poems, 2002; The Mystical Exercycle, 2002; The Pocket Book, 2003; Henry's Gift, 2003; Takes on Bill Evans, 2003; More Takes on Bill Evans, 2003; The Dorset Poems, 2003, The Modigliani/Montparnasse Poems 2003, Retirement Blues 2003, The Ultimate Pessimist 2003, Two Jazz Poems 2004, Jimmy Abbey Stays for the Drum Circle 2004, The Spirit of the Struggle 2005, New Orleans, Chicago, and Points Elsewhere 2006, Open Thy Effing Ears (Please) 2006; contrib. to periodicals. *Address:* c/o Department of English, California State University at Long Beach, Long Beach, CA 90840, USA. *Telephone:* (542) 985-5285 (office). *E-mail:* glocklin@csulb.edu (office). *Website:* www.geraldlocklin.com (home).

LOCKRIDGE, Ernest Hugh, BA, MA, PhD; American academic, novelist and artist; b. 28 Nov. 1938, Bloomington, IN; m. Laurel Richardson 1981; two s. three d. *Education:* Indiana Univ., Yale Univ. *Career:* Prof., Yale Univ.

1963–71, Ohio State Univ. 1971–. *Publications:* fiction: Hartspring Blows his Mind 1968, Prince Elmo's Fire 1974, Flying Elbows 1975; non-fiction: 20th Century Studies of the Great Gatsby 1968, Travels with Ernest 2004; contrib. to professional journals. *Honours:* Book-of-the-Month Club Selection 1974, Ohio State Univ. Distinguished Teaching Award 1985. *Address:* 143 W South Street, Worthington, OH 43085, USA. *E-mail:* lockridge.1@osu.edu.

LOCKWOOD, Lewis Henry, BA, MFA, PhD; American musicologist, writer, editor and academic; b. 16 Dec. 1930, New York, NY. *Education:* Queens Coll., CUNY, Princeton Univ. *Career:* Faculty 1958–65, Assoc. Prof. 1965–68, Prof. 1968–80, Chair., Dept of Music 1970–73, Princeton Univ.; Ed., Journal of the American Musicological Soc. 1963–66, Beethoven Forum 1991–; Prof. of Music 1980–2002, Chair Dept of Music 1988–90, Harvard Univ.; Gen. Ed., Studies in Musical Genesis and Structure 1984–98; mem. American Acad. of Arts and Sciences, American Musicological Soc. (pres. 1987–88, hon. mem. 1993–). *Publications:* Music in Renaissance Ferrara, 1400–1505 1984, Beethoven Essays: Studies in Honor of Elliot Forbes (co-ed.) 1984, Essays in Musicology: A Tribute to Alvin Johnson (co-ed.) 1990, Beethoven: Studies in the Creative Process 1992, Beethoven: The Music and the Life 2003; contrib. to scholarly books and journals. *Honours:* Dr hc (Università degli Studi, Ferrara) 1991, (New England Conservatory of Music) 1998;Nat. Endowment for the Humanities Sr Fellowships 1973–74, 1984–85, Guggenheim Fellowship 1977–78; ASCAP Deems Taylor Award 1993, Festschrift published in his honour 1997. *Address:* c/o Department of Music, Harvard University, Cambridge, MA 02138, USA. *E-mail:* llockw@fas.harvard.edu.

LODGE, David John, CBE, PhD, FRSL; British writer and academic; *Professor Emeritus of English Literature, University of Birmingham*; b. 28 Jan. 1935, London, England; s. of William F. Lodge and Rosalie M. Lodge (née Murphy); m. Mary Frances Jacob 1959; two s. one d. *Education:* St Joseph's Acad., Blackheath and Univ. Coll., London. *Career:* asst, British Council, London 1959–60; Asst Lecturer in English, Univ. of Birmingham 1960–62, Lecturer 1963–71, Sr Lecturer 1971–73, Reader 1973–76, Prof. of English Literature 1976–87, Hon. Prof. 1987–2000, Prof. Emer. 2001–; Chair. Booker Prize Cttee 1989; Harkness Commonwealth Fellow, 1964–65; Visiting Assoc. Prof. Univ. of Calif. at Berkeley 1969; Henfield Writing Fellow, Univ. of E Anglia 1977; Fellow, Univ. Coll. London 1982, Goldsmith's Coll. 1992. *Publications:* fiction: The Picturegoers 1960, Ginger, You're Barmy 1962, The British Museum is Falling Down 1965, Out of the Shelter 1970, Changing Places: A Tale of Two Campuses 1975, How Far Can You Go? (aka Souls and Bodies) (Whitbread Book of Year Award) 1980, Small World: An Academic Romance 1984, Nice Work (Sunday Express Book of the Year Award) 1988, The Writing Game (play) 1991, Paradise News 1991, Therapy 1995, Home Truths (novella) 1999, Thinks... (novel) 2001, Author, Author 2004; non-fiction: Language of Fiction 1966, Graham Greene 1966, The Novelist at the Crossroads and Other Essays on Fiction and Criticism 1971, Evelyn Waugh 1971, Twentieth-Century Literary Criticism: A Reader (ed.) 1972, The Modes of Modern Writing: Metaphor, Metonymy and the Typology of Modern Literature 1977, Working with Structuralism: Essays and Reviews on Nineteenth- and Twentieth Century Literature 1981, Write On: Occasional Essays 1986, Modern Criticism and Theory: A Reader (ed.) 1988, After Bakhtin: Essays on Fiction and Criticism 1990, The Art of Fiction: Illustrated from Classic and Modern Texts 1992, The Practice of Writing: Essays, Lectures, Reviews, and a Diary 1996, Consciousness and the Novel 2002, The Year of Henry James 2006. *Honours:* Chevalier, Ordre des Arts et des Lettres 1997; Yorkshire Post Fiction Prize 1975, Hawthornden Prize 1976, RTS Award for Best Drama Serial 1990. *Address:* c/o Department of English, University of Birmingham, Birmingham, B15 2TT, England (office). *Telephone:* (121) 414-5670 (office). *Fax:* (121) 414-5668 (office). *E-mail:* english@bham.ac.uk (office). *Website:* www.english.bham.ac.uk (office).

LOEWE, Michael Arthur Nathan, MA, PhD; British academic (retd) and writer; b. 2 Nov. 1922, Oxford. *Education:* Magdalen Coll., Oxford, Univ. of London, Univ. of Cambridge. *Career:* Lecturer in History of the Far East, Univ. of London 1956–63; Lecturer in Chinese Studies, Univ. of Cambridge 1963–90. *Publications:* Imperial China: The Historical Background to the Modern Age 1966, Records of Han Administration (two vols) 1967, Everyday Life in Early Imperial China During the Han Period, 202 BC–AD 220 1968, Crisis and Conflict in Han China, 104 BC–AD 9 1974, Ancient Cosmologies (ed. with Carmen Blacker) 1975, Ways to Paradise: The Chinese Quest for Immortality 1979, Divination and Oracles (ed. with Carmen Blacker) 1981, Chinese Ideas of Life and Death: Faith, Myth, and Reason in the Han Period (202 BC–AD 220) 1982, The Ch'in and Han Empires, 221 BC–AD 220, Vol. 1 of The Cambridge History of China (ed. with Denis Twichett) 1986, The Pride That Was China 1990, Early Chinese Texts: A Bibliographical Guide 1993, Divination, Mythology and Monarchy in Han China 1994, The Cambridge History of Ancient China (ed. with E. Shaughnessy) 1999, A Biographical Dictionary of the Qin, Former Han and Xin Periods 2000, The Men Who Governed Han China 2004, The Government of the Qin and Han Empires 221 BCE–220 CE 2006; contrib. to scholarly publications. *Honours:* Fellow, Soc. of Antiquaries, 1972; Fellow, Clare Hall, 1968–90; Foreign Hon. Mem., American Acad. of Arts and Sciences, 2002. *Address:* Willow House, Grantchester, Cambridge CB3 9NF, England.

LÖFFELHOLZ, Thomas, DrJur; German journalist and editor; *Editor, Die Welt*. *Career:* Chair. German Press Asscn, Bonn 1982–83; Chief Ed. Stuttgarter Zeitung 1983–95; Ed., then Chief Ed. Die Welt 1995–98, re-apptd. Ed. 2001–. *Honours:* Chevalier Ordre de la Couronne (Belgium); Karl Bräuer Prize 1981, Ludwig Erhard Prize 1984, Franz Karl Maier Prize 1992, Theodor Wolff Prize 1972, 1998, Bundesverdienstkreuz (First Class) 1999. *Address:* Die Welt, Axel-Springer-Strasse 65, 10888 Berlin, Germany. *Telephone:* (30) 25910. *Fax:* (30) 251606. *Website:* www.welt.de.

LÖFGREN, Lars, PhD; Swedish theatre, film and television director, playwright and poet; *Lord Chamberlain*; b. 6 Sept. 1935, The Arctic Circle; m. Anna-Karin Gillberg 1963; one s. two d. *Education:* Gustavus Adolphus Coll., USA, Stanford Univ., USA, Sorbonne, France, Uppsala Univ., Sweden. *Career:* Dir Royal Dramatic Theatre of Sweden 1985–97, Nordic Museum 1997–2001; Lord Chamberlain 1999–. *Publications:* various plays, filmscripts, TV scripts, poetry, novels, svensk teater — Artistry of the Swedish Theater 2003. *Honours:* Lord-in-Waiting to His Majesty the King; Commdr de l'Orde de la Légion d'Honneur 2001; Royal Prize of Swedish Acad. 1996. *Address:* The Office of the Marshal of the Court of the Royal Palace, 11130 Stockholm (office); Sjötullsbacken 27, 11525 Stockholm Sweden (home). *Telephone:* (8) 402–6000 (office); (8) 855822 (home). *E-mail:* lars.lofgren@pof.se (home).

LOGAN, Mark (see Nicole, Christopher Robin)

LOGUE, Christopher John, CBE; British writer and poet; b. 23 Nov. 1926, Southsea; s. of John Logue and Molly Logue (née Chapman); m. Rosemary Hill 1985. *Education:* Prior Park Coll., Bath and Portsmouth Grammar School. *Screenplays:* The End of Arthur's Marriage 1965, Savage Messiah 1972, Crusoe (based on Defoe's novel, with Walon Green) 1989. *Recordings:* Red Bird (poetry and jazz, with Tony Kinsey and Bill Le Sage) 1960, Songs from the Establishment 1962, The Death of Patroclus 1963, Audiologue (recordings 1958–98) 2001. *Film roles:* Swinburne in Ken Russell's Dante's Inferno 1966, John Ball in John Irvin's The Peasant's Revolt 1969, Cardinal Richelieu in Ken Russell's The Devils 1970; also TV and stage roles. *Publications:* poetry: Wand & Quadrant 1953, Devil, Maggot & Son 1954, The Weakdream Sonnets 1955, The Man Who Told His Love: 20 Poems Based on P. Neruda's 'Los Cantos d'amores' 1958, Songs 1959, Songs from 'The Lily-White Boys' 1960, Patrocleia 1962, Pax 1967, The Establishment Songs 1966, The Girls 1969, New Numbers 1969, Abecedary 1977, Ode to the Dodo 1981, War Music 1981, Fluff 1984, Kings 1991, The Husbands 1994, Selected Poems 1996, Prince Charming: A Memoir 1999, Logue's Homer: War Music 2001, All Day Permanent Red 2003; plays: The Trial of Cob & Leach 1959, The Lily-White Boys (with Harry Cookson) 1959, Antigone 1961, The Seven Deadly Sins 1986; other: Lust, by Count Plamiro Vicarion (ed.) 1955, Count Palmiro Vicarion's Book of Limericks (ed.) 1959, The Arrival of the Poet in the City: A Treatment for a Film 1964, True Stories 1966, The Children's Book of Comic Verse (ed.) 1979, The Bumper Book of True Stories 1980, London in Verse (ed.) 1982, Sweet & Sour: An Anthology of Comic Verse (ed.) 1983, The Oxford Book of Pseuds (ed.) 1983, The Children's Book of Children's Rhymes (ed.) 1986, Cold Calls: War Music Continued (Whitbread Prize for Poetry) 2005; contrib. to Private Eye, The Times, Sunday Times. *Honours:* First Wilfred Owen Award for Poetry 1998, Civil List Pension for Services to Literature 2002. *Address:* 41 Camberwell Grove, London, SE5 8JA, England.

LOMAS, Herbert, MA; British poet, critic and translator; b. 7 Feb. 1924, Yorkshire; m. Mary Marshall Phelps 1968; one s. one d. *Education:* Univ. of Liverpool. *Career:* teacher, Spetsai, Greece, 1950–51; Lecturer, later Sr Lecturer, Univ. of Helsinki, 1952–65; Sr Lecturer, Borough Road Coll. 1966–72, Prin. Lecturer 1972–82; mem., Soc. of Authors, Finnish Acad., Finnish Literary Soc.; Pres., Suffolk Poetry Soc. 1999–. *Publications:* Chimpanzees are Blameless Creatures, 1969; Who Needs Money?, 1972; Private and Confidential, 1974; Public Footpath, 1981; Fire in the Garden, 1984; Letters in the Dark, 1986; Trouble, 1992; Selected Poems, 1995; A Useless Passion, 1998; The Vale of Todmorden, 2003. Translations: Territorial Song, 1991; Contemporary Finnish Poetry, 1991; Fugue, 1992; Wings of Hope and Daring, 1992; The Eyes of the Fingertips are Opening, 1993; Black and Red, 1993; Narcissus in Winter, 1994; The Year of the Hare, 1994; Two Sequences for Kuhmo, 1994; In Wandering Hall, 1995; Selected Poems, Eeva-Lisa Manner, 1997; Three Finnish Poets, 1999; A Tenant Here, 1999; Gaia, A Musicl for Children, 2000;Not Before Sundown, 2003 (republished in USA as Troll: A Love Story 2004). Contributions: Reviews, journals, and magazines. *Honours:* Kt First Class, Order of the White Rose of Finland, 1991; Prize, Guinness Poetry Competition; Cholmondeley Award; Poetry Book Society Biennial Translation Award; : Finnish State Prize for Translation 1991. *Address:* North Gable, 30 Crag Path, Aldeburgh, Suffolk IP15 5BS, England. *E-mail:* herbert@hlomas.freeserve.co.uk. *Website:* www.hlomas.freeserve.co .uk (home).

LOMAX, Marion (see Bolam, Robyn)

LOMPERIS, Timothy, MA, PhD; American academic and writer; *Professor of Political Science, St Louis University*; b. 6 March 1947, Guntur, India; m. Ana Maria Turner 1976; one s. one d. *Education:* Augustana Coll., School of Advanced Int. Studies, Johns Hopkins Univ., Duke Univ. *Career:* Instructor and Asst Prof., Louisiana State Univ. 1980–84; Visiting Asst Prof., Duke Univ., 1983–84, Asst Prof. of Political Science 1984–94; John M. Olin Postdoctoral Fellow, Harvard Univ., 1985–86; Fellow, Woodrow Wilson Int. Center for Scholars, Washington, DC 1988–89; Assoc. Prof. of Political Science, United States Military Acad., West Point, New York, 1994–96; Prof. of Political Science, St Louis Univ. 1996–, also Chair. Dept of Political Science 1996–2004. *Publications:* The War Everyone Lost – and Won: America's Intervention in Viet Nam's Twin Struggles 1984, Hindu Influence on Greek Philosophy: The Odyssey of the Soul from the Upanishads to Plato 1984,

'Reading the Wind': The Literature of the Vietnam War 1987, From People's War to People's Rule: Insurgency, Intervention, and the Lessons of Vietnam 1996; contribs to scholarly journals, book chapters. *Honours:* United States Army Bronze Star, 1973; Vietnamese Army Staff Medal First Class, 1973; Presidential Outstanding Community Achievement Award for Vietnam Era Veterans, Chapel Hill, NC, 1979; Helen Dwight Reid Award, American Political Science Asscn, 1982; Civilian Superior Service Award, United States Military Acad., West Point, New York, 1996, Faculty Excellence Award, St Louis Univ. 2004. *Address:* Department of Political Science, St Louis University, St Louis, MO 63103, USA (office). *Telephone:* (314) 977-3044 (office). *E-mail:* lomperis@slu.edu (office).

LONDON, Joan; Australian writer; b. 1948, Perth, WA. *Publications:* Sister Ships (short stories) (Age Book of the Year, Western Australia Week Literary Award) 1986, Letter to Constantine (short stories) (Steele Rudd Award, West Australian Premier's Award for Fiction) 1994, Gilgamesh (novel) (Age Book of the Year for Fiction 2002) 2001, The New Dark Age (short stories) 2004. *Address:* c/o Pan Macmillan Australia, Level 18, St Martin's Tower, 31 Market Street, Sydney, NSW 2000, Australia.

LONG, Robert Emmet, BA, MA, PhD; American literary critic and writer; b. 7 June 1934, Oswego, NY, USA. *Education:* Columbia Univ., Syracuse Univ. *Career:* Instructor, SUNY 1962–64; Asst Prof., Queens Coll., CUNY 1968–71. *Publications:* The Achieving of the Great Gatsby: F. Scott Fitzgerald 1920–25, 1979; The Great Succession: Henry James and the Legacy of Hawthorne, 1979; Henry James: The Early Novels, 1983; John O'Hara, 1983; Nathanael West, 1985; Barbara Pym, 1986; James Thurber, 1988; James Fenimore Cooper, 1990; Ingmar Bergman: Film and Stage, 1994; The Films of Merchant Ivory, 1999; Broadway, the Golden Years: Jerome Robbins and the Great Choreographers and Dirs, 1940 to the Present, 2001; John Huston: Interviews, 2001; George Cukor; Interviews, 2001. Editor: American Education, 1985; Drugs and American Society, 1985; Vietnam, Ten Years After, 1986; Mexico, 1986; The Farm Crisis, 1987; The Problem of Waste Disposal, 1988; AIDS, 1989; The Welfare Debate, 1989; Energy and Conservation, 1989; Japan and the USA, 1990; Censorship, 1990; The Crisis in Health Care, 1991; The State of US Education, 1991; The Reunification of Germany, 1992; Immigration to the United States, 1992; Drugs in America, 1993; Banking Scandals: The S&L and BCCI, 1993; Religious Cults in America, 1994; Criminal Sentencing, 1995; Suicide, 1995; Immigration, 1996; Affirmative Action, 1996; Multiculturalism, 1997; Right to Privacy, 1997; First Impressions: Observations on Theater and Books 2003; An Enlarging Vision: Early Essays and Stories 2003; James Ivory in Conversation 2005; Gallagher Horse 2005; Liv Ullmann: Interviews (Ed.) 2005, Working in the Theatre (ed., four vols) 2006; contrib. several hundred articles to magazines, journals and newspapers. *Address:* 254 South Third Street, Fulton, NY 13069, USA.

LONG, Robert Hill, BA, MFA; American academic, poet and writer; b. 23 Nov. 1952, Raleigh, NC; m. Sandra Morgen 1980, one s. one d. *Education:* Davidson College, Warren Wilson College. *Career:* Visiting Lecturer, Clark University, University of Hartford, Smith College, University of Connecticut at Torrington, 1987–91; Senior Lecturer in Creative Writing, University of Oregon, 1991–; mem. Associated Writing Programs. *Publications:* The Power to Die (poems), 1987; The Work of the Bow (poems), 1997; The Effigies (fiction), 1998. Contributions: various anthologies and journals. *Honours:* Aspen Writers' Conference Poetry Fellowship, 1981; First Prize, North Carolina Poetry Award, 1986; Grand Prize, A Living Culture in Durham Anthology, 1986; North Carolina Arts Council Literary Fellowship, 1986; National Endowment for the Arts Fellowship, 1988; Cleveland State University Poetry Center Prize, 1995; Oregon Arts Commission Literary Fellowship, 1997. *Address:* c/o Program in Creative Writing, University of Oregon, Eugene, OR 97403, USA.

LONGLEY, Edna; British poet, academic and critic; *Emerita Professor, Queen's University;* m. Michael Longley. *Education:* Trinity Coll., Dublin. *Career:* Lecturer 1964–76, Sr Lecturer 1976–87, Reader 1987–91, Prof. 1991–2002, Emerita Prof. 2002–, School of English, Queen's Univ., Belfast; editorial bd mem., Fortnight and Yeats Annual. *Publications:* poetry: Poetry in the Wars 1986, Alice in Wormland: Selected Poems 1990, From Kathleen to Anorexia 1990, The Living Stream: Literature and Revisionism in Ireland 1994; editor: Language Not to Be Betrayed (with others) 1985, The Biggest Egg in the World 1987, Yeats Annual: That Accusing Eye, Yeats and his Irish Readers (with others) 1996, The Bloodaxe Book of 20th Century Poetry from Britain and Ireland (with others) 2000; contrib. reviews to TLS, The Irish Times, Poetry Review, Thumbscrew, Metre, BBC Radio. *Address:* c/o Bloodaxe Books Ltd, Highgreen, Tarset, Northumberland NE48 1RP, England. *Website:* www.bloodaxebooks.com.

LONGLEY, Michael George, BA; Northern Irish poet; b. 27 July 1939, Belfast; m. Edna Broderick 1964; one s. two d. *Education:* Royal Belfast Academical Institution, Trinity Coll. Dublin. *Career:* teacher, Avoca School, Blackrock 1962–63, Belfast High School and Erith Secondary School 1963–64, Royal Belfast Academical Institution 1964–69; Asst Dir, Arts Council of Northern Ireland, Belfast 1970–91. *Publications:* poetry: Ten Poems 1965, Room To Rhyme (with Seamus Heaney and David Hammond) 1968, Secret Marriages: Nine Short Poems 1968, Three Regional Voices (with Barry Tebb and Ian Chrichton Smith) 1968, No Continuing City: Poems 1963–1968 1969, Lares 1972, An Exploded View: Poems 1968–72 1973, Fishing in the Sky 1975, Man Lying on a Wall 1976, The Echo Gate: Poems 1975–1978 1979, Selected

Poems 1963–1980 1980, Patchwork 1981, Poems 1963–1983 1985, Gorse Fires 1991, The Ghost Orchid 1995, Selected Poems 1998, The Weather in Japan (T. S. Eliot Prize) 2000, Snow Water 2004, Collected Poems 2006; editor: Causeway: The Arts in Ulster 1971, Under the Moon, Over the Stars: Young People's Writing from Ulster 1971, Selected Poems by Louis MacNeice 1988; contrib. to periodicals. *Honours:* Hon. DLitt (Queen's Univ., Belfast) 1995; Eric Gregory Award 1965, Commonwealth Poetry Prize 1985, Whitbread Poetry Award 1991, Hawthornden Prize 2000, Irish Times Poetry Prize 2000, Queen's Gold Medal for Poetry 2001. *Address:* 32 Osborne Gardens, Malone, Belfast 9, Northern Ireland.

LONGMATE, Norman Richard, BA, MA, FRHistS; British writer; b. 15 Dec. 1925, Newbury, Berkshire, England. *Education:* Worcester Coll., Oxford. *Career:* Leader Writer, Evening Standard, 1952; Feature Writer, Daily Mirror, 1953–56; Schools Radio Producer, 1963–65, Senior, subsequently Chief Asst, BBC Secretariat, 1965–83; mem. Oxford Society; Society of Authors; Fortress Study Group; United Kingdom Fortification Club; Historical Asscn; Ramblers Asscn; Society of Sussex Downsmen; Prayer Book Society. *Publications:* A Socialist Anthology (ed.), 1953; Oxford Triumphant, 1955; King Cholera, 1966; The Waterdrinkers, 1968; Alive and Well, 1970; How We Lived Then, 1971; If Britain had Fallen, 1972; The Workhouse, 1974; The Real Dad's Army, 1974; The GI's, 1975; Milestones in Working Class History, 1975; Air Raid, 1976; When We Won the War, 1977; The Hungry Mills, 1978; The Doodlebugs, 1981; The Bombers, 1982; The Breadstealers, 1984; Hitler's Rockets, 1985; Defending the Island from Caesar to the Armada, 1989.

LONGWORTH, Philip, MA; British/Canadian historian; b. 17 Feb. 1933, London. *Education:* Balliol Coll., Oxford. *Career:* Prof. of History, McGill Univ., Montréal 1984–2003. *Publications:* A Hero of Our Time, by Lermontov (trans.), 1962; The Art of Victory, 1965; The Unending Vigil, 1967; The Cossacks, 1969; The Three Empresses, 1971; The Rise and Fall of Venice, 1974; Alexis, Tsar of All the Russias, 1984; The Making of Eastern Europe, 1992 (2nd Edn 1997); The Rise and Fall of Russia's Empires: From Prehistory to Putin 2005; Contributions to periodicals. *Address:* L. A. M. Heath & Co, 6 Warwick Court, London, WC1R 5DV, England (office). *E-mail:* prlongworth@virgin.net (office). *Website:* www.philiplongworth.com (office).

LONGYEAR, Barry B.; American writer; b. 12 May 1942, Harrisburg, PA. *Publications:* City of Baraboo, 1980; Manifest Destiny (short stories), 1980; Circus World (short stories), 1980; Elephant Song, 1981; The Tomorrow Testament, 1983; It Came from Schenectady, 1984; Sea of Glass, 1986; Enemy Mine, 1988; Saint MaryBlue, 1988; Naked Came the Robot, 1988; The God Box, 1989; Infinity Hold, 1989; The Homecoming, 1989; Slag Like Me, 1994; The Change, 1994; Yesterday's Tomorrow, 1997; The Enemy Papers, 1998.

LOPATE, Phillip, BA, PhD; American writer and poet; *Professor of English, Hofstra University;* b. 16 Nov. 1943, New York, NY; m. Cheryl Cipriani 1990; one c. *Education:* Columbia Coll., Union Inst. *Career:* Assoc. Prof. of English, Univ. of Houston 1980–88; Assoc. Prof. of Creative Writing, Columbia Univ. 1988–90; Prof. of English, Bennington Coll. 1990, Hofstra Univ. 1991–. *Publications:* fiction: Confessions of Summer 1979, The Rug Merchant 1987; poetry: The Eyes Don't Always Want to Stay Open 1972, The Daily Round 1976; non-fiction: Being with Children (memoir) 1975, Journal of a Living Experiment (ed.) 1979, Bachelorhood (essays) 1981, The Art of the Personal Essay (ed.) 1994, Against Joie de Vivre (essays) 1989, Portrait of My Body (essays) 1996, The Anchor Essay Annual (ed.) 1997–99, Totally, Tenderly, Tragically (film criticism) 1998, Writing New York (ed.) 1998, Getting Personal 2003, Waterfront 2003, Rudy Burckhardt (biog.) 2003; contrib. to anthologies, newspapers, reviews, quarterlies, journals and magazines. *Honours:* Guggenheim Fellowship, Nat. Endowment for the Arts grants, New York Foundation for the Arts grants, New York Public Library Center for Scholars and Writers Fellowship; Christopher Medallion, Texas Inst. of Letters Award. *Address:* 402 Sackett Street, New York, NY 11231, USA. *E-mail:* plopate@aol.com (home).

LOPES, Henri; Republic of the Congo author and politician; *Ambassador to France, Portugal, Spain, United Kingdom and Vatican City;* b. 12 Sept. 1937, Léopoldville, Belgian Congo (now Kinshasa, Democratic Republic of the Congo); s. of Jean-Marie Lopes and Micheline Vulturi; m. Nirva Pasbeau 1961; one s. three d. *Education:* France. *Career:* Minister of Nat. Educ. 1968–71, of Foreign Affairs 1971–73; mem. Political Bureau, Congolese Labour Party 1973; Prime Minister and Minister of Planning 1973–75, of Finance 1977–80; UNESCO Asst Dir-Gen. for Programme Support 1982–86, UNESCO Asst Dir-Gen. for Culture and Communication 1986–90, for Culture 1990–94, for Foreign Affairs 1994–95, Deputy Dir-Gen. 1996–98; Amb. to France (with responsibility for Portugal, Spain, the UK and the Vatican City) 1998–; mem. Haut Conseil de la Francophonie. *Publications:* Tribaliques (short stories), La Nouvelle Romance (novel), Learning to be (with others), Sans tam-tam (novel) 1977, Le Pleurer Rire (novel) 1982, Le Chercheur d'Afriques (novel) 1990, Sur l'autre Rive (novel) 1992, Le Lys et le flamboyant (novel) 1997. *Honours:* Chevalier, Légion d'Honneur, Commdr du Mérite Congolais, etc.; Prix littéraire de l'Afrique noire 1972, Prix SIMBA de littérature 1978, Prix de littérature du Président (Congo), Prix de l'Acad. de Bretagne et des Pays de la Loire 1990, Grand Prix de la Francophonie de l'Académie Française 1993. *Address:* Embassy of the Republic of the Congo, 37 bis rue Paul Valéry, 75116 Paris, Cedex 16, France (office). *Telephone:* 1-45-00-60-57. *Fax:* 1-40-67-17-33.

LOPEZ, Barry Holstun, BA, MA; American writer; b. 6 Jan. 1945, Port Chester, NY; s. of Adrian Bernard and Mary Frances (Holstun) Lopez. *Education:* Univ. of Notre Dame. *Career:* mem. PEN American Center. *Publications include:* Desert Notes 1976, Giving Birth to Thunder 1978, River Notes 1978, Of Wolves and Men (John Burroughs Medal 1979, Christopher Medal 1979, Pacific NW Booksellers Award 1979) 1978, Winter Count 1981, Arctic Dreams (Nat. Book Award 1987, Christopher Medal 1987, Pacific NW Booksellers Award 1987, Frances Fuller Victor Award 1987) 1986, Crossing Open Ground 1988, Crow and Weasel 1990, The Rediscovery of North America 1991, Field Notes (Pacific NW Booksellers Award 1995, Critics' Choice Award 1996) 1994, About this Life: Journeys on the Threshold of Memory 1998, Light Action in the Caribbean 2000, Resistance (H. L. Davis Award 2005) 2004, Vintage Lopez 2004; contrib. to many periodicals. *Honours:* Fellow, The Explorers Club 2002; Hon. LDH (Whittier Coll.) 1988, (Univ. of Portland) 1994, (Texas Tech. Univ.) 2000, (Utah State Univ.) 2002; numerous awards including American Acad. of Arts and Letters Award 1986, Guggenheim Fellowship 1987, Lannan Foundation Award 1990. *Literary Agent:* Steven Barclay Agency, 12 Western Avenue, Petaluma, CA 94952, USA. *Telephone:* (707) 773-0654. *Fax:* (707) 778-1868. *Website:* www.barclayagency.com.

LOPEZ, Tony, BA, PhD; British academic, poet and writer; b. 5 Nov. 1950, London, England; m. Sara Louise Banham 1985, one s. one d. *Education:* University of Essex, Gonville & Caius College, Cambridge. *Career:* Lecturer in English, University of Leicester, 1986–87, University of Edinburgh, 1987–89; Lecturer to Reader in Poetry, University of Plymouth, 1989–. *Publications:* Snapshots, 1976; Change, 1978; The English Disease, 1979; A Handbook of British Birds, 1982; Abstract and Delicious, 1983; The Poetry of W. S. Graham, 1989; A Theory of Surplus Labour, 1990; Stress Management, 1994; Negative Equity, 1995; False Memory, 1996. Contributions: anthologies and periodicals. *Honours:* Blundel Award 1990, Wingate Scholarship 1996.

LOPEZ, Veronica; Chilean editor and diplomatist; *Cultural Attaché, Washington DC;* b. 1946. *Career:* began career as journalist 1972; Ed. Contigo (women's magazine) 1974; co-f. Cosas (women's magazine) 1976; co-f. Semana (weekly news magazine), Bogotá, Colombia 1981; co-f. Caras (cultural magazine) 1988, Ed.-in-Chief 1988–96; Nieman Fellow Harvard Univ., USA 1996–97; Ed. The Saturday Magazine of El Mercurio newspaper 1997–2001; Cultural Attaché Embassy of Chile, Washington, DC 2001–. *Address:* Embassy of Chile, 1732 Massachusetts Avenue, NW, Washington, DC 20036, USA (office). *Telephone:* (202) 785-1746 (office). *Fax:* (202) 887-5579 (office). *E-mail:* embassy@embassyofchile.org (office). *Website:* www .embassyofchile.org (office).

LORD, Graham John, BA; British writer; b. 16 Feb. 1943, Umtali, Southern Rhodesia (now Zimbabwe); s of the late Harold Reginald Lord and Ida Frances McDowall; m. Jane Carruthers 1962 (died 2000) two d.; pnr Juliet Lewis. *Education:* Falcon Coll., Essexvale, Bulawayo, Southern Rhodesia, Univ. of Cambridge. *Career:* Literary Ed. Sunday Express, London 1969–92; Originator, Sunday Express Book of the Year Award 1987, Judge 1987–92; Ed. Raconteur short story magazine 1994–95. *Publications:* Marshmallow Pie 1970, A Roof Under Your Feet 1973, The Spider and the Fly 1974, God and All His Angels 1976, The Nostradamus Horoscope 1981, Time Out of Mind 1986, Ghosts of King Solomon's Mines 1991, Just the One: The Wives and Times of Jeffrey Bernard 1992, A Party to Die For 1997, James Herriot: The Life of a Country Vet 1997, Sorry, We're Going to have to Let You Go 1999, Dick Francis: A Racing Life 1999, Arthur Lowe 2002, Niv: The Authorised Biography of David Niven 2003, John Mortimer: The Devil's Advocate 2005, Joan Collins 2007; contrib. to newspapers. *E-mail:* pelicans@caribsurf.com (office). *Website:* www.graham-lord.com.

LORIGA, Ray; Spanish writer, screenwriter and film director; b. 1967, Madrid. *Films include:* Live Flesh (writer, with Pedro Almodóvar) 1997, La pistola de mi hermano (Dir) 1997, Todos los aviones del mundo (writer) 2001, El Séptimo día (writer) 2004, Ausentes (writer) 2005, Teresa, el cuerpo de Cristo (Dir) 2007. *Publications include:* Lo Peor de todo 1993, Heroes 1994, My Brother's Gun: A Novel of Disposable Lives, Immediate Fame and a Big Black Automatic 1997, Tokyo Doesn't Love Us Anymore 2004; contrib. to Crime Hamper. *Address:* c/o Canongate Books, 14 High Street, Edinburgh, EH1 1TE, Scotland.

LORRIMER, Claire (see Clark, Patricia Denise)

LOSHAK, Victor Grigoryevich; Russian journalist; *Editor-in-Chief, Ogoniok;* b. 20 April 1952, Zaporozhye, Ukraine; s. of Grigory Abramovich Loshak and Anna Davydovna Loshak; m. Marina Devovna Loshak; one d. *Education:* Odessa State Univ. *Career:* corresp. for various Odessa newspapers 1973–83; special corresp. Izvestia 1983–86; political observer Moskovskye Novosti 1986–91, First Deputy Ed. 1991–92, Ed.-in-Chief 1992–2003; Ed.-in-Chief Ogoniok (periodical) 2003–; broadcaster for Kultura (TV channel); mem. Int. Inst. of Press (Vice-Pres. Russian br.). *Honours:* Prize of Journalists' Union of Moscow, Order of Honour. *Address:* Ogoniok, Krasnokazarmennaya str. pb. 14, 111250 Moscow, Russia (office). *Telephone:* (495) 540-47-10 (office). *Fax:* (495) 775-41-06 (office). *E-mail:* pochta@ovarpress.ru (office). *Website:* www .ogoniok.com (office).

LOTT, Bret, BA, MFA; American academic and writer; b. 8 Oct. 1958, Los Angeles, CA; m. Melanie Kai Swank 1980, two s. *Education:* California State University at Long Beach, University of Massachusetts. *Career:* reporter, Daily Commercial News, Los Angeles, 1980–81; Instructor in Remedial English, Ohio State University, Columbus, 1984–86; Asst Prof. of English, College of Charleston, 1986–; mem. Associated Writing Programs; Poets and Writers. *Publications:* The Man Who Owned Vermont, 1987; A Stranger's House, 1988; A Dream of Old Leaves, 1989; The Hunt Club, 1997. Contributions: anthologies and periodicals. *Honours:* Awards and fellowships.

LOTT, Tim; British writer and broadcaster; b. 1956, London. *Education:* Harlow Coll. and LSE. *Career:* journalist, Sounds magazine, City Limits magazine; television producer; panellist, Newsnight Review (BBC2) 2001–. *Publications:* The Scent of Dried Roses (memoir) 1996, White City Blue (Whitbread First Novel Award) 1999, Rumours of a Hurricane (novel) 2002, The Love Secrets of Don Juan (novel) 2003, The Seymour Tapes 2005, Fearless (juvenile) 2007; contrib. 'What Young Men Do', Granta 62 1998. *Honours:* J.R. Ackerley Prize for Autobiography. *Address:* c/o Viking, Penguin Books Ltd, 80 Strand, London, WC2R 0RL, England. *Website:* www.penguin.co.uk.

LOUW, Raymond; South African publishing executive; *Editor and Publisher, Southern Africa Report;* b. 13 Oct. 1926, Cape Town; s. of George K. E. Louw and Helen K. Louw (née Finlay); m. Jean Ramsay Byres 1950; two s. one d. *Education:* Parktown High School, Johannesburg. *Career:* reporter on Rand Daily Mail 1946–50, Worthing Herald 1951–52, North-Western Evening Mail 1953–54, Westminster Press Provincial Newspapers (London) 1955–56; Night News Ed. Rand Daily Mail 1958–59, News Ed. 1960–65, Ed. 1966–77; News Ed. Sunday Times 1959–60; Chair. SA Morning Newspaper Group 1975–77; Gen. Man. SA Associated Newspapers 1977–82; Ed. and Publr Southern Africa Report 1982–; Chair. Media Defence Fund 1989–94, Campaign for Open Media 1985–94 (now merged as Freedom of Expression Inst., Chair. 1994–96); New Era Schools Trust; Africa Consultant, World Press Freedom Cttee 2003–; mem. Task Group on Govt Communications 1996; mem. Exec. Bd, Int. Press Inst., London, 1979–87, Fellow 1994; mem. Independent Media Comm. 1994; chosen by Int. Press Inst. to travel to Cameroon to make plea for release from jail of Pius Njawe (Ed. of Le Messager) 1998; mem. IPI delegations to the Pres. of Indonesia 2000, Zimbabwean Govt 2001, Israeli Govt 2003, Ethiopian Govt 2004 on media freedom issues. *Publications:* Four Days in Lusaka – Whites from 'Home' in talks with the ANC 1989, Report on the media situation in South Africa (for UNESCO) 1994; narrative for Nelson Mandela Pictorial Biography by Peter Magubane 1996; Undue Restriction: Laws Impacting on Media Freedom in the SADC (Ed.); numerous papers and articles on the media and press freedom. *Honours:* Pringle Medal for services to journalism 1976, 1992. *Address:* Southern Africa Report, PO Box 261579, Excom, Johannesburg 2023; 23 Duncombe Road, Forest Town, Johannesburg 2193, South Africa (home). *Telephone:* (11) 646-8790. *Fax:* (11) 646-6085. *E-mail:* rlouw@sn.apc.org. *Website:* www.sareport.co.za (office).

LOVE, William F., BA, MBA; American writer; b. 20 Dec. 1932, Oklahoma City, OK; m. Joyce Mary Athman 1970; two d. *Education:* St John's Univ., Collegeville, Minnesota, Univ. of Chicago. *Career:* mem. Authors' Guild, Int. Asscn of Crime Writers, MWA, PEN Midwest, Private Eye Writers of America, Soc. of Midland Authors. *Publications:* The Chartreuse Clue 1990, The Fundamentals of Murder 1991, Bloody Ten 1992.

LØVEID, Cecilie Meyer; Norwegian playwright and poet; b. 21 Aug. 1951, Mysen; d. of Erik Løveid and Ingrid Meyer; m. Bjørn H. Ianke 1978; one s. two d. *Education:* arts and crafts school in Bergen and studies in graphic design, theatre history and drama. *Career:* mem. editorial staff, Profil (magazine) 1969; Sec. Norsk Forfattersentrum, Vestlandsardelingen 1974; Teacher, Writing Arts Centre, Bergen 1986; mem. Literary Council, Den norske Fordatterforening 1987. *Publications:* Most (novel) 1972, Sug (novel) 1979, Måkespisere (radio play) 1982, Balansedame (play) 1986, Maria Q. (play) 1991, Rhindøtrene (play) 1996. *Honours:* Prix Italia 1982; Aschehons Prize; Donblass Prize.

LOVELACE, Col Merline A., BA, MS; American fmr air force officer and writer; b. 9 Sept. 1946, Northampton, Mass; d. of Merlin S. and Alyce S. Thoma; m. Cary A. Lovelace 1970. *Education:* Ripon Coll., Troy State Univ., Middlebury Coll., Princeton Univ., Kennedy School of Govt, Harvard Univ., Squadron Officers' School, Armed Forces Staff Coll., Air War Coll. *Career:* served to Col, USAF 1968–91; novelist, mainly romances 1991–; mem. Romance Writers of America (Pres. Oklahoma Chapter). *Publications:* Bits and Pieces 1993, Maggie and Her Colonel 1994, Alena 1994, Sweet Song of Love 1994, Dreams and Schemes 1994, Siren's Call 1994, Somewhere in Time 1994, His Lady's Ransom 1995, Night of the Jaguar 1995, Cowboy and the Cossack 1995, Undercover Man 1996, Perfect Double 1996, Lady of the Upper Kingdom 1996, Line of Duty 1996, Beauty and the Bodyguard 1996, Halloween Honeymoon 1996, Wrong Bride, Right Groom 1996, The 14th and Forever 1997, Duty and Dishonor 1997, Countess in Buckskin 1998, Return to Sender 1998, Call of Duty 1998, The Tiger's Bride 1998, If A Man Answers 1998, A Drop of Frankincense 1998, The Mercenary and the New Mom 1999, His First Father's Day 1999, River Rising 1999, Undercover Groom 1999, A Man of His Word 1999, Mistaken Identity 2000, Some Like It Hot 2000, The Harder They Fall 2000, Mismatched Hearts 2000, Final Approach to Forever 2000, Dark Side of Dawn 2001, The Horse Soldier 2001, The Spy Who Loved Him 2001, The Major's Wife 2001: Twice in a Lifetime 2001, The Colonel's Daughter 2002, Hot As Ice 2002, Texas Hero 2002, Undercover Ops 2002, The Captain's Woman 2003, After Midnight 2003, Texas Now and Forever 2003, To Love A Thief 2003, A Military Affair 2003, A Savage Beauty 2003, A Question of Intent 2003, Full Throttle 2004, The Right Stuff 2004, Sailor's Moon 2004, Untamed 2004, A Bridge for Christmas 2004,

The First Mistake 2005, The Middle Sin 2005, The Last Bullet 2005, Eye of the Beholder 2005, Diamonds Can Be Deadly 2006, Devlin and the Deep Blue Sea 2006, Closer Encounters 2006. *Honours:* Bronze Star, Legion of Merit with one Oak Leaf Cluster, Defense Meritorious Service Medal; Distinguished Grad., Squadron Officers' School, Air War Coll., Southwest Writers Workshop Prize for Best Historical Novel 1992, Best Romance, Romantic Times 1993, 2002, Romance Writers of America RITA Award 2001, Oklahoma Writer of the Year 1998, Oklahoma Woman Veteran of the Year 2000. *Address:* 2325 Tuttington, Oklahoma City, OK 73170, USA. *E-mail:* lovelace@swbell.net (home). *Website:* www.merlinelovelace.com.

LOVELL, Sir (Alfred Charles) Bernard, Kt, OBE, PhD, MSc, FRS; British radio astronomer; b. 31 Aug. 1913, Oldland Common, Glos.; s. of Gilbert Lovell and Emily Laura Lovell (née Adams); m. Mary Joyce Chesterman 1937 (died 1993); two s. three d. *Education:* Bristol Univ. *Career:* Asst Lecturer in Physics, Univ. of Manchester 1936–39, Lecturer 1945–47, Sr Lecturer 1947–49, Reader 1949–51, Prof. of Radio Astronomy 1951–81, Emer. Prof. 1981–; with Telecommunications Research Est. 1939–45; Founder and Dir Nuffield Radio Astronomy Labs, Jodrell Bank 1945–81; Fellow, Royal Soc. 1955; Pres. Royal Astronomical Soc. 1969–71, British Asscn 1974–75; Vice-Pres. Int. Astronomical Union 1970–76; mem. Aeronautical Research Council 1955–58, Science Research Council 1965–70; Pres. Guild of Church Musicians 1976–89; Master Worshipful Co. of Musicians 1986–87. *Publications:* Science and Civilisation 1939, World Power Resources and Social Development 1945, Radio Astronomy 1952, Meteor Astronomy 1954, The Exploration of Space by Radio 1957, The Individual and the Universe (The Reith Lectures 1958), The Exploration of Outer Space 1962, Discovering the Universe 1963, Our Present Knowledge of the Universe 1967; Ed. (with Tom Margerison) The Explosion of Science: The Physical Universe 1967, The Story of Jodrell Bank 1968, The Origins and International Economics of Space Exploration 1973, Out of the Zenith: Jodrell Bank 1957–1970 1973, Man's Relation to the Universe 1975, P. M. S. Blackett – A Biographical Memoir 1976, In the Centre of Immensities 1978, Emerging Cosmology 1981, The Jodrell Bank Telescopes 1985, Voice of the Universe 1987, Pathways to the Universe (with Sir Francis Graham-Smith) 1988, Astronomer by Chance 1990, Echoes of War 1991. *Honours:* Hon. Foreign mem. American Acad. of Arts and Sciences 1955; Hon. mem. New York Acad. of Sciences 1960, Royal Northern Coll. of Music; Hon. Fellow Royal Swedish Acad. 1962, Inst. of Electrical Engineers 1967, Inst. of Physics 1975; Hon. Freeman City of Manchester 1977; Ordre du Mérite pour la Recherche et l'Invention 1962; Polish Order of Merit 1975; Hon. LLD (Edin.) 1961, (Calgary) 1966, (Liverpool) 1999; Hon. DSc (Leicester) 1961, (Leeds) 1966, (Bath, London) 1967, (Bristol) 1970; Hon. DUniv (Stirling) 1974, (Surrey) 1975; Royal Medal of Royal Soc. 1960, Daniel and Florence Guggenheim Int. Astronautics Award 1961. Maitland Silver Medal, Inst. of Structural Engineers 1964, Churchill Gold Medal, Soc. of Engineers 1964, Benjamin Franklin Medal, Royal Soc. of Arts 1980, Gold Medal, Royal Astronomical Soc. 1981. *Address:* The Quinta, Swettenham, nr Congleton, Cheshire, CW12 2LD, England (home). *Telephone:* (1477) 571254. *Fax:* (1477) 571954.

LOVELL, Mary Sybilla, FRGS; British writer; b. 23 Oct. 1941, Prestatyn, N Wales; m. 2nd Geoffrey A. H. Watts 1991; one s. two step-s. two step-d. *Career:* mem. Soc. of Authors, R. S. Surtees Soc. (vice-pres. 1980–). *Publications:* Hunting Pageant 1980, Cats as Pets 1982, Boys Book of Boats 1983, Straight on Till Morning 1987, The Splendid Outcast 1988, The Sound of Wings 1989, Cast No Shadow 1991, A Scandalous Life 1995, The Rebel Heart 1996, A Rage to Live 1998, The Mitford Girls 2001, Bound to a Star 2004, Bess of Hardwick 2005. *Address:* Stroat House, Stroat, Gloucestershire NP6 7LR, England. *E-mail:* sybil@stroat24.fsnet.co.uk. *Website:* www.marylovell.com.

LOVELOCK, James Ephraim, CH, CBE, PhD, DSc, FRS; British scientist, inventor, writer and academic; *Honorary Visiting Fellow, Green College, Oxford;* b. 26 July 1919, Letchworth Garden City; s. of Tom Arthur Lovelock and Nellie Ann Elizabeth Lovelock (née March); m. 1st Helen Mary Hyslop 1942 (died 1989); two s. two d.; m. 2nd Sandra Jean Orchard 1991. *Education:* Manchester Univ. and London School of Hygiene and Tropical Medicine. *Career:* staff scientist, Nat. Inst. for Medical Research 1941–61; Prof. of Chem. Baylor Univ. Coll. of Medicine, Tex., USA 1961–64; independent scientist 1964–; Hon. Visiting Fellow, Green Coll., Oxford; Fellow, Harvard Univ. 1954–55, Yale Univ. 1958–59; Visiting Prof., Univ. of Reading 1967–90; Pres. Marine Biology Asscn 1986–90. *Publications:* Gaia: A New Look at Life on Earth 1979, The Great Extinction (co-author) 1983, The Greening of Mars (co-author) 1984; The Ages of Gaia 1988, Gaia: The Practical Science of Planetary Medicine 1991, Homage to Gaia: The Life of an Independent Scientist 2000, The Revenge of Gaia 2007. *Honours:* Hon. Visiting Fellow, Green Coll. Oxford 1994–; Norbert Gerbier Prize of the World Meteorological Asscn 1988, Dr A. H. Heineken Prize for the Environment, Royal Netherlands Acad. of Arts and Sciences 1990, Volvo Environment Prize 1996, Nonino Prize 1996, The Blue Planet Prize 1997. *Address:* Coombe Mill, St Giles on the Heath, Launceston, Cornwall, PL15 9RY, England.

LOVESEY, Peter, (Peter Lear), BA; British writer; b. 10 Sept. 1936, Whitton, Middx; m. Jacqueline Ruth Lewis 1959; one s. one d. *Education:* Univ. of Reading. *Career:* mem. Crime Writers Asscn of GB (chair. 1991–92), Detection Club, Soc. of Authors. *Publications:* The Kings of Distance, 1968; Wobble to Death, 1970; The Detective Wore Silk Drawers, 1971; Abracadaver, 1972; Mad Hatters Holiday, 1973; Invitation to a Dynamite Party, 1974; A Case of Spirits, 1975; Swing, Swing Together, 1976; Goldengirl, 1977; Waxwork, 1978; Official Centenary History of the Amateur Athletic Asscn, 1979; Spider Girl,

1980; The False Inspector Dew, 1982; Keystone, 1983; Butchers (short stories), 1985; The Secret of Spandau, 1986; Rough Cider, 1986; Bertie and the Tinman, 1987; On the Edge, 1989; Bertie and the Seven Bodies, 1990; The Last Detective, 1991; Diamond Solitaire, 1992; Bertie and the Crime of Passion, 1993; The Crime of Miss Oyster Brown (short stories), 1994; The Summons, 1995; Bloodhounds, 1996; Upon a Dark Night, 1997; Do Not Exceed the Stated Dose (short stories), 1998; The Vault, 1999; The Reaper, 2000; Diamond Dust, 2002; The Sedgemoor Strangler and Other Stories of Crime, 2002; The House Sitter, 2003; The Circle 2005, The Secret Hangman 2007. *Honours:* Macmillan/Panther First Crime Novel Award, 1970; CWA Silver Dagger, 1978, 1995, 1996 and Gold Dagger, 1982 and Cartier Diamond Dagger, 2000; Grand Prix de Littérature Policière, 1985; Prix du Roman D'Aventures, 1987; Anthony Award, 1992; Macavity Award 1997, 2004. *Literary Agent:* Vanessa Holt Ltd, 59 Crescent Road, Leigh-on-Sea, Essex SS9 2PF, England.

LOW(-WESO), Denise, MA, MFA, PhD; American poet, writer, academic and administrator; *Interim Dean of Humanities and Arts, Haskell Indian Nations University;* b. (Denise Lea Dotson), 9 May 1949, Emporia, Kan.; d. of William Francis Dotson and Dorothy Dotson; m. Thomas F. Weso; two s. one step-d. *Education:* Univ. of Kansas, Wichita State Univ. *Career:* Asst Instructor, Univ. of Kansas 1970–72, Lecturer 1977–84, Visiting Lecturer 1988; Temp. Instructor, Kansas State Univ. 1975–77; part-time Instructor, Washburn Univ., Topeka, Kan. 1982–84; Instructor of Humanities, Haskell Indian Nations Univ., Lawrence, Kan. 1984–, Chair. English Dept 2002–04, currently Interim Dean of Humanities and Arts; Visiting Prof., Univ. of Richmond 2005; Poet Laureate of State of Kansas 2007–09; mem. Associated Writing Programs, Modern Language Asscn, Poets and Writers, Imagination & Place Cttee, Lawrence Arts Center. *Publications:* Dragon Kite 1981, Quilting 1984, Spring Geese and Other Poems 1984, Learning the Language of Rivers 1987, Starwater 1988, Selective Amnesia: Stiletto I 1988, Vanishing Point 1991, Tulip Elegies: An Alchemy of Writing 1993, Touching the Sky: Essays 1994, New and Selected Poems: 1980–99 1999, Thailand Journal 2003, Teaching Leslie Maron Silko's Ceremony (co-ed.), Words of a Prairie Alchemist: Essays 2006; contrib. to anthologies, books, reviews, quarterlies, journals, and magazines. *Honours:* several grants and fellowships. *Address:* Haskell Indian Nations University, Lawrence, KS 66046, USA (office). *Telephone:* (785) 749-8431 (office). *E-mail:* dlow@haskell.edu (office). *Website:* www.haskell.edu (office). deniselow.blogspot.com.

LOW, Lois Dorothea, (Zoe Cass, Dorothy Mackie Low, Lois Paxton); British writer; b. 15 July 1916, Edinburgh, Scotland. *Education:* Edinburgh Ladies' Coll. *Career:* mem. CWA, Romantic Novelists' Asscn (chair. 1969–71), Soc. of Authors. *Publications:* Isle for a Stranger, 1962; Dear Liar, 1963; A Ripple on the Water, 1964; The Intruder, 1965; A House in the Country, 1968; The Man Who Died Twice, 1969; To Burgundy and Back, 1970; The Quiet Sound of Fear, 1971; Who Goes There?, 1972; Island of the Seven Hills, 1974; The Silver Leopard, 1976; A Twist in the Silk, 1980; The Man in the Shadows, 1983.

LOW, Rachael, BSc, PhD; British film historian; b. 6 July 1923, London, England. *Education:* LSE. *Career:* researcher, British Film Inst., London 1945–48; Gulbenkian Research Fellow 1968–71, Fellow Commoner 1983, Lucy Cavendish Coll., Cambridge. *Publications:* History of the British Film 1896–1906 1948, Films of Comment and Persuasion of the 1930s 1979, Documentary and Educational Films of the 1930s 1979, History of the British Film (with Roger Manvell) 1906–1914 1949, 1914–1918 1950, 1918–1929 1971, 1929–1939 Vols I and II 1979, Vol. III 1985. *Address:* c/o Routledge (Media and Cultural Studies), Building 4, Park Square, Milton Park, Abingdon, OX14 4RN, England.

LOW, Robert Nicholas, BA; British journalist and writer; b. 15 Aug. 1948, Addlestone, Surrey, England; m. Angela Levin 1983, one s. *Education:* Fitzwilliam College, Cambridge. *Career:* teacher, University of Chile, La Serena, 1970–72; Journalist, Birmingham Post & Mail, 1973–77; The Observer, 1977–93; Senior Ed.-Deputy Ed., British Edition, 1994–98, European Bureau Chief, 1998–, Reader's Digest. *Publications:* The Kidnap Business (with Mark Bles), 1987; The Observer Book of Profiles (ed.), 1991; La Pasionaria, The Spanish Firebrand, 1992; W. G.: A Life of W. G. Grace, 1997. *Literary Agent:* Curtis Brown Ltd, Haymarket House, 28–29 Haymarket, London, SW1Y 4SP, England. *Telephone:* (20) 7393-4400. *Fax:* (20) 7393-4401. *E-mail:* info@curtisbrown.co.uk. *Website:* www.curtisbrown.co.uk. *Address:* 33 Canfield Gardens, London, NW6 3JP, England (home). *E-mail:* bob.low@readersdigest.co.uk.

LOWDEN, Desmond Scott; British writer; b. 27 Sept. 1937, Winchester, Hampshire, England; m. 1962, one s. one d. *Career:* mem. CWA. *Publications:* Bandersnatch, 1969; The Boondocks, 1972; Bellman and True, 1975; Boudapesti 3, 1979; Sunspot, 1981; Cry Havoc, 1984; The Shadow Run, 1989; Chain, 1990. *Honours:* CWA Silver Dagger Award 1989.

LOWE, Barry; Australian playwright, writer and scriptwriter; b. 16 May 1947, Sydney, NSW; pnr Walter Figallo 1972. *Career:* mem. Australian Writers' Guild, Australian Soc. of Authors. *Publications:* plays: Writers Camp, first performed, 1982; Tokyo Rose, 1989; The Death of Peter Pan, 1989; Seeing Things, 1994; Relative Merits, 1994; The Extraordinary Annual General Meeting of the Size-Queen Club, 1996. Contributions: various publications.

LOWE, John Evelyn, FRSA, FSA; British writer; b. 23 April 1928, London; m. 1st Susan Sanderson 1956; two s. one d.; m. 2nd Yuki Nomura 1989; one d.

Education: New Coll., Oxford, 1950–52. *Career:* Assoc. Ed., Collins Crime Club, 1953–54; Ed., Faber Furniture Series, 1954–56; Deputy Story Ed., Pinewood Studios, 1956–57; Visiting Prof., British Cultural Studies Doshisha Univ., Kyoto, Japan, 1979–81; Literary Ed., Kansai Time Out Magazine, 1985–89; Visiting Prof., Int. Research Centre for Japanese Studies, Kyoto 2001–02. *Publications:* Thomas Chippendale, 1955; Cream Coloured Earthenware, 1958; Japanese Crafts, 1983; Into Japan, 1985; Into China, 1986; Corsica – A Traveller's Guide, 1988; A Surrealist Life – Edward James, 1991; A Short Guide to the Kyoto Museum of Archaeology, 1991; Glimpses of Kyoto Life, 1996; The Warden – A Portrait of John Sparrow, 1998; Old Kyoto, A Short Social History, 2000. Contributions: Encyclopaedia Britannica; Oxford Junior Encyclopaedia; New Dictionary of National Biography; American Scholar; Country Life; Listener; Connoisseur; Apollo; Others. *Honours:* Hon. Fellow, RCA. *Address:* 2 rue Jean Guiton, 47300 Villeneuve sur Lot, France (home). *Telephone:* (5) 53 41 72 53 (home).

LOWE, Stephen, BA; British playwright; *Artistic Director, Meeting Ground Theatre, Nottingham;* b. (Stephen James Wright), 1 Dec. 1947, Nottingham, England; s. of Harry Wright and Minnie Wright; m. 1st Tina Barclay; one s.; m. 2nd Tanya Myers; two d. *Education:* Univ. of Birmingham. *Career:* Sr Tutor in Writing for Performance, Dartington Coll. of Arts Performance 1978–82; Resident Playwright, Riverside Studios, London 1982–84; Sr Tutor, Univ. of Birmingham 1987–88; mem. Nottingham Trent Univ. Advisory Bd to Theatre Design Degree 1987–; Chair. East Midlands Arts 2001–02; Trustee and Gov. Arts Council England, Chair. Arts Council England, East Midlands, 2002–; mem. Theatre Writers Union, Writers Guild, PEN. *Plays:* more than 40 plays for the theatre. *Radio:* Empty Bed Blues (BBC Radio 4) 2006. *Television:* numerous films, including adaptations. *Publications:* Cards 1983, Moving Pictures and Other Plays 1985, Body and Soul in Peace Plays (two vols) 1985, 1990, Divine Gossip/Tibetan Inroads 1988, Ragged Trousered Philanthropists 1991, Revelations 2004. Spirit of the Man 2005, Touched 2006; contribs books and journals. *Honours:* George Devine Award for Playwriting 1977. *Literary Agent:* c/o Sara Stroud, Judy Daish Associates, 2 St Charles Place, London, W10 6EG, England. *Telephone:* (20) 8964-8811. *E-mail:* steph@stephenlowe.co.uk (office). *Website:* www.meetinggroundtheatre.org.uk (office); www.stephenlowe.co.uk.

LOWELL, Susan Deborah, BA, MA, PhD; American writer; b. 27 Oct. 1950, Chihuahua, Mexico; m. William Ross Humphreys 1975, two d. *Education:* Stanford University, Princeton University. *Career:* mem. Southern Arizona Society of Authors. *Publications:* Ganado Red: A Novella and Stories, 1988; I am Lavinia Cumming, 1993. *Honours:* Milkweed Editions National Fiction Prize, 1988; Mountain and Plains Booksellers Assen Regional Book Award, Children's Writing, 1994. *Address:* c/o Rio Nuevo Publishers, Treasure Chest Books, PO Box 5250, Tucson, AZ 85703, USA.

LOWERY, Joanne, AB, MA; American educator, writer and editor; b. 30 July 1945, Cleveland, OH; m. Stephen Paul Lowery 1968 (divorced 1988); one s. one d. *Education:* University of Michigan, University of Wisconsin. *Career:* part-time Instructor of English, Elgin College, 1986–91; College of DuPage, Glen Ellyn, 1991–96, St Mary's College, Notre Dame, 1997–98; Poetry Ed., Black Dirt, literary magazine, 1994–99. *Publications:* Coming to This, 1990; Corinth, 1990; Heroics, 1996; Double Feature, 2000. Contributions: Magazines. *Honours:* New Letters Literary Award, 1993. Address 412 Evelyn Ave, Kalamazoo, MI 49001, USA.

LOWNIE, Andrew James Hamilton, MA, MSc; British literary agent, writer and editor; b. 11 Nov. 1961, Kenya; m. Angela Doyle 1998; one s. one d. *Education:* Magdalene Coll., Cambridge, Univ. of Edinburgh, Coll. of Law, London. *Career:* mem. John Farquharson Literary Agents 1985–86, Dir 1986–88; Dir Andrew Lownie Literary Agency Ltd 1988–; Partner, Denniston and Lownie 1991–93; Dir Thistle Publishing 1996–; mem. Assen of Authors' Agents, Soc. of Authors; Sec. The Biographer's Club 1998–; mem. Exec. Cttee PEN 2000–04. *Publications:* North American Spies 1992, Edinburgh Literary Guide 1992, John Buchan: The Presbyterian Cavalier 1995, John Buchan's Collected Poems (ed.) 1996, The Complete Short Stories of John Buchan, Vols 1–3 (ed.) 1997–98, The Literary Companion to Edinburgh 2000, The Edinburgh Literary Companion 2005; contribs books and periodicals. *Honours:* English Speaking Union Scholarship 1979–80. *Address:* 36 Great Smith Street, London SW1P 3BU, England (home). *Telephone:* (20) 7222-7574 (office). *Fax:* (20) 7222-7576 (office). *E-mail:* lownie@globalnet.co.uk (office). *Website:* www.andrewlownie.co.uk (office).

LOWRY, Beverly Fey, BA; American writer; b. 10 Aug. 1938, Memphis, TN; m. Glenn Lowry 1960, two s. *Education:* Univ. of Mississippi, Memphis State Univ. *Career:* fmr Lecturer, Univs of Houston, Montana, and Alabama; currently Dir, Creative Nonfiction Studies, George Mason Univ., Va. *Publications:* Come Back, Lolly Ray 1977, Emma Blue 1978, Daddy's Girl 1981, The Perfect Sonya 1987, Breaking Gentle 1988, Crossed Over: The True Story of the Houston Pickax Murders 1992, The Track of Real Desire 1994, Harriet Tubman: Imagining a Life 2007; contrib. to newspapers and magazines. *Honours:* Richard Wright Literary Excellence Award 2007. *Address:* Graduate Creative Writing Program, George Mason University, 4400 University Drive, Fairfax, VA 22030 USA (office). *Telephone:* (703) 993-1180 (office). *E-mail:* writing@gmu.edu (office). *Website:* creativewriting.gmu.edu (office).

LOWRY, Lois, BA; American writer; b. 20 March 1937, Honolulu, HI; m. Donald Grey Lowry 1956 (divorced 1977); two s. two d. *Education:* Brown Univ., Univ. of Southern Maine. *Publications:* children's books: A Summer to Die 1977, Find a Stranger, Say Goodbye 1978, Anastasia Krupnik 1979, Autumn Street 1979, Anastasia Again! 1981, Anastasia at Your Service 1982, Taking Care of Terrific 1983, Anastasia Ask Your Analyst 1984, Us and Uncle Fraud 1984, One Hundredth Thing About Caroline 1985, Anastasia on her Own 1985, Switcharound 1985, Anastasia Has the Answers 1986, Rabble Starkey 1987, Anastasia's Chosen Career 1987, All About Sam 1988, Number the Stars 1989, Your Move J.P.! 1990, Anastasia at This Address 1991, Attaboy Sam! 1992, The Giver 1993, Anastasia Absolutely 1995, See You Around, Sam 1996, Stay! Keeper's Story 1997, Looking Back 1998, Zooman Sam 1999, Gathering Blue 2000. *Honours:* Int. Reading Asscn Children's Literature Award 1978, American Library Asscn Notable Book Citation 1980, Boston Globe-Horn Book Award 1987, Nat. Jewish Book Award 1990, Newbery Medals 1990, 1994, American Library Asscn Margaret A. Edwards Award for Lifetime Achievement 2007. *Address:* 205 Brattle Street, Cambridge, MA 02138, USA.

LUCARELLI, Carlo; Italian novelist; b. 26 Oct. 1960, Parma. *Career:* Co-Ed., Stile libero Noir; singer of group, Progetto K; Ed., Incubatoio 16 (online); Lecturer in Creative Writing, Scuola Holden di Alessandro Baricco, Turin; mem. Italian chapter of AIEP (Int. Asscn Police Writers), Associazione Scrittori-Bologna. *Radio:* Radio Bellablù (scriptwriter, for RadioTre). *Plays:* Radiogiallo (Teatro Comunale, Mordano) 1989, Il Delitto di Via Marconi (Teatro Comunale, Mordano) 1991, Finestra sul Cortile (Teatro Comunale, Mordano) 1993, Viva l'Itaglia 1994, Asasini!!! 1997, Via delle Oche (Teatro delle Moline, Bologna) 1999, La Profezia (Teatro Comunale, Mordano) 2001, Belfagor (Teatro Comunale, Mordano) 2001, Delitto a Teatro (Teatro Duse, Bologna) 2002. *Publications:* Compagni di sangue (with Michele Giuttari), Almost Blue, Carta bianca 1990, L'estate torbida 1991, Falange Armata 1993, Indagine non autorizzata (Premio Alberto Tedeschi) 1993, Vorrei essere il pilota di uno zero 1994, Nikita 1994, Il Giorno del lupo 1994, Lupo Mannaro 1995, Via delle Oche (Premio Mistery) 1996, Guernica 1996, Febbre Gialla 1997, Autosole 1998, Il Trillo del diavolo 1998, L'Isola dell'Angelo Caduto (Premio Franco Fedeli 2000) 1999, Mistero in Blu 1999, Un Giorno dopo l'altro 2000, Laura di Rimini 2001, Medical Thriller (with Eraldo Baldini and Giampiero Rigosi) 2002, Misteri d'Italia - i casi di Blu Notte 2002, Serial Killer - Storie di ossessione omicida (with Massimo Picozzi) 2003, Il Lato sinistro del cuore 2003, La Scena del crimine 2005, Tracce criminali (with Massimo Picozzi) 2006. *Address:* c/o Giulio Einaudi Editore, Via Biancamano 2, 10121 Turin, Italy. *E-mail:* eirights@einaudi.it. *Website:* www.carlolucarelli.net.

LUCAS, Celia, BA; British writer; b. 23 Oct. 1938, Bristol, England; m. Ian Skidmore 1971. *Education:* St Hilda's College, Oxford. *Career:* mem. Welsh Acad. 1989–. *Publications:* Prisoners of Santo Tomas, 1975; Steel Town Cats, 1987; Glyndwr Country (with Ian Skidmore), 1988; Anglesey Rambles (with Ian Skidmore), 1989; The Adventures of Marmaduke Purr Cat, 1990; The Terrible Tale of Tiggy Two, 1995; Madoc's Prickly Problem, 2000. Contributions: numerous journals and magazines. *Honours:* Tir Na N-Og Award for Junior Fiction 1988, Irma Chilton Award for Junior Fiction 1995.

LUCAS, Craig, BFA; American playwright and screenwriter; b. 30 April 1951, Atlanta, Ga; s. of Charles Samuel Lucas and Eleanore Alltmont Lucas. *Education:* Boston Univ. *Career:* Rockefeller and Guggenheim Fellowships; mem. Dramatists' Guild, PEN, Writers' Guild of America. *Plays:* Missing Persons 1980, Reckless 1983, Blue Window 1984, Prelude to a Kiss 1987 and The Scare 1989, God's Heart 1994, The Dying Gaul 1996, Savage Light (with David Schulner) 1996. *Musicals:* Marry Me a Little (anthology of songs by Stephen Sondheim) 1981, Three Postcards (music and lyrics by Craig Carnelia) 1987, The Light in the Piazza 2004. *Films:* Blue Window 1987, Longtime Companion 1990, Prelude to a Kiss 1991, Reckless 1995, Secret Lives of Dentists 2002, The Dying Gaul 2005. *Honours:* Sundance Audience Award, Obie and Outer Critics' Award, Los Angeles Drama Critics' Award, two Tony nominations. *Address:* c/o Peter Franklin, William Morris Agency, 1325 Aveue of the Americas, New York, NY 10019, USA. *E-mail:* craig.lucas@mac.com (home).

LUCAS, Georges, LenD; French publisher; b. 29 Aug. 1915, Rennes; s. of René and Madeleine (Bazin) Lucas; m. Evelyne Torres 1941; one s. *Career:* Man. Dir and Pres. Livraria Bertrand-Amadora, Lisbon 1948–75; Pres. Franco-Portuguese Chamber of Commerce, Lisbon 1963–72; mem. Bd Editions Robert Laffont 1967–75, Man. Dir 1976–79; Vice-Pres. and Man. Dir Banque Franco-Portuguaise d'Outre-Mer 1966–73; Chair. and Man.-Dir Librairie Larousse 1979–83, Adviser 1984–86; Conseiller Nat. du Commerce Extérieur 1973–86. *Honours:* Chevalier, Légion d'honneur, Croix de Guerre. *Address:* 5 avenue Emile Deschanel, 75007 Paris, France.

LUCAS, John, BA, PhD, FRSA; British academic, poet, writer and publisher; *Professor Emeritus, Loughborough University and NottinghamTrent University;* b. 26 June 1937, Exeter, Devon; m. 1961; one s. one d. *Education:* Univ. of Reading. *Career:* Asst Lecturer, Univ. of Reading, 1961–64; Lecturer, Sr Lecturer, Reader, Univ. of Nottingham, 1964–77; Visiting Prof., Univ. of Maryland and Indiana Univ., 1967–68; Prof. of English, Loughborough Univ. 1977–96, Prof. Emer. 1996–; Research Prof., Nottingham Trent Univ. 1996–2003, Prof. Emer. 2003–; Lord Byron Visiting Prof., Univ. of Athens, 1984–85; Publr, Shoestring Press, 1994–; mem. John Clare Soc., Poetry Book Soc. (Chair. 1988–92), Robert Bloomfield Soc. *Publications:* over 30 books of a critical and scholarly nature, including studies of Dickens, Arnold Bennett, the 1920s, and romantic and modern poetry; About Nottingham, 1971; A Brief

Bestiary, 1972; Egils Saga: Versions of the Poems, 1975; The Days of the Week, 1983; Studying Grosz on the Bus, 1989; Flying to Romania, 1992; One for the Piano, 1997; The Radical Twenties, 1997; On the Track: Poems, 2000; A World Perhaps: New and Selected Poems, 2002; Starting to Explain: Essays on 20th-Century British and Irish Poetry, 2003; The Long and the Short of It 2004, Flute Music 2006, Shakespeare's Second Tetralogy 2007; contrib. to anthologies, newspapers, reviews; BBC Radio 3 and 4. Honours: Poetry Prize for Best First Full Vol. of Poetry, Aldeburgh Festival, 1990. Address: 19 Devonshire Avenue, Beeston, Nottingham NG9 1BS, England. Telephone: (115) 9251827 (office).

LUCAS, John Randolph, MA, FBA; British academic (retd) and writer; b. 18 June 1929, England; s. of the late E. de G. Lucas and J. M. Lucas; m. Morar Portal 1961, two s. two d. Education: St Mary's College, Winchester, Balliol College, Oxford. Career: Junior Research Fellow, 1953–56, Fellow and Tutor, 1960–96, Merton College, Oxford; Fellow and Asst Tutor, Corpus Christi College, Cambridge, 1956–59; Jane Eliza Procter Visiting Fellow, Princeton University, 1957–58; Leverhulme Research Fellow, Leeds University, 1959–60; Giffford Lecturer, University of Edinburgh, 1971–73; Margaret Harris Lecturer, University of Dundee, 1981; Harry Jelema Lecturer, Calvin College, Grand Rapids, 1987; Reader in Philosophy, University of Oxford, 1990–96; mem. British Acad., fellow; British Society for the Philosophy of Science, pres., 1991–93. Publications: Principles of Politics, 1966; The Concept of Probability, 1970; The Freedom of the Will, 1970; The Nature of Mind, 1972; The Development of Mind, 1973; A Treatise on Time and Space, 1973; Essays on Freedom and Grace, 1976; Democracy and Participation, 1976; On Justice, 1980; Space, Time and Causality, 1985; The Future, 1989; Spacetime and Electromagnetism, 1990; Responsibility, 1993; Ethical Economics, 1996; The Conceptual Roots of Mathematics, 1999, Reason and Reality 2006; contrib. to scholarly journals. Address: Lambrook House, East Lambrook, Somerset TA13 5HW, England. E-mail: john.lucas@merton.ox.ac.uk. Website: users.ox .ac.uk/~jrlucas.

LUCAS, Stephen E., MA, PhD; American academic and writer; Evjue-Bascom Professor in the Humanities, University of Wisconsin at Madison; b. 5 Oct. 1946, White Plains, NY; m. Patricia Vore 1969; two s. Education: Univ. of California at Santa Barbara, Pennsylvania State Univ. Career: Asst Prof., Univ. of Wisconsin at Madison 1972–76, Assoc. Prof. 1976–82, Prof. 1982–, Evjue-Bascom Prof. in the Humanities 2001–; Visiting Assoc. Prof., Univ. of Virginia, 1979; mem. Int. Soc. for the History of Rhetoric, Org. of American Historians, Nat. Communication Asscn. Publications: Portents of Rebellion: Rhetoric and Revolution in Philadelphia 1765–1776 1976, The Art of Public Speaking 1983, George Washington: The Wisdom of an American Patriot 1998; contribs to scholarly books and journals. Honours: Hon. Prof., Univ. of Int. Business and Econs, Beijing 2001, J. Jeffrey Auer Lecturer, Indiana Univ. 1988; Nat. Communication Asscn Golden Anniversary Book Award 1977, Nat. Communication Asscn Golden Anniversary Monograph Award 1999, Donald H. Ecroyd Award for Outstanding Teaching in Higher Education, Nat. Communication Asscn 2001, Text and Academic Authors Asscn Textbook Excellence Award 2004, William Holmes McGuffey Award 2004. Address: Department of Communication Arts, University of Wisconsin at Madison, Madison, WI 53706, USA (office). Telephone: (608) 262-2543 (office).

LUCE, Henry, III, BA; American publisher, journalist and foundation administrator; Chairman Emeritus, The Henry Luce Foundation; b. 28 April 1925, New York; s. of Henry R. Luce and Lila Hotz Tyng; m. 1st Patricia Potter 1947 (divorced 1954); one s. one d.; m. 2nd Claire McGill 1960 (died 1971); three step-s.; m. 3rd Nancy Bryan Cassiday 1975 (died 1987); two step-s. (one deceased); m. 4th Leila Eliott Burton Hadley 1990; two step-s. two step-d. Education: Brooks School and Yale Univ. Career: served USNR 1943–46; Commdr's Asst, Hoover Comm. on Org. Exec. Branch of Govt 1948–49; Reporter, Cleveland Press 1949–51; Washington Corresp. Time Inc. 1951–53, Time writer 1953–55, Head New Bldg Dept 1956–60, Asst to Publr 1960–61, Circulation Dir Fortune and Architectural Forum 1961–64, House and Home 1962–64, Vice-Pres. 1964–80, Chief London Bureau 1966–68, Publr Fortune 1968–69, Publr Time 1969–72; Vice-Pres. for Corporate Planning and Dir Time Inc. 1967–89; Dir Time Warner Inc. 1989–96; Pres. and CEO Henry Luce Foundation 1958–90, Chair. and CEO 1990–2002, Chair. Emer. 2002–; Pres. Asscn of American Corresps in London 1968; Pres. The New Museum of Contemporary Art 1977–98; Chair. American Security Systems Inc.; mem. American Council for UN Univ., Foreign Policy Asscn (Gov., Medal 1997); Trustee, Eisenhower Exchange Fellowships, Princeton Theological Seminary, Center of Theological Inquiry, Coll. of Wooster, China Inst. in America, A Christian Ministry in the Nat. Parks, New York Historical Soc.; Pres. The Pilgrims; Chair. American Russian Youth Orchestra; Dir Nat. Cttee on US–China Relations, Fishers Island Devt Co. Honours: Hon. LHD (St Michael's Coll., Long Island Univ., Pratt Inst.); Hon. LLD (Coll. of Wooster); Hon. DLitt (Cen. Philippine Univ.); Dr hc (Mapuce Inst. of Tech.); American Asscn of Museums Medal for Distinguished Philanthropy 1994, Cen. Park Conservancy Frederick Law Olmstead Award 1996, St Nicholas Soc. Medal 1998, Augustine Graham Medal, Brooklyn Museum of Art 2000, Conrado Benitez Medal, Philippine Univ. for Women 2000. Address: Suite 1500, 720 Fifth Avenue, New York, NY 10019 (office); Mill Hill Road, Mill Neck, NY 11765 (home); 4 Sutton Place, New York, NY 10022, USA. Telephone: (212) 582-5531 (office); (516) 922-0356 (home); (212) 759-8640. Fax: (212) 246-1867 (office); (212) 759-6831 (home). E-mail: hl@hluce.org (office). Website: www.hluce.org (office).

LUCIE-SMITH, (John) Edward (McKenzie), MA, FRSL; British art critic and poet; b. 27 Feb. 1933, Kingston, Jamaica; s. of John Dudley Lucie-Smith and Mary Lushington. Education: King's School, Canterbury, Merton Coll. Oxford. Career: officer RAF 1954–56; fmrly worked in advertising and as freelance journalist and broadcaster; contributes to The Times, Sunday Times, Independent, Mail-on-Sunday, Spectator, New Statesman, Evening Standard, Encounter, London Magazine, Illustrated London News; mem. Acad. de Poésie Européenne. Exhibitions: photographs: Art Kiosk (Brussels) 1999, Galena Toni Benin (Barcelona) 2000, Rosenfeld Gallery (Tel Aviv) 2001. Publications as sole author include: A Tropical Childhood and Other Poems 1961, Confessions and Histories 1964, What is a Painting? 1966, Thinking About Art 1968, Towards Silence 1968, Movements in Art Since 1945 1969, Art in Britain 69–70 1970, A Concise History of French Painting 1971, Symbolist Art 1972, Eroticism in Western Art 1972, The First London Catalogue 1974, The Well Wishers 1974, The Burnt Child (autobiog.) 1975, The Invented Eye (early photography) 1975, World of the Makers 1975, Joan of Arc 1976, Fantin-Latour 1977, The Dark Pageant (novel) 1977, Art Today 1977, A Concise History of Furniture 1979, Super Realism 1979, Cultural Calendar of the Twentieth Century 1979, Art in the Seventies 1980, The Story of Craft 1981, The Body 1981, A History of Industrial Design 1983, Art Terms: An Illustrated Dictionary 1984, Art in the Thirties 1985, American Art Now 1985, Lives of the Great Twentieth Century Artists 1986, Sculpture Since 1945 1987, Art in the Eighties 1990, Art Deco Painting 1990, Fletcher Benton 1990, Jean Rustin 1991, Harry Holland 1992, Art and Civilisation 1992, Andres Nagel 1992, Wendy Taylor 1992, Alexander 1992, British Art Now 1993, Race, Sex and Gender: Issues in Contemporary Art 1994, American Realism 1994, Art Today 1995, Visual Arts in the Twentieth Century 1996, Arts Erotica: an Arousing History of Erotic Art 1997, Adam 1998, Stone 1998, Zoo 1998, Judy Chicago: an American Vision 2000, Flesh and Stone 2000, Changing Shape (poems) 2002; has edited numerous anthologies. Address: c/o Rogers, Coleridge and White, 20 Powis Mews, London, W11 1JN, England.

LUCKLESS, John (see Irving, Clifford Michael)

LUDWIKOWSKI, Rett Ryszard, LLM, PhD, Habil.; American (b. Polish) academic and writer; Professor of Law and Director, Comparative and International Law Institute, Catholic University of America; b. 6 Nov. 1943, Skawina-Kraków, Poland; m. Anna Ludwikowski 1995; one s. one d. Education: Jagiellonian Univ., Kraków. Career: Sr Lecturer, Jagiellonian Univ., Kraków 1967–71, Adjunct Prof. 1971–76, Asst Prof. 1976–81, Assoc. Prof. of Law 1981, Sr Fulbright Scholar 1997; Visiting Prof., Elizabethtown Coll., Pennsylvania 1982–83, Alfred Univ. 1983; Visiting Scholar, Hoover Inst., Stanford Univ. 1983, Max Planck Inst., Hamburg, 1990; Visiting Prof. of Politics, Catholic Univ. of America, Washington, DC 1984, Visiting Prof. of Law 1985, Ordinary Prof. of Law 1986–, Dir Comparative and Int. Law Inst. 1987–. Publications: The Crisis of Communism: Its Meaning, Origins and Phases, 1986; Continuity and Change in Poland, 1991; Constitutionalism and Human Rights (ed. with Kenneth Thompson), 1991; The Beginning of the Constitutional Era: A Comparative Study of the First American and European Constitution (with William Fox Jr), 1993; Constitution Making in the Countries of Former Soviet Dominance, 1996; Regulations of International Trade and Business, 2 vols, 1996, 1998; Comparative Constitutional Law, 2000, Comparative Rights and Fundamental Freedoms Vol. I (with Gisbert Flanz, Man. Ed.) 2002, International Trade 2006; contribs to scholarly books and journals. Honours: Officer, Medal of Merits (Poland); various grants and awards. Address: Columbus School of Law, Catholic University of America, Washington, DC 20064, USA (office). Telephone: (202) 319-5140 (office). Fax: (202) 319-4459 (office). E-mail: ludwikowski@law.edu (office).

LUEBKE, Frederick Carl, BS, MA, PhD; American academic and writer; b. 26 Jan. 1927, Reedsburg, WI. Education: Concordia University, River Forest, IL, Claremont Graduate University, University of Nebraska. Career: Assoc. Prof., 1968–72, Prof., 1972–87, Charles Mach Distinguished Prof. of History, 1987–94, Prof. Emeritus, 1994–, University of Nebraska; Ed., Great Plains Quarterly 1980–84; Dir, Center for Great Plains Studies, 1983–88. Publications: Immigrants and Politics, 1969; Ethnic Voters and the Election of Lincoln (ed.), 1971; Bonds of Loyalty: German-Americans and World War I, 1974; The Great Plains: Environment and Culture (ed.), 1979; Ethnicity on the Great Plains (ed.), 1980; Vision and Refuge: Essays on the Literature of the Great Plains (co-ed.), 1981; Mapping the North American Plains (co-ed.), 1987; Germans in Brazil: A Comparative History of Cultural Conflict During World War I, 1987; Germans in the New World: Essays in the History of Immigration, 1990; A Harmony of the Arts: The Nebraska State Capital (ed.), 1990; Nebraska: An Illustrated History, 1995; European Immigration in the American West: Community Histories (ed.), 1998. Contributions: Professional journals.

LUELLEN, Valentina (see Polley, Judith Anne)

LUHRMANN, Bazmark (Baz) Anthony; Australian film and theatre director; b. 17 Sept. 1962, NSW; s. of Leonard and Barbara Luhrmann; m. Catherine Martin 1997; one d. Education: Narrabeen High School, Sydney. Career: theatre work with Peter Brook; owns Bazmark Inq. production co., Sydney; acting roles in films The Winter of Our Dreams 1982, The Dark Room 1984; directed advertisement for Chanel No.5 2004. Recording: Something for Everybody (concept album, including track Everybody's Free To Wear Sunscreen) (Platinum Album, Australia, Gold Album, USA). Films: Strictly Ballroom 1992 (Cannes Film Festival Prix de la Jeunesse, Toronto Film

Festival People's Choice Award, Chicago Film Festival Award for Best Feature Film), La Bohème (TV) 1993, Romeo + Juliet 1996, Moulin Rouge 2001 (numerous awards including Golden Globe, Producers' Guild of America Film of the Year, Hollywood Film Festival Best Movie). *Plays:* Strictly Ballroom, Haircut. *Operas directed:* La Bohème, Sydney 1990, New York 2002–03, San Francisco 2002, A Midsummer Night's Dream, Sydney 1993. *Television includes:* A Country Practice (actor) 1981–82. *Screenplays written:* Strictly Ballroom 1992, Romeo + Juliet 1996, Moulin Rouge (also story) 2001. *Literary Agent:* Bazmark Inq, PO Box 430, Kings Cross, NSW 1340, Australia; c/o Robert Newman, The Endeavor Agency, 9601 Wilshire Blvd., 10th Floor, Beverly Hills, CA 90212, USA. *Telephone:* (2) 9361-6668. *Fax:* (2) 9361-6667. *Website:* www.bazmark.com.

LUHRMANN, Tanya Marie, BA, MPhil, PhD; American academic and writer; *Professor of Anthropology, Stanford University;* b. 24 Feb. 1959, Dayton, OH. *Education:* Harvard Univ., Univ. of Cambridge. *Career:* Research Fellow, Christ's Coll., Cambridge 1985–89; Assoc. Prof. of Anthropology, Univ. of California at San Diego 1989–98, Prof. of Anthropology 1998–07; Prof. Cttee on Human Development, Univ. of Chicago 2000–07; Prof. of Anthropology, Stanford Univ. 2007–; mem. American Anthropology Asscn, Soc. for Psychological Anthropology, Royal Anthropological Inst. *Publications:* Persuasions of the Witch's Craft 1989, The Good Parsi 1996, Of Two Minds: The Growing Disorder in American Society 2000; contribs to professional journals. *Honours:* Bowdoin Prize 1981, Nat. Science Foundation Graduate Fellow 1982–85, Emanuel Miller Prize 1983, Partingdon Prize 1985, Stirling Prize 1986, Fulbright Award 1990, Turner Prize 2000. *Address:* Building 10, Main Quad, Stanford University, Stanford, CA 60637, USA (office).

LUKACS, John Adalbert, PhD; American academic (retd) and historian; b. 31 Jan. 1924, Budapest, Hungary; m. 1st Helen Schofield 1953 (died 1970); one s. one d.; m. 2nd Stephanie Harvey 1974 (died 2003); m. 3rd Pamela Hall 2005. *Education:* Palatine Joseph Univ., Budapest. *Career:* Prof. of History, Chestnut Hill Coll., Philadelphia 1947–94, Chair. Dept of History 1947–93; Visiting Prof., La Salle Coll. 1949–82, Columbia Univ. 1954–55, Univ. of Toulouse 1964–65, Univ. of Pennsylvania 1964, 1967, 1968, 1995–97, Johns Hopkins Univ. 1970–71, Fletcher School of Law and Diplomacy 1971–72, Princeton Univ. 1988, Univ. of Budapest 1991, Univ. of Pennsylvania 1994–96; Fellow Soc. of American Historians; mem. American Catholic History Asscn (pres. 1977), American Philosophical Soc. *Publications:* The Great Powers and Eastern Europe 1953, A History of the Cold War 1961, The Decline and Rise of Europe 1965, Historical Consciousness 1968, The Passing of the Modern Age 1970, The Last European War, 1939–41 1976, 1945: Year Zero 1978, Philadelphia: Patricians and Philistines, 1900–1950 1981, Outgrowing Democracy: A Historical Interpretation of the US in the 20th Century 1984, Budapest 1900 1988, Confessions of an Original Sinner 1990, The Duel: Hitler vs. Churchill, 10 May–31 August 1940 1991, The End of the 20th Century and the End of the Modern Age 1993, Destinations Past 1994, George P. Kennan and the Origins of Containment: The Kennan/Lukacs Correspondence 1997, The Hitler of History 1997, A Thread of Years 1998, Five Days in London 1999, At the End of an Age 2002, Churchill: Visionary, Statesman, Historian 2002, A New Republic 2004, Democracy and Populism 2005, The Remembered Past 2005, June 1941: Hitler and Stalin 2006, George Kennan: A Study of Character 2007; contrib. many scholarly journals. *Honours:* three hon. doctorates; Ingersoll Prize 1991; Order of Merit, Republic of Hungary 1994, Ordre of the Corvinus Chain 2001. *Address:* 129 Valley Park Road, Phoenixville, PA 19460, USA (home). *Telephone:* (610) 933-7495 (home). *Fax:* (610) 917-0871 (home).

LUKAS, Richard Conrad, MA, PhD; American historian and academic; b. 29 Aug. 1937, Lynn, Massachusetts. *Education:* Florida State Univ. *Career:* Research Consultant, US Air Force Historical Archives, 1957–58; Asst Prof., Tennessee Tech. Univ., Cookeville 1963–66, Assoc. Prof. 1966–69, Prof. 1969–83, Univ. Prof. of History 1983–89; Prof. Wright State Univ., Lake Campus 1989–92; Adjunct Prof. Univ. of South Florida, Fort Myers 1993–96; Consultant (documentary films) Zegota: A Time to Remember 1997, Burning Questions 1998. *Publications:* Eagles East: The Army Air Forces and the Soviet Union 1941–45 1970, From Metternich to the Beatles (ed.) 1973, The Strange Allies: The United States and Poland 1941–45 1978, Bitter Legacy: Polish-American Relations in the Wake of World War II 1982, Forgotten Holocaust: The Poles under German Occupation 1986, Out of the Inferno: Poles Remember the Holocaust 1989, Did the Children Cry?: Hitler's War Against Jewish and Polish Children 1994, Forgotten Survivors: Polish Christians Remember the Nazi Occupation 2004. *Honours:* Polonia Restituta 1988; Hon. DHumLitt 1987; American Inst. of Aeronautics and Astronautics History Book Award 1971, American Council for Polish Culture Cultural Achievement Award 1994, Janusz Korczak Literary Award 1996, Waclaw Jedrzejewicz History Award 2000, Kosciuszko Foundation's Joseph Slotkowski Achievement Award 2001. *Address:* 5894 N W 26th Lane, Ocala, FL 34482, USA. *E-mail:* marich@webtv.net.

LUKER, Nicholas John Lydgate, MA, PhD; British academic, writer, editor and translator; *Senior Lecturer in Russian, University of Nottingham;* b. 26 Jan. 1945, Leeds; one s. *Education:* Hertford Coll., Oxford, Univ. of Grenoble, Univ. of Nottingham. *Career:* Lecturer, Univ. of Nottingham 1970–88, Sr Lecturer in Russian 1988–; various visiting lectureships and fellowships in Australia, New Zealand and USA; mem. British Asscn of Slavists. *Publications:* Alexander Grin 1973, The Seeker of Adventure, by Alexander Grin (trans. with B. Scherr) 1978, A I Kuprin 1978, The Forgotten Visionary 1982,

An Anthology of Russian Neo-Realism: The 'Znanie' School of Maxim Gorky (ed. and trans.) 1982, Fifty Years On: Gorky and His Time (ed.) 1987, Alexander Grin: Selected Short Stories (ed. and trans.) 1987, From Furmanov to Sholokhov: An Anthology of the Classics of Socialist Realism (ed. and trans.) 1988, In Defence of a Reputation: Essays on the Early Prose of Mikhail Artsybashev 1990, The Russian Short Story 1900–1917 (ed.) 1991, Urban Romances, by Yuri Miloslavsky (ed. and co-trans.) 1994, After the Watershed: Russian Prose 1917–1927 (ed.) 1996, Out of the Shadows: Neglected Works in Soviet Prose (ed.) 2003; contrib. to numerous scholarly journals. *Address:* c/o Department of Russian and Slavonic Studies, University of Nottingham, Nottingham NG7 2RD, England. *Telephone:* (115) 9515151 (office). *E-mail:* nicholas.luker@nottingham.ac.uk (office).

LUKYANOV, Anatoliy Ivanovich, DJurSc; Russian politician and poet; b. 7 May 1930; m.; one d. *Education:* Moscow Univ. *Career:* mem. CPSU 1955–91; mem. CP of Russian Fed. 1992–; Chief Consultant on Legal Comm. of USSR Council of Ministers 1956–61; Deputy Head of Dept of Presidium of USSR Supreme Soviet 1969–76, Head of Secr. 1977–83; mem. of editorial staff of Sovietskoe Gosudarstvo i Pravo 1978; mem. Cen. Auditing Comm. CPSU 1981–86, 1986–89; Deputy of RSFSR Supreme Soviet 1984–91; Head of Gen. Dept of Cen. Cttee CPSU 1985–87, Sec. of Cen. Cttee 1987–88; Cand. mem. Political Bureau 1988–90; First Vice-Chair. of Presidium, USSR Supreme Soviet 1988–90, Chair. 1990–91; Chief Adviser on Legal Reform in USSR 1986–89; mem. Cen. Cttee CPSU 1986–91; People's Deputy of USSR 1989–91; arrested 1991 following failed coup d'état; charged with conspiracy Jan. 1992; released on bail Dec. 1992, on trial 1993–94; mem. State Duma (Parl.) 1993–2003, mem. Cttee for Legis. and Judicial Reform 1994, Chair. 1996–99; Chair. Cttee for State Org. 2000–2002; mem. Presidium, Cen. Exec. Cttee CP of Russian Fed. *Publications include:* many articles and books on Soviet legal system and Soviet constitution, three vols of poetry (under pseudonym A. Osenev). *Address:* c/o Communist Party of the Russian Federation, per. M. Sukharevskii 3/1, 103051 Moscow, Russia. *Telephone:* (495) 928–71–29. *Fax:* (495) 292-90-50.

LUMSDEN, Lynne Ann; American publishing executive; b. 30 July 1947, Battle Creek, Mich.; d. of Arthur Lumsden and Ruth Pandy; m. Jon Harden 1986; one d. *Education:* Univ. of Paris, Sarah Lawrence Coll., City Grad. Center and New York Univ. *Career:* copy ed., Harcourt, Brace, Jovanovich, New York 1970–71; ed., Appleton-Century Crofts, New York 1971–73; Coll. Div. Prentice Hall 1974–78, Sr Ed. Coll. Div. 1978–81; Asst Vice-Pres. and Ed.-in-Chief, Spectrum Books 1981–82, Vice-Pres. and Editorial Dir, Gen. Publishing Div. 1982–85; Exec. Vice-Pres., Publr and co-owner, Dodd, Mead & Co., Inc. New York 1985–89; owner, Chair. JBH Communications Inc. Hartford, Conn. 1989–; Publr Hartford News and Southside Media 1989–. *Address:* JBH Communications Inc., 99 Hammer Street, Suite A, Hartford, CT 06114, USA (office).

LUND, Gerald Niels, BA, MS; American educator (retd) and writer; b. 12 Sept. 1939, Fountain Green, UT; m. Lynn Stanard 1963; three s. four d. *Education:* Brigham Young Univ., Pepperdine Coll., Univ. of Judaism. *Career:* educator 1965–99; mem. Asscn of Mormon Letters, Hon. Lifetime mem. 1997. *Publications:* The Coming of the Lord 1971, This is Your World 1973, One in Thine Hand 1981, The Alliance 1983, Leverage Point 1986, The Freedom Factor 1987, The Work and the Glory (nine vols) 1990–2000 (also made into a film), The Kingdom and the Crown (three vols) 2000, 2002, 2003, Fire of the Covenant 2001, The Scholarly Writings of Gerald N. Lund 2002; contribs to monographs and periodicals. *Honours:* Best Novel Awards, Asscn of Mormon Letters 1991, 1993, Frankie and John K. Orton 1994, LDS Ind. Booksellers Asscn Awards 1994, 1997, 2000, 2001. *Address:* 47 E. South Temple Street, Salt Lake City, UT 89150-1700 (home); PO Box 30178, Salt Lake City, UT 84130, USA (home).

LUNN, Janet Louise Swoboda; Canadian writer and editor; b. 28 Dec. 1928, Dallas, TX, USA; d. of Herman A. and Margaret Swoboda; m. Richard Lunn 1950; four s. one d. *Education:* Queen's Univ., Ont. *Career:* literary consultant, Ginn and Co. 1968–78; Children's Ed. Clarke, Irwin and Co. 1972–75; conducted writers' workshops with Ontario Arts Council; Writer-in-Residence, Regina Public Library 1982–83, Kitchener Public Library 1988; mem. Bd Dirs The Canadian Children's Book Centre 1990–93, (Vice-Pres. 1990), IBBY Canada 1989; Second Vice-Chair. Writers' Union of Canada 1979–80, Vice-Chair. 1983–84, Chair. 1984–85; mem. Canadian Soc. of Children's Authors, Illustrators and Performers, PEN Int. *Publications include:* The County (jtly) 1967, Double Spell (first published as Twin Spell 1968), Larger Than Life 1979, The Twelve Dancing Princesses (IODE Toronto Br. Children's Book Award) 1979, The Root Cellar (Book of the Year, Canadian Library Asscn 1982, Booklist's Reviewers' Choice, Teachers' Choice, American Nat. Council of Teachers of English 1983, Honour List Int. Bd of Books for Young People 1984, chosen in Jr High Category, California Young Reader Medal programme 1988), Shadow in Hawthorn Bay (Children's Book Award, Canadian Library Asscn, Young Adult Book of the Year Award, Saskatchewan Library Asscn, Children's Book of the Year, IODE Nat. Chapter, Honour List, Int. Bd of Books for Young People 1984, one of 40 books of the year, Int. Children's Library, Munich, Germany 1986), Amos's Sweater (Ruth Schwartz Award, Canadian Booksellers' Asscn 1989, Amelia Frances Howard Gibbon Award, Gov-Gen's Award) 1988, Duck Cakes for Sale 1989, One Hundred Shining Candles 1990, The Story of Canada for Children 1992, The Hollow Tree, Umbrella Birthday, Mr and Mrs Hat, Come to the Fair 1997, Charlotte 1998. *Honours:* Order of Ontario 1996; Hon. LLD (Queen's) 1992; Hon.

Diploma (Loyalist Coll., Belville, Ont.) 1993. *Address:* 115–3260 Southgate Road, Ottawa, Ontario, K1V 8W9, Canada. *E-mail:* janetlunn@sympatico.ca. *Website:* www.keith-n.com/jlunn.

LUPOFF, Richard Allen, BA; American writer; b. 21 Feb. 1935, New York, NY; m. Patricia Enid Loring 1958; two s. one d. *Education:* Univ. of Miami at Coral Gables. *Career:* Ed., Canaveral Press 1963–70; Contributing Ed., Crawdaddy Magazine 1968–71, Science Fiction Eye 1988–90; Ed., Canyon Press 1986–. *Publications:* Edgar Rice Burroughs: Master of Adventure 1965, All in Color for a Dime 1971, Sword of the Demon 1977, Space War Blues 1978, Sun's End 1984, Circumpolar! 1984, Lovecrafts Book 1985, The Forever City 1987, The Comic Book Killer 1988, The Classic Car Killer 1992, The Bessie Blue Killer 1994, The Sepia Siren Killer 1994, The Cover Girl Killer 1995, Master of Adventure: The Worlds of Edgar Rice Burroughs 2005; contrib. Ramparts, Los Angeles Times, Washington Post, San Francisco Chronicle, New York Times, Magazine of Fantasy and Science Fiction. *Honours:* Hugo Award 1963. *Address:* c/o University of Nebraska Press, 1111 Lincoln Mall, Lincoln, NE 68588-0630, USA.

LURAGHI, Raimondo, MD, PhD; Italian academic and writer; *Professor Emeritus of American History, University of Genoa*; b. 16 Aug. 1921, Milan; m. 1950; one s. one d. *Education:* Univ. of Turin, Univ. of Rome. *Career:* Prof. of History, Junior Coll. 1954–64; Prof. of American History, Univ. of Genoa 1964–96, Emeritus Prof. 1996–; mem. Italian Asscn for Military History (pres.). *Publications:* Storia della Guerra Civile Americana 1966, Gli Stati Uniti 1972, The Rise and Fall of the Plantation South 1975, Marinai del Sud 1993, A History of the Confederate Navy 1861–1865 1995; contrib. to Italian, French, American and Chinese historical magazines. *Honours:* Gold Medal of the Pres. of the Italian Republic, Arts and Sciences 1999. *Address:* Corso Regina Margherita 155, 10122 Turin, Italy (home). *Telephone:* (1) 4374678. *E-mail:* luraghiraimondo@libero.it (home).

LURIE, Alison, AB; American novelist and academic; *Whiton Professor of American Literature, Cornell University*; b. 3 Sept. 1926, Chicago, IL; d. of Harry Lawrence and Bernice Stewart Lurie; m. 1st Jonathon Peale Bishop 1948 (divorced 1985); three s.; m. 2nd Edward Hower 1996. *Education:* Radcliffe Coll., Mass. *Career:* Editorial Asst Oxford University Press 1946; worked as receptionist and secretary; Lecturer in English, Cornell Univ. 1969–73, Adjunct Assoc. Prof. 1973–76, Assoc. Prof. 1976–79, Whiton Prof. of American Literature 1979–; Yaddo Foundation Fellow 1963, 1964, 1966, 1984, Guggenheim Fellow 1965, Rockefeller Foundation Fellow 1967. *Publications:* V. R. Lang: a Memoir 1959, Love and Friendship 1962, The Nowhere City 1965, Imaginary Friends 1967, Real People 1969, The War Between the Tates 1974, Only Children 1979, Clever Gretchen and Other Forgotten Folktales (juvenile) 1980, The The Heavenly Zoo (juvenile) 1980, Fabulous Beasts (juvenile) 1981, Foreign Affairs 1984 (Pulitzer Prize in Fiction 1985), The Man with a Shattered World 1987, The Truth about Lorin Jones 1988, Women and Ghosts 1994, The Last Resort 1998, Familiar Spirits 2001, Truth and Consequences 2005; non-fiction: The Language of Clothes 1981, Don't Tell the Grown Ups, Subversive Children's Literature (essays) 1990, Boys and Girls Forever: Reflections on Children's Classics (essays) 2003. *Honours:* New York State Cultural Council Foundation Grant 1972; American Acad. of Arts and Letters Literature Award 1978, Prix Femina Étranger 1989, Parents' Choice Foundation Award 1996. *Literary Agent:* AP Watt Ltd, 20 John Street, London, WC1N 2DR, England. *Address:* Department of English, 263 Goldwin Smith Hall, Cornell University, Ithaca, New York, NY 14853-3201, USA (office). *Telephone:* (607) 255-4235 (office). *E-mail:* al28@cornell.edu (office). *Website:* www.people.cornell.edu/pages/al28 (office).

LURIE, Morris; Australian writer; b. 30 Oct. 1938, Melbourne, Vic. *Career:* Writer-in-Residence, Latrobe Univ. 1984, Holmesglen Tafe 1992. *Publications:* novels: Rappaport 1966, The London Jungle Adventures of Charlie Hope 1968, Rappaport's Revenge 1973, Flying Home 1978, Seven Books for Grossman 1983, Madness 1991; short stories: Happy Times 1969, Inside the Wardrobe 1975, Running Nicely 1979, Dirty Friends 1981, Outrageous Behaviour 1984, The Night We Ate the Sparrow 1985, Two Brothers Running (also wrote screenplay) 1990, The String 1995, Welcome to Tangier 1997, The Secret Strength of Children 2001; children's books: The Twenty-Seventh Annual African Hippopotamus Race 1969, Arlo the Dandy Lion 1971, The Story of Imelda Who Was Small 1984, Night-Night! 1986, What's That Noise? What's That Sound? 1991, Racing the Moon 1993, Zeeks Alive! 1997, Boy in a Storm at Sea 1997; autobiography: Whole Life 1987; contributions to Virginia Quarterly Review, The New Yorker, The New York Times, Antaeus, The Times, Punch, Telegraph Magazine, The Age (Australia); stories broadcast and plays telecast. *Honours:* State of Victoria Short Story Award 1973, National Book Council Selection 1980, Children's Book Council Honour Book 1983, Bicentennial Banjo Award 1988, Patrick White Award 2006. *Address:* 141 Woodhouse Grove, Box Hill North, Vic. 3129, Australia. *Telephone:* (3) 9890-7435 (home).

LUSTIG, Arnošt; American (b. Czech) writer and academic; *Professor Emeritus of Literature, American University*; b. 21 Dec. 1926, Prague; s. of Emil Lustig and Terezie Lustig (née Löwy); m. Věra Weislitz 1949; one s. one d. *Education:* Coll. of Political and Social Sciences, Prague. *Career:* in concentration camps at Terezín (Theresienstadt), Auschwitz-Birkenau and Buchenwald, Second World War; Radio Prague corresp. in Arab-Israeli war 1948, 1949; Radio Prague reporter 1948–58; Ed. Mladý svět (weekly) 1958–59, screenplay writer for Studio Barandov 1960–68, for Jadran-Film Yugoslavia 1969–70; naturalized American citizen 1979; mem. Cen. Cttee Union of Czechoslovak Writers 1963–69, mem. Presidium 1963–69; mem. Int. Writing Program 1970–71; Visiting Lecturer, Univ. of Iowa 1971–72; Visiting Prof., Drake Univ., Iowa 1972–73; Prof. of Literature, American Univ., Washington, DC 1973–2005, Prof. Emer. 2005–; Visiting Prof. in Cooperation with Charles Univ., Prague, Univs of New Orleans and Michigan, summer courses 1993; Lecturer, J. Škvorecký Literary Acad. 2000–. *Screenplays:* Names for which there are no people (Prague) 1960, Theresienstadt (Prague) 1965, Stolen Childhood (Italy) 1966, Triumph of Memory (PBS) 1984, Precious Legacy (USA) 1984, Fighter (USA) 2000, Tanga (Prague) 2002. *Films:* Europa (co-author; autobiographical documentary) 1998, Fighter (autobiographical documentary) 2000. *Publications:* fiction: Démanty noci (short stories, trans. as Diamonds of the Night) 1958, Blue Day (story) 1960, Night and Hope (short stories) 1958, Modlitba za Kateřinu Horovitzovou (novel, translated as A Prayer for Katerina Horovitzova) 1965, Dita Saxova (novel) 1962, The Street of Lost Brothers (short stories) 1962, Prague Crossroads 1964, The Man the Size of a Stamp (radio plays) 1965, Nobody will be Humiliated (stories) 1965, The White Birches in Autumn (novel) 1966, Bitter Smell of Almonds (novel) (translated as Indecent Dreams) 1968, Darling (novel) 1969, Darkness Casts No Shadow (novel) 1976, Children of the Holocaust (three vols, collected stories) 1977–78, The Holocaust and the Film Arts (essay with Josef Lustig) 1980, The Precious Legacy (screenplay for documentary) 1984, The Unloved (from the diary of 17-year-old Pearl Sch., novel) 1985, Indecent Dreams (collection of novellas) 1988, Street of Lost Brothers (short stories) 1990, Colette, Girl from Antwerp (novel) 1993, Tanga, Girl from Hamburg (novel) 1993, Leah, Girl from Antwerp (translated as Waiting for Leah 2005), Porges (novel) 1995, Friends (novel) 1995, House of the Echo Returned (novel) 1995, Chasm (novel) 1996, Beautiful Green Eyes 1997, Fire on the Water (three novellas) 1998, Initiation 2001, Bitter Smell of Almonds (three vols of collected stories) 2001, Collected Works (eight vols) 1992–2002, Lustig ist Gott, Gott ist Lustig 2001, House of Returned Echo 2002; non-fiction: text for symphonic poem Night and Hope (with Otmar Macha) 1963, The Beadle of Prague (text for a cantata) 1983; Answers (two interviews) 2002, Essays 2002, 3×18, portraits and observations (interviews) 2002, Confession (four CD autobiog.) 2005. *Honours:* Hon. Pres. Franz Kafka Soc., Prague 1990–; Hon. mem. Club of Czech Writers 1999–; Hon. DHL (Spertus Coll. of Judaica, Chicago) 1986; Klement Gottwald State Prize 1967, B'nai B'rith Prize 1974, Nat. Jewish Book Award 1980, 1986, Emmy Award, The Nat. Acad. of Television Arts and Sciences 1986, Publishers Weekly Literary Prize, USA 1991, Karel Čapek Literary Prize, Prague PEN Club Int. 1996, Medal of Merit, Czech Repub. 2000, American Acad. of Arts and Letters 2004. *Address:* 4000 Tunlaw Road, NW, Apartment 825, Washington, DC 20007, USA (home). *Telephone:* (202) 885-2984 (office); (202) 338-5357 (home); (420) 736227001 (mobile). *Fax:* (202) 885-2938 (office).

LUTTWAK, Edward Nicolae, PhD; American academic, international consultant and writer; *Senior Fellow, Center for Strategic and International Studies, Georgetown University*; b. 4 Nov. 1942, Arad, Romania; s. of Joseph Luttwak and Clara Baruch; m. Dalya Iaari 1970; one s. one d. *Education:* elementary schools in Palermo and Milan, Carmel Coll., Wallingford, UK, London School of Econs and Johns Hopkins Univ. *Career:* Lecturer, Univ. of Bath, UK 1965–67; Consultant, Walter J. Levy SA (London) 1967–68; Visiting Prof. Johns Hopkins Univ. 1974–76; Sr Fellow, Georgetown Univ. Center for Strategic and Int. Studies 1977–87, Burke Chair. of Strategy 1987–92, Sr Fellow 1992–; Consultant to Office of Sec. of Defense 1975, to Policy Planning Council, Dept of State 1981, Nat. Security Council 1987, Dept of Defense 1987, to Govts of Italy, Korea, Spain; Prin., Edward N. Luttwak Inc. Int. Consultants 1981–; Int. Assoc. Inst. of Fiscal and Monetary Policy, Japan Ministry of Finance (Okurasho); mem. editorial Bd of The American Scholar, Journal of Strategic Studies, The National Interest, Géopolitique, The Washington Quarterly, Orbis. *Publications:* Coup d'Etat 1968, Dictionary of Modern War 1972, The Israeli Army 1975, The Political Uses of Sea Power 1976, The Grand Strategy of the Roman Empire 1978, Strategy and Politics: Collected Essays 1979, The Grand Strategy of the Soviet Union 1983, The Pentagon and the Art of War 1985, Strategy and History: collected essays 1985, International Security Yearbook 1984/85 (with Barry M. Brechman) 1985, On the Meaning of Victory 1986, Strategy: The Logic of War and Peace 1987, The Dictionary of Modern War (with Stuart Koehl) 1991, The Endangered American Dream 1993, Il Fantasma della Povertà (co-author) 1996, Cose è davvero la Democrazia 1996, La Renaissance de la puissance aérienne stratégique 1998, Turbo-Capitalism 1999, Il Libro della Libertà 2000, Strategy: The Logic of War and Peace (ed.) 2002; his books have been translated into 14 languages. *Honours:* Nimitz Lectureship, Univ. of Calif. 1987, Tanner Lecturer, Yale Univ. 1989, Rosenstiel Lecturer, Grinner Coll. 1992. *Address:* Center for Strategic and International Studies, 1800 K Street, NW, Washington, DC 20006, USA. *Telephone:* (301) 656-1972 (office); (202) 775-3145. *Fax:* (202) 775-3199.

LUTZ, John Thomas; American writer; b. 11 Sept. 1939, Dallas, TX; m. Barbara Jean Bradley 1958; one s. two d. *Education:* Meramac Community Coll. *Career:* mem. MWA (fmr. pres.); Private Eye Writers of America (mem. bd of dirs, fmr pres.). *Film:* Single White Female (adapted from novel). *Publications:* The Truth of the Matter 1971, Buyer Beware 1976, Bonegrinder 1977, Lazarus Man 1979, Jericho Man 1980, The Shadow Man 1981, Exiled (with Steven Greene) 1982, Nightlines 1985, The Right to Sing the Blues 1986, Tropical Heat 1986, Ride the Lightning (short story) 1987, Scorcher 1987, Kiss (Private Eye Writers of America Shamus Award) 1988, Shadowtown 1988,

Time Exposure 1989, Flame 1990, Diamond Eyes 1990, SWF Seeks Same 1990, Bloodfire 1991, Hot 1992, Dancing with the Dead 1992, Spark 1993, Shadows Everywhere (short stories) 1994, Thicker Than Blood 1994, Death by Jury 1995, Torch 1995, Burn 1996, Lightning 1996, Final Seconds (with David August) 1998, Oops! 1998, Until You are Dead (short stories) 1998, The Nudger Dilemmas (short stories) 2001, The Night Caller 2001, The Night Watcher 2002, The Night Spider 2003, Endless Road 2003, Darker Than Night 2004, Fear the Night 2005; contrib. to anthologies and magazines. *Honours:* MWA Scroll 1981, 2003, Private Eye Writers of America Shamus Award 1982, MWA Edgar Award 1983, Private Eye Writers of America Life Achievement Award 1995, Short Mystery Fiction Soc. Golden Derringer Lifetime Achievement Award 2000. *Address:* 880 Providence Avenue, Webster Groves, MO 63119, USA. *Telephone:* (314) 968-4989 (office). *Fax:* (314) 962-0402. *E-mail:* jlutz65151@aol.com (office).

LUX, Thomas, BA; American poet and teacher; b. 10 Dec. 1946, Northampton, MA; m. Jean Kilbourne 1983; one d. *Education:* Emerson Coll., Boston and Univ. of Iowa. *Career:* Managing Ed., Iowa Review 1971–72, Ploughshares 1973; poet-in-residence, Emerson Coll. 1972–75; Faculty, Sarah Lawrence Coll. 1975, Warren Wilson Coll. 1980–, Columbia Univ. 1980–. *Publications:* The Land Sighted 1970, Memory's Handgrenade 1972, The Glassblower's Breath 1976, Sunday 1979, Like a Wide Anvil from the Moon the Light 1980, Massachusetts 1981, Tarantulas on the Lifebuoy 1983, Half Promised Land 1986, Sunday: Poems 1989, The Drowned River 1990, A Boat in the Forest 1992, Pecked to Death by Swans 1993, Split Horizon 1994, The Sanity of Earth and Grass (ed. with Jane Cooper and Sylvia Winner) 1994, The Cradle Place 2004. *Honours:* Bread Loaf Scholarship 1970, MacDowell Colony Fellowships 1973, 1974, 1976, 1978, 1980, 1982, Nat. Endowment for the Arts grants 1976, 1981, 1988, Guggenheim Fellowship 1988, Kingsley Tufts Poetry Award 1995. *Address:* c/o Houghton Mifflin, 222 Berkeley Street, Fifth Floor, Boston, MA 02116-3764, USA.

LUXON, Thomas H., BA, AM, PhD; American educator and writer; b. 26 April 1954, Darby, PA; m. 1st Nancy Ellen Gray 1980 (divorced 1985); m. 2nd Ivy Schweitzer 1988; one s. one d. *Education:* Brown University, University of Chicago. *Career:* William Rainey Harper Instructor, University of Chicago, 1984–85; Visiting Asst Prof. of English, St Lawrence University, Canton, New York, 1985–86; Asst Prof. of English, Franklin and Marshall College, Lancaster, Pennsylvania, 1987–88; Assoc. Prof. of English, 1988–, Dept Vice-Chair, 1994–96, Dartmouth College, Hanover, NH; mem. John Bunyan Society of North America; MLA of America; Milton Society of America. *Publications:* Literal Figures: Puritan Allegory and the Reformation, 1995; Milton and Manliness: Friends and Lovers, 1999. Contributions: Prose Studies: Literature, History, Theory. *Honours:* Fellow, National Endowment for the Humanities 1985–86.

LYKIARD, Alexis Constantine, BA, MA; British poet, writer and translator; b. 2 Jan. 1940, Athens, Greece. *Education:* King's Coll., Cambridge. *Career:* Creative Writing Tutor, Arvon Foundation 1974–; writer-in-residence, Sutton Central Library 1976–77, Loughborough Art College 1982–83, Tavistock, Devon Libraries 1983–85, HMP Channings Wood 1988–89, HMP Haslar 1993–94; mem. Soc. of Authors. *Publications:* Lobsters 1961, Journey of the Alchemist 1963, The Summer Ghosts 1964, Wholly Communion (ed.) 1965, Zones 1966, Paros Poems 1967, A Sleeping Partner 1967, Robe of Skin 1969, Strange Alphabet 1970, Best Horror Stories of J. Sheridan Le Fanu (ed.) 1970, Eight Lovesongs 1972, The Stump 1973, Greek Images 1973, Lifelines 1973, Instrument of Pleasure 1974, Last Throes 1976, Milesian Fables 1976, A Morden Tower Reading 1976, The Drive North 1977, New Stories 2 (ed.) 1977, Scrubbers 1983, Cat Kin 1985, Out of Exile 1986, Safe Levels 1990, Living Jazz 1991, Beautiful is Enough 1992, Omnibus Occasions 1995, Selected Poems 1956–96 1997, Jean Rhys Revisited 2000, Skeleton Keys 2003, Jean Rhys Afterwords 2006, Judging By Disappearances 2007; many French translations including Apollinaire, Aragon, Artaud, Lautréamont, Jarry, etc. *Honours:* C. Day Lewis Fellowship 1976; Arts Council Awards 1973, 1978. *Address:* 77 Latimer Road, Exeter, Devon EX4 7JP, England.

LYNCH, Frances (see Compton, David Guy)

LYNCH, John, MA, PhD, FRHistS; British historian and academic; *Professor Emeritus of Latin American History, University of London;* b. 11 Jan. 1927, Boldon. *Education:* Univ. of Edinburgh, Univ. of London. *Career:* Lecturer in History, Univ. of Liverpool 1954–61; Lecturer, Reader and Prof. of Latin American History, Univ. Coll. London 1961–74, Prof. of Latin American History and Dir Inst. of Latin American Studies, Univ. of London 1974–87, Prof. Emer. 1987–. *Publications:* Spanish Colonial Administration 1782–1810: The Intendant System in the Viceroyalty of the Río de la Plata 1958, Spain Under the Habsburgs (two vols) 1964, 1967, The Origins of the Latin American Revolutions 1808–1826 (with R. A. Humphreys) 1965, The Spanish American Revolutions 1808–1826 1973, Argentine Dictator: Juan Manuel de Rosas 1829–1852 1981, The Cambridge History of Latin America (with others), Vol. 3 1985, Vol. 4 1986, Bourbon Spain 1700–1808 1989, Caudillos in

Spanish America 1800–1850 1992, Latin American Revolutions 1808–1826: Old and New World Origins 1994, Massacre in the Pampas 1872: Britain and Argentina in the Age of Migration 1998, Latin America Between Colony and Nation 2001, UNESCO Historia General de América Latina, Vol. V (with others) 2003. *Honours:* Encomienda Isabel La Católica, Spain 1988, Order of Andrés Bello, First Class, (Venezuela) 1995; Dr hc (Seville) 1990. *Address:* 8 Templars Crescent, London, N3 3QS, England. *E-mail:* johnlynch53@msn .com (home).

LYNCH, Thomas; American writer, poet and funeral director; b. 16 Oct. 1948, Detroit, MI; four c. *Publications:* Skating with Heather Grace (poems), 1986; Grimalkin and Other Poems, 1994; The Undertaking: Life Studies from the Dismal Trade (non-fiction), 1997; Still Life in Milford (poems), 1998; Bodies in Motion and at Rest (poems), 2000. *Address:* 404 East Liberty, Milford, MI 48381, USA. *E-mail:* thoslynch@aol.com.

LYNN, Jonathan, MA; British theatre and film director, actor and writer; b. 3 April 1943, Bath, England. *Education:* Pembroke College, Cambridge. *Career:* Artistic Dir, Cambridge Theatre Co, 1976–81; Company Dir, National Theatre, 1987. *Publications:* A Proper Man, 1976; The Complete Yes Minister, 1984; Yes Prime Minister, Vol. I, 1986; Yes Prime Minister, Vol. II, 1987; Mayday, 1993. Other: various screenplays and television series.

LYNTON, Ann (see Rayner, Claire Berenice)

LYNTON, Harriet Ronken, AB; American writer; b. 22 May 1920, Rochester, Minn.; m. Rolf P. Lynton 1955; one s. two d. *Education:* Radcliffe Coll. *Career:* mem. Faculty, Harvard Business School 1945–54; consultant, Indonesia, India, Botswana, Sri Lanka 1955–90; mem. N Carolina Writers Network. *Publications:* Administering Changes 1952, Training for Human Relations 1954, The Days of the Beloved 1974, My Dear Nawab Sahib 1991, Born to Dance 1995, The Sawdust House 2005, Mission to Kabul 2006; contribs to The Homesteaders, Potpourri, The Literary Arts. *Address:* 458 Fearrington Post, Pittsboro, NC 27312, USA. *Telephone:* (919) 542-0020 (home). *Fax:* (919) 542-0020 (home). *E-mail:* ronlynton@gmail.com (home).

LYONS, Arthur, BA; American writer; b. 5 Jan. 1946, Los Angeles, CA; m. Marie Lyons. *Education:* University of California, Santa Barbara. *Publications:* The Second Coming: Satanism in America, 1970; The Dead Are Discreet, 1974; All God's Children, 1975; The Killing Floor, 1976; Dead Ringer, 1977; Castles Burning, 1979; Hard Trade, 1981; At the Hands of Another, 1983; Three With a Bullet, 1985; Fast Fade, 1987; Unnatural Causes (with Thomas Noguchi), 1988; Satan Wants You, 1988; Other Poeple's Money, 1989; Physical Evidence (with Thomas Noguchi), 1990; The Blue Sense (with Marcello Truzzi), 1991; False Pretences, 1993.

LYONS, Elena (see Fairburn, Eleanor M.)

LYONS, Garry Fairfax, BA, MA; British dramatist; b. 5 July 1956, Kingston-upon-Thames, England; m. Ruth Caroline Willis 1985; one s. one d. *Education:* Univ. of York, Univ. of Leeds. *Career:* playwright-in-residence, Major Road Theatre Co 1983; Fellow in Theatre, Univ. of Bradford 1984–88; mem. Theatre Writers' Union. *Productions include:* Echoes from the Valley 1983, Mohicans 1984, St Vitus' Boogie 1985, Urban Jungle 1985, The Green Violinist 1986, Irish Night 1987, Divided Kingdoms 1989, The People Museum 1989, Dream Kitchen 1992, Frankie and Tommy 1992, Wicked Year 1994. *Literary Agent:* International Creative Management, 4–6 Soho Square, London, W1D 3PZ, England.

LYTTELTON, Humphrey Richard Adeane; British bandleader and journalist; b. 23 May 1921, Eton, Bucks.; s. of the late Hon. George William Lyttelton; m. 1st Patricia Mary Braithwaite 1948 (divorced 1952); one d.; m. 2nd Elizabeth Jill Richardson 1952; two s. one d. *Education:* Sunningdale School, Eton Coll. *Career:* served with Grenadier Guards 1941–46; Camberwell Art School 1947–48; mem., George Webb's Dixielanders 1947; formed own band 1948; cartoonist for London Daily Mail 1949–53; freelance journalist 1953–; leader Humphrey Lyttelton Band 1953–; formed own label Calligraph Records 1984–; contrib. Melody Maker 1954–2001, Reynolds News 1955–62, Sunday Citizen 1962–67, Harpers and Queen (restaurant column) 1968–76, Punch; compère BBC jazz programmes: Jazz Scene, Jazz Club, Jazz 625 (TV); frequent TV appearances; Chair. 'I'm Sorry I Haven't a Clue', BBC Radio 4 1972–; Pres. Soc. for Italic Handwriting 1990–. *Publications:* I Play as I Please 1954, Second Chorus 1958, Take it from the Top 1975, The Best of Jazz–Basin Street to Harlem 1978, Humphrey Lyttelton's Jazz and Big Band Quiz 1979, The Best of Jazz 2–Enter the Giants 1981, Why No Beethoven? The diary of a vagrant musician 1984, The Best of Jazz 1998, It Just Occurred to Me... An Autobiographical Scrapbook 2006. *Honours:* Hon. DLitt (Warwick) 1987, (Loughborough) 1988; Hon. DMus (Durham) 1989, (Keele) 1992; Hon. Prof. of Music Keele Univ. 1993. *Address:* BBC, Broadcasting House, Portland Place, London, W1A 4WW; Alyn Close, Barnet Road, Arkley, Herts., EN5 3LS, England (home). *Telephone:* (20) 7580-4468 (London).

M

MA, Jian; Chinese writer; b. 1953, Qingdao; one d. (from previous m.); pnr Flora Drew; one s. one d. *Career:* left Beijing for Hong Kong 1987, shortly before his books were banned in China; moved to Europe 1997, now lives in London. *Publications (in translation):* Red Dust (memoir) (Thomas Cook Travel Book Award 2002) 2001, The Noodle Maker (novel) 2004, Stick Out Your Tongue (short stories) 2006. *Address:* c/o Vintage, Random House, 20 Vauxhall Bridge Road, London, SW1V 2SA, England (office).

MAALOUF, Amin; Lebanese writer; b. 25 Feb. 1949, Beirut; m. Andrée Abouchdid 1971; three c. *Education:* Université Saint-Joseph, Beirut and Université de Lyon. *Career:* journalist, an-Nahar 1971–76, Economia 1976–77; Ed. Jeune Afrique 1978–79, 1982–84. *Publications:* Les Croisades vues par les Arabes 1983, Léon l'Africain 1986, Samarcande 1988, Les Jardins de lumière 1991, Le Premier siècle après Béatrice 1992, Le Rocher de Tanios 1993, Les Echelles du Levant 1996, Les Identités meurtrières 1998, Le Périple de Baldassare 2000, L'Amour de Loin (opera libretto) 2001, Origines 2004, Adriana Mater (opera libretto) 2005. *Honours:* Prix France-Liban 1986, Grand Prix de l'Unicef 1991, Prix Goncourt 1993, Premio Nonino 1997, Premio Elio Vittorini 1997, Prix européen de l'essai 1998, Premio Grinzane Cavour 2001, Premio Antonio de Sancha 2003, Prix Méditerranée 2004. *Address:* c/o Editions Grasset, 61 rue des Saints-Pères, 75006 Paris, France (office).

MABANCKOU, Alain, DEA; Republic of Congo writer; b. 24 Feb. 1966, s. of the late Kimangou Roger and Pauline Kengué. *Education:* Univ. of Paris – Dauphine (Paris IX). *Career:* adviser Lyonnaise des Eaux (now SUEZ) 1992–2002; writer-in-residence Univ. of Michigan at Ann Arbor 2001, Asst Prof. of Francophone Literature 2002–06; Visiting Prof. Dept of French and Francophone Studies UCLA 2006–. *Publications:* poetry: Au jour le jour 1993, L'Usure des lendemains (Prix Jean-Christophe de la Société des Poètes françaises) 1995, La Légende de l'errance 1995, Les Arbres aussi versent des larmes 1997, Quand le coq annoncera l'aube d'un autre jour... 1999, Tant que les arbres s'enracineront dans la terre 2004; novels: Et Dieu seul sait comment je dors 2001, Les Petits-fils nègres de Vercingétorix 2002, African Psycho 2003, Bleu Blanc Rouge (Grand prix littéraire d'Afrique noire) 1998, Verre Cassé (also adapted for theatre) (Prix des Cinq continents de la Francophonie, Prix Ouest-France/Etonnants Voyageurs, Prix RFO du livre) 2005, Mémoires de porc-épic (Prix Renaudot, Prix Aliénor d'Aquitaine, Prix de la rentrée littéraire française) 2006; prose: L'Enterrement de ma mère (essay); contrib. short stories and articles to anthologies, newspapers and magazines, including Transfuge. *Honours:* Fellow in Humanities Council and French and Italian Dept, Princeton Univ.. *Address:* c/o Editions Le Seuil, 27 rue Jacob, 75261 Paris cedex 06, France (office). *Website:* www.alainmabanckou .net.

MABBETT, Ian William, MA, DPhil; British historian and academic; *Professor Emeritus, Aichi Bunkyo University;* b. 27 April 1939, London; m. Jacqueline Diana June Towns 1971; two d. *Education:* Univ. of Oxford. *Career:* faculty, Monash Univ., Melbourne, Australia; Prof., Aichi Bunkyo Univ., Aichi, Japan 2000–02, Prof. Emer. 2002–; Pres. IXth World Sanskrit Conf. 1994; mem. Inst. for Advanced Study, Princeton, NJ, USA 2005–06. *Publications:* A Short History of India 1968, Modern China, The Mirage of Modernity 1985, Kings and Emperors of Asia 1985, Patterns of Kingship and Authority in Traditional Asia (ed.) 1985, The Khmers (co-author) 1995, Sociology of Early Buddhism (co-author) 2003, Writing History Essays: A Student's Guide 2007; contrib. to Hemisphere (Canberra), Asian Pacific Quarterly (Seoul), History Today (London) The Cambridge History of Southeast Asia. *Honours:* Asiatic Soc. Gold Medal 1999. *Address:* Monash Asia Institute, Building 11, Monash University, Clayton, Vic. 3800, Australia (office). *Website:* www.arts.monash.edu.au/mai (office).

MABEY, Richard Thomas, BA, MA; British writer and broadcaster; b. 20 Feb. 1941, Berkhamsted, Hertfordshire, England. *Education:* St Catherine's Coll., Oxford. *Career:* Sr Ed., Penguin Books 1966–73; mem. Botanical Soc. of British Isles (council 1981–83), Nature Conservancy (council 1982–86), London Wildlife Trust (pres. 1982–92), Plantlife (advisory council 1990–), Open Spaces Soc. (vice-pres. 2003–), Richard Jefferies Soc. (pres. 1996–98), Norfolk and Norwich Naturalists' Soc. (pres. 2005–06). *Publications:* The Pop Process 1969, Food for Free 1972, Unofficial Countryside 1973, Street Flowers 1976, Plants with a Purpose 1977, The Common Ground 1980, The Flowering of Britain 1980, In a Green Shade 1983, Oak and Company 1983, Frampton Flora 1985, Gilbert White 1986, The Flowering of Kew 1988, Home Country 1990, Whistling in the Dark 1993, Oxford Book of Nature Writing (ed.) 1995, Flora Britannica 1996, Nature Cure 2005, Birds Britannica (with Mark Cocker) 2005; contrib. to Times, Telegraph, Sunday Times, Observer, Guardian, Nature, Modern Painters, Independent. *Honours:* Hon. DSc (St Andrews) 1997; TES Information Book Award 1977, New York Acad. of Sciences Children's Book Award 1984, Whitbread Biography Award 1986, Nat. Book Award 1997. *Address:* Sheil Land Associates, 43 Doughty Street, London, WC1N 2LF, England.

McADAM, Douglas John, BA, MA, PhD; American academic and writer; *Professor of Sociology, Stanford University;* b. 31 Aug. 1951, Pasadena, CA; m. Tracy Lynn Stevens 1988. *Education:* Occidental Coll., Los Angeles, SUNY at Stony Brook. *Career:* instructor, Occidental Coll., Los Angeles 1975, SUNY at Stony Brook 1977–79; Asst Prof., George Mason Univ., Fairfax, Virginia 1979–82; Asst Prof. 1983–86, Assoc. Prof. 1986–90, Prof. of Sociology 1990–98, Univ. of Arizona; Fellow, Center for Advanced Study in the Behavioral Sciences 1991–92, 1997–98, Udall Center for Studies in Public Policy 1994–95; Hollingshead Lecturer, Yale Univ. 1997; Prof. of Sociology 1998–, Dir Center for Advanced Study in the Behavioral Sciences 2001–, Stanford Univ.; mem. American Sociological Asscn, Sociological Research Asscn; elected mem. American Acad. of Arts and Sciences 2003. *Publications:* The Politics of Privacy (with James Rule, Linda Stearns and David Uglow) 1980, Political Process and the Development of Black Insurgency 1930–1970 1982, Freedom Summer 1988, Collective Behavior and Social Movements (with Gary Marx) 1994, Comparative Perspectives on Social Movements: Political Opportunities, Mobilizing Structures, and Cultural Framings (ed. with John McCarthy and Mayer Zald) 1996, Social Movements: Readings on Their Emergence, Mobilization and Dynamics (with David Snow) 1996, How Movements Matter: Theoretical and Comparative Studies on the Consequences of Social Movements (ed. with Marco Giugni and Charles Tilly) 1998, From Contention to Democracy (ed. with Marco Guigni and Charles Tilly) 1999, Dynamics of Contention (with Sydney Tarrow and Charles Tilly) 2001, Silence and Voice in the Study of Contentious Politics (with others) 2001, Social Movements and Networks (ed with Mario Diani) 2003; contrib. to scholarly books and professional journals. *Honours:* Guggenheim Fellowship 1984–85, Gustavus Myers Center Outstanding Book 1988, C. Wright Mills Award 1990. *Address:* c/o Department of Sociology, Stanford University, Stanford, CA 94305, USA.

MacALAN, Peter (see Ellis, Peter Berresford)

McALLISTER, Casey (see Battin, B. W.)

MacAULAY, David Alexander, BArch; British/American writer and illustrator; b. 2 Dec. 1946, Burton-on-Trent, England; m. 1st Janice Elizabeth Michel 1970 (divorced); one d.; m. 2nd Ruth Marris 1978 (divorced); m. 3rd Charlotte Valerie. *Education:* Rhode Island School of Design. *Publications:* Cathedral: The Story of Its Construction, 1973; City: A Story of Roman Planning and Construction, 1974; Pyramid, 1975; Underground, 1976; Castle, 1977; Great Movements in Architecture, 1978; Motel of the Mysteries, 1979; Unbuilding, 1980; Electricity, 1983; Mill, 1983; BAAA, 1985; Why the Chicken Crossed the Road, 1987; The Way Things Work, 1988; Black and White, 1990; Ship, 1993; Shortcut, 1995. *Honours:* Caldecott Honor Books, 1973, 1977; Christopher Medal, 1991. *Address:* c/o Houghton Mifflin Co, 222 Berkeley Street, Boston, MA 02116, USA.

McAULEY, James John; Irish academic and poet; b. 8 Jan. 1936, Dublin; m. Deirdre O'Sullivan 1982. *Education:* Univ. Coll. Dublin, Univ. of Arkansas, Fayetteville. *Career:* Ed., Dolmen Press, Dublin 1960–66; Prof., Eastern Washington Univ., Cheney 1978–; Dir, Eastern Washington Univ. Press 1993. *Publications:* poetry: Observations 1960, A New Address 1965, Draft Balance Sheet 1970, Home and Away 1974, After the Blizzard 1975, The Exile's Recurring Nightmare 1975, Recital, Poems, 1975–80 1982, The Exile's Book of Hours 1982, Coming and Going: New and Selected Poems, 1968–88 1989, Meditations, with Distractions: Poems 1988–98 2001, New and Selected Poems 2005; play: The Revolution 1966; libretto: Praise 1981. *Honours:* NEA grant 1972, Washington Governor's Award 1976. *Address:* c/o The Dedalus Press, 13 Moyclare Road, Baldoyle, Dublin 13, Republic of Ireland (office). *Telephone:* (1) 8392034 (office). *E-mail:* editor@dedaluspress.com (office). *Website:* www.dedaluspress.com (office).

McAULEY, Paul J., BSc, PhD; British biologist and writer; b. 23 April 1955, Stroud, Gloucestershire, England. *Education:* Univ. of Bristol. *Publications:* Four Hundred Billion Stars 1988, Secret Harmonies 1989, Eternal Light 1991, The King of the Hill and Other Stories 1991, In Dreams (ed. with Kim Newman) 1992, Red Dust 1993, Pasquale's Angel 1994, Fairyland 1995, The Invisible Country 1996, Child of the River 1997, Ancients of Days 1998, Shrine of Stars 1999, The Secret of Life 2001, Whole Wide World 2001, White Devils 2004, Mind's Eye 2005, Players 2007; contrib. to magazines. *Honours:* Philip K. Dick Memorial Award for Best New Novel 1989, Arthur C. Clarke Award for Best British Novel 1995, Sidewise Award 1995, British Fantasy Soc. Short Story Award 1995, John W. Campbell Award 1996. *Literary Agent:* Antony Harwood Ltd, Office 109, Riverbank House, 1 Putney Bridge Approach, London, SW6 3JD, England.

MAC AVOY, Roberta Ann, BA; American writer; b. 13 Dec. 1949, Cleveland, Ohio. *Education:* Case Western Reserve University. *Publications:* Tea with the Black Dragon, Damiano, 1983; Damiano's Lute, Raphael, 1984; The Book of Kells (co-author), 1985; Twisting the Rope, 1986; The Grey Horse, 1987; The Third Eagle, 1989; Lens of the World, 1990.

McBRIDE, James; American writer, journalist and musician; b. New York, NY; m.; two c. *Education:* Oberlin Conservatory of Music, OH, Columbia Univ., NY. *Career:* fmr staff writer, Washington Post, People magazine, Boston Globe; songwriter for artists, including Anita Baker, Grover Washington Jr, Gary Burton; mem. Nat. Council on the Arts. *Publications:* The Color of Water: A Black Man's Tribute to his White Mother 1996, Autobiography of Quincy Jones (with Quincy Jones) 2001, Miracle at St Anna

2002; contrib. to Essence, Rolling Stone, New York Times. *Honours:* Dr hc (Whitman Coll., Coll. of New Jersey); Ansfield-Wolf Book Award for Literary Excellence 1997. *Address:* c/o Bloomsbury Publishing PLC, 38 Soho Square, London, W1V 5DF, England. *Website:* www.jamesmcbride.com.

McBRIDE, Jule, BA, MFA; American writer; b. 27 Oct. 1959, Charleston, West Virginia. *Education:* West Virginia State College, University of Pittsburgh. *Publications:* Wild Card Wedding, 1993; Baby Trap, 1993; The Wrong Wife, 1994; The Baby and the Bodyguard, 1994; Bride of the Badlands, 1995; The Baby Maker, 1995; The Bounty Hunter's Baby, 1996; Baby Romeo, 1996; Cole in My Stocking, 1996; Mission: Motherhood, 1997; Verdict: Parenthood, 1997; Wed to a Stranger, 1997; Who's Been Sleeping in My Bed?, 1997; Diagnosis: Daddy, 1998; How the West Was Wed, 1998; AKA: Marriage, 1998; Smoochin' Santas, 1998; Santa Slept Over, 1999; The Strong Silent Type, 1999. Contributions: anthologies. *Honours:* Reviewer's Choice Award for Best Series Romance, Romantic Times, 1993. *Literary Agent:* Karen Solem, Writers House Inc, 21 W 26th Street, New York, NY 10010, USA.

McBRIEN, Rev. Richard Peter, MA, STD; American academic; *Crowley-O'Brien Professor of Theology, University of Notre Dame;* b. 19 Aug. 1936, Hartford, Conn.; s. of the late Thomas H. McBrien and Catherine Botticelli. *Education:* St Thomas Seminary, Bloomfield, Conn., St John Seminary, Brighton, Mass. and Pontifical Gregorian Univ., Rome. *Career:* Prof. of Theology and Dean of Studies Pope John XXIII Nat. Seminary, Weston, Mass. 1965–70; Prof. Boston Coll., Newton, Mass. 1970–80; Chair. Dept of Theology, Univ. of Notre Dame, Ind. 1980–91, Crowley-O'Brien Prof. of Theology 1980–. *Publications:* Do We Need the Church? 1969, Church: The Continuing Quest 1970, The Remaking of the Church 1973, Catholicism (2 vols) (Christopher Award 1981) 1980, Caesar's Coin: Religion and Politics in America 1987, Report on the Church: Catholicism since Vatican II 1992, Catholicism (new edn) 1994, The HarperCollins Encyclopedia of Catholicism (Gen. Ed.) 1995, Responses to 101 Questions on the Church 1996, Lives of the Popes: The Pontiffs from St Peter to John Paul II 1997, Lives of the Saints: From Mary and St Francis of Assisi to John XXIII and Mother Teresa 2001. *Honours:* John Courtney Murray Award, Catholic Theology Soc. of America 1976. *Address:* Department of Theology, University of Notre Dame, 130 Malloy Hall, Notre Dame, IN 46556, USA. *Telephone:* (574) 631-5151. *E-mail:* rmcbrien@nd.edu (office). *Website:* www.nd.edu/~theo/faculty/mcbrien.html (office).

McCABE, Patrick; Irish writer; b. 27 March 1955, Clones, Co. Monaghan; m. Margot Quinn 1981; two d. *Education:* St Patrick's Teacher Training Coll., Dublin. *Career:* fmr teacher of disabled children. *Play:* has written plays for BBC radio, Frank Pig Says Hello (stage play, based on novel The Butcher Boy). *Film screenplay:* The Butcher Boy (co-writer). *Publications:* The Adventures of Shay Mouse 1985, Music on Clinton Street 1986, Carn 1989, The Butcher Boy (Irish Times/Aer Lingus Fiction Prize) 1992, Frank Pig Says Hello (play based on The Butcher Boy) 1992, The Dead School 1995, Breakfast on Pluto 1997, Mondo Desperado 1998, Emerald Gems of Ireland 2000, Call Me the Breeze 2003, Winterwood 2006; contrib. to anthologies, periodicals. *Honours:* Irish Press Hennessy Award 1979, Sunday Independent Arts Award. *Address:* c/o Picador, Pan Macmillan Publishers, 20 New Wharf Road, London, N1 9RR, England.

McCAFFREY, Anne Inez, BA; American writer; b. 1 April 1926, Cambridge, Mass; m. Wright Johnson 1950 (divorced 1970); two s. one d. *Education:* Radcliffe Coll., Univ. of Dublin. *Career:* mem. Authors' Guild, MWA, Novelists' Ink, PEN (Ireland), Science Fiction and Fantasy Writers of America (SWFA). *Publications:* Restoree 1967, Dragonflight (graphic novel) 1968, The Ship Who Sang 1969, Decision at Doona 1969, Alchemy and Academe (ed.) 1970, Dragonquest: Being the Further Adventures of the Dragonriders of Pern 1971, Mark of Merlin 1971, Ring of Fear 1971, To Ride Pegasus (short stories) 1973, Cooking Out of This World (ed.) 1973, Kilternan Legacy 1975, A Time When 1975, Dragonsong 1976, Dragonsinger 1977, Get Off the Unicorn (short stories) 1977, The White Dragon 1978, Dinosaur Planet 1979, Dragondrums 1979, The Worlds of Anne McCaffrey 1981, Crystal Singer 1982, The Coelura 1983, Moreta: Dragonlady of Pern 1983, Dinosaur Planet Survivors 1984, Habit is an Old Horse (short stories) 1984, Stitch in Snow 1984, The Girl Who Heard Dragons (short stories) 1985, Killashandra 1985, Nerilka's Story 1986, The Year of the Lucy 1986, The Lady (aka The Carradyne Touch) 1987, Dragonsdawn 1988, People of Pern 1988, The Renegades of Pern 1989, The Dragonlover's Guide to Pern (with Jody-Lynn Nye) 1989, Pegasus in Flight 1990, Sassinak (with Elizabeth Moon) 1990, The Death of Sleep (with Jody-Lynn Nye) 1990, The Rowan 1990, Crisis on Doona (with Jody Lynn Nye) 1991, Generation Warriors 1991, Rescue Run 1991, All The Weyrs of Pern 1991, Three Women 1992, Crystal Line 1992, The Partnership (with Margaret Ball) 1992, The Ship Who Searched (with Mercedes Lackey) 1992, Damia 1992, The Planet Pirates (with Elizabeth Moon and Jody Lynn Nye) 1993, The City Who Fought (with S. M. Stirling) 1993, Powers That Be (with Elizabeth Ann Scarborough) 1993, Damia's Children 1993, The Dolphin's Bell: A Tale of Pern 1993, The Chronicles of Pern: First Fall (short stories) 1993, Power Lines (with Elizabeth Ann Scarborough) 1994, The Ship Who Won (with Jody-Lynn Nye) 1994, Treaty Planet 1994, Lyon's Pride 1994, The Dolphins of Pern 1994, Treaty at Doona 1994, Dragons 1994, An Exchange of Gifts 1995, Power Play (with Elizabeth Ann Scarborough) 1995, Freedom's Landing 1995, A Diversity of Dragons (children's fiction with Richard Woods) 1995, Serve It Forth: Cooking with Anne McCaffrey (co-ed. with John Betancourt) 1996, No One Noticed the Cat 1996, Space Opera (co-ed. with Elizabeth Ann Scarborough) 1996, Black Horses for the King 1996, Acorna: The Unicorn Girl (with Margaret Ball) 1997, Red Star Rising (short stories) 1997, Freedom's Choice 1997, The Ship Avenged (with S. M. Stirling) 1997, Freedom's Challenge 1998, If Wishes Were Horses 1998, Dragonseye 1998, Masterharper of Pern 1998, Acorna's People (with Elizabeth Ann Scarborough) 1999, Acorna's Quest (with Margaret Ball) 1999, Nimisha's Ship 1999, The Tower and the Hive 1999, Pegasus in Space 2000, Acorna's World (with Elizabeth Ann Scarborough) 2000, The Skies of Pern 2001, Freedom's Ransom 2002, Dragon's Kin (with Todd McCaffrey) 2003; contrib. to anthologies and periodicals. *Honours:* World Science Fiction Soc. Hugo Award 1967, SFWA Nebula Award 1968, E. E. Smith Award 1975, Ditmar Award 1979, Eurocon/Streso Award 1979, Gandalf Award 1979, Barlog Award 1980, Golden PEN Award 1981, Science Fiction Book Club Awards 1986, 1989, 1991, 1992, 1993, School Library Journal Margaret A. Edwards Lifetime Achievement Award for Outstanding Literature for Young Adults 1999, Cthulu Award, British Science Fiction Asscn 2000, Futura Award 2004, Writers of the Future: Lifetime Achievement 2004, SFWA Grand Master 2005. *Address:* Dragonhold Underhill, Timmore Lane, Newcastle, Co. Wicklow, Ireland (office). *Telephone:* (1) 2819936. *E-mail:* anneinez@eircom.net. *Website:* www.annemccaffrey.org.

McCALL, Carolyn, BA, MA; British media executive; *Chief Executive, Guardian Media Group PLC;* b. 13 Sept. 1961; m.; three c. *Education:* Univ. of Kent, Univ. of London. *Career:* teacher Holland Park School 1982–84; risk analyst Costain Group PLC 1984–86; planner, Guardian Newspapers Ltd (GNL) 1986–88, Advertisement Exec. 1988–89, Advertisement Man. 1989–91, Product Development Man. 1991–92, Display Advertisement Man. 1992, Advertisement Dir Wired UK 1992–94, Deputy Advertisement Dir 1994–95, Advertisement Dir 1995–97, Commercial Dir 1997–98 (with responsibility for internet strategy – launched Guardian Unlimited 1999), Deputy Man. Dir 1998–2000, CEO of GNL 2000–06, and Dir of the Bd of Guardian Media Group PLC (GMG) 2000–, Chief Exec. GMG 2006–; Non-Exec. Dir, New Look Group PLC 1999–2004, Tesco PLC 2005–; Chair. gender equality and diversity org., Opportunity Now 2005–; trustee educational charity, Tools for Schools 2000–05. *Address:* Guardian Media Group PLC, 75 Farringdon Road, London, EC1M 3JY, England (office). *Website:* www.gmgplc.co.uk (office).

McCALL, Christina, BA; Canadian writer and editor; b. 29 Jan. 1935, Toronto, ON; m. 1st Peter Charles Newman 1959 (divorced 1977); m. 2nd Stephen Clarkson 1978; three d. *Education:* Jarvis Coll. Inst., Toronto, Victoria Coll., Univ. of Toronto. *Career:* staff, Maclean's 1956–58, Assoc. Ed. 1971–74; Assoc. Ed., Chatelaine, then Ottawa Ed. 1958–62; Ottawa Ed.,Saturday Night 1967–70, Exec. Ed. 1976, Contributing Ed. 1980–88, 1994–; National Reporter, Globe and Mail 1974–76. *Publications:* The Man from Oxbow 1967, Grits: An Intimate Portrait of the Liberal Party 1982, Trudeau and Our Times (co-author), Vol. 1 The Magnificent Obsession 1990, Vol. 2 The Heroic Delusion 1994, Pearson: The Unlikely Gladiator 1999. *Honours:* Univ. of Toronto Southam Fellowship in Journalism 1977, Nat. Magazine Award Gold Medal 1981, Canadian Authors' Asscn Book of the Year Award 1983, Governor-General's Award for Non-Fiction 1990, John W. Dafoe Prize 1995. *Address:* 59 Lowther Avenue, Toronto, ON M5R 1C5, Canada. *Telephone:* (416) 925-3596. *Fax:* (416) 925-9171.

McCALL SMITH, Alexander, CBE; British writer; *Emeritus Professor of Medical Law, University of Edinburgh;* b. 1948, Southern Rhodesia (now Zimbabwe); m. Elizabeth; two d. *Career:* currently Emer. Prof. of Medical Law, Univ. of Edinburgh; fmr mem. Human Genetics Comm. (fmr Vice-Chair.), UNESCO Int. Bioethics Comm., British Medical Journal Ethics Cttee (fmr Chair.), Roslin Inst. Ethics Cttee (fmr Chair.). *Publications:* fiction: The No. 1 Ladies' Detective Agency 1998, Tears of the Giraffe 2000, Morality for Beautiful Girls 2001, The Kalahari Typing School for Men 2002, The Full Cupboard of Life (Saga Award for Wit) 2003, At the Villa of Reduced Circumstances 2003, Portuguese Irregular Verbs 2003, In the Company of Cheerful Ladies 2004, 44 Scotland Street (serialized in The Scotsman) 2004, The Sunday Philosophy Club 2004, The 2½ Pillars of Wisdom 2004, Friends, Lovers, Chocolate 2005, Blue Shoes and Happiness 2006, Dream Angus: The Celtic God of Dreams 2006, Love Over Scotland 2007, The World According to Bertie 2007, The Right Attitude to Rain 2007; non-fiction: Law and Medical Ethics (with J. K. Mason) 1983, The Duty to Rescue: The Jurisprudence of Aid (with Michael A. Menlowe) 1993, Forensic Aspects of Sleep (with C. Shapiro) 1997, Justice and the Prosecution of Old Crimes: Balancing Legal, Psychological, and Moral Concerns (with Daniel W. Shuman) 2000, The Criminal Law of Botswana; children's fiction includes: White Hippo 1980, The Perfect Hamburger 1982, Jeffrey's Joke Machine 1990, The Five Lost Aunts of Harriet Bean 1990, Marzipan Max 1991, Uncle Gangster 1991, The Spaghetti Tangle 1992, Harriet Bean and the League of Cheats 1991, The Ice-Cream Bicycle 1992, Akimbo and the Lions 1992, The Doughnut Ring 1992, Springy Jane 1992, The Princess Trick 1992, The Cowgirl Aunt of Harriet Bean 1993, My Chameleon Uncle 1993, The Muscle Machine 1993, Paddy and the Ratcatcher 1994, The Banana Machine 1994, Akimbo and the Crocodile Man 1995, Billy Rubbish 1995, The Watermelon Boys 1996, Calculator Annie 1996, The Bubblegum Tree 1996, Bursting Balloons Mystery 1997, The Popcorn Pirates 1999, Chocolate Money Mystery 1999; short story collections: Children of Wax: African Folk Tales 1991, Heavenly Date and Other Stories (revised edn as Heavenly Date: And Other Flirtations) 1995, The Girl Who Married a Lion (short stories) 2004, One City (contrib.) 2006. *Honours:* DIur hc (Univ. of Edinburgh) 2007; British Books Awards Author of the Year 2004, Booksellers Asscn Author of the Year 2004, Waterstone's Author of the Year 2004. *Literary*

Agent: David Higham Associates, 5–8 Lower John Street, Golden Square, London, W1F 9HA, England. *Website:* www.alexandermccallsmith.co.uk.

McCANN, Colum; Irish writer; b. 1965; m. Allison Hawke. *Education:* Clonkeen Coll., Dublin Inst. of Technology and Univ. of Texas at Austin, USA. *Publications:* Fishing the Sloe-Black River 1993, Songdogs 1995, This Side of Brightness 1998, Everything in This Country Must 2000, Dancer 2003, Zoli 2006; contrib. to books and newspapers. *Honours:* Hennessy/Sunday Tribune Award for Best First Fiction, Best New Writer 1991, Rooney Prize for Irish Literature 1994, Irish Book of the Year 2000, Princess Grace Memorial Literary Award 2002, Esquire Magazine Writer of the Year 2003, Sunday Independent Hughes & Hughes Irish Novel of the Year 2003. *Address:* c/o Weidenfeld & Nicolson, Orion House, 5 Upper Saint Martin's Lane, London, WC2H 9EA, England.

McCARRY, Charles; American journalist, government official, editor and writer; b. 14 June 1930, Pittsfield, Mass; m. Nancy Neill 1953; four s. *Career:* reporter and Ed. Lisbon Evening Journal, OH 1952–55; reporter and columnist, Youngstown Vindicator, OH 1955–56; Asst to US Sec. of Labor, Washington, DC 1956–57; Operations Officer, CIA 1958–67; Ed.-at-Large, National Geographic magazine 1983–90. *Publications:* fiction: The Miernik Dossier 1973, The Tears of Autumn 1975, The Secret Lovers 1977, The Better Angels 1979, The Last Supper 1983, The Bride of the Wilderness 1988, Second Sight 1991, Shelley's Heart 1995, Lucky Bastard 1998, Old Boys 2004, Christopher's Ghosts 2007; non-fiction: Citizen Nader 1972, Double Eagle 1979, Isles of the Caribbean (co-author) 1979, The Great Southwest 1980, Caveat (with Alexander M. Haig, Jr) 1983, For the Record (with Donald T. Regan) 1988, Inner Circles: How America Changed the World (with Alexander M. Haig, Jr) 1992; contrib. to periodicals. *Address:* c/o Weidenfeld and Nicholson, 5 Upper St Martin's Lane, London, WC2H 9EA, England.

McCARTHY, Cormac; American writer; b. 1933, Rhode Island; s. of Charles Joseph McCarthy and Gladys McGrail; m. 1st Lee Holleman 1961 (divorced); one s.; m. 2nd Annie DeLisle (divorced); m. 3rd Jennifer Winkley 1998. *Education:* Univ. of Tennessee. *Career:* USAF 1953–57; MacArthur Fellowship 1981; Guggenheim Fellowship; Rockefeller Fellowship. *Play:* The Stonemason 1994. *Publications:* novels: The Orchard Keeper 1965, Outer Dark 1968, Child of God 1973, Suttree 1979, Blood Meridian 1985, All the Pretty Horses (Vol. 1 of The Bouden Trilogy) 1992, The Crossing (Vol. 2 of The Bouden Trilogy) 1994, Cities of the Plain (Vol. 3 of The Bouden Trilogy) 1998, No Country for Old Men 2005, The Road (Pulitzer Prize for Fiction 2007) 2006. *Address:* 1011 N Mesa Street, El Paso, TX 79902, USA.

MacCARTHY, Fiona, MA, FRSL; British biographer and cultural historian; b. 23 Jan. 1940, London, England; m. 1st Ian White-Thomson 1961 (divorced 1966); m. 2nd David Mellor 1966; one s. one d. *Education:* Wycombe Abbey School, Univ. of Oxford. *Career:* Design Correspondent The Guardian 1963–70; Women's Ed. Evening Standard 1970–71; reviewer The Times 1981–91, The Observer 1991–2000; mem. PEN Club, RSL. *Publications:* The Simple Life: C. R. Ashbee in the Cotswolds 1981, The Omega Workshops: Decorative Arts of Bloomsbury 1984, Eric Gill 1989, William Morris: A Life for our Time 1994, Stanley Spencer 1997, Byron: Life and Legend 2002, Last Curtsey: The End of the Debutantes 2006; contrib. to Guardian, TLS, New York Review of Books. *Honours:* Hon. DLitt (Sheffield) 1996, Dr hc (Sheffield Hallam) 2001; RSA Bicentenary Medal 1987, Hon. Fellowship Royal Coll. of Art 1989, Wolfson History Prize 1995, Sr Fellowship Royal Coll. of Art 1997. *Address:* The Round Building, Hathersage, Sheffield, S32 1BA, England (office). *Telephone:* (1433) 650220 (office). *Fax:* (1433) 650944 (office). *E-mail:* fionamacarthy@davidmellordesign.co.uk (office).

McCARTHY, Gary, BS, MS; American writer; b. 23 Jan. 1943, South Gate, CA; m. Virginia Kurzwell 1969; one s. three d. *Education:* California State University, University of Nevada. *Career:* Labour Economist, State of Nevada, Carson City, 1970–77; Economist, Copley International Corp, La Jolla, CA, 1977–79. *Publications:* The Derby Man, 1976; Showdown at Snakegrass Junction, 1978; The First Sheriff, 1979; Mustang Fever, 1980; The Pony Express War, 1980; Winds of Gold, 1980; Silver Shot, 1981; Explosion at Donner Pass, 1981; The Legend of the Lone Ranger, 1981; North Chase, 1982; Rebel of Bodie, 1982; The Rail Warriors, 1983; Silver Winds, 1983; Wind River, 1984; Powder River, 1985; The Last Buffalo Hunt, 1985; Mando, 1986; The Mustangers, 1987; Transcontinental, 1987; Sodbuster, 1988; Blood Brothers, 1989; Gringo Amigo, 1990; Whiskey Creek, 1992; The American River, 1992; Comstock Camels, 1993; The Gila River, 1993; Yosemite, 1995; Grand Canyon, 1996; Mesa Verde, 1997.

McCARTHY, Patrick A., BA, MA, PhD; American academic and writer; *Chairman, English Department, University of Miami at Coral Gables*; b. 12 July 1945, Charlottesville, VA; m. 1st; three c.; m. 2nd Yolanda A. Armstrong 1997. *Education:* Univ. of Virginia, Univ. of Wisconsin at Milwaukee. *Career:* instructor in English, Murray State Univ., Ky 1968–69, William Paterson Coll. of New Jersey 1973–74, Broome Community Coll., Binghamton, NY 1975–76; Visiting Prof. of English, State Univ. of NY at Binghamton 1974–75; Asst Prof., Univ. of Miami at Coral Gables 1976–81, Assoc. Prof. 1981–84, Prof. of English 1984–2005, Acting Chair. History Dept 2002–03, Chair. English Dept 2005–. *Publications:* The Riddles of 'Finnegans Wake' 1980, Olaf Stapledon 1982, Critical Essays on Samuel Beckett (ed.) 1986, The Legacy of Olaf Stapledon: Critical Essays and an Unpublished Manuscript (ed. with Charles Elkins and Martin H. Greenberg) 1989, 'Ulysses': Portals of Discovery 1990, Critical Essays on James Joyce's 'Finnegans Wake' (ed.) 1992, Forests of Symbols: World, Text and Self in Malcolm Lowry's Fiction 1994, Malcolm Lowry's La Mordida: A Scholarly Edition (ed.) 1996, Joyce/Lowry: Critical Perspectives (ed. with Paul Tiessen) 1997, Star Maker (ed.) 2004, Joyce, Family, 'Finnegans Wake' 2005. *Address:* Department of English, University of Miami, Coral Gables, FL 33124-4632, USA (office). *E-mail:* p.mccarthy@miami.edu (office).

McCARTHY, Wil, BS; American engineer and writer; b. 16 Sept. 1966, Princeton, NJ; m. 1st Kumiko McCarthy (divorced 1990); m. 2nd Cathy Polk; one s. *Education:* University of Colorado, Boulder. *Career:* Space Launch Systems Engineer, 1988–97, Flight Systems Engineer, 1997–, Lockheed-Martin Corporation, Denver, CO; Creative Writing Instructor, Colorado Free University and Jefferson Adult and Continuing Education Programme; mem. SFWA; North Colorado Writers Workshop, former Pres. *Publications:* Aggressor Six, 1994; A Midnight Clear (co-author), 1994; Flies from the Amber, 1995; Murder in the Solid State, 1996; The Fall of Sirius, 1996; Bloom, 1998. Contributions: anthologies; Periodicals including: Colorado Engineer; Aboriginal SF; Interzone; Analog; Isaac Asimov's Science Fiction Magazine; ComputerEdge; SF Age; SFWA Bulletin. *Address:* c/o Lockheed-Martin Astronautics, PO Box 179, Denver, CO 80201, USA.

McCARTHY, William Edward John, BA, PhD; British writer; b. 30 July 1925, London, England. *Education:* Ruskin College, Merton College, Oxford, Nuffield College, Oxford. *Career:* Research Fellow, Nuffield College, 1959–63; Staff Lecturer, Tutor, Industrial Relations, 1964–65, Fellow, Nuffield College and Centre for Management Studies, 1968–, University of Oxford; Dir of Research, Royal Commission on Trade and Unions and Employers Asscn, London, 1965–68; Senior Economic Adviser, Dept of Employment, 1968–70; Special Adviser, European Economic Commission, 1974–75. *Publications:* The Future of the Unions, 1962; The Closed Shop in Britain, 1964; The Role of Shop Stewards in British Industrial Relations: A Survey of Existing Information and Research, 1966; Disputes Procedures in Britain (with Arthur Ivor Marsh), 1966; Employers' Associations: The Results of Two Studies (with V. G. Munns), 1967; The Role of Government in Industrial Relations, Shop Stewards and Workshop Relations: The Results of a Study, 1968; Industrial Relations in Britain: A Guide for Management and Unions (ed.), 1969; The Reform of Collective Bargaining: A Series of Case Studies, 1971; Trade Unions, 1972; Coming to Terms with Trade Unions (with A. J. Collier), 1972; Management by Agreement (with N. D. Ellis), 1973; Wage Inflation and Wage Leadership (with J. F. O'Brien and V. C. Dowd), 1975; Making Whitley Work, 1977; Change in Trade Unions (co-author), 1981; Strikes in Post War Britain (with J. W. Durcun), 1985; Freedom at Work, 1985; The Future of Industrial Democracy, 1988; Employee Relations Audits (co-author), 1992; Legal Intervention in Industrial Relations (ed.), 1992; New Labour at Work, 1997; Fairness at Work and Trade Union Recognition, 1998. *Address:* 4 William Orchard Close, Old Headington, Oxford, England.

McCAUGHREAN, Geraldine, BEd; British writer; b. 6 June 1951, Enfield; m. John McCaughrean; one d. *Education:* Christ Church Coll. of Educ., Canterbury. *Plays:* Dazzling Medusa, Polka Children's Theatre 2006, Not the End of The World, Bristol Old Vic 2006. *Publications:* juvenile: A Little Lower than the Angels (Whitbread Children's Book Award 1987), A Pack of Lies (Carnegie Medal, Guardian Children's Fiction Award 1988), Gold Dust (Whitbread Children's Book Award 1994), Plundering Paradise (Smarties Book Prize Bronze Award 1996), Forever X (UK Reading Asscn Children's Book Award 1998) The Stones Are Hatching, The Kite Rider (Smarties Book Prize Bronze Award 2001), Stop the Train (Smarties Book Prize Bronze Award) 2002, Show Stopper! 2003, Jalopy 2003, Not the End of the World (Whitbread Children's Book Award 2005) 2004, The White Darkness 2005, Peter Pan in Scarlet (the official sequel to J. M. Barrie's 'Peter Pan', commissioned by Great Ormond Street Hospital, London) 2006, Peter Pan and the Shadow Thieves 2007; illustrated books: Saint George and the Dragon, Little Angel, Unicorns, Unicorns, Never Let Go, Beauty and the Beast, The Nutcracker, Grandma Chicken Legs, How the Reindeer Got Their Antlers, My Grandmother's Clock, Bright Penny, Jesse Tree, One Thousand and One Arabian Nights, The Canterbury Tales, El CID, The Odyssey, Moby Dick, A Pilgrim's Progress, Myths and Legends of the World (The Golden Hoard, The Silver Treasure, The Bronze Cauldron, The Crystal Pool, Golden Myths and Legends of the World, Silver Myths and Legends of the World, Greek Myths, Greek Gods and Goddesses, Roman Myths, The Greeks on Stage), Starry Tales, Love and Friendship, King Arthur, On the Day the World Began, Tales of Robin Hood, Britannia, Brave Magic, The Quest of Isis, Gilgamesh the Hero, Dog Days 2003, Hercules 2003, Perseus 2003, The Orchard Book of Roman Myths 2004, Theseus 2004, Odysseus 2004, Peter Pan in Scarlet 2006; other: plays and radio plays, poems, books for younger children; adult fiction: The Maypole 1989, Fires' Astonishment 1990, Vainglory 1991, Lovesong 1996, The Ideal Wife 1997; contrib. short stories to anthologies. *Literary Agent:* David Higham Associates Ltd, 5–8 Lower John Street, Golden Square, London, W1F 9HA, England. *Telephone:* (20) 7434-5900. *Fax:* (20) 7437-1072. *E-mail:* dha@davidhigham.co.uk. *Website:* www.davidhigham.co.uk; www.geraldinemccaughrean.co.uk.

McCAULEY, Martin, BA, PhD; British academic and writer; b. 18 Oct. 1934, Omagh, Northern Ireland; s. of Isaac Edmund McCauley and Levena McCauley (née Anderson); m Marta (née Kring); one s. *Education:* Univ. of London. *Career:* Sr Lecturer in Soviet and East European Studies, School of Slavonic and East European Studies, Univ. Coll. London 1968–91, Sr Lecturer in Politics 1991–98, Chair. Dept of Social Sciences 1993–96; mem. Economic and Social Research Council, Politics and Society Group; mem. Royal Inst. of Chartered Surveyors. *Publications:* The Russian Revolution and the Soviet State 1917–1921 (ed.) 1975, Khrushchev and the Development of Soviet Agriculture: The Virgin Land Programme 1953–64 1976, Communist Power in Europe 1944–1949 (ed. and contrib.) 1977, Marxism-Leninism in the German Democratic Republic: The Socialist Unity Party (SED) 1978, The Stalin File 1979, The Soviet Union Since 1917 1981, Stalin and Stalinism 1983, Origins of the Cold War 1983, The Soviet Union Since Brezhnev (ed. and contrib.) 1983, The German Democratic Republic Since 1945 1984, Octobrists to Bolsheviks: Imperial Russia 1905–1917 1984, Leadership and Succession in the Soviet Union, East Europe and China (ed. and contrib.) 1985, The Origins of the Modern Russian State 1855–1881 (with Peter Waldron) 1986, The Soviet Union under Gorbachev (ed.) 1987, Gorbachev and Perestroika (ed.) 1990, Khrushchev 1991, The Soviet Union 1917–1991 1991, Directory of Russian MPs (ed.) 1993, Longman Biographical Directory of Decision Makers in Russia and the Successor States (ed.) 1994, Who's Who in Russia and the Soviet Union 1997, Russia 1917–1941 1997, Longman Companion to Russia since 1914 1997, Gorbachev 1998, America, Russia and the Cold War 1949–1991 1998, Afghanistan and Central Asia 2001, Bandits, Gangsters and the Mafia: Russia, the CIS and the Baltic States 2002, The Origins of the Cold War 1941–1949 2003, Stalin and Stalinism 2003, Russia, America and the Cold War 1949–1991 2004; contrib. to professional journals. *Address:* School of Slavonic and East European Studies, University College London, Senate House, Malet Street, London, WC1E 7HU, England (office). *Telephone:* (20) 8445-2286 (home). *Fax:* (20) 8445-2236 (home). *E-mail:* andermccauley@hotmail.com (home).

McCLANE, Kenneth Anderson, Jr, AB, MA, MFA; American academic, poet and eriter; b. 19 Feb. 1951, New York, NY; m. Rochelle Evette Woods 1983. *Education:* Cornell University. *Career:* Instructor, Colby College, 1974–75; Luce Visiting Prof., Williams College, 1983; Assoc. Prof., 1983–89, Prof., 1989–93, W. E. B. DuBois Prof., 1993–, Cornell University; Visiting Prof., Wayne State University, 1987, University of Michigan, 1989, Washington University, 1991; mem. Associated Writing Programs; Poets and Writers. *Publications:* Take Five: Collected Poems, 1988; Walls: Essays 1985–90, 1991. Contributions: journals. *Honours:* George Harmon Coxe Award, 1973; Corson Morrison Poetry Prize, 1973. *Address:* c/o Department of English, Cornell University, Rockefeller Hall, Ithaca, NY 14853, USA.

McCLARY, Susan Kaye, BMus, MA, PhD; American academic and writer; *Professor of Musicology, University of California at Los Angeles*; b. 2 Oct. 1946, St Louis, MO. *Education:* Southern Illinois Univ., Harvard Univ. *Career:* Lecturer, Trinity Coll., Hartford, CT 1977; Asst Prof. 1977–83, Assoc. Prof. 1983–90, Prof. of Musicology 1990–92, Univ. of Minnesota; Prof. of Musicology, McGill Univ. 1992–94, Univ. of California at Los Angeles 1994–; Ernest Bloch Visiting Prof., Univ. of California at Berkeley 1993; mem. American Musicological Soc. *Publications:* The Transition from Modal to Tonal Organization in the Works of Monteverdi 1976, Music and Society: The Politics of Composition, Performance and Reception (ed. with R. Leppert) 1987, Feminine Endings: Music, Gender, and Sexuality 1991, Georges Bizet: Carmen 1992, Conventional Wisdom: The Content of Musical Form 2000; contrib. to scholarly books and journals. *Honours:* John D. and Catherine T. MacArthur Foundation Fellowship 1995. *Address:* c/o Department of Musicology, University of California at Los Angeles, Los Angeles, CA 90095, USA.

McCLATCHY, Joseph Donald, Jr, AB, PhD; American poet, writer and editor; b. 12 Aug. 1945, Bryn Mawr, Pennsylvania. *Education:* Georgetown University, Yale University. *Career:* Instructor, LaSalle College, Philadelphia, 1968–71; Assoc. Ed., Four Quarters, 1968–72; Asst Prof., Yale University, 1974–81; Poetry Ed., 1980–91, Ed., 1991–, The Yale Review; Lecturer in Creative Writing, Princeton University, 1981–93; Prof. of English, Yale Univ., 2002–; mem. American Acad. of Arts and Letters; American Acad. of Arts and Sciences; International PEN; Acad. of American Poets, chancellor, 1996–2003. *Publications:* Anne Sexton: The Artist and Her Critics, 1978; Scenes from Another Life (poems), 1981; Stars Principal (poems), 1986; James Merrill: Recitative: Prose (ed.), 1986; Kilim (poems), 1987; Poets on Painters: Essays on the Art of Painting by Twentieth-Century Poets (ed.), 1988; White Paper: On Contemporary American Poetry, 1989; The Rest of the Way (poems), 1990; The Vintage Book of Contemporary American Poetry (ed.), 1990; Woman in White: Selected Poems of Emily Dickinson (ed.), 1991; The Vintage Book of Contemporary World Poetry (ed.), 1996; Ten Commandments (poems), 1998; Twenty Questions (essays), 1998; Hazmat (poems), 2002; Selected Poems of Edna St Vincent Millay, 2003; Division of Spoils (poems), 2003. Contributions: anthologies and magazines. *Honours:* Woodrow Wilson Fellowship, 1967–68; O. Henry Award, 1972; Ingram Merrill Foundation Grant, 1979; Michener Award, 1982; Gordon Barber Memorial Award, 1984, Melville Cane Award, 1991, Poetry Society of America; Eunice Tietjens Memorial Prize, 1985, Oscar Blumenthal Prize, 1988, Levinson Prize, 1990, Poetry Magazine; Witter Bynner Poetry Prize, 1985, Award in Literature, 1991, American Acad. of Arts and Letters; National Endowment for the Arts Fellowship, 1986; Guggenheim Fellowship, 1988; Acad. of American Poets Fellowship, 1991. *Address:* 15 Grand Street, Stonington, CT 06378, USA.

McCLURE, Gillian Mary, BA; British children's writer and illustrator; b. (Gillian Mary Coltman), 29 Oct. 1948, Bradford, England; three s. *Education:* Horsham High School for Girls, Bristol Univ., Moray House. *Career:* mem. CWIG Soc. of Authors (cttee mem. 1989–95), PLR Advisory Cttee 1992; Royal

Literary Fund Writing Fellow, Kent Univ. 2005–; Escalator Judge and Mentor, New Writing Partnership 2006–. *Publications:* The Emperor's Singing Bird 1974, Prickly Pig 1976, Fly Home McDoo 1979, What's The Time Rory Wolf? 1982, Tog The Ribber (illustrator, by Paul Coltman) 1985, What Happened To The Picnic? 1986, Witch Watch (illustrator, by Paul Coltman) 1989, Cat Flap 1990, Tinker Jim (illustrator, by Paul Coltman) 1992, The Christmas Donkey 1993, Norse Myths (illustrator, by Kevin Crossley-Holland) 1993, Poems That Go Bump In The Night 1994, The Little White Hen (illustrator, by Philippa Pearce) 1995, Selkie (Parent's Guide to Children's Media Award, USA 2000) 1999, Tom Finger 2001, Bruna (illustrator, by Anne Cottringer) 2003, Mario's Angels (illustrator, by Mary Arrigan) 2006. *Honours:* US Parents' Guide to Children's Media Award 2000. *Address:* 9 Trafalgar Street, Cambridge, CB4 1ET (home); Curtis Brown Ltd, Haymarket House, 28–29 Haymarket, London, SW1Y 4SP, England (office). *Telephone:* (20) 7393-4400 (office). *Fax:* (20) 7393-4401 (office). *E-mail:* gillianmcclure@ntlworld.com (home); info@curtisbrown.co.uk (office). *Website:* www.gillianmcclure.com.

McCLURE, Michael Thomas, BA; American academic, poet, dramatist and writer; b. 20 Oct. 1932, Marysville, KS; m. Joanna Kinnison 1954; one d. *Education:* University of Wichita, University of Arizona, San Francisco State College. *Career:* Asst Prof., 1962–77, Assoc. Prof., 1977–78, Prof., 1978–, California College of Arts and Crafts, Oakland; Playwright-in-Residence, American Conservatory Theatre, San Francisco, 1975; Assoc. Fellow, Pierson College, Yale University, 1982. *Publications:* Poetry: Passage, 1956; For Artaud, 1959; Hymns to St Geryon and Other Poems, 1959; The New Book: A Book of Torture, 1961; Dark Brown, 1961; Ghost Tantras, 1964; 13 Mad Sonnets, 1964; Hail Thee Who Play, 1968; The Sermons of Jean Harlow and the Curses of Billy the Kid, 1969; Star, 1971; The Book of Joanna, 1973; Rare Angel (writ with raven's blood), 1974; September Blackberries, 1974; Jaguar Skies, 1975; Antechamber and Other Poems, 1978; The Book of Benjamin, 1982; Fragments of Perseus, 1983; Selected Poems, 1986; Rebel Lions, 1991; Simple Eyes and Other Poems, 1994. Plays: The Growl, in Four in Hand, 1964; The Blossom, or, Billy the Kid, 1967; The Beard, 1967; The Shell, 1968; The Cherub, 1970; Gargoyle Cartoons (11 plays), 1971; The Mammals, 1972; The Grabbing of the Fairy, 1973; Gorf, 1976; General Gorgeous, 1975; Goethe: Ein Fragment, 1978; The Velvet Edge, 1982; The Beard and VKTMs: Two Plays, 1985. Fiction: The Mad Club, 1970; The Adept, 1971. Other: Meat Science Essays, 1963; Freewheelin' Frank, Secretary of the Angels, as Told to Michael McClure by Frank Reynolds, 1967; Scratching the Beat Surface, 1982; Specks, 1985; Lighting the Corners: On Art, Nature, and the Visionary: Essays and Interviews, 1993. *Honours:* National Endowment for the Arts Grants, 1967, 1974; Guggenheim Fellowship, 1971; Magic Theatre Alfred Jarry Award, 1974; Rockefeller Foundation Fellowship, 1975; Obie Award, 1978. *Website:* www.thing.net/~grist/l&d/mcclure/mcclure.htm.

MACCOBY, Michael, BA, PhD; American consultant and writer; b. 5 March 1933, Mt Vernon, NY; m. Sandylee Weille 1959; one s. three d. *Education:* Harvard Univ., New Coll., Oxford, Univ. of Chicago, Mexican Inst. of Psychoanalysis. *Career:* mem. PEN, Signet Soc., Cosmos, American Psychological Asscn, American Anthropological Asscn, Nat. Acad. of Public Administration. *Publications:* Social Change and Character in Mexico and the United States 1970, Social Character in a Mexican Village (with E. Fromm) 1970, The Gamesman 1977, The Leader 1981, Why Work 1988, Sweden at the Edge 1991, A Prophetic Analyst (with M. Cortina) 1996, Agents of Change (with C. Heckscher, R. Ramirez, P. E. Tixier) 2003, The Productive Narcissist 2003. *Honours:* Woodrow Wilson Fellowship 1954, Fellow Center for Advanced Study in the Behavioral Sciences 1968, McKinsey Award 2000. *Address:* 4825 Linnean Avenue NW, Washington, DC 20008, USA (office). *Telephone:* (202) 895-8922 (office). *Fax:* (202) 895-8923 (office). *E-mail:* michael@maccoby.com. *Website:* www.maccoby.com.

McCOLLEY, Diane Kelsey, AB, PhD; American academic and writer; b. 9 Feb. 1934, Riverside, CA; m. Robert M. McColley 1958; one s. five d. *Education:* Univ. of California at Berkeley, Univ. of Illinois at Urbana-Champaign. *Career:* Teaching Asst, 1966–74, Visiting Lecturer, 1975–78, Univ. of Illinois at Urbana-Champaign; Asst Prof., 1979–84, Assoc. Prof., 1984–93, Prof. of English, 1993–2002, Distinguished Prof. Emer. 2002–, Camden College of Arts and Sciences, Rutgers Univ.; Visiting Fellow, Lucy Cavendish College, Univ. of Cambridge, 1990; mem. Asscn for the Study of Literature and the Environment, Asscn of Univ. Profs of English, Milton Soc. of America, (Pres. 1990, Honoured Scholar 1999). *Publications:* Milton's Eve, 1983; A Gust for Paradise: Milton's Eden and the Visual Arts, 1993; Poetry and Music in Seventeenth-Century England, 1997. Contributions: scholarly books and journals. *Honours:* Nat. Endowment for the Humanities Fellowship, 1989–90; American Philosophical Soc. Research Grant, 1990; James Holly Hanford Award, Milton Soc. of America, 1993; Mellon Fellowship, Huntingdon Library 1999–2000; Clark Library Fellowship 2000. *Address:* 1050 14th Street, Santa Rosa, CA 95404, USA (home). *Telephone:* (707) 528-7678. *E-mail:* mccolley@camden.rutgers.edu.

McCONCHIE, Lyn, (Jan Bishop, Elizabeth Underwood); New Zealand writer; b. 3 April 1946, Auckland. *Career:* Justice Dept, Agriculture and Fisheries Dept, Probation Dept; mem. SFWA, CWA, FAW, NZSA. *Publications:* Farming Daze (as Elizabeth Underwood), 1993; The Key of the Kelian, 1995; The Lonely Troll (also as) The Troll's New Jersey, 1997; Tales From the Marrigan Trade House, 1998; Ciara's Song, 1998; The Troll and the Taniwha, 1998. Contributions: New Zealand Cat Fancy Yearbook; Disinformation.

Honours: Australasion Medal, 1992; New York Public Library Best Books for Teenagers Listing, 1995; Music Medallion, 1996, 1997. *Literary Agent:* Sternig and Bryne, USA. *Address:* Farside Farm, R. D. Norsewood 5491, New Zealand.

McCONICA, James Kelsey, OC, MA, DPhil, FRHistS, FRSC, FBA; Canadian academic; *President, Pontifical Institute of Mediaeval Studies*; b. 24 April 1930, Luseland, SK. *Education:* Univ. of Saskatchewan, Univ. of Oxford, Univ. of Toronto. *Career:* instructor, Univ. of Saskatchewan 1956–57, Asst Prof. 1957–62; Assoc. Prof., Pontifical Inst. of Mediaeval Studies (PIMS), Toronto 1967–70, Prof. of History 1971–90, Prof. Emer. 1990–, Pres. 1996–; Ordained Roman Catholic Priest 1968; Visiting Fellow, All Souls Coll., Oxford 1969–71, 1977, Special Ford Lecturer 1977, Research Fellow 1978–84, 1990–97, Academic Dean 1990–92; Fellow, Davis Center for Historical Studies, Princeton Univ. 1971; Prof., Univ. of Toronto 1972–90; Pres., Univ. of St Michael's Coll., Toronto 1984–90; mem. American Soc. for Reformation Research, Canadian Soc. for Renaissance Studies, Oxford Historical Soc., Renaissance Soc. of America; foreign mem. Royal Belgian Acad. *Publications:* English Humanists and Reformation Politics under Henry VIII and Edward VI 1965, The Correspondence of Erasmus (ed.), Vol. III 1976, Vol. IV 1977, Thomas More: A Short Biography 1977, The History of the University of Oxford (ed.), Vol. III 1986, Erasmus 1991; contrib. to books and professional journals. *Honours:* Hon. Fellow Exeter Coll. Oxford 2002; Hon. LLD (Saskatchewan) 1986, (St Francis Xavier) 1999, (Regina) 1999, Hon. DLitt (Windsor) 1989, Hon. DUniv (St Paul) 2002; Rhodes Scholar 1951, Guggenheim Fellowship 1969–70, Killiam Sr Research Scholar 1976–77. *Address:* Pontifical Institute of Mediaeval Studies, 59 Queen's Park Crescent East, Toronto, ON M5S 2C4, Canada (office). *Telephone:* (416) 926-7288 (office). *Fax:* (416) 926-7292 (office). *E-mail:* james.mcconica@utoronto.ca (office). *Website:* www.pims.ca (office).

McCONKEY, James Rodney, MA, PhD; American academic and writer; *Professor Emeritus, Cornell University*; b. 2 Sept. 1921, Lakewood, OH; m. Gladys Jean Voorhees 1944; three s. *Education:* Cleveland Coll., Western Reserve Univ., Univ. of Iowa. *Career:* Asst Prof. to Assoc. Prof., Morehead State Coll., Ky 1950–56; Dir Morehead Writer's Workshop 1951–56, Antioch Seminar in Writing and Publishing, Yellow Springs, OH 1957–60; Asst Prof. to Assoc. Prof., Cornell Univ. 1956–62, Prof. of English 1962–87, Goldwin Smith Prof. of English Literature 1987–92, Prof. Emer. 1992–; mem. PEN. *Publications:* The Novels of E. M. Forster 1957, The Structure of Prose (ed.) 1963, Night Stand 1965, Crossroads: An Autobiographical Novel 1968, A Journal to Sahalin (novel) 1971, The Tree House Confessions (novel) 1979, Court of Memory 1983, To a Distant Island (novel) 1984, Chekhov and Our Age: Responses to Chekhov by American Writers and Scholars (ed.) 1984, Kayo: The Authentic and Annotated Autobiographical Novel from Outer Space 1987, Rowan's Progress 1992, Stories from My Life with the Other Animals 1993, The Anatomy of Memory (ed.) 1996, The Telescope in the Parlor (essays) 2004; contrib. to magazines. *Honours:* Eugene Saxton Literary Fellow 1962–63, Nat. Endowment for the Arts Essay Award 1967, Ohioana Book Award 1969, Guggenheim Fellowship 1969–70, American Acad. of Arts and Letters Award 1979. *Address:* 402 Aiken Road, Trumansburg, NY 14886, USA. *E-mail:* jrm9@cornell.edu.

McCONNELL, Will (see SNODGRASS, W. D.)

McCORMICK, A. (see Lewis-Smith, Anne Elizabeth)

McCORMICK, John Owen, BA, MA, PhD; American writer; *Professor of Comparative Literature Emeritus, Rutgers University*; b. 20 Sept. 1918, Thief River Falls, MN; m. Mairi MacInnes 1954; three s. one d. *Education:* Univ. of Minnesota, Harvard Univ. *Career:* Sr Tutor and Teaching Asst, Harvard Univ. 1946–51; Lecturer, Salzburg Seminar in American Studies, Austria 1951–52; Lecturer of American Studies, Free Univ. of Berlin 1952–53, Prof. 1954–59; Prof. of Comparative Literature, Rutgers Univ., New Brunswick, NJ 1959–, currently Prof. Emer. *Publications:* Catastrophe and Imagination 1957, Versions of Censorship (with Mairi MacInnes) 1962, The Complete Aficionado 1967, The Middle Distance: A Comparative History of American Imaginative Literature, 1919–1932 1971, Fiction as Knowledge: The Modern Post-Romantic Novel 1975, George Santayana: A Biography 1987, Sallies of the Mind: Essays of Francis Fergusson (ed. with G. Core) 1997, Seagoing: Memoir 2000, Santayana 2003; contrib. to numerous magazines, journals and reviews. *Honours:* Longview Award for Non-Fiction 1960, Guggenheim Fellowships 1964–65, 1980–81, Nat. Endowment for the Humanities Sr Fellow 1983–84, American Acad. and Inst. of Arts and Letters Prize 1988.

McCOURT, Frank; Irish writer; b. 1931, New York, USA; s. of Malachy McCourt and Angela McCourt. *Career:* moved to Ireland in 1935; taught in New York City public schools for 27 years; with brother, Malachy, performed a two-person musical review based on their life as young men in Ireland. *Publications:* Angela's Ashes (Pulitzer Prize 1997, Nat. Book Critics' Circle Award 1997, Los Angeles Times Book Award 1997) 1996, 'Tis: A Memoir 1999, Teacher Man 2005. *Address:* c/o Author Mail, Seventh Floor, HarperCollins Publishers Inc., 10 E 53rd Street, New York, NY 10022, USA (office).

McCOURT, James, BA; American writer; b. 4 July 1941, New York, NY. *Education:* Manhattan College, New York University, Yale University. *Publications:* Mawrdew Czgowchuz, 1975; Kaye Wayfaring, 1984; Time Remaining, 1993; Delancey's Way, 2000. Contributions: anthologies and

magazines. *Literary Agent:* Elaine Markson, 44 Greenwich Avenue, New York, NY 10011, USA.

McCRACKEN, Elizabeth, BA, MA, MFA, MS; American writer and teacher; b. 1966. *Education:* Boston University, University of Iowa. *Career:* Adjunct Asst Lecturer, Drexel University and Evening College, Philadelphia, 1991–92; Mem., Writing Committee, 1993–, Instructor, Summer Program, 1996–98, Fine Arts Work Center, Provincetown; Community Writing Instructor, Sommerville Arts Council, 1995, 1996; Writing Instructor, Iowa Summer Writing Festival, 1997, 1998; Writer-in-Residence, Western Michigan University, 1998. *Publications:* Here's Your Hat What's Your Hurry?, 1993; The Giant's House, 1996; Niagara Falls All Over Again, 2001. Contributions: anthologies and periodicals. *Honours:* James Michener Grant, 1990; Fine Arts Work Centre Fellowships, Provincetown, 1990–91, 1992–93; National Endowment for the Arts Fellowship, 1992; MacDowell Colony Fellowship, 1993; Notable Book of the Year, American Library Asscn, 1996; Discovery Award, Barnes and Noble, 1997; Harold D. Vursell Memorial Award, American Acad. of Arts and Letters, 1997; Guggenheim Fellowship, 1998. *Address:* PO Box 441702, Somerville, MA 02144, USA. *E-mail:* mccrake@world.std.com.

McCRACKEN, Kathleen Luanne, PhD; Canadian poet and literary critic; *Lecturer in American Studies, University of Ulster at Jordanstown*; b. 26 Oct. 1960, Dundalk, Ont.; d. of Robert Ivan and Shirley Marguerite McCracken. *Education:* York Univ. and Univ. of Toronto, Ont. *Career:* Teaching Asst, Course Dir and Lecturer Univ. of Toronto and Ryerson Polytechnic Inst. 1985–89; Course Dir Dept of English, York Univ. 1988–89; Postdoctoral Fellowship, Social Sciences and Humanities Research Council, Univ. Coll. Dublin, Ireland 1989–91; Lecturer in American Studies Univ. of Ulster at Jordanstown, Belfast, NI 1992–; has presented papers at confs in Canada, Ireland and USA; Ontario Arts Council Writers' Grantee (four times); Univ. of Toronto Open Fellowship; Ontario Grad. Scholarships; mem. League of Canadian Poets, Modern Language Asscn, Anglo-Irish Literature. *Publications include:* Reflections 1978, Into Celebration 1980, The Constancy of Objects 1980, Reflections: A Creative History of the One-Room Schoolhouse in Proton Township (jtly) 1978, A Geography of Souls 2002; poetry and literary criticism published in various Canadian, American, Irish and British journals. *Address:* Faculty of Humanities, University of Ulster at Jordanstown, Shore Road, Newtownabbey, Co. Antrim, BT37 0QB, Northern Ireland (office). *Telephone:* (2890) 366192 (office). *Fax:* (2090) 852611 (office). *E-mail:* kl.mccracken@ulster.ac.uk.

McCRAW, Thomas Kincaid, BA, MA, PhD; American academic, writer and editor; b. 11 Sept. 1940, Corinth, Mississippi; m. Susan Morehead 1962; one s. one d. *Education:* University of Mississippi, University of Wisconsin. *Career:* Asst Prof., 1970–74, Assoc. Prof., 1974–78, University of Texas at Austin; Newcomen Fellow, 1973–74, Visiting Assoc. Prof., 1976–78, Prof., 1978–89, Isidor Straus Prof. of Business History, 1989–, Harvard University; Ed., Business History Review, 1994–; mem. American Economic Asscn; Business History Conference, trustee, 1986–95, pres., 1989; Economic History Asscn; Massachusetts Historical Society; Organization of American Historians. *Publications:* Morgan Versus Lilienthal: The Feud Within the TVA, 1970; TVA and the Power Fight, 1933–39, 1971; Regulation in Perspective: Historical Essays (ed.), 1981; Prophets of Regulation, 1984; America Versus Japan (ed.), 1986; The Essential Alfred Chandler (ed.), 1988; Management Past and Present (co-author), 1996; Creating Modern Capitalism (ed.), 1997; The Intellectual Venture Capitalist: John H. McArthur and the Work of the Harvard Business School, 1980–1995 (co-ed.), 1999; American Business, 1920–2000: How It Worked, 2000. Contributions: scholarly books and journals. *Honours:* Woodrow Wilson Fellow, 1966–67; William P. Lyons Master's Essays Award, Loyola University, Chicago, 1969; Younger Humanist Award, National Endowment for the Humanities, 1975; Pulitzer Prize in History, 1985; Thomas Newcomen Book Award, 1986; Inducted, Alumni Hall of Fame, University of Mississippi, 1986. *Address:* c/o Harvard University Business School, Soldiers Field, Boston, MA 02163, USA.

McCREADY, Jack (see Powell, Talmage)

McCREDIE, Andrew Dalgarno, AM, MA, DPhil, FAHA; Australian academic; b. 3 Sept. 1930, Sydney; s. of Harold A. McCredie and Marjorie C. McCredie (née Dalgarno); m. Xenia Rosner 1965; one d. *Education:* Univ. of Sydney, Royal Acad. of Music, London, Univs of Copenhagen, Stockholm, Hamburg. *Career:* Sr Research Fellow, Univ. of Adelaide 1965–69, Sr Lecturer in Musicology 1970–73, Reader in Musicology 1974–77, Prof. 1978–94, Prof. Emer. 1994–; Adjunct Prof. Monash Univ. 1997–; Hon. Visiting Prof. Univ. of Queensland (Brisbane) 1997–; Visiting Lecturer, Univs of Amsterdam, Utrecht 1964, Western Australia 1970, City Univ. of New York 1974, Yale, Pennsylvania 1977, Ljubljana, Bologna, Marburg, Frankfurt, Kraków, Warsaw 1978, Copenhagen, Belfast (Queen's Univ.), Hamburg, Munich, Zentral Inst. für Musikforschung (Berlin), Berne, Basle, Zurich 1983, Melbourne, Stockholm, Tübingen 1986, Heidelberg, Saarbrücken, Queen's Univ., Kingston, Ont., Brandeis (Boston), City Univ. of New York, NSW (Sydney) 1987, Munich, Braunschweig 1988, Wolfenbüttel, Mainz, Edmonton, Calgary, Saskatoon, London (Ont.), Toronto 1989, Cardiff 1992, Cologne 1994, Zagreb 1994, Dresden (1994, 1996), Cologne Weimar (2001), Louvain (2002); mem. Council Int. Musicological Soc. 1977–87; Mem. Inst. for Advanced Musical Studies, King's Coll. Univ., London 1993; Adviser Musica Antiqua Europae Orientalis 1977–; Advisory Corresp.; appointments with Int. Review of Aesthetics and Sociology of Music 1981–, Current Musicology 1987–, Studies in Music 1980. *Publications:* Musical Composition in Australia (3 vols) 1969, Karl Amadeus Hartmann: Catalogue of all his works with biography 1981 (trans. German), Miscellanea Musicologica, Adelaide (ed.) 1966–94, Paperbacks on Musicology (Gen. Ed.) 1978–, From Colonel Light into the Footlights: The Performing Arts in South Australia from 1836 to the Present 1988, Clemens von Franckenstein 1991, Ludwig Thuille 1993, Karl Amadeus Hartmann 1995, Werner Egle 1997. *Honours:* Edward J. Dent Medal 1974, Paderewski Medal-Bydgoszcz Philharmonia 1982, Australian Centennial Medal 2004. *Address:* Tintorettostrasse 1, 80638 Munich, Germany; 13/18 Lansell Road, Toorak, Vic. 3142, Australia (home). *Telephone:* (89) 178-2325 (Germany); (3) 9826-6348 (Australia) (home).

McCRORIE, Edward Pollitt, PhD; American academic, poet and translator; b. 19 Nov. 1936, Central Falls, RI; m. 1995. *Education:* Brown Univ. *Career:* Prof. of English, Providence College, RI. *Publications:* After a Cremation (poems), 1974; The Aeneid of Virgil (trans.), 1995. Contributions: journals. *Address:* c/o Department of English, Providence College, Providence, RI 02918, USA.

McCRUM, (John) Robert, MA; British writer and newspaper editor; b. 7 July 1953, s. of Michael William McCrum and Christine Mary Kathleen fforde; m. 1st Olivia Timbs (divorced 1984); m. 2nd Sarah Lyall 1995; two d. *Education:* Sherborne School, Corpus Christi Coll., Cambridge and Univ. of Pennsylvania. *Career:* house reader Chatto & Windus 1977–79; Editorial Dir Faber and Faber Ltd 1979–89, Ed.-in-Chief 1990–96; Literary Ed. Observer newspaper 1996–; scriptwriter and co-producer The Story of English TV series 1980–86. *Publications:* In the Secret State 1980, A Loss of Heart 1982, The Fabulous Englishman 1984, The Story of English 1986, The World is a Banana 1988, Mainland 1991, The Psychological Moment 1993, Suspicion 1996, My Year Off 1998, Wodehouse: A Life (biog.) 2004. *Honours:* Tony Godwin Prize 1979, Peabody Award 1986, Emmy Award 1987. *Address:* The Observer, 119 Farringdon Road, London, EC1R 3ER, England.

McCRYSTAL, Cahal (Cal); Northern Irish journalist, writer, critic and broadcaster; b. 20 Dec. 1935, Belfast; m. Stella Doyle 1958; three s. *Education:* St Mary's Coll., Dundalk, St Malachy's Coll., Belfast. *Career:* fmrly reporter Northern Herald, labour correspondent Belfast Telegraph; crime reporter, chief reporter, foreign correspondent, New York Bureau Chief, News Ed., Foreign Features Ed. and columnist, Sunday Times, London; sr writer and columnist, Independent on Sunday; sr writer, The Observer; literary critic, Financial Times, Independent on Sunday; mem. editorial bd British Journalism Review. *Publications:* Watergate: The Full Inside Story (co-author) 1973, Reflections on a Quiet Rebel 1997; contrib. to Vanity Fair, British Magazines, Poetry Ireland Review and British Journalism Review. *Honours:* various journalism awards, Belfast Arts Council Literary Award 1998. *Literary Agent:* Greene & Heaton Ltd, 37 Goldhawk Road, London, W12 8QQ, England.

McCULLAGH, Sheila Kathleen, MBE, MA; British writer; b. 3 Dec. 1920, Surrey, England. *Education:* Bedford Froebel College, Univ. of Leeds. *Career:* Lecturer, Univ. of Leeds Institute of Education, 1949–57; mem. Society of Authors. *Publications:* Pirate Books, 1957–64; Tales and Adventures, 1961; Dragon Books, 1963–70; One, Two, Three and Away, 1964–92; Tim Books, 1974–83; Into New Worlds, 1974; Hummingbirds, 1976–92; Whizzbang Adventurers, 1980; Buccaneers, 1980; New Buccaneers, 1984; Where Wild Geese Fly, 1981; Puddle Lane, 1985–88; The Sea Shore (and other information books), 1992. *Literary Agent:* AP Watt Ltd, 20 John Street, London WC1N 2DR, England. *Address:* 27 Royal Crescent, Bath, NE Somerset BA1 2LT, England.

MacCULLOCH, Diarmaid, MA, DipTheol, DD, PhD, FRHistS, FSA, FBA; British academic, writer and editor; *Professor of the History of the Church, St Cross College, Oxford;* b. 31 Oct. 1951, Folkestone, Kent. *Education:* Univs of Cambridge, Liverpool and Oxford. *Career:* Jr Research Fellow, Churchill Coll. Cambridge 1976–78; Tutor in History, Wesley Coll. Bristol 1978–90; Lecturer in Theology, Univ. of Bristol 1978–95; Lecturer in Theology, St Cross Coll. Oxford 1995–97, Sr Tutor 1996–2000, Prof. of the History of the Church 1997–; Co-Ed. Journal of Ecclesiastical History 1995–. *Publications:* The Chorography of Suffolk (ed.) 1976, Suffolk and the Tudors: Politics and Religion in an English County, 1500–1600 1986, Groundwork of Christian History 1987, How to Read Church History, Vol. II (with J. Comby) 1988, The Later Reformation in England, 1547–1603 1990, The Reign of Henry VIII: Politics, Policy, and Piety (ed.) 1995, Thomas Cranmer: A Life 1996, Tudor Rebellions (with Anthony Fletcher, 4th edn) 2004, Tudor Church Militant: Edward VI and the Protestant Reformation 2000, Reformation: Europe's House Divided 1490–1700 (US title: The Reformation: A History 2004) 2003; contrib. to learned books and journals. *Honours:* Royal Historical Soc. Whitfield Prize 1986, Duff Cooper Prize 1996, Whitbread Biography Prize 1996, James Tait Black Memorial Prize 1996, Wolfson History Prize 2004, British Acad. Prize 2004, Non-Fiction Award, Nat. Book Critics Circle of America 2004. *Address:* St Cross College, Oxford, OX1 3LW, England (office).

McCULLOUGH, Colleen; Australian author; b. 1 June 1937, Wellington, NSW; m. Ric Robinson 1984. *Education:* Holy Cross Coll., Woollahra, Sydney Univ., Inst. of Child Health, London Univ. *Career:* trained as neuroscientist and worked in Sydney and English hospitals; researcher lecturer Dept of Neurology, Yale Univ. Medical School, USA 1967–77; moved to Norfolk Island, S Pacific 1979; mem. New York Acad. of Sciences, Bd of Visitors Int. Programs Center Dept of Political Science, Univ. of Oklahoma; Fellow American Assen for the Advancement of Science; fmr Patron Gerontology Foundation of

Australia; currently Patron Macular Degeneration Foundation of Australia. *Publications:* novels: Tim 1974, The Thorn Birds 1977, An Indecent Obsession 1981, A Creed for the Third Millennium 1985, The Ladies of Missalonghi 1987, The First Man in Rome 1990, The Grass Crown 1991, Fortune's Favourites 1993, Caesar's Women 1996, Caesar 1997, The Song of Troy 1998, Morgan's Run 2000, The October Horse 2002, The Touch 2003, Angel Puss 2004, On, Off 2006; non-fiction: Cooking with Colleen McCullough and Jean Easthope 1982, Roden Cutler, VC – The Biography 1998 (aka The Courage and the Will 1999). *Honours:* Hon. Founding Gov. Prince of Wales Medical Research Inst.; Hon. DLitt (Macquarie) 1993; designated one of Australia's Living National Treasures. *Address:* 'Out Yenna', Norfolk Island, Oceania (via Australia). *Fax:* (6723) 23313.

McCULLOUGH, David Gaub, BA; American historian and writer; b. 7 July 1933, Pittsburgh, PA; m. Rosalee Ingram Barnes 1954; three s. two d. *Education:* Yale Univ. *Career:* Ed., Time Inc., New York 1956–61, United States Information Agency, Washington, DC 1961–64, American Heritage Publishing Co., New York 1964–70; Scholar-in-Residence, Univ. of New Mexico 1979, Wesleyan Univ. 1982, 1983; Visiting Prof., Cornell Univ. 1989; Marian McFadden Memorial Lecturer, Indianapolis-Marion County Public Library 2002; mem. Jefferson Legacy Foundation, Nat. Trust for Historic Preservation, Soc. of American Historians, Harry S. Truman Library Inst. *Television:* host, Smithsonian World 1984–88, The American Experience 1988– (both PBS). *Publications:* The Great Bridge 1972, The Path Between the Seas 1977, The Johnstown Flood 1978, Mornings on Horseback 1981, Brave Companions 1991, Truman 1992, John Adams 2001, 1776 2005, The Course of Human Events 2005. *Honours:* various hon. doctorates; Nat. Book Award for History 1978, Samuel Eliot Morison Award 1978, Cornelius Ryan Award 1978, Francis Parkman Prize 1978, 1993, Los Angeles Times Prize for Biography 1981, American Book Award for Biography 1982, Pulitzer Prize in Biography 1993, 2002, Harry S. Truman Public Service Award 1993, Pennsylvania Governor's Award for Excellence 1993, St Louis Literary Award 1993, Pennsylvania Soc. Gold Medal Award 1994, Nat. Book Foundation Medal for Distinguished Contributions to American Letters 1995. *Literary Agent:* Janklow & Nesbit Associates, 445 Park Avenue, New York, NY 10022, USA. *Website:* www.davidmccullough.com.

McCULLOUGH, Kenneth (Ken), BA, MFA; American poet, writer and teacher; b. 18 July 1943, Staten Island, NY. *Education:* University of Delaware, University of Iowa. *Career:* Teacher, Montana State University, 1970–75, University of Iowa, 1983–95, Kirkwood Community College, Cedar Rapids, 1987, St Mary's University, Winona, Minnesota, 1996; Writer-in-Residence, South Carolina ETV Network, 1975–78; Participant, Artist-in-the-Schools Program, Iowa Arts Council, 1981–96; mem. Associated Writing Programs; Assen of American University Profs; National Assen of College Academic Advisers; Renaissance Artists and Writers Assen and Renaissance International; Rocky Mountain MLA; SFWA. *Publications:* Poetry: The Easy Wreckage, 1971; Migrations, 1972; Creosote, 1976; Elegy for Old Anna, 1985; Travelling Light, 1987; Sycamore Oriole, 1991; Walking Backwards, 1997. Contributions: numerous publications. *Honours:* Acad. of American Poets Award, 1966; Second Place, Ark River Awards, 1972; Helene Wurlitzer Foundation of New Mexico Residencies, 1973, 1994; National Endowment for the Arts Fellowship, 1974; Second Prize, Sri Chinmoy Poetry Awards, 1980; Writers' Voice Capricorn Book Award, 1985; Second Place, Pablo Neruda Award, Nimrod magazine 1990; Third Prize, Kudzu Poetry Contest, 1990; Ucross Foundation Residency, WY, 1991; Witter Bynner Foundation for Poetry Grant, 1993; Iowa Arts Council Grants, 1994, 1996.

McCULLY, Emily Arnold, (Emily Arnold), BA, MA; American writer and illustrator; b. 7 Jan. 1939, Galesburg, IL; two s. *Education:* Brown University, Columbia University. *Career:* mem. PEN Society; Authors' Guild. *Publications:* A Craving, 1982; Picnic, 1985; Life Drawing, 1986; Mirette on the High Wire, 1992; The Amazing Felix, 1993; Little Kit, or, the Industrious Flea Circus Girl, 1995; The Pirate Queen, 1995. *Honours:* O. Henry Award Collection, 1977; Caldecott Award, 1993. *Literary Agent:* Harriet Wasserman, 137 E 36th Street, New York, NY 10026, USA.

McCUNN, Ruthanne Lum, BA, DipEd; American writer; b. 21 Feb. 1946, San Francisco, CA; m. Donald H. McCunn 1965. *Education:* Univ. of Texas at Austin, San Francisco State Coll. *Career:* Guest Lecturer, Univ. of California at Santa Cruz 1988, Cornell Univ. 1989, Univ. of San Francisco 1993, 1996; mem. American Civil Liberties Union, Amnesty Int., Chinese for Affirmative Action, Chinese Historical Soc., Int. Inst. of San Francisco. *Play:* Wooden Fish Songs: A Concert Reading 1998. *Publications:* An Illustrated History of the Chinese in America 1979, Thousand Pieces of Gold 1981, Pie-Biter 1983, Sole Survivor 1985, Chinese American Portraits: Personal Histories, 1828–1888 1988, Chinese Proverbs 1991, Wooden Fish Songs 1995, The Moon Pearl 2000; contrib. to journals. *Honours:* Before Columbus Foundation American Book Award 1984, Southwestern Booksellers Assen Best Non-Fiction Adventure Book 1985, Choice Best Non-Fiction Book Citation 1989, Nat. Women's Political Caucus Distinguished Achievement Award 1991, Women's Heritage Museums Jeanne Fair McDonnell Best Fiction Award 1997. *Address:* 1007 Castro, San Francisco, CA 94114, USA (home). *Website:* www.mccunn.com.

McDERMOTT, Alice, BA, MA; American writer; b. 27 June 1953, Long Island, NY; m. David Armstrong; two c. *Education:* SUNY, Univ. of New Hampshire. *Career:* mem. staff Houghton Mifflin publrs; writer, short stories published in Ms, Redbook, Seventeen and Mademoiselle magazines; teacher writing workshops American Univ. (DC); mem. Associated Writing Programs, PEN, Poets and Writers, Writers' Guild. *Publications:* A Bigamist's Daughter 1982, That Night 1987, At Weddings and Wakes 1991, Charming Billy (Nat. Book Award) 1998, Child of My Heart 2002, After This 2006. *Honours:* Whiting Writers Award 1987. *Address:* c/o Bloomsbury Publishing PLC, 36 Soho Square, London, W1D 3QY, England (office).

McDEVITT, Jack, BA, MA; American writer; b. 14 April 1935, Philadelphia, Pa; s. of John McDevitt and Elizabeth McDevitt; m. Maureen McAdams 1967; two s. one d. *Education:* La Salle Coll., Wesleyan Univ. *Career:* mem. Science Fiction and Fantasy Writers of America, US Chess Fed., Mil. Officers Asscn of America. *Publications:* Time Travelers Never Die (Best Novella Award), The Hercules Text 1986, A Talent for War 1989, The Engines of God 1994, Ancient Shores 1996, Standard Candles 1996, Eternity Road 1997, Moonfall 1998, Infinity Beach 2000, Deepsix (Southeastern Science Fiction Achievement Award for Best Novel 2002) 2001, Chindi 2002, Omega (John W. Campbell Memorial Award for Best Novel 2004) 2003, Polaris 2004, Seeker (Southeastern Science Fiction Achievement Award for Best Novel 2005) 2005, Odyssey 2006; contrib. to various publs. *Honours:* Philip K. Dick Special Award 1986, UPC Grand Prize 1992, Homer Award 1997, Southeastern Science Fiction Achievement Lifetime Achievement Award 2006. *Address:* 57 Sunset Blvd, Brunswick, GA 31525, USA (office). *E-mail:* cryptic@gate.net (office). *Website:* www.sfwa.org/mentors/McDevitt (office).

McDONAGH, Martin; Irish playwright; b. 1970, London, England. *Career:* fmr resident playwright, Royal Nat. Theatre, London. *Plays:* The Beauty Queen of Leenane 1996, The Cripple of Inishmaan 1997, The Lonesome West 1997, A Skull In Connemara 1997, The Lieutenant of Inishmore 2001, The Pillowman 2003. *Publications:* Plays One 1999, Plays Two 2004. *Honours:* Evening Standard Award for Most Promising Playwright, Tony Awards, USA, Olivier Award for Best New Comedy 2003, for Best New Play 2004. *Address:* The Rod Hall Agency Ltd, 3 Charlotte Mews, London, W1T 4DZ, England. *Telephone:* (20) 7637-0706. *Fax:* (20) 7637-0807. *E-mail:* office@rodhallagency .com. *Website:* www.rodhallagency.com.

MacDONALD, Alastair A., BLitt, MA, PhD; British academic, poet and writer; *Professor of English Emeritus, Memorial University;* b. 24 Oct. 1920, Aberlour, Scotland. *Education:* Univ. of Aberdeen, Christ Church, Oxford, Univ. of Manchester. *Career:* Temp. Sr English Master, King William's Coll., Isle of Man 1953; Prof. of English 1955–87, Prof. Emeritus 1992–, Memorial Univ., NF, Canada; various poetry readings; mem. League of Canadian Poets, Scottish Poetry Library Asscn, Writers' Alliance of Newfoundland and Labrador. *Publications:* poetry: Between Something and Something 1970, Shape Enduring Mind 1974, A Different Lens 1981, Towards the Mystery 1985, A Figure on the Move 1991, Landscapes of Time: New, Uncollected, and Selected Poems 1994, If More Winters, Or This the Last 2003; novel: Flavian's Fortune 1985; prose and criticism; contrib. to various anthologies, reviews, journals and magazines. *Honours:* Best Poem Canadian Author and Bookman 1972, New Voices in American Poetry 1973, First Prize for Poetry 1976, Hon. Mention 1978, Second Prize for Poetry 1982, Newfoundland Government Arts and Letters Competition. *Address:* c/o Department of English, Arts and Administration Bldg, Memorial University, St John's, NL A1C 5S7 (office); Apt 701, 7 Tiffany Lane, St John's, NL A1A 4B7,, Canada (home). *Telephone:* (709) 754-4844 (home).

MacDONALD, Cynthia, BA, MA; American poet and lecturer; b. 2 Feb. 1928, New York, NY; m. E. C. Macdonald 1954 (divorced 1975); one s. one d. *Education:* Bennington College, Vermont, Mannes College of Music, New York, Sarah Lawrence College. *Career:* Asst Prof., 1970–74, Assoc. Prof. and Acting Dean of Studies, 1974–75, Sarah Lawrence College; Prof., Johns Hopkins University, 1975–79; Consultant, 1977–78, Co-Dir, Writing Program, 1979–, University of Houston; Guest Lecturer at various universities, colleges, seminars, etc; mem. American Society of Composers, Authors, and Publishers; Associated Writing Programs. *Publications:* Amputations, 1972; Transplants, 1976; Pruning the Annuals, 1976; (W)holes, 1980; Alternate Means of Transport, 1985; Living Wills: New and Selected Poems, 1991; I Can't Remember, 1997. Contributions: anthologies and other publications. *Honours:* MacDowell Colony Grant, 1970; National Endowment for the Arts Grants, 1973, 1979; Yaddo Foundation Grants, 1974, 1976, 1979; CAPS Grant, 1976; American Acad. and Institute of Arts and Letters Award, 1977; Rockefeller Foundation Fellow, 1978. *Address:* c/o Alfred A. Knopf Inc, 1745 Broadway, Suite 81, New York, NY 10019–4305, USA.

McDONALD, Forrest, PhD; American academic; *Distinguished Research Professor, University of Alabama;* b. 7 Jan. 1927, Orange, Tex.; s. of John Forrest and Myra M. McGill; m. Ellen Shapiro 1963; five c. *Education:* Orange High School and Univ. of Tex. (Austin). *Career:* State Historical Soc. of Wis. 1953–58; Assoc. Prof., Brown Univ. 1959–64, Prof. 1964–67; Prof., Wayne State Univ. 1967–76; Prof., Univ. of Ala 1976–87, Distinguished Research Prof. 1976, 1987–; J. P. Harrison Visiting Prof., Coll. of William and Mary 1986–87; Jefferson Lecturer Nat. Endowment for the Humanities 1987; Guggenheim Fellow 1962–63; mem. American Antiquarian Soc., Philadelphia Soc., The Historical Soc. *Publications:* We The People: The Economic Origins of the Constitution 1958, Insull 1962, E Pluribus Unum: The Formation of the American Republic 1965, Presidency of George Washington 1974, The Phaeton Ride 1974, Presidency of Thomas Jefferson 1976, Alexander Hamilton: A Biography 1980, A Constitutional History of the United States 1982, Novus Ordo Seclorum: The Intellectual Origins of the Constitution

1985, Requiem: Variations on Eighteenth-Century Themes 1988, The American Presidency: An Intellectual History 1994, States' Rights and the Union 2000, Recovering the Past: A Historian's Memoir 2004. *Honours:* George Washington Medal (Freedom's Foundation) 1980, Frances Tavern Book Award 1980, American Revolution Round Table Book Award 1986, 16th Jefferson Lecturer in the Humanities (Nat. Endowment for the Humanities) 1987, Ingersoll Prize, Richard M. Weaver Award 1990, Salvatori Award for Academic Excellence 1992. *Address:* P.O. Box 155, Coker, AL 35452, USA. *Telephone:* (205) 339-0317.

McDONALD, Gregory Christopher, BA; American writer; b. 15 Feb. 1937, Shrewsbury, MA; m. 1st Susan Aiken 1963 (divorced 1990); two s.; m. 2nd Cheryle Higgins 2001. *Education:* Harvard Univ. *Career:* critic, Boston Globe 1966–73; mem. Authors' Guild, CWA, Dramatists' Guild, MWA (pres. 1985–86), Writers' Guild of America. *Publications:* fiction: Running Scared 1964, Fletch 1974, Confess, Fletch 1976, Flynn 1977, Love Among the Mashed Potatoes 1978, Fletch's Fortune 1978, Fletch Forever 1978, Who Took Tony Rinaldi? 1980, Fletch and the Widow Bradley 1981, The Buck Passes Flynn 1981, Fletch's Moxie 1982, Fletch and the Man Who 1983, Carioca Fletch 1984, Flynn's In 1984, Fletch Won 1985, Safekeeping 1985, Fletch, Too 1986, Fletch Chronicle (three vols) 1986–88, A World Too Wide 1987, Exits and Entrances 1988, Merely Players 1988, The Brave 1991, Son of Fletch 1993, Fletch Reflected 1994, Skylar 1995, Skylar in Yankeeland 1997, Flynn's World 2003; non-fiction: The Education of Gregory McDonald 1985; editor: Last Laughs 1986. *Honours:* MWA Edgar Allan Poe Awards 1975, 1977, Tennessee Asscn of Federal Executives Humanitarian of the Year Award 1989, Nat. Asscn of Social Workers Citizen of the Year Award 1990, Roger William Straus Award 1990, Alex Haley Award 1992. *Literary Agent:* c/o Arthur Greene Esquire, 101 Park Avenue, New York, NY 10178, USA. *Website:* www .gregorymcdonald.com.

MACDONALD, Hugh John, MA, PhD, FRCM; British musicologist and academic; *Avis Blewett Professor of Music, Washington University, St Louis;* b. 31 Jan. 1940, Newbury, Berkshire; m. 1st Naomi Butterworth 1963; one s. three d.; m. 2nd Elizabeth Babb 1979; one s. *Education:* Pembroke Coll., Cambridge. *Career:* Lecturer in Music, Univ. of Cambridge 1966–71, Univ. of Oxford 1971–80; Visiting Prof., Indiana Univ. 1979; Gardiner Prof. of Music, Univ. of Glasgow 1980–87; Avis Blewett Prof. of Music, Washington Univ., St Louis 1987–. *Publications:* New Berlioz Edition (gen. ed., complete works) 1965–2006, Berlioz Orchestral Music 1969, Skryabin 1978, Berlioz 1982, Berlioz: Correspondance générale (ed.) Vol. 4 1984, Vol. 5 1989, Vol. 6 1995, Vol. 7 2001, Vol. 8 2002, Selected Letters of Berlioz 1995, Berlioz's Orchestration Treatise 2002; contrib. to The New Grove Dictionary of Music and Musicians, The New Grove Dictionary of Opera, many journals. *Honours:* Szymanowski Medal 1982, Grand Prix de Littérature Musicale Charles Cros 1985, 1996. *Address:* c/o Department of Music, Washington University, St Louis, MO 63130, USA (office).

McDONALD, Ian A., FRSL; Trinidadian poet, writer, dramatist and editor; *Chief Executive Officer, Sugar Association of the Caribbean;* b. 18 April 1933, St Augustine, Trinidad; m. Mary Angela Callender 1984; three s. *Education:* Queen's Royal Coll., Trinidad, Univ. of Cambridge, UK. *Career:* CEO, Sugar Asscn of the Caribbean 2000–; Dir, Theatre Co of Guyana, Georgetown 1981–; Ed., Kyk-Over-Al West Indian literary journal 1984–; Chair., Demerara Publishers 1988–; CEO, Sugar Asscn of the Caribbean 2000–. *Films:* The Humming Bird Tree (BBC film) 1992. *Publications:* The Tramping Man (play) 1969, The Humming Bird Tree (novel) 1969, Selected Poems 1983, Mercy Ward 1988, Essequibo 1992, Jaffo the Calypsonian (poems) 1994, Between Silence and Silence (poems), The Heinemann Book of Caribbean Poetry (co-ed.) 1994, The Collected Poems of A. J. Seymour (co-ed.) 2000, Poems by Martin Carter (co-ed.) 2006. *Honours:* Hon. DLitt (Univ. of the West Indies) 1997; Golden Arrow of Achievement (Guyana Nat. Award) 1987. *Address:* c/o Demerara Sugar Terminal, River View, Ruimveldt, Georgetown, Guyana (home). *Telephone:* 2272051 (office). *Fax:* 2266104 (office). *E-mail:* dstgsc@ guyana.net.gy (office).

MacDONALD, Malcolm (see Ross-MacDonald, Malcolm John)

MACDONALD, Marianne, BA, BLitt, PhD; Canadian writer; b. 9 July 1934, Kenora, ON; m. Erik Korn 1958 (divorced 1998); two s. *Education:* McGill Univ., Univ. of Oxford, Univ. of Keele. *Career:* Lecturer in English, Univ. of Toronto 1960–62; Lecturer in American Studies, Univ. of Keele 1964–69; Principal Lecturer in English, Middlesex Polytechnic 1972–86; mem. CWA, Crime Writers of Canada, Sisters in Crime. *Publications:* fiction: Death's Autograph 1996, Ghost Walk 1997, Smoke Screen 1999, Road Kill 2000, Blood Lies 2001, Die Once 2002, Three Monkeys 2005; juvenile fiction: Black Bass Rock 1952, Smugglers Cove 1955, The Treasure of Ur 1958, The Pirate Queen 1991, The Eighty-Nine Pennies of Emma Jones 1992, The Witch Repair 1995; non-fiction: The State of Literary Theory Today (ed.) 1982, Ezra Pound: purpose/form/meaning 1983, Ezra Pound and History (ed.) 1985. *Honours:* Woodrow Wilson Fellowship 1954–55. *Literary Agent:* David Higham Associates, 5–8 Lower John Street, Golden Square, London, W1F 9HA, England. *Website:* www.marianne-macdonald.com.

MacDONALD, Sharman, MA; British writer, playwright and screenwriter; b. 8 Feb. 1951, Glasgow; d. of Joseph Henry Hosgood MacDonald and Janet Rewat Macdonald (née Williams); m. Will Knightly 1976; one s. one d. *Education:* Hutchesons' Girls' Grammar School, Glasgow, George Watson's Ladies' Coll., Edinburgh and Univ. of Edinburgh. *Career:* actress with 7:84 at

Royal Court Theatre 1972–84; Thames TV Writer-in-Residence 1985. *Plays:* When I Was A Girl I Used To Scream And Shout 1984, The Brave 1987, When We Were Women 1987, All Things Nice 1990, Shades 1992, The Girl with Red Hair (Lyceum Theatre, Edinburgh) 2005. *Film screenplays:* Wild Flowers 1988, The Winter Guest 1995, Borders of Paradise 1995, After Juliet 1999. *Radio:* Sea Urchins (adapted for stage 1998), Gladly My Cross-Eyed Bear 2000. *Opera libretto:* Hey Persephone! 1998. *Publications:* novels: The Beast 1984, Night, Night 1987. *Honours:* London Evening Standard Award for Most Promising Playwright 1984. *Literary Agent:* c/o Faber and Faber Ltd, 3 Queen Square, London, WC1N 3AU; c/o Alan Brodie, 211 Piccadilly, London, W1V 9LD, England.

McDONALD, Sir Trevor, Kt, OBE; British journalist; *Broadcast Journalist, Independent Television News (UK)*; b. 16 Aug. 1939, Trinidad; m.; two s. one d. *Career:* worked on newspapers, radio and TV, Trinidad 1960–69; Producer BBC Caribbean Service and World Service, London 1969–73; reporter Ind. TV News 1973–78, sports corresp. 1978–80, diplomatic corresp. 1980–87, newscaster 1982–87, Diplomatic Ed. Channel Four News 1987–89, newscaster News at 5.40 1989–90, News at Ten 1990–99, ITV Evening News 1999–2000, ITV News at Ten 2001–04, News at 10.30 2004–05; Chair. Better English Campaign 1995–97, Nuffield Language Inquiry 1998–2000; Gov. English-Speaking Union of the Commonwealth 2000–; Pres. European Year of Languages 2000; Chancellor South Bank Univ. 1999–. *Publications:* Clive Lloyd: A Biography 1985, Vivian Richards: A Biography 1987, Queen and Commonwealth 1989, Fortunate Circumstances (autobiog.) 1993, Favourite Poems 1997, World of Poetry 1999. *Honours:* Hon. Fellow Liverpool John Moores Univ. 1998; Hon. DLitt (South Bank) 1994, (Plymouth) 1995, (Southampton Inst.) 1997, (Nottingham) 1997; Dr hc (Surrey) 1997, (Open Univ.) 1997; Hon. LLD (Univ. of West Indies) 1996; Newscaster of the Year TV and Radio Industries Club 1993, 1997, 1999; Gold Medal, Royal TV Soc. 1998, Richard Dimbleby Award for outstanding contrib. to TV, BAFTA 1999, Royal Television Soc. lifetime achievement award 2005. *Address:* c/o ITN, 200 Gray's Inn Road, London, WC1X 8XZ, England. *Telephone:* (20) 7833-3000 (office).

McDONALD, Walter Robert, BA, MA, PhD; American academic, poet and writer; b. 18 July 1934, Lubbock, TX; m. Carol Ham 1959; two s. one d. *Education:* Texas Technological College, University of Iowa. *Career:* Faculties, US Air Force Acad., University of Colorado, Texas Tech University; Paul W. Horn Prof. of English and Poet-in-Residence, Texas Tech University, Lubbock; mem. Texas Asscn of Creative Writing Teachers; PEN; Poetry Society of America; Assoc. Writing Programs; Texas Institute of Letters, councillor; Conference of College Teachers of English of Texas. *Publications:* Poetry: Caliban in Blue, 1976; One Thing Leads to Another, 1978; Anything, Anything, 1980; Working Against Time, 1981; Burning the Fence, 1981; Witching on Hardscrabble, 1985; Flying Dutchman, 1987; After the Noise of Saigon, 1988; Rafting the Brazos, 1988. Fiction: A Band of Brothers: Stories of Vietnam, 1989; Night Landings, 1989; The Digs in Escondido Canyon, 1991; All That Matters: The Texas Plains in Photographs and Poems, 1992; Where Skies Are Not Cloudy, 1993; Counting Survivors, 1995. Contributions: numerous journals and magazines. *Honours:* Poetry Awards, Texas Institute of Letters, 1976, 1985, 1987; George Elliston Poetry Prize, 1987; Juniper Prize, 1988; Western Heritage Awards for Poetry, National Cowboy Hall of Fame, 1990, 1992; 1993. *Address:* Department of English, Texas Tech University, Lubbock, TX 79409, USA.

MacDONOGH, Giles Malachy Maximilian, BA, MA; British writer and journalist; b. 6 April 1955, London, England. *Education:* Balliol College, Oxford, University of Oxford, École des Hautes Études Pratiques, France. *Career:* freelance journalist, 1983–; Ed., Made in France, 1984; columnist, Financial Times, 1989–; mem. International PEN; Octagon of Wine Writers. *Publications:* A Palate in Revolution: Grimod de La Reynière and the Almanach des Gourmands, 1987; A Good German: Adam von Trott zu Solz, 1990; The Wine and Food of Austria, 1992; Brillat Savarin: The Judge and his Stomach, 1992; Syrah Grenache, Mourvèdre, 1992; Prussia, the Perversion of an Idea, 1994; Berlin, 1997; The Last Kaiser: The Life of Wilhelm II, 2001. Contributions: Reference works, books, and periodicals. *Honours:* Glenfiddich Special Award, 1988. *Literary Agent:* Curtis Brown Ltd, Haymarket House, 28–29 Haymarket, London, SW1Y 4SP, England. *Telephone:* (20) 7393-4400. *Fax:* (20) 7393-4401. *E-mail:* info@curtisbrown.co.uk. *Website:* www.curtisbrown.co.uk.

MacDOUGALL, Ruth Doan, BEd; American writer; b. 19 March 1939, Laconia, NH; m. Donald K. MacDougall 1957. *Education:* Bennington Coll., Keene State Coll. *Career:* mem. NH Writers' Project. *Publications:* The Lilting House 1965, The Cost of Living 1971, One Minus One 1971, The Cheerleader 1973, Wife and Mother 1976, Aunt Pleasantine 1978, The Flowers of the Forest 1981, A Lovely Time Was Had By All 1982, Snowy 1993, The Cheerleader: 25th Anniversary Edition 1998, A Woman Who Loved Lindbergh 2001, Henrietta Snow 2004, Fifty Hikes in the White Mountains 2004, Fifty More Hikes in New Hampshire 2006; contrib. book reviews to New York Times Book Review, Newsday and others. *Honours:* winner PEN Syndicated Fiction Project 1983, 1984, 1985, NH Writers' Project Lifetime Achievement Award 2005, Keene State Coll. Alumni Achievement Award 2006. *Address:* 285 Range Road, Center Sandwich, NH 03227, USA. *Website:* www.ruthdoanmacdougall.com.

McDOUGALL, Walter Allan, BA, MA, PhD; American academic and writer; *Professor of History and Alloy-Ansin Professor of International Relations,*

University of Pennsylvania; b. 3 Dec. 1946, Washington, DC; m. 2nd Jonna van Zanten 1988; two c. *Education:* Amherst Coll., Univ. of Chicago. *Career:* US Army, Viet Nam 1968–70; Asst Prof., Univ. of California, Berkeley 1975–83, Assoc. Prof. 1983–87, Prof. of History 1987–; Prof. of History and Alloy-Ansin Prof. of Int. Relations, Univ. of Pennsylvania 1988–; Sr Fellow and Dir Center for America and the West, Foreign Policy Research Inst., Phila 1991–; Ed. Orbis, 1999–2001; mem. American Church Union, Pumpkin Papers Irregulars. *Publications:* France's Rhineland Diplomacy 1914–1924: The Last Bid for a Balance of Power in Europe 1978, The Grenada Papers (co-ed. with Paul Seabury) 1984, Social Sciences and Space Exploration: New Directions for University Instruction (contrib.) 1984, ...The Heavens and the Earth: A Political History of the Space Age 1985, Let the Sea Make a Noise 1993, Promised Land, Crusader State: The American Encounter with the World Since 1776 1997; contribs to numerous articles and reviews to periodicals. *Honours:* Pulitzer Prize for History 1986, Visiting Scholar, Hoover Inst. 1986, One of America's Ten Best College Profs, Insight 1987, Dexter Prize for Best Book, Soc. for the History of Tech. 1987. *Address:* 208 College Hall, University of Pennsylvania, Philadelphia, PA 19104-6379, USA (office). *Telephone:* (215) 898-2185 (office); (215) 898-0452 (office). *Fax:* (215) 573-2089 (office). *E-mail:* wamcd@sas.upenn.edu (office). *Website:* www.history.upenn.edu/faculty/mcdougall.htm (office).

MacDOWELL, Douglas Maurice, MA, DLitt, FRSE, FBA; British academic and writer; *Professor of Greek Emeritus, University of Glasgow*; b. 8 March 1931, London, England; s. of Maurice Alfred MacDowell and Dorothy Jean MacDowell (née Allan). *Education:* Highgate School, London, Balliol Coll., Oxford. *Career:* Asst Lecturer, Lecturer, Sr Lecturer, Reader in Greek and Latin, Univ. of Manchester 1958–71; Visiting Fellow, Merton Coll. Oxford 1969; Prof. of Greek 1971–2001, Prof. Emeritus 2001–, Univ. of Glasgow. *Publications:* Andokides: On the Mysteries (ed.) 1962, Athenian Homicide Law 1963, Aristophanes: Wasps (ed.) 1971, The Law in Classical Athens 1978, Spartan Law 1986, Demosthenes: Against Meidias (ed.) 1990, Aristophanes and Athens 1995, Antiphon and Andocides (with M. Gagarin) 1998, Demosthenes: On the False Embassy (ed.) 2000, Demosthenes: Speeches 27–38 (trans.) 2004. *Address:* c/o Department of Classics, University of Glasgow, Glasgow, G12 8QQ, Scotland (office). *Telephone:* (141) 330-5256 (office).

MacDOWELL, John (see Parks, Timothy Harold)

McDOWELL, John Henry, MA, FBA, FAAS; British academic; b. 7 March 1942, Boksburg, South Africa; s. of Sir Henry McDowell and Norah (née Douthwaite) McDowell; m. Andrea Lehrke 1977. *Education:* St John's Coll. Johannesburg, Univ. Coll. of Rhodesia and Nyasaland, New Coll., Oxford. *Career:* Fellow, Praelector in Philosophy, Univ. Coll. Oxford 1966–86; Prof. of Philosophy, Univ. of Pittsburgh 1986–88, Univ. Prof. 1988–. *Publications:* Ed. (with Gareth Evans) Truth and Meaning, Ed. (with Philip Pettit) Subject, Thought and Context, Mind and World, Mind, Value and Reality, Meaning, Knowledge and Reality; trans. of Plato, Theaetetus. *Address:* Department of Philosophy, University of Pittsburgh, Pittsburgh, PA 15260, USA. *Telephone:* (412) 624-5792.

McELDOWNEY, Eugene, BA; Irish writer and journalist; b. 27 June 1943, Belfast, Northern Ireland; m. Maura Magill 1970; one s. one d. *Education:* St Mary's Grammar School, Belfast, Queen's Univ., Belfast. *Career:* journalist, Night Ed., Irish Times, Dublin 1972–; mem. Nat. Union of Journalists, Howth Singing Circle and Goilin Club, Dublin. *Publications:* A Kind of Homecoming 1994, A Stone of the Heart 1995, The Sad Case of Harpo Higgins 1996, Murder at Piper's Gut 1997, The Faloorie Man 1999, Stella's Story 2002, Hotel Las Flores 2005, The Beach Bar (writing as Kate McCabe) 2006. *Address:* c/o Imrie and Dervis, 7 Carlton Mansions, Holmleigh Road, London, N16 5PX, England.

McELROY, Colleen Johnson, BS, MS, PhD; American academic, poet and writer; b. 30 Oct. 1935, St Louis, MO; m. (divorced); one s. one d. *Education:* Kansas State University, University of Washington, Seattle. *Career:* Ed., Dark Waters, 1973–79; Prof., University of Washington, Seattle, 1973–. *Publications:* Music From Home, 1976; The Halls of Montezuma, 1979; The New Voice, 1979; Winters Without Snow, 1979; Lie and Say You Love Me, 1981; Queen of the Ebony Isles, 1984; Jesus and Fat Tuesday, 1987; What Madness Brought Me Here, 1990. Contributions: various journals. *Address:* c/o Creative Writing Program, Department of English, University of Washington, Seattle, WA 98195, USA.

McELROY, Joseph Prince, BA, MA, PhD; American writer; b. 21 Aug. 1930, New York, NY. *Education:* Williams College, Columbia University. *Publications:* A Smuggler's Bible, 1966; Hind's Kidnap, 1969; Ancient History, 1971; Lookout Cartridge, 1974; Plus, 1977; Ship Rock, 1980; Women and Men, 1987; Actress in the House, 2003. *Address:* c/o Georges Borchardt, 136 E 57th Street, New York, NY 10022, USA.

McELROY, Lee (see Kelton, Elmer Stephen)

MACER-STORY, Eugenia, BS, MFA; American writer, dramatist and poet; b. 20 Jan. 1945, Minneapolis, MN; m. Leon A. Story 1970 (divorced 1975); one s. *Education:* Northwestern Univ., Columbia Univ. *Career:* mem. Dramatists' Guild, US Psychotronics Asscn, Poet's House, New York, American Soc. for Psychical Research. *Plays:* Meister Hemmelin 1994, Double or Nothing 1994, Radish 1995, Conquest of the Asteroids 1996, Mister Shooting Star 1997, Wild Dog Casino 1998, Holy Dragonet 1998–99, Old Gaffer from Boise 2000, Redecoration According to Currier 2000, Ars Chronicon Sylvestre 2002, Just

45 Minutes from Paradise 2004, other one-act plays 2000–04. *Publications:* Congratulations: The UFO Reality 1978, Angels of Time: Astrological Magic 1981, Du Fu Man Chu Meets the Lonesome Cowboy: Sorcery and the UFO Experience 1991, Legacy of Daedalus 1995, Cattle Bones and Coke Machines (anthology) 1995, The Dark Frontier 1997, Crossing Jungle River (poems) 1998, Troll: Other Interdimensional Invasions (short stories) 2000, Vanishing Questions (poems) 2000, Carrying Thunder 2002, Doing Business in the Adrondocks (metaphysical travelogue) 2002, The Merry Piper's Hollow Hills (chapbook) 2004, Struck by Green Lightning, aka Project Midas (novel) 2004; contrib. to numerous publications. *Honours:* Shubert Fellowship 1968. *Address:* Magick Mirror Communications, PO Box 741, JAF Bldg, New York, NY 10116, USA.

McEWAN, Ian Russell, CBE, MA, FRSL; British writer; b. 21 June 1948, Aldershot, Hants.; s. of the late David McEwan and Rose Moore; m. 1st Penny Allen 1982 (divorced 1995); two s. and two step-d.; m. 2nd Annalena McAfee 1997. *Education:* Woolverstone Hall, Univs of Sussex and E Anglia. *Screenplays:* The Imitation Game & Other Plays 1981, The Ploughman's Lunch 1985, Sour Sweet 1989. *Publications:* novels: The Cement Garden 1978, The Comfort of Strangers 1981, Rose Blanche (juvenile) 1985, The Child in Time (Whitbread Novel of the Year 1987, Prix Fémina Etranger 1993) 1987, The Innocent 1989, Black Dogs 1992, The Daydreamer (juvenile) 1994, Enduring Love 1997, Amsterdam (Booker Prize for Fiction 1998) 1998, Atonement (WHSmith Literary Award 2002, Nat. Book Critics Circle Fiction Award 2002, Los Angeles Times Prize for Fiction 2003, Santiago Prize for the European Novel 2004) 2001, Saturday (James Tait Black Memorial Prize 2006) 2005, On Chesil Beach 2007; short stories: First Love, Last Rites (Somerset Maugham Award 1976) 1975, In Between the Sheets 1978; libretto: Or Shall We Die? 1983. *Leisure interest:* hiking. *Honours:* Hon. Fellow American Acad. of Arts and Sciences 1997; Hon. DPhil (Sussex) 1989, (E Anglia) 1993, (London) 1998; Primo Letteraria, Prato 1982, Shakespeare Prize, Germany 1999. *Address:* c/o Jonathan Cape, Random Century House, 20 Vauxhall Bridge Road, London, SW1V 2SA, England. *Website:* www.ianmcewan.com.

McFARLAND, Ronald Earl, AA, BA, MA, PhD; American academic, poet and writer; b. 22 Sept. 1942, Bellaire, OH; m. Elsie Roseland Watson 1966; one s. two d. *Education:* Brevard Junior College, Florida State University, University of Illinois. *Career:* Teaching Asst, Florida State University, 1964–65, University of Illinois, 1967–70; Instructor, Sam Houston State College, 1965–67; Asst Prof., Assoc. Prof., 1970–79, Prof. of English, 1979–, University of Idaho; Idaho State Writer-in-Residence, 1984–85; Exchange Prof., Ohio University, 1985–86; mem. Acad. of American Poets; Hemingway Society; Pacific Northwest American Studies Asscn. *Publications:* Poetry: Certain Women, 1977; Composting at Forty, 1984; The Haunting Familiarity of Things, 1993; Stranger in Town, 2000; The Hemingway Poems, 2000; The Mad Waitress Poems, 2000; Ballygloves, 2000. Fiction: Catching First Light (short stories), 2001. Non-Fiction: The Villanelle: Evolution of a Poetic Form, 1988; David Wagoner, 1989; Norman Maclean, 1993; Tess Gallagher, 1995; The World of David Wagoner, 1997; Understanding James Welch, 2000. Editor: Eight Idaho Poets, 1979; James Welch, 1987; Norman Maclean (with Hugh Nichols), 1988; Idaho's Poetry: A Centennial Anthology (with William Studebaker), 1988; Deep Down Things: Poems of the Inland Pacific Northwest (with Franz Schneider and Kornel Skovajsa), 1990. Contributions: scholarly books and journals, poetry anthologies, reviews, quarterlies, and periodicals. *Honours:* National Endowment for the Arts Grant, 1978; Asscn for the Humanities in Idaho Grant, 1983; Burlington-Northern Faculty Achievement Award, 1990; Alumni Award for Faculty Excellence, 1991; Distinguished Alumnus, Brevard Community College, 1996; University of Idaho Faculty Award for Creative Excellence, 2002. *Address:* Department of English, University of Idaho, Moscow, ID 83844-1102, USA. *Telephone:* (208) 885-6937.

MacFARLANE, Robert; British writer and academic; b. 1976, Nottingham. *Education:* Nottingham High School, Emmanuel Coll., Cambridge. *Career:* Fellow, Emmanuel Coll., Cambridge. *Publications:* Mountains of the Mind: A History of a Fascination (Guardian First Book Award, Somerset Maugham Award 2004) 2003, Wild Eyed 2005; contrib. to The Sunday Times, The Observer, TLS, The Spectator, Evening Standard. *Literary Agent:* Toby Eady Associates Ltd, Third Floor, 9 Orme Court, London, W2 4RL, England. *Telephone:* (20) 7792-0092. *Fax:* (20) 7792-0879. *E-mail:* toby@tobyeady .demon.co.uk. *Website:* www.tobyeadyassociates.co.uk. *Address:* c/o Emmanuel College, University of Cambridge, St Andrew's Street, Cambridge, CB2 3AP, England.

McFEELY, William Shield, BA, MA, PhD; American academic and writer; b. 25 Sept. 1930, New York, NY; m. Mary Drake 1952; one s. two d. *Education:* Amherst College, Yale University. *Career:* Asst Prof., 1966–69, Assoc. Prof., 1969–70, Yale University; Prof. of History, 1970–80, Rodman Prof. of History, 1980–82, Andrew W. Mellon Prof. in the Humanities, 1982–86, Mount Holyoke College; Visiting Prof., University College London, 1978–79, Amherst College, 1980–81; Visiting Prof., 1984–85, John J. McCloy Prof., 1988–89, University of Massachusetts; Richard B. Russell Prof. of American History, 1986–94, Abraham Baldwin Prof. of the Humanities, 1994–, University of Georgia; mem. American Historical Asscn; Authors' Guild; Century Asscn; Organization of American Historians; PEN; Southern Historical Asscn. *Publications:* Yankee Stepfather: General O. O. Howard and the Freedmen, 1968; The Black Man in the Land of Equality (with Thomas J. Ladenburg), 1969; Grant: A Biography, 1981; Ulysses S. Grant: Memoirs and Selected Letters 1839–1865 (ed. with Mary Drake McFeely), 1990; Frederick Douglass,

1991; Sapelo's People: A Long Walk into Freedom, 1994, Portrait: A Life of Thomas Eakins (biog.) 2006. *Honours:* Morse Fellow, 1968–69; Fellow, ACLS, 1974–75; Pulitzer Prize in Biography, 1982; Francis Parkman Prize, 1982; Guggenheim Fellowship, 1982–83; National Endowment for the Humanities Grant, 1986–87; Avery O. Craven Award, 1992; Lincoln Prize, 1992.

McGARRY, Jean, BA, MA; American writer and teacher; b. 18 June 1952, Providence, RI. *Education:* Harvard University, Johns Hopkins University. *Career:* teacher, Johns Hopkins University; mem. Associated Writing Programs. *Publications:* Airs of Providence, 1985; The Very Rich Hours, 1987; The Courage of Girls, 1992. Contributions: Antioch Review; Southern Review; Southwest Review; Sulfur; New Orleans Review. *Honours:* Short Fiction Prize, Southern Review-Louisiana State University, 1985. *Address:* The Writing Seminars, Johns Hopkins University, Baltimore, MD 21218, USA. *E-mail:* mcgarry@jhu.edu.

McGINN, Bernard John, BA, STL, PhD; American academic, writer, translator and editor; *Naomi Shenstone Donnelley Professor Emeritus, Divinity School, University of Chicago;* b. 19 Aug. 1937, Yonkers, NY; m. Patricia Ferris 1971; two s. *Education:* St Joseph's Seminary and College, Yonkers, NY, Pontifical Gregorian University, Rome, Columbia University, University of Munich, Brandeis University. *Career:* Lecturer Regis College, Weston, Massachusetts 1966–67; Instructor Catholic University of America, Washington, DC 1968–69; Instructor 1969–70, Asst Prof. 1970–75, Assoc. Prof. 1975–78, Prof. of Historical Theology and the History of Christianity 1978–, Naomi Shenstone Donnelley Prof. 1992–2003, Emer. 2003–, Divinity School, University of Chicago; mem. American Society of Church History, pres. 1995–; Eckhart Society; International Society for the Promotion of Eriugenean Studies, pres.; Medieval Acad. of America, fellow 1994–; National Humanities Centre, USA, fellow 1999–2000. *Publications:* The Golden Chain: A Study in the Theological Anthropology of Isaac of Stella 1972, The Crusades 1973, Visions of the End: Apocalyptic Traditions in the Middle Ages 1979, The Calabrian Abbot: Joachim of Fiore in the History of Western Thought 1985, The Presence of God: A History of Christian Mysticism, 3 vols 1991, 1994, 1998, Apocalypticism in the Western Tradition 1994, Antichrist: Two Thousand Years of the Human Fascination with Evil 1994; translator: Apocalyptic Spirituality 1979, Meister Eckhart: The Essential Sermons, Commentaries, Treatises and Defense (with Edmund Colledge) 1981, Meister Eckhart: Teacher and Preacher (with Frank Tobin and Elvira Borgstadt) 1986; editor: Three Treatises on Man: A Cistercian Anthropology 1977, Christian Spirituality: Origins to the Twelfth Century (with John Meyendorff and Jean Leclercq) 1985, Christian Spirituality: High Middle Ages and Reformation (with Jill Raitt and John Meyendorff) 1987, Mystical Union and Monotheistic Faith: An Ecumenical Doctrine (with Moshe Idel) 1989, God and Creation: An Ecumenical Symposium (with David B. Burrell) 1990, The Apocalypse in the Middle Ages (with Richard K. Emmerson) 1992, Meister Eckhart and the Beguine Mystics: Hadewijch of Brabant, Mechthild of Magdeburg, and Marguerite Porete 1994, Eriugena: East and West: Papers of the Eighth International Colloquium of the Society for the Promotion of Eriugenean Studies: Chicago and Notre Dame, 18–20 October 1991 (with Willemiem Otten) 1994, The Encyclopedia of Apocalypticism, Vol. 2: Apocalypticism in Western History and Cultures 1998; contrib. articles in many books and journals. *Honours:* Fulbright-Hays Research Fellowship 1967–68, Research Fellow, Institute for Advanced Studies, Hebrew University, Jerusalem 1988–89, and Institute for Ecumenical and Cultural Research, St John's University 1992. *Address:* 5701 S Kenwood, Chicago, IL 60637, USA.

McGINN, Colin, MA, BPhil; British academic; *Professor, Department of Philosophy, Rutgers University;* b. 10 March 1950, s. of Joseph McGinn and June McGinn; one s. *Education:* Manchester and Oxford Univs. *Career:* lecturer, Univ. Coll. London 1974–85; Wilde Reader in Mental Philosophy, Oxford Univ. 1985–90; Prof., Rutgers Univ., USA 1990–. *Publications:* The Character of Mind 1981, The Subjective View 1982, Wittgenstein on Meaning 1984, Mental Content 1989, The Problem of Consciousness 1991, The Space Trap 1992, Moral Literacy 1992, Problems in Philosophy 1993, Mindsight: Image, Dream, Meaning 2005. *Honours:* John Locke Prize 1973. *Address:* Rutgers University, PO Box 2101, New Brunswick, NY 08903 (office); 270 West End Avenue, Apt 9E, New York, NY 10023, USA. *Telephone:* (908) 932-1766 (office). *Website:* www.philosophy.rutgers.edu (office).

McGINNISS, Joe, BS; American writer; b. 9 Dec. 1942, New York, NY. *Education:* Holy Cross College. *Career:* newspaper reporter 1964–68. *Publications:* The Selling of the President, 1968; The Dream Team, 1972; Heroes, 1976; Going to Extremes, 1980; Fatal Vision, 1983; Blind Faith, 1989; Cruel Doubt, 1991; Last Brother, 1993; The Miracle of Castel di Sangro, 1999. *Address:* c/o Elaine Koster, 55 Central Park W, Suite 6, New York, NY 10023, USA.

McGONIGAL, James, MA, MPhil, PhD; British educator and poet; *Professor of English in Education, University of Glasgow;* b. 20 May 1947, Dumfries, Scotland; m. Mary Alexander 1970; one s. three d. *Education:* Univ. of Glasgow. *Career:* high school English teacher 1971–84; coll. lecturer 1985–91; Head, Dept of Language and Literature, St Andrew's Coll. of Educ., Glasgow 1992–2003; Prof. of English in Educ., Univ. of Glasgow 2004–; mem. Council Asscn for Scottish Literary Studies; Ed. SCROLL (Scottish Cultural Review of Language and Literature) Rodopi, Amsterdam and New York. *Publications:* A Sort of Hot Scotland: New Writing Scotland 12 (with A. L. Kennedy) 1994,

Last Things First: New Writing Scotland 13 (with A. L. Kennedy) 1995, Sons of Ezra: British Poets and Ezra Pound (with M. Alexander) 1995, Full Strength Angels: New Writing Scotland 14 (with K. Jamie) 1996, Driven Home: Selected Poems 1998, Across the Water: 'Irishness' in Contemporary Scottish Literature (co-ed.) 2000, Scottish Religious Poems: From Columba to the Present (co-ed.) 2000, The Star You Steer By: Basil Bunting and British Modernism (co-ed.) 2000, Passage/An Pasaíste: Poems in Scots and Irish 2004. *Address:* Department of Curriculum Studies, Faculty of Education, University of Glasgow, 11 Eldon Street, Glasgow, G3 6NH, Scotland (office). *E-mail:* j.mcgonigal@educ.gla.ac.uk (office).

McGOUGH, Roger Joseph, CBE, MA, DLitt, FRSL; British poet and children's writer; b. 9 Nov. 1937, Liverpool; s. of Roger McGough and Mary McGarry; m. 1st Thelma Monaghan 1970 (divorced 1980); m. 2nd Hilary Clough 1986; three s. one d. *Education:* St Mary's Coll., Liverpool, Hull Univ. *Career:* Poetry Fellow Univ. of Loughborough 1973–75; writer-in-residence Western Australia Coll. of Educ., Perth 1986, Univ. of Hamburg 1994; Vice-Pres. The Poetry Society 1996– (mem. Exec. Council 1989–93); Fellow John Moores Univ. 1999; Trustee Chelsea Arts Club 1987–, fmr Chair.; Freeman City of Liverpool 2001. *Music:* wrote and performed Top Twenty hits Lily the Pink and Thank U Very Much 1968–69. *Plays include:* The Sound Collector and My Dad's a Fire-eater (for children); wrote lyrics for Broadway production of The Wind in the Willows 1984. *Plays for radio include:* Summer with Monika, FX, Walking the Dog. *Television:* Kurt, Mungo, B. P. and Me (Thames Television) 1985, The Elements (Channel 4) (Royal Television Soc. Award) 1993. *Publications:* The Mersey Sound (with Brian Patten and Adrian Henri) 1967, Watchwords 1969, After the Merrymaking 1971, Out of Sequence 1972, Gig 1972, Sporting Relations 1974, In the Glassroom 1976, Summer with Monika 1978, Holiday on Death Row 1979, Unlucky for Some 1981, Waving at Trains 1982, Melting into the Foreground 1986, Blazing Fruit: Selected Poems 1967–1987 1989, You at the Back 1991, Defying Gravity 1992, The Spotted Unicorn 1998, The Way Things Are 1999, Everyday Eclipses 2002, Collected Poems of Roger McGough 2003, Said and Done (memoir) 2005, Selected Poems 2006; for children: Mr Noselighter 1977, The Great Smile Robbery 1982, Sky in the Pie 1983, The Stowaways 1986, Noah's Ark 1986, Nailing the Shadow 1987, An Imaginary Menagerie 1988, Helen Highwater 1989, Counting by Numbers 1989, Pillow Talk 1990, The Lighthouse That Ran Away 1991, My Dad's a Fire-eater 1992, Another Custard Pie 1993, Lucky 1993, Stinkers Ahoy! 1995, The Magic Fountain 1995, The Kite and Caitlin 1996, Bad Bad Cats 1997, Until I Met Dudley 1998, Good Enough to Eat 2002, Moonthief 2002, The Bees' Knees 2002, Dotty Inventions 2002, What On Earth Can It Be? 2003; editor: Strictly Private 1981, The Kingfisher Book of Comic Verse 1986, The Kingfisher Books of Poems About Love 1997, The Ring of Words (anthology) 1998, Wicked Poems 2002, All the Best 2002, Sensational (anthology) 2004. *Honours:* Hon. Prof. Thames Valley Univ. 1993; Hon. MA (Nene Coll.) 1998, Hon. DLitt (Hull Univ.) 2004, (Univ. of Surrey) 2006; Signal Award 1984, 1998, BAFTA Awards 1984, 1992, Cholmondeley Award 1998, Centre for Literacy in Primary Educ. Award for Best Book of Poetry for Children 2004, 2005. *Literary Agent:* PFD, Drury House, 34–43 Russell Street, London, WC2B 5HA, England. *Telephone:* (20) 7344-1000. *Fax:* (20) 7836-9539. *E-mail:* personal@rogermcgough.org.uk (office). *Website:* www.rogermcgough.org.uk.

McGOVERN, Ann, BA; American writer, poet, collage artist and lecturer; b. 25 May 1930, New York, NY; m. Martin L. Scheiner 1970 (died 1992); three s. one d. *Education:* Univ. of New Mexico. *Career:* Publr The Privileged Traveler 1986–90; mem. Explorers Club, PEN, Authors' Guild, Soc. of Children's Book Writers, Women's Forum. *Publications include:* If You Lived in Colonial Times 1964, Too Much Noise 1967, Stone Soup 1968, The Secret Soldier 1975, Sharks 1976, Shark Lady, The Adventures of Eugenie Clark 1978, Playing with Penguins and Other Adventures in Antarctica 1994, Lady in the Box 1997, Adventures of the Shark Lady Eugenie Clark Around the World 1998; contrib. to Signature, Saturday Review, poetry in various literary magazines. *Honours:* Nat. Science Teachers Assn Outstanding Science Books 1976, 1979, 1984, 1993, Scholastic Publishing Inc. Author of the Year 1978, Cuffie Award 1998, First Prize, Artella's Poetry Contest. *Address:* 30 E 62nd Street, New York, NY 10021, USA.

MacGOWAN, Christopher John, BA, MA, PhD; British academic, writer and editor; *Professor of English, College of William and Mary, Williamsburg*; b. 6 Aug. 1948, London, England; m. Catherine Levesque 1988. *Education:* King's Coll., Cambridge, Princeton Univ., USA. *Career:* teaching assistantship, Pennsylvania State Univ. 1976–77; Research Asst, The Writings of Henry D. Thoreau 1981–83; Asst Prof. 1984–90, Assoc. Prof. 1990–96, Prof. 1996–, Coll. of William and Mary, Williamsburg, Virginia; mem. MLA, William Carlos Williams Soc. (pres. 1989–91). *Publications:* William Carlos Williams' Early Poetry: The Visual Arts Background 1984, The Collected Poems of William Carlos Williams, Vol. I 1909–1939 (co-ed.) 1986, Vol. II 1939–1962 (ed.) 1988, William Carlos Williams' Paterson (ed.) 1992, The Letters of Denise Levertov and William Carlos Williams (ed.) 1998, Poetry for Young People: William Carlos Williams (ed.), Twentieth-Century American Poetry 2003; contrib. to reference works and journals. *Honours:* King's Coll., Cambridge James Prize 1976, 1977, Princeton Univ. Graduate Fellowship 1977–81, Coll. of William and Mary summer grants 1985, 1987, 1989, Nat. Endowment for the Humanities summer stipend 1986, and Fellowship 1990–91. *Address:* c/o Department of English, College of William and Mary, Williamsburg, VA 23187, USA (office).

McGRATH, Alister Edgar, BA, BD, MA, DD, DPhil, FRSA; British academic and writer; *Professor of Historical Theology, University of Oxford*; b. 23 Jan. 1953, Belfast, Northern Ireland; m. Joanna Ruth Collicutt 1980; one s. one d. *Education:* University of Oxford. *Career:* Curate, St Leonards Parish Church, Wollaton, Nottingham, 1980–83; Lecturer in Historical and Systematic Theology 1983–95, Prin. 1995–2004, Wycliffe Hall, Oxford; mem. Faculty of Theology, 1983–, Univ. Research Lecturer in Theology, 1993–99, Prof. of Historical Theology, Univ. of Oxford 1999–; Research Prof. of Systematic Theology, Regent Coll., Vancouver, BC 1993–97. *Publications:* Luther's Theology of the Cross, 1985; Iustitia Dei: A History of the Christian Doctrine of Justification, 1986; The Intellectual Origins of the European Reformation, 1987; Reformation Thought: An Introduction, 1988; Explaining Your Faith Without Losing Your Friends, 1989, revised edn as Explaining Your Faith, 1996; A Life of John Calvin, 1990; The Genesis of Doctrine, 1990; Making Sense of the Cross, 1992; What Was God Doing on the Cross?, 1992; The Dilemma of Self-Esteem: The Cross and Christian Confidence, 1992; Suffering, 1992; Understanding Doctrine: Its Relevance and Purpose for Today, 1992; The Blackwell Encyclopedia of Modern Christian Thought (ed.), 1993; The Renewal of Anglicanism, 1993; Intellectuals Don't Need God and Other Modern Myths: Building Bridges to Faith Through Apologetics, 1993; The Making of Modern German Christology, 1750–1990, 1994; Spirituality in an Age of Change: Rediscovering the Spirit of the Reformers, 1994; Christian Theology: An Introduction, 1994; How Shall We Reach Them? (with Michael Green), 1995; Evangelicalism and the Future of Christianity, 1995; Beyond the Quiet Time: Practical Evangelical Spirituality, 1995; Suffering and God, 1995; The Christian Theology Reader (ed.), 1995; A Passion for Truth: The Intellectual Coherence of Evangelicalism, 1996; An Introduction to Christianity, 1997; The NIV Bible Companion: A Basic Commentary on the Old and New Testaments, 1997; J. I. Packer: A Biography (UK edn as To Know and Serve God), 1997; The Foundations of Dialogue in Science and Religion, 1998; Historical Theology: An Introduction to the History of Christian Thought, 1998; 'I Believe': Exploring the Apostles' Creed, 1998; Christian Spirituality: An Introduction, 1999; The Unknown God: Searching for Spiritual Fulfilment, 1999; Science and Religion: An Introduction, 1999; The Hodder Dictionary of Bible Themes (gen. ed.), 1999; The NIV Thematic Reference Bible (gen. ed.), 1999; Christian Literature: An Anthology (ed.), 2000; The J. I. Packer Collection (ed.), 2000; The Journey: A Pilgrim in the Lands of the Spirit, 2000; In the Beginning: The Story of the King James Bible, 2001; The Reenchantment of Nature: Science, Religion and the Human Sense of Wonder 2003, The Twilight of Atheism 2004, Dawkins' God 2004, The Dawkins Delusion? (with Joanna Collicutt McGrath) 2007. *Address:* c/o Wycliffe Hall, 54 Banbury Road, Oxford OX2 6PW, England.

McGRATH, Patrick, BA; British writer; b. 7 Feb. 1950, London, England; m. Maria Aitken. *Education:* Univ. of London and Simon Fraser Univ., Burnaby, BC. *Career:* Managing Ed., Speech Technology magazine 1982–87. *Publications:* The Lewis and Clark Expedition 1985, Blood and Water and Other Tales (short story collection) 1988, The Grotesque (novel) 1989, New York Life or, Friends and Others 1990, Spider (novel and screenplay) 1990, Dr Haggard's Disease (novel) 1993, Asylum (novel) 1996, Martha Peake: A Novel of the Revolution (novel) 2000, Port Mungo (novel) 2004, Ghost Town: Tales of Manhattan Then and Now (non-fiction) 2005; contrib. to periodicals. *Literary Agent:* c/o Deborah Rogers, Rogers, Coleridge & White, 20 Powis Mews, London, W11 1JN, England. *Telephone:* (20) 7221-3717. *Fax:* (20) 7229-9084.

MacGREGOR, David Roy, BA, MA, ARIBA, FRHistS; British writer; b. 26 Aug. 1925, London, England; m. Patricia Margaret Aline Purcell-Gilpin 1962. *Education:* Trinity College, Cambridge, Hammersmith School of Building. *Career:* mem. Soc. of Nautical Research (council mem. 1959–63, 1965–69, 1974–77, 1980–85, hon. vice-pres. 1985), Maritime Trust. *Publications:* The Tea Clippers, 1952; The China Bird, 1961; Fast Sailing Ships 1775–1875, 1973; Clipper Ships, 1977; Merchant Sailing Ships 1775–1815, 1980; Merchant Sailing Ships 1815–1850, 1984; Merchant Sailing Ships 1858–1875, 1984. Contributions: Mariner's Mirror; Journal of Nautical Archaeology. *Honours:* Gold Medal, Daily Express 1973. *Address:* 99 Lonsdale Road, London SW13 9DA, England.

McGREGOR, Iona, BA; British writer; b. 7 Feb. 1929, Aldershot, England. *Education:* University of Bristol. *Career:* mem. Scottish PEN. *Publications:* Fiction: Death Wore a Diadem, 1989; Alice in Shadowtime, 1992. Children's Fiction: An Edinburgh Reel, 1968; The Popinjay, 1969; The Burning Hill, 1970; The Tree of Liberty, 1972; The Snake and the Olive, 1974. Non-Fiction: Edinburgh and Eastern Lowlands, 1979; Wallace and Bruce, 1986; Importance of Being Earnest, 1987; Huckleberry Finn, 1988. *Honours:* Writer's Bursary, Scottish Arts Council, 1989.

McGUANE, Thomas Francis, III, BA, MFA; American writer; b. 11 Dec. 1939, Wyandotte, MI; m. 1st Portia Rebecca Crockett 1962 (divorced 1975); one s.; m. 2nd Margot Kidder 1976 (divorced 1977); one d.; m. 3rd Laurie Buffett 1977; one step-d. one d. *Education:* Univ. of Michigan, Olivet Coll., Michigan State Univ., Yale Univ., Stanford Univ. *Publications:* The Sporting Club 1969, The Bushwacked Piano 1971, Ninety-Two in the Shade 1973, Panama 1977, An Outside Chance: Essays on Sports (revised edn as An Outside Chance: Classic and New Essays on Sports) 1980, Nobody's Angel 1982, In the Crazies: Book and Portfolio 1984, Something to Be Desired 1984, To Skin a Cat 1986, Silent Seasons: Twenty-One Fishing Stories 1988, Keep the Change 1989, Nothing but Blue Skies 1992, Some Horses 1999, The Cadence of Grass 2002, Gallatin Canyon 2006. *Honours:* Wallace Stegner

Fellowship Stanford Univ. 1966–67, Dr hc (Montana State Univ.) 1993, (Rocky Mountain Coll.) 1995; American Acad. of Arts and Letters Richard and Hinda Rosenthal Foundation Award 1971. *Address:* PO Box 25, McLeod, MT 59052, USA.

McGUCKIAN, Medbh, BA, MA; Northern Irish poet and teacher; b. 12 Aug. 1950, Belfast; m. John McGuckian 1977; three s. one d. *Education:* Queen's Univ., Belfast. *Career:* teacher, Dominican Convent, Fortwilliam Park, Belfast 1974; instructor, St Patrick's Coll., Knock, Belfast 1975–; writer-in-residence, Queen's Univ., Belfast 1986–88. *Publications:* poetry: Single Ladies: Sixteen Poems 1980, Portrait of Joanna 1980, Trio Poetry (with Damian Gorman and Douglas Marshall) 1981, The Flower Master 1982, The Greenhouse 1983, Venus and the Rain 1984, The Big Striped Golfing Umbrella: Poems by Young People from Northern Ireland (ed.) 1985, On Ballycastle Beach 1988, Two Women, Two Shores 1989, Marconi's Cottage 1991, The Flower Master and Other Poems 1993, Captain Lavender 1994, Drawing Ballerinas 2001, The Face of the Earth 2004. *Honours:* Nat. Poetry Competition Prize 1979, Eric Gregory Award 1980, Rooney Prize 1982, Ireland Arts Council Award 1982, Alice Hunt Bartlett Award 1983, Cheltenham Literature Festival Poetry Competition Prize 1989. *Address:* c/o Gallery Press, Oldcastle, County Meath, Ireland.

McGUINNESS, Frank, MPhil.; Irish playwright and academic; *Lecturer in English Literature, University College Dublin;* b. 29 July 1953, Buncrana, Donegal; s. of Patrick McGuinness and Celine McGuinness. *Education:* University Coll. Dublin. *Career:* Lecturer in English, Univ. of Ulster, Coleraine 1977–79, Univ. Coll. Dublin 1979–80, St Patrick's Coll., Maynooth 1984–97; Writer-in-Residence, School of English and Drama, Univ. Coll. Dublin 1997–; Dir Abbey Theatre, Dublin 1992–96. *Publications:* The Factory Girls 1982, Observe the Sons of Ulster Marching towards the Somme 1985, Baglady 1985, Innocence 1986, Rosmersholm, A Version 1987, Scout 1987, Yerma: A Version 1987, Carthaginians 1988, The Hen House 1989, Peer Gynt, A Version 1989, Mary and Lizzie 1989, Three Sisters, A Version 1990, The Bread Man 1990, The Threepenny Opera, A Version 1991, Someone Who'll Watch Over Me 1992, The Bird Sanctuary 1994, Hedda Gabler, A Version 1994, Uncle Vanya, A Version 1995, Booterstown: Poems 1995, Selected Plays: Vol. I 1996, The Dazzling Dark: Introduction 1996, A Doll's House: A Version 1996, The Caucasian Chalk Circle: A Version 1997, Electra: A Version 1997, Mutabilitie 1997, Dancing at Lughnasa: A Screenplay 1998, The Storm: A Version 1998, Dolly West's Kitchen 1999, The Sea With No Ships: Poems 1999, Miss Julie: A Version 2000, The Barbaric Comedies 2000, Gates of Gold 2002, The Stone Jug (poems) 2003, Hecuba 2004, Speaking Like Magpies 2005, Phaedra 2006, There Came a Gypsy Riding 2007, Ghosts (A Version) 2007, Supper With Judas 2007. *Honours:* Officier des Arts et Lettres; Hon. DLitt (Ulster) 2000; Harvey's Award, Evening Standard Drama Award, Ewart-Biggs Peace Prize, Cheltenham Literary Prize, Fringe First, Irish American Literary Prize 1992, Independent on Sunday Best Play 1992, New York Drama Critics' Award 1993, Writers' Guild Award 1993, Tony Award for Best Revival 1997. *Address:* School of English and Drama, Department of Anglo-Irish Literature, University College Dublin, Belfield, Dublin 4, Ireland (office). *Telephone:* (1) 7168420 (office). *E-mail:* englishanddrama@ucd.ie (office). *Website:* www.ucd.ie/englishanddrama (office).

McGURN, Barrett, AB; American writer; b. 6 Aug. 1914, New York, NY; m. Janice Ann McLaughlin 1962; five s. one d. *Education:* Fordham Univ., New York. *Career:* reporter New York and Paris Herald Tribune 1935–66; Bureau Chief Herald Tribune, Rome, Paris, Moscow 1946–62; mem. Overseas Press Club of America (pres. 1963–65), Foreign Press Asscn in Italy (pres. 1961, 1962), Nat. Press Club, Cosmos Club (Washington, DC). *Publications:* Decade in Europe 1958, A Reporter Looks at the Vatican 1960, A Reporter Looks at American Catholicism 1966, America's Court, The Supreme Court and the People 1997, Pilgrim's Guide to Rome 1999, Yank, The Army Weekly, Covering the Greatest Generation 2004; contrib. to Reader's Digest, Catholic Digest, Commonweal, Colliers, Yank. *Honours:* Hon. DLitt (Fordham Univ.) 1958; Long Island Univ. Polk Award 1956, Overseas Press Club Award 1957; Cavaliere Ufficiale, Italian Nat. Order of Merit 1961, Meritorious Honor Award, US State Dept 1971. *Address:* 5229 Duvall Drive, Bethesda, MD 20816-1875, USA. *Telephone:* (301) 229-7439. *E-mail:* jmcgurn@erols.com.

McGWIRE, Michael Kane, OBE, BSc; British writer, fmr Royal Navy Commander, fmr academic and foreign policy analyst; b. 9 Dec. 1924, Madras (now Chennai), India; m. Helen Jean Scott 1952; two s. three d. *Education:* Royal Naval Coll., Dartmouth and Univ. of Wales. *Career:* officer, Royal Navy 1942–67; Prof., Dalhousie Univ. 1971–79; Sr Fellow, Brookings Institution, Washington, DC 1979–90; Visiting Prof., Univ. of Cambridge 1990–93; Hon. Prof. of Int. Politics, Univ. of Wales 1997. *Publications:* Military Objectives and Soviet Foreign Policy 1987, Perestroika and Soviet National Security 1991, NATO Expansion and European Security 1997; editor: Soviet Naval Developments 1973, Soviet Naval Policy 1975, Soviet Naval Influence 1977; contrib. to over 40 books and numerous journals, most recently Int. Affairs. *Address:* Hayes, Durlston, Swanage, Dorset BH19 2JF, England.

McHUGH, Heather, BA, MA; American academic, poet, writer and translator; *Professor of English, University of Washington;* b. 20 Aug. 1948, San Diego, CA; m. Nikolai Popov. *Education:* Radcliffe Coll., Harvard Univ., Univ. of Denver. *Career:* Assoc. Prof., SUNY at Binghamton 1974–83; Core Faculty, MFA Program for Writers, Goddard Coll., later Warren Wilson Coll. 1976–; Milliman Distinguished Writer-in-Residence and Prof. of English, Univ. of

Washington 1984–; Holloway Lecturer in Poetry, Univ. of California at Berkeley 1987; Visiting Prof., Univ. of Iowa 1991–92, 1995, Univ. of California at Los Angeles 1994, Univ. of California at Irvine 1994; Coal-Royalty Chair in Poetry, Univ. of Alabama, Tuscaloosa 1992; Elliston Prof. of Poetry, Univ. of Cincinnati 1993; Visiting Lecturer, Univ. of Bergen, Norway 1994; mem. Acad. of American Poets (bd of chancellors 1999–), American Acad. of Arts and Sciences. *Publications:* poetry: Dangers 1977, A World of Difference 1981, To the Quick 1987, Shades 1988, Hinge & Sign: Poems 1968–1993 1994, The Father of the Predicaments (Poems 1993–1998) 1999, Eyeshot 2003; essays: Broken English: Poetry and Partiality 1993; translator: D'Apres Tout: Poems by Jean Follain 1981, Because the Sea is Black: Poems by Blaga Dimitrova (with Niko Boris) 1989; other: Where Are They Now? (with Tom Phillips) 1990, Glottal Stop: 101 Poems by Paul Celan (with Nikolai Popov); contrib. to many anthologies and journals. *Honours:* National Endowment for the Arts Grants 1974, 1979, 1981, Pushcart Prizes 1978 et seq, Guggenheim Fellowship 1989, Woodrow Wilson Nat. Poetry Fellow 1992–93, Daniel A. Pollack Prize, Harvard Univ. and Harvard Coll. Library 1995, Bingham Prize, Boston Book Review 1995, TLS Int. Book of the Year List 1995, Lila Wallace/Reader's Digest Writing Award 1996–99, O. D. Hardison Award 1998, PEN Voelker Prize 2000. *Address:* c/o Department of English, Box 354330, University of Washington, Seattle, WA 98195, USA.

McILVANNEY, William, MA; Scottish writer and poet; b. 25 Nov. 1936, Kilmarnock, Ayrshire. *Education:* Univ. of Glasgow. *Career:* English teacher 1960–75. *Publications:* novels: Remedy is None (Geoffrey Faber Memorial Prize 1967) 1966, A Gift from Nessus (Scottish Arts Council Book Award) 1968, Docherty (Whitbread Novel Award, Scottish Arts Council Book Award) 1975, Laidlaw (CWA Macallan Silver Dagger for Fiction) 1977, The Papers of Tony Veitch (CWA Macallan Silver Dagger for Fiction) 1983, The Big Man 1985, In Through the Head 1988, Strange Loyalties 1991, The Kiln (Saltire Soc. Scottish Book of the Year Award) 1996, Weekend 2006; poetry: The Longships in Harbour: Poems 1970, Landscapes and Figures (poems to accompany eight etchings by Norman Ackroyd) 1973, These Words: Weddings and After (essay and poems) 1984, Walking Wounded (Glasgow Herald People's Prize 1990) 1989, Surviving the Shipwreck (poems and essays) 1991; non-fiction: Shades of Grey: Glasgow 1956–1987 1990. *Address:* c/o Sceptre, 338 Euston Road, London, NW1 3BH, England (office).

McINERNEY, Jay; American writer; b. 1955; m. 1st Linda Rossiter; m. 2nd Merry Raymond; m. 3rd Helen Bransford 1991; one s. one d. *Education:* Williams Univ. *Publications include:* Bright Lights, Big City 1984, Ransom 1986, Story of My Life 1988, Brightness Falls 1992, The Last of the Savages 1996, Model Behavior 1998, How It Ended 2000, The Good Life (novel) 2006, A Hedonist in the Cellar: Adventures in Wine 2006. *Address:* c/o Bloomsbury Publishing Plc, 36 Soho Square, London, W1D 3QY, England.

McINNIS, (Harry) Donald, AB; American writer and dramatist; b. 18 April 1916, Worcester, MA; m. Marjorie E. Graber 1948; two s. two d. *Education:* Clark University, American University, Johns Hopkins University. *Career:* mem. Australian Writers Guild; US Dramatists Guild. *Publications:* The Running Years, 1986; Cobwebs and Twigs, 1990; Will – Man from Stratford (play), 1992; New Work No Lines (play), 1994. *Honours:* special awards, US Government, Government of Guatemala, Republic of Korea. *Address:* 22 Chauvel Circle, Chapman, ACT 2611, Australia.

McINTOSH, Fiona; British (b. Australian) magazine editor; m.; two d. *Career:* worked on Melbourne Herald; moved to UK, where London correspondent for Australian newspapers; feature writer, Daily Mirror newspaper, later Ed. women's page and Deputy Features Ed.; Ed. Company magazine 1995–98; Ed. Elle magazine from 1998, including launch Ed. Elle Girl magazine 2001; fmr Ed. ES magazine; launch Ed.-in-Chief Grazia magazine 2005–. *Address:* Grazia, Endeavour House, 189 Shaftesbury Avenue, London, WC2H 8JD, England (office). *Website:* www.graziamagazine.co.uk.

MacINTYRE, Alasdair, BA, MA; British philosopher, academic and writer; *Research Professor of Philosophy, University of Notre Dame;* b. 12 Jan. 1929, Glasgow, Scotland. *Education:* Queen Mary Coll., London, Manchester Univ., Univ. of Oxford. *Career:* Lecturer, Manchester Univ. 1951–57, Leeds Univ. 1957–61; Research Fellow, Nuffield Coll., Oxford 1961–62; Sr Fellow, Princeton Univ. 1962–63; Fellow, Univ. Coll., Oxford 1963–66; Riddell Lecturer, Univ. of Newcastle upon Tyne 1964; Bampton Lecturer, Columbia Univ. 1966; Prof. of the History of Ideas, Brandeis Univ. 1969–72; Dean Coll. of Liberal Arts 1972–73, Prof. of Philosophy and Political Science 1972–80, Boston Univ.; Henry Luce Prof., Wellesley Coll. 1980–82; W. Alton Jones Prof., Vanderbilt Univ. 1982–88; Gifford Lecturer, Univ. of Edinburgh 1988; Henry Luce Scholar, Yale Univ. 1988–89; McMahon/Hank Prof. 1988–94, Research Prof. of Philosophy 2000–, Univ. of Notre Dame, IN; Prof. of Arts and Sciences, Duke Univ. 1995–2000; mem. American Acad. of Arts and Sciences, British Acad. (corresponding mem.). *Publications:* Marxism and Christianity 1953, The Unconscious 1957, Short History of Ethics 1966, Against the Self-Images of the Age 1971, After Virtue: A Study in Moral Theory 1981, Whose Justice? Which Rationality? 1988, Three Rival Versions of Moral Enquiry 1990, First Principles, Final Ends and Contemporary Philosophy 1990, Dependent-Rational Animals 1999. *Honours:* hon. mem. Royal Irish Acad. *Address:* c/o Philosophy Department, University of Notre Dame, Notre Dame, IN 46556, USA.

McINTYRE, Ian James, BA, MA; British writer and broadcaster; b. 9 Dec. 1931, Banchory, Kincardineshire, Scotland; m. Leik Sommerfelt Vogt 1954;

two s. two d. *Education:* St John's Coll., Cambridge, College of Europe, Bruges, Belgium. *Career:* Ed. At Home and Abroad 1959; Programme Services Officer, ITA 1961; Dir of Information Research, Scottish Conservative Cen. Office 1964–70, contested Roxburgh, Selkirk and Peebles 1966; writer, broadcaster 1970–76; Main Presenter Analysis programme, BBC Radio 4 1970–76, Controller BBC Radio 4 1976–78, BBC Radio 3 1978–87; Assoc. Ed. The Times, London, 1989–90. *Radio includes:* writer and presenter of several BBC Radio 3 programmes including Yanks & Limeys. *Publications:* The Proud Doers: Israel After Twenty Years 1968, Words: Reflections on the Uses of Language (ed. and contrib.) 1975, Dogfight: The Transatlantic Battle over Airbus 1992, The Expense of Glory: A Life of John Reith 1993, Dirt and Deity: A Life of Robert Burns 1996, Garrick 1999, Joshua Reynolds: The Life and Times of the First President of the Royal Academy 2003; contribs to The Listener, The Times, The Independent. *Honours:* Theatre Book Prize 1999. *Address:* Spylaw House, Newlands Avenue, Radlett, Herts., WD7 8EL, England (home). *Telephone:* (1923) 543532 (home). *E-mail:* ian.mcintyre@waitrose.com (home).

MACINTYRE, Stuart Forbes, MA, PhD; Australian academic and writer; *Ernest Scott Professor of History, University of Melbourne;* b. 21 April 1947, Melbourne, Vic.; m. 1st Margaret Joan Geddes 1970; m. 2nd Martha Adele Bruton 1976; two d. *Education:* Univ. of Melbourne, Monash Univ., Univ. of Cambridge. *Career:* Tutor in History, Murdoch Univ., Perth 1976, Lecturer in History 1979; Research Fellow, St John's Coll., Cambridge 1977–78; Lecturer, Univ. of Melbourne 1980–84, Sr Lecturer 1984–86, Reader in History 1987–90, Ernest Scott Prof. 1990–, Dean Faculty of Arts 1999–; mem. Acad. of the Social Sciences in Australia, Australian Acad. of the Humanities. *Publications:* A Proletarian Science: Marxism in Britain 1917–1933 1980, Little Moscows 1980, Militant: The Life and Times of Paddy Troy 1983, Ormond College Centenary Essays (ed.) 1983, Making History (ed.) 1984, Winners and Losers: The Pursuit of Social Justice in Australian History 1985, The Oxford History of Australia, Vol. IV 1986, Foundations of Arbitration (ed.) 1989, The Labour Experiment 1989, Through White Eyes (ed.) 1990, A Colonial Liberalism: The Lost World of Three Victorian Visionaries 1990, A History for a Nation 1995, The Discovery of Australian History (ed.) 1995, The Reds: The Communist Party of Australia, from Origins to Illegality 1998, The Oxford Companion to Australian History (ed.) 1998, A Concise History of Australia 1999, True Believers (ed.) 2001, A Short History of the University of Melbourne 2003, The History Wars 2003, The Historian's Conscience (ed.) 2004, The New Province for Law and Order (ed.) 2004; contrib. to professional journals. *Address:* c/o Department of History, University of Melbourne, Parkville, Vic. 3052 (office); 10 Ferriman Street, W Brunswick, Vic. 3055, Australia (home). *Telephone:* (3) 83445242 (office); (3) 93802650 (home). *E-mail:* s.macintyre@unimelb.edn.au (office).

McIVER, Susan Bertha, BA, MSc, PhD; Canadian (b. American) writer and biologist; b. 6 Nov. 1940, Hutchinson, KS; d. of Ernest D. McIver and Thelma Faye McIver (née McCrory). *Education:* Univ. of California at Riverside and Washington State Univ. *Career:* Research Scientist, Asst Prof. of Parasitology Univ. of Toronto, Canada 1967–72, Assoc. Prof. of Microbiology and Parasitology 1972–80, Prof. of Zoology and of Microbiology 1980–84; Prof., Chair. of Environmental Biology Univ. of Guelph, ON, Canada 1984–90; Consultant in Entomology US Army 1975–79, 1986–89; Consultant Study Group on Tropical Medicine and Parasitology, NIH 1983–85; full-time writer 1990–; Coroner BC Coroners Service 1993–2003; Dir Women-in-Crisis 1980–87, Chair. 1988–89; mem. Entomological Soc., Biological Council of Canada, Entomological Soc. of America, Canadian Soc. of Zoology, American Soc. of Parasitology, Canadian Microscopic Soc., Mosquito Control Asscn; Int. Fellowship in Tropical Medicine 1973; Medical Research Council Fellowship 1978. *Publications include:* Medical Nightmares: The Human Face of Error 2001; more than 100 scientific research papers and articles 1964–90 and numerous short stories 1990–; approx. 600 articles on agriculture and civic affairs for gen. public in newspapers and magazines. *Honours:* C. Gordon Hewitt Award, Entomological Soc. of Canada 1978, 125th Confed. Anniversary Silver Medal for Contribs to Community, Compatriots and Canada. *Address:* POB 968, Penticton, BC V2A 7N7 (office); 10214 Haddrell Avenue, Summerland, BC V0H 1Z8, Canada (home). *Telephone:* (250) 494-9081 (office). *Fax:* (250) 494-9081 (office). *E-mail:* smciver@shaw.ca.

MACK, William P., BS; American naval officer (retd) and writer; b. 6 Aug. 1915, Hillsboro, IL; m. Ruth McMillian 1939, one s. one d. *Education:* US Naval Acad., National War College, George Washington University. *Career:* US Naval Officer, 1935–75; Deputy Asst Secretary of Defense, 1968–71. *Publications:* Non-Fiction: Naval Officers Guide, 1958; Naval Customs, Traditions and Usage, 1978; Command at Sea, 1980. Fiction: South to Java, 1988; Pursuit of the Sea Wolf, 1991; Checkfire, 1992; New Guinea, 1993; Straits of Messina, 1994; Lieutenant Christopher Captain Kulburnie. Contributions: various publications. *Honours:* Alfred Thayer Mahan Award for Literary Excellence, Navy League, 1982.

McKAY, Donald Fleming, BA, MA, PhD; Canadian poet, writer and editor; b. 25 June 1942, Owen Sound, ON; m. (divorced); one s. one d. *Education:* Bishop's University, University of Ontario, University College, Swansea, Wales. *Career:* teacher, University of New Brunswick, 1990–96; Ed., The Fiddlehead; mem. League of Canadian Poets; PEN; Writers' Union of Canada. *Publications:* Air Occupies Space, 1973; Long Sault, 1975; Lependu, 1978; Lightning Ball Bait, 1980; Birding, or Desire, 1983; Sanding Down This Rocking Chair on a Windy Night, 1987; Night Field, 1991; Apparatus, 1997;

Another Gravity, 2000. Contributions: periodicals. *Honours:* Canadian Authors' Asscn Award for Poetry, 1983; Governor-General's Award for Poetry, 1991; National Magazine Award for Poetry, 1991. *Address:* 434 Richmond Avenue, Victoria, BC V8S 3Y4, Canada.

MACKAY, James Alexander, (Ian Angus, William Finlay, Bruce Garden, Alex Matheson, Peter Whittington), MA, DLitt; British author and journalist; b. 21 Nov. 1936, Inverness, Scotland; m. 1st Mary Patricia Jackson 1960 (divorced 1972); one s. one d.; m. 2nd Renate Finlay-Freundlich 1992. *Education:* Glasgow University. *Career:* Philatelic Columnist The New Daily 1962–67; Columnist Financial Times 1967–85; Ed.-in-Chief IPC Stamp Encyclopaedia 1968–72; Antiques Advisory Ed. Ward Lock 1972–79; Ed. The Burns Chronicle 1977–91, The Postal Annual 1978–90, The Burnsian 1986–89, Seaby Coin and Medal Bulletin 1990–92, Coin Yearbook 1994–, Medal Yearbook 1995–, Stamp Yearbook 1996–, Banknotes Yearbook 2001–; Consultant Ed. Antiques Today 1992–94, Stamp and Coin Mart 1993–, Coin News 1994–, International Stamp and Exhibition News 1996–; General Ed. Encyclopedia of World Facts 1999–2001; mem. Burns Federation, exec. council 1977–95; Glasgow Philatelic Society, Pres. 2001–02, Sec. 2005–; West of Scotland Numismatic Soc., Sec. 1992–, Pres. 2003–06. *Publications:* The Tapling Collection 1964, Glass Paperweights 1973, The Dictionary of Stamps in Colour 1973, The Dictionary of Western Sculptors in Bronze 1977, The Guinness Book of Stamps Facts and Feats 1982, Complete Works of Robert Burns 1986, Complete Letters of Burns 1987, Burns A–Z: The Complete Word Finder 1990, Burns: A Biography 1992, Vagabond of Verse: A Life of Robert W. Service 1993, William Wallace: Brave Heart 1994, The Eye Who Never Slept: A Life of Allan Pinkerton 1995, Michael Collins: A Life 1996, Sounds Out of Silence: A Life of Alexander Graham Bell 1997, Thomas Lipton 1998, John Paul Jones 1998, Clans and Tartans of Scotland 2000, Fans 2000, Scotland's Posts 2001, Glasgow's Other River 2001, Antiques at a Glance, four vols 2002, Soldiering on St Kilda 2002, Collect British Coins 2004, Stamps and Stamp Collecting 2005, Glasgow: A History and a Celebration 2005, Coins and Coin Collecting 2006, St Kilda Steamers 2006; contrib. to numerous publications. *Honours:* Silver Medal Amphilex Amsterdam 1965; Vermeil Medals Spellman Foundation, USA 1982, 1987, 1990, Thomas Field Award for Services to Irish Philatelic Literature 1983, Saltire Book of the Year 1993, Gold Medal American Philatelic Society 1998. *Address:* 67 Braidpark Drive, Glasgow, G46 6LY, Scotland.

MACKAY, Shena, FRSL; British writer; b. 6 June 1944, Edinburgh, Scotland; d. of Benjamin Mackey and Morag Mackey (née Carmichael); m. Robin Brown 1964 (divorced 1982); three d. *Education:* Tonbridge Girls' Grammar School, Kent and Kidbrooke Comprehensive, London. *Career:* began career working in antique shop, Chancery Lane, London. *Publications:* Dust Falls on Eugene Schlumberger 1964, Toddler on the Run 1964, Music Upstairs 1965, Old Crow 1967, An Advent Calendar 1971, Babies in Rhinestones 1983, A Bowl of Cherries 1984, Redhill Rococo 1986, Dreams of Dead Women's Handbags 1987, Dunedin 1992, The Laughing Academy 1993, Such Devoted Sisters (ed) 1993, Collected Stories 1994, The Orchard on Fire 1996, Friendship (ed) 1997, The Artist's Widow 1998, The World's Smallest Unicorn 1999, Heligoland 2003. *Honours:* Hon. Visiting Prof. to MA in Writing, Univ. of Middlesex 2000–03; Fawcett Prize 1987, Scottish Arts Council Awards, Soc. of Authors Award. *Literary Agent:* c/o Rogers, Coleridge & White Literary Agency, 20 Powis Mews, London, W11 1JN, England. *Telephone:* (20) 7221-3717. *Fax:* (20) 7229-9084. *Website:* www.rcwlitagency.co.uk.

MACKAY, Simon (see Nicole, Christopher Robin)

McKEAN, John Maule Laurie, BArch, MA, ARIBA; British academic and writer; *Professor of Architecture, University of Brighton;* b. 7 Nov. 1943, Glasgow, Scotland; m. Mary Tetlow; two s. one d. *Education:* Univs of Strathclyde and Essex. *Career:* architect in practice 1966–67, 1969–71; Teacher of Architectural Design, Univ. of Ceylon 1968–69, Univ. of East London, 1976–80, Univ. of North London 1980–90; Teacher of Design and Architectural History, Univ. of North London 1983–88, Univ. of Middlesex 1984–88; Dir of Interior Architecture, Univ. of Brighton 1990–95, Prof. of Architecture 1996–; mem. Critics' Circle of Int. Asscn of Architects, 1990. *Publications:* Architecture of the Western World (co-author) 1980, Learning from Segal 1989, Royal Festival Hall 1991, Crystal Palace 1994, Leicester Engineering Building 1994, Alexander Thomson (co-author) 1995, The Parthenon 1996, C. R. Mackintosh (co-author) 1996, Mackintosh Pocket Guide (8th edition) 1998, C.R. Mackintosh: Architect, Artist, Icon 2000, Giancarlo De Carlo, Layered Places 2004, La Modernite Critique autour du CIAM9 (co-author) 2006, The Man-Made Future (co-author) 2007; contribs to Architects' Journal, Building Design, Spazio e Società, Milan, Architectural History, Journal of Architecture. *Honours:* two AIA Int. Book Awards 1994, 1995, Architects' Journal Books of the Year 2001, 2004. *Address:* The New Banister Fletcher Project, 140 Dyke Road, Brighton, East Sussex, BN1 5PA, England (office). *E-mail:* NBF@clara.co.uk (office).

McKEE, David, (Roc Almirall, Violet Easton); British children's writer and illustrator; b. Devon. *Education:* Plymouth Art Coll. *Career:* started career drawing cartoons for Punch, Reader's Digest, Times Educational Supplement; created popular children's characters for books and TV, including Mr Benn, King Rollo, Elmer the Patchwork Elephant; co-founder King Rollo Films; illustrated numerous Paddington Bear books. *Television:* Mr Benn (series), King Rollo (series), also co-writer Towser, Spot the Dog children's series. *Publications include:* Two Can Toucan 1964, Tusk Tusk 1978, Not Now,

Bernard 1980, I Hate My Teddybear 1982, King Rollo and the Letter 1984, Two Monsters 1985, The Hill and the Rock 1985, The Sad Story of Veronica 1987, Snow Woman 1987, Who's a Clever Baby Then? 1988, The Monster and the Teddy Bear 1989, Zebra's Hiccups 1991, Elmer 1989, Elmer Again 1991, Elmer on Stilts 1993, The School Bus Comes at 8 o'clock 1993, Isabel's Noisy Tummy 1994, Elmer and Wilbur 1994, Elmer in the Snow 1995, Charlotte's Piggy Bank 1996, Elmer and the Wind 1997, Prince Peter and the Teddy Bear 1997, Elmer Plays Hide and Seek 1998, Elmer and the Lost Teddy 1999, Mary's Secret 1999, Elmer and the Stranger 2000, Elmer and Grandpa Eldo 2001, King Rollo and the New Stockings 2001, Mr Benn – Gladiator 2001, Elmer's Concert 2001, Elmer and Butterfly 2002, Elmer's New Friend 2002, Elmer and the Hippos 2003, The Adventures of Charmin the Bear 2003, Who is Mrs Green? 2003, The Conquerors 2004, Charlotte's Piggy Bank 2004, Three Monsters 2005, Four Red Apples 2006. *Address:* c/o Andersen Press Publicity Department, 20 Vauxhall Bridge Road, London, SW1V 2SA, England (office). *E-mail:* andersenpress@randomhouse.co.uk (office).

McKEE, Louis, BA; American poet, writer and editor; b. 31 July 1951, Philadelphia, PA; m. Christine Caruso 1978 (divorced 1982). *Education:* LaSalle Coll., Temple Univ. *Career:* Ed., Painted Bride Quarterly 1984–88, One Trick Pony 1997–; Co-Ed., Axe Factory Review 1984–; mem. Acad. of American Poets, PEN, Poetry Soc. of America, Poets and Writers. *Publications:* Schuylkill Country 1982, The True Speed of Things 1984, Safe Water 1986, No Matter 1987, Oranges 1989, Angelus 1990, Three Poems 1993, River Architecture: Poems from Here and There: Selected Poems, 1973–1993 1999, Right as Rain 2000, Greatest Hits 1973–2003 2003, Near Occasions of Sin 2006; contrib. to anthologies, reviews, quarterlies and journals. *Address:* 8460 Frankford Avenue, Philadelphia, PA 19136, USA. *E-mail:* lmckee4148@aol.com.

McKENNA, Patricia Ann (see Goedicke, Patricia)

MacKENNEY, Richard, BA, PhD, FRHistS; British historian and educator; b. 2 April 1953, Aylesbury, Buckinghamshire, England. *Education:* Queens' College, Cambridge, University of Edinburgh. *Career:* Sr Lecturer in History, University of Edinburgh. *Publications:* Tradesmen and Traders: The World of the Guilds in Venice and Europe, c. 1250–c. 1650, 1987; The City-State, 1500–1700: Republican Liberty in an Age of Princely Power, 1989; Sixteenth-Century Europe: Expansion and Conflict, 1993; Renaissance Italians, 1300–1600, 1997. Contributions: various specialised articles to journals and periodicals. *Honours:* Graduate Fellow, Rotary Foundation, Rotary International, 1975–76. *Literary Agent:* David Higham Associates, 5–8 Lower John Street, Golden Square, London W1F 9HA, England. *Address:* Department of History, University of Edinburgh, William Robertson Building, George Square, Edinburgh EH8 9JY, Scotland.

MacKENZIE, David, AB, MA, PhD; American academic; *Professor of History Emeritus, University of North Carolina at Greensboro*; b. 10 June 1927, Rochester, NY; m. Patricia Williams 1953; three s. *Education:* Univ. of Rochester, Columbia Univ. *Career:* Prof. of History, US Merchant Marine Acad. 1953–58, Princeton Univ. 1959–61, Wells Coll. 1961–68; Prof. of History, Univ. of North Carolina, Greensboro 1969–2000, Prof. Emer. 2000–. *Publications:* The Serbs and Russian Pan-Slavism 1875–1878 1967, The Lion of Tashkent: The Career of General M. G. Cherniaev 1974, Ilija Garasanin: The Balkan Bismarck 1985, Ilija Garasanin Drzavnik i Diplomata 1987, Apis: The Congenial Conspirator 1989, Imperial Dreams/Harsh Realities: Tsarist Russian Foreign Policy, 1815–1917 1993, From Messianism to Collapse: Soviet Foreign Policy 1917–1991 1994, The Black Hand on Trial: Salonika 1917 1995, Violent Solutions: Revolutions, Nationalism, and Secret Societies in Europe to 1918 1996, Serbs and Russians 1996, Solunski proces 1997, Exonerating the Black Hand 1917–1953 1999, Obnova Solunshog procesa 2001, Count N. P. Ignat'ev: Father of Lies? 2002, A History of Russia, the Soviet Union and Beyond (sixth edn) 2002, Russia and the USSR in the Twentieth Century (fourth edn) 2002, One Foot in Russia, the Other in Yugoslavia: a Memoir 2003, Jovan Ristic, Evropski Drzavnik 2004, Jovan Ristic, European Diplomat 2006, Jovan Marinovic 2006, Miloran Milovanovic: Talented and Peace Loving Serbian Diplomat; contrib. to books and professional journals. *Address:* 870 Library Tower, University of North Carolina, Greensboro, NC (office); 1000 Fairmont Street, Greensboro, NC 27401, USA (home). *Telephone:* (336) 275-1229 (home). *Fax:* (336) 334-5910 (office).

McKEOWN, Tom S., MA, MFA; American poet, writing consultant and college instructor; b. 29 Sept. 1937, Evanston, IL; m. Patricia Haebig 1989; one s. one d. *Education:* Univ. of Michigan, Vermont Coll. *Career:* teacher, Alpena Community Coll. 1962–64, Univ. of Wisconsin, Oshkosh 1964–68; writer-in-residence, Stephens Coll. 1968–74; poet-in-residence, Savannah Coll. of Art and Design 1982–83, Univ. of Wisconsin, Oshkosh 1983–87, Univ. of Wisconsin at Madison 1989–94; ind. consultant in writing 1999–. *Performances:* Circle of the Eye (Carnegie Hall 1979, Library of Congress 1979); Poetry Readings (Journalism Club, Moscow 1979, Leningrad 1979, Tallinn 1979). *Art:* August Garden (acrylic on canvas) 1992. *Publications:* The Luminous Revolver 1973, The House of Water 1974, Driving to New Mexico 1974, Certain Minutes 1978, Circle of the Eye 1982, Three Hundred Tigers 1994, The Oceans in the Sleepwalker's Hands 2007; contrib. to newspapers, reviews and magazines. *Honours:* Avery Hopwood Award 1968, Wisconsin Arts Fellowship 1980.

McKERNAN, Llewellyn McKinnie, MA; American poet and children's writer; b. 12 July 1941, Hampton, AR; m. John Joseph McKernan 1967; one d. *Education:* Hendrix College, University of Arkansas, Brown University. *Career:* Instructor of English, Georgia Southern College, 1966–67; Adjunct Prof. of English, Marshall University, 1980–86, 1991; Prof. of English, St Mary's College, 1989; mem. West Virginia Writers; Poetry Society of West Virginia; Society of Children's Book Writers and Illustrators. *Publications:* Short and Simple Annals 1979, More Songs of Gladness 1987, Bird Alphabet 1988, Many Waters 1993, This is the Day and This is the Night 1994, Llewellyn McKernan's Greatest Hit 2005; contributions: Reviews and journals. *Honours:* Third Prize, Chester H. Jones National Poetry Competition, 1982; West Virginia Humanities Artist Grant, 1983; Second Prize, National Founders Award Contest, NFSPS, 1994. *Address:* Route 10, PO Box 4639B, Barboursville, WV 25504, USA.

MACKERRAS, Colin Patrick, BA, MLitt, PhD, FAHA; Australian academic, writer and editor; *Professor Emeritus, Department of International Business and Asian Studies, Griffith University*; b. 26 Aug. 1939, Sydney, NSW; m. Alyce Barbara Brazier 1963; two s. three d. *Education:* Univ. of Melbourne, Australian Nat. Univ., Univ. of Cambridge. *Career:* Foreign Expert, Beijing Inst. of Foreign Languages 1964–66, Beijing Foreign Studies Univ. 1986, 2005; Research Scholar, Australian Nat. Univ. 1966–69, Research Fellow 1969–73, Sr Research Fellow 1973; Prof., School of Modern Asian Studies, Griffith Univ. 1974–2004, Chair. School of Modern Asian Studies 1979–85, Head School of Modern Asian Studies 1988–89, 1996–2000, Prof. Emer., Dept of Int. Business and Asian Studies 2004–; mem. Asian Studies Asscn of Australia (Pres. 1992–95), Chinese Studies Asscn (Pres. 1991–93), Queensland History Teachers Asscn; Ed.-in-Chief Asian Ethnicity (journal). *Publications:* From Fear to Friendship: Australia's Policies Towards the People's Republic of China 1966–1982 (with Edmund S. K. Fung) 1985, Western Images of China 1989, Portaits of China 1989, Dragon's Tongue: Communicating in Chinese (with Peter Chang, Yu Hsiu-ching and Alyce Mackerras, two vols) 1990–91, Chinese Drama: A Historical Survey 1990, The Cambridge Handbook of Contemporary China (with Amanda Yorke) 1991, Unlocking Australia's Language Potential: Profiles of Nine Key Languages in Australia, Vol. 2: Chinese (with Doug Smith, Ng Bee Chin, and Kam Louie) 1993, China Since 1978: Reform, Modernisation, and 'Socialism with Chinese Characteristics' (with Pradeep Taneja and Graham Young) 1994, China's Minorities: Integration and Modernization in the Twentieth Century 1994, China's Minority Cultures: Identities and Integration Since 1912 1995, Peking Opera 1997, China in Transformation 1900–1949 1998, The New Cambridge Handbook of Contemporary China 2001, China's Ethnic Minorities and Globalisation 2003; editor: Essays on the Sources for Chinese History (with Donald Leslie and Wang Gungwu) 1973, China: The Impact of Revolution: A Survey of Twentieth Century China 1976, Chinese Theater from its Origins to the Present Day 1983, Marxism in Asia (with Nick Knight) 1985, Drama in the People's Republic of China (with Constantine Tung) 1987, Chinese Language Teaching and its Application (with Hugh Dunn) 1987, Contemporary Vietnam: Perspectives from Australia (with Robert Cribb and Allan Healy) 1988, Eastern Asia: An Introductory History 1992, Asia Since 1945: History Through Documents 1992, China in Revolution: History Through Documents 1993, Imperialism, Colonialism and Nationalism in East Asia: History Through Documents 1994, Australia and China: Partners in Asia 1996, Dictionary of the Politics of the People's Republic of China (with Donald H. McMillen and Andrew Watson) 1998, Culture and Society in the Asia-Pacific (with Richard Maidment) 1998, Sinophiles and Sinophones, Western Views of China: An Anthology 2000, Ethnicity in Asia 2003; contrib. to various scholarly books and journals. *Honours:* co-recipient United Nations Asscn of Australia Gold Citation for the Media Peace Prize 1981, Albert Einstein Int. Acad. Foundation Cross of Merit Award 1993, Medal for Outstanding Contributions to Australia-China Cultural Relations 1999, Centenary Medal Australia 2003. *Address:* c/o School of International Business and Asian Studies, Griffith University, Nathan, Qld 4111, Australia (office). *Telephone:* (7) 3735-7446 (office); (7) 3735-1647 (home). *Fax:* (7) 3875-5111 (office); (7) 3390-1641 (home). *E-mail:* c.mackerras@griffith.edu.au (office); colinmackerras@hotmail.com (home).

MACKESY, Piers Gerald, BA, DPhil, DLitt, FBA; British historian and writer; *Emeritus Fellow, Pembroke College, University of Oxford*; b. 15 Sept. 1924, Cults, Aberdeenshire, Scotland; s. of Maj.-Gen. P. J. Mackesy, CB, DSO, MC and Dorothy Cook. *Education:* Christ Church, Oxford, Oriel Coll., Oxford. *Career:* Harkness Fellow, Harvard Univ. 1953–54; Fellow 1954–87, Emeritus 1988–, Pembroke Coll., Oxford; Visiting Fellow, Inst. for Advanced Study, Princeton, NJ 1961–62; Visiting Prof., California Inst. of Technology 1966; mem. Nat. Army Museum (council mem. 1983–92), Soc. for Army Historical Research (council mem. 1985–94). *Publications:* The War in the Mediterranean 1803–1810 1957, The War for America 1775–1783 1964, Statesmen at War: The Strategy of Overthrow 1798–1799 1974, The Coward of Minden: The Affair of Lord George Sackville 1979, War without Victory: The Downfall of Pitt 1799–1802 1984, British Victory in Egypt, 1801: The End of Napoleon's Conquest 1995. *Honours:* Templer Medal 1995. *Address:* Westerton Farmhouse, Dess, by Aboyne, Aberdeenshire AB34 5AY, Scotland (home). *Telephone:* (13398) 84415.

MACKEY, James Patrick, BA, LPh, BD, STL, DD, PhD; Irish philosopher, theologian and academic; *Visiting Professor, Trinity College Dublin*; b. 9 Feb. 1934, Ireland; s. of Peter Mackey and Esther Morrissey; m. Noelle Quinlan

1973; one s. one d. *Education:* Mount St Joseph Coll., Nat. Univ. of Ireland, Pontifical Univ., Maynooth and Queen's Univ., Belfast. *Career:* ordained priest 1958; Lecturer in Philosophy, Queen's Univ., Belfast 1960–66; Lecturer in Philosophy and Theology, St John's Coll., Waterford 1966–69; Assoc. Prof. of Philosophical and Systematic Theology, Univ. of San Francisco, USA 1969–73, Prof. 1973–79; Visiting Prof., Univ. of California, Berkeley, USA 1974–75; Thomas Chalmers Prof. of Theology, Univ. of Edin., UK 1979–99, Dean of Faculty of Divinity 1984–88, Dir Grad. School and Assoc. Dean 1995–98, Prof. Emer. 1999–, Fellow, Faculty of Divinity 1999–2002; Visiting Prof., Univ. of Dublin Trinity Coll. 2000–; curricular consultant, Univ. Coll., Cork 2000–04; Visiting Prof., Dartmouth Coll., NH, USA 1989, Univ. of San Francisco 1990; mem. Ind. Assessment Panel and jt author of Report on NI Policing Bd 2005; Dir Derry City Int. Conf. on the Cultures of Europe 1992; Ed. Studies in World Christianity 1995–2001. *Television:* scripted and presented series The Hall of Mirrors 1984, The Gods of War 1986. *Publications:* Life and Grace 1966, Morals, Law and Authority (ed.) 1969, The Problems of Religious Faith 1974, Jesus, The Man and the Myth 1979, The Christian Experience of God as Trinity 1983, Religious Imagination (ed.) 1986, Modern Theology 1987, An Introduction to Celtic Christianity 1989, Power and Christian Ethics 1994, The Cultures of Europe (ed.) 1994, The Critique of Theological Reason 2000, Religion and Politics in Ireland at the Turn of the Millennium (ed.) 2003, Christianity and Creation 2006, The Scientist and the Theologian 2007. *Honours:* British Acad. Research Scholarship 1964–65. *Address:* School of Religions and Theology, Trinity College, Dublin 2 (office); 15 Glenville Park, Dunmore Road, Waterford, Ireland (home). *Telephone:* (1) 6081297 (office); (51) 844624 (home). *E-mail:* jpmackey_ie@yahoo.co.uk (home).

MACKEY, Mary, (Kate Clemens), BA, MA, PhD; American writer, poet and academic; *Professor of English, California State University;* b. 21 Jan. 1945, Indianapolis, Ind.; d. of John Mackey and Jean Mackey; partner, Angus Wright. *Education:* Harvard Coll., Univ. of Michigan. *Career:* Asst Prof. 1972–76, Assoc. Prof. 1976–80, Prof. of English 1980–, currently Writer-in-Residence, California State Univ. at Sacramento; mem. Feminist Writers' Guild, Nat. Book Critics' Circle, PEN American Center West (Pres. 1989–92), Writers' Guild of America, Northern Calif. Book Reviewers Asscn, Authors' Guild. *Publications:* fiction: Immersion 1972, McCarthy's List 1979, The Last Warrior Queen 1983, A Grand Passion 1986, The Kindness of Strangers 1988, Season of Shadows 1991, The Year the Horses Came 1993, The Horses at the Gate 1996, The Fires of Spring 1998, The Stand In (as Kate Clemens) 2003, Sweet Revenge (as Kate Clemens) 2004; poetry: Split Ends 1974, One Night Stand 1977, Skin Deep 1978, The Dear Dance of Eros 1987, Breaking the Fever 2006; other: Chance Music (ed. with Mary MacArthur) 1977; contrib. to periodicals. *Honours:* Woodrow Wilson Fellowship 1966–67, Virginia Center for the Creative Arts Fellowship 1999, 2002. *Literary Agent:* c/o Barbara Lowenstein, Lowenstein-Yost Literary Agency, 121 W 27th Street, Suite 601, New York, NY 10001, USA. *Telephone:* (212) 236-8196 (office). *Address:* Department of English, California State University at Sacramento, Sacramento, CA 95819, USA (office). *Telephone:* (916) 278-6586 (office). *Fax:* (916) 278-5410 (office). *E-mail:* mackeym@mindspring.com. *Website:* www.marymackey.com.

MACKEY, Nathaniel, AB, PhD; American academic, poet, writer and editor; *Professor, University of California at Santa Cruz;* b. 25 Oct. 1947, Miami, FL; m. Pascale Gaitet 1991; one d. one step-s. *Education:* Princeton Univ., Stanford Univ. *Career:* Asst Prof., Univ. of Wisconsin at Madison 1974–76; Ed., Hambone literary magazine 1974–; Asst Prof. and Dir of Black Studies, Univ. of Southern California at Los Angeles 1976–79; Visiting Prof., Occidental Coll. 1979; Asst Prof., Bd of Studies in Literature and American Studies Program, Univ. of California at Santa Cruz 1979–81, Assoc. Prof. 1981–87, Prof. 1987–; writer-in-residence, Washington, DC Project for the Arts 1986, Inst. of American Indian Arts, Santa Fe, NM 1987, 1988, Brown Univ. 1990, Intersection for the Arts, San Francisco 1991; faculty mem., Naropa Inst., Boulder summers 1991, 1993; Visiting Foreign Artist, Kootenay School of Writing, Vancouver, BC 1994; mem. Acad. of American Poets (bd of chancellors 2001–). *Publications:* poetry: Four for Trane 1978, Septet for the End of Time 1983, Eroding Witness 1985, Outlandish 1992, School of Udhra 1993, Song of the Andoumboulou: 18–20 1994, Whatsaid Serif 1998; fiction: From a Broken Bottle Traces of Perfume Still Emanate Vol. I: Bedouin Hornbook 1986, Vol. II: Djbot Baghostus's Run 1993, Splay Anthem (Nat. Book Award for Poetry) 2006; non-fiction: Discrepant Engagement: Dissonance, Cross-Culturality and Experimental Writing 1993; other: Moment's Notice: Jazz in Poetry and Prose (ed. with Art Lange) 1993, Strick: Song of the Andoumboulou 16–25 (poems with musical accompaniment) 1995; contrib. to anthologies, scholarly journals and magazines. *Honours:* Co-ordinating Council of Literary Magazines Editor's Grant 1985, Whiting Writer's Award 1993. *Address:* c/o New Directions Publishing, 80 Eighth Avenue, New York, NY 10011, USA. *E-mail:* editorial@ndbooks.com.

MACKIE, John (see Levinson, Leonard)

MacKINNON, Catharine Alice, BA, JD, PhD; American academic, writer and lawyer; *Elizabeth A. Long Professor of Law, University of Michigan Law School;* b. 7 Oct. 1946, Minneapolis, Minn.; d. of George E. MacKinnon and Elizabeth Davis MacKinnon. *Education:* Smith Coll., Yale Univ., Yale Law School. *Career:* Asst Prof. of Law, Univ. of Minnesota 1982–84; Prof. of Law, York Univ., Toronto 1988–90; Prof. of Law, Univ. of Michigan at Ann Arbor 1990–, Elizabeth A. Long Prof. of Law, Univ. of Michigan Law School; Visiting

Prof., Univ. of Chicago 1997–2004; Fellow, Center for Advanced Study, Standford 2005–06; Fellow, AAAS 2005. *Achievement:* one of the most widely cited legal scholars writing in the English language. *Publications:* Sexual Harrassment of Working Women: A Case of Sex Discrimination 1979, Feminism Unmodified: Discourses on Life and Law 1987, Pornography and Civil Rights: A New Day for Women's Equality (with Andrea Dworkin) 1988, Toward a Feminist Theory of the State 1989, Only Words 1993, In Harm's Way: The Pornography Civil Rights Hearings (with Andrea Dworkin) 1998, Sex Equality 2001, Directions in Sexual Harassment Law (with Reva Siegel) 2002, Women's Lives, Men's Laws 2005, Are Women Human? 2006; contribs to journals. *Honours:* several hon. degrees; Smith Medal, Wilber Lucius Cross Medal, Yale, American Bar Foundation Distinguished Research Award 2007. *Address:* University of Michigan Law School, 625 S State Street, Ann Arbor, MI 48109-1215, USA. *Telephone:* (734) 647-3595 (office). *E-mail:* camtwo@umich.edu (office).

McKINSTRY, Nancy, BA, MBA; American publishing executive; *CEO and Chairman of the Executive Board, Wolters Kluwer NV;* b. 1959; m. *Education:* Univ. of Rhode Island, Kingston and Columbia Univ., New York. *Career:* held man. positions with Booz Allen Hamilton (int. man.-consulting firm) 1980s; held a succession of man. positions with Wolters Kluwer cos in North America 1991–99, Vice-Pres. Product Man. and Sr Officer for CCH Inc. and Asst Vice-Pres. Electronic Products Div. for CCH –1996, Pres. and CEO CCH Legal Information Services 1996, CEO Wolters Kluwer's operations in North America –2001, mem. Exec. Bd Wolters Kluwer NV 2001–, Chair. Exec. Bd Wolters Kluwer NV, responsible for Wolters Kluwer's Divs, Business Devt, Strategy and Tech. 2001–03, CEO and Chair. Exec. Bd 2003–; CEO SCP Communications (medical information co.) 1999; mem. Bd of Dirs Ericsson 2004–, MortgageIT; mem. Bd of Dirs American Chamber of Commerce in the Netherlands 2004–, Tias Business School; mem. Advisory Bd Univ. of Rhode Island, mem. University Club. *Honours:* Hon. LLD (Univ. of Rhode Island); ranked by Fortune magazine as one of 50 Most Powerful Women in Business outside the US (fourth) 2003, (fourth) 2004, (seventh) 2005, (eighth) 2006, ranked by Forbes magazine amongst 100 Most Powerful Women (69th) 2004, (45th) 2005, (67th) 2006, ranked eighth by the Financial Times amongst Top 25 Businesswomen in Europe 2006. *Address:* Wolters Kluwer NV, Apollolaan 153, PO Box 75248, 1070 AE, Amsterdam, The Netherlands (office). *Telephone:* (20) 6070400 (office). *Fax:* (20) 6070490 (office). *E-mail:* info@wolterskluwer.com (office). *Website:* www.wolterskluwer.com (office).

McKISSACK, Frederick Lemuel, BS; American writer; b. 12 Aug. 1939, Nashville, TN; m. Patricia McKissack 1964; three s. *Education:* Tennessee Agricultural and Industrial State Univ. *Career:* fmrly civil engineer. *Publications:* with Patricia McKissack: Abram, Abram, Where Are We Going? 1984, A Long Hard Journey: The Story of the Pullman Porter (Coretta Scott King Award) 1990, Martin Luther King, Jr: Man of Peace 1991, Carter G. Woodson: The Father of Black History 1991, Sojourner Truth: Ain't I a Woman (Boston Globe Horn Book Award for Non-Fiction 1993, Coretta Scott King Award 1993) 1992, Jesse Owens: Olympic Star 1992, Paul Robeson: A Voice to Remember 1992, Langston Hughes: Great American Poet 1992, African-American Inventors 1994, Black Diamond (Coretta Scott King Award) 1994, Christmas in the Big House, Christmas in the Quarters (Coretta Scott King Award 1995, ABC Children's Booksellers Choices Award 1995) 1994, George Washington Carver: The Peanut Scientist 1994, Red-Tail Angels: The Story of the Tuskegee Airmen of World War II (Carter G. Woodson Outstanding Merit Book 1996) 1995, Rebels Against Slavery: American Slave Revolts (Coretta Scott King Award 1997) 1996, Let My People Go (with illustrations by James E. Ransome) 1998, Young, Black and Determined: a biography of Lorraine Hansberry 1998, Black Hands, White Sails: The Story of African-American Whalers (Carter G. Woodson Book Award 2000, Coretta Scott King Award 2000, Soc. of Midland Authors Book Award for Juvenile Non-fiction 2000) 1999, Bugs! 2000, Nzingha: Warrior Queen of Matamba 2000, Ida B. Wells-Barnett: A Voice Against Violence (Soc. of School Librarians Int. Book Award) 2001, Messy Bessey's Garden (with illustrations by Dana Regan) 2002, Ralph J. Bunche: Peacemaker 2002, Satchel Paige: The Best Arm in Baseball 2002, Zora Neale Hurston, Writer and Storyteller 2002, Hard Labor: The First African Americans 1619 2004. *Honours:* Jane Addams Children's Book Award, 1990; Boston Globe/Horn Book Award, 1993. *Address:* c/o Scholastic, 557 Broadway, New York, NY 10012, USA.

McKISSACK, Patricia L'Ann Carwell, BA, MA; American writer; b. 9 Aug. 1944, Smyrna, TN; m. Frederick Lemuel McKissack 1964; three s. *Education:* Tennessee Agricultural and Industrial State Univ., Webster Univ. *Career:* fmrly teacher and children's book ed. *Publications:* The Inca 1985, Flossie & the Fox 1986, A Picture of Freedom: The Diary of Clotee, a Slave Girl, Belmont Plantation, Virginia, 1859, The Dark Thirty: Southern Tales of the Super-natural (Coretta Scott King Award 1993, John Newbery Medal 1993) 1992, Run Away Home 1997, Ma Dear's Aprons (with illustrations by Floyd Cooper) 1997, Can You Imagine (with photographs by Myles Pinkney) 1997, Color Me Dark 2000, The Honest-to-Goodness Truth (with illustrations by Giselle Potter) (Soc. of School Librarians Int. Book Award 2000, Storytelling World Award 2001) 2000, Nzingha: Warrior Queen of Matamba 2000, Goin' Someplace Special (with illustrations by Jerry Pinkney) (Coretta Scott King Award 2002, ABC Children's Booksellers Choices Award 2002) 2001; with Frederick McKissack: Abram, Abram, Where Are We Going? 1984, A Long Hard Journey: The Story of the Pullman Porter (Coretta Scott King Award) 1990, Martin Luther King, Jr: Man of Peace 1991, Carter G. Woodson: The

Father of Black History 1991, Sojourner Truth: Ain't I a Woman (Boston Globe Horn Book Award for Non-Fiction 1993, Coretta Scott King Award 1993) 1992, Jesse Owens: Olympic Star 1992, Paul Robeson: A Voice to Remember 1992, Langston Hughes: Great American Poet 1992, African-American Inventors 1994, Black Diamond (Coretta Scott King Award) 1994, Christmas in the Big House, Christmas in the Quarters (Coretta Scott King Award 1995, ABC Children's Booksellers Choices Award 1995) 1994, George Washington Carver: The Peanut Scientist 1994, Red-Tail Angels: The Story of the Tuskegee Airmen of World War II (Carter G. Woodson Outstanding Merit Book 1996) 1995, Rebels Against Slavery: American Slave Revolts (Coretta Scott King Award 1997) 1996, Let My People Go (with illustrations by James E. Ransome) 1998, Young, Black and Determined: a biography of Lorraine Hansberry 1998, Black Hands, White Sails: The Story of African-American Whalers (Carter G. Woodson Book Award 2000, Coretta Scott King Award 2000, Soc. of Midland Authors Book Award for Juvenile Non-fiction 2000) 1999, Bugs! 2000, Nzingha: Warrior Queen of Matamba 2000, Ida B. Wells-Barnett: A Voice Against Violence (Soc. of School Librarians Int. Book Award) 2001, Messy Bessey's Garden (with illustrations by Dana Regan) 2002, Ralph J. Bunche: Peacemaker 2002, Satchel Paige: The Best Arm in Baseball 2002, Zora Neale Hurston, Writer and Storyteller 2002, Hard Labor: The First African Americans 1619 2004. Honours: Jane Addams Children's Book Award 1990, Boston Globe/Horn Book Award 1993. Address: c/o Scholastic, 557 Broadway, New York, NY 10012, USA.

MACKRELL, Judith, BA, DPhil; British journalist; b. 26 Oct. 1954, London; m. Simon Henson 1977; two s. Education: Univs of York and Oxford. Career: fmr Lecturer in English Literature; Dance Critic The Independent 1986–95, The Guardian 1995–; regular broadcasts for TV and radio. Publications: Out of Line: The History of British New Dance 1992, Reading Dance 1995, Life in Dance (with Darcey Bussell) 1998, Oxford Dictionary of Dance (jtly) 2000. Honours: Hon. Fellow, Laban Cen. Address: The Guardian, 119 Farringdon Road, London, EC1, England (office). Telephone: (20) 7249-5553 (office). E-mail: judith.mackrell@guardian.co.uk (office).

McKUEN, Rod; American writer and composer; b. 29 April 1933, Oakland, Calif. Career: has appeared in numerous films, concerts and on TV, composer of film scores and background music for TV shows; composer-lyricist of many songs; Pres. of numerous record and book cos; mem. Bd of Dirs American Nat. Theater of Ballet, Animal Concern; mem. Bd of Govs Nat. Acad. of Recording Arts and Sciences; mem. American Soc. of Composers, Authors and Publishers (ASCAP), Writers Guild, AFTRA, MPA, NARAS; Pres. of American Guild of Variety Artists (AGVA); mem. Bd of Dirs Calif. Music Theater. Works include: Symphony Number One, Concerto for Guitar and Orchestra, Concerto for Four Harpsichords, Seascapes for Piano and Orchestra, Adagio for Harp and Strings, Piano Variations, Concerto Number Three for Piano and Orchestra 1972, The Plains of My Country (ballet) 1972, The City (orchestral suite) 1973, Ballad of Distances (orchestral suite) 1973, Bicentennial Ballet 1975, Symphony Number Three 1975, over 200 record albums. Film scores: Joanna 1968, The Prime of Miss Jean Brodie 1969, Me, Natalie 1969, A Boy Named Charlie Brown 1970, Come to Your Senses 1971, Scandalous John 1971, Wildflowers 1971, The Borrowers 1973, Lisa Bright and Dark 1973, Awareness of Emily 1976, The Unknown War 1979, Man to Himself 1980, Portrait of Rod McKuen 1982, Death Rides this Trail 1983, The Living End 1983, The Beach 1984. Publications: And Autumn Came 1954, Stanyan Street and Other Sorrows 1966, Listen to the Warm 1967, Twelve Years of Christmas 1968, In Someone's Shadow 1969, With Love 1970, Caught in the Quiet 1970, Fields of Wonder 1971, The Carols of Christmas 1971, And to Each Season 1972, Beyond the Boardwalk 1972, Come to Me in Silence 1973, America–An Affirmation 1974, Seasons in the Sun 1974, Alone, Moment to Moment 1974, The McKuen Omnibus 1975, Celebrations of the Heart 1975, My Country 200 1975, I'm Strong but I Like Roses, Sleep Warm, Beyond the Boardwalk 1976, The Sea Around Me... The Hills Above 1976, Finding My Father (biographical) 1977, Coming Close to Earth 1977, Hand in Hand... 1977, Love's Been Good to Me 1979, We Touch the Sky 1979, Looking for a Friend 1980, An Outstretched Hand 1980, The Power Bright and Shining 1980, Too Many Midnights 1981, Rod McKuen's Book of Days 1981, The Beautiful Strangers 1981, The Works of Rod McKuen, Vol. 1, Poetry 1982, Watch for the Wind... 1982, Rod McKuen – 1984 Book of Days 1983, The Sound of Solitude 1983, Suspension Bridge 1984, Another Beautiful Day 1985, Valentines 1985, Intervals 1986. Honours: Grand Prix du Disque 1966, 1974, 1975, 1982, Golden Globe 1969, Motion Picture Daily Award 1969, LA Shrine Club Award 1975, Freedoms Foundation 1975, Horatio Alger Award 1976, Brandeis Univ. Literary Trust Award 1981, Freedoms Foundation Patriot Medal 1981, Salvation Army Man of the Year 1983, Rose d'Or, Cannes 1986, Myasthenia Gravis Community Service Award 1986. Address: PO Box 2783, Los Angeles, CA 90028, USA.

McLAREN, Colin Andrew, BA, MPhil, DipArch; British writer; b. 14 Dec. 1940, Middlesex, England; one s. one d. Education: University of London. Career: Librarian, Univ. of Aberdeen –1999; mem. Society of Authors. Publications: Rattus Rex, 1978; Crows in a Winter Landscape, 1979; Mother of the Free, 1980; A Twister over the Thames, 1981; The Warriors under the Stone, 1983; Crown and Gown: An Illustrated History of the University of Aberdeen (with J. J. Carter), 1994; Rare and Fair: A Visitor's History of Aberdeen University Library, 1995. Contributions: BBC Radio 3 and 4. Honours: Society of Authors Award for Best Adaptation, 1986.

McLAREN, John David, BEd, MA, PhD; Australian academic, writer and editor; Professor Emeritus, Victoria University; b. 7 Nov. 1932, Melbourne,

Vic. Education: Univ. of Melbourne, Monash Univ. Career: Assoc. Ed. Overland 1966–93, Ed. 1993–97, Consulting Ed. 1997–; Head, Dept of Gen. Studies, Darling Downs Inst. of Advanced Educ. 1972–75, Dept of Humanities 1975–76, Foundation Chair., School of the Arts 1973–76; Head, Dept of Humanities, Footscray Inst. of Tech. 1976–89; Ed. Australian Book Review 1978–86; Prin. Lecturer, Footscray Inst. of Tech./Victoria Univ. of Tech. 1989–91; Prof. of Humanities, Victoria Univ. 1991–97, Hon. Prof. 1997–2001, Prof. Emer. 2001–; mem. Asscn for the Study of Australian Literature, Australian Studies Asscn for South Asia (Vice-Pres. 1997–), South Pacific Asscn for Commonwealth Language and Literature Studies. Publications: Our Troubled Schools 1968, Dictionary of Australian Education 1974, Australian Literature: An Historical Introduction 1989, The New Pacific Literatures: Culture and Environment in the European Pacific 1993, Prophet from the Desert: Critical Essays on Patrick White (ed.) 1995, Writing in Hope and in Fear: Postwar Australian Literature as Politics, 1945–72 1996, States of Imagination 2001, Free Radicals 2003, Not in Tranquillity 2005; contribs to scholarly books and journals. Honours: Hon. Life Mem. Int. Australian Studies Asscn; Fulbright Sr Scholar 1990, Australian Research Council Research Grants 1991, 1993, 1996, 2006, Humanities Research Centre Scholar, ANU 1994. Address: Victoria University, PO Box 14428, MCMC, Melbourne, Vic. 8001, Australia (office). E-mail: john.mclaren@vu.edu.au (office).

MacLAVERTY, Bernard, BA, DipEd; Irish writer and dramatist; Creative Writing Teacher, Research Institute of Irish and Scottish Studies, Aberdeen; b. 14 Sept. 1942, Belfast; s. of John MacLaverty and Mary MacLaverty; m. Madeline McGuckin 1967; one s. three d. Education: Queen's Univ., Belfast. Career: fmrly medical lab. technician, English teacher; fmr Writer-in-Residence Univ. of Aberdeen; mem. Aosdána. Television: plays: My Dear Palestrina 1980, Phonefun Limited 1982, The Daily Woman 1986, Sometime in August 1989; documentary: Hostages 1992; adaptation: The Real Charlotte, by Somerville and Ross 1989. Screenplays: Cal 1984, Lamb 1985, Bye-Child (short film, also dir) 2003. Radio plays: My Dear Palestrina 1980, Secrets 1981, No Joke 1983, The Break 1988, Some Surrender 1988, Lamb 1992, Grace Notes 2003. Publications: novels: Lamb 1980, Cal 1983, Grace Notes 1997, The Anatomy School 2001; short story collections: Secrets and Other Stories 1977, A Time to Dance and Other Stories 1982, The Great Profundo and Other Stories 1987, Walking the Dog and Other Stories 1994, Matters of Life & Death and Other Stories 2006; juvenile fiction: A Man in Search of a Pet 1978, Andrew McAndrew 1988. Honours: Northern Ireland and Scottish Arts Councils Awards, Irish Sunday Independent Award 1983, London Evening Standard Award for Screenplay 1984, jt winner Scottish Writer of the Year 1988, Soc. of Authors Travelling Scholarship 1994, Saltire Scottish Book of the Year Award 1997, Stakis Scottish Writer of the Year, Whitbread Novel of the Year, Creative Scotland Award 2003; Best First Dir, BAFTA Scotland 2004. Literary Agent: c/o Gill Coleridge, Rogers, Coleridge & White, 20 Powis Mews, London, W11 1JN, England. Telephone: (20) 7221-3717. Fax: (20) 7229-9084. E-mail: info@rcwlitagency.co.uk. Website: www.rcwlitagency.co.uk; www.bernardmaclaverty.com.

MacLEAN, Arthur (see Tubb, Edwin Charles)

MacLEAN, Rory, BA; Canadian author and broadcaster; b. 5 Nov. 1954, Vancouver, BC; m. Katrin Latta 1992; one s. Education: Upper Canada Coll., Toronto, Ryerson Univ., Toronto. Career: mem. Exec. Cttee English PEN. Radio: Itchy Feet, Out-takes, Following Durrell, Building Icarus, Magic Bus (all for BBC). Publications: Stalin's Nose 1992, The Oatmeal Ark 1996, Under the Dragon 1998, Next Exit Magic Kingdom 2000, Falling for Icarus 2004, Magic Bus 2006. Honours: Canada Council Independent Travel Writing Award, Yorkshire Post Best First Book Award, Arts Council of England Writers' Award 1998; awards for short films at Cannes Int. Festival du Film Amateur, Los Angeles Filmex, Mannheim and Canadian Television Commercials Festival. Literary Agent: c/o Peter Straus, Rogers, Coleridge & White Literary Agency, 20 Powis Mews, London, W11 1JN, England. Telephone: (20) 7221-3717. Fax: (20) 7229-9084. Website: www.rcwlitagency.co.uk; www.rorymaclean.com (office).

McLELLAN, David Thorburn, LLB, MA, DPhil; British academic and writer; Professor of Political Theory, Goldsmiths College, London; b. 10 Feb. 1940, Hertford, Herts.; m. Annie Brassart 1967; two d. Education: St John's Coll., Oxford. Career: fmr Prof. of Political Theory, Univ. of Kent; Fellow and Prof. of Political Theory, Goldsmiths Coll., London. Publications: The Young Hegelians and Karl Marx 1969, Karl Marx: His Life and Thought 1974, Engels 1977, Marxism After Marx 1980, Ideology 1986, Marxism and Religion 1987, Simone Weil: Utopian Pessimist 1989, Unto Caesar: The Political Importance of Christianity 1993, Political Christianity 1997, Karl Marx: A Biography 2006; contrib. to professional journals. Address: 13 Ivy Lane, Canterbury, Kent, CT1 1TU, England (home).

MacLENNAN, Murdoch; British newspaper executive; CEO, Telegraph Group Ltd.. Career: started career as graduate trainee The Scotsman newspaper; Production Dir Scottish Daily Record and Sunday Mail 1982–84; Dir of Production Mirror Group 1984–85; Production and Tech. Dir Express Newspapers 1985–89, Man. Dir 1989–92; Group Operations Dir Mirror Group Newspapers and Man. Dir Scottish Daily Record and Sunday Mail 1992–94; Group Man. Dir Associated Newspapers 1994–2004; CEO Telegraph Group Ltd 2004–; fmr Pres. IFRA (newspaper publishers' asscn); Chair. Press Asscn Remuneration Cttee; Vice-Pres. and Appeals Chair.

Newspaper Press Fund; Companion Inst. of Man.; Freeman of the City of London. *Honours:* Dr hc (Paisley). *Address:* Telegraph Group Ltd, 1 Canada Square, Canary Wharf, London, E14 5DT, England (office). *Telephone:* (20) 7538-5000 (office). *Fax:* (20) 7513-2512 (office). *Website:* www.pressoffice .telegraph.co.uk.

MACLEOD, Alison; British writer; b. 12 April 1920, Hendon, Middlesex, England. *Publications:* The Heretics (aka The Heretic) 1965, The Hireling (aka The Trusted Servant) 1968, City of Light (aka No Need of the Sun) 1969, The Muscovite 1971, The Jesuit (aka Prisoner of the Queen) 1972, The Portingale 1976, The Death of Uncle Joe 1997. *Address:* Room 27, Mary Feilding Guild, 1 View Road, London, N6 4DU, England. *Telephone:* (20) 8347-7257.

MacLEOD, Alistair, BA, BEd, MA, PhD; Canadian writer and academic; *Professor of English Emeritus, University of Windsor;* b. 20 July 1936, North Battleford, SK; m. Anita MacLellan 1971; six s. *Education:* Nova Scotia Teachers College, St Francis Xavier University, University of New Brunswick, University of Notre Dame. *Career:* Prof. of English, Nova Scotia Teachers College, 1961–63; Faculty, Indiana University at Fort Wayne, 1966–69; Prof. of English, 1969–2000, Prof. Emeritus, 2000–, University of Windsor. *Publications:* The Lost Salt Gift of Blood, 1976; As Birds Bring Forth the Sun and Other Stories, 1986; No Great Mischief, 2000; Island, 2000. Contributions: anthologies and periodicals. *Honours:* Hon. doctorates, St Francis Xavier University, 1987, University College, Cape Breton, 1991; Best Book of the Year, Publisher's Weekly, 1988; International IMPAC Dublin Literary Award, 2001. *Address:* c/o Department of English, University of Windsor, Windsor, ON N9B 3P4, Canada.

McLEOD, Joseph Bertram, BA; Canadian poet, dramatist, teacher, artistic director and farmer; b. 21 Oct. 1929, Hamilton, ON; m. Susan Maslak; one s. one d. *Education:* McMaster University, University of Toronto. *Career:* Artistic Dir, Peterborough Summer Theatre and Minkler Theatre, Seneca College; mem. League of Canadian Poets; PEN International; Writers Union of Canada. *Publications:* Poetry: Conversations with Maria, 1974; Collected Citizen, 1976; And the Rivers Our Blood, 1977; Cleaning the Bones, 1977; Protect My House, 1977; Greendream: Collected and New Poems, 1982; Shorter Chinese Lyrics, 1984; Rim Poems, 1990; From the Fringe of China. Plays: Sam Slick, 1985. Contributions: anthologies; Periodicals, including: Canadian Forum; Cardinal; Bitterroot; Fiddlehead; Four Quarters; Inscape; North; Poet and Critic; Poetry Australia; Poetry Florida; Quixote; Trace. *Honours:* Canada Council Award; Ontario Arts Council Award. *Address:* 25 Prince Arthur Road, Toronto, ON, M5R 1B2, Canada.

McLEOD, Wallace Edmond, BA, AM, PhD; Canadian academic and writer; *Professor of Classics Emeritus, Victoria College, Toronto;* b. 30 May 1931, East York, ON; m. Elizabeth Marion Staples 1957; three s. one d. *Education:* Univ. of Toronto, Harvard Univ. *Career:* instructor, Trinity Coll., Hartford, CT 1955–56, Univ. of British Columbia 1959–61; Lecturer, Univ. of Western Ontario 1961–62; Special Lecturer, Victoria Coll., Univ. of Toronto 1962–63; Asst Prof. 1963–66, Assoc. Prof. 1966–74, Anson Jones Lecturer 1984, Prof. of Classics 1974–96, Prof. Emeritus 1996–, ANZMRC Lecturer 1997, Inaugural Sam Houston Lecturer 1998, Walter Calloway Lecturer 2002, John Ross Robertson Lecturer 2005; mem. Freemason, Philalethes Soc. (pres. 1992), Soc. of Blue Friars, Grand Abbot, Classical Asscn of Canada, American Philological Asscn, Archaeological Inst. of America. *Publications:* Composite Bows from the Tomb of Tut'ankhamun 1970, Beyond the Pillars: More Light on Freemasony (ed. and contrib.) 1973, Meeting the Challenge: The Lodge Officer at Work (ed. and contrib.) 1976, The Sufferings of John Coustos (ed.) 1979, Whence Come We?: Freemasonry in Ontario 1764–1980 (ed. and contrib.) 1980, Self Bows and Other Archery Tackle from the Tomb of Tut'ankhamun 1982, The Old Gothic Constitutions (ed.) 1985, The Old Charges 1986, A Candid Disquisition (ed.) 1989, For the Cause of Good 1990, The Grand Design: Selected Masonic Addresses and Papers 1991, The Quest for Light: Selected Masonic Addresses 1997, Freemasonry on Both Sides of the Atlantic: Essays Concerning the Craft in the British Isles, Europe, the United States, and Mexico (assoc. ed.) 2002, A Daily Advancement in Masonic Knowledge: The Collected Blue Friar Lectures (ed. and contrib.) 2003; contrib. to numerous books and journals. *Honours:* Philalethes Certificate of Literature 1984. *Address:* c/o Victoria College, University of Toronto, 73 Queen's Park, Toronto, ON M5S 1K7 (office); 399 St Clements Avenue, Toronto, ON M5N 1M2, Canada (home). *Telephone:* (416) 585-4488 (office). *Fax:* (416) 585-4584 (office). *E-mail:* w.mcleod@utoronto.ca (office).

McLERRAN, Alice, BA, MS, MPH, PhD; American writer; b. 24 June 1933, West Point, NY; m. Larry Dean McLerran 1976; two s. one d. *Education:* Univ. of California, Harvard School of Public Health. *Career:* mem. Authors' Guild, Soc. of Children's Book Writers and Illustrators. *Publications:* The Mountain that Loved a Bird 1985, Secrets 1990, Roxaboxen 1991, I Want to go Home 1992, Dreamsong 1992, Hugs 1993, Kisses 1993, The Ghost Dance 1995, The Year of the Ranch 1996, The Legacy of Roxaboxen: A Collection of Voices 1998, Dragonfly 2000. *Honours:* Southwest Book Award 1991, Notable Children's Trade Book in Field of Social Studies 1996, 1997, Ariz. Library Asscn Judy Goddard Children's Author Award 2005. *Address:* 70 S Country Road, Bellport, NY 11713, USA. *E-mail:* alicemclerran@mac.com (home). *Website:* www.alicemclerran.com.

McLOUGHLIN, Merrill, BA; American journalist; b. 6 Jan. 1945, Skowhegan, Maine; d. of Comerford W. and Elizabeth M. McLoughlin; m. Michael A. Ruby 1986. *Education:* Smith Coll. *Career:* Educ. Ed. Newsweek Magazine 1973–78, Tech. Writer 1978–1982, Nat. Affairs Ed. 1982–1986; Asst Man. Ed. US News & World Report 1986–89, Co-Ed 1989; now freelance journalist in Milwaukee, Wis. *Publication:* The Impeachment and Trial of President Clinton 1999, A Good Fight (with sarah Brady) 2002.

McMANUS, (I.) Chris; British author and academic. *Career:* fmrly at Univ. Coll. London, Imperial Coll. School of Medicine; Prof. of Psychology and Medical Education, Dept of Psychology, Univ. of London 1997; Assoc. Ed. of Laterality 1995–2000; Assoc. Ed., British Journal of Psychology; editorial bd mem., Journal of Health Psychology, Psychology – Health and Medicine, Developmental Neuropsychology, Perception, Medical Education. *Publications:* Psychology in Medicine 1992, Right Hand Left Hand (Aventis Prize 2003) 2002; contrib. to British Journal of Psychology, British Medical Journal, Journal of Hygiene, The Lancet, Nature, New Scientist, Perception, Times Higher Education Supplement, TLS. *Honours:* Wellcome Trust Prize 2002. *Address:* Royal Free & University College Medical School, University College London, Centre for Health Informatics & Multiprofessional Education, Fourth Floor, Holborn Union Building, The Archway Campus, Highgate Hill, London, N19 3UA, England. *Telephone:* (20) 7288-3378. *Fax:* (20) 7288-3322. *E-mail:* i.mcmanus@chime.ucl.ac.uk. *Website:* www.chime.ucl.ac.uk/~rmhiicm; www .righthandlefthand.com.

McMANUS, James, BA, MA; American poet, writer and teacher; b. 22 March 1951, New York, NY; m. Jennifer Arra 1992; one s. three d. *Education:* Univ. of Illinois at Chicago. *Career:* faculty mem., School of the Art Inst., Chicago 1981–; mem. Associated Writing Programs, PEN. *Publications:* Going to the Sun (novel) 1996, Positive Fifth Street (non-fiction) 2003, Physical: An American Checkup 2006. *Honours:* Guggenheim Fellowship 1994–95. *Address:* 544 Sterling Road, Kenilworth, IL 60043 (home); School of the Art Institute, 37 S Wabash, Chicago, IL 60603, USA (office). *Telephone:* (847) 256-4109 (home). *E-mail:* arramc@msn.com (home); jmcmanus@saic.edu (office).

McMANUS, Jason Donald, BA, MPA; American journalist; b. 3 March 1934, Mission, Kan.; s. of John A. McManus and Stella F. Gosney; m. 1st Patricia A. Paulson 1958 (divorced 1966); one s.; m. 2nd Deborah H. Murphy 1973; two d. *Education:* Davidson Coll., Princeton Univ. and Univ. of Oxford (Rhodes Scholar). *Career:* Common Market Bureau Chief, Time Magazine, Paris 1962–64; Assoc. Ed. Time Magazine, New York 1964–68, Sr Ed. 1968–75, Asst Man. Ed. 1975–78, Exec. Ed. 1978–83; Corporate Ed. Time Inc. 1983–85; Man. Ed. Time Magazine 1985–87; Ed.-in-Chief, Time Inc. 1987–95. *Honours:* Hon. LittD (Davidson Coll.) 1979.

McMASTER, Juliet Sylvia, BA, MA, PhD; Canadian academic and writer; *University Professor Emerita, University of Alberta;* b. 2 Aug. 1937, Kisumu, Kenya; m. Rowland McMaster 1968; one s. one d. *Education:* St Anne's Coll., Oxford, Univ. of Alberta. *Career:* Asst Prof., Univ. of Alberta 1965–70, Assoc. Prof. 1970–76, Prof. 1976–86, Univ. Prof. 1986–, Univ. Prof. Emer. 2000–; Gen. Ed. Juvenilia Press 1994–; mem. Jane Austen Soc. of N America, Asscn of Canadian Univ. Teachers of English. *Publications:* Thackeray: The Major Novels 1971, Jane Austen's Achievement 1976, Trollope's Palliser Novels 1978, Jane Austen on Love 1978, The Novel from Sterne to James 1981, Dickens the Designer 1987, The Beautifull Cassandra 1993, Jane Austen the Novelist 1995, Cambridge Companion to Jane Austen (co-ed.) 1997, Reading the Body in the Eighteenth-Century Novel 2004; contrib. to 19th-Century Fiction, Victorian Studies, Modern Language Quarterly, English Studies in Canada. *Honours:* Canada Council Post-Doctoral Fellowship 1969–70, Guggenheim Fellowship 1976–77, McCalla Professorship 1982–83, Univ. of Alberta Research Prize 1986, Killam Research Fellowship 1987–88, Molson Prize 1994. *Address:* Department of English, University of Alberta, Edmonton, AB T6G 2E5, Canada (office). *Telephone:* (780) 436-5284 (home). *Fax:* (780) 492-8142 (office). *E-mail:* juliet.mcmaster@ualberta.ca (office). *Website:* www.arts.ualberta.ca/~jchook (office).

McMASTER, Susan, (S. M. Page), BA; Canadian poet and editor; b. 11 Aug. 1950, Toronto, ON; m. Ian McMaster 1969; two d. *Education:* Carleton Univ., Ottawa Teachers' Coll., gained Ont. Teacher's Certificate. *Career:* Founding Ed. magazine for women, Branching Out 1973–75; Sr Book Ed., Nat. Gallery of Canada 1989–98, 2002–; Ed.-in-Chief Vernissage 1999–2002; mem. League of Canadian Poets, PEN, Writers' Union of Canada, Writers' Trust (Canada). *Recordings:* Audio tape (with Sugarbeat) 1997, Sugar Beat music and poetry (CD) 1999, Geode music and poetry (CD) 2000, Until the Light Bends (CD) 2004. *Publications:* Pass This Way Again (co-author) 1983, Dark Galaxies 1986, North/South (co-author) 1987, Dangerous Graces (ed.) 1987, Women and Language (ed.) 1990, Two Women Talking, Erin Mouré and Bronwen Wallace 1991, Illegitimate Positions (ed.) 1991, The Hummingbird Murders 1992, Learning to Ride 1994, Dangerous Times (ed.) 1996, Uncommon Prayer 1997, Siolence: Poets on Violence and Silence (ed.) 1998, Waging Peace: Poetry and Political Action (ed.) 2002, La Deriva del Pianeta/World Shift (in English with Italian trans.) 2003, Until the Light Bends 2004; other: Wordmusic (with First Draft) 1987; contrib. to magazines, journals, broadcasts, scripts and anthologies. *Honours:* various awards from Canada Council for the Arts, Ontario Arts Council, Regional Municipality of Ottawa Carleton. *Address:* 43 Belmont Avenue, Ottawa, ON K1S 0T9, Canada. *E-mail:* smcmaster@ncf.ca.

McMILLAN, James Coriolanus, MA; British journalist; b. 30 Oct. 1925, England; m. Doreen Smith 1953; three s. one d. *Education:* Univ. of Glasgow. *Publications:* The Glass Lie 1964, American Take-Over 1967, Anatomy of Scotland 1969, The Honours Game 1970, Roots of Corruption 1971, British

Genius (with Peter Grosvenor) 1972, The Way We Were 1900–1950 (trilogy) 1977–80, Five Men at Nuremberg 1984, The Dunlop Story 1989, From Finchley to the World – Margaret Thatcher 1990. *Address:* Thurleston, Fairmile Park Road, Cobham, Surrey KT11 2PL, England.

MacMILLAN, Margaret Olwen, OC, BA, BPhil, DPhil, FRSL; Canadian university administrator, historian and writer; *Warden, St Antony's College Oxford*; b. Dec. 1943, Toronto, Ont. *Education:* Univ. of Toronto, St Antony's Coll., Oxford, UK. *Career:* Prof. of History, Ryerson Univ., Toronto 1975–2002; Provost and Vice Chancellor, Trinity Coll., Univ. of Toronto 2002–07; Warden St Antony's Coll., Oxford 2007–; Ed. International Journal 1995–2003; Sr Fellow, Massey Coll., Univ. of Toronto. *Publications:* Women of the Raj 1988, Canada and NATO: Uneasy Past, Uncertain Future 1990, Peacemakers: Six Months that Changed the World 2001, Paris 1919 2002, Parties Long Estranged: Canada and Australia in the 20th Century (co-ed.) 2003, Canada's House: Rideau Hall and the Invention of a Canadian Home (with Marjorie Harris and Anne L. Desjardins) 2004, Seize the Hour: When Nixon Met Mao 2006, Nixon and Mao 2007. *Honours:* Hon. Fellow, St Antony's Coll. Oxford; Gov.-Gen.'s Literary Award 2003, BBC 4 Samuel Johnson Prize for Non-Fiction, Duff Cooper Award, Hessell-Tiltman Prize. *Address:* Office of the Warden, St Antony's College, 62 Woodstock Road, Oxford, OX2 6JF, England (office). *Telephone:* (1865) 284700 (office). *Fax:* (1865) 274526 (office). *E-mail:* margaret.macmillan@sant.ox.ac.uk (office). *Website:* www.sant.ox.ac.uk (office).

McMILLAN, Terry, BA; American writer; b. 1952, Port Huron, MI; one s. *Education:* Univ. of Calif. at Berkeley and Columbia Univ. Film School. *Career:* fmr Sec.; guest columnist 'Hers' column, New York Times; book reviewer for New York Times Book Review, Atlanta Constitution, Philadelphia Inquirer; fmr Assoc. Prof. of English Univ. of Arizona; fmr Visiting Prof. in Creative Writing, Univ. of Wyoming, Stanford Univ.; Prof. Univ. of Arizona 1988–91; Fiction Judge Nat. Book Awards 1990; Nat. Endowment for the Arts Fellow 1988; Doubleday/Columbia Univ. Literary Fellow; Fellow Yaddo Artist Colony, Macdowell Colony. *Publications:* Mama (Nat. Book Award, Before Columbus Foundation) 1987, Disappearing Acts 1989, Breaking Ice (ed) 1990, Waiting To Exhale 1995 (co-writer screenplay), How Stella Got Her Groove Back 1996, A Day Late and a Dollar Short 2002, The Interruption of Everything 2003. *Address:* c/o Viking Studio Books, 375 Hudson Street, New York, NY 10014-3657, USA.

McMILLEN, Neil Raymond, BA, MA, PhD; American academic and writer; *Professor Emeritus, University of Southern Mississippi, Hattiesburg*; b. 2 Jan. 1939, Lake Odessa, MI; m. Beverly J. Smith 1960; one s., one d. *Education:* Univ. of Southern Mississippi, Vanderbilt Univ. *Career:* Asst Prof. of History, Ball State Univ., Muncie 1967–69; Asst Prof., Univ. of Southern Mississippi, Hattiesburg 1969–70, Assoc. Prof. 1970–78, Prof. of History 1978–2001, Prof. Emer. 2001–. *Publications:* The Citizens' Council: Organized Resistance to the Second Reconstruction 1971, Thomas Jefferson: Philosopher of Freedom 1973, Dark Journey: Black Mississippians in the Age of Jim Crow 1989, A Synopsis of American History (with Charles Bolton, eighth edn) 1997, Remaking Dixie: The Impact of World War II on the American South (ed.) 1997. *Honours:* Bancroft Prize 1990. *Address:* 509 Bay Street, Hattiesburg, MS 39401, USA (home). *Telephone:* (601) 544-8047 (home). *E-mail:* nmcmillen@aol.com (home).

MacMULLEN, Ramsay, AB, AM, PhD; American retd academic, writer and publisher; b. 3 March 1928, New York, NY; m. 1st Edith Merriman Nye 1954 (divorced 1991); two s. two d.; m. 2nd Margaret McNeill 1992. *Education:* Harvard University. *Career:* Instructor to Asst Prof., University of Oregon, 1956–61; Assoc. Prof. to Prof., 1961–67, Chair., Dept of Classics, 1965–66, Brandeis University; Fellow, Institute for Advanced Study, Princeton, NJ, 1964–65; Prof., 1967–93, Chair., Dept of History, 1970–72, Dunham Prof. of History and Classics, 1979–93, Master, Calhoun College, 1984–90, Yale University; mem. Asscn of Ancient Historians, pres., 1978–81; Friends of Ancient History; Society for the Promotion of Roman Studies. *Publications:* Soldier and Civilian in the Later Roman Empire, 1963; Enemies of the Roman Order, 1966; Constantine, 1969; Roman Social Relations, 1974; Roman Government's Response to Crisis, 1976; Paganism in the Roman Empire, 1981; Christianizing the Roman Empire, 1984; Corruption and the Decline of Rome, 1988; Changes in the Roman Empire, 1990; Paganism and Christianity (with E. N. Lane), 1992; Christianity and Paganism, 1997; Sisters of the Brush, 1997; Romanisation in the Time of Augustus, 2001; Sarah's Choice, 1828–32, 2001; Feeling in History, Ancient and Modern, 2003. Contributions: professional journals. *Honours:* Fulbright Fellowship, 1960–61; Porter Prize, College Art Asscn, 1964; Guggenheim Fellowship, 1964; Senior Fellow, National Endowment for the Humanities, 1974–75; Lifetime Award for Scholarly Distinction, American Historical Asscn, 2000. *Address:* 25 Temple Court, New Haven, CT 06511, USA. *E-mail:* ramsay.macmullen@yale.edu.

McMULLEN, Sean Christopher, MA; Australian writer; b. 21 Dec. 1948, Sale, Vic.; one d. *Education:* Univ. of Melbourne, Canberra Coll. of Adult Educ., Latrobe Univ., Deakin Univ. *Career:* computer systems analyst, Bureau of Meteorology 1981–; speaker to various groups; mem. SFWA. *Publications:* Call to the Edge 1992, Voices in the Light 1994, Mirror Sun Rising 1995, The Centurion's Empire 1998, Souls in the Great Machine 1999, The Miocene Arrow 2000, Eyes of the Calculor 2001, Voyage of the Shadowmoon 2002, Glass Dragons 2004; Non-Fiction: Strange Constellations: A History of Australian Science Fiction (with Russell Blackford and Van Ikin)

1999; contributions: anthologies, including Year's Best Science Fiction 2005; Periodicals, including: Eidolon; Sirius; Aurealis; Analog Science Fiction and Fact; Magazine of Fantasy and Science Fiction; Interzone. *Honours:* Writing Prize, World Science Fiction Convention, 1985; Ditmar Awards 1991, 1992, 1996; William Atheling Awards 1992, 1993, 1996, 1998, 2000; Aurealis Awards 1998, 2000, 2003; Analog Readers Award 2002; Nova Fantasy KA Award 2003. *Literary Agent:* Chris Lotts, Ralph M. Vicinaga Ltd, 303 W 18th Street, New York, NY 10010, USA. *Address:* PO Box 2653, Melbourne, Vic. 3001, Australia (home). *Telephone:* (4) 11439847 (home). *E-mail:* scm@unite .com.au (home). *Website:* www.bdsonline.ne/seanmcmullen (home).

McMURTRY, Larry Jeff; American writer; b. 3 June 1936, Wichita Falls, Tex.; s. of William Jefferson McMurtry and Hazel McIver; m. Josephine Ballard 1959 (divorced 1966); one s. *Television includes:* co-writer and co-producer with Diana Ossana of CBS mini-series Streets of Laredo and ABC mini-series Dead Man's Walk 1996. *Publications:* Horseman Pass By (aka Hud) 1961, Leaving Cheyenne 1963, The Last Picture Show 1966, In a Narrow Grave (essays) 1968, Moving On 1970, All My Friends Are Going to be Strangers 1972, It's Always We Rambled (essay) 1974, Terms of Endearment 1975, Somebody's Darling 1978, Cadillac Jack 1982, The Desert Rose 1983, Lonesome Dove 1985, Texasville 1987, Film Flam: Essay on Hollywood 1987, Anything for Billy 1988, Some Can Whistle 1989, Buffalo Girls 1990, The Evening Star 1992, Streets of Laredo 1993, Pretty Boy Floyd (with Diana Ossana) 1993, The Late Child 1995, Dead Man's Walk 1995, Zeke and Ned (novel, with Diana Ossana) 1996, Comanche Moon 1997, Duane's Depressed 1998, Walter Benjamin at the Dairy Queen 1999, Boone's Lick 2000, Sin Killer: The Berrybender Narratives, Book One 2002, The Wandering Hill: The Berrybender Narratives, Book Two 2003, Folly and Glory: The Berrybender Narratives, Book Three 2004, Loop Group 2004, When the Light Goes 2007. *Address:* Saria Co. Inc., 2509 North Campbell Avenue, Suite 95, Tucson, AZ 85719, USA (office).

McNAB, Andy; British writer; b. 1959. *Career:* joined the army 1976, mem. 22 SAS Regiment, B Squadron 1984–93; writer 1993–; currently Dir, security co. running a specialist training course for individuals working in hostile environments. *Publications:* adult fiction: Remote Control 1997, Crisis Four 1999, Firewall 2000, Last Light 2001, Liberation Day 2002, Dark Winter 2003, Deep Black 2004, Aggressor 2005, Recoil 2006; juvenile fiction: Boy Soldier (with Robert Rigby) 2005, Payback (with Robert Rigby) 2005, Avenger (with Robert Rigby) 2006; non-fiction: Bravo Two Zero (autobiog.) 1993, Immediate Action (autobiog.) 1995. *Honours:* DCM, MM. *Address:* c/o Transworld, 61–63 Uxbridge Road, London, W5 5SA, England. *Website:* www.booksattransworld .co.uk/andymcnab/home.htm.

McNAIR, Wesley, MA, MLitt; American academic and poet; *Professor Emeritus and Writer in Residence, University of Maine at Farmington*; b. 19 June 1941, Newport, NH; m. Diane Reed McNair 1962; three s. one d. *Education:* Keene State Coll., Middlebury Coll. *Career:* Assoc. Prof., Colby Sawyer Coll. 1968–87; Sr Fulbright Prof., Catholic Univ. of Chile 1977–78; Visiting Prof., Dartmouth Coll. 1984, Colby Coll. 2000–01; Assoc. Prof. to Prof., Univ. of Maine at Farmington 1987–98, Prof. Emer. and Writer in Residence 2005–; mem. nominating jury, Pulitzer Prize 2001, 2004. *Publications:* The Town of No 1989, Twelve Journeys in Maine 1992, My Brother Running 1993, Talking in the Dark 1998, Mapping the Heart: Reflections on Place and Poetry 2002, Fire: Poems, 2002 (Jane Kenyon Award 2004), A Place on Water (essays, co-author) 2004, The Ghosts of You and Me 2006; anthologies: The Quotable Moose (Ed.) 1994, The Maine Poets (Ed.) 2003, Contemporary Maine Fiction (Ed.) 2005; contributions: anthologies, reviews, quarterlies, and journals. *Honours:* Nat. Endowment for the Humanities Fellowship in Literature, 1970–71; Nat. Endowment for the Arts Fellowships, 1980, 1990; Devins Award, 1984; Eunice Tietjens Prize, 1984; Guggenheim Fellowship, 1986; Pushcart Prize, 1986; Robert Frost Prize 1987; New England Emmy Award, 1991; Rockefeller Residency, Bellagio, Italy 1993, 2005; Theodore Roethke Prize, 1993; Yankee Magazine Poetry Prize, 1995; Sarah Josepha Hale Medal, 1997, Ind. Book Publishers Award 2006, US Artists' Ford Fellowship 2006. *Address:* c/o Department of Humanities, University of Maine at Farmington, Farmington, ME 04938 (office); RFD 2, Box 790, Merridgewick, ME 04957, USA (home). *Fax:* (207) 587-4241 (home). *E-mail:* wesleymcnair@yahoo.com (home). *Website:* www.wesleymcnair.com (home).

McNALLY, Terrence; American playwright; b. 3 Nov. 1939, St Petersburg, FL. *Career:* Stage Man., Actors Studio, New York 1961; tutor 1961–62; film critic, The Seventh Art 1963–65; Asst Ed., Columbia Coll. Today 1965–66. *Publications:* Apple Pie, Sweet Eros Next and Other Plays 1969, Three Plays: Cuba Si!, Bringing It All Back Home, Last Gasps 1970, Where Has Tommy Flowers Gone? 1972, Bad Habits: Ravenswood and Dunelawn 1974, The Ritz and Other Plays 1976, The Rink 1985, And Things That Go Bump in the Night 1990, Frankie and Jonny in the Clair de Lune 1990, Kiss of the Spider Woman (with John Kander and Fred Ebb) 1992, Lips Together, Teeth Apart 1992, Until Your Heart Stops 1993, Love! Valour! Compassion! 1994, Masterclass 1995, Ragtime (with Stephen Flaherty and Lynn Ahrens) 1997, Corpus Christi 1998, Dead Man Walking (libretto) 2000, The Stendhal Syndrome 2003, Some Men 2006, Deuce 2007. *Honours:* Stanley Award 1962, Obie Award 1974, American Acad. of Arts and Letters Citation, Nat. Inst. of Arts and Letters Citation, Four Tony Awards, Pulitzer Award, two Guggenheim Awards. *Address:* 218 W 10th Street, New York, NY 10014, USA.

McNAMARA, Eugene Joseph, BA, MA, PhD; American academic, editor, poet and writer; b. 18 March 1930, Oak Park, IL; m. Margaret Lindstrom 1952; four s. one d. *Education:* DePaul University, Northwestern University. *Career:* Ed., University of Windsor Review, 1965–, Mainline, 1967–72, Sesame Press, 1973–80; Prof. of English, University of Windsor. *Publications:* Poetry: For the Mean Time, 1965; Outerings, 1970; Dillinger Poems, 1970; Love Scenes, 1971; Passages, 1972; Screens, 1977; Forcing the Field, 1980; Call it a Day, 1984. Short Stories: Salt, 1977; Search for Sarah Grace, 1978; Spectral Evidence, 1985; The Moving Light, 1986. Contributions: Queens Quarterly; Saturday Night; Chicago; Quarry; Denver Quarterly. *Address:* 166 Randolph Place, Windsor, ON N9B 2T3, Canada.

McNAMARA, Robert James, MA, PhD; American academic and poet; *Senior Lecturer in English, University of Washington, Seattle*; b. 28 March 1950, New York, NY; s. of James McNamara and Doris Maier; m. Judith Lightfoot 1993; one d. *Education:* Amherst Coll., Colorado State Univ., Univ. of Washington, Seattle. *Career:* Founder-Ed., L'Epervier Press 1977; Sr Lecturer in English, Univ. of Washington, Seattle 1985–; mem. Acad. of American Poets, PEN West. *Publications:* Second Messengers 1990; contrib. to anthologies, reviews, quarterlies and journals. *Honours:* Nat. Endowment for the Arts Fellowship 1987–88, Fulbright grant, Jadavpur Univ., Kolkata, India 1993. *Address:* c/o Department of English, Box 354330, University of Washington, Seattle, WA 98195, USA (office). *Telephone:* (206) 543-7131 (office). *E-mail:* rmcnamara@u .washington.edu (office). *Website:* faculty.washington.edu/rmcnamar (office).

MacNEACAIL, Aonghas; Scottish writer and poet; b. 7 June 1942, Uig, Isle of Skye; m. Gerda Stevenson 1980; one s. *Education:* University of Glasgow. *Career:* Writing Fellowships, The Gaelic College, Isle of Skye, 1977–79, An Comunn Gaidhealachm Oban, 1979–81, Ross-Cromarty District Council, 1988–90; mem. Scottish Poetry Library Asscn, council mem., 1984–. *Publications:* Poetry Quintet, 1976; Imaginary Wounds, 1980; Sireadh Bradain Sicir/ Seeking Wise Salmon, 1983; An Cathadh Mor/The Great Snowbattle, 1984; An Seachnadh/The Avoiding, 1986; Rocker and Water, 1990. Contributions: many publications. *Honours:* Grampian TV Gaelic Poetry Award; Diamond Jubilee Award, Scottish Asscn for the Speaking of Verse, 1985; An Comunn Gaidhealach Literary Award, 1985. *E-mail:* aonghasd@smo.uhi.ac.uk.

McNEILL, Daniel Richard, AB, JD; American writer; b. 1 June 1947, San Francisco, CA; m. Rosalind Gold 1984. *Education:* University of California at Berkeley, Harvard Law School. *Career:* mem. Authors' Guild. *Publications:* Fuzzy Logic, 1993; The Face, 1998. *Honours:* Los Angeles Times Book Prize in Science and Technology 1993. *Address:* c/o Author Mail, Grand Central Publishing, 237 Park Avenue, New York, NY 10017, USA.

McNEISH, James, BA; New Zealand writer; b. 23 Oct. 1931, Auckland. *Education:* University of Auckland. *Career:* Writer-in-Residence, Berlin Kunstler-program 1983; Research Fellow Nat. Library of New Zealand 1999. *Publications:* Tavern in the Town, 1957; Fire Under the Ashes, 1965; Mackenzie, 1970; The Mackenzie Affair, 1972; Larks in a Paradise (co-author), 1974; The Glass Zoo, 1976; As for the Godwits, 1977; Art of the Pacific (with Brian Brake), 1980; Belonging: Conversations in Israel, 1980; Joy, 1982; Walking on My Feet, 1983; The Man from Nowhere: A Berlin Diary, 1985; Lovelock, 1986; Penelope's Island, 1990; The Man from Nowhere and Other Prose, 1991; My Name is Paradiso 1995, Mr Halliday and the Circus Master 1996, The Mask of Sanity: the Bain Murders 1997, An Albatross Too Many 1998, Dance of the Peacocks: New Zealanders in Exile in the Time of Hitler and Mao Tse-tung 2003. *Address:* c/o Michael Gifkins, POB 6496, Auckland, New Zealand; POB 10628, Wellington. *Telephone:* (4) 473-1813 (home). *Fax:* (4) 499-7837 (home). *E-mail:* michael.gifkins@xtra.co.nz.

McNICHOLAS, Conor, BA; British journalist; *Editor, NME*; b. 1973, Bradford, West Yorkshire, England; m. Susan McNicholas; one s. *Education:* Manchester Victoria Univ. *Career:* staff mem. CD Rom Magazine 1994–95, Escape magazine 1995–96; Features Ed., Ministry magazine 1996–97; account exec., Powerhouse PR 1997–98; News Ed., Mixmag 1998–2001; Ed., Muzik 2001–02, NME (New Musical Express) 2002–; Cttee mem. BSME. *Honours:* PPA Award for Consumer Magazine Editor of the Year, BSME Award for Entertainment Magazine Ed. of the Year. *Address:* New Musical Express, IPC Specialist Group, 25th Floor, King's Reach Tower, Stamford Street, London, SE1 9LS, England (office). *Telephone:* (20) 7261-6472 (office). *E-mail:* editor@nme.com (office). *Website:* www.nme.com (office).

McPHEE, John Angus, AB; American academic and writer; *Professor of Journalism, Princeton University*; b. 8 March 1931, Princeton, NJ; m. 1st Pryde Brown 1957; four d.; m. 2nd Yolanda Whitman 1972; two step-s. two step-d. *Education:* Princeton Univ., Univ. of Cambridge. *Career:* dramatist, Robert Montgomery Presents Television Programme 1955–57; Assoc. Ed., Time magazine, New York 1957–64; staff writer, The New Yorker magazine 1965–; Ferris Prof. of Journalism, Princeton Univ. 1975–; Fellow Geological Soc. of America; mem. American Acad. of Arts and Letters. *Publications:* A Sense of Where You Are 1965, The Headmaster 1966, Oranges 1967, The Pine Barrens 1968, A Roomful of Hovings 1969, The Crofter and the Laird 1969, Levels of the Game 1970, Encounters with the Archdruid 1972, Wimbledon: A Celebration 1972, The Deltoid Pumpkin Seed 1973, The Curve of Binding Energy 1974, Pieces of the Frame 1975, The Survival of the Bark Canoe 1975, The John McPhee Reader 1977, Coming into the Country 1977, Giving Good Weight 1979, Alaska: Images of the Country (with Galen Rowell) 1981, Basin and Range 1981, In Suspect Terrain 1983, La Place de la Concorde Suisse 1984, Table of Contents 1985, Rising from the Plains 1986, Outcroppings

1988, The Control of Nature 1989, Looking for a Ship 1990, Assembling California 1993, The Ransom of Russian Art 1994, The Second John McPhee Reader 1996, Irons in the Fire 1997, Annals of the Former World 1998, The Founding Fish 2002, Uncommon Carriers 2006. *Honours:* various hon. doctorates; American Acad. and Inst. of Arts and Letters Award 1977, Princeton Univ. Woodrow Wilson Award 1982, American Asscn of Petroleum Geologists Journalism Award 1982, 1986, United States Geological Survey John Wesley Powell Award 1988, American Geophysical Union Walter Sullivan Award 1993, Pulitzer Prize for Non-Fiction 1999, Geological Soc. of America Public Service Award 2002, Acad. of Natural Sciences for Distinction in Natural History Art Gold Medal 2005. *Address:* 475 Drake's Corner Road, Princeton, NJ 08540, USA.

McPHERSON, Conor; Irish dramatist; b. 6 Aug. 1971, Dublin. *Education:* Univ. Coll., Dublin. *Career:* writer-in-residence, Bush Theatre, London 1996; co-f., Fly by Night Theatre Co. Dublin. *Plays:* Taking Stock 1989, Michelle Pfeiffer 1990, Scenes Federal 1991, Radio Play 1992, A Light in the Window of Industry 1993, Rum & Vodka 1994, The Good Thief 1994, The Stars Lose Their Glory 1994, Inventing Fortune's Wheel 1994, This Lime Tree Bower 1995, The Weir (Laurence Olivier Award) 1997, St Nicholas 1997, Dublin Carol 2000, Port Authority 2001, Come on Over 2001, Shining City 2004, The Seafarer 2006. *Films:* I Went Down (writer) (San Sebastian Film Festival Best Screenplay Award) 1997, Endgame (TV, dir) 2000, Saltwater (writer, dir) 2000, The Actors (writer, dir) 2003. *Honours:* Evening Standard Most Promising Playwright Award 1997, Stewart Parker Trust Award 1995, Guiness/National Theatre Ingenuity Award, Outer Critics Circle Award for Best Play, George Devine Award for Best New Play in London. *Literary Agent:* Curtis Brown Group Ltd, Haymarket House, 28–29 Haymarket, London, SW1Y 4SP, England. *E-mail:* cb@curtisbrown.co.uk. *Website:* www .curtisbrown.co.uk.

McPHERSON, James A., BA, LLB, MFA; American academic and writer; *Professor of English, University of Iowa*; b. 16 Sept. 1943, Savannah, GA; m. (divorced); one d. *Education:* Morris Brown Coll., Harvard Law School, Univ. of Iowa. *Career:* Rhetoric Program and Law School, Univ. of Iowa 1968–69; Lecturer, Univ. of California at Santa Cruz 1969–72; Asst Prof., Morgan State Univ. 1975–76; Assoc. Prof., Univ. of Virginia, Charlottesville 1976–81; Visiting Scholar, Yale Law School, New Haven 1978; Prof. of English, Writers' Workshop, Univ. of Iowa 1981–; Lecturer, Meiji Univ., Tsuda Coll., Chiba Univ. 1989–90, Japan; Fellow Center for Advanced Studies, Stanford Univ. 1997–98, 2002–03; mem. American Civil Liberties Union, PEN, Writers' Guild, Nat. Asscn for the Advancement of Colored People, American Acad. of Arts and Sciences. *Publications:* Hue and Cry 1969, Railroad 1976, Elbow Room 1977, Crabcakes 1998, A Region Not Home 1999; contrib. to Atlantic, Harvard Advocate, Ploughshares, Nimrod, New York Times, Esquire, Reader's Digest, Washington Post, World Literature Today, Doubletake, Harper's. *Honours:* Guggenheim Fellowship 1973, Pulitzer Prize for Fiction 1978, MacArthur Prize Fellows Award 1981, Univ. of Iowa Award for Excellence in Teaching 1990, Soc. of Southern Journalists Green Eyeshades Award for Excellence in Print Commentary 1994. *Address:* 102 Dey House, 507 S. Clinton Street, Iowa City, IA 52242-1000 (office); 711 Rundell Street, Iowa City, IA 52240, USA (home). *Telephone:* (319) 335-0416 (office); (319) 338-3136 (home). *Fax:* (319) 335-0420 (office).

McPHERSON, James Munro, PhD; American historian, academic and writer; *George Henry Davis '86 Professor Emeritus of History, Princeton University*; b. 11 Oct. 1936, Valley City, ND; s. of James M. McPherson and Miriam O. McPherson; m. Patricia Rasche 1957; one d. *Education:* Gustavus Adolphus Coll. and Johns Hopkins Univ. *Career:* Instructor Princeton Univ. 1962–65, Asst Prof. 1965–66, Assoc. Prof. 1966–72, Prof. of History 1972–82, Edwards Prof. of American History 1982–91, George Henry Davis '86 Prof. of American History 1991, now Prof. Emer.; Pres. Soc. of American Historians 2000–; Woodrow Wilson Fellow and Danforth Fellow 1958–62; Guggenheim Fellow 1967–68; Huntingdon Library-Nat. Endowment for the Humanities Fellowship 1977–78; Center for Advanced Study in the Behavioural Sciences Fellowship 1982–83; Huntington Seaver Fellow 1987–88; Jefferson Lecture 2000; Pres. American Historical Asscn 2003. *Publications:* The Struggle for Equality: Abolitionists and the Negro in the Civil War and Reconstruction 1964, The Negro's Civil War 1965, Marching Toward Freedom 1968, The Anti-Slavery Crusade in America (co-ed, 59 vols) 1969, Blacks in America (essays) 1971, The Abolitionist Legacy 1975, Ordeal by Fire: The Civil War and Reconstruction 1982, Religion, Race and Reconstruction (essays, co-ed) 1982, Battle Cry of Freedom: The Civil War Era 1988, Battle Chronicles of the Civil War (ed, six vols) 1989, Abraham Lincoln and the Second American Revolution 1991, Images of the Civil War 1992, Gettysburg 1993, What They Fought For 1861–1865 1994, The Atlas of the Civil War 1994, What They Fought For 1861–1865 1994, Drawn With the Sword: Reflections on the American Civil War 1996, The American Heritage New History of the Civil War (ed) 1996, For Cause and Comrades: Why Men Fought in the Civil War 1997, Lamson of the Gettysburg: The Civil War Letters of Lt Roswell H. Lamson, US Navy 1997, Is Blood Thicker Than Water? Crises of Nationalism in the Modern World 1998, The Encyclopedia of Civil War Biographies (ed, three vols) 1999, To the Best of My Ability: The American Presidents (ed) 2000, Crossroads of Freedom: Antietam, The Battle That Changed the Course of the Civil War 2002, Hallowed Ground: A Walk at Gettysburg 2003, The Illustrated Battle Cry of Freedom 2003, Into the West (juvenile) 2006; contrib. to reference works, scholarly books and professional journals. *Honours:*

Anisfield-Wolf Prize in Race Relations 1965, Pulitzer Prize in History 1989, Christopher Award 1989, Best Book Award, American Military Inst. 1989, Lincoln Prize 1998, Theodore and Franklin D. Roosevelt Prize in Naval History 1998, Pritzker Military Library Literature Award for lifetime achievement in military writing 2007. *Address:* Department of History, 226 Dickinson Hall, Princeton University, Princeton, NJ 08544 (office); 15 Randall Road, Princeton, NJ 08540, USA (home). *Telephone:* (609)258-4173 (office); (609) 924-9226 (home). *E-mail:* jmcphers@princeton.edu (office). *Website:* his .princeton.edu (office).

McPHERSON, Sandra Jean, BA; American academic and poet; *Professor of English, University of California at Davis*; b. 2 Aug. 1943, San Jose, CA; m. 1st Henry D. Carlile 1966 (divorced 1985); one d.; m. 2nd Walter D. Pavlich 1995 (died 2002). *Education:* San Jose State Univ., Univ. of Washington. *Career:* Visiting Lecturer, Univ. of Iowa 1974–76, 1978–80; Holloway Lecturer, Univ. of California, Berkeley 1981; teacher, Oregon Writers' Workshop, Portland 1981–85; Prof. of English, Univ. of California, Davis 1985–; Ed. and Publr Swan Scythe Press 1999–. *Publications:* Elegies for the Hot Season 1970, Radiation 1973, The Year of Our Birth 1978, Patron Happiness 1983, Streamers 1988, The God of Indeterminacy 1993, Edge Effect 1996, The Spaces Between Birds 1996, A Visit to Civilisation 2002; contrib. to periodicals. *Honours:* Ingram Merrill Foundation grants 1972, 1984, Nat. Endowment for the Arts grants 1974, 1980, 1985, Guggenheim Fellowship 1976, Oregon Arts Comm. Fellowship 1984, American Acad. and Inst. of Art and Letters Award 1987. *Address:* c/o Department of English, University of California, Davis, CA 95616, USA (office). *Telephone:* (530) 752-8519 (office). *E-mail:* sjmcpherson@ucdavis.edu (office). *Website:* www.english.ucdavis.edu/ Faculty/mcpherson/mcpherson.html (office); www.swanscythe.com (home).

McQUAIN, Jeffrey Hunter, AA, BA, MA, PhD; American writer, researcher and word historian; b. 23 Nov. 1955, Frederick, MD. *Education:* Montgomery College, University of Maryland, American University. *Career:* researcher to William Safire, New York Times 1983–; mem. MLA. *Publications:* The Elements of English, 1986; Guide to Good Word Usage, 1989; Power Language, 1996; Coined by Shakespeare, 1998; Never Enough Words, 1999; Homegrown English, 2002; Coined by God, 2003; The Bard on the Brain, 2003. Contributions: New York Times Magazine. *Honours:* Words From Home Award 1996. *Address:* PO Box 4008, Rockville, MD 20849, USA.

McQUEEN, Priscilla (Cilla) Muriel, MA; New Zealand poet and artist; b. 22 Jan. 1949, Birmingham, England; m. Ralph Hotere 1974 (divorced 1986); one d. *Education:* Otago University, Dunedin, New Zealand. *Career:* mem. Australasian Performing Rights Assen; PEN. *Publications:* Homing In, 1982; Anti Gravity, 1984; Wild Sweets, 1986; Benzina, 1988; Berlin Diary, 1990; Crikey, 1994. Contributions: various publications. *Honours:* New Zealand Book Awards for Poetry, 1983, 1989, 1991; Fulbright Visiting Writers Fellowship, 1985; Robert Burns Fellowships, 1985, 1986; Australia-New Zealand Exchange Writers' Fellowship, 1987; Goethe Institute Scholarship, Berlin, 1988. *Address:* 33 Skibo Street, Kew, Dunedin, New Zealand.

McRAE, Hamish Malcolm Donald, MA; British journalist and writer; b. 20 Oct. 1943, Barnstaple, Devon, England; m. Frances Annes Cairncross 1971; two d. *Education:* Fettes Coll., Edinburgh, Trinity Coll., Dublin. *Career:* Ed. Euromoney 1972, Business and City, The Independent 1989; Financial Ed. The Guardian 1975; Assoc. Ed. The Independent 1991. *Publications:* Capital City – London as a Financial Centre (with Frances Cairncross) 1973, The Second Great Crash (with Frances Cairncross) 1975, Japan's Role in the Emerging Global Securities Market 1985, The World in 2020 1994; contrib. to numerous magazines and journals. *Honours:* Wincott Foundation Financial Journalist of the Year 1979, Amex Bank Review Essays Special Merit Award 1987, Periodical Publishers Assen Award for Columnist of the Year 1996, David Watt Prize 2005, Business and Financial Journalist of the Year, British Press Awards 2006. *Address:* The Independent, 191 Marsh Wall, London, E14 9RS (office); 6 Canonbury Lane, London, N1 2AP, England (home). *Telephone:* (20) 7005-2635 (office). *E-mail:* h.mcrae@independent.co.uk (office).

McSHARRY, Deirdre Mary; Irish journalist, editor and curator; b. 4 April 1932, London, England; d. of the late Dr John McSharry and Mary O'Brien; m. Ian Coulter Smyth. *Education:* Dominican Convent, Wicklow, Trinity Coll., Dublin Univ. *Career:* actress at Gate Theatre, Dublin 1953–55; freelance with The Irish Times 1953; mem. staff Evening Herald, Dublin 1955–56; with bookshop Metropolitan Museum of Art, New York 1956; Reporter Women's Wear Daily, New York 1956–58; mem. staff Woman's Own 1959–62; Fashion Ed. Evening News 1962; Woman's Ed. Daily Express 1963–66; Fashion Ed. The Sun 1967–71; Fashion Ed. Cosmopolitan 1972, Ed. 1973–85; Ed.-in-Chief Country Living 1986–89; Consultant Nat. Magazine Co. and Magazine Div. The Hearst Corpn 1990–92; Ed. Countryside magazine, New York 1991–92; Chair. Bath Friends of The American Museum in Britain, Bath; mem. Council of the American Museum, Council of the Bath Festivals Trust 2002; Trustee The American Museum (in Britain) 2002–04. *Art Exhibitions (as curator):* Inspirations – The Textile Tradition (The American Museum) 2001, Quilt Bonanza (The American Museum) 2003. *Publication:* Inspirations: The Textile Tradition Then and Now (American Museum Catalogue) 2001. *Honours:* Ed. of the Year (Periodical Publrs Assen) 1981, 1987, Mark Boxer Award: Editor's Ed. 1991. *Address:* Southfield House, 16 High Street, Rode, BA11 6NZ, England. *Telephone:* (1373) 831263 (home). *Fax:* (1373) 831263 (home). *E-mail:* deirdre.mcsharry@btopenworld.com.

MACSOVSZKY, Peter, DipEd, MA; Slovak teacher and writer; b. 4 Nov. 1966. *Education:* Teacher Training Coll., Mitra, Univ. of Constantine the Philosopher. *Career:* mem. Obec Slovensky Spisovatelov. *Publications:* Strach z Utopie (trans. as Fear of Utopia) 1994, Ambit 1995, Somrak Cudnosti (trans. as The Dusk of Chastity) 1996, Cvicna Pitva (trans. as Training Autopsy) 1997, A'lbonctan (trans. as False Pathology) 1998.

MacTHÒMAIS, Ruaraidh (see Thomson, Derick Smith)

McTRUSTRY, Christifor John; Australian screenwriter and novelist; b. 29 Oct. 1960, Wellington, NSW; m. Patricia Rose Dravine 1986; one s. one d. *Education:* Bachelor of Creative Arts, 1989, Master of Creative Arts, 1990, University of Wollongong. *Career:* mem. Australian Writers Guild; Australian National Playwrights Centre; Australian Society of Authors; MWA; Crime Writers Assen of Australia. *Publications:* The Cat Burglar, 1995; The Card Shark, 1996; Axeman!, 1997; Frankenkid, 1997; George and the Dragon, 1997; Susie Smelly-Feet, 1997. Other: Television and radio series. *Address:* 22 Stanleigh Crescent, West Wollongong, NSW 2500, Australia.

MacVEY, John Wishart, BA; Scottish writer; b. 19 Jan. 1923, Kelso. *Education:* diploma in applied chemistry, University of Strathclyde, Open University, Milton Keynes. *Career:* fmr technical information officer. *Publications:* Speaking of Space (with C. P. Snow, B. Lovell and P. Moore), 1962; Alone in the Universe?, 1963; Journey to Alpha Centauri, 1965; How We Will Reach the Stars, 1969; Whispers from Space, 1973; Interstellar Travel: Past, Present and Future, 1977; Space Weapons/Space War, 1979; Where We Will Go When the Sun Dies?, 1980; Colonizing Other Worlds, 1984; Time Travel, 1987. *Address:* Mellendean, 15 Adair Avenue, Saltcoats, Ayrshire KA21 5QS, Scotland.

McWHIRTER, George, BA, MA; Canadian writer, poet, translator and academic; *Professor Emeritus, University of British Columbia*; b. 26 Sept. 1939, Belfast, Northern Ireland; m. Angela Mairead Coid 1963; one s. one d. *Education:* Queen's Univ., Univ. of British Columbia. *Career:* asst teacher, Kilkeel Secondary 1962–64, Bangor Grammar School 1964–65; instructor, Escuela de Idiomas, Univ. of Barcelona 1965–66; teacher, Alberni District Secondary School 1966–68; Visiting Lecturer, Univ. of BC 1970–71, Asst Prof. 1971–76, Assoc. Prof. 1976–82, Prof. 1982–2004, Prof. Emer. 2004–; Co-Ed.-in-Chief, Prism International Magazine 1977, Advisory Ed. 1978–; Prof., Univ. of British Columbia 1970–, Head of Creative Writing 1983–93; mem. League of Canadian Poets, Writers' Union of Canada, PEN, Literary Trans Assen of Canada. *Publications:* Catalan Poems 1971, Bodyworks 1974, Queen of the Sea 1976, God's Eye 1981, Coming to Grips with Lucy 1982, Fire Before Dark 1983, Paula Lake 1984, Cage 1987, The Selected Poems of José Emilio Pacheco (ed. and trans.) 1987, The Listeners 1991, A Bad Day to be Winning 1992, A Staircase for All Souls 1993, Incubus: The Dark Side of the Light 1995, Musical Dogs 1996, Fab 1997, Where Words Like Monarchs Fly (ed. and trans.) 1998, Ovid in Saskatchewan 1998, Eyes to See Otherwise: The Selected Poems of Homero Aridjis, 1960–2000 (co-ed. and trans.) 2001, The Book of Contradictions (poems) 2002; contrib. to numerous magazines and journals. *Honours:* McMillan Prize 1969, Commonwealth Poetry Prize 1972, F. R. Scott Prize 1988, Ethel Wilson Fiction Prize 1988, Univ. of British Columbia Killan Prize for Teaching 1998, Killan Prize for Mentoring 2004, winner League of Canadian Poets Canadian Poetry Chapbook Competition 1998. *Address:* 4637 W 13th Avenue, Vancouver, BC V6R 2V6, Canada.

McWILLIAM, Candia Frances Juliet, BA; British writer; b. 1 July 1955, Edin.; d. of Colin McWilliam and Margaret McWilliam; m. 1st Quentin Gerard Carew Wallop (now Earl of Portsmouth) 1981; one s. one d.; m. 2nd Fram Dinshaw; one s. *Education:* Sherborne School, Dorset and Girton Coll., Cambridge. *Publications:* novels: A Cast of Knives 1988, A Little Stranger 1989, Debatable Land 1994; short stories: Wait till I Tell You 1997. *Address:* 21 Beaumont Buildings, Oxford, OX1 2LL, England. *Telephone:* (1865) 511931. *Fax:* (1865) 553326. *E-mail:* cleminol@hotmail.com.

MADDEN, David, BS, MA; American educator, writer, critic, editor and poet and dramatist; b. 25 July 1933, Knoxville, TN; m. Roberta Margaret Young 1956; one s. *Education:* Univ. of Tennessee, San Francisco State Coll., Yale Drama School. *Career:* faculty, Appalachian State Teachers Coll., Boone, NC 1957–58, Centre Coll. 1964–66, Ohio Univ. 1966–68; Asst Ed., Kenyon Review 1964–66; writer-in-residence, Louisiana State Univ. 1968–92, Dir Creative Writing Program 1992–94, and US Civil War Center 1992–99, Alumni Prof. 1994, Donald and Veliva Crumbley Prof. of Creative Writing 2000; mem. Associated Writing Programs, Authors' League. *Publications:* fiction: The Beautiful Greed 1961, Cassandra Singing 1969, The Shadow Knows 1970, Brothers in Confidence 1972, Bijou 1974, The Suicide's Wife 1978, Pleasure-Dome 1979, On the Big Wind 1980, The New Orleans of Possibilities 1982, Sharpshooter 1995; non-fiction: Wright Morris 1964, The Poetic Image in 6 Genres 1969, James M. Cain 1970, Creative Choices: A Spectrum of Quality and Technique in Fiction 1975, Harlequin's Stick: Charlie's Cane: A Comparative Study of Commedia dell' arte and Silent Slapstick Comedy 1975, A Primer of the Novel: For Readers & Writers 1980, Writer's Revisions (with Richard Powers) 1981, Cain's Craft 1986, Revising Fiction 1988, The Fiction Tutor 1990, editor: Proletarian Writers of the Thirties 1968, Tough Guy Writers of the Thirties 1968, American Dreams, American Nightmares 1970, Rediscoveries 1971, The Popular Culture Explosion (with Ray B. Browne) 1972, The Contemporary Literary Scene (assoc. ed.) 1973, Nathanael West: The Cheaters and the Cheated 1973, Remembering James Agee 1974, Studies in the Short Story (fourth–sixth edns) 1975–84, Rediscoveries II (with

Peggy Bach) 1988, The World of Fiction 1990, Eight Classic American Novels 1990, Classics of Civil War Fiction 1991, Beyond the Battlefield (ed.), A Pocketful of Prose: Vintage 1992, A Pocketful of Prose: Contemporary 1992, A Pocketful of Plays 1995, A Pocketful of Poems 1995, The Legacy of Robert Penn Warner 2000, Thomas Wolfe's Civil War 2004, Losses of the Sultana 2004, Touching the Web of Southern Novelists 2006; contrib. poems, plays, essays and short stories to various publications. *Honours:* John Golden Fellow in Playwriting 1959, Rockefeller Foundation grant in fiction 1969, Nat. Council on the Arts Award 1970, Robert Penn Warren Fiction Award 2005. *Address:* 614 Park Blvd, Baton Rouge, LA 70806, USA.

MADDOX, Carl (see Tubb, Edwin Charles)

MADDOX, Sir John Royden, Kt; British writer and publishing editor; b. 27 Nov. 1925, s. of A. J. Maddox and M. E. Maddox; m. 1st Nancy Fanning (died 1960); one s. one d.; m. 2nd Brenda Power Murphy 1960; one s. one d. *Education:* Christ Church, Oxford, King's Coll., London. *Career:* asst lecturer, then lecturer in Theoretical Physics, Manchester Univ. 1949–55; science corresp. The Guardian 1955–64; Affiliate, Rockefeller Inst., New York 1962–63; Asst Dir Nuffield Foundation and Co-ordinator Nuffield Foundation Science Teaching Project 1964–66; Man. Dir Macmillan Journals Ltd 1970–72; Dir Macmillan & Co. Ltd 1968–73; Chair. Maddox Editorial Ltd 1972–74; Dir Nuffield Foundation 1975–80; Ed. Nature 1966–73, 1980–96; mem. Crickadarn and Gwendwr Community Council 1981–. *Publications:* The Spread of Nuclear Weapons (jtly) 1962, Revolution in Biology 1964, The Doomsday Syndrome 1972, Beyond the Energy Crisis 1975, What Remains to be Discovered 1987. *Honours:* Hon. Fellow Royal Soc. 2000; Hon. DTech (Surrey) 1982, Hon. DSc (Univ. of E Anglia) 1992, (Liverpool) 1994. *Address:* 9 Pitt Street, London, W8 4NX, England (home). *Telephone:* (20) 7937-8981 (office); (20) 7937-9750 (home). *E-mail:* j.maddox@btopenworld.com (office).

MADELEY, John, BA; British writer and broadcaster; b. 14 July 1934, Salford, England; m. Alison Madeley 1962; one s. one d. *Education:* Univ. of Manchester. *Career:* broadcaster, BBC and Deutsche Welle. *Publications:* Human Rights Begin with Breakfast 1981, Diego Garcia: Contrast to the Falklands 1982, When Aid is No Help 1991, Trade and the Poor 1992, Big Business, Poor People: The Impact of Transnational Corporations on the World Poor 1999, Hungry for Trade: How the Poor Pay for Free Trade 2000, Food for All: The Need for a New Agriculture 2001, A People's World: Alternatives to Economic Globalization 2003, 100 Ways to Make Poverty History 2005; contrib. to newspapers and magazines. *Address:* 19 Woodford Close, Caversham, Reading, Berkshire RG4 7HN, England (office). *Telephone:* (1189) 476063 (office). *E-mail:* madeleyjohn@aol.com (office). *Website:* www .johnmadeley.co.uk (office).

MADGETT, Naomi Long, BA, MEd, PhD; American poet, publisher and academic; b. 5 July 1923, Norfolk, VA; m. Leonard P. Andrews Sr. *Education:* Virginia State Coll., Wayne State Univ., Int. Inst. for Advanced Studies. *Career:* Research Assoc., Oakland Univ.; Lecturer in English, Univ. of Michigan; Assoc. Prof. to Prof. of English Emeritus, Eastern Michigan Univ.; Publisher; Ed., Lotus Press. *Publications:* Songs to a Phantom Nightingale, 1941; One and the Many, 1956; Star by Star, 1965; Pink Ladies in the Afternoon, 1972; Exits and Entrances, 1978; Phantom Nightingale, 1981; A Student's Guide to Creative Writing, 1990. Contributions: numerous anthologies and journals.

MADSEN, Richard Paul, BD, MTh, MA, PhD; American academic and writer; *Professor of Sociology, University of California at San Diego;* b. 2 April 1941, Alameda, Calif.; m. Judith Rosselli 1974. *Education:* Maryknoll Coll., Glen Ellyn, Ill., Maryknoll Seminary, Ossining, NY, Harvard Univ. *Career:* ordained Roman Catholic priest 1968; Maryknoll missioner, Taiwan 1968–71; left priesthood 1974; Lecturer in Sociology, Harvard Univ. 1977–78; Asst Prof., Univ. of California at San Diego, La Jolla 1978–83, Assoc. Prof. 1983–85, Prof. of Sociology 1985–; mem. American Sociological Asscn, Asscn of Asian Studies, Governing Council for China and Inner Asia 1989–91. *Publications:* Chen Village: The Recent History of a Peasant Community in Mao's China (with Anita Chan and Jonathan Unger) 1984, revised edn as Chen Village Under Mao and Deng 1992, Morality and Power in a Chinese Village 1984, Habits of the Heart: Individualism in American Life (with Robert N. Bellah, William M. Sullivan, Ann Swidler and Steven M. Tipton) 1985, Individualism and Commitment in American Life: A Habits of the Heart Reader (with Robert N. Bellah, William M. Sullivan, Ann Swidler and Steven M. Tipton) 1987, Unofficial China (ed. with Perry Link and Paul Pickowicz) 1989, The Good Society (with Robert N. Bellah, William M. Sullivan, Ann Swidler and Steven M. Tipton) 1991, China and the American Dream: A Moral Inquiry 1995, China's Catholics: Tragedy and Hope in a Emerging Civil Society 1998, Meaning and Modernity: Religion, Polity and Self (with William M. Sullivan, Ann Swidler and Steven M. Tipton) 2002, Popular China: Unofficial Culture in a Globalising Society (with Perry Link and Paul Pickowicz) 2002, The Many and the One: Religious and Secular Perspectives in Ethical Pluralism in the Modern World (with Tracy B. Strong) 2003; contribs to journals. *Honours:* C. Wright Mills Award, Soc. for the Study of Social Problems 1985, Current Interest Book Award, Los Angeles Times 1985, Book Award, Asscn of Logos Bookstores 1986. *Address:* c/o Department of Sociology, University of California at San Diego, La Jolla, CA 92093, USA (office).

MAGANI, Mohamed; Algerian writer. *Career:* exiled 1995–2002; Lecturer Univ. of Algiers 2002–; founder and Dir Algerian PEN Club, elected to bd Int.

PEN 2005–. *Publications:* novels: La Faille du ciel (Grand Prix Littéraire International de la Ville d'Alger) 1983, Esthétique de boucher (The Aesthetic of the Butcher) 1998, Un Temps berlinois 2001, Le Refuge des ruines 2002, Une Guerre se meurt 2004; short stories: An Icelandic Dream 1993, Please Pardon our Appearance Whilst we Redress the Window Display 1995; contrib. to Freedom to Publish, Responsibility for a Human Right 1998, Metronome journal. *Address:* B2/59 cité Rabia Tahar, Bab Ezzouar, Algiers, Algeria (office). *E-mail:* mohmagani@yahoo.fr.

MAGDALEN, I. I. (see Botsford, Keith)

MAGEE, Bryan, MA; British author and broadcaster; b. 12 April 1930, London; s. of Frederick Magee and Sheila Lynch; m. Ingrid Söderlund 1954 (died 1986); one d. *Education:* Christ's Hosp., Lycée Hôche, Versailles, Keble Coll. Oxford and Yale Univ. *Career:* Army Intelligence Corps 1948–49; TV reporter This Week; music and theatre critic Musical Times and The Listener; Lecturer in Philosophy, Balliol Coll. Oxford 1970–71; Visiting Fellow, All Souls Coll. Oxford 1973–74; MP for Leyton 1974–83; Pres. Critics Circle of GB 1983–84; Hon. Sr Research Fellow, King's Coll. London 1984–94, Visiting Prof. 1994–2000; Hon. Fellow, Queen Mary Coll. London 1988–; Fellow, Queen Mary and Westfield Coll. London 1989–; Visiting Fellow Wolfson Coll. Oxford 1991–94, New Coll. Oxford 1995, Merton Coll. Oxford 1998, St. Catherine's Coll. Oxford 2000, Peterhouse Cambridge 2001, Clare Hall Cambridge (Life Mem.) 2004; Visiting Prof. Univ. of Otago, Dunedin, New Zealand 2006; also at Yale, Harvard, Sydney, LSE; newspaper columnist; mem. Arts Council of GB and Chair. Music Panel 1993–94; mem. Soc. of Authors. *Television:* Men of Ideas 1978, The Great Philosophers 1987. *Publications:* Crucifixion and Other Poems 1951, Go West Young Man 1958, The New Radicalism 1962, The Democratic Revolution 1964, Towards 2000 1965, One in Twenty 1966, The Television Interviewer 1966, Aspects of Wagner 1968 (revised edn 1988), Modern British Philosophy 1971 (re-issued as Talking Philosophy 2001), Popper 1973, Facing Death 1977, Men of Ideas 1978, The Philosophy of Schopenhauer 1983, 1997, The Great Philosophers 1987, On Blindness 1995 (re-issued as Sight Unseen 1998), Confessions of a Philosopher 1997, The Story of Philosophy 1998, Wagner and Philosophy 2000, Clouds of Glory: A Hoxton Childhood (J. R. Ackerley Prize for autobiography) 2003, Growing Up In a War 2007. *Honours:* Hon. Fellow Keble Coll. Oxford 1994–; Hon. DLitt (Univ. of Leicester) 2005; Silver Medal, Royal TV Soc. 1978, J.R. Ackerley Prize for Autobiography 2004. *Address:* Wolfson College, Oxford, OX2 6UD, England (office).

MAGEE, Wesley (Wes) Leonard Johnston; British poet and writer; b. 20 July 1939, Greenock, Scotland; m. Janet Elizabeth Parkhouse 1967; one s. one d. *Education:* Goldsmiths Coll., Univ. of London, Univ. of Bristol. *Career:* mem. Poetry Soc. of Great Britain, Philip Larkin Soc.; Cole Scholar, FL 1985. *Publications:* over 80 books for children 1972–; contribs: reviews and journals. *Honours:* New Poets Award 1972, Poetry Book Soc. Recommendation 1978, Children's Poetry Bookshelf Choice 2001, Poetry Archive (recording) 2004. *Address:* Crag View Cottage, Thorgill, Rosedale, North Yorkshire YO18 8SG, England (home). *Telephone:* (1751) 417633 (home). *E-mail:* wes@wesmagee .fsnet.co.uk (home).

MAGER, Donald Northrop; American academic, poet and writer; b. 24 Aug. 1942, Santa Rita, NM; m. Barbara Feldman (divorced); two s.; pnr William McDowell. *Education:* BA, Drake University, 1964; MA, Creative Writing, Syracuse University, 1966; PhD, English Literature, Wayne State University, 1986. *Career:* Instructor, Syracuse University; Assoc. Prof., Johnson C. Smith University; mem. MLA. *Publications:* Poetry: To Track the Wounded One: A Journal, 1988; Glosses: Twenty-four Preludes and Etudes, 1995; That Which is Owed to Death, 1998; Borderings, 1998; Good Turns, 2001; Akhmatova (opera libretto), 2002; Elegance of the Ungraspable, 2003. Contributions: anthologies, books, reviews, quarterlies, journals, and magazines. *Honours:* First Prize, Hallmark Competition, 1965; Approach Magazines Award, 1978; Tompkings Award First Prize for Poetry, Wayne State University, 1986; First Prize, The Lyricist Statewide Poetry Competition, Campbell University, 1992; Assoc. Artist Residency, Atlantic Center for the Arts, New Smyrna Beach, FL, 1994; Winner, Union County Writers Club Chapbook Contest, 1998. *Address:* c/o Johnson C. Smith University, UPO 2441, Charlotte, NC 28216, USA.

MAGNUSSON, Sigurdur A., BA; Icelandic writer and poet; b. 31 March 1928, Reykjavík; m. 1st (divorced); m. 2nd (divorced); two s. three d. *Education:* Univ. of Iceland, Univ. of Copenhagen, Univ. of Athens, Univ. of Stockholm, New School for Social Research, New York. *Career:* Literary and Drama Critic, Morgunbladid, 1956–67; Ed.-in-Chief, Samvinnan, 1967–74; mem., Int. Writing Programme, Univ. of Iowa, 1976, 1977; mem., Int. Artists' Programme, West Berlin, 1979–80; mem., Jury, Nordic Council Prize for Literature, 1990–98; mem. Amnesty Int. (Chair., 1988–89, 1993–95), mem. Greek-Icelandic Soc. (Chair. 1985–88), Soc. of Icelandic Drama Critics (Chair. 1963–71), Writers' Union of Iceland (Chair. 1971–78, Hon. mem. 1994–); Hon. mem. Union of Translators and Interpreters. *Plays:* Visiting (Nat. Theatre, 1962). *Publications:* in English: Northern Sphinx: Iceland and the Icelanders from the Settlement to the Present, 1977; Iceland: Country and People, 1978; The Iceland Horse, 1978; The Postwar Poetry of Iceland, 1982; Icelandic Writing Today, 1982; Iceland Crucible: A Modern Artistic Renaissance, 1985; The Icelanders, 1990; Iceland: Isle of Light, 1995; 33 books in Icelandic; 32 translations into Icelandic from English, Danish, German and Greek; contrib. to professional journals. *Honours:* Golden Cross of Phoenix, Greece, 1955; Cultural Council Prize for Best Play, 1961, and Best Novel, 1980; European

Jean Monnet Prize for Literature, 1995. *Address:* Fjolugata 23, 101 Reykjavik, Iceland. *Telephone:* 552-5922 (home). *E-mail:* sambar@isl.is (home).

MAGORIAN, James, BS, MS; American poet and writer; b. 24 April 1942, Palisade, NE. *Education:* Univ. of Nebraska, Illinois State Univ., Univ. of Oxford, Harvard Univ. *Publications:* poetry: Hitchhiker in Hall County 1968, The Garden of Epicurus 1971, Safe Passage 1977, Phases of the Moon 1978, Tap Dancing on a Tightrope 1981, Taxidermy Lessons 1982, The Walden Pond Caper 1983, The Emily Dickinson Jogging Book 1984, Weighing the Sun's Light 1985, The Hideout of the Sigmund Freud Gang 1987, Borderlands 1992, The Yellowstone Meditations 1996, Haymarket Square 1998, Littorals 2004, Voices 2006; fiction: America First 1992, The Man Who Wore Layers of Clothing in the Winter 1994, Hearts of Gold 1996, Souvenir Pillows From Mars 1996; also children's books; contrib. to reviews, quarterlies and journals. *Address:* 2626 North 49th Street, # 402, Lincoln, NE 68504, USA.

MAGORIAN, Michelle Jane, Dip; British writer and actress; b. 6 Nov. 1947, Southsea, Portsmouth, Hants.; d. of William Magorian and Freda Magorian; m. Peter Keith Venner 1987 (divorced 1998); two s. *Education:* Rose Bruford Coll. of Speech and Drama, Kent, École Internationale de Mime Marcel Marceau, Paris. *Career:* mem. PEN, British Actors' Equity. *Publications:* fiction: Goodnight Mister Tom (also libretto for musical 2001) 1981, Back Home 1984, A Little Love Song 1991, Cuckoo in the Nest 1994, A Spoonful of Jam 1998; poetry: Waiting for My Shorts to Dry 1989, Orange Paw Marks 1991; short stories: In Deep Water 1992, Be Yourself 2003; libretti: Hello Life! 2004, Tinsel 2004; contrib. to Puffin Post. *Honours:* Guardian Award for Children's Fiction, UK 1981, Int. Reading Asscn Children's Award, USA 1982, American Library Asscn Notable Children's Books 1982, American Library Asscn Best Book for Young Adults 1982, American Library Asscn Young Adult Reviewers' Choice 1982, Western Australia Young Readers Book Award 1983, 1987, BAFTA Award 1999; Hon. DLitt. *Literary Agent:* Rogers, Coleridge & White Ltd, 20 Powis Mews, London, W11 1JN, England. *E-mail:* patw@rcwlitagency.co.uk.

MAGRIS, Claudio; Italian journalist, writer and academic; *Professor of German Language and Literature, University of Trieste;* b. 10 April 1939, Trieste; s. of Duilio Magris and Pia de Grisogono Magris; m. Marisa Madieri 1964; two s. *Education:* Univ. of Turin. *Career:* Lecturer in German Language and Literature, Univ. of Trieste 1968–70, Turin 1970–78, Trieste 1978–; mem. Deutsche Akad. für Sprache und Dichtung (Darmstadt), Österreichische Akad. der Wissenschaften, Accad. delle Scienze di Torino, Ateneo Veneto, Akad. der Wissenschaften (Göttingen). *Publications:* Il Mito absburgico nella letteratura austriaca moderna 1963, 1988, Wilhelm Heinse 1968, Lontano da dove. Joseph Roth e la tradizione ebraico-orientale 1971, Dietro le parole 1978, Itaca e oltre 1982, Trieste. Un'identità di frontiera 1982, 1987, L'anello di Clarisse 1984, Illazioni su una sciabola 1984, Danubio 1986 (trans. in numerous languages), Stadelmann 1988, Microcosmi 1997, Utopia e disincanto 1999, Telling Tales (contrib. to charity anthology) 2004; numerous essays and book reviews in Corriere della Sera and other European newspapers and periodicals; trans. Ibsen, Kleist, Schnitzler, Büchner. *Honours:* Debenedetti 1972, Val di Comino 1978, Goethe Medaille 1980, Aquileia 1983, Premiolino 1983, San Giusto d'Oro 1984, Musil Medaille der Stadt Klagenfurt 1984, Bagutta 1987, Accad. dei Lincei 1987, Marotta 1987, Città di Modena 1987, Antico Fattore 1988, Juan Carlos I 1989, Premio Strega 1997, Premio Chiara alla Carriera 1999, Premio Würth per la Cultura Europea 1999, Premio Grinzane Piemonte 1999, Medaglia d'Oro della Cultura della Scuola e dell' Arte 1999, Premio Sikken 2000, Premio Nietsche 2000, Premium Erasmianum 2001, Leipziger Buchpreis zur Europäischen Verständigung 2001, Osterreichisches Ehrenkreuz für Wissenschaft und Kunst (First Class), Prince of Asturias Prize for Letters 2004. *Address:* Università degli Studi Trieste, Piazzale Europa 1, 34127 Trieste; Via Carpaccio 2, Trieste, Italy. *Telephone:* (040) 6767111 (office); (040) 305428. *Fax:* (040) 6763093 (office); (040) 314455.

MAGRS, Paul, BA, MA, PhD; British writer and academic; *Senior Lecturer in Creative Writing, Manchester Metropolitan University;* b. 12 Nov. 1969, Jarrow, Tyne and Wear, England. *Education:* Univ. of Lancaster. *Career:* teacher of creative writing from 1993; fmr Lecturer and creative writing organizer, Univ. of East Anglia, Norwich seven years; currently Sr Lecturer in Creative Writing, Manchester Metropolitan Univ. *Publications:* fiction: Marked for Life 1995, Playing Out (short stories) 1997, Does it Show? 1997, Could it be Magic? 1998, Dr Who: The Scarlet Empress 1998, Dr Who: The Blue Angel 1999, Modern Love 2000, Dr Who: Verdigris 2000, All the Rage 2001, Dr Who: Mad Dogs and Englishmen 2002, Strange Boy 2002, Aisles 2003, Hands Up! 2003, To the Devil: A Diva! 2004, The Good, the Bat and the Ugly 2004, Exchange 2006, Never the Bride 2006. *Address:* Department of English, Manchester Metropolitan University, Geoffrey Manton Building Room 461, Rosamond Street West (off Oxford Road), Manchester, M15 6LL, England (office). *E-mail:* p.magrs@mmu.ac.uk (office).

MAHAPATRA, Jayanta, BSc, MSc, LLD; Indian poet, writer and editor; b. 22 Oct. 1928, Cuttack, Orissa; m. Jyotsna Rani Das 1951; one s. *Education:* Univ. of Cambridge, Utkal Univ., Patna Univ. *Career:* lecturer, reader 1950–86; poet-in-residence, Rockefeller Foundation Conference Center, Bellagio, Italy 1986; Poetry Ed., The Telegraph, Kolkata 1994–98; Ed., Lipi 1998; Ed., Chandrabhaga magazine, Cuttack 2000–. *Publications:* Close the Sky 1971, Svayamvara and Other Poems 1971, A Rain of Rites 1976, Waiting 1979, Relationship 1980, The False Start 1980, Life Signs 1983, Dispossessed Nests

1984, Selected Poems 1987, Burden of Waves and Fruit 1988, Temple 1989, A Whiteness of Bone 1992, The Best of Jayanta Mahapatra 1995, Shadow Space 1997, The Green Gardener 1997, Bare Face 2001, Random Descent 2005, Door of Paper 2006; various children's stories and translations; contrib. to reviews, quarterlies and journals. *Honours:* Jacob Glatstein Memorial Award, Chicago 1975, Nat. Acad. of Letters Award, New Delhi 1981, El consejo nacional para la cultura y las artes, Mexico 1994, Gangadhar Nat. Award for Poetry 1994, Jaidayal Harmony Award 1994. *Address:* Tinkonia Bagicha, Cuttack 753 001, Orissa, India. *Telephone:* (671) 2417434.

MAHARIDGE, Dale Dimitro; American writer and university lecturer; b. 24 Oct. 1956, Cleveland, OH. *Education:* Cleveland State University, Cuyahoga Community College. *Career:* staff, Gazette, Medina, OH 1977–78; journalist, Sacramento Bee, CA 1980–91; Asst Prof., Columbia University 1991–92; Lecturer, Stanford University 1992–; mem. Sierra Club. *Publications:* Journey to Nowhere: The Saga of the New Underclass, 1985; And Their Children After Them: The Legacy of 'Let Us Now Praise Famous Men', James Agee, Walker Evans, and the Rise and Fall of Cotton in the South, 1989; Yosemite: A Landscape of Life, 1990; The Last Great American Hobo, 1993; The Coming White Minority: California, Multiculturalism, and the Nation's Future, 1999; Homeland (with Michael Williams) 2004; contrib. to periodicals. *Honours:* World Hunger Award, New York City, 1987; Lucius W. Nieman Fellowship, Harvard University, 1988; Pulitzer Prize for General Non-Fiction, 1990; Pope Foundation Award, 1994; Freedom Forum Profs' Publishing Program Grant, 1995; Social Justice Journalism Award, Hunter College, CUNY, 2001. *Address:* c/o Department of Communications, Stanford University, Stanford, CA 94305, USA.

MAHER, Terence Anthony; British bookseller and publisher; *Chairman, Maher Booksellers Ltd;* b. 5 Dec. 1935, Manchester; s. of the late Herbert Maher and Lillian Maher; m. Barbara Grunbaum 1960; three s. *Education:* Xaverian Coll., Manchester. *Career:* Controller, Carborundum Co. Ltd 1961–69; Dir Corp. Finance, First Nat. Finance Corpn 1969–72; f. Pentos PLC 1972, Chair., CEO –1993; Chair. and CEO Dillons Bookstores 1977–93; Athena Int. 1980–93, Ryman 1987–93; Chair. The Chalford Publishing Co. Ltd 1994–98, Maher Booksellers Ltd 1995–, Race Dynamics Ltd 1998–; Founder Trustee of Liberal Democrats 1988; mem. Advisory Council on Libraries 1997–98; Fellow, Chartered Asscn of Certified Accountants. *Achievement:* led successful campaign to abolish price control on books in UK. *Publications:* Counterblast (co-author) 1965, Effective Politics (co-author) 1966, Against My Better Judgement (autobiog.) 1994, Unfinished Business (fiction) 2003, Grumpy Old Liberal – A Political Rant 2005. *Address:* 33 Clarence Terrace, Regent's Park, London, NW1 4RD; The Old House, Whichford, nr Shipston on Stour, Warwicks., CV36 5PG, England. *Telephone:* (20) 7723-4254 (London); (1608) 684-614 (Whichford).

MAHJOUB, Jamal; British/Sudanese novelist; b. 1960, London. *Education:* Comboni Coll., Sudan, Atlantic Coll., S Wales, Univ. of Sheffield, England. *Publications:* Navigation of a Rainmaker 1989, Wings of Dust 1994, In the Hour of Signs 1996, The Carrier 1998, Travelling with Djinns 2003, Nubian Indigo 2006, The Drift Latitudes 2006. *Honours:* The Guardian/Heinemann African Story Award 1993, Pris de L'Astrolabe 2004, Premio Mario Vargas Llosa 2006. *Literary Agent:* Aitken Alexander Associates Ltd, 18–21 Cavaye Place, London, SW10 9PT, England. *Telephone:* (20) 7373-8672. *Fax:* (20) 7373-6002. *E-mail:* reception@aitkenalexander.co.uk. *Website:* www.aitkenalexander.co.uk.

MAHON, Derek, BA; Northern Irish poet, critic and editor; b. 23 Nov. 1941, Belfast, Northern Ireland. *Education:* Belfast Institute, Trinity College, Dublin. *Career:* Drama Critic, Ed., Poetry Ed., New Statesman, 1981–; Poet-in-Residences. *Publications:* Twelve Poems, 1965; Night-Crossing, 1968; Lives, 1972; The Man Who Built His City in Snow, 1972; The Snow Party, 1975; Light Music, 1977; The Sea in Winter, 1979; Poems 1962–1978, 1979; Courtyards in Delft, 1981; The Hunt by Night, 1982; A Kensington Notebook, 1984; Antarctica, 1986; Selected Poems, 1991; The Yaddo Letter, 1992; The Hudson Letter, 1995; Collected Poems, 1999; Harbour Lights, 2005; Selected Poems 2006. Editor: Modern Irish Poetry, 1972; The Penguin Book of Contemporary Irish Poetry, 1990. *Honours:* Irish American Foundation Award, Lannan Foundation Award, American Ireland Fund Literary Award, Eric Gregory Award, David Cohen Prize 2007. *Literary Agent:* Rogers, Coleridge & White Ltd, 20 Powis Mews, London W11 1JN, England.

MAHY, Margaret Mary, BA; New Zealand writer; b. 21 March 1936, d. of Francis George Mahy and Helen May Penlington; two d. *Career:* Asst Librarian, Petone Public Library 1959; Asst Children's Librarian, Christchurch Public Library 1960, Children's Librarian 1977; Librarian in charge of school requests, School Library Service, Christchurch Br. 1967; writer 1980–. *Publications include:* Picture books: The Dragon of an Ordinary Family 1969, Mrs Discombobulous 1969, Pillycock's Shop 1969, The Little Witch 1970, The Princes and the Clown 1971, The Boy with Two Shadows 1971, The Man Whose Mother Was a Pirate 1971, The Rare Spotted Birthday Party 1974, The Ultra-Violet Catastrophe 1975, The Wind Between the Stars 1976, The Boy Who was Followed Home 1977, Jam 1985, The Great White Maneating Shark 1989; Short stories: Nonstop Nonsense 1977, The Great Piratical Rumbustification 1982, The Librarian and the Robbers 1978, The Chewing-Gum Rescue 1982, The Birthday Burglar and a Very Wicked Headmistress 1984, Wibble Wobble 1984, The Spider in the Shower 1984, The Downhill Crocodile Whizz 1986, The Three Wishes 1986, The Door in the Air 1988, Tick Tock Tales 1994;

Jr fiction: The Bus Under the Leaves 1975, The Pirate Uncle 1977, Raging Robots and Unruly Uncles 1981, The Adventures of a Kite 1985, Sophie's Singing Mother 1985, A Very Happy Bathday 1985, Clever Hamburger 1985, The Man Who Enjoyed Grumbling 1986, The Pop Group 1986, The Terrible Topsy-Turvy Tissy-Tossy Tangle 1986, Mr Rumfitt 1986, My Wonderful Aunt 1986, The Blood and Thunder Adventure on Hurricane Peak 1989, The Cousins Quartet (4 books) 1994, Maddigan's Fantasia 2006; School books: The Crocodile's Christmas Jandals 1982, The Bubbling Crocodile 1983, Shopping with a Crocodile 1983, The Great Grumbler and the Wonder Tree 1984, Fantail Fantail 1984, The Crocodile's Christmas Thongs 1985, Horraka-potchin 1985; also books for older children and for children learning to read. Honours: Carnegie Medal 1982, Esther Glen Medal. Address: No. 1 RD, Lyttleton, New Zealand. Telephone: (3) 299-703.

MAIDEN, Jennifer Margaret, BA; Australian poet and writer; b. 7 April 1949, Penrith, NSW. Education: Macquarie Univ. Publications: Tactics 1974, The Occupying Forces 1975, The Problem of Evil 1975, Birthstones 1978, The Border Loss 1979, For the Left Hand 1981, The Terms 1982, The Trust 1988, Play with Knives 1990, Selected Poems of Jennifer Maiden 1990, Acoustic Shadow 1993, Mines 1999, Friendly Fire 2005; contrib. to numerous newspapers and magazines. Honours: several Australia Council Fellowships and grants, Grenfell Henry Lawson Award 1979, NSW Premier's Prizes 1991, 2000, Victorian Premier's Prize 1991, Christopher Brennan Award for Lifetime Achievement 1999. Address: PO Box 4, Penrith, NSW 2751, Australia.

MAIER, Paul Luther, MA, MDiv, PhD; American academic; Russell II Seibert Professor of Ancient History, Western Michigan University; b. 31 May 1930, St Louis, Mo.; s. of Dr Walter A. Maier and Hulda Augusta Eickhofrf; m. Joan M. Ludtke 1967; four d. Education: Harvard Univ., Concordia Seminary, St Louis, Univ. of Heidelberg, Germany, Univ. of Basel, Switzerland. Career: Campus Chaplain 1958–99, Russell II Seibert Prof. of Ancient History, Western Michigan Univ. 1960–. Films: Jesus: Legend or Lord?, The Odyssey of St Paul and Christianity: The First Three Centuries (three four-hour video series). Publications: A Man Spoke, A World Listened: The Story of Walter A Maier 1963, Pontius Pilate 1968, First Christmas 1971, First Easter 1973, First Christians 1976, The Best of Walter A. Maier (ed.) 1980, The Flames of Rome 1981, Josephus: The Jewish War (ed.) 1982, Josephus: The Essential Writings (ed. and trans.) 1988, In the Fullness of Time 1991, A Skeleton in God's Closet 1994, Josephus: The Essential Works (ed. and trans.) 1995, Eusebius: The Church History (ed. and trans.) 1999, More Than a Skeleton 2003, The Da Vinci Code – Fact or Fiction? (with H. Hanegraaf) 2004; juvenile: The Very First Christmas 1998, The Very First Easter 2000, The Very First Christians 2001, Martin Luther – A Man Who Changed the World 2004; contrib. to many professional journals. Honours: Hon. LittD (Concordia Seminary) 1995; Hon. LLD (Concordia Univ.) 2000; Western Michigan Univ. Alumni Award for Teaching Excellence 1974, and Distinguished Faculty Scholar 1981, Outstanding Educator in America 1974–75, Council for the Advancement and Support of Education Prof. of the Year 1984, Michigan Acad. of Sciences, Arts and Letters Citation 1985, ECPA Gold Medallion Book Award 1989, 1999, Concordia Univ. Christus in Mundo Award 2001, The Wittenberg Award 2001. Address: Department of History, Western Michigan University, Kalamazoo, MI 49008, USA (office). Telephone: (269) 387-4816 (office). Fax: (269) 387-4651 (office). E-mail: maier@wmich.edu (office).

MAILER, Norman Kingsley, BS; American writer; b. 31 Jan. 1923, Long Branch, NJ; s. of Isaac Barnett Mailer and Fanny Schneider; m. 1st Beatrice Silverman 1944 (divorced 1952); one d.; m. 2nd Adele Morales 1954 (divorced 1962); two d.; m. 3rd Lady Jeanne Campbell 1962 (divorced 1963); one d.; m. 4th Beverly Rentz Bentley 1963 (divorced 1980); two s. one d.; m. 5th Carol Stevens (divorced); one d.; m. 6th Norris Church 1980; one s. Education: Harvard Univ. Career: served in US Army 1944–46; co-f. New York weekly, Village Voice 1955; mem. editorial bd Dissent magazine 1953–69, American Acad. of Arts and Letters 1984–; Pres. of PEN (US Chapter) 1984–86. Films directed: Wild 90 1967, Beyond the Law 1967, Maidstone 1968, Tough Guys Don't Dance 1987. Film appearance: Ragtime 1981. Publications: The Naked and The Dead 1948, Barbary Shore 1951, The Deer Park 1955 (dramatized 1967), Advertisements for Myself 1959, Deaths for the Ladies (poems) 1962, The Presidential Papers 1963, An American Dream 1964, Cannibals and Christians 1966, Why are we in Vietnam?: A Novel 1967, The Armies of the Night 1968, Miami and the Siege of Chicago 1968, Moonshot 1969, A Fire on the Moon 1970, The Prisoner of Sex 1971, Existential Errands 1972, St George and the Godfather 1972, Marilyn 1973, The Faith of Graffiti 1974, The Fight 1975, Some Honourable Men 1976, Genius and Lust–A Journey Through the Writings of Henry Miller 1976, A Transit to Narcissus 1978, The Executioner's Song 1979, Of Women and Their Elegance 1980, The Essential Mailer (selections) 1982, Pieces and Pontifications 1982, Ancient Evenings (novel) 1983, Tough Guys Don't Dance (novel) 1984, Harlot's Ghost (novel) 1991, Oswald's Tale 1995, Portrait of Picasso as a Young Man 1995, The Gospel According to the Son 1997, The Time of Our Time 1998, The Spooky Art: Thoughts on Writing 2003, Why Are We At War? 2003, The Castle in the Forest 2007; contribs to numerous magazines. Honours: Nat. Book Award for Arts and Letters 1969, Pulitzer Prize for Non-Fiction 1969, for Fiction 1980, McDowell Colony Annual Award for outstanding service to the arts 1973, Nat. Book Foundation lifetime achievement medal 2005. Address: c/o American Academy of Arts and Letters, 633 West 155th Street, New York, NY 10032, USA (office).

MAILLARD, Keith; Canadian writer, poet and academic; Professor of Creative Writing, University of British Columbia; b. 28 Feb. 1942, Wheeling, WV; m.; two d. Education: West Virginia Univ., Vancouver Community Coll. Career: Instructor, Univ. of British Columbia 1980–89, Asst Prof. 1989–94, Assoc. Prof., Prof. of Creative Writing 1994–. Publications: novels: Two Strand River 1976, Alex Driving South 1980, The Knife in My Hands 1981, Cutting Through 1982, Motet 1989, Light in the Company of Women 1993, Hazard Zones 1995, Gloria 1999, The Clarinet Polka 2003; poetry: Dementia Americana 1994; contribs to newspapers, reviews, journals and anthology. Honours: Ethel Wilson Fiction Prize 1990, Gerald Lampert Prize for Best First Book of Poetry, League of Canadian Poets 1995. Address: UBC Creative Writing Program, Buchanan Room E462, 1866 Main Mall, University of British Columbia, Vancouver, BC V6T 1Z1, Canada (office). E-mail: maillard@interchange.ubc.ca (office).

MAILLET, Antonine, PC, CC, OQ, ONB, LèsL, MA, DèsL; Canadian author and dramatist; b. 10 May 1929, Bouctouche, NB. Education: Collège de Notre-Dame d'Acadie, Moncton, University of Moncton, University of Montréal, Université Laval. Career: Teacher, University of Moncton, 1965–67, Collège des Jesuites, Québec, 1968–69, Université Laval, 1971–74, University of Montréal, 1974–75; Visiting Prof., University of California at Berkeley, 1983, SUNY at Albany, 1985; mem. Académie canadienne-française; Asscn des Écrivains de Langue Française; PEN; Queen's Privy Council for Canada; Royal Society of Canada; Société des Gens de Lettres de France. Publications: Pointe-aux-Coques 1958, On a mangé la dune 1962, La Sagouine 1971, Don l'Original 1972, Par derrière chez mon père 1972, Mariaagélas 1973, Emmanuel a Joseph a Davit 1975, La Cordes-de-bois 1977, Pélagie-la-Charrette (trans. as Pélagie: The Return to a Homeland) 1979, Cent ans dans les bois 1981, La Gribouille 1982, Crache-a-Pic (trans. as The Devil is Loose) 1984, Le Huitième jour (trans. as On the Eighth Day) 1986, L'Oursiade 1990, Les Confessions de Jeanne de Valois 1992, Le Foire de la Saint-Barthélmy (trans. from Ben Jonson) 1994, L'Ile-sux-Puces 1996, Le Chemin St-Jacques (novel) 1996, Chronique d'une sorcière de vent (novel) 1999, Madame Perfecta 2001; many plays. Honours: Governor-General's Award for Fiction 1972, Prix France-Canada 1975, Prix Goncourt, France 1979; Officier des Palmes académiques françaises 1980, Officier, Ordre des Arts et des Lettres, France 1985, Commdr, Ordre du mérite culturel de Monaco 1993; several hon. doctorates. Address: 735 Antonine Maillet Avenue, Montréal, QC H2V 2Y4, Canada.

MAINE, David (see Avice, Claude Pierre Marie)

MAIR, (Alexander) Craig, BA; Scottish educator and writer; b. 3 May 1948, Glasgow; m. Anne Olizar 1970; two s. one d. Education: Stirling Univ. Career: mem. Scottish Society of Antiquaries, fellow; Educational Institute of Scotland; various local history groups. Publications: A Time in Turkey, 1973; A Star for Seamen, 1978; The Lighthouse Boy, 1981; Britain at War 1914–18, 1982; Mercat Cross and Tolbooth, 1988; David Angus, 1989; Stirling, The Royal Burgh, 1990; The Incorporation of Glasgow Maltmen: A History, 1990.

MAIRS, Nancy Pedrick, AB, MFA, PhD; American writer; b. 23 July 1943, Long Beach, Calif.; m. George Anthony Mairs 1963; one s. one d. Education: Wheaton Coll., Mass, Univ. of Arizona. Career: mem. Authors' Guild, Poets and Writers, Nat. Women's Studies Asscn. Publications: Instead it is Winter 1977, In All the Rooms of the Yellow House 1984, Plaintext 1986, Remembering the Bone House 1989, Carnal Acts 1990, Ordinary Time 1993, Voice Lessons 1994, Waist High in the World 1996, A Troubled Guest 2001; contrib. to American Voice, MSS, Tri Quarterly. Honours: Western States Book Award 1984, Nat. Endowment for the Arts Fellowship 1991, Soros Foundation Award 1999. Address: 579 S Third Avenue, Tucson, AZ 85701, USA. E-mail: nancymairs@msn.com. Website: www.nancymairs.com.

MAJA-PEARCE, Adewale, BA, MA; British researcher, writer and poet; b. 3 June 1953, London, England. Education: University of Wales, Swansea and SOAS, London. Career: Researcher, Index on Censorship, London, 1986–; Consultant, Heinemann International, Oxford, 1986–94; mem. PEN; Society of Authors. Publications: Christopher Okigbo: Collected Poems (ed.), 1986; In My Father's Country: A Nigerian Journey (non-fiction), 1987; Loyalties (short stories), 1987; How Many Miles to Babylon? (non-fiction), 1990; The Heinemann Book of African Poetry in English (ed.), 1990; Who's Afraid of Wole Soyinka?: Essays on Censorship, 1991; A Mask Dancing: Nigerian Novelists of the Eighties, 1992. Contributions: various periodicals.

MAJDALANI, Charif; French/Lebanese writer; b. 1960, Beirut. Education: Université de Aix-en-Provence, France. Career: literary critic, L'Orient-Express 1995–98; fmrly taught at Univ. of Balamand; Chair of Dept of French Literature, Univ. Saint-Joseph, Beirut, Lebanon 1999–. Publications: Petit traité des mélanges 2002, Histoire de la grande maison (novel) 2005. Address: Université Saint Joseph, rue de Damas, BP 17-5208, Mar Mikhaël, Beirut 1104 2020, Lebanon (office).

MAJOR, André; Canadian writer and poet; b. 22 April 1942, Montréal, QC; m. Ginette Lepage 1970, one s. one d. Education: Collège de Montréal, Collège des Eudistes. Publications: Fiction: Nouvelles, 1963; Le Cabochon, 1964; La chair de poule, 1965; Le Vent du diable, 1968; L'Épouvantail, 1974, English trans. as The Scarecrows of Saint-Emmanuel, 1977; L'Épidéme, 1975, English trans. as Inspector Therrien, 1980; Les Rescapés, 1976, English trans. as Man on the Run, 1984; La folle d'Elvis, English trans. as Hooked on Elvis, 1983;

L'hiver au coeur, 1987, English trans. as The Winter of the Heart, 1989; La vie provisoire, 1995, English trans. as A Provisional Life, 1997. Poetry: Le froid se meurt, 1961; Holocauste à 2 voix, 1961; Poèmes pour durer, 1969. Other: Journal: Le Sourire d'Anton ou l'adieu au roman (1975–92), 2001. *Honours:* Gov.-Gen.'s Literary Award, 1977; Prix Canada-Communauté française de Belgique, 1991; Prix Études françaises, 2001.

MAJOR, Clarence, PhD; American novelist, poet, painter and academic; *Professor of English, University of California, Davis;* b. 31 Dec. 1936, Atlanta, Ga; s. of Clarence Major and Inez Huff; m. Pamela Ritter 1980. *Education:* Union Graduate School, Yellow Springs and Cincinnati, Ohio, Univ. of the State of New York, Albany. *Career:* Prof., Dept of English, Univ. of California, Davis 1989–; has given lectures in USA, Europe and in N and W Africa. *Exhibitions include:* Kresge Art Museum, East Lansing, Mich. Natsoulas Art Gallery, Davis, Calif., Gayles Art Gallery Chicago, Sarah Lawrence Coll., NY, First Nat. Bank, Boulder, Colo. Schacknow Museum of Art, Plantation Florida, Exploding Head Gallery and Phoenix Gallery, Sacramento, Calif., Hamilton Club Art Gallery, Paterson, NJ, John Natsoulas Art Gallery, Davis, Calif., Main Street Gallery, Winters, Calif., on-line galleries:art-avisen-avk, Denmark, Saatchi Gallery, London, artvitae, yourart. *Publications:* novels: All-Night Visitors 1969, NO 1973, Reflex and Bone Structure 1975, Emergency Exit 1979, My Amputations (Western States Book Award for Fiction) 1986, Such was the Season 1987, Painted Turtle: Woman with Guitar 1988; short stories: Fun and Games 1990, Calling the Wind: Twentieth Century African-American Short Stories 1993, Dirty Bird Blues 1996, All-Night Visitors (new version) 1998; poetry: Swallow the Lake 1970, Symptoms and Madness 1971, Private Line 1971, The Cotton Club 1972, The Syncopated Cakewalk 1974, Inside Diameter: The France Poems 1985, Surfaces and Masks 1987, Some Observations of a Stranger at Zuni in the Latter Part of the Century 1989, The Garden Thrives, Twentieth Century African-American Poetry 1995, Configurations: New and Selected Poems 1958–98, 1998, Waiting for Sweet Baby 2002; non-fiction: Dictionary of Afro-American Slang 1970, The Dark and Feeling: Black American Writers and their Work 1974, Juba to Jive: A Dictionary of African-American Slang 1994, Necessary Distance: Essays and Criticism 2001, Come by Here: My Mother's Life 2002, Conversations with Clarence Major, Clarence Major and His Art; numerous works in anthologies and periodicals. *Honours:* Fulbright Fellowship, Pushcart Prize, Nat. Council on the Arts Award, Int. Writers' Hall of Fame, Gwendolyn Brooks Foundation Award, Chicago State Univ., Western States Book Award, Sister Circle Book Award. *Address:* Department of English, 281 Voorhies Hall, University of California, Davis, CA 95616, USA (office). *Telephone:* (916) 752-5677 (office). *E-mail:* clmajor@ucdavis.edu (office). *Website:* wwwenglish.ucdavis.edu/faculty/cmajor/cmajor.htm (office); www.clarencemajor.com.

MAJOR, Devorah; American poet, novelist, performer, lecturer and editor; *Adjunct Professor, California College of the Arts;* b. San Francisco, CA; one s. one d. *Career:* poet-in-residence, San Francisco Fine Arts Museum; Mediator, California Lawyer for the Arts; Poet Laureate of San Francisco; composer (with Guillermo Galindo), Trade Routes 2005; Adjunct Prof. Calif. Coll. of the Arts 2004–; poetry performances with jazz music as 'Daughters of Yam'; tours of England and Wales, Italy, France and Bosnia. *Publications:* novels: An Open Weave 1995, Brown Glass Windows 2002; poetry: Travelling Women (with Opal Palmer Adisa) 1989, Street Smarts 1996; other: Where River Meets Ocean 2003, With More Than Tongue 2003, The Other Side of the Postcard (ed.) 2005. *Honours:* inducted into San Francisco State Univ. Hall of Fame 2004; PEN Oakland/Josephine Miles Award 1997, First Novelist Award from American Library Asscn Black Caucus 1997. *Address:* POB 423634, San Francisco, CA 94142, USA (home). *E-mail:* devmajor@pacbell.net (home). *Website:* www.daughtersofyam.com (home).

MAJOR, Kevin Gerald, BSc; Canadian writer; b. 12 Sept. 1949, Stephenville, NF; m. Anne Crawford 1982, two s. *Education:* Memorial University, St John's, NF. *Career:* mem. Writers' Union of Canada. *Publications:* Far from Shore 1980, Thirty-Six Exposures 1984, Dear Bruce Springsteen 1987, Blood Red Ochre 1989, Eating Between the Lines 1991, Diana: My Autobiography 1993, No Man's Land 1995, Gaffer: A Novel of Newfoundland 1997, The House of Wooden Santas 1997, Eh? to Zed: A Canadian Abecedarium 2000, As Near to Heaven by Sea: A History of Newfoundland and Labrador 2001, Ann and Seamus 2003. *Honours:* Book of the Year Award, Canadian Asscn of Children's Librarians 1978, Canada Council Award for Children's Literature 1978, Canadian Young Adult Book Award 1980, Book of the Year Award for Children, Canadian Library Asscn 1991, Vicky Metcalf Award 1992, Mr Christie Award 1998. *Address:* 27 Poplar Avenue, St John's, NF A1B 1C7, Canada.

MAKANIN, Vladimir Semenovich; Russian writer; b. 13 March 1937, Orsk, Orenburg Region. *Education:* Moscow Univ., Higher Workshop for Scenario Writers and Film Dirs. *Career:* started writing 1965. *Publications include:* Straight Line 1965, Air-Vent, Portrait and Around (novel) 1976, Story about an Old Settlement (collection of short stories) 1974, Voices 1982, River with a Fast Current 1983, Where the Skies Meet the Hills 1987, One and One 1987, Subject of Averaging 1992, The Loss: A Novella and Two Stories (Writings from an Unbound Europe), Baize-Covered Table with Decanter 1993, Quasi 1993, Captives 1996, Escape Hatch and The Long Road Ahead: Two Novellas 1998, Underground, or a Hero of Our Time 1998, Letter A 2000, A Good Love Story 2000. *Honours:* Russian Booker Prize 1993, Pushkin Prize 1998, Penne Prize, Italy 1999, Russian State Prize 2000. *Address:* Novinski

Boulevard 16, Apartment 14, 121069 Moscow, Russia. *Telephone:* (495) 291-92-53. *Fax:* (495) 781-01-82. *E-mail:* vmakanin@hotmail.com.

MAKARA, Mpho 'Mampeke, BA, MA; Lesotho writer, teacher and student guidance counsellor; b. 28 Oct. 1954, Quthing; d. of the late Tefo Stephen and Malesia Maria (née Masilo) Moroeng; m. Thabo Makara 1977; two d. one s. *Education:* Morija Girls' Training Coll., Nat. Univ. of Lesotho and Univ. of Bath (UK). *Career:* Primary school teacher 1974–77; Asst Teacher 1982–85, Deputy Head 1987, Teacher, Counsellor of the Lower School, Machabeng Coll. 1987, Co-ordinator Middle Years Programme 2000–. *Publications:* plays: Mali A Llelana 1986, Ke Fahliloe 1990, Sehaeso I 1991, II 1993, III 1994; Novel: Mohanusa 1996; short stories: Sepettele, Materaseng 1997; Poetry: U Elsang Uena 2002; has also written language courses. *Address:* Machabeng College, International School of Lesotho, POB 1570, Maseru; POB 15291, Maseru 100, Lesotho. *Telephone:* 315480. *Fax:* 316109. *E-mail:* machabhm@lesoff.co.za. *Website:* www.lesoff.co.za/machab.

MAKINE, Andreï; French/Russian writer; b. 1957, Siberia; s. of Maria Stepanovna Dolina. *Career:* worked as teacher of literature in Novgorod; emigrated from USSR to France 1987, writes in French. *Publications:* A Hero's Daughter (in trans.), Au Temps du Fleuve Amour (trans. as Once Upon the River Love) 1994, Le Testament Français (trans. as Dreams of My Russian Summers) (Prix Goncourt, Prix Médicis Étranger) 1995, The Crime of Olga Arbelina (in trans.) 1999, Requiem for a Lost Empire (in trans.) 2001, A Life's Music (in trans.) 2002, The Earth and Sky of Jacques Dorme (in trans.) 2005, The Woman Who Waited (in trans.) 2006. *Address:* c/o Arcade Publishing, 141 Fifth Avenue, Eighth Floor, New York, NY 10010, USA.

MAKINSON, John, BA; British publishing executive; *Chairman and Chief Executive, Penguin Group;* m.; two c. *Education:* Univ. of Cambridge. *Career:* journalist Reuters (London, Paris and Frankfurt offices) 1976–79; journalist, later Ed. Lex column Financial Times 1979–86; Vice-Chair. Saatchi & Saatchi US holding co. 1986–89; co-founder and head of consultancy Makinson Cowell 1989–94; Man. Dir Financial Times 1994–96; Chief Financial Officer, Pearson Group 1996–2002, mem. bd of dirs 2002–; Chair. Penguin Group 2001–, also CEO 2002–; Dir and Co-Chair. International Rescue Cttee (UK); Chair., Interactive Data Corporation; Non-Exec. Dir George Weston Ltd, Canada, and Recoletos Grupo de Comunicacion SA, Spain. *Address:* Penguin Group, 80 Strand, London, WC2R 0RL, England. *Website:* www.penguin.com.

MALASHENKO, Igor Yevgenyevich, CandPhilSc; Russian journalist; b. 2 Oct. 1954, Moscow; m. Yelena Pivovarova; two d. *Education:* Moscow State Univ. *Career:* jr, sr researcher, Inst. of USA and Canada USSR Acad. of Sciences 1980–89, research in problems of the concept of nuclear deterrence and public opinion; staff-mem. Int. Div. Cen. Cttee CPSU, admin. of Pres. Gorbachev March–Dec. 1991; political Dir TV & Radio Co. Ostankino 1992–93; Pres. and Dir-Gen. Ind. TV Co. NTV 1993–, Pres. NTV-Telemost Holding 1998; First Deputy Chair. Bd of Dirs Media-Most Co. 1998–2001; adviser to Pres. of Russia on public relations problems, mem. election campaign staff of Boris Yeltsin 1996. *Honours:* Prize of Russian Union of Journalists 1994. *Address:* NTV-Telemost, Academica Koroleva str. 19, 127427 Moscow, Russia. *Telephone:* (495) 215-15-88 (office).

MALEH, Edmond Amran al-; Moroccan writer; b. 30 March 1917, Safi. *Career:* writes in Arabic, French and Hebrew. *Publications:* Citadelles du désert (with Philippe Lafond), Parcours immobile (novel) 1980, Aïlen, ou, La Nuit du récit 1983, Mille ans, un jour (novel) 1986, Jean Genet, Le Captif amoureux 1988, Le Retour d'Abou el Haki (novel) 1990, L'Oeil et la main 1993, Abner Abounour (novel) 1995, Le Café bleu 1998, Essaouira, cité heureuse (jtly) 2000, Asilah des jardins sur les murs 2000. *Honours:* Grand Prix du Maroc 1996. *Address:* c/o André Dimanche, 10 cours Jean-Ballard, 13001 Marseille, France (office).

MALHERBE, René Cornelis; Dutch publisher; b. 22 Aug. 1942, 's-Hertogenbosch; s. of G. Malherbe and R. Algra; m. Renate Emma van de Venne 1966; two s. one d. *Career:* qualified as electro-tech. engineer; with Philips Medical Equipment 1960–62, with Smeets Printing Weert 1964–66, Cargill Marketing, London and Eindhoven 1966–68, Marketing & Promotion, Eindhoven 1968–74, M & P Publishing Weert 1974–86; Dir Malherbe Group Publishing Weert 1986–.

MALIK, Zubeida; British journalist; *Reporter, Today Programme, BBC Radio 4;* *Career:* Producer, Output Ed. then Reporter, Today Programme, BBC Radio 4 1997–; conducted investigative reports on children dealing drugs and Damilola Taylor case; reported on war inside Afghanistan for three months 2001; first British broadcaster and only woman to interview the Taliban during war on terrorism; one of first journalists to uncover training camps in UK; conducted high-profile interviews with leader of Hamas Sheikh Yassin, Kofi Annan, Tony Blair, Pres. Musharaff, Archbishop Tutu; reported from Nigeria, Israel and Saudi Arabia; first woman journalist for the BBC to report on the Haaj from inside Mecca and Medina. *Honours:* Foreign Press Asscn Young Journalist of the Year 2000, Best Radio News Journalist, Ethnic Multicultural Media Awards (EMMAs) 2001, 2002, Asian Women of Achievement Media Personality of the Year Award 2002, Radio and TV Media Personality, Carlton Multicultural Achievement Awards 2003. *Address:* c/o Today Programme, BBC Radio 4, Room 9630, Stage Six, Television Centre, Wood Lane, London, W12 7RJ, England (office).

MALLET-JONES, Françoise; French novelist; b. 6 July 1930, Antwerp, Belgium. *Education:* Bryn Mawr Coll., Pennsylvania, Sorbonne, University of

Paris. *Career:* reader, Grasset Publishers 1965–. *Publications:* Into the Labyrinth, 1951; The Red Room, 1955; Cordelia and Other Stories, 1956; House of Lies, 1956; Café Celeste, 1958; The Favourite, 1961; Signs and Wonders, 1966; The Witches: Three Tales of Sorcery, 1968; The Underground Game, 1973; Allegra, 1976; Le Rire de Laura, 1985; La Tristesse du cerf-volant, 1988; Adriana Sposa, 1989; Divine, 1991. *Other:* French version of Shelagh Delaney's play A Taste of Honey, 1960; A Letter to Myself, 1964; The Paper House, 1970; Juliette Greco, 1975; Marie-Paule Belle, 1987. *Honours:* Ordre National du Mérite 1986.

MALLON, Maurus Edward, BEd, MA; British teacher, writer and dramatist; b. 10 July 1932, Greenock, Scotland; s. of Peter and Agnes Mallon. *Education:* Univ. of Glasgow, Univ. of Manitoba, Winnipeg. *Career:* mem. Living Authors' Soc., Nat. Writers' Asscn (USA), PEN Canada. *Publications:* Basileus 1971, The Opal 1973, Pegaso 1975, Way of the Magus 1978, Anogia 1980, Bammer McPhie 1984, Treasure Mountain 1986, Postcards 1991, Ex Novo Mundo (short stories) 1992, Compendulum 1993, A Matter of Conscience (play) 1994. *Address:* PO Box 331, Deep River, ON K0J 1P0, Canada (home). *Telephone:* (613) 584-3293 (home).

MALLON, Thomas, BA, MA, PhD; American writer and academic; b. 2 Nov. 1951, Glen Cove, NY; s. of Arthur Mallon and Caroline Mallon (née Moruzzi). *Education:* Brown Univ., Harvard Univ. *Career:* fmr Literary Ed., GQ; fmr Prof. of English, Vassar Coll.; fmr Deputy Chair. Nat. Endowment for the Humanities; Visiting Scholar, St Edmund's Coll., Cambridge, England. *Publications:* Edmund Blunden 1983, A Book of One's Own: People and Their Diaries 1984, Arts and Sciences: A Seventies Seduction 1988, Stolen Words: Forays into the Origins and Ravages of Plagarism 1989, Aurora 7 1991, Rockets and Rodeos and Other American Spectacles 1993, Henry and Clara 1994, Dewey Defeats Truman 1997, Two Moons 2001, Mrs Paine's Garage 2002, Bandbox 2004, Fellow Travelers 2007; contrib. to GQ, Harper's, The New Yorker, American Scholar, Yale Review Architectural Digest, New York Times Book Review, The Washington Post Book World. *Honours:* Rockefeller Fellowship 1986, Guggenheim Fellowship 2000; Ingram Merrill Award 1994, Nat. Book Critics Circle Award for Reviewing 1998. *Address:* c/o Pantheon, Random House Inc., 1745 Broadway, New York, NY 10019, USA (office). *E-mail:* tvmallon@aol.com (home).

MALMSTEN, Bodil; Swedish poet and writer; b. 1944, Jämtland. *Education:* Acad. of Fine Arts, Stockholm. *Career:* writer for children, for TV and radio; moved to Brittany, France 2000; involved in art educ., tranlating, directing plays for the stage. *Publications:* Dvärgen Gustaf (poems) 1977, Damen, det brinner! (poems) 1984, Paddan & branden (poems) 1987, B-ställningar 1987, Ett bloss för Bodil Malmsten, dikter 1977–1987 (poems) 1988, Svartvita bilder 1988, Nåd & onåd (poems) 1989, Nefertiti i Berlin 1990, Det är ingen ordning på mina papper 1991, Landet utan lov 1991, Inte med den eld jag har nu. dikt för annan dam 1993, Den dagen kastanjerna slår ut är jag långt härifrån 1994, Dikter 1977–1990 (poems) 1991, Samlade dikter (poems) 1995, En julsaga 1993 1993, Tulipomani (novella) 1995, Nästa som rör mig 1996, Under-gångarens sånger (novella) 1998, Det finns inga lyckopiller 2000, Priset på vatten i Finistère (trans. as The Price of Water in Finistère) 2001, Det är fortfarande ingen ordning på mina papper 2003, Mitt första liv (autobiog.) 2004, Press Star (play) 2005, För att Lämna röstmedddelande Tryck Syjärna (novel) 2005. *Honours:* winner of around 20 Swedish literary awards, including Tilldelad Aniara Prize 1996, Ivar Lo Prize 2006. *Address:* c/o The Harvill Press, Random House, 20 Vauxhall Bridge Road, London, SW1V 2SA, England. *E-mail:* bodil@wanadoo.fr. *Website:* www.finistere.se.

MALOUF, David George Joseph, AO, BA; Australian writer and poet; b. 20 March 1934, Brisbane, Qld; s. of G. Malouf. *Education:* Brisbane Grammar School and Univ. of Queensland. *Publications include:* poetry: Bicycle and other poems 1970, Neighbours in a Thicket 1974, First Things Last 1981, Selected Poems 1991, Poems 1959–89 1992; novels: Johnno 1975, An Imaginary Life 1978, Child's Play 1982, Fly Away Peter 1982, Harland's Half Acre 1984, 12 Edmonstone Street 1985, The Great World 1990, Remembering Babylon 1993, The Conversations at Curlow Creek 1996, Dream Stuff 2000; short stories: Antipodes, Every Move You Make 2007; play: Blood Relations 1987; opera librettos: Voss 1986, Mer de Glace 1991, Baa Baa Black Sheep 1993, Jane Eyre 2000. *Honours:* Hon. Fellow, Australian Acad. of the Humanities; Gold Medal, Australian Literature Soc. 1974, 1982, Age Book of the Year, NSW Premier's Award for Fiction, Vance Palmer Award, Pascal Prize, Commonwealth Writers' Prize and Prix Femina Etranger, for The Great World 1991, inaugural IMPAC Dublin Literary Award 1993; named Neustadt Int. Prize for Literature, Oklahoma Univ. 2000, many other awards. *Literary Agent:* c/o Rogers, Coleridge & White, 20 Powis Mews, London, W11 1JN, England. *Telephone:* (20) 7221-3717. *Fax:* (20) 7229-9084. *Address:* c/o Barbara Mobbs, 35A Sutherland Crescent, Darling Point, Sydney, NSW 2027 (office); 53 Myrtle Street, Chippendale, NSW 2008, Australia (home).

MALZBERG, Barry Norman, AB; American writer; b. 24 July 1939, New York, NY. *Education:* Syracuse Univ. *Career:* pseudonyms include Mike Barry, Francine de Natale, Claudine Dumas, Mel Johnson, Lew W. Mason, K. M. O'Donnell, Gerrold Watkins. *Publications:* Screen 1968, Oracle of the Thousand Hands 1968, The Empty People 1969, Final War and Other Fantasies 1969, Dwellers of the Deep 1970, Confessions of Westchester County 1971, The Falling Astronauts 1971, Gather in the Hall of the Planets 1971, In My Parents' Bedroom 1971, In the Pocket and Other SF Stories 1971, Universe Day 1971, Beyond Apollo (John W. Campbell Memorial Award for

Best Novel 1973) 1972, Overlay 1972, The Men Inside 1972, Revelations 1972, Phase IV 1973, Herovit's World 1973, In the Enclosure 1973, Tactics of Conquest 1973, The Destruction of the Temple 1974, On a Planet Alien 1974, The Sodom and Gomorrah Business 1974, Guernica Night 1974, The Day of the Burning 1974, Underlay 1974, Out from Ganymede 1974, The Many Worlds of Barry Malzberg 1975, The Best of Barry N. Malzberg 1975, The Gamesman 1975, Galaxies 1975, Conversations 1975, Down Here in the Dream Quarter 1976, The Running of Beasts (with Bill Pronzini) 1976, Chorale 1976, Scop 1976, The Last Transaction 1977, Acts of Mercy (with Bill Pronzini) 1977, Night of Screams (with Bill Pronzini) 1979, Malzberg at Large 1979, Prose Bowl (with Bill Pronzini) 1980, The Man Who Loved the Midnight Lady: A Collection 1980, The Cross of Fire 1982, The Engines of the Night: Science Fiction in the Eighties (essays) 1982, The Remaking of Sigmund Freud 1985, The Passage of the Light: The Recursive Science Fiction of Barry N. Malzberg (with Tony Lewis and Mike Resnick) 1994, In the Stone House 2000, Shiva and Other Stories 2001, Problems Solved (with Bill Pronzini) 2003, Breakfast in the Ruins 2007; contrib. short stories to numerous magazines and anthologies.

MAMONOVA, Tatyana; Russian author, academic, poet and activist; *President, Woman and Earth;* m. Gennday Shikarioff; one s. *Education:* Harvard Univ. *Career:* literary journalist, critic for Aurora Publications; post-doctoral fellow at the Bunting Inst. at Harvard Univ.; founder, Woman & Russia Almanac and org. 1979, currently Pres.; Ed.-in-Chief, Succes d'Estime 2000–. *Publications:* non-fiction: Women and Russia 1984, Russian Women's Studies: Essays on Sexism in Soviet Culture 1989, Woman and Earth 1990–2005, Women's Glasnost versus Glasnost: Stopping Russian Backlash 1994, Succes d'estime 2000–07, Album Around the World 2005, 2006, 2007. Woman and Earth Almanac 2007. *Honours:* Diamond Homer Trophy for Famous Poet 1998, Living Legacy Award by Int. Women's Centre of San Diego 2002, Heart of Danko (Russia) 2006. *Address:* Woman & Earth, 467 Central Park W, Suite 7F, New York, NY 10025, USA; Woman and Earth fka Woman and Russia, Dekabristov Street 7–12, St Petersburg 190000, Russia (home). *Telephone:* (212) 866-8130 (office). *Fax:* (212) 866-8130 (office). *Website:* www.dorsai.org/~womearth; www.womanandearth.com.

MAMET, David Alan, BA; American playwright, screenwriter and director; b. 30 Nov. 1947, Chicago; s. of Bernard Morris Mamet and Lenore June Mamet (née Silver); m. 1st Lindsay Crouse 1971 (divorced); m. 2nd Rebecca Pidgeon 1991. *Education:* Goddard Coll., Plainfield, Vt. *Career:* Artist-in-Residence, Goddard Coll. 1971–73; Artistic Dir St Nicholas Theatre Co., Chicago 1973–75; Guest Lecturer, Univ. of Chicago 1975, 1979, NY Univ. 1981; Assoc. Artistic Dir Goodman Theatre, Chicago 1978; Assoc. Prof. of Film, Columbia Univ. 1988. *Films directed:* House of Games 1986, Things Change 1987, Homicide 1991. *Works include:* The Duck Variations 1971, Sexual Perversity in Chicago 1973 (Village Voice Obie Award 1976), The Reunion 1973, Squirrels 1974, American Buffalo (Village Voice Obie Award 1976) 1976, (New York Drama Critics Circle Award 1977), A Life in the Theatre 1976, The Water Engine 1976, The Woods 1977, Lone Canoe 1978, Prairie du Chien 1978, Lakeboat 1980, Donny March 1981, Edmond 1982 (Village Voice Obie Award 1983), The Disappearance of the Jews 1983, The Shawl 1985, Glengarry Glen Ross (Pulitzer prize for Drama, New York Drama Critics Circle award) 1984, Speed-the-Plow 1987, Bobby, Gould in Hell 1989, The Old Neighborhood 1991, Oleanna 1992, Ricky Jay and his 52 Assistants 1994, The Village (novel) 1994, Death Defying Acts 1996, Boston Marriage 1999, The Wicked Son 2006; screenplays: The Postman Always Rings Twice 1979, The Verdict 1980, The Untouchables 1986, House of Games 1986, Things Change (with Shel Silverstein) 1987, We're No Angels 1987, A Life in the Theatre (also dir) 1989, Oh Hell! 1991, Homicide 1991, Hoffa 1991, Glengarry Glen Ross 1992, The Rising Sun 1992, Oleanna 1994, The Edge 1996, The Spanish Prisoner 1996, Wag the Dog 1997, State and Main 2000, The Winslow Bo 1999, Boston Marriage 2001, Heist 2001, Hannibal 2001, Spartan 2004; children's books: Mr Warm and Cold 1985, The Owl (with Lindsay Crouse) 1987, The Winslow Bay 1999; essays: Writing in Restaurants 1986, Some Freaks 1989, On Directing Film 1990, The Hero Pony 1990, The Cabin 1992, A Whore's Profession (also screenplay adaptation) 1993, The Cryptogram 1994, Passover 1995, Make-Believe Town: Essays and Remembrances 1996, Plays 1996, Plays 2 1996, The Duck and the Goat 1996, The Old Religion 1996, True and False 1996, The Old Neighborhood 1998, Jafsie and John Henry 2000, Bambi vs Godzilla (non-fiction) 2007. *Honours:* Hon. DLitt (Dartmouth Coll.) 1996; recipient Outer Critics Circle Award for contrib. to American theatre 1978. *Address:* c/o Howard Rosenstone, Rosenstone/Wender Agency, 38 East 29th Street, 10th Floor, New York, NY 10016, USA.

MAMLEYEV, Yuri; Russian writer, playwright, poet and philosopher; b. 11 Dec. 1931, Moscow; m. Farida Mamleyev 1973. *Education:* Forestry Inst., Moscow. *Career:* mem. French PEN Centre, Russian PEN Centre, Russian Union of Writers, Russian Union of Playwrights. *Publications:* The Sky Above Hell 1980, Iznanka Gogena 1982, Chatouny 1986, Zhivaja Smert 1986, Derniere Comedie 1988, Golos iz Nichto 1990, Utopi Moyu Golovu 1990, Vechnyi dom 1991, Der Murder aus dem Nichts 1992, Izbzannoe 1993, Die Letzte Komödie 1994, Shatuny 1996, Union Mistice 1997, Chernoe zerkalo 1998, J. M. Chatouny 1998, Der Tod des Erotomanen 1999, Moskovski Gambit 1999, Bluzhdajusheje Vremia 2001, Chernoe zerkalo 2001, Bunt luny 2001, Mir i khokhot 2003; contrib. to periodicals. *Honours:* Int. Pushkin Award of Alfred Töpfer, Hamburg, Germany 2000, Andrei Belyi Prize 2001. *Address:*

142 rue Legendre, 75017 Paris, France; Apt 132, Michuzinski Prospect 37, Poccus Mockba, Moscow 117607, Russia.

MANA, Samira Al, BA; Iraqi writer and editor; b. 25 Dec. 1935, Basra; m. Salah Niazi 1959, two d. *Education:* Univ. of Baghdad, Ealing Tech. Coll., UK. *Career:* Asst Ed. Alightrab Al-Adabi (Literature of the Exiled) 1985–2002; mem. PEN Club; read one of her stories at Int. Author Festival, Toronto, Canada. *Play:* Only a Half 1984 (reading on stage sponsored by Int. Women Playwrights Centre and Baffalo State Univ., NY, USA 1990). *Publications:* novels: The Forerunners and the Newcomers 1972, A London Sequel 1979, The Umbilical Cord 1990, The Oppressors 1997, Look at Me... Look at Me Only 2002 (English trans. 2005); short story collections: The Song 1976, The Soul and Other Stories 1999; contrib. to Alightrab Al-Adabi; many short stories in Arabic magazines; trans in Dutch and English periodicals. *Address:* 46 Tudor Drive, Kingston-Upon-Thames, Surrey, KT2 5PZ, England (home). *E-mail:* almananiazi@supanet.com (home). *Website:* alightirab.cjb.net.

MANCHESTER, Rt Rev. Seán; British author and Catholic prelate; *Bishop of Glastonbury*; b. 15 July 1944, Nottingham, England. *Education:* Doctor of Pastoral Ministry, Coll. David's Coll. *Career:* diaconated 1990, ordained priest 1990, consecrated Bishop 1991; founder and Pres. Vampire Research Soc. 1970; Superior Gen. Ordo Sancti Graal 1973; Exec. Dir Holy Grail Outreach Ministry to those in Cults and the Occult 1988; Chair. Soc. of St George 1990; Primate Ecclesia Apostolica Jesu Christi 1991; Bishop of Glastonbury 1993; Presiding Bishop, British Old Catholic Church 2000; Founder Sacerdotal Soc. of the Precious Blood 2002; Patron Guardians Against Satanic Pollution 1990. *Publications:* From Satan to Christ: A Story of Salvation 1988, The Highgate Vampire: The Infernal World of the Undead Unearthed at London's Highgate Cemetery 1991, Mad, Bad and Dangerous to Know: The Life of Lady Caroline Lamb 1992, The Grail Church: Its Ancient Tradition and Renewed Flowering 1995, The Vampire Hunter's Handbook: A Concise Vampirological Guide 1997, Carmel: A Vampire Tale 2000, Stray Ghosts: A Fragment of a Memoir 2003. *Honours:* Kt Commdr, Order of St George Companion, Holy Order of St Michael and St George, Companion, Order of the Sangreal. *Address:* 17 Pen-y-Bryn, Old Colwyn, Clwyd, LL29 9UU, Wales. *Website:* groups.msn.com/BishopSeanManchester; www.holygrail-church.fsnet.co.uk.

MANDEL, Oscar, BA, MA, PhD; American academic, writer, dramatist, poet and translator and art historian; *Professor Emeritus, California Institute of Technology*; b. 24 Aug. 1926, Antwerp, Belgium; m. Adriana Schizzano 1960. *Education:* New York Univ., Columbia Univ., Ohio State Univ. *Career:* faculty mem. Univ. of Nebraska 1955–60; Fulbright Lecturer, Univ. of Amsterdam 1960–61; Assoc. Prof., California Inst. of Tech., Pasadena 1961–65, Prof. of Humanities 1965–, now Prof. Emer.; mem. Dramatists' Guild, Modern Language Asscn, Soc. des Auteurs et Compositeurs Dramatiques. *Publications:* poetry: Simplicities 1974, Collected Lyrics and Epigrams 1981, Where is the light? – Poems 1955–2005; plays: The Fatal French Dentist 1967, Collected Plays (Vols One and Two) 1970, 1972, The Rebels of Nantucket: A Romantic Comedy of the American Revolution 1976, The Kukkurrik Fables: 43 mini-plays for all media 1987, revised and augmented edn 2004, Sigismund, Prince of Poland: A Baroque Entertainment 1988, The Virgin and the Unicorn: Four Plays by Oscar Mandel 1993, Reinventions: Four Plays After Homer, Cervantes, Calderon and Marivaux 2002, L'Arc de Philocète 2002, Amphitryon, ou le cocu béni 2003, Le Triomphe d'Agamemnon 2003; fiction: Chi Po and the Sorcerer: A Chinese Tale for Children and Philosophers 1964, The Gobble-Up Stories (fables) 1967, Amphitryon (adaptation of Molière's comedy) 1976; non-fiction: A Definition of Tragedy (literary theory) 1961, The Theater of Don Juan (thematic history, anthology) 1963, Annotations to Vanity Fair (notes) 1981, Philoctetes and the Fall of Troy: Plays, Documents, Iconography, Interpretations 1982, The Book of Elaborations (essays) 1985, August von Kotzebue: The Comedy, the Man 1990, The Art of Alessandro Magnasco: An Essay in the Recovery of Meaning 1994, The Cheerfulness of Dutch Art: A Rescue Operation 1996, Fundamentals and the Art of Poetry 1997; translations: Seven Comedies by Marivaux 1968, Five Comedies of Medieval France 1970, The Land of Upside Down by Ludwig Tieck 1978, Thomas Corneille's Ariadne 1982, The Theatre of Don Juan: A Collection of Plays and Views, 1630–1963 1986, Prosper Mérimée: Plays on Hispanic Themes (with annotations) 2003; contrib. to scholarly journals. *Address:* Division of Humanities and Social Sciences, California Institute of Technology, Pasadena, CA 91125, USA (office). *Telephone:* (626) 395-4078 (office). *Fax:* (626) 432-1726 (office). *E-mail:* om@hss.caltech.edu (office). *Website:* www.oscarmandel.com.

MANDELA, Nelson Rolihlahla; South African politician, lawyer, international affairs consultant and fmr head of state; b. 1918, Umtata, Transkei; s. of Chief of Tembu tribe; m. 1st Evelyn Mandela 1944 (divorced 1957, died 2004); four c. (three deceased); m. 2nd Winnie Mandela 1958 (divorced 1996); two d.; m. 3rd Graca Machel (widow of the late Pres. Machel of Mozambique) 1998. *Education:* Univ. Coll. of Fort Hare, Univ. of the Witwatersrand. *Career:* legal practice, Johannesburg 1952; Nat. organizer African Nat. Congress (ANC); on trial for treason 1956–61 (acquitted 1961); arrested 1962, sentenced to five years' imprisonment Nov. 1962; on trial for further charges 1963–64, sentenced to life imprisonment June 1964; released Feb. 1990; Deputy Pres. ANC 1990–91, Pres. 1991–97, mem. Nat. Exec. Cttee 1991–; Pres. of South Africa 1994–99; Chancellor Univ. of the North 1992–; Jt Pres. United World Colls 1995–. *Publications:* No Easy Walk to Freedom 1965, How Far We Slaves Have Come: South Africa and Cuba in Today's World (with Fidel Castro) 1991, Nelson Mandela Speaks: Forging a Non-Racial Democratic South Africa 1993, Long Walk to Freedom 1994. *Honours:* Hon. Fellow Magdalene Coll., Cambridge 2001; Hon. Freeman of London; Freedom of City of Glasgow 1981; Hon. Citizen of Rome 1983; Freeman of Dublin 1988; Hon. Bencher Lincoln's Inn 1994; Hon. QC 2000; Order of the Niger 1990; Hon. LLD (Nat. Univ. of Lesotho) 1979, (City Coll. of City Univ. of New York) 1983, (Lancaster) 1984, (Strathclyde) 1985, (Calcutta) 1986, (Harare) 1987, (Kent) 1992, Hon. DLitt (Texas Southern Univ.) 1991; Dr hc (Complutense) 1991; Hon. DCL (Oxford) 1996, Cambridge (1996); Hon. LLD (London) 1996, Bristol (1996), (Nottingham) 1996, (Warwick) 1996, (De Montfort) 1996, (Glasgow Caledonian) 1996; Jawaharlal Nehru Award (India) 1979, Bruno Kreisky Prize for Human Rights 1981, Simon Bolivar Int. Prize (UNESCO) 1983, Third World Prize 1985, Sakharov Prize 1988, Gaddafi Human Rights Prize 1989, Bharat Ratna (India) 1990, Jt winner Houphouët Prize (UNESCO) 1991, Nishan-e-Pakistan 1992, Asturias Prize 1992, Liberty Medal (USA) 1993; shared Nobel Prize for Peace 1993; Mandela-Fulbright Prize 1993, Tun Abdul Razak Award 1994, Anne Frank Medal 1994, Int. Freedom Award 2000, Johannesburg Freedom of the City Award 2004, Amnesty Int. Amb. of Conscience Award 2006. *Address:* c/o ANC, 51 Plein Street, Johannesburg 2001, South Africa (office). *Telephone:* (11) 3307000 (office). *Fax:* (11) 3360302 (office). *E-mail:* info@anc.org.za (office).

MANDELBAUM, Michael, MA, PhD; American academic and writer; *Senior Fellow, Council on Foreign Relations*. *Education:* Yale Univ., King's Coll. Cambridge, UK, Harvard Univ. *Career:* mem. Faculty, Harvard Univ., MA, Columbia Univ., NY, US Naval Acad., Annapolis 1975–90; Christian A. Herter Prof. of American Foreign Policy, Nitze School of Advanced Int. Studies, Johns Hopkins Univ. 1990–, Dir of American Foreign Policy Program; currently Sr Fellow, Council on Foreign Relations; Assoc. Dir Aspen Inst. Congressional Project on American Relations with the Fmr Communist World; foreign affairs columnist Newsday. *Publications:* The Nuclear Question: The United States and Nuclear Weapons, 1946–1976 1979, The Nuclear Revolution: International Politics Before and After Hiroshima 1981, The Nuclear Future 1983, Reagan and Gorbachev (co-author) 1987, The Fate of Nations: The Search for National Security in the 19th and 20th Centuries 1988, Making Markets: Economic Transformation in Eastern Europe and the Post-Soviet States (co-ed.) 1993, The Global Rivals (co-author) 1988, Western Approaches to the Soviet Union (ed.) 1988, The Rise of Nations in the Soviet Union (ed.) 1991, Central Asia and the World (ed.) 1994, The Strategic Quadrangle: Russia, China, Japan and the United States in East Asia (ed.) 1995, The Dawn of Peace in Europe 1996, Postcommunism: Four Perspectives (co-ed.) 1996, The Social Safety Net in Postcommunist Europe (co-ed.) 1997, The New Russian Foreign Policy (ed.) 1998, The New European Diasporas (ed.) 2000, The Ideas that Conquered the World: Peace, Democracy and Free Markets in the Twenty-First Century 2002, The Meaning of Sports: Why Americans Watch Baseball, Football and Basketball and What They See When They Do 2004, The Case for Goliath: How America Acts as the World's Government in the Twenty-First Century 2007; numerous articles in professional journals. *Address:* Council on Foreign Relations, 1779 Massachusetts Avenue, NW, Washington, DC 20036, USA (office). *Telephone:* (202) 663-5669 (office). *Fax:* (202) 986-2984 (office). *E-mail:* dcmeetings@cfr.org (office). *Website:* www.cfr.org (office).

MANDLER, Peter, BA, PhD; American historian; b. 29 Jan. 1958, Boston, Mass; m. Ruth Ehrlich 1987; one s. one d. *Education:* Magdalen College, Oxford, Harvard University. *Career:* Asst Prof., Princeton University, 1984–91; Senior Lecturer, 1991–95, Reader, 1995–97, Prof., 1997–, London Guildhall University; mem. Royal Historical Society, hon. sec., 1998–. *Publications:* Aristocratic Government in the Age of Reform, 1990; The Uses of Charity (ed.), 1990; After the Victorians (co-ed.), 1994; The Fall and Rise of the Stately Home, 1997. Contributions: journals, magazines and newspapers.

MANEA, Norman, MS; American writer and academic; *Frances Flournoy Professor of European Culture, Bard College*; b. 19 July 1936, Suceava, Romania; m. Josette-Cella Boiangiu 1969. *Education:* Inst. of Construction, Faculty of Hydrotechnology, Bucharest. *Career:* Int. Acad. Fellow, Bard Coll. 1989–92, Frances Flournoy Prof. of European Culture 1992–, currently Writer-in-Residence; numerous lectures; mem. Berlin Acad. of Art 2006. *Publications:* fiction: Noaptea pe latura lunga 1969, Captivi 1970, Atrium 1974, Primele porti 1975, Cartea fiului 1976, Zilele si jocul 1977, Octombrie, ora opt (trans. as October, Eight O'Clock) 1981, Plicul Negru (trans. as The Black Envelope) 1986, Compulsory Happiness 1993; other: Anii de ucenicie ai lui August Prostul 1979, Pe contur 1984, On Clowns: The Dictator and the Artist 1992, Casa melcului 1999, Le Retour du Hooligan (The Hooligan's Return, Prix Medicis Entranger 2006) 2003; contrib. to anthologies, periodicals and television. *Honours:* Literary Prize Asscn of Bucharest Writers 1979, Deutscher Akademischer Austauschdienst grant, Berlin 1987, Fulbright Scholarship 1988, Bard Coll. Int. Acad. for Scholarship and the Arts Fellowship 1989–92, Guggenheim Fellowship 1992, John D. and Catherine T. MacArthur Foundation Fellowship 1992, Nat. Jewish Book Award Jewish Book Council/Jewish Welfare Board 1993, New York Public Library Literary Lion Award 1993, Int. Nonino Prize for Literature 2001, Napoli Prize for Int. Fiction 2004. *Address:* Bard College, Annandale-on-Hudson, NY, 12504, USA (office).

MANES, Christopher, BA, MA, JD; American writer; b. 24 May 1957, Chicago, IL; one d. *Education:* University of California, University of Wisconsin. *Career:* mem. California State Bar Asscn; Writers Guild. *Publications:* Place of the Wild, 1994; Post Modernism and Environmental

Philosophy, 1994. Contributions: Reference works, books, journals and magazines.

MANFREDI, Valerio Massimo; Italian archaeologist, academic and writer; *Professor of Archaeology, Bocconi University*; b. 1943. *Career:* specialist in topography of the ancient world; has taken part in many archaeological excavations in Italy and abroad; has taught at Università Cattolica, Milan, Venice Univ., Loyola Univ., Chicago and Ecole Pratique des Hautes Etudes, Paris, currently Prof. of Archaeology Bocconi Univ., Milan; corresp. on antiquities for publs Panorama and Il Messaggero. *Television:* Stargate (LA7–TV). *Publications include:* Xenophon's Anabasis (translator), Lo Scudo di Talos, Palladion, Il Faraone delle Sabbie, L'Oracolo, Le Paludi di Hesperia, La Torre della Solitudine, Alexandros: Child of a Dream, Alexander: The Sands of Amon, Alexander: The Ends of the Earth, The Talisman of Troy 2003, Chimaira Akropolis, L'ultima Legione (The Last Legion: Spartan), Il Tiranno (trans. as Tyrant), Empire of Dragons 2006. *Honours:* Commendatore della Repubblica; Premio Rhegium Julii, Premio Hemingway 2004. *Address:* Laura Grandi (Agent), Via Caradosso 12, 20123, Milan (office); Via delle Grazie 31, 41010, Piumazzo, Modema, Italy (home). *Telephone:* 059-931519 (home). *Fax:* 059-931519 (home). *E-mail:* toilos@tim.it (home).

MANGUEL, Alberto; Canadian (b. Argentine) writer, editor and translator; b. 1948, Buenos Aires, Argentina. *Career:* Fellow, Simon Guggenheim Foundation, S. Fischer Stiftung. *Publications:* (in English) novels: News from a Foreign Country Came (McKitterick Prize 1992) 1991, Stevenson Under the Palm Trees 2004; collections: In Another Part of the Forest: The Flamingo Anthology of Gay Literature (with Craig Stephenson) 1968, The Gates of Paradise: The Flamingo Anthology of Erotic Literature 1969, Black Water: The Flamingo Anthology of Fantastic Literature 1990; non-fiction: The Dictionary of Imaginary Places 1980, Into the Looking-Glass Wood: Essays on Books, Reading and the World 1985, A History of Reading (TLS Int. Book of the Year, Prix Médicis 1998) 1996, Reading Pictures 2001, A Reading Diary 2005, With Borges 2006; ed. of numerous anthologies, many translations. *Honours:* Officier, Ordre des Arts et des Lettres; Premio Lanacion 1971, Harbourfront Festival Prize 1992, Canadian Authors' Asscn Prize 1992, Prix France-Culture 2000, Premio German Sánchez Ruiperez 2002, Prix Poitou-Charentes 2004, Prix Roger Caillois 2004. *Literary Agent:* Guillermo Schavelzon Agency, Calle Muntaner 330, 08 Barcelona, Spain. *Telephone:* (93) 2011310 (office). *Fax:* (93) 2006886 (office). *E-mail:* guillermo@schavelzon.com (office).

MANHIRE, William (Bill), BA, MLitt, MPhil; New Zealand poet, writer and academic; *Professor of Creative Writing and English Literature, Victoria University of Wellington*; b. 27 Dec. 1946, Invercargill; s. of Jack Manhire and Madeline Mary Manhire; m. Barbara Marion McLeod 1970; one s. one d. *Education:* S Otago Dist High School, Otago Boys' High School, Univ. of Otago at Dunedin, Univ. Coll., London, UK. *Career:* Lecturer in English, Vic. Univ., Wellington 1973, f. influential creative writing programme 1976, Prof. of Creative Writing and English Literature 1997–; Dir Int. Inst. of Modern Letters 2001–; Fiction Ed. Victoria Univ. Press 1976–96; Fulbright Visiting Prof. in NZ Studies, Georgetown Univ., USA Jan.–June 1999; inaugural Te Mata Estate New Zealand Poet Laureate 1997–99; Nuffield Fellowship 1981. *Publications:* Malady 1970, The Elaboration 1972, Song Cycle 1975, How to Take Your Clothes Off at the Picnic 1977, Dawn/Water 1980, Good Looks 1982, Locating the Beloved and Other Stories 1983, Zoetropes: Poems 1972–82 1984, Maurice Gee 1986, The Brain of Katherine Mansfield 1988, The New Land: A Picture Book 1990, The Old Man's Example 1990, Milky Way Bar 1991, An Amazing Week in New Zealand 1993, Fault 1994, South Pacific 1994, Hoosh 1995, My Sunshine 1996, Songs of My Life 1996, Sheet Music: Poems 1967–1982 1996, Mutes and Earthquakes 1997, What to Call Your Child 1999, Doubtful Sounds: Essays and Interviews 2000, Collected Poems 2001, Collected Poems 2001, Under the Influence (memoir) 2003, Lifted (poems) 2005, Pine 2005; editor: New Zealand Listener Short Stories Vol. 1 1977, Vol. 2 1978, Some Other Country: New Zealand's Best Short Stories (with Marion McLeod) 1984, Six by Six 1989, Soho Square 1991, 100 New Zealand Poems 1994, Denis Glover: Selected Poems 1995, Spectacular Babies (with Karen Anderson) 2001, The Wide White Page: Writers Imagine Antarctica 2004, 121 New Zealand Poems 2006, The Goose Bath 2006. *Honours:* Companion NZ Order of Merit; Hon. DLitt (Otago); NZ Book Award 1977, 1984, 1992, 1996, Montana Book Award 1994, Katherine Mansfield Fellowship 2004, NZAF Arts Laureate 2005, Montana NZ Book Award 2006. *Address:* Creative Writing Programme, International Institute of Modern Letters, Victoria University of Wellington, PO Box 600, Wellington, New Zealand (office). *Telephone:* (4) 463-6808 (office). *Fax:* (4) 463-6865 (office). *E-mail:* bill.manhire@vuw.ac.nz (office). *Website:* www.vuw.ac.nz/modernletters (office).

MANJI, Irshad, BA; Canadian writer and broadcaster. *Education:* Univ. of British Columbia. *Career:* fmr aide to an MP, press sec. to Ontario Minister for Women's Issues, and speechwriter for first female leader of a Canadian political party; fmrly nat. affairs editorialist Ottawa Citizen newspaper; prod./host Queer Television (Toronto's Citytv) (Gemini Award for Best Edited Information Show) 1998–2001; hosts Big Ideas (TV Ontario); Pres. VERB TV channel; fmrly writer-in-residence Univ. of Toronto's Hart House; mem. inter-faith ed bd Seventeen magazine. *Publications:* Risking Utopia: On the Edge of a New Democracy 1997, The Trouble with Islam Today: A Muslim's Call for Reform in her Faith 2005. *Honours:* Gov.-Gen.'s Award 1990, MS Magazine Feminist for the 21st Century. *E-mail:* irshad@muslim-refusenik.com. *Website:* www.muslim-refusenik.com.

MANKELL, Henning; Swedish playwright and writer; b. 3 Feb. 1948, Stockholm; m. 3rd Eva Bergman 1998; four s. *Career:* merchant seaman 1964–66; Dir Teatro Avenida, Maputo, Mozambique 1987–. *Plays include:* The Amusement Park 1068, Tale on the Beach of Time 1997. *Publications include:* fiction: Vettvillingen 1977, Fångvårdskolonin som försvann 1979, Dödsbrickan 1980, En seglares död 1981, Daisy Sisters 1982, Sagan om Isidor 1984, Leopardens Öga 1990, Comédia infantil 1995, Vindens Son 2000, Tea-bag 2001, Djup 2004, Italienska Skor 2006; crime fiction: Mördare utan ansikte (Faceless Killers) 1991, Hundarna i Rīga (The Dogs of Rīga) 1992, Den vita lejoninnan (The White Lioness) 1993, Mannen som log (The Man Who Smiled) 1994, Villospår (Sidetracked) 1995, Den femte kvinnan (The Fifth Woman) 1996, Steget efter (One Step Behind) 1997, Brandvägg (Firewall) 1998, Pyramiden 1999, Danslärarens återkomst (The Return of the Dancing Master) 1999, Kennedys Hjärna 2000, Innan Frosten (Before the Frost) 2002; juvenile fiction: Sandmålaren 1974, Hunden som Sprang mot en Stjärna 1990, Skuggorna Växer i Skymningen 1991, Katten som Älskade Regn 1992, Eldens Hemlighet 1995, Pojken som sov med snö i sin säng 1996, Resan till Världens Ände 1998, Eldens Gåta 2001, Eldens Vrede (The Wrath of the Fire) 2005; essays: Jag dör, men minnet lever, I sand och i lera 1999. *Honours:* Swedish Mystery Acad. Prize 1991, German Crime Prize 1999, Macallan CWA Golden Dagger Award 2001, Author of the Year, Germany 2002, Premio Pepe Carvalho, Spain 2007. *Address:* c/o Leopard förlag AB, S:t Paulsgatan 11, 118 46 Stockholm, Sweden (office). *E-mail:* info@leopardforlag.se (office). *Website:* www.henningmankell.com.

MANLOW, James; British poet and novelist; b. 1978, Hertfordshire, England. *Education:* Univ. of East Anglia. *Publication:* Attraction (novel) 2004. *Literary Agent:* c/o John Murray Ltd, Hodder Headline, 338 Euston Road, London, NW1 3BH, England. *Website:* www.johnmurray.co.uk.

MANN, Anthony Phillip, MA; British writer and theatre director; b. 7 Aug. 1942, North Allerton, Yorkshire, England. *Education:* Manchester Univ., Humboldt State Univ., CA. *Career:* Trustee, New Zealand Players, 1992; mem. PEN, New Zealand, British Soc. of Dowsers, New Zealand Asscn for Drama in Educ. *Publications:* Eye of the Queen 1982, Master of Paxwax 1986, Fall of the Families 1987, Pioneers 1988, Wulfsyarn – A Mosaic 1990, A Land Fit For Heroes, Vol. 1, Into the Wild Wood, 1993, Vol. 2, Stand Alone Stan, 1994, Vol. 3, The Dragon Wakes, 1995, Vol. 4, The Burning Forest, 1996; contributions: books. *Honours:* Personal Chair. in Drama, Victoria University of Wellington, 1997. *Address:* 22 Bruce Avenue, Brooklyn, Wellington, New Zealand.

MANN, Christopher (Chris) Michael Zithulele, BA, MA; South African poet, writer and dramatist; *Ad Hominem Professor of Poetry, Rhodes University*; b. 6 April 1948, Port Elizabeth; m. Julia Georgina Skeen 1981; one s. one d. *Education:* Univ. of the Witwatersrand, Univ. of Oxford, Univ. of London. *Career:* Research Assoc. Inst. for the Study of English in Africa, Rhodes Univ., Grahamstown 1995–, Ad Hominem Prof. of Poetry 2005–07. *Recording:* Walking on Gravity 2004. *Publications:* First Poems 1977, A New Book of South African Verse (ed. with Guy Butler) 1979, New Shades 1982, Kites 1990, Mann Alive (video and book) 1992, South Africans: A Series of Portrait Poems 1995, Heartlands: A Series of Place Poems 2002, In Praise of the Shades 2003, Lifelines 2005; plays: The Sand Labyrinth 2001, Mahoon's Testimony 1995, The Horn of Plenty: A Series of Painting-Poems (with Julia Skeen, artist) 1997, Frail Care: A Play in Verse 1997, The Roman Centurion's Good Friday, Cathedral of St Michael and St George 1999, Thuthula 2003, Walking on Gravity 2004; contrib. to numerous journals and magazines. *Honours:* Newdigate Prize, Olive Schreiner Award, South African Performing Arts Council Playwright Award, Eastern Cape Premier's Award for Literature 2002; Hon. DLitt (Univ. of Durban-Westville) 1993. *Address:* 19 Frances Street, Grahamstown, 6140 (home); c/o Institute for the Study of English in Africa, Rhodes University, Grahamstown, 6139, South Africa (office). *Telephone:* (46) 622-6093 (office). *Fax:* (46) 603-8566 (office). *E-mail:* c.mann@ru.ac.za (office).

MANN, Emily Betsy, BA, MFA; American writer, theatre director and playwright; *Artistic Director, McCarter Theatre*; b. 12 April 1952, Boston, Mass; d. of Arthur Mann and Sylvia Mann (née Blut); m. Gary Mailman; one s. from previous m. *Education:* Harvard Univ., Univ. of Minnesota. *Career:* Resident Dir Guthrie Theater, Minneapolis 1976–79; Dir Brooklyn Acad. of Music Theater Co., Brooklyn, NY 1980–81; freelance writer and dir, New York 1981–90; Artistic Dir McCarter Theatre, Princeton, NJ 1990–; mem. Soc. of Stage Dirs and Choreographers, Theater Communications Group, New Dramatists, PEN, Writer's Guild; mem. Exec. Bd Dramatists' Guild. *Plays directed include:* Suddenly Last Summer, Loeb Drama Center 1971, The Bull Gets the Matador Once in a Lifetime, Agassiz Theater 1972, Macbeth, Loeb Drama Center 1973, Matrix, Guthrie Theater 1975, The Birthday Party, Guthrie Theater 1975, Cold, Guthrie Theater 1976, Ashes, Guthrie 2 Theater 1977, Cincinnati Playhouse 1980, Annulla, Guthrie Theater 1977, New Theater of Brooklyn 1989, Dark Pony and Reunion, Guthrie Theater 1978, The Farm, Actors Theater of St Paul 1978, On Mount Chimborazo, Guthrie 2 Theater, 1978, Surprise Surprise, Guthrie 2 Theater 1978, The Roads in Germany, Theater in the Round 1978, The Glass Menagerie, Guthrie Theater 1979, McCarter Theatre 1990, He and She, Brooklyn Acad. of Music 1980, Still Life (Obie Award), Goodman Theater 1980, American Place Theater 1981, Dwarfman Master of a Million Shapes, Goodman Theater 1981, A Doll's House, Oregon Contemporary Theater 1982, Hartford Stage Co. 1986, Through the Leaves, Empty Space Theater 1983, A Weekend Near Madison, Astor Place Theater 1983, The Value of Names, Hartford Stage Co. 1984,

Execution of Justice, Guthrie Theater 1985, Virginia Theater (Broadway) 1986, Hedda Gabbler, La Jolla Playhouse 1987, Betsey Brown, American Music Theater Festival 1989, McCarter Theatre 1991, Miss Julie, McCarter Theatre 1992, Three Sisters, McCarter Theatre 1992, Cat on a Hot Tin Roof, McCarter Theatre 1992, Twilight: Los Angeles 1992 (LA Nat. Asscn for the Advancement of Colored People (NAACP) Award for Best Dir), Mark Taper Forum/McCarter Theatre 1993, The Perfectionist, McCarter Theatre 1993, The Matchmaker, McCarter Theatre 1994, Having our Say, McCarter Theatre 1995, Booth Theater (Broadway) 1995, The Mai, McCarter Theatre 1996, Betrayal, McCarter Theatre 1997, The House of Bernarda Alba, McCarter Theatre 1997, Safe as Houses, McCarter Theatre 1998, Meshugah, McCarter Theatre 1998, Fool for Love, McCarter Theatre 1999, The Cherry Orchard, McCarter Theatre 2000, Romeo and Juliet, McCarter Theatre 2001, Because He Can, McCarter Theatre 2001, All Over, McCarter Theatre and Roundabout Theater Co. 2002, The Tempest, McCarter Theatre 2003, Anna in the Tropics, McCarter Theatre/Broadway 2003, Last of the Boys, McCarter Theatre 2004, The Bells, McCarter Theatre 2005, Miss Witherspoon, McCarter Theatre/Playwright's Horizons 2005. *Plays translated and adapted include:* Nights and Days (Les nuits et les jours, Pierre Laville) 1985, Miss Julie 1992, The House of Bernarda Alba 1997, Meshugah 1998, Uncle Vanya 2003. *Plays included in publications:* New Plays USA 1, New Plays 3, Coming to Terms: American Plays and the Vietnam War 1985, The Ten Best Plays of 1986, Out Front 1988, Testimonies: Four Plays by Emily Mann (Theater Communications Group Inc.) 1997. *Publications include:* plays: Annulla Allen: The Autobiography of a Survivor 1977, Still Life (six Obie Awards 1981, Fringe First Award 1985) 1982, Execution of Justice (Helen Hayes Award, Bay Area Theater Critics Circle Award, HBO/USA Award, Playwriting Award Women's Cttee Dramatists Guild for Dramatizing Issues of Conscience) 1986, Having Our Say: The Delaney Sisters' First 100 Years (LA NAACP Award for Best Play) 1994, Greensboro: A Requiem 1996; musicals: Betsey Brown: A Rhythm and Blues Musical (co-author with Ntozake Shange); screenplays: Fanny Kelly (unproduced) 1981, You Strike a Woman, You Strike a Rock: The Story of Winnie Mandela (unproduced mini-series) 1988, The Greensboro Massacre (unproduced) 1992, Having Our Say (Christopher Award, Peabody Award) 1999, Political Stages (co-ed.) 2002. *Honours:* BUSH Fellowship 1975–76, Obie Awards for Directing 1981, 2002, Obie Award for Playwriting 1981, New Drama Forum Asscn Rosamond Gilder Award 1983, NEA Asscns Grant 1984, Tony Award for Outstanding Regional Theater 1984, Guggenheim Fellowship 1985, McKnight Fellowship 1985, CAPS Award 1985, NEA Playwrights Fellowship 1986, Brandeis Univ. Women of Achievement Award 1995, Douglass Coll. of NJ Woman of Achievement Award 1996, Rosamond Gilder Award for Outstanding Achievement in the Theater 1999, Harvard Univ. Alumnae Recognition Award 1999, Nat. Conf. for Community and Justice Award 2004, Leader of the Year Award, Princeton Regional Chamber of Commerce 2005. *Address:* McCarter Theatre, 91 University Place, Princeton, NJ 08540-5121, USA (office). *Telephone:* (609) 258-6502 (office). *Fax:* (609) 497-0369 (office). *E-mail:* emann@mccarter.org (office). *Website:* www.mccarter.org.

MANN, James, BA; American political analyst and journalist; *Author-in-Residence, Paul H. Nitze School of Advanced International Studies, Johns Hopkins University. Education:* Harvard Univ. *Career:* Supreme Court corresp. Los Angeles Times 1978, Chief of Beijing Bureau 1984–87, fmr diplomatic corresp. and foreign affairs columnist –2001; fmr Guest Scholar, Woodrow Wilson Int. Center for Scholars and Sr Writer-in-Residence, Int. Security Program, Center for Strategic and Int. Studies (CSIS); currently Author-in-Residence School of Advanced Int. Studies, Johns Hopkins Univ. and Fellow Foreign Policy Inst.; commentator All Things Considered radio program PBS; contrib. LA Times; mem. Council on Foreign Relations. *Publications:* Beijing Jeep 1989, About Face: A History of America's Curious Relationship with China from Nixon to Clinton (New York Public Library Helen Bernstein Award 2000, Asia-Pacific Prize) 1999, Rise of the Vulcans: The History of Bush's War Cabinet 2004. *Honours:* Edwin M. Hood Award 1993, 1999, Edward Weintal Prize 1999. *Address:* Paul H. Nitze School of Advanced International Studies, Foreign Policy Institute, Johns Hopkins University, 1619 Massachusetts Avenue, NW, Washington, DC 20036, USA (office). *Telephone:* (202) 663-5600 (office). *Fax:* (202) 663-5656 (office). *Website:* www.sais-jhu.edu/centers/fpi/index.html (office).

MANNING, Ned; Australian playwright and actor. *Television appearances:* Young Ramsay 1980, Prisoner: Cell Block H 1981, A Country Practice 1990, The Brides of Christ 1991, Heartbreak High 1994. *Plays as writer:* Us or Them 1984, Close to the Bone 1994, Kingaroy (with Martin Buzacott) 1996, Luck of the Draw 2000. *Address:* c/o Currency Press Pty Ltd, PO Box 2287, Strawberry Hills, NSW 2012, Australia. *E-mail:* enquiries@currency.com.au. *Website:* www.currency.com.au.

MANNING, Paul; American author; b. 22 Nov. 1912, Pasadena, CA; m. Louise Margaret Windels 1947, four s. *Education:* Occidental College, Los Angeles. *Career:* Ed., Time-Life, New York City, 1937–38, Everyweek, 1939; Chief European Correspondent in London, Newspaper Enterprise Asscn and Scripps Howard Newspaper Group, 1939–42; Joined Edward R. Murrow as CBS News Commentator from London, England, 1942; Only journalist to witness and broadcast both German surrender ceremonies, Reims, France, and Japanese surrender aboard USS Missouri, Tokyo Bay; mem. Eighth Air Force Historical Society. *Publications:* Mr England: Biography of Winston Churchill, 1941; Martin Bormann: Nazi in Exile, 1986; Hirohito: The War

Years, 1986; The Silent War: KGB Against the West, 1987; Years of War, 1988. Contributions: New York Times; Reader's Digest; Saturday Evening Post; Articles to numerous journals including 8th Air Force News. *Honours:* Special Citations, Secretary of War Robert Patterson and Secretary of Navy James Forrestal.

MANNING, Phillip, BS, PhD; American science writer; b. 8 July 1936, Atlanta, Ga; m. Diane Karraker 1960; one s. one d. *Education:* The Citadel, Univ. of North Carolina at Chapel Hill. *Career:* mem. Nat. Asscn of Science Writers, Nat. Book Critics Circle. *Publications:* Afoot in the South 1993, Palmetto Journal 1995, Orange Blossom Trails 1997, Islands of Hope 1999; contrib. of more than 150 articles to Backpacker, Field & Stream, and others. *Honours:* Nat. Outdoor Book Award 1999. *Address:* 315 East Rosemary Street, Chapel Hill, NC 27514, USA (home). *E-mail:* pvmanning@mindspring.com (home). *Website:* www.scibooks.org.

MANNING, Robert Joseph; American journalist; *President and Editor-in-Chief, Bobcat Books Inc.*; b. 25 Dec. 1919, Binghamton, NY; s. of Joseph James Manning and Agnes Pauline Brown; m. 1st Margaret Marinda Raymond 1944 (died 1984); three s.; m. 2nd Theresa Slomkowski 1987. *Career:* US Army service 1942–43; Nieman Fellow, Harvard Univ. 1945–46; State Dept and White House Corresp. United Press. 1944–46, Chief UN Corresp. United Press. 1946–49; Writer, Time magazine 1949–55, Senior Ed. 1955–58, Chief, London Bureau, Time, Life, Fortune, Sports Illustrated magazines 1958–61; Sunday Ed., New York Herald Tribune 1961–62; Asst Sec. of State for Public Affairs, US Dept of State 1962–64; Exec. Ed. Atlantic Monthly 1964–66, Ed.-in-Chief 1966–80; Vice-Pres. Atlantic Monthly Co. 1966–80; Ed.-in-Chief Boston Publishing Co. 1981–87; Pres., Ed.-in-Chief Bobcat Books Inc., Boston 1987–; Fellow, Kennedy Inst. of Politics, Harvard Univ. 1980; mem. AAAS. *Publications include:* Who We Are 1976, The Swamp Root Chronicle 1992, The Vietnam Experience (25 vols). *Honours:* Dr hc (Tufts Univ.), (St Lawrence Univ.). *Address:* 1200 Washington Street, Apt 507, Boston, MA 02118, USA. *E-mail:* bobcat1225@rcn.com (office).

MANOR, Jason (see Hall, Oakley Maxwell)

MANOTTI, Dominique; French novelist; b. 1942, Paris. *Career:* fmr teacher of history in schools; currently teacher of economic history, Université de Paris VIII—Vincennes à St-Denis. *Publications:* Sombre Sentier (Premier roman 1995) 1995, A nos chevaux! 1997, Kop 1998, Nos fantastiques années fric (Prix Mystère de la Critique 2002, Prix du roman noir du Festival de Cognac 2002) 2001, Le corps noir 2004. *Address:* Université de Paris VIII—Vincennes à St-Denis, 2 rue de la Liberté, 93526 St Denis Cedex 02, France (office).

MANSEL, Philip Robert Rhys, MA, PhD, FRHistS; British writer; b. 19 Oct. 1951, London, England. *Education:* Balliol Coll., Oxford, Univ. Coll. London. *Career:* Ed. The Court Historian, Newsletter of the Soc. for Court Studies 1995; mem. Soc. for Court Studies; Fellow, Inst. of Historical Research 2001, Comité d'Honneur, Centre de Recherche, Chateau de Versailles 2005. *Publications:* Louis XVIII 1981, Pillars of Monarchy 1984, Sultans in Splendour: The Last Years of the Ottoman World 1988, The Court of France 1789–1830 1989, Charles Joseph de Ligne 1992, Constantinople 1995, The French Emigrés in Europe 1789–1814 1999, Paris Between Empires 1814–1852 2001, Prince of Europe: The Life of Charles-Joseph de Ligne 1735–1814 2003, Dressed to Rule 2005; contrib. to Apollo, History Today, International Herald Tribune, Spectator, TLS, Guardian. *Address:* 13 Prince of Wales Terrace, London, W8 5PG, England. *E-mail:* philipmansel@compuserve.com.

MANSELL, Chris, BEc; Australian poet and writer; b. 1 March 1953, Sydney, NSW; m. Steven G. Sturgess 1986; one s. one d. *Education:* Univ. of Sydney. *Career:* residencies include Curtin Univ., 1985, Univ. of Southern Queensland, 1990, K. S. Prichard Centre, 1992, Bundanon, 1996; Lecturer, Univ. of Wollongong, 1987–89, Univ. of Western Sydney, 1989–91; mem. Australian Society of Authors; Poets Union. *Publications:* Delta, 1978; Head, Heart and Stone, 1982; Redshift/Blueshift, 1988; Shining Like a Jinx, 1992; Day Easy Sunlight Fine, 1995; Fickle Brat, 2002; Stalking the Rainbow, 2002. Contributions: many reviews, quarterlies and magazines. *Honours:* Amelia Chapbook Award, 1987; Queensland Premier's Prize for Poetry, 1993. *Address:* PO Box 94, Berry, NSW 2535, Australia. *E-mail:* info@chrismansell.com. *Website:* www.chrismansell.com.

MANSER, Martin Hugh, BA, MPhil; British editor and language trainer; b. 11 Jan. 1952, Bromley, England; m. Yusandra Tun 1979; one s. one d. *Education:* Univ. of York, CNAA. *Publications:* Concise Book of Bible Quotations, 1982; A Dictionary of Everyday Idioms, 1983; Listening to God, 1984; Pocket Thesaurus of English Words, 1984; Children's Dictionary, 1984; Macmillan Student's Dictionary, 1985; Penguin Wordmaster Dictionary, 1987; Guinness Book of Words, 1988; Dictionary of Eponyms, 1988; Visual Dictionary, Bloomsbury Good Word Guide, 1988; Printing and Publishing Terms, 1988; Marketing Terms, 1988; Guinness Book of Words, 1988; Bible Promises: Outlines for Christian Living, 1989; Oxford Learner's Pocket Dictionary; Get To the Roots: A Dictionary of Words and Phrase Origins, 1992; The Lion Book of Bible Quotations, 1992; Oxford Learner's Pocket Dictionary with Illustrations, 1992; Guide to Better English, 1994; Chambers Compact Thesaurus, 1994; Bloomsbury Key to English Usage, 1994; Collins Gem Daily Guidance, 1995; NIV Thematic Study Bible, 1996; Chambers English Thesaurus, 1997; Dictionary of Bible Themes, 1997; NIV Shorter Concordance, 1997; Guide to English Grammar, 1998; Crash Course in Christian Teaching, 1998; Dictionary of the Bible, 1998; Christian Prayer, 1998; Bible Stories, 1999; Millennium Quiz Book (ed.), 1999; I Never Knew That Was in the Bible, 1999; Pub Quiz Book, 1999; Trivia Quiz Book, 1999; Children's Dictionary, 1999; Lion Bible Quotation Collection, 1999; New Penguin English Thesaurus (joint ed.), 2000; The Westminster Collection of Christian Quotations (compiler), 2001; Heinemann English Dictionary (man. ed.), fifth edn, 2001; NIV Comprehensive Concordance (consultant ed.), 2001; Writer's Manual (joint ed.), 2002; Dictionary of Foreign Words and Phrases, 2002; Dictionary of Proverbs, 2002; Eagle Handbook of Bible Prayers (joint ed.), 2002; Holy Bible: NRSV Cross-Reference Edition (man. ed.), 2003; A Treasury of Psalms (compiler), 2003; Dictionary of Classical and Biblical Allusions (ed.), 2003; The Joy of Christmas (co-author), 2003; Bible A–Z (co-author), 2004; The Chambers Thesaurus (ed.), 2004; Best Loved Hymns, Poems and Readings (compiler), 2004; The Really Useful Concise English Dictionary (ed.), 2004; Dictionary of Saints (ed.), 2004; Best Loved Christmas Carols, Readings and Poetry (compiler), 2005, Collins Dictionary of the Bible (compiler) 2005, Walking with God: 365 Promises and Prayers from the Bible for Every Day of the Year (compiler) 2005, Facts on File Guide to Good Writing (co-author) 2005, Facts on File Guide to Style (co-author) 2006, Wordsworth Book of Hymns (compiler) 2006, Collins Dictionary for Writers and Editors (jt ed.) 2006, Wordsworth Thesaurus (ed.) 2006, Wordsworth Dictionary of Proverbs (ed.) 2006, Wordsworth Dictionary of Idioms (ed.) 2006, Pocket Writer's Handbook (ed.) 2006, Thematic Dictionary 1 (compiler) 2006, Thematic Dictionary 2 (compiler) 2006. *Address:* 102 Northern Road, Aylesbury, Bucks HP19 9QY, England. *Website:* www.martinmanser.com (office).

MANSFIELD, Sir Peter, Kt, BSc, PhD, FRS; British physicist and academic; *Professor Emeritus in Residence, University of Nottingham;* b. 9 Oct. 1933, London; s. of the late S. G. Mansfield and R. L. Mansfield; m. Jean M. Kibble 1962; two d. *Education:* William Penn School, Peckham and Queen Mary Coll., London, Univ. of London. *Career:* Research Assoc. Dept of Physics, Univ. of Ill. 1962; lecturer, Univ. of Nottingham 1964, Sr Lecturer 1967, Reader 1970, Prof. of Physics 1979–94, Prof. Emer. in Residence 1995–; MRC Professorial Fellow 1983–88; Sr Visitor, Max Planck Inst. for Medical Research, Heidelberg 1972–73; Fellow, Queen Mary Coll. 1985; Pres. Soc. of Magnetic Resonance in Medicine 1987–88. *Publications:* NMR Imaging in Biomedicine 1982, NMR Imaging (co-ed.) 1990, MRI in Medicine 1995; some 200 scientific publs in learned journals. *Honours:* Hon. FRCR 1992; Hon. FInstP 1996; Hon. mem. British Inst. of Radiology (BIR) 1993; Hon. DrMed (Strasbourg) 1995; Hon. DSc (Univ. of Kent at Canterbury) 1996; Royal Soc. Wellcome Foundation Gold Medal and Prize 1985, Duddell Medal, Inst. of Physics 1988, Royal Soc. Mullard Medal 1990, ISMAR Prize 1992, Barclay Medal, BJR 1993, Gold Medal, European Asscn of Radiology 1995, Garmisch-Partenkirchen Prize for MRI 1995, Rank Prize 1997, Nobel Prize for Medicine (jtly) 2003; several other awards. *Address:* Magnetic Resonance Centre, Department of Physics and Astronomy, University of Nottingham, NG7 2RD, England. *Telephone:* (115) 9514740 (office). *Fax:* (115) 9515166 (office). *E-mail:* pamela.davies@nottingham.ac.uk (office). *Website:* www.magres.nottingham .ac.uk/~mansfield.

MANTEL, Hilary Mary, CBE, BJur, FRSL; British writer; b. 6 July 1952, Hadfield, Derbyshire; d. of Henry Thompson and Margaret Mary Thompson; m. Gerald McEwen 1973. *Education:* Harrytown Convent, Cheshire, London School of Econs, Sheffield Univ. *Radio:* The Giant, O'Brien (drama) 2002, Learning to Talk (5 plays) 2003. *Publications:* Every Day is Mother's Day 1985, Vacant Possession 1986, Eight Months on Ghazzah Street 1988, Fludd (Winifred Holtby Memorial Award, Southern Arts Literature Prize, Cheltenham Festival Prize) 1989, A Place of Greater Safety (Sunday Express Book of the Year Award 1993) 1992, A Change of Climate 1994, An Experiment in Love (Hawthornden Prize 1996) 1995, The Giant, O'Brien 1998, Giving up the Ghost 2003, Learning to Talk 2003, Beyond Black 2005. *Literary Agent:* A. M. Heath & Co., 79 St Martin's Lane, London, WC2N 4AA, England.

MANWARING, Randle Gilbert, MA; British poet and writer; b. 3 May 1912, London, England; m. Betty Violet Rout 1941, three s. one d. *Education:* University of Keele. *Career:* mem. Downland Poets, chair., 1981–83; Kent and Sussex Poetry Society; Society of Authors; Society of Sussex Authors. *Publications:* The Heart of This People, 1954; Satires and Salvation, 1960; Christian Guide to Daily Work, 1963; Under the Magnolia Tree, 1965; Slave to No Sect and Other Poems, 1966; Crossroads of the Year, 1975; Insurance, 1976; From the Four Winds, 1976; In a Time of Unbelief, 1977; The Swifts of Maggiore, 1981; The Run of the Downs, 1984; Collected Poems, 1986; A Study of Hymn Writing and Hymn-singing in the Christian Church, 1990; Some Late Lark Singing, 1992; Love So Amazing, 1995; The Swallow, The Fox and the Cuckoo, 1997; Trade Winds, 2001; From Controversy to Co-Existence, 2002. Contributions: reviews, quarterlies, and magazines.

MAPLE, Gordon Extra, FRSL; British writer and dramatist; b. 6 Aug. 1932, Jersey, Channel Islands; m. Mabel Atkinson-Frayn 1953, one s. one d. *Career:* mem. BPM, Oxford Yec. *Publications:* Limeade, 1963; Here's a Funny Thing, 1964; Dog, 1967; Elephant, 1968; Tortoise, 1974; Singo, 1975; Napoleon Has Feet, 1977; Pink Circle, 1984; Chateau Schloss, 1985; Popeye, 1985; Keeping in Front (memoirs), 1986; Sour Grapes (with Miles Whittier), 1986; Yet Another Falklands Film, 1987. *Honours:* Evening Standard Awards, 1964, 1973; SWEAT Award, 1986.

MARAINI, Dacia; Italian writer; b. 13 Nov. 1936, d. of Fosco Maraini and Alliata Topazia. *Education:* Collegio S.S. Annunziata, Florence and Rome. *Publications:* La Vacanza 1962, L'Età del Malessere 1962, Crudeltà All' Aria Aperta (poems) 1966, A Memoria (novel) 1967, La famiglia normale (one-act play) 1967, Il ricatto a teatro (play) 1968, Memoirs of a Female Thief 1973, Donna in Guerra (novel) 1975, Mangiami Pure (poems) 1980, I Sogni di Clitennestra (5 plays) 1981, Lettere a Marina (novel) 1981, Lezioni d'Amore (6 plays) 1982, Dimenticato di Dimenticare (poems) 1983, Isolina (novel) 1985, Devour me too (short stories) 1987, La Bionda, la bruna e l'asino (essays) 1987, La Lunga Vita di Marianna Ucria (novel) 1990, Bagheria (novel) 1993, Voci (novel) 1994, Buio (short stories) 1999, Fare Teatro (play) 2000. *Honours:* Prix Formentor for L'Età del Malessere (The Age of Discontent) 1962. *Address:* Via Beccaria 18, 00196 Rome, Italy. *Telephone:* 3611795.

MARANGOU, Niki; Cypriot writer; b. 23 May 1948, Limassol; d. of George Marangos and Kaety Chasapis; m. 1st Michael Attalides 1970 (divorced 1975); one d.; m. 2nd Constantin Candounas 1999. *Education:* studied in Nicosia and Free Univ. (Berlin, Germany). *Career:* Dramaturgist Nicosia State Theatre 1975–85; Dir Kochlias Bookshop, Nicosia 1980–; regular newspaper columnist; seven exhibitions of painting; participated in Biennale of Graphic Arts, Ljubljana 1993, Alexandria 1996; State Prize for Poetry 1981, 1987, State Prize for Prose 1990, Cavafy Prize for Poetry in Alexandria 1998, Biannual State Prize for Prose 2000. *Publications:* Ta Apo Kipon 1981, Arhi Indiktou 1987, Mia Strosi Ammou 1991, Paramythia tis Kyprou (Fairy Tales from Cyprus) 1994, Is the Panther Alive? 1998, Recipes for Katerina 2000, Und sie feierten Hochzeit, Romisini 2000, Selections from the Divan 2001, Doctor from Vienna 2003, Seven Tales from Cyprus 2003, Divan 2005, Doctor of Bneha, Sofia 2005, Din Famagusta la Vienna 2005, O Tsangaris ne o vasilias 2005. *Address:* Ioanni Metaxa 14, Ayios Dometios, Nicosia, Cyprus. *Telephone:* (22) 761766. *Fax:* (22) 766258. *E-mail:* kochlias@spidernet.com.cy. *Website:* www .marangou.com.

MARBER, Patrick; British writer and director; b. 19 Sept. 1964, London; s. of Brian Marber and Angela Benjamin; m. Debra Gillett; one s. *Education:* Wadham Coll., Oxford. *Plays directed and/or written include:* Dealer's Choice 1995, Blue Remembered Hills 1996, '1953' 1996, Closer 1997, The Old Neighbourhood 1998, The Caretaker 2000, Howard Katz 2001. *Television work includes:* The Day Today, Paul Calf Video Diary, Knowing Me Knowing You, 3 Fights 2 Weddings and a Funeral, The Curator, After Miss Julie. *Publications include:* Dealer's Choice 1995, After Miss Julie 1996, Closer 1997, Howard Katz 2001. *Honours:* Evening Standard Award for Best Comedy 1995, Writers' Guild Award for Best West End Play 1995 (both for Dealer's Choice), Evening Standard Best Comedy Award 1997, Critics' Circle Award for Best Play 1997, Olivier Award 1998, New York Drama Critics' Award 1999 (all four for Closer). *Address:* c/o Judy Daish Associates Ltd, 2 St Charles Place, London, W10 6EG, England. *Telephone:* (20) 8964-8811. *Fax:* (20) 8964-8966.

MARCEAU, Félicien, (pseudonym of Louis Carette); French writer; b. 16 Sept. 1913, Cortenberg, Belgium; s. of Louis Carette and Marie Lefèvre; m. 2nd Bianca Licenziati 1953. *Education:* Coll. de la Sainte Trinité à Louvain and Univ. de Louvain. *Career:* mem. Acad. Française 1975. *Publications:* Novels: Chasseneuil 1948, L'Homme du Roi 1952, Bergère Légère 1953, Creezy 1969, Le corps de mon ennemi 1975, Appelez-moi Mademoiselle 1984, La Carriole du Père Juniet 1985, Les passions partagées 1987, Un Oiseau dans le Ciel 1989, Les ingénus 1992, La Terrasse de Lucrezia 1993, Le Voyage de noces de Figaro 1994, La grande fille 1997, La Fille du Pharaon 1998, L'affiche 2000; plays: L'oeuf 1956, La bonne soupe 1958, La preuve par quatre 1965, Un jour j'ai rencontré la vérité 1967, Le babour 1969, L'ouvre-boîte 1972, L'homme en question 1973, A nous de jouer 1979; essays: Balzac et son monde 1955, Le roman en liberté 1977, Une insolente liberté: Les aventures de Casanova 1983, L'Imagination est une science exacte 1998; memoirs: Les années courtes 1968. *Honours:* Prix Interallié for Les élans du coeur 1955, Prix Goncourt for Creezy 1969, Prix Prince Pierre de Monaco 1974; Grand Prix du Théâtre 1975; Officier Légion d'honneur, Ordre nat. du Mérite, Commdr des Arts et des Lettres. *Address:* c/o Les Editions Gallimard, 5 rue Sébastien-Bottin, 75007 Paris; Academie Française, 23 quai de Conti, 75006 Paris, France. *Telephone:* 1-49-54-42-00; 1-44-41-43-06.

MARCH, Jessica (see Africano, Lillian)

MARCHANT, Anyda, (Sarah Aldridge), AB, MA, LLB; American writer and publisher; b. 27 Jan. 1911, Rio de Janeiro, Brazil. *Education:* Nat. Univ. (now part of George Washington Univ.), Washington, DC. *Career:* admitted to the bars of Virginia, District of Columbia, and US Supreme Court; staff, Law Library, Library of Congress, Washington, DC 1940–45, Assoc. in law firm of Covington and Burling, Washington DC 1948–51; Bureau of Foreign and Domestic Commerce, US Dept of Commerce, Washington, DC 1951–53, Int. Bank for Reconstruction and Development, Washington, DC 1954–73; co-founder, Naiad Press 1974, A & M Books 1995. *Publications:* The Latecomer 1974, Tottie: A Tale of the Sixties 1975, Cytherea's Breath 1976, All True Lovers 1978, The Nesting Place 1982, Madame Aurora 1983, Misfortune's Friend 1985, Magdalena 1987, Keep to me Stranger 1989, A Flight of Angels 1992, Michaela 1994, Amantha 1995, Nina in the Wilderness 1997, O, Mistress Mine 2003; contrib. to books and journals. *Honours:* Nat. Women's Music Festival, Bloomington, IN Jeanine Rae Award 1992. . *Address:* 212 Laurel Street, Rehoboth Beach, DE 19971, USA (office). *Telephone:* (800) 489-7662 (office); (302) 227-2893 (home). *Website:* www.sarahaldridge.com (office).

MARCINKEVIČIUS, Justinas; Lithuanian poet, playwright and translator; b. 10 March 1930, Važatkiemis, Lithuania; s. of Motiejus Marcinkevičius and Ieva Marcinkevičius; m. Genovaitė Kalvaitytė 1955; two d. *Education:* Univ. of Vilnius. *Career:* began literary career 1953; fmr Vice-Chair. Bd Union of Lithuanian Writers; mem. CPSU 1957–90; USSR People's Deputy 1989–91; mem. Lithuanian Acad. of Science 1990, Lithuanian Council of Culture and Art 1991. *Publications include:* I Ask to Speak 1955, The Twentieth Spring 1955, The Pine that Laughed 1961, Blood and Ashes 1961, Hands that Share out the Bread 1963, The Wall 1965, Mindaugas 1968, The Cathedral 1971, Mazhvidas 1977, The Tender Touch of Life 1978, The Only Land 1984, For the Living and the Dead 1988, Lullaby to the Homeland and the Mother 1992, By the Rye and by the Hearth 1993, Poems from the Diary 1993, The Harmony of the Flowing River 1995. *Honours:* Order of the Grand Duke Gediminas; awards include State Prizes (twice), People's Poet of Lithuania, J. G. Horder Award 1997, Polish PEN Centre Award 1997, Santarvė Award 1999. *Address:* Mildos gve. 33, Apt 6, 2055 Vilnius, Lithuania. *Telephone:* (2) 740162.

MARCUS, Emilie, BA, PhD; American; *Editor, Cell*; b. 1960. *Education:* Wesleyan Univ., Univ. of Yale, Salk Inst., CA. *Career:* fmr Ed., Neuron; Ed., Cell 2003–. *Address:* Cell, Cell Press, 600 Technology Square, Fifth Floor, Cambridge, MA 02139, USA (office). *E-mail:* emarcus@cell.com. *Website:* www.cell.com.

MARCUS, Ruth Barcan, BA, MA, PhD; American academic and author; *Senior Research Scholar, Reuben Post Halleck, Emerita, Yale University*; b. 2 Aug. 1921, New York; d. of Samuel Barcan and Rose Post; m. Jules A. Marcus 1942 (divorced 1976); two s. two d. *Education:* New York and Yale Univs. *Career:* Research Assoc. Inst. for Human Relations, Yale Univ. 1945–47; Assoc. Prof. Roosevelt Univ. 1959–64; Prof. and Chair. Dept of Philosophy, Univ. of Ill. 1964–70; Prof. Northwestern Univ. 1970–73; Reuben Post Halleck Prof. of Philosophy, Yale Univ. 1973–93, Sr Research Scholar 1994–, now Senior Research Scholar, Reuben Post Halleck, Emer.; Visiting Distinguished Prof., Univ. of Calif., Irvine 1994–99; Adviser, Oxford Univ. Press New York 1980–90; Guggenheim Fellow 1953–54; NSF Fellow 1963–64; Fellow, Center for Advanced Studies, Stanford Univ. 1979, Inst. for Advanced Study in the Humanities, Univ. of Edin. 1983, Wolfson Coll. Oxford 1985, 1986, Clare Hall, Cambridge 1988 (Perm. mem. Common Room); Fellow, American Acad. of Arts and Sciences; mem. and Pres. Inst. Int. de Philosophie, Paris 1990–93, Hon. Pres. 1993–; Chair. Nat. Bd of Officers, American Philosophical Asscn 1977–83; Pres. Asscn for Symbolic Logic 1983–86; Pres. Elizabethan Club 1988–90; mem. Council on Philosophical Studies (Pres. 1988–), Steering Cttee, Fed. Int. Soc. de Philosophie 1985–99; mem. numerous editorial bds. *Publications:* The Logical Enterprise (ed. with A. Anderson and R. Martin) 1975, Logic Methodology and Philosophy of Science (ed.) 1986, Modalities 1993, 1995; articles in professional journals. *Honours:* Hon. DHumLitt (Illinois) 1995; Medal, Coll. de France 1986, Wilbur Cross Medal, Yale Univ. 2000. *Address:* Department of Philosophy, Box 208306, Yale University, New Haven, CT 06520, USA (office). *Telephone:* (203) 432-1672. *Fax:* (203) 432-7950 (office). *E-mail:* ruth.marcus@yale.edu (office). *Website:* www.yale.edu/philos (office).

MARCUS, Steven, AB, PhD; American academic and writer; b. 13 Dec. 1928, New York, NY; m. Gertrud Lenzer 1966; one s. *Education:* Columbia Univ. *Career:* Prof. of English, Columbia Univ. 1966–, George Delacorte Prof. of Humanities 1976–, Chair Dept of English and Comparative Literature 1977–80, 1985–90, Vice-Pres. School of Arts and Sciences 1993–95, Dean Columbia Coll. 1993–95; Fellow Center for Advanced Studies in the Behavioural Sciences 1972–73; Dir of Planning, Nat. Humanities Center 1974–76, Chair of the Exec. Cttee, Bd of Dirs 1976–80; Chair Lionel Trilling Seminars 1976–80; Fellow Acad. of Literary Studies, American Acad. of Arts and Sciences; mem. American Acad. of Psychoanalysis, American Psychoanalytic Asscn, Inst. for Psychoanalytic Teaching and Research. *Publications:* Dickens: From Pickwick to Dombey, 1965; Other Victorians, 1966; Engels, Manchester and the Working Class, 1974; Representations: Essays on Literature and Society, 1976; Doing Good (with others), 1978; Freud and the Culture of Psychoanalysis, 1984. Editor: The Life and Work of Sigmund Freud (with Lionel Trilling), 1960; The World of Modern Fiction, 2 vols, 1968; The Continental Op, 1974; Medicine and Western Civilization (with David Rothman), 1995. Contributions: Professional journals and to general periodicals. *Honours:* Guggenheim Fellowship, 1967–68; Rockefeller Foundation Fellowship, 1980–81; National Humanities Center Fellowship, 1980–82; Fulbright Fellowship, 1982–84; Hon. DHL, Clark University, 1985. *Address:* c/o Department of English and Comparative Literature, Columbia University, New York, NY 10027, USA.

MARDELL, Mark Ian, BA; British journalist; *Europe Editor, BBC News*; b. 10 Sept. 1957, s. of Donald Mardell and Maureen Mardell; m. Joanne Veale 1990; two s. one d. *Education:* Priory School, Banstead, Epsom Coll. and Univ. of Kent at Canterbury. *Career:* journalist Radio Tees, Teesside 1980–82, Radio Aire, Leeds 1982; Industrial Ed. Independent Radio News, London 1983–87; reporter Sharp End (Channel 4) 1987–89; worked for BBC from 1988, Political Correspondent 1988–93, Political Ed. Newsnight 1993–2000, Political Correspondent BBC News at Six 2000–03, Chief Political Correspondent BBC News 2003–05, Europe Ed. 2005–. *Television programmes:* presenter This Week (BBC 1). *Radio programmes:* Judgement Day (Radio 4 short story) 2004, occasional presenter World at One, Broadcasting House (both BBC Radio 4). *Publication:* How to Get On in TV (juvenile) 2001. *Address:* BBC TV Centre, Wood Lane, London, W12 7RJ, England. *Website:* www.bbc.co.uk.

MARFEY, Anne, PhD; Danish writer and academic; b. 19 Feb. 1927, Copenhagen; m. Dr Peter Marfey 1964 (deceased); one s. one d. *Education:* Danish Teachers' Coll., Copenhagen, Columbia Univ., Pacific Western Univ., HI. *Career:* Adjunct Lecturer in Danish, SUNY at Albany; Lecturer, NY State Conf. for Early Childhood; Rep. for Danes Worldwide, Albany Area; mem. Danish Writers Guild; Bd Mem., UN Albany, US-China Friendship Asscn, Albany, New York Acad. of Sciences 1997, American Asscn of Univ. Women 1998. *Publications:* Learning to Write, 1961; Vejen til hurtigere Laesning, 1962; Svante, 1965; Las Bedre, 1966; Amerikanere, 1967; Telefontraden, 1968; Skal Skal ikke, 1969; How Parents Can Help Their Child with Reading, 1976; Rose's Adventure, 1989; Moderne Dansk, 1989; The Duckboat, The Pump, The Pine Tree, 1994; The Chipmunk, 1994; The Miracle of Learning, 1997; The Ugly Carrot, 2002, Callaway The Cat, Callaway The Cat Disappears, Poems in the National Library of Poetry. *Address:* 9 Tudor Road, Albany, NY 12203, USA. *Telephone:* (518) 482-6145.

MARGOLIN, Phillip Michael, BA, JD; American lawyer and writer; b. 20 April 1944, New York, NY; m. Doreen Stamm 1968, one s. one d. *Education:* American University, New York University. *Career:* Law Clerk to the Chief Judge, Oregon Court of Appeals, 1970–71; Deputy District Attorney and Special Agent for Multnomah County, OR, 1971–72; Partner, Nash & Margolin, 1974–80, Margolin & Margolin, 1986–96, Portland, OR; mem. MWA; National Asscn of Criminal Defense Lawyers; Oregon Criminal Defense Lawyers Asscn; Oregon State Bar Asscn. *Publications:* Heartstone, 1978; The Last Innocent Man, 1981; Gone, but Not Forgotten, 1993; After Dark, 1995; The Burning Man, 1996; The Undertaker's Widow, 1998; Wild Justice, 2000. Contributions: Professional journals, anthologies and periodicals.

MARGOSHES, Dave, BA, MFA; American writer and poet; b. 8 July 1941, New Brunswick, NJ; m. Ilya Silbar 1963. *Education:* Univ. of Iowa. *Career:* instructor, numerous writers' workshops and creative writing courses; Writer-in-Residence, Univ. of Winnipeg 1995–96, Saskatoon Public Library 2001–02. *Publications:* Third Impressions (short stories with Barry Dempster and Don Dickinson) 1982, Small Regrets (short stories) 1986, Walking at Brighton (poems) 1988, Northwest Passage (poems) 1990, Nine Lives (short stories) 1991, Saskatchewan 1992, Long Distance Calls (short stories) 1996, Fables of Creation (short stories) 1997, Tommy Douglas: Building the New Society (biog.) 1999, We Who Seek: A Love Story (novella) 1999, I'm Frankie Sterne (novel) 2000, Purity of Absence (poems) 2001, Drowning Man (novel) 2003; contrib. to numerous anthologies, journals and magazines. *Honours:* Canadian Author and Bookman Poem of the Year Award 1980, Saskatchewan Writers' Guild Long Manuscript Award 1990, Second Prize, League of Canadian Poets' Nat. Poetry Contest 1991, Stephen Leacock Award for Poetry 1996, John V. Hicks Award for Fiction 2001, City of Regina Writing Award 2004. *Address:* 2922 19th Avenue, Regina, SK S4T 1X5, Canada (home). *Telephone:* (306) 522-9429 (office). *E-mail:* dmargos@sasktel.net (home).

MARIANI, Paul Louis, BA, MA, PhD; American academic, writer, biographer and poet; *University Professor of English, Boston College*; b. 29 Feb. 1940, New York, NY; s. of the late Paul Patrick Mariani and Harriet Green Mariani; m. Eileen Spinosa 1963; three s. *Education:* Manhattan Coll., Colgate Univ., Grad. School and Univ. Center, CUNY. *Career:* Asst Prof., John Jay Coll. of Criminal Justice, CUNY 1967–68; Asst Prof., Univ. of Massachusetts, Amherst 1968–71, Assoc. Prof. 1971–75, Prof. 1975–85, Distinguished Univ. Prof. 1985–; Univ. Prof. of English, Boston Coll. 2000–; Robert Frost Fellow, Bread Loaf Writers' Conf. 1980, Faculty 1982, 1983, 1984, Robert Frost Prof. 1983, Visiting Lecturer 1986, School of English Poetry Staff 1985–96; Dir The Glen, Colorado Springs 1995, 1996, 1998, The Image Conf. 2004, 2005, 2006; Poetry Ed. America Magazine 2000–06; mem. Acad. of American Poets, Poetry Soc. of America. *Publications:* poetry: Timing Devices 1979, Crossing Cocytus 1982, Prime Mover 1985, Salvage Operations: New and Selected Poems 1990, The Great Wheel 1996, Deaths and Transfigurations: Poems (designed and illustrated by Barry Moser) 2005; prose: William Carlos Williams: A New World Naked 1981, Dream Song: The Life of John Berryman 1990, Lost Puritan: A Life of Robert Lowell 1994, The Broken Tower: A Life of Hart Crane 1999, Thirty Days: On Retreat with the Exercises of St Ignatius 2002, God and the Imagination: On Poets, Poetry and the Ineffable 2002, The Havoc and the Glory: The Life and Times of Gerard Manley Hopkins 2007; contrib. to books and journals. *Honours:* Hon. DHL (Manhattan Coll.) 1998, (The Elms Coll.) 2001; Nat. Endowment for the Humanities Fellowships 1972–73, 1981–82, New Jersey Writers' Award 1982, New York Times Notable Books 1982, 1994, 1999, Univ. of Massachusetts Chancellor's Medal 1984, Nat. Endowment for the Arts Fellowship 1984, Prairie Schooner Choice Awards 1989, 1995, Ohioana Award 2000, Catholic Press Asscn Award for Popular Presentation of the Catholic Faith 2003. *Address:* PO Box M, Montague, MA 01351, USA (home). *Telephone:* (617) 552-3177 (office); (413) 367-2820 (home). *Fax:* (413) 367-0358 (home). *E-mail:* pmariani@english.umass.edu (office); paul.mariani@bc.edu (office).

MARÍAS FRANCO, Javier; Spanish writer and translator; b. 20 Sept. 1951, Madrid; s. of Julián Marías Aguilera and the late Dolores Franco Manera. *Education:* Institución Libre de Enseñanza, Colegio Estudio, Universidad Complutense de Madrid. *Career:* trans. and writer of film screenplays 1969–; Ed. Alfaguara 1974; lecturer at various univs worldwide; mem. Int. Parliament of Writers (exec. council 2001–). *Publications:* novels: Los dominios del lobo 1971, Travesía del horizonte 1972, El Monarca del tiempo

1978, El hombre sentimental (Premio Herralde de Novela, Premio Ennio Flaiano 2000) 1986, El Siglo 1982, Todas las almas (Premio Ciudad de Barcelona) 1989, Corazón tan blanco (Premio de la Crítica 1993, Prix L'Oeil et la Lettre 1993, Int. IMPAC Prize 1997) 1992, Mañana en la batalla piensa en mí (Premio Fastenrath de la Real Academia Española de la Lengua 1995, Premio Internacional de Novela Rómulo Gallegos 1995, Prix Fémina Étranger, France 1996, Premio Arzobispo Juan de San Clemente 1995, Premio Letterario Internazionale Mondello-Cittá di Palermo 1998) 1994, Negra espalda del tiempo 1998, Tu rostro mañana, 1. Fiebre y lanza (Premio Salambó 2003) 2002, Your Face Tomorrow 2: Dance and Dream 2006; other fiction: Gospel (screenplay) 1969, Mientras ellas duermen (short stories) 1990, Cuando fui mortal (short stories) 1996, Mala índole (short story) 1998; non-fiction: Pasiones pasadas (articles and essays) 1991, Vidas escritas (articles) 1992, Literatura y fantasma (articles and essays) 1993, Vida del fantasma (articles) 1995, Si yo amaneciera otra vez (articles and poems) 1997, Miramientos (articles) 1997, Mano de sombra (articles) 1997, Desde que te vi morir (articles and poems) 1999, Seré amado cuando falte (articles) 1999, Salvajes y sentimentales (articles) 2000, A veces un caballero (articles) 2001; numerous translations; contrib. to anthologies, including Cuentos únicos 1989, El hombre que parecia no querer nada 1996; contrib. to journals and newspapers, including El País, El Diario de Barcelona, Hiperión, Revista de Occidente. Honours: Chevalier, Ordre des Arts et des Lettres, Premio Comunidad de Madrid 1998; Premio Nacional de Traducción (for translation of Tristram Shandy) 1979, Alberto Moravia Int. Prize, Rome 2000, Grinzane Cavour prize, Turin 2000. Address: Mercedes Casanovas Agencia Literaria, Iradier 24, 08017 Barcelona, Spain (office). Website: www.javiermarias.es.

MARINEAU, Michele, BA; Canadian writer and translator; b. 12 Aug. 1955, Montréal, QC; m. (divorced); one s. one d. Education: University of Montréal. Career: mem. Union des écrivaines et des écrivains québécois; Corporation Professionnelle des Traducteurs et Interprétes Agréés du Québec; Asscn des Traducteurs Litteraires du Canada; Communication-Jeunesse. Publications: Cassiopée ou L'été Polonais, 1988; L'été des Baleines, 1989; L'Homme du Cheshire, 1990; Pourquoi pas Istambul?, 1991; La Route de Chlifa, 1992. Honours: Prix du Gouverneur Général, 1988, 1993; Prix, Brive-Montréal, 1993; Prix, Alvine-Bélisle, 1993. Address: 4405 rue de Brebeuf, Montréal, QC H2J 3K8, Canada.

MARININA, Col. Aleksandra Borisovna, PhD; Russian writer and fmr criminologist; b. (Marina Anatolyevna Alekseyeva), 16 June 1957, Lviv, Ukraine; m. Col Sergey Zatochny. Education: Moscow State Univ. Career: fmr mem. of staff Acad. of Internal Affairs; began writing detective stories 1991–; mem. of staff Moscow Inst. of Justice, Ministry of Internal Affairs 1994–97. Films for television: Kamenskaya (48 episodes). Publications: Death and Some Love, Ghost of Music, Stolen Dream, I Died Yesterday, Men's Game, Forced Murderer, Black List, Requiem, When Gods Laugh, He Who Knows (vols 1–2), and numerous others. Address: Verhnaya Krasnoselskaya str. 9, Apt 44, 107140 Moscow, Russia (home). Address: COP Literary Agency, Zhukovskogo str. 4, Apt 29, 103062 Moscow (office); Verhnaya Krasnoselskaya str. 9, Apt 44, 107140 Moscow, Russia (home). Telephone: (495) 928-84-56 (office); (495) 975-45-35 (home). Fax: (495) 928-84-56 (office). E-mail: alexandra@marinina.ru (office). Website: www.marinina.ru (home).

MARINOS, Yannis, BA; Greek journalist; b. 20 July 1930, Hermoupolis. Education: Univ. of Athens. Career: journalist, To Vima (daily) 1953–65; journalist, Economicos Tachydromos, Ed.-in-Chief 1956, Ed. and Dir 1964–96, consultant/columnist 1996–; political commentator in Ta Nea (daily) 1972–75; columnist, To Vima (daily political journal) 1992–; commentator for many radio and TV stations in Greece; mem. European Parl. 1999–2004; Deputy Nea Democratia and European Popular Party 1999–; mem. Bd Lambrakis Research Foundation, Org. of Music Hall of Athens. Publications: The Palestinian Problem and Cyprus 1975, For a Change Towards Better 1983, Greece in Crisis 1987, Common Sense 1993. Honours: Hon. PhD (Aristotelian Univ. Salonika) 1999; more than 30 awards including Best European Journalist of 1989 (EC Comm. and Asscn of European Journalists) and awards from UN and Athens Acad. Address: 9 Merlin Street, Athens 106 71 (office); 2 Kontziade Street, Piraeus 185 37, Greece (home). Telephone: (210) 3641828 (office); (210) 4526823 (home). Fax: (210) 3641839. E-mail: jmarinos@dolnet.gr (office).

MARIZ, Linda Catherine French, (Linda French), BA, MA; American novelist; b. 27 Nov. 1948, New Orleans, LA; m. George Eric Mariz 1970, one s. one d. Education: University of Missouri, Columbia, Western Washington University. Career: Creative Writing Instructor, Western Washington University, 1994; mem. Sisters in Crime; International Asscn of Crime Writers; Washington Commission for the Humanities. Publications: as Linda Mariz: Body English, 1992; Snake Dance, 1992; as Linda French: Talking Rain, 1998; Coffee to Die For, 1998; Steeped in Murder, 1999. Contributions: Cash Buyer (story) in Reader, I Murdered Him Too (anthology), 1995. Address: 708 17th Street, Bellingham, WA 98225, USA.

MARKHAM, Edward Archibald, BA, FRSL; British editor, poet, writer, dramatist and academic; b. 1 Oct. 1939, Montserrat. Education: Univ. of Wales, Lampeter, Univ. of East Anglia, Univ. of London. Career: Lecturer, Abraham Moss Centre, Manchester 1976–78; Asst Ed., Ambit Magazine, London 1980–85; Ed., Artrage 1985–87, Sheffield Thursday 1992–2000; writer-in-residence, Univ. of Ulster, Coleraine 1988–91; Prof., Sheffield Hallam Univ. 1991–2005; Int. Writer, Fellow Trinity Coll., Dublin 2006.

Plays: The Masterpiece 1964, The Private Life of the Public Man 1970, Dropping Out is Violence 1971, Dreamers 2001. Publications: poetry: Human Rites: Selected Poems, 1970–82 1983, Living in Disguise 1986, Towards the End of a Century 1989, Letter from Ulster and the Hugo Poems 1993, Misapprehensions 1995, A Rough Climate 2002, John Lewis & Co 2003, Hinterland (ed.) 1989, Plant Care: A Festschrift for Mimi Khalvati (ed.) 2004; short story collections: Something Unusual 1986, Ten Stories 1994, Taking the Drawing Room Through Customs: Selected Stories 2002, Meet Me in Mozambique 2005, At Home With Miss Vanesa 2006; other prose: The Penguin Book of Caribbean Short Stories (ed.) 1996, A Papua New Guinea Sojourn: More Pleasures of Exile (memoir) 1998, Marking Time (novel) 1999, At Home with Miss Vanesa (novel) 2006. Honours: C. Day-Lewis Fellowship 1980–81, Government of Montserrat Certificate of Honour 1997. Address: c/o Anvil Press Poetry Ltd, Neptune House, 70 Royal Hill, London, SE10 8RF, England.

MARKHAM, Jehane; British poet and playwright; b. 12 Feb. 1949, Sussex, England; m.; three s. Education: Cen. School of Art. Career: mem. Poetry Book Soc., Highgate Literary and Scientific Soc., Poetry Soc. Publications: poetry: The Captain's Death 1975, Ten Poems 1993, Virago New Poets 1993, Twenty Poems 1999, My Mother, Myself (audio) 2001, Between Sessions and Beyond the Couch 2002, In the Company of Poets 2003; radio plays: More Cherry Cake 1980, Thanksgiving 1984, The Bell Jar, Frost in May; television play: Nina 1978; theatre plays: One White Day 1976, The Birth of Pleasure 1997; contribs. to Women's Press, Longmans Study, Sunday Times, BBC 2 Epilogue, Bananas Literary Magazine, Camden Voices, Independent, Observer, Acorn, Ambit, New Statesman, Cork Literary Review, Wild Cards (anthology) 1999, Between Sessions and On the Couch 2002. Honours: winner BBC Radio 4 Open Book Paradelle Competition 2002. Literary Agent: c/o Emily Hayward, Sheil Land Associates, 52 Doughty Street, London, WC1N 2LS, England. Address: 56 Lady Somerset Road, London, NW5 1TU, England. Website: www.roughwinds.co.uk.

MARKHAM, Marion Margaret, BS; American writer; b. 12 June 1929, Chicago, IL; m. Robert Bailey Markham 1955, two d. Education: Northwestern University. Career: mem. Society of Midland Authors, MWA, Authors' Guild of America, Society of Children's Book Writers. Publications: Escape from Velos, 1981; The Halloween Candy Mystery, 1982; The Christmas Present Mystery, 1984; The Thanksgiving Day Parade Mystery, 1986; The Birthday Party Mystery, 1989; The April Fool's Day Mystery, 1991; The Valentine's Day Mystery, 1992.

MARKISH, David; Russian/Israeli writer; b. 24 Sept. 1938, Moscow, Russia; m. Nathalie Laskina 1990; two s. Education: Gorky Literary Inst., Moscow. Publications: Five Close to the Sky 1966, A New World for Simon Ashkenazy 1976, The Cock 1980, Forward 1980, Jesters 1983, The Dog 1984, In the Shadow of a Big Stone 1986, The Field 1989, The Garnet Shaft 1990, My Enemy Cat 1991, To Be Like Others 2000, To Become Lutov 2001, The White Circle 2004. Honours: seven Israeli Literary Awards, British Book League Award, Int. Literary Award of Ukraine, Machabeli Literary Award of Georgia. Address: Erez 65, Or-Ehuda, Israel (home). E-mail: markishd@bezeqint.net (office).

MARKOVIĆ, Predrag; Serbian politician and publisher; b. 7 Dec. 1955, Cepure. Education: Univ. of Belgrade. Career: Ed. Student, Vreme (newspapers), Vidici (magazine); Owner Stubovi kulture publishing house 1993–; Pres. G17 PLUS Man. Bd 2000–01, Pres. Political Council, mem. Exec. Bd 2001–02, Vice-Pres. G17 PLUS party 2003–; Pres. Nat. Ass. of Serbia 2004–; Acting Pres. of Serbia March–July 2004; fmr Pres. Asscn of Publrs of Serbia and Montenegro; mem. PEN, Serbian Literary Soc. Publications: Morali su doći nasmejani lavovi 1983, Otemenost duše 1989. Address: G17 PLUS, Trg Republike 5, 11000 Belgrade, Serbia (office). Telephone: (11) 3344930 (office). Fax: (11) 3344459 (office). Website: www.g17plus.org.yu (office).

MARKS, Stanley; Australian writer and dramatist; b. 1929, London, England; m. Eve Mass; one s. one d. (deceased). Education: Univ. of Melbourne (did not complete course). Career: journalist and foreign corresp., Australia, UK, USA, Canada; Originator-Writer, MS cartoon series, Australian and NZ newspapers, 1975–80; Ed. Journal of Melbourne Holocaust Centre; mem. Australian Soc. of Authors. Publications: God Gave You One Face 1964, Graham is an Aboriginal Boy 1968, Fifty Years of Achievement 1972, Animal Olympics 1972, Rarua Lives in Papua New Guinea 1974, Ketut Lives in Bali 1976, St Kilda Sketchbook 1980, Malvern Sketchbook 1981, Welcome to Australia 1981, Out and About in Melbourne 1988, Reflections 1994, St Kilda Heritage Sketchbook 1995; essay in anthology Memory Guide My Hand 1994; contribs to newspapers and journals. Honours: Australia Day Award 1993, Australia Day Citizen of the Year for the large municipality of Glen Eira 1994, B'nai B'nai Menorah Award 1994. Address: 348 Bambra Road, South Caulfield, Melbourne, Vic. 3162, Australia. Telephone: (3) 9578-6697 (home). Fax: (3) 9578-5197 (home). E-mail: smar4858@bigpond.net.au (home).

MARKWORT, Helmut; German journalist, publisher, editor and presenter; Publisher, Editor-in-Chief and CEO, Focus Magazine; b. 8 Dec. 1936, Darmstadt; s. of August Markwort and Else Markwort (née Volz). Career: started in journalism 1956, various posts in local media –1966; founder Ed.-in-Chief of several magazines and radio stations; Publr, Ed.-in-Chief and CEO Focus Magazine 1993–; Man. Focus TV 1996–; Publr Focus Money 2000–; Head of Bd Tomorrow Focus AG 2001–, Playboy Publishing Deutschland AG 2002–; presenter Bookmark 2004. Honours: Nat. Merit Cross (1st Class) 1999;

'Horizont Mann der Medien' Award 1983, 1993, Advertising Age 'Marketing Superstar' 1994, Hildegard von Bingen Award for Journalism, BDS Mittelstandspreis Award, Bavarian's Merit Medal 1996, Premio Capo Circeo 2004. *Address:* Focus Magazine, Arabella str. 23, 81925 Munich, Germany (office). *Fax:* (89) 92502026 (office). *Website:* www.focus.de (office).

MARLATT, Daphne Shirley; Canadian poet and writer; b. 11 July 1942, Melbourne, Vic., Australia; m. Gordon Alan Marlatt 1963 (divorced 1970); one s. *Education:* BA, English and Creative Writing, University of British Columbia, 1964; MA, Comparative Literature, Indiana University, 1968. *Career:* Co-Ed., Tessera (Journal), 1983–91; Special Lecturer in Creative Writing, University of Saskatchewan, 1998–99; mem. Writers' Union of Canada. *Publications:* Frames of a Story, 1968; Leaf/Leaf/s, 1969; Rings, 1971; Vancouver Poems, 1972; Steveston, 1974; Our Lives, 1975; Steveston Recollected: A Japanese-Canadian History (with M. Koizumi), 1975; Zócalo, 1977; Opening Doors: Vancouver's East End (with Carole Itter), 1979; What Matters, 1980; Selected Writing: Net Work, 1980; How Hug a Stone, 1983; Touch to My Tongue, 1984; Double Negative (with Betsy Warland), 1988; Ana Historic, 1988; Salvage, 1991; Ghost Works, 1993; Taken, 1996; Readings from the Labyrinth, 1998; This Tremor Love Is, 2001. *Address:* Simon Fraser University, English Department, 8888 University Drive, Burnaby, BC Canada V5A 1S6, USA (office). *E-mail:* dmarlatt@sfu.ca (office).

MARLIN, Henry (see Giggal, Kenneth)

MARLOW, Joyce; British author; b. 27 Dec. 1929, Manchester, England. *Education:* Whalley Range High School, Manchester. *Career:* professional actress 1950–65; author 1964–. *Publications:* The Man with the Glove 1964, A Time to Die 1966, Billy Goes to War 1967, The House on the Cliffs 1968, The Peterloo Massacre 1969, The Tolpuddle Martyrs 1971, Captain Boycott and the Irish 1973, The Life and Times of George I 1973, The Uncrowned Queen of Ireland 1975, Mr and Mrs Gladstone 1977, Kings and Queens of Britain 1977, Kessie 1985, Sarah 1987, Anne 1989, Industrial Tribunals and Appeals 1991, Virago Book of Women of the Great War 1998, Virago Book of Votes for Women 2000. *Literary Agent:* c/o Sara Menguc (literary agent). *E-mail:* saramenguc@aol.com. *Address:* 3 Spring Bank, New Mills, High Peak, SK22 4AS, England (home). *Telephone:* (1663) 742600 (home). *E-mail:* joyce.marlow@firenet.uk.net (home).

MARLOWE, Hugh (see Patterson, Harry)

MARLOWE, Stephen, (Andrew Frazer, Milton Lesser, Jason Ridgway, C. H. Thames), AB; American author; b. 7 Aug. 1928, New York, NY; m. 1st Leigh Lang 1950; m. 2nd Ann Humbert 1964, two d. *Education:* College of William and Mary. *Career:* Writer-in-Residence, College of William and Mary, 1974–75, 1980–81. *Publications include:* novels: The Shining, 1963; Colossus, 1972; The Valkyrie Encounter, 1978; The Memoirs of Christopher Columbus, 1987; The Death and Life of Miguel de Cervantes, 1991; The Lighthouse at the End of the World, 1995. *Honours:* Prix Gutenberg du Livre, 1988; Life Achievement Award, Private Eye Writers of America, 1997.

MARMOT, Sir Michael Gideon, Kt, MBBS, PhD, FFPHM, FRCP, FAcMedSci; British academic and director of health research; *Director, International Institute for Society and Health and Professor of Epidemiology and Public Health, University College London;* b. 26 Jan. 1945, s. of Nathan Marmot and Alice Marmot (née Weiner); m. Alexandra Naomi Ferster 1971; two s. one d. *Education:* Univ. of Sydney and Univ. of California, Berkeley. *Career:* Resident Medical Officer, Royal Prince Alfred Hosp. 1969–70; Fellowship in Thoracic Medicine 1970–71; Resident Fellow and Lecturer Univ. of Calif., Berkeley 1971–76 (fellowships from Berkeley and American Heart Asscn); Lecturer then Sr Lecturer in Epidemiology, London School of Hygiene and Tropical Medicine, Univ. Coll. London 1976–85, Prof. of Epidemiology and Public Health Medicine 1985–; Dir Int. Centre for Health and Society, Univ. Coll. London 1994–; Hon. Consultant in Public Health Medicine, Bloomsbury and Islington Dist Health Authority 1985–; Visiting Prof. Royal Soc. of Medicine 1987; MRC Research Professorship 1995; Chair. Comm. on Social Determinants of Health, WHO 2004–; mem. Faculty of Community Medicine; Foreign Assoc. mem. Inst. of Medicine (Nat. Acads of Sciences). *Publications:* Status Syndrome (Bloomsbury and Times Holt) 2004; numerous articles in learned journals. *Honours:* Hon. MD (Univ. of Sydney) 2006; Balzan Prize for Epidemiology 2004, Harveian Oration 2006. *Address:* Department of Epidemiology and Public Health, University College London, 1–19 Torrington Place, London, WC1E 6BT (office); Wildwood Cottage, 17 North End, London, NW3 7HK, England (home). *Telephone:* (20) 7679-1717 (office). *Fax:* (20) 7813-0242 (office). *E-mail:* m.marmot@ucl.ac.uk (office). *Website:* www.ucl.ac.uk/epidemiology/staff/marmot (office); www.ucl.ac.uk/iish (office).

MARNY, Dominique Antoinette Nicole; French novelist, screenwriter and journalist; b. 21 Feb. 1948, Neuilly; m. Michel Marny 1970 (divorced); one d. *Career:* mem. PEN Club. *Publications:* Crystal Palace, 1985; Les orages desirés, 1988; Les fous de lumière, 1991; Les desirs et les jours, 1993; Les courtisanes, 1994; Les belles de Cocteau, 1995. Contributions: Madame Figaro; Vogue; Marie France. *Honours:* Prix Madame Europe 1993.

MAROWITZ, Charles; American writer; b. 26 Jan. 1934, New York; m. Jane Elizabeth Allsop 1980. *Career:* Artistic Dir, Malibu Stage Co, Texas Stage Co; West Coast Correspondent, Theatre Week Magazine; Senior Ed., Matzoh Ball Gazette; Theatre Critic, Los Angeles Village View; Guest Artist-in-Residence, California State University, Long Beach, CA, 1997; mem. Dramatists Guild; Writers Guild; Asscn of Literary Scholars and Critics. *Publications:* The Method as Means, 1961; The Marowitz Hamlet, 1966; The Shrew, 1972; Artaud at Rodez, 1975; Confessions of a Counterfeit Critic, 1976; The Marowitz Shakespeare, 1980; Act of Being, 1980; Sex Wars, 1983; Sherlock's Last Case, 1984; Prospero's Staff, 1986; Potboilers, 1986; Recycling Shakespeare, 1990; Burnt Bridges, 1991; Directing the Action, 1992; Cyrano de Bergerac (trans.), 1995; Alarums and Excursions, 1996; The Other Way: An Alternative Approach to Acting and Directing, 1998; Boulevard Comedies, 2000; Stage Dust, 2001; Roar of the Canon; Kott and Marowitz on Shakespeare (with Jan Kott), 2002. Contributions: newspapers, journals and magazines. *Honours:* Order of Purple Sash, 1965; Whitbread Award, 1967; First Prize, Louis B. Mayer Award, 1984. *Address:* 3058 Sequit Drive, Malibu, CA 90265, USA.

MARQUAND, David Ian, FBA, FRHistS, FRSA; British academic, author and fmr politician; *Visiting Fellow, Department of Politics, University of Oxford;* b. 20 Sept. 1934, Cardiff, Wales; s. of Rt Hon. Hilary Marquand and Rachel Marquand; m. Judith M. Reed 1959; one s. one d. *Education:* Emanuel School, Magdalen Coll., Oxford, St Antony's Coll., Oxford, Univ. of California, Berkeley, USA. *Career:* Sr Scholar, St Antony's Coll. Oxford 1957–58; Teaching Asst, Univ. of California 1958–59; editorial writer, The Guardian 1959–61; Research Fellow, St Antony's Coll. Oxford 1962–64, Hon. Fellow; Lecturer in Politics, Univ. of Sussex 1964–66; MP (Labour) for Ashfield, Notts. 1966–77; del. to Council of Europe and WEU assemblies 1970–73; Opposition Spokesman on Treasury Affairs 1971–72; Chief Adviser, Sec.-Gen. EC 1977–78; Prof. of Contemporary History and Politics, Univ. of Salford 1978–91; Prof. of Politics, Univ. of Sheffield 1991–96, Dir Political Economy Research Centre 1993–96, Hon. Prof. 1997–; Prin. Mansfield Coll. Oxford 1996–2002, Hon. Fellow; Visiting Fellow, Dept of Politics, Univ. of Oxford 2002–; Jt Ed. The Political Quarterly 1987–96. *Publications:* Ramsay Macdonald 1973, Parliament for Europe 1979, The Unprincipled Society 1988, The Progressive Dilemma 1991, The New Reckoning 1997, Religion and Democracy 2000, Decline of the Public 2004. *Honours:* Hon. DLitt (Salford, Sheffield); Hon. Dr of Political Science (Bologna); George Orwell Memorial Prize 1979, Isaiah Berlin Prize for Lifetime Achievement in Political Studies. *Address:* Department of Politics and International Relations, Manor Road, University of Oxford, Oxford, OX1 3UQ (office); Mansfield College, Oxford, OX1 3TF, England (office). *Telephone:* (1865) 751026 (office). *Fax:* (1865) 278725 (office). *E-mail:* david.marquand@politics.ox.ac.uk (office). *Website:* www.politics.ox.ac.uk (office).

MÁRQUEZ, Gabriel García (see GARCÍA MÁRQUEZ, Gabriel)

MARR, Andrew William Stevenson, BA; British journalist; b. 31 July 1959, Glasgow, Scotland; s. of Donald Marr and Valerie Marr; m. Jackie Ashley 1987; one s. two d. *Education:* Dundee High School, Craigflower School, Loretto School, Trinity Hall, Cambridge. *Career:* gen. reporter, business reporter The Scotsman 1982–84; Parl. Corresp. 1984–86, Political Ed. 1988; Political Ed. The Economist 1988–92; Political Corresp. The Independent 1986–88, Chief Commentator 1992–96, Ed. 1996–98, Ed.-in-Chief 1998; columnist The Express and The Observer 1998; Political Ed. BBC 2000–05; presenter Start the Week, BBC Radio 4 2002–; presenter morning interview programme, Sunday AM (BBC) 2005–; Chair. Jury Bd Samuel Johnson Prize for Non-Fiction 2001. *Publications:* The Battle for Scotland 1992, Ruling Britannia 1996, The Day Britain Died 2000, My Trade: A Short History of British Journalism 2004, A History of Modern Britain (also TV series) 2007. *Honours:* What The Papers Say Award for Columnist of the Year 1995, British Press Award for Columnist of the Year 1995, Creative Freedom Award for Journalist of the Year 2000, Channel 4 Political Awards Journalist Award 2001, Royal Television Soc. Television Journalism Award for specialist journalism 2001, Voice of the Listener and Viewer Award for Best Individual Contributor on TV 2002, BAFTA Richard Dimbleby Award 2004. *Address:* Room 3200, BBC Television Centre, Wood Lane, London, W12 7RJ, England (office). *Website:* www.bbc.co.uk (office).

MARR, David; Australian journalist, writer and television producer. *Career:* worked on TV programme, Four Corners (ABC); feature writer, Sydney Morning Herald. *Publications:* Barwick, 1981; The Ivanov Trail; Patrick White—A Life, 1991; Patrick White—Letters, 1994; The High Price of Heaven (essays), 1999; Dark Victory: The Story of The Tampa (with Marian Wilkinson), 2002. *Honours:* NSW Premier's Literary Award, 1981; numerous literary awards. *Literary Agent:* Australian Literary Management, 2A Booth Street, Balmain, NSW 2041, Australia. *Address:* c/o Allen & Unwin, PO Box 8500, St Leonards, NSW 1590, Australia.

MARR, William Wei-Yi, (Fei Ma), MS, PhD; American/Chinese engineer (retd), poet, editor and artist; b. 3 Sept. 1936, China; m. Jane Jy Chyun Liu 1962; two s. *Education:* Taipei Inst. of Technology, Marquette Univ., Univ. of Wisconsin. *Career:* fmr researcher, Argonne Nat. Lab., Chicago; editorial adviser, The Chinese Poetry International, New World Poetry; adviser, Chinese Writers Asscn of Greater Chicago, Asscn of Modern Chinese Literature and Arts of N America; mem. Chinese Artists Asscn of N America, Illinois State Poetry Soc. (Pres. 1993–95), Li Poetry Soc., New Poetry, Beijing (Vice-Pres. 1994–2000), Poets' Club of Chicago. *Exhibitions:* several solo and group exhbns of artworks (paintings and sculptures) in the Chicago area and on the Internet. *Publications:* In the Windy City 1975, Selected Poems 1983, White Horse 1984, Selected Poems of Fei Ma 1985, The Galloping Hoofs 1986, Road 1987, Selected Short Poems 1991, Fly Spirit 1992, Selected Poems 1994, Autumn Window 1995, A Microscopic World 1998, Not All Flowers Need to

Bear Fruit 2000, The Collected Poems of Fei Ma 2000, Selected Poems of William Marr 2003, The Awakening of Worldly Desires (Selected Essays) 2005; poems have been included in more than 100 anthologies and textbooks and translated into ten languages; contrib. to periodicals and magazines. *Honours:* Wu Cho Liu Poetry Award 1982, Li Poetry Trans. Award 1982, and Poetry Award 1984. *E-mail:* marrfei@yahoo.com. *Website:* wmarr9.home .comcast.net/bmz.htm.

MARRECO, Anne (see Wignall, Anne)

MARRODÁN, Mario Ángel, LicenDer, LicenFil; Spanish writer, critic and poet; b. 7 June 1932, Portugalete, Vizcaya; m. Mercedes Gómez Estíbaliz 1961; two s. *Career:* mem. Asociación Española de Críticos de Arte, Asociación Española de Críticos Literarios, Asociación Colegial de Escritores de España, Int. Asscn of Art Critics, Soc. of Basque Studies, Fraternity of the Béret, Real Sociedad Bascongada de Amigos del País. *Publications:* more than 300 books, including vols of essays, art criticism and poetry; 300 poetas cantan a Bilbao 2000; contribs to magazines and journals; more than 2000 collaborations. *Honours:* Golden Seagull, Royal Basque Soc. of Friends of the Nation. *Address:* Apdo de Correos 16, 48920 Portugalete, Vizcaya, Spain. *Telephone:* (6) 78474684 (Mobile) (office); (94) 4614221 (home).

MARS-JONES, Adam; British writer; b. 1954, s. of the late Sir William Mars-Jones. *Education:* Westminster School, Trinity Hall, Cambridge and Univ. of Virginia, USA. *Career:* film critic, The Independent 1989–97, The Times 1999–2001. *Publications:* Lantern Lecture (short stories) 1981, Mae West is Dead 1983, The Darker Proof (with Edmund White) 1987, Monopolies of Loss 1992, The Waters of Thirst (novel) 1993, Blind Bitter Happiness (essays) 1997. *Honours:* Somerset Maugham Award 1982. *Address:* 38 Oakbank Grove, Herne Hill, London, SE24 0AJ, England (home).

MARSDEN, George M., BA, BD, MA, PhD; American academic and writer; *Francis A. McAnaney Professor of History, University of Notre Dame;* b. 25 Feb. 1939, Harrisburg, Pennyslvania; m. Lucie Commeret, 30 March 1969, one s. one d. *Education:* Haverford Coll., Westminster Theological Seminary, Yale Univ. *Career:* instructor, Asst, and Assoc. Prof. 1965–74, Prof. 1974–86, Calvin Coll., Grand Rapids; Assoc. Ed., Christian Scholar's Review 1970–77; Visiting Prof. of Church History, Trinity Evangelical Divinty School, Deerfield, IL 1976–77; Ed., The Reformed Journal 1980–90; Visiting Prof. of History, Univ. of California at Berkeley 1986, 1990; Prof. of the History of Christianity in America, Divinity School, Duke Univ. 1986–92; Francis A. McAnaney Prof. of History, Univ. of Notre Dame 1992–; mem. American Soc. of Church History (pres. 1992), Inst. for the Study of American Evangelicals (advisory council). *Publications:* The Evangelical Mind and the New School Presbyterian Experience 1970, A Christian View of History? (ed. with Frank Roberts) 1975, Fundamentalism and American Culture: The Shaping of Twentieth-Century Evangelicalism, 1870–1925 1980, Eerdman's Handbook to the History of Christianity in America (co-ed.) 1983, The Search for Christian America (with Mark A. Noll and Nathan O. Hatch) 1983, Evangelicalism and Modern America (ed.) 1984, Reforming Fundamentalism: Fuller Seminary and the New Evangelicalism 1987, Religion and American Culture 1990, Understanding Fundamentalism and Evangelicalism 1991, The Seculariza-tion of the Academy (ed. with Bradley J. Longfield) 1992, The Soul of the American University 1994, The Outrageous Idea of Christian Scholarship 1997, Jonathan Edwards: A Life (Soc. for Eighteenth Century Studies Annibel Jenkins Prize 2002–04, Bancroft Prize 2004, Org. of American Historians Merle Curti Award 2004, Historical Soc. Eugene Genovese Prize 2004, John Pollock Award for Christian Biography 2004, Christianity Today Book Award for History and Biography 2004) 2003; contrib. to many scholarly books and journals. *Honours:* Younger Humanists Fellowship, Nat. Endowment for the Humanities 1971–72, Fellow, Calvin Center for Christian Scholarship 1979–80, Book of the Year Citations, Eternity magazine 1981, 1988, Calvin Research Fellowship 1982–83, J. Howard Pew Freedom Trust Grant 1988–92, Guggenheim Fellowship 1995. *Address:* c/o Department of History, University of Notre Dame, Notre Dame, IN 46556, USA.

MARSDEN, Peter Richard Valentine, FSA; British archaeologist and writer; b. 29 April 1940, Twickenham, Middlesex, England; m. Frances Elizabeth Mager 1979, two s. one d. *Education:* Kilburn Polytechnic, University of Oxford. *Career:* mem. Institute of Field Archaeologists. *Publications:* Londinium, 1971; The Wreck of the Amsterdam, 1974; Roman London, 1980; The Marsden Family of Paythorne and Nelson, 1981; The Roman Forum Site in London, 1987; The Historic Shipwrecks of South-East England, 1987. Contributions: Geographical Magazine; Independent; TLS; Illustrated London News; Telegraph Colour Magazine; various academic journals.

MARSDEN, Sir Simon Neville Llewelyn, Bt; British writer and photo-grapher; b. 1 Dec. 1948, Lincoln, England; m. Caroline Stanton 1984; one s. one d. *Education:* Ampleforth Coll., Yorkshire, Sorbonne, Univ. of Paris. *Career:* mem. Chelsea Arts Club, Arthur Machen Soc. *Film:* The Twilight Hour (drama/documentary). *Publications:* In Ruins 1980, The Haunted Realm 1986, Visions of Poe 1988, Phantoms of the Isles 1990, The Journal of a Ghost Hunter 1994, Beyond the Wall: The Lost World of East Germany 1999, Venice, City of Haunting Dreams 2001, The Twilight Hour 2003, This Spectred Isle 2005, La France Hantée (Haunted France) 2006. *Honours:* Arts Council of Great Britain Awards 1975, 1976. *Address:* The Presbytery, Hainton, Market Rasen, Lincolnshire LN8 6LR, England. *Telephone:* (1507) 313646 (office). *Fax:* (1507) 313646 (office). *E-mail:* info@marsdenarchive.com (office).

Website: www.simonmarsden.co.uk (office); www.marsdenarchive.com (office).

MARSÉ, Juan Faneca Roca; Spanish writer; b. 8 Jan. 1933, Barcelona. *Publications:* Encerrados con un solo juguete 1961, Esta cara de la luna 1962, Ultimatas tardes con Teresa 1966, La oscura historia de la prima Montse 1970, Si te dicen que caí 1973, Confidencias de un chorizo 1977, La muchacha de las bragas de oro 1978, Un día volveré (trans. as One Day I Will Return) 1982, La ronda de Guinardó 1984, La fuga del Rio Lobo (trans. as The Flight of Wolf River) 1985, Teniente Bravo 1987, El amante bilingüe 1990, El embrujo de Shangai (trans. as The Bewitchment of Shanghai) 1993, Las mujeres de Juanito Marés 1997, Rabos de Lagartija (trans. as Lizard Tails) 2000; contrib. to Dietario de Posguerra 1998. *Honours:* Planeta Prize 1978, European Literature Prize 1994. *Address:* c/o Harvill Secker, 20 Vauxhall Bridge Road, London, SW1V 2SA, England.

MARSHALL, Jack; American writer and poet; b. 25 Feb. 1937, New York, NY. *Education:* Brooklyn Public Schools. *Publications:* The Darkest Con-tinent, 1967; Bearings, 1970; Floats, 1972; Bits of Thirst, 1974; Bits of Thirst and Other Poems and Translations, 1976; Arriving on the Playing Fields of Paradise, 1983; Arabian Nights, 1986; Sesame, 1993.

MARSHALL, Owen, DipEd, MA; New Zealand writer; b. (Owen Marshall Jones), 17 Aug. 1941, Te Kuiti; m. Jacqueline Hill 1965; two d. *Education:* Univ. of Canterbury, Christchurch Teachers' Coll. *Career:* Adjunct Prof., Univ. of Canterbury 2005–. *Publications:* Supper Waltz Wilson 1979, The Master of Big Jingles 1982, The Day Hemingway Died 1984, The Lynx Hunter 1987, The Divided World 1989, Tomorrow We Save the Orphans 1991, A Many Coated Man 1995, Coming Home in the Dark 1995, The Best of Owen Marshall 1997, Harlequin Rex 1999, When Gravity Snaps 2002, Essential New Zealand Short Stories (ed.) 2002, Watch of Gryphons 2005; contrib. to numerous magazines and journals. *Honours:* Hon. DLitt (Univ. of Canter-bury) 2002; New Zealand Literary Fund Scholarship in Letters 1988, Robert Burns Fellowship 1992, ONZM 2000, Creative New Zealand Arts Fellowship. *Address:* 10 Morgans Road, Timaru, New Zealand.

MARSHALL, Paule, BA; American writer; b. 9 April 1929, New York, NY; m. 1st Kenneth E. Marshall 1957 (divorced 1963); one s.; m. 2nd Nourry Menard 1970. *Education:* Brooklyn College, CUNY. *Career:* staff mem., Our World magazine 1953–56. *Publications:* Brown Girl, Brownstones, 1959; Soul Clap Hands and Sing, 1962; The Chosen Place, The Timeless People, 1969; Praisesong for the Widows, 1983; Reena and Other Stories, 1983; Daughters, 1991; The Fisher King, 2000. Contributions: anthologies and periodicals. *Honours:* Guggenheim Fellowship, 1961; John D. and Catherine T. MacArthur Foundation Fellowship, 1992.

MARSHALL, Penelope Jane Clucas, BA; British journalist; b. 7 Nov. 1962, Addlestone; d. of the late Alan and of Mary (née Hanlin) Marshall; m. Tim Ewart 1991; three d. *Education:* LSE. *Career:* Foreign Corresp. for ITN (Ind. TV News), Moscow coverage 1990, Bosnia coverage 1992, Defence and Diplomatic Corresp. 1994–, S Africa Corresp. 1999–2001; Visiting Prof., City Univ., London. *Honours:* BAFTA Award 1992, Royal TV Soc. Award, Gold, Silver and Bronze Medals, New York. *Address:* City University, Northampton Square, London, EC14 0HB, England (office). *Telephone:* (20) 7430-4411 (office). *Fax:* (20) 430-4687 (office). *E-mail:* pennymarshall@btinternet.com (office).

MARTEL, Yann; Canadian writer; b. 1963, Spain. *Education:* Trent Univ. *Career:* grew up in Alaska, BC, Costa Rica, France, Ont. and Mexico; fmr tree planter, dishwasher, security guard; became professional writer 1990. *Publications:* Facts Behind the Helsinki Roccamatios (short stories) (Journey Prize) 1993, Self (novel) 1996, Life of Pi (novel) (Hugh MacLennan Prize for Fiction 2001, Man Booker Prize 2002) 2001, We Ate the Children Last (short stories) 2004. *Address:* c/o Knopf Canada, Random House of Canada Ltd, One Toronto Street, Unit 300, Toronto, ON M5C 2VC, Canada (office). *Telephone:* (416) 364-4449 (office). *Fax:* (416) 364-6863 (office). *Website:* www .randomhouse.ca (office).

MARTELL, Owen; Welsh novelist; b. 1976, Exeter, England. *Career:* writer-in-residence School of Welsh, Cardiff Univ. *Publications:* Cadw dy ffydd, brawd (novel, Gomer First Novel Prize, Arts Council of Wales Book of the Year 2001) 2000, Dyn yr Eiliad (novel) 2003. *Address:* c/o School of Welsh, Cardiff University, Cardiff, CF10 3XW, Wales.

MARTELLA, Maureen; Irish writer; b. 28 Jan. 1947, Dublin; m. Antonio Martella; three s. one d. *Education:* St Brigid's Coll., Co. Dublin. *Publications:* Are You the Other Listener? (poems), Bugger Bucharest (novel) 1995, Maddy Goes to Holywood (novel) 1999, Annie's New Life (novel) 2000, A Perfect Partnership (novel) 2004, Friends & Lovers (novel) 2007; contribs to Woman's Way (Dublin), radio documentaries (RTE Radio), Sunday Miscellany (RTE Radio). *Address:* Nunsland, Naas, Co. Kildare, Ireland (home). *Website:* www .maureenmartella.com.

MARTI, René; Swiss writer, poet and journalist; b. 7 Nov. 1926, Frauenfeld; m. Elizabeth Wahrenberger 1955, one s. two d. *Education:* Commercial School, Lausanne, Cambridge Proficiency Class, Polytechnic School, London, Univ. of Konstanz. *Career:* mem. PEN of Switzerland and other literary organizations; Regensburger Schriftstellergruppe intern., Turmbund Innsbruck, Verband Kath. Schriftsteller Oesterreichs, PEN German-speaking Writers Abroad, London, Freier deutscher Autorenverband, Autoren der

Schweiz, Interessengemeinschaft deutschsprachiger Autoren (IGdA), Zürcher Schriftstelleryerband, Berner Schriftstellerverband, Präsidium des Internat, Bodenseeclubs, Konstanz. *Publications:* Das unauslöschliche Licht 1954, Dom des Herzens 1967, Die fünf Unbekannten (with others) 1970, Der unsichtbare Kreis 1975, Weg an Weg 1979, Besuche dich in der Natur (with Lili Keller) 1983, Gedichte zum Verschenken (with Lili Keller) 1984, Stationen 1986, Die verbrannten Schreie 1989, Gib allem ein bisschen Zeit (with Brigitta Weiss) 1993, Rückblicke 1996, Spatenstich für die Rose (with Magdalena Obergfell) 2001, Atrium: 28 poems set to music by eight composers 2006; contribs to more than 200 anthologies, to newspapers, magazines and for radio. *Honours:* several publishing grants, AWMM Lyric Poetry Prize, Luxemburg 1985, Lyrikpreis der Nationalbibliothek des deutschsprachigen Gedichts in München für ein unter Tausenden von Einsendungen hervorragendes Gedicht, welches in einzigartigem Einfallsreichtum ein herausragendes Sprachkunstwerk darstelle (Gedicht 'Zum blauen Abschied'), Ehrenpräsident der IGdA, Anerkennungspreis für Literatur der Stadt Frauenfeld 2006. *Address:* Haus am Herterberg, Haldenstrasse 5, 8500 Frauenfeld, Switzerland. *Telephone:* 721 43 74 (office).

MARTIN, Alexander George, MA, DipArts; American writer; b. 8 Nov. 1953, Baltimore, MD; m. 1979, two s. *Education:* University of Cambridge, University College, Cardiff. *Career:* mem. Society of Authors. *Publications:* Boris the Tomato, 1984; Snow on the Stinker, 1988; The General Interruptor, 1989; Modern Poetry, 1990; Modern Short Stories, 1991. *Honours:* Betty Trask Award 1988.

MARTIN, David Alfred, DipEd, BSc, PhD; British academic, writer and priest; *Professor of Sociology Emeritus, London School of Economics and Political Science;* b. 30 June 1929, London, England; m. 1st Daphne Sylvia Treherne 1953; one s.; m. 2nd Bernice Thompson 1962; two s. one d. *Education:* Westminster Coll., Univ. of London, LSE. *Career:* Asst Lecturer, Sheffield Univ. 1961–62; Lecturer 1962–67, Reader 1967–71, Prof. of Sociology 1971–89, Prof. Emeritus 1989–, LSE; Ordained Deacon 1983, Priest 1984; Scurlock Prof. of Human Values, Southern Methodist Univ., Dallas 1986–90; Sr Professorial Fellow, later Int. Fellow, Inst. for the Study of Economic Culture, Boston Univ. 1990–; Hon. Prof., Lancaster Univ. 1993–2006; Adjunct Prof. Liverpool Hope Univ. 2006–; various visiting lectureships; mem. Int. Conference of the Sociology of Religion (pres. 1975–83). *Publications:* Pacifism 1965, A Sociology of English Religion 1967, The Religious and the Secular 1969, Tracts Against the Times 1973, A General Theory of Secularisation 1978, Dilemmas of Contemporary Religion 1978, Crisis for Cranmer and King James (ed.) 1978, The Breaking of the Image 1980, Theology and Sociology (co-ed.) 1980, No Alternative (co-ed.) 1981, Unholy Warfare (co-ed.) 1983, Divinity in a Grain of Bread 1989, Tongues of Fire 1990, The Forbidden Revolution 1996, Reflections on Sociology and Theology 1997, Does Christianity Cause Wars? 1997, Pentecostalism 2000, The World Their Parish 2001, Christian Language in the Secular City 2002, Christian Language and its Mutations 2002, Christian Language in the Secular City 2002, On Secularization 2005; contrib. to journals. *Honours:* Hon. Asst Priest, Guildford Cathedral 1983–, Hon. DTheol (Univ. of Helsinki) 2000. *Address:* Cripplegate Cottage, 174 St John's Road, Woking, Surrey GU21 7PQ, England (home). *Telephone:* (1483) 762134 (home).

MARTIN, George Whitney, BA, LLB; American writer; b. 25 Jan. 1926, New York. *Education:* Harvard Coll., Trinity Coll., Cambridge, Univ. of Virginia Law School. *Career:* practised law 1955–59; writer 1959–. *Publications:* The Damrosch Dynasty, America's First Family of Music 1983, Verdi, His Music, Life and Times (fourth edn) 1992, Aspects of Verdi (second edn) 1993, Verdi at The Golden Gate, Opera and San Francisco in the Gold Rush Years 1993, The Opera Companion (fifth edn) 1997, Twentieth Century Opera, A Guide 1999, CCB: The Life and Century of Charles C. Burlingham, New York's First Citizen 1858–1959 (US Supreme Court Historical Soc. Erwin N. Griswold Award 2006) 2005; contrib. numerous articles on Verdi and his operas in The Opera Quarterly. *Address:* 53 Crosslands Drive, Kennett Square, PA 19348, USA. *Telephone:* (610) 388-0529 (office). *Fax:* (610) 388-0241 (office). *Website:* www.georgewmartin.com.

MARTIN, Jay Herbert, BA, MA, PhD; American psychoanalyst, academic, author and editor; *Edward S. Gould Professor of Humanities and Professor of Government, Claremont McKenna College;* b. 30 Oct. 1935, Newark, NJ; m. Helen Bernadette Saldini 1956, one s. two d. *Education:* Columbia Univ., Ohio State Univ., Southern California Psychoanalytic Inst. *Career:* Instructor in English, Pennsylvania State Univ. 1957–58; Instructor in English and American Studies, Yale Univ. 1960–64, Asst Prof. 1964–67, Assoc. Prof. 1967–68; Prof. of English, American Studies and Comparative Culture, Univ. of California at Irvine 1968–79, Lecturer and Clinical Supervisor in Psychiatry and Human Behaviour 1978–95; Leo S. Bing Prof. of English and American Literature, Univ. of Southern California at Los Angeles 1979–96; Edward S. Gould Prof. of Humanities and Prof. of Govt, Claremont McKenna Coll. and Claremont Graduate Univ., CA 1996–; Dai Ho Chun Distinguished Visiting Prof., Univ. of Hawaii (Honolulu) 2000–01; mem. American Psychoanalytic Asscn, Authors' Guild, Int. Psychoanalytic Asscn, MLA. *Publications:* Winfield Townley Scott (ed) 1961, Conrad Aiken: A Life of His Art 1962, Harvests of Change: American Literature 1865–1914 1967, A Collection of Critical Essays on 'The Waste Land' (ed.) 1968, Nathanael West: The Art of His Life 1970, Robert Lowell 1970, Twentieth-Century Views of Nathanael West: A Collection of Critical Essays (ed.) 1972, A Singer in the Dawn: Reinterpretations of Paul Laurance Dunbar 1975, A Dunbar Reader

(ed. with Gossie H. Hudson) 1975, Always Merry and Bright: The Life of Henry Miller: An Unauthorized Biography 1978, Winter Dreams: An American in Moscow 1979, Economic Depression and American Humor (ed.) 1984, Who Am I This Time?: Uncovering the Fictive Personality 1988, A Corresponding Leap of Love: Henry Miller, Lying and Dying 1996, Henry Miller's Dream Song 1996, Swallowing Tigers Whole: Conceptions of the Desirable in American Life and Education 1997, Journey to Heavenly Mountain 2002, The Education of John Dewey 2003, Baseball and Other Games 2005. *Contributions:* scholarly books, professional journals and literary periodicals. *Honours:* American Philosophical Society Fellowship 1966, Guggenheim Fellowship 1966–67, Rockefeller Foundation Senior Fellowship in the Humanities 1977–78, National Endowment for the Humanities Senior Research Grant 1983–84, Research Fellow Rockefeller Study Center Bellagio Italy 1985–86, Burlington Northern Foundation Award for Outstanding Scholarship 1989, Durfee Fellowship to China 2000, University of Southern California at Los Angeles Distinguished Emer. Prof. Award 2001, Research Fellow Bogliasco (Italy) Foundation 2004. *Address:* 748 Via Santo Tomas, Claremont, CA 91711 (home); Claremont McKenna College, 850 N Columbia Avenue, Claremont, CA 91711, USA (office). *Telephone:* (909) 398-0193 (home); (909) 607-3184 (office). *Fax:* (909) 398-1352 (home); (909) 621-8419 (office). *E-mail:* helenjay@comcast.net (home); jmartin@ claremontmckenna.edu (office). *Website:* www.mckenna.edu (office).

MARTIN, Sir Laurence Woodward, Kt, MA, PhD, DL; British academic; *Professor Emeritus, University of Newcastle upon Tyne;* b. 30 July 1928, St Austell, Cornwall; s. of Leonard Martin and Florence Mary Woodward; m. Betty Parnall 1951; one s. one d. *Education:* St Austell Grammar School, Christ's Coll., Cambridge, Yale Univ. *Career:* RAF Flying Officer 1948–51; Asst Prof. MIT 1956–61; Assoc. Prof. Johns Hopkins Univ. 1961–64; Prof. Univ. of Wales 1964–68, King's Coll. London 1968–78; Vice-Chancellor Univ. of Newcastle 1978–90, Emer. Prof. 1991–; Arleigh Burke Chair in Strategy Center for Strategic and Int. Studies, Washington, DC 1998–2000; Visiting Prof. Univ. of Wales 1985–90; Dir Royal Inst. of Int. Affairs 1991–96; Fellow, King's Coll., London; Lees Knowles Lecturer, Cambridge; Reith Lecturer BBC. *Radio:* Reith Lectures 1981. *Publications:* Peace Without Victory 1958, The Sea in Modern Strategy 1967, Arms and Strategy 1973, The Two Edged Sword 1982, The Changing Face of Nuclear War 1987, British Foreign Policy (jtly) 1997. *Honours:* Hon. DCL (Newcastle) 1991. *Address:* University of Newcastle upon Tyne, Newcastle, NE1 7RU (office); 35, Witley Court, Coram Street, London, WC1N 1HP, England (home). *E-mail:* lmartin@csis.org (office).

MARTIN, (Roy) Peter, (James Melville), MBE, BA, MA; British writer; b. 5 Jan. 1931, London, England; two s. *Education:* Birkbeck Coll., London, Tübingen Univ., Germany. *Career:* crime fiction reviewer, Hampstead, Highgate Express 1983–2000; mem. CWA, Detection Club. *Publications:* 13 Superintendent Otani mysteries, The Imperial Way 1986, A Tarnished Phoenix 1990, The Chrysanthemum Throne 1997. *Literary Agent:* Curtis Brown Ltd, Haymarket House, 28–29 Haymarket, London, SW1Y 4SP, England. *Telephone:* (20) 7393-4400. *Fax:* (20) 7393-4401. *E-mail:* info@ curtisbrown.co.uk. *Website:* www.curtisbrown.co.uk.

MARTIN, Philip John Talbot, BA; Australian retd lecturer and poet; b. 28 March 1931, Melbourne, Vic. *Education:* University of Melbourne. *Career:* Tutor to Senior Tutor in English, University of Melbourne, 1960–62; Lecturer in English, Australian National University, 1963; Lecturer to Senior Lecturer, Monash University, 1964–88. *Publications:* Poetry: Voice Unaccompanied, 1970; A Bone Flute, 1974; From Sweden, 1979; A Flag for the Wind, 1982; New and Selected Poems, 1988. Other: Shakespeare's Sonnets: Self Love and Art (criticism), 1972; Lars Gustafsson: The Stillness of the World Before Bach (trans.), 1988. *Contributions:* 7 anthologies, 1986–98; Age; Australian; Carleton Miscellany; Helix; Meanjin; New Hungarian Quarterly; Poetry USA; Quadrant; Southerly; TLS. *Address:* 25/9 Nicholson Street, Balmain 2041, NSW, Australia.

MARTIN, Ralph Guy, BJ; American writer; b. 4 March 1920, Chicago, IL; m. Marjorie Jean Pastel 1944, one s. two d. *Education:* University of Missouri. *Career:* Managing Ed., Box Elder News Journal, Brigham, Utah, 1941; Assoc. Ed., The New Republic, New York City, 1945–48, Newsweek magazine, New York City, 1953–55; Exec. Ed., House Beautiful, New York City, 1955–57; mem. Authors' Guild; Century Asscn; Dramatists Guild; Overseas Press Club. *Publications:* Boy from Nebraska, 1946; The Best is None too Good, 1948; Eleanor Roosevelt: Her Life in Pictures (with Richard Harrity), 1958; The Human Side of FDR (with Richard Harrity), 1959; Front Runner, Dark Horse (with Ed Plaut), 1960; Money, Money, Money (with Morton Stone), 1961; Man of Destiny: Charles de Gaulle (with Richard Harrity), 1962; World War II: From D-Day to VE-Day (with Richard Harrity), 1962; The Three Lives of Helen Keller (with Richard Harrity), 1962; Ballots and Bandwagons, 1964; The Bosses, 1964; President from Missouri, 1964; Skin Deep, 1964; World War II: Pearl Harbor to VJ-Day, 1965; Wizard of Wall Street, 1965; The GI War: 1941–1945, 1967; A Man for All People: Hubert H. Humphrey, 1968; Jennie: The Life of Lady Randolph Churchill (two vols) 1969, 1971; Lincoln Center for the Performing Arts, 1971; The Woman He Loved: The Story of the Duke and Duchess of Windsor, 1973; Cissy: The Life of Elenor Medill Patterson, 1979; A Hero of Our Time: An Intimate Study of the Kennedy Years, 1983; Charles and Diana, 1985; Golda: Golda Meir, the Romantic Years, 1988; Henry and Clare: An Intimate Portrait of the Luces, 1991; Seeds of Destruction: Joe Kennedy and His Sons, 1995. *Contributions:* books and periodicals.

MARTIN, Rhona Madeline; British writer and artist; b. 3 June 1922, London, England; m. 1st Peter Wilfrid Alcock 1941 (divorced); two d.; m. 2nd Thomas Edward Neighbour. *Career:* part-time Tutor in Creative Writing, Univ. of Sussex 1986–91; mem. Romantic Novelists Asscn, Soc. of Authors, PEN, Friends of the Arvon Foundation, Soc. of Limners. *Publications:* Gallows Wedding 1978, Mango Walk 1981, The Unicorn Summer 1984, Goodbye Sally 1987, Writing Historical Fiction 1988; contrib. to London Evening News, South East Arts Review, Cosmopolitan, Prima. *Honours:* Georgette Heyer Historical Novel Award 1978. *Address:* 25 Henwood Crescent, Pembury, Kent TN2 4LJ, England.

MARTIN, Ruth (see Rayner, Claire Berenice)

MARTIN, Valerie; American writer; b. 1948, Missouri. *Publications:* Love: Short Stories 1976, Set in Motion (novel) 1978, Alexandra (novel) 1980, A Recent Martyr (novel) 1987, The Consolation of Nature and Other Stories 1988, Mary Reilly (novel) 1990, The Great Divorce (novel) 1994, Italian Fever (novel) 1999, Salvation: Scenes from the Life of St Francis (biog.) 2001, Property (novel) (Orange Prize for Fiction) 2003, The Unfinished Novel and Other Stories 2006. *Address:* c/o Alfred A. Knopf, 299 Park Avenue, Fourth Floor, New York, NY 10171, USA (office).

MARTIN, Victoria Carolyn; British writer; b. 22 May 1945, Windsor, Berkshire, England; m. Tom Storey 1969, four d. *Education:* Winkfield Place, Berks, Byam Shaw School of Art. *Publications:* September Song 1970, Windmill Years 1975, Seeds of the Sun 1980, Opposite House 1984, Tigers of the Night 1985, Obey the Moon 1987; contrib. to Woman, Woman's Own, Woman's Realm, Woman's Journal, Good Housekeeping, Woman's Weekly, Redbook, Honey 1967–87. *Address:* Newells Farm House, Lower Beeding, Horsham, Sussex RH13 6LN, England (home). *Telephone:* (1403) 891326 (home). *Fax:* (1403) 891530 (home). *E-mail:* vicky.storey@btinternet.com (home).

MARTINAC, Paula, BA, MA; American writer and editor; b. 30 July 1954, Pittsburgh, PA; pnr Katie Hogan. *Education:* Chatham College, Pittsburgh, College of William and Mary. *Career:* Asst Curator, West Virginia State Museum, Charleston, 1979–82; Production Ed., Prentice-Hall Inc, Englewood Cliffs, NJ, 1982–85; Mem., Editorial Collective, Womanews, 1982–85; Production Dir, Feminist Press, CUNY, 1985–94; Ed., 1988–90, Mem., Editorial Board, 1990–92, Conditions magazine, New York; Curator, In Our Own Write reading series, New York City Lesbian and Gay Community Services Center, 1988–90; Panelist, Cultural Council Foundation, New York City, 1991. *Publications:* The One You Call Sister: New Women's Fiction (ed., contributor), 1989; Out of Time (novel), 1990; Home Movies, 1993; k d lang, 1996; Chicken (novel), 1997; The Queerest Places: A National Guide to Gay and Lesbian Historic Sites, 1997; The Lesbian and Gay Book of Love and Marriage: Creating the Stories of Our Lives, 1998. Contributions: books and periodicals including: Focus: A Journal for Lesbians; Conditions; Binnewater Tides; Sinister Wisdom; Queer City; Art and Understanding; Blithe House Quarterly. *Honours:* Lambda Literary Award for Lesbian Fiction, 1990; Puffin Foundation Grant, 1990; Best Book for Teens Citation, New York Public Library, 1997.

MARTÍNEZ, Guillermo, PhD; Argentine writer; *Professor of Mathematics, University of Buenos Aires*; b. 29 July 1962, Bahía Blanca. *Education:* Univ. Nacional del Sur, Bahía Blanca, Univ. of Buenos Aires, Univ. of Oxford, UK. *Career:* graduate asst (Jefe de Trabajos Prácticos) Univ. of Buenos Aires 1985–91, Prof. of Mathematics 1991–; reviewer, literary collaborator Radar, Página 12 1997, Clarín and La Nación 1998–; Visiting Lecturer St Anthony's Coll., Oxford, Literary Week, Hamburg, Univ. del Nordeste, Chaco, literary festival in Segovia, Spain, book fair in Buenos Aires; Latin American Eminent Scholar Chair of Columbus State Univ.; numerous grants. *Publications:* La jungla sin bestias (Nat. Roberto Arlt Short Story Prize) 1982, Infierno Grande (short stories, trans. as Vast Hell) (Fondo Nacional de las Artes First Prize 1988) 1989, Acerca de Roderer (novel, trans. as Regarding Roderer) 1993, La mujer del maestro (novel, trans. as The Woman of the Master) 1998, Borges y la matemática (essays) 2003, Crímenes imperceptibles (novel, aka Los crímenes de Oxford, trans. as The Oxford Murders) (Premio Planeta) 2003, La fórmula de la immortalidad (essays and articles) 2005; contrib. numerous articles, essays and reviews to anthologies and periodicals. *Honours:* Bienal de Arte Joven Short Story Award 1989. *Literary Agent:* Carmen Balcells Agency, Diagonal 580, Barcelona, Spain. *E-mail:* infogmartinez@yahoo.com.ar. *Website:* www.guillermomartinez.8m.net.

MARTÍNEZ, Tomás Eloy, MA; Argentine novelist, essayist, journalist and academic; *Professor and Director, Latin American Studies Program, Rutgers University*; b. 1934, Tucumán. *Education:* Univ. of Tucumán, Univ. of Paris VII. *Career:* film critic La Nación, Buenos Aires 1957–61; production chief Primera Plana, Buenos Aires 1962–69; European correspondent based in Paris, Abril 1969–70; Ed. Panorama 1970–72, cultural supplement of La Opinión 1972–75; Literary Ed. El Nacional, Caracas 1975–77, Consultant Ed. 1977–78; f. and production chief El Diario de Caracas 1979; co-f. Siglo 21, Guadalajara 1991; founder and Ed. literary supplement, Primer Plano for Página/12, Buenos Aires 1991–95; columnist La Nación, Buenos Aires 1996–, New York Times Syndicate 1996–; numerous conferences, courses in univs throughout Europe and America; Prof. Univ. of Maryland 1984–87; currently Distinguished Prof. and Dir of Latin American Studies programme Rutgers Univ., NJ; Fellow Woodrow Wilson Center for Int. Scholars, Washington, DC, Guggenheim Foundation, Kellogg Inst., Univ. of Notre-Dame, IN. *Screenplays*

include: (with Augusto Roa Bastos) El último piso 1962, El terrorista 1962, El demonio en la sangre 1964, La Madre María 1974. *Publications:* Estructuras del cine argentino (essay) 1961, Sagrado (novel) 1969, La pasión según Trelew (non-fiction) 1974, Los testigos de afuera (essay) 1978, Lugar común la muerte (short stories) 1979, El retrato del artista enmascarado (essay) 1982, La novela de Perón 1985, La mano del amo 1991, Santa Evita 1995, Las memorias del General (novel) 1996, El suelo argentino (non-fiction) 1999, Ficciones verdaderas (short stories) 2000, El vuelo de la reina 2002, El cantor de Tango 2004; numerous essays. *Honours:* Dr hc (John F. Kennedy Univ., Buenos Aires), (Univ. of Tucumán); Premio Alfaguara de Novela 2002. *Address:* Spanish and Portuguese Department, Rutgers University, 105 George Street, New Brunswick, NJ 08901, USA (office). *Telephone:* (732) 932-9412, ext. 27 (office). *E-mail:* eloy@rci.rutgers.edu. *Website:* span-port.rutgers.edu (office).

MARTONE, Michael, AB, MA; American academic, writer and poet; *Professor, University of Alabama*; b. 22 Aug. 1955, Fort Wayne, IN; m. Theresa Pappas 1984. *Education:* Butler Univ., Indianapolis, Indiana Univ., Johns Hopkins Univ. *Career:* Asst Prof. 1980–83, Assoc. Prof. 1983–87, Iowa State Univ.; Ed., Poet and Critic magazine 1981–86; Contributing Ed., North American Review 1984–; Briggs-Copeland Lecturer on Fiction 1987–89, Briggs-Copeland Asst Prof. on Fiction 1989–91, Harvard Univ.; Assoc. Prof. of English 1991–96, Syracuse Univ.; Prof., Dir Program for Creative Writing 1996–, Univ. of Alabama; mem. Associated Writing Programs, Nat. Writers' Union, PEN. *Publications:* fiction: Alive and Dead in Indiana 1984, Safety Patrol 1988, Fort Wayne is Seventh on Hitler's List 1990, Pensees: The Thoughts of Dan Quayle 1994, Seeing Eye 1995, The Blue Guide to Indiana 2001, Michael Martone 2005; prose poems: At a Loss 1977, Return to Powers 1985, The Sex Lives of the Fantastic Four; other: The Flatness and Other Landscapes (essays) 1999, Unconventions (essays) 2006; editor: A Place of Sense: Essays in Search of the Midwest 1988, Townships: Pieces of the Midwest 1992, The Scribner Anthology of Contemporary Short Fiction 1999, Extreme 2004, Michael Martone 2005, Unconventions 2005, Rules of Thumb (ed.) 2006; contrib. to various books and journals. *Honours:* Nat. Endowment for the Arts Fellowships 1983, 1988, Black Ice magazine Margaret Jones Fiction Prize 1987, Ingram Merrill Foundation Award 1989, Pushcart Prize 1990, second place Thin Air Fiction Contest 1998, honorable mention 32 Pages Chapbook Contest 1998, Associated Writing Programs Award for Non-Fiction 1998, Best American Essays 2005. *Address:* PO Box 21179, Tuscaloosa, AL 35402, USA.

MARTY, Martin E., MDiv, PhD, STM; American academic and ecclesiastic; *Fairfax M. Cone Distinguished Service Professor Emeritus of the History of Modern Christianity, Divinity School, University of Chicago*; b. 5 Feb. 1928, West Point, Neb.; s. of Emil A. Marty and Anne Louise Wuerdemann Marty; m. 1st Elsa Schumacher 1952 (died 1981); seven c.; m. 2nd Harriet Lindemann 1982. *Education:* Concordia Seminary, St Louis, Lutheran School of Theology, Chicago and Univ. of Chicago. *Career:* Lutheran Minister 1952–63; Prof. of History of Modern Christianity Univ. of Chicago 1963–, Fairfax M. Cone Distinguished Service Prof. 1978–98, now Emer.; Assoc. Ed. The Christian Century 1956–85, Sr Ed. 1985–98; Sr Scholar in Residence, Park Ridge Center 1985, Pres. 1985–89; Pres. American Soc. of Church History 1971, American Catholic History Asscn 1981, American Acad. of Religion 1988; Dir Fundamentalism project American Acad. of Arts and Sciences 1988–, The Public Religion Project 1996–99; Fellow, AAAS, Soc. of American Historians. *Publications:* many books and numerous articles on religious history, theology and cultural criticism. *Honours:* more than 70 hon. degrees; Nat. Book Award for Righteous Empire 1972, Nat. Medal Humanities 1997. *Address:* 239 Scottswood Road, Riverside, IL 60546 (home); University of Chicago Divinity School, 1025 East 58th Street, Swift Hall, Chicago, IL 60637, USA (office). *E-mail:* memarty@aol.com (home). *Website:* divinity.uchicago.edu/faculty/profile_mmarty (office); marty-center.uchicago.edu (office).

MARX, Arthur; American screenwriter, playwright and author; b. 21 July 1921, New York, NY. *Education:* University of Southern California, Los Angeles. *Career:* mem. Authors' Guild; Dramatists Guild; International Asscn of Crime Writers; Writers Guild of America. *Publications:* The Ordeal of Willie Brown, 1951; Life with Groucho (biog.), 1954; Not as a Crocodile (short stories), 1958; The Impossible Years (play), 1965; Minnie's Boys (play), 1970; Son of Groucho (autobiog.), 1972; Everybody Loves Somebody Sometime, Especially Himself (biog.), 1974; Sugar and Spice (play), 1974; My Daughter's Rated X (play), 1975; Goldwyn, 1976; Red Skelton (biog.), 1979; Groucho: A Life in Revue (play), 1986; The Nine Lives of Mickey Rooney (biog.), 1986; The Ghost and Mrs Muir (play), 1987; My Life with Groucho (biog.), 1988; Set to Kill (mystery novel), 1993; The Secret Life of Bob Hope (biog.), 1993. Contributions: Los Angeles Magazine; Cigar Aficionado.

MARX, Michael William, BA, MFA, MA; American writer, publisher and teacher; b. 11 Jan. 1951, Philadelphia, PA; m. Ilsun Kang, one s. two d. *Education:* Hobart and William Smith Colleges, New York, New York University, Indiana State University. *Career:* Teacher, Indiana State University, 1999–, Lake Land College, Danville, IL, 2000–, Ivy Tech State College, Terre Haute, Indiana, 2001–. *Publications:* A War Ends, 1985; Eric Greenfield – Middle American, 1987; Justus – A Upopia, 1999. Contributions: newspapers, magazines and journals. *E-mail:* michael@michaelmarx.com.

MASCHLER, Thomas Michael; British publisher; *Managing Director and Publisher, Jonathan Cape Ltd*; b. 16 Aug. 1933, Berlin; s. of Kurt Leo Maschler and Rita Masseron; m. 1st Fay Coventry 1970 (divorced 1987); one s.

two d.; m. 2nd Regina Kulinicz 1988. *Education:* Leighton Park School, Reading. *Career:* Production Asst, André Deutsch 1955–56; Ed., MacGibbon and Kee 1956–58; Fiction Ed., Penguin Books 1958–60; Editorial Dir, Jonathan Cape Ltd 1960–70, Man. Dir 1960–, Chair. 1970–91, Publr 1991–; Dir Random House 1987. *Film:* The French Lieutenant's Woman (assoc. producer) 1981. *Publications:* Declarations (ed.) 1957, New English Dramatists series (ed.) 1959–63, Publisher (memoir) 2005. *Address:* Jonathan Cape Ltd, Random House, 20 Vauxhall Bridge Road, London, SW1V 2SA, England (office). *Telephone:* (20) 7840-8400 (office). *Fax:* (20) 7233-6117 (office). *Website:* www.randomhouse.co.uk (office).

MASLOW, Jonathan Evan, BA, MS; American writer; b. 4 Aug. 1948, Long Branch, NJ; m. Liliya Khobotkova 1992. *Education:* Marlboro College, VT, Columbia University Graduate School of Journalism. *Career:* staff reporter, Cape May County Herald, 1997–2002; Asst City Ed., Herald, 2002–; mem. Authors' Guild. *Publications:* The Owl Papers, 1983; Bird of Life, Bird of Death: A Political Ornithology of Central America, 1986; Sacred Horses: Memoirs of a Turkmen Cowboy, 1994; Torrid Zone: Six Stories of the Gulf Coast, 1995; Footsteps in the Jungle, 1996; Skulls (poems written to accompany Leonard Baskin woodcuts), 2002. Other: A Tramp in the Darien (screenplay), 1990; Geldi: Horsemen of the Turkmen Steppes (screenplay), 1993. Contributions: Magazines and reviews. *Honours:* George Varsell Award, American Acad. of Arts and Letters, 1988; Guggenheim Fellowship, 1989–90; John Heinz Fellowship in Environmental Journalism, 1999; Knight International Press Fund Fellowship, 2001.

MASŁOWSKA, Dorota; Polish writer; b. 3 July 1983, Wejcherowo. *Publication:* White and Red (novel, in trans.) (Polityka Prize) 2003. *Address:* c/o Atlantic Books, Ormond House, 26–27 Boswell Street, London, WC1N 3JZ, England.

MASON, Bobbie Ann, PhD; American writer; *Writer in Residence, University of Kentucky;* b. 1 May 1940, Mayfield, KY; d. of Wilburn Arnett and Christy Lee Mason; m. Roger Rawlings 1969. *Education:* Univs of Kentucky and Connecticut and Binghamton Univ., NY. *Career:* short stories have appeared in numerous journals including The New Yorker, Harper's, The North American Review, The Washington Post Magazine, The Atlantic, The Boston Globe Magazine, The Paris Review, Oxford American, DoubleTake; contrib. to journals Esquire and Vanity Fair; Prof. Mansfield Coll., Pa 1972–79; Grantee Nat. Endowment for the Arts 1983, Pennsylvania Arts Council 1983, 1989; Guggenheim Fellow 1984; Writer in Residence, Univ. of Kentucky 2001–. *Publications include:* Shiloh and Other Stories (Ernest Hemingway Foundation Award 1982, Award of American Acad. and Inst. for Arts and Letters 1984) 1982, In Country (Award for Cultural Contrib. to the Arts, Vietnam Veterans of America 1989, made into feature film 1989) 1985, Spence + Lila 1988, Love Life 1989, Feather Crowns (Southern Book Award) 1993, Midnight Magic 1998, Clear Springs (shortlisted for Pulitzer Prize) 1999, Zigzagging Down A Wild Trail (Southern Book Award) 2001, Elvis Presley (Kentucky Literary Award) 2003, An Atomic Romance 2005, Nancy Culpepper 2006. *Honours:* several short story awards 1981–; Appalachian Medallion Award, Univ. of Charleston 1991, Corrington Award 2005. *Literary Agent:* c/o Amanda Urban, International Creative Management, 40 West 57th Street, New York, NY 10019, USA.

MASON, Connie; American writer; b. 22 April 1930, Niles, MI; m. Lewis G. Mason 1950; one s. two d. *Career:* author of historical romance fiction. *Publications:* Tender Fury 1984, Caress and Conquer 1985, For Honor's Sake 1985, Promised Splendour 1986, My Lady Vixen 1986, Desert Ecstasy 1987, Wild is my Heart 1987, Bold Land, Bold Love 1988, Tempt the Devil 1988, Beyond the Horizon 1989, Love me with Fury 1989, Wild Love, Wild Land 1989, Promise Me Forever 1990, Brave Land, Brave Love 1990, Surrender to the Fury 1990, A Frontier Christmas 1990, Ice and Rapture 1991, A Promise of Thunder 1991, Lord of the Night 1991, Treasures of the Heart 1992, Wilderness Christmas 1992, Tears Like Rain 1993, Wind Rider 1993, Their First Noel 1993, Sierra 1994, Christmas Miracle 1994, The Lion's Bride 1994, Taken by You 1996, Pure Temptation 1996, A Love to Cherish 1996, Flame 1997, Shadow Walker 1997, To Love a Stranger 1997, Sheik 1998, Viking 1998, Swept Away 1998, To Tame a Renegade 1998, Pirate 1998, Gunslinger 1999, To Tempt a Rogue 1999, The Outlaws: Rafe 2000, A Taste of Sin 2000, The Outlaws: Jess 2000, A Breath of Scandal 2001, The Outlaws: Sam 2001, The Dragon Lord 2001, A Touch so Wicked 2002, The Rogue and the Hellion 2002, Lionheart 2002, Seduced by a Rogue 2003, The Laird of Stonehaven 2003, The Last Rogue 2004, The Pirate Prince 2004, Gypsyhover 2005, Falcon's Honor 2005. *Honours:* Career Storyteller of the Year 1992, Romantic Times Achievement Award 1994. *Address:* PO Box 2908, Portland, OR 97208-2908, USA (office).

MASON, David James, BA, MA, PhD; American academic, poet, critic and writer; *Associate Professor of English, The Colorado College;* b. 11 Dec. 1954, Bellingham, WA; m. Anne Lennox 1988; one step-d. *Education:* Colorado Coll., Univ. of Rochester. *Career:* Visiting Instructor, Colorado Coll. 1983, 1987, Visiting Prof. 1986, 1987, 1988, 1994, Asst Prof. 1998–2000, Assoc. Prof. 2000–; instructor, Univ. of Rochester 1986–88; Asst Prof., Moorhead State Univ. 1989–93, Assoc. Prof. 1993–98. *Publications:* Blackened Peaches 1989, Small Elegies 1990, The Buried Houses 1991, Questions at Christmas 1994, Three Characters from a Lost Home 1995, The Country I Remember 1996, Land Without Grief 1996, Rebel Angeles: 25 Poets of the New Formalism (ed. with Mark Jarman) 1996, Kalamitsi 1997, The Poetry of Life and the Life of

Poetry (essays) 2000, Western Wind: An Introduction to Poetry (co-ed.) 2000, Twentieth Century American Poetry (co-ed.) 2004, Twentieth Century American Poetics (co-ed.) 2004, Arrivals (poems) 2004; contrib. to books, reviews, quarterlies and journals. *Honours:* Nicholas Roerich Poetry Prize 1991, Poetry Soc. of America Alice Fay Di Castagnola Award 1993, Carnegie Foundation for the Advancement of Teaching and Council for Advancement and Support of Education Minnesota Prof. of the Year 1994, Hon. DHL (Colorado Coll.) 1996, Fulbright Artist-in-Residence Fellowship, Greece 1997. *Address:* 1131 Paradise Valley Drive, Woodland Park, CO 80863, USA (home). *Telephone:* (719) 389-6502 (office); (719) 686-1191 (home). *Fax:* (719) 389-6833 (office). *E-mail:* dmason@coloradocollege.edu.

MASON, Francis Kenneth, FRHistS; British editor, writer, archivist and researcher; b. 4 Sept. 1928, London, England. *Education:* Royal Air Force Coll., Cranwell. *Career:* Ed., Flying Review Int. 1963–64; Managing Dir, Profile Publications Ltd 1964–67, Alban Book Services Ltd, Watton, Norfolk; Managing Ed., Guiness Superlatives Ltd, Enfield, Middlesex 1968–71. *Publications:* author 91 books and ed. of numerous others 1961–96; contrib. to radio and television. *Honours:* Int. History Diploma, Aero Club of France, Paris 1973, Founder Fellowship, Canadian Guild of Authors 1988. *Address:* 68 Hunter's Oak, Watton, Thetford, Norfolk IP25 6HL, England. *E-mail:* alanfoster@con-brio.com.

MASON, Haydn Trevor, BA, AM, DPhil; British academic and writer; *Professor Emeritus and Senior Research Fellow, University of Bristol;* b. 12 Jan. 1929, Saundersfoot, Pembrokeshire, Wales; s. of Herbert Mason and Margaret Mason; m. 1st Gretchen Reger 1955 (divorced 1982); one s., one d.; m. 2nd Adrienne Mary Barnes 1982. *Education:* Univ. Coll. of Wales, Middlebury Coll., Vermont, Jesus Coll., Oxford. *Career:* instructor, Princeton Univ., USA 1954–57; Lecturer, Univ. of Reading 1964–65, Reader 1965–67; Prof. of European Literature, Univ. of East Anglia 1967–79; Ed. Studies on Voltaire and the Eighteenth Century 1977–95; Prof. of French Literature, Univ. of Paris III 1979–81; Prof. of French, Univ. of Bristol 1981–94, Prof. Emer. and Sr Research Fellow 1994–; Scholar-in-Residence, Univ. of Maryland 1986; Gen. Ed. Complete Works of Voltaire 1998–2001; Pres. Modern Humanities Research Asscn 1999; mem. Asscn of Univ. Profs of French (Chair. 1981–82), Soc. for French Studies (Pres. 1982–84), British Soc. for Eighteenth-Century Studies (Pres. 1984–86), Int. Soc. for Eighteenth-Century Studies (Pres. 1991–95), Voltaire Foundation (Dir 1977–97, Chair. 1989–93). *Publications:* Pierre Bayle and Voltaire 1963, Marivaux: Les Fausses Confidences (ed.) 1964, Leibniz-Arnauld Correspondence (trans. and ed.) 1967, Voltaire: Zadig and Other Stories (ed.) 1971, Voltaire 1974, Voltaire: A Life 1981, French Writers and Their Society 1715–1800 1982, Cyrano de Bergerac: L'Autre Monde 1984, Voltaire: Discours en vers sur l'homme (ed.) 1991, Candide: Optimism Demolished 1992, Candide (ed.) 1995, Voltaire: Micromégas and Other Short Fictions 2002, Le Mondain (ed.) 2003, Zadig (ed.) 2004. *Honours:* Hon. Fellow, British Soc. for Eighteenth-Century Studies 2006; Médaille d'Argent de la Ville de Paris 1989, Jt Prizewinner, European Humanities Research Centre Philosophical Dialogue Competition 1998; Officier, Ordre des Palmes académiques 1985. *Address:* Department of French, University of Bristol, Bristol, BS8 1TE (office); 11 Goldney Avenue, Bristol, BS8 4RA, England (home).

MASON, Sarah J., (Hamilton Crane), MA; British novelist; b. 18 Dec. 1949, Bishop's Stortford, Herts., England; m. William G. Welland 1976. *Education:* St Andrews Univ., Scotland. *Career:* mem. CWA, Soc. of Authors. *Publications:* Let's Talk of Wills 1985, Murder in the Maze (Trewley and Stone series) 1993, Frozen Stiff (Trewley and Stone series) 1993, Corpse in the Kitchen (Trewley and Stone series) 1993, Dying Breath (Trewley and Stone series) 1994, Sew Easy to Kill (Trewley and Stone series) 1996, Seeing is Deceiving (Trewley and Stone series) 1997, Death on her Doorstep 2003; as Hamilton Crane: Miss Seeton Cracks the Case 1991, Miss Seeton Paints the Town 1991, Hands Up, Miss Seeton 1992, Miss Seeton by Moonlight 1992, Miss Seeton Rocks the Cradle 1992, Miss Seeton Goes to Bat 1993, Miss Seeton Plants Suspicion 1993, Miss Seeton Rules 1994, Starring Miss Seeton 1994, Miss Seeton Undercover 1994, Sold to Miss Seeton 1995, Sweet Miss Seeton 1996, Bonjour Miss Seeton 1997, Miss Seeton's Finest Hour 1999. *Literary Agent:* c/o Curtis Brown Ltd, Haymarket House, 28–29 Haymarket, London, SW1Y 4SP, England. *Telephone:* (20) 7393-4400. *Fax:* (20) 7393-4401. *E-mail:* info@curtisbrown.co.uk. *Website:* www.curtisbrown.co.uk. *E-mail:* sarahjmason@waitrose.com (home).

MASON, Stanley Allen, MA; Canadian editor, translator, poet and dramatist; b. 16 April 1917, Blairmore, AB; m. Cloris Ielmini 1944; one d. *Education:* Oriel College, Oxford. *Career:* Technical Trans., 1943–63; Literary Ed., Graphis Magazine, 1963–83; Ed., Elements, Dow Chemical Europe house organ, 1969–75. *Publications:* Modern English Structures (with Ronald Ridout), four vols, 1968–72; A Necklace of Words (poems), 1975; A Reef of Honours (poems), 1983; Send Out the Dove (play), 1986; The Alps, by Albrecht von Haller (trans.), 1987; The Everlasting Snow (poems), 1993; Collected Poems, 1993; A German Treasury (anthology, trans.), 1993–95. Contributions: many publications. *Honours:* Borestone Mountain Poetry Award; Living Playwright Award.

MASSIE, Allan Johnstone, BA, FRSL; British author; b. 19 Oct. 1938, Singapore; m. Alison Agnes Graham Langlands 1973; two s. one d. *Education:* Trinity Coll., Glenalmond and Trinity Coll., Cambridge. *Career:* fiction reviewer, The Scotsman, 1976–; Creative Writing Fellow, Univ. of Edinburgh,

1982–84, Univ. of Glasgow and Univ. of Strathclyde, 1985–86; Columnist, Glasgow Herald, 1985–88, Sunday Times Scotland, 1987–, Daily Telegraph, 1991–; mem. Scottish Arts Council. *Publications:* Fiction: Change and Decay in All Around I See, 1978; The Last Peacock, 1980; The Death of Men, 1981; One Night in Winter, 1984; Augustus: The Memoirs of the Emperor, 1986; A Question of Loyalties, 1989; The Hanging Tree, 1990; Tiberius: The Memoirs of an Emperor, 1991; The Sins of the Father, 1991; These Enchanted Woods, 1993; Caesar, 1993; The Ragged Lion, 1994; King David, 1995; Arthur the King, 2003; Caligula, 2003, The Thistle and the Rose 2005. Other: Muriel Spark, 1979; Ill Met by Gaslight: Five Edinburgh Murders, 1980; The Caesars, 1983; Edinburgh and the Borders: In Verse (ed.), 1983; A Portrait of Scottish Rugby, 1984; Eisenstadt: Aberdeen, Portrait of a City, 1984; Colette: The Woman, the Writer and the Myth, 1986; 101 Great Scots, 1987; PEN New Fiction: Thirty-Two Short Stories (ed.), 1987; How Should Health Services be Financed? A Patient's View, 1988; The Novelist's View of the Market Economy, 1988; Byron's Travels, 1988; Glasgow: Portraits of a City, 1989; The Novel Today: A Critical Guide to the British Novel, 1970–1989, 1990; Edinburgh, 1994. Contributions: periodicals. *Honours:* Niven Award, 1981; Scottish Arts Council Award, 1982. *Literary Agent:* Curtis Brown Group Ltd, Haymarket House, 28–29 Haymarket, London SW1Y 4SP, England. *Address:* Thirladean House, Selkirk TD7 5LU, Scotland.

MASSIE, Robert Kinloch, BA; American writer; b. 5 Jan. 1929, Lexington, KY; m. 1st Suzanne L. Rohrbach 1954 (divorced 1990); one s. two d.; m. 2nd Deborah L. Karl 1992; one s. two d. *Education:* Yale Univ., Univ. of Oxford. *Career:* reporter, Collier's magazine, New York 1955–56; writer, Newsweek magazine, New York 1956–62, USA-1 magazine, New York 1962, Saturday Evening Post, New York 1962–65; Ferris Prof. of Journalism, Princeton Univ. 1977, 1985; Mellon Prof. in the Humanities, Tulane Univ. 1981; mem. Authors' Guild of America, PEN, Soc. of American Historians. *Publications:* Nicholas and Alexandra 1967, Journey 1976, Peter the Great: His Life and World 1980, Dreadnought: Britain, Germany and the Coming of the Great War 1991, The Romanovs: The Final Chapter 1995, Castles of Steel: Britain, Germany and the Winning of the Great War at Sea 2004; contrib. to periodicals. *Honours:* Christopher Award 1976, Pulitzer Prize for Biography 1981. *Address:* 60 West Clinton Avenue, Irvington, NY 10533, USA.

MASSON, Jeffrey Moussaieff, BA, PhD; American writer, editor and translator; b. (Jeffrey Lloyd Masson), 28 March 1941, Chicago, IL; m. Leila Siller; one d. two s. *Education:* Harvard Univ. *Career:* Instructor in Religious Studies, Brown Univ., 1967–68; Asst Prof. of Sanskrit and Indian Studies, 1969–70, Assoc. Prof., 1970–75, Prof., 1976–80, Univ. of Toronto; Visiting Prof. of Sanskrit, 1978–79, Research Assoc., Dept of South and Southeast Asian Studies, 1981–92, Visiting Lecturer, Graduate School of Journalism, 1994, Univ. of California at Berkeley; Projects Dir, Sigmund Freud Archives, New York, 1980–81; Visiting Part-time Lecturer in Journalism, Univ. of Michigan, 1993. *Publications:* Santarasa and Abhinvagupta's Philosophy of Aesthetics (with M. V. Patwardhan), 1969; Avimaraka: Love's Enchanted World (with D. D. Kosambi), 1970; Aesthetic Rapture: The Rasadhyaya of the Natyasastra (with M. V. Patwardhan), two vols, 1970; The Oceanic Feeling: The Origins of Religious Sentiment in Ancient India, 1980; Love Poems from the Ancient Sanskrit (with W. S. Merwin), 1981, revised edn as The Peacock's Egg, 1983; The Assault on Truth: Freud's Suppression of the Seduction Theory, 1984; Complete Letters of Sigmund Freud to Wilhelm Fuess, 1887–1904 (ed. and trans.), 1985; A Dark Science: Women, Sexuality and Psychiatry in the Nineteenth Century, 1987; Against Therapy: Emotional Tyranny and the Myth of Psychological Healing, 1988; The Dhvanyaloka of Anandavardhana with the Locana of Abhinavagupta (co-ed. and co-trans.), 1990; Final Analysis: The Making and Unmaking of a Psychoanalyst, 1991; My Father's Guru: A Journey Through Spirituality and Disillusion, 1992; When Elephants Weep: The Emotional Lives of Animals (with Susan McCarthy), 1994; Lost Prince: The Unsolved Mystery of Kaspar Hauser, 1996; Dogs Never Lie About Love: The Emotional World of Dogs, 1997; The Emperor's Embrace: The Evolution of Fatherhood, 1999; Dogs Have the Strangest Friends and Other True Stories of Animal Feelings, 1999; The Nine Emotional Lives of Cats, 2002; The Pig Who Sang to the Moon: The Emotional World of Farm Animals, 2003; The Pig Who Sang to the Moon 2004; contrib. articles to Atlantic Monthly, International Journal of Psycho-Analysis, New York Times. *Honours:* Hon. Fellow, Dept of Philosophy, Univ. of Auckland. *Literary Agent:* Elaine Markson Literary Agency, 44 Greenwich Avenue, New York, NY 10011, USA. *Address:* PO Box 25930, St Heliers, Auckland, New Zealand.

MASTER, Simon Harcourt; British publisher; b. 10 April 1944, Caterham; s. of Humphrey R. Master and Rachel B. Plumbly; m. Georgina M. C. Batsford 1969; two s. *Education:* Ardingly Coll. Sussex. *Career:* Publishing Dir Pan Books Ltd 1973–80, Man. Dir 1980–87; Chief Exec. Random House UK and Exec. Vice-Pres. Random House Int. Group 1987–89, Group Man. Dir Random Century Group 1989–90, Group Deputy Chair. 1989–, Chair., CEO Gen. Books Div., Random House UK 1992–; Chair., Arrow Books 1990–92; Dir (non-exec.) HMSO 1990–95; mem. Council Publrs Asscn 1989–95 (Vice-Pres. 1995–96, 2000–2001, Pres. 1996–97, 2001–02). *Address:* Flat 1, St George's Mansions, Causton Street, London, SW1P 4RZ, England (home). *Telephone:* (20) 7630-7121 (home).

MASTERS, Hilary Thomas, AB; American writer and academic; *Professor of English and Creative Writing, Carnegie Mellon University;* b. 3 Feb. 1928, Kansas City, MO; m. 1st Polly Jo McCulloch 1955 (divorced 1986); one s. two d.; m. 2nd Kathleen E. George 1994. *Education:* Davidson Coll., Brown Univ.

Career: Ed. and Publisher Hyde Park Record newspaper, New York 1956–59; Prof. of English and Creative Writing, Carnegie Mellon Univ. 1983–; several visiting univ. positions; mem. Associated Writing Programs, Authors' Guild, Authors' League of America, PEN Center New York. *Publications:* The Common Pasture 1967, An American Marriage 1969, Palace of Strangers 1971, Last Stands: Notes from Memory 1982, Clemmons 1985, Hammertown Tales 1986, Cooper 1987, Manuscript for Murder 1987, Strickland 1989, Success: New and Selected Stories 1992, Home is the Exile 1996, In Montaigne's Tower 2000, Shadows on a Wall 2005, Elegy for Sam Emerson 2006; contrib. to anthologies and periodicals. *Honours:* Yaddo Fellowships 1980, 1982, 2000, Fulbright Lecturer to Finland 1983, Time magazine Ed.'s Choice 1984, Los Angeles Times Notable Novel 1990, Sewanee Review Monroe Spears Prize 1997, Balch Prize for Fiction 1998, Anchor Best Essays 1998, Best American Essays 1999, American Acad. of Arts and Letters Award for Literature 2003. *Address:* c/o Department of English, Carnegie Mellon University, Pittsburgh, PA 15213, USA.

MASTORAKI, Jenny; Greek poet and translator; b. 1949, Athens. *Education:* Athens Univ. *Publications:* The Legend of Saint Youth 1971, Tolls 1972, Kin 1979, Tales of the Deep 1983, With a Crown of Life 1989; contrib. to The Rehearsal of Misunderstanding: Three Collections by Contemporary Greek Women Poets 1998.

MATAR, Hisham; Libyan writer; b. 1970, New York, NY, USA. *Publications:* Amorous/Amatory: Poems 1998, In the Country of Men (novel) (Commonwealth Writers' Prize Best First Book – Europe and South Asia 2007) 2006. *Address:* c/o Penguin Books Ltd, 80 Strand, London, WC2R 0RL, England (office).

MATAR, Salim; Iraqi writer and journalist. *Career:* left Iraq 1978; has lived in Syria and Italy, now in Geneva, Switzerland. *Publications include (in translation):* The Woman of the Flask (novel) (al-Naqid Award) 1990, The Dialogue of Identities. *Address:* c/o The American University in Cairo Press, 113 Sharia Kasr el Aini Street, Cairo, Egypt. *Website:* www.salimmatar.com.

MATAS, Carol Rosaline, BA; Canadian writer; b. 14 Nov. 1949, Winnipeg, MB; d. of Roy Matas and Ruth Matas; m. Per K. Brask 1977; one s. one d. *Education:* Univ. of Western Ontario, Actors' Lab, London, UK. *Career:* Visiting Prof., Bemidji State Univ. Minnesota; Creative Writing Instructor, Continuing Educ. Div., Univ. of Winnipeg; mem. International PEN, Manitoba Writers Guild, Soc. of Children's Book Writers and Illustrators, Writer's Union of Canada. *Publications:* The D.N.A Dimension 1982, The Fusion Factor 1986, Zanu 1986, Me, Myself and I 1987, Lisa (aka Lisa's War) 1987, Jesper (aka Code Name Kris) 1989, Adventure in Legoland 1991, The Race 1991, Sworn Enemies 1993, Safari Adventure in Legoland 1993, Daniel's Story 1993, The Lost Locket 1994, The Burning Time 1994, Of Two Minds (with Perry Nodelman) 1994, The Primrose Path 1995, After the War 1996, More Minds (with Perry Nodelman) 1996, The Freak 1997, The Garden 1997, Greater Than Angels 1998, Telling 1998, Out of Their Minds 1998, Cloning Miranda 1999, In My Enemy's House 1999, Meeting of Minds 1999, Rebecca 2000, The War Within 2001, The Second Clone 2001, Sparks Fly Upwards 2001, Gotcha! Rosie in New York City 2003, Playball! Rosie in Chicago 2003, Action! Rosie in LA 2004, Turned Away 2005, The Dark Clone 2005. *Honours:* many awards and citations for young people's literature. *Literary Agent:* c/o David Bennett, TLA Inc., 72 Glengowan Road, Toronto, ON M4N 1G4, Canada. *Telephone:* (416) 488-9214. *Fax:* (416) 488-4531. *E-mail:* david@tla1 .com. *Website:* www.tla1.com; www.carolmatas.com.

MATESIS, Pavlos; Greek novelist, playwright and translator; b. Greece. *Publications:* fiction: The Ancient of the Days, Always Well, Sylvan Substances, The Daughter (Greek Critics Award) 1990, Contemporary Greek Theatre Vol. 2 (four plays) 2002. *Address:* c/o Arcadia Books, 15-16 Nassau Street, London, W1W 7AB, England (office).

MATHESON, Alex (see Mackay, James Alexander)

MATHESON, Richard Burton, BA; American writer and dramatist; b. 20 Feb. 1926, Allendale, NJ; m. Ruth Ann Woodson 1952, two s. two d. *Education:* University of Missouri. *Career:* mem. Dramatists' Guild, Writers' Guild. *Publications:* Novels: Someone is Bleeding, 1953; Fury on Sunday, 1953; I Am Legend, 1954; The Shrinking Man, 1956; A Stir of Echoes, 1958; Ride the Nightmare, 1959; The Beardless Warriors, 1960; Hell House, 1971; Bid Time Return, 1975; What Dreams May Come, 1978; Earthbound, 1982; Through Channels, 1989; Journal of the Gun Years, 1991; The Gunfight, 1993; 7 Steps to Midnight, 1993; Shadow on the Sun, 1994; The Memoirs of Wild Bill Hickock, 1995; Now You See It..., 1995; Passion Play, 2000; Hunger and Thirst, 2000. Other: Born of Man and Woman: Tales of Science Fiction and Fantasy, 1954; The Shores of Space, 1957; Shock: Thirteen Tales to Thrill and Terrify, 1961; Shock II, 1964; Shock III, 1966; Shock Waves, 1970; By the Gun: Six from Richard Matheson, 1993; Shadow on the Sun, 1993; The Path, 1993; The Memoirs of Wild Bill Harris, 1996; The Twilight Zone Scripts of Richard Matheson, 1998; Hunger and Thirst, 2000; Camp Pleasant, 2001; ABU and the 7 Marvels, 2002; Hunted Past Reason, 2002; A Primer of Reality, 2002. Non-Fiction: The Path: Metaphysics for the '90s, 1993; Robert Bloch: Appreciations of the Master (ed. with Ricia Mainhardt), 1995; Mediums Rare, 2000. Other: many screenplays. *Honours:* Hugo Award, World Science Fiction Convention, 1958; Writers' Guild Awards, 1960, 1974; World Fantasy Award, 1976, and Life Achievement Award, 1984; Bram Stoker Award, 1990.

MATHEWS, Harry; American writer, poet, editor and translator; b. 14 Feb. 1930, New York, NY. *Education:* Princeton Univ., Harvard Univ., L'École Normale de Musique, Paris. *Career:* writes under pseudonym, Harry Mathews; mem. Ouvroir de Littérature Potentielle (Oulipo), France. *Publications:* prose: The Conversions 1962, The Tlooth 1966, The Sinking of the Odradek Stadium and Other Novels 1975, Selected Declarations of Dependence 1977, Country Cooking and Other Stories 1980, Cigarettes 1987, The Orchard (memoirs) 1988, Twenty Lines a Day 1988, Singular Pleasures 1988, The American Experience 1991, Immeasurable Distances (criticism) 1991, The Journalist 1994, Oulipo Compendium (co-ed.) 1998, Sainte Catherine 2000, The Human Country 2002, The Case of the Persevering Maltese: Collected Essays 2003, My Life in CIA: A Chronicle of 1973 2005; poetry: The Planisphere 1974, Trial Impressions 1977, Armenian Papers 1987, Out of Bounds 1989, A Mid-Season Sky 1992; contrib. to numerous anthologies, reviews, quarterlies and journals. *Honours:* Nat. Endowment for the Arts grant 1982, American Acad. and Inst. of Arts and Letters Award 1991. *Literary Agent:* Maxine Groffsky, 2 Fifth Avenue, New York, NY 10011, USA. *E-mail:* hmathews2@cs.com.

MATHIAS, Roland Glyn, BA, BLitt, MA; British poet and writer; b. 4 Sept. 1915, Talybont-on-Usk, Breconshire, Wales; m. Mary (Molly) Hawes 1944; one s. two d. *Education:* Jesus Coll., Oxford. *Career:* schoolmaster; Ed., The Anglo-Welsh Review 1961–76; Extra-Mural Lecturer, Univ. Coll., Cardiff 1970–77; Visiting Prof., Univ. of Alabama at Birmingham 1971; mem. Welsh Arts Council (chair. literature cttee 1976–79). *Publications:* poetry: Break in Harvest 1946, The Roses of Tretower 1952, The Flooded Valley 1960, Absalom in the Tree 1971, Snipe's Castle 1979, Burning Brambles 1983, A Field at Vallorcines 1996, The Collected Poems of Roland Mathias 2002; short stories: The Eleven Men of Eppynt 1956; non-fiction: Whitsun Riot 1963, Vernon Watkins 1974, John Cowper Powys as Poet 1979, A Ride Through the Wood 1985, Anglo-Welsh Literature: An Illustrated History 1987, The Collected Short Stories of Roland Mathias 2001; contrib. to many literary journals and periodicals. *Honours:* Hon. DHL (Georgetown Univ., Washington, DC) 1985. *Address:* Deffrobani, 5 Maescelyn, Brecon, Powys LD3 7NL, Wales.

MATHIS-EDDY, Darlene, PhD; American poet and academic; *Adjunct Professor, Core Program and College Seminar Program, University of Notre Dame*; b. 19 March 1937, Elkhart, Ind.; d. of the late William Eugene Mathis and Fern Roose Paulmer Mathis; m. Spencer Livingston Eddy, Jr 1964 (died 1971). *Education:* Goshen Coll. and Rutgers Univ. *Career:* Instructor in English, Douglass Coll. 1962–64; Instructor in English, Rutgers Univ. 1964, 1965, Rutgers Univ. Coll. (Adult Educ.) 1967; Asst Prof. in English, Ball State Univ. 1967–71, Assoc. Prof. 1971–75, Prof. 1975–99, Poet-in-Residence 1989–93, Prof. Emer., English and Humanities 1999–, Ralph S. Whitinger Lecturer, Ball State Univ. Honors Coll. 1998–99; Adjunct Prof., Core Program and Coll. Seminar Program, Univ. of Notre Dame, Ind. 2001–; Consulting Ed. Blue Unicorn 1995–; Founding Ed. The Hedge Row Press 1995–; mem. Comm. on Women for the Nat. Council of Teachers of English 1976–79; Poetry Ed. BSU Forum; Vice-Pres. Programs, American Asscn of Univ. Women, Elkhart Br. *Publications:* Leaf Threads, Wind Rhymes 1986, The Worlds of King Lear 1971, Weathering 1992, Reflections: Studies in Light 1993; Contributing Ed. Snowy Egret 1988–90; numerous poems in literary reviews; book reviews and essays in numerous journals; articles in American Literature, English Language Notes, etc. *Honours:* Woodrow Wilson Nat. Fellow 1959–62, Rutgers Univ. Grad. Honors and Honors Dissertation Fellow 1964–65, 1966–67, Notable Woodrow Wilson Nat. Fellow 1991; numerous creative arts, creative teaching, research grants and awards. *Address:* 346 O'Shaughnessy Hall, College Seminar Program, University of Notre Dame, Notre Dame, IN 46556-5639 (office); 1840 West Cobblestone Boulevard, Elkhart, IN 46514-4961, USA (home). *Telephone:* (574) 631-5378 (office); (574) 266-4394 (home). *Website:* www.nd.edu/~collegeseminar (office).

MATRAY, James Irving, BA, MA, PhD; American academic and writer; *Professor of History, California State University, Chico*; b. 6 Dec. 1948, Chicago, IL; m. Mary Karin Heine 1971; one s. one d. *Education:* Lake Forest Coll., Univ. of Virginia. *Career:* Visiting Asst Prof. 1980–82, Asst Prof. 1982–87, Assoc. Prof. 1987–92, Prof. of History 1992–2002, New Mexico State Univ.; Visiting Assoc. Prof. of History, Univ. of Southern California 1988–89; Distinguished Visiting Scholar, Kyung Hee Univ., Seoul 1990; Dept Chair, Prof. of History, California State Univ., Chico 2002–; mem. American Historical Asscn, Soc. for Historians of American Foreign Relations; mem. Bd of Eds, Diplomatic History 2005–07. *Publications:* The Reluctant Crusade: American Foreign Policy in Korea 1941–1950 1985, Historical Dictionary of the Korean War 1991, Korea and the Cold War: Division, Destruction, and Disarmament (ed. with Kim Chull-Baum) 1993, Japan's Emergence as a Global Power 2000, East Asia and the United States: An Encyclopedia of Relations Since 1784, Korea Divided: The 38th Parallel and the DMZ; contrib. to many scholarly books and journals. *Honours:* several research grants, Soc. for Historians of American Relations Stuart L. Bernath Article Award (co-recipient) 1980, Best Reference Book Award, Library Journal 1992, Outstanding Academic Book Award, Choice 1992 recipient Bautzer Advancement 2003. *Address:* 246 Eagle Nest Drive, Chico, CA 95928, USA.

MATSON, Clive, MFA; American writer and teacher; *Instructor in Creative Writing, University of California extension at Berkeley*; b. 13 March 1941, Los Angeles, CA; m. Gail Ford 1993; one s. *Education:* Univ. of Chicago, Columbia Univ. *Career:* Instructor in Creative Writing, Univ. of Calif. extension at Berkeley 1985–. *Publications:* Mainline to the Heart 1966, Space Age 1969, Heroin 1972, On the Inside 1982, Equal in Desire 1983, Hourglass 1987, Breath of Inspiration (essay) 1987, Let the Crazy Child Write 1998, Squish Boots 2002, An Eye for an Eye Makes the Whole World Blind: Poets on 9/11 (ed. with Allen Cohen) 2002; contrib. to anthologies and journals. *Honours:* Columbia Univ. Graduate Writing Fellowship 1987–88, PEN Oakland Josephine Miles Nat. Literary Award 2003. *Address:* 472 44th Street, Oakland, CA 94609, USA (office). *Telephone:* (510) 654-6495 (office). *E-mail:* clive@matson-food.com (office). *Website:* www.matson-food.com (office).

MATTESON, Stefanie Newton, BA; American writer; b. 9 Oct. 1946, Hackensack, NJ; m. 1st David Bruce Matteson 1971 (divorced 1994); one s. one d.; m. 2nd Richard Leon Grocholski 1994 (divorced 2002). *Education:* Skidmore Coll., Saratoga Springs, NY, Boston Univ., School of Public Communications. *Career:* mem. MWA (dir New York chapter 1996–97), Sisters in Crime. *Publications:* Murder at the Spa 1990, Murder at Teatime 1991, Murder on the Cliff 1991, Murder on the Silk Road 1992, Murder at the Falls 1993, Murder on High 1994, Murder Among the Angels 1996, Murder Under the Palms 1997. *Address:* Dominick Abel Literary Agency, 146 W 82nd Street, No. 1B, New York, NY 10024, USA (office). *Telephone:* (908) 719-7779 (home).

MATTHEW, Christopher Charles Forrest, MA; British novelist, journalist and broadcaster; b. 8 May 1939, London, England; m. Wendy Mary Matthew 1979; two s. one d. *Education:* St Peter's Coll., Oxford. *Career:* Ed. Times Travel Guide 1972–73; columnist, Punch 1983–88; restaurant critic, Vogue (UK) 1983–86; book and TV reviewer, Daily Mail; mem. Soc. of Authors, Chelsea Arts Club. *Publications:* A Different World: Stories of Great Hotels 1976, Diary of a Somebody 1978, Loosely Engaged 1980, The Long Haired Boy 1980, The Crisp Report 1981, Three Men in a Boat (with Benny Green) 1982, The Junket Man 1983, How to Survive Middle Age 1983, Family Matters 1987, The Amber Room 1995, A Nightingale Sang in Fernhurst Road 1998, Now We Are Sixty 1999, Knocking On 2001, Now We Are Sixty (and a bit) 2003, Summoned by Balls 2005; contrib. to newspapers, magazines and TV. *Literary Agent:* c/o Christopher Little Literary Agency, 10 Eel Brook Studios, 125 Moore Park Road, London, SW6 4PS, England. *Telephone:* (20) 7736-4455. *Fax:* (20) 7736-4490. *E-mail:* info@christopherlittle.net. *Website:* www.christopherlittle.net. *Address:* 35 Drayton Gardens, London, SW10 9RY, England. *E-mail:* cmatt@onetel.com.

MATTHEWS, Patricia Anne, (P. A. Brisco, Patty Brisco, Laura Wylie); American writer; b. 1 July 1927, San Fernando, CA; m. 1st Marvin Owen Brisco 1946 (divorced 1961); two s.; m. 2nd Clayton Hartly Matthews 1971. *Education:* California State Univ., Los Angeles. *Career:* mem. Romantic Writers Asscn, MWA, Sisters in Crime, Novelists Ink. *Publications:* Merry's Treasure 1969, The Other People 1970, The House of Candles 1973, Mist of Evil 1976, Love's Avenging Heart 1977, Love Forever More 1977, Love's Wildest Promise 1978, Raging Rapids 1978, Love's Daring Dream 1978, Love's Magic Moment 1979, Love's Many Faces 1979, Love's Pagan Heart 1979, Love's Golden Destiny 1979, The Night Visitor 1979, Love's Raging Tide 1980, Love's Bold Journey 1980, Love's Sweet Agony 1980, Midnight Whispers (with Clayton Matthews) 1981, Tides of Love 1981, Embers of Dawn 1982, Empire (with Clayton Matthews) 1982, Flames of Glory 1983, Dancer of Dreams 1984, Gambler in Love 1984, Midnight Lavender (with Clayton Matthews) 1985, Tame the Restless Heart 1986, Destruction at Dawn 1986, Twister 1986, Enchanted 1987, Thursday and the Lady 1987, Mirrors 1988, Oasis 1989, The Dreaming Tree 1989, Sapphire 1989, The Death of Love 1990, The Unquiet 1991, The Scent of Fear (with Clayton Matthews) 1992, Vision of Death (with Clayton Matthews) 1992, Taste of Evil (with Clayton Matthews) 1993, The Sound of Murder (with Clayton Matthews) 1994, Touch of Terror 1995, Dead Man Riding 1999, Secret of Secco Canyon 1999, Death in the Desert 2000, Rendezvous at Midnight 2004; contrib. to anthologies and magazines. *Honours:* West Coast Review of Books Porgie Award 1979, Silver Medal 1983, Bronze Medal 1983; Romantic Times Team Writing Award (with Clayton Hartly Matthews) 1983, Reviewers' Choice Awards for Best Historical Gothic 1986–87, Affaire de Coeur Silver Pen Readers Award 1989. *Literary Agent:* Pinder, Lane & Garon-Brooke Associates Ltd, 159 W 53rd Street, Suite 14, New York, NY 10019, USA.

MATTHIAS, John Edward, BA, MA; American academic, poet, writer and translator; *Professor, University of Notre Dame*; b. 5 Sept. 1941, Columbus, OH; m. Diana Clare Jocelyn 1967; two c. *Education:* Ohio State Univ., Stanford Univ., Univ. of London. *Career:* Asst Prof. 1967–73, Assoc. Prof. 1973–80, Prof. 1980–, Univ. of Notre Dame; Visiting Fellow in Poetry 1976–77, Assoc. 1977–, Clare Hall, Cambridge; Visiting Prof., Skidmore Coll. 1978, Univ. of Chicago 1980; mem. American Literary Trans Asscn, PEN American Center, Poetry Soc. of America. *Publications:* Bucyrus 1971, 23 Modern Poets (ed.) 1971, Turns 1975, Crossing 1979, Five American Poets (ed.) 1979, Contemporary Swedish Poetry (trans. with Goran Printz-Pahlson) 1979, Barthory and Lermontov 1980, Northern Summer: New and Selected Poems 1984, David Jones: Man and Poet 1989, Tva Dikter 1989, A Gathering of Ways 1991, Reading Old Friends 1992, Selected Works of David Jones 1993, Swimming at Midnight: Selected Shorter Poems 1995, Beltane at Aphelion: Collected Longer Poems 1995; contrib. to numerous anthologies, reviews, quarterlies and journals. *Honours:* Fulbright Grant 1966, Swedish Inst. Trans. Award 1977–78, Columbia Univ. Trans. Award 1978, Ingram Merrill Foundation Awards 1984, 1990, Soc. of Midland Authors Poetry Award 1986, Soc. for the Study of Midwestern Literature Poetry Prize 1986, Slobodan Janovic Literary Prize 1989, Poetry Soc. of America George Bogin Memorial

Award 1990, Lilly Endowment grant 1991–92, Ohio Library Asscn Poetry Award 1996. *Address:* c/o Department of English, University of Notre Dame, Notre Dame, IN 46556, USA.

MATTHIESSEN, Peter, BA; American writer and editor; *Founding Editor, The Paris Review;* b. 22 May 1927, New York; s. of Erard A. Matthiessen and Elizabeth (née Carey) Matthiessen; m. 1st Patricia Southgate 1951 (divorced); m. 2nd Deborah Love 1963 (died 1972); three s. one d.; m. 3rd Maria Eckhart 1980. *Education:* Sorbonne, Paris, Yale Univ. *Career:* co-founder and now Founding Ed. The Paris Review 1953–; ordained a Zen Monk 1981; fmr corresp., New Yorker; Trustee New York Zoological Soc. 1965–78; mem. American Acad. of Arts and Letters 1974–, Nat. Inst. of Arts and Science 1986–. *Publications:* Race Rock 1954, Partisans 1955, Raditzer 1960, Wildlife in America 1959, The Cloud Forest 1961, Under the Mountain Wall 1963, At Play in the Fields of the Lord 1965, The Shore Birds of North America 1967, Oomingmak: The Expedition to the Musk Ox Island in the Bering Sea 1967, Sal si puedes 1969, Blue Meridian 1971, The Tree Where Man Was Born 1972, The Wind Birds 1973, Far Tortuga 1975, The Snow Leopard 1978, Sand Rivers 1981, In the Spirit of the Crazy Horse 1983, Indian Country 1984, Midnight Turning Grey 1984, Nine-Headed Dragon River 1986, Men's Lives 1986, Partisans 1987, On the River Styx 1989, Killing Mr Watson 1990, African Silences 1991, Baikal 1992, African Silences 1992, Baikal 1992, Shadows of Africa 1992, East of Lo Monthang: In the Land of Mustang 1995, Lost Man's River 1997, Bone by Bone (novel) 1999, Tigers in the Snow 2000, Peter Matthiessen Reader: Non Fiction 1959-1991 2000, An African Trilogy 2000, Sal si Puedes – Cesar Chávez and the New American Revolution 2000, Birds of Heaven: Travels with Cranes 2001, Ends of the Earth: Voyages to Antarctica 2003. *Honours:* Atlantic Prize 1950, American Acad. of Arts and Letters Award 1963, National Book Award 1978, John Burroughs Medal 1981, African Wildlife Leadership Foundation Award 1982, Gold Medal for Distinction in Natural History 1985, Orion-John Hay Award 1999, Soc. of Conservation Biologists Award 1999, Heinz Award for Arts and Humanities 2000, Lannan Lifetime Achievement Award 2002, Harvard Nat. History Museum Roger Tory Peterson Medal 2003. *Address:* The Paris Review, 541 East 72 Street, New York, NY 10021, USA (office). *Website:* www.parisreview.com (office).

MATTINGLEY, Christobel Rosemary, AM, BA; Australian writer; b. 26 Oct. 1931, Adelaide, S Australia; d. of Arthur Raymond Shepley and Isabelle Margaret Mary Shepley; m. Cecil David Mattingley 1953; two s. one d. *Education:* Presbyterian Ladies' Coll., Pymble, NSW, The Friends' School, Hobart, Tasmania, Univ. of Tasmania Library Training School, State Library of Victoria. *Career:* librarian 1951–57, 1966–74; freelance writer, lecturer, ed., researcher 1975–; Assoc., Library Asscn of Australia 1971; Patron Soc. of Women Writers 1998–. *Film scripts:* Children's Libraries 1979, Woman Artists of Australia 1980. *Publications include:* Windmill at Magpie Creek 1971, Tiger's Milk 1974, The Battle of the Galah Trees 1974, The Great Ballagundi Damper Bake 1975, Rummage 1981, The Magic Saddle 1983, The Angel with a Mouth Organ 1984, The Miracle Tree 1985, Survival in Our Own Land: Aboriginal Experiences in South Australia since 1836 1988, The Butcher, the Beagle and the Dog Catcher 1990, Tucker's Mob 1992, The Sack 1993, No Gun for Asmir 1993, The Race 1995, Asmir in Vienna 1995, Escape from Sarajevo 1996, Ginger 1997, Daniel's Secret 1997, Work Wanted 1998, Hurry up Alice 1998, Cockawun and Cockatoo 1999, First Friend 2000, King of the Wilderness 2001, Ruby of Trowutta 2003, Nest Egg, Battle Order 204 2007; contrib. to Australian Library Journal, New Zealand Libraries, Land-fall, Reading Time, Classroom, Magpies, Something About the Author Autobiography Series, National Library of Australia News, Word of Mouth. *Honours:* Hon. DUniv (South Australia) 1995; Christobel Mattingley Young Writers' Award inaugurated by City of S Perth, WA 1987, Advance Australia Award 1990, Pheme Tanner Award, La Trobe Univ. 1999, Lifetime Recogni-tion Award 2004. *Literary Agent:* c/o Curtis Brown, 2 Boundary Street, Paddington, NSW 2021, Australia. *Telephone:* (2) 9331-5301. *E-mail:* fiona@curtisbrown.com.au. *Website:* www.curtisbrown.com.au. *Address:* 10 Rose-bank Terrace, Stonyfell, S Australia 5066, Australia.

MATURA, Mustapha; Trinidadian playwright; b. 1939. *Plays:* Black Pieces (ICA, London) 1970, As Time Goes By (Traverse Theatre, Edinburgh) 1971, Bakerloo Line (Almost Free, London) 1972, Nice (Almost Free, London) 1973, Play Mas (Royal Court, London) 1974, Black Slaves, White Chains (Royal Court Theatre Upstairs, London) 1975, Bread (Young Vic, London) 1976, Rum An' Coca Cola (Royal Court, London) 1976, Another Tuesday (ICA, London) 1978, More, More (ICA, London) 1978, Independence (Bush Theatre, London) 1979, Welcome Home Jacko (Factory, London) 1979, A Dying Business (Riverside Studios, London) 1980, Meetings (Phoenix Theatre, New York) 1981, One Rule (Riverside Studios, London) 1981, The Playboy of the West Indies (Oxford) 1984, The Trinidad Sisters (Donmar Warehouse, London) 1988, The Coup: A Play of Revolutionary Dreams (London) 1991, A Small World (Southwark Playhouse, London) 1996. *Television writing:* No Problem (sitcom, Channel 4) 1983. *Literary Agent:* Judy Daish Associates Ltd, 2 St Charles Place, London, W10 6EG, England. *Telephone:* (20) 8964-8811. *Fax:* (20) 8964-8966. *E-mail:* emily@judydaish.demon.co.uk.

MATURA, Thaddee, LicTh; French/Canadian Franciscan monk, theologian and scholar; b. 24 Oct. 1922, Zalesie Wielkie, Poland. *Education:* Pontificio Ateneo Antoniano, Rome, Studio Biblico Francescano, Jerusalem. *Career:* entered Franciscan Order 1940; mem. Tantur Ecumenical Inst., Jerusalem 1973–75; religious counsellor, all cloistered monasteries, France 1981–90. *Publications:* Célibat et communauté: Les Fondements évangéliques de la vie religieuse (trans. as Celibacy and Community: The Gospel Foundation for Religious Life) 1967, La Vie religieuse au tournant (trans. as The Crisis of Religious Life) 1971, Readings in Franciscanism (ed. with Dacian Francis Bluma) 1972, La Naissance d'un charisme (trans. as The Birth of a Movement) 1973, Le Projet évangélique de François d'Assise aujourd-hui (trans. as The Gospel Life of Francis of Assisi Today) 1977, Le Radicalisme évangélique (trans. as Gospel Radicalism) 1978, Franz von Assisi (with Anton Rotzetter, trans. as Gospel Living: Francis of Assisi Yesterday and Today) 1981, François d'Assise, Ecrits (with Theophile Desbonnets) 1981, Suivre Jésus 1983, Claire d'Assise, Ecrits (with Marie-France Becker) 1985, Une Absence ardente 1988, Dieu le Père trés saint 1990, Chants de terre étrangere 1991, Prier 15 jours avec François d'Assise (trans. as A Dwelling Place for the Most High) 1994, François d'Assise 'auteur spirituel' (trans. as Francis of Assisi: The Message in his Writings) 1996, François d'Assise, maître de vie spirituelle (trans. as Francis of Assisi, Writer and Spiritual Master) 2000. *Address:* 33 rue de la Porte-Evèque, 84000 Avignon, France. *Telephone:* (4) 32-76-86-55. *E-mail:* thaddee.matura@wanadoo.fr (home).

MATVEJEVIC, Predrag; Croatian writer; b. 1932, Mostar. *Career:* frm Prof. of French Literature, Zagreb Univ., Prof. of Comparative Literatures, Sorbonne, Paris; currently teaches at New Sorbonne, Paris, and Slavic Studies, La Sapienza Univ., Rome; Vice-Pres., Int. PEN, London; Pres., Foundation Laboratori Mediterraneo, Naples; f. mem. Sarajevo Asscn (Paris and Rome). *Publications:* Pour une poétique de l'événement, 1979; Breviario Mediterraneo, 1987; Epistolario dell'altra Europa, 1992; Sarajevo Motta, 1995; Ex Jugoslavia. Diario di una guerra, 1995; Golfo di Venezia; Mondo Ex - Confessioni, 1996; Tra asilo ed esilio, 1998; Il Mediterraneo e l'Europa lezioni al College de France, 1998; I signori della guerra, 1999; Isolario mediterraneo, 2000. *Honours:* European Essay Prize 1992, French European Book Prize 1993, Légion d'honneur. *Address:* c/o International PEN, 9–10 Charterhouse Bldgs, Goswell Road, London, EC1M 7AT, England. *E-mail:* matvejevic@mclink.it. *Website:* giardini.sm/matvejevic.

MATVEYEVA, Novella Nikolaevna; Russian poet and chansonnier; b. 7 Oct. 1934, Pushkin, nr Leningrad; d. of Nikolai Nikolaevich Matveye-Bodryi and Nadejda Timofeevna Matveyeva (Orleneva); m. Ivan Semyonovich Kiuru 1963. *Recordings:* A Gipsy Girl 1966, What a Strong Wind! 1966, Poems and Songs 1973, A Princess on a Peascod 1980, A Trail is my Home 1982, (with Ivan Kiuru) The Music of Light 1984, My Small Raven 1985, Ballads 1985, A Red-haired Girl 1986, The Unseverable Circle 1991, (with I. Kiuru) The Poetic Dialogue 1993, (with I. Kiuru) Hosanna to Skhodnya 1993, Sonnets to Dashkova 1994, Minuet 1994. *Publications:* Lirika 1961, Little Ship 1963, Selected Lyrics 1964, The Soul of Things 1966, Reflection of a Sunbeam 1966, School for Swallows 1973, River 1978, The Song's Law 1983, The Land of the Surf 1983, Rabbit's Village 1984, Selected Works 1986, Praising the Labour 1987, An Unseverable Circle 1988, Poems 1988; (play) The Foretelling of an Eagle (in Theatre magazine) 1988. *Address:* Kammergerski per. 2, Apt. 42, 103009 Moscow, Russia. *Telephone:* (495) 292-33-61.

MAUGARLONNE, Mathurin (see George, François)

MAUPIN, Armistead Jones, Jr; American writer; b. 13 May 1944, s. of Armistead Jones Maupin and the late Diana Jane (née Barton) Maupin. *Education:* Univ. of North Carolina. *Career:* reporter, News and Courier, Charleston, SC 1970–71; Associated Press, San Francisco 1971–72; Account Exec. Lowry Russom and Leeper Public Relations 1973; columnist, Pacific Sun Magazine 1974; publicist, San Francisco Opera 1975; serialist, San Francisco Chronicle 1976–77, 1981, 1983; Commentator K.R.O.N.-TV San Francisco 1979; serialist, San Francisco Examiner 1986; Exec. Producer Armistead Maupin's Tales of the City 1993; contrib. to New York Times, Los Angeles Times and others. *Film:* The Night Listener (adapted from his book, exec. prod.) 2006. *Publications:* Tales of the City (Big Gay Read Award 2006) 1978, More Tales of the City 1980, Further Tales of the City 1982, Babycakes 1984, Significant Others 1987, Sure of You 1989, 28 Barbary Lane 1990, Back to Barbary Lane 1991, Maybe the Moon 1992, The Essential Clive Baker (co-author) 1999, The Night Listener 2000, Michael Tolliver Lives 2007; librettist: Heart's Desire 1990. *Honours:* numerous awards, including: Freedom Leader-ship Award, Freedoms Foundation 1972, Communications Award, Metropo-litan Elections Comm., LA 1989, Exceptional Achievement Award, American Libraries Asscn 1990, Outstanding Miniseries Award, Gay and Lesbian Alliance Against Defamation 1994. *Address:* c/o Literary Bent, PO Box 4109990, Suite 528, San Francisco, CA 94141 (office); c/o Amanda Urban, 40 West 57th Street, Floor 16, New York, NY 10019, USA. *E-mail:* inquiries@literarybent.cor (office).

MAVOR, Elizabeth Osborne; British author; b. 17 Dec. 1927, Glasgow, Scotland. *Education:* St Andrews, and St Leonard's and St Anne's Colleges, Oxford. *Publications:* Summer in the Greenhouse, 1959; The Temple of Flora, 1961; The Virgin Mistress: A Biography of the Duchess of Kingston (aka The Virgin Mistress: A Study in Survival: The Life of the Duchess of Kingston) 1964; The Redoubt, 1967; The Ladies of Llangollen: A Study in Romantic Friendship, 1971; A Green Equinox, 1973; Life with the Ladies of Llangollen, 1984; The Grand Tour of William Beckford, 1986; The White Solitaire, 1988; The American Journals of Fanny Kemble, 1990; The Grand Tours of Katherine Wilmot, France 1801–3 and Russia 1805–7, 1992; The Captain's Wife, The South American Journals of Maria Graham 1821–23, 1993. *Literary Agent:* Curtis Brown Ltd, Haymarket House, 28–29 Haymarket, London,

SW1Y 4SP, England. *Telephone:* (20) 7393-4400. *Fax:* (20) 7393-4401. *E-mail:* info@curtisbrown.co.uk. *Website:* www.curtisbrown.co.uk.

MAXWELL, Catherine (Cathy) Fern, BA; American writer; b. 17 July 1953, Memphis, TN; m. Kevin M. Maxwell 1979; one s. two d. *Education:* Washington Univ. *Publications:* All Things Beautiful 1994, Treasured Vows 1996, You and No Other 1996, Falling in Love Again 1997. *Honours:* co-recipient first place award Reader's Voice Best Read of 1994, Romantic Times Award for Best Historical Love and Laughter 1996. *Literary Agent:* Rowland-Axelrod, 510 E 23rd Street, Suite 8-G, New York, NY 10010-5020, USA. *Address:* PO Box 1532, Midlothian, VA 23113, USA. *E-mail:* CathyMaxwell@ msn.com.

MAXWELL, Douglas; British playwright; b. 1974. *Plays:* The Chameleon's Play 1997, The Crusader 1998, Helmet 1999, Our Bad Magnet 2000, Decky Does a Bronco 2001, Variety 2002. *Honours:* Fringe First, Edinburgh Festival. *Literary Agent:* PFD, Drury House, 34–43 Russell Street, London, WC2B 5HA, England. *Telephone:* (20) 7344-1000. *Fax:* (20) 7836-9543. *Website:* www.pfd.co.uk.

MAXWELL, Glyn Meurig, BA, MA; British poet, writer and editor; b. 7 Nov. 1962, Welwyn Garden City, Hertfordshire, England. *Education:* Worcester Coll., Oxford, Boston Univ., USA. *Career:* mem. PEN, Poetry Soc. *Publications:* Tale of the Mayor's Son (poems) 1990, Out of the Rain (poems) 1992, Gnyss the Magnificent: Three Verse Plays 1993, Blue Burneau (novel) 1994, Rest for the Wicked (poems) 1995, The Breakage 1998, Time's Fool 2001, The Sugar Mile (poems) 2005; contrib. to reviews, journals and magazines. *Honours:* Poetry Book Society Choice 1990, and Recommendation 1992, Eric Gregory Award 1991, Somerset Maugham Award 1993. *Address:* c/o Bloodaxe Books Ltd, Highgreen, Tarset, Northumberland NE48 1RP, England.

MAXWELL, Gordon Stirling, MA, FRSA; British archaeologist; b. 21 March 1938, Edinburgh, Scotland; m. Kathleen Mary King 1961, two d. *Education:* University of St Andrews. *Career:* Curatorial Officer, Royal Commission for Ancient and Historical Monuments, Scotland, 1964–; Fellow Soc. of Antiquaries of London, Soc. of Antiquaries of Scotland. *Publications:* The Impact of Aerial Reconnaissance on Archaeology (ed.), 1983; Rome's Northwest Frontier: The Antonine Wall, 1983; The Romans in Scotland, 1989; A Battle Lost: Romans and Caledonians at Mons Graupius, 1990. Contributions: Britannia; Proceedings of the Society of Antiquaries of Scotland; Glasgow Archaeological Journal.

MAXWELL, Ian, MA; British/French publisher; b. 15 June 1956, Maisons-Laffitte, France; s. of the late (Ian) Robert Maxwell and of Elisabeth Meynard; brother of Kevin Maxwell; m. 1st Laura Plumb 1991 (divorced 1998); m. 2nd Tara Dudley Smith 1999. *Education:* Marlborough Coll. and Balliol Coll., Oxford. *Career:* Man. Dir Pergamon Press France 1980–81; Jt Man. Dir Pergamon Pres. GmbH 1980; Marketing Dir Pergamon Press Inc. 1982–83; Dir Sales Devt BPCC PLC 1985–86; Dir Group Marketing BPCC PLC (now Maxwell Communication Corpn PLC) 1986; Chair. Agence Centrale de Presse, Paris 1986–89; Dir TFI TV station, Paris 1987–89; CEO Maxwell Pergamon Publrs 1988–89; Jt Man. Dir Maxwell Communication Corpn 1988–91; Acting Chair. Mirror Group Newspapers 1991; Dir New York Daily News –1991; Telemonde Holdings 1997–; publishing consultant Westbourne Communications Ltd 1993; Publr Maximov Publs Ltd. 1995–; Chair. Derby Co. Football Club 1984–87, Vice-Chair. 1987–91; mem. Nat. Theatre Devt Council 1986; Pres. Club d'Investissement Media 1988.

MAXWELL, John (see Freemantle, Brian Harry)

MAXWELL, Patricia Anne, (Jennifer Blake, Maxine Patrick, Patricia Ponder, Elizabeth Trehearne); American writer and poet; b. 9 March 1942, Winn Parish, LA; m. Jerry R. Maxwell 1957; two s. two d. *Career:* writer-in-residence, Univ. of Northeastern Louisiana; mem. Nat. League of American Pen Women, Romance Writers of America. *Publications include:* Love's Wild Desire, 1977; Tender Betrayal, 1979; The Storm and the Splendor, 1979; Golden Fancy, 1980; Embrace and Conquer, 1981; Royal Seduction, 1983; Surrender in Moonlight, 1984; Midnight Waltz, 1985; Fierce Eden, 1985; Royal Passion, 1986; Prisoner of Desire, 1986; Southern Rapture, 1987; Louisiana Dawn, 1987; Perfume of Paradise, 1988; Love and Smoke, 1989; Spanish Serenade, 1990; Joy and Anger, 1991; Wildest Dreams, 1992; Arrow to the Heart, 1993; Shameless, 1994; Silver-Tongued Devil, 1996; Tigress, 1996; Garden of Scandal, 1997. Contributions: anthologies and periodicals. *Honours:* Best Historical Romance Novelist of the Year, 1985; Reviewer's Choices, 1984, 1995, Romantic Times; Golden Treasure Award, Romance Writers of America, 1987; Romance Hall of Fame, Affaire de Coeur, 1995; Frank Waters Award for Writing Excellence, 1997. *Literary Agent:* Richard Curtis Associates Inc., 171 E 74th Street, Second Floor, New York, NY 10021, USA. *Website:* www.curtisagency.com.

MAY, Derwent James, British writer and journalist; b. 29 April 1930, Eastbourne, Sussex, England; m. Yolanta Izabella Sypniewska; one s. one d. *Education:* Lincoln Coll., Oxford. *Career:* theatre and film critic Continental Daily Mail, Paris 1952–53; Lecturer in English Univ. of Indonesia 1955–58; Sr Lecturer in English Univs of Łódź and Warsaw 1959–63; chief leader writer TLS 1963–65; Literary Ed. The Listener 1965–86; Literary and Arts Ed. Sunday Telegraph 1986–90, The European 1990–91; European Arts Ed. The Times 1992–; mem., Booker Prize jury 1978, Hawthornden Prize cttee 1987–; mem. Beefsteak Club, Garrick Club. *Publications:* fiction: The Professionals 1964, Dear Parson 1969, The Laughter in Djakarta 1973, A Revenger's

Comedy 1979; non-fiction: Proust 1983, The Times Nature Diary 1983, Hannah Arendt 1986, The New Times Nature Diary 1993, Feather Reports 1996, Critical Times: The History of the Times Literary Supplement 2001, How To Attract Birds to Your Garden 2001, The Times: A Year in Nature Notes 2004; contrib. to Encounter, Hudson Review. *Address:* 45 Burghley Road, London, NW5 1UH, England.

MAY, Gita, MA, PhD; American academic and writer; b. 16 Sept. 1929, Brussels, Belgium; m. Irving May 1947. *Education:* Hunter Coll., CUNY, Columbia Univ. *Career:* Prof. of French and Chair Dept of French, Columbia Univ. 1968–94; Pres. American Soc. for 18th Century Studies 1985–86; Gen. Ed., The Age of Revolution and Romanticism 1990–; mem. Société Française d'Étude du 18e Siècle, Société Diderot, North American Soc. for the Study of Rousseau, MLA (exec. council 1980–83); mem. editorial bds, including Romanic Review 1959–, French Review 1975–86, 1998–, Women in French Studies 2000–. *Publications:* Diderot Studies III (ed. with O. Fellows) 1961, Madame Roland and the Age of Revolution 1970, Stendhal and the Age of Napoleon 1977, Diderot: Essais sur la peinture, Vol. XIV of his complete works (ed.) 1984, Pensées détachées sur la peinture 1995, Rebecca West 1996, Anita Brookner 1997, Graham Swift 1999; contrib. to Dictionary of Literary Biography 2003, Voltaire's Candide 2003, Elisabeth Vigée Le Brun: The Odyssey of an Artist in an Age of Revolution 2005; other books and professional journals. *Honours:* Guggenheim Fellowship 1964, Officier, Ordre des Palmes Académiques 1981, Nat. Endowment for the Humanities Sr Fellow 1971, Columbia Univ. Van Amringe Distinguished Book Award 1971, named Outstanding Mentor by Women in French Studies 2003, honoured by American Soc. for 18th Century Studies as one of its great teachers. *Address:* c/o Department of French, Columbia University, 516 Philosophy Hall, New York, NY 10027, USA (office). *Telephone:* (212) 854-3905 (office); (212) 864-5997 (home). *Fax:* (212) 854-5863 (office). *E-mail:* gm9@columbia.edu.

MAY, Julian, (Lee N. Falconer, Ian Thorne); American writer and editor; b. 10 July 1931, Chicago, IL; m. Thaddeus E. Ditky 1953 (died 1991); two s. one d. *Career:* science ed. for a Chicago encyclopedia publisher 1953–57; co-founder (with Ted Ditky) Publication Associates 1957–. *Publications include:* Dune Roller (short story) 1951, Star of Wonder (short story) 1953, Robots and Thinking Machines (non-fiction) 1961, Land Beneath the Sea 1972, The Many Colored Land (Pliocene Exiles series) 1981, The Golden Torc (Pliocene Exiles series) 1982, The Nonborn King (Pliocene Exiles series) 1983, The Adversary (Pliocene Exiles series) 1984, Intervention (Intervention series) 1987, The Surveillance (Intervention series) 1988, Metaconcert (Intervention series) 1988, Black Trillium (with Marion Zimmer Bradley and Andre Norton) 1990, Jack the Bodiless (Galactic Milieu series) 1991, Blood Trillium (with Marion Zimmer Bradley and Andre Norton) 1992, Golden Trillium (with Marion Zimmer Bradley and Andre Norton) 1993, Diamond Mask (Galactic Milieu series) 1994, Magnificat (Galactic Milieu series) 1996, Sky Trillium 1997, Perseus Spur (Rampart World series) 1998, Orion Arm (Rampart World series) 1999, Sagittarius Whorl (Rampart World series) 2001, Conqueror's Moon (Boreal Moon series) 2003, Ironcrown Moon (Boreal Moon series) 2004, Sorcerer's Moon (Boreal Moon series) 2005; as Lee N. Falconer: The Gazeteer of the Hyborian World of Conan 1977; as Ian Thorne (adaptations): Frankenstein 1977, King Kong 1977, The Wolf Man 1977, Godzilla 1977, Dracula 1977, Mad Scientists 1977, The Loch Ness Monster 1978, Murders in the Rue Morgue 1978, Bigfoot 1978, Bermuda Triangle (with Howard Schroeder) 1978, Ancient Astronauts (co-author) 1978, Monster Tales of Native Americans (with Barbara Howell Furan) 1978, UFOs 1978, Creature from the Black Lagoon 1981, The Mummy 1982, Frankenstein Meets Wolfman 1982, Deadly Mantis 1982, The Blob 1982, It Came from Outer Space 1982, Phantom of the Opera 1987, Invisible Man 1987. *Address:* PO Box 851, Mercer Island, WA 98040, USA.

MAY, Naomi Young, DFA; British novelist, journalist and painter; b. 27 March 1934, Glasgow, Scotland; m. Nigel May 1964; two s. one d. *Education:* Slade School of Fine Art, London and Univ. of London. *Career:* mem. PEN. *Publications:* At Home 1969, radio adaptation 1987, The Adventurer 1970, Troubles 1976; contrib. to anthologies, newspapers and magazines. *Honours:* Slade School of Fine Art History of Art Prize. *Address:* 6 Lion Gate Gardens, Richmond, Surrey TW9 2DF, England.

MAY, Baron (Life Peer), cr. 2001, of Oxford in the County of Oxfordshire; **Robert McCredie May,** Kt, AC, PhD, FRS, FAAS; Australian biologist and academic; b. 1 Aug. 1936, Sydney; s. of Henry W. May and Kathleen M. McCredie; m. Judith Feiner 1962; one d. *Education:* Sydney Boys' High School, Univ. of Sydney. *Career:* Gordon MacKay Lecturer in Applied Math., Harvard Univ. 1959–61; at Univ. of Sydney 1962–73, Sr Lecturer in Theoretical Physics 1962–64, Reader 1964–69, Personal Chair 1969–73; Class of 1877 Prof. of Biology, Princeton Univ. 1973–88, Chair. Univ. Research Bd 1977–88; Royal Soc. Research Prof., Dept of Zoology, Oxford Univ. and Imperial Coll., London 1988–; Chief Scientific Adviser to UK Govt and Head, Office of Science and Tech. 1995–2000; Pres. Royal Soc. 2000–05; mem. Australian Acad. of Sciences 1991–, Academia Europaea 1994–; Fellow Merton Coll., Oxford 1988–; foreign mem. NAS 1992–; Trustee British Museum 1989–, Royal Botanic Gardens, Kew 1991–95, WWF (UK) 1990–94, Nuffield Foundation 1993–; Croonian Lecturer, Hitchcock Lecturer, John M. Prather Lecturer. *Publications:* Stability and Complexity in Model Ecosystems 1973, Exploitation of Marine Communities (ed.) 1974, Theoretical Ecology: Principles and Applications (ed.) 1976, Population Biology of Infectious Diseases (ed.) 1982, Exploitation of Marine Ecosystems (ed.)

1984, Perspectives in Ecological Theory (ed.) 1989, Population Regulation and Dynamics (ed.) 1990, Infectious Diseases of Humans: Transmission and Control (with R. M. Anderson) 1991, Large Scale Ecology and Conservation Biology 1994, Extinction Rates 1995, Evolution of Biological Diversity 1999, Virus Dynamics: the Mathematical Foundations of Immunology and Virology (with Martin Nowak) 2000. *Honours:* numerous hon. degrees; Crafoord Prize, Royal Swedish Acad. 1996, Balzan Prize 1998; MacArthur Award, Weldon Memorial Prize, Edgeworth David Medal. *Address:* c/o House of Lords, London, SW1A 0PW, England (office).

MAY, Sarah, BA; British writer; b. (Sarah Hutchinson), 1972, Northumberland; m.; two s. *Education:* Univs of London and Lancaster. *Publications:* novels: The Nudist Colony 1999, Spanish City 2002, The Internationals 2003, The Rise and Fall of the Queen of Suburbia 2006. *Honours:* Amazon.co.uk Writers' Bursary 2001. *Address:* c/o Chatto & Windus, 20 Vauxhall Bridge Road, London, SW1V 2SA, England. *Telephone:* (20) 7840-8540. *Fax:* (20) 7233-6117. *Website:* www.randomhouse.com.

MAY, Stephen James, (Julian Poole), AA, BA, MA, DLitt; American writer and academic; b. 10 Sept. 1946, Toronto, Ont. Canada; m. Caroline Casteel 1972; one s. *Education:* El Camino Coll., California State Univ. at Carson, Int. Univ., Mumbai. *Career:* Instructor in English, Colorado Northwestern Coll. 1992–98; Visiting Prof. of English, Univ. of Northern Colorado 1999–; currently Visiting Prof. of English and Literature, Front Range Community Coll., Fort Collins, Colo; mem. Colorado Authors' League, James Michener Soc., Soc. of Southwestern Authors, Western Writers of America, World Literary Acad., Zane Grey Soc. *Publications:* Pilgrimage: A Journey Through Colorado's History and Culture 1987, Intruders in the Dust 1988, Fire from the Skies 1990, Footloose on the Santa Fe Trail 1992, A Land Observed 1993, Zane Grey: Romancing the West 1997, Maverick Heart: The Further Adventures of Zane Grey 2000, Rascals 2001, James A. Michener: A Writer's Journey 2005; contrib. to Denver Post, Frontier Rocky Mountain News, Southwest Art, Artists of the Rockies, National Geographic. *Honours:* Western Writers of America Non-Fiction Award 2001, Colorado Authors' League Non-Fiction Award 2001. *Address:* 731 Peregrine Run, Fort Collins, CO 80524, USA. *E-mail:* stepkm@msn.com.

MAYER, Bernadette; American poet and writer; b. 12 May 1945, New York, NY; one s. two d. *Education:* New School for Social Research, New York. *Career:* Resident Dir, St Mark's Poetry Project, Greenwich Village, 1980–84; various workshops. *Publications:* Ceremony Latin, 1964; Story, 1968; Moving, 1971; The Basketball Article (with Anne Waldman), 1975; Memory, 1975; Studying Hunger, 1975; Poetry, 1976; Eruditio Ex Memoria, 1977; The Golden Book of Words, 1978; Midwinter Day, 1982; Incidents Reports Sonnets, 1984; Utopia, 1984; Mutual Aid, 1985; The Art of Science Writing (with Dales Worsley), 1989; Sonnets, 1989; The Formal Field of Kissing, 1990; A Bernadette Mayer Reader, 1992; The Desires of Mothers to Please Others in Letters, 1994. Contributions: anthologies.

MAYER, Christian, (Carl Amery); German writer; b. 9 April 1922, Munich; s. of Dr Anton Mayer and Anna Mayer (née Schneller); m. Marijane Gerth 1950; three s. two d. *Education:* Humanistisches Gymnasium, Freising and Passau, Univ. of Munich and Catholic Univ. of America, Washington, DC. *Career:* freelance author 1949–; Dir of City Libraries, Munich 1967–71; mem., fmr Chair. German Writers' Asscn; co-founder German Literary Fund 1980; Chair. E. F. Schumachergesellschaft 1980; Pres. PEN Centre of FRG 1989–90. *Publications:* novels: Der Wettbewerb 1954, Die Grosse Deutsche Tour 1958, Das Königsprojekt 1974, Der Untergang der Stadt Passau 1975, An den Feuern der Leyermark 1979, Die Wallfahrer 1986, Das Geheimnis der Krypta 1990; essays: Die Kapitulation 1963, Fragen an Welt und Kirche 1967, Das Ende der Vorsehung 1972, Natur als Politik 1976, Leb Wohl Geliebtes Volk der Bayern 1980, G. K. Chesterton oder Der Kampf gegen die Kälte 1981, Die Botschaft des Jahrtausends 1994, Hitler als Vorläufer 1998, Global Exit 2002; various radio essays, radio plays, translations, etc. *Honours:* Fed. Cross of Merit, First Class; Literary Prize, City of Munich 1991. *Address:* Drächslstrasse 7, 81541 Munich, Germany. *Telephone:* (89) 486134. *Fax:* (89) 4801997 (home). *E-mail:* carl.amery@t-online.de.

MAYER, Peter, BA, MA; American/British book publisher; *President, Overlook Press, New York; Gerald Duckworth Publishers, London*; b. 28 March 1936, Hampstead, London, England; s. of Alfred Mayer and Lee Mayer; one d. *Education:* Columbia Univ., New York, Christ Church, Oxford. *Career:* Grad. Fellow, Indiana Univ.; Fulbright Fellow, Freie Universität Berlin 1959; worked with Orion Press before joining Avon books for 14 years; Publr and Pres. Pocketbooks 1976–78; Chief. Exec. Penguin Books Ltd, London 1978–96, later Chair. Penguin USA; exec. positions with The Overlook Press (co-f. with his father 1970) 1996–, acquired Ardis Publrs 2001, Duckworth Publrs 2003, Nonesuch Press 2005; mem. Bd Asscn of American Publrs –2003, Bd Frankfurt Bookfair Fellowship, Bd Nat. Book Foundation –2003), New York Univ. Publrs Advisory Bd, Scholastic Bd of Dirs, German Book Office. *Publications:* An Idea is Like a Bird 1963, The Pacifist Conscience (ed.) 1966. *Honours:* Chevalier and Officier, Ordre des Arts et des Lettres 1996; Most Distinguished Publr of the Year 1995, Foundation of Publrs' and Booksellers' Asscn's in India Award for Oustanding Contrib. to Int. Publishing 1996. *Address:* Duckworth Publishers, 90–93 Cowcross Street, London, EC1M 6BF, England (office); The Overlook Press, 141 Wooster Street, New York, NY 10012, USA. *Telephone:* (20) 7490-7300 (London) (office); (212) 673-2223 (New York) (office). *Fax:* (20) 7490-0080 (London) (office); (212) 673-2296 (New York)

(office). *E-mail:* info@duckworth-publishers.co.uk (office); sales@overlookpress.com (office). *Website:* www.ducknet.co.uk (office); www.overlookpress.com (office).

MAYER, Robert, BA, MS; American writer; b. 24 Feb. 1939, New York, NY; m. La Donna Cocilovo 1989; one step-d. *Education:* City College, CUNY, Columbia University. *Career:* reporter and columnist, Newsday, 1961–71; Managing Ed., Santa Fe Reporter, 1988–90. *Publications:* Superfolks, 1977; The Execution, 1979; Midge and Decker, 1982; Sweet Salt, 1984; The Grace of Shortstops, 1984; The Search, 1986; The Dreams of Ada, 1987; I, JFK, 1989. Contributions: Vanity Fair; New York Magazine; Travel and Leisure; Rocky Mountain Magazine; New Mexico Magazine; Santa Fe Reporter; Newsday. *Honours:* National Headliner Award, 1968; Mike Berger Awards, 1969, 1971.

MAYER-KOENIG, Wolfgang; Austrian poet, writer, editor and academic; *Editor, LOG literary magazine*; b. 28 March 1946, Vienna. *Education:* Univs of Vienna, Saarbrücken and Los Angeles. *Career:* univ. Prof. 1987–; Ed. int. literary magazine, LOG; mem. Acad. Tiberina, Acad. Burckhardt St Gallen, Acad. Consentina, Acad. Europa; mem. Austrian Writers' Asscn (bd mem.), PEN, Robert-Musil Archive Asscn (vice-pres. 1975–), Europa Literaturkreis Kapfenberg. *Publications:* Sichtbare Pavilions 1969, Stichmarken 1970, Texte und Bilder 1972, Sprache-Politik-Aggression 1975, Texte und Zeichnungen 1975, Psychologie und Literatursprache 1976, Language-Politics-Agression 1977, Italienreisen Goethes 1978, Robert Musils Moglichkeitsstil 1979, In den Armen unseres Waerters 1980, Chagrin non dechiffré 1986, A Hatalom bonyolult Angyala 1988, Underestimated Deep 1989, A Complicated Angel 1989, Responsibility of Writing: Contributions to a Modern Grammar 1990, Risks of Writing 1991, Verzögerung des Vertrauens 1995, Colloquios nel Cuarto 1996, Fire and Ice 1996, Mirror Wading 1996, Verkannte Tiefe 1996, Grammatik der Modernen Poesie 1996, Behind Desires Deficits 1997, Confessions of an Angry Loving European 1999, Another Place for Victory 2000, Visiting 2001, The Three Dolphins 2004, The Necessary Doubt 2005, The Adoption 2005; contrib. to various publications. *Honours:* Officer Order of Merit, Egypt 1974, Commander Order of St Agatha, San Marino 1982, Ordre du Mérite Africain 1983, Chevalier, Ordre des Arts et des Lettres 1987, Golden Cross Order of Eagle of Tyrol 1988, Papal Lateran Cross first class, Grand Cross of Honour, Govt of Carinthia 1993, Cross of merit first class of Lilienfeld 1984, Cross of Merit of Greek Orthodox Papal Patriarch of Alexandria, Egypt, Star of Peace, Rome, Italy; Theodor Körner Prize for Poetry 1974, Austrian Cross of Honour for Science and Arts 1974, Cross of Honour, Lower Austria 1982, Int. ARC Golden medal of merit 1983, Premio Prometeo Aureo Lazio, Vienna Art Foundation Prize, New Century Award, Int. Peace Prize 2005. *Address:* Hernalser Guertel 41, 1170 Vienna (office); Haubenbiglstrasse 1A, 1190 Vienna, Austria (home). *Telephone:* 223652306 (office); 6643570361 (home). *Fax:* 13707620 (home). *E-mail:* univ.prof.mayer-koenig@aon.at (home).

MAYHAR, Ardath, (Frank Cannon, Frances Hurst, John Killdeer); American writer, poet, editor and instructor; b. 20 Feb. 1930, Timpson, TX; m. Joe E. Mayhar June 1958. *Education:* self-educated. *Career:* mem. SFWA, Western Writers of America, Novelists Ink, writing instructor. *Publications include:* How the Gods Wove in Kyrannon 1979, Soul Singer of Tyrnos 1981, Runes of the Lyre 1982, Lords of the Triple Moons 1983, The World Ends in Hickory Hollow 1985, A Place of Silver Silence 1987, Texas Gunsmoke 1988, Far Horizons 1994, Island in the Swamp 1994, Hunters of the Plains 1995, High Mountain Winter 1996, Riddles and Dreams Images 2003; contribs to quarterlies and magazines. *Honours:* awards and prizes for fiction and poetry. *Address:* 533 CR 486, Chireno, TX 75937, USA (office). *Telephone:* (936) 362-2913 (home). *Fax:* (936) 362-2517 (home). *E-mail:* ardathm@netdot.com. *Website:* w2.netdot.com/ardat.html (office); www.renebooks.com.

MAYNE, Richard John, MA, PhD; British writer and broadcaster; b. 2 April 1926, London, England; m. 1st Margot Ellingworth Lyon; m. 2nd Jocelyn Mudie Ferguson; two d. *Education:* Trinity Coll., Cambridge. *Career:* Rome Correspondent New Statesman 1953–54; Official of the European Community, Luxembourg and Brussels 1956–63; Personal Asst to Jean Monnet, Paris 1963–66; Paris Correspondent 1963–73, Co-Ed. 1990–94, Encounter; Visiting Prof. Univ. of Chicago 1970; Dir Federal Trust, London 1971–73; Head UK Offices of the European Commission, London 1973–79; film critic Sunday Telegraph, London 1987–89, The European 1990–98; mem. Soc. of Authors, Royal Inst. of Int. Affairs, Federal Trust for Education and Research. *Publications:* The Community of Europe 1962, The Institutions of the European Community 1968, The Recovery of Europe 1970, The Europeans 1972, Europe Tomorrow (ed.) 1972, The New Atlantic Challenge (ed.) 1975, The Memoirs of Jean Monnet (trans.) 1978, Postwar: The Dawn of Today's Europe 1983, Western Europe: A Handbook (ed.) 1987, Federal Union: The Pioneers (with John Pinder) 1990, Europe: A History of its Peoples (trans.) 1990, History of Europe (trans.) 1993, A History of Civilizations (trans.) 1994, The Language of Sailing 2000, In Victory, Magnanimity, in Peace Goodwill: A History of Wilton Park 2003, Cross Channel Currents: 100 Years of the Entente Cordiale (co-ed.) 2004, Nuances 2006; contrib. to newspapers and magazines. *Honours:* Scott-Moncrieff Prize for Trans. from French 1978, Officier, Ordre des Arts et des Lettres 2002. *Address:* Albany Cottage, 24 Park Village East, Regent's Park, London, NW1 7PZ, England. *Telephone:* (20) 7387-6654 (home). *Fax:* (20) 7383-3004 (home).

MAYNE, Seymour, BA, MA, PhD; Canadian academic, poet, writer, editor and translator; *Professor of English, University of Ottawa*; b. 18 May 1944,

Montréal, QC. *Education:* McGill Univ., Univ. of British Columbia. *Career:* Lecturer, Univ. of British Columbia 1972; Lecturer, Univ. of Ottawa 1973, Asst Prof. 1973–78, Assoc. Prof. 1978–85, Prof. of English 1985–; Visiting Prof., Hebrew Univ. of Jerusalem 1979–80, Visiting Prof. and Scholar 1983–84, 1992, Writer-in-Residence 1987–88; Visiting Prof., Concordia Univ., Montréal 1982–83, Univ. of La Laguna, Spain 1993; Adjunct Research Prof., Carleton Univ. 2002–05; Contributing Ed. Viewpoints 1982–90, Poetry Ed. 1990–95; Contributing Ed. Tel-Aviv Review 1989–96, Poet Lore 1992–2000, Jerusalem Review 1997–2001; Founder and Consulting Ed. Bywords 1990–2004, Graffito 1994–2000. *Publications:* That Monocycle the Moon 1964, Tiptoeing on the Mount 1965, From the Portals of Mouseholes 1966, Manimals 1969, Mouth 1970, For Stems of Light 1971, Face 1971, Name 1975, Diasporas 1977, The Impossible Promised Land: Poems New and Selected 1981, Children of Abel 1986, Diversions 1987, Six Ottawa Poets (with others) 1990, Killing Time 1992, The Song of Moses and Other Poems 1995, Five-O'Clock Shadows (with others) 1996, Dragon Trees 1997, City of the Hidden 1998, Carbon Filter 1999, Light Industry 2000, Hail: Word Sonnets 2002, Cinque Foil (with others) 2003, Ricochet: Word Sonnets 2004, El Viejo Sofá Azul 2004, Foreplay: An Anthology of Word Sonnets (co-ed.) 2004; ed. or co-ed. of 13 other books 1968–97; trans. or co-trans. of eight books 1974–98; contrib. to anthologies, books, journals, reviews and quarterlies. *Honours:* numerous grants and fellowships, Chester Macnaghten First Prize in Creative Writing 1962, J. I. Segal Prize in English-French Literature 1974, York Poetry Workshop Award 1975, American Literary Trans Asscn Poetry Trans. Award 1990, Jewish Book Cttee Prize 1994, Louis L. Lockshin Memorial Award 1997, Fuerstenberg-Aaron Prize 2000, Capital Educators' Award 2003, Excellence in Educ. Prize 2005. *Address:* Department of English, Faculty of Arts, University of Ottawa, PO Box 450, Station A, Ottawa, ON K1N 6N5, Canada (office). *Telephone:* (613) 562-5764 (office). *Fax:* (613) 562-5990 (office).

MAYO, Wendell, Jr, BS, BA, MFA, PhD; American academic and writer; *Professor of English, Bowling Green State University;* b. 16 Aug. 1953, Corpus Christi, Tex.; s. of Wendell Mayo and Blanche Soledad Durant; m. Deborah Masonis 1982. *Education:* Ohio State Univ., Ohio Univ., Univ. of Toledo, Vermont Coll. *Career:* Asst Prof. of English, Indiana Univ., Purdue Univ., Fort Wayne 1991–94; Asst Prof. of Creative Writing and Literature, Univ. of Southwestern Louisiana, Lafayette 1994–96; Asst Prof. of Creative Writing and Literature, then Assoc. Prof., then Prof. of English, Bowling Green State Univ., OH 1996–; mem. Bd Dirs American Professional Partnership for Lithuanian Educ. (APPLE) 1999–2001, Div. Chair. Language Arts, APPLE 1995–; mem. Associated Writing Programs; Fellow, Millay Colony for the Arts 1992, Master Fellow, Indiana Arts Comm. 1992, Yado Fellow 1992, 1994, 1996, Fellow, Edward F. Albee Foundation 1993. *Publications:* Centaur of the North (short stories) 1996, In Lithuanian Wood (novel), B Horror and Other Stories 1999, Vilko Valanda (short stories); contrib. to various reviews, quarterlies and magazines, including Harvard Review, Prairie Schooner, Western Humanities Review, Missouri Review, New Letters, The Yale Review, North American Review, Threepenny Review, and to anthologies, including City Wilds, 100% Pure Florida Fiction. *Honours:* First Prize for Fiction, Mississippi Valley Review 1995, New Delta Review 1996, Univ. of New Mexico Premio Aztlan 1997, Nat. Endowment for the Arts grant 2001, Fulbright grant 2002. *Address:* Department of English, Creative Writing Program, Bowling Green State University, Bowling Green, OH 43403 (office). *Telephone:* (419) 823-7005 (office). *Fax:* (419) 372-6805 (office). *E-mail:* wmayo@bgnet.bgsu.edu (office). *Website:* personal.bgsu.edu/~wmayo/ (home).

MAYRÖCKER, Friederike; Austrian writer and poet; b. 20 Dec. 1924, Vienna; d. of Franz and Friederike Mayröcker. *Education:* secondary school and teacher training Coll., Vienna. *Career:* English teacher 1946–68; first book published 1956; freelance writer 1969–; about 70 publications (prose, poetry, radio plays and children's books). *Recordings:* Sprech Klavier, Umarmungen. *Publications include:* Lorifari 1956, Die Abschiede, Gute Nacht, guten Morgen, Magische Blätter (four vols), Reise durch die Nacht, Das Herzzerreißende der Dinge, Winterglück, Mein Herz mein Zimmer mein Name, Gesammelte Prosa, Stilleben, Das besessere Alter, Ausgewählte Gedichte 1944–78, Lektion, Notizen auf einem Kamel (poems) 1996, five vols of Magische Blätter, mein Arbeitstirol, Die kommunizierenden Gefäsze 2003, Requiem für Ernst Jandl, Gesammelte Gedichte, Und ich schüttelte einen Liebling; play: Nada–Nichts. *Honours:* Dr hc; Österreichischer Würdigungspreis für Literatur 1975, Literature Prize (City of Vienna) 1977, Großes Österreichisches Staatspreis für Literatur, Roswitha-von-Gandersheim Preis, Austrian Insignia for Arts and Letters, Friedrich-Hölderlin-Preis 1993, Manuskripte-Preis 1994, Großer Literaturpreis der Bayerischen Akad. der Schönen Künste 1996, Georg-Büchner-Preis 2001, Premio Internazionale, Camaiore, Italy 2003. *Address:* Zentagasse 16/40, 1050 Vienna, Austria. *Telephone:* (1) 545-66-60. *Fax:* (1) 545-66-60.

MAYSON, Marina (see Rogers, Rosemary)

MAZER, Norma Fox; American writer; b. 15 May 1931, New York, NY; m. Harry Mazer 1950, one s. three d. *Education:* Antioch College, Syracuse University. *Publications:* I Trissy, 1971; A Figure of Speech, 1973; Saturday, The Twelfth of October, 1975; Dear Bill, Remember Me, 1976; The Solid Gold Kid, 1977; Up in Seth's Room, 1979; Mrs Fish, Ape and Me and the Dump Queen, 1980; Taking Terri Mueller, 1981; When We First Met, 1982; Summer Girls, Love Boys, and Other Stories, 1982; Someone To Love, 1983; Supergirl, 1984; Downtown, 1984; A, My Name is Ami, 1986; Three Sisters, 1986; B, My Name is Bunny, 1987; After the Rain, 1987; Silver, 1988; Heartbeat, 1989; Babyface, 1989; C, My Name is Cal, 1990; D, My Name is Danita, 1991; Bright Days, Stupid Nights, 1992; E, My Name is Emily, 1991; Out of Control, 1993. *Contributions:* English Journal; Alan Review; The Writer; Signal; Writing; Redbook; Playgirl; Voice; Ingenue. *Address:* Brown Gulf Road, Jamesville, NY 13078, USA.

MAZLISH, Bruce, MA, PhD; American historian and writer; *Professor of History Emeritus, Massachusetts Institute of Technology;* b. 15 Sept. 1923, New York, NY; m. 1st; three s., one d.; m. 2nd Neva Goodwin 1988. *Education:* Columbia Univ. *Career:* Instructor, Univ. of Maine 1946–48, Columbia Univ. 1949–50; Instructor, MIT 1950–53, Faculty 1955–, Prof. of History 1965–2004, Chair. History Section 1965–70, Head Dept of Humanities 1974–79, now Prof. of History Emer.; Dir American School, Madrid 1953–55; mem. American Acad. of Arts and Sciences, fellow; mem. bd of dirs, Rockefeller Family Fund 1987–97, Toynbee Prize Foundation (Pres. 1999–). *Publications:* The Western Intellectual Tradition (with J. Bronowski) 1960, The Riddle of History 1966, In Search of Nixon 1972, James and John Stuart Mill: Father and Son in the 19th Century 1975, The Revolutionary Ascetic 1976, Kissinger: The European Mind in American Policy 1976, The Meaning of Karl Marx 1984, A New Science: The Breakdown of Connections and the Birth of Sociology 1989, The Leader, the Led and the Psyche 1990, The Fourth Discontinuity: The Co-Evolution of Humans and Machines 1993, The Uncertain Sciences 1998, Civilization and Its Contexts 2004; editor: Psychoanalysis and History 1963, The Railroad and the Space Program: An Exploration in Historical Analogy 1965, Conceptualizing Global History (with Ralph Bultjens) 1993, Progress: Fact or Illusion? (with Leo Marx) 1996, The Global History Reader (with Akira Iriye) 2005; contrib. to professional journals. *Honours:* Clement Staff Essay Award 1968, Toynbee Prize 1986–87. *Address:* 11 Lowell Street, Cambridge, MA 02138, USA.

MAZOWER, Mark, BA, MA, PhD; British historian, academic and writer; *Professor of History, Birkbeck College, London. Education:* Univ. of Oxford, UK and Johns Hopkins Univ., USA. *Career:* Prof. of History, Birkbeck Coll., London; Prof. of History and Dir Center for Int. History, Columbia Univ.; Visiting Scholar Minda de Gunzburg Center for European Studies, Harvard Univ. *Publications:* Greece and the Inter-War Economic Crisis 1991, Inside Hitler's Greece: The Experience of Occupation 1941–44 (Fraenkel Prize in Contemporary History, Longman/History Today Book of the Year) 1993, The Policing of Politics in the Twentieth Century (ed.) 1997, Dark Continent: Europe's 20th Century 1998, After the War was Over: Reconstructing the Family, Nation and State in Greece 1943–60 2000, The Balkans 2000, Ideologies and National Identities: The Case of Twentieth-Century South-Eastern Europe (co-ed.) 2003, Salonica, City of Ghosts (Runciman Award) 2005; contrib. to The Nation, Financial Times. *Address:* School of History, Classics and Archaeology, Birkbeck College, Malet Street, London, WC1E 7HX, England (office); Columbia University, 503 Fayerweather Hall, 2960 Broadway, New York, NY 10027-6902, USA (office). *E-mail:* m.mazower@bbk .ac.uk (office); mm2669@columbia.edu (office). *Website:* www.bbk.ac.uk; www .columbia.edu; mazower.com.

MAZUR, Grace Dane, BA, MFA, PhD; American writer; b. 22 April 1944, Boston, MA; m. Barry C. Mazur; one s. *Education:* Harvard Coll., Harvard Univ., Warren Wilson Coll. *Career:* teacher, Harvard Univ. Extension School 1996–. *Publications:* Silk (short stories) 1996, Trespass (novel) 1998; contrib. to reviews and journals. *Honours:* Bread Loaf Literary Fellowship. *Address:* c/o Writers House, 21 W 26th Street, New York, NY 10010, USA.

MAZZANTINI, Margaret; Italian writer and actress; b. 27 Oct. 1961, Dublin, Ireland; m. Sergio Castellitto; three c. *Education:* Accademia di Arte Drammatica, Rome. *Films as actress:* Un caso di coscienza 1983, Lucas 1988, Nulla ci può fermare 1988, L'assassina 1989, Una fredda mattina di maggio 1990, Quando le montagne finiscono 1994, Paesaggio con figure 1995, Il cielo è sempre più blu 1995, Festival 1996, Il barbiere di rio 1996, Libero burro 1998. *Television as actress:* Antropophagus 1980, La voce 1982, Un delitto 1983, Venezia salvata 1985, Cheri 1985, Sentimental 1987, Cuore di mamma 1987, Duel of Love 1990, Cane sciolto II 1990, Eurocops 1990, Kaminsky, un flic a Moscou (series) 1991, Promo 1992. *Plays as actress:* Ifigenia 1982, Venezia salvata 1982–83, Le tre sorelle 1984–85, L'onesto Jago 1984–85, L'Alcade di Zalamea 1984–85, La signora Giulia 1985–86, Antigone 1986, Faust 1987, Mon Faust 1987, Bambino 1988, Praga magica-Valeria 1989, A piedi nudi nel parco 1992–93, Colpi bassi 1994, Manola 1994, 1995, 1996, 1998. *Publications:* Il catino di zinco (novel) (Premio Selezione Campiello, Premio Opera Prima Rapallo-Carige) 1994, Manola (play) 1994, Libero burro (screenplay) 1999, Non ti muovere (novel) (Premio Città di Bari-Costiera del Lavante-Pinuccio Tatarella 2001, Premio Strega 2002, Premio Rapallo-Carige 2002, Premio Grinzane-Cavour 2002) 2001, Zorro: Un eremita sul marciapiede (novel) 2002. *Honours:* Premio UBU for best young actress 1984, Maschera d'oro IDI 1985, Premio Biglietto d'oro 1994. *E-mail:* margaret_mazzantini@yahoo.it. *Website:* www.margaretmazzantini.com.

MAZZARELLA, David; American newspaper editor; *Editorial Director, Stars and Stripes;* b. 1938. *Career:* with Assoc. Press, Lisbon, New York, Rome 1962–70; with Daily American, Rome 1971–75, Gannett News, Washington, DC 1976–77, The Bridgewater, Bridgewater, NJ 1977–83; Ed., Sr Vice-Pres. USA Today –1999; Ombudsman Stars and Stripes (newspaper for American military services) 2000–01, Ed. Dir 2001–. *Address:* Stars and Stripes, 529 14th Street NW, Suite 350, Washington, DC 20450, USA. *Telephone:* (202)

761-0900. *Fax:* (202) 761-089. *E-mail:* mazzarellad@stripes.osd.mil. *Website:* www.stripes.com.

MAZZARO, Jerome Louis; American academic, poet, writer and editor; b. 25 Nov. 1934, Detroit, Michigan. *Education:* AB, Wayne University, 1954; MA, University of Iowa, 1956; PhD, Wayne State University, 1963. *Career:* Instructor, University of Detroit, 1958–61; Ed., Fresco, 1960–61, Modern Poetry Studies, 1970–79; Asst Prof., SUNY at Cortland, 1962–64; Asst Ed., North American Review, 1963–65, Noetics, 1964–65; Prof. of English and Comparative Literature, SUNY at Buffalo, 1964–96; Contributing Ed., Salmagundi, 1967–97, American Poetry Review, 1972–, Italian-American, 1974–88; Poetry Ed., Helios, 1977–79; mem. Dante Society of America; Mark Twain Society. *Publications:* The Achievement of Robert Lowell, 1939–1959, 1960; Juvenal: Satires (trans.), 1965; The Poetic Themes of Robert Lowell, 1965; Changing the Windows (poems), 1966; Modern American Poetry (ed.), 1970; Transformation in the Renaissance English Lyric, 1970; Profile of Robert Lowell (ed.), 1971; Profile of William Carlos Williams (ed.), 1971; William Carlos Williams: The Later Poetry, 1973; Postmodern American Poetry, 1980; The Figure of Dante: An Essay on the 'Vita Nuova', 1981; The Caves of Love (poems), 1985; Rubbings (poems), 1985; John Logan: The Collected Poems (ed. with Al Poulin), 1989; John Logan: The Collected Fiction (ed.), 1991; Mind Plays: Luigi Pirandello's Theatre, 2000; Robert Lowell and Ovid, 2001; War Games (fiction), 2001; Robert Lowell and America, 2002; Weathering the Changes (poems), 2002; Memory and Making, 2003. Contributions: Reference works, books and journals. *Honours:* Guggenheim Fellowship, 1964–65; Hadley Fellowship, 1979–80. *Address:* 392 Central Park W, Apartment 11J, New York, NY 10025, USA.

MDA, Zanemvula Kizito Gatyeni (Zakes), PhD; South African playwright, novelist, poet and painter; *Professor of Creative Writing, Ohio University;* b. 1948, Herschel District, Eastern Cape Province; s. of the late Ashby Peter Solomzi Mda and Nompumelelo Rose Mda. *Education:* Ohio Univ., Univ. of Capetown. *Career:* lived with family in exile in Basotholand Protectorate (later became Lesotho) 1964–80; wrote first plays in English while still at high school; worked as teacher, bank clerk and in marketing during law studies; studied theatre in USA then returned to Lesotho 1985; worked with Lesotho Nat. Broadcasting Corpn Television Project; also Dir Theatre-for-Development Project, Univ. of Lesotho; f. Marotholi Travelling Theatre; Lecturer in English, Nat. Univ. of Lesotho, Full Prof. and Head of English Dept 1991; taught at US univs 1991–94; writer-in-residence Univ. of Durham, UK 1991; research fellow Yale Univ. 1992; Visiting Prof. School of Dramatic Art, Witwatersrand Univ., S Africa 1995; now Prof. of Creative Writing Ohio Univ.; Dir Southern African Multimedia AIDS Trust, Johannesburg. *Publications:* plays: We Shall Sing for the Fatherland and Other Plays (Amstel Playwright of the Year Award) 1980, The Road (Christina Crawford Award of American Theatre Asscn 1984) 1982, The Plays of Zakes Mda 1990, The Nun's Romantic Story 1991, The Dying Screams of the Moon 1992, Four Works (Joys of War, And the Girls in their Sunday Dresses, Banned, The Final Dance) 1993; novels: Ways of Dying 1995, She Plays with the Darkness 1995, The Heart of Redness 2001, The Madonna of Excelsior 2002, The Whale Caller 2005; prose: When People Play People (development communication through theatre) 1993, Melville 67 (novella) 1998, Penny and Puffy (juvenile, with Mpapa Mokhoane) 2000, Fools, Bells and the Habit of Eating (three satires); poetry: Bits of Debris 1986; contrib. short stories to anthologies and articles to academic journals and newspapers. *Honours:* American Library Asscn Notable Book 2005, Commonwealth Writers' Prize (Africa region) 2005, Zora Neale Hurston/Richard Wright Legacy Award 2005. *Literary Agent:* Blake Friedmann Literary, Film and Television Agency, 122 Arlington Road, London, NW1 7HP, England. *Telephone:* (20) 7284-0408. *Fax:* (20) 7284-0442.

MEAD, Matthew; British poet and translator; b. 12 Sept. 1924, Buckinghamshire, England. *Career:* Ed., Satis Magazine, Edinburgh 1960–62. *Publications:* A Poem in Nine Parts 1960, Identities 1964, Kleinigkeiten 1966, Identities and Other Poems 1967, Penguin Modern Poets 16 (with Harry Guest and J. Beeching) 1970, In the Eyes of the People 1973, Minusland 1977, The Midday Muse 1979, A Roman in Cologne 1986, A Sestina at the End of Socialism 1996, A Dozen Villanelles 1999, The Sentences of Death 2000, Walking Out of the World 2003; also numerous trans. from German (with Ruth Mead). *Address:* c/o Anvil Press, Neptune House, 70 Royal Hill, London, SE10 8RF, England.

MEADES, Jonathan Turner; British journalist, writer and broadcaster; b. 21 Jan. 1947, Salisbury, Wiltshire, England; m. 1st Sally Dorothee Renee Brown 1980 (divorced); two d.; m. 2nd Frances Anne Bentley 1988 (divorced); two d.; m. 3rd Colette Claudine Forder 2003. *Education:* King's Coll., Taunton, RADA, Univ. of Bordeaux. *Career:* Ed., Event 1981–82; Features Ed., Tatler 1982–85; restaurant critic The Times 1986–2001, columnist 2002–05. *Television:* The Victorian House, Abroad in Britain, Further Abroad, Jerry Building, Even Further Abroad, Travels with Pevsner: Worcestershire, Meades Eats, Heart Bypass, Victoria Died in 1901 and is Still Alive Today, tvSSFBM, Abroad Again (i), Joe Building, Abroad Again (ii). *Publications:* This is Their Life 1979, An Illustrated Atlas of the World's Great Buildings 1980, Filthy English 1984, Peter Knows What Dick Likes 1989, Pompey 1993, The Fowler Family Business 2001, Incest and Morris Dancing 2002; contrib. to Times, Sunday Times, Observer, Independent. *Honours:* Essay Prize, Paris Int. Art Film Festival 1994, Glenfiddich Awards 1986, 1990, 1996. *Literary Agent:* Capel and Land, 24 Wardour Street, London, W1D 6PS, England. *E-mail:* jtm.juvarra@orange.fr (home).

MEARS, Gillian, BA; Australian writer; b. 21 July 1964, Lismore, NSW. *Career:* mem. Australian Society of Authors. *Publications:* Ride a Cock Horse (short stories) 1989, Fineflour (short stories) 1990, The Mint Lawn 1991, The Grass Sister 1995, Collected Stories 1997, Paradise Is a Place (essay) 1997, A Map of the Gardens (short stories) 2002; contrib. to periodicals. *Honours:* Commonwealth Writers Regional First Book Prize 1989, Regional Best Book Prize 1996, Australian/Vogel Award 1991, Steele Rudd Award 2003. *Literary Agent:* Barbara Mobbs, PO Box 126, Edgecliff, NSW 2027, Australia. *E-mail:* bmobbs@pogo.com.au.

MEASHAM, Donald Charles, BA, MPhil; British teacher (retd), writer and editor; b. 19 Jan. 1932, Birmingham, England; m. Joan Doreen Barry 1954, one s. one d. *Education:* Birmingham University, Nottingham University. *Career:* Founding Ed. 1983, Company Secretary, Co-Ed., 1988–2001, Staple New Writing. *Publications:* Leaving, 1965; Fourteen, 1965; English Now and Then, 1965; Larger Than Life, 1967; Quattordicenni, 1967; The Personal Element, 1967; Lawrence and the Real England, 1985; Ruskin: The Last Chapter, 1989; Twenty Years of Twentieth Century Poetry, 2001, Jane Austen out of the blue 2006; contrib. to periodicals. *Address:* Tor Cottage, 81 Cavendish Road, Matlock, Derbyshire DE4 3HD, England.

MECKEL, Christoph; German author, poet and graphic artist; b. 12 June 1935, Berlin. *Education:* studied in Freiburg, Paris and Munich. *Career:* mem. Acad. of Science and Literature, Mainz; Akademie für Sprache und Dichtung eV, Darmstadt; PEN. *Publications:* Manifest der Toten, 1960; Im Land der Umbramauten, 1961; Wildnisse, 1962; Die Drummheit liefert uns ans Messer: Zeitgespräch in zehn Sonetten (with Volker von Törne), 1967; Bockshorn, 1973; Wen es angeht, 1974; Komödie der Hölle, 3 vols, 1979, 1984, 1987; Suchbild: Über meinen Vater, 1980; Ein roter Faden, 1983; Das Buch Jubal, 1987; Das Buch Shiralee, 1989; Von den Luftgeschäften der Poesie, 1989; Die Messingstadt, 1991; Gesang vom unterbrochenen Satz, 1995. *Honours:* Rainer Maria Rilke Prize, 1979; Georg Trakl Prize, 1982; Literature Prize, Kassel, 1993.

MEDDEB, Abdelwahab; Tunisian poet, novelist and translator; *Professor of Comparative Literature, Université de Paris X (Paris-Nanterre);* b. 1946, Tunis. *Career:* Prof. of Comparative Literature, Université de Paris X (Paris-Nanterre); fmr Visiting Prof. Yale Univ.; Ed. Dédale literary journal; curator West by East exhibition, Centre for Contemporary Culture, Barcelona 2005. *Publications:* Talismano (novel) 1976, Tombeau d'Ibn Arabi (poems) 1987, Phantasia (novel) 1989, Le Dits de Bistami 1989, Récit de l'exil occidental 1993, Les 99 stations de Yale (poems) 1995, Aya dans les villes 1999, Matière des oiseaux 2001, La Maladie de l'Islam (non-fiction) 2002, Ibn Arabis Grab 2004; contrib. to Banipal magazine. *Address:* Université de Paris X (Paris-Nanterre), 200 avenue de la République, Paris 92001, Nanterre Cedex, France (office). *Telephone:* 1-40-97-56-30 (office). *E-mail:* Abdelwahab.Meddeb@u-paris10.fr (office). *Website:* www.u-paris10.fr.

MEDEIROS, Teresa, AA; American writer; b. 26 Oct. 1962, Heidelberg, Germany; m. Michael Medeiros 1984. *Education:* Madisonville Community Coll. *Career:* mem. Kentucky Romance Writers, Novelists Inc, Romance Writers of America. *Publications:* Lady of Conquest, 1989; Shadows and Lace, 1990; Heather and Velvet, 1991; Once an Angel, 1993; A Whisper of Roses, 1993; Thief of Hearts, 1994; Fairest of Them All, 1995; Breath of Magic, 1996; Touch of Enchantment, 1997; Nobody's Darling, 1998; Charming the Prince, 1999; The Bride and the Beast, 2000. *Address:* 239 Crossbar Court, Hopkinsville, KY 42240, USA.

MEDOFF, Mark Howard, BA, MA; American dramatist and screenwriter; b. 18 March 1940, Mount Carmel, IL; m. Stephanie Thorne, three d. *Education:* University of Miami, Coral Gables, Stanford University. *Career:* mem. Actors Equity Asscn; Screen Actors Guild; Writers Guild of America. *Publications:* Plays: When You Comin' Back, Red Ryder?, 1973; Children of a Lesser God, 1979; The Majestic Kid, 1981; The Hands of Its Enemy, 1984; The Heart Outright, 1986; Big Mary, 1989; Stumps, 1989; Stephanie Hero, 1990; Kringle's Window, 1991. Film Scripts: Good Guys Wear Black, 1977; When You Comin' Back, Red Ryder?, 1978; Off Beat, 1985; Apology, 1986; Children of a Lesser God, 1987; Clara's Heart, 1988; City of Joy, 1992. Contributions: periodicals. *Honours:* Obie Award, 1974; Drama Desk Awards, 1974, 1980; New York Outer Critics Circle Awards, 1974, 1980; Guggenheim Fellowship, 1974–75; Antoinette Perry Award, 1980; Governor's Award for Excellence in the Arts, State of New Mexico, 1980; Distinguished Alumnus, University of Miami, 1987; California Media Access Award, 1988.

MEDVED, Michael, BA, MFA; American film critic, writer and broadcaster; b. 3 Oct. 1948, Philadelphia, Pennsylvania; m. 1st Nancy Harris Herman 1972 (divorced 1983); m. 2nd Diane Elvenstar 1985; one s. two d. *Education:* Yale University, California State University at San Francisco. *Career:* Political Speech Writer, 1970–73; Creative Dir, Advertising, Anrick Inc, Oakland, CA, 1973–74; Co-Founder and Pres., Pacific Jewish Center, Venice, CA, 1977–94; On-Air Film Critic, People Now, Cable News Network, 1980–83; Pres., Emanuel Streisand School, Venice, CA, 1980–85; On-Air Film Critic and Co-Host, Sneak Previews, PBS-TV, 1985–96; Chief Film Critic, New York Post, 1993–98; Radio Talk Show Host, Seattle, Washington, 1996–; Nationally Syndicated Radio Host, SRN Radio Network, 1998–; mem. American Federation of Television and Radio Artists; Writers Guild of America. *Publications:* What Really Happened to the Class of '65?, 1976; The 50 Worst Films of All Time (with Harry Medved), 1978; The Shadow Presidents, 1979; The Golden Turkey Awards (with Harry Medved), 1980; Hospital, 1983; The

Hollywood Hall of Shame (with Harry Medved), 1984; Son of Golden Turkey Awards (with Harry Medved), 1986; Hollywood vs America, 1992; Saving Childhood (with Diane Medved), 1998. Contributions: periodicals. *Address:* c/o KV1, 1809 Seventh Avenue, Suite 200, Seattle, WA 98101, USA.

MEDVEDEV, Roy Aleksandrovich, PhD; Russian historian and sociologist; b. 14 Nov. 1925, Tbilisi; s. of Aleksandr Romanovich Medvedev and Yulia Medvedeva; twin brother of Zhores Medvedev (q.v.); m. Galina A. Gaidina 1956; one s. *Education:* Leningrad State Univ., Acad. of Pedagogical Sciences of USSR. *Career:* mem. CPSU –1969, 1989–91; worker at mil. factory 1943–46; teacher of history, Ural Secondary School 1951–53; Dir of Secondary School in Leningrad region 1954–56; Deputy to Ed.-in-Chief of Publishing House of Pedagogical Literature, Moscow 1957–59; Head of Dept, Research Inst. of Vocational Educ., Acad. of Pedagogical Sciences of USSR 1960–70, Senior Scientist 1970–71; freelance author 1972–; People's Deputy of USSR, mem. Supreme Soviet of USSR 1989–91; mem. Cen. Cttee CPSU 1990–91; Co-Chair. Socialist Party of Labour 1991–2003. *Publications:* Vocational Education in Secondary School 1960, Faut-il réhabiliter Staline? 1969, A Question of Madness (with Zhores Medvedev) 1971, Let History Judge 1972, On Socialist Democracy 1975, Qui a écrit le 'Don Paisible'? 1975, La Révolution d'octobre était-elle inéluctable? 1975, Solschenizyn und die Sowjetische Linke 1976, Khrushchev–The Years in Power (with Zhores Medvedev) 1976, Political Essays 1976, Problems in the Literary Biography of Mikhail Sholokhov 1977, Samizdat Register 1978, Philip Mironov and the Russian Civil War (with S. Starikov) 1978, The October Revolution 1979, On Stalin and Stalinism 1979, On Soviet Dissent 1980, Nikolai Bukharin–The Last Years 1980, Leninism and Western Socialism 1981, An End to Silence 1982, Khrushchev 1983, All Stalin's Men 1984, China and Superpowers 1986, L'URSS che cambia (with G. Chiesa) 1987, Time of Change (with G. Chiesa) 1990, Brezhnev: A Political Biography 1991, Gensek s Lybianki: A Political Portrait of Andropov 1993, 1917. The Russian Revolution 1997, Capitalism in Russia? 1998, The Unknown Andropov 1998, Post-Soviet Russia 2000, The Unknown Stalin (with Zhores Medvedev) 2001, Putin 2004, Solzhenitsyn and Sakharov (with Zhores Medvedev) 2004, Moscow Model of Yuri Luzhkov 2005; and over 400 professional and general articles. *Address:* c/o Z. A. Medvedev, 4 Osborn Gardens, London, NW7 1DY, England; Abonnement Post Box 258, 125475 Moscow A-475; Dybenko str 2 apt 20, 125475 Moscow A-475, Russia (home). *Telephone:* (495) 451-12-84 (home).

MEDVEDEV, Zhores Aleksandrovich, PhD; British/Russian biologist; b. 14 Nov. 1925, Tbilisi; s. of Aleksandr Romanovich Medvedev and Yulia Medvedeva; twin brother of Roy Medvedev (q.v.); m. Margarita Nikolayevna Buzina 1951; two s. *Education:* Timiriazev Acad. of Agricultural Sciences, Moscow, Inst. of Plant Physiology, USSR Acad. of Sciences. *Career:* joined Soviet Army 1943, served at front as a pvt.; Scientist, later Sr Scientist, Dept of Agrochemistry and Biochemistry, Timiriazev Acad. 1951–62; Head of Lab., Molecular Radiobiology, Inst. of Medical Radiology, Obninsk 1963–69; Sr Scientist All-Union Scientific Research Inst. of Physiology and Biochemistry of Farm Animals, Borovsk 1970–72; Sr Scientist, Nat. Inst. for Medical Research, London 1973–92; mem. New York Acad. of Sciences, American Gerontological Soc., Biochemical Soc., Genetic Soc.; Soviet citizenship restored 1990. *Publications:* Protein Biosynthesis and Problems of Heredity, Development and Ageing 1963, Molecular-Genetic Mechanisms of Development 1968, The Rise and Fall of T. D. Lysenko 1969, The Medvedev Papers 1970, A Question of Madness (with Roy Medvedev) 1971, Ten Years After 1973, Khrushchev–The Years in Power (with Roy Medvedev) 1976, Soviet Science 1978, The Nuclear Disaster in the Urals 1979, Andropov 1983, Gorbachev 1986, Soviet Agriculture 1987, The Legacy of Chernobyl 1990, The Unknown Stalin (with Roy Medvedev) 2001; Stalin and the Jewish Problem 2003, Solzhenitsyn and Sakharov (with Roy Medvedev) 2004; and over 400 papers and articles on gerontology, genetics, biochemistry, environment, history and other topics. *Honours:* Book award of the Moscow Naturalist Soc. 1965, Aging Research Award of US Aging Assen 1984, René Schubert Preis in Gerontology 1985. *Address:* 4 Osborn Gardens, London, NW7 1DY, England (home). *Telephone:* (20) 8346-4158 (home). *E-mail:* zhmedvedev@yahoo.co.uk (home).

MEEK, James; British writer and journalist; b. 7 Dec. 1962, London. *Career:* newspaper reporter 1985–; writer for The Guardian, in fmr Soviet Union 1991–99, in London 1999–. *Publications:* novels: Mcfarlane Boils the Sea 1989, Drivetime 1995, The People's Act of Love (RSL Ondaatje Prize 2006) 2005; short story collections: Last Orders 1992, The Museum of Doubt 2000; contrib. to LRB, Granta. *Literary Agent:* c/o AP Watt Ltd, 20 John Street, London, WC1N 2DR, England. *Telephone:* (20) 7405-6774. *Fax:* (20) 7831-2154. *E-mail:* apw@apwatt.co.uk. *Website:* www.apwatt.co.uk. *Address:* c/o Canongate Books, 14 High Street, Edinburgh, EH1 1TE, Scotland. *E-mail:* customerservices@canongate.co.uk.

MEEK, Jay, BA, MA; American academic and poet; *Professor Emeritus, University of North Dakota*; b. 23 Aug. 1937, Grand Rapids, MI; m. Martha George 1966; one d. *Education:* Univ. of Michigan, Syracuse Univ. *Career:* faculty, Wake Forest Univ. 1977–80, Sarah Lawrence Coll. 1980–82; Assoc. Prof., MIT 1982–83; writer-in-residence, Memphis State Univ. 1984; Prof., Univ. of North Dakota 1985–2004, Prof. Emeritus 2004–. *Publications:* The Week the Dirigible Came 1976, Drawing on the Walls 1980, Earthly Purposes 1984, Stations 1989, Windows 1994, Headlands: New and Selected Poems 1997, The Memphis Letters (novel) 2002, Trains in Winter 2004; contrib. to journals and magazines. *Honours:* NEA Award 1972–73, Guggenheim

Fellowship 1985–86, Bush Artist Fellowship 1989. *Address:* 3149 34th Avenue South, Minneapolis, MN 55406, USA (home). *Telephone:* (612) 729-0260 (home).

MEGGED, Aharon; Polish writer; b. 10 Aug. 1920, Wloclawek; m. Eda Zoritte 1946; two s. *Career:* Ed. MASSA 1953–55; Literary Ed. Lamerchav Daily 1955–68; Cultural Attaché, Israel Embassy, London 1968–71; columnist, Davar Daily 1971–85; mem. Israel PEN Centre (Pres. 1980–87), Hebrew Acad. 1982–. *Publications:* Hedva and I 1953, Fortunes of a Fool 1960, Living on the Dead 1965, The Short Life 1971, The Bat 1975, Asahel 1978, Heinz, His Son and the Evil Spirit 1979, Journey in the Month of Av 1980, The Flying Camel and the Golden Hump 1982, The Turbulent Zone (essays) 1985, Foiglmann 1987, The Writing Desk (literary essays) 1988, Anat's Day of Illumination 1992, Longing for Olga 1994, Iniquity 1996, Love-Flowers from the Holy Land 1998, Persephone Remembers 2000, Until Evening 2001, Beautiful Milisinda 2002, Yolam's Vengeance 2003; plays: Hedva and I 1955, Hannah Senesh 1963, Genesis 1965, The High Season 1968; contribs to Atlantic Monthly, Encounter, Midstream, Listener, Moment, Present Tense, Partisan Review, Ariel. *Honours:* Brenner Prize 1960, Bialik Prize 1973, Present Tense, New York 1983, Agnon Prize 1997, Wizo-Paris Prize 1998, Prime Minister's Prize 1998, Pres.'s Prize 2001, Israel Prize for Literature 2003. *Literary Agent:* c/o Lipman Ag, Marienberg Str. 23, PO Box 572, 8044 Zürich, Switzerland. *Address:* 8 Pa'amoni Street, Tel-Aviv 62918, Israel. *Telephone:* (3) 6021680. *Fax:* (3) 6022408. *E-mail:* meged1@zahav.net.il.

MEHREN, Stein; Norwegian poet, novelist and playwright; b. 16 May 1935, Oslo. *Education:* Univ. of Oslo. *Career:* also renowned as a painter. *Publications include:* poetry: Gjennom stillheten en natt (Through the Silence One Night) 1960, Mot en verden av lys (Norwegian Critics' Prize for Literature) 1963, Gobelin Europa (Goblin Europe) 1965, Den store søndagsfrikosten (The Great Sunday Breakfast) 1976, Evighet, vårt flyktigste stoff 1994, Hotell Memory 1996, Kjærlighetsdikt 1997, Nattmaskin (Nightmachine) 1998, Utvalgte dikt 1999, Ark 2000, Den siste ildlender 2002, Imperiet lukker seg 2005, Nye bilder, tidlige dikt (New Paintings, Early Poems) 2005, Call from a Dark Star 2006. *Honours:* Dagbladets lyrikkpris i 1966, Kulturrådets bokpris 1966, 1969, Doublougprisen 1971, Nordic Council Literature Prize 1971, 1978, 1982, 1984, 1993, 2005, Fritt Ord-prisen 1978, Det norske Akademi for Sprog og Litteraturs pris 1987, Anders Jahres Pris 1993. *Literary Agent:* Aschehoug Agency, POB 363 Sentrum, 0102 Oslo, Norway.

MEHROTRA, Sri Ram, MA, PhD; Indian writer and educator; b. 23 June 1931, Anantram, Etawah, Uttar Pradesh; m. Eva Mehrotra 1957. *Education:* Univ. of Allahabad, Univ. of London. *Career:* Lecturer, Univ. of London 1962; Fellow, Indian Inst. of Advanced Study, Shimla 1971–79; Prof., Himachal Pradesh Univ. 1972; Visiting Prof., Univ. of Wisconsin 1974; Visiting Fellow, St John's Coll., Cambridge 1983–84; Nehru Prof., MD Univ. 1992–96. *Publications:* India and the Commonwealth, 1885–1929 1965, The Emergence of the Indian National Congress 1971, The Commonwealth and the Nation 1978, Towards India's Freedom and Partition 1979, A History of the Indian National Congress, Vol. 1 1885–1918 1995, Selected Writings of Allan Octavian Hume (1829–1867) Vol. 1 (co-ed.) 2004; contrib. to scholarly journals. *Address:* Seva, Kenfield Estate, Ambedkar Chowk, Shimla, HP 171004, India (home). *Telephone:* (0177) 2656615 (home); 09816 136171 (mobile). *E-mail:* srirammehrotra@yahoo.com (home).

MEHTA, Gita; Indian writer; b. 1943, Delhi; m. Ajai Singh 'Sonny' Mehta; one s. *Education:* Univ. of Cambridge. *Career:* Dir, documentaries about India for BBC, NBC. *Publications:* Karma Cola: Marketing The Mystic East 1979, Raj (novel) 1989, A River Sutra (novel) 1993, Snakes and Ladders: Glimpses of Modern India (essays) 1997, Mountain Sutra 1999; contrib. essay 'Unborn', in Clemente 1999. *Address:* c/o Random House, 1745 Broadway, 15-3, New York, NY 10019, USA.

MEHTA, Ajai Singh (Sonny); American (b. Indian) publishing company executive; *Chairman and Editor-in-Chief, Knopf Publishing Group*; b. 1942, India; m. Gita Mehta; one s. *Education:* Lawrence School, Sanawar, and Univ. of Cambridge. *Career:* fmrly with Pan and Picador Publs, UK; Pres. Alfred A. Knopf Div. of Random House (now Knopf Publishing Group, New York 1987–, now Chair. and Ed.-in-Chief. *Address:* Alfred A. Knopf Inc., 1745 Broadway, New York, NY 10019, USA. *Website:* www.randomhouse.com/knopf.

MEHTA, Ved (Parkash), MA; American (naturalized) writer and academic; b. 21 March 1934, Lahore, Pakistan (fmrly British India); s. of Amolak Ram and Shanti Mehta (née Mehra); m. Linn Cary 1983; two d. *Education:* Arkansas School for the Blind, Pomona Coll., Calif., Balliol Coll., Oxford, UK, Harvard Univ. *Career:* staff writer, New Yorker magazine 1961–94; Visiting Scholar, Case Western Reserve 1974; Visiting Prof. of Literature, Bard Coll. 1985, 1986; Noble Foundation Visiting Coll. of Art and Cultural History, Sarah Lawrence Coll. 1988; Fellow, New York Inst. for the Humanities 1988–92; Visiting Fellow (Literature), Balliol Coll., Oxford 1988–89; Visiting Prof. of English, New York Univ. 1989–90; Rosenkrantz Chair in Writing, Yale Univ. 1990–93, Lecturer in History 1990, 1991, 1992, Lecturer in English 1991–93; Assoc. Fellow, Berkeley Coll. (a constituent of Yale Coll.) 1988–, Residential Fellow 1990–93; Arnold Bernhard Visiting Prof. of English and History, Williams Coll. 1994; Randolph Visiting Distinguished Prof. of English and History, Vassar Coll., NY 1994–96; Sr Fellow, Freedom Forum, Media Studies Center and Visiting Scholar, Columbia Univ., New York 1996–97; Fellow, Center for Advanced Study in Behavioral Sciences 1997–98; mem.

Council on Foreign Relations 1979–, Usage Panel, American Heritage Dictionary 1982. *Television:* writer and narrator of documentary film, Chachaji: My Poor Relation (DuPont Columbia Award for Excellence in Broadcast Journalism 1977–78) (PBS) 1978, (BBC) 1980. *Publications:* Face to Face (Secondary Educ. Annual Book Award 1958, serial reading on BBC Light Programme 1958, dramatization on BBC Home Programme 1959) 1957, Walking the Indian Streets 1960, Fly and the Fly Bottle 1963, Delinquent Chacha (novel) 1967, Portrait of India 1970, John Is Easy to Please 1971, Mahatma Gandhi and His Apostles 1977, The New India 1978, Photographs of Chachaji 1980, A Family Affair: India Under Three Prime Ministers 1982, Three Stories of the Raj (fiction) 1986, Rajiv Gandhi and Rama's Kingdom 1995, A Ved Mehta Reader: The Craft of the Essay 1998; Continents of Exile (autobiography): Daddyji 1972, Mamaji, 1979, Vedi 1982 (serial reading on BBC Book at Bedtime 1990), The Ledge Between the Streams 1984, Sound-Shadows of the New World 1986, The Stolen Light 1989, Up at Oxford 1993, Remembering Mr. Shawn's New Yorker 1998, All For Love 2001, Dark Harbor 2003, The Red Letters (concluding volume) 2004. *Honours:* Hon. Fellow, Balliol Coll. Oxford 1999; Hon. DLtrs (Pomona Coll.) 1972, (Williams Coll.) 1986; Hon. DLitt (Bard Coll.) 1982; Hon. DUniv (Stirling, Scotland) 1988; Hon. LHD (Bowdoin) 1995; Hazen Fellow 1956–59, Harvard Prize Fellow 1959–60, Residential Fellow, Eliot House 1959–61, Guggenheim Fellow 1971–72, 1977–78, Ford Foundation Travel and Study Grantee 1971–76, Public Policy Grantee 1979–82, MacArthur Prize Fellow 1982–87, Asscn of Indians in America Award 1978, Signet Medal, Harvard Univ. 1983, Distinguished Service Award, Asian/Pacific American Library Asscn 1986, New York City Mayor's Liberty Medal 1986, Centenary Barrows Award, Pomona Coll. 1987, New York Public Library Literary Lion Medal 1990, and Literary Lion Centennial Medal 1996, New York State Asian-American Heritage Month Award 1991, South Asian Literary Asscn Lifetime Achievement Award 2004. *Fax:* (212) 472-7220 (home). *E-mail:* vedmehta@aol.com (home). *Website:* www.vedmehta.com.

MEIDINGER-GEISE, Inge, DPhil; German writer; b. 16 March 1923, Berlin; d. of the late Kurt Geise and Irene Geise (née Minsberg); m. Konrad Meidinger 1946 (died 1979). *Education:* Univs of Berlin and Erlangen. *Career:* has written over 50 books including essays, poems, radio plays and historical works 1954–; Chair. Die Kogge (European Asscn of Writers) 1967–88, Hon. Chair. 1988–; mem. PEN (Germany). *Publications include:* Sündenbrand (plays) 1976, Alle Katzen sind nicht grau (short stories) 1982, Menuett in Schwarz (short stories) 1990, Bodenpreise (novel) 1993. *Honours:* awards include Kulturpreis Erlangen 1972, Literaturpreis Mölle (Sweden) 1979 and Wolfram-von-Eschenbach-Preis 1988. *Address:* Schobertweg 1A, 91056 Erlangen, Germany. *Telephone:* (9131) 41307.

MEIGHAN, Roland, DSocSc, PhD, FRSA; British writer, publisher and consultant; b. 29 May 1937, Sutton Coldfield, England; m. Janet Meighan; one s. two step-s. *Career:* various school teaching positions; Lecturer, then Sr Lecturer in Educ., Univ. of Birmingham; Special Prof. of Educ., Univ. of Nottingham; ind. writer and consultant; Founder and Dir Educational Heretics Press; Dir and Trustee Centre for Personalised Educ. Trust. *Publications:* Flexischooling 1988, Theory and Practice of Regressive Education 1993, The Freethinkers' Guide to the Educational Universe 1994, John Holt: Personalised Education and the Reconstruction of Schooling 1995, The Next Learning System 1997, The Next Learning System: Pieces of the Jigsaw 2000, Learning Unlimited 2001, Natural Learning and the Natural Curriculum 2001, John Holt: Personalised Learning Instead of Uninvited Teaching 2002, A Sociology of Educating (fifth edn) 2007, Damage Limitation: Trying to Reduce the Harm Schools do to Children 2004, Comparing Learning Systems: The Good, the Bad, the Ugly and the Counterproductive 2005; contrib. to Natural Parent Magazine, Observer, Yorkshire Post, Times Educational Supplement. *Address:* 113 Arundel Drive, Bramcote, Nottingham NG9 3FQ, England (office). *Telephone:* (115) 925-7261 (office). *Fax:* (115) 925-7261 (office). *Website:* www.edheretics.gn.apc.org (office).

MEINER, Richard; German publisher; b. 8 April 1918, Dresden; s. of Felix Meiner and Elisabeth Meiner (née Gensel); m. Ursula Ehlert 1947; one s. one d. *Career:* mil. service 1937–45; f. Richard Meiner Verlag, Hamburg 1948–64; Dir Verlage Felix Meiner 1964–81, Felix Meiner Verlag GmbH, Hamburg 1981–98. *Publications:* Verlegerische Betreuung der Philosophischen Bibliothek, Corpus Philosophorum Teutonicorum Medii Aevi, G.W.F. Hegel, Gesammelte Werke, Krit. Ausgabe, G.W.F. Hegel, Vorlesungen, Kant-Forschungen, Nicolai de Cusa Opera omnia. Krit. Ausgabe, Handbuch PRAGMATIK, Studien zum achtzehnten Jahrhundert und weitere philosophische Reihen und Einzelmonographien. *Honours:* Mil. Medal; Gold Medal of Union of German Booksellers 1983; Medal of Honour of German Bücherei Leipzig 1987; Hon. Fellow German Soc. for Philosophy in Germany 1988; Bundesverdienstkreuz I. Klasse 1989. *Address:* c/o Felix Meiner Verlag GmbH, Richardstrasse 47, 22081 Hamburg, Germany.

MEINKE, Peter, AB, MA, PhD; American academic (retd), poet and writer; b. 29 Dec. 1932, New York, NY; m. Jeanne Clark 1957; two s. two d. *Education:* Hamilton Coll., Univ. of Michigan, Univ. of Minnesota. *Career:* Asst Prof., Hamline Univ., St Paul, Minnesota 1961–66; Prof. of Literature and Dir of the Writing Workshop, Eckerd Coll., St Petersburg, FL 1966–93; Fulbright Sr Lecturer, Univ. of Warsaw 1978–79; Visiting Distinguished Writer, Univ. of Hawaii 1993, Univ. of North Carolina, Greensboro 1996; Fellow, Le Château de Lavigny, Switzerland 1998; Darden Chair in Creative Writing, Old Dominion Univ., Norfolk, VA 2003–05; several writer-in-residencies; mem.

Acad. of American Poets, Poetry Soc. of America. *Publications:* Lines from Neuchâtel 1974, The Night Train and the Golden Bird 1977, The Rat Poems 1978, Trying to Surprise God 1981, The Piano Tuner 1986, Underneath the Lantern 1987, Night Watch on the Chesapeake 1987, Far from Home 1988, Liquid Paper: New and Selected Poems 1991, Scars 1996, Campocorto 1996, The Shape of Poetry 1999, Zinc Fingers 2000, Greatest Hits 2001, The Contracted World 2006; contrib. to periodicals. *Honours:* first prize Olivet Sonnet Competition 1966, Nat. Endowment for the Arts Fellowships 1974, 1989, Poetry Soc. of America Gustav Davidson Memorial Award 1976, Poetry Soc. of America Lucille Medwick Memorial Award 1984, Flannery O'Connor Award 1986, Poetry Soc. of America Emily Dickinson Award 1992, Paumanok Poetry Award 1993, Fine Arts Work Center, Provincetown Master Artist's Fellowship 1995, Southeast Booksellers Asscn) Award for Poetry 2000. *Address:* 147 Wildwood Lane SE, St Petersburg, FL 33705, USA (home). *Telephone:* (727) 896-1862 (home). *E-mail:* meinkep@eckerd.edu (home).

MELCHETT, Sonia (see Sinclair, Sonia Elizabeth)

MELCHIOR, Ib Jorgen; American writer, dramatist and director; b. 17 Sept. 1917, Copenhagen, Denmark; s. of Lauritz and Inger Melchior; m. 1st Kate Hathaway 1942 (divorced 1960); one s.; m. 2nd Cleo Baldon 1964; one step.s. *Education:* Stenhus Coll., Univ. of Copenhagen. *Career:* writer, dir, over 500 live and filmed TV episodes, 12 feature films, 60 documentary films 1959–76; mem. Authors' Guild, Dirs Guild of America, Manuscript Soc., Writers' Guild of America, Acad. of Science Fiction. *Films include:* Live Fast, Die Young (writer) 1958, The Angry Red Planet (writer and dir) 1960, Reptilicus (writer) 1961, Journey to the Seventh Planet (writer) 1962, Robinson Crusoe on Mars (writer) 1964, The Time Travelers (writer and dir) 1964, Terrore nello spazio (writer) 1965, Ambush Bay (writer) 1966, Death Race 2000 (writer) 1975. *Television includes:* The Perry Como Show (series dir) 1948, The March of Medicine (series dir) 1958, Men Into Space (series writer) 1959, The Outer Limits (series writer) 1963. *Publications:* Order of Battle 1972, Sleeper Agent 1975, The Haigerloch Project 1977, The Watchdogs of Abaddon 1979, The Marcus Device 1980, Hour of Vengeance (stage play, Shakespeare Soc. of America Hamlet Award 1982) 1982, Eva 1984, V-3 1985, Code Name: Grand Guignol 1987, Steps and Stairways 1989, Quest 1990, Hitler's Werewolves 1991, Case by Case 1993, Reflections on the Pool 1997, Lauritz Melchior: The Golden Years of Bayreuth 2003. *Honours:* Golden Scroll 1976, Outstanding American-Scandinavian 1995, Bronze Star, King Christian X Medal, Denmark, Knight Commander, Militant Order of St Brigitte, Sweden. *Address:* 8228 Marmont Lane, Los Angeles, CA 90069, USA. *E-mail:* ijmelchior@aol.com (office).

MELDRUM, James (see Broxholme, John Franklin)

MELEAGROU, Evie (Ivi), BA; Cypriot writer; b. 27 May 1928, Nicosia; d. of Efstathios Hadjidemetriou and Euridice Akritas; m. Ioannis Meleagros 1952; two d. one s. *Education:* Pancyprian Gymnasium (Nicosia), Athenerum Inst. (Athens), Ecole de St Joseph (Nicosia) and Univ. of London (UK). *Career:* Secondary school teacher of English and French 1947–52; broadcaster 1952–55; Ed. Cyprus Chronicles literary magazine 1960–72, George Seferis' works 1969–72; Pres. Pancyprian Women's Asscn 1974–81; Official Rep. World Writers' Conf. 1965, Panhellenic Congress on the Status of Women 1975, TV discussion on Cyprus, Greece 1984; public speaker on Cyprus in many countries; numerous TV appearances in UK, USA, Norway, Lebanon, France, etc; First Prize Pancyprian Short Story Competition 1952, Pancyprian Novella Competition 1957, Cyprus Nat. Novel Award 1970, 1981, Hellenic Nat. Novel Award 1981. *Publications:* Solomos Family 1957, Anonymous City (short stories) 1963, Eastern Mediterranean 1969, Conversation With Che 1970, Penultimate Era 1980, Persona is the Unknown Cypriot Woman (essays and poetry) 1994, The Virgin Plunge in the Ocean Depths (short stories and novellas) 1996; short stories have been translated into English, German, Russian and Hungarian. *Address:* 22 Mesolongi St, Nicosia 100, Cyprus. *Telephone:* (2) 463507.

MELECKI, Maciej; Polish poet and screenwriter; b. 1969. *Career:* works at the Mikolów Institute; co-ed., Arcadia journal. *Publications:* poetry: Zachodzenie za siebie (Behind the Self), 1993; Te sprawy (Such Things), 1995; Niebezpiecznie blisko (Dangerously Close), 1996; Dalsze zajecia (Further Goings Behind), 1998; Zimni ogrodnicy (Mid-May Cold Spell), 1999; Przypadki i odmiany (Cases and Declensions), 2001. Screenplays: Wojaczek (co-writer), 1997; Autsajder, 2000; Dzien Oszusta, 2000. Contributions: Chicago Review; anthologies: Inny Swit, 1994; Macie swoich poetów, 1995, 1997; Dlugie pozegnanie, 1997; Antologia wspólczesnej poezji polskiej, 2000; 14, 44, 2000.

MELFI, Mary, BA, MLS; Canadian author, poet and dramatist; b. 10 June 1951, near Rome, Italy; m. George Nemeth 1975, two s. *Education:* Loyola College, Concordia University, McGill University. *Publications:* The Dance, the Cage and the Horse (poems), 1976; A Queen Is Holding a Mummified Cat (poems), 1982; A Bride in Three Acts (poems), 1983; A Dialogue with Masks (novella), 1985; The O Canada Poems, 1986; A Season in Beware (poems), 1989; Infertility Rites (novel), 1991; Ubu: The Witch Who Would Be Rich (children's novel), 1994; Sex Therapy (play), 1996; Painting Moments, Art, AIDS and Nick Palazzo (ed.), 1998; Stages: Selected Poems, 1998; Office Politics (poems), 1999. Contributions: many reviews, quarterlies and journals. *Honours:* Canada Council Arts Grants, 1981–82, 1982–83; Québec Arts Council Grants, 1993–94, 1996–97; Canadian Heritage Grant, 1995. *Address:* c/o Guernica Editions, PO Box 117, Station P, Toronto, ON M5S 2S6, Canada.

MELINESCU, Gabriela; Romanian poet, editor, essayist and translator; b. 16 Aug. 1942, Bucharest. *Education:* Univ. of Philology, Bucharest. *Career:* began career as Ed. Femeia and Luceafarul magazines; based in Sweden 1975–; trans. of works by Swedenborg, Strindberg, Brigitta Trotzig, Goran Sonevi. *Publications:* poetry: Ceremonie de iarna 1965, Fiintele abstracte 1967, Interiorul legii 1968, Boala de origine divina 1970, Juramantul de saracie, castitate si supunere (Writers' Union Prize) 1972, Inginarea lumiir 1972, Impotriva celui drag 1975, Zeul fecunditatii 1977, Oglinda femeii 1986, Lumina spre lumina 1993; prose: Jurnal suedez Vols I–III, Bobinocarii 1969, Catargul cu doua corabii (juvenile) 1969, Viata cere viata (jtly) (non-fiction) 1975, Copiii rabdarii 1979, Lupii urca in cer 1981, Vrajitorul din Gallipoli 1986, Regina strazii 1988, Omul pasare (Swedish Acad. De Nio Prize) 1991; contrib. to Crossing Boundaries: An International Anthology of Women's Experiences in Sport 1999. *Honours:* Albert Bonniers Prize 2002, Nichita Stanescu Prize 2002, Inst. of Romanian Culture Prize 2004.

MELLAH, Fawzi; Tunisian writer and sociologist; b. 1946. *Career:* based in Geneva, Switzerland; has acted as legal consultant to immigrants. *Plays:* Néron, ou Les oiseaux de passage 1973, Palais de non-retour 1975. *Publications:* novels: Elissa la reine vagabonde 1988, Le Conclave des pleureuses 1997, Entre chien et loup 1997; non-fiction: De lunité arabe: essai d'interprétation critique 1985, Clandestins en méditerranée 2001. *Address:* c/o Éditions Cérès, 6 rue Alain Savary, Le Belvédère, Tunis 1002, Tunisia. *E-mail:* info@ceres-editions.com.

MELLERS, Wilfrid Howard, OBE, MA, DMus, DPhil; British composer, writer and academic; *Professor Emeritus of Music, University of York*; b. 26 April 1914, Leamington; s. of Percy Wilfrid Mellers and Hilda Maria Lawrence; m. 1st Vera Hobbs 1940; m. 2nd Peggy Pauline Lewis 1950 (divorced 1975); two d.; m. 3rd Robin Hildyard 1987. *Education:* Leamington Coll. and Downing Coll. Cambridge. *Career:* Supervisor in English Studies and Lecturer in Music, Downing Coll. Cambridge 1945–48; Staff Tutor in Music, Extramural Dept, Univ. of Birmingham 1948–60; Distinguished Andrew Mellon Visiting Prof. of Music, Univ. of Pittsburgh, USA 1960–63; Prof. and Head of Dept of Music, Univ. of York 1964–81, now Emer.; Part-time Prof., Guildhall School of Music, London, City Univ., London and Keele Univ. 1981–; many compositions and books published. *Music:* one full-scale opera, two chamber operas. *Publications:* François Couperin and the French Classical Tradition 1950, Man and His Music 1957, Music in a New Found Land (themes and developments in American music) 1964, Harmonious Meeting 1964, Twilight of the Gods: The Beatles in Retrospect 1973, Bach and the Dance of God 1981, Beethoven and the Voice of God 1984, A Darker Shade of Pale: A Backdrop to Bob Dylan 1984, Angels of the Night: Women Jazz and Pop Singers in the Twentieth Century 1986, The Masks of Orpheus 1986, Vaughan Williams and the Vision of Albion 1988, Le Jardin Retrouvé: Homage to Federico Mompou 1989, The Music of Percy Grainger 1992, The Music of Francis Poulenc 1993, Between Old Worlds and New 1997, Singing in the Wilderness 2001, Celestial Music 2002. *Honours:* Hon. DPhil (City Univ.) 1981. *Address:* Oliver Sheldon House, 17 Aldwark, York, YO1 7BX, England (office). *Telephone:* (1904) 638686. *Fax:* (1904) 638686 (home).

MELLING, John Kennedy, FRSA; English drama critic, editor, writer, lecturer and broadcaster and chartered accountant; b. 11 Jan. 1927, Westcliff-on-Sea, Essex; s. of John Robert Melling and Ivy Edith May Melling (née Woolmer). *Education:* Thirsk School, Westcliff High School for Boys. *Career:* drama critic The Stage 1957–90; theatre correspondent Essex Countryside 1966–77; drama critic Fur Weekly News 1968–73; Ed. The Liveryman Magazine 1970–75; Antiques Correspondent, Evening Echo 1971–74; Ed. Chivers Black Dagger Series of Crime Classics 1986–91; radio crime book critic BBC London 1984–85, BBC Essex 1987; Fellow Inst. of Taxation; Fellow Faculty of Building; mem. BAFTA, CWA (cttee mem. 1985–88), Cookery and Food Asscn, Marylebone Rifle and Pistol Club, American Federation of Police (int. life vice-pres.). *Radio:* conducted interview with Alfred Hitchcock (BBC) 1966. *Publications:* Discovering Lost Theatres 1969, Southend Playhouses from 1793 1969, Discovering Theatre Ephemera 1974, Discovering London's Guilds and Liveries 1973, She Shall Have Murder 1987, Murder in the Library (ed.) 1987, Crime Writers' Handbook of Practical Information (ed.) 1989, Gwendoline Butler: Inventor of the Women's Police Procedural 1993, Alchemy of Murder 1993, Murder Done to Death 1996, Scaling the High C's (with John L. Brecknock) 1996, A Little Manual of Etiquette for Gentlemen 2004, The Constructors – Genesis and Growth 2004, A Little Manual of Etiquette for Ladies 2006; plays: George... From Caroline 1971, The Toast Is... (series) 1979–84, Old Christmas, Diarists' Pleasures 1982, Murder at St Dunstan's 1983; contrib. to newspapers and journals; regular columnist Crime Time 1996–2002. *Honours:* Master Worshipful Company of Poulters 1980–81; Knight Grand Cross, Order of St Michael, Knight Order of St Basil 1984; CWA Award for Outstanding Services 1989, American Law Enforcement Officers Asscn Medal of Honor 1984. *Address:* 44A Tranquil Vale, Blackheath, London, SE3 0BD; 85 Chalkwell Avenue, Westcliff-on-Sea, Essex SS0 8NL, England. *Telephone:* (20) 8852-9230; (1702) 476012 (home). *Fax:* (20) 8852-9230.

MELLOR, David Hugh, MA, MEng, MS, PhD, ScD, FBA, FAHA; British philosopher and academic; *Professor Emeritus of Philosophy, University of Cambridge*; b. 10 July 1938, London; s. of S. D. Mellor and E. N. Mellor (née Hughes). *Education:* Newcastle Royal Grammar School, Manchester Grammar School and Pembroke Coll., Cambridge. *Career:* Harkness Fellowship in Chem. Eng, Univ. of Minnesota, USA 1960–62, MIT School of Chem. Eng Practice 1962; Tech. Officer, ICI 1962–63; research student in philosophy 1963–68; Fellow, Pembroke Coll., Cambridge 1964–70; Fellow, Darwin Coll., Cambridge 1971–2005, Vice-Master 1983–87; Asst Lecturer in Philosophy, Univ. of Cambridge 1965–70, Lecturer 1970–83, Reader in Metaphysics 1983–86, Prof. of Philosophy 1986–99, Prof. Emer. 1999–, Pro-Vice-Chancellor 2000–01; Hon. Prof. of Philosophy, Univ. of Keele 1989–92; Visiting Fellow in Philosophy, ANU 1975; Radcliffe Fellow in Philosophy 1978–80; Visiting Prof., Auckland Univ., NZ 1985; Pres. British Soc. for the Philosophy of Science 1985–87, Aristotelian Soc. 1992–93. *Publications:* The Matter of Chance 1971, Real Time 1981, Matters of Metaphysics 1991, The Facts of Causation 1995, Real Time II 1998, Probability: A Philosophical Introduction 2005; numerous articles on philosophy of science, metaphysics and philosophy of mind. *Honours:* Hon. PhD (Lund) 1997. *Address:* 25 Orchard Street, Cambridge, CB1 1JS, England (home). *Telephone:* (1223) 740017 (home). *Fax:* (1223) 740017 (home). *E-mail:* dhm11@cam.ac.uk (home). *Website:* people.pwf.cam.ac.uk/dhm11 (office).

MELO, Patrícia; Brazilian playwright, writer and screenwriter; b. 1962, Assis, São Paulo. *Screenplays:* Colônia Cecília (TV film) 1989, Traição (with others) 1998, Bufo & Spallanzani 2001, O Xangô de Baker Street 2001, O Homem do Ano 2003. *Publications:* novels: Acqua Toffana 1994, O Matador (trans. as The Killer) (Deux Océans Prize, France 1997, Deutscher Krimi Prize, Germany) 1995, Elogio da Mentira (trans. as In Praise of Lies) 1998, Inferno 2000, Valsa Negra (trans. as Black Waltz) 2003. *Address:* c/o Departamento Editorial, Editoria Companhia das Letras, Rua Bandeira Paulista 702, cj. 32, São Paulo, SP 04532-002, Brazil. *Website:* www.companhiadasletras.com.br.

MELTZER, David; American poet, writer, teacher, editor and musician; b. 17 Feb. 1937, Rochester, NY; m. Christina Meyer 1958, one s. three d. *Education:* Los Angeles City College, University of California at Los Angeles. *Career:* Ed., Maya, 1966–71, Tree magazine and Tree Books, 1970–; Faculty, Graduate Poetics Program, 1980–, Chair, Undergraduate Writing and Literature Program, Humanities, 1988–, New College of California, San Francisco. *Publications:* Poetry: Poems (with Donald Schenker), 1957; Ragas, 1959; The Clown, 1960; Station, 1964; The Blackest Rose, 1964; Oyez!, 1965; The Process, 1965; In Hope I Offer a Fire Wheel, 1965; The Dark Continent, 1967; Nature Poem, 1967; Santamaya (with Jack Shoemaker), 1968; Round the Poem Box: Rustic and Domestic Home Movies for Stan and Jane Brakhage, 1969; Yesod, 1969; From Eden Book, 1969; Abulafia Song, 1969; Greenspeech, 1970; Luna, 1970; Letters and Numbers, 1970; Bronx Lil/Head of Lilian S.A.C., 1970; 32 Beams of Light, 1970; Knots, 1971; Bark: A Polemic, 1973; Hero/Lil, 1973; Tens: Selected Poems 1961–1971, 1973; The Eyes, the Blood, 1973; French Broom, 1973; Blue Rags, 1974; Harps, 1975; Six, 1976; Bolero, 1976; The Art, the Veil, 1981; The Name: Selected Poetry 1973–1983, 1984; Arrows: Selected Poetry 1957–1992, 1994; No Eyes: Lester Young, 2001. Fiction: Orf, 1968; The Agency, 1968; The Agent, 1968; How Many Blocks in the Pile?, 1968; Lovely, 1969; Healer, 1969; Out, 1969; Glue Factory, 1969; The Martyr, 1969; Star, 1970; The Agency Trilogy, 1994; Under, 2000. Other: We All Have Something to Say to Each Other: Being an Essay Entitled 'Patchen' and Four Poems, 1962; Introduction to the Outsiders, 1962; Bazascope Mother, 1964; Journal of the Birth, 1967; Isla Vista Notes: Fragmentary, Apocalyptic, Didactic Contradictions, 1970; Two-way Mirror: A Poetry Note-Book, 1977; San Francisco Beat: Talking With the Poets, 2002. Editor: Journal for the Protection of All Beings 1 and 3 (with Lawrence Ferlinghetti and Michael McClure), 2 vols, 1961, 1969; The San Francisco Poets, 1971, revised as Golden Gate, 1976; Birth: An Anthology, 1973; The Secret Garden: An Anthology in the Kabbalah, 1976; Death, 1984; Reading Jazz: The White Invention of Jazz, 1993; Writing Jazz, 1997. *Honours:* Council of Literary Magazine Grants, 1972, 1981; National Endowment for the Arts Grants, 1974, 1975; Tombstone Award for Poetry, James Ryan Morris Memorial Foundation, 1992.

MELVILLE, James (see Martin, (Roy) Peter)

MELVILLE, Jennie (see Butler, Gwendoline Williams)

MEMMI, Albert; French writer; b. 15 Dec. 1920, Tunis; s. of François Memmi and Marguerite née Sarfati; m. Germaine Dubach 1946; three c. *Education:* Lycée Carnot, Tunis, Univ. of Algiers and Univ. de Paris à la Sorbonne. *Career:* Teacher, Lycée Carnot, Tunis 1953, Teacher of Philosophy, Tunis 1955; Dir Psychological Centre, Tunis 1953–57; moved to France 1956; attached to Centre Nat. de la recherche Scientifique 1957, Researcher, CNRS, Paris 1959–; Chargé de conférences, Ecole pratique des hautes études 1958, Asst Prof. 1959–66, Prof. 1966–70; Prof., Inst. de Psychanalyse, Paris 1968–; Prof. Univ. of Paris 1970–, Dir Social Sciences Dept 1973–76, Dir Anthropological Lab.; mem. Acad. des Sciences d'Outre-mer; Vice-Pres. Pen-Club 1976-79; Managing Agent, Syndicat des Écrivains de Langue Française (SELF) 1981; Vice-Pres. Comité Nat. Laïcité-République 1991; mem. Comité de patronage du MRAP; mem. Ligne Internationale Contre le Racisme et l'Anti-sémitisme (LICRA); Hon. Cttee Mem. l'Union Rationaliste, Comité Culturel Tunisien en France 1995; Scientific Cttee Mem. Chaiers Francophones d'Europe Centre-Orientale 1996; Cttee Mem. sponsoring Association des Anciens Elèves du Lycée Carnot de Tunis 1996; Hon. Mem. Association des Etudes Françaises en Afrique Australe 1996; Advisory mem., Institut des Études Transrégionales du Centre d'Études, Int. Study Centre, Princeton Univ. 1995; mem. l' Acad. des Sciences d'Outremer, l'Academia Internazionale, l' Acad. de la Méditerranée. *Publications include:* novels: Le Statue de Sel (trans. as The Pillar of Salt) 1953, Strangers 1955, Agar 1955, Le Scorpion

1969, Le Désert 1977, Le Pharaon 1988; poems: Le Mirliton du ciel 1990, short stories: Le nomade immobile 2000, Térésa et autre femmes 2004; non-fiction: Portrait du colonisé 1957, Portrait d'un Juif 1962, Anthologie des écrivains Maghrebins 1964, 1969, Anthologie des écrivains nord-africains 1965, Les français et le racisme 1965, The Liberation of the Jew 1966, Dominated Man 1968, Decolonisation 1970, Juifs et Arabes 1974, Entretien 1975, La terre intérieure 1976, La dependance 1979, Le racisme 1982, Ce que je crois 1984, Les écrivains francophones du Maghreb 1985, L'Écriture colorée 1986, Bonheurs 1992, A contre-courants 1993, Ah, quel bonheur 1995, Le Juif et l'autre 1995, L'Exercice du bonheur 1996, Le Buveur et l'amoureux 1996, Feu sur 40 idées recues 1999, Dictionnaire à l'usage des incrédules 2002, Portrait du décolonisé, arabo-musulman et de quelques autres 2004, contrib. to Le onde 1989–94, Le Figaro 1995, New York Times, L'Action. Honours: Officier Légion d'honneur; Commdr Ordre de Nichan Iftikhar; Officier Palmes académiques, Officier Arts et Lettres, Officier Ordre République Tunisienne; Chevalier des affaires culturelles du Burkina Faso; Dr hc (Ben Gurion) 1999, (Beer Schéba); Hon. Prof. Walker Aims Univ., Washington Univ., l'école des H.E.C.; Prix de Carthage 1953, Prix Fénéon 1953, Prix Simba 1978, Prix de l'Union Rationaliste 1994, Grand Prix Littéraire de l'Afrique du Nord, Grand Prix Littéraire du Maghreb 1995, Prix littéraire Tunisie-France 1999, Chalom du Crif 2000, Grand Prix de la ville de Bari 2000, Prix de l'Afrique méditeranéenne 2002, Prix de la Fondation Ignacio Silone 2003, Grand Prix de la Francophonie décerné par l'Académie Française 2004. Address: 5 rue Saint Merri, 75004 Paris, France. Telephone: 1-40-29-08-31. Fax: 1-42-74-25-22.

MEMMOTT, David R., BA; American editor, writer and poet; b. 10 Dec. 1948, Grand Rapids, MI; m. Susan A. Memmott 1974; one d. Education: Eastern Oregon State University. Career: Man. Ed., 1986–90, Contributing Ed., 1990, 1997, Ice River: Magazine of Speculative Writing; mem. Council for Literature of the Fantastic; Institute for Noetic Sciences. Publications: Alpha Gallery: Selections from the Fantastic Small Press (poetry ed.), 1991; House on Fire: Poetry and Collage, 1992; The Larger Earth: Descending Notes of a Grounded Astronaut (poems), 1996; Within the Walls of Jericho (poems), 1998; Shadow Bones (short stories), 1999. Honours: Co-ordinating Council of Literary Magazines Grant, 1988; Oregon Arts Commission Grants, 1988, 1989; Fishtrap Fellow, 1990; Rhysling Award, 1990; Literary Arts Inc Fellowships, 1995, 2000. Address: 1003 Y Avenue, PO Box 3235, La Grande, OR 97850, USA.

MÉNARD, Jean-François; French writer and translator; b. 1948, Paris. Career: translator 1980–, including J.K. Rowling's Harry Potter series, Eoin Colfer's Artemis Fowl series, and other authors' works, including Martin Amis, Malcolm J. Bosse, Roald Dahl, Jerome K. Jerome. Publications include: Le Voleur de chapeaux et autres contes pour la semaine 1980, Quinze millions pour un fantôme 1980, Calebasse d'étoiles, Haïti Blues: echo poèmes, De l'autre bord de l'eau 1994, Fromage ou dessin 1994, Jimmy Lalouette 1995, Le Vagabond du Middle West 1995, D'écume au vent la vie 1996, La Belle anglaise a disparu 1996, La Ville du désert et de l'eau 1997, La Sorcière Mangetout (with Alex Sanders) 1998, L'Oiseau de malheur 1998, Le Soleil sur l'ardoise 1999, Du balai la sorcière (with Alex Sanders) 1999, Les Pieds de la sorcière (with Alex Sanders) 1999, Léger goût d'orange sure 2000, Dehors la sorcière (juvenile) 2001, Brumes en lumière 2002. Address: c/o Éditions Gallimard-Jeunesse, 5 rue Sébastien-Bottin, 75328 Paris, cedex 07, France. E-mail: litterature@gallimard-jeunesse.fr.

MENDES, David (Bob); Belgian writer and poet; b. 15 May 1928, Antwerp. Career: mem. Flemish Writers' Guild; PEN Club. Publications include: Day of Shame, 1988; The Chunnel Syndrome, 1989; The Fourth Sura, 1990; The Fraud Hunters, 1991; Vengeance, 1992; Races/Riots, 1993; Link, 1994; Merciless, 1995; The Power of Fire, 1996; The Power of Ice, 1998; Taste of Freedom, 1999; Dirty Dancing, 2000; Blood Feud, 2001. Honours: Golden Noose Awards, 1993, 1997; Dutch Award for Best Thriller (twice); Cultural Award, Schoten, 2000. Literary Agent: Dan Wright, Ann Wright Literary Agency, 136 E 56th Street, New York, NY 10022, USA. Address: Wezelsebaan 191, 2900 Schoten, Belgium. E-mail: bob.mendes@pandora.be. Website: www.mendes.be.

MENDOZA, Eduardo; Spanish writer; b. 11 Jan. 1943, Barcelona. Education: Hermanos Maristas school, studied law. Career: lawyer in Barcelona 1968–72; translator UN, New York 1973–78; Lecturer in Faculty of Translation and Interpretation, Universidad Pompeu Fabra, Barcelona 1995–96. Publications: La verdad sobre el caso Savolta (Premio de la Crítica) 1975, El misterio de la cripta embrujada (novel) 1978, El laberinto de las aceitunas (novel) 1982, La ciudad de los prodigios (novel) (Premio Ciudad de Barcelona 1987, Lire magazine Book of the Year, France 1988) 1986, Nueva York 1986, La isla inaudita 1989, Barcelona modernista (with Cristina Mendoza) 1989, Sin noticias de Gurb (originally serialised in El País) 1990, Restauraciò (play) 1990, El año del diluvio 1992, Una comedia ligera (Prix du meilleur livre étranger, France 1998) 1996, La aventura del tocador de señoras (novel) (Gremio de Libreros de Madrid Premio al Mejor Libro del Año 2002) 2001, Baroja, la contradicción (biog.) 2001, El último trayecto de Horacio Dos (novel, originally serialised in El País) 2002, Mauricio o la elecciones primarias 2006. Address: c/o Editorial Seix Barral, Avda Diagonal 662–664, 7°, Barcelona 08034, Spain (office). E-mail: editorial@seix-barral.es. Website: www.clubcultura.com/clubliteratura/clubescritores/mendoza.

MENDOZA, Mario, BA, MA; Colombian novelist; b. 1964, Bogotá. Education: Univ. of Bogotá, Fundación José Ortega y Gasset, Toledo, Spain. Publications: La ciudad de los umbrales 1992, La travesía del vidente (short stories) 1995, Scorpio City 1998, Relato de un asesino 2001, Satanás 2003. Honours: Premio Nacional de Literatura, Instituto Distrital de Cultura y Turismo 1995. Address: c/o Seix Barral, Avda Diagonal 662–664, 7°, Barcelona 08034, Spain (office).

MENKES-SPANIER, Suzy Peta, OBE, MA; British journalist and writer; Fashion Editor, International Herald Tribune; b. 24 Dec. 1943, Beaconsfield; d. of Edouard Menkes and Betty Curtis Menkes (née Lightfoot); m. David Spanier (died 2000); three s. one d. (deceased). Education: Brighton and Hove High School and Newnham Coll., Cambridge. Career: jr reporter The Times 1966–69, Fashion Ed. 1979–87; Fashion Ed. The Evening Standard 1968–77; Women's Ed. Daily Express 1977–79; Fashion Ed. The Independent 1987–88, Int. Herald Tribune 1988–; writes column in the Tribune. Publications include: The Royal Jewels 1985, The Windsor Style 1987, Queen and Country 1992. Honours: Freedom, City of Milan 1986, City of London 1987; British Press Awards Commendations 1983, 1984, Eugenia Sheppard Award for Fashion Journalism, Council of Fashion Designers of America; Chevalier, Legion d'Honneur 2005. Address: c/o International Herald Tribune, 6 bis rue des Graviers, 92521 Neuilly Cedex, France (office). Telephone: (1) 41-43-94-28 (office). Fax: (1) 41-43-93-38 (office). E-mail: smenkes@iht.com (office). Website: iht.com (office).

MERCHANT, Carolyn, MA, PhD; American environmental historian and academic; b. 12 July 1936, Rochester, NY. Education: Vassar Coll., Univ. of Wisconsin. Career: fmr Chair. Dept of Conservation and Resource Studies, now Prof. of Environmental History, Philosophy and Ethics, Univ. of California at Berkeley; Ecofeminist Scholar, Murdoch Univ., Western Australia 1991; various consultantships, lectureships; Pres. American Soc. for Environmental History 2001–03; has served on exec. and advisory bds of the History of Science Soc., Asscn for the Study of Literature and the Environment, and the journals: Environmental History, Environmental Ethics, Ethics and the Environment, International Journal of Ecoforestry, Organization and Environment; Fellow, Center for Advanced Study in the Behavioural Sciences, Stanfors 1978, American Council of Learned Socs. Publications: The Death of Nature: Women, Ecology and the Scientific Revolution 1980, Ecological Revolutions: Nature, Gender, and Science in New England 1989, Radical Ecology: The Search for a Livable World 1992, Major Problems in American Environmental History: Documents and Essays (ed.) 1993, Key Concepts in Critical Theory: Ecology (ed.) 1994, Earthcare: Women and the Environment 1996, Green Versus Gold: Sources in California's Environmental History (ed.) 1998, Columbia Guide to American Environmental History 2002, Reinventing Eden: The Fate of Nature in Western Culture 2003, Encyclopedia of World Environmental History (co-ed with John McNeill and Shepard Krech III) 2004; contrib. to scholarly journals. Honours: Dr hc (Umeå Univ., Sweden) 1995; NSF grants 1976–78, Nat. Endowment for the Humanities grants 1977, 1981–83, ACLS Fellowship 1978, Fulbright Sr Scholar, Umeå, Sweden 1984, Guggenheim Fellowship 1995, MacArthur Fellow in Ecological Humanities, Nat. Humanities Center 2001. Address: Department of Environmental Science Policy and Management, University of California, 138 Giannini Hall, Berkeley, CA 94720-3312, USA (office). Telephone: (510) 642-0326 (office). E-mail: merchant@nature.berkeley.edu (office). Website: ecohhistory.org (office).

MEREDITH, Christopher Laurence, BA; British novelist, poet, academic and translator; Senior Lecturer in Creative Writing, University of Glamorgan; b. 15 Dec. 1954, Tredegar, Wales; s. of Emrys Meredith and Joyce Meredith; m. V. Smythe 1981; two s. Education: Univ. Coll. Wales, Aberystwyth, Swansea Univ. Career: Sr Lecturer in Creative Writing, Univ. of Glamorgan 1993–; Fellow Yr Academi Gymreig (English language section), Soc. of Authors. Publications: poetry: This 1984, Snaring Heaven 1990, The Meaning of Flight 2005; novels: Shifts 1988, Griffri 1991, Sidereal Time 1998; for children: Nadolig bob Dydd 2000; translation from Welsh: Melog by Mihangel Morgan 2005; contrib. to literary magazines in Wales, England and the USA. Honours: Eric Gregory Award 1984, Welsh Arts Council Young Writer's Prize 1985, and Fiction Prize 1989, Arts Council Bursaries 1988, 1995. Address: c/o Seren Books, Norton Street, Bridgend, Mid Glamorgan, Wales.

MEREDITH, Gwenyth Valmai, OBE, BA; Australian playwright (retd); b. 18 Nov. 1907, NSW; d. of George and Florence Meredith; m. Ainsworth Harrison 1938. Education: Sydney Girls' High School and Univ. of Sydney. Career: freelance writer; scriptwriter Australian Broadcasting Comm. 1942–76, cr. radio serials The Lawsons and Blue Hills; Propr Chelsea Book Club, Sydney 1932–39. Publications include: novels: The Lawsons, Blue Hills, Beyond Blue Hills, Into the Sun; travel book: Inns and Outs (jtly with Ainsworth Harrison); plays: Wives Have Their Uses, Great Inheritance. Address: Unit 45, Kenilworth Gardens, Kangaloon Road, Bowral, NSW 2576, Australia.

MERNISSI, Fatema, PhD; Moroccan sociologist and writer; b. 1941, Fez. Education: Univ. of Paris (Sorbonne) and in the USA. Career: sociologist, feminist and expert in the Koran; Prof. Univ. Mohammed V, Rabat. Publications include: The Veil and the Male Elite: A Feminist Interpretation of Women's Rights in Islam 1992, Islam and Democracy: Fear of the Modern World 1994, The Forgotten Queens of Islam 1994, Dreams of Trespass: Tales of a Harem Girlhood 1994, Fear of Modernity or The Political Harem, Women's Rebellion and Islamic Memory 1996, Dreams on the Threshold, Les

Ait Débrouille 1997, Scheherazade Goes West 2001, Beyond the Veil: Male-Female Dynamics in Muslim Society 2003, Les Sindbads Marocains: Voyage dans le Maroc civique 2004. *Address:* University Mohammed V, BP 554, 3 rue Michelifen, Agdal, Rabat, Morocco. *E-mail:* fatema@mernissi.net. *Website:* www.mernissi.net.

MERRILL, Christopher Lyall, BA, MA; American poet, writer, editor, translator and academic; *Director of the International Writing Program, University of Iowa*; b. 24 Feb. 1957, Northampton, MA; m. Lisa Ellen Gowdy 1983; two d. *Education:* Middlebury Coll., Univ. of Washington at Seattle. *Career:* Dir Santa Fe Writers' Conference 1987–90; Founder-Dir Taos Conference on Writing and the Natural World 1987–92, Santa Fe Literary Center 1988–92; General Ed. Peregrine Smith Poetry Series 1987–; Poetry Ed. Orion Magazine 1993–; freelance journalist 1987–95; William H. Jenks Chair in Contemporary Letters, Coll. of the Holy Cross 1995–2000; Visiting Lecturer, Chatham Coll. 1999–2000; Prof. of English, Univ. of Iowa 2000–, Dir Int. Writing Program 2000–; literary critic, The World (Public Radio International) 2000–; mem. Acad. of American Poets, Authors' Guild, PEN American Center. *Publications:* Workbook (poems) 1988, Fevers and Tides (poems) 1989, The Forgotten Language: Contemporary Poets and Nature (ed.) 1991, From the Faraway Nearby: Georgia O'Keefe as Icon (co-ed. with Ellen Bradbury) 1992, The Grass of Another Country: A Journey Through the World of Soccer 1993, Watch Fire (poems) 1994, Anxious Moments, by Aleš Debeljak (trans.) 1994, The Old Bridge: The Third Balkan War and the Age of the Refugee 1995, What Will Suffice: Contemporary American Poets on the Art of Poetry (co-ed. with Christopher Buckley) 1995, The Forest of Speaking Trees: An Essay on Poetry 1996, Your Final Pleasure: An Essay on Reading 1996, The Four Questions of Melancholy: New and Selected Poems of Tomaz Šalamun (ed.) 1996, The Way to the Salt Marsh: A John Hay Reader (ed.) 1998, Only the Nails Remain: Scenes from the Balkan Wars 1999, Brilliant Water (poems) 2001, The City and the Child, by Aleš Debeljak (trans.) 2003, Things of the Hidden God: Journey to the Holy Mountain 2005; contrib. to many periodicals. *Honours:* Chevelier, Ordre des Arts et des Lettres 2006; Univ. of Utah Sherman Brown Neff Fellowship 1986–87, Bread Loaf Writers' Conf. John Ciardi Fellow in Poetry 1989, Pushcart Prize in Poetry 1990, Ingram Merrill Foundation Award in Poetry 1991, Prairie Schooner Readers' Choice Award in Poetry 1992, Acad. of American Poets Peter I. B. Lavan Younger Poets Award 1993, Slovenian Ministry of Culture Trans. Award 1997, The Bosnian Stecak Writers' Asscn of Bosnia-Herzegovina Annual Literary Award 2001, Kostas Kyrzias Foundation Hon. Int. Literary Award 2005. *Address:* International Writing Program, Shambaugh House, University of Iowa, 430 N Clinton Street, Iowa City, IA 52242-2020 (office); 216 McLean Street, Iowa City, IA 52242, USA (home). *Telephone:* (319) 335-2609 (office). *Fax:* (319) 335-3843 (office). *E-mail:* christopher-merrill@uiowa.edu (office). *Website:* www.christophermerrillbooks.com.

MERRIN, Jeredith, BS, MA, PhD; American academic, writer and poet; *Professor of English, Ohio State University, Columbus*; b. 9 April 1944, California; one d. *Education:* Iowa State University, San Jose State University, University of California at Berkeley. *Career:* Instructor, Gifted Program, University of California at Berkeley, 1983–85; Asst Prof., 1987–93, Assoc. Prof., 1993–97, Prof. of English, 1997–, Ohio State University, Columbus; MacDowell Artists Colony residencies 1999, 2001; presenter, workshops and poetry readings. *Publications:* An Enabling Humility: Marianne Moore, Elizabeth Bishop, and the Uses of Tradition, 1990; Shift (poems), 1996; Bat Ode (poems), 2001. Contributions: books, anthologies, reviews, quarterlies and journals. *Honours:* Lilly Foundation Fellow, 1988–89; Regdale Artists Colony Residencies, 1990, 1991, 1996; Fellow, Skidmore College, 1993; Elizabeth Gee Award for Research on Women, 1993; National Endowment for the Humanities Grants, 1995, 1997, Ohio Arts Council Grant for Poetry 2005. *Address:* c/o Department of English, Ohio State University, 164 W 17th Ave, Columbus, OH 43210, USA. *E-mail:* merrin.1@osu.edu (office). *Website:* www.jeredithmerrin.com.

MERTZ, Barbara Louise Gross, (Barbara Michaels, Elizabeth Peters), PhD; American writer; b. 29 Sept. 1927, Canton, IL; m. (divorced); one s. one d. *Education:* Univ. of Chicago. *Career:* mem. ACWL (pres. 1991–94); mem. advisory bd, KMT: A Modern Journal of Ancient Egypt; mem. advisory bd, The Writer. *Publications:* Temples Tombs & Hieroglyphs 1964, Red Land Black Land 1966, The Master of Blacktower 1966, Sons of the Wolf 1967, The Jackal's Head 1968, Ammie Come Home 1968, Prince of Darkness 1969, The Camelot Caper 1969, The Dark on the Other Side 1970, The Crying Child 1971, The Night of 400 Rabbits 1971, Greygallows 1972, The Seventh Sinner 1972, Witch 1973, Borrower of the Night 1973, House of Many Shadows 1974, Murders of Richard III 1974, Sea King's Daughter 1975, Crocodile on the Sandbank 1975, Patriot's Dream 1976, Legend in Green Velvet 1976, Wings of the Falcon 1977, Devil-May-Care 1977, Wait For What Will Come 1978, Street of the Five Moons 1978, The Walker in the Shadows 1979, Summer of the Dragon 1979, The Wizard's Daughter 1980, The Love Talker 1980, The Curse of the Pharaohs 1981, Someone in the House 1981, The Copenhagen Connection 1982, Black Rainbow 1982, Silhouette in Scarlet 1983, Here I Stay 1983, Die for Love 1984, The Grey Beginning 1984, The Mummy Case 1985, Be Buried in the Rain 1985, Lion in the Valley 1986, Shattered Silk 1986, Trojan Gold 1987, Search the Shadows 1987, Deeds of the Disturber 1988, Naked Once More 1989, Smoke and Mirrors 1989, Into the Darkness 1990, The Last Camel Died at Noon 1991, Vanish with the Rose 1992, Houses of Stone 1993, The Snake the Crocodile and the Dog 1992, Night Train to

Memphis 1994, Stitches in Time 1995, The Hippopotamus Pool 1996, The Dancing Floor 1997, Seeing a Large Cat 1997, The Ape Who Guards the Balance 1998, Other Worlds 1999, The Falcon at the Portal 1999, He Shall Thunder in the Sky 2000, Lord of the Silent 2001, The Golden One 2002, Children of the Storm 2003, Amelia Peabody's Egypt: A Compendium 2003, Guardian of the Horizon 2004, The Serpent on the Crown 2005; contrib. to reference works and periodicals. *Honours:* Hon. DHumLitt (Hood Coll.) 1992; Lifetime Achievement Award, Bouchercon 1986, Agatha Best Novel 1992, MWA Grand Master Award 1998, Agatha Best Non-Fiction 2003. *Address:* c/o Dominick Abel, 146 W 82nd Street, No. 1B, New York, NY 10024, USA (office). *Website:* www.mpmbooks.com (office).

MERVILLON, Pol-Jean (see Nadaus, Roland)

MERWIN, William Stanley, AB; American poet, dramatist, writer and translator; b. 30 Sept. 1927, New York, NY; m. Diane Whalley 1954. *Education:* Princeton Univ. *Career:* playwright-in-residence Poet's Theatre, Cambridge, MA 1956–57; Poetry Ed. The Nation 1962; Assoc., Theatre de la Citié, Lyons 1964–65; Special Consultant in Poetry, Library of Congress, Washington, DC 1999; Acad. of American Poets Fellowship 1973; mem. Acad. of American Poets, American Acad. of Arts and Letters. *Publications:* poetry: A Mask for Janus 1952, The Dancing Bears 1954, Green with Beasts 1956, The Drunk in the Furnace 1960, The Moving Target 1963, The Lice 1967, Three Poems 1968, Animae 1969, The Carrier of Ladders 1970, Signs 1971, Writings to an Unfinished Accompaniment 1973, The First Four Books of Poems 1975, Three Poems 1975, The Compass Flower 1977, Feathers from the Hill 1978, Finding the Islands 1982, Opening the Hand 1983, The Rain in the Trees 1988, Selected Poems 1988, Travels 1993, The Vixen 1996, The Folding Cliffs 1998, Migration: New and Selected Poems (Nat. Book Award for Poetry) 2005, Present Company 2005; plays: Darkling Child (with Dido Milroy) 1956, Favor Island 1957, The Gilded West 1961, adaptations of five other plays; other: A New Right Arm, West Wind: Supplement of American Poetry (ed.) 1961, The Miner's Pale Children 1970, Houses and Travellers 1977, Unframed Originals: Recollections 1982, Regions of Memory: Uncollected Prose 1949–1982 1987, The Essential Wyatt (ed.) 1989, The Lost Upland 1993, The Ends of the Earth (essays) 2005, Summer Doorways (memoir) 2005; translator: Selected Translations 1948–1968 1968, Selected Translations 1968–1978 1979, Sir Gawain and the Green Knight: A New Verse Translation 2004. *Honours:* Yale Series of Younger Poets Award 1952, Bess Hokin Prize 1962, Ford Foundation grant 1964, Harriet Monroe Memorial Prize 1967, PEN Translation Prize 1969, Rockefeller Foundation grant 1969, Pulitzer Prize in Poetry 1971, Shelley Memorial Award 1974, NEA grant 1978, Bollingen Prize 1979, Aiken Taylor Award 1990, Maurice English Award 1990, Dorothea Tanning Prize 1994, Lenore Marshall Award 1994, Ruth Lilly Poetry Prize 1998. *Literary Agent:* Steven Barclay Agency, 12 Western Avenue, Petaluma, CA 94952, USA. *Telephone:* (707) 773-0654. *Fax:* (707) 778-1868. *Website:* www.barclayagency.com.

MESERVE, Walter Joseph; American academic, editor and writer; b. 10 March 1923, Portland, Maine; m. 1st; two s. two d.; m. 2nd Mollie Ann Lacey 1981. *Education:* Portland Junior College, 1941–42; AB, Bates College, Lewiston, Maine, 1947; MA, Boston University, 1948; PhD, University of Washington, 1952. *Career:* Instructor to Prof., University of Kansas, 1951–68; Prof. of Dramatic Literature and Theory, 1968–88, Dir, Institute for American Theatre Studies, 1983–88, Indiana University; Vice-Pres., Feedback Services, New York City, Brooklin, Maine, 1983–; Ed.-in-Chief, Feedback Theatre-books, 1985–; Distinguished Prof., 1988–93, Distinguished Prof. Emeritus, 1993–, Graduate School and Univ. Center, PhD Programs in Theatre and English, CUNY; Co-Ed., American Drama and Theatre journal, 1989–93; mem. Cosmos Club. *Publications:* The Complete Plays of W. D. Howells (ed.), 1960; Outline History of American Drama, 1965; American Satiric Comedies (co-ed.), 1969; Robert E. Sherwood, 1970; Modern Drama from Communist China (co-ed.), 1970; Studies in Death of a Salesman (ed.), 1972; Modern Literature from China (co-ed.), 1974; An Emerging Entertainment: The Drama of the American People to 1828, 1977; The Revels History of Drama in English, Vol. VIII: American Drama (co-author), 1977; Cry Woolf (co-author), 1982; Heralds of Promise: The Drama of the American People During the Age of Jackson 1829–1849, 1986; Who's Where in the American Theatre (co-ed.), 1990; A Chronological Outline of World Theatre (co-author), 1992; The Theatre Lover's Cookbook (co-ed.), 1992; Musical Theatre Cookbook (co-ed.), 1993. *Honours:* National Endowment for the Humanities Fellowships, 1974–75, 1983–84, 1988–89; Rockefeller Foundation Fellowship, 1979; Guggenheim Fellowship, 1984–85. *Address:* PO Box 174, Brooklin, ME 04616, USA.

MESSENT, Peter Browning, BA, MA, PhD; British academic; *Professor of Modern American Literature, University of Nottingham*; b. 24 Oct. 1946, Wimbledon, England; m. 1st Brenda 1972 (divorced); one s. one d.; m. 2nd Carin 1994. *Education:* Univ. of Manchester, Univ. of Nottingham. *Career:* temporary lecturer, Univ. of Manchester 1972–73; Lecturer, Univ. of Nottingham 1973–94, Sr Lecturer in American and Canadian Studies 1994–95, Reader in Modern American Literature 1995–99, Prof. of Modern American Literature 1999–; mem. British Asscn for American Studies, Mark Twain Circle, Hemingway Soc. *Publications:* Twentieth Century Views: Literature of the Occult (ed.) 1981, New Readings of the American Novel 1990, Ernest Hemingway 1992, Henry James: Selected Tales (ed.) 1992, Mark Twain 1997, Criminal Proceedings (ed.) 1997, The Short Works of Mark Twain: A Critical Study 2001, A Companion to Mark Twain (co-ed.) 2005, The

Civil War Letters of Joseph Hopkins Twichell (co-ed.) 2005, Cambridge Introduction to Mark Twain 2007; contrib. to books, journals and magazines. *Address:* School of American and Canadian Studies, University of Nottingham, Nottingham, NG7 2RD, England (office). *Telephone:* (115) 951-4265 (office). *Fax:* (115) 951-4270 (office). *E-mail:* peter.messent@nottingham.ac.uk (office). *Website:* www.nottingham.ac.uk/american (office).

MESSER, Thomas Maria, MA; American museum director; b. 9 Feb. 1920, Bratislava, Czechoslovakia; s. of Richard Messer and Agatha (Albrecht) Messer; m. Remedios García Villa 1948. *Education:* Thiel Coll. (Greenville, Pa), Boston, Paris and Harvard Univs. *Career:* Dir, Roswell Museum, New Mexico 1949–52; Dir American Fed. of Arts, New York 1952–56, Trustee and First Vice-Pres. 1972–75; Dir Inst. of Contemporary Art, Boston 1956–61; Dir Solomon R. Guggenheim Museum, New York 1961–88; Pres. Asscn of Art Museum Dirs 1974–75 (Hon. mem. 1988–); Chair. Int. Cttee for Museums and Collections of Modern Art, Int. Council of Museums 1974–77, Hon. Chair. 1977–; Chair. Int. Exhbns Cttee 1976–78, US/ICOM (Nat. Cttee of Int. Council of Museums) 1979–81; Adjunct Prof. of Art History, Harvard Univ. 1960; Barnard Coll. 1965, 1971; Sr Fellow, Center for Advanced Studies, Wesleyan Univ. 1966; Trustee Center for Inter-American Relations (now Americas Soc.) 1974–, Exec. Council Int. Council of Museums 1983–85; Vice-Chair. US Int. Council of Museums Cttee of American Asscn of Museums, Washington, DC 1979–81; Pres. MacDowell Colony Inc. 1977–80; Dir Solomon R. Guggenheim Foundation 1980–90, Trustee 1985–90, Dir Emer. 1988–; mem. Advisory Bd, Palazzo Grassi Venice 1986–97; Trustee Fontana Foundation, Milan 1988–; Chair. Arts Int., Inst. of Int. Educ. 1988–90; Trustee, Inst. of Int. Educ. 1991–99, Hon. Trustee 1999–, Fontana Foundation 1996–; Curatorships Schirn Kunsthalle, Frankfurt 1988–99, Sr Adviser La Caixa Foundation, Barcelona 1990–94; Visiting Prof. Frankfurt Goethe Univ. 1991–; fmr mem. Museum Advisory Panel of Nat. Endowment for the Arts, Art Advisory Panel to Commr of Internal Revenue Service 1974–77; mem. Council Nat. Gallery of the Czech Repub. 1994–99; Trustee Isamo Noguchi Foundation, New York and Tokyo 1998–. *Major retrospective exhibitions at the Guggenheim Museum include:* Edvard Munch, Vasily Kandinsky, Egon Schiele, Paul Klee and Alberto Giacometti. *Publications:* The Emergent Decade: Latin American Painters and Paintings in the 1960s 1966, Edvard Munch 1973, Vasily Kandinsky 1997; museum catalogues on Vasily Kandinsky, Paul Klee, Edvard Munch, Egon Schiele, etc.; articles and contributions to numerous art journals. *Honours:* Hon. mem. Inst. of Int. Educ. 1999–; Dr Fine Arts hc (Univ. of Mass.), (Thisk Coll. Greenville USA), (Univ. of Arts, Philadelphia); Kt, Royal Order of St Olav (Norway); Officer's Cross of Order of Merit (FRG) 1975; Officer of Order of Leopold II (Belgium) 1978, Officier Légion d'honneur 1989, Austrian Cross of Honour for Science and Art 1981, Goethe Medal 1990. *Address:* 205 E 77th Street, New York, NY 10021; 303 E 57th Street, New York, NY 10022 (office); 35 Sutton Place, New York, NY 10022, USA (home). *Telephone:* (212) 486-1393 (office); (212) 355-8611 (home); (212) 249-2727. *Fax:* (212) 249-2727 (office). *E-mail:* tmmesser@aol.com (office).

MESTAS, Jean-Paul, BA, LLB; French poet, writer and translator; b. 15 Nov. 1925, Paris; m. Christiane Schoubrenner 1977, two s. one d. *Education:* Institute of Political Studies, Paris. *Career:* mem. International Acad., Chennai, fellow; International Poetry, Republic of Korea; International Writers and Artists, board of research. *Publications:* various poems, essays and translations 1965–95; contrib. to many anthologies and periodicals. *Honours:* Excellence in Poetry, International Poet, New York, 1982; Premio de la Cultura, Palermo, 1991; Prix Marcel Beguey, Bergerac, 1992.

MESTROVIC, Stjepan, BA, PhD; American academic, writer and editor; *Professor of Sociology, Texas A & M University*; b. 12 March 1955, Croatia; two d. *Education:* Harvard Univ., Syracuse Univ. *Career:* Prof. of Sociology, Texas A & M Univ., College Station, USA 1990–; Series Ed. Postmodern Social Futures, Eastern Europe; mem. American Sociological Asscn, Schopenhauer Soc. *Publications:* Emile Durkheim and the Reformation of Sociology 1988, The Coming Fin de Siècle: An Application of Durkheim's Sociology to Modernity and Postmodernity 1991, Durkheim and Postmodern Culture 1992, The Road from Paradise: The Possibility of Democracy in Eastern Europe 1993, Habits of the Balkan Heart: Social Character and the Fall of Communism 1993, The Barbarian Temperament: Towards a Postmodern Critical Theory 1993, The Balkanization of the West: The Confluence of Postmodernism with Postcommunism 1994, Genocide after Emotion: The Postemotional Balkan War 1996, This Time We Knew: Western Responses to Genocide in Bosnia (co-ed.) 1996, The Conceit of Innocence: How the Conscience of the West Was Lost in the War against Bosnia 1997, Postemotional Society 1997, Anthony Giddens: The Last Modernist 1998, Veblen on Theory, Culture and Society 2004, The Trials of Abu Ghraib 2006. *Honours:* Fellow, Nat. Endowment for the Humanities 1986–87, Fulbright Fellow in Croatia 1992–93. *Address:* Department of Sociology, Texas A & M University, College Station, TX 77843-4351, USA (office). *E-mail:* mestrovic@neo.tamu.edu (office). *Website:* sociweb.tamu.edu (office).

METCALF, John Wesley, CM, BA; Canadian author and editor; *Editor, Canadian Notes and Queries*; b. 12 Nov. 1938, Carlisle, UK; s. of Thomas Metcalf and Gladys Moore; m. Myrna Teitelbaum 1975; three s. three d. *Education:* Beckenham and Penge Grammar School and Univ. of Bristol. *Career:* emigrated to Canada 1962; Writer-in-Residence, Univs of NB 1972–73, Loyola of Montreal 1976, Ottawa 1977, Concordia Univ. Montreal 1980–81, Univ. of Bologna 1985; Sr Ed. Porcupine's Quill Press 1989–, Ed. Canadian Notes and Queries (literary magazine) 1997–; Sr Ed. Biblioasis Press 2005–. *Publications:* The Lady Who Sold Furniture 1970, The Teeth of My Father 1975, Girl in Gingham 1978, Selected Stories 1982, Kicking Against the Pricks 1982, Adult Entertainment 1986, What is a Canadian Literature? 1988, Volleys 1990, How Stories Mean 1992, Shooting the Stars 1992, Freedom from Culture: Selected Essays 1982–1992 1994, Acts of Kindness and of Love (jtly) 1995, Forde Abroad 2003, An Aesthetic Underground 2003, Standing Stones: The Best Stories of John Metcalf 2004. *Address:* 128 Lewis Street, Ottawa, ON K2P 0S7, Canada. *Telephone:* (613) 233-3200. *Website:* www.biblioasis.com.

METZGER, Deena, BA, MA, PhD; American writer, poet, playwright, teacher and healer; b. 17 Sept. 1936, New York, NY; m. 1st H. Reed Metzger 1957; m. 2nd Michael Ortiz Hill 1987; two s. *Education:* Brooklyn College, CUNY, University of California, International College, Los Angeles. *Career:* Prof., Los Angeles Valley College, 1966–69, 1973–74, 1975–79; Faculty, California Institute of the Arts, 1970–75; International Lecturer, Teacher of Writing, Supervision and Training of Healers in the Ethical, Creative and Spiritual Aspects of Healing, 1997–. *Publications:* Skin Shadows/Silence, 1976; Dark Milk, 1978; The Book of Hags, 1978; The Axis Mundi Poems, 1981; What Dinah Thought, 1989; Looking for the Face of God, 1989; A Sabbath Among the Ruins, 1992; Writing for Your Life: A Guide and Companion to the Inner Worlds, 1992; Tree: Essays and Pieces (co-ed.), 1997; Intimate Nature: Women's Bond with Animals (co-ed.), 1998, The Other Hand 1999, Entering the Ghost River: Meditations on the Theory and Practice of Healing 2001, Doors: A Fiction for Jazz Horn 2004, Dreams Against the State (play) 2005. *Address:* PO Box 186, Topanga, CA 90290, USA.

METZGER, Henry, AB, MD, FAAS; American (b. German) scientific researcher; b. 23 March 1932, Mainz, Germany; s. of Paul Alfred Metzger and Anne (Daniel) Metzger; m. Deborah Stashower 1957; two s. one d. *Education:* Univ. of Rochester, Columbia Univ. *Career:* emigrated to USA 1938; Intern, then Asst Resident, Col-Presbyterian Medical Center 1957–59; Research Assoc., NIAMD, NIH 1959–61, Medical Officer, Arthritis and Rheumatism Branch, Bethesda, MD 1963–73, Chief, Section on Chemical Immunology 1973–, Chief, Arthritis and Rheumatism Branch, Nat. Inst. of Arthritis and Musculoskeletal and Skin Diseases 1983–94, Dir Intramural Research Program 1987–98; Fellow Helen Hay Whitney Foundation, Dept of Biology, Univ. of Calif., San Diego 1961–63; Pres. American Asscn of Immunologists 1991–92; Pres. Int. Union of Immunological Socs 1992–95; mem. Health Research Council BMFT, German Govt 1994–97; mem. NAS. *Publications:* over 200 scientific papers and contribs to scientific journals. *Honours:* Hon. mem. Chilean and French Socs of Immunology; several awards. *Address:* 3410 Taylor Street, Chevy Chase, MD 20815, USA (home).

MEWSHAW, Michael, MA, PhD; American author and poet; b. 19 Feb. 1943, Washington, DC; m. Linda Kirby 1967, two s. *Education:* University of Virginia. *Career:* Instructor, 1970, Visiting Writer, 1989–91, University of Virginia; Asst Prof. of English, University of Massachusetts, 1970–71; Asst Prof. to Assoc. Prof. of English, University of Texas, Austin, 1973–83; Visiting Artist, 1975–76, Writer-in-Residence, 1977–78, American Acad., Rome; mem. PEN; Society of Fellows of the American Acad. in Rome; Texas Institute of Letters; US Tennis Writers Asscn. *Publications:* Fiction: Man in Motion, 1970; Waking Slow, 1972; The Troll, 1974; Earthly Bread, 1976; Land Without Shadow, 1979; Year of the Gun, 1984; Blackballed, 1986; True Crime, 1991. Non-Fiction: Life for Death, 1980; Short Circuit, 1983; Money to Burn: The True Story of the Benson Family Murders, 1987; Playing Away: Roman Holidays and Other Mediterranean Encounters, 1988; Ladies of the Court: Grace and Disgrace on the Women's Tennis Tour, 1993. Contributions: newspapers and magazines. *Honours:* Fulbright Fellowship, 1968–69; William Rainey Fellowship, 1970; National Endowment for the Arts Fellowship, 1974–75; Carr Collins Awards for Best Book of Non-Fiction, 1980, 1983; Guggenheim Fellowship, 1981–82; Book of the Year Award, Tennis Week, 1993.

MEYER, Kai; German novelist; b. 1969. *Career:* fmr journalist; freelance author 1995–, writing mainly for young adults; co-creator of fantasy role-playing game, Engel. *Publications:* Der schwarze Storch (trans. as The Black Stork) 1999, Die Rückkehr des Hexenmeisters (trans. as The Wizard's Return) 1999, Die Katakomben des Damiano (trans. as Damiano's Catacombs) 1999, Der Dornenmann (trans. as The Thorn Man) 1999, Jenseits des Jarhtausands (trans. as Beyond the Millennium) 1999, Teuflisches Halloween (trans. as A Diabolic Halloween) 2000, Dämonen der Tiefe (trans. as Demons of the Depth) 2000, Die Nacht der lebenden Scheuchen (trans. as The Night of the Living Scarecrows) 2000, Schattenengel (trans. as Shadow Angel) 2000, Tor Zwischen den Welten (trans. as Gateway Between Two Worlds) 2001, Die Fliessende Königin (trans. as The Flowing Queen 2005) (Marsh Award for Children's Literature in Translation 2007) 2001, Mondwanderer (trans. as Moon Wanderer) 2002, Das Steinerne Licht (trans. as The Stone Light) 2002, Das Gläserne Wort (trans. as The Glass Word) 2002, Die Wellenläufer (trans. as The Wave Runners) 2003, Die Muschelmagier (trans. as The Shell Magicians) 2004, Die Wasserweber (trans. as The Water Weavers) 2004, Das Buch Von Eden (The Book of Eden) 2004, Frostfeuer (trans. as Frostfire) (Corine Award for Books for Children and Adolescents) 2005, Seide und Schwert (trans. as Silk and Sword) 2006, Lanze und Licht (trans. as Lance and Light) 2007, Drache und Diamant 2007; also Pandoramicum (comic book), screenplays. *Address:* c/o Egmont Books, 239 Kensington High Street, London, W8 6SA, England (office). *E-mail:* info@egmont.co.uk. *Website:* www.kaimeyer.com.

MEYER, Lynn (see Slavitt, David Rytman)

MEYERS, Carol, AB, MA, PhD; American archaeologist, academic and writer; *Mary Grace Wilson Professor, Duke University*; b. 26 Nov. 1942, Wilkes-Barre, PA; d. of Dr Harry J. Lyons and Irene W. Lyons; m. Eric Meyers 1964; two d. *Education:* Wellesley Coll., Hebrew Union Coll. Biblical and Archaeological School, Jerusalem and Hebrew Univ. of Jerusalem, Israel, Brandeis Univ. *Career:* Lecturer, Univ. of North Carolina at Chapel Hill 1975, part-time Lecturer 1976–77, Visiting Asst Prof. 1979; Asst Prof., Duke Univ. 1977–84, Assoc. Prof. 1984–90, Prof. 1990–, Mary Grace Wilson Prof. of Religion 2002–; Assoc. Dir Meiron Excavation Project 1978–; Co-Dir Jt Sepphoris Project 1984–92, Sepphoris Regional Project 1992–99, Sr Advisor, Sepphoris Acropolis Project 1999–; Visiting Faculty, MA Program in Judaic Studies, Univ. of Connecticut 1994–; mem. Center of Theological Inquiry, Princeton 1991–, American Acad. of Religion, American Schools of Oriental Research, Archaeological Inst. of America, Asscn for Jewish Studies, British School of Archaeology in Jerusalem, Catholic Biblical Assen, Center for Cross-Cultural Research on Women, Oxford, UK, Israel Exploration Soc., Palestine Exploration Soc., Soc. for Values in Higher Educ., Soc. of Biblical Literature, Wellesley Coll. Center for Research on Women, Women's Assen of Ancient Near Eastern Studies; Assoc. Ed. Semeia 1990–96, Bulletin of the American Schools of Oriental Research 1997–2006; Consulting Ed. (on Genesis and Exodus, for gender language) Contemporary Torah: A Gender-Sensitive Adaptation of the JPS Translation, for Dictionary of the Bible, for Jesus and His World: An Archaeological and Cultural Dictionary; mem. Editorial Bd and Consulting Ed. Women's Commentary on the Torah; mem. Editorial Bd Jewish Women: A Comprehensive Historical Encyclopedia, Library of Hebrew Bible/Old Testament Studies (fmr Journal for the Study of the Old Testament Supplement); many consultant positions. *Television:* documentaries on archaeology and the Bible. *Publications:* The Tabernacle Menorah: A Synthetic Study of a Symbol from the Biblical Cult 1976; Excavations at Ancient Meiron: Upper Galilee, Israel 1971–72, 1974–75, 1977 (with E. M. Meyers and J. F. Strange) 1981, The Word of the Lord Shall Go Forth (co-ed. with M. O'Connor) 1983, Haggai, Zechariah 1–8 (with E. Meyers) 1987, Discovering Eve: Ancient Israelite Women in Context 1988, Excavations at the Ancient Synagogue of Gush Halav (with E. Meyers) 1990, Sepphoris (with E. Netzer and E. Meyers) 1992, Zechariah 9–14 (with E. Meyers) 1993, Ethics and Politics in the Hebrew Bible (co-ed. with D. A. Knight) 1995, Community, Identity, and Ideology: Social Science Approaches to the Hebrew Bible (co-ed. with C. W. Carter) 1996, Sepphoris in Galilee: Cross-Currents of Culture (co-ed. with R. Nagy, E. M. Meyers and Z. Weiss) 1996, Families in Ancient Israel (with L. G. Perdue, J. Blenkinsopp and J. J. Collins) 1997, Women in Scripture: A Dictionary of Named and Unnamed Women in the Hebrew Bible, the Apocryphal/Deuterocanonical Books, and the New Testament (co-ed. with T. Craven and R. S. Kraemer) 2000, Households and Holiness: The Religious Culture of Israelite Women 2005, Exodus 2005; contribs to scholarly books and professional journals. *Honours:* various grants; Thayer Fellow, Albright Inst. 1975–76, Nat. Endowment for the Humanities Fellowships 1982–83, 1990–91, Howard Foundation Fellowship 1985–86, Int. Corresp. Fellow, Ingeborg Rennert Center for Jerusalem Studies, Bar Ilan Univ., Israel 1998–, Severinghaus Award 1991, Wellesley Coll. Alumnae Achievement Award 1999, Educ. Endowment Award, Women's Inst. for Continuing Jewish Educ. 2001. *Address:* Department of Religion, Duke University, Box 90964, Durham, NC 27708-0964, USA (office). *Telephone:* (919) 660-3514 (office). *Fax:* (919) 660-3530 (office). *E-mail:* carol@duke.edu (office). *Website:* www.duke.edu/religion/ugrad/undergraduates.html (office).

MEYERS, Jeffrey, MA, PhD, FRSL; American writer; b. 1 April 1939, New York, NY. *Education:* Univ. of Michigan, Univ. of California at Berkeley. *Publications:* Fiction and the Colonial Experience 1973, The Wounded Spirit: A Study of Seven Pillars of Wisdom 1973, T. E. Lawrence: A Bibliography 1975, A Reader's Guide to George Orwell 1975, George Orwell: The Critical Heritage 1975, Painting and the Novel 1975, A Fever at the Core 1976, George Orwell: An Annotated Bibliography of Criticism 1977, Married to Genius 1977, Homosexuality and Literature, 1890–1930 1977, Katherine Mansfield: A Biography 1978, The Enemy: A Biography of Wyndham Lewis 1980, Wyndham Lewis: A Revaluation 1980, D. H. Lawrence and the Experience of Italy 1982, Hemingway: The Critical Heritage 1982, Disease and the Novel, 1860–1960 1984, Hemingway: A Biography 1985, D. H. Lawrence and Tradition 1985, The Craft of Literary Biography 1985, The Legacy of D. H. Lawrence 1987, Manic Power: Robert Lowell and his Circle 1987, Robert Lowell: Interviews and Memoirs 1988, The Biographer's Art 1989, The Spirit of Biography 1989, T. E. Lawrence: Soldier, Writer, Legend 1989, Graham Greene: A Revaluation 1989, D. H. Lawrence: A Biography 1990, Joseph Conrad: A Biography 1991, Edgar Allan Poe: His Life and Legacy 1992, Scott Fitzgerald: A Biography 1994, Edmund Wilson: A Biography 1995, Robert Frost: A Biography 1996, Bogart: A Life in Hollywood 1997, Gary Cooper: American Hero 1998, Orwell: Wintry Conscience of a Generation 2000, Privileged Moments: Encounters with Writers 2000, Hemingway: Life into Art 2000, The Sir Arthur Conan Doyle Reader 2002, Inherited Risk: Errol and Sean Flynn in Hollywood and Vietnam 2002, Somerset Maugham: A Life 2004, The Somerset Maugham Reader 2004, Impressionist Quartet: The Intimate Genius of Manet and Morisot, Degas and Cassatt 2005, Married to Genius 2005, Modigliani: A Life 2006. *Honours:* awards from American Council of Learned Socs, Huntington Library; Fulbright Fellowship, Guggenheim Fellowship. *Address:* 84 Stratford Road, Kensington, CA 94707, USA. *E-mail:* vjmeyers@nothingbutnet.net.

MEYNELL, Hugo Anthony, BA, PhD; British/Canadian academic and writer; b. 23 March 1936, Derbyshire, England; m. Jenifer Routledge 1969; three d. one adopted s. *Education:* King's Coll., Cambridge. *Career:* Lecturer, Univ. of Leeds 1961–81; Visiting Prof., Emory Univ. 1978; Prof. of Religious Studies, Univ. of Calgary 1981–98; mem. Canadian Philosophical Assen, Canadian Soc. for Religious Studies, RSC. *Publications:* Sense, Nonsense and Christianity 1964, Grace versus Nature 1966, The New Theology and Modern Theologians 1967, God and the World 1971, An Introduction to the Philosophy of Bernard Lonergan 1976, Freud, Marx and Morals 1981, The Intelligible Universe: A Cosmological Argument 1982, The Nature of Aesthetic Value 1986, The Theology of Bernard Lonergan 1986, The Art of Handel's Operas 1986, Is Christianity True? 1994, Redirecting Philosophy 1998, Postmodernism and the New Enlightenment 2001; contrib. to scholarly journals. *Address:* # 309, 1320 Eighth Avenue SE, Calgary, AB T2G 0M9, Canada (home). *Telephone:* (403) 283-3320 (home). *E-mail:* hugomeynell@shaw.ca (home).

MEZHIROV, Aleksandr Petrovich; Russian poet; b. 26 Sept. 1923, Moscow; s. of Pyotr Izraelevich Mezhirov and Yelizaveta Semyonovna Mezhirova; m. Yelena Yaschenko; one d. *Education:* Moscow Univ. *Career:* served in Soviet Army 1941–45; Prof. in Literary Inst., Moscow 1966–91. *Publications:* more than 50 vols of poetry, including Long is the Road 1947, Returns 1955, Poems and Translations 1962, Ladoga Ice 1965, Selected Works (2 Vols) 1981, The Blind Turning 1983, The Outline of Things 1984, Prose in Poetry 1985, Bormotucha 1990, The What That Has No Name 1995, Ground Wind 1997, Apologia of a Circus 1997; trans. Georgian and Lithuanian poetry, articles, critical reviews, essays on history of Russian econs. *Honours:* State Prize for Poetry 1986, Georgian State Prize 1989.

MIALL, Robert (see Burke, John Frederick)

MIAN MIAN; Chinese writer; b. 1970, Shanghai. *Career:* started writing aged 16; DJ, Cotton Club, Shanghai 1996; music promoter and dance party organizer 1997–; contributor of short stories and novellas to Chinese literary magazines, including Xiaoshuo Jie 1997–; books banned in China 2000–02; columnist for Hong Kong independent newspaper, Apple Daily, and for fashion magazines 2002–. *Publications:* La La La (short stories) 1997, Candy (novel) 2000, Every Good Child Deserves Candy (short stories) 2000, Acid Lover (short stories) 2000, Social Dance (short stories) 2002, Panda Sex (novel) 2005. *E-mail:* nanawang@mianmian.com. *Website:* www.modernsky.com; www.mianmian.com.

MICHAELS, Anne, BA; Canadian poet, novelist, writer and teacher; *Professor of Creative Writing, University of Toronto*; b. 15 April 1958, Toronto, Ont. *Education:* Univ. of Toronto. *Career:* many workshops and guest residencies; Prof. of Creative Writing, Univ. of Toronto 1988–; mem. League of Canadian Poets, Writers' Union of Canada, PEN Canada. *Publications:* poetry: The Weight of Oranges 1986 (Commonwealth Poetry Prize for the Americas), Miner's Pond 1991 (Canadian Authors' Assen Award for Poetry), Skin Divers 1999; fiction: Fugitive Pieces (several awards including Trillium Award, Beatrice and Martin Fischer Award, Orange Prize for Fiction, Guardian Fiction Award) 1997; fiction translated into 30 languages; contrib. to numerous anthologies, reviews and magazines. *Honours:* Epstein Award for Poetry 1980, 1986, 1991, Nat. Magazine Award for Poetry 1991, Chapter/Books in Canada First Novel Award 1997, Lannan Prize 1997, H. H. Wingate Award 1997, Harry Ribalow Award 1998, Acerbi Prize 2001. *Address:* c/o McClelland and Stewart Inc., 75 Sherbourne Street, 5th floor, Toronto, ON M5A 2P9, Canada; c/o Bloomsbury Publishing, 38 Soho Square, London, W1D 3HB, England.

MICHAELS, Barbara (see Mertz, Barbara Louise Gross)

MICHAELS, Kristin (see Williams, Jeanne)

MICHEL, Caroline; British literary agent and fmr publisher; *Managing Director, William Morris Agency (UK) Ltd*; m. Matthew Evans (later Lord Evans of Temple Guiting) 1991; two s. one d. *Education:* Univ. of Edinburgh. *Career:* worked at poetry magazine, Agenda; Publicity Dept Chatto & Windus from 1981; founder and Dir Bloomsbury Publishing; Man. Dir Granta Books; worked at Orion; Deputy Man. Dir and Deputy Publisher of CCV division of Random House, and Publisher Vintage (Random House imprint) 1993–2003; Man. Dir and Publisher HarperPress (division of HarperCollins Publishers) 2003–05; Man. Dir William Morris Agency (UK) Ltd 2005–; Gov. British Film Inst.; mem. exec. cttee English PEN 2006; fmr mem. Man Booker Prize cttee. *Address:* William Morris Agency, 52–53 Poland Street, London, W1F 7LX, England (office). *Website:* www.wma.com (office).

MICHEL, Pauline, LèsL; Canadian poet, writer and songwriter; b. 1944, Asbestos, PQ. *Education:* Univ. of Sherbrooke, École normale Marguerite Bourgeois and Laval Univ. *Career:* fmr teacher Cegep de Sherbrooke, Université du Québec à Montréal; numerous poetry and song tours and recitals in Canada, Africa, France; Parl. Poet Laureate 2004–06; mem. Union des écrivaines et des écrivains Québécois. *Writing for television:* À la Claire Fontaine, Hello Moineau (lyricist), L'animagerie, La Maison de Ouimzie, Le Château des enfants, Passe-Partout, Télé-Ressources, You-hou; scripts for broadcasts with Radio-Canada, Télé-Métropole, TV Ontario and Télé-Québec. *Films:* consultant on La Caresse d'une ride (film), Les Cheveux en quatre (documentary), Les héritières d'Esther Blondin (video of own work). *Recordings:* Au coeur d'la vie 1979, Contrastes 1980, Hello moineau 1985, Le tour du monde 2000. *Publications include:* L'assiette-à-tourmente (novella), Le tour du monde (songbook), On perd la boule (play), Farfelu ou Les Sens ensorceleurs (play and lyrics), Les yeux d'eau (novel) 1975, Mirage (novel) 1978, La poupée abandonnée (multimedia) (Prix Adate) 1980, Sors de ta cage (lyrics to musical) 1984, Hello Moineau (songbook) 1985, Demeurez dans mon amour 1987, Livret de chants (songbook) 1987, Voyez comme ils s'aiment (songbook) 1988, L'oeil sauvage (poems) 1988, Cannelle et pruneau dans les feuilles de thé 1992, Le papillon de Vénus (novel) 1999, Au fil de l'autre (play) 2004, Funambule/Tightrope 2006, Frissons d'enfants (short stories) 2006; contrib. novellas and poems to anthologies. *Honours:* Ministry of Cultural Affairs grant, Canadian Embassy in Paris bursary 1980; winner Québec en chansons. *Address:* 3315, Ridgewood Avenue, Apartment 6, Montréal, Québec H3V 1BY (home); c/o Broken Jaw Press Inc., PO Box 596, Stn A, Fredericton, NB E3B 5A6, Canada. *Telephone:* (514) 344-0588 (home). *E-mail:* pmichel@aei.ca (home).

MICHEL, Sandra Seaton, BA; American writer, poet and editor; b. 30 Jan. 1935, Hancock, Mich.; m. Philip R. Michel 1956; three s. one d. *Education:* Stanford Univ. *Career:* Ed., Lenape Publishing 1973–78; teacher, Coast Episcopal Schools 1982–84; Delaware State Arts Council and Nat. Endowment for the Arts Residency Artist in Creative Writing 1974–79, 1984–2004; Ed., Highland Publishing House 1996–2002; mem. Bd Dirs Mobius, The Poetry Magazine 1998–2005; mem. Nat. League of American Pen Women (Historian 2004–06, Vice-Pres. 2006–08), Soc. of Children's Book Writers and Illustrators, Nat. Fed. of Press Women. *Publications:* books: My Name is Jaybird 1972, No More Someday 1973, From the Peninsula South 1980, Thomas, My Brother 1981, Visions to Keep 1990. *Honours:* First State Writers Nat. Bicentennial Poetry Award 1976, First Place, Contra Costa County Fair Nat. Poetry Contest 1979, Distinguished Service Award, Lutheran Community Services Bd, Wilmington 1994–95, First Place, Nat. League of American Pen Women Children's Short Story Award 1998. *Address:* 3 Lanark Drive, Wilmington, DE 19803, USA (home). *E-mail:* sandramichel@verizon.net (home).

MICKLETHWAIT, John; British journalist and writer; *Editor-in-Chief, The Economist. Education:* Magdalen Coll., Oxford. *Career:* fmrly with Chase Manhattan Bank; joined The Economist 1987, as Media Correspondent, then established Los Angeles office 1990–93, Ed. business section 1993–97, New York Bureau Chief 1997–99, US Ed. 1999–2006, Ed.-in-Chief 2006–. *Publications:* The Witch Doctors (with Adrian Wooldridge) (Financial Times/Booz Allen Global Business Book Award 1997) 1996, A Future Perfect: The Challenge and Hidden Promise of Globalisation (with Adrian Wooldridge) 2000, The Company: A Short History of a Revolutionary Idea (with Adrian Wooldridge) 2003, The Right Nation (with Adrian Wooldridge) 2004; contrib. articles to the New York Times, Los Angeles Times, Wall Street Journal, Guardian, Spectator and the New Statesman, Boston Globe. *Honours:* Harold Wincott Press Award for Young Financial Journalist 1989. *Address:* The Economist, 25 St James's Street, London, SW1A 1HG, England (office). *Website:* www.economist.com (office).

MIDDLEBROOK, Diane Wood, AB, MA, PhD, FRSL; American academic, writer, poet and biographer; b. 16 April 1939, Pocatello, Ida; m. 1st Jonathan Middlebrook 1963 (annulled 1972); one d.; m. 2nd Carl Djerassi 1985. *Education:* Whitman Coll., Walla Walla Coll., Wash., Univ. of Washington, Yale Univ. *Career:* Asst Prof., Stanford Univ. 1966–73, Assoc. Prof. 1974–83, Dir Center for Research on Women 1977–79, Assoc. Dean of Undergraduate Studies 1979–82, Prof. of English 1983–2002, Chair. Program in Feminist Studies 1985–88, Howard H. and Jessie T. Watkins Univ. Prof. 1985–90; Visiting Assoc. Prof., Rutgers Univ. 1973; mem. Chadwyck-Healey LION (Literature Online), mem. Editorial Bd 1997–; Trustee Djerassi Resident Artists Program 1980–96, Chair. Bd 1994; mem. Advisory Bd Humanities West 1997–, Investigative Reporters and Eds 1995–, Modern Language Assocn 1966–, Biographers' Club, London 1999–, California Classical Assocn 1999–, Int. Assocn of Univ. Profs of English 1999–2003, Royal Soc. for the Encouragement of the Arts, Mfg & Commerce 2003; Fellow, Bunting Inst., Radcliffe Coll. 1982–83, Stanford Humanities Center 1983–84, Rockefeller Study Center, Bellagio, Italy 1990. *Publications:* Walt Whitman and Wallace Stevens 1974, Worlds Into Words: Understanding Modern Poems 1980, Gin Considered as a Demon (poems) 1983, Coming to Light: American Women Poets (co-ed. with Marilyn Yalom) 1985, Selected Poems of Anne Sexton (co-ed. with Diana Hume George) 1988, Anne Sexton: A Biography 1991, Suits Me: The Double Life of Billy Tipton 1998, Her Husband: Hughes & Plath, a Marriage 2003; contribs to books, anthologies and journals, including poems, articles and reviews. *Honours:* Hon. mem. Christ's Coll., Cambridge, UK; Hon. DLitt (Kenyon Coll.) 1999, (Univ. of Massachusetts at Dartmouth) 2005; Woodrow Wilson Fellowship 1961, Albert S. Cook Memorial Prize for Poetry 1962, Theron Rockwell Field Prize for Doctoral Dissertation Yale Univ. 1968, Acad. of American Poets Prize 1965, Dean's Award for Distinguished Teaching, Stanford Nat.. 1977, Walter J. Gores Award for Excellence in Teaching, Stanford Univ. 1987, National Endowment for the Humanities Fellowship 1982–83, Guggenheim Fellowship 1988–89, Commonwealth Club of California Gold Medal for Non-Fiction 1992. *Address:* 1101 Green Street, No. 1501, San Francisco, CA 94109, USA (home). *E-mail:* dwm@stanford.edu (office). *Website:* www.dianemiddlebrook.com.

MIDDLETON, (John) Christopher, MA, DPhil; British academic; *David J. Bruton Centennial Professor Emeritus of Modern Languages, University of Texas;* b. 10 June 1926, Truro; s. of Hubert S. Middleton and Dorothy M. Miller; m. 1953 (divorced); one s. two d. *Education:* Felsted School and Merton Coll. Oxford. *Career:* Lektor in English, Univ. of Zürich 1952–55; Asst Lecturer in German, King's Coll. Univ. of London 1955–57, Lecturer 1957–66; Prof. of Germanic Languages and Literature Univ. of Texas 1966–98, David J. Bruton Centennial Emer. Prof. 1998–. *Publications:* Torse 3, poems 1948–61 1962, Nonsequences/Selfpoems 1965, Our Flowers and Nice Bones 1969, The Lonely Suppers of W.V. Balloon 1975, Carminalenia 1980, 111 Poems 1983, Two-Horse Wagon Going By 1986, Selected Writings 1989, The Balcony Tree 1992, Some Dogs 1993, Andalusian Poems 1993, Intimate Chronicles 1996, The Swallow Diver 1997, Twenty Tropes for Doctor Dark 2000, The Word Pavilion and Selected Poems 2001, Of the Mortal Fire 2003, The Anti-Basilisk 2005; prose: Pataxanadu and Other Prose 1977, Serpentine 1985, In the Mirror of the Eighth King 1999, Crypto-Topographia 2002; trans: Ohne Hass und Fahne (with W. Deppe and H. Schönherr) 1958, Modern German Poetry 1910–60 (with M. Hamburger) 1962, Germany Writing Today 1967, Selected Poems, by Georg Trakl 1968, Selected Letters, by Friedrich Nietzsche 1969, Selected Poems, by Friedrich Hölderlin and Eduard Mörike 1972, Selected Poems of Goethe 1983, Slected Stories, by Robert Walser 1983, Andalusian Poems (with Leticia Garza-Falcón) 1993, Faint Harps and Silver Voices: Selected Translations 2000; essays and other writings. *Honours:* Sir Geoffrey Faber Memorial Prize 1964, Guggenheim Poetry Fellowship 1974–75, Nat. Endowment for Humanities Poetry Fellowship 1980, Tieck-Schlegel Trans Prize 1985, Max Geilinger Stiftung Prize 1987, Soeurette Diehl Fraser Award for Trans, Texas Inst. of Letters 1993, Camargo Foundation Fellow 1999. *Address:* 1112 W 11th Street, Apt 201, Austin, TX 78703 (home); Department of Germanic Studies, University of Texas, Austin, TX 78712, USA (office). *Telephone:* (512) 471-4123 (office). *Website:* www.utexas.edu/depts/german/faculty/middleton.html (office).

MIDDLETON, Osman Edward; New Zealand author; b. 25 March 1925, Christchurch; m. 1949 (divorced); one s. one d. *Education:* Auckland Univ. Coll., 1946, 1948; Univ. of Paris, 1955–56. *Career:* Robert Burns Fellow, Univ. of Otago, 1970–71; Visiting Lecturer, Univs of Canterbury, 1971, Zürich, Frankfurt, Giessen, Kiel, Erlangen, Regensburg, Turin, Bologna, Pisa, Venice, Rome, 1983; Writer-in-Residence, Michael Karolyi Memorial Foundation, Vence, France, 1983; mem. cttee, New Zealand Assocn of the Blind and Partially Blind (now Assocn of Blind Citizens of New Zealand) 1970–95. *Publications:* 10 Stories, 1953; The Stone and Other Stories, 1959; From the River to the Tide (children's), 1962; A Walk on the Beach, 1964; The Loners, 1972; Selected Stories, 1976; Confessions of an Ocelot, 1979; The Big Room and Other Stories, 1998. Contributions: anthologies world-wide; numerous magazines and journals. *Honours:* Achievement Award, 1959, Scholarship in Letters, 1965, New Zealand Literary Fund; Second New Zealand Katherine Mansfield Award, 1960; Hubert Church Prose Award, 1964; Jt Winner, New Zealand Prose Fiction Award, 1976; Jt Winner, John Cowie Reid Short Story Award 1989, Janet Frame Award 2006. *Address:* 20 Clifford Street, Dalmore, Dunedin, New Zealand.

MIDDLETON, Stanley, BA, MEd, FRSL; British writer and schoolteacher (retd); b. 1 Aug. 1919, Bulwell, Nottingham; s. of Thomas Middleton and Elizabeth Ann Middleton (née Burdett); m. Margaret Shirley Charnley (née Welch) 1951; two d. *Education:* Bulwell St Mary's School, Bulwell Highbury School, High Pavement School, Nottingham, Nottingham Univ. Coll., Univ. of Nottingham. *Career:* fmr English teacher; fmr Head of English High Pavement Coll., Nottingham, retd 1981; Judith Wilson Fellow Emmanuel Coll., Cambridge 1982–83. *Radio Plays include:* The Captain from Nottingham (BBC), A Little Music at Night (BBC). *Publications:* A Short Answer 1958, Harris's Requiem 1960, A Serious Woman 1961, The Just Exchange 1962, Two's Company 1963, Him They Compelled 1964, The Golden Evening 1968, Wages of Virtue 1969, Brazen Prison 1971, Holiday (Booker Prize) 1974, Still Waters 1976, Two Brothers 1978, In a Strange Land 1979, The Other Side 1980, Blind Understanding 1982, Entry into Jerusalem 1983, The Daysman 1984, Valley of Decision 1985, An After Dinner's Sleep 1986, After a Fashion 1987, Recovery 1988, Vacant Places 1989, Changes & Chances 1990, Beginning to End 1991, A Place to Stand 1992, Married Past Redemption 1993, Catalysts 1994, Toward the Sea 1995, Live and Learn 1996, Brief Hours 1997, Against the Dark 1997, Necessary Ends 1999, Small Change 2000, Love in the Provinces 2002, Brief Garlands 2004, Sterner Stuff 2005, Mother's Boy 2006. *Honours:* Hon. MA (Nottingham) 1975, Hon. MUniv (Open) 1995, Hon. DLitt (De Montfort) 1998, (Nottingham Trent) 2000. *Address:* 42 Caledon Road, Sherwood, Nottingham, NG5 2NG, England. *Telephone:* (115) 962-3085.

MIELI, Paolo; Italian journalist; b. 25 Feb. 1949, Milan; m. Barbara Parodi Delfino; two s. *Education:* classical lycée and univ. *Career:* Asst to Chair of History of Political Parties, Univ. of Rome; Corresp., Political Commentator at Home, Head of Cultural Desk and then Cen. Man. Ed., Espresso (weekly) 1967–85; worked for La Repubblica 1985–86; Leader Writer, La Stampa 1986–90, Ed.-in-Chief 1990–92; Ed. Corriere della Sera 1992–97; apptd Pres. RAI (Radiotelevisione Italiana) March 2003 (resgnd after five days); mem. Bd Govs Storia Illustrata, Pagina and has collaborated with Tempi Moderni, Questi Istituzioni, Mondo operaio. *Publications:* Litigo a Sinistra, Il Socialismo Diviso, Storia del Partito Socialista Negli Anni della Repubblica, Le Storie – La Storia 1999, Storia e Politica: Risorgimento, fascismo e comunismo 2001. *Honours:* Premio Spoleto 1990; Premio Mediterraneo 1991, Premio Alfio Russo 1995. *Address:* Via Medaglie d'Oro 391, Rome 00136, Italy (home).

MIÉVILLE, China, BA, MA, PhD; British writer; b. 6 Sept. 1972, London. *Education:* Univ. of Cambridge, LSE. *Career:* fmrly taught English in Egypt; Frank Knox Fellowship, Harvard Univ. *Publications:* novels: King Rat 1998,

Perdido Street Station (Arthur C. Clarke Award 2001, British Fantasy Award 2001) 2000, The Scar 2002, The Tain 2002, Iron Council 2004, Looking for Jake: Stories 2005, Un Lun Dun (for children) 2007. *Address:* c/o Pan Macmillan, 20 New Wharf Road, London, N1 9RR, England. *Website:* www .panmacmillan.com/Features/China.

MIHAILOVICH, Vasa D., MA, PhD; American retd academic, writer and poet; b. 12 Aug. 1926, Prokuplje, Yugoslavia; m. Branka 1957; two s. *Education:* Wayne State Univ., Univ. of Calif. at Berkeley. *Career:* Instructor, 1961–63, Asst Prof., 1963–68, Assoc. Prof., 1968–75, Prof. of Slavic Languages and Literatures, 1975–95, University of NC at Chapel Hill; mem. Asscn of Writers of Serbia. *Publications:* Library of Literary Criticism: Modern Slavic Literatures, 2 vols, 1972, 1976; Introduction to Yugoslav Literature, 1973; A Comprehensive Bibliography of Yugoslav Literature in English, 1976; Contemporary Yugoslav Poetry, 1977; Stari i Novi Vilajet, 1977; Bdenja, 1980; Emigranti i Druge Price, 1980; Krugovi na Vodi, 1982; U Tudjem Pristanistu, 1988; Serbian Poetry From the Beginnings to the Present, 1988; Litija Malih Praznika, 1990; Na Brisanom Prostoru, 1994; Bozic u Starom Kraju, 1994; Dictionary of Literary Biography: South Slavic Writers, 2 vols, 1994, 1997; Songs of the Serbian People: From the Collections of Vuk St Karadzic, 1997; Rasejano Slovo/The Scattered Word, 1997; Braca i Druge Price, 1997; Sesta Rukovet, 2002; Elze i Druge Price, 2002; Vrane na Snegu, 2002; Jagnje i Vuk, 2003; Darovi: Sna 2001; Tango, Poems in Prose, 2004; Belly Dancer and Other Stories, 2004; Anthology of Serbian Literature 2004. Contributions: Books Abroad/World Literature Today; Saturday Review; Serbian Studies; Slavic and East European Journal; Slavic Review. *Honours:* Serbian PEN Center, 1988; Zlatni Prsten, 1994; Vukova Zaduzbina, 1997; Povelja Rastko Petrovic, 1998; Vukova nagrada 2003; Povelja Arsenije Carnojevic 2004; In a Foreign Harbor: Essays in Honour of Vasa D. Mihailovich, 2000. *Address:* 821 Emory Drive, Chapel Hill, NC 27517, USA (home). *Telephone:* (919) 942-5261 (home). *Fax:* (919) 942-5261 (home). *E-mail:* vamih@aol.com (home).

MIKHAIL, Dunya, MA; Iraqi writer and poet; *Teacher of Arabic, Wayne State University;* b. 1965. *Education:* Univ. of Baghdad, Wayne State Univ. *Career:* Literary Ed. The Baghdad Observer 1988–95; Man. Dir Al-Mashreq Co. for Press, Amman, Jordan 1995–96; facing increasing threats from Iraqi authorities for her writing, fled to USA in late 1990s; currently teacher of Arabic, Wayne State Univ.; Dir Iraqi American Center humanitarian org. *Publications in translation include:* poetry: Bleeding of the Sea 1986, The Songs of Absence 1993, Almost Music 1997, Diary of a Wave Outside the Sea 1999, The War Works Hard 2000; contrib. poems to anthologies, magazines and newspapers, including Le Poème Arabe Moderne, Iraqi Poetry Today, The Post-Gibran Anthology of New Arab-American Writing, New Arab Poetry, The Poetry of Arab Women: A Contemporary Anthology, Poetry International, Modern Poetry in Translation, The Times. *Honours:* UN Human Rights Award for Freedom of Writing 2001. *E-mail:* DMik139729@aol.com. *Website:* www.dunyamikhail.com.

MIKHAIL, Edward Halim, BA, BEd, DES, PhD; Canadian academic and writer; *Professor Emeritus of English, University of Lethbridge;* b. 29 June 1926, Cairo, Egypt. *Education:* Univ. of Cairo, Trinity Coll., Dublin, Univ. of Sheffield. *Career:* Lecturer to Asst Prof., Univ. of Cairo 1949–66; Assoc. Prof. Univ. of Lethbridge 1966–72, Prof. of English Literature 1972–, now Emer. *Publications:* The Social and Cultural Setting of the 1890s, 1969; John Galsworthy the Dramatist, 1971; Comedy and Tragedy: A Bibliography of Criticism, 1972; Sean O'Casey: A Bibliography of Criticism, 1972; A Bibliography of Modern Irish Drama 1899–1970, 1972; Dissertations on Anglo-Irish Drama, 1973; The Sting and the Twinkle: Conversations with Sean O'Casey (co-ed.), 1974; J. M. Synge: A Bibliography of Criticism, 1975; Contemporary British Drama 1950–1976: An Annotated Critical Bibliography, 1976; W. B. Yeats: Interviews and Recollections, 1977; J. M. Synge: Interviews and Recollections, 1977; English Drama 1900–1950, 1977; Lady Gregory: Interviews and Recollections, 1977; Oscar Wilde: An Annotated Bibliography of Criticism, 1978; A Research Guide to Modern Irish Dramatists, 1979; Oscar Wilde: Interviews and Recollections, 1979; The Art of Brendan Behan, 1979; Brendan Behan: An Annotated Bibliography of Criticism, 1980; An Annotated Bibliography of Modern Anglo-Irish Drama, 1982; Brendan Behan: Interviews and Recollections, 1982; Lady Gregory: An Annotated Bibliography of Criticism, 1982; Sean O'Casey and His Critics, 1985; The Abbey Theatre, 1987; Sheridan: Interviews and Recollections, 1989; James Joyce: Interviews and Recollections, 1990; The Letters of Brendan Behan, 1991; Goldsmith: Interviews and Recollections, 1993; Dictionary of Appropriate Adjectives, 1994; contrib. to journals. *Address:* No. 115, 100-2 Avenue S, Lethbridge, AB T1J OB5, Canada.

MIKHALKOV, Sergey Vladimirovich; Russian playwright, poet and children's writer; b. 13 March 1913, Moscow; m. 1st Natalia Konchalovskaya (deceased); two s.; m. 2nd. *Education:* Literary Inst., Moscow. *Career:* began writing 1928, verses for children 1935; co-author (with El-Registan) Soviet Anthem 1943; mem. CPSU 1950–91; Chief Ed. Fitil 1962–; First Sec. Moscow Br., RSFSR Union of Writers 1965–70, Chair. of Union 1970–91; Deputy to Supreme Soviet of RSFSR 1967–70, to USSR Supreme Soviet 1970–89; author Anthem of Russian Fed. (new version) 2000; mem. Comm. for Youth Affairs, Soviet of Nationalities; fmr Corresp. mem. Acad. of Pedagogical Sciences 1970. *Film script:* Frontovye podrugi (Frontline Friends) 1941. *Plays:* Tom Kenti (after Mark Twain) 1938, Krasnyi galstuk (Red Neckerchief), Selected Works 1947, Ilya Golovin, Ya khochu domoi (I Want to Go Home) 1949, Raki

(Lobsters) 1952, Zaika-Zaznaika 1955, Sombrero 1958, Pamyatnik Sebe (A Monument to Oneself) 1958, Dikari (Campers) 1959, Collected Works (4 vols) 1964, Green Grasshopper 1964, We Are Together, My Friend and I 1967, In the Museum of Lenin 1968, Fables 1970, Disobedience Day 1971, The Funny Bone (articles) 1971, Collected Works (3 vols) 1970–71, Selected Works 1973, Slap in the Face 1974, Bibliographical Index 1975, The Scum 1975, The Lodger 1977, Echo 1980, Almighty Kings 1983, Fables 1987, A Choice for Children (English trans.) 1988. *Publications:* Dyadya Styopa (Uncle Steve) 1936 and Collected Works (poems, stories, plays) in two vols. *Honours:* Order For Service to Fatherland (Second Class) 2003; numerous awards. *Address:* Tchaikovskogo str. 28/35, Apt 67, 121069 Moscow, Russia. *Telephone:* (495) 291-78-15.

MIKHAYLOVA, Lilyana; Bulgarian screenwriter and author; b. 11 May 1939, Plovdiv; m. Mladen Denew 1968; one s. *Education:* Univ. of Sofia. *Career:* teacher 1962–68; journalist 1968–74; Chief Ed. in a publishing house 1974–90. *Films include:* Solistat (The Soloist) 1980, Otkoga te chakam (It's Nice to See You) 1984, Grehat na Maltitza (Sin of Maltitza) 1985. *Television includes:* Dom za nashite deca (Home for Our Children) 1987, Neizchezvashtite (People, Who Never Disappear) 1988, Bashti i sinove (Fathers and Sons) 1990, Yosif i Mariya (Joseph and Maria) 1995. *Honours:* First Prize Varna Int. Film Festival 1974, 1984, Nat. Award for Contemporary Literature 1984, Sofia Award for Literature 1986. *Address:* Brest 11, Sofia 1126, Bulgaria. *Telephone:* (2) 66-32-32.

MIKI, Taku; Japanese novelist and poet; b. 13 May 1935, Tokyo. *Career:* involved in publication of Han (Inundation) and Shi soshiki (Poetry Organization) magazines. *Publications:* poetry: Tokyô gozen sanji (3am in Tokyo) 1959, Wa ga kidirando (My Kiddyland) 1971; novels: Hiwa (The Siskin) (Akutagawa Award) 1972, Furueru shita (With Quivering Tongue) 1974, Karera ga hashirinuketa hi (The Day They Went the Distance) 1978, Gyosha no aki (The Charioteer in Autumn) 1985, Koguma-za no otoko (The Man from the Little Dipper) 1989, Hadashi to kaigara (Naked Feet and Seashell) (Yomiuri Prize) 1999; prose: Tokyo bishiteki hokô (Microscopic Strolls Through Tokyo, essays) 1975, Kotoba no suru shigoto (The Work Words Do, criticism) 1975, Potapota (Drip, Drip, juvenile) 1984, Roji (Alley, short stories) (Tanizaki Jun'ichiro Prize) 1997. *Address:* c/o Shueisha Incorporated, 5–10, 2 Chome, Hitotsubashi, Chiyoda-ku, Tokyo 101 50, Japan.

MIKLOWITZ, Gloria, BA; American writer; b. 18 May 1927, New York, NY; m. Julius Miklowitz 1948; two s. *Education:* Hunter Coll., CUNY, Univ. of Michigan, New York Univ. *Career:* Instructor, Pasadena City Coll. 1970–80; mem. Soc. of Children's Book Writers and Illustrators. *Publications:* some 70 books for children 1964–; contrib. to newspapers, journals and magazines. *Honours:* Western Australia Young Book Award 1984, Bucks Herald for Teens Publrs' Award 1990, Wyoming Soaring Eagle Award 1993, Sugarman Family Award for Best Book for Children on a Jewish Theme 1999. *Address:* 5255 Vista Miguel Drive, La Canada, CA 91011, USA (home). *Telephone:* (818) 952-3382 (home). *E-mail:* glow7@aol.com (home).

MILES, John (Jack) Russiano, LittB, PhB, PhD; American journalist and critic; b. 30 July 1942, Chicago, IL; m. Jacqueline Russiano 1980; one d. *Education:* Xavier Univ., Cincinnati, Pontifical Gregorian Univ., Rome, Hebrew Univ., Jerusalem, Harvard Univ. *Career:* Asst Prof., Loyola Univ., Chicago 1970–74; Asst Dir, Scholars Press, Missoula, MT 1974–75; Post-doctoral Fellow, Univ. of Chicago 1975–76; Ed., Doubleday & Co., New York 1976–78; Exec. Ed., Univ. of California Press at Berkeley 1978–85; Book Ed. 1985–91, mem. editorial bd 1991–95, Los Angeles Times; Dir, Humanities Center, Claremont Graduate School, CA 1995–97; Visiting Prof. Calif. Inst. of Tech. 1997–98; Sr Adviser to the Pres. J. Paul Getty Trust 1998–; mem. American Acad. of Religion, Amnesty Int., Nat. Books Critics Circle (pres. 1990–92), PEN. *Publications:* Retroversion and Text Criticism 1984, God: A Biography 1995, Christ: A Crisis in the Life of God 2001; contrib. to many periodicals. *Honours:* Guggenheim Fellowship 1990–91, Pulitzer Prize in Biography 1996, MacArthur Fellow 2003–(07). *Address:* 1200 Getty Center Drive, Suite 1100, Los Angeles, CA 90049-1688, USA. *Website:* www .JackMiles.com.

MILLAR, Sir Ronald Graeme; British dramatist, screenwriter and author; b. 12 Nov. 1919, Reading, England. *Education:* King's Coll., Cambridge. *Career:* screenwriter in Hollywood, USA 1948–54. *Publications:* Plays: Frieda, 1946; Champagne for Delilah, 1948; Waiting for Gillian, 1954; The Bride and the Bachelor, 1956; The More the Merrier, 1960; The Bride Comes Back, 1960; The Affair (after C. P. Snow), 1961; The New Men (after C. P. Snow), 1962; The Masters (after C. P. Snow), 1963; Number 10, 1967; Abelard and Heloise, 1970; The Case in Question (after C. P. Snow), 1975; A Coat of Varnish (after C. P. Snow), 1982. Musicals: Robert and Elizabeth, 1964; On the Level, 1966. Autobiography: A View from the Wings, 1993.

MILLER, Alexander (Alex) McPhee, BA, DipEd; Australian author; b. 27 Dec. 1936, London, England; m. 1st Anne Roslyn Neil 1962 (divorced 1983); one s. one d.; m. 2nd Stephanie Ann Pullin 1983. *Education:* Univ. of Melbourne, Hawthorn Inst. *Career:* Visiting Fellow, La Trobe Univ. 1994–; mem. Australian Soc. of Authors, Fellowship of Australian Writers. *Publications:* Watching the Climbers on the Mountain 1988, The Tivington Nott 1989, The Ancestor Game (Miles Franklin Award, Commonwealth Writers Prize 1993) 1992, The Sitters 1995, Conditions of Faith 2000, Journey to the Stone Country (Miles Franklin Award 2003) 2002; plays: Kitty Howard 1978, The Exiles 1981; contrib. to newspapers, journals and periodicals. *Honours:* Braille

Book of the Year Award 1990, Barbara Ramsden Award, Fellowship of Australian Writers 1993. *Address:* c/o Hodder & Stoughton, 338 Euston Road, London, NW1 3BH, England.

MILLER, Andrew; British writer; b. 29 April 1960, Bristol, England. *Publications:* Ingenious Pain 1997, Casanova 1998, Oxygen 2001, The Optimists 2005. *Honours:* James Tait Black Memorial Prize for Fiction 1997, Int. IMPAC Dublin Literary Award 1999, Grinzane Cavour Prize, Italy. *Literary Agent:* Sheil Land Associates, 43 Doughty Street, London, WC1N 2LF, England.

MILLER(-POGACAR), Anesa, BA, MA, PhD; American writer, poet, editor, translator and educator; b. 8 June 1954, Wichita, KS; m. 1st Timothy Pogacar 1980 (divorced 1990); m. 2nd Jack Panksepp 1991; two d. *Education:* Occidental College, University of Kansas. *Career:* Instructor in Russian Language and Literature, University of Kansas, 1979–83, Bowling Green State University, Ohio, 1986–94; Ed., Memorial Foundation for Lost Children, 1994–. *Publications:* After the Future: Paradoxes of Postmodernism and Contemporary Russian Culture (trans. and ed.), 1995; Re-Entering the Sign: Articulating New Russian Culture (co-ed.), 1995; A Road Beyond Loss: Three Cycles of Poems and an Epilogue, 1995. Contributions: periodicals.

MILLER, Arthur I., BS, PhD; American academic and writer; *Emeritus Professor of History and Philosophy of Science, University College London.* *Education:* City Coll. of New York and Massachusetts Inst. of Technology. *Career:* Visiting Prof., École Pratique des Hautes Études, Paris 1977; fmr Assoc. Ed., American Journal of Physics; Vice-Chair. Division of History of Physics, American Physical Soc. 1983–84 Chair. 1984–85; Prof. of History and Philosophy of Science, Univ. Coll. London, now Emeritus Prof.; Dir Int. History of Physics School, Ettore Majorana Centre for Scientific Culture, Erice, Sicily; Fellow American Physical Soc.; Corresponding Fellow Académie Internationale d'Histoire des Sciences; mem. Int. Acad. of the History of Science. *Television:* presenter Einstein (WGBH NOVA production). *Publications:* Albert Einstein's Special Theory of Relativity: Emergence (1905) and Early Interpretation (1905–1911) 1981, Imagery in Scientific Thought: Creating 20th-Century Physics 1984, Frontiers of Physics: 1900–1911 1986, Sixty-Two Years of Uncertainty: Historical, Philosophical and Physical Inquiries into the Foundations of Quantum Mechanics (ed.) 1990, Early Quantum Electrodynamics: A Source Book 1994, Insights of Genius: Imagery and Creativity in Science and Art 1996, Einstein and Picasso: Space, Time and the Beauty that Causes Havoc 2001, Empire of the Stars: Friendship, Obsession and Betrayal in the Quest for Black Holes 2005. *Honours:* fellowships and grants from American Council of Learned Socs, American Philosophical Soc., Centre Nat. de la Recherche Scientifique, Fritz Thyssen Stiftung, John Simon Guggenheim Memorial Foundation, Nat. Endowment for the Humanities, Nat. Science Foundation. *Address:* Department of Science and Technology Studies, University College London, Gower Street, London, WC1E 6BT, England. *E-mail:* a.miller@ucl.ac.uk.

MILLER, Edmund, BA, MA, PhD; American academic, poet and writer; *Chairman, English Department, C. W. Post Campus of Long Island University;* b. 18 July 1943, Queens, NY; s. of Edmund Miller Jr and Eugenia Marie Miller (née Andreani). *Education:* C. W. Post Campus, Long Island Univ., Ohio State Univ., State Univ. of NY at Stony Brook. *Career:* Lecturer, Ohio State Univ. 1968–69; Instructor, Rockhurst Coll. 1969–71; Asst Prof., Temple Univ. 1977–78, Illinois State Univ. 1979–80; Assoc. Prof., Hofstra Univ. 1980–81; Asst Prof., C. W. Post Campus, Long Island Univ. 1981–86, Assoc. Prof. 1986–90, Prof. 1990–, Chair. Dept of English 1993; mem. Conf. on Christianity and Literature, Lewis Carroll Soc. of N America (Life Mem.), Milton Soc. of America, Modern Language Asscn. *Publications:* poetry: Fucking Animals: A Book of Poems 1973, The Nadine Poems 1973, Winter 1975, A Rider of Currents 1986, The Happiness Cure and Other Poems 1993, Leavings 1995, The Go-Go Boy Sonnets: Men of the New York Club Scene 2005; non-fiction: Drudgerie Divine: The Rhetoric of God and Man in George Herbert 1979, Exercises in Style 1980, Like Season'd Timber: New Essays on George Herbert (co-ed. with Robert DiYanni) 1987, George Herbert's Kinships: An Ahnentafel with Annotations 1993; fiction: Night Times 2000; contrib. to books and journals. *Address:* Department of English, C. W. Post Campus, Long Island University, Brookville, NY 11548, USA (office). *Telephone:* (516) 299-2391 (office). *Fax:* (516) 299-2997 (office). *E-mail:* edmund.miller@liu.edu (office).

MILLER, Hugh; British writer; b. 27 April 1937, Wishaw, Lanarkshire, Scotland. *Education:* Univ. of Glasgow; Stow Coll.; London Polytechnic. *Publications:* A Pocketful of Miracles, 1969; Secrets of Gambling, 1970; Professional Presentations, 1971; The Open City, 1973; Levels, 1973; Drop Out, 1973; Short Circuit, 1973; Koran's Legacy, 1973; Kingpin, 1974; Double Deal, 1974; Feedback, 1974; Ambulance, 1975; The Dissector, 1976; A Soft Breeze from Hell, 1976; The Saviour, 1977; The Rejuvenators, Terminal 3, 1978; Olympic Bronze, 1979; Head of State, 1979; District Nurse, 1984; Honour a Physician, 1985; Eastenders, 1986; Teen Eastenders, 1986; Snow on the Wind, 1987; Silent Witnesses, 1988; The Paradise Club, 1989; An Echo of Justice, 1990; Home Ground, 1990; Skin Deep, 1992; Scotland Yard (co-author), 1993; Unquiet Minds, 1994; Proclaimed in Blood, 1995; Prime Target, 1996; Ballykissangel, 1997; Borrowed Time, 1997; Forensic Fingerprints, 1998; Charlie's Case Notes, 1999; Secrets of the Dead, 2000; Crimewatch Solved, 2001; What the Corpse Revealed, 2002, Mindset 2003. *Literary Agent:* Lucas Alexander Whitley Ltd, 14 Vernon Street, London, W14 0RJ, England.

MILLER, Ian (see Milne, John Frederick)

MILLER, Sir Jonathan Wolfe, Kt, CBE, MB, BCh, FRA; British stage director, film director, physician and writer; b. 21 July 1934, London; s. of the late Emanuel Miller; m. Helen Rachel Collet 1956; two s. one d. *Education:* St Paul's School, St John's Coll., Cambridge and Univ. Coll. Hosp. Medical School, London. *Career:* co-author of and appeared in Beyond the Fringe 1961–64; Dir John Osborne's Under Plain Cover, Royal Court Theatre 1962, Robert Lowell's The Old Glory, New York 1964 and Prometheus Bound, Yale Drama School 1967; Dir at Nottingham Playhouse 1968–69; Dir Oxford and Cambridge Shakespeare Co. production of Twelfth Night on tour in USA 1969; Research Fellow in the History of Medicine, Univ. Coll., London 1970–73; Assoc. Dir Nat. Theatre 1973–75; mem. Arts Council 1975–76; Visiting Prof. in Drama, Westfield Coll., Univ. of London 1977–; Exec. Producer Shakespeare TV series 1979–81; Artistic Dir Old Vic 1988–90; Research Fellow in Neuropsychology, Univ. of Sussex; Fellow, Univ. Coll. London 1981–; mem. American Acad. of Arts and Sciences. *Productions:* for Nat. Theatre, London: The Merchant of Venice 1970, Danton's Death 1971, The School for Scandal 1972, The Marriage of Figaro 1974, The Wind in the Willows 1990; other productions The Tempest, London 1970, Prometheus Bound, London 1971, The Taming of the Shrew, Chichester 1972, The Seagull, Chichester 1973, The Malcontent, Nottingham 1973, Arden Must Die (opera) 1973, The Family in Love, Greenwich Season 1974, The Importance of Being Earnest 1975, The Cunning Little Vixen (opera) 1975, All's Well That Ends Well, Measure For Measure, Greenwich Season 1975, Three Sisters 1977, The Marriage of Figaro (ENO) 1978, Arabella (opera) 1980, Falstaff (opera) 1980, 1981, Otello (opera) 1982, Rigoletto (opera) 1982, 1984, Fidelio (opera) 1982, 1983, Don Giovanni (opera) 1985, The Mikado (opera) 1986, Tosca (opera) 1986, Long Day's Journey into Night 1986, Taming of the Shrew 1987, The Tempest 1988, Turn of the Screw 1989, King Lear 1989, The Liar 1989, La Fanciulla del West (opera) 1991, Marriage of Figaro (opera), Manon Lescaut (opera), Die Gezeichneten (opera) 1992, Maria Stuarda (opera), Capriccio (opera), Fedora (opera), Bach's St Matthew Passion 1993, Der Rosenkavalier (opera), Anna Bolena (opera), Falstaff (opera), L'Incoronazione di Poppea (opera), La Bohème (opera) 1994, Così fan Tutte (opera) 1995, Carmen (opera) 1995, Pelléas et Mélisande (opera) 1995, She Stoops to Conquer, London 1995, A Midsummer Night's Dream, London 1996, The Rake's Progress, New York 1997, Ariadne auf Naxos, Maggio Musicale, Florence 1997, Falstaff, Berlin State Opera 1998, The Beggar's Opera 1999, Tamerlano, Sadler's Wells, Paris and Halle 2001, Acis and Galatea, Holland Park Opera, London 2003, Jenufa, Glimmerglass Opera 2006, The Cherry Orchard, Sheffield Crucible 2007. *Films:* Take a Girl Like You 1969 and several films for television including Whistle and I'll Come to You 1967, Alice in Wonderland 1966, The Body in Question (series) 1978, Henry the Sixth, part one 1983, States of Mind (series) 1983, Subsequent Performances 1986, The Emperor 1987, Jonathan Miller's Opera Works (series) 1997, Brief History of Disbelief (series) 2005. *Art exhibition:* Mirror Image, National Gallery, London 1998. *Publications:* McLuhan 1971, Freud: The Man, his World, his Influence (ed.) 1972, The Body in Question 1978, Subsequent Performances 1986, The Don Giovanni Book: Myths of Seduction and Betrayal (ed.) 1990, On Reflection 1998. *Honours:* Hon. Fellow, St John's Coll. Cambridge, Royal Coll. of Physicians 1997, Royal Coll. of Physicians (Edin.) 1998; Dr hc (Open Univ.) 1983, Hon. DLitt (Leicester) 1981, (Kent) 1985, (Leeds) 1996, (Cambridge) 1996; Dir of the Year, Soc. of West End Theatre Awards 1976, Royal Television Soc. Silver Medal 1981, Royal Soc. of Arts Albert Medal 1992. *Literary Agent:* IMG Artists, 616 Chiswick High Road, London, W4 5RX, England. *E-mail:* cdyer@imgartists.com. *Website:* www.imgartists.com.

MILLER, Karl Fergus Connor, FRSL; British academic, writer and editor; b. 2 Aug. 1931, s. of William Miller and Marion Miller; m. Jane Elisabeth Collet 1956; two s. one d. *Education:* Royal High School, Edinburgh and Downing Coll., Cambridge. *Career:* Asst Prin., HM Treasury 1956–57; BBC TV producer 1957–58; Literary Ed. The Spectator 1958–61, New Statesman 1961–67; Ed. The Listener 1967–73; Lord Northcliffe Prof. of Modern English Literature, Univ. Coll., London 1974–92; Ed. London Review of Books 1979–89, Co-Ed. 1989–92. *Publications:* Poetry from Cambridge 1952–54 (ed.) 1955, Writing in England Today: The Last Fifteen Years (ed.) 1968, Memoirs of a Modern Scotland (ed.) 1970, A Listener Anthology, August 1967–June 1970 (ed.) 1970, A Second Listener Anthology (ed.) 1973, Cockburn's Millennium 1975, Robert Burns (ed.) 1981, Doubles: Studies in Literary History 1985, Authors 1989, Rebecca's Vest (autobiog.) 1993, Boswell and Hyde 1995, Dark Horses (autobiog.) 1998, Electric Shepherd: A Likeness of James Hogg 2003. *Honours:* James Tait Black Prize 1975, Scottish Arts Council Book Award 1993. *Address:* 26 Limerston Street, London, SW10 0HH, England. *Telephone:* (20) 7351-1994.

MILLER, Leslie Adrienne, BA, MA, MFA, PhD; American poet and academic; b. 22 Oct. 1956, Medina, OH. *Education:* Stephens College, University of Missouri, University of Iowa, University of Houston. *Career:* Dir, Creative Writing Program, Stephens College, 1983–87; Visiting Writer, University of Oregon, 1990; Assoc. Prof. of English, University of St Thomas, 1991–; mem. Associated Writing Programs; MLA; Poetry Society of America; Poets and Writers. *Publications:* Hanging on the Sunburned Arm of Some Homeboy (with Matthew Graham), 1982; No River, 1987; Staying Up for Love, 1990; Ungodliness, 1994; Yesterday Had a Man In It, 1998. Contributions: anthologies, reviews, quarterlies, and journals. *Honours:* National Endowment for the Arts Fellowship, 1989; John and Becky Moores Fellowship,

University of Houston, 1990; Goethe-Institut Cultural Exchange Fellowship, Berlin, 1992; Loft-McKnight Award in Poetry, 1993, and Award of Distinction, 1998. *Address:* Department of English, Mail # JRC 333, University of St Thomas, St Paul, MN 55105-1096, USA. *Telephone:* (651) 962-5604. *E-mail:* lamiller@stthomas.edu. *Website:* www.lesliemillerpoet.com.

MILLER, Marc William, BS; American writer; b. 29 Aug. 1947, Annapolis, MD; m. Darlene File 1981, one s. one d. *Education:* University of Illinois. *Career:* Contributing Ed., Fire and Movement Magazine, 1977–84; Staff, Grenadier Magazine, 1977–79, Journal of the Traveller's Aid Society, 1979–85, Challenge Magazine, 1986–92; mem. Acad. of Adventure Gaming Arts and Sciences; Game Designer's Guild; SFWA. *Publications:* Traveller, 1977; Imperium, 1977; 2300 AD, 1986; Mega Traveller, 1988; Mega Traveller II, Quest for the Ancients, 1991; Spellbound, 1992. Contributions: journals.

MILLER, Sue, BA, MA; American writer; b. 29 Nov. 1943; m. 1st (divorced); one s.; m. 2nd Doug Bauer (divorced 2001). *Education:* Radcliffe Coll., Harvard Univ., Boston Univ., Wesleyan Univ. *Career:* mem. PEN, PEN New England (chair. 1999–2003). *Publications:* The Good Mother 1986, Inventing the Abbotts and Other Stories 1987, Family Pictures: A Novel 1990, For Love 1993, The Distinguished Guest 1995, While I Was Gone: A Novel 1999, The World Below 2001, The Story of My Father 2003, Lost in the Forest 2005. *Honours:* MacDowell Colony Fellowship, Guggenheim Fellowship, Radcliffe Inst. of Advanced Study 2001. *Literary Agent:* Maxine Groffsky Literary Agency, 2 Fifth Avenue, New York, NY 10011, USA. *Address:* c/o Bloomsbury, 38 Soho Square, London, W1D 3HB, England.

MILLETT, Katherine (Kate) Murray, PhD; American artist and writer; b. 14 Sept. 1934, St Paul, Minn.; m. Fumio Yoshimura 1965. *Education:* Univ. of Minnesota, St Hilda's Coll., Univ. of Oxford, UK and Columbia Univ. *Career:* Sculptor, Tokyo 1961–63; teacher, Barnard Coll. 1964–68; Distinguished Visiting Prof., Sacramento State Coll., Calif. 1973–; f. Women's Art Colony Farm (now Millett Farm), Poughkeepsie, NY; mem. Congress of Racial Equality 1965–. *Exhibitions include:* Minami Gallery, Tokyo, Judson Gallery 1967, Soho Gallery, New York 1976, 1978 1980, 1982, 1984, 1986, Women's Bldg, Los Angeles 1977, Andre Wanters Gallery, New York 1977, Chuck Levitan Gallery, New York, deVille Galerie, New Orleans, Emmy Gallery, Berlin 1977. *Publications include:* Sexual Politics 1970, The Prostitution Papers 1973, Flying 1974, Sita 1977, The Basement 1979, Going to Iran 1982, The Loony Bin Trip 1990, The Politics of Cruelty 1994, AD 1995, Mother Millett 2001. *Address:* Millett Farm, 20 Old Overlook Road, Poughkeepsie, NY 12603; Apt 5E, 59 East 4th Street, New York, NY 10003–7104, USA (office). *Telephone:* (845) 473-9267. *Website:* www.katemillett.com.

MILLHAUSER, Steven, BA; American author; b. 3 Aug. 1943, New York, NY; m. Cathy Allis 1986, one s. one d. *Education:* Columbia College, Brown University. *Publications:* Edwin Mullhouse: The Life and Death of an American Writer, 1972; Portrait of a Romantic, 1976; In the Penny Arcade, 1986; From the Realm of Morpheus, 1986; The Barnum Museum, 1990; Little Kingdoms, 1993; The Knife Thrower and Other Stories, 1998. *Honours:* Prix Médicis Étranger 1975, Award in Literature 1987.

MILLHISER, Marlys Joy, BA, MA; American writer; b. 27 May 1938, Charles City, IA; m. David Millhiser 1960, one s. one d. *Education:* University of Iowa, University of Colorado. *Career:* mem. Authors' Guild; Colorado Authors League; MWA; Sisters in Crime; Western Writers of America. *Publications:* Michael's Wife, 1972; Nella Waits, 1974; Willing Hostage, 1976; The Mirror, 1978; Nightmare Country, 1981; The Threshold, 1984; Murder at Moot Point, 1992; Death of the Office Witch, 1993; Murder in a Hot Flash, 1995. Contributions: Magazines. *Honours:* Top Hand Awards 1975, 1985.

MILLINGTON, Barry John, BA; British music journalist and writer; b. 1 Nov. 1951, Hadleigh, England; m. Deborah Jane Calland 1996. *Education:* Clare Coll., Cambridge. *Career:* editorial staff mem., The New Grove Dictionary of Music and Musicians 1975–76; criticism for Musical Times and newspapers, notably The Times 1977–82, 1988–2001; Reviews Ed. for BBC Music Magazine 1992–2002; Chief Music Critic, Evening Standard 2002–; founder and Artistic Dir, Hampstead and Highgate Festival 1999–2003; dramaturgical adviser on new production of Lohengrin at Bayreuth Festival 1999; mem. Royal Musical Asscn, Critics Circle. *Publications:* Wagner 1984, Selected Letters of Richard Wagner (trans. and ed. with S. Spencer) 1987, The Wagner Compendium: A Guide to Wagner's Life and Music (ed.) 1992, Wagner in Performance (ed. with S. Spencer) 1992, Wagner's Ring of the Nibelung: A Companion (ed. with S. Spencer) 1993, The New Grove Wagner 2002; contrib. to Oxford Illustrated History of Opera 1994, The New Grove Dictionary of Opera 1992, The New Grove Dictionary of Music and Musicians (revised edn) 2001; with Roger Parker and Julian Rushton: The New Grove Guide to Wagner 2006, The New Grove Guide to Verdi 2006, The New Grove Guide to Mozart and his Operas 2006; numerous other publications in newspapers and periodicals. *Address:* 50 Denman Drive South, London, NW11 6 RH, England (home). *E-mail:* bmillin397@aol.com (office).

MILLS, Kyle; American novelist; b. 1966. *Publications:* Rising Phoenix, 1997; Storming Heaven, 1998; Free Fall, 2000; Burn Factor, 2001; Sphere of Influence, 2002; Smoke Screen, 2003, Fade 2006, The Second Horseman, 2006. *Address:* PO Box 8036, 618 Hillside Drive, Jackson, WY, 83002 USA (home). *E-mail:* author@kylemills.com (home). *Website:* www.kylemills.com (home).

MILLS, Magnus; British writer; b. 1954, Birmingham. *Education:* Wolverhampton Polytechnic. *Publications:* novels: The Restraint of Beasts 1998, All Quiet on the Orient Express 1999, Three to See the King 2001, The Scheme for Full Employment 2003, Explorers of the New Century 2005; short story collections: Only When the Sun Shines Brightly 1999; contrib. to The Independent, The Verb (BBC Radio 3), Front Row (BBC Radio 4). *Address:* c/o Bloomsbury Publishing Plc, 36 Soho Square, London, W1D 3QY, England.

MILLS, Ralph Joseph, Jr, MA, PhD; American academic, poet and writer; *Professor of English Emeritus, Lake Forest College;* b. 16 Dec. 1931, Chicago, IL; m. Helen Daggett Harvey 1959; one s. two d. *Education:* Lake Forest Coll., Northwestern Univ., Univ. of Oxford. *Career:* Instructor, 1959–61, Asst Prof., 1962–65, University of Chicago; Assoc. Prof., 1965–67, Prof. of English, 1967–97, Prof. Emeritus, 1997–, University of Illinois at Chicago. *Publications:* poetry: Door to the Sun, 1974; A Man to His Shadow, 1975; Night Road, 1978; Living with Distance, 1979; With No Answer, 1980; March Light, 1983; For a Day, 1985; Each Branch: Poems 1976–1985, 1986; A While, 1989; A Window in Air, 1993; In Wind's Edge, 1997; Grasses Standing: Selected Poems, 2000. Other: Contemporary American Poetry, 1965; On the Poet and His Craft: Selected Prose of Theodore Roethke (ed.), 1965; Edith Sitwell: A Critical Essay, 1966; Kathleen Raine: A Critical Essay, 1967; Creation's Very Self: On the Personal Element in Recent American Poetry, 1969; Cry of the Human: Essays on Contemporary American Poetry, 1975; Essays on Poetry 2004. Contributions: books and journals. *Honours:* English-Speaking Union Fellowship, 1956–57; Illinois Arts Council Awards for Poetry, 1979, 1983, 1984; Society of Midland Authors Prize for Poetry, 1980; Carl Sandburg Prize for Poetry, 1984; William Carlos Williams Prize, Poetry Society of America, 2002. *Address:* 110 South Fairview Avenue, Park Ridge, IL 60068 (home); 1451 N Astor Street, Chicago, IL 60610, USA.

MILNE, John Frederick, (Ian Miller), BA; British writer and scriptwriter; b. 20 Sept. 1952, Bermondsey, England; m. Sarah Laetitia Beresford Verity 1983, two s. *Education:* St Joseph's Acad., Blackheath, Chelsea School of Art, Ravensborne School of Art. *Career:* book reviewer and feature writer for the Daily Telegraph and Time Out; mem. Writers' Guild. *Television:* Futurecast (Channel 4) 2001; screen credits include A Mind to Kill 1994, Waking the Dead (BBC 1), The Bill (ITV). *Publications:* Tyro 1981, London Fields 1982, Wet Wickets and Dusty Balls 1982, Dead Birds 1984, Out of the Blue 1985, Shadow Play 1986, Daddy's Girl 1988, Alive and Kicking 1998. *Honours:* John Llewelyn Rhys Prize 1985, Writers' Guild Award 1991, Edgar, Mystery Writers of America 1998. *Literary Agent:* The Agency, 24 Pottery Lane, Holland Park, London, W11 4LZ, England. *E-mail:* john.milne@shu.ac.uk.

MILTNER, Robert F., BA, MEd, PhD; American writer, poet and educator; b. 25 Feb. 1949, Cleveland, OH; m. 1st Linda Smith 1975 (divorced 1996); m. 2nd Mari Artzner Wolf 1996 (divorced 2002); one s. one d. *Education:* Xavier University, John Carroll University, Kent State University. *Career:* English Teacher, private religious high schools, Denver, CO, 1975–77, including Dept Head, Parma, Ohio, 1977–87; Co-ordinator for Developmental Education, 1987–93, 1993–95, Instructor in English, 1987–95, Dir, Writing Center, 1990–92, 1995–97, Asst Prof. of English, 1998–, Kent State University, Stark Campus, Canton, Ohio; Instructor in English, Walsh University, Canton, 1993–94; mem. Associated Writing Programs; American Assen of University Profs. *Publications:* The Seamless Serial Hour (poems), 1993; Against the Simple (poems), 1995; On the Off Ramp (poems), 1996; Ghost of a Chance (poems), 2002; Four Crows on a Phone Line (poems), 2002; A Box of Light (prose poems), 2002; Curriculum materials. Contributions: New York Quarterly; English Journal; Chiron Review; Ohioana Quarterly; Mid-American Review; Birmingham Poetry Review. *Honours:* Wick Poetry Chapbook Award, 1994. *E-mail:* rmiltner@stark.kent.edu.

MIN, Anchee, BFA, MFA; Chinese novelist; b. 1957, Shanghai; m.; one d. *Education:* Univ. of Illinois, Chicago Inst. of Arts. *Career:* born and raised in Communist China, during the Cultural Revolution; fmly worked as a peasant in the rural areas of the country, later in the Chinese film industry; moved to USA in 1984. *Publications:* Red Azalea (memoir) (New York Times Notable Book 1995) 1994, Katherine (novel) 1995, Becoming Madame Mao (novel) 2000, Wild Ginger (novel) 2002, Empress Orchid (novel) 2004. *Literary Agent:* Steven Barclay Agency, 12 Western Avenue, Petaluma, CA 94952, USA. *Telephone:* (707) 773-0654. *Fax:* (707) 778-1868. *Website:* www.barclayagency.com.

MINARIK, John Paul, BS, BA; American poet, writer and engineer; b. 6 Nov. 1947, McKeesport, PA; s. of Rudolph Andrew and Pauline Anne Minarik; m. 1st Marcia Margaret Tarasovic 1978 (divorced 1987); two d.; m. 2nd Susan Kay Minarik 1988 (divorced 2005); one s. *Education:* Carnegie Mellon Univ., Univ. of Pittsburgh. *Career:* engineer, United Steel Corpn 1966–71; Instructor, Community Coll. of Allegheny County 1977–83; teaching consultant, Univ. of Pittsburgh 1978–96; Poet-in-the-Schools, Pennsylvania Council on the Arts 1979–83; project engineer-consultant, Economy Industrial Corpn 1981–82; Chief Engineer, New Directions 1989–96; founder-Ed., Acad. of Prison Arts; Advisory Ed., Greenfield Review Press; poetry readings; mem. American Soc. of Mechanical Engineers. *Publications:* (book) 1974, Patterns in the Dusk 1978, Past the Unknown, Remembered Gate 1981, Kicking Their Heels with Freedom (ed.) 1982; contrib. to over 100 newspapers in the USA, journals including American Ethnic, Backspace, Caprice, Carnegie Mellon Magazine, Confrontation, Gravida, Greenfield Review, Happiness Holding Tank, Hyacinths and Biscuits, Interstate, Joint Conference, Journal of

Popular Culture, Mill Hunk Herald, New Orleans Review, Nitty-Gritty, Old Main, Painted Bride Quarterly, Pittsburgh and Tri-State Area Poets, Prison Writing Review, Poetry Society of America Bulletin, Small Pond, Sunday Clothes; poems read on Monitoradio, Voice of America, WQED-FM and WYEP, and at Three Rivers Arts Festival and American Wind Symphony. *Honours:* hon. mention PEN Writing Award 1976–77, Carnegie Magazine Best Book of the Year Citation 1982, poetry and prose writing contest winner, Pennsylvania Dept of Corrections 1985, 1988. *Address:* 1600 Walters Mill Road, APO-580, Somerset, PA 15510-0005, USA.

MINATOYA, Lydia, BA, MA, PhD; American writer; b. 8 Nov. 1950, New York, NY; one s. *Education:* Saint Lawrence University, George Washington University, University of Maryland. *Publications:* Talking to High Monks in the Snow, 1992; The Strangeness of Beauty, 1999. *Honours:* PEN Jerard Fund Award, 1991; American Library Asscn Notable Book, 1992; New York Public Library Notable Book, 1992; Pacific Northwest Booksellers Award, 1993.

MINEAR, Richard Hoffman, MA, PhD; American academic and writer; *Professor of History, University of Massachusetts;* b. 31 Dec. 1938, Evanston, IL; m. Edith Christian 1962; two s. *Education:* Yale Univ., Harvard Univ. *Career:* Asst Prof., Ohio State Univ. 1967–70; Assoc. Prof. of History, Univ. of Mass. 1970–75, Prof. 1975–; mem. Asscn for Asian Studies. *Publications:* Japanese Tradition and Western Law, 1970; Victors' Justice, 1971; Through Japanese Eyes, 1974; Requiem for Battleship Yamato by Yoshida Mitsuru (ed. and trans.), 1985; Hiroshima: Three Witnesses, 1990; Black Eggs by Kurihara Sadako (ed. and trans.), 1994; When we say 'Hiroshima', 1999; Dr Seuss Goes to War, 1999; Japan's Past, Japan's Future: One Historian's Odyssey by Ienaga Saburo (ed. and trans.), 2000, The Scars of War: Tokyo during World War II, Writings of Takeyama Michio 2007; contrib. to professional journals and general magazines. *Address:* c/o Department of History, University of Massachusetts, Amherst, MA 01003, USA (office).

MINGHELLA, Anthony, CBE; British director and playwright; b. 6 Jan. 1954, Isle of Wight; s. of Eddie Minghella and Gloria Minghella; m. Carolyn Choa; one s. and one d. from previous marriage. *Education:* St John's Coll., Sandown High School, Univ. of Hull. *Career:* fmr drama lecturer, Univ. of Hull; f. Mirage Enterprises (film co.); Chair. Bd of Govs BFI. *Films:* Truly, Madly, Deeply (dir, writer) 1991, Mr Wonderful (dir) 1993, The English Patient (dir, screenplay writer) (Acad. Award for Best Dir, BAFTA for Best Adapted Screenplay) 1997, The Talented Mr Ripley (dir, screenplay writer) 1999, Iris (exec. producer) 2001, Heaven (exec. producer) 2002, The Quiet American (exec. producer) 2002, Cold Mountain (dir, screenplay writer) 2003, Breaking and Entering 2006. *Writing for television:* Maybury (series creator) 1981, What If It's Raining 1985, Boon (series) 1986, Inspector Morse (series, numerous episodes) 1987, The Storyteller (series) 1987, Living with Dinosaurs 1989. *Theatre:* One 1992, Driven to Distraction: A Case for Inspector Morse 1994, Two 1997, Madama Butterfly (opera for ENO, Coliseum, London) 2005. *Opera:* Madam Butterfly, Royal Opera House, Covent Garden 2005. *Publications:* Whale Music 1983, Made in Bangkok 1986, Jim Henson's Storyteller 1988, Interior—Room, Exterior—City 1989, Minghella on Minghella 2005. *Honours:* Hon. DLitt (Hull) 1997; First Hon. Freeman, Isle of Wight 1997. *Address:* MacCartendale & Holton, 1640 Fifth Street, Suite 05, Santa Monica, CA 90401, USA (office); c/o British Film Institute, National Film Theatre, Belvedere Road, South Bank, Waterloo, London, SE1 8XT, England. *E-mail:* anthony.minghella@bfi.org.uk. *Website:* www.bfi.org.uk.

MINOGUE, Valerie Pearson, BA, MLitt; British academic, writer and editor; b. 26 April 1931, Llanelli, S Wales; m. Kenneth Robert Minogue 1954 (divorced 2000); one s. one d. *Education:* Girton Coll., Cambridge. *Career:* Asst Lecturer, Univ. Coll., Cardiff 1952–53; contrib. to Cambridge Italian Dictionary 1956–61; Lecturer, Queen Mary Coll., London 1963–74, Sr Lecturer 1975–81; Prof., Univ. of Wales, Swansea 1981–88, Research Prof. 1988–96, Prof. Emer. 1996–; Founding Ed. Romance Studies 1982–98, Gen. Ed. 1998–2003; mem. Modern Humanities Research Asscn, Soc. for French Studies, Romance Studies Inst., Émile Zola Soc., Soc. des Dix-Neuviémistes, Soc. Marguerite Duras du Royaume Uni. *Publications:* Proust: Du Côté de chez Swann 1973, Nathalie Sarraute: The War of the Words 1981, Zola: L'Assommoir 1991, Eight texts, Pléiade Oeuvres complètes of Nathalie Sarraute (ed., with notes and critical essays) 1996; contributions to Quadrant, Literary Review, Modern Language Review, French Studies, Romance Studies, Forum for Modern Language Studies, New Novel Review, Revue des Sciences Humaines, Times Literary Supplement, Esprit Créateur, Theatre Research International, Critique; numerous chapters in books. *Honours:* Mary Elizabeth Ponsonby Prize for French Literature 1952. *Address:* 23 Richford Street, London, W6 7HJ, England (home). *E-mail:* v.minogue@ukonline.co.uk (home).

MINOT, Susan Anderson, BA, MFA; American writer; b. 7 Dec. 1956, Boston, MA; m. Davis McHenry 1988 (divorced). *Education:* Brown Univ., Columbia Univ. *Publications:* Monkeys, 1986; Lust & Other Stories, 1989; Folly, 1992; Evening, 1998; Rapture, 2002. *Contributions:* New Yorker; Grand Street; Paris Review; Mademoiselle; Harper's; GQ; New England Monthly; Conde Nasts Traveler; Esquire; New York Times Magazine; Atlantic Monthly. *Honours:* Prix Fémina Etranger 1987.

MINTER, David Lee, BA, MA, BD, PhD; American academic and writer; b. 20 March 1935, Midland, TX. *Education:* North Texas State University, Yale University. *Career:* Lecturer, University of Hamburg, 1965–66, Yale University, 1966–67; Asst Prof., 1967–69, Assoc. Prof. 1969–74, Prof., 1974–80,

1991–, Rice University; Prof., Dean of Emory College, Vice-Pres. for Arts and Sciences, Emory University, 1981–90. *Publications:* The Interpreted Design as a Structural Principle in American Prose, 1969; William Faulkner: His Life and Work, 1980; The Harper American Literature, 1986; The Norton Critical Edn of The Sound and the Fury, 1987; A Cultural History of the American Novel: Henry James to William Faulkner, 1994; Faulkner's Questioning Narratives: Fiction of His Major Phase 1929–1942, 2001. Contributions: Professional journals.

MIOT, Jean Louis Yves Marie; French journalist; b. 30 July 1939, Châteauroux (Indre); s. of René Miot and Madeleine Moreau; two s. three d. *Education:* Lycée Jean Giraudoux de Châteauroux and Univ. de Poitiers. *Career:* Ed. Centre Presse, Poitiers 1964–68; journalist, French Antilles 1968–70; Ed.-in-Chief, later Political Dir Havre-Presse 1970–74; Man. Dir France Antilles Martinique Guadeloupe, launched France-Guyane (weekly) 1974–76; Head, Legis. Elections Service, Le Figaro 1977–78; Man. Dir Berry Républicain, Bourges 1978; Dir Groupe de Presse Robert Hersant 1978–79; Political corresp. L'Aurore 1979–80; mem. Man. Bd Société de Gestion and Assoc. Dir Le Figaro 1980–93; Pres. Advisory Bd Le Figaro 1993–96; Pres. Syndicat de la Presse Parisienne 1986–96; Pres. Féd. Nat. de la Presse Française 1993–96; Pres. Agence-France-Presse (AFP) 1996–99, Syndicat des agences de presse de nouvelles (SANOV) 1996–99; Pres.-Dir Gen. Codalie, Financière-CDP and CD-Presse 1999–; mem. Conseil Econ. et Social 1993–96, Comm. de réflexion sur la justice 1997; Dir Société Financière de Radio-Diffusion (SOFIRAD) 1995; many other professional appointments. *Honours:* Chevalier, Légion d'honneur, Officier de l'Etoile Civique, Officer, Order of Lion (Senegal). *Address:* SARL Codalie, 59 avenue Victor Hugo, 75116 Paris (office); CD-Presse, 3 chemin du Clos, 95650 Puiseux-Pontoise (office); 10 rue Maître Albert, 75005 Paris, France (home). *E-mail:* janmio@wanadoo.fr (home).

MIRABELLI, Eugene, BA, MA, PhD; American writer and academic; *Professor Emeritus, State University of New York at Albany;* b. 3 Feb. 1931, Arlington, Mass; s. of Eugene Miabelli and Josephine Miabelli; m. Margaret Anne Black 1959; one s. two d. *Education:* Harvard Univ., Johns Hopkins Univ. *Career:* Faculty, Williams Coll. 1960–64, State Univ. of NY at Albany 1965–95; mem. Bd and Officer, non-profit Alternative Literary Programs; mem. Authors' Guild, PEN American Center. *Publications:* The Burning Air 1959, The Way In 1968, No Resting Place 1972, The World at Noon 1994, The Language Nobody Speaks 1999, The Passion of Terri Heart 2004; contribs to numerous fiction and non-fiction book reviews and articles in various publs. *Honours:* Rockefeller Foundation Grant 1969.

MISTRY, Rohinton, BA, BSc; Canadian author; b. 3 July 1952, Bombay (now Mumbai), India; m. Freny Elavia 1975. *Education:* St Xavier's High School, Bombay, Univ. of Bombay, Univ. of Toronto and York Univ., Canada. *Career:* moved to Canada 1975; bank clerk, Toronto 1975–85; began writing short stories 1982; writings have been translated into more than 25 languages. *Publications include:* Tales from Firozsha Baag (short stories) 1987, Such a Long Journey (novel) 1991, A Fine Balance (novel) 1995, Family Matters (novel) 2002; essays and articles in various languages and periodicals. *Honours:* Hon. PhD (Ottawa) 1996, (Toronto) 1999, (York) 2003; Gov.-Gen.'s Award for Fiction 1991, Commonwealth Writers' Prize for Best Book 1992, 1996, First Novel Award, W.H. Smith/Books in Canada 1992, Giller Prize 1995, Winifred Holtby Prize, RSL 1996, Los Angeles Times Fiction Prize 1997, ALOA Prize for Asscn Fiction (Denmark) 1997, Kiriyama Pacific Rim Book Prize for Fiction 2002, Canadian Authors' Asscn Award for Fiction 2003, Guggenheim Fellowship 2005. *Literary Agent:* Bruce Westwood, Westwood Creative Artists Ltd, 94 Harbord Street, Toronto, ON M5S 1G6, Canada.

MITAL, Christine Marie Michelle, LèsL, MA; French journalist; b. 24 April 1946, Lyons; d. of Antoine and Lucette Riboud; m. Gérard Mital 1969; two s. *Education:* Univ. of Lyons and Inst. d'Etudes Politiques de Paris. *Career:* Ed on France Soir 1971–72, Informations 1973; Ed. on Nouvel Economiste 1974–76, Head Social Section 1976–79; Ed. on L'Expansion 1979–85, Sr Reporter 1985–87, Deputy Ed.-in-Chief 1990, Ed-in-Chief then Deputy Editorial Dir 1991–99; Co-Dir Le Monde des Affaires (supplement to Le Monde) 1987–88; Ed-in-Chief Le Nouvel Observateur 2000–; Asst Ed-in-Chief Capital 1999–. *Address:* Le Nouvel Observateur, 10–12 place de la Bourse, 75002 Paris, France.

MITCHARD, Jacquelyn, BA; American writer; b. 10 Dec. 1953, Chicago, IL; m. Dan Allegretti 1981 (died 1993); five c. *Education:* Rockford Coll. *Career:* reporter, Man. Ed., Pioneer Press, Chicago, 1976–79; Metro reporter and columnist, Milwaukee Journal, 1984–88; syndicated columnist. *Publications:* non-fiction: Jane Addams: Pioneer in Social Reform and Activist for World Peace 1991, Jane Addams: Peace Activist (co-author) 1992; novels: Mother Less Child: The Love Story of a Family 1985, The Deep End of the Ocean 1996, A Theory of Relativity 2001, Still Summer 2007; other: screenplays. *Honours:* Maggie Awards for Public Service Magazine Journalism, 1993, 1994; Parenting Network Public Awareness Award, 1997; Milwaukee Press Club Headliner Award, 1997; Anne Powers Award for Fiction, Council of Wisconsin Writers, 1997.

MITCHELL, Adrian; British poet and playwright; b. 24 Oct. 1932, London; s. of James Mitchell and Kathleen Mitchell. *Education:* Christ Church, Oxford. *Career:* left journalism in 1966; since then has written novels and numerous plays for stage and TV for both children and adults; has performed his poems world-wide. *Films:* Man Friday 1975, The Tragedy of King Real 1982. *Music:*

The Ledge (opera libretto) 1961, Houdini (opera libretto) 1977, Start Again (oratorio) 1998, The Princess Robot (opera libretto) 2003. *Plays:* Tyger and Tyger Two, Man Friday, Mind Your Head, A Seventh Man, White Suit Blues, Uppendown Money, Hoagy, In the Unlikely Event, Satie Day/Night, The Pied Piper, The Snow Queen, Jemima Puddleduck, The Siege, The Heroes, The Lion, the Witch and the Wardrobe, The Mammoth Sails Tonight, Alice in Wonderland and Through the Looking Glass, Peter Rabbit, Tom Kitten, Robin Hood and Marian, King of Shadows, The Fear Brigade. *Radio plays:* Animals Can't Laugh, White Suit Blues, Anna on Anna; poetry: Paradise Lost and Paradise Regained; five programmes on Brecht's poetry 1998. *Television:* Man Friday 1972, Daft as a Brush 1975, Glad Day 1978, Pieces of Peace 1992. *Publications:* novels: If You See Me Comin', The Bodyguard, Wartime; plays: Plays with Songs; poetry: Out Loud, Heart on the Left, Blue Coffee, All Shook Up, The Shadow Knows; for children: Robin Hood and Maid Marian, Nobody Rides the Unicorn, Maudie and the Green Children, Zoo of Dreams; also adaptations of numerous foreign plays. *Honours:* Dr hc (Univ. of N London); Fellowships at Univ. of Lancaster 1967–69, Wesleyan Coll. 1972, Univ. of Cambridge 1980–81, Royal Soc. of Literature 1987, Gold Medal, Theatre of Poetry, Varna, Bulgaria, Shadow Poet Laureate (apptd by Red Pepper magazine). *Literary Agent:* c/o PFD, Drury House, 34–43 Russell Street, London, WC2B 5HA, England. *Telephone:* (20) 7344-1000. *Website:* www.pfd .co.uk.

MITCHELL, Chris, BA; Australian journalist and editor; *Editor-in-Chief, The Australian*; b. 13 Oct. 1956, Brisbane; pnr Christine Jackman; two s. one d. *Education:* Padua Coll., Brisbane and Univ. of Queensland. *Career:* journalist with The Telegraph, Brisbane 1973–79, The Townsville Bulletin 1979–81, The Daily Telegraph, Sydney 1981, The Australian Financial Review; Chief Sub-Ed., Night Ed., Deputy Ed., The Australian 1984–92, Ed. 1992–95; Ed.-in-Chief, The Courier Mail and The Sunday Mail, Queensland 1995–2002; fmr Ed.-in-Chief, Queensland Newspapers; Ed.-in-Chief The Australian 2002–. *Address:* The Australian, PO Box 4245, Sydney 2001, Australia (office). *Telephone:* (2) 9288-2302 (office). *Fax:* (2) 9288-2912 (office). *Website:* www.theaustralian.com.au (office).

MITCHELL, David, MA; British writer; b. Jan. 1969, Southport; m. Keiko Mitchell; one d. *Education:* Univ. of Kent. *Career:* worked in Waterstone's, Canterbury 1990–91; taught English in Japan 1994–2002. *Publications:* Ghostwritten (Mail on Sunday/John Llewellyn Rhys Prize, James Tait Black Memorial Prize) 1999, Number9Dream 2001, Cloud Atlas (British Book Awards for Richard & Judy Best Read of the Year 2005, South Bank Show Literary Fiction Award, Geoffrey Faber Memorial Prize 2005) 2004, Black Swan Green 2006. *Honours:* one of Granta's Best of Young British Novelists 2003. *Address:* c/o Sceptre, Hodder Headline Ltd, 338 Euston Road, London, NW1 3BH, England.

MITCHELL, David John, MA; British writer; b. 24 Jan. 1924, London, England; m. 1955; one s. *Education:* Bradfield Coll., Berkshire, Trinity Coll., Oxford. *Career:* staff writer Picture Post 1947–52; mem. Soc. of Authors. *Publications:* Women on the Warpath 1966, The Fighting Pankhursts 1967, 1919 Red Mirage 1970, Pirates 1976, Queen Christabel 1977, The Jesuits: A History 1980, The Spanish Civil War 1982, Travellers in Spain 1990, The Spanish Attraction (ed.) 2001; contrib. to newspapers and magazines. *Honours:* Civil List Pension for services to literature 1998. *Address:* 20 Mountacre Close, Sydenham Hill, London, SE26 6SX, England (home). *Telephone:* (20) 8670-5992 (home).

MITCHELL, Jerome, MA, PhD; American academic and writer; b. 7 Oct. 1935, Chattanooga, Tenn. *Education:* Emory Univ., Univ. of Bonn, Germany, Duke Univ. *Career:* Asst Prof., Univ. of Illinois, 1965–67; Assoc. Prof., Univ. of Georgia 1967–72, Prof. 1972–97; Fulbright Guest Prof., Univ. of Bonn, 1972–73; Visiting Exchange Prof., Univ. of Erlangen, 1975; Richard Merton Guest Prof., Univ. of Regensburg, 1978–79. *Publications:* Thomas Hoccleve: A Study in Early 15th Century English Poetic, 1968; Hoccleve's Works: The Minor Poems, 1970; Chaucer: The Love Poet, 1973; The Walter Scott Operas, 1977; Scott, Chaucer and Medieval Romance, 1987; Old and Middle English Literature, 1994; More Scott Operas, 1996. Contributions: various scholarly journals. *Address:* PO Box 1268, Athens, GA 30603, USA.

MITCHELL, Julian, BA; British author; b. 1 May 1935, Epping, Essex, England; s. of the late William Moncur Mitchell and Christine Mitchell (née Browne). *Education:* Winchester and Wadham Coll., Oxford. *Career:* mem. Literature Panel, Arts Council 1966–69, Welsh Arts Council 1988–92. *Publications:* novels: Imaginary Toys 1961, A Disturbing Influence 1962, As Far As You Can Go 1963, The White Father 1964, A Circle of Friends 1966, The Undiscovered Country 1968; Biography: Jennie: Lady Randolph Churchill (with Peregrine Churchill), A Disgraceful Anomaly 2003; Plays: Half Life 1977, The Enemy Within 1980, Another Country 1981 (SWET Award 1982, filmed 1984), Francis 1983, After Aida (or Verdi's Messiah) 1986, Falling over England 1994, August 1994 (adapted from Uncle Vanya, filmed 1995). *Art exhibition:* Curator, Joshua Gosselin in Wales, Chepstow 2003. *Films:* Arabesque 1965, Vincent and Theo 1990, Wilde 1997; television plays and adaptations; translation of Pirandello's Henry IV. *Television:* more than 50 TV plays. *Honours:* John Llewellyn Rhys Prize 1965; Somerset Maugham Award 1966. *Address:* 47 Draycott Place, London, SW3 3DB, England. *Telephone:* (20) 7589-1933.

MITCHELL, Kenneth Ronald, OC, BA, MA; Canadian academic, writer and dramatist; *Professor, University of Regina*; b. 13 Dec. 1940, Moose Jaw, SK; m.

Jeanne Shami 1983; four s. one d. *Education:* Univ. of Saskatchewan. *Career:* instructorUniv. of Regina 1967–70, Prof. 1984–2005; Visiting Prof., Univ. of Beijing 1980–81, Foreign Affairs Coll., Beijing 1986–87; mem. Canadian Asscn of Univ. Teachers, Playwrights' Union of Canada. *Publications:* Wandering Rafferty 1972, The Meadowlark Connection 1975, Everybody Gets Something Here 1977, Cruel Tears (co-author) 1977, Horizon: Writings of the Canadian Prairie (ed.) 1977, The Con Man 1979, Davin 1979, Sinclair Ross 1981, Ken Mitchell Country 1984, Gone the Burning Sun 1985, Through the Nan Da Gate 1986, Witches and Idiots 1990, The Plainsman 1992, Stones of the Dalai Lama 1993, The Heroic Adventures of Donny Coyote 2003, The Jazz Province 2005. *Honours:* Ottawa Little Theatre Prize 1971, Canadian Authors' Asscn Award for Best Canadian Play 1985. *Address:* 209 Angus Crescent, Regina, SK S4T 6N3, Canada.

MITCHELL, Roger Sherman, AB, MA, PhD; American poet and teacher; b. 8 Feb. 1935, Boston, MA; two d. *Education:* Harvard College, University of Colorado, Manchester University. *Career:* Ed., Minnesota Review, 1973–81; Dir, Writers Conferences, 1975–85, Creative Writing Program, 1978–96, Indiana University; mem. Associated Writing Programs. *Publications:* Letters from Siberia, 1971; Moving, 1976; A Clear Space on a Cold Day, 1986; Adirondack, 1988; Clear Pond, 1991; The Word for Everything, 1996; Braid, 1997; Savage Baggage, 2001. Contributions: periodicals. *Honours:* Abby M. Copps Award, 1971; Midland Poetry Award, 1972; Borestone Mountain Award, 1973; PEN Award, 1977; Arvon Foundation Awards, 1985, 1987; National Endowment for the Arts Fellowships, 1986, 2001; Chester H. Jones Award, 1987.

MITCHELL, Susanna Ryland; British writer; b. 8 April 1941, Newry, Northern Ireland; m. Charles Donald Mitchell 1965, two d. *Education:* University of Cambridge. *Publications:* The Token, 1984; The Christening, 1986; The Colour of His Hair, 1994. *Literary Agent:* Curtis Brown Ltd, Haymarket House, 28–29 Haymarket, London, SW1Y 4SP, England. *Telephone:* (20) 7393-4400. *Fax:* (20) 7393-4401. *E-mail:* info@curtisbrown.co .uk. *Website:* www.curtisbrown.co.uk. *Address:* 63 Cloudesley Road, London N1 0EL, England (home).

MITCHELL, William John Thomas, BA, MA, PhD; American academic, editor and writer; *Gaylord Donnelley Distinguished Service Professor, University of Chicago*; b. 24 March 1942, Anaheim, CA; m. Janice Misurell 1968; one s. one d. *Education:* Michigan State Univ., Johns Hopkins Univ. *Career:* Ed., Critical Inquiry 1979–; Prof. of English and Art History, Chair Dept of English Univ. of Chicago 1989–92; Fairchild Distinguished Scholar, Cal Tech 1994; Berg Prof., New York Univ. 1998, 2000; Maclean Visiting Prof., Colorado Coll. 2001; Hawke Prof., Univ. of South Australia 2001; mem. Acad. of Literary Studies, MLA, PEN. *Publications:* Blake's Composite Art 1977, The Language of Images 1980, The Politics of Interpretation 1983, Against Theory 1985, Iconology 1986, Art and the Public Sphere 1993, Landscape and Power 1993, Picture Theory 1994, The Last Dinosaur Book: The Life and Times of a Cultural Icon 1998, What Do Pictures Want? 2005; contrib. to professional journals and general periodicals. *Honours:* American Philosophical Soc. Essay Prize 1968, Nat. Endowment for the Humanities Fellowships 1978, 1986, Guggenheim Fellowship 1983, Gaylord Donnelley Distinguished Service Professorship 1989, Coll. Art Asscn's Charles Rufus Morey Prize for Distinguished Book in Art History 1996, Univ. of Chicago Press Laing Prize for Picture Theory 1997, American Acad. in Berlin Berlin Prize Fellow 2002, Hon. Fellow Wissenschaftskolleg zu Berlin 2004–05, Leverhulme Prof., UK 2006. *Address:* c/o Dept of English and Art History, University of Chicago, 1050 E 59th Street, Chicago, IL 60637, USA (office). *Telephone:* (773) 702-8475 (office). *Fax:* (772) 702-3397 (office). *E-mail:* wjtm@uchicago.edu (office).

MITSON, Eileen Nora; British author; b. 22 Sept. 1930, Langley, Essex; m. Arthur Samuel Mitson 1951; two d. (one deceased). *Education:* Cambridge Technical Coll. and School of Art. *Career:* columnist, Christian Woman magazine, later Woman Alive Magazine 1982–94. *Publications:* Beyond the Shadows 1968, Amazon Adventure 1969, The Inside Room 1973, A Kind of Freedom 1976, Reaching for God 1978, Creativity (co-author) 1985, Songs of Freedom 2005. *Address:* 39 Oaklands, Hamilton Road, Reading, Berkshire RG1 5RN, England (home). *Telephone:* (118) 926-4144 (home).

MITTMAN, Stephanie, BA; American writer and artist; b. 15 April 1950, New York, NY; m. Alan Mittman 1969; one s. one d. *Education:* Ithaca Coll. *Career:* mem. Authors' Guild, Novelists Inc., Romance Writers of America. *Publications:* Bridge to Yesterday, 1995; A Taste of Honey, 1995; The Marriage Bed, 1996; Sweeter than Wine, 1997; The Courtship, 1997; A Kiss to Dream On, 1998; Head Over Heels, 1999; A Heart Full of Miracles, 2000. Contributions: anthologies. *Honours:* Best Sweet Historical Award, American Online Romance Reader Awards, 1995; Reviewer's Choice Certificate of Excellence, Romantic Times, 1996; Best Americana Historical Romance Award, Romantic Times, 1997; Career Achievement Award, Romantic Times, 1997. *Address:* c/o MLGW, 190 Willis Avenue, Mineola, NY 11501, USA. *E-mail:* smittman@tweny.rr.com.

MIYAMOTO, Teru; Japanese novelist; b. 6 March 1947, Kobe. *Education:* Otemon Gakuin Univ. *Career:* began career as advertising copywriter. *Publications:* Doro no Kawa (River of Mud) (Dazai Osamu Prize) 1977, Hoterugawa (Firefly River) (Akutagawa Prize) 1978, Maborosi no Hikari (Illusory Light) 1979, Kinshu (trans. as Kinshu: Autumn Brocade) 1982, Yumemidori no hitobito (The People of Dream Street) 1989. *Address:* c/o New

Directions Publishing Corporation, 80 Eighth Avenue, New York, NY 10011, USA. *E-mail:* editorial@ndbooks.com.

MIZUMURA, Minae; Japanese novelist; b. 1951, Tokyo; m. *Education:* Yale Coll., Yale Univ. *Career:* teacher at Princeton Univ., Univ. of Michigan, Stanford Univ.; mem. Int. Writing Program at Univ. of Iowa 2003. *Publications:* Zoku Meian (trans. Light and Darkness Continued) 1990, Shishosetsu from Left to Right (trans. An I-Novel from Left to Right) 1995, Tegami - Shiori wo Suete 1998, Honkaku Shosetsu (trans. An Orthodox Novel) 2002. *Honours:* Japan Foundation Fellowship 1983; Geijutsu Sensho Award 1991, Noma Award 1995, Yomiuri Literary Award 2002. *Address:* International Writing Program, University of Iowa, 100 Shambaugh House, 430 N Clinton Street, Iowa City, IA 52242, USA. *Telephone:* (319) 335-0128. *E-mail:* iwp@uiowa.edu. *Website:* wwwuiowa.edu/~iwp.

MLECHIN, Leonid M.; Russian journalist and writer; b. 12 June 1957; m.; one s. *Education:* Moscow State Univ. *Career:* staff, head of division, Deputy Ed.-in-Chief weekly Novoye Vremya 1979–93; Deputy Ed.-in-Chief newspaper Izvestia 1993–96; political reviewer All-Russian State Cttee on Radio and Television 1996–97; writer and narrator Particular Dossier (TV-Tsentr) 1997–. *Publications include:* more than 20 books, including detective stories, novels, historical non-fiction, and biographies of Yevgeny Primakov and the chairmen of the KGB. *Address:* TV-Tsentr, ul. B. Tatarskaya 33/1, Moscow 113184, Russia (office). *Telephone:* (495) 215-18-12 (office); (495) 217-75-50 (office).

MNATSAKANOVA, Elizaveta Arkad'evna; Russian poet and teacher; b. 1922, Baku, Azerbaijan. *Education:* Moscow Conservatory, Moscow State Univ. *Career:* teacher of literature, Universität Wien, Austria. *Publications include:* Shagi i vzdokhi: Chetyre knigi stikhov 1982, Perm': Izdatel'stvo Permskogo gosudarstvennogo universiteta 1994, Velikoe tikhoe more ('The Great Quiet Sea: 10 poems in memory of Anne N. Segodnia) 1996, Vita breve. *Honours:* Oden Literary Prize. *Address:* c/o Universität Wien, Dr Karl Luegerring 1, 1010 Vienna, Austria.

MO, Timothy; British author; b. 30 Dec. 1950, Hong Kong; s. of Peter Mo Wan Lung and Barbara Helena Falkingham. *Education:* Mill Hill School and St John's Coll., Univ. of Oxford. *Career:* fmrly worked for Times Educational Supplement and New Statesman; fmr reporter for Boxing News and PAYE clerk. *Publications include:* The Monkey King 1979 (Geoffrey Faber Memorial Prize 1979), Sour Sweet 1982, An Insular Possession 1986, The Redundancy of Courage 1991 (E. M. Forster Award 1992), Brownout on Breadfruit Boulevard 1995, Renegade or Halo 2 1999 (James Tait Black Memorial Prize 1999). *Honours:* Hawthornden Prize. *Address:* c/o Paddleless Press, BCM Paddleless, London, WC1N 3XX, England. *Telephone:* timothymo@eudoramail.com.

MO, Yan; Chinese novelist; b. (Guan Moye), 1955, Gaomi, Shandong Prov. *Education:* PLA Acad. of Arts, Beijing Normal Univ. *Career:* joined PLA 1976. *Publications:* Red Sorghum, Garlic Ballads 2002, Thirteen Steps, The Herbivora Family, Jiuguo, Shifu You'll Do Anything for a Laugh, Big Breasts and Wide Hips 2006. *Literary Agent:* c/o Publicity, 375 Hudson Street, New York, NY 10014, USA.

MOAT, John, MA; British author and poet; b. 11 Sept. 1936, India; m. 1962; one s. one d. *Education:* Univ. of Oxford. *Publications:* 6d per Annum 1966, Heorot (novel) 1968, A Standard of Verse 1969, Thunder of Grass 1970, The Tugen and the Toot (novel) 1973, The Ballad of the Leat 1974, Bartonwood (children's) 1978, Fiesta and the Fox Reviews and His Prophecy 1979, The Way to Write (with John Fairfax) 1981, Skeleton Key 1982, Mai's Wedding (novel) 1983, Welcombe Overtunes 1987, The Missing Moon 1988, Firewater and the Miraculous Mandarin 1990, Practice 1994, The Valley (poems and drawings) 1998, 100 Poems 1998, Rain (short stories) 2000, Hermes & Magdalen (poetry and related prints) 2004, The Founding of Arvon (memoir) 2006. *Address:* Crenham Mill, Hartland, North Devon, EX39 6HN, England. *Website:* www.johnmoat.co.uk.

MODIANO, Patrick Jean; French novelist; b. 30 July 1945, Boulogne-Billancourt; s. of Albert Modiano and Luisa Colpyn; m. Dominique Zehrfuss 1970; two d. *Education:* schools in Biarritz, Chamonix, Deauville, Thônes, Barbizon, coll. in Paris. *Publications:* La place de l'étoile 1968, La ronde de nuit 1969, Les boulevards de ceinture 1972, Lacombe Lucien (screenplay) 1973, La polka (play) 1974, Villa triste (novel) 1975, Interrogatoire d'Emmanuel Berl 1976, Livret de famille (novel) 1977, Rue des boutiques obscures 1978, Une jeunesse 1981, Memory Lane 1981, De si braves garçons (novel) 1982, Poupée blonde 1983, Quartier perdu 1985, Dimanches d'août 1986, Une aventure de Choura 1986, La fiancée de Choura 1987, Remise de peine (novel) 1988, Catherine Certitude 1988, Vestiaire de l'enfance (novel) 1989, Voyage de noces 1990, Fleurs de ruine 1991, Un cirque passe (novel) 1992, Chien de Printemps 1993, Du plus loin de l'oubli 1995, Dora Bruder 1997, Des inconnues 1999, La petite bijou 2001, Accident Nocturne 2003, Un Pedigree 2005. *Honours:* Prix Roger Nimier 1968, Prix Felix Fénéon 1969, Grand Prix de l'Académie française 1972, Prix Goncourt 1978; Chevalier des Arts et des Lettres; prix Pierre de Monaco 1984; Grand prix du Roman de la Ville de Paris 1994, Grand prix de littérature Paul Morand de l'Académie française 2000. *Address:* c/o Editions Gallimard, 5 rue Sébastien Bottin, 75007 Paris, France.

MOFFAT, Gwen; British writer; b. 3 July 1924, Brighton, Sussex; m. 1st Gordon Moffat 1948; one d.; m. 2nd John Rodney Lees 1956. *Education:* Hove Co. Grammar School. *Career:* mem. Crime Writers' Asscn, Soc. of Authors,

Pinnacle Club. *Radio:* short stories and talks. *Publications:* Space Below My Feet 1961, Two Star Red 1964, On My Home Ground 1968, Survival Count 1972, Lady With a Cool Eye 1973, Deviant Death 1973, The Corpse Road 1974, Hard Option 1975, Miss Pink at the Edge of the World 1975, Over the Sea to Death 1976, A Short Time to Live 1976, Persons Unknown 1978, Hard Road West 1981, The Buckskin Girl 1982, Die Like a Dog 1982, Last Chance Country 1983, Grizzly Trail 1984, Snare 1987, The Stone Hawk 1989, The Storm Seekers 1989, Rage 1990, The Raptor Zone 1990, Pit Bull 1991, Veronica's Sisters 1992, The Outside Edge 1993, Cue the Battered Wife 1994, The Lost Girls 1998, A Wreath of Dead Moths 1998, Running Dogs 1999, Private Sins 1999, Quicksand 2001, Retribution 2002, Man Trap 2003, Dying for Love 2005; contribs: short stories, features and series for newspapers and magazines; reviews for Shots E magazine. *Address:* c/o Juliet Burton Literary Agency, 2 Clifton Avenue, London, W12 9DR, England. *Telephone:* (20) 8762-0148. *Fax:* (20) 8743-8765. *E-mail:* juliet.burton@btinternet.com. *Website:* www.twbooks.co.uk/authors/gmoffat.html.

MOFFEIT, Tony A., BSc, MLS; American librarian and poet; b. 14 March 1942, Claremont, OK. *Education:* Oklahoma State University, University of Oklahoma. *Career:* Asst Dir, Library, 1980–, Poet-in-Residence, 1986–95, University of Southern Colorado; Dir, Pueblo Poetry Project, 1980–; mem. American Library Asscn. *Publications:* La Nortenita, 1983; Outlaw Blues, 1983; Shooting Chant, 1984; Coyote Blues, 1985; Hank Williams Blues, 1985; The Spider Who Walked Underground, 1985; Black Cat Bone, 1986; Dancing With the Ghosts of the Dead, 1986; Pueblo Blues, 1986; Boogie Alley, 1989; Luminous Animal, 1989; Poetry is Dangerous, the Poet is an Outlaw, 1995. Contributions: journals and magazines. *Honours:* Jack Kerouac Award, 1986; National Endowment for the Arts Fellowship, 1992.

MOFFETT, Judith, BA, MA, PhD; American poet, writer and teacher; b. 30 Aug. 1942, Louisville, KY; m. Edward B. Irving 1983. *Education:* Hanover College, IN, Colorado State University, University of Wisconsin at Madison, University of Pennsylvania. *Career:* Fulbright Lecturer, University of Lund, Sweden, 1967–68; Asst Prof., Behrend College, Pennsylvania State University, 1971–75; Visiting Lecturer, University of Iowa, 1977–78; Visiting Lecturer, 1978–79, Asst Prof., 1979–86, Adjunct Asst Prof., 1986–88, Adjunct Assoc. Prof., 1988–93, Adjunct Prof. of English, 1993–94, University of Pennsylvania. *Publications:* Poetry: Keeping Time, 1976; Whinny Moor Crossing, 1984. Fiction: Pennterra, 1987; The Ragged World, 1991; Time, Like an Ever-Rolling Stream, 1992; Two That Came True, 1992. Other: James Merrill: An Introduction to the Poetry, 1984; Homestead Year: Back to the Land in Suburbia, 1995. *Honours:* Fulbright Grants, 1967, 1973; American Philosophical Society Grant, 1973; Eunice Tiejens Memorial Prize, 1973; Borestone Mountain Poetry Prize, 1976; Levinson Prize, 1976; Ingram Merrill Foundation Grants, 1977, 1980, 1989; Columbia University Trans. Prize, 1978; Bread Loaf Writers Conference Tennessee Williams Fellowship, 1978; Swedish Acad. Trans. Prize, 1982; National Endowment for the Humanities Trans. Fellowship, 1983; National Endowment for the Arts Fellowship, 1984; Swedish Acad. Trans. Grant, 1993.

MOGGACH, Deborah, BA, DipEd, FRSL; British writer; b. 28 June 1948, London; d. of Richard Hough and Helen Charlotte Hough; m. Anthony Moggach 1971 (divorced); one s. one d. *Education:* Camden School for Girls, Univ. of Bristol, Univ. of London. *Career:* Chair. Soc. of Authors 1999–2001; mem. PEN. *Television:* (dramas) To Have and To Hold 1986, Stolen 1990, Goggle-Eyes (adaptation) 1993 (Writers' Guild Award for Best Adapted TV Serial), Seesaw 1998, Close Relations 1998, Love in a Cold Climate (adaptation) 2001, Final Demand 2003. *Film:* Pride and Prejudice (adaptation) 2005. *Play:* Double Take. *Publications:* novels: You Must Be Sisters 1978, Close to Home 1979, A Quiet Drink 1980, Hot Water Man 1982, Porky 1983, To Have and To Hold 1986, Driving in the Dark 1988, Stolen 1990, The Stand-in 1991, The Ex-Wives 1993, Seesaw 1996, Close Relations 1997, Tulip Fever 1999, Final Demand 2001, These Foolish Things 2004, In the Dark 2007; short stories: Smile 1987, Changing Babies 1995. *Literary Agent:* Curtis Brown, 28–29 Haymarket, London, SW1Y 4SP, England. *Telephone:* (20) 7396-6600. *Fax:* (20) 7396-0110.

MOHAIMEED, Yousef al-; Saudi Arabian writer; b. 1964, Riyadh. *Career:* Cultural Ed. literary journal, Al-Yamama. *Publications include:* novels: Traps of Scent 2003, The Bottle; contrib. to journals, including Banipal. *Address:* Al-Yamama, POB 851, Riyadh 11421, Saudi Arabia (office); c/o Riad El-Rayyes Books, Sanayeh, Union Bldg, Beirut, Lebanon. *E-mail:* info@elrayyesbooks.com.

MOHN, Reinhard; German publisher; *Chairman Emeritus, Bertelsmann AG*; b. 29 June 1921; m. Elisabeth Mohn 1982. *Career:* army service 1939–43; POW in N Africa and USA 1943–46; Pres. and CEO Bertelsmann AG 1947–81, Chair. Supervisory Bd 1981–91, now Chair. Emer.; Founder, mem. Cttee Bertelsmann Foundation, Chair. 1991–98. *Publications:* Success Through Partnership 1988, Humanity Wins 2000. *Address:* Bertelsmann AG, Carl-Bertelsmann-Strasse 270, 33311 Gütersloh, Germany. *Telephone:* (5241) 800 (office). *Fax:* (5241) 809662 (office). *Website:* www.bertelsmann.de (office).

MOHRT, Michel, LenD; French writer and editor; b. 28 April 1914, Morlaix; s. of Fernand Mohrt and Amélie Mohrt (née Gélébart); m. Françoise Jarrier 1955; one s. *Education:* Law School, Rennes. *Career:* lawyer, Marseilles Bar – 1942; Prof., Yale Univ., Smith Coll., UCLA, USA 1947–52; Ed. and Head English Trans Section Les Editions Gallimard 1952–; mem. Acad. française 1985. *Art Exhibition:* Aquarelles Expositions (Galeries des Orfèvres Paris).

Publications: novels: Le répit, Mon royaume pour un cheval 1949, Les nomades, le serviteur fidèle, La prison maritime (Grand Prix du roman de l' Acad. française 1962) 1961, La campagne d'Italie 1965, L'ours des Adirondacks 1969, Deux Indiennes à Paris 1974, Les moyens du bord 1975, La guerre civile 1986, Le Télésiège 1989, Un soir à Londres 1991, On liquide et on s'en va 1992, L'Ile des fous 1999; essays: Les intellectuels devant la défaite de 1870, Montherlant, homme libre 1943, Le nouveau roman américain 1956, L'air du large 1969, L'air du large II 1988; plays: Un jeu d'enfer 1970, La maison du père 1979, Vers l'Ouest 1988, L'Air du temps 1991. *Honours:* Officier, Légion d'honneur, Croix de guerre; Grand Prix de la Critique littéraire 1970, Grand Prix de Littérature de l' Acad. française 1983. *Address:* c/o Editions Gallimard, 5 rue Sébastien-Bottin, 75007 Paris; 4 bis rue du Cherche-Midi, 75006 Paris, France (home). *Telephone:* 1-42-22-42-12 (home).

MOI, Toril, PhD; Norwegian academic and writer; *James B. Duke Professor of Literature and Romance Studies, Duke University;* b. 28 Nov. 1953, Farsund; d. of Georg Seval Moi and Nora Moi; m. David Leon Paletz 1999. *Education:* Bergen Univ. *Career:* fmr teacher at Univ. of Bergen and Univ. of Oxford, UK; James B. Duke Prof. of Literature and Romance Studies, Duke Univ., Durham, NC. *Publications include:* Sexual/Textual Politics: Feminist Literary Theory 1985, Simone de Beauvoir: The Making of an Intellectual Woman 1994, What is a Woman? and Other Essays 1999, Henrik Ibsen and the Birth of Modernisim 2006; editor: The Kristeva Reader 1986, French Feminist Thought 1987; articles on feminist theory, psychoanalytic theory, French phenomenology and ordinary language philosophy. *Honours:* Guggenheim Fellowship 2001. *Address:* Literature Program, Duke University, Box 90670, Durham, NC 27708-0670, USA (office). *Telephone:* (919) 681-4971 (office). *Fax:* (919) 684-3598 (office). *E-mail:* toril@duke.edu (office). *Website:* fds.duke.edu/db/aas/Literature/faculty/toril (office).

MOJTABAI, Ann Grace, MA, MS; American author and educator; b. 8 June 1937, Brooklyn, NY; m. Fathollah Motabai 1960 (divorced 1966); one s. one d. *Education:* Antioch Coll.; Columbia Univ.y. *Career:* Lecturer in Philosophy, Hunter Coll., CUNY, 1966–68; Briggs-Copeland Lecturer on English, Harvard Univ. 1978–83; Writer-in-Residence, Univ. of Tulsa, 1983–; mem. Mark Twain Soc., PEN. Texas Inst. of Letters. *Publications:* Mundome, 1974; The 400 Eels of Sigmund Freud, 1976; A Stopping Place, 1979; Autumn, 1982; Blessed Assurance, 1986; Ordinary Time, 1989; Called Out, 1994; Soon, 1998. Contributions: New York Times Book Review; New Republic; Philosophy Today; Philosophical Journal. *Honours:* Radcliffe Institute Fellow, 1976–78; Guggenheim Fellowship, 1981–82; Richard and Hinda Rosenthal Award, American Acad. and Inst. of Arts and Letters, 1983; Lillian Smith Award, Southern Regional Council, 1986; Award in Literature, American Acad. of Arts and Letters, 1993. *Address:* 2329 Woodside, Amarillo, TX 79124-1036, USA. *E-mail:* agmojtabai@aol.com.

MOKEDDEM, Malika; Algerian novelist and physician; b. 1949, Kenadsa. *Education:* studied medicine in France. *Career:* currently based in France, worked as general practitioner focusing on health needs of immigrant North African community, Montpellier. *Publications:* novels: le Siècle des sauterelles (Century of Locusts) (ADELF Prix Afrique–Méditerranée) 1992, L'Interdite (The Forbidden Women) (Prix Méditerranée, Perpignan) 1994, Des rêves et des assassins (Of Dreams and Assassins) 1995, Les Hommes qui marchent 1997, La Nuit de la lézarde 1998, N'zid 2001, La Transe des insoumis 2003, Mes hommes 2005. *Address:* c/o Éditions Grasset & Fasquelle, 61 rue des Saints-Pères, Paris 75006, France. *E-mail:* dfanelli@grasset.fr.

MOKYR, Joel, BA, PhD; Dutch/American academic and writer; *Robert H. Strotz Professor of Arts and Sciences, Northwestern University;* b. 26 July 1946, Leyden, The Netherlands; m. Margalit B. Moky 1969; two d. *Education:* Hebrew Univ., Yale Univ. *Career:* Robert H. Strotz Prof. of Arts and Sciences, NW Univ.; Sackler Prof., Eitan Berglas School of Econs., Tel Aviv Univ.; Fellow, American Acad. of Arts and Sciences, 1996; Pres. Economic History Asscn 2003–04; Foreign Mem. Royal Dutch Acad. of Sciences 2001–, Accademia Nazionale dei Lincei (Social Science Section) 2004–. *Publications:* Industrialization in the Low Countries, 1976; Why Ireland Starved, 1983; The Lever of Riches, 1990; The British Industrial Revolution, 1993; The Gifts of Athena, 2002; Oxford Encyclopedia of Economic History (Ed.-in-Chief), 2003. *Address:* Department of Economics, Northwestern University, 2003 Sheridan Road, Evanston, IL 60208, USA (office). *Telephone:* (847) 491-5693 (office). *Fax:* (847) 491-7001 (office). *Website:* www.faculty.econ.northwestern.edu/facullty/mokyr (office).

MOLCHANOV, Vladimir Kyrillovich; Russian journalist; b. 7 Oct. 1950, Moscow; s. of Kyrill Molchanov; m. Consuella Segura; one d. *Education:* Moscow State Univ. *Career:* with Press Agency Novosti 1973–86; observer USSR State Cttee for TV and Radio 1987–91; artistic Dir studio of independent co. REN-TV 1991–, Observer Reuter-TV 1994–; regular appearances in his own TV programmes Before and After Midnight 1987–93, Before and After 1994–, Panorama 2000–, Longer than Age 2000–; mem. Acad. of Russian TV, Acad. of Natural Sciences. *Publications:* TV films: Remembrance, I, You, He and She, People and Years, Zone, I Still Have More Addresses, Tied with One Chain, August of 1991 (screenplays), Retribution Must Come (M. Gorky Prize 1982). *Honours:* Prize of Journalists' Union as the Best TV Journalist 1990 and other awards. *Address:* REN-TV, Zubovsky blvd 17, Moscow, Russia. *Telephone:* (495) 255-90-77 (office).

MOLE, John Douglas, MA; British poet and critic; b. 12 Oct. 1941, Taunton, Somerset; m. Mary Norman 1968; two s. *Education:* Magdalene Coll.,

Cambridge. *Career:* teacher, Haberdashers' School, Elstree 1964–73; Exchange Teacher, Riverdale School, New York 1969–70; Head, Dept of English, Verulam School 1973–81, St Albans School 1981–98; Poet-in-Residence, Magdalene Coll. Cambridge 1996; Visiting Poet, Univ. of Hertfordshire 1998–2003; Poet to the City of London 1999–; Pres. Ver Poets, Toddington Poetry Soc.; mem. Soc. of Authors. *Publications:* poetry: Feeding the Lake 1981, In and Out of the Apple 1984, Homing 1987, Boo to a Goose 1987, The Mad Parrot's Countdown 1989, Catching the Spider 1990, The Conjuror's Rabbit 1992, Depending on the Light 1993, Selected Poems 1995, Hot Air 1996, Copy Cat (for children) 1997, The Dummy's Dilemma 1999, For the Moment 2000, The Wonder Dish 2002, Counting the Chimes: New & Selected Poems 2004; other: Passing Judgements: Poetry in the Eighties 1989, Poetry (ed.) 1945–80, Figures of Speech (ed.) 2000; contribs to newspapers, reviews, and magazines. *Honours:* Hon. DLitt (Hertfordshire) 2004; Eric Gregory Award 1970, Signal Award for Outstanding Contrib. to Children's Poetry 1988, Cholmondeley Award 1994. *Address:* 11 Hill Street, St Albans, Herts., AL3 4QS, England (home). *Telephone:* (1727) 857153 (home). *E-mail:* john_mole@bigfoot.com (home).

MOLINA, Silvia; Mexican novelist; b. 11 Oct. 1946, México, DF. *Publications:* La mañana debe seguir gris (Gray Skies Tomorrow) 1977, La familia vino del norte 1987, Imagen de Héctor 1990, Un hombre cerca 1993, El amor que me juraste (The Love You Promised Me) 1999. *Honours:* Xavier Villarrutia Prize 1977. *Address:* c/o Curbstone Press, 321 Jackson Street, Willimantic, CT 06226-1738, USA. *E-mail:* info@curbstone.org. *Website:* www.curbstone.org.

MOLLENKOTT, Virginia Ramey, MA, PhD; American academic, writer and editor; *Professor Emerita of English, William Paterson University;* b. 28 Jan. 1932, Philadelphia, PA; d. of Robert Franklin Ramey and May Lotz; m. Friedrich H. Mollenkott 1954 (divorced 1973); one s. *Education:* Bob Jones Univ., Temple Univ., New York Univ. *Career:* Chair. Dept of English, Shelton Coll. 1955–63, Nyack Coll. 1963–67; Assoc. Prof., William Paterson Univ. 1967–74, Prof. of English 1974–97, Chair. Dept of English 1972–76, Prof. Emer. 1997–; Life mem. Milton Soc. of America, Modern Language Asscn, Evangelical and Ecumentical Women's Caucus. *Publications:* Adamant and Stone Chips: A Christian Humanist Approach to Knowledge 1967, In Search of Balance 1969, Adam Among the Television Trees: An Anthology of Verse by Contemporary Christian Poets (ed.) 1971, Women, Men and the Bible 1976, Speech, Silence, Action 1980, Is the Homosexual My Neighbor? (with L. D. Scanzoni) 1978, The Divine Feminine: Biblical Imagery of God as Female 1983, Views from the Intersection (with Catherine Barry) 1984, Women of Faith in Dialogue (ed.) 1987, Sensuous Spirituality: Out from Fundamentalism 1992, Omnigender: A Trans-Religious Approach 2001, Transgender Journeys (with V. Sheridan) 2003; contrib. to numerous journals and reviews; The Witness (contributing ed.) 1994–. *Honours:* Hon. Dr of Ministry (Samaritan Coll.) 1989; Penfield Fellow 1973, Andiron Award 1964, Founders Day Award 1964, New York Univ., New Jersey Lesbian and Gay Coalition Achievement Award 1992, SAGE (Sr Action in a Gay Environment) Lifetime Achievement Award 1999, Lambda Literary Award 2002. *Address:* 11 Yearling Trail, Hewitt, NJ 07421, USA. *Telephone:* (973) 853-4281 (office). *E-mail:* jstvrm@warwick.net (home). *Website:* www.virginiarameymollenkott.com.

MOLLOY, Michael John; British journalist, editor and writer; b. 22 Dec. 1940, England; m. Sandra June Foley 1964, three d. *Education:* Ealing School of Art. *Career:* staff, 1962–70, Asst Ed., 1970–75, Deputy Ed., 1975, Ed., 1975–85, Daily Mirror; Dir, 1976–90, Ed.-in-Chief, 1985–90, Mirror Group Newspapers; Ed., Sunday Mirror, 1986–88. *Publications:* The Black Dwarf, 1985; The Kid from Riga, 1987; The Harlot of Jericho, 1989; The Century, 1990; The Gallery, 1991; Sweet Sixteen, 1992; Cat's Paw, 1993; Home Before Dark, 1994; Dogsbody, 1995.

MOLTMANN, Jürgen, DTheol; German theologian and academic; *Professor and Rector, Wuppertal Church University;* b. 8 April 1926, Hamburg; m. Dr. Elisabeth Moltmann-Wendel; four d. *Career:* POW during Second World War; with Dept of Theology, Univ. of Göttingen 1948–52, Prof. of Theology 1957–; fmr Minister, Bremen; Prof. and Rector Wuppertal Church Univ. 1958–; co-ed. Deutsch-Polnische Hefte 1959–68; Visiting Prof. in USA 1967–68; Dir CONCILIUM 1979–94. *Publications:* Christliche Petzel und das Calvinismus in Bremen 1958, Prädestination und Perseveranz 1961, Anfänge Dialektische Theologie 1963, Theologie der Hoffnung (Theology of Hope) (Isle of Elba Literary Prize) 1964, Mensch 1971, Der gekreuzigte Gott (The Crucified God) 1972, Der Sprache der Befreiung 1972, Das Experiment Hoffnung 1974, Kirche in der Kraft des Geistes 1975, Zukunft der Schöpfung 1977, Trinität und Reich Gottes 1980, Gott in der Schöpfung (God in Creation) 1985, Das Weg Jesu Christi (The Way of Jesus Christ) 1989, Der Geist des Lebens (The Spirit of Life) 1991, Das Kommen Gottes (The Coming of God) (Grawemeyer Religion Award) 1995, Experiences in Theology 1999, Science and Wisdom 2002, In the End – the Beginning: The Life of Hope 2004. *Honours:* Italian Prize of Literature, Isle of Elba 1971, Amos Comenius Medal, Bethlehem, Pa 1992, Ernst Bloch Prize of the City of Ludwigshafen 1995, Grawemeyer Award on Religion, Louisville, Ky 2000 Dr hc (Duke Univ.), (Bethlehem Theological Seminary), (Kalamazoo Coll.), (Raday Kolleg, Budapest), (St Andrews Univ.), (Emory Univ.), (Univ. of Leuven), (Univ. of Iasi), (Nottingham Univ.), (Managua, Nicaragua). *Address:* Liebermeister Strasse 12, 72076 Tübingen, Germany.

MOMADAY, Navarre Scott; American writer, painter and academic; b. 27 Feb. 1934, Lawton, Oklahoma; m. Regina Heitzer 1978; four d. *Education:* BA, University of New Mexico, 1958; MA, 1960, PhD, 1963, Stanford University. *Career:* Visiting Prof., Columbia University, Princeton University, 1979; Writer-in-Residence, Southeastern University, 1985, Aspen Writers Conference, 1986; mem. PEN. *Publications:* House Made of Dawn, 1968; The Way to Rainy Mountain, 1969; The Names, 1976; The Gourd Dancer, 1976; The Ancient Child, 1989; In the Presence of the Sun, 1992; Enchanted Circle, 1993; The Native Americans (with Linda Hozan), 1993; The Man Made of Words, 1997. *Honours:* Pulitzer Prize in Fiction, 1969; Premio Mondello, Italy, 1979; Hon. Degrees, various universities. *Literary Agent:* Julian Bach Literary Agency, 22 East 71st Street, New York, NY 10021, USA.

MOMEN, Wendi, PhD, JP; British publisher and religious organization official; *Representative, Office of External Affairs, UK Bahá'í Community*; b. 21 Oct. 1950, Hollywood, Calif., USA; d. of Robert Wirtshafter and Carol Allen (née Morris); m. Moojan Momen 1971; one s. one d. *Education:* London School of Econs. *Career:* Ed. George Ronald publishing co., Oxford 1979–; editorial services OneWorld Publications, Oxford 1989–95, Intellect Books, Oxford 1991–2000; Chair. Man. Exec. Bahá'í Publishing Trust (UK) 1989–94, Ed. 1991–, Asst Ed. The Bahá'í Encyclopedia, Bahá'í Publishing Trust, USA 1991–94; mem. Nat. Spiritual Ass. of the Bahá'ís of the UK 1982–2004, Treas. 1984–90, 2001–04, Chair. 1990–2000, Asst Sec. 2000–01, now Rep. Office of External Affairs, UK Bahá'í Community and Office for the Advancement of Women 2005–; Pres. European Bahá'ís Business Forum 1991–2002, Chair. 2003–, Asst Sec.-Gen. 2002–; JP Biggleswade (now Bedford) Petty Sessional Div. 1982–, Court Chair. 1994–; Dir (non-exec.) Beds. Family Health Services Authority 1990–94, 1999–2001; Dir (non-exec.) Beds. Heartlands Primary Care Trust 2003–05; mem. Int. Steering Cttee Global Women sector of Global Forum 1994, Bedford Council of Faiths 2002– (Chair. 2007–); Trustee One World Trust 1997– (Chair. 2002–), BASED-UK 1997– (Chair. 1997–), Multi-Faith Centre (Derby Univ.) 2000–, Bedfordshire and Luton Community Foundation. *Television:* programmes for Broomsticks Productions, Tonga 1994–96. *Publications:* Call Me Ridvan 1982, Family Worship 1989, A Basic Bahá'í Dictionary 1989, Jewels (series) 1994, Meditation 1996, I'm a Bahá'í, Basic Bahá'í Chronology (with Glenn Cameron) 1996, To Be a Mother 1999, Paradise Created (with Brenton Edwards) 2001, To Be a Father 2002, The Devotional Meeting 2003, Understanding the Bahá'í Faith (with Moojan Momen) 2005; numerous conf. papers. *Address:* Wixamtree, Sand Lane, Northill, nr Biggleswade, Beds., SG18 9AD, England (home). *Telephone:* (1767) 627626 (home). *Fax:* (1767) 627626 (home). *E-mail:* wendi@northill .demon.co.uk (home). *Website:* www.northill.demon.co.uk (home).

MOMI, Balbir Singh, MA, PhD; Indian teacher (retd), writer, dramatist, editor and translator; b. 20 Nov. 1935, Amagarh; m. Baldev Kaur 1954, four d. *Education:* Panjab Univ., Chandigarh. *Career:* Lecturer and Research Asst, GND University, Amritsar, 1974–76; Literary Ed., Perdesi Canafi Ajit Punjab, Toronto, 1982–97; mem. International Cultural Forum, India and Canada, senior international vice-pres., 1993–. *Publications:* novels, short stories, plays and translations; contrib. to many publications. *Honours:* various literary awards.

MOMPLE, Lilia, BA; Mozambican writer; b. 1935; m. *Education:* studied social work in Portugal. *Career:* Sec.-Gen., Mozambique Writers' Asscn, 1995–2001, Pres., 1997–99; mem., UNESCO Exec. Council. *Publications:* No One Killed Suhara 1988, The Eyes of the Green Cobra 1997, Muhupitit Alima (screenplay) 1988, Neighbours: The Story of a Murder 1995, Celina's Banquet (novel) 2001.

MONACO, James Frederick, BA, MA; American writer and publisher; b. 15 Nov. 1942, New York, NY; s. of George C. Monaco and Susanne Monaco (née Hirshland); m. Susan R. Schenker 1976; two s. one d. *Education:* Muhlenberg Coll., Columbia Univ. *Career:* mem. Bd Dirs Copyright Clearance Center Inc. 2002–; mem. Authors' Guild, Writers' Guild. *Publications:* How to Read a Film 1977 (multimedia edn) 2000, American Film Now 1979, The New Wave 1976, Media Culture 1977, Celebrity 1977, Connoisseur's Guide to the Movies 1985, The International Encyclopedia of Film 1991, The Movie Guide 1992, Cinemania: Interactive Movie Guide 1992, Dictionary of New Media 1999; contrib. to numerous publs. *Address:* UNET 2 Corporation, 80 East 11th Street, New York, NY 10003, USA (office). *Telephone:* (212) 777-5463 (office). *Fax:* (212) 777-5534 (office). *E-mail:* jmonaco@unet.net (office). *Website:* jamesmonaco.com.

MONÉNEMBO, Tierno; Guinean writer; b. (Thierno Saïdou Diallo), 1947. *Career:* has lived in Senegal, Algeria, Morocco; living in France 1973–; fmr teacher of biochemistry; writer-in-residence Chateau La Napoule 1992. *Publications:* novels: Les Crapauds-brousse (The Bush Toads) 1979, Un Rêve utile 1991, Un Attiéké pour Elgass 1993, Pelourinho 1995, Cinéma 1997, Les Écailles du ciel 1997, L'Aîné des orphelins (The Oldest Orphan) 2000, Peuls 2004; contrib. to Notre Librairie, Forum for Modern Language Studies. *Address:* c/o Editions du Seuil, 27 rue Jacob, Paris 75006, France. *E-mail:* contact@seuil.com.

MONETTE, Madeleine, MA; Canadian writer; b. 3 Oct. 1951, Montréal, QC; m. William R. Leggio 1979. *Education:* TV of Québec. *Career:* mem. Québec Writers Union, PEN. *Publications:* Le Double Suspect 1980, English trans. as Doubly Suspect 2000, Petites Violences 1982, Fuites et Poursuites 1982, Plages 1986, L'Aventure, la Mesaventure 1987, Amandes et melon 1991, Nouvelles de Montréal 1992, La Femme furieuse 1997, Nouvelles d'Amérique

1998, Ligne de métro 2002; contribs to periodicals. *Honours:* Robert-Cliche Award 1980, grants from Canadian Council of Arts, Conseil des Arts et des Lettres du Québec, and Fonds Gabrielle-Roy. *Address:* 2 Charlton Street, 11K, New York, NY 10014, USA (home). *E-mail:* mmonet@aol.com (home).

MONEY, David Charles, BSc, FRGS; British teacher (retd) and writer; b. 5 Oct. 1918, Oxford, England; m. Madge Matthews 1945, one s. *Education:* St John's College, Oxford. *Career:* mem. Farmer's Club. *Publications:* Human Geography, 1954; Climate, Soils and Vegetation, 1965; The Earth's Surface, 1970; Patterns of Settlement, 1972; Environmental Systems (series), 1978–82; Foundations of Geography, 1987; Climate and Environmental Systems, 1988; China – The Land and the People, 1984; China Today, 1987; Australia Today, 1988; Environmental Issues – The Global Consequences, 1994; China in Change, 1996; The Vocation of Bachan Singh, 1997; Weather and Climate, 2000. *Honours:* hon. mem. Geographical Asscn.

MONEY, Keith; New Zealand author, artist and photographer; b. 1934, Auckland. *Publications:* Salute the Horse 1960, The Horseman in Our Midst 1963, The Equestrian World 1963, The Art of the Royal Ballet 1964, The Art of Margot Fonteyn 1965, The Royal Ballet Today 1968, Fonteyn: The Making of a Legend 1973, John Curry 1978, Anna Pavlova: Her Life and Art 1982, The Bedside Book of Old Fashioned Roses 1985, Some Other Sea: The Life of Rupert Brooke 1988–89, Margot, assoluta 1993, Fonteyn and Nureyev: The Great Years 1994; Other: Screenplays. Contributions: anthologies, journals, and magazines. *E-mail:* fairprospectimprint@ihug.co.nz. *Website:* www .fairprospect.co.nz.

MONGRAIN, Serg; Canadian writer, poet and photographer; b. 15 Jan. 1948, Trois Rivières, QC. *Education:* Mathematical Université du Québec. *Career:* mem. Union des écrivains et des écrivains québécois. *Publications:* L'Oeil du l'idée, 1988; Le calcul des heures, 1993; L'objet des sens, 1996; Brouillard, 1999; Le Poème déshabillé, 2000; Gladys, 2001. As Photographer: Lis: écris, 1981; L'image titre, 1981; Agrestes, 1988; Québec Kerouak Blues, 1998. Other: many exhibition catalogues in art. Contributions: periodicals.

MONK, Lorraine Althea Constance, OC, MA, LLD, DLitt, FDCA, ESFIAP; Canadian writer and producer of photographic books and exhibitions; *Founder, Photographers for Peace*; b. Montréal, PQ; d. of Edwin and Eileen Marion (née Nurse) Spurrell; m. John McCaughan Monk; two s. two d. *Education:* McGill Univ. *Career:* Exec. Dir Canadian Museum of Photography; Exec. Dir Still Photography Div., Nat. Film Bd of Canada. *Publications include:* A Year of the Land 1967, Ces visages qui sont en pays 1967, Stones of History 1967, Call Them Canadians 1968, A Time To Dream – Reveries en couleurs 1971, The Female Eye 1975, Between Friends (Gold Medal Int. Book Fair, Leipzig, Germany) 1977, Robert Bourdeau Monograph 1979, Image (series), Signature (series), Canada With Love 1982, Celebrate our City 1983, Ontario: A Loving Look 1984, Photographs That Changed the World 1989, Canada: Romancing the Land 1996, These Things We Hold Dear – An Album of Photographic Memories (producer) 2000, Moritz Liebling 2002, Hannah: A Story about the Journey of a Lifetime 2003. *Honours:* Centennial Medal 1967, Fed. Int. de l'art photographique Excellence of Service Award, Nat. Asscn of Photographic Art Gold Medal, Leipzig Book Fair Silver Medal 1975, First Prize, Int. Craftsman Guild 1983. *Address:* 176 Balmoral Avenue, Toronto, Ontario, M4V 1J6, Canada. *Telephone:* (416) 929-9357 (also fax) (home). *E-mail:* lorrainemonk@sympatico.ca.

MONNIER, Claude Michel, PhD; Swiss journalist; *Adviser to General Management, Edipresse Suisse SA*; b. 23 March 1938, Rwankéri, Rwanda; s. of Henri Monnier and Olga Monnier; m. Estela Troncoso Balandrán 1958; two s. *Education:* Univs of Geneva and Mexico, Grad. Inst. of Int. Studies, Geneva. *Career:* educational tour in Asia and America 1956–58; Research Fellow, Swiss Nat. Fund for Scientific Research, Tokyo 1958–66; Tokyo Corresp. Journal de Genève 1963–66, Foreign Ed. 1966–70, Ed.-in-Chief 1970–80; Ed. Le Temps Stratégique, Genève 1982–2001; mem. Bd French-speaking Swiss TV and radio 1989–2000; mem. Academic Council, Univ. of Lausanne 1998–2005, Bd Médias and Société Foundation, Geneva; Adviser to Gen. Man. Edipresse Suisse SA 2001–. *Publications:* Les Américains et sa Majesté l'Empereur: Etude du conflit culturel d'où naquit la constitution japonaise de 1946 1967, Alerte, citoyens! 1989, L'année du Big-Bang 1990, La terre en a marre 1991, La déprime, ça suffit! 1992, Dieu, que la crise est jolie! 1993, Les Rouges nous manquent 1994, La bonté qui tue 1995, Envie de bouffer du lion 1996, Programme d'un agitateur 1997, Le temps des règlements de compte 1998, Le Culte suspect de l'action 1999, La trahison de l'an 2000 2000, Morts de trouille 2001, Il faut nous faire soigner! 2002, Où est ta victoire, George W. 2003, La Suisse devient folle 2004, Et maintenant, on fait quoi? 2005. *Address:* Chemin de Saussac 2, 1256 Troinex, Geneva, Switzerland (home). *Telephone:* (22) 322-34-92 (office); (22) 343-95-55 (home). *Fax:* (22) 343-95-55 (home).

MONTAG, Tom, BA; American poet, writer, editor and publisher; b. 31 Aug. 1947, Fort Dodge, IA. *Education:* Dominican Coll. of Racine. *Career:* Ed., publisher, Monday Morning Press, Milwaukee 1971–, Margins Books 1974–. *Publications:* Wooden Nickel 1972, Twelve Poems 1972, Measurers 1972, To Leave This Place 1972, Making Hay 1973, The Urban Ecosystem: A Holistic Approach (ed. with F. Stearns) 1974, Making Hay and Other Poems 1975, Ninety Notes Toward Partial Images and Lover Prints 1976, Concerns: Essays and Reviews 1977, Letters Home 1978, The Essential Ben Zen 1992. *Address:* c/o Sparrow Press, 193 Waldron Street, West Lafayette, IN 47906, USA.

MONTAGUE, John Patrick, BA, MA, MFA; Irish poet, writer and lecturer; b. 28 Feb. 1929, New York, NY, USA. *Education:* Univ. Coll., Dublin, Yale Univ. and Univ. of Iowa. *Career:* Lecturer in Poetry, Univ. Coll., Cork. *Publications:* Forms of Exile 1958, The Old People 1960, Poisoned Lands and Other Poems 1961, The Dolmen Miscellany of Irish Writing (ed.) 1962, Death of a Chieftain and Other Stories 1964, All Legendary Obstacles 1966, Patriotic Suite 1966, A Tribute to Austin Clarke on his Seventieth Birthday, 9th May 1966 (ed. with Liam Miller) 1966, Home Again 1967, A Chosen Light 1967, Hymn to the New Omagh Road 1968, The Bread God: A Lecture, with illustrations in Verse 1968, A New Siege 1969, The Planter and the Gael (with J. Hewitt) 1970, Tides 1970, Small Secrets 1972, The Rough Field (play) 1972, The Cave of Night 1974, O'Riada's Farewell 1974, The Faber Book of Irish Verse (ed.) 1974, A Slow Dance 1975, The Great Cloak 1978, Selected Poems 1982, The Dead Kingdom 1984, Mount Eagle 1989, Smashing the Piano (poems) 1999, Drunken Sailor (poems) 2004. *Address:* c/o The Gallery Press, Loughcrew, Oldcastle, County Meath, Ireland.

MONTAZAM, Mir Ali Asghar, MA, PhD; Iranian/British academic, historian and writer; *Head, CARSI International;* b. 25 Sept. 1935, Tabriz; s. of Sayyid Hassan Mousavi-Harzandi and Ismat; m. Zakieh 1974; two d. *Education:* Middle East Coll., Beirut, American Univ. of Beirut, Lebanon and Univ. of Tehran. *Career:* Islamologist and life-long activist in advocating reform of Islam; Head, CARSI International (Centre for Advice and Research Services on Islam-Related Issues of Int. Concern) 2004–. *Publications include:* non-fiction: Politics of Religion in the Middle East 1988, The Life and Times of Ayatollah Khomeini 1994, Iran and Ayatollah Khomeini 1997, Islam and Mullahcracy in Iran 2000, Islam in Iran: The Background to the Rule of Anarchy and Despotism in the Country's Islamic Past and Present 2003, Islam, The West and Mullahcracy in Iran: Egalitarian Principles of Islamic Government, Islam's Pagan Code of Punishments, Historical Roots of Despotism in Muslim Communities, Anglo-American Foreign Policies in the Islamic Countries 2005, The Life and Legacy of Prophet Muhammad: A Solution to the Dilemma: 'War on Terror' 2007; novel: The Strange Death of a Dream 1998. *Address:* c/o 5 Elsie Lane Court, Westbourne Park Villas, London, W2 5EF, England (office). *Fax:* (20) 7727-7388 (office). *E-mail:* montazam100@hotmail.co.uk (office). *Website:* montazam-islam.tripod.com (office).

MONTEJO, Eugenio; Venezuelan poet and writer; b. 1938, Caracas. *Education:* Univ. of Harvard, USA. *Film appearance:* 21 Grams 2003. *Publications:* poetry: Elegos 1967, Muerte y memoria 1972, Algunas palabras 1976, Terredad 1978, Trópico absoluto 1982, Alfabeto del mundo 1986, Adiós al siglo XX 1992, El azul de la tierra 1997, Partitura de la cigarra 1999, Tiempo transfigurado 2001, The Trees: Selected Poems 1967–2004 (in trans.) 2004; essays: La ventana oblicua 1974. *Honours:* Nat. Prize for Literature 1998. *Address:* c/o Salt Publishing, PO Box 937, Great Wilbraham, Cambridge, CB1 5JX, England. *E-mail:* info@saltpublishing.com. *Website:* www.saltpublishing.com.

MONTEJO, Victor; Guatemalan writer and lecturer; b. 1951. *Career:* Prof. of Anthropology, Univ. of California at Davis. *Publications include:* El Q'Amil: El Hombre Rayo (trans. as Man of Lightning) 1984, Testimony: Death of a Guatemalan Village 1987, The Bird Who Cleans the World 1992, Voices from Exile: Violence and Survival in Modern Maya History 1999. *Literary Agent:* c/o Curbstone Press, 321 Jackson Street, Willimantic, CT 06226-1738, USA. *E-mail:* info@curbstone.org. *Website:* www.curbstone.org.

MONTELEONE, Thomas Francis, BS, MA; American writer and dramatist; b. 14 April 1946, Baltimore, MD; m. Elizabeth; two s. one d. *Education:* Univ. of Maryland. *Career:* writes for television; mem. SFWA, Horror Writers of America. *Publications:* fiction: Seeds of Change 1975, The Time Connection 1976, The Time-Swept City 1977, The Secret Sea 1979, Dragonstar (with David F. Bischoff) 1980, Guardian 1980, Night Things 1980, Ozymandias 1981, Dark Stars and Other Illuminations (short stories) 1981, Day of the Dragonstar (with David F. Bischoff) 1983, Night Trains 1984, Random Access Messages of the Computer Age 1984, Microworlds 1985, Night of the Dragonstar (with David F. Bischoff) 1985, The Crooked House (with John DeChancie) 1987, Fantasma 1987, Lyrica: A Novel of Horror and Desire 1987, The Magnificent Gallery 1987, Borderlands (ed.) 1988, Dragonstar Destiny (with David F. Bischoff) 1989, Borderlands 2 (ed.) 1991, Borderlands 3 (ed.) 1992, The Blood of the Lamb (Bram Stoker Award 1993) 1992, Borderlands 4 (ed., with Elizabeth Monteleone) 1993, The Resurrectionist 1995, Between Floors 1997, Night of Broken Souls 1997, The Reckoning 1999, Eyes of the Virgin 2002, Rough Beasts and Other Mutations (short stories) 2003, From the Borderlands (ed.) 2004, Fearful Symmetries 2004; non-fiction: The Arts and Beyond: Visions of Man's Aesthetic Future 1987, The Mothers and Fathers Italian Association 2003, The Complete Idiot's Guide to Writing a Novel 2004; contrib. to anthologies and magazines. *Honours:* Nebula Awards 1976, 1977, Gabriel Award 1984, Int. Film and TV Festival Bronze Award, New York 1984. *Literary Agent:* Howard Morhaim Literary Agency, 11 John Street, Suite 407, New York, NY 10038, USA.

MONTGOMERY, David John, BA; British newspaper executive; *Executive Chairman, Mecom Group plc;* b. 6 Nov. 1948, Bangor, Northern Ireland; s. of William John Montgomery and Margaret Jean Montgomery; m. 1st Susan Frances Buchanan Russell 1971 (divorced 1987); m. 2nd Heidi Kingstone 1989 (divorced 1997); m. 3rd Sophie, Countess of Woolton 1997. *Education:* Queen's Univ., Belfast. *Career:* Sub-Ed., Daily Mirror London, Manchester 1973–76,

Asst Chief Sub-Ed. 1976–80; Chief Sub-Ed. The Sun 1980; Asst Ed. Sunday People 1982; Asst Ed. News of the World 1984, Ed. 1985–87; Ed. Today 1987–91 (Newspaper of the Year 1988); Man. Dir News UK 1987–91; Chief Exec. London Live TV 1991–92, Dir 1991–92; Chief Exec. Mirror Group 1992–99; Dir Satellite Television PLC 1986–91, News Group Newspapers 1986–91, Donohue Inc. 1992–95, Newspaper Publishing 1994–98, Scottish Media Group 1995–99, Press Asscn 1996–99; Founder and Exec. Chair. Mecom Group plc 2000–; Chair. Tri-Mex Group PLC 1999–, Yava 2000–, Africa Lakes PLC 2000–, Integrated Educ. Fund Devt Bd, NI 2000–, Espresso 2001–; with other investors acquired Berliner Verlag (Berliner Zeitung and Berliner Kurier newspapers), Germany, Chair. Supervisory Bd 2005–. *Address:* Mecom Group plc, Empire House, 175 Piccadilly, London, W1J 9EN (office); ALC, 7–10 Chandos Street, London, W1G 9DQ; 15 Collingham Gardens, London, SW5 0HS, England. *Telephone:* (20) 7491-6660 (Mecom) (office); (20) 7323-5440 (office); (20) 7373-1982 (home). *Fax:* (20) 7491-6666 (Mecom) (office). *E-mail:* info@mecom.co.uk (office); dmontgomery@tri-mex.com (office). *Website:* www.mecom.co.uk (office); www.berlinonline.de/berliner-zeitung (office).

MONTGOMERY, Marion H., Jr, AB, MA; American academic, writer and poet; *Emeritus Professor of English, University of Georgia;* b. 16 April 1925, Thomaston, GA; m. Dorothy Carlisle 1952; one s., four d. *Education:* Univ. of Georgia; Creative Writing Workshop, Univ. of Iowa. *Career:* Asst Dir, Univ. of Georgia Press 1950–52; Business Man., Georgia Review 1951–53; Instructor, Darlington School for Boys 1953–54; Instructor, University of Georgia 1954–60, Asst Prof. 1960–67, Assoc. Prof. 1967–70, Prof. of English 1970, now Prof. Emer.; Writer-in-Residence, Converse Coll. 1963. *Publications:* fiction: The Wandering of Desire 1962, Darrell 1964, Ye Olde Bluebird 1967, Fugitive 1974; poetry: Dry Lightening 1960, Stones from the Rubble 1965, The Gull and Other Georgia Scenes 1969; non-fiction: Ezra Pound: A Critical Essay 1970, T. S. Eliot: An Essay on the American Magus 1970, The Reflective Journey Toward Order: Essays on Dante, Wordsworth, Eliot and Others 1973, Eliot's Reflective Journey to the Garden 1978, The Prophetic Poet and the Spirit of the Age, Vol. 1, Why Flannery O'Connor Stayed Home 1980, Vol. II, Why Poe Drank Liquor 1983, Vol. III, Why Hawthorne Was Melancholy 1984, Possum, and Other Receipts for the Recovery of 'Southern' Being 1987, The Trouble with You Innerleckchuls 1988, The Men I Have Chosen for Fathers: Literary and Philosophical Passages 1990, Liberal Arts and Community: The Feeding of the Larger Body 1990, Virtue and Modern Shadows of Turning: Preliminary Agitations 1990, Romantic Confusions of the Good: Beauty as Truth, Truth Beauty 1997, Concerning Intellectual Philandering: Poets and Philosophers, Priests and Politicians 1998, Making: The Proper Habit of Our Being 1999, The Truth of Things: Liberal Arts and the Recovery of Reality 1999, Romancing Reality: Homo Viator and the Scandal of Beauty 2000, John Crowe Ransom and Allen Tate: At Odds About the Ends of History and the Mystery of Nature 2003, Eudora Welty and Walker Percy: The Concept of Home in Their Lives and Literature 2004, On Matters Southern: Essays About Literature and Culture 1964–2000 (ed. Michael Jordan) 2005, Hillbilly Thomist: Flannery O'Connor, St Thomas and the Limits of Art (2 Vols) 2006, With Walker Percy at the Tupperware Party, In Company with Dostoevsky, Marcel, Eliot, O'Connor and Others 2007; contrib. to anthologies and magazines. *Honours:* Eugene Saxton Memorial Award 1960, Georgia Writers' Asscn Literary Achievement in Fiction 1964, Georgia Writers' Asscn Literary Achievement Award in Poetry 1970, Earhart Foundation Fellowship 1973–74, Stanley W. Lindberg Award 2001, Intercollegiate Studies Inst. Gerhart Niemeyer Award 2003. *Address:* PO Box 115, Crawford, GA 30630, USA.

MOODY, Rick, BA, MFA; American writer and editor; b. (Hiram F. Moody III), 18 Oct. 1961, New York, NY. *Education:* Brown Univ., Columbia Univ. *Career:* founder mem., The Wingdale Community Singers; collaboration with experimental group, One Ring Zero. *Recording:* The Wingdale Community Singers (album) 2005. *Publications:* Garden State: A Novel 1991, The Ice Storm 1994, The Ring of Brightest Angels Around Heaven (short stories) 1995, Demonology 2001, The Black Veil (memoir) 2002, The Diviners 2006, Right Livelihoods: Three Novellas 2007; contrib. to various periodicals. *Honours:* Ed.'s Book Award, Pushcart Press 1991. *Address:* c/o Little, Brown & Co., 1271 Avenue of the Americas, New York, NY 10020, USA (office).

MOONEY, Bel, BA; British writer and broadcaster; b. 8 Oct. 1946, Liverpool; m. Jonathan Dimbleby 1968 (divorced 2006); one s. one d. *Education:* Univ. Coll. London. *Career:* columnist, Daily Mirror, 1979–80, Sunday Times, 1982–83, The Listener, 1984–86, The Times 2005–; TV interview series, TV films and radio programmes; Gov., Bristol Polytechnic, 1989–91. *Radio:* presenter of Devout Sceptics, BBC Radio 4. *Publications:* fiction: The Windsurf Boy 1983, The Anderson Question 1985, The Fourth of July 1988, Lost Footsteps 1993, Intimate Letters 1997, The Invasion of Sand 2005; children's books: Liza's Yellow Boat 1980, I Don't Want To! 1985, The Stove Haunting 1986, I Can't Find It! 1988, It's Not Fair! 1989, A Flower of Jet 1990, But You Promised! 1990, Why Not? 1990, I Know! 1991, The Voices of Silence 1994, I'm Scared! 1994, I Wish! 1995, The Mouse with Many Rooms 1995, Why Me? 1996, I'm Bored! 1997, Joining the Rainbow 1997, The Green Man 1997, It's not my Fault 1999, So What! 2002, Kitty's Friends 2003, Mr Tubs is Lost 2004, Who Loves Mr Tibs 2006, Like Mother, Like Daughter (ed.) 2006; other: The Year of the Child 1979, Differences of Opinion 1984, Father Kissmass and Mother Claws (with Gerald Scarfe) 1985, Bel Mooney's Somerset 1989, From this Day Forward 1989, Perspectives for Living 1992, Devout Sceptics 2003.

Honours: Fellow, Univ. Coll. London, 1994, Liverpool John Moores Univ. 2002; Hon. DLitt (Bath Univ.), 1998. *Literary Agent:* David Higham Associates, 5–8 Lower John Street, Golden Square, London, W1F 9HA, England. *Website:* www.belmooney.co.uk.

MOORCOCK, Michael John, (Edward P. Bradbury, Desmond Read); British novelist; b. 18 Dec. 1939, London; s. of Arthur Moorcock and June Moorcock; m. 1st Hilary Bailey 1963 (divorced 1978); one s. two d.; m. 2nd Jill Riches 1978 (divorced 1983 m. 3rd Linda M. Steele 1983. *Education:* Michael Hall School, Sussex. *Career:* worked as musician and journalist; Ed. Outlaws Own 1951–53, Tarzan Adventures 1957–59, Sexton Blake Library 1959–61, Current Topics 1961–62; Ed. New Worlds 1963–96, Consulting Ed. 1996–. *Films:* The Final Programme 1973, The Land that Time Forgot 1975. *Records:* Warrior on the Edge of Time (Hawkwind) 1975, The New World's Fair 1975, The Brothel in Rosenstrasse 1982, Roller Coaster Holiday 2004. *Publications include:* The Eternal Champion sequence 1963–98, Behold the Man (Nebula Award 1967) 1968, Condition of Muzak (Guardian Fiction Prize 1977) 1976, Gloriana (World Fantasy Award 1979) 1977, Byzantium Endures 1981, The Laughter of Carthage 1984, Mother London 1988, Jerusalem Commands 1992, Blood 1994, The War Amongst Angels 1996, Tales from the Texas Woods 1997, King of the City 2000, Silverheart (co-author) 2000, London Bone 2001, The Dreamthief's Daughter 2001, The Skrayling Tree 2003, The Lives and Times of Jerry Cornelius 2004, Wizardry and Wild Romance 2004, The White Wolf's Son 2005, The Vengeance of Rome 2006. *Honours:* August Derleith Prize, World Fantasy Lifetime Achievement Award 2000, Science Fiction Hall of Fame 2002, Priz Utopiales 2004. *Address:* c/o Morham Literary, 30 Pierrepont Street, Brooklyn, NY 11201, USA (office); PO Box 1230, Bastrop, TX 78602, USA (home); c/o Hoffman, 77 Boulevard St Michel, 75005 Paris, France. *Telephone:* (718) 222-8400 (office). *Fax:* (512) 321-5000 (office). *E-mail:* mjm@multiverse.org (office). *Website:* www.moorcocks weeklymiscellany (office).

MOORE, Ann S., BSc, MBA; American publisher and media executive; *Chairman and CEO, Time Inc.*; b. 1950, McLean, Va; m. Donovan Moore; one s. *Education:* Vanderbilt Univ., Nashville, Harvard Univ. Business School. *Career:* financial analyst, Time Inc. 1978, served in various exec. positions including Publr and Pres. People magazine (est. spin-offs Teen People, Instyle, Real Simple, People en Español 2001), cr. Sports Illustrated for Kids 1989, Exec. Vice-Pres. Time Inc. 2001–02, Chair. and CEO 2002–, responsible for Time magazine, People, Fortune, Money, Entertainment Weekly and 135 other titles (first woman in position); mem. Bd of Dirs Avon Products Inc., Wallace Foundation. *Honours:* Adweek's Publishing Exec. of the Year 1998, MIN Magazine's Consumer Magazine Player of the Year 1999, named one of Advertising Age's Women to Watch 2001, ranked by Fortune magazine amongst 50 Most Powerful Women in Business in the US 1998–2001, (11th) 2002, (13th) 2003, (13th) 2004, (13th) 2005, (15th) 2006, first Annual AOL Time Warner Civic Leadership Award 2003, ranked by Forbes magazine amongst 100 Most Powerful Women (20th) 2004, (38th) 2005, (53rd) 2006. *Address:* Time Inc., Rockefeller Plaza, New York, NY 10019, USA (office). *Telephone:* (212) 484-8000 (office). *Website:* www.timewarner.com (office).

MOORE, Charles Hilary, MA; British journalist; *Group Consulting Editor, The Daily Telegraph (UK)*; b. 31 Oct. 1956, Hastings; s. of Richard Moore and Ann Moore; m. Caroline Baxter 1981; twin s. and d. *Education:* Eton Coll. and Trinity Coll. Cambridge. *Career:* editorial staff, Daily Telegraph 1979–81, leader writer 1981–83; Asst Ed. and Political Columnist, The Spectator 1983–84, Ed. 1984–90, fortnightly columnist ('Another Voice') 1990–95; weekly columnist, Daily Express 1987–90; Deputy Ed. Daily Telegraph 1990–92; Ed. Sunday Telegraph 1992–95, Daily Telegraph 1995–2003, Group Consulting Ed. Daily Telegraph (UK) 2003–; Chair. Policy Exchange; Trustee T. E. Utley Memorial Fund, Benenden Council, ShareGift. *Publications:* 1936 (co-ed. with C. Hawtree) 1986, The Church in Crisis (with A. N. Wilson and G. Stamp) 1986, A Tory Seer: The Selected Journalism of T. E. Utley (co-ed. with S. Heffer) 1986. *Address:* c/o Daily Telegraph, 11 Buckinghham Palace Road, London, SW1 0DT, England (office).

MOORE, Christopher Hugh, BA, MA; Canadian historian and writer; b. 9 June 1950, Stoke-on-Trent, England; m. Louise Brophy 1977. *Education:* Univ. of British Columbia, Univ. of Ottawa. *Career:* mem. Writers' Union of Canada, Canadian Historical Asscn, Ontario Historical Soc., Heritage Canada Foundation. *Publications:* Louisbourg Portraits 1982, The Loyalists 1984, The Illustrated History of Canada (co-author) 1987; also school texts, historical guidebooks, educational software programmes and radio documentaries; contrib. to numerous scholarly journals and magazines. *Honours:* Governor-General's Award for Non-Fiction 1982, Canadian Historical Asscn Award of Merit 1984, Secretary of State's Prize for Excellence in Canadian Studies 1985. *E-mail:* cmed@sympatico.ca. *Website:* www.christophermoore.ca.

MOORE, Eric (see Bruton, Eric)

MOORE, Capt. John Evelyn, RN, FRGS; British editor, author and retd naval officer; b. 1 Nov. 1921, Sant' Ilario, Italy; s. of William John Moore and Evelyn Elizabeth (née Hooper); m. 1st Joan Pardoe 1945; one s. two d.; m. 2nd Barbara Kerry. *Education:* Sherborne School, Dorset. *Career:* entered RN 1939, specialized in hydrographic surveying, then submarines: commanded HM Submarines Totem, Alaric, Tradewind, Tactician, Telemachus; RN staff course 1950–51; Commdr 1957; attached to Turkish Naval Staff 1958–60; subsequently Plans Div., Admiralty, 1st Submarine Squadron, then 7th Submarine Squadron in command; Capt. 1967; served as Chief of Staff, C-in-C

Naval Home Command; Defence Intelligence Staff; retd list at own request 1972; Ed. Jane's Fighting Ships 1972–87; Ed. Jane's Naval Review 1982–87. *Publications:* Jane's Major Warships 1973, The Soviet Navy Today 1975, Submarine Development 1976, Soviet War Machine (jtly) 1976, Encyclopaedia of World's Warships 1978, World War 3 1978, Seapower and Politics 1979, Warships of the Royal Navy 1979, Warships of the Soviet Navy 1981, Submarine Warfare: Today and Tomorrow (jtly) 1986; ed. The Impact of Polaris 1999. *Honours:* Hon. Prof. of Int. Relations, Aberdeen Univ. 1987–90, St Andrews Univ. 1990–92. *Address:* 1 Ridgelands Close, Eastbourne, East Sussex, BN20 8EP, England. *Telephone:* (1323) 638836.

MOORE, Lorrie, BA, MFA; American academic and writer; *Professor of English, University of Wisconsin at Madison*; b. 13 Jan. 1957, Glens Falls, NY. *Education:* St Lawrence Univ., Cornell Univ. *Career:* Lecturer in English, Cornell Univ. 1982–84; Asst Prof., Univ. of Wisconsin at Madison 1984–87, Assoc. Prof. 1987–91, Prof. of English 1991–; mem. Associated Writing Programs (AWP), Authors' Guild, PEN. *Publications:* Self-Help, 1985; Anagrams, 1986; The Forgotten Helper, 1987; Like Life, 1990; I Know Some Things: Stories About Childhood by Contemporary Writers (ed.), 1992; Birds of America, 1998. Contributions: periodicals including New Yorker, New York Review of Books. *Honours:* Guggenheim Fellowship 1991, Irish Times Int. Prize for Literature 1999, Nat. Book Critics' Circle Nominee 1999, Rea Prize for the Short Story 2004. *Address:* c/o Department of English, University of Wisconsin at Madison, Madison, WI 53706, USA.

MOORE, Michael; American writer, film-maker and political commentator; b. 1954, Davison, Mich. *Education:* Davison High School. *Career:* elected to Davison, Mich. school bd aged 18; active in student politics; began career as journalist with The Flint Voice, later Ed., expanded into The Mich. Voice; Ed. Mother Jones magazine, San Francisco 1986–88. *Television includes:* Pets or Meat: The Return to Flint 1992, TV Nation (NBC series) 1994–95, 1997, And Justice for All (dir) 1998, The Awful Truth (series) 1999. *Films:* Roger and Me (writer, dir, producer) 1989, Canadian Bacon (writer, producer, dir) 1994, The Big One (dir) 1997, Bowling for Columbine (screenwriter, dir, producer; Jury Award, Cannes Film Festival 2003, Acad. Award for Best Documentary 2003) 2002, Fahrenheit 9/11 (dir; Palme d'Or, Cannes Film Festival, US People's Choice Award for Best Film 2005) 2004, Sicko 2007. *Film appearances:* Pony Express 1953, Lucky Number 1999, EdTV 1999. *Publications:* Downsize This!: Random Threats from an Unarmed America 1996, Stupid White Men (Book of the Year, British Book Awards 2003) 2001, Adventures in a TV Nation (with Kathleen Glynn) 2002, Dude, Where's My Country? 2003, Will They Ever Trust Us Again?: Letters from the War Zone 2004. *Address:* c/o Random House Inc., 1745 Broadway, Suite B1, New York, NY 10019-4305, USA (office). *E-mail:* mike@michaelmoore.com. *Website:* www.michaelmoore.com.

MOORE, Sir Patrick Alfred Caldwell-, Kt (see Caldwell-Moore, Sir Patrick Alfred, Kt)

MOORE, Susanna; American writer; b. 9 Dec. 1948, Bryn Mawr, PA; m., one d. *Publications:* My Old Sweetheart 1982, The Whiteness of Bones 1989, Sleeping Beauties 1993, In the Cut 1995, One Last Look 2003, I Myself Have Seen It 2003, The Big Girls 2007. *Honours:* PEN/Ernest Hemingway Citation, American Acad. of Arts and Letters Sue Kaufman Prize 1983. *Address:* The Gernert Company, 136 East 57th Street, New York, NY 10022, USA (office). *Telephone:* (212) 838-3402 (office).

MOOREHEAD, Caroline Mary, OBE, BA, FRSL; British journalist and writer; b. 28 Oct. 1944, London, England. *Education:* Univ. of London. *Career:* reporter, Time magazine, Rome 1968–69; feature writer, Telegraph Magazine, London 1969–70, The Times, London 1973–88; Features Ed., Times Educational Supplement 1970–73; human rights columnist, The Independent 1988–93. *Publications:* Myths and Legends of Britain (ed. and trans.) 1968, Helping: A Guide to Voluntary Work 1975, Fortune's Hostages 1980, Sidney Bernstein: A Biography 1983, Freya Stark: A Biography 1985, Troublesome People: Enemies of War 1916–1986 1987, Over the Rim of the World: The Letters of Freya Stark (ed.) 1988, Betrayed: Children in the Modern World 1988, Bertrand Russell: A Life 1992, The Lost Treasures of Troy 1996, 6 Dunant's Dream: War, Switzerland and the Red Crown 1998, Iris Origo: A Life 1999, Martha Gellhorn: A Life 2003, Human Cargo 2005, Letters of Martha Gellhorn (ed.) 2006; contrib. to newspapers and magazines. *Literary Agent:* c/o Clare Alexander, Aitken Alexander Associates, 18–21 Cavaye Place, London, SW10 9PT, England. *Telephone:* (20) 7373-8672. *Fax:* (20) 7373-6002. *E-mail:* reception@aitkenalexander.co.uk. *Website:* www.aitkenalexander.co.uk. *E-mail:* cmmoorehead@clara.co.uk (home).

MOORHOUSE, Frank; Australian writer; b. 21 Dec. 1938, Nowra, Qld. *Education:* University of Queensland, WEA. *Career:* Pres., Australian Society of Authors 1979–82; Chair. Copyright Council of Australia 1985; mem. Groucho Club, London; AM. *Publications:* Futility and Other Animals 1969, The Americans, Baby 1972, The Electrical Experience 1974, Conference-Ville 1976, Tales of Mystery and Romance 1977, Days of Wine and Rage 1980, Room Service 1986, Forty-Seventeen 1988, Lateshows 1990, Dark Palace 2000, Satanic Killings 2006; contrib. to Bulletin. *Honours:* Henry Lawson Short Story Prize 1970, National Award for Fiction 1975, Awgie Award 1976, Gold Medal for Literature, Australian Literary 1989, Miles Franklin Award 2001.

MOORHOUSE, Geoffrey, FRSL; British writer; b. 29 Nov. 1931, Bolton, Lancs.; s. of William Heald and Gladys Heald (née Hoyle, subsequently Moorhouse) and step-s. of Richard Moorhouse; m. 1st Janet Marion Murray

1956; two s. two d. (one deceased); m. 2nd Barbara Jane Woodward 1974 (divorced 1978); m. 3rd Marilyn Isobel Edwards 1983 (divorced 1996). *Education:* Bury Grammar School. *Career:* RN 1950–52; editorial staff, Bolton Evening News 1952–54, Grey River Argus, NZ, Auckland Star, and Christchurch Star-Sun 1954–56, News Chronicle 1957, Guardian, Manchester 1958–70 (Chief Features Writer 1963–70); full-time author 1970–; rode camels across the Sahara Desert 1972–73; deep-sea fisherman, Gloucester, Mass, USA 1976–77. *Publications:* The Other England 1964, The Press 1964, Against All Reason 1969, Calcutta 1971, The Missionaries 1973, The Fearful Void 1974, The Diplomats 1977, The Boat and the Town 1979, The Best-Loved Game (Cricket Soc. Award) 1979, India Britannica 1983, Lord's 1983, To the Frontier (Thomas Cook Award) 1984, Imperial City: The Rise and Rise of New York 1988, At the George 1989, Apples in the Snow 1990, Hell's Foundations: A Town, Its Myths and Gallipoli 1992, Om: An Indian Pilgrimage 1993, A People's Game: The Centenary History of Rugby League Football 1895–1995 1995, Sun Dancing: A Medieval Vision 1997, Sydney: The Story of a City 1999, The Pilgrimage of Grace: The Rebellion That Shook Henry VIII's Throne 2002, Great Harry's Navy: How Henry VIII Gave England Seapower 2005; contrib. to newspapers and magazines in UK and USA. *Honours:* Hon. DLitt (Warwick) 2006; Cricket Soc. Award 1979, Thomas Cook Award 1984. *Address:* Park House, Gayle, nr Hawes, N Yorks., DL8 3RT, England (home). *Telephone:* (1969) 667456 (office). *Fax:* (1969) 667456 (office).

MORAVCOVÁ, Jana, PhD; Czech writer and translator; b. 8 May 1937, Černčice; d. of Jindřich and Anna Moravec; m. Bohumil Neumann 1959; one d. *Education:* Charles Univ., Prague. *Career:* writer and trans. from Russian and Spanish; publishing house Ed. 1959–; Ed.-in-Chief Int. Asscn of Crime Writers' Czech Section; has written over 30 novels and collections of poetry; numerous awards for literature. *Radio:* Interview with Butterfly (drama) 2003. *Publications include:* Club of Unmistakables 1973, Snow Circle 1974, Still Life With Citadel 1978, Silent Cormorant 1979, Second Glass 1990, Fear Has Long Legs 1992, Holidays With Monica 1994, Fixdictionary 1996, J. Petrovická (biog.) 1999, Cases of a Kind Detective 2000, Thirteen Colours of Love 2000, Killer 2002, Murder in Spa Luhacovice 2004, Death Doesn't Wear Glasses 2005. *Address:* Podolská 1487, 147 00 Prague 4, Czech Republic (home). *Telephone:* (2) 44460015 (home).

MORENCY, Pierre, OC, BA, LèsL; Canadian poet, writer and dramatist; b. 8 May 1942, Lauzon, QC. *Education:* Collège de Lévis, Université Laval, Québec. *Career:* broadcaster; co-founder, Estuaire poetry journal; mem. PEN Club, Union des écrivaines et des écrivains québécois. *Publications:* Lieu de naissance 1973, Le temps des oiseaux 1975, Torrentiel 1978, Effets personnels 1987, L'oeil américain: Histories naturelles du Nouveau Monde 1989, Lumière des oiseaux: Histoires naturelles du Nouveau Monde 1992, Les paroles qui marchent dans la nuit 1994, La vie entière 1996, A l'heure du loup 2004, Poèmes (1966–1986) 2004, Chez les oiseaux 2004. *Honours:* Chevalier, Ordre des Arts et des Lettres, Officier, Ordre du Canada 2003, Chevalier, Ordre National du Québec 2005; Prix Alain Grandbois 1987, Prix Québec-Paris 1988, Prix Ludger Duvernay 1991, Prix France Québec 1992, Prix Athanase-David 2000, Prix Guillevic 2003. *Address:* 155 Avenue Laurier, QC G1R 2K8, Canada.

MORENO, Armando, LM, LL, PhD; Portuguese academic, physician, writer, poet and dramatist; b. 19 Dec. 1932, Porto; m. Maria Guinot Moreno 1987. *Education:* Faculdade Medicina, Porto. *Career:* academic, physician –2005 (retd); mem. many professional and literary organizations. *Publications:* A Chamada (short stories) 1982, As Carreiras 1982, O Bojador 1982, Historias Quase Clinicas (short stories, three vols) 1982, 1984, 1988, Cais do Sodre (short stories) 1988, O Animal Que deupla Mente 1993, Contos Oeirenses (short stories) 1994, A Governaçao pela Competencia 1995, O Mundo Fascinante da Medicina (12 vols, illustrated) 1997, Disseram que Já É Tarde (short stories) 2003, Glória e Suicídio (literary study) 2003, As Fezes (literary study) 2003, História da Ortopedia Portuguesa 2003, Ética em Tecnologias da Saúde (literary study) 2004, Fingindo Poesia (poems) 2004, Ética em Medicina (literary study) 2005, O Terceiro Túnel (romance) 2006; also medical books, poetry, plays and television series; contrib. to periodicals. *Honours:* drama and fiction awards. *Address:* Rua Almirante Matos Moreira 7, 2775 Carcavelos, Portugal (home). *Telephone:* 214578739. *Fax:* 214578739.

MORETON, John (see Cohen, Morton Norton)

MORGAN, Abi; British playwright; b. 1969, Cardiff, S Glamorgan, Wales. *Plays:* Skinned 1998, Splendour 2000, Tender 2001, Tiny Dynamite 2002. *Television drama:* Sex Traffic (serial for Granada TV/Channel 4) (BAFTA Award for Best Drama Serial 2005) 2004. *Address:* c/o Faber and Faber Ltd, 3 Queen Square, London, WC1N 3AU, England.

MORGAN, Edmund Sears, AB, PhD; American historian and academic; *Sterling Professor Emeritus, Yale University;* b. 17 Jan. 1916, Minneapolis; s. of Edmund Morris Morgan and Elsie Sears Smith; m. 1st Helen Theresa Mayer 1939; two d.; m. 2nd Marie Caskey 1983. *Education:* Harvard Univ. *Career:* radiation laboratory instrument maker, Massachusetts Inst. of Technology 1942–45; Instructor, Univ. of Chicago 1945–46; Asst Prof., Brown Univ. 1946–49, Assoc. Prof. 1949–51, Prof. 1951–55, Acting Dean of the Graduate School 1951–52; Research Fellow, Huntington Library 1952–53; Prof., Yale Univ. 1955–65, Sterling Prof. 1965–86, Sterling Professor Emeritus 1986–; Johnson Research Prof., Univ. of Wisconsin 1968–69; Trustee, Smith Coll. 1984–89; mem. editorial bd, Northeast Quarterly; Chair. of Bd, The Benjamin Franklin Papers; mem. American Acad. of Arts and Sciences, American Antiquarian Soc., American Philosophical Soc., British Acad., Colonial Soc. of Massachusetts, Massachusetts Historical Soc., Organization of American Historians (pres. 1971–72), Royal Historical Soc. *Publications:* The Puritan Family 1942, Virginians at Home 1953, The Stamp Act Crisis (with Helen M. Morgan) 1953, The Birth of the Republic 1956, The Puritan Dilemma 1958, The Gentle Puritan 1962, Visible Saints 1963, Roger Williams 1967, So What About History 1969, American Slavery, American Freedom (Soc. of American Historians Francis Parkman Prize, Southern Historical Asscn Charles S. Sydnor Prize, American Historical Asscn Albert J. Beveridge Award) 1975, The Challenge of the American Revolution 1976, The Meaning of Independence 1976, The Genius of George Washington 1980, Inventing the People: The Rise of Popular Sovereignty in England and America (Columbia Univ. Bancroft Prize in American History 1989) 1988, Benjamin Franklin 2002, The Genuine Article 2004. *Honours:* Yale Chapter of Phi Beta Kappa William Clyde DeVane Medal 1971, Douglas Adair Memorial Award for scholarship in early American history 1972, American Historical Asscn Distinguished Scholar Award 1986, Nat. Humanities Medal 2000, Pulitzer Special Citation 2006. *Address:* c/o Department of History, Yale University, PO Box 208324, New Haven, CT 06520-8324, USA (office). *E-mail:* edmund.morgan@yale.edu (office).

MORGAN, Edwin George, OBE, MA; Scottish poet, writer, translator and academic; *The Scots Makar (National Poet of Scotland);* b. 27 April 1920, Glasgow. *Education:* Rutherglen Acad., High School of Glasgow, Univ. of Glasgow. *Career:* RAMC 1940–46; Asst Lecturer, Univ. of Glasgow 1947–50, Lecturer 1950–65, Senior Lecturer 1965–71, Reader 1971–75, Titular Prof. of English 1975–80, Prof. Emeritus 1980–; Visiting Prof., Univ. of Strathclyde 1987–90; Hon. Prof., Univ. Coll., Wales 1991–95; Poet Laureate of Glasgow 1997–2006; The Scots Makar (Nat. Poet of Scotland) 2004–(07); has trans poetry from Hungarian, Italian, French, German, Russian, Spanish and Anglo-Saxon. *Plays:* various plays and opera librettos. *Publications:* poetry: The Vision of Cathkin Braes 1952, The Cape of Good Hope 1955, Starryveldt 1965, Scotch Mist 1965, Sealwear 1966, Emergent Poems 1967, The Second Life 1968, Gnomes 1968, Proverbfolder 1969, Penguin Modern Poets 15 (with Alan Bold and Edward Brathwaite) 1969, The Horseman's Word: A Sequence of Concrete Poems 1970, Twelve Songs 1970, The Dolphin's Song 1971, Glasgow Sonnets 1972, Instamatic Poems 1972, The Whittrick: A Poem in Eight Dialogues 1973, From Glasgow to Saturn 1973, The New Divan 1977, Colour Poems 1978, Star Gate: Science Fiction Poems 1979, Poems of Thirty Years 1982, Grafts/Takes 1983, Sonnets from Scotland 1984, Selected Poems 1985, From the Video Box 1986, Newspoems 1987, Themes on a Variation 1988, Tales from Limerick Zoo 1988, Collected Poems 1990, Hold Hands Among the Atoms 1991, Sweeping Out the Dark 1994, Virtual and Other Realities 1997, Demon 1999, New Selected Poems 2000, Cathures 2002, Love and a Life 2003, Tales from Baron Munchausen 2005, The Play of Gilgamesh 2006, A Book of Lives 2007; prose/editor: Collins Albatross Book of Longer Poems: English and American Poetry from the Fourteenth Century to the Present Day (ed.) 1963, Scottish Poetry 1–6 (co-ed.) 1966–72, New English Dramatists 14 (ed.) 1970, Essays 1974, East European Poets 1976, Hugh MacDiarmid 1976, Scottish Satirical Verse (ed.) 1980, Twentieth Century Scottish Classics 1987, Nothing Not Giving Messages (interviews) 1990, Crossing the Border: Essays in Scottish Literature 1990, Language, Poetry and Language Poetry 1990, Collected Translations 1996, Evening Will Come They Will Sew the Blue Sail 1991, James Thomson: The City of Dreadful Night (ed.) 1993. *Honours:* Cholmondeley Award for Poetry 1968, Scottish Arts Council Book Awards 1968, 1973, 1975, 1977, 1978, 1983, 1984, 1991, 1992, Hungarian PEN Memorial Medal 1972, Soros Translation Award 1985, Queen's Gold Medal for Poetry 2000, Saltire Soc. and Scottish Arts Council Lifetime Achievement Award 2003. *Address:* Clarence Court, 234 Crow Road, Glasgow, G11 7PD, Scotland (home). *Website:* www.edwinmorgan.com (home).

MORGAN, Mihangel (see Morgan-Finch, Mihangel Ioan)

MORGAN, Piers Stefan; British journalist; b. 30 March 1965, Guildford; s. of Anthony Pughe-Morgan and Gabrielle Oliver; m. Marion E. Shalloe 1991; three s. *Education:* Cumnor House Preparatory School, Chailey School, Sussex, Lewes Priory Sixth Form Coll. and Harlow Journalism Coll. *Career:* reporter, Surrey and S London newspapers 1987–89; Showbusiness Ed. The Sun 1989–94; Ed. The News of the World 1994–95, Daily Mirror (later The Mirror) 1995–2004; co-founder Press Gazette Ltd, owner of Press Gazette 2005–; Editorial Dir newspaper for children, First News 2006–. *Television:* presenter, The Importance of Being Famous (Channel 4) 2004, Morgan & Platell (Channel 4) 2005–. *Publications:* Private Lives of the Stars 1990, Secret Lives of the Stars 1991, Phillip Schofield, To Dream a Dream 1992, Take That, Our Story 1993, Take That: On the Road 1994, The Insider (memoir) 2005, Don't You Know Who I Am? 2007. *Honours:* Atex Award for Nat. Newspaper Ed. of Year 1994, What the Papers Say Newspaper of the Year Award 2001, GQ Ed. of the Year 2002, British Press Awards Newspaper of the Year 2002. *Literary Agent:* William Morris Agency Inc., 52–53 Poland Street, London, W1F 7LX, England. *Telephone:* (20) 7534-6800. *Fax:* (20) 7534-6900. *Website:* www.pressgazette.co.uk; www.firstnews.co.uk.

MORGAN, Robert, BA, MFA; American academic, poet and writer; *Kappa Alpha Professor of English, Cornell University;* b. 3 Oct. 1944, Hendersonville, NC; m. Nancy K. Bullock 1965; one s. two d. *Education:* Emory Coll., Oxford; NC State Univ., Raleigh; Univ. of NC at Chapel Hill; Univ. of NC at Greensboro. *Career:* Instructor, Salem Coll., Winston-Salem, NC, 1968–69;

Lecturer, Cornell Univ. 1971–73, Asst Prof. 1973–78, Assoc. Prof. 1978–84, Prof. 1984–92, Kappa Alpha Prof. of English 1992–. *Publications:* poetry: Zirconia Poems, 1969; The Voice in the Crosshairs, 1971; Red Owl, 1972; Land Diving, 1976; Trunk & Thicket, 1978; Groundwork, 1979; Bronze Age, 1981; At the Edge of the Orchard Country, 1987; Sigodlin, 1990; Green River: New and Selected Poems, 1991; Wild Peavines: Poems 1996. Fiction: The Blue Valleys: A Collection of Stories, 1989; The Mountains Won't Remember Us and Other Stories, 1992; The Hinterlands: A Mountain Tale in Three Parts, 1994; The Truest Pleasure, 1995; Gap Creek, 1999; The Balm of Gilead Trec: New and Selected Stories, 1999; Topsoil Road, 2000; This Rock, 2001; Brave Enemies: A Novel of the American Revolution, 2003; The Strange Attractor: New and Selected Poems, 2004. Non-Fiction: Good Measure: Essays, Interviews and Notes on Poetry, 1993. *Honours:* National Endowment for the Arts Fellowships, 1968, 1974, 1981, 1987; Southern Poetry Review Prize, 1975; Eunice Tietjens Award, 1979; Jacaranda Review Fiction Prize, 1988; Guggenheim Fellowship, 1988–89; Amon Liner Prize, 1989; James G. Hanes Poetry Prize, 1991; North Carolina Award in Literature, 1991; Southern Book Award, 2000; Fellowship of Southern Writers 2005–. *Address:* 1608 Hanshaw Road, Ithaca, NY 14853 (home); c/o Department of English, Goldwin Smith Hall, Cornell University, Ithaca, NY 14853, USA (office). *Telephone:* (607) 255-3503 (office). *Fax:* (607) 255-6661 (office). *E-mail:* rrm4@cornell.edu (office). *Website:* www.people.cornell.edu/pages/rrm4 (office).

MORGAN, Robin Evonne; American magazine editor and feminist writer; b. 29 Jan. 1941, Lake Worth, Fla; one c. *Education:* Columbia Univ., New York. *Career:* Freelance book ed 1961–69; Ed. Grove Press 1967–70; Ed. and Columnist, World Ms Magazine, New York 1974–87; Ed.-in-Chief 1990–93; Int. Consulting Ed. 1993–; Visiting Chair. and Guest Prof., New Coll., Sarasota, FL 1973; Distinguished Visiting Scholar and Lecturer, Centre for Critical Analysis of Contemporary Culture, Rutgers Univ. 1987; Special Consultant UN Cttee, UN Convention to End All Forms of Discrimination Against Women, Brazil 1987; Special Adviser to Gen. Ass. Conf. on Gender, UN Int. School 1985–86; organized first feminist demonstration against Miss America Pageant 1968; Co-Founder and mem. Bd of Dirs Feminist Women's Health Network, Nat. Battered Women's Refuge Network, Nat. Network Rape Crisis Centers, Women's Media Center; Founder Sisterhood Is Global Inst. (int. think-tank) 1984, Officer 1989–97, Chair. Advisory Bd 1997–; Founding mem. Nat. Museum of Women in Arts; mem. Bd of Dirs Women's Foreign Policy Council; mem. Feminist Writers' Guild, Media Women, Women's Action Alliance, N America Feminist Coalition, Pan Arab Feminist Solidarity Asscn; Grantee Writer-in-Residence Yaddo 1980, Nat. Endowment for Arts 1979–80, Ford Foundation 1982, 1983, 1984. *Publications include:* Sisterhood is Powerful: An Anthology of Writings from the Women's Liberation Movement (also compiler and ed) 1970, Monster 1972, Lady of the Beasts (poetry) 1976, Going Too Far: The Personal Chronicle of a Feminist 1978, The Anatomy of Freedom: Feminism, Physics and Global Politics 1982, Sisterhood is Global: The International Women's Movement Anthology (also compiler and ed.) 1984, Dry Your Smile: A Novel 1987, The Demon Lover: On the Sexuality of Terrorism 1989, The Mer-Child: A New Legend (poetry) 1990, Saturday's Child: A Memoir 2000, The Burning Time 2006, Fighting Words: A Tool Kit for Combating the Religious Right 2006. *Honours:* Hon. DHL (Connecticut) 1992; Front Page Award, Wonder Woman Award 1982, National Endowment for the Arts Prize (Poetry) and numerous other awards. *Address:* c/o Nation Books, 245 West 17th Street, 11th floor, New York, NY 10011, USA. *E-mail:* info@RobinMorgan.us. *Website:* www.robinmorgan.us.

MORGAN, Robin Richard; British journalist, editor and writer; b. 16 Sept. 1953, Stourbridge, England; two s. one d. *Career:* fmrly Ed.-in-Chief Sunday Express, editorial dir designate The Readers Digest; Ed., The Sunday Times Magazine 1995–; Non-Exec. Dir, Totally Plc 2005–. *Publications:* The Falklands War (co-author), 1982; Bullion (co-author), 1983; Rainbow Warrior (co-author), 1986; Manpower (ed.), 1986; Ambush (co-author), 1988; Book of Movie Biographies (co-ed.), 1997. *Honours:* Campaigning Journalist of the Year 1982, 1983. *Address:* c/o Sunday Times Magazine, 1 Pennington Street, London, E1 9XW, England.

MORGAN, Rozanne (see Gentle, Mary Rosalyn)

MORGAN, Susan Margaret, MA; British journalist; b. 7 Feb. 1944, Exeter; d. of Frederick Morgan and H. M. Morgan. *Education:* Redland High School for Girls, Univ. Coll. of Wales, Aberystwyth and Univ. of Essex. *Career:* teacher, Univ. of Qusqo, Cuzco, Peru 1966–68; Simultaneous Interpreter, Geneva 1968–70; freelance journalist and writer, Cen. America, N Africa, Middle East, UK 1970–. *Publication:* In Search of the Assassin (also film documentary 1988) 1991. *Address:* Garden Flat, 22 Belsize Gardens, London NW3 4LH, England. *Telephone:* (20) 7483-2817.

MORGAN-FINCH, Mihangel Ioan, (Mihangel Morgan), BA, PhD; British academic, writer and poet; b. 7 Dec. 1959, Aberdare, Wales. *Education:* University of Wales. *Career:* mem. Gorsedd Beirdd; Ynys Prydain. *Publications:* Diflaniad Fy Fi, 1988; Beth Yw Rhif Ffon Duw, 1991; Hen Lwybr A Storiau Eraill, 1992; Saith Pechod Marwol, 1993; Dirgel Ddyn, 1993; Te Gyda'r Frenhines, 1994; Tair Ochr Geiniog, 1996. Contributions: several publications. *Honours:* Prose Medal, Eisteddfod, 1993.

MORIARTY, Marilyn Frances, BA, MA, PhD; American academic, writer and poet; b. 6 Jan. 1953, Fort Jackson, SC. *Education:* University of Edinburgh, University of Florida, University of California at Irvine. *Career:* Instructor in Rhetoric and Composition, Saddleback Community College, Mission Viejo, CA, 1985–86; Fellow, University of California at Irvine, 1991, National Humanities Center, 1994; Asst Prof., 1992–98, Assoc. Prof. of English, 1998–, Hollins University, Roanoke, VA. *Publications:* Critical Architecture and Contemporary Culture (co-ed.), 1994; Writing Science Through Critical Thinking, 1997; Moses Unchained, 1998. Contributions: periodicals. *Honours:* First Place Award, University of Utah Novella Contest, 1987; Katherine Anne Porter Prize for Fiction, Arts and Humanities Council, Tulsa, 1990; Creative Non-Fiction Prize, Associated Writing Programs, 1996; Peregrine Prize for Short Fiction, Amberst Writers and Artists Press, 1997. *Address:* PO Box 9535, Hollins University, Roanoke, VA 24020, USA. *E-mail:* moriarty@hollins.edu.

MÖRING, Marcel; Dutch novelist; b. 5 Sept. 1957, Enschede. *Publications:* Mendels erfenis 1990, Betaaldag 1991, Het grote verlangen (The Great Longing) 1992, De Kotzker 1993, Bederf is de weg van alle vlees (Decay is the Way of All Flesh, novella) 1994, Het derde testament 1995, In Babylon 1997, Nachtzwemmen 1998, Modelvliegen (The Dream Room) 2001, Dis (Dis) 2006. *Honours:* Geertjan Lubberhuizen Prize for Best Debut 1990, AKO Prize 1992, two Golden Owl awards 1998, Aga Khan Prize 2000. *Literary Agent:* AP Watt Ltd, 20 John Street, London, WC1N 2DR, England. *Website:* www.marcelmoring.com.

MORITS, Yunna Petrovna; Russian poet; b. 2 June 1937, Kiev, Ukraine; m. Yuri Grigor'yevich Vasil'yev; one s. *Education:* Gorky Literary Inst. *Career:* began publishing poetry 1954; has participated in int. poetry festivals London, Cambridge, Toronto, Rotterdam etc.; has made recordings of recitations of her poetry; mem. Russian PEN, Exec. Cttee, Russian Acad. of Natural Sciences. *Publications:* eleven collections of poetry (trans. in many languages), including The Vine 1970, With Unbleached Thread 1974, By Light of Life 1977, The Third Eye 1980, Selected Poems 1982, The Blue Flame 1985, On This High Shore 1987, In the Den of Vice 1990, The Face 2000, In This Way 2000, By the Law to the Postman Hello 2005, and six books for children including The Great Secret for a Small Company 1987, A Bunch of Cats 1997, Move Your Ears 2003; poems appeared in journal Oktyabr 1993–97; also short stories, essays, scripts for animated cartoons. *Honours:* Golden Rose, Italy 1996, Triumph Prize, Russia 2000, A. D. Sakharov Prize for Civil Courage of Writer 2004. *Address:* Astrakhansky per. 5, Apt 76, 129010 Moscow, Russia (home). *Telephone:* (495) 680-08-16 (home). *E-mail:* morits@owl.ru (home).

MORITZ, Albert Frank, BA, MA, PhD; Canadian poet and writer; b. 15 April 1947, Niles, OH, USA; m. Theresa Carrothers; one s. *Education:* Marquette University. *Career:* Northrop Frye Visiting Lecturer in Poetry, University of Toronto, 1993–94. *Publications:* Here, 1975; Signs and Certainties, 1979; Music and Exile, 1980; Black Orchid, 1981; The Pocket Canada (with Theresa Moritz), 1982; Canada Illustrated: The Art of Nineteenth-Century Engraving, 1982; Between the Root and the Flower, 1982; The Visitation, 1983; America the Picturesque: The Art of Nineteenth-Century Engraving, 1983; Stephen Leacock: A Biography (with Theresa Moritz), 1987; Song of Fear, 1992; The Ruined Cottage, 1993; Mahoning, 1994; Phantoms in the Ark, 1994. Contributions: periodicals. *Honours:* American Acad. of Arts and Letters Award, 1991; Guggenheim Fellowship, 1993; Ingram Merrill Foundation Fellowship, 1993–94. *Address:* 14 Alpha Avenue, Toronto, ON M4X 1J3, USA. *E-mail:* tmoritz@chass.utoronto.ca.

MORLAND, Dick (see Hill, Reginald Charles)

MORLEY, Patricia Marlow, BA, MA, PhD; Canadian writer and educator; b. 25 May 1929, Toronto, ON; m. Lawrence W. Morley (divorced); three s. one d. *Education:* University of Toronto, Carleton University, University of Ottawa. *Career:* Asst Prof. of English, 1972–75, Assoc. Prof., 1975–80, Fellow, 1979–89, Prof. of English and Canadian Studies, 1980–89, Lifetime Hon. Fellow, 1989–, Simone de Beauvoir Institute, Concordia University, Montréal; mem. Writer's Union of Canada. *Publications:* The Mystery of Unity: Theme and Technique in the Novels of Patrick White, 1972; The Immoral Moralists: Hugh MacLennan and Leonard Cohen, 1972; Robertson Davies: Profiles in Canadian Drama, 1977; The Comedians: Hugh Hood and Rudy Wiebe, 1977; Morley Callaghan, 1978; Kurelek: A Biography, 1986; Margaret Laurence: The Long Journey Home, 1991; As Though Life Mattered: Leo Kennedy's Story, 1994; The Mountain is Moving: Japanese Women's Lives, 1999. Contributions: Professional and mainstream journals. *Honours:* Ottawa-Carleton Literary Award, 1988; Hon. Doctor of Sacred Letters, Thorneloe College, Laurentian University, 1992.

MORPURGO, Michael, OBE; British writer; b. 5 Oct. 1943, St Albans, Hertfordshire; m. Clare Morpurgo. *Career:* co-f., Farms for City Children project; Children's Laureate 2003–05; Writer-in-Residence, The Savoy Hotel, London 2007. *Publications include:* Beyond the Rainbow Warrior, Billy the Kid, Black Queen, Colly's Barn, Conker, Dear Olly, Escape from Shangri-La, Farm Boy, Friend or Foe, From Hearabout Hill, Grania O'Malley, Joan of Arc, Kensuke's Kingdom, King of the Cloud Forests, Long Way Home, Marble Crusher, Mr Nobody's Eyes, My Friend Walter, Out of the Ashes, Red Eyes at Night, Sam's Duck, Snakes and Ladders, The Butterfly Lion, The Nine Lives of Montezuma, The Rainbow Bear, The Sleeping Sword, The War of Jenkins' Ear, The White Horse of Zennor, The Wreck of the Zanzibar, Toro! Toro!, Twist of Gold, Waiting for Anya, War Horse, Wartman, Who's a Big Bully Then?, Why the Whales Came, Wombat Goes Walkabout, The Last Wolf 2002, Private Peaceful (Prix Sorcières for children's novel, France, Blue Peter Book Award 2005) 2003, The Amazing Story of Adolphus Tips 2005, Alone on a Wide Wide Sea 2006, On Angel Wings 2006. *Honours:* Whitbread Children's Book Award

1995, Smarties Book Prize 1996, Bronze Prize in 6–8 years group 2003, Children's Book Awards 1996, 2000, 2002. *Address:* c/o Farms for City Children, Nethercott House, Iddesleigh, Winkleigh, Devon EX19 8BG, England.

MORRALL, Clare; British writer and music teacher; b. 1952, Exeter, England; two c. *Publications:* Astonishing Splashes of Colour 2003, Natural Flights of the Human Mind 2006. *Literary Agent:* The Marsh Agency, 11 Dover Street, London, W1S 4LJ, England. *Telephone:* (20) 7399-2800. *Fax:* (20) 7399-2801. *Website:* www.marsh-agency.co.uk.

MORRELL, David, BA, MA, PhD; Canadian writer; b. 24 April 1943, Kitchener, ON; m. Donna Maziarz 1965; one s. (deceased) one d. *Education:* Univ. of Waterloo, Pennsylvania State Univ. *Career:* Asst Prof. 1970–74, Assoc. Prof. 1974–77, Prof. of American Literature 1977–86, Univ. of Iowa; mem. Horror Writers of America, Writers' Guild of America, Int. Thriller Writers organization (co-pres.). *Publications:* fiction: First Blood 1972, Testament 1975, Last Reveille 1977, The Totem 1979, Blood Oath 1982, The Hundred-Year Christmas 1983, The Brotherhood of the Rose 1984, The Fraternity of the Stone 1985, Rambo (First Blood Part II) 1985, The League of Night and Fog 1987, Rambo III 1988, The Fifth Profession 1990, The Covenant of the Flame 1991, Assumed Identity 1993, Desperate Measures 1994, Extreme Denial 1996, Double Image 1998, Black Evening 1999, Burnt Sienna 2000, Long Lost 2002, The Protector 2003, Nightscape 2004, Creepers 2005; non-fiction: John Barth: An Introduction 1976, Fireflies: A Father's Tale of Love and Loss 1988, American Fiction, American Myth: Essays by Philip Young 2000, Lessons from a Lifetime of Writing: A Novelist Looks at his Craft 2002; contrib. to journals and magazines. *Honours:* hon. life mem. Special Operations Asscn, Asscn of Former Intelligence Officers; Friends of American Writers Distinguished Recognition Award 1972, Horror Writers of America Best Novella Awards 1989, 1991. *Address:* c/o Henry Morrison, PO Box 235, Beford Hills, NY 10507, USA. *Website:* www.davidmorrell.net.

MORRILL, Rev. John Stephen, DPhil, FBA; British historian and academic; *Professor of British and Irish History, University of Cambridge;* b. 12 June 1946, Manchester; s. of William Henry Morrill and Marjorie Morrill (née Ashton); m. Frances Mead 1968; four d. *Education:* Altrincham Grammar School, Trinity Coll., Oxford. *Career:* Research Fellow, Trinity Coll. Oxford 1970–74, Hon. Fellow 2006–; Lecturer in History, Univ. of Stirling 1974–75; Fellow, Selwyn Coll. Cambridge 1975–, Sr Tutor 1989–92, Vice-Master 1994–2005; Lecturer in History, Cambridge Univ. 1975–92, Reader in Early Modern History 1992–98, Prof. of British and Irish History 1998–; mem. Council, Royal Historical Soc. 1988–92, Vice-Pres. 1992–96; Chair. Communications and Activities Cttee, British Acad. 1998–, mem. Council 1998–, Vice-Pres. 2000–02; mem. and Trustee Arts and Humanities Research Council 2000–04, Chair. Rescue Cttee 2001–04; ordained Perm. Deacon, RC Diocese of East Anglia 1996; mem. Acad. of Finland 2001. *Publications:* Cheshire 1630–1660 1974, The Revolt of the Provinces 1976, Reactions to the English Civil War 1981, Oliver Cromwell and the English Revolution 1989, The Impact of the English Civil War 1991, Revolution and Restoration 1992, The Nature of the English Revolution 1992, The British Problem 1534–1707 1996, The Oxford Illustrated History of Tudor and Stuart Britain 1996, Revolt in the Provinces 1998, Soldiers and Statesmen of the English Revolution (jtly) 1998; 40 articles in learned journals. *Honours:* Hon. DLitt (Univ. of East Anglia) 2001; Hon. DUniv (Surrey) 2001. *Address:* Selwyn College, Cambridge, CB3 9DQ (office); 1 Bradford's Close, Bottisham, Cambridge, CB5 9DW, England (home). *Telephone:* (1223) 335895 (office); (1223) 811822 (home). *Fax:* (1223) 335837 (office). *E-mail:* jsm1000@cam.ac.uk (office).

MORRIS, Desmond John, DPhil; British zoologist; b. 24 Jan. 1928, Purton, Wilts.; s. of Capt. Harry Howe Morris and Marjorie (née Hunt) Morris; m. Ramona Joy Baulch 1952; one s. *Education:* Dauntsey's School, Wilts., Birmingham Univ. and Oxford Univ. *Career:* zoological research worker Univ. of Oxford 1954–56; Head of Granada TV; Head of Film Unit Zoological Soc. of London 1956–59, Curator of Mammals 1959–67; Dir Inst. of Contemporary Arts, London 1967–68; Research Fellow at Wolfson Coll., Oxford 1973–81; privately engaged in writing books on animal and human behaviour 1968–73, 1981–2006 and making television programmes; artist; mem. Scientific Fellow Zoological Soc. of London. *Television:* Zootime (Granada) 1956–67, Life in the Animal World (BBC) 1965–67, The Human Race (Thames TV) 1982, The Animals Roadshow (BBC) 1987–89, The Animal Contract 1989, Animal Country 1991–95, The Human Animal 1994, The Human Sexes 1997. *Solo exhibitions include:* Swindon Museum and Art Gallery 1976, Galerie D'Eendt Amsterdam 1978, Mayor Gallery London 1987, 1989, 1991, 1994, 1997, 1999, Keitelman Gallery Brussels, 1998, Jessy Van der Velde Gallery Antwerp 1998, Museum of Modern Art, Antwerp 2002, Solomon Gallery Dublin 2004, Madrid 2005 and many others. *Publications:* The Reproductive Behaviour of the Ten-spined Stickleback 1958, The Story of Congo 1958, Curious Creatures 1961, The Biology of Art 1962, Apes and Monkeys 1964, The Mammals: A Guide to the Living Species 1965, The Big Cats 1965, Men and Snakes (with Ramona Morris) 1965, Zootime 1966, Men and Apes (with Ramona Morris) 1966, Men and Pandas (with Ramona Morris) 1966, Primate Ethology (Editor) 1967, The Naked Ape 1967, The Human Zoo 1969, Patterns of Reproductive Behaviour 1970, Intimate Behaviour 1971, Manwatching: A Field-Guide to Human Behaviour 1977, Gestures, Their Origins and Distribution 1979, Animal Days (autobiog.) 1979, The Giant Panda 1981, The Soccer Tribe 1981, Inrock (fiction) 1983, The Book of Ages 1983, The Art of Ancient Cyprus 1985, Bodywatching 1985, The Illustrated Naked Ape 1986, Dogwatching 1986,

Catwatching 1986, The Secret Surrealist 1987, Catlore 1987, The Human Nestbuilders 1988, The Animals Roadshow 1988, Horsewatching 1988, The Animal Contract 1990, Animal-Watching 1990, Babywatching 1991, Christmas Watching 1992, The World of Animals 1993, The Naked Ape Trilogy 1994, The Human Animal 1994, Body Talk: A World Guide to Gestures 1994, The Illustrated Catwatching 1994, Illustrated Babywatching 1995, Catworld: A Feline Encyclopedia 1996, Illustrated Dogwatching 1996, The Human Sexes 1997, Illustrated Horse-Watching 1998, Cool Cats: The 100 Cat Breeds of the World 1999, Body Guards: Protective Amulets and Charms 1999, Cosmetic Behaviour and the Naked Ape 1999, The Naked Eye 2000, Dogs, a Dictionary of Dog Breeds 2001, People-Watching 2002, The Silent Language 2004, The Nature of Happiness 2004, The Naked Woman: A Study of the Female Body 2004, Watching: Encounters with Humans and Other Animals (autobiog.) 2006. *Honours:* Hon. DSc (Reading) 1998. *Address:* c/o Jonathan Cape, 20 Vauxhall Bridge Road, London, SW1V 2SA, England. *Fax:* (1865) 512103. *E-mail:* dmorris@ukstudio.org. *Website:* www.desmond-morris.com.

MORRIS, Edmund; American writer; b. 27 May 1940, Nairobi, Kenya. *Education:* Rhodes Univ. *Publications:* The Rise of Theodore Roosevelt (Pulitzer Prize in Biography 1980) 1979, Dutch: A Memoir of Ronald Reagan 1999, Theodore Rex 2001, Beethoven: The Universal Composer 2005. *Honours:* Pulitzer Prize 1980, American Book Award 1980, Los Angeles Times Book Award for Biography 2002. *Address:* 222 Central Park S, New York, NY 10019, USA.

MORRIS, James Humphry (see Morris, Jan)

MORRIS, Jan, (James Humphry Morris), CBE, MA, FRSL; British writer; b. 2 Oct. 1926, Somerset, England. *Education:* Christ Church Coll., Oxford. *Career:* editorial staff, the Times 1951–56, The Guardian 1957–62; Commonwealth Fellowship, USA 1954; mem. Yr Academi Gymreig, Gorsedd of Bards, Welsh Nat. Eisteddfod. *Publications:* as James Morris: Coast to Coast (aka I Saw the USA) 1956, Sultan in Oman 1957, The Market of Seleukia (aka Islam Inflamed: A Middle East Picture) 1957, Coronation Everest 1958, South African Winter 1958, The Hashemite Kings 1959, Venice 1960, South America 1961, The Upstairs Donkey (juvenile) 1962, The World Bank: A Prospect (aka The Road to Huddersfield: A Journey to Five Continents) 1963, Cities 1963, The Outriders: A Liberal View of Britain 1963, The Presence of Spain 1964, Oxford 1965, Pax Britannica: The Climax of an Empire 1968, The Great Port: A Passage through New York 1969, Places 1972, Heaven's Command: An Imperial Progress 1973, Farewell the Trumpets: An Imperial Retreat 1978; as Jan Morris: Conundrum 1974, Travels 1976, The Oxford Book of Oxford 1978, Destinations: Essays from 'Rolling Stone' 1980, The Venetian Empire: A Sea Voyage 1980, My Favourite Stories of Wales 1980, The Small Oxford Book of Wales, Wales The First Place, A Venetian Bestiary 1982, The Spectacle of Empire 1982, Stones of Empire: The Buildings of the Raj 1983, Journeys 1984, The Matter of Wales: Epic Views of a Small Country 1984, Among the Cities 1985, Last Letters from Hav: Notes from a Lost City 1985, Stones of Empire: The Buildings of the Raj 1986, Scotland, The Place of Visions 1986, Manhattan, '45 1987, Hong Kong: Xianggang 1988, Pleasures of a Tangled Life 1989, Ireland Your Only Place 1990, City to City 1990, O Canada 1992, Sydney 1992, Locations 1992, Travels with Virginia Woolf (ed.) 1993, A Machynlleth Triad 1994, Fisher's Face 1995, The Princeship of Wales 1995, The World of Venice 1995, 50 Years of Europe 1997, Hong Kong: Epilogue to an Empire 1997, Lincoln: A Foreigner's Quest 1999, Our First Leader 2000, A Writer's House in Wales 2001, Trieste and the Meaning of Nowhere 2001, A Writer's World: Travels 1950–2000 2003, Hav (fiction) 2006, Portmeirion (with others) 2006. *Honours:* Hon. Fellow, Univ. Coll. Wales, Univ. of Wales, Bangor; Hon. FRIBA; Hon. Student, Christ Church Oxon.; Dr hc (Univ. of Wales) 1993, (Univ. of Glamorgan) 1996. *Literary Agent:* c/o AP Watt Ltd, 20 John Street, London, WC1N 2DR, England. *Telephone:* (20) 7405-6774. *Fax:* (20) 7831-2154. *E-mail:* apw@apwatt.co.uk. *Website:* www.apwatt.co.uk. *Address:* Trefan Morys, Llanystumdwy, Gwynedd LL52 0LP, Wales (home). *Telephone:* (1766) 522222 (home). *E-mail:* janmorris1@msn.com (home).

MORRIS, Janet Ellen, (Casey Prescott, Daniel Stryker); American writer; b. 25 May 1946, Boston, MA; m. 31 Oct. 1970. *Career:* mem. SFWA; MWA; New York Acad. of Science; National Intelligence Study Center; Asscn of Old Crows. *Publications:* Silistra Quartet, 1976–78, 1983–84; Dream Dance Trilogy, 1980–83; I the Sun, 1984; Heroes in Hell, 10 vols, 1984–88; Beyond Sanctuary, 3 vols, 1985–86; Warlord, 1986; The Little Helliad, 1986; Outpassage, 1987; Kill Ratio, 1987; City at the Edge of Time, 1988; Tempus Vabound, 1989; Target (with David Drake), 1989; Warrior's Edge, 1990; Threshold, 1991; Trust Territory, 1992; American Warrior, 1992; The Stalk, 1994. Contributions: various publications. *Honours:* Hellva Award for Best Novel, 1985.

MORRIS, Mark, (J. M. Morris), BA; British writer; b. 15 June 1963, Bolsover, Derbyshire; m. Nel Whatmore 1990; one s. one d. *Education:* Trinity and All Saints Coll., Horsforth, Leeds. *Career:* mem. British Fantasy Soc. *Publications:* fiction: Toady 1989, Stitch 1991, The Immaculate 1992, The Secret of Anatomy 1994, Close to the Bone (short stories) 1995, Mr Bad Face 1996, Longbarrow 1997, Doctor Who: The Bodysnatchers 1997, Genesis 1999, Doctor Who: Deep Blue 1999, The Dogs 2001, The Uglimen 2002, Fiddleback (as J. M. Morris) 2002, Nowhere Near An Angel 2005, Stumps 2005; works included in numerous anthologies; contrib. to several magazines including Fear, Interzone, Million, SFX, The Third Alternative, The Dark Side, Me,

Skeleton Crew, Beyond, Subterranean. *Literary Agent:* PFD, Drury House, 34–43 Russell Street, London, WC2B 5HA, England.

MORRIS, Mary, BA, MA, MPhil; American writer; *Professor, Sarah Lawrence College;* b. 14 May 1947, Chicago, Ill.; m. Larry O'Connor 1989; one d. *Education:* Tufts Coll., Columbia Univ. *Career:* teacher, Princeton Univ. 1980–87, 1991–94, New York Univ. 1988–94, Sarah Lawrence Coll. 1994–; mem. American PEN, Authors' Guild, Friends of the American Acad. in Rome. *Publications:* Vanishing Animals 1978, The Bus of Dreams 1985, Nothing to Declare: Memoirs of a Woman Travelling Alone 1989, The Waiting Room 1991, Wall to Wall: From Beijing to Berlin by Rail 1992, A Mother's Love 1993, Maiden Voyages 1993, House Arrest 1996, The Lifeguard 1997, Angels and Aliens 1998, Acts of God 2000, Revenge 2004; contribs to periodicals. *Honours:* Guggenheim Fellowship 1980, Rome Prize 1981. *Literary Agent:* Ellen Levine, Trident Media Group, 41 Madison Avenue, New York, NY 10010, USA. *E-mail:* mmorris348@yahoo.com. *Website:* www.marymorris.net.

MORRIS, Mary Joan McGarry; American writer; b. 1943, Meriden, CT; m. Michael Morris 1962; one s. four d. *Education:* Univ. of Vermont, Univ. of Massachusetts. *Publications:* Vanished 1988, A Dangerous Woman 1991, Songs in Ordinary Time 1995, Fiona Range 2000, A Hole in the Universe 2004, The Last Mother, 2005; contrib. to periodicals. *Literary Agent:* Naggar Literary Agency, 216 E 75th Street, New York, NY 10021, USA.

MORRIS, Sara (see Burke, John Frederick)

MORRIS, Stephen; British artist, poet and writer; b. 14 Aug. 1935, Smethwick; m. 1963 (divorced 1989); one s. two d. *Education:* Moseley Art School, Fircroft Coll., Marie Borgs Folk High School, Univs of Cardiff and Leicester. *Career:* ed. student newspaper, Univ. of Cardiff 1961–62; Asst Lecturer, Univ. of Wolverhampton 1967–69, Lecturer 1969–72, Sr Lecturer 1972–86; full-time artist 1986–; commissioned by British Art Medal Soc. to produce a medal 2003. *Film:* To Forgive the Unforgivable 1996. *Exhibitions:* 60 solo exhbns of painting and sculpture. *Publications:* poetry: The Revolutionary 1972, The Kingfisher Catcher 1974, Death of a Clown 1976, The Moment of Truth 1978, Too Long at the Circus 1980, Rolling Dice 1986, To Forgive the Unforgivable 1997, Twelve 1998, Limbus of the Moon 2005; other: Lord of Death (play) 1963; contribs to Guardian, Observer, Peace News, Rolling Stone, Sunday Times, Tribune. *Honours:* elected to be a Companion of the Guild of St George 2001. *Address:* 4 rue Las Cours, Aspiran, L'Herault 34800, France (home). *E-mail:* palehorse-publishing@hotmail.com (office); morris.stephen@wanadoo.fr (home). *Website:* www.stephen-morris.net.

MORRISON, Bill, LLB; British playwright and theatre director; b. 22 Jan. 1940, Ballymoney, Northern Ireland; m. (divorced); one s. one d. *Education:* Queen's University, Belfast. *Career:* Resident Playwright, Victoria Theatre, Stoke-on-Trent, 1968–71; Everyman Theatre, Liverpool, 1976–79; Assoc. Dir, 1981–83, Artistic Dir, 1983–85, Liverpool Playhouse. *Publications:* Stage Plays: Patrick's Day, 1971; Flying Blind, 1979; Scrap, 1982; Cavern of Dreams (with Carol Ann Duffy), 1984; Be Bop a Lula, 1988; A Love Song for Ulster, 1993; Drive On, 1996. Radio and Stage Plays: Sam Slade is Missing, 1971; The Love of Lady Margaret, 1972; Ellen Cassidy, 1975; The Emperor of Ice Cream, 1977; Blues in a Flat, 1989; The Little Sister, 1990. Radio Plays: The Great Gun-Running Episode, 1973; Simpson and Son, 1977; Maguire, 1978; The Spring of Memory, 1981; Affair, 1991; Three Steps to Heaven, 1992; Waiting for Lefty, 1994; Murder at the Cameo, 1996. Television Plays: McKinley and Sarah, 1974; Joggers, 1979; Potatohead Blues, 1980; Shergar, 1986; A Safe House, 1990; Force of Duty, 1992; C'mon Everybody, 1996; A Love Song for Ulster, 1999. *Honours:* Rye Radio Award for Best Programme 1981.

MORRISON, (Philip) Blake, BA, MA, PhD, FRSL; British author, poet and dramatist; *Professor of Creative and Life Writing, Goldsmith's College;* b. 8 Oct. 1950, Burnley, Lancs.; m. Katherine Ann Drake 1976; two s. one d. *Education:* Univ. of Nottingham, McMaster Univ., Canada, Univ. Coll., London. *Career:* Poetry and Fiction Ed. Times Literary Supplement 1978–81; Deputy Literary Ed. The Observer 1981–86, Literary Ed. 1987–89; Literary Ed. The Independent on Sunday 1990–94; Prof. of Creative Writing, Goldsmiths Coll., London 2003–. *Publications:* The Movement: English Poetry and Fiction of the 1950s 1980, Seamus Heaney 1982, Penguin Book of Contemporary British Poetry (ed. with Andrew Motion) 1982, Dark Glasses (poems) 1984, The Ballad of the Yorkshire Ripper and Other Poems 1987, The Yellow House (juvenile) 1987, And When Did You Last See Your Father? (memoir) 1993, The Cracked Pot: A Play, after Heinrich von Kleist 1996, As If: A Crime, a Trial, a Question of Childhood 1997, Too True (essays and stories) 1998, Dr Ox's Experiment (libretto) 1998, Selected Poems 1999, The Justification of Johann Gutenberg (novel) 2000, Things My Mother Never Told Me (memoir) 2002, Oedipus/Antigone (drama) 2003. *Honours:* Eric Gregory Award 1980, Somerset Maugham Award 1984, Dylan Thomas Prize 1985, E. M. Forster Award 1988, J. R. Ackerley Prize 1994. *Address:* 54 Blackheath Park, London, SE3 9SJ, England (office). *Telephone:* (20) 7919-7514 (office). *E-mail:* blakemorr@aol.com (office).

MORRISON, Dorothy Jean Allison, MA, DipEd, FSA; Scottish author and lecturer; b. 17 Feb. 1933, Glasgow; m. James F. T. Morrison 1955; one s. one d. *Education:* Univ. of Glasgow. *Career:* Principal Teacher of History, Montrose Acad., 1968–73; Lecturer in History, Dundee Coll. of Educ., 1973–83; Adviser to Scottish History series, History at Hand series, Scotland's War series, Scottish TV; mem. Church and Nation Cttee, Church of Scotland, 1996–; Netherbow Council for the Arts, Church of Scotland, 2000. *Publications:* Old

Age, 1972; Young People, 1973; Health and Hospitals, 1973; The Civilian War (with M. Cuthbert), 1975; Travelling in China, 1977; The Romans in Britain, 1978; Billy Leaves Home, 1979; Story of Scotland (with J. Halliday), I, 1979, 1980, II, 1982; The Great War, 1914–18, 1981; Historical Sources for Schools, I Agriculture, 1982; History Around You, 1983; People of Scotland, I, 1983, II, 1985; Ancient Greeks (with John Morrison), 1984; Handbook on Money Management, 1985; Modern China, 1987; The Rise of Modern China, 1988; Montrose Old Church – A History, 1991; Scotland's War, 1992; A Sense of History – Castles, 1994; Ancient Scotland, 1996; The Wars of Independence, 1996; Changed Days in Montrose (with Isobel Reynolds), 1999; The Lifeboat: 200 Years of Service, 2000; Rural Schools in Angus (with Isobel Reynolds), 2003. *Address:* Craigview House, Usan, Montrose, Angus, DD10 9SD, Scotland. *Telephone:* (1674) 672639 (home). *Fax:* (1674) 672639 (home). *E-mail:* d.j.morrison@talk21.com (home).

MORRISON, Sally, BSc; Australian writer; b. 29 June 1946, Sydney, NSW; one s. *Education:* Australian National University. *Career:* mem. Fellowship of Australian Writers; Australian Society of Authors; Victorian Writers Centre. *Publications:* Who's Taking You to the Dance? (novel), 1979; I Am a Boat (short stories), 1989; Mad Meg (novel), 1994. Contributions: Bulletin; Australian Literary Supplement; Overland; Quadrant; Island; Sydney Morning Herald; Age Monthly Review. *Honours:* Project Assistance Grants, Victorian Ministry of the Arts, 1988, 1993, 1994; Writer's Grants, Australia Council Literary Board, 1990, 1991, 1992; National Book Council Banjo Award for Fiction, 1995.

MORRISON, Toni, MA; American novelist and academic; *Goheen Professor in the Humanities, Program in Creative Writing, Princeton University;* b. (Chloe Anthony Wofford), 18 Feb. 1931, Lorain, Ohio; d. of George Wofford and Ella Ramah (Willis) Wofford; m. Harold Morrison 1958 (divorced 1964); two c. *Education:* Lorain High School, Howard Univ., Cornell Univ. *Career:* taught English and Humanities, Tex. Southern Univ. 1955–57, Howard Univ. 1957–64; Ed., then Sr Ed. Random House, New York 1965–85; Assoc. Prof. of English, State Univ. of New York 1971–72, Schweitzer Prof. of the Humanities 1984–89; Robert F. Goheen Prof. of the Humanities, Princeton Univ. 1989–; Visiting Lecturer Yale Univ. 1976–77, Bard Coll. 1986–88; Clark Lecturer Trinity Cambridge 1990; Massey Lecturer Harvard Univ. 1990; mem. Council, Authors Guild, American Acad. of Arts and Sciences, American Acad. of Arts and Letters, Authors League of America, Nat. Council on the Arts. *Publications:* The Bluest Eye 1970, Sula 1974, The Black Book (ed) 1974, Song of Solomon 1977, Tar Baby 1983, Dreaming Emmett (play) 1986, Beloved 1987 (Pulitzer Prize and Robert F. Kennedy Book Award 1988), Jazz 1992, Playing in the Dark: Whiteness and the Literary Imagination (lectures) 1992, Race-ing Justice, En-gendering Power (ed, essays) 1992, Honey and Rue (song cycle) 1993, Nobel Prize Speech 1994, Birth of a Nation'hood: Gaze, Script and Spectacle in the O. J. Simpson Trial 1997, Paradise 1998, Collected Essays of James Baldwin (ed) 1998, Love 2003; co-author, for children: The Big Box (poems) 1999, The Book of Mean People 2002, The Ant or the Grasshopper, The Lion or the Mouse 2003. *Honours:* Commdr Ordre des Arts et des Lettres; Ohioana Book Award 1975, American Acad. and Inst. of Arts and Letters Award 1977, Nat. Book Critics Circle Awards 1977, 1997, NY State Gov.'s Arts Award 1987, Nobel Prize for Literature 1993, Nat. Book Foundation Medal 1995, Nat. Humanities Medal 2000. *Literary Agent:* Suzanne Gluck, International Creative Management, 40 57th Street West, New York, NY 10019, USA. *Address:* Princeton University, Program in Creative Writing Program, 185 Nassau Street, Princeton, NJ 08544, USA. *Telephone:* (609) 258-8561. *Fax:* (609) 258-2230. . *Website:* www.princeton.edu/~visarts/cre.html.

MORRISON, Anthony (Tony) James, BSc; British writer; *Director, South American Pictures;* b. 5 July 1936, Gosport; m. Elizabeth Marion Davies 1965; one s. one d. *Education:* Univ. of Bristol. *Career:* Partner, South American Pictures; Dir, Nonesuch Expeditions Ltd. *Publications:* Steps to a Fortune (co-author) 1967, Animal Migration 1973, Land Above the Clouds 1974, The Andes 1976, Pathways to the Gods 1978, Lizzie: A Victorian Lady's Amazon Adventure (co-ed.) 1985, The Mystery of the Nasca Lines 1987, Margaret Mee: In Search of Flowers of the Amazon (ed.) 1988, QOSQO: Navel of the World 1995, Peru: Country of Contrasts 2001. *Address:* 48 Station Road, Woodbridge, Suffolk IP12 4AT, England. *Telephone:* (1394) 383963 (office). *E-mail:* editor@nonesuchinfo.info (office). *Website:* www.nonesuchinfo.info (office).

MORTIMER, Sir John Clifford, Kt, CBE, QC, FRSL; British author, barrister and playwright; b. 21 April 1923, Hampstead, London; s. of Clifford and Katherine (née Smith) Mortimer; m. 1st Penelope Fletcher (Penelope Mortimer) 1949 (divorced 1972); one s. one d.; m. 2nd Penelope Gollop; two d. *Education:* Harrow, Brasenose Coll., Oxford. *Career:* called to the Bar 1948, Master of the Bench, Inner Temple 1975; mem. Bd of Nat. Theatre 1968–; Chair. Council Royal Soc. of Literature 1989; Chair. Council Royal Court Theatre 1990–2002, Pres. 2004–; Pres. Howard League for Penal Reform 1991–. *Plays include:* The Wrong Side of the Park 1960, Two Stars for Comfort 1962, The Judge 1967, A Voyage Round My Father 1970 (adapted for TV 1982, Int. Emmy Award), I, Claudius (adaptation from Robert Graves) 1972, Collaborators 1973, Mr. Luby's Fear of Heaven (radio) 1976, Heaven and Hell 1976, The Bells of Hell 1977, The Lady from Maxim's (trans. from Feydeau) 1977, Flea in Her Ear, A Little Hotel on the Side (trans. from Feydeau), TV adaptations of Rumpole of the Bailey (six series), Brideshead Revisited 1981, Unity Mitford 1981, The Ebony Tower 1984, adaptation of Die Fledermaus 1989, (TV) A Christmas Carol 1994, Naked Justice 2001, Hock and Soda Water 2001; Under the Hammer (TV series) 1993. *Publications:* novels:

Charade 1947, Rumming Park 1948, Answer Yes or No 1950, Like Men Betrayed 1953, Three Winters 1956, The Narrowing Stream 1958, Will Shakespeare 1977, Rumpole of the Bailey 1978, The Trials of Rumpole 1979, Rumpole's Return 1981, Rumpole and the Golden Thread 1983, Paradise Postponed 1985, Rumpole's Last Case 1987, Rumpole and the Age of Miracles 1988, Summer's Lease 1988, Rumpole à la Carte 1990, Titmuss Regained 1990, Dunster 1992, Rumpole on Trial 1992, The Best of Rumpole 1993, Rumpole and the Angel of Death 1995, Rumpole and the Younger Generation 1996, Felix in the Underworld 1997, Rumpole's Return 1997, The Third Rumpole Omnibus 1997, The Sound of Trumpets 1998, Rumpole Rests His Case 2001, Rumpole and the Primrose Path (short stories) 2002, Rumpole and The Penge Bungalow Murders 2002, Quite Honestly 2005; trans. Die Fledermaus 1988; other: Clinging to the Wreckage (autobiog.) 1982, In Character 1983, Character Parts (interviews) 1986, Great Law and Order Stories 1991, The Oxford Book of Villains 1992; Murderers and Other Friends (autobiog.) 1993, The Summer of a Dormouse (autobiog.) 2000, Where There's a Will 2003; numerous articles in magazines. Honours: Hon. LLD (Susquehanna Univ.) 1985, Dr hc (Exeter) 1986, Hon. DLitt (St Andrews) 1987, (Nottingham) 1989, Hon. DUniv (Brunel) 1990; British Acad. Writers' Award 1979, 1980, British Book Award for Lifetime Achievement 2005. Address: Turville Heath Cottage, Henley on Thames, Oxon., RG9 6JY, England. Telephone: (1491) 638237 (home). Fax: (1491) 638861 (home).

MORTON, Colin Todd, MA; Canadian novelist, poet and editor; b. 26 July 1948, Toronto, ON; m. Mary Lee Bragg 1969; one s. Education: Univs of Calgary and Alberta. Career: Creative Writing Instructor, Algonquin Coll. 1993–94; Writer-in-Residence, Concordia Coll. 1995–96, Connecticut Coll. 1997; mem. League of Canadian Poets (Vice-Pres. 2000–01). Play: The Cabbage of Paradise 1988. Film: Primiti Too Taa 1987. Publications: poetry: In Transit 1981, This Won't Last Forever 1985, Word/Music (cassette with First Draft) 1986, North/South (with A. McClure and S. McMaster) 1987, The Merzbook: Kurt Schwitters Poems 1987, Two Decades: From A Century of Inventions 1987, How to Be Born Again 1992, Coastlines of the Archipelago 2000, Dance, Misery 2003; novel: Oceans Apart 1995; contribs to reviews and journals; anthologies, including Capital Poets 1989, In the Clear 1998, Vintage '94 1995, Waging Peace 2002, In Fine Form 2005. Honours: Third Prize, CBC Radio Literary Competition 1984, Archibald Lampman Award 1986, Best Soundtrack, ASIFA East Film Festival, New York 1988, Bronze Apple, Nat. Educational Film and Video Festival 1988, Second Prizes for prose poem, Short Grain Contest 1989, postcard fiction 1990, Archibald Lampman Award for Poetry 2001. Address: 40 Grove Avenue, Ottawa, ON, K1S 3A6, Canada. E-mail: cmorton@sympatico.ca (home). Website: www3.sympatico.ca/cmorton.

MORTON, Frederic, BS, MA; American/Austrian author; b. 5 Oct. 1924, Vienna, Austria; m. Marcia Colman 1957; one d. Education: Coll. of the City of New York, New School for Social Research, New York. Career: mem. Authors' Guild, PEN Club. Publications: The Rothschilds (also Broadway musical 1972) 1962, A Nervous Splendour (also musical, premiered in Budapest 2006) 1978, The Forever Street 1987, Thunder at Twilight 1991, Runaway Waltz 2005; contributions: newspapers and journals. Honours: Author of the Year Award, Anti Defamation League, USA 1963; City of Vienna Gold Medal of Honour 2001; Cross of Honour in Arts and Letters, Repub. of Austria 2003. Literary Agent: Lantz Office Ltd, 200 W 57th Street, Suite 503, New York, NY 10019, USA. Telephone: (212) 873-9266 (office). Fax: (212) 721-6938 (office).

MORTON, G. L. (see Fryer, Jonathan)

MORTON, Henry (Harry) Albert, BA, BEd, MA, PhD; New Zealand academic (retd) and writer; b. 20 July 1925, Gladstone, MB, Canada. Education: University of Manitoba, University of Cambridge, University of Otago, New Zealand. Career: mem. Blenheim Club; New Zealand Society of Authors; Royal New Zealand Airforce Asscn. Publications: And Now New Zealand, 1969; The Wind Commands, 1975; Which Way New Zealand, 1975; Why Not Together?, 1978; The Whale's Wake, 1982; The Farthest Corner, 1988. Honours: Sir James Wattie Award, Book of the Year, 1976.

MOSES, Daniel David, BA, MFA; Canadian writer, dramatist and poet; b. 18 Feb. 1952, Ohsweken, ON. Education: York University, University of British Columbia. Career: Instructor in Creative Writing, University of British Columbia, 1990; Instructor in Playwrighting, Graduate Drama Centre, University of Toronto, 1992; Resident Artist, Banff Centre for the Arts, 1993; Writer-in-Residence, University of Western Ontario, 1994, University of Windsor, 1995–96; mem. League of Canadian Poets; Playwrights Union of Canada; Writers' Guild of Canada; Writers' Union of Canada. Publications: Plays: The Dreaming Beauty, 1989; Coyote City, 1991; Almighty Voice and His Wife, 1992; The Indian Medicine Shows, 1995. Poetry: Delicate Bodies, 1980; The White Line. Other: An Anthology of Canadian Native Literature in English (co-ed.), 1992. Honours: First Prize, Theatre Canada National Playwrighting Competition, 1990; Winner, New Play Centre Playwrighting Competition, 1994.

MOSLEY, Nicholas (see Ravensdale, 3rd Baron)

MOSLEY, Walter; American writer; b. 1952, Los Angeles; m. Joy Kellman 1987 (divorced). Education: Goddard Coll., Johnson State Coll., City Coll. CUNY. Career: Artist-in-Residence Africana Studies Inst., NY Univ. 1996; mem. Bd of Dirs Nat. Book Awards, Poetry Soc. of America; past Pres. MWA. Publications include: Devil in a Blue Dress (Shamus Award) 1990, A Red

Death 1991, White Butterfly 1992, Black Betty 1994, RL's Dream 1995, A Little Yellow Dog 1996, Gone Fishin' 1997, Always Outnumbered, Always Outgunned 1997, Blue Light 1998, Walkin' the Dog 1999, Fearless Jones 2001, Futureland: Nine Stories of an Imminent Future 2001, Bad Boy Brawly Brown 2002, Fear Itself 2003, Six Easy Pieces (short stories) 2003, What Next: An African American Initiative Toward World Peace 2003, The Man in My Basement 2004, Little Scarlet 2004, Cinnamon Kiss 2005, 47 (for young adults) 2006, Fortunate Son 2006, Killing Johnny Fry 2007; contribs to New York Times, Library of Contemporary Thought, New Yorker, GQ, Esquire, USA Weekend, Los Angeles Times Magazine, Savoy. Honours: American Library Asscn Literary Award 1996, O. Henry Award 1996, Anisfield Wolf Award 1996, TransAfrica Int. Literary Prize 1998. Address: W. W. Norton, 500 Fifth Avenue, Floor 6, New York, NY 10110, USA (office). Website: www.waltermosley.com.

MOSS, Norman Bernard; British writer and journalist; b. 30 Sept. 1928, London; m. Hilary Sesta 1963; two s. Education: Hamilton Coll., New York. Career: Staff Journalist with newspapers, news agencies and radio networks; mem. Int. Inst. of Strategic Studies, Soc. of Authors, Royal Inst. of Int. Affairs. Publications: Men Who Play God – The Story of the Hydrogen Bomb, 1968; A British-American Dictionary, 1972; The Pleasures of Deception, 1976; The Politics of Uranium, 1982; Klaus Fuchs: The Man Who Stole the Atom Bomb, 1987; Managing the Planet, 2000; 19 Weeks: America, Britain and the Fateful Summer of 1940, 2003. Honours: Magazine Writer of the Year, Periodical Publishers Asscn 1982. Address: 21 Rylett Crescent, London, W12 9RP, England. E-mail: normanmoss@aol.com (office).

MOSSE, Kate, BA, MA, FRSA; British writer and broadcaster; Co-founder, Orange Prize for Fiction; b. 20 Oct. 1961, Chichester; m. Greg Mosse; two c. Education: Chichester High School for Girls, New Coll., Oxford. Career: fmr publisher, Random House; Deputy Dir, Chichester Festival Theatre, W Sussex 1998–2001; co-founder and Hon. Dir, Orange Prize for Fiction 1996–; Chair., Orange Futures initiative; creator and writer-in-residence of creative writing and reading website, www.labyrinth.co.uk; Co-Dir, Mosse Associates, provider of creative writing workshops; judge of numerous literary competitions and awards; Trustee, Arts & Business; mem. Inst. of Dirs, South West Sussex Arts Group, Arts Council of England South East (council mem.). Radio: The Business of the Arts (series, BBC Radio 4), guest presenter Saturday Review (BBC Radio 4). Television: presenter Readers and Writers Roadshow (BBC4). Publications: fiction: Eskimo Kissing 1996, Crucifix Lane 1998, Labyrinth (British Book Awards Richard and Judy Best Read of the Year 2006) 2005; non-fiction: Becoming a Mother 1993, The House: Behind the Scenes at the Royal Opera House, Covent Garden 1995; contrib. short stories and articles to magazines and newspapers. Honours: European Woman of Achievement for contribution to the arts 2000. Address: c/o Arts & Business, Nutmeg House, 60 Gainsford Street, Butler's Wharf, London, SE1 2NY, England. Website: www.mosselabyrinth.co.uk; www.orangeprize.co.uk.

MOSTEGHANEMI, Ahlam, BA, PhD; Algerian poet and novelist; b. 13 April 1953, Algiers; d. of Mohammed Chérif. Education: Univ. of Algiers, Sorbonne Univ., Paris, France. Career: worked for Centre Arabe de Documentation et d'Information, Paris, France; broadcast daily programme on poetry on Algerian radio; wrote for the Ech-Chaâb newspaper. Publications: Aâla marfaâ el-ayam (poems, trans. as Au hâvre des jours) 1973, Kitaba fi lahdat ouâr (poems, trans. as L'Écriture dans un moment de nudité) 1976, Femmes et écritures (essays) 1985, Zakirat al-jassed (novel, trans. as Memory in the Flesh) (Naguib Mahfouz Medal for Literature) 1985, Faoud al-hawess (novel, trans. as Chaos of the Senses) 1997, Akhadib samaka (poems, trans. as Mensonges d'un poisson) 1993, Aber Sereer (novel) 2003. Address: POB 113, 5734 Beruit, Lebanon. E-mail: ahlem2@mosteghanemi.com.

MOTION, Andrew Peter, MLitt, FRSA; British biographer and poet; Poet Laureate; b. 26 Oct. 1952, London, England; s. of Andrew R. Motion and Catherine G. Motion; m. 1st Joanna J. Powell 1973 (divorced 1983); m. 2nd Janet Elisabeth Dalley 1985; two s. one d. Education: Radley Coll. and Univ. Coll., Oxford. Career: Lecturer in English, Univ. of Hull 1977–81; Ed. Poetry Review 1981–83; Poetry Ed. Chatto & Windus 1983–89, Editorial Dir 1985–87; Prof. of Creative Writing Univ. of E Anglia, Norwich 1995–2003; Chair. Literature Advisory Panel Arts Council of England 1996–98; Poet Laureate 1999–; Chair of Creative Writing, Royal Holloway Coll., University Coll. London 2003–; mem. Poetry Soc. (vice-pres.). Publications: poetry collections: The Pleasure Steamers 1978, Independence 1981, The Penguin Book of Contemporary British Poetry (ed., anthology) 1982, Secret Narratives 1983, Dangerous Play (Rhys Memorial Prize) 1984, Natural Causes 1987, Love in a Life 1991, The Price of Everything 1994, Salt Water 1997, Selected Poems 1996–97 1998, Public Property 2001, Here to Eternity: An Anthology of Poetry (ed.) 2001; poems as Poet Laureate: Remember This: An Elegy on the Death of HM Queen Elizabeth The Queen Mother 2002, A Hymn for the Golden Jubilee 2002, On the Record (for Prince William's 21st birthday) 2003, Spring Wedding (for the wedding of Prince Charles and Camilla Parker Bowles) 2005, The Golden Rule (anthem for 80th birthday of HM Queen Elizabeth II, with music by Sir Peter Maxwell-Davies) 2006; non-fiction: The Poetry of Edward Thomas 1981, Philip Larkin 1982, The Lamberts (Somerset Maugham Award 1987) 1986, Philip Larkin: A Writer's Life 1993, William Barnes Selected Poems (ed.) 1994, Keats 1997, Wainewright the Poisoner 2000, In the Blood: A Memoir of my Childhood 2006; fiction: The Pale Companion 1989, Famous for the Creatures 1991, The Invention of Dr Cake 2003; other: additional texts for a performance of Haydn's Seven Last Words of

Our Saviour on the Cross 2003. *Honours:* Hon. DLitt (Hull) 1996, (Exeter) 1999, (Brunel) 2000, (A.P.U.) 2001, (Open Univ.) 2002; Arvon/Observer Prize 1982, Dylan Thomas Award 1987, Whitbread Biography Award 1993. *Address:* c/o Faber & Faber, 3 Queen Square, London, WC1N 3AU, England.

MOTT, Michael Charles Alston, BA; British academic, writer and poet; *Professor Emeritus, Bowling Green State University;* b. 8 Dec. 1930, London; m. 1st Margaret Ann Watt 1961 (died 1990); two d.; m. 2nd Emma Lou Powers 1992. *Education:* Central School of Arts and Crafts, London, Law Soc., London, Univ. of London, Courtauld Inst. and Warburg Inst., London. *Career:* Ed., Air Freight 1954–59, Thames and Hudson Publrs 1961–64; Asst Ed. Adam International Review 1956–66, The Geographical Magazine 1964–66; Poetry Ed., The Kenyon Review 1966–70; Visiting Prof. and Writer-in-Residence, Kenyon Coll. 1966–70, SUNY at Buffalo 1968, Concordia Univ., Montréal, QC, Canada 1970, 1974, Emory Univ. 1970–77, Coll. of William and Mary 1978–79, 1985–86; Prof. of English, Bowling Green State Univ. 1980–92, Prof. Emer. 1992–; mem. Amnesty Int., British Lichen Soc., RGS. *Publications:* fiction: The Notebooks of Susan Berry 1962, Master Entrick 1964, Helmet and Wasps 1964, The Blind Cross 1968; poetry: Absence of Unicorns, Presence of Lions 1977, Counting the Grasses 1980, Corday 1986, Piero di Cosimo: The World of Infinite Possibility 1990, Taino 1992, Woman and the Sea: Selected Poems 1999; The World of Richard Dadd, 2005; non-fiction: The Seven Mountains of Thomas Merton 1984; contrib. to journals and newspapers. *Honours:* Hon. DLitt (St Mary's Coll., Notre Dame) 1983; Governor's Award in Fine Arts, State of Georgia 1974, Guggenheim Fellowship 1979–80, Christopher Award 1984, Ohioana Book Award 1985, Olscamp Research Award 1985, Nancy Dasher Book Award 1985, Fortsam Award 1999, Allen Tate Award in Poetry 2002, Robert E. Lee and Ruth I. Wilson Poetry Book Award 2004. *Address:* 122 The Colony, Williamsburg, VA 23185, USA (office). *Telephone:* (757) 220-1042 (office).

MOTTA, Federico; Italian publisher; *Managing Director, Federico Motta Editore;* b. Milan. *Career:* Man. Dir Federico Motta Editore; Pres. Associazione Italiana Editori. *Honours:* Officier, Ordre des Arts et des Lettres 2003. *Address:* Gruppo Editoriale Motta, Via Branda Castiglioni 7, 20156 Milan, Italy. *E-mail:* info@mottaeditore.it. *Website:* www.mottaeditore.it.

MOUGEOTTE, Etienne Pierre Albert; French journalist; b. 1 March 1940, La Rochefoucauld; s. of Jean Mougeotte and Marcelle Thonon; m. Françoise Duprilot 1972; one s. two d. *Education:* Lycée Buffon, Lycée Henri-IV, Paris, Inst. d'études politiques de Paris, Inst. Français de presse. *Career:* reporter, France-Inter 1965-66, Beirut Corresp. 1966–67; Ed. Europe Numéro 1 1968–69; Chief Reporter, Asst Ed.-in-Chief Information Première (TV) 1969–72; Producer l'Actualité en question 1972; journalist Radio-Télé Luxembourg 1972–73; Ed.-in-Chief Europe 1 1973, News Dir 1974–81; monthly contrib. Paradoxes 1974–; Editorial Dir Journal du Dimanche 1981–83, Télé 7 Jours 1983–87; Dir Gen. Broadcasting TF1 1987–89, Dir Gen. 1987–89, Vice-Pres. Broadcasting 1989–; Vice-Pres. French Fed. of Press Agencies 1975–81; mem. Interprofessional communication group (Gic) 1985–87; Pres. Nat. Videocommunication Syndicate 1982–87, TF1 Films, Tricom; Dir TF1 1991–; Pres. TF1 Films Productions; Dir TFI Films 1991–, Pres. TFI Films and TFI Digital 2000–. *Honours:* Officier Légion d'honneur; Ordre nat. du Mérite. *Address:* TF1, 1 quai du Point-du-Jour, 92656 Boulogne-Billancourt Cedex, France.

MOUNT, (William Robert) Ferdinand, BA, FRSL; British writer and journalist; b. 2 July 1939, London; s. of the late Robert Mount and Julia Mount; m. Julia Margaret Lucas 1968; two s. (one deceased), one d. *Education:* Eton Coll., Christ Church, Oxford. *Career:* Political Ed. The Spectator 1977–82, 1985, Literary Ed. 1984–85; Head Prime Minister's Policy Unit 1982–84; Dir, Centre for Policy Studies 1984–91; Political Columnist The Standard 1980–82, The Times 1984–85, Daily Telegraph 1985–90; Ed. Times Literary Supplement 1991–2002; Sr Columnist The Sunday Times 2002–04; Vice-Chair. Power Comm. 2004–05; mem. RSL (mem. of Council 2002–05). *Publications:* Very Like a Whale 1967, The Theatre of Politics 1972, The Man Who Rode Ampersand 1975, The Clique 1978, The Subversive Family 1982, The Selkirk Strip 1987, Of Love and Asthma 1991 (Hawthornden Prize 1992), The British Constitution Now 1992, Communism 1992, Umbrella 1994, The Liquidator 1995, Jem (and Sam) 1998, Fairness 2001, Mind the Gap: The New Class Divide in Britain 2004, Heads You Win 2004, The Condor's Head 2007. *Honours:* Hon. Fellow (Univ. of Wales, Lampeter) 2002. *Address:* 17 Ripplevale Grove, London, N1 1HS, England. *Telephone:* (20) 7607-5398.

MOWAT, Farley McGill, OC, BA; Canadian writer; b. 12 May 1921, Belleville, Ont.; s. of Angus Mowat and Helen Mowat (née Thomson); m. 1st Frances Mowat 1947; two s.; m. 2nd Claire Mowat 1963. *Education:* Toronto Univ. *Career:* served in the Canadian Army 1939–45; Arctic exploration 1947–49; full-time writer 1950–. *Publications:* People of The Deer 1952, The Regiment 1955, Lost in The Barrens 1956, The Dog Who Wouldn't Be 1957, Coppermine Journey 1958, The Grey Seas Under 1958, The Desperate People 1959, Ordeal by Ice 1960, Owls in the Family 1961, The Serpent's Coil 1961, The Black Joke 1962, Never Cry Wolf 1963, Westviking 1965, The Curse of the Viking Grave 1966, Canada North 1967, The Polar Passion 1967, This Rock Within the Sea 1968, The Boat Who Wouldn't Float 1969, Sibir 1970, A Whale for the Killing 1972, Tundra 1973, Wake of the Great Sealers (with David Blackwood) 1973, The Snow Walker 1975, Canada North Now 1976, And No Birds Sang 1979, The World of Farley Mowat 1980, Sea of Slaughter 1984, My Discovery of America 1985, Virunga (Woman in the Mist, USA) 1987, The New Founde

Land 1989, Rescue the Earth 1990, My Father's Son 1992, Born Naked 1993, Aftermath 1995, A Farley Mowat Reader 1997; TV documentary: Sea of Slaughter 1990, The Farfarers 1998, Walking on the Land 2000. *Honours:* Hon. DLitt (Laurentian Univ.) 1970, (Univ. of Victoria) 1982, (Lakehead Univ.) 1986, (Univ. Coll. of Cape Breton) 1996; Hon. DLaws (Lethbridge, Toronto, Prince Edward Island, Queen's Univ.); Hon. DH (McMaster Univ., Hamilton) 1994; Hon. LLD (Queen's Univ.) 1995; Fourth Nat. Prize for Foreign Literature Books, Beiyue Literature and Art Publishing House, People's Repub. of China 1999; Gov.-Gen.'s Award, Canadian Centennial Medal, Leacock Medal for Humour, Hans Christian Andersen Award, Anisfield Wolf Award, Mark Twain Award, Gemini Award (Best Documentary Script), Award of Excellence (Atlantic Film Festival) 1990, Canadian Achievers Award, Take Back the Nation Award, Council of Canadians 1991, Author's Award, Author of the Year, Foundation for Advancement of Canadian Letters 1993. *Address:* c/o Writers Union of Canada, 24 Ryerson Avenue, Toronto, Ont., M4T 2P3 (office); 18 King Street, Port Hope, Ont., L1A 2R4, Canada.

MOYERS, William (Bill) D., FAAS; American journalist and broadcaster; *Executive Editor, Public Affairs Television, Inc.;* b. 5 June 1934, Hugo, Okla; s. of Henry Moyers and Ruby Johnson; m. Judith Davidson 1954; two s. one d. *Education:* Univ. of Texas, Edinburgh Univ. and Southwestern Baptist Theological Seminary. *Career:* Exec. Asst to Senator Lyndon Johnson 1959–60; Assoc. Dir US Peace Corps 1961–63, Deputy Dir 1963; Special Asst to Pres. Johnson 1963–66, Press Sec. to Pres. 1965–66; Publr of Newsday, Long Island, NY 1966–70; host of This Week, weekly current affairs TV programme 1970; Ed.-in-Chief Bill Moyers Journal, Public Broadcasting Service 1971–76, 1978–81; Contrib. Newsweek 1974–76; Chief Corresp. CBS Reports 1976–78, Sr News Analyst, CBS News 1981–86; Exec. Ed. Public Affairs TV Inc. 1987–; news analyst, NBC News 1995–; Pres. Florence and John Schumann Foundation 1991–; mem. American Philosophical Soc. *Publications:* Listening to America 1971, The Secret Government 1988, Joseph Campbell and the Power of Myth 1988, A World of Ideas 1989, Healing and the Mind 1993, Genesis: A Living Conversion 1996, Fooling with Words 1999. *Honours:* Emmy Awards 1983–90, Gold Baton Award 1991, 1999, American Jewish Cttee Religious Liberty Award 1995, Walter Cronkite Award 1995, Fred Friendly First Amendment Award 1995, Charles Frankel Prize 1997, George Peabody Award 2000. *Address:* Public Affairs Television Inc., 450 West 33rd Street, New York, NY 10001, USA.

MOYES, Jojo; British writer and journalist; b. 1969, London; m.; two c. *Career:* fmr arts and media correspondent, The Independent newspaper; contrib. to Woman's Hour (BBC Radio 4). *Publications:* Sheltering Rain 2002, Foreign Fruit (aka Windfallen) (RNA Novel of the Year 2004) 2003, The Peacock Emporium 2004, Silver Bay 2007. *Literary Agent:* Sheila Crowley, AP Watt Ltd, 20 John Street, London, WC1N 2DR, England. *Telephone:* (20) 7405-6774. *Fax:* (20) 7831-2154. *E-mail:* apw@apwatt.co.uk. *Website:* www .apwatt.co.uk.

MPHAHLELE, Ezekiel (Es'kia), MA, PhD, DLitt; South African writer; *Professor Emeritus of African Literature, University of Witwatersrand;* b. 17 Dec. 1919, Marabastad; s. of Moses Mphahlele and Eva Mphahlele; m. Rebecca Nnana Mphahlele 1945; four s. one d. *Education:* Univ. of South Africa, Pretoria. *Career:* teacher of English and Afrikaans, Orlando High School, Johannesburg 1942–52; Fiction Ed. Drum magazine 1955–57; Lecturer in English Literature, Dept of Extra-Mural Studies, Univ. Coll., Ibadan, Nigeria 1957–61; Dir African Programme, Int. Asscn for Cultural Freedom, Paris 1961–63; Dir Chem-chemi Creative Centre, Nairobi, Kenya 1963–65; Lecturer, Univ. Coll., Nairobi 1965–66, Univ. of Denver 1966–74, Univ. of Pennsylvania 1974–77; circuit schools inspector Lebowa 1978; Educ. Adviser and Chair. of Bd Funda Centre, Soweto 1986–; Researcher African Studies Inst., Univ. of Witwatersrand 1979, Prof. of African Literature 1979–88, Head of African Literature 1983–88, Prof. Emer. 1988–; fmr Dir Council for Black Educ. *Publications:* Man Must Live and Other Stories 1947, Down Second Avenue (autobiog.) 1959, The Living Dead and Other Stories 1961, The African Image (essays) 1962, Modern African Stories (ed. with E. Komey) 1964, African Writing Today (ed.) 1967, In Corner B and Other Stories 1967, The Wanderers (novel) 1971, Voices in the Whirlwind and other essays 1972, Chirundu (novel) 1979, The Unbroken Song 1981, Bury Me at the Marketplace 1984, Father Come Home (novel) 1984, Afrika My Music: An Autobiography 1957–1983 1984, Let's Talk Writing, Prose (creative writing guide), Let's Talk Writing, Poetry (creative writing guide), The Story of African Literature 1986, Renewal Time 1989, Telling Tales (contrib. to charity anthology) 2004. *Honours:* numerous hon. degrees. *Address:* c/o African Studies Institute, University of the Witwatersrand, Johannesburg 2001, South Africa (office); 5444, Zone 5, Pimville, Johannesburg, South Africa (home). *Telephone:* (11) 9332273 (home).

MTSHALI, Oswald (Joseph) Mbuyiseni; South African poet and journalist; b. 1940, KwaBhanya, N Natal. *Education:* Columbia Univ., USA. *Career:* travelled to Johannesburg aged 18 to enrol at the Univ. of Witwatersrand, but was refused because of separate univs legislation; worked as messenger in Soweto; studied in USA, returning to S Africa 1980; fmr Vice-Principal, Pace Coll., Soweto; . fmr Adjunct Prof., New York City Coll. of Tech., teaching African folklore and modern African history. *Publications:* Sounds of a Cowhide Drum (poems) 1971, Poems: The Soweto I Love 1977, Fireflames (poems) 1980; contrib. to journals, newspapers and anthologies, including The

Classic, New Coin, The Purple Renoster, Ophir. *Honours:* Poetry Int. Award, London 1973, Olive Schreiner Prize for Literature 1975.

MU XIN; Chinese writer, poet and painter; b. (Sun Pu), 1927, Wuzhen, Zhejiang Prov. *Education:* Shanghai Fine Arts Inst. *Career:* imprisoned three times during Cultural Revolution; many manuscripts and paintings destroyed by authorities; moved to USA 1982. *Exhibitions:* The Art of Mu Xin: Landscape Paintings and Prison Notes (toured galleries including Smart Museum of Art, Chicago 2002, Asia Soc., New York 2003, Yale Univ. Art Gallery, Harvard Univ. Art Gallery), other exhbns at World Econ. Forum, China Business Summit 2004. *Publications:* Sanwen Yiji 1983, Qionmeika Suixianglu 1986, Wensha Muyuan (short stories) 1988, Xibanya Sankeshu (poems) 1988, Jixing Panduan (essays) 1988, Suli Zhi Wang (prose poems) 1994, Balong (poems) 1998, Wo fenfen de qingyu (poems) 1998, Hui wu zhong (poems) 1998, Malage Jihua (essays) 1999, Tongqing zhongduanlu (short stories) 1999. *Address:* c/o Elizabeth Wang Gallery, 800 Fifth Avenue at 61st Street, New York, NY 10021-7216, USA (office). *E-mail:* ewanggallery@aol.com (office). *Website:* www.elizabethwanggallery.com (office).

MUAMBA, Muepu; Democratic Republic of the Congo journalist, writer and poet; b. 23 Nov. 1946, Tshilundu. *Education:* Institut St Ferdinand, Jernappes, Belgium. *Career:* mem. Maison Africaine de la Poesie Internationale, Dakar; Royal African Society, London; Société Française des Gens de Lettres, Paris; Union Internale des Journalistes et de la Presse de la Langue Française, Paris. *Publications:* Afrika in eigener Sache (essays with Jochen Klicker and Klaus Paysan), 1980; Devoir d'ingerence, 1988; Moi Qui T'Amour, 1997; Ma Terre d'O, 1999. Contributions: various anthologies and periodicals.

MUBARAK, Rabia'; Moroccan writer; *Professor, Université Mohammed V Souissi;* b. 1940. *Career:* currently Prof., Université Mohammed V Souissi, Rabat. *Publications include:* Attayyibun (The Good Ones) 1972, Dar wa Dukhkhan (A House and Smoke) 1975, Rufqata Assilah'i wa Lqamar (In the Company of Weapons and the Moon) 1976, Arrih' Ashshatwiyya (The Winter Rain) 1977, Rih'alat Al-H'asad wa Al-H'ubb (Voyage of Harvest and Love) 1983, Badru Zamanihi (Full Moon of his Time) 1984, Burju Assua'ud (Tower of Fortunes) 1990; other: short stories, plays, novels, children's books, psychological studies on childhood. *Address:* c/o Université Mohammed V Souissi, BP 8007, N. U. Agdal, Rabat, Morocco.

MUDIMBE, Valentin Yves, DèsL; Democratic Republic of the Congo academic and writer; *Newman Ivey White Professor of Literature, Duke University.* *Education:* Univ. of Louvain, Univ. of Paris–VII, France. *Career:* fmr Lecturer, Univs of Louvain, Paris-Nanterre, Zaïre and Haverford Coll.; specialist in phenomenology and structuralism; Prof., Literature Program, Stanford Univ. 1994–2000; currently Newman Ivey White Prof. of Literature, Duke Univ., NC, USA; Gen.-Sec. Soc. for African Philosophy in N America (SAPINA); Chair. Bd African Philosophy, Univ. of London, Int. Africa Inst., SOAS; discussant, The Crossing Conf., Inst. St Eugène de Mazenod, Kinshasa 2002. *Publications include:* L'odeur du père 1982, The Invention of Africa 1988, Parables and Fables 1991, The Idea of Africa 1994, Tales of Faith 1997; Ed.: The Surreptitious Speech 1992, The American Society of French Philosophy, Nations, Identities, Cultures 1997, Diaspora and Immigration 1999; Co-Ed.: Africa and the Disciplines 1993, Le corps glorieux des mots et des êtres 1994; seventy articles; three collections of poetry. *Address:* Duke University, Literature Program, 115 Art Museum, Box 90670, Durham, NC 27708, USA (office). *Telephone:* (919) 684-4240 (office). *E-mail:* vmudimbe@duke.edu (office). *Website:* fds.duke.edu/db/aas/Literature/faculty/vmudimbe (office).

MUEHL, Lois Baker, BA, MA; American academic (retd), writer and poet; b. 29 April 1920, Oak Park, IL; m. Siegmar Muehl 1944; two s. two d. *Education:* Oberlin Coll., Univ. of Iowa. *Career:* fmr Assoc. Prof. of Rhetoric; mem. Iowa Poetry Asscn, Univ. Women's Writers Group. *Publications:* My Name is… 1959, Worst Room in the School 1961, The Hidden Year of Devlin Bates 1967, Winter Holiday Brainteasers 1979, A Reading Approach to Rhetoric 1983, Trading Cultures in the Classroom (with Siegmar Muehl) 1993, Talkable Tales 1993; poems; contrib. to scholarly journals and general magazines. *Honours:* Old Gold Creative Fellowship 1970, Community Service Commendation, Merced, California 1984, grand prize Poetry Guild Contest 1997, Lyrical Iowa Poetry Prize for humour 2005. *Address:* 701 Oaknoll Drive, Iowa City, IA 52246, USA.

MUELLER, Lisel, BA; American poet, writer and translator; b. 8 Feb. 1924, Hamburg, Germany; m. Paul E. Mueller 1943; two d. *Education:* Univ. of Evansville, Indiana Univ. *Career:* instructor in poetry, Elmhurst Coll. 1969–72; associated with poets in the schools programme 1972–77; Visiting Prof., Goddard Coll. and Warren Wilson Coll. 1977–86. *Publications:* poetry: Dependencies 1965, Life of a Queen 1970, The Private Life 1976, Voices from the Forest 1977, The Need to Hold Still 1980, Second Language 1986, Waving from Shore 1989, Learning to Play by Ear (essays and poetry) 1990, Alive Together 1996; contrib. to anthologies and journals. *Honours:* Dr hc (Lake Forest Coll.) 1985; Friends of Literature Robert M. Ferguson Memorial Award 1966, Helen Bullis Awards 1974, 1977, Lamont Poetry Selection 1975, Emily Clark Balch Award 1976, Nat. Book Award 1981, Nat. Endowment for the Arts Fellowship 1990, Carl Sandburg Award 1990, Pulitzer Prize for Poetry 1997, Ruth Lilly Poetry Prize 2002. *Address:* c/o Louisiana State University Press, PO Box 25053, Baton Rouge, LA 70894-5053, USA.

MUGGESON, Margaret Elizabeth, (Margaret Dickinson, Everatt Jackson); British writer; b. 30 April 1942, Gainsborough, Lincolnshire, England; m. Dennis Muggeson 1964, two d. *Education:* Lincoln College of Technology. *Career:* mem. Romantic Novelists Asscn. *Publications:* Pride of the Courtneys 1968, Brackenbeck 1969, Portrait of Jonathan 1970, The Road to Hell (as Everatt Jackson) 1975, Abbeyford Trilogy 1981, Lifeboat! 1983, Beloved Enemy 1984, Plough the Furrow 1994, Sow the Seed 1995, Reap the Harvest 1996, The Miller's Daughter 1997, Chaff Upon the Wind 1998, The Fisher Lass 1999, The Tulip Girl 2000, The River Folk 2001, Tangled Threads 2002, Twisted Strands 2003, Red Sky in the Morning 2004, Without Sun 2005, Wish Me Luck 2007. *Address:* 17 Seacroft Drive, Skegness, Lincolnshire PE25 3AP, England.

MÜHRINGER, Doris Agathe Annemarie; Austrian poet and writer; b. 18 Sept. 1920, Graz. *Career:* mem. Asscn of Austrian Writers; Kogge; PEN; Poium. *Publications:* Gedichte I, 1957, II, 1969, III, 1976, IV, 1984; Tag, mein Jahr (with H. Valencak), 1983; Das hatten die Ratten vom Schatten: Ein Lachbuch, 1989; Reisen wir (poems), 1995; Aber ietzt zögerst etu Späte Gedichte, 1999. Contributions: numerous literary magazines, domestic and foreign. *Honours:* Georg Trakl Prize, 1954; Award of Achievement, Vienna, 1961; Lyric Prize of Steiermark, 1973; Austrian State Scholarship, 1976; Award of Achievement, Board of Austrian Litera-Mechana, 1984; Grosser Literturpreis des Landes Steiermark, 1985.

MUIR, Richard, MA, PhD; British writer, photographer, lecturer, editor and researcher; b. 18 June 1943, Yorkshire; m.; one s. *Education:* Univ. of Aberdeen. *Career:* Ed. Nat. Trust Regional Histories and Countryside Comm. Nat. Park Series; founder LANDSCAPES Journal 2000; Hon. Research Fellow in Geography and Environment, Univ. of Aberdeen; self-employed landscape historian and archaeologist. *Publications include:* Modern Political Geography 1975, Hedgerows: Their History and Wildlife (with N. Muir) 1987, Old Yorkshire 1987, The Countryside Encyclopaedia 1988, Fields (with Nina Muir) 1989, Portraits of the Past 1989, The Dales of Yorkshire 1991, The Villages of England 1992, The Coastlines of Britain 1993, Political Geography: A New Introduction 1997, The Yorkshire Countryside: A Landscape History 1997, Approaches to Landscape 1999, The New Reading the Landscape 2000, Landscape Detective 2001, Landscape Encyclopaedia 2004, Ancient Trees, Living Landscapes 2005, Valley of Ghosts 2006; contrib. to academic journals and general periodicals. *Honours:* Yorkshire Arts Literary Prize 1982–83, hon. life mem. Yorkshire Dales Soc. 2004–. *Address:* 20 Stray Walk, Harrogate, Yorkshire HG2 8HU, England. *Telephone:* (1423) 529343 (home). *E-mail:* richard.muir1@btinternet.com. *Website:* www.richardmuir.net.

MUJAHID, Jamila; Afghan journalist and broadcaster; *President, Afghanistan Women in Media Network;* b. Kabul; m. Sayed Amin; five c. *Education:* in Afghanistan. *Career:* broadcaster with Radio-Television Afghanistan from 1980, evening news broadcaster on TV and radio 1985–96; worked for NGOs during Taleban regime; first female broadcaster to appear on Radio-Television Afghanistan announcing the departure of the Taleban 2001; Pres., Afghanistan Women in Media Network, Kabul 2002–, publishing monthly magazine, Hefat and running 'The Voice of Afghan Women' radio station (Dir of radio station 2003, relaunched 2005–); Ed., Malalai women's magazine 2003–. *Address:* Afghanistan Women in Media Network, Afghan Media and Culture Centre, Behind Ministry of Planning, Malik Ashgar Crossroads, Kabul, Kabul Province, Afghanistan.

MUJICA, Barbara, AB, MA, PhD; American academic and writer; *Professor of Spanish, Georgetown University;* b. 25 Dec. 1943, Los Angeles, Calif.; m. Mauro E. Mujica 1966; one s. two d. *Education:* Univ. of California at Los Angeles, Middlebury Grad. School, Paris, New York Univ. *Career:* Teacher of French, UCLA Extension Div. 1963–64; Assoc. Ed. of Modern Languages, Harcourt Brace Jovanovich, New York City 1966–73; Instructor, Baruch College, CUNY 1973–74; Asst Prof. of Romance Languages 1974; Asst Prof., Georgetown Univ. 1974–79, Assoc. Prof. 1979–91, Prof. of Spanish 1991–; Ed. Comedia Performance; mem. American Asscn of Teachers of Spanish and Portuguese, American Asscn of Univ. Profs, American Council on the Teaching of Foreign Languages, Asscn for Hispanic Classical Theater (Pres.), Feministas Unidas, Modern Language Asscn, Washington Ind. Writers, Writer's Center, S Atlantic Modern Language Asscn, Golden Age Division (Sec. 1999, Pres. 2000), PEN International, Nat. Writers Union, Asociación de Escritoras de España y las Américas. *Publications:* scholarly: Readings in Spanish Literature (co-ed. with Anthony Zahareas) 1975, Calderón's Characters: An Existential Point of View 1983, Expanding the Curriculum in Foreign Language Classes: Spanish and Contemporary Affairs (with William Cressey and Mark Goldin) 1983, Iberian Pastoral Characters 1986, Texto y espectáculo: Selected Proceedings of the Symposium on Spanish Golden Age Theater 1987, 1989, Texto y vida: Introducción a la literatura española 1990, Antología de literatura española, Vol. I, La Edad Media (with Amanda Curry) 1991, Vol. II, Renacimiento y Siglo de Oro 1991, Vol. III, Siglos XVIII y XIX (with Eva Florensa) 1999, Et in Arcadia Ego: Essays on Death in the Pastoral Novel (with Bruno Damiani) 1990, Texto y vida: Introducción a la literatura hispanoamericana 1992, Looking at the Comedia in the Year of the Quincentennial co-(ed. with Sharon Voros) 1993, Premio Nóbel: Once grandes escritores del mundo hispánico (ed.) 1997, Books of the Americas: Reviews and Interviews from Americas Magazine 1990–1991 1997, El texto puesto en escena (ed. with Anita Stoll) 2000, Hispanomundo 2001, Early Modern Spanish Women Writers 2004, Teresa de Jesús: Espiritualidad y feminismo 2006. Other: The Deaths of Don Bernardo (novel) 1990, Sanchez across the

Street (short stories) 1997, Far from My Mother's Home (short stories) 1999, Frida (novel) (Trailblazers Award, Dialogue on Diversity 2004) 2001, Affirmative Actions (novel) 2006 Sister Teresa 2007; contrib. to anthologies, scholarly publs and the popular press. *Honours:* Poets and Writers Recognition for Fiction, New York 1984, One of Best Fifty Op Ed Pieces of the Decade, New York Times 1990, Winner, E.L. Doctorow Int. Fiction Contest 1992, Pangolin Prize for Best Short Story of 1998, Theodore Christian Hoepfner Award for Short Fiction 2002. *Address:* Department of Spanish and Portuguese, Georgetown University, Box 571039, Washington, DC 20057, USA (office). *E-mail:* mujica@georgetown.edu (office). *Website:* www.barbaramujica.com.

MUKHERJEE, Bharati, BA, MA, PhD; American (b. Indian) academic and writer; *Professor, English Department, University of California, Berkeley*; b. 27 July 1940, Kolkata; s. of Sudhir Lal Mukherjee and Bina Banerjee; m. Clark Blaise 1963; two s. *Education:* Univs of Calcutta, Baroda and Iowa. *Career:* Prof. of English, McGill Univ.; lecturer, Skidmore Coll.; Lecturer in Literature and Creative Writing, Queen's Coll., New York; Prof. Univ. of Calif. at Berkeley 1990–. *Publications:* The Tiger's Daughter 1971, The Tiger's Daughter and Wife 1975, Days and Nights in Calcutta (with Clark Blaise) 1977, Darkness 1985, The Sorrow and the Terror (with Clark Blaise) 1987, The Middleman and Other Stories (Nat. Book Critics Circle Award for Fiction) 1988, Jasmine 1989, The Holder of the World 1993, Leave it to Me 1996, Desirable Daughters 2002, The Tree Bride 2004. *Address:* English Department, University of California, 334 Wheeler Hall, Berkeley, CA 94720 (office); 130 Rivoli Street, San Francisco, CA 94117, USA. *Telephone:* (510) 642-2765 (office); (415) 681-0345. *Fax:* (415) 759-9810. *E-mail:* mukhster@aol.com. *Website:* english.berkeley.edu (office).

MUKUNDAN, M.; Indian short story writer and novelist; b. 10 Sept. 1942, Mayyazhi, Mahe, Kerala. *Career:* Malayalam writer; Deputy Cultural Attaché, French Embassy in New Delhi, India. *Publications:* novels and collections of short stories incl.: Delhi (novel), 1969; Mayyazhi Puzhayude Theerangalil (On the Banks of the Mayyazhi); Daivathinte Vikrithikal (God's Mischief); Appam Chudunna Kunkiyamma; Lesli Achante Kadangal; Ee Lokam Athiloru Manushyan; Nrittam (Dance); Adithyanum Radhayum Mattu Chilarum; Oru Dalit Yuvathiyude Kadanakatha; Nirtham; Haridwaril Manikal Muzhangunnu (The Bells are Tolling in Haridwar); Kesavante Vilapanghal. Contributions: Mathrubhumi; various periodicals. *Honours:* NV Prize; Crossword Award; Kerala State Award; Kendra Sahitya Academi Awards, 1989, 1994; Chevalier, Ordre des Arts et des Lettres, 1998; Katha Award, 2003.

MULDOON, Paul Benedict, BA, FRSL; Irish poet and academic; *Howard G.B. Clark '21 University Professor in the Humanities and Professor of the Council of the Humanities and Creative Writing, Princeton University*; b. 20 June 1951, Portadown, NI; s. of Patrick Muldoon and Brigid Regan; m. Jean Hanff Korelitz 1987; one s. one d. *Education:* St Patrick's Coll., Armagh, Queen's Univ., Belfast. *Career:* radio and TV producer, BBC NI 1973–86; has taught at Univs of Cambridge, East Anglia, Columbia Univ., New York, Univ. of California, Berkeley, Univ. of Massachusetts 1986–; Lecturer, Princeton Univ., NJ 1987–88, 1990–95, Dir Creative Writing Program 1993, Prof. 1995–, Howard G.B. Clark Prof. in the Humanities and Prof. of Council of Humanities and Creative Writing 1998–; Visiting Prof., Univ. of Massachusetts 1989–90, Bread Loaf School of English 1997–; mem. Aosdána, Poetry Soc. of GB (Pres. 1996–), American Acad. of Arts and Sciences 2000. *Publications:* poetry: Knowing My Place 1971, New Weather 1973, Spirit of Dawn 1975, Mules 1977, Names and Addresses 1978, Immram 1980, Why Brownlee Left 1980, Out of Siberia 1982, Quoof 1983, The Wishbone 1984, Selected Poems 1968–83 1986, Meeting the British 1987, Madoc: A Mystery 1990, Incantata 1994, The Prince of the Quotidian 1994, The Annals of Chile (T.S. Eliot Prize) 1995; Kerry Slides 1996, New Selected Poems 1968–1994 1996, Hopewell Haiku 1997, The Bangle (Slight Return) 1998, Hay (poems) 1999, Poems 1968–1998 2001, Horse Latitudes 2006; for children: The O-O's Party 1981, The Last Thesaurus 1995, The Noctuary of Narcissus Batt 1997; other: Monkeys (TV play) 1989, Shining Brow (opera libretto) 1993, Six Honest Serving Men (play) 1995, Bandanna (opera libretto) 1999, To Ireland, I (essays) 2000; ed.: The Scrake of Dawn 1979, The Faber Book of Contemporary Irish Poetry 1986, The Essential Byron 1989, Moy Sand and Gravel (Pulitzer Prize for Poetry) 2002; trans.: The Astrakhan Cloak, by Nuala Ni Dhomhnaill 1993, The Birds, by Aristophanes (with Richard Martin) 1999. *Honours:* Hon. Prof. of Poetry, Univ. of Oxford 1999–2004; Eric Gregory Award 1972, Sir Geoffrey Faber Memorial Awards 1980, 1991, Guggenheim Fellowship 1990, American Acad. of Arts and Letters Award for Literature 1996, Irish Times Poetry Prize 1997, Pulitzer Prize for Poetry 2003, Griffin Prize 2003, Shakespeare Prize 2004. *Address:* Creative Writing Program, Room 122, 185 Nassau Street, Princeton University, Princeton, NJ 08544, USA (office). *Telephone:* (609) 258-4708 (office). *E-mail:* muldoon@princeton.edu (office). *Website:* www.princeton.edu/~visarts/Paul1 (office); www.paulmuldoon.net (home).

MULISCH, Harry; Dutch novelist, poet and dramatist; b. 29 July 1927, Haarlem. *Education:* Haarlem Lyceum. *Publications:* Archibald Strohalm (novel) 1952, Tussen hamer en aambeeld (novella) 1952, Chantage op het leven (short story) 1953, De Diamant (novel) 1954, De Sprong der Paarden en de Zoete Zee (novel) 1955, Het mirakel (short stories) 1955, Het Zwarte licht (novel) 1957, Manifesten (essays) 1958, Het Stenen Bruidsbed (novel) 1959, Tanchelijn (play) 1960, Voer voor Psychologen (autobiog.) 1961, Wenken voor de bescherming van uw gezin en uzelf, tijdens de Jongste Dag (essays) 1961, De Knop (play) 1961, De Zaak 40/61 (non-fiction) 1963, Bericht aan de Rattenkoning (essay) 1966, Wenken voor de Jongste Dag (essays) 1967, Het woord bij de daad (essays) 1968, Reconstructie (essays) 1969, De Verteller (novel) 1970, Paralipomena Orphica (essays) 1970, De Verteller verteld: Kommentaar, Katalogus, Kuriosa en een Katastrofestuk (essay) 1971, De Toekomst van gisteren (essay) 1972, Oidipous Oidipous (play) 1972, Woorden, woorden, woorden (poems) 1973, De Vogels (poems) 1974, Tegenlicht (poems) 1975, Twee Vrouwen (novel) 1975, Kind en Kraai (poems) 1975, Mijn Getijdenboek (autobiog.) 1975, Oude Lucht (short stories) 1977, De Aanslag (novel) 1982, Opus Gran (poems) 1982, De Kamer (short stories) 1984, Hoogste Tijd (novel) 1985, De Pupil (novel) 1987, De Elementen (novel) 1988, De Ontdekking van de Hemel (novel) 1992, De Procedure (novel) 1999, Het Theater, de brief en de waarheid (novel) 2000, Siegfried (novel) 2001. *Honours:* Knight, Order of Orange Nassau 1977. *Address:* Van Miereveldstraat 1, 1071 DW Amsterdam, Netherlands. *E-mail:* info@mulisch.nl. *Website:* www.mulisch.nl.

MULLER, Marcia, BA, MA; American writer and editor; b. 28 Sept. 1944, Detroit, MI; m. 1st Frederick T. Guilson Jr 1967 (divorced 1981); m. 2nd Bill Pronzini 1992. *Education:* Univ. of Michigan. *Publications:* Edwin of the Iron Shoes, 1977; Ask the Cards a Question, 1982; The Cheshire Cat's Eye, 1983; The Tree of Death, 1983; Games to Keep the Dark Away, 1984; Leave a Message for Willie, 1984; Double (with Bill Pronzini), 1984; The Legend of Slain Soldiers, 1985; There's Nothing to Be Afraid of, 1985; Beyond the Grave (with Bill Pronzini), 1986; The Cavalier in White, 1986; The Lighthouse (with Bill Pronzini), 1987; Eye of the Storm (with Bill Prozini), 1988; There Hangs the Knife, 1988; Dark Star, 1989; The Shape of Dread, 1989; There's Something in a Sunday, 1989; Trophies and Dead Things, 1990; Deceptions, 1991; Where Echoes Live, 1991; Pennies on a Dead Woman's Eyes, 1992; The Wall, 1993; Wolf in the Shadows, 1993; Till the Butchers Cut Him Down, 1994; A Wild and Lonely Place, 1995; The McCone Files: The Complete Sharon McCone Stories, 1995; The Broken Promise Land, 1996; Both Ends of the Night, 1997; While Other People Sleep, 1998; Duo (with Bill Pronzini), 1998; A Walk Through the Fire, 1999; Listen to the Silence, 2000; McCone and Friends, 2000; Point Deception, 2001; Dead Midnight, 2002. Editor: several anthologies. *Honours:* American Mystery Award, 1989; Shamus Award, 1991, Life Achievement Award, 1993, Private Eye Writers of America; Anthony Boucher Awards, 1994, 1996; Lifetime Achievement in Suspense Award, Romantic Times, 1999.

MULLIN, Christopher John, LLB; British politician and writer; b. 12 Dec. 1947, Chelmsford, Essex; m. Nguyen Thi Ngoc 1987; two d. *Education:* Univ. of Hull. *Career:* sub-ed., BBC World Service 1974–78; Ed. Tribune 1982–84; MP (Labour), Sunderland S 1987–; Chair. Home Affairs Select Cttee 1997–99, 2001–03; Under-Sec., Dept of the Environment 1999–2001, Dept of Int. Devt 2001, Foreign Office 2003–05. *Publications:* fiction: A Very British Coup 1982, The Last Man Out of Saigon 1986, The Year of the Fire Monkey 1991; non-fiction: Error of Judgement: The Truth About the Birmingham Bombings 1986, 1997. *Honours:* Hon. LLD (City of London). *Literary Agent:* PFD, Drury House, 34–43 Russell Street, London, WC2B 5HA, England. *Telephone:* (20) 7344-1000. *Fax:* (20) 7836-9539. *E-mail:* info@pfd.co.uk. *Website:* www.pfd.co.uk. *Address:* House of Commons, Westminster, London, SW1A 0AA, England (office). *Telephone:* (191) 567-2848 (office). *Fax:* (191) 510-1063 (office). *E-mail:* mullinc@parliament.uk (office). *Website:* www.chrismullinmp.co.uk (office).

MUNGOSHI, Charles Muzuva; Zimbabwean writer, poet and playwright; b. 2 Dec. 1947, Chivhu; m. Jesesi Jaboon 1976; four s. one d. *Education:* secondary school. *Career:* clerk in bookshop, Harare 1969–74; Ed. with the Literature Bureau 1974–81; Dir and Ed. publisher in Zimbabwe 1981–88; Writer-in-Residence, Univ. of Zimbabwe 1985–87; Visiting Arts Fellow, Univ. of Durham 1990; Writer-in-Residence Univ. of Florida, Gainesville (USA) 2000. *Film:* The Axe (writer and Dir) 1999. *Publications:* (novels) Makunun'unu Maodzamwoyo (in Shona) 1970, Waiting for the Rain 1975, Ndiko Kupindana Kwamazuva (in Shona) 1975, Kunyarara Hakusi Kutaura? (in Shona) 1983; (short stories) Coming of the Dry Season 1972, Some Kinds of Wounds 1980, Setting Sun and Rolling World 1987, One Day Long Ago: Tales from a Shona Childhood (folk tales) 1991, Walking Still 1997; (poetry) The Milkman Doesn't Only Deliver Milk 1981. *Honours:* Hon. DLitt (Zimbabwe) 2004; Noma Award for Publishing in Africa, Book Centre/PEN Award, Commonwealth Writers Award (Africa Region). *Address:* P.O. Box 1688, Harare (office); 47/6156 Uta Crescent, Zengeza 1, Chitungwiza, Zimbabwe. *E-mail:* muzuva47@yahoo.com.

MUNONYE, John Okechukwu, ON, CertEd; Nigerian novelist; b. 22 April 1929, Akokwa; m. Regina Nwokeji 1957, one s. one d. *Education:* University of London. *Career:* Chief Inspector of Education, East Central State, 1973–76, Imo State, 1976–77. *Publications:* The Only Son, 1966; Obi, 1969; Oil Man of Obange, 1971; A Wreath for Maidens, 1973; A Dancer of Fortune, 1974; Bridge to a Wedding, 1978. Short Stories: Silent Child, 1973; Pack Pack Pack, 1977; Man of Wealth, 1981; On a Sunday Morning, 1982; Rogues, 1985.

MUNRO, Alice, BA; Canadian writer; b. 10 July 1931, Wingham, Ont.; d. of Robert E. Laidlaw and Anne Chamney; m. 1st James A. Munro 1951 (divorced 1976); three d.; m. 2nd Gerald Fremlin 1976. *Education:* Univ. of Western Ont. *Publications:* Dance of the Happy Shades 1968 (Gov.-Gen.'s Award for Literature 1968), A Place for Everything 1970, Lives of Girls and Women 1971, Something I've Been Meaning to Tell You 1974, Who Do You Think You Are? (aka The Beggar Maid) 1978, The Moons of Jupiter 1982, The Progress of

Love 1986, Friend of My Youth 1990, Open Secrets 1994, Selected Stories 1996, The Love of A Good Woman 1998, Hateship, Friendship, Courtship, Loveship, Marriage 2001, Runaway (short stories) 2005, The View from Castle Rock 2006. *Honours:* Gov.-Gen.'s Award for Literature 1978, 1986, Canadian Booksellers' Award 1972, Marian Engel Award 1986, Canada-Australia Literary Prize 1994, Lannan Literary Award 1995, WH Smith Literary Award 1996, Fiction Prize, Nat. Book Critics Circle 1999, Giller Prize 1999, O. Henry Award 2001. *Address:* The Writers' Shop, 1325 Avenue of the Americas, Floor 16, New York, NY 10019, USA (office); PO Box 1133, Clinton, ON, N0M 1L0, Canada (home).

MUNRO, David Mackenzie, BSc, PhD, FRGS, FRSA; British geographer, editor and writer; *Director and Secretary, Royal Scottish Geographical Society*; b. 28 May 1950, Glasgow, Scotland. *Education:* Univ. of Edinburgh. *Career:* Research Assoc., then Research Fellow, Univ. of Edinburgh 1979–96; Dir and Sec., Royal Scottish Geographical Soc. 1996–; consultant, Times Atlas of the World 2000; Fellow Soc. of Antiquaries of Scotland; Trustee, South Georgia Heritage Trust; UK Rep., UN Group of Experts on Geographical Names; mem. Michael Bruce Trust (Chair.), Nat. Trust for Scotland (council mem.), Permanent Cttee on Geographical Names for British Official Use (Chair.). *Publications:* Chambers World Gazetteer (ed.) 1988, Ecology and Environment in Belize (ed.) 1989, A World Record of Major Conflict Areas (with Alan J. Day) 1990, The Hutchinson Guide to the World (assoc. ed.) 1990, Loch Leven and the River Leven: A Landscape Transformed 1994, The Oxford Dictionary of the World (ed.) 1995; contrib. to reference works and journals. *Honours:* Scotia Centenary Medal 2005. *Address:* c/o Royal Scottish Geographical Society, 40 George Street, Glasgow, G1 1QE, Scotland (office). *Telephone:* (141) 552-3330 (office). *Fax:* (141) 552-3331 (office). *E-mail:* rsgs@strath.ac.uk (office). *Website:* www.rsgs.org.uk (office).

MUNRO, J. Richard, BA; American publishing executive; b. 1931; m. *Education:* Colgate, Columbia and New York Univs. *Career:* joined Time Inc. 1957; Pres. Pioneer Press Inc. (Time subsidiary) 1969; Publr Sports Illustrated 1969–71; Vice-Pres. Time Inc. 1971–75, Group Vice-Pres. for Video 1975–79, Exec. Vice-Pres. 1979–80, Pres. 1980–86, CEO 1980–90, Chair. 1986–90, Chair. Exec. Comm. 1990–96, also Dir; Chair. Genentech Inc. 1997; mem. Bd of Chancellors Juvenile Diabetes Research Foundation Int. (JDRF); fmr Dir IBM Corpn; Trustee RAND Corpn 1984-1994. *Honours:* Hon. LittD (Richmond Univ.) 1983; Purple Heart with two Clusters. *Address:* c/o Board of Chancellors, Juvenile Diabetes Research Foundation International, 120 Wall Street, New York, NY 10005-4001, USA.

MUNRO, John Murchison, BA, PhD; American university administrator and writer; b. 29 Aug. 1932, Wallasey, Cheshire, England; m. Hertha Ingrid Bertha Lipp 1956, two s. two d. *Education:* University of Durham, Washington University, St Louis. *Career:* part-time Instructor of English, Washington University, St Louis, 1956–60; Instructor, University of North Carolina, 1960–63; Asst Prof., University of Toronto, Canada, 1963–65; Prof., American University of Beirut, Lebanon, 1965–87; Dir, Outreach Services, Prof. of Mass Communications, 1987–, Assoc. Dean for External Affairs, 1990–97, American University, Cairo, Egypt; Contributing Ed., Cairo Times, 1997–; Media Consultant, NSCE, Cairo, 1998–. *Publications:* English Poetry in Transition, 1968; Arthur Symons, 1969; The Decadent Poets of the 1890s, 1970; Selected Poems of Theo Marzials, 1974; James Elroy Flecker, 1976; A Mutual Concern: The Story of the American University of Beirut, 1977; Cyprus: Between Venus and Mars (with Z. Khuri), 1984; Selected Letters of Arthur Symons (with Karl Beckson), 1988; Theatre of the Absurd: Lebanon, 1982–88, 1989. Contributions: scholarly journals and general periodicals. *Honours:* Fulbright Research Award, University of California, Los Angeles, 1987.

MUNRO, Rona, MA; British playwright; b. 7 Sept. 1959, Aberdeen, Scotland. *Education:* Univ. of Edinburgh. *Career:* Literary Assoc., Hampstead Theatre, London 1996. *Plays:* Stick Granny on the Roofrack, The Band and the Whimper (Stage Traffic Theatre Co.) 1982, The Salesman (Stage Traffic Theatre) 1982, Fugue (Traverse Theatre, Edinburgh) 1983, Touchwood (Guizer Theatre) 1984, The Bus (Scottish Youth Theatre) 1984, Ghost Story (Thron Theatre, Glasgow) 1985, Watching Waiters (Offstage Theatre) 1985, Piper's Cave (Soho Poly Theatre, London) 1985, Dust and Dreams 1986, The Biggest Party in the World 1986, The Way to Go Home (The Upstairs, London) 1987, Winners 1987, Off the Road 1988, Saturday at the Commodore (Sabhal Mor Ostaig, Isle of Skye) 1989, Bold Girls (Hampstead Theatre, London) 1990, Your Turn to Clean the Stair (Traverse Theatre, Edinburgh) 1992, The Maiden Stone (Hampstead Theatre, London) 1996, Haunted (Traverse Theatre, Edinburgh) 1999, Snake (Hampstead Theatre, London) 1999, Iron (Traverse Theatre, Edinburgh) 2002, Gilt (Tron Theatre, Glasgow) 2003, Catch a Falling Star! (Theatre Royal) 2004, Women on the Verge of a T Junction (Theatre Royal) 2004, Strawberries in January 2006. *Honours:* Evening Standard Award 1991. *Literary Agent:* International Creative Management, 4–6 Soho Square, London, W1D 3PZ, England. *E-mail:* admin@icmlondon.co.uk; www.icmtalent.com.

MURA, David Alan, BA, MFA; American poet, writer and teacher; b. 17 June 1952, Great Lakes, IL; m. Susan Sencer 1983; one d. *Education:* Grinnell Coll., Univ. of Minnesota, Vermont Coll. *Career:* Instructor 1979–85, Assoc. Dir of the Literature Program 1982–84, Writers and Artists-in-the-Schools, St Paul, Minnesota; faculty mem., The Loft, St Paul, Minnesota 1984–; Instructor, St Olaf Coll. 1990–91; Visiting Prof., Univ. of Oregon 1991; various poetry readings; mem. Asian-American Renaissance Conference, Center for Arts

Criticism (pres. 1991–92), Jerome Foundation, Playwrights' Center. *Publications:* A Male Grief: Notes on Pornography and Addiction 1987, After We Lost Our Way (poems) 1989, Turning Japanese 1991, The Colors of Desire (poems) 1995, Where the Body Meets Memory 1996; contrib. to anthologies and magazines. *Honours:* Fanny Fay Wood Memorial Prize, Acad. of American Poets 1977, US/Japan Creative Artist Fellow 1984, Nat. Endowment for the Arts Fellowships 1985, 1993, Discovery/Nation Award 1987, Nat. Poetry Series Contest 1988, Pushcart Prize 1990, Minnesota State Arts Board Grant and Fellowship 1991, New York Times Notable Book of the Year 1991, Loft McKnight Award of Distinction 1992, Lila Wallace Reader's Digest Writers' Award 1995, Hon. DHumLitt (Cornell Coll.) 1997. *Address:* 1920 E River Terrace, Minneapolis, MN 55414, USA.

MURAKAMI, Haruki, BA; Japanese writer; b. 12 Jan. 1949, Kyoto; m. Yoko Takahashi 1971. *Education:* Kobe High School, Waseda Univ. *Career:* owner Peter Cat jazz club, Tokyo 1974–81; began writing in 1978, lived in Europe 1986–89, USA 1991–95; Visiting Scholar, Princeton Univ. 1991–93; Una's Lecturer in the Humanities, Univ. of Calif., Berkeley 1992; Writer-in-Residence, Tufts Univ. 1993–95, Harvard Univ. 2005–06. *Publications:* fiction: Hear the Wind Sing (Gunzo Literature Award for Budding Writers) 1979, Pinball 1980, A Wild Sheep Chase (Noma Literary Award for New Writers) 1982, Hard-Boiled Wonderland and The End of the World (Junichi Tanizaki Award) 1985, Norwegian Wood 1987, Dance Dance Dance 1988, South of the Border, West of the Sun 1992, Wind-Up Bird Chronicle (Yomiuri Literary Award 1996) 1994–95, Sputnik Sweetheart 1999, Kafka on the Shore 2002, After Dark 2004, After Dark 2007; short stories: Slow Boat to China 1983, A Perfect day for Kangaloos 1983, Dead Heat 1985, The Elephant Vanishes 1986, TV People 1990, Phantoms of Lexington 1998, After the Quake 2000, Blind Willow, Sleeping Woman (Frank O'Connor Int. Short Story Award) 2006; non-fiction: Underground 1997, The Place That was Promised (Kuwahara Takeo Award) 1998; essays: A Young Reader's Guide to Short Fiction 1997; has translated works by F. Scott Fitzgerald, Raymond Carver, Truman Capote, Paul Theroux, John Irving, J. D. Salinger. *Literary Agent:* ICM, 40 West 57th Street, New York, NY 10019, USA. *Telephone:* (212) 556-5600. *Website:* www.icmtalent.com.

MURAKAMI, Ryunosuke (Ryū); Japanese writer and film director; b. 19 Feb. 1952, Sasebo City, Nagasaki; m. Tazuko Takahashi 1976. *Career:* fmr rock band drummer, TV talk show host; writer and film-maker 1976–. *Films:* adaptations of many of his novels, including Almost Transparent Blue (writer and dir) 1978, Daijôbu, mai furendo (writer and dir) 1983, Raffles Hotel (writer and dir) 1989, Topâzu (writer and dir) 1992, Ôdishon (writer) 1999, Kyoko (writer and dir) 2000, Hashire! Ichiro (from novel Hashire! Takahashi) 2001. *Publications:* novels: Kagirinaku tōmei ni chikai burrū (trans. as Almost Transparent Blue) (Akutagawa Prize, Gunzou Prize) 1976, Hashire! Takahashi, Ôdishon, Topâzu (trans. as Tokyo Decadence), Raffles Hotel, Daijôbu, mai furendo (trans. as All Right, My Friend), Kyoko (trans. as Because of You), 69 1987, Coin Locker Babies 1995, In the Miso Soup (Yomiuri Literary Award 1998) 1997, Exodus (serialised) 1998–99, Piercing 2007; non-fiction: Ano kane de nani ga kaeta ka 2003. *Address:* c/o Kodansha International Ltd, Otowa YK Building, 1-17-14 Otowa, Bunkyo-ku, Tokyo 112-8652, Japan.

MURDOCH, (Keith) Rupert, AC; American (b. Australian) publisher, broadcaster and media business developer; *Chairman and CEO, News Corporation*; b. 11 March 1931, Melbourne, Victoria; s. of the late Sir Keith Murdoch and of Dame Elisabeth Murdoch; m. 1st Patricia Booker (divorced); one d.; m. 2nd Anna Maria Torv 1967 (divorced); two s. one d.; m. 3rd Wendi Deng 1999; two d. *Education:* Geelong Grammar School, Victoria and Worcester Coll., Oxford. *Career:* inherited Adelaide News 1954; has since built up News Corporation (Group CEO 1979–, Chair. 1991–); has acquired newspapers, broadcasting and other interests in Australia, UK, USA, Latin America, Europe and Asia, including: Australia – newspapers: The Australian (nat.), Daily Telegraph, Sunday Telegraph, Daily Mirror (Sydney), Sunday Sun (Brisbane), The News and Sunday Mail (Adelaide), The Sunday Times (Perth); USA – New York Post; UK – newspapers: Sun, News of the World (nat., acquired 1969); acquired Times Newspapers Ltd 1981, group includes The Times, The Sunday Times, The Times Literary Supplement, The Times Educational Supplement, The Times Higher Education Supplement; Dir Times Newspapers Holdings 1981–, Chair. 1982–90, 1994–; magazines: Weekly Standard (US politics); film: Fox Filmed Entertainment; TV: British Sky Broadcasting (UK), STAR (Asia), Fox Broadcasting Co., Fox Cable Networks; other interests include lifestyle portal MySpace.com, book publr HarperCollins and ownership of 35 US TV stations; Chair. and CEO Fox Entertainment Group USA 1992–. *Honours:* Commdr of the White Rose (First Class) 1985; Kt, Order of St Gregory the Great 1998. *Address:* News International, 1 Virginia Street, London, E98 1EX, England (office); News Corporation Ltd, 2 Holt Street, Surry Hills, Sydney, NSW 2010, Australia (office); News Corporation, 1211 Avenue of the Americas, New York, NY 10036, USA (office). *Telephone:* (2) 9288-3000 (Sydney) (office); (212) 852-7017 (New York) (office). *Fax:* (2) 9288-3292 (Sydney) (office); (212) 852-7145 (New York) (office). *Website:* www.newscorp.com (office).

MURÍN, Gustav, PhD; Slovak writer; b. 9 April 1959, Bratislava; m. Jana Murín; two d. *Education:* Comenius Univ., Bratislava. *Career:* founder samizdat Voice of the Boiler Room 1989–92; int. readings, presentations and conferences; mem. Slovak PEN Centre (sec. 1995–97, pres. 2000–04), Slovak Syndicate of Journalists, World Innovation Foundation. *Publications in translation include:* The Case of a Buried Cemetery (novella) 1986, Summer

Favors Lovers (short stories) 1990, Comebacks from Light (short stories) 1990, Substitutional End of the World (essays) 1992, Instinct Contra Culture (essay) 1994, Orgasmodromes (essays and articles) 1997, Proppe and others (fiction in electronic form) 1997, How Are You (novel) 1998, Animals, Me and Other (Prose) (short stories) 1998, Just Like the Gods (essay) 2001, And You Will Become Gods (essays) 2002; co-author of nine story collections, 12 radio dramas, TV documentaries, screenplays; contrib. over 990 articles in newspapers and magazines. *Honours:* Hon. Fellow in Writing Univ. of Iowa 1995; Best Slovak Story 1979, Best Czech and Slovak Story 1981, Best Czech and Slovak Novella 1986, Special Prize in Slovak Radio Drama 1988, Slovenské pohľady magazine Best Essay of the Year 1996, E. E. Kisch Award 2003, Fifik's Children Jury Award 2005. *Address:* J. Hagaru 17, 83151 Bratislava, Slovakia (home). *Telephone:* (2) 5441-5603 (office); (2) 4488-4237 (home). *E-mail:* murin@m2.fedu.uniba.sk (office); murinsk@yahoo.com (home).

MURNANE, Gerald; Australian writer; b. 1939, Melbourne, Vic.; m.; three s. *Education:* BA, University of Melbourne, 1969. *Career:* Lecturer, Victoria College, Melbourne; Senior Lecturer, Deakin University, Melbourne. *Publications:* Tamarisk Row, 1974; A Lifetime on Clouds, 1976; The Plains, 1982; Landscape with Landscape, 1985; Inland, 1988; Velvet Waters (short stories), 1990; Emerald Blue (short stories), 1995, Invisible Yet Enduring Lilacs (essays) 2005. *Honours:* Patrick White Literary Award, 1999. *Literary Agent:* Golvan Arts, PO Box 766, Kew, Vic. 3101, Australia. *Address:* 2 Falcon Road, Macleod, Vic. 3085, Australia (home). *Telephone:* (3) 9459-3472 (home).

MURPHEY, Rhoads, AB, MA, PhD; American academic and writer; b. 13 Aug. 1919, Philadelphia, PA; m. 1st Katherine Elizabeth Quinn 1942 (died 1950); one s. one d.; m. 2nd Eleanor Taylor Albertson 1952; one s. one d. *Education:* Harvard University. *Career:* Asst Prof. of Geography, Ohio State University, 1950–51; Asst Prof. to Prof. of Geography, University of Washington, 1952–64; Prof. of Asian Studies and History, University of Michigan, Ann Arbor, 1964–; mem. Asscn of American Geographers; Asscn for Asian Studies, pres., 1987–88; American Historical Asscn. *Publications:* Shanghai: Key to Modern China, 1953; A New China Policy (with others), 1967; An Introduction to Geography, 1969; The Scope of Geography, 1969; The Treaty Ports and China's Modernization, 1970; China Meets the West, 1975; The Mozartian Historian (with others), 1976; The Outsiders, 1977; The Fading of the Maoist Vision, 1980; Civilizations of the World (with others), 1990; A History of Asia, 1992; East Asia: A New History, 1996. Contributions: scholarly books and journals. *Honours:* Ford Foundation Fellowship, 1955–56; Guggenheim Fellowship, 1966–67; National Endowment for the Humanities Fellowship, 1972–73; Hons Award, Asscn of American Geographers, 1980.

MURPHY, Caryle Marie, BA; American journalist; b. 16 Nov. 1946, Hartford, Conn.; d. of Thomas Joseph Murphy and Muriel Kathryn Murphy (née McCarthy). *Education:* Jeanne d'Arc Acad. High School, Milton, Mass, Trinity Coll. and Johns Hopkins School for Advanced Int. Studies. *Career:* English and history teacher, Nyeri, Kenya 1968–70; Staff Reporter, Brockton Enterprise, Brockton, Mass 1972–73; Freelance Foreign Corresp., Angola 1974–76; joined Washington Post 1976, Foreign Corresp. for S Africa 1977–82, Staff Reporter, Washington, DC 1982–89, Middle East Corresp. 1989–94, currently covers religion; Edward R Murrow Fellow, Council on Foreign Relations 1994–95. *Publications:* Passion for Islam: Shaping the Modern Middle East: The Egyptian Experience 2002. *Honours:* awards for reporting from Kuwait following its invasion by Iraqi troops 1990 include Int. Women's Media Foundation Award for Courage in Journalism 1990, George Polk Award for Foreign Reporting, Long Island Univ. 1990, Pulitzer Prize for Int. Reporting 1991, Edward Weintal Journalism Prize for Diplomatic Reporting 1991. *Address:* The Washington Post, 1150 15th Street, NW, Washington, DC 20071, USA. *Telephone:* (202) 334-7400. *Fax:* (202) 334-5547. *Website:* www.washingtonpost.com.

MURPHY, Clive, BA, LLB, ARSL; Irish writer, poet and editor; b. 28 Nov. 1935, Liverpool, England. *Education:* Trinity Coll., Dublin. *Career:* Solicitor, Incorporated Law Soc. of Ireland 1958; mem. PEN, Soc. of Authors. *Publications:* novels: Freedom for Mr Mildew 1975, Nigel Someone 1975, Summer Overtures 1976; poetry: Sour Grapes 2000, Cave Canem 2002, Orts and All 2003, Lust and Malice 2005; compiler or ed. of 10 autobiographies 1978–94; contrib. to anthologies and magazines. *Honours:* co-winner Adam Int. Review First Novel Competition 1968. *Address:* 132 Brick Lane, London, E1 6RU, England (office). *Telephone:* (20) 7247-6626 (office). *Website:* clivemurphy.org (office).

MURPHY, Dervla Mary; Irish author and critic; b. 28 Nov. 1931, Cappoquin; d. of Fergus Murphy and Kathleen Rochfort-Dowling; one d. *Education:* Ursuline Convent, Waterford. *Publications:* Full Tilt 1965, Tibetan Foothold 1966, The Waiting Land 1967, In Ethiopia with a Mule 1968, On a Shoestring to Coorg 1976, Where the Indus is Young 1977, A Place Apart 1978, Wheels Within Wheels 1979, Race to the Finish? 1981, Eight Feet in the Andes 1983, Muddling Through in Madagascar 1985, Ireland 1985, Tales from Two Cities 1987, Cameroon with Egbert 1989, Transylvania and Beyond 1992, The Ukimwi Road 1993, South from the Limpopo 1997, Visiting Rwanda 1998, One Foot in Laos 1999, Through the Embers of Chaos: Balkan Journeys 2002, Through Siberia by Accident 2005, Silverland: A Winter Journey Beyond the Urals 2006. *Honours:* American Irish Foundation Literary Award 1975, Ewart-Biggs Memorial Prize 1978, Irish American Cultural Inst. Literary Award 1985. *Address:* Lismore, Co. Waterford, Ireland.

MURPHY, Jill; British writer and illustrator; b. 1949, Wimbledon, London; one s. *Education:* Chelsea Coll. of Art, Croydon and Camberwell Schools of Art. *Career:* fmr nanny, now writer of jr fiction and illustrator. *Publications include:* My Teddy 1973, The Worst Witch 1975, Peace at Last 1980, The Worst Witch Strikes Again 1981, A Bad Spell for the Worst Witch 1982, On the Way Home 1982, Whatever Next! 1983, Geoffrey Strangeways 1985, Baby Bear's Press-out Book 1985, Five Minutes' Peace 1986, All in One Piece 1987, Worlds Apart 1989, A Piece of Cake 1989, The Christmas Babies 1992, The Worst Witch All at Sea 1993, A Quiet Night In 1993, The Last Noo-noo 1995, All For One 2002, The Worst Witch Saves the Day 2005. *Address:* c/o Walker Books, 87 Vauxhall Walk, London, SE11 5HJ, England.

MURPHY, Richard, BA, MA, FRSL; Irish poet and author; b. 6 Aug. 1927, Co. Mayo; s. of the late Sir William Murphy; m. Patricia Avis 1955 (divorced 1959); one d. *Education:* Magdalen Coll., Oxford, Univ. of Paris (Sorbonne). *Career:* various visiting positions, including Univ. of Virginia, USA 1965, Univ. of Reading, UK 1968, Bard Coll., Annandale-on-Hudson, New York 1972–74, Princeton Univ., USA 1974–75, Univ. of Iowa, USA 1976–77, Syracuse Univ., USA 1977–78, Catholic Univ. of America, Washington, DC 1983, Pacific Lutheran Univ., Tacoma, Wash., USA 1985, Wichita State Univ., USA 1987; Compton Lecturer in Poetry, Univ. of Hull, UK 1969; O'Connor Prof. of Literature, Colgate Univ., NY, USA 1971; Distinguished Visiting Poet, Univ. of Tulsa, Okla, USA 1992–95; mem. Aosdána, Ireland. *Publications:* The Archaeology of Love 1955, Sailing to an Island 1963, The Battle of Aughrim 1968, High Island 1974, The Price of Stone 1985, The Mirror Wall 1989, New Selected Poems 1989, Collected Poems 2000, The Kick: A Memoir 2002, The Kick: a Life among Writers 2003; contrib. to various periodicals. *Honours:* several poetry awards. *Address:* c/o Granta Books, 2–3 Hanover Yard, Noel Road, London, N1 8BE, England; 51 Rio Street, Knysna, WC 6571, South Africa (home). *Telephone:* (44) 3827152 (office). *E-mail:* rmurphy@iafrica.com (home).

MURPHY, Thomas (Tom); Irish playwright and theatre director; b. 23 Feb. 1935, Tuam, Co. Galway; s. of John (Jack) Murphy and Winifred Shaughnessy; m. Mary Lindisfarne Hamilton-Hippisley 1966; two s. one d. *Education:* Tuam Vocational School, Vocational Teachers' Training Coll., Dublin. *Career:* metalwork teacher 1957–62; playwright and theatre Dir 1962–; Writer-in-Asscn Druid Theatre Co., Galway 1983–86, Abbey Theatre 1986–89; Tom Murphy at the Abbey (Irish Nat. Theatre), six-play season 2001; Mem. Irish Acad. of Letters, Aosdána. *Stage plays:* On the Outside 1959, A Whistle in the Dark 1961, A Crucial Week in the Life of a Grocer's Assistant 1966, The Orphans 1968, Famine 1968, The Morning After Optimism 1971, The White House 1972, The Vicar of Wakefield (adaptation) 1974, On the Inside 1974, The Sanctuary Lamp 1975, The J. Arthur Maginnis Story 1976, The Blue Macushla 1980, The Informer (adaptation) 1981, The Gigli Concert 1983, Conversations on a Homecoming 1985, Bailegangaire 1985, A Thief of a Christmas 1986, Too Late for Logic 1989, The Patriot Game 1991, She Stoops to Folly 1995, The Wake 1998, Too Late for Logic 1998, The House 2000, The Cherry Orchard 2003, The Drunkard 2003, Alice Trilogy 2005. *Publications:* The Seduction of Morality (novel) 1994. *Honours:* Hon. DLitt (Dublin) 1998, (Galway NUI) 2000; Irish Acad. of Letters Award 1972, Harveys Award 1983, 1985, Sunday Tribune Arts Award 1985, Independent Newspapers Award 1983, 1989, Drama-Logue Critics' Award 1995, Irish Times ESB Theatre Awards Special Tribute 1997, 2000. *Address:* Alexandra Cann Representation, 2 St Thomas Square, Newport, Isle of Wight PO30 1SN, England (office); 4 Garville Road, Dublin 6, Ireland (home). *Telephone:* (1983) 556866 (office). *E-mail:* alex@alexandracann.co.uk (office).

MURPHY, Walter Francis, AB, AM, PhD; American academic and writer; *McCormick Professor of Jurisprudence Emeritus, Princeton University*; b. 21 Nov. 1929, Charleston, SC; m. Mary Therese Dolan 1952; two d. *Education:* Univ. of Notre Dame, George Washington Univ., Univ. of Chicago. *Career:* Research Fellow, Brookings Institution, Washington, DC 1957–58; Asst Prof. 1958–61, Assoc. Prof. 1961–65, Prof. of Politics 1965–95, McCormick Prof. of Jurisprudence 1968–95, Prof. Emeritus 1995–, Princeton Univ.; Fellow American Acad. of Arts and Sciences; mem. American Political Science Asscn. *Publications:* Courts, Judges and Politics (ed. with C. Herman Pritchett, Lee Epstein and Jack Knight) 1961, Congress and the Court 1962, American Democracy (co-author, fourth–tenth edns) 1963–83, Elements of Judicial Strategy 1964, Wiretapping on Trial 1965, Modern American Democracy (with M. N. Danielson) 1969, The Study of Public Law (with Joseph Tanenaus) 1972, Public Evaluations of Constitutional Courts (co-author) 1974, Comparative Constitutional Law (co-author) 1977, The Vicar of Christ (fiction) 1979, Basic Cases in Constitutional Law (ed. with W. D. Lockard) 1980, The Roman Enigma (fiction) 1981, Upon This Rock (fiction) 1986, American Constitutional Interpretation (with J. Fleming, S. A. Barber and S. Macedo, third edn) 2003, Constitutional Democracy 2006; contrib. to professional journals. *Honours:* Distinguished Service Cross, Purple Heart, Birkhead Award 1958, Merriam-Cobb-Hughes Award 1963, Guggenheim Fellowship 1973–74, Nat. Endowment for the Humanities Fellowship 1978–79, Chicago Foundation for Literature Award 1980, American Political Science Asscn (Law and Courts Section) Lifetime Achievement Award 1995. *Address:* 1533 Eagle Ridge Drive NE, Albuquerque, NM 87122, USA. *Telephone:* (505) 828-3587 (office). *E-mail:* wmurphy37@comcast.net.

MURRAY, Denis James, OBE; British journalist; b. 7 May 1951, s. of the late James Murray and Helen Murray; m. Joyce Linehan 1978; two s. two d. *Education:* St Malachy's Coll. Belfast, Trinity Coll. Dublin, Queen's Univ.

Belfast. *Career:* grad. trainee, Belfast Telegraph 1975–77, also reporter; Belfast Reporter, Radio Telefís Éireann 1977–82; Dublin Corresp. BBC 1982–84, NI Political Corresp. 1984–88, Ireland Corresp. 1988–. *Address:* c/o BBC, Ormeau Avenue, Belfast, BT2 8HQ, Northern Ireland. *Telephone:* (28) 9033-8000.

MURRAY, Douglas; British journalist and biographer; b. 1979. *Education:* Eton Public School, Magdalen Coll., Oxford. *Publications:* Bosie: A Biography of Lord Alfred Douglas 2000, Neo-Conservatism: Why We Need It 2006. *Literary Agent:* c/o Hodder and Stoughton General, 338 Euston Road, London, NW1 3BH, England. *Website:* www.hodderheadline.co.uk.

MURRAY, Frances (see Booth, Rosemary)

MURRAY, John; British novelist; b. 1950, Cumbria; m.; one d. *Career:* founder and co-ed., Panurge 1984. *Publications:* novels: Samarkand 1985, Kin 1986, Radio Activity 1993, John Dory 2001, Jazz, etc. 2003, Murphy's Favourite Channels 2004; short story collection: Pleasure 1987. *Honours:* Dylan Thomas Award 1988, winner of creative category Lakeland Book of the Year 2002. *Literary Agent:* c/o Independent Northern Publishers, Flambard Press, PO Box 990, Newcastle upon Tyne, NE99 2US, England. *E-mail:* info@northernpublishers.co.uk. *Website:* www.flambardpress.co.uk.

MURRAY, John R.; British publisher and author. *Education:* Univ. of Oxford. *Career:* fmr Chair. John Murray (Publrs) Ltd (bought by Hodder Headline 2002). *Publications include:* Old Chestnuts Warmed Up (ed.) 2002. *Address:* c/o 50 Albemarle Street, London, W1S 4BD, England (office).

MURRAY, Leslie (Les) Allan, BA, AO; Australian poet; b. 17 Oct. 1938, Nabiac, NSW; s. of the late Cecil Allan Murray and Miriam Pauline Murray (née Arnall); m. Valerie Gina Morelli 1962; three s. two d. *Education:* Univ. of Sydney. *Career:* translator Australian Nat. Univ. 1963–67; in Prime Minister's Dept 1970–71; acting ed., Poetry Australia 1973–80; ed. New Oxford Book of Australian Verse 1985–97; literary ed., Quadrant 1989–. *Publications:* The Ilex Tree (with Geoffrey Lehmann) 1965, The Weatherboard Cathedral 1969, Poems Against Economics 1972, Collected Poems 1976, Selected Poems: The Vernacular Republic 1979, The Boys Who Stole the Funeral (verse novel) 1980, Selected Poems 1986, Dog Fox Field 1990, The Paperbark Tree (selected prose) 1991, Translations from the Natural World 1992, Fivefathers (ed.) 1995, Subhuman Redneck Poems 1996, A Working Forest (prose) 1997, Fredy Neptune (verse novel) 1998, Conscious & Verbal 1999, Learning Human – New Selected Poems 2001, Poems the Size of Photographs 2002, New Collected Poems 2003, The Best Australian Poems (ed.) 2004, The Biplane Houses 2006. *Honours:* Petrarca Prize, Germany 1995, T. S. Eliot Prize 1997, Queen's Gold Medal for Poetry 1999, Mondello Prize (Italy) 2004. *Literary Agent:* Margaret Connolly & Associates, 16 Winton Street, Warrawee, NSW 2074, Australia.

MURRELL, John; Canadian dramatist and translator; b. 15 Oct. 1945, Lubbock, TX, USA. *Education:* BFA, Southwestern University, Georgetown, Texas, 1966; BEd, University of Calgary, 1969. *Career:* Playwright-in-Residence, Alberta Theatre Project, 1975–76; Assoc. Dir, Stratford Festival, 1977–78; Dramaturg, Theatre Calgary, 1981–82; Head, Playwright's Colony, Banff Centre School of Fine Art, 1986, Theatre Section, Canada Council, 1988–92. *Publications:* Haydn's Head, 1973; Power in the Blood, 1975; Teaser (with Kenneth Dyba), 1975; Arena, 1975; A Great Noise, a Great Light, 1976; Memoir, 1977; Waiting for the Parade, 1980; Farther West, 1986; New World, 1986; October, 1988; Democracy, 1992; Faraway Nearby, 1995. *Honours:* Clifford E. Lee Playwrighting Award, 1975. *Address:* c/o Talonbooks, No. 104-3100 Production Way, Burnaby, BC V5A 4R4, Canada.

MURTAGH, Peter, MA; Irish journalist; b. 9 April 1953, Dublin; s. of Thomas Murtagh and Olive de Lacy; m. Moira Gutteridge 1988; one s. one d. *Education:* The High School, Dublin and Trinity Coll. Dublin. *Career:* reporter, The Irish Times 1981–84; Ed. Insight, The Sunday Times, London 1985; reporter, Deputy Foreign Ed. and News Ed. The Guardian, London 1986–94; Ed. The Sunday Tribune, Dublin 1994–97. *Publications:* The Boss: Charles J. Haughey in Government (with J. Joyce) 1983, Blind Justice: The Sallins Mail Train Robbery (with J. Joyce) 1984, The Rape of Greece 1994. *Honours:* Journalist of the Year, Ireland 1983; Reporter of the Year, UK 1986. *Address:* Penhanboon, Somerby Road, Greystones, Co. Wicklow, Ireland (home). *Fax:* (1) 6615302 (office).

MUSCHG, Adolf, PhD; Swiss writer, dramatist and academic; b. 13 May 1934, Zollikon. *Education:* Zürich, Cambridge, England. *Career:* Prof., Eidgenössische Technische Hochschule, Zürich 1970–. *Publications:* Im Sommer des Hasen, 1965; Fremdkörper, 1968; Das Kerbelgericht, 1969; Die Aufgeregten von Goethe, 1971; Liebesgeschichten, 1972; Albissers Grund, 1974; Kellers Abend, 1975; Gottfried Keller, 1977; Baiyun oder die Freundschaftsgesellschaft, 1980; Literatur als Therapie?, 1981; Das Licht und der Schlüssel, 1984; Der rote Ritter, 1993; Nur ausziehen wollte sie sich nicht, 1995. *Honours:* Hermann Hesse Prize, 1974; Literature Prize, Zürich, 1984; Carl Zuckmayer Medal, 1990; Georg Büchner Prize, 1994. *Address:* Hasenackerstrasse 24, 8708 Männedorf, Switzerland.

MUSGRAVE, Susan; Canadian writer; b. 12 March 1951, Santa Cruz, CA, USA; d. of Edward Lindsay and Judith Bradfield (née Stevens) Musgrave; m. Stephen Douglas Reid 1982; two d. *Career:* Writer since the age of 16; Bi-weekly Columnist Toronto Star, Vancouver Sun; book reviewer CBC Journal; Writer-in-Residence Univ. of Waterloo 1983–85, Univ. of New Brunswick 1985, Univ. of W. Ontario 1992–93; teacher of English Arvon Foundation 1975, 1980, Univ. of Waterloo 1983–84, Kootenay School of Writing 1986, Camosun Coll., Victoria 1988–91; frequent judge and jury mem. of poetry competitions; Toronto Univ. Presidential Writer-in-Residence Fellowship 1995; Nat. Magazine Award (Silver) 1981; b. p. nichol Poetry Chapbook Award 1991; CBC/Tilden Award for Poetry 1996; Vicky Metcalf Short Story Editors Award 1996. *Publications include:* Poetry: Songs of the Sea-Witch 1970, Entrance of the Celebrant 1972, Grave-Dirt and Selected Strawberries 1973, Gullband 1974, The Impstone 1976, Kiskatinaw Songs 1977, Selected Strawberries and Other Poems 1977, Becky Swan's Book 1978, A Man to Marry, A Man to Bury 1979, Tarts and Muggers: Poems New and Selected 1982, Cocktails at the Mausoleum 1985, Kestrel and Leonardo 1990, In The Small Hours of the Rain 1991, The Embalmer's Art 1992, Forcing the Narcissus 1994, Things That Keep and Do Not Change 1999, What the Small Day Cannot Hold 2000; Novels: The Charcoal Burners 1980, Hag Head 1980, The Dancing Chicken 1987, Dreams Are More Real than Bathtubs 1998; Essays: Great Musgrave 1989; has written numerous articles and poems for periodicals and anthologies. *Address:* PO Box 2421, Station Main, Sidney, BC V8L 3Y3, Canada.

MUSGROVE, Frank, BA, PhD, FRSA; British academic and writer; *Sarah Fielden Professor of Education Emeritus, University of Manchester;* b. 16 Dec. 1922, Nottingham, England; m. Dorothy Ellen Nicholls; one d. *Education:* Magdalen Coll., Oxford, Univ. of Nottingham. *Career:* Lecturer Univ. of Leicester 1957–62; Sr Lecturer Univ. of Leeds 1963–65; Prof. of Research in Education Univ. of Bradford 1965–70; Sarah Fielden Prof. of Education 1970–82, Prof. Emeritus 1982–, Univ. of Manchester; Co-Ed. Research in Education 1971–76; various guest lectureships; mem. Royal Anthropological Inst. *Publications:* The Migratory Elite 1963, Youth and the Social Order 1964, The Family, Education and Society 1966, Society and the Teacher's Role (with P. H. Taylor) 1969, Patterns of Power and Authority in English Education 1971, Ecstasy and Holiness 1974, Margins of the Mind 1977, School and the Social Order 1979, Education and Anthropology 1982, The North of England: A History from Roman Times to the Present 1990, Dresden and the Heavy Bombers 2005; contrib. to professional journals. *Honours:* Hon. DLitt (Open Univ.) 1982; Chancellor's Lecturer, Univ. of Wellington, NZ 1970, Hon. Prof. Univ. of Hull 1985–88. *Address:* Dib Scar, The Cedar Grove, Beverley, East Yorkshire HU17 7EP, England (home). *Telephone:* (1482) 868799 (home).

MUSHKETIK, Yuri Mikhailovich; Ukrainian writer; b. 21 March 1929, Verkiivka, Chernigiv Region; s. of Mikhail Petrovich Mushketik and Uliana Onufriivna Mushketik; m. Lina Sergiivna Mushketik (née Lushnikova); two d. *Education:* Kiev State Univ. *Career:* mem. CPSU 1951–91; Chair. Bd Union of Writers of Ukraine 1987–; Ed.-in- Chief Dnipro journal; Chair. Nat. Cttee of UNESCO; first works published 1952. *Publications include:* Fires in the Middle of the Night 1959, Black Bread 1960, The Heart and the Stone 1961, Drop of Blood 1964, A Bridge Across the Night 1975, White Shadow 1975, Position 1979, Pain 1981, The Boundary 1987, Selected Works (2 vols) 1989, Hetman's Treasure (novel) 1993, Brother Against Brother (novel) 1995. *Honours:* T. Shevchenko Ukrainian State Prize 1980. *Address:* Suvorova Str. 3, Apt. 10, 252010 Kiev, Ukraine. *Telephone:* (44) 290-80-04.

MUSICANT, Ivan Martin, BA; American naval historian; b. 18 Dec. 1943, New York, NY; m. Gretchen Granlund Musicant 1982, one s. *Education:* Bemidji State University. *Publications:* United States Armored Cruisers: A Design and Operational History, 1985; Battleship At War: The Epic Story of the USS Washington, 1986; The Banana Wars: United States Military Intervention in Latin America, 1990; Divided Waters: The Naval History of the Civil War, 1995; Empire by Default: The Spanish-American War, 1998. Contributions: journals, reviews, periodicals and quarterlies. *Honours:* Samuel Eliot Morison Awards for Naval Literature, 1987, 1998.

MUSKE-DUKES, Carol Anne; American poet, writer and academic; b. 17 Dec. 1945, St Paul, Minn.; m. David Dukes 1983 (died 2000); one step-s. one d. *Education:* BA, English, Creighton University, Omaha, 1967; MA, English, California State University, San Francisco, 1970. *Career:* Founder-Writing Program Dir, Art Without Walls, New York, 1971–84; Lecturer, New School for Social Research, New York City, 1975; Asst Prof., University of New Hampshire, 1978–79; Visiting Writer, 1978, Visiting Poet, 1983, 1993, University of California at Irvine; Adjunct Prof., Columbia University, 1979–81; Visiting Poet, Iowa Writers' Workshop, 1980; Jenny McKean Moore Lecturer, George Washington University, 1980–81; Writer-in-Residence, University of Virginia, 1981; Lecturer, 1984–88, Asst Prof., 1989–91, Assoc. Prof., 1991–93, Prof., 1993–, Founder-Dir, PhD Program in Creative Writing and Literature, 1999–, University of Southern California, Los Angeles; Visiting Fiction Writer, University of California, Los Angeles, 1989; mem. Poetry Society of America, West, program dir and pres., 1992–94. *Publications:* Poetry: Camouflage, 1975; Skylight, 1981; Wyndmere, 1985; Applause, 1989; Red Trousseau, 1993; An Octave Above Thunder: Selected and New Poems, 1997. Fiction: Dear Digby, 1989; Saving St Germ, 1993; Life After Death, 2001; Married to the Icepick Killer: A Poet in Hollywood, 2002. Non-Fiction: Women and Poetry (essays), 1997. Contributions: numerous anthologies and journals. *Honours:* Dylan Thomas Poetry Award, 1973; Pushcart Prizes, 1978, 1988–89, 1992–93, 1998; Alice Fay di Castagnola Award, Poetry Society of America, 1979; Guggenheim Fellowship, 1981; National Endowment for the Arts Grant, 1984; Ingram Merrill Foundation Fellowship, 1988; New York Times Most Notable Book Citation, 1993; Alumni Achievement Award, Creighton University, 1996; Witter Bynner Award, Library of

Congress, Washington, DC, 1997–98. *Literary Agent:* Aaron Priest Literary Agency, 708 Third Avenue, 23rd Floor, New York, NY 10017, USA. *Address:* c/o Dept of English, University of Southern California, Los Angeles, CA 90095, USA.

MUTAFCHIEVA, Vera, PhD; Bulgarian writer, historian and academic; b. 28 March 1929, Sofia; d. of Petar and Nadia (née Tritonova) Mutafchiev; m. 1st Jossif Krapchev 1950 (divorced 1956); m. 2nd Atanas Slavov 1961 (divorced 1967); two d. *Education:* Univ. of Sofia. *Career:* Sr Researcher in Ottoman History, Inst. of History, Sofia 1958–63, Inst. of Balkan Studies 1963–79; Prof. Inst. of Literature 1979–91, Inst. of Demographic Studies, Acad. of Sciences 1991, Univ. of Sofia 1991; Dir Language and Ancient Civilization Centre 1979–80, Bulgarian Inst. of Research, Austria 1980–82; Sec. Union of Bulgarian Writers 1982–86. *Publications include:* 12 novels, several plays, numerous essays, monographs and translations; has published 67 scientific studies 1952–92. *Honours:* Dr hc (New Bulgarian Univ.) 2000; Gottfried von Herder Preis, Hamburg, Vienna 1980, State Prize 1982, Paissii Hilendarsky Award 2000. *Address:* c/o Balkani Publishers, 47 A Tsarigradsko Chaussee, Block B, Floor 2, Sofia 1124, Bulgaria (office). *Telephone:* (2) 944-50-39 (office). *Fax:* (2) 944-50-48 (office). *E-mail:* balkani@infotel.bg (office). *Website:* balkani .dir.bg (office).

MUTIS, Alvaro; Colombian poet and novelist; b. 25 Aug. 1923, Bogotá; m. Mireya Durán; three s. *Publications:* poetry: La balanza, 1948; Los elementos del desastre, 1953; Reseñas de los Hospitales de Ultramar, 1955; Los Trabajos Perdidos, 1965; Summa de Maqroll el Gaviero, 1973; Caravansary, 1981; Los emisarios, 1984; Crónica regia y alabanza del reino, 1985; Un homenaje y siete nocturnos, 1986. Novels: Diario de Lecumberri, 1960; La mansión de Araucaíma, 1973; La verdadera historia del flautista de Hammelin, 1982; La Nieve del Almirante; Ilona llega con la lluvia, 1987; Un bel morir, 1989; La última escala del Tramp Steamer, 1989; La muerte del estratega, 1990; Amirbar, 1990; Abdul Bashur, soñador de navíos, 1991; Tríptico de mar y tierra, 1993. Essays: Contextos para Maqroll, 1997; De lecturas y algo del mundo, 1999; Caminos y encuentros de Maqroll el Gaviero, 2001. *Honours:* Premio Nacional de Letras, 1974; Premio Nacional de Poesía, 1983; Premio de la Crítica 'Los Abriles', 1985; Comendador de la Orden del Águila Azteca, Mexico, 1988; Premio Xavier Villaurrutia, Mexico, 1988; Dr hc, Universidad del Valle, Colombia, 1988; Commdr., Ordre des Arts et des Lettres, France, 1989; Prix Médicis Étranger, France, 1989; Nonino Prize, Italy, 1990; Ordre nat. du Mérite, France, 1993; Roger Caillois Prize, France, 1993; Gran Cruz de la Orden de Boyacá, 1993; Gran Cruz de la Orden de Alfonso X el Sabio, Spain, 1996; Grinzane-Cavour Prize, Italy, 1997; Premio Príncipe de Asturias de las Letras, Spain, 1997; Premio Reina Sofía de Poesía Iberoamericana, Spain, 1997; Rossone d'Oro Prize, Italy, 1997; Trieste Poetry Prize, Italy, 2000; Premio Cervantes, Spain, 2001; Neustadt Prize, 2002.

MWANGI, Meja; Kenyan novelist; b. 1948, Nanyuki. *Education:* Kenyatta Coll. *Career:* soundman, TV ORTF 1972–73; film librarian, British Council 1974–75; Fellow in Writing, Iowa Univ. 1975–76; also film dir, casting agent and location manager. *Publications:* Kill Me Quick 1973, Carcase for Hounds 1974, Going Down River Road 1976, The Cockroach Dance 1979, The Bushtrackers 1980, Bread of Sorrow 1987, Weapon for Hunger 1989, The Return of Shaka 1990, Striving for the Wind 1990, The Last Plague 2000; also children's books, plays. *Honours:* Jomo Kenyatta Prize 1974.

MYERS, Margaret Jane (Dee Dee), BS; American broadcaster, magazine editor and fmr government official; *President, Dee Dee Myers & Associates;* b. 1 Sept. 1961, Quonset Point, RI; d. of Stephen George Myers and Judith Ann Burleigh; one d. *Education:* Univ. of Santa Clara. *Career:* Press Asst Mondale for Pres. Campaign, LA 1984, to deputy Senator Art Torres, LA 1985; Deputy Press Sec. to Mayor Tom Bradley, LA 1985–87, Tom Bradley for Gov. Campaign 1986; Calif. Press Sec. Dukakis for Pres. Campaign, LA 1988; Press Sec. Feinstein for Gov. Campaign, LA and San Francisco 1989–90; Campaign Dir Jordan for Mayor Campaign, San Francisco 1991; Press Sec. Clinton for Pres. Campaign, Little Rock 1991–92, White House, Washington 1993–94; Co-Host Equal Time, CNBC, Washington 1995–97; Contributing Ed. Vanity Fair magazine, Washington 1995–; founder and Pres. Dee Dee Myers & Associates; mem. Bd Trustees, Calif. State Univ. 1999–2004 (Vice-Chair. 2000–01); lecturer on politics, current affairs and women's issues; consultant to NBC TV drama The West Wing;. *Honours:* Robert F. Kennedy Award, Emerson Coll., Boston 1993. *Address:* c/o Vanity Fair, Condé Nast Publications, 4 Times Square, 17th Floor, New York, NY 10036, USA (office). *Website:* www .vanityfair.com (office).

MYERS, Jack Elliot, BA, MFA; American academic, poet and writer; b. 29 Nov. 1941, Lynn, MA; m. 1st Nancy 1967; m. 2nd Willa 1981; m. 3rd Thea 1993, three s. one d. *Education:* University of Massachusetts, Boston, University of Iowa. *Career:* Asst Prof., 1975–81, Assoc. Prof., 1982–88, Prof. of English, 1988–, Dir, Creative Writing Program, 1990–94, Southern Methodist University, Dallas; Poetry Ed., Fiction International, 1978–80, Cimarron Review, 1989–91; Faculty, MFA Program in Writing, Vermont College, 1981–; Distinguished Poet-in-Residence, Wichita State University, 1992; Distinguished Visiting Writer, University of Idaho, 1993; Distinguished

Writer-in-Residence, Northeast Louisiana University, 1995; mem. Associated Writing Programs; PEN; Texas Assn of Creative Writing Teachers; Texas Institute of Letters. *Publications:* Poetry: Black Sun Abraxas, 1970; Will It Burn, 1974; The Family War, 1977; I'm Amazed That You're Still Singing, 1981; Coming to the Surface, 1984; As Long as You're Happy, 1986; Blindsided, 1993; Human Being, 1997. Other: A Trout in the Milk: A Composite Portrait of Richard Hugo, 1980; New American Poets of the 80s (ed. with Roger Weingarten), 1984; The Longman Dictionary of Poetic Terms, 1985; A Profile of Twentieth-Century American Poetry (ed. with David Wojahn), 1991; New American Poets of the 90s (ed. with Roger Weingarten), 1991; Leaning House Poets, Vol. 1 (ed. with Mark Elliott), 1996; One On One, 1999. Contributions: anthologies, reviews, quarterlies, journals, and magazines. *Honours:* Acad. of American Poets Award, 1972; Texas Institute of Letters Poetry Awards, 1978, 1993; Yaddo Fellowship, 1978; National Endowment for the Arts Fellowships, 1982–83, 1986–87; Winner, National Poetry Series Open Competition, 1985; Southern Methodist University Author's Award, 1987.

MYERSON, Julie, BA; British writer and journalist; b. 1960, Nottingham; m. Jonathan Myerson; three c. *Education:* Univ. of Bristol. *Career:* staff mem., Royal Nat. Theatre, London; publicist, columnist, broadcaster, panellist on Newsnight Review (BBC2). *Publications include:* novels: Sleepwalking 1994, The Touch 1996, Me and the Fatman 1998, Laura Blundy 2000, Something Might Happen 2003, Not a Games Person 2005, The Story of You 2006; non-fiction: Home: The Story of Everyone Who Ever Lived in Our House 2004. *Honours:* Elle talent contest 1993. *Address:* c/o Yellow Jersey Press, Random House, 20 Vauxhall Bridge Road, London, SW1V 2SA, England.

MYNERS, Paul, FRSA; British publishing executive; *Chairman, Guardian Media Group;* b. 1 April 1948; m.; five c. *Education:* Univ. of London. *Career:* finance writer, Daily Telegraph –1974; N. M. Rothschild 1974–85; CEO Gartmore Investment Man. 1985–87, Chair. 1987–2001; Deputy Chair. Powergen 1999–2001; Exec. Dir Nat. Westminster Bank 1999–2000; Dir City Disputes Panel, Financial Reporting Council, Lloyds of London Investment Cttee; Chair. Guardian Media Group 2001–; Dir (non-exec.) mmO₂2001–, Bank of NY, Marks & Spencer 2002, interim Chair. June 2004–; Chair. Tate St Ives; mem. Royal Acad. Trust, United Response. *Address:* Guardian Media Group, 75 Farringdon Road, London, EC1M 3JX (office); Gartmore House, 8 Fenchurch Place, London, EC3M 4PH, England. *Telephone:* (20) 7278-2332 (Guardian) (office); (20) 7782-2000. *Fax:* (20) 7242-0679 (Guardian) (office). *Website:* www.gmgplc.co.uk.

MYRDAL, Jan; Swedish writer; b. 19 July 1927, Stockholm; s. of the late Gunnar Myrdal and Alva Reimer; m. 1st Nadja Wiking 1948; m. 2nd Maj Liedberg 1953; m. 3rd Gun Kessle 1956; one s. one d. *Career:* Sunday columnist (politics, culture) Stockholms-Tidningen 1963–66, Aftonbladet 1966–72; Chair. and Publr Folket i Bild/Kulturfront 1971–72, columnist 1972–. *Works include:* films: Myglaren 1966, Hjalparen 1968, Balzac or The Triumphs of Realism 1975, Mexico: Art and Revolution 1991; TV documentaries: Democratic Kampuchea 1978–79, Guerilla Base Area of Democratic Kampuchea 1979, China 1979, 20 films on history of political caricature and posters 1975–87. *Publications:* (in Swedish) novels: Hemkomst 1954, Jubelvår 1955, Att bli och vara 1956, Badrumskranen 1957, Karriär 1975, Barndom 1982, En annan värld 1984; drama: Folkets Hus 1953, Moraliteter 1967, Garderingar 1969, B. Olsen 1972; travel: Resa i Afghanistan 1960, Bortom berg och öknar 1962, Turkmenistan 1966, En världsbild (co-author) 1977, Sidenvägen 1977, Indien väntar 1980; politics: Kina: Revolutionen går vidare 1970, Albansk utmaning 1970, Ett 50-tal 1972, lag utan ordning, Kinesiska frågor, Tyska frågor 1976, Kina efter Mao Tse-tung 1977, Kampuchea och kriget 1978, Kampuchea hösten 1979, Den albanska utmaningen 1968–86, 1987, Mexico, Dröm och längtan 1996; art: Bartom Bergen 1983; essays: Söndagsmorgon 1965, Skriftställning 1968, Skriftställning II 1969, Skriftställning III 1970, Skriftställning IV 1973, V 1975, Klartexter 1978, Skriftställning X 1978, Balzac und der Realismus (in German) 1978, Strindberg och Balzac 1981, Ord och Avsikt 1986, Det nya Stor, Tyskland 1993; autobiography: Rescontra 1962, Samtida bekännelser 1964, Inför nedräkningen 1993, När morgondagarna sjöng 1994, En kärlek 1998, Maj: En kärlek 1998; art: Ansikte av sten, Angkor 1968, Ondskan tar form 1976; Dussinet fullt 1981, Den trettonde 1983, Franska revolutionens bilder 1989, 5 ar av frihet 1830–35 1991, När Västerlandet tradde fram 1992, André Gill 1995, Drömmen om det goda samhallet; Kinesiska affischer 1966–1976 1996; wine: Jan Myrdal on vin 1999; biography: Johan August Strindberg 2000; (in English) Report from a Chinese Village 1965, Chinese Journey 1965, Confessions of a Disloyal European 1968, Angkor: an essay on art and imperialism 1970, China: The Revolution Continued 1971, Gates to Asia 1971, Albania Defiant 1976, The Silk Road 1979, China Notebook 1975–78 1979, Return to a Chinese Village 1984, India Waits 1984, Childhood 1991, Another World 1993, 12 Going on 13 1995. *Honours:* Hon. DLit (Upsala Coll., NJ) 1980; Hon. PhD (Nankai Univ., China) 1993; Chevalier, Ordre des Arts et Lettres 1990. *Address:* Kalvängen 70 D, 739 91 Skinnskatteberg, Sweden. *Telephone:* (223) 51-012. *Fax:* (223) 51-007. *E-mail:* myrdal@myrdal.pp.se (office).

N

NAAMANI, Houda an-, LLB; Lebanese poet; b. Damascus, Syria; two s. *Education:* Lycée-Français, Franciscan School, Univ. of Damascus and Cornell Univ., New York, USA. *Career:* fmr lawyer; writer 1970–. *Publications include:* Ilayka 1970, Anamili... Laa 1971, Qasidat Hub 1973, Adhkuru Kuntu Nuqtah Kuntu Da'ira 1978, Haa Tatadahraju 'ala al'Thalj 1982, Ru'ya 'ala 'Arsh 1989, Huda... Ana al-Haq 1990, I Was a Point. I Was a Circle (trans.) 1993. *E-mail:* naamanih@terra.net.lb.

NÁDAS, Péter; Hungarian novelist, essayist and playwright; b. 1942, Budapest. *Publications:* A biblia (short stories), 1967; Kulcskereso játék (short stories), 1969; Egy családregény vége (The End of a Family Story, novel), 1977; Takarítás (play), 1977; Találkozás (play), 1979; Leírás, 1980; Temetés, 1980; Nézotér, 1983; Emlékiratok könyve (A Book of Memories), 1986; Játéktér, 1988; Égi és földi szerelem, 1991; Talált cetli, 1992; A Lovely Tale of Photography (in trans.), 1999; Valamennyi fény, 2000; Love (in trans.), 2001. *Honours:* Prize for Hungarian Art, 1989; Austrian State Prize for European Literature, 1991; Vilenica International Prize for Literature, 1998. *Address:* c/o Twisted Spoon Press, PO Box 21, Preslova 12, 150 00 Prague 5, Czech Republic (office).

NADAUS, Roland, (Pol-Jean Mervillon); French writer and poet; b. 28 Nov. 1945, Paris; m. Simone Moris 1967, one d. *Career:* mem. PEN Club of France. *Publications:* Maison de Paroles, 1969; Journal: Vrac, 1981; Je ne Tutoie que Dieu et ma femme (poems), 1992; Dictionnaire initiatique de l'orant, 1993; L'homme que tuèrent les mouches, 1996. Contributions: journals. *Honours:* Prix Gustave Gasser 1993.

NADER, Ralph; American lawyer, author and consumer advocate; b. 27 Feb. 1934, Winsted, Conn.; s. of Nadra Nader and Rose Bouziane. *Education:* Princeton and Harvard Univs. *Career:* admitted to Conn. Bar 1958, Mass. Bar 1959, also US Supreme Court; US Army 1959; law practice in Hartford, Conn. 1959–; Lecturer in History and Govt, Univ. of Hartford 1961–63; founder and fmr Head of Public Citizen Inc. 1980; Lecturer, Princeton Univ. 1967–68; Co-founder Princeton Project 55 1989; launched political movt Democracy Rising 2001; presidential cand. 2000, 2004; mem. ABA; f. Clean Water Action Project, Disability Rights Center, Public Interest Research Groups (PIRGs), Center for Study of Responsive Law, Center for Auto Safety, Pension Rights Center, Project for Corporate Responsibility; Contributing Ed. Ladies Home Journal 1973–81, syndicated columnist 'In the Public Interest' 1972–; f. The Multi-national Monitor (monthly magazine). *Film appearance:* (as himself) Fun with Dick and Jane 2005. *Publications:* Unsafe at Any Speed 1965, Who Runs Congress? 1972, The Consumer and Corporate Accountability 1974, Taming the Giant Corporation (co-author) 1976, The Menace of Atomic Energy (with John Abbotts) 1979, The Lemon Book 1980, Who's Poisoning America? 1981, The Big Boys 1986, Winning the Insurance Game (co-author) 1990, Good Works 1993, No Contest: Corporate Lawyers and the Perversion of Justice in America 1996, The Ralph Nader Reader 2000. *Honours:* Woodrow Wilson Award (Princeton Univ.) 1972. *Address:* Democracy Rising, POB 18485, Washington, DC 20036, USA. *Website:* www.democracyrising.us; www.nader .org.

NADICH, Judah, AB, MA, DHL; American rabbi and writer; b. 13 May 1912, Baltimore, MD; m. Martha Hadassah Ribalow 1947, three d. *Education:* College of New York, Jewish Theological Seminary of America, Columbia University. *Career:* mem. Jewish Book Council of America (pres. 1970–72), Rabbinical Assembly (pres. 1972–74). *Publications:* Eisenhower and the Jews, 1953; Menachem Ribalow: The Flowering of Modern Hebrew Literature (trans.), 1957; Louis Ginzberg: Al Halakhah Ve-Aggadah (ed.), 1960; Jewish Legends of the Second Commonwealth, 1983; Legends of the Rabbis, 1994; Rabbi Akiba and His Contemporaries, 1998. Contributions: Reference works, books, and journals. *Honours:* Croix de Guerre 1945, Aleh, Israel 1985.

NADOLNY, Sten, DPhil; German writer; b. 29 July 1942, Zehdenick/Havel. *Publications:* Netzkarte 1981, Die Entdeckung der Langsamkeit 1983, Selim oder die Gabe der Rede 1990, Das Erzählen und die guten Absichten 1990, Ein Gott der Frechheit 1994, Er oder ich 1999, Ullsteinroman 2003. *Honours:* Ingeborg Bachmann Prize 1980, Hans Fallada Prize 1985, Vallombrosa Prize, Florence 1986, Ernst Hoferichter Prize 1995. *Literary Agent:* Agence Hoffman, Bechsteinstrasse 2, 80804 Munich, Germany. *Telephone:* (89) 308 48 07. *Fax:* (89) 308 21 08.

NAFEH, Ibrahim; Egyptian journalist; *President, Arab Journalists' Union*; b. 1934, Suez; m.; two c. *Career:* diplomatic corresp., Cairo Radio 1956–60; Econ. Ed. Al-Gumhuriya newspaper 1960–62; Econ. Ed. Al-Ahram newspaper 1962–67, Head Econ. Dept 1974–75, Chief Ed. 1975, then Chair. and Ed.-in-Chief; Middle East specialist in IBRD, Information Dept 1971–73; currently Pres. Arab Journalists' Union. *Publication:* Translation into Arabic of Lester Pearson's Report: Partners in Development 1971. *Address:* c/o Al-Ahram, Sharia al Galaa, Cairo 11511, Egypt.

NAFISI, Azar, PhD; Iranian writer and academic; b. 1962; m.; one d. *Education:* Oklahoma Univ., USA. *Career:* fmrly teacher, Tehran Univ., Allemeh Tabatabai Univ.; fmrly visiting fellow, Oxford Univ.; currently Dir of the Dialogue Project, School of Advanced Int. Studies, Johns Hopkins Univ., Washington, DC, USA. *Publications:* Anti-Terra: A Study of Vladimir Nabokov's Novels 1994, Reading 'Lolita' in Tehran: A Memoir in Books 2003; contrib. numerous chapters and articles on promotion of democracy, human rights in Muslim societies, women's rights, literature, culture. *Address:* The Paul H. Nitze School of Advanced International Studies, Johns Hopkins University, The Nitze Building, 1740 Massachusetts Avenue, Washington, DC 20036, USA.

NAFTALI, Ben (see Offen, Yehuda)

NAGATSUKA, Ryuji; Japanese academic and writer; b. 20 April 1924, Nagoya; m. 1949. *Education:* Univ. of Tokyo. *Career:* Prof., Nihon Univ. 1968–; mem. Asscn Internationale des Critiques Littéraires, Paris. *Publications:* Napoleon tel qu'il était 1969, J'étais un kamikaze 1972, George Sand, sa vie et ses oeuvres 1977, Napoleon (two vols) 1986, Talleyrand 1990; contrib. to Yomiuri Shimbun. *Honours:* Prix Pierre Mille 1972, Prix Senghor 1973. *Address:* 7-6-37 Oizumigakuen-cho, Nerima-ku, Tokyo, Japan.

NAGEL, Paul Chester, BA, MA, PhD; American historian and writer; b. 14 Aug. 1926, Independence, MO; m. Joan Peterson 1948; three s. *Education:* Univ. of Minnesota. *Career:* historian, Strategic Air Command, US Air Force, Omaha, 1951–53; Asst Prof., Augustana Coll., Sioux Falls, SD 1953–54; Asst Prof. to Assoc. Prof., Eastern Kentucky Univ., Richmond 1954–61; Visiting Prof., Amherst Coll. 1957–58, Vanderbilt Univ. 1959, Univ. of Minnesota 1964; Faculty, Univ. of Kentucky 1961–65, Prof. of History 1965–69, Dean, Coll. of Arts and Sciences 1965–69; Special Asst to Pres. for Academic Affairs, Univ. of Missouri 1969–71, Prof. of History 1969–78, Vice-Pres. for Academic Affairs 1971–74; Prof. of History and Head of Dept of History, Univ. of Georgia 1978–80; Dir, Virginia Historical Soc., Richmond 1981–85; Distinguished Lee Scholar, Lee Memorial Foundation 1986–90; Visiting Scholar, Duke Univ. 1991–92, Univ. of Minnesota 1992–, Carleton Coll. 1993–; mem. Colonial Williamsburg Foundation (Trustee 1983–95), Mass Historical Soc., Pilgrim Soc., Soc. of American Historians, Southern Historical Asscn (Pres. 1984–85). *Publications:* One Nation Indivisible: The Union in American Thought 1776–1861 1964, This Sacred Trust: American Nationality 1798–1898 1971, Missouri: A History 1977, Descent from Glory: Four Generations of the John Adams Family 1983, Extraordinary Lives: The Art and Craft of American Biography (co-author) 1986, The Adams Women: Abigail and Louisa Adams, Their Sisters and Daughters 1987, George Caleb Bingham (co-author) 1989, The Lees of Virginia: Seven Generations of an American Family 1990, Massachusetts and the New Nation (co-author) 1992, John Quincy Adams: A Public Life, A Private Life 1997, The German Migration to Missouri 2002, George Caleb Bingham: Missouri's Famed Painter and Forgotten Politician 2005; contribs to professional journals and general publications. *Honours:* Best Book Award 1977, Book of the Month Club Main Selection 1983, Laureate of Virginia 1988, American Soc. of Colonial Dames Book Award 1998, Best Biography Award 1999. *Address:* 1425 10th Avenue S, Apt 655, Minneapolis, MN 55404, USA (home).

NAGEL, Thomas, PhD; American academic; *Professor of Philosophy and Law, School of Law, New York University*; b. 4 July 1937, Belgrade, Serbia; s. of Walter Nagel and Carolyn Baer Nagel; m. 1st Doris Blum 1968 (divorced 1972); m. 2nd Anne Hollander 1979. *Education:* Cornell and Harvard Univs and Univ. of Oxford, UK. *Career:* Asst Prof. of Philosophy, Univ. of Calif., Berkeley 1963–66; Asst Prof. of Philosophy, Princeton Univ. 1966–69, Assoc. Prof. 1969–72, Prof. 1972–80; Prof., New York Univ. 1980–, Prof. of Philosophy and Law 1986–; Fellow, American Acad. of Arts and Sciences, British Acad. *Publications:* The Possibility of Altruism 1970, Mortal Questions 1979, The View from Nowhere 1986, What Does It All Mean? 1987, Equality and Partiality 1991, Other Minds 1995, The Last Word 1997. *Address:* New York University Law School, 40 Washington Square South, New York, NY 10012, USA. *Telephone:* (212) 998-6225. *Fax:* (212) 995-4526.

NAGY, Paul, BA, DipArts; Hungarian writer; b. 23 Aug. 1934. *Education:* studied in Hungary and at Sorbonne, University of Paris. *Career:* co-founder, Atelier Hongrois, 1962, p'ART video review, 1987; mem. Union des écrivains français; Union des écrivains hongrois. *Publications:* Les faineants de Hampstead, 1969; SadisfactionS, 1977; Journal in-time, I, 1984, II, 1994; Points de Repères 'Postmodernes': Lyotard, Habermas, Derrida, 1993; Les genres nouveaux de la littérature, 1995; Sacrés Grecs!, 1998; Le texte inaccessible, 1999, Recueil d'essais 2005; contrib. to several publications. *Honours:* Prix Attila József, Budapest, 2000. *Address:* 141 avenue Jean Jaurès, 92120 Montrouge, France (home). *E-mail:* nagypal@free.fr (home).

NAGY, Phyllis; American playwright and screenwriter; b. 7 Nov. 1960, New York; d.of Peter Thomas Nagy and Virginia Marie nagy (née Sottile). *Career:* debut at Royal Court Theatre, London, fmr Writer-in-Residence; currently commissioned to write plays for Nat. Theatre, Royal Shakespeare Co., Royal Court Theatre, London; playwrighting fellowships from Nat. Endowment of the Arts, McKnight Foundation, New York Foundation for the Arts. *Plays include:* Butterfly Kiss, Entering Queens, Girl Bar, Plaza Delores, The Scarlet Letter, Trip's Crinch, Weldon Rising, The Strip, Disappeared, Never Land. *Screenplays include:* Found in the Street 2004, Mrs. Harris 2005 (also dir). *Address:* c/o Mel Kenyan, Casarotto Ramsay Ltd, 60–66 Wardour Street, London, W1V 3HP, England; c/o Joyce Ketay, 1501 Broadway, Suite 1910, New York, NY 10036, USA. *Telephone:* (20) 7287-4450. *Fax:* (20) 7287-9128.

NAHAL, Chaman, MA, PhD; Indian writer; b. 2 Aug. 1927, Sialkot. *Education:* Delhi University, University of Nottingham. *Career:* mem. Dept of English, Delhi University 1963–; columnist, Talking About Books, The Indian Express newspaper 1966–73; Assoc. Prof. of English, Long Island University, New York, USA 1968–70. *Publications:* The Weird Dances (short stories), 1965; A Conversation with J. Kristnamurti, 1965; D. H. Lawrence: An Eastern View, 1970; Drugs and the Other Self (ed.), 1971; The Narrative Pattern in Ernest Hemingway's Fiction, 1971; The New Literatures in English, 1985; The Bhagavad-Gita: A New Rendering, 1987. Fiction: My True Faces, 1973; Azadi, 1975; Into Another Dawn, 1977; The English Queens, 1979; The Crown and the Loincloth, 1982; Sunrise in Fiji, 1988; The Salt of Life, 1990; Silent Life: Memoirs of a Writer 2005. *Address:* c/o Roli Books, M-75, Greater Kailash-II Market, New Delhi 110 048, India (office).

NAIDOO, Beverley, PhD; South African/British writer and educationalist; b. 21 May 1943, Johannesburg, South Africa; d. of Ralph Henry Trewhela and Evelyn Levison; m. Nandhagopaul Naidoo 1969; one s. one d. *Education:* Univs of Witwatersrand, York and Southampton. *Career:* NGO worker, SA 1964; detained without trial, SA 1964; teacher, London then Dorset, UK 1969–89; educ. adviser on English and cultural diversity, Dorset 1990–97; writer 1985–; held int. writers' workshops 1991–. *Plays:* The Playground, Polka Theatre, London 2004. *Radio:* The Other Side of Truth (BBC) 2003. *Publications:* Censoring Reality: An Examination of Non-fiction Books on South Africa 1985, Journey to Jo'burg 1985, Chain of Fire 1989, Through Whose Eyes? Exploring Racism: Reader, Text and Context 1992, Letang and Julie (series – illustrator Petra Rohr-Rouendaal) 1994, No Turning Back 1995, Where is Zami? (illustrator Petra Rohr-Rouendaal) 1998, The Other Side of Truth 2000, Out of Bounds 2001, Baba's Gift (with Maya Naidoo, illustrator Karin Littlewood) 2003, The Great Tug of War and Other Stories 2003, Web of Lies 2004, Burn My Heart 2007. *Honours:* Hon. Visiting Fellow, School of Educ., Univ. of Southampton 1992–2006; Hon. DLitt (Southampton) 2002; Hon. DUniv (Open Univ.) 2003; The Other Award, UK 1985, Child Study Children's Book Cttee Award, USA 1986, 1998, Vlag en Wimpel Award, Netherlands 1991, African Studies Asscn Africana Children's Book Award, USA 1998, 2004, Arts Council Writer's Award, UK 1999, Smarties Silver Medal for Children's Books, UK 2000, Carnegie Medal for Children's Literature, UK 2000, Jane Addams Book Award, USA 2002, 2004. *Address:* c/o Hilary Delamere, The Agency, 24 Pottery Lane, London, W11 4LZ, England (office). *Telephone:* (20) 7727-1346 (office). *Fax:* (20) 7727-9037 (office). *E-mail:* info@theagency.co.uk (office). *Website:* www.beverleynaidoo.com (office).

NAIFEH, Steven Woodward, AB, MA, JD; American writer; b. 19 June 1952, Tehran, Iran. *Education:* Princeton University, Harvard University. *Publications:* Culture Making: Money, Success, and the New York Art World, 1976; Moving Up in Style (with Gregory White Smith), 1980; Gene Davis, 1981; How to Make Love to a Woman, 1982; What Every Client Needs to Know About Using a Lawyer, 1982; The Bargain Hunter's Guide to Art Collecting, 1982; Why Can't Men Open Up?: Overcoming Men's Fear of Intimacy, 1984; The Mormon Murders: A True Story of Greed, Forgery, Deceit, and Death, 1988; Jackson Pollack: An American Saga, 1989; The Best Lawyers in America (ed. with Gregory White Smith), 1990; The Best Doctors in America (ed. with Gregory White Smith), 1992; Final Justice: The True Story of the Richest Man Ever Tried for Murder, 1993; A Stranger in the Family: A True Story of Murder, Madness, and Unconditional Love, 1995; On a Street Called Easy, In a Cottage Called Joye, 1996; Making Miracles Happen, 1997. *Honours:* Pulitzer Prize for Biography 1991. *Address:* Woodward/White, Inc., 129 First Avenue, SW, Aiken, SC 29801, USA. *E-mail:* info@bestlawyers.com.

NAIPAUL, Sir V(idiadhar) S(urajprasad), Kt, CLit, BA, FRSL; Trinidadian-born writer; b. 17 Aug. 1932, Chaguanas; m. 1st Patricia Ann Hale 1955 (died 1996); m. 2nd Nadira Khannum Alvi 1996; one d. (adopted). *Education:* Queen's Royal Coll., Port-of-Spain and Univ. Coll. Oxford. *Career:* for two years freelance broadcaster with the BBC, producing programmes for the Caribbean area; fiction reviewer on New Statesman 1958–61; grant from Trinidad Govt to travel in Caribbean and S America 1961; in India 1962–63, 1975, 1988–89, in Uganda 1965–66, in USA 1969, 1978–79, 1987–88, in Argentina 1972, 1973–74, 1977, 1991, in Venezuela 1977, 1985, in Iran, Pakistan, Malaysia and Indonesia 1979–80, 1995; mem. Soc. of Authors. *Publications:* The Mystic Masseur 1957, The Suffrage of Elvira 1958, Miguel Street 1959, A House for Mr Biswas 1961, The Middle Passage 1962, Mr Stone and the Knights Companion 1963, An Area of Darkness 1964, The Mimic Men 1967, A Flag on the Island 1967 (collection of short stories), The Loss of El Dorado 1969, In a Free State 1971, The Overcrowded Barracoon (essays) 1972, Guerrillas 1975, India: A Wounded Civilization 1977, A Bend in the River 1979, A Congo Diary 1980, The Return of Eva Perón 1980, Among the Believers 1981, Finding the Centre 1984, The Enigma of Arrival 1987, A Turn In The South 1989, India: A Million Mutinies Now 1990, A Way in the World 1994, Beyond Belief 1998, Letters Between a Father and Son 1999, Reading and Writing: a Personal Account 2000, Half a Life 2001, Literary Occasions 2004, Magic Seeds 2004. *Honours:* Hon. DLitt (Univ. of the W Indies, St Augustine) 1975, (St Andrews) 1979, (Columbia) 1981, (Cambridge) 1983, (London) 1988, (Oxford) 1992; John Llewelyn Rhys Memorial Prize 1958, Somerset Maugham Award 1961, Phoenix Trust Award 1962, Hawthornden Prize 1964, W. H. Smith Award 1968, Booker Prize 1971, Jerusalem Prize 1983, Ingersoll Prize 1986, David Cohen British Literature Prize 1993, Nobel Prize for Literature 2001. *Address:* Aitken Alexander Associates Ltd, 18–21 Cavaye Place, London, SW10 9PT, England. *Telephone:* (20) 7373-8672. *Fax:* (20) 7373-6002. *E-mail:* reception@aitkenalexander.co.uk. *Website:* www.aitkenalexander.co.uk.

NAIRN, Tom, PhD; British academic and writer; *Professor of Nationalism and Cultural Diversity, Globalism Research Institute, Royal Melbourne Institute of Technology (RMIT). Education:* Univs of Edinburgh, Oxford, and Rome, Italy. *Career:* taught at Univ. of Birmingham and Hornsey Coll. of Art, London 1960s; Sr Research Fellow, Transnational Inst., Amsterdam, Netherlands 1973–79; worked for Scottish TV as writer-producer with Agenda Productions 1980s before returning to acad. life; worked with Ernest Gellner at Cen. European Univ., Prague, Czechoslovakia; f. Nationalism Studies degree at Grad. School, Univ. of Edinburgh 1995–2000; taught at Monash Univ., Australia 2001–02; Prof. of Nationalism and Cultural Diversity, Globalism Research Inst., Royal Melbourne Inst. of Tech. (RMIT Univ.) 2002–. *Publications include:* The Break-Up of Britain: Crisis and Neo-Nationalism, Atlantic Europe, The Left Against Europe, The Enchanted Glass: Britain and its Monarchy, After Britain: New Labour and the Return of Scotland, Faces of Nationalism: Janus Revisited, The Beginning of the End (with Angelo Quattrocchi), Pariah, Counter-Clockwise: Renegotiating Britain 2002. *Address:* Globalism Research Institute, Royal Melbourne Institute of Technology, 124 La Trobe Street, Melbourne, Vic. 3000, Australia (office). *Telephone:* (3) 9925-9586 (office). *Website:* www.rmit.edu.au/globalism (office).

NAJJAR, Alexandre; Lebanese writer and poet; b. 5 Feb. 1967, s. of Roger Najjar. *Career:* lawyer; literary critic for two French-language magazines. *Publications:* narratives: La Honte du survivant 1989, Comme un aigle en dérive 1993, L'École de la guerre 1999; novels: Les Exilés du Caucase 1995, L'Astronome 1997, Athina 2000, Lady Virus 2002, Le Roman de Beyrouth 2005; non-fiction: Pérennité de la littérature libanaise d'expression française, L'Administration de la Société Anonyme Libanaise 1998, Le Procureur de l'Empire: Ernest Pinard (1822–1909) 2001, Le Crapaud 2001, Kahlil Gibran, L'auteur du Prophète (biog.) 2002, De Gaulle et le Liban, Vers l'Orient compliqué (1929–1931) 2002, De Gaulle et le Liban, de la Guerre à l'Indépendance (1941–1943) 2004, Le Mousquetaire 2004; poems: Khiam 2000, A quoi rêvent les statues? 1989. *Honours:* Bourse de l'Ecrivain Fondation Hachette 1990, Prix de Poésie de la Ville de Paris 1990, Prix du Palais littéraire 1994, Prix littéraire de l'Asie French-speaking Writers' Asscn 1996, France-Liban Prize 1998, Amsterdam Prize 1999. *Address:* c/o Editions Plon, 76 rue Bonaparte, 75006 Paris, France. *E-mail:* alexandre@najjar.org. *Website:* www.najjar.org.

NAJŽAR-FLEGER, Dora, PhD; Croatian dentist, academic, writer, poet and journalist; b. 10 Oct. 1931, Sv Petar Orehovec; d. of Antun Najžar and Marija Najžar; m. Branko Fleger 1958; one d. one s. *Education:* Univ. of Zagreb School of Dentistry. *Career:* Dentist 1957–60; Asst Dental Pathology Dept, Univ. of Zagreb 1960–71, Asst Prof. 1972–86, apptd Head Dept of Operative Dentistry and Endodontics Dental Clinic 1981, Head Dept of Dental Pathology 1982–91, Full Prof. 1987–98; Pres. Dental Pathology Section, Croatian Medical Asscn 1986–89; Post-doctoral Fellow, Univ. of British Columbia, Vancouver, Canada 1982–83. *Publications:* Accidents in Dental Practice (contrib.) 1988, Lexicon of Dentistry (contrib.) 1990, Preventive Programs in Dentistry (contrib.) 1990, Operative Dentistry (contrib.) 1992; contribs to professional journals 1962–99, newspapers and literary journals 2000–. *Honours:* awards from Croatian Medical Asscn 1974, 1986, 1997. *Address:* Novomarofska 37, 10000 Zagreb, Croatia (home). *Telephone:* (1) 3021780 (home). *E-mail:* dora.najzar-fleger@zg.htnet.hr (home).

NAKAE, Toshitada; Japanese journalist; b. 4 Oct. 1929, Chiba City; m. Yohko Nakae 1959; three s. *Education:* Tokyo Univ. *Career:* local reporter Asahi Shimbun 1953–58, econ. reporter 1958–72, Econ. Ed. 1972–76, Asst Man. Ed. 1976–78, Man. Ed. 1978–83, Dir 1982–97, Pres. 1989–96, Special Adviser 1996–; Pres. Japan Newspaper Publrs' and Eds' Asscn 1991–95. *Publications:* (in English trans.) Cities 1966, The Pulitzer Prize Story 1970, The News Media 1971, The Economy of Cities 1971. *Honours:* Commdr des Arts et des Lettres 1994. *Address:* 1-11-1-401 Hamadayama, Suginami-ku, Tokyo, Japan. *Telephone:* (3) 3302-7087. *Fax:* (3) 3302-7087 (home).

NAMJOSHI, Suniti, PhD; Canadian/British writer; b. 20 April 1941, Bombay (now Mumbai), India; d. of Manohar Namjoshi and Sarojini Namjoshi (née Naik Nimbalkar). *Education:* Univ. of Pune, India and McGill Univ., Montréal. *Career:* fmr academic in Canada; lives and writes in Devon. *Publications:* Feminist Fables 1981, 1994, Saint Suniti and the Dragon 1994, Building Babel 1996, Goja 2000, Sycorax 2006, several 'Aditi' children's books. *Address:* Grindon Cottage, Combpyne Lane, Rousdon, nr Lyme Regis, DT7 3XW, England. *Telephone:* (1297) 443422. *Fax:* (1297) 443422. *E-mail:* suniti@freeuk.com.

NANDA, Bal Ram, MA; Indian historian and writer; b. 11 Oct. 1917, Rawalpindi; m. Janak Khosla 1946, two s. *Education:* University of Punjab, Lahore. *Career:* Dir, Nehru Memorial Museum and Library, New Delhi, 1965–79; mem. Institute for Defence Studies and Analyses, New Delhi; Authors' Guild of India; Indian International Centre. *Publications:* Mahatma Gandhi: A Biography, 1958; The Nehrus, Motilal and Jawaharlal, 1962; Gandhi: A Pictorial Biography, 1972; Gokhale: The Indian Moderates and the British Raj, 1977; Jawaharlal Nehru: A Pictorial Biography, 1980; Gandhi and His Critics, 1986; Gandhi, Pan-Islamism, Imperialism and Nationalism in India, 1989; In Gandhi's Footsteps: Life and Times of Jamnalal Bajaj, 1990; Jawaharal Nehru: Rebel and Statesman, 1996; The Making of a Nation:

India's Road to Independence, 1998, In Search of Gandhi 2002, Witness to Partition 2003. *Editor:* Socialism in India, 1972; Indian Foreign Policy: The Nehru Years, 1975; Science and Technology in India, 1977; Essays in Modern Indian History, 1980; Selected Works of Gobind Ballabh Pant, Vols 1–18, 1993–2002; Mahatma Gandhi: 125 Years, 1995. *Contributions:* numerous newspapers, magazines and journals. *Honours:* Rockefeller Fellowship, 1964; National Fellowship, Indian Council of Social Science Research, New Delhi, 1979; Dadabhai Naoroji Memorial Prize, 1981; Padma Vibhushan 2003. *Address:* S-174 Panchshila Park, New Delhi 110017, India.

NAPELS, Stella (see Van De Laar, Waltherus Antonius Bernardinus)

NAPIER, William (Bill) McDonald, PhD, FRAS; British astronomer and writer; b. 29 June 1940, Perth, Scotland; m. Nancy Miller Baillie 1965; one s. one d. *Career:* mem. Int. Astronomical Union, Spaceguard UK, Cttee on Space Research, European Astronomical Soc. *Publications:* The Cosmic Serpent 1982, The Cosmic Winter 1990, The Origin of Comets 1990, Nemesis (novel) 1998, Revelation (novel) 2000, The Lure (novel) 2002, Shattered Icon (novel) 2004; contrib. to New Scientist, Astronomy Today. *Honours:* Hon. Prof., Univ. of Wales, Cardiff 2001; jt recipient Arthur Beer Memorial Prize 1986–87.

NARAYAMA, Fujio; Japanese writer and poet; b. 13 June 1948, Iwate. *Education:* Toho Gakuen Junior College, Tokyo. *Career:* mem. Japan Writers Asscn; MWA; Mystery Writers of Japan; Sino-Japanese Cultural Exchange Society. *Publications:* Manhattan Ballad, 1977; Sanctuary of Evil, 1979; Lay Traps in the Winter, 1981; The Scarred Bullet, 1989; Neverending Night, 1992. *Honours:* Iwate Arts Festival Awards, 1967, 1969; All Yomimono New Writer's Award, 1975.

NASAW, David, PhD; American writer and historian; *Distinguished Professor of History, City University of New York. Education:* Columbia Univ. *Career:* Distinguished Prof. of History, Graduate Center, City Univ. of New York; historical consultant for television documentaries. *Publications:* Schooled to Order: A Social History of Public Schooling in United States 1979, Children of the City: At Work and at Play 1985, Going Out: The Rise and Fall of Public Amusements 1993, The Chief: The Life of William Randolph Hearst 2000, Andrew Carnegie 2006; articles include: Learning to go to the Movies, in American Heritage (Nov. 1993), Teaching Cultural History to Graduate Students, in Radical History Review (Fall 1996), Cities of Light, Landscapes of Pleasure, in Landscapes of Modernity (ed. by Oliver Zunz and David Ward) 1992; contrib. to New Yorker, The Nation, Traveler and other periodicals. *Honours:* Bancroft Prize 2000, J. Anthony Lucas Prize 2000. *Address:* The Graduate Center, The City University of New York, 365 Fifth Avenue, New York, NY 10016-4309, USA (office). *Telephone:* (212) 817-8431 (office). *E-mail:* dnasaw@gc.cuny.edu (office).

NASH, Gary Baring, BA, PhD; American academic and writer; b. 27 July 1933, Philadelphia, PA; m. 1st Mary Workum 1955 (divorced); one s. three d.; m. 2nd Cynthia Shelton 1981. *Education:* Princeton University. *Career:* Asst to the Dean, Graduate School, 1959–61, Instructor, 1964–65, Asst Prof., 1965–66, Princeton University; Asst Prof., 1966–68, Assoc. Prof., 1969–72, Prof. of History, 1972–, Dean, Undergraduate Curriculum Development, 1984–91, University of California at Los Angeles; Assoc. Dir., 1988–94, Dir, 1994–, National Center for History in the Schools; Co-Chair., National History Studies Project, 1992–96; mem. American Antiquarian Soc.; American Historical Asscn; Institute of Early American History and Culture; Organization of American Historians, pres., 1994–95; Soc. of American Historians, American Philosophical Soc. *Publications:* Quakers and Politics: Pennsylvania, 1681–1726, 1968; Class and Society in Early America, 1970; The Great Fear: Race in the Mind of America (ed. with Richard Weiss), 1970; Red, White, and Black; The Peoples of Early America, 1974; The Urban Crucible: Social Change, Political Consciousness, and the Origins of the American Revolution, 1979; Struggle and Survival in Colonial America (ed. with David Sweet), 1980; The Private Side of American History (co-ed.), 2 vols, 1975, 1979; The American People: Creating a Nation and a Society (with J. R. Jeffrey), 2 vols, 1985, 1989; Retracing the Past, 2 vols, 1985, 1989; Race, Class and Politics: Essays on American Colonial and Revolutionary Society, 1986; Forging Freedom: The Formation of Philadelphia's Black Community, 1720–1840, 1988; Race and Revolution, 1990; Freedom by Degrees: Emancipation and Its Aftermath in Pennsylvania (with Jean R. Soderlund), 1991; American Odyssey: The United States in the 20th Century, 1991; History on Trial: Culture Wars and the Teaching of the Past (with Charlotte Crabtree and Ross Dunn), 1997; Forbidden Love: The Secret History of Mixed-Race America, 1999; First City: Philadelphia and the Forging of Historical Memory 2002, Landmarks of the American Revolution 2003, African American Lives: The Struggle for Freedom (co-author) 2005, The Unknown American Revolution: The Unruly Birth of Democracy and the Struggle to Create America 2005, The Forgotten Fifth: African Americans in the Age of Revolution 2006; contrib. to professional journals. *Honours:* Guggenheim Fellowship, 1969–70; ACLS Fellowship, 1973–74. *Address:* 1336 Las Canoas Road, Pacific Palisades, CA 90272, USA. *Telephone:* (310) 825-4702 (office); (310) 454-5824 (home). *Fax:* (310) 454-1808 (home). *E-mail:* gnash@ucla.edu (home).

NASHASHIBI, Nassiriddin; Palestinian journalist; b. 1924. *Education:* American Univ. of Beirut. *Career:* Arab Office, Jerusalem 1945–47; Chief Chamberlain, Amman, Jordan 1951; Dir Gen. Hashemite Broadcasting 1952; Ed. Akhbar al Youm, Cairo; Chief Ed. Al-Gumhuriyah, 1959–65; Rep. of the Arab League 1965–67; Diplomatic Ed. Al-Ahram; freelance journalist in Europe and the Middle East; Diplomatic Commentator, Jordanian, Israeli and

other Middle Eastern TV stations. *Publications:* What Happened in the Middle East 1958, Political Short Stories 1959, Return Ticket to Palestine 1960, Some Sand 1962, An Arab in China 1964, Roving Ambassador 1970, The Ink is Very Black 1976 and 40 other books. *Honours:* Order of Independence, Jordan; Order of the Jordanian Star. *Address:* 55 Avenue de Champel, Geneva, Switzerland; PO Box 1897 Jerusalem 91017, Israel; 26 Lowndes Street, London, SW1, England. *Telephone:* (22) 3463763 (Geneva) (office); (20) 7235-1427 (London) (office).

NASIR, Agha, MA; Pakistani television executive and playwright; *Executive Director, Geo TV Network;* b. 9 Feb. 1937, Meerut, UP, India; s. of Ali Ahmad Khan and Ghafari Begum; m. Safia Sultana 1957; one s. two d. *Education:* Karachi Univ. *Career:* Programmes Man. Pakistani TV 1967–68, Additional Gen. Man. 1967, Gen. Man. 1969–72, Dir Programmes Admin. 1972–86, Deputy Man. Dir 1986–87, Man. Dir 1987–88; Man. Dir Nat. Film Devt Corpn 1979; Dir-Gen. Pakistan Broadcasting Corpn 1989–92; Chief Exec. Shalimar Recording and Broadcasting Co. 1992–97; media consultant 1997–; Exec. Dir Geo TV Network 1998–. *Radio:* has written a large number of features and plays for radio and produced more than 500 programmes. *Television:* has written more than 20 plays for TV and has produced about 100. *Publications:* Saat Dramay (plays), Television Dramey (TV plays), Gumshuda Log (collection of articles), Gulshan-e-Yaad. *Honours:* recipient of numerous awards for radio and TV plays; Pride of Performance Award from Pres. of Pakistan for services in field of broadcasting 1993. *Address:* Geo TV Network, 40 Blue Area, Fazal-ul-huq Road, Islamabad (office); House No. 23, Street No. 3, F-8/3, Islamabad, Pakistan (home). *Telephone:* (51) 2263685 (home); (51) 2852619 (home). *Fax:* (51) 2827396 (office); (51) 2263685 (home). *E-mail:* agha .nasir@geo.tv (office).

NASIRI, Buthaina al; Iraqi short story writer and publisher; b. 1947. *Education:* Univ. of Baghdad Coll. of Arts. *Career:* moved to Cairo, Egypt 1979, where she runs a publishing house specializing in the works of Iraqi writers under UN sanctions. *Publications:* five short story collections in Arabic; Final Night (in trans.) 2003. *Address:* c/o The American University in Cairo Press, 113 Sharia Kasr el Aini Street, Cairo, Egypt. *E-mail:* aucpress@ aucegypt.edu. *Website:* www.aucpress.com.

NASRALLAH, Emily, BA; Lebanese writer and journalist; b. 6 July 1931, Kfeir; d. of Daoud Abi Rashed and Lutfa Abou Nasr; m. Philip Nasrallah 1957; two s. two d. *Education:* Shoueifat Nat. Coll., Beirut Univ. Coll. and American Univ. of Beirut. *Career:* mem. writing staff Al-Sayyad magazine and Al-Anwar newspaper 1955–70; Cultural and Public Relations Consultant Beirut Univ. Coll. 1973–75; Feature Writer and Ed. Fayruz Magazine 1981–87; ECWA Del. to UN Women's Forum on Population and Devt, New York, USA 1974; writer and women's rights activist, one of the Beirut Decentrist women writers; participated in Olympics Authors' Festival, Calgary, Canada 1988; panellist and guest reader PEN Int. Congress, Toronto and Montréal, Canada 1989. *Publications:* (in Arabic): novels: Birds of September (translated into several languages, Laureate Best Novel, Said Akl Prize, Friends of the Book Prize) 1962, The Oleander Tree 1968, The Bondaged (translated into German 1996) 1974, Those Memories 1980, Flight Against Time (translated into several languages) 1981, Sleeping Ember 1995; short story collections: Island of Illusion 1973, The Source 1978, The Woman in Seventeen Stories 1983, The Lost Mill 1984, Forgotten Papers, Black and White, Our Daily Bread 1990, A House Not Her Own 1992, Stations of Departure 1996, Gypsy Nights 1998; non-fiction: Pioneer Women, from East and West (six vols) 1986, Recollections of Start-up of Journalist Career (memoirs), Southern Winds (essay) (Poet Said Akl Prize 2002) 2002; children's books: The Resplendent Flower (novel) 1975, Little Shadi (reading book) 1977, A Cat's Diary (novel) (LIBBY Children's Book Prize 1998) 1997, Days Recounted (short story collection) 1997, On a Snow Carpet, Anda the Fool. *Honours:* Fayruz Magazine Prize for Outstanding Literary Works 1983, Khalil Gibran Prize, Arab Heritage Union, Australia 1991. *Address:* Osman Building, Ain-el-Tineh, Off Verdun Street, Beirut, Lebanon. *Telephone:* (1) 862483. *Fax:* (1) 862483. *E-mail:* pnsralah@ cyberia.net.lb. *Website:* www.emilynasrallah.com.

NASREEN, Taslima; Bangladeshi feminist, writer and doctor; b. 25 Aug. 1962, Mymensingh, E Pakistan (now Bangladesh); d. of Royab Ali; m. 3rd (divorced). *Education:* Mymensingh Medical Coll., Dhaka Univ. *Career:* practised as a gynaecologist 1986–93; columnist Ajker Kagoj 1989; books banned in Bangladesh and Indian state of W Bengal, fatwa (death threat) pronounced against her 1993; left Bangladesh to live in self-imposed exile in Sweden 1994, later in Germany, USA and France; conducting research into women's rights in Islamic countries Harvard Univ. 2003–04; has published 16 books. *Publications include:* Laija (Shame) (novel) 1993, Nirbachito Kolam, Nosto meyer nosto goddo, choto choto dukkho kotha (selected columns), Opoppokkho, Bhromor koio gia, Sodh, Fera (Return), Nirbachito Kobita, Amar Meyebela, Utal Hawa 2002, Dwihkandita (Split in Two, autobiog.) 2003. *Honours:* Dr hc (Ghent Univ., Belgium) 1995; Ananda Puroshkar, India 1992, Kurt Tukholsky Prize, Sweden 1994, Feminist of the Year, USA 1994, Human Rights Award, French Govt 1994, Edit de Nantes Award, France 1994, Monismanien Prize, Sweden 1995, Sakharov Prize, European Parl. 1995, Int. Humanist Award, Int. Humanist and Ethical Union 1996. *Address:* c/o Penguin Books India Pvt. Ltd, #11 Community Centre, Panchsheel Park, New Delhi 110 017, India.

NASSAR, Eugene Paul, BA, MA, PhD; American academic, writer and poet; b. 20 June 1935, Utica, NY; m. Karen Nocian 1969, one s. two d. *Education:*

Kenyon College, Worcester College, Oxford, Cornell University. *Career:* Instructor in English, Hamilton College, 1962–64; Asst Prof., 1964–66, Assoc. Prof., 1966–71, Prof. of English, 1971–, Utica College, Syracuse University; Dir, Ethnic Heritage Studies Center. *Publications:* Wallace Stevens: An Anatomy of Figuration, 1965; The Rape of Cinderella: Essays in Literary Continuity, 1970; Selections from a Prose Poem: East Utica, 1971; The Cantos of Ezra Pound: The Lyric Mode, 1975; Wind of the Land: Two Prose Poems, 1979; Essays: Critical and Metacritical, 1983; Illustrations to Dante's Inferno, 1994; A Walk Around the Block: Literary Texts and Social Contexts, 1999. Editor: several books. Contributions: various publications. *Honours:* NEH Fellowship 1972. *Address:* 918 Arthur Street, Utica, NY 13501, USA.

NASTA, Susheila, MA, DLitt, FRSA; British literary critic, teacher, broadcaster and editor; *Editor, Wasafiri*; b. 16 Oct. 1953, Wallington, Surrey; d. of Kanayalal Nasta and Winnifred Nasta; m.; one s. one d. *Education:* Univ. of Kent, Univ. of London. *Career:* lived in India, Holland and Germany before returning to Great Britain 1960s; held academic posts at Univ. of Cambridge; Sr Lecturer, School of English and Drama Queen Mary, Univ. of London – 1998, founding-course dir MA in Nat. and Int. Literatures in English Inst. of English Studies –1998, currently Sr Visiting Research Fellow and Assoc. Fellow Inst. of English Studies; Reader in Literature, Open Univ. 1998–; Founding Ed. Wasafiri literary journal; mem. exec. cttee Commonwealth Writers Prize; judge for many literary prizes, including British Book Awards Nibbies Prize. *Radio:* plays: Highway in the Sun, El Dorado: West One. *Publications include:* Critical Perspectives on Sam Selvon 1988, Motherlands: Women's Writing from Africa, the Caribbean and South Asia (ed.) 1991, Tiger's Triumph 1995, Reading the 'New' Literatures in a Postcolonial Era (ed.) 2000, Home Truths: Fictions of the South Asian Diaspora in Britain 2002, Writing Across Worlds (ed.) 2004. *Address:* Literature Department, Faculty of Arts, The Open University, Walton Hall, Milton Keynes, MK7 6AA (office); Wasafiri: The Open University in London, 1–11 Hawley Crescent, London, NW1 8NP, England (office). *Telephone:* (1908) 652092 (Milton Keynes) (office). *E-mail:* s.m.nasta@open.ac.uk (office); wasafiri@open.ac.uk (office). *Website:* www.wasafiri.org (office).

NATHAN, Leonard Edward, BA, MA, PhD; American academic (retd), poet, writer and translator; b. 8 Nov. 1924, Los Angeles, Calif.; s. of Israel 'Jack' Nathan and Florence Nathan (née Rosenberg); m. Carol G. Nash 1949; one s. two d. *Education:* Univ. of California, Berkeley. *Career:* Instructor, Modesto Junior Coll., Calif. 1954–60; Prof., Univ. of California, Berkeley 1961–91, Chair. Dept of Rhetoric 1968–72, Prof. Emer. 1991–. *Publications:* poetry: Glad and Sorry Seasons 1963, The Matchmaker's Lament 1967, The Day the Perfect Speakers Left 1969, Flight Plan 1971, Without Wishing 1973, Coup and Other Poems 1975, The Likeness: Poems Out of India 1975, Returning Your Call 1975, Teachings of Grandfather Fox 1976, Lost Distance 1978, Dear Blood 1980, Holding Patterns 1982, Carrying On: New and Selected Poems 1985, The Potato Eaters 1999, Tears of the Old Magician 2003, Restarting the World 2006; prose: The Tragic Drama of W. B. Yeats: Figures in Dance 1963, The Poet's Work: An Introduction to Czesław Miłosz (with Arthur Quinn) 1991, Diary of a Left-Handed Bird Watcher 1996; translator: First Person, Second Person, by 'Agyeya' (with the author) 1971, Grace and Mercy in Her Wild Hair, by Ramprasad Sen (with Clinton Seely) 1982, Songs of Something Else, by Gunnar Ekelof (with James Larson) 1985, Happy as a Dog's Tail, by Anna Swir (with Czesław Miłosz) 1985, With the Skin, by Aleksander Wat (with Czesław Miłosz) 1989, Talking to My Body, by Anna Swir (with Czesław Miłosz) 1996; contrib. to reviews, journals and magazines. *Honours:* Phalen Award for Narrative Poetry 1955, Longview Foundation Award for Poetry 1962, Creative Arts Fellowships, University of California 1963–64, 1973–74, American Institute of Indian Studies Fellowship 1967–68, National Institute of Arts and Letters Award 1971, Guggenheim Fellowship 1976–77, Commonwealth Club of California, Medals for Poetry 1976, 1980, 1999. *Address:* 275 Los Ranchitos Road, San Rafael, CA 94903, USA (home). *E-mail:* lenathan@berkeley.edu.

NATHAN, Robert Stuart, BA; American writer; b. 13 Aug. 1948, Johnstown, PA. *Education:* Amherst College. *Career:* Producer, Law and Order series, NBC-TV. *Publications:* Amusement Park, 1977; Rising Higher, 1981; The Religion, 1982; The Legend, 1986; The White Tiger, 1988; In the Deep Woods, 1989. Other: In the Deep Woods (television film), 1992. Contributions: periodicals and national public radio.

NATSUKI, Shizuko; Japanese novelist; b. (Shizuko Idemitsu), 21 Dec. 1938, Tokyo; m. Yoshihide Idemitsu 1963; one s. one d. *Education:* Keio Univ. *Career:* screenplay for Only I Know (Japanese TV); followed by numerous novels, short stories and screenplays. *Films:* Tragedy of W 1984. *Plays:* novels adapted for the stage: Tragedy of W 1993, Actress X 1994. *Works adapted for television include:* The Angel Vanishes 1972 and more than 200 others. *Publications:* 39 novels including The Angel Vanishes 1970, Disappearance 1973, Murder at Mt. Fuji 1984, Dome 1986, The Third Lady 1987, Portal of the Wind 1990, Mariko 1999, The Punishment 2001, and about 240 novelettes and short stories. *Honours:* Mystery Writers of Japan Prize 1973, Prix du Roman d'Aventures (France) 1989, Nishinippon Shinsbeen Cultural Award 1999, Fukuoka Prefecture Cultural Award 2001. *Address:* 2-6-1 Ooike, Minami-ku, Fukuoka-shi 815-0073, Japan. *Telephone:* (92) 553-1893. *Fax:* (92) 552-0181.

NATSUME, Fusanosuke; Japanese Manga researcher and critic; b. 1950, Tokyo. *Education:* Aoyama Gakuin Univ. *Career:* fmrly worked in publishing; Manga critic and historian; gives lectures worldwide; columnist Shunkan

Asahi magazine 1982–91. *Television:* Natsume Fusanosuke's 'Class' (weekly programme, NHK TV) 1987–89. *Publications:* Tezuka Osamu no Bouken (The Adventure of Tezuka Osamu), Manga/Sekai/Senryaku (Manga/World/Strategy), Natsume Fusanosuke no mangagaku (Natsume Fusanosuke's Mangalogy) 1985, Tezuka Osamu wa doko ni iru (Where is Tezuka Osamu?) 1992.

NATUSCH, Sheila Ellen, MA; British/New Zealand writer and illustrator; b. 14 Feb. 1926, Invercargill, New Zealand; m. Gilbert G. Natusch 1950. *Education:* Otago Univ. *Career:* worked in Nat. Library of NZ, Old Dominion Museum, New Zealand Correspondence School; produces her own paperbacks (Nestegg Books); has produced numerous illustrations for her own and others' books 1980s–. *Publications:* Stewart Island (with N. S. Seaward) 1951, Native Plants 1956, Native Rock 1959, Animals of New Zealand 1967, A Bunch of Wild Orchids 1968, New Zealand Mosses 1969, Brother Wohlers: A Biography 1969, On the Edge of the Bush: Women in Early Southland 1976, Hell and High Water: A German Occupation of the Chatham Islands 1843–1910 1977, The Cruise of the Acheron: Her Majesty's Steam Vessel on Survey in New Zealand Waters 1848–1851 1978, The Roaring Forties 1978, Fortnight in Iceland 1979, Wild Fare for Wilderness Foragers 1979, Pop Kelp and Poha Bags 1980, A Pocketful of Pebbles 1983, Southward Ho!: The Search for a Southern Edinburgh 1844 1985, Granny Gurton's Garden (with Lois Chambers) 1987, William Swainson: The Anatomy of a Nineteenth-Century Naturalist 1987, Roy Traill of Stewart Island 1991, An Island Called Home 1992, The Natural World of the Traills: An Investigation into Some of the 19th Century Naturalists of a Particular Family in Scotland and the Colonies 1996, Ruapuke Visited 1998, My Dear Friend Tuckett, Vol. I 1998, Vol. II 1999, Wellington Awash 2000, Pop Kelp 2000, Rugged Shores 2001, Out of our Tree 2001, The Salty Shore 2003, Letters from Jean 2004; contrib. to books, periodicals and dictionaries of biog. *Honours:* NZ Order of Merit 2007; Hubert Church Award, PEN New Zealand 1969. *Address:* 46 Owhiro Bay Parade, Wellington 6023, New Zealand. *Telephone:* (4) 3836645.

NAUGHTIE, (Alexander) James, MA; British journalist; b. 9 Aug. 1951, Aberdeen, Scotland; s. of Alexander Naughtie and Isabella Naughtie; m. Eleanor Updale 1986; one s. two d. *Education:* Univ. of Aberdeen and Univ. of Syracuse, NY, USA. *Career:* journalist, The Scotsman (newspaper) 1977–84, The Guardian 1984–88, also Chief Political Corresp.; Presenter The World at One, BBC Radio 1988–94, The Proms, BBC Radio and TV 1991–, Today, BBC Radio 4 1994–, Book Club BBC Radio 4 1998–; mem. Council Gresham Coll. 1997–. *Publications:* The Rivals 2001, The Accidental American: Tony Blair and the Presidency 2004. *Honours:* Hon. LLD (Aberdeen), (St Andrews); Hon. DUniv (Stirling). *Address:* BBC News Centre, London, W12 8QT, England. *Telephone:* (20) 8624-9644.

NAUMANN, Michael, DPhil; German publisher; *Editor-in-Chief, Die Zeit*; b. 8 Dec. 1941, Köthen; s. of Eduard Naumann and Ursula Naumann (née Schönfeld); m. Christa Wessel 1969 (divorced); one s. one d. *Education:* Univ. of Munich and Queen's Coll., Oxford, UK. *Career:* Asst Prof., Univ. of Bochum 1971–76; Florey Scholar, Queen's Coll. Oxford 1976–78; Ed., Foreign Corresp. Die Zeit, Hamburg 1978–82; Sr Foreign Ed. Der Spiegel, Hamburg 1982–84; Publr Rowohlt Verlag, Reinbek 1984–95; Pres. and CEO Henry Holt and Co., New York 1996–; Minister of State for Culture 1998–2000; Ed.-in-Chief Die Zeit 2001–. *Publications:* Der Abbau einer Verkehrten Welt 1969, Amerika liegt in Kalifornien 1983, Strukturwandel des Heroismus 1984, Die Geschichte ist offen 1990, Die schönste Form der Freiheit 2001. *Honours:* Commdr Légion d'honneur. *Address:* Die Zeit, Pressehaus, Speersort 1, 20095 Hamburg, Germany (office). *Telephone:* (40) 32800 (office); (40) 327111. *Website:* www.zeit.de (office).

NAUMOFF, Lawrence Jay, BA; American author; *Professor of Creative Writing, University of North Carolina at Chapel Hill*; b. 23 July 1946, Charlotte, NC; m. (divorced); one s. *Education:* Univ. of N Carolina at Chapel Hill. *Career:* Prof. of Creative Writing, Univ. of N Carolina at Chapel Hill 2000–. *Publications:* The Night of the Weeping Women 1988, Rootie Kazootie 1990, Taller Women 1992, Silk Hope, NC 1994, A Plan for Women 1997, A Southern Tragedy, in Crimson and Yellow 2005; contribs to various literary magazines, short stories. *Honours:* Thomas Wolfe Memorial Award 1969, Nat. Endowment for the Arts Grant, 1970, Whiting Foundation Writers' Award 1990. *Address:* 1240 Epps Clark Road, Siler City, NC 27344, USA.

NAVASKY, Victor Saul, AB, LLB; American writer and editor; *Publisher and Editorial Director, The Nation*; b. 5 July 1932, New York; s. of Macy Navasky and Esther Goldberg; m. Anne Landey Strongin 1966; one s. two d. *Education:* Swarthmore Coll., Yale Univ. Law School. *Career:* Special Asst to Gov. G. Mennen Williams, Mich. 1959–60; Founding Ed. and Publr Monocle quarterly 1961–65; Ed. New York Times Magazine 1970–72, wrote monthly column (In Cold Print) for The New York Times Book Review; Ed.-in-Chief The Nation magazine 1978–94, Editorial Dir and Publr 1995–; George Delacorte Prof. of Magazine Journalism, Grad. School of Journalism, Columbia Univ. 1999–, Dir Delacorte Center of Magazines; Visiting Scholar, Russell Sage Foundation 1975–76; Ferris Visiting Prof. of Journalism, Princeton Univ. 1976–77; Visiting Prof. of Social Change, Swarthmore Coll. 1982; Fellow, John F. Kennedy School of Govt, Harvard Univ. 1994, Freedom Forum Media Studies Center 1995; has taught at numerous colls and univs; mem. Man. Bd Swarthmore Coll. 1991–94; fmr mem. Bd Authors' Guild, Cttee to Protect Journalists; fmr mem. Bd of Govs New School for Social Research; fmr Vice-Pres. PEN. *Play:* Starr's Last Tape (with Richard R. Lingeman) 1999. *Publications:* Kennedy Justice 1971, Naming Names (Nat. Book Award 1981)

1980, The Experts Speak – The Definitive Compendium of Authoritative Misinformation (co-ed. with C. Cerf, published in UK as Wish I Hadn't Said That!) 1984, The Best of the Nation (with Katrina van den Heuvel), A Matter of Opinion 2005; numerous articles and reviews published in magazines and journals of opinion. *Honours:* numerous hon. degrees; Guggenheim Fellow 1975–76, Carey McWilliams Award, American Political Science Asscn 2001. *Address:* The Nation, 33 Irving Place, 8th Floor, New York, NY 10003 (office); 33 W 67th Street, New York, NY 10023, USA (home). *Telephone:* (212) 209-5411 (office). *Fax:* (212) 982-9000 (office). *E-mail:* vic@thenation.com (office). *Website:* thenation.com (office).

NAVON, Robert, BA, MS, MA, PhD; American editor, poet, writer and philosopher; b. 18 May 1954, New York, NY. *Education:* Lehman College, CUNY, SUNY at Geneseo, New School for Social Research, New York City, University of New Mexico. *Career:* mem. Society of Ancient Greek Philosophy; American Philosophical Asscn. *Publications:* Patterns of the Universe, 1977; Autumn Songs: Poems, 1983; The Pythagorean Writings, 1986; Healing of Man and Woman, 1989; Harmony of the Spheres, 1991; Cosmic Patterns, Vol. I, 1993; Great Works of Philosophy, 7 vols (ed.). *Honours:* New York State Regents Scholar, 1971; Intern, Platform Asscn, 1980.

NAYLOR, Gloria, BA, MA; American author; b. 25 Jan. 1950, New York, NY. *Education:* Brooklyn College, CUNY, Yale University. *Career:* Writer-in-Residence, Cummington Community of the Arts, 1983; Visiting Prof., George Washington University, 1983–84, Princeton University, 1986–87, Boston University, 1987; United States Information Agency Cultural Exchange Lecturer, India, 1985; Visiting Writer, New York University, 1986; Fannie Hurst Visiting Prof., Brandeis University, 1988; Senior Fellow, Society for the Humanities, Cornell University, 1988; Pres., One Way Productions films, New York City, 1990–. *Publications:* The Women of Brewster Place: A Novel in Seven Stories, 1982; Lindin Hills, 1985; Mama Day, 1988; Bailey's Cafe, 1992; Children of the Night: The Best Short Stories by Black Writers, 1967 to the Present (ed.), 1995; The Men of Brewster Place, 1998. Contributions: magazines. *Honours:* National Book Award for Best First Novel, 1983; Distinguished Writer Award, Mid-Atlantic Writers Asscn, 1983; National Endowment for the Arts Fellowship, 1985; Candace Award, National Coalition of 100 Black Women, 1986; Guggenheiim Fellowship, 1988; Lillian Smith Award, 1989.

NAYLOR, Phyllis, BA; American writer; b. 4 Jan. 1933, Anderson, IN. *Education:* Joliet Junior College, American University. *Publications:* over 126 books for adults or children 1965–. *Honours:* American Library Asscn Newbery Medal 1992, Edgar Allan Poe Mystery Writers Award, Christopher Award, Mark Twain Award and others. *Address:* 9910 Holmhurst Road, Bethesda, MD 20817, USA.

NAYLOR, Thomas Herbert, BS, MBA, PhD; American academic and writer; *Founder, Second Vermont Republic;* b. 30 May 1936, Jackson, Miss.; m. Magdalena Raczkowska 1985; one s. one d. *Education:* Millsaps Coll., Columbia Univ., New York, Indiana Univ., Tulane Univ. *Career:* Instructor, Tulane Univ. 1961–63; Asst Prof., Duke Univ. 1964–66, Assoc. Prof. 1966–68, Prof. of Econs 1968–93, Prof. Emer. 1994–; Visiting Prof., Univ. of Wisconsin, 1969–70, Middlebury Coll. 1993–94, Univ. of Vermont, 1994–96; Pres. Social Systems Inc. 1971–80; Man. Dir Naylor Group 1980; Founder Second Vermont Repub. (Vermont's independence movt). *Publications:* Linear Programming (with Eugene Byrne) 1963, Computer Simulation Techniques (with Joseph L. Balintfy, Donald S. Burdick and King Chu) 1966, Microeconomics and Decision Models of the Firm (with John Vernon) 1969, Computer Simulation Experiments with Models of Economic Systems 1971, Corporate Planning Models 1979, Strategic Planning Management 1980, Managerial Economics: Corporate Economics and Strategy (with John M. Vernon and Kenneth Wertz) 1983, The Corporate Strategy Matrix 1986, The Gorbachev Strategy 1988, The Cold War Legacy 1991, The Search for Meaning 1994, The Abandoned Generation: Rethinking Higher Education (with William H. Willimon) 1995, The Search for Meaning in the Workplace (with Rolf Osterberg and William H. Willimon) 1996, Downsizing the USA 1997, Affluenza 2001, The Vermont Manifesto 2003; contrib. to scholarly books and journals. *Address:* 202 Stockbridge Road, Charlotte, VT 05445, USA (office). *Telephone:* (802) 425-4133 (office). *Website:* www.vermontrepublic.org (office).

NDEBELE, Njabulo Simakahle, PhD; South African academic, writer and university administrator; *Vice-Chancellor, University of Cape Town;* b. 4 July 1948, Johannesburg; m. Kathleen Mpho; one s. two d. *Education:* Univs of Botswana, Lesotho and Swaziland, Cambridge Univ., UK. *Career:* Head of Dept, Nat. Univ. of Lesotho, Dean of Humanities Faculty 1987, Pro-Vice-Chancellor 1988; Chair. and Head of Dept of African Literature, Wits Univ.; Vice-Rector, Univ. of the Western Cape; Vice-Chancellor and Prin., Univ. of the North, Scholar in Residence, Ford Foundation; Vice-Chancellor, Univ. of Cape Town July 2000–; Chair. S African Broadcasting Policy Project, Ministry of Post, Telecommunications and Broadcasting, S African Univs Vice-Chancellors' Asscn –2000; mem. Exec. Bd AA4, AC4. *Publications:* Fools and Other Stories 1983, Bonolo and the Peach Tree 1991, Rediscovery of the Ordinary 1991, The Prophetess 1992, Sarah, Rings and I 1993, South African Literature and Culture: Rediscovery of the Ordinary 1994, Death of a Son 1996, The Cry of Winnie Mandela (novel) 2004, Telling Tales (contrib. to charity anthology) 2004. *Honours:* Dr hc (Natal Univ., Chicago State Univ., Vrije Univ. Amsterdam, Soka Univ. Japan); Lincoln Univ. President's Award, Nat. Univ. of Lesotho Fiftieth Anniversary Distinguished Service Award,

NOMA Award for Publishing in Africa 1984, Sanlam Award for Outstanding Fiction, Pringle Prize for Outstanding Criticism. *Address:* University of Cape Town, Private Bag, Rondebosch 7701, Cape Town (office); Glenara, Burg Road, Rondebosch 7700, Cape Town, South Africa (home). *Telephone:* (21) 6502105, (21) 6502106 (office). *Fax:* (21) 6892440 (office). *E-mail:* vc@bremner .uct.ac.za (office). *Website:* www.uct.ac.za (office).

NDIAYE, Marie; French writer; b. 1967, Pithiviers; m. Jean-Yves Cendrey; three c. *Education:* Sorbonne, Univ. of Paris. *Plays:* Hilda (Grand Prix de la Critique 2001) 1999, Providence 2001, Papa doit manger 2003, Les Serpents 2004, Rien d'humain 2004. *Publications:* Quant au riche avenir (novel) 1985, Comédie classique (novel) 1987, La Femme changée en bûche (novel) 1989, En famille (novel) 1991, Un Temps de saison (novel) 1994, La Sorcière (novel) 1996, La Naufragée (text to pictures by J. M. W. Turner) 1999, Rosie Carpe (novel) (Prix Fémina) 2001, Tous mes amis (short stories) 2004, Autoportrait en vert 2005; also children's fiction. *Honours:* Académie de France grant for residency at Villa Médicis, Rome. *Address:* c/o Les Éditions de Minuit, 7 rue Bernard-Palissy, 75006 Paris, France (office). *E-mail:* presse@ leseditionsdeminuit.fr (office).

NDIBE, Okey A.; Nigerian poet and writer; b. 1960, Yola; m. Sheri Fafunwa-Ndibe; three c. *Career:* fmr magazine ed.; moved to USA, 1988; f. ed., African Commentary magazine; Visiting Writer-in-Residence, Asst Prof. of English, Connecticut College; weekly column, Nigerian newspaper, Guardian. *Publications:* Arrows of Rain, 2000. Contributions: An Anthology of New West African Poets; essays in numerous magazines.

NEATE, Patrick; British writer and journalist; b. London, England. *Publications:* Musungu Jim and the Great Chief Tuloko 2000, Twelve Bar Blues 2001, The London Pigeon Wars 2003, Where You're At: Notes from the Frontline of a Hip Hop Planet 2004, City of Tiny Lights 2005; contrib. to Q, The Face, Mixmag, Sky, The Washington Post, Building, Hospital Doctor, Doctor, Minx, The Times, The Telegraph, Marie-Claire, The Sunday Times, The Guardian, Harpers and Queen, The Sunday Tribune, The Standard, Time Out, Tatler. *Honours:* Whitbread Novel Award 2001. *Address:* c/o Penguin Books Ltd, 80 Strand, London, WC2R 0RL, England. *Website:* www .patrickneate.com.

NEEDLE, Jan, (Frank Kippax), BA; British writer; b. 8 Feb. 1943, Holybourne, England. *Education:* Victoria Univ. of Manchester. *Publications:* fiction for adults: Wild Wood (illustrated by William Rushton) 1981, The Scar (aka Underbelly, as Frank Kippax) 1990, The Butcher's Bill (as Frank Kippax) 1991, Other People's Blood (as Frank Kippax) 1992, Fear of Night and Darkness (as Frank Kippax) 1993, A Fine Boy for Killing 2002, The Wicked Trade 2003, The Spithead Nymph 2004, Undertaker's Wind 2006; fiction for children: Albeson and the Germans 1977, My Mate Shofiq 1978, A Fine Boy for Killing 1979, Rottenteeth (illustrated by Roy Bentley) 1979, A Sense of Shame and Other Stories 1980, The Bee Rustlers (illustrated by Paul Wright) 1980, The Size Spies (illustrated by Roy Bentley) 1980, Losers Weepers (illustrated by Jane Bottomley) 1981, Piggy in the Middle 1982, Another Fine Mess (illustrated by Roy Bentley) 1982, Going Out 1983, A Pitiful Place and Other Stories 1984, Tucker's Luck 1984, A Game of Soldiers 1985, Behind the Bike Sheds 1985, Great Days at Grange Hill 1985, Tucker in Control 1985, Skeleton at School (illustrated by Robert Bartelt) 1987, Uncle in the Attic (illustrated by Robert Bartelt) 1987, Wagstaffe the Wind-Up Boy (illustrated by Roy Bentley) 1987, In the Doghouse (illustrated by Robert Bartelt) 1988, The Sleeping Party (illustrated by Robert Bartelt) 1988, The Thief 1989, Mad Scramble (illustrated by Kate Aldous) 1990, The War of the Worms (illustrated by Kay Widdowson) 1992, Wagstaffe and the Life of Crime (illustrated by Roy Bentley) 1992, Bogeymen (illustrated by Liz Tofts) 1992, The Bully 1993. *Address:* Rye Top, Knowl Top Lane, Uppermill, Oldham, OL3 6LQ, England. *E-mail:* jan@janneedle.com. *Website:* www.janneedle.com.

NEEDLEMAN, Jacob, PhD; American academic; *Professor of Philosophy, San Francisco State University;* b. 6 Oct. 1934, Philadelphia; s. of Benjamin Needleman and Ida Needleman; m. 1st Carla Satzman 1959 (divorced 1989); one s. one d.; m. 2nd Gail Anderson 1990. *Education:* Research Assoc., Rockefeller Inst., New York 1960–61, Harvard Coll., Yale Univ. *Career:* Assoc. Prof. of Philosophy, San Francisco State Univ. 1962–66, Prof. 1967–; Dir Center for the Study of New Religions, Grad. Theological Union, Berkeley, Calif. 1977–83; Vice-Pres. Audio Literature Co. 1987–; Rockefeller Humanities Fellow, Fulbright Scholar. *Publications:* The New Religions 1970, A Sense of the Cosmos 1975, Lost Christianity 1980, The Heart of Philosophy 1982, The Way of the Physician 1985, Sorcerers 1986, Money and the Meaning of Life 1991, A Little Book on Love 1996, Time and the Soul 1998, The American Soul 2002, The Wisdom of Love 2005, Why Can't We Be Good 2007. *Address:* San Francisco State University, Department of Philosophy, 1600 Holloway Avenue, San Francisco, CA 94132, USA (office). *Telephone:* (415) 338-1596 (office). *E-mail:* jneedle@sfsu.edu (office). *Website:* www .jacobneedleman.com (office).

NEELY, Mark Edward, Jr, BA, PhD; American writer, editor and academic; b. 10 Nov. 1944, Amarillo, TX; m. Sylvia Eakes 1966. *Education:* Yale University. *Career:* Dir, Louis A Warren Lincoln Library and Museum, Fort Wayne, Indiana; Visiting Instructor, Iowa State University, 1971–72; Ed., Lincoln Lore, 1973–; Prof., St Louis University; mem. Abraham Lincoln Asscn; Indiana Asscn of Historians, pres., 1987–88; Society of Indiana Archivists, pres., 1980–81. *Publications:* The Abraham Lincoln Encyclopedia, 1981; The Lincoln Image: Abraham Lincoln and the Popular Print (with Harold Holzer and Gabor S. Boritt), 1984; The Insanity File: The Case of Mary Todd Lincoln (with R. Gerald McMurty), 1986; The Confederate Image: Prints of the Lost Cause, 1987; The Lincoln Family Album: Photographs from the Personal Collection of a Historic American Family, 1990; The Fate of Liberty: Abraham Lincoln and Civil Liberties, 1991; The Last Best Hope on Earth: Abraham Lincoln and the Promise of America, 1993; Mine Eyes Have Seen the Glory: The Civil War in American Art (with Harold Holzer), 1993. *Honours:* Pulitzer Prize for History, 1992. *Address:* c/o Dept of History, St Louis University, 221 N Grand Avenue, St Louis, MO 63103, USA.

NEESER, Andreas, DipEd; Swiss teacher, writer and poet; b. 25 Jan. 1964, Schlossrued. *Education:* Univ. of Zürich. *Career:* mem. PEN Switzerland, Swiss Writers' Union, Zürich. *Publications:* Schattensprünge (novel) 1995, Treibholz (poems) 1997. *Honours:* grants.

NEGRI, Antonio; Italian political philosopher and writer; b. 1933. *Career:* fmrly Lecturer in Political Science Univ. of Paris, Prof. of Political Science Univ. of Padua. *Publications include (in translation):* Revolution Retrieved: Selected Writings on Marx, Keynes, Capitalist Crisis and New Social Subjects 1967–1983 1988, Marx beyond Marx 1979, The Savage Anomaly 1981, Communists Like Us (with Felix Guattari) 1985, The Politics of Subversion 1986, Labor of Dionysus (with Michael Hardt) 1994, Empire 2000, Time for Revolution, Constituent Power; contrib. essays to numerous publications. *Address:* c/o Penguin Books Ltd, 80 Strand, London, WC2R 0RL, England. *Website:* www.antonionegri.com.

NEHAMAS, Alexander, BA, PhD; Spanish academic and writer; b. 22 March 1946, Athens, Greece; m. Susan Glimcher 1983; one s. *Education:* Swarthmore Coll., Princeton Univ. *Career:* Asst Prof. 1971–76, Assoc. Prof. 1976–81, Prof. of Philosophy 1981–86, Univ. of Pittsburgh; Visiting Fellow 1978–79, Prof. of Philosophy 1988, 1990–, Edmund N. Carpenter II Class of 1943 Prof. in the Humanities 1989–, Prof. of Comparative Literature 1990–, Princeton Univ.; Mills Prof. of Philosophy 1983, Sather Prof. of Classical Literature 1993, Univ. of California at Berkeley; Visiting Scholar 1983–84, Prof. of Philosophy 1986–90, Univ. of Pennsylvania; mem. American Acad. of Arts and Sciences, American Soc. for Aesthetics, Modern Greek Studies Asscn, North American Nietzsche Soc., American Philosophical Asscn, British Soc. for Aesthetics. *Publications:* Nietzsche: Life as Literature, 1985; Plato's 'Symposium' (trans. and ed. with Paul Woodruff), 1989; Aristotle's 'Rhetoric': Philosophical Essays (co-ed. with D. J. Furley), 1994; Plato's 'Phaedrus' (trans. and ed. with Paul Woodruff), 1995; The Art of Living: Socratic Reflections from Plato to Foucault, 1998; Virtues of Authenticity: Essays on Plato and Socrates, 1999. Contributions: books and professional journals. *Honours:* National Endowment for the Humanities Fellowship, 1978–79; Guggenheim Fellowship, 1983–84; Romanell-Phi Beta Kappa Prof. in Philosophy, 1990–91; Hon. DPhil, University of Athens, 1993; Phi Beta Kappa Visiting Scholar, 1995; Howard T. Behrman Award for Distinguished Achievement in the Humanities, Princeton University, 1999; Award for Distinguished Achievement, Acad. of Athens, 2000; International Nietzshe Prize, 2001, Mellon Distinguished Achievement in the Humanities Award 2001. *Address:* 692 Pretty Brook Road, Princeton, NJ 08540, USA.

NEIL, Andrew Ferguson, MA, FRSA; British publisher, broadcaster and editor; *Publisher, Press Holdings*; b. 21 May 1949, Scotland; s. of James Neil and Mary Ferguson. *Education:* Paisley Grammar School, Univ. of Glasgow. *Career:* with Conservative Party Research Dept 1971–73; with The Economist 1973–83, Ulster Political then Industrial Corresp. 1973–79, American Corresp. 1979–82, UK Ed. 1982–83; Ed. The Sunday Times 1983–94; Exec. Ed. Fox TV News, USA 1994; Exec. Chair. Sky TV 1988–90; Publr The Scotsman, Scotland on Sunday, Edinburgh Evening News 1996–2006; Publr, The Business 1999–; regular anchorman and TV commentator UK and USA; anchorman, The Daily Politics (BBC 2) and This Week (BBC 1), Contrib. Ed. Vanity Fair, New York 1994–; Chief Exec. The Spectator magazine, Apollo magazine, handbag.com 2004–; Chair. World Media Rights 2005–; f. Glenburn Enterprises; writer, speaker and broadcaster 1994–; Lord Rector Univ. of St Andrews 1999–2002. *Publications:* The Cable Revolution 1982, Britain's Free Press: Does It Have One? 1989, Full Disclosure 1996, British Excellence 1999, 2000, 2001. *Honours:* Hon. DLit (Napier Univ.) 1998; Hon. DUniv (Paisley) 2001; Hon. LLD (St Andrews) 2002. *Address:* Glenburn Enterprises, PO Box 584, London, SW7 3QY, England (office). *Telephone:* (20) 7581-1655 (office). *E-mail:* afneil@aol.com (office).

NEILL, William, MA; Scottish teacher (retd), poet and writer; b. (Uilleam Neill), 22 Feb. 1922, Prestwick, Ayrshire; m. 1st; two d.; m. 2nd Doris Marie Walker 1970. *Education:* Univ. of Edinburgh. *Career:* mem. PEN Int. (Scottish Branch). *Publications:* Scotland's Castle, 1970; Poems, 1970; Four Points of a Saltire (co-author), 1970; Despatches Home, 1972; Galloway Landscape, 1981; Cnù a Mogail, 1983; Wild Places, 1985; Blossom, Berry, Fall, 1986; Making Tracks, 1991; Straight Lines, 1922; Tales from the Odyssey, 1992; Selected Poems 1969–92, 1994; Caledonian Cramboclink, 2001. Contributions: various publications, BBC Scotland, and BBC Radio 4. *Honours:* Bardic Crown, National Gaelic MOD, 1969; Sloan Verse Prize, 1970; Grierson Prize, 1970; Scottish Arts Council Book Award, 1985. *Address:* Burnside, Crossmichael, Castle Douglas, Kirkcudbrightshire DG7 3AP, Scotland.

NEILSON, Anthony; Scottish playwright and theatre director. *Plays:* Welfare My Lovely (Traverse Theatre, Edinburgh), Heredity (Royal Court Theatre, London), White Trash (Nat. Theatre Studio, London), Normal (Edinburgh Festival) 1991, Penetrator (Traverse Theatre, Edinburgh) 1993,

The Year of the Family (Finborough Theatre, London) 1994, The Night Before Christmas (Finborough Theatre Red Room, London) 1995, Hoover Bag (Young Vic Theatre, London) 1996, The Censor (Finborough Theatre Red Room, London) (Writers' Guild Award for Best Fringe Play) 1997, Edward Gant's Amazing Feats of Loneliness (Theatre Royal, Plymouth) 2002, Stitching (Traverse Theatre, Edinburgh) 2002, The Lying Kind (Royal Court Theatre Downstairs) 2002, Twisted (theatre workshop, Edinburgh Festival) 2003, The Wonderful World of Dissocia (Tron, Glasgow) 2004, The Menu (work in progress, Nat. Theatre, London) 2006, Home (Edinburgh Queens Hall) 2006. *Other Productions include:* The Death of Klinghoffer (by John Adams; dir, Edinburgh Int. Festival and Scottish Opera) 2005. *Television includes:* Deeper Still (ten-minute film for Channel 4, also dir), A Terrible Coldness (for Granada), 'Bible John' (episode of In Suspicious Circumstances). *Film:* The Debt Collector 1999. *Radio plays include:* The Colours of the King's Rose (BBC Scotland Radio) 1988, A Fluttering of Wings. *Literary Agent:* Julia Tyrrell Management, 57 Greenham Road, London, N10 1LN, England. *Telephone:* (20) 8374-0575. *Fax:* (20) 8374-5800. *E-mail:* julia@jtmanagement.co.uk. *Website:* www.jtmanagement.co.uk.

NELSON, Antonya; American writer and academic; b. 6 Jan. 1961, Wichita, KS; m. Robert L. Boswell 1984; two s. *Education:* BA, University of Kansas, 1983; MFA, University of Arizona, 1986. *Career:* Asst Prof., 1989–95, Assoc. Prof. of English, 1995–, New Mexico State University. *Publications:* The Expendables, 1990; In the Land of Men, 1992; Family Terrorists: A Novella and Seven Stories, 1994; Talking in Bed, 1996; Nobody's Girl: A Novel, 1998; Living to Tell: A Novel, 2000; Some Fun: Stories and a Novella 2006; contrib. to anthologies and periodicals. *Honours:* Nelson Algren Award, 1988, Heartland Award, 1996, Chicago Tribune; Flannery O'Connor Award, 1990; American Library Asscn Award, 2000; Guggenheim Fellowship, 2000–01. *Address:* c/o Department of English, New Mexico State University, Las Cruces, NM 88003, USA.

NELSON, Marilyn, (Marilyn Nelson Waniek), BA, MA, PhD; American academic, poet and translator; *Professor Emerita of English, University of Connecticut*; b. 26 April 1946, Cleveland, OH; one s. one d. *Education:* Univ. of California at Davis, Univ. of Pennsylvania, Univ. of Minnesota. *Career:* Visiting Asst Prof., Reed Coll., Portland, OR 1971–72; Asst Prof., St Olaf Coll., Northfield, MN 1973–78; Instructor, Univ. of Hamburg, Germany 1977; Asst Prof. to Prof. of English, Univ. of Connecticut at Storrs 1978–, now Prof. Emer.; faculty, MFA Program, New York Univ. 1988, 1994, Vermont Coll. 1991; Elliston Poet-in-Residence, Univ. of Cincinnati 1994; Writer-in-Residence, Vanderbilt Univ. 1999; Visiting Prof., US Mil. Acad., West Point 2000; Connecticut Poet Laureate 2001–; f. writers' colony, Soul Mountain Retreat 2004; mem. Associated Writing Programs, Poetry Soc. of America, Soc. for the Study of Multi-Ethnic Literature of the USA, Soc. for Values in Higher Educ. *Publications:* For the Body 1978, The Cat Walked Through the Casserole (with Pamela Espeland) 1984, Mama's Promises 1985, The Homeplace (Annisfield-Wolf Award 1992) 1990, Partial Truth 1992, Magnificat 1995, The Fields of Praise: New and Selected Poems (The Poets Prize 1998) 1997, Carver: A Life in Poems 2001, Triolets for Triolet (chapbook), Fortune's Bones 2004, A Wreath for Emmett Till 2005, The Cachoiera Tales 2005, The Thirteenth Month (trans of the poems of Danish poet Inge Pedersen) 2006, The Ladder (trans. of a verse narrative for children by Danish poet Halfdan Rasmussen) 2006, The Freedom Business 2006, Miss Crandall's School for Young Ladies and Little Misses of Color 2007; contribs to books and journals. *Honours:* Commdr's Award for Public Service, Dept of the Army; Kent Fellowship 1976, National Endowment for the Arts Fellowships 1981, 1990, Danish Ministry of Culture Grant 1984, Connecticut Arts Award 1990, Individual Artist Grant, Connecticut Commission for the Arts 1990, Fulbright Teaching Fellow 1995, Contemplative Practices Fellowship 1999, Guggenheim Fellowship 2001, Boston Globe/Horn Book Award 2001, Newbery Honor Book 2002, Coretta Scott King Honor Book 2002, Flora Stieglitz Strauss Award 2002, Poet Laureate, State of Connecticut 2001–. *Address:* University of Connecticut, Department of English, Box U-4025, 215 Glenbrook Road, Storrs, CT 06269-4025 (office); Soul Mountain Retreat, PO Box 1071, Old Lyme, CT 06371 USA. *E-mail:* marilyn.nelson@uconn.edu (office); soulmountainretreat@yahoo.com. *Website:* english.uconn.edu/site_files/html/main.html (office); web.uconn.edu/mnelson/mainframe/index.html (office); www.soulmountainretreat.com.

NELSON, Martha, BA; American editor; *Editor, People Group*; b. 13 Aug. 1952, Pierre, S Dakota. *Education:* Barnard Coll. *Career:* fmrly staff ed., Ms magazine, Man. Ed. Signs: Journal of Women in Culture & Society, Ed.-in-Chief Women's Sports & Fitness, Ed.-in-Chief Savvy magazine; joined Time Inc. as Consulting Ed. Who Weekly, Sydney, Australia 1992, then Asst Man. Ed. People Magazine; left to co-found InStyle magazine 1994–2002; returned to Time Inc. as Man. Ed. People Magazine 2002–06, Ed. People Group 2006–. *Honours:* Corporate Citizen Award, The Actors' Fund 2003, ranked by Forbes magazine amongst 100 Most Powerful Women (92nd) 2004, (92nd) 2005, (98th) 2006. *Address:* Time Inc., 1271 Avenue of the Americas, New York, NY 10020-1393, USA (office). *Telephone:* (212) 522-1212 (office). *Fax:* (212) 467-0979 (office). *Website:* www.people.com (office).

NELSON, Richard, BA; American dramatist and screenwriter; b. 17 Oct. 1950, Chicago, IL. *Education:* Hamilton College. *Career:* Literary Man., BAM Theatre Co, Brooklyn, 1979–81; Assoc. Dir, Goodman Theatre, Chicago, 1980–83; Dramaturg, Guthrie Theatre, Minneapolis, 1981–82. *Publications:* The Vienna Notes (in Word Plays I), 1980; Il Campiello (adaptation), 1981; An

American Comedy and Other Plays, 1984; Between East and West (in New Plays USA 3), 1986; Principia Scriptoriae, 1986; Strictly Dishonorable and Other Lost American Plays (ed.), 1986; Rip Van Winkle, 1986; Jungle Coup (in Plays from Playwrights Horizons), 1987; Accidental Death of an Anarchist (adaptation), 1987.

NESBØ, Jo; Norwegian writer. *Publications:* Vleermuisman 1997, Roodborstje (trans. as The Redbreast 2006) 2003, Wraakuur 2004, Zes seconden te laat 2005. *Address:* c/o Harvill Secker, Random House, 20 Vauxhall Bridge Road, London, SW1V 2SA, England.

NETTL, Bruno, BA, MA, PhD; American musicologist and writer; *Professor of Music and Anthropology Emeritus, University of Illinois*; b. 14 March 1930, Prague, Czechoslovakia; m. Wanda Maria White 1952; two d. *Education:* Indiana Univ., Univ. of Michigan Ann Arbor. *Career:* instructor in music 1953–54, Asst Prof. of Music 1954–56, 1959–64, Music Librarian 1958–64, Wayne State Univ., Detroit; Ed., Ethnomusicology 1961–65, 1988–2002, Yearbook of the Int. Folk Music Council 1975–77; Assoc. Prof. of Music 1965–67, Prof. of Music and Anthropology 1967–92, Prof. Emeritus 1992–, Chair Division of Musicology 1967–72, 1975–77, 1982–85, Univ. of Illinois, Urbana; numerous visiting lectureships and professorships, including Visiting Prof. of Music Harvard Univ. 1990, Distinguished Albert Seay Prof. of Music Colorado Coll. 1992, Visiting Hill Prof. of Music Univ. of Minnesota 1995, Benedict Distinguished Visiting Prof. of Music Carleton Coll. 1996; mem. American Acad. of Arts and Sciences, Coll. Music Soc., Int. Council for Traditional Music, Int. Musicological Soc., Soc. of Ethnomusicology (pres. 1969–71, hon. mem. 2001). *Publications:* North American Indian Musical Styles 1954, Music in Primitive Culture 1956, An Introduction to Folk Music in the United States (third edn, revised by H. Myers, as Folk Music in the United States: An Introduction 1976) 1960, Cheremis Musical Styles 1960, Reference Materials in Ethnomusicology 1961, Theory and Method in Ethnomusicology 1964, Folk and Traditional Music of the Western Continents 1965, Daramad of Chahargah: A Study in the Performance Practice of Persian Music (with B. Foltin Jr) 1972, Contemporary Music and Music Cultures (with C. Hamm and R. Byrnside) 1975, Eight Urban Musical Cultures: Tradition and Change (ed.) 1978, The Study of Ethnomusicology: 29 Issues and Concepts 1983, The Western Impact on World Music: Change, Adaptation, and Survival 1985, The Radif of Persian Music: Studies of Structure and Cultural Context 1987, Blackfoot Musical Thought: Comparative Perspectives 1989, Comparative Musicology and Anthropology in Music: Essays on the History of Ethnomusicology (ed. with P. Bohlman) 1991, Excursions in World Music (with others) 1992, Community of Music: An Ethnographical Seminar in Champaign-Urbana (ed. with others) 1993, Heartland Excursions: Ethnomusicological Reflections on Schools of Music 1995, In the Course of Performance: Studies in the World of Musical Improvisation (ed. with M. Russell) 1998, Encounters in Ethnomusicology 2002. *Honours:* Hon. LHD (Univ. of Chicago) 1993, (Univ. of Illinois) 1996, (Carleton Coll.) 2000, (Kenyon Coll.) 2002;hon. mem. American Musicological Soc. 1995; Koizumi Prize in Ethnomusicology, Tokyo 1994. *Address:* c/o University of Illinois, Department for Performing Arts, EPASW Bldg, 1040 W Harrison Street, MC-255, Chicago, IL 60607; 1423 Cambridge Drive, Champaign, IL 61821, USA.

NEUBERGER, Baroness (Life Peer), cr. 2004; **Rabbi Julia Babette Sarah**, DBE, MA; British rabbi, public health official, writer, politician and broadcaster; b. 27 Feb. 1950, London; d. of the late Walter Schwab and Alice Schwab; m. Anthony John Neuberger 1973; one s. one d. *Education:* South Hampstead High School, Newnham Coll. Cambridge and Leo Baeck Coll. London. *Career:* Rabbi, S London Liberal Synagogue 1977–89; Lecturer and Assoc. Fellow, Leo Baeck Coll. 1979–97; Assoc. Newnham Coll. Cambridge 1983–96; Sec. and Chief Exec. The King's Fund 1997–2004; Chancellor Univ. of Ulster 1994–2000; Chair. Rabbinic Conf. Union of Liberal and Progressive Synagogues 1983–85; Camden and Islington Community Health Services NHS Trust 1993–97; mem. Policy Planning Group, Inst. of Jewish Affairs 1986–90, NHS Complaints Review 1993–94, Gen. Medical Council 1993–2001, Council, Univ. Coll. London 1993–97, MRC 1995–2000, Council, Save the Children Fund 1995–96; Visiting Fellow, King's Fund Inst. 1989–91; Chair. Patients Assen 1988–91, Royal Coll. of Nursing Comm. on Health Service; mem. Nat. Cttee Social Democratic Party 1982–88, Funding Review of BBC 1999, Cttee on Standards in Public Life 2001–04; Civil Service Commr 2001–02; mem. Bd of Visitors, Memorial Church, Harvard Univ. 1994–2000, Bloomberg Prof. of Philanthropy and Public Policy, Divinity School 2006; Trustee Runnymede Trust 1990–97, Imperial War Museum 1999–, British Council, Booker Prize Foundation; other public and charitable appointments; Harkness Fellow, Commonwealth Fund of New York; Visiting Fellow, Harvard Medical School 1991–92. *Television:* Presenter, Choices (BBC) 1986, 1987. *Publications:* The Story of Judaism 1986, Days of Decision (ed., four vols) 1987, Caring for Dying Patients of Different Faiths 1987, Whatever's Happening to Women? 1991, A Necessary End (co-ed. with John White) 1991, Ethics and Healthcare: The Role of Research Ethics Committees in the UK 1992, The Things That Matter 1993, On Being Jewish 1995, Dying Well: A Health Professional's Guide to Enabling a Better Death 1999, Hidden Assets: Values and Decision-Making in the NHS Today (co-ed. with Bill New) 2002, The Moral State We're In 2005; contribs to various books on cultural, religious and ethical factors in nursing; contribs journals and newspapers, including Nursing Times, Jewish Chronicle, Times, Irish Times, The Independent, Guardian, Telegraph, Sunday Express, Mail on Sunday, Evening Standard. *Honours:* Hon. Fellow, City and Guilds Inst., Mansfield

Coll. Oxford; Hon. FRCP 2004; Hon. Fellow, Royal Coll. of Gen. Practioners; Dr hc (Open Univ., City Univ. London, Humberside, Ulster, Stirling, Oxford Brookes, Teesside, Nottingham, Queen's Belfast, Aberdeen). *Address:* House of Lords, Westminster, London, SW1 0PW (office). *Telephone:* (1206) 503130 (PA Paola Churchill) (office); (20) 7428-9895 (home); (7711) 386974 (mobile). *Fax:* (1206) 503130 (office); (20) 7813-2030 (home). *E-mail:* paolachurchill@hotmail.com (office); jneuberger@blueyonder.co.uk (home).

NEUGEBOREN, Jay Michael, BA, MA; American writer and academic; b. 30 May 1938, New York, NY; m. 1st Betsey Bendorf 1964 (divorced); two s. one d.; m. 2nd Judy Karasik 1985 (divorced 1987). *Education:* Columbia Univ., New York, Indiana Univ. *Career:* Preceptor in English, Columbia Univ. 1964–66; Visiting Writer, Stanford Univ., Calif. 1966–67; Asst Prof., State Univ. of NY at Albany 1969–70; Prof. and Writer-in-Residence, Univ. of Massachusetts at Amherst 1971–2001; mem. Authors' Guild, PEN, Writers' Guild. *Publications:* Big Man 1966, Listen Ruben Fontanez 1968, Corky's Brother 1969, Parentheses: An Autobiographical Journey 1970, Sam's Legacy 1974, An Orphan's Tale 1976, The Stolen Jew 1981, Before My Life Began 1985, Poli: A Mexican Boy in Early Texas 1989, Don't Worry About the Kids: Stories 1997, Imagining Robert: My Brother, Madness, and Survival: A Memoir 1997, Transforming Madness: New Lives for People Living With Mental Illness 1999, Open Heart: A Patient's Story of Life-Saving Medicine and Life-Giving Friendship 2003, News from the New American Diaspora and Other Tales of Exile 2005; contribs to many anthologies and periodicals. *Honours:* Transatlantic Review Novella Award 1967, National Endowment for the Arts Fellowships 1972–73, 1989–90, Guggenheim Fellowship 1978–79, Kenneth B. Smilen/Present Tense Award for Best Novel 1982, Edward Lewis Wallant Prize for Best Novel 1985, Ken Book Award, National Alliance for the Mentally Ill 2000. *Literary Agent:* c/o Richard Parks, 138 East 16th Street, New York, NY 10003, USA. *Address:* 532 West 111th Street #65, New York City, NY 10025, USA (home). *E-mail:* jneug@earthlink.net (home).

NEUHÄUSER CANUTO, Mary Helen; American artist, playwright and author; b. 17 Feb. 1943, San Antonio, Tex.; d. of Gotthelf Friedrich and Edna Earl Neuhäuser (née Walling); m. Federico Andrea Canuto 1972 (divorced 1981). *Education:* Bethesda-Chevy Chase High School, Catholic Univ., Carnegie Mellon Univ., Studio Nera Simi and Univ. of Florence, Italy. *Career:* group and one-woman exhbns include Potters House Gallery, Washington, DC, Martha Washington Library, Alexandria, Va, Nat. Cathedral, Washington, DC, Nat. Museum of Fine Arts, Washington, DC, Smithsonian Inst., Washington, DC, Corcoran Gallery of Art, Veerhoff Galleries, Washington, DC, Capricorn Galleries, Bethesda, Md, Lorenz Gallery, Bethesda, Art and Design Gallery, Chantilly, Va, Seloff Art Gallery, Brownsville, Tex., Dellinger Gallery, Alexandria, VA, Thirty-Year Retrospective, Friendship Gallery, Chevy Chase, Md 1989; official portrait comms include FBI Bldg, House of Reps Bldg, Trinity Coll., Sidwell Friends School, Washington, DC; contribs to newspapers including The Washington Post, The Evening Star, Capitol Hill Roll Call; poet and writer for Democratic Presidential Campaign 1988; First Place The Washington Post (Portraits) 1961, 1964; portraits of Robert Frost and J. F. Kennedy for The Washington Post. *Plays:* The Great Sin 1993, Awkwright and Murgatroyd 1994, Threatened by Hitler – My Father's Crusade Against Nazi Subversion in America 2002, Crusade (screenplay) 2005. *Honours:* numerous awards for portraits and abstract paintings 1961–76.

NEUHOFF, Eric; French writer and journalist; b. 1956. *Publications:* Des gens impossibles 1986, Lettre ouverte à François Truffaut 1987, Les Hanches de Laetitia 1989, Actualités françaises 1992, Comme hier 1993, Pas trop près de l'écran 1993, Michel Déon 1994, Barbe à Papa 1996, La Petite française (Prix Interallié) 1997, Champagne! 1998, La Séance du mercredi à 14 heures 1998, Précautions d'usage 2001, Un Bien fou (Grand Prix du Roman) 2001, Rendez-vous à Samarra 2005, Folie dans la famille 2005, Histoire de Franck 2005. *Address:* c/o Albin Michel, 22 rue Huyghers, 75680 Paris Cédex 14, France.

NEUMEYER, Peter Florian, BA, MA, PhD; American academic and writer; *Professor Emeritus, San Diego State University*; b. 4 Aug. 1929, Munich, Germany; m. Helen Wight Snell 1952; three s. *Education:* Univ. of California at Berkeley. *Career:* Asst Prof., Harvard Univ. 1963–69; Assoc. Prof., State Univ. of New York at Stony Brook 1969–75; Prof. and Chair Dept of English, West Virginia Univ. 1975–78; Prof. 1978–95, Prof. Emeritus 1995–, San Diego State Univ. *Publications:* Kafka's The Castle 1969, Donald and the... 1969, Donald Has a Difficulty 1970, The Faithful Fish 1971, Elements of Fiction (co-ed.) 1974, Homage to John Clare 1980, Image and Maker (co-ed.) 1984, The Phantom of the Opera (adaptation) 1988, The Annotated Charlotte's Web 1994; contrib. to journals. *Address:* 45 Marguerita Road, Kensington, CA 94707, USA.

NEVILLE, Robert Cummings, BA, MA, PhD; American academic and author; *Executive Director, The Danielsen Institute, Dean of Marsh Chapel and University Chaplain, Boston University*; b. 1 May 1939, St Louis, MO; m. Elizabeth E. Neville 1963, three d. *Education:* Yale University. *Career:* Instructor, Yale University, 1963–65; Visiting Lecturer and Instructor, Wesleyan University, 1964–65; Asst Prof., 1965–68, Assoc. Prof., 1968–73, Fordham University; Assoc. for the Behavioral Sciences, Institute of Society, Ethics, and the Life Sciences, Hastings-on-Hudson, New York, 1971–73; Assoc. Prof., 1971–74, Prof. of Philosophy, 1974–77, SUNY at Purchase; Adjunct Prof. of Religious Studies and Research Prof., 1977–78, Prof. of

Philosophy and Prof. of Religious Studies, 1978–87, SUNY at Stony Brook; Prof., Depts of Religion and Philosophy and School of Theology, Boston University 1987–2003, Dean School of Theology 1988–2003, Dean of Marsh Chapel and Univ. Chaplain 2003–06, Exec. Dir The Danielsen Inst. 2005–(08); mem. American Acad. of Religion, pres. 1992; American Philosophical Asscn; American Theological Society (pres. 2005–06); Boston Theological Society; Institute of Society, Ethics, and the Life Sciences; Society for Studies of Process Philosophies; Society of Philosophers in America; International Society for Chinese Philosophy, pres., 1993; Metaphysical Society of America, pres., 1989. *Publications:* God the Creator: On the Transendence and Prescence of God, 1968; The Cosmology of Freedom, 1974; Soldier, Sage, Saint, 1978; Creativity and God: A Challenge to Process Theology, 1980; Reconstruction of Thinking, 1981; The Tao and the Daimon: Segments of a Religious Enquiry, 1982; The Puritan Smile, 1987; Recovery of the Measure, 1989; Behind the Masks of God, 1991; A Theology Primer, 1991; The Highroad Around Modernism, 1992; Eternity's and Time's Flow, 1993; Normative Cultures, 1995; The Truth of Broken Symbols, 1996; The God Who Beckons, 1999; Boston Confucianism, 2000; Symbols of Jesus, 2002; Religion in Late Modernity, 2002, Preaching the Gospel without Cosy Answers 2005, The Scope and Truth of Theology 2006; editor: Operating on the Mind: The Psychosurgery Conflict (with Willard Gaylin and Joel Meister), 1975; Encyclopedia of Bioethics (assoc. ed.), 1978; New Essays in Metaphysics, 1987; The Recovery of Philosophy in America (with Thomas Kasulis), 1997; The Human Condition, 2001; Ultimate Realities, 2001; Religious Truth, 2001. Contributions: books, professional journals, and periodicals. *Address:* 5 Cliff Road, Milton, MA 02186, USA (home). *E-mail:* rneville@bu.edu (office).

NEVINS, Francis Michael, Jr, AB, JD; American academic and writer; *Professor Emeritus, St Louis University School of Law;* b. 6 Jan. 1943, Bayonne, NJ; m. 1st Muriel Walter 1966 (divorced 1978); m. 2nd Patricia Brooks 1982. *Education:* St Peter's Coll., New York Univ. *Career:* admitted to the New Jersey Bar 1967; Asst Prof. St Louis Univ. School of Law 1971–75, Assoc. Prof. 1975–78, Prof. 1978–2005, Prof. Emer. 2005–. *Publications:* fiction: Publish and Perish 1975, Corrupt and Ensnare 1978, The 120-Hour Clock 1986, The Ninety Million Dollar Mouse 1987, Into the Same River Twice 1996, Beneficiaries' Requiem 2000, Night of Silken Snow and Other Stories 2001, Leap Day and Other Stories 2003; non-fiction: Detectionary (co-author) 1971, Royal Bloodline: Ellery Queen, Author and Detective 1974, Missouri Probate: Intestacy, Wills and Basic Administration 1983, The Films of Hopalong Cassidy 1988, Cornell Woolrich: First You Dream, Then You Die 1988, Bar-20: The Life of Clarence E. Mulford, Creator of Hopalong Cassidy 1993, Joseph H. Lewis: Overview, Interview and Filmography 1998, The Films of the Cisco Kid 1998, Paul Landres: A Director's Stories 2000, The Sound of Detection 2001; editor/co-editor (fiction): Nightwebs 1971, The Good Old Stuff 1983, Exeunt Murderers 1983, Buffet for Unwelcome Guests 1983, More Good Old Stuff 1985, Carnival of Crime 1985, Hitchcock in Prime Time 1985, The Best of Ellery Queen 1985, Leopold's Way 1985, The Adventures of Henry Turnbuckle 1987, Better Mousetraps 1988, Mr President – Private Eye 1988, Death on Television 1989, Little Boxes of Bewilderment 1989, The Night My Friend 1991, Night and Fear 2003, Tonight, Somewhere in New York 2005; editor/co-editor (non-fiction): The Mystery Writer's Art 1970, Mutiplying Villainies 1973, The Anthony Boucher Chronicles (three vols) 2001–02, one vol. edn 2005, The Keeler Keyhole Collection 2005. *Honours:* MWA Edgar Awards 1975, 1988. *Address:* 7045 Cornell, University City, MO 63130, USA (office). *E-mail:* nevinsfm@slu.edu (office).

NEWBERY, Linda; British writer and children's writer; b. 12 Aug. 1952, Romford, Essex, England; m. *Publications include:* Run with the Hare 1988, Hard and Fast 1990, Some Other War 1990, The Kind Ghosts 1991, The Wearing of the Green 1992, Riddle Me This 1993, Smoke Cat 1995, The Shouting Wind 1995, A Fear of Heights 1996, The Cliff Path 1996, Whistling Jack 1997, The Big Animal Ghost Book 1999, The Nowhere Girl 1999, Flightsend 1999, The Cat with Two Names 2000, The Little Mermaid 2001, The Damage Done 2001, Windfall 2002, Break Time 2002, The Shell House 2002, Sisterland 2003, Polly's March 2004, At the Firefly Gate 2004, Lost Boy 2005, Set in Stone (Costa Children's Book of the Year (fmrly the Whitbread Prize) 2007) 2006, Catcall 2006. *Literary Agent:* c/o Maggie Noach Literary Agency, 22 Dorville Crescent, London, W6 0HJ, England. *Telephone:* (20) 8748-8057. *Fax:* (20) 8748-2926. *E-mail:* m-noach@dircon.co.uk. *E-mail:* linda@lindanewbery.co.uk. *Website:* www.lindanewbery.co.uk.

NEWBOULD, Brian Raby, BA, BMus, MA; British writer and academic; *Professor Emeritus of Music, University of Hull;* b. 26 Feb. 1936, Kettering, Northants.; m. 1st Anne Leicester 1960; one s. one d.; m. 2nd Ann Airton 1976; one d. *Education:* Univ. of Bristol. *Career:* Lecturer, Royal Scottish Acad. of Music, Glasgow 1960–65, Univ. of Leeds 1965–79; Prof. of Music, Univ. of Hull 1979–2001, Prof. Emeritus 2001–; numerous talks/discussions on nat. radio, lectures with live illustrations by Allegri String Quartet, Chilingirian String Quartet, the Lindsays, London Mozart Trio, Jyväskylä Sinfonia. *Artistic achievements:* realizations of Schubert's Symphonies No. 7 in E 1979, No. 10 in D 1981, completion of Schubert's Symphony No. 8 in B minor 1982, orchestration of Schubert's other symphonic fragments, completions of Schubert's String Trio String Trio in B flat 2000, Piano Sonata in C 2003; Patrick for narrator and small orchestra, completion of fragmentary Klavierstück 1995, transcription for clarinet and string quartet of Arpeggione Sonata 1996. *Publications:* Musical Analysis in the Sixth Form, Music to an Unpurged Ear 1981, Schubert and the Symphony: A New Perspective 1992,

Schubert: The Music and the Man 1997, Schubert Studies (ed.) 1998, Schubert the Progressive (ed.) 2003; contrib. to Musical Times, Music & Letters, 19th-Century Music, Current Musicology Music Review, Musiktheorie, Schubert-Jahrbuch, Schubert durch die Brille, The Schubertian, BBC Music Magazine, The Guardian, The Scotsman, Glasgow Herald, Daily Telegraph, Radio Times, Jewish Echo, Classic CD, Classical Music, Ovation, Journal of the Conductors' Guild, Beethoven Newsletter, Nieuwsbrief Franz-Schubert Stichting, Meddelelse Franz Schubert Selskabet Danmark, Music Teacher. *Honours:* Hon. Vice-Pres. Schubert Inst. (UK), Hon. Pres. Sheffield Gramophone Soc. *Address:* c/o Department of Music, University of Hull, Hull, HU6 7RX, England (office). *E-mail:* B.R.Newbould@hull.ac.uk (office). *Website:* www.briannewbould.co.uk.

NEWCOMER, James William; American academic, writer and poet; b. 14 March 1912, Gibsonburg, OH; m. 1946; one s. two d. *Education:* PhB, Kenyon College; MA, University of Michigan; PhD, University of Iowa. *Publications:* Non-Fiction: Maria Edgeworth the Novelist, 1967; Maria Edgeworth, 1973; The Grand Duchy of Luxembourg, 1984; Lady Morgan the Novelist, 1990; Luxembourg, 1995; The Nationhood of Luxembourg, 1996. Poetry: The Merton Barn Poems, 1979; The Resonance of Grace, 1984. Contributions: journals and periodicals. *Honours:* Commander, Order of Merit, Hon. Mem., L'Institut Grand-Ducal, Grand Duchy of Luxembourg. *Address:* 1100 Elizabeth Blvd, Fort Worth, TX 76110, USA.

NEWHOUSE, Samuel I., Jr; American publishing executive; *Chairman and CEO, Advance Publications, Inc.;* b. 1928; m. Victoria Newhouse. *Career:* took over father's Staten Island Advance co. 1922 and built newspaper and magazine chain; Chair. Condé Nast Publs Inc., New York and Chair., CEO Advance Publs Inc., New York; fmr mem. Bd NY Museum of Modern Art. *Honours:* Henry Johnson Fisher Award, Magazine Publishers' Asscn 1985. *Address:* Advance Publications, Inc. 950 Fingerboard Road, Staten Island, NY 10305, USA. *Telephone:* (212) 286-2860. *Fax:* (212) 981-1456. *Website:* www.advance.net.

NEWLAND, Courttia; British writer and playwright; b. 1973, London. *Career:* resident playwright, Post Office Theatre 2000–. *Plays:* Euripides' Women of Troy 1999, The Far Side 2000, Mother's Day 2002, B Is For Black 2003. *Publications:* novels: The Scholar 1997, Society Within 1999, IC3 (co-ed.) 2001, Snakeskin 2002; contrib. to Disco 2000, New Writers 8, Afrobeat, Time Out Book of Short Stories Vol. 2, England Calling, Voices for Peace. *Address:* c/o Abacus, Brettenham House, Lancaster Place, London, WC2E 7EN, England.

NEWMAN, Andrea, BA, MA; British writer; b. 7 Feb. 1938, Dover, England; m. (divorced). *Education:* University of London. *Career:* mem. PEN, Writers' Guild. *Publications:* A Share of the World, 1964; Mirage, 1965; The Cage, 1966; Three Into Two Won't Go, 1967; Alexa, 1968; A Bouquet of Barbed Wire, 1969; Another Bouquet, 1977; An Evil Streak, 1977; Mackenzie, 1980; A Sense of Guilt, 1988; Triangles, 1990; A Gift of Poison, 1991; Imogen's Face (TV script), 1998; Pretending to be Judith (TV script), 2001. Contributions: Magazines and television.

NEWMAN, Aubrey Norris, BA, MA, DPhil; British academic and writer; b. 14 Dec. 1927, London, England. *Education:* University of Glasgow, Wadham College, Oxford. *Career:* Research Fellow, Bedford College, University of London, 1954–55; Prof. of History, University of Leicester; mem. Jewish Historical Soc. of England (pres. 1977–79). *Publications:* The Parliamentary Diary of Sir Edward Knatchbull, 1722–1730, 1963; The Stanhopes of Chevening: A Family Biography, 1969; The United Synagogue, 1870–1970, 1977; The Jewish East End, 1840–1939, 1981; The Board of Deputin, 1760–1985: A Brief Survey, 1987; The World Turned Inside Out: New Views on George II, 1988. *Address:* c/o School of Historical Studies, University of Leicester, University Road, Leicester, LE1 7RH, England (office).

NEWMAN, Edwin Harold; American journalist; b. 25 Jan. 1919, New York; s. of Myron Newman and Rose Parker Newman; m. Rigel Grell 1944; one d. *Education:* Univ. of Wisconsin, Louisiana State Univ. *Career:* Washington Bureau, Int. News Service 1941, United Press 1941–42, 1945–46; USN 1942–45; CBS News, Washington, DC 1947–49; freelance, London 1949–52; NBC News, London Bureau 1952–, Rome Bureau 1957–58, Paris Bureau 1958–61; Corresp. and Commentator, NBC News, New York 1961–83; Moderator of Presidential Cand. debates Ford-Carter 1976, Reagan-Mondale 1984; Columnist, King Features Syndicate 1984–89; freelance journalist and lecturer; appeared as self in numerous TV comedy series and films including The Pelican Brief and Spies Like Us. *Publications:* Strictly Speaking 1974, A Civil Tongue 1976, Sunday Punch 1979, I Must Say 1988; articles for Punch, Esquire, Atlantic, Harper's, New York Times, Saturday Review, Chicago Tribune, TV Guide, Sports Illustrated. *Honours:* Chevalier, Légion d'honneur and other decorations; Peabody Award, Overseas Press Club Award, Emmy Award, Univ. of Mo. School of Journalism Award. *Address:* c/o Richard Fulton Inc., 66 Richfield Street, Plainview, NY 11803, USA.

NEWMAN, Gordon F.; British writer, dramatist and producer; b. 19 May 1947; two s. *Career:* mem. Writers' Guild. *Publications:* Sir, You Bastard 1970, Billy: A Family Tragedy 1971, You Nice Bastard 1972, The Player and the Guest 1972, The Split 1973, Three Professional Ladies 1973, The Price 1974, The Streetfighter 1975, The Guvnor 1977, The List 1980, The Obsession 1980, Charlie and Joanna 1981, The Men With the Guns 1982, Law and Order 1983,

Set a Thief 1986, The Testing Ground 1987, Trading the Future 1992, Circle of Poison 1995; plays: Operation Bad Apple 1982, An Honourable Trade 1986, The Testing Ground 1989; screenplay: Number One 1984; television plays: Law and Order 1978, Billy 1979, The Nation's Health 1983, Here Is the News 1989, Black and Blue 1992, The Healer 1994, Judge John Deed (series) 2000–06, New Street Law (series) 2006. *Honours:* Writer's Awards, BAFTA 1992, Best Drama 1995, Golden Knight 1999. *Literary Agent:* Talent Media Group, Oxford House, 76 Oxford Street, London, W1D 1BS, England. *Address:* 47 Palace Gardens Terrace, London, W8 4SB, England (home). *E-mail:* gordon .newman@bbc.co.uk (office).

NEWMAN, Jay, FRSC; Canadian/American academic and writer; *Professor of Philosophy, University of Guelph;* b. 28 Feb. 1948, Brooklyn, NY, USA; s. of Louis Newman and Kate Newman. *Education:* BA, Brooklyn College, CUNY, 1968; MA, Brown University, 1969; PhD, York University, 1971. *Career:* Lecturer, University of Guelph 1971–72, Asst Prof. 1972–77, Assoc. Prof. 1977–82, Prof. of Philosophy 1982–; Pres. Canadian Theological Soc. 1990–91. *Publications:* Foundations of Religious Tolerance, 1982; The Mental Philosophy of John Henry Newman, 1986; Fanatics and Hypocrites, 1986; The Journalist in Plato's Cave, 1989; Competition in Religious Life, 1989; On Religious Freedom, 1991; Religion vs Television: Competitors in Cultural Context, 1996; Religion and Technology: A Study in the Philosophy of Culture, 1997; Inauthentic Culture and Its Philosophical Critics, 1997; Biblical Religion and Family Values: A Problem in the Philosophy of Culture, 2001; contrib. articles and reviews. *Honours:* several grants; Distinguished Alumnus Award, Brooklyn College, CUNY, 1988, Pres.'s Distinguished Prof. Award Univ. of Guelph 2001. *Address:* 313–19 Woodlawn Road East, Guelph, Ont., N1H 7B1, Canada (home). *Telephone:* (519) 824-4120 (office); (519) 821-1944 (home). *Fax:* (519) 837-8634 (office).

NEWMAN, John Kevin, BA, MA, PhD; British academic and writer; b. 17 Aug. 1928, Bradford, Yorks.; m. Frances M. Stickney 1970, one s. two d. *Education:* Univ. of Oxford, Univ. of Bristol. *Career:* Classics Master, St Francis Xavier Coll., Liverpool 1952–54, Downside School, Somerset 1955–69; faculty mem., Univ. of Illinois, Urbana 1969–, Prof. of Classics 1980–; Ed., Illinois Classical Studies 1982–87. *Publications:* Augustus and the New Poetry 1967, The Concept of Vates in Augustan Poetry 1967, Latin Compositions 1976, Golden Violence 1976, Dislocated: An American Carnival 1977, Pindar's Art 1984, The Classical Epic Tradition 1986, Roman Catullus 1990, Lelio Guidiccioni, Latin Poems 1992, Horace-Bénédict de Saussure (with A. V. Carozzi) 1995, Augustan Propertius 1997, de Saussure on Geography (with A. V. Carozzi) 2003, Troy's Children 2005. *Honours:* Silver Medals, Vatican City 1960, 1962, 1965, 1997. *Address:* 703 W Delaware Avenue, Urbana, IL 61801, USA. *E-mail:* j-newman@uiuc.edu.

NEWMAN, Lesléa, BS; American writer, poet and teacher; b. 5 Nov. 1955, New York, NY. *Education:* University of Vermont, Naropa Institute. *Career:* teacher, women's writing workshops; mem. Authors' Guild; Authors League of America; Poets and Writers. *Publications:* Good Enough to Eat, 1986; Love Me Like You Mean It, 1987; A Letter to Harvey Milk, 1988; Heather Has Two Mommies, 1989; Bubbe Meisehs by Shayneh Maidelehs, 1989; Secrets, 1990; In Every Laugh a Tear, 1992; Writing from the Heart, 1992; Every Woman's Dream, 1994; Fat Chance, 1994; Too Far Away to Touch, 1995; A Loving Testimony: Remembering Loved Ones Lost to AIDS, 1995; The Femme Mystique, 1995; Remember That, 1996; My Lover is a Woman: Contemporary Lesbian Love Poems, 1996; Out of the Closet and Nothing to Wear, 1997; Matzo Ball Moon, 1998; Still Life With Buddy, 1998; Girls Will Be Girls, 2000; Signs of Love, 2000; Cats, Cats, Cats!, 2001; She Loves Me, She Loves Me Not (short stories), 2002; Dogs, Dogs, Dogs!, 2002; Runaway Dreidel, 2002; Felicia's Favourite Story, 2002. Contributions: Magazines. *Honours:* Massachusetts Artists Fellowship in Poetry, 1989; National Endowment for the Arts Fellowship, 1997. *Address:* PO Box 815, Northampton, MA 01061, USA.

NEWMAN, Paul Nigel; British author, poet and editor; *Editor, Abraxas;* b. 12 Oct. 1945, Bristol. *Education:* Weston Super-Mare Tech. Coll., St Paul's Coll., Cheltenham. *Career:* founder and Ed. Abraxas: A Journal of Literature, Philosophy and Ideas 1991–. *Publications:* Channel Passage 1975, The Hill of the Dragon 1979, Channel Portraits 1980, Grandeur and Decay 1981, Somerset Villages 1986, Bath 1986, Bristol 1987, Gods and Graven Images 1987, Spiders and Outsiders 1989, The Meads of Love 1994, Murder as an Antidote for Boredom 1996, In Many Ways Frogs (poems with A. R. Lamb) 1997, Lost Gods of Albion 1998, A History of Terror 2000, That Summer in Lamorna (script commissioned by Cornwall Film Fund) 2003, Galahad (novel) (Peninsula Prize 2003) 2004, Aleister Crowley and the Cult of Pan (critical study) 2004, The Tregerthen Horror: Aleister Crowley, D.H. Lawrence and Peter Warlock in Cornwall 2005, entries on terror and literary history in Scribner's World Dictionary of Ideas 2005; contribs to Time Out travel guides, Writers' Monthly, 3rd Stone, British Archaeology, South West Arts, Westwords, Cornish Review, Psychopoetica, The Journal, Ramraid Extraordinaire, Story Cellar, Dreams from a Stranger's Café, The Cerne Giant: Antiquity on Trial, The Dreamt Sea: An Anthology of Anglo-Cornish Poetry 1928–2004. *Address:* 57 Eastbourne Road, St Austell, Cornwall, England.

NEWMAN, Peter Charles, CC, CD; Canadian author and journalist; b. 10 May 1929, Vienna, Austria; s. of Oscar Newman and Wanda Newman; m. 1st Christina McCall (divorced); m. 2nd Camilla J. Turner 1978; two d.; m. 3rd Alvy Björklund 1992. *Education:* Upper Canada Coll., Toronto, Univ. of Toronto and McGill Univ. *Career:* Asst Ed. The Financial Post 1951–55;

Ottawa Ed. Maclean's 1955–64; Ottawa Ed. Toronto Daily Star 1964–69, Ed.-in-Chief 1969–71; Ed.-in-Chief, Maclean's 1971–82, Sr Contributing Ed. 1982–; Dir Maclean Hunter Ltd 1972–83, Key Radio Ltd 1983–; Prof. Creative Writing, Univ. of Victoria 1985–90; Prof. Creative Writing, Univ. of British Columbia. *Publications:* Flame of Power 1959, Renegade in Power 1963, The Distemper of Our Times 1968, Home Country 1973, The Canadian Establishment: Vol. I 1975, Bronfman Dynasty 1978, The Acquisitors – The Canadian Establishment: Vol. II 1981, The Establishment Man 1982, True North – Not Strong and Free 1983, Debrett's Illustrated Guide to the Canadian Establishment 1983, Company of Adventurers 1985, Caesars of the Wilderness 1987, Sometimes A Great Nation 1988, Empire of Bay 1989, Merchant Princes 1991, The Canadian Revolution 1995, Defining Moments 1996, Titans: How the New Canadian Establishment Seized Power 1998. *Honours:* several honours and awards including Kt Commdr Order of St Lazarus; Hon. LLD (Brock) 1974, (Wilfrid Laurier) 1983, (Royal Mil. Coll.) 1986, (Queens) 1986; Hon. DLitt (York) 1975, (British Columbia) 1998. *Address:* One Mount Pleasant Road, Toronto, M4Y 2Y5, Canada. *Telephone:* (604) 222-8274 (office); (604) 222-8274 (home). *Fax:* (604) 222-8275 (office). *E-mail:* petercnewman@home.com (home).

NEWMAN, Rachel, BA; American magazine editor; b. 1 May 1938, Walden, Mass; d. of Maurice Newman and Eythe Brenda Newman (née Techell); m. Herbert Bleiweiss 1973. *Education:* Pennsylvania State Univ. and New School of Interior Design. *Career:* Accessories Ed. Women's Wear Daily, New York 1964–65; Designer and Publicist, Grandoe Glove Corpn, New York 1965–67; Assoc. Ed. McCall's Sportswear and Dress Merchandiser magazine, New York 1967, Man. Ed. McCall's You-Do-It Home Decorating 1968–70; Man. Ed. Ladies Home Journal Needle and Craft magazine, New York 1970–72; Ed.-in-Chief American Home Crafts, New York 1972–77; Fashion Dir Good Housekeeping, New York 1977–78, Dir of Home Bldg and Decorating 1978–82; Ed. Country Living 1979–1998; Founding Ed. Country Cooking 1985–90, Dream Homes 1989–2000, Country Kitchens 1990–93, Country Living Gardener 1993–2000, Healthy Living 1996–2000; mem. American Soc. of Magazine Editors; Fellow, Pennsylvania State Univ. Alumni 1986. *Publications:* Living with Folk Art, Country Look and How to Get It, Country Gardens, Country Quilts, Country Decorating, Country Kitchens, Country Christmas, New Country Kitchens. *Honours:* Distinguished Alumni Pennsylvania State Univ. 1988. *Address:* c/o Country Living, 224 W 57th Street, New York, NY 10019-3203, USA (office). *E-mail:* Rachelsfree@aol.com.

NEYREY, Jerome Henry, BA, MA, PhL, MDiv, MTh, PhD, STL; American writer, academic, editor and priest; b. 5 Jan. 1940, New Orleans, LA. *Education:* St Louis University, Regis College, Toronto, Yale University, Weston School of Theology. *Career:* Ordained Roman Catholic Priest, 1970; Faculty, Weston School of Theology, 1977–92; Assoc. Ed., New Testament Abstracts, 1977–81, Catholic Biblical Quarterly, 1983–91, 1994–, Biblical Theology Bulletin, 1986–, Hervormde Teologiese Studies, 1995–, Journal for the Study of the New Testament, 1997–; Visiting Prof., Pontifical Biblical Institute, Rome, 1989; Prof., University of Notre Dame, IN, 1992–; mem. Catholic Biblical Asscn; Society of Biblical Literature; The Context Group: Project on the Bible in Its Cultural Environment, charter mem., 1989–. *Publications:* First Timothy, Second Timothy, Titus, James, First Peter, Second Peter, Jude, Vol. Nine, Collegeville Bible Commentary, 1983; Christ is Community, 1985; The Passion Narrative in St Luke, 1985; The Resurrection Stories, 1988; Calling Jesus Names (with Bruce Malina), 1988; An Ideology of Revolt: John's Christology in Social-Science Perspective, 1988; Paul, In Other Words: A Cultural Reading of His Letters, 1990; The Social World of Luke–Acts: Models for Interpretation (ed.), 1991; Peter and Jude, Anchor Bible Commentary, 1993; Portraits of Paul: An Archaeology of Ancient Personality (with Bruce Malina), 1996; Honor and Shame in the Gospel of Matthew, 1998. Contributions: Catholic Biblical Quarterly; Journal of Biblical Literature; Biblica; Novum Testamentum; New Testament Studies; Journal for the Study of the New Testament; Journal for the Study of Judaism. *Honours:* Bannan Fellowship, Santa Clara University, 1984–85; Young Scholars Grant, 1984; ATS Grant, 1989; Lilly Foundation, 1989; Plowshares, 1990. *Address:* c/o Department of Theology, University of Notre Dame, Notre Dame, IN 46556, USA. *E-mail:* neyrey.1@nd.edu. *Website:* www.nd.edu/~jneyreyl.

NGANANG, Patrice, PhD; Cameroon writer; *Associate Professor of French and German, Shippensburg University;* b. 17 March 1970, Yaoundé. *Education:* Univ. of Yaoundé, Univ. of Frankfurt, Germany–. *Career:* Assoc. Prof. of French and German, Shippensburg Univ. 2000–. *Publications:* Histoire d'un enfant Quatr' Z'yeux (short story, Prix CREPLA 1986), elobi (poetry collection) 1995, Promesse des fleurs (novel) 1997, Interkulturalität und Bearbeitung: Untersuchung zu Soyinka und Brecht (literary criticism) 1998, Temps de chien (novel) (Grand Prix Littéraire de l'Afrique Noire) 2001, La joie de vivre (novel) 2003, L'Invention du beau regard 2005, Le principe dissident (essay) 2005, La chanson du joggeur (novel, serialised in Le Messager newspaper) 2005; short stories, essays and articles on African literature and film. *Honours:* Prix Marguerite Yourcenar for Francophone writers living in the USA . *Address:* c/o Editions Gallimard, 5 rue Sébastien-Bottin, 75328 Paris Cedex 7, France.

NGEMA, Mbongeni; South African writer, producer and composer; b. 1955, Hlabisa; m. Leleti Khumalo (separated). *Career:* mem. Gibson Kente's acting co., f. Cttee Artists; est. S African struggle theatre on London and New York stages 1981. *Plays:* Woza Albert! (with Percy Mtwa and Barney Simon) 1981, Asinamali 1986, Sarafina! 1987, Township Fever 1989, Sarafina 2! 1996, The

Zulu 2000. *Recordings:* Sarafina! 1990, Time to Unite 1990, Woza My Fohlaza 1998, AmaNyida 2002, Best of Mbongeni Ngema 2002. *Publications:* Voices of Sarafina! Songs of Hope and Freedom 1988; contrib. to Woza Afrika!: A Collection of South African Plays 1986, Where is the Way: Song and Struggle in South Africa 1990. *Address:* c/o Skotaville Publishers, PO Box 32483, Braamfontein, South Africa.

NÍ CHUILLEANÁIN, Eiléan, BLitt, MA; Irish poet and lecturer; b. 28 Nov. 1942, Cork; d. of Cormac Ó Cuilleanáin and Eilis Dillon; m. Macdara Woods 1978; one s. *Education:* Univ. Coll. Cork and Lady Margaret Hall, Oxford. *Career:* Lecturer, Trinity Coll., Dublin 1966–, then Assoc. Prof. in English; Co-founder Cyphers literary magazine 1975–; mem. Aosdána. *Publications include:* Irish Women: Image and Achievement 1985; poems: The Second Voyage (2nd edn) 1986, The Magdalene Sermon 1989, The Brazen Serpent 1994, The Girl Who Married the Reindeer 2001. *Honours:* Irish Times Poetry Prize 1966, Patrick Kavanagh Prize 1973, O'Shaughnessy Prize for Poetry 1993. *Address:* Department of English, University of Dublin Trinity College, Dublin 2 (office); 3 Selskar Terrace, Dublin 6, Ireland (home). *Telephone:* (1) 772941 (office). *Fax:* (1) 6717114 (office).

NÍ DHOMHNAILL, Nuala, BA; Irish poet; b. 16 Feb. 1952, St Helens, Lancs., England; d. of Séamus Ó Dhomhnaill and Eibhlín Ní Fhiannachta; m. Dogan Leflef 1973; one s. three d. *Education:* Laurel Hill Convent, Limerick and Univ. Coll., Cork. *Career:* travel overseas 1973–80; writer-in-residence Univ. Coll., Cork 1992–93; Visiting Prof. New York Univ., 1998, Villanova Univ. 2001; Ireland Prof. of Poetry 2002–04; mem. Aosdána, Irish Writers' Union, Poetry Ireland. *Publications:* An Dealg Droighinn 1981, Feár Suaithinseach 1984, Raven Introductions (with others) 1984, Selected Poems/Rogha Danta 1986, Pharoah's Daughter 1990, Feís 1991, The Astrakhan Cloak 1992, Jumping Off Shadows: Selected Contemporary Irish Poets (ed. with Greg Delanty) 1995, Cead Aighnis 1998, In the Heart of Europe: Poems for Bosnia 1998, The Water Horse 1999; contribs to many anthologies and magazines. *Honours:* Oireachtas Poetry Awards, 1982, 1989, 1990, 1998; Irish Arts Council Awards, 1985, 1988; Irish American O'Shaughnessy Award 1988, Ireland Fund Literary Prize 1991. *Address:* c/o The Gallery Press, Loughcrew, Oldcastle, County Meath, Ireland. *E-mail:* contactus@gallerypress.com.

NIAZI, Mohammad Munir Khan, BA; Pakistani poet; b. 1928, Khanpur. *Education:* SE Coll., Bahawalpur, Diyal Singh Coll., Lahore. *Career:* writes poems in Urdu and Punjabi; founder Saat Rang weekly publ., Sahiwal 1949, al-Misal 1960; wrote songs for films 1960s; has worked for Lahore TV. *Publications:* Urdu poetry: Taiz Hawa Aur Tanha Phool, Jungle mein Dhanak, Dushmanoon Kai Darmiyan Sham, Mah-e-Munir, Ek Musalsal; Punjabi poetry: Safar di Raat, Char Chup Cheezan, Rasta Dasan Walay Tarey; poetry in trans.: A Cry in the Wilderness 2001; contrib. to Selected New Punjabi Literature in English Translation. *Honours:* Pres.'s Award for Pride of Performance 1992, Sitara-i-Imtiaz 1998, 2005, Kamal-e-fun Award 2002, al-Muftah Award 2003. *Address:* 43-B Block 1, Sector B-i, Lahore Township, Lahore, Pakistan (home).

NICHOLLS, Christine Stephanie, BA, MA, DPhil; British editor and writer; b. 23 Jan. 1943, Bury, Lancs.; d. of Christopher James Metcalfe and Olive Metcalfe (née Kennedy); m. Anthony James Nicholls 1966; two d. one s. *Education:* Kenya High School, Lady Margaret Hall, Oxford, St Antony's Coll., Oxford. *Career:* Henry Charles Chapman Research Fellow Inst. of Commonwealth Studies, Univ. of London 1968–69; freelance writer for BBC 1970–74, Research Asst 1975–76; Jt Ed., Dictionary of Nat. Biography 1977–89, Ed. 1989–95; Ed. Sutton Pocket Biographies 1996–; Assoc. Fellow, St Antony's Coll., Oxford 1990–. *Publications:* The Swahili Coast 1971, Cataract (with Philip Awdry) 1985, Power: A Political History of the 20th Century 1990, Dictionary of National Biography Missing Persons 1986–90 (ed.) 1993, 1996, The Hutchinson Encyclopedia of Biography 1996, David Livingstone 1998, The History of St Antony's College, Oxford 1950–2000 2000, Elspeth Huxley: A Biography 2002, Red Strangers – The Whites of Kenya 2005. *Address:* 27 Davenant Road, Oxford, OX2 8BU, England. *Telephone:* (1865) 511320. *E-mail:* christine.nicholls@lineone.net (office).

NICHOLS, Grace; Guyanese writer and poet; b. 18 Jan. 1950, d. of the late Iris Nichols; pnr John Agard; two d. *Education:* Univ. of Guyana, Georgetown. *Career:* moved to UK 1976; poet-in-residence Tate Britain, London 2002–. *Publications:* Trust You, Wriggly 1980, I is a Long Memoried Woman (Commonwealth Poetry Prize 1983) 1983, Leslyn in London 1984, The Fat Black Woman's Poems 1984, The Discovery 1986, Whole of a Morning Sky 1986, Come on into my Tropical Garden 1988, Black Poetry (ed.) 1988, Lazy Thoughts of a Lazy Woman and Other Poems 1989, Can I Buy a Slice of Sky? (ed.) 1991, No Hickory Dickory Dock (with John Agard) 1991, Give Yourself a Hug 1994, A Caribbean Dozen (ed.) 1994, Sunris 1996, Asana and the Animals 1997, The Poet Cat (children's book) 2000, Paint Me a Poem 2004, Startling the Flying Fish 2006. *Honours:* Arts Council Bursary 1988, Guyana Prize for Poetry 1996. *Literary Agent:* Curtis Brown Ltd, Haymarket House, 28–29 Haymarket, London, SW1Y 4SP, England.

NICHOLS, John Treadwell, BA; American writer; b. 23 July 1940, Berkeley, CA; m. (divorced); one s. one d. *Education:* Hamilton College. *Career:* Visiting Prof., University of New Mexico, 1992, 1993. *Publications:* The Sterile Cuckoo, 1965; The Wizard of Loneliness, 1966; The Milagro Beanfield War, 1974; The Magic Journey, 1978; If Mountains Die, 1979; A Ghost in the Music, 1979; The Nirvana Blues, 1981; The Last Beautiful Days of Autumn, 1982; In Praise of Mountain Lions (with Edward Abbey), 1984; On the Mesa, 1986; American Blood, 1987; A Fragile Beauty: John Nichol's Milagro Country, 1987; The Sky's the Limit: A Defense of the Earth, 1990; An Elegy for September, 1992; Keep It Simple: A Defense of the Earth, 1992; Conjugal Bliss: A Comedy of Marital Arts, 1994; Dancing on the Stones: Selected Essays, 2000; An American Child Supreme: The Education of a Liberation Ecologist, 2001; The Voice of the Butterfly: A Novel, 2001, The Empanada Brotherhood 2007; contrib. to periodicals. *Honours:* Hon. doctorates (Colo Coll.) 1989, (Hamilton Coll.) 2000, Univ. of New Mexico) 2000; New Mexico Gov.'s Award 1981, Frank Waters Award 2003, Wallace Stegner Award 2004. *Address:* PO Box 1165, Taos, NM 87571, USA.

NICHOLS, Leigh (see Koontz, Dean Ray)

NICHOLS, Peter Richard, FRSL; British playwright; b. 31 July 1927, Bristol; s. of the late Richard G. Nichols and of Violet A. Poole; m. Thelma Reed 1960; one s. two d. (and one d. deceased). *Education:* Bristol Grammar School, Bristol Old Vic School and Trent Park Training Coll. *Career:* actor, mostly in repertory 1950–55; schoolteacher 1958–60; mem. Arts Council Drama Panel 1973–75; Playwright-in-Residence, Guthrie Theatre, Minneapolis; Visiting Writer, Nanyang Coll., Singapore 1994; directed revivals of Joe Egg and Forget-me-not Lane (Greenwich), National Health (Guthrie, Minneapolis) and first productions of Born in the Gardens (Bristol), A Piece of My Mind (Southampton), Blue Murder (Bristol), Nicholodeon (Bristol). *Plays:* A Day in the Death of Joe Egg 1967, The National Health 1969, Forget-me-Not Lane 1971, Chez Nous 1973, The Freeway 1974, Privates on Parade 1977, Born in the Gardens 1979, Passion Play 1980, Poppy (musical) 1982, A Piece of My Mind 1986, Blue Murder 1995, So Long Life 2000, Nicholodeon 2000. *Films:* Catch Us If You Can 1965, Georgy Girl 1967, Joe Egg 1971, The National Health 1973, Privates on Parade 1983. *Television:* plays include Walk on the Grass 1959, Promenade 1960, Ben Spray 1961, The Reception 1961, The Big Boys 1961, Continuity Man 1963, Ben Again 1963, The Heart of the Country 1963, The Hooded Terror 1963, When the Wind Blows 1964, The Brick Umbrella 1968, Daddy Kiss It Better 1968, The Gorge 1968, Hearts and Flowers 1971, The Common 1973 and Greeks Bearing Gifts (in the Inspector Morse series). *Publications:* Feeling You're Behind (memoirs) 1984, Nichols: Plays One and Two 1991, Diary 1969–71, Diary Selection 2000; all listed plays published separately; archive now available in Manuscripts Dept, British Library. *Honours:* Tony Award, New York 1985; several SWET and four Evening Standard Drama Awards, Ivor Novello Award for Best Musical 1977. *Literary Agent:* Alan Brodie Representation, Fairgate House, 6th Floor, 78 New Oxford Street, London, WC1A 1HB, England. *Address:* 22 Belsize Park Gardens, London, NW3 4LH, England. *Telephone:* (20) 7079-7990 (office). *E-mail:* info@alanbrodie.com (office).

NICHOLS, Roger David Edward, MA; British writer and broadcaster; b. 6 April 1939, Ely, Cambridgeshire, England; m. Sarah Edwards 1964; two s. one d. *Education:* Worcester College, Oxford. *Career:* Master, St Michael's College, Tenbury, 1966–73; Lecturer, Open University, 1974–80, University of Birmingham, 1974–80. *Publications:* Debussy, 1973; Through Greek Eyes (with Kenneth McLeish), 1974; Messiaen, 1975; Through Roman Eyes (with Kenneth McLeish), 1976; Ravel, 1977; Greek Everyday Life (with Sarah Nichols), 1978; Ravel Remembered, 1987; Debussy: Letters (ed. and trans.), 1987; Claude Debussy: Pelléas et Mélisande (with Richard Langham Smith), 1989; Debussy Remembered, 1992; The Life of Debussy, 1998; The Harlequin Years: Music in Paris 1917–1929, 2002. *Address:* The School House, The Square, Kington, Herefordshire HR5 3BA, England. *E-mail:* roger.nichols@iname.com.

NICHOLS, (Joanna) Ruth; Canadian theologian and writer; b. 4 March 1948, Toronto, ON; m. W. N. Houston 1974. *Education:* BA, University of British Columbia; MA, Religious Studies, 1972, PhD, Theology, 1977, McMaster University. *Publications:* Ceremony of Innocence, 1969; A Walk Out of the World, 1969; The Marrow of the World, 1972; Song of the Pearl, 1976; The Left-handed Spirit, 1978; The Burning of the Rose, 1989; What Dangers Deep: A Story of Philip Sidney, 1992. *Honours:* Shankar International Literary Contest Awards, 1963, 1965; Woodrow Wilson Fellowship, 1968; Fellow, 1971–72, Research Fellow, 1978, Canada Council; Gold Medal, Canadian Asscn of Children's Librarians, 1972.

NICHOLSON, Christina (see Nicole, Christopher Robin)

NICHOLSON, Geoffrey (Geoff) Joseph, MA; British writer; b. 4 March 1953, Sheffield, Yorks. *Education:* Gonville and Caius Coll., Cambridge, Univ. of Essex, Colchester. *Publications:* Street Sleeper, 1987; The Knot Garden, 1989; What We Did On Our Holidays, 1990; Hunters and Gatherers, 1991; Big Noises, 1991; The Food Chain, 1992; Day Trips to the Desert, 1992; The Errol Flynn Novel, 1993; Still Life with Volkswagens, 1994; Everything and More, 1994; Footsucker, 1995; Bleeding London, 1997; Flesh Guitar, 1998; Female Ruins, 1999; Bedlam Burning, 2000; Frank Lloyd Wright, A Beginner's Guide, 2002; Andy Warhol, A Beginner's Guide, 2002, The Hollywood Dodo 2004, Sex Collectors 2006; contrib. to Ambit magazine; Grand Street; Tiger Dreams; Night; Twenty Under 35; A Book of Two Halves; The Guardian; Independent; Village Voice; New York Times Book Review; Salon.Com. *Literary Agent:* AP Watt Ltd, 20 John Street, London, WC1N 2DR, England.

NICHOLSON, Michael Thomas, OBE, MA; British foreign correspondent and writer; b. 9 Jan. 1937, Romford, Essex, England; m. Diana Margaret Slater 1968, two s. two d. *Education:* Univ. of Leicester. *Publications:* Partridge Kite, 1978; Red Joker, 1979; December Ultimatum, 1981; Across the

Limpoto, 1985; Pilgrims Rest, 1987; Measure of Danger, 1991; Natasha's Story, 1993.

NICHOLSON, Robin (see Nicole, Christopher Robin)

NICHOLSON, William; British author and screenwriter; b. 1948; m.; three c. *Education:* Univ. of Cambridge. *Career:* documentary maker and producer, BBC Television, mid-1970s to mid-1980s; screenwriter for television and film. *Television screenplays:* Shadowlands 1985, Sweet as You Are 1987, Life Story 1987, A Private Matter 1992, Crime of the Century 1996. *Film screenplays:* The Vision 1987, Sarafina! 1992, Shadowlands 1993, Nell 1994, First Knight 1995, Firelight 1997, Gladiator 2000. *Publications:* novels: The Seventh Level 1979, The Society of Others 2004; juvenile novels: The Wind Singer (Wind on Fire trilogy, book one) (Nestlé Smarties Book Prize) 2000, Slaves of the Mastery (Wind on Fire trilogy, book two) 2001, Firesong (Wind on Fire trilogy, book three) 2002, Seeker (Noble Warriors trilogy, book one) 2005, Jango (Noble Warriors trilogy, book two) 2006. *Literary Agent:* PFD, Drury House, 34–43 Russell Street, London, WC2B 5HA, England. *Telephone:* (20) 7344-1000. *Fax:* (20) 7836-9543. *Website:* www.pfd.co.uk.

NICOL, Michael George, BA; South African writer, poet and journalist; b. 17 Nov. 1951, Cape Town; one s. one d. *Education:* University of South Africa. *Career:* reporter, To The Point, Johannesburg, 1974–76, The Star, Johannesburg, 1976–79; Ed., African Wildlife, Johannesburg, 1979–81; Freelance Journalist, 1981–85; Asst to the Ed., Leadership, Cape Town, 1986–88; Writer, Journalist, 1989–. *Publications:* Among the Souvenirs (poems), 1979; The Powers That Be (novel), 1989; A Good-Looking Corpse (history), 1991; This Day and Age (novel), 1992; This Sad Place (poems), 1993; Horseman (novel), 1994; The Waiting Country (memoir), 1995; The Ibis Tapestry (novel), 1998; Bra Henry (novella for young adults), 1998; The Invisible Line: The Life and Photography of Ken Oosterbroek (biog.), 1998. Contributions: The Guardian; New Statesman; London Magazine. *Honours:* Ingrid Jonker Award 1980.

NICOLE, Christopher Robin, (Daniel Adams, Leslie Arlen, Robin Cade, Peter Grange, Nicholas Grant, Caroline Gray, Mark Logan, Simon MacKay, Max Marlowe, Christina Nicholson, Robin Nicholson, Alan Savage, Alison York, Andrew York); Guyanese novelist; b. 7 Dec. 1930, Georgetown; m. Diana Bachmann 1982; four s., three d. *Education:* Harrison Coll., Barbados; Queen's Coll., Guyana. *Career:* mem. Soc. of Authors, Literary Guild of America, Mark Twain Soc.; Fellow, Canadian Bankers Asscn. *Publications:* as Christopher Nicole: West Indian Cricket 1957, Off White 1958, Shadows in the Jungle 196, Ratoon 1962, Dark Noon 1963, Amyot's Cay 1964, Blood Amyot 1964, The Amyot Crime 1965, The West Indies 1965, White Boy 1966, The Self Lovers 1968, The Thunder and the Shouting 1969, The Longest Pleasure, 1970, The Face of Evil 1971, A Beginner's Guide to Chess 1973, Heroes 1972, Lord of the Golden Fan 1973, Caribee 1974, The Devil's Own 1975, Mistress of Darkness 1976, Black Dawn 1977, Sunset 1978, The Secret Memoirs of Lord Byron 1979, Haggard 1980, Haggard's Inheritance 1981, The Young Haggards 1982, The Crimson Pagoda 1983, The Sun Rises 1983, The Scarlet Princess 1984, The Sun in Splendour 1984, Black Majesty 1984, Red Dawn 1985, The Sun on Fire 1985, Days of Wine and Roses 1986, The Ship With No Name 1986, Old Glory 1986, The Sea and the Sand 1986, The Titans 1987, The Regiment 1987, Iron Ships, Iron Men 1987, Wind of Destiny 1987, The High Country 1987, The Command 1988, Resumption 1988, Raging Sea, Searing Sky 1988, The Happy Valley 1988, Singpura 1988, The Last Battle 1989, The Triumph 1989, The Passion and the Glory 1989, Dragon's Blood 1989, Sword of Fortune 1990, Dark Sun 1990, Sword of Empire 1991, Bloody Sunrise 1993, Bloody Sunset 1994, Courtesan 1995, The Seeds of Power 1995, The Masters 1995, The Crimson Tide 1995, A Woman of Her Time 1996, The Red Gods 1996, The Scarlet Generation 1997, Death of a Tyrant 1997, The Trade 1997, Shadows in the Sun 1998, Guns in the Desert 1998, Prelude to War 1999, To All Eternity 1999, The Quest 1999, Be Not Afraid 2000, Commando 2000, The Cause 2001, The Tiger 2001, The Search 2001, Ransom Island 2001, Poor Darling 2002, The Pursuit 2002, Demon 2003 The Voyage 2003, The Followers 2004, A Fearful Thing 2005, The Falls of Death 2005, Them That Sleep 2005, The Angel from Hell 2006; as Daniel Adams: Brothers and Enemies 1982, Defiant Loves 1983; as Leslie Arlen: Love and Honour 1980, War and Passion 1981, Fate and Dreams 1982, Hope and Glory 1983, Rage and Desire 1984, Fortune and Fury 1985; as Robin Cade: The Fear Dealers 1974; as Peter Grange: King Creols 1966, The Devil's Emissary 1968, The Tumult at the Gate 1971, The Golden Goddess 1973; as Nicholas Grant: Khan 1993, Siblings 1995; as Alan Savage: Ottoman 1990, The Eight Banners 1991, Mogul 1991, The Last Bannerman 1992, Queen of Night 1992, Eleanor of Aquitaine 1995, Queen of Love 1995, The Sword and the Scalpel 1996, The Sword and the Jungle 1996, The Sword and the Prison 1997, Stop Rommel 1997, Afrika Crops 1998, The Traitor Within 1998, Queen of Fury 2000, Queen of Destiny 2001, Partisan 2001, Murder's Art 2002, Battleground 2002, Queen of the Sun (in German) 2002, The Killing Ground 2003, Queen of Warriors (in German) 2003, Queen of Mountains (in German) 2003, Resistance 2003, The Game of Treachery 2004, The Legacy of Hate 2004, Queen of Lovers 2004, The Brightest Day 2005, Blue Yonder 2005, Death in the Sky 2006; as Caroline Gray: First Class 1984, So Grand 1984, White Rani 1986, Victoria's Walk 1986, The Third Life 1988, Shadow of Death 1989, Blue Water, Black Death 1991, Spares 1993, The Daughter 1992, Golden Girl 1992, Spawn of the Devil 1993, Sword of the Devil 1994, Death of the Devil 1995, Crossbow 1996, Masquerade 1997, The Promised Lane 1997, The Phoenix 1997, The Torrent 1998, The Inheritance 1998; as Mark Logan: Tricolour 1976, Guillotine 1977,

Brumaire 1978; as Simon MacKay: The Seas of Fortune 1983, The Rivals 1984; as Robin Nicholson: The Power and the Passion 1977, The Savage Sands 1978, The Queen of Paris 1978, Hitler's Woman 1981; as Andrew York: The Eliminator 1966, The Co-Ordinator 1967, The Predator 1968, Operation Destruct 1969, The Deviator 1969, The Dominator 1969, Operation Manhunt 1970, Where the Cavern Ends 1971, The Infiltrator 1971, Operation Neptune 1971, The Expurgator 1972, The Captivator 1973, The Fascinator 1975, Dark Passage 1976, Tallant for Trouble 1977, Tallant for Disaster 1978, The Fire and the Rope 1979, The Scented Sword 1980, Tallant for Terror 1995; as Max Marlow with Diana Bachmann: Her Name will be Faith 1988, The Red Death 1990, Arctic Peril 1990, Meltdown 1990, The Growth 1993, Where the River Rises 1994, Shadow at Evening 1994, The Burning Rocks 1996, Children of Hell 1996, Dry 1996; other: Refugees (drama) 1987; contribs to numerous journals and magazines. *Address:* Marlow House, St Jacques, St Peter Port, Guernsey, GY1 1SW, Channel Islands. *Telephone:* (1481) 710896 (office); (1481) 722543 (home). *E-mail:* christopher.nicole@tiscali.co.uk.

NICOLOPULOS, Thania; Brazilian poet and writer; b. 12 Jan. 1924, Pernambuco; d. of Elias Nicolopulos Pablopulos and Georgina (née Joanides) Reissis; m. Ricardo Farias Rosas 1942; one s. one d. *Education:* La Prensa, Mexico. *Career:* freelance writer 1960–; founder and Ed. Centro Editorial Mexicano Osiris 1974; Fellow Altrusas, Red Cross, Fed. of Int. Volunteers; mem. Asscn Escritores Poetas Mexicanos, Soc. Autores Compositores, Anthropology Museum of Mexico. *Publications:* Interpretación de los Sueños 1965, El Mágico Lenguaje de los Sueños 1967, Antologí del Pensamiento 1973, Tlaltelolco Presente 1974, El Despertar de los Sentidos 1975, Metáforas y Paradijas 1975, Un album de poesie musicale 1979, Interpretación de las Manos 1980, Sebastiana la Medium 1981, El Verano de la Vida 1982, La Ofrenda 1983, Remonicencias 1983, Poesía Haiku en español 1990. *Address:* Sierra Ventana 545, 11000 México, DF, Mexico.

NIEMI, Mikael; Swedish writer and poet; b. 1959. *Plays:* Man måste kunna försvara sig (Radioteater) 1988, Ulosveisu (Tornedalsteatern) 1991, Specialaren (Lule Stassteater) 1992, Ska hon vara snygg eller oneurotisk (Radioteater) 1993, Kuppari (Tornedalsteatern) 1994, Innan det rasar (Teater Normlösa) 1994, Ulkojärvi cabaré (Radioteater) 1995–96, Elsa Laula (Sydsamisk Teater) 1996, Bondänger (comedy series for SvT) 1997, Samerevy (Dolgi Teater, Kiruna) 1997, Konsten att begrava en kärring (Upsala Stadsteater) 1998, Kalla tjejer och varma killar (Tornedalsteatern) 2000, Hej Hitler (Lule Stassteater) 2000, Min pappa är knivjonglör (ToTe, Kiruna) 2000, Dansa din djävul (Tornedalsteatern) 2001, En ö i Valhall (S. Ölands Musikteater) 2001, Tahto rautanen on (Tornedalsteatern) 2002. *Publications:* Näsblod under högmässan (poems) 1988, Mitt i skallen! (non-fiction) 1988, Änglar med mausergevär (poems) 1989, Med rötter häruppe (non-fiction) 1989, Kyrkdjävulen (juvenile fiction) 1994, Blodsugarna (juvenile fiction) 1997, Populärmusik från Vittula (novel, Popular Music from Vittula, aka Popular Music) (Augustpriset) 2000, Svålhålet (short stories) 2004, Astrotruckers (short stories) 2007. *Honours:* Tidningen Vis litteraturpris 2000, Årets Norrbottning 2000, Din bok - vårt val 2000, Årets Bok, Månadens boks pris 2002, Piratenpriset 2002. *Address:* c/o Norstedts, PO Box 2052, 103 12 Stockholm, Sweden.

NIFFENEGGER, Audrey, BFA, MFA; American novelist and visual artist; b. 13 June 1963, South Haven, MI. *Education:* School of the Art Inst. of Chicago, Northwestern Univ. *Career:* Prof., Columbia Coll., Chicago Centre (Interdisciplinary Book Arts, MFA program); Ragdale Foundation Fellowship 1996–2003, Illinois Art Council Fellowship in Prose 2000. *Publications:* The Time Traveler's Wife (novel) (British Book Awards Sainsbury's Popular Fiction Award 2006) 2003, The Three Incestuous Sisters 2005, The Adventures 2006. *Literary Agent:* c/o MacAdam/Cage Publishing, 1900 Wazee Street, Suite 210, Denver, CO 80202, USA. *Telephone:* (303) 753-7565. *Fax:* (303) 753-7566. *Website:* www.macadamcage.com.

NIGG, Joseph Eugene, (John Topsell), BA, MFA, PhD; American editor and writer; b. 27 Oct. 1938, Davenport, Ia; s. of Joseph John Nigg and Hollis Ellen Nigg; m. 1st Gayle Madsen 1960 (divorced 1979); two s. (one deceased); m. 2nd Esther Muzzillo 1989. *Education:* Kent State Univ., Univ. of Iowa, Univ. of Denver. *Career:* Asst Ed. Essays in Literature 1974–75; Assoc. Ed. Liniger's Real Estate 1979–85; Fiction Ed. Wayland Press 1985–92; mem. Colorado Authors' League. *Television:* participant and historical consultant, Ancient Mysteries' Dragons segment 1997; on Myths and Legends DVD 2001. *Publications:* The Book of Gryphons 1982, The Strength of Lions and the Flight of Eagles 1982, A Guide to the Imaginary Birds of the World 1984, Winegold 1985, The Great Balloon Festival 1989, Wonder Beasts 1995, The Book of Fabulous Beasts 1998, The Book of Dragons and Other Mythical Beasts 2002, How to Raise and Keep a Dragon 2006; contribs to various journals and magazines. *Honours:* Non-Fiction Book of the Year Awards, Colorado Authors League 1983, 1985, 1989, 1996, 2003, Mary Chase Author of the Year, Rocky Mountain Writers' Guild 1984. *Address:* 1114 Clayton Street, Denver, CO 80206, USA (home). *Telephone:* (303) 322-2175 (home). *E-mail:* jegryphon@aol.com (home); joe@josephnigg.com (home). *Website:* JosephNigg.com.

NIGHTINGALE, (William) Benedict Herbert, BA; British writer and theatre critic; b. 14 May 1939, London; s. of R. E. Nightingale and Hon. Mrs Nightingale (née Gardner); m. Anne B. Redmon 1964; two s. one d. *Education:* Charterhouse School, Magdalene Coll., Cambridge and Univ. of Pennsylvania. *Career:* gen. writer, The Guardian 1963–66; Literary Ed. New Society

1966–67; Theatre Critic, New Statesman 1968–86; Prof. of English, Theatre and Drama Univ. of Mich. 1986–89; Chief Drama Critic The Times 1990–; Sunday Theatre Critic, New York Times 1983–84. *Publications:* Charities 1972, Fifty British Plays 1982, Fifth Row Center 1986, The Future of the Theatre 1998; numerous articles on cultural and theatrical matters in British and American journals. *Address:* 40 Broomhouse Road, London, SW6 3QX, England.

NIKLANDER, Hannu, MA; Finnish poet, writer and critic; b. 1951, Helsinki; m. Kirsti Salmi-Niklander; one s. one d. *Education:* Univ. of Helsinki. *Career:* mem. Bd Union of Finnish Writers 2001–03, 2005–. *Publications:* Poetry: Kotiinpäin 1974, Maakuntalaulu 1979, Kauniisti Niiaava Tytär 1983, Suksien Surujuhla 1985, Muodonmuutoksia 1987, Vackert Nigande Dotter 1989; fiction: Kenkää enolle (short stories, with Anja Kauranen and Kosti Sironen) 1983, Öinen Kävely (short stories) 1989, Sairaskertomuksia (short stories) 1994, Aurinko Katsoo Taakseen (novel) 1999, Leskimiehen Kevät (short stories) 2000, Radan varrella varjo (novel) 2003; non-fiction: Kössi Kaatran Elämää Ja Lohjalaisvaiheita (essays) 1982, Kahvilavieraan Muistiinpanot (essays) 1987, Tuokiokuvia Euroopasta (essays) 1990, Vaahteranlehti Ja Vaakunalilja 1996; contrib. to Länsi-Uusimaa, Karkkilan Seutu, Karkkilan Tienoo, Kul Hunrivihkot, Helsingin Sanomat, Etelä-Suomen Sanomat, Suomenmaa, Kirjastolehti, Suomen Luonto, Parnasso, Kanava, Kaltio. *Honours:* Poetry Prize of NVL 1971, Nuoren Voiman Liitto Poetry Award 1971, State Award for Literature 1999. *Address:* c/o Atena Kustannus Oy, Pl 436, 40101 Jyväskylä (office); Fagerkulla 75, 03600 Karkkila, Finland (home). *E-mail:* hannu.niklander@kolumbus.fi (home).

NIMIER, Marie; French writer; b. 1957, Paris. *Publications:* novels: Sirène 1985, La Girafe 1987, L'Hypnotisme à la portée de tous (trans. as Hypnotism Made Easy) 1992, La caresse 1994, Celui qui court derrière loiseau 1996, Sabine Weiss: Des enfants 1997, La Nouvelle pornographie 2000; contrib. to Fictions contemporaines au féminin 2002. *Address:* c/o Editions Gallimard, 5 rue Sébastien-Bottin, 75328, Paris, France.

NISBET, Jim; American writer and poet; b. 20 Jan. 1947. *Publications:* Poems for a Lady, 1978; Gnachos for Bishop Berkeley, 1980; The Gourmet (novel), 1980; Morpho (with Alaistair Johnston), 1982; The Visitor, 1984; Lethal Injection (novel), 1987; Death Puppet (novel), 1989; Laminating the Conic Frustum, 1991; Small Apt, 1992; Ulysses' Dog, 1993; Sous le Signe de la Razoir, 1994.

NISBET, Robin George Murdoch, MA, FBA; British classical scholar; b. 21 May 1925, Glasgow; s. of Robert George Nisbet and Agnes Thomson Husband; m. Anne Wood 1969 (died 2004). *Education:* Glasgow Acad., Glasgow Univ. and Balliol Coll. Oxford. *Career:* Fellow and Tutor in Classics, Corpus Christi Coll. Oxford 1952–70, Prof. of Latin 1970–92. *Publications:* Commentary on Cicero, In Pisonem 1961, Horace, Odes I, II (with M. Hubbard) 1970, 1978, III (with N. Rudd) 2004, Collected Papers on Latin Literature 1995. *Honours:* Hon. Fellow Balliol Coll. 1989, Corpus Christi Coll. 1992; Kenyon Medal, British Acad. 1997. *Address:* 80 Abingdon Road, Cumnor, Oxon., OX2 9QW, England (home). *Telephone:* (1865) 862482 (home).

NISH, Ian Hill, CBE; British academic and writer; b. 3 June 1926, Edinburgh, Scotland; m. Rona Margaret Speirs 1965; two d. *Education:* Univ. of Edinburgh, 1943–51; Univ. of London, 1951–56. *Career:* Univ. of Sydney, NSW, Australia, 1957–62, LSE, England, 1962–91; mem. European Assen of Japanese Studies (Pres. 1985–88), British Assen of Japanese Studies (Pres. 1978). *Publications:* Anglo-Japanese Alliance, 1966; The Story of Japan, 1968; Alliance in Decline, 1972; Japanese Foreign Policy, 1978; Anglo-Japanese Alienation 1919–52, 1982; Origins of the Russo-Japanese War, 1986; Contemporary European Writing on Japan, 1988; Japan's Struggle with Internationalism, 1931–33, 1993; The Iwakura Mission in America and Europe, 1998; Collected Writings, Part I, 2001, Part II, 2002, Japanese Foreign Policy in the Interwar Period 2002. *Honours:* Hon. mem. Japan Acad. 2007; Order of the Rising Sun, Japan 1991; Japan Foundation Award 1991. *Address:* Oakdene, 33 Charlwood Drive, Oxshott, Surrey, KT22 0HB, England.

NISSABOURI, Mostafa; Moroccan poet and editor; b. 1943, Casablanca. *Career:* co-founder and Ed. of journals, Poésie Toute 1964, Eaux Vives 1965, Souffles, Intégral; Dir Éditions Archimédia; mem. Bd House of Poetry, Morocco; mem. The Book of Hope and World Healing Book. *Publications:* Plus haute mémoire 1968, La Mille et deuxieme nuit 1975, Approaching the Wilderness 2001; contrib. to Aufgabe, Banipal. *Address:* c/o Editions al-Manar, Art Point France, Catherine Plassart, 6 rue Gimelli, 83000 Toulon, France.

NITCHIE, George Wilson, BA, MA, PhD; American academic, writer and poet; b. 19 May 1921, Chicago, IL; m. Laura Margaret Woodard 1947; three d. *Education:* Middlebury College, Columbia University. *Career:* Instructor, 1947–50, Asst Prof., 1950–59, Assoc. Prof., 1959–66, Prof. of English, 1966–86, Chair., Dept of English, 1972–79, Prof. Emeritus, 1986–, Simmons College; mem. American Assen of University Profs. *Publications:* Human Values in the Poetry of Robert Frost, 1960; Marianne Moore: An Introduction to the Poetry, 1969. Contributions: various critical essays in scholarly journals and poems in many publications.

NIU, Han; Chinese poet; b. (Shi Chenghan), 23 Oct. 1923, Dingxiang, Shanxi Prov.; m. Wu Ping; one s. one d. *Education:* Northwest Univ. *Career:* fmrly Sec. Research Dept Renmin Univ.; Dir Cultural and Educational Office,

Political Dept of Northeast Air Force; Exec. Assoc. Chief Ed. Chinese Literature; Chief Ed. Historical Records of New Literature Movt; Dir Editorial Office of May 4th Literature; Sr Ed. People's Publishing House. *Publications:* Motherland, In Front of the Motherland, Coloured Life, Hot Spring, Love and Songs, Earthworm and Feather, Selected Lyric Poems of Niu Han, Notes Taken While Learning to Write Poems, A Sonambulist's Talk on Poetry 2001, Spaciousness Afar-off 2005. *Honours:* Creative Literary Works Award 1981–82, Literary Stick Prize for Nation's Best New Poem (Macedonia) 2003, China Central TV Poet of the Year 2006. *Address:* 203 Gate 6 Building 309 Balizhuang Beili, Beijing 100025 (home); People's Literature Publishing House, 166 Chaoyangmen Nei Dajie, Beijing 100705, People's Republic of China (office). *Telephone:* (10) 85836410 (home); (10) 65138394 (office). *Fax:* (10) 65138394 (office). *E-mail:* fangjia2001@yahoo.com.cn (home).

NIVEN, Larry, BA; American science-fiction writer; b. (Laurence Van Cott Niven), 30 April 1938, Los Angeles, CA; m. Marilyn Joyce Wisowaty 1969. *Education:* Washburn Univ., KS. *Career:* first published story, 'The Coldest Place' appeared in Dec. 1964 issue, World of If. *Publications:* Known Space series: The World of Ptavvs 1966, Neutron Star (Hugo Award for Best Short Story 1967) 1966, A Gift From Earth 1968, The Shape of Space (short story collection) 1969, Ringworld (Nebula Award for Best Novel 1970, Hugo Award for Best Novel 1971, Locus Award for Best Novel 1970, Ditmar Award, Australia 1972) 1970, All the Myriad Ways (short story collection) 1971, Inconstant Moon (Hugo Award for Best Short Story 1972) 1971, Protector (originally published in Galaxy Magazine as 'The Adults') (Ditmar Award, Australia) 1973, Tales of Known Space (short story collection) 1975, The Long Arm of Gil Hamilton (short story collection) 1976, The Convergent Series (short story collection) (Locus Award for single author collection 1980) 1979, The Ringworld Engineers 1980, The Patchwork Girl (short story collection) 1980, Niven's Laws (short story collection) 1984, Limits (short story collection) 1985, N-Space (short story collection) 1990, Playgrounds of the Mind (short story collection) 1991, Bridging the Galaxies (short story collection) 1993, Crashlander (short story collection) 1994, The Ringworld Throne 1996, Ringworld's Children 2004; other books: The Flying Sorcerers (with David Gerrold) 1971, The Flight of the Horse 1973, The Hole Man (Hugo Award for Best Short Story 1975) 1974, A Hole in Space 1974, The Mote In God's Eye (with Jerry Pournelle) 1974, Inferno (with Jerry Pournelle) 1975, The Borderland of Sol (Hugo Award for Best Short Story 1976) 1975, A World Out of Time 1976, The Magic Goes Away 1977, Lucifer's Hammer (with Jerry Pournelle) 1977, Dream Park (with Steven Barnes) 1981, Oath of Fealty (with Jerry Pournelle) 1981, The Descent of Anansi (with Steven Barnes) 1982, The Integral Trees (Locus Award for Best Novel) 1984, Footfall (with Jerry Pournelle) 1985, The Legacy of Heorot (with Jerry Pournelle and Steven Barnes) 1987, The Smoke Ring 1987, The Barsoom Project (with Steven Barnes) 1989, Achilles' Choice (with Steven Barnes) 1991, Dream Park: The Voodoo Game (aka The California Voodoo Game) (with Steven Barnes) 1991, Fallen Angels (with Jerry Pournelle and Michael Flynn) (Prometheus Award for Best Novel 1992, Seiun Award, Japan 1998) 1991, The Gripping Hand (aka The Moat Around Murcheson's Eye) (with Jerry Pournelle) 1993, Rainbow Mars 1999, Saturn's Race (with Steven Barnes) 2000, The Burning City (with Jerry Pournelle) 2000, The Missing Mass (Locus Award for Best Short Story) 2001; contrib. numerous short stories to books and magazines. *Honours:* Hon. DLitt (Washburn Univ.) 1984; New England Science Fiction Asscn Edward E. Smith Memorial Award for Imaginative Fiction 'Skylark Award' 1973, San Diego Comic Convention Inkpot Award 1979, 5 Science Fiction Achievement Awards. *Address:* c/o Orbit, Brettenham House, Lancaster Place, London, WC2E 7EN, England. *E-mail:* organlegger@earthlink.net (home).

NIXON, Colin Harry; British poet and writer; b. 9 March 1939, London; m. Betty Morgan 1967; three d. *Education:* Univ. of London. *Career:* civil servant, 1960–99; Disablement Resettlement Officer 1974–83; ACAS Conciliation Officer 1983–99. *Publications:* Roads, 1975; Geography of Love, 1977; With All Angles Equal, 1980; The Bright Idea, 1983. Contributions: anthologies, including: Spongers, 1984; Affirming Flame, 1989; Poetry Street 3, 1991; Red Candle Treasury, 1948–1998, 1998; The Art of Haiku 2000, 2000; Periodicals, including: Outposts; Tribune; Countryman; Cricketer. *Honours:* George Camp Memorial Poetry Prizes 1975, 1983, First Prize Civil Service Poetry 1978. *Address:* 72 Barmouth Road, Wandsworth Common, London, SW18 2DS, England.

NKOSI, Lewis, DipLit; South African writer and critic; b. 5 Dec. 1936, Natal. *Education:* M. C. Sultan Technical Coll., Harvard Univ., Univ. of London, Univ. of Sussex. *Career:* staff mem. on Zulu newspaper, Ilange Lae Natal, Durban 1955–56, Drum magazine and Golden City Post, Johannesburg 1956–60, South African Information Bulletin, Paris 1962–68; radio producer, BBC Transcription Centre, London 1962–64; Literary Ed., New African magazine, London 1965–68; Prof. of Literature, Univ. of Wyoming, USA 1997–98, Univ. of California at Irvine, univs in Zambia and Warsaw, Poland. *Publications:* The Rhythm of Violence (play) 1964, Home and Exile (essays) 1965, The Transplanted Heart: Essays on South Africa (essays) 1975, Tasks and Masks: Themes and Styles of African Literature (essays) 1981, Mating Birds (novel) 1986, Underground People (novel) 1994, The Black Psychiatrist (play) 2001, Mandela's Ego (novel) 2006. *Honours:* Univ. of London Leverhulme Visiting Fellowship. *Address:* c/o Kwela Books, PO Box 6525, Roggebaai 8012, South Africa. *E-mail:* kwela@kwela.com.

NOAKES, Vivien, MA, DPhil, FRSL; British writer; b. 16 Feb. 1937, Twickenham; m. Michael Noakes 1960; two s. one d. *Education:* Manchester

Coll., Oxford and Somerville Coll., Oxford. *Career:* Judge, RSL W.H. Heinemann Award 1999–2004, Winifred Holtby Prize 1999–2003; mem. Soc. of Authors, PEN. *Publications:* Edward Lear: The Life of a Wanderer 1968, For Lovers of Edward Lear 1978, Scenes from Victorian Life 1979, Edward Lear 1812–1888, The Catalogue of the Royal Acad. Exhbn 1985, The Selected Letters of Edward Lear 1988, The Painter Edward Lear 1991, The Imperial War Museum Catalogue of Isaac Rosenberg 1998, The Daily Life of the Queen: An Artist's Diary 2000, Edward Lear: The Complete Verse and Other Nonsense (ed.) 2001, revised edn as Edward Lear: The Complete Nonsense and Other Verse 2002, The Poems and Plays of Isaac Rosenberg (ed.) 2004; contribs to The Times, Times Literary Supplement, Daily Telegraph, New Scientist, Punch, Harvard Magazine, Tennyson Research Bulletin. *Literary Agent:* Watson, Little Ltd, Lymehouse Studios, 38 Georgiana Street, London, NW1 0EB, England. *Address:* 146 Hamilton Terrace, London, NW8 9UX, England (home). *Telephone:* (20) 7328-6754 (home). *E-mail:* mail@vivien -noakes.co.uk. *Website:* www.vivien-noakes.co.uk.

NOBBS, David Gordon, BA; British writer; b. 13 March 1935, Orpington, Kent; m. 1st Mary Jane Goddard 1968 (divorced 1998); two step-s. one step-d.; m. 2nd Susan Sutcliffe 1998; one step-d. *Education:* Marlborough College, St John's College, Cambridge. *Publications:* The Itinerant Lodger, 1965; Ostrich Country, 1967; A Piece of the Sky is Missing, 1968; The Fall and Rise of Reginald Perrin, 1975; The Return of Reginald Perrin, 1977; The Better World of Reginald Perrin, 1978; Second From Last in the Sack Race, 1983; A Bit of a Do, 1986; Pratt of the Argus, 1988; Fair Dos, 1990; The Cucumber Man, 1994; The Legacy of Reginald Perrin, 1995; Going Gently, 2000; I Didn't Get Where I Am Today (autobiog.), 2003; Sex and Other Changes 2004. *Address:* 10 Iron Bridge House, Bridge Approach, London, NW1 8BD, England.

NOBLE, Denis, CBE, PhD, FRS; British scientist and academic; b. 16 Nov. 1936, London; s. of George Noble and Ethel Rutherford; m. Susan Jennifer Barfield 1965; one s. (adopted) one d. *Education:* Emanuel School and Univ. Coll. London. *Career:* Asst Lecturer, Univ. Coll. London 1961–63; Fellow, Lecturer and Tutor in Physiology, Balliol Coll. Oxford 1963–84, Praefectus, Balliol Grad. Centre 1971–89, Burdon Sanderson Prof. of Cardiovascular Physiology, Univ. of Oxford 1984–2004, Professorial Fellow 1984–2004; Visiting Prof., Univ. of Alberta 1969–70; Ed., Progress in Biophysics 1967–; Founder Dir, Oxsoft Ltd 1984–, Physiome Sciences Inc. 1994–; Chair., Jt Dental Cttee 1984–90; Pres. Medical Section, British Asscn 1992; Gen.-Sec., Int. Union of Physiological Sciences 1993–2001; Hon. Sec., Physiological Soc. 1974–80, Foreign Sec. 1986–92; Fellow, University Coll. London 1986; Founder Fellow, Acad. of Medical Sciences 1998; Adjunct Prof., Xi'an Jiaotong Univ., China 2003–07; Visiting Prof., Osaka Univ., Japan 2006. *Publications:* Initiation of the Heartbeat 1975, Electric Current Flow in Excitable Cells 1975, Electrophysiology of Single Cardiac Cells 1987, Goals, No Goals and Own Goals 1989, Sodium-Calcium Exchange 1989, Logic of Life 1993, Ionic Channels and the Effect of Taurine on the Heart 1993, Ethics of Life 1997, The Music of Life 2006; scientific papers mostly in Journal of Physiology. *Honours:* Hon. DSc (Sheffield Univ.) 2004, Dr hc (Bordeaux) 2005 Hon. FRCP; Hon. mem. Acad. de Medécine de Belgique, American Physiological Soc., Academia Europaea 1989, Japanese Physiological Soc. 1998, The Physiological Soc. 1999; Darwin Lecturer, British Asscn 1966, Scientific Medal, Zoological Soc. 1970, Nahum Lecturer, Yale Univ. 1977, British Heart Foundation Gold Medal and Prize 1985, Lloyd Roberts Lecturer 1987, Bowden Lecturer 1988, Alderdale Wyld Lecturer 1988, Pierre Rijlant Prize, Belgian Royal Acad. 1991, Baly Medal, Royal Coll. of Physicians 1993, Pavlov Medal Russian Acad. of Science 2004, Hodgkin-Huxley-Katz Prize, Physiological Soc. 2004, Mackenzie Prize, British Cardiac Soc. 2005. *Address:* University Laboratory of Physiology, Parks Road, Oxford, OX1 3PT (office); 49 Old Road, Oxford, OX3 7JZ, England. *Telephone:* (1865) 272533 (office); (1865) 762237 (home). *Fax:* (1865) 272554 (office). *E-mail:* denis.noble@physiol.ox.ac.uk (office). *Website:* www.physiol.ox.ac.uk (office).

NOEL, Lise, BA, LèsL, MA, PhD; Canadian writer and columnist; b. 19 April 1944, Montréal, QC. *Education:* University of Montréal, University of Aix-en-Provence, France. *Publications:* Intolerance: The Parameters of Oppression 1994, Le Devoir, Mariage Homosexuel: Les Termes du Débat 2003; contributions to Critère, Liberté, Possibles, Service Social. *Honours:* Hach-ette-Larousse 1967, Governor-General's Award for Non-Fiction 1989, Myers Centre Award for the Study of Human Rights in North America 1994. *Address:* 2608 Chemin Cote Sainte Catherine, Montréal, QC H3T 1B4, Canada.

NOËL-HUME, Ivor, (Richard Akerman), OBE; British archaeologist and writer; b. 1927, London. *Education:* St Lawrence College, Kent. *Career:* archaeologist, Guildhall Museum Corp, London, 1949–57; Chief Archaeologist, 1957–64, Dir, Dept of Archaeology, 1964–72, Resident Archaeologist, 1972–87, Colonial Williamsburg; Research Assoc., Smithsonian Institution, Washington, DC, 1959–; Guest Curator, Steuben Glass Co, 1990; Dir, Roanoke Project, 1991–93; Chair., Jamestown Rediscovery Advisory Board, 1994–95; mem. American Antiquarian Society; Society of Antiquaries, London, fellow; Society of Historical Archaeology; Society for Post-Medieval Archaeology; Virginia Archeological Society. *Publications:* Archaeology in Britain, 1953; Tortoises, Terrapins and Turtles (with Audrey Noël-Hume), 1954; Treasure in the Thames, 1956; Great Moments in Archaeology, 1957; Here Lies Virginia, 1963; 1775: Another Part of the Field, 1966; Historical Archaeology, 1969; Artifacts of Early America, 1970; All the Best Rubbish, 1974; Early English Delftware, 1977; Martin's Hundred, 1982; The Virginia Adventure, 1994;

Shipwreck: History from the Bermuda Reeds, 1995; In Search of This and That, 1995; If These Pots Could Talk, 2001, Civilized Men 2006, Something from the Cellar 2006. Films: Doorway to the Past, 1968; The Williamsburg File, 1976; Search for a Century, 1981. Contributions: Professional journals. *Honours:* Award for Historical Archaeology, University of South Carolina, 1975; Hon. Doctor of Humane Letters, University of Pennsylvania, 1976; College of William and Mary, Williamsberg, VA, 1983; Achievement Award, National Society of the Daughters of the Founders and Patriots of America, 1989, National Society of the Daughters of the American Colonists, 1990. *Address:* 2 West Circle, Williamsburg, VA 23185, USA. *E-mail:* thamesis1@ msn.com.

NOKES, David, MA, PhD, FRSL; British biographer, screenwriter and academic; *Professor of English Literature, King's College, London. Career:* currently Prof. of English Literature King's Coll., London. *Television adaptations:* The Count of Solar 1991, Clarissa 1991, The Tenant of Wildfell Hall 1996, Frankenstein: Birth of a Monster 2003. *Publications:* non-fiction: Fielding's Joseph Andrews 1987, Raillery and Rage: Study of Eighteenth Century Satire 1987; biographies: Jonathan Swift, A Hypocrite Reversed (James Tait Black Memorial Prize for Biography) 1985, John Gay, A Profession of Friendship 1995, Jane Austen 1997; novel: The Nightingale Papers 2005. *Address:* Department of English Language and Literature, King's College, Strand, London, WC2R 2LS, England. *E-mail:* david.nokes@ kcl.ac.uk.

NOLAN, Patrick, MA, PhD; American academic, writer and dramatist; b. 2 Jan. 1933, New York, NY; three s. *Education:* Univ. of Detroit, Bryn Mawr Coll. *Career:* instructor, Univ. of Detroit; Prof., Villanova Univ.; mem. Writers' Guild of America (West), Dramatists' Guild. *Film screenplays:* Hourglass Moment 1969, Jericho Mile 1978. *Plays:* Chameleons 1981, Midnight Rainbows 1991. *Honours:* Emmy Award 1979, Philadelphia Magazine citation for teaching excellence 1980. *Address:* c/o Department of English, Villanova University, Villanova, PA 19085, USA.

NOLAN, William Francis, (Frank Anmar, Mike Cahill, F. E. Edwards, Michael Phillips); American writer and poet; b. 6 March 1928, Kansas City, MO. *Education:* Kansas City Art Institute, San Diego State College, Los Angeles City College. *Publications:* Barney Oldfield, 1961; Phil Hall: Yankee Champion, 1962; Impact 20 (short stories), 1963; John Huston: King Rebel, 1965; Sinners and Superman, 1965; Death is for Losers, 1968; Dashiell Hammett: A Casebook, 1969; Alien Horizons (short stories), 1974; Hemingway: Last Days of the Lion, 1974; Wonderworlds (short stories), 1977; Hammett: A Life on the Edge, 1983; Things Beyond Midnight (short stories), 1984; Dark Encounters (poems), 1986; Logan: A Trilogy, 1986; How to Write Horror Fiction, 1990; Six in Darkness (short stories), 1993; Night Shapes (short stories), 1993.

NONHEBEL, Clare, BA; British writer; b. 7 Nov. 1953, London; m. Robin Nonhebel 1975. *Education:* Univ. of Warwick. *Career:* mem. MENSA. *Publications:* Cold Showers, 1985; The Partisan, 1986; Incentives, 1988; Healed and Souled, 1988; Child's Play, 1991; Eldred Jones, Lulubelle and the Most High (novel), 1998; Don't Ask Me to Believe (non-fiction), 1998; Far From Home, (non-fiction), 1999; Healing for Life (non-fiction), 2000. Contributions: newspapers, journals, and magazines. *Honours:* Joint Winner, Betty Trask Award, 1984.

NOONAN, Peggy, BA; American writer; *Contributing Editor, The Wall Street Journal;* b. 7 Sept. 1950, Brooklyn, NY; d. of James J. and Mary Jane (née Byrne) Noonan; m. Richard Rahn 1985 (divorced); one s. *Education:* Fairleigh Dickson Univ. (Rutherford, NJ). *Career:* Adjuster Aetna Insurance Co., Newark, NJ until 1970; scriptwriter, producer and later Editorial Dir WEEI (CBS), Boston; Writer, Ed. CBS 1977–81, writer radio commentaries 1981–84; Adjunct Prof. of Journalism, NY Univ. 1978–79; speech writer and special asst to Pres. Ronald Reagan 1984–86; chief speech writer for Pres. George Bush 1988; adviser Bush–Quayle 1992 presidential campaign; columnist Mirabella Magazine, New York Times, Forbes Magazine, Newsweek 1990–92; currently Contributing Ed. Wall Street Journal, Time magazine, Good Housekeeping magazine; mem. Bd of Dirs Manhattan Inst. *Publications:* I Am Often Booed Because of Who My Friends Are, What I Saw at the Revolution: A Political Life in the Reagan Era 1990, Life, Liberty and the Pursuit of Happiness 1994, The Case Against Hillary Clinton 2000, When Character was King: A Story of Ronald Reagan 2001, A Heart, a Cross and a Flag 2003. *Honours:* Dr hc (Fairleigh Dickinson) 1990, (Adelphi Univ.), (St. John Fisher Coll.); Esquire Magazine Achievement Award 1984, Republican Nat. Women's Club Award for Journalism 1992. *Address:* c/o The Wall Street Journal, 200 Liberty Street, New York, NY 10281, USA. *Telephone:* (212) 416-2000. *Website:* www .opinionjournal.com/columnists/pnoonan; www.peggynoonan.com.

NOOTEBOOM, Cornelis (Cees) Johannes Jacobus Maria; Dutch writer and poet; b. 31 July 1933, The Hague. *Publications:* fiction: Philip en de anderen (Anne Frank-prijs 1957) 1954, De verliefde gevangene 1958, De koning is dood 1961, De ridder is gestorven (Lucy B. en C. W. van der Hoogtprijs 1963) 1963, Rituelen (F. Bordewijkprijs 1981, Mobil Pegasus Literatuurprijs 1982) 1980, Een lied van schijn en wezen 1981, Mokusei 1982, In Nederland (Multatuliprijs 1985) 1984, De Boeddha achter de schutting. Aan de oever van de Chaophraya 1986, Ina Rilke 1991, Allerzielen 1998, Paradijs Verloren 2004; plays: De zwanen van de Theems (ANV-Visser Neerlandia-prijs 1960) 1959, Gyges en Kandaules. Een koningsdrama 1982; poetry: De doden zoeben een huis 1956, Koude gedichten 1959, Het zwarte gedicht 1960, Ibicenzer gedicht (Poëzieprijs van de gemeente Amsterdam) 1960, Gesloten gedichten (Poëzieprijs van de gemeente Amsterdam 1965) 1964, Gemaakte gedichten 1970, Open als een schelp – dicht als een steen (Jan Campertprijs 1978) 1978, Aas 1982, Vuurtijd, Ijstijd. Gedichten 1955–1983 1984, Het gezicht van het oog 1989, Zo kon het zijn (Gedichtendagprijzen 2000) 1999, Bitterzoet, honderd gedichten van vroeger en zeventien nieuwe 2000; non-fiction: Een middag in Bruay 1963, Een nacht in Tunesië 1965, Een ochtend in Bahia 1968, De Parijse beroerte 1968, Bitter Bolivia, Maanland Mali 1971, Een avond in Isfahan 1978, Waar je gevallen bent, blijf je 1983, De zucht naar het Westen 1985, De wereld een reiziger 1989, Berlijnse notities 1990, Vreemd water 1991, Het volgende verhaal 1991, De omweg naar Santiago (Preis für Reiseliteratur des Landes Tirol 1996) 1992, Zurbaránk 1992, De ontvoering van Europa (essay) 1993, De koning van Suriname 1993, Van de lente de dauw. Oosterse reizen 1995, De filosoof zonder ogen: Europese reizen 1997, Terugkeer naar Berlijn 1997. *Honours:* hon. mem. Modern Language Asscn, USA 1997; Chevalier, Légion d'honneur 1991; Hon. DLitt (Katholieke Universiteit Brussel) 1998; Prijs van de dagbladjournalistiek 1969, Cestoda-prijs 1982, Preis zum 3 Oktober 1990, Constantijn Huygensprijs 1992, Hugo Ball Preis 1993, Aristeion Prijs 1993, Premio Grinzane Cavour 1994, Dirk Martens-prijs 1994, Goethe-prijs 2002, Oostenrijkse staatsprijs 2002, P. C. Hooftprijs 2004. *Address:* c/o Arbeiderspers, Herengracht 370-372, 1016 CH Amsterdam, The Netherlands.

NORÉN, Lars; Swedish playwright and director; b. 9 May 1944, Stockholm; s. of Matti Norén and Britt Norén; m. 1st Titti Mörk 1979; m. 2nd Charlott Neuhauser 1993; two d. *Career:* started career as a poet; wrote first play 1968; has written 55 plays, performed world-wide. *Plays include:* Courage to Kill 1978, Munich-Athens 1981, Night is Day's Mother 1982, Comedians 1985, Hebriana 1987, Autumn and Winter 1987, And Give Us the Shadows 1988, Trick or Treat 1989, Lost and Found 1991, Leaves in Vallombrosa 1992, Blood 1994, Some Kind of Hades 1994, The Clinic 1995, Personkrets 3:1 1997, 7:3 1998, The Shadow Boys 1991. *Honours:* De Nio's Pris 1985, Expressens Reviewers' Prize 1993, Pilot Prize 1994 and many other prizes and awards. *Address:* c/o Ulla Orre, Draken Teaterförlag, Södermannagatan 27 NB, 11640 Stockholm (Agent); Östermalmsgatan 33, S-11426 Stockholm, Sweden, (home). *Telephone:* (8) 642-71-06 (Agent). *Fax:* (8) 643-81-08. *E-mail:* draken@mbox307.swipnet.se (office). *Website:* home.swipnet.se/draken (office).

NORFOLK, Lawrence; British writer; b. 1963, London, England. *Publications:* novels: Lemprière's Dictionary, 1991; The Pope's Rhinoceros, 1997; In the Shape of a Boar, 2000; editor of anthologies.

NORFOLK, Mark, Postgraduate Dip. Film Studies; British playwright and filmmaker; b. Croydon, Surrey. *Education:* Univ. of Wales, Cardiff. *Career:* Co-Founder, Prussia Lane Productions Ltd. *Plays:* Fair as the Dark Get 1998, Buy Your Leave 1998, Knock Down Ginger 2000, Wrong Place 2003, Fess Up 2003. *Radio:* Medium Risk (BBC Radio 3) 2005. *Films:* Love is Not Enough (also screenplay) 2001, Crossing Bridges (also screenplay) 2004. *Publication:* contrib. to Black Filmmaker Magazine 2001–. *Honours:* Production Award, London Film and Video Devt Agency 1999, Champion of Culture Award 2003. *Literary Agent:* Prussia Lane Productions Ltd, 1A Upper Brockley Road, London, SE4 1SY, England. *Telephone:* (20) 8692-6618. *Fax:* (20) 8692-6618. *E-mail:* mail@prussialane.freeserve.co.uk. *Website:* www.prussialane.com; www.pruzz.com.

NORLING, Bernard, BA, MA, PhD; American academic (retd) and writer; b. 23 Feb. 1924, Hunters, WA; m. Mary Pupo 1948. *Education:* Gonzaga University, University of Notre Dame. *Career:* Instructor, 1952–55, Asst Prof., 1955–61, Assoc. Prof., 1961–71, Prof. of History, 1971–86, University of Notre Dame; mem. Indiana Asscn of Historians; Michiana Historians, pres., 1972. *Publications:* Towards a Better Understanding of History, 1960; Timeless Problems in History, 1970; Understanding History Through the American Experience, 1976; Return to Freedom, 1983; Behind Japanese Lines, 1986; The Nazi Impact on a German Village, 1993; Lapham's Raiders, 1996; The Intrepid Guerrillas of North Luzon, 1999. Contributions: Magazines and journals. *Honours:* University of Notre Dame Best Teacher of Freshman Award 1968.

NORMAN, Barry Leslie, CBE; British writer and broadcaster; b. 21 Aug. 1933, London; s. of Leslie Norman and Elizabeth Norman; m. Diana Narracott 1957; two d. *Education:* Highgate School, London. *Career:* Entertainment Ed. Daily Mail, London 1969–71; weekly columnist The Guardian 1971–80; Writer and Presenter of BBC 1 Film 1973–81, 1983–98, The Hollywood Greats 1977–79, 1984, The British Greats 1980, Omnibus 1982, Film Greats 1985, Talking Pictures 1988, Barry Norman's Film Night, BSkyB 1998–2001; Radio 4 Today 1974–76, Going Places 1977–81, Breakaway 1979–80. *Publications:* Novels: The Matter of Mandrake 1967, The Hounds of Sparta 1968, End Product 1975, A Series of Defeats 1977, To Nick a Good Body 1978, Have a Nice Day 1981, Sticky Wicket 1984, The Birddog Tape 1992, The Mickey Mouse Affair 1995, Death on Sunset 1998; non-fiction: Tales of the Redundance Kid 1975, The Hollywood Greats 1979, The Movie Greats 1981, The Film Greats 1985, Talking Pictures 1987, The Good Night In Guide 1992, 100 Best Films of the Century 1992, And Why Not? (autobiog.) 2002. *Honours:* Hon. DLitt (E Anglia) 1991, (Herts.) 1996; Richard Dimbleby Award, BAFTA 1981, Columnist of the Year Award 1990. *Address:* c/o Curtis Brown Ltd, Haymarket House, 28–29 Haymarket, London, SW1Y 4SP, England. *Telephone:* (20) 7396-6600.

NORMAN, Geraldine Lucia, (Geraldine Keen, Florence Place), MA; British journalist and writer; *UK Representative, State Hermitage Museum, St Petersburg;* b. (Geraldine Lucia Keen), 13 May 1940, Wales; m. Frank Norman, July 1971. *Education:* St Anne's Coll., Oxford, Univ. of California at Los Angeles, USA. *Career:* Sale Room Corresp., The Times 1969–87; Art Market Corresp., The Independent 1987–95; UK Rep., State Hermitage Museum, St Petersburg 2001–, Ed. Hermitage Magazine 2002–05. *Publications:* The Sale of Works of Art (as Geraldine Keen) 1971, 19th Century Painters and Paintings: A Dictionary 1977, The Fake's Progress (co-author) 1977, The Tom Keating Catalogue (ed.) 1977, Mrs Harper's Niece (as Florence Place) 1982, Biedermeier Painting 1987, Top Collectors of the World (co-author) 1993, The Hermitage: The Biography of a Great Museum 1997; contrib. to newspapers. *Honours:* Russian State Medal 'In memory of St Petersburg's 300th Anniversary'; News Reporter of the Year 1976. *Address:* 5 Seaford Court, 220 Great Portland Street, London, W1, England (home). *Telephone:* (20) 7387-6067 (office). *Fax:* (20) 7383-3470 (office).

NORMAN, John; American academic, writer and poet; b. 20 July 1912, Syracuse, NY; m. Mary Lynott 1948; four d. *Education:* BA, 1935, MA, 1938, Syracuse University; PhD, Clark University, 1942. *Publications:* Edward Gibbon Wakefield: A Political Reappraisal, 1963; Labor and Politics in Libya and Arab Africa, 1965; Life Lines: A Volume of Verse, 1997. Contributions: anthologies, reference books, and journals. *Honours:* World Poetry Prize, 1991. *Address:* 94 Cooper Road, John's Pond, Ridgefield, CT 06877, USA.

NORMAN, Marsha, BA, MAT; American playwright and writer; b. 21 Sept. 1947, Louisville, KY; d. of Billie Williams and Bertha Conley; m. 1st Michael Norman (divorced 1974); m. 2nd Dann C. Byck Jr 1978 (divorced); m. 3rd Timothy Dykman; one s. one d. *Education:* Agnes Scott Coll. and Univ. of Louisville. *Career:* Rockefeller playwright-in-residence grantee 1979–80; American Acad. and Inst. for Arts and Letters grantee. *Plays:* Getting Out 1977, Third and Oak 1978, Circus Valentine 1979, The Holdup 1980, 'Night, Mother 1982, Traveler in the Dark 1984, Sarah and Abraham 1987, The Secret Garden (musical) 1991, Loving Daniel Boone 1992, The Red Shoes 1992, Trudy Blue 1995. *Television plays:* It's the Willingness 1978, In Trouble at Fifteen 1980, The Laundromat 1985, The Pool Hall 1989, Face of a Stranger 1991. *Publications:* The Fortune Teller (novel) 1987; books of lyrics; plays. *Honours:* Pulitzer Prize for Drama 1983; Tony Award 1991; many other awards and prizes.

NORMANBY, 5th Marquis of, cr. 1838 Constantine Edmund Walter Phipps, MA; British company director and writer; b. 24 Feb. 1954, Whitby, North Yorkshire, England; m. Nicola St Aubyn (née Shulman) 1990; two s. two d. *Education:* Worcester Coll., Oxford, City Univ., London. *Publications:* Careful with the Sharks 1985, Among the Thin Ghosts 1989; other: The Day's Work by Rudyard Kipling (ed.) 1988. *Address:* Mulgrave Castle, Whitby, YO21 3RJ, England.

NORRELL, Gregory T., BS, PhD; American writer, poet and publisher; b. 24 Nov. 1960, Tallahassee, FL; m. Karen Norrell 1980 (divorced 1995); one s. one d. *Education:* State University of West Georgia, SUNY at Albany. *Career:* Publisher, Dandelion Press and Dandelion Media, Idaho Falls, 1955–; Owner, Dandelion Studios, Dandelion Multimedia Recording Division; mem. Acad. of American Poets; Web Poets Society, founder. *Publications:* 'Til Death Do Us Part (short stories), 1997; 95 Windows: An Unofficial Poetry Collection from the Microsoft Network, 1997; Amongst the Shadows (poems), 1997; The River of No Return (novel), 1998; Impact (novel), 1999. *Address:* 1935 E 113 South Street, Idaho Falls, ID 83404, USA. *E-mail:* dandelion@dandelion-multimedia.com.

NORRIS, Geoffrey, BA, ARCM; British critic and musicologist; *Chief Music Critic, The Daily Telegraph;* b. 19 Sept. 1947, London. *Education:* Univ. of Durham, Univ. of Liverpool, Inst. of Theatre, Music and Cinematography, Leningrad. *Career:* music critic, The Daily Telegraph 1983, chief music critic 1995–, also for The Times; Lecturer in Music History, Royal Northern Coll. of Music 1975–77; Commissioning Ed., New Oxford Companion to Music 1977–83; Prof., Rachmaninoff Music Inst., Tambov, Russia 2005–; mem Royal Musical Asscn, The Critics' Circle. *Publications include:* Encyclopedia of Opera (co-author) 1976, Rachmaninoff 1976, Shostakovich: The Man and his Music (co-author) 1982, A Catalogue of the Compositions of S. Rachmaninov (co-author) 1982; contrib. to New Grove Dictionary of Music and Musicians 1980, 2001, Musical Times, Music Quarterly, Tempo, Music and Letters, BBC broadcasts. *Address:* The Daily Telegraph, 1 Canada Square, Canary Wharf, London, E14 5DT, England (office).

NORRIS, Kathleen, BA; American poet and writer; b. 27 July 1947, Washington, DC; m. David J. Dwyer. *Education:* Bennington Coll. *Career:* Poet-in-Residence, North Dakota Arts Council, 1979–92; Oblate, Benedictine Order, 1986–; mem. National Book Critics Circle; Poetry Society of America. *Publications:* Poetry: Falling Off, 1971; From South Dakota: Four Poems, 1978; The Middle of the World, 1981; How I Came to Drink My Grandmother's Piano: Some Benedictine Poems, 1989; The Year of Common Things, 1990; The Astronomy of Love, 1994; Little Girls in Church, 1995. Other: Dakota: A Spiritual Geography, 1993; The Cloister Walk, 1996; Amazing Grace: A Vocabulary of Faith, 1998; The Quotidian Mysteries, 1998. Editor: Leaving New York: Writers Look Back, 1995. Contributions: anthologies and periodicals. *Honours:* Big Table Poetry Series Younger Poets Award, 1971; Creative Artists Public Service Programme Grant, New York State, 1972; Fine Arts Work Centre Fellowship, Provincetown, Massachusetts, 1972; Bush Foundation Grant, 1993; Guggenheim Foundation Grant, 1994; Western Libraries Asscn Award, 1995. *Literary Agent:* Steven Barclay Agency, 12 Western Avenue, Petaluma, CA 94952, USA. *Telephone:* (707) 773-0654. *Fax:* (707) 778-1868. *Website:* www.barclayagency.com. *Address:* PO Box 570, Lemmon, SD 57638, USA.

NORRIS, Ken, BA, MA, PhD; American academic and poet; b. 3 April 1951, New York, NY; two d. *Education:* SUNY at Stony Brook, Concordia University, McGill University. *Career:* Prof. of Canadian Literature, University of Maine, 1985–; mem. League of Canadian Poets; Writers' Union of Canada. *Publications:* Vegetables, 1975; The Perfect Accident, 1978; Autokinesis, 1980; Whirlwinds, 1983; The Better Part of Heaven, 1984; Islands, 1986; Report: Books 1–4, 1988, 8–11, 1993; In the House of No, 1991; Full Sun: Selected Poems, 1992; The Music, 1995; Odes, 1997; Limbo Road, 1998. Contributions: various reviews, journals, and periodicals. *Honours:* Third Prize, CBC Literary Competition 1986.

NORSE, Harold George, BA, MA; American academic, writer and poet; b. 6 July 1916, New York, NY. *Education:* Brooklyn Coll., CUNY, New York Univ. *Career:* instructor, Cooper Union Coll., New York 1949–52, Lion School of English, Rome, Italy 1956–57, United States Information Service School, Naples, Italy 1958–59; Instructor in Creative Writing, San Jose State Univ., CA 1973–75; Prof. in Creative Writing, New Coll. of California 1994–95; mem. PEN. *Publications:* The Roman Sonnets of Giuseppe Gioacchino Belli (trans.) 1960, Karma Circuit (poems) 1967, Hotel Nirvana (poems) 1974, Carnivorous Saint (poems) 1977, Mysteries of Magritte (poems) 1984, Love Poems 1986, Memoirs of a Bastard Angel (autobiog.) 1989, Seismic Events (poems) 1993; contrib. to journals and magazines. *Honours:* Nat. Endowment for the Arts Fellowship 1974, R. H. de Young Museum grant 1974, Nat. Poetry Asscn Lifetime Achievement Award in Poetry 1991. *Address:* 157 Albion Street, San Francisco, CA 94110, USA.

NORTH, Anthony (see Koontz, Dean Ray)

NORTH, Elizabeth Stewart, BA; British author and teacher; b. 20 Aug. 1932, Hampshire, England. *Education:* University of Leeds. *Career:* Writer-in-Residence, Bretton Hall College of Higher Education, 1984–85. *Publications:* Make Thee an Ark (radio play), 1969; Wife Swopping (radio play), 1969; The Least and Vilest Things (novel), 1971; Pelican Rising (novel), 1975; Enough Blue Sky (novel), 1977; Everything in the Garden (novel), 1978; Florence Avenue (novel), 1980; Dames (novel), 1981; Ancient Enemies (novel), 1982; The Real Tess (radio feature), 1984; Jude the Obscure (adaptation for radio), 1985.

NORTH, John David, BSc, MA, DPhil, DLitt, FBA; British academic; *Senior Research Associate, Museum of the History of Science, University of Oxford*; b. 19 May 1934, Cheltenham; s. of J. E. North and G. A. North; m. Marion J. Pizzey; one s. two d. *Education:* Merton Coll. Oxford and Univ. of London. *Career:* Nuffield Foundation Research Fellow Univ. of Oxford 1963–68, Museum of History of Science, Univ. of Oxford 1968–77; Visiting Prof. of History of Science, Århus Univ., Demark 1974; Prof. of the History of Philosophy and the Exact Sciences, Univ. of Groningen, Netherlands 1977–99, Prof. Emer. 1999–; currently Sr Research Assoc., Museum of the History of Science, Univ. of Oxford; Visiting Prof. at univs in Germany, Denmark and USA; Dean of the Cen. Interfaculty 1981–84, 1991–93; Secrétaire Perpétuel, Acad. int. d'histoire des sciences, Paris 1983–89, Secrétaire Perpétuel Honoraire 1990–; mem. Royal Netherlands Acad. (mem. Council 1990–93), Deutsche Akad. der Naturforscher Leopoldina; Foreign mem. Royal Danish Acad.; Corresp. Fellow, British Acad. 1992–2001, Ordinary Fellow 2001–. *Publications:* The Measure of the Universe 1965, Richard of Wallingford (three vols) 1976, The Light of Nature (ed.) 1985, Horoscopes and History 1986, Chaucer's Universe 1988, Stars, Minds and Fate 1989, The Universal Frame 1989, The Fontana History of Astronomy and Cosmology 1994, Stonehenge: Neolithic Man and the Cosmos 1996, The Ambassadors' Secret: Holbein and the World of the Renaissance 2002, God's Clockmaker: Richard of Wallingford and the Invention of Time 2005. *Honours:* Kt, Order of the Netherlands Lion 1999; Koyré Medal, Acad. Int. d'Histoire des Sciences 1989. *Address:* 28 Chalfont Road, Oxford, OX2 6TH, England. *Telephone:* (1865) 558458.

NORTH, Kate (see Lloyd, Kathleen Annie)

NORTHCUTT, Wayne, MA, PhD; American academic and writer; b. 5 July 1944, New Orleans, LA. *Education:* California State Univ., Long Beach, Univ. of California, Irvine. *Career:* teaching asst, Univ. of California, Irvine 1969–72, Teaching Assoc. 1973–74, 1979–80, Lecturer 1972–73, Asst Prof. 1975–78, Monterey Inst. of Int. Studies, Calif.; Lecturer, Schiller Coll., Paris, France 1978; Asst Prof., Niagara Univ. 1980–83, Assoc. Prof. 1983–88, Prof. of History 1988–; Foreign Expert, Chinese People's Univ., Beijing 1983; Adjunct Prof. of History, State Univ. of New York at Buffalo 1993. *Publications:* The French Socialist and Communist Party Under the Fifth Republic 1958–1981: From Opposition to Power 1985, Historical Dictionary of the French Fourth and Fifth Republics 1946–1991 (ed.-in-chief) 1992, Mitterrand: A Political Biography 1992, The Regions of France: A Reference Guide to History and Culture 1996; contribs to scholarly books and journals. *Honours:* numerous research grants and fellowships. *Address:* c/o Department of History, Niagara University, PO Box 1932, Niagara, NY 14109, USA (office).

NORTON, Augustus Richard, BA, MA, PhD; American academic and writer; *Professor of Anthropology and International Relations, Boston University*; b.

New York, NY. *Education:* Univ. of Miami, Defense Language Inst., Monterey, Calif., Univ. of Chicago 1984. *Career:* Asst Prof. of Mil. Science, Univ. of Illinois-Chicago Circle Campus 1974–78, Adjunct Asst Prof. of Political Science 1975–77; Adjunct Asst Prof. of Political Science, Old Dominion Univ. 1979–80; Asst Prof., US Mil. Acad., West Point, NY 1981–84, Assoc. Prof. of Int. Studies 1984, Perm. Assoc. Prof. of Comparative Politics 1984–90, Prof. of Political Science 1990–93; Visiting Assoc. Prof. of Political Science, Univ. of Texas at Austin 1986; Visiting Research Prof., New York Univ. 1992–95; Prof. of Anthropology and Int. Relations, Boston Univ. 1993–; Distinguished Visiting Fellow, Oxford Centre for Islamic Studies 2000; Distinguished Visiting Scholar, al-Ahram Center for Strategic Studies, Cairo, Egypt 2006–07; Advisor, Baker-Hamilton Comm., Iraq Study Group 2006; mem. American Political Science Asscn, Asscn for Middle East Women's Studies, Council on Foreign Relations, Middle East Studies Asscn. *Publications:* Studies in Nuclear Terrorism (sr ed. and contrib.) 1979, International Terrorism: An Annotated Bibliography and Research Guide (sr ed.) 1980, The Emergence of a New Lebanon: Fantasy or Reality? (co-author) 1984, NATO: A Bibliography and Resource Guide (sr ed.) 1985, Touring Nam: The Vietnam War Reader (co-ed. and contrib.) 1985, Amal and the Shi'a: Struggle for the Soul of Lebanon 1987, The International Relations of the Palestine Liberation Organization (sr ed. and contrib.) 1989, UN Peacekeepers: Soldiers with a Difference 1990, Political Tides in the Arab World 1992, Civil Society in the Middle East (ed., two vols) 1995–96, 2005, Al-Amn fi al-sharq al-awsat: Tujahat jdida (ed. and contrib.) 1999, Hizballah: Extremist Ideals vs Mundane Politics 2000, Hezbollah: A Short History 2007; contrib. to reference works, scholarly books, professional journals and non-specialist publs, including Survival, Foreign Policy, Current History, The Nation, New Outlook, New Leader, Middle East Journal. *Honours:* Legion of Merit; various grants and fellowships; Outstanding Academic Book Citation, Choice 1980. *Address:* Department of International Relations, Boston University, 152 Bay State Road, Boston, MA 02215, USA (office). *Telephone:* (617) 353-9279 (office). *Fax:* (617) 353-9290 (office); (508) 653-9258 (home). *E-mail:* arn@bu.edu (office). *Website:* www.people.bu.edu/arn (office).

NORTON, Rictor Carl, BA, MA, PhD; American editor and writer; b. 25 June 1945, Friendship, NY; s. of Arnold C. Norton and Marion Norton (née Anderson); partner, David W. Allen. *Education:* Florida Southern Coll., Florida State Univ. *Career:* Instructor, Florida State Univ. 1970–72; Research Ed. Gay News, London 1974–78; Foreign Rights Man. Western Publishing Co., London, 1979–90; freelance since 1990; mem. Int. William Beckford Soc., Nat. Trust, Royal Horticultural Soc., Alpine Garden Soc., London Natural History Soc., Royal Soc. for the Protection of Birds. *Publications:* The Homosexual Literary Tradition: An Interpretation 1974, College English 36 (co-ed.) 1974, Mother Clap's Molly House: The Gay Subculture in England, 1700–1830 1992, revised 2nd edn 2006, The Myth of the Modern Homosexual: Queer History and the Search for Cultural Unity 1997, My Dear Boy: Gay Love Letters Through the Centuries (ed.) 1998, The Mistress of Udolpho: The Life of Ann Radcliffe 1999, Gothic Readings 2000, Eighteenth-Century British Erotica (ed.) 2002, 2004; contribs to The Male Homosexual in Literature: A Bibliography, Oxford Dictionary of National Biography, Essays to Gay Roots, Vols 1 and 2; contrib. of articles to scholarly journals and periodicals, including American Imago, Renascence, Yearbook of Comparative and General Literature, London Journal, Gay News, Gay Sunshine, Advocate; columns and book reviews to periodicals. *Address:* 29 Huddleston Road, Tufnell Park, London, N7 0AD, England (home). *Telephone:* (20) 7607-2035 (office). *E-mail:* norton@infopt.demon.co.uk (home). *Website:* www.infopt.demon.co.uk (office).

NORWICH, 2nd Viscount, cr. 1952, of Aldwick; **John Julius (Cooper),** CVO, FRSL, FRGS; British author and broadcaster; b. 15 Sept. 1929, London; s. of 1st Viscount Norwich, PC, GCMG, DSO and of the late Lady Diana Cooper; m. 1st Anne Clifford 1952 (divorced 1985); one s. one d.; m. 2nd Mollie Philipps 1989. *Education:* Upper Canada Coll. Toronto, Eton Coll., Univ. of Strasbourg, France and New Coll., Oxford. *Career:* entered Foreign Office 1952; Third Sec. Belgrade 1955–57; Second Sec. Beirut 1957–60; Foreign Office and British del. to Disarmament Conf. Geneva 1960–64; Chair. British Theatre Museum 1966–71, Venice in Peril Fund 1970–99, World Monuments Fund in Britain 1994–; mem. Exec. Cttee Nat. Trust 1969–95; mem. Franco-British Council 1972–79; mem. Bd ENO 1977–81; Ed. New Shell Guides to Britain 1987–91; Dir Robclif Productions Ltd 1991–94; has made over 30 documentary films for TV, mainly on history and architecture; mem. Soc. of Authors, fellow. *Television:* has made some 30 documentary films for TV, mainly on history and architecture. *Publications:* as John Julius Norwich: Mount Athos (with R. Sitwell) 1966, The Normans in the South 1967, Sahara 1968, The Kingdom in the Sun 1970, Great Architecture of the World (ed.) 1975, A History of Venice Vol. I 1977, Vol. II 1981, Christmas Crackers 1970–79 1980, Britain's Heritage (ed.) 1982, The Italian World (ed.) 1983, Fifty Years of Glyndebourne 1985, A Taste for Travel (anthology) 1985, The Architecture of Southern England 1985, Byzantium, the Early Centuries 1988, More Christmas Crackers 1980–89 1990, Venice: a Traveller's Companion 1990, The Oxford Illustrated Encyclopaedia of the Arts, Vol. V (ed.) 1990, Byzantium: The Apogee 1991, Byzantium: Decline and Fall 1995, The Twelve Days of Christmas 1998, Shakespeare's Kings 1999, Still More Christmas Crackers 1990–99 2000, Paradise of Cities 2003, The Middle Sea 2007. *Honours:* Commendatore, Ordine al Merito della Repubblica Italiana; Commendatore della Solidarità Italiana; Hadrian Award, World Monuments Fund, New York 2005. *Address:* 24 Blomfield Road, London, W9 1AD, England. *Telephone:* (20) 7286-5050. *Fax:* (20) 7266-2561. *E-mail:* jjnorwich@dial.pipex.com (home).

NOTHOMB, Amélie; Belgian writer; b. 13 Aug. 1967, Kobe, Japan; d. of Patrick Nothomb. *Education:* Université Libre de Bruxelles. *Publications include:* Hygiène de l'assassin 1992, Le Sabotage amoureux 1993, Les Combustibles 1994, Les Catallinaires 1995, Péplum 1996, Attentat 1997, Mercure 1998, Stupeur et tremblements (Grand Prix du Roman, Acad. française) (trans. as Fear and Trembling) 1999, Métaphysique des tubes (trans. as The Character of Rain) 2000, Cosmétique de l'ennemi 2001, Robert des noms propres (trans. as The Book of Proper Names) 2002, Biographie de la faim (trans. as The Life of Hunger) 2004, Acide Sulfurique 2005. *Honours:* Prix Rene-Fallet, Prix Alain Fournier (two times).

NOTLEY, Alice, BA, MFA; American poet and writer; b. 8 Nov. 1945, Bisbee, AZ; m. 1st Ted Berrigan 1972 (died 1983); two s.; m. 2nd Douglas Oliver 1988. *Education:* Barnard College, University of Iowa. *Publications:* Poetry: 165 Meeting House Lane, 1971; Phoebe Light, 1973; Incidentals in the Days World, 1973; For Frank O'Hara's Birthday, 1976; Alice Ordered Me to be Made: Poems 1975, 1976; A Diamond Necklace, 1977; Songs for the Unborn Second Baby, 1979; When I Was Alive, 1980; Waltzing Matilda, 1981; How Spring Comes, 1981; Three Zero, Turning Thirty (with Andrei Codrescu), 1982; Sorrento, 1984; Margaret and Dusty, 1985; Parts of a Wedding, 1986; At Night the States, 1988; Selected Poems of Alice Notely, 1993. Other: Doctor Williams' Heiresses: A Lecture, 1980; Tell Me Again, 1981; Homer's 'Art', 1990; The Scarlet Cabinet: A Compendium of Books (with Douglas Oliver), 1992. Contributions: various publications. *Honours:* National Endowment for the Arts grant, 1979; Poetry Center Award, 1981; General Electric Foundation Award, 1983; Fund for Poetry Awards, 1987, 1989.

NOURISSIER, François; French writer and journalist; b. 18 May 1927, Paris; s. of Paul E. E. Nourissier and Renée Heens; m. 1st Marie-Thérèse Sobesky 1949; two s.; m. 2nd Cécile Muhlstein 1962; one d. *Education:* Lycée St Louis, Lycée Louis-le-Grand, Paris, Ecole libre des Sciences Politiques, Paris and Faculté de Droit, Paris. *Career:* mem. staff Secours Catholique Int. and worked with Int. Refugee Org. 1949–51; Dir Chalet Int. des Etudiants, Combloux (World Univ. Service) 1951–52; Sec.-Gen. Editions Denoël 1952–56; Ed.-in-Chief La Parisienne (review) 1956–58; Literary Adviser to Editions Grasset 1958–95; Literary Dir Vogue (French) 1964–66, Contributing Ed. Vogue (American) 1964–; Literary Critic Les Nouvelles littéraires 1963–72; Cinema Critic L'Express 1970–72; Literary Critic Le Point 1972–, Le Figaro 1975–, Figaro-Magazine 1978–; mem. l'Acad. Goncourt 1977, Sec.-Gen. 1983–96, Pres. 1996–2002. *Publications:* L'eau grise (novel) 1951, Lorca (essay) 1955, Les orphelins d'Auteuil (novel) 1956, Le corps de Diane (novel) 1957, Portrait d'un indifférent 1957, Bleu comme la nuit 1958, Un petit bourgeois 1964, Une histoire française 1966, Les Français (essay) 1967, Le maître de maison 1968, The French (trans. of Les Français) 1970, Cartier-Bresson's France 1971, La crève (novel) 1970, Allemande (novel) 1973, Lettre à mon chien (essay) 1975, Lettre ouverte à Jacques Chirac (essay) 1977, Le musée de l'homme (essay) 1979, L'empire des nuages (novel) 1981, La fête des pères (novel) 1986, En avant, calme et droit (novel) 1987, Bratislava (essay) 1990, Autos Graphie (essay) 1990, Le Gardien des ruines (novel) 1992, Mauvais genre (essay) 1994, Le Bar de l'escadrille (novel) 1997, Les Plus belles histoires d'amour (anthology) 1997, A défaut de génie (autobiog.) 2000. *Honours:* Prix Félix Fénéon 1952, Grand Prix de la Guilde du Livre 1965 (Swiss), Grand Prix du Roman de l'Acad. française 1966, Prix Fémina 1970, Prix Prince Pierre de Monaco 1975; Grand Prix de la Ville de Paris 1987, Prix Mondial Cino Del Duca 2002; Commdr, Légion d'honneur, Commdr, Ordre nat. du Mérite, Commdr des Arts et des Lettres. *Address:* c/o Editions Grasset, 61 rue des Saints-Pères, 75006 Paris, France (office); Gallimard, 5 rue Sébastien Bottin, 75007 Paris.

NOVA, Craig, BA, MFA; American writer; b. 5 July 1945, Los Angeles, CA; m. Christina Barnes 1977, two c. *Education:* University of California at Berkeley, Columbia University. *Publications:* Turkey Hash, 1972; The Geek, 1975; Incandescence, 1978; The Good Son, 1982; The Congressman's Daughter, 1986; Tornado Alley, 1989; Trombone, 1992; The Book of Dreams, 1994; The Universal Door, 1997. *Honours:* National Endowment for the Arts Fellowships, 1973, 1975, 1985; Guggenheim Fellowship, 1977.

NOVÁK, Jan, MA; American (b. Czechoslovakian) author; b. 4 April 1953, Kolín, Czechoslovakia. *Education:* Univ. of Chicago. *Career:* moved to USA aged 17. *Film screenplays:* Valmont (script consultant), Septej (Whisper) 1996, Bájecná léta pod psa (The Wonderful Years That Sucked) 1997, Ax Murder in St Petersburg (Astorka Theatre, Bratislava) 2001, 3x12 (documentary, also prod.) 2004, Citizen Václav Havel Goes on Vacation (documentary, also prod.) 2005. *Publications:* Zatím dobrý (So Far So Good) (Book of the Year Magnesia Litera Awards 2005) 2004, The Willys Dream Kit (fiction) (Sandburg Prize for Chicago's Book of the Year), Commies, Spooks, Gypsies, Crooks & Poets (non-fiction) (Sandburg Prize for Chicago's Book of the Year) 1995, The Grand Life (novel), Turnaround (autobiog. of Milos Forman, co-author); also trans.

NOVAK, Maximillian Erwin, PhD, DPhil; American academic, writer and editor; *Distinguished Professor Emeritus of English, University of California at Los Angeles*; b. 26 March 1930, New York, NY; m. Estelle Gershgoren 1966, two s. one d. *Education:* Univ. of California at Los Angeles, St John's Coll., Oxford, UK. *Career:* Asst Prof. of English, Univ. of Michigan, 1958–62; Prof. of English, UCLA 1962–2001, Prof. Emer. 2001–; mem. American Soc. of 18th Century Studies; MLA. *Publications:* Economics and the Fiction of Daniel Defoe 1962, Defoe and the Nature of Man 1963, Congreve 1970, Realism, Myth and History in the Fiction of Daniel Defoe 1983, Eighteenth-Century English Literature 1983, The Stoke Newington Defoe, Vol. 1 1999, Vol. 2 2000, Daniel Defoe, Master of Fictions 2001; Ed.: The Works of John Dryden, Vol. X 1971, Vol. XIII 1984, The Wild Man Within 1972, English Literature in the Age of Disguise 1977, Passionate Encounters 2000, Enchanted Ground 2004, Approaches to Robinson Crusoe 2005; contribs to scholarly books and journals. *Honours:* Fulbright Fellowship 1955–57, Guggenheim Fellowships 1965–66, 1985–86, American Philosophical Soc. Fellowship 1979, Nat. Endowment for the Humanities Fellowship, 1980–81, Beinecke Library Fellow 1991; Pres.'s Fellow, Univ. of California 1991–, Huntington Library Fellow 1991–, Clark Literary Prof. 2003–04. *Address:* 451 S El Camino Drive, Beverly Hills, CA 90212, USA (home). *Telephone:* (310) 825-4173 (office); (310) 552-0433 (home). *Fax:* (310) 552-3709 (home). *E-mail:* novak@humnet.ucla.edu (office).

NOVAK, Michael, BT, MA; American theologian and writer; *George Frederick Jewett Scholar in Religion, Philosophy and Public Policy, American Enterprise Institute*; b. 9 Sept. 1933, Johnstown, Pa; s. of Michael J. Novak and Irene Sakmar; m. Karen R. Laub 1963; one s. two d. *Education:* Stonehill Coll., North Easton, Mass. and Gregorian Univ., Rome. *Career:* Teaching Fellow, Harvard Univ. 1961–63; Asst Prof. of Humanities, Stanford Univ. 1965–68; Assoc. Prof. of Philosophy and Religious Studies, State Univ. of NY, Old Westbury 1969–71; Assoc. Dir Humanities, Rockefeller Foundation 1973–74; Ledden-Watson Distinguished Prof. of Religion, Syracuse Univ. 1976–78; Resident Scholar American Enterprise Inst. 1978–, George Frederick Jewett Prof. of Religion, Philosophy, and Public Policy 1983–, Dir Social and Political Studies 1987–; Visiting Prof., Univ. of Notre Dame 1987–88; columnist, The Nat. Review 1979–86, Forbes Magazine 1989–; f., Publr Crisis 1982–95, Ed.-in-Chief 1993–95; mem. Bd for Int. Broadcasting 1983; Judge, Nat. Book Awards, DuPont Awards in Broadcast Journalism; Head, US Del. to UN Human Rights Comm., Geneva 1981, 1982, to CSCE, Berne 1996; other public appointments. *Publications include:* Belief and Unbelief 1965, The Rise of the Unmeltable Ethnics 1972, Choosing Our King 1974, The Spirit of Democratic Capitalism 1982, Freedom with Justice: Catholic Social Thought and Liberal Institutions 1984, Taking Glasnost Seriously 1988, Free Persons and the Common Good 1989, This Hemisphere of Liberty 1990, The Catholic Ethic and the Spirit of Capitalism 1993, Business as a Calling 1996, The Experience of Nothingness 1998, Tell Me Why 1998, On Cultivating Liberty 1999, A Free Society Reader (ed.) 2000, Three in One 2001, On Two Wings 2002, The Universal Hunger for Liberty 2004, Washington's God 2006 and more than 500 articles in journals. *Honours:* Kt of Malta; several hon. degrees; Freedom Award, Coalition for a Democratic Majority 1979, George Washington Honor Medal, Freedom Foundation 1984, Angel Award 1985, Ellis Island Medal of Honor 1986, Templeton Prize 1994, Bratislava Medal 1998, Boyer Award 1999, Masaryk Medal 2000, Econs Medal, Inst. of Italian Mans and Entrepreneurs 2000. *Address:* American Enterprise Institute, 1150 17th Street, NW, Washington, DC 20036, USA. *Telephone:* (202) 862-5839. *Fax:* (202) 862-5821 (office). *E-mail:* mnovak@aei.org (office). *Website:* www .aei.org (office).

NOWRA, Louis; Australian writer and scriptwriter; b. 12 Dec. 1950. *Publications:* Albert Names Edward 1975, The Misery of Beauty (fiction) 1976, The Cheated 1977, Inner Voices 1978, Visions 1979, Inside the Island 1981, The Precious Woman 1981, The Song Room 1982, Sunrise 1983, The Golden Age 1985, Palu 1987, Capricornia 1988, The Watchtower 1992, Summer of the Aliens 1992, Cosi (play) 1992, (screenplay) 1996, Radiance (play) 1993, The Temple 1993, Crow 1994, The Incorruptible 1995, Red Nights 1997, Twisted (play) 1997, The Jungle 1998, Language of the Gods 1999, The Twelfth of Never (memoir) 1999, Byzantine Flowers 2000, Radiance (film and play) 2000, In the Gutter... Looking at the Stars (co-ed.) 2000, Abaza 2001, Warne's World 2002, Walkabout (non-fiction) 2003, Shooting the Moon (memoir) 2004, Chihuahuas, Women and Me 2005. *Honours:* Prix Italia 1990, Australia/Canada Award 1993. *Literary Agent:* HLA Management, PO Box 1536, Strawberry Hills, NSW 2012, Australia. *Telephone:* (2) 9310-4948. *Fax:* (2) 9310-4113. *E-mail:* hla@hlamgt.com.au. *Website:* www.hlamgt.com .au.

NOYES, Stanley Tinning, BA, MA; American writer and poet; b. 7 April 1924, San Francisco, CA; m. Nancy Black 1949, two s. one d. *Education:* University of California, Berkeley. *Career:* mem. PEN American Center. *Publications:* No Flowers for a Clown (novel), 1961; Shadowbox (novel), 1970; Faces and Spirits (poems), 1974; Beyond the Mountains (poems), 1979; The Commander of Dead Leaves (poems), 1984; Los Comanches: The Horse People, 1751–1845, 1993; Comanches in the New West: Historic Photographs, 1895–1908, 1999, Annus Mirabilis: A Peripatetic Calendar (poems) 2003. Contributions: Reviews and quarterlies. *Honours:* MacDowell Fellow 1967. *Address:* 634 E Garcia, Santa Fe, NM 87505, USA.

NUDELSTEJER, Sergio; Mexican journalist and writer; b. 24 Feb. 1924, Warsaw, Poland; m. Tosia Malamud. *Education:* National University of Mexico. *Publications:* Theodor Herzl: Prophet of Our Times, 1961; The Rebellion of Silence, 1971; Albert Einstein: A Man in His Time, 1980; Franz Kafka: Conscience of an Era, 1983; Rosario Castellanos: The Voice, the Word, the Memory (anthology), 1984; Borges: Getting Near to His Literary Work, 1987; Elias Canetti: The Language of Passion, 1990; Spies of God: Authors at the End of the Century, 1992; Stefan Zweig: The Conscience of Man, 1992; Everlasting Voices: Latin American Writers, 1996; Jerusalem: 3000 Years of History, 1997. Contributions: periodicals.

NUMMI, Lassi; Finnish writer, poet and journalist; b. 9 Oct. 1928, Helsinki; m. Pirkko Aho 1959; two s. *Education:* Univ. of Helsinki. *Career:* State Prof. of Art 1990–95; mem. Finnish Writers' Union (pres. 1969–72, hon. mem. 1982–), PEN Centre Finland (pres. 1983–88). *Publications include:* Collected Poems 1978, 1998, Requiem 1990, Grandfather's Poems 1999, Mediterranean 2000, Existing for Each Other 2003. *Honours:* Hon. PhD 1986, Hon. DTh 2000; State Literary Prizes 1950, 1964, 1968, 1978, 1983, Pro Finlandia Medal 1972, Savonia Prize 1990, Suometar Journalist Prize 1990. *Address:* Ulvilantie 11 BA, 00350 Helsinki, Finland (home). *Telephone:* (9) 553494 (home). *Fax:* (9) 506 2905 (home).

NUNN, Frederick McKinley, BA, MA, PhD; American academic and writer; b. 29 Oct. 1937, Portland, OR; m. 1st Tey Diana Rebolledo 1960 (divorced 1973); one d.; m. 2nd Susan Karant Boles 1974, one d. *Education:* University of Oregon, University of New Mexico. *Career:* Asst Prof., 1965–67, Assoc. Prof., 1967–72, Prof. of History, 1972–, Portland State University, Oregon. *Publications:* Chilean Politics, 1920–31: The Honorable Mission of the Armed Forces, 1970; The Military in Chilean History: Essays on Civil-Military Relations, 1810–1973, 1976; Yesterday's Soldiers: European Military Professionalism in South America, 1890–1940, 1983; The Time of the Generals: Latin American Professional Militarism in World Perspective, 1992. Contributions: professional journals.

NUSSBAUM, Martha Craven, MA, PhD; American academic; *Ernst Freund Distinguished Service Professor of Law and Ethics, University of Chicago*; b. 6 May 1947, New York, NY; d. of George Craven and Betty Craven; m. Alan J. Nussbaum 1969 (divorced 1987); one d. *Education:* New York and Harvard Univs. *Career:* Jr Fellow, Soc. of Fellows, Harvard Univ. 1972–75, Asst Prof. of Philosophy and Classics 1975–80, Assoc. Prof. 1980–83; Assoc. Prof. of Philosophy and Classics, Brown Univ. 1984–85, Prof. of Philosophy, Classics and Comparative Literature 1985–87, David Benedict Prof. 1987–89, Prof. 1989–95; Visiting Prof. of Law, Univ. of Chicago 1994, Prof. of Law and Ethics 1995–96, Prof. of Philosophy 1995–, Prof. of Divinity 1995–, Ernst Freund Prof. of Law and Ethics 1996–, Assoc. mem. Classics Dept 1996–, Assoc. mem. Dept of Political Science 2003–, Founder and Coordinator, Center for Comparative Constitutionalism 2002–; Visiting Prof. Jawaharlal Nehru Univ., New Delhi, India 2004; Fellow, American Acad. of Arts and Science; mem. American Philosophical Asscn (Chair. Cttee on Status of Women 1994–97). *Publications:* Aristotle's De Motu Animalium 1978, Language and Logic (ed.) 1983, The Fragility of Goodness 1986, Love's Knowledge 1990, Essays on Aristotle's De Anima (ed. with A. Rorty) 1992, The Therapy of Desire 1994, The Quality of Life (ed. with A. Sen) 1993, Passions and Perceptions (ed. with J. Brunschwig) 1993, Women, Culture and Development (ed. with J. Glover) 1995, Poetic Justice 1996, For Love of Country 1996, Cultivating Humanity 1997, Sex and Social Justice 1998, Hiding from Humanity: Disgust, Shame and the Law 2004. *Honours:* Brandeis Creative Arts Award 1990, PEN Spielvogel-Diamondstein Award 1991, NY Univ. Distinguished Alumni Award 2000, Grawwmeyer Award in Educ. 2002, Barnard Medal of Distinction 2003; many other awards. *Address:* 520 Law Quad, Law School, University of Chicago, 1111 East 60th Street, Chicago, IL 60637, USA (office). *Telephone:* (773) 702-3470 (office). *Fax:* (773) 702-0730 (office). *E-mail:* martha_nussbaum@law.uchicago.edu (office). *Website:* www.law.uchicago.edu/faculty/nussbaum (office).

NWAPA, Flora; Nigerian author; b. 1931. *Education:* Univ. College Ibadan, Edinburgh Univ. *Career:* fmrly, Women's Education Officer, Calabar, teacher of English and geography, Queen's School, Enugu, Asst Registrar, Univ. of Lagos; fmr mem., East Central State Exec. Council, Commissioner for Lands, Survey and Urban Development; first Nigerian woman to be published. *Publications:* Efuru, 1966; Idu, 1970; Emeka: Driver's Guard, 1972; Wives at War and Other Stories, 1992; One is Enough, 1992; This is Lagos and Other Stories, 1992; Never Again, 1992; Women Are Different, 1995.

NYE, Joseph Samuel, Jr, BA, PhD; American political scientist, academic and fmr government official; *Distinguished Service Professor, Harvard University*; b. 19 Jan. 1937, s. of Joseph Nye and Else Ashwell; m. Molly Harding 1961; three s. *Education:* Princeton, Oxford and Harvard Univs. *Career:* Prof. of Govt Harvard Univ. 1969–, also Dir Centre for Int. Affairs 1989–93; Deputy Under-Sec. Dept of State, Washington, DC 1977–79, Chair. Nat. Intelligence Council 1992–; Asst Sec. of Defense for Int. Security Affairs 1994–95, Dean and Don K. Price Prof. of Public Policy, John F. Kennedy School of Govt 1995–2004, Distinguished Service Prof. 2004–; mem. Trilateral Comm.; Fellow, American Acad. of Arts and Sciences, Aspen Inst.; mem. Council, Int. Inst. of Strategic Studies; mem. Council on Foreign Relations. *Publications:* Power and Independence (co-author) 1977, The Making of America's Soviet Policy (ed. and co-author) 1984, Hawks, Doves and Owls (co-author and ed.) 1985, Nuclear Ethics 1986, Fateful Visions (co-ed.) 1988,

Bound to Lead: The Changing Nature of American Power (co-ed.) 1990, Understanding International Conflicts: An Introduction to Theory and History 1993 (fourth ed. 2002), Governance in a Globalizing World 2000, The Paradox of American Power 2002, Soft Power: The Means to Success in World Politics 2004, Power in a Global Information Age 2004, The Power Game (novel) 2004. *Honours:* Dept of State Distinguished Honor Award 1979, Intelligence Distinguished Service Award 1994, Dept of Defense Distinguished Service Medal 1995, Charles E. Merriman Award, American Political Science Asscn 2003, Woodrow Wilson Award, Princeton Univ. 2004. *Address:* Harvard University, John F. Kennedy School of Government, 79 John F. Kennedy Street, Cambridge, MA 02138, USA (office). *Telephone:* (617) 495-1123 (office). *Fax:* (617) 495-8963 (office). *E-mail:* joseph_nye@harvard.edu (office). *Website:* www.ksgfaculty.harvard.edu/Joseph_Nye (office).

NYE, Naomi Shihab, BA; Palestinian/American poet and writer; b. 1952, St Louis, MO; m. Michael Nye; one s. *Education:* Trinity Univ., San Antonio. *Career:* has travelled twice to Middle East and Asia for the US Information Agency promoting int. goodwill through the arts; fmr Lannan Fellow, Guggenheim Fellow, Wittner Bynner Fellow; columnist Organica. *Publications:* poetry: Different Ways to Pray 1980, On the Edge of the Sky 1981, Hugging the Jukebox 1982, Yellow Glove 1986, Travel Alarm 1993, The Children of Nigh 1993, Red Suitcase 1994, Words Under the Words 1995, Fuel 1998, What Have You Lost? 1999, Come with Me: Poems for a Journey (juvenile) 2000, 19 Varieties of Gazelle: Poems of the Middle East 2002, You and Yours (Isabella Gardner Award) 2005, A Maze Me: Poems for Girls 2005; juvenile fiction: Sitti's Secrets 1994, Benito's Dream Bottle 1995, Lullaby Raft 1997, Habibi 2001, Baby Radar 2003, Going Going 2005; editor: This Same Sky 1992, The Tree is Older Than You Are: A Bilingual Gathering of Poems and Stories from Mexico (co-ed.) 1995, I Feel a Little Jumpy Around You 1996, Salting the Ocean: 100 Poems by Young Poets 2001, The Flag of Childhood: Poems from the Middle East 2002, Is This Forever or What? 2004; other prose: Never in a Hurry (essays) 1996, Mint Snowball (short stories) 2001. *Honours:* Texas Inst. of Letters Prize, Carity Randall Prize, Int. Poetry Forum Award. *Literary Agent:* Steven Barclay Agency, 12 Western Avenue, Petaluma, CA 94952, USA. *Telephone:* (707) 773-0654. *Fax:* (707) 778-1868. *E-mail:* steven@barclayagency.com. *Website:* www.barclayagency.com.

NYE, Robert, FRSL; British poet, novelist and critic; b. 15 March 1939, London; s. of Oswald William Nye and Frances Dorothy Weller; m. 1st Judith Pratt 1959 (divorced 1967); three s.; m. 2nd Aileen Campbell 1968; one d. one step-s. one step-d. *Education:* Southend High School. *Career:* freelance writer 1961–; contributes critical articles and reviews to British periodicals, including The Times and The Scotsman; Poetry Critic, The Times 1971–96. *Publications include:* (poetry) Juvenilia 1 1961, Juvenilia 2 1963, Darker Ends 1969, Agnus Dei 1973, Two Prayers 1974, Five Dreams 1974, Divisions on a Ground 1976, A Collection of Poems 1955–1988 1989, 14 Poems 1994, Henry James and Other Poems 1995, Collected Poems 1995, 1998, The Rain and the Glass: 99 Poems, New and Selected 2005, Sixteen Poems 2005; (novels) Doubtfire 1967, Falstaff 1976, Merlin 1978, Faust 1980, The Voyage of the Destiny 1982, The Facts of Life and Other Fictions 1983, The Memoirs of Lord Byron 1989, The Life and Death of My Lord Gilles de Rais 1990, Mrs. Shakespeare: The Complete Works 1993, The Late Mr. Shakespeare 1998, and several children's books, plays: ed.: A Choice of Sir Walter Ralegh's Verse 1972, William Barnes of Dorset: A Selection of his Poems 1973, A Choice of Swinburne's Verse 1973, The English Sermon 1750–1850 1976, The Faber Book of Sonnets 1976, PEN New Poetry I 1986, First Awakenings: The Early Poems of Laura Riding (co-ed.) 1992, A Selection of the Poems of Laura Riding 1993, Some Poems by Ernest Dowson 2006. *Honours:* Eric Gregory Award 1963, Guardian Fiction Prize 1976, Hawthornden Prize 1977, Soc. of Authors Travelling Scholarship 1991, Authors' Foundation Award 2003. *Literary Agent:* c/o Curtis Brown Ltd, 28–29 Haymarket, London, SW1Y 4SP, England. *Telephone:* (20) 7393-4400. *Fax:* (20) 7393-4401. *E-mail:* cb@curtisbrown.co.uk. *Website:* www.curtisbrown.co.uk.

NYSTROM, Debra, BA, MFA; American poet, writer and academic; b. 12 July 1954, Pierre, SD. *Education:* University of South Dakota, Boston University, Goddard College, University of Virginia. *Career:* Faculty in Creative Writing, University of Virginia, 1984–; mem. Associated Writing Programs; Poetry Society of America. *Publications:* A Quarter Turn, 1991; Torn Sky, 2003. Contributions: various anthologies, reviews, quarterlies, and journals. *Honours:* Virginia Commission for the Arts Prizes for Poetry, 1987, 1997; Balch Prize for Poetry, Virginia Quarterly Review, 1991; James Boatwright Prizes for Poetry, Shenandoah, 1994, 2000; Borders Books/HEART Prize, 2002. *Address:* University of Virginia, Department of English, 219 Bryan Hall, PO Box 400121, Charlottesville, VA 22904-4121, USA.

O

OAKLEY, Ann, MA, PhD; British sociologist and writer; *Director, Social Science Research Unit, Institute of Education, University of London*; b. 17 Jan. 1944, d. of Richard Titmus; m. Robin Oakley (divorced); three c. *Education:* Chiswick Polytechnic and Somerville Coll., Oxford. *Career:* Research Fellow, Bedford Coll., Univ. of London 1974–79, Univ. of Oxford 1979–84; Deputy Dir Thomas Coram Research Unit, Univ. of London 1985–90; Prof. of Sociology and Social Policy, Dir Social Science Research Unit, Inst. of Educ., Univ. of London 1991–2005, Founding Dir Social Science Research Unit 2005–. *Publications include:* novels: The Men's Room (adapted for TV 1991) 1988; as Rosamund Clay: Only Angels Forget 1990; as Ann Oakley: Matilda's Mistake 1991, The Secret Lives of Eleanor Jenkinson 1992, Scenes Orginating in the Garden of Eden 1993, A Proper Holiday 1996, Overheads 1999; two short stories; non-fiction: Sex, Gender and Society 1972, Housewife 1974, The Sociology of Housework 1974, The Rights and Wrongs of Women (co-ed. with J. Mitchell) 1976, Becoming a Mother (also published as From Here to Maternity 1981) 1979, Women Confined: Towards a Sociology of Childbirth 1980, Subject Women 1981, Miscarriage (with A. McPherson and H. Roberts) 1984, The Captured Womb: A History of the Medical Care of Pregnant Women 1984, Taking it Like a Woman 1984, What is Feminism? (co-ed. with J. Mitchell) 1986, Telling the Truth About Jerusalem: Selected Essays 1986, Helpers in Childbirth: Midwifery Today (with S. Houd) 1990, Social Support and Motherhood: The Natural History of a Research Project 1992, Essays on Women, Medicine and Health 1993, Young People, Health and Family Life (with others) 1994, The Politics of the Welfare State (co-ed. with A.S. Williams) 1994, Evaluating Social Interventions: A Report on Two Workshops (co-ed. with H. Roberts) 1996, Man and Wife: Richard and Kay Titmus, My Parents' Early Years 1996, Who's Afraid of Feminism? (co-ed. with J. Mitchell) 1997, The Gift Relationship: From Human Blood to Social Policy (co-ed. with J. Ashton) 1997, Welfare Research: A Critical Review (co-ed. with F. Williams and J. Popay) 1998, Experiments in Knowing: Gender and Method in the Social Sciences 2000, Welfare and Being: Richard Titmuss's Contribution to Social Policy (co-ed. with P. Alcock and H. Glennerster) 2001, Gender on Planet Earth 2002, The Ann Oakley Reader 2005. *Honours:* Hon. Prof., Univ. Coll. London 1996–; Hon. Fellow, Somerville Coll., Oxford 2001–; Hon. DLitt (Salford) 1995. *Address:* Social Science Research Unit, Institute of Education, 18 Woburn Square, London, WC1H 0NR (office); c/o Tessa Sayle Agency, Bickerton House, 25–27 Bickerton Road, London, N19 5JT, England. *Telephone:* (20) 7612-6391 (Inst. of Educ.) (office). *Fax:* (20) 7612-6400 (Inst.ofEduc.) (office). *E-mail:* a.oakley@ioe.ac.uk (office). *Website:* www.ioe.ac.uk/SSRU (office); www.annoakley.co.uk (home).

OANDASAN, William Cortes, BA, MA, MFA; American poet and editor; b. 17 Jan. 1947, Santa Rosa, CA; m. 1973, two d. *Career:* Ed., A Publications, 1976–; Senior Ed., American Indian Culture and Research Journal, 1981–86; Instructor, English Dept, University of Orleans, Louisiana State University, 1988–90; mem. Associated Writing Programs; MLA; Society for the Study of Multi-Ethnic Literatures; Asscn for the Study of American Indian Literatures; National Asscn of Ethnic Studies; Philological Society of the Pacific Coast. *Publications:* Moving Inland, 1983; Round Valley Songs, 1984; Summer Night, 1989. Contributions: anthologies, reviews and journals, including: Colorado Review; Southern California Anthology; California Courier; American Indian Culture and Research Journal; Approaches to Teaching World Literature; Harper's Anthology of 20th Century Native American Poetry. *Honours:* Publishing Grant, National Endowment for the Arts, 1977; American Book Award, 1985; Summer Scholar Award for Writers, 1989; Research Council Grant, 1989.

OATES, Joyce Carol, (Rosamond Smith), MA; American writer, poet, publisher and academic; *Roger S. Berlind '52 Professor in the Humanities, Princeton University*; b. 16 June 1938, Lockport, NY; d. of Frederic J. Oates and Caroline Bush; m. Raymond J. Smith 1961. *Education:* Syracuse Univ. and Univ. of Wis. *Career:* instructor 1961–65, Univ. of Detroit, Asst Prof. of English 1965–67; faculty mem. Dept of English, Univ. of Windsor, Ont. 1967–78; publr (with Raymond Joseph Smith), Ontario Review 1974–; Writer-in-Residence, Princeton Univ. 1978–81, Prof. 1987–, currently Roger S. Berlind '52 Prof. in the Humanities; mem. American Acad., Inst. of Arts and Letters; Guggenheim Fellow 1967–68. *Plays:* Three Plays: Ontological Proof of My Existence, Miracle Play, The Triumph of the Spider Monkey 1980, Twelve Plays 1991, The Perfectionist and Other Plays 1995. *Publications:* novels: With Shuddering Fall 1964, A Garden of Earthly Delights 1967, Expensive People 1968, Them 1969, Wonderland 1971, Do With Me What You Will 1973, The Assassins: A Book of Hours 1975, Childworld 1976, Son of the Morning 1978, Unholy Loves 1979, Cybele 1979, Bellefleur 1980, A Sentimental Education 1981, Angel of Light 1981, A Bloodsmoor Romance 1982, Mysteries of Winterthurn 1984, Solstice 1985, Marya: A Life 1986, You Must Remember This 1987, American Appetites 1989, Because it is Bitter and Because it is my Heart 1990, Black Water 1992, Foxfire 1993, What I Lived For 1994, Zombie 1995, First Love: A Gothic Tale 1996, We Were the Mulvaneys 1996, Man Crazy 1997, My Heart Laid Bare 1998, Come Meet Muffin 1998, The Collector of Hearts 1999, Broke Heart Blues 1999, Blonde: A Novel 2000, Middle Age: A Romance 2002, I'll Take You There 2002, Big Mouth and Ugly Girl 2002, The Tattooed Girl 2004, Rape: A Love Story 2004, I Am No One You Know 2004, The Falls 2004, Mother, Missing 2005, The Gravedigger's Daughter 2007;

short story collections: By the North Gate 1963, Upon the Sweeping Flood and Other Stories 1966, The Wheel of Love 1970, Cupid and Psyche 1970, Marriages and Infidelities 1972, A Posthumous Sketch 1973, The Girl 1974, Plagiarized Material 1974, The Goddess and Other Women 1974, Where Are You Going, Where Have You Been?: Stories of Young America 1974, The Hungry Ghosts: Seven Allusive Comedies 1974, The Seduction and Other Stories 1975, The Poisoned Kiss and Other Stories from the Portuguese 1975, The Triumph of the Spider Monkey 1976, Crossing the Border 1976, Night-Side 1977, The Step-Father 1978, All the Good People I've Left Behind 1979, Queen of the Night 1979, The Lamb of Abyssalia 1979, A Middle-Class Education 1980, A Sentimental Education 1980, Last Day 1984, Wild Saturday and Other Stories 1984, Wild Nights 1985, Raven's Wing 1986, The Assignation 1988, Heat and Other Stories 1991, Where Is Here? 1992, Haunted Tales of the Grotesque 1994, Faithless: Tales of Transgression 2001, The Female of the Species 2006, High Lonesome: New & Selected Stories 1966–2006 2006; poetry: Women in Love and Other Poems 1968, Anonymous Sins and Other Poems 1969, Them (Nat. Book Award 1970) 1969, Love and its Derangements 1970, Wooded Forms 1972, Angel Fire 1973, Dreaming America and Other Poems 1973, The Fabulous Beasts 1975, Seasons of Peril 1977, Women Whose Lives are Food, Men Whose Lives are Money 1978, Celestial Timepiece 1980, Nightless Nights: Nine Poems 1981, Invisible Women: New and Selected Poems 1970–1982 1982, Luxury of Sin 1984, The Time Traveller: Poems 1983–1989 1989; non-fiction: The Edge of Impossibility: Tragic Forms in Literature 1972, The Hostile Sun: The Poetry of D. H. Lawrence 1973, New Heaven, New Earth: The Visionary Experience in Literature 1974, The Stone Orchard 1980, Contraries: Essays 1981, The Profane Art: Essays and Reviews 1983, Funland 1983, On Boxing 1987, (Woman) Writer: Occasions and Opportunities 1988, George Bellows: American Artist (biog.) 1995, The Faith of a Writer: Life, Craft, Art 2004, Black Girl/White Girl 2006; editor: Scenes from American Life: Contemporary Short Fiction 1973, The Best American Short Stories 1979 (with Shannon Ravenel) 1979, Night Walks: A Bedside Companion 1982, First Person Singular: Writers on Their Craft 1983, Story: Fictions Past and Present (with Boyd Litzinger) 1985, Reading the Fights (with Daniel Halpern) 1988, The Oxford Book of American Short Stories 1993, The Best American Mystery Stories 2006; as Rosamond Smith: The Lives of the Twins 1987, Kindred Passions 1988, Soul-Mate 1989, Nemesis 1990, Snake Eyes 1992, You Can't Catch Me 1995, Double Delight 1997, Starr Bright Will Be With You Soon 1999, The Barrens 2001, Beasts 2003; fiction in nat. magazines. *Honours:* O. Henry Prize Story Award 1967, 1968, Rea Award for Short Story 1990, Elmer Holmes Bukst Award 1990. *Address:* Department of Creative Writing, Princeton University, 185 Nassau Street, Princeton, NJ 08544 (office); c/o John Hawkins, 71 West 23rd Street, Suite 1600, New York, NY 10010, USA. *Website:* www.princeton.edu/~visarts/cwr.

OATES, Stephen Baery, BA, MA, PhD; American academic and writer; *Paul Murray Kendall Professor Emeritus of Biography and Professor Emeritus of History, University of Massachusetts at Amherst*; b. 5 Jan. 1936, Pampa, TX; m. 1st; one s. one d.; m. 2nd Marie Philips. *Education:* Univ. of Texas at Austin. *Career:* instructor 1964–67, Asst Prof. 1967–68, Arlington State Coll.; Asst Prof. 1968–70, Assoc. Prof. 1970–71, Prof. of History 1971–80, Adjunct Prof. of English 1980–85, Paul Murray Kendall Prof. of Biography 1985–, Univ. of Massachusetts at Amherst; various guest lectureships; Fellow Texas State Historical Asscn 1968; Fellow Texas Inst. of Letters 1969; mem. American Antiquarian Soc., Soc. of American Historians. *Publications:* Confederate Cavalry West of the River 1961, John Salmon Ford: Rip Ford's Texas (ed.) 1963, The Republic of Texas (gen. ed.) 1968, Visions of Glory, Texas on the Southwestern Frontier 1970, To Purge This Land with Blood: A Biography of John Brown 1970, Portrait of America (ed.): Vol. I From the European Discovery to the End of Reconstruction, Vol. II From Reconstruction to the Present 1973, The Fires of Jubilee: Nat Turner's Fierce Rebellion 1975, With Malice Toward None: The Life of Abraham Lincoln 1977, Our Fiery Trial: Abraham Lincoln, John Brown, and the Civil War Era 1979, Let the Trumpet Sound: The Life of Martin Luther King Jr 1982, Abraham Lincoln: The Man Behind the Myths 1984, Biography as High Adventure: Life-Writers Speak on Their Art (ed.) 1986, William Faulkner: The Man and the Artist, a Biography 1987, A Woman of Valor: Clara Barton and the Civil War 1994, The Approaching Fury: Voices of the Storm, 1820–1861 1997, The Whirlwind of War: Voices of the Storm, 1861–1865 1998; contrib. to professional journals. *Honours:* Guggenheim Fellowship 1972, Christopher Awards 1977, 1982, New York Civil War Round Table Barondess/Lincoln Award 1978, Nat. Endowment for the Humanities Fellow 1978, Robert F. Kennedy Memorial Book Award 1983, Inst. for Advanced Studies in the Humanities Fellow 1984, New England History Teachers Asscn Kidger Award 1992, Chicago Civil War Round Table Nevins-Freeman Award 1993. *Address:* 10 Bridle Path, Amherst, MA 01002, USA.

OBA, Minako; Japanese writer; b. 1930, Tokyo; m. *Career:* d. of naval doctor, family moved frequently during 1940s, lived outside Hiroshima by end of World War II, conscripted to care for bomb victims; moved with her husband to Alaska, USA 1959–70; travelled extensively alone in Europe; publ. of her short story Sanbiki no kani (Three Crabs) brought instant acclaim as writer in Japan 1968; many of her works have been translated into French and English.

Publications: novels: Garakuta hakubutsukan (The Garbage Museum) (14th Women's Literature Prize 1976), Urashimaso (Urashima Grass) 1977, Katachi mo naku (Shapeless) (Tanizaki Prize 1982); short stories: Sanbiki no kani (Three Crabs) (Gunzo Literary Prize 1968, Akutagawa Prize 1968) 1968, Kozu no nai e (Formless Painting) 1968, Niji to ukihashi (The rainbow and the Floating Bridge) 1968, Kiri no tabi (Journey Through Mist), Hugusa (Fireweed), Aoi kitsune (Pale Fox); numerous poems and essays.

O'BALANCE, Edgar; Irish writer; b. 17 July 1918, Dalkey, County Dublin; m. 1st Mary Edington-Gee 1949 (died 1969); two s. one d.; m. 2nd Kathleen Barbara Tanner 1972. *Education:* studied in Ireland. *Career:* mem. Military Commentators Circle. *Publications:* The Arab-Israeli War, 1956; The Sinai Campaign, 1956; The Story of the French Foreign Legion, 1961; The Red Army of China, 1962; The Indo-China War 1945–1954, 1964; The Red Army of Russia, 1964; The Greek Civil War 1948–1960, 1966; The Algerian Insurrection 1954–1962, 1967; The Third Arab-Israeli War 1967, 1972; The Kurdish Revolt 1961–1970, 1973; Arab Guerrilla Power, 1974; The Electronic War in the Middle East 1968–1970, 1974; The Wars in Vietnam 1954–1972, 1975; The Secret War in the Sudan 1955–1972, 1977; No Victor, No Vanquished, 1978; The Language of Violence, 1979; Terror in Ireland, 1979; The Tracks of the Bear, 1982; The Gulf War, 1988; The Cyanide War, 1989; Terrorism in the 1980s, 1989; Wars in Afghanistan: 1839–1990, 1991; Civil War in Bosnia: 1992–1994; The Kurdish Struggle: 1920–94, 1995; Islamic Fundamentalist Terrorism, 1996; Wars in the Caucasus: 1990–95, 1996.

O'BRIEN, Alison D., AB, PhD; American scientist and writer; *Professor, Uniformed Services University of the Health Sciences. Education:* Univ. of California at Davis, Ohio State Univ. *Career:* Prof. and Chair of Dept of Microbiology and Immunology, Uniformed Services Univ. of the Health Sciences. *Publications include:* co-author: Bacterial Toxins: Friends or Foes? 1999, Microbiology: A Centenary Perspective 1999; co-editor: Escherichia coli and Other Shiga Toxins Producing E.coli 1998, Comparative Pathogenicity of E.coli 2003. *Address:* Department of Microbiology and Immunology, Uniformed Services University of the Health Sciences, 4301 Jones Bridge Road, Bethesda, MD 20814, USA (office). *Fax:* (301) 295-3773 (office). *E-mail:* aobrien@usuhs.mil (office). *Website:* www.usuhs.mil (office).

O'BRIEN, Conor Cruise, (Donat O'Donnell), PhD; Irish writer and diplomatist; b. 3 Nov. 1917, Dublin; s. of Francis Cruise O'Brien and Katherine Sheehy; m. 1st Christine H. Foster 1939 (divorced 1962); one s. one d. (and one d. deceased); m. 2nd Maire MacEntee 1962; one s. one d. (both adopted). *Education:* Sandford Park School, Dublin, Trinity Coll., Dublin. *Career:* entered Dept of External Affairs of Ireland 1944, Counsellor, Paris 1955–56, Head UN Section and mem. Irish Del. to UN 1956–60, Asst Sec.-Gen., Dept of External Affairs of Ireland 1960; Rep. of Sec.-Gen. of UN in Katanga, Congo (later Shaba, Zaïre) May-Dec. 1961; Vice-Chancellor, Univ. of Ghana 1962–65; Regent's Prof. and Holder of Albert Schweitzer Chair in Humanities, New York Univ. 1965–69; mem. Dáil Eireann (House of Reps) for Dublin (Labour) 1969–77; Minister for Posts and Telegraphs 1973–77; resgnd from Labour Party; Senator for Dublin Univ. 1977–79; Ed.-in-Chief The Observer, London 1978–81, Consultant Ed. 1981; Contributing Ed. The Atlantic, Boston; Pro-Chancellor Univ. of Dublin 1973–; Visiting Fellow, Nuffield Coll., Oxford 1973–75; Fellow, St Catherine's Coll., Oxford 1978; Visiting Prof. Dartmouth Coll., USA 1984–85; mem. Royal Irish Acad. *Publications:* Maria Cross (under pseudonym Donat O'Donnell) 1952, Parnell and his Party 1957, The Shaping of Modern Ireland (ed.) 1959, To Katanga and Back 1962, Conflicting Concepts of the United Nations 1964, Writers and Politics 1965, The United Nations: Sacred Drama 1967, Murderous Angels (play) 1968, Power and Consciousness (ed.) 1969, Conor Cruise O'Brien Introduces Ireland 1969, Edmund Burke's Reflections on the Revolution in France (ed.) 1969, Camus 1969, A Concise History of Ireland (with Máire Cruise O'Brien) 1972, The Suspecting Glance 1972, States of Ireland 1972, Herod's Reflections on Political Violence 1978, Neighbours: Ewart-Biggs memorial lectures 1978–79 1980, The Siege: the Saga of Israel and Zionism 1986, Passion and Cunning 1988, God Land: Reflections on Religion and Nationalism 1988, The Great Melody: A Thematic Biography of Edmund Burke 1992, Ancestral Voices 1994, On the Eve of the Millennium 1996, The Long Affair: Thomas Jefferson and the French Revolution 1996, Memoir: My Life and Themes 1998. *Honours:* Hon. DLitt (Bradford) 1971, (Ghana) 1974, (Edin.) 1976, (Nice) 1978, (Liverpool) 1987; Hon. LLD (Glasgow) 1990; Valiant for Truth Media Award 1979. *Address:* Whitewater, Howth Summit, Dublin, Ireland. *Telephone:* (1) 8322474.

O'BRIEN, Edna; Irish writer; b. Tuamgraney, Co. Clare; d. of Michael O'Brien and Lena Cleary; m. Ernest Gébler 1954 (divorced 1964); two s. *Education:* convents, Pharmaceutical Coll. of Ireland. *Career:* engaged in writing from an early age. *Publications include:* The Country Girls 1960 (film 1983), The Lonely Girl 1962, Girls in Their Married Bliss 1963, August is a Wicked Month 1964, Casualties of Peace 1966, The Love Object 1968, A Pagan Place 1970 (play 1971), Night 1972, A Scandalous Woman (short stories) 1974, Mother Ireland 1976, Johnny I Hardly Knew You (novel) 1977, Arabian Days 1977, Mrs. Reinhardt and other stories 1978, Virginia (play) 1979, Mrs. Reinhardt (adapted for TV) 1981, The Dazzle (children's book), Returning: A Collection of New Tales 1982, A Christmas Treat 1982, A Fanatic Heart (Selected Stories) 1985, Madame Bovary (play) 1987, Vanishing Ireland 1987, Tales for the Telling (children's book) 1987, The High Road (novel) 1988, On the Bone (poetry) 1989, Scandalous Woman and Other Stories 1990, Lantern Slides (stories) 1990, Time and Tide (novel) 1992, House of Splendid Isolation (novel) 1994, Down By the River (novel) 1997, Maud Gonne (screenplay) 1996, James Joyce 1999, Wild Decembers 1999, In the Forest (novel) 2002, Iphigenia (play) 2003, Triptych (play) 2004, The Light of Evening (novel) 2006. *Honours:* Hon. DLitt (Queen's) 1999; Yorkshire Post Novel Award 1971, Kingsley Amis Award, Writers' Guild of GB Award 1993, European Prize for Literature 1995, American Nat. Arts Gold Medal. *Address:* c/o David Godwin Associates, 55 Monmouth Street, London, WC2H 9DG, England. *Telephone:* (20) 7240-9992.

O'BRIEN, Sean Patrick, BA, MA, PGCE; British writer and poet; b. 19 Dec. 1952, London, England. *Education:* Selwyn Coll., Cambridge, Univ. of Birmingham, Univ. of Hull, Univ. of Leeds. *Career:* Fellow in Creative Writing, Univ. of Dundee 1989–91; Northern Arts Literary Fellow 1992–94; Visiting Writer, Univ. of Odense, Denmark 1996, Hokudai Univ., Sapporo, Japan 1997; Lecturer in Writing, Sheffield Hallam Univ. 1998–; Writer-in-Residence, Univ. of Leeds 1999. *Publications:* The Indoor Park 1983, The Frighteners 1987, Boundary Beach 1989, HMS Glasshouse 1991, Ghost Train (Forward Prize for Best Collection) 1995, The Deregulated Muse: Essays on Contemporary Poetry in Britain and Ireland 1998, The Firebox: Poetry in Britain and Ireland after 1945 (ed.) 1998, Downriver (Forward Prize for Best Collection) 2001, Cousin Coat: Selected Poems 1976–2001 2002, The Birds: A New Verse Version of Aristophanes' Birds 2002, Keepers of the Flame 2003, Inferno: A Verse Version of Dante's Inferno 2006, Manifest 2007; plays: Laughter When We're Dead, My Last Barmaid; contrib. to anthologies, newspapers, reviews and radio. *Honours:* Eric Gregory Award 1979, Somerset Maugham Award 1984, Cholmondeley Award 1988, Arts Council Writer's Bursary 1992, E. M. Forster Award 1993, Forward Prize for Best Poem (for 'Fantasia on a Theme of James Wright') 2006, Northern Rock Foundation Award 2007. *Literary Agent:* Aitken Alexander Associates Ltd, 18–21 Cavaye Place, London, SW10 9PT, England. *Telephone:* (20) 7373-8672. *Fax:* (20) 7373-6002. *E-mail:* reception@aitkenalexander.co.uk. *Website:* www.aitkenalexander.co.uk.

O'BRIEN, (William) Timothy (Tim), BA; American writer; b. 1 Oct. 1946, Austin, MN; m. Anne O'Brien. *Education:* Macalester Coll., Harvard Univ. *Career:* currently faculty mem. Dept of English, Texas State Univ. at San Marcos. *Publications:* If I Die in a Combat Zone, Box Me Up and Ship Me Home 1973, Northern Lights 1975, Going After Cacciato 1978, The Nuclear Age 1981, The Things They Carried: A Work of Fiction (Prix du Meilleur Livre Étranger, France 1993, Soc. of American Historians James Fenimore Cooper Prize) 1990, In the Lake of Woods 1994, Tomcat in Love 1998, July July 2002; contrib. short stories to Esquire, Harper's, Atlantic, Playboy, Granta, GQ and The New Yorker. *Honours:* O. Henry Memorial Awards 1976, 1978, Nat. Book Award 1979, Vietnam Veterans of America Award 1987, Chicago Tribune Heartland Prize 1990, Guggenheim Foundation fellowship, NEA fellowship. *Address:* Department of English, Texas State University, 601 University Drive, San Marcos, TX 78666, USA (office). *E-mail:* mfinearts@txstate.edu (office).

OBSTFELD, Raymond, (Pike Bishop, Jason Frost, Don Pendleton, Carl Stevens), BA, MA; American academic, writer, poet, dramatist and screenwriter; b. 22 Jan. 1952, Williamsport, PA. *Education:* Johnston College, University of Redlands, and University of California at Davis. *Career:* Lecturer to Asst Prof. of English, Orange Coast College, 1976–; mem. MWA. *Publications:* fiction: The Golden Fleece, 1979; Dead-End Option, 1980; Dead Heat, 1981; Dead Bolt, 1982; The Remington Factor, 1985; Masked Dog, 1986; Redtooth, 1987; Brainchild, 1987; The Whippin Boy, 1988; as Pike Bishop: Diamondback, 1983; Judgement at Poisoned Well, 1983; as Jason Frost: Warlord series, 1983–85; Invasion USA, 1985; as Don Pendleton: Bloodsport, 1982; Flesh Wounds, 1983; Savannah Swingsaw, 1985; The Fire Eaters, 1986; as Carl Stevens: The Centaur Conspiracy, 1983; Ride of the Razorback, 1984. Poetry: The Cat With Half a Face, 1978. Contributions: anthologies and other publications.

OCKRENT, Christine; Belgian journalist; *Editor-in-Chief and Presenter, France Europe Express*; b. 24 April 1944, Brussels, Belgium; d. of Roger Ockrent and Greta Bastenie; m. Bernard Kouchner; one s. *Education:* Collège Sévigné, Paris, Cambridge Univ., England and Institut d'Etudes Politiques de Paris. *Career:* journalist, Information Office, EEC 1965–66; researcher, NBC News, USA 1967–68; producer and journalist, CBS News, USA 1968–77; journalist and producer, FR3, France 1976–80; Ed. and Anchor, news programme on Antenne 2 1980–85; Chief Ed. RTL 1985–86; Deputy Dir-Gen. TF1 1986–87; Ed., anchor and producer, news programmes on Antenne 2 1988–92, on France 3 1992–95; Chief Ed. L'Express 1995–96; Deputy Dir BFM 1996–2000; Ed.-in-Chief Dimanche Soir programme France 3 1996–98; Ed.-in-Chief and Presenter France Europe Express 1997–; Pres. BFMbiz.com; columnist La Provence, Dimanche CH. *Publications:* Dans le secret des princes 1986, Duel 1988, Les uns et les autres 1993, Portraits d'ici et d'ailleurs 1994, La Mémoire du cœur 1997, Les Grands patrons (jtly) 1998, L'Europe racontée à mon fils, de Jules César à l'euro 1999, La double vie d'Hillary Clinton 2000, Françoise 2003. *Honours:* Chevalier de la Légion d'honneur 2000. *Address:* France 3, esplanade Henri de France, 75907 Paris cedex 15, France. *Website:* www.bfmbiz.com.

O'CONNELL, Richard James, BS, MA; American academic, poet and translator; *Professor Emeritus, Temple University*; b. 25 Oct. 1928, New York, NY. *Education:* Temple Univ., Johns Hopkins Univ. *Career:* Instructor, Temple Univ. 1957–61, Asst Prof. 1961–69, Assoc. Prof. 1969–86, Sr Assoc. Prof. 1986–93, Prof. Emer. 1993–; Fulbright Lecturer, Univ. of Brazil, Rio de

Janeiro 1960, Univ. of Navarre, Pamplona, Spain 1962–63; Guest Lecturer, Johns Hopkins Univ. 1961–74; Poet-in-the-Schools, Pennsylvania Council for the Arts 1971–73; mem. Associated Writing Programs, MLA, PEN. *Play:* System Klam 2000 (performed at Off-Broadway Theatre, Fort Lauderdale, Fla 1998). *Publications:* From an Interior Silence 1961, Cries of Flesh and Stone 1962, New Poems and Translations 1963, Brazilian Happenings 1966, Terrane 1967, Thirty Epigrams 1971, Hudson's Fourth Voyage 1978, Temple Poems 1985, Hanging Tough 1986, Battle Poems 1987, Selected Epigrams 1990, Lives of the Poets 1990, The Caliban Poems 1992, RetroWorlds 1993, Simulations 1993, Voyages 1995, The Bright Tower 1997, American Obits 2001, Fractals 2002, Dawn Crossing 2003. Translator: various works, including: Irish Monastic Poems 1975, Middle English Poems 1976, More Irish Poems 1976, Epigrams from Martial 1976, The Epigrams of Luxorius 1984, New Epigrams from Martial 1991. *Honours:* Contemporary Poetry Press Prize 1972. *Address:* 1147 Hillsboro Mile, Suite 510, Hillsboro Beach, FL 33062, USA (home). *Telephone:* (954) 426-8906 (home). *Fax:* (954) 426-8906 (home). *E-mail:* rocon100@comcast.net (home).

O'CONNOR, Joseph, BA, MA; Irish writer, playwright and critic; b. 20 Sept. 1963, Glenageary, Co. Dublin. *Education:* Univ. Coll., Dublin, Univ. of Oxford, Univ. of Leeds. *Plays:* Red Roses and Petrol 1995. *Publications:* novels: Cowboys and Indians 1991, Desperadoes 1995, The Salesman 1998, Inishowen 2000, The Last of the Irish Males 2001, Star of the Sea (Irish Post Literature Award 2004) 2002, Redemption Falls 2007; biography: Even the Olives are Bleeding: The Life and Times of Charles Donnelly 1992; contrib. and columnist for The Sunday Tribune. *Honours:* Hennessy Award. *Address:* c/o Random House UK Ltd, 20 Vauxhall Bridge Road, London, SW1V 2SA, England (office).

Ó'CURRAOIN, Seán, NT, BA, MA, LLB; Irish fmr parliamentary translator, poet and teacher; b. Connemara, Co. Galway; s. of James Curran and Mary Barnacle. *Education:* St Patrick's Training Coll, Drumcondra. *Career:* fmr Chief Translator, Irish Parl.; linguistic researcher and Asst Ed. on Ó Dónaill's Irish-English Dictionary; Asst Ed. Béalocdeas (Journal of the Folklore of Ireland Soc.); fmr Prin. Glenicmurrin Nat. School, Connemara, Colehill Nat. School and Colehill Boys' Nat. School, Streamstown, Co. Westmeath; fmr teacher Suckeen Nat. School, Galway and St Peter's Nat. School, Walkinstow, Dublin; mem. Irish Trans' Asscn, Folklore of Ireland Soc. *Publications:* Soilse ar na Dumhchannaí 1985, Beairtle 1985, Tinte Sionnaigh (short stories) 1985, De Ghlaschloch an Oileáin (biog. of Máirtín O'Cadhain) 1987, Iascairín Chloch na Cora 2000, Cloch na Cainte (poems) 2003, Boscaí (short stories) 2003; contrib. to Comhar, Feasta, Innti. *Honours:* Hon. MPhil (Trinity Coll., Dublin) 2004; Michael Hartnett Poetry Award 2004. *Address:* 18 Ascaill Verbena, Bóthar Chill Bharróg, Baile Átha Cliath 13, Ireland (home).

ODA, Makoto; Japanese author; b. 2 June 1932, Osaka; m. Hyon Sune 1982; one d. *Education:* Univ. of Tokyo, Harvard Univ., USA. *Career:* mem. Japanese PEN. *Publications:* Japanese Intellectuals (essay, trans. as Les Intellectuels Japonais 1979) 1964, HIROSHIMA (novel, trans. as The H: A Hiroshima Novel 1990, dramatised and broadcast by BBC 1995) 1981, Far From Vietnam (novel) 1992, Thought on the Earthquake and War (critical essay) 1996, Demokratia (critical essay) 1997, Osaka Symphony (novel) 1997, Stomping on Aboji (short stories) 1998, Gyokusai (novel, trans. as The Breaking Jewel 2003, dramatised and broadcast by BBC World Service 2005) 1998, Deep Sound (novel) 2002, Children's War (short stories) 2003, The Japanese Spirit (critical essay) 2004, Thoughts and Words (collection of critical essays) 2005. *Honours:* Lotus Prize, Afro-Asian Writers Asscn 1987, Kawabata Yasunari Literary Prize 1997. *Address:* 1-41-801 Ohama-cho, Nishinomiya, Japan.

ODDOUL, Haggag Hassan; Egyptian writer; b. 1944, Alexandria. *Career:* fmr construction worker on the Aswan High Dam; fmrly served in the armed forces. *Publications include:* Nights of Musk (State Prize for Short Stories 1990). *Honours:* Sawiris Foundation Award for Best Egyptian Novel 2005. *Address:* c/o BANIPAL, PO Box 22300, London, W13 8ZQ, England (office).

ØDEGÅRD, Knut, LittD; Norwegian poet, writer, critic and diplomatist; *Norwegian Consul General, Republic of Macedonia*; b. 6 Nov. 1945, Molde; m. Thorgerdur Ingólfsdóttir 1981; two d. *Education:* Univ. of Oslo. *Career:* poetry critic Aftenposten newspaper 1968–; Man. Dir Scandinavian Centre, Nordens Hus, Reykjavík 1984–89; Pres. Norwegian Festival of Int. Literature 1992–; Consul Republic of Slovakia 1995–97; Consul Gen. Republic of Macedonia 1997–; Pres. Bjørnstjerne Bjørnson Acad., Norwegian Acad. of Literature and Freedom of Expression 2003–; mem. Acad. of Norwegian Language, Icelandic Soc. of Authors, Literary Acad. of Romania, Norwegian Soc. of Authors, European Acad. of Poetry. *Publications include:* poetry: Bee-buzz, Salmon Leap 1968, Cinema Operator 1991, Ventriloquy 1994, Selected Poems 1995, Missa 1998, The Stephensen House 2003; books of prose and essays, a play, and two non-fiction books about Iceland 1992, 1998. *Honours:* Norwegian State Scholar for Life 1989–; knighted by Pres. of Iceland 1987, Grand Kt Commdr, Order of the Icelandic Falcon 1993, Int. Order of Merit 1993, Kt, Norwegian Order of Literature 1995, knighted by King of Norway 1998. *Literary Agent:* c/o J. W. Cappelen, Oslo, Norway. *Address:* Postboks 326, 6401 Molde, Norway. *Telephone:* 71-21-59-91 (office). *E-mail:* knut.odegard@moldenett.no.

ODELL, Peter Randon, BA, MA, PhD, FRSA, FRGS, FEI; British academic and writer; *Professor Emeritus, Erasmus University, Rotterdam*; b. 1 July 1930, Coalville, England; m. Jean Mary McKintosh 1957; two s. two d. *Education:* Univ. of Birmingham, Fletcher School of Law and Diplomacy, Cambridge, USA. *Career:* Economist, Shell International Petroleum Co. 1958–61; Lecturer 1961–65, Senior Lecturer 1965–68, Visiting Prof. 1983–2001, LSE; Prof. of Economic Geography 1968–81, Dir, Centre for Int. Energy Studies 1981–91, Prof. Emeritus 1991–, Erasmus Univ., Rotterdam; Stamp Memorial Lecturer, Univ. of London 1975; Prof., Coll. of Europe, Bruges 1983–90; Scholar-in-Residence, Rockefeller Centre, Bellagio, Italy 1984; European Ed., Energy Journal 1988–90; Killam Visiting Scholar, Univ. of Calgary, Canada 1989; Visiting Scholar, Univ. of Plymouth 1996–2003; Fellow, Inst. of Energy 1973–. *Publications:* An Economic Geography of Oil 1963, Oil: The New Commanding Height 1966, Natural Gas in Western Europe: A Case Study in the Economic Geography of Energy Resources 1969, Oil and World Power: A Geographical Interpretation 1970, Economies and Societies in Latin America (with D. A. Preston) 1973, Energy: Needs and Resources 1974, The North Sea Oil Province (with K. E. Rosing) 1975, The West European Energy Economy: The Case for Self-Sufficiency 1976, The Optimal Development of the North Sea Oilfields (with K. E. Rosing) 1976, The Pressures of Oil: A Strategy for Economic Revival (with L. Vallenilla) 1978, British Offshore Oil Policy: A Radical Alternative 1980, The Future of Oil 1980–2080 (with K. E. Rosing) 1980, Energie: Geen Probleem? (with J. A. van Reijn) 1981, The International Oil Industry: An Interdisciplinary Perspective (ed. with J. Rees) 1986, Energy in Europe: Resources and Choices 1990, Global and Regional Energy Supplies: Recent Fictions and Fallacies Revisited 1991, The New Europe: Energy Resources and Choices 1998, Fossil Fuel Reserves in the 21st Century 1999, Oil and Gas: Crises and Controversies 1961–2000, Vol. 1: Global Issues 2001, Vol. 2: Europe's Entanglement 2002, Why Carbon Fuels Will Dominate the 21st Century's Global Energy Economy 2004. *Honours:* Canadian Council Fellow 1978, Int. Asscn for Energy Economics Prize 1991, Royal Scottish Geographical Soc. Centenary Medal 1993. *Address:* 22A Compton Road, London, N1 2PB, England. *Telephone:* (20) 7359-8199. *E-mail:* peter@odell.u-net.com.

ODELL, Robin Ian; British writer; b. 19 Dec. 1935, Totton, Hants.; m. Joan Bartholomew, 19 Sept. 1959. *Career:* mem. Paternosters, Our Society. *Publications:* Jack the Ripper in Fact and Fiction, 1965; Exhumation of a Murder, 1975; Jack the Ripper: Summing-up and Verdict (with Colin Wilson), 1977; The Murderers' Who's Who (with J. H. H. Gaute), 1979; Lady Killers 1980; Murder Whatdunit, 1982; Murder Whereabouts, 1986; Dad Help Me Please (with Christopher Berry-Dee), 1990; A Question of Evidence, 1992; The Long Drop, 1993; Landmarks in Twentieth Century Murder, 1995; The International Murderer's Who's Who, 1996. Contributions: Crimes and Punishment; The Criminologist. *Honours:* Hon. Fellow, Chartered Inst. of Water and Environmental Man. 2003; FCC Watts Memorial Prize 1957, Edgar Award, MWA 1980. *Address:* 11 Red House Drive, Sonning Common, Reading, RG4 9NT, England. *Telephone:* (118) 972-3532 (office). *Fax:* (118) 972-3532 (office). *E-mail:* bobodell@compuserve.com.

ODONE, Cristina, MA; Italian journalist and writer; b. 11 Nov. 1960, Nairobi, Kenya; d. of Augusto Odone and Ulla Sjöström. *Education:* Oxford Univ. *Career:* Vice-Pres. Odone Assocs. consultancy, Washington; Ed. The Catholic Herald, UK 1992–96; Diary journalist The Times 1991–; TV reviewer Daily Telegraph 1996–98; Deputy Ed. The New Statesman 1998–; columnist Observer. *Publications:* The Shrine 1996, Renewal 1997, A Perfect Wife 1997, A Married Man 1997, The Dilemmas of Harriet Carew 2007. *Address:* New Statesman, Victoria Station House, 7th Floor, 191 Victoria Street, London, SW1E 5NE (office); Capel & Land, 29 Wardour Street, London, W10 6PS, England. *Telephone:* (20) 7828-1232 (office); (20) 7734-2414 (Capel & Land). *Fax:* (20) 7828-1881 (office). *E-mail:* info@newstatesman.co.uk (office).

O'DONNELL, Donat (see O'Brien, Conor Cruise)

O'DONNELL, M. R. (see Ross-Macdonald, Malcolm John)

O'DONNELL, Mary Elizabeth Eugenie, BA, DipHigherEd; Irish writer, poet, critic, lecturer and broadcaster and essayist; b. 3 April 1954, Monaghan; m. Martin Nugent 1977; one d. *Education:* Maynooth Coll. *Career:* Writer-in-Residence, Univ. Coll., Dublin, and Co. Laois 1995; teacher of creative writing, Univ. of Iowa Summer Writing Programme, USA, Trinity Coll., Dublin 1998–2000; mem. Poetry Ireland, Aosdana (the Irish 'Acad.'). *Publications:* Reading the Sunflowers in September (poems) 1990, Strong Pagans and Other Stories 1991, The Light-Makers (novel) (Best New Irish Novel, Sunday Tribune Award 1992) 1992, Spiderwoman's Third Avenue Rhapsody (poems) 1993, Virgin and the Boy (novel) 1996, Unlegendary Heroes (poems) 1998, The Elysium Testament (novel) 1999, September Elegies (poems) 2003, The Place of Miracles (new and selected poems) 2005, New Island 2006; contribs to anthologies, reviews, quarterlies and periodicals. *Honours:* Second Prize, Patrick Kavanagh Poetry Award 1986, Second Prize, Bloodaxe Nat. Poetry Competition 1986, Allingham Poetry Award 1988, Jameson Short Story Award, Listowel 1990, prize-winner, V. S. Pritchett Short Story Award 2000. *Address:* Rook Hollow, Newtownmacabe, Maynooth, Co. Kildare, Ireland (home). *Telephone:* (1) 6272204 (office). *E-mail:* maryelizabeth@eircom.net (home). *Website:* www.maryodonnell.com.

O'DONNELL, Peter, (Madeleine Brent); British author; b. 11 April 1920, London. *Education:* Catford Central School, London. *Career:* writer of Strip Cartoons, Garth 1953–66, Tug Transom 1954–66, Romeo Brown 1956–62, Modesty Blaise 1963–2001. *Publications:* Modesty Blaise, 1965; Sabre-Tooth, 1966; I, Lucifer, 1967; A Taste for Death, 1969; The Impossible Virgin, 1971; Pieces of Modesty (short stories), 1972; The Silver Mistress, 1973; Murder

Most Logical (play), 1974; Last Day in Limbo, 1976; Dragon's Claw, 1978; The Xanadu Talisman, 1981; The Night of Morningstar, 1982; Dead Man's Handle, 1985; Cobra Trap, 1996. As Madeleine Brent: Tregaron's Daughter, 1971; Moonraker's Bride, 1973; Kirkby's Changeling, 1975; Merlin's Keep, 1977; The Capricorn Stone, 1979; The Long Masquerade, 1981; A Heritage of Shadows, 1983; Stormswift, 1984; Golden Urchin, 1986. *Address:* 49 Sussex Square, Brighton BN2 1GE, England.

O'DONOGHUE, (James) Bernard, MA, BPhil; Irish academic and poet; b. 14 Dec. 1945, Cullen, Co. Cork; m. Heather MacKinnon 1977; one s. two d. *Education:* Lincoln Coll., Oxford. *Career:* Lecturer and Tutor in English, Magdalen Coll., Oxford, 1971–95; Fellow in English, Wadham Coll., Oxford, 1995–; Poetry Reviewer, TLS, Irish Times; mem. Poetry Soc., London, 1984–; FRSL, 1999; Fellow, English Soc., 1999. *Publications:* Razorblades and Pencils, 1984; Poaching Rights, 1987; The Weakness, 1991; Gunpowder, 1995; Here Nor There, 1999; Outliving, 2003; Sir Gawain and the Green Knight (trans.), 2006. *Honours:* Southern Arts Literature Prize, 1991; Whitbread Poetry Award, 1995. *Address:* Wadham College, Oxford OX1 3PN, England.

O'DONOHOE, Nick; American writer and academic; b. 31 Oct. 1952, Charles City, IA; m. Lynn Anne Evans 1978. *Education:* BA, Carleton College, 1975; PhD, Syracuse University, 1983. *Career:* Instructor, 1981–83, Asst Prof., 1983–, Virginia Polytechnic Institute and State University, Blacksburg; mem. MWA. *Publications:* April Snow, 1984; Wind Chill, 1985; Open Season, 1986; Too, Too Solid Flesh, 1989; The Magic and the Healing, 1994; Under the Healing Sign, 1995; The Healing of Crossroads, 1996. *Address:* c/o Ace Books, 375 Hudson Street, New York, NY 10014, USA.

O'DRISCOLL, Dennis; Irish editor and poet; b. 1 Jan. 1954, Thurles, County Tipperary; m. Julie O'Callaghan 1985. *Education:* Univ. Coll., Dublin. *Career:* studied law; Literary Organizer, Dublin Arts Festival 1977–79; Ed., Poetry Ireland Review 1986–87. *Publications:* poetry: Kist 1982, Hidden Extras 1987, Long Story Short 1993, The Bottom Line 1994, Quality Time 1997, Weather Permitting (Lannan LiteraryAward) 1999, Exemplary Damages 2002, New and Selected Poems 2004, Fifty O'Clock 2005, Reality Check 2007; prose: The First Ten Years: Dublin Arts Festival Poetry (co-ed.) 1979, As The Poet Said (selection of columns) 1997, Troubled Thoughts, Majestic Dreams: Selected Prose Writings 2001, The Bloodaxe Book of Poetry Quotations 2006. *Honours:* Irish Arts Council Bursaries, American Acad. of Arts and Letters E. M. Forster Award 2005, O'Shaughnessy Prize for Poetry 2006. *Address:* c/o Anvil Press Poetry Ltd, Neptune House, 70 Royal Hill, London, SE10 8RF, England. *Telephone:* (1) 7024257.

ŌE, Kenzaburō, BA; Japanese writer; b. 31 Jan. 1935, Ehime, Shikoku; m. Yukari Itami 1960; two s. one d. *Education:* Tokyo Univ. *Career:* first stories published 1957; first full-length novel Pluck The Flowers, Gun The Kids 1958; represented young Japanese writers at Peking (now Beijing) 1960; travelled to Russia and Western Europe writing a series of essays on Youth in the West 1961. *Publications:* fiction: Shisha no ogori (trans. as The Catch) (Japanese Soc. for the Promotion of Literature Akutagawa Prize) 1958, Memushiri kouchi (trans. as Nip the Buds, Shoot the Kids) 1958, Miru mae ni tobe 1958, Our Age (in trans.) 1959, Screams (in trans.) 1962, The Perverts (in trans.) 1963, Nichijo seikatsu no boken 1963, Kojinteki na taiken (trans. as A Personal Matter) 1964, Adventures in Daily Life (in trans.) 1964, Man'en gannen no futtoburu (trans. as The Silent Cry) 1967, Football in The First Year of Mannen (in trans.) 1967, Pinchi ranna chosho (trans. as The Pinch Runner Memorandum) 1976, Warera no kyoki o iki nobiru michi o 1969, Shosetsu no hoho 1978, Natsukashii toshi e no tegami 1986, M/T to mori no fushigi no monogatari 1986, A Healing Family (in trans.) 1996, A Quiet Life (in trans.) 1998, Rouse Up, O Young Men of the New Age (in trans.) 2002, Somersault (in trans.) 2003, Telling Tales (contrib. to charity anthology) 2004; non-fiction: Hiroshima noto (trans. as Hiroshima Notes) 1963, Okinawa noto 1970, Chiryo noto 1990, Japan, the Ambiguous and Myself (the Nobel Prize speech and other lectures) 1995. *Honours:* Commdr, Légion d'Honneur 2002; Shinchosha Literary Prize 1964, Tanizaka Prize 1967, Europelia Arts Festival Literary Prize 1989, Nobel Prize for Literature 1994. *Address:* Marion Boyars Publishers Ltd, 24 Lacy Road, London, SW15 1NL, England (office); 585 Seijomachi, Setagaya-ku, Tokyo, Japan. *Telephone:* 482-7192.

O'FAOLÁIN, Julia, MA, FRSL; Irish writer; b. 1932, London; d. of Sean and Eileen (née Gould) O'Faoláin; m. Lauro R. Martines 1957; one s. *Education:* Sacred Heart Convent, Monkstown, Co. Dublin, Univs of Dublin, Paris (Sorbonne) and Rome. *Career:* writer and translator 1968–; Dir Susan Smith Blackburn Prize; mem. Aosdána, Soc. of Authors. *Publications include:* We Might See Sights! and Other Stories 1968, Godded and Codded, Man in the Cellar, Women in the Wall, No Country for Young Men 1980, The Obedient Wife, The Irish Signorina, Daughters of Passion 1982, The Judas Cloth 1992, Not in God's Image (co-ed.), Women in History from the Greeks to the Victorians (co-ed.), Ercoli e il Guardiano Nollurno 1999. *Literary Agent:* c/o Rogers, Coleridge and White Ltd, 20 Powis Mews, London, W11 1JN, England. *Telephone:* (20) 7221-3717 (office).

O'FARRELL, John; British scriptwriter and writer; b. 27 March 1962, Maidenhead, Berkshire, England; m.; two c. *Education:* Univ. of Exeter. *Career:* newspaper columnist, The Independent, The Guardian. *Writing for radio:* Week Ending (BBC Radio 4) 1987–92, Peter Dickson's Nightcap (BBC Radio 2) 1987–89, A Look Back at the Nineties (BBC Radio 4) 1992–93. *Radio:* as performer: The News Quiz (BBC Radio 4), We've Been Here Before (BBC

Radio 4). *Writing for television:* Spitting Image (ITV) 1989–95, Brian Conley: This Way Up (ITV) 1990, Smith and Jones (TalkBack/BBC1) 1990–93, Clive Anderson Talks Back (Hat Trick/Channel 4) 1993–95, Room 101 (Hat Trick/BBC2) 1994–97, Have I Got News For You (Hat Trick/BBC2) 1994–99, The Peter Principle (Hat Trick/BBC1) 1995–2000, Never Mind The Horrocks (Hat Trick/Channel 4) 1996, The Best Show in the World... Probably (BBC1) 1998. *Television appearances:* The 11 O'Clock Show (TalkBack/Channel 4) 2000, Grumpy Old Men (BBC2) 2003. *Publications:* non-fiction: Things Can Only Get Better 1998, Global Village Idiot 2001, I Blame the Scapegoats 2003, An Utterly Impartial History of Britain (Or 2000 Years of Upper Class Idiots in Charge) 2007; fiction: The Best A Man Can Get 2000, This is Your Life 2002, May Contain Nuts 2005. *Address:* c/o Random House UK Ltd, 20 Vauxhall Bridge Road, London, SW1V 2SA, England. *Website:* www.randomhouse.co.uk.

O'FARRELL, Maggie, BA; Northern Irish novelist; b. 1972; pnr William Sutcliffe; one s. *Education:* Univ. of Cambridge. *Career:* fmr journalist. *Publications:* After You'd Gone (Betty Trask Prize 2001) 2000, My Lover's Lover 2002, The Distance Between Us (Soc. of Authors Somerset Maugham Award 2005) 2004, The Vanishing Act of Esme Lennox 2006. *Address:* c/o Hodder Headline Ltd, 338 Euston Road, London, NW1 3BH, England.

OFFEN, Yehuda, (Huri Halim, Ben Naftali), BA, MA; Israeli writer and poet; b. 4 April 1922, Altona, Germany; m. Tova Arbisser 1946; one d. *Education:* Univ. of London, Hebrew Univ. of Jerusalem. *Career:* Sr Ed., Al Hamishmar, Daily Guardian 1960–80; mem. ACUM (Soc. of Authors, Composers and Editors in Israel), Hebrew Writers Asscn (Israel), Int. Acad. of Poets (USA), Int. Federation of Journalists (Brussels), Nat. Federation of Israeli Journalists, PEN Centre (Israel). *Publications:* L'Lo L'An 1961, Har Vakhol 1963, Lo Agadat Khoref 1969, Nofim P'nima 1979, B'Magal Sagur (short stories) 1979, N'Vilat Vered 1983, Shirim Bir'hov Ayaif 1984, P'Gishot Me'ever Lazman 1986, Massekhet Av 1986, Stoning on the Cross Road (short stories) 1988, Who Once Begot a Star 1990, Silly Soil 1992, Back to Germany 1994. *Honours:* ACUM Prizes for Literature 1961, 1979, 1984, Talpir Prize for Literature 1979, Efrat Prize for Poetry 1989. *Address:* c/o Acum Ltd, 9 Tuval Street, POB 1704, Ramat-Gan 52117, Israel.

O'FIANNACHTA, Pádraig, BA, MA, PhD, MRIA; Irish academic, poet, writer and editor; b. 20 Feb. 1927, Co. Kerry. *Education:* St Patrick's Coll., Maynooth, Nat. Univ. of Ireland, Univ. College, Cork, Pontifical Univ., Maynooth. *Career:* Lecturer, St Patrick's Coll., Maynooth 1959–60, Prof. of Early Irish and Lecturer in Welsh 1960–81, Prof. of Modern Irish 1981–92; mem. Cumann na Sagart, Oireachtas (also Pres.) 1985, Poetry Ireland. *Publications:* Ponc 1966, Ruin 1969, Feoirlingi Fileata 1972, Donn Bo 1976, An Bíobla Naofa (ed. and trans.) 1981, Spaisteoireacht 1982, Deora De 1987, Léim An Dá Míle 1999, An Dá Shaul 2004; contribs to various publs. *Honours:* Hon. DPh (Maynooth) 1995; Hon. DLittHum (SHU) 2004; Douglas Hyde Prize for Literature 1969, Monsignor 1998. *Address:* Dingle, Tralee, Co. Kerry, Ireland. *Telephone:* (66) 9151208 (home). *Fax:* (66) 151183 (home).

O'FLAHERTY, Patrick Augustine, BA, MA, PhD; Canadian academic and writer; *Professor Emeritus, Memorial University;* b. 6 Oct. 1939, Long Beach, NF. *Education:* Memorial Univ., St John's, NF, Univ. of London. *Career:* Prof. 1965–95, Head Dept of English 1981–86, Prof. Emeritus 1997–, Memorial Univ.; mem. Writers' Union of Canada. *Publications:* The Rock Observed 1979, Part of the Main: An Illustrated History of Newfoundland and Labrador (with Peter Neary) 1983, Summer of the Greater Yellowlags 1987, Priest of God 1989, A Small Place in the Sun 1989, Come Near at Your Peril: A Visitor's Guide to the Island of Newfoundland 1992, Benny's Island 1994, Reminiscences of J. P. Howley: Selected Years (co-ed.) 1997, Old Newfoundland: A History to 1843 1999; contrib. to numerous publications. *Address:* PO Box 2676, St John's, NF A1C 6K1, Canada (office).

OGAWA, Kunio; Japanese writer; b. 21 Dec. 1927, Shizuoka Pref. *Education:* Tokyo Univ. *Publications:* Seido jidai (The Bronze Age) 1957, Kokoromo no kishi 1972, Itsumin (Recluse) 1986, Hashissu gangu (The Hashish Gang). *Honours:* Kawabata Yasunari Prize 1986, Yomiuri Prize 1998.

OGDEN, Hugh, BA, MA, PhD; American academic, poet and writer; b. 11 March 1937, Erie, PA; m. Ruth Simpson 1960, one s. two d. *Education:* Haverford Coll., New York UN, UN of Michigan. *Career:* Teaching Asst, Univ. of Michigan 1961–65, Instructor 1965–67; Asst Prof., Trinity Coll., Hartford, CT 1967–75, Assoc. Prof. 1975–91, Prof. 1991–; mem. Associated Writing Programs, Poetry Soc. of America, Poets and Writers. *Publications:* Looking for History 1991, Two Road and this Spring 1993, Windfalls 1996, Gift 1998, Natural Things 1998, Bringing a Fiv Straight Down 2005; contribs to reviews, quarterlies and journals. *Honours:* Connecticut Comm. on the Arts Poetry Project Grant 1990, 2003, Nat. Endowment for the Arts grant 1993. *Address:* Department of English, Trinity College, Hartford, CT 06106, USA (office).

OGDEN, Margaret Astrid Lindholm, (Megan Lindholm, Robin Hobb); American writer; b. 1952, Oakland, CA; m.; four c. *Education:* Univ. of Denver. *Publications:* as Megan Lindholm: Harpy's Flight 1983, The Windsingers 1984, The Limbreth Gate 1984, The Wizard of the Pigeons 1986, The Reindeer People 1988, Wolf's Brother 1988, Luck of the Wheels 1989, Cloven Hooves 1991, Gypsy (with Steven Brust) 1992, Alien Earth 1992; as Robin Hobb: The Assassin's Apprentice 1995, Royal Assassin 1996, Assassin's Quest 1997, Ship of Magic 1998, The Mad Ship 1999, Ship of Destiny 2000, Fool's Fate 2003, Shaman's Crossing 2005, Forest Mage 2006, Renegade's Magic 2007; contrib.

to anthologies and periodicals. *Address:* c/o Bantam Books, 1540 Broadway, New York, NY 10036, USA.

OGG, Wilson Reid, AB, JD; American social scientist, philosopher, lawyer and poet, lyricist, educator and judge; *Curator in Residence, Pinebrook and CEO, Pinebrook Press*; b. 26 Feb. 1928, Alhambra, Calif.; s. of James Brooks Ogg and Mary Newton Wilson. *Education:* Univ. of California. *Career:* mem. California State Bar; Psychology Instructor, US Armed Forces Inst., Taegu, Repub. of Korea 1953–54; English Instructor, Taegu English Language Inst. 1954; Trustee Sec. First Unitarian Church of Berkeley 1957–58; Research Attorney, Continuing Educ. of the Bar, Univ. of California 1958–63; Vice-Pres. International House Asscn 1961–62; Pres. Bd and Chair. California Soc. for Physical Study 1963–65; pvt. law practice 1955–; Dir of Admissions, Int. Soc. for Philosophical Enquiry 1981–84; currently Curator in Residence, Pinebrook, CEO Pinebrook Press; mem. San Francisco Bar Asscn, American Mensa, ASCAP, International Acad. of Law and Sciences, World Diplomatic Acad., Scientific Faculty, Cambridge, UK, Faculty Club, Univ. of California at Berkeley, New York Acad. of Sciences. *Publications:* The Enfolding Universe 1995, Constitutional Law, Constitutional Crisis Facing American Democracy 2005, Collective Essay 2005; contrib. to poems in various anthologies and articles in journals. *Honours:* Cultural Doctorate (World Univ.); Hon. DD (Univ. of Life Church) 1969; Dr hc in Religious Humanities 1970; Commendation Ribbon W. Medal Pendant. *Address:* Pinebrook at Bret Harte Way, 8 Bret Harte Way, Berkeley, CA 94708; 1104 Keith Avenue, Berkeley, CA 94708, USA (home). *Telephone:* (510) 845-7155 (home). *Fax:* (510) 540-6052 (home). *E-mail:* wilsonogg@cal.berkeley.edu (office); wilsonogg@comcast.net (home). *Website:* wilsonogg.com.

O'GRADY, Desmond James Bernard, MA, PhD; Irish poet, writer, translator and academic; b. 27 Aug. 1935, Limerick City; one s. two d. *Education:* Jesuit Coll., Limerick, Cistercian Coll., Roscrea, Univ. Coll., Dublin, Harvard Univ., USA. *Career:* secondary school teacher, univ. prof. 1955–82; poetry readings in Ireland, UK, France, Italy, Germany, Greece, Egypt, Sweden, Hungary, Czechoslovakia, Yugoslavia, USA, Canada; selected poems translated into Croatian, Hebrew, German, Italian, Spanish; Distinguished Visiting Prof. and Poet-in-Residence, American Univ., Cairo, Egypt, Univ. of Alexandria, Egypt; Distinguished Visiting Poet, Stockholm, Sweden; Founding mem. and Fellow, Aosdána; mem. Irish Acad. of Arts and Letters. *Publications:* Chords and Orchestrations 1956, Reilly 1961, Prof. Kelleher and the Charles River 1964, Separazioni 1965, The Dark Edge of Europe 1967, The Dying Gaul 1968, Off Licence (trans.) 1968, Hellas 1971, Separations 1973, Stations 1976, Sing Me Creation 1977, The Gododdin (trans.) 1977, A Limerick Rake (trans.) 1978, The Headgear of the Tribe 1979, His Skaldcrane's Nest 1979, Grecian Glances (trans.) 1981, Alexandria Notebook 1989, The Seven Arab Odes (trans.) 1990, Tipperary 1991, Ten Modern Arab Poets (trans.) 1992, My Fields This Springtime 1993, Alternative Manners (trans.) 1993, Trawling Tradition: Collected Translations 1954–1994 1994, Il Galata Morente 1996, The Road Taken: Poems 1956–1996 1996, The Golden Odes of Love (trans.) 1997, C. P. Cavafy: Selected Poems (trans.) 1998, The Wandering Celt 2001, The Battle of Kinsale 1601 2002, The Song of Songs (trans.) 2002, The Wide World (a casebook) 2003, Croatia My Love (trans.) 2003, Summer Harvest: a poem with Matthew Garden 2004, Pegasus 2005, Kurdish Poems of Love and Liberty (trans.) 2005, On My Way, Poems 2006, My Alexandria, Poems and Prose Diary 2006; prose memoirs: Ezra Pound, Patrick Kavanagh, Samuel Beckett, Olga Rudge, Anna Akhmatova; essays: on poetry, poets, translating poetry; contrib. to The Norton Anthology of Modern Poetry 1973, The Norton World Poetry 1998, Archeology of Literature 2004, all anthologies of modern Irish poetry, numerous magazines. *Honours:* Patrick and Catherine Kavanagh Fellowship Award 2004. *Address:* Rincurran Cottage, Kinsale, Co. Cork, Ireland. *Telephone:* (21) 4772898 (office). *E-mail:* bandonbooks@eircom.ie (office).

O'GRADY, Tom, BA, MA; American poet, writer, dramatist, translator and editor and vintner; *Adjunct Professor of English, Hampden-Sydney College*; b. 26 Aug. 1943, Baltimore, MD; m. Bronwyn Southworth; two s. *Education:* Univ. of Baltimore, Johns Hopkins Univ., Univ. of Delaware. *Career:* teacher of writing and literature, various colls and univs 1966–96; Adjunct Prof. of English and Poet-in-Residence, Hampden-Sydney Coll. 1974–; Founder-Ed. The Hampden-Sydney Poetry Review 1975–; numerous lectures and poetry readings. *Publications:* poetry: Unicorn Evils 1973, Establishing a Vineyard 1977, Photo-Graphs 1980, The Farmville Elegies 1981, In the Room of the Just Born 1989, Carvings of the Moon 1992, Sun, Moon, and Stars 1996; prose: Shaking the Tree: A Book of Works and Days 1993, The Same Earth, The Same Sky: New and Selected Poems and Translations 2002; editor: The Hampden-Sydney Poetry Anthology 1990; contribs to anthologies, newspapers, journals and magazines; also trans. stage and TV plays. *Honours:* Leache Prize for Poetry 1975, Co-ordinating Council of Literary Magazine Ed.'s Award 1977, Merit Award 1977, Mettauer Research Award 1984, Trustees Award 1986, Hampden-Sydney Coll. Virginia Prize for Poetry 1989, Nat. Foundation for Advancement in the Arts Teacher of the Arts Award 1989–90, Virginia Center for the Arts Fellowship residency 1995, Henrico Theater Co. Prize 1997, Virginia Comm. for the Arts Poetry Fellowship 2001–02. *Address:* Rose Bower Vineyard, PO Box 126, Hampden-Sydney, VA 23943, USA (home). *Telephone:* (434) 223-8209 (home). *Fax:* (434) 223-3508 (home). *E-mail:* tograd y@hsc.edu (office).

O'HAGAN, Andrew; British writer; b. 1968, Glasgow, Scotland. *Education:* Univ. of Strathclyde. *Career:* Contributing Ed., London Review of Books; columnist, Daily Telegraph. *Publications:* The Missing (non-fiction) 1995, Calling Bible John (radio adaptation of an excerpt from The Missing) 1996, Our Fathers (novel) 1999, The End of British Farming (non-fiction) 2001, New Writing 11 (ed.) 2002, Personality (novel, James Tait Black Memorial Prize for Fiction 2004) 2003, Be Near Me (novel) 2006; contrib. to London Review of Books, New York Review of Books, The New Yorker, The Weekenders (anthology) 2001. *Honours:* Winifred Holtby Memorial Prize 1999, BAFTA Award 1996, E.M. Forster Award, American Acad. of Arts and Letters, James Tait Black Memorial Prize 2004. *Literary Agent:* AP Watt Ltd, 20 John Street, London, WC1N 2DR, England. *E-mail:* edit@lrb.co.uk (office).

OHLSSON, Per Evald Torbjörn; Swedish journalist and author; *Senior Columnist, Sydvenska Dagbladet*; b. 3 March 1958, Malmö; s. of Ulla Ohlsson and Torsten Ohlsson; m. Maria Rydqvist-Ohlsson 1989; one s. *Education:* Univ. of Lund. *Career:* Ed. Lundagard 1980–81; editorial writer, Expressen, Stockholm 1981–85; New York Corresp., Sydvenska Dagbladet 1985–88, Ed.-in-Chief 1990–2005, Sr Columnist 2005–. *Publications:* Over There – Banden Över Atlanten 1992, Gudarnas Ö 1993, 100 År Av Tillväxt 1994. *Honours:* Soderberg Foundation Prize for Journalism 1998. *Address:* Sydvenska Dagbladet, 205 05 Malmö, Sweden (office). *Telephone:* 40-28-12-00 (office). *Fax:* 40-28-13-86 (office). *E-mail:* per.t.ohlsson@sydsvenskan.se (office).

OHNEMUS, Günter; German writer, translator and critic; b. 1946. *Publications include:* Siebenundsechzig Ansichten einer Frau 1995, Der Tiger auf deiner Schulter (trans. as The Tiger on your Shoulder) 1998, Reise in die Angst 2002, The Russian Passenger 2004. *Honours:* Tukan-Award, Alfred Kerr Award. *Address:* c/o Bitter Lemon Press, 37 Arundel Gardens, London, W11 2LW, England. *E-mail:* fvh@bitterlemonpress.com. *Website:* www.bitterlemonpress.com.

OJAIDE, Tanure, BA, MA, PhD; Nigerian poet, writer and academic; b. 24 April 1948, Okpara Island, Nigeria; m. Anne Numuoja 1976; five c. *Education:* Federal Government College, Warri, University of Ibadan, Syracuse University, USA. *Career:* Teacher of English, Federal Government College, Warri, 1973–75; Lecturer in English and Communication, Petroleum Training Institute, Effurun, 1975–77; Lecturer, 1977–85, Senior Lecturer, 1985–87, Reader, 1987–89, University of Maiduguri; Visiting Johnston Prof. of Third World Literatures, Whitman College, Walla Walla, WA, 1989–90; Asst Prof., 1990–93, Assoc. Prof., 1993–98, Prof. of African-American and African Studies, 1998–, University of North Carolina at Charlotte; National Endowment for the Humanities Prof., Albright College, Reading, PA, 1996–97; mem. African Literature Asscn; African Studies Asscn; Associated Writing Programs; Asscn of Nigerian Authors; International Asscn of University Profs of English; International Black Writers, Charlotte, NC; MLA of America; North Carolina Writers' Network. *Publications:* Poetry: Children of Iroko and Other Poems, 1973; Labyrinths of the Delta, 1986; The Eagle's Vision, 1987; Poems, 1988; The Endless Song, 1989; The Fate of Vultures and Other Poems, 1990; The Blood of Peace, 1991; Daydream of Ants, 1997; Delta Blues and Home Songs, 1998; Invoking the Warrior Spirit: New and Selected Poems, 1999; Cannons for the Brave, 1999; When It No Longer Matters Where You Live, 1999; In the Kingdom of Songs: A Trilogy of Poems, 1995–2000, 2001. Other: Yono Urhobo: Obe Rerha (with S. S. Ugheteni), 1981; The Poetry of Wole Soyinka, 1994; Poetic Imagination in Black Africa: Essays on African Poetry, 1996; Great Boys: An African Childhood, 1998; The New African Poetry: An Anthology (ed. with Tijan M. Sallah), 1999; Texts and Contexts: Culture, Society, and Politics in Modern African Literature (with Joseph Obi), 2001; God and his Medicine Men: Short Stories, 2002. Contributions: books, anthologies, magazines and journals. *Honours:* Africa Regional Winner, Commonwealth Poetry Prize, 1987; Overall Winner, BBC Arts and Africa Poetry Award, 1988; Asscn of Nigerian Authors' Portey Prizes, 1988, 1994; All-Africa Okigbo Prizes for Poetry, 1988, 1997; Fellow, Headlands Center for the Arts, Sausalito, CA, 1994; National Endowment for the Humanities Fellowship, 1999–2000; Residency, Bellagio Center for Scholars and Artists, 2001. *Address:* c/o African-American and African Studies Dept, University of North Carolina at Charlotte, Charlotte, NC 28223, USA. *E-mail:* tojadie@email.uncc.edu.

OKAI, Atukwei; Ghanaian poet and academic; b. 1941, Accra; m.; one d. *Education:* Gorky Literary Inst., Moscow, Univ. of London. *Career:* teacher in Russian literature, Univ. of Ghana; faculty mem., Inst. of African Studies, Legon; exec., Pan-African Writers' Asscn (PAWA). *Publications:* poetry: Flowerfall 1969, The Oath of the Fontomfrom and Other Poems 1971, Lorgorligi Logarithms 1974, The Anthill in the Sea 1988. *Literary Agent:* c/o Pan-African Writers' Association, PAWA House, Roman Ridge, POB C456, Accra, Ghana. *Telephone:* (21) 773 062. *Fax:* (21) 773 042. *E-mail:* pawa@ghana.com.

O'KANE, Maggie, BA; Irish journalist; *Foreign Correspondent, The Guardian, and Editorial Director, Guardian Films*; b. 8 June 1962, Ardglas, Co. Down, Northern Ireland; d. of Peter O'Kane and Maura McNeil; m. John Mullin 1995; one s. *Education:* Loreto Convent (Balbriggan, Co. Dublin), Univ. Coll. Dublin, Coll. de Journalistes en Europe, Paris and Coll. of Commerce, Dublin. *Career:* reporter on Irish TV 1982–84, for Sunday Tribune newspaper 1984–87; reporter, TV Producer and Presenter 1987–89; Foreign Corresp. and Feature Writer, The Guardian 1989–; has reported from world trouble spots: Eastern Europe 1989–91, Baghdad 1991, Kurdistan 1991–92, Yugoslavia 1992–94, Bosnia, Haiti, Cuba 1994–96, Afghanistan, Cambodia, Kosovo, Yugoslavia 2000, etc.; writer and presenter various TV documentaries. *Films:*

(documentaries) Milosevic: Puppet Master of the Balkans (Channel 4) (Royal TV Soc. Documentary of the Year 1993), Bloody Bosnia (Royal TV Soc. Documentary of the Year 1994), Looking for Karadzic (Guardian Films) (European Journalist of the Year 2002). *Publications:* A Woman's World: Beyond the Headlines 1996, Mozambique. *Honours:* Journalist of the Year 1992, Foreign Corresp. of the Year 1992, Reporter of the Year (commended) (jt award) 1994, Amnesty Int. Foreign Corresp. of the Year 1993, James Cameron Award for Journalism 1996, European Journalist of the Year 2002, 2003. *Address:* The Guardian, 119 Farringdon Road, London, EC1R 3ER, England. *Telephone:* (20) 7278-2332. *Fax:* (20) 7239-9787. *E-mail:* maggie.okane@ guardian.co.uk.

OKAWA, Ryuho; Japanese religious leader; *Leader, Kofuku-no-Kagaku*; b. 7 July 1956, Tokushima Pref. *Education:* Univ. of Tokyo, Graduate Center, City Univ. of New York, USA. *Career:* attained enlightenment 23 March 1981, realized his identity as El Cantare, saviour of humanity; f. Kofuku-no-Kagaku (Inst. for Research in Human Happiness) 1986; holds numerous open lecture sessions with large audiences that are broadcast by satellite throughout Japan. *Publications:* more than 400 books including The Starting Point of Happiness – A Practical and Intuitive Guide to Discovering Love, Wisdom, and Faith, Love, Nurture, and Forgive – A Handbook on Adding New Richness in Your Life, An Unshakeable Mind – How to Cope with Life's Difficulties and Turn Them into Food for Your Soul 2002, A Revolution of Happiness – The Power of Thought to Change the Future, The 'Inability to Attain Happiness' Syndrome – Say Good-bye to a Life of Gloom, Work and Love – Become a True Leader in the Business World, Invincible Thinking – Become a Master of Your Own Destiny. *Address:* c/o Lantern Books, 1 Union Square West, Suite 201, New York, NY 10003, USA (office).

OKRI, Ben, OBE, FRSL, FRSA; Nigerian/British author and poet; b. 15 March 1959, Minna; s. of Silver Okri and Grace Okri. *Education:* John Donne's School, Peckham, London, Children's Home School, Sapele, Nigeria, Christ High School, Ibadan, Urhobo Coll., Warri and Univ. of Essex, UK. *Career:* staff writer and librarian, Afriscope magazine 1978; Poetry Ed. West Africa magazine 1983–86; broadcaster with BBC 1983–85; Fellow Commoner in Creative Arts, Trinity Coll. Cambridge 1991–93; mem. Int. PEN, a Vice-Pres. English Centre of Int. PEN 1997–; mem. Bd Royal Nat. Theatre of GB 1999–2006; mem. Soc. of Authors, RSL (mem. of Council 1999–2004). *Play:* In Exilus (The Studio, Royal Nat. Theatre of GB) 2001. *Television:* Great Railway Journey: London to Arcadia 1996. *Publications:* Flowers and Shadows 1980, The Landscapes Within 1982, Incidents at the Shrine 1986, Stars of the New Curfew 1988, The Famished Road (Booker Prize) 1991, An African Elegy (vol. of poems) 1992, Songs of Enchantment 1993, Astonishing the Gods 1995, Birds of Heaven (essays) 1996, Dangerous Love (novel) 1996, A Way of Being Free (non-fiction) 1997, Infinite Riches (novel) 1998, Mental Fight (epic poem) 1999, In Arcadia (novel) 2002, Starbook (novel) 2007; poems, essays, short stories. *Honours:* Hon. DLitt (Westminster) 1997, (Essex) 2002, (Exeter) 2004; Commonwealth Prize for Africa 1987, Paris Review Aga Khan Prize for Fiction 1987, Premio Letterario Internazionale, Chianti Ruffino-Antico Fattore 1992, Premio Grinzane Cavour 1994, The Crystal Award (World Econ. Forum, Switzerland) 1995, Premio Palmi 2000. *Address:* c/o Orion Books, Orion House, 5 Upper St Martin's Lane, London, WC2H 9EA, England.

OLAFSSON, Olaf, BSc; Icelandic writer; *Executive Vice-President, Time Warner Digital Media*; b. 1962, Reykjavík. *Education:* Brandeis Univ. *Career:* various positions at Sony Corpn 1985–91, founder, Pres. and CEO Sony Interactive Entertainment 1991–97; fmr Pres. and mem. of bd Advanta Corpn; apptd Vice-Chair. Time Warner Digital Media, now Exec. Vice Pres. *Publications:* Absolution 1994, The Journey Home 2000, Walking into the Night 2003. *Address:* Time Warner Inc., One Time Warner Center, New York, NY 10019-8016, USA.

OLASKY, Marvin, BA, MA, PhD; American academic, writer and editor; *Professor of Journalism, University of Texas at Austin*; b. 12 June 1950, Malden, MA; m. Susan Northway 1976; four s. *Education:* Yale Univ., Univ. of Michigan. *Career:* reporter and corresp., Boston Globe 1970–71, 1973; reporter, Bulletin, Bend, Ore. 1971–72; Lecturer, San Diego State Univ. 1976–77; Academic Affairs Co-ordinator and Speechwriter, Du Pont Co., Wilmington, Del. 1978–83; Asst Prof., Univ. of Texas at Austin 1983–88, Assoc. Prof. 1988–93, Prof. of Journalism 1993–; Bradley Resident Scholar, Heritage Foundation 1989–90; Resident Scholar, Americans United for Life 1990–91; Ed. Philanthropy, Culture and Society 1991–94; Ed.-at-Large, World 1991–94, Ed. 1994–2001 Ed.-in-Chief 2001–; Sr Fellow, Acton Inst. 1999; mem. Nat. Asscn of Scholars. *Publications:* Corporate Public Relations: A New Historical Perspective 1987, Patterns of Corporate Philanthropy: Public Affairs and the Forbes 100 1987, Turning Point: A Christian Worldview Declaration (with Herbert Schlossberg) 1987, Prodigal Press: The Anti-Christian Bias of the News Media 1988, The Press and Abortion, 1838–1988 1988, More Than Kindness: A Compassionate Approach to Childbearing (with Susan Olasky) 1990, Central Ideas in the Development of American Journalism 1991, The Tragedy of American Compassion 1992, Abortion Rites: A Social History of Abortion in America 1992, Philanthropically Correct: The Story of the Council on Foundations 1993, Loving Your Neighbor: A Principled Guide to Charity 1995, Fighting for Liberty and Virtue: Political and Cultural Wars in Eighteenth-Century America 1995, Renewing American Compassion 1996, Telling the Truth: How to Revitalize Christian Journalism 1996, Whirled Views: Tracking Today's Culture Storms (with Joel Belz) 1997, The American Leadership Tradition: Moral Vision from Washington to Clinton 1999, revised edn as The American Leadership Tradition: The Inevitable Impact of a Leader's Faith on a Nation's Destiny 2000, Compassionate Conservatism: What It Is, What It Does, and How It Can Transform America 2000, Standing for Christ in a Modern Babylon 2003, The Religions Next Door 2004, Monkey Business (with John Perry) 2005, Scimitar's Edge 2006, The Politics of Disaster 200; contrib. to periodicals. *Address:* c/o Department of Journalism, University of Texas at Austin, Austin, TX 78712, USA (office). *Telephone:* (512) 471-7908 (office). *Fax:* (512) 471-7979 (office). *E-mail:* molasky@aol.com (office). *Website:* www.worldmag.com (office).

OLDKNOW, Antony, BA, PhD; American poet, writer, literary translator and academic; *Professor of Literature, Eastern New Mexico University*; b. 15 Aug. 1939, Peterborough, England. *Education:* Univ. of Leeds, Univ. of Edinburgh, Univ. of North Dakota, USA. *Career:* Ed., Publisher, Scopcraeft Press Inc 1966–; travelling writer, The Plains Book Bus 1979–81; writer-in-residence, Wisconsin Arts Board 1980–83; poetry staff, Cottonwood 1984–87; Prof. of Literature, Eastern New Mexico Univ. 1987–; Assoc. Ed., Blackwater Quarterly 1993. *Publications:* Lost Allegory 1967, Tomcats and Tigertails 1968, The Road of the Lord 1969, Anthem for Rusty Saw and Blue Sky 1975, Consolations for Beggars 1978, Miniature Clouds 1982, Ten Small Songs 1985, Clara d'Ellébeuse (trans.) 1992, The Villages and Other Poems (trans.) 1993, The Passion Play and Nine Other Ghost Stories 2006; contrib. short stories and articles to anthologies, reviews, journals and magazines. *Address:* Department of Languages and Literature, Eastern New Mexico University, Portales, NM 88130 (office); POB 1091, Portales, NM 88130-1091, USA (home). *Telephone:* (505) 562-2688 (office); (505) 359-0901 (home). *Fax:* (505) 562-2142 (home). *E-mail:* antony.oldknow@enmu.edu (office); oldknowa@msn .com (home).

OLDS, Sharon, BA, PhD; American poet and academic; b. 19 Nov. 1942, San Francisco, CA. *Education:* Stanford Univ., Columbia Univ. *Career:* Lecturer-in-Residence on Poetry, Theodor Herzl Inst., New York 1976–80; Adjunct Prof. 1983–90, Dir 1988–91, Assoc. Prof. 1990–, Graduate Program in Creative Writing, New York Univ.; Fanny Hurst Chair in Literature, Brandeis Univ. 1986–87; New York State Poet 1998–2000. *Publications:* Satan Says 1980, The Dead and the Living 1984, The Gold Cell 1987, The Matter of This World: New and Selected Poems 1987, The Sign of Saturn 1991, The Father 1992, The Wellspring 1996, Blood, Tin, Straw 1999, The Unswept Room 2002, Selected Poems 2006. *Honours:* Creative Arts Public Service Award 1978, Madeline Sadin Award 1978, Guggenheim Fellowship 1981–82, NEA Fellowship 1982–83, Lamont Prize 1984, National Book Critics Circle Award 1985, Lila Wallace-Reader's Digest Fellowship 1993–96. *Address:* c/o Department of English, New York University, 19 University Place, New York, NY 10003, USA.

OLDSEY, Bernard Stanley, BA, MA, PhD; American academic (retd), editor and writer; b. 18 Feb. 1923, Wilkes-Barre, PA; m. Ann Marie Re 1946; one s. one d. *Education:* Pennsylvania State University. *Career:* Instructor to Assoc. Prof. of English, Pennsylvania State University, 1951–69; Senior Fulbright Prof. of American Literature, Universidad de Zaragoza, Spain, 1964–65; Prof. of English, West Chester University of Pennsylvania, 1969–90; Ed., College Literature, 1974–90; Prof., University of Innsbruck, Austria, 1986; mem. Authors' Guild. *Publications:* From Fact to Judgment, 1957; The Art of William Golding, 1967; The Spanish Season (novel), 1970; Hemingway's Hidden Craft, 1979; Ernest Hemingway: Papers of a Writer (ed.), 1981; British Novelists, 1930–1960, 1983; Critical Essays on George Orwell, 1985; The Mayfield Story, 1999; The Snows of Yesteryear (novel), 2001. *Address:* 520 William Ebbs Lane, West Chester, PA 19380, USA. *Telephone:* (610) 436-4223. *E-mail:* oldbern@aol.com.

O'LEARY, Patsy Baker, BS, MA; American writer, poet and teacher; b. 23 Sept. 1937, NC; m. Denis L. O'Leary 1962 (divorced 1979); one d. *Education:* East Carolina College, California State University at Northridge. *Career:* Instructor in Creative Writing, Pitt Community College, 1980–; Lecturer in English, 1980–81, and Communications, 1990–95, East Carolina University; mem. National Writers' Union; Poets and Writers; North Carolina Writers Network; Southeastern Writers Asscn. *Publications:* With Wings as Eagles (novel), 1997; Phoenix (poem); A Voice Heard in Ramah (short story). *Honours:* First Place Awards for article, 1981, 1982, for novel-in-progress, 1981, 1982, for inspirational poem, 1983, Council of Authors and Journalists; First Place Award for short story, Tar Heel Writer's Roundtable, 1984; Award established in her honour, Pitt Community College, 1989. *Address:* 310 Baytree Drive, Greenville, NC 27858, USA.

OLIVER, (Symmes) Chadwick; American writer; b. 30 March 1928, Cincinnati, OH; m. Betty Jane Jenkins 1952; one s. one d. *Publications:* Shadows in the Sun, 1954; Another Kind (short stories), 1955; The Winds of Time, 1957; Unearthly Neighbors, 1960; Ecology and Cultural Continuity as Contributing Factors in the Social Organization of the Plains Indians, 1962; The Wolf is My Brother (western novel), 1967; The Shores of Another Sea, 1971; The Edge of Forever (short stories), 1971; Giants in the Dust, 1976; Cultural Anthropology: The Discovery of Humanity, 1980; Broken Eagle, 1989. *Honours:* Western Heritage Award for Best Novel, 1989. *Address:* 301 Eanes Road, Austin, TX 78746, USA.

OLIVER, Douglas Dunlop, BA, MA; British poet, novelist and prosodist; b. 14 Sept. 1937, Southampton, England; m. 1st Janet Hughes 1962; m. 2nd Alice Notley 1988; two d. two step-s. *Education:* University of Essex. *Career:* Journalist, newspapers in England, Agence France-Presse, Paris, 1959–72;

University Lecturer, Literature, English, various, 1975–; Editorial Board, Franco-British Studies; Co-Ed., Gare du Nord Magazine. *Publications:* Oppo Hectic, 1969; The Harmless Building, 1973; In the Cave of Succession, 1974; The Diagram Poems, 1979; The Infant and the Pearl, 1985; Kind, 1987; Poetry and Narrative in Performance, 1989; Three Variations on the Theme of Harm, 1990; Penniless Politics, 1991; The Scarlet Cabinet (with Alice Notley), 1992; Selected Poems, 1996; Penguin Modern Poets 10, 1996. Contributions: anthologies including: A Various Art, 1987; The New British Poetry 1968–1988, 1988; numerous poems, articles, fiction, to magazines and journals. *Honours:* Eastern Arts Grant, 1977; South-East Arts Grant, 1987; Fund for Poetry Grants, 1990, 1991; Judith E. Wilson Lecturer, University of Cambridge, 1995.

OLIVER, Mary; American poet and educator; b. 10 Sept. 1935, Cleveland, OH. *Education:* Ohio State Univ., Vassar Coll. *Career:* Mather Visiting Prof., Case Western Reserve Univ. 1980, 1982; Poet-in-Residence, Bucknell Univ. 1986; Elliston Visiting Prof., Univ. of Cincinnati 1986; Margaret Banister Writer-in-Residence, Sweet Briar Coll. 1991–95; William Blackburn Visiting Prof. of Creative Writing, Duke Univ. 1995; Catharine Osgood Foster Prof., Bennington Coll. 1996–; mem. PEN. *Publications:* No Voyage, and Other Poems 1963, The River Styx, Ohio, and Other Poems 1972, The Night Traveler 1978, Twelve Moons 1978, Sleeping in the Forest 1979, American Primitive 1983, Dream Work 1986, Provincetown 1987, House of Light 1990, New and Selected Poems 1992, A Poetry Handbook 1994, White Pine: Poems and Prose Poems 1994, Blue Pastures 1995, West Wind 1997, Rules for the Dance 1998, Winter Hours 1999, The Leaf and the Cloud 2000, What Do We Know 2002, Owls and Other Fantasies 2003, Long Life 2004, Why I Wake Early 2004, Blue Iris 2004; contrib. to periodicals in the USA and UK. *Honours:* Poetry Society of America First Prize 1962; Devil's Advocate Award 1968; Shelley Memorial Award 1972; National Endowment for the Arts Fellowship 1972–73; Alice Fay di Castagnola Award 1973; Guggenheim Fellowship 1980–81; American Acad. and Institute of Arts and Letters Award 1983; Pulitzer Prize in Poetry 1984; Christopher Award 1991; L. L. Winship Award 1991; National Book Award for Poetry 1992; Lannan Literary Award 1998. *Literary Agent:* Molly Malone Cook Literary Agency, Box 619, Provincetown, MA 02657, USA.

OLIVER, Roland Anthony, PhD, FBA; British writer and Africanist; b. 30 March 1923, Srinagar, Kashmir; s. of Douglas Gifford Oliver and Lorimer Janet Donaldson; m. 1st Caroline Linehan 1947 (died 1983); one d.; m. 2nd Suzanne Miers 1990. *Education:* Univ. of Cambridge. *Career:* Lecturer, SOAS, Univ. of London 1948–49, 1950–57, Reader 1958–63, Prof. of African History 1963–86, Hon. Fellow 1992; organized first confs on history and archaeology of Africa, London Univ. 1953, 1957, 1961; gounder and Ed. Journal of African History 1960–73; Pres. British Inst. in E Africa 1981–93; Chair. Minority Rights Group 1976–92. *Publications:* The Missionary Factor in East Africa 1952, Sir Harry Johnston and the Scramble for Africa 1957, The Dawn of African History 1961, Short History of Africa (with J. D. Fage) 1962, History of East Africa (with G. Mathew) 1963, Africa Since 1800 (with A. Atmore) 1967, Africa in the Iron Age (with B. M. Fagan) 1975, The African Middle Ages 1400–1800 (with A. Atmore) 1980, The African Experience 1991, The Realms of Gold 1997, Medieval Africa (with A. Atmore) 2001; Gen. Ed. Cambridge History of Africa (eight vols) 1975–86. *Honours:* Distinguished Africanist Award, American African Studies Asscn 1989, African Studies Asscn of the UK 2004. *Address:* Frilsham Woodhouse, near Thatcham, Berkshire RG18 9XB, England. *Telephone:* (1635) 201407. *Fax:* (1635) 202716.

OLMSTEAD, Andrea Louise, BM, MA; American musicologist; *Christopher Hogwood Research Fellow, Handel and Haydn Society*; b. 5 Sept. 1948, Dayton, OH; m. Larry Thomas Bell 1982. *Education:* Hartt Coll. of Music, New York Univ. *Career:* faculty, The Juilliard School 1972–80, Boston Conservatory 1981–2004; Christopher Hogwood Research Fellow Handel and Haydn Soc. 2005–. *Publications:* Roger Sessions and His Music 1985, Conversations with Roger Sessions 1987, The New Grove 20th Century American Masters 1987, The Correspondence of Roger Sessions 1992, Juilliard: A History 1999; contrib. to Journal of the Arnold Schoenberg Institute, American Music, Musical Quarterly, Tempo, Musical America, Perspectives of New Music, Music Library Association Notes, Journal of Musicology. *Honours:* three Nat. Endowment for the Humanities grants 1989, 1992, 2000, Outstanding Academic Book, Choice 1986, Outstanding Teacher of the Year Boston Conservatory 2000, 2004. *Address:* 73 Hemenway Street, Apt 501, Boston, MA 02115, USA (home). *Telephone:* (617) 262-1775 (home). *E-mail:* andrea.olmstead@gmail.com (home). *Website:* www.andreaolmstead.com.

OLSEN, Lance, BA, MFA, MA, PhD; American writer, poet and critic; b. 14 Oct. 1956; m. Andrea Hirsch, 3 Jan. 1981. *Education:* Univs of Wisconsin, Iowa and Virginia. *Career:* Prof. of Creative Writing and Contemporary Fiction, Univ. of Idaho 1996–2001; Writer-in-Residence, State of Idaho 1996–98; Fulbright Scholar, Turku, Finland 2000; Chair. Bd of Dirs Fiction Collective Two 2001–. *Publications:* Ellipse of Uncertainty 1987, Circus of the Mind in Motion 1990, Live From Earth 1991, William Gibson 1992, My Dates With Franz 1993, Natural Selections (poems with Jeff Worley) 1993, Scherzi I Believe 1994, Tonguing the Zeitgeist 1994, Lolita 1995, Burnt 1996, Time Famine 1996, Rebel Yell: A Short Guide to Fiction Writing 1998, Sewing Shut My Eyes 2000, Freaknest 2000, Girl Imagined By Chance 2002, Hideous Beauties 2003, 10:01 2005, Nietzsche's Kisses 2006; contrib. to journals and magazines. *Honours:* Nat. Endowment of the Arts 2006. *Website:* www.lanceolsen.com.

OLSEN, Theodore Victor, (Joshua Stark, Christopher Storm, Cass Willoughby), BSc; American writer; b. 25 April 1932, Rhinelander, Wisconsin; m. Beverly Butler 1976. *Education:* University of Wisconsin. *Career:* mem. Western Writers of America. *Publications:* Haven of the Hunted, 1956; The Rhinelander Story, 1957; The Man from Nowhere, 1959; McGivern, 1960; High Lawless, 1960; Gunswift, 1960; Ramrod Rider, 1960; Brand of the Star, 1961; Brothers of the Sword, 1962; Savage Sierra, 1962; The Young Duke, 1963; Break the Young Land, 1964; The Sex Rebels, 1964; A Man Called Brazos, 1964; Canyon of the Gun, 1965; Campus Motel, 1965; The Stalking Moon, 1965; The Hard Men, 1966; Autumn Passion, 1966; Bitter Grass, 1967; The Lockhart Breed, 1967; Blizzard Pass, 1968; Arrow in the Sun, 1969; Keno, 1970; A Man Named Yuma, 1971; Eye of the Wolf, 1971; There Was a Season, 1973; Mission to the West, 1973; Run to the Mountain, 1974; Track the Man Down, 1975; Day of the Buzzard, 1976; Westward They Rode, 1976; Bonner's Stallion, 1977; Rattlesnake, 1979; Roots of the North, 1979; Allegories for One Man's Moods, 1979; Our First Hundred Years, 1981; Blood of the Breed, 1982; Birth of a City, 1983; Red is the River, 1983; Lazlo's Strike, 1983; Lonesome Gun, 1985; Blood Rage, 1987; A Killer is Waiting, 1988; Under the Gun, 1989; The Burning Sky, 1991; The Golden Chance, 1992. Contributions: 20 short stories in Ranch Romances, 1956–57. *Honours:* Award of Merit, State Historical Society of Wisconsin, 1983; Western Writers of America Spur Award for Best Western Paperback Novel, 1992.

OLSON, Peter, AB, MBA, JD; American publishing executive; *Chairman and CEO, Random House Inc.*; b. 1 May 1950, Chicago, Ill.; m. 1st (divorced); three c.; m. 2nd Candice Carpenter 2001. *Education:* Harvard Univ., Cambridge, Mass, Harvard Business School, Harvard Law School. *Career:* Assoc. Attorney, Baker & Botts (law firm), Washington, DC 1976–77; Assoc. Attorney, Hamada & Matsumoto (law firm), Tokyo, Japan 1977–79; Officer, Int. Div. Dresdner Bank, Frankfurt am Main, Germany 1979–81, Deputy Man. Corp. Business Dept, Tokyo Br. 1981–84, Man. Credit Dept, Tokyo Br. 1984–87, Vice-Pres. Planning Dept, Treasury Div., Frankfurt 1987–88; Man. Bertelsmann AG Corp. Office, Gütersloh, Germany 1988–89; Sr Vice-Pres. Doubleday Book & Music Clubs, Inc., Garden City, NY, USA 1989–90, Pres. Bertelsmann, Inc., New York, USA 1990–92; Exec. Vice-Pres. and Chief Financial Officer Bantam Doubleday Dell Publishing Group, New York 1992–94; Chair. and CEO Bertelsmann Book Group North America, New York 1994–98 (mem. Bertelsmann Book AG Exec. Bd); Chair. and CEO Random House, Inc., New York 1998– (mem. Bertelsmann Book AG Exec. Bd), mem. Bd Bertelsmann AG 2001–. *Honours:* Detur Prize; Phi Beta Kappa. *Address:* Random House, Inc., 1745 Broadway, New York, NY 10019, USA (office). *Telephone:* (212) 782-9000 (office). *Fax:* (212) 302-7985 (office). *Website:* www.randomhouse.com (office).

OLSON, Merle Theodore (Toby), BA, MA; American academic (retd), writer and poet; b. 17 Aug. 1937, Berwyn, IL. *Education:* Occidental Coll., Los Angeles, Long Island Univ. *Career:* Assoc. Dir Aspen Writers' Workshop 1964–67; Asst Prof., Long Island Univ. 1966–74; Faculty, New School for Social Research, New York City 1967–75; Prof. of English, Temple Univ., Phila 1975–2000. *Publications:* fiction: The Life of Jesus 1976, Seaview 1982, The Woman Who Escaped From Shame 1986, Utah 1987, Dorit in Lesbos 1990, The Pool 1991, Reading 1992, At Sea 1993, Write Letter to Billy 2000 The Blond Box 2003 The Bitter Half 2006, poetry: Maps 1969, Worms Into Nails 1969, The Hawk-Foot Poems 1969, The Brand 1969, Pig's Book 1970, Vectors 1972, Fishing 1973, The Wrestler and Other Poems 1974, City 1974, Changing Appearances: Poems 1965–1975 1975, Home 1976, Three and One 1976, Doctor Miriam 1977, Aesthetics 1978, The Florence Poems 1978, Birdsongs 1980, Two Standards 1982, Still/Quiet 1982, Sitting in Gusevik 1983, We Are the Fire 1984, Unfinished Building 1993, Human Nature 2000; editor: Writing Talks: Views on Teaching Writing from Across the Professions (with Muffy E. A. Siegel) 1983; opera libretti: Dorit 1994, Chihuahua 1999, contribs to numerous anthologies, newspapers, and magazines. *Honours:* CAPS Award in Poetry, New York State 1974, Pennsylvania Council on the Arts Fellowship 1983, PEN/Faulkner Award for Fiction 1983, Guggenheim Fellowship 1985, Nat. Endowment for the Arts Fellowship 1985, Yaddo Fellowships 1985, 1986, Rockefeller Foundation Fellowship, Bellagio, Italy 1987, Creative Achievement Award, Temple Univ. 1990, PENN/Book Philadelphia Award for Fiction 1990. *Address:* 275 S 19th Street, Philadelphia, PA 19103, USA (home). *Telephone:* (215) 732-8296 (office); (508) 487-0882 (office). *E-mail:* toby.olson@verizon.net (office).

OLUDHE-MACGOYE, Marjorie Phyllis, BA, MA; Kenyan writer and poet; b. 21 Oct. 1928, Southampton, England; m. D. G. W. Oludhe-Macgoye 1960 (died 1990); three s. one d. *Education:* Univ. of London. *Publications:* Growing Up at Lina School (children's) 1971, Murder in Majengo (novel) 1972, Song of Nyarloka and Other Poems 1977, Coming to Birth (novel) 1986, The Story of Kenya (history) 1986, The Present Moment (novel) 1987, Street Life (novella) 1988, Victoria and Murder in Majengo 1993, Homing In (novel) 1994, Moral Issues in Kenya 1996, Chira (novel) 1997, The Black Hand Gang (children's) 1997, Make It Sing and Other Poems 1998, A Farm Called Kishinev (novel) 2005, Further Adventures of the Black Hand Gang (children's) 2005, The Black Hand Gang Grow Up (children's) 2006; contribs to anthologies, reviews, and journals. *Honours:* BBC Arts in Africa Poetry Award 1982, Sinclair Prize for Fiction 1986. *Address:* PO Box 70344, Nairobi 00400, Kenya.

O'MALLEY, Mary; British playwright; b. 19 March 1941, Bushey, Hertfordshire, England. *Career:* Writer-in-Residence, Royal Court Theatre 1977. *Publications:* Superscum, 1972; A 'Nevolent Society, 1974; Oh If Ever a Man

Suffered, 1975; Once a Catholic, 1977; Look out, Here Comes Trouble, 1978; Talk of the Devil, 1986. *Honours:* Evening Standard Award 1978.

OMOTOSO, Kole, BA, PhD; Nigerian writer. *Education:* Univ. of Ibadau, Univ. of Edinburgh, Scotland. *Career:* Lecturer, Dept of Arabic and Islamic Studies, Univ. of Ibadau, 1972–76; Senior Lecturer, Head of Dept of Dramatic Arts, Dir of the Univ. of Ife Theatre, Univ. of Ife, Ile-Ife, 1976–88; Visiting Prof., Dept of English Studies, Univ. of Stirling, Scotland, 1989–90; Visiting Prof., Dept of English, National Univ. of Lesotho Roma, Lesotho, Aug.–Dec. 1990; worked with Tawala Theatre, London, England, 1991; Prof. of English, Univ. of the Western Cape, Cape Town, 1991–2000; Second Prof. and Researcher of Drama, Univ. of Stellenbosch, 2001–. *Publications:* Fiction: The Edifice, 1972; The Combat, 1972; Just Before Dawn, 1988. Non-Fiction: The Theatrical into Theatre: A Study of Drama in the English-speaking Caribbean, 1982; Achebe or Soyinka?: A Re-interpretation and a Study in Contrasts, 1995. Other: Short story collection, plays, historical narratives. Contributions: numerous articles. *Address:* University of Stellenbosch, Private Bag XI, Matieland 7602, South Africa. *E-mail:* bankole@yebo.co.za.

ONDAATJE, Michael; Canadian author; b. 12 Sept. 1943, Colombo, Sri Lanka; s. of Philip Mervyn Ondaatje and Enid Doris Gratiaen; m. Linda Spalding; two s. *Education:* Dulwich Coll. London, Queen's Univ. and Univ. of Toronto, Canada. *Publications include:* poetry: The Dainty Monsters 1967, The Man with Seven Toes 1968, There's a Trick with a Knife I'm Learning to Do 1979, Secular Love 1984, The Cinnamon Peeler 1991, Handwriting 1998; fiction: The Collected Works of Billy the Kid, Coming Through Slaughter, Running in the Family, In the Skin of a Lion, The English Patient (shared the Booker Prize for Fiction 1992), Anil's Ghost (Prix Medicis) 2000, Divisadero 2007. *Address:* 2275 Bayview Avenue, Toronto, Ont., N4N 3M6, Canada.

ONDERDONK, Andrew Bruce, BA, MS, PhD; American medical scientist and academic; *Editor-in-Chief, Journal of Clinical Microbiology;* b. 5 July 1947, Hartfod, Conn.; m. Juliet Onderdonk; one s. two d. *Education:* MacMurray Coll., Univ. of Missouri. *Career:* Prof. of Pathology, Harvard Medical School; Dir of Clinical Microbiology, Channing Lab. at Brigham and Women's Hosp.; Pres. Int. Soc. for Anaerobic Bacteria; Ed.-in-Chief, Journal of Clinical Microbiology. *Television:* programme on Lyme Disease, NBC Today Show 1986. *Publications:* 20 book chapters, three medical educ. movies, three patents and more than 160 peer-reviewed publs. *Honours:* Hon. MS (Harvard); Distinguished Alumni Award, MacMurray Coll., Phalen Award, Crohn's and Colitis Foundation of America. *Address:* Journal of Clinical Microbiology, American Society for Microbiology, 1752 N Street NW, Washington, DC 20036-2904, USA (office). *Telephone:* (617) 732-7372 (office). *Fax:* (617) 731-1541 (office). *E-mail:* aonderdonk@partners.org (office); onderdonk@aol.com (home). *Website:* jcm.asm.org (office).

O'NEILL, Gilda, BA, MA; British writer and historian; b. 1951, Bethnal Green, London; m. *Education:* Open Univ., North East London Polytechnic, Univ. of Kent. *Publications:* novels: The Cockney Girl 1992, Whitechapel Girl 1993, The Bells of Bow 1994, Just Around the Corner 1995, Cissie Flowers 1996, Dream On 1997, The Lights of London 1998, Playing Around 2000, Getting There 2001, Sins of their Fathers 2002, Make Us Traitors 2004, Of Woman Born 2004; non-fiction: Pull No More Bines: Hop-Picking Memories of a Vanished Way of Life 1990, A Night Out with the Girls: Women Having a Good Time 1993, My East End: Memories of Life in Cockney London 1999, Our Street: East End Life in the Second World War 2003, The Good Old Days: Crime, Murder and Mayhem in Victorian London 2006, Lost Voices: Memories of a Vanished Way of Life 2006. *Honours:* Dr hc (East London Univ.). *Address:* c/o William Heinemann, 20 Vauxhall Bridge Road, London, SW1V 2SA, England. *Website:* www.randomhouse.co.uk.

O'NEILL, Joseph, BA; Irish writer and barrister; b. 23 Feb. 1964, Cork; m. Sally Singer 1994. *Education:* Girton College, Cambridge. *Career:* barrister 1990–. *Publications:* This is the Life, 1991; The Breezes, 1995; Bood-Dark Track, 2001. Contributions: Reviews and articles in: TLS; Spectator; Literary Review. *Address:* c/o Granta Books, 2/3 Hanover Yard, Noel Road, London N1 8BE, England.

O'NEILL, Michael Stephen Charles, BA, DPhil; British academic, writer, poet and editor; *Professor of English, University of Durham;* b. 2 Sept. 1953, Aldershot, Hants.; m. Rosemary Ann McKendrick 1977; one s. one d. *Education:* Exeter Coll., Oxford. *Career:* Lecturer, Univ. of Durham 1979–91, Sr Lecturer 1991–93, Reader 1993–95, Prof. of English 1995–, Head, Dept of English 1997–2000, 2002–05, Dir, Inst. of Advanced Study 2006–; Co-Founder and Ed. Poetry Durham 1982–94; Fellow, English Asscn 2000–. *Publications:* The Human Mind's Imaginings: Conflict and Achievement in Shelley's Poetry, 1989; Percy Bysshe Shelley: A Literary Life, 1989; The Stripped Bed (poems), 1990; Auden, MacNeice, Spender: The Thirties Poetry (with Gareth Reeves), 1992; Percy Bysshe Shelley (ed.), 1993; The 'Defence of Poetry' Fair Copies (ed.), 1994; Keats: Bicentenary Readings (ed.), 1997; Fair-Copy Manuscripts of Shelley's Poems in American and European Libraries (ed. with Donald H. Reiman), 1997; Romanticism and the Self-Conscious Poem, 1997; Literature of the Romantic Period: A Bibliographical Guide (ed.), 1998; Shelley: The Major Works (ed. with Zachary Leader), 2003; A Routledge Literary Sourcebook on the Poems of W. B. Yeats (ed.) 2004; Romanticism: Critical Concepts, 4 Vols (ed. with Mark Sandy) 2006; contribs to books and journals. *Honours:* Eric Gregory Award 1983, Cholmondeley Award for Poets 1990. *Address:* Department of English Studies, University of Durham, Hallgarth House, 77 Hallgarth Street, Durham, DH1 3AY, England (office). *E-mail:* m.s.o'neill@dw.ac.uk (office).

O'NEILL, Paul; Canadian author; b. 26 Oct. 1928, St John's, NF. *Education:* National Acad. of Theatre Arts, New York. *Career:* mem. Canadian Authors Asscn; Canadian Radio Producers Asscn; Newfoundland and Labrador Arts Council, chair., 1988–89; Newfoundland Writers Guild; Writers Union of Canada. *Publications:* Spindrift and Morning Light, 1968; The City in Your Pocket, 1974; The Oldest City, 1975; Seaport Legacy, 1976; Legends of a Lost Tribe, 1976; Breakers, 1982; The Seat Imperial, 1983; A Sound of Seagulls, 1984; Upon This Rock, 1984. Other: Radio and stage plays; Television and film scripts. Contributions: many periodicals. *Honours:* Literary Heritage Award, Newfoundland Historical Society; Robert Weaver Award, National Radio Producers Asscn of Canada, 1986; Hon. Doctor of Laws, Memorial University of Newfoundland, 1988; Order of Canada, 1990; Newfoundland and Labrador Arts Hall of Honour, 1991; Canada Commemorative Medal, 1992.

O'NEILL, Robert John, AO, MA, BE, DPhil, FASSA; Australian historian and army officer; b. 5 Nov. 1936, Melbourne; s. of Joseph Henry O'Neill and Janet Gibbon O'Neill; m. Sally Margaret Burnard 1965; two d. *Education:* Scotch Coll. Melbourne, Royal Mil. Coll. of Australia, Melbourne Univ., Brasenose Coll. Oxford. *Career:* served in Australian army 1955–68, Fifth Bn Royal Australian Regt, Vietnam (despatches) 1966–67, Maj. 1967–68 (resgnd); Rhodes scholar, Vic. 1961; Official Australian Historian for the Korean War 1969–82; Head Strategic and Defence Studies Centre, ANU 1971–82; Dir IISS, London 1982–87, Chair. Council 1996–2001; Chichele Prof. of the History of War Oxford Univ. 1987–2001; Dir Grad. Studies Modern History Faculty, Oxford 1990–92; Fellow All Souls Coll. Oxford 1987; Sr Fellow in Int. Relations ANU 1969–77, Professorial Fellow 1977–82; Trustee Imperial War Museum 1990–, Deputy Chair. 1996–98, Chair. 1998–2001; Gov. Ditchley Foundation 1989–, Int. Peace Acad. 1990–; Chair. Bd Centre for Defence Studies and Bd Centre for Australian Studies, Univ. of London 1990–95; Dir The Shell Transport and Trading Co. 1992– and two mutual funds of Capital Group, LA 1992–; mem. Advisory Bd Investment Co. of America 1988–; mem. Commonwealth War Graves Comm. 1990, The Rhodes Trust 1995–. *Publications:* The German Army and the Nazi Party 1933–39 1966, Vietnam Task 1966, General Giap: politician and strategist 1969, (ed.) The Strategic Nuclear Balance 1975, (ed.) The Defence of Australia: fundamental new aspects 1977, (ed.) Insecurity: the spread of weapons in the Indian and Pacific Oceans 1978, (co-ed.) Australian Dictionary of Biography Vols 7–12, 1891–1939, 1979–91, (co-ed.) New Directions in Strategic Thinking 1981, Australia in the Korean War 1950–53: Vol. I Strategy and Diplomacy 1981, Vol. II Combat Operations 1985, (co-ed.) Australian Defence Policy for the 1980s 1982, (ed.) Security in East Asia 1984, (ed.) The Conduct of East–West Relations in the 1980s 1985, (ed.) New Technology and Western Security Policy 1985, (ed.) Doctrine, the Alliance and Arms Control 1986, (ed.) East Asia, the West and International Security 1987, (ed.) Security in the Mediterranean 1989, (co-ed.) The West and the Third World 1990, (co-ed.) Securing Peace in Europe 1945–62 1992, (co-ed.) War, Strategy and International Politics 1992, Alternative Nuclear Futures 1999; articles in numerous journals. *Honours:* Hon. Fellow Brasenose Coll. Oxford; Hon. Col 5th (V) Bn, The Royal Greenjackets 1993–99; Hon. DL (ANU) 2001.

ONG, Han; Philippine playwright and novelist; b. 1968. *Career:* moved to USA 1984–. *Plays:* The LA Plays: In A Lonely Country and A Short List of Alternate Places (Almeida, London) 1993, Middle Finger 2001, The Suitcase Trilogy 2006. *Publications:* Fixer Chao (novel) 2001, The Disinherited (novel) 2004. *Honours:* MacArthur Fellowship 1997, Guggenheim Fellowship 2005. *Literary Agent:* c/o Susan Bergholz Literary Services, 17 West 10th Street #5, New York, NY 10011, USA.

ONWUEME, Osonye Tess, (Tess Akaeke Onwueme, Tess Osonye Onwueme); Nigeria dramatist, novelist and academic; b. 8 Sept. 1955; m. Obika Gray 1998; two s. three d. *Education:* BA, Education, 1979, MA, Literature, 1982, University of Ife; PhD, African Drama, University of Benin, 1988. *Career:* Lecturer, University of Ife, 1980–82; Asst Prof., Federal University of Technology, Owerri, 1982–87; Assoc. Prof. and Head, Performing Arts Dept, Imo State University, 1986–88; Assoc. Prof., Montclair State University, NJ, 1990–92; Wayne State University, Detroit, 1990–98; Prof. of English and Africana Studies, Vassar College, 1992–93; Distinguished Prof. of Cultural Diversity and Prof. of English, University of Wisconsin at Eau Claire, 1994–; mem. African Literature Asscn; African Studies Asscn; Asscn of Nigerian Authors; International Women Playwrights Asscn; Organization of Women Writers of African Descent; PEN International. *Publications:* A Hen Too Soon, 1983; The Broken Calabash, 1984; The Desert Encroaches, 1985; Ban Empty Barn, 1986; A Scent of Onions, 1986; Mirror for Campus, 1987; The Reign of Wazobia, 1988; Legacies, 1989; Riot in Heaven, 1996; The Missing Face, 1997; Tell it to Women, 1997; Shakara: Dance Hall Queen, 2000; Why the Elephant Has No Butt, 2000; Then She Said It: An Epic Drama, 2002; What Mama Said, 2003. Contributions: periodicals. *Honours:* Drama Prizes, Asscn of Nigerian Authors, 1985, 1995, 2001; Distinguished Authors Award, Ife International Bookfair, 1988; Ford Foundation Award, 2000. *Literary Agent:* Kimberly Crank, 1019 Huebsh Street, Eau Claire, WI 54701, USA. *Address:* c/o Dept of English, University of Wisconsin at Eau Claire, Eau Claire, WI 54701, USA.

ONYEAMA, Charles Dillibe Ejiofor; Nigerian publisher, writer and journalist; b. 6 Jan. 1951, Enugu; m. 1st Ethel Ekwueme 1984, four s.; m.

2nd Nneka Okwu; two d. *Education:* Eton Coll., Premier School of Journalism, London, England. *Career:* mem. Bd of Dirs, Star Printing and Publishing Co. Ltd 1992–94; Man. Dir, Delta Publications (Nigeria) Ltd; Pres. Delta Book Club 1981–; mem. Local Govt Caretaker Cttee, Udi, Enugu State 1994–96. *Publications:* Nigger at Eton 1972, John Bull's Nigger 1974, Sex is a Nigger's Game 1975, The Book of Black Man's Humour 1975, I'm the Greatest 1975, Juju 1976, Secret Society 1977, Revenge of the Medicine Man 1978, The Return 1978, Night Demon 1979, Female Target 1980, The Rules of the Game 1980, The Story of an African God 1982, Modern Messiah 1983, Godfathers of Voodoo 1985, African Legend 1985, Correct English 1986, Notes of a So-Called Afro-Saxon 1988, A Message to My Compatriots 1997, The Boomerang 1998, The Joys of African Humour 2000, The New Man 2002, The Joys of Ibo Humour 2003, And The Last Shall Be First 2006; contrib. to Books and Bookmen, Spectator, The Times, Daily Express, Sunday Express, Drum, West Africa, Roots, The Guardian, Evening News. *Address:* 8B Byron Onyeama Close, New Haven, PO Box 1172, Enugu, Enugu State, Nigeria. *Telephone:* (42) 256595 (home). *E-mail:* dillibeonyeama@yahoo.com.

ONYEFULU, Ifeoma, DipMan.; British/Nigerian author and photographer; b. 30 March 1959, Onitsha; m. Roger Malbert 1988; two s. *Education:* Seven Sisters Coll., London. *Publications:* A is for Africa 1993, Emeka's Gift 1994, Chidi Only Likes Blue 1997, One Big Family 1996, My Grandfather is a Magician 1998, Ebele's Favourite 1999, A Triangle for Adaora 2000, And Saying Goodbye 2001, Welcome Dede 2003, Here Comes the Bride 2004, African Christmas 2005, Ikenna Goes to Nigeria 2007. *Honours:* Notable Book Award (USA), Children's Africana Book Award 2005. *Address:* 15 Bickerton Road, London, N19 5JU, England.

OOKA, Makoto; Japanese poet, writer and academic; b. 16 Feb. 1931, Mishima City; s. of Hiroshi Ooka and Ayako Ooka; m. Kaneko Aizawa 1957; one s. one d. *Education:* Tokyo Nat. Univ. *Career:* journalist with Yomiuri (newspaper), foreign news section 1953–63; Asst Prof., Meiji Univ., Tokyo 1965–70, Prof. 1970–87; Pres. Japan Poets' Asscn 1979–81; Prof., Nat. Univ. for Fine Arts and Music 1988–93; Soshitsu Sen XV Distinguished Lecturer in Japanese Culture and Visiting Fellow, Donald Keene Center of Japanese Culture, Columbia Univ. 2000; Pres. Japan PEN Club 1989–93; mem. Int. Advisory Bd of Poetry Int., Rotterdam; mem. Japan Art Acad. 1995–. *Publications:* poetry: Memories and the Present 1956, For a Girl in Springtime 1978, City of Water 1981, Odes to the Waters of my Hometown 1989, The Afternoon in the Earthly Paradise 1992, The Last Will of Fire 1995; Criticism: The Banquet and the Solitary Mind, Aesthetics of Japanese Poetry 1978; English translations: Japanese Poetry; Past and Present, A Poet's Anthology 1979–, an anthological series for the newspaper Asahi, A String Around Autumn 1982, A Play of Mirrors: Eight Major Poets of Modern Japan (co-ed) 1987, Elegy and Benediction 1991, The Colours of Poetry – Essays on Classic Japanese Verse 1991, What the Kite Thinks, a linked poem with three American poets 1994, The Range of Japanese Poetry 1994, Beneath the Sleepless Tossing of the Planets 1995, The Poetry and Poetics of Ancient Japan 1997, Love Songs from the Man'yoshu: Selections from a Japanese Classic 2000; French translations: Poèmes de tous les jours 1993, Propos sur le vent et autres poèmes 1995, Poésie et Poétique du Japon Ancien 1995, Dans l'Océan du Silence 1998, Citadelle de Lumière 2002. *Honours:* Officier des Arts et Lettres; Order of Cultural Merit 2003; Yomiuri Prize for Literature, Kikuchi Kan Prize, Hanatsubaki Prize for Poetry, Golden Wreath Prize, Struga Poetry Evenings Macedonia 1996, Asahi Prize 1996, Japanese Art Acad. Imperial Award 1996, Person of Cultural Merit 1997, Japan Foundation Prize 2002. *Address:* 2-18-1-2606, Iidabashi, Chiyoda-ku, Tokyo 102-0072, Japan.

OPIE, Iona Margaret Balfour, CBE, FBA; British writer and folklorist; b. 13 Oct. 1923, d. of the late Sir Robert Archibald and Olive Cant; m. Peter Mason Opie 1943 (died 1982); two s. one d. *Education:* Sandecotes School (Parkstone). *Career:* Served with meteorological section of Women's Auxiliary Air Force (WAAF) 1941–43; writer and folklorist 1947–; Hon. mem. Folklore Soc. 1974. *Publications:* I Saw Esau (jtly) 1947, The Oxford Dictionary of Nursery Rhymes (jtly) 1951, The Oxford Nursery Rhyme Book (jtly) 1955, Christmas Party Games (jtly) 1957, The Lore and Language of Schoolchildren (jtly) 1959, Puffin Book of Nursery Rhymes (jtly, European Prize City of Caorle, Italy) 1963, Children's Games in Street and Playground (jtly, Chicago Folklore Prize) 1969, The Oxford Book of Children's Verse (jtly) 1973, The Classic Fairy Tales (jtly) 1974, A Nursery Companion (jtly) 1980, The Oxford Book of Narrative Verse 1983, The Singing Game (Katharine Briggs Folklore Award, Rose Mary Crawshay Prize, Children's Literature Asscn Book Award) 1985, Tail Feathers From Mother Goose 1988, The Treasures of Childhood (co-ed) 1989, A Dictionary of Superstitions 1989, Babies: an unsentimental anthology (jtly) 1990, The People in the Playground 1993, My Very First Mother Goose 1996, Here Comes Mother Goose 1999. *Honours:* Hon. MA (Oxon) 1962, (Open) 1987, Hon. DLitt (Southampton) 1987, (Nottingham) 1991 Jt recipient Coote-Lake Medal 1960. *Address:* Mells House, Farnham Road, West Liss, Hants., GU33 6JQ, England. *Telephone:* (1730) 893309.

O'REILLY, Kenneth, BA, MA, PhD; American historian and writer; b. 24 Oct. 1951, New York, NY; m. Maureen Alice Moore 1976, three s. *Education:* University of Detroit, Central Michigan University, Marquette University. *Career:* Prof. of History, University of Alaska, Anchorage, 1983–; Writer. *Publications:* Hoover and the Un-Americans: The FBI, HUAC, and the Red Menace, 1983; 'Racial Matters': The FBI's Secret File on Black America, 1960–1972, 1989; Black Americans: The FBI Files, 1994; Nixon's Piano:

Presidents and Racial Politics from Washington to Clinton, 1995. *Address:* 18728 Snowy Plover, Anchorage, AK 99516, USA.

ORFALEA, Gregory Michael, AB, MFA; American academic; *Assistant Professor and Director, Center for Writing, Pitzer College*; b. 9 Aug. 1949, Los Angeles, Calif.; m. Eileen Rogers 1984; three s. *Education:* Georgetown University, University of Alaska. *Career:* Reporter, Northern Virginia Sun, 1971–72; Prof., Santa Barbara City College, Calif., 1974–76; Ed., Political Focus, 1979–81, Small Business Administration, 1985–91, Resolution Trust Corporation, 1991–95, Federal Deposit Insurance Corporation, 1995–96, Comptroller of the Currency, 1996–97, Freddie Mac, 1997–, Substance Abuse and Mental Health Services 1998–2004; Asst Prof. and Dir Center for Writing, Pitzer Coll. 2004–; mem. American PEN. *Publications:* Before the Flames, 1988; The Capital of Solitude, 1988; Grape Leaves, 1988; Imagining America: Stories of the Promised Land, 1991; Messengers of the Lost Battalion, 1997; Up All Night 2004, The Arab Americans 2005. Contributions: Washington Post; TriQuarterly; Cleveland Plain-Dealer; Christian Science Monitor, Los Angeles Times. *Honours:* California Arts Council Award, 1976; American Middle East Peace Research Award, 1983; District of Columbia Commission on the Arts and Humanities Awards, 1991, 1993. *Address:* Pitzer College, 1050 N Mills Avenue, Claremont, CA 91711, USA (office). *Telephone:* (909) 607-3766 (office). *Fax:* (909) 607-7880 (office). *E-mail:* gregory-orfalea@pitzer.edu (office). *Website:* www.pitzer.edu (office).

ORGEL, Doris, (), BA; American children's writer; b. (Doris Adelberg), 15 Feb. 1929, Vienna, Austria; m. Shelley Orgel 1949, two s. one d. *Education:* Barnard College. *Career:* Sr Staff Writer, Ed., Publications and Media Group, Bank Sheer College of Education, 1961–. *Publications:* Sarah's Room, 1963; The Devil in Vienna, 1978; My War with Mrs Galloway, 1985; Whiskers Once and Always, 1986; Midnight Soup and a Witch's Hat, 1987; Starring Becky Suslow, 1989; Nobodies and Somebodies, 1991; Next Time I Will, 1993; The Mouse Who Wanted To Marry, 1993; Ariadne, Awake, 1994. Young Adult Fiction: Risking Love, 1985; Crack in the Heart, 1989. Other: Some 30 works. Contributions: Cricket magazine.

O'RIORDAN, Marie, BA, MA; British magazine editor; *Editor, Marie Claire magazine*; b. 1960, Dublin, Ireland. *Education:* Univ. Coll., Dublin. *Career:* fmr Ed. More!; Ed. Elle magazine 1996–99; Group Publishing Dir EMAP Elan 1999–2001; Ed. Marie Claire 2001–. *Honours:* EMAP Editor of the Year 1996, IPC Editor of the Year 2003. *Address:* Marie Claire, European Magazines Ltd, 13th Floor, King's Reach Tower, Stamford Street, London, SE1 9LS, England (office). *Telephone:* (20) 7261-5177 (office). *Fax:* (20) 7261-5277 (office).

ORLANDERSMITH, Dael; American playwright and performer; b. Harlem, NY. *Stage appearances:* Macbeth, Romeo and Juliet, Raisin in the Sun, Goin' for Dolo, US, European and Australian tours with the Nuyorican Poets' Cafe, Leftover Life to Kill (solo show). *Plays written:* Beauty's Daughter 1993, Liar Liar 1994, Monster, The Gimmick 1997, Yellowman 2002. *Publications:* Lone Dancer Underground (novel). *Honours:* OBIE Award 1994, New York Foundation for the Arts Fellowship, Helen Merrill Award for Emerging Playwrights. *Address:* c/o Random House Inc, 1745 Broadway, Third Floor, New York, NY 10019, USA. *Website:* www.randomhouse.com.

ORLEDGE, Robert Francis Nicholas, MA, PhD; British academic, author, editor and orchestrator; *Professor Emeritus of Music, University of Liverpool*; b. 5 Jan. 1948, Bath, Somerset. *Education:* Assoc., Royal Coll. of Organists 1964; Clare Coll., Cambridge; Univ. of Cambridge. *Career:* Prof. of Music, Univ. of Liverpool –2004, Prof. Emer. 2004–; mem. Royal Musical Asscn, Centre de Documentation Claude Debussy, Asscn des Amis de Charles Koechlin, Fondation Erik Satie. *Music:* completion and orchestration of Debussy's opera The Fall of the House of Usherand Debussy's ballet No-ja-li ou Le Palais du Silence. *Publications:* Gabriel Fauré 1979, Debussy and the Theatre 1982, Charles Koechlin (1867–1950): His Life and Works 1989, Satie the Composer 1990, Satie Remembered 1995; contrib. to Music and Letters, Musical Quarterly, Musical Times, Music Review, Current Musicology, Journal of the Royal Musical Association. *Address:* 6 Dorset Gardens, Brighton, BN2 1RL, England (home). *Telephone:* (1273) 698384 (home). *E-mail:* robertorledge@aol.com (home).

ORMEROD, Roger; British author; b. 17 April 1920, Wolverhampton, Staffordshire, England. *Publications:* Time to Kill, 1974; The Silence of the Night, 1974; Full Fury, 1975; A Spoonful of Luger, 1975; Sealed with a Loving Kill, 1976; The Colour of Fear, 1976; A Glimpse of Death, 1976; Too Late for the Funeral, 1977; The Murder Come to Mind, 1977; A Dip into Murder, 1978; The Weight of Evidence, 1978; The Bright Face of Danger, 1979; The Amnesia Trap, 1979; Cart Before the Hearse, 1979; More Dead than Alive, 1980; Double Take, 1980; One Breathless Hour, 1981; Face Value, 1983; Seeing Red, 1984; The Hanging Doll Murder, 1984; Dead Ringer, 1985; Still Life with Pistol, 1986; A Death to Remember, 1986; An Alibi Too Soon, 1987; The Second Jeopardy, 1987; An Open Window, 1988; By Death Possessed, 1988; Guilt on the Lily, 1990; Death of an Innocent, 1989; No Sign of Life, 1990; Hung in the Blance, 1990; Farewell Gesture, 1990.

ORMESSON, Comte Jean d'; French writer, journalist and international official; b. 16 June 1925, s. of Marquis d'Ormesson; nephew of late Comte Wladimir d'Ormesson; m. Françoise Béghin 1962; one d. *Education:* Ecole Normale Supérieure. *Career:* Deputy Sec.-Gen. Int. Council for Philosophy and Humanistic studies (UNESCO) 1950–71, Sec.-Gen. 1971; staff of various Govt ministers 1958–66; Deputy Ed. Diogène (int. journal) 1952–72, mem.

Man. Cttee 1971–; mem. Council ORTF 1960–62, Programme Cttee 1973; mem. Control Comm. of Cinema 1962–69; mem. Editorial Cttee Editions Gallimard 1972–74; Ed.-in-Chief, Columnist, Le Figaro 1974–77, Dir-Gen. 1976, leader writer, columnist 1977–; mem. Acad. Française 1973; Pres., Soc. des amis de Jules Romains 1974–. *Publications:* L'amour est un plaisir 1956, Du côté de chez Jean 1959, Un amour pour rien 1960, Au revoir et merci 1966, Les illusions de la mer 1968, La gloire de l'empire (Grand Prix du Roman (Acad. Française) 1971, Au plaisir de Dieu 1974, Le vagabond qui passe sous une ombrelle trouée 1978, Dieu, sa vie, son oeuvre 1981, Mon dernier rêve sera pour vous 1982, Jean qui grogne et Jean qui rit 1984, Le vent du soir 1985, Tous les hommes en sont fous 1985, Bonheur à San Miniato 1987, Garçon de quoi écrire (jtly.) 1989 (prix de Mémorial 1990), Histoire du juif errant 1991, Tant que vous penserez à moi, entretien avec Emmanuel Berl 1992, La Douane de mer 1994, Presque rien sur presque tout 1996, Casimir mène la grande vie 1997, Une autre histoire de la littérature française 1997, Le rapport Gabriel (Prix Jean Giono) 1999, Voyez comme on danse 2001, C'était bien 2003, Une Fête en Larmes 2005; numerous articles in Le Figaro, Le Monde, France-Soir, Paris Match, etc. *Honours:* Officier, Légion d'honneur, Commdr des Arts et Lettres, Officier, Ordre nat. du Mérite, Chevalier des Palmes académiques. *Address:* c/o Le Figaro, 37 rue du Louvre, Paris 75001 (office); 1 rue Miollis, 75015 Paris (office); 10 avenue du Parc-Saint-James, 92200 Neuilly-sur-Seine, France (home).

ORMSBY, Frank, BA, MA; Northern Irish poet, writer and editor; b. 30 Oct. 1947, Enniskillen, Co. Fermanagh. *Education:* Queen's University, Belfast. *Career:* Ed., The Honest Ulsterman, 1969–89. *Publications:* A Store of Candles, 1977; Poets from the North of Ireland (ed.), 1979; A Northern Spring, 1986; Northern Windows: An Anthology of Ulster Autobiography (ed.), 1987; The Long Embrace: Twentieth Century Irish Love Poems (ed.), 1987; Thine in Storm and Calm: An Amanda McKittrick Ros Reader (ed.), 1988; The Collected Poems of John Hewitt (ed.), 1991; A Rage for Order: Poetry of the Northern Ireland Troubles (ed.), 1992; The Ghost Train, 1995; The Hip Flask: Short Poems from Ireland (ed.), 2000, The Blackbird's Nest: An Anthology of Poetry from Queen's University Belfast (ed.) 2006, John Hewitt: Selected Poems (ed. with Michael Longley) 2007. *Address:* 33 North Circular Road, Belfast, BT15 5HD, Northern Ireland.

O'ROURKE, Patrick Jake, BA, MA; American writer and editor; b. 14 Nov. 1947, Toledo, OH; m. 1st Amy Lumet 1990 (divorced 1992); m. 2nd Christina Mallon 1995; one s. two d. *Education:* Miami Univ., Oxford, OH, Johns Hopkins Univ., Baltimore, Md. *Career:* writer, National Lampoon 1972–81, Ed.-in-Chief 1978–81; Correspondent, Rolling Stone 1985–2001, Atlantic Monthly 2001–. *Publications:* Modern Manners 1983, The Bachelor Home Companion 1987, Republican Party Reptile 1987, Holidays in Hell 1989, Parliament of Whores 1991, Give War a Chance 1992, All the Trouble in the World 1994, Age and Guile 1995, Eat the Rich 1998, The CEO of the Sofa 2001, Peace Kills (essays) 2004, On 'The Wealth of Nations' 2007; contribs to periodicals. *Address:* c/o Atlantic Monthly, 77 N Washington Street, Boston, MA 02114, USA.

ORR, Gregory Simpson, BA, MFA; American academic, poet and writer; b. 3 Feb. 1947, Albany, NY; m. Trisha Winer 1973, two d. *Education:* Antioch College, Columbia University. *Career:* Asst Prof., 1975–80, Assoc. Prof., 1980–88, Prof. of English, 1988–, University of Virginia; Poetry Consultant, Virginia Quarterly Review, 1976–; Visiting Writer, University of Hawaii at Manoa, 1982. *Publications:* Poetry: Burning the Empty Nests, 1973; Gathering the Bones Together, 1975; Salt Wings, 1980; The Red House, 1980; We Must Make a Kingdom of It, 1986; New and Selected Poems, 1988; City of Salt, 1995. Non-Fiction: Stanley Kunitz: An Introduction to the Poetry, 1985; Richer Entanglements: Essays and Notes on Poetry and Poems, 1993. *Honours:* Acad. of American Poets Prize, 1970; YM-YWHA Discovery Award, 1970; Bread Loaf Writers Conference Transatlantic Review Award, 1976; Guggenheim Fellowship, 1977; National Endowment for the Arts Fellowships, 1978, 1989; Fulbright Grant, 1983.

ORSENNA, Erik (see Arnoult, Erik)

ORSZÁG-LAND, Thomas; Hungarian/British poet and foreign correspondent; b. 12 Jan. 1938, Budapest, Hungary. *Career:* mem. Foreign Press Asscn, Royal Inst. of Int. Affairs, Soc. of Authors; Fellow Int. PEN. *Publications:* Berlin Proposal 1990, Free Women 1991, Tales of Matriarchy 1998; translations: Bluebeard's Castle, by Balázs/Bartók 1988, Splendid Stags, by Bartók 1992, 33 Poems by Radnoti 1992, Holocaust Testimony, by Mezei 1995; contribs to newspapers and reviews. *Address:* PO Box 1213, London, N6 5HZ, England (office).

ORTIZ, Simon Joseph; American poet and writer; b. 27 May 1941, Albuquerque, NM; m. Marlene Foster 1981 (divorced 1984); three c. *Education:* Fort Lewis College, University of New Mexico, University of Iowa. *Career:* Instructor, San Diego State University, 1974, Institute of American Arts, Santa Fe, New Mexico, 1974, Navajo Community College, Tsaile, AZ, 1975–77, College of Marin, Kentfield, CA, 1976–79, University of New Mexico, Albuquerque, 1979–81, Sinte Gleska College, Mission, SD, 1985–86, Lewis and Clark College, Portland, Oregon, 1990; Consulting Ed., Navajo Comunity College Press, Tsaile, 1982–83; Pueblo of Acoma Press, Acoma, New Mexico, 1982–84; Arts Co-ordinator, Metropolitan Arts Commission, Portland, Oregon, 1990. *Publications:* Naked in the Wind (poems), 1971; Going for the Rain (poems), 1976; A Good Journey (poems), 1977; Howbah Indians (short stories), 1978; Song, Poetry, Language (essays), 1978; Fight

Back: For the Sake of the People, For the Sake of the Land (poems and prose), 1980; From Sand Creek: Rising in This Heart Which is Our America (poems), 1981; A Poem is a Journey, 1981; The Importance of Childhood, 1982; Fightin': New and Collected Stories, 1983; Woven Stone: A 3-in-1 Volume of Poetry and Prose, 1991; After and Before the Lightning (poems), 1994. Editor: Califa: The California Poetry (co-ed.), 1978; A Ceremony of Brotherhood (co-ed.), 1980; Earth Power Coming (anthology of Native American short fiction), 1983. Contributions: various anthologies and textbooks. *Honours:* National Endowment for the Arts Discovery Award, 1969, and Fellowship, 1981; Honored Poet, White House Salute to Poetry and American Poets, 1980; New Mexico Humanities Council Humanitarian Award for Literary Achievement, 1989.

OSBORN, Karen, BA, MFA; American novelist and poet; b. 26 April 1954, Chicago, IL; m. Michael Jenkins 1983; two d. *Education:* Hollins College, University of Arkansas at Fayetteville. *Career:* Poet, Arkansas Poetry in the Schools 1979–83, Dir 1982–83; Instructor of English, Clemson University, 1983–87; part-time Instructor of English, University of Kentucky 1988–93; various workshops and readings. *Publications:* Patchwork, 1991; Between Earth and Sky, 1996; The River Road, 2003. Contributions: numerous anthologies, including: Jumping Pond: Poems and Stories from the Ozarks; Cardinal: A Contemporary Anthology; Hollins Anthology; Poems to numerous periodicals, including: Artemis; Mid American Review; Seattle Review; Tar River Poetry; Embers; Southern Review; Kansas Quarterly; Poet Lore; Passages North; Montana Review; Centennial Review; Wisconsin Review. *Honours:* Hollins Literary Festival Awards for Poetry, for Fiction, 1979; Nancy Thorp Prize for Poetry, 1979; Mary Vincent Long Award, Distinguished Literary Achievement, 1979; Kentucky Foundation for Women Grant, 1991; Al Smith Artists Fellowship Award for Fiction, Kentucky Arts Council, 1991; New York Times Notable Book, 1991.

OSBORNE, Charles Thomas, FRSL; Australian/British writer, critic and poet; *Opera Critic, Jewish Chronicle*; b. 24 Nov. 1927, Brisbane, Qld; partner, Kenneth Thomson 2006. *Education:* Griffith Univ., studied with Archie Day, Irene Fletcher, Vido Luppi and Browning Mummery. *Career:* Asst Ed., London Magazine 1957–66; Asst Literary Dir, Arts Council of GB 1966–71, Literary Dir 1971–86; Opera Critic, Jewish Chronicle 1985–; Chief Theatre Critic, Daily Telegraph 1986–92; mem. Editorial Bd Opera magazine; mem. Critics' Circle, PEN. *Publications:* The Gentle Planet 1957, Opera 66 1966, Swansong 1968, The Complete Operas of Verdi 1969, Letters of Giuseppe Verdi (ed.) 1971, The Concert Song Companion 1974, Wagner and his World 1977, The Complete Operas of Mozart 1978, W. H. Auden: The Life of a Poet 1980, The Dictionary of Opera 1983, Letter to W. H. Auden and Other Poems 1984, Giving It Way 1986, The Operas of Richard Strauss 1988, The Complete Operas of Richard Wagner 1990, The Bel Canto Operas of Rossini, Donizetti and Verdi 1994, The Pink Danube 1998, The Opera Lover's Companion 2004; contribs to anthologies, newspapers and journals, including Opera, London Magazine, Spectator, Times Literary Supplement, Encounter, New Statesman, Observer, Sunday Times. *Honours:* Hon. DUniv; Gold Medal 1993. *Address:* 125 St George's Road, London, SE1 6HY, England (home). *Telephone:* (20) 7928-1534 (home). *Fax:* (20) 7401-9099 (home).

OSBORNE, Margaret (Maggie) Ellen; American writer; b. 10 June 1941, Los Angeles, CA; m. George M. Osborne II 1972, one s. *Publications:* Alexa, 1980; Salem's Daughter, 1981; Portrait in Passion, 1981; Yankee Princess, 1982; Rage to Love, 1983; Flight of Fancy, 1984; Castles and Fairy Tales, 1986; Winter Magic, 1986; The Heart Club, 1987; Where There's Smoke, 1987; Chase the Heart, 1987; Heart's Desire, 1988; Dear Santa, 1989; Partners (with Carolyn Bransford), 1989; Jigsaw, 1990; American Pie, 1990; Lady Reluctant, 1991; Emerald Rain, 1991; Happy New Year Darling, 1992; Murder By the Book, 1992; The Pirate and His Lady, 1992; Cache Poor, 1993; A Wish and a Kiss, 1993; The Accidental Princess, 1994; The Drop in Bride, 1994; The Wives of Bowie Stone, 1994; Silver Lining, 2000; I Do, I Do, I Do, 2000.

OSBORNE, Mary Pope, BA; American writer; b. 20 May 1949, Fort Sill, OK; m. Will Osborne 1976. *Education:* University of North Carolina. *Career:* mem. Pres., Authors' Guild Inc., 1993–97. *Publications:* Run, Run, As Fast As You Can, 1982; Love Always, Blue, 1983; Best Wishes, Joe Brady, 1984; Mo to the Rescue, 1985; Last One Home, 1986; Beauty and the Beast, 1987; Christopher Columbus, Admiral of the Ocean Sea, 1987; Pandora's Box, 1987; Jason and the Argonauts, 1988; The Deadly Power of Medusa (with Will Osborne), 1988; Favorite Greek Myths, 1989; A Visit to Sleep's House, 1989; Mo and His Friends, 1989; American Tall Tales, 1990; Moonhorse, 1991; Spider Kane Series, 1992; Magic Tree House Series 1993–2004; Mermaid Tales, 1993; Molly and the Prince, 1994; Haunted Waters, 1994; Favourite Norse Myths, 1996; One World, Many Religions, 1996; Rockinghorse Christmas, 1997; Favourite Medieval Tales, 1998; Standing in the Light, 1998; The Life of Jesus, 1998, Adaline Falling Star 2000, My Secret War 2001, My Brother's Keeper 2001, After the Rain 2001, Kate and the Beanstalk 2001, The Brave Little Seamstress 2002, New York's Bravest 2002, Happy Birthday, America 2003, Tales from the Odyssey Series 2002–2005. *Honours:* Distinguished Alumnus Award, University of North Carolina, 1994. *Literary Agent:* Brandt & Hochman Literary Agents Inc., 1501 Broadway, New York, NY 10036, USA.

OSERS, Ewald, BA, FRSL; Czech poet, writer and translator; b. 13 May 1917, Prague; m. Mary Harman 1942; one s. one d. *Education:* Univ. of Prague, Univ. of London, UK. *Career:* Editorial Dir, Babel 1979–87; Fellow, Int. PEN, English Centre; mem. Poetry Soc., Soc. of Authors. *Publications:* poetry: Wish You Were Here 1976, Arrive Where We Started 1995, Snows of Yesteryear: An

Autobiography 2004, Golden City: Poems of Prague 2004; trans. of more than 150 books, including 42 vols of poetry; contrib. to magazines. *Honours:* Cyril and Methodius Order, First Class, Bulgaria 1987, Officer's Cross of Merit, Germany 1991, Order of Merit, Czech Repub. 1997; Hon. DrPhil (Palacky Univ., Olomouc) 1990; European Poetry Translator's Prize 1987, Vitezlaw Nezval Medal, Czechoslovakia 1987, Golden Pen, Macedonia 1988, Jan Masaryk Award 2001, Premia Bohemica 2001. *Address:* 33 Reades Lane, Sonning Common, Reading, Berks., RG4 9LL, England (home). *Telephone:* (118) 972-3196 (home). *Fax:* (118) 972-4950 (home). *E-mail:* osers@aol.com (home).

O'SIADHAIL, Micheal, BA, MLitt; Irish poet and writer; b. 12 Jan. 1947, Dublin; m. Brid Carroll 1970. *Education:* Trinity Coll., Dublin, Univ. of Oslo, Norway. *Career:* Lecturer, Trinity Coll., Dublin 1969–73; Prof., Dublin Inst. for Advanced Studies, 1974–87; Visiting Prof., Univ. of Iceland 1982; Ed. Poetry Ireland Review 1989–91; mem. Ireland's Advisory Cttee on Cultural Relations 1990–97; Founder-mem. Aosdána 1982–; mem. Arts Council of Ireland 1988–93, Bd Dublin Int. Writers' Festival; Founder-Chair. Ireland Literary Exchange 1992–99. *Publications:* poetry: Springnight 1983, The Image Wheel 1985, The Naked Flame (song cycle) 1987, The Chosen Garden 1990, Hail! Madam Jazz: New and Selected Poems 1992, Summerfest (song cycle) 1993, A Fragile City 1995, Our Double Time 1998, Poems 1975–1995 1999, Earlsfort Suite (three poems) 2000, The Gossamer Wall: Poems in Witness to the Holocaust 2002, Dublin Spring (song cycle) 2002, Love Life 2005, Globe 2007; other: Learning Irish 1980, Modern Irish 1989. *Honours:* Irish-American Cultural Prize for Poetry 1982, Poetry Book of the Year, Sunday Tribune 1992, Marten Toonder Prize for Literature 1998, Wingate Jewish Quarterly Literary Award Special Recommendation 2003. *Address:* 5 Trimleston Avenue, Booterstown, Co. Dublin, Ireland. *Website:* www.osiadhail.com.

OSTEN, Suzanne Carlota; Swedish playwright and theatre and film director; b. 20 June 1944, Stockholm; d. of Carl Otto Osten and Gud Osten; m.; one d. *Education:* Lund Univ. *Career:* started directing while a student 1963; ran fringe theatre group performing in schools, prisons, public areas, etc.; joined City Theatre, Stockholm 1971; f. Unga Klara Stadsteatern ind. repertory co. 1975; has written and directed over 30 plays, numerous radio and TV productions; began directing films 1980; Prof. Dramatic Inst. 1995–. *Films include:* Mamma – Our Life is Now 1982, The Mozart Brothers (Guldbagge Award for Direction 1986) 1986, Lethal Film 1988, Guardian Angel 1990, Speak Up It's So Dark 1992, Only You and Me 1994, Carmen's Revenge 1996. *Honours:* Nat. Theatre Critics Prize 1982, Paris-Creteil Prize 1993; several other awards and prizes. *Address:* Upplandsgt. 19, 113 60 Stockholm, Sweden. *Telephone:* (8) 32-54-23.

OSTRIKER, Alicia Suskin, BA, MA, PhD; American academic, poet and writer; *Faculty Member, New England College Poetry MFA Program;* b. 11 Nov. 1937, New York, NY; m. Jeremiah P. Ostriker 1958; one s. two d. *Education:* Brandeis Univ., Univ. of Wisconsin. *Career:* Asst Prof., Rutgers Univ. 1965–68, Assoc. Prof. 1968–72, Prof. of English and Creative Writing 1972–2004; mem. Faculty, New England Coll. low-residency Poetry MFA Program 2004–; mem. Modern Language Asscn, PEN, Bd Govs Poetry Soc. of America 1988–91. *Publications:* poetry: Songs 1969, Once More Out of Darkness and Other Poems 1974, A Dream of Springtime: Poems, 1970–77 1978, The Mother-Child Papers 1980, A Woman Under the Surface 1983, The Imaginary Lover 1986, Green Age 1989, The Crack in Everything 1996, The Little Space: Poems Selected and New 1968–1998 1998, The Volcano Sequence 2002, No Heaven 2005; criticism: Vision and Verse in William Blake 1965, Writing Like a Woman 1982, Stealing the Language 1986, Feminist Revision and the Bible 1993, The Nakedness of the Fathers: Biblical Visions and Revisions 1994, Dancing at the Devil's Party: Essays on Poetry, Politics and the Erotic 2000; contrib. to professional journals and general publs. *Honours:* National Endowment for the Arts Fellowship 1977, Guggenheim Fellowship 1984–85, William Carlos Williams Prize, Poetry Society of America 1986, Strousse Poetry Prize, Prairie Schooner 1987, Anna Rosenberg Poetry Award 1994, Paterson Poetry Prize 1996, San Francisco State Poetry Center Award 1997, Bookman News Book of the Year 1998. *Address:* 33 Philip Drive, Princeton, NJ 08540, USA (home). *E-mail:* ostriker@rci.rutgers.edu (home).

OSTROM, Hans Ansgar, BA, MA, PhD; American academic, writer and poet; b. 29 Jan. 1954, Grass Valley, CA; m. Jacquelyn Bacon 1983, one s. *Education:* University of California at Davis. *Career:* faculty mem., University of California at Davis, 1977–80, 1981–83; Visiting Lecturer in American Studies, Johannes Gutenberg University, Mainz, 1980–81; Prof. of English, University of Puget Sound, Tacoma, Washington, 1983–; Fulbright Senior Lecturer, University of Uppsala, 1994; mem. American Asscn of University Profs; Conference on College Composition and Communication; MLA; National Book Critics Circle; National Council of Teachers of English. *Publications:* The Living Language: A Reader (co-ed.), 1984; Leigh Hunt: A Reference Guide (with Tim Lulofs), 1985; Spectrum: A Reader (co-ed.), 1987; Lives and Moments: An Introduction to Short Fiction, 1991; Three to Get Ready (novel), 1991; Langston Hughes: A Study of the Short Fiction, 1993; Colors of a Different Horse (ed. with Wendy Bishop), 1994; Water's Night (poems with Wendy Bishop), 1994; Genres of Writing: Mapping the Territories of Discourse (ed. with Wendy Bishop), 1997; The Coast Starlight (poems), 1998. Contributions: books, journals, reviews, and magazines. *Honours:* First Prize, Harvest Awards, University of Houston, 1978; Grand Prize, Ina Coolbrith Memorial Award, 1979; First Prize, Warren Eyster Competition, New Delta Review,

1985; Second Prize, Redbook Magazine Annual Fiction Contest, 1985; John Lantz Fellowship, University of Puget Sound, 1996–97.

O'SULLIVAN, John, OBE, BA; British editor and journalist; b. 25 April 1942, Liverpool; s. of Alfred M. O'Sullivan and Margaret (née Corner) O'Sullivan. *Education:* Univ. of London. *Career:* jr tutor, Swinton Conservative Coll. 1965–67, Sr Tutor 1967–69; Ed. Swinton Journal 1967–69; London Corresp. Irish Radio and TV 1970–72; editorial writer and parl. sketchwriter, Daily Telegraph 1972–79; Ed. Policy Review 1979–83; Asst Ed. Daily Telegraph 1983–84; columnist, The Times 1984–86, Assoc. Ed. 1986–87; Editorial Page Ed. New York Post 1984–86; Ed. Nat. Review 1988–97, Ed.-at-Large 1998–; columnist, Sunday Telegraph 1988–; Dir of Studies Heritage Foundation 1979–83; Special Adviser to the Prime Minister 1987–88; Founder, Co-Chair. The New Atlantic Initiative 1996–; Conservative parl. cand. 1970; mem. Exec. Advisory Bd Margaret Thatcher Foundation, Advisory Council Social Affairs Unit, Hon. Bd Civic Inst., Prague; Fellow Inst. of Politics, Harvard Univ. 1983. *Address:* National Review, 215 Lexington Avenue, New York, NY 10016, USA. *Telephone:* (212) 679-7330.

O'SULLIVAN, Sally Angela, BA; British magazine editor; b. 26 July 1949, d. of Lorraine and Joan Connell; m. 1st Thaddeus O'Sullivan 1973 (divorced); m. 2nd Charles Wilson 1980 (divorced); one s. one d. *Education:* Ancaster House School and Trinity Coll. Dublin. *Career:* Deputy Ed. Woman's World 1977–78; Women's Ed. Daily Record 1980, Sunday Standard 1981; Ed. Options 1982–88; Launch Ed. Country Homes & Interiors 1986; Ed. She 1989, Harpers & Queen 1989–91, Good Housekeeping 1991–95; Ed.-in-Chief Ideal Home, Homes and Ideas, Women and Home, Homes and Gardens, Country Homes and Interiors, Beautiful Homes, Living, etc. magazines 1996–98; Chief Exec. Cabal Communications 1998–2003; Editorial Dir Highbury House PLC 2003–; Dir (non-exec.) London Transport 1995–2001, Anglian Water 1996–2001; mem. Broadcasting Standards Council 1994–, Nuffield Council of Bioethics 1995–99. *Honours:* Magazine Ed. of the Year 1986, 1994. *Address:* Highbury House, 1–3 Highbury Station Road, London, N1 1SE, England.

O'SULLIVAN, Vincent Gerard, BLitt, MA; New Zealand poet, writer, dramatist and editor; b. 28 Sept. 1937, Auckland. *Education:* University of Auckland, Lincoln College, Oxford. *Publications:* In Quiet, 1956; Opinions: Chapters on Gissing, Rolfe, Wilde, Unicorn, 1959; Our Burning Time, 1965; Revenants, 1969; An Anthology of Twentieth Century New Zealand Poetry (ed.), 1970; Bearings, 1973; New Zealand Poetry in the Sixties, 1973; Katherine Mansfield's New Zealand, 1975; New Zealand Short Stories (ed.), 1975; From the Indian Funeral, 1976; James K. Baxter, 1976; Miracle: A Romance, 1976; Butcher & Co, 1977; The Boy, the Bridge, the River, 1978; Brother Jonathan, Brother Kafka, 1980; Dandy Edison for Lunch and Other Stories, 1981; The Rose Ballroom and Other Poems, 1982; The Butcher Papers, 1982; The Oxford Book of New Zealand Writing Since 1945 (ed. with MacDonald P. Jackson), 1983; The Collected Letters of Katherine Mansfield (ed. with Margaret Scott), three vols, 1984–96; Shuriken (play), 1985; Survivals, 1986; The Pilate Tapes, 1986; Poems of Katherine Mansfield (ed.), 1988; Jones and Jones (play), 1989; Billy, 1990; The Snow in Spain, 1990; Palms and Minarets: Selected Stories, 1992; Selected Poems, 1992; The Oxford Book of New Zealand Short Stories (ed.), 1994; Believers to the Bright Coast, 1998. *Honours:* Jessie Mackay Award, 1965; Farmers Poetry Prize, 1967; New Zealand Book Award, 1981.

OSWALD, Debra; Australian playwright and writer; two s. *Education:* Australian Nat. Univ., Australian Film and Television School. *Plays:* Going Under 1983, Dags 1986, Lumps 1993, Gary's House 1996, Sweet Road 2000, Mr Bailey's Minder 2004. *Writing for television:* Police Rescue, Palace of Dreams, Bananas in Pyjamas, Sweet and Sour, Dancing Daze, The Secret Life of Us. *Publications include:* juvenile fiction: The Return of the Baked Bean 1990, Nathan and the Ice Rockets 1998, Frank and the Emergency Joke 2000, The Redback Leftovers 2000, The Fifth Quest 2002. *Literary Agent:* RGM Associates, PO Box 128, Surry Hills, NSW 2010, Australia. *Telephone:* (2) 9281-3911. *Fax:* (2) 9281-4705. *E-mail:* info@rgm.com.au. *Website:* www.rgm.com.au.

OTCHAKOVSKY-LAURENS, Paul, LenD; French publisher; b. 10 Oct. 1944, Valreas, Vaucluse; s. of Zelman Otchakovsky and Odette Labaume; adopted s. of Berthe Laurens; m. Monique Pierret 1970; one s. one d. *Education:* Coll. and Lycée de Sablé sur Sarthe, Coll. Montalembert de Courbevoie, Coll. St Croix de Neuilly and Faculté de Droit, Paris. *Career:* Reader, Editions Christian Bourgois 1969–70; Dir of Collection, Editions Flammarion 1970–77; Dir of Collections, then Dir of Dept Editions Hachette 1977–82; Pres. Dir-Gen. Editions P.O.L. 1983–. *Honours:* Commdr Ordre des Arts et des Lettres, Chevalier Légion d'honneur. *Address:* Editions P.O.L., 33 rue Saint-André-des-Arts, 75006 Paris, France. *Telephone:* 1-43-54-21-20. *E-mail:* otchakov@pol-editeur.fr (office).

OTOIU, Adrian, PhD; Romanian writer and poet; *Lecturer in English and American Literature, North University of Baia Mare.* *Education:* Baia Mare Coll. of Arts, Baia Mare Univ., Babes-Bolyai Univ., Cluj-Napoca. *Career:* school teacher Oradea 1981–87; children's theatre instructor 1987–1990, teacher of English Baia Mare 1990–92; Asst Lecturer North Univ. of Baia Mare 1992–95, Lecturer in English and American Literature 1995–; has participated in numerous conferences, seminars and symposia worldwide; numerous grants; mem. Writers' Union of Romania, European Soc. for the Study of English, Asscn of Professional Writers of Romania (ASPRO). *Publications:* Coaja lucrurilor sau Dansînd cu Jupuita (novel, The Skin of the Matter or Dancing with the Flayed) (Writers' Union of Romania Award for Debut in Prose, ASPRO Best Book of the Year, The Typewriter Nat. Award, Baia Mare City Council Book of the Year) 1996, Chei fierbinti pentru ferestre moi (short stories, Hot Keys for Soft Windows) (Maramures Co. Council Book of Fiction) 1998, Tourism in Maramures (co-author) 1998, Stingacii si enormitati (short stories, Enormities and Left-handed Stuff) 1999, Trafic de frontiera (critical essay, Frontier Traffic) 2000, Ochiul bifurcat, limba sasie (critical essay, The Forked Eye, the Squinting Tongue) 2003, Under Eastern Eyes: Cross-Cultural Refractions (essays) 2003; translation: At Swim-Two-Birds by Flann O'Brien (Ireland Literature Exchange Translation Bursary) 2005; contrib. to anthologies, journals and magazines. *Address:* Universitatea de Nord din Baia Mare, Catedra de Limbi Moderne, 62/A Victor Babes Street, 430083 Baia Mare, Maramures, Romania.

OTOMO, Katsuhiro; Japanese animator and manga artist; b. 14 April 1954, Tome-gun, Miyagi Pref.; m. Yoko Otomo. *Education:* Sanuma High School. *Career:* following high school, moved to Tokyo to work in manga industry, wrote short strips for Action comics, including Prosper Merimee's short novel Mateo Falcone (retitled A Gun Report) 1973; began Fireball series (unfinished) introducing themes that later became his trademark 1979; serialization of Domu (A Child's Dream) graphic novel was his first major success, selling over half a million copies 1980–82, won Science Fiction Grand Prix 1983 (first ever manga recipient); began work on his masterpiece Akira which took 10 years and over 2,000 pages to complete, animated film version released in 1988 (greatest box office success in Japan that year). *Films:* genre filmography: Koko Erotopia: Akai seifuku (scriptwriter) 1979, Shuffle (comic strip Run) 1981, Jiyu o warera (dir) 1982, Crusher Joe (special character designer) 1983, Harmagedon: Genam taisen (Armageddon: The Great Battle with Genma) (animator, character designer) 1983, Meikyu monogatari (Labyrinth Tales) (segment scriptwriter, dir and character designer) 1987, Roboto kanibauru (segment dir) 1987, Akira (scriptwriter, dir) 1988, Akira Production Report (performed as himself) 1988, Fushigi monogatari: Hachi neko wa yoku asagata kaette kuru (scriptwriter) 1988, Rojin Z (Oldman Z) (scriptwriter) 1991, Warudo apaatoment hora (World Apartment Horror) (dir) 1991, Memories (exec. producer, scriptwriter, dir, art dir) 1995, Perfect Blue (supervisor) 1997, Spriggan (gen. supervisor) 1998, Metoroporisu (Metropolis) (scriptwriter, storyboard artist) 2001, Animax Special: The Making of Metropolis (performed as himself) 2002, Steamboy (dir) 2004; non-genre filmography: Give Us Guns (dir) 1981, So What (scriptwriter) 1988. *Address:* c/o Toho Co. Ltd, 1-2-1 Yurako-cho, Chiyoda-ku, Tokyo 100-8415, Japan (office).

OTTEN, Charlotte Fennema, AB, MA, PhD; American academic (retd), poet and writer; b. 1 March 1926, Chicago, IL; m. Robert T. Otten 1948; two s. *Education:* Calvin College, Grand Rapids, Michigan State University. *Career:* Assoc. Prof. of English, Grand Valley State University, Allendale, Michigan 1971–77; Lecturer on Women and Literature, University of Michigan Extension Center 1972; Prof. of English, Calvin College, Grand Rapids 1977–91; mem. Milton Society of America; MLA; Shakespeare Asscn of America; Society for Literature and Science; Society for Textual Scholarship; Society of Children's Book Writers and Illustrators. *Publications:* Environ'd with Eternity: God, Poems, and Plants in Sixteenth and Seventeenth Century England 1985, A Lycanthropy Reader: Werewolves in Western Culture 1986, The Voice of the Narrator in Children's Literature (ed. with Gary D. Schmidt) 1989, English Women's Voices 1540–1700 1992, The Virago Book of Birth Poetry 1993, The Book of Birth Poetry 1995, January Rides the Wind 1997, The Literary Werewolf: An Anthology 2002, Something Sweeter than Honey 2002, Home in a Wildermere Fort 2006; contrib. to scholarly books and journals and poetry journals. *Honours:* several grants and fellowships; Editors' Choice, Booklist 1997. *Address:* c/o Department of English, Calvin College, 3201 Burton Street, SE, Grand Rapids, MI 49546, USA (office).

OUELLETTE, (Marie Léonne) Francine, DFA; Canadian writer; b. 11 March 1947, Montréal, Québec; one d. *Career:* mem. Union des écrivaines et des écrivains québécois. *Publications:* Au Nom du Père et du Fils, 1984; Le Sorcier, 1985; Sire Gaby du Lac, 1989; Les Ailes du Destin, 1992; Le Grand Blanc, 1993; L'Oiseau Invisible, 1994; BIP, 1995, Feu: La Rivière Profanée Vol. 1 2004, Feu: L'Etranger Vol. 2 2005. *Honours:* France-Québec, Jean Hamelin, 1986; Prix, Du Grand Public, 1993. *Address:* PO Box 30, 1044 ch Presquîle, Lac des Iles, QC J0W 1J0, Canada. *Telephone:* (819) 597-2597 (home). *Fax:* (819) 597-2597 (home).

OUETTAR, Tahar; Algerian writer and media executive; *President, Al Jahidia;* b. 1936. *Education:* Ulemas Asscn school. *Career:* fmr journalist with Liwa'u Al Barlaman At-tunissi (standard of Tunisian Parl., co-founder) and Al Sabah newspaper; published first short stories in Arabic 1955, in Tunisian Al Sabah and Al Aamal newspapers, Al Nida and Al fikr magazines; founder Ed. ind. Algeria's first weekly newspaper Al Ahrar, Constantine 1962 and Al Jamahir in Algiers 1963 (later banned); founder Al-Shaab cultural weekly 1973 (banned in 1974); founder Al-Tabyiin and Al-Qasida magazines 1990; Gen. Dir Algerian Nat. Radio 1991–92; Pres. Al Jahidia cultural asscn 1989–; joined Nat. Liberation Front (FLN) 1956, mem. nat. comm. for information, insp. and militant 1963–84, when forced to retire. *Publications:* short stories: Dukhan fi Qalbi (A Smoke in my Heart) 1961, At-Taana:t (The Blows) 1971, Al Shuhada' ya'udun hadha al usbu' (The Martyrs Return This Week) 1974; novels: Al Laz (The Ace) 1974, Al Zilzal (The Earthquake) 1974, Al hawwat wa al qasr (The Fisherman and the Palace) 1974, Ars baghl (The Wedding of a Mule) 1983, Al Ushq wa Al Mawt fi Al Zaman Al Harachi (Love and Death in

the Harrachi Time) 1982, Tajriba fi Al Ushq (A Love Experience) 1989, Rommana 1971, Al sham'aa wa al Dahaliz (The Candle and the Corridors) 1995, Al Waliyu al Tahar ya'udu ila maqamihi al zakiy (St Tahir Returns to his Holy Shrine) 1999, Al Waliyu al Tahar yarfa'u yadahu bi-du'aa (The Holy Man Prays) 2005; plays and trans. *Address:* c/o El Khabar, Maison de Presse 'Abdelkader Safir', 2 rue Farid Zouioueche, Kouba, Algiers, Algeria.

OUOLOGUEM, Yambo, (Utto Rodolph), DScS; Malian writer and poet; b. 1940, Bandiagary, Dogon, French Sudan (now Mali). *Career:* teacher, Lycée de Charenton, Paris 1964–66. *Publications:* Le Devoir de violence (Bound to Violence), 1968; Lettre ouverte à la France-nègre, 1969; Les Milles et un bibles du sexe (as Utto Rodolph), 1969; Terres du Soleil (with others), 1971. Contributions: Nouvelle somme. *Honours:* Prix Théophraste-Renaudot 1968.

OUŘEDNÍK, Patrik; Czech poet and author; b. 23 April 1957, Prague. *Career:* fmr bookseller, warehouseman, postman and medical orderly; moved to France 1984; fmr reader Robert Laffont publishing house; Visiting Lecturer on Czech Literature, Univs of Toulouse, Rennes, Carcassonne 1988–93; literary ed. L'Autre Europe (quarterly) 1986–. *Publications include:* Šmírbuch jazyka českého: Slovník nekonvenční češtiny (non-fiction, Rough-book of the Czech Language: A Dictionary of Unconventional Czech) 1988, Anebo (poems) 1992, Aniž jest co nového pod sluncem: Slova, rčení a úsloví biblického původu (non-fiction, No New Thing Under the Sun: Words, Phrases and Sayings of Biblical Origin) 1994, Pojednání o případném pití vína (Treatise on the appropriate drinking of wine) 1995, Rok čtyřiadvacet (novel, Year Twenty-Four) 1995, Neřkuli (poems, Let Alone) 1996, Europeana: Stručné dějiny dvacátého věku (novel, Europeana: A brief history of the 20th century) (Lidové Noviny Book of the Year) 2001; also translations of works of François Rabelais, Samuel Beckett and others; contrib. to Encyclopaedia Universalis, Dictionnaire des auteurs, Dictionnaire des oeuvres littéraires. *Honours:* Czech Literary Fund Award.

OUTERS, Jean-Luc; Belgian writer; b. 5 March 1949. *Publications:* L'ordre du jour (novel) 1987, Avec le temps (essay) 1993, Corps de métier (novel) 1993, La place du mort (novel) 1995, La compagnie des eaux (novel) 2001, Le bureau de l'heure (novel) 2004; contrib. numerous articles in Le Soir, La Libre Belgique, Libération. *Honours:* Prix Rossel 1993, Prix AT&T 1995. *Address:* c/o Actes Sud, BP 38, 13633 Arles Cedex, France.

OUTRAM, Richard Daley, BA; Canadian poet and publisher; b. 9 April 1930, Oshawa, ON; m. Barbara Howard 1957. *Education:* Victoria Coll., Univ. of Toronto. *Career:* co-founder (with Barbara Howard), The Gauntlet Press 1959; reading and exhibition of published work, Nat. Library of Canada 1986; mem. PEN Canada, Arts and Letters Club of Toronto. *Publications:* Eight Poems, 1959; Exsulate, Jubilate, 1966; Creatures, 1972; Seer, 1973; Thresholds, 1974; Locus, 1974; Turns and Other Poems, 1975; Arbor, 1976; The Promise of Light, 1979; Selected Poems 1960–1980, 1984; Man in Love, 1985; Benedict Abroad, 1988; Hiram and Jenny, 1989; Mogul Recollected, 1993; Around and About the Toronto Islands, 1993; Peripatetics, 1994; Tradecraft, 1994; Eros Descending, 1995. *Honours:* City of Toronto Book Award 1999. *Address:* 226 Roslin Avenue, Toronto, ON M4N 1Z6, Canada.

OVADIA, Salomone (Moni); Italian playwright, singer and actor; *Artistic Director, Mittelfest;* b. 1946, Plovdiv, Bulgaria. *Education:* Milan Univ. *Career:* fmr mem. of band, Almanacco Popolare; founder mem., Gruppo Folk Internazionale 1972; founder mem., Theather Orchestra 1990–; Artistic Dir, Mittelfest, Cividale del Friuli 2004–. *Stage productions include:* Oylem Goylem 1990, Dybbuk 1995, Taibele e il suo demone 1995, Diario ironico dall'esilio 1995, Ballata di fine millennio 1996, Pallida madre, tenera sorella 1996, Il Caso Kafka 1997, Trieste, ebrei e dintorni 1998, Mame, mamele, mamma, mamà... 1998, Joss Rakover si rivolge a Dio 1999, Il Banchiere errante 2001, L'Armata a cavallo 2003. *Publications:* Perché no? 1996, Oylem Goylem 1998, L'ebreo che ride 1998, La porta di sion 1999, Ballata di fine millennio 1999, Speriamo che tenga 2001, Le Baladin du monde yiddish 2002, Vai a te stesso 2002, Contro l'idolatria 2005, Lavoratori di tutto il mondo ridete 2007. *Address:* c/o Oylem Goylem Produzioni, via Savona 52, 20154 Milan, Italy (office). *E-mail:* oylemgoylem@tiscali.it. *Website:* www.moniovadia.it.

OVENDEN, Graham Stuart, MA, ARCA, ARCM; British art historian, artist and poet; b. 11 Feb. 1943, Alresford, Hants.; s. of the late Henry Ovenden and Gwendoline D. Hill; m. Ann. D. Gilmore 1969; one s. one d. *Education:* Alresford Dames School, Itchen Grammar School, Southampton, Southampton Coll. of Art, Royal Coll. of Music and Royal Coll. of Art. *Career:* corresp. and critic, Architecture Design Magazine; Founder mem. South West Acad. of Fine and Applied Art. *Publications:* Illustrators of Alice 1971, Victorian Children 1972, Clementina, Lady Harwarden 1973, Pre-Raphaelite Photography 1972, Victorian Erotic Photography 1973, Aspects of Lolita 1975, A Victorian Album (with Lord David Cecil) 1976, Satirical Poems and Others 1983, The Marble Mirror (poems) 1984, Lewis Carroll Photographer 1984; Graham Ovenden... A Monograph with Essays by Laurie Lee, etc. 1987, Sold With All Faults (poems) 1991; photographs: Alphonse Mucha 1973, Hill & Adamson 1973, Graham Ovenden – Childhood Streets (Photographs 1956–64) 1998; contribs on art to numerous journals. *Address:* Barley Splatt, Panters Bridge, Mount, nr Bodmin, Cornwall, England.

OVERY, Paul Vivian, BA, MA; British art critic, art historian and writer; *Senior Research Fellow, Middlesex University;* b. 14 Feb. 1940, Dorchester; s. of Arthur Overy and Joan Major; m. Tag Gronberg 1992. *Education:* King's Coll., Cambridge. *Career:* art critic, The Listener, London 1966–68; The

Financial Times, London 1968–70; Literary Ed., New Society, London 1970–71; Chief Art Critic, The Times, London 1973–78; freelance critic and writer 1978–; Reader in the History and Theory of Modernism, Middlesex Univ. 1997–2005, Sr Research Fellow 2005–; Leverhulme Research Fellowship 1984–85; mem. Nat. Union of Journalists, Soc. of Authors, Int. Asscn of Art Critics. *Publications:* Edouard Manet 1967, De Stijl 1969, Kandinsky: The Language of the Eye 1969, Paul Neagu: A Generative Context 1981, The Rietveld Schroder House (co-author) 1988, De Stijl: Art, Architecture, Design 1991, The Complete Rietveld Furniture (with Peter Vöge) 1993, The Cell in the City (essay in Cubism and Architecture) 1997, Norman Foster: 30 Colours (co-author) 1998, White Walls, White Shins (essay on cosmopolitan Modernism) 2005, The Restoration of Modern Life (essay in The Modern Period Room) 2006; contrib. to periodicals and journals. *Literary Agent:* c/o Johnson & Alcock Ltd, Clerkenwell House, 45–47 Clerkenwell Green, London, EC1R 0HT, England. *Address:* 92 South Hill Park, London, NW3 2SN, England (home).

OVERY, Richard James, PhD, FRHistS, FBA, FRSA; British historian and academic; *Professor of History, University of Exeter*; b. 23 Dec. 1947, London; s. of James Herbert Overy and Margaret Grace Overy (née Sutherland); m. 1st Tessa Coles 1969 (divorced 1976); m. 2nd Jane Giddens 1979 (divorced 1992); m. 3rd Kim Turner 1992 (divorced 2004); one s. four d. *Education:* Sexey's Blackford Grammar School, Somerset, Gonville and Caius Coll., Cambridge. *Career:* Research Fellow, Churchill Coll., Cambridge 1972–73; Fellow and Coll. Lecturer, Queen's Coll., Cambridge 1973–79; Asst Univ. Lecturer, Univ. of Cambridge 1976–79; Lecturer in History, King's Coll., London 1980–88, Reader in History 1988–92, Prof. of Modern History 1992–2004, Fellow 2003–; Prof. of History, Univ. of Exeter 2004–. *Publications:* William Morris, Viscount Nuffield 1976, The Air War 1939–1945 1980, The Nazi Economic Recovery 1982, Goering: The Iron Man 1984, The Origins of the Second World War 1987, The Road to War 1989, War and Economy in the Third Reich 1994, The Interwar Crisis 1919–1939 1994, Why the Allies Won 1995, The Penguin Atlas of the Third Reich 1996, The Times Atlas of the Twentieth Century 1996, Bomber Command 1939–1945 1997, Russia's War 1998, The Times History of the World (Gen. Ed.) 1999, The Battle 2000, Interrogations: The Nazi Elite in Allied Lands 1945 2001, The Dictators: Hitler's Germany and Stalin's Russia (Second Prize, Wolfson Prize for History 2004, Hessell-Tiltman Prize for History (jtly) 2005) 2004; contrib. to scholarly books and professional journals. *Honours:* T.S. Ashton Prize 1983, Cass Prize for Business History 1987, Samuel Eliot Morison Prize for lifetime contrib. to mil. history, Soc. for Mil. History 2001. *Address:* School of Humanities and Social Science, Amory Building, Rennes Drive, Exeter, Devon, EX4 4RJ, England (office). *Fax:* (1392) 263291 (office). *E-mail:* R.Overy@ex.ac.uk (office). *Website:* www.ex.ac.uk/shipss/history/index.php (office).

OVESEN, Ellis, MA; American poet, writer, artist and composer; b. 18 July 1923, New Effington, SD; m. Thor Lowe Smith 1949, two s. *Education:* University of Wisconsin, San Jose State University. *Career:* Teacher of English, University of Wisconsin, 1946–48, San Jose State University, 1962–63; Teaching Poetry, 1963–90; mem. National Writers Club; California Writers Club; Poetry Society of America; California State Poetry Society. *Publications:* Gloried Grass, 1970; Haloed Paths, 1973; To Those Who Love, 1974; The Last Hour: Lives Touch, 1975; A Time for Singing, 1977; A Book of Praises, 1977; Beloved I, 1980, II, 1990; The Green Madonna, 1984; The Flowers of God, 1985; The Keeper of the Word, 1985; The Wing Brush, 1986; The Year of the Snake, 1989; The Year of the Horse, 1990. Contributions: Poet India; Los Altos Town Crier; Paisley Moon; Fresh Hot Bread; Samvedana; Plowman. *Honours:* Los Altos Hills Poet, 1976–90; Hon. Doctorate, World Acad. of Arts and Culture, 1986; Dame of Merit, Knights of Malta, 1988; Golden Poet Awards, 1988, 1989, 1991; Research Fellow, 1992.

OWEN, Deborah; American/British literary agent; *Founder and Literary Agent, Deborah Owen Ltd*; b. 8 July 1942, NY; d. of the late Kyrill Schabert and Mary Babcock Smith; m. David Anthony Llewellyn Owen (now Lord Owen) 1968; two s. one d. *Career:* Founder and Literary Agent Deborah Owen Ltd 1971; Vice-Pres. Cttee Asscn of Authors' Agents 1991–94; mem. Bd of Dirs Viva radio 1993, Advisory Bd London Symphony Orchestra, Fulbright Comm. *Address:* Deborah Owen Ltd, 78 Narrow Street, Limehouse, London, E14 8BP, England (office). *Telephone:* (20) 7987-5119 (office).

OWEN, Sir Geoffrey David, Kt, MA; British newspaper editor and academic; b. 16 April 1934, s. of L. G. Owen; m. 1st Dorothy J. Owen 1961 (died 1991); two s. one d.; m. 2nd Miriam Marianna Gross 1993. *Education:* Rugby School and Balliol Coll., Oxford. *Career:* joined Financial Times as feature writer and Industrial Corresp. 1958, US Corresp. 1961, industrial 1967; Exec. Industrial Reorganization Corpn 1967–69; Dir of Admin, Overseas Div. of British Leyland Int. 1969, Dir of Personnel and Admin 1972; Deputy Ed. Financial Times 1974–80, Ed. 1981–90; Dir Business Policy Programme, Centre for Econ. Performance, LSE 1991–98, Sr Fellow Inter-disciplinary Inst. of Man. 1998–; mem. Council Foundation for Mfg and Industries 1993–; Chair. Wincott Foundation 1998–; Dir Laird Group 2000–. *Publications:* Industry in the USA 1966, From Empire to Europe 1999. *Address:* London School of Economics and Political Science, Houghton Street, London, WC2A 2AE, England. *Telephone:* (20) 7405-7686. *Fax:* (20) 7242-0392. *Website:* www.lse.ac.uk (office).

OWEN, Jan Jarrold, BA, ALAA; Australian poet and writer; b. 18 Aug. 1940, Adelaide, SA; two s. one d. *Education:* University of Adelaide. *Career:* Writer-

in-Residence, Venice Studio of the Literature Board of the Australian Council, 1989, Tasmanian State Institute of Technology, 1990, Brisbane Grammar School, 1993, Tasmanian Writers Union, 1993, B. R. Whiting Library, Rome, 1994, Rimbun Dahan, Kuala Lumpur, 1997–98; mem. South Australian Writers' Centre. *Publications:* Boy With a Telescope, 1986; Fingerprints on Light, 1990; Blackberry Season, 1993; Night Rainbows, 1994. Contributions: newspapers and magazines. *Honours:* Ian Mudie Prize, 1982; Jessie Litchfield Prize, 1984; Grenfell Henry Lawson Prize, 1985; Harri Jones Memorial Prize, 1986; Anne Elder Award, 1987; Mary Gilmore Prize, 1987; Wesley Michel Wright Poetry Prize, 1992.

OWEN, Ursula Margaret, OBE, MA; British publishing executive; *Editor-in-Chief and CEO, Index on Censorship*; b. 21 Jan. 1937, Oxford; d. of Werner and Emma Sachs; m. Roger Owen 1960 (divorced 1977); one d.; partner Frank Kermode. *Education:* Putney High School, St Hugh's Coll., Oxford and Bedford Coll., Univ. of London. *Career:* social worker and researcher into social issues 1960–69; Ed. Barrie and Jenkins Ltd publrs; Founder-mem. Virago Press 1973, Editorial Dir and Jt Man. Dir 1974–90, Non-Exec. Dir 1990–95; Cultural Policy Adviser to Lab. Party, Dir Hamlyn Fund 1990–92; joined Index on Censorship 1990, Ed. in Chief and CEO 1993–; mem. Bd New Statesman magazine 1985–90, Cttee Royal Literary Fund 1990–94; Chair. Educ. Extra 1992–2000; Adviser, Hay on Wye Festival of Literature; Gov. Parliament Hill School 1993–2003, South Bank Centre 2003–. *Publications:* Fathers: Reflections by Daughters (ed.) 1984, Whose Cities? (co-ed.) 1990. *Address:* Index, 6–8 Amwell Street, London, EC1R 1UQ (office); 1C Spencer Rise, London, NW5 1AR, England (home). *Telephone:* (20) 7278-2313 (office); (20) 7485-9060 (home). *Fax:* (20) 7278-1868 (office). *E-mail:* ursula@indexoncensorship.org (office); ursulaibook@freeuk.net (home). *Website:* www.indexonline.org (office).

OWENS, Agnes; British writer; b. 24 May 1926, Milngavie, Scotland; m. Patrick Owens 1964, three s. four d. *Career:* mem. Scottish PEN Centre. *Publications:* Gentlemen of the West, 1985; Lean Tales, 1985; Like Birds in the Wildnerness, 1986; A Working Mother, 1994; People Like That, 1996; For the Love of Willie, 1998; Bad Attitudes, 2003.

OWENS, John Edwin, BA, PhD, FRSA; British political scientist; *Professor of United States Government and Politics, University of Westminster, London*; b. 13 June 1948, Widnes, Cheshire, England; m. Margaret Owens 1971; one s. one d. *Education:* Univ. of Reading, Univ. of Warwick, Univ. of Essex. *Career:* Lecturer, Central London Polytechnic, 1978–85, Univ. of Essex, 1985–86; Senior Lecturer, 1986–98, Reader, 1998–2002, Prof. of United States Govt and Politics, 2002–, Univ. of Westminster, London; mem., Editorial Boards, Presidential Studies Quarterly, Journal of Legislative Studies, Politics and Policy; mem. Political Studies Asscn, UK; Legislative Studies Section, American Political Science Asscn; International Political Science Asscn; British Asscn of American Studies. *Publications:* After Full Employment (with John Kearne), 1986; Congress and the Presidency: Institutional Politics in a Separated System (with Michael Foley), 1996; The Republican Takeover of Congress (with Dean McSweeney), 1998; Political Leadership in Context (with Erwin C. Hargrove), 2003. Contributions: American Review of Politics; British Journal of Political Science; Journal of Legislative Studies; Political Studies; Politics and Policy; Roll Call; Times Higher Educational Supplement. *Address:* Centre for the Study of Democracy, University of Westminster, 32–38 Wells Street, London W1T 3UW, England (office). *E-mail:* owensj@westminster.ac.uk (office).

OWENS, Rochelle; American poet, dramatist, critic, academic and translator; *Adjunct Professor, University of Oklahoma at Norman*; b. 2 April 1936, New York, NY; m. 1st David Owens 1956 (divorced 1959); m. 2nd George Economou 1962. *Education:* New School for Social Research, New York, Univ. of Montréal, Alliance Française, Paris, New York. *Career:* Visiting Lecturer, Univ. of California at San Diego 1982; writer-in-residence, Brown Univ. 1989; Adjunct Prof., Univ. of Oklahoma at Norman 1993–; poet- and playwright-in-residence, Deep South Writers Conference, Univ. of Southwestern Louisiana 1997; mem. ASCAP, Dramatists' Guild. *Publications:* poetry: Not Be Essence That Cannot Be 1961, Four Young Lady Poets (with others) 1962, Salt and Core 1968, I Am the Babe of Joseph Stalin's Daughter: Poems 1961–1971 1972, Poems From Joe's Garage 1973, The Joe 82 Creation Poems 1974, The Joe Chronicles, Part 2 1979, Shemuel 1979, French Light 1984, Constructs 1985, W. C. Fields in French Light 1986, How Much Paint Does the Painting Need 1988, Black Chalk 1992, Rubbed Stones and Other Poems 1994, New and Selected Poems, 1961–1996 1997, Luca: Discourse on Life and Death 2001; plays: Futz and What Came After 1968, The Karl Marx Play and Others 1974, Emma Instigated Me 1976, The Widow and the Colonel 1977, Mountain Rites 1978, Chucky's Hunch 1982, The Passers by Liliane Atlan (trans.) 1993, Plays by Rochelle Owens: Collection of 4 Plays 2000; editor: Spontaneous Combustion: Eight New American Plays 1972; contrib. to anthologies and journals. *Honours:* Rockefeller Grants 1965, 1976, Obie Awards 1965, 1967, 1982, Yale School of Drama Fellowship 1968, American Broadcasting Corporation Fellowship 1968, Guggenheim Fellowship 1971, Nat. Endowment for the Arts Award 1976, Villager Award 1982, Franco-Anglais Festival de Poésie, Paris 1991, Rockefeller Foundation Resident Scholar, Bellagio, Italy 1993, Oklahoma Centre for the Book Award 1998. *Address:* 1401 Magnolia, Norman, OK 73072, USA.

OXLEY, William; British poet, writer, philosopher and translator; b. 29 April 1939, Manchester; m. Patricia Holmes 1963; two d. *Education:* Manchester

Coll. of Commerce. *Career:* accountant, part-time gardener and actor 1956–76; freelance poet and writer 1976–; fmr mem. Gen. Council Poetry Soc.; fmr Asst Ed. Acumen; Founder Long Poem Group (co-ed. of its newsletter); dubbed "Britain's first Europoet" 1980s. *Publications:* The Dark Structures 1967, New Workings 1969, Passages from Time: Poems from a Life 1971, The Icon Poems 1972, Sixteen Days in Autumn (travel) 1972, Opera Vetera 1973, Mirrors of the Sea 1973, Eve Free 1974, Mundane Shell 1975, Superficies 1976, The Exile 1979, The Notebook of Hephaestus and Other Poems 1981, Poems of a Black Orpheus 1981, The Synopthegms of a Prophet 1981, The Idea and Its Imminence 1982, Of Human Consciousness 1982, The Cauldron of Inspiration 1983, A Map of Time 1984, The Triviad and Other Satires 1984, The Inner Tapestry 1985, Vitalism and Celebration 1987, The Mansands Trilogy 1988, Mad Tom on Tower Hill 1988, The Patient Reconstruction of Paradise 1991, Forest Sequence 1991, In the Drift of Words 1992, The Playboy 1992, Cardboard Troy 1993, The Hallsands Tragedy 1993, Collected Longer Poems 1994, Completing the Picture (ed.) 1995, The Green Crayon Man 1997, No Accounting for Paradise (autobiog.) 1999, Firework Planet (children's) 2000, Reclaiming the Lyre: New and Selected Poems 2001, Modern Poets of Europe (co-ed.) 2003, Namaste: Nepal Poems 2004, London Visions 2005; contrib. to anthologies, magazines and journals including The Scotsman, New Statesman, The London Magazine, Stand, The Independent, The Spectator, The Observer in the UK and Sparrow, The Formalist in the USA. *Honours:* Millennium Year of the Artist Poet-in-Residence for Torbay, S Devon 2000–01, Echoes of Gilgamesh magazine Award for online long poem (Over the Hills of Hampstead) 2002. *Address:* 6 The Mount, Furzeham, Brixham, South Devon TQ5 8QY, England (home). *Telephone:* (1803) 851098 (home). *Fax:* (1803) 851098 (home). *E-mail:* pwoxley@aol.com (home).

OYUUN, Eredenebatiin, PhD; Mongolian theatre producer and writer; b. 27 Dec. 1918, Ulan Bator; d. of Erdenebat and Tsetseg; m. Col Purev 1935 (died 1951); one s. one d. *Education:* Mongolian State Univ. *Career:* Trans., Asst Theatre Producer 1934–52, Theatre Producer 1957–80; now retd, researching into the history of the theatre; State Prize Laureate 1946; title of People's Actress conferred 1959. *Publications:* plays: I don't go there, The Love, My Beautiful Mother; has written more than ten plays and 30 short stories, and translated over 40 plays into Mongolian. *Address:* State Drama Theatre, Ulan Bator, Mongolia; Central Post Office, POB 265, Ulan Bator, Mongolia.

OZ, Amos, BA; Israeli writer; b. 4 May 1939, Jerusalem; m. Nily Zuckermann 1960; one s. two d. *Education:* Hebrew Univ. Jerusalem. *Career:* Kibbutz Hulda 1957–86; teacher of literature and philosophy, Hulda High School and Givat Brenner Regional High School 1963–86; Visiting Fellow, St Cross Coll. Oxford 1969–70; Writer-in-residence Hebrew Univ. Jerusalem 1975; Visiting Prof. Univ. of Calif. at LA (Berkeley); Writer-in-Residence and Prof. of Literature Colorado Coll., Colorado Springs 1984–85; Prof. of Hebrew Literature, Ben Gurion Univ. 1987–, Agnon Chair in Modern Hebrew 1990–; Visiting Prof. of Literature, Writer in Residence, Boston Univ. 1987; Writer-in-Residence, Hebrew Univ. 1990– and Prof of Literature, Princeton Univ. 1997, Weidenfeld Visiting Prof. of European Comparative Literature St Anne's Coll., Oxford 1998. *Publications:* novels: Elsewhere, Perhaps 1966, My Michael 1968, Touch the Water, Touch the Wind 1973, A Perfect Peace 1982, Black Box 1987, To Know a Woman 1989, The Third Condition (Fima) 1991, The Same Sea 1991, Don't Call It Night 1994, Panther in the Basement 1995; novellas and short stories: Where the Jackals Howl 1965, Unto Death 1971,

Different People (selected anthology) 1974, The Hill of Evil Counsel 1976, Soumchi (children's story) 1978, Telling Tales (contrib. to charity anthology) 2004; essays: Under this Blazing Light 1979, In the Land of Israel 1983, The Slopes of Lebanon 1987, Report of the Situation (in German) 1992, Israel, Palestine and Peace 1994, A Story Begins 1996, All Our Hopes 1998, But These Are Two Different Wars 2002; other: A Tale of Love and Darkness (memoir) (The Jewish Quarterly Wingate Literary Prize for non-fiction 2005) 2002. *Honours:* Officier, Ordre des Arts et des Lettres; Kt's Cross, Légion d'honneur 1997; Dr hc (Hebrew Union Coll., Cincinnati, OH and Jerusalem) 1988, (Western New England Coll.) 1988, (Tel-Aviv) 1992; Holon Prize 1965, Brenner Prize 1976, Zeev Award for Children's Books 1978, Bernstein Prize 1983, Bialik Prize 1986, Wingate Prize, London 1988, Prix Femina, Paris 1989 (for novel Black Box), German Publrs' Int. Peace Prize 1992, Luchs Prize for Children's Books (Germany) 1993, Hamore Prize 1993, Israeli Prize for Literature 1998, Freedom of Speech Prize, Writers' Union of Norway 2002, Int. Medal of Tolerance, Polish Ecumenical Council 2002, Goethe Cultural Prize, Frankfurt, Germany 2005, Premio Príncipe de Asturias (for literature) 2007. *Address:* Ben Gurion University of the Negev, PO Box 653, Beersheva 84105, Israel. *Telephone:* (8) 6461111. *Fax:* (8) 6237682. *E-mail:* acsec@bgumail.bgu.ac.il (office). *Website:* www.bgu.ac.il (office).

OZICK, Cynthia, MA; American writer and poet; b. 17 April 1928, New York, NY; d. of William Ozick and Celia Regelson; m. Bernard Hallote 1952; one d. *Education:* New York Univ. and Ohio State Univ. *Career:* mem. PEN, Authors' League, American Acad. of Arts and Sciences, American Acad. of Arts and Letters; Founder mem. Acad. Universelle des Cultures; Guggenheim Fellow 1982. *Publications:* Trust 1966, The Pagan Rabbi and Other Stories 1971, Bloodshed and Three Novellas 1976, Levitation: Five Fictions 1982, Art & Ardor: Essays 1983, The Cannibal Galaxy 1983, The Messiah of Stockholm 1987, Metaphor & Memory: Essays 1989, The Shawl 1989, Epodes: First Poems 1992, What Henry James Knew, and Other Essays on Writers 1993, Blue Light (play) 1994, Portrait of the Artist as a Bad Character and Other Essays on Writing 1995, The Shawl (novel) 1996, Fame & Folly: Essays 1996, The Puttermesser Papers (novel) 1997, The Best American Essays (ed.) 1998, Quarrel & Quandary (essays) 2000, Heir to the Glimmering World (novel published as The Bear Boy in UK) 2004, Collected Stories 2006, A Din in the Head: Essays 2006; contrib. fiction to numerous periodicals and anthologies including New Criterion, New Yorker, Harper's, Partisan Review, Yale Review, New York Times Magazine, Best American Short Stories, O. Henry Prize Stories, Best American Essays, The Oxford Book of Jewish Short Stories, The Norton Anthology of Jewish American Literature. *Honours:* Hon. degrees (Yeshiva) 1984, (Hebrew Union Coll.) 1984, (Williams Coll.) 1986, (Hunter Coll.) 1987, (Jewish Theological Seminary) 1988, (Adelphi) 1988, (State Univ. of NY) 1989, (Brandeis) 1990, (Bard Coll.) 1991, (Spertus Coll.) 1991, (Seton Hall Univ.) 1999, (Rutgers Univ.) 1999, (Asheville) 2000, (New York) 2001, (Bar-Ilan) 2002, (Baltimore Hebrew Univ.) 2004, (Georgetown) 2007; Mildred and Harold Strauss Living Award, American Acad. of Arts and Letters 1983; Rea Award for short story 1986, PEN/Spiegel-Diamonstein Award for the Art of the Essay 1997, Harold Washington Literary Award, City of Chicago 1997, John Cheever Award 1999, Lotos Club Medal of Merit 2000, Lannan Foundation Award 2000, Nat. Critics' Circle Award for Criticism 2001, Koret Foundation Award for Literary Studies 2001, Mary McCarthy Award, Bard Coll. 2007. *Fax:* (914) 654-6583.

P

PACK, Robert, BA, MA; American academic, poet and writer; *Abernathy Professor, Middlebury College, Vermont*; b. 29 May 1929, New York, NY; m. 1st Isabelle Miller 1950; m. 2nd Patricia Powell 1961; two s. one d. *Education:* Dartmouth Coll., Columbia Univ. *Career:* teacher, Barnard Coll. 1957–64; Abernathy Prof., Middlebury Coll., Vermont 1970–; Dir, Bread Loaf Writers Conferences 1973–. *Publications:* poetry: The Irony of Joy 1955, A Stranger's Privilege 1959, Guarded by Women 1963, Selected Poems 1964, Home from the Cemetery 1969, Nothing But Light 1972, Keeping Watch 1976, Waking to My Name: New and Selected Poems 1980, Faces in a Single Tree: A Cycle of Monologues 1984, Clayfield Rejoices, Clayfield Laments: A Sequence of Poems 1987, Before It Vanishes: A Packet for Prof. Pagels 1989, Fathering the Map: New and Selected Later Poems 1993; other: Wallace Stevens: An Approach to his Poetry and Thought 1958, Affirming Limits: Essays on Morality, Choice and Poetic Form 1985, The Long View: Essays on the Discipline of Hope and Poetic Craft 1991; editor: The New Poets of England and America (with Donald Hall and Louis Simpson) 1957, Poems of Doubt and Belief: An Anthology of Modern Religious Poetry (with Tom Driver) 1964, Literature for Composition on the Theme of Innocence and Experience (with Marcus Klein) 1966, Short Stories: Classic, Modern, Contemporary (with Marcus Klein) 1967, Keats: Selected Letters 1974, The Bread Loaf Anthology of Contemporary American Poetry (with Sydney Lea and Jay Parini) 1985, The Bread Loaf Anthology of Contemporary American Short Stories (with Jay Parini, two vols) 1987, 1989, Poems for a Small Planet: An Anthology of Nature Poetry (with Jay Parini) 1993. *Honours:* Fulbright Fellowship 1956, American Acad. of Arts and Letters grant 1957, Borestone Mountain Poetry Award 1964, Nat. Endowment for the Arts grant 1968. *Address:* c/o Middlebury College, Middlebury, VT 05742, USA.

PACKER, Zuwena Z., BA, MA, MFA; American writer; b. 12 Jan. 1973, Chicago. *Education:* Yale Univ., Johns Hopkins Univ. *Career:* fmr teacher of English and Creative Writing in Baltimore; fmr Stegner Fellow and Jones Lecturer, Stanford Univ.; currently Sr Visiting Prof. of Creative Writing, Calif. Coll. of the Arts. *Publications:* Drinking Coffee Elsewhere (short stories) 2003. *Honours:* Whiting Writer's Award, Rona Jaffe Foundation Writers Award, Ms Giles Whiting Award, Billingham Review Award; Guggenheim Fellowship 2005. *Address:* c/o Writing and Literature Program, California College of the Arts, 1111 Eighth Street, San Francisco, CA 94107-2247, USA. *Telephone:* (415) 703-9500. *Website:* www.cca.edu/academics/writingliterature.

PADEL, Ruth, BA, PhD, FRSL; British poet, writer and journalist; b. 8 May 1946, London, England; one d. *Education:* Univ. of Oxford. *Career:* mem. PEN, Royal Zoological Soc., Soc. of Authors. *Publications:* poetry: Alibi 1985, Summer Snow 1990, Angel 1993, Fusewire 1996, Rembrandt Would Have Loved You 1998, Voodoo Shop 2002, The Soho Leopard 2004; non-fiction: In and Out of the Mind 1992, Whom Gods Destroy 1995, I'm a Man 2000, 52 Ways of Looking at a Poem 2002, Tigers in Red Weather 2005, The Poem and the Journey: And Sixty Poems to Read Along the Way 2007. *Honours:* Nat. Poetry Competition First Prize 1996, Poetry Book Soc. Recommendation 1993, 2002, Choice 1998, 2004, Cholmondley Award 2004. *Literary Agent:* Conville and Walsh, 2 Ganton Street, London, W1F 7GL, England.

PADFIELD, Peter Lawrence Notton; British author and historian; b. 3 April 1932, Kolkata, India; m. Dorothy Jean Yarwood 1960, one s. two d. *Career:* mem. Society for Nautical Research. *Publications:* The Sea is a Magic Carpet, 1960; The Titanic and the Californian, 1965; An Agony of Collisions, 1966; Aim Straight: A Biography of Admiral Sir Percy Scott, 1966; Broke and the Shannon: A Biography of Admiral Sir Philip Broke, 1968; The Battleship Era, 1972; Guns at Sea: A History of Naval Gunnery, 1973; The Great Naval Race: Anglo-German Naval Rivalry 1900–1914, 1974; Nelson's War, 1978; Tide of Empires: Decisive Naval Campaigns in the Rise of the West, Vol. I 1481–1654, 1979, Vol. II 1654–1763, 1982; Rule Britannia: The Victorian and Edwardian Navy, 1981; Beneath the Houseflag of the P & O, 1982; Dönitz, The Last Führer, 1984; Armada, 1988; Himmler, Reichsführer SS, 1990; Hess: Flight for the Führer, 1991, revised edn as Hess: The Führer's Disciple, 1993; War Beneath the Sea: Submarine Conflict 1939–1945, 1995; Maritime Supremacy and the Opening of the Western Mind: Naval Campaigns that Shaped the Modern World 1588–1782, 1999. Fiction: The Lion's Claw, 1978; The Unquiet Gods, 1980; Gold Chains of Empire, 1982; Salt and Steel, 1986. *Literary Agent:* The Andrew Lownie Literary Agency Ltd, 36 Great Smith Street, London SW1P 3BU, England. *E-mail:* mail@andrewlownie.co.uk.

PADGAONKAR, Dileep, PhD; Indian journalist; *Consulting Editor and Columnist, Times of India*; b. 1 May 1944, Pune; s. of Vasant Padgaonkar and Shakuntala Padgaonkar (née Kattakar); m. Latika Tawadey 1968; two s. *Education:* Fergusson Coll., Pune, Institut des Hautes Etudes Ciné-matographiques, Sorbonne, France. *Career:* Paris Corresp., The Times of India 1968–73; Asst Ed., Bombay and Delhi 1973–78, Assoc. Ed. and Exec. Ed. The Times of India Group 1986–88, Ed. 1988–94, Dir (Corp.) and Exec. Man. Ed. 1998–2002, Consulting Ed. and Columnist 2002–; f. Asia Pacific Communication Assocs 1994; Information Chief for Asia and Pacific, UNESCO 1978–81; Deputy Dir Office of Public Information, Paris 1981–85, Acting Dir 1985–86, Acting Dir Communication Sector 1986; Presenter Question Time India, BBC World. *Television:* presenter, BBC World's Question Time India panel discussion programme. *Publication:* When Bombay Burned (ed.) 1993. *Honours:* Chevalier, Legion d'honneur 2001. *Address:* The Times of India, Times House, 7 Bahadur Shah Zafar Marg, New Delhi 110002 (office); C-313, Defence Colony, New Delhi 110024, India (home). *Telephone:* (11) 3312277 (office); (11) 4697949 (home). *Fax:* (11) 3323346. *Website:* www.timesofindia.com (office).

PADMANABHAN, Neela, BSc, BSc (Eng), FIE; Indian engineer (retd), poet and writer; b. 26 April 1938, Trivandrum; s. of Neelakanta Pillai and Janaki Ammal; m. U. Krishnammal 1963; one s. three d. *Education:* Kerala Univ. *Career:* joined Kerala State Electricity Bd as Jr Engineer 1963, retd as Deputy Chief Eng. 1993; mem. Bd of Studies Kerala Univ. 1985–89; mem. Authors' Guild of India, PEN, Poetry Soc. of India, Sahitya Akademi (exec. cttee 1998–2002). *Publications:* Talaimuraikal (novel, trans. as Generations) 1968, Pallikondapuram (novel, trans. as The City Where God Sleeps) 1970, Filekal (novel) 1973, Bothayil Karainthavarkal, Uravugal (novel, trans. as Relations) (Rajah Sir Annamalai Chettiar Award 1977) 1975, Neela Padmanabhan Kavithaikal (poems) 1975, Min ulakam (novel, trans. as World of Power) 1976, Anubhavankal (novel, trans. as Experiences) 1977, Samar (novel, trans. as Agitation) 1977, Vattathin Veliye (novel, trans. as Beyond the Circle) 1980, Surrender and Other Poems 1982, Naa Kaakka (poems) 1984, Therodum Veedhi (novel) (Government of Tamilnadu Award) 1987, Peyarilenna (poems) 1993, Koondinul Pakshikal (novel) 1995, Neela Padmanabhan 148 Kavithai-kal (poems) 2003; 10 short story collections, 7 essay collections; contrib. to many publications. *Honours:* Tamilannai Prize 1987, Lily Deva Sikamani Award 1994, Tiruppur Tamilsangham Award 1995, Ulloorparameswaraiyer Poetry Award 2001, Sahitya Akademi Award for Translation 2003, Bhasha Bharathi Samman Award 2003–04. *Address:* Nilakant 39/1870 Kuriyathi Bypass Road, Manacaud PO, Thiruvanantha Puram 695009, Kerala, India (home). *Telephone:* (471) 2476060 (home). *E-mail:* neelapadmanabham1@rediffmail.com (home). *Website:* m-blog.com/padmanabhan (home).

PADOVANO, Anthony Thomas, BA, MA, PhL, PhD; American academic and writer; *Distinguished Professor of Literature and Philosophy, Ramapo College of New Jersey*; b. 18 Sept. 1934, Harrison, NJ, USA; m. Theresa P. Lackamp 1974; three s. one d. *Education:* Seton Hall Univ., Pontifical Gregorian Univ., Rome, St Thomas Pontifical Int. Univ., Rome, New York Univ., Fordham Univ. *Career:* Prof. of Systematic Theology, Darlington School of Theology, Mahwah, NJ, 1962–74; Prof. of Literature and Philosophy, Ramapo Coll. of New Jersey 1971–, now Distinguished Prof.; various visiting professorships; mem. Catholic Theological Society of America; International Federation of Married Priests; International Thomas Merton Society; Priests for Equality. *Publications:* The Cross of Christ, The Measure of the World, 1962; The Estranged God, 1966; Who Is Christ?, 1967; Belief in Human Life, 1969; American Culture and the Quest for Christ, 1970; Dawn Without Darkness, 1971; Free to Be Faithful, 1972; Eden and Easter, 1974; A Case for Worship, 1975; Presence and Structure, 1975; America: Its People, Its Promise, 1975; The Human Journey: Thomas Merton, Symbol of a Century 1982, Trilogy 1982, Contemplation and Compassion, 1984; Winter Rain: A Play in One Act and Six Scenes, 1985; His Name is John: A Play in Four Acts, 1986; Christmas to Calvary, 1987; Love and Destiny, 1987; Summer Lightning: A Play in Four Acts and Four Seasons, 1988; Conscience and Conflict, 1989; Reform and Renewal: Essays on Authority, Ministry and Social Justice, 1990; A Celebration of Life, 1990; The Church Today: Belonging and Believing, 1990; Scripture in the Street, 1992; A Retreat with Thomas Merton: Biography as Spiritual Journey, 1995; Hope is a Dialogue, 1998; Resistance and Renewal 2002, Life Choices 2004; contrib. to books and periodicals. *Honours:* awards and citations; all professional and personal papers retained in the archives of the Univ. of Notre Dame, IN. *Address:* c/o School of American and International Studies, Ramapo College of New Jersey, Mahwah, NJ 07430 (office); 9 Millstone Drive, Morris Plains, NJ 07950, USA (home). *Telephone:* (201) 684-7430 (office). *E-mail:* apadovan@ramapo.edu (office); tpadovan@optonline.net (home). *Website:* apadovano.com (home).

PADURA FUENTES, Leonardo, BA; Cuban novelist, essayist and critic; b. 1955, Havana. *Education:* Havana Univ. *Career:* fmr investigative journalist. *Publications include:* Con la espada y la pluma: Comentarios al Inca Garcilaso (literary criticism), Lo real maravilloso: creación y realidad (literary criticism), El viaje más largo, La cultura y la revolucion cubana: conversaciones en La Habana, La novela de mi vida, La puerta de Alcalá y otras cacerías, Pasado perfecto (vol. one of Las cuatro estaciones quartet) 1991, Vientos de cuaresma (vol. two of Las cuatro estaciones quartet) 1994, Máscaras (vol. three of Las cuatro estaciones quartet) (Premio Café Gijón) 1997, Paisaje de otoño (vol. four of Las cuatro estaciones quartet) (Int. Asscn of Crime Writers Premio Hammett 1998) 1998, Adios Hemingway (novella), La neblina del ayer. *Address:* c/o Canongate Books, 14 High Street, Edinburgh, EH1 1TE, Scotland.

PAGE, Bruce; British journalist; b. 1 Dec. 1936, London; s. of Roger Page and Amy B. Page; m. 1st Anne Gillison 1964 (divorced 1969); m. 2nd Anne L. Darnborough 1969; one s. one d. *Education:* Melbourne High School and Melbourne Univ., Australia. *Career:* trained as journalist, Melbourne Herald 1956–60; Evening Standard, London 1960–62; Daily Herald, London 1962–64; various exec. posts, Sunday Times, London 1964–76; Assoc. Ed. Daily Express

1977; Ed. New Statesman 1978–82; Dir Direct Image Systems and Communications 1992–95; various awards for journalism. *Publications:* co-author: Philby, the Spy who Betrayed a Generation, An American Melodrama, Do You Sincerely Want to be Rich?, Destination Disaster, Ulster (contrib.), The Yom Kippur War, The British Press; author: The Murdoch Archipelago 2003. *Honours:* British Newspaper Hall of Fame 2005. *Address:* c/o PFD Limited, Drury House, 34–43 Russell Street, London WC2B 5HA (office); Beach House, Shingle Streeet, Shottisham, Suffolk, IP12 3BE, England (home). *Telephone:* (1394) 411427 (home); (7771) 641018 (mobile). *E-mail:* bruce@pages.dircon.co.uk (office).

PAGE, Clarence, BS; American journalist and columnist; b. 2 June 1947, Dayton, OH; m. Lisa Johnson Cole 1987. *Education:* Ohio University. *Career:* reporter and Asst City Ed., Chicago Tribune 1969–80, columnist and editorial bd mem. 1984–; Dir Dept of Community Affairs, WBBM-TV 1980–82; syndicated columnist; many television appearances. *Publications:* contrib. to various periodicals. *Honours:* James P. McGuire Award 1987, Pulitzer Prize for Commentary 1989.

PAGE, Geoffrey Donald, BA, DipEd; Australian poet, writer and educator; b. 7 July 1940, Grafton, NSW; one s. *Education:* Univ. of New England, Armidale, NSW. *Career:* Head, Dept of English, Narrabundah Coll., Canberra 1974–2001; Writer-in-Residence, Univ. of Wollongong, NSW 1982, Curtin Univ. 1990, Edith Cowan Univ. 1993; mem. Australian Soc. of Authors. *Publications:* The Question 1971, Smalltown Memorials 1975, Collecting the Weather 1978, Cassandra Paddocks 1980, Clairvoyant in Autumn 1983, Shadows from Wire: Poems and Photographs of Australians in the Great War Australian War Memorial (ed.) 1983, Benton's Conviction 1985, Century of Clouds: Selected Poems of Guillaume Apollinaire (co-trans. with Wendy Coutts) 1985, Collected Lives 1986, Smiling in English, Smoking in French 1987, Footwork 1988, Winter Vision 1989, Invisible Histories 1990, Selected Poems 1991, Gravel Corners 1992, On the Move (ed.) 1992, Human Interest 1994, Reader's Guide to Contemporary Australian Poetry 1995, The Great Forgetting 1996, The Secret 1997, Bernie McGann: A Life in Jazz 1998, Collateral Damage 1999, The Scarring 1999, Darker and Lighter 2001, Day after Day: Selected Poems of Salvatore Quasimodo (co-trans. with R. F. Brissenden and Loredana Nardi-Ford) 2002, Drumming on Water 2003, The Indigo Book of Modern Australian Sonnets 2003, My Mother's God 2003, Cartes Postales 2004, Freehold 2005, Agnostic Skies 2006; contrib. to newspapers and magazines. *Honours:* Australia Council Literature Board Grants 1974, 1983, 1987, 1989, 1992, 1997, 2000, Queensland Premier's Prize 1990, Patrick White Literary Award 2001, ACT Poetry Award 2004. *Address:* 8/40 Leahy Close, Narrabundah, ACT 2604, Australia (home). *E-mail:* geoffdpage@ozemail.com.au (home).

PAGE, Jeremy Neil, BA, MA, DipRSA; British educator, poet and editor; b. 23 Feb. 1958, Folkestone, Kent, England. *Education:* University of Warwick, University of Bristol. *Career:* Ed., The Frogmore Papers 1983–; teacher and trainer 1984–, Dir of Studies, Int. House, London 1995–; founder, Frogmore Poetry Prize 1987; teacher, Academia Britannica, Arezzo, Italy 1987–88; Series Ed., Crabflower Pamphlets 1990–; Deputy Dir Sussex Language Inst., Univ. of Sussex. *Publications:* Bliss (poems) 1989, Secret Dormitories (poems) 1993, Think Ahead To First Certificate Workbook (with Jon Naunton) 1993, Poetry South East 2000 (ed.) 2000, The Alternative Version (poems) 2001, Search (with Janet Hardy-Gould) 2002, The Norwood Mystery (adaptation) 2006. *Honours:* Acad. of Paraphysical Science Grand Transcendent Knight Salamander 1992. *Address:* Sussex Language Institute, University of Sussex, Falmer, Brighton, East Sussex BN1 9SH, England (office). *E-mail:* J.N.Page@sussex.ac.uk (office).

PAGE, Katherine Hall, AB, EdM, DEd; American writer; b. 9 July 1947, New Jersey, USA; m. Alan Hein 1975; one s. *Education:* Wellesley College, Tufts University, Harvard University. *Career:* mem. Mystery Readers International; MWA; Authors' Guild; Sisters in Crime; American Crime Writers League; Society of Children's Bookwriters and Illustrators; International Asscn of Crime Writers; Boston Author's Club; Brontë Society; Agatha Christie Society. *Publications:* The Body in the Belfry, 1990; The Body in the Bouillon, 1991; The Body in the Kelp, 1991; The Body in the Vestibule, 1992; The Body in the Cast, 1993; The Body in the Basement, 1994; The Body in the Bog, 1996; The Body in the Fjord, 1997; The Body in the Bookcase, 1998; The Body in the Big Apple, 1999; The Body in the Moonlight, 2001, The Body in the Bonfire 2002, The Body in the Lighthouse 2003, The Body in the Attic 2004, The Body in the Snowdrift 2005; children's fiction: Christie and Company, 1996; Christie and Company Down East, 1997; Christie and Company in the Year of the Dragon, 1998; Bon Voyage Christie and Company, 1999. *Honours:* Agatha for Best First Domestic Mystery 1991, Agatha for Best Short Story 2002. *Literary Agent:* Sanford J. Greenburger Associates Inc, 55 Fifth Avenue, New York, NY 10003, USA. *Website:* www.katherine-hall-page.org.

PAGE, Louise, BA; British playwright; b. 7 March 1955, London, England. *Education:* University of Birmingham. *Career:* Resident Playwright, Royal Court Theatre, 1982–83. *Publications:* Want Ad, 1977; Glasshouse, 1977; Tissue, 1978; Lucy, 1979; Hearing, 1979; Flaws, 1980; House Wives, 1981; Salonika, 1982; Real Estate, 1984; Golden Girls, 1984; Beauty and the Beast, 1985; Diplomatic Wives, 1989; Adam Wasxa Gardener, 1991; Like to Live, 1992; Hawks and Doves, 1992. Other: Radio and television plays. *Honours:* George Devine Award 1982.

PAGE, Norman; British academic and writer; b. 8 May 1930, Kettering, Northamptonshire, England; m. Jean Hampton 1958; three s. one d. *Education:* BA, 1951, MA, 1955, Emmanuel College, Cambridge; PhD, University of Leeds, 1968. *Career:* Principal Lecturer in English, Ripon College of Education, Yorkshire, 1960–69; Asst Prof., 1969–70, Assoc. Prof., 1970–75, Prof. of English, 1975–85, University of Alberta; Prof. of Modern English Literature, University of Nottingham, 1985–; mem. Royal Society of Canada, fellow; Thomas Hardy Society; Vice-Pres., Newstead Abbey Byron Society; Vice-Pres., Tennyson Society. *Publications:* The Language of Jane Austen, 1972; Speech in the English Novel, 1973; Thomas Hardy, 1977; A. E. Housman: A Critical Biography, 1983; A Kipling Companion, 1984; E. M. Forster, 1988; Tennyson: An Illustrated Life, 1992; Auden and Isherwood: The Berlin Years, 1998; Oxford Reader's Companion to Hardy, 2000. Contributions: London Magazine; London Review of Books; Literary Review. *Honours:* Guggenheim Fellowship, 1979; University of Alberta Research Prize, 1983. *Address:* 23 Braunston Road, Oakham, Rutland LE15 6LD, England.

PAGE, Patricia Kathleen, (Judith Cape), CC, OBE; Canadian writer and painter; b. 23 Nov. 1916, UK; d. of the late Lionel F. and Rose Laura (née Whitehouse) Page; William Arthur Irwin 1950. *Education:* St Hilda's School for Girls (Calgary). *Career:* solo exhbns in Mexico and Canada, numerous group exhbns; works featured in collections including Nat. Gallery of Canada and The Art Gallery of Ontario; subject of film Still Waters 1991, of two-part sound feature The White Glass 1996; Symposium Trent Univ. 2002. *Recording:* The Filled Pen (poetry readings) 2005. *Publications:* The Sun and The Moon 1944, As Ten as Twenty 1946, The Metal and the Flower 1954, Cry Ararat! – Poems New and Selected 1967, The Sun and The Moon and Other Fictions 1973, Poems – Selected and New 1974, To Say the Least (ed) 1979, Evening Dance of the Grey Flies 1981, The Travelling Musicians (text) 1984, The Glass Air 1985, Brazilian Journal (Hubert Evens Prize, British Columbia Book Awards 1988) 1987, A Flask of Sea Water 1989, The Glass Air (poems) 1991, The Travelling Musicians (children's book) 1991, Unless the Eye Catch Fire 1994, The Goat that Flew 1994, Hologram – A Book of Glosas (poems) 1994, A Children's Hymn (with music by Harry Somers), The Malahat Review (special issue) 1996, The Hidden Room – Collected Poems 1997, Alphabetical (poem) 1998, Compass Rose (poems in Italian trans) 1998, A Somewhat Irregular Renga (jtly) (for the CBC) 1999, An Invisible Reality (text (poems) for oratorio by Derek Holman) 2000, A Children's Millennium Song (with music by Oscar Peterson) 2000, And Once More Saw the Stars – Four Poems for Two Voices (letters and poems) 2001, A Kind of Fiction (short stories) 2001, Planet Earth, Poems New and Selected 2002, Porcupine's Quill 2002, A Grain of Sand 2003, Cosmologies 2003; numerous poems, short stories, essays, art criticism, drawings in various nat. and int. magazines and anthologies. *Honours:* Mem. Order of British Columbia 2003 Hon. DLitt (Victoria) 1985, (Guelph) 1990, (Trento) 1998, (Winnipeg) 2000, (Trent) 2004; Hon. LLD (Calgary) 1989, (Simon Fraser) 1990; Oscar Blumenthal Award 1944, Gov.-Gen.'s Award for Poetry 1954, Nat. Magazine Gold Award 1985, Canadian Authors' Asscn Literary Award for Poetry 1986, Banff Centre Nat. Award 1989, Tribute at the Vancouver Writers' Festival 2000, Distinguished Writer, Banff 2002, Terasen Lifetime Achievement Award 2004, Lt Gov.'s Award for Literary Excellence 2004. *Address:* 3260 Exeter Road, Victoria, BC V8R 6H6, Canada (home).

PAGE, Robin; British writer; b. 3 May 1943, Cambridgeshire, England. *Publications:* Down with the Poor, 1971; The Benefits Racket, 1972; Down Among the Dossers, 1973; The Decline of an English Village, 1974; The Hunter and the Hunted, 1977; Weather Forecasting: The Country Way, 1977; Cures and Remedies: The Country, 1978; Weeds: The Country Way, 1979; Animal Cures: The Country Way, 1979; The Journal of a Country Parish, 1980; Journeys into Britain, 1982; The Country Way of Love, 1983; The Wildlife of the Royal Estates, 1984; Count One to Ten, 1986; The Fox's Tale, 1986; The Duchy of Cornwall, 1987; The Fox and the Orchid, 1987; The Twitcher's Guide to British Birds, 1989. *Address:* Bird's Farm, Barton, Cambridgeshire, England.

PAGE, S. M. (see McMaster, Susan)

PAGE, Stephen; British publisher; b. 1965. *Education:* Bristol Univ. *Career:* bookseller Sherratt & Hughes, Croydon 1987–88; marketing exec. Longman 1988–90; retail sales manager Transworld 1990–94; Sales Dir Fourth Estate 1994–2000, Man. Dir, then (after takeover by Harper Collins) group sales and marketing dir Harper Collins 2000; CEO Faber & Faber Ltd 2001–04, CEO and Publisher 2004–; Pres. Publishers Asscn 2006–. *Address:* Faber and Faber Ltd, 3 Queen Square, London, WC1N 3AU, England. *Telephone:* (20) 7465-0045 (office). *Fax:* (20) 7465-0034 (office). *E-mail:* contact@faber.co.uk (office). *Website:* www.faber.co.uk (office).

PAGELS, Elaine Hiesey, PhD; American writer and academic; *Harrington Spear Paine Professor of Religion, Princeton University;* b. 13 Feb. 1943, Palo Alto, CA; m 1st Heinz R. Pagels 1969 (died 1988); two s. (one died 1987) one d.; m. 2nd Kent Greenawalt 1995. *Education:* Stanford and Harvard Univs. *Career:* Asst Prof., Barnard Coll., Columbia Univ. 1970–74, then Assoc. Prof., later Prof. of Religion and Head of Dept of Religion 1974–82; Harrington Spear Paine Prof. of Religion, Princeton Univ. 1982–; mem. American Acad. of Religion, Biblical Theologians Club, Soc. of Biblical Literature; Aspen Inst. of Humanistic Studies Mellon Fellow 1974, Hazen Fellow 1975, Rockefeller Foundation Fellowship 1978, Guggenheim Fellowship 1979, John D. and Catherine T. MacArthur Foundation Fellowship 1981. *Publications:* The

Johannine Gospel in Gnostic Exegesis: Heracleon's Commentary on John 1973, The Gnostic Paul: Gnostic Exegesis of the Pauline Letters 1975, The Gnostic Gospels (Nat. Book Critics' Circle Award, Nat. Book Award 1980) 1979, The Gnostic Jesus and Early Christian Politics 1981, Adam, Eve and the Serpent 1988, The Origin of Satan: The New Testament Origins of Christianity's Demonization of Jews, Pagans and Heretics 1995, Beyond Belief: The Secret Gospel of Thomas 2003, Reading Judas: The Gospel of Judas and the Shaping of Christianity (with Karen L. King) 2007; contrib. to various scholarly books and journals. *Honours:* National Endowment for the Humanities grant 1972. *Address:* Princeton University, Department of Religion, 1879 Hall, Room 240, Princeton, NJ 08544-1006, USA (office). *Telephone:* (609) 258-4484 (office). *E-mail:* pagels@princeton.edu (office). *Website:* www.princeton.edu/~religion (office).

PAGLIA, Camille, BA, MPhil, PhD; American academic and writer; *University Professor of Humanities and Media Studies, University of the Arts;* b. 2 April 1947, Endicott, NY; d. of Pasquale Paglia and Lydia Paglia. *Education:* State Univ of New York at Binghamton, Yale Univ. *Career:* Faculty mem. Bennington Coll. 1972–80; Visiting Lecturer, Wesleyan Univ. 1980, Yale Univ. 1980–84; Asst Prof., Phil. Coll. of Performing Arts (now Univ. of the Arts) 1984–87, Assoc. Prof. 1987–91, Prof. of Humanities 1991–2000; Univ. Prof. of Humanities and Media Studies 2000–; columnist Salon.com 1995–2001; Contributing Ed. Interview magazine 2001–. *Publications:* Sexual Personae: Art and Decadence from Nefertiti to Emily Dickinson 1990, Sex, Art and American Culture: Essays 1992, Vamps and Tramps: New Essays 1994, Alfred Hitchcock's The Birds 1998, Break, Blow, Burn: Camille Paglia Reads Forty-Three of the World's Best Poems 2005. *Address:* University of the Arts, 320 South Broad Street, Philadelphia, PA 19102, USA. *Telephone:* (212) 421-1700 (agent) (office); (215) 717-6265. *Fax:* (212) 980-3671 (agent). *Website:* www.uarts.edu (office).

PAIGE, Richard (see Koontz, Dean Ray)

PAIGE, Robin (see Albert, Susan Wittig)

PAINTER, John, ThL, ThSchol, BD, PhD, FAHA; Australian academic and writer; *Professor of Theology, Charles Sturt University;* b. 22 Sept. 1935, Bellingen, NSW; m. Gillian Gray 1963; two d. *Education:* Australian Coll. of Theology, Univs of London and Durham, UK. *Career:* Tutor, St John's Coll. Durham 1965–68; Assoc. Prof., Univ. of Cape Town, SA 1971–76; Assoc. Prof. and Reader, Latrobe Univ., Melbourne 1977–97; Prof. of Theology, St Mark's School of Theology, Charles Sturt Univ., Canberra 1997–. *Publications:* John: Witness and Theologian 1975, Theology and Hermeneutics: Rudolf Bultmann's Interpretation of the History of Jesus 1987, The Quest for the Messiah 1991, Worlds in Conflict 1997, Just James, The Brother of Jesus in History and Tradition 1997, 1, 2, and 3 John 2002; contrib. to New Testament Studies, Journal for the Study of the New Testament, Scottish Journal of Theology. *Honours:* Centenary Medal 2003. *Address:* St Mark's School of Theology, Charles Sturt University, 15 Blackhall Street, Barton, ACT 2600 (office); PO Box 321, Jamison Centre, Macquarie, ACT 2614, Australia (home). *Telephone:* (2) 6273-1572 (office). *Fax:* (2) 6273-4067 (office). *E-mail:* jpainter@csu.edu.au (office).

PAKENHAM, Thomas Francis Dermot, BA; British historian and writer; b. 14 Aug. 1933, s. of 7th Earl of Longford and Elizabeth, Countess of Longford (succeeded father as 8th Earl of Longford 2001, but does not use title); m. Valerie 1964; two s. two d. *Education:* Dragon School, Oxford, Belvedere Coll., Dublin, Ampleforth Coll., York, Magdalen Coll., Oxford. *Career:* travelled in Nr East and Ethiopia 1955–56; freelance writer 1956–58; editorial staff mem., Times Educational Supplement 1958–60, Sunday Telegraph 1961, The Observer 1961–64; Chair. Ladbroke Asscn 1988–91; mem., Victorian Soc. (co-founder 1958–, cttee mem. 1958–64) Historic Irish Tourist Houses and Gardens Asscn (co-founder, cttee mem. 1968–72), British-Irish Asscn (treas. 1972–2002, chair. 2002–), Christopher Ewart-Biggs Memorial Trust (sec., co-founder 1976–), Irish Tree Soc. (founder and chair. 1990–); sr assoc. mem. St Antony's Coll., Oxford 1979–81. *Publications:* non-fiction: The Mountains of Rasselas: an Ethiopian Adventure 1959, The Year of Liberty: History of the Great Irish Rebellion of 1798 1969, The Boer War (Cheltenham Prize 1980) 1979, Dublin: A Traveller's Companion (with Valerie Pakenham) 1988, The Scramble for Africa (Alan Paton Memorial Prize 1992, WHSmith Award 1992) 1991, Meetings with Remarkable Trees 1996, Remarkable Trees of the World 2002, Mythic Woods: The World's Most Remarkable Forests 2004, Remarkable Baobab 2004, In Search of Remarkable Trees 2007. *Honours:* Hon. DLitt (Ulster) 1992. *Address:* 111 Elgin Crescent, London, W11 2JF, England; Tullynally, Castlepollard, Westmeath, Ireland.

PALAHNIUK, Chuck; American novelist and essayist; b. 21 Feb. 1962, Pasco, WA. *Education:* Univ. of Oregon. *Publications:* novels: Fight Club 1996, Invisible Monsters 1999, Survivor 2000, Lullaby 2002, Nana 2003, Diary 2003, Haunted: a Novel in Stories 2005, Rant 2007; short story collections: Choke 2001, Fugitives and Refugees: A Walk through Portland, Oregon 2003, Stranger than Fiction: True Stories 2004, Non-Fiction 2004; contrib. to Bikini, Black Book, Gear, The Guardian, The Stranger. *Address:* c/o Random House, 20 Vauxhall Bridge Road, London, SW1V 2SA, England.

PALČINSKAITE, Violeta; Lithuanian writer; b. 20 Nov. 1943; m. (divorced). *Education:* Univ. of Vilnius. *Career:* first book of poetry published 1961; first children's play performed by Lithuanian State Youth Theatre 1966. *Film scripts include:* Andrius, Train to Bulzibar, The Iron Princess. *Publications*

include: Stairs (poetry) 1985, The Dolls of the Old City (children's poetry) 1987, I am Going After Summer (plays) 1988, A Spotted Snail of Dreamland 1997, Window-Sills Over an Alley (collection of poetry and plays for children) 2003. *Honours:* Gold Medal Int. Children's Film Festival, Italy 1982, Int. Bd on Books for Young People Honours List 1988. *Address:* Antakalnio 8-3, 10308 Vilnius, Lithuania (home). *Telephone:* (5) 2625628 (home). *E-mail:* violpalc@ takas.lt (home).

PALEI, Marina Anatolevna; Dutch (b. Russian) writer and physician; b. (Marina Anatolevna Spivak), 1955, Leningrad (now St Petersburg); m. (divorced); one s. *Education:* State Medical Acad., Leningrad, Inst. of Literature, Moscow. *Career:* model at the Mukhina Fine Arts Inst., Leningrad; joined amateur theatre group; lecturer and speaker across Europe 1992–; writer-in-residence Italy, Germany, USA, Sweden, Scotland, Greece; mem. Russian Soc. of Authors, Russian PEN, Netherlands Soc. of Authors. *Publications include:* Pominovenie (translated as Remembrance) 1990, Evgesha i Annushka (translated as Evgesha and Annushka) 1990, Kabiriia s Obvodnogo kanala (translated as Cabiria of the Obvodny Canal) 1991; short story collections: Otdelenie propashchikh (translated as The Lost Souls' Division) 1991, Die Cabiria vom Umleitungskanal 1992, Iz zhizni avtoovetchikov (translated as From the Life of Answering Machines) 1993, Herinnerd huis 1995, Cabiria di Pietroburgo 1996, Rückwärtsgang der Sonne 1997, The Wind-Field 1998, The Long Distance, or the Slavic Accent 2000, The Lunch 2000; contrib. to numerous nat. and int. journals and anthologies. *Honours:* Rockefeller Foundation Grant, awards from Limbus Press (Russia), The Prince Bernhard Foundation (The Netherlands), Graz – The Cultural Capital of Europe 2003. *Literary Agent:* Bettina Nibbe, Nibbe & Wiedling Literary Agency, Rumfordstrasse 10, 80469, Munich, Germany. *Telephone:* (89) 290-840-12. *Fax:* (89) 290-840-50. *E-mail:* nibbe@nibbe-wiedling.de. *Website:* www .nibbe-wiedling.de. *E-mail:* marinapalei@yahoo.co.uk (home). *Website:* www .synthart.com/silvana/LICA%20RUSSKOJ%20LIT%20WEB.

PALEY, Grace; American writer, poet and teacher; b. 11 Dec. 1922, The Bronx, New York, NY; d. of Isaac Goodside and Manya Ridnik Goodside; m. 1st Jess Paley 1942 (divorced); one s. one d.; m. 2nd Robert Nicholls 1972. *Education:* Hunter Coll., CUNY and New York Univ. *Career:* teaching staff Sarah Lawrence Coll. 1966–88, Columbia Univ., New York 1984, also at Syracuse Univ. and City Coll., CUNY; New York State first official author 1989–91; Poet Laureate State of Vermont 2003–; mem. Inst. of American Writers, American Acad. of Arts and Letters; Guggenheim Fellowship 1961, NEA Sr Fellowship 1987. *Publications:* The Little Disturbances of Man: Stories of Women and Men at Love 1959, Enormous Changes at the Last Minute (fiction) 1974, Later the Same Day (short stories) 1984, Leaning Forward (poems) 1985, Long Walks and Intimate Talks (poems and stories) 1991, New and Selected Poems 1992, Begin Again: Collected Poems 1993, The Collected Stories 1994, Just As I Thought 1998; contrib. to books, anthologies and magazines. *Honours:* Nat. Inst. of Arts and Letters Award 1970, New York State Writers' Inst. Edith Wharton Citation of Merit 1986, Vermont Governor's Award for Excellence in the Arts 1993. *Address:* PO Box 620, Thetford Hill, VT 05074, USA.

PALIN, Michael Edward, CBE, BA; British actor, writer and traveller; b. 5 May 1943, Sheffield, Yorks.; s. of the late Edward Palin and Mary Palin; m. Helen M. Gibbins 1966; two s. one d. *Education:* Birkdale School, Sheffield, Shrewsbury School, Brasenose Coll. Oxford. *Career:* Pres. Transport 2000. *Television:* actor and writer: Monty Python's Flying Circus, BBC TV 1969–74, Ripping Yarns, BBC TV 1976–79; actor: Three Men in a Boat, BBC 1975: writer: East of Ipswich, BBC TV 1987, Number 27, BBC TV, The Weekend (play for stage) 1994; TV series: contrib. to Great Railway Journeys of the World, BBC TV 1980, 1993; presenter Around the World in 80 Days 1989, Pole to Pole 1992, Palin's Column 1994, Full Circle 1997, Michael Palin's Hemingway Adventure 1999, Sahara 2002, Himalaya with Michael Palin 2004, Michael Palin and the Mystery of Hammershoi 2005; art documentaries (presenter); Palin on Redpath 1997, The Bright Side of Life 2000, The Ladies Who Loved Matisse 2003. *Musical theatre:* Monty Python's Spamalot 2006. *Films:* actor and co-author: And Now for Something Completely Different 1970, Monty Python and the Holy Grail 1974, Monty Python's Life of Brian 1979, Time Bandits 1980, Monty Python's 'The Meaning of Life' 1982; actor, writer and co-producer: The Missionary 1982; actor, co-scriptwriter: American Friends 1991; actor: Jabberwocky 1976, A Private Function 1984, Brazil 1985, A Fish Called Wanda 1988 (Best Supporting Film Actor, BAFTA Award 1988), GBH (Channel 4 TV) 1991, Fierce Creatures 1997. *Publications include:* Monty Python's Big Red Book 1970, Monty Python's Brand New Book 1973, Montypythonscrapbook 1979, Dr Fegg's Encyclopaedia of All World Knowledge 1984, Limericks 1985, Around the World in 80 Days 1989, Pole to Pole 1992, Hemingway's Chair 1995, Full Circle 1997, Michael Palin's Hemingway Adventure 1999, Sahara 2002, The Pythons Autobiography (co-author) 2003, Himalaya (British Book Award for TV & Film Book of the Year 2005) 2004, Diaries 1969–1979: The Python Years 2006; for children: Small Harry and the Toothache Pills 1981, The Mirrorstone 1986, The Cyril Stories 1986. *Honours:* Dr hc (Sheffield) 1992, (Queen's, Belfast) 2000; Michael Balcon Award for outstanding contrib. to cinema (with Monty Python), BAFTA 1987, Travel Writer of the Year, British Book Awards 1993, Lifetime Achievement Award, British Comedy Awards 2002, BCA Illustrated Book of the Year Award 2002, BAFTA Special Award for Outstanding Contrib. to TV 2005. *Literary Agent:* Mayday Management, 34 Tavistock Street, London, WC2E 7PB, England. *Telephone:* (20) 7497-1100. *Fax:* (20) 7497-1133.

PALING, Chris, BA; British writer and radio producer; b. 7 Dec. 1956, Derby, England; m. Julie Fiona 1979; one s. one d. *Education:* Sussex Univ. *Publications:* After the Raid, Deserters, Morning All Day, The Silent Sentry, Newton's Swing 2000, The Repentant Morning 2003, A Town by the Sea 2005; contrib. to Literary Review, Punch, Independent Magazine, Spectator. *Literary Agent:* Rogers, Coleridge & White Ltd, 20 Powis Mews, London, W11 1JN, England.

PALLEY, Julian, BA, MA, PhD; American academic, poet and translator; b. 16 Sept. 1925, Atlantic City, NJ; m. Shirley Wilson 1950, four s. *Education:* Mexico City College, University of Arizona, University of New Mexico. *Career:* Instructor, Rutgers University, 1956–59; Assoc. Prof., Arizona State University, 1959–62, University of Oregon, 1962–66; Prof. of Spanish Literature, University of California at Irvine, 1966–; mem. California State Poetry Society. *Publications:* Spinoza's Stone, 1976; Bestiary, 1987; Pictures at an Exhibition, 1989; Family Portraits, 1994. Other: several trans. Contributions: reviews, quarterlies, and journals. *Honours:* Arizona Quarterly Poetry Prize, 1956; Jefferson Poetry Prize, 1976.

PALMA, Milagros, DèsL; French (b. Nicaraguan) anthropologist, writer and publisher; *Professor, University of Caen*; b. 26 March 1949, León, Nicaragua; d. of Alicia Guzmán. *Education:* León, Paris and Univ. of Paris X (Paris-Nanterre). *Career:* Ed. Indigo and Côté-Femmes Publrs 1989–. *Publications:* Palabra mítica de la Gente del Agua 1983, El Cóndor, dimensión mítica del Ave Sagrada (2nd edn) 1984, Los viajeros de la Gran Anaconda, Le ventre de la grande femme de l'Amazonie 1986, La mujer es puro cuento 1987, Senderos Míticos de Nicaragua, Revolución tranquila de Santos, Diablos y Diablitos 1988, Nicaragua: Once mil. vírgenes 1988, Bodas de cenizas (novel) 1990, Le ver et le fruit ou L'apprentissage de la féminité en Amérique latine 1991, Desencanto al amanecer (novel) 1995, Le pacte 1998, Un Latino-américain à Paris (novel) 2005. *Honours:* Maison des Ecrivains grant for foreign writers 1987, Prix José Marti UNESCO 1998. *Address:* Côté-Femmes, 39 bis Avenue Gambetta, 75020 Paris, France. *Telephone:* (1) 43-79-74-79. *Fax:* (1) 43-79-46-87. *E-mail:* indigo-cf@wanadoo.fr.

PALMER, Alan Warwick, MA, MLitt, FRSL; British writer; b. 28 Sept. 1926, Ilford, Essex, England; m. Veronica Mary Cordell 1951. *Education:* Oriel Coll., Oxford. *Career:* Asst Master Highgate School, London 1951–53, Sr History Master 1953–69. *Publications:* A Dictionary of Modern History, 1789–1945 1962, Independent Eastern Europe: A History (with C. A. Macartney) 1962, Yugoslavia 1964, The Gardeners of Salonika 1965, Napoleon in Russia 1967, The Lands Between: A History of East Central Europe Since the Congress of Vienna 1970, Metternich 1972, The Life and Times of George VI 1972, Russia in War and Peace 1972, Alexander I: Tsar of War and Peace 1974, Age of Optimism 1974, Nations and Empires (ed.) 1974, Frederick the Great 1974, Bismark 1976, Kings and Queens of England 1976, Quotations in History: A Dictionary of Historical Quotations, *c.* 800 AD to the Present (with Victoria Palmer) 1976, The Kaiser: Warlord of the Second Reich 1978, Princes of Wales 1979, The Facts on File Dictionary of 20th Century History 1979, The Penguin Dictionary of Twentieth-Century History 1979, Who's Who in Modern History 1980, Who's Who in Shakespeare's England (with Veronica Palmer) 1981, The Chancelleries of Europe 1983, Royal England: A Historical Gazetteer (with Veronica Palmer) 1983, An Encyclopedia of Napoleon's Europe 1984, Crowned Cousins: The Anglo-German Royal Connection 1985, The Banner of Battle: The Story of the Crimean War 1987, Who's Who in Bloomsbury (with Veronica Palmer) 1987, The East End: Four Centuries of London Life 1989, The Chronology of British History (with Veronica Palmer) 1992, The Decline and Fall of the Ottoman Empire 1992, Twilight of the Habsburgs: The Life and Times of Emperor Francis Joseph 1995, Dictionary of the British Empire and Commonwealth 1996, The Pimlico Chronology of British History: From 250,000 BC to the Present (with Veronica Palmer) 1996, Who's Who in World Politics: From 1860 to the Present Day 1996, Victory 1918 2000, Fictional Minds 2005; contribs to journals. *Address:* c/o Carroll & Graf Publishers, 245 West 17th Street, 11th floor, New York, NY 10011-5300, USA. *Telephone:* (212) 981-9919. *Fax:* (646) 375-2571.

PALMER, Diana (see Kyle, Susan Eloise Spaeth)

PALMER, Frank Robert, MA, DLitt, FBA; British academic; *Professor Emeritus of Linguistic Science, University of Reading*; b. 9 April 1922, Westerleigh, Glos.; s. of George Samuel Palmer and Gertrude Lilian Palmer (née Newman); m. Jean Elisabeth Moore 1948; three s. two d. *Education:* Bristol Grammar School, New Coll., Oxford, Merton Coll., Oxford. *Career:* Lecturer in Linguistics, SOAS, Univ. of London 1950–60; Prof. of Linguistics, Univ. Coll. of North Wales, Bangor 1960–65; Prof. of Linguistic Science, Univ. of Reading 1965–87, Dean, Faculty of Letters and Social Sciences 1969–72, Prof. Emer. 1987–; Vice-Pres., Philological Soc.; Chair. Linguistics Assen (GB) 1965–68, Ed. Journal of Linguistics 1969–79, Linguistic Soc. of America Prof., Buffalo, USA 1971; Distinguished Visiting Prof. Univ. of Delaware, Newark, USA 1982; mem. Academia Europaea 1992. *Publications:* The Morphology of the Tigre Noun 1962, A Linguistic Study of the English Verb 1965, Selected Papers of J. R. Firth (1951–58) (ed.) 1968, Prosodic Analysis (ed.) 1970, Grammar 1971, 1984, The English Verb 1974, 1987, Semantics 1976, 1981, Modality and the English Modals 1979, 1990, Mood and Modality 1986, 2001, Studies in the History of Western Linguistics in Honour of R. H. Robins (co-ed.) 1986, Grammatical Roles and Relations 1994, Grammar and Meaning: Essays in Honour of Sir John Lyons (ed.) 1995, Modality in Contemporary English (co-ed.) 2003, English Modality in Perspective (co-ed.) 2004. *Honours:* Hon. DLitt 1997. *Address:* 'Whitethorns', Roundabout Lane, Winnersh, Wokingham, Berks., RG41 5AD, England (home). *Telephone:* (118) 978-6214 (home). *E-mail:* llspalmf@reading.ac.uk (home).

PALMER, John, BA; Canadian playwright and theatre and film director; *Course Instructor, Ryerson University, Toronto*; b. 13 May 1943, Sydney, NS. *Education:* Carleton Univ., Ottawa. *Career:* Assoc. Dir dramaturg Factory Theatre, Toronto 1970–73; Co-founder, Co-Artistic Dir and Literary Man. Toronto Free Theatre 1972–76; teacher/dir/playwright Juilliard School, New York 1979–81; resident playwright, Nat. Theatre School of Canada, Montreal 1993–94, Course Dir 1990–2003; Course Dir York Univ., Toronto 1991–93, Directing Course Instructor, Ryerson Univ., Toronto 2003–; teacher, Workman Theatre Project, Queen St Mental Health Centre, Toronto 1993–. *Films:* Sugar (writer, dir) (Best Feature, Toronto Lesbian and Gay Film Festival) 2004. *Publications:* 2 Plays: The End, and A Day at the Beach 1991, Before the Guns, Memories for my Brother Part I, Dangerous Traditions: Four Passe-Muraille Plays 1992, Henrik Ibsen on the Necessity of Producing Norwegian Drama 1992–93, Singapore 2001; contrib. to various publs. *Address:* 32 Monteith Street, Toronto, ON M4Y 1K7, Canada. *Telephone:* (416) 967-7455. *E-mail:* jpadd09@sympatico.ca; jp@darsmedia.com.

PALMER, (George) Michael, BA, MA; American poet, writer and translator; b. 11 May 1943, New York; m. Cathy Simon 1972; one d. *Education:* Harvard Univ. *Career:* has lectured at colls and univs in USA and Europe; collaborates on dance works and with numerous composers and performance artists; contributing ed. Facture magazine; Visiting Prof. Cardiff Univ. 2004; chancellor American Acad. of Poets. *Publications:* Plan of the City of O 1971, Blake's Newton 1972, C's Songs 1973, The Circular Gates 1974, Without Music 1977, Transparency of the Mirror 1980, Alogon 1980, Notes for Echo Lake 1981, Code of Signals: Recent Writings in Poetics (ed.) 1983, First Figure 1984, Songs for Sarah 1987, Sun 1988, For a Reading 1988, An Alphabet Underground 1993, At Passages 1995 (America Award for Poetry), The Lion Bridge 1998, The Danish Notebook 1998, The Promises of Glass 2000, Codes Appearing: Poems 1979–1988 2001, Fatal 2003, Company of Moths (poems) 2005; other: trans, ed. of books; contributions to many anthologies, books and journals. *Honours:* two Nat. Endowment for the Arts Fellowships, Guggenheim Fellowship, Lila Wallace Readers Digest Fund Writer's Award 1992–94, Shelley Memorial Award of the Poetry Soc. of America 2001. *Address:* 265 Jersey Street, San Francisco, CA 94114, USA.

PAMUK, Orhan; Turkish novelist; b. 7 June 1952, Istanbul; m. Aylin Turegen 1982 (divorced 2001); one d. *Education:* Robert Coll., Istanbul Technical Univ., Inst. of Journalism at Istanbul Univ. *Career:* jury mem. Cannes Film Festival 2007. *Publications:* Cevdet Bey ve Ogullari (Cevdet Bey and His Sons) 1983, Sessiz Ev (The Quiet House) 1983, Beyaz Kale (trans. as The White Castle) 1985, Kara Kitap (trans. as The Black Book) 1990, Gizli Yuz (screenplay of Kara Kitap) 1992, Yeni Hayat (trans. as The New Life) 1995, My Name is Red (trans.) (IMPAC Dublin Literary Award 2003) 2000, Istanbul 2003, Snow (trans.) 2004, Istanbul: Memories of a City 2006, Istanbul: City of a Hundred Names 2007; contrib. to various newspapers and magazines. *Honours:* Milliyet Press Novel Contest, first prize 1979, Orhan Kemal Novel Prize 1983, Madarali Novel Prize 1984, Prix de la Découverte Européenne 1991, Nobel Prize in Literature 2006. *Address:* Klodfarer Cad 7, Cagaloglu, Istanbul, 34400, Turkey (office).

PANICHAS, George Andrew, FRSA, MA, PhD, LittD; American writer and academic; *Professor Emeritus of English, University of Maryland*; b. 21 May 1930, Springfield, Mass; s. of Andrew Panichas and Fannie Dracouli Panichas. *Education:* Springfield Classical High School, American Int. Coll., Trinity Coll. and Nottingham Univ., England. *Career:* Instructor in English, Univ. of Maryland 1962, Asst Prof. 1963, Assoc. Prof. 1966, Prof. 1968–92, now Prof. Emer.; Co-Dir of Conf. "Irving Babbitt: Fifty Years Later" 1983; mem. Richard M. Weaver Fellowship Awards Cttee 1983–88; Academic Bd Nat. Humanities Inst. 1985–, Advisory Bd Humanitas 1993–; Editorial Adviser, Modern Age: A Quarterly Review 1972–77, Assoc. Ed. 1978–83, Ed. 1984–; mem. Advisory Bd Continuity: A Journal of History 1984; Ingersoll Prizes Jury Panel 1986. *Publications:* Adventure in Consciousness: The Meaning of D. H. Lawrence's Religious Quest 1964, Renaissance and Modern Essays: Presented to Vivian de Sola Pinto in Celebration of his Seventieth Birthday (ed. with G. R. Hibbard and A. Rodway) 1966, Epicurus 1967, Mansions of the Spirit: Essays in Literature and Religion (ed.) 1967, Promise of Greatness: The War of 1914–1918 (ed.) 1968, The Politics of Twentieth-Century Novelists (ed.) 1971, The Reverent Discipline: Essays in Literary Criticism and Culture 1974, The Burden of Vision: Dostoevsky's Spiritual Art 1977, The Simone Weil Reader (ed.) 1977, Irving Babbitt: Representative Writings (ed.) 1981, The Courage of Judgment: Essays in Criticism, Culture and Society 1982, Irving Babbitt in Our Time (ed. with C. G. Ryn) 1986, Modern Age: The First Twenty-Five Years. A Selection (ed.) 1988, The Critic as Conservator: Essays in Literature, Society and Culture 1992, In Continuity: The Last Essays of Austin Warren (ed.) 1996, The Critical Legacy of Irving Babbitt: An Appreciation 1999, Growing Wings to Overcome Gravity: Criticism as the Pursuit of Virtue 1999, Joseph Conrad: His Moral Vision 2005, The Essential Russell Kirk: Selected Essays (ed.) 2007; also numerous articles, trans. and reviews for books and journals published in USA and Europe. *Honours:* Earhart Foundation Award 1982, Henry Regnery Award 2003. *Address:* 4313 Knox Road, Apartment 402, College Park, MD 20740, USA (home). *Telephone:* (301) 779-1436 (office).

PANKIN, Boris Dmitriyevich; Russian diplomatist (retd) and essayist; b. 20 Feb. 1931, Frunze (now Bishkek); m.; two s. one d. *Education:* Moscow State Univ. *Career:* journalist and literary critic 1957–; Ed. Komsomolskaya Pravda 1965–73; Chair. Bd USSR Copyright Agency 1973–82; USSR Amb. to Sweden 1982–90, to Czechoslovakia 1990–91; Foreign Minister Aug.–Dec. 1991; Russian Amb. to UK 1991–94; now living in Sweden. *Publications:* Severe Literature, Time and Word, Boundaries and Books, The Last 100 Days of the Soviet Union, Four I of Konstantin Simonov. *Honours:* USSR State Prize 1982. *Telephone:* (46) 880-7871.

PANNENBERG, Wolfhart Ulrich, DTheol, FBA; German academic; *Professor Emeritus, University of Munich;* b. 2 Oct. 1928, Stettin; s. of Kurt B.S. Pannenberg and Irmgard Pannenberg; m. Hilke Sabine Schütte 1954. *Education:* Univ. of Heidelberg. *Career:* ordained as Lutheran Minister 1956; Privatdozent, Heidelberg 1955–58; Prof. of Systematic Theology, Univ. of Wuppertal 1958–61; Prof., Univ. of Mainz 1961–67; Prof., Univ. of Munich 1967–94, Prof. Emer. 1994–, fmr Head, Inst. of Ecumenical Theology; mem. Bavarian Acad. of Sciences. *Publications:* Offenbarung als Geschichte (translated as Revelation as History) 1961, Was ist der Mensch?: Die Anthropologie der Gegenwart im Lichte der Theologie (translated as What is Man?) 1962, Grundzüge der Christologie (translated as Jesus: God and Man) 1964, Grundfragen systematischer Theologie (two vols, translated as Basic Questions in Theology) 1967, 1980, Theology and the Kingdom of God 1969, Spirit, Faith and Church (with Carl E. Braaten and Avery Dulles) 1970, Thesen zur Theologie der Kirche 1970, Das Glaubensbekenntnis (translated as The Apostles' Creed in the Light of Today's Questions) 1972, Gottesgedanke und menschliche Freiheit (translated as The Idea of God and Human Freedom) 1972, Wissenschaftstheorie und Theologie (translated as Theology and the Philosophy of Science) 1973, Glaube und Wirklichkeit (translated as Faith and Reality) 1975, Ethik und Ekklesiologie 1977, Human Nature, Election and History 1977, Anthropologie in Theologischer Perspektive (translated as Anthropology in Theological Perspective) 1983, Christian Spirituality 1983, Christentum in Einer Säkularisierten Welt (translated as Christianity in a Secularized World) 1988, Systematische Theologie (three vols, translated as Systematic Theology) 1988–93, Metaphysik und Gottesgedanke (translated as Metaphysics and the Idea of God) 1988, An Introduction to Systematic Theology 1991, Toward a Theology of Nature: Essays on Science and Faith 1993, Grundlagen der Ethik 1996, Theologie und Philosophie 1996, Problemgeschichte der neueren Evangelischen Theologie in Deutschland 1997, Beiträge zur systematischen Theologie (three vols) 1999–2000, Beiträge zur Ethik 2004. *Honours:* Hon. DD (Glasgow) 1972, (Manchester) 1977, (Trinity Coll. Dublin) 1979, (St Andrews) 1993, (Cambridge) 1997, (Comillas, Madrid) 1999. *Telephone:* (89) 21803482 (office); (89) 855915 (home).

PANYCH, Morris Stephen, BFA; Canadian dramatist, writer, actor and director; b. 30 June 1952, Calgary, AB. *Education:* NAIT, Edmonton, Univ. of British Columbia. *Publications:* Last Call 1983, 7 Stories 1990, The Ends of the Earth 1993, Other Schools of Thought 1994, Vigil 1995, Lawrence and Holloman 1998, Girl in the Goldfish Bowl 2002, Earshot 2004, The Dishwashers 2005, What Lies Before Us 2007, Benevolence 2007. *Honours:* six Jessie Awards, Vancouver Theatre, five Dora Mavor Moore Awards, Toronto Theatre, two Gov.-Gen.'s Awards for English Drama 1994, 2004. *Literary Agent:* c/o Gary Goddard Agency, 305 10 St Mary Street, Toronto, ON M4Y 1P9, Canada. *Telephone:* (416) 928-0299. *Fax:* (416) 924-9593. *E-mail:* goddard@canadafilm.com.

PAOLINI, Christopher; American children's writer; b. Montana. *Publications:* Inheritance Trilogy: Book I: Eragon 2002, Book II: Eldest (Quill Book Award for Young Adult/Teen 2006) 2005. *Literary Agent:* Simon Lipskar, Writers' House, 21 W 26th Street, New York, NY 10010, USA. *Website:* www.alagaesia.com.

PAOLUCCI, Anne, BA, MA, PhD; American retd academic, poet, writer, dramatist and editor; *President, Council on National Literatures;* b. Rome, Italy; m. Henry Paolucci (deceased). *Education:* Barnard College, Columbia University. *Career:* Instructor 1959–61, Asst Prof. 1961–69, City College CUNY; Fulbright Lecturer American Drama University of Naples 1965–67; Research Prof. 1969–75, Prof. of English 1969–97, Chair Dept of English 1974–75, 1982–91, Dir Doctor of Arts Degree Program in English 1982–96, St John's University, Jamaica, New York; Founder, Publisher, and Ed.-in-Chief, Review of National Literatures 1970–; Founder-Pres. Council on National Literatures 1974–; mem. Nat. Council on the Humanities 1986–93; mem. American Comparative Literature Asscn; CUNY board of trustees 1996–, chair. 1997–; Dante Society of America; Dramatists Guild; Hegel Society of America; International Comparative Literature Asscn; MLA; PEN American Center; Pirandello Society of America, pres. 1972–95; Renaissance Asscn of America; Renaissance Institute of America; Shakespeare Asscn of America; World Centre for Shakespeare Studies. *Publications:* poetry: Poems Written for Sbek's Mummies, Marie Menken, and Other Important People, Places, and Things 1977, Riding the Mast Where It Swings 1980, Gorbachev in Concert (and Other Poems) 1991, Queensboro Bridge (and Other Poems) 1995; fiction: Eight Short Stories 1977, Sepia Tones: Seven Short Stories 1985, Terminal Degrees 1997, Do Me A Favor (and Other Stories) 2002, In Wolf's Clothing 2003; non-fiction: Hegel on Tragedy (with Henry Paolucci) 1962, A Short History of American Drama 1966, Eugene O'Neill, Arthur Miller, Edward Albee 1967, From Tension to Tonic: The Plays of Edward Albee 1972, Pirandello's Theater: The Recovery of the Stage for Dramatic Art 1974, Dante and the 'Quest for Eloquence' in the Vernacular Languages of India (with

Henry Paolucci) 1984, The Women in Dante's Divine Comedy and Spenser's Faerie Queene 1984; plays: Minions of the Race 1978 (video 2003), Cipango! 1986 (video 1990); editor: Dante's Influence on American Writers 1977; trans.: Selected Poems of Giacomo Leopardi 2004; contrib. to numerous books, reviews and journals. *Honours:* Fulbright Scholarship, Italy 1951–52; Woodbridge Hon. Fellowship Columbia University 1961–62; Writer-in-Residence, Yaddo 1965; ACLS Grant 1978; Commendatore Order of Merit, Italy 1992; Gold Medal, Canada 1991; Hon. Degree in Humane Letters, Lehman College, CUNY 1995. *Address:* CNL/Anne and Henry Paolucci International Conference Center, 68–02 Metropolitan Avenue, Middle Village, NY 11379, USA (office). *Telephone:* (718) 821-3916 (office). *Website:* www.annehenrypaolucci.com.

PAPALEO, Joseph, BA, MA; American academic and writer; b. 13 Jan. 1926, New York, NY; m., four s. *Education:* Sarah Lawrence College, University of Florence, Italy, Columbia University. *Career:* Teacher, Fieldston Prep School, 1952–60; Prof. of Literature and Writing, Sarah Lawrence College, 1960–68, 1969–92; Guest Prof., Laboratorio de Cibernetica, Naples, Italy, 1968–69; mem. Authors' Guild; Italian American Writers Asscn; American Asscn of University Profs. *Publications:* All the Comforts (novel), 1968; Out of Place (novel), 1971; Picasso at Ninety One, 1988; several short stories; contrib. to journals and magazines. *Honours:* Guggenheim Fellowship, 1974; Ramapo College Poetry Prize, 1986.

PAPINEAU, David Calder, BA, BSc, PhD; British philosopher, academic and writer; *Professor, King's College, London;* b. 30 Sept. 1947, Como, Italy; m. Rose Wild 1986; one s. one d. *Education:* Univ. of Natal, Univ. of Cambridge. *Career:* Prof., King's College, London 1990–; mem. British Soc. for the Philosophy of Science, Pres. 1993–95. *Publications:* For Science in the Social Sciences 1978, Theory and Meaning 1979, Reality and Representation 1987, Philosophical Naturalism 1993, Introducing Consciousness 2000, Thinking About Consciousness 2002, The Roots of Reason. *Address:* Department of Philosophy, King's College, Strand, London, WC2R 2LS, England (office). *Website:* www.kcl.ac.uk/philosophy (office).

PARES, Marion, (Judith Campbell, Anthony Grant); British writer; b. 7 Nov. 1914, West Farleigh, Kent, England; m. Humphrey Pares 1937, four d. *Publications:* Family Pony, 1962; The Queen Rides, 1965; Horses in the Sun, 1966; Police Horse, 1967; World of Horses, 1969; World of Ponies, 1970; Anne: Portrait of a Princess, 1970; Family on Horseback (with N. Toyne), 1971; Princess Anne and Her Horses, 1971; Elizabeth and Philip, 1972; The Campions, 1973; Royalty on Horseback, 1974; The World of Horses, 1975; Anne and Mark, 1976; Queen Elizabeth II, 1979; The Mutant, 1980; Charles: A Prince of His Time, 1980; The Royal Partners, 1982; Royal Horses, 1983.

PARETSKY, Sara N., MBA, PhD; American writer; b. 8 June 1947, Ames, IA; d. of David Paretsky and Mary E. Edwards; m. S. Courtenay Wright 1976; three c. *Education:* Univs of Kansas and Chicago. *Career:* Man. Urban Research Center, Chicago 1971–74, CNA Insurance Co., Chicago 1977–85; writer of crime novels 1985–; Pres. Sisters in Crime, Chicago 1986–88; Dir Nat. Abortion Rights Action League, Ill. 1987–; mem. Crime Writers' Asscn. *Publications include:* Indemnity Only 1982, Deadlock (Friends of American Writers Prize 1985) 1984, Killing Orders 1986, Bitter Medicine 1987, Toxic Shock (British Crime Writers Asscn Silver Dagger for Fiction 1988) 1987, Blood Shot 1988, Burn Marks 1990, Guardian Angel 1992, A Woman's Eye (ed.) 1992, Tunnel Vision 1994, Women on the Case 1997, Hard Time 2000, Total Recall 2002, Blacklist 2003 (British Crime Writers Asscn Gold Dagger for Fiction 2004), Fire Sale 2006; numerous short stories and articles. *Honours:* several hon. degrees, Ms Magazine Woman of the Year 1987, CWA Silver Dagger Award 1988, Diamond Dagger for Lifetime Achievement, British Crime Writers Asscn 2002. *Literary Agent:* 1507 East 53rd Street, #302, Chicago, IL 60615; c/o Dominick Abel Literary Agency, Inc., 146 West 82nd Street, 1B, New York, NY 12546, USA. *E-mail:* viwarshawski@mindspring.com; dominick@dalainc.com. *Website:* www.saraparetsky.com.

PARINI, Jay Lee, AB, BPhil, PhD; American writer, poet, literary critic and academic; b. 2 April 1948, Pittston, PA; m. Devon Stacey Jersild 1981; three s. *Education:* Lafayette Coll., Univ. of St Andrews, Scotland. *Career:* Faculty, Dartmouth Coll. 1975–82; co-founder, New England Review 1976; Prof. of English, Middlebury Coll. 1982–, currently Dir Creative Writing Programme. *Publications:* fiction: The Love Run 1980, The Patch Boys 1986, The Last Station 1990, Bay of Arrows 1992, Benjamin's Crossing 1997, The Apprentice Lover 2002; poetry: Singing in Time 1972, Anthracite Country 1982, Town Life 1988, House of Days 1988; non-fiction: Theodore Roethke: An American Romantic 1979, An Invitation to Poetry 1988, John Steinbeck: A Biography 1995, Some Necessary Angels (essays) 1998, Robert Frost 1999, One Matchless Time: A Life of William Faulkner 2005; editor: Gore Vidal: Writer Against the Grain 1992, The Columbia History of American Poetry 1993, The Columbia Anthology of American Poetry 1995, The Norton Book of American Autobiography 1999. *Address:* c/o English Department, Munroe Hall 118, Middlebury College, Middlebury, VT 05753, USA.

PARIS, Bernard Jay, AB, PhD; American academic (retd) and writer; b. 19 Aug. 1931, Baltimore, Md; m. Shirley Helen Freedman 1949, one s. one d. *Education:* Johns Hopkins Univ. *Career:* Instructor, Lehigh Univ. 1956–60; Asst Prof., Michigan State Univ. 1960–64, Assoc. Prof. 1964–67, Prof. 1967–81; Prof. of English, Univ. of Florida 1981–96; Dir Inst. for Psychological Study of the Arts 1985–92, Int. Karen Horney Soc. 1991–; mem. MLA of America, Scientific Assoc., American Acad. of Psychoanalysis. *Publications:*

Experiments in Life: George Eliot's Quest for Values 1965, A Psychological Approach to Fiction: Studies in Thackeray, Stendhal, George Eliot, Dostoevsky and Conrad 1974, Character and Conflict in Jane Austen's Novels 1978, Third Force Psychology and the Study of Literature (ed.) 1986, Shakespeare's Personality (co-ed.) 1989, Bargains with Fate: Psychological Crises and Conflicts in Shakespeare and His Plays 1991, Character as a Subversive Force in Shakespeare: The History and the Roman Plays 1991, Karen Horney: A Psychoanalyst's Search for Self-Understanding 1994, Imagined Human Beings: A Psychological Approach to Character and Conflict in Literature 1997, The Therapeutic Process, by Karen Horney (ed.) 1999, The Unknown Karen Horney, by Karen Horney (ed.) 2000, Rereading George Eliot: Changing Responses to Her Experiments in Life 2003, Conrad's Charlie Marlow: A New Approach to Heart of Darkness and Lord Jim 2005; contrib. to numerous scholarly and literary journals. *Honours:* Hon. mem. American Inst. for Psychoanalysis, Asscn for the Advancement of Psychoanalysis; Nat. Endowment for the Humanities Fellow 1969, Guggenheim Fellowship 1974. *Address:* 1430 NW 94th Street, Gainesville, FL 32606, USA. *E-mail:* bjparis@ufl.edu.

PARISI, Joseph Anthony, BA, MA, PhD; American editor, writer, poet and consultant; b. 18 Nov. 1944, Duluth, MN. *Education:* Coll. of St Thomas, St Paul, Minnesota, Univ. of Chicago. *Career:* Instructor to Asst Prof. of English, Roosevelt Univ., Chicago 1969–78; Assoc. Ed., Poetry Magazine, Chicago 1976–83, Acting Ed. 1983–85, Ed. 1985–2003; Visiting and Adjunct Asst Prof. of English, Univ. of Illinois at Chicago 1978–87; consultant, American Library Asscn 1980–; Chair., Ruth Lilly Poetry Prize 1986–2003, and Fellowships 1989–2003; Prod., writer and host, Poets in Person, Nat. Public Radio 1991; Exec. Dir Modern Poetry Asscn (now The Poetry Foundation) 1996–2003. *Publications:* The Poetry Anthology 1912–1977: Sixty-five Years of America's Most Distinguished Verse Magazine (ed. with Daryl Hine) 1978, Voices & Visions: Viewer's Guide 1987, Marianne Moore: The Art of a Modernist (ed.) 1989, Poets in Person: Listener's Guide 1992, Dear Editor: A History of Poetry in Letters: The First Fifty Years 1912–1962 (co-ed.) 2002, The Poetry Anthology 1912–2002 (co-ed.) 2002; contributions to reference books, scholarly journals and literary publications. *Honours:* Everett Helm Travelling Fellowship 1999, Guggenheim Fellowship 2000, Fellow Churchill Coll., Cambridge 2002. *Address:* 3440 N Lake Shore Drive, Chicago, IL 60657, USA. *Telephone:* (773) 525-3116 (home).

PARK, Linda Sue, MA; American writer; b. 25 March 1960, Urbana, Ill.; d. of Ed Park and Susie Park; m. 1983; one s. one d. *Education:* Stanford Univ., Trinity Coll. Dublin, Ireland, Univ. of London. *Career:* worked as writer in public-relations dept of Amoco Oil Co. 1981–83; taught English as second language, London, UK 1984–86, Brooklyn Coll. 1990, Rochester Inst. of Tech.'s English Language Center 1993; began writing children's books 1997. *Publications include:* Seesaw Girl 1999, The Kite Fighters 2000, A Single Shard (American Library Asscn John Newbery Medal 2002) 2001, When My Name Was Keoko 2002; contribs to Cricket, Contemporary Poetry and Alsop Review. *Address:* Author Mail, c/o Houghton Mifflin Children's Books, 8th Floor, 222 Berkeley Street, Boston, MA 02116-3764, USA. *Website:* www.lindasuepark.com.

PARK, Yongsoo; South Korean/American filmmaker and novelist; m. *Career:* lives in New York, USA. *Film:* Free Country the Movie (writer, dir) 1996, Antigone 5000. *Play:* Free Country (Asian American Theater Co.) 1997. *Publications:* novels: Boy Genius (Kiriyama Prize notable book) 2002, Las Cucarachas 2004. *Honours:* Asian American Writers' Workshop Van Lier Fellowship. *Address:* c/o Akashic Books, PO Box 1456, New York, NY 10009, USA (office). *E-mail:* akashic7@aol.com (office).

PARKER, Rev. David C., MTheol, DipTh, ThD; British theologian and educator; *Edward Cadbury Professor of Theology, University of Birmingham*; b. 4 July 1953, Boston, Lincolnshire; m. Karen Parker, two s. two d. *Education:* Univs of St Andrews and Cambridge and Univ. of Leiden, Netherlands. *Career:* curate, Christian churches, London 1977–80, Oxon. 1980–85; Theological Coll. Tutor, Birmingham, 1985–93; Lecturer and Reader, Univ. of Birmingham, Prof. in Theology, Dir Inst. for Textual Criticism and Electronic Editing 2002–, Edward Cadbury Prof of Theology 2005–; Co-Ed., Int. Greek New Testament Project; mem. Studiorum Novi Testamenti Societas, Co-Chair. Textual Criticism Seminar, Soc. of Biblical Literature. *Publications:* Codex Bezae: An Early Christian Manuscript and Its Text 1992, The Gospel of John: The Papyri 1995, The Living Text of the Gospels 1997, Calvin: Commentary on Romans (with T. H. L. Parker) 1999, The Gospel of John: The Majuscule Manuscripts 2005. *Address:* Centre for the Editing of Texts in Religion, Graduate Institute for Theology and Religion, University of Birmingham, Elmfield House, Bristol Road, Birmingham, B29 6LQ, England (office). *Telephone:* (121) 415-8341 (office). *E-mail:* d.c.parker@bham.ac.uk (office). *Website:* www.theology.bham.ac.uk/parker.html (office).

PARKER, Gordon; British author and playwright; b. 28 Feb. 1940, Newcastle upon Tyne. *Education:* Newcastle Polytechnic (HND in Mechanical Eng). *Career:* book reviewer, BBC Radio and ITV. *Publications:* The Darkness of the Morning 1975, Lightning in May 1976, The Pool 1978, Action of the Tiger 1981; radio plays: The Seance 1978, God Protect the Lonely Widow 1982. *Address:* 14 Thornhill Close, Seaton Delaval, Northumberland NE25 0JS, England (home). *Telephone:* (191) 237-7333 (home). *E-mail:* delavallad14@aol.com (home).

PARKER, Gwendolyn McDougald, BA, JD, LLM; American writer; b. 9 June 1950, Durham, NC. *Education:* Radcliffe College, New York Univ. School of Law. *Publications:* These Same Long Bones, 1994; Trespassing, My Sojourn in the Halls of Privilege, 1997. *Honours:* New York Times Notable Book of the Year citation 1994.

PARKER, Peter Robert Nevill, BA, FRSL; British writer; b. 2 June 1954, Hereford, England. *Education:* Univ. Coll. London. *Career:* exec. cttee mem., English PEN 1994–97; trustee 1994–, Chair. 1998–2000, PEN Literary Foundation; Assoc. Ed., Oxford Dictionary of National Biography 1996–; Trustee London Library 1998–. *Publications:* The Old Lie 1987, Ackerley 1989, The Reader's Companion to the Twentieth-Century Novel (ed.) 1994, The Reader's Companion to Twentieth-Century Writers (ed.) 1995, Isherwood: A Life 2004; contrib. to Daily Telegraph, Independent, Sunday Times, Hortus. *Literary Agent:* Rogers, Coleridge & White, 20 Powis Mews, London, W11 1JN, England.

PARKER, Robert Brown, PhD; American writer; b. 17 Sept. 1932, Springfield, Mass.; s. of Carroll Snow Parker and Mary Pauline (née Murphy) Parker; m. Joan Hall 1956; two s. *Education:* Colby Coll., Boston Univ. *Career:* served with US Army 1954–56; Co-Chair. Parker-Farman Co. 1960-62; lecturer Boston Univ. 1962–64; mem. faculty Lowell State Coll., Mass. 1964–66; lecturer Suffolk Univ. 1965–66; mem. faculty Bridgewater State Coll. 1966–68; Asst Prof. of English Northeastern Univ., Boston 1968–73, Assoc. Prof. 1973–76, Prof. 1976–79; screenwriter with Joan Parker 1985–; mem. Writers Guild of America. Screenwriting includes: Spenser: For Hire 1985–88 (series), Blues for Buder 1988, High Rise 1988, A Man Called Hawk (series) 1989–90, Spenser: Ceremony 1993, Spenser: Pale Kings and Princes 1993, Spenser: Small Vices 1999. *Publications include:* Promised Land 1976 (Edgar Allan Poe Award for Best Novel, Mystery Writers of America 1976), Three Weeks in Spring (with Joan Parker) 1978, A Savage Place 1981, Surrogate: A Spenser Short Story 1982, Love and Glory 1983, Parker on Writing 1985, Pale Kings and Princes 1987, Poodle Springs (with Raymond Chandler) 1989, Stardust 1990, A Year at the Races 1990, Paper Doll 1993, All Our Yesterdays 1994, Spenser's Boston 1994, Thin Air 1995, Chance 1996, Small Vices 1997, Night Passage 1997, Sudden Mischief 1998, Trouble in Paradise 1998, Family Honor 1999, Hush Money 1999, Hugger Mugger 2001, School Days 2005, Sea Change 2006, Dream Girl 2006. *Honours:* Hon. DLitt (Northeastern Univ.) 1987.

PARKER, Robert M., Jr, BA, LLB; American writer and wine critic; *Publisher, The Wine Advocate*; b. 23 July 1947, Baltimore, Md; m. Patricia Parker 1969; one d. *Education:* Univ. of Maryland. *Career:* attorney, Sr Attorney and later Asst Gen. Counsel for Farm Credits, Bank of Baltimore 1973–84; Founder, Writer and Publr The Wine Advocate 1978–; Contributing Ed. Food and Wine Magazine; wine critic for L'Express magazine (first non-French holder of post). *Publications include:* Bordeaux (Glenfiddich Award 1986, Int. Asscn of Cooking Professionals Award for second edn 1992, Goldene Feder Award (Germany) for third edn 1993, Moët-Hennessy Wine and Vine Communication Award for French edn 1993) 1985, Parker's Wine Buyer's Guide 1987, The Wines of the Rhône Valley and Provence (Tastemaker's Award, USA 1989, Wine Guild's Wine Book of the Year Award, UK 1989) 1987, Burgundy (Moët-Hennessy Wine and Vine Communication Award for French edn 1993) 1990; contribs to The Field. *Honours:* Hon. Citizen of Châteauneuf du Pape 1995; Chevalier, Ordre nat. du Mérite 1993, Chevalier, Légion d'honneur 1999; Loyola Coll. Marylander of the Year Award 1992, James Beard Foundation Wine and Spirits Professional of 1997. *Address:* The Wine Advocate, Inc., PO Box 311, Monkton, MD 21111, USA (office). *Telephone:* (410) 329-6477 (office). *Fax:* (410) 357-4504 (office). *E-mail:* wineadvocate@erobertparker.com (office). *Website:* www.erobertparker.com (office).

PARKER, Trey; American screenwriter, film director and producer; b. (Randolph Severn Parker III), 19 Oct. 1969, Conifer, CO. *Career:* collaborated with Matt Stone on short animation, Jesus vs Frosty 1992, later remade as animated Christmas card for FoxLab, titled The Spirit of Christmas 1995; co-creator and Exec. Prod., South Park animation (with Matt Stone) 1997–, and other films and TV series. *Films:* Jesus vs Frosty (writer, dir, prod.) 1992, American History (writer, dir) (Student Acad. Award) 1992, Your Studio and You (writer, dir) 1995, The Spirit of Christmas (writer, dir, prod.) 1995, For Goodness Sake II (dir) 1996, Alferd Packer: The Musical (aka Cannibal! The Musical) (writer, dir, prod.) 1996, Orgazmo (writer, dir, prod.) 1997, South Park: Bigger Longer & Uncut (writer, dir, prod.) (Los Angeles Film Critics Award, New York Film Critics Award, MTV Movie Award) 1999, How's Your News? (exec. prod.) 1999, Team America: World Police (writer, dir, prod.) 2004. *Film appearances:* BASEketball 1998, provides voices for many characters in his animation films and television series. *Television:* South Park (series writer, dir, prod.) 1997–, That's My Bush! (series writer, dir, prod.) 2001. *Recordings:* albums: Chef Aid: The South Park Album, South Park: Bigger, Longer and Uncut (soundtrack), Mr Hankey's Christmas Classics, Timmy and the Lords of the Underworld. *Address:* c/o Paramount Studios, 5555 Melrose Avenue, Hollywood, CA 90038, USA. *E-mail:* news@southparkstudios.com. *Website:* www.southparkstudios.com.

PARKES, Roger Graham, DipAgr; British novelist and scriptwriter; b. 15 Oct. 1933, Chingford, Essex, England; m. Tessa Isabella McLean 1964, one s. one d. *Career:* staff writer, Farming Express, Scottish Daily Express, 1959–63; Ed., Farming Express, 1963; staff script ed. for drama, BBC TV, London, 1964–70; mem. Writers Guild of Great Britain; Magistrates Asscn. *Publica-*

tions: Death Mask, 1970; Line of Fire, 1971; The Guardians, 1973; The Dark Number, 1973; The Fourth Monkey, 1978; Alice Ray Morton's Cookham, 1981; Them and Us, 1985; Riot, 1986; Y-E-S, 1986; An Abuse of Justice, 1988; Troublemakers, 1990; Gamelord, 1991; The Wages of Sin, 1992. Contributions: Daily Express; Sunday Express. *Honours:* Grand Prix de Littérature, Paris, 1974. *Address:* Cartlands Cottage, Kings Lane, Cookham Dean, Berkshire SL6 9AY, England (home).

PARKHOMENKO, Sergey Borisovich; Russian journalist; b. 13 March 1964, Moscow; m.; two s. *Education:* Moscow State Univ. *Career:* Head of Div. Teatre (magazine) 1985–90; political observer Nezavisimaya Gazeta 1990–92; mem. Bd Segodnya (newspaper) 1993–95; co-founder Moscow Charter for Journalists 1994; Ed.-in-Chief Itogi (magazine) 1996–2001, IT Weekly (journal) 2002, Real Itogi 2002, now ind. journalist.

PARKIN, Andrew Terence Leonard, (Jiang An Dao), BA, MA, PhD; British/Canadian poet and critic; *Honorary Senior Tutor, Shaw College, Chinese University of Hong Kong;* b. (Terence Leonard Parkin), 30 June 1937, Birmingham, England; s. of F. S. Parkin and M. P. M. Stansfield; m. 1st Christine George 1959; one s.; m. 2nd Françoise Lentsch 1990. *Education:* Pembroke Coll., Cambridge, Univ. of Bristol. *Career:* Ed. Canadian Journal of Irish Studies, 1974–89; Prof. of English, Univ. of British Columbia; Prof. of English, Chinese Univ. of Hong Kong, Prof. Emer. and Hon. Sr Tutor, Shaw Coll. 2001–; Distinguished Research Assoc., Faculty of Int. Affairs, Le Havre Univ., France; mem. Canadian Asscn for Irish Studies (Hon. Life Mem.), League of Canadian Poets, Cambridge Club of Paris, Writers' Union of Canada, Soc. des Anglicistes de l'Enseignement Supérieur, Paris Asscn for Decorative and Fine Arts (Cttee mem.); read poems accompanied by pianist Isabelle Le Goux at Institut Polonais, Paris 2006. *Exhibition:* suite of 12 poems read with Chinese trans. at Opening of Art Exhbn of Chan Hang 2006, poems relating to his paintings, at Chinese Univ. of Hong Kong. *Radio:* two series of Poetry on the Air for RTHK 1987. *Publications:* Stage One: A Canadian Scenebook, 1973; The Dramatic Imagination of W. B. Yeats, 1978; Shaw's Caesar and Cleopatra, 1980; Dion Boucicault: Selected Plays, 1987; Dancers in a Web, 1987; Yeats's Herne's Egg, 1991; Yokohama Days, Kyoto Nights, 1991; File on Nichols, 1993; Hong Kong Poems (with L. Wong) 1997; The Humanities (ed.), 2001; Shakespeare Global/Local: The Hong Kong Imaginary in Transcultural Production (co-ed. with K. K. Tam and Terry Yip), 2002; The Rendez-Vous: Poems of Multicultural Experience, 2003, Shaw Sights and Sounds: A Collection of Painting and Poetry (with C. Hang and L. Wong) 2006; contribs; more than 100 essays and reviews in scholarly journals; more than 30 radio broadcasts; two TV interviews; 200 poems; poems anthologized in VS: 12 Hong Kong Poets 1993, Tolo Lights 1993, Tolo Lights 1994, First Hong Kong International Poetry Festival anthology 1997, City Voices 2003, Hong Kong: Poems/Gedichte 2006. *Honours:* Hon. Adviser, Chinese Acad. of Social Sciences, Beijing 2000–; First Prize, Martini Rossi Sonnet Competition 1985, Most Distinguished Ed. of a Learned Journal 1989. *Address:* 52 rue du Rendez-vous, Paris 75012, France (home). *Telephone:* 1-40-04-96-91 (home). *E-mail:* andrew.parkin@wanadoo.fr (home).

PARKS, Suzan-Lori, BA; American playwright; b. 10 May 1963, Fort Knox, Ky; m. Paul Oscher. *Education:* John Carroll School, Mount Holyoke Coll. *Career:* Guggenheim Foundation Fellow 2000. *Plays include:* The Sinner's Place 1984, Imperceptible Mutabilities in the Third Kingdom (OBIE Award for Best New American Play) 1989, Betting on the Dust Commander 1990, The Death of the Last Black Man in the Whole Entire World 1990, Devotees in the Garden of Love 1992, The America Play 1994, Venus 1996, In the Blood 1999, Fucking A 2000, Topdog/Underdog (Pulitzer Prize for Drama 2002) 2001, 365 Days/365 Plays 2006. *Plays for radio:* Pickling 1990, Third Kingdom 1990, Locomotive 1991. *Screenplays:* Girl 6 1996, Their Eyes Were Watching God 2005. *Publication:* Getting Mother's Body: A Novel 2003. *Honours:* MacArthur Foundation Award 2001, Eugene McDermott Award in the Arts, Council for the Arts at MIT 2006. *Address:* c/o Steven Barclay Agency, 12 Western Avenue, Petaluma, CA 94952, USA. *Telephone:* (707) 773-0654. *Fax:* (707) 778-1868. *E-mail:* steven@barclayagency.com.

PARKS, Timothy Harold, (John MacDowell), BA, MA; British writer, educator and translator; b. 19 Dec. 1954, Manchester, England. *Education:* Univ. of Cambridge and Harvard Univ. *Career:* mem. Authors' Soc. *Publications:* novels: Tongues of Flame 1985, Loving Roger 1986, Home Thoughts 1987, Family Planning 1989, Cara Massimina 1990, Goodness 1991, Italian Neighbours 1992, Juggling the Stars 1993, Shear 1993, Mimi's Ghost 1995, An Italian Education 1996, Europa 1997, Adultery and Other Diversions 1999, Destiny 2000, A Season with Verona 2002, Judge Savage 2003, Rapids 2005, Cleaver 2006; short stories: Keeping Distance 1988, The Room 1992; non-fiction: Translating Style: The English and their Italian Translations 1999, Hell and Back: Reflections on Writers and Writing from Dante to Rushdie 2001, Medici Money: Banking, Metaphysics and Art in Fifteenth-Century Florence 2005; numerous translations from Italian; contrib. numerous articles, reviews and talks to BBC Radio 3. *Honours:* Somerset Maugham Award 1986, Betty Trask Prize 1986, Rhys Prize 1986, John Floria Prize for Best Translation from Italian. *Literary Agent:* Curtis Brown Ltd, Haymarket House, 28–29 Haymarket, London, SW1Y 4SP, England. *Telephone:* (20) 7393-4400. *Fax:* (20) 7393-4401. *E-mail:* info@curtisbrown.co.uk. *Website:* www.curtisbrown.co.uk.

PARMET, Herbert Samuel, BS, MA; American academic and writer; b. 28 Sept. 1929, New York, NY; m. Joan Kronish 1948, one d. *Education:* SUNY at Oswego, Queens College, CUNY, Columbia University. *Career:* Prof. of History, 1968–83, Distinguished Prof. of History, 1983–95, Prof. Emeritus, 1995–, Graduate School and University Center, CUNY; Consultant, ABC-TV, New York City, 1983, KERA-TV, Dallas, 1986–91, WGBH-TV, Boston, 1988–91; mem. American Historical Asscn; Authors' Guild; Authors League; Organization of American Historians; Society of American Historians, fellow. *Publications:* Aaron Burr: Portrait of an Ambitious Man, 1967; Never Again: A President Runs for a Third Term, 1968; Eisenhower and the American Crusades, 1972; The Democrats: The Years after FDR, 1976; Jack: The Struggles of John F. Kennedy, 1980; JFK: The Presidency of John F. Kennedy, 1983; Richard Nixon and His America, 1990; George Bush: The Life of a Lone Star Yankee, 1997; Presidential Power: From the New Deal to the New Right, 2002. Contributions: Professional journals. *Honours:* National Endowment for the Humanities grant 1987.

PARODI, Anton Gaetano; Italian journalist and playwright; b. 19 May 1923, Castanzaro Lido (Calabria); s. of Luigi Parodi and Grazia Scicchitano; m. Piera Somino 1952; two c. *Education:* Università degli Studi, Turin and Genoa. *Career:* journalist 1945–; professional journalist 1947–; corresp. of Unità, Budapest 1964–. *Plays include:* Il gatto, Il nostro scandalo quotidiano, L'ex-maggiore Hermann Grotz, Adolfo o della nagia, Filippo l'Impostore, Una corda per il figlio di Abele, Quel pomeriggio di domenica, Dialoghi intorno ad un'uovo, Una storia della notte, Pioggia d'estate, Cielo di pietra, I giorni dell'Arca, Quello che dicono. *Honours:* Premio nazionale di teatro Riccione 1959, 1965, Premio nazionale di teatro dei giovani 1947 and numerous other prizes.

PARQUE, Richard Anthony, BA, MA; American writer, poet and teacher; b. 8 Oct. 1935, Los Angeles, CA; m. Vo Thi Lan 1975, three s. *Education:* California State University, Los Angeles, University of Redlands. *Career:* mem. Authors' Guild; Acad. of American Poets. *Publications:* Sweet Vietnam, 1984; Hellbound, 1986; Firefight, 1987; Flight of the Phantom, 1988; A Distant Thunder, 1989. Contributions: journals, magazines and newspapers. *Honours:* Bay Area Poets Award, 1989; Viet Nam novels have been placed in the Colorado State University Vietnam War Collection.

PARRA, Nicanor; Chilean poet; b. 5 Sept. 1914, San Fabián; s. of Nicanor P. Parra and Clara S. Navarrete; m. 1st Ana Troncoso 1948; m. 2nd Inga Palmen; seven c. *Education:* Univ. de Chile, Brown Univ., USA and Oxford. *Career:* Prof. of Theoretical Mechanics, Univ. de Chile 1964–; has given poetry readings in LA, Moscow, Leningrad, Havana, Lima, Ayacucho, Cuzco. *Publications:* poetry: Cancionero sin nombre 1937, Poemas y antipoemas 1954, La cueca larga 1958, Antipoems 1958, Versos de salón 1962, Discursos (with Pablo Neruda) 1962, Manifiesto 1963, Deux Poèmes (bilingual) 1964, Antología (also in Russian) 1965, Antología de la Poesía Soviética Rusa (bilingual) 1965, Canciones Rusas 1967, Defensa de Violeta Parra 1967, Artefactos 1972, Sermones y prédicas del Cristo de Elqui 1977, Nuevos sermones y prédicas del Cristo de Elqui 1979, El anti-Lázaro 1981, Poema y antipoema de Eduardo Frei 1982, Cachureos, ecopoemas, guatapiques, últimas prédicas 1983, Chistes para desorientar a la policía 1983, Coplas de Navidad 1983, Poesía política 1983, Hojas de Parra 1985, Poemas para combatir la calvicie 1993, Páginas en blanco 2001, Lear Rey & Mendigo 2004; scientific works: La Evolución del Concepto de Masa 1958, Fundamentos de la Física (trans. of Foundation of Physics by Profs Lindsay and Margenau) 1967, Obra Gruesa 1969, Los profesores, 1971. *Honours:* Premio Municipal de Poesía, Santiago 1937, 1954, Premio Nacional de Literatura 1969. *Address:* Julia Bernstein, Parcela 272, Lareina, Santiago, Chile.

PARRINDER, (John) Patrick, MA, PhD; British academic and literary critic; *Professor of English, University of Reading;* b. 11 Oct. 1944, Wadebridge, Cornwall, England; two d. *Education:* Christ's Coll. and Darwin Coll., Cambridge. *Career:* Fellow, King's Coll., Cambridge 1967–74; Lecturer, Univ. of Reading 1974–80, Reader 1980–86, Prof. of English 1986–; mem. H. G. Wells Soc., Science Fiction Foundation, Soc. of Authors; Fellow, English Asscn 2001. *Publications:* H. G. Wells 1970, Authors and Authority 1977, Science Fiction: Its Criticism and Teaching 1980, James Joyce 1984, The Failure of Theory 1987, Shadows of the Future 1995; ed.: H. G. Wells: The Critical Heritage 1972, Science Fiction: A Critical Guide 1979, Learning from Other Worlds 2000, Nation and Novel: The English Novel from its Origins to the Present Day 2006; contribs to London Review of Books and many academic journals. *Honours:* Pres.'s Award, World Science Fiction 1987, Leverhulme Major Research Fellowship 2001–04. *Address:* School of English and American Literature, University of Reading, PO Box 218, Reading, Berks., RG6 6AA (office); 82 Hillfield Avenue, Crouch End, London, N8 7DN, England (home). *Telephone:* (118) 378-8360 (office); (20) 8340-6355 (home). *E-mail:* j.p.parrinder@reading.ac.uk (office).

PARRIS, Matthew; British writer and broadcaster; b. 7 Aug. 1949, Johannesburg, S Africa; s. of Leslie F. Parris and Theresa E. Parris (née Littler). *Education:* Waterford School, Swaziland, Clare Coll., Cambridge and Yale Univ. *Career:* FCO 1974–76; with Conservative Research Dept 1976–79; MP (Conservative) for W Derbyshire 1979–86; presenter Weekend World 1986–88; Parl. Sketch Writer for The Times 1988–2001; columnist for The Times 1988–, for The Spectator 1992–; mem. Broadcasting Standards Council 1992–97. *Publications:* Chance Witness (memoir) 2001, A Castle in Spain 2005; various books about travel, politics, insult, abuse and scandal. *Honours:* various awards for writing and journalism. *Address:* The Spout, Gratton,

Bakewell, Derbyshire, DE45 1LN, England; c/o The Times, Pennington Street, London, E1 9XN.

PARROTT, Jasper William, BA; British impresario and agent; b. 8 Sept. 1944, Stockholm, Sweden; s. of the late Prof. Sir Cecil Parrott and of Lady Parrott; m. Cristina Ortiz; two d. *Education:* Tonbridge School, Peterhouse Cambridge. *Career:* joined Ibbs and Tillett Ltd 1965–69; f. Harrison Parrott Ltd 1969, Chair. and Man. Dir 1987–; Dir Japan Festival 1991, Swiss Festival in UK 1991; Dir Rambert Dance Co. 1993–98; Hon. Trustee Kew Foundation, Royal Botanical Gardens 1991–; Co-Dir Simdi Mew, Turkish Festival of Arts, Berlin 2004; Int. Adviser, Sakip Sabanci Museum, Istanbul 2004; Dir Polyarts UK 2004–. *Publication:* Beyond Frontiers: Vladimir Ashkenazy. *Address:* Harrison Parrott, 12 Penzance Place, London, W11 4PA, England (office). *Telephone:* (20) 7229-9166 (office). *Fax:* (20) 7221-5042 (office). *E-mail:* info@harrisonparrott.co.uk (office). *Website:* www.harrisonparrott.com (office).

PARRY, Graham, MA, PhD, FSA; British academic and author; *Professor Emeritus of English, University of York*; b. 5 Jan. 1940, Sutton Coldfield; m. Barbara Henry, 4 Nov. 1967. *Education:* Pembroke Coll., Cambridge, Columbia Univ., New York, USA. *Career:* Preceptor, Columbia Univ. 1962–65; Asst Prof., Univ. of British Columbia, Canada 1965–67, Visiting Prof. 1993–94; Lecturer in English, Univ. of Leeds 1967–76; Visiting Prof., Université de Toulouse, France 1972–73, City Coll., CUNY 1975–76, Doshisha Univ., Japan 1981–82, 1997–98; Lecturer in English 1977, then Prof. of Renaissance Literature, Univ. of York, now Prof. Emer. *Publications:* Lady Mary Wroth's Urania 1975, The Pre-Raphaelite Image: Style and Subject 1848–56 1978, Hollar's England: A Mid-Seventeenth Century View 1980, The Golden Age Restor'd: The Culture of the Stuart Court 1603–1642 1981, Seventeenth-Century Poetry: The Social Context 1985, The Seventeenth Century: The Intellectual and Cultural Context of English Literature 1603–1700 1989, The Trophies of Time: English Antiquarians of the Seventeenth Century 1995, The Life and Letters of John Talman 1997, Milton and the Terms of Liberty (ed. with J. Raymond) 2002, Glory, Laud and Honour: the Arts of the Anglican Counter-Reformation 2006. *Address:* Department of English and Related Literature, University of York, Heslington, York, YO10 5DD, Yorks. (office); 28 Micklefield Lane, Rawdon, Leeds, England (home). *Telephone:* (1904) 433330. *E-mail:* gp8@york.ac.uk (office).

PARSONS, Nigel; British media executive; *Managing Director, Al Jazeera International. Career:* started career as newspaper journalist, working for Cambridge Evening News, New Zealand Herald; worked in radio, Radio Television Hong Kong (RTHK), then news desks of BBC Radio 1, 2, 3, 4 and BBC World Service; cameraman (Central and S America), United Press International Television News (UPITN), later this became Worldwide Television News (WTN); also freelance contrib. to Daily Telegraph, BBC World Service, ABC Radio (USA), ABC Radio (Australia), CBC Radio (Canada); News Desk Ed., WTN 1985; Operations Dir, founding European Business Channel (EBC), Zurich, Switzerland 1988; Man. of re-launch as news and business channel, Telecampione, Italy; Regional Exec. (Eastern European and fmr USSR markets), WTN, then Vice-Pres. Europe; Dir of Associated Press Television News (APTN, created when Associated Press bought WTN); Man. Dir, Al Jazeera International 2004–, English-language news channel f. 2005, broadcasting 2006–. *Address:* Al Jazeera International, PO Box 23127, Doha, Qatar (office). *E-mail:* press.int@aljazeera.net (office). *Website:* english.aljazeera.net (office).

PARSONS, Tony; British writer. *Publications:* Man and Boy 1999, One for My Baby 2001, Man and Wife 2002, The Family Way 2004, Stories We Could Tell 2005. *Honours:* Butler and Tanner Book of the Year 2001, Nielsen BookScan and the Times Platinum Book Award, British Book Awards 2002.

PASCHEN, Elise Maria, BA, MPhil, DPhil; American arts administrator and poet; b. 4 Jan. 1959, Chicago, IL. *Education:* Harvard University, University of Oxford. *Career:* Exec. Dir, Poetry Society of America; mem. National Arts Club. *Publications:* Houses: Coasts, 1985; Infidelities, 1996. Contributions: Reviews, journals, and magazines. *Honours:* Lloyd McKim Garrison Medal for Poetry, Harvard University, 1982; Joan Grey Untermyer Poetry Prize, Harvard University/Radcliffe College, 1982; Richard Selig Prize for Poetry, Magdalen College, Oxford, 1984; Nicholas Roerich Poetry Prize, 1996.

PATCHETT, Ann, BA, MFA; American writer; b. 2 Dec. 1963, Los Angeles, CA. *Education:* Sarah Lawrence Coll. and Univ. of Iowa Writers' Workshop. *Career:* writer-in-residence Allegheny Coll. 1989–90; Yaddo Fellow 1990; Millay Fellow 1990; Resident Fellow, Fine Arts Work Center, Provincetown 1990–91; Visiting Asst Prof. Murray State Univ. 1992; Bunting Fellow, Mary Ingram Bunting Inst., Radcliffe Coll. 1993; Guggenheim Fellowship 1994. *Publications:* The Patron Saint of Liars (Univ. of Iowa James A. Michener/Copernicus Award for a book in progress 1989, American Library Asscn Notable Book 1992) 1992, Taft (Janet Heidinger Kafka Prize) 1994, The Magician's Assistant 1997, Bel Canto (PEN/Faulkner Award 2002, Orange Prize 2002) 2001, Truth and Beauty (biog.) 2004, Run 2007; contrib. to anthologies and to periodicals, including The New York Times Magazine, Chicago Tribune, Boston Globe, Vogue, GQ, Elle, Gourmet. *Honours:* Nashville Banner Tenn. Writer of the Year Award 1994. *Address:* c/o Carol Fass Ivy Publishing, 201 E 50th Street, New York, NY 10022, USA (office). *Website:* www.annpatchett.com (office).

PATERSON, Alistair Ian, (Ian Hughes), BA, DipEd; New Zealand poet, writer and educational consultant; b. 28 Feb. 1929, Nelson; m. 1984, two s. three d. *Education:* University of New Zealand, University of Auckland. *Career:* Royal New Zealand Navy, 1954–74; Dean of General Studies, New Zealand Police, 1974–78; Tertiary Inspector, New Zealand Dept of Education, 1979–89; Educational Consultant, 1990–; mem. PEN, Wellington Poetry Society. *Publications:* Caves in the Hills, 1965; Birds Flying, 1973; Cities and Strangers, 1976; The Toledo Room: A Poem for Voices, 1978; 15 Contemporary New Zealand Poets (ed.), 1980; Qu'appelle, 1982; The New Poetry, 1982; Incantations for Warriors, 1982; Oedipus Rex, 1986; Short Stories from New Zealand (ed.), 1988; How to be a Millionaire by Next Wednesday (novel), 1994. Contributions: various publications. *Honours:* Fulbright Fellowship, 1977; John Cowie Reid Award, University of Auckland, 1982; Katherine Mansfield Award for Fiction, 1993; New Zealand Creative Writing Grant, 1995.

PATERSON, Donald (Don); British poet, editor and musician; b. 30 Oct. 1963, Dundee, Scotland. *Career:* writer-in-residence, Dundee Univ. 1993–95; Poetry Ed. Picador Ltd; Lecturer in School of English, Univ. of St Andrew's. *Publications:* Nil Nil 1993, God's Gift to Women (T. S. Eliot Prize) 1997, The Eyes 1999, The White Lie: New and Selected Poetry 2001, Landing Light (T. S. Eliot Prize, Whitbread Award for Poetry) 2003, The Book of Shadows 2004, Orpheus (trans.) 2006, The Blind Eye 2007; ed. of numerous anthologies and collections. *Honours:* Eric Gregory Trust Fund Award 1990, Arvon/Observer International Poetry Competition 1993, Forward Poetry Prize 1993, Scottish Arts Council Book Awards 1993, 1997, 1999, Geoffrey Faber Memorial Prize 1998. *Address:* c/o Faber and Faber, 3 Queen Square, London, WC1N 3AU, England (office).

PATERSON, Katherine Womeldorf; American children's writer; b. 31 Oct. 1932, Qing Jiang, People's Republic of China; m. John Paterson 1962; four c. *Education:* King Coll., Bristol, TN and Union Theological Seminary, New York. *Publications:* novels: Bridge to Terabithia (Newbery Medal 1978, Lewis Carroll Shelf Award 1978, Janusz Korczak Medal, Poland 1981, Silver Pencil Award, Netherlands 1981, Grand Prix des Jeunes Lecturs, France 1986, Colorado Blue Spruce Young Adult Book Award 1986), Come Sing, Jimmy Jo, Flip-Flop Girl, The Great Gilly Hopkins (Nat. Book Award 1979, Newbery Honor Award 1979, Jane Addams Children's Book Award 1979, Christopher Award 1979), Jacob Have I Loved (Newbery Medal 1981), Jip, his Story (Scott O'Dell Award for Historical Fiction 1997), Lyddie (Int. Bd of Books for Young People Honor Book 1994, IBBY Honor Book), The Master Puppeteer (Nat. Book Award for Children's Literature 1977, MWA Edgar Allen Poe Special Award 1977), Of Nightingales that Weep (Children's Literature Asscn Phoenix Award 1994), Park's Quest, Preacher's Boy (Jefferson Cup of Virginia Library Asscn), Rebels of the Heavenly Kingdom, The Same Stuff as Stars (Paterson Prize 2003, Jane Addams Award 2003, Judy Lopez Memorial Award 2003), Sign of the Chrysanthemum; picture books: The Angel and the Donkey, Blueberries for the Queen, Celia and the Sweet, Sweet Water, The King's Equal, The Tale of the Mandarin Ducks (Boston Globe/Horn Book Picture Book Award 1991), The Wide-Awake Princess; non-fiction: Consider the Lilies, Gates of Excellence, Images of God, The Invisible Child, A Sense of Wonder, The Spying Heart, Who Am I?. *Honours:* Dr hc (St Mary of the Woods, IN), (Univ. of Maryland), (Hope Coll., Holland, MI), (Otterbein Coll., OH), (Presbyterian Coll., SC), (King Coll., TN), (Norwich Univ., VT), (St Michael's Coll., VT), (Shenandoah Coll. and Conservatory, VA), (Washington and Lee Univ., VA), (Mount Saint Vincent Univ., Halifax, Canada); Union Theological Seminary Union Medal, New York, Univ. of Southern Mississippi Medallion 1983, Univ. of Minnesota Kerlan Award 1983, Keene State Coll. Children's Literature Award 1987, Catholic Library Asscn Regina Medal 1988, New England Book Award 1992, Tulsa Public Library Anne V. Zarrow Award 1993, Education Press Friend of Education Award 1993, Hans Christian Andersen Medal for Writing 1998, New York Public Library Lion 1998, Library of Congress Living Legend Award 2000, Boston Public Library Literary Light 2000, Astrid Lindgren Memorial Award 2006. *Address:* c/o Clarion Books, 215 Park Avenue S, New York, NY 10003, USA. *Website:* www.terabithia.com.

PATERSON, Stuart A.; British writer, poet and editor; b. 31 Jan. 1966, Truro, Cornwall, England. *Education:* Stirling Univ. *Career:* founder-Ed., Spectrum review, 1990–96; Scottish Arts Council Writer-in-Residence, Dumfries and Galloway Region, 1996–98; mem. Kilmarnock North West Writers Group, founder; Artists for Independence; Scottish Poetry Library; Scottish National Party. *Publications:* Mulaney of Larne and Other Poems, 1991; Saving Graces, 1997. Contributions: anthologies, reviews, newspapers and journals. *Honours:* Eric Gregory Award, 1992; Scottish Arts Council Writer's Bursary, 1993.

PATON WALSH, Jill, CBE, MA, DipEd, FRSL; British writer; b. 29 April 1937, d. of John Llewelyn Bliss and Patricia Paula DuBern; m. 1st Anthony Paton Walsh 1961 (deceased); two d. one s; m. 2nd John Townsend. *Education:* St Michael's Coll., Finchley and St Anne's Coll., Oxford. *Career:* teacher 1959–62; Arts Council Creative Writing Fellow, Brighton Polytechnic 1976–78; Gertrude Clark Whitall Memorial Lecturer, Library of Congress, USA 1978; Visiting Faculty mem., Center for Children's Literature, Simmons Coll., Boston, MA, USA; Judge Whitbread Literary Award 1984; Chair. Cambridge Cttee, Children's Writers' and Illustrators' Group; Adjunct British Bd of Children's Literature, New England. *Publications include:* general fiction: Farewell, Great King 1972, Lapsing 1986, A School for Lovers 1989, The Wyndham Case 1993, Knowledge of Angels 1994, A Piece of Justice 1995, A Desert in Bohemia 2001, A Presumption of Death 2003, Debts of Dishonour 2006, The Bad Quarto 2007; children's books: Hengest's Tale 1966, The Dolphin Crossing 1967, Wordhoard (jtly) 1969, Fireweed (Book World Festival

Award) 1970, Goldengrove 1972, Toolmaker 1973, The Dawnstone 1973, The Emperor's Winding Sheet (jtly, Whitbread Prize) 1974, The Butty Boy 1975, The Island Sunrise: pre-historic Britain (non-fiction) 1975, Unleaving (Boston Globe/Horn Book Award) 1976, Crossing to Salamis, The Walls of Athens, and Persian Gold 1977–78, A Chance Child 1978, The Green Book 1981, Babylon 1982, Lost and Found 1984, A Parcel of Patterns (Universe Prize) 1984, Gaffer Samson's Luck (Smarties Prize Grand Prix 1984) 1985, Five Tides 1986, Torch 1987, Birdy and the Ghosties 1989, Can I Play? (series of four titles) 1990, Grace 1992, When Grandma Came 1992, Little Pepi and the Secret Names 1994, Connie Came to Play 1995, Thomas and the Tinners 1995, When I Was Little Like You 1997. *Address:* c/o David Higham Associates, 5–8 Lower John Street, Golden Square, London, W1R 4HA, England.

PATRICK, Maxine (see Maxwell, Patricia Anne)

PATRICK, Susan (see Clark, Patricia Denise)

PATRICK, William (see Haining, Peter Alexander)

PATTEN, Brian, FRSL; British poet and author; b. 7 Feb. 1946, Liverpool; s. of Ireen Stella Bevan. *Career:* Regents Lecturer, Univ. of California at San Diego; performance work and lectures worldwide for British Council. *Radio:* History of 20th-Century Poetry for Children, BBC Radio 2000, The Dittisham Nativity, BBC Radio 2005. *Publications include:* poetry: The Mersey Sound 1967, Little Johnny's Confession 1967, The Home Coming 1969, Notes to the Hurrying Man 1969, At Four O'Clock in the Morning 1971, Walking Out: The Early Poems of Brian Patten 1971, Love Poems 1981, New Volume 1983, Gargling With Jelly 1985, Storm Damage 1988, Grinning Jack: Selected Poems 1990, Thawing Frozen Frogs 1990, Armada 1996; (ed) Clare's Countryside: A Book of John Clare 1981; children's: Grizzelda Frizzle and Other Stories 1992, The Magic Bicycle 1993, Impossible Parents 1994, Frognapped! and Other Stories 1994, The Utter Nutters 1995, The Blue and Green Ark 1999, Juggling with Gerbils 2000, Little Hotchpotch 2000, Impossible Parents Go Green; (ed) The Puffin Book of 20th Century Children's Verse 1991, The Story Giant 2001, Ben's Magic Telescope 2003, Selected Poems 2007, New Collected Love Poems 2007. *Honours:* Freedom of City of Liverpool 2000; Hon. Fellow, John Moores Univ. 2002; Cholmondeley Award for Poetry 2002. *Literary Agent:* c/o Rogers, Coleridge & White Literary Agency, 20 Powis Mews, London, W11 1JN, England. *Telephone:* (20) 7221-3717. *Fax:* (20) 7229-9084. *Website:* www.rcwlitagency.co.uk.

PATTEN OF BARNES, Baron (Life Peer), cr. 2005, of Barnes in the London Borough of Richmond; **Christopher Francis Patten,** CH, PC; British politician; *Chancellor, University of Oxford;* b. 12 May 1944, s. of the late Francis Joseph Patten and Joan McCarthy; m. Mary Lavender Thornton 1971; three d. *Education:* St Benedict's School, Ealing, Balliol Coll., Oxford. *Career:* worked in Conservative Party Research Dept 1966–70, Dir 1974–79; seconded to Cabinet Office 1970; at Home Office, then personal asst to Lord Carrington, Party Chair. 1972–74; MP for Bath 1979–92; Parl. Pvt. Sec. (PPS) to Leader of the House 1979–81, to Social Services Sec. 1981–83; Parl. Under-Sec. for Northern Ireland 1983–85; Minister of State for Educ. 1985–86; Overseas Devt Minister 1986–89; Sec. of State for the Environment 1989–90; Chancellor of the Duchy of Lancaster and Chair. of the Conservative Party 1990–92; Gov. of Hong Kong 1992–97; Chair. Comm. charged with reform of Royal Ulster Constabulary 1998–99; Chancellor Newcastle Univ. 1999–, Univ. of Oxford 2003–; EU Commr for External Relations 1999–2004; Dir Ind. Newspapers 1998–99. *Publications:* The Tory Case 1983, East and West 1998, Not Quite the Diplomat: Home Truths About World Affairs 2005. *Honours:* Hon. FRCP (Edin.) 1994; Hon. Fellow Balliol Coll., Oxford 1999; Hon. DCL (Newcastle) 1999; Coolidge Travelling Scholarship, USA 1965. *Address:* House of Lords, London, SW1A 0PW, England. *Telephone:* (20) 7219-3000.

PATTERSON, Glenn, BA, MA; Northern Irish writer; *Creative Writing Fellow, Seamus Heaney Centre for Poetry, Queen's University Belfast;* b. 9 Aug. 1961, Belfast; m. Ali Fitzgibbon 1995. *Education:* Univ. of East Anglia. *Career:* writer-in-the-community, Arts Council, Northern Ireland 1989–91; Creative Writing Fellow, Univ. of East Anglia 1992; writer-in-residence, Univ. Coll., Cork 1993–94; Queen's Univ., Belfast 1994–97; currently Creative Writing Fellow Seamus Heaney Centre for Poetry, Queen's Univ., Belfast; mem. Arts Council Northern Ireland (bd mem. 1996–2000), Soc. of Authors, Tyrone Guthrie Centre (bd mem. 2004–). *Publications:* novels: Burning Your Own 1988, Fat Lad 1992, Black Night at Big Thunder Mountain 1995, The International 1999, Number 5 2003, That Which Was 2004. *Honours:* Betty Trask Prize 1988, Rooney Prize for Irish Literature 1988. *Address:* c/o Hamish Hamilton, Penguin Books Ltd, 80 Strand, London, WC2R 0RL, England.

PATTERSON, Henry (Harry), (Martin Fallon, James Graham, Jack Higgins, Hugh Marlowe), BSc (Soc.), FRSA; British/Irish novelist; b. 27 July 1929, Newcastle upon Tyne; s. of Henry Patterson and Rita Higgins Bell; m. 1st Amy Margaret Hewitt 1958 (divorced 1984); one s. three d.; m. 2nd Denise Leslie Ann Palmer 1985. *Education:* Roundhay School, Leeds, Beckett Park Coll. for Teachers, London School of Econs. *Career:* NCO, The Blues 1947–50, tried numerous jobs including clerk and circus tent hand 1950–58; schoolmaster, lecturer in liberal studies, Leeds Polytechnic, Sr Lecturer in Educ., James Graham Coll. and Tutor in School Practice, Leeds Univ. 1958–72; fulltime writer from age of 41. *Publications:* as Martin Fallon: The Testament of Caspar Schultz 1962, Year of the Tiger 1963, The Keys to Hell 1965, Midnight Never Comes 1966, Dark Side of the Street 1967, A Fine Night for Dying 1969, Day of Judgement 1978; as Hugh Marlowe: Seven Pillars to Hell 1963,

Passage by Night 1964, A Candle for the Dead (aka The Violent Enemy) 1966; as James Graham: A Game for Heroes 1970, The Wrath of God 1971, The Khufra Run 1972, The Run to Morning 1974; as Harry Patterson: Sad Wind from the Sea 1959, Cry of the Hunter 1960, The Thousand Faces of Night 1961, Comes the Dark Stranger 1962, Wrath of the Lion 1963, Pay the Devil 1963, The Dark Side of the Island 1963, A Phoenix in Blood 1964, Thunder at Noon (aka Dillinger) 1964, The Graveyard Shift 1965, Iron Tiger 1966, Brought in Dead 1967, Hell is Always Today 1968, Toll for the Brave 1971, To Catch a King (aka The Judas Gate) 1979; as Jack Higgins: East of Desolation 1968, In the Hour Before Midnight 1969, Night Judgement at Sinos 1970, The Last Place God Made 1971, The Savage Day 1972, The Eagle has Landed 1975, Storm Warning 1976, The Valhalla Exchange 1976, A Prayer for the Dying 1977, Solo (aka The Creatan Lover) 1980, Luciano's Luck 1981, Touch the Devil 1982, Exocet 1983, Confessional 1985, Night of the Fox 1986, Walking Wounded (play) 1987, Memoirs of a Dance Hall Romeo 1989, A Season in Hell 1989, Cold Harbour 1989, The Eagle Has Flown 1990, Eye of the Storm (aka Midnight Man) 1992, Thunder Point 1993, On Dangerous Ground 1994, Angel of Death 1995, Sheba 1995, Drink With the Devil 1996, The President's Daughter 1996, The Violent Enemy 1997, Flight of Eagles 1998, The White House Connection 1999, Day of Reckoning 1999, Midnight Runner 2001, Edge of Danger 2001, The Keys of Hell 2002, Bad Company 2003, Without Mercy 2005. *Honours:* Hon. DUniv (Leeds Metropolitan Univ.) 1995. *Literary Agent:* Ed Victor Ltd, 6 Bayley Street, London, WC1B 3HB, England.

PATTERSON, James, BA, MA; American writer and fmr advertising executive; b. 22 March 1947, Newburgh, NY; m.; one s. *Education:* Manhattan Coll., Vanderbilt Univ. *Career:* wrote first novel 1976; joined J. Walter Thompson as jr copywriter 1971, subsequently Exec. Creative Dir, CEO, Chair. 1990–96. *Publications:* The Thomas Berryman Number (MWA Edgar Award) 1976, The Season of the Machete 1977, The Jericho Commandment (aka See How They Run) 1979, Virgin 1980, Black Market 1986, The Midnight Club 1989, The Day America Told the Truth: What People Really Believe About Everything that Matters (non-fiction, with Peter Kim) 1991, Along Came a Spider 1993, The Second American Revolution 1994, Kiss the Girls 1995, Hide & Seek 1996, Jack & Jill 1996, Miracle on the 17th Green (with Peter de Jonge) 1996, Cat & Mouse 1997, When the Wind Blows 1998, Pop Goes the Weasel 1999, Cradle and All (revised version of Virgin) 2000, Roses are Red 2000, Suzanne's Diary for Nicholas 2001, 1st to Die 2001, Violets are Blue 2001, 2nd Chance (with Andrew Gross) 2002, Four Blind Mice 2002, The Beach House (with Peter de Jonge) 2002, The Jester 2003, The Lake House 2003, The Big Bad Wolf 2003, 3rd Degree 2003, Sam's Letters to Jennifer 2004, London Bridges 2004, Honeymoon 2005, 4th of July 2005, Mary Mary 2005, Maximum Ride: The Angel Past 2005, The 5th Horseman (with Maxine Paetro) 2006, Judge and Jury 2006, Lifeguard (with Andrew Gross) 2006, Thriller (short stories) (ed) 2006, Maximum Ride: School's Out Forever (with Peter De Jonge) 2006, Cross 2006, Step on a Crack (with Michael Ledwidge) 2007, The Beach Road (with Peter De Jonge) 2007, The 6th Target (with Maxine Paetro) 2007, Maximum Ride: Saving the World and Other Extreme Sports (children's fiction) 2007, The Quickie (with Michael Ledwidge) 2007. *Address:* c/o Little, Brown and Company, 1271 Avenue of the Americas, New York, NY 10020, USA. *Website:* www.jamespatterson.com.

PATTERSON, (Horace) Orlando Lloyd; Jamaican academic and writer; *John Cowles Professor of Sociology, Harvard University;* b. 5 June 1940. *Education:* BSc, University of the West Indies 1962; PhD, LSE 1965. *Career:* Prof. of Sociology 1971–, John Cowles Prof. of Sociology 1993, Harvard University; Assoc. Ed., American Sociological Review 1989–92; mem. American Acad. of Arts and Sciences, fellow; American Sociological Asscn. *Publications:* fiction: The Children of Sisyphus 1964, An Absence of Ruins 1967, Die the Long Day 1972; non-fiction: The Sociology of Slavery: Jamaica 1655–1838 1967, Ethnic Chauvinism: The Reactionary Impulse 1977, Slavery and Social Death: A Comparative Study 1982, Freedom 1991, The Ordeal of Integration: Progress and Resentment in America's 'Racial' Crisis 1997, Rituals of Blood: The Consequences of Slavery in Two American Centuries 1999; contributions to books and professional journals. *Honours:* Best Novel in English Award, Dakar Festival of Negro Arts 1965, Co-Winner, Ralph Bunche Award, American Political Science Asscn 1983, Distinguished Contribution to Scholarship Award, American Sociological Asscn 1983, Walter Channing Cabot Faculty Prizes, Harvard University 1983, 1997, National Book Award for Non-Fiction 1991, University of California at Los Angeles Medal 1992; Order of Distinction, Government of Jamaica 1999; Hon. Doctor of Humane Letters (New School University) 2000, (Chicago) 2002. *Address:* c/o Department of Sociology, Harvard University, 520 William James Hall, 33 Kirkland Street, Cambridge, MA 02138, USA. *E-mail:* opatters@fas.harvard.edu (office).

PATTERSON, Richard North, BA, JD; American novelist; b. 22 Feb. 1947, Berkeley, CA; m. Laurie Anderson Patterson 1993; four s. two d. *Education:* Ohio Wesleyan Univ., Case Western Reserve Law School. *Career:* mem. PEN (bd of dirs). *Publications:* The Lasko Tangent 1979, The Outside Man 1981, Escape the Night 1983, Private Screening 1985, Degree of Guilt 1993, Eyes of a Child 1995, The Final Judgement 1995, Silent Witness 1997, When the Wind Blows 1998, Protect and Defend 2000, Balance of Power 2003, Conviction 2005, Exile 2007; contrib. to magazines, journals and newspapers. *Honours:* Edgar Allan Poe Award 1979, French Grand Prix de Littérature Policière 1995, Case Western Reserve Univ. Pres.'s Award to Distinguished Alumni

1997. *Address:* c/o Random House, 1745 Broadway, New York, NY 10019, USA.

PATTISON, Robert, AB, MA, PhD; American academic and writer; b. 28 Oct. 1945, Orange, NJ. *Education:* Yale and Columbia Univs, Univ. of Sussex, UK. *Career:* Adjunct Lecturer, Richmond Coll., CUNY 1974, Adjunct Instructor, Queensborough Community Coll., CUNY 1974–75; Instructor of English, St Vincent's Coll., St John's Univ., New York 1975–77; Prof. of English, Southampton Coll., Long Island Univ., New York 1978–2004, Co-ordinator of the English and Writing Programme 1992–2004; Prof. of English, Long Island Univ., Brooklyn 2005–; Pres. Southampton Coll. Fed. of Teachers 1981–83, 1985–86, 1996–2001, 2003–04. *Publications:* The Child Figure in English Literature 1978, Tennyson and Tradition 1980, On Literacy 1982, The Triumph of Vulgarity 1987, The Great Dissent: John Henry Newman and the Liberal Heresy 1991; contrib. to Nation, ADE Bulletin, University of Toronto Quarterly, Mosaic, New York Times, Dickens Studies Newsletter; various edited vols. *Honours:* Long Island Univ. Trustees Awards for Scholarship 1979, 1985, Rockefeller Foundation Fellowship 1980–81, Guggenheim Fellowship 1986–87. *Address:* Humanities Division, Southampton College, Southampton, NY 11968, USA (office). *Telephone:* (631) 287-8421 (office). *Fax:* (631) 287-8120 (office). *E-mail:* robert.pattison@liu.edu (office).

PAUL, Jeremy; British writer; b. 29 July 1939, Bexhill, Sussex; m. Patricia Garwood 1960; four d. *Education:* King's, Canterbury and St Edmund Hall, Oxford. *Career:* mem. Writers' Guild of GB. *Television plays, series and adaptations include:* Upstairs, Downstairs 1971–75, Country Matters 1972, The Duchess of Duke Street 1976, Danger, UXB 1977, A Walk in the Forest 1980, The Flipside of Dominick Hide (with Alan Gibson) 1980, Sorrell and Son 1983, By the Sword Divided 1985, The Adventures, Return and Memoirs of Sherlock Holmes 1984–94, Lovejoy 1991–94, Hetty Wainthropp Investigates 1996–98, Midsomer Murders 2001. *Plays:* David Going Out 1971, Manoeuvres 1971, The Little Match Girl (with Strachan and Stewart) 1976, Visitors (with Carey Harrison) 1980, The Secret of Sherlock Holmes 1988, The Watcher 1989, Dead Easy 2006. *Film screenplay:* Countess Dracula 1970. *Publication:* Sing Willow 2002. *Address:* 4 Seymer Place, Swanage, Dorset BH19 2AJ, England (home). *E-mail:* jeremy@jpaulwriting.com (home). *Website:* www.jeremypaul.org.uk.

PAULIN, Thomas (Tom) Neilson, BA, BLitt; British poet, critic and academic; b. 25 Jan. 1949, Leeds, Yorkshire, England; m. Munjiet Kaut Khosa 1973; two s. *Education:* Univ. of Hull, Lincoln Coll., Oxford. *Career:* Lecturer Univ. of Nottingham 1972–89, Reader in Poetry 1989–94; G. M. Young Lecturer in English Literature Univ. of Oxford 1994–; Fellow Hertford Coll., Oxford 1994–. *Television:* panel mem. Newsnight Review (BBC 2). *Publications:* poetry: Theoretical Locations 1975, A State of Justice 1977, Personal Column 1978, The Strange Museum 1980, The Book of Juniper 1981, Liberty Tree 1983, The Argument at Great Tew 1985, Fivemiletown 1987, Selected Poems 1972–90 1993, Walking a Line 1994, The Wind Dog 1999, The Invasion Handbook 2002, The Road to Inver 2004; non-fiction: Thomas Hardy: The Poetry of Perception 1975, Ireland and the English Crisis 1984, The Faber Book of Political Verse (ed.) 1986, Hard Lines 3 (co-ed.) 1987, Minotaur: Poetry and the Nation State 1992, Writing to the Moment: Selected Critical Essays 1996, The Day Star of Liberty: William Hazlitt's Radical Style (biog.) 1998, Crusoe's Secret: The Aesthetics of Dissent 2005. *Honours:* Eric Gregory Award 1978, Somerset Maugham Award 1978, Faber Memorial Prize 1982, Fulbright Scholarship 1983–84. *Address:* c/o Faber and Faber, 3 Queen Square, London, WC1N 3AU, England.

PAULSEN, Nancy; American publishing executive. *Career:* fmr Ed.-in-Chief Puffin Books, Publr 1991–94; fmr Sr Ed. Viking Children's Books; Pres. and Publr G.P. Putnam's Sons Books for Young Readers 1994–, Dial Books for Young Readers 1998–. *Publications include:* All That You Are (co-author) 2000, Miracle's Boys (co-author) 2000, Belly Button Boy 2000, Forging Freedom 2000, Hope Was Here 2000. *Address:* G.P. Putnam's Sons Children's Books, Penguin USA, 375 Hudson Street, New York, NY 10014, USA (office). *Website:* www.penguinputnam.com (office).

PAULSON, Ronald Howard, BA, PhD; American academic and writer; *Mayer Professor Emeritus of Humanities, Johns Hopkins University*; b. 27 May 1930, Bottineau, ND; m. Barbara Lee Appleton 1957 (divorced 1982); one s. one d. *Education:* Yale Univ. *Career:* Instructor, Univ. of Illinois 1958–59, Asst Prof. 1959–62, Assoc. Prof. 1962–63; Prof. of English, Johns Hopkins Univ. 1967–75, Chair. Dept of English 1968–75, Andrew W. Mellon Prof. of Humanities 1973–75, Mayer Prof. of Humanities 1984– (Mayer Prof. Emer. 2005–), Chair. Dept of Humanities 1985–91; Prof. of English, Yale Univ. 1975–84; mem. American Soc. of 18th Century Studies, Pres. 1986–87; Fellow, American Acad. of Arts and Sciences. *Publications:* Theme and Structure in Swift's Tale of a Tub 1960, Fielding: The Critical Heritage (ed. with Thomas Lockwood) 1962, Fielding: 20th Century Views (ed.) 1962, Hogarth's Graphic Works 1965, The Fictions of Satire 1967, Satire and the Novel 1967, Satire: Modern Essays in Criticism 1971, Hogarth: His Life, Art and Times 1971, Rowlandson: A New Interpretation 1972, Emblem and Expression: Meaning in Eighteenth Century English Art 1975, The Art of Hogarth 1975, Popular and Polite Art in the Age of Hogarth and Fielding 1979, Literary Landscape: Turner and Constable 1982, Book and Painting: Shakespeare, Milton and the Bible 1983, Representations of Revolution 1983, Breaking and Remaking 1989, Figure and Abstraction in Contemporary Painting 1990, Hogarth: Vol. I, The Making of the Modern Moral Subject 1991, Vol. II, High Art and Low 1992, Vol. III, Art and Politics 1993, The Beautiful, Novel and Strange: Aesthetics and Heterodoxy 1996, The Analysis of Beauty (ed.) 1997, Don Quixote in England: The Aesthetics of Laughter 1998, The Life of Henry Fielding: A Critical Biography 2000, Hogarth's Harlot: Parody in Enlightenment England 2003; contrib. to professional journals. *Honours:* Guggenheim Fellowships 1965–66, 1986–87, Nat. Endowment for the Humanities Fellow 1977–78. *Address:* 2722 St Paul Street, Baltimore, MD 21218, USA (home). *Telephone:* (410) 366-7454 (home). *E-mail:* pauls_r@jhu.edu (home).

PAVIĆ, Milorad, DPhil; Serbian poet, novelist and historian; b. 15 Oct. 1929, Belgrade; m. 1st Branka Pavić; one s. one d.; m. 2nd Jasmina Mihailović. *Education:* Belgrade Univ. and Univ. of Zagreb. *Career:* journalist, Radio Belgrade 1958–63, Prosveta Publrs 1963–74; Prof., Dean, Faculty of Philosophy, Novy Sad Univ. 1974–82; Prof., Belgrade Univ. 1982–94; Lecturer, Univ. of Paris (Sorbonne); works trans. into 30 languages; mem. Serbian Acad. of Sciences and Arts. *Plays:* adaptation of the novel Dictionary of the Khazars, Forever and a Day 1993, Triple Bed, Glass Snail 2002. *Publications:* Vojislav Ilic (1860–1894) 1961, Vojislav Ilic, njegovo vreme i delo (non-fiction) 1962, Palimpsesti (poems) 1967, Istorija srpske knjizevnosti baroknog doba (non-fiction) 1970, Mesecev kamen (poems) 1971, Vojislav Ilic i evropsko pesnistvo 1971, Gavril Stefanovic Venclovic 1972, Gvozdena zavesa (short stories, trans. as The Iron Curtain) 1973, Jezicko pamcenje i pesnicki oblik 1976, Konji svetoga Marka (short stories, trans. as St Mark's Horses) 1976, Istorija srpske knjizevnosti klasicizma i predromantizma 1979, Ruski hrt/Borzoi (short stories, trans. as Borzoi) 1979, Nove beogradske price 1981, Duse se kupaju poslednji put 1982, Radjanje nove srpske knjizevnosti (non-fiction) 1983, Hazarski recnik (novel, trans. as Dictionary of the Khazars) 1984, Istorija, stalez i stil 1985, Izabrana dela 1985, Predeo slikan cajem (novel, trans. as Landscape Painted with Tea) 1988, Izvrnuta rukavica (short stories, trans. as The Inverted Glove) 1989, Kratka istorija Beograda 1990, Unutrasnja strana vetra ili roman o Heri i Leandru (novel, trans. as The Inner Side of the Wind) 1991, Istorija srpske knjizevnosti 1991, Pozorisni jelovnik za uvek i dan vise (trans. as Forever and a Day) 1993, Poslednja ljubav u Carigradu (novel, trans. as The Last Love in Constantinople) 1994, Sesir od riblje koze 1996, Stakleni puz 1998, Zvezdani plast (novel) 2001, Sedam smrtnih grehova (novel) 2002, Nevidljivo ogledalo - Sareni hleb (children's novel, trans. as Invisible Mirror and Multicoloured Bread) 2002, Unikat (novel, trans. as Unique Item) 2004, Plava sveska (catalogue of endings to accompany Unikat) 2004, Interaktivne drame (collection of plays) 2004, Love Story in Two Tales (with Jasmina Mihajlović) 2004, Prica koja jeubila Emiliju Knor (trans. as The Tale that Killed Emily Knorr), Roman Kaodrzava i drugi ogledi 2005, Svadba u kupatilu vesela igra u sedam slika 2005; contrib. numerous articles and essays. *Honours:* Hon. Prof., Natalia Nesterovoj Univ., Moscow 2006 Zepter Int. Award for Literature, Warsaw 2005. *Address:* Brace Baruh 2, Belgrade, Serbia. *E-mail:* mpavic@eunet.yu. *Website:* www.khazars.com.

PAVLÍČEK, František, PhD; Czech playwright; b. 20 Nov. 1923, Lukov, Zlín Dist; s. of František Pavlíček and Růžena Šmídová; m. 1st Alena Břízová 1971, one s. one d.; m. 2nd Eva Košlerová 1991. *Education:* Charles Univ., Prague. *Career:* Script Ed.-in-Chief, Czechoslovak Film Co. 1956–65; Dir Theatre Na Vino-hradech 1965–70, signed Charter 77, served long-term prison sentence; Dir-Gen. Czechoslovak Radio, Prague 1990–91. *Plays for stage and TV include:* The Little Mermaid 1992, In Praise of Debauchery 1994, Muž v pozadí (Mastermind) 1995; 20 screenplays, including Labyrint srdce (The Labyrinth of the Heart) 1961, Horouci srdce 1962, Peter und das Einmaleins mit ser Sieben 1962, Marketá Lazarová 1967, Tony, tobe preskocilo 1968, Babicka 1971, Tri orisky pro Popelku (Three Wishes for Cinderella) 1974, Královský slib 2001; 80 radio plays and The End of the Patriarchate (novel) 1992, Zrcadlení (The Reflection) 1997. *Honours:* Medal of Merit (Second Grade) 2002; Czechoslovak State Prize 1968. *Address:* K. Brance 1012/19, 150 00 Prague 5, Czech Republic (home). *Telephone:* (235) 521799.

PAVLYCHKO, Dmytro Vasylovych; Ukrainian poet and politician; b. 28 Sept. 1929, Ivano-Frankivsk; s. of Vasyl Pavlychko and Paraska Bojchuk. *Education:* Lviv Univ. *Career:* started publishing in early 1950s; mem. CPSU 1954–88; keen advocate of de-Stalinization from 1962; f. Taras Shevchenko Ukrainian Language Soc. 1988, for protection of language; Chair. Inaugural Congress of the Popular Movt of the Ukraine for Perestroika (Rukh); Deputy to Ukrainian Supreme Soviet 1990; Chair. Parl. Cttee for Int. Affairs 1991; Amb. to Slovakia 1995–98, to Poland 1999–2003. *Publications include:* My Land 1955, The Day 1960, Bread and Banner 1968, Sonnets 1978, Turned to the Future 1986, Repentance Psalms 1994, Nostalgia 1998. *Address:* c/o Ministry of Foreign Affairs, pl. Mykhailivska 1, 01018 Kiev, Ukraine (office). *Telephone:* (44) 21-28-33 (office). *Fax:* (44) 226-31-69 (office).

PAXMAN, Jeremy Dickson, MA; British broadcast journalist and writer; *Presenter, Newsnight*; b. 11 May 1950, Leeds; s. of Arthur Keith Paxman and Joan McKay Dickson; one s. two d. *Education:* Malvern Coll., St Catharine's Coll., Cambridge. *Career:* journalist, Northern Ireland 1973–77; reporter, BBC TV Tonight and Panorama programmes 1977–85, presenter BBC TV Breakfast Time 1986–89, Newsnight 1989–, Univ. Challenge 1994–, Start the Week, Radio 4, 1998–2002; Fellow St Edmund Hall, Oxford, St Catharine's Coll. Cambridge 2001; Vice-Pres. The Wild Trout Trust (WTT) 2004–. *Publications:* A Higher Form of Killing (co-author) 1982, Through the Volcanoes 1985, Friends in High Places 1990, Fish, Fishing and the Meaning of Life 1994, The Compleat Angler 1996, The English 1998, The Political Animal 2002, On Royalty 2006; numerous articles in newspapers and magazines. *Honours:* Dr hc (Leeds, Bradford) 1999; Royal TV Soc. Award for Int. Reporting, Richard Dimbleby Award, BAFTA 1996, 2000, Interview of the Year, Royal TV Soc. 1997, 1998, 2001, Voice of the Viewer and Listener Presenter of the Year 1994, 1997, Variety Club Media Personality of the Year 1999. *Address:* c/o BBC, Broadcasting House, Portland Place, London, W1A 1AA, England. *Website:* news.bbc.co.uk/1/hi/programmes/newsnight.

PAXSON, Diana Lucile, BA, MA; American writer and editor; b. 20 Feb. 1943, Detroit, MI; d. of Edwin Woolman Paxson and Mary Harrington Paxson; m. Donald C. Studebaker 1968, two s. *Education:* Mills College, University of California at Berkeley. *Career:* Ordained Minister, Fellowship of the Spiral Path 1982; Elder, The Troth, Covenant of the Goddess; Ed., Idunna journal 1996–; mem. SFWA. *Publications:* fiction: Lady of Light 1982, Lady of Darkness 1983, Brisingamen 1984, Silverhair the Wanderer 1986, White Mare, Red Stallion 1986, The Earthstone 1987, The Paradise Tree 1987, The Sea Star 1988, The White Raven 1988, The Wind Crystal 1990, Lady of Darkness 1990, The Serpent's Tooth 1991, The Wolf and the Raven 1993, Master of Earth and Water 1993, The Shield Between the Worlds 1994, Sword of Fire and Shadow 1995, The Dragons of the Rhine 1995, The Lord of Horses 1996, Priestess of Avalon 2000, The Hallowed Isle 2001, Ancestors of Avalon 2004, The Golden Hill of Westria 2006, Ravens of Avalon 2007; non-fiction: Celestial Wisdom 2003, Taking Up the Reins 2005, Essential Asatra 2006; contrib. articles to Sagewoman magazine, short stories in various publications. *Address:* PO Box 472, Berkeley, CA 94701, USA. *E-mail:* diana@westria .org (home). *Website:* www.westria.org.

PAXTON, Lois (see Low, Lois Dorothea)

PAYNE, Alexander, BA, MFA; American film director and screenwriter; b. 1961, Omaha, Neb.; m. Sandra Oh 2003. *Education:* Stanford Univ. and UCLA. *Career:* began making films aged six; employee Universal Pictures; completed several shorts for Propaganda Films and screened on Playboy Channel; feature film debut with Citizen Ruth (co-wrote screenplay with Jim Taylor) 1996. *Films include:* The Passion of Martin (thesis film, dir) 1989, Inside Out (dir and screenwriter) 1992, Citizen Ruth (dir and screenwriter) (First Prize, Munich Film Festival) 1996, Election (dir and co-screenwriter with Jim Taylor) (Best Screenplay Award: WGA, New York Film Critics' Circle and Ind. Spirit, Best Film and Best Dir, Ind. Spirit Awards) 1999, Jurassic Park III (screenplay) 2001, About Schmidt (dir and co-screenwriter with Jim Taylor) (Best Movie of the Year, Los Angeles Film Critics' Asscn 2002, Golden Globe for Best Screenplay 2003) 2002, Sideways (dir) (Los Angeles Film Critics' Asscn Best Movie of the Year, Golden Globe Award for Best Screenplay 2005, BAFTA Award for Best Adapted Screenplay 2005, Writers' Guild of America Award for best adapted screenplay 2005, Acad. Award for Best Adapted Screenplay 2005, Independent Spirit Awards for Best Dir, Best Screenplay 2005) 2004. *Address:* c/o New Line Cinema Corporation, 116 North Robertson Boulevard, Los Angeles, CA 90048, USA (office).

PAYNE, (William) David; American writer; b. 13 April 1955, Henderson, NC. *Publications:* Confessions of a Taoist on Wall Street: A Chinese American Romance, 1984; Early from the Dance, 1989; Ruin Creek, 1993; Gravesend Light, 2000. *Honours:* Houghton Mifflin Company Fellowship 1984. *Literary Agent:* Janklow & Nesbit Associates, 445 Park Avenue, New York, NY 10022, USA.

PAZ MARTÍNEZ, (Arsenio) Senel, BA; Cuban writer and screenwriter; b. 1950, Fomento. *Education:* Universidad de La Habana. *Publications include:* El niño aquel (short stories), Entre sus cuentos figuran ese niño 1980, El rey en el jardín (novel) (Premio de la Crítica Literaria 1985) 1983, Mentiras adorables (play), El lobo, el bosque y el hombre nuevo (novel) 1991, Fresa y chocolate (screenplay, from El lobo, el bosque y el hombre nuevo) 1994, Las Hermanas, En el cielo con diamantes (novel) 2007. *Honours:* Premio Juan Rulfo de Literatura, Medalla Alejo Carpentier 1999.

PEACE, David; British writer; b. 1967, Ossett, W Yorks.; m.; two c. *Education:* Manchester Polytechnic. *Career:* taught English in Istanbul and Tokyo 1993–2001. *Publications:* novels: Red Riding quartet: Nineteen Seventy-Four 1999, Nineteen Seventy-Seven 2000, Nineteen Eighty 2001, Nineteen Eighty-Three 2002, GB84 (James Tait Black Prize for Fiction 2005) 2004, The Damned Utd 2006. *Honours:* one of Granta magazine's 20 Best of Young British Novelists 2003. *Address:* c/o Faber and Faber Ltd, 3 Queen Square, London, WC1N 3AU, England.

PEACOCK, Molly, BA, MA; American/Canadian writer and poet; b. (Mary Peacock), 30 June 1947, Buffalo, NY; d. of Edward Frank Peacock and Pauline Ruth Wright; m. Michael Groden 1992. *Education:* Harpur Coll., State Univ. of New York (SUNY) at Binghamton, Johns Hopkins Univ. *Career:* Lecturer, SUNY at Binghamton 1975–76, Univ. of Delaware 1978–79; Writer-in-Residence, Delaware State Arts Council 1978–81, Univ. of Western Ontario 1995–96, English Faculty, Friends Seminary, New York 1981–87; Visiting Poet, Hofstra Univ. 1986, Columbia Univ. 1986, 1992, Carlow Coll. 1993; Poet-in-Residence, Bucknell Univ. 1993, Bennington Coll. 2001, American Poets' Corner, Cathedral of St John the Divine, New York 2000–05; mem. Grad. Faculty, Spalding Univ. 2002–; Contributing Writer, House & Garden, 1996–2001; Regents Lecturer, Univ. of California at Riverside 1998; mem. Acad. of American Poets, Associated Writing Programs, PEN, Poetry Soc. of America (Pres. 1989–95). *Works include:* The Shimmering Verge: A One-Woman Show in Poems 2003. *Publications:* poetry: And Live Apart 1980, Raw Heaven 1984, Take Heart 1989, Original Love 1995, Cornucopia 2002; other:

Paradise, Piece by Piece (literary memoir) 1998, How to Read a Poem... and Start a Poetry Circle 1999; ed.: Poetry in Motion: 100 Poems from the Subways and Buses (with Elise Paschen and Neil Neches) 1996, The Private I: Privacy in a Public Age (essays) 2001; contribs to anthologies, reviews, quarterlies, journals, and magazines. *Honours:* MacDowell Colony Fellowships 1975–76, 1979, 1982, 1985, 1989, Danforth Foundation Fellowships 1976–77, Yaddo Fellowships 1980, 1982, Ingram Merrill Foundation Awards 1981, 1986, New Virginia Review Fellowship 1983; PEN/Nat. Endowment for the Arts Fiction Award 1984, New York Foundation for the Arts Grant 1985, 1989, Nat. Endowment for the Arts Grant 1990. *Address:* 109 Front Street E, No. 1041, Toronto, Ont. M5A 4P7, Canada (home). *Telephone:* (212) 677-3535; (414) 866-8779 (home); (416) 774-8779 (mobile). *Fax:* (414) 866-8780 (home). *E-mail:* molly@mollypeacock.org. *Website:* www.mollypeacock.org.

PEARCE, Mary Emily; British writer; b. 7 Dec. 1932, London, England. *Career:* mem. Society of Authors. *Publications:* Apple Tree Lean Down, 1973; Jack Mercybright, 1974; The Sorrowing Wind, 1975; Cast a Long Shadow, 1977; The Land Endures, 1978; Seedtime and Harvest, 1980; Polsinney Harbour, 1983; The Two Farms, 1985; The Old House at Railes, 1993.

PEARLMAN, Daniel D., BA, MA, PhD; American academic and writer; *Professor Emeritus, University of Rhode Island;* b. 22 July 1935, New York, NY; one d. *Education:* Brooklyn Coll., CUNY, Columbia Univ., New York. *Career:* positions at Brooklyn Coll., Univ. of Ariz., Monmouth Coll., NJ, Univ. of Seville, Lehman Coll. 1958–76; Dept Chair. Univ. of Idaho 1976–80; Prof., Univ. of Rhode Island 1980–2005, Dept Chair. 1980–83, Prof. Emer. 2005–. *Publications:* The Barb of Time: On the Unity of Ezra Pound's Cantos 1969, Guide to Rapid Revision (eighth edn) 2002, Letter Perfect: An ABC for Business Writers 1985, The Final Dream and Other Fictions 1995, Black Flames (novel) 1997, The Best Known Man in the World (short stories) 2001, Memini (novel) 2003; contrib. to science fiction magazines and anthologies, including Amazing Stories, Synergy, Semiotext SF, Simulations: 15 Tales of Virtual Reality, Imaginings: An Anthology of Long Short Fiction, short stories to literary journals, including Florida Review, New England Review/Bread Loaf Quarterly, Quarterly West. *Address:* c/o Department of English, University of Rhode Island, Kingston, RI 02881, USA.

PEARLSTINE, Norman, LLB; American journalist; *Senior Advisor, Carlyle Group;* b. 4 Oct. 1942, Philadelphia; s. of Raymond Pearlstine and Gladys Pearlstine (née Cohen); m. Nancy Colbert Friday 1988. *Education:* Haverford Coll., Univ. of Pennsylvania. *Career:* staff reporter, Wall Street Journal, Dallas, Detroit, LA 1968–73; Tokyo Bureau Chief 1973–76, Man. Ed. Asian Wall Street Journal, Hong Kong 1976–78; Exec. Ed. Forbes Magazine, LA 1978–80; Nat. News Ed. Wall Street Journal, New York 1980–82, Ed. and Publr Wall Street Journal Europe, Brussels 1982–83, Man. Ed. and Vice-Pres. Wall Street Journal, New York 1983–91, Exec. Ed. 1991–92; Pres. and CEO Friday Holdings L.P., New York 1993–94; Ed.-in-Chief Time Inc. 1995–2006, now Sr Advisor to Time Warner; Sr Advisor to global telecommunications and media team, The Carlyle Group 2006–; mem. New York Historical Soc., Council on Foreign Relations. *Honours:* Ed. of Year Award, Nat. Press Foundation 1989. *Address:* The Carlyle Group, 1001 Pennsylvania Avenue, NW, Washington, DC 20004-2505, USA (office). *Telephone:* (202) 729-5626 (office). *Fax:* (202) 347-1818 (office). *Website:* www.carlyle.com (office).

PEARSALL, Derek Albert, MA; British academic and writer; *Gurney Professor Emeritus of English, Harvard University;* b. 28 Aug. 1931, Birmingham, England; m. Rosemary Elvidge 1952; two s. three d. *Education:* Univ. of Birmingham. *Career:* Asst Lecturer, then Lecturer, King's Coll. London 1959–65; Lecturer, then Sr Lecturer, then Reader, Univ. of York 1965–76, Prof. 1976–87; Visiting Prof., Harvard Univ., USA 1985–87, Gurney Prof. of English 1987–2000, Prof. Emer. 2000–; Pres. New Chaucer Soc. 1988–90; mem. Early English Text Soc. (Council mem.), Modern Humanities Research Asscn (Pres. 2004–05); Fellow, Medieval Acad. of America, American Acad. of Arts and Sciences. *Publications:* John Lydgate 1970, Landscapes and Seasons of the Medieval World (with Elizabeth Salter) 1973, Old English and Middle English Poetry 1977, Langland's Piers Plowman: An Edition of the C-Text 1978, The Canterbury Tales: A Critical Study 1985, The Life of Geoffrey Chaucer: A Critical Biography 1992, John Lydgate (1371–1449): A Bio-bibliography 1997, Chaucer to Spenser: An Anthology of Writings in English 1375–1575 1999, Gothic Europe 1200–1450 2001, Arthurian Romance: A Short Introduction 2003. *Address:* 4 Clifton Dale, York, YO30 6LJ, England (home). *E-mail:* derek@apearsall.fsnet.co.uk (home).

PEARSE, Lesley Margaret; British novelist; b. 24 Feb. 1945, Rochester, Kent, England; three d. *Education:* Northbrook School, Lee, London. *Career:* mem. Romantic Writers Asscn, RNA, West Country Writers Asscn. *Publications:* Georgia 1993, Tara 1994, Charity 1995, Ellie 1996, Camellia 1997, Rosie 1998, Charlie 1999, Never Look Back 2000, Trust Me 2001, Father Unknown 2002, Till We Meet Again 2002, Remember Me 2003, Secrets 2004, A Lesser Evil 2005, Hope 2006. *Literary Agent:* c/o Penguin Books Ltd, 80 Strand, London, WC2R 0RL, England.

PEARSON, Ridley; American author; b. 13 March 1953, Glen Cove, NY. *Education:* University of Kansas, Brown University. *Career:* mem. Writers Guild of America; MWA; Authors' Guild; International Asscn of Crime Writers. *Publications:* Never Look Back, 1985; Blood of the Albatross, 1986; The Seizing of Yankee Green Mall, 1987; Undercurrents, 1988; Probable Cause, 1990; Hard Fall, 1992; The Angel Maker, 1993; No Witnesses, 1994; Chain of Evidence, 1995; Beyond Recognition, 1997; The Pied Piper, 1998; The

First Victim, 1999; Middle of Nowhere, 2000; Parallel Lies, 2001; The Art of Deception, 2002, Dead Aim (as Wendell McCall) 2007. *Honours:* Fulbright Fellow 1990–91. *Address:* PO Box 715, Boise, ID 83701, USA.

PEARSON, Thomas Reid, BA, MA; American writer; b. 27 March 1956, Winston-Salem, NC. *Education:* North Carolina State Univ., Pennsylvania State Univ. *Publications:* A Short History of a Small Place 1985, Off for the Sweet Hereafter 1986, The Last of How It Was 1987, Call and Response 1989, Gospel Hour 1991, Cry Me a River 1993, Blue Ridge 2000, True Cross 2004. *Literary Agent:* Young Agency, 156 Fifth Avenue, New York, NY 10010, USA.

PECK, Dale; American writer and critic; b. 1967, Long Island, NY. *Education:* Drew Univ., NJ and Columbia Univ. *Career:* book reviewer, Village Voice Literary Supplement, London Book Review, New York Times; currently creative writing teacher, New School, New York. *Publications:* Fucking Martin (novel, aka Martin and John) 1993, The Law of Enclosures (novel) 1996, Now It's Time to Say Goodbye (novel) 1998, What We Lost (memoir) 2003, A Story of my Father's Childhood 2003, Hatchet Jobs (criticism) 2004; juvenile: Drift House: The First Voyage 2005. *Honours:* Guggenheim Fellowship. *Address:* c/o Houghton Mifflin Publishing, 222 Berkeley Street, Boston, MA 02116, USA.

PECKER, David J., CPA; American publishing executive; *Chairman and CEO, American Media, Inc.*; b. 24 Sept. 1951; m. Karen Balan 1987. *Education:* Pace and New York Univs. *Career:* fmrly Sr Auditor Price Waterhouse & Co.; fmrly Man. Financial Reporting Diamandis Communications Inc., also Dir Financial Reporting, Dir Accounting, Asst Controller; Exec. Vice-Pres. Hachette Magazines Inc. 1990–91, Pres. 1991–92, Pres., CEO 1992–99, Chair. and CEO American Media Inc. 1999–; mem. Fashion Group's Int. Advisory Bd, NY City Partnership Cttee, American Man. Asscn; mem. Bd Dirs Pace Univ., Drug Enforcement Agents Foundation 1995–. *Address:* American Media Inc., 1000 American Media Way, Boca Raton, FL 33431-1000, USA (office). *Telephone:* (561) 997-7733 (office). *Fax:* (561) 272-8411 (office). *Website:* www.nationalenquirer.com (office).

PECKHAM, Morse; American academic, writer and editor; b. 17 Aug. 1914, Yonkers, NY. *Education:* BA, University of Rochester, 1935; MA, 1938, PhD, 1947, Princeton University. *Career:* Instructor, 1946–47, Asst Prof. 1948–49, Rutgers University; Asst Prof., 1949–52, Assoc. Prof., 1952–61, Dir, Institute for Humanistic Education for Business Executives, 1953–54, University Press, 1953–55, Prof., 1961–67, University of Pennsylvania, Philadelphia; Distinguished Prof. of English and Comparative Literature, 1967–80, Distinguished Prof. Emeritus, 1980–, University of South Carolina, Columbia. *Publications:* On the Origin of Species: A Variorum Text, by Charles Darwin (ed.), 1959; Humanistic Education for Business Executives: An Essay in General Education, 1960; Word, Meaning, Poem: An Anthology of Poetry (ed. with Seymour Chapman), 1961; Beyond the Tragic Vision: The Quest for Identity in the Nineteenth Century, 1962; Man's Rage for Chaos: Biology, Behaviour and the Arts, 1965; Romanticism: The Culture of the Nineteenth Century (ed.), 1965; Paracelsus, by Robert Browning (ed.), 1969; Art and Pornography: An Experiment in Explanation, 1969; The Triumph of Romanticism: Speculation on Some Heroes of a Culture Crisis, 1970; Pippa Passes, by Robert Browning (ed.), 1971; Luria, by Robert Browning (ed.), 1973; Romanticism and Behaviour: Collected Essays II, 1976; Sordello, by Robert Browning (ed.), 1977; Explanation and Power: The Control of Human Behavior, 1979; Romanticism and Ideology, 1985; The Birth of Romanticism, 1986.

PEDEN, W(illiam) Creighton, BA, BD, MA, PhD; American academic, writer and editor; *Fuller E. Calloway Professor Emeritus of Philosophy, Augusta State University*; b. 25 July 1935, Concord, NC; m. 2nd Harriet McKnight Peden 1978; two d. one step-s. *Education:* Davidson Coll., NC, Univ. of Chicago, St Andrews Univ., Scotland. *Career:* founding faculty mem., Florida Presbyterian Coll. 1960–61; Asst Prof., St Andrews Coll. 1964–65; Prof., Radford Coll., VA 1965–68; Chair Dept of Philosophy, Millikin Univ., Decatur, IL 1968–69; Visiting Prof., Iliff School of Theology 1969, 1973, 1978, Univ. of Glasgow 1982–83, Vrije Univ., Amsterdam 1991; Fuller E. Calloway Prof. of Philosophy, Augusta Coll., later Augusta State Univ., GA 1969–93, Prof. Emeritus 1993–; founding Ed., Journal of Social Philosophy 1970–83; founding Co-Ed., American Journal of Theology and Philosophy 1980–91; Exec. Dir, Highlands Inst. for American Religious Thought 1987–92, Pres. 1992–98; Scholar-in-Residence, Univ. of Copenhagen 1988; mem. American Acad. of Religion, American Philosophical Asscn, North American Soc. for Social Philosophy, Social Philosophy Research Inst., Soc. for the Advancement of American Philosophy, Soc. of Religious Humanism. *Publications:* Wieman's Empirical Process Philosophy 1977, Whitehead's View of Reality (with Charles Hartshorne) 1981, The Chicago School: Voices of Liberal Religious Thought 1987, The Philosopher of Free Religion: Francis Ellingwood Abbot, 1836–1903 1992, Civil War Pulpit to World's Parliament of Religion: The Thought of William James Potter, 1829–1893 1996; editor: Philosophical Reflections on Education and Society (with Donald Chapman) 1978, Critical Issues in Philosophy of Education (with Donald Chapman) 1979, Philosophy for a Changing Society 1983, Philosophical Essays on Ideas of a Good Society 1988, Freedom, Equality and Social Change 1989, God, Values and Empiricism 1989, Revolution, Violence and Equality 1990, Terrorism, Justice and Social Values 1990, The American Constitutional Experiment 1991, Communitarianism, Liberalism and Social Responsibility 1991, Rights, Justice and Community 1992, The Bill of Rights: Bicentennial Reflections 1993, Freedom, Dharma and Rights 1993, New Essays in Religious Naturalism (with Larry E. Axel) 1993, Essays and Sermons of William James Potter (1829–1893), Unitarian Minister and Freethinker (with Everett J. Tarbox Jr, two vols) 1993, The Chicago School of Theology: Pioneers in Religious Inquiry (with J. Stone, two vols) 1996, The Collected Essays of Francis Ellingwood Abbot (1836–1903): American Philosopher and Free Religionist (with Everett J. Tarbox Jr, four vols) 1996, Essays and Sermons of William James Potter (1929–1893): Unitarian Minister and Freethinker (with Everett J. Tarbox Jr, two vols) 2003, A Good Person in a World Made Good: Albert Eustace Haydon 1880–1975 2005, Works of Albert Eustace Haydon 1880–1975 (three vols, co-ed.) 2006, Meditations on Man 2006; contrib. to Dictionary of Modern American Philosophers 1860–1960 2005, scholarly books and journals. *Honours:* Fellow Soc. of Philosophers in America. *Address:* PO Box 2009, Bonnie Drive, Highlands, NC 28741, USA.

PEDRAM, Abdul Latif; Afghan poet, writer and journalist; b. 1963, Badakhstan. *Career:* taught journalism 1989–91; Deputy Ed.-in-Chief, Haghighat-e Enghelab-e Sor, Ed.-in-Chief, Theoretical supplement 1982–85; f. and Ed.-in-Chief, Shora journal 1988–89; Deputy Dir, Hakim Nasser Khosrow Balki Foundation Library, Baghlan (Ed.-in-Chief, Hojjat foundation journal, f., foundation newletter, Kian) 1996–98; Lecturer of Literary Critique, Thought and Poetry, Univ. of Baghlan, Pol-i Khomri 1996–98; founder National Congress Party of Afghanistan 2004 (ran for Pres. 2004); mem. bd of eds, Peyvand journal. *Publications:* poetry: Naqshi dar abgineh va baran (A Figure in Crystal and Rain) 1979, Lahzehay-e massloub (Crucified Moments) 1983, She'rhay-e enzeva (Poems of Solitude) 1984, Khatabeh az sakouyeh hendo-koush (A Letter from the Hend and Koush) 1988, Mo'alegheye hashtom (The Eighth Moalegheh) 1988, Ta'reef-e talkh-e mandan 1999; prose: Delavaraneh kuhestan (The Brave Men from the Mountains) 1979, Safarnomeyeh Czechoslovaqui (My Travels in Czechoslovakia) 1980, Chand nokteh beh sheeveyeh tarh (A Few Points Told in Rough) 1983, Darssyahey journalism (Lessons in Journalism, two vols) 1988, Chahar magholeyeh falsafi (Four Philosophical Essays) 1990, Afateh ideology (The Evil of Ideology) 1996, Dar zarurateh jodayee deen az siasat (About the Necessity of Separation of Religion from Politics) 1996; contrib. numerous articles in newspapers and journals, including Erfan, Avaz, Jowandun, Iness, Hevad. *Honours:* hon. mem. Int. Parliament of Writers, Asscn of the Persian Speakers of the World Peyvand; Reporters sans Frontières grant 1998, Human Rights Watch Hellman-Helmet Prize 1999.

PEDRETTI, Erica; Swiss writer and artist; b. Feb. 1930, Šternberk (Czechoslovakia, now Czech Repub.); m. Gian Pedretti 1952; five c. *Education:* Schule für Gestaltung, Zürich. *Career:* lived in Switzerland 1945–50, USA 1950–74, Switzerland 1974–; Corresp. mem. Deutschen Akad. für Sprache und Dichtung, Darmstadt 1998–. *Publications:* Harmloses, bitte 1970, Heiliger Sebastian, Valerie oder das Unerzogene Auge 1986, Engste Heimat 1995, Zerhümmerung 1996, Kuckuckskind 1998, Heute. Ein Tagebuch 2002. *Honours:* Bachmann-Preis 1984, Großer Literatur-Preis des Kantons Bern 1990, Berliner-Preis, Bobrowski-Medaille 1994, M. L. Kaschnitz-Preis 1996, Kunstpreis der Stadt Biel 1996, Mitteleuropäischer Literaturpreis Vilenica, Slowenien 1999, Kunstpreis des Kantons Graubünden 1999. *Address:* c/o Prof. Dr Marcel Baumgartner, Institut für Kunstgeschichte, Justus-Liebig-Universität Gießen, Otto-Behaghel-Straße 10 G, 35394 Gießen, Germany; 4 chemin de Beausite, 2520 La Neuveville, Switzerland. *Telephone:* (38) 513561. *E-mail:* Marcel.Baumgartner@kunst.geschichte.uni-giessen.de. *Website:* www.erica-pedretti.de.

PEERY, Janet, BA, MFA; American writer, book reviewer and teacher; b. 18 July 1948, Wichita, KS; m. 1st William Peery 1976 (divorced 1988); three d.; m. 2nd Cy Bolton 1994. *Education:* Wichita State University. *Career:* teacher of fiction, Warren Wilson College, Sweet Briar College, Old Dominion University. *Publications:* Alligator Dance (short stories), 1993; The River Beyond the World (novel), 1996. Contributions: Reviews, quarterlies and journals, including: New Virginia Review; Shenandoah; Black Warrior Review; Chattahoochee Review; Kansas Quarterly; Southwest Review; Quarterly West; Los Angeles Times; Washington Post Book World. *Honours:* Writers at Work Fellowship, 1990; National Endowment for the Arts Fellowship, 1990; Goodheart Prizes, Washington and Lee University, 1991, 1992; Seaton Award, Kansas Quarterly, 1992; Whiting Writers' Award, 1992; Rosenthal Award, American Acad. of Arts and Letters, 1993. *Address:* Old Dominion University, Department of English, Norfolk, VA 23529, USA. *E-mail:* jpeery@odu.edu.

PEET, Mal; British children's writer; m. Elspeth Graham; three c. *Publications include:* novels: Keeper (Branford-Boase Award 2004) 2003, Tamar (Carnegie Medal 2006) 2005, The Penalty 2006. *Address:* c/o Walker Books, 87 Vauxhall Walk, London, SE11 5HJ, England.

PELECANOS, George Peter; American journalist, writer and screenwriter; b. 18 Feb. 1957, Washington, DC; m.; three c. *Career:* Los Angeles Times Book Award 2003, Int. Crime Novel of the Year in France, Germany and Japan. *Television:* The Wire (writer and story ed., HBO). *Publications:* novels: A Firing Offense 1992, Nick's Trip 1993, Shoedog 1994, Down by the River 1995, The Big Blowdown 1996, The Sweet Forever 1999, King Suckerman 2000, Shame the Devil 2000, Right as Rain 2001, Hard Revolution 2002, Hell to Pay 2002, Soul Circus 2003, Drama City 2005, The Night Gardener 2006; contrib. to Esquire, GQ, The Washington Post. *Address:* c/o The Orion Publishing

Group Ltd, 5 Upper St Martin's Lane, London, WC2H 9EA, England. *Website:* www.orionbooks.co.uk.

PELEVIN, Viktor Olegovich; Russian writer; b. 27 Nov. 1962, Moscow. *Education:* Moscow Power Engineering Inst., Gorky Inst. of Literature, Moscow. *Career:* army service; corresp. Face-to-Face journal 1989–90; journal Science and Religion; author of numerous novels and stories. *Publications include:* (most in trans.) Omon Ra (novel) 1996, Vera Pavlovna's Ninth Dream, Reconstructor, Prince of Gosplan, The Yellow Arrow (novella) 1996, Ivan Kublakhanov, Generation, Babylon, The Blue Lantern (short stories) (Russian Booker Prize 1997), The Life of Insects 1998, Crystal World, A Werewolf Problem in Central Russia (short stories) 1998, Chapayev and Pustota (Buddha's Little Finger, aka Babylon) 2000, The Clay Machine-Gun (novel), Generation P 1999, Homo Zapiens (aka Generation P) 2002, Dialectic for the Transitional Phase From Nowhere to Nowhere 2003, The Sacred Book of Werewolf 2006. *Honours:* Wanderer Prize 1995, Nonino Literary Prize 2001, Robert Schönefeld Prize 2000, 2001, Grigoriev Prize 2004. *Literary Agent:* c/o Aragi Inc., 143 West 27th Street, #4F, New York, NY 10001, USA. *E-mail:* queries@aragi.net (office).

PELLETIER, Chantal; French writer and screenwriter; b. 1949, Lyon. *Writing for television:* En cas de bonheur (TF1) 1989, Divisé par deux (adaptation, Antenne 2) 1990, Carré d'as (FR2) 1992, Le prix d'une femme (FR3) 1994, Danger d'aimer (FR3) 1998. *Publications include:* novels: Supermarché rayon boucher 1990, Le fils d'Ariadne 1992, Le squatt 1996, La vande tuera 1997, Éros et Thalasso 1998, Le Chant du bouc 2000, Troubles fêtes 2001, More is Less (in trans.) 2002, La visite 2003, Eddy Mitchell. *Address:* c/o Éditions Gallimard, 5 rue Sébastien-Bottin, 75328 Paris, France. *Website:* www.gallimard.fr.

PEMBERTON, Margaret, BA; British writer; b. 10 April 1943, Bradford, England; m., one s. four d. *Career:* mem. CWA, Romantic Novelists' Asscn, PEN, Soc. of Authors. *Publications:* Harlot 1981, Lion of Languedoc 1981, The Flower Garden 1982, Silver Shadows, Golden Dreams 1985, Never Leave Me 1986, Multitude of Sins 1988, White Christmas in Saigon 1990, An Embarrassment of Riches 1992, Zadruga 1993, Moonflower Madness 1993, Tapestry of Fear 1994, The Londoners 1995, Magnolia Square 1996, Yorkshire Rose 1996, Coronation Summer 1997, A Many Splendoured Thing 2002, The Four of Us 2004; as Maggie Hudson: Tell Me No Secrets 1998, Fast Women 1999, Looking for Mr Big 2000, Nowhere to Run 2001. *Address:* Oak Tree House, 188 Courtlands Avenue, Lee, London, SE12 8JD, England. *Website:* mpwriteruk@ntlworld.com.

PENCHEVA, Stanka Michaylova; Bulgarian writer; b. 9 July 1929, Sliven; d. of Michael Penchev and Maria Pencheva; m. 1st Kliment Tzachev 1951 (divorced 1965); m. 2nd Georgy Bourmov 1984 (died 1991); one d. *Education:* Univ. of Sofia. *Career:* Journalist and Literary Ed. Bulgarsko Radio 1950–55, Septemvri magazine 1959–75, Otechestvo magazine 1975–86; trans. three books of poetry; writer of 26 anthologies of poetry, an autobiographical novel, a short novel for children and three books of essays, including one on the contemporary Bulgarian woman 1952–2004; mem. Union of Bulgarian Writers. *Publications include:* A Baker's Dozen (ed, anthology of 13 Bulgarian women poets) 1990. *Honours:* Union of Bulgarian Writers award for poetry 1970, 2002. *Address:* 1113 Sofia, 20-3 Tintyava Str, Entr G, Bulgaria. *Telephone:* (2) 72-86-01.

PENDLETON, Don (see Obstfeld, Raymond)

PENHALL, Joe; British playwright; b. 1968, Thames Ditton. *Career:* Chief Reporter, Hammersmith Guardian 1992–94; Writer in Residence Royal Nat. Theatre 1995. *Plays:* Some Voices 1994, Pale Horse 1995, Love and Understanding 1997, The Bullet 1998, Blue/Orange 2000, Dumb Show 2004, Landscape with Weapon 2006. *Film:* Enduring Love (screen adaptation), Some Voices (screenplay). *Television:* The Long Firm (screen adaptation for BBC). *Publications:* Methuen Plays I. *Honours:* John Whiting Award 1995, Evening Standard Award Best Play 2000, Critics Circle Best Play 2001, Olivier Award Best Play 2001. *Address:* c/o Methuen Publishing Ltd, 215 Vauxhall Bridge Road, London, SW1V 1EL, England. *Website:* www.methuen.co.uk.

PENNAC, Daniel, MA; French novelist; b. (Daniel Pennacchioni), 1 Dec. 1944, Casablanca, Morocco. *Education:* Univ. of Nice. *Career:* teacher in secondary schools in Soissons and Paris 1969–95. *Publications:* juvenile fiction: Le Grand Rex 1980, Cabot caboche 1982, L'Oeil du loup 1984, Au bonheur des ogres 1985, La Fée carabine 1987, La Petite marchande de prose (Prix Inter 1990) 1989, Kamo et moi 1992, Kamo, l'agnece Babel 1992, Kamo, l'idée du siècle 1993, Sang pour sang, le réveil des vampires 1993, Miro: le tour du ciel Pennac 1994, Monsieur Malaussène 1995, Monsieur Malaussène au théatre 1996, Vercors d'en haut 1996, La Réserve naturelle des Hauts Plateaux 1996, Messieurs les enfants 1997, Des chrétiens et des maures 1999, Lévasion Kamo 1997, Aux fruits de la passion 2000, Le Dictateur et le hamac (trans. as The Dictator and the Hammock) 2003, Merci 2004; non-fiction: Comme un roman (essay) 1992, Nemo par Pennac 2006. *Address:* c/o Éditions Gallimard-Jeunesse, 5 rue Sébastien-Bottin, 75328 Paris cedex 07, France (office).

PENROSE, Sir Roger, Kt, OM, PhD, FRS; British mathematician and academic; *Professor Emeritus of Mathematics, University of Oxford;* b. 8 Aug. 1931, Colchester; s. of Lionel Penrose; m. 1st Joan Wedge 1959 (divorced 1981), three s.; m. 2nd Vanessa Thomas 1988. *Education:* Univ. Coll. School,

Univ. Coll. London and St John's Coll. Cambridge. *Career:* Asst Lecturer, Bedford Coll. London 1956–57; Research Fellow, St John's Coll. Cambridge 1957–60; NATO Research Fellow, Princeton and Syracuse Univs 1959–61; Research Assoc. King's Coll. London 1961–63; Visiting Assoc. Prof. Univ. of Tex. Austin 1963–64; Reader, Birkbeck Coll. London 1964–66, Prof. of Applied Math. 1966–73; Rouse Ball Prof. of Math. Univ. of Oxford 1973–98, Prof. Emer. 1998–; Gresham Prof. of Geometry, Gresham Coll. 1998; Fellow, Univ. Coll. London 1975; Hon. Fellow, St John's Coll. Cambridge 1987; Visiting Prof. Yeshiva, Princeton and Cornell Univs 1966–67, 1969; Lovett Prof. Rice Univ. Houston 1983–87; Distinguished Prof. of Physics and Math. Syracuse Univ. 1987–93, Francis and Helen Pentz Distinguished Prof. of Physics and Math., Pa State Univ. 1993–; mem. London Math. Soc., Cambridge Philosophical Soc., Inst. for Math. and its Applications, Int. Soc. for Gen. Relativity and Gravitation; Fellow Birkbeck Coll. 1998, Inst. of Physics 1999; Foreign Assoc. Nat. Acad. of Sciences, USA 1998. *Publications:* Techniques of Differential Topology in Relativity 1973, Spinors and Space-time (with W. Rindler), (Vol. I) 1984, (Vol. II) 1986, The Emperor's New Mind 1989, The Nature of Space and Time (with S. W. Hawking) 1996, The Large, the Small and the Human Mind 1997, White Mars (with B. Aldiss) 1999, The Road to Reality: A Complete Guide to the Laws of the Universe 2004; articles in scientific journals. *Honours:* Dr hc, (New Brunswick) 1992, (Surrey) 1993, (Bath) 1994, (London) 1995, (Glasgow) 1996, (Essex) 1996, (St Andrew's) 1997, (Santiniketon) 1998, Hon. DUniv (Open Univ.) 1998; Adams Prize (Cambridge Univ.) 1966–67, Dannie Heinemann Prize (American Physics Soc. and American Inst. of Physics) 1971, Eddington Medal (with S. W. Hawking) (Royal Astronomical Soc.) 1975, Royal Medal (Royal Soc.) 1985, Wolf Foundation Prize for Physics (with S. W. Hawking) 1988, Dirac Medal and Prize, Inst. of Physics 1989, Einstein Medal 1990, Science Book Prize 1990, Naylor Prize, London Math. Soc. 1991. *Address:* Mathematical Institute, 24–29 St Giles, Oxford, OX1 3LB, England (office). *Telephone:* (1865) 270501 (office). *Fax:* (1865) 273583 (office). *E-mail:* rouse@maths.ox.ac.uk (office). *Website:* www.maths.ox.ac.uk (office).

PEONIDOU, Elli; Cypriot writer; b. 21 Nov. 1940; m. Panos Peonides 1963; one s. one d. *Education:* Charokopios Coll., Athens. *Career:* has written nine books of poetry, 16 children's books, three novels and several other works; works published in Bulgaria, Czech Repub., Slovenia, Slovakia, France, Poland, Hungary, Russia, Yugoslavia and Germany; two children's plays staged in Cyprus and abroad; mem. Hon. List IBBY, Basel (Switzerland) 2002. *Honours:* Repub. of Cyprus Awards 1978, 1980, 1984, 1997, 2001, 2004, Asscn of Children's Books Awards 1987, 1991, 1992, 1993, 2000, awards for books 1994, 1996, for plays 1994, State Prize for Novel 1997, 2001, 2004. *Address:* 14 M Parides Street, 3091 Limassol, Cyprus. *Telephone:* (5) 354142. *E-mail:* peonide@cytanet.com.cy.

PEPETELA; Angolan novelist; b. (Artur Carlos Mauricio Pestana), 1941, Benguela. *Career:* co-f. Centre of Angolan Studies, Algeria; trained as sociologist and Movimento Popular de Libertação de Angola (MPLA) operative, Algeria 1960s; guerilla fighter for seven years, rising to regional commdr in defence of Angola against first S African invasion 1975; Deputy Minister of Education, Angola 1976–82; mem. Angolan Writers' Union. *Play:* A Revolta da casa dos ídolos 1980. *Publications:* A revolta da casa dos ídolos, As aventuras de Ngunga, Muana Puó 1978, Mayombe 1980, O cão e os calús 1985, Yaka 1984, Lueji, o nascimento dum império 1990, A geração da utopia 1992, O desejo de Kianda (trans. as The Return of the Water Spirit) 1995, Parábola do cágado velho 1996, A gloriosa família 1997, Jaime Bunda, agente secreto 2001, Jaime Bunda e a morte do agente americano 2003, Predadores 2005. *Honours:* Nat. Literature Prize 1986, Camões Prize 1997, Rio Branco Order 2002. *Literary Agent:* Dr Ray-Güde Mertin Literarische Agentur, Friedrichstrasse 1, 61348 Bad Homburg, Germany. *Telephone:* 6172-29842. *Fax:* 6172-29771. *E-mail:* info@mertin-litag.de. *Website:* www.mertin-litag.de.

PEPPE, Rodney Darrell; British writer and artist; b. 24 June 1934, Eastbourne, E Sussex; m. Tatjana Tekkel 1960; two s. *Education:* Eastbourne School of Art, London Co. Council Cen. School of Art, NDD, Illustration (special subject) and Cen. School Diploma. *Career:* mem. Soc. of Authors. *Television:* Huxley Pig (26 episodes for ITV) 1989, Angelmouse (26 episodes for BBC) 1999. *Publications:* The Alphabet Book 1968, The House That Jack Built 1970, Odd One Out 1974, Henry series 1975–84, The Mice Who Lived in a Shoe 1981, Run Rabbit Run! 1982, The Kettleship Pirates 1983, The Mice and the Flying Basket 1985, The Mice and the Clockwork Bus 1986, Huxley Pig series 1989, The Mice on the Moon 1992, The Mice and the Travel Machine 1993, The Magic Toybox 1996, Gus and Nipper 1996, Hippo Plays Hide and Seek 1997, Angelmouse series 2000, Automata and Mechanical Toys 2002, Toys and Models 2003, Making Mechanical Toys 2005; contribs to periodicals. *Address:* Stoneleigh House, 6 Stoneleigh Drive, Livermead, Torquay, Devon TQ2 6TR, England (home). *Telephone:* (1803) 690794 (home).

PERALTA, Bertalicia; Panamanian poet and writer; b. 1 March 1940, Panama City. *Education:* Universidad de Panamá, Instituto Nacional de Música. *Career:* fmr secondary school teacher; worked in Radio y Televisión Educativa del Ministerio de Educación de Panamá; f. co-Ed. of literary magazine, El Pez Original 1961–68. *Publications:* poetry: Canto de esperanza filial 1962, Sendas fugitivas 1962, Dos poemas 1964, Atrincherado amor 1965, Los Retornos: poesía 1966, Crecimiento (anthology) 1970, Un lugar en la esfera terrestre 1971, Libro de las fábulas 1972, Himno a la alegría 1973, Ragul 1976, Casa Flotante: poesía 1979, Piel de Gallina 1982, Frisos 1983, En tu cuerpo cubierto de flores 1985, Zona de silencio 1987, Invasión USA 1989, Leit Motiv 1989, La única mujer, Concurso de Belleza, Dos Amigos; short stories: Largo en crescendo 1967, Barcarola y otras fantasías incorregibles (Premio Universidad) 1973, Muerto en enero (Instituto Nacional de Cultura Premio Itinerario del Cuento) 1974, Encore y Guayacán de marzo (Instituto Nacional de Cultura Premio Itinerario del Cuento) 1980; juvenile: Puros cuentos 1986, Historia de una nube blanca; contrib. to anthologies and journals.

PERELMAN, Robert (Bob), MA, MFA, PhD; American poet, writer and academic; *Professor, University of Pennsylvania*; b. 2 Dec. 1947, Youngstown, OH; m. Francie Shaw 1975; two s. *Education:* University of Michigan, University of Iowa, University of California. *Career:* Ed., Hills magazine 1973–80; Asst Prof. University of Pennsylvania 1990–95, Assoc. Prof. 1995–2001, Prof. 2001–. *Publications:* Braille, 1975; Seven Works, 1978; aka, 1979; Primer, 1981; To the Reader, 1984; The First World, 1986; Writing/Talks (ed.), 1985; Face Value, 1988; Captive Audience, 1988; Virtual Reality, 1993; The Trouble with Genius: Reading Pound, Joyce, Stein, and Zukovsky, 1994; The Marginalization of Poetry: Language Writings and Literary History, 1996; The Future of Memory 1998, Ten to One 1999, Playing Bodies 2003.

PERES DA COSTA, Suneeta, BA, MFA; Australian playwright and novelist; b. 1976, Sydney, NSW. *Education:* Univ. of Technology, Sydney, Sarah Lawrence Coll., New York, USA, Univ. of Sydney. *Radio plays:* Watermark (ABC Radio), Angelina's Song (ABC Radio), Children See Everything (ABC Radio), Fire and Water (ABC Radio). *Plays:* I am an Island 1995, Free Men 1996, Blood is Blue 1996, The Art of Straying 1998, Klactoveesedstene 2001. *Publication:* Homework (novel) 1999. *Honours:* Sydney Theatre Co.-ICI Young Playwrights' Award 1995, 1996, NSW Ministry for the Arts Philip Parsons Young Playwrights' Award 1996, Ian Reed Foundation Prize for Radio Drama 1998. *Literary Agent:* Tiffany Loehnis, Janklow & Nesbit (UK) Ltd, 33 Drayson Mews, London, W8 4LY, England; RGM Associates, PO Box 128, Surry Hills, NSW 2010, Australia. *Telephone:* (20) 7376-2733 (England); (2) 9281-3911 (Aus.). *Fax:* (20) 7376-2915 (England); (2) 9281-4705 (Aus.). *E-mail:* tifloehnis@janklow.co.uk; info@rgm.com.au. *Website:* www.rgm.com.au.

PÉREZ-REVERTE, Arturo; Spanish journalist and writer; b. 1951, Cartagena. *Career:* journalist, war corresp., Pueblo; war corresp., Spanish nat. TV; elected to Spanish Royal Acad. 2003. *Publications:* El Husar 1986, El maestro de esgrima (translated as The Fencing Master) 1988, La tabla de Flandes (translated as The Flanders Panel) 1990, El club Dumas (translated as The Dumas Club) 1993, La sombra del Aguila 1993, Territorio comanche 1994, Un asunto de honor 1995, Obra breve 1995, La piel del tambor (translated as The Seville Communion; Jean Monnet Prize for European Literature 1997) 1995, El capitán Alatriste (translated as Captain Alatriste) 1996, Limpieza de sangre (translated as Purity of Blood) 1997, El sol de Breda 1998, Patente de corso 1998, La carta esférica (translated as The Nautical Chart) (Prix Beau Livre de l'Académie de Marine Française) 2000, El oro del rey 2000, Con ánimo de ofender 2001, La Reina del Sur (translated as The Queen of the South) 2002, El caballero del jubón amarillo 2003, Cabo Trafalgar 2004, No me cogeréis vivo 2005, El pintor de batallas 2006, Corsarios de Levante 2006; contrib. to Spanish periodicals, including XL Semanal (weekly article). *Honours:* Chevalier, Ordre des Arts et des Lettres (France) 1998, Gran Cruz del Mérito Naval 2005; Grand Prix for Detective Literature (France) 1993, Asturias Prize for Journalism for his coverage of the war in the fmr Yugoslavia for TV 1993, Ondas Prize for Radio de España's La Ley de la Calle 1993. *Literary Agent:* c/o RDC Agencia Literaria, Fernando VI 13–15, 3° derecha, 28004 Madrid, Spain. *Telephone:* (91) 308-55-85. *Fax:* (91) 308-56-00. *E-mail:* rdc@rdclitera.com. *Website:* www.capitanalatriste.com.

PERKINS, Emily; New Zealand novelist; b. 1970, Christchurch. *Education:* New Zealand Drama School, Victoria Univ. *Career:* fmr TV actor. *Publications:* Not her Real Name (short stories) (Geoffrey Faber Memorial Prize for Fiction) 1996, Leave Before You Go (novel) 1998, The Picnic Virgin (ed.) 2000, The New Girl (novel) 2001. *Literary Agent:* c/o Georgia Garrett, AP Watt Ltd, 20 John Street, London, WC1N 2DR, England. *Telephone:* (20) 7405-6774. *Fax:* (20) 7831-2154. *E-mail:* apw@apwatt.co.uk. *Website:* www.apwatt.co.uk.

PERKINS, George Burton, AB, MA, PhD; American editor and writer; b. 16 Aug. 1930, Lowell, Mass; m. Barbara Miller 1964; three d. *Education:* Tufts Coll., Duke Univ., Cornell Univ. *Career:* Duke Univ. Fellow 1953–54, Cornell Univ. Fellow 1954–55; Teaching Asst, Cornell Univ. 1955–57; Asst Prof. Washington Univ. 1957–60, Baldwin-Wallace Coll. 1960–63, Farleigh Dickinson Univ. 1963–66; Lecturer in American Literature, Univ. of Edinburgh 1966–67, Fellow, Inst. for Advanced Studies in the Humanities 1981; Prof., Eastern Michigan Univ. 1967–2001; Gen. Ed. Journal of Narrative Technique 1970–92; mem. various professional orgs. *Publications:* Writing Clear Prose 1964, The Theory of the American Novel 1970, Realistic American Short Fiction 1972, American Poetic Theory 1972, The American Tradition in Literature (with B. Perkins), 11th edn 2006, The Practical Imagination (with Frye and Baker) 1985, Contemporary American Literature (with B. Perkins) 1991, Harper Collins Reader's Encyclopedia of American Literature (with Perkins and Leininger) 2002, Kaleidoscope (with B. Perkins) 1993, Women's Work (with Perkins and Warhol) 1994, The Harper Handbook to Literature (with Frye, Baker and Perkins) 1997, A Season in New South Wales 1998; contribs to professional journals. *Honours:* Distinguished Faculty Award, Eastern Michigan Univ. 1978, Sr Fulbright Scholar, Univ. of Newcastle, Australia 1989. *Address:* 1316 King George Blvd, Ann Arbor, MI 48108, USA

(home). *Telephone:* (734) 971-1893 (home). *E-mail:* george.perkins@emich.edu (office). *Website:* www.georgeperkins.net.

PERKINS, Michael; American writer and editor; b. 3 Nov. 1942, Lansing, MI; m. 1st Renie (Shoemaker) McCune 1968, one s. two d.; 2nd Sondra Howell 2004. *Education:* New School for Social Research, New York, Ohio University, Athens, City College, CUNY. *Career:* Ed., Tompkins Square Press 1966–68, Croton Press Ltd 1969–72, Ulster Arts Magazine 1978–79; Program Dir, Woodstock Guild 1985–95, Woodstock Library 1985–; Sr Ed., Masquerade Books, New York 1992–98; panelist, Thayer/Ross Prize, SUNY 1997; mem. advisory bd and contributor, Encyclopedia of Erotic Literature 2007; mem. Authors' Guild, National Book Critics Circle. *Publications:* Evil Companions 1968, Down Here 1969, The Secret Record 1977, The Persistence of Desire 1977, The Good Parts 1994, Gift of Choice 1994, Dark Matter 1996, Coming Up (ed.) 1996, Burn 2002, I Could Walk All Day 2002, Praise in the Ears of Clouds 2005; contrib. to reviews and periodicals. *Address:* 750 Ohayo Mountt Road, Glenford, NY 12433, USA (home). *Telephone:* (845) 657-6439 (home).

PERLIS, Vivian, BMus, MMus; American musicologist, musician and writer; b. 26 April 1928, New York, NY. *Education:* University of Michigan, Philadelphia Acad. of Music, Columbia University. *Career:* Reference Librarian, Music Library, 1967–72, Senior Research Assoc. and Founder, Oral History, American Music Project, 1972–, School of Music, Yale University; Lecturer, University of Southern California at Los Angeles, 1974–75; Visiting Senior Research Fellow, Brooklyn College, CUNY, 1976–77; Visiting Lecturer, Wesleyan University, 1992–93. *Publications:* Charles Ives Remembered: An Oral History, 1974; An Ives Celebration: Papers and Panels of the Charles Ives Centennial Festival-Conference (with H. Wiley Hitchcock), 1977; Two Men for Modern Music, 1978; The Charles Ives Papers, 1983; Copland: 1900 through 1942 (with Aaron Copland), 1984; Copland: Since 1943 (with Aaron Copland), 1989. Contributions: many publications and television documentaries. *Honours:* Charles Ives Award, National Institute of Arts and Letters, 1971; Otto Kinkeldey Award, American Musicological Society, 1975; ASCAP-Deems Taylor Award, 1985; Guggenheim Fellowship, 1987; Irving Lowens Award, Sonneck Society, 1991. *Address:* 139 Goodill Road, Weston, CT 06883, USA. *E-mail:* vperlis@optonline.net.

PERREIN, Michèle Marie-Claude; French writer; b. 30 Oct. 1929, La Réole; d. of Roger Barbe and Anne-Blanche Perrein; m. Jacques Laurent (divorced). *Education:* Univ. of Bordeaux, Centre de Formation des Journalistes. *Career:* literary contrib. to periodicals Arts-Spectacles, La Parisienne, Marie-Claire, La vie judiciaire, Votre beauté, Le point, F. magazine, Les nouvelles littéraires. *Plays:* L'Hôtel Racine 1966, a+b+c = la Clinique d'anticipation 1971, L'alter-auto 1971; film collaborator La vérité 1959. *Publications:* La sensitive 1956, Le soleil dans l'oeil 1957, Barbastre 1960, La flemme 1961, Le cercle 1962, Le petit Jules 1965, M'oiselle S, la Chineuse 1970, La partie de plaisir 1971, Le buveur de Garonne 1973, Le mâle aimant 1975, Gemma lapidaire 1976, Entre chienne et louve 1978, Comme une fourmi cavalière 1980, Ave Caesar 1982, Les cotonniers de Bassalane 1984, La Margagne 1989. *Address:* c/o Grasset et Fasqualle, 61 rue des Saints-pères, 75006 Paris, France (office).

PERRETT, Bryan, (R. Eldworth); British author and military historian; b. 9 July 1934, Liverpool; m. Anne Catherine Trench 1966. *Education:* Liverpool College. *Career:* served in regular and territorial regts Royal Armoured Corps 1952–71; Defence Correspondent to Liverpool Echo during Falklands War and Gulf War; mem. Rotary Club of Ormskirk. *Television:* scripts for Fighting the Iron Fist (series). *Publications:* The Czar's British Squadron (with A. Lord) 1981, A History of Blitzkrieg 1983, Knights of the Black Cross: Hitler's Panzerwaffe and its Leaders 1986, Desert Warfare 1988, Encyclopaedia of the Second World War (with Ian Hogg) 1989, Canopy of War 1990, Liverpool: A City at War 1990, Last Stand: Famous Battles Against the Odds 1991, The Battle Book: Crucial Conflicts in History from 1469 BC to the Present 1992, At All Costs: Stories of Impossible Victories 1993, Seize and Hold: Master Strokes of the Battlefield 1994, Iron Fist: Crucial Armoured Engagements 1995, Against All Odds! More Dramatic Last Stand Actions 1995, Impossible Victories: Ten Unlikely Battlefield Successes 1996, The Real Hornblower: The Life and Times of Admiral Sir James Gordon, GCB 1998, The Taste of Battle 2000, The Changing Face of Battle 2000, Gunboat! 2000, Last Convoy 2000, Beach Assault 2000, Heroes of the Hour 2001, My Story: Trafalgar 2002, My Story: The Crimea 2002, My Story: Waterloo 2003, For Valour: Victoria Cross and Medal of Honour Battles 2003, My Story: D Day 2004, My Story: U-Boat Hunter 2005; contrib. to War Monthly, Military History, World War Investigator, War in Peace (partwork), The Elite (partwork), Battleground Geography and the History of Warfare, British Military Greats. *Literary Agent:* Watson Little Ltd, Lymehouse Studios, 38 Georgiana Street, London NW1 0EB, England. *Address:* 7 Maple Avenue, Burscough, Ormskirk, Lancashire L40 5SL, England (home). *Telephone:* (1704) 892598 (home). *E-mail:* bbperrett@aol.com (home).

PERRIAM, Wendy Angela, BA, MA; British writer and poet; *Creative Writing Tutor, Morley College*; b. 23 Feb. 1940, London, England; d. of Edward Brech and Irene Thompson; m. 1st 1964; one d., m. 2nd John Alan Perriam 1974. *Education:* St Anne's Coll., Oxford, Univ. of Oxford, London School of Econs. *Career:* advertising copywriter 1962–73; Creative Writing Tutor, Morley Coll., Lambeth 2003–; mem. British Actors Equity Asscn, PEN, Soc. of Authors. *Publications:* Absinthe for Elevenses 1980, Cuckoo 1981, After Purple 1982, Born of Woman 1983, The Stillness The Dancing 1985, Sin City

1987, Devils, for a Change 1989, Fifty-Minute Hour 1990, Bird Inside 1992, Michael, Michael 1993, Breaking and Entering 1994, Coupling 1996, Second Skin 1998, Lying 2000, Dreams, Demons and Desire 2001, Tread Softly 2002, Virgin in the Gym and Other Stories 2004, Laughter Class and Other Stories 2006, The Biggest Female in the World and Other Stories 2007; contribs to anthologies, newspapers and magazines. *Literary Agent:* Curtis Brown Ltd, Haymarket House, 28–29 Haymarket, London, SW1Y 4SP, England. *Telephone:* (20) 7393-4400. *Fax:* (20) 7393-4401. *E-mail:* info@curtisbrown.co.uk. *Website:* www.curtisbrown.co.uk; www.wendyperriam.com (home).

PERRICK, Penny; British novelist and critic; b. 30 June 1941, London; m. Clive Labovitch 1962 (divorced 1973); one s. one d. *Education:* S Hampstead High School, London, Alliance Française, Paris. *Career:* feature writer, Vogue magazine, 1959–62; columnist, The Sun 1974–79, The Times 1983–89; Fiction Ed., The Sunday Times 1989–95; mem. Society of Authors, RSL, English PEN. *Publications:* Malina, 1993; Impossible Things, 1995; Evermore, 1997, Something to Hide 2007; contrib. to Times; Sunday Times; Country Homes and Interiors; You Magazine; The Irish Times; The Irish Tatler; Gardens Illustrated. *Address:* Parnells, The Quay, Roundstone, Connemara, Co. Galway, Ireland.

PERRIE, Walter, MA, MPhil; British poet, author and critic; b. 5 June 1949, Lanarkshire, Scotland; s. of James Perrie and Jean Gray Perrie. *Education:* Univs of Edinburgh and Stirling. *Career:* Ed. Chapman 1970–75; Scottish-Canadian Exchange Fellow, Univ. of British Columbia, Canada 1984–85; Man. Ed. Margin: International Arts Quarterly, 1985–90; Ed. FRAS Publications 2004–, Co-Ed. FRAS: A Scottish Literary Magazine 2004; part-time Lecturer in Philosophy and Creative Writing Perth Coll. 2000–; Stirling Writing Fellow, Univ. of Stirling 1991. *Publications:* Metaphysics and Poetry (with Hugh MacDiarmid) 1974, Poem on a Winter Night 1976, A Lamentation for the Children 1977, By Moon and Sun 1980, Out of Conflict 1982, Concerning the Dragon 1984, Roads that Move: A Journey Through Eastern Europe 1991, Thirteen Lucky Poems 1991, From Milady's Wood and Other Poems 1997, The Light in Strathearn (poems) 2000, Caravanserai: Poems 2004, Decagon: Selected Poems 1995–2005 2005, Rhapsody of the Red Cliff (poems) 2006, As Far As Thales – Beginning Philosophy 2006, The King of France is Bald: Philosophy and Meaning 2007; contribs to journals and periodicals. *Honours:* Scottish Arts Council Bursaries 1976, 1983, 1994, 1999, and Book Awards 1976, 1983, Eric Gregory Award 1978, Ingram Merrill Foundation Award 1987, Soc. of Authors Travelling Scholarship 2000. *Address:* 10 Croft Place, Dunning, Perthshire, PH2 0SB, Scotland (home).

PERRY, John Curtis, BA, MA, PhD; American academic and writer; b. 18 July 1930, Orange, NJ; m. Sarah Hollis French 1957, five c. *Education:* Yale University, Harvard University. *Career:* Instructor, 1962–64, Asst Prof. of History, 1964–66, Connecticut College; Asst Prof., 1966–68, Assoc. Prof., 1968–74, Prof. of History, 1974–80, Acting Dir, College Library, 1975–76, Carleton College; Visiting Research Assoc., Fairbank Center, 1976–79, Japan Institute, 1979–80, Assoc. in Research, 1980–, Harvard University; Henry Willard Denison Prof. of History, 1981–, Organizer-Dir, Fletcher North Pacific Seminars, 1985–97, Fletcher School of Law and Diplomacy, Tufts University; mem. American Historical Asscn; Asscn for Asian Studies; Japan Society. *Publications:* Beneath the Eagle's Wings: Americans in Occupied Japan, 1980; Sentimental Imperialists: The American East Asian Experience (with James C. Thomson Jr and Peter W. Stanley), 1981; Facing West: Americans and the Opening of the Pacific, 1994; The Flight of the Romanovs: A Family Saga (with Constantine Pleshakov), 1999. Contributions: scholarly books, journals, newspapers, radio and television. *Honours:* Research Grants, NIRA, 1986–87, Nippon Foundation, 1998–2001, Japan Economic Foundation, 2000–; Order of the Sacred Treasure, Japan, 1991.

PERRY, Ritchie, (John Allen), BA; British teacher and author; b. 7 Jan. 1942, King's Lynn, Norfolk, England. *Education:* St John's College, Oxford. *Publications:* The Fall Guy, 1972; Nowhere Man, US edn as A Hard Man to Kill, 1973; Ticket to Ride, 1973; Holiday with a Vengeance, 1974; Your Money and Your Wife, 1975; One Good Death Deserves Another, 1976; Dead End, 1977; Brazil: The Land and Its People, 1977; Copacabana Stud (as John Allen), 1977; Dutch Courage, 1978; Bishop's Pawn, 1979; Up Tight (as John Allen), 1979; Grand Slam, 1980; Fool's Mate, 1981; Foul Up, 1982; MacAllister, 1984; Kolwezi, 1985; Presumed Dead, 1988; Comeback, 1991. Children's Books: George H. Ghastly, 1982; George H. Ghastly to the Rescue, 1982; George H. Ghastly and the Little Horror, 1985; Fenella Fang, 1986; Fenella Fang and the Great Escape, 1987; Fenella Fang and the Wicked Witch, 1989; The Creepy Tale, 1989; Fenalla Fang and the Time Machine, 1991; The Runton Werewolf, 1994.

PERUTZ, Kathrin, BA, MA; American author; b. 1 July 1939, New York, NY. *Education:* Barnard College, New York University. *Career:* Exec. Dir, Contact Program Inc.; mem. PEN, Authors' Guild. *Publications:* The Garden, 1962; A House on the Sound, 1964; The Ghosts, 1966; Mother is a Country: A Popular Fantasy, 1968; Beyond the Looking Glass: America's Beauty Culture, 1970; Marriage is Hell: The Marriage Fallacy, 1972; Reigning Passions, 1978; Writing for Love and Money, 1991. Also as Johanna Kingsley: Scents, 1985; Faces, 1987.

PESETSKY, Bette, BA, MFA; American writer; b. 16 Nov. 1932, Milwaukee, WI; m. Irwin Pesetsky 1956; one s. *Education:* Washington Univ., Univ. of Iowa. *Career:* mem. PEN. *Publications:* Stories Up to a Point, 1982; Author from a Savage People, 1983; Midnight Sweets, 1988; Digs, 1988; Confessions of a Bad Girl, 1989; Late Night Muse, 1991; Cast a Spell, 1993. Contributions: New Yorker; Vanity Fair; Ms; Vogue; Paris Review; Ontario Review; Stand. *Honours:* Creative Writing Fellowship, National Endowment for the Arts, 1979–80; Creative Writing Public Service Award, New York Council for the Arts, 1980–81. *Address:* Hilltop Park, Dobbs Ferry, NY 10522, USA.

PESSL, Marisha; American novelist; b. 1977; m. *Education:* Northwestern Univ., Chicago and Columbia Univ., New York. *Publications:* Special Topics in Calamity Physics (novel) (one of New York Times Ed.'s Choice five best works of fiction) 2006. *Address:* c/o Penguin Publicity, 80 Strand, London, WC2R 0RL, England (office). *Website:* www.marishapessl.com.

PETERFREUND, Stuart Samuel, BA, MFA, PhD; American academic and poet; *Associate Dean for Curriculum and Faculty Affairs, Division of Adult and Continuing Education, Northeastern University*; b. 30 June 1945, New York, NY; m. 1st Carol Jean Litzler 1981 (divorced 1997); one d.; m. 2nd Christina Sieber 2001. *Education:* Cornell Univ., Univ. of California at Irvine, Columbia Univ., Univ. of Washington. *Career:* Lecturer, Univ. of Puget Sound 1975; Asst Prof., Univ. of Arkansas at Little Rock 1975–78; Asst Prof., Dept of English, Northeastern Univ. 1978–82, Assoc. Prof. 1982–91, Prof. of English and Chair 1991–99, Prof. of English 1999–, Assoc. Dean for Curriculum and Faculty Affairs, Div. of Adult and Continuing Educ. 2005–; mem. American Soc. for Eighteenth-Century Studies, British Soc. for History of Science, Byron Soc., History of Science Soc., Interdisciplinary Nineteenth-Century Studies, Int. Asscn for Philosophy and Literature, Keats-Shelley Asscn of America, MLA, Poets and Writers, Soc. for Literature and Science (Pres. 1995–97), Wordsworth-Coleridge Asscn. *Publications:* poetry: The Hanged Knife and Other Poems 1970, Harder than Rain 1977, Interstatements 1986; other: William Blake in the Age of Newton: Essays on Literature as Art and Science 1998, Shelley Among Others: The Play of the Intertext and the Idea of Language 2002; ed.: Critical Theory and the Teaching of Literature 1985, Culture/Criticism/Ideology 1986, Literature and Science: Theory and Practice 1990; contribs to scholarly books, professional journals, poetry anthologies and reviews. *Honours:* grants; fellowships; First Prize in Poetry, Writers' Digest Competition, 1970; Poet-in-Residence, Southern Literary Festival, 1977; First Prize, Worcester County Poetry Asscn Contest, 1989; Third Prize, Abiko Journal Poetry Contest, 1994; Third Prize, Anna Davidson Rosenberg Award for Poems on the Jewish Experience, 1996. *Address:* Department of English, Northeastern University, 406 Holmes Hall, 360 Huntington Avenue, Boston, MA 02115, USA. *Telephone:* (617) 373-7013 (office); (617) 864-0053 (home). *Fax:* (617) 373-3325 (office). *E-mail:* s.peterfreund@neu.edu (office).

PETERKIEWICZ, Jerzy, MA, PhD; British academic, poet, writer and dramatist; b. 29 Sept. 1916, Fabianki, Poland. *Education:* University of Warsaw, University of St Andrews, Scotland, King's College, London. *Career:* Lecturer, then Reader, 1952–72, Head, Dept of East European Languages and Literature, 1972–77, Prof. of Polish Language and Literature, 1972–79, University of London. *Publications:* Prowincja 1936, Wiersze i poematy 1938, Pogrzeb Europy 1946, The Knotted Cord 1953, Loot and Loyalty 1955, Polish Prose and Verse 1956, Antologia liryki angielskiej 1958, Future to Let 1958, Isolation 1959, Five Centuries of Polish Poetry (with Burns Singer) 1960, revised edn (also with Jon Stallworthy) 1970, The Quick and the Dead 1961, That Angel Burning at My Left Side 1963, Poematy Londynskie 1965, Inner Circle 1966, Green Flows the Bile 1969, The Other Side of Silence: The Poet at the Limits of Language 1970, The Third Adam 1975, Easter Vigil and Other Poems, by Karol Wojtyla (Pope John Paul II) (ed. and trans.) 1979, Kula magiczna 1980; Collected Poems, by Karol Wojtyla (Pope John Paul II) (ed. and trans.) 1982, Poezje Wybrane 1986, Literatura polska w perspektywie europejskiej (essays trans. from English) 1986, Modlitwy intelektu 1988, Messianic Prophecy: a case for reappraisal 1991, In the Scales of Fate (autobiog.) 1993, Wiersze dobrzynskie 1994, The Place Within: The Poetry of Pope John Paul II (ed. and trans.) 1994, Metropolitan Idyll (bilingual Edn) 1998, Poezje-poems by Karel Wojtyla (Pope John Paul II) (trans.) 1998, Slowa sa bez Poreczy (Poems 1935–56) 1998, Cyprian Norwid: Poems, Letters, Drawings (ed. and trans. with Christine Brooke-Rose) 2000, John Paul II: Roman Triptych (ed. and trans.) 2003. Contributions: numerous periodicals and BBC3. *Honours:* Commander, Cross, Order of Polonia Restituta, 1995.

PETERS, Andrew Fusek; British/Czech poet and children's writer; b. Prague, Czechoslovakia. *Career:* grew up in London; vocalist, didgeridu player and collaborator with Tim Juckes in the band Colour People; composer with Ben Rodway; radio work includes features for Talking Poetry (BBC Radio 4), children's poetry for BBC Radio 5, Poetry Please (BBC Radio 4); television work includes Wham Bam Strawberry Jam (BBC1), Carlton Country (Carlton Central), Heart of the Country (Carlton); mem. Nat. Asscn of Writers in Education, Poetry Soc., Poetry Soc. Poetryclass Team. *Plays:* with Polly Peters: Twisted, Much Ado About Clubbing, Angelcake, Dragon Chaser. *Publications include:* juvenile fiction: When I Come to the Dark Country 1997, The Moon is on the Microphone 1997, The Barefoot Book of Strange and Spooky Stories 1997, May the Angels be With Us: Poems of Life, Love, AIDS and Death 1999, Sadderday and Funday (with Polly Peters) 2001, Plays with Attitude (collection of plays, with Polly Peters) 2001, Poems with Attitude: Uncensored 2002, Ed and the Witchblood 2003, Dragon and Mousie 2003, Hubble Bubble 2003, Monkey's Clever Tale 2003, The Tiger and the Wise Man 2004; editor: Sheep Don't Go To School 1999, The Upside Down Frown 1999, The Unidentified Frying Omelette 2000, Out of Order 2002, The Dog Ate My Bus Pass (co-ed.) 2004, Love, Hate and My Best Mate (co-ed.) 2004; contrib. to Poems About Festivals 2000, Poems About Seasons 2000. *Address:* The Old

Chapel, Lydbury North, Shropshire SY7 8AU, England; c/o Bloodaxe Books Ltd, Highgreen, Tarset, Northumberland NE48 1RP, England (office). *E-mail:* andrew@tallpoet.com. *Website:* www.tallpoet.com.

PETERS, Catherine Lisette, MA; British academic and writer; b. 30 Sept. 1930, London, England; m. 1st John Glyn Barton 1952, four s. (one deceased); m. 2nd Anthony Storr 1970. *Education:* Univ. of Oxford. *Career:* Ed., Jonathan Cape, 1960–74; Lecturer in English, Somerville College, Oxford, 1981–92; mem. Wilkie Collins Society; Society of Authors; FRSL; International PEN. *Publications:* Thackeray's Universe, 1987; The King of Inventors: A Life of Wilkie Collins, 1991; Charles Dickens, 1998; Byron, 2000. Contributions: books and journals. *Literary Agent:* PFD, Drury House, 34–43 Russell Street, London, WC2B 5HA, England. *Address:* 4 Murray Court, 80 Banbury Road, Oxford, OX2 6LQ, England (home). *E-mail:* catherine.peters@ell.ox.ac.uk (home).

PETERS, Elizabeth (see Mertz, Barbara Louise Gross)

PETERS, Janis; Latvian diplomatist, writer and poet; b. 30 June 1939, Liepāja Region; s. of Janis Peters and Zelma Peters; m. Baiba Kalniņa 1969; one s. *Career:* started as journalist in Latvian newspapers, later freelance; Chair. Bd of Latvian Writers' Union 1985–89; participant democratic movt for independence; Chair. Org. Cttee People's Front of Latvia 1988; USSR People's Deputy 1989–90; Perm. Rep. of Council of Ministers of Latvia to Russia 1990–91, then Amb. to Russian Fed. 1991–97; mem. govt del. to negotiations with Russia 1992–. *Publications:* more than 30 books of poetry, prose and essays in Latvian, Russian and English. *Honours:* Hon. mem. Latvian Acad. of Sciences 1990–, Latvian Univ. 1991–; Cavaliere di San Marco 1993. *Address:* Vesetas Str. 8, Apt 12, 1013 Rīga, Latvia; c/o Latvijas vestnieciba (Embassy of Latvia in Russia), Ul. Chapligina 3, Moscow 103062, Russia. *Telephone:* (095) 925-27-07 (Moscow); 6237-0774 (Rīga); 6733-9350 (Rīga). *Fax:* (095) 923-9295 (Moscow).

PETERS, Lance; Australian author, dramatist and screenwriter; b. 8 May 1934, Auckland, New Zealand; m. Laura Chiang 1981, two s. two d. *Career:* hon. life mem. Australian Writers' Guild (pres. 1970–72); mem. Australian Soc. of Authors, Writers' Guild of Great Britain, BAFTA. *Publications:* Carry On Emmannuelle, 1978; The Dirty Half Mile, 1981; Cut-Throat Alley, 1982; Enemy Territory, 1988; God's Executioner, 1988; The Civilian War Zone, 1989; The Red Collar Gang, 1989; The Dirty Half Mile (Again), 1989; Gross Misconduct, 1993; Savior in the Grave, 1994. Other: Assault with a Deadly Weapon (play); 5 screenplays; many television comedies, documentaries. Contributions: numerous popular magazines.

PETERS, Lenrie Leopold Wilfred, MA, FRCS; Gambian physician and writer; *Surgeon Specialist, Westfield Clinic;* b. 1 Sept. 1932, Banjul; s. of Lenrie Peters and Keria Peters; m. (divorced). *Education:* Boys' High School, Banjul, Prince of Wales Secondary School, Freetown, Sierra Leone, Trinity Coll., Cambridge, UK, Univ. Coll. Hospital, London. *Career:* surgeon specialist, Westfield Clinic, Banjul 1972–; farmer, Chair. and Chief Exec. Farato Farms Export Ltd 1981–99; Chair. Colloquium Cttee, Lagos 1977, Bd of Govs Gambia Coll. 1979–87, W African Examinations Council 1988–91, Nat. Consultative Cttee The Gambia 1995–; Fellow Int. Coll. of Surgeons 1992; Distinguished Friend of W African Examinations Council. *Publications:* Poems 1964, The Second Round (novel) 1965, Satellites (poems) 1967, Katchikali (poems) 1971, Selected Poetry 1981; contrib. to many anthologies. *Honours:* Officer of Repub. of The Gambia. *Address:* PO Box 142, Banjul, Gambia (home). *Telephone:* 392219 (office); 495419 (home). *Fax:* 495419.

PETERS, Margot McCullough, BA, MA, PhD; American academic and writer; *Professor Emerita, University of Wisconsin at Whitewater;* b. 13 May 1933, Wausau, Wisconsin; m. Peter Ridgway Jordan 1981; one s. one d. *Education:* Univ. of Wisconsin at Madison. *Career:* Asst Prof. of English Northland Coll., Ashland, Wisconsin 1963–66; Asst Prof. 1969–74, Assoc. Prof. 1974–77, Prof. of English 1977–91, Prof. Emerita 1991–, Univ. of Wisconsin at Whitewater; Kathe Tappe Vernon Prof. of Biography, Dartmouth Coll. 1978; mem. Authors' Guild, Brontë Soc., Mark Twain Soc., Bernard Shaw Soc., Wisconsin Center for the Book, Int. Shaw Soc. *Publications:* Charlotte Brontë: Style in the Novel 1973, Unquiet Soul: A Biography of Charlotte Brontë 1975, Bernard Shaw and the Actresses 1980, Mrs Pat: The Life of Mrs Patrick Campbell 1984, The House of Barrymore 1990, Wild Justice (as Margret Pierce) 1995, May Sarton: A Biography 1997, Design for Living: Alfred Lunt and Lynn Fontanne 2003; contributions to professional journals, newspapers, reviews and periodicals. *Honours:* Friends of American Writers Award for Best Prose Work 1975, ACLS Fellow 1976–77, George R. Freedley Memorial Awards 1980, 1984, Banta Awards 1981, 1985, Guggenheim Fellowship 1988–89, Wisconsin Institute for Research in the Humanities Grant 1988–89, English-Speaking Union Ambassador Award 1991, Wisconsin Library Asscn Distinguished Achievement Awards 1991, 1998 Outstanding Achievement Award 2004, Triangle Book Publishers Judy Gran Award 1998. *Address:* 511 College Street, Lake Mills, WI 53551, USA. *E-mail:* margot@gdinet.com.

PETERS, Michael Adrian, BA, DipEd, MA, PhD, FRSA; New Zealand academic and writer; *Research Professor, University of Glasgow;* b. 4 Sept. 1948, Wellington; m. Christine Athlone Besley 1996; two s. *Education:* Victoria Univ. of Wellington, Christchurch Coll. of Education, Univ. of Auckland. *Career:* secondary teacher, Linwood High School 1973–78; Head of Geography, Longbay High School 1979–80; private consultant 1981–89; Lecturer in Education, Univ. of Canterbury 1990–92; Sr Lecturer 1993–95, Assoc. Prof.

1996–2000, Prof. 2000–, Univ. of Auckland; Research Prof., Univ. of Glasgow 2000–; Adjunct Prof. of Communication Studies, Auckland Univ. of Technology 2001–; Ed., educational, philosophy and theory journals, policy futures in education, e-learning online journals; mem. Humanities Soc. of New Zealand (council 1997–98), RSA. *Publications:* Education and the Postmodern Condition 1995, Poststructuralism, Politics and Education 1996, Critical Theory, Poststructuralism and the Social Context 1996, Cultural Politics and the University 1997, Virtual Technologies and Tertiary Education 1998, Naming the Multiple: Poststructuralism and Education 1998, Wittgenstein: Philosophy, Postmodernism, Pedagogy (with James Marshall) 1999, Individualism and Community: Education and Social Policy in the Postmodern Condition (with James Marshall) 1999, University Futures and the Politics of Reform (with Peter Roberts) 1999, Nietzsche's Legacy for Education: Past and Present Values (with James Marshall and Paul Smeyers) 2001, Poststructuralism, Marxism and Neoliberalism: Between Politics and Theory 2001, Richard Rorty: Education, Philosophy and Politics (with Paulo Ghiraldelli), Heidegger, Education and Modernity 2002, Critical Theory and the Human Condition: Founders and Praxis (with Colin Lankshear and Mark Olssen) 2003, Derrida, Deconstruction and Education: Ethics of Pedagogy and Research (with Peter Trifonas) 2004; contrib. to journals. *Honours:* Postgraduate Scholarship, Univ. of Auckland 1981, Macmillan Brown Lectures Univ. of Canterbury 2000. *Address:* c/o Faculty of Education, University of Glasgow, St Andrews Bldg, 11 Eldon Road, Glasgow, G3 6NH, Scotland. *Telephone:* (141) 330-3636 (office). *Fax:* (141) 330-5451 (office). *E-mail:* m.peters@educ.gla.ac.uk (office). *Website:* www.gla.ac.uk/~map6p/index .html.

PETERS, Richard (see Haining, Peter Alexander)

PETERS, Richard Stanley, BA, PhD; British academic and writer; b. 31 Oct. 1919, Missouri, India; m. Margaret Lee Duncan 1943; one s. two d. *Education:* Clifton College, Bristol, Queen's College, Oxford, Birkbeck College, London. *Career:* part-time Lecturer, 1946–49, full-time Lecturer, 1949–58, Reader in Philosophy, 1958–62, Birkbeck College, London; Visiting Prof., Harvard University, 1961, University of Auckland, 1975; Prof. of the Philosophy of Education, 1962–82, Prof. Emeritus, 1982–, University of London; Part-time Lecturer, Bedford College, London, and LSE, 1966; Visiting Fellow, Australian National University, Canberra, 1969. *Publications:* Ethics and Education, 1945; Brett's History of Psychology, revised edn, 1953; Hobbes, 1956; The Concept of Motivation, 1958; Social Principles and the Democratic State (with S. I. Benn), 1959; Authority, Responsibility and Education, 1960; Ethics and Education, 1966; The Concept of Education (ed.), 1967; Perspectives on Plowden (ed.), 1969; The Logic of Education (with P. H. Hirst), 1970; Hobbes and Rousseau (ed. with M. Cranston), 1971; Education and the Development of Reason (ed. with R. F. Dearden and P. H. Hirst), 1972; Reason and Compassion, 1973; The Philosophy of Education (ed.), 1973; Psychology and Ethical Development, 1974; Nature and Conduct (ed.), 1975; The Role of the Head (ed.), 1976; Education and the Education of Teachers, 1977; John Dewey Reconsidered (ed.), 1977; Essays on Education, 1981; Moral Development and Moral Education, 1981.

PETERS, Robert Louis, BA, MA, PhD; American academic, poet and writer; b. 20 Oct. 1924, Eagle River, WI; m. (divorced); three s. one d. *Education:* University of Wisconsin at Madison. *Career:* Instructor, University of Idaho, 1952–53, Boston University, 1953–55; Asst Prof., Ohio Wesleyan University, 1955–58; Assoc. Prof., Wayne State University, 1958–63; Prof. of English, University of California at Riverside, 1963–68, and Irvine, 1968–94; mem. American Society for Aesthetics; PEN; Writer's Guild. *Publications:* The Drowned Man to the Fish, 1978; Picnic in the Snow: Ludwig of Bavaria, 1982; What Dillinger Meant to Me, 1983; Hawker, 1984; Kane, 1985; Ludwig of Bavaria: Poems and a Play, 1986; The Blood Countess: Poems and a Play, 1987; Haydon, 1988; Brueghel's Pigs, 1989; Poems: Selected and New, 1992; Goodnight Paul: Poems, 1992; Snapshots for a Serial Killer: A Fiction and Play, 1992; Zapped: 3 Novellas, 1993; Nell: A Woman from Eagle River, 1994; Lili Marlene: A Memoir of World War II, 1995; Familial Love: Poems, 2001. Other: Victorians in Literature and Art, 1961; The Crowns of Apollo: Swinburne's Principles of Literature and Art, 1965; The Letters of John Addington Symonds (co-ed., 3 vols) 1967–69; Letter to a Tutor: The Tennyson Family Letters to Henry Graham Dakyns (ed.), 1988. Contributions: professional journals. *Honours:* Guggenheim Fellowship, 1966–67; Yaddo, MacDowell Colony, and Ossabaw Island Project Fellowships, 1973–74; National Endowment for the Arts Grant, 1974.

PETERSEN, Peter James, AB, MA, PhD; American writer and teacher; b. 23 Oct. 1941, Santa Rosa, CA; m. Marian Braun 1964, two d. *Education:* Stanford University, San Francisco State University, University of New Mexico. *Career:* English Instructor, Shasta College; mem. Society of Children's Bookwriters and Illustrators. *Publications:* Would You Settle for Improbable 1981, Nobody Else Can Walk It for You 1982, Going for the Big One 1986, Good-bye to Good Ol'Charlie 1987, The Freshman Detective Blues 1987, I Hate Camping 1991, Liars 1992, The Sub 1993, I Hate Company 1994, White Water 1997, Can You Keep A Secret 1997, My Worst Friend 1998, I Hate Weddings 2000, Rising Water 2002, rob&sara.com 2004. *Honours:* National Endowment for the Humanities Fellowship 1976–77, William Allen White Award, Children's Crown Award. *Address:* 1243 Pueblo Court, Redding, CA 96001, USA. *E-mail:* pjpetersen@charter.net.

PETERSON, Robert, BA, MA; American writer and poet; b. 2 June 1924, Denver, CO; one d. *Education:* Univ. of California, Berkeley, San Francisco State Coll. *Career:* writer-in-residence, Reed Coll., Portland, Oregon 1969–71; mem. Marin Poetry Soc. *Publications:* Home for the Night, 1962; The Binnacle, 1967; Wondering Where You Are, 1969; Lone Rider, 1976; Under Sealed Orders, 1976; Leaving Taos, 1981; The Only Piano Player in La Paz, 1985; Waiting for Garbo: 44 Ghazals, 1987; All The Time in the World, 1996. *Honours:* Nat. Endowment for the Arts grant 1967, Amy Lowell Travelling Fellowship 1972–73.

PETKOVA, Wania, (Katidja Sadik), DLit; Bulgarian poet and journalist; b. 10 July 1954, Sofia; m.; one d. one s. *Education:* Cuba, Bulgaria and Inst. Gamal Abdel Nasser, Dar es Salaam. *Career:* fmr diplomat, postings included Sudan; journalist Trud (newspaper); interpreter and poet. *Publications include:* Salt Winds, Sinner, The Black Dove, Bullets in the Sand; 32 books of poetry, short stories and essays published. *Honours:* numerous Bulgarian and int. awards for poetry including two Pres. Awards, Bulgaria 2005, Union of Bulgarian Writers Award 2005. *Address:* Complex Hippodroma, Block 134, entry 5, Sofia (office); Complx 'Goze Delchev', Block 109, Entry 1, 2nd Floor, 1404 Sofia, Bulgaria (home). *Telephone:* (2) 859-37-82 (home). *Fax:* (2) 859-63-54 (home).

PETRAKIS, Harry Mark; American writer; b. 5 June 1923, St Louis, MO,; m. Diane Perparos 1945; three s. *Education:* University of Illinois. *Career:* teacher, writing workshops; McGuffey Visiting Lecturer, Ohio University, 1971; Writer-in-Residence, Chicago Public Library, 1976–77, Chicago Board of Education, 1978–79; Kazantzakis Prof., San Francisco State University, 1992; mem. Authors' Guild; PEN; Writers Guild of America, West. *Publications:* Lion at My Heart, 1959; The Odyssey of Kostas Volakis, 1963; Pericles on 31st Street, 1965; The Founder's Touch, 1965; A Dream of Kings, 1966; The Waves of Night, 1969; Stelmark: A Family Recollection, 1970; In the Land of Morning, 1973; The Hour of the Bell, 1976; A Petrakis Reader: 28 Stories, 1978; Nick the Greek, 1979; Days of Vengeance, 1983; Reflections on a Writer's Life and Work, 1983; Collected Stories, 1986; Ghost of the Sun, 1990; Tales of the Heart, 1999; Twilight of the Ice, 2002. Contributions: various magazines. *Honours:* Carl Sandburg Award; Ellis Island Medal of Honour, 1995. *Address:* 80 East Road, Dune Acres, Chesterton, IN 46304, USA.

PETREU, Marta; Romanian editor, essayist and poet; *Professor of Philosophy, Babes-Bolyai University of Cluj;* b. (Rodica Marta Vartic), 1955. *Education:* Univ. Babes-Bolyai, Cluj, Univ. of Bucharest. *Career:* teacher of philosophy Emil Racovita school, Cluj 1980–90; Ed. Steaua magazine 1990; Ed. Apostrof magazine 1990–; Lecturer in Philosophy Babes-Bolyai Univ. of Cluj 1992–2001, Prof. of Philosophy 2001–; residency Ledig House Int. Writers' Colony Ghent, New York 1998; mem. Echinox literary group, Writers' Union of Romania, Apostrof Cultural Foundation (f. mem.). *Publications:* Aduceti verbele (poems) (Premiul Uniunii Scriitorilor) 1981, Dimineata tinerelor doamne (poems) 1983, Loc psihic (poems) 1991, Teze neterminate (essays) 1991, Poeme nerusinate (poems) 1993, Jocurile manierismului logic (essay) 1995, Cartea miniei (poems) 1997, Apocalipsa dupa Marta (poems) 1999, Un trecut deocheat sau Schimbarea la fata a Romaniei 1999, Ionescu in tara tatalui (Centrul Cultural Francez Premiul Henri Jacquier) 2001, Falanga (poems) 2001, Filosofia lui Caragiale 2003; editor of numerous vols; contrib. poems to anthologies and journals, including Sulfur, Partisan Review, Compost, Mississippi Review, The Bitter Oleander, Salt Hill, The Alembic, The Literary Review, Transylvanian Voices, Massachusetts Review, Beacons, Paper Street, and essays and articles to journals and other publs. *Honours:* Poesis magazine prize 1993, Premiul Salonului de Carte Oradea 1993, Contemporanul magazine Premiul George Bacovia 1993, Premiul Uniunii Scriitorilor 1997, Premiul Nichita Stanescu 1998, Premiul Salonului Nat. de Carte, Cluj 1998, Kenneth Rexroth Memorial Trans. Prize 1999, Human Rights Watch Hellman/Hammett grant 2001. *Address:* Facultatea de Istorie si Filosofie, Universitatea Babeş-Bolyai, Str. M. Kogălniceanu 1, 3400 Cluj-Napoca, Romania.

PETRIE, Paul James, BA, MA, PhD; American academic (retd) and poet; b. 1 July 1928, Detroit, MI; m. Sylvia Spencer 1954, one s. two d. *Education:* Wayne State Univ., Univ. of Iowa. *Career:* Assoc. Prof., Peru State University, 1958–59; Instructor to Prof. of English, University of Rhode Island, 1959–90. *Publications:* Confessions of a Non-Conformist, 1963; The Race With Time and the Devil, 1965; From Under the Hill of Night, 1969; The Academy of Goodbye, 1974; Light From the Furnace Rising, 1978; Not Seeing is Believing, 1983; Strange Gravity, 1985; The Runners, 1988, Rooms of Grace: New and Selected Poems 2005; contrib. to newspapers, reviews, quarterlies, journals, and magazines. *Honours:* Scholarly Achievement Award, University of Rhode Island, 1983; Catholic Press Award, 1985; Arts Achievement Award, Wayne State University, 1990. *Address:* 200 Dendron Road, Peace Dale, RI 02879, USA (home). *Telephone:* (401) 783-8644 (home).

PETROBELLI, Pierluigi, BLitt, MFA; Italian musicologist and writer; b. 18 Oct. 1932, Padua; s. of Giuseppe Petrobelli and Carolina Talpo. *Education:* Univ. of Rome, Princeton Univ., Harvard Univ. and Summer School, Univ. of California at Berkeley, USA. *Career:* Ed. Rivista Italiana di Musicologia 1968–71, Studi verdiani 1981–; teaching asst, Univ. of Parma 1968–70, Assoc. Prof. of Music History 1970–72; librarian and teacher of music history, Rossini Conservatory, Pesaro 1970–73; Lecturer in Music, King's Coll., London, UK 1973–77; Reader in Musicology, Univ. of London 1978–80; Dir Istituto di Studi Verdiani, Parma 1980–89, Istituto Nazionale di Studi Verdiani, Parma 1989–; Prof. of Music History, Univ. of Perugia 1981–83, Univ. of Rome 'La Sapienza'

1983–2005; Chair of Italian Culture, Univ. of California at Berkeley 1988; Lauro de Bosis Lecturer in the History of Italian Civilization, Harvard Univ. 1996; Visitante distinguido, Univ. of Cordoba, Argentina; mem. External Advisory Bd, Faculty of Music, Univ. of Oxford, UK, Advisory Bd, Forschungsinstitut für Musiktheater, Univ. of Bayreuth, Thurn, Germany; mem. Accad. Nazionale dei Lincei, Academia Europaea; Corresp. mem. American Musicological Soc.; Foreign Hon. mem. Royal Musical Asscn, UK. *Publications:* Thematic Catalog of an 18th-Century Collection of Italian Instrumental Music (held in the Music Library, Univ. of California at Berkeley, with V. Duckles and M. Elmer) 1963, Giuseppe Tartini: le fonti biografiche 1968, Mozart's Il re pastore (critical edn, with Wolfgang Rehm) 1984, Carteggio Verdi-Ricordi 1880–1881 (co-ed.) 1988, Tartini, le sue idee e il suo tempo 1992, Music in the Theater: Essays on Verdi and Other Composers 1994, Italian edn 1998; contribs to scholarly books and professional journals. *Honours:* Hon. mem. Akad. der Mozartforschung, Salzburg. *Address:* 34 via di San Anselmo, 00153 Rome, Italy (home). *Telephone:* (0521) 286044 (office); (06) 5750433 (home). *Fax:* (0521) 287949 (office). *E-mail:* petrobel@rmcisadu .let.uniromat.it (office); direzione@studioerdiani.it (office).

PETROSKI, Catherine, BA, MA; American writer; b. 1939, St Louis, Mo.; m. Henry Petroski 1966; one s. one d. *Education:* MacMurray Coll., Univ. of Illinois. *Career:* mem. Authors' Guild, Nat. Book Critics' Circle. *Publications:* Gravity and Other Stories 1981, Beautiful My Mane is the Wind 1983, The Summer That Lasted Forever 1984, A Bride's Passage: Susan Hathorn's Year Under Sail 1997; contrib. to reviews, quarterlies and periodicals. *Honours:* Hon. DLitt (MacMurray Coll.) 1984; Nat. Endowment for the Arts Fellowships 1978–79, 1983–84; Berlin Prize 1960, Texas Inst. of Letters Prize 1976, PEN Syndicated Fiction Prizes 1983–85, 1988, O. Henry Award 1989, John Lyman Book Award 1997. *Address:* 3910 Plymouth Road, Durham, NC 27707, USA (home).

PETROSKI, Henry, BME, MS, PhD; American academic, engineer, historian and writer; *Vesic Professor of Civil Engineering, Duke University;* b. 6 Feb. 1942, New York, USA; m. Catherine Ann Groom 1966; one s. one d. *Education:* Manhattan Coll., Univ. of Illinois. *Career:* Instructor, Univ. of Illinois 1965–68; Asst Prof., Univ. of Texas at Austin 1968–74; Engineer, Argonne Nat. Lab. 1975–80; Assoc. Prof. of Civil Eng, Duke Univ. 1980–87, Dir Grad. Studies 1981–86, Prof. 1987–93, Chair, Dept of Civil and Environmental Eng 1991–2000, Aleksandar S. Vesic Prof. 1993–, Prof. of History 1995–; mem. American Soc. of Civil Engineers, American Soc. of Mechanical Engineers, Nat. Acad. of Eng, American Acad. of Arts and Sciences, American Philosophical Soc. *Television:* writer and presenter of To Engineer is Human (50-minute documentary for BBC) 1987. *Publications:* To Engineer is Human 1985, Beyond Engineering 1986, The Pencil 1990, The Evolution of Useful Things 1992, Design Paradigms 1994, Engineers of Dreams 1995, Invention by Design 1996, Remaking the World 1997, The Book on the Bookshelf 1999, Paperboy: Confessions of a Future Engineer (memoir) 2002, Small Things Considered 2003, Pushing the Limits 2004, Success Through Failure 2006; contribs to professional journals, including American Scientist. *Honours:* Dr hc (Clarkson Univ.) 1990, (Trinity Coll.) 1997, (Valparaiso Univ.) 1999, (Manhattan Coll.) 2003; Nat. Endowment for the Humanities Fellowship 1987–88, Guggenheim Fellowship 1990–91, Best Book Award in Engineering, American Asscn of University Presses 1994. *Address:* School of Engineering, Duke University, PO Box 90287, Durham, NC 27708, USA (office). *Telephone:* (919) 660-5203 (office). *Fax:* (919) 660-5219 (office).

PETRUSHEVSKAYA, Liudmila Stefanovna; Russian author, playwright and poet; b. 26 May 1938, Moscow; d. of Stefan Antonovitsh Petrushevskij and Valentina Nikolaevna Jakovleva; m. 1st Evgenij Kharatian; one s.; m. 2nd Boris Pavlov; one s. one d. *Education:* Moscow Univ. *Career:* newspaper and radio journalist 1957–73; started writing short stories 1968, plays and folk tales 1971; stage productions and publ. of works were forbidden for many years; first underground performance 1975, first official performance, Tallinn 1979; mem. Bayerische Akad. der Schönen Kunste 1997. *Plays include:* Two Windows 1971, Music Lessons 1973, Cinzano 1973, Love 1974, The Landing 1974, Andante 1975, The Execution, A Glass of Water, Smirnova's Birthday 1977–78, Three Girls in Blue 1980, Colombina's Flat 1981, Moscow Choir 1984, The Golden Goddess 1986, The Wedding Night 1990, The Men's Quarters 1992; co-author of screenplay Tale of Tales (prize for best animated film of all time, Los Angeles 1980). *Publications:* Immortal Love 1988, Songs of the 20th Century 1988, On the Way to the God Eros 1993, The Mystery of the House 1993; (children's books) Vasilli's Treatment 1991, Once Upon a Time There Was a Trrrr! 1994, Real Fairy Tales 1997, The Alphabet's Tale 1997; Complete Works (5 vols) 1996, The Girl's House 1998, Find Me, My Dream 2000. *Honours:* Int. A. Pushkin Prize (Germany) 1991, prizes for the best short story of the year from Ogoniok 1988, 1989 and Oktiabr 1993, 1996, Grand Prize for play The Time: Night, Annual All-Russian Theatre Festival of Solo Theatre, Perm 1995, Moscow-Penne Prize (Russia/Italy) 1996. *Address:* Staroslobodsky per. 2A, Apt 20, 107113 Moscow, Russia. *Telephone:* (495) 269-74-48. *Fax:* (495) 269-74-48.

PETTERSON, Per; Norwegian writer; b. 18 July 1952, Hemnes. *Career:* fmr librarian, bookseller. *Publications:* Aske i munnen, sand i skoa (short stories) 1987, Ekkoland (novel) 1989, Det er griet for meg (novel) 1992, Til Sibir (novel, trans. as To Siberia) 1996, I kjølvannet (novel, trans. as In the Wake) 2000, Ut å stjæle hester (novel, trans. as Out Stealing Horses) (Independent Foreign Fiction Prize 2006, Impac Award (jtly) 2007) 2003. *Address:* c/o Harvill Press, 20 Vauxhall Bridge Road, London, SW1V 2SA, England (office).

PETTIFER, Julian, MA; British writer and broadcaster; b. 21 July 1935, Malmesbury. *Education:* St John's College, Cambridge. *Career:* TV Reporter, Writer, Presenter, Southern TV 1958–62; Tonight 1962–64, 24 Hours 1964–69, Panorama 1969–75, BBC; Presenter, Cuba – 25 Years of Revolution, series 1984, Host, Busman's Holiday 1985–86, ITV; numerous TV documentaries including: Vietnam War Without End 1970, The World About Us 1976, The Spirit of 76 1976, Diamonds in the Sky 1979, Nature Watch, 5 series 1981–90, Automania 1984, The Living Isles 1986, Africawatch 1989, Missionaries 1990, BBC Crossing Continents 2001–; BBC Assignment 1993–94; BBC Correspondent 1994–95; mem. Royal Society for Nature Conservation (vice-pres. 1992–), RSPB (pres. 1994–2000, 2004–). *Publications:* Diamonds in the Sky: A Social History of Air Travel (co-author), 1979; Nature Watch (co-author), 1981; Automania (co-author), 1984; The Nature Watchers (co-author), 1985; Missionaries (co-author), 1990; Nature Watch (co-author), 1994. *Honours:* Reporter of the Year Award, Guild of Television Dirs and Producers, 1968; Royal Geographical Society Cherry Kearton Award for Wildlife Films, 1990; Royal Scottish Geographical Society Mungo Park Award, 1995. *Literary Agent:* Curtis Brown Ltd, Haymarket House, 28–29 Haymarket, London, SW1Y 4SP, England. *Telephone:* (20) 7393-4400. *Fax:* (20) 7393-4401. *E-mail:* info@curtisbrown.co.uk. *Website:* www.curtisbrown.co.uk.

PETTIT, Philip Noel, PhD; Irish philosopher and academic; *L. S. Rockefeller University Professor of Politics and Human Values, Princeton University;* b. 20 Dec. 1945, Ballinasloe, Ireland; s. of Michael A. Pettit and Bridget C. Molony; m. Eileen McNally 1978; two s. *Education:* Maynooth Coll., Nat. Univ. of Ireland, Queen's Univ. Belfast, Northern Ireland. *Career:* Lecturer, Univ. Coll. Dublin 1968–72, 1975–77; Research Fellow, Trinity Hall Cambridge, UK 1972–75; Prof. of Philosophy, Univ. of Bradford, UK 1977–83; Professorial Fellow, Research School of Social Sciences, ANU, Canberra, Australia 1983–89, Prof. of Social and Political Theory 1989–2002; Visiting Prof. of Philosophy, Columbia Univ., New York, USA 1997–2001; William Nelson Cromwell Prof. of Politics, Princeton Univ., USA 2002, currently L. S. Rockefeller Univ. Prof. of Politics and Human Values; Assoc. Faculty Mem. Dept of Philosophy; Fellow Acad. of Social Sciences, Australia, Australian Acad. of Humanities. *Publications:* Concept of Structuralism 1975, Judging Justice 1980, Semantics and Social Science (with G. Macdonald) 1981, Not Just Deserts: A Republican Theory of Criminal Justice (with J. Braithwaite) 1990, The Common Mind: An Essay on Psychology, Society and Politics 1992, Republicanism: A Theory of Freedom and Government 1997, A Theory of Freedom: From the Psychology to the Politics of Agency 2001, Rules, Reasons and Norms: Selected Essays 2002, Penser en Société 2003, Mind, Morality, and Explanation: Selected Collaborations (co-author) 2004, The Economy of Esteem (with Geoffrey Brennan) 2004. *Honours:* Hon. Mem. Italian Soc. for Analytical Philosophy; Hon. DLitt (Nat. Univ. of Ireland) 2000, Hon. PhD (Univ. of Crete) 2005; Univ. Medal, Univ. of Helsinki 1992. *Address:* UCHV, 308 Marx Hall, Princeton University, Princeton, NJ 08544-1012 (office); 16 College Road, Princeton, NJ 08540, USA (home). *Telephone:* (609) 258-4759 (office); (609) 924-3664 (home). *E-mail:* ppettit@princeton.edu (office). *Website:* www.princeton.edu/~ppettit (office).

PETTY, William Henry, CBE, BSc, MA, DLitt; British educator (retd) and poet; b. 7 Sept. 1921, Bradford, Yorks., England; m. Margaret Elaine Bastow 1948; one s. two d. *Education:* Peterhouse, Cambridge, Univs of London and Kent. *Career:* admin., teaching and lecturing posts, London, Doncaster, N and W Ridings of Yorks., Kent 1945–73; Chief Educ. Officer, Kent 1973–84; Chair. Govs Christ Church Univ. Coll., Canterbury 1992–94; mem. Poetry Soc., English Asscn, Soc. of Educ. Officers (Pres. 1981–82). *Publications:* No Bold Comfort 1957, Conquest 1967, Educational Administration (co-author) 1980, Executive Summaries (booklets) 1984–90, Springfield: Pieces of the Past 1994, Genius Loci (with Robert Roberts) 1995, The Louvre Imperial 1997, Interpretations of History 2000, No-one Listening 2002, Breaking Time 2005, Hi-jacked in China with Jane Austen 2006; contrib. to various anthologies, reviews, quarterlies and journals. *Honours:* Cheltenham Festival of Literature Prize 1968, Camden Festival of Music and the Arts Prize 1969, Greenwood Prize, Poetry Soc. 1978, Lake Aske Memorial Award 1980, Swanage Festival of Literature Prize 1995, Ali Competition Prize 1995, Kent Fed. of Writers Prize 1995, White Cliffs Prize 2000, Envoi Prize 2004, Ottaker/Faber local prize 2004, Essex Literary Festival Prize 2006, Newark Poetry Prize 2007. *Address:* Willow Bank, Moat Road, Headcorn, Kent, TN27 9NT, England (home). *Telephone:* (1622) 890087 (home).

PEYSER, Joan Gilbert, BA, MA; American musicologist and writer; b. 12 June 1931, New York, NY. *Education:* Barnard Coll., Columbia Univ. *Career:* Ed., The Musical Quarterly 1977–84; regular contrib. to the Sunday New York Times 1966–85; mem. American Musicological Soc., Music Critics Asscn, PEN. *Publications:* The New Music: The Sense Behind the Sound 1970, revised second edn as Twentieth Century Music: The Sense Behind the Sound 1980, Boulez: Composer, Conductor, Enigma 1976, The Orchestra: Origins and Transformations (Ed., First Prize Humanities Category, Prof. and Scholarly Publ. Div. Asscn of American Publishers) 1986, Bernstein: A Biography 1987, The Memory of All That: The Life of George Gershwin 1993, The Music of My Time (essays) 1995, To Boulez and Beyond: Music in Europe Since the Rite of Spring 1999; contrib. to periodicals and journals. *Honours:* five ASCAP/Deems Taylor Awards. *Address:* 19 Charlton Street, New York, NY 10014, USA. *Telephone:* (212) 675-5066. *Fax:* (212) 675-9544.

PEYTON, Kathleen Wendy, (Kathleen Herald, K. M. Peyton), ATD; British writer; b. 2 Aug. 1929, Birmingham; d. of William Joseph and Ivy Kathleen Herald; m. Michael Peyton 1950; two d. *Education:* Wimbledon High School and Manchester School of Art. *Career:* art teacher, Northampton 1953–55; writer 1947–. *Publications:* as Kathleen Herald: Sabre, the Horse from the Sea 1947, The Mandrake 1949, Crab the Roan 1953; as K. M. Peyton: North to Adventure 1959, Stormcock Meets Trouble 1961, The Hard Way Home 1962, Windfall 1963, Brownsea Silver 1964, The Maplin Bird (New York Herald Tribune Award 1965) 1964, The Plan for Birdsmarsh 1965, Thunder in the Sky 1966, Flambards Trilogy (Guardian Award 1970), Vol. I: Flambards 1967, Vol. II: The Edge of the Cloud (Carnegie Medal) 1969, Vol. III: Flambards in Summer 1969, Fly-by-Night 1968, Pennington's Seventeenth Summer 1970, The Beethoven Medal 1971, The Pattern of Roses 1972, Pennington's Heir 1973, The Team 1975, The Right-Hand Man 1977, Prove Yourself a Hero 1977, A Midsummer Night's Death 1978, Marion's Angels 1979, Flambards Divided 1981, Dear Fred 1981, Going Home 1983, Who Sir? Me Sir? 1983, The Last Ditch 1984, Froggett's Revenge 1985, The Sound of Distant Cheering 1986, Downhill All the Way 1988, Darkling 1989, Skylark 1989, No Roses Round the Door 1990, Poor Badger 1991, Late to Smile 1992, The Boy Who Wasn't There 1992, The Wild Boy and Queen Moon 1993, Snowfall 1994, The Swallow Tale 1995, Swallow Summer 1995, Unquiet Spirits 1997, Firehead 1998, Swallow the Star 1998, Blind Beauty 1999, Small Gains 2003, Greater Gains 2005, Blue Skies ad Gunfire 2006, Minna's Ride 2007. *Address:* Rookery Cottage, N Fambridge, Chelmsford, Essex CM3 6LP, England. *Telephone:* (1621) 828545. *Fax:* (1621) 828545.

PEYTON, Richard (see Haining, Peter Alexander)

PFAFF, William; American writer and journalist; *Columnist, Tribune Media Services, The Tribune Company;* m. Carolyn Cleary; two c. *Education:* Univ. of Notre Dame, Ind. *Career:* Asst Ed. Commonweal magazine, New York 1949–55; Writer, ABC News 1955–57; Exec. Free Europe Cttee 1957–61; Sr Mem. Hudson Inst., New York 1961–75, Deputy Dir Hudson Research Europe, Paris 1971–78; freelance writer 1978–; syndicated columnist International Herald Tribune 1978–; Contrib. New Yorker magazine 1971–92, also New York Review of Books, Harper's Magazine, Foreign Affairs, The National Interest, The Observer, London, Commentaire, Paris, etc. *Publications include:* The New Politics (with Edmund Stillman) 1960, The Politics of Hysteria (with Edmund Stillman) 1964, Power and Impotence (with Edmund Stillman) 1966, Condemned to Freedom 1971; published in Best American Essays: The Lay Intellectual (autobiog. essay) 1987, Barbarian Sentiments: How the American Century Ends (Prix Jean-Jacques Rousseau, Geneva) 1989, The Wrath of Nations 1993, Barbarian Sentiments: America in the New Century 2000, Fear Anger and Failure 2004, The Bullet's Song: Romantic Violence and Utopia 2004. *Honours:* Rockefeller Foundation Grant 1962; Hon. LLD (Univ. of Notre Dame) 1992 Prix de l'Annuaire Français de Relations Internationales 2004. *Address:* 23/25 Rue de Lisbonne, 7608 Paris Cedex, France (office). *Telephone:* 1-43-59-05-66 (office). *Fax:* 1-43-59-09-98 (office). *E-mail:* wpfaff@wanadoo.fr (office). *Website:* www.williampfaff.com (office).

PHELAN, Thomas (Tom) J., BA, MA; Irish writer; b. 5 Nov. 1940, Mountmellick, Co. Laois, Ireland; m. Patricia Mansfield 1991, two s. *Education:* St Patrick's Seminary, Carlow, Univ. of Seattle. *Career:* Priest; fmrly worked in insurance and farming; Asst Prof. of English, Harriman Coll., New York; mem. Poets and Writers, My Irish History Roundtable, American Conf. for Irish Studies. *Publications:* In the Season of the Daisies 1993, Iscariot 1995, Derrycloney 1999, The Canal Bridge 2005. *E-mail:* Glanvil3@aol.com (office). *Website:* www.tomphelan.net.

PHILIP, Marlene Nourbese, BSc, MA, LLB; Trinidad and Tobago/Canadian poet, writer and lawyer; b. 3 Feb. 1947, Tobago; m. Paul Chamberlain 1978, three c. *Education:* University of the West Indies, University of Western Ontario. *Publications:* Thorns, 1980; Salmon Courage, 1983; Harriet's Daughter, 1988; She Tries Her Tongue, Her Silence Softly Breaks, 1989; Looking for Livingstone: An Odyssey of Silence, 1991; Frontiers: Essays and Writings on Racism and Culture, 1992; Showing Grit: Showboating North of the 44th Parallel, 1993. *Honours:* Casa de las Americas Prize for Poetry, 1988; Toronto Book Award for Fiction, 1990; Max and Greta Abel Award for Multicultural Literature, 1990; Guggenheim Fellowship, 1990; Toronto Arts Award, 1995. *E-mail:* nourbese@nourbese.com. *Website:* www.nourbese.com.

PHILIPPE, Cécile; French novelist and playwright. *Plays include:* Ruptures, Qui est cette femme?, Dis leur, C'est trop, La Mémoire longue, Le bonheur va bien, Audition, Zapping, Non-lieu, Bavardages. *Publications include:* Petites histoires horizontales 1997, Nouvelles histoires horizontales 1999, Don Juan, père et fils 1999, Je ne suis là pour personne (Prix Charles Exbrayat 2003) 2002, Le Magané 2003, Salut Lulu! 2003, Tous les hommes sont des pères Noël 2004. *Address:* c/o Editions Mercure de France, 26 rue de Condé, 75006 Paris, France.

PHILLIPS, Adam; British psychoanalyst and writer. *Career:* fmr Principal Child Psychotherapist, Charing Cross Hospital, London; Series Ed., Penguin translations of Sigmund Freud's work. *Publications:* On Kissing, Tickling and Being Bored: Psychoanalytic Essays on the Unexamined Life 1993, On Flirtation 1994, Terrors and Experts 1995, Monogamy 1996, The Beast in the Nursery 1998, Darwin's Worms: On Life Stories and Death Stories 2000, Promises Promises: Essays on Psychoanalysis and Literature 2000, Houdini's Box: The Art of Escape 2001, Psychoanalysis 2001, Equals 2002, Going Sane 2005, Side Effects 2006. *Address:* c/o Faber and Faber Ltd, 3 Queen Square, London, WC1N 3AU, England (office).

PHILLIPS, Carl, BA, MAT, MA; American academic, poet and writer; *Professor, Washington University, St Louis*; b. 23 July 1959, Everett, WA. *Education:* Harvard Univ., Univ. of Massachusetts at Amherst, Boston Univ. *Career:* poet-in-residence 1993–94, Asst Prof. 1994–96, Assoc. Prof. 1996–2000, Dir Writing Program 1996–98, 2000–, Prof. 2000–, Washington Univ., St Louis; Visiting Asst Prof., Harvard Univ. 1995–96; Faculty, Warren Wilson Coll. 1997–; Visiting Writer-in-Residence, Univ. of Iowa 1998; mem. Acad. of American Poets, Associated Writing Programs, MLA, PEN American Center, Poetry Soc. of America. *Publications:* In the Blood 1992, Cortège 1995, From the Devotions 1998, Pastoral 2000, The Tether 2001, Rock Harbor 2002; contrib. to many anthologies, reviews, quarterlies and journals. *Honours:* Samuel French Morse Poetry Prize 1992, Acad. of American Poets Prize 1993, Guggenheim Fellowship 1997–98, Witter Bynner Fellowship 1997–98, Pushcart Prizes 1998, 2001, Lambda Literary Award in Poetry 2001, American Acad. of Arts and Letters Award in Literature 2001, Kingsley Tufts Poetry Prize 2002. *Address:* 1026 Fairmount Avenue, St Louis, MO 63139, USA.

PHILLIPS, Caryl, BA, FRSL; British/Saint Christopher and Nevis writer and academic; *Professor of English, Yale University*; b. 13 March 1958, St Kitts, West Indies. *Education:* The Queen's Coll., Oxford. *Career:* Writer-in-Residence, The Factory Arts Centre, London 1980–82, Univ. of Mysore, India 1987, Univ. of Stockholm 1989; visiting writer, Amherst Coll., Mass., USA 1990–92, Writer-in-Residence and Co-Dir Creative Writing Center 1992–94, Prof. of English 1994–97, Prof. of English and Writer-in-Residence 1997–98; Prof. of English and Henry R. Luce Prof. of Migration and Social Order, Barnard Coll., Columbia Univ., New York 1998–2005, Dir of Initiatives in the Humanities 2003–05; Prof. of English, Yale Univ. 2005–; writing instructor, Arvon Foundation, UK 1983–; Visiting Prof. of Humanities, Univ. of W Indies, Barbados 1999–2000; Exec. Sec., N American Network of Cities of Asylum 2005–; Consultant Ed. Faber Inc., Boston 1992–94; Contributing Ed. Bomb Magazine, New York 1993–; Consultant Ed. Graywolf Press, Minneapolis 1994–; Dir Heartland Productions Ltd 1994–2000; Advisory Ed. Wasifiri Magazine, London 1995–; Series Ed. Faber and Faber, London 1996–2000; mem. Arts Council of GB Drama Panel 1982–85, British Film Inst. Production Bd 1985–88, Bd, The Bush Theatre, London 1985–89; mem. English PEN 1997, Writers' Guild (UK) 1997, American PEN, council mem. 1998; Hon. Sr mem. Univ. of Kent 1988–; Fellow New York Public Library 2002–03. *Films:* Playing Away 1986, The Mystic Masseur 2001. *Plays:* Strange Fruit 1980, Where There is Darkness 1982, The Shelter 1983. *Radio:* plays: The Wasted Years (BBC Giles Cooper Award for Best Radio Play of the Year) 1984, Crossing the River 1985, The Prince of Africa 1987, Writing Fiction 1991, A Kind of Home 2004, Hotel Cristobel 2005; several documentaries. *Television:* The Final Passage (Channel 4) 1996. *Publications:* fiction: The Final Passage (Malcolm X Prize for Literature) 1985, A State of Independence 1986, Higher Ground 1989, Cambridge (Sunday Times Young Writer of the Year Award) 1991, Crossing the River (James Tait Black Memorial Prize) 1993, The Nature of Blood 1997, A Distant Shore (Commonwealth Writers Prize 2004) 2003, Dancing in the Dark 2005; non-fiction: The European Tribe (Martin Luther King Memorial Prize) 1987, The Atlantic Sound 2000, A New World Order: Selected Essays 2001; editor: Extravagant Strangers 1997, The Right Set: A Tennis Anthology 1999. *Honours:* Hon. AM (Amherst Coll.) 1995; Hon. DUniv (Leeds Metropolitan) 1997, (York) 2003; Hon. DLitt (Leeds) 2003; Hon. MA (Yale) 2006; British Council 50th Anniversary Fellowship 1984, Guggenheim Fellowship 1992; Lannan Literary Award 1994. *Literary Agent:* c/o Georgia Garrett, A.P. Watt Ltd, 20 John Street, London, WC1N 2DR, England. *Telephone:* (20) 7282-3106 (office). *Fax:* (20) 7282-3142 (office). *E-mail:* apw@apwatt.co.uk. *Website:* www.carylphillips.com.

PHILLIPS, Edward O., BA, LLL, AMT, MA; Canadian teacher and writer; b. 26 Nov. 1931, Montréal, QC. *Education:* McGill University, University of Montréal, Harvard University, Boston University. *Career:* mem. Canadian Writers Union; PEN. *Publications:* Sunday's Child, 1981; Where There's a Will, 1984; Buried on Sunday, 1986; Hope Springs Eternal, 1988; Sunday Best, 1990; The Landlady's Niece, 1992; The Mice Will Play, 1996; Working on Sunday, 1998; No Early Birds, 2001. Contributions: Short stories to various Canadian journals. *Honours:* Arthur Ellis Award 1986.

PHILLIPS, Jayne Anne, BA, MFA; American writer; b. 19 July 1952, Buckhannon, WV; m. Mark Brian Stockman 1985; one s. two step-s. *Education:* West Virginia University, University of Iowa. *Career:* Adjunct Assoc. Prof. of English, Boston University, 1982–; Fanny Howe Chair of Letters, Brandeis University, 1986–87; mem. Authors' Guild; Authors League of America; PEN. *Publications:* Sweethearts, 1976; Counting, 1978; Black Tickets, 1979; How Mickey Made It, 1981; Machine Dreams, 1984; Fast Lanes, 1984; Shelter, 1994; Motherkind, 2000. *Honours:* Pushcart Prizes, 1977, 1979, 1983; Fels Award in Fiction, Co-ordinating Council of Literary Magazines, 1978; National Endowment for the Arts Fellowships, 1978, 1985; St Lawrence Award for Fiction, 1979; Sue Kaufman Award for Fiction, American Acad. and Institute of Arts and Letters, 1980; O. Henry Award, 1980; Bunting Institute Fellowship, Radcliffe College, 1981; Notable Book Citation, American Library Asscn, 1984; Best Book Citation, New York Times, 1984.

PHILLIPS, Kate, BA, MA, PhD; American writer; b. 30 July 1966, Pomona, CA; m., two c. *Education:* Dartmouth College, Harvard University. *Career:* Teacher, Beijing Normal University, People's Republic of China, 1988–89; Grant Writer, Newsletter Ed., Irish Immigration Center, Boston, 1992–95. *Publications:* White Rabbit, 1996; Helen Hunt Jackson: A Literary Life, 2003.

PHILLIPS, Louis, BA, MA; American academic, writer, dramatist and poet; b. 15 June 1942, Lowell, MA; m. Patricia L. Ranard 1971, two s. *Education:* Stetson University, University of North Carolina at Chapel Hill, CUNY. *Career:* Prof. of Humanities, School of Visual Arts, New York, 1977–. *Publications:* The Man Who Stole the Atlantic Ocean, 1971; Theodore Jonathon Wainwright is Going to Bomb the Pentagon, 1973; The Time, the Hour, the Solitariness of the Place, 1986; A Dream of Countries Where No One Dare Live, 1994; The Hot Corner, 1997. Contributions: The Georgia Review; Massachusetts Review; Chicago Review; Regular Columnist for The Armchair Detective; Shakespeare Bulletin. *Address:* 375 Riverside Drive, Apt 14C, New York, NY 10025, USA.

PHILLIPS, Michael (see Nolan, William Francis)

PHILLIPS, Mike, OBE, BA, PhD; British writer and broadcaster; *Cross Cultural Consultant, Tate Britain*; b. Georgetown, Guyana. *Education:* Univ. of London, Univ. of Essex, Goldsmiths Coll., London. *Career:* journalist and broadcaster BBC 1972–83; fmr Lecturer in Media Studies Univ. of Westminster; full-time writer 1992–; Curator Tate Britain 2005–06, Cross Cultural Consultant 2006–. *Opera:* Bridgetower (with Julian Joseph), City of London Festival 2007. *Publications:* Community Work and Racism (non-fiction) 1982, Smell of the Coast 1987, Blood Rights (novel, also adapted for TV) 1989, The Late Candidate (novel) (CWA Macallan Silver Dagger for Fiction) 1990, Boyz 'n' the Hood 1991, Notting Hill in the Sixties (non-fiction) 1991, Point of Darkness (novel) 1994, An Image to Die For (novel) 1995, The Dancing Face (novel) 1997, Windrush: The Irresistible Rise of Multi-Racial Britain (non-fiction, co-author) 1998, A Shadow of Myself (novel) 2000, London Crossings: A Biography of Black Britain (essays and stories) 2001, The Name You Once Gave Me 2006. *Address:* Trustee, HCF, 7 Holbein Place, London, SW1W 8NR, England. *E-mail:* mpushkin2@aol.com (home).

PHILLIPS, Robert Schaeffer, BA, MA; American academic, poet and writer; b. 2 Feb. 1938, Milford, DE; m. Judith Anne Bloomingdale, 16 June 1962, one s. *Education:* Syracuse University. *Career:* Instructor, New School for Social Research, New York City, 1966–68, Belle Levine Arts Center, 1968–69; Poetry Review Ed., Modern Poetry Studies, 1969–73; Prof. of English, 1991–, Dir, Creative Writing Program, 1991–96, John and Rebecca Moores University Scholar, 1998–(2006), University of Houston; Poetry Reviewer, Houston Post, 1992–95, Houston Chronicle, 1995–; mem. Acad. of American Poets; American PEN Center, board of dirs; Asscn of Literary Scholars and Critics; English-Speaking Union; Friends of Poets and Writers; National Book Critics Circle; Poetry Society of America; South Central MLA; Texas Institute of Letters, councillor; The Poets' Prize, chair. *Publications:* Poetry: Inner Weather, 1966; The Pregnant Man, 1978; Running on Empty, 1981; Personal Accounts: New and Selected Poems, 1966–1986, 1986; The Wounded Angel, 1987; Face to Face, 1993; Breakdown Lane, 1994; Spinach Days, 2000; Interviews: The Madness of Art, 2003. Fiction: The Land of the Lost Content, 1970; Public Landing Revisited, 1992; News About People You Know, 2002. Criticism: Aspects of Alice (ed.), 1971; The Confessional Poets, 1973; Denton Welch, 1974; William Goyen, 1978, Are Those Real Poems, or Did You Write Them Yourself? (essays) 2005. Contributions: many anthologies, reviews, quarterlies, and journals. *Honours:* American Acad. and Institute of Arts and Letters Award, 1987; Arents Pioneer Medal, Syracuse University, 1988; Greenwood Award, 1993; New York Times Notable Book of the Year Citations, 1994, 2000; Fort Concho Literary Festival Fiction Prize, 1994. *Address:* 1903 Banks Street, Houston, TX 77098 (home); c/o Creative Writing Program, Department of English, University of Houston, Houston, TX 77204, USA (office). *Telephone:* (713) 526-6263 (home); (713) 743-2951 (office). *E-mail:* cwbobphillips@yahoo.com.

PHILLIPS, Warren Henry, BA; American publisher and newspaper executive; b. 28 June 1926, New York City; s. of Abraham and Juliette Phillips; m. Barbara Anne Thomas 1951; three d. *Education:* Queens Coll. *Career:* Copyreader Wall Street Journal 1947–48, Foreign Corresp., Germany 1949–50, Chief, London Bureau 1950–51, Foreign Ed. 1951–53, News Ed. 1953–54, Man. Ed. Midwest Edition 1954–57, Man. Ed. Wall Street Journal 1957–65, Publr 1975–88; Exec. Ed. Dow Jones & Co. 1965–70; Vice-Pres. and Gen. Man. Dow Jones & Co. Inc. 1970–71, Editorial Dir 1971–88, Exec. Vice-Pres. 1972, Pres. 1972–79, CEO 1975–90, Chair. 1978–91, mem. Bd of Dirs 1972–97, Dir Emer. 1997–; Pres. American Council on Educ. for Journalism 1971–73; Co-Publr Bridge Works Publishing Co. 1992–; mem. Bd of Dirs Public Broadcasting Service 1991–97; Pres. American Soc. of Newspaper Eds 1975–76; mem. Pulitzer Prizes Bd 1977–87; Trustee, Columbia Univ. 1980–93, Trustee Emer. 1993–; mem. Visitors' Cttee Kennedy School of Govt, Harvard Univ. 1984–90, 1992–97; mem. Corp. Advisory Bd Queens Coll. 1986–90, Foundation Bd of Trustees 1990–97. *Publication:* China: Behind the Mask (with Robert Keatley) 1973. *Honours:* Hon. LHD (Pace) 1982, (Queens Coll.) 1987, (Long Island) 1987; Hon. JD (Portland) 1973. *Address:* Bridge Works Publishing, PO Box 1798, Bridgehampton, NY 11932, USA (office). *Telephone:* (631) 537-3418. *Fax:* (631) 537-5092.

PHILLIPS, Will (see Williamson, Philip G.)

PHILLIS, Sir Robert Weston, Kt, BA, FRSA, FRTS; British media executive; b. 3 Dec. 1945, Croydon; s. of Francis W. Phillis and Gertrude G. Phillis; m. Jean Derham 1966; three s. *Education:* John Ruskin Grammar School and Univ. of Nottingham. *Career:* apprentice, printing industry 1961–65; Thomson Regional Newspapers Ltd 1968–69; British Printing Corpn Ltd 1969–71; lecturer in industrial relations, Univ. of Edin. and Scottish Business

School 1971–75; Visiting Fellow, Univ. of Nairobi 1974; Personnel Dir, later Man. Dir Sun Printers Ltd 1976–79; Man. Dir Independent TV Publs Ltd 1979–82; Man. Dir Cen. Independent TV PLC 1981–87, Dir (non-exec.) 1987–91; Group Man. Dir Carlton Communications PLC 1987–91; Chief Exec. Independent TV News (ITN) 1991–93; Man. Dir BBC World Service 1993–94, Deputy Dir-Gen. BBC 1993–97, Chair. BBC Worldwide 1994–97; Chief Exec. Guardian Media Group 1997–2006, Non-Exec. Dir 2006–; Chair. ITV Network Programming Cttee 1984–86, ITV Film Purchase Group 1985–87, Zenith Productions 1984–91, Trader Media Group Ltd 2001–; Dir (non-exec.) ITN Ltd 1982–87, ITV 2005–; Dir and Trustee TV Trust for the Environment, Teaching Awards Trust 2001–; Vice-Chair. (Int.), Int. Council, Nat. Acad. of TV Arts and Sciences 1994–97 (Life Fellow), (Dir 1985–93); Vice-Pres. European Broadcasting Union 1996–97; Hon. Prof. Univ. of Stirling 1997; Fellow Royal Television Soc. 1993 (Chair. 1989–92, Vice-Pres. 1994, currently Pres.); Trustee Nat. Film and TV School Foundation. *Honours:* Hon. DLitt (Salford Univ.) 1999; Hon. DLit (City Univ.) 2000; Hon. DLitt (Nottingham Univ.) 2003. *Address:* c/o Guardian Media Group, 75 Farringdon Road, London, England (office). *E-mail:* bob.phillis@gmgplc.co.uk (office).

PICANO, Felice, BA; American writer and poet; b. 22 Feb. 1944, New York, NY. *Education:* Queens College, CUNY. *Career:* mem. PEN Club; Writers Guild of America; Authors' Guild; Publishing Triangle. *Publications:* Smart as the Devil, 1975; Eyes, 1976; Deformity Lover and Other Poems, 1977; The Lure, 1979; Late in the Season, 1980; An Asian Minor, 1981; Slashed to Ribbons in Defense of Love and Other Stories, 1982; House of Cards, 1984; Ambidextrous, 1985; Men Who Loved Me, 1989; To the Seventh Power, 1989; The New Joy of Gay Sex, 1992; Dryland's End, 1995; Like People in History, 1995. Contributions: Men on Men; Violet Quill Reader; numerous magazines and journals. *Honours:* PEN Syndicated Short Fiction Award; Chapbook Award, Poetry Society of America.

PICARD, Barbara Leonie; British author; b. 4 Dec. 1917, Richmond, Surrey, England. *Publications:* Ransom for a Knight, 1956; Lost John, 1962; One is One, 1965; The Young Pretenders, 1966; Twice Seven Tales, 1968; Three Ancient Kings, 1972; Tales of Ancient Persia, revised edn, 1993; The Iliad, 1991; The Odyssey, 1991; French Legends, Tales and Fairy Stories, 1992; German Hero-sagas and Folk-tales, 1993; Tales of the Norse Gods, 1994; Selected Fairy Tales, 1994; The Deceivers, 1996; The Midsummer Bride, 1999.

PICARD, Robert George, BA, MA, PhD; American writer; b. 15 July 1951, Pasadena, CA; m. Elizabeth Carpelan 1979, two d. one s. *Education:* Loma Linda University, California State University, Fullerton, University of Missouri. *Career:* Ed., Journal of Media Economics, 1988–97; Assoc. Ed., Political Communication and Persuasion, 1989–91. *Publications:* The Press and the Decline of Democracy, 1985; Press Concentration and Monopoly, 1988; The Ravens of Odin: The Press in the Nordic Nations, 1988; In the Camera's Eye: News Coverage of Terrorist Events, 1991; Media Portrayals of Terrorism: Functions and Meaning of News Coverage, 1993; The Cable Networks Handbook, 1993; Joint Operating Agreements: The Newspaper Preservation Act and its Application, 1993; The Newspaper Publishing Industry, 1997.

PICHASKE, David Richard, BA, MA, PhD; American academic, poet, writer and editor; *Professor of English, Southwest State University;* b. 2 Sept. 1943, Kenmore, NY; m. 1st Elaine Ezekian 1968 (divorced 1988); one s. one d.; m. 2nd Michelle Payne 1991. *Education:* Wittenberg Univ., Ohio Univ. *Career:* Assoc. Prof. of English, Bradley Polytechnical Institute, Peoria, IL 1970–80; Ed., Spoon River Quarterly 1977–; Prof. of English, Southwest State University, Marshall, MN 1980–; Sr Fulbright Lecturer, Łódź, Poland 1989–91, Rīga, Latvia 1997–98, Ulaanbaatar, Mongolia 2003; Publisher-Ed. Spoon River Poetry Press, Plains Press, Ellis Press 1976–. *Publications:* Beowulf to Beatles: Approaches to Poetry, 1972; Writing Sense: A Handbook of Composition, 1975; Chaucer's Literary Pilgrimage: Movement in the Canterbury Tales, 1978; A Generation in Motion: Popular Music and Culture in the 1960s, 1979; Beowulf to Beatles and Beyond: The Varieties of Poetry, 1980; The Poetry of Rock, 1981; The Jubilee Diary: April 10 1980–April 19 1981, 1982; Salem/Peoria, 1883–1982, 1982; Bringing the Humanities to the Countryside: Access to the Humanities in Western Minnesota (ed. with Gerrit Groen), 1985; Tales from Two Rivers (ed. with John E. Halwas), Vol. 4, 1987; Visiting the Father and Other Poems, 1987; Late Harvest: Rural American Writing (ed.), 1991; Poland in Transition, 1989–1991, 1994; Exercises Against Retirement (poems), 1995; Southwest Minnesota: The Land and the People, 2000; UB03 2003, A Place Called Home 2003, Harassment: A Novel of Ideas 2003, Hallelujah Anyway 2004, Rooted: Six Midwest Writers of Place 2006; contrib. to reviews, quarterlies and journals. *Address:* c/o Department of English, Southwest State University, Marshall, MN 56258, USA (office). *Telephone:* (507) 537-6463 (office); (320) 564-2424 (home). *E-mail:* pichasked@hotmail.com (home).

PICKARD, Tom, (Thomas Marriner Pickard); British writer, poet and documentary film-maker; b. 7 Jan. 1946, Newcastle upon Tyne, England; divorced 2003; two s. one d. *Career:* Arts Council writer-in-residence, Univ. of Warwick 1979–80; George Oppen Memorial Lecture 2004. *Libretto:* The Ballad of Jamie Allan, for composer John Harte, performed and commissioned by Sage Gateshead 2005, recorded 2007. *Publications:* High on the Walls 1967, New Human Unisphere 1969, The Order of Chance 1971, Guttersnipe 1972, Dancing Under Fire 1973, Hero Dust: New and Selected Poems 1979, OK Tree 1980, The Jarrow March 1982, Custom and Exile 1985, We Make Ships 1989,

Tiepin Eros: New and Selected Poems 1994, Fuckwind: New Poems and Songs 1999, Hole in the Wall: New and Selected Poems 2001, The Dark Months of May 2004, The Ballad of Jamie Allan 2007; other: television plays and documentaries; contributions: Chicago Review, London Magazine, Northern Review, Sniper Logic, David Jones Journal. *Literary Agent:* Judy Daish Associates, 2 St Charles Place, London, W10 6EG, England. *Telephone:* (20) 8964-8811. *E-mail:* tompickard@onetel.com (home).

PICKERING, Paul Granville, BA; British novelist and playwright; b. 9 May 1952, Rotherham, England; m. Alison Beckett 1983, one d. *Education:* Leicester University. *Career:* mem. Society of Authors. *Publications:* Wild About Harry, 1985; Perfect English, 1986; The Blue Gate of Babylon, 1989; Charlie Peace, 1991. Plays: After Hamlet, 1994; Walk Her Home. 1999. Contributions: Times; Sunday Times; Independent; Anthologies. *Address:* c/o Mic Cheetham, 11–12 Dover St, London W1X 3PH, England. *E-mail:* ryetrip@aol.com.

PICOULT, Jodi, AB, MA; American writer; b. 1967, Long Island, NY; m. Tim Van Leer; three c. *Education:* Univ. of Princeton. *Publications:* novels: Songs of the Humpback Whale: A Novel in Five Voices 1992, Harvesting the Heart 1993, Picture Perfect 1995, Mercy 1996, Keeping Faith 1999, Pact: A Love Story 1999, Plain Truth 2000, Salem Falls 2001, Second Glance 2003, Falling to Earth 2004, My Sister's Keeper 2004, Vanishing Acts 2005, Perfect Match 2005, The Tenth Circle 2006, Mercy 2006, Nineteen Minutes 2007; author of 5 issues of Wonder Woman comic 2007. *Honours:* New England Bookseller Award for Fiction 2003. *Address:* c/o Hodder Headline, 338 Euston Road, London, NW1 3BH, England. *Website:* www.jodipicoult.com.

PIELMEIER, John, BA, MFA; American dramatist and actor; b. 3 Feb. 1949, Altoona, PA; m. Irene O'Brian 1982. *Education:* Catholic University of America, Pennsylvania State University. *Career:* mem. Writers Guild of America; Dramatists Guild; American Federation of Television and Radio Artists; Actors Equity Asscn. *Publications:* Agnes of God, 1983; Haunted Lives (A Witches Brew, A Ghost Story, A Gothic Tale), 1984. *Honours:* Christopher Award, 1984; Humanitas Award, 1984.

PIERARD, Richard Victor, BA, MA, PhD; American academic and writer; b. 29 May 1934, Chicago, IL; m. Charlene Burdett 1957; one s. one d. *Education:* California State Univ., Los Angeles, Univ. of Hamburg, Univ. of Iowa. *Career:* instructor, Univ. of Iowa 1964; Asst Prof. 1964–67, Assoc. Prof. 1967–72, Prof. of History 1972–2000, Indiana State Univ., Terre Haute; Research Fellow, Univ. of Aberdeen 1978; Fulbright Prof., Univ. of Frankfurt 1984–85, Univ. of Halle 1989–90; mem. American Historical Soc., American Soc. of Church History, American Soc. of Missiology, Baptist World Alliance (Baptist Heritage study cttee 1990–2000), Evangelical Theological Soc. (pres. 1985), Greater Terre Haute Church Federation (pres. 1987–88), Int. Asscn of Mission Studies, American Baptist Historical Soc. (bd of mans). *Publications:* Protest and Politics: Christianity and Contemporary Affairs (with Robert G. Clouse and Robert D. Linder), 1968; The Unequal Yoke: Evangelical Christianity and Political Conservatism, 1970; The Cross and the Flag (ed. with Robert G. Clouse and Robert D. Linder), 1972; Politics: A Case for Christian Action (with Robert D. Linder), 1973; The Twilight of the Saints: Christianity and Civil Religion in Modern America (with Robert D. Linder), 1977; Streams of Civilization, Vol. II (with Robert G. Clouse), 1980; Bibliography on the Religious Right in America, 1986; Civil Religion and the Presidency (with Robert D. Linder), 1988; Two Kingdoms: The Church and Culture Through the Ages (with Robert G. Clouse and E. M. Yamauchi), 1993; The Revolution of the Candles (with Joerg Swoboda), 1996; The New Millennium Manual (with Robert G. Clouse and Robert N. Hosdck), 1999. Contributions: many books, reference works, and professional journals. *Honours:* Research and Creativity Award, Indiana State Univ. 1994.

PIERCE, Meredith Ann, AA, BA, MA; American writer; b. 5 July 1958, Seattle, WA. *Education:* University of Florida. *Career:* mem. Authors' Guild; SFWA. *Publications:* The Darkangel, 1982; A Gathering of Gargoyles, 1984; The Woman Who Loved Reindeer, 1985; Birth of the Firebringer, 1985; Where the Wild Geese Go, 1988; Rampion, 1989; The Pearl of the Soul of the World, 1990. Contributions: magazines. *Honours:* several citations and awards for children's and young adult literature.

PIERCY, Marge, MA; American novelist, poet and essayist; b. 31 March 1936, Detroit, Mich.; d. of Robert Douglas Piercy and Bert Bernice Piercy (née Bunnin); m. Ira Wood 1982. *Education:* Univ. of Mich. and Northwestern Univ. *Career:* instructor, Gary Extension, Indiana Univ. 1960–62; Poet-in-Residence, Univ. of Kansas 1971; Distinguished Visiting Lecturer, Thomas Jefferson Coll., Grand Valley State Coll. 1975, 1976, 1978, 1980; mem. staff, Fine Arts Work Center, Provincetown, Mass 1976–77; Visiting Faculty, Women's Writers' Conf., Cazenovia, NY 1976, 1978, 1980; Fiction Writer-in-Residence, Holy Cross Univ., Worcester, Mass 1976; Purdue Univ. Summer Write-In 1977; Butler Chair of Letters, State Univ. of NY at Buffalo 1977; poetry and fiction workshops at Writers' Conf., Univ. of Indiana, Bloomington 1977, 1980; poetry, Writers' Conf., Vanderbilt Univ., Nashville, Tenn. 1981; Visiting Faculty, Women's Writers' Conf., Hartwick Coll. 1979, 1981, 1984; poetry and fiction, Lake Superior Writers' Conf. 1984; Fiction Writer-in-Residence, Ohio State Univ. 1986; Elliston Poetry Fellow, Univ. of Cincinnati 1986; master-class in poetry, Omega Inst. for Holistic Studies 1990, 1991, 1994; DeRoy Distinguished Visiting Prof., Univ. of Michigan 1992; Thunder Bay Writers' Conf. 1994; Univ. of N Dakota Writers' Conf. 1995; Florida Suncoast Writers' Conf. 1996; Hassayampa Summer Inst. for Creative

Writing, Prescott, Ariz. 1998, 2000, 2002, 2004, 2006; Washington Library Association Conf., Spokane, Wash. 2001; Bilgray Scholar-in-Residence, Temple Emmanuel Residency, Univ. of Arizona 2001; Residency and Silver Memorial Lecture, Temple Israel, Duluth, Minn. 2002; mini-residency, Trinity Coll., San Antonio, Tex. 2003; Writers in Residence, World Fellowship Center, Conway, NH 2005; mem. Advisory Bd Eastern Massachusetts Abortion Fund 1999–, Advisory Bd FEMSPEC: An Interdisciplinary Feminist Journal 1998–2004, Advisory Bd The Poetry Center at Passaic Co. Community Coll. 2004–, Advisory Bd Carrie A. Seaman Animal Shelter 2005–, Artists Grants Panel in Poetry 2006; Ed. Leapfrog Press 1997–; Poetry Ed. Lilith 2000–; Fiction Ed. Seattle Review 2003–. *Recording:* Louder We Can't Hear You (Yet!): The Political Poems of Marge Piercy 2004. *Publications:* Breaking Camp 1968, Hard Loving 1969, Going Down Fast 1969, Dance the Eagle to Sleep 1970, Small Changes 1973, To Be of Use 1973, Living in the Open 1976, Woman on the Edge of Time 1976, The High Cost of Living 1978, Vida 1980, The Moon is Always Female 1980, Braided Lives 1982, Circles on the Water 1982, Stone, Paper, Knife 1983, My Mother's Body 1985, Gone to Soldiers 1988, Available Light 1988 (May Sarton Award 1991), Summer People 1989, He, She and It 1991, Body of Glass 1991 (Arthur C. Clarke Award 1993), Mars and Her Children 1992, The Longings of Women 1994, Eight Chambers of the Heart 1995, City of Darkness, City of Light 1996, What Are Big Girls Made Of? 1997, Storm Tide 1998, Early Grrrl 1999, The Art of Blessing the Day 1999, Three Women 1999, So You Want to Write: How to Master the Craft of Writing Fiction and the Personal Narrative (with Ira Wood) 2001, 2005, Sleeping with Cats, A Memoir 2002, The Third Child 2003, Colors Passing Through Us 2003, Sex Wars 2005, The Crooked Inheritance 2006. *Honours:* Honorary Doctor of Letters, Lesley College; Honorary Doctor of Letters, Bridgewater State College; Honorary Degree of Doctorate of Humane Letters, Eastern Connecticut State University, 2005; Doctor of Human Letters, honoris causa Hebrew Union College, 2004; Rhode Island School of Design Faculty Asscn Medal, Borestone Mountain Poetry Award (twice), Avery Hopwood Contest, Orion Scott Award in Humanities, Lucinda Goodrich Downs Scholar, James B. Angell Scholar, Sheaffer-PEN/New England Award for Literary Excellence, Calapooya Coll. 1986, 1990, Carolyn Kizer Poetry Prize, Literary Award, Gov. of Mass Comm. on Status of Women 1974, Nat. Endowment for the Arts Award 1978, Golden Rose Poetry Prize 1990, The Golden Rose, New England Poetry Club 1990, May Sarton Award, New England Poetry Club 1991, Barbara Bradley Award, New England Poetry Club 1992, Brit ha-Dorot Award, The Shalom Center 1992, Arthur C. Clarke Award for Best Science Fiction Novel published in UK 1993, American Library Asscn Notable Book Award 1997, Notable Book Award 1997, Paterson Poetry Prize 2000, Paterson Award for Literary Achievement 2004. *Address:* PO Box 1473, Wellfleet, MA 02667, USA (home). *Telephone:* (508) 349-3163 (office). *E-mail:* hagolem@c4.net (office). *Website:* www.margepiercy.com (office).

PIERPOINT, Katherine, BA; British writer and poet; b. 1961, Northampton. *Education:* Univ. of Exeter. *Publications:* Truffle Beds 1995, Moon Apple 2001. *Honours:* Somerset Maugham Award 1996, Sunday Times Young Writer of the Year 1996, Royal Literary Fund Writing Fellowship 2004–06, Arts Council Writers' Award 2004. *Website:* www.faber.co.uk.

PIERRE, D. B. C. (Dirty But Clean); Mexican/Australian novelist; b. (Peter Finlay), 1961, Australia. *Publication:* Vernon God Little (Man Booker Prize, Bollinger Everyman Woodhouse Award, Whitbread Prize for first novel) 2003, Ludmila's Broken English 2006. *Address:* c/o Faber and Faber, 3 Queen Square, London, WC1 3AU, England.

PIGLIA, Ricardo; Argentine writer and academic; *Walter S. Carpenter Professor of Literature, Princeton University;* b. 1941, Adrogué, Buenos Aires. *Career:* Prof. of Romance Literatures, Princeton Univ., USA, currently Walter S. Carpenter Prof. of Literature. *Publications:* Artificial Respiration 1994, Assumed Name 1996, Absent City 2000, Money to Burn 2003, El Ultimo Lector 2005. *Address:* Guillermo Schavelzon and Associates, Muntaner 339, 5°, Barcelona 08021, Spain. *E-mail:* info@schavelzon.com. *Website:* www.granta.com.

PIGOTT, Mark, (David Riggs), BA, PhD; American biographer and academic; m. *Education:* Univ. of Harvard. *Career:* Asst Prof., Stanford Univ. 1970–85; Prof., School of Humanities and Sciences, Stanford Univ. 1985–. *Publications:* as David Riggs: Ben Jonson: A Life 1989, The World of Christopher Marlowe 2004. *Honours:* Frank Knox Fellowship 1963–64, Nat. Endowment for the Humanities and Stanford Humanities Centre Fellowships, Guggenheim Foundation Fellowship. *Address:* School of Humanities and Sciences, Stanford University, Stanford, CA 94305, USA.

PIKE, Charles R. (see Harknett, Terry)

PILCHER, Rosamunde, (Jane Fraser), OBE; British writer; b. 22 Sept. 1924, Lelant, Cornwall; m. Graham Pilcher 1946; four c. *Publications:* A Secret to Tell 1955, April 1957, On My Own 1965, Sleeping Tiger 1967, Another View 1969, The End of the Summer 1971, Snow in April 1972, The Empty House 1973, The Day of the Storm 1975, Under Gemini 1976, Wild Mountain Thyme 1979, The Carousel 1982, Voices in Summer 1984, The Blue Bedroom and Other Stories 1985, The Shell Seekers 1987, September 1990, Blackberry Days 1991, Flowers in the Rain and Other Stories 1991, Coming Home (Romantic Novelists Asscn Novelist of the Year 1996) 1995, Winter Solstice 2000; as Jane Fraser: Halfway to the Moon 1949, The Brown Fields 1951, Dangerous Intruder 1951, Young Bar 1952, A Day Like Spring 1953, Dear Tom 1954, Bridge of Corvie 1956, A Family Affair 1958, A Long Way from Home 1963, The Keeper's House 1963; contrib. to Woman and Home, Good Housekeeping. *Honours:* Deutscher Videopreis 1996, Bunte magazine Bambi Award 1997, Goldene Kamera Award, Hörzu 1998. *Address:* Penrowan, Longforgan, Dundee, DD2 5ET, Scotland (home).

PILGER, John Richard; Australian journalist, filmmaker and writer; b. Sydney, NSW; s. of Claude Pilger and Elsie Pilger (née Marheine); m. (divorced); one s. one d. *Education:* Sydney High School, Journalism Cadet Training, Australian Consolidated Press. *Career:* journalist, Sydney Daily/Sunday Telegraph 1958–62, Reuters, London 1962; feature writer, columnist and Foreign Corresp. (latterly Chief Foreign Corresp.), Daily Mirror, London 1963–86; columnist, New Statesman, London 1991–; freelance contrib., The Guardian, London, The Independent, London, New York Times, Melbourne Age, The Nation, New York, South China Morning Post, Hong Kong, Aftonbladet, Sweden; documentary filmmaker, Granada TV, UK 1969–71, Associated Television 1972–80, Central/Carlton/Granada Television, UK 1980–; credited with alerting much of int. community to horrors of Pol Pot régime in Cambodia, also occupation of Timor-Leste; Visiting Fellow, Deakin Univ., Australia 1995; Frank H. T. Rhodes Visiting Prof., Cornell Univ., USA 2003–. *Exhibitions:* Reporting the World: John Pilger's Great Eyewitness Photographers, The Barbican Summer Exhbn 2001. *Feature film:* The Last Day 1983. *Documentary films include:* Cambodia: Year Zero 1979 (and four other films on Cambodia), The Quiet Mutiny 1970, Japan Behind the Mask 1986, The Last Dream 1988, Death of a Nation 1994, Flying the Flag: Arming the World 1994, Inside Burma 1996, Breaking The Mirror: The Murdoch Effect 1997, Apartheid Did Not Die 1998, Welcome to Australia 1999, Paying the Price: Killing the Children of Iraq 2000, The New Rulers of the World 2001, Palestine Is Still The Issue 2002, Breaking the Silence: Truth and Lies in the War on Terror 2003, Stealing a Nation 2004, The War on Democracy 2007. *Publications:* The Last Day 1975, Aftermath: The Struggle of Cambodia and Vietnam 1981, The Outsiders 1983, Heroes 1986, A Secret Country 1989, Distant Voices 1992, Hidden Agendas 1998, Reporting the World: John Pilger's Great Eyewitness Photographers 2001, The New Rulers of the World 2002, Tell Me No Lies: Investigative Journalism and its Triumphs (ed) 2004, Freedom Next Time 2006. *Honours:* Hon. DLitt (Staffordshire Univ.) 1994; Hon. PhD (Dublin City Univ.) 1995, (Kingston) 1999, (Open Univ.); Hon. DArts (Oxford Brookes Univ.) 1997; Hon. DrIur (St Andrews) 1999; Hon. DUniv (Open Univ.) 2001; Descriptive Writer of the Year, UK 1966, Journalist of the Year, UK 1967, 1979, Int. Reporter of the Year, UK 1970, Reporter of the Year, UK 1974, BAFTA Richard Dimbleby Award 1991, US Acad. Award (Emmy) 1991, Reporteurs sans frontières, France 1993, George Foster Peabody Award, USA 1992, Sophie Prize for Human Rights 2003, Royal TV Soc. Award 2005. *Address:* 57 Hambalt Road, London, SW4 9EQ, England. *Telephone:* (20) 8673-2848. *Fax:* (20) 8772-0235. *E-mail:* jpmarheine@hotmail.com (home). *Website:* www.johnpilger.com.

PILIKIAN, Hovhanness Israel, BSc, MA; British theatre director, writer, composer, academic and film maker; *Group Executive Director, SHE Management;* b. 15 April 1942, Nineveh-Mosul, Iraq; s. of Israel and Tefarik Pilikian; m. 1st Gail Rademacher (divorced 1992, died 2000); two s. one d.; m. 2nd Clarice Stephens 1993; one s. two d. *Education:* Univ. of Munich, Univ. of London, Royal Acad. of Dramatic Art, Open Univ., American Univ. of Beirut. *Career:* has directed more than 40 plays (specializing in classical Greek drama); cr. Hanano Mask Theatre Co. 1970, Cervantes Players (first all-black actors' co. in Europe), London 1971; f. Spice of Life Theatre Club 1980, Bloomsbury Theatre Club 1982; Consultant, Cheltenham Int. Guitar Music Festival 2001; mem. Acad. Bd City Lit Inst. 2000–; Group Exec. Dir SHE Management, London 2004–; Fellow, Royal Anthropological Inst., Deutscher Akademischer Austauschdienst; life mem. Swedenborg Soc. of GB, Univ. of London Convocation Governing Bd; mem. Turner Soc.; Visiting Prof., State Univ. of Yerevan, Dutch Drama Center, Slade School of Art, Cen. School of Art and Design, Yerevan Inst. of Literature, Armenian Acad. of Sciences; regular columnist, Gibrahayer weekly internet magazine 2005–. *Films:* The New Supremes in London 1986, A King of Arabia 1987. *Plays directed include:* Euripides' Electra (Greenwich Theatre, London) 1971, Euripides' Medea (Yvonne Arnaud Theatre) 1971, William Alfred's Agamemnon (McCarthur Theater, Princeton Univ.) 1973, Sophocles' Oedipus Tyrannus (Chichester Festival Theatre) 1974, Schiller's Die Räuber (Roundhouse) 1975, King Lear (Nat. Theatre of Iceland) 1977, Fat Hamlet (Shaw Theatre, London) 1993. *Music:* Clarice de Lune 2003, Katya's Baby Or Lenin's Revolution 2005. *Achievements:* organized and produced first ever season of Armenian Cinema for the Nat. Film Theatre, London 1981; Armenian Cinema weeks in Venice 1983, Paris 1986, Montreal 2000. *Publications include:* My Hamlet 1961, An Armenian Symphony and Other Poems 1980, Armenian Cinema, A Source Book 1981, Flower of Japanese Theatre 1984, Aspects of Armenian History 1986; contrib. to Society Matters (Open Univ. newspaper), Encyclopedia Britannica. *Honours:* Adamian Award for Lifetime Achievement, Ministry of Culture of Armenian SSR 1985, Calouste Gulbenkian Foundation Scholar (LSE) 1990, Wandsworth Council Business Award 2004. *E-mail:* profpilikian@hotmail.com. *Website:* pilikian.blogspot.com.

PILLING, Christopher Robert, BA; British writer, poet, translator and playwright; b. 20 April 1936, Birmingham; m. Sylvia Hill 1960; one s. two d. *Education:* Univ. of Poitiers, France, Univ. of Leeds, Loughborough Coll. *Career:* English Asst, École Normale, Moulins, France 1957–58; teacher of French and Physical Educ., Wirral Grammar School, Cheshire, 1959–61, King Edward's School for Boys, Birmingham, 1961–62; teacher of French and athletics, and House Master, Ackworth School, Yorkshire, 1962–73; reviewer, Times Literary Supplement 1973–74; Head of Modern Languages and Housemaster, Knottingley High School, West Yorkshire, 1973–78; Tutor, Dept of Adult Educ., Univ. of Newcastle upon Tyne 1978–80; Head of French, Keswick School, Cumbria 1980–88; mem. Cumbrian Poets (Co-founder and Sec.), Soc. of Authors, Translators' Assⁿ, Cercle Édouard et Tristan Corbière, North Cumbria Playwrights, Les Amis de Max Jacob, Slate (New Writing Cumbria), Cumbria Cultural Skills Partnership. *Publications:* Snakes and Girls 1970, In All the Spaces on All the Lines 1971, Foreign Bodies 1992, Cross Your Legs and Wish 1994, These Jaundiced Loves, by Tristan Corbière (trans.) 1995, The Lobster Can Wait 1998, In the Pink 1999, The Dice Cup, by Max Jacob (translated with David Kennedy) 2000, The Ghosts of Greta Hall (with Colin Fleming) 2001, Tree Time 2003, Emperor on a Lady's Bicycle 2003, Love at the Full, by Lucien Becker (trans.) 2003; contribs to books, anthologies, reviews, quarterlies, journals and newspapers. *Honours:* New Poets Award 1970, Arts Council Grants 1971, 1977, Kate Collingwood Award 1983, Northern Arts Writers' Award 1985, and Tyrone Guthrie Centre Residency 1994, Lauréat du Concours Européen de Création Littéraire, Centre Culturel du Brabant Wallon, Belgium 1992, European Poetry Trans' Network Residencies 1995, 1998, European Comm. Residency, Collège Int. des Traducteurs Littéraires, Arles 1996, Hawthornden Fellowship 1998, Translator Residency, British Centre for Literary Trans., Univ. of East Anglia 2000. *Address:* 25 High Hill, Keswick, Cumbria CA12 5NY, England.

PILON, Jean-Guy, OC, LLB, CQ; Canadian poet; b. 12 Nov. 1930, St Polycarpe; s. of Arthur Pilon and Alida Besner; m. 2nd Denise Viens 1988; two s. from 1st marriage. *Education:* Univ. de Montreal. *Career:* founded Liberté (review) 1959, Ed. 1959–79; Head of Cultural Programmes and Producer Radio-Canada 1970–88; Les Ecrits (literary review); mem. Académie des lettres du Québec 1982, Royal Soc. of Canada 1967–. *Publications (poems):* La fiancée du matin 1953, Les cloîtres de l'été 1954, L'homme et le jour 1957, La mouette et le large 1960, Recours au pays 1961, Pour saluer une ville 1963, Comme eau retenue 1969 (enlarged edn 1985), Saisons pour la continuelle 1969, Silences pour une souveraine 1972. *Honours:* Prix de Poésie du Québec 1956, Louise Labé (Paris) 1969, France-Canada 1969, van Lerberghe (Paris) 1969, du Gouverneur gén. du Canada 1970, Athanase-David 1984, Prix littéraire int. de la Paix (PEN Club Quebec) 1991; Ordre du Canada 1986, Chevalier Ordre Nat. du Québec 1987, Officier Ordre des Arts et des Lettres (France) 1992. *Address:* 5724 Côte St-Antoine, Montreal, PQ, H4A 1R9, Canada.

PINCHER, (Henry) Chapman, BSc; British writer; b. 29 March 1914, Ambala, India; m. 1st; one d. one s.; m. 2nd Constance Wolstenholme 1965. *Career:* Defence, Science and Medical Ed., Daily Express 1946–73; Chief Defence Correspondent, Beaverbrook Newspapers 1972–79; freelance journalist and author; Fellow King's Coll. London 1979; elected Prof. Moscow Acad. for Defence, Security and Law Enforcement 2005–. *Publications:* non-fiction: Breeding of Farm Animals 1946, A Study of Fishes 1947, Into the Atomic Age 1947, Spotlight on Animals 1950, Evolution 1950, It's Fun Finding Out (with Bernard Wicksteed) 1950, Sleep and How to Get More of It 1954, Sex in Our Time 1973, Inside Story 1978, Their Trade is Treachery 1981, Too Secret Too Long 1984, The Secret Offensive 1985, Traitors: The Labyrinth of Treason 1987, A Web of Deception 1987, The Truth about Dirty Tricks 1991, One Dog and her Man 1991, Pastoral Symphony 1993, A Box of Chocolates 1993, Life's a Bitch! 1996, Tight Lines! 1997; fiction: Not with a Bang 1965, The Giantkiller 1967, The Penthouse Conspirators 1970, The Skeleton at the Villa Wolkonsky 1975, The Eye of the Tornado 1976, The Four Horses 1978, Dirty Tricks 1980, The Private World of St John Terrapin 1982, Contamination 1989. *Honours:* ; Order of the Great Victory (Russia) 2006; Hon. DLitt (Univ. of Newcastle upon Tyne) 1979; Granada Award for Journalist of the Year 1964, Reporter of the Decade 1966. *Address:* The Church House, 16 Church Street, Kintbury, Near Hungerford, Berkshire RG7 9TR, England. *Telephone:* (1488) 658397 (office).

PINCIO, Tommaso; Italian writer; b. 1963, Rome. *Publications:* novels: M 1999, Lo Spazio Sfinito 2000, Un amore dell'Altro Mondo (trans. as Love Shaped Story) 2002; contrib. to Il Manifesto, Nuovi Argomenti. *Address:* c/o Flamingo, 77–85 Fulham Palace Road, London, W6 8JB, England. *Website:* www.harpercollins.co.uk.

PINEAU, Gisèle; French writer; b. 1956, Paris. *Education:* Université de Nanterre, Centre Hospitalier de Villejuif. *Career:* also psychiatric nurse; currently Ed. Mercure de France. *Publications:* Un papillon dans la cité 1992, La Grande drive des esprits 1993, L'espérance-macadam 1995, L'exil selon Julia 1996, L'âme prêtée aux oiseaux 1998, Guadeloupe: Découverte 1998, Caraïbes sur Seine 2000, C'est la règle 2002, Chair piment (Prix des hémisphères Chantal Lapicque 2003) 2002, Les colères du Volcan 2004, Case mensonge, numéro 153 2004, Guadeloupe d'Antan 2005, Fleur de Barbarie (Prix Rosine Perrier 2006) 2005, Mes Quatre Femmes; many essays and short stories; contrib. to various publications. *Honours:* Prix Écritures d'Iles 1987, Prix Carbet de la Caraïbe 1993, Grand Prix des Lectrices de Elle 1994, Oscar Littérature du Conseil de la Guadeloupe 1996, Prix RFO Radio Télévision Française 1996, Grande Prix du Livre de Jeunesse de la Martinique 1996. *Address:* c/o Editions Mercure de France, 26 rue de Condé, 75006 Paris (office); c/o Éditions Gallimard, 5 rue Sébastien-Bottin, 75328 Paris, Cédex 07 (office); Hall 18, 3 rue du Général Séré de Rivières, 75014 Paris, France (home). *Telephone:* 6-19-59-89-02 (office); 1-45-42-62-08 (home). *E-mail:* giselepineau@yahoo.fr (home).

PINGEL, Velande Regnia, BA, MA, PhD; American retd academic, writer, poet, composer and artist; b. (Martha Mary Pingel), 10 Sept. 1923, New York, NY; d. of Regnar S. A. (von) Pingel and Ella Charlotte Pries; m. Bert Raymond Taylor Jr 1961 (died 2003). *Career:* Instructor, Paul Smiths Coll., New York 1946–47; Asst Prof., East Carolina Univ., NC 1947–58; Prof. and Head Dept of Humanities, Colorado Woman's Coll. 1958–66; Visiting Prof., St Mary's Univ., TX 1966–69; Prof., Middle Georgia Coll. 1969–72; Prof. and writer-in-residence, Hong Kong Baptist Coll. 1974–84; Retreat Facilitator in Poetry and Fiction, WordCraft by Lan 1984–; recently began series of workshops and retreats in meditation techniques and grief ministry; mem. Acad. of American Poets, American Philosophical Assⁿ, Nat. Authors' Registry. *Music:* Pale Violet & Gold (song) 1961, Hemisphere Happenings: San Antonio Commemorative Suite for organ 1968, Night Passage (song) 1968, Seasons (song) 1975, Impressions, eight tone-poems for piano 2000–05. *Art:* numerous works in various media. *Publications:* An American Utilitarian 1948, Catalyst 1951, Mood Montage 1968, Immortal Dancer 1968, Mode and Muse in a New Generation 1979, Homilies in the Marketplace 1996, Copper Flowers 1996, Walking Songs 1997, Zbyx 1997, Tales from the Archetypal World 1998, Flowing Water, Singing Sand 1999, Between the Lines 1999, The Zodiac Affair 2000, Gallery 2001, The Shining Kingdom (trans. of Sollyse Egne, by Helga P. Marstrand) 2004, Inner Worlds: Meditations 2005; contrib. to anthologies, periodicals, radio and television. *Honours:* Int. Mark Twain Soc. Certificate 1947, Order of the Danne Brog Miniature Medal 1951, Gold Medal Freedoms Foundation 1953, Writer's Digest Rhymed Poetry Contest Certificate 1994. *Address:* 910 Marion Street, No. 505, Seattle, WA 98104-1272, USA (home). *Telephone:* (206) 621-1376 (home).

PINKER, Steven, BA, PhD; American psychologist, scientist, writer and academic; *Johnstone Family Professor of Psychology, Harvard University;* b. 18 Sept. 1954, Montreal, Canada; s. of Harry Pinker and Roslyn Pinker; m. Ilavenil Subbiah 1995. *Education:* McGill Univ., Canada, Harvard Univ. *Career:* Asst Prof., Harvard Univ. 1980–81, Johnstone Family Prof. of Psychology 2003–; Asst Prof., Stanford Univ. 1981–82; Asst Prof., MIT 1982–85, Assoc. Prof., Dept of Brain and Cognitive Sciences 1985–89, Prof. 1989–, Peter de Florez Prof. 2000–03, Margaret MacVicar Fellow 2000–, Co-Dir Center for Cognitive Science 1985–94, Dir McDonnell-Pew Center for Cognitive Neuroscience 1994–99; Assoc. Ed. Cognition. *Publications include:* Language Learnability and Language Development 1984, Visual Cognition (ed.) 1985, Connections and Symbols (ed. with J. Mehler) 1988, Learnability and Cognition: The Acquisition of Argument Structure 1989, The Language Instinct 1994 (William James Book Prize, American Psychological Assⁿ 1995), How the Mind Works 1997 (William James Book Prize, American Psychological Assⁿ 1999), Words and Rules: The Ingredients of Language 1999, The Blank Slate: The Modern Denial of Human Nature 2002; contribs to Animal Learning and Behavior, Annals of the New York Academy of Sciences, Behavioral and Brain Sciences, Canadian Journal of Psychology, Child Development, Cognition, Cognitive Psychology, Cognitive Science, Communication and Cognition, Journal of Child Language, Journal of Cognitive Neuroscience, Journal of Experimental Psychology, Journal of Mental Imagery, Journal of Psycholinguistic Research, Journal of Verbal Learning and Verbal Behavior, Language and Cognitive Processes, Language, Lingua, Memory and Cognition, Monographs of the Society for Research in Child Development, Nature, New York Times, The New Yorker, Papers and Reports in Child Language, Psychological Science, Science, Slate, Time, Trends in Cognitive Science, Trends in Neurosciences, Visual Cognition. *Honours:* Hon. DSc (McGill) 1999; Hon. DPhil (Tel-Aviv) 2003; Hon. DUniv (Surrey) 2003; Distinguished Scientific Award for Early Career Contribution to Psychology, American Psychological Assⁿ 1984, Boyd R. McCandless Young Scientist Award, Div. of Developmental Psychology, American Psychological Assⁿ 1986, Troland Research Award NAS 1993, Linguistics, Language and the Public Interest Award, Linguistics Soc. of America 1997, Los Angeles Times Book Prize in Science and Technology 1998, Golden Plate Award, American Acad. of Achievement 1999, Humanist Laureate Int. Acad. of Humanism 2001. *Literary Agent:* The Lavin Agency, 872 Massachusetts Avenue, Cambridge, MA 02139, USA. *Address:* Department of Psychology, Harvard University, William James Hall, 33 Kirkland Street, Cambridge, MA 02138, USA (office). *Website:* pinker.wjh.harvard.edu (office).

PINNER, David John; British writer and dramatist; b. 6 Oct. 1940, Peterborough, England; m. Catherine 1965, one s. one d. *Education:* RADA. *Publications:* plays: Dickon, 1965; Fanghorn, 1966; The Drums of Snow, 1969; Corgi, 1969; The Potsdam Quartet, 1973; An Evening with the GLC, 1974; The Last Englishman, 1975; Lucifer's Fair, 1979; Screwball, 1985; The Teddy Bears' Picnic, 1988; Cartoon; Hereward the Wake; Shakebag; Revelations; The Sins of the Mother; Lenin in Love, 2000. Television Plays: Juliet and Romeo, 1975; 2 Crown Courts, 1978; The Potsdam Quartet, 1980; The Sea Horse. Novels: Ritual, 1967; With My Body, 1968; There'll Always Be an England, 1984. Non-Fiction: Newton's Darkness: Two Dramatic Views (with Carl Djerassi), 2003.

PINNEY, Lucy Catherine, BA; British writer and journalist; b. 25 July 1952, London, England; m. Charles Pinney 1975 (divorced 2000); two s. one d. *Education:* York Univ. *Career:* columnist, The Times. *Publications:* The Pink Stallion 1988, Tender Moth 1994, A Country Wife 2004; contrib. to Sunday Times, Observer, Daily Mail, Telegraph, Company, Cosmopolitan, Country Living, Country Homes and Interiors, She. *Address:* Egremont Farm,

Payhembury, Honiton, Devon EX14 0JA, England. *E-mail:* lucy@egremont.eurobell.co.uk.

PINNOCK, Winsome, BA, MA; British playwright; b. 1961, London, England. *Education:* Goldsmiths Coll. London, Birkbeck Coll. London. *Career:* playwright-in-residence, Tricycle Theatre, Kilburn 1990, Royal Court Theatre, London 1991, Clean Break Theatre Co. 1994. *Plays:* The Wind of Change 1987, Leave Taking (Liverpool Playhouse) 1988, Picture Palace 1988, A Rock in Water 1989, A Hero's Welcome 1989, Talking in Tongues 1991, One Under (Tricycle, London) 2005. *Television plays:* episodes in South of the Border and Chalkface Series. *Film screenplay:* Bitter Harvest. *Honours:* Thames TV Award 1991, George Devine Award 1991. *Literary Agent:* Lemon, Unna and Durbridge, 24 Pottery Lane, Holland Park, London, W11 4LZ, England.

PIÑON, Nélida, BPhil; Brazilian writer, journalist and academic; b. 3 May 1937, Vila Isabel, Río de Janeiro; d. of Lino Piñon Muiños and Olívia Carmen Cuiñas Piñon. *Education:* Pontificial Catholic Univ., Rio de Janeiro and Columbia Univs, USA. *Career:* Chair. in Creative Writing, Fed. Univ. of Rio de Janeiro 1970, Dr Henry King Stanford Chair. in Humanities, Univ. of Miami 1990–2003; visiting writer, Columbia Univ. 1978, Johns Hopkins Univ. 1988, Georgetown Univ., Washington 1999, Harvard Univ., USA 2001; has lectured at univs in France, Spain and Peru; mem. Brazilian Acad. of Letters (Chair. 1996–97) 1989–; corresponding mem. Acad. of Sciences of Lisbon; elected mem. Brazilian Acad. of Philosophy 2004–. *Publications:* Guia-mapa de Gabriel Arcanjo (novel, trans. as Guide Map of Archangel Gabriel) 1961, Madeira feita cruz (novel) 1963, Tempo das frutas (short stories, trans. as Season of Fruit) 1966, Fundador (novel, trans. as Founder, Walmap Prize) 1969, A casa da paixão (novel, trans. as The House of Passion, Mario Andrade Prize) 1972, Sala de armas (short stories, trans. as Weapons Room) 1973, Tebas do meu coração (novel, trans. as Thebes of my Heart) 1974, A força do destino (novel, trans. as The Force of Destiny) 1977, O calor das coisas (short stories) 1980, A república dos sonhos (novel, trans. as The Republic of Dreams) (Asscn of Art Critics' Award) 1984, A doce canção de Caetana (novel) 1987, O pão de cada dia (articles) 1994, A roda do vento (juvenile novel) 1996, Até amanhã, outra vez (short stories) 1999, O cortejo do divino, O ritual da arte (literary criticism), O Presumível Coração da América (articles) 2002, Vozes do Deserto (Prêmio Jabuti 2005) 2004. *Honours:* Order of Río Branco, Cruzeiro do Sul, Medalha Mérito Cultural, Brazil, Aguila Medal, Mexico, Dom Afonso Henriques Medal, Portugal, Lazo de Dama Medal, Spain, Gabriela Mistral Medal and Grand Officer, Order of Cultural Merit, Chile, Chevalier des Arts et des Lettres, France, Order of Feminine Merit, Brazil 2004,; Dr hc (Florida Atlantic Univ.) 1996, (Univ. of Poitiers, France) 1997, (Univ. of Santiago de Compostela) 1998, (Rutgers Univ., USA) 1998, (Univ. of Montréal, Canada) 2004; Pen Club Award, Juan Rulfo Literary Award 1995, Don Alfonso Enrique Medal, Portugal, Gabriella Mistral Medal, Chile, Isabel la Católica Award 2000, Jorge Isaacs Ibero-American Narrative Award 2001, Rosalía de Castro Award 2002, Menéndez Pelayo Int. Prize 2003, Puterbaugh Felow 2004, Prince of Asturias Award for Literature 2005. *Address:* Av. Epitácio Pessoa, no. 4956, ap. 801, Lagoa, CEP 22471-001 (home); c/o Editora Record, Rua Argentina 171, São Cristóvão, Rio de Janeiro, RJ CEP 20921-380, Brazil (office). *Telephone:* (21) 2537-2996 (home); (21) 2535-3385 (office). *Fax:* (21) 2537-1108 (home). *E-mail:* pinonproducoes@terra.com.br (office). *Website:* www.nelidapinon.com.br.

PINSKER, Sanford, BA, PhD; American academic, writer and poet; *Shadek Professor of Humanities, Franklin and Marshall College*; b. 28 Sept. 1941, Washington, Pennsylvania; m. Ann Getson 1968; one s. one d. *Education:* Washington and Jefferson Coll., Univ. of Washington. *Career:* Asst Prof. 1967–74, Assoc. Prof. 1974–84, Prof. 1984–88, Shadek Prof. of Humanities 1988–, Franklin and Marshall Coll.; Visiting Prof., Univ. of California at Riverside 1973, 1975; Fulbright Sr Lecturer, Belgium 1984–85, Spain 1990–91; Pennsylvania Humanist 1985–87, 1990–91, 1996–97; Ed., Academic Questions 1995–; mem. Nat. Book Critics Circle. *Publications:* The Schlemiel as Metaphor: Studies in the Yiddish and American-Jewish Novel, 1971; The Comedy That 'Hoits': An Essay on the Fiction of Philip Roth, 1975; Still Life and Other Poems, 1975; The Languages of Joseph Conrad, 1978; Between Two Worlds: The American Novel in the 1960s, 1978; Philip Roth: Critical Essays, 1982; Memory Breaks Off and Other Poems, 1984; Conversations with Contemporary American Writers, 1985; Whales at Play and Other Poems of Travel, 1986; Three Pacific Northwest Poets: Stafford, Hugo, and Wagoner, 1987; The Uncompromising Fictions of Cynthia Ozick, 1987; Bearing the Bad News: Contemporary American Literature and Culture, 1990; Understanding Joseph Heller, 1991; Jewish-American Literature and Culture: An Encyclopedia (ed. with Jack Fischel), 1992; Jewish-American Fiction, 1917–1987, 1992; Sketches of Spain (poems), 1992; The Catcher in the Rye: Innocence Under Pressure, 1993; Oedipus Meets the Press and Other Tragi-Comedies of Our Time, 1996. Contributions: Articles, stories, poems, and reviews in numerous publications. *Address:* 700 N Pine Street, Lancaster, PA 17603, USA.

PINSKY, Robert Neal, PhD; American poet and academic; *Professor of Creative Writing, Boston University*; b. 20 Oct. 1940, Long Branch, NJ; s. of Milford Simon Pinsky and Sylvia Pinsky (née Eisenberg); m. Ellen Jane Bailey 1961; three d. *Education:* Rutgers Univ., Stanford Univ. *Career:* taught English Univ. of Chicago 1967–68, Wellesley Coll. 1968–80; Prof. of English Univ. of Calif., Berkeley 1980–89; Prof. Boston Univ. 1980–89, Prof. of Creative Writing 1989–; Poet Laureate of USA 1997–2000; Visiting Lecturer, Harvard Univ.; Hurst Prof. Washington Univ., St Louis; Poetry Ed. New Repub. magazine 1978, Slate Magazine 1994–2000; Guggenheim Fellow 1980; mem. AAAS. *Publications:* Landor's Poetry 1968, Sadness and Happiness 1975, The Situation of Poetry 1977, An Explanation of America 1980, History of my Heart 1980, Poetry and the World 1988, The Want Bone 1990, The Inferno of Dante 1994, The Figured Wheel: New and Collected Poems 1966–96 1996, The Sounds of Poetry 1998, The Handbook of Heartbreak 1998, Americans' Favorite Poems 2000, Jersey Rain 2000. *Honours:* Artist's Award, American Acad. of Arts and Letters 1979, Saxifrage Prize 1980, William Carlos Williams Prize 1984, Shelley Memorial Award 1996, Harold Washington Literary Award 1999. *Address:* Department of English, Boston University, 236 Bay State Road, Boston, MA 02215, USA (office). *Telephone:* (617) 353-2506 (office). *E-mail:* rpinsky@bu.edu (office). *Website:* www.bu.edu/english (office).

PINTER, Frances Mercedes Judith, PhD; American/British publisher; *CEO, International House Trust*; b. 13 June 1949, Venezuela; d. of George Pinter and Vera Hirschenhauser Pinter; m. David Percy 1985. *Education:* Univ. Coll., London. *Career:* Research Officer, Centre for Criminological Research, Univ. of Oxford, UK 1976–79; Man. Dir Pinter Publrs 1979–94; Chair. Ind. Publrs Guild 1979–82, Publrs Asscn E European Task Force 1990–; Man. Dir Cen. European Univ. Press 1994–96; Chair. Bd of Trustees, Int. House 2001, CEO Int. House Trust 2002–06; Deputy Chair. Book Devt Council 1985–89; mem. Bd UK Publrs Asscn 1987–92, IBIS Information Services 1988–90, Libra Books 1991–; Exec. Dir Centre for Publishing Devt 1994–, Open Soc. Inst. 1994–99; Visiting Fellow, LSE 2000–01, 2006–. *Address:* 1 Belsize Avenue, London, NW3 4BL, England (home). *Telephone:* (20) 7431-7849 (office). *E-mail:* frances@pinter.org.uk (office).

PINTER, Harold, CH, CBE, CLit, FRSL; British playwright, writer and poet; b. 10 Oct. 1930, London; s. of J. Pinter; m. 1st Vivien Merchant 1956 (divorced 1980, died 1982); one s.; m. 2nd Lady Antonia Fraser (q.v.) 1980. *Education:* Hackney Downs Grammar School, London. *Career:* actor mainly in English and Irish prov. repertory 1949–58; playwright 1957–; Assoc. Dir Nat. Theatre 1973–83; Dir United British Artists 1983–85; Jt Ed. Publr Greville Press 1988–; bd mem. Cricket World 1989–; BAFTA Fellowship 1997. *Film:* Mansfield Park 1999. *Plays:* The Room 1957, The Dumb Waiter 1957, The Birthday Party 1957, A Slight Ache 1958, The Hothouse 1958, The Caretaker 1959, A Night Out 1959, Night School 1960, The Dwarfs 1960, The Collection 1961, The Lover 1962, Tea Party (TV play) 1965, The Homecoming 1964, The Basement (TV play) 1966, Landscape 1967, Silence 1968, Night (one act play) 1969, Old Times 1970, Monologue (one act play) 1972, No Man's Land 1974, Betrayal 1978, Family Voices 1980, Other Places 1982, A Kind of Alaska 1982, Victoria Station 1982, One for the Road 1984, Mountain Language 1988, The New World Order 1991, Party Time 1991, Moonlight 1993, Ashes to Ashes 1996, Celebration 2000, Remembrance of Things Past 2000, Press Conference (sketch) 2002. *Screenplays:* The Caretaker 1962, The Servant 1962, The Pumpkin Eater 1963, The Quiller Memorandum 1965, Accident 1966, The Birthday Party 1967, The Go-Between 1969, Langrishe Go Down 1970, A la Recherche du Temps Perdu 1972, The Last Tycoon 1974, The French Lieutenant's Woman 1980, Betrayal 1981, Victory 1982, Turtle Diary 1984, The Handmaid's Tale 1987, Reunion 1988, The Heat of the Day 1988, The Comfort of Strangers 1989, The Trial 1989. *Plays directed:* The Man in the Glass Booth, London 1967, NY 1968, Exiles 1970, 1971, Butley 1971, (film) 1973, Next of Kin 1974, Otherwise Engaged 1975, The Rear Column 1978, Close of Play 1979, Quartermaine's Terms 1981, Incident at Tulse Hill 1982, The Trojan War Will Not Take Place 1983, The Common Pursuit 1984, Sweet Bird of Youth 1985, Circe and Bravo 1986, Vanilla 1990, The New World Order 1991, Party Time 1991, Party Time (TV) 1992, Oleanna 1993, Ashes to Ashes 1996, Twelve Angry Men 1996, The Late Middle Classes 1999, Celebration 2000, The Room 2000, No Man's Land 2001. *Television:* A Night Out 1960, Huis Clos 1965, The Basement 1967, Rogue Male 1976, Lanerishe, Go Down 1978, The Birthday Party 1987, Breaking the Code 1997, Catastrophe 2000, Wit 2000. *Publications:* Poems and Prose 1949–77 1978, The Proust Screenplay (with Joseph Losey and Barbara Bray) 1978, Collected Poems and Prose 1986, 100 Poems by 100 Poets (co-ed.) 1986, The Dwarfs (novel) 1990, Various Voices: prose, poetry, politics 1948–1998 1999, Politics 1948–1998 1999, Cancer Cells (poem) 2002, War (poetry) 2003. *Honours:* Chevalier, Légion d'honneur 2007; Hon. Fellow (Queen Mary Coll.) 1987; Hon. DLitt (Reading) 1970, (Birmingham) 1971, (Glasgow) 1974, (East Anglia) 1974, (Stirling) 1979, (Brown) 1982, (Hull) 1986, (Sussex) 1990, (Bristol) 1998, Hon. Degree (Turin) 2002; Shakespeare Prize, Hamburg 1973, Austrian Prize for European Literature 1973, Pirandello Prize 1980, Commonwealth Award for Dramatic Arts, Washington, DC 1981, Donatello Prize 1982, Chilean Order of Merit 1992, David Cohen British Literature Prize 1995, Special Olivier Award 1995, Molière d'Honneur, Paris 1997, Sunday Times Award for Literary Excellence 1997, RSL Companion of Literature 1998, Critics' Circle Award for Distinguished Service to the Arts 2000, Brianza Poetry Prize, Italy 2000, South Bank Show Award for Outstanding Achievement in the Arts 2001, S. T. Dupont Golden Pen Award 2001, Premio Fiesole ai Maestri del Cinema, Italy 2001, Laurea ad honorem, Univ. of Florence 2001, World Leaders Award Toronto 2001, Hermann Kesten Medallion, German PEN, Berlin 2001, Wilfred Owen Award 2004, Special Award, Evening Standard Theatre Awards 2004, Nobel Prize in Literature 2005. *Literary Agent:* Judy Daish Associates, 2 St Charles Place, London, W10 6EG, England. *Website:* www.haroldpinter.org.

PINTO CORREIA, Clara, PhD; Portuguese writer and scientist; b. 30 Jan. 1960, Lisbon. *Education:* Portugal and USA. *Career:* journalist; researcher on developmental biology; writes for various newspapers and magazine; contributes to various radio and television programmes. *Publications:* Agrião 1984, Adeus Princesa (Goodbye Princess) 1987, The Ovary of Eve, Secondary Messengers 1999, Return of the Crazy Bird: The Sad, Strange Tale of the Dodo 2003; numerous other publs including short stories, children's books, histories of science and an opera libretto. *Address:* c/o University of Chicago Press, 1427 East 60th Street, Chicago, IL 60637, USA.

PIONTEK, Heinz; German writer; b. 15 Nov. 1925, Kreuzburg, Silesia; s. of Robert Piontek and Marie Piontek (née Seja); m. Gisela Dallmann 1951. *Education:* Theologisch-Philosophische Hochschule, Dillingen. *Career:* mem. Bavarian Acad. of Fine Arts 1960–, Central PEN of Fed. Repub. of Germany. *Publications:* Die Furt (poems) 1952, Die Rauchfahne (poems) 1953, Vor Augen (stories) 1955, Wassermarken (poems) 1957, Buchstab-Zauberstab (essays) 1959, Aus meines Herzens Grunde (anthology) 1959, John Keats: Poems (trans.) 1960, Mit einer Kranichfeder (poems) 1962, Kastanien aus dem Feuer (stories) 1963, Windrichtungen (journey reports) 1963, Neue deutsche Erzählgedichte (anthology) 1964, Klartext (poems) 1966, Die mittleren Jahre (novel) 1967, Liebeserklärungen in Prosa (essays) 1969, Männer, die Gedichte machen (essays) 1970, Die Erzählungen (stories) 1971, Tot oder lebendig (poems) 1971, Deutsche Gedichte seit 1960 (anthology) 1972, Helle Tage anderswo (travel reports) 1973, Gesammelte Gedichte (collected poems) 1974, Dichterleben (novel) 1976, Wintertage-Sommernächte (collected stories) 1977, Juttas Neffe (novel) 1979, Vorkriegszeit (poetry cycle) 1980, Was mich nicht loslässt (poems) 1981, Lieb', Leid und Zeit und Ewigkeit (anthology) 1981, Zeit meines Lebens (autobiog. vol. 1) 1984, Werke in sechs Bänden (collected works) 1985, Helldunkel (poems) 1987, Stunde der Überlebenden (autobiog. vol. 2) 1989, Werkauswahl in 2 Bänden (poems and stories) 1990, Nach Markus (story) 1991, Morgenwache (poems) 1991, Goethe unterwegs in Schlesien (almost a novel) 1993, Dichterleben (novel, new composition) 1995, Neue Umlaufbahn (poems) 1998, Schattenlinie (trans. of novel by Joseph Courad) 1999, Texte und Bilder-Catalogue of Exposition (drawing) 2001. *Honours:* Berlin Prize for Literature 1957, Andreas Gryphius Prize, Esslingen 1957, Rom-Preis, Villa Massimo 1960, Münchner Literatur Preis 1967, Eichendorff-Preis 1971, Tukan-Preis 1971, Literatur-Preis des Kulturkreises im BDI 1974, Georg-Büchner-Preis 1976, Werner-Egk-Preis 1981, Oberschlesischer Kulturpreis 1984, Bundesverdienstkreuz (1st Class) 1985, Grosser Kultur-Preis Schlesien des Landes Niedersachsen 1991, Bayerischer Verdienstorden 1992, Villa-Massimo-Preis 1995. *Address:* Dülfer Strasse 97, 80995 Munich, Germany.

PIPER, Christa, MA; German painter and writer. *Education:* Kunst Schüle Westerd, Frankfurt/Main. *Career:* paintings and drawings exhibited in Germany, fmr GDR, Austria, Switzerland, Israel, People's Repub. of China, Monaco, Norway; Producer lyric/sound/dance collage Wieviel Erde braucht das Mensch 1984. *Publications include:* illustrated poems: Alltag 1969, Der Übermensch (Persiflage auf die Menschen im Jahr 3000) 1970, Spiel zu zweit 1976; novels: Trotzdem Christine 1984, Im Zeichen der Rose 1984, Nimm dir dein Leben 1986, Die Wolke und der Regenbogen 1991, Wenn Dr Wieder 'Anion' Sagst 1998; work featured in calendars and catalogues. *Honours:* Study Prize Heussenstammschen Stiftung, Frankfurt 1984. *Address:* Koselstr 19, 60318 Frankfurt am Main, Germany. *Telephone:* (69) 557899.

PIPES, Richard, BA, MA, PhD; American academic and writer; *Frank B. Baird Jr Professor of History Emeritus, Harvard University*; b. 11 July 1923, Cieszyn, Poland; s. of Mark Pipes and Sophia Pipes; m. Irene Eugenia Roth 1946; two s. *Education:* Muskingum Coll., Cornell Univ., Harvard Univ. *Career:* faculty, Russian Research Center, Harvard Univ. 1950–, Prof. of History 1958–, Assoc. Dir 1962–64, Dir 1968–73, Frank B. Baird Jr Prof. of History 1975–96, Frank B. Baird Jr Prof. of History Emeritus 1996–; Visiting Asst Prof. of History, Univ. of California at Berkeley 1955–56; Fellow, Center for Advanced Study in the Behavioural Sciences, Stanford, CA 1969–70; Sr Consultant, Stanford Research Inst. 1973–78; Dir, East European and Soviet Affairs, Nat. Security Council 1981–82; Fellow, American Acad. of Arts and Sciences 1965–; mem. Council on Foreign Relations; foreign mem. Polish Acad. of Arts and Sciences (PAU) 1996–. *Publications:* Formation of the Soviet Union, 1954; Karamzin's Memoir on Ancient and Modern Russia, 1959; The Russian Intelligentsia (ed.), 1961; Social Democracy and the St Petersburg Labor Movement, 1963; Of the Russe Commonwealth (1591), by Giles Fletcher (ed. with John Fine), 1966; Revolutionary Russia (ed.), 1968; Europe Since 1815, 1970; Struve: Liberal on the Left, 1870–1905, 1970; P. B. Struve: Collected Works in Fifteen Vols (ed.), 1973; Russia Under the Old Regime, 1974; Soviet Strategy in Europe (ed.), 1976; Struve: Liberal on the Right, 1905–1944, 1980; U.S.–Soviet Relations in the Era of Détente, 1981; Survival is Not Enough, 1984; Russia Observed, 1989; The Russian Revolution, 1990; Communism: The Vanished Specter, 1993; Russia Under the Bolshevik Regime, 1994; A Concise History of the Russian Revolution, 1995; The Unknown Lenin: From the Secret Archive (ed.), 1996; Three 'Whys' of the Russian Revolution, 1996; Property & Freedom, 1999; Land-Tenure in Pre-Roman Antiquity and its Political Consequences, 2001; Communism: A History, 2001; The Degaev Affair, 2003; Vixi: Memoirs of a Non-Belonger, 2003, Russian Conservatism and its Critics 2006; contributions: scholarly books and journals. *Honours:* George Louis Beer Prize, American Historical Asscn, 1955; Guggenheim Fellowships, 1956, 1965; Fellow, ACLS, 1965; Hon. doctorates, Adelphi College, 1991, Muskingum College, 1998, University of

Silesia, 1994; Walter Channing Cabot Fellow, Harvard University, 1990–91; Commander's Cross of Merit, Poland, 1996; Hon. Citizen, 1997, Hon. Consul, 1997–, Republic of Georgia. *Address:* 17 Berkeley Street, Cambridge, MA 02138, USA (home). *Telephone:* (617) 492-0727 (home). *E-mail:* rpipes23@aol.com (home).

PIRIE, David Tarbat; British dramatist and writer; b. 4 Dec. 1946, Dundee, Scotland; m. Judith Harris 1983, one s. one d. *Education:* Univ. of York, Univ. of London. *Career:* tutor; film critic and Ed., Time Out Magazine 1980–84; mem. Soho House, London 1990. *Film screenplays:* Rainy Day Women 1984, Wild Things 1988, Black Easter 1993, Element of Doubt 1996. *Television screenplays:* Never Come Back (BBC serial) 1989, Ashenden (BBC serial) 1990, Natural Lies (serial) 1991, The Woman in White (adaptation) 1997, Murder Rooms: The Dark Beginnings of Sherlock Holmes 2000, Murder Rooms 2: The Safe House 2002. *Publications:* Heritage of Horror 1974, Mystery Story 1980, Anatomy of the Movies 1981, The Patient's Eyes 2001, The Night Calls 2002; contrib. to various journals. *Honours:* New York Festival Drama Prize 1985, Chicago Film Festival Best TV Network Series Prize 1990 and Best TV Feature Film Prize 1996, Crimescene/Sherlock Holmes Magazine/NFT Award for Best TV Detective Series 2002. *Literary Agent:* The Agency, 24 Pottery Lane, Holland Park, London, W11 4LZ, England.

PIRSIG, Robert Maynard, BA, MA; American author; b. 6 Sept. 1928, Minneapolis, MN; m. 1st Nancy Ann James 1954 (divorced 1978); two s.; m. 2nd Wendy Kimball 1978; one d. *Education:* Univ. of Minnesota. *Publications:* Zen and the Art of Motorcycle Maintenance: An Inquiry into Values 1974, Lila: An Inquiry into Morals 1991. *Honours:* Guggenheim Fellowship 1974, AAAL Award 1979.

PITCHER, Harvey John, BA; British writer; b. 26 Aug. 1936, London, England. *Education:* Univ. of Oxford. *Publications:* Understanding the Russians 1964, The Chekhov Play: A New Interpretation 1973, When Miss Emmie was in Russia 1977, Chekhov's Leading Lady 1979, Chekhov: The Early Stories, 1883–1888 (with Patrick Miles) 1982, The Smiths of Moscow 1984, Lily: An Anglo-Russian Romance 1987, Muir and Mirrielees: The Scottish Partnership that Became a Household Name in Russia 1994, Witnesses of the Russian Revolution 1994, Chekhov: The Comic Stories 1998, If Only We Could Know: An Interpretation of Chekhov, by Vladimir Kataev (ed. and trans.) 2002; contrib. to magazines and journals, including TLS. *Address:* 37 Bernard Road, Cromer, Norfolk NR27 9AW, England.

PITMAN, Jennifer (Jenny) Susan, OBE; British consultant and fmr racehorse trainer and writer; b. (Jennifer Susan Harvey), 11 June 1946, Leicester; d. of George Harvey and Mary Harvey; m. 1st Richard Pitman 1965 (annulled); two s.; m. 2nd David Stait 1997. *Education:* Sarson Secondary Girls' School. *Career:* Nat. Hunt trainer 1975–99; Dir Jenny Pitman Racing Ltd 1975–99; Racing and Media Consultant, DJS Racing 1999–; winners include: Watafella (Midlands Nat. 1977), Bueche Giorod (Ferguson Gold Cup 1980), Corbiere (Welsh Nat. 1982, Grand Nat. 1983), Burrough Hill Lad (Anthony Mildmay Peter Cazalet Gold Cup 1983, Welsh Nat. 1983, Cheltenham Gold Cup 1984, King George VI Gold Cup 1984, Hennessey Gold Cup 1984), Smith's Man (Whitbread Trophy 1985), Stears By (Anthony Mildmay Peter Cazalet Gold Cup 1986, Welsh Nat. 1986), Gainsay (Ritz Club Chase 1987, Sporting Life Weekend Chase 1987), Willsford (Midlands Nat. 1990), Crumpet Delite (Philip Cornes Saddle of Gold Final 1988), Garrison Savannah (Sun Alliance Chase 1990, Cheltenham Gold Cup 1991), Wonder Man (Welsh Champion Hurdle 1991), Don Valentino (Welsh Champion Hurdle 1992), Superior Finish (Anthony Mildmay Peter Cazalet Gold Cup 1993), Royal Athlete (Grand Nat. 1995), Willsford (County Hurdle 1989, Scottish Nat. 1995), Mudahim (Irish Nat. 1995), Nathen Lad (Sun Alliance Chase 1996), Indefence (Supreme Novice Hurdler 1996), Master Tribe (Ladbroke Hurdler Leopardstown 1997), Princeful (Stayers Hurdle Cheltenham 1998), Smiths Cracker (Philip Cornes Saddle of Gold Final 1998); first woman to train Grand Nat. winner 1983. *Publications:* Glorious Uncertainty (autobiog.) 1984, Jenny Pitman: The Autobiography 1999; novels: On the Edge 2002, Double Deal 2002, The Dilemma 2003, The Vendetta 2004, The Inheritance 2005. *Honours:* numerous awards including Racing Personality of the Year, Golden Spurs 1983, Commonwealth Sports Award 1983, 1984, Piper Heidsieck Trainer of the Year 1983–84, 1989–90, Variety Club of GB Sportswoman of the Year 1984, BBC East Midlands Lifetime Achievement Award 2005. *Address:* Owls Barn, Kintbury, Hungerford, Berks., RG17 9SX, England (office). *Telephone:* (1488) 668774 (office); (1488) 669191 (home). *Fax:* (1488) 668999 (office). *E-mail:* jpr@owlsbarn.fsbusiness.co.uk (office).

PITT, David George, BA, MA, PhD; Canadian academic (retd) and writer; b. 12 Dec. 1921, Musgravetown, NF; m. Marion Woolfrey 1946, one s. one d. *Education:* Mt Allison Univ., Univ. of Toronto. *Career:* Prof. of English Literature, Memorial Univ. of Newfoundland 1949–83; mem. Assscn of Canadian Univ. Teachers of English, Humanities Assscn of Canada. *Publications:* Elements of Literacy 1964, Windows of Agates 1966, Critical Views on Canadian Writers: E. J. Pratt 1969, Toward the First Spike: The Evolution of a Poet 1982, Goodly Heritage 1984, E. J. Pratt: The Truant Years 1984, E. J. Pratt: The Master Years 1987, Tales from the Outer Fringe 1990. *Honours:* Hon. LLD (Mt Allison Univ.) 1989, Hon. DLitt (Memorial Univ.) 2005; Univ. of British Columbia Medal for Biography 1984, Newfoundland Arts Council Artist of the Year 1988. *Address:* 7 Chestnut Place, St John's, NF A1B 2T1, Canada.

PITT, Ingrid; British actress and writer; b. 21 Nov. 1937. *Education:* Goethe Schule, Berlin, Germany. *Career:* acting career began with Berliner Ensemble; defected from fmr GDR to USA 1962; joined Spanish Nat. Theatre 1966, toured USA; int. film debut in Where Eagles Dare 1968; writer 1980–; formed Monaco Films Ltd 1987, Co-Dir. *Films include:* The Vampire Lovers, The House That Dripped Blood, Wild Geese 2, Countess Dracula 1971, Nobody Ordered Love, The Omegans, The Wicker Man, El Lobo, Who Dares Wins 1983, Parker, Requiem, Underworld 1987, Innocent Heroes 1988, Green Fingers 2000, The Asylum 2000, Green Fingers 2000, Dominator (voice) 2003, Minotaur 2005, Sea of Dust 2005, The Scary Movie Show 2005, Crumpet 2006. *Publications include:* Cuckoo Run 1980, Katarina 1985, The Perons (jtly), Eva's Spell (jtly) 1986, Pitt of Horror, Hisako San, Bertie the Bus, Dragonhunter, Bertie to the Rescue, The Bedside Companion for Vampire Lovers, The Bedside Companion for Ghosthunters, The Ingrid Pitt Book of Murder, Torture and Depravity, Life's a Scream (autobiog.). *Honours:* Mar del Plata Best Actress Award, Baltimore Best Supporting Actress Award. *Literary Agent:* c/o Barry Langford, Langford Associates, 17 Westfields Avenue, London, SW13 0AT, England. *Telephone:* (20) 8878-7148. *E-mail:* info@pittofhorror.com (home). *Website:* www.pittofhorror.com (home).

PITT-KETHLEY, (Helen) Fiona, BA; British writer and poet; b. 21 Nov. 1954, Edgware, Middlesex, England; m. James Plaskett; one s. *Education:* Chelsea School of Art. *Publications:* London, 1984; Rome, 1985; The Tower of Glass, 1985; Gesta, 1986; Sky Ray Lolly, 1986; Private Parts, 1987; Journeys to the Underworld, 1988; The Perfect Man, 1989; The Misfortunes of Nigel, 1991; The Literary Companion to Sex, 1992; The Maiden's Progress, 1992; Too Hot to Handle, 1992; Dogs, 1993; The Pan Principle, 1994; The Literary Companion to Low Life, 1995; Double Act, 1996; Memo from a Muse, 1999; Red Light Districts of the World, 2000; Baker's Dozen, 2000; My Schooling (autobiog.), 2000. Contributions: numerous newspapers and magazines. *Honours:* Calouste Gulbenkian Award 1995.

PITTOCK, Murray George Hornby, MA, DPhil, FRSE, FRSA, FEA, FRHistS, FSAScot; British academic, writer and editor; *Professor of Scottish and Romantic Literature, University of Manchester*; b. 5 Jan. 1962; m. Anne Grace Thornton Martin 1989; two d. *Education:* Univs of Glasgow and Oxford. *Career:* British Acad. Postdoctoral Fellow, Univ. of Aberdeen 1988–89; Lecturer and Reader, Dept of English Literature, Univ. of Edinburgh 1994–96; Co-Ed. Scottish Studies Review 2000–; Prof. in Literature, Univ. of Strathclyde 1996–2003, Head, Dept of Literature 1997–2000; Prof. of Scottish and Romantic Literature, Univ. of Manchester 2003–, Chair. Dept of English and American Studies 2003–04, Deputy Head School of Arts, Histories and Cultures 2004–; Assoc. Ed. New Dictionary of National Biography. *Publications:* The Invention of Scotland 1991, Spectrum of Decadence: The Literature of the 1890s 1993, Poetry and Jacobite Politics in Eighteenth-Century Britain and Ireland 1994, The Myth of the Jacobite Clans 1995, Inventing and Resisting Britain 1997, Jacobitism 1998, Celtic Identity and the British Image 1999, Scottish Nationality 2001, The Jacobite Relics of Scotland 2002, 2003, A New History of Scotland 2003, The Edinburgh History of Scottish Literature (co-ed.) 2006; contribs scholarly books and journals. *Honours:* various research grants; Royal Soc. of Edinburgh BP Humanities Research Prize, 1992–93, Chatterton Lecturer, British Acad. 2002. *Address:* School of Arts, Histories and Cultures, University of Manchester, Manchester, M13 9PL, England (office).

PIVOT, Bernard; French journalist; b. 5 May 1935, Lyons; s. of Charles Pivot and Marie-Louise Pivot (née Dumas); m. Monique Dupuis 1959; two d. *Education:* Centre de formation des Journalistes. *Career:* on staff of Figaro littéraire, then Literary Ed.; Figaro 1958–74; Chronique pour sourire, on Europe 1 1970–73; Columnist, Le Point 1974–77; producer and presenter of Ouvrez les guillemets 1973–74, Apostrophes, Channel 2 1975–90, Bouillon de culture 1991–2001; Ed. Lire 1975–93; Dir Sofica Créations 1986–; mem. Conseil supérieur de la langue française 1989–; Pres. Grévin Acad. 2001–; mem. Académie Goncourt 2004. *Publications:* L'Amour en vogue (novel) 1959, La vie oh là là! 1966, Les critiques littéraires 1968, Beaujolaises 1978, Le Football en vert 1980, Le Métier de lire. Réponses à Pierre Nora 1990, Remontrances à la ménagère de moins de cinquante ans (essay) 1998. *Honours:* Chevalier du Mérite agricole; Grand Prix de la Critique l' Acad. française 1983, Prix Louise Weiss, Bibliothèque Nat. 1989, Prix de la langue française décerne à la Foire 2000. *Address:* France 2, 7 esplanade Henri de France, 75907 Paris Cedex 15; Les Jonnerys, 69430 Quincié-en-Beaujolais, France (home).

PIZZEY, Erin Patria Margaret; British writer and campaigner; b. 19 Feb. 1939, People's Repub. of China; d. of Cyril Edward Antony Carney and Ruth Patricia Carney (née Balfour-Last); m. John Leo Pizzey 1961 (divorced 1979); one s. one d. *Education:* Leweston Manor, Dorset. *Career:* protests on behalf of women and children's rights led to several court appearances; Founder first Shelter for Battered Wives and their children 1971; toured USA to help set up shelters 1974, New Zealand 1978; now writer; works as trans. to Japanese, Russian, Greek, Portuguese, Polish, Latvian, Hebrew, Italian; contribs to The New Statesman, The Sunday Times, Cosmopolitan and to other int. magazines; resident expert on family violence on Phil Donahue Show, TV 1982; gave evidence to Attorney-Gen's Task Force on Family Violence, USA 1984; Guest of Honour at conf. of Int. Supreme Court Judges, Rome 1994; Lunch of Honour on Capitol Hill, Washington, DC, sponsored by Congresswomen; lecture tours, New Zealand 1978, USA 1979. *Publications:* non-fiction: Scream Quietly or the Neighbours Will Hear (also film 1979) 1974, Infernal Child (autobiog.) 1978, The Slut's Cookbook (jtly) 1981, Prone to Violence 1982, Erin Pizzey Collects 1983; fiction: The Watershed 1983, In the Shadow 1984, The Pleasure Palace 1986, First Lady 1987, The Consul General's Daughter 1988, The Snow Leopard of Shanghai 1989, Other Lovers 1991, Swimming with Dolphins, For the Love of a Stranger, Kisses, The Wicked World of Women 1996, The Fame Game 1999; short stories: The Man in the Blue Van, The Frangipani Tree, Addictions, Dancing, Sand. *Honours:* numerous awards including Diploma of Honour, Int. Order of Volunteers for Peace, Italy 1981, Nancy Astor Award for Journalism 1983, Distinguished Leadership Award, World Congress of Victimology 1987, St Valentino Palm d'Oro Int. Award for Literature, Italy 1994. *Address:* Flat 5, 29 Lebanon Park, Twickenham, TW1 3DH, England (home). *Telephone:* (20) 8241-6541 (home). *E-mail:* erin.pizzey@blueyonder.co.uk (home).

PLACE, Florence (see Norman, Geraldine Lucia)

PLAICE, Stephen James, BA, MPhil; British writer, poet and librettist; b. 9 Sept. 1951, Watford, Herts.; m. Marcia Bellamy; three c. *Education:* Univ. of Sussex, Univ. of Marburg, Germany, Univ. of Zürich, Switzerland. *Career:* Writer-in-Residence, HM Prison, Lewes 1987–94; Artistic Dir Alarmist Theatre 1987–2002; Ed. Printer's Devil 1990–2002. *Plays:* Trunks 1993, The Last Post 1994, Home Truths 1995, Nemesis 2006. *Opera libretti:* Misper 1997, Zoë 2000, The Io Passion 2004, Tangier Tattoo 2005, School4Lovers 2006, Daddy Cool 2006, The Finnish Prisoner 2007. *Films:* The Last Post 1996, Zoë 2000. *Television:* The Bill, Dream Team, Ballykissangel. *Publications:* Rumours of Cousins 1983, Over the Rollers 1992. *Literary Agent:* c/o Gavin Plumley, Macnaughton Lord 2000 Ltd, 19 Margravine Gardens, London, W6 8RL, England. *Telephone:* (20) 8741-0606. *Fax:* (20) 8741-7443. *E-mail:* gavin@ml2000.org.uk. *Website:* www.ml200.org.uk. *Address:* 83 Stanford Road, Brighton, East Sussex, BN1 5PR, England (home). *Telephone:* (1273) 700849 (home). *E-mail:* cultureshock@ntlworld.com (home). *Website:* www.stephenplaice.co.uk (home).

PLAIN, Belva; American writer; b. 9 Oct. 1919, New York, NY; m. Irving Plain 1941 (died 1982); three c. *Education:* Barnard Coll., Columbia Univ. *Publications:* Evergreen 1978, Random Winds 1980, Eden Burning 1982, Crescent City 1984, The Golden Cup 1987, Tapestry 1988, Blessings 1989, Harvest 1990, Treasures 1992, Whispers 1993, Daybreak 1994, The Carousel 1995, Promises 1996, Secrecy 1997, Homecoming 1997, Legacy of Silence 1998, Fortune's Hand 1999, After the Fire 2000, Looking Back 2001, Her Father's House 2002. *Literary Agent:* Janklow & Nesbit Associates, 445 Park Avenue, New York, NY 10022, USA. *Address:* c/o Delacourte Press, 1540 Broadway, New York, NY 10036, USA. *Telephone:* (973) 912-9884 (home).

PLANCHON, Roger; French theatrical director and playwright; b. 12 Sept. 1931, Saint-Chamond; s. of Emile Planchon and Augusta Planchon (née Nogier); m. Colette Dompietrini 1958; two s. *Career:* bank clerk 1947–49; Founder Théâtre de la Comédie, Lyon 1951; Co-Dir Théâtre de la Cité, Villeurbanne 1957–72; Dir Théâtre Nat. Populaire 1972–2005; Pres. Fondation Molière 1987–; aims to popularize the theatre by extending its units and recreating the classics within a modern social context; Pres. Rhône-Alpes Cinéma. *Film roles include:* Le grand frère 1982, Danton 1983, Un amour interdit, La septième Cible 1984, Camile Claudel 1988, Radio Corbeau 1989, Jean Galmot, aventurier 1990, L'année de l'éveil 1991, Louis, enfant roi 1992. *Films written and directed:* Dandin 1987, Louis, enfant roi 1992, Lautrec 1998. *Plays:* has directed and acted in over 60 plays by Shakespeare, Molière, Racine, Marivaux, Brecht, Adamov, Vinaver, Dubillard and himself, most recently: Ionesco 1983, L'avare 1986, George Dandin 1987, Andromaque (dir) 1989, Le vieil hiver 1990, Fragile forêt 1990, Les libertins 1994, No Man's Land 1994, Occupe-toi d'Amélie! 1995, Le radeau de la Méduse 1995, La tour de Nesle 1996, Le triomphe de l'amour 1996, Les démons et la Dame de Chez Maxim 1998. *Publications:* plays: La remise 1961, Patte blanche 1965, Bleus, blancs, rouges ou les Libertins 1967, Dans le vent 1968, L'infâme 1969, La langue au chat 1972, Le cochon noir (Prix Ibsen 1974) 1973, Gilles de Rais 1976, Fragile Forêt 1991, Le radeau de la Méduse 1995, L'avare 2001. *Honours:* Chevalier de la Légion d'honneur, des Arts et Lettres; Croix de guerre; Prix Georges Lherminier du Syndicat de la critique dramatique 1986, 1998. *Address:* Studio 24, 24 bis rue Emile Decorps, 69100 Villeurbanne, France.

PLANTE, David Robert, BA, FRSL; American writer; b. 4 March 1940, Providence, RI. *Education:* University of Louvain, Belgium, Boston College. *Career:* Writer-in-Residence, University of Tulsa, 1979–82; Visiting Fellow, University of Cambridge, 1984–85; L'Université de Québec à Montréal, 1990; Gorky Institute of Literature, Moscow, 1991; Prof., Columbia University, 1998–. *Publications:* Fiction: The Ghost of Henry James, 1970; Slides, 1971; Relatives, 1974; The Darkness of the Body, 1974; Figures in Bright Air, 1976; The Family, 1978; The Country, 1981; The Woods, 1982; The Foreigner, 1984; The Catholic, 1986; The Native, 1988; The Accident, 1991; Annunciation, 1994; The Age of Terror, 1999. Non-Fiction: Difficult Women: A Memoir of Three, 1983. Contributions: anthologies and magazines. *Honours:* Henfield Fellow, University of East Anglia, 1975; British Arts Council Grant, 1977; Guggenheim Fellowship, 1983; American Acad. and Institute of Arts and Letters Award, 1983; Senior Mem., King's College, Cambridge.

PLANTINGA, Alvin, AB, MA, PhD; American academic and writer; *John A. O'Brien Professor of Philosophy, University of Notre Dame*; b. 15 Nov. 1932, Ann Arbor, MI; m. Kathleen Ann DeBoer 1955; two s. two d. *Education:* Calvin Coll., Grand Rapids, Univ. of Michigan and Yale Univ. *Career:* Instructor,

Yale Univ. 1957–58; Assoc. Prof., Wayne State Univ. 1958–63; Prof., Calvin Coll. 1963–82; Fellow, Center for Advanced Study in the Behavioral Sciences 1968–69; Visiting Fellow, Balliol Coll., Oxford 1975–76; John A. O'Brien Prof. of Philosophy 1982–, Dir Center for Philosophy of Religion 1983–, Univ. of Notre Dame, IN; Gifford Lecturer, Aberdeen Univ. 1987; Fellow American Acad. of Arts and Sciences 1975; Gifford Lecturer 2005; mem. American Philosophical Asscn, Soc. of Christian Philosophers (pres. 1983–86). *Publications:* God and Other Minds 1967, The Nature of Necessity 1974, God, Freedom, and Evil 1974, Does God Have a Nature? 1980, Faith and Rationality 1983, Warrant: The Current Debate 1993, Warrant and Proper Function 1993, The Analytic Theist 1998, Warranted Christian Belief 2000, Essays in the Metaphysics of Modality 2003. *Honours:* Guggenheim Fellowship 1971–72, Nat. Endowment for the Humanities Fellowships 1975–76, 1987, 1995–96, hon. doctorates. *Address:* c/o Department of Philosophy, University of Notre Dame, Notre Dame, IN 46556, USA (office).

PLANTINGA, Leon Brooks, BA, MMus, PhD; American musicologist, academic and writer; *Professor of Music, Yale University*; b. 25 March 1935, Ann Arbor, MI. *Education:* Calvin Coll., Michigan State Univ., Yale Univ. *Career:* Faculty 1963–74, Prof. 1974–, Acting Chair Dept of Music 1978–79, Chair Dept of Music 1979–86, Dir Division of Humanities 1991–97, Yale Univ.; mem. American Musicological Soc. *Publications:* Schumann as Critic 1967, Muzio Clementi: His Life and Music 1977, Romantic Music: A History of Musical Style in Nineteenth-Century Europe 1984, Anthology of Romantic Music 1984, Beethoven's Concertos: History, Style, Performance 1999; contrib. to scholarly books and journals. *Honours:* ASCAP-Deems Taylor Award 1985. *Address:* c/o Department of Music, Yale University, PO Box 208310, New Haven, CT 06520, USA. *E-mail:* leon.plantinga@yale.edu.

PLATELL, Amanda, BA; Australian newspaper executive. *Career:* fmr mem. staff Perth Daily News; moved to London 1986; joined Today newspaper, later Features Production Ed., then Deputy Ed.; fmr mem. staff London Daily News; Group Man. Dir Mirror Group Newspapers (MGN) 1995–96, Head of Promotions for MGN Titles, mem. subsidiary MGN Bd, Group Man. Dir and Acting Ed. Sunday Mirror 1996–97; Ed. Sunday Express 1998–99; Head of Media, Conservative Party 1999–2001. *Television:* presenter, Morgan & Platell (Channel 4) 2005–. *Publication:* Scandal 1999. *Address:* c/o Channel 4 Television, 124 Horseferry Road, London, SW1P 2TX, England.

PLATER, Alan Frederick, CBE, FRSL, FRSA; British writer; b. 15 April 1935, Jarrow-on-Tyne; s. of Herbert Richard Plater and Isabella Scott Plater; m. 1st Shirley Johnson 1958 (divorced 1985); two s. one d.; m. 2nd Shirley Rubinstein 1986; three step-s. *Education:* Kingston High School and King's Coll. Newcastle-upon-Tyne. *Career:* trained as architect; full-time writer 1960–; has written extensively for radio, TV, films and theatre, also for The Guardian, Listener, New Statesman, etc.; Co.-Chair. Writers' Guild of GB 1986–87, Pres. 1991–95; Visiting Prof., Univ. of Bournemouth 2001–. *Plays include:* A Smashing Day, Close the Coalhouse Door, And a Little Love Besides, Swallows on the Water, Trinity Tales, The Fosdyke Saga, Fosdyke Two, On Your Way, Riley!, Skyhooks, A Foot on the Earth, Prez, Rent Party (musical), Sweet Sorrow, Going Home, I Thought I Heard a Rustling, Shooting the Legend, All Credit to the Lads, Peggy for You, Tales From the Backyard, Only a Matter of Time, Barriers. *Films include:* The Virgin and the Gypsy, It Shouldn't Happen to a Vet, Priest of Love, Keep the Aspidistra Flying. *Radio includes:* Only a Matter of Time, Time Added on for Injuries, The Devil's Music. *Television includes:* series: Z Cars, Softly Softly, The Beiderbecke Trilogy; adaptations: The Barchester Chronicles, Fortunes of War, A Very British Coup, Campion, A Day in Summer, A Few Selected Exits, Oliver's Travels, Dalziel and Pascoe; recent plays: Doggin' Around, The Last of the Blonde Bombshells. *Publications:* The Beiderbecke Affair 1985, The Beiderbecke Tapes 1986, Misterioso 1987, The Beiderbecke Connection 1992, Oliver's Travels 1994, Doggin' Around 2006; plays and shorter pieces in various anthologies. *Honours:* Hon. Fellow, Humberside Coll. of Educ. 1983; Hon. DLitt (Hull) 1985; Hon. DCL (Northumbria) 1997; Royal TV Soc. Writers' Award 1988, BAFTA Writers' Award 1988, BAFTA Dennis Potter Award 2005, and many other awards. *Literary Agent:* Alexandra Cann Representation, 12 Abingdon Road, London, W8 6AF, England. *Telephone:* (20) 7938-4002.

PLATH, James Walter, BA, MA, PhD; American writer, editor and educator; b. 29 Oct. 1950, Chicago, IL; three s. three d. *Education:* California State University at Chico, University of Wisconsin-Milwaukee. *Career:* Prof. of English, Illinois Wesleyan University; mem. Acad. of American Poets; Fitzgerald Society; Fulbright Asscn; Hemingway Society; Illinois College Press Asscn; Society of Midland Authors. *Publications:* Conversations With John Updike, 1994; Courbet, On the Rocks, 1994; Remembering Ernest Hemingway, 1999. Contributions: anthologies, reviews, periodicals, journals, quarterlies, magazines and newspapers. *Honours:* Fulbright Scholar; Ed.'s Award, Council of Literary Magazines and Presses, 1990; Pantagraph Award for Teaching Excellence 2004. *Address:* c/o Department of English, Illinois Wesleyan University, Bloomington, IL 61702-2900, USA.

PLATT, Charles Michael, (Aston Cantwell, Robert Clarke, Charlotte Prentiss); British writer; b. 26 April 1945, London, England; one d. *Education:* Univ. of Cambridge, London Coll. of Printing. *Publications:* fiction: Garbage World 1967, The Gas 1968, The City Dwellers (aka Twilight of the City) 1970, Highway Sandwiches (collection, with T. M. Disch and M. Hacker) 1970, Planet of the Voles 1971, The Power and the Pain 1971, The Image Job 1971, Outdoor Survival 1976, Sweet Evil 1977, Love's Savage Embrace (as Charlotte Prentiss) 1981, Double Delight (as Aston Cantwell) 1983, Tease for Two (as Aston Cantwell) 1983, Less Than Human (as Robert Clarke) 1986, Plasm 1987, Free Zone 1988, Soma 1989, The Silicon Man 1991, Children of the Ice (as Charlotte Prentiss) 1993, People of the Mesa (as Charlotte Prentiss) 1994, Children of the Sun (as Charlotte Prentiss) 1995, Protektor 1996, The Island Tribe (as Charlotte Prentiss) 1997, The Ocean Tribe (as Charlotte Prentiss) 1999, Loose Canon 2001; editor: New Worlds 6 (ed. with M. Moorcock) 1973, New Worlds 7 (ed. with H. Bailey) 1974; non-fiction: Who Writes Science Fiction? (aka The Dream Makers) 1976, Dream Makers: The Uncommon People Who Write Science Fiction 1980, Micromania 1984, How to be a Happy Cat 1986, When You Can Live Twice as Long, What Will You Do? 1989, Anarchy Online: Netsex / Netcrime 1996. *E-mail:* other@platt.us. *Website:* www.davidpascal.com/charlesplatt.

PLATT, Stephen (Steve), BSc (Econ); British journalist; b. 29 Sept. 1954, Stoke-on-Trent; s. of Kenneth Platt and Joyce Pritchard; one d. by Diane Louise Paice. *Education:* Longton High School, Stoke On Trent, Wade Deacon School, Widnes and London School of Econs. *Career:* teacher, Moss Brook Special School, Widnes 1972–73; Dir Self Help Housing Resource Library, Polytechnic of N London 1977–80; co-ordinator, Islington Community Housing 1980–83; freelance writer and journalist 1983–; News Ed., subsequently Acting Ed. New Society 1986–88; Ed. Midweek 1988–89, Enjoying the Countryside 1988–; Ed. New Statesman and Society 1991–96; Contributing Ed. Channel 4 TV 1996–; Website and Contributing Ed. Time Team 1999– (BAFTA Award for Interactive Entertainment 2002); Dispatches Website Ed. 1999–. *Honours:* UKGLO Award for Outstanding Achievement 1999. *Address:* 46 Tufnell Park Road, London, N7 0DT, England. *Telephone:* (20) 7263-4185. *Fax:* (870) 124-5850 (home). *E-mail:* mail@steveplatt.net (home). *Website:* www.steveplatt.net (office).

PLENEL, Edwy; French journalist; b. 31 Aug. 1952, Nantes; s. of Alain Plenel and Michèle Bertreux; m. Nicole Lapierre; one d. *Education:* Institut d'études politiques, Paris. *Career:* journalist Rouge 1976–78, Matin de Paris 1980; joined Le Monde 1980, Educ. Ed. 1980–82, Legal columnist 1982–90, Reporter 1991, Head Legal Dept 1992–94, Chief Ed. 1994–95, Asst Editorial Dir 1995–96, Ed. 1996–2000, Ed.-in-Chief 2000–04 (resgnd). *Publications:* L'Effet Le Pen 1984, La République inachevée: l'État et l'école en France 1985, Mourir à Ouvéa: le tournant calédonien 1988, Voyage avec Colomb 1991, La République menacée: dix ans d'effet Le Pen 1992, La Part d'ombre 1992, Un temps de chien 1994, Les Mots volés 1997, L'Epreuve 1999, Secrets de jeunesse 2001, La Découverte du monde 2002, Procès 2006. *Address:* c/o Le Monde, 21 bis rue Claude Bernard, 75242 Paris Cedex, France (office).

PLORITIS, Marios; Greek academic, writer, journalist and director; *Professor of Philosophy, Athens University*; b. 19 Jan. 1919, Piraeus; m. *Education:* Athens Univ. *Career:* Founder-mem. Art Theatre 1942; film and theatre reviewer 1945–67; Dir Niki Newspaper 1962–63; Dir Theatro Review 1965–67; Prof. at Art Theatre Dramatic School 1957–67; Dir Courrier de la Resistance Grecque, Paris 1968–69; Prof. Univ. Paris VIII 1970–72; Prof. of Philosophy, Athens Univ. 1991–; fmr Chair. Union of Greek Film Reviewers, Greek Center of Theatre, Soc. of Authors; has translated into Greek more than 120 plays and has directed more than 30 plays. *Publications include:* Masks 1967, Dynasties and Tyrants 1974, Politics 1980, Brecht and Hitler 1984, Art, Language and Power 1989. *Address:* Panepistimiopolis, Zografon, 157 71 (office); Athinisin Ethnikon Kai Kapodistriakon Panepistimion, Odos Panepistimiou 30, 106 79 Athens, Greece (home). *Telephone:* (1) 3614301. *Fax:* (1) 3602145. *Website:* www.uoa.gr (office).

PLUMLY, Stanley Ross, BA, MA; American poet and academic; b. 23 May 1939, Barnesville, OH. *Education:* Wilmington College, Ohio University. *Career:* Instructor in Creative Writing, Louisiana State University, 1968–70; Ed., Ohio Review, 1970–75, Iowa Review, 1976–78; Prof. of English, Ohio University, 1970–74, University of Houston, 1979–; Visiting lecturer at several universities. *Publications:* In the Outer Dark, 1970; How the Plains Indians Got Horses, 1973; Giraffe, 1973; Out-of-the-Body Travel, 1977; Summer Celestial, 1983; Boy on the Step, 1989; The Marriage in the Trees, 1997; The New Bread Loaf Anthology of Contemporary American Poetry (ed. with Michael Collier), 1999; Now That My Father Lies Down Beside Me: New and Selected Poems, 1970–2000, 2000. Contributions: periodicals. *Honours:* Delmore Schwartz Memorial Award, 1973; Guggenheim Fellowhip, 1973; National Endowment for the Arts Grant, 1977.

PODHORETZ, John, AB; American writer and editor; b. 18 April 1961, NY; s. of Norman Podhoretz (q.v.) and Midge (née Rosenthal) Podhoretz; m. Elisabeth Hickey 1996. *Education:* Univ. of Chicago. *Career:* Exec. News Ed. Insight Magazine 1985–87; contrib. US News and World Report 1987–88; speechwriter to Pres. of USA 1988–89; Asst Man. Ed. Washington Times 1989–91; Sr Fellow Hudson Inst. 1991–94; TV critic NY Post 1994–95, now columnist; Deputy Ed. The Weekly Standard 1995–97. *Publication:* Hell of a Ride: Backstage at the White House Follies 1989–93 1993. *Honours:* J.C. Penney/Mo. Award for Excellence in Feature Sections 1990. *Address:* New York Post, 1211 Avenue of the Americas, 10th Floor, New York, NY 10036-8790, USA (office). *Telephone:* (212) 930-8000 (office). *Website:* www.nypost.com (office).

PODHORETZ, Norman, BA, MA, BHL; American writer and editor; *Editor-at-Large, Commentary*; b. 16 Jan. 1930, Brooklyn, NY; s. of Julius Podhoretz and Helen Podhoretz (née Woliner); m. Midge R. Decter 1956; one s. (John

Podhoretz) three d. *Education:* Columbia Univ., Jewish Theological Seminary and Univ. of Cambridge. *Career:* Assoc. Ed. Commentary 1956–58, Ed.-in-Chief 1960–95, Ed.-at-Large 1995–; Ed.-in-Chief, Looking Glass Library 1959–60; Chair. New Directions Advisory Comm. US Information Agency 1981–87; mem. Council on Foreign Relations, Comm. on the Present Danger, Comm. for the Free World; Sr Fellow, Hudson Inst. 1995–; Fulbright Fellow 1950–51; Kellett Fellow 1950–53. *Publications:* Doings and Undoings, The Fifties and After in American Writing 1964, Making It 1968, Breaking Ranks 1979, The Present Danger 1980, Why We Were in Vietnam 1982, The Bloody Crossroads 1986, Ex-Friends 1999, My Love Affair with America 2000, The Prophets: Who They Were, What They Are 2002, Norman Podhoretz Reader 2004, World War IV 2007. *Honours:* Hon. LLD (Jewish Theological Seminary); Hon. LHD (Hamilton Coll.), (Boston) 1995, (Adelphi) 1996; Hon. DHumLitt (Yeshiva) 1991; Presidential Medal of Freedom 2004. *Address:* Commentary, 165 East 56th Street, New York, NY 10022, USA (office). *Telephone:* (212) 891-6735 (office). *Fax:* (212) 891-6700 (office). *E-mail:* nhp30@hotmail.com (office). *Website:* www.commentarymagazine.com (office).

POHL, Frederik James MacCreigh; American writer and editor; b. 26 Nov. 1919, New York, NY. *Career:* Book Ed. and Assoc. Circulation Man., Popular Science Co, New York City 1946–49; Literary Agent, New York City 1949–53; Ed., Galaxy Publishing Co, New York City 1960–69; Exec. Ed., Ace Books, New York City 1971–72; Science Fiction Ed., Bantam Books, New York City 1973–79; mem. Authors' Guild; SFWA, pres. 1974–76; World Science Fiction, pres. 1980–82. *Publications:* author or ed. of over 45 books 1953–98; The Boy Who Would Live Forever 2004. *Address:* c/o World, 855 S Harvard Drive, Palatine, IL 60067, USA.

POIRIER, Richard, BA, MA, PhD; American literary critic, academic and editor; b. 9 Sept. 1925, Gloucester, MA. *Education:* Univ. of Paris, Amherst Coll., Yale Univ., Univ. of Cambridge, Harvard Univ. *Career:* faculty, Williams Coll. 1950–52, Harvard Univ. 1955–62; Prof. of English and American Literature Rutgers Univ. 1962–96; Ed., Partisan Review 1963–71, Raritan Quarterly (founder) 1980–2002; Vice-Pres. and founder, Library of America 1980–, currently Chair. Emer.; mem. Poets, Playwrights, Editors, Essayists and Novelists, American Acad. of Arts and Letters, American Acad. of Arts and Sciences. *Publications:* Comic Sense of Henry James 1960, In Defense of Reading (co-ed.) 1962, A World Elsewhere 1966, The Performing Self 1971, Norman Mailer 1976, Robert Frost: The Work of Knowing 1977, The Renewal of Literature 1987, Poetry and Pragmatism 1992, Trying it Out in America: Literary and Other Performances 1999; contrib. to Daedalus, New Republic, Partisan Review, New York Review, London Review of Books, TLS. *Honours:* Hon. HHD (Amherst Coll.) 1978; Fulbright Fellow 1952, Bollingen Fellow 1963, Guggenheim Fellowship 1967, Nat. Endowment for the Humanities Fellow 1972, American Acad. of Arts and Letters Award 1980, New York Public Library Literary Lion 1992. *Address:* 104 W 70th Street, 9B, New York, NY 10023 (home); Library of America, 14 East 60th Street, NY 10022, USA (office). *Telephone:* (212) 496-2709 (home); (212) 308-3360 (office). *Fax:* (212) 750-8352 (office).

POIVRE D'ARVOR, Patrick, LenD; French journalist and radio and television presenter; b. 20 Sept. 1947, Reims (Marne); s. of Jacques Poivre and Madeleine France Jeuge; m. Véronique Courcoux 1971; six c. (two deceased). *Education:* Lycée Georges-Clemenceau, Reims, Instituts d'études politiques, Strasbourg and Paris, Faculties of Law, Strasbourg, Paris and Reims, Ecole des langues orientales vivantes. *Career:* Special Corresp., France-Inter 1971, journalist 1971–74, Head Political Dept 1975–76, Deputy Chief Ed., Antenne 2 1976–83, Presenter, evening news programme 1976–83, 1987–, Deputy Dir News 1989–; Leader-writer Paris-Match, Journal du Dimanche 1983–91; Producer and Compère, A nous deux, Antenne 2 1983–86, A la folie, TF1 1986–88; Compère, Tous en Scène, Canal Plus 1984–85; Compère and Producer Ex libris 1988–; Compère Vol de nuit 1999–; Presenter and Producer magazine programme Le Droit de savoir, TF1 1990–94. *Publications:* Mai 68-Mai 78 1978, Les Enfants de l'aube 1982, Deux amants 1984, Le Roman de Virginie 1985, Les Derniers trains de rêve 1986, La Traversée du miroir 1986, Rencontres 1987, Les Femmes de ma vie 1988, L'Homme d'images 1992, Lettres à l'absente 1993, Les Loups et la bergerie 1994, Elle n'était pas d'ici 1995, Anthologie des plus beaux poèmes d'amour 1995, Un héros de passage 1996, Lettre ouverte aux violeurs de vie privée 1997, Une trahison amoureuse 1997, La fin du monde (collection) 1998, Petit homme 1999, Les rats de garde (collection) 2000, L'Irrésolu 2000 (Prix Interallié), Un enfant 2001, Courriers de nuit (collection) 2002, J'ai aimé une reine 2003, Coureurs des morts (collection) 2003, La Mort de don Juan (Prix Maurice-Genevoix 2205) 2004. *Honours:* Chevalier des Arts et Lettres, Chevalier de l'Ordre National du Mérite, Chevalier de la Légion d'Honneur; Prix Interallié 2000, Prix des Lettres du Livre de Poche 2003, Prix Cyrano 2004. *Address:* TF1, 1 quai du Point du Jour, 92656 Boulogne Cedex, France. *Telephone:* (1) 41-41-23-28 (office). *Fax:* (1) 41-41-19-63 (office). *Website:* tf1.lci.fr/infos/jt_tf1/siteppda (office).

POLAND, Dorothy Elizabeth Hayward, (Alison Farely, Jane Hammond); British writer; b. 3 May 1937, Barry, Wales. *Publications:* As Alison Farely: The Shadows of Evil, 1963; Plunder Island, 1964; High Treason, 1966; Throne of Wrath, 1967; Crown of Splendour, 1968; The Lion and the Wolf, 1969; Last Roar of the Lion, 1969; Leopard From Anjou, 1970; King Wolf, 1974; Kingdom under Tyranny, 1974; Last Howl of the Wolf, 1975; The Cardinal's Nieces, 1976; The Tempestuous Countess, 1976; Archduchess Arrogance, 1980; Scheming Spanish Queen, 1981; Spain for Mariana, 1982. As Jane Hammond: The Hell Raisers of Wycombe, 1970; Fire and the Sword, 1971; The Golden Courtesan, 1975; Shadow of the Headsman, 1975; The Doomtower, 1975; Witch of the White House, 1976; Gunpowder Treason, 1976; The Red Queen, 1976; The Queen's Assassin, 1977; The Silver Madonna, 1977; Conspirator's Moonlight, 1977; Woman of Vengeance, 1977; The Admiral's Lady, 1978; The Secret of Petherick, 1982; The Massingham Topaz, 1983; Beware the King's Enchantress, 1983; Moon in Aries, 1984; Eagle's Talon, 1984; Death in the New Forest, 1984; One Voyage Too Far, 2003. *Address:* Horizons, 99 Dock View Road, Barry, Glamorgan, Wales. *E-mail:* polandangelcake@aol.com.

POLE, Jack Richon, PhD, FBA, FRHistS; British historian, writer and academic; *Profesor Emeritus of American History, University of Oxford; Fellow Emeritus, St Catherine's College, Oxford*; b. 14 March 1922, London; s. of Joseph Pole and Phoebe Rickards; m. Marilyn Mitchell 1952 (divorced 1988); one s. two d. *Education:* King Alfred School, London, King's Coll. London, Queen's Coll. Oxford and Princeton Univ., USA. *Career:* served in army, rank of Capt. 1941–46; Instructor in History, Princeton Univ. 1952–53; Asst Lecturer, then Lecturer in American History, Univ. Coll. London 1953–63; Reader in American History and Govt, Cambridge Univ. and Fellow of Churchill Coll. 1963–79, Vice-Master of Churchill Coll. 1975–78; Rhodes Prof. of American History and Insts, Univ. of Oxford and Fellow, St Catherine's Coll., Oxford 1979–89, Fellow Emer. 1989–, Prof. Emer.; Visiting Prof., Univ. of Calif., Berkeley 1960–61, Ghana Univ. 1966, Univ. Chicago 1969, Univ. Beijing 1984, William and Mary Law School 1991; Goleib Fellow, New York Univ. Law School 1990; mem. Selden Soc., MCC; Hon. Fellow, King Alfred School Soc. *Exhibition:* paintings and pastels, Wolfson Coll., Oxford 2001, The Theatre, Chipping Norton 2004. *Publications:* Abraham Lincoln and the Working Classes of Britain 1959, Abraham Lincoln 1964, Political Representation in England and the Origins of the American Republic 1966, The Advance of Democracy (ed.) 1967, The Seventeenth Century: The Origins of Legislative Power 1969, The Revolution in America (ed.) 1971, The Meanings of American History (co-ed.) 1971, Foundations of American Independence 1972, The Decision for American Independence 1975, The Idea of Union 1977, The Pursuit of Equality in American History 1978, (revised and enlarged edn) 1993, Paths to the American Past 1979, The Gift of Government: Political Responsibility from the English Restoration to American Independence 1983, Colonial British America (co-ed.) 1984, The American Constitution: For and Against (ed.) 1987, The Blackwell Encyclopedia of the American Revolution (co-ed.) 1991, Freedom of Speech: Right or Privilege? 1998, Blackwell Companion to the American Revolution 2000, The Federalist (ed.) 2005; series co-ed. Early America: History, Context, Culture; contrib. to reference works and professional journals. *Honours:* Hon. Vice-Pres. British Nineteenth Century Historians 2000–, Hon. Foreign Mem. American Historical Asscn 2002, Hon. Vice Pres. Int. Comm. for the History of Representative and Parliamentary Insts 1991–2001; New Jersey Prize Princeton Univ. 1953, Ramsdell Award, Southern Historical Asscn 1959. *Address:* St Catherine's College, Oxford, OX1 3UJ (office); 20 Divinity Road, Oxford, OX4 1LJ, England (home). *Telephone:* (1865) 271757 (office); (1865) 246950 (home). *Fax:* (1865) 271768 (office). *E-mail:* jack.pole@ntlworld.com (home).

POLIAKOFF, Stephen, CBE; British playwright and film director; b. 1 Dec. 1952, London; s. of the late Alexander Poliakoff and Ina Montagu; m. Sandy Welch 1983; one d. one s. *Education:* Westminster School and Univ. of Cambridge. *Theatre:* Clever Soldiers 1974, The Carnation Gang 1974, Hitting Town 1975, City Sugar 1976, Strawberry Fields (Nat. Theatre) 1978, Shout Across the River (RSC) 1978, The Summer Party 1980, Favourite Nights 1981, Breaking the Silence (RSC) 1984, Coming in to Land (Nat. Theatre) 1987, Playing with Trains (RSC) 1989, Siena Red 1992, Sweet Panic (Hampstead) 1996, Blinded by the Sun (Nat. Theatre) 1996 (Critics' Circle Best Play Award), Talk of the City (RSC) 1998, Remember This (Nat. Theatre) 1999. *Films:* Runners (original story and screenplay) 1983, Hidden City 1988, Close My Eyes (Best British Film Award, Evening Standard) 1991, Century 1993. *Television:* Stronger Than the Sun 1977, Bloody Kids (aka One Joke Too Many, USA) 1979, Caught on a Train (BAFTA Award) 1980, A Természet lágy ölén 1981, Soft Targets 1982, Die doppelte Welt 1985, She's Been Away (Venice Film Festival Prize) 1989, Frontiers 1996, Food of Love 1998, The Tribe 1998, Shooting the Past (Prix Italia) 1999, Perfect Strangers 2001, The Lost Prince 2003, Friends and Crocodiles 2006, Gideon's Daughter 2006. *Publications:* Plays One 1989, Plays Two 1994, Plays Three 1998, Sweet Panic and Blinded by the Sun, Talk of the City, Shooting the Past, Remember This. *Address:* 33 Devonia Road, London, N1 8JQ, England. *Telephone:* (20) 7354-2695.

POLING-KEMPES, Lesley Ann, BA; American writer; b. 9 March 1954, Batavia, NY; m. James Kempes 1976, one s. one d. *Education:* University of New Mexico. *Publications:* Harvey Girls: Women Who Opened the West, 1989; Canyon of Remembering, 1996; Valley of Shining Stone: The Story of Abiquiu, 1997, Ghost Ranch: A History 2005. Contributions: Puerta del Sol; Writer's Forum 16; Best of the West 3; Higher Elevations; New Mexico Magazine. *Honours:* Zia Award for Excellence, New Mexico Press Women, 1991. *Address:* PO Box 36, Abiquiu, NM 87510, USA. *Telephone:* (505) 685-4579.

POLITO, Robert, BA, PhD; American writer and poet; b. 27 Oct. 1951, Boston, MA; m. Kristine M. Harris 1987. *Education:* Boston Coll., Harvard Univ. *Career:* faculty mem., Harvard University, 1976–81, Wellesley College, 1981–89, New York University, 1990–92, New School for Social Research, New York City, 1992–. *Publications:* Fireworks: The Lost Writings of Jim

Thompson (ed.), 1988; A Reader's Guide to James Morrill's The Changing Light at Sandover, 1994; Doubles (poems), 1995; Savage Art: A Biography of Jim Thompson, 1995. Contributions: newspapers and magazines. *Honours:* National Book Critics Circle Award 1995.

POLKINGHORNE, Rev. Canon John Charlton, Kt, KBE, MA, PhD, ScD, FRS; British ecclesiastic and physicist; b. 16 Oct. 1930, Weston-super-Mare; s. of George B. Polkinghorne and Dorothy E. Charlton; m. Ruth I. Martin 1955; two s. one d. *Education:* Perse School, Cambridge, Trinity Coll. Cambridge and Westcott House, Cambridge. *Career:* Commonwealth Fund Fellow Calif. Inst. of Tech. 1955–56; Lecturer, Univ. of Edin. 1956–58; Lecturer, Univ. of Cambridge 1958–65, Reader 1965–68, Prof. of Math. Physics 1968–79; Fellow, Trinity Coll. Cambridge 1954–86; ordained deacon 1981, priest 1982; Curate, St Andrew's, Chesterton 1981–82, St Michael & All Angels, Bedminster 1982–84; Vicar of St Cosmus and St Damian in the Blean 1984–86; Fellow and Dean, Trinity Hall, Cambridge 1986–89, Hon. Fellow 1989–; Pres. Queens' Coll. Cambridge 1989–96, Fellow 1996–, Hon. Fellow 1996–; Canon Theologian, Liverpool Cathedral 1994–2005; Six Preacher, Canterbury Cathedral 1996–; mem. Church of England Doctrine Comm. 1989–95, Human Genetics Advisory Comm. 1996–99, General Synod 1999–2000, Human Genetics Comm. 2000–02; Hon. Fellow, St Edmund's Coll., Cambridge 2002;. *Publications:* The Analytic S-Matrix (jointly) 1966, The Particle Play 1979, Models of High Energy Processes 1980, The Way the World Is 1983, The Quantum World 1984, One World 1986, Science and Creation 1988, Science and Providence 1989, Rochester Roundabout 1989, Reason and Reality 1991, Science and Christian Belief 1994, Quarks, Chaos and Christianity 1994, Serious Talk 1995, Scientists as Theologians 1996, Beyond Science 1996, Searching for Truth 1996, Belief in God in an Age of Science 1998, Science and Theology 1998, Faith, Science and Understanding 2000, The End of the World and the Ends of God (ed with M. Welker) 2000, Faith in the Living God (with M. Welker) 2001, The Work of Love (ed.) 2001, The God of Hope and the End of the World 2002, Quantum Theory: A Very Short Introduction 2002, Living with Hope 2003, Science and the Trinity 2004, Exploring Reality 2005, Quntum Physics and Theology 2007. *Honours:* Hon. Prof. of Theoretical Physics, Univ. of Kent 1984–89; Hon. DD (Kent) 1994, (Durham) 1999; Hon. DSc (Exeter) 1994, (Leicester) 1995, (Marquette) 2003; Hon. DHum (Hong Kong Baptist) 2006; Templeton Prize 2002. *Address:* Queens' College, Cambridge, CB3 9ET, England.

POLKINHORN, Harry, BA, MA, PhD; American writer, poet, editor and translator; b. 3 March 1945, Calexico, CA; m. Armida Romero 1986 (divorced 1991); one d. *Education:* University of California at Berkeley, San Diego State University, New York University. *Publications:* Excisions (poems), 1976; Radix Zero (poems), 1981; Volvox (poems), 1981; El Libro de Calo: Pachuco Slang Dictionary, 1983, revised edn as El Libro de Calo: Chicano Slang Dictionary (co-author), 1986; Travelling with Women (fiction), 1983; Anaesthesia (poems), 1985; Bridges of Skin Money (visual poems), 1986; Summary Dissolution (visual poems), 1988; Jerome Rothenberg: A Descriptive Bibliography, 1988; Lorenia La Rosa: A Travelogue (fiction), 1989; Begging for Remission (poems), 1989; Teraphim (visual poems), 1995; Mount Soledad (poems), 1996; Throat Shadow (poems), 1997; Blueshift (poems), 1998. Other: Ed. or co-ed. of several publications; Trans. Contributions: periodicals, including: American Book Review; Afterimage; Poetics Journal; Photostatic; Moody Street Irregulars; Smile; Uno Más Uno; Score; Tempus Fugit; La Poire d'Angoisse; Sink; Kaldron. *Address:* PO Box 927428, San Diego, CA 92192, USA. *E-mail:* hpolkinh@mail.sdsu.edu.

POLLAND, Madelaine Angela, (Frances Adrian); Irish writer; b. 31 May 1918, Kinsale, County Cork. *Publications:* Children of the Red King, 1961; Beorn the Proud, 1962; The White Twilight, 1962; Chuiraquimba and the Black Robes, 1962; City of the Golden House, 1963; The Queen's Blessing, 1963; Flame over Tara, 1964; Thicker Than Water, 1964; Mission to Cathay, 1965; Queen Without Crown, 1965; Deirdre, 1967; The Little Spot of Bother, 1967, US edn as Minutes of a Murder; To Tell My People, 1968; Stranger in the Hills, 1968; Random Army, 1969, US edn as Shattered Summer; To Kill a King, 1970; Alhambra, 1970; A Family Affair, 1971; Package to Spain, 1971; Daughter to Poseidon, 1972, US edn as Daughter of the Sea; Prince of the Double Axe, 1976; Double Shadow (as Francis Adrian), 1977; Sabrina, 1979; All Their Kingdoms, 1981; The Heart Speaks Many Ways, 1982; No Price Too High, 1984; As It Was in the Beginning, 1987; Rich Man's Flowers, 1990; The Pomegranate House, 1992.

POLLARD, Eve; British newspaper editor; b. 25 Dec. 1945, d. of Ivor Pollard and Mimi Pollard; m. 1st Barry L. D. Winkleman 1968 (divorced 1978); one d.; m. 2nd Sir Nicholas M. Lloyd 1978; one s. *Career:* Fashion Ed. Honey 1967–68; Fashion Ed. Daily Mirror Magazine 1968–69, top feature writer 1969–70, Women's Ed. Sunday Mirror 1971–81, Ed. (and responsible for launch of Sunday Mirror Magazine) 1988–91; Women's Ed. Observer Magazine 1970–71; Asst Ed. Sunday People 1981–83; Features Ed., Presenter TV-AM 1983–85; Ed., Elle USA (and launched magazine, New York) 1985–86, Sunday magazine News of the World 1986, You magazine Mail on Sunday 1986–88, Sunday Express and Sunday Express Magazine 1991–94; f. Wedding Magazine 1999; TV Presenter The Truth About Women; Founder and fmr Chair. Women in Journalism 1995 (now Hon. Pres.); Vice-Chair. WOW (Wellbeing of Women) 2003–; Visiting Fellow, Bournemouth Univ. 1995–; mem. English Tourism Council (fmrly English Tourist Bd) 1993–2000, Competition Comm. Newspaper Takeover Panel 2001–; Ed. of the Year, Focus Awards 1991. *Publications:* Jackie: Biography of Mrs J. K. Onassis

1971, Splash! 1995, Best of Enemies 1996, Double Trouble 1997, Unfinished Business 1998. *Address:* c/o Wellbeing of Women, 27 Sussex Place, Regent's Park, London, NW1 4SP, England.

POLLARD, Jane, (Jane Jackson, Dana James); British writer; b. 22 Nov. 1944, Goole, Yorkshire, England; m. 3rd Michael Pollard 1992; two s. one d. *Career:* mem. Authors Asscn, Soc. of Authors, Historical Novel Soc. *Publications:* Harlyn Tremayne 1984, Doctor in The Andes 1984, Desert Flower 1986, Doctor in New Guinea 1986, Rough Waters 1986, The Marati Legacy 1986, The Eagle and the Sun 1986, The Consul's Daughter 1986, Heart of Glass 1987, Tarik's Mountain 1988, Snowfire 1988, Pool of Dreaming 1988, Dark Moon Rising 1989, Love's Ransom 1989, A Tempting Shore 1992, Bay of Rainbows 1993, Deadly Feast 1997, A Place of Birds 1997, The Iron Road 1999, Eye of the Wind 2001, Tide of Fortune 2004, Dangerous Waters 2006, The Chain Garden 2006; contrib. to periodicals, radio and television. *Literary Agent:* Dorian Literary Agency, Upper Thornehill, 27 Church Road, St Marychurch, Torquay, TQ1 4QY, England. *Address:* 32 Cogos Park, Comfort Road, Mylor, Falmouth, Cornwall TR11 5SF, England.

POLLARD, John Richard Thornhill, TD, MA, MLitt; British academic and writer; b. 5 April 1914, Exeter, Devon, England; m. Shirley Holt 1952; one s. three d. *Education:* Hereford High School, The King's School, Ottery-St-Mary, Univ. Coll., Exeter and Exeter Coll., Oxford. *Career:* Classics Master, Herne Bay Coll. 1938–39; Capt., Devonshire Regt and King's African Rifles 1939–45; Asst in Classics, St Andrews Univ. 1948–49; Lecturer in Classics, Univ. Coll. of N Wales, Bangor 1949–66, Sr Lecturer in Classics 1966–88 (retd). *Publications:* Journey to the Styx 1955, Adventure Begins in Kenya 1957, Africa for Adventure 1961, African Zoo Man 1963, Wolves and Werewolves 1964, Helen of Troy 1965, Seers, Shrines and Sirens 1965, The Long Safari 1967, Virgil: The Aeneid Appreciation (with C. Day-Lewis) 1969, Birds in Greek Life and Myth 1977, Divination and Oracles: Greece, Civilization of the Ancient Mediterranean 1988, No County to Compare 1994; contrib. Greek Mythology and Greek Religion, in Encyclopaedia Britannica.

POLLEY, Jacob, MA; British poet and screenwriter; b. 1975, Carlisle, Cumbria. *Education:* Univ. of Lancaster. *Career:* writer-in-residence, The Wordsworth Trust 2002. *Film:* Flickerman and the Ivory-Skinned Woman (co-author). *Publications:* poetry: Salvage 2000, The Brink 2003. *Honours:* Arts Council of England/BBC Radio 4 First Verse Award 2002, Soc. of Authors Eric Gregory Award 2002. *Address:* c/o Picador Publishing, 20 New Wharf Road, London, N1 9RR, England.

POLLEY, Judith Anne, (Helen Kent, Valentina Luellen, Judith Stewart); British author; b. 15 Sept. 1938, London, England; m. Roy Edward Polley 1959, one s. *Education:* High School, Belgravia and Maida Vale, London. *Career:* founding mem. English Romantic Novelists' Asscn. *Publications include:* To Touch the Stars, 1980; Beloved Enemy, 1980; Don't Run From Love, 1981; Moonshadow, 1981; Prince of Deception, 1981; Beloved Adversary, 1981; Shadow of the Eagle, 1982; Silver Salamander, 1982; The Wind of Change, 1982; The Measure of Love, 1983; The Peaceful Homecoming, 1983; The Valley of Tears, 1984; Moonflower, 1984; Elusive Flame of Love, 1984; Mistress of Tanglewood, 1984; Black Ravenswood, 1985; The Lord of Darkness, 1985; Devil of Talland, 1985; Passionate Pirate, 1986; Where the Heart Leads, 1986; Love the Avenger, 1986; The Devil's Touch, 1987; My Lady Melisande, 1987; Dark Star, 1988; Love and Pride (Book 1), 1988; The Web of Love (Book 2), 1989; Winter Embers, Summer Fire, 1991; To Please a Lady, 1992; One Love, 1993; Hostage of Love, 1994; many foreign edns and trans. Contributions: Woman's Weekly Library; Woman's Realm; Woman's Weekly Fiction series; Museum of Peace and Solidarity, Samarkand, Uzbekistan.

POLLITT, Katha, BA, MFA; American writer, poet and editor; b. 14 Oct. 1949, New York, NY; m. (divorced) one c. *Education:* Harvard Univ., Columbia Univ. *Career:* Literary Ed., The Nation 1982–84, Contributing Ed. 1986–92, Assoc. Ed. 1992–; Jr Fellow Council of Humanities, Princeton Univ. 1984; Lecturer, New School for Social Research, New York 1986–90, Poetry Center, 92nd Street YMHA and WYHA, New York 1986–95. *Publications:* Antarctic Traveller 1982, Reasonable Creatures: Essays on Women and Feminism 1994; contrib. to journals and periodicals. *Honours:* National Book Critics Circle Award 1983, Acad. of American Poets I. B. Lavan Younger Poet's Award 1984, NEA grant 1984, Guggenheim Fellowship 1987, Whiting Fellowship 1993. *Address:* c/o The Nation, 33 Irving Place, New York, NY 10003, USA (office).

POLLOCK, Rev. John Charles, BA, MA; British clergyman and writer; b. 9 Oct. 1923, London, England; m. Anne Barrett-Lennard 1949. *Education:* Trinity Coll., Cambridge. *Career:* Asst Master, Wellington Coll., Berkshire 1947–49; Ordained Anglican Deacon 1951, Priest 1952; Curate St Paul's Church, Portman Square, London 1951–53; Rector Horsington, Somerset 1953–58; Ed. The Churchman (quarterly) 1953–58; mem. English Speaking Union Club. *Publications:* Candidate for Truth 1950, A Cambridge Movement 1953, The Cambridge Seven 1955, Way to Glory: The Life of Havelock of Lucknow 1957, Shadows Fall Apart 1958, The Good Seed 1959, Earth's Remotest End 1960, Hudson Taylor and Maria 1962, Moody Without Sankey 1963, The Keswick Story 1964, The Christians from Siberia 1964, Billy Graham 1966, The Apostle: A Life of Paul (revised edn as Paul the Apostle) 1969, Victims of the Long March 1970, A Foreign Devil in China: The Life of Nelson Bell 1971, George Whitefield and the Great Awakening (revised edn as Whitfield: The Evangelist) 1972, Wilberforce (revised edn as Wilberforce: God's Statesman) (Clapham Prize) 1977, Billy Graham: Evangelist to the World 1979, The Siberian Seven 1979, Amazing Grace: John Newton's Story (revised edn as Newton: The Liberator) 1981, The Master: A Life of Jesus (revised edn as Jesus: The Master) 1984, Billy Graham: Highlights of the Story 1984, Shaftesbury: The Poor Man's Earl (revised edn as Shaftesbury: The Reformer) 1985, A Fistful of Heroes: Great Reformers and Evangelists 1988, John Wesley (revised edn as Wesley: The Preacher) 1989, On Fire for God: Great Missionary Pioneers 1990, Fear No Foe: A Brother's Story 1992, Gordon: The Man Behind the Legend 1993, Kitchener: The Road to Omdurman 1998, Kitchener: Saviour of the Nation 2000, Kitchener (comprising The Road to Omdurman and Saviour of the Nation) 2001, The Billy Graham Story 2004, Abolition! The Ex-Slave Trader and the Little Abolitionist 2007; contrib. to reference works incl. Oxford DNB and religious periodicals. *Honours:* Hon. DLitt (Samford Univ., USA) 2002; Samford Univ. created the John Pollock Award for Christian Biography in his name 1999, Gordon Coll. Clapham Prize, USA 2002. *Address:* Rose Ash House, South Molton, Devon EX36 4RB, England (home). *Telephone:* (1769) 550403.

POLOMÉ, Edgar Ghislain Charles; American academic and writer; b. 31 July 1920, Brussels, Belgium; m. 1st Julia Joséphine Schwindt 1944 (died 1975); one s. one d.; m. 2nd Barbara Baker Harris 1980 (divorced 1991); m. 3rd Sharon Looper Rankin 1991. *Education:* BA, 1940, PhD, 1949, Free University of Brussels; MA, Catholic University of Louvain, 1943. *Career:* Prof. of Germanic Languages, Athénée Adolphe Max, Brussels, 1942–56; Prof. of Linguistics, University of the Belgian Congo, 1956–61; Visiting Assoc. Prof., 1961–62, Prof. of Germanic, Oriental and African Languages and Literatures, 1961–90, Dir, Center for Asian Studies, 1962–72, Christie and Stanley Adams Jr Centennial Prof. of Liberal Arts, 1984–98, Prof. Emeritus, 1998–, University of Texas at Austin; Co-Ed., 1973–, Managing Ed., 1987–, Journal of Indo-European Studies; Co-Ed., Mankind Quarterly, 1980–; mem. American Anthropological Assocn; American Institute of Indian Studies; American Oriental Society; Indogermanische Gesellschaft; Linguistics Society of America; MLA; Societas Linguistica Europea; Société de Linguistique de Paris; Hon. Mem., Belgian Asscn for Celtic Studies. *Publications:* Swahili Language Handbook, 1967; Language Surveys in the Developing Nations (ed. with Sirarpi Ohannessian and Charles Ferguson), 1974; Linguistics and Literary Studies in Honor of Archibald A. Hill (ed. with M. A. Jazayery and Werner Winter), 1976; Language in Tanzania (ed. with C. P. Hill), 1980; Man and the Ultimate: A Symposium (ed.), 1980; The Indo-Europeans in the Fourth and Third Millennia (ed.), 1982; Language, Society and Paleoculture, 1982; Essays on Germanic Religion, 1989; Guide to Language Change (ed.), 1990; Reconstructing Languages and Cultures (ed.), 1992; Indo-European Religion after Dumézil (co-ed.), 1996; Festschrift J. Puhvel (co-ed.), 1997. Contributions: scholarly books and professional journals. *Honours:* Fulbright-Hays Scholar, University of Kiel, 1968; First Sociolinguistic Prize, University of Umeå, Sweden, 1988. *Address:* 2701 Rock Terrace Drive, Austin, TX 78704, USA.

POLONSKY, Antony Barry, BA, MA, DPhil; South African academic and writer; b. 23 Sept. 1940, Johannesburg. *Education:* University of the Witwatersrand, University of Oxford. *Career:* Lecturer in East European History, University of Glasgow, 1968–70; Lecturer in International History, LSE, 1970–, University of London, 1981–. *Publications:* Politics in Independent Poland, 1972; The Little Dictator, 1975; The Great Powers and the Polish Question, 1976; The Beginnings of Communist Rule in Poland (with B. Druckier), 1978; The History of Poland since 1863 (co-author), 1981; My Brother's Keeper?: Recent Polish Debates on the Holocaust, 1990; Jews in Eastern Poland and the USSR (ed. with Norman Davies), 1991; From Shtetl to Socialism: Studies from Polin, 1994. Contributions: professional journals. *Address:* Brandeis University, 415 South Street, Waltham, MA 02454-9110, USA. *E-mail:* polonsky@brandeis.edu.

PONDER, Patricia (see Maxwell, Patricia Anne)

PONIATOWSKA, Elena; Mexican writer and journalist; b. 19 May 1932, Paris, France. *Career:* mem. exec. bd, Int. Center for Writing and Translation, Univ. of California at Irvine. *Publications include:* Hasta no verte Jesús mío 1969, Ay vida, no me mereces de noche vienes 1974, Quendo Diego te Abreza Quiela 1978, Fuerte es el silencio 1982, Lilus Kikus 1982, Domingo siete 1983, Dear Diego 1986, Nada, nadie: Las voces del temblor 1988, Compañeros de México: Women Photograph Women 1990, Todo México 1990, Frida Kahlo: The Camera Seduced 1992, Luz y luna, las lunitas 1996, Tinisima 1996, Guerrero vieja 1997, Todo empezó el domingo 1998, Octavio Paz, las palabras del árbol 1998, Paseo de la Reforma 1998, El Niño: Children of the Streets, Mexico City 1999, La casa en Mango Street 1999, Cuentos Méxicanos 1999, La noche de Tlatelolco 1999, Las soldaderas 2000, La piel del cielo 2001, Here's To You Jesusa 2001, Cartas de Alvaro Mutis a Elena Poniatowska 2002, Tlapaleria 2003. *Honours:* Nat. Mexican Award for Journalism 1979. *Address:* International Center for Writing and Translation, School of Humanities, 172 Humanities Instruction Building, University of California, Irvine, CA 92697-3380, USA.

PONOMAREVA, Ksenya Yuryevna; Russian journalist; b. 19 Sept. 1961, Moscow; m.; one s. one d. *Education:* Moscow State Univ. *Career:* schoolteacher 1984–86, teacher of Slavic languages Diplomatic Acad. 1986–88; on staff Kommersant Publrs 1988–95, Deputy Ed. Kommersaut Daily 1992–93; Ed.-in-Chief Revisor (magazine) 1993–95; First Deputy Dir Information and Political Broadcasting Russian Public TV 1995–96; concurrently gen. producer information programmes 1996–97; mem. Bd of Dirs Russian Public TV 1996–, Dir-Gen. 1997–98, resigned in protest against political activity of broadcaster S. Dorenko; Deputy Head of election campaign of Vladimir Putin. *Address:* Akademika Koroleva str. 12, 127000 Moscow, Russia (office). *Telephone:* (495) 217-98-38 (office); (495) 215-18-95 (office).

POOLE, Josephine (see Helyar, Jane Penelope Josephine)

POOLE, Julian (see May, Stephen James)

POOLE, Margaret (Peggy) Barbara, (Terry Roche, Margaret Thornton); British broadcaster, poet and writer; b. 8 March 1925, Petham, Kent, England; m. Reginald Poole 1949 (died 1994); three d. *Education:* Benenden School. *Career:* co-organizer Jabberwocky 1968–86; Producer-Presenter First Heard poetry programme, BBC Radio Merseyside 1976–88; Poetry Consultant, BBC Network Northwest 1988–96; contributor, Writers' News; tutor, Writers' News Home Study Poetry Course; adjudicator, Writers' News Competitions, Southport Open Poetry Competition 2004; mem. Poetry Soc., Soc. of Women Writers and Journalists. *Recordings include:* album: Polishing Pans 2003. *Publications:* Never a Put-up Job 1970, Cherry Stones and Other Poems 1983, No Wilderness in Them 1984, Midnight Walk 1986, Hesitations 1990, Trusting the Rainbow 1994, From the Tide's Edge 1999, Polishing Pans 2001, Selected Poems 2003; editor (anthologies): Windfall (co-ed.) 1994, Poet's England: Cumbria 1995, Marigolds Grow Wild on Platforms 1996, Perceptions 2000; contrib. to various anthologies, children's anthologies, other publs. *Honours:* first prize Waltham Forest Competition 1987, winner Lancaster Litfest 1987, 1991, 2002, first prize Southport Open 1989, winner LACE Competition 1992, winner Sandburg-Livesey Award 1999. *Address:* 36 Hilbre Court, West Kirby, Wirral, Merseyside CH48 3JU, England (home). *Telephone:* (151) 625-8957. *E-mail:* peggypoole@hilbrecourt.fsnet.co.uk.

POOLE, Richard Arthur, MA; British novelist, poet, translator and literary critic; b. 1 Jan. 1945, Yorks., England; m. Sandra Pauline Smart 1970; one s. *Education:* Univ. Coll. of N Wales. *Career:* Tutor in English Literature, Coleg Harlech 1970–2001; Ed. Poetry Wales, 1992–96; mem. Welsh Acad. *Publications:* Goings and Other Poems 1978, Words Before Midnight 1981, Richard Hughes, Novelist (literary biog.) 1987, Natural Histories 1989, Autobiographies and Explorations 1994, That Fool July 2003, Jewel and Thorn (novel) 2005, The Brass Key (novel) 2006; contrib. to many reviews and journals. *Honours:* Fellow, Welsh Acad. *Website:* www.richardpoole.net.

POPE, Pamela Mary Alison; British writer; b. 26 April 1931, Lowestoft, Suffolk, England; m. Ronald Pope 1954; two d. *Career:* mem. Romantic Novelists Asscn; Society of Women Writers and Journalists. *Publications:* The Magnolia Seige, 1982; The Candleberry Tree, 1982; Eden's Law, 1983; The Wind in the East, 1989; The Rich Pass By, 1990; Neither Angels Nor Demons, 1992; A Collar of Jewels, 1994. Contributions: Good Housekeeping; Woman; Woman's Realm; Vanity Fair; True; Loving; Hampshire Magazine; Hampshire Life; London Evening News.

POPESCU, Dumitru Radu; Romanian writer; b. 19 Aug. 1935, Păusa Village, Bihor Co. *Education:* Colls of Medicine and Philology, Cluj. *Career:* reporter, literary magazine Steaua 1956–69; Ed.-in-Chief literary magazine Tribuna 1969–82, Contemporanul 1982; Alt. mem. Cen. Cttee Romanian CP 1968–79, mem. 1979–90; Chair. Romanian Writers' Union 1980–90; Corresp. mem. Romanian Acad. 1997–; in custody Jan. 1990. *Publications:* collections of short stories: Fuga (Flight) 1958, Fata de la miazăzi (A Girl from the South) 1964, Somnul pământului (The Earth's Sleep) 1965, Dor (Longing) 1966, Umbrela de soare (The Parasol) 1967, Prea mic pentru un război așa de mare (Too Little for Such a Big War) 1969, Duios Anastasia trecea (Tenderly Anastasia Passed) 1967, Leul albastru (The Blue Lion) 1981, The Ice Bridge 1980, the Lame Hare 1981, God in the Kitchen 1994, Truman Capote and Nicolae 1995; novels: Zilele săptămînii (Weekdays) 1959, Vara oltenilor (The Oltenians' Summer) 1964, F 1964, Vînătoarea regală (Royal Hunt) 1973, O bere pentru calul meu (A Beer for My Horse) 1974, Ploile de dincolo de vreme (Rains beyond Time) 1976, Împăratul norilor (Emperor of the Clouds) 1976; plays: Vara imposibilei iubiri (The Summer of Impossible Love) 1966, Vis (Dream) 1968, Acești îngeri triști (Those Sad Angels) 1969, Pisica în noaptea Anului nou (Cat on the New Year's Eve) 1970, Pasărea Shakespeare (The Shakespeare Bird) 1973, Rezervația de pelicani (The Pelican Reservation) 1983, Iepurele șchiop (The Lame Rabbit) 1980, Orasul îngerilor (The Angel's City) 1985, Powder Mill 1989, The Bride with False Eyelashes 1994, Love is like a Scab 1995; poems: Ciinele de fosfor (The Phosphorus Dog) 1981; essays: Virgule (Commas) 1978, Galaxy 1994, Ophelia's Complex 1998. *Honours:* Prize of the Writers' Union 1964, 1969, 1974, 1977, 1980, Prize of the Romanian Acad. 1970, Grand Prize for Balkan Writers 1998, Writers' Union Prize 1994, Writers' Asscn of Bucharest Prize 1997, Grand Prize Camil Petrescu 1994. *Address:* c/o Romania Academy, 125 Calea Victoriei, sector 1, 71102 Bucharest, Romania. *Telephone:* (21) 2128640. *Fax:* (21) 2116608. *E-mail:* esimion@acad.ro.

PORAD, Francine Joy, BFA; American poet and painter; b. 3 Sept. 1929, Seattle, WA; m. Bernard L. Porad 1949, three s. three d. *Education:* University of Washington. *Career:* Ed., Brussels Sprout haiku journal, 1988–95; Red Moon Anthologies, 1996; mem. Asscn of International Renku; Haiku Society of America, pres., 1993–95; National League of American Pen Women. *Publications:* many poetry books, including: Pen and Inklings, 1986; After Autumn Rain, 1987; Free of Clouds, 1989; Round Renga Round, 1990; A Mural of Leaves, 1991; Joy is My Middle Name, 1993; Waterways, 1995; Extended Wings, 1996; Fog Lifting, 1997; Let's Count the Trees (edited by Le Roy Gorman), 1998; Cur*rent, Linked Haiku, 1998; Other Rens, 2000; The

Perfect Worry-stone, 2000; Other Rens, Book 2 plus Book 3, 2000; Trio of Wrens, 2000; To Find the Words (anthology, co-ed.). Contributions: Haiku journals world-wide. *Honours:* Cicada Chapbook Award, 1990; International Tanka Awards, 1991, 1992, 1993; First Prize, Poetry Society of Japan International Tanka Competition, 1993; Haiku Society of America Merit Book Awards, 1994, 2000; Haiku Oregon Pen Women Award, 1995. *Address:* 6944 SE 33rd, Mercer Island, WA 98040, USA. *E-mail:* poradf@aol.com.

PORRITT, Sir Jonathon Espie, 2nd Bt, cr. 1963, CBE, BA; British environmentalist; *Founding Director, Forum for the Future*; b. 6 July 1950, London; s. of the late Lord Porritt; m. Sarah Staniforth 1986; two d. *Education:* Eton Coll. and Magdalen Coll. Oxford. *Career:* school teacher, London 1975–84; Head of English, Burlington Danes School, London 1980–84; Chair. Ecology Party 1979–80, 1982–84; parl. cand. at gen. elections in 1979, 1983; Dir Friends of the Earth 1984–90; Founder and Dir Forum for the Future 1996–; Chair. UK Sustainable Devt Comm. 2000–; mem. Bd South West Regional Devt Agency 2000; Co-Dir Prince of Wales Business and Environment Programme. *Publications:* Seeing Green: The Politics of Ecology 1984, Friends of the Earth Handbook 1987, The Coming of the Greens 1988, Save the Earth (ed.) 1990, Where on Earth are We Going? 1991, Captain Eco (for children) 1991, Playing Safe: Science and the Environment 2000, Capitalism as if the World Matters 2005. *Address:* 9 Imperial Square, Cheltenham, Glos., GL50 IQB; 9 Lypiatt Terrace, Cheltenham, Glos., GL50 2SX, England (home). *Telephone:* (1242) 262737 (office). *Fax:* (1242) 262757 (office). *E-mail:* a.paintin@forumforthefuture.org.uk (office).

PORTER, Andrew Brian, MA; British music critic; *Music Critic, Times Literary Supplement*; b. 26 Aug. 1928, Cape Town, South Africa; s. of Andrew Ferdinand and Vera Sybil Porter (née Bloxham). *Education:* Diocesan Coll., Rondebosch, Cape Town, Univ. Coll., Oxford. *Career:* music critic, The Financial Times 1950–74; Ed. The Musical Times 1960–67; music critic, The New Yorker 1972–92, The Observer 1992–97, Times Literary Supplement 1997–; Visiting Fellow, All Souls Coll., Oxford 1973–74; Bloch Prof., Univ. of Calif., Berkeley 1981; Corresp. mem. American Musicological Soc. 1993. *Opera:* librettos for The Tempest 1985, The Song of Majnun 1991 and numerous trans. *Publications:* A Musical Season 1974, Wagner's Ring 1976, Music of Three Seasons 1974–77 1978, Music of Three More Seasons 1977–80 1981, Musical Events: A Chronicle 1980–1983 1987, Musical Events: A Chronicle 1983–1986 1989, Verdi's Macbeth: A Sourcebook (ed. with David Rosen) 1984, A Music Critic Remembers 2000; contrib. to Music and Letters, Musical Quarterly, Musical Times, Proceedings of the Royal Musical Association, Atti del Congresso Internazionale di Studi Verdiani. *Honours:* ASCAP–Deems Taylor Award 1975, 1978, 1982, Nat. Music Theater Award 1988, Words on Music: Essays in Honour of Andrew Porter on the Occasion of His 75th Birthday (co-ed. by David Rosen and Claire Brook) 2003. *Address:* 9 Pembroke Walk, London, W8 6PQ, England.

PORTER, Anna Maria, OC, MA; Canadian (b. Hungarian) publishing executive; b. Budapest; d. of Steven and Maria (née Racz) Szigethy; m. Julian Porter 1971; two d. *Education:* Univ. of Canterbury, Christchurch, NZ. *Career:* mem. staff Cassell and Co., UK, Collier Macmillan Ltd, London 1967–69, Toronto 1970; Pres. and Publr McClelland-Bantam Ltd (Seal Books) until 1982, Pres. 1987–92; Publr, CEO and Dir Key Porter Books Ltd 1982–2005; Chair. Doubleday Canada 1986–91; Dir Key Publrs, Alliance Communications Ltd, Young Naturalists Foundation, Imperial Life Assurance Co., People's Jewelry Ltd, Conf. Bd of Canada, WWF—World Wide Fund for Nature, Canada; mem. Advisory Bd Schulich School of Business; mem. Soulpepper Theatre Company Advisory Council, Interval House Capital Campaign Cttee; mem. Bd of Govs York Univ. 2004–; mem. Asscn of Canadian Publrs, Asscn for Export of Canadian Books, UNICEF (advisory), Information Highway Council. *Publications:* Hidden Agenda 1985, Mortal Sins 1987, The Bookfair Murders 1997. *Honours:* Dr hc (Ryerson Univ.) (St. Mary's Univ.), (Univ. of Toronto), (Law Soc. of Upper Canada). *Address:* c/o York University, 4700 Keele Street, Toronto, ON M3J 1P3, Canada (office). *Website:* www .yorku.ca (office).

PORTER, Bernard John, MA, PhD; British historian and writer; *Professor Emeritus of Modern History, University of Newcastle*; b. 5 Feb. 1941, Essex, England; m. Deirdre O'Hara 1972 (divorced 1996); one s. two d.; partner, Kajsa Ohrlander. *Education:* Corpus Christi Coll., Cambridge. *Career:* Fellow, Corpus Christi Coll., Cambridge 1966–68; Lecturer, Univ. of Hull 1968–78, Sr Lecturer 1978–87, Reader 1987–92; Prof. of Modern History, Univ. of Newcastle 1992–2002, Prof. Emer. 2002–; Visiting Prof., Yale Univ., USA 1999–2000, Univ. of Sydney, Australia 2006; part-time Prof., Univ. of Stockholm, Sweden 2007. *Publications:* Critics of Empire: British Radical Attitudes to Colonialism in Africa 1896–1914 1968, The Lion's Share: A Short History of British Imperialism 1850–1970 1976, The Refugee Question in Mid-Victorian Politics 1979, Britain, Europe and the World 1850–1982: Delusions of Grandeur 1983, The Origins of the Vigilant State: The London Metropolitan Police Special Branch Before the First World War 1987, Plots and Paranoia: A History of Political Espionage in Britain 1790–1988 1989, Britannia's Burden: The Political Development of Britain 1857–1990 1994, The Absent-Minded Imperialists 2004, Empire and Superempire 2006; contrib. to professional journals. *Honours:* Hon. Prof., Univ. of Sydney 2007; Morris D. Forkosch Prize, American Historical Asscn 2005. *Address:* 29 Salisbury Street, Hull, HU5 3HA, England (home); Kantarellvägen 26, 122–63 Enskede, Sweden (home). *Telephone:* (1482) 494415 (England) (home); (8) 649-4379 (Sweden) (home). *E-mail:* bernard.porter@kajsa.karoo.co.uk (home).

PORTER, Brian Ernest, BSc, PhD, FRHistS; British academic and writer; b. 5 Feb. 1928, Seasalter, Kent, England. *Education:* LSE. *Career:* Lecturer in Political Science, University of Khartoum, 1963–65; Lecturer, 1965–71, Senior Lecturer in International Politics, 1971–85, University College, Aberystwyth; Acting Vice-Counsel, Muscat, 1967; Hon. Lecturer in International Relations, University of Kent, Canterbury, 1984–; mem. Royal Institute of International Affairs. *Publications:* Britain and the Rise of Communist China, 1967; The Aberystwyth Papers: International Politics 1919–1969 (ed.), 1972; The Reason of States (co-author), 1982; Home Fires and Foreign Fields: British Social and Military Experience in the First World War (co-author), 1985; The Condition of States (co-author), 1991; Martin Wight's International Theory: The Three Traditions (co-ed.), 1991. *Honours:* Gladstone Memorial Essay Prize, 1956; Mrs Foster Watson Memorial Prize, 1962–67.

PORTER, Burton Frederick, BA, PhD; American academic and writer; *Professor of Philosophy, Western New England College, Springfield*; b. 22 June 1936, New York, NY; m. 1st Susan Jane Porter 1966 (divorced 1974); one d.; m. 2nd Barbara Taylor Metcalf 1980; one s. one step-d. *Education:* Univ. of Maryland, Univ. of Oxford, England and St Andrews Univ., Scotland. *Career:* Asst Prof., Univ. of Maryland Overseas Division, London 1966–69; Assoc. Prof., King's Coll., Wilkes-Barre, PA 1969–71; Dept Chair and Prof. of Philosophy, Russell Sage Coll., Troy, NY 1971–87; Head Humanities and Communications Dept, Drexel Univ. 1987–91; Dean of Arts and Sciences 1991–99, Prof. of Philosophy 1999–, Western New England Coll., Springfield, MA; mem. American Philosophical Asscn. *Publications:* Deity and Morality 1968, Philosophy: A Literary and Conceptual Approach 1974, Personal Philosophy: Perspectives on Living 1976, The Good Life: Alternatives in Ethics 1980, Reasons for Living: A Basic Ethics 1988, Religion and Reason 1993, The Voice of Reason 2001, Philosophy Through Fiction and Film 2003, The Head and the Heart 2006; contrib. to professional journals. *Honours:* Outstanding Educator of America 1973. *Address:* c/o Department of Communications and Humanities, Western New England College, Springfield, MA 01119 (office); 72 Belchertown Road, Amherst, MA 01002, USA (home). *Telephone:* (413) 782-1760 (office); (413) 256-4524 (home). *E-mail:* bporter@ wnec.edu (office); bfporter@rcn.com (home).

PORTER, Joshua Roy; British theologian and writer; b. 1921, England. *Career:* Fellow, Chaplain and Tutor, Oriel Coll., Oxford and Univ. Lecturer in Theology, Univ. of Oxford 1949–62; Canon and Prebendary of Wightring, Chichester Cathedral and Theological Lecturer 1965–88, mem. Wiccamical Canon and Prebendary of Exceit 1988–2001; Prof. of Theology and Head of Dept, Univ. of Exeter 1962–86, Dean, Faculty of Arts 1968–71; mem. Soc. for Old Testament Study (Pres. 1983), Soc. of Biblical Literature, Folklore Soc. (Pres. 1976–79), Prayer Book Soc. (Vice-Chair. 1987–96). *Publications:* Eight Oxford Poets (with J. Heath-Stubbs and S. Keyes) 1941, Poetry from Oxford in War-Time (with W. Bell) 1944, World in the Heart 1944, Promise and Fulfilment (with F.F. Bruce) 1963, Moses and Monarchy 1963, The Extended Family in the Old Testament 1967, A Source Book of the Bible for Teachers (with R.C. Walton) 1970, Proclamation and Presence (ed. with J.I. Durham) 1970, The Non-Juring Bishops 1973, The Journey to the Other World (with H.R.E. Davidson) 1975, The Book of Leviticus 1976, Animals in Folklore (ed. with W.D.M. Russell) 1978, The Monarchy, the Crown and the Church 1978, Tradition and Interpretation (with G.W. Anderson) 1979, A Basic Introduction to the Old Testament (with R.C. Walton) 1980, Folklore Studies in the Twentieth Century (co-ed.) 1980, Divination and Oracles (with M. Loewe and C. Blacker) 1981, The Folklore of Ghosts (with H.R.E. Davidson) 1981, Israel's Prophetic Tradition (co-author) 1982, Tracts for Our Times (co-author) 1983, The Hero in Tradition and Folklore (with C. Blacker) 1984, Arabia and the Gulf: From Traditional Society to Modern States (with I. Netton) 1986, Schöpfung und Befreiung (co-author) 1989, Synodical Government in the Church of England 1990, Christianity and Conservatism (co-author) 1990, Oil of Gladness 1993, Boundaries and Thresholds (with H.R.E. Davidson) 1993, World Mythology 1993, The Illustrated Guide to the Bible 1995, Jesus Christ: The Jesus of History, the Christ of Faith 1999, The First and Second Prayer Books of Edward VI (ed.) 1999, The Lost Bible 2001, Supernatural Enemies (with H.R.E. Davidson) 2001, The New Illustrated Companion to the Bible 2003, Bell of Chichester (with Paul Foster) 2004. *Address:* 36 Theberton Street, Barnsbury, London, N1 OQX, England (home).

PORTER, Peter Neville Frederick, FRSL; Australian poet, writer and broadcaster; b. 16 Feb. 1929, Brisbane, Qld; s. of William R. Porter and Marion Main; m. 1st Jannice Henry 1961 (died 1974); two d.; m. 2nd Christine Berg 1991. *Education:* Church of England Grammar School Brisbane and Toowoomba Grammar School. *Career:* fmr journalist in Brisbane; came to UK 1951; worked as clerk, bookseller and advertising writer; full-time writer and broadcaster 1968–. *Publications:* Once Bitten, Twice Bitten 1961, Penguin Modern Poets, No. 2 1962, Poems, Ancient and Modern 1964, A Porter Folio 1969, The Last of England 1970, Preaching to the Converted 1972, After Martial (trans.) 1972, Jonah (with A. Boyd) 1973, The Lady and the Unicorn (with A. Boyd) 1975, Living in a Calm Country 1975, New Poetry I (co-ed.) 1975, The Cost of Seriousness 1978, English Subtitles 1981, Collected Poems (Duff Cooper Prize) 1983, Fast Forward 1984, Narcissus (with A. Boyd) 1985, The Automatic Oracle (Whitbread Poetry Award) 1987, Mars (with A. Boyd) 1988, A Porter Selected 1989, Possible Worlds 1989, The Chair of Babel 1992, Millennial Fables 1995, New Writing (ed. with A. S. Byatt) 1997, The Oxford Book of Modern Verse (ed.) 1997, The Shared Heritage: Australian and English Literature 1997, The Oxford Book of Modern Australian Verse (ed.)

1997, Dragons in Their Pleasant Places 1997, Collected Poems 1961–1999 (two vols) 1999, Max is Missing (Forward Poetry Prize 2002) 2001, Saving from the Wreck: Essays on Poetry 2001, Rivers 2002, Afterburner 2004, Eighteen Poems 2007; contrib. to various publications. *Honours:* Hon. DLitt (Melbourne) 1985, (Loughborough) 1987, (Sydney) 1999, (Queensland) 2001, Queen's Gold Medal for Poetry 2002. *Address:* 42 Cleveland Square, London, W2 6DA, England (home). *Telephone:* (20) 7262-4289 (home). *Fax:* (20) 7262-4289 (home). *E-mail:* peter.porter3@btopenworld.com (home).

PORTIS, Charles McColl, BA; American writer; b. 28 Dec. 1933, El Dorado, AR. *Education:* Univ. of Arkansas. *Publications:* fiction: Norwood 1966, True Grit 1968, The Dog of the South 1979, Masters of Atlantis 1985, Gringos 1991. *Address:* 7417 Kingwood, Little Rock, AR 72207, USA.

PORTWAY, Christopher John, TD, FRGS; British travel writer and author; b. 30 Oct. 1923, Halstead, Essex; m. Jaroslava Krupickova 1957; one s. one d. *Education:* Felsted School, Essex. *Publications:* Journey to Dana 1955, The Pregnant Unicorn 1969, All Exits Barred 1971, Corner Seat 1972, Lost Vengeance 1973, Double Circuit 1974, The Tirana Assignment 1974, The Anarchy Pedlars 1976, The Great Railway Adventure 1983, Journey Along the Spine of the Andes 1984, The Great Travelling Adventure 1985, Czechmate 1987, Indian Odyssey 1993, A Kenyan Adventure 1993, Pedal for Your Life 1996, A Good Pair of Legs 1999, The World Commuter 2001, Flat Feet and Full Steam 2004; contrib. to periodicals. *Honours:* Winston Churchill Fellow 1993. *Address:* 22 Tower Road, Brighton, BN2 0GF, England (home). *Telephone:* (1273) 682783 (home). *Fax:* (1273) 682783 (home). *E-mail:* christopher.portway@tesco.net.

POSNER, Gerald, BA, JD; American attorney and writer; b. 20 May 1954, San Francisco, CA; m. Trisha D. Levene 1984. *Education:* University of California, Hastings College of Law. *Career:* mem. National Writers Union; Authors' Guild; PEN. *Publications:* Mengele: The Complete Story, 1986; Warlords of Crime, 1988; Bio-Assassins, 1989; Hitler's Children, 1991; Case Closed, 1993; Citizen Perot, 1996; Killing the Dream, 1998. Contributions: New York Times; New Yorker; Chicago Tribune; US News & World Report; Talk Magazine.

POSTE, George, CBE, PhD, FRS, FRCVS, FRCPath, BVSc; British research scientist, business executive and academic; *Del E. Webb Distinguished Professor of Biology and Director, Biodesign Institute, Arizona State University*; b. 30 April 1944, Polegate, Sussex; s. of the late John H. Poste and of Kathleen B. Poste; m. Linda Suhler 1992; one s. two d. *Education:* Bristol Univ. *Career:* lecturer Royal Post grad. Medical School, Univ. of London 1969–72, Sr. Lecturer 1974; Assoc. Prof. of Experimental Pathology, State Univ. of New York (SUNY) Buffalo 1972–74, Principal Cancer Research Scientist and Prof. of Cell and Molecular Biology 1975–80; Vice-Pres. and Dir of Research Smith Kline & French Labs, Philadelphia, Pa 1980–83, Vice-Pres. Research and Devt Technologies 1983–86, Vice-Pres. Worldwide Research and Preclinical Devt 1987–88, Pres. Research and Devt 1988–89, Exec. Vice-Pres. Research and Devt SmithKline Beecham Pharmaceuticals 1989–91, Pres. Research and Devt 1991–97, Chief Science and Tech. Officer 1997–99; CEO Health Tech. Networks 2000–; partner Care Capital, Princeton 2000–; Research Prof. Univ. of Pa 1981–, Univ. of Tex. Medical Center 1986–; Fleming Fellow Lincoln Coll. Oxford 1995; William Pitt Fellow Pembroke Coll. Cambridge 1996–; Distinguished Visiting, Fellow, Hoover Inst., Stanford Univ. 2000–; Del E. Webb Distinguished Prof. of Biology and Dir Biodesign Inst. Arizona State Univ. 2003–; Chair. (non-exec.) Orchid Biosciences, Princeton NJ; mem. Bd of Dirs Exelixis, Monsanto; mem. Defense Science Bd of US Dept of Defense, Chair. Task Force on Bioterrorism; mem. NAS Working Group on Defense Against Bioweapons; mem. Human Genetics Advisory Cttee 1996–; mem. Bd Govs Center for Molecular Medicine and Genetics, Stanford Univ. 1992–; mem. Alliance for Ageing 1992–97; Jt Ed. Cell Surface Reviews 1976–83, New Horizons in Therapeutics 1984–; mem. Council on Foreign Relations 2004–. *Publications:* numerous reviews and papers in learned journals. *Honours:* Hon. FRCP 1993; Hon. Fellow Univ. Coll. London 1993; Hon. DSc 1987, (Sussex) 1999; Hon. LLD (Bristol) 1995, (Dundee) 1998. *Address:* Biodesign Institute, Arizona State University, PO Box 875001, Tempe, AZ 85287-5001, USA (office). *Telephone:* (480) 727-8662 (office). *Fax:* (480) 965-2765 (office). *E-mail:* george.poste@asu.edu (office). *Website:* www.biodesign.org (office).

POSTER, Jem, MA, PhD; British poet, novelist, academic and fmr archaeologist; *Professor of Creative Writing, University of Aberystwyth*; b. 3 Nov. 1949, Cambridge, England; m.; two c. *Education:* Univs of Cambridge and Nottingham. *Career:* Prof. of Creative Writing, Univ. of Aberystwyth 2003–; mem. Welsh Acad. *Publications:* poetry: Brought to Light 2001; novels: Courting Shadows 2002, Rifling Paradise 2006; criticism: The Thirties Poets 1993. *Address:* Department of English, University of Aberystwyth, Aberystwyth, Ceredigion, SY23 3DY, Wales (office). *Telephone:* (1970) 621578 (office). *E-mail:* jem.poster@aber.ac.uk (office).

POTAPOV, Alexander Serafimovich, CandPhil; Russian journalist; *Editor-in-Chief, Trud newspaper*; b. 6 Feb. 1936, Oktyabry, Kharkov Region, Ukraine; m.; one s. *Education:* Vilnius State Univ., Lithuania. *Career:* contrib. Leninskaya Smena (newspaper) 1958–66; Head of Dept, Deputy Ed.-in-Chief Belgorodskaya Pravda (newspaper) 1966–73; Head of Dept Belgorod Regional Exec. CPSU Cttee 1973–75; Ed. Belgorodskaya Pravda 1975–76; instructor CPSU Cen. Cttee 1976–78, 1981–85; Ed.-in-Chief Trud (Labour) newspaper 1985–; People's Deputy of Russian Fed., mem. Cttee of Supreme Soviet of Russian Fed. on Problems of Glasnost and Human Rights –1993. *Address:* Trud, Nastas'yinsky per. 4, 103792 Moscow, Russia (office). *Telephone:* (495) 299-39-06 (office). *Fax:* (495) 299-47-40 (office). *E-mail:* letter@trud.ru (office). *Website:* www.trud.ru (office).

POTTER, Jeremy Ronald, MA; British writer and publisher; b. 25 April 1922, London, England; m. 1950, one s. one d. *Education:* Queen's College, Oxford. *Publications:* Good King Richard?, 1983; Pretenders, 1986; Independent Television in Britain, Vol. 3: Politics and Control 1968–80, 1989 and Vol. 4: Companies and Programmes 1968–80, 1990; Tennis and Oxford, 1994. Fiction: Hazard Chase, 1964; Death in Office, 1965; Foul Play, 1967; The Dance of Death, 1968; A Trail of Blood, 1970; Going West, 1972; Disgrace and Favour, 1975; Death in the Forest, 1977; The Primrose Hill Murder, 1992; The Mystery of the Campden Wonder, 1995.

POTTS, Robert; British writer. *Education:* Univ. of Oxford. *Career:* fmrly Politics Ed. TLS; Poetry Critic, The Guardian; judge, Geoffrey Faber Memorial Prize 1998; Jt Ed. Poetry Review 2002–05. *Publications:* contrib. to The Times, The Observer, Atlantic Monthly, London Magazine, Literary Review, Scribners' British Writers' Series, BBC Radio London. *Address:* c/o The Guardian, 119 Farringdon Road, London, EC1R 3ER, England. *E-mail:* review@observer.co.uk. *Website:* www.guardian.co.uk.

POULIN, Gabrielle, MA, DLitt; Canadian writer and poet; b. 21 June 1929, St Prosper, QC. *Education:* University of Montréal, University of Sherbrooke. *Career:* Writer-in-Residence, Ottawa Public Library, 1988; mem. Union des écrivaines et des écrivains québécois. *Publications:* Les Miroirs d'un poète: Image et reflets de Paul Éluard 1969, Cogne la caboche 1979, English trans. as All the Way Home 1984, L'age de l'interrogation 1937–52 1980, Un cri trop grand (novel) 1980, Les Mensonges d'Isabelle (novel) 1983, La couronne d'oubli (novel) 1990, Petites fugues pour une saison sèche (poems) 1991, Nocturnes de l'oeil (poems) 1993, Le livre de déraison (novel) 1994, Mon père aussi était horloger (poems) 1996, Qu'est-ce qui passe ici si tard? (novel) 1998, La vie l'écriture (memoir) 2000, Ombres et lueurs (poems) 2003. Contributions: periodicals. *Honours:* Swiss Embassy Prize 1967, 11 Arts Council of Canada Grants 1968–83, 1985, Champlain Literary Prize 1979, Carleton Literary Prize, Ottawa 1983, Alliance Française Literary Prize 1984, Salon du Livre de Toronto Literary Prize 1994. *Address:* 1997 Avenue Quincy, Ottawa, ON K1J 6B4, Canada. *E-mail:* gabriellepoilin@rogers.com (home).

POULIN, Jacques; Canadian writer; b. 23 Sept. 1937, Saint-Gédéon-de-Beauce, QC. *Education:* Université Laval. *Career:* mem. Union des écrivaines et des écrivains québécois. *Publications:* Mon cheval pour un royaume (trans. as My Horse for a Kingdom) 1967, Jimmy 1969, La Coeur de la baleine bleue (trans. as The Heart of the Blue Whale) 1970, Faites de beaux rêves 1974, Les Grandes marées (trans. as Spring Tides) 1978, La Tournée d'automne 1993. *Honours:* Prix de La Presse 1974, Gov.-Gen.'s Literary Award 1978, Prix Athanase-David 1995.

POURNELLE, Jerry Eugene, (Wade Curtis), BS, MS, PhD; American writer and academic; b. 7 Aug. 1933, Shreveport, LA. *Education:* University of Iowa, University of Washington. *Career:* mem. Operations Research Society of America, fellow; American Asscn for the Advancement of Science, fellow; SFWA, pres., 1974. *Publications:* Red Heroin (as Wade Curtis), 1969; The Strategy of Technology: Winning the Decisive War (with Stefan Possony), 1970; Red Dragon (as Wade Curtis), 1971; A Spaceship for the King, 1973; Escape From the Planet of the Apes (novelization of screenplay), 1973; The Mote in God's Eye (with Larry Niven), 1974; 20/20 Vision (ed.), 1974; Birth of Fire, 1976; Inferno (with Larry Niven), 1976; West of Honor, 1976; High Justice (short stories), 1977; The Mercenary, 1977; Lucifer's Hammer (with Larry Niven), 1977; Exiles to Glory, 1978; Black Holes (ed.), 1979; A Step Further Out (non-fiction), 1980; Janisseries, 1980; Oath of Fealty (with Larry Niven), 1981; Clan and Crown (with Roland Green), 1982; There Will Be War (co-ed.), 1983; Mutual Assured Survival (with Dean Ing), 1984; Men of War (co-ed.), 1984; Blood and Iron (co-ed.), 1984; Day of the Tyrant (co-ed.), 1985; Footfall (with Larry Niven), 1985; Warriors (co-ed.), 1986; Imperial Stars: The Stars at War, Republic and Empire (co-ed.), 2 vols, 1986–87; Guns of Darkness (co-ed.), 1987; Storms of Victory (with Roland Green), 1987; Legacy of Hereot (with Larry Niven), 1987; Prince of Mercenaries, 1989; The Gripping Hand (with Larry Niven), 1993.

POWELL, Neil Ashton, BA, MPhil; British writer and poet; b. 11 Feb. 1948, London, England; s. of Ian Otho James Powell and Dulcie Delia Powell (née Lloyd). *Education:* Sevenoaks School, Univ. of Warwick. *Career:* teacher Kimbolton School 1971–74, St Christopher School, Letchworth 1974–78, Head of English 1978–86; bookshop owner 1986–90; writer and editor 1990–; mem. Soc. of Authors. *Publications:* Suffolk Poems 1975, At the Edge 1977, Carpenters of Light 1979, Out of Time 1979, A Season of Calm Weather 1982, Selected Poems of Fulke Greville (ed.) 1990, True Colours: New and Selected Poems 1991, Unreal City 1992, The Stones on Thorpeness Beach 1994, Roy Fuller: Writer and Society 1995, Gay Love Poetry (ed.) 1997, The Language of Jazz 1997, Selected Poems 1998, George Crabbe: An English Life 2004, A Halfway House 2004; contrib. to anthologies, newspapers, reviews and journals. *Honours:* Eric Gregory Award 1969. *Literary Agent:* c/o Carcanet Press, Fourth Floor, Alliance House, 30 Cross Street, Manchester M2 7AQ, England. *Telephone:* (161) 834-8730. *Address:* 32 Bridge Street, Bungay, Suffolk NR35 1HD, England (home). *Telephone:* (1986) 893248 (home).

POWELL, Padgett, BA, MA; American academic and writer; b. 25 April 1952, Gainesville, FL; m. Sidney Wade 1984, two d. *Education:* Coll. of Charleston, Univ. of Houston. *Career:* Prof. of Creative Writing, Univ. of Florida, Gainesville 1984–; mem. PEN,Authors' Guild, Writers' Guild of America (East). *Publications:* Edisto (novel) 1984, A Woman Named Drown (novel) 1987, Typical (short stories) 1991, Edisto Revisited (novel) 1996, Aliens of Affection (short stories) 1998, Mrs Hollingsworth's Men (novel) 2000; contrib. to periodicals, including Harper's Magazine, New Yorker, Paris Review, Travel and Leisure, Esquire. *Honours:* Time Magazine Best Book Citation 1984, Whiting Foundation Writers' Award 1986, American Acad. and Inst. of Arts and Letters Rome Fellowship in Literature 1987. *Address:* Turlington Hall 4211E, Department of English, University of Florida, Gainesville, FL 32611, USA (office). *E-mail:* powell@english.ufl.edu (office).

POWELL, Talmage, (Jack McCready); American writer; b. 4 Oct. 1920, Hendersonville, NC. *Education:* University of North Carolina. *Publications:* Cabins & Castles, 1981; Western Ghosts, 1990; New England Ghosts, 1990; Murder for Halloween, 1994; Encyclopedia Mysteriosa, 1994; Wild Game, 1994; Six-Gun Ladies: Stories of Women on the American Western Frontier, 1996. Contributions: anthologies, films, and television.

POWER, Susan, JD, MFA; American writer; b. 12 Oct. 1961, Chicago, IL. *Education:* Radcliffe College, Harvard University Law School, University of Iowa Writers' Workshop. *Career:* mem. Standing Rock Sioux Reservation. *Publications:* Fiction: The Grass Dancer, 1994; Strong Heart Society, 1997. Contributions: journals including: Atlantic Monthly; Paris Review; Ploughshares; Story; Short stories to anthologies. *Honours:* Award for First Fiction, Ernest Hemingway Foundation, 1995; Iowa Arts Fellowship; James Michener Fellowship; Bunting Institute Fellowship; Alfred Hodder Fellowship; Other fellowships.

POWERS, M. L. (see Tubb, Edwin Charles)

POWERS, Richard; American writer; b. 1957; m. Jane Powers. *Career:* teacher of creative writing, Univ. of Illinois. *Publications:* Three Farmers on Their Way to a Dance (Richard and Hinda Rosenthal Foundation Award, American Acad. and Inst. of Arts and Letters, PEN/Hemingway Foundation special citation) 1985, Prisoner's Dilemma 1988, The Gold Bug Variations 1991, Operation Wandering Soul 1993, Galatea 2.2 1995, Gain (American Soc. of Historians James Fenimore Cooper Prize 1999) 1998, Plowing the Dark (American Acad. and Inst. of Arts and Letters Vursell Prize) 2000, The Time of Our Singing (WHSmith Literary Award 2004) 2003, The Echo Maker (Nat. Book Award for Fiction) 2006; contrib. to journals and magazines. *Honours:* John D. and Catherine T. MacArthur Foundation grant 1989. *Literary Agent:* Gunther Stuhlmann, Box 276, Beckett, MA 01223, USA.

POWERS, Thomas Moore, BA; American writer and editor; b. 12 Dec. 1940, New York, NY; m. Candace Molloy 1965; three d. *Education:* Yale University. *Career:* reporter, Rome Daily American, 1965–67, United Press International, 1967–70; Ed.-Founding Partner, Steerforth Press, South Royalton, Vermont, 1993–; mem. Council on Foreign Relations; PEN American Center. *Publications:* Diana: The Making of a Terrorist, 1971; The War at Home, 1973; The Man Who Kept the Secrets: Richard Helms and the CIA, 1979; Thinking About the Next War, 1982; Total War: What It Is, How It Got That Way, 1988; Heisenberg's War: The Secret History of the German Bomb, 1993; The Confirmation, 2000; Intelligence Wars: American Secret History from Hitler to Al Qaeda, 2003. Contributions: New York Review of Books; London Review of Books. *Honours:* Pulitzer Prize for National Reporting, 1971. *Address:* 106 Chelsea Street, South Royalton, VT 05068, USA.

POWNALL, David, BA, FRSL; British author and dramatist; b. 19 May 1938, Liverpool, England; m. 1st Glenys Elsie Jones 1961 (divorced); one s.; m. 2nd Mary Ellen Ray 1981; one s.; m. 3rd Alex Sutton 1993; one s. *Education:* Univ. of Keele. *Career:* Resident Writer, Century Theatre 1970–72; Resident Playwright, Duke's Playhouse, Lancaster 1972–75; Founder-Resident Writer, Paines Plough Theatre, London 1975–80. *Publications:* fiction: The Raining Tree War 1974, African Horse 1975, The Dream of Chief Crazy Horse 1975, God Perkins 1977, Light on a Honeycomb 1978, Beloved Latitudes 1981, The White Cutter 1989, The Gardener 1990, Stagg and His Mother 1991, The Sphinx and the Sybarites 1994, The Catalogue of Men; plays: more than 25 stage plays 1969–98, including Master Class, Beef, An Audience Called Edouard; radio and TV plays. *Honours:* Hon. DLitt (Keele) 2001; Edinburgh Festival Fringe Awards 1976, 1977, Giles Cooper Awards 1981, 1985, John Whiting Award, Arts Council of GB 1982, Sony Gold and Silver Awards for Original Radio Drama 1994, 1995, 1996. *Literary Agent:* Johnson & Alcock Ltd, Clerkenwell House, 45–47 Clerkenwell Green, London, EC1R 0HT, England.

POYER, Joseph (Joe) John, BA; American writer, editor and publisher; b. 30 Nov. 1939, Battle Creek, MI; m. Bonnie Prichard 1987. *Education:* Michigan State Univ. *Career:* Publisher and Ed., Safe and Secure Living, International Military Review, International Naval Review 1990–93. *Publications:* fiction: North Cape 1968, Balkan Assignment 1971, Chinese Agenda 1972, Shooting of the Green 1973, The Contract 1978, Tunnel War 1979, Vengeance 10 1980, Devoted Friends 1982, Time of War (two vols) 1983, 1985; non-fiction: The 45–70 Springfield 1991, US Winchester Trench and Riot Guns 1993, Pocket Guide 45–70 Springfield 1994, The M1 Garand, 1936 to 1957 1995, The SKS Carbine 1997, The M14-type Rifles 1997, The SAFN Battle Rifle 1998, The Swedish Mauser Rifles 1999, The M16/AR15 Rifles 2000, The Model 1903 Springfield Rifle and its Variations 2001, The American Krag Rifle and Carbine 2002, Swiss Magazine Loading Rifles 1869–1958 2003, The AK-47 and AK-74 Rifles and Their Variations 2004; contrib. to journals. *Address:* PO Box 1027, Tustin, CA 92681, USA.

PRABHAKAR, Vishnu; Indian writer and poet; b. 1912. *Career:* writes in Hindi. *Publications:* Ardhanarishwara (novel, trans. as The Androgynous God or Shiva) (Sahitya Akademi Award), Awara Masiha (biog., trans. as The Great Vagabond) 1974; several short stories, novels, plays and travelogues. *Honours:* Parampara Award for contrib. to Hindi literature 2004, Padma Bhushan Award 2004. *Address:* c/o BR Publishing Corporation, 1 Ansari Road, Darya Ganj, New Delhi 2, India.

PRABHJOT KAUR; Indian poet and politician; b. (Matia), 6 July 1924, Langaryal; d. of Nidhan Singh and Rajinder Kaur; m. Brig. Narenderpal Singh 1948; two d. *Education:* Khalsa Coll. for Women, Lahore and Punjab Univ. *Career:* first collected poems published 1943 (aged sixteen); represented India at numerous int. literary confs; mem. Legis. Council, Punjab 1966; Ed. Vikendrit; mem. Sahitya Akademi (Nat. Acad. of Letters), Exec. Bd 1978; mem. Cen. Comm. for UNESCO, Nat. Writers Cttee of India; Fellow Emer., Govt of India. *Television:* Ishak Shara Kee Nata (musical play). *Publications:* 50 books, including: Poems: Supne Sadhran 1949, Do Rang 1951, Pankheru 1956, Lala (in Persian) 1958, Bankapasi 1958, Pabbi 1962, Khari 1967, Plateau (French) 1968, Wad-darshi Sheesha 1972, Madhiantar 1974, Chandra Yug 1978, Dreams Die Young 1979, Shadows and Light (Bulgarian) 1980, Him Hans 1982, Samrup 1982, Ishq Shara Ki Nata 1983, Shadows (English and Danish) 1985, Charam Serma, Men Tapu Mukhatab Han–Manas Man the Gagan Mokla (collected poems in four vols); Short Stories: Kinke 1952, Aman de Na 1956, Zindgi de Kujh Pal 1982, Main Amanat Naheen (Hindi), Kuntith, Casket (English); autobiog.: Jeena vi 9k Ada Hai (two vols). *Honours:* received honours of Sahitya Shiromani 1964 and Padma Shri 1967; title of Rajya Kavi (Poet Laureate) conferred by Punjab Govt 1964, Sahitya Akademi Award 1964, Golden Laurel Leaves, United Poets Int., Philippines 1967, Grand Prix de la Rose de la France 1968, Most Distinguished Order of Poetry, World Poetry Soc. Intercontinental, USA 1974; Woman of the Year, UPLI, Philippines 1975, Sewa Sifti Award 1980, NIF Cultural Award 1982, Josh Kenya Award 1982, Delhi State Award 1983, Safdar Hashmi Award. *Address:* D-203, Defence Colony, New Delhi 110024, India. *Telephone:* 4622756; 4626045.

PRADO, Benjamin; Spanish writer and poet; b. 1961, Madrid. *Publications:* poems: Cobijo contra la tormenta (Hiperión Prize) 1995, Todos nosotros 1998; novels: Raro 1995, Dónde crees que vas y quién te crees que eres 1996, Nunca le des la mano a un pistolero zurdo (trans. as Never Shake Hands with a Left-handed Gunman) 1996, Alguien se acerca 1998, No solo el fuego (trans. as Not Only Fire) (Premio Andalucía de Novela) 1999, La nieve está vacía (trans. as Snow is Silent) 2000, Los nombres de Antígona (biog.) 2001. *Address:* c/o Faber and Faber Ltd, 3 Queen Square, London, WC1N 3AU, England.

PRADO FREITAS, Adélia Luzia; Brazilian poet and writer; b. 13 Dec. 1935, Divinópolis, Minas Gerais; d. of João do Prado Filho and Ana Clotilde Corrêa; m. José Assunção de Freitas; three s. two d. *Education:* Faculty of Philosophy, Science and Letters, Divinópolis. *Career:* teacher of religious education and philosophy in schools and colls 1955–79; full-time writer aged 40; Head of Cultural Division, Municipal Office of Education and Culture, Divinópolis 1983–88. *Publications:* poetry: Bagagem 1976, O coração disparado (Prêmio Jabuti da Câmara Brasileira do Livro) 1978, Terra de Santa Cruz 1981, O pelicano 1987, A faca no peito 1988, Oráculos de maio 1999; prose: Solte os cachorros 1979, Cacos para um vitral 1980, Os componentes da banda 1984, O homem da mão seca 1994, Manuscritos de Felipa 1999, Filandras 2001, Quero Minha Mãe 2005; contrib. to anthologies and journals.

PRALL, Stuart Edward, BA, MA, PhD, FRHistS; American academic and writer; *Professor Emeritus of History, City University of New York;* b. 2 June 1929, Saginaw, MI; m. Naomi Shafer 1958; one s. one d. *Education:* Michigan State Univ., Univ. of Rhode Island, Univ. of Manchester, England and Columbia Univ. *Career:* Queens Coll. and Graduate School and Univ. Center, CUNY 1955–58, 1960–2001; Newark State Coll., NJ 1958–60; Exec. Officer PhD Program in History, Graduate School and Univ. Center, CUNY 1988–94, Prof. Emer. 2001–; mem. North American Conference on British Studies. *Publications:* The Agitation for Law Reform during the Puritan Revolution, 1640–1660 1966, The Puritan Revolution: A Documentary History 1968, The Bloodless Revolution: England, 1688 1972, A History of England 1991, Church and State in Tudor and Stuart England 1993, The Puritan Revolution and the English Civil War 2002; contrib. to The Development of Equity in Tudor England, American Journal of Legal History. *Honours:* Univ. of Manchester Fulbright Scholar 1953–54. *Address:* 7050 Owl's Nest Terrace, Bradenton, FL 34203, USA (home); 27 Wildwood Lane, Bethel, NB E5C 3W1, Canada (home). *Telephone:* (941) 739-0198 (USA) (home); (506) 755-9197 (Canada) (home).

PRANTERA, Amanda; British author; b. 23 April 1942, England. *Publications:* Strange Loop, 1984; The Cabalist, 1985; Conversations with Lord Byron on Perversion, 163 Years After His Lordship's Death, 1987; The Side of the Moon, 1991; Pronto-Zoe, 1992; The Young Italians, 1993; Spoiler, 2003.

PRASHAD, Vijay, PhD; Indian/American writer and journalist; b. Kolkata, India. *Education:* Univ. of Chicago, USA. *Career:* Assoc. Prof. and Dir International Studies Program, Trinity College, Hartford, CT, USA; Ed., Amerasia Journal; mem. Center for Third World Organizing (board mem.);

Forum of Indian Leftists (co-founder). *Publications:* The Karma of Brown Folk, 2000; Untouchable Freedom: A Social History of a Dalit Community, 2000; Everybody was Kung Fu Fighting: Afro-Asian Connections and the Myth of Cultural Purity, 2002; The American Scheme: Three Essays, 2002; War Against the Planet: The Fifth Afghan War, Imperialism and Other Assorted Fundamentalism, 2002; Fat Cats and Running Dogs: The Enron Stage of Capitalism, 2002; Keeping Up with the Dow Joneses: Stocks, Jails, Welfare, 2003. Contributions: Colorlines; Himal South Asia; Frontline; www.truthindia.com; Little India; ZNET. *Address:* c/o Trinity College, Hartford, CT 06106, USA (office). *Telephone:* (870) 297-2518 (office). *E-mail:* vijay.prashad@mail.cc.trincoll.edu.

PRATCHETT, Terence (Terry) David John, OBE; British writer; b. 28 April 1948, Beaconsfield, Bucks.; m. Lyn Marian Purves 1968; one d. *Career:* journalist 1965–80; Press Officer Cen. Electricity Generating Bd 1980–87; Chair. Soc. of Authors 1994–95. *Publications:* Discworld series: The Dark Side of the Sun 1976, Strata 1981, The Colour of Magic 1983, The Light Fantastic 1986, Equal Rites 1987, Mort 1987, Sourcery 1989, Wyrd Sisters 1988, Pyramids (BSFA Award for best novel) 1989, Eric 1989, Guards! Guards! 1989, Moving Pictures 1990, Reaper Man 1991, Witches Abroad 1991, Small Gods 1992, Lords and Ladies 1993, Men at Arms 1993, The Streets of Ankh-Morpork (with Stephen Briggs) 1993, Soul Music 1994, Interesting Times 1994, The Discworld Companion (with Stephen Briggs) 1994, Maskerade 1995, Discworld Map (with Stephen Briggs) 1995, Feet of Clay 1996, Hogfather 1996, The Pratchett Portfolio (with Paul Kidby) 1996, Jingo 1997, The Last Continent 1998, Carpe Jugulum 1998, A Tourist Guide to Lancre (with Stephen Briggs and Paul Kidby) 1998, The Fifth Elephant 1999, Death's Domain (with Paul Kidby) 1999, The Truth 2000, Nanny Ogg's Cookbook (with Stephen Briggs, Tina Hannan and Paul Kidby) 2000, The Last Hero 2001, Thief of Time 2001, Night Watch 2002, The Science of the Discworld I, II, III (with others) 2002, Monstrous Regiment 2003, The Wee Free Men 2003, A Hat Full of Sky 2004, Going Postal 2004, Thud! 2005, Where's My Cow 2005, Wintersmith 2006; other fiction: The Carpet People 1971, The Unadulterated Cat (with Gray Jolliffe) 1989, Truckers 1989, Diggers 1990, Wings 1990, Good Omens: The Nice and Accurate Predictions of Agnes Nutter, Witch (with Neil Gaiman) 1990, Only You Can Save Mankind 1992, Johnny and the Dead 1993, Johnny and the Bomb 1996, The Amazing Maurice and his Educated Rodents (Carnegie Medal) 2001; screenplay: Terry Pratchett's Hogfather (BAFTA Award 2007) 2006; other: short stories. *Honours:* Hon. DLitt (Warwick) 1999. *Literary Agent:* c/o Colin Smythe, PO Box 6, Gerrards Cross, Bucks., SL9 8XA, England. *Telephone:* (1753) 886000. *Website:* www.terrypratchettbooks.com.

PRATLEY, Gerald Arthur, OC; British/Canadian writer and teacher; b. 3 Sept. 1923, London, England; three d. *Education:* Queen's University. *Career:* co-founder and Pres., Toronto Film Society, 1948–55; Film Critic, Commentator and Broadcaster, CBC Network Radio, Toronto, 1948–75; Chair., Toronto and District Film Council, 1952–57; Dir ., Canadian Film Institute, Ottawa, 1958–60; Film Time, CFRB Radio, 1965–70; Dir, Film Programming, Centennial Commission, Ottawa, 1966–67; Dir, Programmer, Little Cinema, Toronto, 1968–69; Chair., International Jury, Canadian Film Awards, 1968–78; Founder, Dir, Ontario Film Institute, 1968–90; University teaching positions, 1968–99; Film Critic, Canada AM, 1970–75; Dir, Stratford International Film Festival, Stratford, Ontario, 1970–76; Programmer, Moderator, International Film Week, Bowling Green State University, Ohio, 1992–99; Ministry of Citizenship, Judge, Ceremonial, 1996–2002; Assoc. Ed., Kinema, University of Waterloo, 1993–; mem. Arts and Letters Club; St Georges Society; Royal Commonwealth Society; Churchill Society; Canadian Motion Picture Pioneers; Writers' Guild of Canada; Toronto Press Club; Acad. of Canadian Cinema and Television. *Publications:* The Cinema of John Frankenheimer, 1970; The Cinema of Otto Preminger, 1972; The Cinema of David Lean, 1973; The Cinema of John Huston, 1975; Torn Sprockets: The Uncertain Projection of the Canadian Film, 1987; The Films of John Frankenheimer, 1998. Contributions: periodicals. *Honours:* Order of Canada, 1984; ACTRA Writers' Guild, The Writers' Block, 'A Friend of Canadian Screenwriters Through the Years', Toronto, 1987; Hon. DLitt, York University, Toronto, 1991; Canada 125th Anniversary Commemorative Medal, 1992; Canadian Film Celebration Achievement Award, Calgary, 1992; Hon. Doctorates of Letters, University of Waterloo, 1993, Bowling Green State University, 1994; Toronto Film Critics' Asscn Award for 'Outstanding Contribution to the Advancement of Cinema', 1998; Canadian Acad. of Cinema and Television, Special Genie Award, 2001. *Address:* 350 Front Street, Apt 606, Belleville, ON K8N 5M5, Canada.

PRAWER, Siegbert Salomon, MA, DLitt, PhD, LittD, FBA; British university teacher and author (retd); b. 15 Feb. 1925, Cologne, Germany; s. of Marcus Prawer and Eleonora Prawer; brother of Ruth Prawer Jhabvala (q.v.); m. Helga Alice Schaefer 1949; one s. two d. (and one s. deceased). *Education:* King Henry VIII School, Coventry, Jesus Coll., Christ's Coll. Cambridge. *Career:* Adelaide Stoll Research Student, Christ's Coll. Cambridge 1947–48; Asst Lecturer, then Lecturer, then Sr Lecturer, Univ. of Birmingham 1948–63; Prof. of German, Westfield Coll., London Univ. 1964–69; Taylor Prof. of German Language and Literature, Oxford 1969–86, Prof. Emer. 1986–; Co-editor, Oxford Germanic Studies 1971–75, Anglica Germanica 1973–79; Fulbright Exchange Scholar, Columbia Univ. 1956; Visiting Prof. City Coll., New York 1956–57, Univ. of Chicago 1963–64, Harvard Univ. 1968, Hamburg Univ. 1969, Univ. of Calif. at Irvine 1975, Otago Univ., NZ 1976, Univ. of Pittsburgh 1977, Australian Nat. Univ., Canberra 1980, Brandeis Univ.

1981–82; Resident Fellow, Knox Coll., Dunedin, NZ 1976; Fellow Queen's Coll. Oxford 1969–86, Supernumerary Fellow 1986–90, Hon. Fellow 1990, Dean of Degrees 1976–93; Pres. British Comparative Literature Asscn 1984–87, Hon. Fellow 1989; Corresp. Fellow German Acad. of Literature 1989; Pres. English Goethe Soc. 1992–95, Vice-Pres. 1995–. *Exhibitions:* drawings on exhbn Queen's Coll. and St Edmund Hall, Oxford and many other insts. *Publications:* German Lyric Poetry 1952, Mörike und seine Leser 1960, Heine's Buch der Lieder: A Critical Study 1960, Heine: The Tragic Satirist 1962, The Penguin Book of Lieder 1964, The Uncanny in Literature (inaugural lecture) 1965, Heine's Shakespeare, a Study in Contexts (inaugural lecture) 1970, Comparative Literary Studies: An Introduction 1973, Karl Marx and World Literature 1976, Caligari's Children: The Film as Tale of Terror 1980, Heine's Jewish Comedy: A Study of His Portraits of Jews and Judaism 1983, Coalsmoke and Englishmen 1984, A. N. Stencl–Poet of Whitechapel 1984, Frankenstein's Island–England and the English in the Writings of Heinrich Heine 1986, Israel at Vanity Fair: Jews and Judaism in the Writings of W. M. Thackeray 1992, Breeches and Metaphysics, Thackeray's German Discourse 1997, W. M. Thackeray's European Sketch Books: A Study of Literary and Graphic Portraiture 2000, The Blue Angel 2002, Werner Herzog's Nosferatu 2004, Between Two Worlds: The Jewish Presence in German and Austrian Film 1910–1933 2005; edited: The Penguin Book of Lieder 1964, Essays in German Language, Culture and Society (with R. H. Thomas and L. W. Forster) 1969, The Romantic Period in Germany 1970, Seventeen Modern German Poets 1971; screenplay: Das Kabinett des Dr Caligari (ed and introduction); numerous articles on German, English and comparative literature. *Honours:* Hon. Dir London Univ. Inst. of Germanic Studies 1967–69, Hon. Fellow 1986; Hon. mem. Modern Languages Asscn of America 1986; Hon. Fellow Jesus Coll. Cambridge 1996–; Hon. DPhil (Cologne) 1985; Hon. DLitt (Birmingham) 1988; Goethe Medal 1973, Gold Medal, German Goethe Soc. 1995; Isaac Deutscher Memorial Prize 1977, Gundolf-Prize of the German Acad. 1986. *Address:* The Queen's College, Oxford, OX1 4AW, England (office). *Telephone:* (1865) 279121 (office); (1865) 557614 (home).

PRENTISS, Charlotte (see Platt, Charles Michael)

PRESCOTT, Casey (see Morris, Janet Ellen)

PRESCOTT, Richard Chambers; American poet and writer; b. 1 April 1952, Houston, Tex.; m. Sarah Elisabeth Grace 1981. *Publications:* The Sage 1975, Moonstar 1975, Neuf Songes (Nine Dreams) 1976, The Carouse of Soma 1977, Lions and Kings 1977, Allah Wake Up 1978, Night Reaper 1979, Dragon Tales 1983, Dragon Dreams 1986, Dragon Prayers 1988, Dragon Songs 1988, Dragon Maker 1989, Dragon Thoughts 1990, Tales of Recognition 1991, Kings and Sages 1991, Dragon Sight: A Cremation Poem 1992, Three Waves 1992, Years of Wonder 1992, Dream Appearances 1992, Remembrance, Recognition and Return 1992, Spare Advice 1992, The Imperishable 1993, The Dark Deitess 1993, Disturbing Delights: Waves of the Great Goddess 1993, The Immortal: Racopa and the Rooms of Light 1993, Hanging Baskets 1993, Writer's Block and Other Gray Matters 1993, The Resurrection of Quantum Joe 1993, The Horse and the Carriage 1993, Kalee Bhava: The Goddess and Her Moods 1995, Because of Atma 1995, The Skills of Kalee 1995, Measuring Sky without Ground 1996, Kalee: The Allayer of Sorrows 1996, The Goddess and the God Man 1996, Living Sakti: Attempting Quick Knowing in Perpetual Perception and Continuous Becoming 1997, The Mirage and the Mirror 1998, Inherent Solutions to Spiritual Obscurations 1999, The Ancient Method 1999, Quantum Kamakala 2000; contrib. of articles and essays to professional publs. *Address:* 8617 188th Street SW, Edmonds, WA 98026, USA.

PRESNYAKOV, Oleg; Russian playwright; b. Sverdlovsk, Siberia. *Career:* taught literary theory and psychology, Ekaterinburg; co-f., Gorky Urals State Univ. youth theatre; writes and produces plays with brother, Vladimir Presnyakov; connected with New Writing Project, Russia. *Publications:* with Vladimir Presnyakov: Set-2, We Shall Overcome 2002, Terrorism 2002, Plenniye Dukhi (Captive Spirits) 2003, Playing the Victim 2003. *Literary Agent:* Judy Daish Associates Ltd, 2 St Charles Place, London, W10 6EG, England. *Telephone:* (20) 8964-8811. *Fax:* (20) 8964-8966.

PRESNYAKOV, Vladimir; Russian playwright; b. Sverdlovsk, Siberia. *Career:* taught literary theory and psychology, Ekaterinburg; co-f., Gorky Urals State Univ. youth theatre; writes and produces plays with brother, Oleg Presnyakov; connected with New Writing Project, Russia. *Publications:* with Oleg Presnyakov: Set-2, We Shall Overcome 2002, Terrorism 2002, Plenniye Dukhi (Captive Spirits) 2003, Playing the Victim 2003. *Literary Agent:* Judy Daish Associates Ltd, 2 St Charles Place, London, W10 6EG, England. *Telephone:* (20) 8964-8811. *Fax:* (20) 8964-8966.

PRESTON, Ivy Alice Kinross; New Zealand writer; b. 11 Nov. 1913, Timaru, Canterbury; m. Percival Edward James Preston 1937, two s. two d. *Career:* mem. South Canterbury Writers Guild; New Zealand Women Writers Society; South Island Writers Asscn; Romance Writers of America; Romantic Novelists Asscn, London. *Publications:* The Silver Stream (autobiog.), 1958; Hospital on the Hill, 1967; Voyage of Destiny, 1974; The House Above the Bay, 1976; Fair Accuser, 1985; Stranger From the Sea, 1987. Other: 40 romance novels. Contributions: many publications.

PRESTON, Paul, CBE, MA, DPhil, FRHistS, FBA; British academic; *Prince of Asturias Professor of Contemporary Spanish History, London School of Economics;* b. 21 July 1946, Liverpool; s. of Charles R. Preston and Alice Hoskisson; m. Gabrielle P. Ashford-Hodges 1983; two s. *Education:* St

Edward's Coll. Liverpool, Oriel Coll. Oxford and Univ. of Reading. *Career:* Research Fellow, Centre for Mediterranean Studies, Rome 1973–74; Lecturer in History, Univ. of Reading 1974–75; Lecturer in Modern History, Queen Mary Coll. London 1975–79, Reader 1979–85, Prof. of History 1985–91; Prof. of Int. History, LSE 1991–94, Prince of Asturias Prof. of Contemporary Spanish History 1994–; regular contrib. to Times Literary Supplement; columnist in ABC, Diario 16 and El País, Madrid. *Publications:* The Coming of the Spanish Civil War 1978, The Triumph of Democracy in Spain 1986, The Spanish Civil War 1986, The Politics of Revenge 1990, Franco: A Biography 1993, Comrades: Portraits from the Spanish Civil War 1999, Doves of War: Four Women of Spain 2003, Juan Carlos: A People's King 2004. *Honours:* Comendador, Orden del Mérito Civil (Spain) 1987, Caballero Gran Cruz de la Orden de Isabel la Católica 2006; Yorkshire Post Book of the Year 1994, Así fue – La Historia rescatada Prize 1998, Premi Internacional Ramon Llull, Catalan Govt 2005, Trias Fargas Non-Fiction Prize 2006, Marcel Proust Chair of European Acad. 2006. *Address:* Department of International History, London School of Economics, Houghton Street, London, WC2A 2AE (office). *Telephone:* (20) 7955-7107 (office). *Fax:* (20) 8482-9865 (home). *E-mail:* p.preston@lse.ac.uk (office). *Website:* www.lse.ac.uk (office).

PRESTON, Peter John, MA; British journalist; b. 23 May 1938, Barrow-upon-Soar, Leicestershire; s. of John Whittle Preston and Kathlyn Preston (née Chell); m. Jean Mary Burrell 1962; two s. two d. *Education:* Loughborough Grammar School and St John's Coll. Oxford. *Career:* editorial trainee, Liverpool Daily Post 1960–63; Political Reporter, The Guardian 1963–64, Educ. Corresp. 1965–66, Diary Ed. 1966–68, Features Ed. 1968–72, Production Ed. 1972–75, Ed. The Guardian 1975–95, Ed.-in-Chief 1995, Ed.-in-Chief The Observer 1995–96, Editorial Dir Guardian Media Group 1996–98; Co-Dir Guardian Foundation 1997–; mem. Scott Trust 1976–; Chair. Int. Press Inst. 1995–97, Asscn of British Eds 1996–99; mem. UNESCO Advisory Group on Press Freedom 2000–04; Gov. British Asscn for Cen. and Eastern Europe 2000–. *Publications:* Dunblane: Reflecting Tragedy 1996, The 51st State 1998, Bess 1999. *Honours:* Hon. DLitt (Loughborough) 1982, (E Anglia), (City Univ.) 1997, (Leicester) 2003; Hon. Fellow (St John's Coll. Oxford) 2003; What the Papers Say Award for Lifetime Achievement 2006. *Address:* The Guardian, 119 Farringdon Road, London, EC1R 3ER, England. *Telephone:* (20) 7278-2332. *Website:* www.guardian.co.uk (office).

PRESTON, Richard McCann, BA, PhD; American writer; b. 5 Aug. 1954, Cambridge, MA; m. 1985. *Education:* Pomona Coll., Princeton Univ. *Career:* Lecturer in English, Princeton Univ. 1983; Visiting Fellow, Princeton Univ. Council of the Humanities 1994–95; mem. Authors' Guild. *Publications:* First Light 1987, American Steel 1991, The Hot Zone 1994, The Cobra Event 1998, The Demon in the Freezer 2003, The Boat of Dreams 2003, The Wild Trees: A Story of Passion and Daring 2007; contrib. to newspapers and magazines. *Honours:* American Inst. of Physics Science Writing Award 1988, Asteroid 3686 named 'Preston' 1989, AAAS Westinghouse Award 1992, MIT McDermott Award 1993. *Address:* c/o Author mail, Random House, 20 Vauxhall Bridge Road, London, SW1V 2SA, England (office). *Website:* www.richardpreston.net.

PREUSS, Paul F., BA; American writer; b. 7 March 1942, Albany, GA; m. 1st Marsha May Pettit 1963, one d.; m. 2nd Karen Reiser 1973; m. 3rd Debra Turner 1993. *Education:* Yale Univ. *Career:* mem. Northern California Science Writers Asscn; SFWA; Bay Area Book Reviewers' Asscn. *Publications:* The Gates of Heaven, 1980; Re-entry, 1981; Broken Symmetries, 1983; Human Error, 1985; Venus Prime series (with Arthur C. Clarke), 1987–91; Starfire, 1988; The Ultimate Dinosaur, 1992; Core, 1993; Secret Passages, 1997. Contributions: books and newspapers; New York Review of Science Fiction.

PRICE, (Alan) Anthony, MA; British writer and journalist; b. 16 Aug. 1928, Herts., England; m. Yvonne Ann Stone 1953; two s. one d. *Education:* The King's School, Canterbury, Merton Coll., Oxford. *Career:* Ed. The Oxford Times 1972–88. *Publications:* The Labyrinth Makers 1970, The Alamut Ambush 1971, Colonel Butler's Wolf 1972, October Men 1973, Other Paths to Glory 1974, Our Man in Camelot 1975, War Game 1976, The '44 Vintage 1978, Tomorrow's Ghost 1979, The Hour of the Donkey 1980, Soldier No More 1981, The Old Vengeful 1982, Gunner Kelly 1983, Sion Crossing 1984, Here Be Monsters 1985, For the Good of the State 1986, A New Kind of War 1987, A Prospect of Vengeance 1988, The Memory Trap 1989, The Eyes of the Fleet 1990. *Honours:* CWA Silver Dagger 1970, Gold Dagger 1974, Swedish Acad. of Detection Prize 1978. *Address:* Wayside Cottage, Horton cum Studley, Oxford, OX33 1AW, England (home). *Telephone:* (1865) 351326 (home).

PRICE, Glanville, BA, MA, DUniv; British academic and writer; *Professor Emeritus, University of Wales Aberystwyth*; b. 16 June 1928, Rhaeadr, Wales; m. Christine Winifred Thurston 1954; three s. one d. *Education:* Univ. of Wales Bangor, Université de Paris, France. *Career:* Prof. of French, Univ. of Stirling 1967–72; Prof. of French, Univ. of Wales Aberystwyth 1972–92, Research Prof. 1992–95, Prof. Emer. 1995–; mem. Modern Humanities Research Asscn (Chair. 1979–90), Philological Soc. *Publications:* The Present Position of Minority Languages in Western Europe 1969, The French Language, Present and Past 1971, The Year's Work in Modern Language Studies (co-ed.) 1972–92, William, Count of Orange: Four Old French Epics (ed.) 1975, Romance Linguistics and the Romance Languages (with Kathryn F. Bach) 1977, The Languages of Britain 1984, Ireland and the Celtic Connection 1987, An Introduction to French Pronunciation 1991, (second edn)

2005, The Celtic Connection (ed.) 1992, Hommages offerts à Maria Manoliu (co-ed. with Coman Lupu) 1994, Encyclopedia of the Languages of Europe (ed.) 1998, Languages in Britain and Ireland 2000, A Comprehensive French Grammar 2003; contrib. to professional journals. *Address:* Department of European Languages, University of Wales, Aberystwyth, Ceredigion, SY23 3DY, Wales (office).

PRICE, (Edward) Reynolds; American academic, writer, poet and dramatist; b. 1 Feb. 1933, Macon, NC. *Education:* AB, Duke University, 1955; BLitt, Merton College, Oxford, 1958. *Career:* Faculty, 1958–61, Asst Prof., 1961–68, Assoc. Prof., 1968–72, Prof., 1972–77, James B. Duke Prof., 1977–, Duke University; Writer-in-Residence, University of North Carolina at Chapel Hill, 1965, University of Kansas, 1967, 1969, 1980, University of North Carolina at Greensboro, 1971; Glasgow Prof., Washington and Lee University, 1971; Faculty, Salzburg Seminar, 1977; mem. American Acad. of Arts and Letters. *Publications:* A Long and Happy Life, 1962; The Names and Faces of Heroes, 1963; A Generous Man, 1966; Love and Work, 1968; Permanent Errors, 1970; Things Themselves, 1972; The Surface of Earth, 1975; Early Dark, 1977; A Palpable God, 1978; The Source of Light, 1981; Vital Provisions, 1982; Private Contentment, 1984; Kate Vaiden, 1986; The Laws of Ice, 1986; A Common Room, 1987; Good Hearts, 1988; Clear Pictures, 1989; The Tongues of Angels, 1990; The Use of Fire, 1990; New Music, 1990; The Foreseeable Future, 1991; Conversations with Reynolds Price, 1991; Blue Calhoun, 1993; Full Moon, 1993; The Collected Stories, 1993; A Whole New Life, 1994; The Promise of Rest, 1995; Three Gospels, 1996; Roxanne Slade, 1998. *Honours:* William Faulkner Foundation Award for Notable First Novel, 1962; Sir Walter Raleigh Awards, 1962, 1976, 1981, 1984, 1986; Guggenheim Fellowship, 1964–65; National Endowment for the Arts Fellowship, 1967–68; National Institute of Arts and Letters Award, 1971; Bellamann Foundation Award, 1972; North Carolina Award, 1977; National Book Critics Circle Award, 1986; Elmer H. Bobst Award, 1988; R. Hunt Parker Award, North Carolina Literary and Historical Society, 1991. *Address:* PO Box 99014, Durham, NC 27708, USA.

PRICE, Richard, PhD; British poet, librarian, editor and writer; *Head of Modern British Collections, British Library*; b. 15 Aug. 1966, Reading, England; m. Jacqueline Canning 1990 (divorced 2005); two d. *Education:* Univ. of Strathclyde, Glasgow. *Career:* Head of Modern British Collections, British Library, London 2003–; mem. Poetry Soc. (Council 1998–2002). *Publications:* poetry: Sense and a Minor Fever 1993, Tube Shelter Perspective 1993, Marks & Sparks 1995, Eftirs/Afters (trans of Apollinaire, with Donny O'Rourke) 1996, Hand Held 1997, Perfume and Petrol Fumes 1999, Renfrewshire in Old Photographs (with Raymond Friel) 2000, Frosted, Melted 2002, Lucky Day 2005; prose: The Fabulous Matter of Fact: The Poetics of Neil M. Gunn 1991, César Vallejo: Translations, Transformations, Tributes (ed. with Stephen Watts) 1998, La Nouvelle alliance: Influences francophones sur la littérature ecossaise (ed. with David Kinloch) 2000, The Star You Steer By: Basil Bunting and 'British' Modernism (ed. with James McGonigal) 2000, A Boy in Summer (short stories) 2002; artists' books: Gifthorse (with Ron King) 1999, The Mechanical Word (with Karen Bleitz) 2005; contrib. to Scotland on Sunday, Poetry Review, PN Review, Object Permanence. *Address:* Modern British Collections, British Library, 96 Euston Road, London, NW1 2DB, England (office). *Website:* www.hydrohotel.net (home).

PRICE, Richard; American writer and screenwriter; b. 12 Oct. 1949, New York, NY. *Screenplays include:* The Wanderers 1979, The Color of Money 1986, New York Stories 1989, Sea of Love 1989, Night and the City 1992, Mad Dog and Glory 1993, Kiss of Death 1995, Clockers 1995, Ransom 1996, Shaft 2000, Freedomland 2004. *Television:* The Wire (series writer) 2002. *Publications:* novels: The Wanderers 1975, Bloodbrothers 1978, The Breaks 1983, Clockers 1992, Freedomland 1998, Samaritan 2003. *Address:* c/o Bloomsbury Publishing PLC, 38 Soho Square, London, W1V 5DF, England. *Website:* www.bloomsbury.com.

PRICE, Roger David, BA, DLitt, FRHistS; British historian and writer; *Professor of Modern History, University of Wales, Aberystwyth*; b. 7 Jan. 1944, Port Talbot, S Wales; s. of Godfrey Price and Martha Price; m. Heather Price; one s. three d. *Education:* Univ. of Wales, Univ. Coll. of Swansea. *Career:* Lecturer, Univ. of East Anglia 1968–82, Sr Lecturer 1982–83, Reader in Social History 1984–91, Prof. of European History 1991–94; Prof. of Modern History, Univ. of Wales, Aberystwyth 1993–. *Publications:* The French Second Republic: A Social History 1972, The Economic Modernization of France 1975, Revolution and Reaction: 1848 and the Second French Republic (ed. and contrib.) 1975, 1848 in France 1975, An Economic History of Modern France 1981, The Modernization of Rural France: Communications Networks and Agricultural Market Structures in 19th Century France 1983, A Social History of 19th Century France 1987, The Revolutions of 1848 1989, A Concise History of France 1993, 2005, Documents on the French Revolution of 1848 1996, Napoleon III and the French Second Empire 1997, The French Second Empire: An Anatomy of Political Power 2001, People and Politics in France 1848–1870 2004; contrib. to numerous magazines and journals. *Address:* Department of History and Welsh History, University of Wales, Aberystwyth, Ceredigion, SY23 3DY, Wales (office). *Telephone:* (1970) 627212 (office). *E-mail:* rdp@aber.ac.uk (office).

PRICE, Stanley, MA; British writer and dramatist; b. 12 Aug. 1931, London, England; m. Judy Fenton 1957, one s. *Education:* University of Cambridge. *Career:* mem. Writer's Guild; Dramatists Club. *Publications:* Fiction:

Crusading for Kronk, 1960; A World of Difference, 1961; Just for the Record, 1962; The Biggest Picture, 1964. Stage Plays: Horizontal Hold, 1967; The Starving Rich, 1972; The Two of Me, 1975; Moving, 1980; Why Me?, 1985. Screenplays: Arabesque, 1968; Gold, 1974; Shout at the Devil, 1975. Television Plays: All Things Being Equal, 1970; Exit Laughing, 1971; Minder, 1980; The Kindness of Mrs Radcliffe, 1981; Moving, 1985; Star Quality, series, 1986; Close Relations, 1986–87; The Bretts, 1990. Contributions: Observer; Sunday Telegraph; New York Times; Los Angeles Times; Punch; Plays and Players; New Statesman; Independent; Town.

PRICE, Susan; British children's author; b. 8 July 1955, Brades Row, England. *Career:* mem. Soc. of Authors. *Publications:* Devil's Piper, 1973; Twopence a Tub, 1975; Sticks and Stones, 1976; Home from Home, 1977; Christopher Uptake, 1981; The Carpenter (short stories), 1981; In a Nutshell, 1983; From Where I Stand, 1984; Ghosts at Large, 1984; Odin's Monster, 1986; The Ghost Drum, 1987; The Bone Dog, 1989; Forbidden Doors, 1990; The Sterkarm Handshake, 1998; A Sterkarm Kiss 2004, Odin's Queen 2006. *Honours:* The Other Award, 1975; Carnegie Medal, 1987; The Guardian Children's Fiction Award, 1999. *Address:* c/o Faber and Faber Ltd, 3 Queen Square, London WC1N 3AU, England.

PRICE, Victor, BA; Northern Irish writer and poet; b. 10 April 1930, Newcastle, County Down. *Education:* Queen's Univ., Belfast. *Career:* with the BBC, 1956–90, ending as Head of German Language Service. *Publications:* The Death of Achilles, 1963; The Other Kingdom, 1964; Caliban's Wooing, 1966; The Plays of Georg Büchner, 1971; Two Parts Water (poems), 1980. Contributions: Financial Times; Scotsman; BBC World Service; Deutschland Rundfunk; Channel Four.

PRIEST, Christopher McKenzie; British writer; b. 14 July 1943, Cheadle, Cheshire, England; m. Laura; one s. one d. *Publications:* Indoctrinaire 1970, Fugue for a Darkening Island 1972, Real-Time World (short stories) 1974, Inverted World 1974, The Space Machine 1976, A Dream of Wessex 1977, An Infinite Summer 1979, The Affirmation 1981, The Glamour 1984, The Book on the Edge of Forever (non-fiction) 1984, The Quiet Woman 1990, The Prestige 1995, The Extremes 1998, The Dream Archipelago 1999, The Separation 2002; short stories, TV plays; contrib. to Impulse, New Worlds, New Writings in SF, various anthologies. *Honours:* John W. Campbell Jr Memorial Award for Outstanding British Novel 1972, BSFA Awards for Best Novel 1974, 1999, 2003, for Best Short Story 1979, Ditmar Awards for Best Int. Novel 1977, 1982, Kurd Lasswitz Award for Best Foreign Novel 1988, James Tait Black Memorial Prize for Fiction 1995, World Fantasy Award 1996, Prix Utopia Lifetime Achievement Award 2001, Grand Prix de l'Imaginaire 2001, 2006, Arthur C. Clarke Award 2003. *Literary Agent:* PFD, Drury House, 34–43 Russell Street, London, WC2B 5HA, England. *Telephone:* (20) 7344-1000. *Fax:* (20) 7836-9539. *E-mail:* info@pfd.co.uk. *Website:* www.pfd.co.uk. *E-mail:* cp@ christopher-priest.co.uk (home). *Website:* www.christopher-priest.co.uk.

PRIGENT, Michel; French editor; b. 29 Sept. 1950, Paris; s. of Jean Prigent and Germaine Morvan; m. Elisabeth Depierre 1974; two s. *Education:* Lycées Henri IV and Louis-le-Grand, Ecole Normale Supérieure and Sorbonne, Paris. *Career:* joined Presses Universitaires de France 1974, Sec. to Bd of Dirs 1978, Editorial Dir 1985; Président du Directoire 1994; Pres. Editeurs de Sciences Humaines et Sociales 1984–90. *Publications:* La liberté à refaire 1984, Le héros et l'Etat dans la tragédie de Pierre Corneille 1986. *Honours:* Officier, Ordre nat. du Mérite. *Address:* Presses Universitaires de France, 108 boulevard Saint-Germain, 75006 Paris (office); 17 rue de Tournon, 75006 Paris, France (home). *Telephone:* 1-46-34-12-01 (office).

PRINCE, Alison Mary, DFA, DipEd; British writer and poet; b. 26 March 1931, Kent, England; m. Goronwy Siriol Parry 1957; two s. one d. *Education:* Beckenham Grammar School, Univ. of London, Slade School of Fine Art, Goldsmiths Coll. *Career:* fmr farmer, art teacher and TV scriptwriter; Fellow in Creative Writing, Jordanhill Coll., Glasgow 1988–90; currently writer and illustrator of children's fiction; organizes creative writing workshops in schools in Scotland, sponsored by Scottish Arts Council; Fellow Inst. of Contemporary Scotland; mem. Scottish PEN, Soc. of Authors. *Television:* Trumpton (writer, TV series) 1966–67. *Publications:* juvenile: The Doubting Kind 1974, How's Business 1985, The Ghost Within 1987, The Blue Moon Day 1989, Having Been in the City (poems) 1994, The Witching Tree 1996, The Sherwood Hero (Guardian Children's Fiction Award) 1996, Magic Dad 1997, Fergus, Fabulous Ferret 1997, Screw Loose 1998, Cat Number Three 1999, Dear Del 1999, Second Chance 2000, A Nation Again 2000, Bird Boy 2000, Bumble 2001, Oranges and Murder 2001, The Fortune Teller 2001, My Tudor Queen 2001, Boojer 2002, Turnaround 2002, Spud 2003, Three Blind Eyes 2003, Anne Boleyn and Me 2004, Luck 2004, The Summerhouse 2005, Tower-Block Pony 2004, Smoke 2005; poetry: The Whifflet Train; non-fiction: The Necessary Goat (essays) 1992, Kenneth Grahame: An Innocent in the Wild Wood (biog.) 1994, Hans Christian Andersen: The Fan Dancer (biog.) 1998. *Honours:* Hon. DLitt (Leicester) 2005; Scottish Arts Council Awards for Children's Literature Literary Review Grand Poetry Prize 2001, 2002. *Address:* Burnfoot, Whiting Bay, Isle of Arran KA27 8QL, Scotland. *Telephone:* (1770) 700574. *Fax:* (1770) 700204. *Website:* www.alisonprince.co .uk.

PRINCE, Mona; Egyptian novelist. *Publications:* Three Suitcases for Departure (in Arabic) 2003. *Address:* c/o American University in Cairo, POB 2511, 113 Sharia Kasr El-Aini, Cairo, Egypt.

PRINCE, Peter Alan, BA, MA; British writer and screenwriter; b. 10 May 1942, Bromley, England. *Education:* Univ. of Pennsylvania, Columbia Univ. *Television plays include:* Oppenheimer 1980. *Publications:* Play Things (Soc. of Authors Somerset Maugham Award 1973) 1972, Dogcatcher 1974, Agents of a Foreign Power 1977, The Good Father 1983, Death of a Soap Queen 1990, The Great Circle 1997, Waterloo Story 1999, Adam Runaway 2005; contrib. to periodicals. *Honours:* BAFTA Award 1980, Writers' Guild of Great Britain Award, MWA Special Award. *Address:* c/o Bloomsbury Publishing Plc, 36 Soho Square, London, W1D 3QY; 31 Meteor Street, London, SW11, England.

PRINGLE, Heather Anne, BA, MA; Canadian writer; b. 8 Dec. 1952, Edmonton, AB; m. 1978. *Education:* Univ. of Alberta, Univ. of British Columbia. *Publications:* In Search of Ancient North America 1996, The Mummy Congress 2001, The Master Plan: Himmler's Scholars and the Holocaust 2006; contribs to Science, Discover, Stern, Geo, New Scientist, National Geographic Traveler, Islands, Saturday Night, Canadian Geographic. *Honours:* American Asscn for the Advancement of Science Excellence in Science Journalism Award for Magazines 2001, Nat. Magazine Award 1988, Authors' Award 1992. *Address:* 825 Granville Street, Suite 202, Vancouver, BC V6Z 1K9, Canada. *Website:* www.heatherpringle.com.

PRISTAVKIN, Anatoliy Ignatevich; Russian author and government official; b. 17 Oct. 1931, Lyubertsy, Moscow; m. 1st V. Golubkova 1960 (divorced 1975); one s. one d.; m. 2nd M Berezhnaya 1986; one d. *Education:* Gorky Inst. of Literature. *Career:* first works published 1956; Prof. Gorky Inst. of Literature 1981–; Leader of April Independent Asscn of Writers 1989–; Chair. Comm. for Grace, under Pres. of Russian Fed. 1992–2001; Adviser to the Pres. of Russian Fed. 2002–. *Publications:* Little Stories 1959, A Lyrical Book 1969, A Golden Cloud (Nochevala tuchka zolotaya) 1987, The Small Cuckoos 1989, Ryazanka 1990, The Vine Road 1998, A Valley of Death (Dolina teni smertnoj) 2000. *Honours:* USSR State Prize 1987, Deutsche Jugendliteratur Prize 1991, Druzhba Narodov Literary Prize 1999, Aleksandr-Men Prize 2002. *Address:* 8/4 ul. Ilinka, 103132 Moscow (office); Leningradskij prosp. 26-2, apt 53, 125040 Moscow, Russia (home). *Telephone:* (495) 206-43-60 (office); (495) 212-82-36 (home). *Fax:* (495) 206-43-38 (office).

PRITCHARD, R(obert) John, AB, MA, PhD, LLB, FRHistS; American historian; b. 30 Nov. 1945, Los Angeles, CA; m. 1st Sonia Magbanna Zaide 1969 (divorced 1984); one s. one d.; m. 2nd Lady Selina Elaine Antonia FitzAlan-Howard Lodge 1989. *Education:* University of California, LSE, University of Kent at Canterbury, Inns of Court School of Law, London. *Career:* Lecturer in History, University of Kent, 1990–93; Fellow in War Studies, King's College, London, 1990–93; Simon Senior Research Fellow in History, University of Manchester, 1993–94; Dir, Historical Enterprises, 1993–; Dir, Robert M. Kempner Collegium, 1996–2000; Lecturer in Law, Business Studies and History, Stafford House College, Canterbury 2001–; mem. Middle Temple, 1995–. *Publications:* Reichstag Fire: Ashes of Democracy 1972, Cry Sabotage (co-author) 1972, The Tokyo War Crimes Trial: An International Symposium (co-author) 1984, General History of the Philippines Vol. 1: The American Half-Century 1898–1946 (co-author) 1984, Far Eastern Influences on British Strategy Towards the Great Powers 1937–39 1987, Overview of the Historical Importance of the Tokyo War Trial 1987, Total War: Causes & Courses of the Second World War (co-author) 1989, 1995, Japan and the Second World War (with Lady Toskiko Marks) 1989, Unit 731: The Japanese Army's Secret of Secrets (co-author) 1989, From Pearl Harbour to Hiroshima (co-author), 1993, The Cambridge Encyclopedia of Japan (co-author) 1993, La Déportation: La Système Concentrationnaire Nazi (co-author) 1995, Wada umi no Koe wo Kiku: senso sekinin to Ningen no Tsumi; to no Ma (Harken to the Cries at Our Birth: The Intervals Separating War Responsibility and Crimes of Humanity) (co-author) 1996, The Tokyo Major War Crimes Trial: The Records of the International Military Tribunal for the Far East with an Authoritative Commentary and Comprehensive Guide 1998–, World War II in Asia and the Pacific and the War's Aftermath, with General Themes: A Handbook of Literature and Research (co-author) 1998, Showa Japan: Political, Economic and Social History 1926–1989, II: 1941–1952, Section I: Politics & Economics (co-author) 1999, 1945: War and Peace in the Pacific, Selected Essays (co-author) 1999, The Penguin History of the Second World War 1999, International Criminal Law, III: Enforcement (co-author) 1999, A History of Anglo-Japanese Relations, III: The Military Dimension (co-author) 2003, International Humanitarian Law: Origins, Challenges, Prospects (with John N. Carey and William V. Dunlap), 3 vols, 2003, Encyclopedia of Genocide and Crimes against Humanity (co-author) 2004. *Honours:* many grants and fellowships. *Address:* 11 Charlotte Square, Margate, Kent, CT9 1LR, England.

PRITCHARD, William Harrison, BA, MA, PhD; American academic and author; b. 12 Nov. 1932, Binghamton, NY; m. Marietta Pritchard 1957, three s. *Education:* Amherst College, Columbia University, Harvard University. *Career:* Instructor, 1958–61, Asst Prof., 1961–65, Assoc. Prof., 1965–70, Prof., 1970–, later Henry Clay Folger Prof. of English, Amherst College; Mem., Editorial Board, Hudson Review; mem. Asscn of Literary Scholars and Critics, American Acad. of Arts and Sciences. *Publications:* Wyndham Lewis, 1968; Wyndham Lewis: Profiles in Literature, 1972; W. B. Yeats (ed.), 1972; Seeing Through Everything: English Writers 1918–1940, 1977; Lives of the Modern Poets, 1980; Frost: A Literary Life Reconsidered, 1984; Randall Jarrell: A Literary Life, 1990; Selected Poems of Randall Jarrell (ed.), 1990; Playing It By Ear: Literary Essays and Reviews, 1994; English Papers: A Teaching Life, 1995; Talking Back to Emily Dickinson and Other Essays, 1998; Updike:

America's Man of Letters, 2000; Shelf Life: Literary Essays and Reviews, 2003. Contributions: Boston Sunday Globe; Hudson Review; New York Times Book Review; numerous others. *Honours:* ACLS Junior Fellowship, 1963–64, and Fellowship, 1977–78; Guggenheim Fellowship, 1973–74; National Endowment for the Humanities Fellowships, 1977–78, 1986; Book of essays, Under Criticism, published in his honour, 1998. *Address:* 62 Orchard Street, Amherst, MA 01002, USA.

PROCHÁZKOVÁ, Petra; Czech journalist and humanitarian worker; b. 20 Oct. 1964, Césky Brod. *Education:* Charles Univ., Prague. *Career:* reporter Lidové Noviny newspaper 1989–97, foreign corresp. 1992–97; f. (with Jaromír Štetina) of war reporting agency, Epicentrum 1994; covered events in war zones including Georgia, Afghanistan and Grozny, Chechnya; also reported for Tyden and for Slovak newspaper, SME; began to organize relief efforts for war-ravaged families 2000–, est. shelter for orphans in Grozny; f. humanitarian org., Berkat to bring aid to Chechnya and Afghanistan; now freelance journalist and documentary maker. *Television:* Dark Side of the World (documentary) (Johns Hopkins Univ. SAIS-Novartis Prize for Excellence in Int. Journalism, Washington) 2000. *Publication:* Aluminiová Královna: rusko-cecenská válka ocima žen (The Aluminium Queen: The Russian-Chechen War through the Eyes of Women) 2003. *Honours:* Ferdinand Peroutka Award 1998, K. H. Borovský Prize for extraordinary journalism activities 1999, 2000, Medal of Merit for humanitarian work in Chechnya 2000, Woman of Europe 2001, SVU Andrew Elias Humanitarian and Tolerance Award 2006. *Address:* c/o Berkat, Rumunská 24, 12000 Prague 2, Czech Republic.

PROCTER, Jane Hilary Elizabeth; British journalist; b. London; d. of Gordon H. Procter and Florence Bibby Procter; m. Thomas C. Goldstaub 1985; one s. one d. *Education:* Queen's Coll. Harley St London. *Career:* Fashion Asst Vogue 1974–75; Asst Fashion Ed. Good Housekeeping 1975–77; Acting Fashion Ed. Woman's Journal 1977–78; Fashion Writer Country Life 1978–80; Freelance Fashion Ed. The Times, Daily Express 1980–87; Ed. Tatler 1990–99, Ed. Dir PeopleNews Network 1999–2002. *Publication:* Dress Your Best 1983. *Address:* c/o PeopleNews Network, 77 Dean Street, London, W1D 3SH, England (office). *Telephone:* (20) 7025-1818 (office).

PROKHANOV, Aleksandr Andreevich; Russian writer, journalist and publisher; b. 1938, Moscow. *Education:* Moscow Institute of Aviation. *Career:* fmr correspondent, various Moscow newspapers, publisher, newspaper, Den; Ed., nationalist newspaper, Zavtra. *Publications:* Idu v moi put (I'm Entering My Way, prose), 1971; Kochuiushchaia roza (A Wandering Rose, novel), 1976; Vremia polden (The Time is Noon, novel), 1977; Mesto deistviia (A Place of Action, novel), 1980; Vechnyi gorod (Eternal Town, novel), 1981; Derevo v tsentre Kabula (The Tree in Kabul Downtown, novel), 1982; Risunki batalista (The Sketches of the Battle-pieces Painter, novel), 1985; Angel proletel (An Angel Has Flown, novel), 1991; Poslednii soldat imperii (The Last Soldier of the Empire, novel), 1992; Dvorets (The Palace, novel), 1994; Mr Hexagon, 2001. Contributions: various journals and magazines incl.: Znamia, Lunost, Oktiabr, Nash sovremennik. *Honours:* National Bestseller Prize 2002.

PROSE, Francine, BA, MA; American writer and academic; b. 1 April 1947, New York, NY; m. Howard Michels 1976; two s. *Education:* Radcliffe Coll., Harvard Univ. *Career:* teacher of creative writing, Harvard Univ. 1971–72; Visiting Lecturer in Fiction, Univ. of Arizona at Tucson 1982–84; instructor, Bread Loaf Writers' Conference 1984; fmr faculty mem., MFA Program, Warren Wilson Coll. 1984; Guggenheim and Fulbright fellowships; mem. Associated Writing Programs, PEN. *Publications:* Judah the Pious 1973, The Glorious Ones 1974, Stories From Our Living Past 1974, Marie Laveau 1977, Animal Magnetism 1978, Household Saints 1981, Hungry Hearts 1983, Bigfoot Dreams 1986, Women and Children First and Other Stories 1988, Primitive People 1992, A Peaceable Kingdom 1993, Hunters & Gatherers 1995, Guided Tours of Hell: Novellas 1997, The Demon's Mistake: A Story from Chelm 2000, Blue Angel: A Novel 2000, On Writing Short Stories (with others) 2000, The Lives of the Muses: Nine Women and the Artists They Inspired (non-fiction) 2002, Gluttony (non-fiction) 2003, After (juvenile) 2003, Best New American Voices (ed., anthology) 2005, A Changed Man 2005, Leopold, the Liar of Leipzig (juvenile) 2005, Reading Like a Writer 2006; contrib. to periodicals, including Harper's and the Wall Street Journal. *Honours:* Dir's Fellow, Center for Scholars and Writers at the New York Public Library; Jewish Book Council Award 1973, Mademoiselle MLLE Award 1975, Hartford Jewish Community Center Edgar Lewis Wallant Memorial Award 1984. *Address:* c/o HarperCollins Publishers Inc., 10 E 53rd Street, New York, NY 10022, USA. *Website:* www.francineprose.com.

PROUD, Linda Helena; British writer; b. 9 July 1949, Broxbourne, Herts., England; m. David Smith. *Education:* Coll. of Distributive Trades, London. *Career:* mem. Soc. of Authors. *Publications:* Consider England 1994, Knights of the Grail 1995, Tabernacle for the Sun 1997, 2000 Years 1999, Icons: A Sacred Art 2000, Angels 2001, Pallas and the Centaur 2004. *Honours:* Southern Arts Bursary Fund 1995. *Address:* c/o Godstow Press, 60 Godstow Road, Wolvercote, Oxford, OX2 8NY, England. *Telephone:* (1865) 556215. *E-mail:* info@godstowpress.co.uk. *Website:* www.godstowpress.co.uk.

PROULX, (Edna) Annie, MA; American writer; b. 22 Aug. 1935, Norwich, CT; d. of George Napoleon Proulx and Lois Nellie Gill; m. 1st H. Ridgeley Bullock 1955 (divorced); one d.; m. 2nd James Hamilton Lang 1969 (divorced 1990); three s. *Education:* Univ. of Vermont and Sir George Williams (now Concordia) Univ., Montréal. *Career:* freelance journalist, Vt 1975–87; f. Vershire Behind the Times newspaper, Vershire, Vt; short stories appeared in

Blair & Ketchums Country Journal, Esquire, etc.; Vt Council Arts Fellowship 1989, Ucross Foundation Residency, Wyo. 1990, 1992; mem. PEN; Guggenheim Fellow 1993; active anti-illiteracy campaigner. *Publications:* Heart Songs and Other Stories 1988, Postcards (novel) (PEN/Faulkner Award for Fiction 1993) 1992, The Shipping News (Chicago Tribune Heartland Prize for Fiction, Irish Times Int. Fiction Prize, Nat. Book Award for Fiction, Pulitzer Prize for Fiction 1994) 1993, Accordion Crimes 1996, Best American Short Stories (ed.) 1997, Brokeback Mountain 1998, Close Range: Wyoming Stories 1998, That Old Ace in the Hole 2002, Bad Dirt: Wyoming Stories 2 2004; contrib. numerous articles. *Honours:* Hon. DHumLitt (Maine) 1994; Alumni Achievement Award, Univ. of Vt 1994, New York Public Library Literary Lion 1994, Dos Passos Prize for Literature 1996, American Acad. of Achievement Award 1998, The New Yorker Book Award for Best Fiction 2000, English Speaking Union Amb. Book Award 2000. *Address:* c/o Simon Schuster Inc., 1230 Avenue of the Americas, New York, NY 10020 (office); PO Box 230, Centennial, WY 82055, USA. *Fax:* (307) 742-6159.

PRUNTY, (Eugene) Wyatt; American academic, poet, writer and editor; b. 15 May 1947, Humbolt, TN; m. Barbara Heather Svell 1973; one s. one d. *Education:* BA, University of the South, 1969; MA, Johns Hopkins University, 1973; PhD, Louisiana State University, 1979. *Career:* Instructor in English, Louisiana State University, 1978–79; Asst Prof. to Prof. of English, Virginia Polytechnic Institute and State University, 1978–89; Visiting Writer, Washington and Lee University, 1982–83; Visiting Assoc. and Prof. Johns Hopkins University 1987–89, Elliot Coleman Prof. 1988; Carlton Prof. of English University of the South 1989–; f. Dir Sewanee Writers' Conf.; f. and ed Sewanee Writers' Series; mem. Associated Writing Programs; College English Asscn; English Institute; MLA of America. *Publications:* Poetry: Domestic of the Outer Banks, 1980; The Times Between, 1982; What Women Know, What Men Believe, 1986; Balance as Belief, 1989; The Run of the House, 1993; Since the Noon Mail Stopped, 1997; Unarmed and Dangerous: New and Selected Poems, 1999. Other: Fallen from the Symboled World: Precedents for the New Formalism, 1990; Sewanee Writers on Writing (ed.), 2001. Contributions: anthologies, reviews, quarterlies and journals. *Honours:* Poetry Prize, Sewanee Review 1969; Fellow, Bread Loaf Writers' Conference 1982, Guggenheim Fellowship 2001–02, Rockefeller Foundation residency 2002. *Address:* c/o Department of English, University of the South, Sewanee, TN 37383, USA.

PRUTKOV, Kozma (see Snodgrass, W. D.)

PRYCE-JONES, David, BA, MA; British writer; b. 15 Feb. 1936, Vienna, Austria; m. 1959, one s. two d. *Education:* Magdalen College, Oxford. *Career:* Literary Ed., Time & Tide, 1961, Spectator, 1964; Senior Ed., National Review, New York, 1999; mem. RSL. *Publications:* Owls & Satyrs 1961, The Sands of Summer 1963, Next Generation 1964, Quondam 1965, The Stranger's View 1967, The Hungarian Revolution 1969, Running Away 1969, The Face of Defeat 1971, The England Commune 1973, Unity Mitford 1976, Vienna 1978, Shirley's Guild 1981, Paris in the Third Reich 1983, Cyril Connolly 1984, The Afternoon Sun 1986, The Closed Circle 1989, Inheritance 1992, You Can't Be Too Careful 1993, The War That Never Was 1995, Betrayal 2006, Safe Houses 2007; contrib. to numerous journals and magazines. *Honours:* Wingate Prize 1986, Sunlight Literary Prize 1989. *Address:* Lower Pentwyn, Gwenddwr, Powys LD2 3LQ, Wales.

PRYOR, Boori Monty; Australian writer; b. 12 July 1950, Townsville, Qld. *Publications:* Maybe Tomorrow (with Meme McDonald), 1998; My Girragundji (with Meme McDonald), 1998; The Binna Binna Man (with Meme McDonald), 1999; Reconcilliation, 2000. Contributions: Australian Bookseller and Publisher, 1999; The Bulletin, 2000. *Honours:* Children's Book Council of Australia Book of the Year Award for Younger Readers, 1999; NSW State Literary Award for Younger Readers, 2000, and Book of the Year, 2000, and Ethnic Affairs Commission Award, 2000; Australian Audio Book Awards, Author/Narrator Category winner and Overall Narration Book Winner. *Address:* c/o Penguin Group (Australia), 250 Camberwell Road, Camberwell, Vic. 3124, Australia (office).

PU, Nai-fu; Taiwanese writer; b. Nanjing; m. *Education:* Beijing Russian-Language Jr Coll. *Career:* imprisoned for various periods in labour-reform camps during anti-intellectual campaigns in China; moved to Hong Kong, subsequently to Taiwan 1983. *Publications include:* Romance in the Arctic, The Woman in the Pagoda, Books Without Names (six vols), The Scourge of the Sea, Red in Tooth and Claw.

PULLMAN, Philip, CBE, BA, FRSL; British writer; b. 19 Oct. 1946, Norwich, Norfolk; m. Jude Speller 1970; two s. *Education:* Exeter Coll., Oxford. *Career:* teacher in Oxford 1972–86; part-time Lecturer, Westminster Coll., Oxford 1986–96. *Publications:* One More River 1973, Count Karlstein 1982, The Ruby in the Smoke (Sally Lockhart series) 1985, The Shadow in the Plate 1986, The Shadow in the North (Sally Lockhart series) 1987, Spring-Heeled Jack 1989, The Tiger in the Well (Sally Lockhart series) 1990, The Broken Bridge 1990, The White Mercedes 1992, The Tin Princess (Sally Lockhart series) 1994, The New Cut Gang: Thunderbolt's Waxwork 1994, The New Cut Gang: The Gasfitter's Ball 1995, The Wonderful Story of Aladdin and the Enchanted Lamp 1995, The Firework-Maker's Daughter 1995, Northern Lights (aka The Golden Compass, Vol. I, His Dark Materials trilogy) (Carnegie Medal 1996, Guardian Children's Fiction Prize 1996, British Book Awards Children's Book of the Year 1996, CILIP Carnegie Medal 2007) 1995, Clockwork 1996, The Subtle Knife (Vol. II, His Dark Materials trilogy) 1997, The Butterfly Tattoo

1998, Mossycoat 1998, Detective Stories (ed.) 1998, I Was a Rat! 1999, The Amber Spyglass (Vol. III, His Dark Materials trilogy) (British Book Awards WH Smith Children's Book of the Year, Whitbread Children's Book of the Year Prize 2001, Whitbread Book of the Year Award 2001) 2000, Puss-in-Boots 2000, Sherlock Holmes and the Limehouse Horror 2001, Lyra's Oxford 2003, The Scarecrow and his Servant 2004; contrib. reviews to Times Educational Supplement, The Guardian. *Honours:* Hon. Fellow Univ. of Wales, Bangor; Hon. DLitt (Univ. of East Anglia), (Oxford Brookes Univ.), Hon. DUniv (Univ. of Surrey Roehampton); Booksellers' Asscn/Book Data Author of the Year Award 2001, Booksellers' Asscn Author of the Year 2001, 2002, British Book Awards Author of the Year Award 2002, Whitbread Book of the Year Award 2002. *Literary Agent:* c/o Caradoc King, A. P. Watt Ltd, 20 John Street, London, WC1N 2DR, England. *Telephone:* (20) 7405-6774. *Fax:* (20) 7831-2154. *Website:* www.philip-pullman.com.

PUNTER, David Godfrey, BA, MA, PhD, FRSA, FSA; British academic, writer and poet; *Research Dean of Arts, University of Bristol;* b. 19 Nov. 1949, London, England; m. Caroline Case 1988, one s. two d. *Education:* University of Cambridge. *Career:* Lecturer in English, University of East Anglia, 1973–86; Prof. and Head of Dept, Chinese University of Hong Kong, 1986–88; Prof. of English, University of Stirling, 1988–2000; Prof. of English, University of Bristol, 2000–. *Publications:* The Literature of Terror, 1980; Blake, Hegel and Dialectic, 1981; Romanticism and Ideology, 1982; China and Class, 1985; The Hidden Script, 1985; Introduction to Contemporary Cultural Studies (ed.), 1986; Lost in the Supermarket, 1987; Blake: Selected Poetry and Prose (ed.), 1988; The Romantic Unconscious, 1989; Selected Poems of Philip Larkin (ed.), 1991; Asleep at the Wheel, 1997; Gothic Pathologies, 1998; Spectral Readings (ed.), 1999; Selected Short Stories, 1999; Companion to the Gothic (ed.), 2000; Writing the Passions, 2000; Postcolonial Imaginings, 2000. Contributions: Hundreds of articles, essays, and poems in various publications. *Honours:* Scottish Arts Council Award, Founding Fellow Institute of Contemporary Scotland; Hon. DLitt (Stirling) 1999. *Address:* The Coach House, Church Lane, Backwell, Bristol, BS48 3JJ, England (home). *E-mail:* david.punter@bristol.ac.uk (office).

PURDY, James; American writer and poet; b. 17 July 1923, Freemont, Ohio. *Education:* Univ. of Chicago, Univ. of Puebla, Mexico. *Career:* interpreter and other posts in Cuba, Mexico, Washington, DC. *Publications:* novels: Don't Call Me by My Right Name 1956, 63: Dream Palace 1956, Color of Darkness 1957, Malcolm 1959, The Nephew 1960, Cabot Wright Begins 1963, Eustace Chisholm and the Works 1967, Sleepers in Moon-Crowned Valleys (Part I Jeremy's Version 1970, Part II The House of the Solitary Maggot 1971), I Am Elijah Thrush 1972, In a Shallow Grave 1976, Narrow Rooms 1978, On Glory's Course 1983, Garments The Living Wear 1989, Out With the Stars 1992, Kitty Blue: A Fairytale 1993, Gertrude of Stony Island Avenue 1997; plays: Children is All 1962, A Day After the Fair 1977, How I Became a Shadow (eight plays) 1979, Proud Flesh 1980, Scrap of Paper 1981, The Berry-Picker 1981, Foment 1997; An Oyster is a Wealthy Beast (story and poems) 1967, Mr. Evening 1968 (story and poems), On the Rebound 1970 (story and poems), The Running Sun (poems) 1971, Sunshine is an Only Child (poems) 1973, Lessons and Complaints (poems) 1978, Mourners Below 1981, Dawn 1985, Don't Let the Snow Fall (poem) 1985, In the Hollow of His Hand 1986, The Candles of your Eyes (collected stories) 1987, Are You in the Winter Tree? 1987, The Brooklyn Branding Parlors (poems) 1987, The Room All to Itself (play) 1988, Garments the Living Wear 1989, Collected Poems 1990, Gertrude of Stony Island Avenue 1998, Moe's Villa and Other Stories (fiction) 2000; LP recordings: 63: Dream Palace 1968, Eventide and Other Stories 1969. *Honours:* American Acad. of Arts and Letters Morton Dauwen Zabel Award for Fiction 1993, Oscar Williams and Gene Durwood Award for Poetry 1995. *Address:* 236 Henry Street, Brooklyn, NY 11201, USA. *Telephone:* (718) 858-0015.

PURPURA, Lia, BA, MFA; American poet and teacher; b. 22 Feb. 1964, Long Island, NY; m. Jed Gaylin 1992, one s. *Education:* Oberlin Coll., Iowa Writers' Workshop. *Career:* Dept of Writing and Media, Loyola College, Baltimore, MD, 1990. *Publications:* The Brighter the Veil, 1996; Taste of Ash and Berliner Tagebuch-Poems of Grzegorz Musial, in press; Trans., poems by Katarzyna Borun-Jagodzinska and Krzysztof Piechowicz. Contributions: poems to numerous journals including: American Poetry Review; Antioch Review; Denver Quarterly; Ploughshares; Essays and reviews to several journals including: Willow Springs; Verse. *Honours:* Acad. of American Poets Award, 1986; Teaching and Writing Fellowship, University of Iowa Writers Workshop, 1988–90; Fulbright Fellowship, 1991–92; Blue Mountain Center Residency, 1995; First Prize, Visions International Trans. Prize, 1996; Millay Colony Resident Fellow, 1996.

PURSER, Philip John, MA; British journalist and author; b. 28 Aug. 1925, Letchworth, Herts., England; m. Ann Elizabeth Goodman 1957; one s. two d. *Education:* St Andrews Univ. *Career:* mem. staff, Daily Mail 1951–57; TV Critic, Sunday Telegraph 1961–87; mem. Writers Guild of Great Britain, BAFTA. *Plays:* Calf Love (BBC TV) 1966, Dr Glas (play, from novel by Hjalmar Soderberg, Derby Playhouse) 1970, The One & Only Phyllis Dixey (Thames TV) 1978, Backfischliebe (WDR/NDR, Germany) 1985, Ceremonies of War (BBC Radio 4) 1985. *Publications:* Peregrination 22 1962, Four Days to the Fireworks 1964, The Twentymen 1967, Night of Glass 1968, The Holy Father's

Navy 1971, The Last Great Tram Race 1974, Where is He Now? 1978, A Small Explosion 1979, The One and Only Phyllis Dixey 1978, Halliwell's Television Companion (with Leslie Halliwell) 1982, Shooting the Hero 1990, Poeted: The Final Quest of Edward James 1991, Done Viewing 1992, Lights in the Sky 2005; contribs to numerous magazines and journals. *Address:* 10 The Green, Blakesley, Towcester, Northants., NN12 8RD, England (home). *Telephone:* (1327) 860274 (home). *E-mail:* annphil.purser@btinternet.com (home).

PURVES, Elizabeth (Libby) Mary, OBE, MA; British writer and broadcaster; b. 2 Feb. 1950, London; d. of James Grant and Mary (née Tinsley) Purves; m. Paul Heiney 1980; one s. (deceased) one d. *Education:* Convent of the Sacred Heart, Tunbridge Wells and St Anne's Coll., Oxford. *Career:* BBC local radio, Oxford 1972–76; Reporter Today Programme BBC Radio 4 1976–79, Presenter 1979–81, currently Presenter on Radio 4 and BBC World Service; Presenter BBC TV Choices 1982, BBC Radio Midweek 1984–; Ed. Tatler magazine 1983; Pres. Council for Nat. Parks 2000–01; writer for newspapers and magazines including The Times and Good Housekeeping. *Publications include:* Sailing Weekend Book 1985, Where Did You Leave the Admiral 1987, The English and their Horses (jtly) 1988, How Not to be a Perfect Mother 1988, One Summer's Grace 1990, How Not to Raise a Perfect Child 1991, Casting Off (novel) 1995, A Long Walk in Wintertime (novel) 1996, Grumpers' Farm (with Paul Heiney) 1996, Home Leave (novel) 1997, Holy Smoke 1998, More Lives than One (novel) 1998, Regatta (novel) 1999, Nature's Masterpiece: A Family Survival Book 2000, Passing Go (novel) 2000, Radio: A Love Story 2003, Continental Drift 2003, Love Songs and Lies (novel) 2007. *Address:* c/o Lisa Eveleigh, 26A Rochester Square, London, NW1 9SA, England.

PUTNAM, Hilary, PhD; American academic; *Cogan University Professor Emeritus, Department of Philosophy, Harvard University;* b. 31 July 1926, Chicago, Ill.; s. of Samuel Putnam and Riva Sampson; m. 1st Erna Diesendruck 1948 (divorced 1962); one d.; m. 2nd Ruth A. Hall 1962; two s. one d. *Education:* Cen. High School of Philadelphia, Univ. of Pa, Harvard Univ. and Univ. of Calif. at Los Angeles. *Career:* Asst Prof. of Philosophy, Princeton Univ. 1953–60, Assoc. Prof. 1960–61; Prof. of Philosophy of Science, MIT 1961–65; Prof. of Philosophy, Harvard Univ. 1965, Walter Beverly Pearson Prof. of Mathematical Logic and Modern Math. 1976–, then Cogan University Professor, Emer. 2000–; Guggenheim Fellow 1960–61; Corresp. mem. British Acad.; many other fellowships. *Publications:* Meaning and the Moral Sciences 1978, Reason, Truth and History 1981, Philosophical Papers (3 vols) 1975–83, The Many Faces of Realism 1987, Representation and Reality 1989, Realism with a Human Face 1990, Renewing Philosophy 1992. *Honours:* two hon. degrees. *Address:* Department of Philosophy, Emerson 207, Harvard University, Cambridge, MA 02138 (office); 116 Winchester Road, Arlington, MA 02174, USA (home). *Telephone:* (617) 495-3921 (office). *E-mail:* hputnam@fas.harvard.edu (office). *Website:* emerson.fas.harvard.edu/general.php (office).

PYBUS, Rodney, BA, MA; British writer and poet; b. 5 June 1938, Newcastle upon Tyne; m. Ellen Johnson, 1961; two s. *Education:* Gonville and Caius Coll., Cambridge. *Career:* Lecturer, Macquarie Univ., Australia 1976–79; Literature Officer, Cumbria 1979–81; mem. Soc. of Authors. *Performance:* In Memoriam Milena poems set to music by Jacques Michon and performed Toulouse 2001, Paris 2004. *Publications:* In Memoriam Milena 1973, Bridging Loans 1976, At the Stone Junction 1978, The Loveless Letters 1981, Talitha Cumi 1985, Cicadas in Their Summers: New and Selected Poems 1988, Flying Blues 1994, In Memoriam Milena 1995; contrib. to numerous publs. *Honours:* Poetry Soc. Alice Hunt Bartlett Award 1974, Arts Council Writer's Fellowships 1982–85, Nat. Poetry Competition Awards 1984, 1985, 1988, Hawthornden Fellowship 1988, First Prize, Peterloo Poetry Competition 1989. *Address:* 21 Plough Lane, Sudbury, Suffolk, CO10 2AU, England (home). *E-mail:* rodneypybus@ntlworld.com (home). *Website:* www.rodneypybus.co.uk.

PYLKKÄNEN, Alison, MA; British magazine editor; *Editor-Publisher, Zest magazine;* b. 1963, Maltby, South Yorkshire; d. of Michael Green and Betty Green; m. Jussi Pylkkänen 1986; one s. one d. *Education:* Lady Margaret Hall, Oxford. *Career:* Sub-Ed., Good Housekeeping 1987, Deputy Ed. 1991; Ed. Good Housekeeping's Wedding magazine 1995; Ed. She magazine 1995–2001; Ed. Zest magazine 2001–05, Ed.-Publisher 2005–. *Address:* Zest magazine, National Magazine House, 72 Broadwick Street, London, W1F 9EP, England (office). *Website:* www.zest.co.uk (office).

PYNCHON, Thomas Ruggles, Jr, BA; American novelist; b. 8 May 1937, Glen Cove, NY; s. of Thomas R. Pynchon. *Education:* Cornell Univ. *Career:* fmr editorial writer, Boeing Aircraft Co. *Publications:* V (Faulkner Prize for Best First Novel) 1963, The Crying of Lot 49 (Rosenthal Foundation Award 1967) 1965, Gravity's Rainbow (Nat. Book Award) 1973, Mortality and Mercy in Vienna 1976, Low-Lands 1978, Slow Learner (short stories) 1984, In the Rocket's Red Glare 1986, Vineland 1989, Deadly Sins 1994, Mason & Dixon 1996, Against the Day 2006; contrib. short stories to various publs, including Saturday Evening Post. *Honours:* John D. and Catherine T. MacArthur Foundation Fellowship 1988; American Acad. of Arts and Letters Howells Medal 1975. *Literary Agent:* Melanie Jackson Agency, 915 Broadway, Suite 1009, New York, NY 10010, USA. *Address:* c/o Penguin Books, 250 Madison Avenue, New York, NY 10016, USA.

QIAN, Xinbo; Chinese journalist; b. (Jiarui Qian), 14 Jan. 1923, Jiading Co., Jiangsu Prov.; m. Chen Meixia 1953; one s. one d. *Education:* Yanjing Univ. *Career:* Council mem. of New China News Agency 1982–; Vice-Pres. and Sec.-Gen. of Fed. Journalism Soc. 1984–90; Deputy Dir of Journalism Inst. Acad. of Social Sciences 1982–90. *Publications:* On News' Role of Guidance, Five Historical Periods of Development of Chinese Journalism. *Address:* 6-1-502 Tuanjiehu Beili, Beijing 100026, People's Republic of China. *Telephone:* (10) 85989648.

QUANDT, William Bauer, BA, PhD; American academic and writer; *Professor of Government and Foreign Affairs, University of Virginia*; b. 23 Nov. 1941, Los Angeles, CA; m. 1st Anna Spitzer 1964 (divorced 1980); m. 2nd Helena Cobban 1984, one d. *Education:* Stanford Univ., MIT. *Career:* researcher, Rand Corpn, Santa Monica, CA 1967–72; staff mem. 1972–74, sr staff mem. 1977–79, Nat. Security Council, Washington, DC; Assoc. Prof., Univ. of Pennsylvania 1974–76; Sr Fellow, Brookings Institution, Washington, DC 1979–94; Sr Assoc., Cambridge Energy Research Assocs, MA 1983–90; Prof. of Government and Foreign Affairs, Univ. of Virginia 1994–; mem. Council on Foreign Relations, Middle East Inst., Middle East Studies Asscn (pres. 1987–88), American Acad. of Arts and Sciences. *Publications:* Revolution and Political Leadership: Algeria 1954–68 1969, The Politics of Palestinian Nationalism 1973, Decade of Decisions 1977, Saudi Arabia in the 1980s 1981, Camp David: Peacemaking and Politics 1986, The Middle East: Ten Years After Camp David 1988, The United States and Egypt 1990, Peace Process: American Diplomacy and the Arab–Israeli Conflict Since 1967 1994, The Algerian Crisis (with Andrew Preire) 1996, Between Ballots and Bullets: Algeria's Transition from Authoritarianism 1998; contrib. to professional journals. *Honours:* NDEA Fellow 1963, Social Science Research Council Fellow 1966, Council on Foreign Relations Fellow 1972. *Address:* Department of Politics, University of Virginia, PO Box 400787, Charlottesville, VA 22904-4787, USA. *E-mail:* quandt@virginia.edu. *Website:* www.people.virginia.edu/~wbq8f.

QUARTON, Marjorie; Irish farmer (retd) and writer; b. 25 Oct. 1930, Nenagh, Co. Tipperary; m. John Quarton, one d. *Career:* mem. Irish PEN, Writers' Union. *Publications:* Corporal Jack (novel) 1987, No Harp Like My Own (novel) 1988, Breakfast The Night Before (memoir) 1989, The Cow Watched the Battle (juvenile) 1990, The Other Side of the Island (juvenile) 1991, Renegade (novel) 1991, Saturday's Child (memoir) 1993, One Dog, His Man and His Trials (non-fiction) 1994, The Working Border Collie (non-fiction) 1998. *E-mail:* mquarton@eircom.net.

QUEFFÉLEC, Yann; French writer; b. 4 Sept. 1949, Paris; s. of Henri Queffélec. *Publications include:* Béla Bartok 1881–1945 (biog.) 1981, Le Charme noir 1983, Les Noces barbares (Prix Goncourt) 1985, La Femme sous l'horizon 1988, Le Maître des chimères 1990, Prends garde au loup 1992, Disparue dans la nuit 1994, Bretagne, le soleil se lève à l'ouest 1994, Et la force d'aimer 1996, Happy Birthday Sara 1998, Trente jours à tuer (online interactive novel) 1998, Noir animal, ou la menace 1999, Osmose 2000, Boris après l'amour 2002, Nellys Lachen 2002, La Dégustation 2003, Vert cruel 2003, Moi et toi 2004, Les Affamés 2004, Dora 2004, Vents et marées 2005, Eloge de l'alcool 2005, Ma première femme 2005, L'Amante 2006, Andy Warhol 2006. *Address:* c/o Editions Fayard, 13 rue du Montparnasse, 75006 Paris, France. *E-mail:* presse@editions-fayard.fr.

QUERRY, Ronald (Ron) Burns, BA, MA, PhD; American novelist; b. 22 March 1943, Washington, DC; m. Elaine Stribling Querry, one d. *Education:* Central State Univ., Oklahoma, New Mexico Highlands Univ., Univ. of New Mexico. *Career:* Asst Prof., New Mexico Highlands Univ. 1975–77; Assoc. Prof., Lake Erie Coll. 1979–83; Instructor, Univ. of Oklahoma 1979–83, Visiting Assoc. Prof. and writer-in-residence 1993–; mem. PEN, Native Writers Circle of the Americas, Tucson Pima Copunty Arts Commission. *Publications:* Growing Old at Willie Nelson's Picnic 1983, I See By My Get-Up 1987, Native Americans Struggle for Equality 1992, The Death of Bernadette Lefthand 1993, Bad Medicine 1998. *Honours:* Mountains & Plains Booksellers Award, Border Regional Library Asscn Southwest Book Award. *Address:* c/o Publicity Department, Random House Inc., 1745 Broadway, New York, NY 10019, USA.

QUICK, Barbara, BA; American writer; b. 28 May 1954, Los Angeles, CA; m. John Quick 1988. *Education:* Univ. of California, Santa Cruz. *Publications:* Northern Edge: A Novel of Survival in Alaska's Arctic 1990, The Stolen Child (novel) 1997, Anna Maria Violino: Student of Maestro Vivaldi 2005; contrib. to Ms, New York Times Book Review, Newsweek, People magazine. *Honours:* second place Ina Coolbrith Poetry Prize 1977, citation B. Dalton Bookseller 1990. *Literary Agent:* Felicia Eth Literary Representation, 555 Bryant Street, Suite 350, Palo Alto, CA 94301, USA. *E-mail:* bqwriter@sbcglobal.net. *Website:* www.barbaraquick.com.

QUIGNARD, Pascal Charles Edmond, LicenFil; French writer; b. 23 April 1948, Verneuil-sur-Avre, Eure; s. of Jacques Quignard and Anne Quignard (née Bruneau); one s. *Education:* Lycée de Havre, Lycée de Sèvres and Faculté des Lettres de Nanterre. *Career:* lecturer 1969–77; mem. Cttee of Lecturing 1977–94; Sec.-Gen. for Editorial Devt, Editions Gallimard; Pres. Int. Festival of Opera and Baroque Theatre, Château de Versailles 1990–94; Pres. Concert

des Nations 1990–93. *Publications include:* L'être du balbutiement 1969, Alexandra de Lycophron 1971, La parole de la Délie 1974, Michel Deguy 1975, Echo 1975, Sang 1976, Le lecteur 1976, Hiems 1977, Sarx 1977, Inter aerias fagos 1977, Sur le défaut de terre 1979, Carus 1979, Le secret du domaine 1980, Petits traités (tome I à VIII) 1990, Les tablettes de buis d'Apronenia Avitia 1984, Le vœu de silence (essay) 1985, Une gêne technique à l'égard des fragments 1986, Ethelrude et Wolframm 1986, Le salon de Wurtemberg 1986, La leçon de musique 1987, Les escaliers de Chambord 1989, La raison 1990, Albucius 1990, Tous les matins du monde 1991, Georges de La Tour 1991, La Frontière 1992, Le nom sur le bout de la langue 1993, Le sexe et l'effroi 1994, L'occupation américaine 1994, Rhétorique spéculative 1995, L'amour conjugal 1995, Les septante 1995, La haine de la musique 1996, Vie secrète 1998, Terrasse à Rome (Grand Prix du roman de l' Acad. française 2000) 2000, Albucius 2001, Les ombres errantes (Prix Goncourt 2002) 2002. *Honours:* Chevalier, Légion d'honneur; Prix de la Soc. des gens de lettres for his collected works 1998, Grand prix du roman de la Ville de Paris 1998, Prix de la fondation Prince Pierre de Monaco for his collected works 2000.

QUINNEY, Richard, BS, MA, PhD; American academic and writer; *Professor Emeritus, Northern Illinois University*; b. 16 May 1934, Elkhorn, WI. *Education:* Carroll Coll., Northwestern Univ., Univ. of Wisconsin. *Career:* Instructor, St Lawrence Univ. 1960–62; Asst Prof., Univ. of Kentucky 1962–65; Assoc. Prof. 1965–70, Prof. 1970–73, New York Univ.; Visiting Prof., CUNY 1974–75; Boston Univ. 1975; Visiting Prof. 1975–78, Adjunct Prof. 1978–83, Brown Univ.; Assoc. Ed., Victimology 1976–82, Contemporary Crises 1977–90, California Sociologist 1977–, Critical Sociology 1978–, Western Sociological Review 1982–, Journal of Political and Military Sociology 1984–, Visual Sociology 1991–, Contemporary Justice Review 1997–; Distinguished Visiting Prof. 1978–79, Adjunct Prof. 1980–83, Boston Coll.; Prof., Univ. of Wisconsin at Milwaukee 1980; Prof. of Sociology 1983–97, Prof. Emeritus 1998–, Northern Illinois Univ.; Fellow American Soc. of Criminology 1995; mem. American Sociological Asscn. *Publications:* Criminal Behavior Systems: A Typology (with Marshall B. Clinard) 1967, The Problem of Crime 1970, The Social Reality of Crime 1970, Criminal Justice in America: A Critical Understanding (ed.) 1974, Critique of Legal Order: Crime Control in Capitalist Society 1974, Criminology: Analysis and Critique of Crime in America 1975, Class, State, and Crime: On the Theory and Practice of Criminal Justice 1977, Capitalist Society: Readings for a Critical Sociology (ed.) 1979, Providence: The Reconstruction of Social and Moral Order 1980, Marxism and Law (ed. with Piers Beirne) 1982, Social Existence: Metaphysics, Marxism and the Social Sciences 1982, Criminology as Peacemaking (ed. with Harold E. Pepinsky) 1991, Journey to a Far Place: Autobiographical Reflections 1991, For the Time Being: Ethnography of Everyday Life 1998. *Honours:* American Soc. of Criminology Edwin Sutherland Award 1984, Fulbright Lecture and Research Award Univ. Coll., Galway, Ireland 1986, Western Soc. of Criminology Pres.'s Award 1992, Canterbury Visiting Fellowship Univ. of Canterbury, New Zealand 1993. *Address:* c/o Department of Sociology, Northern Illinois University, 33 Frederick Circle, DeKalb, IL 60115, USA.

QUINTANA, Leroy V., BA, MA; American poet and writer; *Professor of English, San Diego Mesa College*; b. 1944, Alberquerque, NM. *Education:* Univ. of New Mexico, Univ. of Denver, New Mexico State Univ. *Career:* served in Viet Nam war 1967–68; Prof. of English, San Diego Mesa Coll. *Publications include:* Hijo del Pueblo 1976, Sangre 1981, Interrogations 1990, The History of Home 1993, My Hair Turning Gray Among Strangers 1996, The Great Whirl of Exile 1999, La Promesa and other stories 2002. *Honours:* American Book Awards 1981, 1992, Southwest Book Award 1981. *Address:* c/o Curbstone Press, 321 Jackson Street, Willimantic, CT 06226-1738, USA. *E-mail:* info@curbstone.org. *Website:* www.curbstone.org.

QUIRK, Baron (Life Peer), cr. 1994, of Bloomsbury in the London Borough of Camden; **(Charles) Randolph Quirk,** Kt, CBE, PhD, DLitt, LLD, FBA; British academic; b. 12 July 1920, Isle of Man; s. of the late Thomas and Amy Randolph Quirk; m. 1st Jean Williams 1946; two s.; m. 2nd Gabriele Stein 1984. *Education:* Cronk y Voddy School, Douglas High School, Isle of Man, Univ. Coll., London. *Career:* served in RAF 1940–45; Lecturer in English, Univ. Coll. London 1947–54; Commonwealth Fund Fellow, Yale Univ. and Univ. of Mich., USA 1951–52; Reader in English Language and Literature, Univ. of Durham 1954–58, Prof. of English Language 1958–60; Quain Prof. of English, Univ. Coll. London 1960–81; Dir Univ. of London Summer School of English 1962–67; Survey of English Usage 1959–83; mem. Senate, Univ. of London 1970–85 (Chair. Academic Council 1972–75), Court 1972–85; Vice-Chancellor, Univ. of London 1981–85; Pres. Inst. of Linguists 1983–86, British Acad. 1985–89, Coll. of Speech Therapists 1987–91; Gov. British Inst. of Recorded Sound, English-Speaking Union; Chair. Cttee of Enquiry into Speech Therapy Services, British Council English Cttee 1976–80, Hornby Educational Trust 1979–93; mem. BBC Archives Cttee 1979, British Council 1983–91; Trustee Wolfson Foundation 1987–; Lee Kwan Yew Fellow, Singapore 1985–86; Vice-Pres. Foundation of Science and Tech. 1986–90; mem. House of Lords Select Cttee on Science and Tech. 1999–2002; Fellow, King's Coll. London, Queen Mary Coll. London, Univ. Coll. London, Imperial Coll. London, Academia Europaea; Foreign Fellow, Royal Belgian Acad.

Sciences 1975, Royal Swedish Acad. 1986, Finnish Acad. of Sciences 1992, American Acad. of Arts and Sciences 1995. *Publications:* The Concessive Relation in Old English Poetry 1954, Studies in Communication (with A. J. Ayer and others) 1955, An Old English Grammar (with C. L. Wrenn) 1955, Charles Dickens and Appropriate Language 1959, The Teaching of English (with A. H. Smith) 1959, The Study of the Mother-Tongue 1961, The Use of English (with supplements by A. C. Gimson and J. Warburg) 1962, Prosodic and Paralinguistic Features in English (with D. Crystal) 1964, A Common Language (with A. H. Marckwardt) 1964, Investigating Linguistic Acceptability (with J. Svartvik) 1966, Essays on the English Language–Medieval and Modern 1968, Elicitation Experiments in English (with S. Greenbaum) 1970, A Grammar of Contemporary English 1972 (with S. Greenbaum, G. Leech, J. Svartvik) 1972, The English Language and Images of Matter 1972, A University Grammar of English (with S. Greenbaum) 1973, The Linguist and the English Language 1974, Old English Literature: A Practical Introduction (with V. Adams, D. Davy) 1975, A Corpus of English Conversation 1980; contrib. to many others including Charles Dickens (ed. S. Wall) 1970, A New Companion to Shakespeare Studies 1971, The State of the Language (with J. Svartvik) 1980, Style and Communication in the English Language 1982, A Comprehensive Grammar of the English Language (with S. Greenbaum, G. Leech and J. Svartvik) 1985, Words at Work: Lectures on Textual Structure 1986, English in Use (with Gabriele Stein) 1990, A Student's Grammar of the English Language (with S. Greenbaum) 1990, Grammatical and Lexical Variance in English 1995; papers in linguistic and literary journals. *Honours:* Hon. Fellow, Coll. of Speech Therapists, Inst. of Linguists; Hon. Master Gray's Inn Bench 1983; hon. degrees (Lund, Uppsala, Poznań, Nijmegen, Paris, Liège, Helsinki, Prague, Reading, Leicester, Salford, London, Newcastle, Bath, Durham, Essex, Open Univ., Glasgow, Bar-Ilan, Brunel, Bucharest, Sheffield, Richmond Coll., Aston, Copenhagen, Queen Margaret); Jubilee Medal, Inst. of Linguists 1973. *Address:* University College London, Gower Street, London, WC1E 6BT, England (office). *Telephone:* (20) 7219-2226 (office). *Fax:* (20) 7916-2054 (office).

R

RAAB, Lawrence Edward, BA, MA; American academic, poet and writer; b. 8 May 1946, Pittsfield, MA; m. Judith Ann Michaels 1968, one d. *Education:* Middlebury College, Syracuse University. *Career:* Instructor, American University, 1970–71; Lecturer, University of Michigan, 1974; Prof. of English, Williams College, 1976–; Staff, Bread Loaf School of English, 1979–81, Bennington Writer's Conference, 1988, Bread Loaf Writer's Conference, 1994. *Publications:* Poetry: Mysteries of the Horizon, 1972; The Collector of Cold Weather, 1976; Other Children, 1986; What We Don't Know About Each Other, 1993; The Probable World, 2000; Visible Signs: New and Selected Poems, 2003. Contributions: many anthologies, scholarly journals, and periodicals. *Honours:* Acad. of American Poets Prize, 1972; National Endowment for the Arts Fellowships, 1972, 1984; Robert Frost Fellowship, Bread Loaf Writer's Conference, 1973; Yaddo Residencies, 1979–80, 1982, 1984, 1986–90, 1994, 1996, 1998; Bess Hokin Prize, Poetry Magazine, 1983; National Poetry Series Winner, 1992; MacDowell Colony Residencies, 1993, 1995, 1997, 2000.

RABAN, Jonathan, BA, FRSL; British author and critic; b. 14 June 1942, Fakenham, Norfolk; s. of Rev. Peter J. C. P. Raban and Monica Sandison; m. 1st Bridget Johnson (divorced 1970s); m. 2nd Caroline Cuthbert 1985 (divorced 1992); m. 3rd Jean Cara Lenihan 1992 (divorced 1997); one d. *Education:* King's School, Worcester, Peter Symonds School, Winchester, Brockenhurst Grammar and Univ. of Hull. *Career:* Asst Lecturer Univ. Coll. of Wales, Aberystwyth 1965–67; Lecturer in English and American Literature, Univ. of E Anglia 1967–69; professional writer 1969–; emigrated to USA 1990; mem. Soc. of Authors. *Publications:* The Technique of Modern Fiction 1969, Mark Twain: Huckleberry Finn 1969, The Society of the Poem 1971, Soft City 1973, Robert Lowell's Poems (ed.) 1974, Arabia Through the Looking Glass 1979, Old Glory (RSL Heinemann Award and Thomas Cook Award 1982) 1981, Foreign Land (novel) 1985, Coasting 1986, For Love and Money 1987, God, Man & Mrs Thatcher 1989, Hunting Mister Heartbreak (Thomas Cook Award 1991) 1990, The Oxford Book of the Sea (ed.) 1992, Bad Land: An American Romance (Nat. Book Critics Circle Award and PEN/West Creative Nonfiction Award 1997) 1996, Passage to Juneau 1999, Waxwings (novel) 2003, My Holy War: Dispatches from the Home Front 2005, Surveillance (novel) 2006; contribs to Harper's, Esquire, New Republic, New York Review of Books, Outside, Granta, New York Times Book Review, Vogue. *Literary Agent:* Aitken Alexander Associates Ltd, 18–21 Cavaye Place, London, SW10 9PT, England. *Telephone:* (20) 7373-8672. *Fax:* (20) 7373-6002. *E-mail:* reception@aitkenalexander.co.uk. *Website:* www.aitkenalexander.co.uk.

RABE, Berniece, BSEd, MA; American author; b. 11 Jan. 1928, Parma, MO; m. 1946, three s. one d. *Education:* National College, Northern Illinois University, Roosevelt University, Columbia College, Chicago. *Career:* Writing Instructor, Columbia College, Chicago; Consultant, Missouri Council of the Arts; mem. Society of Midland Authors; Off Campus Writers; Fox Valley Writers. *Publications:* Rass, 1973; Naomi, 1975; The Girl Who Had No Name, 1977; The Orphans, 1978; Who's Afraid, 1980; Margaret's Moves, 1987; A Smooth Move, 1987; Rehearsal for the Bigtime, 1988; Where's Chimpy, 1988; Tall Enough to Own the World, 1988; Magic Comes In It's Time, 1993; The Legend of the First Candy Cares, 1994. Other: Two film scripts; Picture books for children. Contributions: Short stories and articles. *Honours:* Honor Book, 1975, Golden Kite Award, 1977, National Society of Children's Book Writers; Midland Author's Award, 1978; Notable Book of the Year, American Library Asscn, 1982; National Children's Choice Award, 1987.

RABE, David William, BA, MA; American dramatist, screenwriter and author; b. 10 March 1940, Dubuque, IA; m. 1st Elizabeth Pan 1969 (divorced); one c.; m. 2nd Jill Clayburgh 1979. *Education:* Loras Coll., Villanova Univ. *Career:* feature writer, Register, New Haven 1969–70; Asst Prof., Villanova Univ. 1970–72. *Publications:* plays: The Basic Training of Pavlo Hummel 1971, Sticks and Bones 1971, The Orphan 1973, In the Boom Boom Room 1973, Burning 1974, Streamers 1976, Goose and Tomtom 1976, Hurlyburly 1984, Those the River Keeps 1990, A Question of Mercy, The Dog Problem, The Black Monk; screenplays: I'm Dancing as Fast as I Can 1982, Streamers 1983, Casualties of War 1989, The Firm 1993; novels: Recital of the Dog 1992, The Crossing Guard 1994; A Primitive Heart (stories). *Honours:* Rockefeller Foundation grant 1969, Associated Press Award 1970, Drama Desk Award 1971, Drama Guild Award 1971, Dramatists' Guild Elizabeth Hull-Kate Warriner Award 1971, Obie Award 1971, Outer Critics' Circle Award 1972, Tony Award 1972, American Acad. of Arts and Letters Awards 1974, 1976, Guggenheim Fellowship 1976, New York Drama Critics' Circle Award 1976. *Address:* c/o Grove-Atlantic, 841 Broadway, Fourth Floor, New York, NY 10003, USA (office).

RABEE, Hayder K. Gafar, BA; Iraqi teacher of calligraphy; b. 22 Feb. 1962, Najaf; m. Ahalam A. al-Zahawi 1986; two s. one d. *Education:* Inst. of Fine Arts. *Career:* calligrapher, Baghdad TV 1982–88; worked as designer, newspapers and magazines 1989–91; teacher, Inst. of Fine Arts, Baghdad 1992–, Head, Calligraphy Dept (evening classes) 1995–; teacher of Arabic Calligraphy, Jordanian Calligraphers' Soc. 1998; Gen. Sec. Iraqi Calligraphers' Soc. 1998–99; mem. Iraqi Plastic Arts Soc. 1996–2002, Iraqi Union of Artists, Iraqi Soc. for Calligraphy Jordanian Calligraphers' Soc., Egyptian Calligraphers' Soc. *Exhibitions:* Breezes from Baghdad, Italy 2001, 2004,

Postal Card Fair, Sharijah Art Museum 2004. *Publication:* Proposed Alphabetic Study for Arabic Calligraphy in Printing 1989. *Honours:* State Trophy for Plastic Arts and Calligraphy 1989, 1999, Gold Medal, 2nd World Festival 1992, Third World Festival 1993, Gold Medal for Creativity, Dar Es-Salaam 1st Nat. Festival 1993, Appreciation Prize, 4th Baghdad Nat. Festival 1998, Appreciation Prize in 5th Int. Competition for Calligraphy, Turkey 2001, a main prizewinner, Int. Meeting for Calligraphy of the Islam World, Tehran 2002. *Address:* al-Waziria, Sec. 301, St. 13 Ho. 50, Baghdad (home); Department of Calligraphy, Institute of Fine Arts, al-Mansur, Baghdad, Iraq (office).

RACHLIN, Nahid, BA; Iranian/American writer and teacher; b. 6 June 1944, Abadan, Iran; m. Howard Rachlin, one d. *Education:* Lindenwood Coll., St Charles, MO and Columbia Univ. *Career:* teacher in New York Univ., School of Continuing Education 1978–90, Marymount Manhattan Coll. 1986–87, Hofstra Univ. 1988–90, Yale Univ. 1989–90, Hunter Coll., CUNY 1990, Barnard Coll. 1991–; mem. PEN. *Publications:* Foreigner 1978, John Murray 1978, Married to a Stranger 1983, Veils 1992; contrib. to reviews, journals and magazines. *Honours:* Doubleday-Columbia Fellowship, Stanford Univ. Stegner Fellowship, NEA grant, Bennet Certificate, PEN Syndicated Fiction Project. *E-mail:* nahidr@rcn.com. *Website:* nahidrachlin.com.

RACIONERO GRAU, Luis; Spanish librarian, academic and writer; b. 1940, Seu d'Urgell, Lleida. *Education:* Univ. of Calif. at Berkeley, USA, Churchill Coll., Cambridge, UK. *Career:* industrial engineer, Barcelona 1965; Prof. of Micro Econs, Faculty of Econ. Sciences and Urban Studies, School of Architecture, Barcelona; fmr Dir Spanish Coll., Paris; Dir-Gen. Biblioteca Nacional, Madrid 2001–04. *Publications include:* Taoista textos de estética 1991, Atenas de Pericles 1993, El arte de escribir 1995, La sonrisa de la Gioconda: Memorias de Leonardo 1999, Filosofias del Underground 2000, El pecado original 2001, Oriente y Occidente 2001, El progreso decadente (Espasa de Ensayo Prize) 2001, El alquimista trouador 2003. *Address:* c/o Editorial Planeta, Córcega 273-277, 08008 Barcelona, Spain.

RADAKOVIĆ, Borivoj; Serbian playwright and writer; b. 1951. *Career:* f. Festival of Alternative Culture, network of new writers and publishers (invites UK and US writers to perform); currently full-time writer Zagreb, Croatia. *Publications:* Sjaj epohe (novel) 1990, Dobro dosli uplavi pakao (play) 1996, Jako, Croatian Nights (ed., anthology) 2005; two collections of short stories, trans. *Address:* c/o Rende, Hadži Đerina 7, II sprat, stan br. 8, 11000 Belgrade, Serbia. *E-mail:* info@rende.co.yu. *Website:* www.rende.co.yu.

RADDEN, Jennifer H., BA, BPhil, DPhil; Australian/American academic and writer; *Professor of Philosophy, University of Massachusetts, Boston*; b. 10 Sept. 1943, Melbourne, Vic. *Education:* Univ. of Melbourne, Univ. of Oxford. *Career:* psychiatric social worker, Melbourne 1966–67, Greenfield, MA, USA 1971–72; Lecturer in Philosophy, Tufts Univ., Medford, MA 1972–74; Lecturer 1975–84, Asst Prof. 1984–89, Assoc. Prof. 1990–97, Prof. of Philosophy 1997–, Chair 2002–07, Univ. of Massachusetts, Boston; Guest Lecturer in Australia 1995, 1996, England 1995, 1999, 2006, Sweden 1996, Denmark 1997; mem., Forensic Psychiatry Group 1992–99, Human Rights Cttee 1996–2000, Massachusetts Mental Health Center and Harvard Medical School; mem. Ethics Cttee, McLean Hospital 1996–; Fellow Harvard Univ. 1991; mem. American Philosophical Asscn, Soc. for Women in Philosophy, Asscn for the Advancement of Philosophy and Psychiatry (exec. bd 1992–2002, pres. 1997–), Soc. for Practical and Professional Ethics. *Publications:* Madness and Reason 1985, Divided Minds and Successive Selves: Ethical Issues in Disorders of Identity and Personality 1996, The Nature of Melancholy (ed.) 2000, The Philosophy of Psychiatry: A Companion (ed.) 2004; contrib. to Philosophical Studies, Current Opinion in Psychiatry, Philosophy and Phenomenological Research, Bioethics, Journal of Social Theory and Practice, Dialogue, Philosophy, Psychiatry and Psychology Review, Harvard Review of Psychiatry. *Address:* Department of Philosophy, University of Massachusetts, Boston, MA 02125, USA (office). *Telephone:* (617) 287-6546 (office). *Fax:* (617) 287-6511 (office). *E-mail:* jennifer.radden@umb.edu.

RADLEY, Sheila (see Robinson, Sheila Mary)

RADZINSKY, Edvard Stanislavovich; Russian dramatist; b. 23 Sept. 1936, Moscow; s. of Stanislav Radzinsky and Sofia Radzinsky; m. 2nd Yelena Timofeyevna Denisova. *Education:* Inst. of History and Archival Science, Moscow. *Plays include:* My Dream is India 1960, You're All of Twenty-Two, you Old Men! 1962, One Hundred and Four Pages on Love 1964, Kolobashkin the Seducer 1967, Socrates 1977, Lunin 1980, I Stand at the Restaurant 1982, Theatre of the Time of Nero and Seneca 1984, Elderly Actress in the Role of Dostoevsky's Wife 1986, Sporting Scenes 1987, Our Decameron 1989. *Television:* author and narrator of TV series Mysteries of History 1997–. *Publications:* novels: The Last of the Romanovs 1989, Our Decameron 1990; non-fiction: The Last Tsar: The Life and Death of Nicholas II 1992, God Save and Restrain Russia 1993, Stalin 1996, Mysteries of History 1997, Mysteries of Love 1998, Fall of Gallant Century 1998, Collected Works (7 Vols) 1998–99, Rasputin 1999, The Theatrical Novel (memoirs) 1999, Alexander II, The Last Great Tsar 2005. *Address:* Usiyevicha Street 8, Apt 96, 125319 Moscow, Russia (home). *E-mail:* edvard@radzinski.ru (office). *Website:* www.radzinski.ru (office).

RADZYMIŃSKA, Józefa, BA; Polish writer; b. Lesznowola; d. of Julian Radzymiński and Helena Ładyńska; m. Franciszek Płodowski 1945; one s. *Education:* Acad. of Political Sciences, Warsaw. *Career:* served in Polish underground army (Armia Krajowa) 1939–45, imprisoned by the Nazis 1941, 1944–45; took part in Warsaw Uprising 1944; lived in Italy, UK and Argentina 1945–62, returned to Poland 1962; mem. PEN, Asscn of Polish Writers 1962. *Publications:* Second Time Ashes, The White Eagle on Río de la Plata, Not Destroyed by Thunder, Independent for Ever; 25 vols of poetry, novels, memoirs and monographs. *Honours:* Polonia Restituta Cross, Armia Krajowa Cross, Warsaw Rising Cross, numerous other medals 1973–83. *Address:* Broniewskiego 14/29, 00 771 Warsaw, Poland. *Telephone:* (22) 39-90-40.

RAE, Hugh Crauford, (James Albany, Robert Crawford, R. B. Houston, Stuart Stern, Jessica Stirling); British novelist; b. 22 Nov. 1935, Glasgow, Scotland; m. Elizabeth Dunn 1960, one d. *Career:* mem. Scottish Asscn of Writers. *Publications:* Skinner, 1965; Night Pillow, 1966; A Few Small Bones, 1968; The Saturday Epic, 1970; Harkfast, 1976; Sullivan, 1978; Haunting at Waverley Falls, 1980; Privileged Strangers, 1982. As Jessica Stirling: The Spoiled Earth, 1974; The Hiring Fair, 1976; The Dark Pasture, 1978; The Deep Well at Noon, 1980; The Blue Evening Gone, 1982; The Gates at Midnight, 1983; Treasures on Earth, 1985; Creature Comforts, 1986; Hearts of Gold, 1987; The Good Provider, 1988; The Asking Price, 1989; The Wise Child, 1990; The Welcome Light, 1991; Lantern for the Dark, 1992; Shadows on the Shore, 1993; The Penny Wedding, 1994; The Marrying Kind, 1995; The Workhouse Girl, 1996; The Island Wife, 1997; Prized Possessions, 2001. As James Albany: Warrior Caste, 1982; Mailed Fist, 1982; Deacon's Dagger, 1982; Close Combat, 1983; Matching Fire, 1983; Last Bastion, 1984; Borneo Story, 1984.

RAE, Simon; British poet, biographer, broadcaster and playwright; b. 1952. *Career:* poet-in-residence, Warwickshire County Cricket Club/Midlands Arts Centre 1999; founder mem., Top Edge Theatre Productions. *Radio:* Poetry Please (presenter, BBC Radio 4), 20,000 Frenchmen under the Sea (writer) 1993, A Memory Lost (writer) 1994, Who Shall Bind the Infinite? (writer) 1995, Not at Dorking (writer) 1996. *Plays:* A Quiet Night In 1999, Grass 2001, Rose 2003. *Publications:* poetry: Faber Introduction 5 1982, Great Tew 1989, Seren Poets 2 1990, Calendar 1990, Soft Targets 1991, Thatcher's Inferno 1992, Listening to the Lake 1993, Allotment 1996, Rapid Response: Poems from The Guardian 1991–1996, The Face of War 1999, Empires 2001, Caught On Paper: Cricket Poems 2002; biography: W.G. Grace: A Life 1998, It's Not Cricket: A History of Skulduggery, Sharp Practice and Downright Cheating in the Noble Game 2001; editor: The Orange Dove of Fiji: Poems for the World Wide Fund for Nature 1989, The Faber Book of Drink, Drinkers and Drinking 1991, The Faber Book of Murder 1994, The Faber Book of Christmas 1996, News That Stays News: The Twentieth Century in Poems 1999; contrib. poetry to anthologies, including Give Me Shelter 1991, Klaonica: Poems for Bosnia 1993, Bearing Witness 1995, The Gift: New Writing for the NHS 2002; contrib. to The Guardian, TLS, The Observer, New Statesman, Poetry Review, London Magazine, Leviathan. *Honours:* Royal Literary Fund Fellow, Warwick Univ. 1999–2001, Oxford Brookes Univ. 2003; Nat. Poetry Competition winner 1999, Southern Arts Literature Bursary, Gregory Award. *Address:* Faber and Faber Ltd, 3 Queen Square, London, WC1N 3AU, England. *Website:* www.faber.co.uk.

RAE-ELLIS, Vivienne, (Antonia Bell), FRGS; Australian writer; b. 23 July 1930, Tasmania, Australia; m. W. F. Ellis 1952; one s. one d. *Career:* mem. Australian Soc. of Authors, RSL, Soc. of Authors, London. *Publications:* Lively Libraries 1975, Trucanini: Queen or Traitor? 1976, Queen Trucanini (with Nancy Cato) 1976, Menace at Oyster Bay 1978, The Tribe With No Feet 1978, Louisa Anne Meredith: A Tigress in Exile 1979, The Cavendish Affair 1980, Black Robinson 1988, True Ghost Stories 1990; contrib. to books, newspapers, journals, radio and TV. *Address:* Gainsborough's House, 17 The Circus, Bath, BA1 2ET, England. *E-mail:* vraellis@gifford.co.uk.

RAFFEL, Burton Nathan; American academic, lawyer, writer, poet and editor and translator; b. 27 April 1928, New York, NY; m. Elizabeth Clare Wilson 1974; three s. three d. *Education:* BA, Brooklyn College, CUNY, 1948; MA, Ohio State Univ., 1949; JD, Yale Univ., 1958. *Career:* Lecturer, Brooklyn College, CUNY, 1950–51; Ed., Foundation News, 1960–63; Instructor, 1964–65, Asst Prof., 1965–66, State Univ. of New York at Stony Brook; Assoc. Prof., State Univ. of New York at Buffalo, 1966–68; Visiting Prof., Haifa Univ., 1968–69, York Univ., Toronto, 1972–75, Emory Univ., 1974; Prof. of English and Classics, Univ. of Texas at Austin, 1969–71; Sr Tutor (Dean), Ontario College of Art, Toronto, 1971–72; Prof. of English, 1975–87, Lecturer in Law, 1986–87, Univ. of Denver; Ed.-in-Chief, Denver Quarterly, 1976–77; Contributing Ed., Humanities Education, 1983–87; Dir, Adirondack Mountain Foundation, 1987–89; Advisory Ed., The Literary Review, 1987–2003; Distinguished Prof. of Humanities and Prof. of English, Univ. of Louisiana at Lafayette, 1989–2003; mem. National Faculty. *Publications:* Non-Fiction: The Development of Modern Indonesian Poetry, 1967; The Forked Tongue: A Study of the Translation Process, 1971; Introduction to Poetry, 1971; Why Re-Create?, 1973; Robert Lowell, 1981; T. S. Eliot, 1982; American Victorians: Explorations in Emotional History, 1984; How to Read a Poem, 1984; Ezra Pound: The Prime Minister of Poetry, 1985; Politicians, Poets and Con Men, 1986; The Art of Translating Poetry, 1988; Artists All: Creativity, the University, and the World, 1991; From Stress to Stress: An Autobiography of English Prosody, 1992; The Art of Translating Prose, 1994; The Annotated Milton, 1999. Fiction: After Such Ignorance, 1986; Founder's Fury (with Elizabeth Raffel), 1988; Founder's Fortune (with Elizabeth Raffel), 1989. Poetry: Mia Poems, 1968; Four Humours, 1979; Changing the Angle of the Sun-Dial, 1984; Grice, 1985; Evenly Distributed Rubble, 1985; Man as a Social Animal, 1986; Beethoven in Denver, and other poems, 1999. Other: numerous trans.; annotated version of Hamlet, 2003. Contributions: professional journals. *Honours:* Frances Steloff Prize for Fiction, 1978; American-French Foundation Trans. Prize, 1991; several grants. *Address:* 203 S Mannering Avenue, Lafayette, LA 70508, USA. *E-mail:* bnraffel@cox-internet.com.

RAGAN, James, BA, PhD; American poet, dramatist and academic; *Professor and Director of Professional Writing Program, University of Southern California;* b. 19 Dec. 1944, Pennsylvania; m. Debora Ann Skovranko 1982; one s. two d. *Education:* Vincent Coll., Ohio Univ. *Career:* Prof. and Dir Professional Writing Program, Univ. of Southern California 1981–; Visiting Prof. CALTECH 1989–; Poet-in-Residence Charles Univ., Prague 1993–; mem. Associated Writing Programs, MLA, Modern Poetry Asscn, PEN, Poetry Soc. of America, Writers' Guild of America, West. *Plays produced:* The Landlord, Saints, Commedia. *Publications:* In the Talking Hours 1979, Womb-Weary 1990, Yevgeny Yevtushenko: The Collected Poems (ed.) 1991, The Hunger Wall 1995, Lusions 1996, The World Shouldering I 2006; contrib. to anthologies, reviews, quarterlies, journals and magazines. *Honours:* hon. mem. Russian Acad. of Arts and Sciences 1997; Hon. DHumLitt (St Vincent Coll.) 1990, (Richmond Univ., London) 2001; Swan Foundation Humanitarian Award, Pittsburgh 1972, Nat. Endowment for the Arts grant 1972, Fulbright Fellow 1985, 1988, co-winner Poetry Soc. of America Gertrude Claytor Award 1987, Ohio Univ. Medal of Merit for Poetry 1990, Poet's Corner, BHTV Telly Award 1996, St Vincent Coll. Phi Kappa Phi Nat. Creative Artist Award 1999, Phi Beta Kappa 2002, and Presidential Medal 2003. *Address:* 1516 Beverwil Drive, Los Angeles, CA 90035, USA.

RAHIMI, Atiq, PhD; Afghan novelist and film-maker; b. 1962, Kabul; m. *Education:* Univ. of Kabul, Sorbonne, France. *Career:* political asylum in France 1985–. *Publications (in translation):* Earth and Ashes 2001, A Thousand Rooms of Dream and Fear 2006. *Address:* c/o Chatto & Windus, Random House, 20 Vauxhall Bridge Road, London, SW1V 2SA, England.

RAINE, Craig Anthony, BA, BPhil; British writer; b. 3 Dec. 1944, Shildon, Co. Durham; s. of Norman Edward and Olive Marie Raine; m. Ann Pasternak Slater 1972; three s. one d. *Education:* Exeter Coll., Oxford. *Career:* Lecturer, Exeter Coll., Oxford 1971–72, 1975–76, Lincoln Coll. 1974–75, Christ Church 1976–79; Books Ed. New Review 1977–78; Ed. Quarto 1979–80; Poetry Ed. New Statesman 1981; Poetry Ed. Faber and Faber Ltd 1981–91; Fellow in English, New Coll. Oxford 1991–; Ed. Areté 1999–. *Publications:* The Onion, Memory 1978, A Martian Sends a Postcard Home 1979, A Free Translation 1981, Rich 1984, The Electrification of the Soviet Union (opera) 1986, A Choice of Kipling's Prose (ed.) 1987, The Prophetic Book 1988, '1953' (play) 1990, Haydn and the Valve Trumpet: Literary Essays 1990, Rudyard Kipling: Selected Poetry (ed.) 1992, History: The Home Movie 1994, Clay. Whereabouts Unknown 1996, New Writing 7 1998, A la recherche du temps perdu 1999, In Defence of T.S. Eliot: Literary Essays (Vol. 2) 2000, Collected Poems 1978–1999 2000, Rudyard Kipling: The Wish House and Other Stories (ed.) 2002, T.S. Eliot 2006. *Honours:* Kelus Prize 1979, Southern Arts Literature Award 1979, Cholmondeley Poetry Award 1983, Sunday Times Award for Literary Excellence 1998. *Address:* New College, Oxford, OX1 3BN, England (office).

RAINES, Howell, MA; American journalist. *Education:* Birmingham-Southern Coll. and Univ. of Alabama. *Career:* journalist, Birmingham Post-Herald 1964, Birmingham (Ala) News 1970; Political Ed. Atlanta Constitution 1971–76, St Petersburg (Fla) Times 1976–78; Nat. Corresp. in Atlanta, NY Times 1978, Atlanta Bureau Chief 1979–81, White House Corresp. 1981–84, Nat. Political Corresp. 1984, Deputy Washington Ed. 1985–87, London Bureau Chief 1987–88, Washington Bureau Chief 1988–93, Editorial Page Ed. 1993–2001, Exec. Ed. 2001–03. *Publications:* My Soul Is Rested 1977, Whiskey Man 1977, Fly Fishing Through the Midlife Crisis 1993. *Honours:* Pulitzer Prize for feature writing 1992. *Address:* c/o The New York Times, 229 W. 43rd Street, New York, NY 10036, USA (office).

RAJAN, Tilottama, BA, MA, PhD, FRSC; American academic, writer and poet; *Canada Research Chair in English and Theory, University of Western Ontario;* b. 1 Feb. 1951, New York, NY. *Education:* Trinity Coll., Toronto, Univ. of Toronto. *Career:* Asst Prof., Huron Coll., Univ. of Western Ontario 1977–80; Asst Prof. 1980–83, Assoc. Prof. 1983–85, Queen's Univ.; Prof., Univ. of Wisconsin at Madison 1985–90; Prof. 1990–, Dir Centre for the Study of Theory and Criticism 1995–2001, Canada Research Chair in English and Theory 2001–, Univ. of Western Ontario; mem. Canadian Comparative Literature Asscn, Univ. of Teachers of English, Keats-Shelley Asscn, MLA of America, North American Soc. for the Study of Romanticism, Wordsworth-Coleridge Asscn. *Publications:* Myth in a Metal Mirror 1967, Dark Interpreter: The Discourse of Romanticism 1980, The Supplement of Reading 1990, Intersections: Nineteenth Century Philosophy and Contemporary Theory 1995, Romanticism, History and the Possibilities of Genre 1998, Deconstruction and the Remainders of Phenomenology: Sartre, Derrida, Foucault, Baudrillard 2002, After Poststructuralism: Writing the Intellectual History of Theory 2002, Idealism Without Absolutes: Philosophy and Romantic Culture (with Arkady Plotnitsky) 2004; contrib. to professional journals. *Honours:* Guggenheim Fellowship 1987–88, Keats-Shelley Asscn of America Distinguished Lifetime Award 2005. *Address:* Department of

English, University of Western Ontario, London, ON N6A 5B8, Canada (office). *Telephone:* (519) 661-2211 (office). *E-mail:* trajan@uwo.ca.

RAJIC, Négovan, BEng, DipEng; Canadian writer; b. 24 June 1923, Belgrade, Yugoslavia; s. of Vladimir Rajic and Zagorka Rajic (née Vuletic); m. Mirjana Knezevic 1970; one s. one d. *Education:* Gymnasium of Belgrade, Univ. of Belgrade, Conservatoire des Arts et Metiers, France. *Career:* fought with Resistance during World War II; settled in France 1947; research engineer, physics laboratory, École Polytechnique de Paris 1956–63; electronics teacher, France 1963–69; settled in Canada 1969; Prof. of Mathematics, Collège de Trois-Rivières –1987; mem. Int. PEN, Asscn of Writers of Québec. *Publications:* Les Hommes-Taupes (trans. as The Mole Men) 1978, Propos d'un vieux radoteur (trans. as The Master of Srappado) 1982, Sept Roses pour une boulangère (trans. as Seven Roses for a Baker) 1987, Service pénitentiaire national (trans. as The Shady Business) 1988, Vers l'autre rive: Adieu Belgrade (novel) (Grand prix culturel de Trois-Rivières 2001) 2000, Le Puits ou histoire sans queue ni tête (play); contrib. numerous articles and short stories to publications. *Honours:* hon. mem. Asscn of Serbian Writers, Belgrade; Prix Esso du Cercle du Livre de France 1978, Prix Air Canada for best short story 1980, Prix Slobodan Yovanovitch, Asscn des écrivains et artistes serbes en éxil 1984, Prix littéraire de Trois-Rivières 1988, Franz Kafka Medal, European Circle, Prague 2000. *Address:* 300 rue Dunant, Trois-Rivières, QC G8Y 2W9, Canada.

RAKOVSZKY, Zsuzsa; Hungarian writer, poet and translator; b. 4 Dec. 1950, Sopron. *Education:* Eötvös Univ., Budapest. *Career:* mem. Hungarian PEN, Hungarian Writers' Asscn. *Publications:* Joslatok es hataridok 1981, Tovabb egy hazzal 1987, Feher-fekete 1991, A kigyo arnyeka (novel) 2002, A hullocsillag eve (novel) 2005; contrib. to Kortars, Jelenkor, Alfold, Holmi, 2000, New Hungarian Quarterly. *Honours:* Graves Prize 1980, Dery Prize 1986, József Attila Prize 1986. *Address:* Torna u 22, Sopron, Hungary. *E-mail:* pap.zoltan@lira.hu.

RAKOWSKI, Andrzej, MA, MSc, PhD, DSc; Polish musicologist and acoustician; *Chair of Musicology, A. Mickiewicz University*; b. 16 June 1931, Warsaw; m. Magdalena Jakobczyk 1972; one s. two d. *Education:* Univ. of Durham, UK, Warsaw Univ. of Technology, Warsaw Univ., State Coll. of Music in Warsaw. *Career:* Prof. of Musical Acoustics 1963–2001, Prof. Emer. 2001–; Pres. 1981–87, Chopin Acad. of Music, Warsaw; part-time Prof., Inst. of Musicology, Warsaw Univ. 1987–2003; Chair. of Musicology, A. Mickiewicz Univ. 1997–; Visiting Prof., McGill Univ., Montreal, Canada 1985, Hebrew Univ., Jerusalem, Israel 1991, Central Inst. for the Deaf, St Louis, Mo., USA 1997–98, Univ. Nova de Lisboa, Portugal 2004; mem. Polish Music Council (Vice-Pres. 1984–89), Union of Polish Composers, Polish Acad. of Sciences (Pres. Acoustical Cttee 1996–), European Soc. for Cognitive Sciences of Music (Pres. 2000–03); Fellow, Acoustical Soc. of America 2001–. *Publications:* Categorical Perception of Pitch in Music 1978, The Access of Children and Youth to Musical Culture 1984, Studies on Pitch and Timbre of Sound in Music (ed.) 1999, Creation and Perception of Sound Sequences in Music (ed.) 2002; contrib. over 100 articles on music perception and music acoustics to int. journals. *Honours:* Golden Cross of Merit 1973, Bachelor's Cross, Order of Polonia Restituta 1983, Officer's Cross 2002. *Address:* Fryderyk Chopin Academy of Music, Okolnik 2, 00-368 Warsaw (office); Pogonowskiego 20, 01-564 Warsaw, Poland (home). *Telephone:* (22) 827-8303 (office); (22) 839-9456 (home). *Fax:* (22) 827-8310 (office). *E-mail:* rakowski@chopin.edu.pl. *Website:* www.chopin.edu.pl/angielskie/osobowe/rakowski.html (office).

RAMA, Carlos M., PhD; Uruguayan writer, lawyer, academic and editor; b. 26 Oct. 1921, Montevideo; s. of Manuel Rama and Carolina Facal; m. Judith Dellepiane 1943; one s. one d. *Education:* Univ. de la República and Univ. de Paris. *Career:* journalist 1940–48, 1972–; Exec. Sec. of Uruguayan Bar Asscn 1940–49; Prof. of Universal History in secondary schools 1944–48; Ed. Nuestro Tiempo 1954–56, Gacetilla Austral 1961–73; Prof. of Sociology and Social Research, Prof. of Contemporary History, Prof. of Theory and Methodology of History, Univ. de la República 1950–72; Prof. of Latin American History, Univ. Autónoma de Barcelona 1973–; Pres. PEN Club Latinoamericano en España; Sec. Gen. Grupo de Estudios Latinoamericanos de Barcelona. *Publications:* La Historia y la Novela 1947, 1963, 1970, 1974, Las ideas socialistas en el siglo XIX 1947, 1949, 1963, 1967, 1976, Ensayo de Sociología Uruguaya 1956, Teoría de la Historia 1959, 1968, 1974, 1980, Las clases sociales en el Uruguay 1960, La Crisis española del siglo XX 1960, 1962, 1976, Itinerario español 1961, 1977, Revolución social y fascismo en el siglo XX 1962, Sociología del Uruguay 1965, 1973, Historia del movimiento obrero y social latinoamericano contemporáneo 1967, 1969, 1976, Los afrouruguayos 1967, 1968, 1969, 1970, Garibaldi y el Uruguay 1968, Uruguay en Crisis 1969, Sociología de América Latina 1970, 1977, Chile, mil días entre la revolución y el fascismo 1974, España, crónica entrañable 1973–77, 1978, Historia de América Latina 1978, Fascismo y anarquismo en la España contemporánea 1979. *Honours:* Commdr, Order of Liberation (Spain), Officier des Palmes académiques (France). *Address:* c/o Monte de Orsá 7, Vallvidrera, Barcelona 17, Spain.

RAMA RAU, Santha; Indian writer; b. 24 Jan. 1923, Madras, Tamil Nadu; d. of the late Sir Benegal Rama Rau and Dhanvanthi Handoo; m. 1st Faubion Bowers 1951 (divorced 1966, died 1999); one s.; m. 2nd Gurdon W Wattles 1970 (died 1995); two step-s. two step-d. *Education:* St Paul's Girls' School, London and Wellesley Coll., USA. *Career:* numerous journeys in Europe, India, America, S. E Asia, Japan and Russia; fmr teacher Hani Freedom School, Tokyo; English teacher at Sarah Lawrence Coll., Bronxville, NY 1971–73. *Plays:* A Passage to India (Oxford Playhouse 1959, West End, London 1960, Broadway, New York 1961). *Television:* A Passage to India 1962. *Publications:* Home to India 1945, East of Home 1950, This is India 1953, Remember the House 1955, View to the South-East 1957, My Russian Journey 1959, A Passage to India (dramatization of E. M. Forster novel) 1962, Gifts of Passage (autobiog.) 1962, The Cooking of India 1969, The Adventuress 1971, A Princess Remembers 1976, An Inheritance 1979; numerous articles and short stories. *Honours:* hon. doctorates from Bates, Brandeis, Roosevelt and Russell Sage Coll.; Achievement Awards from Wellesley Coll., Asia Soc., New York, The Secondary Educ. Bd, NJ, The Asscn of Indians in America. *Address:* 508 Leedville Road, Amenia, NY 12501; 16 Sutton Place, New York, NY 10022, USA. *Telephone:* (845) 373-9124 (Amenia) (office); (212) 755-3684 (New York) (office). *Fax:* (845) 373-7796 (Amenia) (home).

RAMADAN, Tariq, MA, PhD; Swiss academic; *Senior Research Fellow, Lokahi Foundation*; b. 26 Aug. 1962, Geneva; m.; two s. two d. *Education:* Univ. of Geneva. *Career:* taught Islamic Studies and Philosophy at Freiburg Univ.; apptd Prof. of Islamic Studies and Luce Prof. of Religion Conflict and Peacebuilding, Kroc Inst., Univ. of Notre Dame, USA 2004 (visa revoked); Sr Research Fellow, Lokahi Foundation 2004–, Doshisha Univ., Kyoto 2007–; Visiting Prof., St Antony's Coll., Oxford, UK 2004–, Erasmus Univ., Netherlands 2007–; Chair. European Muslim Network, Brussels. *Publications:* To be a European Muslim 1998, Islam, the West, and the Challenges of Modernity 2000, Jihad, Violence, War and Peace in Islam (in French) 2002, Western Muslims and the Future of Islam 2003, Globalisation: Muslim Resistances 2004, Muslims in France: The Way Towards Coexistence 2004, The Life of the Prophet, Lessons from his Life 2006, Radical Reform, Radical Ijtihad 2007, The Messenger 2007, In the Footsteps of the Prophet 2007; contrib. of more than 850 articles, reviews and chapters in books and magazines. *Honours:* One of the Seven Innovators of the 21st Century, Time magazine 2000, One of the 100 People of the Year 2004, European of the Year, European Voice 2006. *Address:* St Antony's College, 62 Woodstock Road, Oxford, OX2 6JF, England (office). *Telephone:* (1865) 284700 (office). *Fax:* (20) 8810-5142 (office). *E-mail:* office@tariqramadan.com (office). *Website:* www.tariqramadan.com (office).

RAMBAUD, Patrick; French writer; b. 21 April 1946, Paris; s. of François Rambaud and Madeleine de Magondeau; m. Pham-thi Tieu Hong 1988. *Career:* mil. service with French AF 1968–69; co-f. Actual magazine 1970–84. *Plays:* Fregoli (with Bernard Haller) (Théâtre nat. de Chaillot 1991. *Publications:* La Saignée 1970, Les Aventures communautaires de Wao-le-Laid (with Michel-Antoine Burnier) 1973, Les Complots de la liberté: 1832 (with Michel-Antoine Burnier) (Prix Alexandre Dumas) 1976, Parodies (with Michel-Antoine Burnier) 1977, 1848 (with Michel-Antoine Burnier) 1977, Le Roland Barthes sans peine (with Michel-Antoine Burnier) 1978, Comme des rats 1980, La Farce des choses et autres parodies (with Michel-Antoine Burnier) 1982, Fric-Frac 1984, La Mort d'un ministre 1985, Frontière suisse (with Jean-Marie Stoerkel) 1986, Comment se tuer sans en avoir l'air 1987, Virginie Q (Prix de l'Insolent) 1988, Le Visage parle (with Bernard Haller) 1988, Bernard Pivot reçoit... 1989, Le Dernier voyage de San Marco 1990, Ubu Président ou L'Imposteur 1990, Les Carnets secrets d'Elena Ceaucescu (with Francis Szpiner) 1990, Les Mirobolantes aventures de Frégoli 1991, Mururoa mon amour 1996, Le Gros secret 1996, Oraisons funèbres des dignitaires politiques qui ont fait leur temps et feignent de l'ignorer (with André Balland) 1996, La Bataille (Grand Prix du Roman de l' Acad. française 1997, Prix Goncourt 1997, Napoleonic Soc. of America Literary Award 2000) 1997, Le Journalisme sans peine (with Michel-Antoine Burnier) 1997, Les Aventures de Mai 1998, Il neigeait (Prix Ciné-Roman 2001) 2000, L'Absent 2003, L'Idiot du village (Prix de la dédicace sonore 2005) 2004. *Honours:* Prix Alexandre Dumas 1976, Prix Lamartine 1981. *Address:* c/o Editions Grasset, 61 rue des Saints-Pères, 75006 Paris, France.

RAMDIN, Ronald Andrew, DipArts, BSc, DLitt, FRHistS, FRSA; Trinidadian historian, biographer, novelist and academic; b. 20 June 1942, Marabella; m. Irma de Freitas 1969, one s. *Education:* New Era Acad. of Drama and Music, University of Middlesex, LSE, University of London. *Career:* First Sec., Whitley Council, British Library 1973–75; Section Exec. Mem., Museums and Galleries Commission; mem. Society of Authors. *Publications:* From Chattel Slave to Wage Earner 1982, Introductory Text: The Black Triangle 1984, The Making of the Black Working Class in Britain 1987, Paul Robeson: The Man and His Mission 1987, World in View: The West Indies 1990, Reimaging Britain: 500 Years of Black and Asian History, The Other Middle Passage 1995, Arising From Bondage: A History of the Indo-Caribbean People 2000; essays: 'Multicultural Britain' in Fragments of British Culture 1998, 'The English Test: Post-War Immigration' in England 1945–2000 2000, Martin Luther King, Jr: Life and Times 2004; contributions to Anglo-British Review, City Limits, Dragon's Teeth, Race Today, Caribbean Times, West Indian Digest, History Workshop Journal, Wasafiri, Dalit Voice, The Hindu. *Honours:* Scarlet Ibis Medal, Gold Award, Trinidad and Tobago High Commission 1990, Hansib, Caribbean Times Community Award 1990. *Address:* c/o The British Library, Oriental and India Office Collections, 96 Euston Road, London NW1 2DB, England (office). *Website:* www.ronramdin.com.

RAMÍREZ MERCADO, Sergio; Nicaraguan politician and author; *President, Movimiento de Renovación Sandinista (MRS)*; b. 5 Aug. 1942, Masatepe, Masaya; s. of late Pedro Ramírez Gutiérrez and Luisa Mercado Gutiérrez; m. Gertrudis Guerrero Mayorga 1964; one s. two d. *Education:*

Univ. Autónoma de Nicaragua. *Career:* was active in revolutionary student movt and founding mem. of Frente Estudiantil Revolucionario 1962; mem. Cen. American Univ. Supreme Council (CSUCA), Costa Rica 1964, Pres. 1968; mem. Int. Comm. of FSLN (Sandinista Liberation Front) 1975; undertook tasks on diplomatic front, propaganda and int. work on behalf of FSLN leading to overthrow of regime 1979; mem. Junta of Nat. Reconstruction Govt 1979–; Vice-Pres. of Nicaragua 1984–90; minority leader, Speaker, Nat. Ass. 1990–94; Pres. Movimiento de Renovación Sandinista (MRS) 1994–, MRS pre-cand. for presidency 1996; co-founder literary journal Ventana. *Publications include:* Cuentos 1963, El cuento centroamericano 1974, Charles Atlas también muere 1976, El cuento nicaragüense 1976, Castigo divino 1988, Confesión de amor 1991, Clave de sol 1992, Cuentos 1994, Oficios compartidos 1994, Un baile de máscaras 1995, Margarita, Está Linda la Mar. *Honours:* Dr hc (Cen. Univ. of Ecuador); Bruno Kreisky Prize 1988, Alfaguara Prize (Madrid) 1998; Chevalier des Arts et des Lettres 1993. *Address:* MRS, Tienda Katty lc. Abajo, Apdo. 24, Managua, Nicaragua. *Telephone:* (2) 78-0279. *Fax:* (2) 78-0268. *Website:* www.sergioramirez.org.ni (office).

RAMKE, Bin, MA, PhD; American academic, editor and poet; b. 19 Feb. 1947, Port Neches, TX; m. 1967, one s. *Education:* Louisiana State Univ., Univ. of New Orleans, Ohio Univ. *Career:* Prof. of English, Columbus Univ., GA 1976–85, Univ. of Denver 1985–; Ed., Contemporary Poetry Series, University of Georgia Press, 1984–; Poetry Ed., The Denver Quarterly 1985–94, Ed. 1994–; mem. Associated Writing Programs, Nat. Book Critics Circle, PEN American Centre. *Publications:* The Difference Between Night and Day, 1978; White Monkeys, 1981; The Language Student, 1987; The Erotic Light of Gardens, 1989; Massacre of the Innocents, 1995. Contributions: reviews, quarterlies, and journals. *Honours:* Yale Younger Poets Award 1977, Texas Inst. of Arts and Letters Award for Poetry 1978, Iowa Poetry Award 1995. *Address:* Sturm Hall 384, University of Denver, Denver, CO 80208, USA (office). *E-mail:* bramke@du.edu (office).

RAMNEFALK, (Sylvia) Marie Louise, DLitt; Swedish poet, essayist and literary critic; b. 21 March 1941, Stockholm. *Education:* Univ. of Stockholm. *Career:* literary critic for several newspapers and magazines, now especially Svenska Dagbladet; mem. Bd Swedish Writers' Union 1979–83, 2006–, Swedish PEN. *Writing for music performance:* Love Love Love (opera libretto after poems by Robert Graves, music by Eskil Hemberg; premiered Rotunda of the Royal Opera, Stockholm) 1973, Någon har jag sett (opera libretto, music by Karólína Eiríksdóttir; premiered Vadstena Acad.) 1988, Det är du (mass, with music by Johannes Johansson; premiered Uppsala Cathedral) 2000, also texts for choral music and solo singing. *Publications:* Modern dramatik, tio analyser (with Gösta Kjellin) 1971, Tre lärodiktare. Studier i Harry Martinsons, Gunnar Ekelöfs och Karl Vennbergs lyrik (diss.) 1974, Enskilt liv pågår (poems) 1975, Robert Graves: Poems, interpretations 1976, Verkligheten gör dig den äran (poems) 1978, Någon har jag sett (poems) 1979, Kungsådra (poems) 1981, Kvinnornas litteraturhistoria (ed. with Anna Westberg) 1981, Sorg (poems) 1982, Levnadskonster. Lyrisk polemik om det Rätta, det Sanna, det Sköna (poems) 1983, Adam i Paradiset (narrative poetry) 1984, Det behövs något underjordiskt som kärlek och musik (selected poems) 1987, Julian såg Gud (narrative poetry) 1992, Älska mig nu! Dikter om kärlek och relationer av ungdomar (poems, ed. with Tom Hedlund) 1994, Författaren, världen, språket. Essäer om litteratur och skrivande (essays) 1996, Mystik – en kärlekshistoria. Richard Rolle, Walter Hilton, Julian av Norwich och Margery Kempe I senmedeltidens England (essays) 1997, Tusen och en natt I–II (stories) 1999, Lugna ner sig till det gråa (poems) 2001; also writes for TV drama, subjects including Esaias Tegnér; contrib. to various periodicals. *Honours:* several scholarships. *Address:* Vastra Valhallavagen 25A, 182 66 Djursholm, Sweden.

RAMOS ROSA, António; Portuguese poet and literary critic; b. 17 Oct. 1924, Faro; m. Agripina Costa Marques 1962; one d. *Career:* Dir literary reviews, Árvore 1951–53, Cassiopeia 1955, Cadernos do Meio-Dia 1958–60. *Publications include:* poetry: Delta seguido de Pela Primeira Vez 1996, Nomes de Ninguém 1997, À Mesa do Vento seguido de As Espirais de Dioniso 1997, A Imobilidade Fulminante 1998; essays: Poesia, Liberdade Livre 1962, A Poesia Moderna e a Interrogação do Real 1979, Incisões Oblíquas 1987, A Parede Azul 1991, As Palavras 2001, Génese 2005. *Honours:* Grand Oficial, Order of Santiago da Espada; Great Cross, Order of Infante Dom Henrique; Prize of Portuguese Centre of Int. Asscn of Literary Critics 1980, PEN Club's Poetry Prize 1980, 2006, Portuguese Asscn of Writers' Grand Prize 1989, Pessoa Prize 1988, International Poetry Prize of Liège Poetry Biennial 1991, European Poet of the Decade (Collège de l'Europe) 1991, Jean Malrieux Prize (Marseille) 1992; Luís Miguel Nava Poetry Prize 2006. *Address:* c/o Roma Editora, Avenida Roma, 129 r/c Esq., 1700-346 Lisbon, Portugal.

RAMPERSAD, Arnold, BA, MA, PhD; American academic and writer; b. 13 Nov. 1941, Trinidad; m. 1985, one c. *Education:* Bowling Green State Univ., Harvard Univ. *Career:* faculty mem. Dept of English, Stanford Univ. 1974–83; faculty mem., Rutgers Univ., Columbia Univ. and Princeton Univ. 1983–98; Sara Hart Kimball Prof. in the Humanities, Stanford Univ. 1998–; MacArthur Foundation Fellowship 1991–96; elected mem. American Acad. of Arts and Sciences, American Philosophical Soc. *Publications:* Melville's Israel Potter: A Pilgrimage and Progress 1969, The Art and Imagination of W. E. B. Dubois 1976, Life of Langston Hughes Vol. I 1902–1941: I Too Sing America 1986, Vol. II 1941–1967: I Dream a World 1988, Slavery and the Literary Imagination (co-ed.) 1989, Days of Grace: A Memoir (with Arthur Ashe) 1993, Jackie Robinson: A Biography 1997, Ralph Ellison: A Biography 2007. *Honours:* Cleveland Foundation Ansfield Wolf Book Award in Race Relations 1987, Phelps Stoke Fund Clarence L. Hotte Prize 1988, American Book Award 1990. *Address:* Department of English, Stanford University, Building 460, Margaret Jacks Hall, Stanford, CA 94305, USA (office). *E-mail:* rampersad@stanford.edu (office).

RAMPLING, Anne (see Rice, Anne)

RAMSAY-BROWN, John Andrew, (Jay Ramsay), BA; British poet, writer, editor and translator; b. 20 April 1958, Guildford, Surrey, England. *Education:* Pembroke College, Oxford, London Institute. *Career:* mem. College of Psychic Studies, London; Poetry Society; Psychosynthesis Education and Trust, London. *Publications:* Psychic Poetry: A Manifesto, 1985; Angels of Fire (co-ed.), 1986; New Spiritual: Selected Poems, 1986; Trwyn Meditations, 1987; The White Poem, 1988; Transformation: The Poetry of Spiritual Consciousness (ed.), 1988; The Great Return, books 1 to 5, 2 vols, 1988; Transmissions, 1989; Strange Days, 1990; Journey to Eden (with Jenny Davis), 1991; For Now (with Geoffrey Godbert), 1991; The Rain, the Rain, 1992; St Patrick's Breastplate, 1992; Tao Te Ching: A New Translation, 1993; I Ching, 1995; Kuan Yin, 1995; Chuang Tzu (with Martin Palmer), 1996; Alchemy: The Art of Transformation, 1996; Earth Ascending: An Anthology of New and Living Poetry (ed.), 1996; Kingdom of the Edge: New and Selected Poems 1980–1998, 1998. Contributions: periodicals.

RAMSEY, Jarold William, BA, PhD; American academic, poet, writer and dramatist; *Professor Emeritus, University of Rochester*; b. 1 Sept. 1937, Bend, OR; m. Dorothy Ann Quinn 1959; one s. two d. *Education:* Univ. of Oregon, Univ. of Washington. *Career:* acting instructor Univ. of Washington 1962–65; Asst Prof. 1965–70, Assoc. Prof. 1970–80, Prof. 1980–97, Prof. Emeritus 1997–, Univ. of Rochester; Visiting Prof. of English Univ. of Victoria, BC 1974, 1975–76; mem. MLA. *Publications:* poetry: The Space Between Us 1970, Love in an Earthquake 1973, Dermographia 1983, Hand-Shadows 1989; plays and libretti: Coyote Goes Upriver (play) 1981, The Lodge of Shadows (cantata with Samuel Adler) 1974; non-fiction: Coyote Was Going There: Indian Literature of the Oregon Country 1977, Reading the Fire: Essays in the Traditional Indian Literature of the Far West 1983; editor: Elizabeth and Melville Jacobs, Nehalem Tillamook Tales 1990, The Stories We Tell: Anthology of Oregon Folk Literature (with Suzi Jones) 1994, New Era: Reflections on the Human and Natural History of Central Oregon 2003; contrib. to anthologies, reviews, quarterlies and journals. *Honours:* Nat. Endowment for the Arts grant 1974, and Fellowship 1975, Ingram Merrill Foundation grant 1975, Don Walker Award for Best Essay on Western Literature 1978, Helen Bullis Award for Poetry 1984, Quarterly Review Int. Poetry Prize 1989. *Address:* 5884 NW Highway, No. 26, Madras, OR 97741, USA. *Telephone:* (541) 475-5390. *E-mail:* JWR_1937@madras.net.

RAND, Peter, MA; American writer; b. 23 Feb. 1942, San Francisco, CA; m. Bliss Inui 1976, one s. *Education:* Johns Hopkins University. *Career:* Fiction Ed., Antaeus, 1970–72; Ed., Washington Monthly, 1973–74; Teaching Fellow, Johns Hopkins University, 1975; Lecturer in English, Columbia University, 1976–91; mem. PEN; Authors' Guild; Poets and Writers; East Asian Institute, Columbia University; Research Assoc., Fairbank Center, Harvard University. *Publications:* Firestorm, 1969; The Time of the Emergency, 1977; The Private Rich, 1984; Gold From Heaven, 1988; Deng Xiaoping: Chronicle of an Empire, by Ruth Ming (ed. and trans. with Nancy Liu and Lawrence R. Sullivan), 1994; China Hands, 1995. Contributions: periodicals. *Honours:* CAPS 1977.

RANDALL, Jeff William, BA; British journalist; *Editor-at-Large, The Daily Telegraph*; b. 3 Oct. 1954, London; s. of Jeffrey Charles Randall and Grace Annie Randall (née Hawkridge); m. Susan Diane Fidler 1986; one d. *Education:* Royal Liberty Grammar School, Romford, Univ. of Nottingham, Univ. of Florida, USA. *Career:* with Hawkins Publrs 1982–85; Asst Ed. Financial Weekly 1985–86; City Corresp. Sunday Telegraph 1986–88; Deputy City Ed. The Sunday Times 1988–89, City Ed. 1989–94, City and Business Ed. 1994–95, Asst Ed. and Sports Ed. 1996–97; Ed. Sunday Business 1997–2001; Business Ed. BBC 2001–05; Ed.-at-Large The Daily Telegraph 2005–; freelance contrib. Daily Telegraph, Euromoney, Sporting Life, Golf World; Dir Times Newspapers 1994–95; Deputy Chair. Financial Dynamics Ltd 1995–96. *Publications:* The Day That Shook the World (co-author). *Honours:* Dr hc (Anglia Polytechnic Univ.) 2001; Financial Journalist of the Year, FT-Analysis 1991, Business Journalist of the Year, London Press Club 2000, Sony Gold Award 2003, Communicator of the Year 2004. *Address:* The Daily Telegraph, 111 Buckingham Palace Road, London, SW1W 0DT, England (office). *Website:* www.telegraph.co.uk (office).

RANDALL, Lisa, PhD; American physicist and academic; *Professor of Physics, Harvard University*. *Education:* Harvard Univ. *Career:* summer research at Smithsonian Astrophysical Observatory 1981, IBM Poughkeepsie 1982, FNAL 1982, Bell Laboratories 1983; Teaching Asst, Physics Dept, Harvard Univ. 1984, Physics Tutor, Adams House 1984–87, Asst Sr Tutor 1985–87; Pres.'s Fellow, Univ. of Calif., Berkeley 1987–89; Postdoctoral Fellow, Lawrence Berkeley Lab. 1989–90; Jr Fellow, Harvard Soc. of Fellows 1990–91; mem. staff MIT and Inst. for Theoretical Physics 1994, Asst Prof. of Physics, MIT 1991–95, Assoc. Prof. 1995–98, Prof. 1998–2001; Prof. of Physics, Princeton Univ. 1998–2000; Prof. of Physics, Harvard Univ. 2001–; Radcliffe Inst. Fellow 2002; Chair Radcliffe Inst. Cosmology and Theoretical Astrophysics Cluster 2003; mem. numerous conference programme and advisory cttees; Ed. Annual Review of Nuclear and Particle Science 1997–, Journal of High Energy Physics 1997–98, 2000–; Assoc. Ed. Nuclear Physics 1999–; John

Harvard Scholarship, Elizabeth Cary Agassiz Scholarship; Bell Laboratories Graduate Research Fellowship for Women; Alfred P. Sloan Foundation Research Fellowship 1992; Fellow, American Acad. of Arts and Science 2004. *Publications include:* Warped Passages 2005; numerous articles in magazines and journals. *Honours:* Westinghouse Science Talent Search Winner, David J. Robbins Prize, Dept of Energy Outstanding Jr Investigator Award 1992, Nat. Science Foundation Young Investigator Award 1992, Premio Caterina Tomassoni e Felice Pietro Chisesi Award 2003, Klopsted Award, American Soc. of Physics Teachers 2006. *Address:* Jefferson 461, 17 Oxford Street, Cambridge, MA 02138, USA (office). *Telephone:* (617) 496-8188 (office). *E-mail:* randall@physics.harvard.edu (office). *Website:* www.physics.harvard .edu/randall.htm (office).

RANDALL, Margaret; American writer, poet, photographer and teacher; b. 6 Dec. 1936, New York, NY; one s. three d. *Career:* Managing Ed., Frontiers: A Journal of Women's Studies, 1990–91; Distinguished Visiting Prof., University of Delaware, 1991; Visiting Prof., Trinity College, Hartford, CT, 1992. *Publications:* Giant of Tears, 1959; Ecstasy is a Number, 1961; Poems of the Glass, 1964; Small Sounds from the Brass Fiddle, 1964; October, 1965; Twenty-Five Stages of My Spine, 1967; Getting Rid of Blue Plastic, 1967; So Many Rooms Has a House But One Roof, 1967; Part of the Solution, 1972; Day's Coming, 1973; With These Hands, 1973; All My Used Parts, Shackles, Fuel, Tenderness and Stars, 1977; Carlota: Poems and Prose from Havana, 1978; We, 1978; A Poetry of Resistance, 1983; The Coming Home Poems, 1986; Albuquerque: Coming Back to the USA, 1986; This is About Incest, 1987; Memory Says Yes, 1988; The Old Cedar Bar, 1992; Dancing with the Doe, 1992; Hunger's Table: The Recipe Poems, 1997. Oral History: Cuban Women Now, 1974; Sandino's Daughters, 1981. Photography: Women Brave in the Face of Danger, 1985; Nicaragua Libre!, 1985. Contributions: anthologies, reviews, journals, and magazines. *Honours:* first prize in photography Nicaraguan Children's Asscn 1983, Creating Ourselves Nat. Art Exhibition 1992.

RANDALL, William Lowell, AB, MDiv, ThM, EdD; Canadian educator and writer; *Associate Professor, Department of Gerontology, St Thomas University;* b. 1 Dec. 1950, Black's Harbour, NB. *Education:* Harvard Univ., Emmanuel Coll., Victoria Univ., Univ. of Cambridge, Princeton Theological Seminary, Univ. of Toronto. *Career:* Minister, United Church of Canada 1979–90; English instructor, Seneca Coll. of Applied Arts and Tech., North York, Ont. 1991–95; Adjunct Lecturer, St Bonaventure Univ. 1992–94; part-time instructor, Univ. of Toronto 1993; seminar facilitator, site leader, Brock Univ. . 1993–95; Visiting Chair, Dept of Gerontology, St Thomas Univ., Fredericton, NB 1995, Research Assoc. 1996–2001, Asst Prof. 2001–05, Assoc. Prof. 2005–, Project Dir, Fredericton 80+ Study 1998–2007; Co-organizer Narrative Matters Conf. 2002–04; mem. Harvard Club of Atlantic Canada, Canadian Asscn on Gerontology. *Publications:* Restorying Our Lives: Personal Growth through Autobiographical Reflection (co-author) 1997, The Stories We Are: An Essay on Self-Creation 1995, Ordinary Wisdom: Biographical Aging and the Journey of Life (co-author) 2001, Reading Our Lives: The Poetics of Growing Old 2007; contrib. of articles to Aging and Biography: Explorations in Adult Development 1996, Journal of Aging Studies 1999, 2006, Narrative Gerontology: Theory, Research and Practice 2001, Rural Social Work 2001, 2005, Critical Advances in Reminiscence 2002, Education and Ageing 2002, Canadian Journal on Aging 2004, Narrative Inquiry 2004, McGill Journal of Education 2005, Theory & Psychology 2007, Encyclopedia of Gerontology 2006, Encyclopedia of Aging 2007. *Honours:* Harvard Univ. Regular Scholarship 1968–72, Emmanuel Coll., Victoria Univ. Wallace, Mitchell and Billes Postgraduate Scholarships 1973–76, United Church of Canada McLeod Scholarship 1989–91. *Address:* c/o Department of Gerontology, St Thomas University, Fredericton, NB, E3B 5G3, Canada (office). *Telephone:* (506) 452-0632 (office). *Fax:* (506) 452-0611 (office). *E-mail:* brandall@stu.ca (office). *Website:* www.stu.ca (office).

RANDHAWA, Ravinder, BA; British writer; b. 25 Jan. 1952, India; d. of Pakhar Singh and Kartar Kaur Randhawa; two d. *Education:* Leamington Coll. for Girls, Leamington Spa. *Career:* came to UK aged seven years; worked for women's groups establishing refuges and resource centres for Asian women 1978–84; Founder Asian Women Writers' Collective 1984; Fellow, Tonybee Hall 2000–02, Project Fellow 2002–04; Fellow, St Mary's Coll., Univ. of Surrey 2006–07; Writing Fellow, Royal Literary Fund, Queen Mary, Univ. of London 2007–08; mem. PEN Int. *Publications:* More to Life than Mr. Right (contrib.) 1986, A Wicked Old Woman 1987, Right of Way (contrib.) 1989, Hari-jan 1992, Flaming Spirit (contrib.) 1994, The Coral Strand 2001. *Honours:* Kathleen Burnett Award 1990. *Address:* Royal Literary Fund's Fellowship Scheme, School of English and Drama, Queen Mary, University of London, Mile End Road, London, E1 4NS, England. *E-mail:* ravi@randhawa .co.uk. *Website:* www.languageandlearning.qmul.ac.uk/elss/study/rlf .html#scheme.

RANKIN, Ian James, (Jack Harvey), OBE, BA; Scottish writer; b. 1960, Cardenden, Fife; m. Miranda; two s. *Education:* Edinburgh Univ. *Career:* mem. CWA, Int. Asscn of Crime Writers. *Recording:* Jackie Leven Said (short story, put to songs by Jackie Leven) 2005. *Publications:* The Flood 1986, Watchman 1988, Death is Not the End 1998, Beggars Banquet (short stories) 2002, Inspector Rebus series: Knots and Crosses 1987, Hide and Seek 1991, Tooth and Nail (aka Wolfjack) 1992, A Good Hanging and Other Stories (short stories) 1992, Strip Jack 1992, The Black Book 1993, Mortal Causes 1994, Let it Bleed 1996, Black and Blue 1997, The Hanging Garden 1998, Dead Souls 1999, Set in Darkness 2000, The Falls 2000, Resurrection Men 2001, A Question of Blood 2003, Fleshmarket Close (British Book Award for Crime Thriller of the Year 2005) 2004, The Naming of the Dead (British Book Award for Crime Thriller of the Year 2007) 2006; as Jack Harvey: Witch Hunt 1993, Bleeding Hearts 1994, Blood Hunt 1995; contrib. to anthologies, including One City 2006. *Honours:* CWA Golden Dagger 1997, Hawthornden Fellow, Chandler-Fulbright Award in Detective Fiction, CWA Dagger for best short story 1994, CWA Cartier Diamond Dagger 2005. *Address:* c/o Orion House, 5 Upper St Martin's Lane, London, WC2H 9EA, England (office). *Website:* www .ianrankin.net.

RANKIN, Robert; British writer; b. 27 July 1949, London; m. *Publications:* The Antipope 1981, The Brentford Triangle 1982, East of Ealing 1984, The Sprouts of Wrath 1984, Armageddon: The Musical 1988, They Came and Ate Us 1991, The Suburban Book of the Dead 1992, The Book of Ultimate Truths 1993, Raiders of the Lost Car Park 1994, The Greatest Show Off Earth 1994, The Most Amazing Man Who Ever Lived 1995, The Garden of Unearthly Delights 1995, A Dog Called Demolition 1996, Nostradamus Ate My Hamster 1996, Sprout Mask Replica 1997, The Brentford Chainstore Massacre 1997, The Dance of the Voodoo Handbag 1998, Apocalypso 1998, Snuff Fiction 1999, Sex and Drugs and Sausage Rolls 1999, Waiting for Godalming 2000, Web Site Story 2001, Fandom of the Operator 2001, The Hollow Chocolate Bunnies of the Apocalypse (SFX Award for Best Book 2003) 2002, The Witches of Chiswick 2003, Knees Up Mother Earth 2004, The Brightonomicon 2004, The Toyminator 2006, The Da-da-di-da-da Code 2007. *Address:* c/o Gollancz, Orion House, 5 Upper Saint Martin's Lane, London, WC2H 9EA, England (office). *Website:* www.sproutlore.com.

RANSFORD, Tessa, OBE, MA, DipEd; British poet, writer and editor; *President, Scottish PEN;* b. 8 July 1938, Mumbai, India; m. 1st Iain Kay Stiven 1959 (divorced 1986); one s. three d.; m. 2nd Callum Macdonald 1989 (deceased). *Education:* Univ. of Edinburgh, Craiglockhart Coll. of Educ. *Career:* cultural activist; Founder School of Poets, Edinburgh 1981–; Dir Scottish Poetry Library 1984–99; Ed. Lines Review 1988–98; freelance poet and adviser 1999–; mem. Scottish Int. PEN (Pres. 2003–), Soc. of Authors; Fellow, Centre for Human Ecology 2003; Royal Literary Fund Writing Fellowship 2001–04, 2006–. *Publications:* Light of the Mind 1980, Fools and Angels 1984, Shadows from the Greater Hill 1987, A Dancing Innocence 1988, Seven Valleys 1991, Medusa Dozen and Other Poems 1994, Scottish Selection 1998, When it Works it Feels Like Play 1998, Indian Selection 2000, Natural Selection 2001, Noteworthy Selection 2002, The Nightingale Question 2004, Shades of Green 2005; contrib. to anthologies, reviews and journals. *Honours:* Hon. Fellow, Inst. for Contemporary Scotland 2000; Hon. mem. Saltire Soc. 1993, Scottish Library Asscn 1999, Scottish Poetry Library 1999; Hon. DUniv (Paisley) 2003; Scottish Arts Council Book Award 1980, Howard Sergeant Award for Services to Poetry 1989, Heritage Soc. of Scotland Annual Award 1996, Soc. of Authors Travelling Scholarship 2001. *Address:* 31 Royal Park Terrace, Edinburgh, EH8 8JA, Scotland (home). *Telephone:* (131) 661-1277 (home). *E-mail:* wisdomfield@talk21.com (home). *Website:* www.wisdomfield .com; www.scottish-pamphlet-poetry.com.

RANSOM, Bill, MA; American writer and poet; b. 6 June 1945, Puyallup, WA; one d. *Education:* Univ. of Washington, Utah State Univ. *Career:* Poetry-in-the-Schools Master Poet, National Endowment for the Arts 1974–77; Foudner Director Port Townsend Writers' Conf.; mem. International Asscn of Machinists and Aerospace Workers, Poetry Society of America, Poets and Writers, Poets, Essayists and Novelists, SFWA. *Publications:* fiction: The Jesus Incident 1979; The Lazarus Effect 1983; The Ascension Factor 1988; Jaguar 1990; Viravax 1993; Burn 1995; poetry: Finding True North 1974; Waving Arms at the Blind 1975; Last Rites 1979; The Single Man Looks at Winter 1983; Last Call 1984; Semaphore 1993, War Baby 2004; other: Learning the Ropes (poems, essays, and short fiction) 1995; contrib. to numerous publications. *Honours:* National Endowment for the Arts Discovery Award 1977. *Address:* 1193 Wood Lane, Grayland, WA 98547, USA.

RANSOM, Jane Reavill, BA, MA; American poet and writer; b. 28 June 1958, Boulder, CO. *Education:* Indiana University, New York University. *Career:* Asst Ed., San Juan Star, 1981–84; National and International News Ed., New York Daily News, 1984–89; Adjunct Prof., New York University, 1991; guest lecturer in creative writing. *Publications:* Without Asking (poems), 1989; Bye-Bye (novel), 1997; Scene of the Crime: Poems, 1997; Missed (essay), 1997. *Honours:* Nicholas Roerich Poetry Prize, Story Line Press, 1989; New York University Press Award, 1997; Fellowships and residencies. *Literary Agent:* Linda Chester Literary Agency, Rockefeller Center, 630 Fifth Avenue, New York, NY 10103, USA.

RÂPEANU, Valeriu; Romanian literary critic, historian and editor; b. 28 Sept. 1931, Ploiestiori, Prahova Co.; s. of Gheorghe Râpeanu and Anastasia Râpeanu; m. Sanda Marinescu 1956; one s. *Education:* Univ. of Bucharest. *Career:* journalist 1954–69; Vice-Chair. of the Romanian Cttee of Radio and TV 1970–72; Dir Mihai Eminescu Publishing House, Bucharest 1972–90; Prof., Faculty of Journalism and Philosophy, Spiru Haret Univ., Bucharest; mem. Romanian Writers' Union; fmr mem. Cen. Cttee Romanian CP; mem. Int. Assoc. of Literary Critics. *Publications:* the monographs George Mihail-Zamfirescu 1958, Al. Vlahuță 1964, Noi și cei dinaintea noastră (Ourselves and Our Predecessors) 1966, Interferențe spirituale (Spiritual Correspondences) 1970, Călător pe două continente (Traveller on Two Continents) 1970, Pe drumurile tradiției (Following Traditions) 1973, Interpretări si înțelesuri

(Interpretations and Significances) 1975, Cultură si istorie (Culture and History) (two vols) 1979, 1981; Tărâmul unde nu ajungi niciodată (The Land You Could Never Reach) 1982, Scriitori dintre cele două războaie (Writers between the two World Wars) 1986, La vie de l'histoire et l'histoire d'une vie 1989, N. Iorga: Opera, Omul, Prietenii 1992, N. Iorga, Mincea Eliade, Nae Ionescu 1993, N. Iorga 1994; vols by Nicolae Iorga, Gh. Brătianu, Al. Kiriţescu, Cella Delavrancea, Marcel Mihalovici, I. G. Duca, Gh.I. Brătianu, George Enescu, C. Rădulescu-Motru, C. Brâncuşi; anthology of Romanian drama; essays on François Mauriac, Jean d'Ormesson, Marcel Proust, Aaron Copland, André Malraux, Jean Cocteau. *Address:* Universitatea Spiru Haret, Strada Ion Ghica nr. 13, Sector 3, Bucharest (office); Str. Mecet 21, Bucharest, Romania. *Telephone:* (21) 3149931 (office). *Fax:* (21) 3149932 (office). *E-mail:* info@spiruharet.ro (office). *Website:* www.spiruharet.ro (office).

RAPHAEL, Frederic Michael, MA, FRSL; American writer; b. 14 Aug. 1931, Chicago, Ill.; s. of Cedric Michael Raphael and Irene Rose Mauser; m. Sylvia Betty Glatt 1955; two s. one d. *Education:* Charterhouse, St John's Coll., Cambridge. *Publications:* novels: Obbligato 1956, The Earlsdon Way 1958, The Limits of Love 1960, A Wild Sunrise 1961, The Graduate's Wife 1962, The Trouble with England 1962, Lindmann 1963, Orchestra and Beginners 1967, Like Men Betrayed 1970, April, June and November 1972, California Time 1975, The Glittering Prizes 1976, Heaven and Earth 1985, After the War 1988, A Wild Surmise 1991, A Double Life 1993, Old Scores 1995, Coast to Coast 1998, All His Sons 1999; short stories: Sleeps Six 1979, Oxbridge Blues 1980, Think of England 1986, The Hidden I (illustrated by Sarah Raphael) 1990, The Latin Lover and Other Stories 1994, biography: Somerset Maugham and his World 1977, Byron 1982; essays: Cracks in the Ice 1979, Of Gods and Men (illustrated by Sarah Raphael) 1992, France, the Four Seasons 1994, The Necessity of Anti-Semitism 1997, Historicism and its Poverty 1998, Karl Popper 1998, Eyes Wide Open 1999, Personal Terms 2001, The Benefits of Doubt 2002, Rough Copy (Personal Terms II) 2004, Cuts and Bruises (Personal Terms III) 2006; translations: Catullus (with K. McLeish) 1976, The Oresteia of Aeschylus 1978, Aeschylus (complete plays, with K. McLeish) 1991, Euripides' Medea (with K. McLeish) 1994, Euripides: Hippolytus, Bacchae (with K. McLeish) 1997, Sophocles Aias (with K. McLeish) 1998, Bacchae 1999; screenplays: Nothing But the Best 1964, Darling (US Acad. Award for Best Original Screenplay) 1965, Far from the Madding Crowd 1967, Two for the Road 1968, Daisy Miller 1974, Rogue Male 1976, Richard's Things 1980, The Man in the Brooks Brothers Shirt (ACE award 1991), Armed Response 1995, Eyes Wide Shut 1998; numerous plays for TV and radio including: The Glittering Prizes (Royal TV Soc. Writer of the Year Award) 1976, From the Greek 1979, The Daedalus Dimension (radio) 1982, Oxbridge Blues 1984, The Thought of Lydia (radio) 1988, After the War 1989, The Empty Jew (radio) 1993, Eyes Wide Open. *Honours:* Lippincott Prize 1961, Prix Simone Genevois 2000. *Address:* c/o David Miller, Rogers, Coleridge & White, 20 Powis Mews, London, W11 1JN, England.

RAPOPORT, Janis, BA; Canadian poet, writer and dramatist; b. 22 June 1946, Toronto, ON; m. 1st; one s. two d.; m. 2nd Douglas Donegani 1980; one d. *Education:* University of Toronto. *Career:* Assoc. Ed., Tamarack Review, 1970–82; Playwright-in-Residence, Tarragon Theatre, 1974–75; Dir, Ethos Cultural Development Foundation, 1981–; Ed., Ethos magazine, 1983–87; Part-time Instructor, Sheridan College, 1984–86; Writer-in-Residence, St Thomas Public Library, 1987, Beeton Public Library, 1988, Dundas Public Library, 1990, North York Public Library, 1991; Instructor, School of Continuing Studies, University of Toronto, 1988–; mem. League of Canadian Poets; Playwrights' Union of Canada; Writers' Guild of Canada; Writers' Union of Canada. *Publications:* Within the Whirling Moment, 1967; Foothills, 1973; Jeremy's Dream, 1974; Landscape (co-ed.), 1977; Dreamgirls, 1979; Imaginings (co-author), 1982; Upon Her Fluent Route, 1992; After Paradise, 1996. Contributions: anthologies, newspapers, magazines, and radio. *Honours:* Canadian Council Arts Award, 1981–82; AIGA Certificate of Excellence, 1983; New York Dirs Club Award, 1983; Outstanding Achievement Award, American Poetry Asscn, 1986; Toronto Arts Council Research and Development Awards, 1990, 1992; Excellence in Teaching Award for Creative Writing, School of Continuing Studies, University of Toronto, 1998.

RASHID, Ahmed; Pakistani journalist and author; *Correspondent, The Daily Telegraph*; b. 1948, Rawalpindi; m.; three c. *Education:* Univ. of Cambridge, UK. *Career:* currently Pakistan, Afghanistan and Cen. Asia Corresp. The Daily Telegraph, Far Eastern Economic Review; writes regularly for several Pakistani newspapers and magazines; broadcaster on TV and radio stations around the world, including BBC World Service, ABC Australia, Radio France Int. and German Radio. *Publications include:* The Resurgence of Central Asia: Islam or Nationalism, Fundamentalism Reborn: Afghanistan and the Taliban, Jihad: The Rise of Militant Islam in Central Asia, Taliban: Islam, Oil and the New Great Game in Central Asia. *Honours:* Nisar Osmani Award for Courage in Journalism, Human Rights Soc. of Pakistan. *Address:* The Daily Telegraph, 1 Canada Square, Canary Wharf, London, E14 5DT, England (office). *Telephone:* (20) 7538-5000 (office). *Fax:* (20) 7513-2506 (office). *E-mail:* dtnews@telegraph.co.uk (office). *Website:* www .telegraph.co.uk (office).

RASPUTIN, Valentin Grigoriyevich; Russian writer; b. 15 March 1937, Ust-Uda (Irkutsk). *Education:* Irkutsk Univ. *Career:* first works published 1961; elected People's Deputy 1989; mem. Presidential Council 1990–91. *Publications:* I Forgot to Ask Lyosha 1961, A Man of This World 1965, Bearskin for Sale 1966, Vasilii and Vasilisa 1967, Deadline 1970, Live and Remember, Stories, 1974, Parting with Matera 1976, Live and Love 1982, Fire 1985, Collected Works (2 vols) 1990, Siberia, Siberia 1991. *Honours:* USSR State Prize 1977, 1987; Hero of Socialist Labour 1987. *Address:* 5th Army Street 67, Apt 68, 664000 Irkutsk, Russia. *Telephone:* (3952) 4-71-00.

RATCLIFFE, Eric Hallam; British poet, writer, editor and physicist (retd) and information scientist (retd); b. 8 Aug. 1918, Teddington, Middx. *Career:* war service 1938–45; Founder-Ed. Ore 1955–95; reviewer, New Hop Int. Online. *Publications include:* The Visitation 1952, The Chronicle of the Green Man 1960, Gleanings for a Daughter of Aeolus 1968, Leo Poems 1972, Commius 1976, Nightguard of the Quaternary 1979, Ballet Class 1986, The Runner of the Seven Valleys 1990, The Ballad of Polly McPoo 1991, Advent 1992, The Golden Heart Man 1993, Fire in the Bush: Poems, 1955–1992 1993, William Ernest Henley (1849–1903): An Introduction 1993, The Caxton of her Age: The Career and Family Background of Emily Faithfull (1835–1895) 1993, Winstanley's Walton, 1649: Events in the Civil War at Walton-on-Thames 1994, Ratcliffe's Megathesaurus 1995, Anthropos 1995, Odette 1995, Sholen 1996, The Millennium of the Magician 1996, The Brussels Griffon 1996, Strange Furlongs 1996, Wellington—A Broad Front 1998, Capabilities of the Alchemical Mind 1999, Cosmologia 2000, Loyal Women 2000, The Ghost with Nine Fathers 2001, No Jam in the Astral 2002, On Baker's Level 2002, The Divine Peter 2002, Desert Voices: A Tribute to Abu'l-Ala 2003, Going for God 2005, Unfinished Business 2005, Islandia 2005, Tghe Ruffian on the Stair 2005; contrib. to anthologies and journals. *Honours:* Baron, Royal Order of the Bohemian Crown 1995. *Address:* 7 The Towers, Stevenage, Hertfordshire SG1 1HE, England (home). *E-mail:* octillion@ntlworld.com (home). *Website:* homepage.ntlworld.com/chessmaster/eric (home).

RATHBONE, Julian, BA; British writer and poet; b. 10 Feb. 1935, London; s. of Christopher Fairrie Rathbone and Decima Doreen Frost. *Education:* Clayesmore School, Magdalene Coll., Cambridge. *Career:* teacher of English, Ankara, London, W Sussex 1959–73; full-time writer 1973–; contrib. The Times, The New Statesman, Literary Review, The Guardian, The Independent, The Sunday Telegraph, TLS. *Publications include:* With My Knives I Know I'm Good 1969, Trip Trap 1972, Kill Cure 1975, Bloody Marvellous 1975, Carnival 1976, King Fisher Lives 1976, Raving Monarchist 1977, Joseph 1979, Euro-killers 1979, Last Resort 1980, Base Case 1981, Spy of the Old School 1982, Watching the Detectives 1983, Wellington's War 1984, Nasty, Very 1984, Lying in State 1985, Greenfinger 1987, The Crystal Contract 1988, The Pandora Option 1990, Dangerous Games 1991, Intimacy 1995, Blame Hitler 1997, The Last English King 1997, Trajectories 1998, Brandenburg Concerto 1998, Sand Blind 2000, Kings of Albion 2000, Accidents Will Happen 2000, Homage 2001, A Very English Agent 2002, As Bad as it Gets 2003, Birth of a Nation 2004, The Mutiny 2007; screenplays, poetry. *Honours:* Swanage Int. Poetry Prize, Crime Writers Short Story Silver Dagger, Deutsche Krimi Preis. *Address:* Sea View, School Road, Thorney Hill, nr Christchurch, Dorset, BH23 8DS, England (home). *Telephone:* (1425) 673313 (home). *Fax:* (1425) 673313 (home). *E-mail:* julianrathbone@btinternet.com (home).

RATHER, Dan, BA; American broadcaster and journalist; b. Oct. 1931, Wharton, Tex.; m. Jean Goebel; one s. one d. *Education:* Sam Houston State Coll., Univ. of Houston, Tex., S Tex. School of Law. *Career:* writer and sports commentator with KSAM-TV; taught journalism for one year at Houston Chronicle; with CBS 1962; with radio station KTRH, Houston for about four years; News and Current Affairs Dir CBS Houston TV affiliate KHOU-TV late 1950s; joined CBS News 1962; Chief London Bureau 1965–66; worked in Viet Nam; White House 1966; anchorman CBS Reports 1974–75; co-anchorman 60 Minutes CBS-TV 1975–81; anchorman Dan Rather Reporting CBS Radio Network 1977–2006; co-ed. show Who's Who CBS-TV 1977; anchorman Midwest desk CBS Nat. election night 1972–80; CBS Nat. Political Consultant 1964–2006; anchorman Man. Ed. CBS Evening News with Dan Rather 1981–2005, co-anchorman 1993–2005; host Dan Rather Reports, HDNet 2006–; anchored numerous CBS News Special Programmes, including coverage of presidential campaigns in 1982 and 1984; as White House corresp. accompanied Pres. on numerous travels, including visits to Middle East, USSR, People's Repub. of China. *Publications:* The Palace Guard 1974 (with Gary Gates), The Camera Never Blinks Twice (with Mickey Herskowitz) 1977, I Remember (with Peter Wyden) 1991, The Camera Never Blinks Twice: The Further Adventures of a Television Journalist 1994. *Honours:* ten Emmy awards; numerous acad. honours; Distinguished Achievement for Broadcasting Award, Univ. of S. Calif. Journalism Alumni Asscn, Bob Considine Award 1983. *Address:* c/o HDNet, 2909 Taylor Street, Dallas, TX 75226, USA (office). *Telephone:* (214) 651-1446 (office). *Website:* www.hd.net (office).

RATNER, Rochelle; American poet, writer and editor; b. 2 Dec. 1948, Atlantic City, NJ; m. Kenneth Thorp 1990. *Career:* poetry columnist, Soho Weekly News 1975–82; Co-Ed. Hand Book 1976–82; Exec. Ed., American Book Review 1978–; small press columnist, Library Journey 1985; poetry consultant, Israel Horizons 1988–97; Ed. New Jersey Online: Reading Room 1995–96; NBCC Board of Dirs 1995–2001; mem. Editorial Bd Marsh Hawk Press 2004–; mem. Authors' Guild, Hudson Valley Writers Guild, Nat. Book Critics Circle, Nat. Writers Union, PEN, Poetry Soc. of America, Poets and Writers. *Publications:* poetry: A Birthday of Waters 1971, False Trees 1973, The Mysteries 1976, Pirate's Song 1976, The Tightrope Walker 1977, Quarry 1978, Combing the Waves 1979, Sea Air in a Grave Ground Hog Turns Toward 1980, Hide and Seek 1980, Practicing to be a Woman: New and Selected Poems 1982, Someday Songs 1992, Zodiac Arrest 1995, Tellings 2003, House and Home 2003, Lady Pinball 2004, Leah 2004, Beggars at the Wall 2006; fiction:

Bobby's Girl 1986, The Lion's Share 1991; non-fiction: Trying to Understand What it Means to be a Feminist: Essays on Women Writers 1984, Bearing Life: Women's Writings on Childlessness (ed.) 2000. *Honours:* Susan Koppelman Award 2000. *Address:* 609 Columbus Avenue, Apt 16F, New York, NY 10024, USA. *E-mail:* rochelleratner@mindspring.com. *Website:* www.rochelleratner .com.

RATUSHINSKAYA, Irina Borisovna; Russian poet; b. 4 March 1954; m. Igor Gerashchenko 1979. *Education:* Odessa Pedagogical Inst. *Career:* teacher Odessa Pedagogical Inst. 1976–83; arrested with husband, Moscow 1981; lost job, arrested again, 17 Sept. 1982, convicted of 'subverting the Soviet regime' and sentenced 5 March 1983 to seven years' hard labour; strict regime prison camp Aug. 1983, released Sept. 1986; settled in UK 1986; f. Democracy and Independence Group April 1989–; poetry appeared in samizdat publs, West European Russian language journals, trans. in American and British press and in USSR 1989–. *Publications include:* Poems (trilingual text) 1984, No, I'm Not Afraid 1986, Off Limits (in Russian) 1986, I Shall Live to See It (in Russian) 1986, Grey Is the Colour of Hope 1989, In the Beginning 1990, The Odessans 1992, Fictions and Lies 1998. *Address:* c/o Vargius Publishing House, Kazakova str. 18, 107005 Moscow, Russia. *Telephone:* (495) 785-09-62.

RAU, Santha Rama (see Rama Rau, Santha)

RAUSING, Sigrid, MSc, PhD; Swedish anthropologist, philanthropist and publisher; b. 1962, Lund; d. of Hans Anders Rausing (q.v.) and Märit Rausing; m. 1st Dennis Hotz; one s.; m. 2nd Eric Abraham 2003. *Education:* Univ. of York, Univ. Coll. London, UK. *Career:* moved to England aged 18; wealth derived from family-owned co. Tetra-Pak, manufacturer of drink cartons; f. Sea Foundation (charitable foundation) 1988; transferred funds to Ruben and Elisabeth Rausing Trust 1995 (changed name to Sigrid Rausing Trust 2003); f. Portobello Books 2005; acquired Granta (magazine and publishing house) 2005–; mem. Bd of Dirs Human Rights Watch, NY, Whitley Laing Foundation, Lisbet Rausing Charitable Fund. *Publications:* History, Memory, and Identity in Post-Soviet Estonia 2004; articles in academic journals. *Honours:* Int. Service Human Rights Award, Global Human Rights Defender Category 2004, Beacon Special Award for Philanthropy 2005, Changing Face of Philanthropy Award, Women's Funding Network 2006. *Address:* The Sigrid Rausing Trust, Eardley House, 4 Uxbridge Street, London, W8 7SY England. *Telephone:* (20) 7908-9870. *Fax:* (20) 7908-9879. *Website:* www.sigrid-rausing-trust.org.

RAVENSDALE, 3rd Baron, cr. 1911, 7th Baronet; **Sir Nicholas Mosley,** Bt, MC; British writer; b. 25 June 1923, London, England; s. of the late Sir Oswald Mosley and of Lady Cynthia Curzon; m. 1st Rosemary Salmond 1947 (divorced 1974, died 1991); three s. one d.; m. 2nd Verity Bailey (née Raymond) 1974; one s. *Education:* Eton, Balliol Coll., Oxford. *Publications:* novels: Spaces of the Dark 1951, The Rainbearers 1955, Corruption 1957, African Switchback 1958, The Life of Raymond Raynes 1961, Meeting Place 1962, Accident 1964, Assassins 1966, Impossible Object (also screenplay) 1968, Natalie, Natalia 1971, Catastrophe Practice (three plays and a novella) 1979, Imago Bird 1980, Serpent 1981, Judith 1986, Hopeful Monsters (Whitbread Book of the Year) 1990, Children of Darkness and Light 1996, The Hesperides Tree 2001, Inventing God 2003, Look at the Dark 2005; non-fiction: Experience and Religion: A Lay Essay in Theology 1965, The Assassination of Trotsky (also screenplay) 1972, Julian Grenfell: His Life and the Times of his Death 1988–1915 (biog.) 1976, Rules of the Game: Sir Oswald and Lady Cynthia Mosley 1896–1933 (biog.) 1982, Beyond the Pale: Sir Oswald Mosley and Family 1933–1980 (biog.) 1983, Efforts at Truth (autobiog.) 1994, Time at War: A Memoir 2006. *Address:* 2 Gloucester Crescent, London, NW1 7DS, England. *Telephone:* (20) 7485-4514.

RAVITCH, Diane Silvers, PhD; American education scholar and academic; *Research Professor of Education, New York University;* b. 1 July 1938, Houston, Tex.; d. of Walter Cracker and Ann Celia Silvers (née Katz); m. Richard Ravitch 1960 (divorced 1986); three s. (one deceased). *Education:* Wellesley Coll. and Columbia Univ. *Career:* Adjunct Asst Prof. of History and Educ., Teachers' Coll., Columbia Univ. 1975–78, Assoc. Prof. 1978–83, Adjunct Prof. 1983–91; Dir Woodrow Wilson Nat. Fellowship Foundation 1987–91; Chair. Educational Excellence Network 1988–91; Asst Sec. Office of Research and Improvement, US Dept of Educ., Washington, DC 1991–93, Counsellor to Sec. of Educ. 1991–93; Visiting Fellow, Brookings Inst. 1993–94, Brown Chair in Educ. Policy 1997–; Sr Research Scholar, New York Univ. 1994–98, Research Prof. in Educ. 1998–; Sr Fellow, Progressive Policy Inst. 1998–2002, Hoover Inst.; Adjunct Fellow, Manhattan Inst. 1996–99; Trustee New York Historical Soc. 1995–98, New York Council on the Humanities 1996–2004; mem. numerous public policy bodies. *Publications:* The Great School Wars: New York City 1805–1973 1974, The Revisionists Revised 1977, Educating and Urban People (co-author) 1981, The Troubled Crusade: American Education 1945–1980 1983, The School and the City (co-author) 1983, Against Mediocrity (co-author) 1984, The Schools We Deserve 1985, Challenges to the Humanities (co-author) 1985, What Do Our 17-Year-Olds Know? (with Chester E. Finn Jr) 1987, The American Reader (co-ed.) 1990, The Democracy Reader (ed. with Abigail Thernstrom) 1992, National Standards in American Education 1995, Debating the Future of American Education (ed.) 1995, Learning from the Past (ed. with Maris Vinovskis) 1995, New Schools for a New Century (ed. with Joseph Viteretti) 1997, Left Back 2000, City Schools (ed.) 2000, The Language Police 2003, Forgotten Heroes of American Education (co-ed.) 2006, The English Reader (co-ed.) 2006; contrib. articles and reviews to scholarly books and professional journals. *Honours:*

Hon. DHumLitt (Williams Coll.) 1984, (Reed Coll.) 1985, (Amherst Coll.) 1986, (State Univ. of New York) 1988, (Ramopo Coll.) 1990, (St Joseph's Coll., NY) 1991; Hon. LHD (Middlebury Coll.) 1997, (Union Coll.) 1998. *Address:* New York University, 82 Washington Square East, New York, NY 10003, USA (office). *Telephone:* (212) 998-5146 (office). *E-mail:* dr19@hyu.edu (office); gardend@aol.com (home). *Website:* www.dianeravitch.com (office).

RAVVIN, Norman, BA, MA, PhD; Canadian novelist and teacher; b. 26 Aug. 1963, Calgary, AB. *Education:* University of British Columbia, University of Toronto. *Career:* Instructor, Concordia University; General Ed., Hungry I Books, 2000–; mem. Writers Guild of Alberta; Asscn of Canadian College and University Teachers of English; MLA of America. *Publications:* Café des Westens (novel) 1991, Sex, Skyscrapers and Standard Yiddish (short stories) 1997, A House of Words: Jewish Writing, Identity and Memory (essays) 1997, Great Stories of the Sea (ed.) 1999, Hidden Canada: An Intimate Travelogue 2001, Not Quite Mainstream: Canadian Jewish Short Stories (ed.) 2001, Lola by Night (novel) 2003. Contributions: anthologies: Fresh Blood: New Canadian Gothic Fiction, The Nelson Introduction to Literature; journals: Canadian Jewish Studies, Canadian Literature, English Studies in Canada, Malcolm Lowry Review, Prairie Fire, Prism International, Studies in Canadian Literature, Wascana Review, West Coast Review, Western Living. *Honours:* K.M. Hunter Emerging Artist Award, Alberta Culture and Multiculturalism New Fiction Award 1990, PhD Fellowship, Social Sciences and Humanities Research Council of Canada. *Address:* c/o Concordia University, Department of Religion, Montréal, QC H3G 1M8, Canada (office).

RAWN, Melanie Robin, BA; American writer; b. 12 June 1954, Santa Monica, CA. *Education:* Scripps College, University of Denver, California State University at Fullerton. *Career:* mem. SFWA. *Publications:* Dragon Prince, 1988, The Star Scroll, 1989, Sunrunner's Fire, 1990; Stronghold, 1990, The Dragon Token, 1992, Skybowl, 1993; The Ruins of Ambrai, 1994; The Golden Key (co-author), 1996; The Mageborn Traitor, 1997. *Website:* www .melanierawn.com.

RAWNSLEY, Andrew Nicholas James, MA, FRSA; British journalist, broadcaster and author; *Associate Editor and Chief Political Columnist, The Observer;* b. 5 Jan. 1962, Leeds; s. of Eric Rawnsley and Barbara Rawnsley (née Butler); m. Jane Leslie Hall 1990; three d. *Education:* Lawrence Sheriff Grammar School, Rugby, Rugby School, Sidney Sussex Coll., Cambridge. *Career:* with BBC 1983–85, The Guardian 1985–93 (political columnist 1987–93); Assoc. Ed. and Chief Political Columnist The Observer 1993–; Presenter Channel 4 TV series A Week in Politics 1989–97, ITV series The Agenda 1996–, Bye Bye Blues 1997, Blair's Year 1998, The Westminster Hour (radio) 1998–, The Unauthorized Biography of the United Kingdom (radio) 1999. *Publication:* Servants of the People: The Inside Story of New Labour (Channel 4/Politico Book of the year 2001) 2000. *Honours:* Student Journalist of the Year 1983, Young Journalist of the Year 1987, Columnist of the Year, What the Papers Say Award 2000, Book of the Year Award, Channel 4/House Magazine Political Awards 2001, Political Journalist of the Year, Channel 4 Political Awards, 2003. *Address:* The Observer, 119 Farringdon Road, London, EC1R 3ER, England. *Telephone:* (20) 7278-2332. *E-mail:* a.rawnsley@ observer.co.uk (office). *Website:* www.observer.co.uk (office).

RAWORTH, Thomas Moore, MA; British poet and writer; b. 19 July 1938, London, England; m. Valerie Murphy; four s. one d. *Education:* Univ. of Essex. *Career:* Poet-in-Residence, Univ. of Essex 1969, Northeastern Univ., Chicago 1973–74, King's Coll., Cambridge 1977–78; Lecturer, Bowling Green State Univ., OH 1972–73; Visiting Lecturer, Univ. of Texas 1974–75, Univ. of Cape Town 1991, Univ. of San Diego 1996; mem. PEN. *Publications:* The Relation Ship 1967, The Big Green Day 1968, A Serial Biography 1969, Lion, Lion 1970, Moving 1971, Act 1973, Ace 1974, Common Sense 1976, Logbook 1977, Sky Tails 1978, Nicht Wahr, Rosie? 1979, Writing 1982, Levre de Poche 1983, Heavy Light 1984, Tottering State: Selected Poems 1963–83 1984, Lazy Left Hand 1986, Visible Shivers 1987, All Fours 1991, Catacoustics 1991, Eternal Sections 1991, Survival 1991, Clean and Well Lit: Selected Poems 1987–1995 1996, Collected Poems 2003, Caller 2006. *Honours:* Alice Hunt Bartlett Prize 1969, Cholmondeley Award 1971, Int. Cttee on Poetry Award, New York 1988. *Address:* 1 Albert Street, Cambridge, CB4 3BE, England. *E-mail:* raworth@ ntlworld.com. *Website:* www.tomraworth.com.

RAWSON, Claude Julien, BA, BLitt, MA; British academic, writer and editor; *Maynard Mack Professor of English, Yale University;* b. 8 Feb. 1935, Shanghai, People's Republic of China; m. Judith Ann Hammond 1959; three s. two d. *Education:* Magdalen Coll., Oxford. *Career:* Lecturer in English, Univ. of Newcastle 1957–65; Lecturer, then Prof., Univ. of Warwick 1965–85, Hon. Prof. 1986–; George Sherburn Prof. of English, Univ. of Illinois 1985–86; George M. Bodman Prof. of English, Yale Univ. 1986–96, Maynard Mack Prof. of English 1996–; Ed., Modern Language Review and Yearbook of English Studies 1974–88; Gen. Ed., Unwin Critical Library 1974–, Blackwell Critical Biographies 1985–; Gen. Ed., Cambridge History of Literary Criticism 1983–; Chair. and Gen. Ed., Yale edn of the Private Papers of James Boswell 1990–2001; Gen. Ed., Cambridge edn of the Works of Jonathan Swift 2001–; Visiting Prof., Univ. of Pennsylvania 1973, Univ. of California, Berkeley 1980; Fellow American Acad. of Arts and Sciences; life mem. MHRA (cttee mem. 1974–88); mem. Int. Soc. for 18th Century Studies, American Soc. for 18th-Century Studies, British Soc. for 18th-Century Studies (pres. 1973–74), Grolier Club. *Publications:* Henry Fielding 1968, Focus Swift 1971, Henry Fielding and the Augustan Ideal 1972, Gulliver and the Gentle Reader 1973,

Fielding: A Critical Anthology 1973, The Character of Swift's Satire 1983, English Satire and the Satiric Tradition 1984, Order from Confusion Sprung 1985, Collected Poems of Thomas Parnell (ed. with F. P. Lock) 1989, Satire and Sentiment 1660–1830 (with F. P. Lock) 1994, Jonathan Swift: A Collection of Critical Essays (ed.) 1995, Cambridge History of Literary Criticism, Vol. 4: The Eighteenth Century (with H. B. Nisbet) 1997, God, Gulliver and Genocide 2001, Basic Writings of Jonathan Swift 2002. *Honours:* Conference of Editors of Learned Journals Certificate of Merit for Distinguished Service 1988, Nat. Endowment of the Humanities grant 1991, Andrew Mellon Fellow of Clark and Huntington Library 1980, 1990, Guggenheim Fellow 1991–92, Sr Faculty Fellow Yale Univ. 1991–92. *Address:* Department of English, Yale University, PO Box 208302, New Haven, CT 06520-8302, USA (office). *E-mail:* claude .rawson@yale.edu (office).

RAY, David Eugene, BA, MA; American academic, poet and writer; *Professor of English Emeritus, University of Missouri*; b. 20 May 1932, Sapulpa, OK; m. Suzanne Judy Morrish 1970; one s. three d. *Education:* Univ. of Chicago. *Career:* instructor, Wright Junior Coll. 1957–58, Northern Illinois Univ. 1958–60; instructor, Cornell Univ. 1960–64; Asst Prof., Reed Coll., Portland, OR 1964–66; Lecturer, Univ. of Iowa 1969–70; Visiting Assoc. Prof., Bowling Green State Univ. 1970–71; Ed., New Letters Magazine 1971–85; Prof. of English 1971–95, Prof. Emeritus 1995–, Univ. of Missouri, Kansas City; Visiting Prof., Syracuse Univ. 1978–79, Univ. of Rajasthan, India 1981–82; Exchange Prof., Univ. of Otago, New Zealand 1987; Visiting Fellow, Univ. of Western Australia 1991; mem. Acad. of American Poets, PEN, Poetry Soc. of America. *Publications:* poetry: X-Rays 1965, Dragging the Main and Other Poems 1968, A Hill in Oklahoma 1972, Gathering Firewood: New Poems and Selected 1974, Enough of Flying: Poems Inspired by the Ghazals of Ghalib 1977, The Tramp's Cup 1978, The Farm in Calabria and Other Poems 1979, The Touched Life 1982, On Wednesday I Cleaned Out My Wallet 1985, Elysium in the Halls of Hell 1986, Sam's Book 1987, The Maharani's New Wall 1989, Not Far From the River 1990, Wool Highways 1993, Kangaroo Paws 1995, Heartstones: New and Selected Poems 1998, Demons in the Diner 1999, One Thousand Years 2004, The Death of Sardanapalus and Other Poems of the Iraq Wars 2004; prose: The Mulberries of Mingo (short stories) 1978, The Endless Search: A Memoir 2003, contrib. to journals and newspapers. *Honours:* William Carlos Williams Awards 1979, 1993, PEN Syndicated Fiction Awards 1982–86, Amelia Magazine Bernice Jennings Award for Traditional Poetry 1987, Maurice English Poetry Award 1988, Passaic Community Coll. Nat. Poetry Award 1989, first prize St Louis Poetry Centre Stanley Hanks Memorial Contest 1990, New England Poetry Club Daniel Varoujan Award 1996, New Millennium Poetry Award 1997, Poetry Centre, Paterson Allen Ginsberg Poetry Award 1997, Explorations magazine Poetry Award 1997, Amelia Magazine Long Poem Award 1998, Richard Snyder Memorial Prize 1999, Flyway Magazine Poetry Award 2000, Nuclear Age Peace Foundation Poetry Award 2001. *Address:* 2033 E 10th Street, Tucson, AZ 85719, USA. *E-mail:* djray@gainusa.com. *Website:* www.davidraypoet.com.

RAY, Robert Henry, BA, PhD; American academic and writer; *Professor of English and Graduate Program Director, Baylor University*; b. 29 April 1940, San Saba, TX; m. Lynette Elizabeth Dittmar 1962, two d. *Education:* Univ. of Texas at Austin. *Career:* Asst Prof. of English 1967–75, Assoc. Prof. of English 1975–85, Prof. of English 1985–, Graduate Program Dir, Baylor Univ.; mem. MLA of America; John Donne Soc. *Publications:* The Herbert Allusion Book 1986, Approaches to Teaching Shakespeare's King Lear 1986, A John Donne Companion 1990, A George Herbert Companion 1995, An Andrew Marvell Companion 1998; contrib. to various publications. *Address:* Department of English, PO Box 97406, Baylor University, Waco, TX 76798, USA. *E-mail:* Robert_Ray@baylor.edu.

RAY, Robert J., BA, MA, PhD; American teacher and writer; b. 15 May 1935, Amarillo, TX; m. 1st Ann Allen (divorced); m. 2nd Margot M. Waale 1983. *Education:* University of Texas, Austin. *Career:* Instructor, 1963–65, Asst Prof., 1965–68, Assoc. Prof., 1968–75, Prof., 1976, Beloit College, Wisconsin; Writing Teacher, Valley College, 1984–88, University of California, Irvine, 1985–88; Adjunct Prof., Chapman College, 1988–; mem. MWA. *Publications:* The Art of Reading: A Handbook on Writing (with Ann Ray), 1968; The Heart of the Game (novel), 1975; Cage of Mirrors (novel), 1980; Small Business: An Entrepreneur's Plan (with L. A. Eckert and J. D. Ryan), 1985; Bloody Murdock (novel), 1987; Murdock for Hire (novel), 1987; The Hitman Cometh (novel), 1988; Dial M for Murder (novel), 1988; Murdock in Xanadu (novel), 1989. *Address:* c/o Random House Inc., 1745 Broadway, New York, NY 10019, USA.

RAYBAN, Chlöe (see Bear, Carolyn Ann)

RAYMOND, Diana Joan; British novelist; b. 25 April 1916, London, England; m. Ernest Raymond 1940; one s. *Education:* Cheltenham Ladies' Coll. *Career:* mem. Soc. of Authors. *Publications:* The Small Rain 1954, Guest of Honour 1960, The Climb 1962, People in the House 1964, Incident on a Summer's Day 1974, Emma Pride 1981, Lily's Daughter 1974, Roundabout 1994, The Sea Family 1997. *Address:* 22 The Pryors, East Heath Road, London, NW3 1BS, England (home).

RAYMOND, Mary (see Keegan, Mary Constance)

RAYMOND, Patrick Ernest; British royal air force officer (retd) and writer; b. 25 Sept. 1924, Cuckfield, Sussex, England; m. Lola Pilpel 1950, one s. *Education:* Art School, Cape Town, South Africa. *Career:* Royal Air Force, rising to Group Captain 1942–77. *Publications:* A City of Scarlet and Gold,

1963; The Lordly Ones, 1965; The Sea Garden, 1970; The Last Soldier, 1974; A Matter of Assassination, 1977; The White War, 1978; The Grand Admiral, 1980; Daniel and Esther, 1989.

RAYNER, Claire Berenice, (Sheila Brandon, Ann Lynton, Ruth Martin), OBE; British writer and broadcaster; b. 22 Jan. 1931, London; m. Desmond Rayner 1957; two s. one d. *Education:* Royal Northern and Guy's Hosps, London. *Career:* nurse and midwife until 1960; writer advice columns in Petticoat, The Sun, The Sunday Mirror 1980–88, Today newspaper, Woman's Own 1966–88, Woman magazine 1988–92; has made numerous radio broadcasts for BBC, LBC radio and Capital Radio, London; many TV appearances including Pebble Mill at One, Kitchen Garden (co-presenter), Claire Rayner's Casebook 1980, 1983, 1984, BBC Breakfast TV, TV-AM Advice Spot 1985, A Problem Shared (British Sky Broadcasting TV), The David Frost Programme; has produced In Company with Claire Rayner, women's health and family life videos; Pres. Gingerbread, The Patient's Assⁿ; Vice-Pres. British Humanist Assⁿ 1999–; fmr mem. Royal Coll. of Nursing Cttee on Ethics; mem. Video Appeals Cttee British Bd of Film Classification, Council Charter 88, Royal Comm. on Funding of Care of the Elderly 1998–99; Assoc. Non-Exec. Dir Royal London Hosps Trust (Barts and the London); Fellow Soc. of Authors; Patron the Terrence Higgins Trust. *Publications include:* fiction: The Hive 1967, The Meddlers 1970, A Time to Heal 1972, The Performers (12 Vol. saga) 1973–1986, Reprise 1980, Family Chorus 1984, The Virus Man 1985, Maddie 1988, The Poppy Chronicles (six vols) 1987–, Omnibus of Three Hospital Novels (reprint, as Sheila Brandon) 1989, Postscripts 1991, Dangerous Things 1992, The Barnabus crime novels 1993, 1994, 1995, 1996, 1997; non-fiction: For Children 1967, Mothercraft (as Ann Lynton) 1967, Woman's Medical Dictionary 1971, People in Love: Modern Guide to Sex in Marriage, Kitchen Garden, four vols, (jtly) 1976, The Body Book 1978, Related to Sex 1979, Claire Rayner's Lifeguide 1980, Baby and Young Child Care 1981, Growing Pains 1984, The Getting Better Book 1985, Safe Sex 1987, The Don't Spoil Your Body Book 1989, How Did I Get Here From There? (autobiog.) 2003; books published in many countries; contribs to Design magazine (journal of the Design Council), nat. newspapers, professional medical journals. *Honours:* Hon. Fellow Univ. of N London 1988; Freeman, City of London 1981; Hon. DUniv (Oxford Brookes) 2000, (Middlesex) 2002; Medical Journalist of the Year 1987, Best Specialist Consumer Columnist of the Year, Publisher Magazine 1988. *Address:* Holly Wood House, Roxborough Avenue, Harrow-on-the-Hill, Middx, HA1 3BU, England. *Telephone:* (20) 8864-9898. *Fax:* (20) 8422-3710. *E-mail:* clairerayner@harrowhill.demon.co.uk.

RAYSON, Hannie, BA; Australian playwright; b. 31 March 1957, Brighton, Melbourne, Vic. *Education:* Univ. of Melbourne, Victoria Coll. of Arts. *Career:* writer-in-residence, various insts; mem. Literature Bd Australia Council 1992–95. *Publications:* Please Return to Sender 1980, Mary 1981, Leave it Till Monday 1984, Room to Move 1985, Hotel Sorrento 1990, SLOTH (television play) 1992, Falling from Grace 1994, Life After George 2001, Inheritance (play) 2003, Scenes from a Separation (play). *Honours:* Australian Writers' Guild Awards 1986, 1991, 2001, New South Wales Premier's Literary Award, Sidney Myer Performing Arts Award 1996, Helpmann Awards for Best Play and Best New Australian Work 2004, Victoria Premier's Literary Award. *Literary Agent:* c/o HLA Management, PO Box 1536, Strawberry Hills, NSW 2012, Australia. *Telephone:* (2) 9310-4948. *Fax:* (2) 9310-4113. *E-mail:* hla@ hlamgt.com.au. *Website:* www.hlamanagement.com.au.

RAZ, Joseph, MA, MJr, DPhil, FBA; British (b. Israeli) philosopher and academic; *Research Professor and Fellow Emeritus, Balliol College, University of Oxford*; b. 21 March 1939. *Education:* Hebrew Univ., Jerusalem and Univ. of Oxford. *Career:* Lecturer, Faculty of Law and Dept of Philosophy, Hebrew Univ. 1967–71, Sr Lecturer 1971–72; Fellow and Tutor in Law, Balliol Coll., Oxford 1972–85, also mem. sub-faculty of philosophy 1977–; Ed. (with Prof. A. M. Honoré), The Clarendon Law Series 1984–92; Prof. of Philosophy of Law, Univ. of Oxford and Fellow, Balliol Coll. 1985–2006, Research Prof. and Fellow Emer. 2006–; Visiting Prof., School of Law, Columbia Univ., New York 1995–2002, Prof., Columbia Univ. Law School 2002–. *Publications:* The Concept of a Legal System 1970, Practical Reason and Norms 1975, The Authority of Law 1979, The Morality of Freedom (W.J.M. Mackenzie Book Prize, Political Studies Assⁿ of the UK, Elaine and David Spitz Book Prize, Conf. for the Study of Political Thought, NewYork) 1986, Ethics in the Public Domain 1994, Engaging Reason 2000, Value, Respect and Attachment 2001, The Practice of Value 2003. *Honours:* Foreign Hon. Mem. American Acad. of Arts and Sciences; Dr hc (Katholieke Univ. Brussels) 1994; first Hector Fix-Zamudio Int. Prize for Legal Research (Univ. Nacional Autonoma de Mexico) 2005. *Address:* Balliol College, Oxford, OX1 3BJ, England (office). *Telephone:* (1865) 277721 (office). *Fax:* (1865) 277803 (office). *E-mail:* joseph.raz@law.ox .ac.uk (office). *Website:* josephnraz.googlepages.com.

READ, Miss (see Saint, Dora Jessie)

READ, Anthony; British writer and dramatist; b. 21 April 1935, Staffs., England; m. Rosemary E. Kirby 1958; two d. *Education:* Queen Mary's Grammar School, Walsall and Central School of Speech and Drama, London. *Career:* Trustee and fmr Chair. Writers' Guild of GB. *Publications:* The Theatre 1964, Operation Lucy (with David Fisher) 1980, Colonel Z (with David Fisher) 1984, The Deadly Embrace (with David Fisher) 1988, Kristallnacht (with David Fisher) 1989, Conspirator (with Ray Bearse) 1991, The Fall of Berlin (with David Fisher) 1992, Berlin: The Biography of a City (with David Fisher) 1994, The Proudest Day: India's Long Road to

Independence (with David Fisher) 1997, The Devil's Disciples: The Lives and Times of Hitler's Inner Circle 2003, The Baker Street Boys: The Case of the Disappearing Detective 2005, The Baker Street Boys: The Case of the Captive Clairvoyant 2006, The Baker Street Boys: The Case of the Ranjipur Ruby 2006 The Baker Street Boys: The Case of the Limehouse Laundry 2007; also more than 200 TV films, plays, series and serials. *Honours:* BAFTA (SFTA) Best Drama Series Award 1966, Pye Colour TV Award 1983, Wingate Literary Prize 1989. *Address:* 7 Cedar Chase, Taplow, Bucks., England (home). *E-mail:* readwrites@msn.com (home).

READ, Desmond (see Moorcock, Michael (John))

READ, Piers Paul, MA, FRSL; British writer; b. 7 March 1941, Beaconsfield, Bucks.; s. of Herbert Edward Read and Margaret Ludwig; m. Emily Albertine Boothby 1967; two s. two d. *Education:* Ampleforth Coll., York and St John's Coll., Cambridge. *Career:* Artist-in-Residence, Ford Foundation, W Berlin 1964; Sub-Ed. Times Literary Supplement, London 1965; Harkness Fellow Commonwealth Fund, New York 1967–68; Council mem. Inst. of Contemporary Arts (ICA), London 1971–75; Cttee of Man. Soc. of Authors, London 1973–76; mem. Literature Panel Arts Council, London 1975–77; Adjunct Prof. of Writing, Columbia Univ., New York 1980; Chair. Catholic Writers' Guild 1992–97; mem. Bd Aid to the Church in Need 1991–; Trustee Catholic Library 1997–; mem. Council RSL 2001–. *Publications:* Game in Heaven with Tussy Marx 1966, The Junkers 1968, Monk Dawson 1969, The Professor's Daughter 1971, The Upstart 1973, Alive: The Story of the Andes Survivors 1974, Polonaise 1976, The Train Robbers 1978, A Married Man 1979, The Villa Golitsyn 1981, The Free Frenchman 1986, A Season in the West 1988, On the Third Day 1990, Quo Vadis? The Subversion of the Catholic Church 1991, Ablaze: The Story of Chernobyl 1993, A Patriot in Berlin 1995, Knights of The Cross 1997, The Templars 1999, Alice in Exile 2001, Alec Guinness: The Authorised Biography 2003, Hell and Other Essays 2006. *Honours:* Sir Geoffrey Faber Memorial Prize 1968, Somerset Maugham Award 1969, Hawthornden Prize 1969, Thomas More Award (USA) 1976, James Tait Black Memorial Prize 1988. *Address:* 50 Portland Road, London, W11 4LG, England (home). *Telephone:* (20) 7460-2499 (office); (20) 7727-5719 (home). *E-mail:* piersread@dial.pipex.com (office).

READE, Hamish (see Gray, Simon James Holliday)

REANEY, James Crerar, OC, BA, MA; Canadian academic, poet and dramatist; *Professor Emeritus, Middlesex College, University of Western Ontario;* b. 1 Sept. 1926, South Easthope, ON; m. 1951; two s. one d. *Education:* Univ. of Toronto. *Career:* faculty mem., Univ. of Manitoba, Winnipeg 1948–60; Prof., Middlesex Coll., Univ. of Western Ontario from 1960, now Prof. Emeritus; mem. Asscn of Canadian Univ. Teachers (pres. 1959–60), Playwright's Union of Canada, League of Canadian Poets. *Publications:* poetry: The Red Heart 1949, A Suit of Nettles 1958, Twelve Letters to a Small Town 1962, The Dance of Death at London 1963, Poems 1972, Selected Shorter and Longer Poems 1975–76, Performance Poems 1990, Souwesto Home 2005; plays: Night Blooming Cereus 1959, The Killdeer 1960, One Masque 1960, The Sun and the Moon 1965, Listen to the Wind 1966, The Canada Tree 1967, Genesis 1968, Masque 1972, The Donnellys: A Trilogy 1973–75, Baldoon 1976, King Whistle 1979, Antler River 1980, Gyroscope 1981, I, the Parade 1982, The Canadian Brothers 1983, Alice Through the Looking Glass (adaptation of Lewis Carroll's book) 1994; opera libretti: The Shivaree (music by John Beckwith) 1982, Crazy to Kill (music by John Beckwith), Scripts 2004; other: The Box Social and Other Stories 1996, The Donnelly Documents: An Ontario Vendetta 2004; contrib. to books, journals and periodicals. *Honours:* Governor-General's Awards 1949, 1958, 1963, Univ. of Alberta Award for Letters 1974. *Address:* 276 Huron Street, London, ON N6A 2J9, Canada (home). *Telephone:* (519) 439-3850.

REARDON, Katherine (Kate) Genevieve; British writer; b. 20 Nov. 1968, New York, USA; d. of P. W. J. Reardon and J. H. A. Wood. *Education:* Cheltenham Ladies' Coll. and Stowe School, Buckingham. *Career:* worked at Vogue magazine, New York 1988–90; apptd Fashion Ed. Tatler Magazine, London 1990, later Fashion Dir; writer The Times 2005–, also Contributing Ed. Vanity Fair. *Address:* The Times, 1 Pennington Street, London, E98 1XY, England. *E-mail:* kate.reardon@thetimes.co.uk. *Website:* www.timesonline.co.uk.

REBOUL, Jacquette Suzanne Danièle, PhD; French librarian and writer; b. 5 Dec. 1937, Valence; d. of Paul and Camille (née Marchal) Reboul. *Education:* Lycée de Jeunes Filles (Valence), Univ. of Paris (Sorbonne) and Ecole Nat Supérieure de Bibliothécaires. *Career:* Librarian Univ. of Rennes Library 1966–70; Librarian Library of the Sorbonne 1970–85, Chief Librarian 1986–98; retd. *Publications:* Le lever de l'aurore 1969, Le vieux Roi 1972, A l'intérieur de la vue 1973, Du bon usage des bibliographies 1973, La nuit scintille 1975, L'apprentie sorcière (Prix Louis Guillaume) 1982, Les cathédrales du savoir ou les bibliothèques universitaires de recherche aux Etats-Unis 1982, La liberté pour l'ombre 1985, Face à face 1986, Critique universitaire et critique créatrice 1986, L'œil du monde 1990, Raison ardente 1992, Cristal 1996, Psyché 2001, Ta Solitude et le Monde 2002, La Mort en Inde 2003. *Honours:* Chevalier de la Légion d'Honneur; Officier des Palmes Académiques;; Prix Louis Guillaume for poetry. *Address:* c/o La Maison des Ecrivains, 53 rue de Verneuil, 75007 Paris, France. *E-mail:* courrier@maison-des-ecrivains.asso.fr (office)

REBUCK, Gail Ruth, CBE, BA, FRSA; British publishing executive; *Chairman and Chief Executive, Random House Group Ltd;* b. 10 Feb. 1952, London; d. of Gordon Rebuck and Mavis Rebuck; m. Philip Gould 1985; two d. *Education:* Lycée Français de Londres, Univ. of Sussex. *Career:* Production Asst, Grisewood & Dempsey (children's book packager) 1975–76; Ed., later Publr Robert Nicholson Publs London Guidebooks 1976–79; Publr Hamlyn Paperbacks 1979–82; Founder Partner Century Publishing Co. Ltd, Publishing Dir Non-Fiction 1982–85, Publr Century Hutchinson 1985–89, Chair. Random House Div., Random Century 1989–91, Chair. and Chief Exec. Random House UK Ltd (now Random House Group) 1991–; mem. COPUS 1995–97, Creative Industries Task Force 1997–2000; Dir (non-exec.) Work Foundation 2001–, BSkyB 2002–; mem. Court Univ. of Sussex 1997–, Council RCA 1999–; Trustee Inst. for Public Policy Research 1993–2003. *Honours:* ranked 25th by the Financial Times amongst Top 25 Businesswomen in Europe 2005. *Address:* The Random House Group Ltd, 20 Vauxhall Bridge Road, London, SW1V 2SA, England (office). *Telephone:* (20) 7840-8886 (office). *Fax:* (20) 7233-6120 (office). *E-mail:* grebuck@randomhouse.co.uk (office). *Website:* www.randomhouse.co.uk.

REDDY, T. Vasudeva, BSc, MA, PGTDE, PhD; Indian educator, writer and poet; b. 21 Dec. 1943, Mittapalem; m. 1970; two s. one d. *Career:* Nat. Fellowship, UGC, N Delhi 1998–2000; mem. Int. Poets' Acad. (Chennai), World Poetry Soc. (CA), ABI (NC). *Publications:* When Grief Rains (poems) 1982, The Vultures (novel) 1983, The Broken Rhythms (poems) 1987, Jane Austen 1987, Jane Austen: Matrix of Matrimony 1987, The Fleeting Bubbles (poems) 1989, Melting Melodies (poems) 1994, Advanced Grammar and Composition in English 1995, Pensive Memories (poems) 2005; contrib. to journals and magazines. *Honours:* Hon. DLitt (WAAC, California) 1987; hon. mem. Research Bd of Advisors, ABI, N Carolina; Int. Eminent Poet Award 1987, Best Teacher Award (univ. level) Govt of Andhra Pradesh 1990, Michael Madhusudan Award 1995. *Address:* Mittapalem, Narasingapuram, Chandragiri, Andhra Pradesh 517 102, India (home). *Telephone:* (877) 2276414. *E-mail:* kumar_kvr@yahoo.com.

REECE, Henry Michael, MA, DPhil; British publisher; *Secretary to the Delegates and CEO, Oxford University Press;* b. 10 Aug. 1953; m. Allison Jane King 1993 (divorced 2005). *Education:* Univs of Bristol and Oxford. *Career:* Tutor in History, Univ. of Exeter 1977–78; Field Sales Ed., Prentice Hall International 1979–82; Academic Sales Man., Simon and Schuster International 1982–84, UK Sales Man. 1984–85, Asst Vice-Pres. 1985–88; Exec. Ed., Allyn & Bacon, USA 1988–91; Man. Dir Pitman Publishing 1991–94; Exec. Dir Longman Group Ltd 1994–95; Exec. Dir Pearson Professional 1995–97; Man. Dir Financial Times Professional 1997–98; CEO Oxford University Press (Sec. to the Delegates and Chair. Group Strategy Cttee 1998–; Dir (non-exec.) Knowledge Pool 2000–01; mem. Publishers' Assen (mem. Council 1999–2004, Pres. 2004–05. *Honours:* Fellow, Jesus Coll. Oxford 1998–. *Address:* Oxford University Press, Great Clarendon Street, Oxford, OX2 6DP, England (office). *Telephone:* (1865) 556767 (office). *Fax:* (1865) 556646 (office). *E-mail:* enquiry@oup.com (office). *Website:* www.oup.com (office).

REED, Ishmael Scott; American writer and poet; b. 22 Feb. 1938, Chattanooga, TN; s. of Bennie S. Reed and Thelma Coleman; m. 1st Priscilla Rose 1960 (divorced 1970); two s.; m. 2nd Carla Blank; one d. *Education:* Univ. of Buffalo. *Career:* co-f. and Dir Reed, Cannon & Johnson Co. 1973–; Assoc. Fellow, Calhoun House, Yale Univ. 1982–; founder (with Al Young) and ed., Quilt magazine 1981–; Guest Lecturer, Univ. of Calif. Berkeley 1968–; mem. usage panel, American Heritage Dictionary; Assoc. Ed. American Book Review; Exec. Producer Personal Problems (video soap opera); collaborator in multimedia Bicentennial mystery, The Lost State of Franklin (winner Poetry in Public Places contest 1975); Chair. Berkeley Arts Comm.; Advisory Chair. Co-ordinating Council of Literary Magazines; Pres. Before Columbus Foundation 1976–; Nat. Endowment for Arts Writing Fellow 1974; Guggenheim Fellow 1975; mem. Authors' Guild of America, PEN. *Publications:* fiction: The Free-Lance Pallbearers 1967, Yellow Back Radio Broke Down 1969, Mumbo Jumbo 1972, The Last Days of Louisiana Red 1974, Flight to Canada 1976, The Terrible Twos 1982, Reckless Eyeballing 1986, Cab Calloway Stands in for the Moon 1986, The Terrible Threes 1989, Japanese By Spring 1993; poetry: Catechism of a Neoamerican Hoodoo Church 1970, Conjure: Selected Poems 1963–1970 1972, Chattanooga 1973, A Secretary to the Spirits 1978, Calafia: The California Poetry (ed.) 1979, New and Collected Poems 1988, New and Collected Poems 1964–2006 2006; non-fiction: The Rise, Fall and...? of Adam Clayton Powell (with others) 1967, 19 Necromancers from Now (ed.) 1970, Yardbird Reader (five vols, ed.) 1971–77, Yardbird Lives! (ed., with Al Young) 1978, Shrovetide in Old New Orleans 1978, Quilt 2–3 (ed., with Al Young, two vols) 1981–82, God Made Alaska for the Indians 1982, Writin' is Fightin': Thirty-Seven Years of Boxing on Paper (ed.) 1988, Ishmael Reed: An Interview 1990, The Before Columbus Foundation Fiction Anthology: Selections from the American Book Awards 1980–1990 (ed., with Kathryn Trueblood and Shawn Wong) 1992, Airin' Dirty Laundry 1993, Multi-America 1996, The Reed Reader (ed.) 2000. *Honours:* Nat. Inst. of Arts and Letters Award 1975, Rosenthal Foundation Award 1975, Michaux Award 1978, ACLU Award 1978. *Address:* c/o Penguin Putnam Inc., 375 Hudson Street, New York, NY 10014, USA.

REED, Jane Barbara, CBE, FRSA; British journalist, editor and publishing executive; *Director, Times Newspapers Limited;* b. 31 March 1940, Letchworth, Herts.; d. of the late William Reed and Gwendoline Reed. *Education:* Royal Masonic School. *Career:* Ed. Woman's Own 1969–79; Publr IPC

Magazines Ltd Women's Monthly Magazines Group 1979–81; Ed.-in-Chief Woman magazine 1981–83; Asst Man. Dir IPC Specialist Educ. and Leisure Group 1983; Man. Dir IPC Holborn Publishing Group 1983–85; Man. Ed. Today newspaper 1985–89; Dir of Corp. Affairs, News Int. PLC 1989–2000; Dir Times Newspapers Ltd; Dir Nat. Acad. of Writing 2001–; fmr Pres. Media Soc.; mem. Council Nat. Literacy Trust; Dir (non-Exec.) Media Trust; Trustee St Katharine & Shadwell Trust. *Publications:* Girl About Town 1965, Kitchen Sink – or Swim? (co-author) 1981. *Honours:* Editor of the Year 1975, 1981, Mark Boxer Award for Lifetime Achievement 2002. *Address:* News International PLC, PO Box 495, 1 Virginia Street, London, E98 1EX (office).

REED, Jeremy, BA; British poet and writer; b. 1951, Jersey, Channel Islands. *Education:* Univ. of Essex, Colchester. *Publications:* poetry: Target 1972, Saints and Psychotics: Poems 1973–74 1974, Vicissitudes 1974, Diseased Near Deceased 1975, Emerald Cat 1975, Ruby Onocentaur 1975, Blue Talaria 1976, Count Bluebeard 1976, Jack's in His Corset 1978, Walk on Through 1980, Bleecker Street 1980, No Refuge Here 1981, A Long Shot to Heaven 1982, A Man Afraid 1982, By the Fisheries 1984, Elegy for Senta 1985, Skies 1985, Border Pass 1986, Selected Poems 1987, Engaging Form 1988, The Escaped Image 1988, Nineties 1990, Diving for Pearls 1990, Red-Haired Android 1992; fiction: The Lipstick Boys 1984, Blue Rock 1987, Madness: The Price of Poetry 1990. *Honours:* Somerset Maugham Award 1985. *Address:* c/o Jonathan Cape Ltd, 20 Vauxhall Bridge Road, London, SW1V 2SA, England.

REEDER, Carolyn, BA, MEd; American writer; b. 16 Nov. 1937, Washington, DC; m. Jack Reeder 1959; one s. one d. *Education:* American Univ. *Career:* mem. Children's Book Guild of Washington, DC (fmr Treas.), Authors' Guild. *Publications:* non-fiction: Shenandoah Heritage (with Jack Reeder) 1978, Shenandoah Vestiges (with Jack Reeder) 1980, Shenandoah Secrets (with Jack Reeder) 1991; juvenile fiction: Shades of Gray 1989, Grandpa's Mountain 1991, Moonshiner's Son 1993, Across the Lines 1997, Foster's War 1998, Captain Kate 1999, Before the Creeks Ran Red 2003, The Secret Project Notebook 2005. *Honours:* Scott O'Dell Award for Historical Fiction 1989, Child Study Asscn Award 1989, American Library Asscn Notable Book 1989, Honour Book for the Jane Addam's Children's Book Award 1989, Notable Trade Book in the Language Arts 1989, Jefferson Cup Award 1990, Int. Reading Asscn Young Adult Choice 1991, Joan G. Sugarman Children's Book Award 1992–93, Hedda Seisler Mason Honor Award 1995. *Address:* 7314 University Avenue, Glen Echo, MD 20812, USA. *Website:* www.reederbooks .com.

REEMAN, Douglas Edward, (Alexander Kent); British writer; b. 15 Oct. 1924, Thames Ditton, Surrey, England; m. Kimberley June Jordan 1985. *Publications:* A Prayer for the Ship 1958, High Water 1959, Send a Gunboat 1960, Dive in the Sun 1961, The Hostile Shore 1962, The Last Raider 1963, With Blood and Iron 1964, HMS Saracen 1965, Path of the Storm 1966, The Deep Silence 1967, The Pride and the Anguish 1968, To Risks Unknown 1969, The Greatest Enemy 1970, Against the Sea 1971, Rendezvous – South Atlantic 1972, Go In and Sink! 1973, The Destroyers 1974, Winged Escort 1975, Surface with Daring 1976, Strike from the Sea 1978, A Ship Must Die 1979, Torpedo Run 1981, Badge of Glory 1982, The First to Land 1984, D-Day: A Personal Reminiscence 1984, The Volunteers 1985, The Iron Pirate 1986, In Danger's Hour 1988, The White Guns 1989, Killing Ground 1991, The Horizon 1993, Sunset 1994, A Dawn Like Thunder 1996, Battlecruiser 1997, Dust on the Sea 1999, For Valour 2000, Twelve Seconds to Live 2002, Knife Edge 2004; as Alexander Kent: To Glory We Steer 1968, Form Line of Battle 1969, Enemy in Sight! 1970, The Flag Captain 1971, Sloop of War 1972, Command a King's Ship 1974, Signal – Close Action! 1974, Richard Bolitho – Midshipman 1975, Passage to Mutiny 1976, In Gallant Company 1977, Midshipman Bolitho and the 'Avenger' 1978, Captain Richard Bolitho, RN 1978, The Inshore Squadron 1978, Stand Into Danger 1980, A Tradition of Victory 1981, Success to the Brave 1983, Colours Aloft! 1986, Honour This Day 1987, With All Despatch 1988, The Only Victor 1990, Beyond the Reef 1992, The Darkening Sea 1993, For My Country's Freedom 1995, Cross of St George 1996, Sword of Honour 1998, Second to None 1999, Relentless Pursuit 2001, Man of War 2003, Band of Brothers 2005, Heart of Oak 2007; contrib. to various journals and magazines. *Literary Agent:* PFD, Drury House, 34–43 Russell Street, London, WC2B 5HA, England.

REES, Rev. D(avid) Ben(jamin), (Ceredig), BA, BD, MA, MSc, PhD, FRHistS; British writer, editor and minister of religion; *Professor of Theology, University of Liverpool*; b. 1 Aug. 1937, Wales; s. of John Rees and Anne Rees; m. 1963; two s. *Education:* Univs of Wales, Liverpool and Salford. *Career:* minister, Presbyterian Church of Wales, Cynon Valley 1962–68, Heathfield Road, Liverpool 1968–; Founder-Sec. Modern Welsh Publs 1963–; part-time Lecturer, Univ. of Liverpool 1970–2001, Prof. of Theology 1998–; Ed. Peace and Reconciliation Magazine 2000–02, Y Bont/Bridge 1997–; Vice-Pres. Wales and the World 1979, Liverpool Welsh Choral Union 2004; mem. Cymmrodorion Soc., Welsh Acad.; Founder-mem. Merseyside Welsh Heritage Soc. 1999. *Publications:* Wales: A Cultural History 1980, Preparation for a Crisis: Adult Education in England and Wales 1945–1980 1981, Liverpool, Welsh and Their Religion 1984, Owen Thomas: A Welsh Preacher in Liverpool 1991, The Welsh of Merseyside 1997, Local and Parliamentary Politics in Liverpool from 1800 to 1911 1999, The Welsh of Merseyside in the Twentieth Century 2001, Vehicles of Grace and Hope (ed.) 2002, The Call and Contribution of Dr Robert Arthur Hughes 2004; contrib. to magazines and newspapers. *Honours:* Ellis Griffith Prize 1979, Paul Harris Fellow 2005. *Address:* 32 Garth Drive, Liverpool, L18 6HW, England (home). *E-mail:* ben@

garthdrive.fsnet.co.uk (home). *Website:* www.welshpublications.co.uk; www .lordsdaywales.co.uk.

REES, Baron (Life Peer), cr. 2005, of Ludlow in the County of Shropshire; **Martin John Rees,** MA, PhD, FRS, OM; British astronomer and academic; *President, The Royal Society*; b. 23 June 1942, s. of Reginald J. Rees and Joan Rees; m. Caroline Humphrey 1986. *Education:* Shrewsbury School and Trinity Coll., Cambridge. *Career:* Fellow, Jesus Coll., Cambridge 1967–69; Research Assoc. Calif. Inst. of Tech. 1967–68, 1971; mem. Inst. for Advanced Study, Princeton 1969–70, Prof. 1982–96; Visiting Prof., Harvard Univ. 1972, 1986–87; Prof., Univ. of Sussex 1972–73; Plumian Prof. of Astronomy and Experimental Philosophy, Univ. of Cambridge 1973–91, Royal Soc. Research Prof. 1992–2002, Prof. of Cosmology and Astrophysics 2004–; Astronomer Royal 1995–; Master Trinity Coll., Cambridge 2004–; Fellow, King's Coll., Cambridge 1969–72, 1973–2003; Visiting Prof., Imperial Coll., London 2001–, Leicester Univ. 2001–; Dir Inst. of Astronomy 1977–82, 1987–91; Regents Fellow, Smithsonian Inst. 1984–88; mem. council Royal Soc. 1983–85, 1993–95, Pres. 2005–; Pres. Royal Astronomical Soc. 1992–94, British Asscn for the Advancement of Science 1994–95; Trustee British Museum 1996–2002, Inst. for Advanced Study, Princeton, USA 1998–, Nat. Endowment for Sciences, Tech. and Arts 1998–2001, Kennedy Memorial Trust 1999–2004, Inst. for Public Policy Research 2001; Foreign Assoc. NAS; mem. Academia Europaea 1989, Pontifical Acad. of Sciences 1990; Foreign mem. American Philosophical Soc., Royal Swedish Acad. of Science, Russian Acad. of Sciences, Norwegian Acad. of Arts and Science, Accad. Lincei (Rome), Royal Netherlands Acad., Finnish Acad. of Arts and Sciences. *Television:* What We Still Don't Know (documentary series, Channel 4) 2004. *Publications:* Perspectives in Astrophysical Cosmology 1995, Gravity's Fatal Attraction (with M. Begelman) 1995, Before the Beginning 1997, Just Six Numbers 1999, Our Cosmic Habitat 2001, Our Final Century? 2003; edited books; articles and reviews in scientific journals and numerous gen. articles. *Honours:* Hon. Fellow, Trinity Coll., Darwin Coll. and Jesus Coll., Cambridge, Indian Acad. of Sciences, Univ. of Wales, Cardiff 1998, Inst. of Physics 2001; Foreign Hon. mem. American Acad. of Arts and Sciences; Officier, Ordre des Arts et des Lettres; Hon. DSc (Sussex) 1990, (Leicester) 1993, (Copenhagen, Keele, Uppsala, Newcastle) 1995, (Toronto) 1997, (Durham) 1999, (Oxford) 2000; Heinemann Prize, American Inst. of Physics 1984, Gold Medal (Royal Astronomical Soc.) 1987, Guthrie Medal, Inst. of Physics 1989, Balzan Prize 1989, Robinson Prize for Cosmology 1990, Bruce Medal, Astronomical Soc. of Pacific 1993, Science Writing Award, American Inst. of Physics 1996, Bower Award (Franklin Inst.) 1998, Rossi Prize, American Astronomical Soc. 2000, Cosmology Prize of Peter Gruber Foundation 2001, Einstein Award, World Cultural Congress 2003, Crafoord Prize, Royal Swedish Acad. 2005, Niels Bohr Medal, UNESCO 2005. *Address:* Trinity College, Cambridge, CB2 1TQ (office); Institute of Astronomy, Madingley Road, Cambridge CB3 0HA, England (office). *Telephone:* (1223) 338412 (office). *E-mail:* mjr@ast.cam.ac.uk (office). *Website:* www.ast.cam.ac.uk/IoA/staff/mjr (office); www.trin.cam.ac .uk/index.php?pageid=172 (office).

REES, Paul; British journalist; *Editor, Q magazine.* *Career:* contrib. to Brum Beat; News Ed., Raw –1995; News Ed., freelance writer, Ed. Kerrang! 1995–2002, Q magazine 2002–. *Address:* Q, Emap Publishing, Mappin House, 4 Winsley Street, London, W1W 8HF, England (office). *E-mail:* paul.rees@ emap.com (office). *Website:* www.q4music.com (office).

REES-MOGG, Baron (Life Peer), cr. 1988, of Hinton Blewett in the County of Avon; **William Rees-Mogg,** Kt; British journalist and publisher; *Chairman, Pickering and Chatto Publishers Ltd*; b. 14 July 1928, Bristol; s. of the late Edmund Fletcher and Beatrice Rees-Mogg (née Warren); m. Gillian Shakespeare Morris 1962; two s. three d. *Education:* Charterhouse and Balliol Coll., Oxford. *Career:* Pres. Oxford Union 1951; Financial Times 1952–60, Chief Leader Writer 1955–60, Asst Ed. 1957–60; City Ed. Sunday Times 1960–61, Political and Econ. Ed. 1961–63, Deputy Ed. 1964–67; Ed. of The Times 1967–81, Dir The Times Ltd 1968–81; Vice-Chair. BBC 1981–86; Chair. Arts Council 1982–89; Chair. Broadcasting Standards Council 1988–93; mem. Exec. Bd Times Newspapers Ltd 1968–81, Dir 1978–81; Dir Gen. Electric Co. 1981–97; Chair. and Propr Pickering and Chatto Publishers Ltd 1983–; Chair. Sidgwick and Jackson 1985–89, Int. Business Communications PLC 1994–98, Fleet Street Publications 1995–; Dir M & G Group 1987, EFG Pvt. Bank and Trust Co. 1993–2005, Value Realization Trust PLC 1996–98, Newsmax Media, Inc., USA 2000–06; columnist, The Times 1992–, The Mail on Sunday 2004–; mem. Int. Cttee Pontifical Council for Culture 1983–87. *Publications:* The Reigning Error: the Crisis of World Inflation 1974, An Humbler Heaven 1977, How to Buy Rare Books 1985, Blood in the Streets (with James Dale Davidson) 1987, The Great Reckoning (with James Dale Davidson) 1992, Picnics on Vesuvius 1992, The Sovereign Individual (with James Dale Davidson) 1997. *Honours:* Hon. LLD (Bath) 1977, (Leeds) 1992. *Address:* Pickering & Chatto Publishers Ltd, 21 Bloomsbury Way, London, WC1A 2TH, England (office). *Telephone:* (20) 7242-2241 (office). *Fax:* (20) 7405-6216 (office). *Website:* www.pickeringchatto.com (office).

REEVE, Franklin Dolier, PhD; American academic, writer, poet, translator and editor; *Professor of Letters Emeritus, Wesleyan University*; b. 18 Sept. 1928, Philadelphia, PA; m. Laura C. Stevenson; seven c. *Education:* Princeton Univ., Columbia Univ. *Career:* Lecturer, Columbia Univ. 1952–61; Exchange Scholar, ACLS-USSR Acad. of Sciences 1961; Prof. of Letters, Wesleyan Univ. 1962–2002, Prof. Emer. 2002–; Visiting Prof., Univ. of Oxford 1964, Columbia Univ. 1988; Visiting Lecturer, Yale Univ. 1974–86, New England Coll. MFA

Program 2003–05; mem. Poetry Soc. of America 1974–94, gov. bd 1978–80, vice-pres. 1980–84, Ed. Poetry Review 1982–84; mem. Poets House, mem. gov. bd 1985–99, sec. 1994–99; mem. Pettee Memorial Library (Trustee), Marlboro Review (advisory bd), New England Poetry Soc. (bd dir). *Performances include:* Alcyone (poetic drama with music by T. L. Reed) 1997, The Urban Stampede (poetic drama with music by Andrew Gant) 2000, The Return of the Blue Cat (poems with improvised jazz trio Exit 59) 2004, The Puzzle Master (poetic drama with music by Eric Chasalow) 2007, The Blue Cat Walks the Earth (poems with music by jazz trio) 2007. *Publications include:* Five Short Novels by Turgenev (trans.) 1961, Anthology of Russian Plays (trans.) 1961, 1963, Aleksandr Blok: Between Image and Idea (non-fiction) 1962, Robert Frost in Russia (non-fiction) 1964, The Russian Novel (non-fiction) 1966, In the Silent Stones (poems) 1968, The Red Machines (fiction) 1968, Just Over the Border (fiction) 1969, The Brother (fiction) 1971, The Blue Cat (poems) 1972, White Colors (fiction) 1973, Nightway (poems) 1987, The White Monk (non-fiction) 1989, The Garden (trans.) 1990, Concrete Music (poems) 1992, The Trouble with Reason (trans.) 1993, A Few Rounds of Old Maid and Other Stories (fiction) 1995, The Moon and Other Failures (poems) 1999, A World You Haven't Seen (poems) 2001, The Urban Stampede and Other Poems 2002, The Return of the Blue Cat (poems) 2005, My Sister Life (fiction) 2005, Lions and Acrobats: Selected Poems (trans.) 2005, North River (fiction) 2006; contrib. to journals and periodicals. *Honours:* Hon. DLit (New England Coll.) 2004; American Acad. of Arts and Letters Award in Literature 1970, PEN Syndicated Fiction Awards 1985, 1986, New England Poetry Soc. Golden Rose 1994, May Sarton Award 2004, Allen Tate Award 2005. *Address:* PO Box 14, Wilmington, VT 05363, USA. *E-mail:* lcsfdr@sover.net (home).

REGÀS, Rosa, BPhil; Spanish writer and journalist; *General Director, Biblioteca Nacional*; b. 1933, Barcelona; m.; five c. *Education:* Barcelona Univ. *Career:* editorial staff with Seix Barral 1964–70, with Edhasa; f. and Publisher, La Gaya Ciencia 1970–, journals Arquitectura Vis, Cuadernos de la Gaya Ciencia 1976–; trans. for UN 1983–94; Head of Culture Dept of Casa de América, part of Foreign Affairs Ministry 1994–98; Gen. Dir Biblioteca Nacional de España 2004–. *Publications include:* fiction: Memoria de Almator (novel) 1991, Azul (novel) (Premio Nadal) 1994, Pobre corazón (short stories) 1996, Barcelona, un día (short stories) 1998, Luna Lunera (novel) (Premio Ciudad de Barcelona) 1999, La canción de Dorotea (novel) (Premio Planeta) 2001, contrib. short stories to anthologies, including Relatos para un fin de milenio 1998, Cuentos solidarios 1999, Mujeres al alba 1999, La paz y la palabra 2003; non-fiction: La cuina de l'ampurdanet (leaflet) 1985, Ginebra (leaflet) 1988, Canciones de amor y de batalla: 1993–1995 (articles) 1995, Viaje a la luz del Cham 1995, Una revolución personal 1997, Desde el mar 1997, España: una nueva mirada (leaflet) 1997, Más canciones 1995–1998 (articles) 1998, La creación, la fantasía y la vida (essay) 1998, Sangre de mi sangre (essay) 1999, Diario de una abuela de verano (biog.) 2004, El valor de la protesta (articles) 2004; contrib. essays to collections, including Retratos literarios 1997, Ser mujer 2000, and to numerous journals and periodicals. *Address:* Biblioteca Nacional, Paseo de Recoletos 20, 28071 Madrid, Spain (office). *E-mail:* directorgeneral@bne.es (office). *Website:* www.bne.es (office).

REGNAULT, François; French philosopher, dramatist and translator; b. Nov. 1938, Paris; s. of Jacques Regnault. *Education:* Lycée Montaigne, Lycée Louis-le-Grand. *Career:* teacher Prytanée Militaire de la Flèche, then Lycée de Reims 1964–70; teacher Dept of Philosophy, Univ. de Vincennes 1970–74, then Dept of Psychoanalysis 1974–; first involvement in theatre 1973; co-f. Compagnie Pandora 1976; Co-Dir Théâtre de la Commune/Pandora, Aubervilliers 1991–97; speech tutor Conservatoire Nat. d'Art dramatique, Paris 1994–2001. *Play:* Corneille's L'Illusion comique (actor, Théâtre de Gennevilliers) 2005. *Publications:* non-fiction: Mais on doit tout oser puisque 1981, Dieu est inconscient 1986, Le Spectateur 1986, Dire le vers (with Jean-Claude Milner) 1987, Le Théâtre et la mer 1989, La Doctrine inouï: Dix leçons sur le théâtre classique français 1996, Conférences d'esthétique lacanienne 1997, L'Une des trois unités 1999, Théâtre-Equinoxes 2001, Théâtre-Solstices 2002, Notre objet a 2003, Le Théâtre de Pandora 1999; translations: Wedekind's L'Eveil du printemps, Ibsen's Peer Gynt 1996, J. M. Synge's Le Baladin du monde occidental; contrib. articles and essays. *Address:* c/o Faculty of Psychology, Université de Paris VIII – Vincennes à St-Denis, 2 rue de la Liberté, 93526 St Denis Cédex, France.

REICH, Robert Bernard, BA, MA, JD; American political economist, academic and fmr government official; *Professor of Public Policy, Goldman School of Public Policy, University of California, Berkeley*; b. 24 June 1946, Scranton, Pa; s. of Edwin Saul and Mildred Dorf Reich (née Freshman); m. Clare Dalton 1973; two s. *Education:* Dartmouth Coll., Univ. of Oxford, UK, Yale Univ. *Career:* Asst Solicitor-Gen., US Dept of Justice, Washington, DC 1974–76; Dir of Policy Planning Fed. Trade Comm., Washington 1976–81; mem. Faculty, John F. Kennedy School of Govt, Harvard Univ. 1981–92; fmr Econ. Adviser to Pres. Bill Clinton; Sec. of Labor 1993–97; Univ. Prof., Maurice B. Hexter Prof. of Social and Econ. Policy, Brandeis Univ. Grad. School for Advanced Studies in Social Welfare 1997–2006; Prof. of Public Policy, Goldman School of Public Policy, Univ. of Calif., Berkeley 2006–; Chair. Biotechnology Section US Office Tech. Assessment, Washington 1990–91; Co-founder and Chair. Editorial Bd The American Prospect 2002–03; mem. Nat. Governing Bd, Common Cause 1982–88; mem. Mass Comm. on Mature Industries 1985–87; mem. Bd of Dirs Business Enterprise Trust 1986–93, Econ. Policy Inst. 1988–93, 2002–03; Trustee Dartmouth Coll. 1988–93; Contributing Ed. The New Republic, Washington 1982–93; Rhodes Scholar 1968. *Publications:* The Next American Frontier 1983, Tales of a New America 1987, The Power of Public Ideas (co-author) 1987, The Work of Nations 1991, Putting People First 1997, Locked in the Cabinet 1997, The Future of Success 2001, Reason: Why Liberals Will Win the Battle for America 2004. *Honours:* Dr hc (Dartmouth Coll.) 1994, (Univ. of New Hampshire) 1997, (Wheaton Coll.) 1998, (Emory Univ.) 1999, (Bates Coll.) 2001, (Grinnell Coll.) 2002; Mass Teachers Asscn Award for Excellence 1997, Lifetime Achievement Award, Nat. Ass. of Voluntary Health and Social Welfare Orgs 1997, Eleanor Roosevelt Award for Public Service, Americans for Democratic Action 2001, Vaclev Havel Humanitarian Prize 2003. *Address:* Richard & Rhoda Goldman School of Public Policy, 301 GSPP Main, 2607 Hearst Avenue, University of California, Berkeley, Berkeley, CA 94720-7320, USA (office). *Telephone:* (510) 642-0551 (office). *E-mail:* rreich@berkeley.edu (office); bob@RobertReich.org. *Website:* gspp.berkeley.edu/people/faculty/reich.htm (office); www.robertreich.org.

REICHS, Kathleen (Kathy), PhD; American writer and forensic anthropologist; b. Chicago; m. Paul Reichs; two d. one s. *Education:* Northwestern Univ. *Career:* forensic anthropologist, Office of the Chief Medical Examiner, Carolina, USA, Laboratoires des Sciences Judiciaires et de Médecine Légale, Canada; mem. Bd of Dirs American Acad. of Forensic Sciences; Prof. of Anthropology, Univ. of N Carolina at Charlotte. *Publications:* Déjà Dead (Ellis Award for Best First Novel) 1997, Death du Jour 1999, Deadly Decisions 2000, Fatal Voyage 2001, Grave Secrets 2002, Bare Bones 2003, Monday Mourning 2004, Cross Bones 2005. *Address:* c/o Random House, 20 Vauxhall Bridge Road, London, SW1V 2SA, England (office). *Website:* www.kathyreichs.com (office).

REID, Alastair, MA; British writer, translator and poet; b. 22 March 1926, Whithorn, Wigtonshire, Scotland. *Education:* Univ. of St Andrews, Scotland. *Career:* visiting lecturer at univs in the UK and USA; staff writer, correspondent, New Yorker 1959–. *Publications:* To Lighten my House 1953, Oddments, Inklings, Omens, Moments 1959, Passwords: Places, Poems, Preoccupations 1963, Mother Goose in Spanish 1967, Corgi Modern Poets in Focus 3 1971, Weathering: Poems and Translations 1978, Whereabouts: Notes on Being a Foreigner 1987, An Alastair Reid Reader 1995, OASES: Poems and Prose 1997; stories for children and trans. from Spanish of Pablo Neruda, Jorge Luis Borges and other writers. *Honours:* Scottish Arts Council Award 1979, PEN Award for Translation 2000. *Address:* c/o The New Yorker, 4 Times Square, New York, NY 10036-6592, USA.

REID, Barbara Jane; Canadian illustrator and writer; b. 16 Nov. 1957, Toronto, Ont.; d. of Robert Johnstone and Dora Ann Reid; m. Ian Robert Crysler 1981; two d. *Education:* Lawrence Park Coll. Inst. and Ont. Coll. of Art. *Career:* author and illustrator of children's books 1980–; mem. Canadian Asscn of Photographers and Illustrators in Communications, Children's Book Centre. *Illustrated works include:* The New Baby Calf 1984, Have You Seen Birds 1986, Sing a Song of Mother Goose 1987, Playing With Plasticene, The Zoe Series 1991, Two By Two 1992, Gifts 1994, The Party 1997, The Golden Goose 2000, The Subway Mouse 2005. *Honours:* Illustration Award, Ind. Order of Daughters of the Empire 1986, Canadian Council Prize 1986, Ruth Schwartz Award for Children's Literature 1986, Elizabeth Cleaver Award 1987, 1993, Ezra Jack Keats Award 1988, Mr Christie Book Award 1991, Amelia Francis Howard Gibbon Award 1995, 1997, Gov-Gen's Award 1997. *Address:* 37 Strathmore Blvd, Toronto, ON M4J 1P1, Canada.

REID, Christina; Northern Irish playwright; b. 12 March 1942, Belfast. *Education:* Queen's Univ., Belfast. *Career:* writer-in-residence, Lyric Theatre, Belfast 1983–84, Young Vic Theatre, London 1988–89. *Plays:* Did You Hear the One About the Irishman? 1980, Tea in a China Cup 1983, Joyriders 1986, The Last of a Dyin' Race 1986, The Belle of the Belfast City 1986, My Name, Shall I Tell You My Name? 1987, Lords, Dukes and Earls 1989, Les Miserables (after Hugo) 1992, Clowns 1996, The King of the Castle 1999, The Gift of the Gab 2004, The Understudy 2003. *Screenplays:* The Last of a Dyin' Race 1987, Streetwise (series of 13 episodes) 1991, Pie in the Sky 1995, Mighty Belfast (based on Joyriders and the sequel, Clowns). *Publications:* Christina Reid: Plays One 1997, The Gift of the Gab 2003; featured in anthologies Best Radio Plays of 1986, New Connections. *Honours:* Ulster TV Drama Award 1980, Giles Cooper Award 1986, George Devine Award 1986. *Literary Agent:* Alan Brodie Representation, Sixth Floor, Fairgate House, 78 New Oxford Street, London, WC1A 1HB, England. *Telephone:* (20) 7079-7990 (office). *Fax:* (20) 7079-7999 (office). *E-mail:* info@alanbrodie.com (office). *Website:* www.alanbrodie.com (office).

REID, Philip (see Ingrams, Richard Reid)

REID BANKS, Lynne (see Banks, Lynne Reid)

REIDY, Carolyn Kroll, AB, MA, PhD; American publishing executive; *President, Adult Publishing Division, Simon and Schuster*; b. (Carolyn Judith Kroll), 2 May 1949, Washington, DC; d. of Henry Kroll and Mildred Kroll; m. Stephen Kroll Reidy 1974. *Education:* Middlebury Coll. Vt and Indiana Univ. *Career:* various positions, Random House, New York 1975–83; Dir of Subsidiary Rights, William Morrow & Co., New York 1983–85; Vice-Pres. Assoc. Publr, Vintage Books, Random House, New York 1985–87; Assoc. Publr, Random House (concurrent with Assoc. Publr and Publr of Vintage Books) 1987–88; Publr, Vintage Books 1987–88, Anchor Books, Doubleday, New York 1988; Pres. and Publr, Avon Books, New York 1988–92; Pres. and Publr, Simon and Schuster Trade Div. 1992–2001, Pres. Adult Publishing

Div., Simon and Schuster 2001–; Dir NAMES Project 1994–98, New York Univ. Center for Publishing 1997–, Literacy Partners, Inc. 1999–, Nat. Book Foundation 2000–. *Honours:* Matrix Award 2002. *Address:* Simon and Schuster, 1230 Avenue of the Americas, New York, NY 10020, USA (office). *Telephone:* (212) 698-7323 (office). *Fax:* (212) 698-7035 (office). *E-mail:* carolyn .reidy@simonandschuster.com (office). *Website:* simonsays.com (office).

REIF, Stefan Clive, MA, PhD, LittD, FRAS; British academic and writer; *Emeritus Professor of Medieval Hebrew Studies and Fellow of St John's College, University of Cambridge*; b. 21 Jan. 1944, Edinburgh, Scotland; m. Shulamit Stekel 1967; one s. one d. *Education:* Univs of London and Cambridge. *Career:* Ed. Cambridge University Library Genizah Series 1978–; Prof. of Medieval Hebrew Studies and Dir of Genizah Research, Univ. of Cambridge –2006, Emer. Prof. 2007–; Fellow, St John's Coll., Cambridge; Fellow, Mekize Nirdamim Soc., Jerusalem; mem. Jewish Historical Soc. of England (fmr Pres.), British Asscn for Jewish Studies (fmr Pres.), Soc. for Old Testament Study. *Publications:* Shabbethai Sofer and his Prayer-book 1979, Interpreting the Hebrew Bible 1981, Published Material from the Cambridge Genizah Collections 1988, Genizah Research after Ninety Years 1992, Judaism and Hebrew Prayer 1993, Hebrew Manuscripts at University of Cambridge Library 1997, A Jewish Archive from Old Cairo 2000, Why Medieval Hebrew Studies 2001, The Cambridge Genizah Collections: Their Contexts and Significance 2002, Problems with Prayers 2006; contrib. over 300 articles in Hebrew and Jewish studies. *Address:* Cambridge University Library, West Road, Cambridge, CB3 9DR, England (office). *Telephone:* (1223) 766370 (office). *Fax:* (1223) 333160 (office). *E-mail:* scr3@ .cam.ac.uk (office). *Website:* www.lib.cam.ac.uk/Taylor-Schechter (office).

REINEROVÁ, Lenka; Czech writer and journalist; b. 17 May 1916, Prague; one d. *Education:* Prague Stephan Gymnasium. *Publications:* Hranice uzavreny 1956, Grenze Geschlossen 1958, Ein für allemal 1962, Barva slunce a noci 1969, Der Ausflug zum Schwanensee 1983, Es began in der Melantrichgasse 1985, Die Premiere 1989, Sklo a porcelan 1991, Das Traumcafe einer Pragerin 1991, Mandelduft 1998, Zu Hause in Prag 2000, Besadresy 2001, Kovàtua uad Prahow 2001, Alle Farben der Sonne und der Nacht 2003, Všechny barvy slunce a noci 2003, Vůně mandli 2004, Praha Bláznivà 2005, Nattisches Prag 2005. *Honours:* Schillerring 1999, Medal for Merit I Class 2001, Ehrenbürgerin der Stadt Prag seit 2002, Goethe Medal 2003. *Address:* c/o Aufbau-Verlag GmbH, Postfach 193, 10105 Berlin, Germany (office); Plseňskà 129, 150 00 Prague, Czech Republic (home). *Telephone:* 25712091 (home).

REINIG, Christa; German writer; b. 6 Aug. 1926, Berlin; d. of Wilhelmine Reinig. *Education:* Humboldt-Univ. of Berlin. *Career:* Curator Märkisches Museum, Kultur-historisches Museum der Stadt Berlin 1958–63; mem. PEN-Zentrum, Bayerische Akad. der Schönen Künste. *Publications include:* poetry: Die Steine für Finisterre 1960, Schwabinger Marterln 1968, Schwalbe von Olevano 1969, Müßiggang ist aller Liebe Anfang 1979, Sämtliche Gedichte 1984; prose: Der Traum meiner Verkommenheit 1961, Drei Schiffe 1965, Orion trat aus dem Haus: Neue Sternbilder 1968, Die himmlische und die irdische Geometrie 1975, Entmannung 1976, Der Wolf und die Witwen 1980, Die Frau im Brunnen 1984, Simsalabim 1999; short stories: Die ewige Schule 1982, Gesammelte Erzählungen 1986, Nobody 1989, Glück und Glas 1991; Das Aquarium (radio play, Kriegsblinden Prize). *Honours:* Literature Prize (Bremen) 1964, Tukan-Preis (Munich) 1969, Verband der deutschen Kritiker Prize 1976, Bundesverdienstkreuz 1976, Literature Grant, Munich 1980, Literature Prize (Südwestfunk—SWF, Baden-Baden) 1984, Literature Prize (Stadt Gandersheim) 1993. *Address:* Bertholdstr 11, 80809 Munich, Germany. *Telephone:* (89) 3512505.

REINSHAGEN, Gerlind; German writer; b. 4 May 1926, Königsberg; d. of Ekkehard Technau and Frieda Technau; m. 1949. *Education:* studies in pharmacy and art, Berlin. *Career:* freelance author of novels, theatre and radio plays, screenplays, poetry, essays and criticism; mem. German PEN; mem. Deutsche Akad. der darstellenden Künste. *Plays:* Doppelkopf 1968, Leben und Tod der Marilyn Monroe 1971, Himmel und Erde 1974, Sonntagskinder 1976, Frühlingsfest 1980, Eisenherz 1982, Die Clownin 1988, Feuerblume 1987, Tanz, Marie! 1989, Die fremde Tochter 1993, Die grüne Tür 1999. *Television:* Doppelkopf 1972, Himmel und Erde 1976, Sonntagskinder 1981. *Radio:* 12 radio plays. *Publications:* novels: Rovinato 1981, Die flüchtige Braut 1984, Zwölf Nächte 1989, Jäger am Rand der Nacht 1993, Am grossen Stern 1996, Göttergeschichte 2000; Gesammelte Stücke (collected pieces) 1986, Joint Venture 2003, Vom Feuer 1988; contribs to theatrical journals and yearbooks etc. *Honours:* Fördergabe Schillerpreis, Baden Württemberg 1974, Mühlheimer Dramatikerpreis 1977, Roswitha von Gandersheim Medaille 1984, Ludwig Mülheimes Preis 1993, Niedersächsischer Kunstpreis 1997, Niedersächsischer Staatspreis 1999. *Address:* Rheingaustrasse 2, 12161 Berlin, Germany. *Telephone:* (30) 8217171.

REISMAN, Heather; Canadian publishing executive; *CEO, Indigo Books & Music Inc.*; b. Montreal; m. Gerald Schwartz; four c. *Education:* McGill Univ. *Career:* Co-Founder and Man. Dir Paradigm Consulting 1979–95; Pres. Cott Corpn 1995–96; Founder, Pres. and CEO Indigo Books, Music and Café, Inc. 1996–2001, Pres. and CEO Indigo Books & Music Inc. (following merger with Chapters Inc. 2001) 2001–; mem. Bd Rogers Cable, Williams-Sonoma Inc.; Dir and Officer Mt Sinai Hosp.; fmr Gov. McGill Univ., Toronto Stock Exchange. *Publications include:* numerous articles on media, communications, manufacturing and retailing. *Address:* Indigo Books & Music Inc., 468 King Street West, Suite 500, Toronto, Ont., M5V 1L8, Canada (office). *Telephone:* (416) 364-4499 (office). *Fax:* (416) 364-0355 (office). *Website:* www.chapters.indigo .ca (office).

REISS, James, MA; American academic, poet, writer and editor; *Professor of English, Miami University at Oxford, OH*; b. 11 July 1941, New York, NY; m. Barbara Eve Klevs 1964 (divorced 1995); two d. *Education:* Univ. of Chicago. *Career:* instructor, Miami Univ., Oxford, OH 1965–69, Asst Prof. of English 1969–73, Assoc. Prof. of English 1973–81, Prof. of English 1981–; Visiting Poet and Assoc. Prof. of English, Queens Coll., CUNY 1975–76; Ed., Miami Univ. Press 1992–; numerous poetry readings; mem. Acad. of American Poets, Poetry Soc. of America. *Publications:* Self-Interviews: James Dickey (co-ed.) 1970, The Breathers (poems) 1974, Express (poems) 1983, The Parable of Fire (poems) 1996, Ten Thousand Good Mornings (poems) 2001, Riff on Six: New and Selected Poems 2003, Greatest Hits: 1970–2005 2005, Facade for a Penny Arcade (novel) 2008; contrib. to many anthologies and periodicals. *Honours:* first prizes Acad. of American Poets 1960, 1962, MacDowell Colony Fellowships 1970, 1974, 1976, 1977, two Borestone Mountain Poetry Awards 1974, Poetry Soc. of America Consuelo Ford Award 1974, Poetry Soc. of America Lucille Medwick Award 1989, Nat. Endowment for the Arts Fellowship 1974–75, Bread Loaf Fellowship 1975, New York State Council on the Arts Creative Artists Public Service Awards 1975–76, Ohio Arts Council grants 1980, 1981, Coll. English Asscn of Ohio Nancy Dasher Book Award 1984, Dorland Mountain Arts Colony Fellow 1991, 1993, 1999, Acad. of American Poets James Laughlin Award 1995, Pushcart Prize 1996, Helen & Laura Krout Memorial Ohioana Poetry Award 2005. *Address:* c/o Department of English, 326 Bachelor Hall, Miami University, Oxford, OH 45056, USA (office).

REISS, Tom; American writer; b. 1964, New York, NY; m.; two d. *Education:* Harvard Coll. and Univ. of Houston. *Career:* fmr teacher and journalist. *Publications:* Fuhrer-Ex: Memoirs of a Former Neo-Nazi (memoir, with Ingo Hasselbach) 1996, The Orientalist 2005; contrib. to newspapers, including The New Yorker, The New York Times, The Wall Street Journal. *Literary Agent:* c/o Svetlana Katz, Janklow & Nesbit Associates, 445 Park Avenue, 13th Floor, New York, NY 10022-2606, USA. *E-mail:* tom@theorientalist.info. *Website:* www.theorientalist.info.

REITER, David Philip, BA, MA, PhD; Australian publisher and writer; b. 30 Jan. 1947, Cleveland, OH, USA; m. Cherie Lorraine Reiter 1992. *Education:* University of Oregon, University of Alberta, Canada, University of Denver. *Career:* Lecturer, Cariboo University College, Canada, 1975–84, University of British Columbia, 1984, British Columbia Institute of Technology, 1984, University of Canberra, Australia, 1986–90. *Publications:* The Snow in Us, 1989; Changing House, 1991; The Cave After Saltwater Tide, 1992. Contributions: Australian, Canadian, US and UK journals. *Honours:* Queensland Premier's Poetry Award, 1989; Imago-QUT Short Story Competition, 1990. *Address:* 9 Kuhler Court, Carindale, Queensland 4152, Australia. *E-mail:* reiter@ipoz.biz. *Website:* members.ozemail.com.au/~reiterdr.

REKAI, Catherine (Kati), OC; Canadian (b. Hungarian) journalist, writer and broadcaster; b. 20 Oct. 1921, Budapest; d. of Desider and Ilona (née Hajdu) Elek; m. Dr John Rekai, CM 1941; two d. *Education:* Maria Terezia Gymnazium, Budapest, Hungary. *Career:* newspaper and radio reporter; Public Relations Consultant Cen. Hosp., Toronto; Dir Canadian Scene Multilanguage News Service, Hungarian-Canadian Chamber of Commerce, Russian and European Studies, Univ. of Toronto, Performing Arts Magazine, Toronto Int. Cultural Exchange Foundation; Vice-Pres. Canadian Ethnic Journalists and Writers Club; mem. Multicultural Advisory Cttee, Toronto History Bd, Writers' Union of Canada (co-chair. Foreign Affairs Cttee), Asscn of Children's Writers and Illustrators, PEN Int., George R. Gardiner Museum, Stratford Festival, Nat. Ballet of Canada, Canadian Opera Co., TMAC-Travel Media Asscn of Canada, Canadian Ethnic Media Asscn; weekly arts commentator for CIAO Radio, Hungarian Hour, Kanadai Magyarsag (int. newspaper), Kaleidoscope magazine. *Puppet shows:* The Great Totem Pole Caper, Tale of Tutenkhamen, The Boy Who Forgot. *Publications include:* plays: The Great Totem Pole Caper (also video), The Boy Who Forgot, The Tale of Tutenkhamen; children's books: (travel book series) The Adventures of Mickey, Taggy, Puppo and Cica and How They Discover... Toronto, Ottawa, Montréal, Kingston, Brockville, The Thousand Island, The Gardiner Museum of Ceramic Art, France, Switzerland, Budapest, Vienna, The Netherlands, Italy and Mickey Taggy, Puppo and Cica Celebrate Toronto 2000, Greece (Prix Saint-Exupéry Francophonie Valeurs Jeunesse, Paris 1988); numerous contribs to newspapers and radio programmes. *Honours:* Kt of St Ladislaus of Hungary 1980, Cross of the Order of Merit (Hungary) 1993; Certificate of Honour for Contribution to Canadian Unity 1981, Rakoczi Foundation Award 1990, Sierhey Khamara Ziniak Award for Excellence in Multilingual Media 1996. *Address:* 21 Dale Avenue, No. 727, Toronto, ON M4W 1K3, Canada. *Telephone:* (416) 922-5841. *Fax:* (416) 921-8322. *E-mail:* j.rekai.rickerd@gmail .com.

REMINI, Robert Vincent, BS, MA, PhD; American historian, academic and writer; *University Historian and Professor of History Emeritus, University of Illinois, Chicago*; b. 17 July 1921; m. Ruth T. Kuhner 1948, one s. two d. *Education:* Fordham University, Columbia University. *Career:* Instructor, 1947–51, Asst Prof., 1951–59, Assoc. Prof. of American History, 1959–65, Fordham University; Prof. of History, 1965–91, Research Prof. of Humanities, 1985–91, Prof. of History Emeritus and Research Prof. of Humanities

Emeritus, 1991–, University Historian, 1997–, University of Illinois at Chicago; mem. American Historical Asscn; Society of Amerian Historians. *Publications:* Martin Van Buren and the Making of the Democratic Party, 1959; The Election of Andrew Jackson, 1963; Andrew Jackson, 1966; Andrew Jackson and the Bank War, 1967; Freedom's Frontiers: The Story of the American People (with James I. Clark), 1975; We the People: A History of the United States (with James I. Clark), 1975; The Revolutionary Age of Jackson, 1976; Andrew Jackson and the Course of American Empire, 1767–1821, 1977; The Era of Good Feelings and the Age of Jackson, 1816–1841 with Edwin A. Miles), 1979; The American People: A History (with Arthur S. Link, Stanley Coben, Douglas Greenberg and Robert McMath), 1981; Andrew Jackson and the Course of American Freedom, 1822–1833, 1981; Andrew Jackson and the Course of American Democracy, 1833–1845, 1984; The Legacy of Andrew Jackson: Essays on Democracy, Indian Removal and Slavery, 1988; The Life of Andrew Jackson, 1988; The Jacksonian Era, 1989; Andrew Jackson: A Bibliography (with Robert O. Rupp), 1991; Henry Clay: Statesman for the Union, 1991; Daniel Webster: The Man and His Time, 1997; The Battle of New Orleans, 1999; The University of Illinois at Chicago: A Pictorial History (with Fred W. Beuttler and Melvin G. Holly), 2000; Andrew Jackson and His Indian Wars, 2001, John Quincy Adams 2002, Joseph Smith 2002. Contributions: scholarly books and journals. *Honours:* Hon. doctorates; Guggenheim Fellowship, 1978–79; Rockefeller Foundation Fellowships, Bellagio, Italy, 1979, 1989; George Washington Medal of Honor, Freedom Foundation, 1982; National Book Award, 1984; Carl Sandburg Award, 1989; Society of Midland Authors Award for Biography, 1992; American Historical Asscn Award for Scholarly Distinction, 2001; Western Writers of America Award, 2002, Chicago Historical Soc. Award for Distinguished Scholarship 2003. *Address:* c/o Department of History, University of Illinois, PO Box 4348, Chicago, IL 60680, USA. *Telephone:* (312) 355-0604 (home). *Fax:* (312) 355-0755 (office). *E-mail:* remini@uic.edu (office).

REMNICK, David J., AB; American journalist, editor and writer; *Editor-in-Chief, The New Yorker;* b. 29 Oct. 1958, Hackensack, NJ; s. of Edward C. Remnick and Barbara (née Seigel) Remnick; m. Esther B. Fein; two s. one d. *Education:* Princeton Univ. *Career:* reporter The Washington Post 1982–91; staff writer The New Yorker 1992–, Ed.-in-Chief 1998–. *Publications:* Lenin's Tomb: The Last Days of the Soviet Empire (Pulitzer Prize for General Nonfiction 1994) 1993, The Devil Problem (and other true stories) 1996, Resurrection: The Struggle for a New Russia 1997, King of the World: Muhammad Ali and the Rise of an American Hero 1998, Life Stories: Profiles from The New Yorker (ed.) 1999, Wonderful Town: Stories from The New Yorker (ed.) 1999, Reporting: Writings from The New Yorker 2006; contrib. to newspapers and periodicals. *Honours:* Livingston Award 1991, George Polk Award 1994, Helen Bernstein Award 1994. *Address:* The New Yorker, 4 Times Square, New York, NY 10036, USA (office). *E-mail:* themail@newyorker.com (office). *Website:* www.newyorker.com (office).

RÉMY, Pierre-Jean (see Angrémy, Jean-Pierre)

RENAUD, (Ernest) Hamilton Jacques; Canadian writer, poet and translator; b. 10 Nov. 1943, Montréal, QC; two s. one d. *Career:* critic and researcher, Radio Canada 1965–67; reporter, Metro-Express, Montréal 1966; critic, Le Devoir, Montréal 1975–78; teacher, creative writing workshop, University of Québec 1980–89; spokesman, Equality Party 1989; researcher, Senator Jacques Hebert 1990. *Publications include:* Electrodes (poems), 1962; Le Casse (short stories), 1964; Clandestines (novel), 1980; L'espace du Diable (short stories), 1989; Les Cycles du Scorpion (poems), 1989; La Constellation du Bouc Emissaire (non-fiction), 1993. Contributions: various publications.

RENAUT, Alain; French philosopher, academic and writer; b. 25 Feb. 1948, Paris; m. Sylvie Mesure 1984. *Education:* École Normale Supérieure, Paris. *Career:* researcher, Institut Raymond Aron, Écoles des Hautes Études en Sciences Sociales, Paris 1984–; Prof., Univ. of Caen 1986–. *Publications:* La Pensée 68: Essais sur l'individualisme contemporain (co-author) 1985, Itinéraires de l'individu 1987, Heidegger et les modernes 1988, L'Ere de l'individu: Contribution à une histoire de la subjectivité 1989, Philosophie du droit (co-author) 1991, Sartre: Le Dernier Philosophe 1995; contrib. to scholarly books and journals. *Address:* 135 avenue Flouquet, 94290 L'Hay-les-Roses, France.

RENDELL OF BABERGH, Baroness (Life Peer), cr. 1997, of Aldeburgh in the County of Suffolk; **Ruth Barbara Rendell,** (Barbara Vine), CBE, FRSL; British crime novelist; b. 17 Feb. 1930, d. of Arthur Grasemann and Ebba Kruse; m. Donald Rendell 1950 (divorced 1975), remarried 1977 (died 1999); one s. *Education:* Loughton County High School. *Publications include:* From Doon with Death 1964, To Fear a Painted Devil 1965, Vanity Dies Hard 1965, A New Lease of Death (aka Sins of the Father) 1967, Wolf to the Slaughter 1967, The Secret House of Death 1968, The Best Man to Die 1969, A Guilty Thing Surprised 1970, No More Dying Then 1971, One Across, Two Down 1971, Murder Being Once Done 1972, Some Lie and Some Die 1973, The Face of Trespass 1974, Shake Hands Forever 1975, A Demon in My View 1976, A Judgement in Stone 1976, A Sleeping Life 1978, Make Death Love Me 1979, The Lake of Darkness 1980, Put on by Cunning (aka Death Notes) 1981, Master of the Moor 1982, The Speaker of Mandarin 1983, The Killing Doll 1984, The Tree of Hands 1984, An Unkindness of Ravens 1985, Live Flesh 1986, Heartstones 1987, Talking to Strange Men 1987, The Veiled One 1988, The Bridesmaid 1989, Mysterious 1990, Going Wrong 1990, The Strawberry Tree 1990, Walking on Water 1991, Kissing the Gunner's Daughter 1992, The

Crocodile Bird 1993, Simisola 1994, Blood Lines 1996, The Keys to the Street 1997, Road Rage 1997, A Sight for Sore Eyes 1998, Harm Done 1999, Babes in the Wood 2002, The Rottweiler 2003, Thirteen Steps Down 2004, End in Tears 2005, The Water's Lovely 2006; as Barbara Vine: A Dark-Adapted Eye 1986, A Fatal Inversion 1987, The House of Stairs 1988, Gallowglass 1990, King Solomon's Carpet 1991, Asta's Book 1993, The Children of Men 1994, No Night is Too Long 1994, The Keys to the Street 1996, The Brimstone Wedding 1996, The Chimney Sweeper's Boy 1998, Grasshopper 2000, The Blood Doctor 2002, The Minotaur 2005, The Water's Lovely 2007; short story collections: The Fallen Curtain 1976, Means of Evil 1979, The Fever Tree 1982, The New Girlfriend 1985, Collected Short Stories 1987, Undermining the Central Line (with Colin Ward) 1989, The Copper Peacock 1991, Blood Lines 1995, Piranha to Scurfy and Other Stories 2001; other: A Warning to the Curious: The Ghost Stories of M. R. James (ed.) 1987, Ruth Rendell's Suffolk 1989, The Reason Why: An Anthology of the Murderous Mind (ed.) 1995, Harm Done (ed.) 2000. *Honours:* Dr hc (Essex) 1990; Arts Council Nat. Book Award for Genre Fiction 1981, Sunday Times Award for Literary Excellence 1990 and other awards. *Address:* 26 Cornwall Terrace Mews, London, NW1 5LL; House of Lords, London, SW1A 0PW, England.

RENÉE, BA; New Zealand playwright and writer; b. (Renée Gertrude Taylor), 19 July 1929, Napier. *Education:* Univ. of Auckland. *Career:* Robert Burns Fellowship, University of Otago, 1989; Writers Fellowship, University of Waikato, New Zealand, 1995. *Publications:* Secrets: Two One-Woman Plays, 1982; Breaking Out, 1982; Setting the Table, 1982; What Did You Do in the War, Mummy?, 1982; Asking For It, 1983; Dancing, 1984; Wednesday to Come, 1984; Groundwork, 1985; Pass It On, 1986; Born to Clean, 1987; Jeannie Once, 1990; Touch of the Sun, 1991; Missionary Position, 1991; The Glass Box, 1992; Tiggy Tiggy Touchwood, 1992; Willy Nilly (novel), 1990; Daisy and Lily, 1993; Does This Make Sense To You?, 1995; The Snowball Waltz (novel), 1997; Let's Write Plays (textbook for schools), 1998; Yin and Tonic (humour), 1998; The Skeleton Woman (novel), 2002. Other: Television plays and short stories. *Honours:* Project Grant, 1991; Queen Elizabeth II Arts Council Scholarship in Letters, 1993.

RENFREW OF KAIMSTHORN, Baron (Life Peer), cr. 1991, of Hurlet in the District of Renfrew; **Andrew Colin Renfrew,** PhD, ScD, FBA, FSA; British archaeologist; *Fellow, McDonald Institute for Archaeological Research, University of Cambridge;* b. 25 July 1937, Stockton-on-Tees; s. of the late Archibald Renfrew and Helena D. Renfrew; m. Jane M. Ewbank 1965; two s. one d. *Education:* St Albans School, St John's Coll., Cambridge and British School of Archaeology, Athens. *Career:* Lecturer in Prehistory and Archaeology, Univ. of Sheffield 1965–70, Sr Lecturer 1970–72, Reader in Prehistory and Archaeology 1972; Prof. of Archaeology and Head of Dept, Univ. of Southampton 1972–81; Disney Prof. of Archaeology, Univ. of Cambridge 1981–2004; Dir McDonald Inst. for Archaeological Research 1990–2004, Fellow 2004–; Fellow, St John's Coll., Cambridge 1981–86; Master Jesus Coll., Cambridge 1986–97, Professorial Fellow 1997–2004, Fellow Emer. 2004–; Foreign Assoc. Nat. Acad. of Sciences, USA; Visiting Lecturer, UCLA 1967; mem. Ancient Monuments Bd for England 1974–84, Royal Comm. on Historical Monuments 1977–87, Historic Buildings and Monuments Comm. for England 1984–86, Ancient Monuments Advisory Cttee 1984–2002, British Nat. Comm. for UNESCO 1984–86; Foreign mem. American Philosophical Asscn 2006; Trustee British Museum 1991–2001. *Publications:* The Emergence of Civilization 1972, Before Civilization 1973, The Explanation of Culture Change (ed.) 1973, British Prehistory (ed.) 1974, Transformations: Mathematical Approaches to Culture Change 1979, Problems in European Prehistory 1979, An Island Polity 1982, Theory and Explanation in Archaeology (ed.) 1982, Approaches to Social Archaeology 1984, The Archaeology of Cult 1985, Peer, Polity Interaction and Socio-Political Change (ed.) 1986, Archaeology and Language: The Puzzle of Indo-European Origins 1987, The Idea of Prehistory (co-author) 1988, Archaeology: Theories, Methods and Practice (co-author) 1991, The Cycladic Spirit 1991, The Archaeology of Mind (co-ed. with E. Zubrow) 1994, Loot, Legitimacy and Ownership 2000, Archaeogenetics (ed.) 2000, Figuring It Out 2003, Archaeology, The Key Concepts (co-ed.) 2005; contribs to Archaeology, Scientific American, Phylogenetic Methods and the Prehistory of Languges (co-ed.) 2006. *Honours:* Hon. FSA (Scotland); Hon. FRSE 2001; Hon. LittD (Sheffield) 1990, (Southampton) 1995, (Edinburgh) 2004, (Liverpool) 2004, (St Andrews) 2006; Dr hc (Faculty of Letters, Univ. of Athens) 1991 Rivers Memorial Medal, British Anthropological Inst. 1979, Sir Joseph Larmor Award 1961, Huxley Memorial Medal, Royal Anthropological Inst. 1991, Prix Int. Fyssen, Fondation Fyssen, Paris 1997, Language and Culture Prize, Univ. of Umeå, Sweden 1998, Rivers Memorial Medal, European Science Foundation Latsis Prize 2003, Bolzan Prize 2004. *Literary Agent:* c/o Curtis Brown Ltd, Haymarket House, 28–29 Haymarket, London, SW1Y 4SP. *Telephone:* (20) 7393-4400. *Fax:* (20) 7393-4401. *Address:* McDonald Institute for Archaeological Research, Downing Street, Cambridge, CB2 3ER; 5a Chaucer Road, Cambridge, CB2 2EB, England (home). *Telephone:* (1223) 333521. *Fax:* (1223) 333536. *E-mail:* des25@cam.ac.uk (office).

RENRICK, D. F. (see Kerner, Fred)

RENTCHNICK, Pierre, MD; Swiss physician and editor; b. 17 July 1923, Geneva; s. of Jacques Rentchnick and Blanche (Spiegel) Rentchnick; m. Paule Adam 1948; one s. *Education:* Univs of Geneva and Paris. *Career:* Ed.-in-Chief, Médecine et Hygiène, Geneva 1956–93, Recent Results in Cancer Research; Ed. Springer, Heidelberg and New York 1962–83, Bulletin de l'Union int. contre le cancer, Geneva 1962–80; f. Kiwanis-Club, Geneva 1966, Pres. 1976–77; f. Int. Soc. for Chemotherapy 1959; Fellow, New York Acad. of Sciences, Medical Soc. of Prague, French Soc. of Infectious Pathology. *Publications:* Esculape chez les Soviets 1954, Klinik und Therapie der Nebenwirkungen 1963, Esculape chez Mao 1973, Ces malades qui nous gouvernent 1976, Les orphelins mènent-ils le monde? 1978, Ces malades qui font l'Histoire 1983, Ces nouveaux malades qui nous gouvernent 1988–96; numerous publs on antibiotics in infectious diseases, on ethical problems, euthanasia etc. *Honours:* Prix Littré (France) 1977. *Address:* La Taupinière, Chemin Bouchattet 8, 1291 Commugny, Vaud, Switzerland. *Telephone:* (22) 7762264. *Fax:* (22) 7765047 (home).

RESCHER, Nicholas, PhD; American philosopher and author; *Professor of Philosophy, University of Pittsburgh;* b. 15 July 1928, Hagen, Germany; s. of Erwin Hans Rescher and Meta Anna Rescher; m. 1st Frances Short 1951 (divorced 1965); one d.; m. 2nd Dorothy Henle 1968; two s. one d. *Education:* Queens Coll., New York, Princeton Univ. *Career:* Assoc. Prof. of Philosophy, Lehigh Univ. 1957–61; Prof., Univ. of Pittsburgh 1961–, Dir Center for Philosophy of Science 1982–89; Consultant RAND Corpn 1954–66, Encyclopaedia Britannica 1963–64, North American Philosophical Publs 1980–; Ed. American Philosophical Quarterly 1964–94; Sec.-Gen. Int. Union of History and Philosophy of Science 1969–75; Pres. American Philosophical Asscn (Eastern Div.) 1989–90, American Catholic Philosophical Asscn 2003–04, American Metaphysical Soc. 2004–05; mem. Academia Europea, Institut Int. de Philosophie, Acad. Int. de Philosophie des Sciences; Guggenheim Fellow 1970–71; visiting lectureships at Univs of Oxford, Munich, Konstanz, Western Ontario and others. *Publications:* more than 90 books including The Coherence Theory of Truth 1973, Methodological Pragmatism 1977, Scientific Progress 1978, The Limits of Science 1984, Ethical Idealism 1987, Rationality 1988, A System of Pragmatic Idealism (three vols) 1992–94, Pluralism 1993, Predicting the Future 1997, Paradoxes 2001, Philosophical Reasoning 2001, Metaphysics 2005, Epistemetrics 2006; numerous articles in many areas of philosophy. *Honours:* Hon. mem. Corpus Christi Coll. Oxford; six hon. degrees; Alexander von Humboldt Prize 1983. *Address:* 1012 Cathedral of Learning, University of Pittsburgh, Pittsburgh, PA 15260 (office); 5818 Aylesboro Avenue, Pittsburgh, PA 15217, USA (home). *Telephone:* (412) 624-5950 (office); (412) 521-6768 (home). *Fax:* (412) 383-7506 (office). *E-mail:* rescher@pitt.edu (office). *Website:* www.pitt.edu/~rescher (office).

RESTAK, Richard Martin, MD; American physician and writer; b. 4 Feb. 1942, Wilmington, DE; m. Carolyn Serbent 1968; three d. *Education:* Georgetown Medical School. *Career:* Consultant, Encyclopedia of Bioethics 1978; Special Contributing Ed., Science Digest 1981–85; mem. editorial bd, Integrative Psychiatry: An International Journal for the Synthesis of Medicine and Psychiatry 1986; mem. American Acad. of Neurology, American Acad. of Psychiatry and the Law, American Psychiatric Asscn, Behavioral Neurology Soc., New York Acad. of Sciences, Int. Neuropsychological Soc., Nat. Book Critics Circle, Int. Brotherhood of Magicians, Philosophical Soc. of Washington. *Publications:* Premeditated Man: Bioethics and the Control of Future Human Life 1975, The Brain: The Last Frontier: Explorations of the Human Mind and Our Future 1979, The Self Seekers 1982, The Brain 1984, The Infant Mind 1986, The Mind 1988, The Brain has a Mind of its Own 1991, Receptors 1994, Modular Brain 1994, Brainscopes 1995, Older and Wiser 1997, The Secret Life of the Brain 2001, Mozart's Brain and the Fighter Pilot 2001, The New Brain 2003, Poe's Heart and the Mountain Climber 2004; contrib. to anthologies, journals and periodicals. *Honours:* Nat. Endowment for the Humanities Fellowship 1976, Nat. Soc. for Medical Research Claude Bernard Science Journalism Award 1976, Gettysburg Coll. Distinguished Alumni Award 1985. *Address:* 1800 R Street NW, Suite C-3, Washington, DC 20009, USA (office). *Telephone:* (202) 462-0455 (office); (202) 362-6547 (home). *Fax:* (202) 462-0340 (office); (202) 686-6993 (home). *E-mail:* neurology -associates@yahoo.com.

RESTON, James Barrett, Jr., BA; American writer; *Senior Scholar, Woodrow Wilson International Center for Scholars;* b. 8 March 1941, New York, NY; m. Denise Brender Leary 1971. *Education:* Univ. of Oxford, Univ. of North Carolina at Chapel Hill. *Career:* reporter, Chicago Daily News 1964–65; Lecturer in Creative Writing, Univ. of North Carolina at Chapel Hill 1971–81; Sr Scholar, Woodrow Wilson Int. Center for Scholars, Washington, DC; mem. Authors' Guild, Dramatists' Guild, PEN; US Tennis Asscn Captain 2001–05. *Plays:* Sherman the Peacemaker 1979, Jonestown Express 1983, Man of the Millennium 1999; also radio and television documentaries and plays. *Publications:* fiction: To Defend, To Destroy 1971, The Knock at Midnight 1975; non-fiction: The Amnesty of John David Herndon 1973, Perfectly Clear: Nixon from Whittier to Watergate (with Frank Mankiewicz) 1973, The Innocence of Joan Little: A Southern Mystery 1977, Our Father Who Art in Hell: The Life and Death of Jim Jones 1981, Sherman's March and Vietnam 1985, The Lone Star: The Life of John Connally 1989, Collision at Home Plate: The Lives of Peter Rose and Bart Giamatti 1991, Galileo: A Life 1994, The Last Apocalypse: Europe at the Year 1000 AD 1998, Warriors of God: Richard the Lionheart and Saladin in the Third Crusade 2001, Dogs of God: Columbus, the Inquisition and the Defeat of the Moors 2005, Fragile Innocence: A Father's Memoir of his Daughter's Courageous Journey 2006; contrib. to various periodicals. *Honours:* Dupont-Columbia Award 1982, Prix Italia, Venice 1982, NEA grant 1982, Valley Forge Award 1985. *Address:* 4714 Hunt Avenue, Chevy Chase, MD 20815, USA.

REVERE, Michael Rigsby; American writer, poet, musician and music teacher; b. 26 July 1951, East Point, GA; pnr Judy Revere; one s. one d. *Education:* Southwestern Community College, Sylva, NC. *Career:* guest lectures, poetry readings and workshops. *Publications:* Spirit Happy (poems), 1974; The Milky Way Poems, 1976; Shotgun Vision (poems), 1977; Fire and Rain (poems), 1998; Lizard Man: Collected Poems 1969–2002 (with original music soundscapes CD), 2002. Contributions: journals and periodicals.

REY, Alain; French lexicographer and linguist; b. 30 Aug. 1928, Pont-du-Château; m. Josette Rey-Debove. *Career:* fmr Prof., Univ. of Indiana, Univ. of Montréal; employed by Paul Robert to produce dictionaries 1952, Editorial Gen. Sec. for Le Robert publications 1956, now Ed.-in-Chief; Co-Dir of collection, Approaches to Semiotics (Berlin-New-York); Co-Dir of German journal, Lexicographie 1985–; Pres. Commission de terminologie, Ministry of Culture and Communication 1997–; two-year collaboration on production of 'Trésor de la Langue Française' for Centre National de la Recherche Scientifique. *Television:* presenter Le mot de la fin (France-Inter) 1995–. *Publications:* as editor: Dictionnaire alphabétique et analogique de la langue française (six vols) 1964, Le Petit Robert 1967, Le Micro-Robert 1971, Le Petit Robert des noms propres 1974, Dictionnaire des expressions et locutions 1979, Grand Robert de la langue française (nine vols) 1985, Dictionnaire historique de la langue française (five vols) 1992, Petit Robert de la langue française 1993, Dictionnaire historique de la langue française en petit format (three vols) 1998, Dictionnaire culturel en langue française (four vols) 2005; as writer: Littré, l'humaniste et les mots (Prix de l'Académie française) 1970, La Lexicologie: lectures 1970, Théories dusigneet du sens (two vols) 1973, La Terminologie 1979; contrib. to numerous books and journals. *Honours:* Commandeur, Ordre des Arts et des Lettres 2005. *Address:* Le Robert, 25 avenue Pierre de Coubertin, 75211 Paris cedex 13, France (office). *Website:* www.lerobert.com (office).

REYES, Carlos, BA, MA, ABD; American poet and teacher; b. 2 June 1935, Marshfield, MO; m. 1st Barbara Ann Hollingsworth 1958 (divorced 1973); one s. three d.; m. 2nd Karen Ann Stoner 1979 (divorced 1992); m. 3rd Elizabeth Atly 1993 (divorced 2003); m. 4th Karen Checkoway 2005. *Education:* Univ. of Oregon, Univ. of Arizona. *Career:* Governor's Advisory Cttee on the Arts, Oregon 1973; Poet to the City of Portland 1978; poet-in-residence various public schools in Oregon and Washington; Ed., Hubbub 1982–90, Ar Mhuin Na Muicea (journal of Irish literature, music, current events) 1995; mem. Portland Poetry Festival Inc. (bd 1974–84), PEN Northwest (co-chair. 1992–93), Mountain Writers Series (bd 1996–2000), Writers-in-Schools 2005–. *Publications:* The Prisoner 1973, The Shingle Weaver's Journal 1980, At Doolin Quay 1982, Nightmarks 1990, A Suitcase Full of Crows 1995, Poemas de la Isla (trans. of Josefina de la Torre) 2000, Puertas Abiertas/ Open Doors (bilingual edn of poems by Edwin Madrid) 2000, Obra Poética Completa de Jorge Carrera Andrade/Complete Poetic Works of Jorge Carrera Andrade (bilingual edn) 2004, At the Edge of the Western Wave (poems) 2004; contrib. to various journals and magazines. *Honours:* Oregon Arts Commission Individual Artist Fellowship 1982, Yaddo Fellowship 1984, Hon. Fellow Fundación Valparaíso, Mojácar, Spain 1998. *Address:* 6034 SE Stephens Street, Portland, OR 97215, USA.

REYN, Evgeny Borisovich; Russian poet and writer; b. 29 Dec. 1935, Leningrad; m. Nadejda Reyn 1989; one s. *Education:* Leningrad Tech. Inst. *Career:* freelance poet published in samizdat magazine Sintaksis and émigré press abroad in magazines Grani, Kovcheg; participated in publication of almanac Metropol; literary debut in Russia 1984; Prof., Moscow M. Gorky Inst. of Literature; mem. Writers' Union, Union of Moscow Writers, Russian PEN Centre. *Television:* Kuprin 1967, The Thcukokkala 1969, The Tenth Chapter 1970, Journeys with Josef Brodsky 1993, Josef Brodsky: The Hatchings to Portrait 1996. *Publications:* The Names of Bridges 1984, Shore Line 1989, The Darkness of Mirrors 1989, Breda 1995, Irretrievable Day 1991, Counter-Clockwise 1992, Nezhnosmo 1993, Selected Poems 1993, The Prognostication 1994, The Top-booty 1995, The Others 1996, The News Stages of the Life of The Moscow Beau Monde 1997, Balkony 1998, Arch over Water 2000, The Remarks of Marathon Man: Inconclusive Memoirs 2003, The Overground Transition 2004, After Our Age 2005, My Best Addressman… 2005, The Poems, Prose, Essays 2006. *Honours:* Peterburg Prize of Arts 'Tsarskoye Selo' 1995, State Prize of Russia in Literature and Art 1996, Ind. Alexander Block Literature Award 1999, Alfred Tepfer Foundation Pushkin Prize (Gamburg, Germany) 2003, State Pushkin Prize in Literature and Art 2004, Grinzane Cavour Prize (Turin, Italy) 2004, Petropol Prize in Literature and Arts, St Peterburg 2005. *Address:* Leningradsky Prospect, 75, Apt 167, 125057 Moscow (home). *Telephone:* (499) 157-20-14 (home). *Fax:* (495) 203-46-78 (office). *E-mail:* Reyne@cnt.ru (home).

REYNOLDS, (Eva Mary) Barbara, PhD; British academic (retd) and writer; *President, Dorothy L. Sayers Society;* b. 13 June 1914, d. of the late Alfred Charles Reynolds; m. 1st Lewis Thorpe 1939 (died 1977); one s. one d.; m. 2nd Kenneth Imeson 1982 (died 1994). *Education:* St Paul's Girls' School and Univ. Coll. London. *Career:* Asst Lecturer in Italian LSE 1937–40; Asst Lecturer in Italian Univ. of Cambridge 1940–45, Lecturer in Italian Literature and Language 1945–62, mem. Senate Council 1961–62; Chief Exec. and Gen. Ed. The Cambridge Italian Dictionary 1948–81; Warden Willoughby Hall, Univ. of Nottingham 1963–69, Reader in Italian Studies 1966–78; Visiting Prof. Univ. of California at Berkeley, USA 1974–75, Wheaton Coll., IL, USA 1977–78, 1982, Trinity Coll. Dublin 1980, 1981, Hope Coll., MI, USA 1982; Hon. Reader in Italian, Univ. of Warwick 1975–80;

Man. Ed. Seven Anglo-American literary review 1980–89; Pres. Dorothy L. Sayers Soc. 1995–. *Publications include:* Tredici Novelle Moderne (jtly) 1947, The Linguistic Writings of Alessandro Manzoni: a textual and chronological reconstruction 1950, The Cambridge Italian Dictionary (vol. I) 1962, (vol. II) 1981, Guido Farina, Painter of Verona (jtly) 1967, Concise Cambridge Italian Dictionary 1975, Cambridge-Signorelli Dizionario 1986, The Translator's Art (co-ed.) 1987, The Passionate Intellect: Dorothy L. Sayers' Encounter with Dante 1989, Dorothy L. Sayers: Her Life and Soul 1993, The Letters of Dorothy L. Sayers (vol. I) 1995, (vol. II) 1997, (vol. III) 1998, (vol. IV) 2000, (vol. V) 2002, Dante: The Poet, the Political Thinker, the Man 2006; several translations of Italian works, including Orlando Furioso vol. I (Int. Literary Prize 1976) 1975, (vol. II) 1977; numerous articles in professional journals. *Honours:* Hon. DLitt (Wheaton Coll.) 1979, (Hope Coll., MI) 1982, (Durham) 1995; Edmund Garner Prize 1964; Silver Medal, Italian Govt 1964, Silver Medal Prov. Admin. of Vicenza 1971, Cavaliere Ufficiale al Merito della Repubblica Italiana 1978. *Address:* 220 Milton Road, Cambridge, CB4 1LQ, England (home). *Telephone:* (1223) 565380 (home). *Fax:* (1223) 424894 (home). *Website:* www.sayers.org.uk (office).

REYNOLDS, David James, BA, MA, PhD, FRHistS; British academic and writer; *Professor of International History, University of Cambridge*; b. 17 Feb. 1952, Orpington, Kent, England; m. Margaret Philpott Ray 1977; one s. *Education:* Univ. of Cambridge. *Career:* Choate Fellow, Harvard Univ. 1973–74, Warren Fellow 1980–81; Research Fellow, Gonville and Caius Coll., Cambridge 1978–80, 1981–83; Fellow, Christ's Coll., Cambridge 1983–; Asst Lecturer in History, Univ. of Cambridge 1984–88, Lecturer 1988–97, Reader in Int. History 1997–2002, Prof. of Int. History 2002–. *Publications:* The Creation of the Anglo-American Alliance, 1937–1941: A Study in Competitive Co-operation 1981, Lord Lothian and Anglo-American Relations, 1939–1940 1983, An Ocean Apart: The Relationship Between Britain and America in the Twentieth Century (with David Dimbleby) 1988, Britannia Overruled: British Policy and World Power in the Twentieth Century 1991, Allies at War: The Soviet, American, and British Experience, 1939–1945 (ed. with Warren F. Kimball and A. O. Chubarian) 1994, Rich Relations: The American Occupation of Britain, 1942–1945 1995, One World Divisible: A Global History Since 1945 2000, From Munich to Pearl Harbor: Roosevelt's America and the Origins of the Second World War 2001, In Command of History: Churchill Fighting and Writing the Second World War (first prize Wolfson Prize for History 2005) 2004; contrib. to scholarly books and journals. *Honours:* Soc. for Historians of American Foreign Relations Bernath Prize 1982, Soc. for Military History Distinguished Book Award 1996. *Address:* c/o Christ's College, Cambridge, CB2 3BU, England (office). *Telephone:* (1223) 334900 (office).

REYNOLDS, Graham, OBE, CVO, BA, FBA; British writer and art historian; b. 10 Jan. 1914, London, England; m. Daphne Dent 1943 (died 2002). *Education:* Queens' Coll., Cambridge. *Career:* Keeper Dept of Prints and Drawings and of Paintings, Victoria & Albert Museum 1959–1974. *Publications:* Nicholas Hilliard and Isaac Oliver 1947, English Portrait Miniatures 1952, Painters of the Victorian Scene 1953, Catalogue of the Constable Collection, Victoria and Albert Museum 1960, Constable, The Natural Painter 1965, Victorian Painting 1966, Turner 1969, Concise History of Watercolour Painting 1972, Catalogue of Portrait Miniatures, Wallace Collection 1980, The Later Paintings and Drawings of John Constable (two vols) 1984, English Water-colours 1988, The Earlier Paintings of John Constable (two vols) 1996, Catalogue of European Portrait Minatures, Metropolitan Museum of Art, New York 1996, The Miniatures in the Collection of HM the Queen, The Sixteenth and Seventeenth Centuries 1999; contrib. to TLS, Burlington Magazine, Apollo, New Departures. *Honours:* Hon. Keeper of Miniatures, Fitzwilliam Museum, Cambridge 1994–; Mitchell Prize 1984. *Address:* The Old Manse, Bradfield St George, Bury St Edmunds, Suffolk, IP30 0AZ, England (home). *Telephone:* (1284) 386610 (home).

REYNOLDS, Keith (Kev) Ronald; British writer, photo journalist and lecturer; b. 7 Dec. 1943, Ingatestone, Essex; m. Linda Sylvia Dodsworth 1967; two d. *Career:* mem. Outdoor Writers' Guild. *Publications:* Walks and Climbs in the Pyrenees 1978, Mountains of the Pyrenees 1982, The Visitor's Guide to Kent 1985, The Weald Way and Vanguard Way 1987, Walks in the Engadine 1988, The Valais 1988, Walking in Kent 1988, Classic Walks in the Pyrenees 1989, Classic Walks in Southern England 1989, The Jura 1989, South Downs Way 1989, Eye on the Hurricane 1989, The Mountains of Europe 1990, Visitors Guide to Kent 1990, The Cotswold Way 1990, Alpine Pass Route 1990, Classic Walks in the Alps 1991, Chamonix to Zermatt 1991, The Bernese Alps 1992, Walking in Ticino 1992, Central Switzerland 1993, Annapurna: A Trekkers' Guide 1993, Walking in Kent, Vol. II 1994, Everest: A Trekkers' Guide 1995, Langtang: A Trekkers Guide 1996, Tour of the Vanoise 1996, Walking in the Alps 1998, Kangchenjunga: A Trekkers' Guide 1999, Walking in Sussex 2000, 100 Hut Walks in the Alps 2000, Manaslu: A Trekkers' Guide 2000, The South Downs Way 2001, The North Downs Way 2001, The Ecrins National Park 2001, Tour of Mont Blanc 2002, The Pyrenees 2004, Alpine Points of View 2004; contrib. to The Great Outdoors, Climber and Hill Walker, Environment Now, Trail Walker, Country Walking, High, The Alpine Journal, The Observer. *Address:* Little Court Cottage, Froghole, Crockham Hill, Edenbridge, Kent, TN8 6TD, England. *E-mail:* kev.reynolds@virgin.net. *Website:* www.kevreynolds.co.uk.

REYNOLDS, Sheri, AB, MFA; American writer; *Ruth and Perry Morgan Chair of Southern Literature, Old Dominion University*; b. 29 Aug. 1967,

Conway, SC. *Education:* Davidson Coll., Virginia Commonwealth Univ. *Career:* fmrly part-time instructor of English, Virginia Commonwealth Univ., Visiting Asst Prof. of English, Coll. of William and Mary; Ruth and Perry Morgan Chair. of Southern Literature, Dept of English, Old Dominion Univ. 2002–, currently Assoc. Prof. in Creative Writing; mem. Authors' Guild. *Play:* Orabelle's Wheelbarrow (Women Playwrights' Initiative Award) 2005. *Publications:* Bitterroot Landing 1994, The Rapture of Canaan 1996, A Gracious Plenty 1997, The Firefly Cloak 2006. *Honours:* Outstanding Faculty Award, Rising Star Award, State Council for Higher Educ. of Virginia 2004. *Address:* c/o Department of English, BAL 204, Old Dominion University, Norfolk, VA 23529, USA (office). *Telephone:* (757) 683-4010 (office). *E-mail:* SReynold@odu.edu. *Website:* www.sherireynolds.com (home).

REYNOLDS, Vernon, MA, PhD; British academic and writer; *Professor Emeritus, University of Oxford*; b. 14 Dec. 1935, Berlin, Germany; m. Frances Glover 1960; one s. one d. *Education:* Univs of London and Oxford. *Career:* academic, primatologist, studying chimpanzees in Uganda and teaching students, principally at Univ. of Oxford; Prof. Emer., Univ. of Oxford; Fellow Emer., Magdalen Coll. Oxford. *Publications:* Budongo: A Forest and its Chimpanzees 1965, The Apes 1967, The Biology of Human Action 1976, The Biology of Religion (with R. Tanner) 1983, Primate Behaviour: Information, Social Knowledge and the Evolution of Culture (with D. Quiatt) 1993, The Chimpanzees of the Budongo Forest 2005. *Address:* Orchard House, West Street, Alfriston, East Sussex, BN26 5UX, England (home). *E-mail:* vreynolds@btopenworld.com (home). *Website:* www.budongo.org.

REZA, (Evelyne Agnès) Yasmina; French novelist, dramatist, screenwriter and actress; b. 1 May 1959, Paris; d. of the late Jean Reza and of Nora (née Heltaï) Reza; one s. one d. *Education:* Lycée de St-Cloud, Paris Univ. X, Nanterre, Ecole Jacques Lecoq. *Stage appearances include:* Le Malade imaginaire 1977, Antigone 1977, Un Sang fort 1977, La Mort de Gaspard Hauser 1978, L'An mil 1980, Le Piège de Méduse 1983, Le Veilleur de nuit 1986, Enorme changement de dernière minute 1989, La Fausse suivante 1990. *Plays directed include:* Birds in the Night 1979, Marie la louve 1981. *Plays written include:* Conversations après un enterrement (Molière Award for Best Author, Prix des Talents nouveaux de la Soc. des auteurs et compositeurs dramatiques, Johnson Foundation prize) 1987, La Traversée de l'hiver 1989, La Métamorphose (adaptation) 1988, 'Art' 1994, L'Homme du hasard 1995, Trois versions de la vie 2000, Une pièce espagnole 2004. *Screenplays written include:* Jusqu'à la nuit (also dir) 1984, Le Goûter chez Niels 1986, A demain 1992, Le Pique-nique de Lulu Kreutz 2000. *Publications:* novels: Hammerklavier 1997, Une Désolation (trans. as Desolation) 1999, Adam Haberberg 2003, Nulle part 2005, Dans la luge d'Arthur Schopenhauer 2005, Le Dieu du carnage 2007. *Honours:* Chevalier, Ordre des Arts et des Lettres; Prix du jeune théâtre Beatrix Dussane-André Roussin de l'Acad. française 1991. *Address:* c/o Marta Andras (Marton Play), 14 rue des Sablons, 75116 Paris, France.

REZVANI, Serge; Russian writer and artist; b. 1928, Tehran, Iran. *Publications include:* Light Years 1971, La Loi humaine 1983, Le Testament amoureux 1984, La Folie tintoretto 1994, Les Années Lula 1998, Enigma 1998, La Cité potemkine 1998, L'Origine du monde 2000. *Literary Agent:* c/o Dedalus Ltd, Langford Lodge, St Judith's Lane, Sawtry, Cambridgeshire PE28 5XE, England. *E-mail:* info@dedalusbooks.com. *Website:* www.dedalusbooks.com.

RHEINSBERG, Anna Rose Anette; German poet and essayist; b. 24 Sept. 1956, Berlin; d. of Joachim and Anneliese Puscheck Rheinsberg; m. 1st Matthias Hoffbauer 1975 (divorced 1979); m. 2nd Mischka Krahl Rheinsberg 1980; one s. *Education:* Friedrichs Gymnasium (Kassel) and Philipps Univ. (Marburg). *Career:* writer and ed.; acted in Anna experimental film, Austria 1980. *Publications:* Bella Donna 1981, Hannah 1982, Alles trutschen (2nd edn) 1989, Wolfskuss 1984, Annakonda 1985, 1986, Marthe und Ruth 1987, Fée 1987, Herzlos 1988, Kriegs/Läufe 1989, Narcisse noir 1990. *Address:* Wehrdaer Weg 43a, 3550 Marburg/Lahn 1, Germany. *Telephone:* (6421) 64375.

RHODES, Richard Lee, BA; American writer; b. 4 July 1937, Kansas City, Kan.; s. of Arthur Rhodes and Georgia Collier Rhodes; m. Ginger Untrif 1993; two c. by previous m. *Education:* East High School, Kansas City, Yale Univ. *Career:* Trustee Andrew Drumm Inst., Independence, Mo. 1990–, Atomic Heritage Foundation 2004–, Cypress Fund 2005–; Fellowships: John Simon Guggenheim Memorial Foundation 1974–75, Nat. Endowment for the Arts 1978, Ford Foundation 1981–83, Alfred P. Sloan Foundation 1985, 1993, 1995, 2001, MacArthur Foundation Program on Peace and Int. Co-operation 1990–91. *Publications:* non-fiction: The Inland Ground: An Evocation of the American Middle West 1970, The Ozarks 1974, Looking for America: A Writer's Odyssey 1979, The Making of the Atomic Bomb (Nat. Book Critics' Circle Award for Gen. Non-fiction, Nat. Book Award for Non-fiction 1987, Pulitzer Prize for Non-fiction 1988) 1987, Farm: A Year in the Life of an American Farmer 1989, A Hole in the World: An American Boyhood 1990, Making Love: An Erotic Odyssey 1992, Nuclear Renewal: Common Sense about Energy 1993, Dark Sun: The Making of the Hydrogen Bomb 1995, How To Write 1995, Trying To Get Some Dignity: Stories of Triumph Over Childhood Abuse (with Ginger Rhodes) 1996, Deadly Feasts: Tracking the Secrets of a Terrifying New Plague 1997, Visions of Technology (ed) 1999, Why They Kill 1999, Masters of Death 2001, John James Audubon: The Making of an American (biog.) 2004, The Audubon Reader (ed) 2006, Arsenals of Folly:

Nuclear Weapons in the Cold War 2007; fiction: The Ungodly 1973, Holy Secrets 1978, The Last Safari 1980, Sons of Earth 1981. *Honours:* Hon. DHumLitt (Westminster Coll., Fulton, Mo.) 1988; Hon. Mem. American Nuclear Soc. 2001. *Address:* c/o Janklow & Nesbit Assocs, 455 Park Avenue, New York, NY 10021, USA (office). *Telephone:* (212) 421-1700 (office). *E-mail:* Rhodes.Today@comcast.net (office). *Website:* www.RichardRhodes.com.

RHONE, Trevor Dave; Jamaican playwright, director and screenwriter; b. 24 March 1940, Kingston; m. Camella King 1974; two s. one d. *Education:* Rose Bruford Coll. of Speech and Drama. *Career:* resident playwright, Barn Theatre, Kingston 1968–75. *Publications:* Old Time Story 1981, Two Can Play 1984. *Honours:* Inst. of Jamaica Silver Musgrave Medal 1972, Gold Musgrave Medal 1988, Commander of the Order of Distinction, Nat. Honour, Jamaica 1980, Acad. Award, Film Canada 1989. *Address:* 1 Haining Mews, Kingston 5, Jamaica.

RI, Kai-sei, (Yi Hoe-song); South Korean writer; b. 1935, Kabata Shinoka. *Education:* Waseda Univ. *Career:* lives in Japan. *Publications include:* (titles translated) Towards the Peak of Our Youth (novel) 1969, The Woman at the Washing Block (novel) (Akutagawa Prize, Japan 1972) 1971.

RIBEIRO, João Ubaldo Osório Pimentel, LLB, MS; Brazilian writer and journalist; b. 23 Jan. 1941, Itaparica, Bahia; s. of Manoel Ribeiro and Maria Felipa Osório Pimentel Ribeiro; m. 1st Maria Beatriz Moreira Caldas 1962; m. 2nd Mônica Maria Roters 1971; m. 3rd Berenice de Carvalho Batella Ribeiro 1982; one s. three d. *Education:* Fed. Univ. of Bahia Law School and School of Admin. and Univ. of Southern California, USA. *Career:* Reporter, Jornal da Bahia, Salvador 1958–59, City Ed. and Columnist 1960–63; Chief Ed. Tribuna da Bahia 1968–73; Columnist O Globo, Rio de Janeiro, O Estado de São Paulo, São Paulo; Editorial-writer Folha de São Paulo 1969–73; Prof. of Political Science, Fed. Univ. of Bahia 1965–71, Catholic Univ of Bahia 1967–71; mem. Brazilian Acad. of Letters. *Publications:* (novels) Setembro Não Tem Sentido 1968, Sargento Getúlio 1971, Vila Real 1980, Viva o Povo Brasileiro 1984, O Sorriso do Lagarto 1989, O Feitiço da Ilha do Pavão 1997, Miséria e Grandeza do Amor de Benedita 2000, Diário do Farol 2002, (short stories) Vencecavalo e o Outro Povo 1973, Livro de Histórias 1983, Ein Brasilianer in Berlin (autobiog.) 1994, Você me mata, Mãe gentil 2004, A gente se acostuma a tudo 2006. *Honours:* Jabuti Prize (Brazilian Book Chamber) 1971, 1984; Golfinho de Ouro (Govt of Rio) and many others. *Address:* c/o Editora Nova Fronteira SA, Rua Bambina 25, 22251-050 Rio de Janeiro, R.J.; Rua General Urquiza, 147/401, 22431-040 Rio de Janeiro, R.J., Brazil (home). *Telephone:* (21) 537-8770 (office); 21) 239-8528 (home). *Fax:* (21) 286-6755.

RIBMAN, Ronald Burt, BBA, MLitt, PhD; American dramatist; b. 28 May 1932, New York, NY; m. Alice Rosen 1967, one s. one d. *Education:* Brooklyn College, CUNY, University of Pittsburgh. *Career:* Asst Prof. of English, Otterbein College, 1962–63; Rockefeller Playwright-in-Residence, Public Theater, 1975; mem. Dramatists Guild. *Publications:* Harry, Noon and Night, 1965; The Journey of the Fifth Horse, 1966; The Ceremony of Innocence, 1967; Passing Through from Exotic Places, 1969; Fingernails Blue as Flowers, 1971; A Break in the Skin, 1972; The Poison Tree, 1976; Cold Storage, 1977; Buck, 1982; Seize the Day, 1985; The Cannibal Masque, 1988; The Rug Merchants of Chaos, 1991; Dream of the Red Spider, 1993. Contributions: films and television. *Honours:* Obie Award, 1966; Rockefeller Foundation Grants, 1966, 1968; Guggenheim Fellowship, 1970; National Endowment for the Arts Fellowship, 1973; Straw Hat Award, 1973; Elizabeth Hull-Kate Warriner Award, 1977; Drama Critics Award, 1977; Playwrights USA Award, 1984.

RIBNIKAR, Jara; Serbian writer; b. 23 Aug. 1912, Hradec, Czech Republic; d. of Emil and Ana Hajek; m. Vladislav Ribnikar 1936; one s. one d. *Education:* Classic Gymnasium (Prague). *Career:* fought with Nat. Liberation Army (Partisans) in Second World War; ed. of works on arts and literature, Yugoslavia publishing house; work translated in USA, Russia, Germany, Bulgaria, Czechoslovakia, Hungary, Romania, UK, Poland; Pres. Yugoslav (now Serbian) PEN; literary awards for short story (Zagreb, Croatia) and film-script (Bosnia). *Publications include:* novels: Jan. Nepomuk (Serbian Writers Asscn Award), I and You and She, Copperskin, Hallucinations, Novel about TM, Switch, Life, No Story 2002; short stories: Life and Story (Yugoslav Award), The Power of Life, Family Stories, Women's Love Stories. *Address:* 11000 Belgrade, Generala Zdanova 32, Serbia. *Telephone:* (11) 334 1468. *E-mail:* vribnika@eunet.yu (home).

RICCI, Nino, MA; Canadian writer; b. 23 Aug. 1959, Leamington; s. of Virginio Ricci and Amelia Ricci (née Ingratta); m. Erika de Vasconcelos 1997. *Education:* York Univ., Toronto, Concordia Univ., Montreal. *Career:* Pres. Canadian Centre, Int. PEN 1995–96. *Publications:* (novels): Lives of the Saints 1990, In a Glass House 1993, Where She Has Gone 1997, Testament 2002. *Honours:* Gov.-Gen.'s Award 1990, Betty Trask Award 1991, Winifred Holtby Award 1991. *Address:* c/o Anne McDermid & Associates, 92 Wilcocks Street, Toronto, Ont., M5S 1C8, Canada.

RICE, Anne, (Anne Rampling, A. N. Roquelaure), BA, MA; American writer; b. 4 Oct. 1941, New Orleans, LA; m. Stan Rice 1961; one s. one d. (deceased). *Education:* Texas Women's Univ., San Francisco State Coll., Univ. of Calif. at Berkeley. *Career:* mem. Authors' Guild. *Publications:* Interview with the Vampire 1976, The Feast of All Saints 1979, Cry to Heaven 1982, The Claiming of Sleeping Beauty (as A. N. Roquelaure) 1983, Beauty's Punishment (as A. N. Roquelaure) 1984, The Vampire Lestat 1985, Exit to Eden (as Anne Rampling) 1985, Beauty's Release (as A. N. Roquelaure) 1985, Belinda

(as Anne Rampling) 1986, The Queen of the Damned 1988, The Mummy, or Ramses the Damned 1989, The Witching Hour 1990, The Tale of the Body Thief 1992, Lasher 1993, Taltos 1994, Memnoch the Devil 1995, Servant of the Bones 1996, Violin 1997, Pandora 1998, Armand 1998, Vittorio the Vampire 1999, Merrick 2000, Blood and Gold 2001, The Master of Rampling Gate (short story) 2002, Blackwood Farm 2002, Blood Canticle 2003, Christ the Lord: Out of Egypt 2005. *Address:* c/o Alfred A. Knopf Inc., 1745 Broadway, Suite B1, New York, NY 10019-4305, USA. *Website:* www.annerice.com.

RICE, Earle Wilmont, Jr; American writer; b. 21 Oct. 1928, Lynn, MA; m. Georgia Joy Black Wood 1958; one s. one d. *Education:* San Jose City Coll., Foothill Coll., Los Altos. *Career:* mem. Soc. of Children's Book Writers and Illustrators, League of World War I Aviation Historians, Cross and Cockade Int., US Naval Inst., Air Force Asscn. *Publications:* fiction: Tiger, Lion, Hawk 1977, The Animals 1979, Fear on Ice 1981, More Than Macho 1981, Death Angel 1981, The Gringo Dies at Dawn 1993; non-fiction: The Cuban Revolution 1995, The Battle of Britain 1996, The Battle of Midway 1996, The Inchon Invasion 1996, The Battle of Belleau Wood 1996, The Attack on Pearl Harbor 1996, The Tet Offensive 1996, The Nuremberg Trials 1996, The Salem Witch Trials 1996, The O. J. Simpson Trial 1996, The Final Solution 1997, Nazi War Criminals 1997, The Battle of the Little Bighorn 1997, Life Among the Great Plains Indians 1997, Life During the Crusades 1997, Life During the Middle Ages 1997, Kamikazes 1999, Strategic Battles of the Pacific 2000, Strategic Battles in Europe 2000, The Bombing of Pearl Harbor 2000, The Third Reich: Demise of the Nazi Dream 2000, The Cold War: Collapse of Communism 2000, Sir Francis Drake: Navigator and Pirate 2003, Normandy 2002, First Battle of the Marne 2002, The Battle of Gettysburg 2002, Claire Chennault, Flying Tiger 2003, Manfred von Richthofen The Red Baron 2003, George S. Patton 2004, Erwin J. E. Rommel 2004, Douglas MacArthur 2004, Korea 1950: Pusan to Chosin 2004, Point of No Return: Tonkin Gulf and the Vietnam War 2004, Alexandra David-Néel: Explorer at the Roof of the World 2004, Great Military Leaders (series ed.) 2004, Ulysses S. Grant: Defender of the Union 2005, Robert E. Lee: First Soldier of the Confederacy 2005, Empire in the East: The Story of Genghis Khan 2005, Adolf Hitler and Nazi Germany 2006; adaptations: Dracula 1995, All Quiet on the Western Front 1995, The Grapes of Wrath 1996; contrib. to California Today, Calliope, PSA Magazine, Pro/Am Hockey Review. *Honours:* Second Place, Children's Book Chapters Category 1993, Third Place 1994, Ninth Hon. Mention Novel Chapter 1994, All in Florida Freelance Writers' Asscn Florida State Writing Competition. *Address:* PO Box 2131, Julian, CA 92036-2131, USA. *E-mail:* ericejr@julian-ca.com.

RICH, Adrienne, AB; American writer; b. 16 May 1929, Baltimore; d. of Arnold Rich and Helen Elizabeth Jones; m. Alfred Conrad (died 1970); three s. *Education:* Radcliffe Coll. *Career:* Teacher, New York Poetry Center 1966–67; Visiting Lecturer, Swarthmore Coll. 1967–69; Adjunct Prof., Columbia Univ. 1967–69; Lecturer, City Coll. of New York 1968–70, Instructor 1970–71, Asst Prof. of English 1971–72, 1974–75; Visiting Prof. of Creative Literature, Brandeis Univ. 1972–73; Prof. of English, Rutgers Univ. 1976–79; Prof.-at-Large, Cornell Univ. 1981–87; Lecturer and Visiting Prof, Scripps Coll. 1983, 1984; Prof. of English and Feminist Studies, Stanford Univ. 1986–93; Marjorie Kovler Visiting Lecturer, Univ. of Chicago 1989; Clark Lecturer, Trinity Coll., Cambridge 2002; Guggenheim Fellow 1952, 1961; MacArthur Fellowship 1994–99. *Publications:* A Change of World 1951, The Diamond Cutters and Other Poems 1955, Snapshots of a Daughter-in-Law 1963, Necessities of Life 1962–65, 1965–68 1969, Leaflets, Poems 1965–68, The Will to Change 1971, Diving into the Wreck 1973, Of Woman Born: Motherhood as Experience and Institution 1976, On Lies, Secrets and Silence: Selected Prose 1966–78 1979, A Wild Patience Has Taken Me This Far: Poems 1978–81 1981, Blood, Bread and Poetry: Selected Prose 1979–85 1986, Your Native Land, Your Life 1986, Time's Power: Poems 1985–88 1989, An Atlas of the Difficult World: Poems 1988–91 1991, Collected Early Poems, 1950–1970 1993, What Is Found There: Notebooks on Poetry and Politics 1993, Dark Fields of the Republic: Poems 1991–95 1995, Midnight Salvage: Poems 1995–1998 1999, Arts of the Possible: Essays and Conversations 2001, Fox: Poems 1998–2000 2001, The Fact of a Doorframe: Poems 1950–2000 2002, The School Among the Ruins: Poems 2000–2004 2004. *Honours:* Hon. LittD (Wheaton Coll.) 1967, (Smith Coll.) 1979, (Brandeis Univ.) 1987, (Wooster Coll.) 1989, (Harvard) 1990, (City Coll. of New York) 1990; Yale Series of Younger Poets Award 1951, Ridgely Torrence Memorial Award, Poetry Soc. of America 1955, Shelley Memorial Award 1971, Nat. Book Award 1974, Ruth Lilly Prize 1987, Brandeis Medal in Poetry 1987, Nat. Poetry Asscn Award 1989, LA Times Book Award 1992, Frost Silver Medal (Poetry Soc. of America) 1992, The Poets' Prize 1993, Acad. of American Poets, Fellowship 1993, Dorothea Tanning Award 1996, Lannan Foundation Literary Award for Lifetime Achievement 1999, Bollingen Prize for Poetry 2003. *Literary Agent:* c/o Steven Barclay Agency, 12 Western Avenue, Petaluma, CA 94952, USA. *Telephone:* (707) 773-0454. *E-mail:* steven@barclayagency.com. *Website:* www.barclayagency.com.

RICH, Alan, AB, MA; American music critic, editor and writer; b. 17 June 1924, Boston, MA. *Education:* Harvard Univ., Univ. of California, Berkeley, studied in Vienna, Austria. *Career:* Asst Music Critic, Boston Herald 1944–45, New York Sun 1947–48; contrib., American Record Guide 1947–61, Saturday Review 1952–53, Musical America 1955–61; music teacher, Univ. of California, Berkeley 1950–58; Programme and Music Dir, Pacifica Foundation FM Radio 1953–61; Asst Music Critic, New York Times 1961–63; Chief Music Critic and Ed., New York-Herald Tribune 1963–66; Music Critic and Ed., New

York World-Journal-Tribune 1966–67; Contributing Ed., Time magazine 1967–68; Music and Drama Critic and Arts Ed., California magazine 1979–83, Contributing Ed. 1983–85; Gen. Ed., Newsweek magazine 1983–87; Music Critic, Los Angeles Herald-Examiner 1987–; teacher, New School for Social Research 1972–75, 1977–79, Univ. of Southern California School of Journalism 1980–82, California Inst. of the Arts 1982–; artist-in-residence, Davis Center for the Performing Arts, CUNY 1975–76. *Publications:* Careers and Opportunities in Music 1964, Music: Mirror of the Arts 1969, Simon and Schuster Listener's Guide to Music (three vols) 1980, The Lincoln Center Story 1984; contrib. numerous articles and reviews to various journals. *Address:* c/o Los Angeles Herald-Examiner, 1111 S Broadway, Los Angeles, CA 90015, USA.

RICH, Elaine Sommers, MA; American writer and poet; b. 8 Feb. 1926, Plevna, IN; m. Ronald L. Rich 1953; three s. one d. *Education:* Goshen Coll., Michigan State Univ. *Career:* instructor, Goshen Coll. 1947–49, 1950–53, Bethel Coll., North Newton, KS 1953–66; Lecturer, Int. Christian Univ., Tokyo 1971–78; columnist, Mennonite Weekly Review 1973–; Adviser to Int. Students, Bluffton Coll., OH 1979–89; Adjunct Prof. of English, Univ. of Findlay, OH 1990–95, Owens Community Coll. 1995–97; mem. Fellowship of Reconciliation, Int. League for Peace and Freedom. *Publications:* Breaking Bread Together (ed.) 1958, Hannah Elizabeth 1964, Tomorrow, Tomorrow, Tomorrow 1966, Am I This Countryside? 1981, Mennonite Women 1683–1983: A Story of God's Faithfulness 1983, Spiritual Elegance: A Biography of Pauline Krehbiel Raid 1987, Prayers for Everyday 1990, Walking Together in Faith (ed.) 1993, Pondered in Her Heart 1998; contrib. to books and journals. *Address:* 112 S Spring Street, Bluffton, OH 45817, USA.

RICH, Frank Hart, Jr, BA; American journalist; b. 2 June 1949, Washington, DC; s. of Frank Hart Rich and Helene Aaronson; m. 1st Gail Winston 1976; two s.; m. 2nd Alexandra Rachelle Witchel 1991. *Education:* Harvard Univ. *Career:* Film Critic and Sr Ed. New Times Magazine 1973–75; Film Critic, New York Post 1975–77; Film and TV Critic, Time Magazine 1977–80; Chief Drama Critic, New York Times 1980–93, Op-Ed. Columnist 1994–; Assoc. Fellow Jonathan Edwards Coll., Yale Univ. 1998–. *Publications:* Hot Seat: Theater Criticism for the New York Times 1980–93 1998, Ghost Light 2000, The Greatest Story Every Sold 2006. *Address:* c/o The New York Times, 229 West 43rd Street, New York, NY 10036, USA.

RICH, Robert R., BA, MD; American microbiologist, immunologist and writer; *Editor-in-Chief, Journal of Immunology. Education:* Oberlin Coll. OH, Univ. of Kansas School of Medicine, Univ. of Washington School of Medicine, Seattle, Nat. Insts of Health, Harvard Medical School. *Career:* Asst Prof, then Assoc. Prof. 1973–78, Head of Immunology section 1977–98, Prof. 1978–95, Vice-Pres. and Dean of Research 1990–98, Distinguished Service Prof. 1995–98, Microbiology and Immunology and Medicine, Baylor Coll. of Medicine; mem. of Immunobiology Study Section, Nat. Insts of Health 1977–81; Investigator, Howard Hughes Medical Inst. 1977–91; Advisory Ed., The Journal of Experimental Medicine 1981–84; mem., Transplantation Biology and Immunology Sub-cttee 1982–86, chair. 1984–86 NIAID; Assoc. Ed., The Journal of Infectious Diseases 1983–88; mem. 1984–88, chair. 1986–88, Nat. Research Cttee for Arthritis Foundation; mem. of bd of dirs 1988–93, chair. 1991, American Board of Allergy and Immunology; editiorial bd mem., The Journal of Clinical Immunology 1989–96; mem. 1989–94, chair. 1993–94, Nat. Multiple Sclerosis Soc. Research Programs Advisory Cttee; mem. of bd of dirs, American Board of Internal Medicine 1990–93; Section Ed. and Deputy Ed. 1991–2002, Ed.-in-Chief 2003–, The Journal of Immunology; mem. of cttee on public affairs 1993–2000, chair. 1994–2000, American Asscn of Immunologists; pres., Clinical Immunology Soc. 1995; mem. of bd of dirs 1998–, pres. and chair. 2001–02, FASEB; Exec. Assoc., Dean/Research and Strategic Initiatives 1998–, Prof. of Medicine, Microbiology and Immunology 1998–, Emory Univ. School of Medicine; Vice-Pres., American Acad. of Allergy, Asthma and Immunology. *Publications:* over 200 publications (some collaborative). *Address:* Journal of Immunology, 9650 Rockville Pike, Bethesda, MD 20814-3998, USA. *Website:* www.jimmunol.org.

RICHARDS, David Adams; Canadian writer; b. 17 Oct. 1950, Newcastle, NB. *Education:* St Thomas University, NB. *Publications:* The Coming of Winter 1974, Blood Ties 1976, Dancers at Night 1978, Lives of Short Duration 1981, Road to the Stilt House 1985, Nights Below Station Street 1988, Evening Snow Will Bring Such Peace 1990, For Those Who Hunt the Wounded Down 1993, Mercy Among the Children 2000, The Bay of Love and Sorrows 2003, River of the Brokenhearted 2004, The Friends of Meager Fortune 2007. *Honours:* Governor-General's Award 1988, Canada Authors Asscn Literary Award 1991, Canada-Australian Literary Award 1992. *Address:* c/o Canada Council, 350 Albert Street, PO Box 1047, Ottawa, ON K1P 5V8, Canada.

RICHARDS, Hubert John, STL, LSS; British academic and writer; b. 25 Dec. 1921, Weilderstadt, Germany; m. 1975, one s. one d. *Education:* Gregorian University, Rome, Biblical Institute, Rome. *Career:* mem. Norfolk Theological Society. *Publications:* The First Christmas: What Really Happened? 1973, The Miracles of Jesus: What Really Happened? 1975, The First Easter: What Really Happened? 1977, Death and After: What Will Really Happen? 1979, What Happens When You Pray? 1980, Pilgrim to the Holy Land 1985, Focus on the Bible 1990, The Gospel According to St Paul 1990, God's Diary 1991, Pilgrim to Rome 1994, Quips and Quotes 1997, Anthology for the Church Year 1998, Philosophy of Religion 1998, The Bible: What Does It Really Say? 1999, Who's Who and What's What in the Bible 1999, More Quips and Quotes 2000,

Jesus: Who Did He Think He Was? 2000, The Bible: 150 Readings 2001; contrib. of regular articles and reviews in various publications. *Address:* 59 Park Lane, Norwich, Norfolk NR2 3EF, England.

RICHARDS, Leigh (see King, Laurie R.)

RICHARDS, Sean (see Haining, Peter Alexander)

RICHARDSON, Joanna, MA, FRSL; British author; b. London; d. of the late Frederick Richardson and Charlotte Richardson (née Benjamin). *Education:* The Downs School, Seaford, Sussex, St Anne's Coll., Oxford. *Career:* mem. Council, RSL 1961–86. *Radio:* numerous interviews, trans. of plays and novels, and feature programmes for Third Programme (now BBC Radio 3) and Home Service (now BBC Radio 4). *Publications:* Fanny Brawne: a biography 1952, Théophile Gautier: his Life and Times 1958, Edward FitzGerald 1960, The Pre-Eminent Victorian: A Study of Tennyson 1962, The Everlasting Spell: A Study of Keats and his Friends 1963, Introduction to Victor Hugo: Choses Vues 1964, Edward Lear 1965, George IV: A Portrait 1966, Creevey and Greville 1967, Princess Mathilde 1969, Verlaine 1971, Enid Starkie 1973, Stendhal: A Critical Biography 1974, Victor Hugo 1976, Zola 1978, Keats and his Circle: An Album of Portraits 1980, The Life and Letters of John Keats 1981, Letters from Lambeth: the Correspondence of the Reynolds Family with John Freeman Milward Dovaston 1808–1815, 1981, Paris Under Siege 1982, Colette 1983, The Brownings 1986, Judith Gautier (first non-French winner Prix Goncourt de la Biographie 1989) 1987, Portrait of a Bonaparte: The Life and Times of Joseph-Napoleon Primoli 1851–1927 1987, Baudelaire 1994; editor: FitzGerald: Selected Works 1962, Essays by Divers Hands 1964, Verlaine Poems (and trans.) 1974, Baudelaire Poems (and trans.) 1975, Gautier, Mademoiselle de Maupin (and trans.) 1981; has contributed to The Times, The Times Literary Supplement, Sunday Times, Spectator, New Statesman, New York Times Book Review, The Washington Post, French Studies, French Studies Bulletin, Modern Language Review, Keats-Shelley Memorial Bulletin, etc. *Honours:* Chevalier, Ordre des Arts et des Lettres. *Literary Agent:* Curtis Brown Group, Haymarket House, 28–29 Haymarket, London, SW1Y 4SP, England. *Telephone:* (20) 7396-6600.

RICHARDSON, Keith, MA; British writer, administrator and fmr journalist; *Trustee, Friends of Europe;* b. 14 June 1936, Wakefield, Yorks.; s. of Gilbert Richardson and Ellen Richardson; m. Sheila Carter 1958; three d. *Education:* Wakefield Grammar School, Univ. Coll., Oxford. *Career:* feature writer, The Financial Times 1960–63; Industrial Ed. and European Corresp. The Sunday Times 1964–68, 1970–83; Production Man. GKN 1969–70; Head of Group Public Affairs, BAT Industries 1983–88; Sec.-Gen. The European Round Table of Industrialists 1988–98; Trustee, Friends of Europe. *Publications:* Monopolies and Mergers 1963, Do it the Hard Way 1971, Daggers in the Forum 1978, Reshaping Europe 1991, Beating the Crisis 1993, Europe Made Simple 1998. *Address:* c/o Friends of Europe. La Maison de l'Europe at the Bibliotheque Solvay, Leipoldpark, 137 Rue Belliard, 1040 Brussels, Belgium (office). *Telephone:* (2) 737-91-45 (office). *Fax:* (2) 738-75-97 (office). *E-mail:* info@friendsofeurope.org (office). *Website:* www.friendsofeurope.org (office).

RICHARDSON, Robert Dale, Jr; AB, PhD; American academic and writer; b. 14 June 1934, Milwaukee, WI; m. 1st Elizabeth Hall 1959 (divorced 1987); m. 2nd Annie Dillard 1988; three d. *Education:* Harvard Univ. *Career:* instructor, Harvard Univ. 1961–63; Asst Prof. 1963–68, Assoc. Prof. 1968–72, Chair Dept of English 1968–73, Prof. of English 1972–87, Assoc. Dean for Graduate Studies 1975–76, Univ. of Denver; Assoc. Ed. 1967–76, 1983–87, Book Review Ed. 1976–83, Denver Quarterly; Visiting Fellow, Huntington Library 1973–74; Visiting Prof., Queens Coll. and Graduate School and Univ. Center, CUNY 1978, Sichuan Univ., People's Republic of China 1983; Prof. of English, Univ. of Colorado 1987; Visiting Lecturer, Yale Univ. 1989; Visiting Prof. of Letters 1990, Adjunct Prof. of Letters 1993–94, Wesleyan Univ.; Assoc. Fellow, Calhoun Coll., Yale Univ. 1997–; mem. American Studies Asscn, Asscn of Literary Scholars and Critics, Authors' Guild, Emerson Soc., Melville Soc., Soc. of American Historians, Soc. for Eighteenth Century Studies, Thoreau Soc. *Publications:* Literature and Film 1969, The Rise of Modern Mythology, 1680–1860 (with B. Feldman) 1972, Myth and Literature in the American Renaissance 1978, Henry Thoreau: A Life of the Mind 1986, Ralph Waldo Emerson: Selected Essays, Lectures and Poems (ed.) 1990, Emerson: The Mind on Fire 1995, Three Centuries of American Poetry (with Allen Mandelbaum) 1999; contrib. to scholarly books and journals. *Honours:* Melcher Prizes 1986, 1995, Guggenheim Fellowship 1990, Francis Parkman Prize 1995, Washington Irving Award for Literary Excellence 1995, Dictionary of Literary Biography Award for a Distinguished Literary Biography 1995, New York Times Book Review Notable Book Citation 1995, American Acad. of Arts and Letters Special Award in Literature 1998, Emerson Soc. Prize 2001, Thoreau Soc. Distinguished Achievement Award 2001, Hon. DHumLitt (Meadville Lombard Theological School) 2003. *Address:* 143 W Margaret Lane, Hillsborough NC 27278, USA. *E-mail:* rrichardson@aol.com.

RICHIE, Donald Steiner, BS; American critic and writer; *Arts Critic, The Japan Times;* b. 17 April 1924, Lima, OH; m. Mary Evans 1961 (divorced 1965). *Education:* Antioch Coll., US Maritime Acad., Columbia Univ. *Career:* film critic, Pacific Stars and Stripes, Tokyo 1947–49; arts critic, Saturday Review of Literature, New York 1950–51, The Nation, New York 1959–61, Newsweek Magazine, New York 1973–76, Time Magazine 1997; film critic, Japan Times, Tokyo 1953–69, literary critic 1972–03, arts critic 1972–; Lecturer in American Literature, Waseda Univ., Tokyo 1954–59; Curator of

Film, Museum of Modern Art, New York 1968–73; Toyoda Chair, Univ. of Michigan 1993; Lecturer in Film, Temple Univ., Tokyo 1996–. *Recording:* A Donald Richie Film Anthology (films directed 1962–68, on DVD). *Publications:* Where Are the Victors? (novel) 1956, The Japanese Film: Art and Industry (with Joseph L. Anderson) 1959, The Japanese Movie: An Illustrated History 1965, The Films of Akira Kurosawa 1965, Companions of the Holiday (novel) 1968, George Stevens: An American Romantic 1970, The Inland Sea 1971, Japanese Cinema 1971, Three Modern Kyogen 1972, Ozu: The Man and his Films 1974, Ji: Signs and Symbols of Japan (with Mana Maeda) 1975, The Japanese Tattoo 1980, Zen Inklings: Some Stories, Fables, Parables, Sermons and Prints with Notes and Commentaries 1982, A Taste of Japan: Food Fact and Fable, What the People Eat, Customs and Etiquette 1985, Viewing Film 1986, Introducing Tokyo 1987, A Lateral View 1987, Different People: Pictures of Some Japanese 1987, Tokyo Nights 1988, Japanese Cinema: An Introduction 1990, The Honorable Visitors 1994, Partial Views 1995, The Temples of Kyoto 1995, Lafcadio Hearn's Japan: An Anthology of his Writings on the Country and its People (ed.) 1997, The Memoirs of the Warrior Kumagai 1999, Tokyo: A View of the City 1999, A Hundred Years of Japanese Film: A Short History and a Selective Guide to Videos and DVDs 2001, The Donald Richie Reader: Fifty Years of Writing on Japan (ed. by Arturo Silva) 2001, The Image Factory: Fads and Fashions in Japan 2003, Japanese Literature Reviewed 2003, Tokyo Story: The Script 2003, A View from the Chuo Line and Other Stories 2004, The Japan Journals 2004. *Honours:* Citations from Govt of Japan 1963, 1970, 1983, Citation from US Nat. Soc. of Film Critics 1970, Kawakita Memorial Foundation Award 1983, Presidential Citation New York Univ. 1989, San Francisco Film Festival Novikoff Award 1990, Tokyo Metropolitan Govt Cultural Award 1993, John D. Rockefeller III Award 1994, Japan Foundation Prize 1995, Japan Soc. Award, New York 2001, Order of the Rising Sun (Gold Rays), Japan 2004; Dr hc (Univ. of Maryland) 1999, (Bard Coll.) 2004. *Address:* Ueno 2, 12.18 (804), Taito-ku, Tokyo 110 0005, Japan.

RICHTER, Harvena, BA, MA, PhD; American academic (retd), writer and poet; b. 13 March 1919, Reading, PA. *Education:* University of New Mexico, New York University. *Career:* Lecturer, New York University 1955–66, University of New Mexico 1969–89; mem. Authors' Guild. *Publications:* The Human Shore, 1959; Virginia Woolf: The Inward Voyage, 1970; Writing to Survive: The Private Notebooks of Conrad Richter, 1988; The Yaddo Elegies and Other Poems, 1995; Green Girls: Poems Early and Late, 1996; The Innocent Island, 1999; Frozen Light: The Crystal Poems, 2002; The Golden Fountains: Sources of Energy and Life, 2002. Contributions: magazines and newspapers. *Honours:* grants and fellowships.

RICKS, Christopher Bruce, BA, BLitt, MA, FBA; British academic and writer; *Professor of Poetry, University of Oxford;* b. 18 Sept. 1933, London; s. of James Bruce Ricks and Gabrielle Roszak; m. 1st Kirsten Jensen 1956 (divorced 1975); two s. two d.; m. 2nd Judith Aronson 1977; one s. two d. *Education:* King Alfred's School, Wantage, Oxon., Balliol Coll., Oxford. *Career:* 2nd Lt Green Howards 1952; Andrew Bradley Jr Research Fellow Balliol Coll. Univ. of Oxford 1957, Fellow Worcester Coll. 1958–68; Prof. of English Bristol Univ. 1968–75; Fellow Christ's Coll., Prof. of English Univ. of Cambridge 1975–86, King Edward VII Prof. of English Literature 1982–86; Prof. of English Boston Univ. 1986–98, Warren Prof. of the Humanities 1998–, Co-Dir Editorial Inst. 1999–; elected Prof. of Poetry, Univ. of Oxford 2004–(09); Visiting Prof. at Univs of Berkeley and Stanford 1965, Smith Coll. 1967, Harvard Univ. 1971, Wesleyan 1974, Brandeis 1977, 1981, 1984, USA; Distinguished Visiting Fellow in Residence, Columbia Univ. 2006; Vice-Pres. Tennyson Soc.; Fellow, American Acad. of Arts and Sciences 1991. *Publications:* Milton's Grand Style 1963, Tennyson 1972, Keats and Embarrassment 1974, The Force of Poetry 1984, T. S. Eliot and Prejudice 1988, Beckett's Dying Words 1993, Essays in Appreciation 1996, Reviewery 2002, Allusion to the Poets 2002, Decisions and Revisions in T. S. Eliot 2003, Dylan's Visions of Sin 2003; editor: Poems and Critics: An Anthology of Poetry and Criticism from Shakespeare to Hardy 1966, A. E. Housman: A Collection of Critical Essays 1968, Alfred Tennyson: Poems 1842 1968, John Milton: Paradise Lost and Paradise Regained 1968, The Poems of Tennyson 1969, The Brownings: Letters and Poetry 1970, English Poetry and Prose 1540–1674 1970, English Drama to 1710 1971, Selected Criticism of Matthew Arnold 1972, The State of the Language (with Leonard Michaels) 1980, The New Oxford Book of Victorian Verse 1987, Collected Poems and Selected Prose of A. E. Housman 1988, The Faber Book of America (with William Vance) 1992, Inventions of the March Hare: Poems 1909–1917 by T. S. Eliot 1996, The Oxford Book of English Verse 1999, Selected Poems of James Henry 2002, Samuel Menashe: New and Selected Poems (Ed.) 2006; contrib. to professional journals. *Honours:* Hon. Fellow, Balliol Coll. 1989, Worcester Coll. 1990, Christ's Coll. Cambridge 1993; Hon. DLitt (Oxford) 1998, (Bristol) 2003; George Orwell Memorial Prize 1979; Beefeater Club Prize for Literature 1980, Distinguished Achievement Award Andrew W. Mellon Foundation 2004. *Address:* 39 Martin Street, Cambridge, MA 02138, USA; Lasborough Cottage, Lasborough Park, Tetbury, Glos., GL8 8UF, England. *Telephone:* (617) 354-7887 (USA); (1666) 890252 (England).

RIDE, Sally, PhD; American astronaut, scientist and academic; *Hibben Professor of Space Science, University of California, San Diego;* b. 26 May 1951, Los Angeles; d. of Dale Ride and Joyce Ride; m. Steven Hawley (divorced). *Education:* Westlake High School, Los Angeles and Stanford Univ. *Career:* astronaut trainee, NASA 1978–79, astronaut 1979–87; on-orbit capsule communicator STS-2 mission, Johnson Space Center, NASA,

Houston; on-orbit capsule communicator STS-3 mission NASA, mission specialist STS-7 1983; Scientific Fellow, Stanford Univ. 1987–89; Dir Calif. Space Inst., Univ. of Calif. at San Diego 1989–96, Prof. of Physics 1989–; Pres. Space.com 1999–2000; co-founder Imaginary Lines Inc., Pres. 2000–; mem. Presidential Comm. on Space Shuttle 1986, Presidential Comm. of Advisers on Science and Tech. 1994–; mem. Bd of Dirs Apple Computer Inc. 1988–90. *Publications:* To Space and Back (with Susan Okie) 1986, Voyager: An Adventure to the Edge of the Solar System (with Tam O'Shaughnessy) 1992, The Third Planet: Exploring the Earth from Space (with Tam O'Shaughnessy) 1994, The Mystery of Mars 1999, Exploring Our Solar System (with Tam O'Shaughnessy) 2003, Space (with Mike Goldsmith) 2005. *Honours:* Jefferson Award for Public Service, von Braun Award, Lindbergh Eagle, two Nat. Space Flight Medal. *Address:* California Space Institute, 9500 Gilman Drive, Dept 0524, University of California at San Diego, La Jolla, CA 92093-0524, USA (office). *Telephone:* (619) 534-5827 (office). *Fax:* (619) 822-1277 (office). *Website:* www.calspace.ucsd.edu (office).

RIDGWAY, Jason (see Marlowe, Stephen)

RIDLEY, Matt, BA, DPhil; British businessman and fmr journalist and writer; b. 1958, Newcastle upon Tyne, England; m. Anya Hurlbert; two c. *Education:* Univ. of Oxford. *Career:* Science Ed. and American Ed., The Economist 1983–92; columnist, Sunday Telegraph, Daily Telegraph 1993–2000; Chair., Int. Centre for Life, Newcastle upon Tyne 1996–2003; Chair., Northern Rock plc; Chair., Northern 2 VCT; Dir, Northern Investors Co. plc. *Publications:* The Red Queen: Sex and the Evolution of Human Nature 1993, The Origins of Virtue: Human Instincts and the Evolution of Co-operation 1996, Genome: The Autobiography of a Species in 23 Chapters 1999, Nature via Nurture: Genes, Experience and What Makes us Human 2003, Francis Crick 2006; contrib. articles and book reviews in The Times, Guardian, TLS, New Statesman, TIME, Newsweek, New York Times, Wall Street Journal, Atlantic Monthly, Discover, Natural History. *Address:* c/o Fourth Estate, 77–85 Fulham Palace Road, London, W6 8JB, England.

RIDPATH, Ian William, FRAS; British writer and broadcaster; b. 1 May 1947, Ilford, Essex. *Career:* mem. Soc. of Authors. *Publications include:* Worlds Beyond 1975, Encyclopedia of Astronomy and Space (ed.) 1976, Messages From the Stars 1978, Stars and Planets 1978, Young Astronomer's Handbook 1981, Hamlyn Encyclopedia of Space 1981, Life Off Earth 1983, Collins Guide to Stars and Planets 1984, Gem Guide to the Night Sky 1985, Secrets of the Sky 1985, A Comet Called Halley 1985, Longman Illustrated Dictionary of Astronomy and Astronautics 1987, Monthly Sky Guide 1987, Star Tales 1989, Norton's Star Atlas (ed.) 1989, Book of the Universe 1991, Atlas of Stars and Planets 1992, Oxford Dictionary of Astronomy (ed.) 1997, Eyewitness Handbook of Stars and Planets 1998, Gem Stars 1999, Collins Encyclopedia of the Universe (gen. ed.) 2001, The Times Space 2002, The Times Universe 2004. *Address:* 48 Otho Court, Brentford Dock, Brentford, Middlesex TW8 8PY, England. *Website:* www.ianridpath.com.

RIDPATH, Michael William Gerrans; British author; b. 7 March 1961, Exeter, England; m. Barbara Nunemaker 1994; one s. two d. *Education:* Merton Coll., Oxford. *Career:* mem. Society of Authors, Managing Cttee; CWA; People of Today. *Publications:* Free to Trade, 1995; Trading Reality, 1996; The Market Maker, 1998; Fatal Error, 2003, See No Evil 2006. *Address:* c/o Blake Friedmann, 37–41 Gower Street, London WC1E 6HH, England.

RIFBJERG, Klaus; Danish author; b. 15 Dec. 1931, Copenhagen; s. of Thorvald Rifbjerg and Lilly Nielsen; m. Inge Merete Gerner 1955; one s. two d. *Education:* Princeton Univ., USA and Univ. of Copenhagen. *Career:* Literary Critic, Information 1955–57, Politiken 1959–65 (Copenhagen daily newspapers); Literary Dir Gyldendal Publrs 1984–92, mem. Bd of Dirs 1992–98; Prof. of Aesthetics, Laererhøjskole, Copenhagen 1986; Prof. of Languages, Copenhagen Business School 2003–; Grant of Honour from the Danish Dramatists 1966, Grant of Honour from the Danish Writers' Guild 1973. *Publications include:* novels: Den Kroniske Uskyld 1958, Operaelsken 1966, Arkivet 1967, Lonni Og Karl 1968, Anna (Jeg) Anna 1970, Marts 1970 1970, Leif den Lykkelige JR. 1971, Til Spanien 1971, Lena Jorgensen, Klintevej 4, 2650 Hvidovre 1971, Brevet til Gerda 1972, R.R. 1972, Spinatfuglene 1973, Dilettanterne 1973, Du skal ikke vaere ked af det Amalia 1974, En hugorm i solen 1974, Vejen ad hvilken 1975, Tak for turen 1975, Kiks 1976, Twist 1976, Et Bortvendt Ansigt 1977, Tango 1978, Dobbeltgœnger 1978, Drengene 1978, Joker 1979, Voksdugshjertet 1979, Det sorte hul 1980, De hellige aber 1981, Maend og Kvinder 1982, Jus 1982, En omvej til Klostret 1983, Falsk Forår 1984, Borte tit 1986, Engel 1987, Rapsodi i blåt 1991; short stories: Og Andre Historier 1964, Rejsende 1969, Den Syende Jomfru 1972, Sommer 1974, Det. Svage Køn 1989; non-fiction: I Medgang Og Modgang 1970, Deres Majestæt! 1977; plays: Gris Pa Gaflen 1962, Hva Skal Vi Lave 1963, Udviklinger 1965, Hvad en Mand Har Brug For 1966, Voks 1968, Ar 1970, Narrene 1971, Svaret Blaeser i Vinden 1971, Det Korte af det lange 1976; poems: Livsfrisen 1979 and several other vols of poetry; 20 radio plays, essays, several film and TV scripts. *Honours:* Dr hc (Lund) 1991, (Odense) 1996; Aarestrup Medal 1964, Danish Critics' Award 1965, Danish Acad. Award 1966, Golden Laurels 1967, Soren Gyldendal Award 1969, Nordic Council Award 1970, PH Prize 1979, Holberg Medal 1979, H. C. Andersen Prize 1988, Johannes V. Jensen Prize 1998, Prize for Nordic Writers, Swedish Acad. 1999, Danish Publicists' Award 2001, Danish Language Soc. Award 2001. *Address:* c/o Gyldendal Publishers, 3 Klareboderne, 1001 Copenhagen, Denmark.

RIGGS, David (see Pigott, Mark)

RIIS, Povl, MD, DM, FRCP; Danish physician, academic and editor; *Chairman, AgeForum;* b. 28 Dec. 1925, Copenhagen; s. of Lars Otto Riis and Eva Elisabeth Riis (née Erdmann); m. Else Harne 1954 (died 1997); one s. three d. *Education:* Univ. of Copenhagen. *Career:* specialist in internal medicine 1960, gastroenterology 1963; Head of Medical Dept B, Gentofte Univ. Hosp. 1963–76; Prof. of Internal Medicine, Univ. of Copenhagen 1974–96 (title and functions preserved externally), Vice-Dean Faculty of Medicine 1979–82; Head of Gastroenterological Dept C, Herlev Co. Hosp. 1976–96; Asst Ed. Journal of the Danish Medical Asscn 1957–67, Chief Ed. 1967–90; Ed. Bibliothek for Laeger 1965–90, Danish Medical Bulletin 1968–90, Nordic Medicine 1984–91; mem. Bd, Danish Soc. for Internal Medicine 1962–67, Danish Anti-Cancer League 1970–75, Danish Soc. for Theoretical and Applied Therapy 1972–77, Int. Union against Cancer 1978–86; mem. Danish Medical Research Council 1968–74, Chair. 1972–74; mem. Danish Science Advisory Bd 1972–74, Co-Chair. 1974; mem. Nordic Scientific Co-ordination Cttee for Medicine 1968–72, Chair. 1970–72; Chair. Nordic Medical Publs Cttee 1970–72; Vice-Pres. European Science Foundation (ESF) 1974–77, mem. Exec. Council 1977–83; Chair. ESF Cttee on Genetic Manipulation 1975–77, Chair. ESF Liaison Cttee on Genetic Manipulation 1977–83; mem. Council for Int. Org. of Medical Sciences Advisory Cttee 1977; mem. Trustees Foundation of 1870 1976, Trier-Hansen Foundation 1977–, Hartmann Prize Cttee 1986–2002, Buhl Olesen Foundation 1982–, Madsen Foundation 1978–, Jakobsen Foundation 1989–, Brinch Foundation 1990–96; Chair. Danish Central Scientific-Ethical Cttee 1979–98, Nat. Medical Bd Danish Red Cross 1985–94, Int. Org. of Inflammatory Bowel Diseases 1986–89; mem. Nat. Cttee on Scientific Misconduct 1992–99; Danish Foreign Office del. Helsinki negotiations, Hamburg 1980; mem. Bd Danish Helsinki Cttee; mem. Nuffield Foundation Working Party on Ethics 1999–2002, Ethical Collegial Council, Danish Dental Asscn 2000–, Ethical Collegial Council, Danish Medical Asscn 2000–03; mem. Medical Advisory Bd NetDoktor 1999–; Evaluator EU 1999–; Adviser Augustinus Foundation 1999–; mem. Int. Cttee of Medical Journal Eds 1980–90, Editorial Bd, Acta Medica Scandinavica, Journal Int. Medicine 1980, Ethics Bd, Danish Medical Asscn 1980–82, WHO European Advisory Cttee for Medical Research 1980–85, Scientific Bd, Danish Nat. Encyclopaedia 1991–2001, Editorial Bd JAMA 1994–; Chair. Nat. Medical Bd of Danish Red Cross; Chair. Nat. Center for First Aid and Health Promotion 1991, AgeForum 1996–, Bd Epidemiological Research, Univ. of Århus 2004–; mem. Preid. Cttee Foundation of Psychiatry 1996–. *Television:* several contribs to Danish Broadcasting System for radio and TV. *Publications:* contrib.: Handbook of Scientific Methodology (in Danish) 1971–, World Medical Association Helsinki Declaration 1975, We Shall All Die – But How? (in Danish) 1977; author: Handbook of Internal Medicine (in Danish) 1968, Grenzen der Forschung 1980; Community and Ethics (in Danish) 1984, Medical Ethics (in Danish) 1985, Ethical Issues in Preventive Medicine 1985, Medical Science and the Advancement of World Health 1985, Bearing and Perspective 1988, The Appleton Consensus 1988, Face Death 1989, Ethics in Health Education 1990, The Future of Medical Journals 1991, Research on Man: Ethics and Law 1991, Scientific Misconduct – Good Scientific Practice 1992, Health Care in Europe after 1992 1992, A Better Health Service – But How? (in Danish), The Culture of General Education 1996, Drugs and Pharmacotherapy 1997, The Time That Followed (in Danish) 1998, Ethics and Clinical Medicine (in Danish) 1998, Can Our Nat Heritage Survive? (in Danish) 1999, Frailty in Aging (in Danish) 1999, Ethics and Evidence-based Pharmacotherapy 2000, Can We Not Do It A Little Better? 2000, In That We Believe 2001, Fraud and Misconduct in Biomedical Research 2001, The Ethics of Research Related to Health Care in Developing Countries 2002; 48 AgeForum publs 1996–2007; Council of Europe, Ethical Eye: Biomedical Research 2004; many articles in medical journals; lyrics to contemporary Danish compositions, trans of lyrics. *Honours:* Hon. Mem. Icelandic Medical Asscn 1978, Swedish Medical Soc., Finnish Medical Soc., Danish Soc. of Gastroenterology 1995 and 2004; Hon. MRCP (UK) 1991; Hon. DMed (Univ. of Odense) 1996, (Gothenburg); Alfred Benzon Prize, August Krogh Prize 1974, Christensen-Ceson Prize 1976, Klein-Prize 1980, Barfred-Pedersen Prize 1980, Hagedorn Prize 1983, Nordic Gastro Prize 1983, Nordic Language Prize in Medicine 1993, Danish Prize of Honour in Research Ethics 2003, National Prize of Honour, JL-Foundation 2005, Medal of Honour, Icelandic Medical History Soc. 2005. *Address:* AgeForum, Skibshusvej 52 B³, 5000, Odense C (office); Nerievej 7, 2900 Hellerup, Denmark (home). *Telephone:* 65484050 (office); 39629688 (home). *Fax:* 65484051 (office); 39629588 (home). *E-mail:* aef@aeldreforum.dk (office). *Website:* www.aeldreforum.dk (office).

RILEY, Denise, PhD; British poet, philosopher and translator; b. 1948, England. *Education:* University of Sussex. *Publications:* Marxism for Infants, 1977; No Fee: A Line or Two for Free, 1979; Some Poems: 1968–1978 (with Wendy Mulford), 1982; War in the Nursery: Theories of the Child and Mother, 1983; Dry Air, 1985; 'Am I That Name?': Feminism and the Category of 'Women' in History, 1988; Poets on Writing: Britain, 1970–1991 (ed.), 1992; Mop Mop Georgette: New and Selected Poems, 1993; Selected Poems, 2001; The Words of Selves: Identification, Solidarity, Irony, 2001.

RILEY, Joan; Jamaican novelist; b. 1958, Hopewell. *Education:* Univ. of Sussex, Univ. of London. *Career:* moved to UK 1976; active career in social work, on which her works draw. *Publications:* The Unbelonging (novel) 1985, Waiting in the Twilight (novel) 1987, Romance (novel) 1988, A Kindness to Children (novel) (MIND Prize 1993) 1992, Leave to Stay: Stories of Exile and Belonging (ed. with Briar Wood) 1996. *Honours:* Voice Award for Fiction 1992.

Address: c/o The Women's Press, 27 Goodge Street, London, W1T 2LD, England.

RIMAWI, Fahid Nimer ar-, BA; Jordanian journalist; *Publisher and Editor-in-Chief, Al Majd;* b. 1942, Palestine; m.; two s. five d. *Education:* Cairo Univ., Egypt. *Career:* Ed. Difa (newspaper) 1965–67; Ed.-in-Chief, Jordan News Agency 1968–70; Sec. Editorial Bd of Afkar (magazine) 1970–73; Dir Investigating Dept of Al-Raiue (newspaper) 1975–76; writer Al-Destour (newspaper) 1978–81; Political Writer, Al-Raiue (newspaper) 1981–85; Corresp. al Talie'ah (magazine) Paris 1982–85; political writer 1985–94; Publr and Ed.-in-Chief Al Majd (weekly). *Publications:* Mawaweel Fi al Layl Al Taweel, short stories in Arabic 1982. *Address:* PO Box 926856, Amman 11190 (office); Dahiyat al-Rashid, Amman, Jordan. *Telephone:* (6) 5530553 (office); (6) 5160615 (home). *Fax:* (6) 553 0352. *E-mail:* almajd@almajd.net (office). *Website:* www.almajd.net (office).

RIMINGTON, Dame Stella, DCB, MA; British civil servant; b. 1935; m. John Rimington 1963; one d. *Education:* Nottingham High School for Girls, Edinburgh Univ. *Career:* Dir-Gen. Security Service 1992–96; Dir (non-exec.) Marks and Spencer 1997–2004, BG PLC 1997–2000, BG Group 2000–, GKR. Group (now Whitehead Mann) 1997–2001; Chair. Inst. of Cancer Research 1997–2001. *Publications:* Intelligence, Security and the Law (non-fiction) 1994, Open Secret (autobiog.) 2001, At Risk (novel) 2004, Secret Asset (novel) 2006, Illegal Action (novel) 2007. *Honours:* Hon. Air Commodore 7006 (VR) Squadron Royal Auxiliary Air Force 1997–2001; Hon. LLB (Nottingham) 1995, (Exeter) 1996, (London Metropolitan Univ.) 2004. *Address:* PO Box 1604, London, SW1P 1XB, England.

RINALDI, Ange-Marie (Angelo); French writer and literary critic; b. 17 June 1940, Bastia; s. of Pierre-François Rinaldi and Antoinette Pietri. *Education:* Lycée de Bastia, Corsica. *Career:* journalist Nice-Matin 1961–68, Paris-Jour 1969–72; Literary Ed. L'Express 1972–98; journalist Nouvel Observateur 1998–; writer 1968–; elected mem. Acad. Française 2001. *Publications:* La Loge du gouverneur (Prix Fénéon) 1969, La Maison des Atlantes (Prix Fémina 1972) 1971, L'Education de l'oubli 1974, Les Dames de France 1977, La Dernière fête de l'empire (Prix Marcel Proust 1981) 1980, Les Jardins du consulat 1985, Les Roses de Pline (Prix Jean Freustié 1988) 1987, La Confession des collines 1990, Les jours ne s'en vont pas longtemps 1993, Dernières nouvelles de la nuit 1997, Service de presse: chroniques 1999, Tou ce que je sais de Marie 2000. *Honours:* Prix Prince Pierre de Monaco 1994, Prix de la Fondation Mumm 1995. *Address:* c/o Le Nouvel Observateur, 10 place de la Bourse, 75002 Paris, France.

RINALDI, Nicholas Michael, AB, MA, PhD; American academic, writer and poet; *Professor, Fairfield University;* b. 2 April 1934, New York, NY; m. Jacqueline Tellier 1959; three s. one d. *Education:* Shrub Oak Coll., Fordham Univ. *Career:* Instructor to Asst Prof., St John's Univ. 1960–65; Lecturer, CUNY 1966; Assoc. Prof., Columbia Univ. 1966; Asst Prof. to Prof., Prof., Fairfield Univ. 1966–; Prof., Univ. of Connecticut 1972; mem. Associated Writing Programs; Poetry Society of America. *Publications:* novels: Bridge Fall Down 1985, The Jukebox Queen of Malta 1999, Between Two Rivers 2004; poetry: The Resurrection of the Snails 1977, We Have Lost Our Fathers 1982, The Luftwaffe in Chaos 1985; contrib. to periodicals and journals, including Virginia Quarterly Review. *Honours:* Joseph P. Slomovich Memorial Award for Poetry, 1979; All Nations Poetry Awards, 1981, 1983; New York Poetry Forum Award, 1983; Eve of St Agnes Poetry Award, 1984; Charles Angoff Literary Award, 1984. *Address:* c/o English Department, Fairfield University, 1073 N Benson Road, Fairfield, CT 06824, USA.

RINDO, Ronald J.; American academic and writer; b. 21 March 1959, Milwaukee, WI; m. Ellen S. Meyer, 13 Oct. 1984, one s. one d. *Education:* BA, Carroll College, 1981; MA, 1984, PhD, 1989, University of Wisconsin, Milwaukee. *Career:* Asst Prof. of English, Birmingham Southern College, AL, 1989–92, University of Wisconsin, Oshkosh, 1992–; mem. MLA; Society for the Study of Midwestern Literature; Wisconsin Council of Teachers of English. *Publications:* Suburban Metaphysics and Other Stories, 1990; Secrets Men Keep (short stories), 1995. Contributions: anthologies, books, reviews and periodicals. *Honours:* Milwaukee Small Press Award, 1989, Wisconsin Writer's Award, Wisconsin Library Asscn, 1990; Bell South Foundation Grant, 1990; Wye Fellow, Aspen Institute, 1991; Wisconsin Humanities Council Grant, 1995. *E-mail:* rindo@uwosh.edu.

RÍOS, Juan; Peruvian poet, dramatist, journalist and critic; b. 28 Sept. 1914, Barranco, Lima; s. of Rogelio Ríos and Victoria Rey (de Ríos); m. Rosa Saco 1946; one d. *Career:* Writers' Fellowship, UNESCO, Europe and Egypt 1960–61; mem. Academia Peruana de la Lengua Correspondiente a la Española. *Publications:* Canción de Siempre 1941, Malstrom 1941, La Pintura Contemporánea en el Perú 1946, Teatro (I) 1961, Ayar Manko 1963, Primera Antología Poética 1982. *Honours:* Nat. Prize for Playwriting 1946, 1950, 1952, 1954, 1960; Nat. Poetry Prize 1948, 1953. *Address:* Bajada de Baños 109, Barranco, Lima 04, Peru. *Telephone:* (14) 671799.

RIPLEY, Michael (Mike) David, BA; British writer and critic; b. 29 Sept. 1952, Huddersfield, England. *Career:* fmr crime fiction critic, Sunday Telegraph, Daily Telegraph, Birmingham Post; co-ed., Fresh Blood anthology series. *Publications:* novels: Just Another Angel 1988, Angel Touch 1989, Angel Hunt 1990, Angel in Arms 1992, Angel City 1994, Angel Confidential 1995, Family of Angels 1996, That Angel Look 1997, Bootlegged Angel 1999, Lights, Camera, Angel 2001, Double Take 2001, Angel Underground 2002,

Angel on the Inside 2003, Angel in the House 2005, Angel's Share 2006. *Honours:* CWA Last Laugh Awards 1989, 1991, Angel Literary Award for Fiction 1990, Sherlock Award 1999.

RISSET, Jacqueline; French poet, writer and translator; *Professor, Università degli Studi di Roma Tre;* b. 1933, Besançon; m. *Education:* École Normale Supérieure de Sèvres, studied in Italy. *Career:* mem. editorial bd of journal, Tel Quel; Prof. in the Faculty of Philosophy and Literature, Università degli Studi di Roma Tre 1979–. *Publications include:* Jeu (poems) 1971, Mors 1977, La Traduction commence (poems) 1978, En voyage 1980, Dante écrivain: ou l'Intelletto d'amore 1982, Sept passages de la vie d'une femme (poems) 1985, L'Amour de loin (poems) 1988, Petits éléments de physique amoureuse (poems) 1991, L'anagramme du désir 1995, Dante, une vie (biog.) 1995, Puissances du sommeil 1997, Les instants 2000; translations into French include Dante's Inferno, Purgatorio and Paradiso (Prix Académie française) 1985–90. *Address:* Università degli Studi di Roma Tre, Facoltà di Lettere e Filosofia, via Ostiense 234, 00144 Rome, Italy (office).

RITTER, Erika, MA; Canadian dramatist and writer; b. 1948, Regina, SK. *Education:* McGill Univ., Montréal and Univ. of Toronto. *Career:* host and broadcaster, CBC Radio 1981–; writer-in-residence, Concordia Univ. 1984; playwright-in-residence, Smith Coll. 1985, Stratford Festival 1985. *Publications:* plays: A Visitor from Charleston 1975, The Splits 1978, Winter, 1671 1979, Automatic Pilot 1980, The Passing Scene 1982, Murder at McQueen 1986, The Road to Hell 1992; prose: Urban Scrawl 1984, Ritter in Residence 1987, The Hidden Life in Humans 1997, The Great Big Book of Guys: Alphabetical Encounters with Men 2004. *Honours:* Chalmers Award 1980, ACTRA Award 1982. *Literary Agent:* c/o Shain Jaffe, Great North Artists, 350 Dupont Street, Toronto, ON M5R 1V9, Canada.

RIVARD, David, BA, MFA; American writer, poet and editor; b. 2 Dec. 1953, Fall River, MA; m. Michaela Sullivan 1982, one d. *Education:* Southeastern Massachusetts University, University of Arizona. *Career:* faculty mem., Dept of English, Tufts University; Poetry Ed., Harvard Review. *Publications:* Torque, 1988; Wise Poison, 1996; Bewitched Playground, 2000. Contributions: periodicals. *Honours:* Fine Arts Work Center Fellowships, Provincetown, Massachusetts, 1984–85, 1986–87; National Endowment for the Arts Fellowships, 1986, 1991; Agnes Lynch Starrett Poetry Prize, University of Pittsburgh, 1987; Pushcart Prize, 1994; Massachusetts Cultural Council Fellow, 1994; James Laughlin Award, Acad. of American Poets, 1996; Guggenheim Fellowship, 2001.

RIVAS, Manuel; Spanish journalist, novelist and poet; b. 1957, A Coruña. *Career:* contributor to Galician literature, co-establishing a number of Galician- and Spanish-language journals. *Publications:* poetry: Libro de Entroido 1979, Balada nas praias do Oeste 1985, Mohicania 1987, Ningún cisne 1989, El pueblo de la noche 1997; novels: Todo ben 1985, Un millón de vacas (Premio de la Crítica) 1989, Os comedores de patacas 1991, En salvaxe compaña 1994, ¿Qué me queres, amor? (Premio Nacional de Narrativa) 1996, Bala perdida 1997, O lapis do carpinteiro 1998, Ela, maldita alma 1999, A man dos paíños 2000, As chamadas perdidas 2002, Contos de Nadal 2004, Os libros arden mal (Premio de los Libreros de Madrid 2007) 2006; essays: El bonsái atlántico 1994, El periodismo es un cuento 1997, Toxos e flores 1999, Galicia Galicia 2001; numerous short stories; contrib. to El País, El Ideal Gallego, Diario de Galicia, La voz de Galicia. *Honours:* Amnesty International Prize (Belgian section), Premio Torrente Ballester, Premio Arcebispo Xoán de San Clemente y el de la Crítica, Premio ONCE – Galicia a la Solidaridad. *Address:* c/o Alfaguara, Santillana Ediciones Generales SL, Calle Torrelaguna 60, 28043 Madrid, Spain (office). *E-mail:* alfaguara@santillana.es (office).

RIVERA-GARZA, Cristina, PhD; Mexican writer, poet and historian; b. 1964, Matamoros, Tamaulipas. *Education:* Nat. Autonomous Univ. of Mexico, Mexico City, Univ. of Houston, TX, USA. *Career:* Assoc. Prof. of Mexican History, San Diego State Univ.; Head of Creative Writing Narrative Program, Centro Cultural Tijuana. *Publications:* La guerra no importa 1991, La más mía 1998, Nadie me verá llorar (trans. as No One Will See Me Cry) 2000, La cresta de Ilion 2002, Ningún reloj cuenta esto 2002, Hombres frágiles 2005; contrib. to Hispanic American Historical Review, Journal of the History of Medicine. *Literary Agent:* c/o Curbstone Press, 321 Jackson Street, Willimantic, CT 06226-1738, USA. *E-mail:* info@curbstone.org. *Website:* www.curbstone.org.

RIVERO CASTAÑEDA, Raúl Ramón; Cuban journalist and poet; b. 1945, Morón, Camagüey; m. Blanca Reyes Castañón. *Education:* Havana Univ. School of Journalism. *Career:* co-founder satirical magazine Caimán Barbudo 1966; Moscow correspondent for govt press agency, Prensa Latina 1973–76, then worked for science and culture service, Cuba; independent journalist 1988–; co-founder and Dir, Cuba Press news agency 1995–2003, contributing to newspapers and journals abroad, including El Nuevo Herald, The Miami Herald, Encounter magazine; correspondent for French press agency, Reporters sans frontières; fmr regional vice-chair. for Cuba, Inter-American Press Asscn Cttee on Freedom of the Press and Information; accused of collaborating with the USA and sentenced to 20 years' imprisonment by govt April 2003, released Nov. 2004; mem. Manuel Márquez Sterling Journalists' Asscn. *Publications:* poems include: Suite de la muerte, Patria 1994, Orden de registro, Oración de septiembre, Foto en La Hanana, Ensayo sobre la tiranía. *Honours:* Reporters sans frontières Fondation de France prize 1997, Inter-American Press Asscn Grand Prize for Press Freedom, Columbia Univ. Graduate School of Journalism Maria Moors Cabot Prize 1999, World Press

Freedom Prize 2004. *Address:* c/o Reporters sans frontières, 5 rue Geoffroy-Marie, 75009 Paris, France. *Telephone:* 1 44 83 84 84. *Fax:* 1 45 23 11 51. *E-mail:* rsf@rsf.org. *Website:* www.rsf.org.

RIX, Timothy John, CBE, BA, CIMgt, FRSA, FInstD; British publisher; *Chairman, Edinburgh University Press;* b. 4 Jan. 1934, Maidenhead, Berks.; s. of the late Howard T. Rix and of Marguerite Selman Rix; m. 1st Wendy E. Wright 1960 (divorced 1967); m. 2nd Gillian Greenwood 1968; one s. two d. *Education:* Radley Coll., Clare Coll., Cambridge and Yale Univ., USA. *Career:* joined Longmans Green & Co. Ltd 1958, Overseas Educ. Publr 1958–61, Publishing Man. Far East and SE Asia 1961–63, Head, English Language Teaching Publishing 1964–68, Div. Man. Dir 1968–72, Jt Man. Dir 1972–76, Chief Exec. Longman Group Ltd 1976–90, Chair. 1984–90; Chair. Addison-Wesley-Longman Group Ltd 1988–89; Chair. Pitman Examinations Inst. 1987–90; Dir Pearson Longman Ltd (now Pearson PLC) 1979–83, Goldcrest Television 1981–83, Yale Univ. Press Ltd, London 1984–, ECIC (Man.) Ltd 1990–92, Blackie & Son Ltd 1990–93, B.H. Blackwell Ltd 1991–95, Geddes and Grosset Ltd 1996–98, Jessica Kingsley Publrs Ltd 1997–, Frances Lincoln Ltd 1997–, Meditech Media Ltd 1997–2003, Scottish Book Source 1999–, Central European Univ. Press 1999–2005; Pres. Publrs' Asscn 1981–83; mem. British Library Bd 1986–96, British Council Bd 1988–97, Health Educ. Authority Bd 1995–99; Chair. Book Trust 1986–88, British Library Centre for the Book 1989–95, Book Marketing Ltd 1990–2003, Soc. of Bookmen 1990–92, British Library Publishing 1992–2003, Book Aid Int. 1994–, Bell Educational Trust 1994–2001, Nat. Book Cttee 1997–2003, Edinburgh Univ. Press 2001–; mem. Oxford Brookes Univ. Devt Cttee 1991–96, Finance Cttee, Oxford Univ. Press 1992–2002, Council, Ranfurly Library Service 1992–94, Advisory Council, Inst. of English Studies, London Univ. 2000–; Gov. English-Speaking Union 1998–2005. *Publications:* articles on publishing in trade journals. *Honours:* Hon. Pres. Independent Publrs' Guild 1993–. *Address:* Top Flat, 27 Wolseley Road, London, N8 8RS, England (home). *Telephone:* (20) 8341-4160 (home). *Fax:* (20) 8341-4160 (home). *E-mail:* tim@rixpublishing.co.uk (home).

ROBB, Graham Macdonald, PhD, FRSL; British writer; b. 2 June 1958, Manchester; m. Margaret Hambrick 1986. *Education:* Univ. of Oxford, Goldsmiths Coll., London and Vanderbilt Univ., Nashville, Tenn., USA. *Career:* British Acad. Fellowship 1987–90. *Publications include:* Le Corsaire – Satan en Silhouette 1985, Baudelaire Lecteur de Balzac 1988, Scènes de la Vie de Bohème (ed.) 1988, Baudelaire (trans.) 1989, La Poésie de Baudelaire et la Poésie Française 1993, Balzac 1994, Unlocking Mallarmé 1996, Victor Hugo: A Biography 1998, Rimbaud 2000, Strangers: Homosexual Love in the 19th Century; contribs to Times Literary Supplement, Daily Telegraph, London Review of Books, New York Times. *Honours:* New York Times Book of the Year 1994, 1999 and 2001, Whitbread Biography of the Year Award 1997, R.S.L. Heinemann Award 1998. *Literary Agent:* Rogers, Coleridge & White Ltd, Powis Mews, London, W11 1JN, England.

ROBB, J. D. (see Roberts, Nora)

ROBBE-GRILLET, Alain; French writer, film-maker and agronomist; b. 18 Aug. 1922, Brest; s. of Gaston Robbe-Grillet and Yvonne Canu; m. Catherine Rstakian 1957. *Education:* Lycée Buffon, Lycée St Louis and Institut Nat. Agronomique, Paris. *Career:* Chargé de Mission, Inst. Nat. de la Statistique 1945–48; Engineer Inst. des Fruits Tropicaux (Guinea, Morocco, Martinique and Guadeloupe) 1949–51; literary adviser, Editions de Minuit 1955–85; teacher, New York Univ. 1972–97; Dir Centre for the Sociology of Literature, Univ. of Brussels 1980–88. *Films:* L'année dernière à Marienbad 1961; films directed: L'immortelle 1963, Trans-Europ-Express 1967, L'homme qui ment 1968, L'Eden et après 1970, Glissements progressifs du plaisir 1974, Le jeu avec le feu 1975, La belle captive 1983, Un bruit qui rend fou 1995. *Publications:* novels: Les gommes 1953, Le voyeur 1955, La jalousie 1957, Dans le labyrinthe 1959, La maison de rendez-vous 1965, Projet pour une révolution à New York 1970, Topologie d'une cité fantôme 1976, La belle captive 1977, Un régicide 1978, Souvenirs du triangle d'or 1978, Djinn 1981, Le miroir qui revient 1984, Angélique ou l'enchantement 1988, Les derniers jours de Corinthe 1994, La Reprise 2001; short stories: Instantanés 1962; essay: Pour un nouveau roman 1964, Le Voyageur 2001. *Honours:* mem. de l' Acad. française 2004; Officier, Légion d'honneur, Ordre nat. du Mérite, des Arts et Lettres; Prix Louis Delluc 1963, Premio Vittorio de Sica 2001. *Address:* Editions de Minuit, 7 rue Bernard-Palissy, 75006 Paris (office); 18 boulevard Maillot, 92200 Neuilly-sur-Seine, France (home). *Telephone:* 1-47-22-31-22 (home). *Fax:* 2-31-77-03-30 (home).

ROBBINS, Kenneth Randall, AA, BSEd, MFA, PhD; American academic, writer and dramatist; *Director, School of the Performing Arts, Louisiana Technical University;* b. 7 Jan. 1944, Douglasville, Ga; m. Dorothy Dodge 1988; one s. one d. *Education:* Young Harris Coll., Georgia Southern Univ., Univ. of Georgia, Southern Illinois Univ. at Carbondale. *Career:* Asst Prof., Jacksonville Univ., Fla 1974–79; Assoc. Prof., Newberry Coll., SC 1977–85, Univ. of S Dakota 1985–98; Dir School of the Performing Arts, Louisiana Tech Univ. 1998–; presenter, Black Hills Writers Conf. 1986–90; mem. Soc. for Study of Southern Literature, Nat. Partners of American Theatre, Asscn of Theatre in Higher Educ.; stage plays have been produced throughout the USA, Canada, Denmark and Japan. *Plays:* Atomic Field, Molly's Rock, Bar None, The Hunger Feast, One Man's Hero, The Audition. *Publications:* The Dallas File (play) 1982, Buttermilk Bottoms (novel) 1987, The Baptism of Howie Cobb (novel) 1995, In the Shelter of the Fold (novel) 2002, Christmas

Stories from Louisiana (co-ed.) 2003, The City of Churches 2004, Christmas on the Great Plains (co-ed.) 2005, Christmas Stories from Georgia (co-ed.) 2005, Matchless (novel) 2006, Dynamite Hill (radio play); contrib. to journals and radio. *Honours:* Toni Morrison Prize for Fiction 1986, Associated Writing Programs Novel Award 1986, Festival of Southern Theatre Awards 1987, 1990, Japan Foundation Arts Fellowship 1995, Louisiana Div. of Arts Theatre Fellowship 2002, Georgia Southern Univ. Coll. of Educ. Alumnus of the Year 2003, Fulbright Scholar to Macedonia 2003. *Address:* School of the Performing Arts, Louisiana Tech University, PO Box 8608, Ruston, LA 71272, USA (office). *Telephone:* (318) 257-2711 (office). *Fax:* (318) 257-4571 (office). *E-mail:* krobbins@latech.edu (office). *Website:* www.latech.edu (office).

ROBBINS, Richard Leroy, AB, MFA; American academic, poet, writer and editor; *Professor, Minnesota State University, Mankato;* b. 27 Aug. 1953, Los Angeles, CA; m. Candace L. Black 1979; two s. *Education:* San Diego State Univ., Univ. of Montana. *Career:* Co-Ed., Cafeteria 1971–81, CutBank and SmokeRoot Press 1977–79, Montana Arts Council anthologies 1979–81; writer-in-residence, Poet-in-the-Schools, Montana Arts Council 1979–81; instructor, Moorhead State Univ. 1981–82, Oregon State Univ. 1982–84; Prof., Minnesota State Univ., Mankato 1984–; Asst Ed., Mankato Poetry Review 1984–; mem. Associated Writing Programs, The Loft, Poetry Soc. of America, Western Literature Asscn. *Publications:* Where We Are: The Montana Poets Anthology (ed. with Lex Runciman) 1978, Toward New Weather 1979, The Invisible Wedding 1984, Famous Persons We Have Known 2000; contrib. to 20 anthologies 1978–, reviews, quarterlies and journals. *Honours:* Portland Review Branford P. Millar Award First Prize in Poetry 1978, Univ. of Montana Frontier Award 1978, Minnesota State Arts Bd Individual Artist Fellowships 1986, 1999, Poetry Soc. of America Robert H. Winner Memorial Award 1988, Nat. Endowment for the Arts Fellowship 1992, McKnight Individual Artist grants 1993, 1996, and Fellowship 1997, Hawthornden Fellowship 1998, Loft Award of Distinction in Poetry 2000. *Address:* c/o Department of English, Minnesota State University, 230 Armstrong Hall, Mankato, MN 56001, USA.

ROBBINS, Tim, BA; American actor, director and screenwriter; b. 16 Oct. 1958, West Covina, Calif.; s. of folk singer Gil Robbins; pnr Susan Sarandon; three c. *Education:* UCLA. *Career:* began career as mem. Theater for the New City; Founder and Artistic Dir The Actors' Gang 1981–; Founder Havoc Inc. (production co.). *Theatre:* as actor: Ubu Roi 1981; as dir: A Midsummer Night's Dream 1984, The Good Woman of Setzuan 1990; as writer, with Adam Simon: Alagazam, After the Dog Wars, Violence: The Misadventures of Spike Spangle, Farmer, Carnage – A Comedy (rep. USA at Edin. Int. Festival, Scotland); as writer: Embedded 2004. *Films as actor:* No Small Affair 1984, Toy Soldiers 1984, The Sure Thing 1985, Fraternity Vacation 1985, Top Gun 1986, Howard the Duck 1986, Five Corners 1987, Bull Durham 1988, Tapeheads 1988, Miss Firecracker 1989, Eric the Viking 1989, Cadillac Man 1990, Twister 1990, Jacob's Ladder 1990, Jungle Fever 1991, The Player 1992, Bob Roberts (also writer and dir) 1992, Amazing Stories: Book Four 1992, Short Cuts 1993, The Hudsucker Proxy 1994, The Shawshank Redemption 1994, Prêt-à-Porter 1994, I.Q. 1994, Dead Man Walking (writer and dir) 1995, Nothing to Lose 1997, Arlington Road 1999, Cradle Will Rock (also writer and dir) 1999, Austin Powers: The Spy Who Shagged Me 1999, Mission to Mars 2000, High Fidelity 2000, Antitrust 2001, Human Nature 2001, The Truth About Charlie 2002, The Day My God Died 2003, Mystic River (Golden Globe for Best Supporting Actor 2004, Critics' Choice Award for Best Supporting Actor 2004, Screen Actors Guild Best Supporting Actor Award 2004, Acad. Award for Best Supporting Actor 2004) 2003, Code 46 2003, The Secret Life of Words 2005, War of the Worlds 2005, La Vida secreta de las palabras 2005, Zathura: A Space Adventure 2005, Catch a Fire 2006, Tenacious D: The Pick of Destiny 2006. *Television:* Queens Supreme (pilot episode and series dir) 2003. *Literary Agent:* Havoc Inc., 16 West 19th Street, 12th Floor, New York, NY 10011; c/o Elaine Goldsmith Thomas, ICM, 40 West 57th Street, New York, NY 10019 (office); The Actors' Gang at The Ivy Substation, 9070 Venice Blvd., Culver City, CA 90232, USA. *Website:* www.theactorsgang.com.

ROBBINS, Tom, BA; American writer; b. 22 July 1936, Blowing Rock, NC; s. of George T. Robbins and Katherine Robinson Robbins; m. 1st Terrie Lunden 1967 (divorced 1972); one s.; m. 2nd Alexa d'Avalon 1987. *Education:* Virginia Commonwealth Univ. and Univ. of Washington. *Career:* operated black market ring in S Korea 1956–57; int. news Times-Dispatch, Richmond, Va 1959–62; Art Critic, The Seattle Times and contrib. to Artforum and Art in America etc. 1962–65; Art Critic, Seattle Magazine 1965–67. *Films:* Even Cowgirls Get the Blues 1994. *Publications:* novels: Another Roadside Attraction 1971, Even Cowgirls Get the Blues 1976, Still Life With Woodpecker 1980, Jitterbug Perfume 1984, Skinny Legs and All 1990, Half Asleep in Frog Pajamas 1994, Fierce Invalids Home from Hot Climates 2000, Villa Incognito 2003, Wild Ducks Flying Backward 2005. *Honours:* Bumbershoot Golden Umbrella for Lifetime Achievement 1998, Writers' Digest 100 Best Writers of the 20th Century 2000. *Address:* PO Box 338, La Conner, WA 98257, USA (home).

RÖBEL, Udo; German editor; *Editor-in-Chief, Bild.de;* b. 20 Jan. 1950, Neustadt, Weinstrasse. *Career:* Restaurant Ed. for Rheinpfalz and Mil. Service Corresp. for DPA and AP 1969–71; mem. editorial staff BILD newspaper, Frankfurt, Kettwig, and Aachen-zum-Schluss 1972–82; Deputy Ed.-in-Chief Express newspaper, Cologne 1983–89; journalistic adviser Heinrich-Bauer-Verlag 1989–92; mem. Chief Editorial Staff BILD 1993–97, Ed.-in-Chief BILD 1998–2000, Ed.-in-Chief Bild.de 2001–. *Honours:* Wächter-

Preis, Deutschen Tagespresse 1985. *Address:* Bild, Axel-Springer-Platz 1, 20355 Hamburg, Germany (office). *Telephone:* (40) 34700 (office). *Fax:* (40) 345811 (office). *Website:* www.bild.de (office).

ROBERSON, John Royster, BA, MA; American editor and writer; b. 7 March 1930, Roanoke, Va; m. Charlene Grace Hale 1966; one s. one d. *Education:* Univ. of Virginia, Univ. of Grenoble, France, US Army Language School, Monterey, Calif. *Career:* Asst to Sr Ed., Holiday 1959–70; copywriter, N.W. Ayer Advertising 1971–76; Assoc. to Sr Staff Ed., Reader's Digest Condensed Books 1976–95; mem. Int. House of Japan, US China People's Friendship Asscn, Science Educ. Centre, Fairfield Co., Conn. (Bd Dirs). *Publications:* China from Manchu to Mao 1699–1976 1980, Japan from Shogun to Sony 1543–1984 1985, Transforming Russia 1692–1991 1992, Japan Meets the West 1998; contrib. to Atlantic, Holiday, Reader's Digest, Studies in Bibliography, Virginia Magazine of History and Biography. *Honours:* Raven Soc., Univ. of Virginia 1950, Rotary International Fellowship, Univ. of Grenoble 1951–52. *Address:* 16 Hassake Road, Old Greenwich, CT 06870, USA.

ROBERTS, Andrew, MA, FRSL; British writer; b. 13 Jan. 1963, London, England. *Education:* Gonville and Caius Coll., Cambridge. *Career:* mem. Beefsteak Club, Univ. Pitt Club, Cambridge, Brooks's. *Publications:* The Holy Fox: A Biography of Lord Halifax 1991, Eminent Churchillians 1994, The Aachen Memorandum 1995, Salibury: Victorian Titan 1999, Napoleon and Wellington 2001, Hitler and Churchill: Secrets of Leadership 2003, What Might Have Been: Leading Historians on Twelve 'What Ifs' of History (ed.) 2004, Waterloo: Napoleon's Last Gamble 2004, A History of the English Speaking Peoples Since 1900 2006; contrib. to Sunday Telegraph, Literary Review. *Honours:* Hon. DHumLitt (Univ. of Westminster, Fulton, MO) 2000. *Literary Agent:* Capel & Land Ltd, 29 Wardour Street, London, W1D 6PS, England. *Address:* 11 Ovington Square, London, SW3 1LH, England. *Website:* www.andrew-roberts.net.

ROBERTS, Brian, DipSoc; British writer; b. 19 March 1930, London, England. *Education:* St Mary's Coll., Twickenham, Univ. of London. *Career:* teacher of English and history 1955–65. *Publications:* Ladies in the Veld 1965, Cecil Rhodes and the Princess 1969, Churchills in Africa 1970, The Diamond Magnates 1972, The Zulu Kings 1974, Kimberley: Turbulent City 1976, The Mad Bad Line: The Family of Lord Alfred Douglas 1981, Randolph: A Study of Churchill's Son 1984, Cecil Rhodes: Flawed Colossus 1987, Those Bloody Women: Three Heroines of the Boer War 1991. *Literary Agent:* c/o Andrew Lownie, 17 Sutherland Street, London, SW1V 4JU, England. *Address:* 7 The Blue House, Market Place, Frome, BA11 1AP, England (home). *Telephone:* (1373) 471581 (home).

ROBERTS, Gregory David; Australian writer; b. 1952, Melbourne, Vic. *Publications:* Shantaram 2003. *Address:* c/o Scribe Publishing, 313 Rathdowne Street, Carlton, Vic. 3053, Australia. *E-mail:* scribe@bigpond.net.au. *Website:* www.scribepub.com.au.

ROBERTS, Irene, (Roberta Carr, Elizabeth Harle, I. M. Roberts, Ivor Roberts, Iris Rowland, Irene Shaw); British writer; b. 27 Sept. 1925, London, England. *Career:* Woman's Page Ed., South Hams Review 1977–79; Tutor in Creative Writing, Kingsbridge Community Coll. 1978–; founder-mem. Romantic Novelists' Asscn. *Publications:* Shadows on the Moon, 1968; Thunder Heights, 1969; Surgeon in Tibet, 1970; Birds Without Bars, 1970; The Shrine of Fire, 1970; Sister at Sea, 1971; Gull Haven, 1971; Moon Over the Temple, 1972; The Golden Pagoda, 1972; Desert Nurse, 1976; Nurse in Nepal, 1976; Stars Above Raffael, 1977; Hawks Burton, 1979; Symphony of Bells, 1980; Nurse Moonlight, 1980; Weave Me a Moonbeam, 1982; Jasmine for a Nurse, 1982; Sister on Leave, 1982; Nurse in the Wilderness, 1983; Moonpearl, 1986; Sea Jade, 1987; Kingdom of the Sun, 1987; Song of the Nile, 1987. Children's Books: Holiday's for Hanbury, 1964; Laughing is for Fun, 1964. As Ivor Roberts: Jump into Hell, 1960; Trial by Water, 1961; Green Hell, 1961. As Iris Rowland: Blue Feathers, 1967; Moon Over Moncrieff, 1969; Star Drift, 1970; Rainbow River, 1970; The Wild Summer, 1970; Orange Blossom for Tara, 1971; Blossoms in the Snow, 1971; Sister Julia, 1972; Golden Bubbles, 1976; Hunter's Dawn, 1977; Golden Triangle, 1978; Forgotten Dreams, 1978; Temptation, 1983; Theresa, 1985. As Roberta Carr: Sea Maiden, 1965; Fire Dragon, 1967; Golden Interlude, 1970. As Elizabeth Harle: Golden Rain, 1964; Gay Rowan, 1965; Sandy, 1967; Spray of Red Roses, 1971; The Silver Summer, 1971; The Burning Flame, 1979; Come to Me Darling, 1983. As Irene Shaw: Moonstone Manor, 1968; US edn as Murder Mansion 1976; The Olive Branch, 1968. As I. M. Roberts: The Throne of the Pharoahs, 1974; Hatsheput, Queeen of the Nile, 1976; Hour of the Tiger, 1985; Jezebel Street, 1994; Limehouse Lady, 1995; More Laughter Than Tears, 1996; London's Pride in Progress, 1997. *Address:* Alpha House, Higher Town, Marlborough, Kingsbridge, South Devon TQ7 3RL, England.

ROBERTS, Ivor (see Roberts, Irene)

ROBERTS, Leonard (Len), BA, MA, PhD; American academic, poet and translator; *Professor of English, Northampton County College;* b. 13 March 1947, Cohoes, NY; m. 1981; two s. one d. *Education:* Siena Coll., Univ. of Dayton, Lehigh Univ. *Career:* Prof. of English, Northampton County Coll. 1974–83, 1986–87, 1989–93, 1995–; Visiting Asst Prof., Lafayette Coll. 1983–85; Visiting Prof., Univ. of Pittsburgh 1984–; Fulbright Scholar, Janus Pannonius Univ., Pécs, Hungary 1988–89, Univ. of Turku, Finland 1994; mem. MLA, Pennsylvania Council on the Arts (advisory bd 1990–), Poetry Soc.

of America, Poets and Writers. *Publications:* poetry: Cohoes Theater 1980, From the Dark 1984, Sweet Ones 1988, Black Wings 1989, Learning About the Heart 1992, Dangerous Angels 1993, The Million Branches: Selected Poems and Interview 1993, Counting the Black Angels 1994, The Trouble-Making Finch 1998, The Silent Singer: New and Selected Poems 2001; translator: The Selected Poems of Sándor Csoóri 1992, Before and After the Fall: New Poems by Sándor Csoóri 2004, The Disappearing Trick 2007; contrib. to anthologies and journals. *Honours:* Pennsylvania Council on the Arts Writing Awards in Poetry 1981, 1986, 1987, 1991, Nat. Endowment for the Arts Awards 1984, 1989, Great Lakes and Prairies Award 1988, Nat. Poetry Series Award 1988, Soros Foundation Poetry Trans. Awards 1989, 1990, 1992, 1997, Guggenheim Fellowship 1990–91, Pushcart Prize 1991, Witter Bynner Poetry Trans. Award 1991–92, winner Silverfish Review Chapbook Competition 1992, first prize Wildwood Poetry Contest 1993, Nat. Endowment for the Humanities Trans. Award 1999, Pennsylvania Council on the Arts Poetry Award 2000. *Address:* 2443 Wassergass Road, Hellertown, PA 18055, USA (office). *Telephone:* (610) 861-5393 (office).

ROBERTS, Michael Symmons; British poet and librettist; b. 1963, Preston, Lancs.; m.; three s. *Education:* Univ. of Oxford. *Career:* joined BBC as radio prod., Cardiff 1989; worked in Manchester and London, also TV scriptwriter and documentary film-maker, fmr Exec. Prod. and Head of Devt for Religion and Ethics; Creative Writing Lecturer, Manchester Metropolitan Univ. *Libretti:* with James McMillan: Chosen, Sun Dogs, Parthenogenesis 2001, The Birds of Rhiannon 2001, Raising Sparks 2002, Quickening 2002, The Sacrifice 2007. *Radio:* poetry (BBC Radio): Anno Domini 1999, A Fearful Symmetry (Sandford St Martin Prize) 2000, Behold the Man 2000, The Wounds 2001, The Hurricane 2002, Last Words 2002, Crossing the Dark Sea 2004; documentaries: The Good Book (Jerusalem Trust Premier Award 2004) 2003, The Cross 2003, Sacred Nation 2004. *Publications:* poetry: Soft Keys (Soc. of Authors Gregory Award) 1993, Raising Sparks 1999, Burning Babylon (Poetry Book Soc. Recommendation, Soc. of Authors K. Blundell Trust Award) 2001, Corpus (Whitbread Poetry Award 2005) 2004; novel: Patrick's Alphabet 2006. *Literary Agent:* David Godwin Associates, 55 Monmouth Street, London, WC2H 9DG, England. *Telephone:* (20) 7240-9992. *E-mail:* assistant@davidgodwinassociates.co.uk. *Website:* www.davidgodwinassociates.co.uk. *Address:* c/o Jonathan Cape, Random House, 20 Vauxhall Bridge Road, London SW1V 2SA, England. *Website:* www.symmonsroberts.com.

ROBERTS, Michèle Brigitte, MA (Oxon.), ALA, FRSL; British novelist and poet; b. 20 May 1949, Herts.; d. of Reginald Roberts and Monique Caulle; m. 1st Howard Burns 1984 (divorced 1987); m. 2nd Jim Latter 1991 (divorced 2004); two step-s. *Education:* Convent Grammar School, Somerville Coll., Oxford and University Coll. London. *Career:* British Council Librarian, Bangkok 1973–74; Poetry Ed. Spare Rib 1974, City Limits 1981–83; Visiting Fellow Univ. of E Anglia 1992, Univ. of Nottingham Trent 1994; Visiting Prof. Univ. of Nottingham Trent 1996–2001; Prof. of Creative Writing, Univ. of E Anglia 2002–; Chair. Literary Cttee British Council 1998–2002; judge, Booker Prize 2001; mem. Soc. of Authors. *Plays:* The Journeywoman 1988, Child-Lover 1995. *Television film:* The Heavenly Twins (Channel 4) 1993. *Publications include:* novels: A Piece of the Night 1978, The Visitation 1983, The Wild Girl 1984, The Book of Mrs Noah 1987, In the Red Kitchen 1990, Daughters of the House 1992, Flesh and Blood 1994, Impossible Saints 1997, Fair Exchange 1999, The Looking-Glass 2000, The Mistressclass 2003, Reader, I Married Him 2005, Paper Houses (autobiog.) 2007; Mind Readings (co-ed.) 1996; short stories: During Mother's Absence 1993, Playing Sardines 2001; essays: Food, Sex and God 1998; poetry: The Mirror of the Mother 1986; plays: Psyche and the Hurricane 1991, Child Lover 1993, All the Selves I Was 1995. *Honours:* Chevalier, Ordre des Arts et des Lettres 2001; Hon. MA (Nene) 1999; WHSmith Literary Award 1993. *Literary Agent:* Aitken Alexander Associates Ltd, 18–21 Cavaye Place, London, SW10 9PT, England. *Telephone:* (20) 7373-8672. *Fax:* (20) 7373-6002. *E-mail:* reception@aitkenalexander.co.uk. *Website:* www.aitkenalexander.co.uk. *Address:* School of English and American Studies, University of East Anglia, Norwich, Norfolk, NR4 7TJ, England (office).

ROBERTS, Nora, (J. D. Robb); American writer; b. 10 Oct. 1950, Silver Spring, MD. *Career:* mem. Romance Writers of America, Novelists Inc. *Publications:* Irish Thoroughbred 1981, Blithe Images 1982, Song of the West 1982, Search for Love 1982, Island of Flowers 1982, The Heart's Victory 1983, From This Day 1983, Her Mother's Keeper 1983, Reflections 1983, Once More with Feeling 1983, Untamed 1983, Dance of Dreams 1983, Tonight and Always 1983, This Magic Moment 1983, Endings and Beginnings 1984, Storm Warning 1984, Sullivan's Woman 1984, Rules of the Game 1984, Less of a Stranger 1984, A Matter of Choice 1984, The Law is a Lady 1984, First Impressions 1984, Opposites Attract 1984, Promise Me Tomorrow 1984, Partners 1985, The Right Path 1985, Boundary Lines 1985, Summer Desserts 1985, Dual Images 1985, Night Moves 1985, Playing the Odds 1985, Tempting Fate 1985, All the Possibilities 1985, One Man's Art 1985, The Art of Deception 1986, One Summer 1986, Treasures Lost, Treasures Found 1986, Risky Business 1986, Lessons Learned 1986, Second Nature 1986, A Will and a Way 1986, Home for Christmas 1986, Affaire Royale 1986, Mind Over Matter 1987, Temptation 1987, Hot Ice 1987, Sacred Sins 1987, For Now, Forever 1987, Command Performance 1987, The Playboy Prince 1987, Brazen Virtue 1988, Local Hero 1988, Irish Rose 1988, The Name of the Game 1988, Rebellion 1988, The Last Honest Woman 1988, Dance to the Piper 1988, Skin Deep 1988, Sweet Revenge 1989, Loving Jack 1989, Best Laid Plans 1989,

Gabriel's Angel 1989, Lawless 1989, Public Secrets 1990, Taming Natasha 1990, Night Shadow 1991, Genuine Lies 1991, With This Ring 1991, Night Shift 1991, Without a Trace 1991, Luring a Lady 1991, Courting Catherine 1991, A Man for Amanda 1991, For the Love of Lilah 1991, Suzannah's Surrender 1991, Carnal Innocence 1992, Unfinished Business 1992, The Welcoming 1992, Honest Illusions 1992, Divine Evil 1992, Captivated 1992, Entranced 1992, Charmed 1992, Second Nature 1993, Private Scandals 1993, Falling for Rachel 1993, Time Was 1993, Times Change 1993, Boundary Lines 1994, Hidden Riches 1994, Nightshade 1994, The Best Mistake 1994, Night Smoke 1994, Born in Fire 1994, Born in Ice 1995, True Betrayals 1995, Born in Shame 1996, Montana Sky 1996, From the Heart 1997, Sanctuary 1997, Holding the Dream 1997, Daring to Dream 1997, Finding the Dream 1997, The Reef 1998, The Winning Hand 1998, Sea Swept 1998, Homeport 1999, The Perfect Neighbor 1999, Megan's Mate 1999, Enchanted 1999, Rising Tides 1999, Inner Harbor 1999, Carolina Moon 2000, The Villa 2001, Heaven and Earth 2001, Three Fates 2002, Chesapeake Blue 2002, Key of Knowledge 2003, Key of Light 2003, Once Upon a Midnight 2003, Birthright 2003, Remember When 2003, Blue Dahlia 2004, Key of Valor 2004, Northern Lights 2005, Angels Fall 2006, Blue Smoke (Quill Award for Romance) 2006, Heart of the Sea 2007; as J. D. Robb: Only Survivors Tell Tales 1990, Naked in Death 1995, Glory in Death 1995, Rapture in Death 1996, Ceremony in Death 1997, Vengeance in Death 1997, Holiday in Death 1998, Immortal in Death 1998, Silent Night 1998, Loyalty in Death 1999, Conspiracy in Death 1999, Witness in Death 2000, Judgment in Death 2000, Seduction in Death 2001, Out of this World 2001, Betrayal in Death 2001, Reunion in Death 2002, Purity in Death 2002, Imitation in Death 2003, Remember When 2003, Portrait in Death 2003, Once Upon a Midnight 2003, Divided in Death 2004, Visions in Death 2004, Memory in Death 2006, Born in Death 2006, Innocent in Death 2007. *Honours:* various Romance Writers of America Awards, named as one of 100 People Who Shape Our World, Time magazine 2007. *Literary Agent:* Writers' House Inc., 21 W 26th Street, New York, NY 10010, USA. *Telephone:* (212) 685-2400. *Fax:* (212) 685-1781. *E-mail:* write2nora@msn.com. *Website:* www.noraroberts.com.

ROBERTS, Yvonne; British journalist and writer; b. 1949; fmr pnr John Pilger; one d.; pnr Stephen Scott; one d. *Education:* Univ. of Warwick. *Career:* with Weekend World 1970s; writer for New Statesman and New Society magazines (now New Statesman and Society) and Guardian and Independent newspapers. *Publications include:* Man Enough 1984, Mad About Women 1994, Every Woman Deserves an Adventure (novel) 1994, The Trouble with Single Women 1997, A History of Insects 2000, Shake 2004. *Address:* c/o David Higham Associates, 5-8 Lower John Street, Golden Square, London, W1F 9HA; c/o Guardian Newspapers Ltd., 119 Farringdon Road, London, EC1R 3ER, England. *E-mail:* yroberts@dial.pipex.com.

ROBERTSON, Barbara, BA, MA; Canadian writer; b. 20 July 1931, Toronto, ON. *Education:* University of Toronto, Queen's University, Kingston. *Publications:* The Wind Has Wings (ed. with M. A. Downie), 1968, revised edn as The New Wind Has Wings, 1984; Wilfrid Laurier: The Great Conciliator, 1971; The Well-Filled Cupboard (with M. A. Downie), 1987, revised edn as The Canadian Treasury of Cooking and Gardening, 1997; Doctor Dwarf and Other Poems for Children (ed. with M. A. Downie), 1990; Ottawa at War: The Grant Dexter Memoranda 1939–1945 (ed. with F. W. Gibson), 1994. Contributions: periodicals.

ROBERTSON, Denise; British writer and broadcaster; b. 9 June 1933, Sunderland, England; m. 1st Alexander Robertson 1960; m. 2nd John Tomlin 1973, five s. *Publications:* Year of Winter, 1986; Land of Lost Content, 1987; Blue Remembered Hills, 1987; Second Wife, 1988; None to Make You Cry, 1989; Remember the Moment, 1990. Contributions: numerous publications. *Honours:* Constable Fiction Trophy 1985.

ROBERTSON, Geoffrey Ronald, QC, BA, LLB, BCL; Australian judge and lawyer; *Master of the Bench, Middle Temple, London;* b. 30 Sept. 1946, Sydney; s. of Francis Robertson and Bernice Beattie; m. Kathy Lette (q.v.) 1990; one s. one d. *Education:* Epping Boys' High School and Univs of Sydney and Oxford. *Career:* Rhodes scholar; solicitor, Allen, Allen & Hemsley 1970; called to bar, Middle Temple, London 1973; QC 1988; Visiting Prof., Univ. of NSW 1979, Univ. of Warwick 1981; leader, Amnesty missions to S Africa 1983–90; consultant on Human Rights to Govt of Australia 1984; Head, Doughty Street Chambers 1990–; Counsel to Royal Comm. on gun-running to Colombian drug cartels 1991; Asst Recorder 1993–99, a Recorder 1999–; Master of Bench, Middle Temple 1997–; Chief Counsel Comm. on Admin. of Justice in Trinidad and Tobago 2000; Appeal Judge, UN Special Court for War Crimes in Sierra Leone 2002–; Chair. Staff Panel on Reform of UN Justice 2006; mem. Exec. Council Justice. *Radio:* Chair. You the Jury (BBC Radio 4). *Plays:* The Trials of Oz (BBC) 1992. *TV series:* Hypotheticals, Granada TV, ABC and Channel 7 (Australia). *Publications:* Reluctant Judas 1976, Obscenity 1979, People Against the Press 1983, Geoffrey Robertson's Hypotheticals 1986, Does Dracula Have AIDS ? 1987, Freedom, The Individual and The Law 1989, The Justice Game 1998, Crimes Against Humanity 1999, Media Law (with A. Nicol) 2002, The Tyrannical Brief 2005. *Honours:* Hon. LLD (Sydney) 2006; Freedom of Information Award 1992. *Address:* Doughty Street Chambers, 11 Doughty Street, London, WC1N 2PL, England (office). *Telephone:* (20) 7404-1313 (office); (20) 7624-3268 (home). *Fax:* (20) 7404-2283 (office); (20) 7624-7146 (home). *E-mail:* g.robertson@doughtystreet.co.uk (office). *Website:* www.doughtystreet.co.uk (office).

ROBERTSON, James; Scottish writer, editor and publisher; b. 1958. *Career:* founder of pamphlet publisher, Kettillonia 1999–; Gen. Ed. of children's book imprint, Itchy Coo; Writer-in-Residence, Scottish Parliament. *Publications:* Close 1991, The Ragged Man's Complaint 1993, A Tongue in Yer Heid (ed.) 1994, Sound Shadow 1995, I Dream of Alfred Hitchcock 1999, The Fanatic (novel) 2000, Fae the Flouers o Evil: Baudelaire in Scots 2001, Stirling Sonnets 2002, A Scots Parliament 2002, Joseph Knight (novel) (Saltire Soc. Book of the Year 2003, Scottish Arts Council Book of the Year 2004) 2003, Voyages of Intent 2005, The Testament of Gideon Mack (novel) 2006. *Address:* Kettillonia, Sidlaw House, South Street, Newtyle, Angus, PH12 8UQ, Scotland (office). *E-mail:* james@kettillonia.co.uk (office). *Website:* www .scotgeog.com.

ROBERTSON, James Irvin, Jr, BA, MA, PhD, LittD; American academic; b. 18 July 1930, Danville, VA; m. Elizabeth Green 1952; two s. one d. *Education:* Randolph-Macon Coll., Emory Univ., Randolph-Macon Coll. *Career:* Assoc. Prof. of History, University of Montana, 1965–67; Prof. of History, 1967–75, C. P. Miles Prof. of History, 1976–92, Alumni Distinguished Prof. of History, 1992–, Virginia Polytechnic Institute and State University; mem. Virginia Historical Society; Organization of American Historians; Southern Historical Asscn; Confederate Memorial Society. *Publications:* The Stonewall Brigade, 1963; The Civil War Letters of General Robert McAllister, 1965; Recollections of a Maryland Confederate Soldier, 1975; Four Years in the Stonewall Brigade, 1978; The 4th Virginia Infantry, 1980; Civil War Sites in Virginia: A Tour-Guide, 1982; The 18th Virginia Infantry, 1983; Tenting Tonight: The Soldiers' View, 1984; General A. P. Hill, 1987; Soldiers Blue and Gray, 1988; Civil War: America Becomes One Nation, 1992; Jackson and Lee: Legends in Gray (with Mort Kunstler), 1995; Stonewall Jackson: The Man, The Soldier, The Legend, 1997. Contributions: More than 150 articles in historical journals and history magazines; Regular appearances in Civil War programmes on television and radio. *Honours:* Freeman-Nevins Award, 1981; Bruce Catton Award, 1983; William E. Wine Award for Teaching Excellence, 1983; A. P. Andrews Memorial Award, 1985; James Robertson Award of Achievement, 1985. *Address:* Department of History, Virginia Polytechnic Institute and State University, Blacksburg, VA 24061, USA.

ROBINETTE, Joseph Allen, BA, MA, PhD; American fmr academic and playwright; b. 8 Feb. 1939, Rockwood, TN; m. Helen M. Seitz 1965, four s. one d. *Education:* Carson-Newman Coll. and Southern Illinois Univ. *Career:* Prof. in Dept of Theatre and Dance, Rowan Coll.; mem. American Soc. of Composers, Authors and Publishers, American Asscn for Theatre in Education, Opera for Youth. *Publications:* The Fabulous Fable Factory 1975, Once Upon a Shoe (play) 1979, Legend of the Sun Child (musical) 1982, Charlotte's Web (dramatisation) 1983, Charlotte's Web (musical with Charles Strouse) 1989, Anne of Green Gables (dramatisation) 1989, The Lion, the Witch and the Wardrobe (dramatisation) 1989, The Trial of Goldilocks (operetta) 1990, Dorothy Meets Alice (musical) 1991, Stuart Little (dramatisation) 1992, The Trumpet of the Swan (dramatisation) 1993, The Adventures of Beatrix Potter and her Friends (musical) 1994, The Littlest Angel (musical) 1994, The Jungle Book (dramatisation) 1995, The Trial of the Big Bad Wolf (play) 1999, Just So Stories (play) 2001, Humpty-Dumpty is Missing (play) 2001, Sarah, Plain and Tall (American Alliance for Theatre and Educ. Award for Best Play 2004) 2003; contrib. to Children's Theatre News, Opera for Youth News. *Honours:* Charlotte Chorpenning Cup, Nat. Children's Playwriting Award 1976, Lifetime Achievement Award Children's Theatre Foundation of America 2006. *Address:* POB 11, Richwood, NJ 08074, USA (home).

ROBINS, Patricia (see Clark, Patricia Denise)

ROBINSON, David Julien, BA; British film critic, festival director and writer; b. 6 Aug. 1930, England. *Education:* King's Coll., Cambridge. *Career:* Assoc. Ed., Sight and Sound, and Ed., Monthly Film Bulletin 1956–58; Programme Dir, Nat. Film Theatre 1959; film critic, Financial Times 1959–74, The Times 1974–92; Dir, Garrett Robinson Co. 1987–88, The Davids Film Co. 1988–, Channel 4 Young Film-maker of the Year Competition, Edinburgh Film Festival 1992–95, Pordenone Silent Film Festival, Italy 1997–; Guest Dir, Edinburgh Film Festival 1989–91. *Publications:* Hollywood in the Twenties 1969, Buster Keaton 1969, The Great Funnies 1972, World Cinema (aka The History of World Cinema) 1973, Chaplin: The Mirror of Opinion 1983, Chaplin: His Life and Art 1985, The Illustrated History of the Cinema (co-ed.) 1986, Music of the Shadows 1990, Masterpieces of Animation 1833–1908 1991, Richard Attenborough 1992, Georges Méliès 1993, Lantern Images: Iconography of the Magic Lantern 1440–1880 1993, Sight and Sound Chronology of the Cinema 1994–95, Musique et cinema muet 1995, Charlot: Entre rires et larmes 1995, Peepshow to Palace 1995, Light and Image: Incunabula of the Motion Picture (co-author) 1996; contrib. to newspapers and periodicals. *Address:* 19 Lansdown Crescent, Bath, BA1 5EX, England. *Telephone:* (1125) 333391. *E-mail:* robinorama@aol.com.

ROBINSON, Derek, (Dirk Robson), MA; British writer; b. 12 April 1932, Bristol, England; m. Sheila Collins 1968. *Education:* Downing Coll., Cambridge. *Career:* nat. service with RAF; advertising copywriter, London and New York; freelance writer. *Publications:* Goshawk Squadron 1971, Rotten With Honour 1973, Kramer's War 1977, The Eldorado Network 1979, Piece of Cake (also televised as mini-series) 1983, War Story 1987, Artillery of Lies 1991, A Good Clean Fight 1993, Rugby: A Player's Guide to the Laws 1995, Hornet's Sting 1999, Kentucky Blues 2002, Damned Good Show 2002, Invasion 1940 2005, Red Rag Blues 2006. *Literary Agent:* David Higham

Associates, 5–8 Lower John Street, Golden Square, London, W1F 9HA, England.

ROBINSON, Jeffrey, BS; American writer; b. 19 Oct. 1945, New York, NY, USA; m. Aline Benayoun 1985; one s. one d. *Education:* Temple Univ., Philadelphia. *Career:* mem. PEN. *Television, radio and screenplays:* The Laundrymen 1996, Same Time Next Week 2000, Tightrope 2002, Rossum's Cyber Café 2003, Sister Banjo 2003, The Real Amos 'n' Andy 2004, Bardot 2005, Notice of Claim 2005, The Confession 2006, I Je t'Aime You 2006, The Wind Off Drumcliffe Bay 2007. *Publications:* Bette Davis – Her Stage and Film Career 1983, Teamwork 1984, The Risk Takers 1985, Pietrov and Other Games (fiction) 1985, Minus Millionaires 1986, The Ginger Jar (fiction) 1986, Yamani – The Inside Story 1988, Rainier and Grace 1989, The Risk Takers – Five Years On 1990, The End of the American Century 1992, The Laundry-men 1994, Bardot – Two Lives 1994, The Margin of the Bulls (fiction) 1995, The Hotel 1996, The Monk's Disciples (fiction) 1996, The Manipulators 1997, A True and Perfect Knight (fiction) 1998, The Merger 2000, Prescription Games 2001, The Sink 2003, Standing Next to History (with Joseph Petro) 2005; contrib. of more than 700 articles and short stories to major magazines and journals world-wide. *Honours:* Overseas Press Club 1984, Benedictine After Dinner Speaker of the Year 1990. *Literary Agent:* Bell-Lomax Agency, James House, 1 Babmaes Street, London, SW1 6HF, England.

ROBINSON, Kim Stanley, BA, MA, PhD; American author; b. 23 March 1952, Waukegan, IL. *Education:* Univ. of California at San Diego, Boston Univ. *Career:* Visiting Lecturer, Univ. of California at San Diego 1982, 1985, Univ. of California at Davis 1982–84, 1985. *Publications:* Black Air (World Fantasy Award 1983) 1982, Icehenge 1984, The Wild Shore (Locus Award 1985) 1984, The Blind Geometer (novella) (Nebula Award for Best Novella 1986) 1985, The Memory of Whiteness 1985, The Planet on the Table (short stories) 1986, Escape from Kathmandu (short stories) 1987, The Gold Coast 1988, Pacific Edge (John W. Campbell Memorial Award for Best Science Fiction Novel 1991) 1990, A Short, Sharp Shock (Locus Award 1991) 1990, Remaking History (short stories) 1991, Red Mars (Nebula Award for Best Novel 1993) 1992, Green Mars (Hugo Award for Best Novel 1994, Locus Award 1994) 1993, Blue Mars (Hugo Award for Best Novel 1997, Locus Award 1997) 1996, Antarctica 1997, Martians (Locus Award 2000) 1999, Vinland the Dream 2002, The Years of Rice and Salt (Locus Award 2003) 2002, Forty Signs of Rain 2004, Fifty Degrees Below 2005, Sixty Days and Counting 2007; other: Future Primitive (ed.) 1982, The Novels of Philip K. Dick 1984, Nebula Awards Showcase (ed.) 2002; contrib. to periodicals and anthologies. *Address:* 17811 Romelle Avenue, Santa Ana, CA 92705, USA.

ROBINSON, Marilynne, PhD; American novelist and essayist; b. 1947, Sandpoint, ID; d. of John J. Summers and Ellen Harris Summers; m.; two s. *Education:* Coeur d'Alene High School, Brown Univ., Univ. of Washington. *Career:* taught at Univ. de Haute Bretagne, Rennes, France 1966–67; writer-in-residence and visiting prof. at numerous colls and univs, including Univ. of Kent, England, Amherst Coll., Univ. of Massachusetts, Skidmore Coll.; mem. of faculty Writers' Workshop 1991–, Univ. of Iowa. *Publications:* House-keeping (novel) (PEN/Hemingway Foundation Award for Best First Novel, Richard and Hilda Rosenthal Award) 1980, Mother Country: Britain, the Welfare State and Nuclear Pollution (non-fiction) 1988, The Death of Adam: Essays on Modern Thought 1998, Puritans and Prigs (non-fiction) 1999, Gilead (fiction) (Nat. Book Critics Circle Award, Pulitzer Prize for Fiction 2005) 2004; contrib. essays and book reviews to Harper's, Paris Review, The New York Times Book Review. *Address:* c/o Virago Press, Brettenham House, Lancaster Place, London, WC2E 7EN, England.

ROBINSON, Nick; British journalist; *Political Editor, BBC*; b. 1963, Macclesfield, Cheshire. *Education:* Cheadle Hulme School, Univ. Coll., Oxford. *Career:* trainee producer on programmes, including Brass Tacks, Newsround, Crimewatch 1986, then Deputy Ed. On the Record, Panorama; fmr presenter Late Night Live and Weekend Breakfast (both on BBC Radio Five Live), Westminster Live (BBC 2); fmr Chief Political Corresp., BBC News 24, presenting Straight Talk and One to One –2002; Political Ed. ITV News 2002–05; columnist of political 'Notebook' in The Times 2003–; Political Ed. BBC 2005–. *Address:* BBC Westminster, 4 Millbank, London, SW1P 3JA, England (office). *Website:* www.bbc.co.uk/nickrobinson (office).

ROBINSON, Robert Henry, MA; British writer and broadcaster; b. 17 Dec. 1927, Liverpool, England; m. Josephine Mary Richard 1958; one s. two d. *Education:* Exeter Coll., Oxford. *Publications:* Landscape With Dead Dons 1956, Inside Robert Robinson 1965, The Conspiracy 1968, The Dog Chairman 1982, Everyman Book of Light Verse (ed.) 1984, Bad Dreams 1989, Prescriptions of a Pox Doctor's Clerk 1991, Skip All That: Memoirs 1996, The Club 2000; contrib. to newspapers, radio and television. *Literary Agent:* Curtis Brown Ltd, Haymarket House, 28–29 Haymarket, London, SW1Y 4SP, England. *Telephone:* (20) 7393-4400. *Fax:* (20) 7393-4401. *E-mail:* info@curtisbrown.co.uk. *Website:* www.curtisbrown.co.uk. *Address:* 16 Cheyne Row, London, SW3, England.

ROBINSON, Sheila Mary, (Sheila Radley, Hester Rowan), BA; British writer; b. 18 Nov. 1928, Cogenhoe, Northamptonshire, England. *Education:* University of London. *Publications:* Overture in Venice, 1976; The Linden Tree, 1977; Death and the Maiden, 1978; Snowfall, 1978; The Chief Inspector's Daughter, 1981; A Talent for Destruction, 1982; Blood on the Happy Highway, 1983; Fate Worse Than Death, 1985; Who Saw Him Die?, 1987; This Way Out,

1989; Cross My Heart and Hope to Die, 1992; Fair Game, 1994; New Blood from Old Bones, 1998.

ROBINSON, Spider, BA; American writer; b. 24 Nov. 1948, New York, NY. *Education:* SUNY at Stony Brook. *Career:* Writer-in-Residence, H.R. MacMillan Space Centre, Vancouver, BC 2006. *Publications:* Telempath (Hugo Award for Best Novella 1976) 1976, Callahan's Crosstime Saloon (American Library Asscn Best Book for Young Adults 1977) 1977, Stardance (with Jeanne Robinson) (Hugo Award for Best Novella 1977, Nebula Award for Best Novella 1977, Locus Award for Best Novella 1977) 1979, Antinomy 1980, Time Travelers Strictly Cash 1981, Mindkiller 1982, Melancholy Elephants 1984, Night of Power 1985, Callahan's Secret 1986, Time Pressure 1987, Callahan and Company 1988, Callahan's Lady 1989, Copyright Violation (novella) 1990, True Minds 1990, Starseed (with Jeanne Robinson) 1991, Kill the Editor (novella) 1991, Lady Slings the Booze 1992, The Callahan Touch 1993, Off the Wall at Callahan's 1994, Starmind 1994, Callahan's Legacy 1996, Lifehouse 1997, User Friendly 1998, Callahan's Key 2001, The Free Lunch 2001, By Any Other Name 2001, God is an Iron and Other Stories 2002, Callahan's Con 2003, The Crazy Years (non-fiction) 2004, Very Bad Deaths 2004, Variable Star (with Robert A. Heinlein) 2006. *Honours:* John W. Campbell Award for Best New Writer 1974, Locus Award for Best Critic 1976, Sydney (Australia) Science Fiction Foundation Pat Terry Memorial Award for Humorous Writing 1977, New England Science Fiction Asscn E.E. Smith Memorial Award for Speculative Fiction 1977, Hugo Award for Best Short Story (for Melancholy Elephants) 1983, Canada Council for the Arts grants 1983, 1984, 1986, 1989, 1992, Nova Scotia Dept of Culture, Recreation & Fitness grants 1983, 1986, BC Ministry of Municipal Affairs, Recreation & Culture grant 1991. *Literary Agent:* c/o Eleanor Wood, Spectrum Literary Agency, 320 Central Park West, Suite 1-D, New York, NY 10025, USA. *E-mail:* spiderweb@shaw.ca. *Website:* www.spiderrobinson.com.

ROBSKI, Oksana; Russian author. *Career:* chat show host. *Publications:* titles in translation: Casual (novel) 2005, Pro Liuboff/on 2005, The Rich Russian's Guide to Sex, Shopping, and Revenge: A Novel.

ROBSON, Dirk (see Robinson, Derek)

ROCHE, William (Billy) Michael; Irish playwright and author; b. 11 Jan. 1949, Wexford. *Career:* singer, The Roach Band 1975–80; playwright-in-residence, Bush Theatre, London 1988; Writer in Asscn with Druid Theatre, Galway 1997, The Abbey Theatre, Dublin 2000. *Publications:* plays: A Handful of Stars 1987, Amphibians 1987, Poor Beast in the Rain 1989, Belfry 1991, The Cavalcaders 1993, On Such As We 2001; other: Tumbling Down (novel) 1986, Trojan Eddie (film script) 1997, Tales from Rain Water Pond 2006. *Honours:* London Theatre Fringe Award 1992, Time Out Award 1992, San Sebastian Film Festival Prize for Trojan Eddie 1997. *Address:* 44 Pineridge, Clonard, Wexford, Ireland.

ROCHE, Denis; French writer, photographer and editor. *Career:* Dir Tel Quel magazine 1962–72; Literary Dir Editions Tchou 1964–70; worked for Editions du Seuil 1971, later as mem. editorial cttee and directing Les Contemporains imprint, cr. Fiction & Cie imprint 1974–; co-f. Les Cahiers de la Photographie publisher 1980–; began exhibiting photographs 1978–. *Photography exhibitions:* solo: Galerie l'oeil, Chateauroux 2000 1978, Canon Photo Galerie, Geneva, Switzerland 1979, Galerie Déclinaisons, Rouen 1980, Centre Culturel franco-italien, Turin, Italy, Inst. Supérieur pour l'étude du langage plastique, Brussels, Belgium 1981, Menées photographiques, Galerie J. et J. Donguy, Paris 1985, Galerie Images Nouvelles, Bordeaux 1986, Musée d'Art moderne, Vienna, Austria, Fulton Co. Public Library, Atlanta, USA, Frankfurter Kunstverein, Germany 1987, Musée de Tijuana, Mexico, Musée d'Art Moderne de Mexico, L'Art des circonstances, Centre culturel français, Cairo, Egypt 1988, Le Mas de l'enfant, Barbentane, Arles, Espace photographique de Paris 1989, Galerie Le Réverbère, Lyon, Artothèque Grand Place, Grenoble 1990, Galerie Maeght, Paris 1991, Alliance française, Lima, Peru, Galerie municipale du Château d'Eau, Toulouse 1992, Artothèque, Vitré 1994, Centre régional de la photographie Nord-Pas-de-Calais, Douchy-les-Mines, Galerie Zeit-Foto Salon, Tokyo, Japan 1995, Il n'y a pas de leçon des Ténèbres, Galerie Le Réverbère, Lyon 1996, Saint-Gervais, Geneva, Switzerland, Galerie J. et J. Donguy, Paris, Encontros da Imagem, Braga, Portugal 1997, Galerie Archi typographies, Bordeaux 1997, Univ. Saint-Esprit de Kaslik, Beirut, Lebanon 1998, Florence ilenri – Denis Roche, Rencontres Int. de la Photographie, Arles 1999, Centre culturel français, Damascus, Syria 2000, Hôpitaux universitaires Belle-Idée, Geneva, Switzerland, La question que je pose, Galerie Le Réverbère, Lyon 2001, Les preuves du temps Musée Nicéphore Niepee, Chalon-sur-Saône, Maison européenne de la photographie, Paris; numerous jt exhbns. *Publications:* Forestière Amazonide 1962, Récits complets 1963, Les Idées centésimales de Miss Elanize 1964, Eros énergumène 1968, Carnac, ou les mésaventures de la narration 1969, 3 Pourrissements poétiques 1972, Le Mécrit 1972, Louve basse 1972, Notre antéfixe 1978, Antéfixe de Françoise Peyrot 1978, Dépôts de savoir et de technique 1980, A quoi sert le lynx? A rien, comme Mozart 1980, Légendes de Denis Roche 1981, La Disparition des lucioles 1982, Conversations avec le temps 1985, A Varèse 1986, Ecrits momentanés chroniques photo du magazine City 1984–87 1988, Photoalies 1988, Prose au devant d'une femme 1988, Lettre ouverte à quelques amis et à un certain nombre de jean-foutres 1988, L'Hexaméron (co-author) 1990, Ellipse et laps 1991, Dans la Maison du Sphinx 1992, La Poésie est inadmissible 1995, L'Embarquement pour Mercure (with Michel Butor) 1996, Le Boîtier de mélancolie, la photographie en 100 photographies (ed.)

(Prix André Malraux) 1999. *Honours:* Grand Prix de Photographie de la Ville de Paris 1997. *Address:* c/o Editions du Seuil, 27 rue Jacob, 75006 Paris, France.

ROCHE, Terry (see Poole, Margaret Barbara)

RODDY, Lee, AA; American writer; b. 22 Aug. 1921, Marion County, IL; m. Cicely Price 1947, one s. one d. *Education:* Los Angeles City College. *Career:* mem. Authors' Guild of America; Authors League; National Society of Children's Book Writers. *Publications:* The Life and Times of Grizzly Adams, 1977; The Lincoln Conspiracy, 1977; Jesus, 1979; Ghost Dog of Stoney Ridge, 1985; Dooger, Grasshopper Hound, 1985; The City Bear's Adventures, 1985; The Hair Pulling Bear Dog, 1985; Secret of the Shark Pit, 1988; Secret of the Sunken Sub, 1989; The Overland Escape, 1989; The Desperate Search, 1989; Danger on Thunder Mountain, 1990; Secret of the Howland Cave, 1990; The Flaming Trap, 1990; Mystery of the Phantom Gold, 1991; The Gold Train Bandits, 1992. Other: several books made into films and television programmes.

RODGERS, Carolyn Marie, BA, MA; American writer, poet, editor and academic; b. 14 Dec. 1942, Chicago, IL. *Education:* Roosevelt Univ., Univ. of Chicago. *Career:* Prof. of Afro-American Literature 1969, Lecturer in English and Co-ordinator of Poetry Workshop 1970, Columbia Coll.; poet-in-residence, Univ. of Washington 1970, Indiana Univ. 1974, Roosevelt Univ. 1983; Founder-Ed., Eden Press 1991, Rare Form newsletter 1994–; Ed., Anthology 1998–2004; Lecturer, Harold Washington Coll.; mem. Gwendolyn Brooks Writing Workshop, Organization of Black American Culture. *Performances* Lincoln Center Inst., New York 2004–05. *Publications:* Paper Soul 1968, Songs of a Blackbird 1970, How I Got Ovah 1976, The Heart as Evergreen 1978, Translation 1980, A Little Lower Than the Angels 1984, Morning Glory 1989, The Religious Poetry of Carolyn M. Rodgers 1993, Daughters of Africa 1993, We're Only Human 1994, Broadsides 1995, A Train Called Judah 1996, Chosen to Believe 1996, Salt: The Salt of the Earth 1999, Windows in Heaven 2005, I Know I've Been Changed 2005; contrib. to journals and magazines. *Honours:* Nat. Endowment for the Arts Award 1970, Conrad Kent Rivers Award 1970, Soc. of Midland Authors Award 1970, Carnegie Writer's Grant 1980, Television Gospel Tribute 1982, PEN grant 1987. *E-mail:* imanijua@aol .com. *Address:* PO Box 804271, Chicago, IL 60680, USA (office). *Telephone:* (773) 484-6167 (office).

RODGERS, Mary Columbro, MA, PhD; American university chancellor and writer; b. 17 April 1925, Autora, OH; d. of Nicola and Nancy (née DeNicola) Columbro; m. Daniel Richard Rodgers 1965; two d. one s. *Education:* Notre Dame Coll., Western Reserve Univ. and Ohio State Univ. *Career:* English teacher, Cleveland, OH 1945–62; Supervisor Ohio State Univ. 1962–64; Asst Prof. of English Univ. of Maryland 1965–66; Assoc. Prof. Trinity Coll. 1967–68; Prof. of English, DC Teachers' Coll. 1968–; Chancellor and Dean American Open Univ. 1965–; Pres. Maryland Nat. Univ. 1972–; Ind. Researcher 2002–; Fellow Catholic Scholars; mem. Poetry Soc. of America, Nat. Council of English Teachers, American Educational Research Asscn. *Publications include:* A Short Course in English Compositions 1976, Chap-book of Children's Literature 1977, Essays and Poems on Life and Literature 1979, Modes and Models: Four Lessons for Young Writers 1981, Open University Structures and Adult Learning 1982, English Pedagogy in the American Open University 1983, Design for Personalized Graduate Degrees in the Urban University 1984, Poet and Pedagogue in Moscow and Leningrad: a travel report 1989, Twelve Lectures in Literary Analysis 1990, Ten Lectures in Literary Production 1990, Analyzing Fact and Fiction 1991, Analyzing Poetry and Drama 1991, A Chapbook of Poetry and Drama Analysis 1992, Convent Poems 1943–61 1993, Catholic Marriage Poems 1962–79 1993, New Design Responses 1945–93 (10 vols) 1993, Catholic Widow with Children Poems 1979–93 1994, Journals: Reflections and Resolves 1984–95 (16 vols) 1995, Biographical Sourcebook: Mary Columbro Rodgers 1969–95 1995, Catholic Teacher Poems 1945–95 1995. *Honours:* Hon. DipEd (California Nat. Open) 1975, Hon. DLitt (California Nat. Open) 1978. *Address:* College Heights Estate, 3916 Commander Drive, Hyattsville, MD 20782, USA.

RODOLPH, Utto (see Ouologuem, Yambo)

RODRIGUES, Louis Jerome, BA, MA, MPhil, PhD; writer, poet and translator; b. 20 July 1938, Chennai, India; m. 1st Malinda Weaving (deceased); one s.; m. 2nd Josefina Bernet Soler 1984; one s. *Education:* University of Chennai, University of London, University of Barcelona. *Career:* Asst Dir, Benedict, Mannheim, 1977; Dir of Studies, Inlingua, Barcelona, 1978–82; Dir, Phoenix, Barcelona, 1982–87; mem. International Asscn of Anglo-Saxonists; RSL; Society of Authors, exec. committee mem., 1988–91, 2003–06; Trans. Asscn; American Literary Trans. Asscn. *Publications:* A Long Time Waiting, 1979; Anglo-Saxon Riddles, 1990; Seven Anglo-Saxon Elegies, 1991; Chiaroscuro, 1991; The Battles of Maldon and Brunanburh, 1991; Anglo-Saxon Verse Runes, 1992; Anglo-Saxon Verse Charms, Maxims and Heroic Legends, 1993; Anglo-Saxon Elegiac Verse, 1994; Anglo-Saxon Didactic Verse, 1995; Three Anglo-Saxon Battle Poems, 1995; Salvador Espriu: Selected Poems (trans.), 1997; Beowulf and the Fight at Finnsburh, Buttercups and Daisies 2006; contrib. to various publications. *Honours:* Poetry Trans. Prize, Catholic University of America, Washington, DC, 1993. *Address:* 132 Wisbech Road, Littleport, Ely, Cambridgeshire CB6 1JJ, England. *E-mail:* louis.rodrigues@ntlworld.com. *Website:* www .louisrodrigues.co.uk.

RODRIGUEZ, Judith Catherine, AM, BA, MA; Australian retd poet, dramatist, librettist, editor and lecturer; b. 13 Feb. 1936, Perth, WA; m. 1st Fabio Rodriguez 1964 (divorced 1981); four c.; m. 2nd Thomas Shapcott 1982. *Education:* Univ. of Queensland, Brisbane, Girton Coll., Cambridge, Univ. of London. *Career:* Lecturer in External Studies, Univ. of Queensland, Brisbane 1959–60; Lecturer in English, Philippa Fawcett Coll. of Education, London 1962–63, Univ. of the West Indies, Jamaica 1963–65, St Mary's Coll. of Education, Twickenham 1966–68, Macarthur Inst. of Higher Education, Milperra, Sydney 1987–88; Lecturer in Professional Writing, Royal Melbourne Inst. of Technology 1988–89, Victoria Coll. 1989–92; teacher of English as a foreign language, St Giles School of English, London 1965–66; Lecturer 1969–75, Sr Lecturer in English 1977–85, La Trobe Univ., Bundoora, Australia; writer-in-residence, Rollins Coll., FL, USA 1986; Sr Lecturer in Professional Writing, Deakin Univ. 1993–2003; Visiting Fellow, Univ. of Madras 2000–04; mem. Australian Soc. of Authors, Melbourne PEN Centre, Victorian Writer's Centre, Melbourne Shakespeare Soc. *Publications:* poetry: Four Poets 1962, Nu-Plastik Fanfare Red 1973, Water Life 1976, Shadow on Glass 1978, Mudcrab at Gambaro's 1980, Witch Heart 1982, Floridian Poems 1986, The House By Water: New and Selected Poems 1988, The Cold 1992, Terror: Poems 2002; play: Poor Johanna (with Robyn Archer) 1994; opera libretto: Lindy 1994; editor: Mrs Noah and the Minoan Queen 1982, Poems Selected from the Australian's 20th Anniversary Competition (with Andrew Taylor) 1985, Modern Swedish Poetry (with Thomas Shapcott) 1985, Collected Poems of Jennifer Rankin 1990; contrib. to numerous publications. *Honours:* Arts Council of Australia Fellowships 1974, 1978, 1983, Government of South Australia Biennial Prize for Literature 1978, Int. PEN Peter Stuyvesant Prize for Poetry 1981, Fellowship of Australian Writers Christopher Brennan Award 1994. *Address:* PO Box 231, Mont Albert, Vic. 3127, Australia (home). *Telephone:* (613) 9898-7889 (home). *Fax:* (613) 9898-7889 (home). *E-mail:* rodju@tpg.com.au (home).

RODRIGUEZ, Luis J.; American poet and writer; b. 1954, El Paso, TX. *Career:* regular speaker and poet at nat. conferences and cultural centres; founder, Tia Chucha Press. *Publications include:* poetry: The Concrete River 1991, Poems Across the Pavement 1993, Trochemoche 1998; How to Make Sure Your Child Behaves 2000, Music of the Mill 2004; short story collections: The Republic of East L.A. 2003; juvenile: La llaman América (trans. as America is her Name) 1998, It Doesn't Have to be This Way 1999; memoirs: Always Running: La Vida Loca: Gang Days in L.A. 1995; contrib. to The Nation, Los Angeles Weekly, America's Review. *Honours:* Carl Sandburg Award for Non-Fiction, Poetry Center Book Award from San Francisco State Univ., PEN Oakland/Josephine Miles Award for Poetry 1991, Skiping Stones Award, Paterson Prize for Books for Young People, Hispanic Heritage Award for Excellence in Literature 1998. *Literary Agent:* Steven Barclay Agency, 12 Western Avenue, Petaluma, CA 94952, USA. *Telephone:* (707) 773-0654. *Fax:* (707) 778-1868. *Website:* www.barclayagency.com.

RODRÍGUEZ RODRÍGUEZ, Martha; Mexican poet; b. 20 Oct. 1939, Chihuahua. *Education:* studies in accountancy. *Career:* made a record 1990. *Honours:* numerous awards for poetry, including Golden Rose Award, Ciudad Juárez 1971, Silver Medal and First Prize for poem El Campesino 1984. *Address:* Calle Colima 415, Departamento 1303, Col Condesa, México, DF 06700, Mexico. *Telephone:* (5) 2112149. *Fax:* (5) 2112149.

RODRIQUEZ, Isaias, PhD; Venezuelan lawyer, poet and politician. *Education:* Univs of Santa Maria and Zulia and Cen. Univ. of Venezuela. *Career:* legal adviser to Ministry of Agric. 1969; consultant to Veterinary Asscn 1971–; Attorney-Gen.; Chief Attorney of Aragua 1990–91; Prof. of Univ. of Carabobo, Vice-Pres. of the Nat. Ass.; Vice-Pres. of Venezuela 1998–2000; regular columnist for El Siglo. *Publications:* legal: New Labour Procedures 1987, Legal Stability in Labour Laws 1993; poetry: Pozo de cabrillas, Con las aspas de todos los molinos, Los tiempos de la sed; contrib. numerous articles. *Address:* Congreso Nacional, Caracas, Venezuela (office).

ROEBUCK, Derek, MA, MCom; British lawyer and writer; b. 22 Jan. 1935, Stalybridge, England; m. Susanna Leonie Hoe 1981; two s. one d. *Education:* Univ. of Oxford, Victoria Univ. of Wellington, NZ. *Career:* mem. Selden Soc. *Publications include:* Credit and Security in Asia (10 vols, with D. E. Allan and M. E. Hiscock) 1973–80, Whores of War: Mercenaries Today (with Wilfred Burchett) 1976, The Background of the Common Law (second edn) 1990, Hong Kong Digest of Contract 1995, Hong Kong Digest of Criminal Law (three vols) 1995–96, Hong Kong Digest of Criminal Procedure (three vols) 1996–97, The Taking of Hong Kong: Charles and Clara Elliot in China Waters (with Susanna Hoe) 1999, A Miscellany of Disputes 2000, Ancient Greek Arbitration 2001, The Charitable Arbitrator: How to Mediate and Arbitrate in Louis XIV's France 2002, Roman Arbitration (with Bruno de Loynes de Fumichon) 2004; contrib. to more than 50 articles on law, history and language. *Address:* 20A Plantation Road, Oxford, OX2 6JD, England.

ROGERS, Evelyn, (Keller Graves), BA, MA; American writer and teacher; b. 30 Aug. 1935, Mobile, AL; m. Jay Rogers 1957, two c. *Education:* North Texas State University, Our Lady of the Lake University. *Career:* mem. Romance Writers of America; National Society of Arts and Letters; Novelists Inc; San Antonio Romance Authors; Opera Guild of San Antonio. *Publications:* Brazen Embrace (co-author) 1987; Rapture's Gamble (co-author) 1987; Desire's Fury (co-author) 1988; Velvet Vixen (co-author) 1988; Lawman's Lady (co-author) 1988; Midnight Sins, 1989; Texas Kiss, 1989; Wanton Slave, 1990; A Love So Wild, 1991; Surrender to the Night, 1991; Sweet Texas Magic, 1992; Desert

Fire, 1992; Desert Heat, 1993; Flame, 1994; Raven, 1995; Angel, 1995; Wicked, 1996; The Forever Bride, 1997; Betrayal, 1997; Hot Temper, 1997; Texas Empires: Crown of Glory, 1998; Golden Man, 1999; Lone Star, 1999; Second Opinion, 1999; Longhorn, 2000; Devil in the Dark, 2001; The Loner, 2001; The Grotto, 2002; The Ghost of Carnal Cove, 2002, Dark of the Moon 2003. Novellas: Cactus and Thistle, 1991; A Christmas Wagon, 1993; Always Paradise, 1994; Gentle Rain, 1995; The Gold Digger, 1997; Something Borrowed, 2000. *Honours:* Prism Award for Best Light Paranormal Novel, Romance Writers of America, Fantasy, Futuristic and Paranormal Chapter, 1997; Texas Gold Award, East Texas Romance Writers of America. *Literary Agent:* Evan Marshall Agency, 6 Tristan Place, Pine Brook, NJ 07058-9445, USA. *Address:* 2722 Belvoir Drive, San Antonio, TX 78230, USA (home).

ROGERS, Floyd (see Spence, William John Duncan)

ROGERS, Ingrid, PhD; German teacher and writer; b. 3 May 1951, Rinteln; m. H. Kendall Rogers 1972, one s. one d. *Education:* DUEL, Sorbonne Nouvelle, Paris, Univ. of Oxford, Philipps Univ., Marburg, Dr of Ministry Bethany Theological Seminary. *Publications:* Tennessee Williams: A Moralist's Answer to the Perils of Life, 1976; Peace Be Unto You, 1983; Swords into Plowshares, 1983; In Search of Refuge, 1984; Glimpses of Clima, 1989; Recollections of East Germany, 1996. *Honours:* Christopher Book Award 1985, Angel Award of Excellence 1985.

ROGERS, Jane Rosalind, BA, PGCE, FRSL; British writer and academic; *Professor of Writing, Sheffield Hallam University;* b. 21 July 1952, London, England; m. Michael Harris 1981; one s. one d. *Education:* New Hall, Cambridge, Univ. of Leicester. *Career:* novelist and radio dramatist; Writer-in-Residence, Northern Coll., Barnsley, S Yorkshire 1985–86, Sheffield Polytechnic 1987–88; Judith E. Wilson Fellow, Cambridge 1991; tutor for MA in writing, Sheffield Hallam Univ. 1994–; mem. Soc. of Authors. *Radio:* Shirley (BBC Radio 4, drama serial) 2002, Island (BBC Radio 4 play) 2002, The Inland Sea (BBC Radio 4) 2005, Lorna Doone (BBC Radio 4) 2005, The Bottle Factory Outing (adaptation, BBC Radio 4) 2006. *Television:* Dawn and the Candidate (Channel 4) 1989, Mr Wroe's Virgins (BBC 2). *Publications:* novels: Separate Tracks 1983, Her Living Image 1984, The Ice is Singing 1987, Mr Wroe's Virgins (also scripted BBC TV serial) 1991, Promised Lands 1995, Island 1999, The Voyage Home 2004; other: Dawn and the Candidate (screenplay) 1989, OUP Good Fiction Guide (ed.) 2001, Ellipsis 2 (short stories) 2006; contrib. to magazines. *Honours:* North West Arts Writers Bursary 1985, Somerset Maugham Award 1985, Samuel Beckett Award 1990, Writers' Guild Award for Best Fiction Book 1996, Arts Council Writers' Bursary 1996, ACE Overseas Writers' Fellowship 2006. *Literary Agent:* c/o Pat Kavanagh, PFD, Drury House, 34–43 Russell Street, London, WC2B 5HA; c/o Norman North, The Agency (London) Ltd, 24 Pottery Lane, Holland Park, London, W11 4LZ, England. *Telephone:* (20) 7344-1000 (PFD); (20) 7727-1346 (The Agency). *Fax:* (20) 7836-9539 (PFD); (20) 7727-9037 (The Agency). *E-mail:* pkavanagh@pfd.co.uk; nnorth@theagency.co.uk. *Website:* www.pfd.co .uk; www.theagency.co.uk. *E-mail:* jane.rogers@btinternet.com (home). *Website:* www.janerogers.org.

ROGERS, Linda Hall, MA; Canadian poet, writer and lecturer; b. 10 Oct. 1944, Port Alice, BC; m. Rick Van Krugel; three s. *Education:* Univ. of British Columbia. *Career:* Lecturer, Univ. of British Columbia, Univ. of Victoria, Camosun Coll., Malaspina Coll.; currently cultural columnist, Focus Magazine; mem. Federation of British Columbia Writers (pres.), League of Canadian Poets, Soc. of Canadian Composers, Writers' Union of Canada, York Univ. Writers in Electronic Residence. *Television:* host, Bookshelf. *Publications:* Some Breath 1978, Queens of the Next Hot Star 1981, I Like to Make a Mess 1985, Witness 1985, Singing Rib 1987, Worm Sandwich 1989, The Magic Flute 1990, Brown Bag Blues 1991, Letters from the Doll Hospital 1992, Hard Candy 1994, The Half Life of Radium 1994, Frankie Zapper and the Disappearing Teacher 1994, Molly Brown is Not a Clown 1996, Love in the Rainforest (selected poems) 1996, Heaven Cake 1997, The Saning 1999, The Broad Canvas: Portraits of Women Artists (non-fiction) 1999, Say My Name (novel) 2000, Rehearsing the Miracle (poems) 2001, P. K. Page: Essays on her Work (ed.) 2001, Al Purdy: Essays on his Work (ed.) 2002, Bill Bissett: Essays on his Work (ed.) 2002, The Bursting Test (poems), Friday Water (fiction) 2003; contrib. to journals, magazines and newspapers. *Honours:* Aya Poetry Prize 1983, Canada Council Arts Awards 1987, 1990, British Columbia Writers Poetry Prize 1989, Cultural Services Award 1990, Alcuin Awards 1991, 2002, Gov.-Gen.'s Centennial Medal for Poetry and Performance 1993, Stephen Leacock Awards for Poetry 1994, 1996, Dorothy Livesay Award for Poetry 1995, Voices Israel Poetry Award 1995, People's Poetry Award 1996, Acorn Rukeyser Award 1999, Cardiff Poetry Prizes 1999, 2001, Canada's People's Poet 2000, Bridport Poetry Prize (UK) 2000, Millennium Award 2000, Prix Anglais (France) 2000, Petra Kenny Award 2001, Monday Award 2004, Arc Poetry Prize 2004. *Address:* 1235 Styles Street, Victoria, BC V9A 3Z6, Canada (home). *Telephone:* (250) 386-8066 (home). *E-mail:* lrogers@ pacificoast.net.

ROGERS, Michael Alan, BA; American journalist, editor and writer; b. 29 Nov. 1950, Santa Monica, CA; m. Donna Rini 2000. *Education:* Stanford University. *Career:* Assoc. Ed., Rolling Stone Magazine, San Francisco, 1972–76; Ed.-at-Large, Outside magazine, San Francisco, 1976–78; Visiting Lecturer in Fiction, University of California at Davis, 1980; Senior Writer, Newsweek magazine, 1983–; Man. Ed., Newsweek InterActive, 1993–97; Exec. Prod., Broadband Division, Washington Post Co, 1995–96; Vice-Pres.,

Washingtonpost.Newsweek Interactive, 1996–; Ed. and Gen. Man., Newsweek.MSNBC.com, 1998–; mem. Authors' Guild; Sierra Club. *Publications:* Mindfogger, 1973; Biohazard, 1977; Do Not Worry About the Bear, 1979; Silicon Valley, 1982; Forbidden Sequence, 1988. Contributions: newspapers and magazines. *Honours:* Distinguished Science Writing Award, American Asscn for the Advancement of Science, 1976; Best Feature Articles Award, Computer Press Asscn, 1987.

ROGERS, Pat, BA, MA, PhD, LittD; British academic and writer; b. 17 March 1938, Beverley, Yorkshire, England. *Education:* Fitzwilliam Coll., Cambridge. *Career:* Fellow, Sidney Sussex Coll., Cambridge 1964–69; Lecturer, King's Coll., London 1969–73; Prof. of English, Univ. Coll. of North Wales, Bangor 1973–76; Univ. of Bristol 1977–86; DeBartolo Chair of the Humanities, Univ. of South Florida, Tampa 1986–. *Publications:* Daniel Defoe: A Tour Through Great Britain 1971, Grub Street: Studies on a Sub-culture (aka Hacks and Dunces) 1972, Daniel Defoe: The Critical Heritage (ed.) 1972, The Augustan Vision: An Introduction to Pope 1976, The Eighteenth Century (ed.) 1978, Henry Fielding: A Biography 1979, Swift: Complete Poems, Literature and Popular Culture in the Eighteenth Century (ed.) 1983, Eighteenth-Century Encounters 1985, The Oxford Illustrated History of English Literature (ed.) 1987, The Economy of Arts in the 18th Century 1989, An Outline of English Literature 1992, Essays on Pope 1993, Johnson and Boswell in Scotland 1993, The Alexander Pope Encyclopedia 2004. *Address:* Department of English, University of South Florida, Tampa, FL 33620, USA.

ROGERS, Rosemary, (Marina Mayson), BA; American writer; b. 7 Dec. 1932, Sri Lanka; m. 1st Summa Navaratnam 1953 (divorced); two s. two d.; m. 2nd Leroy Rogers 1957 (divorced 1964); m. 3rd Christopher M. Kadison 1984. *Career:* mem. Writers Guild of America, Authors' Guild. *Publications:* Sweet Savage Love, 1974; Wildest Heart, 1974; Dark Fires, 1975; Wicked Loving Lies, 1976; The Crowd Pleasers, 1978; The Insiders, 1979; Lost Love, Last Love, 1980; Love Play, 1981; Surrender to Love, 1982; The Wanton, 1984; Bound by Desire, 1988. Contributions: Star Magazine; Good Housekeeping.

ROGNET, Richard; French poet; b. 5 Nov. 1942, Val d'Ajol. *Education:* Ecole Normale d'Instituteurs de Mirecourt, Fac de Lettres, Nancy and Académie Mallarmé. *Career:* teacher 1969–. *Publications include:* (first vol. of poems) 1966, L'Épouse émiettée (Prix Charles-Vildrac) 1978, Petits poèmes en fraude 1980, Recours á l'abandon 1992, Dérive du voyageur (Prix Théophile Gautier 2004) 2003. *Honours:* Prix Louise-Labé 1985, Prix Max-Jacob 1989, Prix Théophile Gautier 1993, Prix Apollinaire 1997, Prix Louis-Montalte 1998, Grand Prix de Poésie de la Société des Gens de Lettres 2002, Prix Alain Bosquet 2005; Chevalier, Ordre des Arts et des Lettres 1994, Chevalier, Ordre des Palmes Académiques 1996. *Address:* c/o Éditions Gallimard, 5 rue Sébastien-Bottin, 75328 Paris, Cédex 07, France.

ROHAN, Michael Scott, (Mike Scott Rohan, Michael Scot), MA; British writer and editor; b. 22 Jan. 1951, Edinburgh, Scotland; m. Deborah Rohan. *Education:* University of Oxford. *Publications:* The Hammer and the Cross (co-author), 1980; Fantastic People (co-author), 1982; First Byte: Choosing and Using a Home Computer, 1983; Run to the Stars, 1983; The BBC Micro Add-On-Guide (co-author), 1985; The Ice King (co-author, aka Burial Rites) 1986; The Anvil of Ice, 1986, The Forge in the Forest, 1987, The Hammer of the Sun, 1988; Chase the Morning, 1990, The Gates of Noon, 1992, The Horns of Tartarus (co-author), 1992; Cloud Castles, 1993; The Lord of the Middle Air, 1994; The Classical Video Guide (ed.), 1994; Maxie's Little Demon, 1997. Contributions: anthologies and periodicals. *Honours:* All-Time Great Fantasy Short Story, Gamemaster International, 1991; William F. Crawford Award for Best First Fantasy Novel, International Asscn for the Fantastic Arts, 1991.

ROHRBACH, Peter Thomas, (James Cody), BA, MA; American writer; b. 27 Feb. 1926, New York, NY; m. Sheila Sheehan 1970, one d. *Education:* Catholic University of America. *Career:* mem. Authors' Guild of America; Poets, Playwrights, Editors, Essayists and Novelists; Washington Independent Writers. *Publications:* 17 books, including: Conversation with Christ, 1981; Stagecoach East, 1983; American Issue, 1985; The Largest Event: World War II, 1993; National Issue, 1994. Contributions: Encyclopedias and periodicals.

ROITFELD, Carine; French magazine editor; *Editor-in-Chief, French Vogue;* b. Paris; d. of Jacques Roitfeld; pnr Christian Restoin; one s. one d. *Career:* fmrly writer, then a stylist for French Elle; freelance stylist, worked with Mario Testino; consultant for Ford at Gucci and YSL six years; Ed.-in-Chief French Vogue 2001–. *Address:* Vogue, 56A rue du Faubourg St Honoré, 75008 Paris, France (office). *E-mail:* pub.magazine@vogueparis.com (office). *Website:* www.vogue.fr.

ROJA, Clarita (see Aguilar, Mila D.)

ROLAND, Alex, BS, MA, PhD; American academic and writer; b. 7 April 1944, Providence, RI; m. 1979, four c. *Education:* US Naval Acad., University of Hawaii, Duke University. *Career:* Historian, National Aeronautics and Space Administration, 1973–81; Assoc. Prof., 1981–87, Prof. of History, 1987–, Chair, Dept of History, 1996–99, Duke University; Harold K. Johnson Visiting Prof. of Military History, US Army War College, 1988–89; Senior Fellow, MIT, 1994–95; mem. Society for Military History; Society for the History of Technology, pres., 1995–96. *Publications:* Underwater Warfare in the Age of Sail, 1978; Model Research: The National Advisory Committee for Aeronautics, 1915–1958, 2 vols, 1985; A Spacefaring People: Perspectives on Early Spaceflight (ed.), 1985; Men in Arms: A History of Warfare and Its Interrelationships with Western Society (with Richard A Preston and Sydney

F. Wise), fifth edn, 1991; Atmospheric Flight (ed. with Peter Galison), 2000; The Military – Industrial Complex, 2001. Contributions: scholarly books and journals. *Honours:* grants and fellowships; Fellow, Dibner Institute, MIT, 1993–94.

ROLIN, Jean; French novelist, journalist and essayist; b. 14 June 1949, Boulogne-Billancourt. *Publications:* Journal de Gand aux Aléoutiennes 1982, L'Or du scaphandrier 1983, Vu sur la mer 1986, La Ligne de front (Prix Albert Londres) 1988, La Frontière belge 1989, Cyrille et Méthode 1994, Joséphine 1994, Zones 1995, L'Organisation (Prix Médicis) 1996, Chemins d'eau 1998, C'était juste cinq heures du soir (with Jean-Christian Bourcart) 1998, Traverses 1999, Campagnes 2000, La Clôture 2001, Dingos—Cherbourg-est/Cherbourg-ouest 2002, La Clôture 2002, Chrétiens 2003, Terminal Frigo 2005, L'Homme qui a vu l'ours: reportages et autres articles 1980–2005 2006. *Address:* c/o Éditions P.O.L., 33 rue Saint-André-des-Arts, 75006 Paris, France.

ROLLS, Eric Charles, AM, FAHA; Australian writer and poet; b. 25 April 1923, Grenfell, NSW; m. 1st Joan Stephenson 1954 (died 1985); two s. one d.; m. 2nd Elaine van Kempen 1988. *Career:* Australian Creative Fellow 1991; mem. Australian Soc. of Authors, Nat. Book Council. *Publications:* Sheaf Tosser 1967, They All Ran Wild 1969, Running Wild 1973, The River 1974, The Green Mosaic 1977, Miss Strawberry Verses 1978, A Million Wild Acres 1981, Celebration of the Senses 1984, Doorways: A Year of the Cumberdeen Diaries 1989, Selected Poetry 1990, Sojourners 1993, From Forest to Sea 1993, Citizens 1996, A Celebration of Food and Wine (three vols) 1997, Australia: A Biography, Vol. 1 2000, Visions of Australia 2002; contrib. to Bulletin, Overland, National Times, Age, Sydney Morning Herald, Independent Monthly, Sun Herald. *Honours:* Dr hc (Univ. of Canberra) 1995; David Myer Trust Award for Poetry 1968, Captain Cook Bicentennial Award for Non-Fiction 1970, John Franklin Award for Children's Books 1974, Braille Book of the Year 1975, The Age Book of the Year 1981, Talking Book of the Year 1982, Centenary Medal 2003. *Address:* PO Box 2038, North Haven, NSW 2443, Australia. *Telephone:* (2) 6559-6888. *Fax:* (2) 6559-6900. *E-mail:* rollsvk@kooee.com.au.

ROLOFF, Michael, BA, MA; American playwright, poet and writer; b. (translator), 19 Dec. 1937, Berlin, Germany. *Education:* Haverford Coll., Pennsylvania, Stanford Univ. *Film screenplays:* Feelings 1982, Darlings and Monsters 1983, Graduation Party 1984. *Plays:* Wolves of Wyoming 1985, Palombe Blue 1985, Schizzohawk 1986. *Publications:* poetry: Headshots 1984, It Won't Grow Back 1985; fiction: Darlings and Monsters Quartet (four vols) 1986; other: numerous trans from German. *Address:* c/o Picador USA, 175 Fifth Avenue, New York, NY 10010, USA.

ROMER, Stephen Charles Mark, PhD; British academic and poet; b. 20 Aug. 1957, Bishops Stortford, Hertfordshire, England; m. Bridget Stevens 1982, one s. *Education:* Radley College, Trinity Hall, Cambridge, Harvard University, British Institute, Paris. *Publications:* The Growing Dark, 1981; Firebird 3, 1985; Idols, 1986; Plato's Ladder, 1992. Contributions: anthologies, journals and periodicals. *Honours:* Gregory Award for Poetry 1985.

ROMERIL, John; Australian playwright; b. 26 Oct. 1945, Melbourne, Vic. *Education:* BA, Monash University, Clayton, 1970. *Career:* Writer-In-Residence, various Australian groups and National University, Singapore, 1974–87. *Publications:* A Nameless Concern, 1968; The Kitchen Table, 1968; The Man from Chicago, 1969; In a Place Like Somewhere Else, 1969; Chicago, Chicago, 1970; Marvellous Melbourne, 1970; Dr Karl's Kure, 1970; Whatever Happened to Realism?, 1971; Rearguard Action, 1971; Hackett Gets Ahead, 1972; Bastardy, 1972; Waltzing Matilda, 1974; The Floating World, 1974; The Golden Holden Show, 1975; The Accidental Poke, 1977; Mickey's Moomba, 1979; Centenary Dance, 1984; The Kelly Dance, 1984; Definitely Not the Last, 1985; Koori Radio, 1987; Top End, and History of Australia (co-author), 1989; Lost Weekend, 1989; Black Cargo, 1991; The Reading Boy, 1991; Working Out, 1991. Other: Television plays. *Honours:* Victorian Government Drama Fellowship, 1988. *Literary Agent:* Almost Managing, PO Box 1034, Carlton, Vic. 3053, Australia.

ROMTVEDT, David William, BA, MFA; American writer and poet; b. 7 June 1950, Portland, OR; m. Margo Brown 1987. *Education:* Reed Coll., Iowa Writers' Workshop. *Career:* State Literature Consultant, WY 1987; Assoc. Prof. of English, Adjunct Assoc. Prof. of American Studies, Univ. of Wyoming; Poet Laureate of Wyoming 2004–. *Publications:* Free and Compulsory for All 1984, Moon 1984, Letters from Mexico 1987, Black Beauty and Kiev the Ukraine 1987, Crossing the River: Poets of the Western US 1987, How Many Horses 1988, A Flower Whose Name I Do Not Know 1992, Crossing Wyoming 1992, Certainty 1996, Windmill: Essays from Four Mile Ranch 1997, Deep West: A Literary Tour of Wyoming (ed.) 2003, Some Church (poems) 2005; contrib. to Paris Review, Canadian Forum, American Poetry Review, Poets and Writers Magazine. *Honours:* NEA Residency Award 1979, NEA Fellowship 1987, Pushcart Prize 1991, Nat. Poetry Series Award 1991, NEA Tri-Nat. Exchange Fellowship 1996, Wyoming Gov.'s Arts Award 2000. *Address:* 457 N Main, Buffalo, WY 82834, USA.

RONAN, Frank; Irish novelist; b. 6 May 1963, New Ross. *Publications:* The Men Who Loved Evelyn Cotton, 1989; A Picnic in Eden, 1991; The Better Angel, 1992; Dixie Chicken, 1994; Handsome Men are Slightly Sunburnt (short stories), 1996; Lovely, 1996; Home, 2002. *Honours:* Irish Times/Aer Lingus Irish Literature Prize 1989. *Literary Agent:* Rogers, Coleridge & White

Ltd, 20 Powis Mews, London W11 1JN, England. *E-mail:* a@frankronan.com. *Website:* www.frankronan.com.

RONAY, Egon, LLD; British publisher and journalist; b. Pozsony, Hungary; m. 2nd Barbara Greenslade 1967; one s. (and two d. by previous marriage). *Education:* School of Piarist Order, Budapest, Univ. of Budapest and Acad. of Commerce, Budapest. *Career:* trained in kitchens of family catering firm and abroad; managed 5 restaurants within family firm; emigrated from Hungary 1946; Gen. Man. 2 restaurant complexes in London before opening own restaurant The Marquee 1952–55; gastronomic and good living columnist, Sunday Times 1986–91 and Sunday Express 1991, weekly columnist on eating out, food, wine and tourism, Daily Telegraph and later Sunday Telegraph 1954–60; weekly column, The Evening News 1968–74; Ed. Egon Ronay's Guide to Eating at the Airport 1992–94; mem. Acad. des Gastronomes (France) 1979; Founder Int. Acad. of Gastronomy; Founder and Pres. British Acad. of Gastronomes; Founder and Ed. the Egon Ronay Guides 1957, Publr and Ed. 1957–85. *Publications:* Egon Ronay's Guides 1957–84 annually, The Unforgettable Dishes of My Life 1989. *Honours:* Médaille de la Ville de Paris 1983, Chevalier de l'Ordre du Mérite Agricole 1987. *Telephone:* (20) 7584-1384 (office). *E-mail:* egon@egonronay.com (office).

ROOKE, Daphne Marie; British writer; b. 6 March 1914, Boksburg, South Africa; d. of Robert Pizzey and Marie Knevitt; m. 1937; one d. *Publications:* A Grove of Fever Trees 1950, Mittee 1951, Ratoons 1953, Wizards Country 1957, Beti 1959, A Lover for Estelle 1961, The Greyling 1962, Diamond Jo 1965, Boy on the Mountain 1969, Margaretha de la Porte 1976, Three Rivers: A Memoir 2003; contrib. to journals. *Honours:* Hon. DLitt (Univ. of Natal) 1997; first prize APB Novel Competition 1946. *Address:* 54 Regatta Court, Oyster Row, Cambridge, CB5 8NS, England (home). *Telephone:* (1223) 314293 (home).

ROOKE, Leon; American writer; b. 11 Sept. 1934, Roanoke Rapids, NC. *Education:* Mars Hill College, NC, University of North Carolina at Chapel Hill. *Career:* writer-in-residence, University of North Carolina, 1965–66, University of Victoria, 1972–73, University of Southwest Minnesota, 1974–75, University of Toronto, 1984–85, University of Western Ontario, 1990–91; Visiting Prof., University of Victoria, 1980–81; mem. PEN; Writers' Union of Canada. *Publications:* Fiction: Last One Home Sleeps in the Yellow Bed, 1968; Vault, 1974; The Broad Back of the Angel, 1977; The Love Parlour, 1977; Fat Woman, 1980; The Magician in Love, 1980; Death Suite, 1982; The Birth Control King of the Upper Volta, 1983; Shakespeare's Dog, 1983; Sing Me No Love Songs I'll Say You No Prayers, 1984; A Bolt of White Cloth, 1984; How I Saved the Province, 1990; The Happiness of Others, 1991; A Good Baby, 1991; Who Do You Love?, 1992; Muffins, 1995. Stage Plays: A Good Baby, 1991; The Coming, 1991; 4 others. Contributions: About 300 short stories in leading North American journals. *Honours:* Canada and Australia Literary Prize, 1981; Best Paperback Novel of the Year, 1981; Governor-General's Award, 1984; North Carolina Award for Literature, 1990. *Website:* www.leonrooke .com.

ROOM, Adrian Richard West, DipEd, MA, FRGS; British writer; b. 27 Sept. 1933, Melksham, England. *Education:* Univ. of Oxford. *Career:* mem. English Place-Name Soc., American Name Soc. *Publications:* Placenames of the World 1974, 2006, Great Britain: A Background Studies English–Russian Dictionary 1978, Room's Dictionary of Confusibles 1979, Place-Name Changes since 1900 1980, Naming Names 1981, Room's Dictionary of Distinguishables 1981, Dictionary of Trade Name Origins 1982, Room's Classical Dictionary 1983, Dictionary of Cryptic Crossword Clues 1983, A Concise Dictionary of Modern Place-Names in Great Britain and Ireland 1983, Dictionary of Changes in Meaning 1986, Dictionary of Coin Names 1988, Dictionary of Dedications 1990, A Name for Your Baby 1992, The Street Names of England 1992, Brewer's Dictionary of Names 1992, Corporate Eponymy 1992, Place-Name Changes 1900–91 1993, The Naming of Animals 1993, African Place-Names 1994, Cassell Dictionary of Proper Names 1994, A Dictionary of Irish Place-Names 1994, Cassell Dictionary of First Names 1995, Brewer's Dictionary of Phrase and Fable (revised edn) 1995, Literally Entitled 1996, An Alphabetical Guide to the Language of Name Studies 1996, Placenames of Russia and the Former Soviet Union 1996, Placenames of the World 1997, Cassell Dictionary of Word Histories 1999, Cassell's Foreign Words and Phrases 2000, Dictionary of Art Titles 2000, Dictionary of Music Titles 2000, Brewer's Dictionary of Modern Phrase and Fable 2000, Encyclopedia of Corporate Names Worldwide 2002, Penguin Dictionary of British Place Names 2003, Dictionary of Pseudonyms 2004, Placenames of France 2004. *Address:* 12 High Street, St Martin's, Stamford, Lincs., PE9 2LF, England (home). *Telephone:* (1780) 752097 (home). *Fax:* (1780) 752097 (home). *E-mail:* adrian-room@msn.com (home).

ROORBACH, Bill; American academic and writer; b. 18 Aug. 1953, Chicago, IL; m. Juliet Brigitte Karelsen 1990; one d. *Education:* BA, Ithaca College, 1976; MFA, Columbia University, 1990. *Career:* Asst Prof. of English, University of Maine at Farmington, 1991–95; Asst Prof., 1995–98, Assoc. Prof. of English, 1998–, Ohio State University; mem. Associated Writing Programs; Authors' Guild; MLA of America. *Publications:* Summers with Juliet, 1992; Writing Life Stories: How to Make Memories into Memoirs, Ideas into Essays, and Life into Literature, 1998; The Art of Truth: A Contemporary Creative Nonfiction Reader (ed.), 2000; Big Bend: Stories, 2001; The Smallest Color, 2001. Contributions: anthologies, magazines, reviews, quarterlies and journals. *Honours:* Ohio Arts Council Grants; Flannery O'Connor Award,

2001. *Address:* c/o Department of English, Ohio State University, Columbus, OH 43210, USA.

ROOT, Deane Leslie; American musicologist, museum curator, teacher, librarian and editor; b. 9 Aug. 1947, Wausau, WI; m. Doris J. Dyen 1972; two d. *Education:* New Coll., Sarasota, FL, Univ. of Illinois. *Career:* faculty, Univ. of Wisconsin 1973; editorial staff, New Grove Dictionary of Music and Musicians 1974–76; Research Assoc., Univ. of Illinois 1976–80; Visiting Research Assoc., Florida State Univ. 1981–82; Curator, Stephen Foster Memorial and Adjunct Asst Prof. in Music, Univ. of Pittsburgh 1982–96, Chair of Music Dept 2002–05; Heinz Chapel Administrator 1983–95; Dir of Cultural Resources 1990–94, Adjunct Assoc. Prof. 1992–96, Prof. of Music, Dir of Center for American Music 1998–, Univ. of Pittsburgh; Pres., Sonneck Soc. for American Music 1989–93; Delegate American Council of Learned Socs 1996–99. *Recordings:* Proud Traditions, Musical Tribute to Pitt. *Publications:* American Popular Stage Music 1860–1880, Music of Florida Historic Sites, Resources of American Music History (co-author), Music of Stephen C. Foster (co-ed.), Nineteenth Century American Musical Theater (series ed., 16 vols) 1994, Voices Across Time: American History Through Song 2004; contrib. to New Grove Dictionary of Music and New Grove Dictionary of American Music, American National Biography, various journals, yearbooks, conference proceedings. *Telephone:* (412) 624-4126. *Fax:* (412) 624-4186. *E-mail:* dlr@ pitt.edu*Address:* Department of Music, University of Pittsburgh, Pittsburgh, PA 15260, USA.

ROOT, William Pitt, BA, MFA; American fmr academic and poet; b. 28 Dec. 1941, Austin, TX; m. Pamela Uschuk 1988, one d. *Education:* University of Washington, University of North Carolina at Greensboro. *Career:* Stegner Fellow, Stanford University, 1967–68; Asst Prof., Michigan State University, 1967–68; Visiting Writer-in-Residence, Amherst College, 1971, University of Southwest Louisiana, 1976, Wichita State University, 1976, University of Montana, 1978, 1980, 1982–85, Pacific Lutheran University, 1990; Prof., Hunter College, CUNY, 1986–2005; Poet Laureate of Tuscon, AZ, 1997–2002. *Publications:* The Storm and Other Poems, 1969; Striking the Dark Air for Music, 1973; A Journey South, 1977; Reasons for Going It on Foot, 1981; In the World's Common Grasses, 1981; Invisible Guests, 1984; Faultdancing, 1986; Trace Elements from a Recurring Kingdom, 1994, A Beauty Warrior: Bruce's Book 2005; contrib. to magazines and periodicals. *Honours:* Acad. of American Poetry Prize, 1967; Rockefeller Foundation Grant, 1969–70; Guggenheim Fellowship, 1970–71; National Endowment for the Arts Grant, 1973–74; Pushcart Awards, 1977, 1980, 1985; US-UK Exchange Artist, 1978–79; Stanley Kunitz Poetry Award, 1981; Guy Owen Poetry Award, 1984. *Address:* 154 Concho Circle, Bayfield, Colorado 81122, USA (home). *Telephone:* (970) 884-3623 (home). *E-mail:* wprpoet@tglobal.net (home).

ROQUELAURE, A. N. (see Rice, Anne)

ROSE, Andrew Wyness, MA, LLM; British barrister and writer; b. 11 Feb. 1944, England. *Education:* Trinity Coll., Cambridge. *Career:* called to Bar, Grays Inn, London 1968, Barrister 1968–; mem. Crimes Club, 'Our Society'. *Publications:* Stinie: Murder on the Common 1985, Scandal at the Savoy 1991, Lethal Witness 2007. *Address:* The Andrew Lownie Literary Agency, 17 Sutherland Street, London, SW1V 4JU, England (office).

ROSE, Daniel Asa, AB; American writer, essayist, poet and editor; b. 20 Nov. 1949, New York, NY; m. 1st Laura Love 1974 (divorced); two s.; m. 2nd Shelley Roth 1993; two s. *Education:* Brown Univ. *Career:* Arts and Culture Ed. The Forward; travel columnist Esquire; sr book reviewer The New York Observer; book reviewer Vanity Fair; Travel Ed. Madison; Ella Baker Fellow 2004. *Publications:* Flipping For It 1987, Small Family with Rooster 1988, Hiding Places: A Father and his Sons Retrace their Family's Escape from the Holocaust 2000; also screenplays, poems, stories, reviews and literary essays; contrib. to The New Yorker, The New York Times Magazine, GQ, Esquire, Playboy. *Honours:* O. Henry Prize 1980, PEN Literary Awards 1987, 1988, Massachusetts Cultural Council Award 1992. *Address:* 138 Bay State Road, Rehoboth, MA 02769, USA.

ROSE, Jacqueline, BA, PhD, Maitrise (Paris-Sorbonne), FBA; British academic and writer; *Professor, School of English and Drama, Queen Mary, University of London*; b. 1949, London; one adopted d. *Education:* St Hilda's Coll., Oxford, Univ. of Paris-Sorbonne, Univ. of London. *Career:* fmr staff mem., Univ. of Sussex; currently Prof. of English Literature, Queen Mary, Univ. of London; participated in London Review of Books forum, The War on Terror 2002. *Films include:* Dangerous Liaison (UK Channel 4) 2002. *Publications include:* Feminine Sexuality (co-ed. with Juliet Mitchell) 1982, The Case of Peter Pan 1984, Sexuality in the Field of Vision 1986, The Haunting of Sylvia Plath 1991, Why War? Psychoanalysis, Politics and the Return to Melanie Klein, The Bucknell Lectures in Literary Theory 1993, Black Hamlet (co-ed. with Saul Dubow) 1996, States of Fantasy, The Oxford Clarendon Lectures 1998, Albertine 2001, On Not Being Able To Sleep: Psychoanalysis and the Modern World 2003, The Question of Zion (Christian Gauss seminars, Princeton Univ.) 2004. *Address:* School of English and Drama, Queen Mary, University of London, Mile End Road, London, E1 4NS (office); c/o Chatto &Windus, Random House UK Ltd, Random House, 20 Vauxhall Bridge Road, London, SW1V 2SA, England. *Telephone:* (20) 7882-5014 (office). *Fax:* (20) 7882-3357 (office). *E-mail:* j.rose@qmul.ac.uk (office). *Website:* www.english.qmul.ac.uk (office).

ROSE, Joel Steven, BA, MFA; American writer; b. 1 March 1948, Los Angeles, CA; m. Catherine Texier; two d. *Education:* Hobart College, Columbia University. *Career:* f., publisher, ed. two literary magazines, The Seneca Review and Between C and D 1988; mem. Co-ordinating Council of Literary Magazines; Poets and Writers; Writers Guild of America. *Publications include:* Kill the Poor (novel, also film) 1988, Love is Strange (co-ed.) 1993, The Big Book of Thugs 1996, Kill Kill Faster Faster 1998, New York Sawed in Half 2001, The Blackest Bird 2007; contrib. to newspapers and magazines. *Honours:* National Endowment for the Arts Award, 1986; New York State Council on the Arts Award, 1986–87. *E-mail:* joeyrose@nyc.rr.com. *Website:* www.joelrosebooks.com.

ROSE, Kenneth Vivian, CBE, MA, FRSL; British writer; b. 15 Nov. 1924, Bradford, Yorkshire, England. *Education:* Repton School, New College, Oxford. *Career:* Asst Master, Eton College, 1948; Editorial Staff, Daily Telegraph, 1952–60; Founder, Writer, Albany Column, Sunday Telegraph, 1961–97. *Publications:* Superior Person: A Portrait of Curzon and his Circle in Late Victorian England, 1969; The Later Cecils, 1975; William Harvey: A Monograph, 1978; King George V, 1983; Kings, Queens and Courtiers: Intimate Portraits of the Royal House of Windsor, 1985; Harold Nicolson, 1992; Elusive Rothschild: The Life of Victor, 3rd Baron, 2003. Contributions: Dictionary of National Biography. *Honours:* Wolfson Award for History, 1983; Whitbread Award for Biography, 1983; Yorkshire Post Biography of the Year Award, 1984.

ROSE, Marion (see Harris, Marion Rose)

ROSE, Mark Allen, AB, BLitt, PhD; American academic and writer; *Professor of English, University of California at Santa Barbara*; b. 4 Aug. 1939, New York, NY; m. Anne Benningham; one s. *Education:* Princeton Univ., Merton Coll., Harvard Univ. *Career:* Instructor to Assoc. Prof. of English, Yale Univ. 1967–74; Prof. of English, Univ. of Illinois 1974–77; Prof. of English, Univ. of California at Santa Barbara 1977–, Assoc. Vice-Chancellor 2001–; Dir, Univ. of California Humanities Research Inst. 1989–94; mem. MLA, Renaissance Soc. of America, Shakespeare Soc. of America. *Publications:* Heroic Love 1968, Golding's Tale 1972, Shakespearean Design 1972, Spenser's Art 1975, Alien Encounters 1981, Authors and Owners 1993; editor: Twentieth Century Views of Science Fiction 1976, Twentieth Century Interpretations of Antony and Cleopatra 1977, Bridges to Science Fiction (with others) 1980, Shakespeare's Early Tragedies 1994, Norton Shakespere Workshop 1997. *Honours:* Woodrow Wilson Fellow 1961, Henry Fellow 1961–62, Dexter Fellow 1966, Morse Fellow 1970–71, Nat. Endowment for the Humanities Fellowships 1979–80, 1990–91. *Address:* 1135 Oriole Road, Montecito, CA 93108, USA. *E-mail:* mrose@english.ucsb.edu.

ROSE, Richard, BA, DPhil, FBA; American writer, academic and consultant; *Professor of Public Policy, University of Aberdeen*; b. 9 April 1933, St Louis, Mo.; s. of Charles Imse Rose and Mary C. Rose; m. Rosemary J. Kenny 1956; two s. one d. *Education:* Clayton High School, Mo., Johns Hopkins Univ., LSE, Oxford. *Career:* worked in political public relations, Miss. Valley 1954–55; reporter, St Louis Post-Dispatch 1955–57; Lecturer in Govt, Univ. of Manchester 1961–66; Prof. of Politics Strathclyde Univ. 1966–82, Prof. of Public Policy and Dir Centre for the Study of Public Policy 1976–2005; Prof. of Public Policy, Univ. of Aberdeen 2005–; Specialist Adviser, House of Commons Public Admin Cttee 2002–03; Consultant Psephologist, The Times, ITV, Daily Telegraph, etc. 1964–; Sec. Cttee on Political Sociology, Int. Sociology Asscn 1970–85; Founding mem. European Consortium for Political Research 1970; mem. US/UK Fulbright Comm. 1971–75; Guggenheim Fellow 1974; Visiting scholar at various insts, Europe, USA, Hong Kong; mem. Home Office Working Party on Electoral Register 1975–77; Co-Founder British Politics Group 1974–; Convenor Work Group on UK Politics, Political Studies Asscn 1976–88; mem. Council Int. Political Science Asscn 1976–82; Tech. Consultant OECD, UNDP, World Bank, Council of Europe, Int. IDEA; Dir SSRC Research Programme, Growth of Govt 1982–86; Ed. Journal of Public Policy 1985–, Chair. 1981–85; Scientific Adviser, New Democracies Barometer, Paul Lazarsfeld Soc., Vienna 1991–; Sr Fellow in Governance, Oxford Internet Inst. 2003–05. *Publications:* numerous books on politics and public policy including Politics in England 1964, People in Politics: Observations Across the Atlantic 1970, Governing Without Consensus: An Irish Perspective 1971, International Almanack of Electoral History (co-author) 1974, The Problem of Party Government 1974, Northern Ireland: A Time of Choice 1976, Managing Presidential Objectives 1976, What is Governing? Purpose and Policy in Washington 1978, Can Government Go Bankrupt? (co-author) 1978, Do Parties Make A Difference 1984, Understanding Big Government 1984, Public Employment in Western Nations (co-author) 1985, Taxation by Political Inertia (co-author) 1987, Ministers and Ministries 1987, Presidents and Prime Ministers, The Postmodern President 1988, Ordinary People in Public Policy 1989, Training With Trainers? How Germany Avoids Britain's Supply-side Bottleneck (co-author) 1990, The Loyalties of Voters (co-author) 1990, Lesson-Drawing in Public Policy 1993 Inheritance in Public Policy (co-author) 1994, What is Europe? 1996, How Russia Votes (co-author) 1997, Democracy and Its Alternatives, Understanding Post-Communist Societies (co-author) 1998, A Society Transformed: Hungary in Time-Space Perspective, International Encyclopedia of Elections (co-author) 2000, The Prime Minister in a Shrinking World 2001, Elections without Order: Russia's Challenge to Vladimir Putin (co-author) 2002, Elections and Parties in New European Democracies 2003, Learning from Comparative Public Policy 2005; hundreds of papers in academic journals. *Honours:* Hon. Vice-Pres. UK Political Studies Asscn; Hon. Fellow American Acad. of Arts and Sciences, Finnish Acad. of Science and Letters, Acad. of Learned Socs in the Social Sciences 2000; Hon. PhD, Örebro Univ. (Sweden); AMEX Prize in Int. Econs 1992, Lasswell Prize for Lifetime Achievement, Policy Studies Org. 1999; Lifetime Achievement Award, UK Political Studies Asscn 1990. *Address:* Centre for the Study of Public Policy, University of Aberdeen, Aberdeen, AB24 3QY (office); 1 East Abercromby Street, Helensburgh, G84 7SP, Scotland (home). *Telephone:* (1436) 672164 (home). *Fax:* (1436) 673125 (home). *E-mail:* richard.rose@abdn.ac.uk (office). *Website:* www.abdn.ac.uk/cspp (office).

ROSEN, Charles, PhD; American pianist and writer; b. 5 May 1927, New York, NY; s. of Irwin Rosen and Anita Gerber. *Education:* Juilliard School of Music, Princeton Univ., Univ. of S. California. *Career:* studied piano with Moriz Rosenthal and Hedwig Kanner-Rosenthal 1938–45; recital début, New York 1951; first complete recording of Debussy Etudes 1951; première of Double Concerto by Elliott Carter, New York 1961; has played recitals and as soloist with orchestras throughout America and Europe; has made over 35 recordings including Stravinsky: Movements with composer conducting 1962, Bach: Art of Fugue, Two Ricercares, Goldberg Variations 1971, Beethoven: Last Six Sonatas 1972, Boulez: Piano Music, Vol. I, Diabelli Variations, Beethoven Concerto No. 4, 1979, Schumann: The Revolutionary Masterpieces, Chopin: 24 Mazurkas 1991; Prof. of Music, State Univ. of NY 1972–90; Guggenheim Fellowship 1974; Messenger Lectures, Cornell Univ. 1975, Bloch Lectures, Univ. of Calif., Berkeley 1977, Gauss Seminars, Princeton Univ. 1978; Norton Prof. of Poetry, Harvard Univ. 1980–81; George Eastman Prof., Balliol Coll., Oxford 1987–88, Prof. of Music and Social Thought, Univ. of Chicago 1988–96. *Publications:* The Classical Style: Haydn, Mozart, Beethoven 1971, Beethoven's Last Six Sonatas 1972, Schoenberg 1975, Sonata Forms 1980, Romanticism and Realism: The Mythology of Nineteenth-Century Art (with Henri Zerner) 1984, The Musical Language of Elliott Carter 1984, Paisir de jouer, plaiser de penser 1993, The Frontiers of Meaning: Three Informal Lectures on Music 1994, The Romantic Generation 1995, Romantic Poets, Critics and Other Madmen 1998, Critical Entertainment: Music Old and New 2000, Beethoven's Piano Sonatas: A Short Companion 2001, Piano Notes 2003; contrib. to books, newspapers and journals. *Honours:* Hon. DMus (Trinity Coll., Dublin 1976, Leeds Univ. 1976, Durham Univ.); Dr hc (Cambridge) 1992; Nat. Book Award 1972, Edison Prize, Netherlands 1974. *Literary Agent:* c/o Owen/White Management, 59 Lansdowne Place, Hove, East Sussex BN3 1FL, England. *Telephone:* (1273) 727127. *Fax:* (1273) 328128. *E-mail:* info@owenwhitemanagement.com. *Website:* www.owenwhitemanagement.com.

ROSEN, Michael, MA; British children's writer, poet, broadcaster and critic; *Children's Laureate*; b. 7 May 1946, Harrow, Middlesex, England. *Education:* Wadham Coll., Oxford, Reading Univ. *Career:* worked for BBC television, on Play School and other children's programmes, BBC radio as presenter, Treasure Islands (Radio 4), Best Worlds (Radio 3), Meridian (World Service), Word of Mouth (Radio 4); Children's Laureate 2007–(09); mem. Poetry Soc. (vice-pres.). *Publications include:* fiction: Backbone (play) (Sunday Times Nat. Union of Students Drama Festival Award 1968) 1969, Everybody Here (Children's Rights Workshop Other Award 1983) 1982, Hairy Tales and Nursery Crimes 1985, Smelly Jelly, Smelly Fish 1986, Under the Bed 1986, Hard-boiled Legs 1987, Spollyollydiddlytiddlyitis 1987, You're Thinking About Doughnuts 1987, Silly Stories (aka Michael Rosen's Horribly Silly Stories) 1988, We're Going on a Bear Hunt (Smarties Best Children's Book of the Year Award 1990, Boston Globe-Horn Book Honor Award, USA 1990, School Library Journal Best Book of the Year, USA 1990, Horn Book Fanfare Title, USA 1990, Japanese Picture Book Award for an Outstanding Picture Book from Abroad 1991) 1989, The Wicked Tricks of Till Owlyglass (re-telling) 1989, The Golem of Old Prague (re-telling) 1990, Clever Cakes 1991, Walking the Bridge of Your Nose (Publishers Weekly Cuffies Award for Best Anthology or Collection, USA 1992) 1992, Burping Bertha 1993, The Man with no Shadow (re-telling) 1994, This is Our House 1996, Snore! (Parent magazine Play and Learn Award 1998) 1998, Mission Ziffoid 1999, Rover 1999, Lovely Old Roly 2002, Oww! 2003, Howler 2004, Michael Rosen's Sad Book 2004, William Shakespeare's Romeo and Juliet (re-telling) 2004, You're Thinking About Tomatoes 2005, Totally Wonderful Miss Plumberry 2006, Mustard, Custard, Grumble Belly and Gravy 2006; poetry for children: Mind Your Own Business 1974, Wouldn't You Like to Know 1977, You Tell Me (with Roger McGough) 1979, You Can't Catch Me (Signal Poetry Award 1982) 1981, Quick, Let's Get Out of Here 1983, Don't Put Mustard in the Custard 1985, The Kingfisher Book of Children's Poetry (anthology ed.) 1985, A Spider Bought a Bicycle (anthology ed.) 1987, The Hypnotiser 1988, The Kingfisher Book of Funny Stories (anthology ed.) 1988, Little Rabbit Foo Foo 1990, A World of Poetry (anthology ed.) 1991, Sonsense Nongs (aka Michael Rosen's Book of Very Silly Poems, anthology ed.) 1992, Poetry for the Very Young (anthology ed.) (Nat. Asscn of Parenting Publications Best Book Award, USA 1993) 1993, A Different Story: Poems from the Past (anthology ed.) 1994, The Zoo at Night 1996, You Wait Till I'm Older Than You (Talkies Award for the Best Poetry Audio Tape of the Year 1998) 1996, Tea in the Sugar Bowl, Potato in my Shoe 1997, Michael Rosen's Book of Nonsense 1997, Classic Poetry (anthology ed.) 1998, Night-Night, Knight (anthology ed.) 1998, Lunch Boxes Don't Fly 1999, Centrally Heated Knickers 1999, Even More Nonsense 2000, Uncle Billy Being Silly 2001, No Breathing in Class 2003, Alphabet Poem (Nat. Literacy WOW Award 2005) 2004; poetry for adults: The Chatto Book of Dissent (ed.) 1991, The Penguin Book of Childhood (ed.) 1994, Carrying the Elephant: A Memoir of Love and Loss 2002, This is Not My Nose 2004, In the Colonie 2005; non-fiction: Did I Hear You Write? 1989, Goodies and Daddies, an A–Z Guide to Fatherhood 1991, A Year With Poetry: Teachers Write About Teaching Poetry (co-ed.) 1997, Shakespeare: His Life and his Work 2001, William Shakespeare in his Times, for our Times 2004, Dickens 2005. *Honours:* Dr hc (Open Univ.) 2005; Glennfiddich Award for the Best Radio Programme on the subject of food (for Treasure Islands Special: Lashings of Ginger Beer) 1996, Eleanor Farjeon Award for distinguished services to children's literature 1997. *Literary Agent:* PFD, Drury House, 34–43 Russell Street, London, WC2B 5HA, England. *Telephone:* (20) 7344-1000. *Website:* www.pfd.co.uk. *E-mail:* michael@michaelrosen.co.uk. *Website:* www.michaelrosen.co.uk.

ROSEN, Norma, BA, MA; American writer and teacher; b. 11 Aug. 1925, New York, NY; m. Robert S. Rosen 1960, one s. one d. *Education:* Mt Holyoke College, Columbia University. *Career:* Teacher of Creative Writing, New School for Social Research, New York City, 1965–69, University of Pennsylvania, 1969, Harvard University, 1971, Yale University, 1984, New York University, 1987–95; mem. PEN; Authors' Guild. *Publications:* Joy to Levine!, 1962; Green, 1967; Touching Evil, 1969; At the Center, 1982; John and Anzia: An American Romance, 1989; Accidents of Influence: Writing as a Woman and a Jew in America (essays), 1992; Biblical Women Unbound: Counter-Tales (narratives), 1996. Contributions: anthologies and other publications.

ROSENBERG, Bruce Alan, BA, MA, PhD; American teacher and writer; b. 27 July 1934, New York, NY; m. Ann Harleman 1981, three s. *Education:* Hofstra University, Pennsylvania State University, Ohio State University. *Career:* mem. Folklore Fellows International. *Publications:* The Art of the American Folk Preacher, 1970; Custer and the Epic of Defeat, 1975; The Code of the West, 1982; The Spy Story, 1987; Can These Bones Live?, 1988; Ian Fleming, 1989; The Neutral Ground, 1995. Contributions: Over 60 professional journals. *Honours:* James Russell Lowell Prize, 1970; Chicago Folklore Prizes, 1970, 1975.

ROSENBERG, Liz; American academic, poet and writer; b. 3 Feb. 1956, Glen Cove, NY; m. David Bosnick 1996; one s. *Education:* BA, Bennington College, 1976; MA, Johns Hopkins University, 1978; PhD, Comparative Literature, SUNY at Binghamton, 1997. *Career:* Assoc. Prof. of English, SUNY at Binghamton; Guest Teacher-Poet, various venues; many poetry readings; mem. Associated Writing Programs; PEN. *Publications:* The Fire Music (poems), 1987; A Book of Days (poems), 1992; Children of Paradise (poems), 1994; Heart and Soul (novel), 1996; The Invisible Ladder (ed.), 1997; Earth-Shattering Poems (ed.), 1998; These Happy Eyes (prose poems), 1999. Contributions: many newspapers, reviews, and journals. *Honours:* Kelloggs Fellow, 1980–82; Pennsylvania Council of the Arts Poetry Grant, 1982; Agnes Starrett Poetry Prize, 1987; Claudia Lewis Poetry Prize, 1997; Best Book for Teens Citation, New York Public Library, 1997; Paterson Prizes for Children's Literature, 1997, 1998. *Address:* c/o Department of English, General Literature, and Rhetoric, State University of New York at Binghamton, PO Box 6000, Binghamton, NY 13902, USA.

ROSENBERG, Nancy Taylor; American writer; b. 9 July 1946, Dallas, TX; m. 1st Calvin S. Kyrme (divorced); two s. one d.; m. 2nd Jerry Rosenberg; two d. *Education:* Gulf Park College, University of California at Los Angeles. *Publications:* Mitigating Circumstances, 1993; Interest of Justice, 1993; The Eyewitness, 1994; First Offense, 1994; California Angel, 1995; Conflict of Interest, 2002.

ROSENBERG, Peter Michael, BSc; British writer; b. 11 July 1958, London, England. *Education:* Univ. of Sussex. *Publications:* The Usurper (co-author) 1988, Kissing Through a Pane of Glass 1993, Touched By a God or Something 1994, Because It Makes My Heart Beat Faster 1995, Daniel's Dream 1996; contribs to journals and magazines. *Honours:* Second Prize, Betty Trask Award 1992. *Literary Agent:* c/o Christopher Little Literary Agency, 10 Eel Brook Studios, 125 Moore Park Road, London, SW6 4PS, England. *E-mail:* peter.rosenberg@virgin.net.

ROSENBLATT, Joseph (Joe); Canadian poet, writer and artist; b. 26 Dec. 1933, Toronto, ON; m. Faye Smith 1970; one s. *Education:* Central Technical School, Toronto, George Brown Coll., Toronto. *Career:* Ed., Jewish Dialog magazine 1969–83; writer-in-residence, Univ. of Western Ontario, London 1979–80, Univ. of Victoria, BC 1980–81, Saskatoon Public Library, Saskatchewan 1985–86; Visiting Lecturer, Univ. of Rome 1987, Univ. of Bologna 1987. *Publications:* The Voyage of the Mood 1960, The LSD Leacock 1963, The Winter of the Luna Moth 1968, Greenbaum 1970, The Bumblebee Dithyramb 1972, Blind Photographer: Poems and Sketches 1973, Dream Craters 1974, Virgins and Vampires 1975, Top Soil 1976, Doctor Anaconda's Solar Fun Club: A Book of Drawings 1977, Loosely Tied Hands: An Experiment in Punk 1978, Snake Oil 1978, The Sleeping Lady 1979, Brides of the Stream 1984, Escape from the Glue Factory: A Memoir of a Paranormal Toronto Childhood in the Late Forties 1985, Poetry Hotel: Selected Poems 1963–1985 1985, The Kissing Goldfish of Siam: A Memoir of Adolescence in the Fifties 1989, Gridi nel Buio 1990, Beds and Consenting Dreamers 1994, The Joe Rosenblatt Reader 1995, The Voluptuos Gardener: The Collected Art and Writing of Joe Rosenblatt 1973–1996 1996; contrib. to many publications. *Honours:* Canada Council Senior Arts Awards 1973, 1976, 1980, 1987, Ontario Arts Council Poetry Award 1970, Gov.-Gen.'s Award for Poetry 1976, British Columbia Book Award for Poetry 1986. *Address:* 221 Elizabeth Avenue, Qualicum Beach, BC V9K IG8, Canada.

ROSENDORFER, Herbert; German novelist and academic; b. 19 Feb. 1934, Bolzano. *Career:* fmr attorney and judge (retd), Prof. of German Literature, Univ. of Munich. *Publications:* novels: Der Ruinenbaumeister (trans. as The Architect of Ruins) 1969, Stephanie und das vorige Leben (trans. as Stephanie or a Previous Existence) 1977, Briefe in die chinesische Vergangenheit (trans. as Letters Back to Ancient China) 1983, Die Nacht der Amazonen 1989, Ein Liebhaber ungerader Zahlen 1994, Die grosse Umwendung: neue Briefe in die chinesische Vergangenheit 1997, Kadon, Ehemaliger Gott 2001. *Honours:* Jean-Paul Prize 1999. *Literary Agent:* c/o Dedalus Ltd, Langford Lodge, St Judith's Lane, Sawtry, Cambridgeshire PE28 5XE, England. *E-mail:* info@dedalusbooks.com. *Website:* www.dedalusbooks.com.

ROSENTHAL, Barbara Ann, BFA, MFA; American writer, artist, photographer and video artist; b. 17 Aug. 1948, New York, NY; two d. *Education:* Carnegie-Mellon University, Queens College, CUNY. *Career:* Ed.-in-Chief, Patterns, 1967–70; Adjunct Lecturer in English, College of Staten Island, CUNY, 1990–. *Publications:* Clues to Myself, 1982; Sensations, 1984; Old Address Book, 1985; Homo Futurus, 1986; In the West of Ireland, 1992; Children's Shoes, 1993; Soul and Psyche, 1999. Contributions: anthologies and journals. *Honours:* various awards and residencies.

ROSENTHAL, Thomas Gabriel, MA, PhD; British publisher, critic and broadcaster; b. 16 July 1935, s. of the late Erwin I. J. Rosenthal and Elisabeth Charlotte Marx; m. Ann Judith Warnford-Davis; two s. *Education:* Perse School, Cambridge and Pembroke Coll., Cambridge. *Career:* served in RA 1954–56; joined Thames and Hudson Ltd 1959, Man. Dir Thames and Hudson Int. 1966; joined Martin Secker and Warburg Ltd as Man. Dir 1971, Dir Heinemann Group of Publrs 1972–84, Man. Dir William Heinemann Int. Ltd 1979–84, Chair. World's Work Ltd 1979–84, Heinemann Zsolnay Ltd 1979–84, Kaye and Ward Ltd 1980–84, William Heinemann, Australia and SA 1981–82, Pres. Heinemann Inc. 1981–84; Jt Man. Dir and Jt Chair. André Deutsch Ltd 1984, CEO 1987–96, Sole Man. Dir and Chair. 1987, Chair. 1984–98; Chair. Frew McKenzie (Antiquarian Booksellers) 1985–93, Bridgewater Press 1997–; Art Critic The Listener 1963–66; Chair. Soc. of Young Publrs 1961–62; mem. Cambridge Univ. Appointments Bd 1967–71, Exec. Cttee Nat. Book League 1971–74, Cttee of Man. Amateur Dramatic Club, Cambridge (also Trustee), Council RCA 1982–87, Exec. Council Inst. of Contemporary Arts 1987–99 (Chair. 1996–99); Trustee Phoenix Trust, Fitzwilliam Museum, Cambridge 2002–; mem. Editorial Bd Logos 1989–93. *Publications:* Monograph on Jack B. Yeats 1964, Monograph on Ivon Hitchens (with Alan Bowness) 1973; A Reader's Guide to European Art History 1962, A Reader's Guide to Modern American Fiction 1963, Monograph on Arthur Boyd (with Ursula Hoff) 1986, The Art of Jack B. Yeats 1993, Sidney Nolan 2002, Paula Rego: The Complete Graphic Works 2004, Joseph Albers: Formulation Articulation 2006; articles in journals and newspapers. *Address:* Flat 7, Huguenot House, 19 Oxendon Street, London, SW1Y 4EH, England (home). *Telephone:* (20) 7839-3589 (home). *Fax:* (20) 7839-0651 (home).

ROSS, Angus (see Giggal, Kenneth)

ROSS, Dennis B., PhD; American academic and fmr government official; *Counsellor and Ziegler Distinguished Fellow, Washington Institute for Near East Policy.* *Education:* UCLA. *Career:* after graduation became Exec. Dir. of program on Soviet International Behavior sponsored by Univ. Calif, Berkeley and Stanford Univ. 1984–86; Dir Near East and S Asian Affairs, Nat. Security Council (during Reagan Admin), Policy Planning Office, State Dept 1989–92, Special Middle East Co-ordinator 1997–2001, helped achieve the 1995 Interim Agreement and brokered the Hebron Accord 1997; currently Distinguished Fellow and Counsellor, Washington Inst. Near East Policy; Chair. Institute for Jewish People Policy Planning, Jerusalem. *Publications include:* The Missing Peace: The Inside Story of the Fight for Middle East Peace 2004, Statecraft: And How to Restore America's Standing in the World 2007; numerous articles in learned journals and newspapers. *Honours:* Hon. DHumLitt (Amherst Coll.) 2002, Dr hc (Jewish Theological Seminary, Syracuse Univ.); UCLA Alumnus of the Year. *Address:* Washington Institute for Near East Policy, 1828 L Street, NW, Suite 1050, Washington, DC 20036, USA (office). *Telephone:* (202) 452-0650 (office). *Fax:* (202) 223-5364 (office). *E-mail:* dennisr@washingtoninstitute.org (office). *Website:* www.washingtoninstitute.org (office).

ROSS, Helaine (see Daniels, Dorothy)

ROSS, Jonathan (see Rossiter, John)

ROSS, Malcolm (see Ross-Macdonald, Malcolm John)

ROSS-MacDONALD, Malcolm John, (Malcolm MacDonald, M. R. O'Donnell, Malcolm Ross); British writer and editor (retd) and designer (retd); b. 29 Feb. 1932, Chipping, Sodbury, Glos., England; m. Ingrid Giehr; two d. *Education:* Falmouth School of Art, Slade School, London. *Career:* Lecturer, Folk Univ., Sweden 1959–61; Exec. Ed., Aldus Books 1962–65; Visiting Lecturer, Hornsey Coll. of Art 1965–69; mem. Authors' Guild, Soc. of Authors. *Publications:* The Big Waves 1962, Macdonald Illustrated Encyclopaedia (exec. ed., ten vols) 1962–65, Spare Part Surgery (co-author) 1968, Machines in Medicine 1969, The Human Heart 1970, World Wildlife Guide 1971, Beyond the Horizon 1971, Every Living Thing 1973, World from Rough Stones 1974, Origin of Johnny 1975, Life in the Future 1976, The Rich are With You Always 1976, Sons of Fortune 1978, Abigail 1979, Goldeneye 1981, The Dukes 1982, Tessa'd'Arblay 1983, In Love and War 1984, Mistress of Pallas 1986, Silver Highways 1987, The Sky with Diamonds 1988, A Notorious Woman 1988, His

Father's Son 1989, An Innocent Woman 1989, Hell Hath No Fury 1990, A Woman Alone 1990, The Captain's Wives 1991, A Woman Scorned 1991, A Woman Possessed 1992, All Desires Known 1993, To the End of her Days 1993, Dancing on Snowflakes 1994, For I Have Sinned 1994, Kernow and Daughter 1994, Crissy's Family 1995, Tomorrow's Tide 1996, The Carringtons of Helston 1997, Like a Diamond 1998, Tamsin Harte 2000, Rose of Nancemellin 2001; contrib. to Sunday Times, New Scientist, Science Journal, Month, Jefferson Encyclopaedia. *Honours:* Romantic Times Historical Novel of the Year, USA 1981. *E-mail:* mirossmac2@eircom.net (home). *Website:* www.malcolmmacdonald.org.

ROSSET, Barnet (Barney) Lee, Jr, PhB; American publisher; b. 28 May 1922, Chicago, IL; s. of Barnet Lee Rosset and Mary R. Rosset (née Tansey); m. 1st Joan Mitchell 1950 (divorced 1952); m. 2nd Hannelore Eckert 1953 (divorced 1957); one s.; m. 3rd Cristine Agnini 1965 (divorced 1979); two c.; m. 4th Elisabeth Krug 1980 (divorced 1991); one d. *Education:* Univ. of Chicago, New School Social Research, New York. *Career:* Publr and Ed. Grove Press Inc. 1951–86, Evergreen Review 1957–73, Blue Moon Books Inc., New York 1987–98, Foxrock Inc. 1995–, Evergreen Review Inc. 1998–; fought for right in court to publish D. H. Lawrence's Lady Chatterley's Lover, Henry Miller's Tropic of Cancer and William Burroughs's Naked Lunch, in the USA; mem. PEN, Overseas Press Club. *Honours:* Commdr, Ordre des Arts et des Lettres 1999; PEN America Center Ninth Pub. citation 1988, Small Press Center Poor Richard's Award 1999, Nat. Book Critics Circle Lifetime Achievement Award 2001, Asscn of American Publrs Curtis Benjamin Award 2001, Paris Review Ann. Hadaha Award 2003. *Address:* 61 Fourth Avenue, New York, NY 10003-5204, USA (office). *Telephone:* (212) 505-6880 (office); (212) 777-2480 (home). *Fax:* (212) 673-1039 (office). *E-mail:* evergreen@nyc.rr.com (office). *Website:* www.evergreenreview.com (office).

ROSSI, Bruno (see Levinson, Leonard)

ROSSITER, John, (Jonathan Ross); British writer; b. 2 March 1916, Devonshire, England. *Education:* preparatory and military schools, Woolwich and Bulford. *Career:* Detective Chief Superintendent, Wiltshire Constabulary 1939–69; Flight Lieutenant, RAF/VR 1943–46; columnist, Wiltshire Courier, Swindon 1963–64; mem. CWA. *Publications:* as Jonathan Ross: The Blood Running Cold 1968, Diminished by Death 1968, Dead at First Hand 1969, The Deadest Thing You Ever Saw 1969, Death's Head 1982, Dead Eye 1983, Dropped Dead 1984, Fate Accomplished 1987, Sudden Departures 1988, A Time for Dying 1989, Daphne Dead and Done For 1990, Murder be Hanged 1992, The Body of a Woman 1994, Murder! Murder! Burning Bright 1996, This Too Too Sullied Flesh 1997; as John Rossiter: The Victims 1971, A Rope for General Dietz 1972, The Manipulators 1973, The Villains 1974, The Golden Virgin 1975, The Man Who Came Back 1978, Dark Flight 1981; contrib. to Police Review. *Literary Agent:* David Higham Associates, 5–8 Lower John Street, Golden Square, London, W1F 9HA, England. *Address:* 3 Leighton Home Farm Court, Wellhead Lane, Westbury, Wilts BA13 3PT, England. *Telephone:* (1373) 826411 (home).

ROSSITER, John (see Crozier, Brian Rossiter)

ROSTON, Murray, MA, PhD; British academic and writer; *Professor of English, Bar-Ilan University*; b. 10 Dec. 1928, London, England. *Education:* Queens' Coll., Cambridge, Queen Mary Coll., London. *Career:* Prof. of English, Bar-Ilan Univ., Ramat Gan, Israel 1956–; Permanent Adjunct Prof., Univ. of California, Los Angeles 1999–. *Publications:* Prophet and Poet: The Bible and the Growth of Romanticism 1965, Biblical Drama in England from the Middle Ages to the Present Day 1968, The Soul of Wit: A Study of John Donne 1974, Milton and the Baroque 1980, Sixteenth-Century English Literature 1982, Renaissance Perspectives in Literature and the Visual Arts 1987, Changing Perspectives in Literature and the Visual Arts, 1650–1820 1990, Victorian Contexts in Literature and the Visual Arts 1995, Modernist Patterns in Literature and the Visual Arts 1999, The Search for Selfhood in Modern Literature 2001; contrib. to professional journals. *Address:* 51 Katznelson Street, Kiryat Ono, Israel.

ROTH, Andrew, BSS, MA; British political correspondent and writer; *Editor, Parliamentary Profiles*; b. 23 April 1919, New York, NY; m. 1st Mathilda Anna Friederich 1949 (divorced 1984); one s. one d.; m. 2nd Antoinette Putnam 2004. *Education:* City Coll., CUNY, Columbia Univ., Harvard Univ. *Career:* Reader, City Coll., CUNY 1939; Research Assoc., Inst. of Pacific Relations 1940, US Naval Intelligence 1940–45; editorial writer, The Nation 1945–46; Foreign Correspondent, Toronto Star Weekly 1946–50; London Correspondent, France Observateur, Sekai, Singapore Standard 1950–60; Ed., Parliamentary Profiles 1953–; Westminster Confidential 1953–; Political Correspondent, Manchester Evening News 1972–84, New Statesman 1984–96; Political Obituarist, The Guardian 1996–; columnist, British Journal of Health Care Services 1996–. *Publications:* Japan Strikes South 1941, French Interests and Policies in the Far East 1942, Dilemma in Japan 1945, The Business Background of MPs 1959, The MPs Chart 1967, Enoch Powell: Tory Tribune 1970, Can Parliament Decide… 1971, Heath and the Heathmen 1972, Lord on the Board 1972, Sir Harold Wilson: Yorkshire Walter Mitty 1977, Parliamentary Profiles, Vols I–IV 1984–85, 1997–2001, 2001–05, New MPs of '92 1992, Mr Nice Guy and his Chums 1993, New MPs of '97 1997, New MPs of '01 2001, New MPs of '05 2005. *Honours:* Hon. PhD (Open Univ.) 1992. *Address:* 34 Somali Road, London, NW2 3RL, England. *Telephone:* (20) 7794-5884 (office); (20) 7435-6673 (home). *Fax:* (20) 7794-5779 (office). *E-mail:* roth@rothprofiles.demon.co.uk (office). *Website:* www.rothprofiles.demon.co.uk.

ROTH, Gerhard Jürgen; Austrian writer and photographer; b. 24 June 1942, Graz; m. 1st Erika Wolfgruber 1963 (divorced 1986); m. 2nd Senta Thonhauser 1995; one s. two d. *Education:* Univ. of Graz Medical School. *Publications:* Die Autobiographie des Albert Einstein 1972, Der Ausbruch des Ersten Weltkriegs und andere Romane 1972, Der Wille zur Krankheit 1973, Der grosse Horizont 1974, Ein Neuer Morgen 1976, Winterreise 1978, Der stille Ozean (trans. as The Calm Ocean) 1980, Circus Saluti 1981, Die schönen Bilder beim Trabrennen 1982, Das Töten des Bussards 1982, Dorfchronik zum Landläufiger Tod 1984, Die Vergessenen 1986, Am Abgrund 1986, Der Untersuchungsrichter: Die Geschichte eines Entwurfs 1988, Die Geschichte der Dunkelheit: Ein Bericht 1991, Eine Reise in das Innere von Wien 1991, Das doppelköpfige Österreich 1995, Der See (trans. as The Lake) 1995, Der Plan 1998, Der Berg 2000, Der Strom (novel) 2002, Das Labyrinth (novel) 2005; various plays, essays, etc. *Honours:* State of Styria Literature Prizes 1972, 1973, 1976, South West German Radio Critic's Prize 1978, City of Hamburg Fellowship 1979–80, Alfrid Döblin Prize 1983, Marie Luise Kaschnitz Prize 1992, Vienna Literary Prize 1992, Peter-Rossegger Prize 1994, Austrian Booksellers Hon. Prize 1994. *Address:* Am Heumarkt 7/4/37, 1030 Vienna, Austria.

ROTH, Philip Milton, MA; American writer; b. 19 March 1933, Newark, NJ; s. of Bess Finkel Roth and the late Herman Roth; m. 1st Margaret Martinson 1959 (died 1968); m. 2nd Claire Bloom 1990 (divorced 1994). *Education:* Bucknell Univ. and Univ. of Chicago. *Career:* in US Army 1955–56; Lecturer in English, Univ. of Chicago 1956–58; Visiting Lecturer, Univ. of Iowa Writers' Workshop 1960–62; Writer-in-Residence, Princeton Univ. 1962–64, Univ. of Pa 1967–80; Distinguished Prof. of Literature, Hunter Coll. 1989–92; Visiting Lecturer, State Univ. of NY, Stony Brook 1967, 1968; Houghton Mifflin Literary Fellow 1959; Guggenheim Fellowship Grant 1959–60, Rockefeller Grant 1965, Ford Foundation Grant 1966; mem. American Acad. of Arts and Letters 1970–. *Publications:* Goodbye Columbus (novella and stories) 1959, Letting Go 1962, When She Was Good 1967, Portnoy's Complaint 1969, Our Gang 1971, The Breast 1972, The Great American Novel 1973, My Life as a Man 1974, Reading Myself and Others (essays) 1975, The Professor of Desire 1977, The Ghost Writer 1979, A Philip Roth Reader 1980, Zuckerman Unbound 1981, The Anatomy Lesson 1983, The Prague Orgy 1985, Zuckerman Bound 1985, The Counterlife (Nat. Book Critics' Circle Award 1987) 1986, The Facts: A Novelist's Autobiography 1988, Deception 1990, Patrimony (Nat. Book Critics' Circle Award 1992) 1991, Operation Shylock (PEN/Faulkner Award) 1993, Sabbath's Theater (Nat. Book Award for Fiction) 1995, American Pastoral (Pulitzer Prize in Fiction 1998) 1997, I Married a Communist (Ambassador Book Award of the English-Speaking Union) 1998, The Human Stain (PEN-Faulkner Award 2001, Prix Médicis Étranger 2002) 2000, The Dying Animal 2001, Shop Talk 2001, The Plot Against America (WHSmith Literary Award 2005) 2004, Everyman 2006. *Honours:* Guggenheim Fellowship 1959; Daroff Award of Jewish Book Council of America 1959, Nat. Inst. of Arts and Letters Award 1959, Nat. Arts Club's Medal of Honor for Literature 1991, Karel Capek Prize 1994, Nat. Medal of Arts 1999, Gold Medal in Fiction, American Acad. of Arts and Letters 2000, Nat. Book Foundation Medal for Distinguished Contribution to American Letters 2002. *Literary Agent:* The Wylie Agency, 250 W 57th Street, Suite 2114, New York, NY 10107, USA.

ROTHE-VALLBONA, Rima Gretel (see VALLBONA, Rima Gretel Rothe)

ROTHENBERG, Jerome Dennis, BA, MA; American academic, poet and writer; *Professor Emeritus, University of California at San Diego*; b. 11 Dec. 1931, New York, NY; m. Diane Brodatz 1952; one s. *Education:* City Coll., CUNY, Univ. of Michigan. *Career:* Prof. of English and Comparative Literature, State Univ. of NY at Binghamton 1986–88; Prof. of Visual Arts and Literature, Univ. of California, San Diego 1988–, now Prof. Emer.; mem. New Wilderness Foundation, PEN International. *Publications:* New Young German Poets 1959, White Sun Black Sun 1960, Technicians of the Sacred 1968, Poems for the Game of Silence: Selected Poems 1971, Shaking the Pumpkin 1972, America Prophecy 1973, Poland/1931 1974, Revolution of the Word 1974, A Big Jewish Book 1977, A Seneca Journal 1978, Numbers and Letters 1980, Vienna Blood 1980, Pre-Faces 1981, That Dada Strain 1983, Symposium of the Whole 1983, 15 Flower World Variations 1984, A Merz Sonata 1985, New Selected Poems, 1970–85 1986, Exiled in the Word 1989, Khurbn and Other Poems 1989, Further Sightings and Conversations 1989, The Lorca Variations 1994, Gematria 1994, An Oracle for Delfi 1995, Poems for the Millennium (two vols) 1995, 1998, Pictures of the Crucifixion 1996, Seedings and Other Poems 1996, The Book Spiritual Instrument 1996, A Paradise of Poets 1999, A Book of the Book 2000, The Case for Memory 2001, A Book of Witness: Spells and Gris-Gris (poems) 2003, María Sabina Selections 2003, A Book of Concealments 2004, 25 Caprichos (after Goya) 2004, Picasso: The Burial of the Count of Orgaz and Other Poems 2004, Writing Through: Translations and Variations 2004, The Burning Babe and Other Poems 2005, China Notes & The Treasures of Dunhuang 2006, Triptych 2007; contrib. to various publs. *Honours:* Nat. Endowment for the Arts Fellowship 1975, Guggenheim Fellowship 1976, American Book Award 1982, PEN Center, USA West Trans. Award 1994, 2002, PEN Oakland Josephine Miles Literary Awards 1994, 1996, Alfonso el Sabio Award for Trans. 2004, PEN American Center Trans. Award 2005, San Diego Library Lifetime Achievement Award 2007. *Address:* Department of Visual Arts, University of California at San

Diego, La Jolla, CA 92093 (office); 1026 San Abella Drive, Encinitas, CA 92024, USA (home). *Telephone:* (760) 436-9923 (home). *Fax:* (760) 436-6381 (home). *E-mail:* jrothenb@ucsd.edu (office); jrothenberg@cox.net (home). *Website:* wings.buffalo.edu/epc/authors/rothenberg (office).

ROTHERMERE, 4th Viscount, cr. 1919, of Hemsted; **Jonathan Harold Esmond Vere Harmsworth,** BA; British newspaper publisher; *Chairman, Daily Mail and General Trust PLC*; b. 3 Dec. 1967, London; s. of the late 3rd Viscount Rothermere and Patricia Evelyn Beverley Brooks; m. Claudia Clemence 1993; one s. three d. *Education:* Gordonstoun School, Scotland, Kent School, Conn., USA, Duke Univ., USA. *Career:* joined Mirror Group 1993; joined Northcliffe Newspapers Group Ltd 1995; Deputy Man. Dir, then Man. Dir Evening Standard 1997; Chair. Assoc. Newspapers Ltd 1998–; Chair. Assoc. New Media 1998, Daily Mail and Gen. Trust PLC 1998–; Pres. Newspaper Press Fund 1999–. *Address:* Daily Mail and General Trust PLC, Room 602, Northcliffe House, 2 Derry Street, London, W8 5TT, England (office). *Telephone:* (20) 7938-6613. *Fax:* (20) 7937-0043. *E-mail:* chairman@chairman.dmgt.co.uk (office).

ROUDINESCO, Elisabeth, DèsL; French historian and writer; b. 10 Sept. 1944, Paris. *Education:* Univ. of Paris and École Pratique des Hautes Études, Paris. *Career:* mem. Société Int. d'histoire de la Psychiatrie et de la Psychanalyse, Paris. *Publications:* Histoire de la Psychanalyse en France, 1885–1985 (two vols) 1982, 1986, Jacques Lacan & Co. 1990, Madness and Revolution 1991, Jacques Lacan: Esquisse d'une vie Histoire d'une Systéme de Pensée 1993, Jacques Lacan 1997, Pourquoi la psychanalyse – Why Psycho-analysis? 1999, De Quoi demain dialogue with Jacques Derrida, trans. as For What Tomorrow: A Dialogue) 2001, La Famille en dèsordre 2002, Philosophes dans la tourmente 2005; contribs to Le Monde 1996–, and to various other publs. *Address:* 89 ave Denfert-Rochereau, 75014 Paris, France. *Telephone:* 1-43-26-89-67. *Fax:* 1-44-07-25-78. *E-mail:* elisabeth.roudinesco@wanadoo.fr (home).

ROUNTREE, Owen (see Kittredge, William Alfred)

ROUSE, Anne Barrett, BA; American poet and writer; *Visiting Writing Fellow, St Mary's College, Queen's University, Belfast*; b. 26 Sept. 1954, Washington, DC. *Education:* Univ. of London. *Career:* Dir, Islington Mind 1992–95; Visiting Writing Fellow, Univ. of Glasgow 2000–02; mem. Poetry Soc., Writers' Guild. *Publications:* Sunset Grill 1993, Timing 1997; contrib. to periodicals. *Honours:* Poetry Book Soc. recommendations 1993, 1997. *Address:* c/o Bloodaxe Books Ltd, Highgreen, Tarset, Northumberland NE48 1RP, England. *Website:* www.annerouse.com.

ROUSSEAU, George Sebastian, BA, MA, PhD; American academic; *Co-Director, Oxford University Centre for the History of Childhood*; b. 23 Feb. 1941, New York, NY. *Education:* Amherst Coll., Princeton Univ. *Career:* Osgood Fellow in English Literature 1965–66, Woodrow Wilson Dissertation Fellow 1966, Princeton Univ.; book reviewer, The New York Times 1967–; instructor, Harvard Univ. 1966–68; Asst Prof. 1968–69, Assoc. Prof. 1969–76, Prof. of English 1976–94, Univ. of California at Los Angeles; Fulbright Resident Prof., West Germany 1970; Hon. Fellow, Wolfson Coll., Cambridge 1974–75; Overseas Fellow, Univ. of Cambridge 1979; Visiting Fellow Commoner, Trinity Coll., Cambridge 1982; Sr Fulbright Resident Scholar, Sir Thomas Browne Inst., Netherlands 1983; Visiting Exchange Prof., King's Coll., Cambridge 1984; Sr Fellow, Nat. Endowment for the Humanities 1986–87; Visiting Fellow and Waynflete Lecturer, Magdalen Coll., Oxford 1993–94; Regius Prof. of English Literature, King's Coll., Univ. of Aberdeen 1994–98; Research Prof. of Humanities, De Montfort Univ. 1999–2002; mem. Faculty of Modern History, Univ. of Oxford 2003–, currently Co-Dir Oxford Univ. Centre for the History of Childhood; mem. many professional organizations. *Publications:* This Long Disease My Life: Alexander Pope and the Sciences (ed. with Marjorie Hope Nicolson) 1968, John Hill's Hypochondriasis 1969, English Poetic Satire: Wyatt to Byron (with N. Rudenstine) 1969, The Augustan Milieu: Essays Presented to Louis A. Landa (ed. with Eric Rothstein) 1970, Tobias Smollett: Bicentennial Essays Presented to Lewis M. Knapp (co-ed.) 1971, Organic Form: The Life of an Idea (ed.) 1972, Goldsmith: The Critical Heritage 1974, The Renaissance Man in the 18th Century 1978, The Ferment of Knowledge: Studies in the Historiography of Eighteenth Century Science (ed. with Roy Porter) 1980, The Letters and Private Papers of Sir John Hill 1981, Tobias Smollett: Essays of Two Decades 1982, Literature and Science (ed.) 1985, Science and the Imagination: The Berkeley Conference (ed.) 1985, Sexual Underworlds of the Enlightenment (ed. with Roy Porter) 1987, The Enduring Legacy: Alexander Pope Tercentenary Essays (ed. with P. Rogers) 1988, Exoticism in the Enlightenment (with Roy Porter) 1990, Perilous Enlightenment: Pre- and Post-Modern Discourses: Sexual, Historical 1991, Enlightenment Crossings: Pre- and Post-Modern Discourses: Anthropological 1991, Enlightenment Borders: Pre- and Post-Modern Discources: Medical, Scientific 1991, Hysteria Before Freud (co-author) 1993, Gout: The Patrician Malady 1998, Framing and Imagining Disease (ed.) 2003, Marguerite Yourcenar: A Biography 2003, Nervous Acts: Essays on Literature, Culture and Sensibility 2004; contrib. to professional journals and general publications. *Honours:* Clifford Prize 1987, Leverhulme Trust Awardee 1999–2001. *Address:* Modern History Research Unit, Radcliffe Infirmary, Block 11–12, University of Oxford, Oxford, OX2 6HE (office); Osterley House, Wellshead, Harwell Village, Oxfordshire OX11 0HD, England (home). *Telephone:* (1865) 224208 (office). *Fax:* (1865) 224173

(office). *E-mail:* george.rousseau@magdalen.oxford.ac.uk (office). *Website:* www.history.ox.ac.uk (office).

ROUX, Jean-Louis, CC; Canadian theatre director, actor and author; b. 18 May 1923, Montreal; s. of Louis Roux and Berthe Leclerc; m. Monique Oligny 1950; one s. *Education:* Coll. Sainte-Marie and Univ. de Montréal. *Career:* mem. Les Compagnons de Saint Laurent theatrical co. 1939–42, Ludmilla Pitoëff theatrical co. 1942–46; mil. training 1942–46; founder, Théâtre d'Essai, Montreal 1951; Sec.-Gen., Théâtre du Nouveau Monde 1953–63 (co-founder 1950), Artistic Dir 1966–82; Dir-Gen. Nat. Theatre School of Canada 1982–87; has appeared in more than 200 roles (in both French and English) on stage (Montreal, Stratford, Paris), TV, cinema and radio and directed more than 50 theatrical productions; apptd to Senate 1994–96; Lt Gov. of Québec 1996; Chair. Canada Council for the Arts 1998–2003; mem. Royal Soc. of Canada 1982–; Life Gov. Nat. Theatre School of Canada. *Honours:* Ordre de la Pléiade 1995, KStJ; Chevalier, Ordre Nat. du Québec 1989; Dr hc (Laval Univ.) 1988, (Univ. of Ottawa) 1995; Hon. LLD (Concordia Univ.) 1993; numerous awards and medals including Molson Award 1977, World Theatre Award 1985. *Address:* 4145 Blueridge Crescent, Apt. 3, Montreal, PQ H3H 1S7, Canada. *Telephone:* (514) 937-2505. *Fax:* (514) 937-5975.

ROWAN, Deirdre (see Williams, Jeanne)

ROWAN, Hester (see Robinson, Sheila Mary)

ROWAN, Patricia Adrienne; British journalist; d. of the late Henry Matthew and Gladys Talintyre; m. Ivan Settle Harris Rowan 1960; one s. *Education:* Harrow Co. Grammar School for Girls. *Career:* journalist, Time and Tide 1952–56, Sunday Express 1956–57, Daily Sketch 1957–58, News Chronicle 1958–60, Granada TV 1961–62, Sunday Times 1962–66, Times Educational Supplement 1972–89, Ed. 1989–97; mem. Bd Nat. Children's Bureau 1997–2003, Research Cttee Teacher Training Agency 1997–2000; Chair. Bd of Trustees, Stroud Valleys Project 2002–. *Publications:* What Sort of Life? 1980, Education – the Wasted Years? (contrib.) 1988. *Honours:* Hon. FRSA 1989; Hon. Fellow Inst. of Educ., Univ. of London 1997. *Address:* Horsley, Stroud, Glos., GL6 0PY, England. *Telephone:* (1453) 833305. *Fax:* (1453) 833305. *E-mail:* prowan@connectfree.co.uk.

ROWBOTHAM, David Harold, AM, BA; Australian poet, writer and journalist; b. 27 Aug. 1924, Toowoomba, Qld; m. Ethel Jessie Matthews 1952; two d. *Education:* Univ. of Queensland. *Career:* RAAF, South Pacific; Commonwealth Literary Fund Lecturer in Australian Literature 1956, 1961, 1964; Arts Ed. 1970–80, Literary Ed. 1980–87, Brisbane Courier-Mail; mem. Australian Soc. of Authors, Fellowship of Australian Writers. *Publications:* poetry: Ploughman and Poet 1954, Inland 1958, All the Room 1964, Bungalow and Hurricane 1967, The Makers of the Ark 1970, The Pen of Feathers 1971, Mighty Like a Harp 1974, Selected Poems 1975, Maydays 1980, New and Selected Poems, 1945–93 1994, The Ebony Gates: New & Wayside Poems 1996, Poems for America 2002; fiction: Town and City 1956, The Man in the Jungle 1964; contrib. to numerous magazines and journals, to numerous anthologies world-wide. *Honours:* Grace Leven Prize 1964, Second Prize for Poetry, New South Wales Captain Cook Bi-Centenary Celebrations Literary Competition 1970, Emeritus Fellowship in Australian Literature, Literature Bd, Australia Council 1989. *Address:* 28 Percival Terrace, Holland Park, Brisbane, Qld 4121, Australia. *Website:* www.qct.com.au/rowbotham.

ROWE, Bridget; British newspaper editor; b. 16 March 1950, d. of Peter Rowe and Myrtle Rowe; m. James Anthony Nolan; one s. *Education:* St Michael's School, Limpsfield. *Career:* Ed. Look Now 1971–76, Women's World 1976–81; Asst Ed. The Sun 1981–82; launched News of the World Sunday magazine 1981–86; Ed. Woman's Own 1986–90, TV Times 1990–91, Sunday Mirror 1991–92, The People 1992–96, Man. Dir 1995–98; Man. Dir Sunday Mirror 1995–98, Ed. 1997–98; Dir of Communications National Magazines 1998–99; Content Dir Yava 2000. *Address:* c/o Jacque Evans Management Ltd, Suite 1, 14 Holmesley Road, London SE23 1PJ, England.

ROWLAND, Iris (see Roberts, Irene)

ROWLAND, Peter Kenneth; British writer; b. 26 July 1938, London, England. *Education:* Univ. of Bristol. *Publications:* The Last Liberal Governments: The Promised Land 1905–1910 1968, The Last Liberal Governments: Unfinished Business 1911–1914 1971, Lloyd George 1975, Macaulay's History of England in the 18th Century (ed.) 1980, Macaulay's History of England from 1485 to 1685 (ed.) 1985, Autobiography of Charles Dickens (ed.) 1988, The Disappearance of Edwin Drood 1991, Thomas Day 1748–1789: Virtue Almost Personified 1996, Just Stylish 1998, Raffles and his Creator 1999, What's Where in the Saturday Books 2002. *Address:* 18 Corbett Road, Wanstead, London, E11 2LD, England.

ROWLANDS, John, (Sion Prysor), MA, DPhil; British novelist, critic and editor; *Professor Emeritus of Welsh, University of Wales*; b. Trawsfynydd, Wales; m. Margaret Eluned; two s. one d. *Education:* Univ. of Wales, Univ. of Oxford. *Career:* Prof. of Welsh, Univ. of Wales, Aberystwyth –2003, Prof. Emer. 2003–. *Publications include:* Lle bo'r gwenyn: Nofel 1960, Yn ol i'w teyrnasoedd: Nofel 1963, Ienctid yw 'Mhechod: Nofel 1965, Llawer is na'r angylion: Nofel 1968, Bydded tywyllwch: Nofel 1969, Arch ym Mhrâg: Nofel 1973, Tician Tician: Nofel, T. Rowland Hughes (criticism) 1975, Y Meddwl a'r Dychmyg Cymreig (gen. series ed.), Cnoi Cil Ar Lenyddiaeth 1989, Ysgrifau Ar Y Nofel 1992, Sglefrio Ar Eiriau 1992, The Bloodaxe Book of Modern Welsh Poetry (co-ed. with Menna Elfyn) 2003. *Honours:* Hon. Prof., Univ. of Wales,

Bangor; Hon. Fellow, Trinity Coll., Carmarthen; Hon. Mem. Gorsedd of Bards. *Address:* Y Goeden Eirin, Dolydd, Caernarfon, Gwynedd, LL54 7EF, Wales (home). *Telephone:* (1286) 830942 (home). *E-mail:* john_rowlands@tiscali.co .uk (home). *Website:* www.ygoedeneirin.co.uk.

ROWLING, Joanne Kathleen (J. K.), OBE, BA; British writer; b. 31 July 1965, Chipping Sodbury, England; d. of Peter Rowling and Anne Rowling; m. 1st (divorced); one d.; m. 2nd Neil Murray 2001; one s. one d. *Education:* Wyedean Comprehensive School, Univ. of Exeter, Moray House Teacher Training Coll. *Publications:* Harry Potter and the Philosopher's Stone (aka Harry Potter and the Sorcerer's Stone) (Smarties Prize, British Book Awards Children's Book of the Year) 1997, Harry Potter and the Chamber of Secrets (Smarties Prize, British Book Awards Children's Book of the Year) 1998, Harry Potter and the Prisoner of Azkaban (Smarties Prize) 1999, Harry Potter and the Goblet of Fire 2000, Quidditch Through the Ages by Kennilworthy Whisp 2001, Fantastic Beasts and Where to Find Them by Newt Scamander 2001, Harry Potter and the Order of the Phoenix (WHSmith People's Choice Fiction Prize 2004) 2003, Harry Potter and the Half-Blood Prince (Quill Book Award for Book of the Year, Best Children's Book, British Book Awards WHSmith Book of the Year 2006, Royal Mail Award for Scottish Children's Books) 2005, Harry Potter and the Deathly Hallows 2007. *Honours:* Hon. DJur (Univ. of Aberdeen) 2006; Premio Príncipe de Asturias 2003, Variety UK Entertainment Personality Award, British Ind. Film Awards 2004, ranked by Forbes magazine amongst 100 Most Powerful Women (85th) 2004, (40th) 2005. *Literary Agent:* c/o Christopher Little Literary Agency, Eel Brook Studios, 125 Moore Park Road, London, SW6 4PS, England. *Telephone:* (20) 7736-4455. *Fax:* (20) 7736-4490. *E-mail:* info@christopherlittle.net. *Website:* www.christopherlittle.net; www.jkrowling.com.

ROY, Arundhati; Indian writer, artist, actress and activist; b. 1960, Bengal; m. 1st Gerard Da Cunha (divorced); m. 2nd Pradeep Krishen. *Education:* Delhi School of Architecture. *Career:* fmrly with Nat. Inst. of Urban Affairs; judge, Cannes Film Festival 2000–; faced charges of inciting violence, attacking a court official and contempt of court for opposing Sardar Sarovar dam project in the Narmada valley 2001. *Screenplays:* In Which Annie Gives It Those Ones (TV) 1988, Electric Moon 1992, DAM/AGE 2002. *Publications:* The God of Small Things (Booker Prize) 1997, The End of Imagination (essay) 1998, The Cost of Living (essays) 1998, The Great Common Good (essay) 1999, War is Peace 2000, The Algebra of Infinite Justice (essays) 2001, Power Politics 2002, The Ordinary Person's Guide to Empire (essays) 2004; contribs to periodicals. *Honours:* Lannan Prize for Cultural Freedom 2002. *Address:* c/o South End Press, 7 Brookline Street, Suite 1, Cambridge, MA 02139-4146, USA; c/o India Ink Publishing Co. Pvt. Ltd, C-1, Soami Nagar, New Delhi 110 017, India.

ROYLE, Nicholas John, BA; British writer; b. 20 March 1963; m. Kate Ryan 1996; one s. one d. *Education:* Queen Mary Coll., London. *Career:* mem. Soc. of Authors. *Publications:* fiction: Counterparts 1993, Saxophone Dreams 1996, The Matter of the Heart 1997, The Director's Cut 2000, Antwerp 2004; ed.: Darklands 1991, Darklands 2 1992, A Book of Two Halves 1996, The Tiger Garden: A Book of Writers' Dreams 1996, The Time Out Book of New York Short Stories 1997, The Agony and the Ecstasy 1998, The Ex Files 1998, Neonlit: The Time Out Book of New Writing 1998, The Time Out Book of Paris Short Stories 1999, Neonlit: The Time Out Book of New Writing Vol. 2 1999, The Time Out Book of London Short Stories Vol. 2 2000, Dreams Never End 2004; contrib. to Independent, Guardian, Time Out, New Statesman, Literary Review. *Literary Agent:* c/o John Saddler, Curtis Brown Ltd, Haymarket House, 28–29 Haymarket, London, SW1Y 4SP, England. *Telephone:* (20) 7393-4400. *Fax:* (20) 7393-4401. *E-mail:* info@curtisbrown.co.uk. *Website:* www .curtisbrown.co.uk. *Address:* 38 Belfield Road, Manchester, M20 6BH, England (home). *Website:* www.nicholasroyle.com.

RÓŻEWICZ, Tadeusz; Polish poet and playwright; b. 9 Oct. 1921, Radomsko. *Education:* Jagiellonian Univ., Kraków. *Career:* fmr factory worker and teacher; mem. Art Acad. of Leipzig; Corresp. mem. Bavarian Acad. of Fine Arts 1982–, Acad. of Arts (GDR). *Plays include:* Kartoteka (The Card Index), Grupa Laokoona (Laocoön's Group), Świadkowie albo nasza mała stabilizacja (The Witnesses), Akt przerywany (The Interrupted Act), Śmieszny staruszek (The Funny Man), Wyszedł z domu (Gone Out), Spaghetti i miecz (Spaghetti and the Sword), Maja córeczka (My Little Daughter), Stara kobieta wysiaduje (The Old Woman Broods), Na czworakach (On All Fours), Do piachu (Down to Sand), Białe małżeństwo (White Marriage), Odejście Głodomora (Starveling's Departure), Na powierzchni poematu i w środku: nowy wybór wierszy, Pułapka (The Trap), Próba rekonstrukcji (Spread Card Index), Kartoteka rozrzucona (The Card Index Scattered). *Prose includes:* Tarcza z pajęczyny, Opowiadania wybrane (Selected Stories), Na powierzchni poematu (They Came to See a Poet) 1991, Płaskorzeźba (Bas-Relief) 1991, Nasz starszy brat 1992, Historia pięciu wierszy 1993. *Publications:* 15 vols of poetry including Niepokój (Faces of Anxiety), Czerwona rękawiczka (The Red Glove), Czas, który idzie (The Time Which Goes On), Równina (The Plain), Srebrny kłos (The Silver Ear), Rozmowa z księciem (Conversation with the Prince), Zielona róża (The Green Rose), Nic w płaszczu Prospera (Nothing in Prosper's Overcoat), Twarz (The Face), Duszyczka (A Little Soul), Poezje (Poetry) 1987, Słowo po słowie (Word by Word) 1994, Zawsze fragment (Always the Fragment) 1996, Zawsze fragment: Recycling (Always the Fragment: Recycling) 1999, Matka odchodzi (The Mother Goes) 2000, Nożyk profesora (The Professor's Knife) 2001, Szara strefa 2002, Wyjście 2004. *Honours:* Order of Banner of Labour (2nd class) 1977, Great Cross of Polonia Restituta Order

1996; Dr hc (Wrocław) 1991, (Silesian Univ., Katowice) 1999, (Jagiellonian Univ.) 2000, (Kraków) 2000, (Warsaw) 2001; State Prize for Poetry 1955, 1956, Literary Prize, City of Cracow 1959, Prize of Minister of Culture and Art 1962, State Prize 1st Class 1966, Austrian Nat. Prize for European Literature 1982, Prize of Minister of Foreign Affairs 1974, 1987, Golden Wreath Prize for Poetry (Yugoslavia) 1987, Władysław Reymont Literary Prize 1999; Home Army Cross, London 1956, Alfred Jurzykowski Foundation Award, New York 1966, Medal of 30th Anniversary of People's Poland 1974, Nike Literary Prize 2000, Premio Librex Montale, Literary Prize (Italy) 2002. *Address:* ul. Promien 16, 51-659 Wrocław, Poland (home). *Telephone:* (71) 3452126 (home). *Fax:* (71) 3452126 (home).

RUBIN, Diana Kwiatkowski, BA, MA; American poet and writer; b. 30 Dec. 1958, New York, NY; m. Paul Rubin 1986, one s. two d. *Education:* Marymount Manhattan Coll., New York Univ. *Career:* mem. Acad. of American Poets. *Publications:* Spirits in Exile 1990, Visions of Enchantment 1991, Dinosauria 1995; contrib. to Poet, Amelia, Wind, Quest, Fox Cry, Voices International. *Honours:* first prize Sparrowgrass Poetry Forum Awards 1998. *Address:* PO Box 398, Piscataway, NJ 08855, USA.

RUBIN, Louis Decimus, Jr, PhD; American writer, academic and publisher; *Professor Emeritus of English, University of North Carolina;* b. 19 Nov. 1923, Charleston, SC; s. of Louis Decimus Rubin, Sr and Janet Weinstein Rubin; m. Eva Maryette Redfield 1951; two s. *Education:* High School of Charleston, Coll. of Charleston, Univ. of Richmond and Johns Hopkins Univ. *Career:* U.S. Army 1943–46; instructor in English Johns Hopkins Univ. 1948–54; Exec. Sec. American Studies Asscn 1954–56 (also fmr Vice-Pres.); Assoc. Ed. News Leader, Richmond, Va 1956–57; Assoc. Prof. of English, Hollins Coll., Prof., Chair. of Dept 1960–67, Prof. of English Univ. of NC 1967–73, Univ. Distinguished Prof. 1973-89, Prof. Emer. 1989–; Visiting Prof. La. State Univ., Univ. of Calif. at Santa Barbara, Harvard Univ.; lecturer, Aix-Marseille at Nice, Kyoto Summer American Studies Seminars; USICA, Austria, Germany; Ed. Southern Literary Studies Series, Louisiana State Univ. Press 1965–90; Co-Ed. Southern Literary Journal 1968–89; co-founder and Editorial Dir Algonquin Books, Chapel Hill 1982–91; fmr Pres. Soc. for Study of Southern Literature; fmr Chair. American Literature Section, Modern Language Asscn; mem. SC Acad. of Authors, Fellowship of Southern Writers. *Publications:* author: Thomas Wolfe: The Weather of His Youth 1955, No Place on Earth 1959, The Faraway Country 1964, The Golden Weather (novel) 1961, The Curious Death of the Novel 1967, The Teller in the Tale 1967, George W. Cable 1969, The Writer in the South 1972, William Elliott Shoots a Bear 1975, The Wary Fugitives 1978, Surfaces of a Diamond (novel) 1981, A Gallery of Southerners 1982, The Even-Tempered Angler 1984, The Edge of the Swamp: a study in the Literature and Society of the Old South 1989, The Mockingbird in the Gum Tree 1991, Small Craft Advisory 1991, The Heat of the Sun (novel) 1995, Babe Ruth's Ghost 1996, Seaports of the South 1998, A Memory of Trains 2000, An Honorable Estate 2001; editor: Southern Renascence 1953, Idea of an American Novel 1961, South 1961, Comic Imagination in American Literature 1973, The Literary South 1979, American South 1980, The History of Southern Literature 1985, An Apple for My Teacher 1986, Algonquin Literary Quiz Book 1990, A Writer's Companion 1995. *Honours:* Hon. DLitt (Richmond, Clemson, Coll. of Charleston, Univ. of the South, Univ. of NC, Ashville, Univ. of NC Chapel Hill); Richard Beale Davis Award for Lifetime Achievement in Southern Letters, Society for Study of Southern Literature 2004. *Address:* 702 Gimghoul Road, Chapel Hill, NC 27514, USA (home).

RUBINA, Dina Ilyinichna; Israeli writer; b. 19 Sept. 1953, Tashkent, Uzbekistan. *Education:* Tashkent State Conservatory. *Career:* music teacher Tashkent Inst. of Culture 1977–90; literary debut in Yunost magazine 1971; emigrated to Israel 1990; book publications, theatrical stagings, film, newspaper editing (Pyatnitza and others); Head Dept of Public and Cultural Relations, The Jewish Agency in Russia 1999–2003. *Films:* Zavtra, kak obychno 1984, Na Verhney Maslovke 2004. *Publications:* The Double-Barrelled Name (short stories) 1990, In Thy Gates 1994, An Intellectual Sat Down on the Road 1995, Here Comes the Messiah 1997, The Escort Angel 1998, The Last Wild Boar from Pontevedra Forest 1998, High Water in Venice 1999, Several Hurried Words of Love (short stories) 2003. *Honours:* Ministry of Culture Award 1982, Arye Dulchin Award (Israel) 1991, Israel Writers' Union Award 1995, Best Book of literary season, France 1996. *Address:* Et Ha'zmir, 11/8, 98491 Maale-Adumim, Israel (home). *Telephone:* 2-5352435 (home). *Fax:* 2-5352435 (home). *E-mail:* web@dinarubina.com (home). *Website:* www.dinarubina.com (home).

RUDKIN, (James) David, MA; British dramatist; *Honorary Professor, University of Wales, Aberystwyth;* b. 29 June 1936, London, England; m. Alexandra Margaret Thompson 1967; two s. (one deceased) two d. *Education:* St Catherine's Coll., Oxford. *Career:* Judith E. Wilson Fellow, Univ. of Cambridge 1984; Visiting Prof. Univ. of Middlesex 2005–; Hon. Prof. Univ. of Wales, Aberystwyth 2006–; mem. Hellenic Soc. *Plays:* Afore Night Come, The Sons of Light, Ashes, The Triumph of Death, The Saxon Shore, Red Sun 2003. *Film screenplays:* Testimony 1987, December Bride 1989, The Woodlanders 1997. *Radio:* Cries from Casement as his Bones are Brought to Dublin, The Love Song of Alfred J. Hitchcock 1993, The Haunting of Mahler 1994. *Television:* Penda's Fen, Artemis 81 1981. *Publications:* Schoenbergs Moses und Aron (trans. for Royal Opera) 1965, Hippolytus (trans. from Euripides) 1980, Peer Gynt (trans. from Ibsen) 1983, Rosmersholm (trans. from Ibsen) 1990, When We Dead Waken (trans. from Ibsen) 1990, Dreyer's Vampyr (monograph) 2005; opera libretti: The Grace of Todd (music by Gordon Crosse) 1969, Inquest of Love (music by Jonathan Harvey) 1993, Broken Strings (music by Param Vir) 1994; contrib. to Drama, Tempo, Encounter, Theatre Research Journal, Vertigo. *Honours:* Evening Standard Most Promising Dramatist Award 1962, John Whiting Drama Award 1974, Obie Award, New York 1977, New York Film Festival Gold Medal for Screenplay 1987, European Film Festival Special Award 1989, Sony Silver Radio Drama Award 1994. *Literary Agent:* c/o Casarotto Ramsay Ltd, Waverley House, 7–12 Noel Street, London, W1F 8GQ, England. *E-mail:* agents@casarotto.uk.com. *Website:* www.davidrudkin.com.

RUDMAN, Mark, BA, MFA; American poet, critic, editor, translator and academic; b. 11 Dec. 1948, New York, NY; m. Madelaine Bates; one s. *Education:* New School for Social Research, Columbia Univ. *Career:* Poetry and Criticism Ed. 1975–, Ed.-in-Chief 1984–, Pequod Journal; writer-in-residence, Univ. of Hawaii 1978, SUNY at Buffalo 1979, Wabash Coll. 1979; Adjunct Lecturer, Queens Coll., CUNY 1980–81; Lecturer, Parsons School of Design 1983; poet-in-residence and Assoc. Prof., York Coll., CUNY 1984–88; Asst Dir and Adjunct Prof., Graduate Creative Writing Program, New York Univ. 1986–; Adjunct Prof., Columbia Univ. 1988–91, 1992–95; poet-in-residence, SUNY at Purchase 1991; Walt Whitman Poet 1998; mem. PEN, Poetry Soc. of America (bd of govs 1984–88). *Publications:* In the Neighboring Cell (poems) 1982, The Mystery in the Garden (chapbook) 1985, By Contraries and Other Poems: 1970–1984, Selected and New 1986, The Ruin Revived (chapbook) 1986, The Nowhere Steps (poems) 1990, Literature and the Visual Arts (ed.) 1990, Diverse Voices: Essays on Poetry 1993, Rider (poems) 1994, Realm of Unknowing: Meditations on Art, Suicide, Uncertainty, and Other Transformations 1995, The Millennium Hotel (poems) 1996, Provoked in Venice (poems) 1999, The Killers (poems) 2000, The Couple 2001, Sundays on the Phone (poems) 2005; translator: Square of Angels, by B. Antonych 1976, My Sister – Life, by Pasternak 1983; contrib. poems and essays to many anthologies and other publications. *Honours:* Acad. of American Poets Award 1971, PEN Trans. Fellowship 1976, Yaddo Residencies 1977, 1983, Co-ordinating Council for Literary Magazines Ed.'s Award 1981, Ingram Merrill Foundation Fellowship 1983–84, Max Hagward Award for Trans. 1984, New York Foundation of the Arts Fellowship 1988, Nat. Book Critics Circle Award in Poetry 1994, NEA Fellowship 1995, Guggenheim Fellowship 1996–97. *Address:* 817 West End Avenue, New York, NY 10025, USA.

RUDMAN, Michael P.; American publishing executive; b. 1950, New York. *Education:* Univ of Michigan and New York Univ. *Career:* Pres. Nat. Learning Corpn, also CEO, Dir; Pres. Delaney Books Inc., also CEO, Dir; Pres. Frank Merriwell Inc., also CEO, Dir; mem. Asscn of American Publishers. *Address:* National Learning Corporation, 212 Michael Drive, Syosset, NY 11791, USA. *Website:* www.passbooks.com.

RUDOLF, Anthony, BA; British poet, writer and translator; b. 6 Sept. 1942, London, England; m. (divorced); one s. one d. *Education:* Trinity Coll., Cambridge, British Inst., Paris. *Career:* Co-founder and Ed. Menard Press, London 1969; Adam Lecturer, King's Coll., London 1990; Pierre Rouve Memorial Lecturer, Sofia 2001; Visiting Lecturer, Faculty of Arts and Humanities, London Metropolitan Univ. 2001–03; Royal Literary Fund Fellow, Univ. of Hertfordshire 2003–05, Univ. of Westminster 2005–06. *Publications:* The Same River Twice 1976, After the Dream: Poems 1964–79 1980, Primo Levi's War Against Oblivion 1990, Mandorla 1999, The Arithmetic of Memory 1999; translations of poetry; contrib. to periodicals and newspapers. *Honours:* Chevalier, Ordre des Arts et Lettres 2004. *Address:* 8 The Oaks, Woodside Avenue, London, N12 8AR, England (home). *E-mail:* anthony.rudolf@virgin.net (home). *Website:* www.menardpress.co.uk.

RUELL, Patrick (see Hill, Reginald Charles)

RUFIN, Jean-Christophe, MD; French writer and doctor; *President, Action Contre la Faim;* b. 28 June 1952, Bourges; s. of Marcel Rufin and Denise Bonneau; one s. two d. *Education:* Lycées Janson-de-Sailly and Claude Bernard, Paris, Pitié-Salpêtrière School of Medicine, Paris. *Career:* Hosp. Intern, Paris 1975–81, Dir of Clinic 1981–83; Medical Dir Action Int. Contre la Faim (ACF, now Action Contre la Faim) 1983–85, Pres. 2003–; Chief of Mission of Sec. of State for Human Rights 1986–88; Cultural Attaché French Embassy in Brazil 1989–90; Vice-Pres. Médécins sans Frontières (MSF) 1991–93; Adviser to Minister of Defence 1993–95; Hospital Dr, Nanterre Hosp. 1994–95; Conference Dir Univ. de Paris-Nord 1993–95; Admin. French Red Cross 1995; Dir of Research Inst. des Relations Int. et Stratégiques (Iris) 1996, later Deputy Dir. *Publications:* Le Piège humanitaire 1986, L'Empire et les nouveaux barbares 1992, La Dictature libérale (Prix Jean-Jacques Rousseau) 1994, L'Aventure humanitaire 1994, L'Abyssin (Prix Goncourt, Prix Méditerranée) 1997, Sauver Ispahan 1998, Les Causes perdues (Prix Bergot, Prix Interallié) 1999, Rouge Brésil (Prix Goncourt) 2001, Globalia 2004. *Honours:* Chevalier des Arts et des Lettres, Chevalier de la Légion d'Honneur. *Address:* 4 rue Niepce, 75014 Paris (office); 73 rue du Cherche-Midi, 75006 Paris, France (home). *E-mail:* acf12@wanadoo.fr (home).

RÚFUS, Milan; Slovak poet, literary historian and essayist; b. 10 Dec. 1928, Závazná Poruba; m.; one d. *Education:* Comenius Univ., Bratislava. *Career:* at Inst. of Slovak Language and Literature Faculty of Philosophy Comenius Univ. 1952–89; Assoc. Prof., Lecturer in Slovak Language and Literature, Inst. Universitario, Naples 1971–72; mem. Club of Ind. Writers of Slovakia. *Publications:* Until We Have Matured 1956, Bells 1968, A Triptych 1969, People of the Mountains 1969, The Table of the Poor 1972, The Cradle 1972, A

Boy is Drawing a Rainbow 1974, Music of Forms (accompanied by paintings by L. Fulla) 1977, Forest (accompanied by photographs by M. Martincek) 1978, Ode to Joy 1981, Severe Bread 1987, A Late Self-Portrait 1993, Reading from Destiny 1996, Dragonfly 1998, Simple One Until the Little Roots of its Hair 2000; children's: Book of Fairy Tales 1975, Saturday Evenings 1979, A Small Well 1985, Silent Fern 1990, Small Prayers 1990, Small Prayers for a Child 1995; essays: Man, Time and Work 1968, Four Epistles to People 1969, On Literature 1974, And What is a Poem 1978, Epistles Old and New 1997, Time of Shy Questions 2001. *Honours:* Tomáš Garrigue Masaryk Order 1990, L'udovít Štúr Order (1st Class) 1993; Hon. LittD (Bratislava); State Prize 1970, Slovak Nat. Prize 1982, World Congress of Slovaks Nat. Prize, Nat. Literature Prize 1996. *Address:* Fialkové údolie 31, 811 01 Bratislava, Slovakia. *Telephone:* (7) 5441-2948.

RUGARLI, Giampaolo; Italian writer; b. 5 Dec. 1932, Naples; s. of Mirko Rugarli and Rubina De Marco; m. Maria Pulci 1985; three c. *Education:* legal studies. *Career:* bank dir since 1972; a dir of Cariplo 1981–85; contrib. Messaggero and Corriere della Sera and other reviews. *Publications:* Il Superlativo assoluto, La troga, Il nido di ghiaccio, Diario di un uomo a disagio, Andromeda e la notte, L'orrore che mi hai dato 1987, Una montagna australiana 1992, Per i pesci non è un problema 1992, I camini delle fate 1993, Il manuale del romanziere (The Novelist's Handbook) 1993, L'infinito, forse 1995, Una gardenia ni capilli 1997, Il bruno dei crepuscoli (Leopardi) 1998, La Viaggiatrici del tram numero 4 2001, Il Cavaliere e la vendita della saggiera 2002, La mia Milano 2003. *Honours:* Premio Bagutta Opera Prima 1987; Premio Capri 1990. *Address:* Via Colle di Giano 62, Olevano Romano 00035, Italy. *Telephone:* (06) 9564518.

RUHM, Gerhard; Austrian writer, poet, dramatist, composer and graphic artist; b. 12 Feb. 1930, Vienna. *Education:* Acad. of Music, Vienna. *Career:* mem. Acad. of Fine Arts, Hamburg. *Publications:* Literarisches Cabaret (with H. Artmann and K. Bayer), 1958–59; hosn rosn baa (with H. Artmann and F. Achleitner), 1959; Kinderoper (with H. Artmann and K. Bayer), 1964; Gesammelte Gedichte, 1970; Gesammelte Theaterstücke 1954–1971, 1972; Erste Folger Kurzer Hörstücker, 1973; Zweite Folge kurzer Hörstücke, 1975, 1975; wald: ein deutsches requiem, 1983; Allein, verlassen, verloren: 3 Kurzhörspiele zum Thema Angst (with R. Hughes and Marie Luise Kaschnitz), 1986; leselieder/visuelle Musik, 1986; botschaft an die zukunft: gesammelte sprechtexte, 1988; Geschlechterdings: Chansons, Romanzen, Gedichte, 1990; Theatertexte, 1990; Mit Messer und Gabel, 1995. *Honours:* Asscn of War Blind Radio Prize 1983, Great Austrian State Prize 1991.

RUHMKORF, Peter; German poet and author; b. 25 Oct. 1929, Dortmund; m. Eva-Marie Titze. *Education:* studied in Hamburg. *Career:* Writer-in-Residence, University of Texas at Austin, 1969–70; Lecturer, University of Essen, 1974, 1991–92, University of Warwick, England, 1977; mem. Deutsche Akademie für Sprache und Dichtung eV, Darmstadt; Freie Akademie der Künste, Hamburg; PEN. *Publications:* Irdisches Vergnügen in g, 1959; Kunstücke: 50 Gedichte nebst einer Anleitung zum Wilderspruch, 1962; Die Jahre die Ihr kennt: Anfälle und Erinnerungen, 1972; Gesammelte Gedichte, 1976; Strömungslehre I: Poesie, 1978; Haltbar bis Ende, 199, 1979; Auf Wiedersehen in Kenilworth: Ein Märchen in dreizehn Kapiteln, 1980; agar agar: zaurzaurim: Zur Naturgeschichte dees Reims und der menschlichen Anklangsnerven, 1981; Hüter des Misthaufens, 1981; Kleine Fleckenkunde, 1981; Bleib erschütterbar und widersteh, 1984; Dintemann und Schindemann, 1987; Einmalig wie wir alle, 1989; Selbst III/88: Aus der Fassung, 1989; Tabu I: Tagebücher 1989–1991, 1995. *Honours:* Erich Kastner Prize, 1979; Arno Schmidt Prize, 1986; Heinrich Heine Prize, 1988; Georg Buchner Prize, 1993.

RUIZ DE GOPEGUI, Belén, (Belén Gopegui), LLB; Spanish writer; b. 1963, Madrid. *Education:* Univ. Autónoma de Madrid. *Film screenplays:* La suerte dormida (with Ángeles González-Sinde) 2003, El principio de Arquímedes 2004. *Play:* El coloquio. *Publications:* La escala de los mapas (novel) (Premio Tigre Juan 1993, Premio Iberoamericano Santiago del Nuevo Extremo 1994) 1992, Tocarnos la cara (novel) 1995, Cualladó: puntos de vista 1995, En desierta playa (short story) 1995, La conquista del aire (novel) 1998, Lo real (novel) 2001, El lado frío de la almohada (novel) 2004. *Address:* c/o Editorial Anagrama SA, Pedró de la Creu 58, 08034 Barcelona, Spain. *E-mail:* anagrama@anagrama-ed.es. *Website:* www.rebelion.org.

RUIZ GUINAZU, Magdalena; Argentine journalist; *President, Asociación Periodistas.* *Career:* career in journalism has spanned 50 years; currently host Magdalena Tempranisimo, Radio Mitre, Buenos Aires; columnist La Nación newspaper; Founder and Pres. Asociación Periodistas (press freedom org.). *Honours:* Int. Women's Media Foundation Lifetime Achievement Award 2003. *Address:* Asociación Periodistas, Piedras 1675, Of. B, (1140) Buenos Aires, Argentina (office). *Telephone:* (411) 4300-6149/9127 (office). *Fax:* (411) 4300-6149/9127 (office). *E-mail:* periodista@asociacionperiodistas.org (office).

RUIZ ZAFÓN, Carlos; Spanish writer and screenwriter; b. 25 Aug. 1964, Barcelona. *Education:* Barcelona Coll. of Jesuits, Sarrià. *Career:* fmr dir of publicity, Lorente Agency; moved to Los Angeles, USA to write screenplays 1994. *Publications:* novels: El príncipe de la niebla 1993, La sombra del viento (trans. as The Shadow of the Wind) (Prix des Amis du Scribe, France 2005, Prix Michelet, France 2005, Nielsen Gold Book Award 2006) 2000. *Honours:* Edebé Prize 1993. *Literary Agent:* Antonia Kerrigan Literary Agency, Travesera de Gracia 22, 4°, 1a, 08021 Barcelona, Spain. *Telephone:* (932) 093 820. *Fax:* (934) 144 328. *E-mail:* info@antoniakerrigan.com.

RULE, Jane Vance, OC, BA; Canadian writer; b. 28 March 1931, Plainfield, NJ; d. of Arthur Richard and Carlotta Jane (née Hink) Rule. *Education:* Palo Alto High School (CA), Mills Coll. (Oakland, CA), Univ. Coll. London (UK) and Stanford Univ. *Career:* Teacher of English Concord Acad, MA 1954–56; Asst Dir Int. House, Univ. of British Columbia, Canada 1958–59, part-time Lecturer 1959–73; subject of film Fiction and Other Truths: A Film About Jane Rule 1995; mem. Writers' Union of Canada, PEN; Phi Beta Kappa. *Publications:* Novels: The Desert of the Heart 1964, This Is Not For You 1971, Against the Season 1971, The Young in One Another's Arms 1977, Contract With the World 1980, Memory Board 1987, After the Fire 1989; Criticism: Lesbian Images 1975; Stories and essays: Theme for Diverse Instruments 1975, Outlander 1981, A Hot-Eyed Moderate 1985, Inland Passage and Other Stories 1985; numerous articles and short stories for journals and anthologies. *Honours:* Order of BC; Hon. DLitt (British Columbia) 1994; Canadian Authors' Asscn Award for Best Novel 1978, Benson and Hedges Award for Best Short Stories 1978, Literary Award, Gay Acad. Union, USA 1978, Award of Merit, The Fund for Human Dignity, USA 1983, BC Gay Lifetime Achievement Award 1996, Talking Book of the Year. *Address:* The Fork Route 1, S19 C17, Galiano, BC V0N 1P0, Canada.

RUMENS, Carol, PGDip, FRSL; British writer and poet; *Professor of Creative Writing, University of Hull*; b. (Carol-Ann Lumley), 10 Dec. 1944, London, England; m. David Rumens 1965 (divorced); two d. *Education:* Univ. of London and Arden School of Theatre, Manchester. *Career:* Writing Fellow Univ. of Kent 1983–85; Northern Arts Writing Fellow 1988–90; Writer-in-Residence, Queen's Univ., Belfast 1991–, Univ. Coll., Cork 1994, Univ. of Stockholm 1999; Creative Writing Tutor, Queen's Univ. Belfast 1995–99; Univ. of Wales, Bangor 2000–; Prof. of Creative Writing, Univ. of Hull 2005–; mem. Int. PEN, Soc. of Authors, The Welsh Academi. *Publications:* A Strange Girl in Bright Colours 1973, Unplayed Music 1981, Scenes from the Gingerbread House 1982, Star Whisper 1983, Direct Dialling 1985, Selected Poems 1987, Plato Park 1987, The Greening of the Snow Beach 1988, From Berlin to Heaven 1989, Thinking of Skins: New and Selected Poems 1993, Best China Sky 1995, The Miracle Diet (with Viv Quillin) 1997, Holding Pattern 1998, Hex 2002, Collected Poems 2004, Poems 1968–2004 2005; contrib. ed. of numerous anthologies; contrib. to periodicals; trans. poems for collections of Russian poetry. *Honours:* Alice Hunt Bartlett Prize (Jt Winner) 1981, Prudence Farmer Award 1983, Cholmondeley Award 1984, First Prize, BT Section, Nat. Poetry Competition 2002, First Prize Peterloo Poetry Competition 2003. *Address:* 100A Tunis Road, London, W12 7EY, England. *Telephone:* (7917) 860326 (home). *E-mail:* c.rumens@hull.ac.uk (office); carol@rumens .fslife.co.uk (office).

RUSBRIDGER, Alan, MA; British journalist; *Editor, The Guardian and Executive Editor, The Observer (UK)*; b. 29 Dec. 1953, Lusaka, Zambia; s. of G. H. Rusbridger and B. E. Rusbridger (née Wickham); m. Lindsay Mackie 1982; two d. *Education:* Cranleigh School, Magdalene Coll., Cambridge. *Career:* reporter Cambridge Evening News 1976–79; reporter The Guardian 1979–82, diary ed. and feature writer 1982–86, special writer 1987–88, launch ed. Weekend Guardian 1988–89, Features Ed. 1989–93, Deputy Ed. 1993–95, Ed. 1995–; TV critic and feature writer The Observer 1986–, Exec. Ed. 1996–; Washington Corresp. London Daily News 1987; Chair. Photographer's Gallery 2001–; mem. Bd Guardian Newspapers Ltd 1994–, Guardian Media Group 1999–; mem. Scott Trust 1997–. *Television:* presenter of What the Papers Say (Granada TV) 1983–94, co-writer (with Ronan Bennett) of Fields of Gold (BBC TV) 2001. *Publications:* New World Order (ed.) 1991, Altered State (ed.) 1992, Guardian Year 1994, The Coldest Day in the Zoo 2004. *Honours:* Ed. of the Year, What the Papers Say Awards (Granada TV) 1996, 2001, Nat. Newspaper Ed., Newspaper Industry Awards 1996, Editor's Ed., Press Gazette 1997, What the Papers Say Judges' Award 2006. *Address:* The Guardian, 119 Farringdon Road, London, EC1R 3ER, England. *Telephone:* (20) 7278-2332. *Fax:* (20) 7239-9997.

RUSH, Norman, BA; American writer; b. 24 Oct. 1933, San Francisco, CA; m. Elsa Scheidt; one s. one d. *Education:* Swarthmore Coll. *Career:* antiquarian book dealer 1960–78; instructor in English and history and Co-Dir of Coll. A, Rockland Community Coll., Suffern, NY 1973–78; Co-Dir US Peace Corps, Botswana 1978–83; mem. PEN American Center. *Publications:* Whites (short stories) 1986, Mating (novel) 1991, Mortals (novel) 2003; contrib. to New York Review of Books, The New Yorker and other periodicals. *Honours:* Aga Khan Prize for the Short Story, NY State Council on Arts Award, Nat. Endowment for the Arts Award, Nat. Book Award, Nat. Acad. of Arts and Letters Rosenthal Award, Rockefeller Foundation Fellowship (Bellagio Residency) 1991, Irish Times/Aer Lingus Int. Fiction Prize 1992. *Address:* 18 High Tor Road, New City, NY 10956, USA. *E-mail:* rush18@optonline.net.

RUSHDIE, Sir (Ahmed) Salman, Kt, MA, FRSL; British writer and academic; *Distinguished Writer-in-Residence, Emory University*; b. 19 June 1947, Bombay (now Mumbai), India; s. of Anis Ahmed and Negin (née Butt) Rushdie; m. 1st Clarissa Luard 1976 (divorced 1987, died 1999); one s.; m. 2nd Marianne Wiggins 1988 (divorced 1993); one step-d.; m. 3rd Elizabeth West 1997 (divorced); one s.; m. 4th Padma Lakshmi 2004. *Education:* Cathedral and John Connon Boys' High School, Bombay, Rugby School, England, King's Coll., Cambridge. *Career:* mem. Footlights revue, Univ. of Cambridge 1965–68; actor, fringe theatre, London 1968–69; advertising copywriter 1969–73; wrote first published novel Grimus 1973–74; part-time advertising copywriter while writing second novel 1976–80; mem. Int. PEN 1981–, Soc. of Authors 1983–, Exec. Cttee Nat. Book League 1983–, Council Inst. of

Contemporary Arts 1985–, British Film Inst. Production Bd 1986–, PEN American Center (pres. 2004–06); as Distinguished Writer in Residence, Emory Univ., Atlanta 2007–; Hon. Prof. MIT 1993; Hon. Spokesman Charter 88 1989; Exec. mem. Camden Cttee for Community Relations 1977–83. *Television film screenplays:* The Painter and the Pest 1985, The Riddle of Midnight 1988. *Publications:* Grimus 1975, Midnight's Children 1981, Shame (Prix du Meilleur Livre Etranger 1984) 1983, The Jaguar Smile: A Nicaraguan Journey 1987, The Satanic Verses 1988, Is Nothing Sacred (lecture) 1990, Haroun and the Sea of Stories (novel) 1990, Imaginary Homelands: Essays and Criticism 1981–91 1991, The Wizard of Oz 1992, East, West (short stories) 1994, The Moor's Last Sigh (novel) 1995, The Vintage Book of Indian Writing 1947–97 (ed. with Elizabeth West) 1997, The Ground Beneath Her Feet 1999, Fury 2001, Step Across the Line: Collected Non-Fiction 1992–2002 2002, Telling Tales (contrib. to charity anthology) 2004, Shalimar the Clown 2005; articles for New York Times, Washington Post, The Times and Sunday Times. *Honours:* Distinguished Fellow in Literature, Univ. of East Anglia 1995, Hon. DLitt (Bard Coll.) 1995; Booker McConnell Prize for Fiction 1981, Arts Council Literature Bursary 1981, English Speaking Union Literary Award 1981, James Tait Black Memorial Book Prize 1981, Kurt Tucholsky Prize Sweden 1992, Booker of Bookers Award 1993, Prix Colette Switzerland 1993, Austrian State Prize for European Literature 1994, Whitbread Fiction Award 1996, British Book Awards Author of the Year 1996, London Int. Writers Award 2002; Commdr., Ordre des Arts et des Lettres 1999. *Literary Agent:* English Department, Emory University, N-302 Callaway Center, Atlanta, GA 30322, USA; Wylie Agency (UK) Ltd, 4–8 Rodney Street, London, N1 9JH, England. *Telephone:* (404) 727-6422 (office). *Fax:* (404) 727-2605 (office). *E-mail:* english@emory.edu (office). *Website:* www.english.emory.edu (office).

RUSHTON, Julian Gordon, BA, MusB, MA, DPhil; British academic and writer; *Professor Emeritus in the School of Music, University of Leeds*; b. 22 May 1941, Cambridge, England; two s. *Education:* Trinity Coll., Cambridge, Magdalen Coll., Oxford. *Career:* Lecturer, Univ. of East Anglia 1968–74; Lecturer in Music and Fellow, King's Coll., Cambridge 1974–81; West Riding Prof. of Music, Univ. of Leeds 1982–2002, Prof. Emer. 2002–; Chair. Editorial Bd, Musica Britannica 1993–; mem. Royal Musical Asscn (Pres. 1994–99), American Musicological Soc. (Corresp. mem.). *Publications:* Berlioz: Huit Scènes de Faust, La Damnation de Faust, Cipriani Potter, Symphony in G minor (ed.), W. A. Mozart: Don Giovanni 1981, The Musical Language of Berlioz 1983, Classical Music: A Concise History 1986, W. A. Mozart: Idomeneo 1993, Berlioz: Roméo et Juliette 1994, Elgar: Enigma Variations 1999, The Music of Berlioz 2001, The Cambridge Companion to Elgar (ed. with Daniel Grimley) 2004, Mozart, an Extraordinary Life 2005, Mozart (The Master Musicians) 2006; with Roger Parker and Barry Millington: The New Grove Guide to Wagner 2006, The New Grove Guide to Verdi 2006, The New Grove Guide to Mozart and his Operas 2006; contrib. to New Grove Dictionary of Music and Musicians, New Grove Dictionary of Opera, other books and professional journals. *Address:* School of Music, University of Leeds, Leeds, LS2 9JT (office); 362 Leymoor Road, Golcar, Huddersfield, HD7 4QF, England (home). *Telephone:* (113) 343-2579 (office); (1484) 649108 (home). *Fax:* (113) 343-2586 (office). *E-mail:* julianrushton@totalise.co.uk (home); j.g.rushton@ leeds.ac.uk (office).

RUSS, Joanna, BA, MFA; American writer and academic; *Professor Emerita, Department of English, University of Washington, Seattle*; b. 22 Feb. 1937, New York; d. of Everett Russ and Bertha Russ (née Zinner). *Education:* Cornell Univ. and Yale Univ. School of Drama. *Career:* taught at Cornell Univ, SUNY at Binghamton, and Univ of Colo; Prof. of English Univ. of Washington, Seattle 1977–, now Prof. Emer. *Publications include:* When It Changed (Nebula Award for Best Short Story) 1972, The Female Man 1975 (Retrospective Tiptree Award 1996), The Two of Them 1978, Kittatinny: A Tale of Magic 1978, On Strike Against God 1980, The Zanzibar Cat (short stories) 1983, Souls (Hugo Gernsback Award for Best Novella, Hugo Award) 1983, Adventures of Alyx (short stories) 1983, How to Suppress Women's Writing (non-fiction) 1983, Extra(Ordinary) People 1984, Magic Mommas, etc (essays) 1985, Other Side of the Moon (short stories) 1987. *Honours:* several awards including Hugo Award, Nebula Award, Locus Poll Award, Hugo Gernsback Award, Retrospective James Tiptree Jr Award (for Female Man) 1996, and San Francisco Chronicle Award. *Address:* c/o English Department, Box 354330, University of Washington, Seattle, WA 98195-4330, USA.

RUSSELL, James (see Harknett, Terry)

RUSSELL, John, CBE, MA; American (b. British) art critic; b. 22 Jan. 1919, Fleet, Hants.; s. of Isaac J. Russell and Harriet E. Russell (née Atkins); m. 1st Alexandrine Apponyi 1945 (divorced 1950); one d.; m. 2nd Vera Poliakoff 1956 (divorced 1971, died 1992); m. 3rd Rosamund Bernier 1975. *Education:* St Paul's School, London, Magdalen Coll., Oxford. *Career:* Hon. Attaché, Tate Gallery, London 1940; with Ministry of Information 1941, Intelligence Div. Admiralty 1942–46; mem. editorial staff Sunday Times, London 1950–78; moved to USA 1974; Art Critic New York Times 1978–90, Chief Art Critic 1982–90, Emer. 1990–; mem. American Acad. of Arts and Letters 1966; Trustee The Hermitage, St Petersburg. *Exhibitions:* organized major exhbn of Vuillard (Montreal), Modigliani, Balthus, Lucian Freud, Pop Art Revisited (with Suzi Gablik) (all at Tate Gallery or Hayward Gallery, London). *Publications include:* Shakespeare's Country 1942, Switzerland 1950, Braque 1959, Erich Kleiber: A Memoir 1956, Paris 1960, Max Ernst 1967, Vuillard 1971, Francis Bacon 1971, Seurat 1965, Henry Moore 1968, The Meanings of Modern Art 1981, (revised 1990), Reading Russell 1989, London 1994,

Matisse: Father and Son 1999; contrib. to Times Literary Supplement 1945–, New York Review of Books 1999–2005, and to numerous books. *Honours:* Hon. Fellow, RA 1989; Hon. mem. Century Asscn, New York 2000; Officier des Arts et Lettres (France); Order of Merit (FRG); Hon. DLitt (Detroit); Empire Grand Medal of Honour, Austria; Guggenheim Fellow 2000. *Address:* 166 East 61st Street, New York, NY 10021, USA (home). *Telephone:* (212) 753-5280. *Fax:* (212) 759-2523.

RUSSELL, Martin James; British writer; b. 25 Sept. 1934, Bromley, Kent, England; s. of Stanley William Russell and Helen Kathleen Russell. *Education:* Bromley Grammar School. *Career:* mem. Crime Writers' Asscn, Detection Club. *Publications:* No Through Road 1965, The Client 1975, Mr T 1977, Death Fuse 1980, Backlash 1981, The Search for Sara 1983, A Domestic Affair 1984, The Darker Side of Death 1985, Prime Target 1985, Dead Heat 1986, The Second Time is Easy 1987, House Arrest 1988, Dummy Run 1989, Mystery Lady 1992, Leisure Pursuit 1993. *Address:* 15 Breckonmead, Wanstead Road, Bromley, Kent, BR1 3BW, England (home). *Telephone:* (20) 8290-0459 (home).

RUSSELL, Mary Doria, BA, MA, PhD; American palaeoanthropologist and novelist; b. 19 Aug. 1950, Elmhurst, IL; d. of Richard Doria and Louise Doria; m. Donald J. Russell 1970; one s. *Education:* Univ. of Illinois, Northeastern Univ., Univ. of Michigan, Case Western Reserve Univ. *Career:* Instructor, Northeastern Univ., Univ. of Michigan 1978–83; invited lecturer various educational insts 1981–84; Prosector, Special Lecturer, Dept of Oral Biology, School of Dentistry, Case Western Reserve Univ., Cleveland, OH 1983, Clinical Instructor 1984–86, Adjunct Prof., Dept of Anthropology 1986; Propr N Coast Tech. Writing, South Euclid, OH 1986–92; mem. Science Fiction and Fantasy Writers of America, Authors' Guild. *Publications:* The Sparrow: A Novel 1996, Children of God: A Novel 1998, A Thread of Grace: A Novel 2005, Dreamers of the Day; A Novel 2008; contrib. to scientific journals and periodicals during career as palaeoanthropologist. *Honours:* Trotter Award for work on bone 1979, 1981, Tiptree Award 1996, BSFA Best Novel 1997, Arthur C. Clarke Award 1997, John W. Campbell Award 1998, Cleveland Arts Council Prize for Literature 1998, American Library Asscn Readers' Choice Award 1999, Kurd Lasswitz Award, Germany 2001, Spectrum Classic Award 2001. *Literary Agent:* Dystel and Goderich Literary Management, 1 Union Square W, New York, NY 10003, USA. *Telephone:* (216) 627-9100. *E-mail:* jane@dystel.com. *Website:* www.dystelandgoderich.com. *E-mail:* mary@marydoriarussell.info. *Website:* www.marydoriarussell.info.

RUSSELL, Paul, AB, MA, MFA, PhD; American academic and writer; b. 1 July 1956, Memphis, Tenn. *Education:* Oberlin Coll., Cornell Univ. *Career:* Asst Prof., Vassar Coll. 1983–90, Assoc. Prof. 1990–96, Prof. of English 1996–; Co-founder and Ed. The Poughkeepsie Review 1987–89. *Publications:* Fiction: The Salt Point 1990, Boys of Life 1991, Sea of Tranquillity 1994, The Coming Storm 1999, War Against the Animals 2003; non-fiction: The Gay 100: A Ranking of the Most Influential Gay Men and Lesbians, Past and Present 1995; contribs to anthologies, journals, and periodicals. *Honours:* Nat. Endowment for the Arts Creative Writers Fellowship 1993, Regional Winner, GRANTA-Best of Young American Novelists 1995, Ferro-Grumley Award for Fiction 2000. *Address:* Department of English, Vassar College, Poughkeepsie, NY 12604, USA (office). *E-mail:* russell@vassar.edu (office).

RUSSELL, Sharman Apt, BS, MFA; American academic and writer; b. 23 July 1954, Edwards Air Force Base, CA; m. Peter Russell 1981, one s. one d. *Education:* Univ. of California at Berkeley, Univ. of Montana. *Career:* Asst Prof. of Writing, later Prof., Western New Mexico Univ., Silver City 1981–; Faculty, MFA Program in Creative Non-Fiction, Antioch Univ., Los Angeles 1997–. *Publications:* Built to Last: An Architectural History of Silver City, New Mexico (with Susan Berry) 1986, Frederick Douglas 1987, Songs of the Fluteplayer: Seasons of Life in the Southwest (Mountain and Plains Booksellers Award 1992, New Mexico Presswomen's Zia Award 1992) 1991, Kill the Cowboy: A Battle of Mythology in the New West 1993, The Humpbacked Fluteplayer 1994, When the Land was Young: Reflections on American Archaeology 1996, The Last Matriarch 2000, Anatomy of a Rose 2001, An Obsession with Butterflies: Our Long Love Affair with a Singular Insect 2003, Hunger: An Unnatural History 2006. *Honours:* Writers at Work Fellowship Winner in Nonfiction, Park City, Utah 1989, Henry Joseph Jackson Award for Non-Fiction, San Francisco 1989, Pushcart Prize (for essay 'Illegal Aliens') 1990, WNMU Research Award in Excellence 2001, Rockefeller Foundation Residency, Bellagio, Italy 2002. *Address:* c/o Department of Humanities, Western New Mexico University, PO Box 680, Silver City, NM 88062, USA.

RUSSELL, William (Willy) Martin; British writer; b. 23 Aug. 1947, s. of William Russell and Margery Russell; m. Ann Seagroatt 1969; one s. two d. *Education:* St Katharine's Coll. of Educ., Liverpool. *Career:* ladies hairdresser 1963–69; teacher 1973–74; Fellow in Creative Writing, Manchester Polytechnic 1977–78; Founder-mem. and Dir Quintet Films; Hon. Dir Liverpool Playhouse; work for theatre includes: Blind Scouse (three short plays) 1971, When the Reds (adaptation) 1972, John, Paul, George, Ringo and Bert (musical) 1974, Breezeblock Park 1975, One for the Road 1976, Stags and Hens 1978, Educating Rita 1979, Blood Brothers (musical) 1983, Our Day Out (musical) 1983, Shirley Valentine 1986; screenplays include: Educating Rita 1981, Shirley Valentine 1988, Dancing Through the Dark 1989; TV and radio plays. *Publications:* Breezeblock Park 1978, One for the Road 1980, Educating Rita 1981, Our Day Out 1984, Stags and Hens 1985, Blood Brothers 1985,

Shirley Valentine 1989, The Wrong Boy (novel) 2000; songs and poetry. *Honours:* Hon. MA (Open Univ.) 1983; Hon. DLit (Liverpool Univ.) 1990. *Address:* c/o Casarotto Company Ltd, National House, 60–66 Wardour Street, London, W1V 3HP, England. *Telephone:* (20) 7287-4450.

RUSSO, Albert, BSc; French writer and poet; b. 26 Feb. 1943, Kamina, Belgian Congo (now Democratic Repub. of the Congo); one s. one d. *Education:* Athéné Royal d'Usumbura, Rwanda-Urundi Collegium Palatinum, Heidelbert, Germany, New York Univ., USA. *Career:* Co-Ed. Paris Transcontinental and Plurilingual Europe; mem. of Jury, Prix de l'Europe 1982–, Neustadt Int. Prize for Literature 1996; mem. Asscn of French Speaking Writers, Authors' Guild of America, PEN. *Publications:* Incandescences 1970, Eclats de malachite 1971, La Pointe du diable 1973, Mosaique New Yorkaise 1975, Albert Russo: An Anthology 1987, Sang Mêlé ou ton Fils Léopold 1990, Le Cap des Illusions 1991, Futureyes/Dans la nuit bleu-fauve 1992, Kaleidoscope 1993, Eclipse sur le Lac Tanganyika 1994, Venetian Thresholds 1995, Painting the Tower of Babel 1996, Zapinette 1996, Poetry and Peanuts (collection) 1997, Zapinette Video (novel) 1998, Mixed Blood (novel) 1999, Eclipse over Lake Tanganyika (novel) 1999, L'amant de mon père (novel) 2000, Zapinette à New York (novel) 2000, Short Stories: Beyond the Great Water, Unmasking Hearts, The Age of the Pearl 2001, Zany: Zapinette New York (novel) 2001, Zapinette chez le Belges (novel) (Prix Jeunesse 2003) 2002, L'amant de mon père: journal romain (novel) 2003, L'ancêtre noire (novel) 2003, Sangue misto (novel) 2003, ROMAdiva (photography and poems) 2004, Le Tour du Monde de la poésie gay (poems) 2004, Chinese Puzzle (photography and poems) 2005, La Tour Shalom (novel) 2005, AfricaSoul (photography and poems) 2005, In France (photography and poems) 2005, The Benevolent American in the Heart of Darkness (three novels) 2005, Oh Zaperetta! (novel) 2005, The Crowded World of Solitude: Vol. I The Collected Stories (Writer's Digest honorable mention 2005) 2005, Vol. II The Collected Poems 2005, Albert Russo: A Poetic Biorgaphy (two vol. biog. with photographs and texts) 2006, Sardinia (photographs) 2006, Body Glorious (photographs) 2006, Pasion de España (photographs) 2007, Italia Nostra (photographs) 2007, City of Lovers/City of Wonder (photographs) 2007, New York at heart (photographs) 2007, Israel at Heart (photographs) 2007, Granada/Costa del Sol/Ronda (photographs) 2007, Sang Mêlé ou ton fils Léoplold (novel) 2007; contrib. to professional journals and BBC World Service; translated into a dozen languages and published in English and French all over the world. *Honours:* Willie Lee Martin Short Story Award 1987, Silver Medal 1985, British Diversity Award 1997, AAS Memorial Trophy for Best Overseas Entry in Poetry 1999, AAS Poetry Prize 2001, Robert Penn Warren Award Editors' Choice 2002, 2004. *Address:* BP 640, 75826 Paris Cedex 17, France. *E-mail:* albert.russo@wanadoo.fr. *Website:* www.albertrusso.com.

RUTKIEWICZ, Ignacy Mikołaj; Polish journalist; *President, Board of the Foundation Press Centre for Central and Eastern Europe*; b. 15 April 1929, Vilna; s. of Józef Rutkiewicz and Maria Rutkiewicz (née Turkułł); m. Wilma Helena Koller 1961; two s. *Education:* Poznań Univ. *Career:* Ed., Ed.-in-Chief Wrocławski Tygodnik Katolicki (weekly) 1953–55; journalist, Zachodnia Agencja Prasowa (ZAP) 1957–66, Polska Agencja Interpress 1967–70; Ed. Odra (monthly) 1961–81, Ed.-in-Chief 1982–90, mem. Editorial Council 1991–; Co-Founder, mem. Editorial Council Więź (monthly), Warsaw 1958–; Pres.-Ed.-in-Chief Polish Press Agency (PAP), Warsaw 1990–92, 1992–94; Adviser to Prime Minister, Warsaw 1994–95; TV journalist TV Centre of Training, Polish TV (TVP) 1994–96; Sec. TV Comm. for Ethics 1996–; Ed.-in-Chief Antena (weekly) 1998; Adviser to Minister of Culture and Arts 1998–99; Sr Ed. On-line News, TVP 1999–; Co-founder and Vice-Pres. Polish-German Asscn, Warsaw 1990–2001; Vice-Pres. Alliance Européenne des Agences de Presse, Zürich 1991–92; mem. Exec. Bd, Asscn of Polish Journalists (SDP) 1980–82, Pres. 1993–95; mem. Council on Media and Information, Pres.'s Office 1993–95; mem. Euroatlantic Asscn 1995–; mem. Bd Foundation Press Centre for Cen. and Eastern Europe 1996–, (Pres. 2001–), Programme Bd Nat. Club of Friends of Lithuania 1996–, Programme Bd Polish Press Agency 1998–2002; Assoc. mem. Orbicom (int. network of UNESCO Chairs in Communications) 2000–. *Publications:* author or co-author of more than 10 books; Transformation of Media and Journalism in Poland 1989–1996 (author and co-ed.), How to be Fair in the Media: Guidelines not only for TV journalists. *Honours:* Kt, Order of Polonia Restituta 1981; City of Wrocław Award 1963, B. Prus Award of SDP 1990, Phil epistémoni Award, Jagiellonian Univ., Kraków 1991. *Address:* Ośrodek Nowe Media TVP, ul. Woronicza 17, 00-999 Warsaw (office), Al. Jerozolimskie 42/55, 00-024 Warsaw, Poland (home). *Telephone:* (22) 5477082 (office); (22) 8275813 (home). *E-mail:* ignacy.rutkiewicz@waw.tvp.pl (office). *Website:* www.wiadomosci.tvp.pl (office).

RUTSALA, Vern, BA, MFA; American writer, poet and teacher; b. 5 Feb. 1934, McCall, ID; m. Joan Colby 1957; two s. one d. *Education:* Reed Coll., Univ. of Iowa. *Career:* mem. PEN, Poetry Soc. of America, Associated Writing Programs. *Publications:* The Window 1964, Small Songs 1969, The Harmful State 1971, Laments 1975, The Journey Begins 1976, Paragraphs 1978, The New Life 1978, Walking Home from the Icehouse 1981, Backtracking 1985, The Mystery of Lost Shoes 1985, Ruined Cities 1987, Selected Poems 1991, Little-Known Sports 1994, Greatest Hits: 1964–2002 2002, A Handbook for Writers 2004, The Moment's Equation 2004, How We Spent Our Time 2006; contrib. to New Yorker, Esquire, Poetry, Hudson Review, Harper's, Atlantic, American Poetry Review, Paris Review. *Honours:* NEA Fellowships 1974, 1979, Northwest Poetry Prize 1976, Guggenheim Fellowship 1982, Carolyn

Kizer Poetry Prizes 1988, 1997, Oregon Arts Commission Masters Fellowship 1990, Hazel Hall Award 1992, Juniper Prize 1993, Arvon Foundation Duncan Lawrie Prize 1994, Richard Snyder Prize 2004, Akron Poetry Prize 2005. *Address:* 2404 NE 24th Avenue, Portland, OR 97212, USA. *Telephone:* (503) 281-5872 (home).

RUTTER, Sir Michael Llewellyn, Kt, CBE, MD, FRS, FRCP, FRCPsych; British academic; *Research Professor, Institute of Psychiatry, King's College London*; b. 15 Aug. 1933, s. of Llewellyn Charles Rutter and Winifred Olive Rutter; m. Marjorie Heys 1958; one s. two d. *Education:* Univ. of Birmingham Medical School, training in paediatrics, neurology and internal medicine 1955–58. *Career:* practised at Maudsley Hosp. 1958–61; Nuffield Medical Travelling Fellow, Albert Einstein Coll. of Medicine, New York 1961–62; scientist with MRC Social Psychology Research Unit 1962–65; Sr Lecturer, then Reader, Univ. of London Inst. of Psychiatry 1966–73, Prof. of Child Psychiatry 1973–98, Research Prof. 1998–, Dir MRC Research Centre for Social, Genetic and Developmental Psychiatry 1994–98; Hon. Dir MRC Child Psychiatry Unit 1984–98; Fellow, Center for Advanced Study in Behavioral Sciences, Stanford Univ. 1979–80; guest lecturer at many insts in Britain and America; Pres. Soc. for Research in Child Devt 1999–2001 (Pres. elect 1997–99); Clinical Vice-Pres. Acad. of Medical Sciences 2004–07. *Publications:* Children of Sick Parents 1966: A Neuropsychiatric Study in Childhood (jtly) 1970, Education, Health and Behaviour (ed. jtly) 1970, Infantile Autism (ed.) 1971, Maternal Deprivation Reassessed (ed.) 1981, The Child with Delayed Speech (jtly) 1972, Helping Troubled Children (jtly) 1975, Cycles of Disadvantage (jtly) 1976; Child Psychiatry (ed. jtly) 1976, (2nd edn as Child and Adolescent Psychiatry 1985), Autism (ed. jtly) 1978, Changing Youth in a Changing Society (jtly) 1979, Fifteen Thousand Hours: Secondary Schools and Their Effect on Children 1979, Scientific Foundations of Developmental Psychiatry (ed.)1981, A Measure of Our Values: Goals and Dilemmas in the Upbringing of Children (jtly) 1983, Lead versus Health (jtly) 1983, Juvenile Delinquency 1983, Developmental Neuropsychiatry (ed.) 1983, Stress, Coping and Development (ed. jtly) 1983, Depression and Young People (ed. jtly) 1986, Studies of Psychosocial Risk: The Power of Longitudinal Data (ed.) 1988, Parenting Breakdown: The Making and Breaking of Inter-generational Links (jtly) 1988, Straight and Devious Pathways from Childhood to Adulthood (ed. jtly) 1990, Biological Risk Factors for Psychosocial Disorders (ed. jtly) 1991, Developing Minds (jtly) 1993, Development Through Life: A Handbook for Clinicians (ed. jtly) 1994, Stress, Risk and Resilience in Children and Adolescents (ed. jtly) 1994, Psychological Disorders in Young People 1995, Antisocial Behaviour by Young People (jtly) 1998, Genes and Behaviour: Nature-Nurture Interplay Explained 2006. *Honours:* Hon. Fellow, British Psychological Soc. 1978, American Acad. of Pediatrics 1981, Royal Soc. of Medicine 1996; Hon. doctorates (Leiden) 1985, (Catholic Univ. of Leuven) 1990, (Birmingham) 1990, (Edin.) 1990, (Chicago) 1991, (Minnesota) 1993, (Jyväskylä) 1996,

(Warwick) 1999, (E. Anglia) 2000. *Address:* Institute of Psychiatry, King's College London, Box 80, De Crespigny Park, London SE5 8AF (office); 190 Court Lane, Dulwich, London, SE21 7ED, England (home). *Telephone:* (20) 7848-0882 (office). *Fax:* j.wickham@iop.kcl.ac.uk (office). *Website:* www.iop.kcl .ac.uk/iopweb/departments/home/?locator=10 (office).

RYAN, Peter Allen, BA, MM; Australian writer and publisher; b. 4 Sept. 1923, Melbourne; s. of Emmett F. Ryan and Alice D. Ryan; m. Gladys A. Davidson 1947; one s. one d. *Education:* Malvern Grammar School, Melbourne and Univ. of Melbourne. *Career:* mil. service 1942–45; Dir United Service Publicity Pty Ltd 1953–57; Public Relations Man., Imperial Chemical Industries of Australia and New Zealand Ltd 1957–61; Asst to Vice-Chancellor, Univ. of Melbourne 1962; Dir Melbourne Univ. Press 1962–88; mem. Solicitors Disciplinary Tribunal 1984–88; Sec. Bd of Examiners for Barristers and Solicitors 1988–; Exec. Officer Vic. Council of Legal Educ. and Admin. Officer Vic. Council of Law Reporting 1989–. *Publications:* Fear Drive My Feet 1959, The Preparation of Manuscripts 1966, Encyclopedia of Papua and New Guinea (gen. ed.) 1972, Redmond Barry 1973, William Macmahon Ball: A Memoir 1989, Black Bonanza, A Landslide of Gold 1991, Lines of Fire: Manning Clark and Other Writings 1997. *Address:* Supreme Court, William Street, Melbourne, Vic. 3000, Australia. *Telephone:* 603-4388.

RYCKMANS, Pierre, (Simon Leys), PhD; Belgian academic and writer; b. 28 Sept. 1935, Brussels; m. Chang Han-fang; three s. one d. *Education:* Univ. of Louvain. *Career:* taught Chinese Literature, ANU, then Prof. of Chinese Studies, Univ. of Sydney 1987–93; Fellow, Australian Acad of Humanities; mem. Acad. Royale de Littérature Française (Brussels) 1991–. *Film:* The Emperor's New Clothes (Dir Alan Taylor, Producer U. Pasolini) 2001, adapted from Simon Leys' The Death of Napoleon. *Publications:* (under pen-name Simon Leys) The Chairman's New Clothes: Mao and the Cultural Revolution 1977, Chinese Shadows 1977, The Burning Forest 1985, La Mort de Napoléon 1986 (English trans. 1991), Les Entretiens de Confucius 1989, L'humeur, l'honneur, l'horreur 1991, The Analects of Confucius 1996, Essais sur la Chine 1998, The View from the Bridge 1996, The Angel and the Octopus 1999, Protée et autres essais 2001, Les Naufragés du Batavia 2003, La Mer dans la littérature française 2003, Les idées des autres 2005, The Wreck of the Batavia 2005; (under own name Pierre Ryckmans) Les Propos sur la peinture de Shitao 1969, La Vie et l'oeuvre de Su Renshan, rebelle, peintre et fou 1970. *Honours:* Officer Ordre de Léopold, Commdr Ordre des Arts et Lettres 1999; Prix Stanislas-Julien (Institut de France), Prix Jean Walter (Acad. Française), The Independent (UK) Foreign Fiction Award 1992, Christina Stead Prize for Fiction (NSW) 1992, Prix Bernheim 1999, Prix Renaudot 2001, Prix Henri Gal (Acad. Française) 2001, Prix Guizot 2004, Prix Femina (100th anniversary) 2004, Prix del Duca (Acad. Française) 2005. *Address:* 6 Bonwick Place, Garran, ACT 2605, Australia. *Fax:* (2) 6281-4887.

S

SAADAWI, Nawal el-, MA, MD; Egyptian writer and physician; b. 27 Oct. 1931, Kafr Tahla; m. 1st Ahmed Helmi (divorced); m. 2nd (divorced); m. 3rd Sherif Hetata 1964; one s. one d. *Education:* Cairo Univ., Columbia Univ., New York, USA. *Career:* novelist and writer, particularly on feminist issues 1956–; worked Rural Health Centre, Tahla 1955–57; Dir-Gen. Ministry of Health 1958–72; writer, High Inst. of Literature and Science 1973–78; psychiatrist 1974–; fmr Ed.-in-Chief, Health magazine; fmr Asst Gen.-Sec. Medical Asscn; fmr researcher, Faculty of Medicine, Ain Shams Univ., Cairo; Founder, Arab Women's Solidarity Asscn (Pres. 1982–91); worked for UN as Dir African Training and Research Center for Women in Ethiopia 1978–80, adviser to UN Econ. Comm. for West Africa, Lebanon. *Publications:* Memoirs of a Woman Doctor 1958, Two Women in One 1968, Women and Sex 1971, She Has No Place in Paradise (short story) 1972, Woman at Point Zero 1975, God Dies by the Nile 1976, The Hidden Face of Eve: Women in the Arab World (non-fiction) 1977, The Circling Song 1977, The Veil (short story) 1978, Death of an Ex-Minister 1979, Memoirs from the Women's Prison 1983, My Travels Around the World 1986, The Fall of the Imam 1987, The Innocence of the Devil 1992, Nawal el-Saadawi in the Dock 1993, The Well of Life and The Thread: Two Short Novels 1993, The Nawal el-Saadawi Reader 1997, A Daughter of Isis: The Autobiography of Nawal el-Saadawi 1999, Walking Through Fire: A Life of Nawal el-Saadawi 2002, The Novel 2005, God Resigns in the Summit Meeting 2007; contrib. to newspapers and magazines. *Honours:* First Degree Decoration of the Republic of Libya 1989; Hon. DUniv (York) 1994; High Council of Literature Award 1974, Short Story Award (Cairo) 1974, Franco-Arab Literary Award (Paris) 1982, Literary Award of Gubran 1988. *Address:* 19 Maahad Nasser, Shoubra, 11241, Cairo, Egypt. *Telephone:* 2022279. *Fax:* 2035001. *E-mail:* shns@tedata.net.eg. *Website:* www.nawalsaadawi.net.

SAAL, Agnès; French civil servant; *Director-General, Bibliothèque nationale de France;* b. 1957, Tunis, Tunisia; one s. two d. *Education:* Institut d'études politiques de Paris and Ecole nationale d'administration, Paris. *Career:* began career at Council d'Etat 1979–80, Ministry of Culture 1983; employee Centre nat de la cinématographie 1990–97; Tech. Adviser to Minister of Culture and Communication 1997–98, Deputy Dir Cabinet 1998–2001; Dir-Gen. Bibliothèque nationale de France 2001–. *Honours:* Officier, Ordre des Arts et des Lettres, Chevalier, Légion d'honneur 2005. *Address:* Bibliotheque nationale de France, quai Francois Mauriac, 75706 Paris Cédex 13 (office); 36 rue des Vignes, 75016 Paris, France (home). *Telephone:* 1-53-79-44-44 (office); 1-45-27-02-71 (home). *Fax:* 1-53-79-40-40 (office). *E-mail:* agnes.saal@bnf.fr (office).

SAALBACH, Astrid; Danish writer; b. 29 Nov. 1955, Elsinore; m. Jens Kaas 1987; two s. *Education:* Nat. School of Theatre (Copenhagen). *Career:* actress at different theatres until 1985; first radio play 1982, first stage play 1986; first collection of short stories 1985, first novel 1987; awards include Statens Kunsfonds Trearige Legat, Kjell Abell Prisen, Preben Harris Rejelegat, Dramatikernes Haderspris, Nørdisk Radiospilspris, Edv Petersens Bibliotekspris, The Holberg Medal, Statens Kunstfonds Livsvarige Legat, Henri Nathansens Fodselsdags Legat. *Publications include:* plays: Fading Colours (TV) 1980, Footmarks in the Sand 1982, The Hidden City 1985, Myung (TV) 1989, Morning and Evening 1993, Blessed Child 1996, Ashes to Ashes, Dust to Dust 1998, The Cold Heart 2001, End of the World (Nordic Theatre Union Nordic Drama Award, Reumert Award for Best Drama) 2004; novels: Who She Is 2000, Fingeren i Flammen (Finger in the Fire) 2005; short stories: The Face of the Moon 1985. *Address:* Holsteinsgade 9, 3 tv, 2100 Copenhagen Ø, Denmark. *Telephone:* 35-38-18-83. *E-mail:* astrid.saalbach@mail.dk (office).

SABATIER, Robert; French writer; b. 17 Aug. 1923, Paris; s. of Pierre Sabatier and Marie Exbrayat; m. Christiane Lesparre 1957. *Career:* fmr manual worker and factory exec.; produced journal La Cassette; mem. Acad. Goncourt. *Publications:* Alain et le nègre 1953, Le marchand de sable 1954, Le goût de la cendre 1955, Les fêtes solaires 1955, Boulevard 1956, Canard au sang 1958, St Vincent de Paul, Dédicace d'un navire 1959, La Sainte-Farce 1960, La mort du figuier 1962, Dessin sur un trottoir 1964, Les poisons délectables (poems) 1965, Le Chinois d'Afrique 1966, Dictionnaire de la mort 1967, Les châteaux de millions d'années (poems) 1969, Les allumettes suédoises 1969, Trois sucettes à la menthe 1972, Noisettes sauvages 1974, Histoire de la poésie française des origines à nos jours (eight vols) 1975, Icare et autres poèmes 1976, Les enfants de l'été 1978, Les fillettes chantantes 1980, L'oiseau de demain 1981, Les années secrètes de la vie d'un homme 1984, David et Olivier 1986, Lecture (poetry) 1987, La souris verte 1990, Le livre de la déraison souriante 1991, Olivier et ses amis 1993, Ecriture (poems) 1993, Le cygne noir 1995, Le lit de la merveille 1997, Les masques et le miroir 1998, Le sourire aux lèvres 2000. *Honours:* Commdr, Légion d'honneur; Commdr, Ordre nat. du Mérite, des Arts et Lettres; Officier du Mérite agricole; Lauréat de la Soc. des gens de lettres 1961; Grand Prix de Poésie de l' Acad. française 1969 for Les châteaux de millions d'années; Antonin-Artaud Prize and Prix Apollinaire for poems Les fêtes solaires 2000. *Address:* 64 boulevard Exelmans, 75016 Paris, France.

SÁBATO, Ernesto; Argentine writer; b. 24 June 1911, Rojas; m. Matilde Kusminsky-Richter; two s. *Education:* Universidad Nacional de la Plata. *Career:* fmr Dir of Cultural Relations, Argentina; has lectured in numerous univs, including Paris, Columbia, Berkeley, Madrid, Warsaw, Bucharest, Bonn, Milan, Pavia, Florence; Pres. Comisión Nacional sobre Desaparición de Personas (CONADEP) 1984; mem. The Club of Rome. *Publications:* Uno y el universo 1945, Hombres y engranajes 1951, Heterodoxia 1953, El escritor y sus fantasmas 1963, Tres aproximaciones a la literatura de nuestro tiempo (essays) 1969, El túnel 1947, Sobre héroes y tumbas 1961, Abaddon el exterminador (novel) 1976, La resistencia, Narrativa completa 1995, Apologias y rechazos 1995, Antes del fin 1999, La Resistencia 2000. *Honours:* Ribbon of Honour, Argentine Soc. of Letters; Prize of the Inst. of Foreign Relations (Stuttgart) 1973, Grand Prize of Argentine Writers' Soc. 1974, Prix Meilleur Livre Etranger for Abaddon el Exterminador (Paris) 1977; Chevalier, Ordre des Arts et des Lettres (France), Chevalier, Légion d'honneur 1978, Gran Cruz de la República Española, Gabriela Mistral Prize 1984, Cervantes Prize, Madrid 1984, Jerusalem Literary Prize 1989. *Address:* Langeri 3135, Santos Lugares, Argentina. *Telephone:* 757-1373.

SABATO, Haim; Israeli writer; b. Cairo, Egypt. *Publications:* Adjusting Sights, Aleppo Tales 2004. *Honours:* Sapir Prize. *Address:* c/o The Toby Press, PO Box 8531, New Milford, CT 06776-8531, USA. *Website:* www.tobypress.com.

SABUROV, Yevgeny Fedorovich, DEconSc; Russian economist and poet; b. 13 Feb. 1946, Crimea; m. Tatiana Petrovna; three d. *Education:* Moscow State Univ. *Career:* researcher econ. inst. in Moscow –1990; Deputy Minister of Educ. of Russian Fed. 1990–91; project leader Programme of Econ. Reform in Russia April–Aug. 1991; Deputy Prime Minister, Minister of Econ. Aug.–Nov. 1991; Dir Cen. for Information and Social Tech. of Russian Govt 1991–94; Deputy Head of Govt of Repub. of Crimea Feb.–Oct. 1994; Prof. Acad. of Econs. 1995–; Chief Consultant, Menatep Bank 1995–; Chair. Bd of Guardians, Inst. for Urban Econs 1996–; Chair. Bd of Dirs. Confidential and Investment Bank 1999–2000, Deputy Chair. 2000–; mem. Acad. of Information, Acad. of Social Sciences; poetry published in Europe since 1970, in Russia since 1990. *Publications:* Gunpowder Conspiracy (poems) 1996, On the Edge of the Lake (selected poems); over 100 articles on problems of econ. reform in Russia; numerous verses in periodicals. *Address:* Confidential and Investment Bank, Sadovnicheskaya 84/3–7, 113035 Moscow, Russia. *Telephone:* (495) 958-24-26. *Fax:* (495) 958-24-28.

SACHAR, Louis; American children's writer; b. 20 March 1954, East Meadow, NY; m. Carla 1985; one d. *Education:* Univ. of California at Berkeley, Hastings Coll. of Law in San Francisco. *Career:* fmr lawyer. *Publications include:* Marvin Redpost series: Kidnapped at Birth?, Why Pick on Me?, Is He A Girl?, Alone in His Teacher's House, Class President, A Flying Birthday Cake?, Super Fast Out of Control!, A Magic Crystal?; Wayside School series: Sideways Stories from Wayside School (Int. Reading Asscn Children's Choice 1979, Children's Book Council Children's Choice 1979) 1977, Wayside School is Falling Down 1989, Wayside School Gets a Little Stranger 1995, Sideways Arithmetic from Wayside School, More Sideways Arithmetic from Wayside School; Johnny's in the Basement 1983, Someday, Angeline 1983, Sixth Grade Secrets 1987, There's a Boy in the Girls' Bathroom (Young Reader's Choice Award 1990) 1987, Dogs Don't Tell Jokes 1991, Monkey Soup 1992, The Boy Who Lost his Face 1997, Holes (Nat. Book Award, New York Times Book Review Notable Children's Book of the Year, New York Times Outstanding Book of the Year, School Library Journal Best Book of the Year, Horn Book Fanfare Honor List, Bulletin Blue Ribbon Book, Publishers Weekly Best Book of the Year, Newbery Award) 1998, Stanley Yelnats' Survival Guide to Camp Green Lake, Small Steps 2006. *Honours:* Parents' Choice Award 1987. *Address:* c/o Scholastic, 557 Broadway, New York, NY 10012, USA. *Website:* www.louissachar.com.

SACHS, Jeffrey David, BA, MA, PhD; American academic and economist; *Quetelet Professor of Sustainable Development and Director, The Earth Institute, Columbia University;* b. 5 Nov. 1954, Detroit, Mich.; s. of Theodore Sachs and Joan Sachs; m. Sonia Ehrlich; one s. two d. *Education:* Harvard Univ. *Career:* Research Assoc. Nat. Bureau of Econ. Research, Cambridge, Mass. 1980–85; Asst Prof. of Econs Harvard Univ. 1980–82, Assoc. Prof. 1982–83, Galen L. Stone Prof. of Int. Trade 1984–2001; Dir Harvard Inst. for Int. Devt 1995–2002, Center for Int. Devt –2002; Quetelet Prof. of Sustainable Devt and Prof. of Health Policy and Man. and Dir The Earth Inst., Columbia Univ. 2002–; adviser, Brookings Inst. Washington, DC 1982–; Special Advisor to UN Sec.-Gen. Kofi Annan on Millennium Devt Goals 2002–06, Dir Millennium Project; Founder and Chair. Exec. Cttee Inst. of Econ. Analysis, Moscow 1993–; Chair. Comm. on Macro econs and Health, WHO 2000–01; Co-Chair. Advisory Bd The Global Competitiveness Report; mem. Int. Financial Insts Advisory Comm., US Congress 1999–2000; econ. adviser to various govts in Latin America, Eastern Europe, the fmr Soviet Union, Asia and Africa, Jubilee 2000 movt; fmr consultant to IMF, World Bank, OECD and UNDP; adviser to Pres. of Bolivia 1986–90; Fellow, World Econometric Soc.; Research Assoc. Nat. Bureau of Econ. Research; syndicated newspaper column appears in more than 50 countries; mem. American Acad. of Arts and Sciences, Harvard Soc. of Fellows, Brookings Panel of Economists, Bd of Advisers, Chinese Economists Soc.; f. Inst. for Econ. Analysis, Moscow; Distinguished Visiting Lecturer to LSE, Oxford Univ., Tel-Aviv, Jakarta, Yale Univ.; BBC Reith Lecturer 2007. *Publications:* Economics of Worldwide Stagflation (with Michael Bruno) 1985, Developing Country Debt and the Economic Performance (Ed.) 1989, Global Linkages: Macroeconomic Interdependence and

Cooperation in the World Economy (with Warwick McKibbin) 1991, Peru's Path to Recovery (with Carlos Paredes) 1991, Macroeconomics in the Global Economy (with Felipe Larrain) 1993, Poland's Jump to the Market Economy 1993, The Transition in Eastern Europe (with Olivier Blanchard and Kenneth Froot) 1994, Russia and the Market Economy (in Russian) 1995, Economic Reform and the Process of Global Integration (with A. Warner) 1995, The Collapse of the Mexican Peso: What Have We Learned? (jtly) 1995, Natural Resource Abundance and Economic Growth (with A. Warner) 1996, The Rule of Law and Economic Reform in Russia (co-ed.) 1997, Economies in Transition (co-Ed.) 1997, The End of Poverty 2005; more than 200 scholarly articles. *Honours:* Commdr's Cross Order of Merit (Poland) 1999; Hon. PhD (St Gallen) 1990, (Universidad del Pacífico, Peru) 1997, (Lingnan Coll., Hong Kong) 1998, (Varna Econs Univ., Bulgaria) 2000, (Iona Coll., New York) 2000; Frank E. Seidman Award in Political Econ. 1991, Berhard Harms Prize (Germany) 2000, Distinguished Public Service Award, Sec. of State's Open Forum 2002, Sargent Shriver Award for Equal Justice 2005. *Address:* The Earth Institute at Columbia University, 405 Low Library, 535 West 116th Street, MC 4335, New York, NY 10027, USA (office). *Telephone:* (212) 854-8704 (office). *Fax:* (212) 854-8702 (office). *E-mail:* director@ei.columbia.edu (office). *Website:* www.earth.columbia.edu/about/director (office).

SACKS, Sir Jonathan Henry, PhD; British rabbi; *Associate President, Conference of European Rabbis;* b. 8 March 1948, London; s. of the late Louis Sacks and of Louisa (née Frumkin) Sacks; m. Elaine Taylor 1970; one s. two d. *Education:* Christ's Coll. Finchley, Gonville & Caius Coll., Cambridge, New Coll., Oxford, London Univ., Jews' Coll., London and Yeshivat Etz Hayyim, London. *Career:* Lecturer in Moral Philosophy, Middx Poly. 1971–73; Lecturer in Jewish Philosophy, Jews' Coll., London 1973–76; in Talmud and Jewish Philosophy 1976–82, Chief Rabbi Lord Jakobovits Prof. (first incumbent) in Modern Jewish Thought 1982–, Dir Rabbinic Faculty 1983–90, Prin. 1984–90; Chief Rabbi of the United Hebrew Congregations of the British Commonwealth of Nations 1991–; Assoc. Pres. Conf. of European Rabbis 2000–; Visiting Prof. of Philosophy Univ. of Essex 1989–90; currently Visiting Prof. of Philosophy Hebrew Univ., Jerusalem and of Theology and Religious Studies King's Coll., London; Rabbi Golders Green Synagogue, London 1978–82, Marble Arch Synagogue, London 1983–90; Ed. Le'ela (journal) 1985–90; mem. CRAC; Presentation Fellow King's Coll., London 1993; Sherman Lecturer, Manchester Univ. 1989, Reith Lecturer 1990, Cook Lecturer 1997. *Publications:* Torah Studies 1986, Tradition and Transition (essays) 1986, Traditional Alternatives 1989, Tradition in an Untraditional Age 1990, The Persistence of Faith (Reith Lecture) 1991, Orthodoxy Confronts Modernity (Ed.) 1991, Crisis and Covenant 1992, One People?: Tradition, Modernity and Jewish Unity 1993, Will We Have Jewish Grandchildren? 1994, Faith in the Future 1995, Community of Faith 1995, The Politics of Hope 1997, Morals and Markets 1999, Celebrating Life 2000, Radical Then Radical Now 2001, The Dignity of Difference: How To Avoid the Clash of Civilizations 2002, The Chief Rabbi's Hagadah 2003, To Heal a Fractured World 2005. *Honours:* Hon. Fellow Gonville and Caius Coll., Cambridge 1993; Hon. DD (Cantab.) 1993, (Archbishop of Canterbury) 2001; Dr hc (Middx Univ.) 1993, (Haifa Univ., Israel) 1996, (Yeshiva Univ., NY) 1997, (St Andrews Univ.) 1998; Hon. LLD (Univ. of Liverpool) 1997; Jerusalem Prize 1995. *Address:* 735 High Road, London, N12 0US, England (office). *Telephone:* (20) 8343-6301 (office). *Fax:* (20) 8343-6310 (office). *E-mail:* info@chiefrabbi.org (office). *Website:* www.chiefrabbi.org (office).

SACKS, Oliver Wolf, BM, BCh; British neurologist and writer; b. 9 July 1933, London; s. of Dr Samuel Sacks and Dr Muriel Elsie (Landau) Sacks. *Education:* St Paul's School, London and Queen's Coll., Oxford. *Career:* Resident, UCLA 1962–65; Consultant Neurologist, Bronx State Hosp., New York 1965–91, Beth Abraham Hosp., Bronx 1965–, Headache Unit, Montefiore Hosp., Bronx 1966–68, several clinics and homes for the aged and chronically ill, New York 1966–; Consultant Neurologist and mem. Medical Advisory Bd, Gilles de la Tourette Syndrome Asscn, New York 1974–; Instructor in Neurology, Albert Einstein Coll. of Medicine, Bronx, New York 1966–75, Asst Clinical Prof. of Neurology 1975–78, Assoc. Clinical Prof. 1978–85, Clinical Prof. 1985–; Fellow American Acad. of Arts and Letters 1996, New York Acad. of Sciences 1999. *Publications:* Migraine 1970, Awakenings 1973, A Leg to Stand On 1984, The Man Who Mistook His Wife For A Hat 1985, Seeing Voices: A Journey Into The World of the Deaf 1989, An Anthropologist on Mars 1995, The Island of the Colourblind 1996, Uncle Tungsten 2001, Oaxaca Journal 2002. *Honours:* Hon. DHumLitt (Georgetown Univ.) 1990, (Staten Island Coll., CUNY) 1991; Hon. DSc (Tufts Univ.) 1991, (New York Medical Coll.) 1991, (Bard Coll.) 1992; Hon. DMedSc (Medical Coll. of Pennsylvania); Hawthornden Prize (for Awakenings) 1975, Felix Marti-Ibanez Book Award for Humanism in Medicine, Special Presidential Award, American Neurological Asscn. 1991, George S. Polk Award 1994, Mainichi Publishing Culture Award (Tokyo) for Best Natural Science Book (Seeing Voices) 1996 and many others. *Address:* 2 Horatio Street, New York, NY 10014, USA. *Telephone:* (212) 633-8373. *Fax:* (212) 633-8928. *Website:* www.oliversacks.com (office).

SADDLEMYER, (Eleanor) Ann, OC, PhD, FRSC, FRSA; Canadian academic, critic, biographer and university administrator; *Adjunct Professor, University of Victoria;* b. 28 Nov. 1932, Prince Albert; d. of Orrin Angus Saddlemyer and Elsie Sarah Saddlemyer (née Ellis). *Education:* Univ. of Saskatchewan, Queen's Univ., Kingston, ON and Bedford Coll., London. *Career:* Lecturer, Univ. of Victoria, BC 1956–57, Instructor 1960–62, Asst Prof. 1962–65, Prof. of English 1971, Adjunct Prof. 1995–; Prof. of English, Victoria Coll., Univ. of

Toronto, Ont. 1971–95, Dir Grad. Centre for the Study of Drama 1972–77, 1985–86, Master of Massey Coll. 1988–95, Master Emer. and Prof. Emer. 1995–; Berg Prof., Univ. of New York, USA 1975; mem. Bd of Dirs Colin Smythe Publishers, UK 1970; Co-founder and Vice-Pres. Bd of Dirs of Theatre Plus, Toronto 1972–84; Chair. Int. Asscn for the Study of Anglo-Irish Literature 1973–76; Founder and Pres. Asscn for Canadian Theatre History 1976–77; Corresp. Scholar, Acad. of Shaw Festival Theatre 1999–; mem. Chancellor's Council Victoria Coll. 1984–; Guggenheim Fellow 1965, 1977. *Publications include:* The World of W. B. Yeats: Essays in Perspective (jtly) 1965, In Defence of Lady Gregory, Playwright 1966, The Plays of J. M. Synge (two vols) 1968, The Plays of Lady Gregory (four vols) 1971, Theatre History in Canada (co-ed) 1980–86, Theatre Business, the Letters of the First Abbey Theatre Directors 1982, The Letters of J. M. Synge (two vols) 1983, 1984, Early Stages – Theatre in Ontario 1800–1914 1990, The World's Classics J. M. Synge 1995, Later Stages: Essays on Theatre in Ontario 1800–1914 1997, Becoming George – The Life of Mrs W. B. Yeats 2002. *Honours:* Hon. LLD (Queen's) 1977; Hon. DLitt (Victoria, McGill) 1989, (Windsor) 1990, (Toronto) 1999, (Concordia) 2000; Prov. of Ont. Distinguished Service Award 1985, British Acad. Rosemary Crawshay Award for Criticism 1986, cr. Ann Saddlemyer Book Prize for Theatre History 1989, YWCA Toronto Woman of the Year Award 1994. *Address:* 10876 Madrona Drive, Sidney, BC V8L 5N9, Canada (home). *Telephone:* (250) 656-9320 (home). *Fax:* (250) 656-9320 (home). *E-mail:* saddlemy@uvic.ca.

SADGROVE, Sidney Henry, (Lee Torrance); English artist, teacher and writer; b. 1920, England. *Career:* mem. Writers Guild of Great Britain. *Publications:* You've Got To Do Something, 1967; A Touch of the Rabbits, 1968; The Suitability Factor, 1968; Stanislaus and the Princess, 1969; A Few Crumbs, 1971; Stanislaus and the Frog, 1972; Paradis Enow, 1972; Stanislaus and the Witch, 1973; The Link, 1975; The Bag, 1977; Half Sick of Shadows, 1977; Bleep, 1977; All in the Mind, 1977; Icary Dicary Doc, 1978, Angel, 1978; Filling, 1979; First Night, 1980; Only on Friday, 1980; Hoodunnit, 1984; Pawn en Prise, 1985; Just for Comfort, 1986; Tiger, 1987; State of Play, 1988; Warren, 1989; Dear Mrs Comfett, 1990. *Address:* Pimp Barn, Withyham, Hartfield, Sussex TN7 4BB, England (home). *Telephone:* (1892) 770486 (home).

SADUR, Nina Nikolayevna; Russian writer and playwright; b. 15 Oct. 1950, Novosibirsk; d. of Nikolai Sadur; one d. *Education:* Moscow Inst. of Culture, Moscow M. Gorky Inst. of Literature. *Career:* literary debut in Sibirskiye Ogni magazine; freelance writer; mem. USSR Writers' Union 1989. *Plays include:* Chardym, My Brother Chichikov, Weird Baba, Move Ahead. *Publications:* New Amazons (collected stories) 1991, Irons and Diamonds (short stories), German (novel). *Address:* Vagrius Publishers, Troitskaya str. 7/1, Bldg 2, 129090 Moscow, Russia (office). *Telephone:* (495) 785-09-63 (office).

ŞAFAK, Elif, PhD; Turkish writer, academic and activist; *Assistant Professor of Near Eastern Studies, University of Arizona;* b. 1971, Strasbourg, France. *Education:* Middle East Tech. Univ. *Career:* currently Asst Prof., Dept of Near Eastern Studies Univ. of Arizona; Visiting Scholar in Women's Studies Univ. of Michigan 2003–04; fmrly taught at Istanbul Bilgi Univ.; activist for women's and minority rights. *Publications:* novels: Kem Gözlere Anadolu 1994, Pinhan (trans. as The Sufi) (Rumi Prize) 1997, Şehrin Aynalari 1999, Mahrem (trans. as The Gaze) (Turkish Writers' Asscn Best Novel of the Year) 2000, Bit Palas (trans. as The Flea Palace) 2002, Araf (trans. as The Saint of Incipient Insanities) 2004, Med-Cezir 2005, Baba ve Piç (trans. as The Bastard of Istanbul) 2006; contrib. reviews to The Economist, San Francisco Chronicle, Boston Globe, The Washington Post and articles to various newspapers in Turkey. *Literary Agent:* Marly Rusoff & Associates Inc., POB 524, Bronxville, NY 10708, USA. *Telephone:* (914) 961-7939 (office); (212) 2454696 (home). *Website:* www.rusoffagency.com.

SAFIEVA, Gulrukhsor, MA; Tajikistan poet and politician; b. 17 Dec. 1947, d. of Nabiev Safi and Halimova Mastura; m. Rajabov Negmat; one s. *Education:* Tajik State Univ., Dushanbe. *Career:* Gen. Ed. Culture of Tajikistan 1987; mem. Supreme Soviet and Int. Comm. 1989–91; Chair. Int. Tajik Cultural Fund 1987; mem. Presidium Russian Culture Fund 1991; Pres. Int. Euro-Asian Acad. of Culture 1994–2003, Acad. of World Poetry, Moscow 1998–2003, PEN-Club of Tajikistan 2000–03. *Publications include:* more than 70 books, including Selected Poems 1983, 1984, 1985, 1987, Women of Mountains 1990, Neizvestniy Khayam (Unknown Khayam), Zan va Jang (Woman and War). *Honours:* Prize, Youth of Tajikistan 1976, Prize, Youth of USSR 1978, Helmut Hammit Award, Nat. Poet of Tajikistan Award. *Address:* Ismoili Somoni #8, Writer's Union, Dushanbe (office); Gogolstr. 18/3, Apt #7, 734001 Dushanbe, Tajikistan (home). *Telephone:* (3772) 24-56-82 (office); (3772) 215062 (home). *Fax:* (3772) 215062 (office).

SAFIRE, William; American journalist and author; *Chairman, The Dana Foundation;* b. 17 Dec. 1929, New York; s. of Oliver C. Safir and Ida Safir (née Panish); m. Helene Belmar Julius 1962; one s. one d. *Education:* Syracuse Univ. *Career:* reporter, New York Herald Tribune Syndicate 1949–51; Corresp. WNBC-WNBT, Europe and Middle East 1951, Radio and TV Producer, WNBC, New York 1954–55; Vice-Pres. Tex McCrary Inc. 1955–60; Pres. Safire Public Relations Inc. 1960–68; Special Asst to Pres. Nixon, Washington 1968–73; Columnist, New York Times, Washington 1973–; Chair. The Dana Foundation 2000–; mem. American Acad. of Arts and Sciences, Pulitzer Bd; Trustee, Syracuse Univ. *Publications:* The Relations Explosion 1963, Plunging into Politics 1964, Safire's Political Dictionary 1968,

Before the Fall 1975, Full Disclosure 1977, Safire's Washington 1980, On Language 1980, What's the Good Word? 1982, Good Advice (with Leonard Safir) 1982, I Stand Corrected 1984, Take My Word for It 1986, Freedom (novel) 1987, You Could Look It Up 1988, Words of Wisdom 1989, Language Maven Strikes Again 1990, Leadership (with Leonard Safir) 1990, Coming to Terms 1991, The First Dissident 1992, Good Advice on Writing (with Leonard Safir) 1992, Lend Me Your Ears 1992, Safire's New Political Dictionary 1993, Quote the Maven 1993, In Love With Norma Loquendi 1994, Sleeper Spy 1995, Watching My Language 1997, Spreading the Word 1999, Scandalmonger 1999, Let A Smile Be Your Umbrella 2001, No Uncertain Times 2003. *Honours:* Pulitzer Prize for Distinguished Commentary 1978, Presidential Medal of Freedom 2006. *Address:* The Dana Foundation, 900 15th Street, NW, Washington, DC 20005, USA (office). *Telephone:* (202) 682-4545 (office). *Fax:* (202) 682-2662 (office). *E-mail:* wsafire@dana.org (office). *Website:* dana.org (office).

SAFRANKO, Mark Peter, BA, MA; American writer and actor; b. 23 Dec. 1950, Trenton, NJ; m. Lorrie Foster 1996; one s. *Education:* St Vincent Coll., Montclair State Univ. *Career:* mem. Dramatists' Guild, Authors' Guild. *Publications:* fiction: The Favor 1987, Hopler's Statement 1998, Hating Olivia 2004; contrib. to South Carolina Review, North Atlantic Review, Paterson Literary Review, New Orleans Review, Ellery Queen's Mystery Magazine. *Address:* 5 Amherst Place, Montclair, NJ 07043, USA.

SAGALAYEV, Eduard Mikhailovich; Russian journalist; b. 3 Oct. 1946, Samarkand; m.; one s. one d. *Education:* Samarkand Univ., Acad. of Social Sciences Cen. Cttee CPSU. *Career:* Dir, Sr Ed. Cttee on TV and Radio Samarkand; on staff, Deputy Exec. Sec. Leninsky Put 1969–72; Exec. Sec. Komsomolets Uzbekistana Tashkent 1972–73; instructor Propaganda Div. Cen. Comsomol Cttee Moscow 1973–75; Deputy Ed.-in-Chief programmes for youth, USSR Cen. TV 1975–80, Ed.-in-Chief 1980–88; Ed.-in-Chief Information section of Cen. TV 1988–90; Dir Gen. Studio Channel IY 1990; First Deputy Chair. All-Union State Radio and TV Corpn 1991–92; Dir Gen. TV Ostankino Jan.–July 1992; Founder and Pres. TV-6, Moscow's first ind. broadcasting co. 1992–96, 1997–; Chair. Russian TV and Broadcasting co. (RTR) 1996–97; now Chair. Bd of Dirs and Pres. Moscow Ind. Broadcasting Corpn, Deputy Chair. Bd of Dirs ORT (Channel 1); Co-Chair. Int. TV and Radio Broadcasting Policies Comm. 1990–97; Dir-Gen. RTR Signal Co.; Chair. Bd of USSR Journalists' Union 1990–91; Chair. Confed. of Journalists' Unions of CIS 1992–97, Pres. Nat. Asscn of TV and Radio Producers of Russia 1995–; mem. Acad. of Russian TV 1995–, Fed. Tenders Comm. 2004–. *Honours:* USSR State Prize 1978; Order of Friendship (twice). *Address:* National Association of TV Producers, Myasnitskaya str. 13/11, 101000 Moscow, Russia. *Telephone:* (495) 924-24-38. *Fax:* (495) 923-23-18.

SAGER, Dirk; German journalist; b. 13 Aug. 1940, Hamburg; m. Irene Dasbach-Sager; one s. one d. *Career:* fmrly with Radio RIAS Berlin; fmr corresp. ZDF TV, East Berlin, Washington DC, Chief of Moscow Office 1990–97, 1998–, of Brandenburg Office 1997–98. *Publication:* Betrogenes Rubland 1996. *Address:* Zweites Deutsches Fernsehen, August-Bebel-Strasse 15-16, 14482 Potsdam, Germany.

SAHGAL, Nayantara; Indian journalist and novelist; b. (Nayantara Pandit), 10 May 1927, Allahabad; d. of Ranjit Sitaram Pandit and Vijaya Lakshmi Pandit; m. 1st Gautam Sahgal 1949 (divorced 1967); one s. two d.; m. 2nd E. N. Mangat Rai 1979. *Education:* Wellesley Coll., USA. *Career:* Adviser English Language Bd, Sahitya Akademi (Nat. Acad. of Letters), New Delhi 1972–75; Scholar-in-Residence, holding creative writing seminar, Southern Methodist Univ., Dallas, Texas 1973, 1977; mem. Indian Del. to UN Gen. Ass. 1978; Vice-Pres. Nat. Exec., People's Union for Civil Liberties 1980–85; Fellow, Radcliffe Inst. (Harvard Univ.) 1976, Wilson Int. Center for Scholars, Washington, DC 1981–82, Nat. Humanities Center, NC 1983–84; mem. jury Commonwealth Writers' Prize 1990, Chair. Eurasia Region 1991; Annie Besant Memorial Lecture (Banaras Hindu Univ.) 1992; Arthur Ravenscroft Memorial Lecture (Univ. of Leeds) 1993; mem. American Acad. of Arts and Sciences 1990. *Publications:* Prison and Chocolate Cake 1954, A Time to Be Happy 1958, From Fear Set Free 1962, This Time of Morning 1965, Storm in Chandigarh 1969, History of the Freedom Movement 1970, The Day in Shadow 1972, A Situation in New Delhi 1977, A Voice for Freedom 1977, Indira Gandhi's Emergence and Style 1978, Indira Gandhi: Her Road to Power 1982, Rich Like Us (Sinclair Prize 1985, Sahitya Akad. Award 1987) 1985, Plans for Departure 1985 (Commonwealth Writers' Prize 1987), Mistaken Identity 1988, Relationship: Extracts from a Correspondence 1994 (co-author), Point of View 1997, Before Freedom: Nehru's Letters to His Sister 1909–47 (ed.) 2000, Lesser Breeds 2003; contrib. to newspapers and magazines including India Today. *Honours:* Foreign Hon. mem. American Acad. Arts and Sciences 1990; Hon. DLitt (Leeds) 1997; Diploma of Honour, Int. Order of Volunteers for Peace, Salsomaggiore, Italy 1982, Sinclair Prize 1985, Doon Ratna Citizens' Council Prize 1992, Wellesley Coll. Alumni Achievement Award 2002, Pride of Doon Award 2002, Woodstock School Alumni Achievement Award 2004. *Address:* 181B Rajpur Road, Dehra Dun, 248009 Uttaranchal, India. *Telephone:* (135) 2734278 (home). *E-mail:* ebd@ebdbooks.com (office).

SAHNI, Peush; Indian surgeon and writer. *Career:* Assoc. Prof. of Dept of Gastrointestinal Surgery and Liver Transplantation, All India Inst. of Medical Sciences; Pres. of Exec. Bd, World Asscn of Medical Editors (WAME) 2004–05. *Publications:* co-author: Brain Death and Organ Transplantation in India 1990, Medical Books in India 1994, GI Surgery Annual

(Vols II–V) 1995–98; contrib. to Diet, Digestion and Diabetes 1986, Scientific Approach to Surgery 1989, Trends in Hepatology 1990, Modern Concepts in Surgery 1992, GI Surgery Annual (Vol. I) 1994; contrib. articles to British Medical Journal, National Medical Journal of India, The Lancet, Hospital Today, British Journal of Surgery, Journal of Tropical Paediatrics. *Address:* WAME, c/o Margaret A. Winker MD, 515 N State Street, Chicago, IL 60610, USA. *E-mail:* peush_sahni@hotmail.com. *Website:* www.wame.com.

SAHU, N. S., MA, PhD; Indian academic and poet; b. 1 Sept. 1939; m. Shanti Sahu 1962; three s. *Career:* Lecturer in English, Dept of Education, Bhilai Steel Plant, Bhilainagar 1972–79; Lecturer 1979–92, Univ. of Gorakhpur, Reader in English 1992–98, Prof. 1998–2000; fmr Visiting Prof. Pt Ravishankar Shukla Univ.; life mem. American Studies Research Centre; mem. Int. Goodwill Soc. of India, Linguistic Soc. of India, Journal of Indian Writings in English. *Publications:* Aspects of Linguistics 1982, T. S. Eliot: The Man as a Poet, Playwright, Prophet and Critic 1988, A Study of the Works of Matthew Arnold 1988, Theatre of Protest and Anger 1988, Toponymy 1989, Christopher Marlowe and Theatre of Cruelty and Violence 1990, An Approach to American Literature 1991, Poems 1996, Whispers at Midnight (poems) 1996, John Keats: A Sensuous Mystic 2003; contrib. to various publications. *Honours:* Gov.'s Nominee as Academician for Le Magnus Univ., Raipur 2003–05. *Address:* Vani-Niketan, 2/955 Kota (West), Raipur 492 010, Chhattisgarh, India. *Telephone:* (771) 2575661 (home). *Fax:* (771) 4061803 (home).

SAID, Ali Ahman, (Adonis); Syrian poet and critic; b. 1930, Kassabin, nr Latakia. *Education:* Tartus, Damascus Univ., Univ. of Beirut, Lebanon. *Career:* moved to Lebanon 1956; Co-Ed., Shiar magazine 1956–63; Publisher, Mawaqif magazine 1968–78; Univ. Prof., commentator in Paris, France. *Publications include:* Songs of Mihyar, the Damascene 1961, The Book of Changes and Migration to the Regions of Day and Night 1965, A Time Between Ashes and Roses 1970, Introduction to Arab Poetry 1971, A Tomb for New York 1971, Singular in the Form of Plural 1974, Further Songs of Mihyar, the Damascene 1975, The Shock of Modernity 1978, The Book of Five Poems 1980, Manifesto of Modernity 1980. *Address:* c/o Gallimard Publishing, 5 rue Sébastien-Bottin, 75328 Paris, France.

SAIL, Lawrence Richard, BA, FRSL; British poet and writer; b. 29 Oct. 1942, London, England; m. 1st Teresa Luke 1966 (divorced 1981); one s. one d.; m. 2nd Helen Bird 1994; two d. *Education:* St John's Coll., Oxford. *Career:* teacher of modern languages, Lenana School, Nairobi 1966–71, Millfield School 1973–74, Blundell's School, Devon 1975–81, Exeter School 1982–91; Ed., South West Review 1981–85; Chair., Arvon Foundation 1990–94; Programme Dir 1991, Co-Dir 1999, Cheltenham Festival of Literature; jury mem., European (Aristeion) Literature Prize 1994–96; mem. Soc. of Authors, Poetry Soc.; mem. Sr Common Room, St John's Coll., Oxford. *Publications:* Opposite Views, 1974; The Drowned River, 1978; The Kingdom of Atlas, 1980; South West Review: A Celebration (ed.), 1985; Devotions, 1987; Aquamarine, 1988; First and Always (ed.), 1988; Out of Land: New and Selected Poems, 1992; Building into Air, 1995; The New Exeter Book of Riddles (co-ed.), 1999; The World Returning, 2002. Contributions: anthologies, magazines and newspapers. *Honours:* Hawthornden Fellowship 1992, Arts Council Writer's Bursary 1993, Cholmondeley Award 2004. *Address:* Richmond Villa, 7 Wonford Road, Exeter, Devon, EX2 4LF, England.

SAINT, Dora Jessie, (Miss Read), MBE; British novelist, short story writer and children's writer; b. 17 April 1913, Surrey, England. *Education:* Homerton Coll. *Career:* mem. Soc. of Authors. *Publications:* Village School, 1955; Village Diary, 1957; Storm in the Village, 1958; Hobby Horse Cottage, 1958; Thrush Green, 1959; Fresh From the Country, 1960; Winter in Thrush Green, 1961; Miss Clare Remembers, 1962; The Market Square, 1966; The Howards of Caxley, 1967; Country Cooking, 1969; News from Thrush Green, 1970; Tyler's Row, 1972; Christmas Mouse, 1973; Battles at Thrush Green, 1975; No Holly for Miss Quinn, 1976; Village Affairs, 1977; Return to Thrush Green, 1978; The White Robin, 1979; Village Centenary, 1980; Gossip From Thrush Green, 1981; A Fortunate Grandchild, 1982; Affairs at Thrush Green, 1983; Summer at Fairacre, 1984; At Home in Thrush Green, 1985; Time Remembered, 1986; The School at Thrush Green, 1987; The World at Thrush Green, 1988; Mrs Pringle, 1989; Friends at Thrush Green, 1990; Changes at Fairacre, 1991; Celebrations at Thrush Green, 1992; Farewell to Fairacre, 1993; Tales From a Village School, 1994; The Year at Thrush Green, 1995; A Peaceful Retirement, 1996.

SAINT-AMAND, Pierre, BA, MA, PhD; American (b. Haitian) academic and writer; *Francis Wayland Professor, Brown University*; b. 22 Feb. 1957, Port-au-Prince, Haiti. *Career:* Asst Prof., Yale Univ. 1981–82, Stanford Univ. 1982–86; Assoc. Prof. 1986–90, Prof. 1990–97, Francis Wayland Prof. 1997–, Brown Univ.; mem. MLA, American Soc. for Eighteenth-Century Studies. *Publications:* Diderot: Le Labyrinthe de la Relation 1984, Séduire ou la Passion des Lumières 1986, Les Lois de L'Hostilité 1992, The Libertine's Progress 1994, The Laws of Hostility 1996; editor: Diderot 1984, Le Roman au dix-huitième siècle 1987, Autonomy in the Age of Enlightenment 1993, Thérèse philosophe 2000, Confession d'une jeune fille 2005. *Honours:* Chevalier, Ordre des Palmes académiques 2001; Guggenheim Fellowship 1989. *Address:* French Studies, Box 1961, Brown University, Providence, RI 02912, USA (office). *E-mail:* psa@brown.edu (office).

ST AUBIN de TERÁN, Lisa Gioconda, (Lisa Duff-Scott), FRSL; British author; *Chief Executive, Radiant Pictures;* b. (Lisa Gioconda Carew), 2 Oct. 1953, London; d. of Jan Rynveld Carew and Joan Mary St Aubin; m. 1st Jaime

Terán 1970 (divorced 1981); one d.; m. 2nd George Macbeth 1981 (divorced 1989, deceased); one s.; m. 3rd Robbie Duff-Scott 1989; one d. *Education:* James Allen's Girls' School, Dulwich. *Career:* travelled widely in France and Italy 1969–71; managed sugar plantation in Venezuelan Andes 1971–78; moved to Italy 1983; fmr Vice-Pres. Umbria Film Festival, now Hon. Pres.; CEO Radiant Pictures 2002– (film production co.). *Screenplays:* The Slow Train to Milan (co-writer), The Hacienda, The Blessing, A Woman Called Solitude, The Moneymaker, The Orange Sicilian (co-writer, animated feature film). *Television:* wrote and presented documentaries Santos to Santa Cruz in Great Railway Journeys series (BBC) 1994, Great Railway Journeys of the World (BBC and PBS). *Radio:* adapted and read (for BBC) Off the Rails 1995, The Bay of Silence 1996. *Publications:* fiction: Keepers of the House 1982, The Slow Train to Milan 1983, The Tiger 1984, The Bay of Silence 1986, Black Idol 1987, The Marble Mountain (short stories) 1989, Joanna 1990, Nocturne 1993, Distant Landscapes (novella) 1995, The Palace 1998, The Virago Book of Wanderlust and Dreams (ed.) 1998, Southpaw (short stories) 1999, Otto: A Novel 2004; poetry: The Streak 1980, The High Place 1985; memoirs: Off the Rails 1989, Venice: The Four Seasons 1992, A Valley in Italy 1994, The Hacienda 1997, My Venezuelan Years 1997, Memory Maps 2001. *Honours:* Somerset Maugham Award 1983, John Llewelyn Rhys Award 1983, Eric Gregory Award for Poetry 1983. *Telephone:* (20) 618-6660 (office). *Fax:* (20) 668-8204 (office)*Address:* Radiant Pictures, 101 Vondelstraat, 1054 GM Amsterdam, Netherlands (office). *E-mail:* lisa@radiantpictures.com (office). *Website:* www.radiantpictures.com (office).

ST AUBYN, Edward; British writer and poet; b. 14 Jan. 1960, London, England; one s., one d. *Education:* Univ. of Oxford. *Publications:* Never Mind 1992, Bad News 1992, Some Hope 1994, On the Edge 1998, The Patrick Melrose Trilogy (omnibus edn of first three novels) 1999, A Clue to the Exit 2000, Mother's Milk (South Bank Show Award for Literature 2007) 2006. *Honours:* Betty Trask Award 1992, South Bank Award for Literature 2007. *Literary Agent:* Aitken Alexander Associates Ltd, 18–21 Cavaye Place, London, SW10 9PT, England. *Telephone:* (20) 7373-8672. *Fax:* (20) 7373-6002. *E-mail:* reception@aitkenalexander.co.uk. *Website:* www .aitkenalexander.co.uk.

ST AUBYN, Giles R., MA, FRSL; British writer; b. 11 March 1925, London, England. *Education:* Trinity Coll., Oxford. *Career:* mem. Soc. of Authors. *Publications:* Lord Macaulay 1952, A Victorian Eminence 1957, The Art of Argument 1957, The Royal George 1963, A World to Win 1968, Infamous Victorians 1971, Edward VII, Prince and King 1979, The Year of Three Kings 1483 1983, Queen Victoria: A Portrait 1991. *Honours:* Lieutenant, Royal Victorian Order 1977. *Literary Agent:* Christopher Sinclair-Stevenson, 3 South Terrace, London, SW7 2TB, England. *Address:* Apt 2, Saumarez Park Manor, Route de Saumarez, Câtel, Guernsey GY5 7TH, Channel Islands (home). *Telephone:* (1481) 251789 (home).

ST CLAIR, William, FRSL; British writer; b. 7 Dec. 1937, London, England; two d. *Education:* St John's Coll., Oxford. *Career:* fmrly, Under-Sec. Her Majesty's Treasury; Fellow Huntington Library, San Marino, CA 1985; Visiting Fellow 1981–82, Fellow All Souls Coll., Oxford 1992–96; Visiting Fellow Commoner 1997, Fellow 1998, Trinity Coll., Cambridge; mem. British Acad. 1992 (council 1997). *Publications:* Lord Elgin and the Marbles 1967, That Greece Might Still Be Free 1972, Trelawny 1978, Policy Evaluation: A Guide for Managers 1988, The Godwins and the Shelleys: The Biography of a Family 1989, Executive Agencies: A Guide to Setting Targets and Judging Performance 1992, Conduct Literature for Women 1500–1640 (ed. with Irmgard Maassen) 2000, Conduct Literature for Women 1640–1710 (ed. with Irmgard Maassen) 2002, Mapping Lives: The Uses of Biography (ed. with Peter France) 2002, The Reading Nation in the Romantic Period 2004, The Road to St Julien 2005, The Grand Slave Emporium: Cape Coast Castle and the British Slave Trade 2006. *Honours:* RSL Heinemann Prize 1973, Time-Life Prize 1990, MacMillan Silver Pen 1990, Thalassa (Greece) 2000. *Address:* Trinity College, Cambridge, CB2 1TQ, England. *E-mail:* ws214@cam.ac.uk.

ST JOHN OF FAWSLEY, Baron (Life Peer), cr. 1987, of Preston in the County of Northampton; **Norman Antony Francis St John-Stevas,** PC, MA, BCL, PhD, FRSL; British politician, barrister, writer and journalist; b. 18 May 1929, s. of the late Stephen Stevas and Kitty St John O'Connor. *Education:* Ratcliffe, Fitzwilliam Coll., Cambridge, Christ Church, Oxford and Yale Univ. *Career:* Barrister, Middle Temple 1952; Lecturer, King's Coll., London 1953–56; Tutor in Jurisprudence, Christ Church, Oxford 1953–55, Merton Coll., Oxford 1955–57; Founder mem. Inst. of Higher European Studies, Bolzano 1955; Legal Adviser to Sir Alan Herbert's Cttee on Book Censorship 1954–59; Legal and Political Corresp., The Economist 1959–64; Conservative MP for Chelmsford 1964–87; Sec. Conservative Party Home Affairs Cttee 1969–72; mem. Fulbright Comm. 1961; mem. Parl. Select Cttee Race Relations and Immigration 1970–72, on Civil List 1971–83, on Foreign Affairs 1983–87; Parl. Under-Sec. for Educ. and Science 1972–73; Minister of State for the Arts 1973–74; Shadow Cabinet 1974–79, Shadow Leader of the House of Commons 1978–79, Opposition Spokesman on Educ. 1974–78, Science 1974–78 and the Arts 1974–79; Chancellor of the Duchy of Lancaster 1979–81; Leader of the House of Commons 1979–81; Minister for the Arts 1979–81; Vice-Chair. Cons. Parl. NI Cttee 1972–87; Vice-Chair. Cons. Group for Europe 1972–75; Chair. Royal Fine Art Comm. 1985–99; Master Emmanuel Coll., Cambridge 1991–96, Life Fellow 1996; Vice-Pres. Theatres Advisory Council 1983; Founder mem. Christian-Social Inst. of Culture, Rome 1969; mem. Council RADA 1983–88, Nat. Soc. for Dance 1983–, Nat. Youth Theatre 1983–

(Patron 1984–), RCA 1985–; Trustee Royal Philharmonic Orch. 1985–88, Decorative Arts Soc. 1984–; Hon. Sec. Fed. of Conservative Students 1971–73; Ed. The Dublin (Wiseman Review) 1961; Romanes Lecturer, Oxford 1987. *Publications:* Obscenity and the Law 1956, Walter Bagehot 1959, Life, Death and the Law 1961, The Right to Life 1963, Law and Morals 1964, The Literary Essays of Walter Bagehot 1965, The Historical Essays of Walter Bagehot 1968, The Agonising Choice 1971, The Political Essays of Walter Bagehot 1974, The Economic Works of Walter Bagehot 1978, Pope John Paul, His Travels and Mission 1982, The Two Cities 1984. *Honours:* Hon. FRIBA; Hon. DD (Susquehanna, Pa) 1983; Hon. DLitt (Schiller) 1985, (Bristol) 1988; Hon. LLD (Leicester) 1991; Hon. DArts (De Montfort) 1996; Silver Jubilee Medal 1977; Kt Grand Cross, St Lazarus of Jerusalem 1963; Cavaliere Ordine al Merito della Repubblica (Italy) 1965, Commendatore 1978; Grand Bailiff Mil. and Hospitaller Order of St Lazarus of Jerusalem. *Address:* Emmanuel College, Cambridge, CB2 3AP (office); 7 Brunswick Place, Regent's Park, London, NW1 4PS; The Old Rectory, Preston Capes, Daventry, Northants., NN11 6TE, England.

SALAMON, Julie, BA, JD; American journalist and critic; m.; two c. *Education:* Tufts Univ., NY Univ. Law School. *Career:* fmr reporter and film critic The Wall Street Journal; writer and TV critic NY Times 2000–; mem. Bd of Dirs Bowery Residents Cttee. *Publications:* The Devil's Candy, The Net of Dreams, White Lies, The Christmas Tree, Facing the Wind: A True Story of Tragedy and Reconciliation 2001, Rambam's Ladder 2003. *Address:* The New York Times, 229 West 43rd Street, New York, NY 10036, USA.

ŠALAMUN, Tomaž, MA; Slovenian poet, writer and academic; *Visiting Professor, University of Pittsburgh;* b. 4 July 1941, Zagreb, Yugoslavia; m. 1st Marusa Krese 1969 (divorced 1975); m. 2nd Metka Krašovec (1979); one s. one d. *Education:* Univ. of Ljubljana, Univ. of Iowa. *Career:* Asst Curator Modern Gallery, Ljubljana 1968–70; Asst Prof. Acad. of Fine Arts, Ljubljana 1970–73; workshops Univ. of Tennessee at Chattanooga 1987–88, 1996; Visiting Writer, Vermont Coll. 1988, Berlin 2003–04, Bogliasco Foundation 2004; Consul, Slovenian Cultural Attaché, New York 1996–97; currently Visiting Prof. Univ. of Pittsburgh, USA; mem. PEN, Slovenian Writers' Asscn. *Publications:* Turbines: Twenty-One Poems 1973, Snow 1973, Pesmi (Poems) 1980, Maske (Masks) 1980, Balada za Metka Krašovec (trans. as A Ballad for Metka Krašovec) 1981, Analogije svetlobe 1982, Glas 1983, Sonet o mleku 1984, Soy realidad 1985, Ljubljanska pomlad 1986, Mera casa 1987, Ziva rana, zivi sok 1988, The Selected Poems of Tomaz Salamun 1988, Otrok in jelen 1990, Painted Desert: Poems 1991, The Shepherd, The Hunter 1992, Ambra 1994, The Four Questions of Melancholy: New and Selected Poems 1997, Crni labod 1997, Knjiga za mojega brata 1997, Homage to Hat and Uncle Guido and Eliot 1998, Morje 1999, Gozd in kelihi 2000, Feast 2000, Ballad for Metka Krašovec 2001, Table 2002, Poker 2003, Od tam 2003, Blackboards 2004, Z Arhilohom po Kikladih 2004, The Book For My Brother 2006; contrib. to anthologies and periodicals. *Honours:* Mladost Prize 1969, residencies at Yaddo 1973–74, 1979, 1986, 1989, MacDowell Colony 1986, Karoly Foundation, Vence, France 1987, Maisons des écrivains étrangers, Saint-Nazaire, France 1996, Civitella Ranieri, Umbertide, Italy 1997, Bogliasco Foundation 2002, Fulbright Fellowship 1987, Jenko Prize 1988, Pushcart Prize 1994, Civitella Ranieri Fellowship 1997, Prešeren Prize 1999, Alta Marea Prize 2002, Festival Prize, Constanta 2004, Europäische Preis für Poesie, Münster (Germany) 2007. *Address:* Dalmatinova 11, 1000 Ljubljana, Slovenia (home). *Telephone:* (1) 2314522 (home). *Fax:* (1) 4304843 (home). *E-mail:* metka.krasovec@siol.net (home).

SALAS SOMMER, Dario, (John Baines), BA; Chilean writer, academic and philosopher; b. 4 March 1935, Santiago. *Education:* Dario Salas Coll., Santiago de Chile, Univ. of Santiago. *Career:* founder, Inst. for Hermetic Philosophy; mem. Authors' Guild of America. *Publications:* Hypsoconciencia 1965, Los Brujos Hablan 1968, El Hombre Estelar 1979, La Ciencia del Amor 1982, Existe la Mujer? 1983, El Desarrollo del Mundo Interno 1984, Moral para el Siglo XXI 1998. *Address:* Institute for Hermetic Philosophy, PO Box 8549, New York, NY 10150, USA (office). *E-mail:* ihpny@ihpny.org (office). *Website:* www.ihpny.org (office).

SALE, (John) Kirkpatrick, BA; American editor and writer; b. 27 June 1937, Ithaca, NY; m. Faith Apfelbaum Sale 1962 (died 1999); two d. *Education:* Cornell Univ., Ithaca. *Career:* Ed. The New Leader 1959–61, New York Times Magazine 1965–68; Ed. The Nation 1981–82, Contributing Ed. 1986–; Dir Middlebury Inst. (MiddleburyInstitute.org); mem. PEN American Center (Bd mem. 1976–97), E. F. Schumacher Soc. (Bd mem. 1980–). *Publications:* SDS 1973, Power Shift 1975, Human Scale 1980, Dwellers in the Land: The Bioregional Vision 1985, The Conquest of Paradise: Christopher Columbus and the Columbian Legacy 1990, The Green Revolution: The American Environmental Movement 1962–1992 1993, Rebels Against the Future: The Luddites and Their War on the Industrial Revolution 1995, The Fire of his Genius: Robert Fulton and the American Dream 2001, Why the Sea is Salt (poems) 2001, After Eden: The Evolution of Human Domination 2006. *Address:* 127 E Mountain Road, Cold Spring, NY 10516, USA (home). *E-mail:* Director@Middleburginstitute.net (office). *Website:* MiddleburyInstitute.org (office).

SALIH, Tayeb; Sudanese writer; b. 1929, Northern Province. *Education:* Univ. of Khartoum. *Career:* fmr Head of Drama, Arabic service, BBC; fmr Dir-Gen. of Information, Qatar; with UNESCO, Paris; contributor to al-Majalla magazine, London. *Publications include:* Mawsim al-Hijra ash-shamal

(Seasons of Migration to the North) 1967, Urs al-Zein (The Wedding of Zein) 1969, Al-rajul al Qubrosi (The Cypriot Man) 1978, Douma Wad Hamid (The Doum Tree of Wad Hamid) 1985, Bandarshah 1996, A Handful of Dates, Dau al-Bayt, Mariud (Bandar Shah). *Literary Agent:* c/o Caroline Dawnay, PFD, Drury House, 34–43 Russell Street, London, WC2B 5HA, England.

SALINGER, Jerome David (J. D.); American writer; b. 1 Jan. 1919, New York, NY; s. of Sol Salinger and Miriam (née Jillich) Salinger; m. 2nd Claire Douglas 1953 (divorced 1967); one s. one d.; m. 3rd Colleen. *Education:* Manhattan public schools, Valley Forge Military Acad., Columbia Univ. *Career:* travelled in Europe 1937–38; army service with 4th Infantry Div. (Staff Sergeant) 1942–46; mem. Légion d'honneur. *Publications:* The Catcher in the Rye (novel) 1951, For Esme with Love and Squalor (short stories, aka Nine Stories) 1953, Franny & Zooey (novel) 1961, Raise High the Roof-Beam, Carpenters and Seymour: An Introduction (novel) 1963, Hapworth 16, 1924 1997; contrib. numerous stories to magazines, mostly in the New Yorker 1948–. *Literary Agent:* Harold Ober Associates Inc., 425 Madison Avenue, New York, NY 10017, USA.

SALIVAROVÁ, Zdena; Canadian (b. Czechoslovakian) writer, publisher and translator; b. 21 Oct. 1933, Prague, Czechoslovakia; m. Josef Škvorecký. *Career:* fmr mem. Magic Lantern Theatre and Paravan Theatre; moved to Canada 1969; f. and Man.'68 Publishers Corpn, Toronto (Canada) 1971–94, publishing Czechoslovakian books banned in Czechoslovakia. *Publications:* Pánská jízda (three novellas, trans. as Gentlemen's Ride) 1968, Honzlová (novel, trans. as Summer in Prague) 1972, Nebe, peklo, ráj (eight novellas, trans. as Ashes, Ashes, All Fall Down) (Egon Hostovský Memorial Prize for best Czech fiction written in exile 1976) 1987, Hnuj zeme (trans. as Manure of the Earth) 1994, Krátké setkání, s vraždou (novel, with Josef Škvorecký, trans. as Brief Encounter, Including a Murder) 1999, Setkání po letech, s vraždou (novel, with Josef Škvorecký, trans. as Encounter Many Years Later, Including a Murder) 2000, Setkání na konci éry, s vraždou (novel, with Josef Škvorecký, trans. as Encounter at the End of an Era, Including a Murder) 2001. *Honours:* Hon. DLit (Toronto); Gold Medal of Masaryk Univ. 1990; Order of the White Lion 1991. *Website:* www.skvorecky.com.

SALMON, Robert; French journalist; b. 6 April 1918, Marseille; s. of Pierre Salmon and Madeleine Blum; m. Anne-Marie Jeanprost 1942; five c. *Education:* Lycée Louis le Grand, Ecole Normale Supérieure and at the Sorbonne. *Career:* Founder Mouvement de Résistance Défense de la France; mem. Comité Parisien de Libération; Leader Paris Div., Mouvement de Libération Nationale; mem. Provisional Consultative Ass. 1944, First Constituent Ass. 1945; Founder Pres. and Dir Gen. France-Soir 1944; fmr Pres. Soc. France-Editions (Elle, Le Journal de Dimanche, Paris-Presse, etc.), Hon. Pres. 1976–; fmr Pres. Soc. de Publications Economiques (Réalités, Connaissance des Arts, Entreprise, etc.); Sec.-Gen. Féd. Nat. de la Presse 1951–77; Hon. Pres. French Cttee Int. Press Inst. 1973; mem. Admin. Council Fondation Nat. des Sciences Politiques 1973–93; Prof. Inst. d'Etudes Politiques, Univ. of Paris and Ecole Nat. d' Admin 1967–88; mem. Haut Conseil de l'audiovisuel 1973–82; mem. Comm. de la République Française pour l' UNESCO 1979–. *Publications:* Le sentiment de l'existence chez Maine de Biran 1943, Notions élémentaires de psychologie 1947, L'organisation actuelle de la presse française 1955, Information et publicité 1956, L'information économique, clé de la prospérité 1963, Chemins Faisant (two vols) 2004. *Honours:* Commdr, Légion d'honneur, Croix de guerre, Rosette de la Résistance, Médaille des évadés. *Address:* 4 rue Berlioz, 75116 Paris, France (home).

SALOM, Philip, BA, DipEd; Australian academic, poet and writer; b. 8 Aug. 1950, Bunbury, WA. *Education:* Curtin University. *Career:* Tutor and Lecturer, Curtin University, 1982–93; Writer-in-Residence, Singapore National University, 1989, B. R. Whiting Library/Studio, Rome, 1992; Lecturer, Murdoch University, 1994–97, Victorian College of the Arts of the University of Melbourne, 2000–01. *Publications:* The Silent Piano, 1980; The Projectionist: Sequence, 1983; Sky Poems, 1987; Barbecue of the Primitives, 1989; Playback, 1991; Tremors, 1992; Feeding the Ghost, 1993; Always Then and Now, 1993; The Rome Air Naked, 1996; New and Selected Poems, 1998; A Creative Life, 2001. *Honours:* Commonwealth Poetry Prizes, 1981, 1987; Western Australian Premier's Prize, 1984, 1988 1992; Australia/New Zealand Literary Exchange Award, 1992; Newcastle Poetry Prize, 1996, 2000. *Address:* PO Box 273, Kerrimuir, Vic. 3129, Australia. *E-mail:* psalom@netspace.net .au.

SALTER, James, BS, MIA; American writer; b. 10 June 1925, New York, NY; m. 1st Ann Altemus 1951 (divorced 1976); two s. three d.; m. 2nd Kay Eldridge 1998. *Education:* West Point, NY, Georgetown Univ., Washington, DC. *Career:* mem. American Acad. of Arts and Letters, PEN USA. *Publications:* The Hunters 1957, The Arm of Flesh 1960, A Sport and a Pastime 1967, Light Years 1976, Solo Faces 1980, Dusk and Other Stories 1989, Burning the Days 1997, Cassada 2000, Bangkok (in French) 2003, Last Night 2005; contribs to Paris Review, Antaeus, Grand Street, Vogue, Esquire. *Honours:* American Acad. of Arts and Letters Grant 1982, PEN-Faulkner Award 1989, Fadiman Medal 2003. *Address:* Box 765, Bridgehampton, NY 11932, USA. *Telephone:* (631) 537-1630 (home). *E-mail:* saltereast@aol.com (home).

SALTER, Mary Jo, BA, MA; American poet, academic and editor; *Emily Dickinson Senior Lecturer in Humanities, Mount Holyoke College;* b. 15 Aug. 1954, Grand Rapids, MI; m. Brad Leithauser 1980; two d. *Education:* Harvard Univ., Univ. of Cambridge. *Career:* Instructor, Harvard Univ. 1978–79; Staff Ed., Atlantic Monthly 1978–80; poet-in-residence, Robert Frost Place 1981; Lecturer in English 1984–, Emily Dickinson Lecturer in Humanities, later Emily Dickinson Sr Lecturer 1995–, Mount Holyoke Coll., South Hadley, MA; Poetry Ed., The New Republic 1992–95; lyricist for songs by Fred Hersch 2004–; mem. PEN, Poetry Soc. of America (vice-pres. 1995–). *Plays:* Falling Bodies 2004. *Publications:* Henry Purcell in Japan 1985, Unfinished Painting 1989, The Moon Comes Home 1989, Sunday Skaters: Poems 1994, A Kiss in Space: Poems 1999, Open Shutters: Poems 2003; contrib. to periodicals. *Honours:* The Nation Discovery Prize 1983, NEA Fellowship 1983–84, Lamont Prize in Poetry 1988, Guggenheim Fellowship 1993, Amy Lowell Scholarship 1995. *Address:* c/o Department of English, Mount Holyoke College, South Hadley, MA 01075, USA. *Website:* www.mtholyoke.edu.

SALTZMAN, Arthur Michael, AB, AM, PhD; American academic and writer; *Professor of English, Missouri Southern State University;* b. 10 Aug. 1953, Chicago, IL; one d. *Education:* Univ. of Illinois. *Career:* Teaching Fellow, Univ. of Illinois 1975–80; Asst Prof., Missouri Southern State Univ. 1981–86, Assoc. Prof. 1986–92, Prof. 1992–; mem. MLA. *Publications:* The Fiction of William Gass: The Consolation of Language 1986, Understanding Raymond Carver 1988, Designs of Darkness in Contemporary American Fiction 1990, The Novel in the Balance 1993, Understanding Nicholson Baker 1999, This Mad 'Instead': Governing Metaphors in Contemporary American Fiction 2000, Objects and Empathy 2001, Nearer 2005; contribs to various professional journals and general periodicals. *Honours:* Missouri Southern Outstanding Teacher Award 1992, Ames Memorial Essay Award 1998, Mid-List Press First Series Creative Non-fiction Award 1999, Nebraska Review Creative Non-Fiction Award 2002, Victor J. Emmett Memorial Award 2003. *Address:* 3235 Connecticut, Joplin, MO 64804, USA.

SALZBERG, Steven, BA, MS, MPhil, PhD; American scientist and writer. *Education:* Univ. of Yale, Univ. of Harvard. *Career:* research scientist and sr knowledge engineer, Applied Expert Systems Inc. 1985–87; Assoc. in Research, Harvard Business School 1988–89; Asst Prof. 1989–96, Assoc. Prof. 1996–99, Research Prof. 1999–, Dept of Computer Science, jt Research Prof. 1999–, Dept of Biology, Johns Hopkins Univ.; Investigator 1997–, Sr Dir of Bio-informatics 1998–, Inst. for Genomic Research. *Publications:* Learning with Nested Generalized Exemplars 1990, Computational Methods in Molecular Biology (ed.), contrib. to Science, Nucleic Acids Research. *Address:* Institute for Genomic Research, 9712 Medical Center Drive, Rockville, MD 20850, USA. *Telephone:* (301) 838-0200. *Fax:* (301) 838-0208. *Website:* www .tigr.org.

SAMADOGHLU, Vagif; Azerbaijani (Azeri) poet; b. 5 June 1939, Baku; s. of the late Samad Vurghun. *Education:* Tchaikovsky Conservatory, Moscow. *Career:* mem. Azerbaijan Milli Majlis (Parl.); Nat. Poet of Azerbaijan 1999; Parl. Rep. to Council of Europe 2001–. *Publications:* poetry: Yoldan telegram 1968, Gunun baxti 1972, Man burdayam, Ilahi 1996, Uzaq Yashil Ada 1999; prose: Baxt uzuyu (drama) 1999, also essays.

SAMARAS, Zoe, BS, MA, PhD; Greek academic; b. 1935, Karpathos; d. of Constantinos and Maria Malaxos; m. Nicholas Samaras 1960 (died 1981); one s. *Education:* Columbia Univ., NY, USA. *Career:* Lecturer in French, Columbia Univ. 1960; Lecturer, City Univ. of New York, USA 1965, Asst Prof. of French and French Literature 1968; Prof. of French Literature and Theory of Literature, Aristotle Univ. of Thessaloniki 1978, Chair. Dept of French Literature 1978–92, Chair. Grad. Program of French Literature; Visiting Prof. of Theory of Literature, Univ. of Athens 1987, 1995, 1998, Prof. Emer. 2002. *Publications include:* The Comic Element of Montaigne's Style 1971, L'Enfant du Taygète 1974, Le Règne de Cronos 1983, Text Perspectives (in Greek) 1987, Montaigne: Espace Voyage Ecriture (ed.) 1995, Approaches bachelardienne des œuvres littéraires (ed.) 1996, Simulation of Theatrical Discourse (in Greek) 1996, Miltos Sahtouris (in Greek) 1997; poetry (in Greek): For Maria 1991, Days of Dryness 1994, The Passage of Eurydice (Best Book Prize) 1997, The Sanctuary of the Sign (in Greek) 2002, Le discours spéculaire 2003; numerous contrib. to professional journals. *Honours:* Officier de l'Ordre nat. du Mérite (France) 1988; Silver Medal of the City of Paris 1988, Montaigne Int. Award 1992, La Verbe et la Scène: Etudes sur la Littérature et le Théâtre en l'Honneur de Zoe Samara, Paris, Champion 2005. *Address:* Aristotle University of Thessaloniki, Faculty of Philosophy, 54124 Thessaloniki (office); Vassilikou 10, 54636 Thessaloniki, Greece (home). *Telephone:* (2310) 997491 (office); (2310) 212418 (home). *Fax:* (2310) 997491 (office). *E-mail:* zsamara@frl.auth.gr (office). *Website:* www.frl.auth.gr (office).

SAMBROOK, (Arthur) James, BA, MA, PhD; British academic and writer; b. 5 Sept. 1931, Nuneaton, Warwicks.; m. Patience Ann Crawford 1961; four s. *Education:* Worcester Coll., Oxford, Univ. of Nottingham. *Career:* Lecturer, St David's Coll., Lampeter, Wales, 1957–64; Lecturer, Univ. of Southampton 1964–71, Sr Lecturer 1971–75, Reader 1975–81, Prof. of English 1981–92, Prof. Emer. 1992–. *Publications:* A Poet Hidden: The Life of R. W. Dixon, 1962; The Scribleriad, etc (ed.), 1967; William Cobbett, 1973; James Thomson: The Seasons (ed.), 1981; English Pastoral Poetry, 1983; The Eighteenth Century: The Intellectual and Cultural Context of English Literature 1700–1789, 1986; Liberty, the Castle of Indolence and Other Poems, 1986; James Thomson 1700–1748: A Life: Biographical, Critical, 1992; William Cowper: The Task and Other Poems (ed.), 1994; With the Rank and Pay of a Sapper, 1998; contrib. to reference books, including the Oxford Dictionary of National Biography, professional journals and general periodicals. *Address:* 36

Bursledon Road, Hedge End, Southampton, SO30 0BX, England. *Telephone:* (1489) 782552 (office). *E-mail:* jamessambrook@hotmail.com (office).

SAMPSON, Fiona Ruth, ARCM, MA, PhD; British poet and editor; *Editor, Poetry Review. Education:* Royal Acad. of Music, Univ. of Oxford and Univ. of Nijmegen, The Netherlands. *Career:* series of residencies in writing in health care in the UK from 1988; AHRB Research Fellow Oxford Brookes Univ. 2002–05; poetry critic for The Irish Times, The Guardian; judge Foyle Young Poet of the Year 2004, Irish Times Poetry Award 2006; Founder Ed. Orient Express 2002–; Ed. Poetry Review 2005–. *Publications:* BirthChart (chapbook) 1992, Picasso's Men 1994, Hotel Casino (chapbook) 1994, The Self on the Page (with C. Hunt) 1998, The Healing Word 1999, Folding the Real 2001, Travel Diary 2004, Creative Writing in Health and Social Care 2004, The Distance Between Us 2005, Writing: Self and Reflexivity (with C. Hunt) 2005, Setting the Echo (chapbook) 2005. *Honours:* Newdigate Prize 1998, Zlaten Prsten (Macedonia) 2004, awards from Arts Council England, Arts Council of Wales, Soc. of Authors and others. *Address:* Poetry Review, Poetry Society, 22 Betterton Street, London, WC2H 9BX, England (office). *Telephone:* (20) 7420-9883 (office). *E-mail:* poetryreview@poetrysociety.org.uk (office). *Website:* www.poetrysociety.org.uk (office); www.writersartists.net (home).

SANCHEZ, Lavinia (see Elmslie, Kenward Gray)

SANCHEZ, Sonia, BA, PhD; American academic, poet, dramatist and writer; b. 9 Sept. 1934, Birmingham, AL; m. Etheridge Knight (divorced); two s. one d. *Education:* Hunter College, CUNY, New York University, Wilberforce University. *Career:* Instructor, San Francisco State College, 1967–69; Lecturer, University of Pittsburgh, 1969–70, Rutgers University, 1970–71; Manhattan Community College, 1971–73, CUNY, 1972; Assoc. Prof., Amherst College, 1972–73, University of Pennsylvania, 1976–77; Assoc. Prof., 1977–79, Prof. of English, 1979–, Temple University. *Publications:* Poetry: Homecoming, 1969; WE a BaddDDD People, 1970; Liberation Poem, 1970; It's a New Day: Poems for Young Brothas and Sistuhs, 1971; Ima Talken bout the Nation of Islam, 1971; Love Poems, 1973; A Blues Book for Blue Black Magical Women, 1974; I've Been a Woman: New and Selected Poems, 1978; Homegirls and Handgrenades, 1984; Under a Soprano Sky, 1987; Wounded in the House of a Friend, 1995. Plays: The Bronx is Next, 1968; Sister Son/ji, 1969; Dirty Hearts '72, 1973; Uh, Uh: But How Do it Free Us?, 1974. Stories: A Sound Investment, 1980. Other: Crisis in Culture, 1983. Editor: Three Hundred Sixty Degrees of Blackness Comin' at You, 1972; We Be Word Sorcerers: 25 Stories by Black Americans, 1973. *Honours:* PEN Award, 1969; American Acad. of Arts and Letters Award, 1970; National Endowment for the Arts Award, 1978; Smith College Tribute to Black Women Award, 1982; Lucretia Mott Award, 1984; Before Columbus Foundation Award, 1985; PEN Fellow, 1993.

SANDEN, Einar, MA, PhD; Estonian writer and historian; b. 8 Sept. 1932, Tallinn; m. Elizabeth Gorell 1994. *Education:* studied in the USA. *Career:* Managing Dir and owner, Boreas Publishing House 1975; Councillor, Estonian Govt in Exile 1975–90; mem. PEN Centre for Writers in Exile, RSL, Asscn of Estonian Writers Abroad, English PEN, Estonian Nat. Council, Asscn for the Advancement of Baltic Studies, USA, Estonian Academic Asscn of War History, Tallinn. *Publications:* Tuul üle Andaluusia 1954, September 1959, Ungari sügis 1959, Viimne veerand veini 1962, KGB kutsub Evet (trans. as KGB Calling Eve) 1968, Mitme näo ja nimega 1978, Loojangul kahine Tallinnast 1979, Süda ja kivid 1982, Võllamäe kavalkaad 1984, Hommikutunnid 2001, Näod ja maskid 2003, Septembri lapsed 2004, Tormi käest Tulemaale 2004, Kolme ilmakaare poole 2005. *Honours:* UPLI Distinguished Freedom Writer, Manila, The Philippines 1968, Fraternity Sakala Cultural Award, Toronto 1984.

SANDERS, (James) Edward; American poet, writer, singer and lecturer; b. 17 Aug. 1939, Kansas City, MO; m. Miriam Kittell 1961; one c. *Education:* BA, New York University, 1964. *Career:* Ed.-Publisher, Fuck You/A Magazine of the Arts, 1962–65; Founder-Lead Singer, The Fugs, satiric folk-rock-theatre group, 1964–69; Owner, Peace Eye Bookstore, New York City, 1964–70; Visiting Prof. of Language and Literature, Bard College, Annadale-on-Hudson, New York, 1979, 1983; Lectures, readings, performances throughout the US and Europe; mem. New York Foundation for the Arts; PEN. *Publications:* Poetry: Poem from Jail, 1963; A Valorium Edition of the Entire Extant Works of Thales!, 1964; King Lord/Queen Freak, 1964; The Toe Queen Poems, 1964; The Fugs' Song Book (with Ken Weaver and Betsy Klein), 1965; Peace Eye, 1965; Egyptian Hieroglyphics, 1973; 20,000 A.D., 1976; The Cutting Prow, 1981; Hymn to Maple Syrup and Other Poems, 1985; Poems for Robin, 1987; Thirsting for Peace in a Raging Century: Selected Poems 1961–1985, 1987; Hymn to the Rebel Cafe: Poems 1987–1991, 1993; Chekhov: A Biography in Verse, 1995. Editor: Poems for Marilyn, 1962. Compiler and Contributor: Bugger: An Anthology of Buttockry, 1964; Despair: poems to come down by, 1964. Fiction: Shards of God: A Novel of the Yippies, 1970; Tales of Beatnik Glory (short stories), 2 vols, 1975, 1990; Fame and Love in New York, 1980. Non-Fiction: The Family: The Story of Charles Manson's Dune Buggy Attack Battalion, 1971; Vote! (with Abbie Hoffman and Jerry Rubin), 1972; Investigative Poetry, 1976; The Z-D Generation, 1981. Other: Musicals: Recordings with The Fugs; Solo recordings. *Honours:* Frank O'Hara Prize, Modern Poetry Asscn, 1967; National Endowment for the Arts Awards, 1966, 1970, Fellowship, 1987–88; Guggenheim Fellowship, 1983–84; American Book Award, 1988. *Address:* PO Box 729, Woodstock, NY 12498, USA.

SANDERS, Louis; French novelist; b. 1964. *Education:* Sorbonne, Univ. of Paris. *Publications (in translation):* Death in the Dordogne 1999, The Englishman's Wife 2000, An Ignoble Profession 2002. *Address:* c/o Serpent's Tail Publishing, 4 Blackstock Mews, London, N4 2BT, England. *E-mail:* info@serpentstail.com.

SANDERS, Noah (see Blount Jr, Roy Alton)

SANDERS, Scott Russell, BA, PhD; American academic and author; b. 26 Oct. 1945, Memphis, TN; m. Ruth Ann McClure 1967, one s. one d. *Education:* Brown University, University of Cambridge. *Career:* Literary Ed., 1969–70, Contributing Ed., 1970–71, Cambridge Reviews; Fiction Ed., Minnesota Review, 1976–80; Fiction Columnist, Chicago Sun-Times, 1977–84; Contributing Ed., North American Review, 1982–; Asst Prof. of English, Indiana University, 1996–. *Publications:* Fiction: Wilderness Plots: Tales About the Settlement of the American Land, 1983; Fetching the Dead (short stories), 1984; Wonders Hidden: Audubon's Early Years (novella), 1984; Terrarium (novel), 1985; Hear the Wind Blow (short stories), 1985; Bad Man Ballad (novel), 1986; The Engineer of Beasts (novel), 1988; The Invisible Country (novel), 1989. Other: D. H. Lawrence: The World of the Major Novels, 1974; Stone Country, 1985, revised edn as In Limestone Country, 1991; Audubon Reader: The Best Writings of John James Audubon, 1986; The Paradise of Bombs (essays), 1987; Secrets of the Universe (essays), 1991; Staying Put: Making a Home in a Restless World, 1993; Writing from the Center (essays), 1995; Hunting for Hope, 1998. Contributions: anthologies, journals, and magazines. *Honours:* Woodrow Wilson Fellowship, 1967–68; National Endowment for the Arts Fellowship, 1983–84; Indiana Arts Commission Master Fellowships, 1984, 1990–91; Lilly Endowment Open Fellowship, 1986–87; Associated Writing Programs Award for Non-Fiction, 1987; PEN Syndicated Fiction Award, 1988; Kenyon Review Award for Literary Excellence, 1991; Guggenheim Fellowship, 1992–93; Ohioana Book Award in Non-Fiction, 1994; Lannan Literary Award in Non-Fiction, 1995.

SANDERSON, Anne Hilary, BA, MA, MLitt; British poet and writer; b. 13 Jan. 1944, Brighton, England; m. Michael Sanderson 1976. *Education:* St Anne's College, Oxford. *Career:* English Lectrice, École Normale Supérieure de Jeunes Filles, University of Paris, 1969–71; Lecturer in European Literature, University of East Anglia, 1972–98; mem. Asscn of Christian Writers; Norwich Writers' Circle; Norwich Poetry Group; Playwrights East. *Publications:* contrib. to anthologies and periodicals, including poems in Poetry Now, Peace & Freedom, Purple Patch, The Poetry Church, Advance! Isthmus, Triumph Herald, Reflections, Tree Spirit, The Firing Squad, All Year Round; articles in Studies on Voltaire & the 18th Century, Jeunesse de Racine, Norwich Papers. *Honours:* Prix Racine 1969, third prize Hilton House Nat. Open Poetry Awards for Collections 1998, 1999.

SANDERSON, John Michael, MA, PhD; British academic and writer; *Professor Emeritus of Economic and Social History, University of East Anglia;* b. 23 Jan. 1939, Glasgow, Scotland. *Education:* Queens' College, Cambridge. *Career:* Prof. of Economic and Social History, University of East Anglia, now Prof. Emer.; General Ed., Cambridge University Press Economic History Society Studies in Economic and Social History Series, 1992–98; Council, Economic History Society, 1994–2000; mem. Economic History Society. *Publications:* The Universities and British Industry, 1850–1970, 1972; The Universities in the 19th Century, 1975; Education, Economic Change and Society in England, 1780–1870, 1983; From Irving to Olivier, A Social History of the Acting Profession in England, 1880–1983, 1984; Educational Opportunity and Social Change in England, 1900–1980s, 1987; The Missing Stratum, Technical School Education in England, 1900–1990s, 1994; Education and Economic Decline, 1870–1990s, 1999; The History of the University of East Anglia, Norwich, 2002. Contributions: Economic History Review; Journal of Contemporary History; Contemporary Record; Business History; Northern History; Past and Present. *Address:* School of History, University of East Anglia, Norwich NR4 7TJ, England (office).

SANDOR, Anna, BA; Canadian (b. Hungarian) screenwriter; b. Budapest, Hungary; d. of Paul and Agnes Elizabeth (née Laszlo) Sandor; m. (divorced); one d. *Education:* Harbord Coll. Inst., Toronto and Univ. of Windsor. *Career:* has lived in USA since 1989; Lecturer in Writing for TV Summer Inst. of Film, Ottawa; held screenwriting workshops; Co-Chair. Crime Writers of Canada 1985–86; mem. Asscn of Canadian TV and Radio Artists (ACTRA) Writers' Council 1985, Acad. of TV Arts and Sciences, Writers' Guild of America and Canada. *TV productions:* films: A Population of One 1980, Charlie Grant's War 1985, The Marriage Bed 1986, Mama's Going to Buy You a Mockingbird 1987–88, Martha, Ruth and Edie 1988, Two Men (Edgar Dale Award for Excellence in Screenwriting 1989) 1988, Tarzan in Manhattan (jtly) 1989, Stolen: One Husband (jtly) 1990, Miss Rose White (Hallmark Hall of Fame) 1992, Family of Strangers (jtly) 1993, For the Love of My Child – The Anissa Ayala Story 1993, Amelia Earhart: The Final Flight 1994, Gift of Love – The Daniel Huffman Story 1999, My Louisiana Sky 2001, Tiger Cruise (jtly) 2004; series:Running Man 1982–83, High Card 1982–83, Seeing Things (jtly) 1983–85, Danger Bay (Gold Medal, New York Int. Film and TV Festival) 1986–88, On the Record, Tarzan (Exec. Producer) 1991; sitcoms: King of Kensington 1975–80, Flappers, Hangin' In. *Honours:* Prix Anik 1981, 1985, 1986, 1989, ACTRA for Best Writer Original Drama Award 1986, Margaret Collier Award for Lifetime Achievement, Canadian Acad. 1986, Chris Plaque for Best Script (Columbus Film Festival) 1989, Humanitas Award 1993, 2002, Writers' Guild of America Award 2001. *Literary Agent:* c/o Steve Weiss,

William Morris Agency, 151 S El Camino Drive, Beverly Hills, CA 90212, USA. *Telephone:* (310) 859-4423.

SANDOZ, (George) Ellis, Jr, BA, MA, PhD; American academic and writer; b. 10 Feb. 1931, New Orleans, LA; m. Therese Alverne Hubley 1957; two s. two d. *Education:* Louisiana State Univ., Univ. of North Carolina, Georgetown Univ., Univ. of Heidelberg, Univ. of Munich. *Career:* Instructor to Prof., Louisiana Polytechnic Inst. 1959–68; Prof. and Head Dept of Political Science, East Texas State Univ. 1968–78; Prof. of Political Science 1978–, Dir Eric Voegelin Inst. for American Renaissance Studies 1987–, Louisiana State Univ.; Fellow Germanistic Soc. of America 1964–65; Henry E. Huntington Library Fellow 1986–87; mem. American Historical Asscn, American Political Science Asscn, Federalist Soc., Organization of American Historians, Philadelphia Soc., Southern Political Science Asscn, Southwestern Political and Social Science Asscns, Eric Voegelin Soc. (founder-sec. 1985–). *Publications:* Political Apocalypse: A Study of Dostoevsky's Grand Inquisitor 1971, Conceived in Liberty: American Individual Rights Today 1978, A Tide of Discontent: The 1980 Elections and Their Meaning (ed.) 1981, The Voegelianian Revolution: A Biographical Introduction 1981, Eric Voegelin's Thought: A Critical Appraisal (ed.) 1982, Election '84: Landslide Without a Mandate? (ed. with Cecil V. Crabb Jr) 1985, A Government of Laws: Political Theory, Religion and the American Founding 1990, Political Sermons of the American Founding Era, 1730–1805 (ed.) 1991, index 1996, Eric Voegelin's Significance for the Modern Mind (ed.) 1991, The Roots of Liberty: Magna Carta, Ancient Constitution, and the Anglo-American Tradition of Rule of Law (ed.) 1993, Politics of Truth and Other Untimely Essays: The Crisis of Civic Consciousness 1999, Republicanism, Religion and the Soul of America 2006; contrib. to The Collected Works of Eric Voegelin (principal ed.) 1986–, and to scholarly books and professional journals. *Honours:* Hon. PhD (Palacky Univ., Olomouc, Czech Republic) 1995; Fulbright Scholar 1964–65, Fulbright 40th Anniversary Distinguished American Scholar, Italy 1987, Distinguished Research Master and Univ. Gold Medal, Louisiana State Univ. 1993, Medal and Rector's Certificate 1994. *Address:* c/o Eric Voegelin Institute for American Renaissance Studies, Louisiana State University, 240 Stubbs Hall, Baton Rouge, LA 70803 (office); 2843 Valcour Aime Avenue, Baton Rouge, LA 70820, USA (home). *E-mail:* esandoz@lsu.edu.

SANDS, Martin (see Burke, John Frederick)

SANDS, Sarah; British editor and writer; *Consulting Editor, The Daily Mail*; b. (Sarah Harvey), 3 May 1961, Cambridge; m. 1st Julian Sands; one s.; m. 2nd Kim Fletcher; two c. *Education:* Goldsmiths Coll., London. *Career:* worked at Kent and Sussex Courier 1983–86; worked at Evening Standard, London, as diary reporter, Ed. of the Londoner's Diary, later Features Ed., then Assoc. Ed. 1986–95; Deputy Ed. The Daily Telegraph 1996–2005, responsible for The Daily Telegraph Saturday edn, Ed. The Sunday Telegraph 2005–06; Consulting Ed. The Daily Mail 2006–. *Publications:* novels: Playing the Game 2003, Hothouse 2005, Chiswick Wives 2006. *Address:* c/o The Daily Mail, Northcliffe House, 2 Derry Street, London, W8 5TT, England.

SANDY, Stephen, BA, MA, PhD; American poet, writer, translator and fmr college teacher; b. 2 Aug. 1934, Minneapolis, MN; m. Virginia Scoville 1969; one s. one d. *Education:* Yale Univ., Harvard Univ. *Career:* Instructor in English 1963–67, Visiting Prof. 1986, 1987, 1988, Harvard Univ.; Visiting Prof. of English, Tokyo Univ. of Foreign Studies 1967–68, Brown Univ. 1968–69; Visiting Prof. of American Literature, Univ. of Tokyo 1967–68; Lecturer in English, Univ. of Rhode Island 1969; mem. Literature Faculty, Bennington Coll. 1969–2001; NEA poet-in-residence, Y Poetry Center, Philadelphia 1985; McGee Prof. of Writing, Davidson Coll. 1994; Sr Fellow in Literature, Fine Arts Work Center, Provincetown 1998; mem. of jury Wallace Stevens Award Jury; various poetry workshops and numerous poetry readings; mem. Acad. of American Poets, Dept of Educ. Javits Fellows Programme, Arts Panel Wesleyan Writers Conf., Marymount Manhattan Writers Conf. *Publications:* Stresses in the Peaceable Kingdom 1967, Roofs 1971, End of the Picaro 1974, The Ravelling of the Novel: Studies in Romantic Fiction from Walpole to Scott 1980, Flight of Steps 1982, Riding to Greylock 1983, To a Mantis 1987, Man in the Open Air 1988, The Epoch 1990, Thanksgiving Over the Water 1992, Vale of Academe: A Prose Poem for Bernard Malamud 1996, Marrow Spoon 1997, The Thread: New and Selected Poems 1998, Black Box 1999, Surface Impressions 2002, Weathers Permitting 2005; contrib. to numerous anthologies, including The Poetry Anthology 1912–2002, New Yorker Book of Poems, New York Times Book of Verse, Poets for Life, Poets Respond to AIDS, Best American Poetry 1995, 1998, Norton Treasury World Poetry; contrib. to numerous journals, including Agenda, Agni, Atlantic Monthly, APR, Boulevard, Grand St, Green Mountains Review, Harpers, The Nation, New Republic, New Yorker, New York Times, Poetry, Poetry London, Salmagundi, Times Literary Supplement, Hudson, Paris, Partisan, Southwest, Virginia Quarterly, Western Humanities, Yale Reviews. *Honours:* Ingram Merrill Foundation Fellowship 1985, Vermont Coll. on the Arts Fellowship 1988, NEA Creative Writing Fellowship 1988, Chubb Life America Fellow, MacDowell Colony 1993, Reader's Digest Residency for Distinguished Writers 1997, Howard Moss Residency for Poetry, Yaddo 1998, Rockefeller Foundation Residency, Bellagio Study and Conference Center 2001, Fulbright Lectureship. *Address:* PO Box 276, Shaftsbury, VT 05262, USA. *E-mail:* ssandy@saver.net (home). *Website:* www.StephenSandy.com.

SANDYS, Elspeth Somerville, ONZ, MA, LTCL, FTCL; New Zealand/British writer and dramatist; b. (Elspeth Sandilands Somerville), 18 March 1940, Timaru, New Zealand; one s. one d. *Education:* Univ. of Auckland. *Career:* Frank Sargeson Fellow, Auckland 1992; Burns Fellow, Otago Univ. 1995; Writer-in-Residence, Waikato Univ. 1998, Tasmanian Writer-in-Residence 2004; mem. Writers Guild, Soc. of Authors. *Play:* Century's Turn (chosen for London Int. Play Festival) 2005. *Publications:* Catch a Falling Star 1978, The Broken Tree 1981, Love and War 1982, Finding Out 1991, Best Friends (short stories) 1993, River Lines 1995, Riding to Jerusalem 1996, Enemy Territory 1997, A Passing Guest (novel) 2002, Masquerade (stage play) 2005, Standing in Line (short stories) (Elena Garro Prize, PEN Int. Short Story Competion, Mexico 2003) 2006; also radio plays and contribs to magazines. *Honours:* awarded Sarah Hosking Writer's Residency in Stratford-upon-Avon 2005–06. *Literary Agent:* MBA Literary Agents Ltd, 62 Grafton Way, London, W1P 5LD, England. *E-mail:* elsp@xtra.co.nz.

SANER, Reginald (Reg) Anthony, BA, MA, PhD; American poet, writer and academic; b. 30 Dec. 1931, Jacksonville, Ill.; m. Anne Costigan 1958; two s. *Education:* St Norbert Coll., Wis., Univ. of Illinois at Urbana, Università per Stranieri, Perugia, Università di Firenze, Florence. *Career:* Asst Instructor, Univ. of Illinois at Urbana 1956–60, Instructor in English 1961–62; Asst Prof., Univ. of Colorado at Boulder 1962–67, Assoc. Prof. 1967–72, Prof. of English 1972–; mem. Dante Soc., PEN, Renaissance Soc., Shakespeare Asscn. *Publications:* poetry: Climbing into the Roots 1976, So This is the Map 1981, Essay on Air 1984, Red Letters 1989; non-fiction: The Four-Cornered Falcon: Essays on the Interior West and the Natural Scene 1993, Reaching Keet Seel: Ruin's Echo and the Anasazi 1998, The Dawn Collector: On My Way to the Natural World 2005; contribs: poems and essays in numerous anthologies and other publs. *Honours:* Fulbright Scholar to Florence, Italy 1960–61, Borestone Mountain Poetry Awards 1971, 1973, Walt Whitman Award 1975, Nat. Endowment for the Arts Creative Writing Fellowship 1976, Pushcart Prize II 1977–78, Colorado Gov.'s Award for Excellence in the Arts 1983, Quarterly Review of Literature Award 1989, Rockefeller Foundation Resident Scholar, Bellagio, Italy 1990, Hazel Barnes Award, Univ. of Colorado 1993, Wallace Stegner Award, Centre of the American West 1997. *Address:* 1925 Vassar, Boulder, CO 80303, USA.

SANGUINETI, Edoardo; Italian writer; b. 9 Dec. 1930, Genoa; s. of Giovanni Sanguineti and Giuseppina Cocchi; m. Luciana Garabello 1954; three s. one d. *Education:* Univ. degli Studi, Turin. *Career:* Prof. of Italian Literature, Univ. of Salerno 1968–74, Genoa 1974–2000; Town Councillor of Genoa 1976–81; mem. Chamber of Deputies 1979–83. *Publications:* Laborintus 1956, Opus metricum 1960, Interpretazione di Malebolge 1961, Tre studi danteschi 1961, Tra liberty e crepuscolarismo 1961, Alberto Moravia 1962, K. e altre cose 1962, Passaggio 1963, Capriccio italiano 1963, Triperuno 1964, Ideologia e linguaggio 1965, Il realismo di Dante 1966, Guido Gozzano 1966, Il Giuoco dell' Oca 1967, Le Baccanti di Euripide (trans.) 1968, Fedra di Seneca (trans.) 1969, T.A.T. 1969, Teatro 1969, Poesia Italiana del Novecento 1969, Il Giuoco del Satyricon 1970, Orlando Furioso (with L. Ronconi) 1970, Renga (with O. Paz, J. Roubaud, C. Tomlinson) 1971, Storie Naturali 1971, Wirrwarr 1972, Catamerone 1974, Le Troiane di Euripide (trans.) 1974, Giornalino 1976, Postkarten 1978, Le Coefore di Eschilo (trans.) 1978, Giornalino secondo 1979, Stracciafoglio 1980, Edipo tiranno di Sofocle (trans.) 1980, Scartabello 1981, Segnalibro 1982, Alfabeto apocalittico 1984, Scribilli 1985, Faust, un travestimento 1985, Novissimum Testamentum 1986, Smorfie 1986, La missione del critico 1987, Bisbidis 1987, Ghirigori 1988, Commedia dell'Inferno 1989, Lettura del Decameron 1989, Senzatitolo 1992, I Sette contro Tebe di Eschilo (trans.) 1992, Dante reazionario 1992, Gazzettini 1993, Per musica 1993, Satyricon di Petronio (trans.) 1993, Opere e introduzione critica 1993, Malebolge (with E. Baj) 1995, Libretto 1995, Per una critica dell'avanguardia poetica (with J. Burgos) 1995, Tracce (with M. Lucchesi) 1995, Minitarjetas 1996, Orlando Furioso, un travestimento ariostesco 1996, Corollario 1997, Il mio amore è come una febbre (with S. Liberovici) 1998, Cose 1999, Don Giovanni di Molière (trans.) 2000, Il chierico organico 2000, Verdi in Technicolor 2001, La Festa delle donne di Aristofane (trans.) 2001, Sei personaggi.com 2001, L'amore delle tre melarance 2001, Atlante del Novecento italiano 2001, L'orologio astronomico 2002, Il gatto lupesco 2002, Carol Rama 2002, Il cerchio di gesso del Caucaso di Brecht (trans.) 2003, Omaggio a Goethe 2003, Omaggio a Shakespeare 2004, Mikrokosmos 2004, Genova per me 2005, L'illusione comica di Corneille (trans.) 2005. *Honours:* Cavaliere di Gran Croce al merito della Repubblica Italiana 1996, Satrape Transcendant Grand Maître O.G.G. du Coll. de Pataphysique 2001. *Address:* Via Pergolesi 20, 16159 Genoa, Italy (home). *Telephone:* (10) 7452050 (home). *Fax:* (10) 7452050 (home).

SANSOM, Ann; British poet and tutor; b. 1951, Doncaster, S Yorkshire; m. Peter Sansom. *Education:* Univ. of Cambridge. *Career:* playwright and writing tutor, Doncaster Women's Centre 1989–; playwright, Yorkshire Women Theatre; residencies for Arvon Foundation and Aldeburgh Poetry Festival. *Publications:* Romance 1994, In Praise of Men and Other People 2003. *Honours:* Arts Council Writer's Award. *Address:* c/o Bloodaxe Books Ltd, Highgreen, Tarset, Northumberland NE48 1RP, England. *Website:* www.bloodaxebooks.com.

SANTOS, Helen (see Griffiths, Helen)

SANTOS, Sherod, BA, MA, MFA, PhD; American academic, poet and writer; *Curators' Distinguished Professor of English, University of Missouri*; b. 9 Sept. 1948, Greenville, SC; m. Lynne Marie McMahon 1976; two s. *Education:* San Diego State Univ., Univ. of California at Irvine, Univ. of Utah. *Career:* Asst

Prof., California State Univ., San Bernardino 1982–83; Poetry Ed., Missouri Review 1983–90; Asst Prof. 1983–86, Assoc. Prof. 1986–92, Curators' Distinguished Prof. of English 2001–, Univ. of Missouri; Robert Frost Poet and Poet-in-Residence, Robert Frost House, Franconia, NH 1984; external examiner and poet-in-residence, Poets' House, Islandmagee, Northern Ireland, summers 1991–98; various poetry readings, lectures and seminars; Nat. Endowment for the Arts Literature Panel mem. 1995; mem. Acad. of American Poets, Associated Writing Programs, PEN American Center, Poetry Soc. of America, Poets and Writers, Robinson Jeffers Soc. *Publications:* Begin, Distance 1981, Accidental Weather 1982, The New Days 1986, The Southern Reaches 1989, The Unsheltering Ground 1990, The City of Women 1993, The Pilot Star Elegies 1998, The Perishing 2003; contrib. to anthologies, journals and magazines. *Honours:* Discovery/The Nation Award 1978, Pushcart Prizes in Poetry 1980, and in the Essay 1994, Poetry magazine Oscar Blumenthal Prize 1981, Ingram Merrill Foundation grant 1982, Delmore Schwartz Memorial Award 1983, Guggenheim Fellowship 1984–85, Nat. Endowment for the Arts grant 1987, Yaddo Center for the Arts Fellowship 1987, Univ. of Missouri Chancellor's Award 1993, British Arts Council Int. Travel Grant to Northern Ireland 1995, American Acad. of Arts and Letters Award in Literature 1999, Theodore Roethke Memorial Prize in Poetry 2002. *Address:* 1238 Sunset Drive, Columbia, MO 65203, USA.

SAPIA, Yvonne, AA, BA, MA, PhD; American academic, poet and writer; b. 10 April 1946, New York, NY. *Education:* Miami-Dade Community College, Florida Atlantic University, University of Florida, Florida State University. *Career:* reporter and Ed., The Village Post newspaper, Miami, 1971–73; Editorial Asst, University of Florida, 1974–76; Resident Poet and Prof. of English, Lake City Community College, FL 1976–. *Publications:* The Fertile Crescent (poems), 1983; Valentino's Hair (poems), 1987; Valentino's Hair (novel), 1991. Contributions: anthologies, reviews, and journals. *Honours:* First Place, Anhinga Press Poetry Chapbook Award, 1983; Third Place, Eve of St Agnes Poetry Competition, 1983; National Endowment for the Arts Fellowship, 1986–87; First Place, Morse Poetry Prize, 1987; Second Prize, Cincinnati Poetry Review Poetry Competition, 1989; Third Place, Apalaches Quarterly Long Poem Contest, 1989; First Place, Nilon Award for Excellence in Minority Fiction, 1991.

SAPOLSKY, Robert M., AB, PhD; American biologist, neuroscientist and writer; *John A. and Cynthia Fry Gunn Professor of Biological Sciences and Professor of Neurology and Neurological Sciences, Stanford University;* b. 1957. *Education:* Harvard Univ., Rockefeller Univ. *Career:* mem. editorial bd of journals, including Journal of Neuroscience, Psychoneuroendocrinology, Stress; Contributing Ed., The Sciences; John A. and Cynthia Fry Gunn Prof. of Biological Sciences and Prof. of Neurology and Neurological Sciences, Stanford Univ.; also Research Assoc. Inst. of Primate Research, Nat. Museum of Kenya. *Publications:* Stress, the Aging Brain and the Mechanisms of Neuron Death 1992, Why Zebras Don't Get Ulcers: An Updated Guide to Stress, Stress-Related Diseases and Coping 1994, The Trouble with Testosterone, and other essays on the biology of the human predicament 1997, A Primate's Memoir (Bay Area Book Reviewers' Award in Non-fiction 2001) 2001, Monkeyluv and Other Essays on Our Lives as Animals 2005; contrib. articles to numerous journals, including American Journal of Physical Anthropology, American Journal of Primatology, Annals of Neurology, Annals of the New York Academy of Sciences, Biological Psychiatry, Brain Research, Endocrinology, Hippocampus, Journal of Cerebral Blood Flow and Metabolism, Journal of Neurochemistry, Journal of Neurophysiology, Journal of Neuroscience, Journal of Neurovirology, Methods in Molecular Medicine, Neuroendocrinology, Neurology, Neurotoxicology, Proceedings of the National Academies of Science, Science, Scientific American, Stress, Stroke, Trends in Neuroscience. *Honours:* Nat. Science Foundation Presidential Young Investigator Award, Soc. for Neuroscience Young Investigator of the Year Award, Biological Psychiatry Soc. Young Investigator of the Year Award, Int. Soc. for Psychoneuro-Endocrinology Young Investigator of the Year Award, Alfred P. Sloan Fellowship, Klingenstein Fellowship in Neuroscience, MacArthur Fellow, Stanford Univ. Bing Award for Teaching Excellence. *Literary Agent:* The Steven Barclay Agency, 12 Western Avenue, Petaluma, CA 94952, USA. *Telephone:* (707) 773-0654. *Fax:* (707) 778-1868. *Website:* www.barclayagency .com.

SARAH, Robyn, BA, DipMus, MA; American poet and writer; b. 6 Oct. 1949, New York, NY. *Education:* McGill Univ., Conservatoire de Musique du Québec. *Publications:* poetry: Shadowplay 1978, The Space Between Sleep and Waking 1981, Three Sestinas 1984, Anyone Skating on that Middle Ground 1984, Becoming Light 1987, The Touchstone: Poems New and Selected 1992, Questions About the Stars 1998, A Day's Grace 2003; fiction: A Nice Gazebo (short stories) 1992, Promise of Shelter (short stories) 1997; non-fiction: Little Eurekas: A Decade's Thoughts on Poetry (literary criticism) 2007. *Address:* c/o Vehicule Press, PO Box 125, place du Parc Station, Montréal, QC H2W 2M9, Canada (office).

SARAMAGO, José; Portuguese writer and poet; b. 16 Nov. 1922, Azinhaga; m. Pilar del Rio; one c. *Education:* principally self-educated. *Publications include:* novels: Terra do pecado 1947, Manual de pintura e caligrafia (trans. as Manual of Painting and Calligraphy) 1976, Levantado do chão 1980, Memorial do convento (trans. as Baltasar and Blimunda) 1982, O ano da morte de Ricardo Reis (trans. as The Year of the Death of Ricardo Reis) 1984, A jangada de pedra (trans. as The Stone Raft) 1986, História do cerco de Lisboa 1989, O Evangelho Segundo Jesus Cristo (trans. as The Gospel According to Jesus Christ) 1991, Ensaio sobre a cegueira (trans. as Blindness) 1995, Todos os nomes (trans. as All the Names) 1999, O Homeru Duplicado (trans. as The Double) 2000, La caverna 2001, Ensaio sobre a Lucidez 2004, As Intermitências da Morte 2005, As Pequenas Memórias 2006, Seeing 2006; short stories: Objecto quase trans. as Quasi Object) 1978, Poética dos cinco sentidos – O ouvido 1979, Telling Tales (contrib. to charity anthology) 2004; poetry: Os poemas possíveis 1966, Provavelmente alegria 1970, O ano de 1993 1975; plays: A noite 1979, Que farei com este livro? 1980, A segunda vida de Francisco de Assisi 1987, In Nomine Dei 1993, Don Giovanni ou O dissoluto absolvido 2005; opera librettos: Blimunda 1990, Divara 1993, Il dissoluto assolto 2005; other writing: Deste mundo e do outro 1971, A bagagem do viajante 1973, O embargo 1973, Os opiniões que o DL teve 1974, Os apontamentos 1976, Viagem a Portugal 1981, Cadernos de Lanzarote 1994–96, O poeta perguntador (ed.) 1979. *Honours:* Prémio da Críticos Portugueses 1979, Prémio Cidade de Lisboa 1980, Prémios PEN Clube Portugues 1982, 1984, Prémio Literario Municipio de Lisboa 1982, Prémio da Critica, Associacão Portuguesa de Criticos, Prémio Don Dinis 1986, Grinzane Cavour Prize 1987, Mondello Prize 1992, Grande Prémio de Romance e Novela da Associacão Portuguesa de Escritores 1992, Brancatti Literary Prize 1992, Flaiano Prize 1992, Prémio Vida Literária da Associacão Portuguesa de Escritores 1993, Prémio Consagracão Soc. Portuguesa de Autores 1995, Luís de Camões Prize 1995, Nobel Prize for Literature 1998. *Address:* Los Topes 3, 35572 Tias, Lanzarote, Canary Islands, Spain; Ray-Güde Mertin, 1 Friedrichstrasse, 61348 Bad Hamburg 1, Germany.

SARDAR, Ziauddin, BSc, MSc, PhD; Pakistani writer; *Editor, Futures journal;* b. 31 Oct. 1951, Dipalpur; m.; three c. *Education:* City Univ., London, UK. *Career:* moved to London as a child; fmr information scientist, Hajj Research Centre of King Abdul Aziz Univ., Jeddah, Saudi Arabia 1975–80; Consulting Ed., Inquiry magazine; reporter, London Weekend Television; established Centre for Future Studies, East-West Univ., Chicago early 1990s; Visiting Prof. of Science and Tech. Policy, Univ. of Middlesex 1994–98; Visiting Prof. of Postcolonial Studies, Dept of Cultural Policy and Man., City Univ., London; freelance programmer and writer 1985–; Ed. monthly journal of policy, planning and futures studies, Futures 1999–; Co-Ed. critical journal, Third Text; Commr Comm. for Equality and Human Rights, 2006–. *Radio:* featured on Today, Broadcast House, PM, Nightline, Belief, Five Live. *Television:* Encounters with Islam (series of four programmes, BBC) 1985, Islamic Conversations (series of six interviews, Channel 4) 1994, Battle for Islam (90-minute documentary, BBC 2) 2005; numerous appearances on Hard Talk, Last Word and other shows. *Publications:* Science, Technology and Development in the Muslim World 1977, Islam: Outline of a Classification Scheme 1979, The Future of Muslim Civilisation 1979, The Touch of Midas: Science, Values and Environment in Islam and the West 1982, Islamic Futures: The Shape of Ideas to Come 1986, The Revenge of Athena: Science, Exploitation and the Third World 1988, Information and the Muslim World 1988, Distorted Imagination: Lessons from the Rushdie Affair (with Merryl Wyn Davies) 1990, Introducing Islam 1992, Barbaric Others: A Manifesto on Western Racism (with Ashis Nandy, Claude Alvarez and Merryl Wyn Davies) 1993, Postmodernism and the Other: New Imperialism of Western Culture 1997, Orientalism 1999, Rescuing All Our Futures: The Future of Futures Studies 1999, Thomas Kuhn and the Science Wars 2000, The A to Z of Postmodern Life: Essays on Global Culture in the Noughties 2002, Aliens R Us: The Other in Science Fiction Cinema (co-ed. with Sean Cubitt) 2002, Why Do People Hate America? (with Merryl Wyn Davies) 2003, Islam, Postmodernism and Other Futures: A Ziauddin Sardar Reader 2004, American Dream, Global Nightmare (with Merryl Wyn Davies) 2004, Desperately Seeking Paradise: Journeys of a Sceptical Muslim 2004, How Do You Know: Reading Ziauddin Sardar on Islam, Science and Cultural Relations 2006, What Do Muslims Believe? 2006; contrib. to New Statesman, The Independent, The Guardian, The Observer, The Times, Nature, New Scientist. *Address:* c/o New Statesman, Third Floor, 52 Grosvenor Gardens, London, SW1W 0AU, England.

SARI, Mohamed; Algerian writer and academic; b. 1958, Ménacer. *Career:* Prof. of Arabic Literature, Univ. of Algiers. *Publications:* novels: As-Sa'ir 1986, 'Ala Djibel ad-Dahra (The Mountains of Dara) 1988, Le Labyrinthe 2001. *Address:* c/o Algerie Litterature/Action, Éditions Marsa, 103 boulevard MacDonald, Paris 75019, France.

SARIF, Shamim; South African/Indian novelist and journalist; b. 24 Sept. 1969, London. *Education:* Univ. of London, Univ. of Boston, USA. *Screenplays include:* The Reader, Food of Love 2001. *Publications:* novels: The World Unseen 2001, Despite the Falling Snow 2004; contrib. to You magazine, American Way. *Honours:* Pendleton May First Novel Award. *Address:* c/o Hodder Headline PLC, 338 Euston Road, London, NW1 3BH, England. *Website:* www.shamimsarif.com.

SARKAR, Anil Kumar, MA, PhD, DLitt; Indian academic and writer; b. 1 Aug. 1912, Ranchi, India; m. Aruna Sarkar 1941 (deceased); one s. three d. *Education:* Patna Univ. *Career:* Prof., Rajendra College, 1940–44; Senior Lecturer, University of Ceylon, Colombo and Perdeniya, 1944–64; Visiting Prof., University of New Mexico, Albuquerque, 1964–65; Full Prof. of Philosophy and West-East Philosophy, 1965–82, California State University, Hayward, USA; Research Dir, Prof. of Asian Studies, 1968–80, Prof. Emeritus, 1980–, California Institute of Integral Studies, San Francisco. *Publications:* An Outline of Whitehead's Philosophy, 1940; Changing Phases of Buddhist Thought, 1968; Whitehead's Four Principles From West-East Perspectives, 1974; Dynamic Facets of Indian Thought, Vol. 1, 1980, Vols 2–4, 1987–88;

Experience in Change and Prospect: Pathways from War to Peace, 1989; Sri Aurobindo's Vision of the Super Mind – Its Indian and Non-Indian Interpreters, 1989; Buddhism and Whitehead's Process Philosophy, 1990; Zero: Its Role and Prospects in Indian Thought and its Impact on Post-Einsteinian Astrophysics, 1992; The Mysteries of Vajrayana Buddhism: From Atisha to Dalai Lama, 1993; Triadic Avenues of India's Cultural Prospects: Philosophy, Physics and Politics, 1995; Shaping of Euro-Indian Philosophy, 1995. Contributions: Indian, US and other journals. *Address:* B/B/12/15-7 Kalyani, Df Nadia, West Bengal, India.

SARKÖZY DE NAGY BOCSA, Nicolas Paul Stéphane; French politician, barrister, civil servant and head of state; *President;* b. 28 Jan. 1955, Paris; s. of Paul Sarközy de Nagy Bocsa and Andrée Mallah; m. 2nd Cecilia Ciganer-Albeniz 1996; one s. (and two s. by previous m.). *Education:* Inst. of Political Studies, Paris, Paris Univ. *Career:* barrister, Paris 1981–87; Assoc., Leibovici Claude Sarközy 1987; mem. RPR Cen. Cttee 1977–, Nat. Del. 1978–79, Nat. Sec. 1988–90, Asst Sec.-Gen. 1990–93; Town Councillor, Neuilly-sur-Seine 1977–83, Mayor 1983–; Pres. Nat. Cttee Jacques Chirac's presidential campaign 1981; Regional Councillor, Ile-de-France 1983–88; RPR Deputy to Nat. Ass. from Hauts-de-Seine 1988–93, 1993–95, 1997–2007; Chief Spokesman of RPR 1997–2007; Minister of the Budget 1993–94, of Communications 1994–95, of the Interior and Security 2002–04, of the Economy, Finance and Industry 2004–05, of the Interior, Internal Security and Local Freedoms 2005–07 (resgnd); Pres. of France 2007–; mem. RPR Political Office 1995, Sec.-Gen. RPR 1998–99, Interim Pres. April–Oct. 1999, Pres. RPR Regional Cttee of Hauts-de-Seine 2000–; Leader RPR-DL List, European Elections 1999; Pres. Union pour un Mouvement Populaire (UMP) 2004–07. *Publications:* Georges Mandel, moine de la politique 1994, Au bout de la passion, l'équilibre (co-author) 1995, Libre 2001, Témoignage 2006. *Honours:* Chevalier, Légion d'honneur. *Address:* Office of the President, Palais de l'Elysée, 55–57 rue du Faubourg Saint Honoré, 75008 Paris, France (office). *Telephone:* 1-42-92-81-00 (office). *Fax:* 1-47-42-24-65 (office). *Website:* www.elysee.fr (office); www .sarkozy.fr.

SARNA, Jonathan Daniel, BHL, BA, MA, MPhil, PhD; American academic and writer; *Joseph H. and Belle R. Braun Professor of American Jewish History, Brandeis University;* b. 10 Jan. 1955, Philadelphia, PA; m. Ruth Langer 1986, one s. one d. *Education:* Hebrew College, Boston, Brandeis University, Yale University. *Career:* Visiting Lecturer, 1979–80, Asst Prof. to Assoc. Prof. of American Jewish History, 1980–90, Hebrew Union College-Jewish Institute of Religion; Dir, American Jewish Experience Curriculum Project, 1982–, Center for the Study of the American Jewish Experience, 1986–90, Boston Jewish History Project, 1992-95; Visiting Asst Prof., University of Cincinnati, 1983–84; Visiting Assoc. Prof., Hebrew University, Jerusalem, 1986–87; Joseph H. and Belle R. Braun Prof. of American Jewish History, Brandeis University 1990–; mem. American Acad. of Religion; American Historical Asscn; American Jewish Historical Society; Asscn for Jewish Studies; Organization of American Historians. *Publications:* Jews in New Haven (ed.), 1978; Mordecai Manuel Noah: Jacksonian Politician and American Jewish Communal Leader, 1979; Jacksonian Jew: The Two Worlds of Mordecai Noah, 1981; Jews and the Founding of the Republic (co-ed.), 1985; The American Jewish Experience: A Reader (ed.), 1986; American Synagogue History: A Bibliography and State-of-the-Field Survey (with Alexandra S. Korros), 1988; JPS: The Americanization of Jewish Culture: A History of the Jewish Publication Society 1888–1988, 1989; The Jews of Cincinnati (with Nancy H. Klein), 1989; A Double Bond: The Constitutional Documents of American Jewry (ed. with Daniel J. Elazar and Rela Geffen Monson), 1992; Ethnic Diversity and Civic Identity: Patterns of Conflict and Cohesion in Cincinnati Since 1820 (with Henry D. Shapiro), 1992; Yuhude Artsot Ha-Berit (with Lloyd Gartner), 1992; Observing America's Jews (ed. with Marshall Sklare), 1993; The Jews of Boston (with Ellen Smith), 1995; Abba Hillel Silver and American Zionism (with Mark A. Raider and Ronald W. Zweig), 1997; Minority Faiths and the American Protestant Mainstream, 1997; Religion and State in the American Jewish Experience (with David G. Dalin), 1997; Women and American Judaism: Historical Perspectives (with Pamela S. Nadel), 2001, American Judaism – A History 2004; Contributions: scholarly books, professional journals and general periodicals. *Honours:* Outstanding Academic Book, Choice, 1998; Benjamin J. Shevach Memorial Prize for Distinguished Leadership in Jewish Education, 2000, Everett Family Foundation Book of the Year Award, Jewsih Book Council 2004, named on Foward List of 50 Most Influential American Jews 2004. *Address:* Department of Near Eastern and Judaic Studies, Brandeis University, Waltham, MA 02454, USA (office). *Telephone:* (781) 736-2977 (office). *Fax:* (781) 736-2070 (office). *E-mail:* sarna@brandeis.edu.

SAROYAN, Aram; American writer, poet and dramatist; b. 25 Sept. 1943, New York, NY; m. Gailyn McClanahan 1968; one s. two d. *Education:* Univ. of Chicago, New York Univ., Columbia Univ. *Play:* At the Beach House (premiere, Los Angeles) 2005. *Publications:* Aram Saroyan 1968, Pages 1969, Words and Photographs 1970, The Street: An Autobiographical Novel 1974, Genesis Angels: The Saga of Lew Welch and the Beat Generation 1979, Last Rites: The Death of William Saroyan 1982, William Saroyan 1983, Trio: Portrait of an Intimate Friendship 1985, The Romantic 1988, Friends in the World: The Education of a Writer 1992, Rancho Mirage: An American Tragedy of Manners, Madness and Murder 1993, Day and Night: Bolinas Poems 1972–81 1998, Starting Out in the Sixties (essays) 2001, Artists in Trouble: New Stories 2001, Day by Day 2002, Complete Minimal Poems 2007; contrib.

to New York Times Book Review, Los Angeles Times Book Review, The Nation, Village Voice, Mother Jones, Paris Review, Shambhala Sun magazine. *Honours:* NEA Poetry Awards 1967, 1968. *Address:* 5482 Village Green, Los Angeles, CA 90016, USA. *Website:* www.aramsaroyan.com.

SARTIN, Pierrette Anne-Marie, LPh; French writer and former administrator; b. 10 Nov. 1911, Guéret, Creuse; d. of Elie and Marcelle (née Refeuille) Sartin; two d. *Education:* Univs of Clermont-Ferrand and Lyon. *Career:* writer 1939–; civil servant 1946–75; Asst to Sec. of State for Civil Aviation 1953; Technical Adviser Comm. on Productivity and Planning 1954–63; Special Adviser on Women and Young People at Work, OECD and BIT 1965–71; Visiting Prof. Univ. of Laval, PQ, Canada 1968, 1980; Vice-Pres. Soc. des gens de lettres 1968; mem. PEN-Club, Asscn Int. des Critiques Littéraires. *Publications include:* novels: Chroniques du Temps Passé (trilogy, prizes from Société des gens de lettres): Souvenirs d'une jeune fille mal rangée 1982, Un enfer bien convenable 1983, L'or de Mathieu Gaumard 1987, Belles-mères 1991; 23 vols of poems 1939–95 (several literary prizes, including Grand Prix, Maison de Poésie for Ce Destin Accepté 1973); Essays: La promotion des femmes (prize from Académie française) 1964, La femme libérée? 1968, Aujourd'hui la femme 1974; other: Kama Kamanda: poète d'exil 1994; writer of numerous informative works. *Honours:* Chevalier de la Légion d'honneur; Hon. LittD (Laval) 1980. *Address:* 10 rue Saint-Lazare, 75009 Paris; 12 Le Prieuré, 77320 La Ferté-Gaucher, France. *Telephone:* (1) 48-74-87-79 (Paris); (1) 64-04-00-81 (La Ferté-Gaucher).

SASO, Akira; Japanese writer and illustrator; b. 1961, Hyogo Pref. *Education:* Ikeda High School, Osaka Kyoiku Univ. and Waseda Univ. *Career:* writer and illustrator of manga comics. *Publications:* Ai ni Isogasii (Busy Love), Oretachi ni Asu ha Naissu (There is No Tomorrow for Us), Shindo (Child Prodigy), Fuji-san. *Honours:* Japan Media Arts Festival Excellence Prize 1998, Tezuka Osamu Cultural Prize 1999. *Address:* c/o Shogakukan Incorporated, 2-3-1, Hitotsubashi, 2-Chome Chiyoda-ku, Tokyo 101-8001, Japan. *Website:* www.shogakukan.co.jp/english/.

SATO, Ken'ichi; Japanese novelist; b. 12 March 1968, Tsuruoka, Yamagata Pref. *Education:* Tohoku Univ. *Publications:* Jaga ni natta otoko (The Man Who Turned into a Jaguar) (Shosetsu Subaru Prize for New Writers) 1993, Oki no kekkon (The Queen's Marriage) (Naoki Prize) 1999.

SATRAPI, Marjane, MA; Iranian writer and illustrator; b. (Marjan Ebrahimi-Ripa), 22 Sept. 1969, Rasht. *Education:* Visual Communication School of Fine Arts, Tehran, École des Arts Decoratifs de Strasbourg, France. *Publications:* Persepolis: The Story of a Childhood (four vols) 1999–2002, Persepolis 2: The Story of a Return (adapted as screenplay 2007, Jury Prize, Cannes Film Festival 2007) 2005, Embroideries 2005; several children's books; contrib. illustrations to French magazines and periodicals. *Address:* c/o Jonathan Cape, Random House UK Ltd, 20 Vauxhall Bridge Road, London, SW1V 2SA, England (office); 13 rue de Thorigny, 75003 Paris, France (home). *Telephone:* (20) 7840-8576 (office); 6 74 99 04 52 (home). *Fax:* 1 42 72 65 15 (home). *E-mail:* marjanesatrapi@yahoo.fr (home).

SATTERTHWAIT, Walter; American writer; b. 23 March 1946, Philadelphia, Pennsylvania; one d. *Education:* Reed College. *Career:* mem. MWA, Private Eye Writers of America. *Publications:* Cocaine Blues, 1980; The Aegean Affair, 1981; Wall of Glass, 1987; Miss Lizzie, 1989; At Ease With the Dead, 1990; Wilde West, 1991; A Flower In the Desert, 1992; The Hanged Man, 1993, UK edn as The Death Card, 1994; Escapade, 1995; Accustomed to the Dark, 1996; Masquerade, 1998. Contributions: Alfred Hitchcock's Mystery Magazine; Santa Fe Reporter. *Honours:* Prix du Roman d'Aventures, France 1996. *E-mail:* wsatterthwait@yahoo.com. *Website:* www.satterthwait.com.

SAUNDERS, Ann Loreille, (Ann Cox-Johnson), MBE, BA, PhD, FSA; British historian; b. 23 May 1930, London, England; m. Bruce Kemp Saunders 1960; one s. one d. (deceased). *Education:* Queen's Coll., London (Plumptre Scholar), Univ. Coll., London, Univ. of Leicester. *Career:* Deputy Librarian, Lambeth Palace 1952–55; Archivist, Marylebone Public Library, London 1956–63; Fellow, Univ. Coll. London 1992; mem. Costume Soc. (Hon. Ed. 1967–), London Topographical Soc. (Hon. Ed. 1975–). *Publications:* London, North of the Thames 1972, London, City and Westminster 1975, Art and Architecture of London 1984, St Martin-in-the-Fields 1989, The Royal Exchange 1991, The Royal Exchange (ed. and co-author) 1997, St Paul's: The History of the Cathedral 2001, The History of the Merchant Taylor's Company (with Matthew Davies) 2004; contrib. to magazines. *Honours:* Prize for Best Specialist Guide Book of the Year, British Tourist Bd 1984. *Address:* 3 Meadway Gate, London, NW11 7LA, England (home). *Telephone:* (20) 8455-2171 (home).

SAUNDERS, George, BSc, MA; American writer; *Associate Professor, Syracuse University;* b. 2 Dec. 1958, Amarillo, TX. *Education:* Colorado School of Mines, Syracuse Univ. *Career:* Visiting Prof. of Creative Writing, Syracuse Univ. 1996–97, Asst Prof. 1997–2001, Assoc. Prof. 2001–. *Publications:* CivilWarLand in Bad Decline (stories) 1996, Pastoralia: Stories 2000, The Very Persistent Gappers of Frip (juvenile) 2000, The Brief and Frightening World of Phil 2005, In Persuasion Nation 2006, The Brief and Frightening Reign of Phil 2006; contrib. to books and periodicals. *Honours:* Nat. Magazine Awards 1994, 1996, 1999, 2003, New York Times Notable Book of the Year Citation 1996, 2000, Lannen Fellowship 2001–02. *Literary Agent:* International Creative Management, 40 W 57th Street, New York, NY 10019, USA.

SAUPER, Hubert, BA; Austrian film director, producer and writer; b. Kitzbühel, Tyrol. *Education:* Univ. of Performing Arts, Vienna, Univ. of Paris VIII. *Films as writer/director:* On the Road with Emil (documentary) (Int. Festival, Würzburg Best Short Film 1994, Prix Max Ophülz for Best Documentary Nexon, France 1995) 1993, So I Sleepwalk in Broad Daylight (also prod.) (Premio da casa da Figueira da Foz, Portugal 1995, Best First Film, Best Film School Production) 1994, Lomographer's Moscow 1995, Kisangani Diary (documentary, also prod.) (seven int. awards) 1998, Alone With Our Stories (documentary) 2000, Darwin's Nightmare (documentary, also prod.) (six int. awards, including European Film Awards Best Documentary and Vienna Film Prize) 2004. *Films as director:* Wer fürchtet sich vorm schwarzen Mann 1988, Era Max 1989, Piraten in Österreich 1990, Blasi, Der 1990, Ich habe die angenehme Aufgabe 1993. *Films as actor:* In the Circle of the Iris, Blue Distance. *E-mail:* hubert.sauper@free.fr. *Website:* www.hubertsauper.com.

SAUR, Klaus Gerhard, DHumLitt; German publisher; *CEO and Partner, Walter de Gruyter Publishing House GmbH*; b. 27 July 1941, Pullach; s. of Karl-Otto Saur and Veronika Saur; m. Lilo Stangel 1977; one s. one d. *Education:* High School, Icking and Commercial High School, Munich. *Career:* Marketing Man. Vulkan-Verlag, Essen 1962; Publishing Man. KG Saur, Munich 1963, Publishing Dir 1966; Pres. KG Saur New York and KG Saur, London 1977–2003; Man. Dir KG Saur Munich 1988–2004, Chair. Bd 2004; CEO and Partner, Walter de Gruyter Publishing House GmbH, Berlin and New York 2005–; founder World Guide to Libraries, Publrs Int. Directory; mem. Bd F.A. Brockhaus Bibliographical Inst. (Mannheim); Vice-Pres. Goethe-Institut, Germany. *Publications:* World Biographical Information System, Pressehandbuch für Exportwerbung, World Guide to Libraries. *Honours:* Hon. Prof., Univ. of Glasgow, Humboldt-Univ. Berlin; Hon. Fellow, Tech. Univ. of Graz; Hon. mem. Austrian Library Asscn 1998, German Library Asscn, Bavarian Acad. of Belle Arts; Senator hc (Ludwig Maximilians Univ., Munich) 1992, (Leipzig) 2001; Bundesverdienstkreuz der Bundesrepublik Deutschland, Officier Ordre des Arts et Lettres (France), Sächsischer Verdienstordern 2002, Bayerischer Verdienstordern 2002; Hon. DPhil (Marburg) 1985, (Ishevsk, Russia) 1997, (Pisa, Italy) 1998, (Simmons Coll., Mass.) 1992; Hon. Medal City of Munich 1988, Hon. Bene Merenti Medal, Bavarian Acad. of Sciences 1997, Helmut-Sontag Award, Asscn of German Libraries 1999, Großes Österreichisches Verdienstkreuz der Wessenschaftund Künste 2003, Max-Hermann-Award, German State Library. *Address:* Verlag Walter de Gruyter, Genthinerstr. 13, 10785 Berlin (office); Beuerbergerstr. 9, 81479 Munich, Germany (home). *Telephone:* (30) 26005312 (office); (89) 74994651 (home). *Fax:* (30) 26005369 (office); (89) 74994652 (home). *E-mail:* klaus.saur@degruyter.com (office). *Website:* www.degruyter.com (office).

SAUVAIN, Philip Arthur, MA, PGCE; British writer; b. 28 March 1933, Burton on Trent, Staffs.; m. June Maureen Spenceley 1963; one s. one d. *Education:* Univ. of Cambridge, Univ. of London. *Career:* Sr Lecturer in Geography, James Graham Coll., Leeds 1963–68; Head of Environmental Studies Dept, Charlotte Mason Coll. of Education, Ambleside 1968–74. *Publications:* A Map Reading Companion 1961, A Geographical Field Study Companion 1964, Exploring Britain (series) 1966, Discovery (series) 1970, Hulton's Practical Geography (series) 1970, Hulton's Lively History (series) 1970, The First Men on the Moon 1972, The Great Wall of China 1972, First Look Book (series) 1973, Breakaway (series) 1973, Exploring the World of Man (series) 1973, Environmental Books (series) 1974, Looking Around Town and Country 1975, A First Look Series (five vols) 1975–78, Imagining the Past: First Series (six vols) 1976, Second Series (six vols) 1979, The British Isles 1980, The Story of Britain Series (four vols) 1980, Britain's Living Heritage 1982, The History of Britain (four vols) 1982, Theatre 1983, Macmillan Junior Geography (four vols) 1983, Hulton New Geographies (five vols) 1983, History Map Books (two vols) 1983, 1985, Hulton New Histories (five vols) 1984–85, France and the French 1985, European and World History, 1815–1919 1985, Modern World History, 1919 Onwards 1985, How History Began 1985, Castles and Crusaders 1986, What to Look For (four vols) 1986, British Economic and Social History (two vols) 1987, Exploring Energy (four vols) 1987, GCSE History Companion Series (three vols) 1988, How We Build (three vols) 1989, The World of Work (three vols) 1989, Skills for Geography 1989, Skills for Standard Grade History 1990, Exploring the Past: Old World 1991, The Way it Works (three vols) 1991, Changing World 1992, Breakthrough: Communications 1992, History Detectives (three vols) 1992–93, Great Battles and Sieges (four vols) 1992–93, Expanding World 1993, The Era of the Second World War 1993, Robert Scott in the Antarctic 1993, Target Geography (14 vols) 1994–95, The Tudors and Stuarts 1995, Britain Since 1930 (four vols) 1995, Geography Detective (four vols) 1995–96, Famous Lives (two vols) 1996, Key Themes of the Twentieth Century 1996, Key Themes of the Twentieth Century: Teacher's Guide 1996, Germany in the Twentieth Century 1997, Vietnam 1997, Easter 1997. *Address:* 70 Finborough Road, Stowmarket, Suffolk, IP14 1PU, England.

SAVAGE, Alan (see Nicole, Christopher Robin)

SAVAGE, Thomas (Tom), BA, MLS; American poet, writer, critic and editor; b. 14 July 1948, New York, NY. *Education:* Brooklyn College, CUNY, Columbia University School of Library Science. *Career:* Teaching Asst, Naropa Institute School of Poetics 1975; Ed., Roof Magazine 1976–78, Gandhabba Magazine 1981–93; Teacher, Words, Music, Words for Poets and Composers, St Mark's Poetry Project 1983–85; Teacher The Poetry Project workshop, Tribes Gallery, NY 2003–04; mem. Co-ordinating Council of Literary Magazines. *Publications:* Personalities 1978, Filling Spaces 1980, Slow Waltz on a Glass Harmonica 1980, Housing Preservation and Development 1988, Processed Words 1990, Out of the World 1991, Political Conditions and Physical States 1993, Brain Surgery (poems) 1999; contributions to magazines and journals. *Honours:* PEN Grant 1978; Co-ordinating Council of Literary Magazines Grant 1981–82; two Fund For Poetry grants. *Address:* 622 E 11th Street, No. 14, New York, NY 10009, USA. *E-mail:* Tsavageshanti@yahoo.com.

SAVATER, Fernando, (Fernando Fernández-Savater Martín), PhD; Spanish philosopher and essayist; *Professor of Philosophy, Universidad Complutense de Madrid*; b. 21 June 1947, San Sebastián. *Education:* Universidad Complutense de Madrid. *Career:* Asst Prof. in faculty of political science, Universidad Autónoma de Madrid –1971; faculty mem. Dept of Ethics, Universidad del País Vasco 1975; Prof. of Philosophy, Universidad Complutense de Madrid 1995; co-Ed. of journal, Claves de Razón Práctica; mem. various peace organizations, including Basta Ya, which recieved the Premio Sajarov for the defence of human rights 2000. *Publications include:* Nihilismo y acción 1970, La filosofía tachada 1970, Apología del sofista y otros sofismas 1973, Ensayo sobre Cioran 1974, Escritos politeístas 1975, De los dioses y del mundo 1975, La infancia recuperada 1976, La filosofía como anhelo de la revolución 1976, Apóstatas razonables 1976, Para la anarquía y otros enfrentamientos 1977, La piedad apasionada 1977, Panfleto contra el Todo 1978, Nietzsche y su obra 1979, El estado y sus criaturas 1979, Criaturas del aire 1979, Caronte aguarda 1981, La tarea del héroe (Premio Nacional de Ensayo 1982) 1981, Impertinencias y desafíos 1981, Invitación a la ética 1982, Sobre vivir 1983, Las razones del antimilitarismo y otras razones 1984, El contenido de la felicidad 1986, Ética como amor propio 1988, Último desembarco: el vente de Sinapia 1988, Humanismo impenitente 1990, La escuela de Platón 1991, Ética para Amador 1991, Política para Amador 1992, Sin contemplaciones 1993, El jardín de las dudas 1993, El contenido de la felicidad 1994, Semearentzako Etika 1996, Ética para o seu fillo 1996, La voluntad disculpada 1996, El valor de educar (essay) 1997, Malos y malditos 1997, Despierta y lee 1998, Diccioanrio filosófico 1999, Las preguntas de la vida 1999, La aventura africana 1999, Idea de Nietzsche 2000, Ética per el meu fill 2000, A rienda suelta 2000, Perdonen las molestias: Crónica de una batalla sin armas contra las armas (collection of essays and articles) 2001, A caballo entre milenios 2001, Caronte aguarda 2001, El dialecto de la vida 2002, Pensamientos arriesgados 2002, El contenido de la felicidad 2002, Palabras cruzadas: una invitación a la filosofía 2003, Mira por dónde: autobiografía razonada 2003, Las preguntas de la vida 2003, Los caminos para la libertad: ética y educación 2003, El gran fraude: sobre terrorismo, nacionalismo y progresismo 2004, Los diez mandamientos en el siglo XX 2004, La libertad como destino 2004, El valor de escollir 2004, Criaturas del aire 2004, El gran laberinto 2005, Jorge Luis Borges (biog.) 2005. *Honours:* Premio Anagrama, Premio Fernando Abril Martorell, Premio Ortega y Gasset for journalism 2000. *Address:* Departamento de Filosofía IV, Facultad de Filosofía, Ciudad Universitaria, 28040 Madrid, Spain (office). *E-mail:* infocom@ucm.es (office).

SAVILLE, Diana; British writer; b. 15 Feb. 1943, London, England; m. 1974. *Education:* St Hugh's College, Oxford. *Publications:* The Observer's Book of British Gardens, 1982; Walled Gardens: Their Planning and Design, 1982; The Illustrated Garden Planter, 1984; Gardens for Small Country Houses, 1984; Colour, 1992; Walls and Screens, 1993; Green and Pleasant Land: A Thousand Years of Poetry (ed.), 1993; The Marriage Bed, 1995; The Honey Makers, 1996; The Hawk Dancer, 1997.

SAVOY, Deirdre, BBA; American author; b. 31 Oct. 1960, New York, NY; m. Carmelo (Frank) La Mantia 1988, one s. one d. *Education:* Baruch College, CUNY. *Publications:* Spellbound, 1999; Always, 2000. *Address:* PO Box 233, New York, NY 10469, USA.

SAVOY, Most Rt Rev. Douglas Eugene (Gene); American cleric, writer, educator and explorer; b. 11 May 1927, Bellingham, Wash.; two s. one d. *Career:* ordained minister 1962; apptd Head Bishop, Int. Community of Christ, Church of the Second Advent 1971; mem. Authors' Guild, Explorers Club (New York), Geographical Soc. (Lima, Peru), Andean Explorers Foundation, Ocean Sailing Club, World Council for Human Rights, Advocates for Religious Rights and Freedoms. *Publications:* Antisuyo: The Search for the Lost Cities of the Amazon 1970, Vilcabamba: Last City of the Incas 1970, The Child Christ 1973, The Decoded New Testament 1974, On the Trail of the Feathered Serpent 1974, The Prophecies of Jamil (seven vols) 1976–83, The Secret Sayings of Jamil: The Image and the World (seven vols) 1976–87, The Essaei Document: Secrets of an Eternal Race 1978, Project X: The Search for the Secrets of Immortality 1977, The Lost Gospel of Jesus: Hidden Teachings of Christ 1978, Miracle of the Second Advent 1984; some 39 texts, 400 audio tapes: Lectures on Religious Systems and Theology, five documentary videos; contribs to various publs. *Honours:* Officer, Order of the Grand Cross, Peru 1989; more than 40 Flag Awards from Andean Explorers Foundation, Explorers Club (New York) 1958–94, Ministry of Industry and Tourism of Peru Silver Hummingbird Award 1987, Andean Explorers Foundation Explorer of the Century Trophy 1988, Medal of Merit Andres Reyes 1989, City of Ica Award, Peru 1995. *Address:* 2025 LaFond Drive, Reno, NV 89509, USA. *E-mail:* gene@genesavoy.org. *Website:* www.genesavoy.org.

SAWYER, Diane, BA; American journalist; *Co-Anchor, Good Morning America, ABC News*; b. 22 Dec. 1945, Glasgow, Ky; d. of E.P. Sawyer and Jean W. Sawyer (née Dunagan); m. Mike Nichols 1988. *Education:* Wellesley

Coll. *Career:* reporter, WLKY-TV, Louisville, Ky 1967–70; Admin. White House Press Office 1970–74; mem. Nixon-Ford transition team 1974–75; Asst to Richard Nixon (fmr US Pres.) 1974, 1975; Gen. Reporter, later State Dept Corresp., CBS News 1978–81, apptd Co-Anchor Morning News 1981, Co-Anchor Early Morning News 1982–84, Corresp. and Co-Ed. 60 Minutes 1984–89; Co-Anchor PrimeTime Live (now Primetime Thursday), ABC News 1989–, Good Morning America 1999–. *Honours:* nine Emmy awards, Nat. Headliner Awards, George Foster Peabody Award for Public Service, Robert F. Kennedy Journalism Award, Special Dupont Award, Ohio State Award, IRTS Lifetime Achievement Award, inducted TV Acad. of Fame 1997, ranked by Forbes magazine amongst 100 Most Powerful Women (26th) 2004, (55th) 2005, (60th) 2006. *Address:* Good Morning America, 147 Columbus Avenue, New York, NY 10023-5900, USA (office). *Telephone:* (212) 456-2060 (office). *Fax:* (212) 456-1246 (office). *Website:* abcnews.go.com/GMA (office).

SAWYER, Robert James, BAA; Canadian writer; b. 29 April 1960, Ottawa, Ontario; m. Carolyn Joan Clink 1984. *Education:* Ryerson Polytechnical Institute. *Career:* mem. Crime Writers of Canada; MWA; SFWA; Writers Union of Canada. *Publications:* Golden Fleece, 1990; Far-Seer, 1992; Fossil Hunter, 1993; Foreigner, 1994; End of an Era, 1994; The Terminal Experiment, 1995. *Honours:* Aurora Award, Canadian Science Fiction and Fantasy Asscn, 1992; Homer Awards, 1992, 1993; Writer's Reserve Grant, Ontario Arts Council, 1993.

SAWYER, Roger Martyn, BA, DipEd, PhD, FRGS; British historian; b. 15 Dec. 1931, Gloucestershire; s. of Charles F. Sawyer and Winifred A. Sawyer (née Martin); m. Diana Margaret Harte 1952, two s. *Education:* University of Wales, University of Southampton. *Career:* Housemaster, Blue Coat School, Edgbaston 1958–60; Deputy Head then Headmaster, Bembridge Prep. School 1960–83; Gov. Wycliffe Coll.; Research Fellow, The Airey Neave Trust, IAPS 1975; mem. Anti-Slavery Int. (Council mem. 1984–98), Bembridge Sailing Club, Old Wycliffian Soc. *Publications:* Casement: The Flawed Hero 1984, Slavery in the Twentieth Century 1986, Children Enslaved 1988, The Island from Within (ed.) 1990, 'We are but Women': Women in Ireland's History 1993, Roger Casement's Diaries 1910: The Black and The White (ed.) 1997; contrib. to Anti-Slavery Reporter, BBC History Magazine, Immigrants and Minorities, South, UN Development Forum. *Honours:* Airey Neave Award 1985. *Address:* Ducie House, Darts Lane, Bembridge, Isle of Wight, PO35 5YH, England. *Telephone:* (1983) 873384.

SAYER, Ian Keith Terence; British writer; b. 30 Oct. 1945, Norwich, Norfolk; three s. three d. *Publications:* Nazi Gold: The Story of the World's Greatest Robbery 1984, America's Secret Army: The Untold Story of the Counter Intelligence Corps 1989, Hitler's Last General: The Case Against Wilhelm Mohnke 1989, Hitler's Bastard: Through Hell and Back in Nazi Germany and Stalin's Russia (ed.) 2003, Hitler and Women: The Love Life of Adolf Hitler 2004; contrib. to Freight News (columnist), Express Magazine (columnist), Sunday Times Magazine. *Address:* Westerlands, Sherbourne Drive, Sunningdale, Berks., SL5 0LG, England. *E-mail:* ian@sayer.net.

SAYLOR, Steven Warren, (Aaron Travis), BA; American writer; b. 23 March 1956, Port Lavaca, TX; pnr Richard K. Solomon (registered 1991). *Education:* Univ. of Texas at Austin. *Career:* mem. MWA. *Publications:* Roman Blood 1991, Arms of Nemesis 1992, Catilina's Riddle 1993, The Venus Throw 1995, A Murder on the Appian Way 1996, House of the Vestals 1997, Rubicon 1999, A Twist at the End (aka Honour the Dead) 2000, Last Seen in Massilia 2000, A Mist of Prophecies 2002, Have You Seen Dawn? 2003, The Judgement of Caesar 2004, A Gladiator Dies Only Once 2005, Roma 2007; as Aaron Travis: Big Shots 1993, Beast of Burden 1993, Slaves of the Empire 1996; contrib. to books and periodicals. *Honours:* MWA Robert L. Fish Memorial Award 1993, Lambda Literary Award 1994. *Address:* c/o Constable & Robinson Ltd, 3 The Lanchester, 162 Fulham Palace Road, London, W6 9ER, England. *E-mail:* steven@stevensaylor.com. *Website:* www.stevensaylor.com.

SCAGLIONE, Aldo Domenico, DLitt; Italian academic and writer; b. 10 Jan. 1925, Turin; m. 1st Jeanne M. Daman 1952 (died 1986); m. 2nd Marie M. Burns 1992. *Education:* University of Turin. *Career:* faculty, University of California at Berkeley, 1952–68; W. R. Kenan Prof., University of North Carolina at Chapel Hill, 1969–87; Prof., 1987–91, Erich Maria Remarque Prof. of Literature, 1991–, New York University; mem. American Asscn for Italian Studies, hon. pres., 1989; Boccaccio Asscn of America, pres., 1980–83; Medieval Acad. of America. *Publications:* Nature and Love in the Late Middle Ages, 1963; Ars Grammatica, 1970; The Classical Theory of Composition, 1972; The Theory of German Word Order, 1981; The Liberal Arts and the Jesuit College System, 1986; Knights at Court, 1991; Essays on the Art of Discourse, 1998. Contributions: professional journals. *Honours:* Knight of the Order of Merit, Republic of Italy; Fulbright Scholar, 1951; Guggenheim Fellowship, 1958; Newbery Fellow, 1964; Fellow, University of Wisconsin Institute for the Humanities, 1981.

SCALAPINO, Robert Anthony, MA, PhD; American academic and writer; *Robson Research Professor Emeritus of Government, University of California at Berkeley;* b. 19 Oct. 1919, Leavenworth, KS; m. Ida Mae Jessen 1941 (died 2005); three d. *Education:* Santa Barbara Coll., Harvard Univ. *Career:* Lecturer, Santa Barbara Coll., 1940–41; Instructor, Harvard Univ., 1948–49; Asst Prof., Univ. of California at Berkeley 1949–51, Assoc. Prof. 1951–56, Chair. Dept of Political Science 1962–65, Robson Research Prof. of Govt 1977–90, Dir Inst. of East Asian Studies 1978–90, Prof. Emer. 1990–; Visiting Lecturer, Peking Univ. 1981, 1985, 1999; Ed. Asian Survey, 1962–96; Head,

US Del. to Second Mongolian Int. Conf. 1990, 1992, 1999; has travelled extensively throughout Asia and the Far East; Founder and first Chair. Nat. Cttee on US–China Relations, now Dir Emer.; Dir Emer. Japan Soc. of Northern California; Co-Chair. Asian Agenda Advisory Group, Asia Soc.; mem. Bd Dirs Asia Foundation (also mem. Bd Trustees), Atlantic Council, Pacific Forum-CSIS, Nat. Bureau of Asian Research; mem. American Political Science Asscn, Asscn for Asian Studies, Council on Foreign Relations (now Dir Emer.), Foreign Policy Asscn, Western Political Science Asscn; Fellow, American Acad. of Arts and Sciences. *Publications:* 509 articles and 38 books or monographs on Asian politics and US Asian policy including: Democracy and the Party Movement in Pre-War Japan 1953, The Chinese Anarchist Movement (with George T. Yu) 1961, Parties and Politics in Contemporary Japan 1962, North Korea Today (ed.) 1963, The Japanese Communist Movement 1920–1966 1967, The Communist Revolution in Asia (ed.) 1969, Communism in Korea (with Chong-Sik Lee) (American Political Science Associations' Woodrow Wilson Award 1974) 1972, Elites in the People's Republic of China (ed.) 1972, Asia and the Road Ahead 1975, The Foreign Policy of Modern Japan (ed. and contrib.) 1977, The United States and Korea: Looking Ahead 1979, North Korea Today: Strategic and Domestic Issues (ed. with Jun-Yop Kim) 1983, The Early Japanese Labor Movement 1984, China and Its Revolutionary Process (with George T. Yu) 1985, Major Power Relations in Northeast Asia 1987, The Politics of Development: Perspectives on Twentieth Century Asia 1989, The Last Leninists: The Uncertain Future of Asia's Communist States 1992. *Honours:* Hon. Prof., Center on Northeast Asian Studies in Mongolia 1997, Peking Univ. 1997; Order of the Sacred Treasure (Japan) 1988, Order of Diplomatic Service Merit; several hon. doctorates; Carnegie Foundation Grant 1951–53, Social Science Research Council Fellow 1952–53, Ford Foundation Grant 1955, Rockefeller Foundation Grants 1956–59 1961, Guggenheim Fellowship 1965–66, Nat. Endowment for the Humanities Grant, Henry Luce Foundation Grant, Earhart Foundation Grant, Woodrow Wilson Award, American Political Science Asscn 1973, Presidential Order (Repub. of Korea) 1990, Berkeley Citation for Distinguished Service to the Univ. of California 1990, Berkeley Fellow 1993, Japan Foundation Award 1998, Friendship Medal, Govt of Mongolia 1999, Berkeley Medal 1999, Medal of Highest Honor, Grad. Inst. of Peace Studies, Kyung Hee Univ., Heung-In Medal, Govt of Korea. *Address:* Institute of East Asian Studies, University of California, 2223 Fulton Street, Room 516, Berkeley, CA 94720 (office); 2850 Buena Vista Way, Berkeley, CA 94708, USA (home). *Telephone:* (510) 643-7062 (office); (510) 644-2633 (home). *Fax:* (510) 643-7062 (office). *E-mail:* halperin@berkeley.edu (office).

SCALES-TRENT, Judy, BA, MA, JD; American academic, writer and poet; b. 1 Oct. 1940, Winston-Salem, NC; one s. *Education:* Oberlin College, Middlebury College, Northwestern University School of Law. *Career:* Adjunct Faculty, Catholic University Law School 1983; Prof. of Law, SUNY at Buffalo 1984–; Visiting Prof. of Law, Univ. Cheikh Anta Diop de Dakar 1990–91, St Mary's University School of Law 1994. *Publications:* Notes of a White Black Woman: Race, Color, Community 1995. Contributions: anthologies, literary periodicals and law journals. *Honours:* Fulbright Award 1990–91, Baldy Center for Law and Social Policy Award, SUNY at Buffalo 1986, 1991–93, William J. Magavern Fellowship 1993. *Address:* 352 Old Meadow Road, East Amherst, NY 14051, USA.

SCALFARI, Eugenio, DIur; Italian editor; b. 6 April 1924, Civitavecchia; m. Simonetta de Benedetti 1959; two d. *Career:* contrib. Il Mondo, L'Europeo 1950–; Promoter Partito Radicale 1958, L'Espresso 1955–, Ed.-in-Chief 1963–68, Man. Dir 1970–75; Promoter La Repubblica 1976–, Ed.-in-Chief 1976–96, Dir 1988–; Deputy to Parl. 1968–72. *Publications:* Rapporto sul Neocapitalismo Italiano, Il Potere Economico in URSS, L'Autunno della Repubblica, Razza Padrona, Interviste ai Potenti, L'Anno di Craxi, La Sera Andavamo in Via Veneto, Incontro con Io, La Morale Perduta, La Ruga Sulla Fronte. *Honours:* Siena Award 1985, Journalist of the Year Award 1986. *Address:* c/o La Repubblica, Piazza dell'Indipendenza 11/B, 00185 Rome, Italy. *Telephone:* (06) 49821.

SCAMMACCA, Nat, BA, MA; American academic (retd), writer and poet; b. 20 July 1924, New York, NY; m. Nina Scammacca 1948, one s. two d. *Education:* Long Island University, New York University, University of Perugia. *Career:* Pilot, US Air Force, India-Burma-China theatre, World War II; Social Worker, Italian Board of Guardians; Prof. of English, British College, Palermo; Ed., Third Page, Trapani Nuova newspaper; mem. Poets and Writers, New York City. *Publications:* Two Worlds (novel), 1980; Schammachanat (Italian and English), 1985; Bye Bye America (short stories), 1986; Cricepeo (Italian and English), 3 vols, 1990; Sikano L'Amerikano! (short stories), 1991; Due Poeti Americani (Italian and English, co-author), 1994; The Hump (World War II stories and poems), 1994. Other: various books and trans. Contributions: anthologies and periodicals. *Honours:* Air Medal, Bronze Star, US Air Force; Taormina City Poetry Prize, 1978; Premio Letterario Sikania Prize, 1988; VII Premio di Poesia Petrosino Prize, 1991.

SCAMMELL, Michael, BA, PhD; British writer and academic; b. 16 Jan. 1935, Lyndhurst, England; m. 2nd Rosemary Nossiff; one s. three d. *Education:* Univ. of Nottingham, Columbia Univ., New York. *Career:* Lecturer in English, Ljubljana Univ., Yugoslavia 1958–59; Columbia Univ. Fellow 1959–61; Lecturer in Russian, Hunter Coll., CUNY 1961–62; Language Supervisor, Programme Asst, BBC, London 1965–67; Ed. Index on Censorship, London 1971–80; Dir Writers and Scholars Educational Trust, London 1971–80; Sr Visiting Fellow, Russian Inst. 1976–84; Fellow, New York Inst.

for the Humanities 1982–84; Chair. Writers in Prison Cttee, International PEN 1976–84; Prof. of Russian Literature, Cornell Univ., Ithaca, NY 1987–94; Prof. of Creative Writing, Columbia Univ. 1994; Pres. American PEN Center 1998–2001; Vice-Pres. International PEN 1986–; mem. Soc. of Authors (Vice-Chair. 1976–79), Translation Assen, English PEN Centre. *Publications:* Blue Guide to Yugoslavia 1969, Russia's Other Writers (ed.) 1970, Alexander Solzhenitsyn 1971, Unofficial Art from the Soviet Union (ed.) 1977, Solzhenitsyn: A Biography 1984, The Solzhenitsyn Files: Secret Soviet Documents Reveal One Man's Fight Against the Monolith (ed.) 1995; translator: Cities and Years 1962, Crime and Punishment 1963, The Gift 1963, The Defense 1964, Childhood, Boyhood and Youth 1964, My Testimony 1969, Nothing is Lost: Selected Poems by Edvard Kochek (with Veno Taufer) 2004; contrib. to periodicals including TLS, The Observer, The Times, Daily Telegraph, London, Sunday Telegraph, London, New York Times Book Review, New York Review of Books, New Republic, Harpers, USA, Los Angeles Times. *Honours:* Los Angeles Times Book Prize for Biography 1985. *Literary Agent:* c/o AP Watt Ltd, 20 John Street, London, WC1N 2DR, England. *Telephone:* (20) 7405-6774. *Fax:* (20) 7831-2154. *E-mail:* apw@apwatt.co.uk. *Website:* www.apwatt.co.uk. *Address:* 605 West 113 Street, Apt 32, New York, NY 10025, USA. *Telephone:* (212) 854-4391 (office). *E-mail:* MS474@columbia.edu (office).

SCANNELL, Vernon, FRSL; British poet, author and broadcaster; b. 23 Jan. 1922. *Education:* Univ. of Leeds. *Career:* served with Gordon Highlanders 1940–45; professional boxer 1946–47; various jobs including teacher, Hazelwood Prep. School 1955–62; Southern Arts Assen Writing Fellowship 1975–76; Visiting Poet, Shrewsbury School 1978–79; Resident Poet, King's School, Canterbury 1979. *Publications:* novels: The Fight 1953, A Lonely Game (for younger readers) 1979, Ring of Truth 1983, Feminine Endings 2000; poetry: The Masks of Love 1960 (Heinemann Award for Literature 1960), A Sense of Danger (co-ed. Ted Hughes and Patricia Beer) 1962; New Poems, A PEN Anthology 1962; Walking Wounded – Poems 1962–65, 1968, Epithets of War – Poems 1965–69, 1969; Mastering the Craft (Poets Today Series) 1970, Pergamon Poets, No. 8 (with J. Silkin) 1970, Selected Poems 1971, The Winter Man – New Poems 1973, The Apple Raid and Other Poems 1974 (Cholmondeley Poetry Prize), The Loving Game 1975, New and Collected Poems 1950–80, 1980, Winterlude and Other Poems 1982, Funeral Games 1987, Soldiering On, Poems of Military Life 1989, A Time for Fires 1991, Collected Poems 1950–1993 1994, The Black and White Days 1996, Views and Distances 2000, Of Love and War, New and Selected Poems 2002, Behind the Lines, Poems 2004; criticism: Not Without Glory – Poets of World War II 1976, How to Enjoy Poetry 1982, How to Enjoy Novels 1984; (autobiography) The Tiger and the Rose 1971, A Proper Gentleman 1977, Argument of Kings 1987, The Drums of Morning – Growing Up in the Thirties 1992; Sporting Literature – An Anthology 1987, The Clever Potato, Poems for Children 1988, Love Shouts and Whispers (poems for children) 1990, Travelling Light (for children) 1991. *Address:* 51 North Street, Otley, West Yorks., LS21 1AH, England. *Telephone:* (1943) 467176.

SCARDINO, Dame Marjorie Morris, DBE, JD, BA; American/British business executive; *CEO, Pearson PLC*; b. 25 Jan. 1947, Flagstaff, Ariz.; d. of Robert Weldon Morris and Beth Lamb Morris; m. Albert James Scardino 1974; two s. one d. *Education:* Baylor Univ., Univ. of San Francisco. *Career:* started career as reporter, Associated Press; Partner, Brannen, Wessels and Searcy law firm, Savannah, Ga 1975–85; Co-founder (with husband) and Publr The Georgia Gazette Co. (won Pulitzer Prize) 1978–85; Pres. The Economist Newspaper Group Inc. 1985–93; Chief Exec. The Economist Group 1993–97; CEO Pearson PLC 1997–; Dir (non-exec.) Nokia Corpn 2001–; mem. Bd of Trustees The MacArthur Foundation, Carter Center, Victoria & Albert Museum. *Honours:* Hon. Fellow London Business School, City and Guilds of London Inst.; Hon. LLD (Exeter); Hon. DHumLitt (New School Univ.); Dr hc (Heriot-Watt), (Brunel); Veuve Clicquot Businesswoman of the Year Award 1998, ranked by Fortune magazine amongst 50 Most Powerful Women in Business outside the US (first) 2001, (first) 2002, (first) 2003, (third) 2004, (third) 2005, (fifth) 2006, ranked by Forbes magazine amongst 100 Most Powerful Women (59th) 2004, (18th) 2005, (31st) 2006. *Address:* Pearson PLC, 80 Strand, London, WC2R 0RL, England (office). *Telephone:* (20) 7010-2300 (office). *Fax:* (20) 7010-6601 (office). *E-mail:* marjorie.scardino@pearson.com (office). *Website:* www.pearson.com (office).

SCARFE, Allan John, BA, DipEd, TPTC; Australian writer; b. 30 March 1931, Caulfield, Vic.; m. Wendy Scarfe 1955; four c. *Publications:* A Corpse in Calcutta 2000, The Dissident Guru 2004; with Wendy Scarfe: A Mouthful of Petals 1967, 1972, Tiger on a Rein 1969, People of India 1972, The Black Australians 1974, Victims or Bludgers?: Case Studies in Poverty in Australia 1974, J. P: his Biography 1975, 1972, Victims or Bludgers?: A Poverty Inquiry for Schools 1978, Labor's Titan: The Story of Percy Brookfield 1878–1921 1983, All That Grief: Migrant Recollections of Greek Resistance to Facism 1941–49 1994, Remembering Jayaprakash 1997, No Taste for Carnage: Alex Sheppard – A Portrait 1913–1997 1998; contrib. to several publications. *Honours:* Australia Literature Boards Grants (with Wendy Scarfe) 1980, 1988. *Address:* 8 Bostock Street, Warrnambool, Vic. 3280, Australia.

SCARFE, Gerald A.; British cartoonist; b. 1 June 1936, London; m. Jane Asher; two s. one d. *Career:* has contributed cartoons to Punch 1960–, Private Eye 1961–, Daily Mail 1966–, The Sunday Times 1967–, Time 1967–; exhibited at Grosvenor Gallery (group exhbns) 1969, 1970, Pavillion d'Humour, Montreal 1969, Expo 1970, Osaka 1970; animation and film directing BBC 1969–; consultant designer and character design for film Hercules 1997. *Solo exhibitions include:* Waddell Gallery, New York 1968, 1970, Vincent Price Gallery, Chicago 1969, Grosvenor Gallery 1969, Nat. Portrait Gallery 1971, Royal Festival Hall 1983, Langton Gallery 1986, Chris Beetles Gallery 1989, Nat. Portrait Gallery 1998–99, Comic Art Gallery, Melbourne, Gerald Scarfe in Southwark 2000. *Television:* dir. and presenter Scarfe on Art, Scarfe on Sex, Scarfe on Class, Scarfe in Paradise; subject of Scarfe and His Work with Disney (South Bank Special). *Theatre design:* Ubu Roi (Traverse Theatre) 1957, What the Butler Saw (Oxford Playhouse) 1980, No End of Blame (Royal Court, London) 1981, Orpheus in the Underworld (English ENO, Coliseum) 1985, Who's a Lucky Boy (Royal Exchange, Manchester) 1985, Born Again 1990, The Magic Flute (LA Opera) 1992, An Absolute Turkey 1993, Mind Millie for Me (Haymarket, London) 1996, Fantastic Mr. Fox (LA Opera) 1998, Peter and the Wolf (Holiday on Ice, Paris and world tour). *Publications:* Gerald Scarfe's People 1966, Indecent Exposure 1973, Expletive Deleted: The Life and Times of Richard Nixon 1974, Gerald Scarfe 1982, Father Kissmass and Mother Claus 1985, Scarfe by Scarfe (autobiog.) 1986, Gerald Scarfe's Seven Deadly Sins 1987, Line of Attack 1988, Scarfeland 1989, Scarfe on Stage 1992, Scarfe Face 1993, Hades: The Truth at Last 1997, Drawing Blood: Forty-five Years of Scarfe Uncensored 2005. *Honours:* Hon. Fellow London Inst. 2001; Hon. LLD (Liverpool) 2001; Zagreb Prize for BBC film Long Drawn Out Trip 1973, BAFTA Award for Scarfe on Scarfe 1987, Olivier Award for Absolute Turkey 1993. *Literary Agent:* London Management, 2–4 Noel Street, London, W1V 3RB, England.

SCARFE, Norman, MBE, MA, FSA; British writer; b. 1 May 1923, Felixstowe. *Education:* Univ. of Oxford. *Career:* served as subaltern, 76th (Highland) Field Regt, RA 1943–46, experienced active service during Normandy landing 1944; Lecturer, Dept of History, Univ. of Leicester 1949–63; Chair., Centre of East Anglia Studies, Univ. of East Anglia, 1989–96; mem. Int. PEN, Suffolk Book League (founder-chair. 1982), Suffolk Records Soc. (founder, hon. gen. ed. 1958–92, pres. 2002). *Publications:* Suffolk, A Shell Guide 1960, Essex, A Shell Guide 1968, The Suffolk Landscape 1972, Cambridgeshire, A Shell Guide 1983, Suffolk in the Middle Ages 1986, A Frenchman's Year in Suffolk (1784) 1988, Innocent Espionage: The La Rochefoucauld Brothers' Tour of England in 1785 1995, Jocelin of Brakelond 1997, To the Highlands in 1786: The Inquisitive Journey of a Young French Aristocrat 2001, Assault Division: A History of the 3rd Division from the Invasion of Normandy to the Surrender of Germany 2004; contribs to Proceedings, Suffolk Institute of Archaeology, Aldeburgh Festival Annual Programme Book, Country Life, The Book Collector, Dictionary of National Biography, The Impact of the Railways on Society in Britain: Essays in Honour of Jack Simmons 2003. *Honours:* Citoyen d'Honneur, Colleville Montgomery 1994; Hon. LittD (Univ. of East Anglia) 1989; East Anglia's History: Studies in Honour of Norman Scarfe (ed by Christopher Harper-Bill, Carole Rawcliffe, Richard Wilson) 2002. *Address:* The Garden Cottage, 3 Burkitt Road, Woodbridge, Suffolk, IP12 4JJ (home); John Welch, Mill Cottage, Chipping Campden, GL55 6JQ, England (office). *Telephone:* (1394) 387058 (home).

SCARFE, Wendy Elizabeth, BA, BLitt, ATTC; Australian writer and poet; b. 21 Nov. 1933, Adelaide, S Australia; m. Allan Scarfe 1955; four c. *Publications:* fiction: The Lotus Throne 1976, Neither Here Nor There 1978, Laura My Alter Ego 1988, The Day They Shot Edward 1991, 1992, 2003, Miranda 1998, Fishing for Strawberries 2001, Jerusha Braddon, Painter 2005; poetry: Shadow and Flowers 1964, 1984, Dragonflies and Edges (with Jeffrey Ronald Keith) 2004; with Allan Scarfe: A Mouthful of Petals 1967, 1972, Tiger on a Rein 1969, People of India 1972, The Black Australians 1974, Victims or Bludgers?: Case Studies in Poverty in Australia 1974, J. P: His Biography 1975, 1997, Victims or Bludgers?: A Poverty Inquiry for Schools 1978, Labor's Titan: The Story of Percy Brookfield, 1878–1921 1983, All That Grief: Migrant Recollections of Greek Resistance to Fascism, 1941–1949 1994, Remembering Jayaprakash 1997, No Taste for Carnage: Alex Sheppard – A Portrait 1913–1997 1998; contrib. to Overland, Australian Short Stories, The Age. *Honours:* Australia Literature Board Grants (with Allan Scarfe) 1980, 1988. *Address:* 8 Bostock Street, Warrnambool, Vic. 3280, Australia.

SCHALLER, George Beals, PhD; American zoologist and academic; *Vice-President, Science and Exploration Program, Wildlife Conservation Society*; b. 26 May 1933, Berlin, Germany; s. of George Ludwig Schaller and Bettina (Byrd) Iwersen; m. Kay Suzanne Morgan 1957; two s. *Education:* Univ. of Alaska, Univ. of Wisconsin. *Career:* Research Assoc., Johns Hopkins Univ., Baltimore 1963–66; research zoologist Wildlife Conservation Soc. 1966–, Dir Int. Conservation Program 1972–88, now Vice-Pres. Science and Exploration Program; Adjunct Assoc. Prof., Rockefeller Univ., New York 1966–; Adjunct Prof. Peking (now Beijing) Univ.; Research Assoc. American Museum of Natural History; Fellow Guggenheim Foundation 1971. *Publications:* The Mountain Gorilla 1963, The Year of the Gorilla 1964, The Deer and the Tiger 1967, The Serengeti Lion 1972 (Nat. Book Award 1973), Mountain Monarchs 1977, Stones of Silence 1980, The Giant Pandas of Wolong (co-author) 1985, The Last Panda 1993, Tibet's Hidden Wilderness 1997, Wildlife of the Tibetan Steppe 1998, Antelopes, Deer and Relatives (co-ed.) 2000. *Honours:* Hon. Dir Explorers' Club 1991; Int. Cosmos Prize, Japan 1996, Tyler Environmental Prize 1997; Gold Medal, World Wildlife Fund 1980; Order of Golden Ark, Netherlands 1978. *Address:* Wildlife Conservation Society, Bronx Park, Bronx, New York, NY 10460, USA (office). *Telephone:* (718) 220-6807 (office). *Fax:* (718) 364-4275 (office). *E-mail:* asiaprogram@wcs.org (office). *Website:* wcs.org (office).

SCHAMA, Simon Michael, CBE, MA; British historian, academic, writer and art critic; *University Professor, Department of History, Columbia University*; b. 13 Feb. 1945, London; s. of the late Arthur Schama and of Gertrude Steinberg; m. Virginia Papaioannou 1983; one s. one d. *Education:* Christ's Coll., Cambridge. *Career:* Fellow and Dir of Studies in History, Christ's Coll., Cambridge 1966–76; Fellow and Tutor in Modern History, Brasenose Coll., Oxford 1976–80; Prof. of History (Mellon Prof. of the Social Sciences), Harvard Univ. 1980; Univ. Prof. Columbia Univ. 1997–; art critic, New Yorker 1995–; Vice-Pres. Poetry Soc. *Television:* Rembrandt: The Public Eye and the Private Gaze (film for BBC) 1992, A History of Britain (series) 2000–01, The Power of Art (series) 2006. *Publications:* Patriots and Liberators: Revolution in the Netherlands 1780–1813 1977, Two Rothschilds and the Land of Israel 1979, The Embarrassment of Riches: An Interpretation of Dutch Culture in the Golden Age 1987, Citizens: A Chronicle of the French Revolution 1989, Dead Certainties (Unwarranted Speculations) 1991, Landscape and Memory 1995, Rembrandt's Eyes 1999, A History of Britain Vol. 1: At the Edge of the World? 3000 BC–AD 1603 2000, Vol. 2: The British Wars 1603–1776 2001, Vol. 3: The Fate of Empire 1776–2001 2002, Hang-Ups: Essays on Painting 2004, Rough Crossings: Britain, the Slaves and the American Revolution 2005, Power of Art 2006. *Honours:* Wolfson Prize 1977, Leo Gershoy Prize (American Historical Asscn) 1978, Nat. Cash Register Book Prize for Non-Fiction (for Citizens) 1990. *Address:* Department of History, 522 Fayerweather Hall, Columbia University, New York, NY 10027, USA (office). *Telephone:* (212) 854-4593 (office). *E-mail:* sms53@columbia.edu (office). *Website:* www .columbia.edu/cu/history (office).

SCHANBERG, Sydney Hillel, BA; American journalist; b. 17 Jan. 1934, Clinton, Mass.; s. of Louis Schanberg and Freda (née Feinberg) Schanberg; two d. *Education:* Harvard Univ. *Career:* joined New York Times 1959, reporter 1960, Bureau Chief, Albany, New York 1967–69, New Delhi, India 1969–73, SE Asia Corresp., Singapore 1973–75, City Ed. 1977–80, Columnist 1981–85; Assoc. Ed., Columnist Newsday newspaper, New York 1986–98; chief investigative unit APBnews.com; currently writes for Village Voice, NY. *Publications:* Death and Life of Dith Pran 1985. *Honours:* numerous awards, including Page One Award for Reporting 1972, George Polk Memorial Award 1972, Overseas Press Club Award 1972, Bob Considine Memorial Award 1975, Pulitzer Prize 1975. *Address:* c/o Village Voice Media, 36 Cooper Square, New York, NY 10003, USA (office). *Telephone:* (212) 475-3300 (office). *Website:* www.villagevoice.com (office).

SCHÄTZING, Frank; German writer; b. 1957, Cologne. *Publications:* Tod und Teufel 1995, Mordshunger 1996, Die dunkle Seite 1997, Keine Angst (short stories) 1997, lauTlos 2000, KölnKrimiSpiel 2001, Der Schwarm 2004, Der Puppenspieler 2005. *Address:* c/o Verlag Kiepenheuer & Witsch, Rondorfer Str. 5, 50968 Köln, Germany. *Website:* www.frank-schaetzing.com.

SCHEIBER, Harry Noel, AB, MA, PhD; American academic, writer and editor; *Stefan A. Riesenfeld Professor of Law and History and Director, Earl Warren Institute for Legal Research, University of California, Berkeley*; b. 1935, New York, NY. *Education:* Columbia Univ., New York, Cornell Univ., Ithaca, NY. *Career:* Instructor to Assoc. Prof., Dartmouth Coll. 1960–68, Prof. of History 1968–71; Fellow, Centre for Advanced Study in the Behavioural Sciences, Stanford, 1967, 1971; Prof. of American History, Univ. of California, San Diego, 1971–80; Prof. of Law, Univ. of California, Berkeley 1980–, Assoc. Dean 1990–93, 1996–99, Stefan A. Riesenfeld Prof. of Law and History 1991–, Dir Center for the Study of Law and Society 2000–01, Earl Warren Inst. for Legal Research 2002–, Sho Sato Program in Japanese and US Law; Fulbright Distinguished Sr Lecturer, Australia 1983; Ed. Yearbook of the California Supreme Court Historical Society 1994–; Visiting Research Prof., Univ. of Uppsala, Sweden 1995; mem. American Historical Asscn, California Supreme Court Historical Soc., Economic History Asscn, Law and Society Asscn, Org. of American Historians, American Acad. of Arts and Sciences 2003–; Fellow, Japan Soc. for the Promotion of Science 2001. *Publications:* The Wilson Administration and Civil Liberties 1960, United States Economic History 1964, America: Purpose and Power (co-author) 1965, The Condition of American Federalism 1966, The Frontier in American Development (co-ed.) 1969, The Old Northwest 1969, The Ohio Canal Era 1820–1861 1969, Black Labor in American History 1972, Agriculture in the Development of the Far West 1975, American Economic History (co-author) 1976, American Law and the Consitutional Order 1978, Perspectives on Federalism (ed.) 1987, Power Divided (co-ed.) 1989, Federalism and the Judicial Mind (ed.) 1993, Legal Culture and the Legal Profession (co-author) 1995, The State and Freedom of Contract 1998, Law of the Sea: The Common Heritage and Emerging Challenges 2000, Inter-Allied Conflicts and Ocean Law, 1945–1952 2001; contribs to professional journals. *Honours:* Hon. MA (Dartmouth Coll.) 1965; Hon. DJur (Uppsala) 1998; Guggenheim Fellowships 1971, 1988, Rockefeller Foundation Fellowship 1979, Nat. Endowment for the Humanities Fellowship 1985–86. *Address:* School of Law, 442 Boalt Hall (North Addition), University of California, Berkeley, CA 94720, USA (office). *Telephone:* (510) 643-9788 (office). *Fax:* (510) 642-2951 (office). *E-mail:* scheiber@law.berkeley.edu (office); hscheiber@law.berkeley.edu (office). *Website:* www.law.berkeley.edu/faculty/profiles/facultyProfile.php?facID=102 (office).

SCHELL, Jonathan, BA; American journalist; b. 21 Aug. 1943, New York; s. of Orville Hickock Schell Jr and Marjorie Bertha; m. Elspeth Schell; two s. one d. *Education:* Putney School, Vt, Harvard Univ. and Int. Christian Univ., Tokyo. *Career:* articles describing Operation Cedar Falls, one of largest US mil. exercises of Vietnam War and other experiences in Vietnam appeared in New Yorker 1967; mem. staff, New Yorker 1968–87; Fellow, Inst. of Politics, Kennedy School of Govt 1987; Visiting Prof. Inst. of Liberal Arts, Emory Univ. Atlanta, Ga 1987, New York Univ. School of Journalism 1988; Ferris Prof. Princeton Univ. 1989; columnist, Newsday and New York Newsday 1990; mem. New York Inst. for the Humanities, New York Univ. 1991–. *Publications:* The Village of Ben Suc 1967, The Military Half: An Account of Destruction in Quang Ngai and Quang Tin 1968, The Time of Illusion 1976, The Fate of the Earth 1982, The Abolition, History in Sherman Park 1987, Observing the Nixon Years: Notes & Comment from the New Yorker on the Vietnam War and the Watergate Crisis 1969–75 1989, The Unconquerable World: Power, Nonviolence and the Will of the People 2004. *Honours:* Melcher Book Award for The Fate of the Earth 1982. *Address:* c/o Allen Lane, Penguin UK, 80 Strand, London, WC2R 0RL, England.

SCHELL, Orville Hickok, BA, MA, PhD; American journalist and writer; *Dean of the Graduate School of Journalism, University of California at Berkeley*; b. 20 May 1940, New York, NY; m.; three s. *Education:* Stanford University, National Taiwan University, Harvard University, University of California at Berkeley. *Career:* Co-Dir, Bay Area Institute, 1968–71; Founder and Ed.-in-Chief, Pacific News Service, 1970–71; China Correspondent, The New Yorker Magazine, 1975; Research Assoc., 1986, Regents' Lecturer, 1990, Dean, Graduate School of Journalism, 1996–, University of California at Berkeley; Visiting Distinguished Prof., Chico State University, 1987; Moderator, Issues and Perspectives on China, Voice of America, 1995–97; mem. Authors' Guild; Council on Foreign Relations; Global Business Network; Human Rights Watch Board, exec. committee; Pacific Council; PEN; National Committee on US-China Relations; World Affairs Council of San Francisco. *Publications:* The China Reader (with Frederick Crews), 1970; Modern China: The Story of a Revolution, 1972; The Town That Fought to Save Itself, 1976; In the People's Republic, 1976; Brown, 1978; Watch Out for the Foreign Guests: China Encounters the West, 1981; Modern Meat: Antibiotics, Hormones and the Pharmaceutical Farm, 1983; To Get Rich is Glorious: China in the 1980s, 1984; Discos and Democracy: China in the Throes of Reform, 1988; Mandate of Heaven: A New Generation of Entrepreneurs, Dissidents, Technocrats, and Bohemiams Grasp for Power in China, 1994; The China Reader: The Reform Years (ed. with David Shambaugh), 1999; Virtual Tibet: The West's Fascination with the Roof of the World, 1999. Contributions: numerous books, reviews, and journals. *Honours:* Alicia Patterson Foundation Journalism Fellowship, 1981; MacDowell Colony Fellowships, 1983, 1986; Guggenheim Fellowship, 1989–90; Emmy Award, 1992; Senior Fellow, Freedom Forum Media Studies Center, Columbia University, 1995; George Foster Peabody Award, 1997. *Literary Agent:* Steven Barclay Agency, 12 Western Avenue, Petaluma, CA 94952, USA. *Telephone:* (707) 773-0654. *Fax:* (707) 778-1868. *Website:* www.barclayagency.com. *Address:* c/o Graduate School of Journalism, University of California at Berkeley, Berkeley, CA 94720, USA.

SCHELLING, Andrew, BA; American poet, writer, translator and ecology activist; *Professor, Naropa University*; b. 14 Jan. 1953, Washington, DC; m. Kristina Loften 1980 (divorced 1993); one d. *Education:* Univ. of California at Santa Cruz. *Career:* Asst Prof., Naropa Univ., Boulder, CO, then Assoc. Prof., Prof. 2006–. *Publications:* Claw Moraine (poems) 1987, Dropping the Bow: Poems from Ancient India (trans.) 1991, Ktaadn's Lamp (poems) 1991, For Love of the Dark One: Songs of Mirabai (trans.) 1993, Moon is a Piece of Tea (poems) 1993, The India Book: Essays and Translations from Indian Asia 1993, Twilight Speech: Essays on Sanskrit and Buddhist Poetics 1993, Two Immortals (essays) 1994, Disembodied Poetics: Annals of the Jack Kerouac School (co-ed.) 1994, Old Growth: Selected Poems and Notebooks, 1986–1994 1995, Songs of the Sons and Daughters of Buddha (co-trans.) 1996, The Road to Ocosingo 1998, The Cane Groves of Narmada River: Erotic Poems from Old India (trans.) 1998, Tea Shack Interior: New and Selected Poetry 2002, Wild Form, Savage Grammar (essays) 2003, Erotic Love Poems from India (trans.) 2004, Two Elk: A High Country Notebook 2005, The Wisdom Anthology of North American Buddhist Poetry (ed.) 2005; contribs to numerous anthologies and periodicals. *Honours:* Acad. of American Poets Landon Prize in Translation 1992, Witter Bynner Foundation for Poetry translation grants 1996, 2001. *Address:* 2529 Sixth Street, Boulder, CO 80304, USA (home). *Telephone:* (303) 546-3508 (office). *E-mail:* schell@ecentral.com (home).

SCHERER, Peter Julian; New Zealand journalist; b. 15 Aug. 1937, Stratford; s. of Arnold F. Scherer and Constance M. White; m. Gaelyn P. Morgan 1964; one s. one d. *Education:* Browns Bay School and Takapuna Grammar School. *Career:* joined New Zealand Herald 1955; mem. later Chief, Wellington Bureau 1960–71; Chair. Parl. Press Gallery 1965; leader-writer, Duty Ed., Business News Ed. 1973–76, Editorial Man. 1977–83, Asst Ed. 1977–85; Ed. New Zealand Herald 1985–96; Dir Community Newspapers Ltd 1972–73, Wilson & Horton Group 1989–96, NZ Press Asscn 1991–96; Chair. NZ Associated Press 1985–90, NZ section, Commonwealth Press Union (CPU) 1989–94; Chair. Planning Cttee, North Health Medical Workforce 1996–97; Councillor, CPU, London 1989–94; mem. NZ Press Council 1988–97, Communications and Media Law Asscn 1990–97; mem. Communications Advisory Council NZ Comm. for UNESCO 1989–94; mem. Bd of Control, Newspaper Publishers Asscn of NZ 1991–96; mem. NZ Nat. Cttee for Security Co-operation in Asia-Pacific 1994–96, NZ Div., Inst. of Dirs 1989–96; other professional appointments; CPU Fellowship 1963. *Honours:* Cowan Prize 1959. *Address:* Apartment C, 25 Ring Terrace, St Mary's Bay, Auckland 1001; 267 School Road, Tomarata, RD4 Wellsford 1242, New Zealand. *Telephone:* (9)

378-9184 (Auckland); (9) 431-5244 (Wellsford). *Fax:* (9) 431-5244 (Wellsford); (9) 378-9184 (Auckland). *E-mail:* gandpscherer@xtra.co.nz (home).

SCHERMBRUCKER, William (Bill) Gerald, BA, PGCE, MA, PhD; Canadian writer, editor and fmr educator; b. 23 July 1938, Eldoret, Kenya; m. 1st Janet I. Lewis 1959 (divorced); m. 2nd Joanne C. Oben 1972 (divorced); m. 3rd Sharon F. Sawatsky 1984; three s. one d. *Education:* Univ. of Cape Town, Univ. of London, Univ. of British Columbia. *Career:* part-time Lecturer, Univ. of East Africa 1963–64; Instructor in English 1968–2000, Instructor Emeritus 2000–, Capilano Coll., North Vancouver; Lecturer, Genessee Community Coll. 1972–73; Ed., The Capilano Review 1977–82; mem. Writers' Union of Canada (nat. council 1999–2003). *Publications:* The Aims and Strategies of Good Writing 1976, Readings for Canadian Writing Students (ed.) 1976, revised edn as The Capilano Reader 1984, Chameleon, and Other Stories 1983, Mimosa 1988, Motortherapy and Other Stories 1993; contrib. to periodicals. *Honours:* several grants, Second Prize, CBC Literary Competition 1980, Ethel Wilson Prize 1988. *Address:* 362 East Point Road, PO Box 53, Saturna BC V0N 2Y0, Canada. *E-mail:* bscherm@capcollege.bc.ca.

SCHEVILL, James Erwin, BS; American academic, poet and playwright; *Professor Emeritus of English, Brown University;* b. 10 June 1920, Berkeley, Calif.; s. of Rudolph Schevill and Margaret Erwin Schevill; m. 1st Helen Shaner 1942; two d.; m. 2nd Margot Blum 1966. *Education:* Harvard and Brown Univs. *Career:* with US Army 1942–46, rank of Capt.; teacher, Calif. Coll. of Arts and Crafts 1951–58, Pres. of Faculty Ass. 1956; San Francisco State Univ. 1959–68, Prof. of English 1968; Prof. of English, Brown Univ. 1969–85, Prof. Emer. 1985–; Pres. Rhode Island Playwrights' Theatre 1984; Co-Dir, Dir Creative Writing Program, Brown Univ. 1972–75; Dir The Poetry Centre, San Francisco State Univ. 1961–68; numerous readings 1960–; adaptor and translator (with A. Hall) of Bertolt Brecht's Galileo 1983; mem. Bd Trinity Square Repertory Co., Providence, Rhode Island 1975–82. *Plays:* High Sinners, Low Angels 1953, The Bloody Tenet 1957, Voices of Mass and Capital A 1962, The Black President and Other Plays 1965, Lovecraft's Follies 1969, Cathedral of Ice 1975, Wastepaper Theatre Anthology (co-ed) 1978, Collected Short Plays 1986, Oppenheimer's Chair 1985, Time of the Hand and the Eye 1986, Shadows of Memory 1989, Mother O or the Last American Mother 1990, The Garden on F Street (with Mary Gail) 1992, The Phantom of Life: A Melville Play 1993, 5 Plays 5 (collection of plays) 1993, Myth of the Docile Woman 1997, To Die Well 1999, Emperor Norton of the USA (opera libretto) 1999, With the Composer, Jerome Rosen. *Publications:* poetry: Tensions 1947, The American Fantasies 1951, The Right To Greet 1955, Selected Poems 1945–59 1959, Private Dooms and Public Destinations: Poems 1945–62 1962, The Stalingrad Elegies 1964, Release 1968, Violence and Glory: Poems 1962–68 1969, The Buddhist Car and Other Characters 1973, Pursuing Elegy 1974, The Mayan Poems 1978, Fire of Eyes: A Guatemalan Sequence 1979, The American Fantasies: Collected Poems 1945–81 1983, Performance Poems 1984, The Invisible Volcano 1985, Collected Poems, Vol. II, 1945–1986, Ambiguous Dancers of Fame 1987, Winter Channels 1994, The Complete American Fantasies 1996, New and Selected Poems 2000. *Other publications:* Sherwood Anderson: His Life and Work (biog.) 1951, Six Historians by Ferdinand Schevill (ed.) 1956, The Roaring Market and the Silent Tomb (biog.) 1956, The Cid (trans.) 1961, Breakout: In Search of New Theatrical Environments 1973, The Arena of Ants (novel) 1976, Bern Porter (A Personal Biography) 1993. *Honours:* Hon. MA (Browns) 1970; Hon. LHD (Rhode Island Coll.) 1986; numerous awards including Ford Foundation Grant in Theatre to work with Joan Littlewood's Theatre Workshop in London 1960–61, William Carlos Williams Award for The Stalingrad Elegies 1965, Guggenheim Fellowship in Poetry 1981, McKnight Fellowship in Playwriting 1984, Literary Award for Plays, American Acad. of Arts and Letters, New York 1991. *Address:* 1309 Oxford Street, Berkeley, CA 94709, USA (home). *Telephone:* (510) 845-2802 (home). *E-mail:* mschevill@aol.com (home).

SCHICKLER, David, MFA; American writer. *Education:* Columbia Univ. *Publications:* fiction: Kissing in Manhattan (novel) 2001, The Smoker (short story for The New Yorker) 2003, Sweet and Vicious (novel) 2004; contrib. to Tin House, Zoetrope. *Address:* c/o Dial Press, Random House Inc, 1745 Broadway, New York, NY 10019, USA. *Website:* www.randomhouse.com.

SCHIFF, James Andrew, AB, MA, PhD; American academic and writer; *Associate Professor, University of Cincinnati;* b. 6 Dec. 1958, Cincinnati, OH; m. 24 June 1989; three s. *Education:* Duke Univ., New York Univ. *Career:* Visiting Instructor, Univ. of Cincinnati 1989–96, Adjunct Asst Prof. 1997–2000, Assoc. Prof. 2000–; mem. NBCC, MLA. *Publications:* Updike's Version: Rewriting The Scarlet Letter 1992, Understanding Reynolds Price 1996, John Updike Revisited 1998, Critical Essays on Reynolds Price 1998, Updike in Cincinnat 2007; contrib. to Southern Review, American Literature, South Atlantic Review, Studies in American Fiction, Critique, Boulevard, Missouri Review. *Address:* 2 Forest Hill Drive, Cincinnati, OH 45208, USA (home). *Telephone:* (513) 556-0930 (office); (513) 871-8219 (home). *Fax:* (513) 556-5960 (office). *E-mail:* james.schiff@uc.edu (office).

SCHIFFRIN, André, MA; American editor and publisher; *Director and Editor-in-Chief, The New Press;* b. 12 June 1935, Paris, France; s. of Jacques Schiffrin and Simone Heymann; m. Maria Elena de la Iglesia 1961; two d. *Education:* Yale Univ. and Univ. of Cambridge. *Career:* with New American Library 1959–63; with Pantheon Books, New York 1962–90, Ed., Ed.-in-Chief, Man. Dir 1969–90; Publr Schocken Books (subsidiary of Pantheon Books Inc.) 1987–90; Pres. Fund for Ind. Publishing 1990–; Dir, Ed.-in-Chief The New

Press, New York 1990–; Visiting Fellow, Davenport Coll. 1977–79; Visiting Lecturer, Yale Univ. 1977, 1979; mem. Council Smithsonian Inst.; mem. Bd of Dirs New York Council for Humanities; mem. Special Cttee American Centre, Paris 1994–; mem. Visting Cttee of Grad. Faculty The New York School 1995–; other professional appts. and affiliations. *Publications include:* L'Edition sans Editeurs 1999, The Business of Books 2000; contribs to professional journals. *Honours:* Hon. Fellow, Trumbull Coll. Yale Univ.; Grinzane Cavour Prize, Italy 2003. *Address:* The New Press, 38 Greene Street, 4th Floor, New York, NY 10013 (office); 250 West 94th Street, New York, NY 10025, USA (home). *Telephone:* (212) 629-8802. *Website:* www.thenewpress.com.

SCHIFRES, Michel Maurice Réné; French journalist; *Vice-President, the Editorial Committee, Le Figaro;* b. 1 May 1946, Orléans; s. of Jacques Schifres and Paulette Mauduit; m. Josiane Gasnier (divorced); two c. *Education:* Lycée du Mans, Lycée de Caen, Faculté des Lettres de Caen, Centre de Formation des Journalistes. *Career:* journalist with Combat 1970–72, with Monde 1972–74; Head of Political Affairs Quotidien de Paris 1974–76; Asst Head of Political Affairs France-Soir 1976; Head of Political Affairs Journal du Dimanche 1977, Editorial Dir 1985–89; mem. Comm. on quality of radio and TV broadcasts 1977–79; Editorial Dir France-Soir 1989–92, Asst Dir-Gen. 1992; Asst Editorial Dir Figaro 1992–98, Man. Ed. 1998–2000, Vice-Pres. Editorial Cttee 2000–; mem. Editorial Cttee La Revue de l'Intelligent 2003–. *Television:* L'Elysée 1988, Ville de Chiens 1989, Un Siecle d'Ecrivain: Jules Romains 1998. *Publications include:* La CFDT des militants 1972, D'une France à l'autre 1974, L'enaklatura 1987, L'Elysée de Mitterrand 1987, La désertion des énarques 1999. *Honours:* Chevalier, ordre nat. du Mérite. *Address:* Le Figaro, 37 rue du Louvre, 75002 Paris (office); 150 avenue Emile Zola, 75015 Paris, France (home). *Telephone:* 1-42-21-29-73 (office); 1-40-58-16-64 (home); 6-07-59-40-91. *Fax:* 1-42-21-63-82 (office). *E-mail:* mschifres@lefigaro.fr (office); mschifres@noos.fr (home).

SCHLAGMAN, Richard Edward, FRSA; British publisher; *Chairman and Publisher, Phaidon Press Ltd;* b. 11 Nov. 1953, London; s. of Jack Schlagman and the late Shirley Schlagman (née Goldston). *Education:* Univ. Coll. School, Hampstead, Brunel Univ. *Career:* Co-Founder, Jt Chair., Man. Dir Interstate Electronics Ltd 1973–86; purchased Bush from Rank Org., renamed IEL Bush Radio Ltd 1981, floated on London Stock Exchange 1984, sold as Bush Radio PLC 1986; acquired Phaidon Press Ltd 1990, Chair. and Publr 1990–; mem. Exec. Cttee Patrons of New Art, Tate Gallery 1994–97, Royal Opera House Trust, Glyndebourne Festival Soc., Designers and Arts Dirs Asscn of UK; Patron Bayreuth, Salzburger Festspiele; Pres. Judd Foundation, MARFA, Texas 1999–2001. *Address:* Phaidon Press Ltd, Regent's Wharf, All Saints Street, London, N1 9PA, England (office). *Telephone:* (20) 7843-1100 (office). *Fax:* (20) 7843-1212 (office). *E-mail:* richard@phaidon.com (office). *Website:* www.phaidon.com (office).

SCHLINK, Bernhard, PhD, JD; German judge, academic and writer; *Professor of Public Law and Legal Philosophy, Humboldt-Universität zu Berlin;* b. 1944, Bethel, nr Bielefeld; s. of the late Prof. Edmund Schlink; m. Hadwig Arnold (divorced 1974); one s. *Education:* Free Univ., West Berlin, Heidelberg, Darmstadt and Bielefeld Univs. *Career:* Prof. of Constitutional and Admin. Law Bonn Univ. 1981–91; Judge Constitutional Law Court of North Rhein-Westphalia, Munster 1987–; Prof. Wolfgang Goethe Univ., Frankfurt 1991–92; Prof. of Public Law and Legal Philosophy Humboldt Univ., Berlin 1992–; fmr judge of Constitutional Court, Bonn; Visiting Prof. of Law Benjamin Cardozo School of Law, Yeshiva Univ., New York 1994–; qualified as masseur in Calif.; began writing crime fiction in 1980s. *Publications:* fiction: Selbs Justiz (with Walter Popp, trans. as Self's Punishment) 1987, Die Gordische Schleife 1988, Selbs Betrug (trans. as Self's Betrayal) 1994, Der Vorleser (trans. as The Reader) 1995, Selbs Mord 2001, Flights of Love (short stories; trans. as Liebesfluchten) 2001, Die Heimkehr 2006; non-fiction: Weimar: A Jurisprudence of Crisis (co-author), several books on constitutional law, fundamental rights and the issue of separation of powers. *Address:* Humboldt-Universität zu Berlin, Lehrstuhl für Öffentliches Recht und Rechtsphilosophie, Juristische Fakultät, Unter den Linden 6, 10099 Berlin, Germany (office). *Telephone:* (30) 20933472 (office). *Fax:* (30) 20933452 (office). *E-mail:* schlink@rewi.hu-berlin.de (office). *Website:* www.rewi.hu-berlin.de/jura/ls/slk/ (office).

SCHLOSSER, Eric; American journalist and writer; b. 1959, Manhattan, NY; m. Shauna; two c. *Education:* Princeton Univ. and Oriel Coll., Oxford. *Career:* fmr scriptwriter; correspondent Atlantic Monthly. *Play:* Americans 1985. *Publications:* Fast Food Nation 2001, Reefer Madness and Other Tales from the American Underworld (Nat. Magazine Award) 2003, Cogs in the Great Machine (collection of articles) 2005, Chew on This 2006, Fast Food Nation 2007; contrib. to numerous magazines. *Address:* c/o Penguin Books Ltd, 80 Strand, London, WC2R 0RL, England.

SCHMIDMAN, Jo Ann, BFA; American theatre director and playwright; b. 18 April 1948, Omaha, NE. *Education:* Boston Univ. *Career:* Producing Artistic Dir, Omaha Magic Theatre, 1968–; Team Mem., Artist-in-Schools, Nebraska Arts Council, 1994. *Plays:* various unpublished but produced plays 1978–93. *Publications:* plays: This Sleep Among Women, 1974; Running Gag, 1980; Astro Bride, 1985; Velveeta Meltdown, 1985; Right Brain (ed. with M. Terry and S. Kimberlain), 1992; Body Leaks (with M. Terry and S. Kimberlain), 1995.

SCHMIDT, Helmut; German politician, economist and publisher; *Co-Publisher, Die Zeit;* b. 23 Dec. 1918, Hamburg; s. of Gustav Schmidt and

Ludovica Schmidt; m. Hannelore Glaser 1942; one d. *Education:* Licht-warkschule and Univ. Hamburg. *Career:* Man. Transport Admin. of State of Hamburg 1949–53; mem. Social Democrat Party 1946–; mem. Bundestag 1953–61, 1965–87; Chair. Social Democrat (SPD) Parl. Party in Bundestag 1967–69; Vice-Chair. SPD 1968–84; Senator (Minister) for Domestic Affairs in Hamburg 1961–65; Minister of Defence 1969–72, for Econ. and Finance July–Dec. 1972, of Finance 1972–74; Fed. Chancellor 1974–82; Co-Publr Die Zeit 1983–. *Publications:* Defence or Retaliation 1962, Beiträge 1967, Strategie des Gleichgewichts (trans. as Balance of Power) 1969, Kontinuität und Konzentration 1976, Als Christ in der politischen Entscheidung 1976, Der Kurs heisst Frieden 1979, Pflicht zur Menschlichkeit 1981, Kunst im Kanzleramt 1982, Freiheit verantworten 1983, Die Weltwirtschaft ist unser Schicksal 1983, Eine Strategie für den Westen (trans. as A Grand Strategy for the West) (Adolphe Bentinck Prize) 1986, Vom deutschen Stolz: Bekenntnisse zur Erfahrung von Kunst 1986, Menschen und Mächte (trans. as Men and Powers) 1987, Die Deutschen und ihre Nachbarn 1990, Mit Augenmass und Weitblick 1990, Einfügen in die Gemeinschaft der Völker 1990, Kindheit und Jugend unter Hitler 1992, Ein Manifest – Weil das Land sich ändern muss (co-author) 1992, Handeln für Deutschland 1993, Jahr der Entscheidung 1994, Was wird aus Deutschland? 1994, Weggefährten 1996, Jahrhundertwende 1998, Allgemeine Erklärung der Menschenpflichten 1998, Globalisierung 1998, Auf der Suche nach einer öffentlichen Moral 1998, Die Selbstbehaup-tung Europas 2000, Hand aufs Herz 2002, Die Mächte der Zukunft 2005. *Honours:* Hon. DCL (Oxford) 1979; Dr hc (Newberry Coll.) 1973, (Johns Hopkins) 1976, (Cambridge) 1976, (Harvard) 1979, (Sorbonne) 1981, (Lou-vain) 1984, (Georgetown) 1986, (Bergamo) 1989, (Tokyo) 1991, (Haifa) 2000, (Potsdam) 2000 and others; European Prize for Statesmanship (FUS Foundation) 1979, Nahum Goldmann Silver Medal 1980, Athinai Prize 1986. *Address:* Die Zeit, Speersort 1, Pressehaus, 20095 Hamburg (office); Bundeskanzler a.D., Deutscher Bundestag, Platz der Republik 1, 11011 Berlin, Germany. *Telephone:* (40) 32800 (office); (30) 22771580. *Fax:* (40) 327111 (office); (30) 22770571. *Website:* www.zeit.de.

SCHMIDT-BLEIBTREU, Ellen; German writer; b. 11 June 1929, Heidel-berg; d. of Hans and Ellen (née Nass) Kesseler; m. Bruno Schmidt-Bleibtreu 1956; one d. one s. *Education:* Univ. of Mainz-Germersheim. *Career:* European Rep. for Arts, Letters and Music, Conseil Int. des Femmes. *Publications:* Jahre m FJ 1950, Kraniche (poems) 1970, Fragmente (poems) 1973, Anthologie de la poésie féminine mondiale (co-ed.) 1973, Ruhestörung (short stories) 1975, Unter dem Windsegel (poems) 1978, Im Schatten der Genius 1981, Kinder aus 14 Ländern (short stories) 1982, Zeitzeichen I (poems) 1983, Deutsche Komponistinnen des 20 Jahrhunderts 1984, Die Schillers, Schillers Lebem (novel) 1986, Klimawechsel (poems) 1989, Begegnung über Grenzen hinweg (short stories) 1993, Zeitzeichen II (poems) 1999, Die Kuhlmanns im Wandel der Zeiten (novel, two vols) 2000; contrib. to newspapers and periodicals. *Honours:* Dr hc (Istituto Europeo di Cultura) 1989; Urban Prize 1976, Literary Union Hon. Prize 1977, Accad. Italia World Culture Prize 1984. *Address:* Pregelstrasse 5, 53127 Bonn, Germany.

SCHMIDT-DECKER, Petra; German songwriter, record producer and writer; b. Berlin; d. of Felix-Peter Schmidt-Decker and Ingeborg Schmidt-Decker (née Lohse). *Education:* acting classes. *Career:* actress on stage, TV and in films for 13 years; songwriter, then Producer of children's records; produced 150 records, including 30 records for Disney and 25 recorded biographies of composers from Vivaldi to Ravel (with Karlheinz Böhm) 1976–92; writer of TV and theatre scripts; leading companion of START Wort-Ton-Bild Verlags GmbH Hamburg, Germany; has worked on Jungle Book and Sesame Street productions. *Achievements include:* one Double Platinum CD, six Platinum CDs, one Triple Gold CD, eighteen Gold CDs. *Publications:* novels: Die jungen Bosse, Unternehmer Portraits 1984, Das große Buch des guten Benehmens 1985, Die Seherin 1996, Der Schildkröteninstinkt, Motivationsbuch 2003; plays: In Between (TV), Casanova bevorzugt (theatre) 1998; short story: Der Verlorene Blitz 2005. *Address:* Papenhuder Str. 42, 22087 Hamburg-Uhlenhorst, Germany. *Telephone:* (40) 2202203. *Fax:* (40) 2202227.

SCHMIDT-NIELSEN, Knut, DPhil; American physiologist and academic; *James B. Duke Professor Emeritus of Physiology, Duke University*; b. 24 Sept. 1915, Norway; s. of Sigval and Signe Torborg (Sturzen-Becker) Schmidt-Nielsen. *Education:* Oslo and Copenhagen Univs. *Career:* Research Fellow Carlsberg Labs., Copenhagen 1941–44; Research Fellow, Univ. of Copenhagen 1944–46; Research Assoc. Swarthmore Coll. Dept of Zoology 1946–48; Research Assoc. Stanford Univ. Dept of Physiology 1948–49; Docent Univ. of Oslo 1947–49; Asst Prof. Univ. of Cincinnati Coll. of Medicine 1949–52; Prof. of Physiology, Dept of Zoology, Duke Univ. 1952–, James B. Duke Prof. of Physiology 1963–now Prof. Emer.; Guggenheim Fellow, Algeria 1953–54; Brody Memorial Lecturer Univ. of Mo. 1962; Harvey Soc. Lecturer 1962 (Hon. mem. 1962); Regents' Lecturer Univ. of Calif. (Davis) 1963; Hans Gadow Lecturer Cambridge Univ. 1971; Visiting Agassiz Prof. Harvard Univ. 1972; Wellcome Prof. in Basic Medical Sciences, Univ. of S.D. 1988; mem. numerous scientific Cttees., including Advisory Bd to the Physiological Research Lab., Scripps Inst. of Oceanography 1963–69, Chair. 1968–69; U.S. Nat. Cttee for Int. Union of Physiological Sciences 1966–78, Vice-Chair. 1969–78; Biomedi-cal Engineering Advisory Cttee, Duke Univ. 1968; Animal Resources Advisory Cttee, Nat. Inst. of Health 1968; mem. Organizing Cttee, First Int. Conf. Comparative Physiology 1972, Pres. 1972–80; mem. Advisory Bd, Bio-Medical Sciences, Inc. 1973–74; Chair. Interunion Comm. on Comparative Physiology

1976–80; Pres. Int. Union of Physiological Sciences 1980–86; mem. Editorial Bd several scientific journals; mem. NAS, Royal Norwegian Soc. of Arts and Science 1973, Royal Danish Acad. 1975; Foreign mem. Royal Soc., London 1986; Foreign Assoc. Acad. des Sciences (France) 1968. *Publications:* Animal Physiology 1960 (trans. in several languages), Desert Animals, Physiological Problems of Heat and Water 1964, How Animals Work 1972, Animal Physiology, Adaptation and Environment 1975 (5th edn 1997), Scaling: Why is Animal Size so Important? 1984, The Camel's Nose: Memoirs of a Curious Scientist 1998; numerous articles. *Honours:* Hon. mem. Deutsche Ornitolo-gen–Gesellschaft 1988, American Soc. of Zoologists 1990; Fellow, American Acad. of Arts and Sciences, NY Acad. of Science, AAAS; Hon. Fellow Zoological Soc. of London 1990; Hon. DMed (Univ. of Lund, Sweden) 1986; Hon. DPhil (Univ. of Trondheim, Norway) 1993; Int. Prize for Biology, Japan Soc. for Promotion of Science 1992. *Address:* Department of Biology, Duke University, Box 90338, Durham, NC 27708-0338, USA (office). *Telephone:* (919) 684-2687 (office). *Fax:* (919) 660-7293 (office). *E-mail:* knut@duke.edu (office). *Website:* fds.duke.edu/db/aas/Biology/faculty/knut (office).

SCHMITTER, Elke; German writer and critic; b. 1961, Krefeld. *Education:* Univ. of Munich. *Career:* Ed. for S. Fischer, Frankfurt/Main; Ed.-in-Chief Die Tageszeitüng; freelance critic for various papers; critic Der Spiegel, Hamburg 2001–. *Publications:* Und grüsse mich nicht ünter den Linden 1998, Frau Sartoris (trans. as Mrs Sartoris) 2000, Leichte Verfehlungen 2002, Kein Spaniel 2005, Veras Tochter 2006;. *Honours:* Niederrheinischer literaturpreis 2000. *Address:* c/o Berlin Verlag/Bloomsbury Greifswalder Sh. 207, 10405, Berlin, Germany (office).

SCHMITZ, Dennis Mathew, BA, MA; American academic and poet; b. 11 Aug. 1937, Dubuque, IA; m. Loretta D'Agostino 1960, two s. three d. *Education:* Loras College, Dubuque, IA, University of Chicago. *Career:* Instructor, Illinois Institute of Technology, Chicago, 1961–62, University of Wisconsin at Milwaukee, 1962–66; Asst Prof., 1966–69, Poet-in-Residence, 1966–, Assoc. Prof., 1969–74, Prof. of English, 1974–, California State University at Sacramento. *Publications:* We Weep for Our Strangeness, 1969; Double Exposures, 1971; Goodwill, Inc, 1976; String, 1980; Singing, 1985; Eden, 1989; About Night: Selected and New Poems, 1993. *Honours:* New York Poetry Center Discovery Award, 1968; National Endowment for the Arts Fellowships, 1976, 1985, 1992; Guggenheim Fellowship, 1978; di Castagnola Award, 1986; Shelley Memorial Award, 1988.

SCHMOOKLER, Andrew Bard, BA, PhD; American teacher, writer and talk radio host; b. 19 April 1946, Long Branch, NJ; m. 1986; two s. one d. *Education:* Harvard Coll., Graduate Theological Union, Univ. of California, Univ. of Chicago, Yale Univ. *Career:* Founder, author, www.NoneSoBlind.org. *Publications:* The Parable of the Tribes: The Problem of Power in Social Evolution, 1984; Out of Weakness: Healing the Wounds that Drive us to War, 1988; Sowing and Reapings: The Cycling of Good and Evil in the Human System, 1989; The Illusion of Choice: How the Market Economy Shapes Our Destiny, 1992; Fools Gold: The Fate of Values in a World of Goods, 1993; Living Posthumously: Confronting the Loss of Vital Powers, 1997; Debating the Good Society: A Quest to Bridge America's Moral Divide, 1999. *Honours:* Erik H. Erikson Prize, Int. Soc. for Political Psychology 1984. *Address:* 1855 Tramway Terrace Loop, NE, Albuquerque, NM 87122, USA. *Telephone:* (505) 856-1221. *E-mail:* andythebard@comcast.net. *Website:* www.NoneSoBlind .org.

SCHNACKENBERG, Gjertrud, BA; American poet and writer; b. 27 Aug. 1953, Tacoma, WA; m. Robert Nozick 1987 (died 2002). *Education:* Mount Holyoke Coll. *Career:* Fellow in Poetry, The Radcliffe Inst. 1979–80; Christensen Fellow, Saint Catherine's Coll., Oxford 1997; Visiting Scholar, Getty Research Inst., J. Paul Getty Museum 2000; Fellow, American Acad. of Arts and Sciences 1996; Guggenheim Fellowship 1987–88. *Publications:* Portraits and Elegies 1982, The Lamplit Answer 1985, A Gilded Lapse of Time 1992, The Throne of Labdacus 2000, Supernatural Love: Poems 1976–1992 2000; contrib. to books and journals. *Honours:* Dr hc (Mount Holyoke Coll.) 1985;Daimler Chrysler Berlin Prize Fellow, American Acad., Berlin 2004; Glascock Award for Poetry 1973, 1974, Acad. of American Poets Lavan Younger Poets Award 1983, American Acad. and Inst. of Arts and Letters Rome Prize 1983–84, Amy Lowell Traveling Prize 1984–85, Nat. Endowment for the Arts grant 1986–87, American Acad. of Arts and Letters Award in Literature 1998, Los Angeles Times Book Prize in Poetry 2001. *Literary Agent:* c/o Farrar, Straus & Giroux Inc., 19 Union Square West, New York, NY 10003, USA.

SCHNAPPER, Dominique, DSc; French writer and sociologist; *Director of Studies, Ecole des Hautes Etudes en Sciences Sociales, Paris*; b. 9 Nov. 1934, Paris; d. of Raymond Aron and Suzanne Gauchon; m. Antoine Schnapper 1958; three c. *Education:* Sorbonne, Paris. *Career:* Prof. Dir of Studies Ecole des Hautes Etudes en Sciences Sociales (Paris) 1980–; mem. Conseil Constitutionnel (French Supreme Court) 2001–10. *Publications:* La Commu-nauté des citoyens 1994, La Rélation a l'autre 1998, Qu'est ce que la citoyénneté? 2000, La Démocratie providentielle 2002, Diasporas et nations 2006. *Honours:* Prix de l'Assemblée Nat. 1994, Balzan Prize for Sociology 2002. *Address:* Maison des Sciences de l'Homme, 54 blvd Raspail, 75007 Paris; Conseil Constitutionnel, 2 rue de Montpensier, 75001 Paris, France (office). *Telephone:* (1) 40-15-30-00 (office). *E-mail:* schnapp@ehess.fr (office).

SCHNECK, Peter; Austrian editor. *Career:* Ed. Philologie im Netz; Vice Pres., Int. Bd on Books for Young People 1998–2002, Pres. 2002–; responsible for children's literature at the Austrian Federal Chancellery's division of literature; Pres., Hans Christian Andersen Awards Jury 1996, 1998; Chair., Austrian Children's Book Award jury. *Address:* Redaktion München, Amerika-Institut, Ludwig-Maximilians-Universität, Schellingstraße 3, 80799 München, Germany. *E-mail:* Peter.Schneck@lrz.uni-muenchen.de.

SCHOEMPERLEN, Diane Mavis, BA; Canadian writer; b. 9 July 1954, Thunder Bay Ont.; one s. *Education:* Lakehead Univ., Ont. *Career:* teacher Kingston School of Writing Queen's Univ. Ontario 1986–93 St Lawrence Coll. Kingston 1987–93 Univ. of Toronto Summer Writers' Workshop 1992; Ed. Coming Attractions, Oberon Press 1994–96. *Publications:* Double Exposures 1984, Frogs and Other Stories 1986, Hockey Night in Canada 1987, The Man of My Dreams 1990, Hockey Night in Canada and Other Stories 1991, In the Language of Love 1994, Forms of Devotion 1998, Our Lady of the Lost and Found 2001, Red Plaid Shirt 2002, Names of the Dead – An Elegy for the Victims of September 11 2004, Forms of Devotion 2006; contribs to anthologies. *Honours:* WGA Award for Short Fiction 1987 Silver Nat. Magazine Award 1989 Gov.-Gen.'s Award for English Fiction 1998,Lakehead Univ. Alumni Honour Award 1999. *Address:* 32 Dunlop Street, Kingston, Ont., K7L 1L2, Canada.

SCHOFIELD, Paul (see Tubb, Edwin Charles)

SCHOLEY, Arthur Edward; British children's writer, playwright, librettist and lyric writer; b. 17 June 1932, Sheffield, Yorks. *Publications:* The Song of Caedmon (with Donald Swann) 1971, Christmas Plays and Ideas for Worship 1973, The Discontented Dervishes 1977, Sallinka and the Golden Bird 1978, Twelve Tales for a Christmas Night 1978, Wacky and His Fuddlejig (with Donald Swann) 1978, Singalive (with Donald Swann) 1978, Herod and the Rooster (with Ronald Chamberlain) 1979, The Dickens Christmas Carol Show 1979, Baboushka (with Donald Swann) 1979, Candletree (with Donald Swann) 1981, Five Plays for Christmas 1981, Four Plays About People 1983, Martin the Cobbler 1983, The Hosanna Kids 1985, Make a Model Christmas Crib 1988, Who'll Be Brother Donkey? 1990, Brendan Ahoy! (with Donald Swann) 1994, The Journey of the Christmas Creatures (with Karen Bradley) 1998, Babaushka 2001, The Paragon Parrot 2002, The Discontented Dervishes 2002. *Address:* 10 Chiltern Court, Pages Hill, London, N10 1EN, England. *E-mail:* arthurscholey@onetel.com. *Website:* www.arthurscholey.co.uk.

SCHOM, Alan Morris, BA, PhD; American writer; b. 9 May 1937, Sterling, IL; m. Juliana Leslie Hill 1963 (divorced 1984); two d. *Education:* University of California at Berkeley, University of Durham. *Career:* Assoc., Dept of History, University of California at Riverside, 1968–69; Asst Prof. of Modern French and European History, Southern Connecticut State University, 1969–76. *Publications:* Lyautey in Morocco: Protectorate Administration, 1912–1925, 1970; Émile Zola: A Bourgeois Rebel, 1988; Trafalgar: Countdown to Battle, 1803–1805, 1989; One Hundred Days: Napoleon's Road to Waterloo, 1992; Napoleon Bonaparte, 1997. Contributions: scholarly journals. *Honours:* Fellow, Hoover Institution on War, Revolution, and Peace, 1982; Grants.

SCHÖNTHAN, Gaby von; German writer and actress; b. 12 Sept. 1926; m. 1st Paul Frischauer 1957 (died 1977); m. 2nd Henry C. Alter 1984. *Education:* Hochschule für Musik und Darstellende Kunst and Reinhardt Seminar (Vienna). *Career:* Actress Theater in der Josefstadt, Vienna, Staatstheater, Wiesbaden and Munich 1944–55. *Publications:* Die Geliebte des Königs 1963, So nah der Liebe 1963, Die Rosen von Malmaison 1966, Madame Casanova 1968, Die Löwin von San Marco 1972, Das Herrenhaus 1977, Zwei ungleiche Schwestern 1979, Wie viele Stunden hat die Nacht 1982, Aunnia 1986. *Address:* 17 Maplewood Ave, Dobbs Ferry, NY 10522, USA.

SCHRAG, Peter, BA; American journalist and editor; b. 24 July 1931, Karlsruhe, Germany. *Education:* Amherst Coll. and Univ. of Massachusetts. *Career:* reporter, El Paso Herald Post, Texas 1953–55; Asst Sec., Amherst Coll. 1956–66; Assoc. Education Ed. 1966–68, Exec. Ed. 1968–73, Saturday Review, New York; Ed., Change, New York 1969–70; Lecturer, Univ. of Massachusetts 1970–72, Univ. of California at Berkeley 1990–; Ed. editorial page, Sacramento Bee, CA 1978–; Contributing Ed., The American Prospect; mem. Nat. Conference of Editorial Writers; Guggenheim Fellowship 1971–72. *Publications:* Voices in the Classroom 1965, Village School Downtown 1967, Out of Place in America 1970, The Decline of the WASP (US edn as The Vanishing American) 1972, The End of the American Future 1973, Test of Loyalty 1974, The Myths of the Hyperative Child (with Diane Divorky) 1975, Mind Control 1978, Paradise Lost: California's Experience, America's Future 1998, Final Test: The Battle for Adequacy in America's Schools 2004; contrib. to newspapers and magazines. *Literary Agent:* Ellen Levine Literary Agency, 15 E 26th Street, Suite 1801, New York, NY 10010, USA. *Address:* c/o Sacramento Bee, 21st and Q Streets, Sacramento, CA 95816, USA.

SCHREINER, Samuel Agnew, Jr, AB; American author; b. 6 June 1921, Mt Lebanon, PA; m. Doris Moon 1945, two d. *Education:* Princeton University. *Publications:* Thine is the Glory, 1975; The Condensed World of the Reader's Digest, 1977; Pleasant Places, 1977; Angelica, 1978; The Possessors and the Possessed, 1980; The Van Alens, 1981; A Place Called Princeton, 1984; The Trials of Mrs Lincoln, 1987; Cycles, 1990; Mayday! Mayday!, 1990; Code of Conduct (with Everett Alvarez), 1992; Henry Clay Frick: The Gospel of Greed, 1995. Contributions: Reader's Digest; Woman's Day; McCalls; Redbook; Parade.

SCHROEDER, Andreas Peter, BA, MA; Canadian writer, poet and translator; *Rogers Communication Co-Chair, University of British Columbia;* b. 26 Nov. 1946, Hoheneggelsen, Germany; m. Sharon Elizabeth Brown; two d. *Education:* University of British Columbia. *Career:* literary critic and columnist, Vancouver Province newspaper 1968–72; co-founder and Ed.-in-Chief, Contemporary Literature in Trans. 1968–83; Lecturer in Creative Writing, Univ. of Victoria 1974–75, Simon Fraser Univ. 1989–90; Writer-in-Residence, Regina Public Library 1980–81, Univ. of Winnipeg 1983–84, Fraser Valley Coll. 1987; Lecturer in Creative Writing 1985–87, Prof., Maclean Hunter Chair in Creative Non-Fiction 1993, then Rogers Communication Co-Chair, Univ. of British Columbia; mem. Writers' Union of Canada, Alliance of Canadian Cinema, Television and Radio Artists, Federation of British Columbia Writers, PEN Club, Saskatchewan Writers' Guild. *Publications:* The Ozone Minotaur 1969, File of Uncertainties (poems) 1971, UNIverse 1971, The Late Man (short stories) 1972, Stories From Pacific and Arctic Canada (co-ed.) 1974, Shaking it Rough (memoir) 1976, Toccata in 'D' (novella) 1984, Dust-Ship Glory (novel) 1986, Word for Word: The Business of Writing in Alberta 1988, The Eleventh Commandment (trans., with Jack Thiessen) 1990, The Mennonites in Canada: A Photographic History 1990, Carved From Wood: Mission, B.C. 1891–1992 1992, Scams, Scandals and Skullduggery 1996, Cheats, Charlatans and Chicanery 1998, Fakes, Frauds and Flimflammery 1999, Scams! 2004, Thieves! 2005; contribs to numerous anthologies, newspapers and magazines. *Honours:* Woodward Memorial Prize for Prose 1969, Canada Council Grants 1969, 1971, 1975, 1979, 1986, 1991, Nat. Film Board of Canada Scriptwriting Prize 1971, Canadian Asscn of Journalists Award for Best Investigative Journalism 1990. *Address:* University of British Columbia Creative Writing Programme, Buchanan Room E462, 1866 Main Mall, Vancouver, BC V6T 1Z1, Canada (office). *Telephone:* (604) 822-6564 (office). *E-mail:* aps@interchange.ubc.ca (office); apschroeder@dccnet.com (home). *Website:* www.creativewriting.ubc.ca (office).

SCHUHL, Jean Jacques; French writer. *Publications:* Rose poussière 1972, Telex No. 1 1976, Ingrid Caven 2000. *Honours:* Goncourt Prize for Literature 2000. *Address:* c/o Editions Gallimard, 5 rue Sébastien Bottin, 75007 Paris, France (office).

SCHULBERG, Budd, LLD; American novelist and scriptwriter; b. 27 March 1914, New York, NY; s. of Benjamin P. Schulberg and Adeline Schulberg (née Jaffe); m. 1st Virginia Ray 1936 (divorced 1942); one d.; m. 2nd Victoria Anderson 1943 (divorced 1964); two s.; m. 3rd Geraldine Brooks 1964 (died 1977); m. 4th Betsy Langman 1979; one s. one d. *Education:* Deerfield Acad. and Dartmouth Coll. *Career:* short-story writer and novelist 1936–; screenwriter for Samuel Goldwyn, David O. Selznick and Walter Wanger, Hollywood, Calif. 1936–40; Lt in USN 1943–46, assigned to Office of Strategic Service; taught writing courses and conducted workshops at various insts in US; mem. Authors Guild, Dramatists Guild, American Civil Liberties Union, American Soc. Composers Authors and Publrs, Sphinx, Writers Guild of America East, Bd of Trustees, Humanitas Prize, Advisory Cttee on Black Participation, John F. Kennedy Center for the Performing Arts; Founder and Dir Watts Writers Workshop 1965–, Frederick Douglass Creative Arts Center, New York 1971–. *Publications:* novels: What Makes Sammy Run? 1941, The Harder They Fall 1947 (screen adaptation 1955), The Disenchanted 1950, Waterfront 1955, Sanctuary V (Prix littéraire du Festival du cinéma américain de Deauville 2005) 1969, Some Faces in the Crowd (short stories) 1953, From the Ashes: Voices of Watts (ed. and author of introduction) 1967, Loser and Still Champion: Muhammad Ali 1972, The Four Seasons of Success 1972, Swan Watch (with Geraldine Brooks) 1975, Everything That Moves 1980, Moving Pictures: Memories of a Hollywood Prince 1981, Writers in America 1983, Love, Action, Laughter and Other Sad Tales (short stories) 1990, Sparring with Hemingway: And Other Legends of the Fight Game 1995, Ringside 2006; plays, films: Winter Carnival (with F. Scott Fitzgerald) 1939, The Pharmacist's Mate 1951, On the Waterfront (Acad. Award and Screen Writers Guild Award for the screenplay) 1954, A Face in the Crowd (German Film Critics Award) 1957, Wind Across the Everglades 1958, The Disenchanted 1958, What Makes Sammy Run? (TV play 1959, stage 1964), Senor Discretion Himself (musical) 1985, A Table at Ciro's 1987, Joe Louis: For All Time (film documentary) 1988; stories and articles in numerous anthologies; contrib. to Newsday Syndicate, Esquire, Saturday Review, Life, Harper's, Playboy, Intellectual Digest, The New Republic, The New YorkerN New York Times Sunday Book Review. *Honours:* numerous awards for writings, numerous humanitarian awards. *Literary Agent:* c/o Miriam Altshuler Literary Agency, RR #1, Box 5, Old Post Road, Red Hook, NY 12571; c/o Mr Mickey Freiberg, 2221 Pelham, Los Angeles, CA 90046, USA. *Telephone:* (631) 288-0564. *Fax:* (631) 288-1495. *Address:* POB 707, Westhampton Beach, NY 11978, USA (home). *Telephone:* (631) 288-1452 (home). *E-mail:* bschulberg@optonline.net (office).

SCHULER, Robert Jordan, BA, MA, PhD; American academic and poet; *Professor of English, University of Wisconsin;* b. 25 June 1939, California; m. Carol Forbis 1963; two s. one d. *Education:* Stanford University, University of California, Berkeley, University of Minnesota. *Career:* Instructor in English, Menlo College, 1965–67; Instructor in Humanities, Shimer College, 1967–77; Prof. of English, University of Wisconsin-Stout, 1978–; mem. Land Use Commission, Town of Menomonie; Land Use Planner, Dunn Co., WI. *Publications:* Axle of the Oak, 1978; Seasonings, 1978; Where is Dancers' Hill?, 1979; Morning Raga, 1980; Red Cedar Scroll, 1981; Origins, 1981; Floating Out of Stone, 1982; Music for Monet, 1984; Grace: A Book of Days,

1995; Journeys Toward the Original Mind, 1995; The Red Cedar Suite, 1999; In Search of Green Dolphin Street, 2003, Dance into Heaven 2005. Contributions: anthologies and periodicals, including: Caliban; Northeast; Tar River Poetry; Longhouse; Dacotah Territory; Wisconsin Acad. Review; Wisconsin Review; North Stone Review; Wisconsin Poetry 1991 Transactions; Hummingbird; Abraxas; Lake Street Review; Inheriting the Earth; Mississippi Valley Review; Coal City Review; Gypsy; Imagining Home, 1995; Ekphrasis; Mid-America Poetry Review, The Blueline Anthology. *Honours:* Hormel Professorship 1995, Fellowship for Poetry, Wisconsin Arts Bd 1997, recipient of grants from Illinois Arts Council, Illinois Humanities Comm., Wisconsin Arts Bd, Wisconsin Humanities Council. *Address:* Department of English and Philosophy, 153-D Harvey Hall, University of Wisconsin-Stout, Menomonie, WI 54751 (office); E4549 479th Avenue, Menomonie, WI 54751, USA (home). *Telephone:* (715) 232-1454 (office); (715) 235-6525 (home). *E-mail:* schulerr@uwstout.edu (office). *Website:* faculty.uwstout.edu/schulerr/index.shtml (office).

SCHULLER, Gunther Alexander; American composer, conductor, music educator and record producer; b. 22 Nov. 1925, New York, NY; s. of Arthur E. Schuller and Elsie (Bernartz) Schuller; m. Marjorie Black 1948 (died 1992); two s. *Education:* St Thomas Choir School, New York, Manhattan School of Music. *Career:* Principal French horn, Cincinnati Symphony Orchestra 1943–45, Metropolitan Opera Orchestra 1945–59; teacher, Manhattan School of Music 1950–63, Yale Univ. 1964–67; Head Composition Dept, Tanglewood 1963–84; Music Dir First Int. Jazz Festival, Washington 1962; active as conductor since mid-1960s with maj. orchestras in Europe and USA; reconstructed and orchestrated Der Gelbe Klang by De Hartmann/Kandinsky; Pres. New England Conservatory of Music 1967–77; Pres. Nat. Music Council 1979–81; Artistic Co-Dir, then Artistic Dir Summer Activities, Boston Symphony Orchestra, Berkshire Music Center, Tanglewood 1969–84, Festival at Sandpoint 1985–98; founder and Pres. Margun Music Inc. 1975–2000, GM Records 1980; mem. American Acad. of Arts and Sciences, American Acad. of Arts and Letters. *Compositions include:* Horn Concerto No. 1 1945, Vertige d'Eros 1946, Concerto for cello and orchestra 1946, Jumpin' in the Future 1946, Quartet for Four Brasses 1947, Oboe Sonata 1947, Duo Concertante for cello and piano 1947, Symphonic Study (Meditation) 1948, Trio for Oboe, Horn, Viola 1948, Symphony for brass and percussion 1950, Fantasy for Unaccompanied Cello 1951, Recitative and Rondo for violin and piano 1953, Dramatic Overture 1951, Five Pieces for Five Horns 1952, Adagio for flute, string trio 1952, Music for Violin, Piano and Percussion 1957, Symbiosis for violin, piano, percussion 1957, String Quartet No. 1 1957, Contours 1958, Woodwind Quintet 1958, Spectra 1958, Concertino for jazz quartet and orchestra 1959, Seven Studies on Themes of Paul Klee 1959, Conversations 1960, Lines and Contrasts for 16 horns 1960, Abstraction for jazz ensemble 1960, Variants on a Theme of Thelonious Monk 1960, Music for Brass Quintet 1960, Contrasts for woodwind quintet and orchestra 1961, Variants (ballet with choreography by Balanchine) 1961, Double Quintet for woodwind and brass quintets 1961, Meditation for concert band 1961, Concerto for piano and orchestra 1962, Journey into Jazz 1962, Fantasy Quartet for four cellos 1963, Threnos for oboe and orchestra 1963, Composition in Three Parts 1963, Five Bagatelles for Orchestra 1964, Five Etudes for orchestra 1964, The Power Within Us 1964, Five Shakespearean Songs for baritone and orchestra 1964, String Quartet No. 2 1965, Symphony 1965, American Triptych (on paintings of Pollock, Davis and Calder) 1965, Sacred Cantata 1966, Gala Music concerto for orchestra 1966, The Visitation (opera) 1966, Movements for flute and strings, Six Renaissance Lyrics, Triplum I 1967, Study in Textures for concert band 1967, Diptych for brass quintet and orchestra 1967, Shapes and Designs 1968, Concerto for double bass and orchestra 1968, Consequents for orchestra 1969, Fisherman and his Wife (opera) 1970, Concerto da Camera No. 1 1971, Capriccio Stravagante 1972, Tre Invenzioni 1972, Three Nocturnes 1973, Five Moods for tuba quartet 1973, Four Soundscapes 1974, Triplum II 1975, Violin Concerto 1976, Concerto No. 2 for horn and orchestra 1976, Diptych for organ 1976, Concerto No. 2 for orchestra 1977, Concerto for contrabassoon and orchestra 1978, Deaï for three orchestras 1978, Sonata Serenata 1978, Octet 1979, Concerto for trumpet and orchestra 1979, Eine Kleine Posaunenmusik 1980, In Praise of Winds symphony for large wind orchestra 1981, Concerto No. 2 for piano and orchestra 1981, Symphony for organ 1981, Concerto Quaternio 1984, Concerto for alto saxophone 1983, Duologue for violin and piano 1983, On Light Wings piano quartet 1984, Piano Trio 1984, Concerto for viola and orchestra 1985, Concerto for bassoon and orchestra 1985, Farbenspiel Concerto No. 3 for orchestra 1985, String Quartet No. 3 1986, Chimeric Images 1988, Concerto for string quartet and orchestra 1988, Concerto for flute and orchestra 1988, Horn Sonata 1988, On Winged Flight: A Divertimento for Band 1989, Chamber Symphony 1989, Five Impromptus for English horn and string quartet 1989, Impromptus and Cadenzas for chamber sextet 1990, Song and Dance for violin and concert band 1990, Concerto for piano three hands 1990, Violin Concerto No. 2 1991, Brass Quintet No. 2 1993, Reminiscences and Reflections 1993, The Past is the Present for orchestra 1994, Sextet for left-hand piano and woodwind quintet 1994, Concerto for organ and orchestra 1994, Mondrian's Vision 1994, Lament for M 1994, Blue Dawn into White Heat concert band 1995, An Arc Ascending 1996, Ohio River Reflections 1998, A Bouquet for Collage 1988, Fantasia Impromptu for flute and harpsichord 2000, Quod Libet for violin, cello, oboe, horn and harp 2001, String Quartet No. 4 2002, Concerto da Camera No. 2 2002, String Trio 2003, Encounters for jazz orchestra and symphony orchestra 2003. *Publications:* Horn Technique 1962, Early Jazz: Its Roots and Musical Development, Vol. I 1968, Musings: The Musical Worlds of Gunther Schuller 1985, The Swing Era: The Development of Jazz 1930–45 1989, The Compleat Conductor 1997. *Honours:* Hon. DMus (Northeastern Univ.) 1967, (Colby Coll.) 1969, (Ill. Univ.) 1970, (Williams Coll.) 1975, (Rutgers Univ.) 1980, (Oberlin Coll.) 1989, (Fla State Univ.) 1991; Creative Arts Award, Brandeis Univ. 1960, Nat. Inst. Arts and Letters Award 1960, Guggenheim Grant 1962, 1963, ASCAP Deems Taylor Award 1970, Rogers and Hammerstein Award 1971, William Schuman Award, Columbia Univ. 1989, McArthur Foundation Fellowship 1991, McArthur'Genius' Award 1994; Gold Medal American Acad. of Arts and Letters 1996, Order of Merit, Germany 1997, Max Rudolf Award 1998, Pulitzer Prize in Music 1999. *Address:* 167 Dudley Road, Newton Center, MA 02459, USA. *Telephone:* (617) 332-6398. *Fax:* (617) 969-1079.

SCHULZ, Max Frederick, AB, MA, PhD; American art curator and writer; *Distinguished Professor Emeritus of English, University of Southern California*; b. 15 Sept. 1923, Cleveland, OH. *Education:* Univs of Chicago, Pittsburgh and Minnesota, Wayne State Univ. *Career:* Prof. of English, Univ. of Southern California at Los Angeles 1963–94, Chair. Dept of English 1968–80, Distinguished Prof. Emer. of English 1994–, Curator of Exhbns, Fisher Gallery 1993–; Fulbright Prof., Univ. of Graz, Austria 1965–66, Univ. of Vienna 1977–78; Resident Scholar, Rockefeller Foundation Study Center, Bellagio, Italy 1978, 1989; Assoc. Ed. Critique Magazine 1971–85; Sr Fellow, Nat. Endowment for the Humanities 1985–86. *Publications:* The Poetic Voices of Coleridge 1963, Radical Sophistication: Studies in Contemporary Jewish-American Novelists 1969, Bruce Jay Friedman 1973, Black Humor Fiction of the Sixties: A Pluralistic Definition of Man and his World 1973, Paradise Preserved: Recreations of Eden in 18th and 19th Century England 1985, The Muses of John Barth: Tradition and Metafiction from Lost in the Funhouse to the Tidewater Tales 1990, Edgar Ewing: The Classical Connection 1993, The Mythic Present of Chagoya, Valdez and Gronk 1995, Crossing Boundaries 1999, Family Pictures/Ecumenical Icons 2001, Human Conditions: Manfred Müller 2003, Albert Contreras: Luminous Scapes and Environments 2005, Contemporary Soliloquies on the Natural World 2005, The Bone and Bird Art of Joyce Cutler-Shaw and Sarah Perry 2007. *Address:* Fisher Gallery, University of Southern California, 126 Harris Hall, 823 Exposition Blvd, Los Angeles, CA 90089-292 (office); 2413 Palm Avenue, Manhattan Beach, CA 90266, USA (home). *Telephone:* (213) 740-4561 (office). *Fax:* (213) 740-7676 (office). *E-mail:* schulz@usc.edu (office). *Website:* www.usc.edu/fishergallery (office).

SCHULZE, Ingo; German writer and journalist; b. 15 Dec. 1962, Dresden; s. of Christa Schulze; m. Natalia; two d. *Education:* Univ. of Jena. *Career:* Dramatic Producer, Theatre of Altenburg 1988–90; founder weekly newspaper in Altenburg 1990–92, weekly newspaper in St Petersburg 1993; writer in Berlin 1993–. *Publications:* 33 Augenblicke des Glücks (Aspekte-Literatur Prize for best debut) 1995, Simple Storys: Ein Roman aus der ostdeutschen Provinz 1998, Von Nasen, Faxen und Ariadnefäden, Fax-Briefe (with Zeichnungen von Helmar Penndorf) 2000, Telling Tales (contrib. to charity anthology) 2004, Neue Leben (novel) 2005, Handy – 13 Geschichten in alter Manier 2007. *Honours:* Ernst Willner Prize 1995, Aspekte Literature Prize 1995, Berlin Literature Prize 1998, Johannes Bobrowski Medal 1998, Joseph Breitbach Prize 2001, Peter Weiss Prize 2006, Thuringia Literature Prize 2007. *Address:* Liselotte-Herrmann-Str. 33, 10407 Berlin, Germany. *Telephone:* (30) 6239662. *E-mail:* writer@ingoschulze.com. *Website:* www.ingoschulze.com.

SCHÜTZ, Helga; German writer; b. 2 Oct. 1937, Falkenhain/Goldberg; one s. one d. (deceased). *Education:* secondary school, Dresden, Arbeiter und Bauernfakultät (ABF) and Hochschule für Film und Fernsehen, Potsdam. *Career:* gardener, Dresden 1951–55; writer of novels, stories and screenplays 1964–. *Publications include:* Jette in Dresden 1977, Vom Glanz der Elbe 1995, Grenze züm Gestrigen Tag 2000, Dahliem im Sand: Mein Markischer Garten 2002, Kuietief im Paradies 2005. *Honours:* Heinrich Mann Preis, Akad. der Künste, Berlin, Theodor Fontane Preis, Potsdam, Stadtschreiber-Preis, Mainz 1991, Literaturpreis, Brandenburg 1992. *Address:* Jägersteig 4, 14482 Potsdam, Germany. *Telephone:* (33) 1708656.

SCHWAB, George D., PhD; American academic and editor; *President, National Committee on American Foreign Policy*; b. 1931, s. of Arkady Schwab and Klara Schwab (née Jacobson); m. Eleonora Storch 1965; three c. *Education:* Columbia Univ. and City Coll. of New York. *Career:* began teaching career at Columbia Univ., New York; joined Dept of History, City Univ. of New York 1960, now Prof. Emer., City Coll. and Grad. Center; Co-founder Nat. Cttee on American Foreign Policy, Pres. 1993–; Ed. American Foreign Policy Interests (journal); mem. Council on Foreign Relations, several cttees of Holocaust Museum, Washington, DC, Latvian Pres.'s Comm. of Int. Historians. *Publications include:* The Challenge of the Exception: An Introduction to the Political Ideas of Carl Schmitt Between 1921 and 1936 (second edn) 1989, Journey to Belfast and London (jtly) 1999; editor: Ideology and Foreign Policy 1981, Eurocommunism 1981, Detente in Historical Perspective 1981, United States Foreign Policy at the Crossroads 1982, 88 2005; translator: Carl Schmitt's Political Theology: Four Chapters on the Concept of Sovereignty 1985, The Leviathan in the State Theory of Thomas Hobbes 1996, The Concept of the Political 1996. *Honours:* Order of the Three Stars (Latvia) 2002; Ellis Island Medal of Honour 1998. *Address:* National Committee on American Foreign Policy, 320 Park Avenue, Eighth Floor, New York, NY 10022, USA (office). *Telephone:* (212) 224-1120 (office). *Fax:* (212)

224-2524 (office). *E-mail:* contact@NCAFP.org (office). *Website:* www.NCAFP.org (office).

SCHWANDT, Stephen William, BA, BS, MA; American educator and writer; b. 5 April 1947, Chippewa Falls, WI; m. Karen Sambo 1970, two s. *Education:* Valparaiso University, St Cloud State University, University of Minnesota, Twin Cities. *Career:* Teacher of Composition and American Literature, Irondale High School, New Brighton, Minnesota, 1974–; Instructor, Concordia College, St Paul, Minnesota, 1975–80, Normandale Community College, 1983–; mem. National Education Asscn; Authors' Guild; Book Critics Circle; National Council for Teachers of English; The Loft. *Publications:* The Last Goodie, 1985; A Risky Game, 1986; Holding Steady, 1988; Guilt Trip, 1990; Funnybone, 1992. Contributions: various newspapers.

SCHWARTZ, Elliott Shelling, AB, MA, EdD; American composer, writer and academic; *Professor of Music Emeritus, Bowdoin College*; b. 19 Jan. 1936, Brooklyn, NY; m. Dorothy Rose Feldman 1960; one s. one d. *Education:* Columbia Univ. *Career:* Instructor, Univ. of Massachusetts 1960–64; Asst Prof. 1964–70, Assoc. Prof. 1970–75, Prof. of Music and Dept Chair from 1975, Bowdoin Coll., Brunswick, ME, now Prof. of Music Emer.; Prof. of Composition, Ohio State Univ. 1985–86, 1988–91; visiting appointments, Trinity Coll. of Music, London (UK) 1967–, Univ. of California, San Diego 1978–79, Robinson Coll., Cambridge (UK) 1993–94, 1998–99, 2007; NEA grants 1978–83, Rockefeller Foundation residencies, Bellagio, Italy 1980, 1989; mem. American Soc. of Univ. Composers, Coll. Music Soc. (past pres.), American Composers' Alliance. *Compositions:* Timepiece 1794 for chamber orchestra 1994, Rainbow for orchestra 1996, Alto Prisms for eight violas 1997, Mehitadel's Serenade for saxophone and orchestra 2001, Rainforest with Birds 2001, Voyager for orchestra 2002, Riverscape 2003, Summer's Journey for concert bands 2005. *Recordings:* Grand Concerto, Extended Piano, Mirrors, Texture for Chamber Orchestras, Concert Piece for Ten Players, Chamber Concerto, Cycles and Gongs, Extended Clarinet, Dream Music with Variations, Celebrations/Reflections for Orchestra, Memorial in Two Parts, Chiaroscuro, Elan, Aerie for six flutes, Equinox for orchestra, Voyager for orchestra, Timepiece 1794 for chamber orchestra. *Publications:* The Symphonies of Ralph Vaughan Williams 1964, Contemporary Composers on Contemporary Music (ed. with Barney Childs) 1967, Electronic Music: A Listener's Guide 1973, Music: Ways of Listening 1982, Music Since 1945: Issues, Materials and Literature (with Daniel Godfrey) 1993; contrib. to professional journals. *Honours:* Guaudeamus Prize (Netherlands) 1970, Maine State Award in the Arts and Humanities 1970. *Address:* PO Box 451, South Freeport, ME 04078, USA. *Telephone:* (207) 725-3320 (office); (207) 865-3722 (home). *Fax:* (207) 725-3748 (office); (207) 865-6652 (home). *E-mail:* eschwart@bowdoin.edu. *Website:* www.schwartzmusic.com.

SCHWARTZ, John Burnham, BA; American writer; b. 8 May 1965, New York, NY. *Education:* Harvard University. *Career:* mem. Authors' Guild. *Publications:* Bicycle Days, 1989; Reservation Road, 1998; Claire Marvel, 2002. Contributions: periodicals, including: New Yorker; New York Times Book Review. *Honours:* Lyndhurst Prize 1991.

SCHWARTZ, Lloyd, BA, MA, PhD; American academic, music critic and poet; b. 29 Nov. 1941, New York, NY. *Education:* Queens College, CUNY, Harvard University. *Career:* Classical Music Ed., Boston Phoenix, 1977–; Assoc. Prof. of English, 1982–86, Dir of Creative Writing, 1982–02, Prof. of English, 1986–94, Frederick S. Troy Prof. of English, 1994–; University of Massachusetts, Boston; Classical Music Critic, Fresh Air, National Public Radio, 1987–; Poetry Commentator, TomPaine.com, 2001–; mem. New England Poetry Club; PEN New England, exec. committee, 1983–98, exec. council, 1998–; Poetry Society of America. *Publications:* These People, 1981; Elizabeth Bishop and Her Art (ed.), 1983; Goodnight, Gracie, 1992; Cairo Traffic, 2000. Contributions: American Review; Best American Poetry, 1991, 1994; Harvard Magazine; New Republic; New York Times; Partisan Review; Pequod; Ploughshares; Poetry; New Yorker; Slate; The Handbook of Heartbreak; Boulevard; Southwest Review; Atlantic Monthly. *Honours:* ASCAP-Deems Taylor Awards, 1980, 1987, 1990; Daniel Varoujan Prize, 1987; Pushcart Prize, 1987; Somerville Arts Council Grants, 1987, 1989; National Endowment for the Arts Fellowship, 1990; Pulitzer Prize in Criticism, 1994.

SCHWARTZ, Lynne Sharon, BA, MA; American author, poet and translator; b. 19 March 1939, New York, NY; m. Harry Schwartz 1957, two d. *Education:* Barnard College, Bryn Mawr College, New York University. *Career:* mem. Authors' Guild; National Book Critics Circle; National Writers Union; PEN American Centre. *Publications:* Rough Strife 1980, Balancing Acts 1981, Disturbances in the Field 1983, Acquainted with the Night (short stories) 1984, We Are Talking About Homes (short stories) 1985, The Melting Pot and Other Subversive Stories 1987, Leaving Brooklyn 1989, Smoke Over Birkenau by Liana Millu (trans.) 1990, A Lynne Sharon Schwartz Reader: Selected Prose and Poetry 1992, The Fatigue Artist 1995, Ruined by Reading: A Life in Books 1996, In the Family Way 1999, Face to Face: A Reader in the World 2000, In Solitary (poems) 2002, A Place to Live and Other Selected Essays of Natalia Ginzburg (trans.) 2002, Referred Pain and Other Stories 2004; contrib. to periodicals. *Honours:* National Endowment for the Arts Fellowships, 1984, 2002; Guggenheim Fellowship, 1985; New York State Foundation for the Arts Fellowship, 1986. *Address:* 50 Morningside Drive, No. 31, New York, NY 10025, USA.

SCHWARZ, Daniel Roger, BA, MA, PhD; American academic, writer and poet; *Professor of English and Stephen H. Weiss Presidential Fellow, Cornell University*; b. 12 May 1941, Rockville Centre, NY; m. 1st Marcia Mitson 1963 (divorced 1986); two s.; m. 2nd Marcia Jacobson 1998. *Education:* Union Coll., Brown Univ. *Career:* Asst Prof., Cornell Univ. 1968–74, Assoc. Prof. 1974–80, Prof. of English 1980–, Stephen H. Weiss Presidential Fellow 1999–; Distinguished Visiting Cooper Prof., Univ. of Arkansas at Little Rock 1988; Citizen's Chair in Literature, Univ. of Hawaii 1992–93; Visiting Eminent Scholar, Univ. of Alabama, Huntsville 1996; Dir, 9 National Endowment for the Humanities Summer Seminars for College and High School Teachers Grants, 1984–93; mem. Int. Asscn of Univ. Profs of English, Soc. for the Study of Narrative Literature (Past Pres.), Modern Language Asscn. *Publications:* Disraeli's Fiction 1979, Conrad: Almayer's Folly to Under Western Eyes 1980, Conrad: The Later Fiction 1982, The Humanistic Heritage: Critical Theories of the English Novel from James to Hillis Miller 1986, Reading Joyce's Ulysses 1987, The Transformation of the English Novel 1890–1930: Studies in Hardy, Conrad, Joyce, Lawrence, Forster and Woolf 1989, The Case for a Humanistic Poetics 1991, Narrative and Representation in the Poetry of Wallace Stevens 1993, Narrative and Culture (ed. with Janice Carlise) 1994, James Joyce's The Dead (ed.) 1994, Joseph Conrad's The Secret Sharer (ed.) 1997, Reconfiguring Modernism: Explorations in the Relationship Between Modern Art and Modern Literature 1997, Imagining the Holocaust 1999, Rereading Conrad 2001, Broadway Boogie Woogie: Damon Runyon and the Making of New York City Culture 2002, Reading the Modern British and Irish Novel, 1890–1940; other: more than 50 poems; contribs to journals and collections. *Honours:* American Philosophical Soc. Grant 1981, US Information Agency Lecturer and Academic Specialist Lecturer, Australia 1993, Cyprus 1999, Italy 2002, Cornell Univ. Russell Distinguished Teaching Award 1998. *Address:* Department of English, 242 Goldwin Smith Hall, Cornell University, Ithaca, NY 14853 (office); 925 Mitchell Street #3, Ithaca, NY 14850, USA (home). *Telephone:* (607) 255-9313 (office); (607) 273-5735 (office). *Fax:* (607) 255-6661 (home). *E-mail:* drs6@cornell.edu (office). *Website:* www.people.cornell.edu/pages/drs6/ (office).

SCHWEIZER, Karl Wolfgang, MA, PhD, FRHistS; American writer and historian; b. 30 June 1946, Mannheim, Germany; m. (divorced); one s. *Education:* Wilfrid Laurier Univ., Univ. of Waterloo, Peterhouse Coll., Cambridge, UK. *Career:* Prof., Bishop's Univ., Lennoxville, Quebec 1976–88; Mellon Fellow, Harvard Univ. 1978; Visiting Lecturer, Univ. of Guelph 1973–74; Research Assoc., Russian Research Center, Ill. 1979–80, 1999; Academic Visitor, LSE 1986, 1994; Visiting Scholar, Queen's Univ., Ont. 1986–87; Visiting Fellow, Darwin Coll., Cambridge 1987, 1994, 2003, Yale Univ. 1994–95, Princeton Univ. 1994–95; Sr Research Assoc., Peterhouse Coll., Cambridge 2004; Chair. Dept of Humanities 1988–93, Prof. Dept of Social Science 1993–2000, Prof. and Chair. Dept of Humanities and Social Science 2000–02, New Jersey Inst. of Technology; Grad. Faculty, Rutgers, The State Univ. of New Jersey at Newark 1993–; Assoc., Center for Global Change and Governance 1995–. *Publications:* The Devonshire Political Diary 1757–1763 (ed.) 1982, Diplomatic Thought 1648–1815 (ed.) 1983, François de Callières: The Art of Diplomacy 1983, Warfare and Tactics in the Eighteenth Century (ed.) 1984, Essays in European History 1648–1815, in Honour of Ragnhild Hatton (ed. with J. Black) 1985, The Origins of War in Early Modern Europe (co-author) 1987, Lord Bute: Essays in Re-Interpretation 1988, Intellectual History: New Perspectives (ed.) 1988, Politics and the Press in Hanoverian Britain (ed. with J. Black) 1989, England, Prussia and the Seven Years War 1989, Cobbett in his Times 1990, Frederick the Great, William Pitt and Lord Bute: Anglo-Prussian Relations 1756–1763 1991, Lord Chatham 1993, François de Callières: Diplomat and Man of Letters 1995, Herbert Butterfield: Essays on the History of Science (ed.) 1998, Hanoverian Britain and Empire (co-author) 1998, British Prime Ministers (co-author) 1999, Seeds of Evil: The Gray/Snyder Murder Case 2001, War, Diplomacy and Politics: The Anglo-Prussian Alliance 1756–1763 2001, Statesmen, Diplomats and the Press: Essays on 18th Century Britain 2003, Influence of Australia's Constitutional Monarchy (ed.) 2003, Parliament and the Press 1688–1939 (ed.) 2005; contrib. to reference works and scholarly books and journals. *Honours:* Adelle Mellen Prize for Distinguished Contributions to Scholarship 1990, New Jersey Writer's Conference Award 1993, Outstanding Academic Book Citations, Choice 1994, 1998, NJIT Teaching Award 2000. *Address:* 49 S Passaic Avenue, Apt 24, Chatham, NJ 07928, USA (home). *E-mail:* schweizer@adm.njit.edu (office).

SCLIAR, Moacyr; Brazilian novelist and physician; b. 23 March 1937, Porto Alegre; s. of José Scliar and Sara Scliar. *Career:* Visiting Prof., Brown Univ. and Univ. of Texas at Austin, USA; mem. Brazilian Acad. of Letters 2003. *Publications include:* Histórias de um Médico em Formação 1962, O Carnaval dos Animais 1968, A Guerra no Bom Fim 1972, O Exército de um Homem Só 1973, Os Deuses de Raque 1975, O Ciclo das águas 1975, A Balada do Falso Messias 1976, Histórias da Terra Trêmula 1976, Mês de Cães Danados 1977, O Anão no Televisor 1979, Doutor Miragem 1979, Os Voluntários 1979, O Centauro no Jardim 1980, Cavalos e Obeliscos (juvenile) 1980, Max e os Felinos 1981, A Festa no Castelo (juvenile) 1982, A Estranha Nação de Rafael Mendes 1983, A massagista japonesa 1984, Os Melhores Contos de Moacyr Scliar 1984, Memórias de um Aprendiz de Escritor (juvenile) 1984, Dez Contos Escolhidos 1984, O Olho Enigmático 1986, A Condição Judaica (essay) 1987, Do Mágico ao Social: a Trajetória da Saúde Pública (essay) 1987, No Caminho dos Sonhos (juvenile) 1988, A orelha de Van Gogh (Prêmio Casa de las Américas, Cuba 1989) 1988, O Tio que Flutuava (juvenile) 1988, Cenas Médicas 1988, Os Cavalos da República (juvenile) 1989, Cenas da Vida Minúscula 1991, Prá Você Eu Conto (juvenile) 1991, Sonhos Tropicais 1992, Se

Eu Fosse Rotschild (essay) 1993, Uma História Só pra Mim 1994, Judaísmo: dispersão e Unidade (essay) 1994, Contos Reunidos 1995, Um Sonho no Caroço de Abacate (juvenile) 1995, O Rio Grande Farroupilha (juvenile) 1995, Oswaldo Cruz (essay) 1996, A Paixão Transformada: História da Medicina na Literatura (essay) 1996, A Majestade do Xingu (Academia Brasileira de Letras Prêmio José Lins do Rego 1998) 1997, O Amante da Madonna 1997, Os Contistas 1997, Histórias para (Quase) Todos os Gostos 1998, Câmera na Mão, o Guarani no Coração (juvenile) 1998, A mulher que escreveu a bíblia 1999, A Colina dos Suspiros (juvenile) 1999, Os Leopardos de Kafka 2000, Livro da Medicina (juvenile) 2000, O Mistério da Casa Verde (juvenile) 2000, Meu Filho, o Doutor: Medicina e Judaísmo na História, na Literatura e no Humor (essay) 2000, A Face Oculta: Inusitadas e Reveladoras Histórias da Medicina (essay) 2000, Porto de Histórias: Mistérios e Crepúsculos de Porto Alegre (essay) 2000, O Ataque do Comando P. Q. (juvenile) 2001, A lingua de tres pontas: cronicas e citacoes sobre a arte de falar mal 2001, O imaginario cotidiano 2001, O sertao vai virar mar (juvenile) 2002, Aquele estranho colega, o meu pai (juvenile) 2002, O irmao que veio de longe (juvenile) 2002, Pai e filho, filho e pai 2002, A linguagem medica 2002, Oswaldo Cruz & Carios Chagas: o nascimento da ciencia no Brasil 2002, Navio das cores (works by Lasar Segall) 2003, Saturno nos Trópicos 2003, Nem uma coisa, nem outra (juvenile) 2003, O navio das cores (juvenile) 2003, Judaismo 2003, Um olhar sobre a saude publica 2003, Mistérios de Porto Alegre 2004, Historias de aprendiz (juvenile) 2004, Um menino chamado Moises (juvenile) 2004, As melhores cronicas de Moacyr Scliar 2004, Na noite do vente, o diamante 2005. *Honours:* Prêmio da Academia Mineira de Letras 1968, Prêmio Joaquim Manoel de Macedo 1974, Prêmio Cidade de Porto Alegre 1976, Prêmio Brasília 1977, Prêmio Guimarães Rosa 1977, Prêmio Erico Verissimo de Romance 1977, Prêmio da Associação de Críticos de Arte 1980, Prêmio Jabuti 1988, 1993, 2000, Prêmio Pen Club do Brasil 1990, Prêmios Açorianos 1997, 2002, Prêmio Mario Quintana 1999. *Address:* Rua Santa Cecilia, AP 901, Porto Alegre, RS 90420-041, Brazil. *E-mail:* mscliar@uol.com.br.

SCOBIE, Stephen Arthur Cross, MA, PhD, FRSC; Canadian academic, poet and writer; b. 31 Dec. 1943, Carnoustie, Scotland; m. Sharon Maureen 1967. *Education:* University of St Andrews, University of British Columbia. *Career:* faculty mem., University of Alberta 1969–80, Prof. 1980–81; Prof. of English, University of Victoria 1981–; Guest Prof. of Canadian Studies, Christian-Albrechts-Universität, Kiel 1990; mem. League of Canadian Poets (vice-pres. 1972–74, 1986–88), Victoria Literary Arts Festival Society (fmr pres.). *Publications:* poetry: Babylondromat, 1966; In the Silence of the Year, 1971; The Birken Tree, 1973; Stone Poems, 1974; The Rooms We Air, 1975; Airloom, 1975; Les toiles n'ont peur de rien, 1979; McAlmon's Chinese Opera, 1980; A Grand Memory for Forgetting, 1981; Expecting Rain, 1985; The Ballad of Isabel Gunn, 1987; Dunino, 1988; Remains, 1990; Ghosts: A Glossary of the Intertext, 1990; Gospel, 1994; Slowly Into Autumn, 1995; Willow, 1995; Taking the Gate: Journey Through Scotland, 1996. Other: Leonard Cohen, 1978; The Maple Laugh Forever: An Anthology of Canadian Comic Poetry (co-ed.), 1981; Alias Bob Dylan, 1991. Contributions: journals and magazines. *Honours:* Governor-General's Award for Poetry 1980.

SCOFIELD, Sandra; American writer; b. 1943, Wichita Falls, Tex. *Publications:* Gringa (New American Fiction Award) 1989, Beyond Deserving (American Book Award, New American Fiction Award) 1991, Walking Dunes 1992, More than Allies 1993, Opal on Dry Ground 1994, A Chance to See Egypt 1996, Plain Seeing 1999. *Honours:* Nat. Endowment for the Arts Creative Writing Fellowship. *Address:* PO Box 3329, Ashland, OR 97520; 107 Bentley Park Loop, Missoula, MT 59801, USA. *Website:* www.sandrascofield.com.

SCOT, Michael (see Rohan, Michael Scott)

SCOTT, Gail, BA; Canadian writer; b. 20 Jan. 1945, Ottawa, Ontario; one d. *Education:* Queen's University, Kingston, Ontario, University of Grenoble. *Career:* Journalist, Montréal Gazette, The Globe and Mail, 1970–79; Writing Instructor, 1981–90; Writer-in-Residence, Concordia University, Montréal, 1991–92, University of Alberta, Edmonton, 1994–95; mem. Union des écrivaines et des écrivains québécois; Writer's Union of Canada. *Publications:* Spare Parts, 1982; Heroine, 1987; La Theorie, un Dimanche, 1988; Spaces Like Stairs, 1989; Serious Hysterics (anthology), 1992; Resurgences (anthology), 1992; Main Brides, 1994. Contributions: journals and other publications.

SCOTT, John A., BA, DipEd; Australian academic, poet and writer; b. 23 April 1948, Littlehampton, Sussex, England. *Education:* Monash University, Vic., Australia. *Career:* Lecturer, Swinburne Institute 1975–80, Canberra College of Advanced Education 1980–89, University of Wollongong, NSW 1989–. *Publications:* The Barbarous Sideshow, 1976; From the Flooded City, 1981; Smoking, 1983; The Quarrel with Ourselves, 1984; Confession, 1984; St Clair, 1986; Blair, 1988; Singles: Shorter Works 1981–1986, 1989; Translation, 1990; What I Have Written, 1993. *Honours:* Poetry Society of Australia Award, 1970; Mattara Poetry Prize, 1984; Wesley Michel Wright Awards, 1985, 1988; Victorian Premier's Prize for Poetry, 1986; ANA Award, Fellowship of Australian Writers, 1990.

SCOTT, John Peter, BSc, PhD; British academic and writer; b. 8 April 1949, London, England; m. Jill Wheatley 1971, one s. one d. *Education:* Kingston Coll. of Technology, Univ. of London, LSE, Univ. of Strathclyde. *Career:* Lecturer, Univ. of Strathclyde 1972–76; Lecturer, Univ. of Leicester 1976–87; Reader 1987–91; Prof. of Sociology 1991–94; Ed., Network Newsletter, British Sociological Asscn 1985–89, Social Studies Review, later Sociology Review 1986–; Prof. of Sociology, Univ. of Essex 1994–; Adjunct Prof., Univ. of Bergen,

Norway 1997–; mem. British Sociological Asscn (sec. 1991–92, chair. 1992–93, treas. 1997–99, pres. 2001–). *Publications:* Corporations, Classes and Capitalism 1979, The Upper Classes 1982, The Anatomy of Scottish Capital (with M. Hughes) 1982, Directors of Industry (with C. Griff) 1984, Networks of Corporate Power (co-ed.) 1985, Capitalist Property and Financial Power 1986, A Matter of Record 1990, The Sociology of Elites (ed., three vols) 1990, Who Rules Britain 1991, Social Network Analysis 1992, Power (ed., three vols) 1994, Poverty and Wealth 1994, Sociological Theory 1995, Stratification and Power 1996, Corporate Business and Capitalist Classes 1997, Class (ed., four vols) 1997, Sociology (with James Fulcher) 1999, Social Structure (with José López) 2000, Power 2000, Critical Concepts: Social Networks (ed., four vols) 2002; contrib. to professional journals and general periodicals. *Honours:* Choice Outstanding Sociology Book of the Year 1995. *Address:* Department of Sociology, University of Essex, Wivenhoe Park, Colchester, Essex CO4 3SQ, England (office). *E-mail:* scottj@essex.ac.uk (office).

SCOTT, Jonathan Henry, BA, PhD; New Zealand historian, writer and poet; b. 22 Jan. 1958, Auckland; m. 1st Sara Bennett 1980 (divorced); m. 2nd Lindsey Bridget Shaw 1986 (divorced 1991); m. 3rd Anne Hanson Pelzel 1995; one s. one d. *Education:* Victoria University of Wellington, Trinity College, Cambridge. *Career:* Research Fellow, Magdalene College, Cambridge, 1985–87; Lecturer in History, Victoria University of Wellington, 1987–88, University of Sheffield, 1989–91; Fellow and Dir of Studies in History, Downing College, Cambridge, 1991–2002; Carroll Amundson Prof. of British History, Univ. of Pittsburgh, 2002–. *Publications:* Algernon Sidney and the English Republic, 1623–1677, 1988; Algernon Sidney and the Restoration Crisis, 1677–1683, 1991; Harry's Absence: Looking for My Father on the Mountain, 1997; England's Troubles: Seventeenth Century English Political Instability in European Context, 2000, Commonwealth Principles: Republican Writing of the English Revolution 2004; contribs to scholarly books and journals, and literary periodicals. *Address:* 3K38 Posvar Hall, University of Pittsburgh, Pittsburgh, PA 15260, USA.

SCOTT, Paul Henderson, MA, MLitt; British essayist, historian, critic and fmr diplomatist; b. 7 Nov. 1920, Edinburgh, Scotland. *Education:* Univ. of Edinburgh. *Career:* mem. Int. PEN, Scottish Centre, Saltire Soc., Asscn for Scottish Literary Studies, Scottish Nat. Party. *Publications:* 1707: The Union of Scotland and England, 1979; Walter Scott and Scotland, 1981; John Galt, 1985; Towards Independence: Essays on Scotland, 1991; Scotland in Europe, 1992; Andrew Fletcher and the Treaty of Union, 1992; Scotland: A Concise Cultural History (ed.), 1993; Defoe in Edinburgh, 1994; Scotland: An Unwon Cause, 1997; Still in Bed with an Elephant, 1998; The Boasted Advantages, 1999; A Twentieth-Century Life, 2002; Scotland Resurgent, 2003, Spirits of the Age (ed.) 2005, The Unions of 1707: Why and How 2006; contrib. to newspapers and journals. *Honours:* Andrew Fletcher Award 1993, Oliver Award 2000. *Address:* 33 Drumsheugh Gardens, Edinburgh, EH3 7RN, Scotland (home). *Telephone:* (131) 225-1038 (home). *Fax:* (131) 225-1038 (home). *E-mail:* scott.fiore@virgin.net (home).

SCOTT, Peter Dale, BA, PhD; Canadian academic and poet; b. 11 Jan. 1929, Montreal, QC; m. Ronna Kabatznick 1993; two s. one d. *Education:* McGill Univ., Institut d'Etudes Politiques, Paris, Univ. College, Oxford. *Career:* Lecturer, McGill Univ. 1955–56; Canadian Foreign Service, Ottawa and Poland 1957–61; Prof. of Speech, Univ. of California at Berkeley 1961–66, Prof. of English 1966–94. *Publications:* poetry: Poems 1952, Rumors of No Law 1981, Coming to Jakarta 1988, Listening to the Candle 1992, Crossing Borders 1994, Minding the Darkness 2000; prose: Deep Politics and the Death of JFK 1993, Drugs, Oil and War 2003. Contributions: Reviews, quarterlies, and periodicals. *Honours:* Dia Art Foundation 1989, Lannan Poetry Award 2002. *Address:* c/o Department of English, University of California, Berkeley, CA 94720, USA. *E-mail:* pdscottweb@hotmail.com. *Website:* www.peterdalescott.net.

SCOTT, Rosie Judy, BA, MA, DCA; New Zealand/Australian writer, counsellor and editor; b. 22 March 1948, Wellington; d. of Dick and Elsie Scott; m. Danny Vendramini 1987; two d. *Education:* Univ. of Auckland and Victoria Univ. (Wellington), Grad. Diploma of Counselling, Inst. of Counselling, Sydney, Grad. Diploma of Drama, Univ. of Auckland). *Career:* numerous jobs including actress, social worker, counsellor, publr, waitress, editor, factory and home worker; now internationally published novelist, essayist and short story writer; fmr Chair. Australian Soc. of Authors, now mem. Perm. Council; fmr Vice-Pres. Sydney PEN; active in various political campaigns. *Publications include:* novels: Glory Days, Nights with Grace, Feral City, Lives on Fire, Movie Dreams, Faith Singer 2001; poetry: Flesh and Blood; short stories: Queen of Love; play: Say Thankyou to the Lady; non-fiction: The Red Heart 1999. *Honours:* Bruce Mason Nat. Times Play Award 1985. *Address:* 21 Darghan Street, Glebe, NSW 2037, Australia. *Telephone:* (2) 9552 14 27. *Fax:* (2) 9660 61 16. *E-mail:* rosie@amaze.net.au.

SCOTT-HERON, Gil; American singer, songwriter and musician (piano); b. 1 April 1949, Chicago, IL. *Education:* Lincoln Univ., PA. *Career:* co-founder, The Midnight Band 1972–; numerous concerts and festival appearances. *Recordings include:* albums: Small Talk At 125th And Lenox 1970, Pieces Of A Man 1971, Free Will 1972, Winter In America (with Brian Jackson) 1973, The First Minute Of A New Day (with the Midnight Band) 1975, From South Africa To South Carolina (with Brian Jackson) 1975, It's Your World (with Brian Jackson) 1976, Bridges (with Brian Jackson) 1977, Secrets (with Brian Jackson) 1978, The Mind Of Gil Scott-Heron 1979, 1980 (with Brian Jackson)

1980, Real Eyes 1980, Reflections 1981, Moving Target 1982, Amnesia Express 1990, Spirits 1994, Minister Of Information 1994, Evolution And Flashback 1999. *Publications:* The Vulture (novel) 1970, Small Talk at 125th and Lenox 1970, The Nigger Factory (novel) 1972, So Far, So Good 1990, Now and Then (poems) 2001. *Address:* c/o Fore-Word Press Ltd., 53 Rodney Street, Liverpool, L1 9ER, England.

SCOTT-JAMES, Anne Eleanor, Lady Lancaster; British journalist and writer; b. 5 April 1913, d. of R. A. Scott-James and Violet Scott-James (née Brooks); m. 1st Macdonald Hastings 1944 (died 1982); one s. one d.; m. 2nd Sir Osbert Lancaster 1967 (died 1986). *Education:* St Paul's Girls' School and Somerville Coll., Oxford. *Career:* mem. editorial staff, Vogue 1934–41; Women's Ed. Picture Post 1941–45, Sunday Express 1953–57; Ed. Harper's Bazaar 1945–51; Women's Adviser Beaverbrook Newspapers 1959–60; Columnist Daily Mail 1960–68; freelance journalist 1968–; mem. Council Royal Horticultural Soc. 1978–82. *Publications:* In the Mink 1952, Down to Earth 1971, Sissinghurst: the making of a garden 1975, The Pleasure Garden (jtly) 1977, The Cottage Garden 1981, Glyndebourne – the Gardens (jtly) 1983, The Language of the Garden: a personal anthology 1984, The Best Plants for Your Garden 1988, The British Museum Book of Flowers (jtly) 1989, Gardening Letters to My Daughter 1990, Sketches from a Life (autobiog.) 1993. *Address:* 78 Cheyne Court, Royal Hospital Road, London, SW3 5TT, England.

SCRIPPS, Charles Edward; American newspaper publisher; b. 27 Jan. 1920, San Diego; s. of Robert Paine and Margaret Lou (née Culbertson) Scripps; m. 1st Louann Copeland 1941 (divorced 1947); m. 2nd Lois Anne MacKay 1949 (died 1990); two s. two d.; m. 3rd Mary Elizabeth Breslin 1993. *Education:* William and Mary Coll. and Pomona Coll. *Career:* Reporter, Cleveland Press, Ohio 1941; Successor-Trustee, Edward W. Scripps Trust 1945, Chair. Bd of Trustees 1948–; Vice Pres., Dir E.W. Scripps Co. 1946, Chair. of Bd 1953–94. *Honours:* named as Great Living Cincinnatian 2003. *Address:* c/o Scripps Howard Foundation, POB 5380, Cincinnati, OH 45201, USA (office). *Telephone:* (513) 977-3035. *Fax:* (513) 977-3800.

SCRUTON, Roger, BA, PhD, FRSL; British philosopher and writer; b. 27 Feb. 1944, Buslingthorpe; s. of John Scruton and Beryl C. Haines; m. 1st Danielle Laffitte 1975 (divorced 1983); m. 2nd Sophie Jeffreys 1996. *Education:* High Wycombe Royal Grammar School, Jesus Coll. Cambridge and Inner Temple, London. *Career:* Fellow, Peterhouse, Cambridge 1969–71; Lecturer in Philosophy, Birkbeck Coll. London 1971–79, Reader 1979–86, Prof. of Aesthetics 1986–92; Prof. of Philosophy, Boston Univ. 1992–95; Founder and Dir The Claridge Press 1987–; Ed. The Salisbury Review 1982–2000. *Publications:* Art and Imagination 1974, The Aesthetics of Architecture 1979, The Meaning of Conservatism 1980, The Politics of Culture and Other Essays 1981, Fortnight's Anger (novel) 1981, A Short History of Modern Philosophy 1982, A Dictionary of Political Thought 1982, The Aesthetic Understanding 1983, Kant 1983, Untimely Tracts 1985, Thinkers of the New Left 1986, Sexual Desire 1986, Spinoza 1987, A Land Held Hostage: Lebanon and the West 1987, The Philosopher on Dover Beach (essays) 1989, Francesca (novel) 1991, A Dove Descending (stories) 1991, Conservative Texts: An Anthology 1991, The Xanthippic Dialogues 1993, Modern Philosophy 1993, The Classical Vernacular 1994, Modern Philosophy 1996, Animal Rights and Wrongs 1996, An Intelligent Person's Guide to Philosophy 1997, The Aesthetics of Music 1997, On Hunting 1998, Town and Country (co-ed.) 1998, An Intelligent Person's Guide To Modern Culture 1998, On Hunting 1999, Perictione in Colophon 2000, England: An Elegy 2000, The West and the Rest: Globalization and the Terrorist Threat 2002, Death-Devoted Heart: Sex and the Sacred in Wagner's Tristan and Isolde 2004, News from Somewhere: On Settling 2004, Gentle Regrets (autobiog.) 2005. *Honours:* Hon. doctorates (Adelphi Univ.) 1995, (Masaryk Univ., Brno, Czech Repub.) 1998; Medal of Merit, First Class (Czech Repub.). *Address:* Sunday Hill Farm, Brinkworth, Wilts., SN15 5AS, England.

SCULLY, Vincent Joseph, Jr, BA, PhD; American art historian, academic and writer; b. 21 Aug. 1920, New Haven, Conn.; m. Catherine Lynn, 30 Dec. 1980, four c. *Education:* Yale Univ. *Career:* Instructor, Yale Univ., Asst Prof., Assoc. Prof. 1947–61, Col John Trumbull Prof. of Art History 1961–83, Sterling Prof. of History of Art 1983–91, Sterling Prof. Emer. 1991–; Host, New World Visions: American Art and the Metropolitan Museum 1650–1914, PBS-TV 1983; Visiting Prof., Univ. of Miami at Coral Gables 1992–97; Mellon Visiting Prof. of History, California Inst. of Tech. 1995; Trustee Nat. Trust for Historic Preservation. *Publications:* The Architectural Heritage of Newport, Rhode Island (with Antoinette Forrester Downing) 1952, The Shingle Style: Architectural Theory and Design from Richardson to the Origins of Wright 1955, revised edn as The Shingle Style and the Stick Style: Architectural Theory and Design from Downing to the Origins of Wright 1971, Frank Lloyd Wright 1960, Modern Archiecture: The Architecture of Democracy 1961, Louis I Kahn 1962, The Earth, the Temple and the Gods: Greek Sacred Architecture 1962, American Architecture and Urbanism 1969, Pueblo Architecture of the Southwest 1971, The Shingle Style Today: or, The Historian's Revenge 1974, Pueblo: Mountain, Village, Dance 1975, Robert Stern (with David Dunster) 1981, Wesleyan: Photographs 1982, Michael Graves, Buildings and Projects, 1966–1981 1982, The Villas of Palladio 1986, The Architecture of the American Summer: The Flowering of the Shingle Style 1987, New World Visions of Household Gods and Sacred Places: American Art and the Metropolitan Museum 1650–1914 1988, The Architecture of Robert Venturi (with others) 1989, The Great Dinosaur Mural at Yale: The Age of Reptiles

(with others) 1990, Architecture: The Natural and the Manmade 1991, French Royal Gardens: The Design of André Le Notre (with Jeannie Baubion-Maclere) 1992, Robert A. M. Stern, Buildings and Projects 1987–1992 1992, Mother's House: The Evolution of Vanna Venturi's House in Chestnut Hill (with Robert Venturi) 1992, Between Two Towers: The Drawings of The School of Miami (with George Hernandez, Catherine Lynn and Teofilo Victoria) 1996, Modern Architecture and Other Essays by Vincent Scully (ed by Neil Levine) 2003, Yale in New Haven: Architecture and Urbanism (with Catherine Lynn, Erik Vogt, Paul Goldberger) 2004; book of essays (selected by Neil Levine). *Honours:* Hon. Mem. AIA; Hon. FRIBA; hon. doctorates; Nat. Endowment for the Humanities Sr Fellowship 1972–73, AIA Medal 1976, Thomas Jefferson Medal, Univ. of Virginia 1982, Topaz Award, Asscn of Collegiate Schools of Architecture/AIA 1986, Literary Lion, New York Public Library 1992, Gov.'s Arts Awards Medal, State of Conn. 1993, American Acad. in Rome Award 1994, Thomas Jefferson Lecturer, Nat. Endowment for the Humanities 1995, chaired professorship est. in his name at Yale Univ. 1997, first recipient of Vincent Scully Prize cr. by Nat. Building Museum, Washington, DC 1999, Vincent J. Scully Jr Visiting Professorship in Architectural History est. at Yale Univ. 2003, Urban Land Inst. J.C. Nichols Prize for Visionary Urban Devt 2003, Nat. Medal of Arts 2004. *Address:* 252 Lawrence Street, New Haven, CT 06511, USA.

SCUPHAM, John Peter, FRSL, BA; British writer and poet; b. 24 Feb. 1933, Liverpool; m. Carola Nance Braunholtz 1957; three s., one d. *Education:* Emmanuel College, Cambridge. *Career:* founder-Publisher, The Mandeville Press. *Publications:* The Snowing Globe, 1972; Prehistories, 1975; The Hinterland, 1977; Summer Places, 1980; Winter Quarters, 1983; Out Late, 1986; The Air Show, 1989; Watching the Perseids, 1990; Selected Poems, 1990; The Ark, 1994; Night Watch, 1999; Collected Poems, 2002. Contributions: anthologies and magazines. *Honours:* Cholmondeley Award for Poetry. *Address:* Old Hall, Norwich Road, South Burlingham, Norfolk, NR13 4EY, England (home). *Telephone:* (1493) 750804 (home).

SEAGRAVE, Sterling; American writer; b. 15 April 1937, Columbus, OH; m. 1st Wendy Law-Yone 1967; m. 2nd Peggy Sawyer 1982, one s. one d. *Education:* University of Miami, University of Mexico, University of Venezuela. *Career:* mem. Authors' Guild. *Publications:* Yellow Rain 1981, Soldiers of Fortune 1981, The Soong Dynasty 1985, The Marcos Dynasty 1988, Dragon Lady 1992, Lords of the Rim 1995, The Yamato Dynasty (with Peggy Seagrave) 1999, Gold Warriors (with Peggy Seagrave) 2002; contributions to Atlantic, Far Eastern Economic Review, Esquire, Time, Smithsonian. *Website:* www.bowstring.net.

SEAL, Basil (see BARNES, Julian Patrick)

SEARLE, Elizabeth, BA, MA; American writer and teacher; b. 13 Jan. 1962, Philadelphia, PA; m. John Hodgkinson 1984. *Education:* Arizona State University, Oberlin College, Brown University. *Career:* Adjunct Lecturer, Oberlin College, 1983–84, Brown University, 1988–89; Instructor, Suffolk University, Boston, 1990–91, University of Massachusetts at Lowell, summers 1990–92; Emerson College, Boston, 1991; mem. PEN, New England; Poets and Writers. *Publications:* My Body to You, 1993; A Four-Sided Bed, 1998. Contributions: anthologies, reviews and periodicals. *Honours:* Roberts Writing Award, 1990; Chelsea Fiction Prize, 1991; Iowa Short Fiction Prize, 1992. *Address:* 18 College Avenue, Arlington, MA 02174, USA. *E-mail:* jhodgkinson@mediaone.net.

SEARLE, John R.; American academic; *Slusser Professor of Philosophy of the Mind and Language, University of California, Berkeley;* b. 1932, Denver, CO; s. of George W. Searle and Hester Beck Searle; m. Dagmar Carboch 1958; two s. *Education:* Univ. of Wisconsin, Univ. of Oxford. *Career:* Prof. of Philosophy Univ. of California, Berkeley from 1959, later Slusser Prof. of Philosophy; Educ. TV series in Calif. 1960–74; involved with student radical movt 1964; adviser to Nixon Admin. on student unrest in univs 1971; Reith Lecturer 1984; Rhodes Scholar 1952; mem. American Acad. of Arts and Sciences 1977–, Nat. Council of Nat. Endowment for Humanities 1992–96, Scholars' Council Library of Congress 2002–. *Publications:* Speech Acts 1969, The Campus War 1972, Expression and Meaning 1979, Intentionality 1983, Minds, Brains and Science 1984, The Foundations of Illocutionary Logic (with D. Vanderveken) 1985, The Rediscovery of the Mind 1992, (On) Searle on Conversation 1992, The Construction of Social Reality 1995, Mystery of Consciousness 1997, Mind, Language and Society 1998, Conversations with John Searle 2001, La Universidad Desafiada 2002, Consciousness and Language 2002, Liberté et Neurobiologie (trans. as Freedom and Neurology) 2004, Mind, A Brief Introduction 2004. *Honours:* Tassan Award 2000, Dean Nicod Prize 2000, Jovellanos Prize 2000, Nat. Humanities Medal 2004; Dr hc (Adelphi) 1993, (Wisconsin) 1994, (Bucharest) 2000, (Torino) 2000, (Lucano) 2003. *Address:* Department of Philosophy, 314 Moses Hall 2390, University of California, Berkeley, CA 94720-2390, USA (office). *Telephone:* (510) 642-3173 (office). *Fax:* (510) 642-5160 (office). *Website:* philosophy.berkeley.edu (office).

SEARLE, Ronald, CBE, RDI, AGI, FRSA; British artist; b. 3 March 1920, Cambridge; s. of the late William James Searle and of Nellie Searle (née Hunt); m. 1st Kaye Webb (divorced 1967, died 1996); one s. one d.; m. 2nd Monica Koenig 1967. *Education:* Central School, Cambridge and Cambridge School of Art. *Career:* first drawings published 1935–39; served with Royal Engineers 1939–46; POW in Japanese camps 1942–45; contrib. to nat. publs 1946; mem. Punch 'Table' 1956; special features artist, Life magazine 1955, Holiday 1957, The New Yorker 1966–, Le Monde 1995–; Designer of medals for the French Mint 1974–, British Art Medal Soc. 1983–; work represented in Victoria and Albert Museum, Imperial War Museum and British Museum, London, Bibliothèque Nationale, Paris and in several German and US museums. *Exhibitions include:* solo: Leicester Galleries, London 1950, 1954, 1957, Kraushaar Gallery, New York 1959, Bianchini Gallery, New York 1963, Kunsthalle, Bremen 1965, in Paris 1966, 1967, 1968, 1969, 1970, 1971, Bibliothèque Nationale 1973, in Munich 1967, 1968, 1969, 1970, 1971, 1973, 1976, 1981, in London 1968, Neue Galerie Wien, Vienna 1985, 1988, Imperial War Museum 1986, Fitzwilliam Museum, Cambridge 1987, Wilhelm Busch Museum, Hanover 1996, Stadtmuseum, Munich 1996, Galerie Martine Gossieaux, Paris 2000; with Monica Searle: Wilhelm Busch Museum, Hanover 2001. *Films designed:* designer of several films including John Gilpin, On the Twelfth Day, Energetically Yours, Germany 1960, Toulouse-Lautrec, Dick Deadeye, or Duty Done 1975; designed animation sequences for films Those Magnificent Men in their Flying Machines 1965, Monte-Carlo or Bust! 1969, Scrooge 1970, Dick Deadeye 1975. *Publications:* Forty Drawings 1946, John Gilpin 1952, Souls in Torment 1953, Rake's Progress 1955, Merry England 1956, Paris Sketchbook 1957, The St Trinian's Story (with Kaye Webb) 1959, USA For Beginners 1959, Russia for Beginners 1960, The Big City 1958 (all with Alex Atkinson), Refugees 1960 1960, Which Way Did He Go? 1961, Escape from the Amazon 1963, From Frozen North to Filthy Lucre 1964, Those Magnificent Men in their Flying Machines 1965, Haven't We Met Before Somewhere? (with Heinz Huber) 1966, Searle's Cats 1967, The Square Egg 1968, Hello—Where Did All the People Go? 1969, Secret Sketchbook 1970, The Second Coming of Toulouse-Lautrec 1970, The Addict 1971, More Cats 1975, Designs for Gilbert and Sullivan 1975, Paris! Paris! (with Irwin Shaw) 1977, Searle's Zodiac 1977, Ronald Searle (monograph) 1978, 1996, The King of Beasts 1980, The Big Fat Cat Book 1982, Illustrated Winespeak 1983, Ronald Searle in Perspective (monograph) 1984, Ronald Searle's Golden Oldies: 1941–1961, 1985, Something in the Cellar 1986, To the Kwai—and Back 1986, Ah Yes, I Remember It Well...: Paris 1961–1975 1987, Non-Sexist Dictionary 1988, Slightly Foxed—But Still Desirable 1989, Carnet de Croquis 1992, The Curse of St Trinian's 1993, Marquis de Sade Meets Goody Two-Shoes 1994, Searle and Searle 2001, Ronald Searle in Le Monde 2002, The Scrapbook Drawings 2005. *Honours:* Chevalier de la Légion d'honneur 2006; Venice, Edin., San Francisco and other film festival awards for film Energetically Yours; LA Art Dirs' Club Medal 1959, Philadelphia Art Dirs' Club Medal 1959, Nat. Cartoonists' Soc. Award 1959, 1960, Gold Medal, III Biennale, Tolentino, Italy 1965, Prix de la Critique Belge 1968, Grand Prix de l'Humour noir (France) 1971, Prix d'Humour, Festival d'Avignon 1971, Medal of French Circus 1971, Prix Int. 'Charles Huard' 1972, La Monnaie de Paris Medal 1974, Bundesrechtsanwaltskammer Award (Germany) 1998. *Literary Agent:* c/o The Sayle Literary Agency, 8B King's Parade, Cambridge, CB2 1SJ, England; c/o Eileen McMahon Agency. *Telephone:* (1223) 303035 (Cambridge). *Fax:* (1223) 301638 (Cambridge). *E-mail:* rcalder@sayleliteraryagency.com; eileenmcmahon@earthlink.net. *Website:* www.ronaldsearle.com.

SEBAG-MONTEFIORE, Simon Jonathan Sebag, MA, FRSL; British writer and historian; b. 27 June 1965, London; m. Santa Montefiore; one s., one d. *Education:* Harrow School, Gonville and Caius Coll., Univ. of Cambridge. *Publications:* novels: King's Parade 1991, My Affair with Stalin 1997; non-fiction: Prince of Princes: The Life of Potemkin 2000, Stalin: The Court of the Red Tsar 2003 (History Book of the Year Prize, British Book Awards 2004), Young Stalin 2007, Catherine the Great & Potemkin 2007. *Literary Agent:* Georgina Capel, Capel & Land, 29 Wardour Street, London, W1V 3HB, England. *Telephone:* (20) 7734-2414. *Website:* simonsebagmontefiore.com.

SEBBAR, Leïla, DèsL; French writer; b. Aflou, Algeria. *Education:* Sorbonne Univ., Paris. *Career:* moved to France aged 17; teacher Lycée Rodin, Paris. *Publications:* novels: Fatima ou les Algériennes au square 1981, Shérazade: 17 ans, brune, frisée, les yeux verts 1982, Le Chinois vert d'Afrique 1984, Parle mon fils, parle à ta mère 1984, Les Carnets de Shérazade 1985, J. H. cherche âme-soeur 1987, Le Fou de Shérazade 1991, Le Silence des rives 1993, La Seine était rouge 1999, Marguerite 2002, Les femmes au bain 2006, L'habit vert 2006, Le ravin de la femme sauvage 2007, Métro 2007; non-fiction: On tue les petites filles 1978, Le Pédophile et la maman 1980, Le Baiser 1997, Soldats 1999, Une Enfance algérienne (ed.) 1999, Lettres parisiennes: histoires d'exil 1999, J'étais enfant en Algérie: Juin 1962 2001, La Jeune fille au balcon 2001, Une Enfance d'ailleurs: 17 écrivains racontent (co-ed.) 2002, Femmes d'Afrique du Nord: cartes postales 1885–1930 (co-ed.) 2002, Je ne parle pas la langue de mon père 2003, Sept filles 2003, Les Algériens au café 2003, Mes algéries en France 2004, Isabelle l'algérienne; juvenile: Ismaël dans la jungle des villes 1986, Lorient-Québec 1991. *Honours:* Chevalier des Arts et Lettres, Chevalier de la Légion d'honneur. *Address:* c/o Éditions Bleu Autour, 11 avenue Pasteur, Saint-Pourçain-sur-Sioule 03500; 13 rue Vergniaud, 75013 Paris, France (home). *Telephone:* 1-45-89-03-32 (home). *E-mail:* dominique .pignon@free.fr (home).

SEBOLD, Alice, MFA; American author; b. Madison, WI. *Education:* Syracuse Univ., Univ. of Houston, Univ. of California at Irvine. *Career:* teacher and lecturer 1984–. *Publications:* Lucky (memoir) 1999, The Lovely Bones (novel) 2002. *Literary Agent:* Steven Barclay Agency, 12 Western Avenue, Petaluma, CA 94952, USA. *Telephone:* (707) 773-0654. *Fax:* (707) 778-1868. *E-mail:* SJBarclay@aol.com.

SECOR, James L., BA, MS, PhD; American writer, dramatist and poet; b. 11 June 1947, Ft Clayton Air Force Base, Panama; one s. *Education:* Towson State Univ., Johns Hopkins Univ., Univ. of Kansas, Bunraku Nat. Puppet Theatre, Osaka. *Career:* teacher, Aoyama Univ. 1990–92, Japan Coll. of the Arts 1992; Tutor, Univ. of Kansas, 1994–99, Johnson County Community Coll. 1995; Ed., Into the Eye 1996–97; mem. Japan Language Teachers' Asscn 1990–92, Lawrence Community Theatre 1997, Acad. of American Poets. *Publications:* Sapl and Nicholas Ferguson: The Legend, 1992; Tanka, Sweetheart, 1996; Tangled in the Net of Ruin, 1996; Statesmanship, 1996; Saving Grace, 1996; A Different Thing to Do, 1996; Tanka, Reflections of Yesterday, 1996; The Crippled Heart of Man, 1997; Social Puissance, 1997; Votive, 1997; Sex Ed, 1997; Tanka, Ages and Stages, 1997; several plays.

SEDAKOVA, Olga Aleksandrovna; Russian poet, translator and essayist; b. 1949, Moscow. *Education:* Moscow State Univ. *Career:* teacher, Inst. of Theory and History of World Culture, Dept of Philosophy, Moscow State Univ. 1991. *Publications include:* Gates, Windows and Arches 1985, Vrata, okna, arki: Izbrannye stikhotvoreni, a 1986, Kitaiskoe puteshestvie: Stely i nadpisi: Starye pesni 1990, Stikhi 1994, Poems and Elegies 2004; contrib. to Silk of Time: Bilingual Selected Poems 1994. *Honours:* European Prize for Poetry 1996. *Address:* c/o University of Bucknell, Moore Avenue, Bucknell, PA 17837, USA. *Website:* www.bucknell.edu.

SEDARIS, David; American playwright and writer; b. 1956, New York, NY. *Career:* made comic debut reading his Santa Land Diaries on Nat. Public Radio's Morning Edn; writes for This American Life (Public Radio Int.). *Plays:* with Amy Sedaris, as The Talent Family: Stump the Host, Stitches, One Woman Shoe (Obie Award), Incident at Cobbler's Knob, The Book of Liz. *Publications include:* Barrel Fever, Children Playing Before a Statue of Hercules: An Anthology of Outstanding Stories, Holidays on Ice 1997, Naked (essays) 1997, Me Talk Pretty One Day (essays) 2000, Dress Your Family in Corduroy and Denim 2004; contrib. essays to Esquire and The New Yorker. *Honours:* Thurber Prize for American Humor 2001, Time magazine Humorist of the Year 2001. *Literary Agent:* The Steven Barclay Agency, 12 Western Avenue, Petaluma, CA 94952, USA. *Telephone:* (707) 773-0654. *Fax:* (707) 778-1868.

SEDGWICK, Fred, MA; British academic and poet; b. 20 Jan. 1945, Dublin, Ireland. *Education:* St Luke's College, Exeter, University of East Anglia at Norwich. *Career:* Head of Downing Primary School, Suffolk. *Publications:* Really in the Dark, 1980; From Another Part of the Island, 1981; A Garland for William Cowper, 1984; The Living Daylights, 1986; Falernian, 1987; This Way, That Way: A Collection of Poems for Schools (ed.), 1989; Lighting Up Time: On Children's Writing, 1990. *Address:* c/o Society of Authors, 84 Drayton Gardens, London SW10 9SB, England.

SEDLEY, Kate (see Clarke, Brenda Margaret Lilian)

SEDLEY, Rt Hon. Sir Stephen John, Kt, PC, BA; British judge and writer; *Lord Justice of Appeal*; b. 9 Oct. 1939, s. of William Sedley and Rachel Sedley; m. 1st Ann Tate 1968 (divorced 1995); one s. two d.; m. 2nd Teresa Chaddock 1996. *Education:* Mill Hill School, Queens' Coll., Cambridge. *Career:* writer, musician, trans. 1961–64; called to Bar, Inner Temple 1964, Bencher 1989, QC 1983; mem. Int. Comm. on Mercenaries, Angola 1976; Visiting Professorial Fellow, Univ. of Warwick 1981; Pres. Nat. Reference Tribunals for the Coalmining Industry 1983–88; Visiting Fellow, Osgoode Hall Law School, Canada 1987, Visiting Prof. 1997; Dir Public Law Project 1989–93; Chair. Sex Discrimination Cttee, Bar Council 1992–95; Judge of the High Court of Justice, Queen's Bench Div. 1992–99; Distinguished Visitor, Hong Kong Univ. 1992; Hon. Prof., Univ. of Wales, Cardiff 1993–, Univ. of Warwick 1994–; Visiting Fellow, Victoria Univ. of Wellington, NZ 1998; Judicial Visitor, Univ. Coll. London 1999–; Pres. British Inst. of Human Rights 2000–, British Tinnitus Asscn 2006–; Chair. British Council Advisory Cttee on Governance 2002–05; mem. Admin. Law Bar Asscn (Hon. Vice-Pres. 1992–), Haldane Soc. (Sec. 1964–69). *Publications include:* Whose Child? 1987, The Making and Remaking of the British Constitution (with Lord Nolan) 1997, Freedom, Law and Justice 1999, Human Rights: A New World or Business as Usual 2000; editor: Seeds of Love (anthology) 1967, A Spark in the Ashes 1992; translator: From Burgos Jail, by Marcos Ana and Vidal de Nicolas 1964; contrib. essays to numerous books, including Freedom of Expression and Freedom of Information 2000, Judicial Review in International Perspective 2000, Discriminating Lawyers 2000; contrib. to periodicals and journals, including Civil Justic Quarterly, Industrial Law Journal, Journal of Law and Society, Journal of Legal Ethics, Law Quarterly Review, London Review of Books, Modern Law Review, Public Law. *Honours:* Hon. Fellow, Inst. for Advanced Legal Studies 1997; Dr hc (North London) 1996; Hon. LLD (Nottingham Trent) 1997, (Bristol) 1999, (Warwick) 1999, (Durham) 2001, (Hull) 2002, (Southampton) 2003. *Address:* Royal Courts of Justice, Strand, London, WC2A 2LL, England (office). *Telephone:* (20) 7947-6000 (office). *Website:* www.hmcourts-service .gov.uk (office).

SEE, Carolyn, (Monica Highland), PhD; American writer; *Professor Emerita, University of California at Los Angeles*; b. 13 Jan. 1934, Pasadena, CA; m. 1st Richard See 1954; m. 2nd Tom Sturak 1960; two d. *Education:* Univ. of California at Los Angeles. *Career:* fmr Prof. of English, UCLA, now Prof. Emer.; mem. PEN Center USA West (pres. 1993–94). *Publications:* as Carolyn See: The Rest is Done with Mirrors 1970, Blue Money 1974, Mothers, Daughters 1977, Rhine Maidens 1980, Golden Days 1985, When Knaves Meet 1988, The Mirrored Hall in the Hollywood Dance Hall 1991, Dreaming: Hard Luck and Good Times in America 1995, The Handyman 1999, There Will Never Be Another You 2006; as Monica Highland: Lotus Land 1983, 1-10 Shanghai Road 1985, Greetings From Southern California 1987, Two Schools of Thought (with John Espey) 1991, Making a Literary Life 2002, Jerusalem 2005; contrib. to newspapers and magazines. *Honours:* Samuel Goldwyn Award 1963, Sidney Hillman Award 1969, NEA grant 1974, Nat. Women's Political Caucus Bread and Roses Award,1988, Vesta Award 1989, Guggenheim Fellowship 1989, Lila Wallace Grant 1993, PEN Center USA West Lifetime Achievement Award 1998. *Address:* 17339 Tramonto, No. 303, Pacific Palisades, CA 90272, USA (office). *Telephone:* (310) 454-7724 (office). *Fax:* (310) 459-8524 (office). *E-mail:* csee@ucla.edu (office).

SEED, Cecile Eugenie (Jenny); South African author; b. 18 May 1930, Cape Town; m. Edward (Ted) Robert Seed 1953, three s. one d. *Publications:* The Great Thirst, 1985; The Great Elephant, 1985; Place Among the Stones, 1987; Hurry, Hurry, Sibusiso, 1988; The Broken Spear, 1989; The Prince of the Bay, 1989; The Big Pumpkin, 1990; Old Grandfather Mantis, 1992; The Hungry People, 1993; A Time to Scatter Stones, 1993; Lucky Boy, 1995; The Strange Large Egg, 1996. *Honours:* MER Award 1987.

SEFTON, Catherine (see Martin Waddell)

SEGAL, Erich, AB, AM, PhD; American academic and writer; b. 16 June 1937, New York, NY; m. Karen James 1975; one s. (deceased) two d. *Education:* Harvard University. *Career:* Teaching Fellow, Harvard University, 1959–63; Visiting Lecturer Yale University 1964–65, Asst Prof. 1965–68, Assoc. Prof. 1968–72, apptd Adjunct Prof. of Classics 1981, now retired; Visiting Prof., University of Munich, 1973, Princeton University, 1974–75, 1981, University of Tel-Aviv, 1976, Dartmouth College, 1976, 1977; Visiting Fellow, 1978–79, Supernumerary Fellow, 1980–, Wolfson College, Oxford; Hon. Research Fellow, University College London, 1983–; mem. Acad. for Literary Studies; American Society of Composers, Authors, and Publishers; Society of Roman Studies, UK; Writers Guild of America. *Publications:* Fiction: Love Story, 1970; Fairy Tale, 1973; Oliver's Story, 1977; Man, Woman and Child, 1980; The Class, 1985; Doctors, 1987; Acts of Faith, 1992; Prizes, 1995; Only Love, 1997. Editor: Euripides: A Collection of Critical Essays, 1968; Scholarship on Plautus, 1965–1976, 1981; Greek Tragedy: Modern Essays in Criticism, 1983, UK edn as Oxford Readings in Greek Tragedy, 1983; Caesar Augustus: Seven Essays (with Fergus Millar), 1984; Plato's Dialogues, 1986; Oxford Readings in Aristophanes, 1996. Editor and Translator: Plautus, 1996, Greek and Roman Comedy 2006. Classics: Roman Laughter: The Comedy of Plautus, 1968; Plautus: Four Comedies, 1996. Other: The Death of Comedy, 2001, Oxford Readings in Menander, Plautus and Terence 2002. Musicals; screenplays. Contributions: various reviews, journals, periodicals, and magazines, including Times Literary Supplement. *Honours:* Chevalier, Légion d'honneur, 1999; Guggenheim Fellowship, 1968; Golden Globe Award, 1971; Humboldt Stiftung Award, West Germany, 1973; Premio Bancarella, Italy, 1986; Prix Littéraire, Deauville, France, 1986; Co-Recipient, Premio San Valentin di Terni Award, 1989. *Address:* c/o Wolfson College, Oxford, OX2 6UD, England.

SEGAL, Lore, BA; American (b. Austrian) writer and fmr academic; b. (Lore Groszmann), 8 March 1928, Vienna, Austria; m. David I. Segal 1960 (deceased); one s. one d. *Education:* Bedford Coll., Univ. of London. *Career:* Prof. Writing Division, School of Arts, Columbia Univ., Princeton Univ., Sarah Lawrence Coll., Bennington Coll.; Prof. of English, Univ. of Illinois, Ohio State Univ., retd 1996. *Publications:* fiction: Other People's Houses 1964, Lucinella 1976, Her First American 1985; children's books: Tell Me a Mitzi 1970, All the Way Home 1973, Tell Me a Trudy 1977, The Story of Mrs Brubeck and How She Looked for Trouble and Where She Found Him 1981, The Story of Mrs Lovewright and Purrless Her Cat 1985, Morris the Artist 2003, Why Mole Shouted 2004, More Mole Stories and Little Gopher Too 2005; translator: Gallows Songs (with W. D. Snodgrass) 1968, The Juniper Tree and Other Tales from Grimm 1973; contrib. to periodicals. *Honours:* Guggenheim Fellowship 1965–66, NEA grant 1982, Nat. Endowment for the Humanities grant 1983, Acad. of Arts and Letters Award 1986, Ohio Arts Council grant 1996. *Address:* 280 Riverside Drive, New York, NY 10025, USA. *Telephone:* (212) 663-1524. *Fax:* (212) 663-1524. *E-mail:* Lore@usa.net.

SEGAL, Ronald Michael, BA; South African/British author; b. 14 July 1932, Cape Town; s. of Leon Segal and Mary Segal; m. Susan Wolff 1962; one s. two d. *Education:* Univ. of Cape Town and Trinity Coll., Cambridge. *Career:* Dir Faculty and Cultural Studies Nat. Union of S African Students 1951–52; Pres. Univ. of Cape Town Council of Univ. Socs 1951; won Philip Francis du Pont Fellowship to Univ. of Virginia (USA) 1955 but returned to S Africa to found Africa South (quarterly) 1956; helped launch economic boycott April 1959; banned by S African Govt July 1959; in England with Africa South in Exile, April 1960–61; Gen. Ed. Penguin African Library 1961–84; Pluto Crime Fiction 1983–86; Hon. Sec. S African Freedom Asscn 1960–61; Convenor, Int. Conf. on Econ. Sanctions against S Africa 1964, Int. Conf. on SW Africa 1966; Visiting Fellow, Center for Study of Democratic Insts, Santa Barbara 1973; Founding Chair. The Walton Soc. 1975–79, Pres. 1979–; Chair. Ruth First Memorial Trust 1983–. *Publications:* The Tokolosh (a fantasy) 1960, Political Africa: A Who's Who of Personalities and Parties 1961, African Profiles 1962, Into Exile 1963, Sanctions Against South Africa (ed.) 1964, The Crisis of India 1965, The Race War 1966, South West Africa: Travesty of Trust (ed.) 1967, America's Receding Future 1968, The Struggle Against History 1971, Whose Jerusalem? The Conflicts of Israel 1973, The Decline and Fall of the American Dollar 1974, The Tragedy of Leon Trotsky 1979, The State of the World Atlas 1981, The New State of the World Atlas 1984, The Book of Business, Money and Power 1987, The Black Diaspora 1995, Islam's Black Slaves 2001.

Address: The Old Manor House, Manor Road, Walton-on-Thames, Surrey, England (home). *Telephone:* (1932) 227766 (office).

SEIDMAN, Hugh, BS, MS, MFA; American writer, poet and teacher; b. 1 Aug. 1940, New York, NY; m. Jayne Holsinger 1990. *Education:* Polytechnic Institute of Brooklyn, Univ. of Minnesota, Columbia Univ. *Career:* Faculty, New School for Social Research, New York, 1976–98; Asst Prof., Washington College, 1979; Visiting Lecturer, Univ. of Wisconsin, 1981, Columbia Univ., 1985; Poet-in-Residence, College of William and Mary, 1982; Visiting Poet, Writers Voice, New York, 1988; mem. American PEN, Authors' Guild, Authors' League, Poetry Soc. of America. *Publications:* Collecting Evidence, 1970; Blood Lord, 1974; Throne/Falcon/Eye, 1982; People Live, They Have Lives, 1992; Selected Poems 1965–1995, 1995; 12 Views of Freetown, 1 View of Bumbuna, 2002, Somebody Stand Up and Sing 2005; contribs to numerous publs. *Honours:* Yale Series of Younger Poets Prize, 1969; National Endowment for the Arts Grant, 1970, and Fellowships, 1972, 1985; Yaddo Fellowships, 1972, 1976, 1986; MacDowell Colony Fellowships, 1974, 1975, 1989; Writers Digest Poetry Prize, 1982; New York Foundation for the Arts Poetry Fellowships, 1990, 2003, Green Rose Prize 2004. *Address:* 463 West Street, No. H822, New York, NY 10014, USA. *Website:* www.hughseidman.com.

SEIDMAN, L(ewis) William, AB, LLB, MBA; American fmr government official, publisher, television broadcaster and consultant; b. 29 April 1921, Grand Rapids, Mich.; s. of Frank Seidman and Esther Lubetsky; m. Sarah Berry 1944; one s. five d. *Education:* Dartmouth Coll., Harvard Univ. and Univ. of Mich. *Career:* army service 1942–46; mem. Mich. Bar 1949, DC Bar 1977; Special Asst for Financial Affairs to Gov. of Mich. 1963–66; Nat. Man. Partner, Seidman & Seidman (certified public accountants) New York 1969–74; Asst for Econ. Affairs to Pres. Gerald Ford 1974–77; Dir Phelps Dodge Corpn New York 1977–82, Vice-Chair. 1980–82; Dean, Coll. of Business Admin. Ariz. State Univ. 1982–85; Chair. Fed. Deposit Insurance Corpn (FDIC) 1985–91; Dirs Fed. Reserve Bank, Chicago, Detroit Br. 1966–70, Chair. 1970; Co-Chair. White House Conf. on Productivity 1983–84; Chair. Resolution Trust Corpn 1989–91; Chief Commentator CNBC-TV 1991–; Publr Bank Director (magazine); mem. Bd of Dirs Pharmaceutical Resources Inc. 2004–, Clark Inc 1998–, Fiserv Inc 1992–, InteliData Techs Corpn, LML Payment Systems Inc. *Publications:* Full Faith and Credit 1993. *Honours:* Bronze Star Medal. *Address:* CNBC, 8th Floor, 1025 Connecticut Avenue, NW, Washington, DC 20036 (office); 825 Audubon Drive, Bradenton, FL 34209, USA (home). *Telephone:* (202) 530-0910 (office). *Fax:* (202) 822-9551 (office). *E-mail:* lws1025@aol.com (office).

SEIERSTAD, Åsne; Norwegian journalist and writer; b. 1970, Oslo. *Education:* Univ. of Oslo. *Career:* staff, ITAR-TASS news agency, Moscow; covered wars in Chechnya, Kosovo, Afghanistan, Iraq for several Scandinavian newspapers 1994–2004; correspondent, Norwegian television news 1998–2000. *Publications:* non-fiction: With Their Backs to the World 2000, The Bookseller of Kabul 2002, A Hundred and One Days: A Baghdad Journal 2004. *Honours:* award for television reporting from Kosovo, Chechnya and Afghanistan; Journalist of the Year, Norway 2003; EMMA Award, London 2004; Bookseller's Prize, Paris, France 2004. *Address:* c/o Virago Press, Brettenham House, Lancaster Place, London, WC2E 7EN, England (office); Tidemands gt. 20, 0260 Oslo, Norway (home). *E-mail:* aaseie@frisurf.no (home). *Website:* www.virago.co.uk (office).

SEIFFERT, Rachel, BA, MLitt; British writer and teacher; b. 1971, Oxford; one s. *Education:* Univs of Bristol and Glasgow. *Career:* fmr Lecturer in English, Univ. of Glasgow. *Publications:* Blue (short story) 1999, The Crossing (short story) 2001, The Dark Room (novel) (LA Times First Fiction Award 2002) 2001, Field Study (short stories) 2004, Afterwards (novel) 2007. *Honours:* PEN David T. K. Wong Award 2001, Betty Trask Prize 2002. *Literary Agent:* c/o Toby Eady Associates Ltd, Third Floor, 9 Orme Court, London, W2 4RL, England. *Telephone:* (20) 7792-0092. *Fax:* (20) 7792-0879. *E-mail:* toby@tobyeady.demon.co.uk. *Website:* www.tobyeadyassociates.co.uk.

SELBERG, Ingrid Maria, BA; American publishing executive; *Publishing Director, Children's Division, Simon & Schuster UK;* b. 13 March 1950, Princeton, NJ; d. of Atle and Hedvig (née Liebermann) Selberg; m. Mustapha Matura; one s., one d. *Education:* Univ. of Columbia (New York). *Career:* Ed Collins Publs 1978–84; Editorial Dir Bantam (UK) 1984–85; Publr Heinemann Young Books, William Heinemann and Methuen Children's Books, London 1986–1995; Man. Dir Dorling Kindersley –1998; Man. Dir Pleasant Company International, HIT Entertainment and Reed Consumer Books; fmrly Vice Pres. UK and Int. Publishing Gullane Entertainment –2002; Publishing Dir Children's Div. Simon & Schuster UK 2003–. *Publications:* Trees and Leaves 1977, Our Changing World 1981, Nature's Hidden World 1983. *Address:* Simon & Schuster UK Ltd Africa House, 64–78 Kingsway, London WC2B 6AH, England (office). *Telephone:* (20) 7316 1900 (office). *Fax:* (20) 7316 0332 (office). *E-mail:* enquiries@simonandschuster.co.uk.

SELBOURNE, David, BA, MA; British writer and playwright; b. 4 June 1937, London. *Education:* Balliol Coll., Oxford, Inner Temple, London. *Career:* mem. Acad. of Savignano, Italy 1994. *Publications:* The Play of William Cooper and Edmund Dew-Nevett 1968, The Two-Backed Beast 1969, Dorabella 1970, Samson and Alison Mary Fagan 1971, The Damned 1971, Class Play 1973, Brook's Dream: The Politics of Theatre 1974, What's Acting? and Think of a Story Quickly! 1977, An Eye to India 1977, An Eye to China 1978, Through the Indian Looking Glass 1982, The Making of a Midsummer Night's Dream 1983,

Against Socialist Illusion: A Radical Argument 1985, In Theory and In Practice: Essays on the Politics of Jayaprakash Narayan 1986, Left Behind: Journeys into British Politics 1987, A Doctor's Life: The Diaries of Hugh Selbourne MD 1960–63 1989, Death of the Dark Hero: Eastern Europe 1987–90 1990, The Spirit of the Age 1993, Not an Englishman: Conversations With Lord Goodman 1993, The Principle of Duty 1994, The City of Light 1997, One Year On: The 'New' Politics and Labour 1998, Moral Evasion 1998, The Losing Battle with Islam 2005; trans.: The City of Light, by Jacob d'Ancona 1997. *Honours:* Officer, Order of Merit of Italian Repub. 2001. *Literary Agent:* c/o Christopher Sinclair-Stevenson, 3 South Terrace, London, SW7, England.

SELBY, Stephen, BA; British playwright; b. 5 June 1952, Darley Dale, Derbyshire; m. Ann Spence 1982; one d. *Education:* Nottingham Trent and Bolton Inst. *Career:* writer, dir, producer, Noc On Theatre 1987–, Hurdles of Time Theatre 1991–; Dramaturgo, La Edel de Oro Theatre Co.; mem. Theatre Writers Union, Camagüey Theatre Dirs Asscn. *Plays:* Better Looking Corpses 1989, Contentious Work 1990, Archie Pearson The One-Legged Shoemaker 1991, Erewash Giants 1993, The Concrete Silver Band 1995, Tontos Sabios y Ladrones Honestos 1996, Dead Letters 2000. *Publication:* Hurdles of Time 1993. *Address:* 53 Percival Road, Sherwood, Nottingham, NG5 2FA, England. *Telephone:* (115) 910-9116 (office). *E-mail:* jam53p@ntlworld.com (office).

SELF, William (Will) Woodward, MA; British writer and cartoonist; *Columnist, The Independent;* b. 26 Sept. 1961, London; s. of Peter John Otter Self and Elaine Rosenbloom; m. 1st Katharine Sylvia Anthony Chancellor 1989 (divorced 1996); one s. one d.; m. 2nd Deborah Jane Orr 1997; two s. *Education:* Christ's Coll., Exeter Coll., Oxford. *Career:* cartoon illustrations appeared in New Statesman and City Limits 1982–88; Publishing Dir Cathedral Publishing 1988–90; Contributing Ed. London Evening Standard magazine 1993–95; columnist, The Observer 1995–97, The Times 1997–99, Ind. on Sunday 2000–, Evening Standard 2002–, The Independent 2003–. *Publications:* short stories: Quantity Theory of Insanity 1991, Grey Area 1994, A Story for Europe 1996, Tough Tough Toys for Tough Tough Boys 1998, Dr Mukti and Other Tales of Woe 2003; novellas: Cock and Bull 1992, The Sweet Smell of Psychosis 1996; novels: My Idea of Fun 1993, Great Apes 1997, How the Dead Live 2000, Perfidious Man 2000, Feeding Frenzy 2001, Dorian 2002, Dr Mukti 2004, The Book of Dave 2006; Junk Mail (selected journalism) 1995, Sore Sites (collected journalism) 2000; collected cartoons 1985. *Honours:* Geoffrey Faber Memorial Prize 1992. *Literary Agent:* The Wylie Agency, 17 Bedford Square, London, WC1B 3BA, England. *Telephone:* (20) 7908-5900.

SELTZER, Joanne, BA, MA; American writer and poet; b. 21 Nov. 1929, Detroit, MI; d. of Samuel Zellman and Ethel Goldstein; m. Stanley Seltzer 1951; one s. three d. *Education:* Univ. of Michigan, Coll. of St Rose. *Career:* mem. American Literary Trans. Asscn, Associated Writing Programs, Poetry Soc. of America, Poets & Writers. *Publications:* Adirondack Lake Poems 1985, Suburban Landscape 1988, Inside Invisible Walls 1989; contribs to journals and magazines and to anthologies including When I Am an Old Woman I Shall Wear Purple. *Honours:* All Nations Poetry Contest Award 1978, World Order of Narrative and Formalist Poets Competitions Prizes 1986, 1988, 1990, 1992, 1993, 1994, 1997, 1998, 2000, Tucumari Literary Review Poetry Contest Award 1989, Amelia Islander Magazine Literary Contest Poetry Prize 1999. *Address:* 2481 McGovern Drive, Schenectady, NY 12309, USA. *E-mail:* Joseltzer@nycap.rr.com.

SELVADURAI, Shyam, BFA; Sri Lankan writer; b. 1965, Colombo. *Education:* York Univ. *Career:* moved with family to Canada aged 19 after 1983 riots in Colombo; writer for TV. *Publications:* Funny Boy (novel) (WHSmith/Books in Canada First Novel Award, Lambda Literary Award for Best Gay Men's Fiction, USA) 1994, Cinnamon Gardens (novel) 1998; contrib. fiction and essays to journals and anthologies. *Address:* c/o McClelland and Steward, 481 University Avenue, Suite 900, Toronto, ON M5G 2E9, Canada. *Website:* www.interlog.com/~funnyboy/.

SELVIDGE, Marla Jean, BA, MA, PhD; American academic and writer; b. 11 Nov. 1948, Grosse Pointe, MI; m. 1st Stephen P. Schierling (divorced 1981); m. 2nd Thomas C. Hemling 1982. *Education:* Fort Wayne Bible College, Wheaton College, IL, St Louis University. *Career:* several college and university positions, 1973–89; Assoc. Ed., Explorations: A Journal for Adventurous Thought, 1986–; Contributing Ed., Spotlight on Teaching, 1993–; Asst Prof. of Religious Studies and Philosophy, Marist College, Poughkeepsie, New York, 1989–90; Assoc. Prof., 1990–94, Dir, Center for Religious Studies, 1990–, Prof. of Religious Studies, 1994–, Central Michigan State University, Warrensburg; Vice-Pres., American Schools of Oriental Research, 1997–; mem. American Acad. of Religion; Society of Biblical Literature; Catholic Biblical Asscn; Central States Society of Biblical Literature, Chair, Sections on New Testament, 1992–94, Chair, Gender Issues, 1994–96; Missouri State Teachers Asscn, Vice-Pres. and Board of Dirs, 1997–. *Publications:* Fundamentalism Today: What Makes It So Attractive? (ed.), 1984; Daughters of Jerusalem, 1987; Woman, Cult, and Miracle Recital, 1990; Discovering Women, 1995; Notorious Voices: The Roots of Feminist Biblical Interpretation, 1996; Violence, Women, and the Bible, 1996; A Feminist Companion to the Bible: The Old Testament in the New Testament (contributor), 1996; Notorious Voices: A Reader, 1997; The New Testament: A Timeless Book for All Peoples, 1998. Contributions: Religious Studies News; Journal of Religious Studies; Marist Working Papers; Journal of Biblical Literature; Catholic Biblical Quarterly; Journal of Theology for Southern Africa; Missouri Chautauqua: Varieties of American Religious Experience. *Honours:* Society of Biblical Literature Award, 1982–83; Grants, William R. Kenan Fund and National Endowment for the Humanities, 1984–87; Educational Communications Award, Connecticut Asscn of Boards of Education, 1988–89; American Mirror Lecturer, 1991–93, Grant, 1992–94, Missouri Humanities Council.

SEMEL, Nava, MA; Israeli author and playwright; b. 15 Sept. 1954; m. Noam Semel, two s. one d. *Education:* Tel-Aviv Univ. *Career:* mem. Israeli Playwright Asscn, Hebrew Writers' Asscn, PEN International Writers, Writers' Asscn. *Publications:* Hat of Glass 1985, Becoming Gershona 1990, Flying Lessons 1995, Night Games 1994, Little Rose of the Mediterranean 1994, Bride on Paper 1996, Liluna 1998, Who Stole the Show? 1999, Awake in my Sleep 2000, And the Rat Laughed (opera libretto) (with composer Ella Milch-Sheriff, Rosenblum Award of Tel-Aviv 2006) 2004, 1000 Calories a Day (screenplay, Israeli TV) 2002, Isra Island (novel) 2005, Beginner's Love (YA book) 2006; plays: An Old Lady 1984, The Child Behind the Eyes 1986, Hunger 1989, An Old Man 2004, The Courage to be Afraid 2004. *Honours:* Inst. for Holocaust Studies Award 1988, Haifa Award 1988, Nat. Jewish Book Award 1991, Israeli Prime Minister's Award for Literature 1996, Best Illustrated Book of the Year, Israel Museum Award 1998. *Address:* 56 Weitzman Street, #13, Tel-Aviv 62155, Israel (home). *Telephone:* (3) 5460514 (home). *Fax:* (3) 5440398 (home). *E-mail:* semel@012.net.il.

SEMMLER, Clement William, MA; Australian broadcaster and writer; b. 23 Dec. 1914, Eastern Well, SA; m. 1st (divorced); one s. one d.; m. 2nd Catherine Helena Wilson 1974; one d. *Education:* University of Adelaide. *Career:* Fellow, College of Fine Arts, University of New South Wales. *Publications:* For the Uncanny Man (essays), 1963; Barcroft Boake, 1965; Literary Australia (ed.), 1965; The Banjo of the Bush, 1966; Kenneth Slessor, 1966; Twentieth Century Australian Literary Criticism (ed.), 1967; The Art of Brian James, 1972; Douglas Stewart, 1974; The ABC-Aunt Sally and the Sacred Cow, 1981; A Frank Hardy Swag (ed.), 1982; The War Diaries of Kenneth Slessor, 1985; The War Dispatches of Kenneth Slessor, 1987; Pictures on the Margin (memoirs), 1991. Contributions: periodicals and journals. *Honours:* DLitt, University of New England, Armidale, 1968; OBE, 1972; AM, 1988.

SEMPRÚN, Jorge; Spanish politician and writer; b. 10 Dec. 1923, Madrid. *Career:* in exile in France following Spanish Civil War; fought in the French Resistance in World War II, captured by Nazis and sent to Buchenwald concentration camp; became leader of proscribed Spanish Communist Party, expelled as deviationist; Minister of Culture 1988–91; mem. Acad. Goncourt. *Publications:* Le Grand Voyage (novel, in French), The Autobiography of Federico Sánchez (under pseudonym), Literature or Life 1998, Le Retour de Carola Neher (play) 1998; screenplays for films: Z, La Guerre est finie, L'aveu. *Honours:* Dr hc (Turin) 1990; Prix Fémina 1969, Prix Fémina Vacaresco 1994, Prix Littéraire des Droits de l'Homme 1995, Jerusalem Prize 1997, Nonino Prize 1999, Goethe Medal 2003. *Address:* c/o Penguin Books, 80 Strand, London, WC2R 0RL, England.

SEN, Amartya Kumar, PhD, FBA; Indian economist; *Lamont University Professor Emeritus and Professor of Economics and Philosophy, Harvard University;* b. 3 Nov. 1933, Santiniketan, Bengal; s. of the late Ashutosh Sen and of Amita Sen; m. 1st Nabaneeta Dev 1960 (divorced 1975); two d.; m. 2nd Eva Colorni 1978 (died 1985); one s. one d.; m. 3rd Emma Rothschild. *Education:* Presidency Coll., Calcutta and Trinity Coll., Cambridge. *Career:* Prof. of Econs, Jadavpur Univ., Calcutta 1956–58; Fellow, Trinity Coll., Cambridge 1957–63; Prof. of Econs, Univ. of Delhi 1963–71, Chair. Dept of Econs 1966–68; Hon. Dir Agricultural Econs Research Centre, Delhi 1966–68, 1969–71; Prof. of Econs, LSE 1971–77, Univ. of Oxford 1977–80, Drummond Prof. of Political Economy 1980–88; Lamont Univ. Prof., Harvard Univ. 1987–98, 2004–, Prof. Emer. 1998–2004, Prof. of Econs and Philosophy 2004–; Master Trinity Coll., Cambridge 1998–2004; Visiting Prof., Univ. of Calif., Berkeley 1964–65, Harvard Univ. 1968–69; Andrew D. White Prof.-at-Large, Cornell Univ. 1978–84; Pres. Int. Econ. Asscn 1986–89; Fellow, Econometric Soc., Pres. 1984. *Publications:* Choice of Techniques: An Aspect of Planned Economic Development 1960, Growth Economics 1970, Collective Choice and Social Welfare 1970, On Economic Inequality 1973, Employment, Technology and Development 1975, Poverty and Famines 1981, Utilitarianism and Beyond (jtly with Bernard Williams) 1982, Choice, Welfare and Measurement 1982, Resources, Values and Development 1984, Commodities and Capabilities 1985, On Ethics and Economics 1987, The Standard of Living 1988, Hunger and Public Action (with Jean Drèze) 1989, Social Security in Developing Countries (jtly) 1991, Inequality Re-examined 1992, The Quality of Life (jtly) 1993, Development as Freedom 1999, The Argumentative Indian: Writings on Indian History, Culture and Identity 2005, Identity and Violence: The Illusion of Destiny 2006; articles in various journals in econs, philosophy and political science. *Honours:* Hon. Prof., Delhi Univ.; Foreign Hon. mem. American Acad. of Arts and Sciences; Hon. Fellow, Inst. of Social Studies, The Hague, Hon. Fellow LSE, Inst. of Devt Studies; Hon. CH 2000; Grand Cross, Order of Scientific Merit (Brazil) 2000; Hon. DLitt (Univ. of Saskatchewan, Canada) 1979, (Visva-Bharati Univ., India) 1983, (Oxford) 1996; Hon. DUniv (Essex) 1984, (Caen) 1987; Hon. DSc (Bath) 1984, (Bologna) 1988; Dr hc (Univ. Catholique de Louvain) 1989, (Padua) 1998; Senator Giovanni Agnelli Inst. Prize for Ethics 1989, Nobel Prize for Econs 1998, UN Econ. and Social Comm. for Asia and the Pacific (UNESCAP) Lifetime Achievement Award 2007. *Address:* Department of Economics, Harvard University, Cambridge, MA 02138, USA (office). *Telephone:* (617) 495-1871 (office). *Fax:* (617) 496-5942 (office). *E-mail:* weiner@fas.harvard.edu (office). *Website:* www.hsph.harvard.edu/facres/senak.html.

SENCIÓN, Viriato; Dominican Republic writer; b. 1941, San José de Ocoa. *Education:* Seminary Santo Tomás de Aquino, Santo Domingo, Crown Inst of Costa Rica, Lehman Coll., CUNY. *Publications:* Los que falsifican la firma de Dios (trans. as They Forged the Signature of God) 1992, La enema Celania y otros cuentos 1994, Los ojos de la montaña 1997. *Address:* c/o Curbstone Press, 321 Jackson Street, Willimantic, CT 06226-1738, USA. *E-mail:* info@curbstone.org. *Website:* www.curbstone.org.

SENDAK, Maurice Bernard, LHD; American illustrator and writer; b. 10 June 1928, New York; s. of Philip Sendak and Sadie (née Schindler) Sendak. *Education:* Art Students League, New York, Boston Univ. *Career:* writer and illustrator of children's books 1951–; Co-Founder, Artistic Dir The Night Kitchen 1990–. *Solo exhibitions include:* Gallery School of Visual Arts, New York 1964, Ashmolean Museum, Oxford 1975, American Cultural Center, Paris 1978. *Publications (writer and illustrator):* Kenny's Window 1956, Very Far Away 1957, The Sign on Rosie's Door 1960, The Nutshell Library 1963, Where the Wild Things Are (Caldecott Medal 1964) 1963, On Books and Pictures 1986, Caldecott and Co. (collection of reviews and articles) 1989, We Are All in the Dumps with Jack and Guy 1993. *Illustrator:* A Hole is to Dig 1952, A Very Special House 1954, I'll Be You and You Be Me 1954, Charlotte and the White Horse 1955, What Do You Say, Dear? 1959, The Moonjumpers 1960, Little Bear's Visit 1962, Schoolmaster Whackwell's Wonderful Sons 1962, Mr. Rabbit and the Lovely Present 1963, The Griffin and the Minor Canon 1963, Nikolenka's Childhood 1963, The Bat-Poet 1964, Lullabies and Night Songs 1965, Hector Protector and As I Went Over the Water 1965, Zlateh the Goat 1966, Higglety Pigglety Pop, Or There Must Be More To Life 1967, In the Night Kitchen 1970, The Animal Family 1965, In The Night Kitchen Coloring Book 1971, Pictures by Maurice Sendak 1971, The Juniper Tree and Other Tales from Grimm 1973, Outside Over There 1981, The Love for Three Oranges (with Frank Corsaro) 1984, Nutcracker (with Ralph Manheim) 1984, The Cunning Little Vixen 1985, Dear Mili 1988, I Saw Esau 1992, The Ubiquitous Pig 1992; Writer, Dir and Lyricist for TV animated special Really Rosie 1975. *Stage designs:* The Magic Flute 1980, The Love for Three Oranges 1984, L'Enfant et les sortilèges 1987, The Cunning Little Vixen (for New York Opera) 1989, Idomeneo (opera) 1990. *Honours:* Hans Christian Andersen Illustrators Award 1970; Nat. Medal of Arts 1997. *Address:* c/o HarperCollins, Children's Division, 1350 Avenue of the Americas, New York, NY 10019, USA.

SENNETT, Richard, FRSA, FRSL; British sociologist, writer and academic; *Professor of Social and Cultural Theory, London School of Economics and Political Science*; b. 1 Jan. 1943, Chicago, IL, USA; m. Saskia Sassen 1987; one step-s. *Education:* Breck School, Univ. of Chicago, Juilliard Conservatory New York, Harvard Univ. *Career:* Lecturer, Yale Univ. 1968–70; Asst Prof., Brandeis Univ. 1970–72; Prof., New York Univ. 1972–98, Prof. of Sociology 2006–; Founder New York Inst. of the Humanities; Prof. of Social and Cultural Theory, LSE 1999–; Bemis Prof. of Sociology, MIT 2005–07; Fellow, American Acad. of Arts and Sciences 1996–. *Publications:* non-fiction: The Uses of Disorder: Personal Identity and City Life 1970, Families Against the City 1970, The Fall of Public Man 1974, Hidden Injuries of Class (with Jonathan Cobb) 1977, The Psychology of Society 1977, Authority 1980, The Conscience of the Eye 1990, Flesh and Stone: The Body and the City in Western Civilisation 1994, The Corrosion of Character 1998, Respect: The Formation of Character in an Age of Inequality 2003; editor: 19th Century Cities: Essays in the New Urban History (with Stephan Thernstrom) 1969, Classic Essays on the Culture of Cities 1969, The Culture of the New Capitalism 2006; memoir: Respect 2003; novels: The Frog Who Dared to Croak 1982, An Evening of Brahms 1984, Palais Royal 1986. *Honours:* Chevalier, Légion d'honneur 1997; Dr hc (Loyola Univ. of America) 2003; Ebert Prize for Sociology 1999, Amalti Prize 2000, American Technological Assen Lynd Prize 2004, Hegel Prize 2006. *Address:* London School of Economics and Political Science, Houghton Street, London, WC2A 2AE, England (office). *Telephone:* (20) 7955-6076 (office). *Fax:* (20) 7955-7697 (office). *E-mail:* r.sennett@lse.ac.uk (office). *Website:* www.lse.ac.uk (office).

SERENY, Gitta, CBE; American (b. Hungarian) writer; b. 13 March 1923, Hungary; d. of Gyula and Margit Sereny; m. Donald Honeyman 1948; one s. one d. *Education:* Vienna Realgymnasium Luithlen, Stonar House School, Sandwich, Kent and Sorbonne, Paris. *Career:* writer and journalist for several newspapers and periodicals including The Times, The Independent, Die Zeit, Dagens Nyheter, NY Review of Books. *Publications:* The Medallion 1957, The Case of Mary Bell 1972, Into that Darkness 1974, The Invisible Children 1984, Albert Speer – His Battle with Truth (James Tait Black Memorial Prize 1995, Duff Cooper Award 1995) 1995, Cries Unheard (The McAllen Gold Dagger for non-fiction crime 1998) 1998, The German Trauma (US title The Healing Wound) 2000. *Honours:* Hon. DLitt (Kingston, England) 2003; Geting and Arets Awards for Best Pocketbooks 1999, 2001, PASS Award, Nat. Council on Crime and Delinquency, USA 1999, Steg Dagermann Prize for Contrib. to Literature, Sweden 2002. *Literary Agent:* The Sayle Literary Agency, Bickerton House, 25–27 Bickerton Road, London, N19 5JT, England. *Telephone:* (20) 7263-8681. *Fax:* (20) 7561-0529. *Address:* 20 Durrels House, Warwick Gardens, London, W14 8QB, England (home).

SERHANE, Abdelhak; Moroccan writer and poet; b. 1950. *Career:* psychology teacher, Université Ibn Tofaïl, Kénitra. *Publications:* novels: Messaouda (Prix Littéraire des Radios Libres 1984) 1983, Les Enfants des rues étroites 1986, Le Soleil des obscurs (Prix Français du Monde Arabe 1993) 1992, Le Deuil des chiens 1998; poetry: L'Ivre poème 1989, Chant d'ortie 1993, La Nuit du secret 1992; non-fiction: L'Amour circoncis 1995, Les Prolétaires de la haine 1995, Le Temps noir 2002; contrib. to Autrement, Librement, Horizons maghrébins, Lamalif, Oualili, Actes du Colloque de Montpellier. *Address:* Université Ibn Tofaïl, BP 242, Kénitra 14000, Morocco (office). *Website:* www.univ-ibntofail.ac.ma.

SERVADIO, Gaia Cecilia, (Gualtiero Maldè); British (b. Italian) writer and journalist; b. 13 Sept. 1938, Padua, Italy; two s. one d. *Education:* St Martin's School of Art, London, Camberwell School of Typography. *Career:* Lecturer, ACI 1970, Manchester Museum 1982; Consultant Ed., Italy 1987; Dir of Debates and Literary Talks, Accad. Italiana 1988–94; Italian Foreign Minister, Australia 1992, India 1995, Canada 2001; corresp., La Stampa 1978–90, Il Corriere della Sera 1990–2000; apptd responsible for External Relations Teatro Masimo Opera House Palermo; Vice-Pres. Foreign Press Assen 1989–94; Gen. Sec. Abbado's Mahler and Second School of Vienna Festival 1981–82; mem. Soc. of Authors, Associazione Culturale Italiana. *TV documentaries for BBC:* Murder by Neglect, Verdi 1992, Damn Nation 2001. *Publications:* Melinda 1968, Don Juan/Salome 1969, Il Metodo 1971, Mafioso 1972, A Siberian Encounter 1972, A Profile of a Mafia Boss 1973, Insider Outsider 1977, To a Different World: La donna nel Rinascimento 1979, Luchino Visconti: A Biography 1981, Il Lamento di Arianna 1985, Una infanzia diversa 1989, The Story of R 1991, Edward Lear's Italian Letters (ed.) 1990, La Vallata 1990, Incontri (essays) 1992, The Real Traviata 1994, La mia Umbria (ed.) 1994, Motya, Uncovering a Lost Civilisation 2000, Rossini: A Life 2003, Woman in the Renaissance 2004, E i Morti Mon Sanno 2005; contrib. to The Observer, The Times, Sunday Times, Sunday Telegraph, Daily Telegraph. *Honours:* Cavaliere Ufficiale della Republica Italiana 1985. *Address:* 31 Bloomfield Terrace, London, SW1W 8RE, England (home). *Telephone:* (20) 7730-4378 (home). *E-mail:* kdd39@dial.pipex.com (office); gaia@gaiaservadio.info (home). *Website:* www.gaiaservadio.info.

SERVAN-SCHREIBER, Jean-Claude, LenD; French media executive and newspaperman; b. 11 April 1918, Paris; s. of the late Robert Servan-Schreiber and Suzanne Crémieux; m. 1st Christiane Laroche 1947 (divorced); m. 2nd Jacqueline Guix de Pinos 1955 (divorced); two s. three d.; m. 3rd Paule Guinet 1983 (divorced). *Education:* Exeter Coll., Oxford and Sorbonne. *Career:* served World War II in Flanders 1940, in Resistance 1941–42, in N Africa 1943, France 1944, Germany 1945; with Les Echos 1946–65, Gen. Man. 1957, Dir 1963–65; Deputy for Paris, Nat. Ass. 1965–67; Asst Sec.-Gen. UNR-UDT 1965; Pres. Rassemblement français pour Israël 1967; Dir-Gen. Régie française de publicité 1968–78; mem. Haut Conseil de l'audiovisuel 1973–81; Pres. Groupe Européen des Régisseurs de Publicité Télévisée 1975–78; mem. Conseil politique, RPR 1977–81; Conseiller du Groupe de Presse L'Expansion 1980–93; Special Adviser Mitsubishi Electric (Europe) 1992–2000; Pres. Inst. Arthur Vernes (Medical and Surgical Center) 1993–. *Honours:* Commdr, Légion d'honneur; Médaille mil.; Commdr Ordre nat. du Mérite; Croix de guerre; Croix du Combattant volontaire de la Résistance; Legion of Merit (USA), etc. *Address:* 147 bis rue d'Alésia, 75014 Paris, France. *Telephone:* (1) 45-39-96-11. *Website:* jcss@wanadoo.fr (home).

SETH, Vikram, CBE, MA, PhD; Indian author and poet; b. 1952, Calcutta (now Kolkata); s. of Premnath Seth and Leila Seth. *Education:* Doon School, India, Tonbridge School, UK, Corpus Christi Coll., Oxford, Stanford Univ., USA, Nanjing Univ., People's Repub. of China. *Career:* Guggenheim Fellowships. *Publications:* Mappings 1980, From Heaven Lake: Travels Through Sinkiang and Tibet 1983, The Humble Administrator's Garden 1985, All You Who Sleep Tonight (trans.) 1985, The Golden Gate: A Novel in Verse 1986, Three Chinese Poets (trans.) 1992, A Suitable Boy (novel) 1993, Arion and the Dolphin (libretto) 1994, Beastly Tales (animal fables) 1994, An Equal Music (novel) 1999, Two Lives (biog.) 2005; several vols of poetry. *Honours:* Hon. Fellow Corpus Christi Coll., Oxford 1994; Chevalier des Arts et des Lettres 2001; Commonwealth Poetry Prize 1986, W.H. Smith Literary Prize 1994, Commonwealth Writers' Prize 1994. *Literary Agent:* c/o Jonny Geller, Curtis Brown, Haymarket House, 28-29 Haymarket, London, London, SW1Y 4SP, England. *Telephone:* (20) 7393-4400 (office). *Fax:* (20) 7393-4401 (office). *E-mail:* cb@curtisbrown.co.uk.

SETTANNI, Harry Eugene, BS, MA, PhD; American academic and writer; b. 8 March 1945, Chicago, IL. *Education:* St Joseph's Univ., Philadelphia, Villanova Univ., St John's Univ., Jamaica, NY. *Career:* Faculty, St Joseph's Univ., Phildelphia 1976–78, 1990–, St John's Univ., Jamaica, NY 1978–82, Holy Family Coll., Philadelphia 1987–. *Publications:* Holism: A Philosophy for Today, Anticipating the Twenty-First Century 1990, What is Man? 1991, The Probabilist Theism of John Stuart Mill 1991, What is Morality? 1992, Five Philosophers: How Their Lives Influenced Their Thought 1992, Scientific Knowledge 1992, What is Freedom of Choice? 1992, The Philosophic Foundation of Paranormal Phenomena 1992, Controversial Questions in Philosophy 1996, Five Primers in the Social Sciences 1996, Essays in Psychology and Epistemology 1996, Knowledge and Reality 1996, Miscellaneous Essays 1996; contrib. to books and journals. *Address:* c/o University Press of America, 4501 Forbes Blvd, Suite 200, Lanham, MD 20706, USA.

SEVERIN, (Giles) Tim, MA, DLitt; British traveller and writer; b. 25 Sept. 1940, s. of Maurice Watkins and Inge Severin; m. Dorothy Virginia Sherman 1966 (divorced 1979); one d. *Education:* Tonbridge School, Keble Coll., Oxford. *Career:* Commonwealth Fellow, USA 1964–66; expeditions: led motorcycle team along Marco Polo's route 1961, canoe and launch down River Mississippi 1965, Brendan Voyage from W Ireland to N America 1977, Sindbad Voyage from Oman to China 1980–81, Jason Voyage from Greece to Soviet Georgia 1984, Ulysses Voyage, Troy to Ithaca 1985, Crusade: on horseback from Belgium to Jerusalem 1987–88, Travels on horseback in Mongolia 1990, China Voyage: bamboo sailing raft Hong Kong-Japan-Pacific 1993, Spice Islands Voyage in Moluccas, E Indonesia 1996, Pacific travels in search of Moby Dick 1998, Latin America travels seeking Robinson Crusoe sources 2000. *Publications:* Tracking Marco Polo 1964, Explorers of the Mississippi 1967, The Golden Antilles 1970, The African Adventure 1973, Vanishing Primitive Man 1973, The Oriental Adventure 1976, The Brendan Voyage 1978, The Sindbad Voyage 1982, The Jason Voyage 1984, The Ulysses Voyage 1987, Crusader 1989, In Search of Genghis Khan 1991, The China Voyage 1994, The Spice Islands Voyage 1997, In Search of Moby Dick 1999, Seeking Robinson Crusoe 2002, Viking: Odinn's Child (novel) 2004, Viking: Sworn Brother 2005, Viking: King's Man 2005. *Honours:* Hon. DLitt (Trinity Coll., Dublin) 1996; Royal Geographical Soc. Gold Medal, Royal Scottish Geographical Soc. Livingstone Medal. *Address:* Inchy Bridge, Timoleague, Co. Cork, Ireland. *Telephone:* (23) 46127. *Fax:* (23) 46233. *E-mail:* timsev@eircom.net (home). *Website:* www .timseverin.net.

SEWARD, Desmond, BA; British writer and historian; b. 22 May 1935, Paris, France. *Education:* St Catharine's Coll., Cambridge. *Publications:* The First Bourbon: Henry IV, King of France and Navarre 1971, The Monks of War: The Military Religious Orders (aka The Monks of War: The First Religious Orders) 1972, The Bourbon Kings of France 1976, Prince of the Renaissance: The Life of François I (aka Prince of the Renaissance: The Golden Life of François I) 1973, Eleanor of Aquitaine: The Mother Queen (aka Eleanor of Aquitaine) 1978, The Hundred Years War: The English in France 1337–1453 1978, Monks and Wine 1979, Marie Antoinette 1981, Richard III: England's Black Legend 1983, Napoleon's Family 1986, Italy's Knights of St George: The Constantinian Order 1986, Henry V as Warlord (aka Henry V: The Scourge of God) 1987, Napoleon and Hitler: A Comparative Biography 1988, Byzantium (co-author) 1989, Brook's: A Social History (co-ed.) 1991, Metternich: The First European 1991, The Dancing Sun: Journeys to the Miracle Shrines 1993, The War of the Roses through the Lives of Five Men and Women of the Fifteenth Century 1995, Sussex 1995, Caravaggio 1998, Eugénie 2004, The Burning of the Vanities: Savonarola and the Borgia Pope 2006; contrib. to periodicals, including History Today; BBC History Magazine. *Honours:* Kt of Malta 1978. *Literary Agent:* The Andrew Lownie Literary Agency, 17 Sutherland Street, London, SW1V 4JU, England.

SEWELL, Stephen, BS; Australian playwright; b. 1953, Sydney, NSW. *Education:* University of Sydney. *Career:* Chair., Australian National Playwrights Centre. *Publications:* The Father We Loved on a Beach by the Sea, 1976; Traitors, 1979; Welcome the Wright World, 1983; The Blind Giant is Dancing, 1983; Burn Victim (with others), 1983; Dreams in an Empty City, 1986; Hate, 1988; Miranda, 1989; Sisters, 1991; King Golgrutha, 1991; In the City of Grand-Daughters, 1993; Dust, 1993. *Honours:* New South Wales Premier's Award 1985. *Literary Agent:* Hilary Linstead & Associates, PO Box 1536, Strawberry Hills, NSW 2012, Australia.

SEYMOUR, Alan; Australian playwright; b. 6 June 1927, Perth, WA. *Publications:* Swamp Creatures, 1958; The One Day of the Year, 1960; The Gaiety of Nations, 1965; A Break in the Music, 1966; The Pope and the Pill, 1968; Oh Grave, Thy Victory, 1973; Structures, 1973; The Wind from the Plain, 1974; The Float, 1980; various radio and television plays. *Fiction:* The One Day of the Year, 1967; The Coming Self-Destruction of the United States, 1969. *Honours:* Australia Council for the Arts grant.

SEYMOUR, Arabella Charlotte Henrietta; British writer; b. 8 Dec. 1948, London, England; one d. *Education:* West Ham Coll. of Technology. *Career:* mem. Soc. of Authors. *Publications:* A Passion in the Blood 1985, Dangerous Deceptions 1986, The Sins of Rebeccah Russell 1988, The End of the Family 1990, No Sad Songs (as Sarah Lyon) 1990, Princess of Darkness 1991, A Woman of Pleasure 1994, Sins of the Mother 1996. *Address:* Sondes House, Patrixbourne, Canterbury, Kent CT4 5DD, England.

SFAR, Joann; French graphic artist and writer; b. 28 Aug. 1971, Nice; m.; two c. *Career:* graphic artist and writer for L'Association publishing house 1996–. *Publications include:* Chasseur-Cueilleur (La vallée des merveilles vol. one), L'Etoile Polaire (L'Homme-Arbre vol. one), Maison Etroite (L'Homme-Arbre vol. two), L'Atroce Abécédaire (Collection Bréal Jeunesse), Monsieur crocodile a beaucoup faim (Collection Bréal Jeunesse), Orang-outan (Collection Bréal Jeunesse), La Sorcière et la petite fille (Collection Bréal Jeunesse), Le Banquet (La Petite bibliothèque philosophique vol. one), Candide (La Petite bibliothèque philosophique vol. two), Les Carnets de Joann Sfar (five vols), Sardine de l'espace (artwork), Pourquoi cette nuit est-elle différente des autres nuits? (Les Olives noires vol. one, text), Adam Arishon (Les Olives noires vol. two, text), Tu ne mangeras pas le chevreau dans le lait de sa mère (Les Olives noires vol. three, text), Héraclès (Socrate Le Demi-Chien vol. one, text), Ulysse (Socrate Le Demi-Chien vol. two, text), L'Académie des Beaux-Arts (Le Minuscule Mousquetaire vol. one), La Philosophie de la Baignoire (Le Minuscule Mousquetaire vol. two), Le Borgne Gauchet, L'Elficologue (Pétrus Barbygère vol. one, artwork), Le Croquemitaine d'écume (Pétrus Barbygère vol. two, artwork), Le Mexicain à deux têtes (Les Dossiers du professeur Bell vol. one), Les Poupées de Jérusalem (Les Dossiers du professeur Bell vol. two), Le Cargo du Roi Singe (Les Dossiers du professeur Bell vol. three), Promenade des anglaises (Les Dossiers du professeur Bell vol. four), Les insoumis (Troll vol. one, with Jean-David Morvan), Le dragon du Donjon (Troll vol. two, with

Jean-David Morvan), Mille et un ennuis (Troll vol. three, with Jean-David Morvan), La Fille du professeur (script), Noyé le poisson, Le Livre des monstres (artwork), Pascin 1–6, La Java bleu (Pascin vol. seven), Jambon et Tartine (Merlin vol. one, script), Merlin contre le Père Noël (Merlin vol. two, script), Merlin va à la plage (Merlin vol. three, script), Merlin : Le roman de la mère de Renart (Merlin vol. four, script), Terra incognita (Les Potamoks vol. one, script), Les fontaines rouges (Les Potamoks vol. two, script), Nous et le désert (Les Potamoks vol. three, script), Donjon (with Lewis Trondheim), Donjon Zénith (with Lewis Trondheim), Donjon Crépuscule (with Lewis Trondheim), Donjon Potron-Minet (with Lewis Trondheim), Donjon Parade (script, with Lewis Trondheim), Cupidon s'en fout (Grand Vampire vol. one), Mortelles en tête (Grand Vampire vol. two), Transatlantique en solitaire (Grand Vampire vol. three), Quai des brunes (Grand Vampire vol. four), La Communauté des magiciens (Grand Vampire vol. five), Le Peuple est un Golem (Grand Vampire vol. six), Les Aventures d'Ossour Hyrsidoux 1994, Le Petit monde du Golem 1998, Petit Vampire va à l'école (Petit Vampire vol. one) 1999, Petit vampire fait du Kung Fu (Petit Vampire vol. two), La Société Protectrice des Chiens (Petit Vampire vol. three), La maison qui avait l'air normale (Petit Vampire vol. four), La soupe de caca (Petit Vampire vol. five), Les pères noel verts (Petit Vampire vol. six), Le rêve de Tokyo (Petit Vampire vol. seven), Urani (La Ville des mauvais rêves vol. one, with David B.) 2000, La Bar-Mitsva (Le Chat du rabbin vol. one) 2002, Le Malka des Lions (Le Chat du rabbin vol. two), L'Exode (Le Chat du rabbin vol. three) 2003, Le Paradis terrestre (Le Chat du rabbin vol. four) 2005, La Conquête de l'Est (Klezmer vol. one) 2005. *Honours:* Angoulême Jury Prize (for Le Chat du rabbin), Prix Goscinny du Meilleur Scénario (for La Fille du professeur), Angoulême Prix Coup de Coeur (for La Fille du professeur), Angoulême Prix de la jeunesse (for Petit Vampire) 2004. *Address:* c/o Pantheon Graphic Novels, 1745 Broadway 15-3, New York, NY 10019, USA. *E-mail:* joannsfar@pastis.org. *Website:* www .pastis.org/joann.

SHAARA, Jeff, BS; American writer; b. 21 Feb. 1952, New Brunswick, NJ; m. Lynne Shaara 1992. *Education:* Florida State University. *Publications:* Gods and Generals, 1996; The Last Full Measure, 1998; The Glorious Cause, 2002. *E-mail:* jshaara@aol.com.

SHABAN NEJAD, Afsaneh, BA; Iranian writer and poet; b. 1963, Shahdad, Kerman; m. Shamsodin Esaie; one s. one d. *Career:* Gen. Ed., children's radio programme 1985; Gen. Ed., children's magazine 1988–91; Literary Ed., jury mem., Poetry Council of Institute for the Intellectual Development of Children and Young Adults. *Publications:* six novels, 13 collections of poetry, 15 short stories, eight short story collections; contrib. several articles in children's magazines. *Honours:* various book and press festival awards 1990–2000; Hon. diploma (Alzahra Univ.), (Ministry of Culture and Islamic Guidance). *Address:* Institute for the Intellectual Development of Children and Young Adults, 24 Khaled Slamboli Street, Tehran, Iran (office).

SHABTAI, Aharon; Israeli poet and translator; b. 1939. *Education:* Hebrew Univ., Sorbonne, Paris, France, Univ. of Cambridge, England. *Career:* currently Lecturer in Hebrew Literature, Tel-Aviv Univ. *Publications include:* poetry: Kibbutz 1973, Domestic Poem 1976, The Book of Nothing 1981, First Lecture 1985, Love 1988, Divorce 1990, Heart 1995, That Wonderful Month of May 1997, Love and Selected Poems (in trans.) 1997, J'accuse 2003; contrib. to Six Israeli Novellas 1999, American Poetry Review, London Review of Books, Parnassus in Review, Ha'aretz. *Honours:* Prime Minister's Prize for Translation 1993. *Address:* Department of Hebrew Literature, Tel-Aviv University, Ramat-Aviv, 69978 Tel-Aviv, Israel.

SHACHOCHIS, Robert (Bob), BA, MA, MFA; American journalist and writer; b. 9 Sept. 1951, West Pittston, Pennsylvania; m. Barbara Petersen, 1976. *Education:* University of Missouri, Columbia, University of Iowa. *Career:* columnist, GQ magazines; Contributing Ed., Outside magazine, Harper's magazine; mem. Poets and Writers. *Publications:* novel: Swimming in the Volcanos 1993; short story collections: Easy in the Islands 1985, The Next New World 1989; contrib. to many periodicals. *Honours:* Nat. Endowment for the Arts Fellowship 1982, American Book Award for First Fiction 1985, Nat. Book Award 1985, Prix de Rome, American Acad. of Arts and Letters 1989.

SHAFAK, Elif (see Şafak, Elif)

SHAFFER, Sir Peter Levin, Kt, CBE, FRSL; British playwright; b. 15 May 1926, Liverpool; s. of Jack Shaffer and Reka Shaffer (née Fredman). *Education:* St Paul's School, London and Trinity Coll., Cambridge. *Career:* with Acquisitions Dept New York Library 1951; returned to England 1954; with Symphonic Music Dept Boosey and Hawkes 1954; Literary Critic, Truth 1956–57; Music Critic Time and Tide 1957; playwright 1957–; Cameron Mackintosh Prof. of Contemporary Theatre, St Catherine's Coll. Oxford 1994–95; mem. European Acad., Yuste 1998–. *Plays:* Five Finger Exercise, London 1958, New York 1959 (film 1962), The Private Ear and The Public Eye, London 1962, USA 1963, The Royal Hunt of the Sun, London 1964, New York 1964, Black Comedy, London 1965, New York 1967, White Lies, New York 1967 (revised as The White Liars, London 1968 and as White Liars, London 1976), The Battle of Shrivings 1970, Equus, London 1973, New York 1974, Amadeus, London 1979, New York 1980, Yonadab 1985, Lettice and Lovage, London 1987, New York 1990, The Gift of the Gorgon 1992; also performed on stage, Chichester, Guildford, Malvern 1996. *Television:* several TV plays including The Salt Land 1955, Balance of Terror. *Film screenplays:* The Royal Hunt of the Sun 1965, Equus 1977, Amadeus 1984 (all adaptations of his plays). *Radio play:* Whom Do I Have the Honour of Addressing? 1989.

Honours: Hon. DLitt (Bath) 1992, (St Andrews) 1999; New York Drama Critics' Circle Award 1959–60 (Five Finger Exercise); Antoinette Perry Award for Best Play and New York Drama Critics' Circle Award 1975 (Equus) and 1981 (Amadeus); Evening Standard Drama Award 1957 (Five Finger Exercise) and 1980 (Amadeus), London Drama Critics' Award; Acad. Award for Best Screenplay (Amadeus) 1984; Hamburg Shakespeare Prize 1987; Best Comedy, Evening Standard Award for Lettice and Lovage 1988. *Literary Agent:* c/o Macnaughton Lord 2000 Ltd, 19 Margravine Gardens, London, W6 8RL, England. *Telephone:* (20) 8741-0606. *Fax:* (20) 8741-7443. *E-mail:* info@ml2000.org.uk. *Website:* www.ml2000.org.uk.

SHAH, Eddy (Selim Jehane); British newspaper publisher and writer; b. 1944, Cambridge; s. of Moochool Shah and Hazel Strange; m. Jennifer Shah; two s. one d. *Education:* several schools including Gordonstoun. *Career:* worked as Asst Stage Man. in Repertory Theatre; also worked in TV and later as space salesman for free newspaper once published by Manchester Evening News; launched Sale and Altrincham Messenger freesheet in 1974, Stockport Messenger 1977, also Propr of Bury Messenger; launched Today newspaper 1986, Chair., CEO 1986–88; launched The Post Oct. 1988 (folded Dec. 1988). *Publications:* Ring of Red Roses (novel) 1991, The Lucy Ghosts 1992, Manchester Blue (novel) 1992, Fallen Angels (novel) 1994. *Address:* c/o Doubleday, 61–63 Uxbridge Road, London, W5 5SA, England.

SHAH, Saira; British/Afghan journalist; b. 1964. *Career:* freelance journalist in Afghanistan, covering guerrilla war against Soviet invasion 1986–89, in Baghdad, Iraq, covering Gulf War 1990–91; journalist with Channel Four News (UK). *TV documentary films:* Beneath the Veil (Int. Documentary Asscn Courage under Fire Award) 2001, Unholy War 2001, Death in Gaza (with James Miller, for Frostbite Films/HBO/Channel 4) (BAFTA Award for Current Affairs 2005) 2004. *Publication:* Storyteller's Daughter 2003. *Address:* c/o Michael Joseph, Penguin UK, 80 Strand, London, WC2R 0RL, England.

SHAKESPEARE, Nicholas; British biographer and novelist; b. 1957, Worcester, England; m.; two s. *Publications:* The Men Who Would Be King: A Look at Royalty in Exile 1984, Londoners 1986, The Vision of Elena Silves (novel) 1989, The High Flyer (novel) 1993, The Dancer Upstairs (novel) 1995, Bruce Chatwin (biog.) 1999, Snowleg (novel) 2004, In Tasmania 2004, Secrets of the Sea (novel) 2007. *Honours:* Somerset Maugham Award 1989, Betty Trask Award 1990, American Libraries Asscn Award 1997, BAFTA for Best Documentary 2001, Broadcasting Press Guild Award for Best Documentary 2001. *Address:* c/o Vintage, Random House, 20 Vauxhall Bridge Road, London, SW1V 2SA, England.

SHALEV, Zeruya, MA; Israeli poet and novelist; *Chief Literary Editor, Keshet Publishing;* b. 1959, Kinneret Kibbutz; m. Eyal Megged. *Career:* began writing aged 6, published collection of poems aged 15; fmr Ed. Keter Publishing House; currently Chief Literary Ed. Keshet Publishing House. *Publications include:* Rakadeti Amadeti (novel, trans. as Dancing, Standing Still) 1993, Hayei Ahavah (novel, trans. as Love Life) (ACUM Prize) 1997, Ba'al Ve Isha (novel, trans. as Husband and Wife) 2000, Yeled Shel Ima (juvenile, trans. as Mama's Best Boy) 2001, Tera (novel, trans. as Late Family) 2005; other: anthology; contrib. poems to numerous journals. *Honours:* Israeli Asscn of Publrs Gold and Platinum Book Prizes 2001, Corine Book Award (Germany) 2001, Amphi Award (France). *Address:* c/o Canongate Books, 14 High Street, Edinburgh, EH1 1TE, Scotland (office). *Telephone:* (131) 557-5111 (office).

SHAMSIE, Kamila, BA, MFA; Pakistani writer; b. 1973, Karachi; d. of Muneeza Shamsie. *Education:* Hamilton Coll., New York, and Univ. of Mass., Amherst, USA. *Career:* teaches creative writing at Hamilton Coll. *Publications include:* In the City by the Sea (Prime Minister's Award for Literature, Pakistan 1999) 1998, Salt and Saffron (Orange's list of 21 Writers for the 21st century) 2000, Kartography 2002, Broken Verses 2005. *Literary Agent:* c/o Victoria Hobbs, AM Heath & Co. Ltd, 79 St Martin's Lane, London, WC2N 4RE, England. *Address:* c/o Hamilton College, 198 College Hill Road, Clinton, NY 13323, USA (office). *E-mail:* kshamsie@hamilton.edu (office).

SHAN, Sa; Chinese writer; b. 26 Oct. 1972, Beijing. *Career:* moved to Paris, France 1990; private sec. for an artist 1994–96; writes in French. *Publications:* novels: Porte de la paix céleste (Prix Goncourt du premier roman) 1997, Les Quatre vies du saule (Prix Cazes) 1999, La Joueuse de Go (Prix Goncourt des lycéens, Kiriyama Prize, USA) 2001, Impératrice 2003, Les Conspirateurs 2005; poetry: four compilations of poems (in Chinese) pre-1990, Le Vent vif et le glaive rapide 2000, Le Miroir du calligraphe (illustrated) 2002. *Honours:* winner nat. youth poetry competition, People's Republic of China. *Address:* c/o Éditions Albin Michel, 22 rue Huyghens, 75014 Paris, France.

SHANGE, Ntozake, MA; American playwright and poet; b. 18 Oct. 1948, Trenton, NJ; d. of Paul Williams and Eloise Williams; m. David Murray 1977 (divorced); one c. *Education:* Barnard Coll. and Univ. of S Calif. *Career:* mem. Faculty, Sonoma State Univ. 1973–75, Mills Coll. 1975, City Coll. of New York 1975, Douglass Coll. 1978; author and actress in For Colored Girls Who Have Considered Suicide/When the Rainbow is Enuf (play) 1976, Where the Mississippi Meets the Amazon (play) 1977; author and dir A Photograph: A Study in Cruelty 1979; dir The Mighty Gents 1979; performing mem. Sounds in Motion Dance Co.; author, An Evening with Diana Ross: The Big Event 1977; Guggenheim Fellow 1981; mem. Nat. Acad. of TV Arts and Sciences, Acad. of American Poets, PEN America etc. *Publications include:* plays:

Melissa and Smith 1976, From Okra to Greens 1978, Spell #7 1979, Black and White Two Dimensional Planes 1979, Boogie Woogie Landscapes 1980, Mouths 1981, A Photograph: Lovers in Motion 1981, Three Views of Mt. Fuji 1987; novels: Sassafrass, Cypress and Indigo 1976, Betsey Brown 1985, The Love Space Demands 1991, I Live in Music 1994, Liliane: Resurrection of the Daughter 1995; poetry: Natural Disasters and Other Festive Occasions 1977, Nappy Edges 1978, Three Pieces 1981, A Daughter's Geography 1983, From Okra to Greens 1984; essays, short stories, non-fiction, adaptations; contribs to magazines and anthologies. *Honours:* recipient of numerous drama and poetry awards. *Address:* c/o St Martin's Press, 175 Fifth Avenue, New York, NY 10010, USA.

SHANLEY, John Patrick; American playwright; b. 1950, Bronx, NY; m. Jayne Haynes (divorced); two s. *Plays:* Saturday Night at the War 1978, George and the Dragon (New York) 1979, Welcome to the Moon (Ensemble Studio Theater, New York) 1982, Danny and the Deep Blue Sea (Waterford, CT) 1983, Savage in Limbo (Eugene O'Neill Theater Center, Waterford, CT) 1984, Down and Out, the dreamer examines the pillow (Waterford, CT) 1985, Italian American Reconciliation (Eugene O'Neill Theater Center, Waterford, CT) 1986, Women of Manhattan (Manhattan Theater Club, New York) 1986, All for Charity (New York) 1987, The Big Funk (New York Shakespeare Festival) 1990, Cellini, Beggars in the House of Plenty (Manhattan Theater Club, New York) 1991, What is this Everything? (New York) 1992, Four Dogs and a Bone (Manhattan Theater Club) 1993, The Wild Goose, Missing Marisa (Humana Festival, Actors' Theatre of Louisville) 1995–96, Kissing Christine (Humana Festival, Actors' Theatre of Louisville) 1995–96, Let's Go Out into the Starry Night 1996, A Lonely Impulse of Delight, Out West, Psychopathia Sexualis (Seattle Repertory Theater) 1998, Where's My Money? 2001, The Red Coat, Dirty Story (Denver Center Theater Co.) 2003, Sailor's Song (Shiva Theater, New York) 2004, Doubt (Manhattan Theater Club, New York) (Pulitzer Prize for Drama 2005, Tony Award for best play 2005) 2004. *Screenplays:* Five Corners (also assoc. prod.) (Special Jury Prize for screenplay, Barcelona Film Festival) 1987, Moonstruck (Writers' Guild Award, Acad. Award for Best Screenplay 1988) 1987, January Man 1989, Joe Versus the Volcano (also dir) 1990, Danny i Roberta (TV play) 1993, Alive 1993, We're Back! A Dinosaur's Story 1993, Congo 1995, Danny and the Deep Blue Sea (book Papillons de nuit) 2002, Live from Baghdad (TV) 2002, The Waltz of the Tulips 2004. *Literary Agent:* Creative Artists Agency, 9830 Wilshire Boulevard, Beverly Hills, CA 90212-1815, USA. *Telephone:* (310) 288-4545. *Fax:* (310) 288-4800.

SHAO, Yanxiang; Chinese poet; b. 10 June 1933, Beijing; s. of Shao Ji and Cheng Ying; m. Xie Wenxiu 1957; one s. one d. *Career:* attached to Radio Beijing as ed. and corresp. 1949; detained in labour camp during Cultural Revolution 1966–77; rehabilitated 1978; Deputy Ed.-in-Chief Shikan magazine 1978. *Publications:* Singing of the City of Beijing 1951, Going to the Faraway Place 1955, To My Comrades 1956, The Campfire in August 1956, A Reed-Pipe 1957, Love Songs to History 1980, At the Faraway Place 1981, In Full Blossom Lake Flowers 1983, Flower Late in Blossom 1984, Collection of Long Lyrics 1985, Essays Written at Mornings and Evenings 1986, 100 Articles with Sorrows and Joys 1986, There's Joy, there's Sorrow 1988, Selected Poems 1992, Written in Little Honeycomb 1993, Catch that Butterfly 1993, Idle Talk 1993, Rewriting the Bible 1993, One's Own Cup 1993, Essay Workshop 1994, Genuine Absurdity and Sham Absurdity 1994, Multum in Parvo 1994, Selected Poems of Shao Yanxiang 1995, Collection of Works by Shao Yanxiang (three vols). *Address:* A15-3-401 Hufang Road, Beijing 100052, People's Republic of China. *Telephone:* (10) 63536604.

SHAPCOTT, Joanne (Jo) Amanda; British poet; b. 24 March 1953, London. *Education:* Trinity Coll. Dublin, St Hilda's Coll. Oxford, Harvard Univ., USA. *Career:* Judith E. Wilson Fellow in Creative Writing, Univ. of Cambridge 1991, Northern Arts Literary Fellow 1998–2000; currently teaches creative writing at Royal Holloway Coll., Univ. of London; Visiting Prof. of Poetry, Univ. of Newcastle 2001–, Univ. of Arts, London; Consulting Ed. Arc Publs. *Publications:* Electroplating the Baby (Commonwealth Poetry Prize for Best First Collection 1989) 1988, Phrase Book 1992, Emergency Kit: Poems for Strange Times 1996, My Life Asleep (Forward Poetry Prize (Best Poetry Collection of the Year 1999)) 1998, Her Book: Poems 1988–98 1998, Tender Taxes 2002, The Transformers: Newcastle/Bloodaxe Poetry Lectures 2007; contributions to: The Times, Sunday Times, New Statesman, Poetry Review, Times Literary Supplement, Verse, Southern Review. *Honours:* South West Arts Literature Award 1982, First Prize, Nat. Poetry Competition 1981, 1991, Commonwealth Prize 1988, New Statesman Prudence Farmer Award 1989, Poetry Book Society Choice 1992, 1998, Cholmondeley Award 2006. *Address:* c/o TriplePA, 15 Connaught Gardens, Forest Hall, Newcastle, Tyne and Wear, NE12 8AT, England. *E-mail:* triplepa@blueyonder.co.uk.

SHAPCOTT, Thomas William, AO, BA; Australian poet, novelist, writer and academic; *Professor Emeritus of Creative Writing, University of Adelaide;* b. 21 March 1935, Ipswich, Qld; s. of Harold Sutton Shapcott and Dorothy Mary Shapcott (née Gillespie); m. 1st Margaret Hodge 1960; m. 2nd Judith Rodriguez 1982; one s. three d. *Education:* Univ. of Queensland. *Career:* Dir Australia Council Literature Board 1983–90; Exec. Dir Nat. Book Council 1992–97; apptd Prof. of Creative Writing, Univ. of Adelaide 1997, now Prof. Emer. *Publications:* poetry: Time on Fire 1961, The Mankind Thing 1963, Sonnets 1960–63, 1963, A Taste of Salt Water 1967, Inwards to the Sun 1969, Fingers at Air 1969, Begin with Walking 1973, Shabbytown Calendar 1975, 7th Avenue Poems 1976, Selected Poems 1978, Make the Old Man Sing 1980,

Welcome! 1983, Travel Dice 1987, Selected Poems 1956–1988 1989, In the Beginning 1990, The City of Home 1995, Chekhov's Mongoose 2001 Beginnings and Endings 2003, Adelaide Lunch Sonnets 2005, The City of Empty Rooms 2005; fiction: The Birthday Gift 1982, White Stag of Exile 1984, Hotel Bellevue 1986, The Search for Galina 1989, Mona's Gift 1993, Theatre of Darkness 1998, Spirit Wrestlers 2004; plays: The 7 Deadly Sins 1970; nonfiction: Twins in the Family: Conversations with Australian Twins 2002; editor: New Impulses in Australian Poetry (with R. Hall) 1967, Australian Poetry Now 1970, Contemporary American and Australian Poetry 1975, Poetry as a Creative Learning Process 1978, The Moment Made Marvellous (anthology) 1998, An Island on Land: Contemporary Macedonian Poetry (ed. and trans. with Ilija Casule) 1999; contribs to newspapers and journals. Honours: Hon. DLitt (Macquarie Univ.) 1989; Grace Leven Prize 1961, Sir Thomas White Memorial Prize 1967, Sidney Myer Charity Trust Awards 1967, 1969, Churchill Fellowship 1972, Canada-Australia Literary Prize 1978, Gold Wreath, Struga Int. Poetry Festival 1989, Christopher Brennan Award for Poetry 1994, NSW Premier's Special Literary Prize 1996, Michel Wesley Wright Award 1996, Patrick White Award 2000. Address: PO Box 231, Mont Albert, Vic. 3127, Australia (home). E-mail: thomas.shapcott@adelaide.edu.au (office).

SHAPIN, Steven, BA, MA, PhD; American writer, historian and sociologist; Franklin A. Ford Professor of the History of Science, Harvard University; b. 11 Sept. 1943, New York, NY; m. Abigail Barrow, 18 March 1989. Education: Reed Coll., Univ. of Pennsylvania. Career: fmr Reader in Science Studies, Edin. Univ., Scotland; fmr Prof. of Sociology, Univ. of California, San Diego; Franklin A. Ford Prof. of the History of Science, Harvard Univ. 2004–. Publications: Natural Order: Historical Studies of Scientific Cultures (co-ed.), 1979; Leviathan and the Air-Pump: Hobbes, Boyle, and the Experimental Life (co-author), 1985; A Social History of Truth: Civility and Science in Seventeenth Century England, 1994; The Scientific Revolution, 1996; Science Incarnate: Historical Embodiments of Natural Knowledge (co-ed.), 1998. Honours: Erasmus Prize 2005. Address: Department of History of Science, Harvard University, Science Center 371, Cambridge, MA 02138, USA (office). Telephone: (617) 384-7997 (office). Fax: (617) 495-3344 (office). E-mail: shapin@fas.harvard.edu (office).

SHAPIRO, Alan R., BA; American academic, poet, writer and translator; b. 18 Feb. 1952, Boston, MA; m. Della Pollock 1984. Education: Brandeis Univ. Career: Jones Lecturer in Creative Writing 1976–79, Visiting Asst Prof. 1981, Stanford Univ.; Lecturer 1979–85, Assoc. Prof. 1985–88, Prof. 1988–89, Northwestern Univ.; poet-in-residence, Univ. of Chicago 1981, 1986, 1988; Visiting Asst Prof. 1985, Visiting Prof. 1989, of Creative Writing, Univ. of California at Irvine; Visiting Prof. of Creative Writing, Boston Univ. 1989; Fannie Hurst Poet-in-Residence, Brandeis Univ. 1989; Prof., Univ. of North Carolina at Greensboro 1989–94; Hurst Prof. of Creative Writing, Washington Univ. 1994; Prof. of English 1995–, Gillian T. Cell Distinguished Term Prof. 2001, currently Kenan Prof., Univ. of North Carolina at Chapel Hill; Richard L. Thomas Prof. of Creative Writing, Kenyon Coll. 2002. Publications: After the Digging (poems) 1981, The Courtesy (poems) 1983, Happy Hour (poems) 1987, Covenant (poems) 1991, In Praise of the Impure: Poetry and the Ethical Imagination: Essays (1980–1991) 1993, Mixed Company (poems) 1996, The Last Happy Occasion (memoir) 1996, Vigil (memoir) 1997, The Dead Alive and Busy (poems) 2000, Selected Poems 2000, Song and Dance (poems) 2002, The Ortesteia (trans.) 2002; contrib. to many anthologies, reviews, quarterlies and journals. Honours: Wallace Stegner Creative Writing Fellowship 1975–76, Acad. of American Poets Award 1976, National Endowment for the Arts Fellowships 1984–85, 1991, Guggenheim Fellowship 1985–86, William Carlos Williams Award, Poetry Society of America 1987, Lila Wallace-Reader's Digest Writers Award 1991, Pushcart Prize 1996, Los Angeles Times Book Award in Poetry 1996, Open Society Institute Arts Fellowship 1999, Kingsley Tufts Poetry Award, Claremont Graduate University 2001. Address: c/o Department of English, Greenlaw Hall, CB #3520, University of North Carolina, Chapel Hill, NC 27599-3520, USA. E-mail: ashapiro@email.unc.edu.

SHAPIRO, David Joel, BA, MA, PhD; American poet, art critic and academic; Professor of Art History, William Paterson University, Wayne; b. 2 Jan. 1947, Newark, NJ; m. Lindsay Stamm 1970; one c. Education: Columbia Univ., Clare Coll., Cambridge. Career: violinist in various orchestras 1963–; Instructor and Asst Prof. of English, Columbia Univ. 1972–80; Visiting Prof., Brooklyn Coll., CUNY 1979, Princeton Univ. 1982–83, Cooper Union, New York Univ. 1980–; Prof. of Art History, William Paterson Univ., Wayne, NJ 1996–; Kellett Fellow Clare Coll., Cambridge 1968–70; Milton Avery Prof., Bard Graduate School of the Arts 1996. Film screenplays: Regular Flavor (with Rudy Burckhardt), Mobile Homes (with Rudy Burckhardt), Daffodils (with Rudy Burckhardt). Publications: poetry: January: A Book of Poems 1965, Poems from Deal 1969, A Man Holding an Acoustic Panel 1971, The Page-Turner 1973, Lateness 1977, To an Idea 1984, House, Blown Apart 1988, After a Lost Original 1990, Burning Interior 2002, Inventory: New and Selected Poems: Frank Lima (ed.) 2004; prose: John Ashbery: An Introduction to the Poetry 1979, Jim Dine: Painting What One Is 1981, Jasper Johns: Drawings 1954–1984 1984, Mondrian Flowers 1990, Alfred Leslie: The Killing Cycle (with Judith Stein) 1991, Keith Haring 2005, After (with Tsibi Geva) 2005, Rabbit/Duck (with Richard Hall); also contrib. prefaces Zhiyman Long 2005, Anne Porter's Poetry 2006, Such Places as Memory. Honours: Bread Loaf Writers Conference Robert Frost Fellowship 1965, Ingram Merrill

Foundation Fellowship 1967, Book-of-the-Month Club Fellowship 1968, Creative Artists Public Service grant 1974, Morton Dauwen Zabel Award 1977, NEA grant 1979, Nat. Endowment for the Humanities Fellowships 1980, Foundation for Contemporary Performance Arts grant 1996. Address: 3001 Henry Hudson Parkway, Riverdale, NY 10463, USA.

SHAPIRO, Harvey, BA, MA; American editor and poet; b. 27 Jan. 1924, Chicago, IL; m. Edna Kaufman 1953; two s. Education: Yale University, Columbia University. Career: Staff, Commentary, 1955–57, The New Yorker, 1955–57; Staff, 1957–64, Deputy Ed., 1983–, New York Times Magazine; Asst Ed., 1964–75, Ed., 1975–83, New York Times Book Review. Publications: The Eye, 1953; The Book, 1955; Mountain Fire Thornbush, 1961; Battle Report, 1966; This World, 1971; Lauds, 1975; Lauds and Nightsounds, 1978; The Light Holds, 1984; National Cold Storage Company: New and Selected Poems, 1988; A Day's Portion, 1994; Selected Poems, 1997. Contributions: periodicals. Honours: Rockefeller Grant for Poetry, 1967. Address: c/o The New York Times Magazine, 229 W 43rd Street, New York, NY 10036, USA.

SHAPIRO, James S., BA, PhD; American writer and academic; Professor of English and Comparative Literature, Columbia University; b. 1955, Brooklyn, New York; m.; one s. Education: Columbia Univ. and Univ. of Chicago. Career: fmrly taught at Dartmouth Coll., Goucher Coll.; faculty mem. Columbia Univ. 1985, now Prof. of English and Comparative Literature; Fulbright Lecturer, Bar Ilan and Tel-Aviv Univs 1988–89; Wanamaker Fellow, The Globe Theatre, London 1998; columnist, Chronicle of Higher Education; Co-Dir two Nat. Endowment for the Humanities Insts on Shakespeare. Publications: Rival Playwrights: Marlowe, Jonson, Shakespeare 1991, The Columbia History of British Poetry (Assoc. Ed.) 1993, The Columbia Anthology of British Poetry (Co-Ed.) 1995, Shakespeare and the Jews (Sixteenth Century Journal Roland A. Bainton Book Prize) 1997, Oberammergau: The Troubling Story of the World's Most Famous Passion Play 2000, 1599: A Year in the Life of William Shakespeare (BBC Four Samuel Johnson Prize for Fiction 2006) 2005. Honours: Nat. Endowment for the Humanities Fellowship for Univ. Teachers, Henry E. Huntington Library Research Fellowship, Memorial Foundation for Jewish Culture Research Fellowship, Hoffman Prize for Distinguished Scholarship on Marlowe. Address: Department of English, Columbia University, 606B Philosophy Hall, 1150 Amsterdam Avenue, New York, NY 10027, USA (office). Telephone: (212) 854-6227 (office). E-mail: js73@columbia.edu (office). Website: www.columbia.edu/cu/english (office).

SHARIF, Osama ash-, BA; Jordanian publisher, journalist and media consultant; Chairman, Media-Arabia; b. 14 June 1960, Jerusalem; s. of Mahmoud al-Sherif and Aida al-Sherif; m. Ghada Yasser Amr 1984; one s. one d. Education: Univ. of Missouri, Columbia, USA. Career: Chief Ed. The Jerusalem Star 1985–88; Pres. Info-Media, Jordan 1989–; Publr, Chief Ed. and weekly columnist, The Star, Jordan 1990–; Publr Arabian Communications & Publishing (ACP) 1994–97, BYTE Middle East 1994–97, Al Tiqaniyyah Wal 'Amal 1995–97; Chief Ed. and Dir General Arabia.com 1999–2002; Chief Ed. Addustour Newspaper 2003–06; Chair. Media-Arabia 2006–; mem. Royal Cttee for the Nat. Agenda, Amman, Jordan 2005. Address: Addustour Newspaper, PO Box 591, University Street, Amman 11118, Jordan (office). Telephone: (6) 5608000 (office). Fax: (6) 5684478 (office). E-mail: osama@mediaarabia.com (office). Website: www.mediaarabia.com (home).

SHARP, Paula, BA, JD; American writer and attorney; b. 12 Nov. 1957, San Diego, CA. Education: Dartmouth College, Columbia University. Career: mem. Asscn of the Bar of the City of New York; Authors' Guild; Lawyers' Guild; PEN. Publications: The Woman Who Was Not All There, 1988; The Imposter: Stories of Netta and Stanley, 1991; Lost in Jersey City, 1993; Crows Over a Wheatfield, 1996; I Loved You All, 2000. Contributions: periodicals. Honours: Distinguished Artist Award, New Jersey Council on the Arts, 1987; Joe Savago New Voice Award, Quality Paperback Book Club, 1988; BANTA Award, 1992; New York Times Notable Book of the Year Citations, 1993, 1996, 2000.

SHARP, Ronald Alan, BA, MA, PhD; American academic, writer and administrator; b. 19 Oct. 1945, Cleveland, OH; m. Inese Brutans 1968, two s. Education: Syracuse University, Kalamazoo College, Instituto Internacional, Madrid, University of Michigan, University of Edinburgh, University of Virginia. Career: Instructor, Western Michigan University, 1968–70; Instructor, 1970–72, Asst Prof., 1974–78, Assoc. Prof., 1978–85, Prof. of English, 1985–90, John Crowe Ransom Prof. of English, 1990–, Assoc. Provost, 1998–99, Provost, 1999–, Acting Pres., 2002–03, Kenyon College; Visiting Prof., Concordia University, 1978; Co-Ed., The Kenyon Review, 1978–82; mem. Keats-Shelley Asscn; MLA; Wordsworth-Coleridge Asscn. Publications: Keats, Skepticism and the Religion of Beauty, 1979; Friendship and Literature: Spirit and Form, 1986; The Norton Book of Friendship (with Eudora Welty), 1991; Reading George Steiner (with Nathan A. Scott Jr), 1994; The Persistence of Poetry: Bicentennial Essays on Keats (with Robert M. Ryan), 1998. Contributions: books and journals. Honours: Ford Foundation Grant, 1971; English Speaking Union Fellowship, 1973; Mellon Grant, 1980; National Endowment for the Humanities Fellowships, 1981–82, 1984, 1985, 1986–87, 1994, 1996, 1998; National Humanities Center Fellowship, 1986–87; various grants.

SHARPE, Thomas (Tom) Ridley, MA; British novelist; b. 30 March 1928, London; s. of Rev. George Coverdale Sharpe and Grace Egerton Sharpe; m. Nancy Anne Looper 1969; three d. Education: Lancing Coll., Pembroke Coll., Univ. of Cambridge. Career: social worker 1952; teacher 1952–56; photographer 1956–61; Lecturer in History, Cambridge Coll. of Arts and Tech. 1963–71; full-time novelist 1971–. *Publications:* Riotous Assembly 1971, Indecent Exposure 1973, Porterhouse Blue 1974, Blott on the Landscape 1975, Wilt 1976, The Great Pursuit 1977, The Throwback 1978, The Wilt Alternative 1979, Ancestral Vices 1980, Vintage Stuff 1982, Wilt on High 1984, Grantchester Grind 1995, The Midden 1996, Wilt in Nowhere 2004. *Honours:* Laureat, Le Grand Prix de l'Humour Noir, Paris 1986. *Address:* 38 Tunwells Lane, Great Shelford, Cambridge, CB2 5LJ, England.

SHATROV, (Marshak) Mikhail Filippovich; Russian dramatist and scriptwriter; b. 3 April 1932, s. of Filipp Semenovich and Cecilia Alexandrovna Marshak; m. Julia Vladimirovna Chernyshova; two d. *Education:* Moscow Mining Inst. *Career:* Pres. and Chair. of Bd of Dirs Zao Moskva-Krasnye Kholmy Co. 1994–; Head of Drama, Theatre, Cinema and TV, Ministry of Culture of the Russian Fed. 2002–; began writing plays in 1955. *Plays include:* In the Name of Revolution 1957, The Peace of Brest Litovsk 1962, The Sixth of July 1963, Przevalsky's Horse 1972, The Dictatorship of Conscience 1986, Further... Further... Further 1988. *Film screenplays include:* Two Lines of Tiny Handwriting 1981, Tehran-43 1981, Maybe (for Vanessa Redgrave) 1993. *Publications:* February (novel) 1988, Maybe 1993. *Honours:* USSR State Prize 1983. *Address:* Serafimovich str. 2, Apt 349, 109072 Moscow, Russia. *Telephone:* (495) 961-22-30 (office); (495) 959-31-68.

SHAW, Brian (see Tubb, Edwin Charles)

SHAW, Irene (see Roberts, Irene)

SHAW, Mark, BS, JD; American author; b. 3 Oct. 1945, Auburn, IN; m. Chris R. Shaw 1989; three step-s. one step-d. *Education:* Purdue University, Indiana University School of Law. *Career:* mem. Writers' Guild. *Publications:* Down for the Count, 1992; Bury Me in a Pot Bunker, 1993; Forever Flying, 1994; The Perfect Yankee, 1995; McKlaus: A Biography, 1996; Statement to Courage, 1997; Diamonds in the Rough, 1998; Larry Legend, 1998.

SHAW, (Veronica) Patricia; Australian writer; b. 1928, Melbourne; m. (divorced); one s. one d. *Education:* Star of the Sea Convent, Melbourne, Melbourne Teachers College. *Publications:* Brother Digger: The Sullivans, 2nd AIF, 1984; Valley of the Lagoons, 1989; River of the Sun, 1991; The Feather and the Stone, 1992; Where the Willows Weep, 1993; Cry of the Rain Bird, 1994; Fires of Fortune, 1995; The Opal Seekers, 1996; The Glittering Fields, 1997, Mango Hill 2007. *Address:* c/o Hachette Livre Australia, Level 17, 207 Kent Street, Sydney NSW 2000, Australia.

SHAWCROSS, William; British journalist, writer and broadcaster; b. 28 May 1946, Sussex; s. of Baron Shawcross; m. 1st Marina Warner 1972 (divorced 1980); one s.; m. 2nd Michal Levin 1981 (divorced); one d.; m. Olga Forte 1993. *Education:* Eton, Univ. Coll., Oxford. *Career:* freelance journalist in Czechoslovakia 1968–69; corresp. for The Sunday Times, London 1969–72; Chair. Article 19, Int. Centre on Censorship 1986–96; mem. bd Int. Crisis Group 1995–; mem. Council of Disasters Emergency Cttee 1998–. *Publications:* Dubček 1970, Crime and Compromise: Janos Kadar and the Politics of Hungary Since Revolution 1974, Sideshow: Kissinger, Nixon and the Destruction of Cambodia 1979, Quality of Mercy: Cambodia, the Holocaust and Modern Conscience 1984, The Shah's Last Ride 1989, Kowtow: A Plea on Behalf of Hong Kong 1989, Murdoch 1992, Cambodia's New Deal 1994, Deliver Us from Evil: Warlords & Peacekeepers in a World of Endless Conflict 2000, Queen and Country 2002, Allies: The United States, Britain, Europe and the War in Iraq (aka Allies: The US, Britain and Europe in the Aftermath of the Iraq War) 2003; contrib. to newspapers and journals. *Literary Agent:* Green & Heaton Ltd, 37 Goldhawk Road, London, W12. *Telephone:* (20) 7289-8089. *Address:* Friston Place, East Dean, East Sussex BN20 0AH, England. *E-mail:* williamshawcross@compuserve.com (office).

SHAYKH, Hanan ash-; Lebanese novelist and playwright; b. 1945, Beirut; m. *Education:* American Coll. for Girls, Cairo. *Career:* journalist, al-Hasna' magazine, an-Nahar newspaper 1968–75. *Publications:* Intihar rajul mayyit 1970, Faras ash-shaytan 1971, Hikayat Zahrah (The Story of Zahra) 1980, 'The Persian Carpet' in Arabic Short Stories 1983, Misk al-ghazal (Women of Sand and Myrrh) 1988, Barid Bayrut (Beirut Blues) 1992, Aknus ash-shams an as-sutuh (I Sweep the Sun off Rooftops, short stories) 1994, Dark Afternoon Tea (play) 1995, Paper Husband (play) 1997, Only in London 2000, Two Women by the Sea (novella) 2003, Hikayati Sharh Yatool (memoir of her mother) 2005, A Fly on the Wall (play) 2007. *Literary Agent:* c/o Deborah Rogers, Rogers, Coleridge & White, 20 Powis Mews, London, W11 1JN, England. *Telephone:* (20) 7221-3717. *Fax:* (20) 7229-9084.

SHEARER, Jill; Australian playwright; b. 14 April 1936, Melbourne, Vic. *Publications:* The Trouble with Gillian, 1974; The Foreman, 1976; The Boat, 1977; The Kite, 1977; Nocturne, 1977; Catherine, 1978; Stephen, 1980; Release Lavinia Stannard, 1980; A Woman Like That, 1986; Shimada, 1987; Comrade, 1987; The Family, 1994. *Honours:* Australia Council Grant, 1987; Arts Queensland Fellowship, 1993. *Address:* c/o The Australian Script Centre, 77 Salamanca Place, Hobart, Tasmania, Australia.

SHEED, Wilfrid John Joseph, MA; American author; b. 27 Dec. 1930, London, England; s. of Francis Joseph Sheed and Maisie (Ward) Sheed; m. 1st Maria Bullitt Dartington 1957 (divorced); three c.; m. 2nd Miriam Ungerer; one s. two d. *Education:* Lincoln Coll., Oxford Univ. *Career:* film reviewer Jubilee magazine 1959–61, Assoc. Ed. 1959–66; drama critic and fmr book critic Commonweal magazine, New York; film critic Esquire magazine

1967–69; Visiting Prof. Princeton Univ. 1970–71; columnist NY Times 1971–; judge and mem. editorial Bd Book of the Month Club 1972–88; Guggenheim Fellow 1971–72; mem. PEN Club. *Publications include:* A Middle Class Education 1961, The Hack 1963, Square's Progress 1965, Office Politics 1966, The Blacking Factory 1968, Max Jamison 1970, The Morning After 1971, People Will Always Be Kind 1973, Three Mobs: Labor, Church and Mafia 1974, Transatlantic Blues 1978, The Good Word 1979, Clare Boothe Luce 1982, Frank and Maisie 1985, The Boys of Winter 1987, Baseball and Lesser Sports 1991, My Life as a Fan 1993, In Love with Daylight 1995, The House That George Built 2007; ed. of G.K. Chesterton's Essays and Poems 1957, 16 Short Novels 1986; contributes articles to popular magazines. *Address:* c/o Random House, Inc., 1745 Broadway, New York, NY 10019, USA (office). *Telephone:* (212) 782-9000 (office). *Website:* www.randomhouse.com (office).

SHEEHAN, Neil, AB; American journalist and author; b. 27 Oct. 1936, Holyoke, Mass.; s. of Cornelius Sheehan and Mary O'Shea; m. Susan Margulies 1965; two d. *Education:* Harvard Univ. *Career:* Viet Nam Bureau Chief, UPI Saigon 1962–64; reporter, New York Times, New York, Jakarta, Saigon, Washington, DC 1964–72; Guggenheim Fellow 1973–74; Adlai Stevenson Fellow 1973–75; Fellow, Lehrman Inst. 1975–76; Rockefeller Foundation Fellow 1976–77; Fellow, Woodrow Wilson Center for Int. Scholars 1979–80; mem. Soc. of American Historians, Acad. of Achievement. *Publications:* The Arnheiter Affair 1972, A Bright Shining Lie: John Paul Vann and America in Viet Nam (chosen by The Modern Library as one of 100 Best Works of Non-Fiction in 20th Century 1999) 1988, After the War Was Over: Hanoi and Saigon 1992; contrib. to The Pentagon Papers 1971; articles and book reviews for popular magazines. *Honours:* Hon. LittD (Columbia Coll., Chicago) 1972; Hon. LHD (American Int. Coll.) 1990, (Lowell Univ.) 1991; recipient of numerous awards for journalism; Nat. Book Award 1988, J.F. Kennedy Award 1989, Pulitzer Prize for non-fiction 1989. *Address:* 4505 Klingle Street, NW, Washington, DC 20016, USA (home).

SHEEHAN, Susan, BA; American writer; b. 24 Aug. 1937, Vienna, Austria; m. Neil Sheehan 1965; one s. two d. *Education:* Wellesley Coll. *Career:* Editorial Researcher, Esquire-Coronet, New York City, 1959–60; Staff, New Yorker magazine, New York City, 1961–; mem. Authors' Guild; Society of American Historians. *Publications:* Ten Vietnamese, 1967; A Welfare Mother, 1976; A Prison and a Prisoner, 1978; Is There No Place on Earth for Me?, 1982; Kate Quinton's Days, 1984; A Missing Plane, 1986; Life for Me Ain't Been No Crystal Stair, 1993. Contributions: many magazines. *Honours:* Guggenheim Fellowship, 1975–76; Sidney Hillman Foundation Award, 1976; Gavel Award, American Bar Asscn, 1978; Woodrow Wilson International Center for Scholars Fellowship, 1981; Individual Reporting Award, National Mental Health Asscn, 1981; Pulitzer Prize for General Non-Fiction, 1983; Feature Writing Award, New York Press Club, 1984; Alumnae Asscn Achievement Award, Wellesley College, 1984; DHL, University of Lowell, 1991; Carroll Kowal Journalism Award, 1993; Public Awareness Award, National Alliance for the Mentally Ill, 1995. *Address:* 4505 Klingle Street NW, Washington, DC 20016, USA.

SHEEHY, Gail Henion, BS; American writer and journalist; b. 27 Nov. 1937, Mamaronick, NY; d. of Harold Merritt Henion and Lillian Rainey Henion (née Paquin); m. 1st Albert F. Sheehy 1960 (divorced 1967); one d. (one adopted); m. 2nd Clay Felker 1984. *Education:* Univ. of Vermont. *Career:* Home Economist, J. C. Penney & Co. 1958–60; Fashion Ed. Rochester Democrat & Chronicle 1961–63; feature writer New York Herald Tribune 1963–66; Contributing Ed. New York magazine 1968–77; Fellow, Journalism School, Columbia Univ. 1970; Political Contributing Ed. Vanity Fair 1984–; has contributed to New York Times Magazine, Parade, New Republic, Washington Point; mem. Advisory Bd Women's Health Initiative, NIH, Eminent Citizens' Comm., UN Int. Conf. on Population and Devt 1994. *Publications include:* Lovesounds 1970, Panthermania: The Clash of Black Against Black in One American City 1971, Speed is of the Essence 1971, Hustling: Prostitution in our Wide-Open Society 1973, Passages: Predictable Crises of Adult Life (trans. to 28 languages) 1976, Pathfinders 1981, Spirit of Survival 1986, Character: America's Search for Leadership 1988, Gorbachev: The Man Who Changed the World 1990, Maggie and Misha (play) 1991, The Silent Passage: Menopause 1992, New Passages 1995, Hillary's Choice 1999, Understanding Men's Passages 1999, Middletown, America 2003. *Honours:* seven Front Page Awards, Newswomen's Club of New York; Nat. Magazine Award, Columbia Univ. 1973; Penney-Missouri Journalism Award, Univ. of Missouri 1975; Anisfield-Wolf Book Award 1986; Best Magazine Writer Award, Washington Journalism Review 1991; New York Public Library Lion 1992. *Address:* c/o Jennifer Joel, International Creative Management (ICM), 40 West 57th Street, New York, NY 10019, USA (office). *Telephone:* (212) 556-6730 (office). *Fax:* (212) 556-5624 (office). *Website:* www.gailsheehy.com; www.seasonedwomansnetwork.com.

SHEERS, Owen; British writer, poet and broadcaster; b. 1974, Suva, Fiji. *Education:* New Coll., Oxford, Univ. of East Anglia. *Career:* fmr writer-in-residence, The Wordsworth Trust; arts presenter for BBC Wales. *Exhibition:* Wales: Dead Or Alive? (with Dan Llewellyn Hall) 2004. *Play:* Unicorns, Almost 2005. *Publications:* poetry: The Blue Book 2000, Skirrid Hill (Soc. of Authors Somerset Maugham Award 2006) 2005; Resistance (novel) 2007; non-fiction: The Dust Diaries (Tir Na N-Og English Language Welsh Book of the Year 2005) 2004. *Honours:* winner Vogue Talent Contest 1999, Eric Gregory Award, Vogue Talent Contest for Young Writers, selected as a Poetry Soc.

Next Generation Poet 2004. *Address:* c/o Faber and Faber Ltd, 3 Queen Square, London, WC1N 3AU, England. *Website:* www.owensheers.co.uk.

SHEIKH, Ahmad ash-; broadcasting executive; *Editor-in-Chief, Aljazeera International.* Career: fmrly worked for BBC; fmr Chair. Dubai Sports channel; currently Ed.-in-Chief, Aljazeera International. *Address:* Aljazeera International, PO Box 23127, Doha, Qatar (office). *Website:* www.aljazeera .net.

SHELDON, Lee (see Lee, Wayne C.)

SHELDON, Roy (see Tubb, Edwin Charles)

SHEN, Peng; Chinese calligrapher, poet, art critic, editor and publisher; b. Sept. 1931, Jiangyin, Jiangsu Prov. *Career:* began to learn poetry, calligraphy and art from an early age; majored in Chinese literature in coll., later studied journalism; Assoc. Ed.-in-Chief People's Fine Arts Press; fmr Vice-Chair. Chinese Calligraphers Asscn, Chair. 2000, now Hon. Pres.; Sr Ed. and Art Counsellor, China Fine Arts Publishing Group; Adjunct Prof., Peking Univ., China Ren Min Univ.; Vice-Pres. and Deputy Chair. Nat. Book Reward Evaluation Cttee; est. Art Museum of ShenPeng Calligraphy in Jiangyin, Jiansu Prov. and Mengjin, Henan Prov.; attended China Art Museum Contemporary Famous Calligraphers Exhbn 2005; organized draft Chinese Calligraphy Development Compendium 2001–2020; Chief Ed. numerous nat. art magazines, including Art China, Chinese Art, Friends of Chinese Fine Art, and Art Guide; Ed. The laws of the People's Republic of China, Carvings Review, Calligraphy, and 500 other magazines; visits to USA, France, Japan, Sweden, USSR, Singapore, Italy, Korea, Malaysia, Canada, Peru, Venezuela, Hong Kong, Macao and Taiwan; mem. Nat. Cttee CPPCC. *Publications:* academic thesis 'Tradition and yihua' (First Prize, Fourth Art Review Reward, China Fed. of Literary and Art Circles), Origins and Branches (Special Award, Fifth Art Review Reward) Criticism on Calligraphy and Art, Shen Peng's Talks on Calligraphy and Art, San Yu Lyrics on Grass, San Yu Lyrics Continues, Collections of San Yu Poems, Anthology of Contemporary Calligraphers – Shen Peng, Selections of Shen Peng's Calligraphy Works, Collections of ShenPeng's Calligraphy (published in Japan), Shenpeng's Calligraphy of BaiJuyi's Works, ShenPeng's Calligraphy of DuFu's Works, Shen Peng's Running Script of 'Front and Back Chibi', Collections of Running Script, Collections of Regular Script, Script of Words about Yue Yang Pavilion, Shen Peng's Script of Nineteen Ancient Poems, Collections of China Art Museum Contemporary Famous Calligraphers Exhibition. *Honours:* Hon. Commr China Fed. of Literary and Art Circles; among first group of experts honoured by State Council of China for Special Contribs, Modeling Art Creation Study Award, China Fed. of Literary and Art Circles 2006, China Calligraphy Lan Ting Lifelong Accomplishment Award, China Fed. of Literary and Art Circles and China Calligraphy Asscn 2006, World Peace and Art Authority Prize, UN Acad. *Address:* People's Fine Arts Press, Beijing, People's Republic of China (office). *Telephone:* (10) 65245237 (home). *Fax:* (10) 65245237 (office).

SHEPARD, James Russell, BA, AM; American academic and author; b. 29 Dec. 1956, Bridgeport, CT. *Education:* Trinity Coll., Hartford, CT, Brown Univ. *Career:* Lecturer, Univ. of Michigan, Ann Arbor, 1980–83; Asst Prof. of English, 1983–90, Instructor in Film, 1988–, Assoc. Prof. of English, 1990–95, J. Leland Miller Prof. of English, 1995–; Writer-in-Residence, Bread Loaf Writers' Conference, 1982–84, 1988–93, 2002, Univ. of Tennessee at Chattanooga, 1988, 1989, Vassar Coll., 1998; Fiction Faculty, MFA Program, Warren Wilson Coll., 1992–; Univ. of California at Irvine, 2002; The Tin House/Sundance Conference, 2003. *Publications:* Fiction: Flights, 1983; Paper Doll, 1986; Lights Out in the Reptile House, 1990; Kiss of the Wolf, 1994; Nosferatu, 1998; Project X, 2004. Short Story Collections: Batting Against Castro, 1996; Love and Hydrogen, 2004. Editor: You've Got to Read This (with Ron Hansen), 1994; Unleashed: Poems by Writers' Dogs (with Amy Hempel), 1995; Writers at the Movies, 2000. Contributions: anthologies, journals, reviews and magazines. *Honours:* Transatlantic Review Award, Henfield Foundation, 1980; David Sokolov Scholar in Fiction, Bread Loaf, 1982; Nelson Bushnell Prize, Williams Coll., 1997.

SHEPARD, Sam; American playwright, actor, director and screenwriter; b. (Samuel Shepard Rogers), 5 Nov. 1943, Fort Sheridan, Ill.; s. of Samuel Shepard Rogers and Jane Schook Rogers; m. O-Lan Johnson Dark 1969 (divorced); one s.; one s. one d. with Jessica Lange. *Education:* Duarte High School, Mount San Antonio Jr Coll. *Television appearances include:* Lily Dale 1996, Purgatory 1999, Hamlet 2000. *Plays include:* Cowboys and Rock Garden (double bill), Chicago, Icarus's Mother and Red Cross (triple bill; Obie Award) 1966, Melodrama Play 1966, The 4-H Club, La Turista (Obie Award) 1967, Forensic and the Navigators (Obie Award) 1968, The Unseen Hand (rock opera) 1969, Cowboy Mouth (with Patti Smith) 1971, The Mad Dog Blues 1971, The Tooth of Crime (Obie Award) 1973, Geography of a Horse Dreamer 1974, Black Dog Beast Bait, Operation Sidewinder, Shaved Splits, Rock Garden (included in Oh! Calcutta!), Curse of the Starving Class (Obie Award) 1978, Buried Child (Pulitzer Prize) 1979, True West 1980, Fool for Love 1982, A Lie of the Mind 1985 (New York Drama Critics Circle Award for Best Play 1986), States of Shock 1991, Simpatico 1994. *Film appearances include:* Days of Heaven 1978, Resurrection 1980, Francis 1982, The Right Stuff 1983, Paris, Texas 1984, Country, Crimes of the Heart, Baby Boom, Defenceless 1989, Voyager 1991, Thunderheart 1992, The Pelican Brief 1994, Safe Passage 1995, The Good Old Boys 1995, Curtain Call 1997, The Only Thrill 1997, Snow Falling on Cedars 1999, One Kill 2000, All the Pretty Horses 2001, Shot in the

Heart 2001, Swordfish 2001, Black Hawk Down 2001, The Pledge 2001, The Notebook 2004, Don't Come Knockin' 2005, Stealth 2005, Walker Payne 2006, Bandidas 2006, The Return 2006, Charlotte's Web (narrator) 2006. *Screenplay:* Zabriskie Point 1970, Paris, Texas (Palme d'Or, Cannes Film Festival 1984), Fool for Love 1985, Far North (also Dir) 1989, Silent Tongue (also Dir) 1994, Don't Come Knockin' 2005. *Publications:* Hawk Moon 1972, Motel Chronicles 1982, A Murder of Crows (novel) 1996, Cruising Paradise (autobiog.) 1996, Great Dream of Heaven (short stories) 2002, The Rolling Thunder Logbook 2005. *Address:* ICM, 10250 Constellation Boulevard, Los Angeles, CA 90067, USA.

SHEPARD, Stephen Benjamin; American journalist, editor and academic; *Dean, Graduate School of Journalism, City University of New York;* b. 20 July 1939, New York; s. of William Shepard and Ruth Shepard (née Tanner); m. Lynn Povich 1979; one s. one d. *Education:* City Coll., NY, Columbia Univ. *Career:* reporter, writer Business Week 1966–75, Exec. Ed. 1982–84, Ed.-in-Chief 1984–2004; Dean, Graduate School of Journalism, CUNY 2005–; Asst Prof., Dir Walter Bagehot Fellowship Program in econs and business journalism, Columbia Univ. 1975–76; Sr Ed. Newsweek 1976–81; Ed. Saturday Review 1981–82; mem. American Soc. of Magazine Eds. (Vice-Pres. 1990–92, Pres. 1992–94), Council on Foreign Relations, Century Asscn; Gov. Soc. of American Business Eds and Writers. *Honours:* Gerald Coeb Foudation Lifetime Achievement Award 1999, Henry Johnson Fisher Award for Magazine Publisher of America 2000, Soc. of American Business Eds and Writers Distinguished Achievement Award 2005. *Address:* Graduate School of Journalism, c/o The Graduate Center, City University of New York, 365 Fifth Avenue, New York, NY 10016-4309 (office); 322 Central Park West, New York, NY 10025, USA (home). *Website:* www.cuny.edu.

SHEPHERD, Robert James, BA, MA; British writer, journalist, television producer and director; *Managing Director, Wide Vision Productions Ltd;* b. 14 Feb. 1949, Solihull, Warwicks. *Education:* Univ. of Kent. *Career:* Leader and Features Writer, Investors Chronicle 1983; mem. Editorial Team and Producer, A Week in Politics 1983–88; Parl. Lobby Corresp. 1984–87; Producer, documentaries and BBC political programmes, Programme Ed. BBC Political Programmes 1997–; Man. Dir Wide Vision Productions Ltd 1991–; mem. Soc. of Authors, Nat. Union of Journalists. *Television:* Series Producer What Has Become of Us? (four-part history of post-War Britain, Channel 4) 1994. *Publications:* Public Opinion and European Integration 1975, A Class Divided 1988, Ireland's Fate 1990, The Power Brokers 1991, Iain Macleod 1994, Enoch Powell: A Biography 1996; contribs to Oxford Companion to 20th-Century British Politics 2002, Oxford Dictionary of National Biography 2004, Political Quarterly, New Statesman, Investors Chronicle, Marxism Today, Guardian, The Times, Irish Independent, Sunday Press, Ireland of the Welcomes, The Spectator, Contemporary History. *Honours:* Prix Stendhal 1993, Reuter Fellowship, Univ. of Oxford 1995. *Literary Agent:* c/o Jonny Pegg, Curtis Brown Ltd, Haymarket House, 28–29 Haymarket, London, SW1Y 4SP, England. *Telephone:* (20) 7393-4400. *Fax:* (20) 7393-4401. *E-mail:* info@curtisbrown.co.uk. *Website:* www.curtisbrown .co.uk.

SHER, Sir Antony, Kt, KBE; British actor, artist and author; b. 14 June 1949, Cape Town, South Africa. *Education:* Webber Douglas Acad. of Dramatic Art. *Career:* numerous appearances at Liverpool Everyman, Nottingham Playhouse, Royal Court Theatre, Nat. Theatre, RSC (RSC Assoc. Artist 1982–) and in West End; directorial debut with Fraser Grace's play Breakfast with Mugabe at The Other Place, Stratford-upon-Avon. *Plays include:* John, Paul, Ringo and Bert (Lyric Theatre), Teeth 'n' Smiles, Cloud Nine, A Prayer for My Daughter (Royal Court Theatre), Goosepimples (Hampstead and Garrick Theatres), King Lear, Tartuffe, Richard III, Merchant of Venice, The Revenger's Tragedy, Hello and Goodbye, Singer, Tamburlaine the Great, Travesties, Cyrano de Bergerac, The Winter's Tale, Macbeth, The Roman Actor, The Malcontent, Othello (RSC), Torch Song Trilogy (Albery Theatre), True West, Arturo Ui, Uncle Vanya, Titus Andronicus (Royal Nat. Theatre), Stanley (Royal Nat. Theatre, Circle in the Square Theater, New York), Mahler's Conversion (Aldwych Theatre), ID (Almeida Theatre) 2003, Primo (Royal Nat. Theatre, London) 2005, (Music Box Theater, New York—Drama Desk and Outer Critics' Circle Awards for Best Solo Performance 2005–06) 2005, Kean (Apollo Theatre) 2007. *Films include:* Yanks 1979, Superman II 1980 (Superman II: The Richard Donner Cut 2006), Mark Gertler: Fragments of a Biography 1981, Shadey 1985, Erik the Viking 1989, The Young Poisoner's Handbook 1995, The Wind in the Willows 1996, Alive and Kicking (aka Indian Summer) 1996, Mrs. Brown 1997, Shakespeare in Love 1998, The Miracle Maker (voice) 2000, Churchill: The Hollywood Years 2004, A Higher Agency 2005. *Television includes:* ITV Playhouse – Cold Harbour, Pickersgill People – The Sheik of Pickersgill 1978, Collision Course 1979, Play for Today – The Out of Town Boys 1979, One Fine Day 1979, The History Man 1981, Tartuffe, or The Impostor 1983, The Dame Edna Experience 1989, Changing Step 1990, The Land of Dreams 1990, The Comic Strip Presents... – The Crying Game 1992, Genghis Cohn 1993, Shakespeare: The Animated Tales – King Richard III (voice) 1994, One Foot in the Grave – Re-arranging the Dust 1995, Look at the State We're In! (mini-series) 1995, Moonstone 1996, The Winter's Tale (as Anthony Sher) 1999, Hornblower: The Frogs and the Lobsters 1999, Macbeth 2001, The Jury (mini-series) 2002, Home 2003, Murphy's Law – Jack's Back 2004, Primo 2005. *Publications:* Year of the King (autobiography) 1986, Middlepost 1988, Characters (paintings and drawings) 1989, Changing Step (screenplay) 1989, The Indoor Boy 1991, Cheap Lives

1995, Woza Shakespeare! (co-written with Gregory Doran) 1996, The Feast 1998, Beside Myself (autobiography) 2001, I.D. (play) 2003, Primo (play) 2005, Primo Time 2005. *Honours:* Hon. DLitt (Liverpool) 1998 (Exeter) 2003, (Warwick) 2007; Best Actor Awards from Drama Magazine and The Evening Standard Awards, for performance as Richard III (RSC) 1985, Olivier Award for Best Actor, Soc. of West End Theatres, for performances as Richard III, as Arnold in Torch Song Trilogy 1985, for Stanley 1997, Best Actor Award, Martini TMA Awards, for performance as Titus Andronicus 1996, Peter Sellers Evening Standard Film Award for performance as Disraeli in Mrs. Brown 1998. *Literary Agent:* c/o Mic Cheetham Literary Agency, 11–12 Dover Street, London, W1S 4LJ, England. *Telephone:* (20) 7495-2002. *Fax:* (20) 7399-2801. *E-mail:* info@miccheetham.com. *Website:* www.miccheetham.com.

SHER, Steven Jay, BA, MA, MFA; American writer and poet; b. 28 Sept. 1949; m. Nancy Green 1978; one s. one d. *Education:* City Coll., CUNY, Univ. of Iowa, Brooklyn Coll., CUNY. *Career:* Dir Creative Writing, Spalding Univ. 1979–81, Oregon State Univ. 1981–86, Univ. of N Carolina at Wilmington 1986–89; Visiting Writer, Western Oregon Univ. 1991–2002, Willamette Univ. 1993, Yeshiva Univ. 2003–, Fashion Inst. of Tech., State Univ. of New York 2003–; mem. Willamette Literary Guild (Pres. 1992–2002). *Publications:* Nickelodeon 1978, Persnickety 1979, Caught in the Revolving Door 1980, Trolley Lives 1985, Man With a Thousand Eyes and Other Stories 1989, Traveler's Advisory 1994, Flying Through Glass 2001, Thirty-Six 2002, At the Willamette 2003; co-editor: Northwest Variety: Personal Essays by 14 Regional Authors 1987; contrib. to anthologies and periodicals. *Honours:* All Nations Poetry Contest 1977, Weymouth Centre Residency 1988, N Carolina Writers' Network Writers and Readers Series Competition 1989, How the Ink Feels Poetry Contest 2001. *Address:* 344 W 87 Street, No. 3R, New York, NY 10024, USA.

SHERKAT, Shahla; Iranian journalist; *Editor, Zanan magazine. Career:* founder, Ed. and Publisher, Zanan (Women) magazine 1991–, writing about women's issues in Iran. *E-mail:* sherkat@zanan.co.ir. *Website:* www.zanan.co.ir.

SHERMAN, Eileen Bluestone, BA, MA; American author, playwright and lyricist; b. 15 May 1951, Atlantic City, NJ; m. Neal Jonathan Sherman 1973, one s. one d. *Education:* Finch College, New York, SUNY at Albany. *Career:* faculty mem., Baker University, Overland Park, KS 1997; mem. Authors' Guild; Dramatists Guild; National League of American Pen Women; Society of Children's Book Writers. *Publications:* The Odd Potato 1984, Monday in Odessa 1986, Independence Avenue 1990, The Violin Players 1998; musicals: The Sabbath Peddler 1987, The Happiest Day in Heaven 1998, Rockwell 1999, You're Not Sandy Koufax 2000, Broadway Sings the Odd Potato 2003; other: The Magic Door (television series) 1987–90, Room 119 (drama) 1997. *Honours:* Outstanding Social Studies Trade Book Award, 1986; National Jewish Book Award for Children's Literature, 1986; Emmy Awards, 1988, 1989; Teacher's Choice Award, 1991; Jessica Cosgrave Award for Career Achievement, Finch College Asscn, 1997; Thorpe Menn Honorable Mention 1999; Sugarman Family Literature Honorable Mention, 1999; First Place, Short Story Category, National League of American Pen Women, Kansas City, 2000.

SHERMAN, Martin; American playwright; b. 1938, New Jersey. *Education:* Boston Univ. *Plays include:* A Solitary Thing 1963, Fat Tuesday 1966, Next Year in Jerusalem 1968, Night Before Paris 1969, Things Went Badly In Westphalia 1971, Passing By 1974, Soaps 1975, Cracks 1975, Rio Grande 1976, Blackout 1978, Bent 1978, Messiah 1982, When She Danced 1985, Madhouse In Goa 1989, Some Sunny Day 1996, Rose 1999, Chain Play 2001, Passage To India 2002, Absolutely! (Perhaps) 2003. *Films include:* The Clothes in the Wardrobe (The Summer House in USA), Indian Summer. *Address:* c/o Casarotto Ramsay and Associates Ltd, National House, 60-65 Wardour Street, London, W1V 3HP, England.

SHERMAN, Susan; American poet, critic and editor. *Career:* founder and Ed., Ikon magazine 1965–69; teacher, Parsons School of Design. *Publications:* Color of the Heart: Writing from Struggle and Change 1959–1990 1990, Shango de Ima (trans.) 1996. *Honours:* New York Foundation for the Arts Fellowship for Poetry 1990, Puffin Foundation Grant 1992, Fellowship from the New York Foundation for the Arts for Creative Non-Fiction Literature 1997. *Address:* c/o Curbstone Press, 321 Jackson Street, Willimantic, CT 06226-1738, USA. *E-mail:* info@curbstone.org. *Website:* www.curbstone.org.

SHERMAN, William (Bill) David, (Pecos Bill, Alvaro de Campos), AB, MA, PhD; American writer, editor, publisher and lecturer; b. 24 Dec. 1940, Philadelphia, Pa; s. of Louis Sherman and Gertrude Sherman (née Benn); m. Barbara Beaumont 1970 (divorced 1978). *Education:* Temple Univ., State Univ. of New York at Buffalo, Dickinson School of Law. *Career:* Teaching Fellow, English Dept, State Univ. of New York at Buffalo 1962–64, 1965–67; Lecturer in Cinema 1967; Lecturer in American Studies, Univ. of Hull, UK 1967–68; Lecturer, English Dept, Univ. Coll. of Wales, Aberystwyth 1969–72; Founder-Ed. and Publr Branch Redd Books and Branch Redd Review 1976–2002; currently freelance lecturer and writer. *Play:* The Case of Ezra Pound (published in Anglo-Welsh Review) 1970. *Film:* Maximus to Himself (co-directed by Theodora Cichy). *Publications:* The Landscape of Contemporary Cinema (with Leon Lewis) 1967, The Cinema of Orson Welles 1967, The Springbok (poems) 1973, The Hard Sidewalk 1974, The Horses of Gwyddno Garanhir 1976, Mermaids I 1977, Heart Attack and Spanish Songs in Mandaine Land 1981, Duchamp's Door 1983, She Wants to Go to Pago-Pago 1986, Mermaids I and II 1986, The Tahitian Journals 1990, A Tale for Tusitala

1993, From the South Seas 1997, Mana of the Moai 2004; contrib. to anthologies, including Matieres d'Angleterre 1984, The Faber Book of Movie Verse 1993, In the Company of Poets 2003; contribs to periodicals, including Fire (Oxfordshire, UK), Spanner, and numerous other small press publs. *Honours:* Poetry Prize, Royal Albert Hall Reading (The Return of the Reforgotten) for co-trans. of Tahitian poet, Henri Hiro 1995. *Address:* 9300 Atlantic Avenue, No. 218, Margate, NJ 08402, USA. *E-mail:* branchredd@yahoo.com.

SHERRIN, Edward (Ned) George, CBE, MA; British director, writer and presenter; b. 18 Feb. 1931, Low Ham, Somerset; s. of Thomas Adam Sherrin and Dorothy Finch Sherrin (née Drewett). *Education:* Sexey's School, Bruton, Exeter Coll., Oxford, Gray's Inn, London. *Career:* Producer, ATV 1955–58, BBC 1958–65; film producer 1965–75; theatre dir 1972–. *Films produced:* The Virgin Soldiers 1968, The National Health 1972. *Theatre:* directed and narrated Side by Side by Sondheim, London 1976–77, New York 1977–78; directed and co-adapted The Ratepayers' Iolanthe, London (Olivier Award 1984) 1984; directed Mr and Mrs Nobody 1987, Jeffrey Bernard is Unwell 1989 (Australia 1992), Same Old Moon, Bookends 1990, Our Song 1992, A Passionate Woman 1994, Salad Days (revival tour) 1995, (Vaudeville Theatre) 1996, Good Grief 1998, A Saint She Aint 1999. *Radio:* presenter Loose Ends (BBC Radio 4) 1985–, Counterpoint (BBC Radio 4) 1985–. *Television:* created That Was The Week That Was (satire programme) 1961. *Publications:* with Caryl Brahms: Cindy-Ella or I Gotta Shoe 1962, Rappel 1910 1964, Benbow Was His Name 1967, Ooh la! la! 1973, After You M. Feydeau 1975; A Small Thing Like an Earthquake 1983, Cutting Edge 1984, Too Dirty for the Windmill 1985; with Neil Shand: 1956 and All That 1986, Loose Neds 1990; Ned Sherrin's Theatrical Anecdotes 1991, Ned Sherrin in his Anecdotage 1993, The Oxford Dictionary of Humorous Quotations 1994, Scratch an Actor (novel) 1996, Sherrin's Year (diary) 1996, Ned Sherrin: The Autobiography 2005. *Address:* 4 Cornwall Mansions, Ashburnham Road, London, SW10 0PE, England. *Telephone:* (20) 7352-7662.

SHERRY, (Michael) Norman, BA, PhD, FRSL; British/American writer and academic; b. 6 July 1935, Tirana, Albania. *Education:* Univ. of Durham, UK, Univ. of Singapore. *Career:* Lecturer in English Literature, Univ. of Singapore 1961–66; Lecturer, Sr Lecturer, Univ. of Liverpool, UK 1966–70; Prof. of English, Univ. of Lancaster, UK 1970–82; Fellow, Humanities Research Center, NC, USA 1982; Mitchell Distinguished Prof. of Literature, Trinity Univ., San Antonio, Tex. 1983–; mem. Savile. *Publications:* Conrad's Eastern World 1966, Jane Austen 1966, Charlotte and Emily Brontë 1969, Conrad's Western World 1971, Conrad and his World 1972, Conrad: The Critical Heritage 1973, Conrad in Conference 1976, The Life of Graham Greene, Vol. 1 1904–39 1989, Vol. 2 1939–55 1994, Vol. 3 1955–1991 2004, Joseph Conrad 1997; ed.: An Outpost of Progress and Heart of Darkness 1973, Lord Jim 1974, Nostromo 1974, The Secret Agent 1974, The Nigger of the Narcissus, Typhoon, Falk and Other Stories 1975, Joseph Conrad: A Commemoration 1976; contrib. to Academic American Encyclopedia, Guardian, Daily Telegraph, Oxford Magazine, Modern Language Review, Review of English Studies, Notes and Queries, BBC, Times Literary Supplement, Observer. *Honours:* Edgar Allan Poe Award 1989, Guggenheim Fellowship 1989–90. *Address:* Trinity University, 1 Trinity Place, San Antonio, TX 78212, USA (office).

SHERWIN, Byron Lee, BS, BHL, MHL, MA, PhD; American academic and author; *Distinguished Service Professor of Jewish Philosophy and Mysticism, Spertus Institute of Jewish Studies;* b. 18 Feb. 1946, New York, NY; m. Judith Rita Schwartz 1972, one s. *Education:* Columbia Univ., Jewish Theological Seminary, New York Univ., Univ. of Chicago. *Career:* Asst Prof., Spertus Inst. of Jewish Studies, Chicago 1970–74, Assoc. Prof. 1974–78, Prof. of Jewish Philosophy and Mysticism 1978–2000, Vice-Pres. for Academic Affairs 1984–2001, Distinguished Service Prof. of Jewish Philosophy and Mysticism 2001–; Visiting Prof., Mundelein Coll. 1974–82; Dir Holocaust Studies Project, Nat. Endowment for the Humanities 1976–78; mem. American Asscn of Univ. Profs, Rabbinical Assembly, American Philosophical Asscn, Authors' Guild. *Publications:* Judaism: The Way of Sanctification (with Samuel H. Dresner) 1978, Abraham Joshua Heschel 1979, Encountering the Holocaust: An Interdisciplinary Survey (ed. with Susan G. Ament) 1979, Garden of the Generations 1981, Jerzy Kosinski: Literary Alarmclock 1982, Mystical Theology and Social Dissent: The Life and Works of Judah Loew of Prague 1982, The Golem Legend: Origins and Implications 1985, Contexts and Content: Higher Jewish Education in the United States 1987, Thank God: Prayers of Jesus and Christians Together 1989, In Partnership with God: Contemporary Jewish Law and Ethics 1990, No Religion is an Island (with Harold Kasimov) 1991, Towards a Jewish Theology 1992, How to Be a Jew: Ethical Teachings of Judaism (with Seymour J. Cohen) 1992, The Spiritual Heritage of Polish Jews 1995, Sparks Amongst the Ashes: The Spiritual Legacy of Polish Jewry 1997, Crafting the Soul 1998, Why Be Good? 1998, John Paul II and Interreligious Dialogue (co-author) 1999, Jewish Ethics for the 21st Century 2000, Creating an Ethical Jewish Life 2001, Golems Among Us 2004, Workers of Wonders 2004, The Cubs and the Kabbalist: A Novel 2006, Kabbalah for the Curious 2006; contrib. to professional journals. *Honours:* Presidential Medal (Poland) 1995; Hon. DHL (Jewish Theological Seminary of America) 1996; Polish Council of Christians and Jews Man of Reconciliation Award 1992. *Address:* Spertus Institute of Jewish Studies, 618 S Michigan Avenue, Chicago, IL 60605, USA (office). *Telephone:* (312) 322-1738 (office). *Fax:* (312) 922-6406 (office). *E-mail:* BSherwin@spertus.edu (office). *Website:* www.spertus.edu (office).

SHIBLI, Adania; Palestinian novelist and academic; *Lecturer, School of Critical Theory and Cultural Studies, University of Nottingham;* b. 13 Aug. 1974. *Education:* Univ. of East London. *Career:* postgraduate researcher, Univ. of East London; currently Lecturer in Cultural Studies, Univ. of Nottingham; Contributing Ed. Zawaya magazine (Lebanon). *Play:* The Error, New Company Theatre, London, Golden Threads, San Francisco. *Films:* Arab (VPRO, Netherlands) 2001, Nazareth 2000 (Ikona TV, Netherlands) (co-writer). *Publications:* Masas (Touching, novel) 2002, Kulluna Ba'eed Bethat al-Meqdar an al-Hubb (We are Equally Far from Love, novel) 2004; contrib. to al-Karmel literary magazine, al-Adaab cultural magazine, Zawaya Cultural Review, Assiwar magazine, Jerusalem Quarterly, PressAsia, Babelmed. *Honours:* Feewaiver Fellowship, Univ. of East London, A. M. Qattan Foundation Young Writers' Award. *E-mail:* adania.shibli@nottingham.ac.uk (office). *Website:* www.nottingham.ac.uk/critical-theory/staff/staff.htm#shibli.

SHIELDS, David, BA, MFA; American writer and academic; *Professor of English, University of Washington at Seattle;* b. 22 July 1956, Los Angeles, CA. *Education:* Brown Univ., Univ. of Iowa. *Career:* Visiting Lecturer in Creative Writing, Univ. of California at Los Angeles 1985; Visiting Asst Prof., St Lawrence Univ., Canton, NY 1985–86, 1987–88; Asst Prof. 1988–92, Assoc. Prof. 1992–97, Prof. of English 1997–, Univ. of Washington at Seattle; Faculty, Warren Wilson Coll., Asheville, NC 1996–; various visiting instructorships; mem. Associated Writing Programs, Authors' Guild, Int. PEN, MLA of America, Poets and Writers, Writers' Guild of America. *Publications:* Heroes: A Novel 1984, Dead Languages: A Novel 1989, Handbook for Drowning; A Novel in Stories 1992, Remote: Reflections on Life in the Shadow of Celebrity 1996, Black Planet: Facing Race During an NBA Season 1999, 'Baseball is Just Baseball': The Understated Ichiro 2004, Enough About You: Adventures in Autobiography 2004, Body Politic: The Great American Sports Machine 2004; contrib. to New York Times Magazine, Harper's, Yale Review, Village Voice, Slate, Salon, McSweeney's. *Honours:* Iowa Writers' Workshop James A. Michener Fellowship 1980–82, San Francisco Foundation James D. Phelan Award 1981, NEA Fellowships 1982, 1991, Ingram-Merrill Foundation Award 1983, PEN Syndicated Fiction Project Competitions 1985, 1988, Bread Loaf Writers' Conference William Sloane Fellowship 1986, New York Foundation for the Arts Fellowship 1988, Commonwealth Club of California Awards Silver Medal 1989, State of Washington Governor's Writers Award 1990, Artist Trust Fellowships for Literature 1991, 2003, PEN/Revson Foundation Fellowship 1992, first prize Web del Sol Creative Non-Fiction Contest 1999, John Simon Guggenheim Memorial Foundation Fellowship 2005–06, Univ. of Washington Simpson Center for Humanities Research Fellowship 2005–06. *Address:* c/o Department of English, University of Washington at Seattle, Seattle, WA 98195, USA. *E-mail:* dshields@davidshields.com. *Website:* www.davidshields.com.

SHILLITOE, Tony, BA, DipEd, BEd; Australian educator; b. 28 March 1955, Tailem Bend; m. Francesca Stropin 2001. *Education:* Flinders University, Hartley CAE. *Career:* mem. Australian Society of Authors. *Publications:* Guardians, 1992; Kingmaker, 1993; Dragon Lords, 1993; The Last Wizard, 1995; The Innkeeper, 1996; Fiction 2 – The Novel, 1996; Jammin', 1997; The Lure, 1998; The Lore Book, 1998; Joy Ride, 1999; Assassin, 1999; Honour, 1999; Introduction to Styles and Conventions, 1999; The Mother Anger, 2000; Virtual God, 2000; The Sculptor, 2000. *E-mail:* tshillitoe@concordia.sa.edu.au.

SHINDLER, Colin, BA, MA, PhD; British film and television producer, screenwriter, academic and novelist; b. 28 June 1949, Bury, Lancs., England; m. N. Lynn White 1972; one s. one d. *Education:* Bury Grammar School, Univ. of Cambridge. *Publications:* Hollywood Goes to War 1979, Buster 1988, Hollywood in Crisis 1996, Manchester United Ruined My Life 1998, High on a Cliff 2000, Fathers, Sons and Football 2001, First Love Second Chance 2003, George Best and 21 Others 2004. *Literary Agent:* Sheil Land Associates, 43 Doughty Street, London, WC1, England.

SHINKAREV, Vladimir; Russian writer, geologist and artist; b. 4 March 1954, Leningrad; s. of N. F. Shinkarev and N.A. Roumiantseva; m.; one d. *Education:* Leningrad Univ., Muhina Coll., Repin Art Acad. *Career:* mem. St Petersburg Union of Artists 1993–. *Paintings:* World Literature (series of paintings), Great Wall of China, Literature Itself 2000. *Publications include:* 'Solovei i stado': Basnia 1988, Mitki 1990, Stikhi, basmi, pesni 1995, Maxim and Fyodor 2002, London 2002, Poznań 1997, Berlin 1998. *Address:* c/o Seagull Publishing House Ltd, 14 Caterham Road, London, SE13 5AR, England (office); Flat 4, 21/9 Bolshaja Monetnaja Ulitsa, St Petersburg 197101, Russian Federation (home). *Telephone:* (7963) 328006 (Mobile) (office); (812) 232-81-56 (home). *Fax:* (20) 8297-0217 (office). *E-mail:* contactseagull@globalnet.co.uk (office); vshinkarev@mail.ru (home). *Website:* www.seagullpublishing.co.uk.

SHINN, Sharon Ruth, BSJ; American writer; b. 28 April 1957, Wichita, KS. *Education:* Northwestern Univ. *Publications:* The Shape-Changer's Wife 1995, Archangel 1996, Jovah's Angel 1997, The Alleluia Files 1998, Wrapt in Crystal 1999, Heart of Gold 2000, Summers at Castle Auburn 2001, Jenna Starborn 2002, Angelica 2003, Angel-Seeker (Reviewer's Choice Award for Best Science Fiction Novel from the Romantic Times 2005) 2004, The Safe-Keeper's Secret 2004, Fallen Angel (novella) in anthology To Weave a Web of Magic 2004, The Sorcerer's Assassin (short story) in anthology Powers of Detection 2004, Mystic and Rider 2005, The Truth Teller's Tale 2005, The Thirteenth House 2006, The Dream Maker's Magic 2006, Dark Moon Defender 2006, When Winter Comes (novella) in anthology The Queen in Winter 2006, Wintermoon Wish (short story) in anthology Firebirds Rising 2006, The Double-Edged Sword in anthology Elemental 2006. *Honours:* Crawford Fantasy Award, Int. Asscn for the Fantastic in the Arts 1996. *Address:* PO Box 6774, Brentwood, MO 63144, USA.

SHIPLER, David Karr, AB; American journalist and writer; b. 3 Dec. 1942, Orange, NJ; m. Deborah S. Isaacs 1966; two s. one d. *Education:* Dartmouth Coll. *Career:* News Clerk 1966–67, News Summary Writer 1967–68, Reporter 1968–73, Foreign Correspondent, Saigon 1973–75, and Moscow 1975–77, Bureau Chief, Moscow 1977–79, and Jerusalem 1979–84, Correspondent, Washington, DC 1985–87, Chief Diplomatic Correspondent 1987–88, The New York Times; Guest Scholar, Brookings Institution 1988–85; Senior Assoc., Carnegie Endowment for International Peace 1988–90; Adjunct Prof., School of International Service, American University, Washington, DC 1990; Ferris Prof. of Journalism and Public Affairs, Princeton University 1990–91; Montgomery Fellow and Visiting Prof. of Govt, Dartmouth Coll. 2003. *Film documentaries:* Arab and Jew: Wounded Spirits in a Promised Land 1989, Arab and Jew: Return to the Promised Land 2002. *Publications:* Russia: Broken Idols, Solemn Dreams 1983, Arab and Jew: Wounded Spirits in a Promised Land 1986, A Country of Strangers: Blacks and Whites in America 1997, The Working Poor: Invisible in America 2004, The Working Poor: Invisible in America 2004; contrib. to newspapers and journals. *Honours:* Distinguished Reporting Award, Society of Silurians 1971; Distinguished Public Affairs Reporting Award, American Political Science Asscn 1971; Co-Winner, George Polk Award 1982; Pulitzer Prize for General Non-Fiction 1987; Alfred DuPont-Columbia University Award for Broadcast Journalism 1990. *Address:* 4005 Thornapple Street, Chevy Chase, MD 20815, USA.

SHIRAISHI, Kazuko; Japanese poet; b. 1931, Vancouver, BC, Canada; m.; one d. *Career:* mem. VOU avant-garde literary group 1948–53; with Kazuo Ono has mounted series of poetry/dance productions. *Publications:* poetic works include Seasons of Sacred Lust (in English) 1978.

SHMELEV, Nikolay Petrovich, DEcon; Russian economist and writer; *Director of the Institute of Europe, Russian Academy of Sciences;* b. 1936, Moscow; m.; one c. *Education:* Moscow Lomonosov State Univ. *Career:* with USSR (now Russian) Acad. of Sciences (RAN) 1958–, first at Inst. of Econs, then Inst. of World Socialist System Econs, researcher, then head of US foreign policy dept Inst. of USA and Canada Studies 1982–92, chief researcher Deputy Dir Inst. of Europe 1993, currently Dir; corresp. mem. RAN 1997, full mem. 2000–; People's Deputy 1989–92; Dir Consultative Council under the Russian Pres. 1991–93; Stockholm Inst. of Econs of the Soviet Union and Eastern Europe, Sweden 1992. *Publications:* 75 monographs and 300 scientific articles; numerous narratives including Pashkov's House, Performance in Honour of Monsieur First Minister; short stories: The Last Floor, It Serves You Right. *Honours:* Order of Honour; Medal for Valiant Labour. *Address:* c/o Institute of Europe, Russian Academy of Sciences, ul. Mokhovaya 11, Bldg 3V, 101999 Moscow, Russia.

SHNEIDMAN, Noah Norman, MPHE, MA, DipREES, PhD; Canadian academic and writer; *Professor Emeritus, University of Toronto;* b. 24 Sept. 1924, Wilno, Poland; m. (divorced); two d. *Education:* Minsk, Warsaw, Univ. of Toronto. *Career:* Lecturer, Univ. of Toronto 1966–71, Asst Prof. 1971–75, Assoc. Prof. 1975–79, Prof. 1979–91, Professor Emeritus 1991–; Distinguished Visiting Prof., McMaster Univ. 1981; mem. Canadian Asscn of Slavists, American Asscn of Teachers of Slavic and East European Languages. *Publications:* Literature and Ideology in Soviet Education 1973, The Soviet Road to Olympus: Theory and Practice of Soviet Physical Culture 1978, Soviet Literature in the 1970s: Artistic Diversity and Ideological Conformity 1979, Dostoevsky and Suicide 1984, Soviet Literature in the 1980s: Decade of Transition 1989, Russian Literature 1988–1994: The End of an Era 1995, Jerusalem of Lithuania: The Rise and Fall of Jewish Vilnius 1998, The Three Tragic Heroes of the Vilnius Ghetto: Witenberg, Sheinbaum, Gens 2002, Russian Literature 1995–2002: On the Threshold of the New Millennium 2004. *Address:* c/o Department of Slavic Language and Literature, University of Toronto, 121 St Joseph Street, Toronto, ON M5S 1J4, Canada (office). *E-mail:* nn.shneidman@utoronto.ca (office).

SHOAF, Richard Allen, BA, MA, PhD; American academic, poet, writer and editor; b. 25 March 1948, Lexington, NC; m. Judith Patricia McNamara 1975; one s. one d. *Education:* Wake Forest University, University of East Anglia, Cornell University. *Career:* Asst Prof. of English, 1977–81, Assoc. Prof. of English, 1982–85, Yale University; Prof. of English, 1986–, Alumni Prof. of English, 1990–93, University of Florida at Gainesville; Founder-Ed., Exemplaria: A Journal of Theory in Medieval and Renaissance Studies, 1989–; Pres., Council of Eds of Learned Journals, 1994–96; mem. Acad. of American Poets; Dante Society of America; John Gower Society; Medieval Acad. of America; MLA of America; South Atlantic MLA. *Publications:* Dante, Chaucer, and the Currency of the Word: Money, Images, and Reference in Late Medieval Poetry 1983, The Poem as Green Girdle: 'Commercium' in Sir Gawain and the Green Knight 1984, Milton, Poet of Duality: A Study of Semiosis in the Poetry and the Prose 1985, Troilus and Criseyde (ed.) 1989, Simple Rules (poems) 1991, Chaucer's Troilus and Criseyde – 'Subgit to alle poesye': Essays in Criticism 1992, The Testament of Love, by Thomas Usk (ed.) 1998, Chaucer's Body: The Anxiety of Circulation in the Canterbury Tales 2001. Contributions: reference works, scholarly books and literary journals. *Honours:* National Endowment for the Humanities Fellowships 1982–83, 1999–2000; Hon. Visiting Scholar, University of Central Florida

1993, Univ. of Berne (Switzerland) 1999. *Address:* POB 117310, University of Florida, Gainesville, FL 32611-7310, USA. *E-mail:* ras@ufl.edu.

SHONE, Richard, BA; British writer and editor; *Editor, The Burlington Magazine;* b. 8 May 1949, Doncaster, Yorkshire, England. *Education:* Clare College, Cambridge. *Career:* Assoc. Ed. 1979–2003, Ed. 2003–, The Burlington Magazine. *Publications:* Bloomsbury Portraits: Vanessa Bell, Duncan Grant, and Their Circle 1976 (revised edn) 1993, The Century of Change: British Painting Since 1900 1977, Vincent van Gogh 1977, Augustus John 1979, The Post-Impressionists 1979, Walter Sickert 1988, Rodrigo Moynihan 1988, Sickert: Paintings (ed. with Wendy Baron) 1992, Sisley 1992, Sensation (co-author) 1997, Sargent to Freud: Modern Paintings in the Beaverbrook Collection (with Ian G. Lumsden) 1998, The Art of Bloomsbury 1999, The Janice H. Levin Collection of French Art 2002; contrib. to art journals and other publications. *Address:* c/o The Burlington Magazine, 14–16 Duke's Road, London, WC1H 9SZ, England (office). *E-mail:* shone@burlington.org.uk (office).

SHREVE, Anita; American writer. *Career:* fmr high school teacher, journalist in Nairobi, Kenya and USA; teacher of writing Amherst Coll. *Publications:* non-fiction: Remaking Motherhood: How Working Mothers are Shaping Our Children's Future 1987, Women Together, Women Alone: The Legacy of the Consciousness-Raising Movement 1989; fiction: Eden Close 1989, Strange Fits of Passion 1991, Where or When 1993, Resistance 1995, The Weight of Water 1997, The Pilot's Wife 1998, Fortune's Rocks 2000, The Last Time They Met 2001, Sea Glass 2002, All He Ever Wanted 2002, Light on Snow 2004, A Wedding in December 2005; contrib. to Quest, US, Newsweek, New York Times Magazine. *Honours:* O. Henry Prize 1975, New York Newspaper Guild Page One Award, PEN/L. L. Winship Award 1998, New England Book Award for fiction 1998. *Address:* c/o Abacus Books, Little, Brown and Co, Brettenham House, Lancaster Place, London, WC2E 7EN, England.

SHREVE, Susan Richards, MA; American writer; b. 2 May 1939, Toledo, OH; d. of Robert Richards and Helen Richards; m. 1st Porter Shreve (divorced 1987); m. 2nd Timothy Seldes 1987; two s. two d. *Education:* Univs of Pennsylvania and Virginia. *Career:* Prof. of English Literature, George Mason Univ., Fairfax, VA 1976–; Visiting Prof., Columbia Univ., New York 1982–, Princeton Univ., NJ 1991, 1992, 1993; Pres. PEN/Faulkner Foundation 1985–; producer The American Voice for TV 1986–; Essayist, MacNeil/Lehrer Newshour. *Publications:* A Fortunate Madness 1974, A Woman Like That 1977, Children of Power 1979, Miracle Play 1981, Dreaming of Heroes 1984, Queen of Hearts 1986, A Country of Strangers 1989, Daughters of the New World 1992, The Train Home 1993, Skin Deep: Women and Race 1995, The Visiting Physician 1995, The Goalie 1996, Narratives on Justice (co-ed.) 1996, Outside the Law 1997, How We Want to Live (co-ed.) 1998, Plum and Jaggers 2000; juvenile: Jonah, The Whale 1997, Ghost Cats 1999, The End of Amanda, The Good 2000. *Honours:* George Washington Univ. Jenny Moore Award 1978, Guggenheim Fellowship 1980, Nat. Endowment for the Arts Fellowship 1982. *Address:* 3319 Newark Street, NW, Washington, DC 20008, USA.

SHRIGLEY, David; British cartoonist; b. 1968, Macclesfield, Cheshire. *Education:* Glasgow School of Art. *Exhibitions include:* Stephen Friedman Gallery, London 1997, Surfacing – Contemporary Drawing, ICA, London 1998, Yvon Lambert Gallery, Paris 1999, Center for Curatorial Studies at Bard College, Annandale-on-Hudson, NY 2001, billboard commission at Gloucester Road Station, London 2004. *Publications:* Slug Trails 1991, Merry Eczema 1992, Blanket of Filth 1994, Enquire Within 1995, Err 1995, Drawings Done Whilst on Phone to Idiot 1996, Blank Page and Other Pages 1998, Why We Got the Sack from the Museum 1998, The Beast is New 1999, Grip 2000, Do Not Bend 2001, Evil Thoughts 2002, Human Achievement 2002, Joy – 22 Postcards 2002, Dirt 2002, Yellow Bird with Worm 2003, Who I Am and What I Want 2003, Rules – 22 Postcards 2004, Kill Your Pets 2004, The Book of Shrigley 2005. *Address:* c/o Redstone Press, 7a St Lawrence Terrace, London, W10 5SU, England. *E-mail:* jr@redstonepress.co.uk. *Website:* www.redstonepress.co.uk.

SHRIVER, Lionel, BA, MFA; American novelist; b. 18 May 1957, Gastonia, NC. *Education:* Barnard Coll., Columbia Univ. *Publications:* The Female of the Species 1987, Checker and the Derailleurs 1988, The Bleeding Heart 1990, Ordinary Decent Criminals 1992, Game Control 1994, A Perfectly Good Family 1996, Double Fault 1997, We Need to Talk About Kevin (Orange Prize 2005) 2003, The Post-Birthday World 2007; contrib. to the Wall Street Journal, The Economist, Philadelphia Enquirer, The Guardian. *Address:* c/o Serpent's Tail, 4 Blackstock Mews, London, N4 2BT, England (office).

SHU, Ting; Chinese poet and writer; b. (Gong Peiyu), 1952, Shima, Zhangzhou City, Fujian Prov.; d. of Shi Mo Gang and Xiu Zhen Yong; m. Chen Zhongyi 1981; one s. *Career:* sent to work in the countryside during the cultural revolution –1973, then worked on construction sites and in factories; published poems in underground literary magazine, Today; mem. Writers' Asscn Fujian 1983– (Vice-Chair. 1985–), Council of Writers' Asscn of China 1985–; Dir Chinese Writers' Union. *Publications:* Shuangweichuan 1982, Shu Ting Shuqing Shixuan 1984, Poesiealbum Shu Ting 1989, Selected Poems of Seven Chinese Poets 1993, Selected Poems: An Authoritative Collection 1994, Mist of My Heart: Selected Poems of Shu Ting 1995. *Address:* 13 Zhonghua Road, Gulangyu, Xiamen City, Fujian Province, 361002, People's Republic of China.

SHUBIN, Seymour, BS; American author; b. 14 Sept. 1921, Philadelphia, PA; m. Gloria Amet 1957, one s. one d. *Education:* Temple University. *Career:* mem. American Society of Authors and Journalists; Authors' Guild; MWA; PEN, American Center. *Publications:* Anyone's My Name, 1953; Manta, 1958; Wellville, USA, 1961; The Captain, 1982; Holy Secrets, 1984; Voices, 1985; Never Quite Dead, 1989; Remember Me Always, 1994; Fury's Children, 1997; My Face Among Strangers, 1999; The Good and the Dead, 2000; A Matter of Fear, 2002. Contributions: Saturday Evening Post; Reader's Digest; Redbook; Family Circle; Story; Ellery Queen's Mystery Magazine; Emergency Medicine; Official Detective Stories Magazine; Perspective in Biology and Medicine. *Honours:* Edgar Allan Poe, Special Award; Special Citation for Fiction, Athenaeum of Philadelphia; Certificate of Honor, Temple University.

SHUKMAN, Harold, MA, DPhil, FRHistS; British academic and writer; *Fellow Emeritus, St Antony's College, Oxford;* b. 23 March 1931, London; m. 1st Ann King Farlow 1956 (divorced 1970); two s. one d.; m. 2nd Barbara King Farlow. *Education:* Univs of Nottingham and Oxford. *Career:* Fellow, St Antony's Coll., Oxford 1961–98, Fellow Emer. 1998–, Lecturer in Modern Russian History 1969–98; mem. Authors' Soc., Translators' Asscn. *Publications:* Lenin and the Russian Revolution 1966, Blackwell's Encyclopedia of the Russian Revolution (ed.) 1988, Andrei Gromyko: Memories (ed. and trans.) 1989, Stalin: Triumph and Tragedy (ed. and trans.) 1991, Lenin: His Life and Legacy (ed. and trans.) 1994, Trotsky: Eternal Revolutionary (ed. and trans.) 1996, Rasputin 1997, The Rise and Fall of the Soviet Empire (ed. and trans.) 1998, The Russian Revolution 1998, Stalin 1999, Agents for Change (ed.), The Winter War (ed.), Secret Classrooms (co-author), Redefining Stalinism (ed.) 2003, War or Revolution 2006, The Russo–Japanese War and the Trans-Siberian Railway 2007; contrib. to professional journals and general periodicals. *Address:* St Antony's College, Oxford, OX2 6JF, England.

SHUKMAN, Henry; British poet and writer; b. 1963, Oxford. *Career:* poet-in-residence, The Wordsworth Trust; book reviewer, New York Times; contributing ed., Conde Nast Traveller. *Publications:* Sons of the Moon: A Journey in the Andes (travel writing) 1990, Travels with my Trombone: A Caribbean Journey (travel writing) 1992, Savage Pilgrims: On the Road to Santa Fe (memoir) 1996, In Doctor No's Garden (poems) 2002, Darien Dogs (short stories) 2003, Sandstorm (novel) 2005, The Lost City (novel) 2007; contrib. to TLS, Daily Telegraph, Iowa Review. *Honours:* Daily Telegraph Arvon Prize, TLS Prize, Tabla Prize, Peterloo Prize, Arts Council Writer's Award, Aldeburgh Festival Prize. *Address:* c/o The Wordsworth Trust, Dove Cottage, Grasmere, Cumbria LA22 9SH, England. *Telephone:* (15394) 35544. *Fax:* (15394) 35748. *E-mail:* enquiries@wordsworth.org.uk. *Website:* www.wordsworth.org.uk.

SHULMAN, Alexandra, OBE; British journalist; *Editor, British Vogue;* b. 13 Nov. 1957, London; d. of Milton Shulman and Drusilla Beyfus; m. Paul Spike 1994; one s. *Education:* St Paul's Girls' School and Univ. of Sussex. *Career:* Sec. Over-21 magazine; Writer and Commissioning Ed., later Features Ed. Tatler 1982–87; Ed. Women's Page, Sunday Telegraph 1987, later Deputy Ed. 7 Days current affairs photo/reportage; Features Ed. Vogue 1988; Ed. GQ 1990; Ed. British Vogue 1992–; Dir Condé Nast Publications 1997–2002; Trustee Nat. Portrait Gallery, London 1999–. *Address:* Condé Nast Publications, Vogue House, Hanover Square, London, W1R 0AD, England (office). *Telephone:* (20) 7499-9080.

SHUPE, Anson David, Jr, BA, MA, PhD; American academic and writer; b. 21 Jan. 1948, Buffalo, NY; m. Janet Ann Klicua 1970, one s. one d. *Education:* Waseda University, Tokyo, College of Wooster, Indiana University. *Career:* Asst Prof., Alfred University, New York, 1975–76; Asst Prof., 1976–78, Assoc. Prof., 1978–86, Prof. of Sociology, 1986, University of Texas at Arlington; Assoc. Ed., Review of Religious Research, 1980, 1992–, Sociological Focus, 1988–90; Visiting Faculty Lecturer, 1985, Lecturer, 1987, Iliff School of Theology, Denver; Prof. of Sociology and Anthropology, 1987–, Chair, Dept of Sociology and Anthropology, 1987–91, Indiana University-Purdue University, Fort Wayne; mem. American Asscn of University Profs; Asscn for the Scientific Study of Religion; Asscn for the Sociology of Religion; North Central Sociological Asscn; Religious Research Asscn; Society for the Scientific Study of Religion. *Publications:* 'Moonies' in America: Cult, Church, and Crusade (with David G. Bromley), 1980; Six Perspectives on New Religions: A Case Study Approach, 1981; Strange Gods: The Great American Cult Scare (with David G. Bromley), 1982; Born Again Politics and the Moral Majority: What Social Surveys Really Show (with William A. Stacey), 1982; The Anti-Cult Movement in America: A Bibliography and Historical Survey (with David G. Bromley and Donna L. Stacey), 1983; Metaphor and Social Control in a Pentecostal Sect (with Tom Craig Darrand), 1984; The Mormon Corporate Empire (with John Heinerman), 1985; A Documentary History of the Anti-Cult Movement (with David G. Bromley), 1986; Violent Men, Violent Couples: The Dynamics of Family Violence (with William A. Stacey and Lonnie R. Hazelwood), 1986; Televangelism: Power and Politics on God's Frontier (with Jeffrey K. Hadden), 1988; The Darker Side of Virtue: Corruption, Scandal and the Mormon Empire, 1991; The Violent Couple (with William A. Stacey and Lonnie R. Hazelwood), 1994; In the Name of All That's Holy: A Theory of Clergy Malfeasance, 1995; Violence, Inequality, and Human Freedom, 1998. Editor: eight vols; contrib. to many scholarly publications. *Honours:* various grants and fellowships; Henry H. H. Remak Scholar, Institute for Advanced Study, Indiana University, 1997–98; Arts and Sciences Distinguished Scholar, Indiana University – Purdue University at Fort Wayne, 1998. *Address:* c/o

Department of Sociology and Anthropology, Indiana University-Purdue University at Fort Wayne, IN 46805, USA.

SHUSTERMAN, Richard Marc, BA, MA, DPhil; American academic and writer; *Dorothy F. Schmidt Eminent Scholar Chair in the Humanities and Professor of Philosophy, Florida Atlantic University*; b. 3 Dec. 1949, Phila, Pa; m. 1st Rivka Nahmani 1970 (divorced 1986); two s. one d.; m. 2nd Erica Ando 2000; one d. *Education:* Hebrew Univ. of Jerusalem, Israel, St John's Coll., Oxford, UK. *Career:* Lecturer, Bezalael Acad. of Art 1980–81; Lecturer, Ben-Gurion Univ. of the Negev, Beersheba, Israel 1980–82, Sr Lecturer in English and Philosophy 1983–87; Visiting Fellow, St John's Coll. Oxford 1984–85; Visiting Assoc. Prof., Temple Univ., Phila 1985–87, Assoc. Prof. of Philosophy 1987–91, Full Prof. 1992–, Chair. Dept of Philosophy 1998–2004; Dir of Studies, École des Hautes Études en Sciences Sociales, Paris 1990, 1993; Dorothy F. Schmidt Eminent Scholar Chair in the Humanities and Prof. of Philosophy, Florida Atlantic Univ., Boco Raton 2005–; Visiting Lecturer, Hebrew Univ. of Jerusalem 1980–82; Visiting Prof., Collège Int. de Philosophie 1990 (Dir of Studies 1995–), Hiroshima Univ., Japan 2002–03, Univ. of Paris, Sorbonne 2006, Univ. of Oslo, Norway 2006; mem. American Philosophical Asscn, American Soc. for Aesthetics (Trustee); literary agent, Witherspoon Assocs. *Publications:* The Object of Literary Criticism 1984, T. S. Eliot and the Philosophy of Criticism 1988, Analytic Aesthetics 1989, The Interpretive Turn: Philosophy, Science, Culture (ed. with D. Hiley and J. Bohman) 1991, Pragmatist Aesthetics: Living Beauty, Rethinking Art 1992, L'Art á L'État Vif 1992, Kunst Leben 1994, Sous l'interprétation 1994, Practicing Philosophy: Pragmatism and the Philosophical Life 1997, La fin de l'éxperience esthétique 1999, Performing Live 2000, Vivre La Philosophie 2001, Philosophie als Lebenspraxis 2001, Surface and Depth 2002, The Range of Pragmatism and the Limits of Philosophy 2004. *Honours:* ACLS Grant 1988, Nat. Endowment for the Humanities Grant 1988 and Fellowship 1990, Sr Fulbright Fellowship 1995–96, Alexander von Humboldt Transcoop Grant 2006–09. *Address:* Florida Atlantic University, Boca Raton, FL 33431–0991, USA (office). *Fax:* (561) 297-2752 (office). *E-mail:* shuster1@fau.edu (office). *Website:* www .artsandletters.fau.edu/humanitieschair (office); www.shusterman.net.

SHUTTLE, Penelope Diane; British writer and poet; b. 12 May 1947, Staines, Middlesex, England; m. Peter Redgrove 1980 (died 2003); one d. *Career:* tutor Poetry School; Hawthornden Fellow. *Publications:* fiction: An Excusable Vengeance 1967, All the Usual Hours of Sleeping 1969, Wailing Monkey Embracing a Tree 1974, The Terrors of Dr Treviles (with Peter Redgrove) 1974, The Glass Cottage 1976, Rainsplitter in the Zodiac Garden 1976, The Mirror of the Giant 1979; poetry: The Hermaphrodite Album (with Peter Redgrove) 1973, The Orchard Upstairs 1980, The Child-Stealer 1983, The Lion From Rio 1986, Adventures With My Horse 1988, Taxing the Rain 1992, Building a City for Jamie 1996, Selected Poems, 1980–1996 1998, A Leaf out of his Book 1999, Redgrove's Wife 2006; non-fiction: The Wise Wound: Menstruation and Everywoman (with Peter Redgrove) 1978, Alchemy for Women (with Peter Redgrove) 1995; numerous pamphlet collections, broadsheets, radio dramas, recordings, readings and television features; contrib. to various publications. *Honours:* Arts Council Awards 1969, 1972, 1985, Greenwood Poetry Prize 1972, E. C. Gregory Award for Poetry 1974. *Literary Agent:* David Higham Associates, 5–8 Lower John Street, Golden Square, London, W1F 9HA, England.

SHYAMALAN, M. Night; Indian film director, screenwriter, actor and producer; b. (Manoj Nelliyattu Shyamalan), 6 Aug. 1970, Pondicherry, Tamil-Nadu Prov.; m. Bhavna 1993; two c. *Education:* New York Univ. *Films:* Praying with Anger (writer, dir, actor, producer) 1992, Wide Awake (writer, dir) 1998, The Sixth Sense (writer, dir, actor) 1999, Stuart Little (screenplay writer) 1999, Unbreakable (writer, dir, actor, producer) 2000, Signs (writer, dir, producer) 2002, The Village (writer, dir, producer) 2004, Lady in the Water (writer, dir, producer) 2006. *Publications:* juvenile: Stuart Finds His Way Home (with Kitty Richards) 1999, Stuart and the Stouts (with Greg Brooker) 2001, Stuart and Snowbell (with Greg Brooker) 2001. *Address:* United Talent Agency, 9560 Wilshire Blvd, Suite 500, Beverly Hills, CA 90212, USA.

SIDDONS, Anne Rivers, BAA; American writer; b. 9 Jan. 1936, Atlanta, GA; m. Heyward L. Siddons 1966; four s. *Education:* Auburn Univ. *Career:* mem. Authors' Guild, Int. Woman's Forum, Woodward Acad. (Oglethorpe Univ.). *Publications:* John Chancellor Makes Me Cry 1975, Heartbreak Hotel 1976, The House Next Door 1978, Fox's Earth 1980, Homeplace 1986, Peachtree Road 1988, King's Oak 1990, Outer Banks 1991, Colony 1992, Hill Towns 1993, Downtown 1994, Fault Lines 1995, Up Island 1997, Low Country 1998, Nora, Nora 2000, Islands 2003, Sweetwater Creek 2005; contrib. to magazines. *Honours:* Hon. DLitt (Oglethorpe Univ.) 1992, (Auburn Univ.) 1997; Georgia Author of the Year Award 1988, Georgia Writers Lifetime Achievement Award 1998. *Address:* 60 Church Street, Charleston, SC 29401-2885, USA.

SIDHWA, Bapsi; American/Pakistani writer and academic; b. 11 Aug. 1939, Karachi; d. of Peshotan Bhandara and of Tehmina Bhandara; m. Nasher Rustam Sidhwa; two d. one s. *Education:* Kinnaird Coll. for Women, Lahore. *Career:* self-published first novel The Crow Eaters 1978; Asst Prof. Creative Writing Programme Univ. of Houston, Texas, USA 1985; Bunting Fellowship Radcliffe Coll., Harvard Univ. 1986; Asst Prof. Writing Div., Columbia Univ., New York 1989; Visiting Scholar Rockefeller Foundation Centre, Bellagio,

Italy 1991; Prof. of English and writer-in-residence Mount Holyoake Coll., S Hadley, Mass. 1997; Fannie Hurst writer-in-residence, Brandeis Univ., Mass. 1998–99; Postcolonial Teaching Fellowship Southampton Univ., UK 2001; Chair. Commonwealth Writers Prize' 1993; mem. Advisory Cttee to Prime Minister Benazir Bhutto on Women's Devt –1996, Punjab Rep., Asian Women's Conf., Alma Ata; Sec. Destitute Women's and Children's Home, Lahore. *Plays:* Sock'em With Honey 1993. *Films:* Earth (film of Ice-Candy-Man aka Cracking India) 1999. *Publications include:* The Crow Eaters 1978 (commercially published 1980), The Bride 1982, Ice-Candy-Man aka Cracking India (Notable Book of the Year, New York Times) 1991, An American Brat 1993, Bapsi Sidhwa Omnibus 2001; numerous short stories and reviews. *Honours:* Sitara-I-Imtiaz 1991, Lila Wallace Reader's Digest Award 1993, Nat. Award for English Literature, Pakistan Acad. of Letters 1991, Patras Bokhari Award for Literature 1992, Excellence in Literature Award, Zoroastrian Congress 2002. *Literary Agent:* PFD, London; Sterling Lord Literistic, New York. *Address:* 5442 Cheena Drive, Houston, TX 77096, USA (home); c/o Oxford University Press, Banglore Town, Shahrah-e-Faisal, Karachi, Pakistan. *Telephone:* (713) 283-0811 (office); (21) 45290259 (Karachi); (42) 6660618 (Lahore). *Website:* hometown.aol.com/BSIDHWA (home).

SIEGEL, Ira Theodore, MBA; American publishing executive; b. 23 Sept. 1944, New York City; s. of David A. Siegel and Rose Minsky; m. Sharon R. Sacks 1965; three d. *Education:* New York and Long Island Univs. *Career:* Business Man. Buttenheim Publishing Co., New York 1965–72; Corp. Vice-Pres. (research) Cahners Publishing Co. (Div. Reed Publishing Co. USA, Boston) 1972–86; Pres. R.R. Bowker Publishing Co. (Div. Reed Publishing, USA, New York) 1986–91, Martindale-Hubbell Div. NJ 1990–91, Reed Reference Publishing 1991–95, Pres., CEO 1993–95; Pres., CEO Lexis-Nexis 1995–97; Pres. edata.com (now seisint) 1999–. *Address:* 16589 Senterra Drive, Delray Beach, FL 33484, USA. *Telephone:* (561) 999-4400 (office); (561) 499-6457 (home). *Fax:* (561) 999-4692 (office). *E-mail:* ira@edata.com (office).

SIEGEL, Robert Harold, BA, MA, PhD; American poet, writer and educator; *Professor Emeritus of English, University of Wisconsin at Milwaukee*; b. 18 Aug. 1939, Oak Park, IL; m. Roberta Ann Hill 1961, three d. *Education:* Wheaton Coll., Johns Hopkins Univ., Harvard Univ. *Career:* Asst Prof. of English, Dartmouth Coll. 1968–75; Lecturer in Creative Writing, Princeton Univ. 1975–76; McManes Visiting Prof., Wheaton Coll. 1976; Asst Prof., Univ. of Wisconsin at Milwaukee 1976–79, Assoc. Prof. 1979–83, Prof. of English 1983–99, Prof. Emer. 1999–; mem. Authors' Guild, Associated Writing Programs, NAS, Asscn of Literary Scholars and Critics, Chrysostom Soc. (Pres. 2004–). *Publications:* fiction: Alpha Centauri 1980, Whalesong 1981, The Kingdom of Wundle 1982, White Whale 1991, The Ice at the End of the World 1994; poetry: The Beasts and the Elders 1973, In a Pig's Eye 1980, The Waters Under the Earth 2005, A Pentecost of Finches: New and Selected Poems 2006; contrib. to anthologies, reviews, quarterlies and journals, including Poetry, Atlantic Monthly, Cream City Review. *Honours:* Foley Award, America magazine 1970, Poetry Magazine Glatstein Prize 1977, Prairie Schooner Poetry Prize 1977, Univ. of Wisconsin grants 1978, 1984, 1988, 1996, 1999, Nat. Endowment for the Arts Fellowship 1980, Ingram Merrill Foundation Award 1979, First Prize, Soc. of Midland Authors 1974, 1981, Friends of Literature Matson Award 1982, Univ. of Wisconsin at Oshkosh School of Library Science Golden Archer Award 1986, Milton Prize in Poetry 1994, EPA Poetry Prize 2003. *Address:* Department of English, University of Wisconsin, Milwaukee, WI 53201, USA (office). *E-mail:* siegelrh@uwm.edu (office). *Website:* www.uwm.edu/Dept/English/faculty/emeriti.html (office).

SIERRA, Javier; Spanish journalist; b. Aug. 1971, Teruel; m. *Education:* Universidad Complutense de Madrid. *Career:* presenter of programme on Radio Heraldo 1983; co-founder of magazine, Año Cero 1989; reporter, later Ed. of magazine, Más Allá de la Ciencia 1992–2005, Ed. at Large 2005–. *Television:* contributor: Crónicas Marcianas (Telecinco) 2000–04, Milenio 3 (Cadena SER), Herrera en la Onda (Onda Cero), La rosa de los vientos (Onda Cero); presenter: El otro lado de la realidad (Telemadrid) 2004. *Publications:* Roswell, secreto de Estado (non-fiction) 1995, La España extraña (non-fiction, with Jesús Callejo) 1997, La dama azul (novel) 1998, Las puertas templarias (novel) 2000, En busca de la Edad de Oro (non-fiction) 2000, El secreto egipcio de Napoleón (novel) 2002, La cena secreta (novel) 2004. *Address:* c/o Grupo Editorial Random House Mondadori SL, Travessera de Gràcia 47–49, 08015 Barcelona, Spain (office). *E-mail:* webmaster@randomhousemondadori.es (office). *Website:* www.javiersierra.com.

SIGAREV, Vassily; Russian playwright; b. 1977, Nizhnii Tagil, Sverdlovsk Oblast. *Plays:* Plasticine (Evening Standard Most Promising Playwright award) 2002, Black Milk 2003, Ladybird 2004. *Honours:* Anti-Booker Prize, Moscow 2001. *Literary Agent:* Judy Daish Associates Ltd, 2 St Charles Place, London, W10 6EG, England. *Telephone:* (20) 8964-8811. *Fax:* (20) 8964-8966.

SILBER, Joan, BA, MA; American writer and teacher; b. 14 June 1945, Millburn, NJ. *Education:* Sarah Lawrence Coll., New York Univ. *Career:* faculty, Sarah Lawrence Coll. 1985–; Visiting Asst Prof., Univ. of Utah 1988; Visiting Lecturer, Boston Univ. 1992; writer-in-residence, Vanderbilt Univ. 1993; mem. Authors' Guild, PEN. *Publications:* Household Words (PEN/Hemingway Award for the Best First Novel 1981) 1980, In the City 1987, In My Other Life 2000, Lucky Us 2001, Ideas of Heaven: A Ring of Stories 2004; contrib. to newspapers, reviews and journals. *Honours:* Guggenheim Fellowship 1984–85, Nat. Endowment for the Arts grant 1986, New York Foundation for the Arts grant 1986, Pushcart Prizes 2000, 2003. *Address:* 43 Bond Street, New York, NY 10012, USA. *E-mail:* jksilber@earthlink.net.

SILKO, Leslie Marmon, BA; American academic, writer and poet; b. 15 March 1948, Laguna Pueblo, Albuquerque, NM; two s. *Education:* Univ. of New Mexico. *Career:* Teacher, Univ. of New Mexico; Prof. of English, Univ. of Arizona at Tucson, 1978–. *Publications:* fiction: Ceremony (novel), 1977; Storyteller (short stories), 1981; Almanac of the Dead (novel), 1991; Yellow Woman and a Beauty of the Spirit (essays), 1993; Gardens in the Dunes (novel), 1999. Poetry: Laguna Woman, 1974. Non-Fiction: Leslie Silko (autobiog.), 1974; The Delicacy and Strength of Lace: Letters Between Leslie Marmon Silko and James Wright (biog.), 1986; Sacred Water: Narratives and Pictures (autobiog.), 1993; Conversations with Leslie Marmon Silko (biog.), 2000. Contributions: New Mexico Quarterly. *Honours:* National Endowment for the Arts Grant, 1974; Chicago Review Poetry Award, 1974; Pushcart Prize, 1977; John D. and Catherine T. MacArthur Foundation Fellowship, 1983. *Website:* literati.net/Silko.

SILLIMAN, Ronald Glenn; American editor and poet; b. 8 May 1946, Pasco, Washington; m. 1st Rochelle Nameroff 1965 (divorced 1972); m. 2nd Krishna Evans 1986; two s. *Education:* Merritt College, San Francisco State College, University of California at Berkeley. *Career:* Ed., Tottel's, 1970–81; Dir of Research and Education, Committee for Prisoner Humanity and Justice, San Rafael, CA, 1972–76; Project Man., Tenderloin Ethnographic Research Project, San Francisco, 1977–78; Dir of Outreach, Central City Hospitality House, San Francisco, 1979–81; Lecturer, University of San Francisco, 1981; Visiting Lecturer, University of California at San Diego, La Jolla, 1982; Writer-in-Residence, New College of California, San Francisco, 1982; Dir of Public Relations and Development, 1982–86, Poet-in-Residence, 1983–90, California Institute of Integral Studies, San Francisco; Exec. Ed., Socialist Review, 1986–89; Managing Ed., Computer Land, 1989–. *Publications:* Poetry: Moon in the Seventh House, 1968; Three Syntactic Fictions for Dennis Schmitz, 1969; Crow, 1971; Mohawk, 1973; Nox, 1974; Sitting Up, Standing Up, Taking Steps, 1978; Ketjak, 1978; Tjanting, 1981; Bart, 1982; ABC, 1983; Paradise, 1985; The Age of Huts, 1986; Lit, 1987; What, 1988; Manifest, 1990; Demo to Ink, 1992; Toner, 1992; Jones, 1993; N/O, 1994; Xing, 1996. Other: A Symposium on Clark Coolidge (ed.), 1978; In the American Tree (ed.), 1986; The New Sentence, 1987. *Honours:* Hart Crane and Alice Crane Williams Award, 1968; Joan Lee Yang Awards, 1970, 1971; National Endowment for the Arts Fellowship, 1979; California Arts Council Grants, 1979, 1980; Poetry Center Book Award, 1985. *Address:* 1819 Curtis, Berkeley, CA 94702, USA.

SILLITOE, Alan; British author; b. 4 March 1928, Nottingham; s. of Christopher Sillitoe and Sabina Burton; m. Ruth Fainlight 1959; one s. one d. *Education:* elementary school, Radford, Nottingham. *Career:* worked in various factories including Raleigh Bicycles, Nottingham 1942–45; air traffic control asst 1945–46; served as wireless operator, RAF, Malaya 1946–49; lived six years in France and Spain; professional writer 1958–; Visiting Prof. of English, DeMontfort Univ., Leicester 1993–97; Fellow, Royal Geographical Soc., Royal Inst. of Navigation. *Film screenplays:* Saturday Night and Sunday Morning, The Loneliness of the Long Distance Runner, The Ragman's Daughter, Counterpoint. *Publications:* novels: Saturday Night and Sunday Morning 1958, The General 1960, Key to the Door 1961, The Death of William Posters 1965, A Tree on Fire 1967, A Start in Life 1970, Travels in Nihilon 1971, Raw Material 1972, The Flame of Life 1974, The Widower's Son 1976, The Storyteller 1979, Her Victory 1982, The Lost Flying Boat 1983, Down From The Hill 1984, Life Goes On 1985, Out of the Whirlpool 1987, The Open Door 1989, Last Loves 1990, Leonard's War: A Love Story 1991, Snowstop 1993, Alligator Playground 1997, The Broken Chariot 1998, The German Numbers Woman 1999, Birthday 2001, A Man of His Time 2004; short story collections: The Loneliness of the Long Distance Runner 1959, The Ragman's Daughter 1963, Guzman, Go Home 1968, Men, Women and Children 1973, The Second Chance 1981, The Far Side of the Street 1988, Collected Stories 1995, New Collected Stories 2004; essays: Mountains and Caverns 1975, The Mentality of the Picaresque Hero 1993, A Flight of Arrows 2004; poetry: The Rats and Other Poems 1960, A Falling Out of Love 1964, Love in the Environs of Voronezh 1968, Barbarians and Other Poems 1974, Storm and Other Poems 1974, Snow on the North Side of Lucifer 1979, Sun Before Departure 1984, Tides and Stone Walls (with Victor Bowley) 1986, Collected Poems 1993; travel writing: Road to Volgograd 1964, Leading the Blind: A Century of Guide Book Travel 1815–1914 1995, The Saxon Shore Way (with Fay Godwin) 1983, Nottinghamshire (with David Sillitoe) 1986; plays: Three Plays 1978; All Citizens are Soldiers 1969 (trans. of Lope de Vega's Fuenteovejuna, with Ruth Fainlight); children's books: The City Adventures of Marmalade Jim 1967, Big John and the Stars 1977, The Incredible Fencing Fleas 1978, Marmalade Jim on the Farm 1980, Marmalade Jim and the Fox 1985, Alligator Playground 1998; autobiography: Life Without Armour 1995. *Honours:* Hon. Fellow, Manchester Polytechnic, De Montfort Univ. 1998; Dr hc (Nottingham Polytechnic) 1990, (Nottingham Univ.) 1994; Hawthornden Prize 1960. *Address:* 14 Ladbroke Terrace, London, W11 3PG, England.

SILMAN, Roberta, BA, MFA; American writer; b. 29 Dec. 1934, New York, NY; m. Robert Silman 14 June 1956. *Education:* Cornell Univ., Sarah Lawrence Coll. *Career:* mem. PEN, Authors' Guild, Poets and Writers. *Publications:* Somebody Else's Child, 1976; Blood Relations, 1977; Boundaries, 1979; The Dream Dredger, 1986; Beginning the World Again, 1990. Contributions: book reviews in The New York Times, Boston Globe, numerous magazines in USA and UK. *Honours:* Child Study Asscn Award, Best Children's Book, 1976; Pen Hemingway Honorable Mention, 1978; Janet Kafka Prizes, 1978, 1980; Guggenheim Fellowship, 1979; National Endowment for the Arts Fellowship, 1983; PEN Syndicated Fiction Project Awards, 1983, 1984, Nat. Magazine Award 1984. *Address:* 18 Larchmont Street, Ardsley, NY 10502, USA. *E-mail:* rsilman@verizon.net (home).

SILVERS, Robert Benjamin, AB; American literary editor; *Editor, The New York Review of Books;* b. 31 Dec. 1929, Mineola, NY. *Education:* Univ. of Chicago, Sorbonne, Ecole Polytechnique, Paris, France. *Career:* Press Sec. to Gov. of Connecticut 1950; US Army service 1950–53; Man. Ed. Paris Review 1954–58; Assoc. Ed. Harper's Magazine 1958–63; Co-founder and Co-Ed. New York Review of Books 1963–; Robert B. Silvers annual lectures at New York Public Library established 2002. *Honours:* Hon. DLit (Harvard) 2007. *Address:* New York Review of Books, 1755 Broadway, 5th Floor, New York, NY 10019-3743, USA (office). *Telephone:* (212) 757-8070 (office). *Fax:* (212) 333-5374 (office). *E-mail:* nyrev@nybooks.com (office). *Website:* www.nybooks.com (office).

SILVIS, Randall Glenn, BS, MEd; American novelist, playwright and screenwriter; b. 15 July 1950, Rimersburg, PA; m. Rita Lynne McCanna 1982; two s. *Education:* Clarion Univ., Indiana Univ. *Career:* James Thurber Writer-in-Residence, Thurber House, Columbus, OH 1989; Visiting Writer, Mercyhurst Coll., Pennsylvania 1989–90, Ohio State Univ. 1991, 1992. *Film screenplays:* An Occasional Hell, Believe the Children, Mr Dream Merchant, Marguerite and the Moon Man, The Algerian. *Publications:* The Luckiest Man in the World, Excelsior, An Occasional Hell, Under the Rainbow, Dead Man Falling, On Night's Shore, Disquiet Heart, Heart So Hungry, Mysticus, In a Town Called Mundomuerto; contrib. to magazines. *Honours:* NEA Fellowship, Drue Heinz Literature Prize, Nat. Playwright Showcase Award, Fulbright Sr Scholar Research grant, Screenwriting Showcase Award. *Address:* PO Box 297, St Petersburg, PA 16054, USA (office). *E-mail:* rsilvis@csonline.net (office). *Website:* www.csonline.net/rsilvis (office).

SIMIC, Charles, BA; American poet, writer and academic; *Professor of English, University of New Hampshire;* b. 9 May 1938, Belgrade, Yugoslavia; s. of George Simic and Helen Matijevich; m. Helen Dubin 1965; one s. one d. *Education:* Oak Park High School, Chicago, Univ. of Chicago and New York Univ. *Career:* arrived in USA 1954; army service 1961–64; worked for Chicago Sun-Times as proofreader; later business Man. Aperture Magazine 1966–69; Lecturer, Calif. State Univ., Hayward 1970–73; Assoc. Prof., later Prof. of English, Univ. of New Hampshire 1973–; first vol. of poems published 1967; elected a Chancellor of The Acad. of American Poets 2000. *Publications include:* poetry: What the Grass Says 1967, Somewhere Among Us A Stone Is Taking Notes 1969, Dismantling the Silence 1971, White 1972, Return to a Place Lit by a Glass of Milk 1974, Biography and a Lament 1976, Charon's Cosmology 1977, Brooms: Selected Poems 1978, School for Dark Thoughts 1978, Classis Ballroom Dances 1980, Shaving at Night 1982, Austerities 1982, Weather Forecast for Utopia and Vicinity: Poems 1967–82 1983, The Chicken Without a Head 1983, Selected Poems 1985, Unending Blues 1986, The World Doesn't End (prose poems) 1989 (Pulitzer Prize for Poetry 1990), In the Room We Share 1990, The Book of Gods and Devils 1990, Selected Poems: 1963–83 1990, Hotel Insomnia 1992, A Wedding in Hell 1994, Walking the Black Cat 1996, Jackstraws 1999, Night Picnic 2001, The Voice at 3:00AM 2003, Selected Poems 1963–2003 (Griffin Int. Poetry Prize) 2005; prose: The Uncertain Certainty 1985, Wonderful Words, Silent Truth 1990, Dimestore Alchemy 1992, The Unemployed Fortune Teller 1994, Orphan Factory (essays) 1997, A Fly in the Soup 2000; ed.: Another Republic: 17 European and South American Writers (with Mark Strand) 1976, The Essential Campion 1988, The Best American Poetry 1992; many trans of French, Serbian, Croatian, Macedonian and Slovenian poetry. *Honours:* PEN Int. Award for Translation 1970, 1980, Guggenheim Fellowship 1972, Nat. Endowment for the Arts Fellowships 1974, 1979, Edgar Allan Poe Award 1975, American Acad. of Arts and Letters Award 1976, Harriet Monroe Poetry Award 1980, Fulbright Fellowship 1982, Ingram Merrill Foundation Fellowship 1983, John D. and Catherine T. MacArthur Foundation Fellowship 1984, Acad. of American Poets Fellowship 1998. *Address:* Department of English, University of New Hampshire, PO Box 192, Durham, NH 03824 (office); PO Box 192, Stafford, NH 03884, USA. *E-mail:* csimic@cisunix.unh.edu (office). *Website:* www.unh.edu/english (office).

SIMIC, Goran; Bosnia and Herzegovina writer, poet and dramatist; b. 20 Oct. 1952, Vlasenica, Yugoslavia; m. Amela Simic 1982; two c. *Education:* Univ. of Sarajevo. *Career:* founder mem. PEN Bosnia-Herzegovina; mem. PEN Canada. *Publications:* poetry: A Period Next to a Circle or A Journey 1976, Vertigo 1977, Mandragora 1982, Selected Poems 1985, A Step into the Dark 1987, Fantasy Book 1989, Sorrow of Sarajevo 1994, Sprinting from the Graveyard 1997, Peace and War 1998, Walking Across the Minefield 1999, Alledaagse Adam 1999, Book of Wondering 2002, Immigrant Blues 2003; theatrical works: Wind in Uniform (comedy), A Fairy Tale About Sarajevo 1994, Europe (libretto) 1995, Three plays for puppets 1998, London Under Siege (libretto) 1999. *Honours:* several Yugoslav awards, Hellman-Hammet grant 1993, PEN Center West Freedom to Write Award, USA 1995, Canada Council grants 1996, 1998. *Address:* 226 Carlton Street, Toronto, ON M5A 2L1, Canada. *Telephone:* (416) 921-5957. *E-mail:* goransimic@aol.com. *Website:* www.angelfire.com/poetry/goransimic.

SIMMERMAN, Jim; American academic and poet; *Regents' Professor, English Department, Northern Arizona University*; b. 5 March 1952, Denver, CO. *Education:* BS, Education, 1973, MA, English, 1976, University of Missouri; MFA, Creative Writing, University of Iowa, 1980. *Career:* Instructor, English Dept, Northern Arizona Univ. 1977–78, Asst Prof. 1983–86, Assoc. Prof. and Dir of Creative Writing 1986–93, Prof. 1993–2003, Regents' Prof. 2003–; mem. Editorial Bd Pushcart Prize Series 1985–; mem. mem. Bd Dirs Associated Writing Programs 1992–95, Sec. 1994–95; mem. Rocky Mountain MLA. *Publications:* Home 1983, Bad Weather 1987, Once Out of Nature 1989, Moon Go Away, I Don't Love You Anymore 1994, Yoyo 1994, Dog Music: Poetry About Dogs (co-ed.) 1996, Kingdom Come 1999, American Children 2005; contribs to anthologies and journals. *Honours:* Arizona Comm. on the Arts Fellowships for Poetry 1983, 1987, Nat. Endowment for the Arts Fellowship 1984, Pushcart Writers' Choice Selection 1984, and Prize 1985, Fine Arts Work Center Poetry Fellowship 1984–85, Best of the Small Presses Book Fair Selection 1990, Hawthornden Fellowship, Scotland 1996. *Address:* English Department, Northern Arizona University, Flagstaff, AZ 86011, USA (office).

SIMMIE, Lois; Canadian writer and poet; b. 11 June 1932, Edam, SK; two s. two d. *Education:* Saskatchewan Business College, University of Saskatchewan. *Career:* Writer-in-Residence, Saskatoon Public Library, 1987–88; Instructor, community colleges; mem. Asscn of Canadian Television and Radio Artists; Canadian Children's Book Centre; Saskatchewan Writers Guild; Writers' Union of Canada. *Publications:* Ghost House, 1976; They Shouldn't Make You Promise That, 1981; Pictures, 1984; Betty Lee Bonner Lives There, 1993; The Secret Lives of Sgt John Wilson: A True Story of Love and Murder, 1995. Contributions: numerous anthologies and periodicals. *Honours:* awards and grants.

SIMMONS, Michael, BA; British writer and editor; b. 17 Oct. 1935, Watford, England; m. Angela Thomson 1963; two s. *Education:* Univ. of Manchester. *Career:* East Europe Correspondent, Financial Times 1968–72; Third World Ed., The Guardian 1978–82, E Europe Corresp. 1982–92, Deputy Ed. Society 1993–97. *Publications:* Berlin: The Dispossessed City 1988; The Unloved Country: A Portrait of the GDR 1989; The Reluctant President: A Life of Václav Havel 1992; Landscapes of Poverty, 1997, On the Edge 2002, Street Credo (ed.) 1999, Getting a Life (ed.) 2001, Hearing Loss: From Stigma to Strategy 2005, Gathering 2005; contribs to various periodicals. *Literary Agent:* c/o The Sayle Agency, 86 King's Parade, Cambridge CB2 1SJ, England.

SIMMONS, Richard D., AB, LLB; American newspaper publisher; b. 30 Dec. 1934, Cambridge, Mass.; m. Mary DeWitt Bleecker 1961; two s. *Education:* Harvard and Columbia Univs. *Career:* admitted to New York Bar; Assoc. Satterlee, Warfield & Stephens 1958–62; Gen. Counsel Giannini Science Corpn 1962–64; Vice-Pres. and Gen. Counsel Southeastern Publishing Service Corpn 1964–69; Counsel Dun & Bradstreet Inc., New York 1969–70, Vice-Pres. and Gen. Counsel 1970–72; Pres. Moody's Investors Service 1973–76, Dun & Bradstreet Inc. 1975–76; Exec. Vice-Pres. Dun & Bradstreet Corpn, New York 1976–78, Dir and Vice-Chair. Bd 1979–81; Pres. and COO The Washington Post Co. 1981–91, now Dir; Pres. Int. Herald Tribune 1989–96. *Address:* 105 N Washington Street, Suite 202, Alexandria, VA 22314, USA.

SIMON, Neil; American playwright; b. 4 July 1927, New York; s. of Irving Simon and Mamie Simon; m. 1st. Joan Baim 1953 (deceased); two d.; m. 2nd Marsha Mason 1973 (divorced); m. 3rd Diane Lander 1987; one d. *Education:* New York Univ. *Career:* wrote for various TV programmes including The Tallulah Bankhead Show 1951, The Phil Silvers Show 1958–59, NBC Special, The Trouble with People 1972. *Plays:* Come Blow Your Horn 1961, Little Me (musical) 1962, Barefoot in the Park 1963, The Odd Couple 1965, Sweet Charity (musical) 1966, The Star-Spangled Girl 1966, Plaza Suite 1968, Promises, Promises (musical) 1968, Last of the Red Hot Lovers 1969, The Gingerbread Lady 1970, The Prisoner of Second Avenue 1971, The Sunshine Boys 1972, The Good Doctor 1973, God's Favorite 1974, California Suite 1976, Chapter Two 1977, They're Playing Our Song 1979, I Ought to be in Pictures 1980, Fools 1981, Little Me (revised version) 1982, Brighton Beach Memoirs 1983, Biloxi Blues 1985, The Odd Couple Female Version 1985, Broadway Bound 1986, Rumors 1988, Lost in Yonkers 1991, Jake's Women 1992, The Goodbye Girl (musical) 1993, Laughter on the 23rd Floor 1993, London Suite 1995. *Screenplays:* After the Fox 1966, Barefoot in the Park 1967, The Odd Couple 1968, The Out-of-Towners 1970, Plaza Suite 1971, The Last of the Red Hot Lovers 1972, The Heartbreak Kid 1973, The Prisoner of Second Avenue 1975, The Sunshine Boys 1975, Murder By Death 1976, The Goodbye Girl 1977, The Cheap Detective 1978, California Suite 1978, Chapter Two 1979, Seems Like Old Times 1980, Only When I Laugh 1981, I Ought to Be in Pictures 1982, Max Dugan Returns 1983, Lonely Guy (adaptation) 1984, The Slugger's Wife 1984, Brighton Beach Memoirs 1986, Biloxi Blues 1988, The Marrying Man 1991, Broadway Bound (TV film) 1992, Lost in Yonkers 1993, Jake's Women (TV film) 1996, London Suite (TV film) 1996; other motion pictures adapted from stage plays: Come Blow Your Horn 1963, Sweet Charity 1969, The Star-Spangled Girl 1971; mem. Dramatists Guild, Writers' Guild of America; many awards including Emmy Award 1957, 1959; Antoinette Perry (Tony) Awards for The Odd Couple 1965, Biloxi Blues 1985 (Best Play), Lost in Yonkers 1991 (Best Play). *Publications:* Rewrites: A Memoir 1996; individual plays. *Honours:* Hon. DHumLitt (Hofstra Univ.) 1981, (Williams Coll.) 1984; Evening Standard Award 1967, Writers' Guild Screen Award for The Odd Couple 1969, Writers' Guild Laurel Award 1979, American Comedy Award for Lifetime Achievement 1989, Pulitzer Prize (for Lost in Yonkers) 1991,

Kennedy Center Mark Twain Prize for American Humor 2006. *Address:* c/o Albert DaSilva, 502 Park Avenue, New York, NY 10022, USA.

SIMON, Sheldon Weiss, BA, MA, PhD; American academic and writer; *Professor of Political Science, Arizona State University*; b. 31 Jan. 1937, St Paul, MN; s. of Blair Simon and Jennie Dim; m. Charlann Lilwin Scheid 1962; one s. *Education:* Univ. of Minnesota, Princeton Univ., Univ. of Geneva, Switzerland. *Career:* Visiting Prof., George Washington Univ. 1965, Univ. of British Columbia 1972–73, 1979–80, Carleton Univ. 1976, Monetary Inst. of Int. Studies 1991, 1996, American Grad. School of Int. Man. 1991–92; Asst Prof., then Prof., Univ. of Kentucky 1966–75; Prof. of Political Science, Arizona State Univ. 1975–, Chair. Dept of Political Science 1975–79, Dir Center for Asian Studies 1980–88; Sr Advisor and Chair. Southeast Asia Studies Group, Nat. Bureau of Asian Research, Seattle and Washington, DC; mem. American Political Science Asscn, Asia Soc., Asscn of Asian Studies, Int. Studies Asscn, US Council for Asia-Pacific Security. *Publications:* The Broken Triangle: Peking, Djakarta and the PKI 1969, War and Politics in Cambodia 1974, Asian Neutralism and US Policy 1975, The Military and Security in the Third World (ed.) 1978, The ASEAN States and Regional Security 1982, The Future of Asian-Pacific Security Collaboration 1988, East Asian Security in the Post-Cold War Era (ed.) 1993, Southeast Asian Security in the New Millennium (ed.) 1996, The Many Faces of Asian Security (ed.) 2001, Religion and Conflict in South and Southeast Asia: Disrupting Violence (ed.) 2007; contribs to scholarly books and journals. *Honours:* US Inst. of Peace Grantee 2001, W. Alton Jones Grantee 2001, Earhart Foundation Grantee (several years), Outstanding Research Award, Nat. Bureau of Asian Research 2005. *Address:* Department of Political Science, Arizona State University, Tempe, AZ 85287-3802, USA (office). *Telephone:* (480) 965-1317 (office). *Fax:* (480) 965-3929 (office). *E-mail:* shells@asu.edu (office).

SIMPSON, Anne; Canadian poet, writer and artist. *Career:* fmr co-ordinator, Writing Centre, St Francis Xavier Univ., NS; writer-in-residence, Univ. of New Brunswick in Fredericton; mem. Writers' Union of Canada. *Publications include:* poetry: Light Falls Through You 2000, Loop (Griffin Poetry Prize 2004) 2003; novels: Canterbury Beach 2001; editor: An Orange from Portugal: Christmas Stories from the Maritimes and Newfoundland 2003. *Honours:* co-winner, The Journey Prize 1997, Lina Chartrand Award 1997, Bliss Carman Poetry Award 1999, Atlantic Poetry Award 2001, Gerard Lampert Award 2001. *Address:* McLelland and Stewart Ltd, 481 University Avenue, Suite 900, Toronto, ON M5G 2E9; c/o The Writers' Union of Canada, 90 Richmond Street E, Suite 200, Toronto, ON M5C 1P1, Canada.

SIMPSON, Dorothy M., BA, DipEd; British writer; b. 20 June 1933, Blaenavon, Monmouthshire, Wales; m. Keith Taylor Simpson 1961, two s. one d. *Education:* Univ. of Bristol. *Career:* teacher of English and French, Dartford Grammar School for Girls, Kent 1955–59, Erith Grammer School, Kent 1959–61; teacher of English, Senacre School, Maidstone, Kent 1961–62; mem. Soc. of Authors, CWA. *Publications:* Harbinger of Fear 1977, The Night She Died 1981, Six Feet Under 1982, Puppet for a Corpse 1983, Close Her Eyes 1984, Last Seen Alive 1985, Dead on Arrival 1986, Element of Doubt 1987, Suspicious Death 1988, Dead by Morning 1989, Doomed to Die 1991, Wake the Dead 1992, No Laughing Matter 1993, A Day for Dying 1995, Once Too Often 1998, Dead and Gone 1999. *Honours:* CWA Silver Dagger 1985. *Literary Agent:* Curtis Brown Ltd, Haymarket House, 28–29 Haymarket, London, SW1Y 4SP, England. *Telephone:* (20) 7393-4400. *Fax:* (20) 7393-4401. *E-mail:* info@curtisbrown.co.uk. *Website:* www.curtisbrown.co.uk.

SIMPSON, Joe, BA; British novelist; b. 13 Aug. 1960, Kuala Lumpur, Malaysia. *Education:* Ampleforth Public School, Yorkshire, Edinburgh Univ. *Publications:* Touching the Void 1988, The Water People 1992, This Game of Ghosts 1993, Storms of Silence 1996, Dark Shadows Falling 1997, The Beckoning Silence 2002. *Honours:* Boardman-Tasker Prize 1988, NCR Non-Fiction Prize 1989, Asscn of Speakers' Clubs Speaker of the Year, Nat. Outdoor Book Awards Literary Category 2003. *Literary Agent:* c/o Vintage Publishing, Random House UK Ltd, 20 Vauxhall Bridge Road, London, SW1V 2SA, England. *Telephone:* (20) 7840-8400. *Fax:* (20) 7233-6117. *Website:* www .randomhouse.co.uk/vintage.

SIMPSON, John Andrew, BA, MA; British linguist and lexicographer; *Chief Editor, The Oxford English Dictionary*; b. 13 Oct. 1953, Cheltenham, Glos.; s. of Robert Morris Simpson and Joan Margaret Simpson (née Sersale); m. Hilary Croxford 1976; two d. *Education:* Univs of York and Reading. *Career:* Editorial Asst, Supplement to The Oxford English Dictionary 1976–79, Sr Ed. 1981–84; Ed. New Words, The Oxford English Dictionary 1984–86, Co-Ed., The Oxford English Dictionary 1986–93, Chief Ed. 1993–; Fellow Kellogg Coll., Oxford 1991–; mem. Faculty of English, Univ. of Oxford 1993–; mem. Exec. Cttee, European Fed. of Nat. Insts for Language 2003– (mem. Steering Cttee 2002–03); Advisory Bd Opera del Vocabolario Italiano 2003–; mem. Philological Soc., Holton Cricket Club. *Publications:* The Concise Oxford Dictionary of Proverbs (ed.) 1982, The Oxford English Dictionary (second edn, co-ed. with Edmund Weiner) 1989, (third edn, online) 2000–, The Oxford Dictionary of Modern Slang (co-ed. with John Ayto) 1992, The Oxford English Dictionary Additions Series (two vols, co-ed. with Edmund Weiner) 1993, Gen. Edn, Vol. Three 1997; contrib. to scholarly books and journals. *Honours:* Hon. DLitt (ANU). *Address:* Oxford English Dictionary, Oxford University Press, Great Clarendon Street, Oxford, OX2 6DF (office); Chestnut Lodge, 7 St Mary's Close, Wheatley, Oxford, OX33 1YP, England (home). *Telephone:*

(1865) 353728 (office). *Fax:* (1865) 353811 (office). *E-mail:* john.simpson@oup.com (office). *Website:* www.oed.com (office).

SIMPSON, John Cody Fidler-, CBE, MA, FRGS; British broadcaster and writer; *World Affairs Editor, BBC*; b. 9 Aug. 1944, Cleveleys; s. of Roy Fidler-Simpson and Joyce Leila Vivien Cody; m. 1st Diane Petteys 1965 (divorced 1996); two d.; m. 2nd Adèle Krüger 1996; one s. *Education:* St Paul's School, London, Magdalene Coll. Cambridge. *Career:* joined BBC 1966, Foreign Corresp. in Dublin, Brussels, Johannesburg 1972–78, Diplomatic Corresp., BBC TV 1978–80, Political Ed. 1980–81, Diplomatic Ed. 1982–88, Foreign Affairs Ed. (now World Affairs Ed.) 1988–; Contributing Ed. The Spectator 1991–95; columnist, Sunday Telegraph 1995–. *Publications:* The Best of Granta 1966, The Disappeared 1985, Behind Iranian Lines 1988, Despatches from the Barricades 1990, From the House of War 1991, The Darkness Crumbles 1992, In the Forests of the Night 1993, Lifting the Veil: Life in Revolutionary Iran 1995, The Oxford Book of Exile 1995, Strange Places, Questionable People (autobiog.) 1998, A Mad World, My Masters 2000, News from No Man's Land: Reporting the World 2002, Days from a Different World: A Memoir of Childhood (autobiog.) 2005, Twenty Tales from the War Zone 2007, Not Quite World's End 2007. *Honours:* Hon. Fellow Magdalene Coll. Cambridge; Hon. DLitt (De Montfort) 1995, (Univ. of E Anglia) 1998; Dr hc (Nottingham) 2000; Golden Nymph Award Cannes 1979, BAFTA Reporter of the Year 1991, 2001, Royal TV Soc. Dimbleby Award 1991, Peabody Award 1998, Emmy Award (for coverage of the fall of Kabul) 2002, Bayeux War Correspondents' Prize 2002, Int. Emmy Award, New York 2002. *Address:* c/o BBC World Affairs Unit, Television Centre, Wood Lane, London, W12 7RJ, England. *Telephone:* (20) 8743-8000. *Fax:* (20) 8743-7591.

SIMPSON, Leo James Pascal; Canadian writer; b. 24 Sept. 1934, Limerick, Ireland; m. Jacqueline Anne Murphy 1964; one d. *Career:* writer-in-residence, Univ. of Ottawa 1973, Univ. of Western Ontario 1978. *Publications:* Arkwright 1971, Peacock Papers 1973, The Lady and the Travelling Salesman 1976, Kowalski's Last Chance 1980, Sailor Man 1996. *Address:* Moodie Cottage, 114 Bridge Street W, Belleville, ON K8P 1J7, Canada.

SIMPSON, Louis Aston Marantz, PhD CD; American writer and academic; *Distinguished Professor Emeritus, State University of New York at Stony Brook*; b. 27 March 1923, Kingston, Jamaica, West Indies; s. of Aston Simpson and Rosalind (Marantz) Simpson; m. 1st Jeanne Rogers 1949 (divorced 1954); one s.; m. 2nd Dorothy Roochvarg 1955 (divorced 1979); one s. one d.; m. 3rd Miriam Bachner (née Butensky) 1985 (divorced 1998). *Education:* Munro Coll., Jamaica, Columbia Univ., New York. *Career:* Assoc. Ed. Bobbs-Merrill Publishing Co., New York 1950–55; Instructor, Asst Prof. Columbia Univ. 1955–59; Prof., Univ. of Calif. at Berkeley 1959–67; Prof. State Univ. of New York at Stony Brook 1967–91, Distinguished Prof. 1991–93, Prof. Emer. 1993–. *Publications:* poetry: The Arrivistes: Poems 1940–49 1949, Good News of Death and Other Poems 1955, The New Poets of England and America (ed.) 1957, A Dream of Governors 1959, At the End of the Open Road 1963, Selected Poems 1965, Adventures of the Letter I 1971, Searching for the Ox 1976, Armidale 1979, Out of Season 1979, Caviare at the Funeral 1980, People Live Here: Selected Poems 1949–83; The Best Hour of the Night 1983; Collected Poems 1988, Wei Wei and Other Poems 1990, In the Room We Share 1990, There You Are 1995, Nombres et poussière 1996, Modern Poets of France (trans.) 1997, Kaviar pä begravningen 1998, The Owner of the House – New Collected Poems 1940–2001 2003; prose: James Hogg: A Critical Study 1962, Riverside Drive 1962, An Introduction to Poetry (ed.) 1967, North of Jamaica 1971, Three on the Tower: The Lives and Works of Ezra Pound, T. S. Eliot and William Carlos Williams 1975, A Revolution in Taste 1978, A Company of Poets 1981, The Character of the Poet 1986, Selected Prose 1989, Ships Going Into the Blue 1994, The King My Father's Wreck 1995, François Villoh – The Legacy and the Testament (trans.) 2000. *Honours:* Hon. DHL (Eastern Mich. Univ.) 1977; Hon. DL (Hampden-Sydney Coll.) 1991; Prix de Rome American Acad. of Rome 1957, Hudson Review Fellowship 1957, Edna St Vincent Millay Award 1960, Guggenheim Fellowships 1962, 1970, ACLS Grant 1963, Pulitzer Prize for Poetry 1964, Columbia Univ. Medal for Excellence 1965, Commonwealth Club of Calif. Poetry Award 1965, American Acad. of Arts and Letters Award 1976, Inst. of Jamaica Centenary Medal 1980, Jewish Book Council Award for Poetry 1981, Elmer Holmes Bobst Award for Poetry 1987, Harold Morton Landon Award for Translation 1997. *Address:* c/o English Department, Stony Brook University, Humanities Bldg., Stony Brook, NY; PO Box 119, Setauket, NY 11733, USA.

SIMPSON, Matthew (Matt) William, CertEd, MA; British academic (retd), poet and writer; b. 13 May 1936, Lancashire; m. Monika Ingrid Weydert 1961; one s. one d. *Education:* Liverpool, Cantab. *Career:* lecturer in English, various schools; Poet-in-Residence, Tasmanian Poetry Festival 1995. *Publications:* Letters to Berlin 1971, A Skye Sequence 1972, Watercolour From an Approved School 1975, Uneasy Vespers 1977, Making Arrangements 1982, See You on the Christmas Tree 1984, Dead Baiting 1989, An Elegy for the Galosherman: New and Selected Poems 1990, The Pigs' Thermal Underwear 1994, To Tasmania with Mrs Meredith 1993, Catching Up With History 1995, Matt, Wes and Pete 1995, On the Right Side of the Earth 1995, Somewhere Down the Line 1998, Cutting the Clouds Towards 1998, Lost Property Box 1998, Getting There 2001, Hugging the Shore (essays) 2003, Nothing Extenuate: A Consideration of Shakespeare's Othello 2003, A Man Forbid: A Consideration of Shakespeare's Macbeth 2003, Wise Hereafter: Observations on Shakespeare's The Tempest 2004, Something of Great Constancy: A Reading of Shakespeare's A Midsummer Night's Dream 2006, So Full of Shapes: A Reading of Shakespeare's Twelfth Night 2006, In Deep (poems) 2006; contributions to reviews, quarterlies and magazines. *Address:* 29 Boundary Drive, Liverpool, L25 0QB, England. *E-mail:* matt.s13@tiscali.co.uk.

SIMPSON, Norman Frederick; British playwright; b. 29 Jan. 1919, London; s. of George Frederick Simpson; m. Joyce Bartlett 1944; one d. *Education:* Emanuel School, London and Birkbeck Coll., Univ. of London. *Career:* teacher in adult educ. –1963; full-time playwright 1963–. *Publications:* plays: A Resounding Tinkle 1958, The Hole 1958, One Way Pendulum (also film) 1959, The Form 1961, The Cresta Run 1965, Some Tall Tinkles 1968; co-author Diamonds for Breakfast (film) 1968, Was He Anyone? 1973; novel: Harry Bleachbaker 1976.

SINCLAIR, Andrew Annandale, BA, PhD, FRSL, FRSA; British writer, historian and film director; b. 21 Jan. 1935, Oxford, England; m. Sonia Melchett 1984; two s. *Education:* Trinity Coll., Cambridge, Harkness Fellow, Harvard Univ., ACLS Fellow, Stanford Univ. *Career:* Founding Fellow, Churchill Coll. 1961–63; Lecturer, Univ. Coll. London 1966–68; Publisher, Lorrimer Publishing 1968–89; Managing Dir, Timon Films Ltd 1968–2007; Fellow Soc. of American Historians 1970. *Films:* Under Milk Wood 1971, Dylan on Dylan 2004. *Publications:* The Breaking of Bumbo, 1959; My Friend Judas, 1959; Prohibition: The Era of Excess, 1961; Gog, 1967; Magog, 1972; Jack: A Biography of Jack London, 1977; The Other Victoria, 1981; King Ludd, 1988; War Like a Wasp, 1989; The War Decade: An Anthology of the 1940s, 1989; The Need to Give, 1990; The Far Corners of the Earth, 1991; The Naked Savage, 1991; The Strength of the Hills, 1991; The Sword and the Grail, 1992; Francis Bacon: His Life and Violent Times, 1993; In Love and Anger, 1994; Jerusalem: The Endless Crusade, 1995; Arts and Cultures: The History of the 50 Years of the Arts Council of Great Britain, 1995; The Discovery of the Grail, 1998; Death by Fame: A Life of Elisabeth, Empress of Austria, 1998; Guevara, 1998; Dylan the Bard: A Life of Dylan Thomas, 1999; The Secret Scroll, 2001; Blood and Kin, 2002; An Anatomy of Terror, 2003, Rosslyn 2005, Viva Che! 2005, The Grail: The Quest for a Legend 2007, The Reivers' Trail 2007; contrib. to Sunday Times, Times, New York Times, Atlantic Monthly. *Honours:* Somerset Maugham Prize 1967, Venice Film Festival Award 1971. *Address:* Flat 20, Millennium House, 132 Grosvenor Road, London, SW1V 3JY, England. *Telephone:* (20) 7976-5454 (home). *Fax:* (20) 7976-6141 (home). *Website:* andrewsinclairtemplar.com (office).

SINCLAIR, Iain MacGregor, BA; British poet and writer; b. 11 June 1943, Cardiff, Wales; m. Anna Hadman 1967; one s. two d. *Education:* Cheltenham Coll., London Coll. of Film Technique, Trinity Coll., Dublin, Courtauld Inst., London. *Publications:* poetry: Back Garden Poems 1970, Muscat's Würm 1972, The Birth Rug 1973, Lud Heat 1975, Brown Clouds 1977, Suicide Bridge 1979, Fluxions 1983, Fresh Eggs and Scalp Metal 1983, Autistic Poses 1985, Significant Wreckage 1988, Selected Poems 1970–87 1989, Jack Elam's Other Eye 1992; fiction: White Chappell, Scarlet Tracings 1987, Downriver 1991 (Encore Award, James Tait Black Memorial Award 1992), Radon Daughters 1994, The Ebbing of the Kraft 1997, Slow Chocolate Autopsy 1997, Landor's Tower 2001, Dining on Stones or, The Middle Ground 2004; non-fiction: Lights Out for the Territory 1997, Liquid City 1998, Rodinsky's Room (with Rachel Lichtenstein) 1999, London Orbital: A Walk Around the M25 2002, Edge of the Orison: In the traces of John Clare's 'Journey Out of Essex' 2005, London: City of Disappearances (ed.) 2006. *Address:* 28 Albion Drive, London, E8 4ET, England.

SINCLAIR, Olga Ellen, (Ellen Clare, Olga Daniels), JP; British writer; b. 23 Jan. 1923, Norfolk; m. Stanley George Sinclair 1945; three s. *Education:* The Convent, Swaffham, Norfolk. *Career:* mem. Soc. of Authors, Romantic Novelists' Asscn, Soc. of Women Journalists, Norwich Writer's Circle (also Pres.). *Publications:* Gypsies 1967, Hearts By the Tower 1968, Bitter Sweet Summer 1970, Dancing in Britain 1970, Children's Games 1972, Toys 1974, My Dear Fugitive 1976, Never Fall in Love 1977, Master of Melthorpe 1979, Gypsy Girl 1981, Ripening Vine 1981, When Wherries Sailed By 1987, Gretna Green: A Romantic History 1989. As Olga Daniels: Lord of Leet Castle 1984, The Gretna Bride 1985, The Bride From Faraway 1987, The Untamed Bride 1988, The Arrogant Cavalier 1991, A Royal Engagement 1999, An Heir for Ashingby 2004, The Countess and the Miner 2005. *Address:* 'Sycamore', 10 Norwich Road, Lingwood, Norfolk NR13 4BH, England. *Telephone:* (1603) 714558 (home). *E-mail:* olga.sinclair21@btinternet.com (home).

SINCLAIR, Sonia Elizabeth, (Sonia Graham, Sonia Melchett); British writer; b. 6 Sept. 1928, Nainital, India; m. 1st Julian Mond (Lord Melchett) (died 1973); one s. two d.; m. 2nd Andrew Sinclair 1984. *Education:* Queen's Secretarial College, Windsor, England. *Career:* mem. Bd of Dirs English Stage Company; fmr magistrate; fmr mem. Bd of Dirs Royal Nat. Theatre, Royal Soc. for the Prevention of Cruelty to Children. *Publications:* as Sonia Graham: Tell Me Honestly (non-fiction) 1964; as Sonia Melchett: Someone is Missing (non-fiction) 1987, Passionate Quests – Five Contemporary Women Travellers 1989, Sons and Mothers 1996; contrib. to periodicals. *Honours:* Prizewinner, Short Story Competition, Raconteur Magazine. *Address:* Flat 20, Millennium House, 132 Grosvenor Road, London SW1V 3JY, England.

SINDEN, Sir Donald Alfred, Kt, CBE, FRSA, DLitt; British actor and author; b. 9 Oct. 1923, Plymouth; s. of Alfred E. Sinden and Mabel A. Sinden (née Fuller); m. Diana Mahony 1948 (died 2004); two s. *Career:* entered theatrical profession with Charles F. Smith's Co., Mobile Entertainments Southern Area 1942; with Leicester Repertory Co. 1945; with Memorial Theatre Co.,

Stratford-upon-Avon 1946–47; with Old Vic and Bristol Old Vic 1948–50; film actor 1952–60; Chair. British Theatre Museum Assen 1971–77, Theatre Museum Advisory Council 1973–80; Pres. Fed. of Playgoers Socs 1968–93, Royal Theatrical Fund 1983–; Vice-Pres. London Appreciation Soc. 1960–; Assoc. Artist, RSC 1967–; mem. Council, British Actors Equity Assen 1966–77 (Trustee 1988–2004), Council, RSA 1972, Advisory Council, V&A Museum 1973–80, Arts Council Drama Panel 1973–77, Leicestershire Educ. Arts Cttee 1974–2004, BBC Archives Advisory Cttee 1975–78, Council, London Acad. of Music and Dramatic Art 1976–, Kent and E Sussex Regional Cttee, Nat. Trust 1978–82, Arts Council 1982–86. *Stage appearances include:* The Heiress 1949–50, Red Letter Day 1951, Odd Man In 1957, Peter Pan 1960, Guilty Party 1961, as Richard Plantagenet in Henry VI (The Wars of the Roses), as Price in Eh!, etc. (RSC) 1963–64, British Council tour of S. America in Dear Liar and Happy Days 1965, There's a Girl in My Soup 1966, as Lord Foppington in The Relapse (RSC) 1967, Not Now Darling 1968, as Malvolio, Henry VIII 1969, as Sir Harcourt Courtly in London Assurance 1972 (toured USA 1974), In Praise of Love 1973, as Stockmann in An Enemy of the People 1975, Habeas Corpus (USA) 1975, as Benedick in Much Ado About Nothing, King Lear (RSC) 1976–77, Shut Your Eyes and Think of England 1977, Othello (RSC) 1979–80, Present Laughter 1981, Uncle Vanya 1982, The School for Scandal 1983 (European tour 1984), Ariadne auf Naxos (ENO) 1983, Two into One 1984, The Scarlet Pimpernel 1985, Major Barbara 1988, Over My Dead Body 1989, Oscar Wilde 1990, Out of Order 1990 (Australian tour 1992), Venus Observed 1991, She Stoops to Conquer 1993, Hamlet 1994, That Good Night 1996, Quartet 1999, The Hollow Crown (tour to Australia and NZ 2002–03, Canada 2004); Dir The Importance of Being Earnest 1987. *Films:* appeared in 23 films including The Cruel Sea, Doctor in the House 1952–60. *Radio includes:* Doctor Gideon Fell (series). *Television series include:* Our Man from St Marks, Two's Company, Discovering English Churches, Never the Twain, Judge John Deed. *Publications:* A Touch of the Memoirs 1982, Laughter in the Second Act 1985, The Everyman Book of Theatrical Anecdotes (ed.) 1987, The English Country Church 1988, Famous Last Words (ed.) 1994. *Honours:* Drama Desk Award (for London Assurance) 1974, Variety Club of GB Stage Actor of 1976 (for King Lear), Evening Standard Drama Award Best Actor (for King Lear) 1977. *Address:* Rats Castle, TN30 7HX, England. *Fax:* (1797) 270230 (office).

SINGER, Alan, BA, PhD; American writer and teacher; b. 18 Oct. 1948, Atlantic City, NJ; m. Nora Pomerantz 1985, two d. *Education:* University of California at Los Angeles, University of Washington. *Career:* Prof. of English, Dir of Graduate Creative Writing Programme, Temple University, Philadelphia, 1980–. *Publications:* The Ox-Breadth (fiction), 1978; A Metaphorics of Fiction (criticism), 1983; The Charnel Image (fiction), 1984; The Subject as Action (criticism), 1994; Memory Wax (fiction), 1996. *Honours:* Grants, Pennsylvania Arts Council. *Address:* 117 Carpenter Lane, Philadelphia, PA 19119, USA. *E-mail:* singerks@fast.net.

SINGER, June Flaum; American writer; b. 17 Jan. 1932, Jersey City, NJ; m. Joseph Singer 1950; one s. three d. *Education:* Ohio State University, Columbus. *Career:* mem. Southern California Society of Women Writers; PEN West; Authors' Guild. *Publications:* The Bluffer's Guide to Interior Decorating, 1972; The Bluffer's Guide to Antiques (US ed.), 1972; The Debutantes, 1981; Star Dreams, 1982; The Movie Set, 1984; The Markoff Women, 1986; The President's Women, 1988; Sex in the Afternoon, 1990; Till the End of Time, 1991; Brilliant Divorces, 1992. *Address:* 12304 Santa Monica Blvd, Los Angeles, CA 90025-2551, USA. *E-mail:* junesinger@aol.com.

SINGER, Marilyn, BA, MA; American children's writer; b. 3 Oct. 1948, New York, NY; m. Steven Aronson 1971. *Education:* Queens College, CUNY, New York University. *Career:* mem. Authors' Guild; PEN American Centre; Society of Children's Book Writers and Illustrators. *Publications:* 53 books, including: The Morgans Dream, 1995; A Wasp is not a Bee, 1995; Deal with a Ghost, 1997; Prairie Dogs Kiss and Lobsters Wave, 1998; Good Day, Good Night, 1998; Stay True, 1998. Contributions: periodicals.

SINGER, Nicky Margaret; British novelist; b. 22 July 1956, Chalfont-St-Peter, England; m. James King-Smith; two s. one d. *Education:* Univ. of Bristol. *Career:* Assoc. Dir of Talks, ICA 1981–83; Programme Consultant, Enigma Television 1984–85; Co-Founder, Co-Dir, Performing Arts Labs 1987–96; Chair. Brighton Festival Literature Cttee 1988–93; mem., ACE Literary Magazines Group 1993–96; bd mem. Printer's Devil 1993–97, South East Arts 2000–02; presenter, Labours of Eve (BBC 2) 1994–95. *Television:* Feather Boy (BBC TV adaptation) (BAFTA children's award for Best Drama 2004). *Plays:* Feather Boy (stage musical adaptation), Nat. Theatre 2006. *Publications:* fiction: To Still the Child 1992, To Have and To Hold 1993, What She Wanted 1996, My Mother's Daughter 1998; children's fiction: Feather Boy (Blue Peter Book of the Year) 2002, Doll 2003, The Innocent's Story 2005; non-fiction: The Tiny Book of Time 1999, The Little Book of the Millennium 1999; contrib. to Printer's Devil, Guardian, Scotsman, Woman's Journal. *Literary Agent:* c/o Clare Conville, Conville and Walsh Ltd, 2 Ganton Street, London, W1F 7QL, England.

SINGER, Peter Albert David, BPhil, MA; Australian philosopher, academic and writer; *DeCamp Professor of Bioethics, Princeton University;* b. 6 July 1946, Melbourne, Vic.; s. of Ernest Singer and Cora Oppenheim; m. Renata Diamond 1968; three d. *Education:* Scotch Coll., Univ. of Melbourne and Univ. Coll., Oxford. *Career:* Radcliffe Lecturer, Univ. Coll., Oxford 1971–73; Visiting Asst Prof., Dept of Philosophy, New York Univ. 1973–74; Sr Lecturer, Dept of Philosophy, La Trobe Univ., Bundoora, Vic., Australia 1974–76; Prof., Dept of Philosophy, Monash Univ., Clayton, Vic. 1977–99, Dir Centre for Human Bioethics 1981–91, Deputy Dir 1992–99; DeCamp Prof. of Bioethics, Princeton Univ., NJ, USA 1999–; Laureate Prof., Centre for Applied Philosophy and Public Ethics, Univ. of Melbourne 2005; various visiting positions in USA, Canada and Italy. *Publications:* Democracy and Disobedience 1973, Animal Rights and Human Obligations (ed. with Thomas Regan) 1975, Animal Liberation: A New Ethics for Our Treatment of Animals 1975, Practical Ethics 1979, Marx 1980, The Expanding Circle: Ethics and Sociobiology 1981, Test-Tube Babies (ed. with William Walters) 1982, Hegel 1983, The Reproduction Revolution: New Ways of Making Babies (with Deane Wells, aka Making Babies: The New Science and Ethics of Conception) 1984, In Defence of Animals (ed.) 1985, Should the Baby Live?: The Problem of Handicapped Infants (with Helga Kuhse) 1985, Applied Ethics (ed.) 1986, Animal Liberation: A Graphic Guide (with Lori Gruen) 1987, Animal Factories (with Jim Mason) 1990, Embryo Experimentation (ed.) 1990, Companion to Ethics (ed.) 1991, How Are We to Live? 1993, The Great Ape Project: Equality Beyond Humanity (ed. with Paola Cavalieri) 1993, Rethinking Life and Death 1994, Ethics (ed.) 1994, The Greens 1996, Ethics into Action 1998, A Companion to Bioethics (with Helga Kuhse) 1998, A Darwinian Left 1999, Writings on an Ethical Life 2000, One World 2002, Pushing Time Away: My Grandfather and the Tragedy of Jewish Vienna 2003, The President of Good and Evil: Taking George W. Bush Seriously 2004, The Moral of the Story (co-ed.) 2005, Eating: What We Eat and Why it Matters (with Jim Mason) 2006. *Address:* University Center for Human Values, 5 Ivy Lane, Princeton, NJ, 08544-1013, USA (office). *Telephone:* (609) 258-2202 (office). *Fax:* (609) 258-1285 (office). *Website:* www.princeton.edu/~psinger (office).

SINGER, Sarah Beth, BA; American poet and writer; b. 4 July 1915, New York, NY; m. Leon E. Singer 1938; one s. one d. *Education:* New York University, New School for Social Research, New York. *Career:* teacher, poetry seminars and workshops, 1968–74, 1981–83; Consulting Ed., Poet Lore, 1976–81; mem. National League of American Penwomen; Poetry Society of America, vice-pres., 1974–78. *Publications:* After the Beginning, 1975; Of Love and Shoes, 1987; The Gathering, 1992; Filtered Images (anthology), 1992. Contributions: anthologies, newspapers and journals. *Honours:* Stephen Vincent Benét Narrative Poetry Awards, 1968, 1971; 5 Poetry Society of America Awards, 1972–76; National League of American Penwomen Awards, 1976–92; Washington Poets Assen Award, 1989; Haiku Award, Brussels Sprouts, 1992.

SINGH, Amritjit, BA, MA, PhD; American academic, writer, translator and editor; *Langston Hughes Professor of English and African American Studies, Ohio University;* b. 20 Oct. 1945, Rawalpindi, India; m. Prem Singh 1968, one s. one d. *Education:* Panjab Univ., Kurukshetra Univ., New York Univ. *Career:* Prof. of English, Univ. of Delhi 1965–68, CUNY 1970–71, 1973–74, New York Univ. 1972–73, Hofstra Univ. 1984–86, Rhode Island Coll. 1986–2006; Langston Hughes Prof. of English and African American Studies, Ohio Univ. 2006–; Sr Fulbright Prof., JFK Inst., Free Univ., Berlin 2002; mem. MELUS (pres. 1994–97), South Asian Literary Assen (pres. 2000–03), USACLALS (pres. 2000–05). *Publications:* The Novels of the Harlem Renaissance 1976, India: An Anthology of Contemporary Writing 1983, The Magic Circle of Henry James 1989, The Harlem Renaissance: Revaluations 1989, Memory, Narrative and Identity 1994, Conversations with Ralph Ellison 1995, Conversations with Ishmael Reed 1995, Memory and Cultural Politics 1996, Postcolonial Theory and the United States 2000, The Collected Writings of Wallace Thurman: A Harlem Renaissance Reader 2003, Interviews with Edward W. Said 2004; contrib. include numerous essays and reviews in American Literature, Indian Literature, African American Studies. *Honours:* Fulbright Fellowship 1968–69, ACLS 1983–84, Nat. Endowment for the Humanities Fellowship 1991–92, Rhode Island Coll. Alumni Faculty Award 2003, MELUS Lifetime Achievement Award 2007. *Address:* Department of English, Ohio University, Athens, OH 45701, USA (office). *Telephone:* (740) 593-2838 (office). *Fax:* (740) 593-2832 (office). *E-mail:* singha@ohio.edu (office).

SINGH, Gopal, PhD; Indian politician, poet and writer; b. 29 Nov. 1919, Serai Niamat Khan, NW Frontier Prov.; s. of Atma Singh and Nanaki Devi; m. 1950; one d. *Career:* nominated MP 1962–68; Amb. to Bulgaria and Caribbean countries 1970–76; Chair. High Power Comm. of Minorities, Scheduled Castes, Scheduled Tribes and other Weaker Sections 1980–84; Gov. Goa, Daman and Diu 1984, of Nagaland 1989; has lectured at univs in UK, USA, Thailand, Egypt, Iran and India; fmr Sec.-Gen. Indian Council for Africa; Chair. Presidium, World Punjabi Congress. *Publications:* first free-verse English trans. of the Sikh Scripture, five books of Punjabi verse, A History of the Sikh People 1469–1978, The Religion of the Sikhs, A History of Punjabi Literature; The Unstruck Melody (poems), The Man Who Never Died (poems), collection of short stories, children's books, an English-Punjabi lexicon, several biogs and books of literary criticism. *Honours:* many awards and decorations.

SINGH, Khushwant, LLB; Indian author; b. Feb. 1915; m. Kaval Malik; one s. one d. *Education:* Government Coll., Lahore, King's Coll. and Inner Temple, London, UK. *Career:* practised at High Court, Lahore 1939–47; joined Indian Ministry of External Affairs 1947; press attaché, Canada then Public Relations Officer, London 1948–51; Ministry of Information and Broadcasting; edited Yojana; Dept of Mass Communication, UNESCO 1954–56; commissioned by Rockefeller Foundation and Muslim Univ., Aligarh, to write a history of the Sikhs 1958; MP 1980–; Ed.-in-Chief The Hindustan Times, New Delhi 1980–83; Visiting Lecturer Hawaii, Oxford, Princeton, Rochester, Swarthmore; numerous TV and radio appearances; Ed. The Illustrated Weekly of India 1969–78. *Publications:* Mark of Vishnu 1949, The Sikhs 1951, Train to Pakistan 1954, Sacred Writings of the Sikhs 1960, I Shall Not Hear the Nightingale 1961, Umrao Jan Ada—Courtesan of Lucknow (trans.) 1961, History of the Sikhs (1769–1839) Vol. I 1962, Ranjit Singh: Maharaja of the Punjab 1962, Fall of the Sikh Kingdom 1962, The Skeleton (trans.) 1963, Land of the Five Rivers (trans.) 1964, History of the Sikhs (1839–Present Day) Vol. II 1965, Khushwant Singh's India 1969, Indira Gandhi Returns 1979, Editor's Page 1980, Iqbal's Dialogue with Allah (trans.) 1981, Punjab Tragedy (with Kuldip Nayar) 1984, Roots of Dissent 1992 and others. *Honours:* Grove Press Award; Mohan Singh Award; Padma Bhushan 1974. *Address:* 49E Sujan Singh Park, New Delhi 110003, India. *Telephone:* (11) 4620159.

SINGH, Simon Lehna, BSc, PhD; British writer, journalist and television producer; b. 19 Sept. 1964, Wellington, Somerset, England. *Education:* Imperial Coll., Cambridge. *Television:* Fermat's Last Theorem (BBC) 1996, The Science of Secrecy (Channel 4) 2000, Funny You Should Ask (Discovery Channel) 2002, Mind Games (BBC4) 2003; worked on Earth Story series and fmr dir and prod., Tomorrow's World (both BBC). *Radio:* Five Numbers (BBC Radio 4) 2001, The Serendipity of Science (BBC Radio 4) 2001, Another Five Numbers (BBC Radio 4) 2003. *Theatre:* Theatre of Science (with Dr Richard Wiseman, Soho Theatre, London) 2005. *Publications:* Fermat's Last Theorem 1997, The Code Book 1999, The Science of Secrecy 2000, Big Bang: the Most Important Scientific Discovery of All Time and Why You Need to Know About It 2004. *Honours:* Vega Award for science broadcasting 2001. *Literary Agent:* Patrick Walsh, Conville and Walsh Ltd, 2 Ganton Street, London, W1F 7QL, England. *Telephone:* (20) 7287-3030. *Fax:* (20) 7287-4545. *E-mail:* patrick@convilleandwalsh.com. *Address:* PO Box 23064, London, W11 3GX, England. *E-mail:* simoncontact@hotmail.com. *Website:* www.simonsingh.com.

SINGLETON, William Dean; American newspaper executive; *Vice-Chairman and CEO, MediaNews Group Inc.*; b. 1 Aug. 1951, Tex.; s. of the late William Hyde Singleton and of Florence E. Myrick Singleton; m. Adrienne Casale 1983; two s. one d. *Career:* Pres. Gloucester Co. Times, N J.; Vice-Chair. and CEO MediaNews Group, Inc. 1988–; Pres., Chair. The Houston Post 1988–95, The Denver Post; Vice-Chair. 27 daily newspapers and 55 non-daily publications including Houston Post, Denver Post, with daily circulation in excess of 1.1 million in 10 states. *Address:* MediaNews Group Inc., 1560 Broadway, Suite 1450, Denver, CO 80202, USA. *Telephone:* (303) 563-6360. *Fax:* (303) 894-9327. *Website:* www.medianewsgroup.com.

SIPHERD, Ray, BA; American writer; b. 27 Aug. 1935, Uniontown, PA; m. Anne Marie Foran 1986. *Education:* Yale University. *Career:* mem. American Society of Composers, Authors and Publishers; Writers Guild of America. *Publications:* The White Kite, 1972; Ernie and Bert's Telephone Call, 1978; The Count's Poem, 1979; Down on the Farm with Grover, 1980; Sherlock Hemlock and the Outer Space Creatures, 1981; Big Bird's Animal Alphabet, 1987; When is My Birthday?, 1988; The Courtship of Peggy McCoy, 1990; The Christmas Store, 1993; Dance of the Scarecrows, 1996; The Audubon Quartet, 1998. *Honours:* Emmy Awards, 1969, 1974, 1985.

SIROF, Harriet Toby, BA; American writer and teacher; b. 18 Oct. 1930, New York, NY; m. 1949, one s. one d. *Education:* New School for Social Research, New York. *Career:* mem. Authors' Guild, Society of Children's Book Writers. *Publications:* A New-Fashioned Love Story, 1977; The IF Machine, 1978; The Junior Encyclopedia of Israel, 1980; Save the Dam!, 1981; That Certain Smile, 1981; The Real World, 1985; Anything You Can Do, 1986; Because She's My Friend, 1993; The Road Back: Living With a Physical Disability, 1993; Bring Back Yesterday, 1996. Contributions: Colorado Review; Descent; Inlet; Maine Review; North American Review; New Orleans Review; Sam Houston Review; San Jose Studies; Woman; Voices of Brooklyn. *Honours:* Junior Literary Guild Selection 1985. *Address:* 792 E 21st Street, New York, NY 11210, USA. *E-mail:* hsirof@aol.com.

SISSAY, Lemn; British poet; b. 1967, Billinge, Manchester. *Career:* various television appearances and radio broadcasts; music collaborations with Leftfield, Izit; Writer-in-Residence, Contact (later Assoc. Artist), Southbank Centre, London 2007. *Recordings:* Blackwise 1988, Homeland (including two poems) 1988, The Flag 1996, Are You Listening 1992, Move On 1993, Earth Flower 1993, Advice For The Living 2000. *Publications:* Perceptions of the Pen 1985, Tender Fingers in a Clenched Fist 1988, Rebel Without Applause, The Fire People: a Collection of Contemporary Black British Poets (ed.) 1998, Morning Breaks in the Elevator 1999, The Emperor's Watchmaker 2000. *Address:* c/o Bloomsbury Publishing Plc, 37 Soho Square, London, W1D 3HB, England.

SISSON, Rosemary Anne, BA, MLit; British writer; b. 13 Oct. 1923, London. *Education:* Univ. Coll. London, Newnham Coll., Cambridge. *Career:* Junior Lecturer, University of Wisconsin, 1949–50; Lecturer, University College London, 1950–53; University of Birmingham, 1953–54; Drama Critic, Stratford-upon-Avon Herald, 1954–57; Trustee, Theatre of Comedy, 1986–; mem. Dramatists Club (hon. sec.), Writers' Guild of Great Britain (pres.), BAFTA. *Television:* The Six Wives of Henry VIII; Elizabeth R; Upstairs, Downstairs. *Publications:* The Exciseman, 1972; The Killer of Horseman's Flats, 1973; The Stratford Story, 1975; Escape From the Dark, 1976; The Queen and the Welshman, 1979; The Manions of America, 1981; Bury Love Deep, 1985; Beneath the Visiting Moon, 1986; The Bretts, 1987; The Young

Indiana Jones Chronicles, 1993–95; Rosemary for Remembrance, 1995; Footstep on the Stair, 1997; First Love, Last Love, 2002; Murder, She Wrote, 2003. Contributions: newspapers and journals. *Honours:* Writers' Guild of Great Britain Laurel Award. *Literary Agent:* c/o Andrew Mann Ltd, 1 Old Compton Street, London, W1S 5PH, England. *Telephone:* (20) 7734-4751. *Fax:* (20) 7287-9264. *E-mail:* manscript@compuserve.com.

SJÖWALL, Maj; Swedish writer and journalist; b. 1935, Malmö; m. Per Wahlöö 1962 (died 1975); two s. *Career:* Ed. at publishing house, Wahlström and Widstrad 1959–61. *Publications:* with Per Wahlöö: Roseanna 1965, Mannen Som Gick Upp i Rök (The Man Who Went up in Smoke) 1966, Mannen på Balkongen (The Man on the Balcony) 1967, Den Skrattande Polisen (The Laughing Policeman) 1968, Brandbilen Som Försvann (The Fire Engine that Disappeared) 1969, Polis, Polis, Potatismos (Murder at the Savoy) 1970, Den Vedervärdige Mannen Från Säffle (The Abominable Man) 1971, Det Slutna Rummet (The Locked Room) 1972, Polismördaren (Cop Killer) 1974, Terroristerna (The Terrorists) 1975, Kvinnan Som Liknade Greta Garbo (with Thomas Ross) 1990.

SKÁRMETA, Antonio; Chilean writer and diplomatist; b. 1940. *Career:* novelist and playwright; Amb. to Germany 2000–01. *Radio:* Voy y Vuelo 2000. *Publications:* Soñé que la nieve ardía 1975, Ardiente paciencia (made into film Il Postino) 1985, Match Ball 1989. *Address:* c/o Ministry of Foreign Affairs, Catedral 1158, Santiago, Chile (office).

SKELLINGS, Edmund, BA, PhD; American academic and poet; b. 12 March 1932, Ludlow, MA; m. Louise Skellings 1962; one d. *Education:* Univ. of Massachusetts, Univ. of Iowa. *Career:* Poet Laureate of Florida 1980–; Dir, Florida Center for Electronic Communication, Florida Atlantic Univ. *Publications:* Duels and Duets 1960, Heart Attacks 1976, Face Value 1977, Showing My Age 1978, Living Proof 1985, Collected Poems 1958–1998 1998. *Honours:* Florida Governor's Award in the Arts 1979, Hon. DFA (Int. Fine Arts Coll.) 1995, Florida Arts Recognition Award 1997. *Address:* 220 SE Second Avenue, Fort Lauderdale, FL 33301, USA.

SKINNER, Ainslie (see Gosling-Hare, Paula Louise)

SKINNER, Gloria Dale, (Charla Cameron, Amelia Grey); American writer; b. 4 Aug. 1951, Graceville, FL; m. Floyd D. Skinner, one s. one d. *Career:* mem. Romance Writers of America; Georgia Romance Writers; Authors' Guild. *Publications:* Passion's Choice, 1990; Georgia Fever, 1992; Tender Trust, 1993; Starlight, 1994; Midnight Fire, 1994; Bewitching, 1995; Ransom, 1996; Juliana, 1997; Cassandra, 1998; Hellion, 1998. As Charla Cameron: Diamond Days, 1991; Sultry Nights, 1992; Glory Nights, 1993. As Amelia Grey: Never a Bride, 2001; A Dash of Scandal, 2002; A Little Mischief, 2003. *Honours:* Romantic Times Love and Laughter Award, Georgia Romance Writers of America Maggie Award. *Address:* 2023 Thomas Drive, Panama City Beach, FL 32408, USA. *E-mail:* gloriadaleskinner@.att.net.

SKINNER, Quentin Robert Duthie, MA, FBA; British historian and academic; *Regius Professor of Modern History, University of Cambridge*; b. 26 Nov. 1940, Oldham; s. of Alexander Skinner and Winifred Skinner (née Duthie); m. 2nd Susan James 1979; one s. one d. *Education:* Bedford School, Gonville and Caius Coll., Cambridge. *Career:* Fellow, Christ's Coll., Cambridge 1962–, Vice-Master 1997–99; Lecturer in History, Univ. of Cambridge 1967–78, Prof. of Political Science 1978–96, Regius Prof. of Modern History, 1996–, Pro-Vice-Chancellor 1999; mem. Inst. of Advanced Study, Princeton, NJ 1974–75, 1976–79; mem. Academia Europaea 1989; Foreign mem. American Acad. of Arts and Sciences 1986, American Philosophical Soc. 1997, Royal Irish Acad. 1999. *Publications:* The Foundations of Modern Political Thought, Vol. I The Renaissance 1978, Vol. II The Age of Reformation 1978, Machiavelli 1981, Philosophy in History (co-ed. and contrib.) 1984, The Return of Grand Theory in the Human Sciences (ed. and contrib.) 1985, The Cambridge History of Renaissance Philosophy (co-ed. and contrib.) 1988, Machiavelli: The Prince (ed. and introduction) 1988, Meaning and Context: Quentin Skinner and His Critics (ed. James Tully) 1988, Machiavelli and Republicanism (co-ed. and contrib.) 1990, Political Discourse in Early-modern Britain (co-ed. and contrib.) 1993, Milton and Republicanism (co-ed.) 1995, Reason and Rhetoric in the Philosophy of Hobbes 1996, Liberty before Liberalism 1998, Visions of Politics, Vol. I Regarding Method 2002, Vol. II Renaissance Virtues 2002, Vol. III Hobbes and Civil Science 2002, Republicanism: A Shared European Heritage (co-ed. and contrib.) Vol. I Republicanism and Constitutionalism in Early Modern Europe 2002, Vol. II The Values of Republicanism in Early Modern Europe 2002, States and Citizens (co-ed. and contrib.) 2003, Thomas Hobbes: Writings on Common Law and Hereditary Right (co-ed.) 2005. *Honours:* Hon. DLitt (Chicago) 1992, (E Anglia) 1992, (Helsinki) 1997, (Oxford) 2000, (Leuven) 2004, (St Andrews) 2005; Wolfson Literary Award 1979, Balzan Prize 2006, Sir Isaiah Berlin Prize 2006. *Address:* Faculty of History, University of Cambridge, West Road, Cambridge, CB3 9EF, England (office). *Telephone:* (1223) 335345 (office). *E-mail:* qrds2@cam.ac.uk (office). *Website:* www.hist.cam.ac.uk/academic_staff/further_details/skinner.html (office).

SKOCPOL, Theda, BA, MA, PhD; American academic and writer; b. 4 May 1947, Detroit, MI; m. William John Skocpol 1967, one s. *Education:* Michigan State University; Harvard University. *Career:* Asst Prof. 1975–78, Assoc. Prof. 1978–81, Prof. of Sociology 1986–94, Prof. of Govt and Sociology 1995–97, Victor S. Thomas Prof. of Government and Sociology 1998, Dir of the Center for American Political Studies 2000–, Harvard University; Mem., Institute for

Advanced Study, Princeton, NJ 1980–81; Assoc. Prof. 1981–84, Prof. of Sociology and Political Science 1984–86, Dir Center for the Study of Industrial Socs 1982–85, University of Chicago; Senior Visiting Scholar, Russell Sage Foundation 1983–84; mem. American Acad. of Arts and Sciences, fellow; American Political Science Asscn, pres. 2002–03; American Sociological Asscn; National Acad. of Social Insurance; Social Science History Asscn, pres. 1996. *Publications:* States and Social Revolutions: A Comparative Analysis of France, Russia, and China 1979, Protecting Soldiers and Mothers: The Political Origins of Social Policy in the United States 1992, Social Revolutions in the Modern World 1994, Social Policy in the United States: Future Possibilities in Historical Perspective 1995, State and Party in America's New Deal 1995, Boomerang: Clinton's Health Security Effort and the Turn Against Government in US Politics 1996, Historical, and Theoretical Perspectives (with John L. Campbell) 1994, States, Social Knowledge, and the Origins of Modern Social Policies (with Dietrich Rueschemeyer) 1996, The New Majority: Toward a Popular Progressive Politics (with Stanley B. Greenberg) 1997, Democracy, Revolution, and History 1998, Civic Engagement in American Democracy (with Morris Fiorina) 1999, The Missing Middle: Working Families and the Future of American Social Policy 2000, Diminished Democracy: From Membership to Management in American Civic Life 2003. Contributions: scholarly books and journals. Editor: Vision and Method in Historical Sociology 1984, Bringing the State Back In (with Peter Evans and Dietrich Rueschemeyer) 1985, The Politics of Social Policy in the United States (with Margaret Weir and Ann Shola Orloff) 1988, American Society and Politics: Institutional. *Honours:* Hon. degrees (Michigan) 1997, (Northwestern) 2002, (Amherst Coll.) 2004C. Wright Mills Award, Soc. for the Study of Social Problems 1979, Award for a Distinguished Contribution to Scholarship 1980, Theory Prize 1986, American Sociological Asscn; Guggenheim Fellowship 1990; Woodrow Wilson Foundation Award 1993; J. David Greenstone Award, American Political Science Asscn 1993; Best Book Award, American Sociological Asscn 1993; Allan Sharlin Memorial Award, Social Science History Asscn 1993; Ralph Waldo Emerson Award 1993, Phi Beta Kappa 1993, Russell Sage Foundation Grant 1996–98, 2000–2001, 2002–05, John D. and Catherine T. MacArthur Foundation Grant 1997–99; Pew Charitable Trusts Grant 1997–2000, Ford Foundation Grants 1998–2000, 2000–01, 2001–05. *Address:* c/o FAS, Harvard University, Cambridge, MA 02138, USA. *Telephone:* (617) 496-0966. *Fax:* (617) 495-0438. *E-mail:* skocpol@fas.harvard.edu. *Website:* www.gov.harvard.edu/Faculty/Bios/Skocpol.

SKRZYNECKI, Peter, OAM, MLitt, MA, BA; Australian poet, writer and lecturer; *Adjunct Associate Professor, School of Humanities, University of Western Sydney*; b. 6 April 1945, Imhert, Germany; m. Kate Magrath; one s. two d. *Education:* Univ. of Sydney, Univ. of New England. *Career:* fmr Lecturer, Univ. of Western Sydney, now Adjunct Assoc. Prof., School of Humanities. *Publications:* poetry: There, Behind the Lids 1970, Headwaters 1972, Immigrant Chronicle 1975, The Aviary: Poems 1975–77, The Polish Immigrant 1982, Night Swim 1989, Easter Sunday 1993, Time's Revenge 2000; fiction: The Wild Dogs, The Beloved Mountain 1988, Rock 'n' Roll Heroes (short stories) 1992, The Cry of the Goldfinch 1996; non-fiction: Joseph's Coat: An Anthology of Multicultural Writing 1985, Influence: Australian Voices (ed.) 1997, The Sparrow Garden (memoir) 2004. *Honours:* Order of Cultural Merit, Poland 1989; Captain Cook Bicentenary Award 1970, Grace Leven Poetry Prize 1972, Henry Lawson Short Story Award 1985. *Address:* 6 Sybil Street, Eastwood, NSW 2122, Australia.

ŠKVORECKÝ, Josef Václav, PhD, FRSC; Czech/Canadian writer, poet and translator; b. 29 Sept. 1924, Náchod; m. Zdena Salivarová 1958. *Education:* Charles Univ., Prague. *Career:* worked as teacher, Secondary Social School; Ed. Anglo-American Dept, Odeon Publishers, Prague 1953–56; Asst Ed.-in-Chief, World Literature Magazine, Prague 1956–59; Chair. Editorial Bd of journal The Flame –1968; emigrated to Canada 1968; founder (with Zdena Škvorecký) and Ed., Sixty-Eight Publishers, Toronto 1972–95; Visiting Lecturer, Univ. of Toronto 1968, 1970, writer-in-residence 1970, Assoc. Prof. 1971–75, Prof. of English and American Literature 1975–90, Prof. Emeritus 1990–; mem. Bd of Consultants to President Havel 1990–91; f. Literary Acad. Josef Škvorecký, Czech Rep. 2000; Guggenheim Fellowship 1980; mem. Authors League of America, Crime Writers of Canada, Int. PEN Club, MWA, Writers' Union of Canada. *Publications:* The Cowards (novel) 1958, The Legend of Emöke (novel) 1963, The Bass Saxophone (two novellas) 1965, Reading Detective Stories 1965, The Seven-Armed Candlestick, The End of the Nylon Age (story) 1967, The Little Lion (novel), They – Which is We 1968, Miss Silver's Past (novel) 1969, The Tank Battalion (novel) 1969, A Tall Tale About America 1970, The Miracle Game (novel) 1972, All the Bright Young Men and Women 1972, Priest Knox's Sins, The End of Lieutenant Borůvka (novel) 1972, The Swell Season 1975, The Engineer of Human Souls (novel) 1977, The New Men and Women (play) 1977, Working Overtime 1979, Do Not Despair (poems) 1979, The Return of Lieutenant Borůvka (novel) 1980, God in Your House (play) 1980, The Girl from Chicago (poems) 1980, Jiri Menzel and the History of the Closely Watched Trains 1982, Scherzo Capriccioso (novel) 1984, Dvořák in Love 1986, Talkin' Moscow Blues 1988, Sadness of Lieutenant Borůvka (novel) 1988, Bitter Jazz (dramatized stories) 1990, The Bride from Texas (novel) 1992, Headed for the Blues (memoir) 1996, Two Murders in My Double Life (novel) 1996, Short Meeting with Murder (with Zdena Škvorecký) 1999, Life and Work 1999, An Inexplicable Story, or the Narrative of Questus Firmus Siculus (novel) 2002, When Eve Was Naked: Stories of a Life's Journey 2002, Pulchra (novel) 2003, Ordinary People (novel) 2004; five full-length film screenplays. *Honours:* Dr hc (Masaryk Univ., Brno) 1991; Hon. Citizen of Prague 1990, hon. mem. Czechoslovak Soc. of Arts and Sciences; Neutstadt Int. Prize for Literature 1980, Gov.-Gen.'s Award for Fiction 1984, City of Toronto Book Award 1985, Echoing Green Foundation Literature Award 1990, State Prize for Literature Czech Repub. 1999, Pangea Foundation Prize Czech Repub. 2001; Order of the White Lion (3rd Grade) Czechoslovakia 1990. *Address:* 487 Sackville Street, Toronto, Ont. M4X 1T6, Canada.

SLADE, Quilla (see Lewis-Smith, Anne Elizabeth)

SLATER, Nigel; British chef and food writer; b. Wolverhampton, West Midlands. *Career:* worked in restaurants from age 16; recipe tester, cook for food photography; Food Ed., Marie Claire magazine 1988; columnist, The Observer 1993–; presenter, Nigel Slater's Real Food (Channel 4) 1998–99. *Publications:* Marie Claire Cookbook 1992, Real Fast Food 1992, Real Fast Puddings 1993, Real Good Food: The Essential Nigel Slater 1995, 30-Minute Suppers 1996, Real Fast Desserts 1997, Real Cooking 1997, Nigel Slater's Real Food 1998, Appetite: So What Do You Want to Eat Today? 2000, Thirst 2002, Toast: The Story of a Boy's Hunger (autobiog.) 2003, The Kitchen Diaries 2005. *Honours:* Food Writer of the Year, André Simon Cookbook of the Year Award 2001. *Address:* c/o Fourth Estate, 77–85 Fulham Palace Road, London, W6 8JB, England.

SLATTA, Richard Wayne, BA, MA, PhD; American academic and writer; *Professor of History, North Carolina State University*; b. 22 Oct. 1947, Powers Lake, ND; m. Maxine P. Atkinson 1982; one s. *Education:* Pacific Lutheran Univ., Tacoma, WA, Portland State Univ., Ore., Univ. of Texas at Austin. *Career:* Visiting Researcher, Instituto Torcuato di Tella, Buenos Aires 1977–78; Visiting Instructor, Univ. of Colorado at Boulder 1979–80; Asst Prof., N Carolina State Univ. 1980–85, Assoc. Prof. 1985–90, Prof. of History 1990–; staff writer, Cowboys and Indians magazine 1994–2002, Persimmon Hill magazine 1994–2001; lecturer, Holland America Lines 2005–; mem. American Historical Asscn, Conference on Latin American History, Western History Asscn, Western Writers of America. *Publications:* Gauchos and the Vanishing Frontier 1983, Bandidos: The Varieties of Latin American Banditry (ed. and contributor) 1987, Cowboys of the Americas 1990, The Cowboy Encyclopedia 1994, Comparing Cowboys and Frontiers 1997, The Mythical West 2001, Simón Bolívar's Quest for Glory 2003, Cowboy: The Illustrated History 2006; contrib. to scholarly and general publs. *Honours:* Hubert Herring Book Prize, Pacific Coast Council on Latin American Studies 1984, Western Heritage Award for Non-Fiction Literature, Nat. Cowboy Hall of Fame 1991, Best Reference Source Citation, Library Journal 1992, Outstanding Reference Source Citation, American Library Asscn 1995. *Address:* Department of History, North Carolina State University, Raleigh, NC 27695-8108, USA (office). *Telephone:* (919) 513-2229 (office). *E-mail:* slatta@ncsu.edu (office). *Website:* social.chass.ncsu.edu/slatta (office); www.cowboyprof.com (home).

SLAUGHTER, Audrey Cecelia; British writer and journalist; b. 17 Jan. 1930, d. of Frederick George Smith and Ethel Louise Smith; m. 1st W. A. Slaughter 1950 (divorced); m. 2nd Charles Vere Wintour 1979 (died 1999). *Education:* Chislehurst High School and Stand Grammar School, Manchester. *Career:* fashion journalist –1960; Ed. Honey magazine 1960–68; Founder Petticoat 1964; columnist Evening News 1968–69; Ed. Vanity Fair 1970–72; Founder, Dir and Ed. Over 21 1972–79; Assoc. Ed. Sunday Times 1979–81, Sunday Express magazine 1981–82; Founder, Ed. Working Woman 1984–86; Lifestyle Ed. The Independent 1986–87;. *Publications:* Non-fiction: Every Man Should Have One (jtly) 1969, Getting Through... 1981, Working Woman's Handbook 1986, Your Brilliant Career 1987; Fiction: Private View 1990, Blooming 1992, Unknown Country 1994. *Honours:* Magazine Ed. of the Year 1966. *Address:* 613 Cross Street, Barnes, London, SW13 0AP, England.

SLAUGHTER, Karin; American writer; b. S Georgia. *Publications:* novels: Grant County series: Blindsighted 2001, Kisscut 2002, A Faint Cold Fear 2003, Indelible 2004, Faithless 2005; Like a Charm (ed., anthology) 2004, Triptych 2006, Skin Privilege 2007; short stories. *Address:* c/o Random House UK Ltd, Random House, 20 Vauxhall Bridge Road, London, SW1V 2SA, England. *E-mail:* authorslaughter@aol.com. *Website:* www.karinslaughter.com.

SLAVITT, David Rytman, (David Benjamin, Henry Lazarus, Lynn Meyer, Henry Sutton), MA; American writer, poet, translator and lecturer; b. 23 March 1935, White Plains, NY; s. of Samuel Slavitt and Adele Slavitt; m. 1st Lynn Meyer 1956 (divorced 1977); two s. one d.; m. 2nd Janet Lee Abrahm 1978. *Education:* Yale and Columbia Univs. *Career:* Instructor in English, Georgia Inst. of Technology, Atlanta 1957–58; writer, Assoc. Ed., Newsweek 1958–65; Visiting Lecturer, Univ. of Maryland 1977; Visiting Assoc. Prof. Temple Univ. 1978–80; Lecturer in English and Comparative Literature, Columbia Univ. 1985–86; teacher of creative writing, Rutgers Univ. 1987; Lecturer in English and Classics, Univ. of Pa 1991–97; Visiting Lecturer in Creative Writing, Princeton Univ. 1996; Lecturer in English, Bennington Coll. 2000–; Assoc. Fellow, Trumbull Coll. Yale Univ.; has lectured widely at US univs and other academic insts. *Publications:* fiction: Rochelle, or Virtue Rewarded 1967, King Saul (play) 1967, Feel Free 1968, The Cardinal Sins (play) 1969, Anagrams 1970, ABCD 1972, The Outer Mongolian 1973, The Killing of the King 1974, King of Hearts 1976, Jo Stern 1978, Cold Comfort 1980, Ringer 1982, Alice at 80 1984, The Agent 1986, The Hussar 1987, Salazar Blinks 1988, Lives of the Saints 1990, Short Stories Are Not Real Life 1991, Turkish Delights 1993, The Cliff 1994, Get Thee to a Nunnery: Two Divertimentos from Shakespeare 1999, Aspects of the Novel: A Novel 2003; as

Henry Sutton: The Exhibitionist 1967, The Voyeur 1968, Vector 1970, The Liberated 1973, The Proposal 1980, Kid's Stuff 2003; as Lynn Meyer: Paperback Thriller 1975; as Henry Lazarus: That Golden Woman 1976; as David Benjamin: The Idol 1979; poetry: Suits for the Dead 1961, The Carnivore 1965, Day Sailing 1968, Child's Play 1972, Vital Signs: New and Selected Poems 1975, Rounding the Horn 1978, Dozens 1981, Big Nose 1983, Adrien Stoutenburg: Land of Superior Mirages: New and Selected Poems (ed.) 1986, The Walls of Thebes 1986, Equinox 1989, Eight Longer Poems 1990, Crossroads 1994, A Gift 1996, Epic and Epigram 1997, A New Pléiade: Seven American Poets 1998, PS3569.L3 1998, Falling from Silence: Poems 2001, Change of Address: Poems, New and Selected 2005, William Henry Harrison and Other Poems 2006; non-fiction: Understanding Social Life: An Introduction to Social Psychology (with Paul F. Secord and Carl W. Backman) 1976, Physicians Observed 1987, Virgil 1991, The Persians of Aeschylus 1998, Three Amusements of Ausonius 1998, The Book of Lamentations 2001, Re Verse: Essays on Poets and Poetry 2005; translator: The Eclogues of Virgil 1971, The Eclogues and the Georgics of Virgil 1972, The Tristia of Ovid 1985, Ovid's Poetry of Exile 1990, Seneca: The Tragedies 1992, The Fables of Avianus 1993, The Metamorphoses of Ovid 1994, The Twelve Minor Prophets 1999, The Voyage of the Argo of Valerius Flaccus 1999, Sonnets of Love and Death of Jean de Sponde 2001, The Elegies of Propertius 2001, The Poetry of Manuel Bandeira 2002, The Regrets of Joachim du Bellay 2004, The Phoenix and Other Translations 2004, Re Verse: Essays on Poets and Poetry 2005, Blue State Blues: A Republican in Cambridge 2006; contrib. book reviews, articles in journals and magazines. *Honours:* Pennsylvania Council on the Arts Award 1985, Nat. Endowment for Arts Fellowship in Translation 1988, Nat. Acad. and Insts. of Arts and Letters Award 1989, Rockefeller Foundation Artist's Residence, Bellagio 1989. *Address:* 35 West Street, #5, Cambridge, MA 02139, USA. *Telephone:* (617) 497-1219. *E-mail:* drslavitt@comcast.net.

SŁAWIŃSKA, Irena Zofia, PhD; Polish dramatist and academic; *Professor Emerita of Drama, Catholic University of Lublin*; b. 30 Aug. 1913, Wilno (now Vilnius, Lithuania); d. of Seweryn Sławiński and Helena (née Kurnatowska) Sławińska. *Education:* Univ. of St Bator, Wilno, Univ. of Paris (Sorbonne) and Nicholas Copernicus Univ. of Toruń. *Career:* manual worker and teacher 1939–45; Assoc. Prof., Nicholas Copernicus Univ. 1945–49; Full Prof. of Drama, Dept of Humanities, Catholic Univ. of Lublin 1950–, currently Emer. Prof.; univ. teacher in Canada 1957, 1982, Brown Univ., RI, USA 1968–69, Univ. of Illinois, USA 1969, Univ. of Fribourg, Switzerland 1979; Yale Univ. Fellowship, USA 1957–58. *Publications:* Le théâtre dans la pensée contemporaine; over 350 studies and articles, 12 books on drama and theatre. *Honours:* numerous scientific awards. *Address:* Catholic University of Lublin, al Racławickie 14, 20-950 Lublin (office); Ul Chopina 29-12, 20-023 Lublin, Poland (home). *Telephone:* (81) 30426 (office); (81) 25195 (home). *Fax:* (81) 30433 (office). *Website:* www.kul.lublin.pl (office).

SLOAN, Carolyn; British journalist and children's writer; b. 15 April 1937, London, England; m. David Hollis 1961 (deceased); two s. *Education:* Harrogate Coll. and tutorial schools in Newcastle and Guildford. *Career:* mem. Soc. of Authors. *Publications:* Carter is a Painter's Cat 1971, Victoria and the Crowded Pocket 1973, The Penguin and the Vacuum Cleaner 1974, Shakespeare, Theatre Cat 1982, Skewer's Garden 1983, Helen Keller 1984, An Elephant for Muthu 1986, The Sea Child 1987, Don't Go Near the Water 1988, Gracie 1994, Incredible Journey 1996, The Rat 1998, Victorian Day 1999; contrib. to newspapers and journals. *Address:* 175 Stoughton Road, Guildford, Surrey GU1 1LQ, England. *E-mail:* carolyn_sloan@btinternet.com.

SLOBODA, Rudolf; Slovak novelist; b. 16 April 1938. *Publications:* novels: Narcis 1965, Britva 1967, Uhorsky rok 1968, Sede ruze 1969, Romaneto Don Juan 1971, Hlboky mier 1976, Hudba 1977, Vernost 1979, Druhy clovek 1981, Rozum 1982, Dni radosti 1982, Strateny raj 1983, Pansky flam 1986, Ursula 1987, Pokus o autoportret 1988, Rubato 1990, Krv 1991, Jesen 1994, Utek z rodnej obce 1992, Herecky 1995, Pamati 1996; other: Vecerna otazka vtakovi (poems) 1977, Hranicny kamen 1989, Armagedon na Grbe (play) 1993. *Address:* POB 8, 90201 Pezinok, Slovakia.

SLOTKIN, Richard Sidney, BA, PhD; American academic and writer; *Olin Professor of English, Wesleyan University*; b. 8 Nov. 1942, New York, NY; m. Iris F. Shupack 1963; one s. *Education:* Brooklyn Coll., CUNY and Brown Univ. *Career:* Asst Prof., Wesleyan Univ., Middletown, CT 1966–73, Assoc. Prof. 1973–76, Prof. 1976–82, Olin Prof. of English 1982–; Fellow Soc. of American Historians; mem. American Asscn of Univ. Profs, American Film Inst., American Historical Asscn, American Studies Asscn, Authors' Guild, Org. of American Historians, PEN. *Publications:* Regeneration Through Violence: The Mythology of the American Frontier, 1600–1860 1973, So Dreadful a Judgement: Puritan Responses to King Philip's War, 1675–1677 (with J. Folsom) 1978, The Crater: A Novel of the Civil War 1980, The Fatal Environment: The Myth of the Frontier in the Age of Industrialization, 1800–1890 1985, The Return of Henry Starr 1988, Gunfighter Nation: The Myth of the Frontier in Twentieth Century America 1992, Abe: A Novel of the Young Lincoln 2000, Lost Battalions: The Great War and the Crisis of American Nationality 2005; contrib. to professional journals. *Honours:* American Historical Asscn Albert J. Beveridge Award 1973, Nat. Endowment for the Humanities Fellowship 1973–74, Rockefeller Foundation Fellowship 1976–77, Little Big Horn Asscn Award 1986, American Studies Asscn Marg C. Turpie Prize 1995, Salon.com Book Award 2000, Michael Shaara Award 2001. *Address:* Department of English, Wesleyan University, Middletown, CT 06459, USA (office).

SLOVO, Gillian; South African novelist; b. 1952, Johannesburg; one d. *Education:* Manchester Univ., England. *Career:* researcher, journalist, film producer. *Publications:* novels: Morbid Symptoms 1984, Death by Analysis 1986, Death Comes Staccato 1987, Ties of Blood 1989, The Betrayal 1991, Facade 1993, Catnap 1994, Close Call 1995, Red Dust 2000, Ice Road 2004; memoirs: Every Secret Thing: My Family, My Country 1997. *Literary Agent:* c/o Little, Brown, Brettenham House, Lancaster Place, London, WC2E 7EN, England. *Telephone:* (20) 7911-8000. *Fax:* (20) 7911-8100. *E-mail:* email.UK@twbg.co.uk. *Website:* www.twbg.co.uk.

SMALL, Michael Ronald, BA, BEd, MA; British teacher, writer and poet; *Teacher, Carey Grammar School, Melbourne*; b. 3 Jan. 1943, Croydon, Surrey. *Education:* Univ. of London, La Trobe Univ., Australia, Univ. of Windsor, Canada. *Career:* teacher of English, Carey Grammar School, Melbourne, Australia 1974–; mem. Victorian Fellowship of Australian Writers, Melbourne Poets' Union. *Publications:* Her Natural Life and Other Stories 1988, Film: A Resource Book for Studying Film as Text (with Brian Keyte) 1994, Unleashed: A History of Footscray Football Club (with John Lack, Chris McConville and Damien Wright) 1996, Urangeline: Voices of Carey 1923–1997 1997; contribs to numerous journals and magazines in Australia and overseas. *Address:* 71 Strabane Avenue, Box Hill North, Vic. 3129, Australia. *Telephone:* (3) 98984303 (home). *E-mail:* michael.small@carey.vic.edu.au (office).

SMALLEY, Stephen Stewart, BA, BD, MA, PhD; British ecclesiastic and writer; *Dean Emeritus, Chester Cathedral*; b. 11 May 1931, London, England; m. Susan Jane Paterson 1974 (died 1995); one s. one d. *Education:* Jesus Coll., Cambridge, Eden Theological Seminary, USA. *Career:* Deacon, Ridley Hall, Cambridge 1958, Priest 1959; Asst Curate, St Paul's, Portman Square, London 1958–60; Chaplain, Peterhouse, Cambridge 1960–63, Acting Dean 1962–63; Lecturer and Sr Lecturer, Univ. of Ibadan, Nigeria 1963–69; Lecturer and Sr Lecturer, Univ. of Manchester 1970–77; Warden of St Anselm Hall 1972–77; Canon Residentiary and Precentor, Coventry Cathedral 1977–86, Vice-Provost 1986; Dean Chester Cathedral 1987–2001, Dean Emer. 2001–; Visiting Prof., Univ. of Chester 2001–; mem. Archbishops' Doctrine Comm. of the Church of England 1981–86; mem. Studiorum Novi Testamenti Societas, Chester City Club, Chester Business Club, Chesire Pitt Club. *Publications:* The Spirit's Power 1972, Christ and Spirit in the New Testament (ed.) 1973, John: Evangelist and Interpreter 1978, 1, 2, 3 John 1984, Thunder and Love: John's Revelation and John's Community 1994, The Revelation of John 2005, Hope for Ever 2005; contrib. to learned journals. *Honours:* Hon. LLD (Liverpool) 2001; Foundation and Lady Kay Scholar, Jesus Coll., Cambridge 1948, 1955, Select Preacher, Univ. of Cambridge 1963–64, Manson Memorial Lecturer, Univ. of Manchester 1986. *Address:* The Old Hall, The Folly, Longborough, Moreton-in-Marsh, Glos., GL56 0QS, England. *Telephone:* (1451) 830238 (home). *E-mail:* stephen@sssss.fsworld.co.uk (office).

SMILEY, Jane Graves, MFA, PhD; American writer and academic; b. 26 Sept. 1949, Los Angeles, CA; d. of James La Verne Smiley and Frances Nuelle (née Graves); m. 1st John Whiston 1970 (divorced); m. 2nd William Silag 1978 (divorced); two d.; m. 3rd Stephen Mark Mortensen 1987 (divorced 1997); one s. *Education:* Vassar Coll. and Univ. of Iowa. *Career:* Asst Prof., Iowa State Univ. Ames 1981–84, Assoc. Prof. 1984–89, Prof. 1989–90, Distinguished Prof. 1992–96; Visiting Prof., Univ. of Iowa 1981, 1987. *Publications:* Barn Blind 1980, At Paradise Gate 1981, Duplicate Keys 1984, The Age of Grief 1987, Catskill Crafts: Artisans of the Catskill Mountains (non-fiction) 1987, The Greenlanders 1988, Ordinary Love and Goodwill 1989, A Thousand Acres (Pulitzer Prize in Fiction 1992, Nat. Book Critics Circle Award 1992, Midland Authors Award 1992, Heartland Prize 1992) 1991, Moo: A Novel 1995, The All-True Travels and Adventures of Lidie Newton 1998, Horse Heaven 2000, Dickens (biog.) 2002, Good Faith 2003, A Year at the Races 2004, Thirteen Ways of Looking at the Novel (non-fiction) 2006, Ten Days in the Hills 2007. *Honours:* Fulbright grant 1976, Nat. Endowment for the Arts grants 1978, 1987, Distinguished Alumni Award Univ. of Iowa 2003; Friends of American Writers Prize 1981, O. Henry Awards 1982, 1985, 1988. *Address:* c/o Molly Friedrick, Department of English, 708 Third Avenue, Floor 23, New York, NY 10017, USA (office).

SMITH, Ali; British writer; b. 1962, Inverness, Scotland. *Education:* Univ. of Aberdeen, Univ. of Cambridge. *Career:* fmr Lecturer, Univ. of Strathclyde; gave lecture on Angela Carter, Nat. Portrait Gallery, London 2004. *Publications:* Free Love and Other Stories (Saltire First Book Award) 1995, Like (novel) 1997, Other Stories and Other Stories 1999, Hotel World (novel) (Encore Prize, Scottish Arts Council Book Award, Scottish Arts Council Book of the Year 2002) 2001, The Whole Story and Other Stories 2003, The Accidental (novel) (Whitbread Novel of the Year 2005) 2004, The Reader 2006; contrib. to TLS, The Scotsman, Guardian. *Honours:* Scottish Arts Council Award 1995. *Address:* c/o Hamish Hamilton, c/o Penguin Books, 80m Strand, London, WC2R 0RL, England.

SMITH, Anthony Charles Hockley, MA; British writer; b. 31 Oct. 1935, Kew, England. *Education:* Univ. of Cambridge. *Career:* Literary Assoc., RSC 1964–74; Sr Research Assoc., Univ. of Birmingham 1965–69; Dir, Cheltenham Festival of Literature 1978–79, 1999; Chair., Playwrights Co. 1979–83; Visiting Prof., Emory Univ., Atlanta, GA 1986, Univ. of Texas 1990–91, 1994; mem. Writers' Guild of Great Britain. *Theatre:* Up the Feeder, Down the Mouth, Bristol Old Vic 1997, The Redcliffe Hermit, Bristol 2005. *Publications:* The Crowd 1965, Zero Summer 1971, Orghast at Persepolis 1972, Paper

Voices 1975, Treatment 1976, The Jericho Gun 1977, Edward and Mrs Simpson 1978, Extra Cover 1981, The Dark Crystal 1982, Wagner 1983, Sebastian the Navigator 1985, Lady Jane 1985, Labyrinth 1986, The Dangerous Memoir of Citizen Sade 2000; 20 plays staged; contrib. to newspapers, magazines, and television. *Honours:* Arts Council Writing Awards 1970–71, 1974–75, 1980, Univ. of Bristol Drama Fellowship 1976–79. *Address:* 21 West Shrubbery, Bristol, BS6 6TA, England.

SMITH, Barbara Herrnstein, MA, PhD; American academic and writer; *Distinguished Professor of English, Brown University*; b. 6 Aug. 1932, New York, NY; m. 1st R. J. Herrnstein 1951 (divorced 1961); m. 2nd T. H. Smith 1964 (divorced 1974); two d. *Education:* Brandeis Univ. *Career:* faculty, Bennington Coll., Vt 1961–73, Univ. of Pennsylvania 1973–87; Braxton Craven Prof. of Comparative Literature and English, Duke Univ. 1987–, Dir Center for Interdisciplinary Studies in Science and Cultural Theory 1999–; Northrop Frye Chair, Univ. of Toronto 1990; Distinguished Prof. of English, Brown Univ. 2003–. *Publications:* Poetic Closure: A Study of How Poems End 1968, On the Margins of Discourse: The Relation of Literature to Language 1978, Contingencies of Value: Alternative Perspectives for Critical Theory 1988, The Politics of Liberal Education (co-ed.) 1991, Belief and Resistance: Dynamics of Contemporary Intellectual Controversy 1997, Mathematics, Science and Postclassical Theory (co-ed.) 1997, Scandalous Knowledge: Science, Truth and the Human 2005; contribs to numerous professional journals. *Address:* Box 90015, Duke University, Durham, NC 27708-0015 (office); Box 1852, Brown University, Providence, RI 02912, USA (office). *Telephone:* (919) 668 1753 (Duke) (office); (919) 684 3970 (Duke) (office); (401) 863-3622 (Brown, fall terms) (office). *Fax:* (919) 684-4871 (Duke) (office). *E-mail:* bhsmith@duke.edu (office); Barbara_H_Smith@brown.edu (office). *Website:* www.duke.edu (office); www.brown.edu (office).

SMITH, Bernard William, PhD; Australian academic; b. 3 Oct. 1916, Sydney; s. of Charles Smith and Rose Anne Tierney; m. 1st Kate Challis 1941 (died 1989); one s. one d.; m. 2nd Margaret Forster 1995. *Education:* Univ. of Sydney, Courtauld and Warburg Inst., London and Australian Nat. Univ., Canberra. *Career:* school teacher, NSW 1935–44, Educ. Officer, Art Gallery, NSW 1944–52; Lecturer, Sr Lecturer, Univ. of Melbourne 1955–63, Reader 1964–66; Art Critic The Age, Melbourne 1963–66; Prof. of Contemporary Art and Dir Power Inst. of Fine Arts, Univ. of Sydney 1967–77, Sr Assoc., Dept of Fine Arts 1977–; Assoc. Prof., Dept Fine Arts, Classical Studies and Archaeology, Univ. of Melbourne 1994–; Pres. Australian Acad. of the Humanities 1977–80. *Publications:* The Advance of Lot and his Brethern 1940, Pompeii 1940, Place, Taste and Tradition 1945, European Vision and the South Pacific 1960, Australian Painting 1962, The Boy Adeodatus 1985, The Art of Captain Cook's Voyages (jt author) 1985–87, The Death of the Artist as Hero 1988, The Critic as Advocate 1989, Imagining the Pacific 1992, Noel Counihan 1994, Poems 1938–1993 1996, Modernism's History 1998, A Pavane for Another Time 2002. *Honours:* Chevalier, Ordre des Arts et Lettres 1977. *Address:* 168 Nicholson Street, Fitzroy, Vic. 3065, Australia. *Telephone:* (3) 9419-7470. *Fax:* (3) 9419-8092. *Website:* www.arts.usyd.edu.au/departs/arthistory/power/institute (office).

SMITH, Bradley F., BA, MA; American writer and fmr teacher; b. 5 Oct. 1931, Seattle, WA; m. 1983; two d. *Education:* Univ. of California at Berkeley. *Career:* mem. Authors' Guild. *Publications:* Adolf Hitler: His Family, Childhood, and Youth 1967, Himmler Geheimreden 1974, Reaching Judgement at Nuremberg 1977, Operation Sunrise (with Elena Agarossi) 1979, The American Road to Nuremberg 1981, The Road to Nuremberg 1981, The Shadow Warriors 1983, The War's Long Shadow 1986, The Ultra-Magic Deals and the Special Relationship, 1940–46 1992, Sharing Secrets with Stalin: Anglo-American Intelligence Co-operation with the USSR 1941–1945 1996; contrib. dozens of articles to newspapers and journals 1959–. *Honours:* Observer Book of the Year 1977. *Address:* 30 Madeira Road, Ventnor, HW1 8UG, Isle of Wight, UK (home); 104 Regents Park Road, London, NW1 8UG, England (office). *Telephone:* (1983) 852-653 (home).

SMITH, Charlie, BA, MFA; American writer, poet and academic; b. 27 June 1947, Moultrie, GA; m. 1st Kathleen Huber 1974 (divorced 1977); m. 2nd Gretchen Mattox 1987 (divorced 1997); m. 3rd Daniela Serowinski 2003. *Education:* Duke University, University of Iowa. *Career:* Lecturer in Humanities and Creative Writing, Princeton University; Writer-in-Residence, University of Alabama, 2000; mem. Acad. of American Poets; International PEN; Poetry Society of America. *Publications:* Fiction: Canaan, 1985; Shine Hawk, 1988; The Lives of the Dead, 1990; Crystal River, 1991; Chimney Rock, 1993; Cheap Ticket to Heaven, 1996. Poetry: Red Roads, 1987; Indistinguishable from the Darkness, 1990; The Palms, 1993; Before and After: Poems, 1995; Heroin and Other Poems, 2000; Women of America, 2004. Contributions: literary journals and periodicals. *Honours:* Aga Khan Prize, Paris Review, 1983; Guggenheim Fellowship, 2000; National Endowment for the Arts Grant, 2000.

SMITH, David (Dave) Jeddie, MA, PhD; American poet, editor and academic; *Elliot Coleman Professor of Poetry, Johns Hopkins University*; b. 19 Dec. 1942, Portsmouth, VA; m. Deloras Smith 1966, one s. two d. *Education:* Univ. of Virginia, Southern Illinois Univ., Ohio Univ. *Career:* Ed. The Back Door: A Poetry Magazine 1970–78, The Southern Review 1990–2002; Instructor in English, Western Michigan Univ. 1973–74; Asst Prof. of English, Cottey Coll. 1974–75; Asst Prof. 1976–79, Assoc. Prof. of English 1979–81, Dir of Creative Writing 1976–81, Univ. of Utah; Poetry Ed.,

Rocky Mountain Review 1978–79, Univ. of Utah Press 1980–90; Visiting Prof. of English, State Univ. of New York at Binghamton 1980–81; Dir of Poetry, Bennington Writers' Conf., VT 1980–87; Assoc. Prof. of English and Dir of Creative Writing, Univ. of Florida 1981–82; Prof. of English, Virginia Commonwealth Univ. 1982–90; Prof. of English, Louisiana State Univ. 1991–97, Hopkins P. Breazeale Prof. of English 1997–98, Boyd Prof. of English 1998–2002; Elliot Coleman Prof. of Poetry, The Writing Seminars, Johns Hopkins Univ. 2002–; mem. Associated Writing Programs, Fellowship of Southern Writers, MLA, Southern MLA. *Publications:* Bull Island 1970, Mean Rufus Throw Down 1973, The Fisherman's Whore 1974, Drunks 1975, Cumberland Station 1977, In Dark, Sudden With Light 1977, Goshawk, Antelope 1979, Blue Spruce 1981, Dream Flights 1981, Homage to Edgar Allan Poe 1981, Onliness (novel) 1981, The Travelling Photographer 1981, The Pure Clear Word: Essays on the Poetry of James Wright 1982, In the House of the Judge 1983, Southern Delights (short stories) 1984, Gray Soldiers 1984, The Morrow Anthology of Younger American Poets (ed.) 1985, The Roundhouse Voices: Selected and New Poems 1985, Local Assays: On Contemporary American Poetry 1985, Cuba Night 1990, The Essential Poe 1992, Night Pleasures: New and Selected Poems 1992, Fate's Kite: Poems 1990–1995 1996, Floating on Solitude: Three Books of Poems 1997, The Wick of Memory: New and Selected Poems 1970–2000 2000, Little Boats: Unsalvaged 2005, Hunting Men: Reflections on a Life in Poetry 2006; contrib. to anthologies, reviews, and journals. *Honours:* Bread Loaf Fellow 1975, NEA Fellowships 1976, 1980, American Acad. of Arts and Letters Award 1979, Guggenheim Fellowship 1981, Ohio Univ. Alumni of the Year 1985, Lyndhurst Fellowship 1987–89, Virginia Poetry Prize 1988. *Address:* The Writing Seminars, 3400 N Charles Street, Baltimore, MD 21218 (office); 14 East Bishops Road, Baltimore, MD 21218, USA (home). *Telephone:* (410) 516-3409 (office). *Fax:* (410) 516-6828 (office). *E-mail:* davesmith@jhu.edu (office).

SMITH, David Lawrence, MA, PhD, FRHistS; British historian and academic; b. 3 Dec. 1963, London. *Education:* Eastbourne Coll., Selwyn Coll., Cambridge. *Career:* Fellow, Selwyn Coll., Cambridge 1988–, Dir of Studies in History 1992–, Admissions Tutor 1992–2003, Praelector 1996–2006, Tutor for Grad. Students 2004–; Affiliated Lecturer in History, Univ. of Cambridge 1995–; Visiting Asst Prof. of History, Univ. of Chicago 1991; Visiting Prof. of History, Kyungpook Nat. Univ., Repub. of Korea 2004; Gov. Eastbourne Coll. 1993–; Trustee Oakham School 2000–; mem. Cambridge History Forum (Pres. 1997–). *Publications:* Oliver Cromwell 1991, Louis XIV 1992, Cambridge Perspectives in History (co-ed.) 1993–, Constitutional Royalism and the Search for Settlement 1994, The Theatrical City (co-ed.) 1995, A History of the Modern British Isles, 1603–1707: The Double Crown 1998, The Stuart Parliaments, 1603–1689 1999, The Early Stuart Kings, 1603–1642 (with Graham E. Seel) 2001, Crown and Parliaments, 1558–1689 (with Graham E. Seel) 2001, Cromwell and the Interregnum (ed.) 2003; contrib. to Historical Journal, Historical Research, Journal of British Studies, Transactions of the Royal Historical Society, Comparative Drama, Parliamentary History, Oxford Dictionary of National Biography (assoc. ed.) 2004. *Honours:* Royal Historical Soc. Alexander Prize 1991, Thirlwall Prize 1991. *Address:* Selwyn College, Cambridge, CB3 9DQ, England (office). *Telephone:* (1223) 335881 (office); (1223) 331962 (home). *Fax:* (1223) 331720 (office). *E-mail:* dls10@cam.ac.uk (office). *Website:* www.hist.cam.ac.uk/academic_staff/further_details/smith-d .html (office).

SMITH, Sir Dudley Gordon; British management consultant, former politician and writer; b. 14 Nov. 1926, Cambridge, England; m. 1st (divorced); one s. two d.; m. 2nd Catherine Amos 1976. *Career:* journalist and Sr Exec., various provincial and national newspapers, 1943–66; Asst News Ed., Sunday Express, 1953–59; MP, Conservative Party, Brentford and Chiswick, 1959–66, Warwick and Leamington, 1968–97; Management Consultant, 1974–; UK Delegate, Council of Europe and Western European Union, 1979–97; Pres., Western European Assembly, 1993–96. *Publications:* They Also Served 1945, Harold Wilson: A Critical Biography 1964. *Honours:* apptd Deputy Lieutenant of Warwickshire 1988, Commander of the Order of Isabela la Católica, Spain 1994.

SMITH, Emma; British writer; b. 21 Aug. 1923, Newquay, Cornwall, England; m. Richard Llewellyn Stewart-Jones 1951 (died 1957); one s. one d. *Publications:* Maiden's Trip, 1948; The Far Cry, 1949; Emily, 1959; Out of Hand, 1963; Emily's Voyage, 1966; No Way of Telling, 1972; The Opportunity of a Lifetime, 1978. Contributions: various magazines. *Honours:* Atlantic Award, 1948; John Llewellyn Rhys Memorial Prize, 1948; James Tait Black Memorial Prize, 1949. *Literary Agent:* Curtis Brown Ltd, Haymarket House, 28–29 Haymarket, London, SW1Y 4SP, England. *Telephone:* (20) 7393-4400. *Fax:* (20) 7393-4401. *E-mail:* info@curtisbrown.co.uk. *Website:* www .curtisbrown.co.uk.

SMITH, Francis Barrymore, PhD, FAHA; Australian historian and academic; b. 16 May 1932, Hughesdale; s. of Francis John Smith and Bertha Smith; m. Ann Stokes 1965; two s. two d. *Education:* Univ. of Melbourne and Cambridge Univ. *Career:* Lecturer in History, Univ. of Melbourne 1962–66; Professorial Fellow in History, Inst. of Advanced Studies, ANU 1974–94, Hancock Prof. of History 1995–98; Ed. Historical Studies 1963–67; Pres. Australian Historical Asscn 1978–80. *Publications:* Making of the Second Reform Bill 1966, Radical Artisan: William James Linton 1973, The People's Health 1830–1910 1979, Florence Nightingale: Reputation and Power 1982, Retreat of Tuberculosis 1987, 'Agent Orange': The Australian Aftermath 1994, G. G. Achilli versus J. H. Newman 2000. *Address:* History Program, Research

School of Social Sciences, Australian National University, Canberra 0200, Australia (office). *Telephone:* (2) 6125-2358 (office). *Fax:* (2) 6125-3969 (office).

SMITH, Gregory Blake, AB, MA, MFA; American academic and writer; *Professor, Carleton College*; b. 24 July 1951, Torrington, CT; m. Martha L. Smith 1987; one s. *Education:* Bowdoin Coll., Boston Univ., Univ. of Iowa. *Career:* currently Prof., Carleton Coll. *Publications:* The Devil in the Dooryard 1986, The Divine Comedy of John Venner 1992, The Pope's Daughter 2005. *Honours:* Stanford Univ. Stegner Fellowship 1985, Nat. Endowment for the Arts Fellowship 1988. *Address:* c/o Department of English, Carleton College, Northfield, MN 55057, USA.

SMITH, Hedrick Laurence, BA; British journalist, writer and academic; b. 9 July 1933, Kilmacolm, Scotland; m. 1st Ann Bickford 1957 (divorced 1985); one s. three d.; m. 2nd Susan Zox 1987. *Education:* Choate School, Williams College, Balliol College, Oxford. *Career:* staff, United Press International, 1959–62; Diplomatic News Correspondent, 1962–64, 1966–71, Middle East Correspondent, 1964–66, Chief, Moscow Bureau, 1971–74, Washington Bureau, 1976–79, Deputy National Ed., 1975–76, Washington Correspondent, 1980–85, New York Times; Panelist, Washington Week in Review, PBS-TV, 1969–95; Visiting Journalist, American Enterprise Institute, 1985–87; Fellow, Foreign Policy Institute, School of Advanced International Studies, Johns Hopkins University, 1989–97; various PBS-TV documentaries; many lectures; mem. Gridiron Club. *Publications:* The Russians, 1975; The Power Game: How Washington Works, 1988; The New Russians, 1990; Rethinking America, 1995. With others: The Pentagon Papers, 1972; Reagan the Man, the President, 1981; Beyond Reagan: The Politics of Upheaval, 1986; Seven Days That Shook the World, 1991. *Honours:* Nieman Fellow, Harvard University, 1969–70; Pulitzer Prize for International Reporting, 1974; Overseas Press Club Award, 1976, and Citation, 1991; George Polk Award, 1990; Gold Baton Award, DuPont-Columbia University, 1990; George Foster Peabody Award, 1991; Hillman Award, 1996; William Allen White Award, University of Kansas, 1996.

SMITH, Lee, BA; American academic and writer; b. 1 Nov. 1944, Grundy, Va; m. 1st James E. Seay 1967 (divorced); two c.; m. 2nd Hal Crowther 1985. *Education:* Hollins Coll., Va. *Career:* Faculty, Dept of English, N Carolina State Univ., Raleigh 1981–, now Prof. Emer.; Fellow, Center for Documentary Studies, Duke Univ. 1991–93; mem. N Carolina Writers' Network, PEN. *Publications:* The Last Day the Dogbushes Bloomed 1968, Something in the Wind 1971, Fancy Strut 1973, Black Mountain Breakdown 1980, Cakewalk (short stories) 1980, Oral History 1983, Family Linen 1985, Fair and Tender Ladies 1988, Me and My Baby View the Eclipse (short stories) 1990, The Devil's Dream 1992, Saving Grace 1994, Christmas Letters 1997, News of the Spirit 1997, The Last Girls 2002, On Agate Hill 2006. *Honours:* O. Henry Awards 1979, 1981, 1984, John Dos Passos Award 1984, Sir Walter Raleigh Award 1984, North Carolina Award for Literature 1985, Lyndhurst Prize 1990–92, Robert Penn Warren Prize 1991, Award in Literature, American Acad. of Arts and Letters 1999. *Address:* c/o MLS, PO Box 534, Efland, NC 27243, USA (office). *E-mail:* info@leesmith.com (office). *Website:* www.leesmith.com.

SMITH, Martin William Cruz, BA; American writer; b. 3 Nov. 1942, Reading, PA; s. of John Smith and Louise Lopez; m. Emily Arnold 1968; two d. one s. *Education:* Univ. of Pennsylvania. *Career:* fmr newspaperman, ed. *Publications:* The Indians Won 1970, Gypsy in Amber 1971, Canto for a Gypsy 1972, Gorky Park 1972, Nightwing 1977, Analog Bullet 1981, Stallion Gate 1986, Polar Star 1989, Red Square 1992, Rose 1996, Havana Bay 1999, December 6 (aka Tokyo Station) 1999, Death by Espionage: Intriguing Stories of Betrayal and Deception 2001, Wolves Eat Dogs 2005, Stalin's Ghost 2007. *Honours:* CWA Golden Dagger Award 1981. *Address:* c/o Pan Macmillan, 20 New Wharf Road, London, N1 9RR, England. *E-mail:* MCSmith@literati.net.

SMITH, Michael Marshall; British writer; b. 3 May 1965, Knutsford, England. *Education:* King's College, Cambridge. *Publications:* Only Forward, 1994; Spares, 1997; One of Us, 1998; What You Make It, 1999. Contributions: anthologies and periodicals. *Honours:* three British Fantasy Awards. *Address:* c/o Ralph M. Vicinanza, 111 Eighth Street, Suite 1501, New York, NY 10011, USA.

SMITH, Patricia Clark, BA, MA, PhD; American writer, poet and academic; b. 14 Feb. 1943, Holyoke, MA; m. 1st Warren S. Smith 1964 (divorced 1976); two s.; m. 2nd John F. Crawford 1988. *Education:* Smith College, Yale University. *Career:* Lecturer in English, Smith College, 1968–69; Asst Prof. of English, Luther College, Decorah, IA, 1969–71; Asst Prof., 1971–82, Assoc. Prof., 1982–96, Prof. of English, 1996–, University of New Mexico. *Publications:* Talking to the Land (poems), 1979; Changing Your Story (poems), 1990; Western Literature in a World Context (co-ed.), two vols, 1995; As Long as the Rivers Flow: The Stories of Nine Native Americans (co-author), 1996. Contributions: anthologies and periodicals.

SMITH, Rosamond (see Oates, Joyce Carol)

SMITH, Sandra Lee, (Sandra Leesmith), BA, MA; American writer and teacher; b. 28 June 1945, San Francisco, CA; m. Edward Leroy Smith, Jr 1967. *Publications:* Loves Miracles (fiction) 1988, Coping with Decision Making 1989, Dream Song (fiction) 1990, Value of Self Control 1990, Drug Abuse Prevention 1995, Flower for Angela (fiction) 1999; contribs to various publs. *Honours:* Silver Pen Award 1990. *Address:* 5433 S Mill Avenue, Tempe, AZ,

USA. *E-mail:* sandraleesmith@cox.net (office). *Website:* www.sandraleesmith.com.

SMITH, Sarah, BA, PhD; American writer; b. 9 Dec. 1947, Boston, MA, USA; m. 1st David Lee Robbins 1974 (divorced 1977); m. 2nd Frederick S. Perry 1979; two s. (one deceased) one d. *Education:* Radcliffe Coll., Slade Film School, Queen Mary Coll., London, UK, Harvard Univ. *Career:* Pres., Ivy Films 1971–75; Asst Prof. of English, Tufts Univ. 1976–82; Field Ed., G. K. Hall 1977–83; Man. of artificial intelligence and computer-aided software engineering firms 1982–90; writer and consultant 1989–; mem. MWA, Webmaster, Sisters in Crime (NE Chapter pres. 1999–2000), Int. Asscn of Crime Writers, PEN, SFWA, Harvard Univ. Signet Soc. *Publications:* Colette at the Movies (non-fiction) 1980, Samuel Richardson: A Reference Guide 1984, King of Space 1991, The Vanished Child 1992, Future Boston (co-author) 1994, The Knowledge of Water 1996, Doll Street 1996, Riders 1996–97, A Citizen of the Country 2000, Chasing Shakespeares 2003, Deceived 2007; contrib. to Bulletin of the Authors' Guild, New York Review of Science Fiction, The Third Degree, Aboriginal, F & SF, Tomorrow, Shudder Again, Best New Horror 5. *Honours:* Susan Anthony Potter Prize 1968, Fulbright Fellow 1968–69, Harvard Prize Fellow 1969–74, Frank Knox Fellow 1972–73, Bowdoin Prize 1975, Mellon Fellow 1979–80, New York Times Notable Book citations 1992, 1996. *Literary Agent:* c/o Christopher Schelling, Ralph Vicinanza Literary Agency, 303 W 18th Street, New York, NY 10011, USA. *Address:* 32 Bowker Street, Brookline, MA 02446-6955, USA. *E-mail:* sarah@sarahsmith.com. *Website:* www.sarahsmith.com.

SMITH, Steven Ross, DipArts; Canadian writer and poet; b. 25 June 1945, Toronto, ON; m. J. Jill Robinson; one s. *Education:* Ryerson Polytechnic Univ. *Career:* writer-in-residence, Wayburn Public Library 1987–88, Saskatoon 1996–97; Exec. Dir Sage Hill Writing Experience 1990–; mem. League of Canadian Poets, Saskatchewan Writers' Guild, Writers' Union of Canada. *Publications:* Ritual Murders 1983, Blind Zone 1985, Sleepwalkers (with Richard Truhlar) 1987, Transient Light 1990, Reading My Father's Book 1995, Fluttertongue (three vols) 1998, 1999, 2005, Ballet of the Speech Organs: Bob Cobbing on Bob Cobbing 1998; contribs to periodicals. *Honours:* Saskatchewan Book Awards Book of the Year 2005. *Address:* 920 Ninth Avenue N, Saskatoon, SK S7K 2Z4, Canada. *E-mail:* steven.ross.smith@sasktel.net.

SMITH, Vivian Brian, MA, PhD, FAHA; Australian academic, poet and editor; b. 3 June 1933, Hobart, Tasmania; m. Sybille Gottwald 1960; one s. two d. *Education:* Univ. of Sydney. *Career:* Lecturer, Univ. of Tasmania 1955–66; Literary Ed. Quadrant magazine, Sydney 1975–90; Reader, Univ. of Sydney 1982–96; mem. Australian Soc. of Authors, PEN. *Publications:* The Other Meaning 1956, An Island South 1967, The Poetry of Robert Lowell 1975, Familiar Places 1978, Tide Country 1982, Tasmania and Australian Poetry 1984, Selected Poems 1995, New Selected Poems 1995, Late News 2000, Patrick White: A Bibliography 2004, Along the Line (poems) 2006, Windchimes: Asia in Australian Poetry (ed.) 2006; contrib. to newspapers and magazines. *Honours:* Grace Leven Prize, New South Wales Premier's Prize 1983, Patrick White Literary Award 1997. *Address:* 19 McLeod Street, Mosman, NSW 2088, Australia. *Telephone:* (2) 9969-1370. *E-mail:* smith@sydney.dialix.com.au.

SMITH, Ward (see Goldsmith, Howard)

SMITH, Wilbur Addison, BComm; British novelist; b. 9 Jan. 1933, Zambia; m. 1st Danielle Antoinette Smith 1971 (died 1999); two s. one d.; m. 2nd Mokhiniso Rakhimova 2000. *Education:* Michaelhouse, Natal and Rhodes Univ. *Career:* business exec. 1954–58; factory owner 1958–64; professional author 1961–. *Publications:* When the Lion Feeds 1964, The Dark of the Sun 1965, The Sound of Thunder 1966, Shout at the Devil 1968, Gold Mine 1970, The Diamond Hunters 1971, The Sunbird 1972, Eagle in the Sky 1974, The Eye of the Tiger 1975, Cry Wolf 1976, A Sparrow Falls 1977, Hungry as the Sea 1978, Wild Justice 1979, A Falcon Flies 1980, Men of Men 1981, The Angels Weep 1982, The Leopard Hunts in Darkness 1984, The Burning Shore 1985, Power of the Sword 1986, Rage 1987, The Courtneys 1987, The Courtneys in Africa 1988, A Time to Die 1989, Golden Fox 1990, Elephant Song 1991, River God 1993, The Seventh Scroll 1995, Birds of Prey 1997, Monsoon 1999, Warlock 2001, Blue Horizon 2003, The Triumph of the Sun 2005, The Quest 2007; contrib. to numerous journals and magazines. *Literary Agent:* c/o Charles Pick Consultancy Ltd, 21 Dagmar Terrace, London, N1 2BN, England. *Telephone:* (20) 7226-2779. *Fax:* (20) 7226-2779. *Website:* www.wilbursmithbooks.com; www.wilbursmith.net.

SMITH, William Jay, BA, MA; American poet, writer and academic; *Professor Emeritus of English, Hollins College*; b. 22 April 1918, Winnfield, LA; m. 1st Barbara Howes 1947 (divorced 1965); two s.; m. 2nd Sonja Haussmann 1966; one step-s. *Education:* Washington Univ., St Louis, Institut de Touraine, Tours, France, Columbia Univ., Wadham Coll., Oxford, Univ. of Florence. *Career:* instructor 1946–47, Visiting Prof. 1973–75, Columbia Univ.; instructor 1951, poet-in-residence and Lecturer 1959–64, 1966–67, Williams Coll.; writer-in-residence 1965–66, Prof. of English 1967–68, 1970–80, Prof. Emeritus 1980–, Hollins Coll., Virginia; consultant in poetry 1968–70, hon. consultant 1970–76, Library of Congress, Washington, DC; Lecturer, Salzburg Seminar in American Studies 1974; Fulbright Lecturer, Moscow State Univ. 1981; poet-in-residence, Cathedral of St John the Divine, New York 1985–88; mem. American Acad. of Arts and Letters (vice-pres. for literature 1986–89). *Publications:* poetry: Poems 1947, Celebration at Dark 1950, Snow

1953, The Stork 1954, Typewriter Birds 1954, The Bead Curtain: Calligrams 1957, The Old Man on the Isthmus 1957, Poems 1947–1957 1957, Prince Souvanna Phouma: An Exchange Between Richard Wilbur and William Jay Smith 1963, Morels 1964, The Tin Can and Other Poems 1966, New and Selected Poems 1970, A Rose for Katherine Anne Porter 1970, At Delphi: For Allen Tate on His Seventy-Fifth Birthday, 19 November 1974 1974, Venice in the Fog 1975, Verses on the Times (with Richard Wilbur) 1978, Journey to the Dead Sea 1979, The Tall Poets 1979, Mr Smith 1980, The Traveler's Tree: New and Selected Poems 1980, Oxford Doggerel 1983, Collected Translations: Italian, French, Spanish, Portuguese 1985, The Tin Can 1988, Journey to the Interior 1988, Plain Talk: Epigrams, Epitaphs, Satires, Nonsense, Occasional, Concrete and Quotidian Poems 1988, Collected Poems 1939–1989 1990, The World Below the Window: Poems 1937–1997 1998, The Cherokee Lottery: A Sequence of Poems 2000, The Girl in Glass: Love Poems 2002, 17 books of poetry for children 1955–90; other: The Spectra Hoax 1961, The Skies of Venice 1961, Children and Poetry: A Selective Bibliography (with Virginia Haviland) 1969, Louise Bogan: A Woman's Words 1972, The Streaks of the Tulip: Selected Criticism 1972, Green 1980, Army Brat: A Memoir 1980. Editor: Herrick 1962, The Golden Journey: Poems for Young People (with Louise Bogan) 1965, Poems from France 1967, Poems from Italy 1972, A Green Place: Modern Poems 1982. Contributions: journals and magazines. Honours: Rhodes Scholar 1947–48, Ford Foundation Fellowship 1964, Henry Bellamann Major Award 1970, National Endowment for the Arts Grant 1972, 1995, National Endowment for the Humanities Grants 1975, 1989, Gold Medal of Labor, Hungary 1978, Ingram Merrill Foundation Grant 1982, Trans. Award, Swedish Acad. 1990, Médaille de Vermeil Acad. Française 1991, Pro Cultura Hungarica Medal 1993, René Vásquez Díaz Prize, Swedish Acad. 1997. Address: 63 Luther Shaw Road, Cummington, MA 01026-9787, USA; 52–56 rue d'Alleray, 75015 Paris, France. Telephone: (413) 634-5546. Fax: (413) 634-5546.

SMITH, Z. Z. (see Westheimer, David)

SMITH, Zadie, FRSL; British writer and poet; b. (Sadie Smith), 27 Oct. 1975, London; m. Nick Laird 2004. Education: Hampstead Comprehensive, Cricklewood and King's Coll., Cambridge. Career: writer-in-residence Inst. of Contemporary Arts, London; Radcliffe Fellow Harvard Univ. 2002–03. Publications: White Teeth (novel) (Guardian First Book Award 2001, Whitbread First Novel Award and Book of the Year 2001, James Tait Memorial Prize for Fiction 2001, Commonwealth Writers' Best First Book Prize 2001) 2000, Piece of Flesh (ed.) 2001, The May Anthologies (ed.) 2001, The Autograph Man (novel) 2002, The Burned Children of America (ed.) 2003, On Beauty (novel) (Commonwealth Writers' Regional Award (Eurasia) for Best Book 2006, Orange Prize for Fiction 2006, Soc. of Authors Somerset Maugham Award 2006)) 2005; contribs to anthologies and periodicals. Honours: Rylands Prize, King's Coll. London, Betty Trask Prize 2001. Literary Agent: c/o A. P. Watt Ltd, 20 John Street, London, WC1N 2DR, England. Telephone: (20) 7405-6774 (office). Fax: (20) 7831-2154 (office). E-mail: zsmith@literati.net (office).

SMITHER, Elizabeth Edwina; New Zealand poet, novelist and short story writer; b. 15 Sept. 1941, New Plymouth; d. of Edwin Russell Harrington and Elsie Irene Bowerman; m. Michael Duncan Smither 1963; three c. Education: Univ. of Victoria, Massey Univ., New Zealand Library School. Career: part-time librarian; Te Mata Estate New Zealand Poet Laureate 2001–03; mem. New Zealand Soc. of Authors. Publications: poetry: Here Come the Clouds 1975, You're Very Seductive William Carlos Williams 1978, The Sarah Train 1980, The Legend of Marcello Mastroianni's Wife 1981, Casanova's Ankle 1981, Shakespeare Virgins 1983, Professor Musgrove's Canary 1986, Gorilla/Guerilla 1986, Animaux 1988, A Pattern of Marching (New Zealand Book Award 1990) 1989, A Cortège of Daughters 1993, The Tudor Style: Poems New and Selected 1993, The Lark Quartet (Montana New Zealand Book Award 2000) 1999, Red Shoes 2003, The Year of Adverbs 2007; novels: First Blood 1983, Brother-love Sister-love 1986, The Sea Between Us 2003, Different Kinds of Pleasure 2006; short story collections: Nights at the Embassy 1990, Mr Fish 1994, The Mathematics of Jane Austen 1997, Listening to the Everly Brothers 2002; other: Tug Brothers (juvenile) 1983, The Seventies Connection (co-ed.) 1987, The Journal Box (journals) 1996. Honours: Mem. NZ Order of Merit 2004; Hon. DLitt (Auckland) 2004; Scholarships in Letters 1987, 1992. Address: 19A Mt View Place, New Plymouth, New Zealand. Telephone: (6) 7512398 (home). E-mail: elizabethsmither@xtra.co.nz (home).

SMITTEN, Richard, BA; American writer; b. 22 April 1940, New York, NY; one d. Education: University of Western Ontario. Publications: Twice Killed, 1987; The Man Who Made it Snow (with Max Mermelstein and Robin Moore), 1990; Godmother, 1990; Bank of Death, 1993; Legal Tender, 1994.

SMYTHE, Colin Peter, BA, MA, LLD, FRSA; British editor, publisher and literary agent; Managing Director, Colin Smythe Ltd; b. 2 March 1942, Maidenhead, Berks.; s. of Wing Commdr Cyril Richard Smythe and Jean Edith Smythe (née Murdoch). Education: Bradfield Coll., Berks., Trinity Coll., Dublin. Career: Man. Dir Colin Smythe Ltd 1965–; mem. The Athenaeum, Beefsteak Club. Publications: Irish Literary Studies series (gen. ed.), Lady Gregory's Writings (general ed.) 1970–, Lady Gregory 1971–, A Guide to Coole Park: Home of Lady Gregory 1973, Lady Gregory: Our Irish Theatre (ed.) 1973, Lady Gregory: Poets and Dreamers (ed.) 1974, Lady Gregory: Seventy Years 1852–1922 (ed.) 1974, The Collected Works of G. W. Russell – AE (gen. ed. with Henry Summerfield) 1978–, Robert Gregory 1881–1918 (ed.) 1981,

Lady Gregory Fifty Years After (co-ed. with Ann Saddlemyer) 1986, Oxford Companion to Irish Literature (assoc. ed.) 1996. Honours: Hon. Mem. Mark Twain Soc.; various orders and decorations, including Officer, Venerable Order of St John of Jerusalem 1987, Kt, Order of Polonia Restituta, Poland 1988, Kt, Order of Our Lady of the Conception of Vila Viçosa, Portugal 1996, S. M. Constantinian Order of St George, Bourbon/Two Sicilies 1990, Kt Commdr of Grace, Kt Commdr, Royal Order of King Francis I 2005; Hon. LLD (Dublin) 1998. Address: PO Box 6, Gerrards Cross, Bucks., SL9 8XA, England (office). Telephone: (1753) 886000 (office). Fax: (1753) 886469 (office). E-mail: cs@colinsmythe.co.uk (office). Website: www.colinsmythe.co.uk (office).

SNEYD, Stephen (Steve) Henry, BSc, MA; British poet and writer; Editor on Poetry, Fantasy Commentator Magazine; b. 20 March 1941, Maidenhead, Berkshire, England; m. Rita Ann Cockburn, 13 March 1964, one s. one d. Career: UK Columnist, Scavenger's Newsletter, USA 1984–99; Contributing Ed. on Poetry, Fantasy Commentator magazine, USA 1992–; mem. Science Fiction Poetry Asscn, Pendragon Arthurian Soc., Castle Studies Group. Publications: poetry: The Legerdemain of Changelings 1979, Two Humps Not One 1980, Discourteous Self-Service 1982, Prug Plac Gamma 1983, Stone Bones (with Pete Presford) 1983, Fifty-Fifty Infinity 1989, Bad News from the Stars 1991, At the Thirteenth Hour 1991, We Are Not Men 1991, What Time Has Use For 1992, A Mile Beyond the Bus 1992, In Coils of Earthen Hold 1994, A Reason for Staying 1999, Gestaltmacher, Gestaltmacher, Make Me a Gestalt 2000, NeoLithon (with John Light) 2001, The Pennine Triangle (with J. F. Haines and J. C. Hartley) 2002, Ahasuerus On Mars 2004, Three Star Chamber 2005; short stories: over 500 published; contrib. to over 1,000 reviews, quarterlies, journals, magazines and websites world-wide; radio and television. Honours: Trend Prize for Peace Poetry 1967, Northern Star Poetry Prize 1983, Diploma di Merito, Accademia Italia 1983, Best Poet, Small Press and Magazine Awards 1986, Paterson Prize 1996, First Prize, Starlife Poetry Contest, USA 1999, Special Prize Diploma, International Cosmopoetry Festival of SARM, Romania 1999. Address: 4 Nowell Place, Almondbury, Huddersfield, West Yorkshire HD5 8PB, England.

SNICKET, Lemony (see Handler, Daniel)

SNIDER, Clifton Mark, BA, MA, PhD; American academic, poet and writer; b. 3 March 1947, Duluth, Minn.; s. of Allan George Snider and Rhoda Marion Tout. Education: Southern California Coll. (now Vanguard Univ.), Costa Mesa, California State Univ., Long Beach, Univ. of New Mexico. Career: Faculty mem., California State Univ., Long Beach 1974–, Long Beach City Coll. 1975–2002. Publications: poetry: Jesse Comes Back 1976, Bad Smoke Good Body 1980, Jesse and his Son 1982, Edwin: A Character in Poems 1984, Blood & Bones 1988, Impervious to Piranhas 1989, The Age of the Mother 1992, The Alchemy of Opposites 2000; other: The Stuff That Dreams are Made on: A Jungian Interpretation of Literature 1991, Loud Whisper (novel) 2000, Bare Roots (novel) 2001, Wrestling with Angels: A Tale of Two Brothers (novel) 2001; contrib. to anthologies, reviews, quarterlies and journals. Honours: Resident Fellow, Yaddo 1978, 1982, Helene Wurlitzer Foundation of New Mexico 1984, 1990, 1998, 2004, 2005, Michael Karolyi Memorial Foundation, Vence, France 1986, 1987, Meritorious Performance and Professional Promise Award, California State Univ. Address: English Department, California State University, Long Beach, 1250 Bellflower Boulevard, Long Beach, CA 90840 (office); 2719 Eucalyptus Avenue, Long Beach, CA 90806, USA (home). Telephone: (562) 985-4247 (office). E-mail: csnider@csulb.edu (office). Website: www.csulb.edu/~csnider.

SNODGRASS, William DeWitt (W. D.), (S. S. Gardons, Will McConnell, Kozma Prutkov), MA, MFA; American poet, critic, translator and academic; b. 5 Jan. 1926, Wilkinsburg, Pa; s. of Bruce DeWitt Snodgrass and Helen J. Murchie; m. 1st Lila Jean Hank 1946 (divorced 1953); one d.; m. 2nd Janice Marie Wilson 1954 (divorced 1966); one s. one step-d.; m. 3rd Camille Rykowski 1967 (divorced 1977); m. 4th Kathleen Brown 1985. Education: State Univ. of Iowa. Career: Instructor, English Dept, Cornell Univ., Ithaca 1955–57, Univ. of Rochester 1957–58; Prof. English Dept, Wayne State Univ. 1959–68; Prof. English and Speech, Syracuse Univ. 1968–76; Distinguished Prof. of Creative Writing and Contemporary Poetry, Univ. of Delaware 1979–94; Visiting Prof., Old Dominion Univ., Norfolk, Va 1978; Leader, Poetry Workshop, Morehead, Kentucky 1955, Yellow Springs, Ohio 1958, 1959; mem. American Acad. of Arts and Letters 1972, Acad. American Poets 1973, Acad. of American Arts and Sciences; Guggenheim Fellow 1972–73. Publications: Heart's Needle 1959, After Experience 1968, In Radical Pursuit (critical essays) 1975, The Führer Bunker (poems) 1977, Six Troubadour Songs (trans. with music), Traditional Hungarian Songs (trans. with music) 1978, If Birds Build with your Hair 1979, The Boy Made of Meat 1983, Six Minnesinger Songs (trans. with music) 1983, Magda Goebbels (poems) 1983, D.D. Byrde Callyng Jennie Wrenn (poem) 1984, The Four Seasons 1984, Remains 1985, The Death of Cock Robin 1987, Selected Poems, 1957–1987 1987, W. D.'s Midnight Carnival 1989, Autumn Variations 1990, Snow Songs 1992, Each in His Season 1993, The Führer Bunker: The Complete Cycle 1995, Selected Translations (poems and songs) 1998, After-Images (autobiographical sketches) 1999, De/Compositions: One Hundred and One Good Poems Gone Wrong (criticism) 2001, To Sound Like Yourself: Essays on Poetry (criticism) 2002, Not for Specialists: New and Selected Poems 2006. Honours: Pulitzer Prize for Poetry 1960, Guinness Prize for Poetry 1961, Coll. of William and Mary Bicentennial Medal 1976, Acad. of American Poets' Harold Morton Landon Trans. Award 1999 and other awards. Address: 3061 Hughes Road, Erieville, NY 13061, USA (home).

SNOW, Jonathan (Jon) George; British television journalist; b. 28 Sept. 1947, s. of the late Rt Rev. George Snow and Joan Snow; partner Madeleine Colvin; two d. *Education:* St Edward's School, Oxford, Univ. of Liverpool. *Career:* Voluntary Service Overseas, Uganda 1967–68; Co-ordinator New Horizon Youth Centre, London 1970–73 (Chair. 1986–); journalist, Independent Radio News, LBC 1973–76; reporter, ITN 1977–83, Washington Corresp. 1983–86, Diplomatic Ed. 1986–89; presenter, Channel Four News 1989–; Visiting Prof. of Broadcast Journalism, Nottingham Trent Univ. 1992–2001, Univ. of Stirling 2002–; Chair. New Horizon Youth Centre 1986–, Prison Reform Trust 1992–96, Media Trust 1995–, Tate Modern Council 1999–; Trustee Noel Buxton Trust 1992–, Nat. Gallery 1999–; Chancellor Oxford Brookes Univ. 2001–. *Publications:* Atlas of Today 1987, Sons and Mothers 1996, Shooting History: A Personal Journey 2004. *Honours:* Hon. DLit (Nottingham Trent) 1994; Monte Carlo Golden Nymph Award, for Eritrea air attack reporting 1979, TV Reporter of the Year, for Afghanistan, Iran and Iraq reporting, Royal Television Soc. (RTS) 1980, Valiant for Truth Award, for El Salvador reporting 1982, Int. Award, for El Salvador reporting, RTS 1982, Home News Award, for Kegworth air crash reporting, RTS 1989, RTS Presenter of the Year 1994, 2002, BAFTA Richard Dimbleby Award 2005. *Address:* Channel Four News, ITN, 200 Gray's Inn Road, London, WC1X 8HB, England. *Telephone:* (20) 7430-4237. *Fax:* (20) 7430-4607. *E-mail:* jon.snow@itn.co.uk (office).

SNYDER, Gary Sherman, BA; American poet, writer and fmr teacher; b. 8 May 1930, San Francisco, CA; m. 1st Alison Gass 1950 (divorced 1952); m. 2nd Joanne Kyger 1960 (divorced 1965); m. 3rd Masa Uehara 1967 (divorced 1987); m. 4th Carole Koda 1991; two s. two step-d. *Education:* Reed Coll., Portland, OR, Indiana Univ., Univ. of California, Berkeley, studied Zen Buddhism and East Asian culture in Japan. *Career:* Prof. of Creative Writing, Univ. of California at Davis 1986–2001; mem. American Acad. of Arts and Letters, American Acad. of Arts and Sciences. *Publications:* poetry: Riprap and Cold Mountain Poems 1959, Myths and Texts 1960, A Range of Poems 1966, Three Worlds, Three Realms, Six Roads 1966, The Back Country 1968, The Blue Sky 1969, Regarding Wave 1970, Manzanita 1971, Plute Creek 1972, The Fudo Trilogy: Spell Against Demons, Smokey the Bear Sutra, The California Water Plan 1973, Turtle Island 1974, All in the Family 1975, Songs for Gaia 1979, Axe Handles 1983, Left Out in the Rain: New Poems 1947–1986 1986, No Nature: New and Selected Poems 1992, Mountains and Rivers Without End 1996, Danger on Peaks 2003, Danger on Peaks 2004; prose: Earth House Hold: Technical Notes and Queries to Fellow Dharma Revolutionaries 1969, The Old Ways: Six Essays 1977, He Who Hunted Birds in His Father's Village: The Dimensions of a Haida Myth 1979, The Real Work: Interviews and Talks 1964–1979 1980, Passage Through India 1984, The Practice of the Wild 1990, A Place in Space 1995; contribs to anthologies. *Honours:* scholarship First Zen Inst. of America 1956, American Acad. of Arts and Letters Award 1966, Bollingen Foundation grant 1966–67, Frank O'Hara Prize 1967, Levinson Prize 1968, Guggenheim Fellowship 1968–69, Pulitzer Prize in Poetry 1975, Bollingen Prize 1997, Masaoka Shiki Int. Haiku Grand Prize 2004. *Address:* 18442 Macnab Cypress Road, Nevada City, CA 95959, USA.

SNYDER, Midori; American writer; b. 1 Jan. 1954, Santa Monica, CA; m. Stephen Haessler 1979, one s. one d. *Education:* University of Wisconsin. *Publications:* Soulstring, 1987; New Moon, 1989; Sadar's Keep, 1991; Beldane's Fire, 1993; The Flight of Michael McBride, 1994; Dinotopia, Hatchling, 1995; The Innamorati, 1998. Contributions: anthologies.

SNYDER, Richard E.; American publisher; b. 6 April 1933, New York; s. of Jack Snyder and Molly Rothman; m. 1st Otilie Freund 1963 (divorced); one s. one d.; m. 2nd Laura Yorke 1992; two s. *Education:* Tufts Univ., Medford. *Career:* sales rep. Simon & Schuster 1961, Vice-Pres. Marketing 1966–69, Vice-Pres. Trade Books 1969–73, Exec. Vice-Pres. Trade and Educ. Admin 1973–75, Pres. and COO 1975–78, Pres. and CEO 1978–86, Chair. and CEO 1986–94, consultant 1994–95; Chair., CEO Golden Books Family Entertainment 1996–2001; Chair. PEN, NY Area 1988; Dir Reliance Group Holdings, Children's Blood Foundation; Trustee NY Presbyterian Hosp.; Founder-mem. Nat. Book Foundation, Nat. Book Awards; mem. Council on Foreign Relations, Wildlife Conservation Soc., Econ. Club of NY. *Address:* c/o Random House Inc., 1745 Broadway, New York, NY 10019, USA (office).

SNYDER, Zilpha Keatley, BA; American writer; b. 11 May 1927, Lemoore, CA; m. 1950; two s. one d. *Education:* Whittier Coll. *Publications:* Season of Ponies 1964, The Velvet Room 1965, Black and Blue Magic 1966, The Egypt Game 1967, The Changeling 1970, The Headless Cupid 1971, The Witches of Worm 1972, The Princess and the Giants 1973, The Truth About Stone Hollow 1974, The Famous Stanley Kidnapping Case 1979, Blair's Nightmare 1984, The Changing Maze 1985, And Condors Danced 1987, Squeak Saves the Day and Other Tooley Tales 1988, Janie's Private Eyes 1989, Libby on Wednesday 1990, Song of the Gargoyle 1991, Fool's Gold 1993, Cat Running 1994, The Trespasser 1995, Castle Court Kids 1995, The Gypsy Game 1997, Gib Rides Home 1998, The Runaways 1999, Gig and the Gray Ghost 2000, Spyhole Secrets 2001, The Ghosts of Rathburn Park 2002, The Unseen 2004. *Honours:* Beatty Award 1995. *Address:* 52 Miller Avenue, Mill Valley, CA 94941, USA.

SOBEL, Dava; American science writer; b. 1947; m. 1st Arthur Klein (divorced); one s. one d.; m. 2nd Alfonso Triggiani. *Education:* State Univ. of NY at Binghamton. *Career:* fmr science reporter, New York Times; reported for several journals including Audubon, Discover, Life, The New Yorker; fmr

Contributing Ed. Harvard Magazine; has lectured at The Smithsonian Inst., The Explorers Club, NASA Goddard Space Flight Center, Folger Shakespeare Library, Los Angeles Public Library, NY Public Library, Royal Geographical Soc. (London); numerous radio and TV appearances; mem. American Asscn of Univ. Women, Planetary Soc.; Fellow, American Geographical Soc. *Publications:* Is Anyone Out There? The Scientific Search for Extraterrestrial Intelligence (with Frank D. Drake) 1992, Longitude (several awards including Harold D. Vursell Memorial Award American Acad. of Arts and Letters 1996, UK Book of the Year 1996, Prix Faubert du Coton, Premio del Mare Circeo) 1995, Galileo's Daughter: A Historical Memoir of Science, Faith, and Love 1999, Letters to Father 2001, The Planets 2005. *Honours:* Hon. DLit (Middlebury Coll., Vt) 2002, (Bath, UK) 2002; Nat. Media Award American Psychological Foundation 1980, Lowell Thomas Award Soc. of American Travel Writers 1992, Gold Medal Council for the Advancement and Support of Educ. 1994, Christopher Award 1999, Los Angeles Times Book Prize 2000, Nat. Science Bd Public Service Award 2001, Bradford Washburn Award Boston Museum of Science 2001, Nathaniel Bowditch Maritime Scholar 2003, Harrison Medal, Worshipful Co. of Clockmakers (UK) 2004. *Literary Agent:* c/o Michael Carlisle, InkWell Management, 521 Fifth Avenue, 26th Floor, New York, NY 10175, USA. *Telephone:* (212) 922-3500.

SOBH, Alawiya; Lebanese literary critic and writer; b. 1955, Beirut. *Education:* Lebanese Nat. Univ., Beirut. *Career:* fmr high school teacher; contributor to daily Beirut newspapers, including Nida' and an-Nahar; Ed. of the cultural section of Arabic women's magazine, al-Hasnaa', Ed.-in-Chief 1986–90; founder Ed.-in-Chief of women's cultural magazine, al-Hasnaa 1998–. *Publications include:* novels: The Stories of Mariam (title in trans.), Dunya Rabia Raihane. *Address:* al-Hasnaa, al-Iktissad Wal-Aamal Group, PO Box 113-6194, Hamra, Beirut 1103 2100, Lebanon (office). *Website:* www.alhasnaa.com.

SOBOL, Joshua; Israeli playwright; b. 1939, Tel-Aviv. *Education:* Sorbonne, Paris, France. *Career:* teacher of aesthetics and dir of theatrical workshops, Tel-Aviv Univ., Kibbutz Teachers' Seminary, Belt Zvi Drama School; currently Visiting Prof. of Theater, Weslyan Univ., USA. *Plays:* Ghetto 1989, Real Time 2002, Eye Witness 2002. *Publications:* Silence (novel) 2005. *Honours:* Evening Standard Award for Best Play 1989. *Address:* c/o Jewish Book Council, PO Box 38247, London, NW3 5YQ, England.

SOHAIL, Khalid, MBBS, FRCP(C); Pakistani/Canadian psychiatrist, writer and poet; b. 9 July 1952, Pakistan. *Education:* studied in Pakistan and Canada. *Career:* Fellow, Royal College of Physicians and Surgeons, Canada; mem. Writers' Forum of Canada, Writers' Union of Canada. *Publications:* Discovering New Highways in Life, 1991; From One Culture to Another, 1992; Literary Encounters, 1992; Pages of My Heart (poems), 1993; A Broken Man (short stories), 1993; Mother Earth is Sad (fiction), 1999; Encounters With Creativity, Insanity and Spirituality, 1999. Contributions: anthologies and journals. *Honours:* Rahul Award, Kolkata 1994. *E-mail:* welcome@drsohail.com. *Website:* www.drsohail.com.

SOKOLOV, Maksim Yur'yevich; Russian journalist; b. 1959, Moscow; m. *Education:* Moscow State Univ. *Career:* worked as programmer in All-Union Centre of Transport, USSR State Cttee on Science and Tech. 1981–83; All-Union Research Inst. of Patent Information 1983–84; All-Union Research Inst. for Man. of Coal Industry 1985–87; Research Inst. of Gen. Plan of Moscow 1988–89; journalist since late 1980s; contrib. Commersant (weekly) 1989–97; political observer, Izvestiya 1998–; publs in newspapers Nezavisimaya Gazeta, Atmoda, Segodnya, magazines Vek XX i Mir, Oktyabr, Soviet Analyst (UK); broadcaster Russian Public TV Co. ORT; commentator, TV programmes; special corresp., Soviet analyst. *Honours:* Gong 94 Journalism prize; Medal for the Defence of Free Russia 1991. *Address:* Izvestiya, Tverskaya str. 18, 103791 Moscow, Russia. *Telephone:* (495) 299-21-22 (office).

SOLLERS, Philippe, (pseudonym of Philippe Joyaux); French author; b. 28 Nov. 1936, Bordeaux; s. of Octave Joyaux and Marcelle Molinié; m. Julia Kristeva 1967; one s. *Education:* Lycées Montesquieu and Montaigne, Bordeaux and Ecole Sainte-Geneviève, Versailles. *Career:* Dir L'Infini (review) 1983–; mem. reading Cttee Editions Gallimard 1990–, Asscn of French Museums 1998–. *Publications:* Une Curieuse Solitude 1958, Le Parc 1961, Drame 1965, Nombres, Logiques 1968, Lois 1972, H 1973, Paradis, Vision à New York 1981, Femmes 1983, Portrait du joueur 1985, Théorie des exceptions 1986, Paradis 2 1986, Le Coeur absolu 1987, Les Surprises de Fragonard 1987, Les Folies françaises 1988, De Kooning, vite 1988, Le Lys d'or 1989, Carnet de nuit 1989, La Fête à Venise 1991, Improvisations 1991, Le Secret 1993, Venise Éternelle 1993, La Guerre du Goût 1994, Femmes, Mythologies (jtly) 1994, Les Passions de Francis Bacon 1996, Sade contre l'Être Suprême 1996, Picasso, le héros 1996, Studio 1997, Casanova, L'admirable (Prix Elsa-Morante 1999) 1998, L'Année du Tigre, Journal de l'année 1998, 1999, L'Oeil de Proust, les dessins de Marcel Proust 1999, Passion fixe 2000, La Divine Comédie 2000, Eloge de L'Infini 2001, L'Etoile des amants 2002. *Honours:* Chevalier Légion d'honneur; Officier, Ordre nat. du Mérite, des Arts et des Lettres; Prix Médicis 1961, Grand Prix du Roman de la Ville de Paris 1988, Prix Paul-Morand (Académie française) 1992. *Address:* L'Infini, 5 rue Sébastien-Bottin, 75007 Paris, France (office).

SOLOMON, Maynard Elliott, BA; American music historian and writer; b. 5 Jan. 1930, New York, NY; m. Eva Georgiana Tevan 1951; two s. one d. *Education:* Brooklyn Coll., CUNY, Columbia Univ., New England Conservatory of Music. *Career:* co-founder, co-owner, Vanguard Recording Soc. Inc

1950–86; teacher, CUNY 1979–81; Visiting Prof., SUNY at Stony Brook 1988–89, Columbia Univ. 1989–90, Harvard Univ. 1991–92, Yale Univ. 1994–95; Scholarly Adviser, Beethoven Archive, Bonn 1995–; Graduate Faculty, Juilliard School 1998–; Assoc. Ed., American Imago 1976; mem. PEN. *Publications:* Marxism and Art 1973, Beethoven 1977, 1998, Myth, Creativity and Psychoanalysis 1978, Beethoven Essays 1988, Mozart: A Life 1995, Some Romantic Images in Beethoven 1998, Late Beethoven: Music, Thought, Imagination 2003; contrib. articles to Beethoven Jahrbuch: Music and Letters, Musical Quarterly: 19th Century Music, Journal of the American Musicological Society. *Honours:* Hon. DMA; ASCAP–Deems Taylor Awards 1978, 1989, 1995, Kinkeldey Award American Musicological Soc. 1989, hon. mem. 1999, 2000. *Address:* 1 W 72nd Street, Apt 56, New York, NY 10023, USA.

SOLOW, Robert Merton, PhD; American economist and academic; *Institute Professor Emeritus and Professor Emeritus of Economics, Massachusetts Institute of Technology*; b. 23 Aug. 1924, Brooklyn, NY; s. of Milton Solow and Hannah Solow; m. Barbara Lewis 1945; two s. one d. *Education:* Harvard Univ. *Career:* Asst Prof. of Statistics, Mass. Inst. of Technology 1950–53, Assoc. Prof. of Econs 1954–57, Prof. of Econs 1958–73, Inst. Prof. 1973–95, Inst. Prof. Emer. 1995–; W. Edwards Deming Prof., New York Univ. 1996; Sr Economist, Council of Econ. Advisers 1961–62; Marshall Lecturer, Univ. of Cambridge, UK 1963–64; De Vries Lecturer, Rotterdam 1963, Wicksell Lecturer, Stockholm 1964; Eastman Visiting Prof., Univ. of Oxford, UK 1968–69; Killian Prize Lecturer, MIT 1978; Geary Lecturer, Univ. of Dublin, Ireland 1980; Overseas Fellow, Churchill Coll., Cambridge 1984; Mitsui Lecturer, Birmingham 1985; Nobel Memorial Lecture, Stockholm 1987 and numerous others in int. academic insts; mem. Nat. Comm. on Tech., Automation and Econ. Progress 1964–65, Presidential Comm. on Income Maintenance 1968–69; mem. Bd of Dirs Fed. Reserve Bank of Boston 1975–81, Chair. 1979–81; Fellow, Center for Advanced Study in Behavioral Sciences 1957–58, Trustee 1982–95; Vice-Pres. American Econ. Asscn 1968, Pres. 1979, Vice-Pres. AAAS 1970; Pres. Econometric Soc. 1964; Trustee Woods Hole Oceanographic Inst. 1988–, Alfred P. Sloan Foundation 1992–, Resources for the Future 1994–96, Urban Inst. 1994–, German Marshall Fund of US 1994–; Pres. Int. Econ. Asscn 1999–2002; mem. Nat. Science Bd 1995–2000; Fellow American Acad. of Arts and Sciences, mem. of Council, NAS 1977–80, mem. 1972–; Corresp. mem. British Acad.; mem. American Philosophical Soc.; Fellow Acad. dei Lincei (Rome); Foundation Fellow, Russell Sage Foundation 2000–. *Publications:* Linear Programming and Economic Analysis 1958, Capital Theory and the Rate of Return 1963, Sources of Unemployment in the United States 1964, Price Expectations and the Behavior of the Price Level 1970, Growth Theory: An Exposition 1970, The Labor Market as a Social Institution 1989, Learning from "Learning by Doing" 1994, A Critical Essay On Modern Macroeconomic Theory (with Frank Hahn) 1995. *Honours:* Orden pour le mérite, Germany 1995; Hon. LLD (Chicago) 1967, (Lehigh) 1977, (Brown) 1972, (Wesleyan) 1982; Hon. LittD (Williams Coll.) 1974, (Rensselaer Polytechnic Inst.) 2003; Dr hc (Paris) 1975, (Geneva) 1982, (Conservatoire Nat. des Arts et Métiers, Paris) 1994, (Buenos Aires) 1999; Hon. DLitt (Warwick) 1976, (Colgate) 1990, (Glasgow) 1992, (Harvard) 1992; Hon. ScD (Tulane) 1983; Hon. DScS (Yale) 1986, (Univ. of Mass., Boston) 1989, (Helsinki) 1990, (Boston Coll.) 1990, (Chile) 1992, (Rutgers Univ.) 1994; Hon. DSc in Business Admin. (Bryant Coll.) 1988; Hon. DEng (Colorado School of Mines) 1996; Hon. DHumLitt (New York) 2006; David A. Wells Prize, Harvard Univ. 1951, John Bates Clark Medal, American Econ. Asscn 1961, Killian Award, MIT 1977, Seidman Award in Political Econ. 1983, Nobel Prize for Econs 1987, Nat. Medal of Science 2000. *Address:* Department of Economics, Massachusetts Institute of Technology E52-383, Cambridge, MA 02139 (office); 528 Lewis Wharf, Boston, MA 02110, USA (home). *Telephone:* (617) 253-5268 (office); (617) 227-4436 (home). *Fax:* (617) 253-0560 (office). *Website:* econ-www.mit.edu (office).

SOLWAY, David, BA, QMA, MA, PhD; Canadian poet, writer, translator and academic (retd); b. 8 Dec. 1941, Montréal, QC; m. Karin Semmler 1980, one d. *Education:* McGill University, Concordia University, University of Sherbrooke, Lajos Kossuth University. *Career:* Lecturer in English Literature, McGill University, 1966–67, Dawson College, 1970–71, John Abbott College, 1971–99; Writer-in-Residence, Concordia University 1999–2000; Assoc. Ed., Books in Canada, 2001–; several visiting university lectureships; mem. International PEN; Union des écrivaines et des écrivains québécois; President's Circle, Univ. of Toronto. *Publications:* Poetry: In My Own Image, 1962; The Crystal Theatre, 1971; Paximalia, 1972; The Egyptian Airforce and Other Poems, 1973; The Road to Arginos, 1976; Anacrusis, 1976; Mephistopheles and the Astronaut, 1979; The Mulberry Men, 1982; Selected Poetry, 1982; Stones in Water, 1983; Modern Marriage, 1987; Bedrock, 1993; Chess Pieces, 1999; The Lover's Progress (dramatized by Rajori Theatre Ensemble, Regina, Vancouver) 2001; The Pallikari of Nesmine Rifat 2005; Director's Cut (essays), 2003; Franklin's Passage (poems), 2003. Other: Four Montréal Poets (ed.), 1973; Education Lost: Reflections on Contemporary Pedagogical Practice, 1989; The Anatomy of Arcadia, 1992; Lying About the Wolf: Essays in Culture and Education, 1997; Random Walks: Essays in Elective Criticism, 1997; Saracen Island: The Poems of Andreas Karavis (trans.), 2000; An Andreas Karavis Companion, 2000; The Turtle Hypodermic of Sickenpods: Liberal Studies in the Corporate Age, 2001. Contributions: many anthologies, reviews, quarterlies and journals, including: The Atlantic Monthly; International Journal of Applied Semiotics; Journal of Modern Greek Studies; Canadian Notes and Queries; Books in Canada; The Sewanee Review. *Honours:* QSPELL Award for Poetry 1988, and for Non-Fiction 1990, Le Grand Prix du Livre de Montréal 2004; various Canada Council Grants. *Address:* 143 Upper McNaughton, Hudson, QC J0P 1H0, Canada (home). *Telephone:* (450) 458-8663. *E-mail:* parmenius@videotron.ca.

SOLZHENITSYN, Aleksandr Isayevich; Russian writer; b. 11 Dec. 1918, Kislovodsk; m. Natalya Reshetovskaya 1940 (divorced, remarried 1957, she died 2003); three s. *Education:* Rostov Univ. and Correspondence Course in Literature, Moscow History and Literature Inst. *Career:* joined Army 1941, attended artillery school, commissioned 1942, served at front as Commdr of Artillery Battery and twice decorated for bravery; sentenced to eight years in a forced labour camp 1945–53; contracted, later cured of cancer; in exile in Siberia 1953–57; officially rehabilitated 1957; taught mathematics at secondary school, Ryazan; expelled from Writers' Union of USSR Nov. 1969; expelled from USSR Feb. 1974, lived in Vt, USA; ended exile as treason charges dropped 1991; returned to Russia, citizenship restored 1994; hosted A Meeting with Solzhenitsyn 1995; mem. American Acad. of Arts and Sciences 1969–, Russian Acad. of Sciences 1997–. *Publications:* One Day in the Life of Ivan Denisovich 1962 (film 1971), Matryona's Home and An Incident at Krechetovka Station 1963 (short stories), For the Good of the Cause 1964 (short story), The First Circle (publ USA and UK 1968), Cancer Ward (USA and UK 1968), The Easter Procession (short story), The Love Girl and the Innocent (play, UK) 1969, Collected Works (6 vols) 1969, 1970, Stories and Prose Poems 1971, August 1914 1971, The Gulag Archipelago Vol. I 1973, Vol. II 1974, Vol. III 1976, Letter to Soviet Leaders 1974, Peace and Aggression 1974, Quiet Flows the Don: The Enigma of a Novel 1974, Candle in the Wind (play), The Oak and the Calf: Sketches of Literary Life in the Soviet Union 1975, The Nobel Prize Lecture 1975, Lenin in Zürich 1975, Détente (with others) 1976, Prussian Nights (poem trans. by Robert Conquest) 1977, Collected Works 1978–, Victory Celebrations, Prisoners (play) 1983, October 1916 1985, The Red Wheel, Live Not by Lies (essay) 1988, August 1914 (second version) 1989, Rebuilding Russia 1990, The Russian Question at the End of the 20th Century 1994, Invisible Allies (addendum to The Oak and the Calf) 1995, November 1916, Russia in Collapse 1998, Two Hundred Years Together (Jews in Russia) (2 vols) 2001–02. *Honours:* Hon. US Citizen 1974; Hon. Fellow, Hoover Inst. on War, Revolution and Peace 1975; Prix du Meilleur Livre Etranger (France) for The First Circle and Cancer Ward 1969, Nobel Prize for Literature 1970, Templeton Prize 1983. *Address:* PO Box 121, Cavendish, VT 05142, USA. *Telephone:* (495) 229-86-39 (Moscow).

SOMERS, Suzanne (see Daniels, Dorothy)

SOMERS COCKS, The Hon. Anna Gwenllian, (Anna Allemandi), MA, FSA; British museum curator, editor, publisher and journalist; b. 18 April 1950, Rome; d. of John Sebastian Somers Cocks and Marjorie Olive Somers Cocks (née Weller); m. 1st Martin Walker 1971 (divorced); m. 2nd John Hardy 1978 (divorced); one s. one d.; m. 3rd Umberto Allemandi. *Education:* abroad and Convent of the Sacred Heart, Woldingham, St Anne's Coll., Oxford and Courtauld Inst., London. *Career:* Asst Keeper Dept of Metal Work, Victoria and Albert Museum, London 1973–85, Dept of Ceramics 1985–87; Ed. The Art Newspaper 1990–94, 1996–2003; Assoc. Publr Umberto Allemandi Publishing srl 1994–2003, Group Ed. Umberto Allemandi e C. srl 2003–; fmr expert adviser to the Nat. Heritage Lottery Fund; Chair. Venice in Peril Fund 1999–; Trustee Gilbert Collection 1999–, Cass Sculpture Foundation 2004–. *Publications:* Victoria and Albert Museum: the making of the collection 1980, Princely Magnificence: Court Jewels of the Renaissance (co-author) 1980, Renaissance Jewels, Gold Boxes and Objets de Vertu in the Thyssen Collection (co-author) 1985. *Honours:* Commendatore, Ordine della Stella della Solidarietà Italiana 2004; Nat. Art Collections Fund Award for Outstanding Achievement in the Arts 1992, Silver Prize, Int. Specialist Magazine, IPD Awards 1996, European Woman of the Year (Arts and Media section) 2006. *Address:* c/o Umberto Allemandi e C, Via Mancini 8, 10131 Turin, Italy. *Telephone:* (011) 8199111 (office). *Fax:* (011) 8193090 (office). *E-mail:* a.allemandi@theartnewspaper.com (office).

SOMMER, Piotr, MA; Polish poet; *Editor-in-Chief, Literatura na Swiecie*; b. 13 April 1948, Walbrzych. *Education:* Univ. of Warsaw. *Career:* taught at several American insts, including Amherst Coll., Wesleyan Univ., Univ. of Notre Dame, Ind.; Ed.-in-Chief, Literatura na Swiecie 1994–. *Publications:* poetry: W krzesle 1977, Pamiatki po nas 1980, Przed snem 1981, Kolejny swiat 1983, Czynnik liryczny 1986, Czynnik liryczny i inne wiersze 1988, Nowe stosunki wyrazów 1997, Piosenka pasterska 1999; essays: Smak detalu i inne ogolniki 1995, Po stykach 2005; editor of anthologies, including Antologia nowej poezji brytyjskiej 1983, Szesciu poetów pólnocnoirlandzkich 1993, Artykuty pochodzenia zagranicznego 1996; contrib. to anthologies, including The Faber Book of Fevers and Frets 1989, Poetry with an Edge 1993; translations of poets, including John Ashbery, Douglas Dunn, D. J. Enright, Seamus Heaney, Michael Longley, Robert Lowell, Derek Mahon, Frank O'Hara, Charles Reznikoff; contrib. to: Chicago Review, Kresy, Literatura na Swiecie, Midrasz, New Yorker, Poetry, Poetry Review, Reg Publica, Threepenny Review, Times Literary Supplement. *Honours:* Iowa Int. Writing Program Fellowship 2002, Nat. Humanities Center Fellowship 2004–05; Barbara Sadowska Memorial Prize 1988, Koscielski Foundation Prize 1988, Polish PEN Prize 1997. *Address:* c/o Bloodaxe Books Ltd, Highgreen, Tarset, Northumberland NE48 1RP, England.

SOMMER, Theo, DPhil; German journalist; *Editor-at-Large, Die Zeit*; b. 10 June 1930, Constance; s. of Theo Sommer and Else Sommer; m. 1st Elda

Tsilenis 1952; two s.; m. 2nd Heide Grenz 1976; two s.; m. 3rd Sabine Grewe 1989; one d. *Education:* Univ of Tübingen, Chicago and Harvard Univs. *Career:* Local Ed. Schwäbisch-Gmünd 1952–54; Foreign Ed. Die Zeit 1958, Deputy Ed. 1968, Ed.-in-Chief 1973–92, Publr 1992–, Ed.-at-Large 2000–; Lecturer in Int. Relations, Univ. of Hamburg 1967–70; Chief of Planning Staff, Ministry of Defence 1969–70; mem. Deutsche Gesellschaft für Auswärtige Politik; mem. Council IISS 1963–76, 1978–87, German Armed Forces Structure Comm. 1970–72, Int. Comm. on the Balkans 1995–96, Ind. Int. Comm. on the Balkans 1999–2000; Deputy Chair. Comm. on the Future on the Bundeswehr 1999–2000; Chair. Comm. Investigating Effects of DU Ammunitions, Radar and Asbestos on German Armed Forces 2002; mem. Indo-German Consultative Group 1992– (Co-Chair. 1996–), German-Japanese Dialogue Forum 1993–; mem. Bd Deutsche Welthungerhilfe 1992–, Max-Bauer Preis 1992–, German-Turkish Foundation 1998–; mem. German Foreign Policy Asscn, IISS, Königswinter Conf., Advisory Council, Mil. History Inst.; Contributing Ed. Newsweek Int. 1968–90; regular contrib. to American, British, Japanese and Korean publs; commentator German TV, radio and moderator of monthly programmes;. *Publications:* Deutschland und Japan zwischen den Mächten (Germany and Japan Between the Powers) 1935–40 1962, Vom Antikominternpakt zum Dreimächtepakt 1962, Reise in ein fernes Land 1964, Ed. Denken an Deutschland 1966, Ed. Schweden-Report 1974, Die chinesische Karte (The Chinese Card) 1979, Allianz in Umbruch (Alliance in Disarray) 1982, Blick zurück in die Zukunft (Look Back into the Future) 1984, Reise ins andere Deutschland (Journey to the Other Germany) 1986, Europa im 21. Jahrhundert 1989, Geschichte der Bonner Republik 1949–99 1999, Der Zukunft entgegen (Toward the Future) 1999, Phoenix Europe. The European Union: Its Progress, Problems and Prospects 2000, Hamburg 2004, 1945: Biographie eines Jahres 2005. *Honours:* Hon. mem. Asscn of Anciens, NATO Defense Coll. 1971, Trilateral Comm. 1993; Fed. Order of Merit (First Class) 1998, Gold Honor Cross, German Armed Forces 2002; Hon. LLD (Univ. of Maryland, USA) 1982; Theoder-Wolf Prize 1966, Int. Communications Award, People's Repub. of China 1991, Columbus Prize 1993. *Address:* Die Zeit, Pressehaus, Speersort 1, 20079 Hamburg (office); 17 Zabelweg, 22359 Hamburg, Germany (home). *Telephone:* (40) 3280240 (office); (40) 6037300 (home). *Fax:* (40) 3280407 (office); (40) 6030044 (home). *E-mail:* sommer@zeit .de (office); tsommer01@aol.com (home). *Website:* www.zeit.de (office); www .theosommer.de.

SOMOZA, José Carlos; Spanish novelist and psychiatrist; b. 1959, Havana, Cuba. *Publications:* Planos (novella) 1994, Langostas (radio play) 1994, Silencio de Blanca (novel) 1996, Miguel Will (play) 1997, La ventana pintada (novel) 1998, Cartas de un asesino insignificante (novel) 1999, Dafne desvanecida (novel) 2000, La caverna de las ideas (trans. as The Athenian Murders, novel) 2000, Clara y la penumbra (novel) 2001. *Honours:* Premio Gabriel Sijé 1994; Premio Margarita Xirgu 1994; Premio Sonrisa Vertical 1996; Premio Miguel de Cervantes de teatro 1997; Premio Café Gijón 1998; Premio Nadal, 2001; Premio de Novela Fernando Lara, 2001; CWA Macallan Gold Dagger, 2002. *Address:* c/o Editorial Planeta, SA, Edifici Planeta, Diagonal 662–664, 08034 Barcelona, Spain. *E-mail:* jcsomoza@clubcultura .com. *Website:* www.clubcultura.com/clubliteratura/clubescritores/somoza/.

SONG, Cathy, BA, MA; American poet, writer and teacher; b. 20 Aug. 1955, Honolulu, HI; m. Douglas M. Davenport 1979. *Education:* University of Hawaii at Manoa, Wellesley College, Boston University. *Career:* Teacher of Poetry, HI, 1987–; Associated with Poets in the Schools programme. *Publications:* Picture Bride 1983, Frameless Windows, Squares of Light 1988, Sister Stew (ed. with Juliet S. Kono) 1991, School Figures 1994, The Land of Bliss 2001. Contributions: various anthologies and journals. *Honours:* Yale Series of Younger Poets Prize 1983, Frederick Book Prize for Poetry 1986, Cades Award for Literature 1988, Hawaii Award for Literature 1993, Shelley Memorial Award, Poetry Society of America 1993, Creative Writing Fellowship, Nat. Endowment for the Arts 1997, Pushcart Prize 1999, The Best American Poetry 2000. *Address:* PO Box 27262 Honolulu, HI 96827, USA.

SONG, Muwen; Chinese publishing executive; b. 1929, Yushu Co., Jilin. *Career:* Chair. Asscn of Chinese Publrs 1993–2000, Hon. Chair. 2000–; Pres. Copyright Research Society; mem. NPC Educ., Science, Culture and Public Health Cttee. *Address:* Publishers' Association of China, 85 Dongsi Nan Dajie, Beijing 100703, People's Republic of China (office). *Telephone:* (10) 65228632 (office). *Fax:* (10) 65228632 (office).

SORESTAD, Glen Allan, BEd, MEd; Canadian writer and poet; b. 21 May 1937, Vancouver, BC; m. Sonia Diane Talpash 1960; three s. one d. *Education:* Univ. of Saskatchewan. *Career:* elementary school teacher 1957–69; sr English teacher 1969–81; Pres. Thistledown Press 1975–2000; first Poet Laureate of Saskatchewan 2000–05; Life mem. League of Canadian Poets, Saskatchewan Writers' Guild, Writers' Union of Canada, League of Canadian Poets. *Publications:* Hold the Rain in Your Hands: Poems Selected and New 1985, Birchbark Meditations 1996, West into Night 1991, Icons of Flesh 1998, Today I Belong to Agnes 2000, Leaving Holds Me Here: Selected Poems 1975–2000 2001, Grasses and Gravestones 2003, Blood and Bone, Ice and Stone 2005; contrib. to numerous newspapers, journals, magazines and periodicals. *Honours:* SWG Founders' Award, Queen's Golden Jubilee Medal 2003. *Address:* 108–835 Heritage Green, Saskatoon, SK S7H 5S5, Canada (home). *Telephone:* (306) 374-1730 (home). *E-mail:* g.sorestad@sasktel.net (home).

SORG, Margarete; German writer and publisher; b. 4 July 1937, Bochum; m.; one d. (Margarete Sorg-Rose). *Education:* Fachhochschule, Frankfurt/ Main. *Career:* freelance writer 1978–; Publr GEDOK-Journal (magazine for the arts) 1986–95, various anthologies of poetry; publishing man. 1999–; organizer literary competitions, mem. Jury, Germany 1998–; Pres. Jury Andreas Gryphius Award for Literature and Nikolaus Lenau Award for Lyric Poetry 1993–96; Pres. Literary Section of Die Künstlergilde e.V. 1993–96, Pres. Künstlergilde Hessen 1993; Pres. Kulturring HDH, Wiesbaden 1995–; Pres. GEDOK Rhein-Main-Taunus cultural man. co. for artists 1995–. *Publications:* Streiflichter (lyric poetry) (2nd edn) 1984, irgendwann der bitteren tollkirsche süße 2002; 55 publs of lyric poetry in anthologies and literary reviews. *Honours:* Verdienstkreuz am Bande des Verdienstordens der Bundesrepublik Deutschland 2004; Second GEDOK Award for Lyric Poetry 1982, Art-GEDOK-Nadel for Meritorious Artistic and Cultural Activities 1995, Pro-arte-Medaille der Künstlergilde e.V. 1998. *Address:* Henkellstr. 3, 65187 Wiesbaden, Germany. *Fax:* 1805060 34445898 (office).

SOROKIN, Vladimir Georgiyevich; Russian author, screenwriter and painter; b. 7 Aug. 1955, Bykovo, Moscow Region; m. Irina Igorevna Sorokina; two d. *Education:* Moscow Inst. of Oil and Gas. *Career:* worked as artist and writer in Moscow underground; was not published in USSR until 1987; mem. Russian PEN Centre; scholarship of Deutsche Akademische Austauschung Dienst 1992. *Plays:* wrote 10 plays 1986–95. *Screenplays:* Moskva 1995, Kopejka 1997, The Four 2000, Cashfire 2002, The Thing 2003, Exit 2004. *Libretto:* opera 'The Children of Rosenthal' by Leonid Desyatnikov (performed at Bolshoi Theatre, Moscow) 2005. *Publications include:* Thirties Love of Marina 1982–84, The Queue (novel) 1983, The Norm 1984, Obelisk (short stories) 1980–84, Roman 1989, Four Stout Hearts (novel) 1991, Blue Lard 1999, The Feast 2001, The Ice (novel) 2002, Bro 2004, Trilogy 2005. *Honours:* Liberty Prize, USA 2005. *Address:* ul. Gubkina, d4 kv 47, 119333 Moscow, Russia (home). *Telephone:* (495) 135-90-76 (home). *E-mail:* sornorma@mtu -net.ru (home). *Website:* www.srkn.ru; www.vladimirsorokin.ru.

SOROS, George; Hungarian investment banker and philanthropist; *Chairman, Soros Fund Management LLC*; b. 12 Aug. 1930, Budapest; m.; five c. *Education:* London School of Econs. *Career:* moved to England 1947; much influenced by work of philosopher Karl Popper; with Singer & Friedlander (merchant bankers), London; moved to Wall Street, New York 1956; set up pvt. mutual fund, Quantum Fund, registered in Curaçao 1969; since 1991 has created other funds, Quasar Int., Quota, Quantum Emerging Growth Fund (merged with Quantum Fund to form Quantum Endowment Fund 2000), Quantum Realty Trust; Pres. and Chair. Soros Fund Man. LLC, New York 1973–; philanthropist since 1979, provided funds to help black students attend Cape Town Univ., SA; Founder Open Soc. Fund (currently Chair. Open Soc. Inst.) 1979, Soros Foundations, Cen. European Univ., Budapest 1992; f. Global Power Investments 1994. *Publication:* The Alchemy of Finance 1987, Opening the Soviet System 1990, Underwriting Democracy 1991, Soros on Soros – Staying Ahead of the Curve (jtly) 1995, The Crisis of Global Capitalism – Open Society Engendered 1998, Open Society – Reforming Global Capitalism 2000, George Soros on Globalization 2002, The Bubble of American Supremacy – Correcting the Misuse of American Power 2004, Soros on Freedom 2006; numerous essays on politics, society and econs in major int. newspapers and magazines. *Honours:* Dr hc (New School for Social Research, Univ. of Oxford, Budapest Univ. of Econs, Yale Univ.); Laurea hc (Univ. of Bologna) 1995. *Address:* Soros Fund Management LLC, 888 7th Avenue, 3300 New York, NY 10106, USA (office); Open Society Institute, 400 West 59th Street, New York, NY 10019. *Telephone:* (212) 548-0600. *Website:* www .georgesoros.com; www.soros.org.

SOSA, Roberto; Honduran writer and poet; b. 18 April 1930, Yoro. *Career:* teacher of literature, Universidad Nacional Autónoma de Honduras; Pres., Honduran Journalists' Union; Ed., Presente (Central American arts and letters review). *Publications:* Los pobres 1969, Un mundo para todos dividido 1971, Prosa armada 1981, Secreto militar 1985, 13 poemas 1987, Obra completa 1990, Diálogo de sombras 1993, Sociedad y poesia: los enmantados 1997, Honduras: Poesia escogida 1998, Piano vacio 2002; in English: Poems 1984, The Difficult Days 1985, The Common Grief 1994, The Return of the River 2002. *Honours:* Adonais Prize, Spain, Casa de las Américas Prize, Cuba. *Address:* c/o Curbstone Press, 321 Jackson Street, Willimantic, CT 06226-1738, USA. *E-mail:* info@curbstone.org. *Website:* www.curbstone.org.

SOTO, Gary, BA, MFA; American writer and poet; b. 12 April 1952, Fresno, CA; m. Carolyn Sadako Oda 1975, one d. *Education:* California State University at Fresno, University of California at Irvine. *Career:* Asst Prof., 1979–85, Assoc. Prof. of English and Ethnic Studies, 1985–92, Part-time Senior Lecturer in English, 1992–93, University of California at Berkeley; Elliston Prof. of Poetry, University of Cincinnati, 1988; Martin Luther King/ Cesar Chavez/Rosa Park Visiting Prof. of English, Wayne State University, 1990. *Publications:* Poetry: The Elements of San Joaquin, 1977; The Tale of Sunlight, 1978; Where Sparrows Work Hard, 1981; Black Hair, 1985; Who Will Know Us?, 1990; A Fire in My Hands, 1990; Home Course in Religion, 1992; Neighborhood Odes, 1992; Canto Familiar/Familiar Song, 1994; New and Selected Poems, 1995; Fearless Fernie, 2002, One Kind of Faith 2003, World's Apart (children's poetry) 2005. Other: Living Up the Street: Narrative Recollections, 1985; Small Faces, 1986; Lesser Evils: Ten Quartets, 1988; California Childhood: Recollections and Stories of the Golden State (ed.), 1988; A Summer Life, 1990; Baseball in April and Other Stories, 1990; Taking Sides, 1991; Pacific Crossing, 1992; The Skirt, 1992; Pieces of the Heart: New

Chicano Fiction (ed.), 1993; Local News, 1993; The Pool Party, 1993; Crazy Weekend, 1994; Jesse, 1994; Boys at Work, 1995; Chato's Kitchen, 1995; Everyday Seductions (ed.), 1995; Summer on Wheels, 1995; The Old Man and His Door, 1996; Snapshots of the Wedding, 1996; Buried Onions, 1997, Chato and the Party Animals (picture book) 1999; Nickel and Dime (novel), 2000; Poetry Lover (novel), 2001; Jessie De La Cruz: A Profile of a United Farm Worker (young adult biog.), 2002; The Effects of Knut Hamsun on a Fresno Boy (essays), 2002; If the Shoe Fits (picture book), 2002, Cesar Chavez – A Hero for Everyone (children's biography) 2003, Amnesia in a Republican (novel) 2004, The Afterlife (novel) 2004, Help Wanted (short story) 2005, Chato Goes Cruzin' (picture book) 2005; contribs to magazines. *Honours:* Discovery/The Nation Prize, 1975; United States Award, International Poetry Forum, 1976; Bess Hokin Prize for Poetry, 1978; Guggenheim Fellowship, 1979–80; National Endowment for the Arts Fellowships, 1981, 1991; Levinson Award, Poetry Magazine, 1984; American Book Award, Before Columbus Foundation, 1985; California Arts Council Fellowship, 1989; Carnegie Medal, 1993; Tomas Rivera Prize, 1996; Hispanic Heritage Award, 1999; Civil Rights Award, National Education Asscn, 1999. *Address:* 43 The Crescent, Berkeley, CA 94708, USA.

SOUEIF, Ahdaf, BA, MA, PhD, FRSL; Egyptian/British writer; b. 23 March 1950, Cairo; d. of Mustapha Soueif and Fatma Moussa; m. Ian Hamilton 1981 (died 2001); two s. *Education:* Cairo Univ., American Univ. in Cairo, Univ. of Lancaster. *Career:* Assoc. Lecturer, Cairo Univ. 1971–79, Lecturer 1979–84; with Cassel, London and Cairo 1978–84; Assoc. Prof., King Saud Univ. 1987–89; with Al-Furqan Islamic Heritage Foundation, London 1989–; mem. Egyptian-British Soc., Egyptian Writers' Union, PEN Egypt, PEN UK, Council for Advancement of Arab–British Understanding, Amnesty Int.; Patron Palestine Solidarity Campaign. *Publications:* Aisha 1983, In the Eye of the Sun 1992, Sandpiper 1996, The Map of Love 1999, Mezzaterra 2004, I Saw Ramallah (trans.) 2004, I Think of You 2007; contrib. to periodicals. *Honours:* Hon. DLitt (Lancaster) 2004, (London Metropolitan) 2004; Cairo Int. Book Fair Award Best Collection of Short Stories 1996. *Literary Agent:* Wylie Agency, 17 Bedford Square, London, WC1B 3JA, England. *Telephone:* (20) 7908-5900. *Fax:* (20) 7908-5901. *E-mail:* mail@wylieagency.co.uk. *Website:* www.wylieagency.co.uk; www.ahdafsoueif.com.

SOULE, Gardner Bosworth, BA, BSc, MSc; American author; b. 16 Dec. 1913, Paris, TX; m. 1st Janie Lee McDowell 1940 (deceased); m. 2nd Mary Muir Dowhing 1994. *Education:* Rice Univ., Columbia Univ. *Career:* Associated Press, 1936–41; US Naval Reserve, 1942–45; Managing Ed., Better Homes & Gardens, 1945–50. *Publications:* Tomorrow's World of Science, 1963; The Maybe Monsters, 1963; The Mystery Monsters, 1965; Trail of the Abominable Snowman, 1965; The Ocean Adventure, 1966; UFO's and IFO's, 1967; Wide Ocean, 1970; Men Who Dared the Sea, 1976; The Long Trail: How Cowboys and Longhorns Opened the West, 1976; Mystery Monsters of the Deep, 1981; Mystery Creatures of the Jungle, 1982; Antarctica, 1985; Christopher Columbus, 1989. Contributions: Popular Science Monthly; United Features; London Express Syndicate; Boy's Life; Illustrated London News. *Honours:* Navy League commendation 1956.

SOULEZ-LARIVIÈRE, Daniel Joseph; French lawyer and writer; b. 19 March 1942, Angers (Maine-et-Loire); s. of Furcy Soulez-Larivière and Suzanne Soulez-Larivière (née Larivière); m. Mathilde-Mahaut Nobecourt 1988; one s. with Michèle Abbaye. *Education:* Lycée Janson-de-Sailly, Collège Stanislas, Paris, Garden City High School, New York, USA, Faculty of Law, Paris and Institut d'Etudes Politiques, Paris. *Career:* lawyer in Paris 1965–; Chargé de mission, Ministry of Equipment and Housing 1966–67; Second Sec. Conférence du stage 1969; mem. Conseil de l'Ordre 1988–90; mem. Consultative Comm. for the Revision of the Constitution 1992–93; mem. Advisory Bd Centre de prospective de la gendarmerie; Municipal Counsellor for Chambellay 1995–; mem. Soc. of French Jurists. *Publications include:* L'avocature 1982, Les juges dans la balance 1987, La réforme des professions juridiques et judiciaires, vingt propositions 1988, Justice pour la justice 1990, Du cirque médiatico-judiciaire et des moyens d'en sortir 1993, Paroles d'avocat 1994, Grand soir pour la justice 1997, Dans l'engrenage de la justice 1998, Lettres à un jeune avocat 1999, La justice à l'épreuve (with Jean-Marie Coulon) 2002, Notre justice 2002. *Honours:* Chevalier de la Légion d'honneur, Ordre nat. du Mérite. *Address:* 22 avenue de la Grande Armée, 75858 Paris Cedex 17 (office); 6 rue des Fougères, 92140 Clamart (home); le Prieuré, 49220 Chambellay, France (home). *Telephone:* 1-47-63-37-22 (office); 1-45-34-56-50 (home). *Fax:* 1-42-67-83-05 (office); 1-46-26-23-65 (office). *E-mail:* dsl@soulezlariviere.com (office).

SOUSTER, Raymond, (John Holmes), OC; Canadian writer and poet; b. 15 Jan. 1921, Toronto, Ont.; s. of Austin Holmes Souster and Norma Rhodesia; m. Rosalia L. Geralde 1947. *Education:* Univ. of Toronto Schools, Humberside Collegiate Inst., Toronto. *Career:* Founding mem. League of Canadian Poets, Chair. 1968–72, Life mem. 1996–. *Publications:* 100 Poems of 19th Century Canada (ed. with D. Lochhead) 1974, Sights and Sounds (ed. with R. Wollatt) 1974, These Loved, These Hated Lands (ed. with R. Wollatt) 1974, The Poetry of W. W. Campbell (ed.) 1978, The Best-Known Poems of Archibald Lampman (ed.) 1979, Collected Poems of Raymond Souster (eight vols) 1980–93, Powassan's Drum: Selected Poems of Duncan Campbell Scott (ed. with D. Lochhead) 1983, Queen City: Toronto in Poems and Pictures (with Bill Brooks) 1984, Windflower: The Selected Poems of Bliss Carmen (ed. with D. Lochhead) 1986, Riding the Long Black Horse 1993, Old Bank Notes 1993, 23 Poems 1993, No Sad Songs Wanted Here 1995, Close to Home 1997, Of Time and

Toronto 2000, Collected Poems 1940–2000 (ten vols) 1990–2004, Let's All Go to the Ball Game 2001; contribs to magazines. *Honours:* Gov.-Gen.'s Award for Poetry in English 1964, Pres.'s Medal, Univ. of Western Ontario 1967, Centennial Medal 1967, City of Toronto Book Award 1979, Queen's Silver Jubilee Medal 1977, Queen's Golden Jubilee Medal 2002. *Address:* 39 Baby Point Road, Toronto, Ont. M6S 2G2, Canada (home). *Telephone:* (416) 462-4028 (home). *E-mail:* lesgreen@sympatico.ca (home).

SOUTHALL, Ivan Francis, AM, DFC; Australian author; b. 8 June 1921, Melbourne; s. of Francis Southall and Rachel Southall (née Voutier); m. 1st Joyce Blackburn 1945 (divorced); one s. three d.; m. 2nd Susan W. Stanton 1976. *Education:* Box Hill Grammar School. *Career:* RAAF 1942–47; self-employed writer 1947–; Emer. Fellowship, Australia Council 1993. *Exhibition:* State Library of Vic. Retrospective Exhbn, 'Southall A to Z' 1998. *Publications:* more than 60 works translated into 22 languages including They Shall Not Pass Unseen 1956, Softly Tread the Brave 1960, Hills End 1962, Ash Road 1965, To the Wild Sky 1967, The Fox Hole 1967, Let the Balloon Go 1968, Bread and Honey 1970, Josh 1971, Head in the Clouds 1972, Fly West 1974, Matt and Jo 1974, What About Tomorrow 1976, King of the Sticks 1979, The Golden Goose 1981, The Long Night Watch 1983, A City out of Sight 1984, Christmas in the Tree 1985, Rachel 1986, Blackbird 1988, The Mysterious World of Marcus Leadbeater 1990, Ziggurat 1997. *Honours:* Australian Children's Book of the Year Award 1966, 1968, 1971, 1976, Australian Picture Book of the Year Award 1969, Carnegie Medal 1972, Whitall Poetry and Literature Lecturer, Library of Congress 1973, May Hill Arbuthnot Honor Lecturer 1974, Nat. Children's Book Award 1986, The Phoenix Award 2003, Dromkeen Medal 2004. *Address:* PO Box 1698, Healesville, Vic. 3777, Australia.

SOWANDE, Bode, MA, PhD; Nigerian playwright and writer; b. 2 May 1948, Kaduna. *Education:* Univ. of Ife, Univ. of Dakar and Univ. of Sheffield. *Career:* Sr Lecturer, Dept of Theatre Arts, Univ. of Ibadan 1977–90. *Publications:* The Night Before, 1972; Lamps in the Night, 1973; Bar Beach Prelude, 1976; A Sanctus for Women, 1976; Afamoko – the Workhorse, 1978; Farewell to Babylon, 1978; Kalakuta Cross Currents, 1979; The Master and the Frauds, 1979; Barabas and the Master Jesus, 1980; Flamingo, 1982; Circus of Freedom Square, 1985; Tornadoes Full of Dreams, 1989; Arede Owo (after L'Avare by Molière), 1990; Mammy-Water's Wedding, 1991; Ajantala-Pinocchio, 1992. Fiction: Our Man the President, 1981; Without a Home, 1982; The Missing Bridesmaid, 1988. Other: My Life in the Bush of Ghosts (stage adaptation of Amos Tutuola's novel), 1995; radio and television plays. *Honours:* Asscn of Nigerian Authors Drama Award, Pan African Writers Asscn Patron of the Arts Award 1993; Chevalier, Ordre des Arts et des Lettres 1991.

SOWELL, Thomas, BA, MA, PhD; American economist and writer; b. 30 June 1930, Gastonia, NC; m. 1st Alma Jean Parr (divorced); m. 2nd Mary; two c. *Education:* Harvard Univ., Columbia Univ., Univ. of Chicago. *Career:* Economist, US Dept of Labor, 1961–62; Instructor in Economics, Douglass College, Rutgers University, 1962–63; Lecturer in Economics, Howard University, 1963–64; Economic Analyst, AT&T, 1964–65; Asst Prof., Cornell University, 1965–69; Assoc. Prof., Brandeis University, 1969–70; Assoc. Prof., 1970–74, Prof. of Economics, 1974–80, University of California at Los Angeles; Fellow, Center for Advanced Study in the Behavioral Sciences, Stanford, CA, 1976–77; Visiting Prof., Amherst College, 1977; Senior Fellow, 1977, Rose and Milton Friedman Senior Fellow in Public Policy, 1980–, Hoover Institution, Stanford University; mem. American Economic Asscn; National Acad. of Education. *Publications:* Economics: Analysis and Issues, 1971; Black Education: Myths and Tragedies, 1972; Say's Law: An Historical Analysis, 1972; Classical Economics Reconsidered, 1974; Affirmative Action: Was It Necessary in Academia?, 1975; Race and Economics, 1975; Patterns of Black Excellence, 1977; Markets and Minorities, 1981; Pink and Brown People, and Other Controversial Essays, 1981; Knowledge and Decision, 1983; Ethnic America: A History, 1983; The Economics and Politics of Race: An International Perspective, 1983; Compassion versus Guilt, and Other Essays, 1984; Marxism: Philosophy and Economics, 1985; Civil Rights: Rhetoric or Reality?, 1985; Education: Assumptions versus History, 1986; A Conflict of Visions: Ideological Origins of Political Struggles, 1987; Judicial Activism Reconsidered, 1989; Preferential Policies: An International Perspective, 1990; Inside American Education: The Decline, the Deception, the Dogmas, 1992; Race and Culture: A World View, 1992; Is Reality Optional?, and Other Essays, 1993; The Vision of the Anointed: Self-Congratulation as a Basis for Social Policy, 1995; Migrations and Cultures: A World View, 1996; Late-talking Children, 1997; Conquests and Cultures: An International History, 1998; Race, Culture, and Equality, 1998; Barbarians Inside the Gates, and Other Controversial Essays, 1999; The Quest for Cosmic Justice, 1999; A Personal Odyssey, 2000; Basic Economics: A Citizen's Guide to the Economy, 2001; Some Thoughts about Writing, 2001. Contributions: books and newspapers.

SOYINKA, Akinwande Oluwole (Wole), BA; Nigerian playwright, lecturer and academic; *Woodruff Emeritus Professor of the Arts, Emory University;* b. 13 July 1934, Abeokuta; s. of Ayo Soyinka and Eniola Soyinka; m.; four c. *Education:* Univ. of Ibadan, Nigeria and Univ. of Leeds, UK. *Career:* worked at Royal Court Theatre, London; Research Fellow in Drama, Univ. of Ibadan 1960–61; Lecturer in English, Univ. of Ife 1962–63; Sr Lecturer in English, Univ. of Lagos 1965–67; political prisoner 1967–69; Artistic Dir and Head Dept of Theatre Arts, Univ. of Ibadan 1969–72; Research Prof. in Dramatic Literature, Univ. of Ife 1972, Prof. of Comparative Literature and Head of

Dept of Dramatic Arts 1976–85; Goldwin Smith Prof. of Africana Studies and Theatre Cornell Univ. 1988–92; passport seized Sept. 1994, living in France; charged with treason March 1997 in absentia; Ed. Ch'Indaba (fmrly Transition) Accra; Artistic Dir Orisun Theatre, 1960 Masks; Literary Ed. Orisun Acting Editions; Pres. Int. Theatre Inst. 1986–; Fellow, Churchill Coll. Cambridge 1973–74; Woodruff Emeritus Prof. of the Arts, Emory Univ., Atlanta 2004–; mem. American Acad. of Arts and Letters, Int. Theatre Inst., Union of Writers of the African Peoples, Nat. Liberation Council of Nigeria; Fellow, Ghana Asscn of Writers, Pan-African Writers Asscn; Chair. Nigeria Road Safety Comm. 1988–91. *Plays:* The Invention 1955, The Lion and the Jewel 1959, The Swamp Dwellers 1959, A Dance of the Forests 1960, The Trials of Brother Jero 1961, The Strong Breed 1962, The Road 1964, Kongi's Harvest 1965, Madmen and Specialists 1971, Before the Blackout 1971, Jero's Metamorphosis 1973, Camwood on the Leaves 1973, The Bacchae of Euripides 1974, Death and the King's Horsemen 1975, Opera Wonyosi 1978, A Play of Giants 1984, Six Plays 1984, Requiem for a Futurologist 1985, From Zia, with Love 1991, A Scourge of Hyacinths (radio play) 1992, The Beatification of Area Boy 1995, King Baabu 2003. *Publications:* novels: The Interpreters 1964, The Forest of a Thousand Daemons (trans.), Season of Anomy 1973; poetry: Idanre and Other Poems 1967, Poems from Prison 1969, A Shuttle in the Crypt 1972, Poems of Black Africa (ed.) 1975, Ogun Abibman 1977, Mandela's Earth and Other Poems 1988, Samarkand and Other Markets I Have Known 2002; non-fiction: The Man Died (prison memoirs) 1972, Myth, Literature and the African World (lectures) 1972, Aké, The Years of Childhood (autobiog.) 1982, Art, Dialogue and Outrage 1988, Isara: A Voyage Round Essay 1990, Continuity and Amnesia 1991, Ibadan: The Pentelemes Years (memoir) 1994, The Open Sore of a Continent, A Personal Narrative of the Nigerian Crisis 1996, The Burden of Memory, The Muse of Forgiveness 1999, Conversations with Wole Soyinka 2001, You Must Set Forth at Dawn: A Memoir 2006. *Honours:* Commdr Légion d'honneur, Commdr Fed. Repub. of Nigeria 1986, Commdr Order of Merit (Italy) 1990; Hon. DLitt (Leeds) 1973, (Yale) 1981, (Morehouse), (Paul Valéry), (Bayreuth), (Ibadan), (Harvard); Hon. DScS (Edin.) 1977; Rockefeller Foundation Grant 1960, John Whiting Drama Prize 1966, Prisoner of Conscience Award, Amnesty Int., Jock Campbell-New Statesman Literary Award 1969, Nobel Prize for Literature 1986, George Benson Medal, RSL 1990, Writers Guild Lifetime Achievement Award 1996, Distinguished Scholar-in-Residence, New York Univ. 1999 and numerous other awards. *Literary Agent:* c/o Deborah Rogers, Rogers, Coleridge & White, 20 Powis Mews, London, W11 1JN, England. *E-mail:* deborahr@rcwlitagency.demon.co.uk. *Address:* c/o PO Box 935, Abeokuta, Ogun State, Nigeria.

SPACKS, Patricia Meyer, BA, MA, PhD; American academic; b. 17 Nov. 1929, San Francisco, CA; one d. *Education:* Rollins College, Yale University, University of California at Berkeley. *Career:* Instructor in English, Indiana University, 1954–56; Instructor in Humanities, University of Florida, 1958–59; Instructor, 1959–61, Asst Prof., 1961–63, Assoc. Prof., 1965–68, Prof. of English, 1968–79, Wellesley College; Prof. of English, 1979–89, Chair., Dept of English, 1985–88, Yale University; Edgar F. Shannon Prof. of English, 1989–, Chair., Dept of English, 1991–96, University of Virginia; mem. MLA, pres., 1994; American Philosophical Society, 1995; ACLS, chair of board, 1997–. *Publications:* The Varied God, 1959; The Insistence of Horror, 1962; 18th Century Poetry (ed.), 1964; John Gay, 1965; Poetry of Vision, 1967; Late Augustan Prose (ed.), 1971; An Argument of Images, 1971; Late Augustan Poetry (ed.), 1973; The Female Imagination, 1975; Imagining a Self, 1976; Contemporary Women Novelists, 1977; The Adolescent Idea, 1981; Gossip, 1985; Desire and Truth, 1990; Boredom: The Literary History of a State of Mind, 1995. *Honours:* American Acad. of Arts and Sciences, 1994.

SPALDING, Esta; American poet and screenwriter; b. Boston, MA. *Career:* based in Vancouver, BC, Canada. *Writing for television:* Da Vinci's Inquest (CBC-TV) 1998–, The Zack Files (Decode Entertainment) 2000, The Eleventh Hour (also story ed., CTV Network) 2002–04. *Film screenplays:* The Republic of Love 2003, Fallen Angels 2003. *Publications:* poetry: Carrying Place 1995, Mere (with Linda Spalding) 2001, Anchoress 2003, The Wife's Account 2004, Lost August 2004. *Address:* c/o Bloodaxe Books Ltd, Highgreen, Tarset, Northumberland NE48 1RP, England. *Website:* www.bloodaxebooks.com.

SPALDING, Frances, CBE, PhD, FRSL; British art historian, critic and writer; *Reader in Art History, University of Newcastle*; b. 16 May 1950, Woldingham, Surrey; d. of Hedley Stinston Crabtree and Margaret Holiday; m. Julian Spalding 1974 (divorced 1991); one s. *Education:* Farringtons School, Kent and Univ. of Nottingham. *Career:* Lecturer Sheffield Polytechnic 1978–88; art historian, critic and biographer (freelance 1989–99), Univ. of Newcastle upon Tyne 2000–; Paul Mellon Sr Research Fellow and Visiting Research Fellow Newnham Coll., Cambridge 2005–06. *Publications include:* Roger Fry: Art and Life 1983, Vanessa Bell 1983, British Art Since 1900 1986, Stevie Smith: A Critical Biography 1988, A Dictionary of Twentieth Century British Painters and Sculpture 1990, Dance Till the Stars Come Down: A Biography of John Minton 1991, Duncan Grant: A Biography 1997, The Tate: A History 1998, Gwen Raverat: Friends, Family & Affections 2001, John Piper in the 1930s – Abstraction on the Beach (with David Fraser Jenkins) 2003, The Bloomsbury Group 2005. *Honours:* Hon. Fellow RCA . *Literary Agent:* Coleridge, Rogers and White, 20 Powis Mews, London, W11 1JN, England. *Telephone:* (20) 7221-3717 (office).

SPARKS, Nicholas; American writer; b. 31 Dec. 1965, Omaha, NE; m. Cathy Cote 1989; three s. two d. *Education:* Univ. of Notre Dame. *Publications:* The Notebook 1996, Message in a Bottle 1998, A Walk to Remember 1999, The Rescue 2000, A Bend in the Road 2001, Nights in Rodanthe 2002, The Guardian 2003, The Wedding 2003, Three Weeks With My Brother (non-fiction) 2004, True Believer 2005, At First Sight 2005, Dear John 2006. *Website:* www.nicholassparks.com.

SPARSHOTT, Francis Edward, BA, MA, FRSC; British philosopher, writer, poet and academic (retd); b. 19 May 1926, Chatham, Kent; m. Kathleen Elizabeth Vaughan 1953; one d. *Education:* Corpus Christi Coll., Oxford. *Career:* Lecturer in Philosophy, Univ. of Toronto 1950–55, Asst Prof. 1955–62, Assoc. Prof. 1962–64, Prof. 1964–91, Univ. Prof. 1982–91, of Philosophy, Victoria Coll., Univ. of Toronto 1964–91; mem. American Society for Aesthetics (Pres. 1981–82), Canadian Classical Asscn, Canadian Philosophical Asscn (Pres. 1975–76), League of Canadian Poets (Pres. 1977–78), PEN International, Canadian Centre. *Publications:* An Enquiry into Goodness and Related Concepts, 1958; The Structure of Aesthetics, 1963; The Concept of Criticism: An Essay, 1967; Looking for Philosophy, 1972; The Theory of the Arts, 1982; Off the Ground: First Steps in the Philosophy of Dance, 1988; Taking Life Seriously: A Study of the Argument of the Nicomachean Ethics, 1994; A Measured Pace: Toward a Philosophical Understanding of the Arts of Dance, 1995; The Future of Aesthetics, 1998. Poetry: A Divided Voice, 1965; A Cardboard Garage, 1969; The Rainy Hills: Verses After a Japanese Fashion, 1979; The Naming of the Beasts, 1979; New Fingers for Old Dikes, 1980; The Cave of Trophonius and Other Poems, 1983; The Hanging Gardens of Etobicoke, 1983; Storms and Screens, 1986; Sculling to Byzantium, 1989; Views from the Zucchini Gazebo, 1994; Home from the Air, 1997; The City Dwellers, 2000, Scoring in Injury Time 2006; contrib. to various books and periodicals. *Honours:* Hon. DLittSac, (Victoria Univ.) 2000; Hon. LLD (Univ. of Toronto) 2000; ACLS Fellowship, 1961–62; Canada Council Fellowship, 1970–71; Killam Research Fellowship, 1977–78; First Prize for Poetry, CBC Radio Literary Competition, 1981; Centennial Medal, Royal Society of Canada, 1982; Connaught Senior Fellowship in the Humanities, 1984–85;. *Address:* 50 Crescentwood Road, Scarborough, Ont. M1N 1E4, Canada.

SPENCE, Alan; British dramatist, writer and poet; b. 5 Dec. 1947, Glasgow, Scotland; m. *Education:* Univ. of Glasgow. *Career:* writer-in-residence, Univ. of Glasgow 1975–77, Traverse Theatre, Edinburgh 1982, Univ. of Edinburgh 1989–92, Univ. of Aberdeen 1996–. *Plays:* Sailmaker 1982, Space Invaders 1983, Changed Days 1991. *Publications:* fiction: It's Colours They Are Fine (short stories) 1977, The Magic Flute (novel) 1990, Stone Garden (short stories) (Scottish Writer of the Year) 1995, The Pure Land 2006; poetry: Plop (15 Haiku) 1970, Glasgow Zen 1981, Seasons of the Heart 2000, Clear Light 2005. *Honours:* Scottish Arts Council Book Awards 1977, 1990, 1996, People's Prize 1996, TMA Martini Prize 1996. *Address:* c/o Canongate Books, 14 High Street, Edinburgh, EH1 1TE, Scotland.

SPENCE, Jonathan Dermot, PhD, CMG; American historian, academic and writer; *Sterling Professor of History, Yale University*; b. 11 Aug. 1936, Surrey, England; s. of Dermot Spence and Muriel Crailsham; m. 1st Helen Alexander 1962 (divorced 1993); two s.; m. 2nd Chin Annping 1993. *Education:* Univ. of Cambridge, UK and Yale Univ. *Career:* Asst Prof. of History, Yale Univ. 1966–71, Prof. 1971–, now Sterling Prof. of History; Visiting Prof. Univ. of Beijing 1987; Pres. American Historial Asscn 2004–[05]; mem. Bd of Govs Yale Univ. Press 1988–; mem. American Acad. of Arts and Sciences, American Philosophical Soc.; Guggenheim Fellow 1979–80; MacArthur Fellow 1987–92. *Publications:* Ts'Ao Yin and The K'Ang-Hsi Emperor 1966, To Change China 1969, Emperor of China 1974, The Death of Woman Wang 1978, The Gate of Heavenly Peace 1981, The Memory Palace of Matteo Ricci 1984, The Question of Hu 1988, The Search for Modern China 1990, Chinese Roundabout 1992, God's Chinese Son 1996, The Chan's Great Continent 1998, Mao Zedong 1999. *Honours:* Hon. LHD (Knox Coll.) 1984, (New Haven) 1989; Hon. LittD (Wheeling Coll.) 1985, (Chinese Univ. of Hong Kong) 1996, (Gettysburg) Coll. 1996, (Union Coll.) 2000, (Beloit Coll.) 2000, (Conn. Coll.) 2000; William C. DeVane Medal, Yale Chapter of Phi Beta Kappa 1978, Los Angeles Times History Prize 1982, Vursell Prize, American Acad. and Inst. of Arts and Letters 1983, Comisso Prize (Italy) 1987; Gelber Literary Prize (Canada) 1991. *Address:* Department of History, Yale University, P.O. Box 208324, New Haven, CT 06520 (office); 691 Forest Road, New Haven, CT 06515, USA (home). *Telephone:* (203) 432-1333 (office). *E-mail:* jonathan.spence@yale.edu (office). *Website:* www.yale.edu/history/faculty/spence.html (office).

SPENCE, William (Bill) John Duncan, (Jessica Blair, Jim Bowden, Kirk Ford, Floyd Rogers); British author; b. 20 April 1923, Middlesborough, England; m. Joan Mary Rhoda Ludley 1944, one s. three d. *Education:* St Mary's Teachers Training College. *Career:* mem. Society of Authors, Romantic Novelists' Asscn. *Publications:* numerous books, including: Romantic Ryedale (with Joan Spence), 1977; Harpooned, 1981; The Medieval Monasteries of Yorkshire (with Joan Spence), 1981; Stories from Yorkshire Monasteries (with Joan Spence), 1992; novels, as Jessica Blair: The Red Shawl, 1993; A Distant Harbour, 1993; Storm Bay, 1994; The Restless Spirit, 1996; The Other Side of the River, 1997; The Seaweed Gatherers, 1998; Portrait of Charlotte, 1999; The Locket, 2000; The Long Way Home, 2001; The Restless Heart, 2001; Time and Tide, 2002; Echoes of the Past, 2003, Secrets of the Sea 2004, Yesterday's Dreams 2005, Reach for Tomorrow 2006, Dangerous Shores 2007; other: 36 Westerns, three war novels.

SPENCER, Elizabeth, AB, MA; American writer; b. 19 July 1921, Carollton, Miss.; d. of James L. Spencer and Mary James McCain; m. John A. B. Rusher

1956 (died 1998). *Education:* Belhaven Coll. and Vanderbilt Univ. *Career:* writer-in-residence, Univ. of N Carolina 1969, Hollins Coll. 1973, Concordia Univ. 1977–78, Adjunct Prof. 1981–86; Visiting Prof. Univ. of NC, Chapel Hill 1986–92; Vice-Chancellor Fellowship of Southern Writers 1993–97; mem. American Acad. of Arts and Letters; Guggenheim Foundation Fellow 1953. *Publications:* Fire in the Morning 1948, This Crooked Way 1952, The Voice at the Back Door 1956, The Light in the Piazza 1960, Knights and Dragons 1965, No Place for an Angel 1967, Ship Island and Other Stories 1968, The Snare 1972, The Stories of Elizabeth Spencer 1981, Marilee 1981, The Salt Line 1984, Jack of Diamonds and Other Stories 1988, For Lease or Sale (play) 1989, On the Gulf 1991, The Night Travellers 1991, Landscapes of the Heart (memoir) 1998, The Southern Woman: New and Selected Fiction 2000; contrib. short stories in magazines and collections. *Honours:* Hon. LittD (Southwestern Univ., Memphis) 1968, (Concordia Univ.) 1987, (Univ. of the South) 1992, (Univ. of NC) 1998, (Belhaven Coll.) 1999; Rosenthal Foundation Award, American Acad. of Arts and Letters 1957; McGraw-Hill Fiction Award 1960, Award of Merit for short story, American Acad. of Arts and Letters 1983, Salem Award for Literature 1992, Dos Passos Award for Fiction 1992, NC Gov.'s Award for Literature 1994, Fortner Award for Literature 1998, Mississippi State Library Asscn Award for Non-fiction 1999, Thomas Wolfe Award, Univ. of NC 2002, NC Hall of Fame 2002, William Faulkner Award for Literary Excellence 2002. *Address:* 402 Longleaf Drive, Chapel Hill, NC 27517, USA (home). *Telephone:* (919) 929-2115 (home). *E-mail:* elizabeth0222@earthlink.net (home). *Website:* www.elizabethspencerwriter.com.

SPENCER, LaVyrle; American writer; b. 17 Aug. 1943, Browerville, MN; m. Daniel F. Spencer 1962, two d. *Education:* High School, Staples, MN. *Publications:* The Fulfillment, 1979; The Endearment, 1982; Hummingbird, 1983; Twice Loved, 1984; Sweet Memories, 1984; A Heart Speaks, 1986; Tears, 1986; Years, 1986; The Gamble, 1987; Separate Bed, 1987; Vows, 1988; Morning Glory, 1988; Bitter Sweet, 1990; Forgiving, 1991; November of the Heart, 1992; Bygones, 1993; Family Blessings, 1994; That Camden Summer, 1996. *Honours:* Romance Writers of America Historical Romance of the Year Awards 1983, 1984, 1985.

SPENCER, Paul, BLitt, MA, DPhil; British social anthropologist and academic; b. 25 March 1932, London; m. Diane Wells; two s. *Education:* Christ's Coll., Cambridge, Wadham Coll., Oxford. *Career:* scientific officer, Tavistock Inst. of Human Relations, London 1962–71; teacher, SOAS, London 1971–97, Hon. Dir Int. African Inst. 1996–2005. *Publications:* The Samburu 1965, Nomads in Alliance 1973, Society and the Dance 1985, The Maasai of Matapato 1988, Anthropology and the Riddle of the Sphinx 1990, The Pastoral Continuum 1998, Time, Space and the Unknown: Maasai Configurations of Power and Providence 2003. *Telephone:* (20) 7898-4420 (office). *Fax:* (20) 7898-4419 (office). *E-mail:* paul.spencer100@virgin.net (home). *Website:* www.iaionthe.net (office).

SPIEGELMAN, Art; American cartoonist, editor and writer; b. 15 Feb. 1948, Stockholm, Sweden; m. Françoise Mouly 1977; two c. *Education:* High School of Art and Design, Manhattan and Harpur Coll., Binghamton, NY. *Career:* creative consultant, artist, designer, ed. and writer, Topps Chewing Gum Inc, New York 1965–87; Ed., Douglas Comix 1972; instructor, San Francisco Acad. of Art 1974–75, New York School of the Visual Arts 1979–86; Contributing Ed., Arcade, The Comics Revue 1975–76; founder-Ed., Raw comics magazine 1980–; staff artist and contributing ed., The New Yorker 1993–2003; Ed., Little Lit series of children's comics anthologies. *Publications as author and illustrator:* The Complete Mr Infinity 1970, The Viper Vicar of Vice, Villainy, and Vickedness 1972, Ace Hole, Midge Detective 1974, The Language of Comics 1974, Breakdowns: From Maus to Now: An Anthology of Strips 1977, Work and Turn 1979, Every Day Has Its Dog 1979, Two-Fisted Painters Action Adventure 1980, Maus: A Survivor's Tale (Pulitzer Prize Special Citation 1992) 1986, Read Yourself Raw (with F. Mouly) 1987, Maus II 1992, The Wild Party (illustrations to book by Joseph Moncure March) 1994, Open Me... I'm a Dog 1997, Jack Cole and Plastic Man: Forms Stretched to Their Limits 2001, In the Shadow of No Towers 2004. *Honours:* Playboy Editorial Award for Best Comic Strip 1982, Joel M. Cavior Award for Jewish Writing 1986, Stripschappening Award for Best Foreign Comics Album 1987, Guggenheim Fellowship 1990, Alpha Art Award, Angoulerne, France 1993. *Literary Agent:* Steven Barclay Agency, 12 Western Avenue, Petaluma, CA 94952, USA. *Telephone:* (707) 773-0654. *Fax:* (707) 778-1868. *Website:* www.barclayagency.com.

SPONG, Rt Rev. John Shelby, AB, MDiv; American ecclesiastic and writer; b. 16 June 1931, Charlotte, NC; s. of John Shelby Spong and Doolie Griffith Spong; m. 1st Joan Lydia Ketner 1952 (died 1988); three d.; m. 2nd Christine Mary Bridger 1990. *Education:* Univ. of North Carolina, Chapel Hill, Virginia Theological Seminary, Alexandria, Va. *Career:* Rector St Joseph's, Durham, NC 1955–57, Calvary Church, Tarboro, NC 1957–65, St John's Church, Lynchburg, Va 1965–69, St Paul's Church, Richmond, Va 1969–76, Bishop, Diocese of Newark, NJ 1976–2000; Pres. NJ Council of Churches; Quatercentenary Fellow, Emmanuel Coll. Cambridge, UK 1992; William Belden Noble Lecturer, Harvard Univ. 2000; Visiting Lecturer, Univ. of The Pacific, Stockton, Calif. 2003; Faculty, Grad. Theological Union, Berkeley, Calif.; columnist for Beliefnet.com 1999–2000, AgoraMedia 2002–, Waterfront Media 2002–; has appeared on all major talk shows in USA, subject of major story by 60 Minutes (CBS), extensive TV appearances in Canada, UK and Australia. *Radio:* Play by Play sportscaster in Tarboro NC and Lynchburg, Va 1960–65.

Publications: Honest Prayer 1973, This Hebrew Lord 1974, 1988, Dialogue: In Search of Jewish-Christian Understanding 1975, Christpower 1975, Life Approaches Death: A Dialogue on Medical Ethics 1976, The Living Commandments 1977, The Easter Moment 1980, Into the Whirlwind 1983, Beyond Moralism 1986, Consciousness and Survival 1987, Living in Sin? 1988, Rescuing the Bible from Fundamentalism 1991, Born of a Woman – A Bishop Rethinks the Virgin Birth and the Place of Women in a Male-Dominated Church 1992, Resurrection: Myth or Reality? 1994, Liberating the Gospels: Reading the Bible with Jewish Eyes 1996, Why Christianity Must Change or Die: A Bishop Speaks to Believers in Exile 1998, Here I Stand: My Struggle for a Christianity of Integrity, Love and Equality 2000, The Bishop's Voice 1999, A New Christianity for a New World 2001, Crossroads – The Sins of Scripture 2005. *Honours:* Hon. DD (Va Theological Seminary), (St Paul's Coll.); Hon. DHL (Muhlenberg Coll.), (Holmes Inst., Chicago) 2004; Quatercentenary Scholar, Emmanuel Coll., Cambridge, UK 1992, David Frederick Strauss Award, Jesus Seminar 1999, Humanist of the Year, New York City 1999, John A. T, Robinson Award 2004. *Literary Agent:* c/o Julie Rae Mitchell, HarperSanFrancisco, 353 Sacramento Street, Suite 500, San Francisco, CA, 94111, USA. *Address:* 24 Puddingstone Road, Morris Plains, NJ 07950, USA (home). *Fax:* (973) 540-9584 (home). *Telephone:* (973) 538-9825 (home). *E-mail:* johnsspong@aol.com (home); cmsctm@aol.com (home). *Website:* www.johnshelbyspong.com (home).

SPOONER, David Eugene, BA, PhD; British writer, poet and naturalist; b. 1 Sept. 1941, West Kirby, Wirral; m. Marion O'Neil 1986; one d. *Education:* Univs of Leeds, Manchester and Bristol. *Career:* Lecturer, Univ. of Kent 1968–73, Manchester Polytechnic 1974–75; Visiting Prof., Pennsylvania State Univ. 1973–74; Head of Publishing, Borderline Press 1976–85; ind. scholar 1986–; Dir Butterfly Conservation, East Scotland; mem. Welsh Acad. Assoc., Asscn Benjamin Constant, Academic Bd London Diplomatic Acad., Thoreau Soc., Nabokov Soc.; est. David Eugene Spooner Foundation Awards for Entomology with Philosophy. *Publications:* Unmakings 1977, The Angelic Fly: The Butterfly in Art 1992, The Metaphysics of Insect Life 1995, Insect into Poem: 20th Century Hispanic Poetry 1999, Creatures of Air: Poetry 1976–2001 2001, Thoreau's Insects 2002, William Blake and Contemporary Science 2004, The Insect-Populated Mind – How Insects Have Influenced the Evolution of Consciousness 2005; contrib. to Iron, Interactions, Tandem, Weighbauk, Revue de Littérature Comparée, Bestia (Fable Society of America), Margin, Corbie Press, Butterfly Conservation News, Butterfly News, Field Studies, Annales Benjamin Constant. *Honours:* American Medal of Honor for Natural History 2004, American Hall of Fame 2005, listed in Great Minds of the 21st Century 2005, Congressional Medal for Literature. *Address:* 96 Halbeath Road, Dunfermline, Fife, KY12 7LR, Scotland. *Telephone:* (1383) 729251. *E-mail:* doctorspooner@tiscali.co.uk. *Website:* www.davidspooner.org; www.davidspooner.freeservers.com.

SPRIGEL, Oliver (see Avice, Claude Pierre Marie)

SPRIGGE, Timothy Lauro Squire, PhD, FRSE; British academic; *Professor Emeritus of Logic and Metaphysics, University of Edinburgh*; b. 14 Jan. 1932, London; s. of Cecil Sprigge and Katriona Sprigge; m. Giglia Gordon 1959; one s. two d. *Education:* Gonville and Caius Coll. Cambridge. *Career:* Lecturer in Philosophy, Univ. Coll. London 1961–63, Univ. of Sussex 1963–70, Reader in Philosophy 1970–79; Prof. of Logic and Metaphysics, Univ. of Edin. 1979–89, Prof. Emer. 1989–, Endowment Fellow 1989–98, Hon. Fellow 1998–2003. *Publications:* Correspondence of Jeremy Bentham, Vols 1 and 2 (ed.) 1968, Facts, Words and Beliefs 1968, Santayana: An Examination of his Philosophy 1974, The Vindication of Absolute Idealism 1983, Theories of Existence 1984, The Rational Foundations of Ethics 1987, James and Bradley: American Truth and British Reality 1993, The God of Metaphysics 2006. *Address:* 'Saffrons', 5 King Henry's Road, Lewes, East Sussex, BN7 1BT, England (home). *Telephone:* (1273) 487541 (home). *E-mail:* lauro@squire1.demon.co.uk (home).

SPRINGER, Nancy, BA; American writer and poet; b. 5 July 1948, Montclair, NJ; m. Joel H. Springer 1969 (divorced 1997); one s. one d. *Education:* Gettysburg Coll. *Career:* personal development plan instructor, University of Pittsburgh, 1983–85; Leisure Learning Instructor, York College, Pennsylvania, 1986–91; Education Instructor, Franklin and Marshall College, 1988–; Instructor of Creative Writing, York College of PA, 1997–1999; Writing Popular Fiction Masters' Degree Program, Seton Hill College, 1998–; mem. Society of Children's Book Writers and Illustrators; Pennwriters, pres., 1992–93. *Publications:* The Sable Moon, 1981; The Black Beast, 1982; The Golden Swan, 1983; Wings of Flame, 1985; Chains of Gold, 1986; A Horse to Love (children's), 1987; Madbond, 1987; Chance and Other Gestures of the Hand of Fate, 1987; The Hex Witch of Seldom, 1988; Not on a White Horse (children's), 1988; Apocalypse, 1989; They're All Named Wildfire (children's), 1989; Red Wizard (children's), 1990; Colt (children's), 1991; The Friendship Song (children's), 1992; The Great Pony Hassle (children's), 1993; Stardark Songs (poems), 1993; Larque on the Wing, 1994; The Boy on a Black Horse (children's), 1994; Metal Angel, 1994; Music of Their Hooves (children's poems), 1994; Toughing It, 1994; Looking for Jamie Bridger (children's), 1995; Fair Peril, 1996; Secret Star (children's), 1997; I Am Mordred, 1998; Sky Rider (children's), 1999; Plumage, 2000; I Am Morgan Le Fay, 2001; Rowan Hood: Outlaw Girl of Sherwood Forest (children's), 2001; Separate Sisters (children's), 2001; Lionclaw: A Tale of Rowan Hood (children's), 2002. Contributions: Magazines and journals. *Honours:* Distinguished Alumna, Gettysburg College, 1987; International Reading Asscn Children's Choice,

1988; Joan Fassler Memorial Book Award, 1992; International Reading Asscn Young Adult's Choice, 1993; Edgar Allan Poe Awards, MWA, 1995, 1996; James Tiptree Jr Award, 1995; Carolyn W. Field Award, 1995; Outstanding Pennsylvania Writer Award. *Literary Agent:* Jean V. Naggar Literary Agency, 216 E 75th Street, New York, NY 10021, USA.

SPRINKLE, Patricia Houck, AB; American writer; b. 13 Nov. 1943, Bluefield, WV; m. Robert William Sprinkle 1970, two s. *Education:* Vassar College. *Career:* mem. MWA, Penwoman, Sisters in Crime (publicity chair.). *Publications:* Fiction: Murder at Markham, 1988; Murder in the Charleston Manner, 1990; Murder on Peachtree Street, 1991; Somebody's Dead in Snellville, 1992; Death of a Dunwoody Matron, 1993; A Mystery Bred in Buckhead, 1994; Deadly Secrets on the St Johns, 1995; When Did We Lose Harriet?, 1997; But Why Shoot the Magistrate?, 1998; The Remember Box, 2000; Carley's Song, 2001. Non-Fiction: Hunger: Understanding the Crisis Through Games, 1980; In God's Image: Meditations for the New Mother, 1988; Housewarmings: For Those Who Make a House a Home, 1992; Women Who Do Too Much: Stress and the Myth of the Superwoman, 1992; Children Who Do Too Little, 1993; A Gift From God, 1994; Women Home Alone: Learning to Thrive, 1996. Contributions: Magazines.

SPROTT, Duncan; British writer; b. 2 Dec. 1952, Ongar, Essex, England. *Education:* Univ. of St Andrews, Fife, Scotland and Heatherley School of Art, London. *Career:* mem. PEN, Soc. of Authors, Egypt Exploration Soc., Soc. of Antiquaries of Scotland, Soc. of Genealogists, Guild of One-Name Studies, Soc. for the Promotion of Hellenic Studies, Soc. for the Promotion of Roman Studies. *Publications:* 1784 (compiler) 1984, The Clopton Hercules (aka The Rise of Mr Warde) 1991, Our Lady of the Potatoes 1995, Sprottichronicon (genealogy) 2000, The Ptolemies: Book 1, The House of the Eagle 2004, Book 2, Daughter of the Crocodile 2006. *Honours:* Arts Council Literature Award 1995. *Literary Agent:* c/o Rogers, Coleridge & White Ltd, 20 Powis Mews, London, W11 1JN, England. *Telephone:* (20) 7221-3717. *Fax:* (20) 7229-9084. *E-mail:* duncansprott@mac.com.

SPUFFORD, Francis; British journalist and writer; b. 1964. *Publications:* I May Be Some Time: Ice and the English Imagination (Writers' Guild Award for Best Non-Fiction Book 1996, Somerset Maugham Award) 1996, Cultural Babbage (ed., essay collection) 1997, The Child that Books Built 2002, Backroom Boys 2003; contrib. to Granta. *Honours:* Sunday Times Young Writer of the Year 1977. *Address:* c/o Faber and Faber Ltd, 3 Queen Square, London, WC1N 3AU, England.

SPURLING, (Susan) Hilary, CBE, BA; British biographer and literary critic; b. 25 Dec. 1940, d. of Gilbert Alexander Forrest and Emily Maureen Forrest (née Armstrong); m. John Spurling 1961; two s. one d. *Education:* Somerville Coll., Oxford. *Career:* theatre critic, The Spectator 1964–69, Literary Ed. 1966–70; book reviewer, The Observer 1969–86, Daily Telegraph 1986–. *Publications:* Ivy When Young: The Early Life of I. Compton-Burnett 1884–1919 1974, Handbook to Anthony Powell's Music of Time 1977, Secrets of A Woman's Heart: The Later Life of I. Compton-Burnett 1920–69 (Duff Cooper Prize 1984, Heinemann Award 1984) 1984, Elinor Fettiplace's Receipt Book 1986, Paul Scott: A Life 1990, Paper Spirits 1992, The Unknown Matisse: 1869–1908 1998, La Grande Thérèse 1999, The Girl From the Fiction Department: A Portrait of Sonia Orwell 2002, Matisse the Master: 1909–1954 (Whitbread Biog. of the Year, Whitbread Book of the Year) 2005. *Honours:* Rose Mary Crawshaw Prize 1974, Heywood Hill Literary Prize for General Achievement 2003. *Literary Agent:* David Higham Associates, 5–8 Lower John Street, Golden Square, London, W1R 4HA, England. *Telephone:* (20) 7437-7888.

SPURLING, John Antony, BA; British dramatist, novelist and art critic; b. 17 July 1936, Kisumu, Kenya; s. of Antony Cuthbert Spurling and Elizabeth Frances Spurling (née Stobart); m. Hilary Forrest 4 April 1961; two s. one d. *Education:* St John's Coll., Oxford. *Career:* Nat. Service with RA 1955–57; Plebiscite Officer, Southern Cameroon 1960–61; Announcer, BBC Radio 1963–66; freelance writer 1966–; Art Critic, New Statesman 1976–88. *Plays:* MacRune's Guevara (as realised by Edward Hotel), In the Heart of the British Museum, Coming Ashore in Guadeloupe, The British Empire trilogy, The Butcher of Baghdad, Heresy. *Publications:* plays: MacRune's Guevara 1969, In the Heart of the British Museum 1971, Shades of Heathcliff and Death of Captain Doughty 1975, The British Empire Part One 1982; fiction: The Ragged End 1989, After Zenda 1995; other: Beckett: A Study of His Plays (with John Fletcher) 1972, revised third edn as Beckett, the Playwright 1985, Graham Greene 1983; contrib. to books, newspapers, periodicals, theatre (17 plays produced, 1969–2004), radio (10 plays, 1976–2002) and television (4 plays, 1970–73). *Honours:* Henfield Writing Fellowship, Univ. of East Anglia 1973. *Address:* c/o Macnaughton Lord 2000 Ltd, 19 Margravine Gardens, London, W6 8RL, England. *Telephone:* (20) 8741-0606 (office). *Fax:* (20) 8741-7443 (office). *E-mail:* info@ml2000.org.uk (office). *Website:* www.ml2000.org.uk.

STABENOW, Dana, BA, MFA; American writer; b. 27 March 1952, Anchorage, AK. *Education:* Univ. of Alaska. *Publications:* Second Star, 1991; A Handful of Stars, 1991; A Cold Day for Murder, 1992; Dead in the Water, 1993; A Fatal Thaw, 1993; A Cold-Blooded Business, 1994; Red Planet Run, 1995; Play with Fire, 1995; Blood Will Tell, 1996; Breakup, 1997; Killing Grounds, 1998; Fire and Ice, 1998; Hunter's Moon, 1999; Out for Blood, 1999; So Sure of Death, 1999; Midnight Come Again, 2000; Nothing Gold Can Stay, 2000; The Singing of the Dead, 2001; A Fine and Bitter Snow, 2002. *Honours:*

MWA Edgar Allan Poe Award 1992. *Literary Agent:* Richard Henshaw Group, 22 West 23rd Street, Fifth Floor, New York, NY 10010, USA. *E-mail:* rhgagents@aol.com. *Website:* www.stabenow.com.

STAFFORD, David Alexander Tetlow, BA, PhD; British historian and writer; b. 10 March 1942, Newcastle upon Tyne, England; m. *Education:* University of Cambridge, University of London. *Career:* Third Sec., 1967–68, Second Sec., 1968, British Foreign Office, London; Research Assoc., Centre of International Studies, LSE, 1968–70; Asst Prof., 1970–76, Assoc. Prof., 1976–82, Prof. of History, 1982–84, University of Victoria, BC; Senior Assoc. Mem., St Antony's College, Oxford, 1976–77; Dir of Studies, 1985–86, Exec. Dir, 1986–92, Canadian Institute of International Affairs, Toronto; Visiting Prof., Institute for Advanced Studies in the Humanities, 1992–2000, Project Dir, Center for Second World War Studies, 2000–, University of Edinburgh. *Publications:* From Anarchism to Reformism: A Study of the Political Activities of Paul Brousse, 1870–90, 1971; Britain and European Resistance, 1940–1945: A Survey of the Special Operations Executive, with Documents, 1980; Camp X: Canada's School for Secret Agents, 1941–1945, 1986; The Silent Game: The Real World of Imaginary Spies, 1988; Spy Wars: Espionage and Canada: From Gouzenko to Glasnost, 1990; Security and Intelligence in a Changing World: New Perspectives for the 1990s (ed. with A. Stuart Farson and Wesley K. Ward), 1991; Churchill and Secret Service, 1998; American-British-Canadian Intelligence Relations, 1939–2000, 2000; Secret Agent: The True Story of the Special Operations Executive, 2000; Roosevelt and Churchill: Men of Secrets, 2000; Spies Beneath Berlin, 2000; Ten Days to D-Day, 2003. Contributions: scholarly journals and general periodicals. *Address:* c/o Centre for Second World War Studies, University of Edinburgh, Edinburgh EH8 9LN, Scotland. *E-mail:* david.stafford@ed.ac.uk.

STAINES, David, BA, AM, PhD; Canadian academic, writer, translator and editor; *Professor of English, University of Ottawa;* b. 8 Aug. 1946, Toronto, Ont. *Education:* Univ. of Toronto, Harvard Univ. *Career:* Asst Prof. of English, Harvard Univ. 1973–78; Hon. Research Fellow, Univ. Coll. London 1977–78; Assoc. Prof., Univ. of Ottawa 1978–85, Prof. of English 1985–, Dean Faculty of Arts 1996–2003; Five Coll. Prof. of Canadian Studies, Smith Coll. 1982–84. *Publications:* The Canadian Imagination: Dimensions of a Literary Culture (ed.) 1977, Tennyson's Camelot: The Idylls of the King and its Medieval Sources 1982, Stephen Leacock: A Reappraisal (ed.) 1986, The Forty-Ninth and Other Parallels: Contemporary Canadian Perspectives (ed.) 1986, The Complete Romances of Chrétien de Troyes (trans.) 1990, Beyond the Provinces: Literary Canada at Century's End 1995, Margaret Laurence: Critical Reflections (ed.) 2001, Northrop Frye: Essays on Canada (ed.) 2003, Marshall McLuhan: Understanding Me (ed.) 2003, The Letters of Stephen Leacock (ed.) 2003; contrib. to professional journals. *Address:* Department of English, University of Ottawa, Ottawa, ON K1N 6N5, Canada (office). *Telephone:* (613) 562-5990 (office). *E-mail:* dstaines@uottawa.ca (office).

STALLWORTHY, Jon Howie, BA, BLitt, FRSL, FBA; British academic, poet and writer; *Senior Research Fellow, Wolfson College, Oxford;* b. 18 Jan. 1935, London, England; m. Gillian Waldock 1960; three c. *Education:* Magdalen Coll., Oxford. *Career:* Ed. 1959–71, Deputy Academic Publisher 1974–77, OUP; Visiting Fellow, All Souls Coll., Oxford 1971–72; John Wendell Anderson Prof. of English Literature, Cornell Univ., Ithaca, NY 1977–86; Reader in English Literature 1986–92, Prof. of English 1992–2000, Univ. of Oxford, Sr Research Fellow Wolfson Coll., Oxford 2000–. *Publications:* poetry: The Earthly Paradise 1958, The Astronomy of Love 1961, Out of Bounds 1963, The Almond Tree 1967, A Day in the City 1967, Root and Branch 1969, Positives 1969, A Dinner of Herbs 1970, Alexander Blok: The Twelve and Other Poems (trans. with France) 1970, Hand in Hand 1974, The Apple Barrel: Selected Poems 1955–63 1974, A Familiar Tree 1978, The Anzac Sonata: Selected Poems 1986, The Guest from the Future 1995, Rounding the Horn: Collected Poems 1998, Body Language 2004; other: Between the Lines: Yeats's Poetry in the Making 1963, Vision and Revision in Yeats's Last Poems 1969, The Penguin Book of Love Poetry (ed.) 1973, Wilfred Owen: A Biography 1974, Poets of the First World War 1974, Boris Pasternak: Selected Poems (trans. with France) 1982, The Complete Poems and Fragments of Wilfred Owen (ed.) 1983, The Oxford Book of War Poetry (ed.) 1984, The Poems of Wilfred Owen (ed.) 1985, First Lines: Poems Written in Youth from Herbert to Heaney (ed.) 1987, Henry Reed: Collected Poems (ed.) 1991, Louis MacNeice 1995, Singing School: The Making of a Poet 1998, Aleksander Blok: Selected Poems (trans. with France) 2000, Anthem for Doomed Youth: Twelve Soldier Poets of the First World War (ed.) 2002; contrib. to professional journals. *Honours:* Duff Cooper Memorial Prize 1974, WHSmith Literary Award 1974, E. M. Forster Award 1975, Southern Arts Literary Prize 1995. *Address:* Wolfson College, Oxford, OX2 6UD, England.

STAMP, Gavin Mark, PhD, FSA; British architectural historian, writer and academic; b. 15 March 1948, Bromley, Kent; s. of Barry Hartnell Stamp and Norah Clare Stamp (née Rich); m. Alexandra Artley 1982; two d. *Education:* Dulwich Coll., London, Gonville and Caius Coll., Cambridge. *Career:* freelance writer and teacher –1990; Lecturer, Mackintosh School of Architecture, Glasgow School of Art 1990–99, Sr Lecturer and Hon. Prof. 1999–2003; Mellon Sr Fellow and Bye Fellow, Gonville and Caius Coll., Cambridge 2003–04; ind. scholar 2004–; Chair. The Twentieth Century Soc. (fmrly The Thirties Soc.) 1983–2007; Founder and Chair. Alexander Thomson Soc. 1991–2003. *Publications:* Robert Weir Schultz and his work for Marquesses of Bute 1981, The Great Perspectivists 1982, The Changing Metropolis 1984, The English House 1860–1914 1986, Telephone Boxes 1989, Greek Thomson (co-ed.) 1994, Alexander 'Greek' Thomson 1999, Edwin Lutyens' Country Houses 2001, An Architect of Promise: George Gilbert Scott Junior and the Late Gothic Revival 2002, Lutyens Abroad (co-ed.) 2002, The Memorial to the Missing of the Somme 2006. *Honours:* Hon. Fellow, Royal Incorporation of Architects of Scotland 1994; Hon. FRIBA 1998. *E-mail:* gavin.stamp@ btopenworld.com (home).

STAMPER, Alex (see Kent, Arthur William Charles)

STANFIELD, Anne (see Coffman, Virginia Edith)

STANG, Peter J., BSc; American writer and academic; b. Nov. 1941, Nürnburg, Germany. *Education:* DePaul Univ., Chicago, Univ. of California at Berkeley. *Career:* Nat. Inst. of Health work at Princeton Univ.; Dept Chair 1989–95, Distinguished Prof. of Chemistry 1992–, Dean of the Coll. of Science, Univ. of Utah; Assoc. Ed. 1982–99, Ed. 1999–, Journal of the American Chemical Soc.; Ed.-in-Chief, Journal of Organic Chemistry 2000–01; elected mem., Nat. Acad. of Sciences 2000. *Publications include:* Metal-catalyzed Cross-Coupling Reactions 1997, Templated Organic Synthesis (co-ed.) 1999. *Honours:* JSPS Fellowship 1995, 1998, Lady Davis Fellowship in Haifa Israel 1986, 1997; Fulbright Hays Sr Scholar to Zagreb, Croatia 1988; Dr hc (Russian Acad. of Sciences), (Lomonosov Moscow State Univ.) 1992, American Chemical Soc. James Flack Norris Award in Physical Organic Chemistry 1998; A. von Humboldt Sr Scientist Award 1977, 1997. *Address:* Department of Chemistry, University of Utah, 315 South 1400 East, Room 2020, Salt Lake City, UT 84112-0850; c/o Journal Publications, American Chemical Society, 2540 Olentangy River Road, PO Box 3330, Columbus, OH 43210, USA. *E-mail:* Stang@chem.utah.edu (office).

STANSKY, Peter David Lyman, BA, MA, PhD, FRHistS; American academic, writer and editor; *Professor Emeritus, Stanford University;* b. 18 Jan. 1932, New York, NY. *Education:* Yale Univ., King's Coll., Cambridge and Harvard Univ. *Career:* Instructor in History 1961–64, Asst Prof. 1964–68, Harvard Univ.; Assoc. Prof. of History 1968–73, Prof. of History 1973–, Frances and Charles Field Prof. of History 1974–2004, Prof. Emer. 2005–, Stanford Univ.; Assoc. Ed., Journal of British Studies 1973–85; Ed., North American Conference on British Studies Bibliographical Series 1977–87; Visiting Fellow, All Souls Coll., Oxford 1979, Christensen Fellow, St Catherine's Coll., Oxford 1983; Co-Ed., Virginia Woolf Miscellany 1984–2002; Fellow, Center for Advanced Study in the Behavioral Sciences 1988–89; various guest lectureships; Fellow American Acad. of Arts and Sciences; mem. American Historical Assccn, Nat. Book Critics Circle (dir 1980–85), North American Conference on British Studies (pres. 1974–76), Soc. for the Promotion of Science and Scholarship (pres.), Virginia Woolf Soc., William Morris Soc. *Publications:* Ambitions and Strategies: The Struggle for the Leadership of the Liberal Party in the 1890s 1964, Journey to the Frontier: Julian Bell and John Cornford, their Lives and the 1930s (with William Abrahams) 1966, The Unknown Orwell (with William Abrahams) 1972, England Since 1867: Continuity and Change 1973, Gladstone: A Progress in Politics 1979, Orwell: The Transformation (with William Abrahams) 1979, William Morris 1983, Redesigning the World 1985, London's Burning (with William Abrahams) 1994, On or About December 1910: Early Bloomsbury and its Intimate World 1996, From William Morris to Sergeant Pepper 1999, Sassoon: The Worlds of Philip and Sybil 2003; editor: The Left and War: The British Labour Party and the First World War 1969, Winston Churchill: A Profile 1973, The Victorian Revolution 1973, Modern British History Series (with Leslie Hume, 18 vols) 1982, On Nineteen Eighty-Four 1983, Modern European History Series (47 vols) 1987–92. *Honours:* Hon. DL (Wittenberg Univ.) 1984; Guggenheim Fellowships 1966–67, 1973–74, ACLS Fellow 1978–79, Nat. Endowment for the Humanities Sr Fellowships 1983, 1998–99. *Address:* c/o Department of History, Stanford University, Stanford, CA 94305, USA (office). *E-mail:* stansky@stanford.edu (office).

STAPLES, Brent, BA, PhD; American writer; b. 1951, Chester, PA. *Education:* Widener Univ. and Univ. of Chicago. *Career:* reporter, Chicago Sun-Times 1982–83; editorial writer, New York Times 1983–. *Publication:* Parallel Time: Growing Up in Black and White (Anisfield Wolff Book Award) 1994. *Honours:* Danforth Fellowship. *Address:* c/o New York Times, 229 W 43rd Street, New York, NY 10036, USA.

STARK, Joshua (see Olsen, Theodore Victor)

STARK, Richard (see Westlake, Donald Edwin)

STARKEY, David Robert, CBE, MA, PhD, FSA, FRHistS; British historian, academic and broadcaster; b. 3 Jan. 1945, Kendal; s. of Robert Starkey and Elsie Lyon. *Education:* Kendal Grammar School, Fitzwilliam Coll. Cambridge. *Career:* Research Fellow, Fitzwilliam Coll. Cambridge 1970–72, Visiting Fellow 1998–2001, Bye-Fellow 2001–06, Hon. Fellow 2006–; Lecturer in History, Dept of Int. History, LSE 1972–98; Visiting Vernon Prof. of Biography, Dartmouth Coll., NH, USA 1987, 1989; British Council Specialist Visitor Australia 1989; contribs to various newspapers; mem. Editorial Bd History Today 1980–, Commemorative Plaques Working Group, English Heritage 1993–2006; Pres. Soc. for Court Studies 1995–2005; Patron, Tory Group for Homosexual Equality 1994–; Historical Adviser to Henry VIII Exhbn, Nat. Maritime Museum, Greenwich 1991; Guest Curator, Elizabeth I Exhbn, Nat. Maritime Museum 2003, Lost Faces – Identity and Discovery in Tudor Royal Portraiture Exhbn, Philip Mould Gallery 2006; mem. Fitzwilliam Soc. (Pres. 2003–04). *Radio:* panellist, The Moral Maze (BBC Radio 4) 1992–2001, presenter, Talk Radio 1995–98. *Television:* presenter/writer, This

Land of England (Channel 4) 1985, Henry VIII (Channel 4) (Indie Documentary Award 2002) 1998, Elizabeth (Channel 4) 2000, The Six Wives of Henry VIII (Channel 4) (New York Festival for int. TV programming and promotion silver medal) 2001, The Unknown Tudors (Channel 4) 2002, Re-Inventing the Royals 2002, Monarchy (Channel 4) 2004–06, Starkey's Last Word (More 4) 2006. *Publications:* This Land of England (with David Souden) 1985, The Reign of Henry VIII: Personalities and Politics 1985–86, Revolution Reassessed: Revisions in the History of Tudor Government and Administration (ed. with Christopher Coleman) 1986, The English Court from the Wars of the Roses to the Civil War (ed.) 1987, Rivals in Power: the Lives and Letters of the Great Tudor Dynasties (ed.) 1990, Henry VIII: A European Court in England 1991, The Inventory of Henry VIII, Vol. 1 (with Philip Ward) 1998, Elizabeth: Apprenticeship 2000 (WHSmith Award for Biog./Autobiog. 2001), Six Wives: The Queens of Henry VIII 2003, Monarchy: the early kings 2004, The History of England: Jane Austen and Charles Dickens 2006, Monarchy: From the Middles Ages to Modernity 2006; numerous articles in learned journals. *Honours:* Hon. Assoc., Rationalist Press Asscn 1995–; Freeman, Worshipful Co. of Barbers 1992, Liveryman 1999; Hon. DLitt (Lancaster) 2004, (Kent) 2006; Medlicott Medal 2001. *Address:* Fitzwilliam College, Cambridge, CB3 0DG (office); 49 Hamilton Park West, London, N5 1AE, England (home). *Telephone:* (1223) 332000 (office). *Website:* www.fitz.cam.ac .uk (office).

STARKOV, Vladislav Andreyevich; Russian journalist; b. 28 Feb. 1940, Tomsk; s. of Andrei Nikolayevich Starkov and Maria Mikhailovna Starkova; m. Yulia Fedorovna Kuznetsova; one d. *Education:* Rostov State Univ. *Career:* researcher and computer engineer USSR Meteorology Centre 1962–73; corresp. Radio Moscow 1973–76; Znaniye Publishing House 1976–79; ed. Mezhdunarodnye Otnosheniya (journal) 1979–80; Ed.-in-Chief Argumenty i Fakty (weekly) 1980–; Head Argumenty i Fakty Publrs 1995–; RSFSR People's Deputy 1990–93. *Address:* AiF, Myasnitskaya str. 42, 101000 Moscow, Russia. *Telephone:* (495) 921-02-34 (office). *Fax:* (495) 925-61-82 (office). *E-mail:* into@aif.ru (office). *Website:* www.aif.ru (office).

STARNES, John Kennett, BA; Canadian diplomat (retd) and writer; b. 5 Feb. 1918, Montréal, QC; m. Helen Gordon Robinson 1941; two s. *Education:* Institut Sillig, Switzerland, Trinity Coll. School, Univ. of Munich, Germany, Bishop's Univ. *Career:* Counsellor, Canadian Embassy, Bonn 1953–56; Chair. Joint Intelligence Cttee, Ottawa 1958–62; Ambassador to the Federal Republic of Germany and Head Military Mission, Berlin 1962–66; Ambassador, United Arab Republic and The Sudan 1966–67; Asst Undersecretary of State for External Affairs 1967–70; Dir-Gen., Royal Canadian Mounted Police Security Service 1970–73; mem. of the council, Int. Inst. for Strategic Studies 1977–85; life mem. Rideau Club; mem. Canadian Writers' Foundation. *Publications:* Deep Sleepers 1981, Scarab 1982, Orion's Belt 1983, The Cornish Hug 1985, Latonya (novel) 1994, Closely Guarded: A Life in Canadian Security and Intelligence (memoir) 1998; contrib. to numerous newspapers, journals and periodicals. *Honours:* hon. mem. Canadian Security Intelligence Service 1987; Centennial Medal 1967, Commemorative Medal for 125th Anniversary of the Confederation of Canada 1992; Hon. DCL (Bishop's Univ.) 1975. *Address:* 420 Mackay Street, Apt 702, Ottawa, ON K1M 2C4, Canada. *Telephone:* (613) 741-3169. *E-mail:* jstarnes@sympatico.ca.

STAROBINSKI, Jean, PhD, MD; Swiss academic and writer; b. 17 Nov. 1920, Geneva; s. of Aron Starobinski and Szayndla Frydman; m. Jaqueline H. Sirman 1954; three s. *Education:* Univs of Geneva and Lausanne. *Career:* Asst Prof. Johns Hopkins Univ. 1953–56, Prof. of French Literature, History of Ideas 1958–85; Pres. Rencontres Int. de Geneva 1965–; mem. Acad. Lincei, British Acad., American Acad. of Arts and Sciences, Deutsche Akad.; Assoc. mem. Acad. des Sciences Morales et Politiques (France), Acad. Royale de Belgique. *Publications:* Jean Jacques Rousseau: la transparence et l'obstacle 1957, The Invention of Liberty (in trans.) 1964, La Relation critique 1970, Words upon Words (in trans.) 1971, 1789: Les Emblemes de la raison 1973, Montaigne en mouvement 1983, Le Remède dans le mal 1989, La Mélancolie au miroir 1989, Largesse 1994, Action et Réaction 1999, Les Enchanteresses 2005; contrib. to newspapers and journals. *Honours:* Soc. of Fellows Johns Hopkins Univ.; Officier, Légion d'honneur 1980; hon. degrees from Univs of Lille 1973, Brussels, Lausanne 1979, Chicago 1986, Columbia (New York) 1987, Montréal 1988, Strasbourg 1988, Neuchâtel 1990, Nantes 1992, Oslo 1994, Turin 1994, Urbino 1995, Cluj 1995, ETH, Zürich 1998; Prix Européen de L'Essai 1983, Balzan Prize 1984, Monaco Prize 1988, Goethe Prize 1994. *Address:* 51 avenue de Champel, 1206 Geneva, Switzerland. *Telephone:* (22) 3209864.

STARR, Paul Elliot, BA, PhD; American academic, writer and editor; b. 12 May 1949, New York, NY; m. Sandra Luire Stein 1981. *Education:* Columbia University, Harvard University. *Career:* Junior Fellow, Harvard Society of Fellows, 1975–78; Asst Prof., Harvard University, 1978–82; Assoc. Prof., 1982–85, Prof. of Sociology, 1985–, Princeton University; Founder-Co-Ed., The American Prospect; Founder, Electronic Policy Network, 1995. *Publications:* The Discarded Army: Veterans After Vietnam, 1974; The Social Transformation of American Medicine, 1983; The Logic of Health-Care Reform, 1992. Contributions: Professional journals. *Honours:* Guggenheim Fellowship, 1981–82; C. Wright Mills Award, 1983; Pulitzer Prize in General Non-Fiction, 1984; Bancroft Prize, 1984.

STARRATT, Thomas, BSc, MEd; American teacher, poet and writer; b. 6 Oct. 1952, Holyoke, MA; m. Patricia Starratt 1994, three s. two d. *Education:*

Plymouth State Teachers College, NH, University of New Hampshire, various graduate courses. *Career:* mem. International Reading Asscn. *Publications:* Nightwatch, 1994; Amsterdam, 1994; Summer on the Lava Plain, 1994; Eye to Your Storm, 1995; Passages, 1995; Excess, 1995; Summer Days, 1995; Amsterdam Revisited, 1995; Washed Up, 1996. Contributions: professional journals.

STASIUK, Andrzej; Polish writer, poet, playwright and publisher; b. 1960, Ukraine; m. *Career:* co-f. and owner, publishing co, Czarne 1996–. *Publications:* Mury Hebronu (The Walls of Hebron, short stories) 1992, Wiersze milosne i nie (Verses (Non-)Amorous) 1994, Opowiesci galicyjskie (Tales of Galicia, short stories) 1994, Bialy kruk (The White Raven, novel) 1995, Przez rzeke (Through the River, short stories) 1996, Dukla (short stories) 1997, Dwie sztuki (telewizyjne) o smierci (Two Television Plays About Death) 1998, Jak zostalem pisarzem (proba biografii intelektualnej) (How I Became a Writer (Attempt at an Intellectual Biography)) 1998, Dziewiec (Nine) 1998, Moje Europa. Dwa eseje o Europie zwanej Srodkowa (My Europe: Two essays on the place called Central Europe, with J. Andruchowicz) 2000, Tekturowy samolot (Model Aeroplane) 2000, Opowiesci wigilijne (Christmas Tales, with Olga Tokarczuk and Jerzy Pilch) 2000, Zima i inne opowiadania (Winter and Other Stories) 2001; contrib. to Gazeta Wyborcza, Tygodnik Powszechny. *Honours:* Foundation of Culture Prize 1994, Koscielski Prize 1995. *Address:* c/o Twisted Spoon Press, PO Box 21, Preslova 12, Prague 5 150-21, Czech Republic (office).

STAUDINGER, Ulrich; German publisher; b. 30 May 1935, Berlin; s. of Wilhelm Staudinger and Elfriede Poth; m. Irmengard Ehrenwirth 1960 (died 1989); one s. two d. *Education:* Volksschule and Realgymnasium. *Career:* publishing training 1954–57; Lingenbrinck Barsortiment, Hamburg 1957–58; Publicity and Sales, Ensslin & Laiblin, Jugendbuchverlag, Reutlingen 1958–59; Production, Carl Hanser Verlag, Munich 1959–60; Dawson & Sons, London 1960; Franz Ehrenwirth Verlag, Munich 1960; partner, Ehrenwirth Verlag, Munich 1964; responsible for purchase of Franz Schneekluth Verlag KG, Darmstadt by Ehrenwirth Verlag 1967 and amalgamation of two companies into single firm 1976; purchased parts of Philosophia Verlag GmbH, Düsseldorf 1978; various professional appointments. *Address:* Asgardstrasse 34, 8000 Munich 81, Germany (home). *Telephone:* (89) 98-63-67 (home).

STAVANS, Ilan; American writer, editor and critic; *Lewis-Sebring Professor in Latin American and Latino Culture, Amherst College*; b. 1961, Mexico. *Career:* teacher, Amherst Coll. 1993–2001, Lewis-Sebring Prof. in Latin American and Latino Culture 2001–; Ed.-in-Chief, Hopscotch: A Cultural Review. *Television:* host, Conversations with Ilan Stavans 2001–06. *Publications include:* Imagining Columbus: The Literary Voyage 1992, La pluma y la máscara 1993, Antihéroes: México y su novela political 1993, Growing Up Latino: Memoirs and Stories (co-author) 1993, La pluma mágica 1994, Bandido, Oscar Zeta Acosta and the Chicano Experience 1995, The Hispanic Condition: Reflections on Culture and Identity in America 1995, Art and Anger: Essays on Politics and the Imagination 1998, The Oxford Book of Jewish Stories 1998, The Oxford Book of Latin American Essays 1998, One-Handed Pianist and Other Stories 1998, Dictionary of Spanglish 1999, The Essential Ilan Stavans 2000, The Inveterate Dreamer: Essays and Conversations on Jewish Culture 2001, The Hispanic Condition: The Power of a People 2001, Wachale! 2001, On Borrowed Words: A Memoir of Language 2001, Riddle of the Catinflas: Essays on Hispanic Popular Culture 2001, Spanglish: The Making of a New American Language 2003, Dictionary Days 2005, The Disappearance 2006, On Love 2007; editor: Tropical Synagogues: Short Stories by Jewish-Latin American Writers 1994, Prospero's Mirror 1998, Poetry of Pablo Neruda 2003, Isaac Bashevis Singer: Collected Stories 2004, Encyclopedia Latino 2005, The Schecken Book of Modern Sephardic Literature 2005, Lengua Fresca 2006, I Explain a Few Things 2007. *Honours:* Guggenheim Fellowship; Latino Literature Prize, Nat. Jewish Book Award. *Address:* Amherst College, Amherst, MA 01002-5000, USA (office). *Telephone:* (513) 542-8201 (office). *Fax:* (513) 542-2759 (office). *E-mail:* istavans@amherst.edu (office). *Website:* www.amherst.edu (office).

STAVE, Bruce Martin, AB, MA, PhD; American historian and academic; *Distinguished Professor Emeritus, University of Connecticut*; b. 17 May 1937, New York, NY; m. Sondra T. Astor 1961; one s. *Education:* Columbia Coll., Columbia Univ., New York, Univ. of Pittsburgh. *Career:* Prof., Univ. of Connecticut 1975–2000, Dir Center for Oral History 1981–, Chair. Dept of History 1985–94, Bd of Trustees Distinguished Prof. 2000–02, Distinguished Prof. Emer. 2002–; Ed. Oral History Review 1996–99; mem. American Historical Asscn, Org. of American Historians, Immigration History Soc., New England Historical Asscn (Pres. 1994–95), Oral History Asscn, New England Asscn of Oral History. *Publications:* The New Deal and the Last Hurrah 1970, Urban Bosses, Machines and Progressive Reformers (ed.) 1972, The Discontented Society (co-co-ed.) 1972, Socialism and the Cities (contributing ed.) 1975, The Making of Urban History 1977, Modern Industrial Cities 1981, Talking About Connecticut (ed.) 1985, Mills and Meadows: A Pictorial History of Northeast Connecticut (co-author) 1991, From the Old Country: An Oral History of European Migration to America (co-author) 1994, Witnesses to Nuremberg: An Oral History of American Participants at the War Crimes Trials (co-author) 1998, Red Brick in the Land of Steady Habits: Creating the University of Connecticut 1881–2006 2006; contrib. to Journal of Urban History, Americana Magazine, International Journal of Oral History. *Honours:* Fulbright Professorships, India 1968–69, Australia, NZ, Philippines 1977, People's Repub. of China 1984–85, Nat. Endowment for the Humanities Fellowship 1974, Asscn for the Study of Connecticut History Homer Babbidge Award 1995, Univ. of Hartford NEH/Harry Jack Gray Distinguished Visiting Humanist 2003. *Address:* 150 Grant Hill Road, Coventry, CT 06238, USA (home). *Telephone:* (860) 486-4578 (office). *Fax:* (860) 486-4582 (office). *E-mail:* bruce.stave@uconn.edu (office). *Website:* www.oralhistory.uconn.edu (office).

STEAD, Christian Karlson (C. K.), ONZ, CBE, MA, PhD, LittD, FRSL; New Zealand writer and academic; *Professor Emeritus of English, University of Auckland*; b. 17 Oct. 1932, Auckland; s. of James Walter Ambrose Stead and Olive Ethel Stead (née Karlson); m. Kathleen Elizabeth Roberts 1955; one s. two d. *Education:* Mt Albert Grammar School, Auckland Univ. Coll. and Auckland Teachers' Coll., Univ. of Bristol, UK. *Career:* Lecturer in English, Univ. of New England, NSW, Australia 1956–57; Michael Hiatt Baker Scholar, Univ. of Bristol 1957–59; Lecturer, Sr Lecturer, Assoc. Prof., Univ. of Auckland 1960–67, Prof. of English 1967–86, Prof. Emer. 1986–; writer 1986–; Nuffield Fellow, Univ. of London 1965, Hon. Fellow, Univ. Coll. London 1977, Sr Visiting Fellow, St John's Coll. Oxford 1996–97; Chair. NZ Literary Fund Advisory Cttee 1972–75, NZ Authors' Fund Cttee 1989–91; mem. NZ PEN (Chair. Auckland br. 1986–89, Nat. Vice-Pres. 1988–90), Creative New Zealand 1999; Fellow, English Asscn. *Publications:* fiction: Smith's Dream 1972, All Visitors Ashore 1984, The Death of the Body 1986, Sister Hollywood 1989, The End of the Century at the End of the World 1992, The Singing Whakapapa 1994, Villa Vittoria 1997, Talking about O'Dwyer 2000, The Secret History of Modernism 2002, Mansfield: a novel 2004, My Name Was Judas 2006; poetry: Whether the Will is Free 1964, Crossing the Bar 1972, Quesada 1975, Walking Westward 1978, Geographies 1982, Poems of a Decade 1983, Paris 1984, Between 1986, Voices 1990, Straw into Gold 1997, The Right Thing 2000, Dog 2002, The Red Tram 2004, The Black River 2007; short story collections: Five for the Symbol 1981, The Blind Blonde with Candles in Her Hair 1998; non-fiction: The New Poetic: Yeats to Eliot 1964, In the Glass Case: Essays on New Zealand Literature 1981, Pound Yeats Eliot and the Modernist Movement 1986, Answering to the Language: Essays on Modern Writers 1990, The Writer at Work 2000, Kin of Place: Essays on 20 New Zealand Writers 2002; editor: Oxford New Zealand Short Stories (2nd series) 1966, Measure for Measure, a Casebook 1971, Letters and Journals of Katherine Mansfield 1977, Collected Stories of Maurice Duggan 1981, The Faber Book of Contemporary South Pacific Stories 1994, Werner Forman's New Zealand 1994. *Honours:* Hon. DLitt (Bristol) 2001; Katherine Mansfield Prize 1960, Jessie Mackay Award for Poetry 1972, Katherine Mansfield Menton Fellowship 1972, New Zealand Book Award for Poetry 1976, New Zealand Book Award for Fiction 1985, 1995, Queen Elizabeth II Arts Council Scholarship in Letters 1988–89, Queens' Medal for Services to NZ Literature 1990, Michael King Fellowship 2005–06. *Address:* 37 Tohunga Crescent, Parnell, Auckland 1001, New Zealand. *Telephone:* (649) 379-9420. *Fax:* (649) 379-9420.

STEADMAN, Ralph Idris; British cartoonist, writer and illustrator; b. 15 May 1936, s. of Raphael Steadman and Gwendoline Steadman; m. 1st Sheila Thwaite 1959 (divorced 1971); two s. two d.; m. 2nd Anna Deverson 1972; one d. *Education:* London School of Printing and Graphic Arts. *Career:* with de Havilland Aircraft Co. 1952; cartoonist, Kemsley (Thomson) Newspapers 1956–59; freelance for Punch, Private Eye, Daily Telegraph during 1960s; political cartoonist, New Statesman 1978–80;; designed set of stamps depicting Halley's Comet 1986; Artist-in-Residence, Leviathan (series of films, BBC 2) 1999; designer of set and costumes, The Crucible, Royal Ballet 2000. *Retrospective exhibitions:* Nat. Theatre 1977, Royal Festival Hall 1984, Wilhelm Busch Museum, Hanover 1988, One on One Gallery, Denver 1997, Warrington Museum 1998, William Havu Gallery, Denver 2000, Boston Art Inst. (Drawing Breath) 2006. *Written and illustrated:* Alice in Wonderland 1967, Alice Through the Looking Glass 1972, Sigmund Freud 1979, A Leg in the Wind and Other Canine Curses 1982, I, Leonardo 1983, That's My Dad 1986, The Big I Am 1988, No Room to Swing a Cat 1989, Near the Bone 1990, Tales of Weirrd 1990, Still Life with Bottle, Whisky According to Ralph Steadman 1994, Jones of Colorado 1998, Gonzo: The Art 1998, little.com 2000, The Joke's Over 2006. *Illustrator:* many books from 1961, including Friendship 1990 (in aid of John McCarthy), Adrian Mitchell, Heart on the Left, Poems 1953–84 1997, Roald Dahl, The Mildenhall Treasure 1999, Doodaa: The Balletic Art of Gavin Twinge 2002. *Publications:* Jelly Book 1968, Still Life with Raspberry: collected drawings 1969, The Little Red Computer 1970, Dogs Bodies 1971, Bumper to Bumper Book 1973, Two Donkeys and the Bridge 1974, Flowers for the Moon 1974, The Watchdog and the Lazy Dog 1974, America: drawings 1975, America: collected drawings 1977 (r.e. Scar Strangled Banger 1987), Between the Eyes 1984, Paranoids 1986, The Grapes of Ralph 1992, Teddy Where Are You? 1994, Bruised Memories: Gonzo, Hunter Thompson and Me 2006. *Honours:* Hon. DLitt (Kent) 1995; Designers and Art Dirs' Asscn Gold Award 1977, Silver Award 1977, Lifetime Achievement Award – Milton Caniff Award, Nat. Cartoonists Soc. (USA) 2005. *Literary Agent:* c/o Nat Sobel, Sobel Weber Associates, Inc., 146 East 19th Street, New York, NY 10003-2404, USA. *Telephone:* (212) 420-8585. *Website:* www.sobelweber.com; www.ralphsteadman.com.

STEANE, John Barry; British music journalist and writer; b. 12 April 1928, Coventry, England. *Education:* Univ. of Cambridge. *Career:* teacher of English, Merchant Taylors' School, Northwood 1952–88; reviewer, Gramophone 1973–, Musical Times 1988–, Opera Now 1989–. *Publications:* Marlowe: A Critical Study 1964, Dekker: The Shoemaker's Holiday (ed.) 1965, Tennyson 1966, Jonson: The Alchemist (ed.) 1967, Marlowe: The Complete Plays 1969,

Nashe: The Unfortunate Traveller and Other Works 1972, The Grand Tradition: Seventy Years of Singing on Record 1973, Opera on Record (co-author, three vols) 1979–85, Song on Record (co-author, two vols) 1986–88, Choral Music on Record 1991, Voices: Singers and Critics 1992, Elisabeth Schwarzkopf: A Career on Record (with Alan Sanders) 1995, Singers of the Century (three vols) 1996, 1998, 2000, The Gramophone and the Voice 1999; contrib. to The New Grove Dictionary of Music and Musicians 1980, 2001, The New Grove Dictionary of Opera 1992. *Address:* 32 Woodland Avenue, Coventry, CV5 6DB, England (home). *Telephone:* (2426) 674842 (home).

STEARNS, Peter Nathaniel, BA, MA, PhD; American academic, writer and editor; *Provost and Professor of History, George Mason University;* b. 3 March 1936, London, England; one s. three d. *Education:* Harvard Univ. *Career:* instructor 1962–63, Asst Prof. 1963–66, Assoc. Prof. 1966–68, Univ. of Chicago; Visiting Assoc. Prof., Northwestern Univ. 1964; Ed.-in-Chief, Journal of Social History 1967–; Prof. of History, Rutgers Univ. 1968–74; Visiting Prof., Sir George Williams Univ. 1970, Univ. of Houston 1978; Heinz Prof. of History 1974–2000, Head Dept of History 1986–92, Dean Coll. of Humanities and Social Sciences 1992–2000, Carnegie Mellon Univ.; Provost and Prof. of History, George Mason Univ. 2000–; mem. American Historical Asscn, American Sociological Asscn, Nat. Council on Social Studies: Social History Asscn (UK), Soc. of French Historical Studies. *Publications:* European Society in Upheaval: Social History Since 1800 1967, Priest and Revolutionary: Lamennais and the Dilemma of French Catholicism 1967, Modern Europe 1789–1914 1969, Revolutionary Syndicalism and French Labor: A Cause Without Rebels 1971, Workers and Protest: The European Labor Movement, the Working Classes, and the Rise of Socialism 1890–1914 (with Harvey Mitchell) 1971, The European Experience Since 1815 1972, 1848: The Revolutionary Tide in Europe 1974, Lives of Labor: Work in Maturing Industrial Society 1975, Old Age in European Society 1977, Paths to Authority: Toward the Formation of the Middle Class Consciousness 1978, Be a Man!: Males in Modern Society 1979, Themes in Modern Social History (with Linda Rosenzweig) 1985, Anger: The Struggle for Emotional Control in America's History (with Carol Stearns) 1986, World History: Patterns of Change and Continuity 1987, Life and Society in the West: The Modern Centuries 1988, World History: Traditions and New Directions 1988, Emotion and Social Change: Toward a New Psychohistory (with Carol Stearns) 1988, Social History and Issues in Consciousness and Cognition (with Andrew Barnes) 1989, Jealousy: The Evolution of an Emotion in American History 1989, World Civilizations (with Michael Adas and Stuart Schwartz) 1991, Meaning Over Memory: Recasting the Teaching of Culture and History 1993, The Industrial Revolution in World History 1993, Encyclopedia of Social History (ed.) 1993, Turbulent Passage: A Global History of the 20th Century (with Michael Adas and Stuart Schwartz) 1994, American Cool: Developing the Twentieth-Century Emotional Style 1994, Discursive Psychology in Practice (with Rom Harré) 1995, Encyclopedia of the Industrial Revolution (ed. with John Hinshaw) 1996, Fat History: Bodies and Beauty in Western Society 1997, Schools and Students in Industrial Society: Japan and the West 1870–1940 1997, World History in Documents: Comparative Perspectives 1998, The Battleground of Desire: The Struggle for Self-Control in Modern America 1999, Gender in World History 2000, Encyclopedia of European Social History (ed.) 2000, Facing Up to Management Faddism (with Margaret Brindle) 2001, Consumerism in World History: The Global Transformation of Desire 2001, Encyclopedia of World History (ed., sixth edn) 2001, Cultures in Motion 2001, Anxious Parents: A History of Modern Childrearing in America 2003, Western Civilization in World History 2003, Thinking History 2004, Global Outrage: The Rise of World Opinion 2005, American Behavioral History 2005; contrib. to reference works, scholarly books and professional journals. *Honours:* Soc. for French Historical Studies Koren Prize 1964, Business History Review Newcomen Special Award 1965, American Philosophical Soc. grant 1967–68, Guggenheim Fellowship 1973–74. *Address:* c/o Office of the Provost, George Mason University, Fairfax, VA 22030, USA.

STEBEL, Sidney Leo, (Leo Bergson, Steve Toron), BA; American novelist and playwright; b. 28 June 1923, Iowa; m. 1st Jan Mary Dingler 1954 (died 1999); one d.; m. 2nd Karen K. Ford 2004. *Education:* Univ. of Southern California, Los Angeles. *Career:* fmrly columnist, Los Angeles Times Sunday Book Review, Los Angeles Herald-Examiner Sunday Book Review; Exec. Script Consultant, South Australian Film Corpn, working on films Picnic at Hanging Rock, Storm Boy; Adjunct Prof., Masters of Professional Writing programme, Univ. of Southern California, Los Angeles 1991–; mem. Australian Writers' Guild, Authors' Guild, PEN Centre (USA West), Writers' Guild of America, Authors' League. *Writing for theatre:* Father Against Sons, Dial 1-4-sex-talk, Next in Line (adaptation of story by Ray Bradbury, Theater West, Los Angeles) 2004. *Screenplays:* Dreams of Marianne (film), Revolution of Antonio De Leon (TV film). *Publications:* The Widowmaster 1967, The Collaborator 1968, The Vanishing Americans (serialized in West magazine as 'Main Street') 1971, The Vorovich Affair 1975, The Shoe Leather Treatment 1983, Spring Thaw 1989, The Boss's Wife 1992, Double Your Creative Power 1996, Rising Star, Setting Sun 2004. *Honours:* Second Place Fiction Award, PEN Center West 1989. *Literary Agent:* Michael Congdon, Don Congdon & Associates, 156 Fifth Avenue, New York, NY 10010, USA. *Telephone:* (212) 645-1229. *E-mail:* dca@doncongdon.com. *Address:* 1963 Mandeville Canyon Road, Los Angeles, CA 90049, USA. *E-mail:* stebel@usc.edu. *Website:* www .slstebel.com.

STEEL, Danielle Fernande Schüelein; American writer; b. 14 Aug. 1950, New York; d. of John Steel and Norma Schüelein-Steel (née Stone); m. 2nd Bill Toth 1977; m. 3rd John A. Traina Jr; four s. five d. *Education:* Lycée Français, Parsons School of Design, New York, Univ. of New York. *Career:* worked as public relations and advertising exec., Manhattan, New York; published first novel 1973, then wrote advertising copy and poems for women's magazines; wrote first bestseller, The Promise 1979. *Publications:* Going Home 1973, Passion's Promise 1977, Now and Forever 1978, Season of Passion 1978, The Promise 1979, Summer's End 1980, The Ring 1980, To Love Again 1981, Palomino 1981, Loving 1981, Remembrance 1981, Love: Poems 1981, A Perfect Stranger 1982, Once in a Lifetime 1982, Crossings 1982, Thurston House 1983, Changes 1983, Full Circle 1984, Having a Baby (contrib., non-fiction) 1984, Family Album 1985, Secrets 1985, Wanderlust 1986, Fine Things 1987, Kaleidoscope 1987, Zoya 1988, Star 1989, Daddy 1989, Heartbeat 1991, Message from Nam 1991, No Greater Love 1991, Jewels 1992, Mixed Blessings 1992, Vanished 1993, Accident 1994, The Gift 1994, Wings 1995, Lightning 1995, Five Days in Paris 1995, Malice 1995, Silent Honor 1996, The Ranch 1996, The Ghost 1997, Special Delivery 1997, His Bright Light (non-fiction) 1998, The Ranch 1998, The Long Road Home 1998, The Klone and I 1998, Mirror Image 1998, Bittersweet 1999, Granny Dan 1999, Irresistible Forces 1999, The Wedding 2000, The House on Hope Street 2000, Journey 2000, Leap of Faith 2001, The Kiss 2001, Lone Eagle 2001, The Cottage 2002, Sunset in St Tropez 2002, Answered Prayers 2002, Dating Game 2003, Johnny Angel 2003, Safe Harbour 2003, Echoes 2004, Toxic Bachelors 2005, The House 2006, Impossible 2006, Miracle 2006, Coming Out 2006, HRH 2006, Bungalow 2 2007; eight children's books, one book of poetry. *Honours:* Officier, Ordre des Arts et Lettres. *Address:* c/o Dell Publishing, 1540 Broadway, New York, NY 10036 (office); PO Box 1637, New York, NY 10156, USA (home).

STEEL, Ronald Lewis, BA, MA; American academic and writer; *Professor of International Relations, University of Southern California at Los Angeles;* b. 25 March 1931, Morris, IL. *Education:* Northwestern Univ., Harvard Univ. *Career:* Vice-Consul, US Foreign Service 1957–58; Ed., Scholastic Magazine 1959–62; Sr Assoc., Carnegie Endowment for Int. Peace 1962–83, Council on Foreign Relations, Washington, DC 2003–04; Visiting Fellow, Yale Univ. 1971–73; Visiting Prof., Univ. of Texas 1977, 1979, 1980, 1985, Wellesley Coll. 1978, Rutgers Univ. 1980, Univ. of California at Los Angeles 1981, Dartmouth Coll. 1983, Princeton Univ. 1984, École des Hautes Études en Sciences Sociales, Paris 2001–02; Fellow, Woodrow Wilson Int. Center for Scholars 1984–85, Wissenschaftskolleg zu Berlin, Germany 1988, American Acad., Berlin 2005; Prof. of Int. Relations, Univ. of Southern California at Los Angeles 1986–; Shapiro Prof. of Int. Relations, George Washington Univ. 1995–97; mem. American Historical Asscn, Soc. of American Historians. *Publications:* The End of Alliance: America and the Future of Europe 1964, Pax Americana 1967, Imperialists and Other Heroes 1971, Walter Lippmann and the American Century 1980, Temptations of a Superpower 1995, In Love with Night: The American Romance with Robert Kennedy 2000; contrib. to professional journals and general publications. *Honours:* Sidney Hillman Prize 1968, Guggenheim Fellowship 1973–74, Los Angeles Times Book Award 1980, Washington Monthly Book Award 1980, Nat. Book Critics Circle Award 1981, Columbia Univ. Bancroft Prize 1981, American Book Award 1981. *Address:* c/o School of International Relations, University of Southern California, Los Angeles, CA 90089, USA. *Telephone:* (213) 740-0774 (office). *E-mail:* steel@usc .edu (office).

STEELE, Shelby, MA, PhD; American academic and writer; b. 1 Jan. 1946, Chicago, IL; m. Rita Steele, two c. *Education:* Coe College, Southern Illinois University, University of Utah. *Career:* Prof. of English, San Jose State University. *Television:* Seven Days in Bensonhurst (television documentary), PBS TV, 1990. *Publications:* The Content of Our Character: A New Vision of Race in America, 1991; Essay Collection, 1993; contributions: newspapers, journals, and magazines. *Honours:* National Book Critics Award 1991.

ŠTEFANKO, Ondrej; Romanian poet, writer and translator; b. 18 March 1949, Timisoara. *Education:* high school, Nadlak. *Career:* elected mem. parl., representing Slovak minority; held leading post in Democratic Union of Slovaks and Czechs in Romania; f. first independent magazine for Slovaks in Romania, Our Efforts; Ed.-in-Chief The Lowland Slovak magazine, and bilingual quarterly Double Mirror/Oglinzi paralele; Chair. Union of Slovak Writers and Artists Living Outside Slovakia; mem. Union of Romanian Writers, Soc. of Slovak Writers, Slovak Writers' Community. *Publications:* poems: Dva hlasy (with I. M. Ambruš) 1977, Stojím pred domom 1980, Rospaky 1983, Dva hlasy II alebo dvojhra pre štyri oči a dve perá (with I. M. Ambruš) 1987, Reptajúca pokora 1993, Zjavenie Jána 1995, Doma 1996, Na priedomí 1997; juvenile: Desat' strelených rozprávok 1986; essays: Šl'achetný erb bláznov 1996; Escape, Foreboding Without Dimensions, A Poet's Greeting, The Safety Belt, Wandering Through a Rusty Landscape; also translations. *Honours:* Romanian Writers' Union Prize, Bucharest 1983, 1995. *Address:* c/o Literarne Informacne Centrum, Nam. SNP 12, 81224 Bratislava, Slovakia. *E-mail:* lic@litcentrum.sk.

STEFFEN, Jonathon Neil, MA; British university teacher, writer, poet and translator; b. 5 Oct. 1958, London, England. *Education:* King's College, Cambridge. *Career:* teacher, University of Heidelberg. *Publications:* Fiction: In Seville, 1985; Meeting the Majors, 1987; Carpe Diem, 1991; Cleopatra, 1994; The Story of Icarus, 1994; At Breakfast, 1995. Poetry: The Soldier and the Soldier's Son, 1986; German Hunting Party, 1987; The Moving Hand, 1994; The Great Days of the Railway, 1994; Apprentice and Master, 1994; St Francis in the Slaughter, 1995. Contributions: Reviews, quarterlies, and magazines. *Honours:* Harper-Wood Travelling Studentship, 1981–82; Hawthornden Creative Writing Fellowship, 1987.

STEFFLER, John Earl, BA, MA; Canadian academic, poet and writer; *Parliamentary Poet Laureate*; b. 13 Nov. 1947, Toronto, ON; one s. one d. *Education:* Univ. of Toronto, Univ. of Guelph. *Career:* Prof. of English, Sir Wilfred Grenfell Coll., Memorial Univ. of Newfoundland, Corner Brook Campus 1975–; Parl. Poet Laureate 2006–(08); mem. League of Canadian Poets, PEN, Writers' Alliance of Newfoundland and Labrador. *Publications:* An Explanation of Yellow 1980, The Grey Islands 1985, The Wreckage of Play 1988, The Afterlife of George Cartwright (novel) (Smithbooks/Books in Canada First Novel Award 1992, Thomas Raddall Atlantic Fiction Award 1992) 1991, That Night We Were Ravenous (poems) (Atlantic Poetry Award) 1998, Helix 2003; contrib. to journals and periodicals. *Honours:* Newfoundland Arts Council Artist of the Year Award 1992, Joseph S. Stauffer Prize 1993, Newfoundland and Labrador Poetry Award 1998, 2003. *Address:* c/o Department of English, Memorial University of Newfoundland, Corner Brook, NL A2H 6PN, Canada (office). *E-mail:* steffler@swgc.mun.ca (office).

STEIGER, Paul, BA; American journalist and editor; *Editor-at-Large, Wall Street Journal*; b. 15 Aug. 1942, Bronx, NY. *Education:* Yale Univ. *Career:* staff writer, LA Times 1968, Econ. Corresp., Washington, DC Bureau 1971–78, apptd Business Ed. 1978; with Wall Street Journal, reporter for San Francisco Bureau 1966–68, Asst Man. Ed. 1983–85, Deputy Man. Ed. 1985–91, Man. Ed. 1991–2007, Ed.-at-Large 2007, also Vice-Pres. Dow Jones & Co.; mem. Pulitzer Prize Bd 1999–, Columbia Grad. School of Journalism Bd of Visitors; Poynter Fellow, Yale Univ. 2001–2. *Publications include:* The '70s Crash and How to Survive It 1970. *Honours:* George Beveridge Ed. of the Year Award 2001, American Soc. of Newspaper Eds' Leadership Award 2002, Gerald Loeb Award, John Hancock Award 2002, Columbia Journalism Award 2002. *Address:* The Wall Street Journal, 200 Liberty Street, New York, NY 10281, USA (office). *Telephone:* (212) 416-2000 (office). *Website:* www.wsj.com (office).

STEIN, Kevin, BS, MA, PhD; American academic, writer, poet and editor; *Caterpillar Professor of English, Bradley University, Peoria*; b. 1 Jan. 1954, Anderson, IN; m. Debra Lang 1979; one s. one d. *Education:* Ball State Univ., Indiana Univ. *Career:* instructor, Ball State Univ. 1978–79; Assoc. Instructor, Indiana Univ. 1980–84; Asst Prof. 1984–88, Assoc. Prof. 1988–94, Prof. of English 1994–2000, Caterpillar Prof. of English 2000–, Bradley Univ., Peoria, IL; Ed. Illinois Writers Review 1988–92; Assoc. Poetry Ed. Crazyhorse 1992–; State of Illinois Poet Laureate 2003; mem. Illinois Writers, MLA. *Publications:* A Field of Wings (poems) 1986, The Figure Our Bodies Make (poems) 1988, James Wright: The Poetry of a Grown Man 1988, A Circus of Want (poems) 1992, Bruised Paradise (poems) 1996, Private Poets: Worldly Acts: Public and Private History in Contemporary American Poetry 1996, Chance Ransom (poems) 2000, Illinois Voices: An Anthology of Twentieth-Century Poetry (ed. with G. E. Murray) 2001, American Ghost Roses (poems) 2005; contrib. to many reviews, quarterlies and journals. *Honours:* Illinois Arts Council Fellowship 1986, Illinois Writers Chapbook Award 1986, Stanley Hanks Chapbook Award 1988, Frederick Bock Prize for Poetry 1987, Faculty Mem. of the Year Bradley Univ. 1989, Nat. Endowment for the Arts Fellowship 1991, Univ. of Missouri Press Devins Award for Poetry 1992, Indiana Review Poetry Prize 1998. *Address:* c/o Department of English, College of Liberal Arts and Sciences, Bradley University, 1501 W Bradley Avenue, Peoria, IL 61625-0258, USA (office). *Telephone:* (309) 677-2480 (office).

STEIN, Peter Gonville, FBA; British legal scholar and academic; *Professor Emeritus and Fellow, Queens' College, Cambridge*; b. 29 May 1926, Liverpool; s. of Walter O. Stein and Effie D. Walker; m. 1st Janet Chamberlain 1953, three d.; m. 2nd Anne Howard 1978; one step-s. *Education:* Liverpool Coll., Gonville and Caius Coll. Cambridge and Univ. of Pavia, Italy. *Career:* served RN 1944–47; admitted solicitor 1951; Prof. of Jurisprudence, Univ. of Aberdeen 1956–68; Regius Prof. of Civil Law, Univ. of Cambridge 1968–93; Prof. Emer. and Fellow Queens' Coll., Cambridge 1968–; mem. Univ. Grants Cttee 1971–76; JP, Cambridge 1970–; Fellow, Winchester Coll. 1976–91; Pres. Soc. of Public Teachers of Law 1980–81; mem. US –UK Educational Comm. 1985–91; Fellow Academia Europaea 1989; Foreign Fellow, Accad. Nazionale dei Lincei, Accad. di Scienze Morali e Politiche di Napoli, Accad. degli Intronati di Siena, Kon. Akad. v. Wetenschappen, Brussels. *Publications:* Regulae Iuris: from juristic rules to legal maxims 1966, Legal Values in Western Society (with J. Shand) 1974, Legal Evolution 1980, Legal Institutions 1984, The Character and Influence of the Roman Civil Law: essays 1988, The Teaching of Roman Law in England around 1200 (with F. de Zulueta) 1990, Notaries Public in England since the Reformation (ed. and contrib.) 1991, Römisches Recht und Europa 1996, Roman Law in European History 1999. *Honours:* Hon. Fellow, Gonville and Caius Coll., Cambridge; Hon. QC 1993; Hon. DrJur (Göttingen) 1980; Dott.Giur. hc (Ferrara) 1990, (Perugia) 2001; Hon. LLD (Aberdeen) 2000; Dr hc (Paris II) 2001. *Address:* Wimpole Cottage, 36 Wimpole Road, Great Eversden, Cambridge, CB3 7HR, England (home). *Telephone:* (1223) 262349 (home). *E-mail:* gonville@waitrose.com (home).

STEIN, Robert A., MA; American writer; b. 5 Aug. 1933, Duluth, MN; m. Betty L. Pavlik 1955, three s. *Education:* University of Iowa. *Career:* Officer and Pilot, US Air Force, 1956–77; Asst Prof., 1964–66, Assoc. Prof., 1966–68, Prof., 1975–77, University of Iowa; Faculty, Division of Writing, Kirkwood Community College, Iowa City and Cedar Rapids, 1984–89; mem. Authors' Guild; Authors' League of America. *Publications:* Fiction: Apollyon, 1985; Death Defied, 1988; The Chase, 1988; The Black Samaritan, 1997; The Vengeance Equation, 2000. Non-Fiction: Statistical Correlations, 1967; Engineers Vs. Other Students: Is There A Difference?, 1967; Whatever Happened to Moe Bushkin?, 1967; Quest for Viability: One Way!, 1976; Threat of Emergency, 1988. *Honours:* five wartime decorations; nine service awards; Outstanding Faculty Award, 1967–68, Lifetime Achievement Award, 1999, University of Iowa; Iowa Authors' Collection, 1985; Minnesota Authors' Collection, 1987; International Literary Award, 1988.

STEINBACH, Meredith Lynn, BGS, MFA; American academic and writer; *Professor of English, Brown University*; b. 18 March 1949, Ames, IA; d. of Christopher Gene Steinbach and Joy Janice Steinbach (née Johnson); m. Charles Ossian Hartman 1979 (divorced 1991); one s. *Education:* Univ. of Iowa. *Career:* Teaching Fellow, Univ. of Iowa 1975–76; Writer-in-Residence, Antioch Coll. 1976–77; Lecturer, Northwestern Univ. 1977–79; Visiting Asst Prof., Univ. of Washington 1979–82; Asst Prof. to Assoc. Prof., Brown Univ. 1983–97, Prof. of English 1997–; mem. PEN, Associated Writing Programs, Amnesty International. *Publications:* novels: Zara 1982, Here Lies the Water 1990, The Birth of the World as We Know It, or Teiresias 1996; fiction collection: Reliable Light 1990; play: In the Realm of Which There Is No Sign; contrib. to Tri-Quarterly Magazine, Antaeus, Massachusetts Review, Antioch Review, Southwest Review, Black Warrior Review, Tuyonui, 13th Moon, Ploughshares. *Honours:* Pushcart Prize, Best of the Small Presses 1977, Nat. Endowment for the Arts Fellowship 1978, Bunting Fellow, Bunting Summer Fellow, Mary Ingraham Bunting Inst., Radcliffe Coll., Harvard 1982–83, Rhode Island Artists Fellowship 1986–87, Rhode Island Award for Excellence in Literature, RI Council on Arts 1986–87, O. Henry Award 1990, Travel Study Grant to France and Greece 1993–94, Thomas J. Watson Travel Grantee, Thomas J. Watson Inst. for Int. Study, France and Greece 1993–94. *Address:* Department of English, Box 1923, Brown University, Providence, RI 02912, USA (office). *E-mail:* meredith_steinbach@brown.edu (office).

STEINECKERT, Gisela; German writer and journalist; b. 13 May 1931, Berlin; m. Wilhelm Penndorf 1973; one d. *Career:* Former social worker, office worker and ed. in Berlin; writer of poetry, novels, essays, songs, prose and films 1957–; Cttee Pres. Demokratisches Frauenbund 1984–90, later Hon. Chair.; Heinrich Heine award 1977; Nat. Preis für Kunst und Literatur 1986. *Address:* Leipziger Str 41, 1080 Berlin, Germany. *Telephone:* (30) 2081948.

STEINEM, Gloria, BA; American writer, journalist and feminist activist; *Consulting Editor, Ms Magazine*; b. 25 March 1934, Toledo; d. of Leo Steinem and Ruth (née Nuneviller) Steinem; m. David Bale 2000. *Education:* Smith Coll. *Career:* Chester Bowles Asian Fellow, India 1957–58; Co-Dir, Dir Ind. Research Service, Cambridge, Mass. and New York 1959–60; editorial asst, contributing, ed., freelance writer various nat. and New York publs 1960–; co-founder New York Magazine, contrib. 1968–72; co-founder Ms Magazine 1972 (Ed. 1971–87, columnist 1980–87, consulting ed. 1987–); feminist lecturer 1969–; active various civil rights and peace campaigns including United Farmworkers, Vietnam War Tax Protest, Cttee for the Legal Defense of Angela Davis and political campaigns of Adlai Stevenson, Robert Kennedy, Eugene McCarthy, Shirley Chisholm, George McGovern; co-founder and Chair Bd Women's Action Alliance 1970–; Convenor, mem. Nat. Advisory Cttee Nat. Women's Political Caucus 1971–; Co-Founder, Pres. Bd Dirs Ms Foundation for Women 1972–; founding mem. Coalition of Labor Union Women; Woodrow Wilson Int. Center for Scholars Fellow 1977. *Publications:* The Thousand Indias 1957, The Beach Book 1963, Outrageous Acts and Everyday Rebellions 1983, Marilyn 1986, Revolution From Within: A Book of Self-Esteem 1992, Moving Beyond Words 1994; contribs to various anthologies. *Honours:* Penney-Missouri Journalism Award 1970, Ohio Gov.'s Award for Journalism 1972, named Woman of the Year, McCall's Magazine 1972, Missouri Honor Medal for Distinguished Service in Journalism 2004. *Address:* c/o Ms Magazine, 433 South Beverly Drive, Beverly Hills, CA 90212, USA (office). *Website:* www.msmagazine.com (office).

STEINER, (Francis) George, DPhil, FBA, FRSL; British writer and scholar; b. 23 April 1929, Paris, France; s. of Dr Steiner and Mrs F. G. Steiner; m. Zara Shakow 1955; one s. one d. *Education:* Univ. of Paris, Univ. of Chicago, Harvard Univ., USA and Balliol Coll. Oxford, UK. *Career:* editorial staff, The Economist, London 1952–56; Fellow, Inst. for Advanced Study, Princeton 1956–58; Gauss Lecturer, Princeton Univ. 1959–60; Fellow and Dir of English Studies, Churchill Coll. Cambridge 1961–69, Extraordinary Fellow 1969–, Pensioner Fellow 1996–; Albert Schweitzer Visiting Prof., New York Univ. 1966–67; Visiting Prof., Yale Univ. 1970–71; Prof. of English and Comparative Literature, Univ. of Geneva 1974–94, Prof. Emer. 1994–; Visiting Prof., Collège de France 1992; First Lord Weidenfeld Visiting Prof. of Comparative Literature, Univ. of Oxford 1994–95; Charles Eliot Norton Prof. of Poetry, Harvard Univ. 2001–02; Pres. The English Assen 1975–76; Corresp. mem. German Acad., Harvard Club, New York. *Publications:* Tolstoy or Dostoevsky: An Essay in the Old Criticism 1958, The Death of Tragedy 1960, Homer: A Collection of Critical Essays (co-ed. with Robert Flagles) 1962, Anno Domini: Three Stories 1964, The Penguin Book of Modern Verse Translation (ed.) 1966, Language and Silence 1967, Extraterritorial 1971, In Bluebeard's

Castle: Some Notes Towards the Re-Definition of Culture 1971, The Sporting Scene: White Knights in Reykjavík 1973, Fields of Force 1974, A Nostalgia for the Absolute (Massey Lectures) 1974, After Babel: Aspects of Language and Translation 1975, Heidegger 1978, On Difficulty and Other Essays 1978, The Portage to San Cristóbal of A.H. 1981, Antigones 1984, George Steiner: A Reader 1984, Real Presences: Is There Anything in What We Say? 1989, Proofs and Three Parables 1992, The Deeps of the Sea 1996, Homer in English 1996, No Passion Spent 1996, Errata: An Examined Life 1998, Grammars of Creation 2001, Lessons of the Masters: The Charles Eliot Morton Lectures 2001–2002 2004. Honours: Hon. mem. American Acad. of Arts and Sciences 1989; Hon. RA (London) 2004; Hon. Fellow, Balliol Coll., Oxford, St Anne's Coll., Oxford; Chevalier, Légion d'honneur; Commdr, Ordre des Arts et des Lettres 2001; Hon. DLitt (East Anglia) 1976, (Louvain) 1979, (Bristol) 1989, (Glasgow, Liège) 1990, (Ulster) 1993, (Kenyon Coll., USA) 1995, (Trinity Coll. Dublin) 1995, (Rome) 1998, (Sorbonne) 1998, (Salamanca) 2002, (Athens) 2004, (London) 2006, (Bologna) 2006; O. Henry Award 1958, Jewish Chronicle Book Award 1968, Zabel Prize of Nat. Inst. of Arts and Letters 1970, Le Prix du Souvenir 1974, Massey Lecturer 1974, Ransom Memorial Lecturer 1976, King Albert Medal of the Royal Belgian Acad. 1982, F.D. Maurice Lecturer, Univ. of London 1984, Leslie Stephen Lecturer, Univ. of Cambridge 1985, Robertson Lecturer, Courtauld Inst., London 1985, W.P. Ker Lecturer, Univ. of Glasgow 1986, Page-Barbour Lecturer, Univ. of Virginia 1987, Gifford Lecturer 1990, Priestley Lecturer, Univ. of Toronto 1995, Prince of Asturias Prize 2001, 2002. Address: 32 Barrow Road, Cambridge, CB2 8AS, England.

STEINMAN, Lisa Jill Malinowski, BA, MFA, PhD; American academic, poet, writer and editor; *Kenan Professor of English, Reed College*; b. 8 April 1950, Willimantic, Conn.; m. James L. Shugrue 1984. *Education:* Cornell Univ., Ithaca, NY. *Career:* Asst Prof., Reed Coll., Portland, Ore. 1976–82, Assoc. Prof. 1982–89, Prof. 1990–93, Kenan Prof. of English 1993–; Poetry Ed. Hubbub Magazine 1983–; Rockefeller Scholar-in-Residence, 92nd Street Y Poetry Center 1987; mem. Associated Writing Programs, Modern Language Assocn, PEN, PEN/Northwest, Poets and Writers, Wallace Stevens Soc., William Carlos Williams Soc. (Pres. 1998–2000). *Publications:* Lost Poems 1976, Made in America: Science, Technology, and American Modernist Poets 1987, All That Comes to Light 1989, A Book of Other Days 1993, Ordinary Songs 1996, Masters of Repetition: Poetry, Culture, and Work 1998, Carslaw's Sequences 2003, An Invitation to Poetry 2007; contrib. to books, anthologies, reviews, quarterlies and journals. *Honours:* Scholar, Bread Loaf Writers Conf. 1981, Oregon Arts Comm. Poetry Fellow 1983, Nat. Endowment for the Arts Fellowship 1984, Pablo Neruda Award, Nimrod Magazine 1987, Rockelfeller Scholar, 92nd Street Y Poetry Center 1987–88, Outstanding Academic Book, Choice 1989, Oregon Book Award, Oregon Inst. of Literary Arts 1993, Nat. Endowment for the Humanities Fellowship 1996, 2006. *Address:* Department of English, Reed College, 3203 SE Woodstock Blvd, Portland, OR 97202 (office); 5344 SE 38th Avenue, Portland, OR 97202, USA (home). *Telephone:* (503) 517-7464 (office). *Fax:* (503) 777-7769 (office). *E-mail:* lisa.steinman@reed.edu (office).

STENGEL, Richard, BA; American editor; *Managing Editor, Time magazine*; b. 2 May 1955, New York, NY; m. Mary Pfaff; two c. *Education:* Princeton Univ. and Christ Church Coll., Oxford, England. *Career:* worked for MSNBC (TV); staff writer, Time magazine, New York 1981–83, Assoc. Ed. 1984–88, sr writer and essayist 1989–98; Ferris Prof. of Journalism, Princeton Univ. 1998–99; Sr Adviser and chief speechwriter for presidential candidate, Bill Bradley 1999; Man. Ed., Time.com 2000, Cultural Ed., Time magazine, then Nat. Ed. and Asst Man. Ed. –2004; Pres. and CEO, Nat. Constitutional Center, Philadelphia 2004–06; Man. Ed., Time magazine 2006–. *Film:* Mandela (prod., documentary) 1995. *Publications:* January Sun: One Day, Three Lives, a South African Town 1990, Long Walk to Freedom (with Nelson Mandela) 1993, You're Too Kind: A Brief History of Flattery 2000; contrib. articles to The New Yorker, The New Republic, New York Times and others. *Address:* Time magazine, Time-Life Building, 1271 Avenue of the Americas, New York, NY 10020, USA (office). *E-mail:* letters@time.com (office). *Website:* www.time.com.

STEPHAN, John Jason, BA, MA, PhD; American academic and historian; *Emeritus Professor of History, University of Hawaii*; b. 8 March 1941, Chicago, IL; m. 1963. *Education:* Harvard Univ., Univ. of London, England. *Career:* Far Eastern Ed., Harvard Review 1962; Visiting Fellow, St Antony's College, Oxford 1977; Prof. of History 1970–2001, Emeritus Prof. of History 2001–, Univ. of Hawaii; Visiting Prof. of History, Stanford Univ. 1986; Research Fellow, Kennan Inst. of Advanced Russian Studies 1987; mem. Authors' Guild, American Historical Asscn, Canadian Historical Asscn; life mem. PEN, Int. House of Japan, American Asscn for the Advancement of Slavic Studies. *Publications:* Sakhalin: A History, 1971; The Kuril Islands: Russo-Japanese Frontier in the Pacific, 1974; The Russian Fascists, 1978; Hawaii Under the Rising Sun, 1984; Soviet-American Horizons in the Pacific (with V. P. Chichkanov), 1986; The Russian Far East: A History, 1994. Contributions: Washington Post; Modern Asian Studies; American Historical Review; Pacific Affairs; Pacific Community; Journal for Asian Studies; New York Times; Siberica; Pacifica; Australian Slavic and East European Studies. *Honours:* Fulbright Fellowship, 1967–68; Japan Culture Trans. Prize, 1973; Japan Foundation Fellowship, 1977; Sanwa Distinguished Scholar, Fletcher School of Law and Diplomacy, Tufts University, 1989; Distinguished Invited Speaker, Canadian Historical Asscn, 1990; Kenneth W. Baldridge Prize,

1996. *Address:* c/o Department of History, University of Hawaii, 2530 Dole Street, Honolulu, HI 96822, USA.

STEPHEN, Ian, BEd; British writer, poet and artist; b. 29 April 1955, Stornoway, Isle of Lewis, Scotland; m. Barbara Ziehm 1984, two s. *Education:* University of Aberdeen. *Career:* Inaugural Robert Louis Stevenson/Christian Salvesen Fellow, Grez-sur-Loing, France, 1995; mem. PEN Scotland. *Plays:* Seven Hunters (dir Gerry Mulgrew) 2003, Brazil 12 Scotland nil (dir Morven Gregor) 2004, The Sked Crew (dir Alison Peebles) 2007. *Publications:* Malin, Hebrides, Minches, 1983; Varying States of Grace, 1989; Siud an T-Eilean (ed.), 1993; Providence II, 1994; Broad Bay, 1997; Green Waters, 1998; Mackerel and Creamola (short stories), 2001, Selected Poems (in English and Czech) 2007; other: numerous exhibitions of poetry/texts with visual arts; contrib. to UK and Australian publications. *Honours:* Scottish Arts Council Bursaries, 1981, 1995; Creative Scotland Award, 2002. *Address:* Sail Loft 2, North Beach, Stornoway, Western Isles HS1 2XN, Scotland. *Telephone:* (1851) 705320. *E-mail:* netloft2@onetel.com.

STEPHENS, Meic, BA, DLitt; Welsh journalist, poet, writer, editor and translator; *Professor Emeritus of Welsh Writing in English, University of Glamorgan*; b. 23 July 1938, Trefforest, Pontypridd, Wales; m. Ruth Wynn Meredith 1965; one s. three d. *Education:* Univ. Coll. of Wales, Aberystwyth, Univ. of Rennes, Univ. Coll. of North Wales, Bangor. *Career:* teacher of French 1962–66, journalist Western Mail 1966–67; Literature Dir, Welsh Arts Council 1967–90; Visiting Prof., Brigham Young Univ., Provo, UT 1991; Lecturer in Journalism, Univ. of Glamorgan 1994–2000, Centre for Journalism Studies, Cardiff Univ. 1998; Prof. of Welsh Writing in English, Univ. of Glamorgan 2001–03, Prof. Emer. 2003–; Literary Ed. Cambria; mem. Gorsedd of Bards, Welsh Acad. *Publications:* Linguistic Minorities in Western Europe, New Companion to the Literature of Wales, A Dictionary of Literary Quotations, The Oxford Literary Guide to Great Britain and Ireland, The Collected Poems of Harri Webb, The Complete Poems of Glyn Jones, The Collected Short Stories of Rhys Davies, The Literary Pilgrim in Wales, Welsh Names for Your Children, Illuminations: An Anthology of Welsh Short Prose, A Semester in Zion: A Journal With Memoirs, Decoding the Hare; translations: Monica, Shadow of the Sickle, Return to Lleifior, The Basques, For the Sake of Wales, The Plum Tree, A White Afternoon, A Militant Muse, No Half-way House; contrib. to various anthologies, reference works and journals. *Honours:* Hon. MA. *Address:* 10 Heol Don, Whitchurch, Cardiff, CF14 2AU, Wales (home). *Telephone:* (2920) 623359 (home). *E-mail:* hwncomanco@hotmail.co.uk (home).

STEPHENS, Michael Gregory, BA, MA, MFA; American writer, poet and dramatist; b. 4 March 1946, USA. *Education:* City College, CUNY and Yale University. *Career:* Lecturer, Columbia University, 1977–91, Princeton University, 1986–91, New York University, 1989–91; Writer-in-Residence and Asst Prof., Fordham University, 1979–85; mem. Associated Writing Programs; PEN; Royal Asiatic Society. *Publications:* Fiction: Season at Coole, 1972; Paragraphs, 1974; Still Life, 1978; Shipping Out, 1979; The Brooklyn Book of the Dead, 1994. Poetry: Alcohol Poems, 1972; Tangun Legend, 1978; After Asia, 1993. Other: Circles End (poems and prose), 1982; The Dramaturgy of Style, 1986; Lost in Seoul: And Other Discoveries on the Korean Peninsula, 1990; Jig and Reels, 1992; Green Dreams: Essays Under the Influence of the Irish, 1994. Plays: A Splendid Occasion in Spring, 1974; Off-Season Rates, 1978; Cloud Dream, 1979; Our Father, 1980; R & R, 1984. Contributions: many newspapers, journals, and magazines. *Honours:* MacDowell Colony Fellowship, 1968; Fletcher Pratt Fellowship, Bread Loaf Writers Conference, 1971; Creative Artists Public Service Fiction Award, 1978; Connecticut Commission on the Arts Grant, 1979; Associated Writing Programs Award in Creative Non-Fiction, 1993.

STEPHENS, Reed (see Donaldson, Stephen Reeder)

STEPHENSON, Hugh; British journalist and academic; *Professor Emeritus, Department of Journalism, City University London*; b. 18 July 1938, Simla, India; s. of the late Sir Hugh Stephenson and Lady Stephenson; m. 1st Auriol Stevens 1962 (divorced 1987); two s. one d.; m. 2nd Diana Eden 1990. *Education:* New Coll. Oxford, Univ. of California, Berkeley, USA. *Career:* served diplomatic service, London and Bonn 1964–68; with The Times, London 1969–81, Ed., The Times Business News 1971–81; Ed. The New Statesman 1982–86; Prof. of Journalism, City Univ. 1986–2003, Prof. Emer. 2003–; Dir History Today Ltd 1981–; Dir European Journalism Centre, Maastricht 1992–, Chair. 1995–2002. *Publications:* The Coming Clash 1972, Mrs. Thatcher's First Year 1980, Claret and Chips 1982, Libel and the Media (with others) 1997. *Address:* Department of Journalism, City University, Northampton Square, London, EC1V 0HB, England (office). *Telephone:* (20) 7040-8221 (office). *Fax:* (20) 7040-8594 (office). *E-mail:* h.stephenson@city.ac.uk (office). *Website:* www.city.ac.uk/journalism (office).

STEPHENSON, Neal, BA; American writer; b. 31 Oct. 1959, Fort Meade, MD. *Education:* Ames High School, IA, Univ. of Boston. *Publications:* novels: The Big U 1984, Zodiac: The Eco-Thriller 1988, Snow Crash 1991, Diamond Age 1995, Cryptonomicon 1999, Quicksilver (Arthur C. Clarke Award 2004) 2003, The Confusion 2004, The System of the World 2004. *Address:* c/o William Heinemann, Random House, 20 Vauxhall Bridge Road, London, SW1V 2SA, England. *Website:* www.randomhouse.co.uk.

STERN, Fritz, PhD; American historian and academic; *University Professor Emeritus, Columbia University*; b. 2 Feb. 1926, Breslau, Germany; s. of Rudolf

A. Stern and Catherine B. Stern; m. 1st Margaret J. Bassett 1947 (divorced 1992); one s. one d.; m. 2nd Elisabeth Niebuhr Sifton 1996. *Education:* Bentley School, New York, Columbia Univ. *Career:* Lecturer and Instructor Columbia Univ. 1946–51; Acting Asst Prof. Cornell Univ. 1951–53; Asst Prof. Columbia Univ. 1953–57, Assoc. Prof. 1957–63, Full Prof. 1963–67, Seth Low Prof. 1967–92, Univ. Prof. 1992–96, Univ. Prof. Emer. 1997–, Provost 1980–83; Visiting Prof. Free Univ. of Berlin 1954, Yale Univ. 1963, Fondation Nationale des Sciences Politiques, Paris 1979; Perm. Visiting Prof. Konstanz Univ. 1966–; Consultant US State Dept 1966–67; Guggenheim Fellowship 1969–70; mem. OECD team on German Educ. 1971–72; Netherlands Inst. for Advanced Study 1972–73; Trustee German Marshall Fund 1981–99, Aspen Inst. Berlin 1983–2000; Sr Adviser, US Embassy, Bonn 1993–94; mem. American Acad. of Arts and Sciences 1969–, Trilateral Comm. 1983–90, American Philosophical Soc. 1988, German-American Academic Council 1993–97; Corresp. mem. Deutsche Akad. für Dichtung und Sprache 1988; Senator, Deutsche Nationalstiftung 1993–. *Publications:* The Politics of Cultural Despair: A Study in the Rise of the Germanic Ideology 1961, Gold and Iron: Bismarck, Bleichroeder and the Building of the German Empire 1977, The Failure of Illiberalism: Essays in the Political Culture of Modern Germany 1972, Dreams and Delusions: The Drama of German History 1987; ed. The Varieties of History from Voltaire to the Present 1956, Der Nationalsozialismus als Versuchung, in Reflexionen Finsterer Zeit 1984, Verspielte Grösse: Essays zur deutschen Geschichte 1996, Das Feine Schweigen: Historische Essays 1999, Einstein's German World 1999, Grandeurs et Defaillances de l'Allemagne du XXème Siècle 2001, Five Germanys I Have Known 2006. *Honours:* Orden pour le Mérite (Germany) 1994; Hon. DLitt (Oxford) 1985; Hon. LLD (New School for Social Research, New York) 1997, (Columbia Univ.) 1998, (Wrocław) 2002; Lionel Trilling Book Award 1977, Lucas Prize (Tübingen) 1984, Kulturpreis Schlesien (Wrocław) 1996, Peace Prize of the German Book Trade 1999, Alexander-von-Humboldt Research Prize 1999, Bruno Snell Medal, Univ. of Hamburg 2002. *Address:* 15 Claremont Avenue, New York, NY 10027, USA. *Telephone:* (212) 666-2891 (home). *Fax:* (212) 316-0370 (home). *E-mail:* fs20@columbia.edu (home).

STERN, Gerald, BA, MA; American poet and teacher; b. 22 Feb. 1925, Pittsburgh, PA; m. Patricia Miller 1952; one s. one d. *Education:* Univ. of Pittsburgh, Columbia Univ. *Career:* Instructor, Temple Univ., Philadelphia 1957–63; Prof., Indiana Univ. of Pennsylvania 1963–67, Somerset County Coll., NJ 1968–82; Visiting Poet, Sarah Lawrence Coll. 1977; Visiting Prof., Univ. of Pittsburgh 1978, Columbia Univ. 1980, Bucknell Univ. 1988, New York Univ. 1989; Faculty Writer's Workshop, Univ. of Iowa 1982–94; Distinguished Chair, Univ. of Alabama 1984; Fanny Hurst Prof., Washington Univ., St Louis 1985; Bain Swiggert Chair, Princeton Univ. 1989; poet-in-residence, Bucknell Univ. 1994; New Jersey Poet Laureate. *Publications:* The Naming of Beasts and Other Poems 1973, Rejoicings 1973, Lucky Life 1977, The Red Coal 1981, Paradise Poems 1984, Lovesick 1987, Leaving Another Kingdom: Selected Poems 1990, Two Long Poems 1990, Bread Without Sugar 1992, Odd Mercy 1995, This Time: New and Selected Poems 1998, Last Blue 2000, American Sonnets 2002, What I Can't Bear Losing: Notes from a Life 2003, Not God After All 2004, Everything is Burning 2005. *Honours:* NEA grants 1976, 1981, 1987, Lamont Poetry Selection Award 1977, Governor's Award, PA 1980, Guggenheim Fellowship 1980, Bess Hokin Award 1980, Bernard F. Connor Award 1981, Melville Cane Award 1982, Jerome J. Shestack Prize 1984, Acad. of American Poets Fellowship 1993, Ruth Lilly Poetry Prize 1996, Nat. Book Award for Poetry 1998, Wallace Stevens Award 2005. *Address:* 89 Clinton Street, Lambertville, NJ 08530, USA. *Telephone:* (609) 397-2562 (home).

STERN, Jane, MFA; American writer; b. 24 Oct. 1946, d. of Milton Grossman and Norma Weyler; m. Michael Stern 1970. *Education:* The Pratt Inst., Brooklyn, NY and Yale Univ. *Career:* writer on popular American culture (co-author with Michael Stern); numerous appearances on radio and TV; co-writer 'Roadfood' column for Gourmet magazine. *Publications include:* Trucker: A Portrait of the Last American Cowboy 1975, Amazing America 1978, Friendly Relations 1979, Auto Ads 1979, Horror Holiday: Secrets of Vacation Survival 1981, Where to Eat in Connecticut: The Very Best Meals and the Very Best Deals 1985, Ambulance Girl: How I Saved Myself by Becoming an EMT 2003; with Michael Stern: Goodfood 1983, Roadfood 1986, Real American Food: Jane and Michael Stern's Coast-to-Coast Cookbook from Yankee Red Flannel Hash and the Ultimate Navajo Taco to Beautiful Swimme 1986, Elvis World 1987, A Taste of America 1988, Sixties People 1990, The Encyclopedia of Bad Taste 1990, American Gourmet: Classic Recipes, Deluxe Delights, Flamboyant Favorites and Swank Company Food from the 50s and 60s 1991, Jane and Michael Stern's Encyclopedia of Pop Culture: An A to Z Guide of Who's Who and What's What, from Aerobics and Bubble Gum to Valley of the Doll 1992, Way Out West 1993, Happy Trails: Our Life Story (with others) 1994, Eat Your Way Across the USA: 500 Diners, Farmland Buffets, Lobster Shacks, Pie Palaces and Other All-American Eateries 1997, Dog Eat Dog: A Very Human Book About Dogs and Dog Shows 1997, Two Puppies 1998, Chili Nation: The Ultimate Chili Cookbook with Recipes from Every State in the Nation 1999, Blue Plate Specials and Blue Ribbon Chefs: The Heart and Soul of America's Great Roadside Restaurants 2001, The Blue Willow Inn Cookbook 2001, El Charro Cafe Cookbook 2002, The Durgin-Park Cookbook: Classic Yankee Cooking in the Shadow of Faneuil Hall 2002, Roadfood: The Coast-to-Coast Guide to 500 of the Best Barbecue Joints, Lobster Shacks, Ice-Rearm Parlors, Highway Diners and Much, Much More 2002, The Louie's Backyard Cookbook 2003, The Harry Caray's Restaurant Cookbook: The Official Home Plate of the Chicago Cubs 2003, The Famous Dutch Kitchen Restaurant Cookbook: Family-Style Diner Delights from the Heart of Pennsylvania 2004, Cooking in the Lowcountry from The Old Post Office Restaurant: Spanish Moss Warm Nights and Fabulous Southern Food 2004, Southern California Cooking from The Cottage: Casual Cuisine from Old La Jolla's Favorite Beachside Bungalow 2004, Southern Country Cooking from the Loveless Cafe: Fried Chicken, Hams and Jams from Nashville's Favorite Cafe 2005, Elegant Comfort Food from Dorset Inn: Traditional Cooking from Vermont's Oldest Continuously-Operating Inn 2005, Two for the Road: Our Love Affair with American Food 2006. *Honours:* three James Beard Awards (for Roadfood column). *Address:* 28 Wayside, West Redding, CT 06896, USA. *Website:* www.roadfood.com.

STERN, Madeleine Bettina, BA, MA; American rare book dealer and writer; b. 1 July 1912, New York, NY. *Education:* Barnard Coll., Columbia Univ. *Career:* mem. Manuscript Soc., Antiquarian Booksellers Asscn of America, MLA, Authors' League. *Publications:* The Life of Margaret Fuller 1942, Louisa May Alcott 1950, Purple Passage: The Life of Mrs Frank Leslie 1953, Imprints on History: Book Publishers and American Frontiers 1956, We the Women: Career Firsts of 19th Century America 1962, The Pantarch: A Biography of Stephen Pearl Andrews 1968, Heads and Headlines: The Phrenological Fowlers 1971, Books and Book People in 19th Century America 1978, Antiquarian Bookselling in the United States: A History 1985, Old Books, Rare Friends: Two Literary Sleuths and Their Shared Passion (with Leona Rostenberg) 1997, Louisa May Alcott: From Blood and Thunder to Hearth and Home 1998, New Worlds in Old Books (with Leona Rostenberg) 1999, Books have their Fates (with Leona Rostenberg) 2001, Bookends (with Leona Rostenberg) 2001, From Revolution to Revolution: Perspectives on Publishing and Bookselling (with Leona Rostenberg) 2002; editor of numerous L. M. Alcott collections; contrib. to numerous publications. *Honours:* Guggenheim Fellowship, Distinguished Barnard Alumna Award and American Printing History Award (jtly). *Address:* 40 E 88th Street, New York, NY 10128, USA. *Telephone:* (212) 831-6628.

STERN, Michael; American writer; m. Jane Stern 1970. *Career:* writer on popular American culture (co-author with Jane Stern); numerous appearances on radio and TV; co-writer 'Roadfood' column for Gourmet magazine. *Publications:* Stern's Guide to Disney Collectibles: Vol. 1 1989, Vol. 2 1990, Collectors' Guide to Disneyana (with David Longest) 1992; with Jane Stern: Goodfood 1983, Roadfood 1986, Real American Food: Jane and Michael Stern's Coast-to-Coast Cookbook from Yankee Red Flannel Hash and the Ultimate Navajo Taco to Beautiful Swimme 1986, Elvis World 1987, A Taste of America 1988, Sixties People 1990, The Encyclopedia of Bad Taste 1990, American Gourmet: Classic Recipes, Deluxe Delights, Flamboyant Favorites and Swank Company Food from the 50s and 60s 1991, Jane and Michael Stern's Encyclopedia of Pop Culture: An A to Z Guide of Who's Who and What's What, from Aerobics and Bubble Gum to Valley of the Doll 1992, Way Out West 1993, Happy Trails: Our Life Story (with others) 1994, Eat Your Way Across the USA: 500 Diners, Farmland Buffets, Lobster Shacks, Pie Palaces and Other All-American Eateries 1997, Dog Eat Dog: A Very Human Book About Dogs and Dog Shows 1997, Two Puppies 1998, Chili Nation: The Ultimate Chili Cookbook with Recipes from Every State in the Nation 1999, Blue Plate Specials and Blue Ribbon Chefs: The Heart and Soul of America's Great Roadside Restaurants 2001, The Blue Willow Inn Cookbook 2001, El Charro Cafe Cookbook 2002, The Durgin-Park Cookbook: Classic Yankee Cooking in the Shadow of Faneuil Hall 2002, Roadfood: The Coast-to-Coast Guide to 500 of the Best Barbecue Joints, Lobster Shacks, Ice-Rearm Parlors, Highway Diners and Much, Much More 2002, The Louie's Backyard Cookbook 2003, The Harry Caray's Restaurant Cookbook: The Official Home Plate of the Chicago Cubs 2003, The Famous Dutch Kitchen Restaurant Cookbook: Family-Style Diner Delights from the Heart of Pennsylvania 2004, Cooking in the Lowcountry from The Old Post Office Restaurant: Spanish Moss Warm Nights and Fabulous Southern Food 2004, Southern California Cooking from The Cottage: Casual Cuisine from Old La Jolla's Favorite Beachside Bungalow 2004, Southern Country Cooking from the Loveless Cafe: Fried Chicken, Hams and Jams from Nashville's Favorite Cafe 2005, Elegant Comfort Food from Dorset Inn: Traditional Cooking from Vermont's Oldest Continuously-Operating Inn 2005, Two for the Road: Our Love Affair with American Food 2006. *Honours:* three James Beard Awards (for Roadfood column). *Address:* 28 Wayside, West Redding, CT 06896, USA. *Website:* www.roadfood.com.

STERN, Richard Gustave, BA, MA, PhD; American writer and academic; b. 25 Feb. 1928, New York, NY; m. 1st Gay Clark; m. 2nd Alane Rollings; three s. one d. *Education:* Univ. of North Carolina, Harvard Univ., Univ. of Iowa. *Career:* mem. American Acad. of Arts and Sciences; Center for Advanced Studies in Behavioural Sciences, fellow. *Publications:* Golk, 1960; Europe or Up and Down with Baggish and Schreiber, 1961; In Any Case, 1962; Stitch, 1965; Other Men's Daughters, 1973; A Father's Words, 1986; The Position of the Body, 1986; Noble Rot Stories, 1949–89, 1989; Shares and Other Fictions, 1992; One Person and Another, 1993; Sistermony, 1995; Pacific Tremors, 2001; What Is What Was, 2002; Almonds to Zhoof (short stories), 2004. Contributions: journals and magazines. *Honours:* Longwood Award, 1954; American Acad. of Arts and Letters Award, 1968; Friends of Literature Award, 1968; Sandburg Award, 1979; Award of Merit for the Novel, 1985; Heartland Prize, 1995. *Literary Agent:* C. A. Rollings, 5455 S Ridgewood

Court, Chicago, IL 60615, USA. *Address:* 1050 E 59th Street, Chicago, IL 60637, USA.

STERN, Steve; American academic and writer; b. 21 Dec. 1947, Memphis, TN. *Education:* BA, Rhodes College, 1970; MFA, University of Arkansas, 1977. *Career:* Visiting Lecturer, University of Wisconsin, 1987; Assoc. Prof. of English, Skidmore College, Saratoga Springs, New York, 1994–. *Publications:* Isaac and the Undertaker's Daughter 1983, The Moon and Ruben Shein 1984, Lazar Malkin Enters Heaven 1986, Mickey and the Golem 1986, Hershel and the Beast 1987, Harry Kaplan's Adventures Underground 1991, Plague of Dreamers 1994, The Wedding Jester (short stories) 1999, The Angel of Forgetfulness (novel) 2005; contrib. to magazines and journals. *Honours:* O. Henry Prize, 1981; Pushcart Writers Choice Award, 1984, and Prizes, 1997, 2000; Edward Lewis Wallant Award, 1988; National Jewish Book Award, 2000. *Address:* c/o Department of English, Skidmore College, Saratoga Springs, NY 12866, USA.

STERN, Stuart (see Rae, Hugh Crauford)

STERNBERG, Robert Jeffrey, BA, PhD; American academic, writer and editor; b. 8 Dec. 1949, Newark, NJ; m. Alejandra Campos 1991; one s. one d. *Education:* Yale Univ., Stanford Univ. *Career:* Asst Prof., 1975–80, Assoc. Prof., 1980–83, Prof., 1983–86, IBM Prof. of Psychology and Education, 1986–, Yale Univ.; Ed., Psychological Bulletin, 1991–96, Contemporary Psychology, 1999–; Ed.-in-Chief, Educational Psychology Series, Lawrence Erlbaum Assocs, 1996–; mem. American Acad. of Arts and Sciences, fellow; American Asscn for the Advancement of Science, fellow; American Educational Research Asscn; American Psychological Society, fellow; International Council of Psychologists; National Asscn for Gifted Children; Psychonomic Society; Society for Research in Child Development; Society of Multivariate Experimental Psychology; American Psychological Asscn, pres., 2003–. *Publications:* Intelligence, Information Processing, and Analogical Reasoning: The Componential Analysis of Human Abilities, 1977; Beyond IQ: A Triarchic Theory of Human Intelligence, 1985; Intelligence Applied: Understanding and Increasing Your Intellectual Skills, 1986; What is Intelligence? (with D. K. Detterman), 1986; The Psychologist's Companion, second edn, 1988; The Triangle of Love, 1988; The Triarchic Mind: A New Theory of Human Intelligence, 1988; Metaphors of Mind: Conceptions of the Nature of Intelligence, 1990; Love the Way You Want It, 1991; Tacit Knowledge Inventory for Managers (with R. K. Wagner), 1991; For Whom Does the Bell Curve Toll?: It Tolls for You, 1995; In Search of the Human Mind, 1995; Defying the Crowd: Cultivating Creativity in a Culture of Conformity (with T. I. Lubart), 1995; Off Track: When Poor Readers Become Learning Disabled (with L. Spear-Swerling), 1996; Cognitive Psychology, 1996; Successful Intelligence, 1996; Introduction to Psychology, 1997; Pathways to Psychology, 1997; Thinking Styles, 1997; Successful Intelligence, 1997; Cupid's Arrow: The Course of Love Through Time, 1998; Love is a Story, 1998; Perspectives on Learning Disabilities: Biological, Cognitive, Contextual (with L. Spear-Swerling), 1999; Our Labeled Children: What Every Parent and Teacher Needs to Know About Learning Disabilities (with E. L. Grigorenko), 1999; Teaching for Successful Intelligence (with E. L. Grigorenko), 2000; Psychology: In Search of the Human Mind, 2001; Educational Psychology (with W. M. Williams), 2001; Dynamic Testing (with E. L. Grigorenko), 2002; Psychology 101½: The Unspoken Rules for Success in Academia, 2004. Other: Ed. of many books. Contributions: numerous scholarly books and journals. *Honours:* Distinguished Scholar Award, National Asscn for Gifted Children, 1985; Outstanding Book Award, 1987, Sylvia Scribner Award, 1996, American Educational Research Asscn; Guggenheim Fellowship, 1985–86; Award for Excellence, Mensa Education and Research Foundation, 1989; Dr hc, Complutense Univ., Madrid, 1994; G. Stanley Hall Distinguished Lecturer, American Psychological Asscn, 1997; E. L. Thorndike Award for Career Achievement in Educational Psychology, 2003. *Address:* c/o Dept of Psychology, Yale University, PO Box 208205, New Haven, CT 06520, USA. *E-mail:* robert.sternberg@yale.edu.

STERNLICHT, Sanford, BS, MA, PhD; American academic, literary critic and poet; *Professor of English, Syracuse University;* b. 20 Sept. 1931, New York, NY; m. Dorothy Hilkert 1956 (died 1977); two s. *Education:* SUNY at Oswego, Colgate Univ., Syracuse Univ. *Career:* instructor 1959–60, Asst Prof. 1960–62, Assoc. Prof. 1962, Prof. of English 1962–72, Prof. of Theatre 1972–86, SUNY at Oswego; Leverhulme Foundation Visiting Fellow, Univ. of York, England 1965–66; Prof. of English, Syracuse Univ. 1986–; Fulbright Sr Specialist and Visiting Prof. of English, Univ. of Pécs, Hungary 2004; Fellow Poetry Soc. of America; mem. MLA, PEN, Shakespeare Asscn of America, American Conference for Irish Studies. *Publications:* poetry: Gull's Way 1961, Love in Pompeii 1967; non-fiction: Uriah Philips Levy: The Blue Star Commodore 1961, The Black Devil of the Bayous: The Life and Times of the United States Steam-Sloop Hartford (with E. M. Jameson) 1970, John Webster's Imagery and the Webster Canon 1974, John Masefield 1977, McKinley's Bulldog: The Battleship Oregon 1977, C. S. Forester 1981, USF Constellation: Yankee Racehorse (with E. M. Jameson) 1981, Padraic Colum 1985, John Galsworthy 1987, R. F. Delderfield 1988, Stevie Smith 1990, Stephen Spender 1992, Siegfried Sassoon 1993, All Things Herriot: James Herriot and his Peaceable Kingdom 1995, Jean Rhys 1996, A Reader's Guide to Modern Irish Drama 1998; editor: Selected Stories of Padraic Colum 1985, Selected Plays of Padraic Colum 1989, In Search of Stevie Smith 1991, New Plays from the Abbey Theatre 1993–1995 1996, Chaim Potok: A Critical Companion 2000, New Plays from the Abbey Theatre, 1996–1998 2001, A Reader's Guide to Modern American Drama 2002, A Student's Companion to Elie Wiesel 2003, The

Tenement Saga: The Lower East Side and Early Jewish American Writers 2004, A Reader's Guide to Modern British Drama 2004; contrib. to books, professional journals and general periodicals. *Honours:* prizes, fellowships and grants, including Sir Evelyn Wrench English-Speaking Union Travel/ Lecture grants 1997, 1998, 1999. *Address:* English Department, Syracuse University, Syracuse, NY 13244 (office); 128 Dorset Road, Syracuse, NY 13210, USA (home). *Telephone:* (315) 443-9480 (office); (315) 472-5639 (home). *E-mail:* svsternl@syr.edu.

STEVENS, Carl (see Obstfeld, Raymond)

STEVENS, Sir Jocelyn Edward Greville, Kt, CVO, FRSA; British publisher; b. 14 Feb. 1932, London; s. of Major C.G.B. Stewart-Stevens and Betty Hulton; m. Jane Armyne Sheffield 1956 (dissolved 1979); one s. two d. (one s. deceased). *Education:* Eton Coll., Cambridge Univ. *Career:* mil. service Rifle Brigade 1950–52; journalist Hulton Press 1955–56; Chair. and Man. Dir Stevens Press Ltd, Ed. Queen Magazine 1957–68; Personal Asst to Chair. Beaverbrook Newspapers 1968, Dir 1971–81, Man. Dir 1974–77; Man. Dir Evening Standard Co. Ltd 1969–72, Daily Express 1972–74; Deputy Chair. and Man. Dir Express Newspapers 1974–81; Ed. and Publr The Magazine 1982–84; Dir Centaur Communications 1982–84; Gov. Imperial Coll. of Science, Tech. and Medicine 1985–92, Winchester School of Art 1986–89; Rector and Vice-Provost RCA 1984–92; Chair. The Silver Trust 1990–93, English Heritage 1992–2000; Deputy Chair. Independent TV Comm. 1991–96; Dir (non-exec.) The TV Corpn 1996–2002, Asprey & Co. –2002, Garrard & Co. –2002; Pres. The Cheyne Walk Trust 1989–93; Chair. The Prince of Wales's Phoenix Trust; Trustee Eureka! The Children's Museum 1990–2000. *Honours:* Hon. DLitt (Loughborough) 1989, (Buckingham) 1998; Hon. FCSD 1990, Sr Fellow RCA 1990. *Address:* 14 Cheyne Walk, London, SW3 5RA, England. *Telephone:* (20) 7351-1141. *Fax:* (20) 7351-7963.

STEVENS, John (see Tubb, Edwin Charles)

STEVENS, Lynsey, (Lynette Desley Howard); Australian writer; b. 28 Sept. 1947, Sherwood, Qld. *Career:* mem. Queensland Writers Centre, Australian Soc. of Authors, Romance Writers of America, Romance Writers of Australia. *Publications:* Ryan's Return, 1981; Terebori's Gold, 1981; Race for Revenge, 1981; Play Our Song Again, 1981; Tropical Knight, 1982; Starting Over, 1982; Man of Vengeance, 1982; Closest Place to Heaven, 1983; Forbidden Wine, 1983; The Ashby Affair, 1983; Lingering Embers, 1984; Leave Yesterday Behind, 1986; But Never Love, 1988; A Rising Passion, 1990; Touched by Desire, 1993; A Physical Affair, 1994; Misteltoe Kisses (in Christmas Journeys), 1994; His Cousin's Wife, 1996; Close Relations, 1997; Male for Christmas, 1998. *Honours:* Arty, Romantic Times, Worldwide Romance 1984. *Address:* PO Box 400, Red Hill, Qld 4259, Australia. *E-mail:* lynsey@ecn.net .au. *Website:* www.lynseystevens.com.

STEVENS, Peter Stanley, BA, MA, PhD; Canadian academic, poet, critic and editor; *Professor, University of Windsor;* b. 17 Nov. 1927, Manchester, England; m. June Sidebotham 1957; one s. two d. *Education:* Univ. of Nottingham, McMaster Univ., Univ. of Saskatchewan. *Career:* Faculty, Hillfield-Strathallan Coll., Hamilton, ON 1957–64; part-time Lecturer, McMaster Univ. 1961–64; Lecturer and Asst Prof., Univ. of Saskatchewan 1964–69; Poetry Ed., Canadian Forum 1968–73, Literary Review of Canada 1994–96; Assoc. Prof. 1969–76, Prof. 1976–93, Univ. of Windsor. *Publications:* Nothing But Spoons 1969, The McGill Movement (ed.) 1969, A Few Myths 1971, Breadcrusts and Glass 1972, Family Feelings and Other Poems 1974, A Momentary Stay 1974, The Dying Sky Like Blood 1974, The Bogman Pavese Tactics 1977, Modern English-Canadian Poetry 1978, Coming Back 1981, Revenge of the Mistresses 1982, Out of the Willow Trees 1986, Miriam Waddington 1987, Swimming in the Afternoon: New and Selected Poems 1992, Dorothy Livesay: Patterns in a Poetic Life 1992, Rip Rap: Yorkshire Ripper Poems 1995, Thinking into the Dark 1997, Attending to This World 1998, States of Mind 2001, Bread from Stones 2002; contrib. to books, reviews and journals. *Address:* 2055 Richmond Street, Windsor, ON N8Y 1L3, Canada.

STEVENSON, Anne Katharine, MA, FRSL; British/American poet and writer; b. 3 Jan. 1933, Cambridge, England; d. of Charles Stevenson and Louise Destler; m. 1st Robin Hitchcock (divorced) 1955; one d.; m. 2nd Mark Elvin (divorced) 1962; two s.; m. 3rd Michael Farley 1979 (divorced); m. 4th Peter David Lucas 1987. *Education:* Univ. High School, Michigan, Univ. of Michigan. *Career:* Literary Fellow Lady Margaret Hall, Oxford 1973; Northern Arts Literary Fellow 1981–82; Writer-in-Residence, Univ. of Edinburgh 1989; mem. FEA, Soc. of Authors, The Welsh Acad. *Publications:* Living in America 1965, Elizabeth Bishop 1966, Reversals 1969, Travelling Behind Glass 1974, Correspondences 1974, Enough of Green 1977, Minute by Glass Minute 1982, The Fiction Makers 1985, Winter Time 1986, Selected Poems 1987, The Other House 1990, Four and a Half Dancing Men 1993, Collected Poems 1996, Bitter Fame: A Life of Sylvia Plath 1998, Five Looks at Elizabeth Bishop 1998, Between the Iceberg and the Ship (literary essays) 1998, Granny Scarecrow 2000, Hearing with My Fingers 2002, A Report from the Border 2003, Poems 1955–2005 2005; contrib. to reviews, journals and magazines. *Honours:* Dr hc (Durham) 2005; fellowships, Major Hopwood Award 1954, Arts Council Award 1974, Poetry Book Soc. Choice 1985, Athena Award 1990, Soc. of Authors Cholmondely Award 1997, Northern Rock Foundation Writers Award 2002. *Address:* c/o Bloodaxe Books, Highgreen, Tarset, NE48 1RP, England. *Website:* www.anne-stevenson.co.uk/poetry.

STEVENSON, David, BA, PhD, DLitt, FRSE; British academic and writer; b. 30 April 1942, Largs, Ayrshire, Scotland; m. Wendy McLeod; two s. *Education:* Univ. of Dublin, Univ. of Glasgow. *Career:* Faculty, Univ. of Aberdeen, Univ. of St Andrews. *Publications:* The Scottish Revolution 1973, Revolution and Counter-Revolution in Scotland 1977, Alastair MacColla and the Highland Problem 1980, Scottish Covenanters and Irish Confederates 1981, The Origins of Freemasonry 1988, The First Freemasons 1988, King or Covenant: Voices from Civil War 1996, Scotland's Last Royal Wedding 1997, Union, Revolution and Religion in 17th Century Scotland 1997, The Beggar's Benison. Sex Clubs of the Scottish Enlightenment and their Rituals 2001, The Hunt for Rob Roy 2003. *Address:* 5 Forgan Way, Newport-on-Tay, Fife, DD6 8JQ, Scotland. *E-mail:* david.stevenson@btinternet.com.

STEWART, Bruce Robert, BA; New Zealand writer and dramatist; b. 4 Sept. 1925, Auckland; m. Ellen Noonan 1950, three s. three d. *Education:* University of Auckland. *Career:* mem. British Film Institute, Writers' Guild of Australia, Writers' Guild of Great Britain (chair. 1979–81), Actors' Equity. *Publications:* A Disorderly Girl, 1980; The Turning Tide, 1980; The Hot and Copper Sky, 1982; Aspects of Therese, 1997; A Bloke Like Jesus, 1998. Other: various plays for stage, radio and television, including Me and My Shadow, 1988; The Gallows in My Garden, 1989; Stars in my Hair, 1990; Speak Low, 1993; Soeur Sourive, 2000. Contributions: newspapers, magazines and journals. *Honours:* MWA Edgar Allan Poe Award 1963, Charles Henry Foyle Award, UK 1968. *Address:* c/o Harvey Unna, 24 Pottery Lane, Holland Park, London W11, England. *E-mail:* hbstewart@beeb.net.

STEWART, Douglas Keith; New Zealand writer and critic; b. 15 Dec. 1950, Kawakana; m. Julie Joy Burgham 1972, one s. two d. *Education:* Northland College, University of Auckland. *Publications:* The New Zealander's Guide to Wine, 1986; The Art Award, 1988; The Wine Handbook, 1988; Rosa Antipodes: The History of Roses in New Zealand, 1994; The Fine Wines of New Zealand, 1995; Kahukura's Net: Maori Influence on Contemporary New Zealand Art, 1999; Euchre (novel), 1999. Contributions: newspapers and magazines.

STEWART, Harold Frederick; Australian poet, writer and translator; b. 14 Dec. 1916, Sydney, NSW. *Education:* University of Sydney. *Career:* broadcaster, Australian Broadcasting Commission; Lecturer, Victorian Council of Adult Education. *Publications:* Poetry: The Darkening Ecliptic (with James McAuley), 1944; Phoenix Wings: Poems 1940–46, 1948; Orpheus and Other Poems, 1956; The Exiled Immortal: A Song Cycle, 1980; By the Old Walls of Kyoto: A Year's Cycle of Landscape Poems with Prose Commentaries, 1981; Collected Poems (with Ern Malley), 1993. Translator: A Net of Fireflies: Japanese Haiku and Haiku Paintings, 1960; A Chime of Windbells: A Year of Japanese Haiku, 1969; Tannisho: Passages Deploring Deviations of Faith (with Bando Shojun), 1980; The Amida Sutra Mandala (with Inagaki Hisao), 1995. *Honours:* Sydney Morning Herald Prize for Poetry, 1951; Australia Council Grant, 1978; Senior Emeritus Writers Fellow, Australia Council, 1982; Christopher Brennan Prize for Poetry, 1988.

STEWART, John, MA, MFA, PhD; American academic and writer; b. 24 Jan. 1933, Trinidad; m. Sandra MacDonald 1969, one s. one d. *Education:* Stanford University, University of Iowa, University of California at Los Angeles. *Career:* University of Illinois; Ohio State University; University of California at Davis. *Publications:* Last Cool Days (novel), 1971; Curving Road (short stories), 1975; For the Ancestors (life history), 1983; Drinkers, Drummers and Decent Folk (narrative ethnography), 1989; Looking for Josephine (short stories), 1998. *Honours:* Winifred Hoztby Memorial Prize 1971.

STEWART, Judith (see Polley, Judith Anne)

STEWART, Martha Helen Kostyra, BA; American editor, writer and business executive; b. 3 Aug. 1941, Jersey City, NJ; d. of Edward Kostyra and Martha Kostyra (née Ruszkowski); m. Andy Stewart 1961 (divorced 1990); one s. *Education:* Barnard Univ. *Career:* fmr model, stockbroker, caterer; owner, Ed.-in-Chief Martha Stewart Living magazine 1990–; Founder, Chair. and CEO Martha Stewart Living Omnimedia 1997–2003, mem. Bd –2004, Founding Editorial Dir (non-exec.) March 2004–; also appears in cooking feature on Today Show; mem. Bd NY Stock Exchange June–Oct. 2002; mem. Bd Revlon Inc. –2004; under investigation for alleged insider trading June 2002, found guilty of conspiracy, making false statements and obstruction of justice March 2004, sentenced to prison and released March 2005, agreed with Securities and Exchange Comm. to settle insider trading charges and to maximum penalty of about $195,000, to a five-year bar from serving as a dir of a public co. and a five-year limitation on the scope of her service as an officer or employee of a public co. Aug. 2006. *Television:* host of TV show Martha 2005–, starred in The Apprentice: Martha Stewart 2005. *Publications include:* (with Elizabeth Hawes) Entertaining 1982, Weddings 1987; (as sole author) Martha Stewart's Hors d'Oeuvres: The Creation and Presentation of Fabulous Finger Food 1984, Martha Stewart's Pies and Tarts 1985, Martha Stewart's Quick Cook Menus 1988, The Wedding Planner 1988, Martha Stewart's Gardening: Month by Month 1991, Martha Stewart's New Old House: Restoration, Renovation, Decoration 1992, Martha Stewart's Christmas 1993, Martha Stewart's Menus for Entertaining 1994, Holidays 1994, The Martha Rules 2005, Martha Stewart's Homekeeping Handbook 2006. *Honours:* ranked by Fortune magazine amongst 50 Most Powerful Women in Business in the US (21st) 2005, (28th) 2006. *Address:* Martha Stewart Living Omnimedia, 11 West 42nd Street, 25th Floor, New York, NY 10036 (office); Martha Stewart, 19 Newton Toke, Suite 6, Westport, CT 06880; c/o Susan Magrino Agency, 40 West 57th Street, 31st Floor, New York, NY 10019; 10 Saugatuck Avenue,

Westport, CT 06880, USA (home). *Telephone:* (212) 827-8000 (office). *Fax:* (212) 827-8204 (office). *Website:* www.marthastewart.com.

STEWART, Lady Mary Florence Elinor, BA, DipEd, MA; British writer and poet; b. 17 Sept. 1916, Sunderland, England; m. Sir Frederick Henry Stewart 1945 (died 2001). *Education:* St Hilda's Coll., Durham Univ. *Career:* Asst Lecturer in English, Durham Univ. 1941–45, part-time Lecturer in English, St Hild's Training Coll., Durham and Durham Univ. 1948–56; mem. PEN. *Publications:* novels: Madam, Will You Talk? 1954, Wildfire at Midnight 1956, Thunder on the Right 1957, Nine Coaches Waiting 1958, My Brother Michael 1959, The Ivy Tree 1961, The Moonspinners 1962, This Rough Magic 1964, Airs Above the Ground 1965, The Gabriel Hounds 1967, The Wind off the Small Isles 1968, The Crystal Cave (Frederick Niven Prize 1971) 1970, The Hollow Hills 1973, Touch Not the Cat 1976, The Last Enchantment 1979, The Wicked Day 1983, Thornyhold 1988, Stormy Petrel 1991, The Prince and the Pilgrim 1995, Rose Cottage 1997; children's fiction: A Walk in Wolf Wood 1970, The Little Broomstick 1971, Ludo and the Star Horse (Scottish Arts Council Award) 1974; poetry: Frost on the Window and Other Poems 1990; contrib. to magazines. *Honours:* Hon. Fellow, Newnham Coll., Cambridge 1986.

STEWART, Paul; British writer; b. 4 June 1955, London, England; m. Julie Stewart; one s. one d. *Education:* Univ. of Lancaster, Univ. of East Anglia, Univ. of Heidelberg. *Publications:* Stormchaser 1999, The Birthday Presents 1999, The Blobheads (eight vols) 2000, Midnight Over Sanctaphrax 2000, Rabbit's Wish 2001, The Curse of the Gloamglozer 2001, The Were-pig 2001, The Last of the Sky Pirates 2002, Muddle Earth 2003, Vox 2003, Freeglader 2004, Fergus Crane (Smarties Gold Medal) 2004, Corby Flood (Smarties Silver Medal) 2005; with Chris Riddell: The Stone Pilot 2006, Clash of the Sky Galleons 2006, Hugo Pepper (with Chris Riddell) 2006. *Literary Agent:* c/o Philippa Milnes-Smith, L. A. W. Ltd, 14 Vernon Street, London, W14 0RJ, England.

STEWART, Rory, OBE, BA, MA; British diplomatist and writer; *Chief Executive Officer, Turquoise Mountain Foundation, Afghanistan;* b. Hong Kong. *Education:* Balliol Coll., Oxford. *Career:* fmrly in British Army; fmr Desk Officer (Japan and Korea), FCO, London; fmr Second Sec. (Political/ Economic), British Embassy in Jakarta, Indonesia; fmr British Representative in Montenegro –2000; walked from Turkey to Bangladesh 2000–02, crossing Iran, Afghanistan, Pakistan, India and Nepal; Deputy Governorate Co-ordinator (Amara/Maysan) and Sr Adviser and Deputy Governorate Co-ordinator (Nasiriyah/Dhi Qar), for the Coalition Provisional Authority, Maysan Province, Iraq 2003–04; Fellow, The Carr Center for Human Rights Policy, Harvard Univ. 2004–05; CEO Turquoise Mountain Foundation, Afghanistan 2005–. *Publications:* The Places in Between (Royal Soc. of Literature Ondaatje Prize 2005) 2004, Occupational Hazards 2006; contrib. to Granta, LRB, New York Times Magazine. *Address:* c/o Pan Macmillan, 20 New Wharf Road, London, N1 9RR, England (office).

STEWART, Susan, BA, MA, PhD; American writer, poet and educator; b. 15 March 1952, York, PA. *Education:* Dickinson College, Johns Hopkins University, University of Pennsylvania. *Career:* Asst Prof., 1978–81, Assoc. Prof., 1981–85, Prof. of English, 1985–, Temple University, Philadelphia, Pennsylvania. *Publications:* Nonsense: Aspects of Intertextuality in Folklore and Literature, 1979; Yellow Stars and Ice (poems), 1981; On Longing: Narratives of the Miniature, the Gigantic, the Souvenir, the Collection, 1984; The Hive: Poems, 1987; Crimes of Writing: Problems in the Containment of Representation, 1991; The Forest (poems), 1995. *Honours:* National Endowment for the Arts Grants, 1981–82, 1984, 1988; Pennsylvania Council on the Arts Grants, 1984, 1988, 1989–90; Guggenheim Foundation Fellowship, 1986–87; Georgia Press Second Book Award, 1987; Temple University Creative Achievement Award, 1991; Senior Scholar, Getty Center for the History of Art and the Humanities, 1995; Lila Wallace-Reader's Digest Writer's Award for Poetry, 1995; Pew Fellowship, 1995.

STIBBE, Mark W. G., BA, MA, PhD; British writer; b. 16 Sept. 1960, London, England; m. Alison Heather Stibbe 1983, two s. one d. *Education:* University of Cambridge, University of Nottingham. *Publications:* John as Storyteller, 1992; The Gospel of John as Literature, 1993; John: A New Biblical Commentary, 1993; A Kingdom of Priests, 1994; John's Gospel, 1994; Explaining Baptism in the Holy Spirit, 1995; O Brave New Church, 1996; Times of Refreshing, 1996; Know Your Spiritual Gifts, 1997. Contributions: numerous articles to Renewal; Anglicans for Renewal; various New Testament journals; Journal of Pentecostal Theology; Soul Survivor. *Honours:* Hon. MA, Hon. DipTh, Hon. PhD.

STIBOROVÁ, Věra; Czech writer; b. 15 Jan. 1926, Písek; m. Jaroslav Putík 1954; one d. *Education:* School of Applied Arts. *Career:* journalist, Lidové Noviny daily newspaper, Prague; journalist, translator Práce daily newspaper; collaborator with various literary magazines –1969; works prohibited in 1969, but many published through Samizdat; labourer and sales rep. 1972–89. *Publications include:* Blue Loves (Literary Award) 1963, The Minute on the Road 1968, Ikariana 1991, Forget, My River 1996, The Day of the Dames 1991, Come Back to Sorrento... 1995. *Address:* Pod Marjánkou 10, 169 00 Prague 6, Czech Republic.

STICKLAND, Caroline Amanda, BA; British writer; b. 10 Oct. 1955, Rinteln, Germany; m. William Stickland 1974, one d. *Education:* University of East Anglia. *Career:* mem. Society of Authors; Mrs Gaskell Society; Thomas Hardy Society. *Publications:* The Standing Hills, 1986; A House of Clay, 1988;

The Darkness of Corn, 1990; An Ancient Hope, 1993; The Darkening Leaf, 1995; The Kindly Ones, 2000. *Honours:* Betty Trask Award, 1985. *Address:* 81 Crock Lane, Bothenhampton, Bridport, Dorset DT6 4DQ, England.

STIGLITZ, Joseph Eugene, PhD, FBA; American economist and academic; *Professor of Economics and Finance, Graduate School of Business, Columbia University*; b. 9 Feb. 1943, Gary, Ind.; s. of Nathaniel D. Stiglitz and Charlotte Fishman; m. Jane Hannaway 1978; two s. two d. *Education:* Amherst Coll., Mass. Inst. of Tech. and Univ. of Cambridge (Fulbright Scholar). *Career:* Prof. of Econs Cowles Foundation, Yale Univ. 1970–74; Visiting Fellow, St Catherine's Coll. Oxford 1973–74; Prof. of Econs Stanford Univ. 1974–76, and Senior Fellow Hoover Inst. 1988–2001, Joan Kenney Prof. of Econs 1992–2001; Oskar Morgenstern Distinguished Fellow, Inst. of Advanced Studies, Princeton 1978–79; Drummond Prof. of Political Econ. Univ. of Oxford 1976–79; Prof. of Econs Princeton Univ. 1979–88; Stern Visiting Prof. Columbia Univ. 2000, Prof. of Econs and Finance, Graduate School of Business, Columbia Univ. 2001–; mem. Pres.'s Council of Econ. Advisers 1993–95, Chair. (mem. of cabinet) 1995–97; Special Adviser to Pres. of World Bank, Sr Vice-Pres. and Chief Economist 1995–2000; Special Adviser, Bell Communications Research, numerous consultancies in public and pvt. sector, editorial Bd memberships etc.; Sr Fellow Brookings Inst. 2000; Fellow American Acad. of Arts and Sciences, NAS, Econometric Soc., American Philosophical Soc., Inst. for Policy Research (Sr Fellow 1991–93); Guggenheim Fellow 1969–70. *Publications include:* Globalization and its Discontents, Economics of the Public Sector 2000, Principles of Economics 1997, Rethinking the East Asia Miracle (co-ed.) 2001, The Roaring Nineties 2003, Making Globalization Work 2006; other books and more than 300 papers in learned journals. *Honours:* Hon. DHL (Amherst Coll.) 1974; Dr hc (Univ. of Leuven), (Ben Gurion Univ.); John Bates Clark Award, American Econ. Asscn 1979; Int. Prize, Acad. Lincei, Rome 1988; UAP Scientific Prize, Paris 1989; Nobel Prize for Econs (jt recepient) 2001, Dr. hc (Oxford) 2004. *Address:* Uris Hall, Room 814, Columbia University, 3022 Broadway, New York, NY 10027, USA (office). *Telephone:* (212) 854-1481 (office). *Fax:* (212) 662-8474 (office). *E-mail:* jes322@columbia.edu (office). *Website:* www-1.gsb.columbia.edu/faculty/jstiglitz/ (office).

STILES, Martha Bennett, BS; American writer; b. 30 March 1933, Manila, Philippines; d. of Forrest Hampton Wells and Jane McClintock Bennett Wells; m. Martin Stiles 1954; one s. *Education:* Univ. of Michigan. *Career:* teacher of creative writing, Univ. of Louisville 1989, Univ. of Kentucky 1989, 1990; mem. Authors Guild, King Library Assocs, Detroit Women Writers, Nature Conservancy. *Publications:* One Among the Indians 1962, The Strange House at Newburyport 1963, Darkness Over the Land 1966, Dougal Looks for Birds 1972, James the Vine Puller 1975 (second edn 1992), The Star in the Forest 1979, Tana and the Useless Monkey 1979, Sarah the Dragon Lady 1986, Kate of Still Waters 1990, Lonesome Road 1998, Island Magic 1999; contrib. to journals and periodicals. *Honours:* James Bryan Hope Award 1951, Avery Hopwood Awards 1956, 1958, Frankfort Arts Foundation Fiction Prizes 1984, 1986, Soc. of Children's Book Writers grant 1988, Al Smith Fellowship, Kentucky Arts Council 1992, 2003, Detroit Women Writers Millenium Contest (Children's Div.) 2000. *Address:* Stockwell Farm, 861 Hume-Bedford Road, Paris, KY 40361, USA. *Telephone:* (859) 987-4158 (office). *E-mail:* mbsparis@msn.com (office). *Website:* mbstiles.spaces.live.com.

STILLINGER, Jack Clifford, BA, MA, PhD; American writer and academic; *Professor Emeritus, University of Illinois*; b. 16 Feb. 1931, Chicago, IL; m. 1st Shirley Louise Van Wormer 1952; two s. two d.; m. 2nd Nina Zippin Baym 1971. *Education:* Univ. of Texas, Northwestern Univ., Harvard Univ. *Career:* Asst Prof., Univ. of Illinois 1958–61, Assoc. Prof. 1961–64, Prof. of English 1964–2001, mem. Center for Advanced Study 1970–, Prof. Emer. 2001–; Ed. Journal of English and Germanic Philology 1961–72; mem. Byron Soc., Keats-Shelley Asscn of America, MLA; Fellow, American Acad. of Arts and Sciences. *Publications:* The Early Draft of John Stuart Mill's Autobiography (ed.) 1961, Anthony Munday's Zelauto (ed.) 1963, William Wordsworth: Selected Poems and Prefaces (ed.) 1965, The Letters of Charles Armitage Brown (ed.) 1966, Twentieth Century Interpretations of Keats's Odes (ed.) 1968, John Stuart Mill: Autobiography and Other Writings (ed.) 1969, The Hoodwinking of Madeline 1971, The Texts of Keats's Poems 1974, The Poems of John Keats (ed.) 1978, Mill's Autobiography and Literary Essays (ed.) 1981, John Keats: Complete Poems (ed.) 1982, The Norton Anthology of English Literature (ed.) 1986, John Keats: Poetry Manuscripts at Harvard 1990, Multiple Authorship and the Myth of Solitary Genius 1991, Coleridge and Textual Instability: The Multiple Versions of the Major Poems 1994, Reading The Eve of St Agnes: The Multiples of Complex Literary Transaction 1999, Romantic Complexity: Keats, Coleridge and Wordsworth 2006; contrib. to professional journals. *Honours:* Nat. Woodrow Wilson Fellow 1953–54, Guggenheim Fellowship 1964–65, Distinguished Scholar Award, Keats-Shelley Asscn of America 1986. *Address:* 806 W Indiana Avenue, Urbana, IL 61801, USA (home). *Telephone:* (217) 367-3999 (home). *E-mail:* jstill@uiuc.edu (home).

STIMSON (SADLER), Tess, MA; British writer; b. 17 July 1966, England; m. Brent Sadler 1993 (divorced 2002); two s. *Education:* St Hilda's College, Oxford. *Career:* Producer, ITN, 1987–91; Adjunct Prof., University of South Florida, 2002–. *Publications:* Yours Till the End (biog.), 1992; Hard News, 1993; Soft Focus, 1995; Pole Position, 1996. *Honours:* Dorothy Whitelock Award 1985, Eleanor Rooke Award 1986. *E-mail:* carole@blakefriedmann.co.uk*E-mail:* tess@tessstimson.com. *Website:* www.tessstimson.com.

STINE, Robert Lawrence (R. L.); American children's writer; b. 1943, Columbus, OH; m. Jane Waldhorn 1969; one s. *Education:* OH State Univ. *Career:* founder and Ed.-in-Chief juvenile magazine, Bananas, writing under pen name Jovial Bob Stine; co-founder, Parachute Press. *Publications:* fiction: Gnasty Gnomes 1981, The Forest of Enchantment: An Advanced Dungeons and Dragons Story 1983, Blind Date 1986, Spaceballs 1987, Twisted 1987, The Babysitter 1989, Phone Calls 1990, Curtains 1990, Off to Sea: A Romance 1991, The Babysitter 2 1991, The Girlfriend 1991, The Snowman 1991, Losers in Space 1991, The Hitchhiker 1992, Hit and Run 1992, Beach House 1992, The First Evil: Cheerleaders 1993, The Dead Girlfriend 1993, Halloween Night 1993, The Time Raider 1994, Call Waiting 1994, I Saw You That Night! 1994, The Beast 1994, The First Horror 1994, The Witness 1995, Superstitious 1995, The Boyfriend 1995, Deadly Experiments of Dr Eeek 1996, Summer Sizzlers 1998, I Am Your Evil Twin 1998, Revenge R Us 1998, Fright Camp 1998, When Good Ghouls Go Bad 2001, Haunted Lighthouse 2003, The Sitter 2003, Eye Candy 2004; fiction series: Fear Street (over 60 titles) 1989–, Goosebumps (over 100 titles, also Give Yourself Goosebumps and Goosebumps 2000 series) 1992–, The Nightmare Room (15 titles) 1998–, Mostly Ghostly (seven titles) 2004–, Rotten School (11 titles) 2005–, Dangerous Girls; non-fiction: The Sick of Being Sick Book 1980, Don't Stand in the Soup: The World's Funniest Guide to Manners 1982, Everything You Need to Survive: First Dates (with Jane Stine) 1983, Everything You Need to Survive: Homework (with Jane Stine) 1983, Everything You Need to Survive: Money Problems (with Jane Stine) 1983, Cool Kids' Guide to Summer Camp 1986, 101 Silly Monster Jokes 1986, 101 Vacation Jokes 1990, 101 School Cafeteria Jokes 1990, Postcard Book 1996, It Came from Ohio: My Life as a Writer 1997, 101 Wacky Kid Jokes 1997. *Honours:* Free Public Library of Philadelphia Champion of Reading Award, Nickelodeon Kids' Choice Award, Disney Adventures Kids' Choice Award. *Address:* Parachute Press 156 Fifth Avenue, Room 302, New York, NY 10010, USA (office). *Website:* www.rlstine.com.

STIRLING, Jessica (see Rae, Hugh Crauford)

STOCKTON, 2nd Earl of; **Alexander Daniel Alan Macmillan,** FBIM, FRSA; British publisher, farmer and politician; b. 10 Oct. 1943, Oswestry; s. of the late Maurice Victor Macmillan (Viscount Macmillan of Ovenden) and of Dame Katherine Macmillan (Viscountess Macmillan of Ovenden), DBE; grandson of the late 1st Earl of Stockton (fmrly, as Harold Macmillan, Prime Minister of UK 1957–63); m. 1st Hélène Birgitte Hamilton 1970 (divorced 1991); one s. two d.; m. 2nd Miranda Elizabeth Louise Nultall 1995. *Education:* Eton Coll. and Paris and Strathclyde Univs. *Career:* Sub-Ed. Glasgow Herald 1963–65; Reporter, Daily Telegraph 1965–67, Foreign Corresp. 1967–68, Chief European Corresp., Sunday Telegraph 1968–70; Dir Birch Grove Estates Ltd 1969–86, Chair. 1983–89; Dir Macmillan and Co. Ltd 1970–76, Deputy Chair. 1976–80, Chair. 1984–90, Pres. 1990–; Chair. Macmillan Publrs Ltd 1980–90 (Pres. 1990–), St Martin's Press, New York 1983–88 (Dir 1974–90), Sidgwick and Jackson 1989–90; mem. European Parl. for SW of England 1999–; Chair. Cen. London Training & Enterprise Council 1990–95; Dir Book Trade Benevolent Soc. 1976–88, Chair. Bookrest Appeal 1978–86; Dir United British Artists Ltd 1984–90 (Chair. 1985–90); mem. Lindemann Fellowship Cttee 1979– (Chair. 1983–), British Inst. of Man. 1981–, Council of Publrs Asscn 1985–88, Carlton Club Political Cttee 1975–88 (Chair. 1984); Gov. Archbishop Tenison's School 1979–86, Merchant Taylor's School 1980–82, 1990–, English Speaking Union 1980–84, 1986–93; Liveryman Worshipful Co. of Merchant Taylors 1972, Court Asst 1987, of Stationers 1973, Master 1991–92. *Honours:* Hon. DLitt (De Montfort) 1993, (Westminster) 1995; Hon. DUniv (Strathclyde) 1993. *Address:* European Parliament, ASP 8E107, Rue Wiertz, 1047 Brussels, Belgium (office); Porters South, 4–6 Crinan Street, London, N1 9XW (office); Hayne Manor, Stowford, Okehampton, Devon, EX20 4DB, England (home). *Telephone:* (2) 284-76-83 (Brussels) (office); (20) 7833-4000 (Porters) (office); (1566) 783563 (home); (20) 7881-8000. *Fax:* (2) 284-96-83 (Brussels) (office); (1566) 783568 (home); (20) 7881-8001. *E-mail:* estockton@europarl.eu.int (office); l.ferguson@macmillan.uk (home). *Website:* www.alexstockton.com (office).

STOKER, Richard, FRAM, ARAM, ARCM; British composer, actor, conductor, writer and poet and painter; b. 8 Nov. 1938, Castleford, Yorks.; s. of the late Capt. Bower Morrell Stoker and Winifred Harling; m. Gillian Patricia Stoker 1986. *Education:* Breadalbane House School, Castleford, Univ. of Huddersfield with Harold Truscott, Coll. of Art, Royal Acad. of Music and Drama, composition with Sir Lennox Berkeley, conducting with Maurice Miles, pvt. study with Nadia Boulanger in Paris, Arthur Benjamin, Eric Fenby, Benjamin Britten. *Career:* performance debut with BBC Home Service 1953, Nat. and Int. Eisteddfods, Wales 1955–58; conducting debut 1956; Asst Librarian, London Symphony Orchestra 1962–63; Prof. of Composition, RAM 1963–87 (tutor 1970–80); composition teacher, St Paul's School 1972–74, Magdalene Coll., Cambridge 1974–76; Ed. The Composer magazine 1969–80; apptd Magistrate, Inner London Comm. 1995–2003, Crown Court 1998–2003; Adjudicator, Royal Philharmonic Soc. Composer's Award, Cyprus Orchestral Composer's Award for the Ministry of Culture 2001–, BBC Composers' Awards; mem. Composers' Guild 1962– (mem. exec. cttee 1969–80); Founder mem. RAM Guild Cttee 1994– (Hon. Treas. 1995–); Founder mem. European-Atlantic Group 1993–; mem. Byron Soc. 1993–2000, Magistrates' Asscn 1995–2003, English and Int. PEN 1996–2005; mem. and Treas. Steering Cttee Lewisham Arts Festival 1990, 1992; Founder mem. Atlantic Council 1993, RSL, Creative Rights Alliance 2001–; concert appearances as pianist including Queen Elizabeth Hall, Purcell Rooms, Leighton House, RAM, Pizza on the Park, Barnet Festival; mem. RAM Guild. *Art:* exhbns, various works in pvt. collections including Trinity Coll. of Music. *Compositions include:* four symphonies 1961, 1976, 1981, 1991; 12 nocturnes; two jazz preludes; overtures: Antic Hay, Feast of Fools, Heroic Overture; three string quartets, three violin sonatas, Partita for Violin and Harp or Piano, Sonatina for Guitar, two piano sonatas, three piano trios, A York Suite for piano, Piano Variations, Piano Concerto, Partita for Clarinet and Piano, Wind Quintet; organ works: Partita, Little Organ Book, Three Improvisations, Symphony; Monologue, Passacagalia, Serenade, Petite Suite, Nocturnal, Festival Suite; choral works and song cycles: Benedictus, Ecce Homo, Proverb, Psalms, Make Me a Willow Cabin, Canticle of the Rose, O Be Joyful, A Landscape of Truth; piano works: Zodiac Variations, Regency Suite, A Poet's Notebook; vocal works: Music That Brings Sweet Sleep, Aspects of Flight, Four Yeats Songs, Four Shakespeare Songs, Johnson Preserv'd (three-act opera), Thérèse Raquin (in preparation), Chinese Canticle, Birthday of the Infanta; music for film and stage includes Troilus and Cressida, Portrait of a Town, Garden Party, My Friend – My Enemy. *Recordings:* appearances on numerous CDs and records. *Films:* appearances include Red Mercury Rising, Woken, Daddy's Girl, Portrait of a Town, Lear and Goncril, The Shrink, Bedtime Story, The Usual, The End of the Line, The Queen, The Da Vinci Code, Ancient Cataclysms, Vagabond Shoes, Encounter, Bouquet, Interval, Home Guard Ron. *Television:* Mary Tudor (four-part series), Comment (Channel 4), Europe, Dirty Weekend in Hospital, Happiness (BBC), Troilus and Cressida. *Radio:* interviews and discussions on BBC Radio Three, Four, World Service, Radio Leeds, New York Times Radio, Radio New York, Wall Street Radio, Radio Algonquin. *Publications:* Portrait of a Town 1970, Words Without Music 1974, Strolling Players 1978, Open Window – Open Door (autobiog.) 1985, Tanglewood (novel) 1990, Between the Lines 1991, Diva (novel) 1992, Collected Short Stories 1993, Sir Thomas Armstrong: A Celebration 1998, Turn Back the Clock 1998, A Passage of Time 1999; contrib. to anthologies, including Triumph, Forward, Outposts, Spotlight, Strolling Players, American Poetry Soc. publs, reviews and articles for periodicals, including Records and Recording, Books and Bookmen, Guardian, Performance, The Magistrate, poems in numerous anthologies and internet publs; contrib. to Oxford Dictionary of Nat. Biography (nine entries) 2004, 2006 (adviser 2003–). *Honours:* BBC Music Award 1952, Eric Coates Award 1962, Dove Prize 1962, Nat. Library of Poetry (USA) Editors' Choice Award 1995, 1996, 1997. *Address:* Ricordi & Co. (London) Ltd, 210 New King's Road, London, SW6 4NZ, England (office). *Telephone:* (20) 7371-7501 (office); (20) 8852-9608 (home); (7906) 843812 (mobile). *Fax:* (20) 7371-7270. *E-mail:* gps5@tutor.open.ac.uk. *Website:* www.britishacademy.com/members/stoker.htm.

STOLTE, Dieter; German television executive, newspaper publisher and academic; b. 18 Sept. 1934, Cologne. *Education:* Univs of Tübingen and Mainz. *Career:* Head of Science Dept, Saarländischer Rundfunk 1961–62; Personal adviser to Dir-Gen. of Zweites Deutsches Fernsehen (ZDF) 1962, Controller, Programme Planning Dept 1967, Programming Dir 1976–82, Dir-Gen. ZDF March 1982–2002; publisher Die Welt and Berliner Morgenpost (newspapers) 2002–05; Dir and Deputy Dir Gen., Südwestfunk 1973; Prof. Univ. of Music and Presentation Arts, Hamburg 1980–; mem. Admin. Council, German Press Agency (dpa), Hamburg, European Broadcasting Union (EBU); Chair. Admin. Council TransTel, Cologne; Chair. Bd Dirs DeutschlandRadio, Cologne; mem. Int. Broadcast Inst., London; mem. Council, Nat. Acad. of TV Arts, New York, Int. Acad. of Arts and Sciences, New York. *Publications:* ed. and co-author of several books on programme concepts and function of television, etc.; several essays on subjects relating to the philosophy of culture and the science of communication. *Honours:* Int. Emmy Directorate Award 1997; Bundesverdienstkreuz, Officer's Cross, Golden Order of Merit (Austria), Bavarian Order of Merit, Hon. Citizen of State of Tenn., USA; Köckritz Prize 1999, Verdienstorden, Berlin 1999, Robert Geissendorfer Prize 2001. *Address:* c/o Axel Springer Verlag AG, Axel-Springer-Platz 1, 20350 Hamburg, Germany.

STOLTZFUS, Ben, BA, MA, PhD; American novelist, translator and academic; *Professor Emeritus, University of California at Riverside*; b. 15 Sept. 1927, Sofia, Bulgaria; m. 1st Elizabeth Burton 1955 (divorced 1975); two s. one d.; m. 2nd Judith Palmer 1975. *Education:* Amherst Coll., Middlebury Coll., Univ. of Paris, Univ. of Wisconsin. *Career:* instructor in French, Smith Coll. 1958–60; Asst Prof. 1960–65, Assoc. Prof. 1965–66, Prof. of French, Comparative Literature and Creative Writing 1967–93, Prof. Emeritus 1993–, Univ. of California at Riverside; mem. MLA of America, ACLA, ALA, Hemingway Soc., Camus Soc., D. H. Lawrence Soc., Poets and Writers, AATF, ICLA. *Publications:* fiction: The Eye of the Needle 1967, Black Lazarus 1972, Red, White, and Blue 1989, Valley of Roses 2003; non-fiction: Alain Robbe-Grillet and the New French Novel 1964, Georges Chenneviere et l'unanimisme 1965, Gide's Eagles (MLA Award) 1969, Gide and Hemingway: Rebels Against God 1978, Alain Robbe-Grillet: The Body of the Text 1985, Alain Robbe-Grillet: Life, Work, and Criticism 1987, Postmodern Poetics: Nouveau Roman and Innovative Fiction 1987, La Belle Captive 1995, Lacan and Literature: Purloined Pretexts (NAAP Gradiva Award 1997) 1996, The Target: Alain Robbe-Grillet and Jasper Johns 2006; contrib. to numerous journals, quarterlies, reviews and magazines. *Honours:* Dr hc (Amherst Coll.) 1974; Fulbright Scholarships 1955–56, 1963–64, Camargo Foundation grants 1983, 1985, Distinguished Emeritus Award 2006. *Address:* c/o Department of Comparative Literature and Foreign Languages, University of California, Riverside, CA 92521, USA (office).

STONE, Joan Elizabeth, BA, MA, PhD; American academic, poet and writer; b. 22 Oct. 1930, Port Angeles, WA; m. James A Black, 30 July 1990, four s., one d. *Education:* University of Washington. *Career:* Visiting Prof. of Poetry, University of Montana, 1974; Dir, Creative Writing Workshop, University of Washington, 1975; Asst Prof. of English, Colorado College, 1977–. *Publications:* The Swimmer and Other Poems, 1975; Alba, 1976; A Letter to Myself to Water, 1981; Our Lady of the Harbor, 1986. Contributions: journals and magazines. *Honours:* Acad. of American Poets Awards, 1969, 1970, 1972; Borestone Mountain Award, 1974.

STONE, Laurie, BA, MA; American writer, columnist and critic; b. 18 Oct. 1946, New York, NY. *Education:* Barnard College, Columbia College. *Career:* Instructor, Hunter and Queens Colls, CUNY 1969–75; writer, Village Voice 1974–, columnist 1987–96; Critic-at-Large, Fresh Air, National Public Radio 1987–90; teacher in the MFA in Creative Writing programme, Fairleigh Dickinson Univ.; mem. International PEN, National Book Critics Circle, Poets and Writers. *Publications:* Starting with Serge (novel), 1990; Laughing in the Dark: A Decade of Subversive Comedy, 1997; Close to the Bone: Memoirs of Hurt, Rage, and Desire, 1998. Contributions: periodicals, radio and television. *Honours:* Kittredge Fund grant, 1984; MacDowell Colony Residencies, 1984, 1989, 1990, 1991; Virginia Center for the Arts Residency, 1990–91; New York Foundation for the Arts Grant, 1993; Nona Balakian Prize, Excellence in Reviewing, National Book Critics Circle, 1996. *Address:* c/o MFA in Creative Writing, Fairleigh Dickinson University, 285 Madison Avenue, M-MS3-01, Madison, NJ 07940, USA (office).

STONE, Matthew (Matt) Richard; American screenwriter, film director and producer; b. 26 May 1971, Houston, TX. *Career:* collaborated with Trey Parker on short animation, Jesus vs Frosty 1992, later remade as animated Christmas card for FoxLab, titled The Spirit of Christmas 1995; co-creator and Exec. Prod., South Park animation (with Trey Parker) 1997–, and other films and TV series. *Films:* Jesus vs Frosty (writer, dir) 1992, Your Studio and You (writer) 1995, The Spirit of Christmas (writer, dir) 1995, Alferd Packer: The Musical (aka Cannibal! The Musical) (writer, prod.) 1996, Orgazmo (writer, dir, prod.) 1997, South Park: Bigger Longer & Uncut (writer, prod.) (Los Angeles Film Critics Award, New York Film Critics Award, MTV Movie Award) 1999, How's Your News? (exec. prod.) 1999, Team America: World Police (writer, prod.) 2004. *Television:* South Park (series writer, dir, prod.) 1997–, That's My Bush! (series writer, prod.) 2001. *Film appearances:* BASEketball 1998, provides voices for many characters in his animation films and television series. *Recordings:* albums: Chef Aid: The South Park Album, South Park: Bigger, Longer and Uncut (soundtrack), Mr Hankey's Christmas Classics, Timmy and the Lords of the Underworld. *Address:* c/o Paramount Studios, 5555 Melrose Avenue, Hollywood, CA 90038, USA. *E-mail:* news@southparkstudios.com. *Website:* www.southparkstudios.com.

STONE, Robert Anthony; American writer; b. 21 Aug. 1937, New York, NY; m. Janice G. Burr 1959; one s. one d. *Education:* New York Univ. *Career:* Editorial Asst, New York Daily News 1958–60; writer, National Mirror, New York 1965–67; writer-in-residence, Princeton Univ. 1971–72; faculty mem., Amherst Coll. 1972–75, 1977–78, Stanford Univ. 1979, Univ. of Hawaii at Manoa 1979–80, Harvard Univ. 1981, Univ. of California at Irvine 1982, New York Univ. 1983, Univ. of California at San Diego 1985, Princeton Univ. 1985, Johns Hopkins Univ. 1993–94, Yale Univ. 1994–; Stegner Fellow Stanford Univ. 1962; mem. PEN. *Publications:* A Hall of Mirrors 1967, Dog Soldiers 1974, A Flag for Sunrise 1981, Images of War 1986, Children of Light 1986, Outerbridge Reach 1992, Bear and his Daughter: Stories 1997, Damascus Gate 1998, Bay of Souls 2003, Prime Green: Remembering the Sixties 2007; contrib. to anthologies and periodicals. *Honours:* William Faulkner Prize 1967, Guggenheim Fellowship 1971, Nat. Book Award 1975, John Dos Passos Prize 1982, American Acad. of Arts and Letters Award 1982, and grant 1988–92, Nat. Endowment for the Humanities Fellow 1983. *Address:* c/o Ecco Press, 10 E 53rd Street, New York, NY 10022, USA.

STOPPARD, Sir Tom, Kt, OM, CBE, FRSL; British writer; b. (Thomas Straussler), 3 July 1937, Zlin, Czechoslovakia; s. of the late Dr Eugene Straussler and Martha Straussler; step-s. of Kenneth Stoppard; m. 1st Jose Ingle 1965 (divorced 1972); two s.; m. 2nd Dr Miriam Moore-Robinson 1972 (divorced 1992); two s. *Education:* Pocklington Grammar School, Yorks. *Career:* Journalist, Bristol 1954–60; freelance journalist, London 1960–64; mem. Cttee of the Free World 1981–; mem. Royal Nat. Theatre Bd 1989–. *Publications:* plays: Rosencrantz and Guildenstern are Dead 1967, The Real Inspector Hound 1968, Enter a Free Man 1968, After Magritte 1970, Dogg's Our Pet 1972, Jumpers 1972, Travesties 1975, Dirty Linen 1976, New-Found-Land 1976, Every Good Boy Deserves Favour (with music by André Previn, 1978, Night and Day 1978, Dogg's Hamlet, Cahoots Macbeth 1979, Undiscovered Country 1980, On the Razzle 1981, The Real Thing 1982, Rough Crossing 1984, Dalliance (adaption of Schnitzler's Liebelei) 1986, Hapgood 1988, Arcadia 1993 (Evening Standard Award for Best Play), Indian Ink 1995, The Invention of Love 1997, The Seagull (trans. 1997), The Coast of Utopia (trilogy: Part One: Voyage, Part Two: Shipwreck, Part Three: Salvage) (Tony Award for Best Play 2007) 2002, Rock 'N' Roll (London Critics' Circle Award for Best New Play 2006) 2006; radio plays: The Dissolution of Dominic Boot 1964, M is for Moon Among Other Things 1964, Albert's Bridge 1967, If You're Glad I'll be Frank 1968, Where Are They Now? 1970, Artist Descending a Staircase 1972, The Dog It Was That Died 1983, In the Native State 1991; short stories: Introduction 2 1963; novel: Lord Malquist and Mr Moon 1966; screenplays: The Romantic Englishwoman (co-author) 1975, Despair 1977;

film scripts: The Human Factor 1979, Brazil (with Terry Gilliam, and Charles McKeown) 1984, Crown 1987, Empire of the Sun 1987, Rosencrantz and Guildenstern are Dead 1989 (also dir), Russia House 1989, Billy Bathgate 1990, Shakespeare in Love (jtly) 1998 (jt winner Acad. Award Best Original Screenplay 1999), Enigma 2001; television plays: Professional Foul 1977, Squaring the Circle 1984, The Television Plays 1965–84 1993; radio: The Plays for Radio 1964–91, 1994. *Honours:* Hon. MLitt (Bristol, Brunel Univs.); Hon. LittD (Leeds Univ.) 1979, (Sussex) 1980, (Warwick) 1981, (London) 1982; Dr hc (Kenyon Coll.) 1984, (York) 1984; John Whiting Award, Arts Council 1967, Italia Prize (radio drama) 1968, New York Drama Critics Best Play Award 1968, Antoinette Perry Award 1968, 1976, Evening Standard Awards 1967, 1972, 1974, 1978, 1982, 1993, 1997, 2006, Sony Award 1991, Olivier Award 1993. *Literary Agent:* PFD, Drury House, 34–43 Russell Street, London, WC2B 5HA, England.

STOREY, David Malcolm; British author and playwright; b. 13 July 1933, Wakefield, Yorkshire; s. of Frank Richmond Storey and Lily (née Cartwright) Storey; m. Barbara Hamilton 1956; two s. two d. *Education:* Queen Elizabeth Grammar School, Wakefield, Wakefield Coll. of Art and Slade School of Art. *Career:* Fellow, Univ. Coll. London 1974. *Publications:* novels: This Sporting Life (Macmillan Award) 1960, Flight into Camden (John Llewellyn Rhys Memorial Prize 1961, Somerset Maugham Award 1963) 1960, Radcliffe 1963, Pasmore (Faber Memorial Prize 1972) 1972, A Temporary Life 1973, Edward 1973, Saville (Booker Prize 1976) 1976, A Prodigal Child 1982, Present Times 1984, A Serious Man 1998, As It Happened 2002, Thin-Ice Skater 2004; plays: The Restoration of Arnold Middleton (Evening Standard Award 1967), In Celebration 1969 (also film), The Contractor (New York Critics' Prize 1974) 1969, Home (Evening Standard Award, New York Critics' Prize) 1970, The Changing Room (New York Critics' Prize) 1971, Cromwell 1973, The Farm 1973, Life Class 1974, Night 1976, Mother's Day 1976, Sisters 1978, Dreams of Leaving 1980, Early Days 1980, The March on Russia 1989, Stages 1992; poems: Storey's Lives: Poems 1951–1991 1992. *Honours:* Los Angeles Drama Critics Award 1969, Writer of the Year Award, Variety Club of GB 1969. *Address:* c/o Jonathan Cape Ltd, Random Century House, 20 Vauxhall Bridge Road, London, SW1V 2SA, England.

STORM, Christopher (see Olsen, Theodore Victor)

STOTHARD, Sir Peter M., Kt, MA; British journalist and newspaper editor; *Editor, The Times Literary Supplement;* b. 28 Feb. 1951, Chelmsford, Essex; s. of Wilfred Stothard and Patricia Savage; m. Sally Ceris Emerson 1980; one s. one d. *Education:* Brentwood School, Essex and Trinity Coll. Oxford. *Career:* journalist, BBC 1974–77; Shell Petroleum 1977–79; business and political writer, Sunday Times 1979–80; Features Ed. and leader writer, The Times 1980–85; Deputy Ed. The Times 1985–92, US Ed. 1989–92, Ed. 1992–2002; Ed. The Times Literary Supplement 2002–. *Publications:* Thirty Days: A Month at the Heart of Blair's War 2003. *Honours:* Hon. Fellow Trinity Coll. Oxford 2000. *Address:* The Times Literary Supplement, Admiral House, 66–68 East Smithfield, London, E1W 1BX, England (office). *Telephone:* (20) 7782-3380. *Website:* www.the-tls.co.uk.

STOTT, Mike; British playwright; b. 2 Jan. 1944, Rochdale, Lancashire, England. *Education:* Univ. of Manchester. *Career:* Resident Writer, Hampstead Theatre Club 1975. *Publications:* Mata Hari, 1965; Erogenous Zone, 1969; Funny Peculiar, 1973; Lenz (after Büchner), 1974; Plays for People Who Don't Move Much, 1974; Midnight, 1974; Other People, 1974; Lorenzaccio (after De Musset), 1976; Followed by Oysters, 1976; Soldiers Talking Cleanly, 1978; The Boston Strangler, 1978; Grandad, 1978; Strangers, 1979; Ducking Out, 1982; Dead Men, 1982; Penine Pleasures, 1984; The Fling, 1984; The Fancy Man, 1988. Other: Radio and television plays.

STOTT, Richard Keith; British journalist; *Political and Current Affairs Columnist, Sunday Mirror;* b. 17 Aug. 1943, Oxford; s. of Fred B. Stott and Bertha Stott; m. Penny Scragg 1970; one s. two d. *Education:* Clifton Coll. Bristol. *Career:* Bucks. Herald 1963–65; Ferrari Press Agency 1965–68; reporter Daily Mirror 1968–79, Features Ed. 1979–81, Asst Ed. 1981; Ed. The People 1984–85, 1990–91; Ed. Daily Mirror 1985–89, 1991–92, Today 1993–95; Political and Current Affairs Columnist, News of the World 1997–2000, Sunday Mirror 2001–. *Publication:* Dogs and Lampposts 2002. *Honours:* British Press Awards Reporter of the Year 1977, What the Papers Say Ed. of the Year 1993. *Address:* 20 Albany Park Road, Kingston-upon-Thames, Surrey, KT2 5SW, England.

STOUT, Robert Joe, BA; American/Mexican writer and poet; b. 3 Feb. 1938, Scottsbluff, Neb.; m. Maureen Ryan 1988; two s. three d. *Education:* Mexico City Coll. *Publications:* Miss Sally 1973, The Trick 1974, Swallowing Dust 1974, Moving Out 1974, The Way to Pinal 1979, They Still Play Baseball the Old Way 1994, The Blood of the Serpent: Mexican Lives 2003; contrib. to Smoke Magazine, The Retired Officer Magazine, Notre Dame Magazine, The Beloit Poetry Journal, The South Dakota Review, Interim, Commonweal. *Address:* Caja Postal 220, La Paz, BCS, CP 23000, Mexico (home). *Telephone:* (612) 122-9277 (home). *Fax:* (612) 122-9277 (home). *E-mail:* bobstout@ journalist.com (home).

STOW, (Julian) Randolph; Australian novelist, writer and poet; b. 28 Nov. 1935, Geraldton, WA. *Education:* Univ. of Western Australia. *Career:* Lecturer in English, Univ. of Leeds, UK 1962, 1968–69, Univ. of Western Australia 1963–64; reviewer, Times Literary Supplement 1976–2002; Harkness Fellow, USA 1964–66. *Libretti:* (to music by Peter Maxwell Davies) Eight Songs for a Mad King 1969, Miss Donnithorne's Maggot 1974. *Publications:* novels: A Haunted Land 1956, The Bystander 1957, To the Islands 1958, Tourmaline 1963, The Merry-Go-Round in the Sea 1965, Midnite 1967, Visitants 1979, The Girl Green as Elderflower 1980, The Suburbs of Hell 1984; poetry: Act One 1957, Outrider: Poems 1956–62 1962, A Counterfeit Silence: Selected Poems 1969, Randolph Stow (omnibus vol.) 1990. *Honours:* Miles Franklin Award 1958, Britannica-Australia Award 1966, Grace Leven Prize 1969, Arts Council of Great Britain bursary 1969, Commonwealth Literary Fund grant 1974, Patrick White Award 1979. *Literary Agent:* Sheil Land Associates, 52 Doughty Street, London, WC1N 2LS, England.

STRACHAN, Hew Francis Anthony, MA, PhD, FRSE; British academic and writer; *Chichele Professor of the History of War, University of Oxford;* b. 1 Sept. 1949, Edinburgh, Scotland; m. 1st Catherine Margaret Blackburn 1971 (divorced 1980); two d.; m. 2nd Pamela Dorothy Tennant 1982; one s. one step-s. one step-d. *Education:* Corpus Christi Coll., Cambridge. *Career:* Research Fellow 1975–78, Fellow 1979–, Dean of Coll. 1981–86, Admissions Tutor 1981–88, Sr Tutor 1989–92, Corpus Christi Coll., Cambridge; Sr Lecturer in War Studies, Royal Military Acad., Sandhurst 1978–79; Prof. of Modern History 1992–2001, Dir Scottish Centre for War Studies 1996–2001, Univ. of Glasgow; Lees Knowles Lecturer, Cambridge 1995; Visiting Prof., Royal Norwegian Air Force Acad. 2000–; Chichele Prof. of the History of War, Univ. of Oxford 2002–; Fellow, All Souls Coll. Oxford; Life Fellow, Corpus Christi Coll. Cambridge 1992; DL, Tweeddale 2006. *Television:* The First World War (series, Channel 4) 2003. *Publications:* British Military Uniforms, 1768–1796 1975, History of Cambridge University Officers' Training Corps 1976, European Armies and the Conduct of War 1983, Wellington's Legacy: The Reform of the British Army 1984, From Waterloo to Balaclava: Tactics, Technology and the British Army, 1815–1854 1985, The Politics of the British Army 1997, The Oxford Illustrated History of the First World War (ed.) 1998, The British Army, Manpower and Society (ed.) 2000, The First World War, Vol. 1 To Arms 2001, Military Lives 2002, The First World War: An Illustrated History 2003, The Outbreak of War 2004, Financing the War 2004, The War in Africa 2004, Big Wars and Small Wars (ed.) 2005; contrib. to learned books and journals. *Honours:* Hon. DUniv (Univ. of Paisley) 2005; Templer Medal 1985, Westminster Medal 1997. *Literary Agent:* David Higham Associates Ltd, 5–8 Lower John Street, Golden Square, London, W1F 9HA, England. *Telephone:* (20) 7434-5900. *Fax:* (20) 7437-1072. *E-mail:* dha@davidhigham .co.uk. *Website:* www.davidhigham.co.uk. *Address:* All Souls College, Oxford, OX1 4AL, England (office). *Telephone:* (1865) 279371 (office). *Fax:* (1865) 279299 (office). *E-mail:* hew.strachan@all-souls.ox.ac.uk (office).

STRAIGHT, Steve; American writer and lecturer; m.; two d. *Career:* fmr Dir of Seminar Series, Sunken Garden Poetry Festival; Prof. of English and Dir of the Poetry Program, Manchester Community Coll.; Dir, Connecticut Poetry Circuit. *Publications:* The Water Carrier (poems) 2002, In a Different Light (novel) 2005. *Address:* c/o Curbstone Press, 321 Jackson Street, Willimantic, CT 06226-1738, USA. *E-mail:* info@curbstone.org. *Website:* www.curbstone .org.

STRAND, Mark, AB, BFA, MA; American poet, writer and academic; *Professor of English and Comparative Literature, Columbia University;* b. 11 April 1934, Summerside, PEI, Canada; m. 1st Antonia Ratensky 1961 (divorced 1973); one d.; m. 2nd Julia Rumsey Garretson 1976 (divorced 1998); one s. *Education:* Antioch Coll., Yale Univ., Univ. of Iowa. *Career:* instructor, Univ. of Iowa 1962–65; Fulbright Lecturer, Univ. of Brazil 1965; Asst Prof., Mount Holyoke Coll. 1966; Visiting Prof., Univ. of Washington 1967, Univ. of Virginia 1977, California State Univ. at Fresno 1977, Univ. of California, Irvine 1978, Wesleyan Univ. 1979–80; Adjunct Prof., Columbia Univ. 1968–70, currently Prof. of English and Comparative Literature; Visiting Lecturer, Yale Prof. 1969–70, Harvard Prof. 1980–81; Assoc. Prof., Brooklyn Coll., CUNY 1971; Bain Swiggett Lecturer, Princeton Prof. 1972; Fanny Hurst Prof. of Poetry, Brandeis Prof. 1973; Prof. 1981–86, Distinguished Prof. 1986–94, Prof. of Utah; Poet Laureate of the USA 1990–91; Elliot Coleman Prof. of Poetry, Johns Hopkins Prof. 1994–97; fmr Andrew MacLeish Distinguished Service Prof., of Chicago; Writer-in-Residence, American Acad., Rome 1982; mem. American Acad. and Inst. of Arts and Letters 1980–, Nat. Acad. of Arts and Sciences 1995–. *Publications:* poetry: Sleeping With One Eye Open 1964, Reasons for Moving 1968, Darker 1970, Halty Ferguson: 18 Poems from the Quechua (trans.) 1971, Rafael Alberti: The Owl's Insomnia (trans.) 1973, The Sargentville Notebook 1973, The Story of Our Lives 1973, Carlos Drummond de Andrade: Souvenir of the Ancient World (trans.) 1976, Another Republic: 17 European and South American Writers (co-ed. with Charles Simic) 1976, The Late Hour 1978, Selected Poems 1980, Travelling in the Family: The Selected Poems of Carlos Drummond de Andrade (trans.) 1986, The Continuous Life 1990, The Best American Poetry (ed.) 1991, Dark Harbor 1993, The Golden Ecco Anthology (ed.) 1994, Blizzard of One (Pulitzer Prize in Poetry 1999) 1998, Man and Camel 2006, New Selected Poems 2007; prose: The Monument 1978, The Planet of Lost Things (juvenile) 1982, The Art of the Real 1983, Mr and Mrs Baby (short stories) 1985, The Night Book (juvenile) 1985, Rembrandt Takes a Walk (juvenile) 1986, William Bailey 1987, Hopper 1994; contrib. of poems, book reviews, art reviews, essays on poetry and painting, and interviews in numerous periodicals, contrib. to numerous anthologies. *Honours:* Fulbright Scholarship to Italy 1960–61, Ingram Merrill Foundation Fellowship 1966, NEA grants 1967–68, 1977–78, Rockefeller Fellowship 1968–69; Edgar Allan Poe Prize 1974, Guggenheim Fellowship 1974–75, Nat. Inst. of Arts and Letters Award 1975, Acad. of American Poets

Fellowship 1979, John D. and Catherine T. MacArthur Foundation Fellowship 1987–92, Utah Gov.'s Award in the Arts 1992, Bobbitt Nat. Prize for Poetry 1992, Bollingen Prize for Poetry 1993, Bingham Prize for Poetry 1998, Pulitzer Prize 1999, Wallace Stevens Award 2004. *Address:* 602 Philosophy Hall, c/o Department of English and Comparative Literature, Columbia University, New York, NY 10027 (office); 2700 Broadway (8B), New York, NY 10025, USA (home). *Telephone:* (212) 854-7468 (office); (646) 478-8704 (home). *E-mail:* ms3091@columbia.edu (office). *Website:* www.columbia.edu/cu/english (home).

STRATTON, Thomas (see De Weese, Thomas Eugene (Gene))

STRAUB, Peter Francis, BA, MA; American writer; b. 2 March 1943, Milwaukee, WI; m. 1966; one s. one d. *Education:* Univ. of Wisconsin, Columbia Univ. *Television:* two appearances as ret. det. Pete Brsaust on One Life To Live 2006. *Publications:* Open Air (poems) 1972, Marriage 1973, Julia 1975, If You Could See Me New 1977, Ghost Story 1979, Shadowland 1980, Floating Dragon 1983, The Talisman (with Stephen King) 1984, Koko 1988, Mystery 1989, Houses Without Doors 1990, The Throat 1993, The Hellfire Club 1996, Mr X 1999, Magic Terror 2000, Black House (with Stephen King) 2001, Conjunctions 39: The New Fabulists (ed.) 2002, Lost Boy Lost Girl 2003, In the Night Room 2004, Tales of H. P. Lovecraft (ed.) 2005; contrib. to TLS, New Statesman, Washington Post. *Honours:* British Fantasy Award 1983, August Derleth Award 1983, World Fantasy Best Novel Awards 1988, 1993, Bram Stoker Awards for Best Novel 1993, 1998, 2000, 2003, 2004, named Grand Master by Horror Writers Asscn (HWA) 1998, HWA Life Achievement Award 2005. *Literary Agent:* c/o The Gernert Co., 136 E 57th Street, New York, NY 10022, USA. *Telephone:* (212) 838-7777. *Address:* 53 W 85th Street, New York, NY 10024, USA (office). *E-mail:* pstraub@nyc.rr.com (office). *Website:* www.peterstraub.net.

STRAUSS, Botho; German playwright and novelist; b. 2 Dec. 1944, Naumburg. *Education:* Cologne and Munich. *Career:* moved with family to Remscheid, Ruhr region; on staff of Theater heute, West Berlin; Dramaturg at Schaubühne Theater, West Berlin 1970–75; mem. PEN. *Plays include:* Die Hypochonder (first play, 1971, winner Hannover Dramaturgie Award), Trilogie des Wiedersehens 1976, Gross und Klein 1978, Kalldeway Farce 1981, Der Park 1983, Das Gleichgewicht 1994, Theaterstücke in zwei Banden 1994. *Publications:* Bekannte Gesichter, gemischte Gefühle (jtly) 1974, Die Widmung (novel) 1979, Rumor (novel) 1980, Paare, Passanten (novel) 1981, Der Junge Mann (novel) 1984, Diese Erinnerung an einen, der nur einen Tag zu Gast War 1985, Die Fremdenführerin 1986, Niemand Anderes (novel) 1987, Besucher 1988, Kongress: Die Kette der Demütigungen 1989, Wohnen Dammern Lügen 1994, Das Partikular 2000, Der Narr und seine Frau heute abend in Pancomedia 2001. *Honours:* Schiller Prize Baden-Württemberg 1977, Literaturpreis, Bayerische Akademie der Schönen Künste 1981, Mülheimer Drama Prize 1982, Jean Paul Prize 1987, Georg Büchner Prize 1989.

STRAUSS, Jennifer, BA, PhD; Australian academic and poet; b. 30 Jan. 1933, Heywood, Vic.; m. Werner Strauss 1958; three s. *Education:* Univ. of Melbourne, Univ. of Glasgow, Monash Univ. *Career:* Sr Lecturer 1971–92, Assoc. Prof. 1992–, Monash Univ.; mem. Premier's Literary Awards Cttee, PEN, Asscn for Study of Australian Literature, Australian Soc. of Authors. *Publications:* Children and Other Strangers 1975, Winter Driving 1981, Middle English Verse: An Anthology (co-ed.) 1985, Labour Ward 1988, Boundary Conditions: The Poetry of Gwen Harwood 1992, The Oxford Book of Australian Love Poems (ed.) 1993, Judith Wright 1995, Tierra del Fuego: New and Selected Poems 1997, Family Ties: Australian Poems of the Family (ed.) 1998, Oxford Literary History of Australia (co-ed.) 1998, Collected Verse of Mary Gilmore Vol. I 1887–1929 (ed.) 2005; contrib. to various publications. *Honours:* Hon. Sr Research Fellow, Monash Univ. 1998. *Address:* 2–12 Tollington Avenue, East Malvern, Vic. 3145, Australia. *Fax:* (3) 9885-8132 (office).

STRAWSON, Galen John, BA, BPhil, MA, DPhil; British philosopher and literary critic; *Professor of Philosophy, University of Reading;* b. 5 Feb. 1952, Oxford, England; s. of Peter Frederick Strawson and Grace Hall (Ann) Martin; m. 1st Jose Said 1974 (divorced 1994); one s. two d.; m. 2nd Anna Vaux 1997 (divorced 2003); two s.; m. 3rd Michelle Montague 2006. *Education:* Univ. of Cambridge, Univ. of Oxford, Ecole Normale Supérieure, Paris. *Career:* Asst Ed. Times Literary Supplement, London 1978–87, Consultant 1987–; Fellow, Jesus Col Oxford 1987–2000; Prof. of Philosophy, Univ. of Reading 2001–; Visiting Fellow, ANU 1993; Visiting Prof., New York Univ. 1997; Rutgers Univ. 2000; Distinguished Prof. of Philosophy, City of New York Grad. Center 2004–; mem. Mind Asscn; Trustee Kennedy Memorial Trust 1998–2003. *Publications:* Freedom and Belief 1986, The Secret Connection 1989, Mental Reality 1994, Consciousness and its Place in Nature 2006; contrib. to TLS, Sunday Times, Observer, Financial Times, Guardian, New York Times Book Review, The Believer, London Review of Books, Independent on Sunday, Mind, American Philosophical Quarterly, Inquiry, Journal of Consciousness Studies, Analysis, Philosophical Studies, Philosophical Topics, Ratio, Philosophical Issues, Philosophy and Phenomenological Research, many books of essays. *Honours:* R. A. Nicholson Prize for Islamic Studies, Cambridge 1971, T. H. Green Prize for Moral Philosophy, Oxford 1983. *Address:* Department of Philosophy, University of Reading, Reading, RG6 6AA, England (office). *Telephone:* (118) 378-8325 (office).

STREET, Pamela; British writer; b. 3 March 1921, Wilton, Wiltshire, England; m. (divorced); one d. *Education:* Salisbury and South Wiltshire College of Further Education. *Publications:* My Father, A. G. Street, 1969; Portrait of Wiltshire, 1971; Arthur Bryant: Portrait of a Historian, 1979; Light of Evening, 1981; The Stepsisters, 1982; Morning Glory, 1982; Portrait of Rose, 1986; The Illustrated Portrait of Wiltshire, 1984; Personal Relations, 1987; The Mill-Race Quartet, 1988; The Timeless Moment, 1988; The Beneficiaries, 1989; Doubtful Company, 1990; Guilty Parties, 1991; Late Harvest, 1991; The Colonel's Son, 1992; Hindsight, 1993; Keeping it Dark, 1994; King's Folly, 1995; The General's Wife, 1996. Contributions: newspapers and magazines.

STREET-PORTER, Janet, FRTS, FRIBA; British journalist, television producer, presenter and newspaper editor; b. 27 Dec. 1946; m. 1st Tim Street-Porter 1967 (divorced 1975); m. 2nd A. M. M. Elliott 1976 (divorced 1978); m. 3rd Frank Cvitanovich (divorced 1988, died 1995). *Education:* Lady Margaret Grammar School and Architectural Asscn. *Career:* columnist and fashion writer, Petticoat Magazine 1968, Daily Mail 1969–71, Evening Standard 1971–73; own show, LBC Radio 1973; presenter, London Weekend Show, London Weekend Television (LWT) 1975; producer and presenter, Saturday Night People (with Clive James q.v. and Russell Harty), The Six O'Clock Show (with Michael Aspel), Around Midnight 1975–85, co-cr. Network 7 (Channel 4) 1987–88; Head, Youth and Entertainment Features, BBC TV 1988–94; Head, Ind. Production for Entertainment 1994; with Mirror Group PLC 1994–95; TV presenter Design Awards, Travels with Pevsner, Coast to Coast, The Midnight Hour 1996–98, As The Crow Flies (series) 1999, Cathedral Calls 2000 (all BBC2), J'Accuse, Internet 1996 (Channel 4), Bloomberg TV 2001–; Ed. The Independent on Sunday 1999–2001, Ed.-at-Large 2001–; Pres. Ramblers' Asscn 1994–97 (now Vice-Pres.), Globetrotters Club 2003–. *Publications:* Scandal 1980, The British Teapot 1981, Coast to Coast 1998, As the Crow Flies 1999, Baggage – My Childhood 2004, Fall Out 2006. *Honours:* Prix Italia 1992, British Acad. Award for Originality 1988. *Website:* janetstreetporter.com.

STRESHINSKY, Shirley, BA; American writer; b. 7 Oct. 1934, Alton, IL; m. Ted Streshinsky 1966 (deceased); one s. one d. *Education:* Univ. of Illinois. *Publications:* And I Alone Survived 1978, Hers the Kingdom 1981, A Time Between 1984, Gift of the Golden Mountain 1988, The Shores of Paradise (novel) 1991, Oats! A Book of Whimsy (with Maria Streshinsky) 1997, John James Audubon: Life and Art in the American Wilderness 1998; contribs to journals and magazines, including travel writing (several awards) and articles on Asia and the Pacific. *Honours:* Best Human Interest Article, Society Magazine Writers' Asscn 1968, Educational Press Award 1968. *Address:* 50 Kenyon Avenue, Kensington, CA 94708, USA (home). *Telephone:* (510) 526-1976 (office). *E-mail:* streshinsky@earthlink.net (home).

STRINGER, Christopher, BSc, PhD, DSc, FRS; British anthropologist, writer and lecturer; *Head of Human Origins, Natural History Museum, London;* b. 31 Dec. 1947, London, England. *Education:* Univs of London and Bristol. *Career:* Anthropologist, Prin. Researcher and Head of Human Origins Group, Natural History Museum, London 1990–; Dir Ancient Human Occupation of Britain project; Visiting Prof., Royal Holloway, Univ. of London. *Publications:* Aspects of Human Evolution (ed.) 1981, The Human Revolution: Behavioral and Biological Perspectives on the Origins of Modern Humans (co-ed.) 1989, Human Evolution: An Illustrated Guide (co-author) 1989, In Search of Neanderthals: Solving the Puzzle of Human Origins (co-author) 1993, The Origin of Modern Humans and the Impact of Chronometric Dating: A Discussion (co-ed.) 1993, African Exodus: The Origins of Modern Humanity (co-author) 1997, The Complete World of Human Evolution (co-author) 2005, Homo Britannicus 2006. *Honours:* Hon. LLD (Univ. of Bristol) 2000; Primate Soc. of Great Britain Osman Hill Medal 1998, Geologists' Asscn Henry Stopes Medal 2000, Royal Anthropological Inst. Rivers Memorial Medal 2004. *Literary Agent:* c/o John Brockman, 5 E 59th Street, New York, NY 10022, USA. *Address:* Natural History Museum, Cromwell Road, London, SW7 5BD, England (office). *Website:* www.nhm.ac.uk (office).

STROHM, Reinhard, PhD, FBA; German musicologist; *Heather Professor of Music, University of Oxford;* b. 4 Aug. 1942, Munich. *Education:* Univ. of Munich and Technical Univ., Berlin with Carl Dahlhaus. *Career:* Lecturer 1975–83, Prof. 1990–96, King's Coll. London; Prof., Yale Univ. 1983–90; Heather Prof. of Music, Univ. of Oxford 1996–; corresponding mem. American Musicological Soc., Göttinger Akad. der Wissenschaften. *Publications:* Hasse, Scarlatti, Rolli 1975, Wagner Collected Edition (co-ed.) 1970–82, Zu Vivaldis Opern schaffen 1975, Italienische Opernarien des Frühen Settecento, 1720–1730 1976, Die Italienische Oper im 18 Jahrhundert 1979, Music in Late Medieval Bruges 1985, Essays on Handel and Italian Opera (contrib.) 1985, Music in Late Medieval Europe 1987, The Rise of European Music, 1380–1500 1993, On the Dignity and the Effects of Music: Two Fifteenth-Century Treatises (with J. D. Cullington) 1996, Dramma per musica: Italian Opera Seria in the Eighteenth Century 1997, Song Composition in the 14th and 15th Centuries: Old and New Questions 1997, The Eighteenth Century Diaspora of Italian Music and Musicians 2001, Music as Concept and Practice in the Late Middle Ages (The New Oxford History of Music, Vol. III, with B. Blackburn) 2001; contrib. to learned books and journals. *Honours:* Royal Musical Asscn Dent Medal 1977. *Address:* c/o Faculty of Music, University of Oxford, St Aldate's, Oxford, OX1 1DB, England. *E-mail:* reinhard.strohm@music.ox.ac.uk.

STRONG, Eithne, BA; Irish writer and poet; b. 23 Feb. 1923, West Limerick; m. Rupert Strong 1943, two s. seven d. *Education:* Trinity College, Dublin. *Career:* mem. Aosdána; Conradh Na Gaeilge; Irish PEN; Irish Writers Union; Poetry Ireland. *Publications:* Poetry: Songs of Living, 1965; Sarah in Passing, 1974; Circt Oibre, 1980; Fuil agus Fallat, 1983; My Darling Neighbour, 1985; Flesh the Greatest Sin, 1989; An Sagart Pinc, 1990; Aoife Faoi Ghlas, 1990; Let Live, 1990; Spatial Nosing, 1993; Nobel, 1998. Fiction: Degrees of Kindred, 1979; The Love Riddle, 1993. Short Fiction: Patterns, 1981. Contributions: anthologies, journals and magazines.

STRONG, Jonathan; American writer and teacher; b. 13 Aug. 1944, Evanston, IL. *Education:* Harvard University. *Career:* faculty, Tufts University; mem. New England Gilbert and Sullivan Society; Sir Arthur Sullivan Society. *Publications:* Tike, 1969; Ourselves, 1971; Elsewhere, 1985; Secret Words, 1992; Companion Pieces, 1993; An Untold Tale, 1993; Offspring, 1995; The Old World, 1997; The Haunts of His Youth, 1999; A Circle Around Her, 2000. Contributions: American Literature; journals and magazines. *Honours:* O. Henry Story Awards, 1967, 1970; Rosenthal Award, 1970; National Endowment for the Arts Award, 1986.

STRONG, Maggie (see Kotker, (Mary) Zane)

STRONG, Sir Roy Colin, Kt, PhD, FSA, FRSL; British historian, writer and fmr museum director; b. 23 Aug. 1935, London; s. of George Edward Clement Strong and Mabel Ada Smart; m. Julia Trevelyan Oman 1971 (died 2003). *Education:* Queen Mary Coll., Univ. of London and Warburg Inst. *Career:* Asst Keeper, Nat. Portrait Gallery, London 1959–67, Dir 1967–73; Dir Victoria and Albert Museum, London 1974–87; Vice-Chair. South Bank Bd (now South Bank Centre) 1985–90; Dir Oman Productions Ltd, Nordstern Fine Art Insurance 1988–2001; organizer of exhbns including The Elizabethan Image (Tate Gallery) 1969, The Destruction of the Country House (Victoria and Albert Museum) 1974, Artists of the Tudor Court (Victoria and Albert Museum) 1983; mem. Arts Council of GB 1983–87 (Chair. Arts Panel 1983–87), Council, RCA 1979–87; Patron, Pallant House, Chichester 1986–; Fellow, Queen Mary Coll., Univ. of London, Royal Soc. of Literature 1999; High Bailiff and Searcher of the Sanctuary of Westminster Abbey 2000–; Pres. Garden History Soc. 2000–. *Publications:* Portraits of Queen Elizabeth I 1963, Leicester's Triumph (with J. A. Van Dorsten) 1964, Holbein and Henry VIII 1967, Tudor and Jacobean Portraits 1969, The English Icon: Elizabethan and Jacobean Portraiture 1969, Elizabeth R (with Julia Trevelyan Oman) 1971, Van Dyck: Charles I on Horseback 1972, Inigo Jones: The Theatre of the Stuart Court (with S. Orgel) 1972, Mary Queen of Scots (with Julia Trevelyan Oman) 1972, Splendour at Court: Renaissance Spectacle and The Theatre of Power 1973, An Early Victorian Album (with Colin Ford) 1974, Nicholas Hilliard 1975, The Cult of Elizabeth: Elizabethan Portraiture and Pageantry 1977, And When Did You Last See Your Father? The Victorian Painter and British History 1978, The Renaissance Garden in England 1979, Britannia Triumphans, Inigo Jones, Rubens and Whitehall Palace 1980, Holbein 1980, The English Miniature (with J. Murdoch, J. Murrell and P. Noon) 1981, The English Year (with Julia Trevelyan Oman) 1982, The English Renaissance Miniature 1983, Artists of the Tudor Court (with J. Murrell) 1983, Glyndebourne, A Celebration (contrib.) 1984, Art and Power, Renaissance Festivals 1450–1650 1984, Strong Points 1985, Henry Prince of Wales and England's Lost Renaissance 1986, C. V. Wedgwood Festschrift (contrib.) 1986, Creating Small Gardens 1986, Gloriana, Portraits of Queen Elizabeth I 1987, The Small Garden Designers Handbook 1987, Cecil Beaton: the Royal Portraits 1988, Creating Small Formal Gardens 1989, Lost Treasures of Britain 1990, A Celebration of Gardens 1991, Small Period Gardens 1992, Royal Gardens 1992, Versace Theatre 1992, William Larkin 1994, A Country Life 1994, Successful Small Gardens 1994, The Tudor and Stuart Monarchy 1995, The Story of Britain 1996, The English Arcadia 1996, Country Life 1897–1997 1997, The Roy Strong Diaries 1967–1987 1997, On Happiness 1997, The Tudor and Stuart Monarchy 1998, The Spirit of Britain 1999, Garden Party 2000, The Artist and the Garden 2000, Ornament in the Small Garden 2001, Feast – A History of Grand Eating 2002, The Laskett – The Story of a Garden 2003, Coronation: A History of Kingship and the British Monarchy 2005, Passions Past and Present 2005; numerous articles in newspapers and periodicals. *Honours:* Hon. MA (Worcester) 2004; Hon. DLitt (Leeds) 1983, (Keele) 1984; Shakespeare Prize (FVS Foundation, Hamburg) 1980, President's Award Royal Photographic Soc. of Great Britain 2003. *Address:* The Laskett, Much Birch, Hereford, HR2 8HZ, England.

STROUSE, Jean, BA; American writer; b. 10 Sept. 1945, Los Angeles, CA. *Education:* Radcliffe College. *Career:* Editorial Asst, New York Review of Books, 1967–69; Ed., Pantheon Books, 1972–75; Book Critic, Newsweek, 1979–83; Phi Beta Kappa Society Visiting Scholar, 1996–97; Ferris Prof. of Journalism, Princeton University, 1998; John J.Rhodes Chair in American Institutions and Public Policy Arizona State Univ. Barrett Honors Coll. 2003; Dir Cullman Center for Scholars and Writers, The New York Public Library 2003–; various lectureships; mem. Soc. of American Historians, Pres. 2001–02, Authors' Guild, PEN. *Publications:* Women and Analysis: Dialogues on Psychoanalytic Views of Femininity (ed. and compiler), 1974; Alice James: A Biography, 1980; Morgan: American Financier, 1999. Contributions: Reviews, journals and magazines. *Honours:* Radcliffe Institute Fellowship, 1976; National Endowment for the Humanities Fellowships, 1976, 1992; Guggenheim Fellowships, 1977, 1986; National Endowment for the Arts Fellowship, 1978; Bancroft Prize, 1981; Ingram Merrill Foundation Grant, 1989; Lila Wallace-Reader's Digest Writing Fellowship, 1993–94; John D. and

Catherine T. MacArthur Foundation Fellowship 2002–(06); Best Book Citations, Los Angeles Times Book Review, New York Post, New York Times Book Review, Washington Post, etc, 1999. *Address:* c/o Georges Borchardt Inc., 136 E 57th Street, New York, NY 10022, USA.

STRUGATSKY, Boris Natanovich, (S. Viticky); Russian science-fiction writer and astronomer; b. 15 April 1933, Leningrad; s. of Natan Strugatsky; m.; one s. *Education:* Leningrad State Univ. *Career:* astronomer's post in Pulkovo Observatory, Leningrad 1955–65; started publishing science-fiction (with his brother) 1957. *Publications:* with A. N. Strugatsky over 25 novels including: The Land of Purple Clouds 1959, The Return 1962, Escape Attempt 1962, The Far-Away Rainbow 1964, Rapacious Things of the Century 1965, The Inhabited Island 1971, The Ugly Swans 1972, Stories 1975, The Forest 1982, The Lame Fortune 1986, One Billion Years Before the End of the World 1988, Collected Works 1991, Burdened by Evil 1988, The Search of Destination 1994, Collected Works 2001. *Honours:* Victor Hugo Prize (France). *Address:* Pobeda Str. 4, Apt 186, 196070 St Petersburg, Russia. *Telephone:* (812) 291-37-55. *E-mail:* bns@tf.ru (home).

STRYKER, Daniel (see Morris, Janet Ellen)

STUART, Dabney, AB, AM; American academic, editor, poet and writer; b. 4 Nov. 1937, Richmond, VA; m. 3rd Sandra Westcott 1983; two s. one d. *Education:* Davidson College, NC, Harvard University. *Career:* Instructor, College of William and Mary, Williamsburg, Virginia, 1961–65; Instructor, 1965–66, Asst Prof., 1966–69, Assoc. Prof., 1969–74, Prof., 1974–91, S Blount Mason Prof. of English, 1991–, Washington and Lee University, Lexington, Virginia; Poetry Ed., 1966–76, Ed.-in-Chief, 1988–95, Shenandoah; Visiting Prof., Middlebury College, 1968–69; McGuffey Chair of Creative Writing, Ohio University, 1972; Visiting Poet, University of Virginia, 1981, 1982–83; Poetry Ed., New Virginia Review, 1983. *Publications:* Poetry: The Diving Bell, 1966; A Particular Place, 1969; Corgi Modern Poets in Focus 3, 1971; The Other Hand, 1974; Friends of Yours, Friends of Mine, 1974; Round and Round: A Triptych, 1977; Rockbridge Poems, 1981; Common Ground, 1982; Don't Look Back, 1987; Narcissus Dreaming, 1990; Light Years: New and Selected Poems, 1994; Second Sight: Poems for Paintings by Carol Cloar, 1996; Long Gone, 1996; Settlers, 1999; Strains of the Old Man, 1999. Fiction: Sweet Lucy Wine: Stories, 1992; The Way to Cobbs Creek, 1997; No Visible Means of Support, 2000. Non-Fiction: Nabokov: The Dimensions of Parody, 1978. *Honours:* Dylan Thomas Prize, Poetry Society of America, 1965; Borestone Mountain Awards, 1969, 1974, 1977; National Endowment for the Arts Grant, 1969, and Fellowships, 1974, 1982; Virginia Governor's Award, 1979; Guggenheim Fellowship, 1987–88; Individual Artists Fellowship, Virginia Commission for the Arts, 1996; Residency, Rockefeller Study Centre, Bellagio, Italy, 2000.

STUBBS, Jean; British writer; b. 23 Oct. 1926, Denton, Lancashire, England; m. 1st Peter Stubbs 1948; one s. one d.; m. 2nd Roy Oliver 1980. *Education:* Manchester School of Art, Loreburn Secretarial Coll., Manchester. *Career:* copywriter, Henry Melland 1964–66; reviewer, Books and Bookmen 1965–76; Writer-in-Residence for Avon 1984; mem. PEN, Soc. of Women Writers and Journalists, Detection Club, Lancashire Writers Asscn, West Country Writers, Soc. of Authors. *Publications:* The Rose Grower 1962, The Travellers 1963, Hanrahan's Colony 1964, The Straw Crown 1966, My Grand Enemy 1967, The Passing Star 1970, The Case of Kitty Ogilvie 1970, An Unknown Welshman 1972, Dear Laura 1973, The Painted Face 1974, The Golden Crucible 1976, Kit's Hill 1979, The Ironmaster 1981, The Vivian Inheritance 1982, The Northern Correspondent 1984, 100 Years Around the Lizard 1985, Great Houses of Cornwall 1987, A Lasting Spring 1987, Like We Used To Be 1989, Summer Secrets 1990, Kelly Park 1992, Charades 1994, The Witching Time 1998, I'm a Stranger Here Myself 2004; contrib. to anthologies and magazines. *Honours:* Tom Gallon Trust Award 1964, Daughter of Mark Twain 1973. *Literary Agent:* MBA Literary Agents Ltd, 62 Grafton Way, London, W1P 5LD, England.

STUDEBAKER, William Vern, BA, MA; American academic, writer and poet; b. 21 May 1947, Salmon, ID; m. Judy Infanger 1969; two s. two d. *Education:* Idaho State Univ., Univ. of Idaho, Sonoma State Univ. *Career:* Asst Prof. 1975–, Chair Dept of English 1980–82, Coll. of Southern Idaho; Commissioner, Idaho Commission on the Arts 1981–86, Dir Honors Program 1990–98; Councilman, Idaho Humanities Council 1996–2002; correspondent Times-News 2000–. *Publications:* Everything Goes Without Saying 1978, The Cleaving 1985, Idaho's Poetry: A Centennial Anthology 1989, The Rat Lady at the Company Dump 1990, Where the Morning Lights' Still Blue: Personal Essays About Idaho 1994, River Religion 1997, Travelers in an Antique Land 1997, Short of a Good Promise 1999, Passions We Desire 2003; contrib. to numerous reviews, quarterlies and journals. *Honours:* Gov. of Ida Commendation for Distinguished Public Service and Outstanding Achievement in the Humanities 2006. *Address:* 2616 East Street, 4000 North Street, Twin Falls, ID 83301, USA.

STÜTZLE, Walther K. A., Dr rer. pol; German journalist; *Permanent Secretary, Ministry of Defence*; b. 29 Nov. 1941, Westerland-Sylt; s. of the late Moritz Stützle and of Annemarie Ruge; m. Dr H. Kauper 1966; two s. two d. *Education:* Westerland High School and Univs of Berlin, Bordeaux and Hamburg. *Career:* researcher, Inst. for Strategic Studies, London 1967–68, Foreign Policy Inst. Bonn 1968–69; Desk Officer, Ministry of Defence, Planning Staff, Bonn 1969–72, Pvt. Sec. and Chef de Cabinet, 1973–76, Head, Planning Staff, Under-Sec. of Defence, Plans and Policy 1976–82; editorial staff, Stuttgarter Zeitung 1983–86; Dir Stockholm Int. Peace

Research Inst. (SIPRI) 1986–91; Ed.-in-Chief Der Tagesspiegel 1994–98; Perm. Sec., Ministry of Defence 1998–. *Publications:* Adenauer und Kennedy in der Berlinkrise 1961–62 1972, Politik und Kräftverhältnis 1983, Europe's Future – Europe's Choices (co-author) 1967, ABM Treaty – To Defend or Not to Defend 1987, SIPRI Yearbook (ed.) 1986–90, From Alliance to Coalition: The Future of Transatlantic Relations (contributor) 2004. *Address:* c/o Ministry of Defence, 10785 Berlin, Stauffenberg-str. 18 (office); Traunsteiner Str. 2, 10781 Berlin, Germany. *Telephone:* (30) 20048120 (office); (30) 2137742 (home).

STYLES, (Frank) Showell, (Glyn Carr), FRGS; British writer; b. 14 March 1908, Four Oaks, Warwickshire, England; m. Kathleen Jane Humphreys 1954; one s. two d. *Career:* Royal Navy 1939–46 (retd as Commander); professional author 1946–76; led two private Arctic expeditions 1952–53; Himalayan expedition 1954. *Publications:* A Tent on Top, 1971; Vincey Joe at Quiberon, 1971; Admiral of England, 1973; A Sword for Mr Fitton, 1975; Mr Fitton's Commission, 1977; The Baltic Convoy, 1979; A Kiss for Captain Hardy, 1979; Centurion Comes Home, 1980; The Quarterdeck Ladder, 1982; Seven-Gun Broadside, 1982; The Malta Frigate, 1983; Mutiny in the Caribbean, 1984; The Lee Shore, 1985; Gun-Brig Captain, 1987; HMS Cracker, 1988; Nelson's Midshipman, 1990; A Ship for Mr Fitton, 1991; The Independent Cruise, 1992; Mr Fitton's Prize, 1993; Mr Fitton and the Black Legion, 1994; Mr Fitton in Command, 1995; The 12-Gun Cutter, 1996, Lieutenant Fitton 1997, Mr Fitton at the Helm 1998, The Martinique Mission 1999, Mr Fitton's Hurricane 2000. Other: First on the Summits, 1970; First up Everest, 1970; The Forbidden Frontiers: A Survey of India from 1765–1949, 1970; Welsh Walks and Legends, 1972; Snowdon Range, 1973; The Mountains of North Wales, 1973; Glyder Range, 1974; Backpacking: A Comprehensive Guide, 1976; Backpacking in the Alps and Pyrenees, 1976; Backpacking in Wales, 1977; Welsh Walks and Legends: South Wales, 1977. As Glyn Carr: Death on Milestone Buttress, 1951; Murder on the Matterhorn, 1951; The Youth Hostel Murders, 1952; The Corpse in the Crevasse, 1952; A Corpse at Camp Two, 1955; Murder of an Owl, 1956; The Ice-Axe Murders, 1958; Swing Away, Climber, 1959; Holiday With Murder, 1961; Death Finds a Foothold, 1962; Lewker in Norway, 1963; Death of a Weirdy, 1965; Lewker in Tirol, 1967; Fat Man's Agony, 1969. *Address:* Trwyn Cae Iago, Borth y Gest, Porthmadog, Gwynedd LL49 9TW, Wales.

STYLIANOU, Petros Savva, PhD; Cypriot politician, journalist and writer; b. 8 June 1933, Kythrea; s. of Savvas and Evanthia Stylianou; m. Voula Tzanetatou 1960; two d. *Education:* Pancyprian Gymnasium, Univs. of Athens and Salonika. *Career:* served with Panhellenic Cttee of the Cyprus Struggle (PEKA) and Nat. Union of Cypriot Univ. Students (EFEK), Pres. EFEK 1953–54; co-founder Dauntless Leaders of the Cypriot Fighters Org. (KARI); joined liberation Movt of Cyprus 1955; imprisoned in Kyrenia Castle 1955; escaped; leader, Nat. Striking Group; sentenced to 15 years' imprisonment 1956, transferred to UK prison, released 1959; mem. Cen. Cttee United Democratic Reconstruction Front (EDMA) 1959; Deputy Sec.-Gen. Cyprus Labour Confed. (SEK) 1959, Sec.-Gen. 1960–62; f. Cyprus Democratic Labour Fed. (DEOK) 1962, Sec.-Gen. 1962–73, Hon. Pres. 1974–; mem. House of Reps 1960–70, 1985–91, Sec. 1960–62; Deputy Minister of Interior 1980–82; Special Adviser to Pres. on Cultural Affairs 1982–85; Mayor of Engomi 1992–; Founder Pancyprian Orgs for Rehabilitation of Spastics, Rehabilitation from Kidney Disease, from Haemophilia and from Myopathy; Pres. Cyprus Historical Museum and Archives. *Publications:* numerous works on poetry, history, etc. *Honours:* numerous awards and prizes from Cyprus, Greece and USA. *Address:* Erecthiou Street, P.O. Box 7504, Engomi (office); Kimonos 10, Engomi, Nicosia, Cyprus (home). *Telephone:* (2) 353240 (office); (2) 445972 (home).

SU, Tong; Chinese writer; b. 23 Jan. 1963, Suzhou, Jiangsu Prov. *Education:* Beijing Normal Univ. *Career:* fmrly Lecturer, Nanjing Acad. of Arts; Ed. Zhongshan Magazine; writer-in-residence Univ. of Iowa Int. Writing Program 2001; mem. Jiangsu Provincial Writers' Asscn. *Publications include:* (titles in translation) The Eighth Is a Bronze Sculpture, The Escape of 1934, The Mournful Dance, The Lives of Women, Wives and Concubines 1990, Raise the Red Lantern (three novellas) 1991, Blush 1994, Rice 1995, Jasmine Woman 2004, My Life as an Emperor 2005. *Address:* Jiangsu Provincial Writers Association, Nanjing, Jiangsu Province, People's Republic of China (office); c/o Faber and Faber Ltd, 3 Queen Square, London, WC1N 3AU, England.

SU, Ye; Chinese writer and film editor; b. 31 Aug. 1949, Honjiang, Hunan Dist; d. of the late Sue Linxun and Wen Zhinan; m. Chen Chunnian 1980 (divorced 1991); one s. *Education:* Jiangsu Jr Coll. of Theatre and Nanjing Univ. *Career:* mem. Jiangsu Song and Dance Ensemble Chorus 1970; narrator, Nanjing Film Studio 1972–79; apptd ed. 1979; writer 1979–; mem. Chinese Writers' Union 1980. *Publications include:* Infatuation (short story) 1982, Ever Hard to Forget 1986, Paper Wild Goose 1988, Ode to the Starry Sky 1991, A Visit to La She's Tea House 1990, Only the Fan-shaped Cliff 1992, Ever Hard to Forget (collected prose) 1992. *Honours:* First Prize for Prose (Youth Magazine) 1982, Fiction Competition (Nanjing Daily) 1983, for Literature (Nanjing Municipal) 1986, Yan Wu Literary Works Solicitation 1988, Gold Cup Award, Spring Breeze Monthly 1988, Second Prize for Literature, Nanjing Municipal 1989, Creation Award, Supplement to Nanjing Daily 1989, Literary Prize, Chinese Writers' Union and China Literary Foundation 1990, Third Prize for Excellent Works, Chinese Newspapers' Supplements 1990, Jinling Full Moon Prose Competition 1991. *Address:* c/o 43 Gulou Lane, Room 701, Nanjing 210008, People's Republic of China.

SUBRAMANIAN, (Mary) Belinda; American poet and editor; b. 6 Sept. 1953, Statesville, NC; m. S. Ramnath 1977; two d. *Education:* BA, Regents College, New York, 1987; MA, California State University, Dominguez Hills, 1990. *Career:* Ed., Gypsy Magazine and Vergin Press, 1983–. *Publications:* Nürnberg Poems, 1983; Heather and Mace, 1985; Eye of the Beast, 1986; Fighting Woman, 1986; Body Parts, 1987; Skin Divers (with Lyn Lifshin), 1988; Halloween, 1989; The Jesuit Poems, 1989; Elephants and Angels, 1991; The Innocents, 1991; A New Geography of Poets, 1992; Finding Reality in Myth, 1996; Notes of a Human Warehouse Engineer, 1998. Contributions: anthologies, journals, and magazines. *Honours:* Winner, Nerve Cowboy Poetry Contest, 1998. *Address:* PO Box 370322, El Paso, TX 79937, USA.

SUKNASKI, Andrew; Canadian editor and poet; b. 30 July 1942, Wood Mountain, Saskatchewan. *Education:* University of British Columbia, Vancouver. *Career:* Ed., Three Legged Coyote, Wood Mountain, 1982–. *Publications:* This Shadow of Eden, 1970; Circles, 1970; Rose Wayn in the East, 1972; Old Mill, 1972; The Zen Pilgrimage, 1972; Four Parts Sand: Concrete Poems, 1972; Wood Mountain Poems, 1973; Suicide Notes, Booke One, 1973; These Fragments I've Gathered for Ezra, 1973; Leaving, 1974; Blind Man's House, 1975; Leaving Wood Mountain, 1975; Octomi, 1976; Almighty Voice, 1977; Moses Beauchamp, 1978; The Ghosts Call You Poor, 1978; Two for Father, 1978; In the Name of Narid: New Poems, 1981; Montage for an Interstellar Cry, 1982; The Land They Gave Away: Selected and New Poems, 1982; Silk Trail, 1985. *Honours:* Canada Council Grants. *Address:* c/o Thistledown Press, 668 East Place, Saskatoon, Saskatchewan S7J 2Z5, Canada.

SULERI GOODYEAR, Sara, BA, MA, PhD; Pakistani/American writer and academic; b. Lahore, Pakistan. *Education:* Kinnaird Coll., Lahore, Punjab Univ., Lahore, Indiana Univ. *Career:* Prof. of English, Yale Univ. 1983–; founding-ed., Yale Journal of Criticism. *Publications:* Meatless Days, 1989; The Rhetoric of English India, 1992; Boys Will Be Boys: A Daughter's Elegy, 2003. Contributions: editorial boards of YJC, The Yale Review, Transition. *Address:* Dept of English, Yale University, 63 High Street, Room 109, PO Box 208302, New Haven, CT 06520-8302, USA. *E-mail:* sara.goodyear@yale.edu.

SULLEROT, Evelyne Annie Henriette, LèsL; French sociologist, journalist and writer; b. 10 Oct. 1924, Montrouge, Seine; d. of André; and Georgette (née Roustain) Pasteur; m. François Sullerot 1946; three s. one d. *Education:* Colls of Compiègne, Royan and Uzès, Free School of Political Sciences, Univs of Paris and Aix-en-Provence. *Career:* Teacher 1947–49; f. French Family Planning Movt 1955, Sec-Gen. 1955–58, then Hon. Pres.; Researcher Centre for Mass Communications, Tech. Coll. 1960–63; teacher French Press Inst. 1963–68; Prof. Free Univ. of Brussels 1966–68; Head Faculty of Letters Univ. of Paris (Nanterre) 1967; Specialist EC 1969–92, ILO 1970; mem. Econ. and Social Council 1974–89; Founder, Pres. Retravailler (Back to Work) Centres; mem. Nat. Advisory Comm. for Human Rights 1986–99; fmr mem. French Comm. UNESCO; Corresp. mem. Acad. des sciences morales et politiques 1999; Officier de la Légion d'Honneur; Commdr de l'Ordre Nat. du Mérite. *Publications:* La presse féminine 1963, La vie des femmes 1964, Demain les femmes 1965, Aspects sociaux de la radiotélévision 1966, Histoire de la presse féminine des origines à 1848 1966, Histoire et sociologie du travail féminin 1968, Le droit de regard, La femme dans le monde moderne 1970, Les françaises aux travail 1973, Les crèches et les équipements d'accueil pour la petite enfance (jtly) 1974, Histoire et mythologie de l'amour 1976, Le fait féminin 1978, L'Aman 1981, Le statut matrimonial et ses conséquences juridiques, fiscales et sociales 1984, Pour le meilleur et sans le pire 1984, L'âge de travailler 1986, L'enveloppe 1987, Quels pères? Quels fils? 1992, Alias 1996, Le grand remue-ménage, la crise de la famille 1997; numerous research papers for UNESCO, OECD, EU, ILO. *Address:* 95 blvd Saint-Michel, 75005 Paris, France.

SULLIVAN, Andrew, PhD; British journalist; b. 20 Aug. 1963, Godstone, Surrey. *Education:* Magdalen Coll., Oxford Univ., Dept of Govt, Harvard Univ., USA. *Career:* intern Centre For Policy Studies, London; intern New Republic magazine 1986, returned to Harvard and taught in Govt Dept 1987, returned as Assoc. Ed. New Republic 1987, Deputy Ed. 1990, Acting Ed. 1991, Ed. 1991–96, now Sr Ed.; contributing writer and columnist New York Times Magazine, contrib. New York Times Book Review, weekly columnist for the Sunday Times of London from late 1990s; est. andrewsullivan.com's Daily Dish blog 2000. *Publication:* Virtually Normal: An Argument About Homosexuality 1995, Love Undetectable: Notes on Friendship, Sex, and Survival 1999, The Conservative Soul 2006. *Address:* c/o New Republic, Suite 600, 1220 19th Street, NW, Washington, DC 20036, USA. *E-mail:* andrewmsullivan@aol.com. *Website:* time.blogs.com/daily_dish.

SULLIVAN, Rosemary, BA, MA, PhD; Canadian academic, writer and poet; b. 29 Aug. 1947, Montréal, QC. *Education:* McGill University, University of Connecticut, University of Sussex. *Career:* faculty, University of Dijon 1972–73, University of Bordeaux 1973–74, University of Victoria, BC 1974–77; Asst Prof. 1977–80, Assoc. Prof. 1980–91, Prof. 1991–, University of Toronto; mem. Amnesty International, Toronto Arts Group for Human Rights (founding mem.). *Publications:* The Garden Master: The Poetry of Theodore Roethke, 1975; The Space a Name Makes, 1986; By Heart: Elizabeth Smart, a Life, 1991; Blue Panic, 1991; Shadow Maker: The Life of Gwendolyn MacEwan, 1995; The Red Shoes: Margaret Atwood Starting Out, 1998; The Bone Ladder: New and Selected Poems, 2000; Labyrinth of Desire: Women, Passion and Romantic Obsession, 2001; Memory-Making: Selected Essays,

2001. Other: Ed. or Co-Ed. of several books. Contributions: many journals and magazines. *Honours:* Gerald Lampert Award for Poetry, 1986; Brascan Silver Medal for Culture, National Magazine Awards, 1986; Guggenheim Fellowship, 1992; Governor-General's Award for Non-Fiction, 1995; City of Toronto Book Award, 1995; Non-Fiction Prize, Canadian Authors' Asscn, 1995; Pres.'s Medal for Biography, Columbia University, 1995; Killam Fellow, 1996; Canada Research Chair, 2000; Connaught Fellowship, 2002. *Address:* c/o Department of English, University of Toronto, 7 King's College Circle, Toronto, ON M5S 3K1, Canada.

SULLIVAN, Thomas William, BA; American writer and teacher; b. 20 Nov. 1940, Highland Park, Mich.; s. of Wilson H. Sullivan and Maud E. Sullivan; one s. one d. *Career:* fmr All-American athlete in two sports, has lived in a dozen countries and been a gambler, a 'Rube Goldberg' innovator, a coach, a teacher, a city commr; currently writes full-time in Minnesota; frequent public speaker; columnist for www.storytellersunplugged.com each 16th of the month; mem. MENSA, Soc. of the Black Bull, Arcadia Mixture. *Publications:* more than 80 novels and short stories, including Diapason (novel) 1978, The Phases of Harry Moon (novel) 1988, Born Burning (novel) 1989, The Martyring (novel) 1998, Dust of Eden (novel) 2004, Second Soul (novel) 2005, The Water Wolf (novel) 2006; essays; contrib. to magazines. *Honours:* Hemingway Days Festival Literary Contest awards 1985, DADA Literary Contest 1985, 1987, listed in All-Time Top 10 Horror Stories for Writer's Digest (The Man Who Drowned Puppies), Catholic Press Journalism Award for short story (The 4th Flight Is Forever) 1996. *Address:* 15215 91st Avenue N, Maple Grove, MN 55369, USA. *E-mail:* mn333mn@earthlink.net. *Website:* .

SULLOWAY, Frank Jones, AB, AM, PhD; American psychologist and science historian; *Visiting Scholar, Institute of Personality and Social Research, University of California, Berkeley;* b. 2 Feb. 1947, Concord, NH; one s. *Education:* Harvard Univ. *Career:* Jr Fellow, Harvard Univ. Soc. of Fellows 1974–77; mem. Inst. for Advanced Study, Princeton, NJ 1977–78; Research Fellow Miller Inst. for Basic Research in Science 1978–80, Research Prof. 1999, Visiting Prof. from 2000, Visiting Scholar Inst. of Personality and Social Research 2001–06, Dept of Psychology, Univ. of California, Berkeley; Research Fellow MIT 1980–81, Visiting Scholar 1989–98; Postdoctoral Fellow, Harvard Univ. 1981–82, Visiting Scholar 1984–89; Research Fellow, Univ. Coll. London, England 1982–84; Vernon Prof. of Biography, Dartmouth Coll. 1986; Fellow Center for Advanced Study in the Behavioral Sciences, Stanford, CA 1998–99; Fellow, American Asscn for the Advancement of Science; Fellow Linnean Soc. of London; mem. American Psychological Asscn, American Psychological Soc., History of Science Soc., Human Behavior and Evolution Soc. *Publications:* Freud, Biologist of the Mind 1979, Darwin and his Finches 1982, Freud and Biology: The Hidden Legacy 1982, Darwin's Conversion 1982, Darwin and the Galapagos 1984, Darwin's Early Intellectual Development 1985, Reassessing Freud's Case Histories 1991, Born to Rebel: Birth Order, Family Dynamics and Creative Lives 1996, Birth Order, Sibling Competition, and Human Behavior 2001; contrib. to professional journals. *Honours:* History of Science Soc. Pfizer Award 1980, Nat. Endowment for the Humanities Fellowship 1980–81, Nat. Science Foundation Fellowship 1981–82, Guggenheim Fellowship 1982–83, John D. and Catherine T. MacArthur Foundation Fellowship 1984–89, American Acad. of Achievement Golden Plate Award 1997, Skeptics Soc. James Randi Award 1997. *Address:* Department of Psychology, 4125 Tolman Hall, University of California, Berkeley, CA 94720, USA. *Telephone:* (510) 642-7139 (office). *Fax:* (510) 643-9336 (office). *E-mail:* sulloway@berkeley.edu (office). *Website:* www.sulloway.org (office).

SULSTON, Sir John Edward, Kt, PhD, FRS; British scientist; b. 27 March 1942, Fulmer; s. of the late Rev. Canon Arthur Edward Aubrey Sulston and Josephine Muriel Frearson Blocksidge; m. Daphne Edith Bate 1966; one s. one d. *Education:* Merchant Taylor's School and Pembroke Coll., Cambridge. *Career:* Postdoctoral Fellowship at the Salk Inst., Calif. 1966–69; staff scientist, MRC Lab. of Molecular Biology, Cambridge 1969–2003; Dir The Sanger Centre 1992–2000; mem. Human Genetics Comm. 2001–; mem. European Molecular Biology Org. 1989–, Academia Europaea 2001–; *Television:* Royal Inst. Christmas Lectures (Channel 4) 2001. *Publications:* The Common Thread – A Story of Science, Politics, Ethics and the Human Genome (jtly) 2002; papers in scientific journals. *Honours:* Hon. Fellow Pembroke Coll., Cambridge 2000, Royal Soc. of Chemisty 2003, Acad. of Medical Sciences 2003, hon. mem. Biochemical Soc. 2002, Physiological Soc. 2002, Freedom of Merchant Taylors' Co. 2004; Hon. DSc (Trinity Coll., Dublin) 2000, (Essex) 2002, (Cambridge) 2003, (Royal Holloway) 2003, (Exeter) 2003, (Newcastle) 2004, Hon. LLD (Dundee) 2005; Officier, Légion d'honneur 2004; W. Alden Spencer Award (jtly) 1986, Gairdner Foundation Award (jtly) 1991, 2002, Darwin Medal, Royal Soc. 1996, Rosenstiel Award jtly) 1998, Pfizer Prize for Innovative Science 2000, Genetics Soc. of America George W. Beadle Medal 2000, Biochemical Soc. Sir Frederick Gowland Hopkins Medal 2000, Edinburgh Medal 2001, City of Medicine Award, Durham, NC 2001, Prince of Asturias Award, Spain 2001, Robert Burns Humanitarian Award 2002, Daily Mirror Pride of Britain Award 2002, Medical Soc. of London Fothergillian Medal 2002, Tel-Aviv Univ. Dan David Prize 2002, General Motors Sloan Prize 2002, Nobel Prize in Physiology or Medicine (jtly) 2002. *Address:* 39 Mingle Lane, Stapleford, Cambridge, CB2 5SY, England (home). *Telephone:* (1223) 842248 (home). *E-mail:* jes@sanger.ac.uk (office).

SULZBERGER, Arthur Ochs; American newspaper executive; b. 5 Feb. 1926, New York; s. of Arthur Hays and Iphigene (née Ochs) Sulzberger; m. 1st Barbara Grant 1948 (divorced 1956); one s. (Arthur Ochs Sulzberger Jr) one

d.; m. 2nd Carol Fox 1956 (died 1995); two d.; m. 3rd Allison Stacey Cowles 1996. *Education:* Columbia Univ. *Career:* US Marine Corps, Second World War and Korean War; joined The New York Times Co., New York 1951, Asst Treas. 1958–63, Pres. 1963–79, Publr 1963–92, Chair., CEO 1992–97, Chair. Emer. 1997–, mem. Bd Dir –2002; Co-Chair. Bd Int. Herald Tribune 1983; Chair. Newspaper Pres. Asscn 1988; Dir, Times Printing Co., Chattanooga, Gapesia Pulp and Paper Co. Ltd of Canada; Trustee Columbia Univ., mem. Coll. Council; Trustee Metropolitan Museum of Art, Chair. Bd of Trustees 1987–99. *Honours:* Hon. LHD (Montclair State Coll.), (Tufts Univ.) 1984; Columbia Journalism Award 1992; Alexander Hamilton Medal 1982, Vermeil Medal (City of Paris) 1992. *Address:* New York Times Co., 229 West 43rd Street, New York, NY 10036, USA. *Telephone:* (212) 556-1234.

SULZBERGER, Arthur Ochs, Jr, BA; American newspaper publisher; *Chairman, The New York Times Company;* b. 22 Sept. 1951, Mount Kisco, NY; s. of Arthur Ochs Sulzberger and Barbara Winslow Grant; m. Gail Gregg 1975; one s. one d. *Education:* Tufts Univ. and Harvard Univ. Business School. *Career:* reporter The Raleigh Times, NC 1974–76; correspondent Associated Press, London, England 1976–78; Washington bureau correspondent, The New York Times 1978–81, city hall reporter 1981, Asst Metro Ed, 1981–82, Group Man. advertising dept 1983–84, sr analyst corporate planning 1985, production co-ordinator 1985–87, Asst Publisher 1987–88, Deputy Publisher 1988–92, Publisher 1992–, Chair. The New York Times Co. 1997–; Chair. Times Square Business Improvement District 1992; Chair. New York Outward Bound Center 2002; bd mem. Newspaper Asscn of America. *Honours:* RIT Isaiah Thomas Award in Publishing 2003. *Address:* The New York Times Company, 229 W 43rd Street, New York, NY 10036, USA (office). *E-mail:* publisher@nytimes.com (office). *Website:* www.nytco.com.

SUMMERTREE, Katonah (see Windsor, Patricia)

SUN, Shuyun; Chinese writer and film and television producer; b. 1963. *Education:* Beijing Univ. and Univ. of Oxford, England. *Career:* film and TV producer, making documentaries for various companies, including the BBC and Channel 4 in the UK, and int. broadcasters. *Television and radio includes:* Half the Sky (TV documentary), The Monk and the Modern Girl (radio programme) (New York Festival World Gold Medal 2004). *Publications:* Ten Thousand Miles Without a Cloud 2003, The Long March 2006. *Address:* c/o HarperCollins, 77–85 Fulham Palace Road, London, W6 8JB, England (office). *E-mail:* contact@harpercollins.co.uk (office).

SUNDERLAND, Eric, CBE, MA, LLD, PhD, FIBiol; British anthropologist and fmr university vice-chancellor; b. 18 March 1930, Ammanford, Carmarthenshire, Wales; s. of Leonard Sunderland and Mary Agnes Davies; m. Jean Patricia Watson 1957; two d. *Education:* Univ. of Wales, Univ. Coll., London. *Career:* Prof. of Anthropology, Univ. of Durham 1971–84, Pro-Vice-Chancellor 1979–84; Prin. Univ. Coll. of N Wales, Bangor 1984–95; Vice-Chancellor Univ. of Wales 1989–91, Prof. Emer. 1995–; Sec.-Gen. Int. Union of Anthropological and Ethnological Sciences (IUAES) 1978–98, Pres. 1998–2003; Pres. Royal Anthropological Inst., London 1989–91; Chair. of Dirs Gregynog Press 1991–; Chair. Local Govt Boundary Comm. for Wales 1994–2001, Chair. Wales Cttee; mem. Bd British Council 1996–2001, Chair. 1996; mem. BBC Broadcasting Council for Wales 1995–2000; Chair. Environment Agency Advisory Cttee for Wales 1996–2000; High Sheriff of Gwynedd 1998–99; DL; Pres. Univ. of Wales, Lampeter 1998–2002; Lord-Lt of Gwynedd 1999–2006; Chair. Wetlands for Wales Project 2001–, Comm. on Local Govt Electoral Arrangements in Wales 2001–02. *Publications:* Elements of Human and Social Geography: Some Anthropological Perspectives 1973, Genetic Variation in Britain (co-ed.) 1973, The Exercise of Intelligence: Biological Pre-conditions for the Operation of Intelligence (co-ed.) 1980, Genetic and Population Studies in Wales (co-ed.) 1986. *Honours:* Hon. mem. Gorsedd of Bards, Royal Nat. Eisteddfod of Wales; Hon. Fellow, Univ. of Wales, Lampeter, Univ. of Wales, Bangor; Gold Medal of IUAES, Zagreb XIIth Int. Congress 1988. *Address:* Y Bryn, Ffriddoedd Road, Bangor, Gwynedd, LL57 2EH, Wales (home). *Telephone:* (1248) 353265 (home). *Fax:* (1248) 355043 (home).

SÜSKIND, Patrick; German author; b. 26 March 1949, Ambach, Bavaria. *Education:* Univ. of Munich. *Career:* fmr teacher; fmr writer for TV. *Publications:* Perfume: The Story of a Murderer (novel) 1979, The Double Bass (play), The Pigeon (novel) 1988, Three Stories and a Reflection; juvenile: The Story of Mr Summer 1991. *Address:* c/o Vintage, Random House, 20 Vauxhall Bridge Road, London, SW1V 2SA, England; c/o Diogenes Verlag AG, Sprecherstr. 8, 8032 Zürich, Switzerland. *Telephone:* (1) 2548511. *Fax:* (1) 2528407.

SUTHERLAND, John Andrew, PhD, FRSL; British academic and writer; b. 9 Oct. 1938, s. of Jack Sutherland and Elizabeth Sutherland (née Salter); m. Guilland Watt 1967; one s. *Education:* Colchester Royal Grammar School, Univs of Leicester and Edinburgh. *Career:* nat. service, 2nd Lt, Suffolk Regt 1958–60; Lecturer in English, Univ. of Edin. 1965–72; Lecturer in English, Univ. Coll. London 1972–84, Lord Northcliffe Prof. of Modern English Literature 1992–2004; columnist, The Guardian. *Publications include:* Thackeray at Work 1974, Victorian Novelists and Publishers 1976, Fiction and the Fiction Industry 1978, Bestsellers 1980, Offensive Literature 1982, The Longman Companion to Victorian Fiction 1989, Mrs Humphry Ward 1992, The Life of Walter Scott: A Critical Biography 1995, Victorian Fiction: Writers, Publishers, Readers 1995, Is Heathcliffe a Murderer? 1996, Can Jane Eyre be Happy? 1997, Where Was Rebecca Shot? 1998, Who Betrays Elizabeth Bennet? 1999, Henry V, War Criminal ? 1999, Last Drink to LA 2000, The

Literary Detective 2000, Literary Lives 2001, Reading the Decades 2002, Stephen Spender: The Authorised Biography 2004, How to Read a Novel: A User's Guide 2006. *Honours:* Hon. DLitt (Leicester) 1998. *Address:* c/o Department of English, University College London, Gower Street, London, WC1E 6BT, England. *Telephone:* (20) 7387-7050.

SUTHERLAND, Margaret; New Zealand writer; b. 16 Sept. 1941, Auckland; m.; two s. two d. *Career:* registered nurse; Literary Fellow, Univ. of Auckland 1981; mem. Australian Soc. of Authors, Fed. of Australian Writers. *Publications:* The Fledgling 1974, Hello, I'm Karen (juvenile) 1974, The Love Contract 1976, Getting Through (aka Dark Places, Deep Regions) 1977, The Fringe of Heaven 1984, The City Far From Home 1992, Is That Love? 1999, The Sea Between 2006; contrib. to journals and magazines. *Honours:* Scholarship in Letters (NZ)1981, Australia Council Writers Fellowships 1992, 1995. *Address:* 10 Council Street, Speers Point, NSW 2284, Australia. *E-mail:* chapsuth@idl.com.au; books@margaretsutherland.com. *Website:* www .margaretsutherland.com.au.

SUTHERLAND-SMITH, James Alfred, BA, MA; British poet, language teaching consultant and translator; b. 17 June 1948, Aberdeen, Scotland; m. Viera Schlosserova 1992; one d. *Education:* Univ. of Leeds, Univ. of Nottingham, Univ. of East Anglia. *Career:* teacher 1974–85; Deputy Head of Education, Saudi Arabian Nat. Guard Signal Corps Training School 1985–86; Head of English Language Unit, Qatar Public Telecom Corpn 1986–88; with the British Council, Lecturer Univ. P. J. Safarik, Slovakia 1989–95, English Language Consultant, E Slovakia 1995–2002, Peacekeeping English Project Man., Serbia and Montenegro 2002–; mem. Soc. of Authors, Asscn of Literary Trans. *Publications:* Four Poetry and Audience Poets, A Poetry Quintet, Trapped Water, A Singer from Sabiya, Naming of the Arrow, The Country of Rumour, Not Waiting for Miracles – 17 Contemporary Slovak Poets, At the Skin Resort 1999, One Hundred Years of Slovak Literature, An Album of Slovak Literature, Cranberry on Ice – Selected Poems of Ivan Laucik, Melancholy Hunter – Selected Poems of Jan Buzassy, Autumnal Furniture – Juraj Briskar, An Album of Slovak Literature 2, New Poetries III, Pomenovat' sip – Selected Poems trans. into Slovak, The Scent of the Unseen – Selected Poems of Mila Haugova, In the Country of Birds 2004, An Album of Slovak Literature 3, And That's the Truth – Selected Poems of Milan Rufus, Salted Snow – Selected Poems of Jozef Leikert, In Search of Beauty (anthology); contrib. to PN Review, BBC Radio 3, Slovak television and radio. *Honours:* Eric Gregory Award, First Prize Peterloo Poetry Competition, Cumberland Review Poetry Competition, Prizewinner National Poetry Competition of Great Britain, TLS Cheltenham Poetry Competition, Cardiff Int. Poetry Competition, Bridport Festival Poetry Competition, Exeter Festival Poetry Competition, Stand Magazine Poetry Competition, Philips Award, San Jose Studies Poetry Award. *Address:* Matuša trenčianského 4, 08001 Prešov, Slovakia. *E-mail:* james_ssmith@yahoo.co.uk.

SUTTON, Henry (see Slavitt, David Rytman)

SUTTON, Penny (see Cartwright, Justin)

SUZUKI, Kôji; Japanese writer; b. 13 May 1957, Hamamatsu, Shizuoka; m.; two d. *Education:* Keio Univ. *Career:* many of his novels have been made into successful films. *Publications:* fiction: Rakuen (Paradise) (Fantasy Novel Award) 1990, Ringu (Ring) 1991, Rasen (Spiral) (Yoshikawa Eiji Young Writer Award 1996) 1995, Loop 1998, Kamigami no Promenade (The Gods' Promenade) 2003, Bâsudei (Birthday) 2004, Honogurai mizu no soko kara (Dark Water) 2004; juvenile fiction includes Namida (Tears); non-fiction: Fusei no Tanjo, Kazoku no Kizuna, Papa-ism. *Address:* c/o HarperCollins Publishers, 77–85 Fulham Palace Road, Hammersmith, London, W6 8JB England.

SVANIDZE, Nikolay Karlovich; Russian journalist; b. 2 April 1955, Moscow; m.; one s. *Education:* Moscow State Univ. *Career:* researcher Inst. of USA and Canada USSR Acad. of Sciences 1978–91; on staff Russian TV 1992–; commentator Information programme Vesti 1991–94; author and narrator Information programmes Contrasts, Mirror 1996–; Deputy Dir Information programmes, Head Studio Information and Analytical programmes 1996–97; Deputy Chair., Chair. All Russian State TV and Radio Co. 1996–98; political observer 1998–; Head news programme Zerkalo (Mirror). *Honours:* Teffi Prize of Russian Acad. of TV for the best information programme. *Address:* Russian TV and Radio Company, Leninsky prosp. 27/2, 125040 Moscow, Russia (office). *Telephone:* (495) 234-85-22 (office).

SVOBODA, Terese, MFA; American poet and writer; b. 5 Sept. 1950, Ogallala, NE; m. Stephen M. Bull 1981, three s. *Education:* Columbia University. *Career:* Rare Manuscript Curator, McGill University, 1969; Co-Producer, PBS-TV series Voices and Visions, 1980–82; Distinguished Visiting Prof., University of Hawaii, 1992; Prof., Sarah Lawrence College, 1993; Williams College, 1998; mem. PEN, Poets and Writers, Poets' House (founder mem., advisory bd mem. 1986–91). *Publications:* poetry: All Aberration, 1985; Laughing Africa, 1990; Mere Mortal, 1995. Fiction: Cannibal, 1995; A Drink Called Paradise, 1999. Contributions: poems, fiction, essays and translations to periodicals. *Honours:* New York Times Book Review Writer's Choice Column Award 1985, Iowa Prize 1990, Bobst Prize 1995.

SWADOS, Elizabeth A., BA; American composer and writer; b. 5 Feb. 1951, Buffalo, NY; d. of Robert O. Swados and Sylvia Swados (née Maisel). *Education:* Bennington Coll., VT. *Career:* Composer and Music Dir Peter Brook, France, Africa, USA 1972–73; Composer-in-Residence, La Mama Experimental Theater Club, New York 1977–; mem. Faculty Carnegie-Mellon Univ., PA 1974, Bard Coll., New York 1976–77, Sarah Lawrence Coll., New York 1976–77; Creative Artists Service Program Grantee 1976. *Compositions include:* theatre scores: Medea 1972, Elektra 1970, Fragments of Trilogy 1974, Trojan Women 1974, The Good Women of Setzuan 1975, The Cherry Orchard 1977, As You Like It 1979, Haggadah 1980, Doonesbury (with Gary Trudeau) 1983, The Tower of Evil 1990, The Mermaid Wakes 1991; film scores: Step By Step 1973, Sky Dance 1979, Seize the Day 1986, Family Sins 1987. *Publications include:* The Girl With the Incredible Feeling 1976, Runaways 1979, Lullaby 1980, Sky Dance 1980, The Beautiful Lady (musical) 1984, Listening Out Loud: Becoming a Composer 1988, The Four of Us 1991, The Myth Man 1994, Flamboyant (novel); for children: Inside Out: A Musical Adventure 1990, Dreamtective: The Dreamy and Daring Adventures of Cobra Kite (Kid Genesis) 1999, Hey You! C'mere! A Poetry Slam 2002, The Animal Rescue Store 2005, My Depression: A Picture Book 2005; other: The Girl With the Incredible Feeling (audio cassette). *Honours:* New York State Arts Council Playwriting Grantee 1977–, Guggenheim Fellow, Ford Fellow, Covenant Fellow, three Obie Awards, Village Voice 1972, Outer Critics' Circle Award 1977, Stephen Spielberg Righteous Person Grantee. *Literary Agent:* c/o Sam Cohn, International Creative Management, 40 West 57th Street, New York, NY 10019, USA. *Telephone:* (212) 556-5600. *E-mail:* classical@icmtalent.com. *Address:* 112 Waverly Place, New York, NY 10011, USA (home). *Website:* www .lizswados.com.

SWAFFORD, Jan Johnson, BA, MMA, DMA; American writer and composer; b. 10 Sept. 1946, Chattanooga, Tenn.; m. Julie Pisano 1973 (divorced 1979). *Education:* Harvard Univ., Yale School of Music, Tanglewood. *Career:* Asst Prof., Boston Univ. School for the Arts 1977–78; Visiting Asst Prof., Hampshire Coll., Amherst 1979–81, Amherst Coll. 1980–81; freelance composer and writer 1981–; Lecturer in English, Tufts Univ.; currently Instructor in Theory, Musicology and Composition, Boston Conservatory. *Compositions:* Passage for piccolo, strings and percussion 1975, Landscape with Traveller for orchestra 1981, Shore Lines for soprano and flute 1982, Labyrinths for violin and cello 1983, Midsummer Variations for piano quintet 1985, Chamber Sinfonietta for chamber orchestra 1988, They Who Hunger for piano quartet 1989, Requiem in Winter for string trio 1991, From the Shadow of the Mountain for string orchestra 2001, They That Mourn for piano trio 2002. *Publications:* The Vintage Guide to Classical Music 1992, The New Guide to Classical Music 1993, Charles Ives: A Life with Music 1996, Johannes Brahms: A Biography 1997; contrib. articles and reviews to Symphony, New England Monthly, Musical America, Slate, Guardian Int.; programme/liner notes for Boston, Chicago and San Francisco Symphonies, and Sony, Naxos and RCA recordings. *Honours:* Massachusetts Artists' Foundation grant 1983, prizewinner, New England Composers' Competition 1984, Harvard-Mellon Fellowship 1988, Nat. Endowment for the Arts Composers Fellow 1991, L.L. Winship-PEN New England Award 1997. *Address:* English Department, Tufts University, 210 East Hall, Medford, MA 02155, USA (office). *E-mail:* JanSwaff@aol.com (home).

SWAN, Gladys, BA, MA; American writer, painter and academic; b. 15 Oct. 1934, New York, NY; m. Richard Swan 1955; two d. *Education:* Western New Mexico Univ., Claremont Graduate School. *Career:* Prof. of English, Franklin Coll. 1969–86; Faculty MFA Program in Creative Writing, Vermont Coll. 1981–96; Distinguished Visiting Writer-in-Residence, Univ. of Texas at El Paso 1984–85; Visiting Prof. of English, Ohio Univ. 1986–87; Assoc. Prof. of English, Univ. of Missouri-Columbia 1987–98; mem. PEN American Center. *Publications:* On the Edge of the Desert 1979, Carnival for the Gods 1986, Of Memory and Desire 1989, Do You Believe in Calbega de Vaca? 1991, Ghost Dance: A Play of Voices 1992, A Visit to Strangers 1996, News From the Volcano 2000, A Garden Amid Fires 2006; contrib. to Kenyon Review, Virginia Quarterly Review, Ohio Review, Writers Forum, Sewanee Review. *Honours:* Lilly Endowment Faculty Open Fellowship 1975–76, Fulbright Sr Lectureship 1988, Lawrence Foundation Award for Fiction 1994, Sewanee Review Tate Prize for Poetry 2001. *Address:* 2601 Lynnwood Drive, Columbia, MO 65203, USA. *E-mail:* swangl@missouri.edu.

SWAN, Susan Jane, BA; Canadian novelist, writer, poet and academic; *Associate Professor of Humanities, York University;* b. 9 June 1945, Midland, ON; m. Barry Haywood 1969 (divorced); one d.; pnr Patrick Crean. *Education:* McGill Univ. *Career:* Assoc. Prof. of Humanities 1989–, Roberts Chair in Canadian Studies 1999–2000, York Univ., Toronto; mem. Writers' Union of Canada, PEN, Scarlet Key. *Film adaptations:* Wives of Bath, Lost and Delirious. *Publications:* Queen of the Silver Blades 1975, Unfit for Paradise 1982, The Biggest Modern Woman of the World 1983, Tesseracts (co-author) 1985, The Last of the Golden Girls 1989, Language in Her Eye (ed.) 1990, Mothers Talk Back (co-ed.) 1991, Slow Hand 1992, The Wives of Bath 1993, Stupid Boys are Good to Relax With 1996, What Casanova Told Me 2004; contrib. many short stories, articles and poems to various publications. *Literary Agent:* c/o Kim Witherspoon, InkWell Management, 521 Fifth Avenue, 26th Floor, Suite 2600, New York, NY 10175, USA. *Telephone:* (212) 922-3500 (ext. 214) (office). *Address:* 213 Brunswick Avenue, Toronto, ON M5S 2M7, Canada (home). *Telephone:* (416) 323-0870 (home). *E-mail:* sswan@yorku.ca (office). *Website:* www.susanswanonline.com.

SWARD, Robert Stuart, BA, MA; American poet, writer and university lecturer; *Poet-in-Residence, University of California at Santa Cruz;* b. 23 June 1933, Chicago, IL; pnr Gloria K. Alford; two s. three d. *Education:* Univ. of Illinois, Univ. of Iowa, Middlebury Coll., Vermont, Univ. of Bristol, UK.

Career: poet-in-residence, Cornell Univ. 1962–64, Univ. of Victoria, BC 1969–73, Univ. of California at Santa Cruz 1987–; writer-in-residence, Foothill Writers' Conf. summers 1988–; writer, Writing Programme, Language Arts Dept, Cabrillo Coll. 1989–2000; Contributing Ed. Blue Moon Review, Perihelion's Writers' Friendship Series, electronic chapbooks 'God is in the Cracks' and 'Rosy Cross Father', and other internet literary publications, including Web Del Sol, locus for literary arts; mem. League of Canadian Poets, Modern Poetry Asscn, Nat. Writers' Union (USA), Writers' Union of Canada. *Recordings:* three albums of poetry. *Publications:* Uncle Dog and Other Poems 1962, Kissing the Dancer and Other Poems 1964, Half a Life's History: New and Selected Poems 1957–83 1983, The Three Roberts (with Robert Zend and Robert Priest) 1985, Four Incarnations: New and Selected Poems 1957–91 1991, Family (with David Swanger, Tilly Shaw and Charles Atkinson) 1994, Earthquake Collage 1995, A Much-Married Man (novel) 1996, Uncivilizing: A Collection of Poems 1997, Rosicrucian in the Basement: Selected Poems 2001, Heavenly Sex: New and Selected Poems 2002, Collected Poems 1957–2004 2004, God is in the Cracks – A Narrative in Voices 2006; contrib. to anthologies, newspapers and magazines. *Honours:* Fulbright Fellowship 1960–61, Guggenheim Fellowship 1965–66, D. H. Lawrence Fellowship 1966, Djerassi Foundation Residency 1990, Villa Montalvo Literary Arts Award for Poetry 1990, Way Cool Site Award for Editing Internet Literary Magazine 1996. *Address:* PO Box 7062, Santa Cruz, CA 95061-7062, USA. *Telephone:* (831) 426-5247 (office). *E-mail:* sward@cruzio.com (office). *Website:* www.robertsward.com.

SWEDE, George, BA, MA; Canadian educator, poet and writer; *Professor of Psychology, Ryerson University, Toronto;* b. 20 Nov. 1940, Riga, Latvia; m. 1st Bonnie Lewis 1964 (divorced 1969); m. 2nd Anita Krumins 1974; two s. *Education:* Univ. of British Columbia, Dalhousie Univ. *Career:* instructor, Vancouver City Coll. 1966–67; instructor 1968–73, Prof. of Psychology 1973–, Ryerson Univ., Toronto; Dir, Poetry and Things 1969–71; Developmental Psychology, Open Coll. 1973–75; Poetry Ed., Poetry Toronto 1980–81; Co-Ed., Writer's Magazine 1982–90; Assoc. Ed., Red Moor Press 2000–; mem. Haiku Canada (co-founder 1977), Haiku Soc. of America, League of Canadian Poets, PEN, Writers' Union of Canada. *Exhibitions include:* Visualog 3, Arternatives, San Luis Obispo, Calif. 1990, Visualog 4, Orange Co. Community Coll., Newburgh, NY 1991, Visualog 4, Mid-Hudson Arts & Science Centre, Poughkeepsie, NY 1991, Friends of St Bride Temporary Type Exhbns, London 2005. *Radio:* numerous interviews; short stories: Memories of Mexico (Quiet Quarter, RTE) 2001. *Television:* interview, Romper Room (CTV) 1986, Japan Air Lines Haiku Contest, (BCTV) 1987, In Conversation With (TV Ontario) 1992. *Publications:* poetry: Tell-Tale Feathers 1978, A Snowman, Headless 1979, As Far as the Sea Can Eye 1979, Flaking Paint 1983, Frozen Breaths 1983, Tick Bird 1983, Bifids 1984, Night Tides 1984, Time is Flies 1984, High Wire Spider 1986, I Throw Stones at the Mountain 1988, Leaping Lizzard 1988, Holes in My Cage 1989, I Want to Lasso Time 1991, Leaving My Loneliness 1992, Five O'Clock Shadows (co-author) 1996, My Shadow Doing Something 1997, Almost Unseen 2000, First Light, First Shadows 2006; editor: The Canadian Haiku Anthology 1979, Cicada Voices 1983, The Universe is One Poem 1990, There Will Always Be a Sky 1993, The Psychology of Art: An Experimental Approach 1994, Tanka Splendour 1998, Global Haiku: Twenty-Five Poets Worldwide (ed.) 2000; non-fiction: The Modern English Haiku 1981, Creativity: A New Psychology 1994; fiction: Moonlit Gold Dust 1979, Quilby: The Porcupine Who Lost His Quills (with Anita Krumins) 1980, Missing Heirloom 1980, Seaside Burglaries 1981, Downhill Theft 1982, Undertow 1982, Dudley and the Birdman 1985, Dudley and the Christmas Thief 1986; contrib. to magazines world-wide. *Honours:* Haiku Soc. of America Book Award 1980, High/Coo Press Chapbook Competition Winner 1982, Museum of Haiku Literature Awards 1983, 1985, 1993, Canadian Children's Book Centre Our Choice Awards 1984, 1985, 1987, 1991, 1992, Third Place, Poetry Soc. of Japan Int. Tanka Contest 1990, First Prize, Mainichi Daily News Haiku in English competition 1993, Second Place, Mainichi 125th Anniversary Haiku Contest 1997, Third Place, Haiku Soc. of America Henderson Haiku Contest 1997, First Prize, The Snapshot Press Tanka Collection Competition 2005. *Address:* 70 London Street, Toronto, ON M6G 1N3, Canada (office). *Telephone:* (416) 534-4584 (home). *E-mail:* gswede@ryerson.ca (office). *Website:* home.primus.ca/~swede (home).

SWEENEY, Matthew, BA; Irish poet and writer; b. 6 Oct. 1952, Co. Donegal; m. Rosemary Barber 1979. *Education:* University College, Dublin, Polytechnic of North London. *Career:* Writer-in-Residence, Farnham College, Surrey, 1984–85, South Bank Centre, 1994–95; Writing Fellowship, University of East Anglia, 1986; Publicist and Events Asst, Poetry Society, 1988–90; Poet-in-Residence, Hereford and Worcester, 1991, National Library for the Blind, 1999; Writer-in-Residence on the Internet, Chadwyck-Healey, 1997–98. *Publications:* A Dream of Maps, 1981; A Round House, 1983; The Lame Waltzer, 1985; The Chinese Dressing Gown, 1987; Blues Shoes, 1989; The Flying Spring Onion, 1992; Cacti, 1992; The Snow Vulture, 1992; Fatso in the Red Suit, 1995; Emergency Kit: Poems for Strange Times (ed. with Jo Shapcott), 1996; Writing Poetry (with John Hartley Williams), 1997; The Bridal Suite, 1997; Penguin Modern Poets 12, 1997; Beyond Bedlam: Poems Written Out of Mental Distress (ed. with Ken Smith), 1997; A Smell of Fish, 2000; Selected Poems, 2002; Fox, 2002. *Honours:* Prudence Farmer Prize, 1984; Cholmondeley Award, 1987; Arts Council Literature Award, 1992; Arts Council of England Writer's Award, 1999. *Address:* Chamissoplatz 8, 10965, Berlin, Germany (home).

SWICK, Marly, BA, MFA, PhD; American writer and academic; b. 26 Nov. 1949, Indianapolis, IN. *Education:* Stanford Univ., American Univ., Univ. of Iowa. *Career:* Prof. of Fiction Writing, Univ. of Nebraska from 1988; fmr teacher of creative writing, Univ. of Nebraska – Lincoln; currently Prof. in the Creative Writing Program, University of Missouri – Columbia. *Publications:* Monogamy (short stories) 1990, The Summer Before the Summer of Love (short stories) 1995, Paper Wings (novel) 1996, Evening News (novel) 1999; contrib. short stories to many magazines, including Atlantic Monthly, Gettysburg Review, Iowa Review, North American Review, Redbook. *Honours:* James Michener Award 1986, Univ. of Wisconsin Creative Writing Inst. Fellowship 1987, NEA grant 1987, Iowa Short Fiction Prize 1990, Gold Chalk Award for teaching excellence. *Address:* Creative Writing Program, University of Missouri – Columbia, 107 Tate Hall, Columbia, MO 65211-1500, USA (office). *E-mail:* marlyswick@yahoo.com (office).

SWIFT, Graham Colin, FRSL; British writer; b. 4 May 1949, London; s. of Lionel Allan Stanley Swift and Sheila Irene Swift (née Bourne). *Education:* Dulwich Coll., Queens' Coll., Cambridge, Univ. of York. *Publications:* (novels) The Sweet Shop Owner 1980, Shuttlecock 1981, Waterland 1983, Out of This World 1988, Ever After 1992, Last Orders 1996, The Light of Day 2003, Tomorrow 2007; (short stories) Learning to Swim and Other Stories 1982; The Magic Wheel (co-ed. with David Profumo) 1986. *Honours:* Hon. Fellow, Queens' Coll. Cambridge 2005; Hon. LittD (East Anglia) 1998; Hon. DUniv (York) 1998; Hon. DLit (London) 2003; Geoffrey Faber Memorial Prize, Guardian Fiction Prize, RSL Winifred Holtby Award 1983, Premio Grinzane Cavour (Italy) 1987, Prix du meilleur livre étranger (France) 1994, Booker Prize, James Tait Black Memorial Prize 1996. *Literary Agent:* c/o AP Watt Ltd, 20 John Street, London, WC1N 2DR, England. *Telephone:* (20) 7405-6774. *Fax:* (20) 7831-2154. *E-mail:* apw@apwatt.co.uk. *Website:* www.apwatt.co.uk.

SWINBURNE, Richard Granville, MA, BPhil, FBA; British academic; *Nolloth Professor Emeritus of the Philosophy of the Christian Religion, University of Oxford;* b. 26 Dec. 1934, Smethwick; s. of William H. Swinburne and Gladys E. Swinburne; m. Monica Holmstrom 1960 (separated 1985); two d. *Education:* Univ. of Oxford. *Career:* Fereday Fellow, St John's Coll., Oxford 1958–61; Leverhulme Research Fellow in History and Philosophy of Science, Univ. of Leeds 1961–63; Lecturer in Philosophy, Univ. of Hull 1963–72; Prof. of Philosophy, Univ. of Keele 1972–84; Nolloth Prof. of the Philosophy of the Christian Religion, Univ. of Oxford 1985–2002, Prof. Emer. 2002–; Visiting Assoc. Prof., Univ. of Maryland 1969–70; Visiting Prof., Syracuse Univ. 1987, Univ. of Rome 2002, Catholic Univ. of Lublin 2002, Yale Univ. 2003, St Louis Univ. 2003. *Publications:* Space and Time 1968, 1981, The Concept of Miracle 1971, An Introduction to Confirmation Theory 1973, The Coherence of Theism 1977, The Existence of God 1979, 2004, Faith and Reason 1981, 2005, The Evolution of the Soul 1986, Responsibility and Atonement 1989, Revelation 1991, 2007, The Christian God 1994, Is There a God? 1996, Providence and the Problem of Evil 1998, Epistemic Justification 2001, The Resurrection of God Incarnate 2003. *Address:* 50 Butler Close, Oxford, OX2 6JG, England (home). *Telephone:* (1865) 514406 (home). *E-mail:* richard.swinburne@oriel.ox.ac.uk (office). *Website:* users.ox.ac.uk/~orie0087 (office).

SYAL, Meera, MBE, BA; British writer and actress; b. 27 June 1963, Wolverhampton; d. of Surendra Syal and Surrinder Syal; m. 1st 1989; one d.; m. 2nd Sanjeev Bhaskar 2005. *Education:* Queen Mary's High School for Girls, Walsall, Univ. of Manchester. *Career:* actress in one-woman comedy One of Us after graduation (Nat. Student Drama Award); fmr actress Royal Court Theatre, London; writer of screenplays and novels; actress and comedienne in theatre, film and on TV; contrib. to The Guardian newspaper. *Plays include:* Serious Money (London and Broadway, New York) 1987, Stitch 1990, Peer Gynt 1990, Bombay Dreams (story to musical) 2001. *Radio includes:* Legal Affairs 1996, Goodness Gracious Me 1996–98, The World as We Know It 1999. *Film appearances include:* Sammie and Rosie Get Laid 1987, A Nice Arrangement, It's Not Unusual, Beautiful Thing 1996, Girls' Night 1997. *Television appearances include:* The Real McCoy (five series) 1990–95, My Sister Wife (BBC series) 1992, Have I Got News For You 1992, 1993, 1999, Sean's Show 1993, The Brain Drain 1993, Absolutely Fabulous 1995, Soldier Soldier 1995, Degrees of Error 1995, Band of Gold 1995, Drop the Dead Donkey 1996, Ruby 1997, Keeping Mum (BBC sitcom) 1997–98, The Book Quiz 1998, Goodness Gracious Me (first UK Asian TV comedy sketch show; co-writer) 1998–2000, Room 101 1999, The Kumars at No. 42 2002–. *Written works include:* A Nice Arrangement (short TV film) 1991, My Sister Wife (TV film; Best TV Drama Award, Comm. for Racial Equality, Awards for Best Actress and Best Screenplay, Asian Film Acad. 1993) 1992, Bhaji on the Beach (film) 1994, Anita and Me (novel and adapted for TV) (Betty Trask Award) 1996, Goodness Gracious Me (comedy sketch TV show; co-writer) 1999, Life isn't all Ha Ha Hee Hee (novel) 1999. *Honours:* Scottish Critics Award for Most Promising Performer 1984, Woman of the Year in the Performing Arts, Cosmopolitan Magazine 1994, Chair.'s Award, Asian Women of Achievement Awards 2002. *Address:* c/o Rochelle Stevens, 2 Terretts Place, Islington, London, N1 1QZ, England (office). *Telephone:* (1973) 417762 (office).

SYLVESTER, Janet, BA, MA, PhD; American poet and academic; b. 5 May 1950, Youngstown, OH; m. James Vandenberg 1973 (divorced 1980). *Education:* Goddard College, University of Utah. *Career:* Faculty, University of South Carolina at Columbia. *Publications:* That Mulberry Wine, 1985; A Visitor at the Gate, 1996; The Mark of Flesh, 1997. Contributions: anthologies, reivews, quarterlies and journals. *Address:* 700 S Holly Street, Columbia, SC 29205, USA. *E-mail:* sylvesterj@garnet.cla.sc.edu.

SZABÓ, Magda; Hungarian writer; b. 5 Oct. 1917, Debrecen; d. of Alex Szabó and Madeleine Jablonczay; m. Tibor Szobotka 1948. *Education:* Lajos Kossuth Univ., Debrecen. *Career:* graduated as a teacher 1940; worked in secondary schools 1940–44, 1950–59; started literary career as poet and has since written novels, plays, radio dramas, essays and film scripts; Eternal Curator Generalis Calvinistic Church in Hungary 2004; mem. Acad. of Sciences of Europe, Hungarian Széchenyi Acad. of Art and Literature; Fellow, Univ. of Iowa. *Film scripts:* Vörös tinta 1959, Tündér Lala 1981. *TV scripts:* A Danaida 1971, Abigél (mini-series) 1978, Az a szép, fényes nap (also play) 1981, Nemkívánatos viszonyok 1997, Szabó Magda és a 'Für Elise' 2004, Régimódi történet (mini-series) 2005. *Publications:* poems: Neszek (Noises); autobiog.: Ókut (Old Well); novels for children: Szigetkék (Island-Blue), Tündér Lala (Lala the Fairy), Abigél (Abigail); novels: Az őz (The Fawn), Fresko (Fresco), Disznótor (Night of Pig-Killing), Pilatus (Pilate), A Danaida (The Danaid), Mózes 1.22 (Genesis 1.22), Katalin utca (Kathleen Street), A szemlélők (The Onlookers), Régimódi történet (Old-Fashioned Story), Az ajtó (The Door), The Moment 1990; plays: Kiálts város (Cry Out, Town!), Az a szép fényes nap (That Bright Beautiful Day), A meráni fiu (The Boy of Meran), A csata (The Battle) 1982, Béla Király (King Béla), A Macskák Szerdája (The Wednesday of the Cats) 1985, Outside the Circle 1980; essays: The Lethargy of the Semigods 1986, The Logic of the Butterfly 1997, The Monologue of Cseke; other: Cakes for Cerberus (short stories). *Honours:* Hon. Citizen of Debrecen; Hon. DPhil; Baumgarten Prize 1949, József Attila Prize 1959, 1972, Kossuth Prize 1978, Getz Corpn Prize (USA) 1992, Szén Ernő Prize for Dramatic Art, Corrinus Chain of King Matthias. *Address:* Julia-utca 3, 1026 Budapest II, Hungary. *Telephone:* (3) 565-013. *Fax:* (3) 565-013.

SZEWC, Piotr; Polish writer and journalist; b. 1961, Zamościu. *Education:* Catholic Univ. of Lublin. *Career:* Ed. of periodical, Nowe Ksiazki (New Books). *Publications include:* Świadectwo 1983, Zagłada 1987, Ocalony na Wschodzie 1991, i Zmierzchy i poranki 2000, Syn kapłana 2001, Bociany nad powiatem 2005.

SZIRTES, George Gabor Nicholas, BA, PhD, FRSL; British (b. Hungarian) poet, writer and translator; *Co-ordinator Creative Writing, Norwich School of Art and Design;* b. (Gábor György Miklós Szirtes), 29 Nov. 1948, Budapest, Hungary; s. of László Szirtes and the late Magdalena Nussbächer; m. Clarissa Upchurch 1970; one s. one d. *Education:* Leeds Coll. of Art, Goldsmith's Coll. of Art. *Career:* settled in UK 1956; taught in various schools 1973–91; currently Co-ordinator Creative Writing, Norwich School of Art and Design; mem. PEN, Soc. of Authors, Bd PBS, British Centre for Literary Trans. *Publications:* poetry: The Slant Door 1979, November and May 1981, The Kissing Place 1982, Short Wave 1984, The Photographer in Winter 1986, Metro 1988, Bridge Passages 1991, Blind Field 1994, Selected Poems 1996, The Red All Over Riddle Book (juvenile) 1997, Portrait of My Father in an English Landscape 1998, The Budapest File 2000, An English Apocalypse 2001, A Modern Bestiary 2004, Reel (Poetry Book Soc. T. S. Eliot Prize 2005) 2004; criticism: The Colonnade of Teeth: Modern Hungarian Poetry (jtly) 1996, The Lost Rider: Hungarian Poetry, 16th–20th Century 1998, New Writing 10 (ed. with Penelope Lively) 2001, An Island Sound: Hungarian Fiction and Poetry Before and Beyond the Iron Curtain (co-ed.) 2004; criticism: Exercise of Power, The Art of Ana Maria Pacheco 2001; several Hungarian works translated into English, including Ottoó Orbán, The Blood of the Walsungss: Selected Poems 1991, Zsuzsa Rakovsky, New Life: Selected Poems 1994, Gyula Krúdy, The Adventures of Sinbad (short stories) 1999, László Krasznahorkai, The Melancholy of Resistance 1999, The Night of Akhenaton: Selected Poems of Ágnes Nemes Nagy 2003, Sándor Márai, Conversation in Bolzano 2004, László Krasznahorkai, War and War 2005, Sándor Márai, Rebels 2007; contrib. to numerous books, anthologies, journals and magazines, various introductions to books. *Honours:* Gold Star of Hungarian Repub. 1991; Geoffrey Faber Memorial Prize 1980, Arts Council Bursary 1984, British Council Fellowship 1985, 1987, 1989, Cholmondeley Award 1987, Dery Prize for Trans. 1991, European Poetry Trans. Prize 1995, George Cushing Award 2001, Soc. of Authors Travelling Scholarship 2002, Leverhulme Research Fellowship 2003–05, Pro Cultura Hungarica Medal 2004, T. S. Eliot Prize 2004, T. S. Eliot Memorial Lecturer 2005, StAnza Lecturer 2006. *Telephone:* (7752) 713533 (mobile). *Address:* 16 Damgate Street, Wymondham, Norfolk, NR8 0BQ, England. *Telephone:* (1953) 603533 (office). *E-mail:* george@georgeszirtes.co.uk (office). *Website:* www.georgeszirtes.co.uk.

SZYMBORSKA, Wisława; Polish poet, translator and literary critic; b. 2 July 1923, Kórnik, nr Poznań. *Education:* Jagiellonian Univ., Kraków. *Career:* first work 'Szukam slowa' (I am Looking for a Word) published in Dziennik Polski daily 1945; Poetry Ed. and columnist, Życie Literackie (weekly) 1953–81; mem. Polish Writers' Asscn 1951–81, 1981–, mem. Gen. Bd 1978–83; poems have been translated into (and published in book form in) English, German, Swedish, Italian, Danish, Hebrew, Hungarian, Czech, Slovakian, Serbo-Croatian, Romanian, Bulgarian and other languages, and have also been published in numeerous foreign anthologies of Polish poetry. *Publications:* poetry: Dlatego żyjemy (That's Why We're Alive) 1952, Pytania zadawane sobie (Questioning Oneself) 1954, Wołanie do Yeti (Calling Out to Yeti) 1957, Sól (Salt) 1962, Sto pociech (No End of Fun) 1967, Wybór wierszy (Selected Poems) 1967, 1973, Poezje 1970, Wszelki wypadek (Could Have) 1972, Wielka liczba (A Large Number) 1976, Poezje wybrane (Selected Poems II), Ludzie na moście (The People on the Bridge) 1986, Koniec i początek 1993, Widok z ziarnkiem piasku (View With a Grain of Sand) 1996, Poems New and Collected 1957–97 1998, Wiersze wybrane (Selected Poems III) 2000, Chwila (A Moment) 2002. *Honours:* Gold Cross of Merit 1955; Hon. DLitt (Poznań) 1995; Nobel Prize for Literature 1996, Goethe Award (Frankfurt) 1991, Herder Award 1995, Polish PEN Club Award 1996. *Address:* Polish Writers' Association, ul. Kanonicza 7, 31-002 Kraków, Poland.

TABBERER, Margaret (Maggie) May, AM; Australian journalist and fashion executive; b. 11 Dec. 1936, d. of A. Trigar; m. (divorced); two d. *Education:* Unley Tech. Coll. *Career:* model 1957–61; Fashion Publicity Promotions, Maggie Tabberer and Assocs 1961–80; fashion writer Sydney Daily Mirror 1965–80; host Maggie Show (Channel Seven Network) 1968–70; Fashion Ed. Australian Women's Weekly 1981–96; Dir Maggie T. Licencing; face of Fox FX Channel 2000–; presenter 'Maggie at Home' 2001–, Fox Biography (Channel 7). *Publication:* Maggie (autobiog.) 1998. *Address:* c/o Harry M. Miller Group, PO Box 313, King's Cross, NSW 1340, Australia (office). *Telephone:* (2) 9356-0000 (office).

TABOR, Herbert, BA, MD; American academic; *Editor, The Journal of Biological Chemistry;* m. Dr Celia White. *Education:* Univ. of Harvard. *Career:* staff, Nat. Inst. of Health 1943–; Ed., The Journal of Biological Chemistry 1970–; elected to Nat. Acad. of Sciences 1977; Pharmocology Section Chief, Laboratory of Biochemical Pharmacology, Bethesda. *Publications include:* Metabolism of Amino Acids and Amines (co-author) 1971, Polyamines (co-author) 1983. *Honours:* Chemical Soc. of Washington Hillebrand Prize (with Dr Celia Tabor) 1986, American Soc. of Biochemistry and Molecular Biology Rose Award 1996. *Address:* The Journal of Biological Chemistry, 9650 Rockville Pike, Bethesda, MD 20814-3997, USA. *E-mail:* htabor@asbmb.faseb.org. *Website:* www.jbc.org.

TABORSKI, Boleslaw, BA, MA; Polish/British poet, writer and translator; b. 7 May 1927, Toruń; s. of Jozef Taborski and Irena Taborski; m. Halina Junghertz 1959; one d. *Education:* Univ. of Bristol. *Career:* Prod. Polish Section 1959–89, Ed. Arts in Action 1985–93, BBC World Service; Visiting Prof., CUNY 1982–; mem. Asscn of Authors, ZAIKS (Warsaw), Asscn of Polish Writers (Warsaw), Council Gallery in the Provinces Foundation (Lublin), Poets' Fraternity (Kraków), Pro Europa Foundation (Warsaw, council mem. 1994–), World Asscn of the Polish Home Army Ex-servicemen (Warsaw), Polish Shakespeare Soc. (Gdańsk), PEN (Warsaw). *Publications:* poetry: Times of Passing 1957, Grains of Night 1958, Crossing the Border 1962, Lesson Continuing 1967, Voice of Silence 1969, Selected Poems 1973, Web of Words 1977, For the Witnesses 1978, Observer of Shadows 1979, Love 1980, A Stranger's Present 1983, Art 1985, The Stillness of Grass 1986, Life and Death 1988, Politics 1990, Shakespeare 1990, Goodnight Nonsense 1991, Survival 1998, Selected Poems 1999, Gniezno Door 2000, A Fragment of Existence 2002, Big Brother's New Era 2004, Plan B 2007; criticism: New Elizabethan Theatre 1967, Byron and the Theatre 1972, The Inner Plays of Karol Wojtyla 1989, My Uprising: Then and Now 1998, All Roads Drive Straight at my Heart (on Karol Wojtyla/John Paul II: essays, reminiscences, poems) 2005; co-author: Crowell's Handbook of Contemporary Drama 1971, Polish Plays in Translation 1983; numerous trans; contrib. to various publications. *Honours:* Polish Writers Asscn Abroad Award 1954, 2006, Jurzykowski Foundation Award, New York 1968, Merit for Polish Culture Badge and Diploma, Warsaw 1970, Koscielski Foundation Award, Geneva 1977, SI Witkiewicz ITI Award, Warsaw 1988, Asscn of Authors Trans. Award, Warsaw 1990, 1995, Societé Europeen de Culture Award, Warsaw 1998, KLIO, History Publishers Award, Warsaw 1998. *Address:* 66 Esmond Road, London, W4 1JF, England (home). *Telephone:* (20) 8994-0501 (home).

TABUCCHI, Antonio; Italian novelist; b. 1943, Vecchiano, Tuscany; m.; one d. one s. *Education:* Univ. of Pisa. *Career:* Chair of Literature, Univ. of Siena; columnist for Italian newspaper, Corriere della Sera, Spanish newspaper, El País; trans. of Fernando Pessoa. *Publications:* Piazza d'Italia (novel) 1975, Il piccolo naviglio (novel) 1978, Il gioco del rovescio (short stories, trans. as Letter from Casablanca) 1981, Donna di Porto Pim (short stories) 1983, Notturno indiano (novel, trans. as Indian Nocturne) 1984, Pessoana minima: escritos sobre Fernando Pessoa (non-fiction) 1984, Piccoli equivoci senza importanza (novel, trans. as Little Misunderstandings of No Importance) 1985, Il filo dell'orizzonte (novel, trans. as The Edge of the Horizon) 1986, I volatili del Beato Angelico (short stories) 1987, Un baule pieno di gente: scritti su Fernando Pessoa (non-fiction) 1990, Requiem, uma alucinação (novel, trans. as Requiem: A Hallucination) 1990, Sogni di sogni (trans. as Dreams of Dreams) 1992, Gli ultimi tre giorni di Fernando Pessoa (trans. as The Last Three Days of Fernando Pessoa) 1994, Sostiene Pereira (novel, trans. as Pereira Declares) 1994, La testa perduta di Damasceno Monteiro (novel, trans. as The Missing Head of Damasceno Monteiro) 1997, Si sta facendo sempre più tardi (novel) 2001, Tristano muore (novel) 2004. *Honours:* Prix Européen Jean Monnet 1994, Prix Médicis Étranger 1987, Leibniz Acad. Nossack Prize 1999, Italian PEN Club Prize. *Address:* c/o W. W. Norton & Company Inc., 500 Fifth Avenue, New York, NY 10110, USA.

TAFDRUP, Pia, BA; Danish poet and writer; b. 29 May 1952, Copenhagen; d. of Finn Tafdrup and Elin Tafdrup; m. Bo Hakon Jørgensen 1978; two s. *Education:* Univ. of Copenhagen. *Career:* Chair. Art Expert Cttee for the Literary Art 1993–95; mem. Danish Literary Acad. 1989–, Danish PEN Centre, Danish Language Council 1991–99, Council of Danish Arts Foundation 2002–. *Dance:* libretto to The Town of Viso 1999. *Plays:* Døden i bjergene (Death in the Mountains) 1988, Jorden er blå (The Earth is Blue) 1992. *Film:* A Portrait Film, Thousandborn (directed by Cæcilia Holbek Trier) 2005. *Radio play:* Døden i bjergene (Death in the Mountains) 1990. *Recording:* Morning Myth from the poem Mythic Morning, Per Nørgård: Mythic Morning. Works for Choir II 2005. *Publications:* poetry: Når der går hul på en engel (When an Angel Breaks her Silence – Poems) 1981, Konstellationer – en antologi af dansk lyrik 1976–1981 (Constellations – An Anthology of Danish Poems) (ed.) 1982, Intetfang (No Hold) – Poems 1982, Den inderste zone (The Innermost Zone) – Poems 1983, Springflod (Spring Tide) 1985, Transformationer. Poesi 1980–1985 (Transformations. Poetry 1980–1985) (ed.) 1985, Hvid feber (White Fever) – Poems 1986, Sekundernes bro (The Bridge of Moments) – Poems 1988, Over vandet går jeg. Skitse til en poetik (Walking Over the Water. An Outline of a Poetics) 1991, Krystalskoven (The Crystal Forest) – Poems 1992, Territorialsang (Territorial Song) – Poems 1994, Dronningeporten (Queen's Gate) – Poems 1998, Tusindfødt (Thousand Born) – Poems 1999, Digte 1981–83 (Poems 1981–83) 1999, Digte 1984–88 (Poems 1984–88) 2000, Digte 1989–98 (Poems 1989–98) 2001, Hvalerne i Paris (The Whales in Paris) – Poems 2002, Tarkovskijs heste (Tarkovský's Horses) – Poems 2006, Springet over skyggen. Udvalgte digte 1981–2006 (Jump Across The Shadow. Selected Poems 1981–2006) 2007; prose: Hengivelsen (Surrender, novel) 2004; translations: Spring Tide 1989, Ten Poems 1989, Dagen ditt ljus. Dikter 1981–1994 1995, Över vattnet går jag 1997, 2002, Drottningporten 2000, La Forêt de Cristal 2000, Tiché vybuchy 2000, Queen's Gate 2001, Kristaini gozd 2004, Bindooumlu 2004, Valama i Paris 2004, Ponte de Focagem do Oceano 2004, Territorial Song (in Hebrew) 2005, A gi seg bort 2005, De koninginne-poort 2006; English versions of poems have appeared in literary journals in UK, USA and Canada; poems have been translated into Swedish, Finnish, Icelandic, Greenlandic, German, Dutch, French, Portuguese, Spanish, Italian, Lithuanian, Macedonian, Polish, Romanian, Slovenian, Slovakian, Russian, Turkish, Hebrew, Arabic and Vietnamese; contrib. to many journals and anthologies. *Honours:* Kt of the Danish Flag Order 2001; Danish State Art Foundation Scholarship for Authors 1984–86, 12 grants 1986–97, Ragna Sidén Foundation Danish Literature Prize for Women 1997, Lifelong Artist's Grant 1998, Nordic Council Literature Prize 1999, Soeren Gyldendal Award 2005, Nordic Prize, Swedish Acad. 2006. *Address:* Rosenvaengets Sideallé 3, 2. th., 2100 Copenhagen Œ (home); c/o Gyldendal, Klareboderne 3, 1001, Copenhagen K, Denmark (office). *Telephone:* 35-43-27-88 (home). *Fax:* 35-43-94-44 (home). *E-mail:* tafdrup@post6.tele.dk (home). *Website:* www .tafdrup.com (home).

TAGLIABUE, John, BA, MA; American fmr college teacher, poet and writer; *Professor Emeritus, Bates College, Maine;* b. 1 July 1923, Cantu, Italy; m. Grace Ten Eyck 1946; two d. *Education:* Columbia Univ. *Career:* teacher, American Univ., Beirut 1945, State Coll. of Washington 1946–47, Alfred Univ., New York 1948–50, Bates Coll., Maine 1953–89; Fulbright Lecturer, Univ. of Pisa 1950–52, Univ. of Tokyo 1958–60, Fudan Univ., Shanghai 1984, Univ. of Indonesia 1993; mem. Acad. of American Poets, PEN, Poetry Soc. of America. *Publications:* Poems 1959, A Japanese Journal 1966, The Buddha Uproar 1970, The Doorless Door 1970, The Great Day 1984, New and Selected Poems 1942–97 1997; contrib. to journals, magazines and periodicals. *Honours:* Fulbright grants, Italy, Japan, China, Indonesia, two grants in Italy, two grants in Japan, writing grants in Bellagio (Italy), Vence (France), Thessaloniki (Greece) and others. *Address:* Wayland Manor, Apt 412, 500 Angell Street, Providence, RI 02906, USA (home). *Telephone:* (401) 272-1766 (home).

TAHER, Bahaa; Egyptian writer; b. 1935, Cairo. *Education:* Univ. of Cairo. *Career:* worked for Egyptian Radio 2 culture channel; mem. Gallery 68 writers' movement; left Egypt to become UN trans., Geneva, Switzerland 1981; later returned to Egypt. *Publications:* short stories: al-Khutuba (The Engagement) 1972, Bi-l-Amsi Halamtu Bi-K 1984, Ana al-Malik Ji'tu 1985, Zahabtu ila Shalala (I Went to a Waterfall) 1996; novels: Sharq al-Nakhila 1985, Qalat Duha 1985, Khalati Safiyya wal-Dayr (novel, trans. as Aunt Safiyya and the Monastery) (Giuseppe Acerbi Prize, Italy 2000) 1991, Al-Hob fi al-Manfa (novel, trans. as Love in Exile) 1995, Wahet al-Ghuroub (Dusk Oasis) 2006; non-fiction: Masrahiyyat: Ard wa-Naqd (analysis of ten Egyptian plays) 1985. *Honours:* State Award of Merit in Literature 1998.

TAILLANDIER, François Antoine Georges, MA; French writer; b. 20 June 1955, Chamalières; s. of Henri Taillandier and Denise Ducher; three c. *Career:* teacher 1980–83; full-time writer 1984–, also contrib. Le Figaro (newspaper), La Montagne (newspaper), L'Humanité (newspaper), L'Atelier du Roman (periodical); Admin., Soc. des Gens de Lettres de France. *Publications:* fiction: Personnages de la rue du Couteau 1984, Tott 1985, Benoît ou les contemporains obscurs 1986, Les Clandestins (Prix Jean-Freustié 1991) 1990, Les Nuits Racine 1992, Fan et le jouet qui n'existe pas (with Charles Barat) 1993, Mémoires de Monte-Cristo 1994, Des hommes qui s'éloignent 1997, Anielka (Grand Prix du roman de l'Académie française 1999) 1999, Le cas Gentile 2001, La Grande Intrigue: Vol. 1 Option Paradis 2005, Vol. 2 Telling 2006; non-fiction: Tous les secrets de l'avenir 1996, Aragon 1997, Journal de Marseille 1999, N6, la route de l'Italie 1999, Les Parents lâcheurs 2001, Borges, une restitution du monde 2002, Pour ou contre Jacques Chirac (with Joseph Macé-Scaron) 2002, Un Autre langue 2004, Balzac (biog.) 2005. *Honours:* Prix Roger Nimier 1992, Acad. française Prix de la critique 1997. *Address:* c/o Editions Stock, 31 rue de Fleurus, 75006 Paris, France (office).

TAIT, Arch, MA, PhD; British translator and academic; b. 6 June 1943, Glasgow, Scotland. *Education:* Trinity Hall, Cambridge. *Career:* Lecturer,

Univ. of East Anglia 1970–83; Ed., Glas: New Russian Writing 1991; Sr Lecturer, Univ. of Birmingham 1997–; mem. Translators' Asscn, Soc. of Authors, British Asscn for Slavonic and East European Studies. *Publications:* Lunacharsky, The Poet Commissar 1984; translator: The Russian Style, by Evgenia Kirichenko 1991, Is Comrade Bulgakov Dead?, by Anatoly Smeliansky 1993, Baize-covered Table with Decanter, by Vladimir Makanin 1995, Skunk: A Life, by Peter Aleshkovsky 1997, Sonechka and Other Stories, by Ludmila Ulitskaya 1997, Under House Arrest, by Yevgeny Kharitonov 1998, Hurramabad, by Andrei Volos 2001, Medea and her Children, by Ludmila Ulitskaya 2002, Putin's Russia, by Anna Politkovskaya 2004, Globalisation and the Future of Mankind, by Gennady Zyuganov 2004, Sonechka: A Novella and Stories, by Ludmila Ulitskaya 2005, also numerous short stories and articles. *E-mail:* arch@russianwriting.com. *Website:* russianwriting.com.

TAKAGI, Nobuko; Japanese novelist; b. 6 April 1946, Yamaguchi Pref. *Education:* Tokyo Women's Christian Univ. *Career:* Special Guest Prof., Dept of Contemporary Asian Cultural Research, Kyushu Univ. Asia Centre. *Publications:* (titles translated) That Narrow Road 1980, A Distant Friend 1981, A Following Wind 1982, To a Friend Embracing the Light (Akutagawa Prize) 1983, Beyond the Shining Sea 1985, Street Corner Justice 1985, Set Sail on a Starry Night: Satsuki's Story 1986, Maze in the Heat of the Day 1988, Deep in the Forest of Swirling Blossoms: Satsuki's Story 1989, Insect Symphony 1989, Hot Letters 1989, Shades of the Land of Dreams 1989, Die the Time Blue 1990, The Tree Where Dwells the Black Noddy 1990, Foggy Meridian 1990, Flowing Elegies 1991, Southern Squall 1991, Flashback: My High Noon 1991, Afternoon of White Light 1992, Not a Confession 1992, Peak Against Colourful Clouds 1992, Forest on the Lake Bed 1993, Ice Fire 1993, Drops Falling from the Milky Way 1993, Heat 1994, The Burning Vine (Shimase Love Award) 1994, Light Through Petals 1995, Parting Letters 1995, Water Veins (Women Literary Award) 1995, A Billion Nights 1995, The Season when Cherry Trees are in Leaf 1996, Swirling Blossom 1996, Love Space 1997, The Colours of the Months 1997, Darkness in Istanbul 1998, Shade of the Orchid 1998, Samoan Illusion 1998, The Translucent Trees (Tanizaki Junichiro Award) 1999, A Prophecy of a Hundred Years 2000, The Burning Tower 2001, Weird Scenery 2001, Mamiko 2001, Hundred Loves of Ephesus 2002, Flowers of Sin 2003, Devil Wind in Naples 2003, Maimai Shinko 2004, Hokkai (Minister of Education, Science and Technology Art Encouragement Prize 2006) 2005; contrib. to Inside and Other Short Fiction 2006. *Address:* Kyushu University Asia Centre, 6-10-1, Hakozaki, Higashi-ku, Fukuoka 812-8581, Japan (office). *E-mail:* asia@isc.kyushu-u.ac.jp (office).

TAKAHASHI, Genichirō; Japanese writer and critic; b. 1951, Onomichi, Hiroshima. *Education:* Yokohama Nat. Univ. *Career:* participated in radical student movt 1960s and early 70s, imprisoned for six months; worked as a labourer until 1981; successful novelist and essayist 1982–; Visiting Fellow Donald Keene Center of Japanese Culture, Columbia Univ., USA 2002. *Publications:* novels: Sayonara Gyangutachi (Gunzō New Writers' Award) (first novel to be translated into English, as Sayonara, Gangsters 2004) 1982, Ōbaa za reinbō (Over the Rainbow) 1984, Oyogu Otoko (The Swimming Man) 1984, Jon Renon tai kaseijin (John Lennon Versus the Martians) 1985, Yūga de kanshōteki Nihon yakkyū (Japanese Baseball: Languid and Happy) (Mishima Yukio Award 1988) 1987, Penguin mura ni hi ga Ochite (Sundown in Penguin Town) 1989, Wakusei P-13 no himitsu (The Secret of Planet 13) 1990, Gosutobasutazu (Ghostbusters) 1997; numerous collections of essays including Bungaku ga konna ni wakatte ii kashira (Is it Okay to Understand Literature So Well?) 1989. *Address:* c/o Vertical, Inc., 257 Park Avenue South, 8th Floor, New York, NY 10010, USA (office). *Telephone:* (212) 529-2350 (office). *E-mail:* info@vertical-inc.com (office). *Website:* www.vertical-inc.com (office).

TAKAHASHI, Takako; Japanese writer; b. 1932, Kyoto; m. Takahashi Kazumi (died 1971). *Education:* Kyoto Univ. *Career:* writer of novels and short stories 1972–1985; trans. of French writers including Mauriac; retd from writing to become a Roman Catholic nun first in Paris, then Japan; returned to writing during 1990s. *Publications:* Sojikei (Congruent Figures) 1972, Sora no hate made (To the End of the Sky) 1973, Botsuraku Fusei (Falling Scenery) 1974, Yuwakusha (The Temptress) 1976, Ningyo no ai (Doll Love) 1976, Ronrii uuman (Lonely Woman, translated 2004) 1977, Ten no Mizumi 1977, Yomigaeri no ie (The House of Rebirth) 1980, Yosoi seya, waga tamashii yo (Gird up Thyself, Oh My Soul) 1982, Ikari no ko (Child of Wrath; winner Yomiuri Prize) 1985, Tochi no Chikara 1992, Takahashi Kazumi to iu hito: Nijugonen no nochi ni 1997, Kirei na hito 2003. *Address:* c/o Columbia University Press, 61 West 62nd Street, New York, NY 10023, USA. *Website:* www.columbia.edu/cu/cup/.

TALBOT, Martin; British journalist; *Editor, Music Week*. *Career:* fmr Ed., Fono magazine –2002; Exec. Ed., Music Week 2002–. *Address:* Music Week, CMP Information Ltd, Ludgate House, 245 Blackfriars Road, London, SE1 9UR, England (office). *Website:* www.musicweek.com.

TALBOT, Michael Owen, BA, BMus, PhD, ARCM, FBA; British writer; *Professor Emeritus of Music, University of Liverpool*; b. 4 Jan. 1943, Luton, Beds.; m. Shirley Mashiane 1970; one s. one d. *Education:* Royal Coll. of Music, London, Clare Coll., Cambridge. *Career:* Lecturer, Univ. of Liverpool 1968–79, Sr Lecturer 1979–83, Reader 1983–86, James and Constance Alsop Prof. of Music 1986–2003, Prof. Emer. of Music 2003–; mem. Royal Musical Asscn, Società Italiana di Musicologia; Corresp. Fellow, Ateneo Veneto. *Publications:* Vivaldi 1978, Albinoni: Leben und Werk 1980, Antonio Vivaldi: A Guide to Research 1988, Tomaso Albinoni: The Venetian Composer and his World 1990, Benedetto Vinaccesi: A Musician in Brescia and Venice in the Age of Corelli 1994, The Sacred Vocal Music of Antonio Vivaldi 1995, Venetian Music in the Age of Vivaldi 1999, The Musical Work: Reality or Invention (ed.) 2000, The Finale in Western Instrumental Music 2001, The Business of Music (ed.) 2002, The Chamber Cantatas of Antonio Vivaldi 2006; contrib. to professional journals, including Early Music, Music and Letters, Music Review, Musical Times, Journal of the Royal Musical Association, Soundings, The Consort, Note d'Archivio, Händel Jahrbuch, Informazioni e Studi Vivaldiani, Studi Vivaldiani, Journal of Eighteenth Century Music, Recercare. *Honours:* Cavaliere del Ordine al Merito (Italy) 1980; Oldman Prize 1990, Serena Medal 1999. *Address:* School of Music, The University of Liverpool, Liverpool, L69 7WW, England (office). *Fax:* (151) 794 3141 (office). *E-mail:* mtalbot@liv.ac.uk (office).

TALBOTT, Strobe; American journalist and fmr government official; *President, Brookings Institution*; b. 25 April 1946, Dayton, Ohio; s. of Nelson S. Talbott and Josephine Large; m. Brooke Lloyd Shearer 1971; two s. *Education:* Hotchkiss School, Connecticut, Yale Univ. and Univ. of Oxford, UK. *Career:* joined Time magazine; Diplomatic Corresp., White House Corresp., Eastern Europe Corresp., Washington Bureau Chief 1984–89, Ed.-at-Large 1989–94; Amb.-at-Large State Dept Feb.–Dec. 1993; Deputy Sec. of State 1994–2001; Pres. The Brookings Inst. 2002–; Rhodes Scholar, Univ. of Oxford 1969; Dir Carnegie Endowment for Int. Peace; mem. Council on Foreign Relations. *Publications:* Khrushchev Remembers 1970, Khrushchev Remembers: The Last Testament (jtly) 1974, Endgame: The Inside Story of Salt II 1979, Deadly Gambits: The Reagan Administration and the Stalemate in Nuclear Arms Control 1984, The Russians and Reagan 1984, Reagan and Gorbachev (jtly) 1987, The Master of the Game: Paul Nitze and the Nuclear Peace 1988, At the Highest Levels: The Inside Story of the End of the Cold War (jtly) 1993, The Age of Terror: America and The World After September 11 (co-ed.) 2001, The Russia Hand: A Memoir of Presidential Diplomacy 2002, Engaging India 2005. *Address:* The Brookings Institution, 1775 Massachusetts Avenue, NW, Washington, DC 20036, USA (office). *Telephone:* (202) 797-6000 (office). *Fax:* (202) 797-6004 (office). *E-mail:* communications@brookings.edu (office). *Website:* www.brookings.edu (office).

TALL, Deborah, BA, MFA; American academic, poet, writer and editor; *Professor, Hobart and William Smith Colleges*; b. 16 March 1951, Washington, DC; m. David Weiss 1979; two d. *Education:* Univ. of Michigan, Goddard Coll. *Career:* Asst Prof., Visiting Fellow in Literature, Univ. of Baltimore 1980–82; Prof. Hobart and William Smith Colls 1982–, Chair Dept of English 1992–94, John Milton Potter Chair in Humanities 2005–; Ed., Seneca Review 1982–; writer-in-residence, Chautauqua Institution, New York 1998; Visiting Poet Cornell Univ. Spring Semester 2003; mem. Acad. of American Poets, Associated Writing Programs, Asscn for the Study of Literature and the Environment, Authors' Guild, PEN, Poetry Soc. of America. *Publications:* Eight Colors Wide 1974, Ninth Life 1982, The Island of the White Cow: Memories of an Irish Island 1986, Come Wind, Come Weather 1988, Taking Note: From Poets' Notebooks (ed. with Stephen Kuusisto and David Weiss, revised edn as The Poet's Notebook) 1991, From Where We Stand: Recovering a Sense of Place 1993, Summons 2000, A Family of Strangers 2006; contrib. to many anthologies, reviews, quarterlies, journals and magazines. *Honours:* Kathryn A. Morton Prize for Poetry 1999, Yaddo Residencies 1982, 1984, 1991, Co-ordinating Council of Literary Magazines Citation of Achievement 1986, Ingram Merrill Foundation grant 1987, MacDowell Colony Residencies 1998, 2004. *Address:* c/o Department of English, Hobart and William Smith Colleges, Geneva, NY 14456, USA (office). *Fax:* (315) 781-3348 (office). *E-mail:* tall@hws.edu. *Website:* www.deborahtall.com (home).

TALLENT, Elizabeth Ann, BA; American writer and academic; *Professor, Stanford University*; b. 8 Aug. 1954, Washington, DC; m. Barry Smoots, 28 Sept. 1975, one s. *Education:* Illinois State Univ. at Normal. *Career:* fmrly taught literature and creative writing, Univ. of California at Irvine, Iowa Writers Workshop, Univ. of California at Davis; Dir of Creative Writing Programme, Stanford Univ. 1994–96, Prof. 1994–; mem. Poets and Writers. *Publications:* Married Men and Magic Tricks (non-fiction) 1982, In Constant Flight (short stories) 1983, Museum Pieces (novel) 1985, Time with Children (short stories) 1987, Honey (short stories) 1993; contrib. to publications, including The New Yorker, Esquire, Harper's, Grand Street, The Paris Review, The Threepenny Review, ZZYZYVA, and in The Best American Short Stories and O. Henry Award collections. *Honours:* Bay Area Book Reviewers Asscn Fiction Award, NEA Fellowship 1992. *Address:* Creative Writing Program, Department of English, Stanford University, Stanford, CA 94305-2087, USA (office). *E-mail:* ryanj@stanford.edu.

TALU, Umur E., BA (Econ); Turkish journalist; b. 7 Aug. 1957, Istanbul; s. of M. Muvakkar and G. Güzin; m. Şule Talu 1987; two d. *Education:* Galatasaray High School and Bosphorus Univ. *Career:* educ. specialist, Railway Workers' Union 1977–78; Int. Econ. Cooperation Sec. Union of Municipalities 1978–80; Econ. Corresp. Günaydin (newspaper) 1980–82; Chief, Econ. Dept Günes (newspaper) 1982–83; Ed. with Cumhuriyet (newspaper) 1983–85; Chief, Econ. Dept Milliyet (newspaper) 1985–86, News Ed. 1986–87, 1988–92, Ed.-in-Chief 1992–94, columnist 1994–; News Ed. Hürriyet (newspaper) 1987–88. *Publications:* Social Democracy in Europe (co-author) 1985, Keynes (trans.) 1986, Mr Uguran's Post Office 1996. *Honours:* Freedom of the Press Award (Turkish Journalists' Asscn) 1996. *Address:* Milliyet, Dogan Medya Centre,

Bagcilar 344554, Istanbul, Turkey. *Telephone:* (212) 5056111. *Fax:* (212) 5056233.

TAMEN, Pedro, LLB; Portuguese foundation executive and poet; b. 1 Dec. 1934, Lisbon; s. of Mário Tamen and Emília Tamen; m. Maria da Graça Seabra Gomes 1975; two s. two d. *Education:* Lisbon Univ. *Career:* Dir Moraes Publishing House 1958–75; Pres. Portuguese PEN Club 1987–90, Vice Pres. 1991–2002; Trustee Calouste Gulbenkian Foundation, Lisbon 1975–2000; mem. Bd Portuguese Asscn of Writers. *Publications:* 12 books of poetry since 1958; Tábua das Matérias (Collected Works) 1991, Depois de Ver 1995, Guião de Caronte 1997, Memória Indescritível 2000, Retábulo das Matérias 2001, Analogia e Dedos 2006. *Honours:* D. Diniz Prize 1981; Grand Prix for Translation 1990; Critics Award 1993; INAPA Prize for Poetry 1993, Nicola Prize for Poetry 1998, Press Poetry Prize 2000, PEN Club Poetry Prize 2000. *Address:* Rua Luís Pastor de Macedo, lote 25, 5° esq., 1750-157 Lisbon, Portugal (home). *E-mail:* ptamen@mail.telepac.pt (home).

TAMER, Zakaria (see Tamir, Zakaria)

TAMIR, Zakaria; Syrian writer and journalist; b. 2 Jan. 1931, Damascus. *Career:* worked at Ministry of Culture 1960–63, 1980–81, Ministry of Information 1967; Ed., al-Mawqef al-Arabi 1963–65, Ed.-in-Chief 1972–75; screenwriter, Jeddah TV, KSA 1965–66; Head of Drama Dept, Syrian TV 1967–70; Ed.-in-Chief, Rafi magazine 1970–71, Osama magazine 1975–77, al-Marifah magazine 1978–80; Managing Ed., al-Dustoor magazine, UK 1981–82, al-Naquid magazine, UK 1988–93; Cultural Ed., at-Tadhamon magazine, UK 1983–88, Riyadh al-Rayes Publisher, UK 1988–93; founder mem. Syrian Writers' Union 1968– (fmr vice-pres.). *Publications:* (titles translated) short story collections: The Neighing of the White Steed 1957, Spring in the Ashes 1963, The Thunder 1970, Why the River Fell Silent 1973, Damascus Fire 1973, Tigers on the Tenth Day 1978, The Flower Spoke to the Bird 1978, Noah's Summons 1994, We Shall Laugh 1998, If! 1998, Sour Grapes 2000, Breaking the Spirit 2002, The Hedgehog 2005; non-fiction: Glories, Arabs, Glories (articles) 1986, The Victim's Satire of his Killer 2003. *Honours:* Sultan Bin Ali al-Owais Cultural Foundation Prize for Fiction 2001; Syrian Order of Merit 2002. *Address:* c/o Quartet Books, 27 Goodge Street, London, WIT 2LD, England (office).

TAMM, Peter; German publisher; b. 12 May 1928, Hamburg; s. of Emil Tamm; m. Ursula Weisshun 1958; one s. four d. *Education:* Univ. of Hamburg. *Career:* Shipping Ed., Hamburger Abendblatt 1948–58; Man. Dir Ullstein GmbH (Publr) Berlin 1960–62; Man. Dir Bild-Zeitung Hamburg 1962–64; Man. Dir Verlagshaus Axel Springer and Ullstein Verlag Berlin 1964–68, Chair. and CEO Axel Springer Verlag 1968–82, Chair. Bd 1982–91; Vice-Pres. Bundesverband Deutscher Zeitungsverleger 1982–91; currently Propr Koehler/Mittler-Verlagsgruppe and Schiffahrtsverlages Hansa, Propr and Dir Scientific Inst. for Maritime and Naval History; mem. Royal Swedish Soc. of Maritime Sciences, Stockholm 1999. *Publication:* Maler der See 1980. *Honours:* Bayerischer Verdienstorden 1976, Bundesverdienstkreuz I. Klasse 1986, Grosses Verdienstkreuz des Verdienst-ordens der Bundesrepublik Deutschland 1993, Cavaliere Ufficiale: Orden für die Verdienste um die Italienische Republik 1994, Hamburger Bürgerpreis 1996, Vasco da Gama Naval Medal 1997, Grosses Verdienstkreuz mit Stern 1998, Seewartmedaille in Silber 1998, Bismarckmedaille in Gold 1999, Gold Ehrenkreuz der Bundeswehr 2001, Professoren-Titel durch die Stadt Hamburg 2002, Commdr Order of the White Rose of Finland 2003, Hamburg Citizen of the Year 2004. *Address:* Elbchaussee 277, 22605 Hamburg, Germany. *Telephone:* (40) 821341 (office). *Fax:* (40) 8226300 (office).

TAN, Amy Ruth, MA, LHD; American writer; b. 19 Feb. 1952, Oakland, Calif.; d. of John Yuehhan and Daisy Ching (née Tu) Tan; m. Louis M. DeMattei 1974. *Education:* San José State Univ., Calif., Univ. of Calif. at Berkeley, Dominican Coll., San Rafael. *Career:* specialist in language devt Alameda Co. Asscn for Mentally Retarded 1976–80; Project Dir MORE, San Francisco 1980–81; freelance writer 1981–88; Marian McFadden Memorial Lecturer, Indianapolis-Marion Co. Public Library 1996. *Film:* The Joy Luck Club (screenwriter, producer) 1993. *Publications:* The Joy Luck Club (Commonwealth Club and Bay Area Book Reviewers' Best Fiction Award 1990) 1989, The Kitchen God's Wife 1991, The Hundred Secret Senses 1995, The Bonesetter's Daughter 2000, Saving Fish from Drowning 2005; for children: The Moon Lady 1992, The Chinese Siamese Cat 1994; non-fiction: The Opposite of Fate: A Book of Musings (autobiog.); numerous short stories and essays. *Honours:* Best American Essays Award 1991. *Literary Agent:* Steven Barclay Agency, 12 Western Avenue, Petaluma, CA 94952, USA. *Telephone:* (707) 773-0654. *Fax:* (707) 778-1868. *Website:* www.barclayagency.com. *Address:* c/o Ballantine Publications Publicity, 201 East 50th Street, New York, NY 10022, USA.

TAN, Hwee Hwee, MA, MFA; Singaporean writer; b. 1974. *Education:* Univs of E Anglia and Oxford, UK, New York Univ., USA. *Career:* short stories have appeared in PEN Int., New Writing; arts corresp. Business Times, Singapore 2001; sr writer Twenty4Seven Magazine 2001; Tamara S. Wanger Fellow, Nat. Univ. of Singapore; currently freelance journalist TIME, Harper's Bazaar, Elle, Far Eastern Economic Review, BBC. *Publications include:* Foreign Bodies 1996, Mammon Inc. 2001. *Honours:* New York Times Fellowship 1997, numerous awards from BBC, Nat. Univ. of Singapore; Young Artist Award from Nat. Arts Council 2003, Singapore Literature Prize 2004 (for Mammon Inc.). *Address:* c/o Michael Joseph, Penguin Books Ltd, 80 The Strand, London, WC2R 0RL, England (office). *E-mail:* hwee_tan@hotmail.com. *Website:* www.geocities.com/hweehwee_tan/index.html.

TANENHAUS, Sam, MA; American editor; *Book Review Editor, The New York Times;* b. 1956; m. Kathryn Bonomi; one c. *Education:* Grinnell Coll., Iowa, Yale Univ. *Career:* fmrly with publicity Farrar, Straus and Giroux; with trade, acad. and crossover books Oxford Univ. Press, Chelsea House; Asst Ed. Op-Ed page The New York Times 1997–99, Ed. Book Review 2004–; contrib. ed. Vanity Fair 1999–2004; mem. jury on biog. Pulitzer Prize Cttee 2000; affiliated writer School of Journalism NYU 2002–03; mem. exec. bd Soc. of American Historians. *Publications:* Literature Unbound: A Guide for the Common Reader 1984, Louis Armstrong: Biography of a Musician 1989, Whittaker Chambers: A Biography (LA Times Book Prize for Biography) 1997; contrib. to Wall Street Journal, Washington Post, Boston Globe, LA Times, New York Times Magazine, National Review, New Criterion, New York Review of Books, New Republic, American Scholar, Commentary. *Honours:* John M. Olin Foundation Award, Bradley Foundation Award, Nat. Endowment of the Humanities grant 1997, Stanford Univ. Hoover Inst. Media Fellow 2000, 2002. *Address:* The New York Times, 229 W 43rd Street, New York, NY 10036, USA (office).

TANIKAWA, Shuntaro; Japanese poet, translator, playwright and scriptwriter; b. 15 Dec. 1931, Tokyo; s. of Tanikawa Tetsuzo. *Career:* made publishing debut with poems in Bungakukai literary journal 1950; has given readings in Moscow, Leningrad, Berlin, Frankfurt, Zürich, Rotterdam, London, and under the auspices of the Japan Soc., Acad. of American Poets, Library of Congress, USA; trans. of Mother Goose and Peanuts comic strips. *Film scripts:* Tokyo orimpikku 1965, Seishun 1968, Kyoto 1969, Nihon to nihonjin 1970, Ai futatabi 1971, Matatabi 1973, Hi no tori 1978. *Publications include:* poetry: Nijuoku konen no kodoku 1952, Rokujuni no sonetto 1953, Utsumuku shonen 1971, Hibi no chizu 1983, Tanikawa Shuntaro Shishu 1995, Kotoba Asobi Uta (juvenile), Kazuki yasuo no omocha bako (with Kazuki Yasuo) 2003, Shagaru to konoha 2005; poetry in trans.: With Silence My Companion 1975, At Midnight in the Kitchen I Just Wanted to Talk to You 1980, The Selected Poems of Shuntaro Tanikawa 1983, Coca-Cola Lessons 1986, Floating the River in Melancholy 1988, Songs of Nonsense 1991, 62 Sonnets 1992, Two Billion Light-Years of Solitude 1996, Naked 1996, Map of Days 1996, Selected Poems 1998, Looking Down 2000, Les Anges de Klee, Naif, On Love, Giving People Poems. *Honours:* Saida Takashi Drama Prize, Noma, Shogakkan, Hana-Tsubaki, Yomiuri literary prizes. *Address:* c/o University of Hawai'i Press, 2840 Kolowalu Street, Honolulu, HI 96822-1888, USA.

TAPPLY, William George, BA, MAT; American writer and academic; *Professor of English and Writer-in-Residence, Clark University;* b. 16 July 1940, Waltham, MA; m. 1st Cynthia Ehrgott 1970 (divorced 1995); one s. two d.; m. 2nd Vicki Stiefel 2004. *Education:* Amherst Coll., Harvard Univ., Tufts Univ. *Career:* Dir of Econ. Educ., Tufts Univ. 1967–68; housemaster and teacher, Lexington High School 1969–90; Contributing Ed., Field and Stream 1988–; Editorial Assoc., Writer's Digest School 1992–; Instructor, Emerson Coll., Clark Univ. 1995–, currently Prof. of English and Writer-in-Residence; Special Corresp., American Angler 1999–; mem. Authors' Guild, Mystery Writers of America, Private Eye Writers of America. *Publications:* fiction: Death at Charity's Point 1984, The Dutch Blue Error 1985, Follow the Sharks 1985, The Marine Corpse 1986, Dead Meat 1987, The Vulgar Boatman 1987, A Void in Hearts 1988, Dead Winter 1989, Client Privilege 1989, The Spotted Cats 1991, Tight Lines 1992, The Snake Eater 1993, The Seventh Enemy 1995, Thicker Than Water (with Linda Barlow) 1995, Close to the Bone 1996, Cutter's Run 1998, Muscle Memory 1999, Scar Tissue 2000, Past Tense 2001, First Light 2001, A Fine Line 2002, Shadow of Death 2003, Second Sight 2004, Bitch Creek 2004, Nervous Water 2005, Out Cold 2006, Gray Ghost 2007, One-Way Ticket 2007, Third Strike 2007; non-fiction: Those Hours Spent Outdoors 1988, Opening Day and Other Neuroses 1990, Home Water Near and Far 1992, Sportsman's Legacy 1993, The Elements of Mystery Fiction 1995, A Fly-Fishing Life 1997, Bass Bug Fishing 1999, Upland Days 2000, Pocket Water 2001, The Orvis Pocket Guide to Fly Fishing for Bass 2001, Gone Fishin' 2004, Trout Eyes 2007. *Honours:* Scribner Crime Novel Award 1984. *Address:* Chickadee Farm, 75 Antrim Road, Hancock, NH 03448, USA (home). *Website:* www.williamgtapply.com.

TARANTINO, Quentin; American film director, actor and screenwriter; b. 27 March 1963, Knoxville, Tenn.; s. of Tony Tarantino and Connie McHugh. *Career:* fmrly worked in Video Archives, Manhattan Beach, Calif. *Films:* My Best Friend's Birthday (actor, dir, prod.) 1987, Reservoir Dogs (actor, dir) 1992, Past Midnight (assoc. prod.) 1992, Siunin Wong Fei-hung tsi titmalau (prod.) 1993, Eddie Presley (actor) 1993, Sleep With Me (actor) 1994, Killing Zoe (exec. prod.) 1994, Somebody to Love (actor) 1994, Pulp Fiction (actor, dir) (Golden Palm Cannes Film Festival) 1994, Destiny Turns on the Radio (actor) 1995, Desperado (actor) 1995, Four Rooms (actor, dir, exec. prod.) 1995, Red Rain (prod.) 1995, Girl 6 (actor) 1996, From Dusk Till Dawn (actor, exec. prod.) 1996, Curdled (actor, exec. prod.) 1996, Jackie Brown (dir) 1997, God Said, 'Ha!' (exec. prod.) 1998, 40 Lashes (dir) 2000, Little Nicky (actor) 2000, Kill Bill Vol. I (dir, prod.) 2003, Kill Bill Vol. II (dir, prod.) 2004, Daltry Calhoun (exec. prod.) 2005, Hostel (exec. prod.) 2005, Freedom's Fury (exec. prod.) 2006, Grindhouse (actor) 2007. *Film screenplays:* My Best Friend's Birthday 1992, Reservoir Dogs 1992, True Romance 1993, Natural Born Killers 1994, Pulp Fiction 1994, Four Rooms (segment: The Man from Hollywood) 1995, From Dusk Till Dawn 1996, Jackie Brown 1997, 40 Lashes (dir) 2000, Kill Bill (also novel) 2003. *Television:* ER (dir, episode 'Motherhood') 1994, Alias (actor, one episode) 2004, CSI: Crime Scene Investigation (dir, writer two episodes) 2005, Alias (actor, four episodes) 2006. *Honours:* Empire Film Award for icon of the decade 2005; Officier, Ordre des Arts et des Lettres. *Address:* William Morris Agency, 1 William Morris Place, Beverly Hills, CA 90212; 6201 Sunset Boulevard, Suite 35, Los Angeles, CA 90028, USA.

TARCHER, Jeremy Phillip, BA; American publisher; b. 2 Jan. 1932, New York; s. of Jack D. Tarcher and Mary Breger Tarcher; m. 1st Shari Lewis 1958 (died 1998); one d.; m. 2nd Judith Paige Mitchell 1999. *Education:* St John's Coll., Annapolis, Md. *Career:* Founder and Pres. Jeremy P. Tarcher Inc., LA 1964–91, Pres. Tarcher/Putnam (after acquisition by Putnam) 1991–96; Vice-Pres. Houghton Mifflin, Boston 1980–83; Chair. Bd Audio Renaissance Tapes, LA 1985–; mem. Bd Trustees The Esalen Inst., Big Sur, Calif. 1986–; Producer Shari Lewis Show, NBC Network 1959–62; Exec. Producer A Picture of U.S. (Emmy Award for Children's Programming) 1976. *Television:* with wife the late Shari Lewis wrote episode (Lights of Zetar) of original Star Trek series 1969. *Address:* 144 South Beverly Drive, Beverly Hills, CA 90212 (office); 1416 Stone Canyon, Bel Air, CA 90077, USA (home). *Telephone:* (310) 274-7207 (office). *Fax:* (310) 274-3611 (office).

TARN, Nathaniel, BA, MA, Dipl CFRE, PhD; American poet, critic, translator, anthropologist and academic; *Professor Emeritus of Poetry, Comparative Literature and Anthropology, Rutgers University*; b. 30 June 1928, Paris, France; m. 1st (divorced); two c.; m. 2nd Janet Rodney 1981. *Education:* Univ. of Cambridge, UK, École des Hautes Études, Univ. of Paris, France, Yale Univ., Univ. of Chicago, London School of Econs and School of Oriental and African Studies, London, UK. *Career:* Visiting Prof., SUNY at Buffalo 1969–70, Princeton Univ. 1969–70, Univ. of Pennsylvania 1976, Jilin Univ., People's Repub. of China 1982; Prof. of Poetry, Comparative Literature and Anthropology, Rutgers Univ. 1970–85, Prof. Emer. 1985–. *Publications:* poetry: Old Savage/Young City 1964, Penguin Modern Poets 7 (with Richard Murphy and Jon Silkin) 1966, Where Babylon Ends 1968, The Beautiful Contradictions 1969, October: A Sequence of Ten Poems Followed by Requiem Pro Duabus Filiis Israel 1969, The Silence 1970, A Nowhere for Vallejo: Choices, October 1971, Lyrics for the Bride of God 1975, Narrative of This Fall 1975, The House of Leaves 1976, From Alaska: The Ground of Our Great Admiration of Nature (with Janet Rodney) 1977, The Microcosm 1977, Birdscapes, with Seaside 1978, The Forest (with Janet Rodney) 1979, Atitlan/Alashka 1979, The Land Songs 1981, Weekends in Mexico 1982, The Desert Mothers 1984, At the Western Gates 1985, Palenque: Selected Poems, 1972–1984 1986, Seeing America First 1989, The Mothers of Matagalpa 1989, Flying the Body 1993, The Architextures 2000, Three Letters from the City: The St Petersburg Poems 1968–1998 2000, Selected Poems, 1950–2000 2002, Dying Trees 2003, Recollections of Being 2004; non-fiction: Views from the Weaving Mountain: Selected Essays in Poetics and Anthropology 1991, Scandals in the House of Birds 1998. *Honours:* Guinness Prize 1963, Wenner Grenn Fellowships 1978, 1980, Commonwealth of Pennsylvania Fellowship 1984, Rockefeller Foundation Fellowship 1988. *Address:* PO Box 8187, Santa Fe, NM 87504, USA.

TARTT, Donna; American writer; b. 1963, Greenwood, Miss. *Education:* Univ. of Miss., Oxford, Bennington Coll., Vt. *Career:* published first sonnet in a Miss. literary review 1976. *Publications:* novels: The Secret History 1992, The Little Friend 2002; short stories include: A Christmas Pageant (Harper's) 1993, A Garter Snake (GQ) 1995, True Crime (audio book) 1996; contrib. articles to magazines. *Honours:* WHSmith Literary Award 2003. *Literary Agent:* Gill Coleridge, Rogers, Coleridge & White Ltd, 20 Powis Mews, London, W11 1JN, England. *Telephone:* (20) 7221-3717. *Fax:* (20) 7229-9084.

TARUSKIN, Richard Filler, PhD; American musicologist, critic and writer; *Professor, University of California at Berkeley*; b. 2 April 1945, New York, NY. *Education:* Columbia Univ. *Career:* Asst Prof. 1975–81, Assoc. Prof. of Music 1981–87, Columbia Univ.; Visiting Prof., Univ. of Pennsylvania 1985; Assoc. Prof. 1986–89, Prof. 1989–, Univ. of California at Berkeley; Hanes-Willis Visiting Prof., Univ. of North Carolina at Chapel Hill 1987; music critic for Opus, New York Times; Fulbright-Hays Traveling Fellowship 1971–72; Guggenheim Fellowship 1987; mem. American Musicological Soc. *Publications include:* Opera and Drama in Russia 1981, Busnoi: The Latin-Texted Works (ed., two vols) 1990, Musorgsky: Eight Essays and an Epilogue 1993, Stravinsky and the Russian Traditions: A Biography of the Works Through Mavra (two vols) 1995, Text and Act: Essays on Music and Performance 1995; contrib. articles on Russian composers and operas in New Grove Dictionary of Opera (four vols) 1992; many articles and reviews in professional journals and general periodicals. *Honours:* Dent Medal, England 1987, ASCAP Deems Taylor Award 1989. *Address:* c/o Department of Music, University of California at Berkeley, Berkeley, CA 94720, USA.

TASHIRO, Kikuo; Japanese newspaper and television executive; b. 22 April 1917. *Education:* Waseda Univ. *Career:* joined Asahi Shimbun 1940; City Ed. 1959; Man. Ed. 1966; Exec. Dir in charge of Editorial Affairs 1969; Pres. Asahi Nat. Broadcasting Co. Ltd (TV Asahi) 1983. *Address:* 6-4-10 Roppongi, Minato-ku, Tokyo 106, Japan (home). *Telephone:* (3) 405-3211 (home).

TATE, James Vincent, BA, MFA; American poet and academic; b. 8 Dec. 1943, Kansas City, MO. *Education:* Univ. of Missouri, Kansas State Univ., Univ. of Iowa. *Career:* Instructor in Creative Writing, Univ. of Iowa 1966–67; Visiting Lecturer, Univ. of California, Berkeley 1967–68; Poetry Ed., Dickinson Review 1967–76; Trustee and Assoc. Ed., Pym-Randall Press

1968–80; Asst Prof. of English, Columbia Univ. 1969–71; Assoc. Prof., then Prof. of English 1971–, Univ. of Massachusetts, Amherst; poet-in-residence, Emerson Coll. 1970–71; Assoc. Ed., Barn Dream Press; mem. Acad. of American Poets (bd of chancellors 2001–). *Publications:* poetry: Cages 1966, The Destination 1967, The Lost Pilot 1967, Notes of Woe: Poems 1968, Camping in the Valley 1968, The Torches 1968, Row with Your Hair 1969, Is There Anything? 1969, Shepherds of the Mist 1969, Amnesia People 1970, Are You Ready Mary Baker Eddy? (with Bill Knot) 1970, Deaf Girl Playing 1970, The Oblivion Ha-Ha 1970, Wrong Songs 1970, Hints to Pilgrims 1971, Absences 1972, Apology for Eating Geoffrey Movius' Hyacinth 1972, Hottentot Ossuary 1974, Viper Jazz 1976, Riven Doggeries 1979, Land of Little Sticks 1981, Constant Defender 1983, Reckoner 1986, Distance from Loved Ones 1990, Selected Poems 1991, Worshipful Company of Fletchers 1993, Shroud of the Gnome 1997, Memoir of the Hawk: Poems 2001, Return to the City of White Donkeys 2004; novel: Lucky Darryl 1977; contrib. to numerous books and periodicals. *Honours:* Yale Younger Poets Award 1966, Nat. Inst. of Arts and Letters Award 1974, Massachusetts Arts and Humanities Fellow 1975, Guggenheim Fellowship 1976, Nat. Endowment for the Arts Fellowship 1980, Pulitzer Prize in Poetry 1992, Nat. Book Award for Poetry 1994. *Address:* Department of English, University of Massachusetts, Amherst, MA 01003, USA.

TAVARES DIAS, Marina; Portuguese publishing executive and writer; b. 25 May 1960, Lisbon. *Career:* journalist on Portugal Hoje, Diario Popular, Diario de Lisboa 1979–; writer 1987–; Publishing Dir Ibis Editores 1990–. *Publications:* Lisboa Desaparecida (Vol. 1) 1987, (Vol. 2) 1990, (Vol. 3) 1992, (Vol. 4) 1994, (Vol. 5) 1996, (Vol. 6) 1998, (Vol. 7) 2001, (Vol. 8) 2003, Photographias de Lisboa 1988, Mario Sá-Carneiro – Fotobiografia 1988, Rossio, Feira da Ladra, A Lisboa de Fernando Pessoa 1990, História de Futebol em Lisboa 2000, History of the Lisbon Trams 2001, Porto Desparecido 2002, Lisboa nos passos de Pessoa 2004, Lisboa Misteriosa 2005. *Honours:* Julio Cezar Machado Award for Journalism 1985, 1986; Julio Castilho Award for Literature 1987. *Address:* Quimera Editores Lda, Rua do Vale Formoso 37, 1949-013 Lisbon (office); Av Almirante Reis 29, 3 Dto, 1100 Lisbon, Portugal (home). *Telephone:* (218) 455950 (office); (218) 530518 (home).

TAWADA, Yoko, MA; Japanese novelist; b. 23 March 1960, Tokyo. *Education:* Waseda Univ., Hamburg Univ. *Career:* based in Germany 1982–, writes in German and Japanese; writer-in-residence Villa Aurora, Pacific Palisades, USA 1997, Univ. of Kentucky 2004; Max Kade Distinguished Visitor and writer-in-residence Foreign Languages and Literatures Section, MIT 1999. *Publications:* Nur da wo du bist da ist nichts (poems and stories) 1987, Das Bad (novel) 1989, Missing Heels (short story) 1991, Wo Europa anfaengt (Where Europe Begins, poems and stories) 1991, Sanninkankei (short stories) 1991, Inumukoiri (The Bridegroom was a Dog, short stories) (Akutagawa-Prize) 1993, Ein Gast (novel) 1993, Arufabetto no kizuguchi (novel) 1993, Tintenfisch auf Reisen (short stories) 1994, Gottoharutotetsudo (short stories) 1996, Talisman (essays) 1996, Seijodensetsu (novel) 1996, Aber die Mandarinen muessen heute abend noch geraubt werden (poems) 1997, Kitunetsuki (poems) 1998, Hikon (novel) 1998, Verwandlungen (essays) 1998, Katakoto no uwagoto (essays) 1999, Hikari to zerachin no raipuchihhi (short stories) 2000, Opium fuer Ovid (novel) 2000, Hinagiku no ocha no baai (short stories) 2000, Yogisha no yakoressha 2002, Kyukeijikan 2002. *Honours:* City of Hamburg Prize in Literature 1990, Gunzo Prize for new writers 1991, Lessing Prize 1994, Adelbert von Chamisso Prize 1996. *E-mail:* tawadaoo@yahoo.co.jp. *Website:* www.tawada.com.

TAWARA, Machi, BA; Japanese poet; b. 1962, Osaka. *Education:* Waseda Univ. *Career:* worked as a high school teacher 1985–89; bestselling writer of tanka poetry 1987–, over three million copies of first collection in print. *Publications:* poetry collections: Sarada kinenbi (Salad Anniversary) (Modern Japanese Poets Asscn Award 1988) 1987, Chokoreeto kakumeri (The Chocolate Revolution) 1997; translations of classic poetry into contemporary Japanese: Man'yoshu (10,000 Leaves), Taketori Monogatori (The Tale of the Bamboo Cutter), Chokoreeto-go yaku midaregami (Tangled Hair in Chocolate Language) 1998; several popular travel and photography books, numerous essays for newspapers and magazines. *Honours:* 32nd Kadokawa Tanka Award 1986. *Address:* c/o Kodansha International Limited, Otowa YK Building, Bunkyo-ku, Tokyo 112-8652, Japan (office).

TAYLOR, Andrew John Robert, BA, MA; British writer; b. 14 Oct. 1951, Stevenage, England; m. Caroline Jane Silverwood 1979; one s. one d. *Education:* Emmanuel Coll., Cambridge, Univ. of London. *Career:* mem. CWA, Soc. of Authors. *Television:* Fallen Angel (adaptation of the Roth Trilogy) 2007. *Publications:* Caroline Minuscule 1982, Waiting for the End of the World 1984, Our Fathers' Lies 1985, An Old School Tie 1986, Freelance Death 1987, The Second Midnight 1987, Blacklist 1988, Blood Relation 1990, Toyshop 1990, The Raven on the Water 1991, The Sleeping Policeman 1992, The Barred Window 1993, Odd Man Out 1993, An Air That Kills 1994, The Mortal Sickness 1995, The Four Last Things 1997, The Lover of the Grave 1997, The Judgement of Strangers 1998, The Suffocating Night 1998, The Office of the Dead 2000, Where Roses Fade 2000, Death's Own Door 2001, Requiem for an Angel 2002, The American Boy 2003, Call the Dying 2004, A Stain on the Silence 2006, Naked to the Hangman 2006; juvenile fiction: Hairline Cracks 1988, Snapshot 1989, Double Exposure 1990, Negative Image 1992, The Invader 1994; contrib. to anthologies, including Perfectly Criminal 1996, Past Crimes 1998. *Honours:* John Creasey Memorial Award 1982, CWA Ellis Peters Historical Dagger 2001, 2003. *Literary Agent:* Sheil Land

Associates, 50 Doughty Street, London, WC1N 2LS, England. *Website:* www .andrew-taylor.co.uk.

TAYLOR, Andrew MacDonald, BA, MA, DLitt; Australian academic, poet and writer; *Emeritus Professor, Edith Cowan University*; b. 19 March 1940, Warnambool, Vic.; m. Beate Josephi 1981; one s. one d. *Education:* University of Melbourne. *Career:* Lockie Fellow, University of Melbourne 1965–68; Lecturer 1971–74, Senior Lecturer 1974–91, Assoc. Prof. 1991–1992, University of Adelaide; Prof., later Emeritus Prof., School of Int. Cultural and Community Studies, Edith Cowan Univ. 1992–; mem. Asscn for the Study of Australian Literature; Australian Society of Authors; PEN. *Publications:* Reading Australian Poetry, 1987; Selected Poems, 1960–85, 1988; Folds in the Map, 1991; Sandstone, 1995; The Stone Threshold, 2001; Götterdämmerung Café, 2001; Collected Poems 2004. Contributions: newspapers, journals, and magazines. *Honours:* several prizes and awards, AM. *Address:* c/o School of International Cultural and Community Studies, Edith Cowan University, Mount Lawley, WA 6050, Australia.

TAYLOR, Beverly White, BAE, MA, PhD; American academic and writer; b. 30 March 1947, Grenada, Miss. *Education:* Univ. of Mississippi, Duke Univ. *Career:* Asst Prof., Univ. of N Carolina at Chapel Hill 1977–84, Assoc. Prof. 1984–92, Prof. of English 1992–; mem. Victorians Inst. (Pres. 1989–90), Tennyson Soc., Browning Inst., MLA, Int. Arthurian Soc. *Publications:* The Return of King Arthur 1983, Arthurian Legend and Literature 1984, Francis Thompson 1987, The Cast of Consciousness 1987, Gender and Discourse in Victorian Literature and Art 1992; contribs to various encyclopaedias and periodicals. *Address:* Department of English, University of North Carolina, Chapel Hill, NC 27599, USA (office). *E-mail:* btaylor@email.unc.edu (office).

TAYLOR, David John, BA, FRSL; British writer; b. 22 Aug. 1960, Norwich, England; m. Rachel Hore 1990; three s. *Education:* Univ. of Oxford. *Publications:* Great Eastern Land (novel) 1986, A Vain Conceit: British Fiction in the 1980s 1989, Other People: Portraits from the Nineties (with Marcus Berkmann) 1990, Real Life (novel) 1992, After the War: The Novel and England Since 1945 1993, English Settlement (novel) 1996, After Bathing at Baxter's (short stories) 1997, Trespass (novel) 1988, Thackeray 1999, The Comedy Man (novel) 2001, Orwell: The Life 2003, Kept: A Victorian Mystery (novel) 2006, On the Corinthian Spirit: The Decline of Amateurism in Sport 2006; contrib. to periodicals including Independent, Guardian, Sunday Times, TLS, Spectator, Private Eye. *Honours:* Grinzane Cavour Prize, Italy 1999, Whitbread Prize for Biography 2003. *Address:* Caraju House, 1 Poplar Avenue, Norwich, NR4 7LD, England (home).

TAYLOR, Graham P.; British children's writer; b. 1961; m.; three c. *Career:* fmr policeman; vicar at Cloughton, North Yorkshire –2004; full-time writer 2004–. *Publications:* Shadowmancer 2003, Wormwood 2004, Tersias 2005, The Curse of Salamander Street 2006. *Address:* c/o Faber and Faber Ltd, 3 Queen Square, London, WC1N 3AU, England. *E-mail:* shadowmancer@ btopenworld.com. *Website:* www.shadowmancer.com.

TAYLOR, H. Baldwin (see Waugh, Hillary Baldwin)

TAYLOR, Henry Splawn, BA, MA; American academic, poet and writer; *Director of the MFA in Creative Writing, American University*; b. 21 June 1942, Loudoun County, VA. *Education:* Univ. of Virginia, Hollins Coll. *Career:* instructor, Roanoke Coll. 1966–68; Asst Prof., Univ. of Utah 1968–71; Contributing Ed., Hollins Critic 1970–; Assoc. Prof. 1971–76, Prof. of Literature 1975–2003, Co-Dir MFA in Creative Writing 1982–, Dir American Studies Program 1983–85, American Univ.; Consulting Ed., Magill's Literary Annual 1972–1985, Poet Lore 1976–84; writer-in-residence, Hollins Coll. 1978; Bd of Advisers 1986–, Poetry Ed. 1988–89, New Virginia Review; Distinguished Poet-in-Residence, Wichita State Univ. 1994; poet-in-residence, Randolph-Macon Women's Coll. 1996; Elliston Poet-in-Residence, Univ. of Cincinnati 2002. *Publications:* poetry: The Horse Show at Midnight: Poems 1966, Breakings 1971, An Afternoon of Pocket Billiards 1975, Desperado 1979, The Flying Change 1985, Understanding Fiction: Poems 1986–96 1996, Brief Candles: 101 Clerihews 2000; other: Magill's (Masterplots) Literary Annual 1972 (ed. with Frank N. Magill) 1972, Poetry: Points of Departure 1974, Magill's (Masterplots) Literary Annual 1973 (assoc. ed.) 1974, Magill's (Masterplots) Literary Annual 1974 (assoc. ed.) 1975, The Water of Light: A Miscellany in Honor of Brewster Ghiselin (ed.) 1976, Compulsory Figures: Essays on Recent American Poets 1992; contrib. to many books, anthologies, reviews and journals. *Honours:* Acad. of American Poets Prizes 1962, 1964, Utah State Inst. of Fine Arts Poetry Prizes co-winner 1969, winner 1971, Nat. Endowment for the Arts Fellowships 1978, 1986, Nat. Endowment for the Humanities research grant 1980–81, American Acad. and Inst. of Arts and Letters Witter Bynner Prize for Poetry 1984, Pulitzer Prize in Poetry 1986, Virginia Cultural Laureate Award 1986, Nat. Foundation for Advancement in the Arts teacher recognition 1995–96, American Acad. of Arts and Letters Michael Braude Light Verse Prize 2002, Aiken Taylor Award in Modern Poetry 2004. *Address:* c/o Department of Literature, American University, Washington, DC 20016, USA.

TAYLOR, John Russell, MA; British writer, editor and academic; *Art Critic, The Times;* b. 19 June 1935, Dover, Kent; s. of Arthur Russell Taylor and Kathleen Mary Taylor (née Picker). *Education:* Dover Grammar School, Jesus Coll. Cambridge, Courtauld Inst. of Art. *Career:* Sub-Ed., Times Educ. Supplement 1959–60; Editorial Asst, Times Literary Supplement 1960–62; Film Critic, The Times 1962–73; Prof., Div. of Cinema, Univ. of Southern Calif., USA 1972–78; Art Critic, The Times 1978–; Ed. Films and Filming 1983–90; Art Critic, Radio Two Arts Programme 1990–. *Television:* Feet Foremost 1968, The Importer 1969, Dracula 1969, Curse of the Mummy 1970, A Letter to David 1971. *Film:* Charles Chaplin Makes The Countess from Hong Kong 1966. *Publications:* Anger and After 1962, Anatomy of a Television Play 1962, Cinema Eye, Cinema Ear 1964, Penguin Dictionary of the Theatre 1966, The Art Nouveau Book in Britain 1966, The Rise and Fall of the Well-Made Play 1967, The Art Dealers 1969, The Hollywood Musical 1971, The Second Wave 1971, Directors and Directions 1975, Hitch 1978, Impressionism 1981, Strangers in Paradise 1983, Ingrid Bergman 1983, Alec Guinness 1984, Vivien Leigh 1984, Hollywood 1940s 1985, Portraits of the British Cinema 1986, Orson Welles 1986, Edward Wolfe 1986, Great Movie Moments 1987, Meninsky 1990, Impressionist Dreams 1990, Liz Taylor 1991, Muriel Pemberton 1993, Ricardo Cinalli 1993, Igor Mitoraj 1993, Claude Monet 1995, Bill Jacklin 1997, The World of Michael Parkes 1998, Antonio Saliola 1998, The Sun is God 1999, Peter Coker 2002, Roberto Barnardi 2002, Zsuzsi Roboz 2005, Adrian George 2006, The Michael Winner of Donald McGill 2006, Carl Laubin 2007; edited: Look Back in Anger: A Casebook 1968, The Pleasure Dome (Graham Greene on Film) 1972, Masterworks of British Cinema 1974. *Address:* c/o The Times, 1 Pennington Street, London, E1 9XN, England. *Telephone:* (20) 7782-5167.

TAYLOR, Julia (Judy) Marie, MBE, FRSA; British writer; b. 12 Aug. 1932, Murton, S Wales; adopted d. of Gladys Spicer Taylor; m. Richard Hough 1980 (died 1999). *Education:* St Paul's Girls' School, London. *Career:* joined The Bodley Head publishing house 1951, Children's Book Ed. 1962–77, Dir 1967–84, Deputy Man. Dir 1971–80; mem. UNICEF Int. Arts Cttee 1968–70, 1976, 1982–83, UK UNICEF Greetings Card Cttee 1982–85; Chair. Children's Book Group 1969–72; mem. Publishers' Asscn Council 1972–78; mem. Book Devt Council 1973–76; Consultant to Penguin Books on Beatrix Potter 1981–87, 1989–92; Assoc. Dir Weston Woods Inst., USA 1984–2002; Consulting Ed. Reinhardt Books 1988–93; Trustee Beatrix Potter Soc. 1985– (Chair. 1990–97, 2000–03), Volunteer Reading Help 2000–04. *Publications include:* Sophie and Jack 1982, My First Year: A Beatrix Potter Baby Book 1983, Sophie and Jack in the Snow 1984, Beatrix Potter: Artist, Storyteller and Countrywoman 1986, Dudley and the Monster 1986, That Naughty Rabbit: Beatrix Potter and Peter Rabbit 1987, My Cat 1987, Dudley Bakes a Cake 1988, Sophie and Jack in the Rain 1989, Beatrix Potter's Letters: A Selection 1989, Letters to Children from Beatrix Potter 1992, Beatrix: A Play (jtly) 1996, Sketches for Friends by Edward Ardizzone (ed.) 2000. *Address:* 31 Meadowbank, Primrose Hill Road, London, NW3 3AY, England. *Telephone:* (20) 7722-5663. *E-mail:* taylor.hough@talk21.com.

TAYLOR, Mark C., BA, PhD; American academic and writer; b. 13 Dec. 1945, Plainfield, NJ; m. Mary-Dinnis Stearns 1968; one s. one d. *Education:* Wesleyan Univ., Harvard Univ., Univ. of Copenhagen. *Career:* Instructor in Religion, Harvard Univ., 1972–73; Asst Prof. of Religion, 1973–78, Assoc. Prof. of Religion, 1978–81, Prof. of Religion, 1981–86, William R. Kenan Jr Prof., 1986–91, Preston S. Parish Third Century Prof. of Religion, 1992–93, Preston S. Parish Prof. of Humanities, 1993–97, Cluett Prof. of Humanities, 1997–, Williams College; Visiting Lecturer in Religion, Smith College, 1981; Visiting Prof. of Architecture and Religion, Columbia Univ., 1994; Visiting Prof., Univ. of Sydney, 1995; William Neal Reynolds Visiting Prof. of Communication Studies, Univ. of North Carolina at Chapel Hill, 1999; Co-Founder, Global Education Network, 1999; Art exhibition, Grave Matters, Mass MOCA, 2002–03; mem. American Acad. of Religion: Hegel Society of America; Society for Phenomenology and Existential Philosophy; Society for Values in Higher Education; Søren Kierkegaard Acad. *Publications:* Kierkegaard's Pseudonymous Authorship: A Study of Time and the Self, 1975; Religion and the Human Image (with Carl Raschke and James Kirk), 1976; Journeys to Selfhood: Hegel and Kierkegaard, 1980; Unfinished: Essays in Honor of Ray L. Hart (ed.), 1981; Deconstructing Theology, 1982; Erring: A Postmodern A/theology, 1984; Deconstruction in Context: Literature and Philosophy, 1986; Altarity, 1987; Tears, 1989; Double Negative (with Michael Heizer), 1992; Disfiguring: Art, Architecture, Religion, 1992; Nots, 1993; Imagologies: Media Philosophy (with Esa Saarinen), 1994; Hiding, 1996; Critical Terms in Religious Studies (ed.), 1998; The Picture in Question: Mark Tansey and the Ends of Representation, 1999; About Religion: Economies of Faith in Virtual Cultures, 1999; The Moment of Complexity: Emerging Network Culture, 2002; Grave Matters, 2002; Confidence Games: Money and Markets in a World Without Redemption, 2003. Contributions: numerous scholarly books and journals. *Honours:* Guggenheim Fellowship, 1978–79; National Humanities Center Fellow, 1982–83; Awards for Excellence, American Acad. of Religion, 1988, 1994; Research Fellow, Graham Foundation for Fine Arts, 1990; Rector's Medal, University of Helsinki, 1993; National College Prof. of the Year, Carnegie Foundation for the Advancement of Teaching, 1995; Distinguished Alumnus Award, Wesleyan University, 1998.

TAYLOR, Theodore Langhans, (Lang Taylor); American writer; b. 23 June 1921, Statesville, NC; m. 1st Gwen Goodwin 1946, two s. one d.; m. 2nd Flora Gray 1982. *Career:* worked for four daily newspapers before writing first book. *Publications:* The Magnificent Mitscher 1954, Fire on the Beaches 1957, The Cay 1968, The Children's War 1971, The Maldonado Miracle 1973, Teetoncey 1974, Jule 1979, The Trouble with Tuck 1981, Battle of the Midway Island 1982, HMS Hood vs Bismarck 1983, Battle in the English Channel 1984, Sweet Friday Island 1984, The Cats of Shambala 1985, Walking Up a Rainbow 1986, The Stalker 1987, The Hostage 1988, Sniper, Monocolo 1989, Tuck

Triumphant 1990, The Weirdo 1991, Maria 1992, To Kill a Leopard 1993, Timothy of the Cay 1993, The Bomb 1996, Rogue Wave 1996, A Sailor Returns 2001, The Boy Who Could Fly Without a Motor 2002, Lord of the Kill 2002, The Flight of Jesse Leroy Brown 2003, Ice Drift 2004, Making Love to Typewriters 2005, Ice Drift 2005; contrib. to Saturday Evening Post, McCall's, Ladies Home Journal, Saturday Review of Literature, Argosy. *Honours:* Lewis Carroll Shelf Award 1970, Jane Addams Peace and Freedom Foundation Award 1970, Western Writers of America Award, George G. Stone Center Award 1974, American Library Asscn Best Book 1980, 1993, 1995, Edgar Allan Poe Award, International Asscn of School Librarians Award 1981. *Address:* 1856 Catalina Street, Laguna Beach, CA 92651, USA. *Telephone:* (949) 494-6294 (office).

TCHUKHONTSEV, Oleg Grigoryevich; Russian poet; b. 8 March 1938, Pavlov Posad, Moscow Region; m. Irina Igorevna Povolotskaya. *Education:* Moscow Pedagogical Inst. *Career:* poetry section, mem. Editorial Bd Novy Mir; published in Druzhba Narodov, Yunost, Molodaya Gvardiya, Novy Mir. *Publications:* From Three Notebooks (cycles Posad, Name, Sparrow's Night) 1976, The Dormer Window 1983, Poetry 1989, By Wind and Heat 1989, Passing Landscape 1997 and other books of poetry; translations of Goethe, Warren, Frost, Kits and numerous other poets. *Honours:* State Prize of Russia 1993. *Address:* Bolshoi Tishinsky per. 12, Apt. 10, 123557 Moscow, Russia (home). *Telephone:* (495) 253-51-95 (home).

TEIŠERSKYTE, Dalia; Lithuanian magazine editor and business executive; b. 27 Nov. 1944, Raseiniai; m. Anatoly Clipkov 1979; two s. *Education:* Vilnius State Univ. *Career:* family deported to Siberia under Communist govt; later worked as woodcutter, maid, in publishing co., as radio Corresp., Dir of art gallery and ed. of newspaper; later established own co.; Chair. and Vice-Pres. Gabija; Pres. Kaunas Businessman; mem. Nat. UNESCO Cttee. *Publications:* five books of poetry and numerous articles in local and other publs. *Address:* Gabija, Kestucio 64, 3000 Kaunas (office); Dainavos 17-3, 3000 Kaunas, Lithuania (home). *Telephone:* (7) 226640 (office); (7) 225616 (home). *Fax:* (7) 201809 (office); (7) 225616 (home).

TEJPAL, Tarun J.; Indian newspaper editor and writer; *CEO and Editor-in-Chief, Tehelka. Career:* over 20 years' experience, including reporter for The Indian Express and The Telegraph, ed. with India Today and India Express Group; has written for numerous int. publications, including The Paris Review, The Guardian, Financial Times and Prospect; co-f. India Ink publishing house; fmr Managing Ed. Outlook news magazine –2000; f., CEO and Ed.-in-Chief Tehelka newspaper 2000–, initially web-only news site, relaunched as nat. weekly newspaper 2004–. *Publication:* The Alchemy of Desire (novel) 2005. *Address:* RST India Ink Publishing Company Ltd, B57 New Rajinder Nagar, New Delhi 110060, India (office). *E-mail:* editor@tehelka .com (office). *Website:* www.tehelka.com (office).

TEKIN, Latife; Turkish writer; b. 1 Jan. 1957, Kayseri; d. of Mustafa and Hatice Erdoğan; m. 1st Ertuğrul Tekin (divorced); one s.; m. 2nd Latif Demirci; one d. *Publications include:* Dear Shameless Death 1983, Berci Kristin Garbage Tales 1984, Night Lessons 1986, Swords By Ice 1989, Signs of Love 1995, El Panuelo Turco 2000. *Address:* Kirechane Gediği Sok 6, Arnavutköy, Istanbul, Turkey. *Telephone:* (1) 2636687. *Fax:* (1) 5139518.

TELEN, Ludmila Olegovna; Russian journalist; *Deputy Editor-in-Chief, The Moscow News Weekly;* b. 2 Oct. 1957, Zhukovsky, Russia; d. of Oleg P. and Elmira F. Telen; m. Valery Vyzhutovich 1980; one s. *Education:* Moscow M. V. Lomonosov State Univ. *Career:* journalist with Komsomolskaya Pravda newspaper 1977–85; Special Corresp. for Socialisticheskaya Industria 1985–89; analyst for Narodny Deputat magazine 1990–91; Political Columnist Moscow News weekly newspaper 1991–, Deputy Ed.; Presenter regular TV programme Political Kitchen 1991–93, Deputy Ed.-in-Chief, The Moscow News Weekly 1995–. *Address:* The Moscow News, 16/2 Tverskaia, 103829 Moscow (office); Chapaevsky, 18/1, 98, Moscow, Russia (home). *Telephone:* (095) 200-38-11 (office). *Fax:* (095) 209-17-28 (office). *E-mail:* telen@mn.ru (office). *Website:* english.mn.ru/english (office).

TELFER, Tracie (see Chaplin, Jenny)

TEMKO, Allan Bernard; American academic, architecture critic and writer; b. 4 Feb. 1926, New York, NY; m. Elizabeth Ostroff 1950; one s. one d. *Education:* AB, Columbia University, 1947; Postgraduate Studies, Sorbonne, University of Paris, 1948–49, 1951–52, University of California at Berkeley, 1949–51. *Career:* Lecturer, Sorbonne, University of Paris, 1953–54, École des Arts et Metiers, Paris, 1954–55; Asst Prof. of Journalism, 1956–62, Lecturer in City Planning and Social Sciences, 1966–70, Lecturer, Graduate School of Journalism, 1991, University of California at Berkeley; West Coast Ed., Architectural Forum, 1959–62; Architecture Critic, 1961–93, Art Ed., 1979–82, San Francisco Chronicle; Prof. of Art, California State University at Hayward, 1971–80; Lecturer in Art, Stanford University, 1981, 1982. *Publications:* Notre Dame de Paris, 1955; Eero Saarinen, 1962; No Way to Build a Ballpark and Other Irreverent Essays on Architecture, 1993. Contributions: newspapers and magazines. *Honours:* Guggenheim Fellowship, 1956–57; Gold Medal, 1956, Silver Medal, 1994, Commonwealth Club of California; Rockefeller Foundation Grant, 1962–63; Manufacturers Hanover/ Art World First Prize in Architectural Criticism, 1986, and Critics' Award, 1987; National Endowment for the Arts Fellowship, 1988; Professional Achievement Award, Society of Professional Journalists, 1988; Pulitzer Prize for Criticism, 1990. *Address:* 1015 Fresno Avenue, Berkeley, CA 94707, USA.

TEMPLE, (Robert) Philip; New Zealand writer; b. 20 March 1939, Yorkshire, England; m. Daphne Evelyn Keen 1965 (divorced); one s. one d. *Career:* Ed., New Zealand Alpine Journal, 1968–70, 1973, Landfall, 1972–75; Assoc. Ed., Katherine Mansfield Memorial Fellowship, Menton, France, 1979; Robert Burns Fellowship, University of Otago, 1980; Berlin Artist's Program Fellowship, 1987; Research Fellow, National Library, New Zealand, 1996–97; mem. PEN, New Zealand Centre, 1970–; New Zealand Society of Authors, pres., 1998–99. *Publications:* The World at Their Feet, 1969; Ways to the Wilderness, 1977; Beak of the Moon, 1981; Sam, 1984; New Zealand Explorers, 1985; Kakapo, 1988; Making Your Vote Count, 1992; Dark of the Moon, 1993; Temple's Guide to the New Zealand Parliament, 1994; Kotuku, 1994; The Book of the Kea, 1996; To Each His Own, 1998. *Honours:* Arts Council Non-Fiction Bursary, 1994; AIM Honour Award, 1995. *Address:* 147a Tomahawk Road, Dunedin, New Zealand.

TEMPLE, Wayne Calhoun, AB, AM, PhD; American historian, archivist and writer; *Chief Deputy Director, Illinois State Archives;* b. 5 Feb. 1924, Richwood, OH; m. Sunderine Wilson Mohn 1979; two step-s. *Education:* Univ. of Illinois, Champaign-Urbana. *Career:* Ed.-in-Chief 1958–73, Editorial Bd 1973–, Lincoln Herald; historical consultant to sculptor, Rebecca Childers Caleel; currently Chief Deputy Dir, Ill. State Archives, Bd of Advisers, The Lincoln Forum; mem. Abraham Lincoln Asscn, Nat. Abraham Lincoln Bicentennial Comm.'s Advisory Cttee. *Publications:* Indian Villages of the Illinois Country 1958–, Campaigning with Grant 1961, Stephen A. Douglas: Freemason 1982, The Building of Lincoln's Home and its Saga 1984, Lincoln's Connections With the Illinois and Michigan Canal 1986, Illinois' Fifth Capitol (with Sunderine Temple) 1988, Abraham Lincoln: From Skeptic to Prophet 1995, Alexander Williamson: Friend of the Lincolns 1997, By Square and Compass: Saga of the Lincoln Home 2002, 'The Taste is in my Mouth a Little...': Lincoln's Victuals and Potables 2004, Abraham Lincoln and Illinois' Fifth Capitol 2006, Lincoln's Travels on the River Queen 2007; contrib. to numerous journals, including the Lincoln Herald. *Honours:* Lincoln Diploma of Honor, National Sesquicentennial Commission Lincoln Medallion, Archbishop Richard Chenevix Trench Award 1999, Lincoln Memorial Univ. Lifetime Achievement Award 2001, Red Cross of Constantine. *Address:* Illinois State Archives, Springfield, IL 62756 (office); 1121 S Fourth Street Court, Springfield, IL 62703, USA (home). *Telephone:* (217) 782-3501 (office). *Fax:* (217) 524-3930 (office).

TEMPLETON, Edith; British writer; b. 7 April 1916, Prague; d. of Louis Gideon and Irma de Szèll; m. 1st W. S. Templeton 1938 (divorced); m. 2nd Edmund Ronald 1956 (died 1984); one s. *Education:* Lycée in Paris and Prague Medical Univ. *Career:* mem. staff, Office of Chief Surgeon, US War Office 1942–45; Conf. and Law-Court Interpreter for British Forces with rank of Capt., Germany 1945–46. *Publications:* Summer in the Country 1950, Living on Yesterday 1951, The Island of Desire 1952, Surprise of Cremona (Book Soc. Choice) 1954, This Charming Pastime 1955, Gordon 1966, Murder in Estoril 1992, The Darts of Cupid and Other Stories 2002; contrib. short stories to The New Yorker 1956–91, Holiday, Atlantic Monthly, Vogue and Harper's Magazine. *Address:* 76 corso Europa, 18012 Bordighera, Italy. *Telephone:* (0184) 261858.

TEMPLETON, Fiona, MA; British theatre director, poet and writer; b. 23 Dec. 1951, Scotland. *Education:* Univ. of Edinburgh, New York Univ., USA. *Career:* mem. Poets and Writers; alumna New Dramatists. *Plays:* You: The City 1988, Recognition 1995, Delirium of Interpretations 1991, L'Ile 2003. *Publications:* Elements of Performance Art 1976, London 1984, You the City 1990, Delirium of Interpretations 1997, Oops the Join 1997, Cells of Release 1997, Hi Cowboy 1997, Delirious of Interpretations 2003; contrib. to anthologies and journals. *Honours:* various grants, fellowships and awards. *Address:* 100 St Mark's Place, No. 7, New York, NY 10009, USA (office). *Website:* www.fionatempleton.org.

TEN BERGE, Hans Cornelis; Dutch poet, writer and editor; b. 24 Dec. 1938. *Career:* Lecturer, Art Acad., Arnhem; Writer-in-Residence, University of Texas, USA, University College London, England, University of Gronigen, Netherlands; Ed., Raster, Grid, literary journals; mem. PEN; Society of Dutch Literature. *Publications:* Poetry: Gedichten, 3 vols 1969, White Shaman 1973, Poetry of the Aztecs 1972, Va-banque 1977, Semblance of Reality 1981, Texas Elegies 1983, Songs of Anxiety and Despair 1988, Materia Prima, Poems 1963–93, Oesters & gestoofde pot (Oysters and Pot Roast) 2001. Fiction: Zelfportret met witte muts 1985, Het geheim van een oppewekt humeur 1986, The Home Loving Traveller 1995, Women, Jealousy and Other Discomforts 1996, De Jaren in Zeedorp (The Sea-Town Years) 1998, Blauwbaards Ontwaken (Bluebeard's Awakening, novel) 2003. Other: The Defence of Poetry, essays, 1988; Prose books; Books of myths and fables of Arctic peoples; numerous poetry trans. Contributions: periodicals. *Honours:* Van der Hoogt Prize 1968, Prose Prize, City of Amsterdam 1971, Multatuli Prize 1987, Constantijn Huÿgens Prize 1996, A. Roland Holst Prize for Poetry 2003. *Address:* c/o Meulenhoff Publishers, PO Box 100, 1000 AC Amsterdam, The Netherlands.

TENNANT, Emma Christina, FRSL; British writer; b. 20 Oct. 1937, d. of 2nd Baron Glenconner and Elizabeth Lady Glenconner; one s. two d. *Education:* St Paul's Girls' School. *Career:* fmr freelance journalist; Founder, Ed. Bananas 1975–78; Gen. Ed. In Verse 1982–, Lives of Modern Women 1985–. *Television includes:* Frankenstein's Baby, Screen One. *Publications:* The Colour of Rain (as Catherine Aydy) 1963, The Time of the Crack 1973, The Last of the

Country House Murders 1975, Hotel de Dream 1976, Bananas Anthology (ed.) 1977, Saturday Night Reader (ed.) 1978, The Bad Sister 1978, Wild Nights 1979, Alice Fell 1980, The Boggart (with M. Rayner) 1981, The Search for Treasure Island 1981, Queen of Stones 1982, Woman Beware Woman 1983, The Ghost Child 1984, Black Marina 1985, The Adventures of Robina by Herself (ed.) 1986, Cycle of the Sun: The House of Hospitalities 1987, A Wedding of Cousins 1988, The Magic Drum 1989, Two Women of London 1989, Faustine 1992, Tess 1993, Pemberley 1993, Emma in Love 1996, An Unequal Marriage 1994, Strangers: A Family Romance 1998, Girlitude 1999, Burnt Diaries 1999, The Ballad of Sylvia and Ted (contrib.) 2001, A House in Corfu 2001, Felony 2002, Corfu Banquet 2003, Heathcliff's Tale 2005, The Harp Lesson 2005, The French Dancer's Bastard 2006. *Honours:* Hon. DLitt (Aberdeen) 1996. *Literary Agent:* c/o Marsh Agency, 12 Dover Street, London, W1S 4LJ, England. *Telephone:* (20) 7399-2800. *Fax:* (20) 7399-2801. *Website:* www.marsh-agency.co.uk.

TEPPERMAN, Jonathan D., BA, MA, LLM; Canadian journalist; *Deputy Managing Editor, Foreign Affairs (journal)*; b. 10 Aug. 1971, Windsor, Ont.; s. of Bill and Rochelle Tepperman. *Education:* Yale Univ., Univ. of Oxford, UK, NYU School of Law. *Career:* fmr speechwriter for US Amb. . to UN 1994–95; journalist writing for Forward 1996, Jerusalem Post 1997; Assoc. Ed. and Production Man. Foreign Affairs (journal of Council on Foreign Relations) 1998–2001, Sr Ed. 2001–04, Deputy Man. Ed. 2004–. *Publications:* numerous contributions to publications including New York Times, Newsweek, LA Times, Christian Science Monitor, Wall Street Journal, New Republic. *Address:* Foreign Affairs, Council on Foreign Relations, The Harold Pratt House, 58 East 68th Street, New York, NY 10021, USA (office). *Telephone:* (212) 434-9512 (office). *Fax:* (212) 434-9800 (office). *E-mail:* jtepperman@cfr.org (office). *Website:* www.cfr.org (office).

TERKEL, Louis (Studs), PhB, JD; American writer, actor and interviewer; b. 16 May 1912, New York, NY; s. of Samuel Terkel and Anna Terkel (née Finkel); m. Ida Goldberg 1939 (died 1999); one s. *Education:* McKinley High School and Univ. of Chicago. *Career:* star TV programme Studs Place 1950–53, radio programme Wax Museum 1945–, Studs Terkel Almanac 1952–, Studs Terkel Show (station WFMT-FM Chicago 1952–97); master of ceremonies, Newport Folk Festival 1959, 1960, Ravinia Musical Festival 1959, Chicago Univ. Folk Festival 1961 and others; Distinguished Scholar in Residence, Chicago History Soc. 1998–; lecturer and film narrator. *Stage appearances include:* Detective Story 1950, A View from the Bridge 1958, Light up the Sky 1959, The Cave Dwellers 1960. *Publications:* Giants of Jazz 1956, Division Street: America 1966, Amazing Grace (play) 1959, Hard Times: An Oral History of the Great Depression 1970, Working: People Talk About What They Do All Day and How They Feel About What They Do 1974, Talking to Myself: A Memoir of My Times 1977, American Dreams: Lost and Found 1980, The Good War: An Oral History of World War II (Pulitzer Prize 1985) 1984, Envelopes of Oral Sound: The Art of Oral Recording (co-author) 1985, The Neon Wilderness (with Nelson Algren) 1986, Chicago 1986, The Great Divide: Second Thoughts on the American Dream 1988, Race: How Blacks and Whites Think and Feel About the American Obsession 1992, Coming of Age: The Story of Our Century by Those Who've Lived It 1995, My American Century 1997, The Spectator: Talk About Movies and Plays with Those Who Made Them 1999, Will the Circle be Unbroken?: Reflections on Death, Rebirth and Hunger for Faith 2001, Hope Dies Last: Keeping the Faith in Difficult Times 2003, And They All Sang: Adventures of an Eclectic Disc Jockey 2005, And They All Sang: The Great Musicians of the 20th Century Talk About Their Music 2006. *Honours:* Prix Italia, UNESCO Award for Best Radio Programme (East–West Values) 1962, Communicator of the Year Award, Chicago Univ. Alumni Asscn 1969, Nat. Humanities Medal 1997. *Address:* c/o Chicago History Society, Clark Street at North Avenue, Chicago, IL 60614, USA. *Website:* www.studsterkel.org.

TERRILL, Ross, BA, PhD; American writer; b. Melbourne, Vic., Australia. *Education:* Wesley Coll., Univ. of Melbourne, Harvard Univ. *Career:* Teaching Fellow, Harvard Univ. 1968–70, Lecturer 1970–74, Research Assoc. in East Asian Studies 1970–, Assoc. Prof. 1974–80; Contributing Ed., Atlantic Monthly 1970–84; Research Fellow, Asia Soc. 1978–79; Visiting Prof., Univ. of Texas 1997–2004. *Publications:* 800,000,000: The Real China 1972, R. H. Tawney and his Times 1973, Flowers on an Iron Tree: Five Cities of China 1975, The Future of China After Mao 1978, Mao 1980, The White Boned Demon 1984, The Australians 1987, China in Our Time 1992, Madam Mao 1999, The Australians: How We Live Now 2000, The New Chinese Empire 2003; contrib. to newspapers and magazines. *Honours:* Frank Knox Memorial Fellowship 1965, Sumner Prize 1970, George Polk Memorial Award 1972, Nat. Magazine Award 1972, LA Times Book Prize 2003. *Address:* PO Box 230772, Astor Station, Boston, MA 02123-0772, USA (home). *Fax:* (617) 496-2420 (office); (617) 445-3115 (office). *E-mail:* rt5789@cs.com (home).

TESSON, Philippe, DèsSc; French journalist; b. 1 March 1928, Wassigny (Aisne); s. of Albert Tesson and Jeanne Ancely; m. Dr Marie-Claude Millet 1969; one s. two d. *Education:* Coll. Stanislas, Inst. of Political Studies, Paris. *Career:* Sec. of Parl. Debates 1957–60; Ed.-in-Chief, Combat 1960–74; candidate in legis. elections 1968; Diarist and Drama Critic, Canard Enchaîné 1970–83; Co-Man. and Dir Soc. d'Editions Scientifiques et Culturelles 1971, Pres. 1980; Dir and Ed.-in-Chief, Quotidien de Paris 1974; Dir Nouvelles Littéraires 1975–83; Drama Critic, L'Express Paris 1986; Dir and Co.-Man. Quotidien du Maire 1988; Animator (TV programme with France 3) A Quel Titre 1994–; Ed. Valeurs actuelles 1994–; Drama Critic Revue des deux

Mondes 1990–, Figaro Magazine 1995–; Dir Avant-scène Théâtre 2001–. *Publication:* De Gaulle 1er 1965, Où est passée l'autorité? 2000. *Honours:* Chevalier, Légion d'honneur. *Address:* 205 boulevard Saint-Germain, 75007 Paris, France (office).

THACKARA, James, BA; American writer; b. 7 Dec. 1944, Los Angeles, CA; m. Davina Laura Anne 1975, one d. *Education:* Harvard Univ. *Film screenplay:* Shogun 1969. *Publications:* America's Children 1984, Ahab's Daughter 1988, The Book of Kings 1999.

THAI, Ho Anh; Vietnamese novelist and diplomatist. *Career:* served in India and the Middle East as a diplomat; Ed., World Affairs Weekly. *Publications include:* Behind the Red Mist: Short Fiction 1988, The Women on the Island 2001; co-editor: Love After War: Contemporary Fiction from Viet Nam 2003. *Address:* c/o Curbstone Press, 321 Jackson Street, Willimantic, CT 06226-1738, USA. *E-mail:* info@curbstone.org.

THALER, M. N. (see Kerner, Fred)

THAMES, C. H. (see Marlowe, Stephen)

THAROOR, Shashi, MA, MALD, PhD; Indian international organization official and writer; b. 9 March 1956, London, UK; s. of Chandran Tharoor and Lily Tharoor; divorced; twin s. *Education:* St Stephen's Coll., Delhi Univ., Tufts Univ. Fletcher School of Law and Diplomacy, USA. *Career:* int. civil servant and professional author; joined UN 1978; with UNHCR, served at Geneva HQ, Head of Office in Singapore; Special Asst for UN Peace-keeping operations; Exec. Asst to UN Sec.-Gen. 1997–98, Dir Communications and Special Projects, Office of the Sec.-Gen. 1998–2000; Interim Head of Dept of Public Information 2001–02, Head and Under-Sec.-Gen. for Public Information 2002–07; mem. Bd of Overseers Fletcher School of Law and Diplomacy, Bd of Trustees Aspen Inst. India, Advisory Bd World Policy Journal, Advisory Bd Virtue Foundation, Advisory Bd Breakthrough (human rights org.); Fellow, New York Inst. of the Humanities. *Publications:* Reasons of State 1981, The Great Indian Novel 1989, The Five Dollar Smile and Other Stories 1990, Show Business 1992, India: From Midnight to the Millennium 1997, Riot 2001, Kerala: God's Own Country 2002, Nehru: The Invention of India 2003, Bookless in Baghdad 2005. *Honours:* Hon. DLitt; Pravasi Bharatiya Samman 2004; Commonwealth Writers' Prize, several journalism and literary awards; named Global Leader of Tomorrow by World Econ. Forum, Davos, Switzerland 1998. *Address:* c/o Department of Public Information, United Nations, New York, NY 10017; c/o Editorial Offices, Arcade Publishing, 141 Fifth Avenue, New York, NY 10010, USA. *E-mail:* tharoor@un.org (office). *Website:* www.shashitharoor.com.

THAYER, Geraldine (see Daniels, Dorothy)

THELWELL, Norman, NDA, ADT; British artist, writer and cartoonist; b. 3 May 1923, Birkenhead, Cheshire, England; m. 1949, one s. one d. *Education:* Liverpool College of Art. *Career:* Art Teacher, Wolverhampton College of Art 1950–57. *Publications:* Angels on Horseback, 1957; Thelwell Country, 1959; A Place of Your Own, 1960; Thelwell in Orbit, 1961; A Leg at Each Corner, 1962; The Penguin Thelwell, 1963; Top Dog, 1964; Thelwell's Riding Academy, 1965; Drawing Ponies, 1966; Up the Garden Path, 1967; The Compleat Tangler, 1967; The Thelwell Book of Leisure, 1968; This Desirable Plot, 1970; The Effluent Society, 1971; Penelope, 1972; Three Sheets in the Wind, 1973; Belt Up, 1975; Thelwell Goes West, 1976; Thelwell's Brat Race, 1978; A Plank Bridge by a Pool, 1979; Thelwell's Gymkhana, 1980; Pony Calvalcade, 1981; A Mill Stone Round My Neck, 1982; Some Damn Fool's Signed the Rubens Again, 1983; Magnificat, 1984; Thelwell's Sporting Prints, 1985; Wrestling with a Pencil, 1986; Play It As It Lies, 1987; Penelope Rides Again, 1988; The Cat's Pyjamas, 1992. Contributions: newspapers, journals, and magazines.

THÉORET, France, BA, MA, PhD; Canadian author, dramatist and poet; b. 1942, Montréal, QC. *Education:* University of Montréal, University of Sherbrooke. *Publications:* Bloody Mary, 1977, English trans., 1991; Une voix pour Odile, 1978, English trans., 1991; Vertiges, 1979, English trans., 1991; Nécessairement putain, 1980, English trans., 1991; Nous parlerons comme on écrit, 1982; Intérieurs, 1984; Entre raison et déraison, 1987; L'homme qui peignait Staline, 1989, English trans. as The Man Who Painted Stalin, 1991; Étrangeté, l'étreinte, 1992; La fiction de l'ange, 1992; Journal pour mémoire, 1993; Laurence, 1996. Contributions: anthologies and other publications.

THEROUX, Paul Edward, BA, FRSL, FRGS; American writer; b. 10 April 1941, Medford, MA; s. of Albert Eugene Theroux and Anne Dittami Theroux; m. 1st Anne Castle 1967 (divorced 1993), two s.; m. 2nd Sheila Donnelly 1995. *Education:* Univ. of Massachusetts. *Career:* lecturer, Univ. of Urbino, Italy 1963, Soche Hill Coll., Malawi 1963–65, Makerere Univ., Kampala, Uganda 1965–68, Univ. of Singapore 1968–71; Writer-in-Residence, Univ. of Va 1972. *Play:* The White Man's Burden 1987. *Screenplay:* Saint Jack 1979. *Publications:* fiction: Waldo 1967, Fong and the Indians 1968, Girls at Play 1969, Murder in Mount Holly 1969, Jungle Lovers 1971, Sinning with Annie 1972, Saint Jack 1973, The Black House 1974, The Family Arsenal 1976, The Consul's File 1977, Picture Palace (Whitbread Award) 1978, A Christmas Card 1978, London Snow 1980, World's End 1980, The Mosquito Coast (James Tait Black Memorial Prize 1982, Yorkshire Post Best Novel Award 1982) 1981, The London Embassy 1982, Doctor Slaughter 1984, O-Zone 1986, My Secret History 1988, Chicago Loop 1990, Dr. DeMarr 1990, Millroy the Magician 1993, My Other Life 1996, Kowloon Tong 1997, Collected Stories 1997,

Collected Short Novels 1998, Hotel Honolulu 2000, The Stranger at the Palazzo d'Oro (short stories) 2002, Telling Tales (contrib. to charity anthology) 2004, Blinding Light 2005, The Elephanta Suite 2007; non-fiction: V. S. Naipaul (criticism) 1973, The Great Railway Bazaar (travel) 1975, The Old Patagonian Express (travel) 1979, The Kingdom by the Sea (travel) 1983, Sailing through China (travel) 1983, Sunrise with Sea Monsters (travel) 1985, Riding the Iron Rooster: By Train Through China (travel) (Thomas Cook Prize for Best Literary Travel Book 1989) 1988, Travelling the World (travel) 1990, The Happy Isles of Oceania: Paddling the Pacific (travel) 1992, The Pillars of Hercules (travel) 1995, Sir Vidia's Shadow: A Friendship Across Five Continents (travel) 1998, Fresh-Air Fiend (travel) 1999, The Worst Journey in the World 2000, Nurse Wolf and Dr Sacks 2000, Dark Star Safari: Overland from Cairo to Cape Town (travel) 2002. *Honours:* Hon. DLitt (Tufts Univ., Trinity Univ.) 1983, (Univ. of Mass.) 1988; Playboy magazine Editorial Awards 1972, 1976, 1977, 1979. *Literary Agent:* Hamish Hamilton Ltd, 80 Strand, London, WC2, England; The Wylie Agency, 250 West 57th Street, New York NY 10107, USA.

THESEN, Sharon, BA, MA; Canadian poet and writer; b. 1 Oct. 1946, Tisdale, Saskatchewan. *Education:* Simon Fraser University. *Career:* teacher, Capilano College, Vancouver, 1976–92; Poetry Ed., Capilano Review, 1978–89. *Publications:* Artemis Hates Romance, 1980; Radio New France Radio, 1981; Holding the Pose, 1983; Confabulations: Poems for Malcolm Lowry, 1984; The Beginning of the Long Dash, 1987; The Pangs of Sunday, 1990; The New Long Poems Anthology (ed.), 1991; Aurora, 1995; A Pair of Scissors, 2000. Contributions: various publications.

THIBAUDEAU, Colleen, BA, MA; Canadian poet and writer; b. 29 Dec. 1925, Toronto, ON; m. James C. Reaney 1951; two s. one d. *Education:* St Thomas Collegiate Inst., Univ. Coll., Univ. of Toronto, Université Catholique de l'ouest, Angers. *Career:* mem. League of Canadian Poets, hon. mem. 1997–; Life Mem. New Democratic Party. *Publications:* poetry: Ten Letters 1975, My Granddaughters Are Combing Out Their Long Hair 1977, The Martha Landscapes 1984, The Artemesia Book: Poems Selected and New 1991, The Patricia Album and Other Poems 1992; contribs include poems and stories in anthologies. *Address:* 276 Huron Street, London, ON N6A 2J9, Canada.

THIELE, Leslie Paul, BA, MA, PhD; Canadian academic and writer; b. 27 Jan. 1959; m. Susan Wapner 1991; two s. *Education:* McGill University, University of Calgary, Princeton University. *Career:* Asst Prof. of Political Science, Swarthmore College, 1989–91; Asst Prof., 1991–95, Assoc. Prof., 1995–98, Prof. of Political Science, Affiliated Faculty Mem., College of Natural Resources and the Environment, 1997–, Head, Dept of Political Science, 1997–2002, University of Florida, Gainesville. *Publications:* Friedrich Nietzsche and the Politics of the Soul: A Study of Heroic Individualism, 1990; Timely Meditations: Martin Heidegger and Postmodern Politics, 1995; Thinking Politics: Perspectives in Ancient, Modern, and Postmodern Political Theory, 1997; Environmentalism for a New Millennium: The Challenge of Coevolution, 1999. Contributions: articles and reviews to periodicals including: Political Theory; Journal of Modern History; International Studies in Philosophy; Environmental Ethics; American Political Science Review. *Honours:* Grants, National Endowment for the Humanities, 1990, 1991; Fellow, Social Science and Humanities Research Council of Canada, 1991–93; Fellow, Social Science Research Council and MacArthur Foundation, 1994–96. *Address:* Department of Political Science, 234 Anderson Hall, University of Florida, Gainesville, FL 32611-7325, USA. *E-mail:* thiele@polisci.ufl.edu.

THIEP, Nguyen Huy; Vietnamese writer; b. 1950, Hanoi. *Publications include:* Crossing the River 2003; contrib. to Today, Sung Huong, Bao Van Nghe, Libération. *Address:* c/o Curbstone Press, 321 Jackson Street, Willimantic, CT 06226-1738, USA. *E-mail:* info@curbstone.org. *Website:* www.curbstone.org.

THINH, (Nguyen) Huu; Vietnamese writer; *Editor-in-Chief, Van Nghue;* b. 15 Feb. 1942, Phu Vinh, Duy Phien, Tam duong, Vinh Phuc. *Education:* Nguyen Du Inst., Cultural Coll. *Career:* fmr soldier, served in the 202nd Regiment as tank driver, squad leader and journalist 1963–75; Head, Poetry Council, Ed.-in-Chief, Van Nghe Quan Doi 1982–90; Ed.-in-Chief, Van Nghue 1990–; mem. Viet Nam Writers' Asscn (bd of dirs, exec. cttee); Deputy Gen. Sec., Viet Nam Writers' Asscn. *Publications include:* poetry: Duong toi thanh pho (trans. as On the Way to the City), Tu chien hao toi thanh pho (trans. as From the Trench to the City), Troung ca bien (trans. as Song of the Sea), The Time Tree: Selected Poems 2003; juvenile: Khi be Hoa ra doi (trans. as When Little Hoa was Born); contrib. to Am vang chien hao (anthology, Echo from the Trench). *Honours:* Van Nghe Prizes 1973, 1976, Viet Nam Writers' Asscn Poetry Awards 1980, 1995. *Address:* c/o Curbstone Press, 321 Jackson Street, Willimantic, CT 06226-1738, USA. *E-mail:* info@curbstone.org. *Website:* www.curbstone.org.

THISELTON, Rev. Canon Anthony Charles, BD, MTh, PhD, DD; British theologian and academic; *Professor Emeritus of Christian Theology, University of Nottingham;* b. 13 July 1937, Woking, Surrey, England; m. Rosemary Stella Harman 1963; two s. one d. *Education:* Univ. of London, Univ. of Sheffield, Univ. of Durham, Archbishop of Canterbury at Lambeth. *Career:* Curate, Holy Trinity Church, Sydenham 1960–63; Lecturer and Tutor, Tyndale Hall, Bristol and Univ. of Bristol 1964–70; Lecturer in Biblical Studies, Univ. of Sheffield 1970–79, Sr Lecturer 1979–85; Prin. St John's Coll., Nottingham 1985–88; Prin. St John's Coll., Durham 1988–92; Prof. of Christian Theology and Head of Dept of Theology, Univ. of Nottingham 1992–2001, Prof. Emer. of Christian Theology 2001–; Canon Theologian of Leicester Cathedral 1993–, and of Southwell 2000–; Visiting Research Prof. in Christian Theology, Chester Univ. Coll. 2003–; mem. Soc. for the Study of Theology (Pres. 1999, 2000), Crown Appointments Comm. 2001–. *Publications:* The Two Horizons 1980, The Responsibility of Hermeneutics (with R. Lundin and C. Walhout) 1985, New Horizons in Hermeneutics 1992, Interpreting God and the Post-Modern Self 1995, The Promise of Hermeneutics (with R. Lundin and C. Walhout) 1999, I Corinthians: A Commentary on the Greek Text 2000, A Concise Encyclopedia of the Philosophy of Religion 2002; contrib. to Journal of Theological Studies, New Testament Studies, Biblical Interpretation, Scottish Journal of Theology, approx. 80 research articles. *Honours:* British Acad. Research Award 1995–96, American Library Asscn Choice of Theology Books 1995. *Address:* Department of Theology, University of Nottingham, University Park, Nottingham, NG7 2RD (office); 390 High Road, Chilwell, Nottingham, NG9 5EG, England (home). *Telephone:* (115) 917-6391 (home). *Fax:* (115) 917-6392 (home). *E-mail:* anthony.thiselton@ntlworld.com (home).

THOM, James Alexander, AB; American novelist; b. 28 May 1933, Gosport, IN; m. Dark Rain 1990. *Education:* Butler Univ., Indianapolis. *Career:* reporter and columnist, The Indianapolis Star 1961–67; Lecturer in Journalism, Indiana Univ. 1978–80; mem. Authors' Guild. *Publications:* Spectator Sport 1978, Long Knife 1979, Follow the River 1981, From Sea to Shining Sea 1984, Staying Out of Hell 1985, Panther in the Sky 1989, The Children of First Man 1994, The Spirit of the Place 1995, Indiana II 1996, The Red Heart 1997, Sign-Talker 2000, Warrior Woman (with Dark Rain) 2003, St Patrick's Battalion 2006; contrib. to magazines. *Honours:* Hon. DHL (Butler Univ.) 1995. *Address:* 6276 W Stogsdill Road, Bloomington, IN 47404, USA.

THOMAS, Audrey Grace, MA; Canadian (b. American) writer; b. 17 Nov. 1935, Binghamton, New York; d. of Donald Earle and Frances Waldron (née Corbett) Callahan; m. Ian Thomas 1959 (divorced 1979); three d. *Education:* The Mary A. Burnham School (Northampton, MA), Smith Coll. and Univ. of British Colombia. *Career:* Teacher of English Language Univ. of Science and Tech., Ghana 1964–66; Visiting Lecturer Univ. of British Columbia 1975–76, Sr Lecturer 1981–82; Visiting Asst Prof. Concordia Univ., Montréal 1978, Visiting Prof. 1989–90; Visiting Prof. Univ. of Victoria 1978–79, 1988; Writer-in-Residence Simon Fraser Univ. 1982, David Thompson Univ. Centre, Nelson, BC 1984, Univ. of Ottawa 1987; Visiting Prof. Dartmouth Coll., Hanover, NH 1994; mem. Nat. Exec. Writers Union of Canada; mem. Canada Council Periodicals Cttee 1980–83, Editorial Collective, Women and Words Anthology 1984; mem. PEN, Amnesty Int.; Canada-Scotland Literary Fellow (Edinburgh) 1985–86; Dr hc (Simon Fraser Univ., Univ. of BC) 1994; Ethel Wilson Award 1985; Marian Engel Award 1987; Canada-Australia Literary Prize 1990. *Publications:* Ten Green Bottles 1967, Mrs Blood 1970, Muchmeyer and Prospero on the Island 1972, Songs My Mother Taught Me 1973, Blown Figures 1975, Ladies and Escorts 1977, Latakia 1979, Two in the Bush and Other Stories 1980, Real Mothers 1981, Intertidal Life (nominated Gov Gen's Award in Fiction) 1984, Goodbye Harold, Good Luck! 1986, The Wild Blue Yonder 1990, Graven Images 1993, The Path of Totality 2001; Radio dramas include: Once Your Submarine Cable is Gone. . . 1973, The Milky Way 1984, The Woman in Black Velvet 1985, Rosa 1987, Shonadithit 1988, Sanctuary 1989, A Day in the Life of Medusa 1989; writer of several articles. *Address:* R R 2, Galiano, BC V0N 1P0, Canada.

THOMAS, Chantal; French essayist; *Director of Research, Centre National de la Recherche Scientifique (CNRS);* b. 1945, Lyon. *Career:* specialist in eighteenth century history; biographical pubns on Sade, Casanova, Thomas Berhard and Marie-Antoinette; debut novel Adieux à la Reine sold over 110,000 copies and translated into German, English, Korean, Greek, Italian, Japanese, Dutch and Portugese 2002; currently Dir of Research, CNRS. *Publications include:* Marquis de Sade: L'Oeil de la letter 1978, Casanova: Un Voyage libertine 1985, The Wicked Queen: The Origins of the Myth of Marie-Antoinette 2001, Coping with Freedom: Reflections on Ephemeral Happiness 2001, Adieux à la Reine (Farewell to the Queen, Prix Femina 2002) 2002. *Address:* CNRS Headquarters, 3, rue Michel-Ange, 75794 Paris cedex 16 (office); c/o Éditions du Seuil, 27 rue Jacob, 75006 Paris, France (office). *Telephone:* 1-44-96-40-00 (CRNS) (office); 1-40-46-50-50 (office). *Fax:* 1-44-96-53-90 (CRNS) (office); 1-40-46-43-00 (office). *E-mail:* contact@seuil.com (office). *Website:* www.cnrs.fr (office).

THOMAS, (David) Craig Owen, MA; British writer; b. 24 Nov. 1942, s. of late John Brinley George Thomas and Gwendoline Megan Thomas (née Owen); m. Jill Lesley White 1967 (died 1987). *Education:* Cardiff High School, Univ. Coll. Cardiff. *Career:* schoolteacher 1966–77; full-time novelist 1977–; mem. Bd Lichfield Int. Arts Festival; mem. Soc. of Authors. *Publications:* Rat Trap 1976, Firefox 1977, Wolfsbane 1978, Snow Falcon 1979, Sea Leopard 1981, Jade Tiger 1982, Firefox Down 1983, The Bear's Tears 1985, Winter Hawk 1987, All the Grey Cats 1988, The Last Raven 1990, There to Here – Ideas of Political Society 1991, A Hooded Crow 1992, Playing with Cobras 1993, A Wild Justice 1995, A Different War 1997, Slipping into the Shadow 1998; (as David Grant) Moscow 5000 1979, Emerald Decision 1980.

THOMAS, Donald Michael, MA; British novelist and poet; b. 27 Jan. 1935, Redruth, Cornwall; s. of Harold Redvers Thomas and Amy Thomas (née Moyle); two s. one d. *Education:* Redruth Grammar School, Univ. High School, Melbourne, New Coll., Oxford. *Career:* English teacher, Teignmouth, Devon

1959–63; Lecturer, Hereford Coll. of Educ. 1963–78; full-time author 1978–. *Publications:* Two Voices 1968, Logan Stone 1971, Love and Other Deaths 1975, Honeymoon Voyage 1978, The Flute-Player 1978, Birthstone 1980, The White Hotel 1981, Dreaming in Bronze 1981, Ararat 1983, Selected Poems 1983, Swallow 1984, Sphinx 1986, Summit 1987, Memories and Hallucinations 1988, Lying Together 1989, Flying in to Love 1992, The Puberty Tree (new and selected poems) 1992, Pictures at an Exhibition 1993, Eating Pavlova 1994, Lady with a Laptop 1996, Alexander Solzhenitsyn (biog.) 1998, Charlotte 2000, Villains' Paradise: A History of Britain's Underworld 2007. *Honours:* Gollancz/Pan Fantasy Prize, PEN Fiction Prize, Cheltenham Prize, Los Angeles Times Fiction Prize. *Address:* The Coach House, Rashleigh Vale, Truro, Cornwall, TR1 1TJ, England. *Telephone:* (1872) 261724. *E-mail:* dmthomas@btconnect.com (home).

THOMAS, Elizabeth Marshall, AB, MA; American writer; b. 13 Sept. 1931, Boston, MA; m. Stephen M. Thomas 1956, one s. one d. *Education:* Radcliffe Coll., George Washington Univ. *Career:* mem. PEN, Soc. of Women Geographers. *Publications:* The Hill People 1953, The Harmless People 1959, Warrior Herdsmen 1966, Reindeer Moon 1987, The Animal Wife 1990, The Old Way 1990, The Hidden Life of Dogs 1993, The Tribe of Tiger: Cats and Their Culture 1994, Certain Poor Shepherds 1996, The Social Lives of Dogs: The Grace of Canine Company 2000, The Old Way: A Story of the First People 2006; contrib. to journals. *Honours:* Hon. DLitt (Franklin Pierce Coll.) 1992; Brandeis Univ. Creative Arts Award 1968, PEN Hemingway Citation 1988, Radcliffe Coll. Alumni Recognition Award 1989. *Address:* 80 E Mountain Road, Peterborough, NH 03458, USA.

THOMAS, F(ranklin) Richard, AB, MA, PhD; American academic, poet and writer; b. 1 Aug. 1940, Evansville, IN; m. Sharon Kay Myers 1962, one s. one d. *Education:* Purdue University, Indiana University. *Career:* Purdue University, 1969–70; Prof., Michigan State University, 1971–; Ed., Centering magazine, 1973–80; Research Assoc., Indiana University, 1978–79. *Publications:* Poetry: Fat Grass, 1970; Alive with You This Day, 1980; Frog Praises Night: Poems with Commentary, 1980; Heart Climbing Stairs, 1986; Corolla, Stamen, and Style, 1986; The Whole Mustery of the Bregn, 1990; Miracles, 1996; Death at Camp Pahoka, 2000. Novel: Prism: The Journal of John Fish, 1992. Criticism: Literary Admirers of Alfred Stieglitz, 1983. Editor: various books including: The Landlocked Heart: Poems from Indiana, 1980; Americans in Denmark: Comparisons of the Two Cultures by Writers, Artists and Teachers, 1990. Contributions: numerous journals and magazines. *Honours:* Fulbright Awards, 1974, 1985; MacDowell Colony Fellowship, 1979; Michigan Council for the Arts Award, 1990; National Writing Project Summer Institute Fellow, 1993.

THOMAS, Helen A., BA; American journalist; b. 4 Aug. 1920, Winchester, Ky; d. of George Thomas and Mary Thomas; m. Douglas B. Cornell. *Education:* Wayne State Univ., Detroit. *Career:* reporter, United Press Int. (UPI) 1943–74, White House Bureau Chief 1974–2000; columnist Hearst Newspapers 2000–; first woman mem. Gridiron Club 1975, apptd Pres. (first woman) 1992; mem. Women's Nat. Press Club, Pres. 1959–60 (William Allen White Journalism Award); mem. American Newspaper Women's Club (fmr Vice-Pres.), White House Corresps Asscn (Pres. 1976). *Publications:* Dateline White House 1975, Front Row at the White House: My Life and Times 2000, Thanks for the Memories, Mr. President: Wit and Wisdom from the Front Row at the White House 2003, Watchdogs of Democracy?: The Waning Washington Press Corps and How It Has Failed the Public 2006. *Honours:* numerous hon. degrees including Hon. LLD (Eastern Michigan State) 1972, (Ferris State Coll.) 1978, (Brown) 1986, (St Bonaventure) 1988, (Franklin Marshall) 1989, (Skidmore Coll., MO) 1992, (Susquehanna) 1993, (Sage Coll., MO) 1994, (Nothwestern) 1995, (Franklin Coll.) 1995; Hon. LHD (Wayne State) 1974, (Detroit) 1979, (Siena Coll.) 2007; Woman of the Year Award, Ladies Home Journal 1975, Fourth Estate Award, Nat. Press Club 1984, Journalism Award, Univ. of Missouri 1990, Al Newharth Award 1990, Ralph McGill Award 1995, Lifetime Achievement Award, White House Corresps Asscn 1998, Nat. Newspaper Asscn Lifetime Award 2002, Intrepid Award, Nat. Org. for Women 2003. *Address:* c/o Nine Speakers Inc., 2501 Calvert Street, NW, Washington, DC 20008-2620, USA (home). *Telephone:* (202) 328-6861. *E-mail:* ninespeakers@usa.net. *Website:* www.helenthomas.org.

THOMAS, Leslie, OBE; British writer; b. 22 March 1931, Newport, Wales; m. 1st; three c.; m. 2nd Diane Thomas; one s. *Career:* mil. service 1949–51; newspaper reporter; Vice-Pres. Barnardo's. *Publications:* novels: This Time Next Week 1964, The Virgin Soldiers 1966, Orange Wednesday 1967, The Love Beach 1968, Come to the War 1969, Arthur McCann and all his Women 1970, His Lordship 1970, Onward Virgin Soldiers 1971, The Man with the Power 1973, Bedtimes 1974, Tropic of Ruislip 1974, Stand Up Virgin Soldiers 1975, Dangerous Davies: The Last Detective 1976, Bare Nell 1977, That Old Gang of Mine 1979, Omerod's Landing 1978, The Magic Army 1981, The Dearest and the Best 1984, The Adventures of Goodnight and Loving 1986, Dangerous in Love 1987, Orders for New York 1989, The Loves and Journeys of Revolving Jones 1991, Arrivals and Departures 1992, Dangerous by Moonlight 1993, Running Away 1994, Kensington Heights 1996, Chloe's Song 1997, Dangerous Davies and the Lonely Hearts Detective Club 1998, Other Times 1999, Waiting for the Day 2003, Dover Beach 2005; non-fiction: Some Lovely Islands 1968, The Hidden Places of Britain 1983, This Time Next Week 1991, My World of Islands 1993, In My Wildest Dreams 2006. *Honours:* Hon. MA (Univ. of Wales), Dr hc (Univ. of Nottingham). *Address:* c/o Arrow Books,

Random House UK, 20 Vauxhall Bridge Road, London, SW1V 2SA, England. *Website:* www.lesliethomas.co.uk.

THOMAS, Richard; British composer and writer; b. 1965. *Education:* Univ. of Cambridge. *Career:* mem. of musical and comic duo Miles & Milner 1987–93; Co-founder and mem. Club Zarathustra 1993–98; Co-founder Kombat Opera 1996. *Compositions:* Jerry Springer: The Opera (music and lyrics, with Stewart Lee) (Evening Standard Theatre Award for Best New Musical 2004) 2001. *Radio:* performer: The Miles & Milner Show (BBC Radio 4) 1991, Rainer Hersch's All Classical Music Explained (BBC Radio 4) 1998. *Television:* performer: Beethoven's Not Dead (Spitting Image/BBC 2) 1992, This Morning With Richard Not Judy (BBC 2) 1998–99, Either/Or (PlayUK) 1999, Attention Scum (BBC Choice/BBC 2) 2001; Musical Dir The Frank Skinner Show (Avalon TV/BBC 1, later ITV) 1995–2001, This Morning With Richard Not Judy (BBC 2) 1998–99, Baddiel & Skinner Unplanned (Avalon TV/ITV) 2000–03, Jerry Springer: The Opera (BBC 2) 2004. *Address:* c/o Avalon, 4A Exmoor Street, London, W10 6BD, England. *Telephone:* (20) 7598-8000.

THOMAS, Rosie, (Janey King), BA; British novelist; b. 22 Oct. 1947, Denbigh, Wales; m. Caradoc King 1975; one s. one d. *Education:* St Hilda's College, Oxford. *Publications:* Love's Choice, 1982; Celebration, 1982; Follies, 1983; Sunrise, 1984; The White Dove, 1985; Strangers, 1986; Bad Girls, Good Women, 1988; A Woman of Our Times, 1990; All My Sins Remembered, 1991; Other People's Marriages, 1993; A Simple Life, 1996; The Potter's House, 2002; Sun at Midnight 2004, Iris and Ruby 2006. *Honours:* Romantic Novel of the Year Award, Romantic Novelists Assscn, 1985, 2007. *Literary Agent:* AP Watt Ltd, 20 John Street, London, WC1N 2DR, England.

THOMAS, Victoria (see De Weese, Thomas Eugene (Gene))

THOMEY, Tedd, BA; American journalist and writer; b. 19 July 1920, Butte, MT; m. Patricia Natalie Bennett 1943, one d. *Education:* Univ. of California. *Career:* Publicity Dir, San Diego State Coll. 1941–42; reporter, San Diego Union-Tribune 1942; reporter, then Asst Editorial Promotion Man., San Francisco Chronicle 1942–43, 1945–48; News Ed. and columnist, Long Beach Press Telegram 1950–; creative writing instructor, Long Beach City Coll.; guest lecturer, Univ. of Southern California; consultant, 20th Century Fox Studios. *Publications:* And Dream of Evil 1954, Jet Pilot 1955, Killer in White 1956, Jet Ace 1958, I Want Out 1959, Flight to Takla-Ma 1961, The Loves of Errol Flynn 1961, The Sadist 1961, Doris Day (biog.) 1962, All the Way 1964, Hollywood Uncensored 1965, Hollywood Confidential 1967, The Comedians 1970, The Glorious Decade 1971, The Big Love (co-author) 1986, The Prodigy Plot 1987; plays: The Big Love (co-author) 1991, Immortal Images 1996; contrib. to many magazines. *Honours:* California Newspaper Publishers Award for Best Front Page. *Address:* 7228 Rosebay Street, Long Beach, CA 90808, USA.

THOMPSON, Ernest Victor; British writer; b. 14 July 1931, London, England; m. Celia Carole Burton 1972; two s. *Career:* mem. West Country Writers Club (vice-pres.), Mevagissey Male Choir (vice-patron), RSL, Cornish Literary Guild (pres. 1998). *Publications:* Chase the Wind 1977, Harvest of the Sun 1978, The Music Makers 1979, Ben Retallick 1980, The Dream Traders 1981, Singing Spears 1982, The Restless Sea 1983, Cry Once Alone 1984, Polrudden 1985, The Stricken Land 1986, Becky 1988, God's Highlander 1988, Lottie Trago 1989, Cassie 1990, Wychwood 1991, Blue Dress Girl 1992, Mistress of Polrudden 1993, The Tolpuddle Woman 1994, Ruddlemoor 1995, Moontide 1996, Cast no Shadows 1997, Mud Huts and Missionaries 1997, Fires of Evening 1998, Somewhere a Bird is Singing 1999, Here, There and Yesterday 1999, Winds of Fortune 2000, Seek a New Dawn 2001, The Lost Years 2002, Paths of Destiny 2003; also various books on Cornish and West Country subjects, contrib. approximately 200 short stories to magazines. *Honours:* Best Historical Novel 1976. *Address:* Parc Franton, Pentewan, St Austell, Cornwall, England. *E-mail:* thompsonev@hotmail.com.

THOMPSON, Jean Louise, AB, MFA; American academic and writer; b. 1 Jan. 1950, Chicago, IL. *Education:* Univ. of Illinois, Bowling Green State Univ. *Career:* Prof. of English, Univ. of Illinois, Urbana 1973–; teacher, Warren Wilson Coll. MFA Program 1988, 1989, 1990; Distinguished Visiting Writer, Wichita State Univ. 1991; Assoc. Prof., San Francisco State Univ. 1992–93. *Publications:* The Gasoline Wars 1979, My Wisdom 1982, Little Faces and Other Stories 1984, The Woman Driver 1985, Who Do You Love? 1999, Wide Blue Yonder 2002, City Boy 2005, Throw Like a Girl 2007; contrib. to various anthologies, journals and magazines. *Honours:* Illinois Arts Council Literary Awards 1976, 1996, NEA Fellowship 1977, Guggenheim Fellowship 1984, Pushcart Prize 1995. *Address:* c/o Simon & Schuster Inc., 1230 Avenue of the Americas, New York, NY 10020, USA. *Website:* www .jeanthompsononline.com.

THOMPSON, Judith Clare Francesca, BA; Canadian playwright; b. 20 Sept. 1954, Montréal, PQ; d. of William and Mary (née Forde) Thompson; m. Gregor Campbell 1983; five c. *Education:* Queen's Univ. and Nat. Theatre School, Montréal. *Career:* numerous workshops 1980–90; Tutor in Playwriting, Univ. of Toronto 1983–84; mem. Playwright's Unit Tarragon Theatre 1984–86; Resident Instructor and Dir Univ. of New Brunswick 1989–90; Assoc. Prof. of Drama, Univ. of Guelph, Ont. 1991–; screenwriter. *Films include:* Lost and Delerious, Perfect Pie. *TV includes:* Turning to Stone (Prix Italia for Best Film Screenplay), Life with Billy (Best Screenplay, Golden Gate Awards, San Francisco) 1992. *Plays include:* The Crackwalker, White Biting

Dog (Gov.-Gen.'s Award), The Other Side of the Dark (Gov.-Gen.'s Award 1990), I Am Yours, Lion in the Streets (an adaptation of 'Hedda Gabler'), Sled, Perfect Pie, Habitat, Capture Me. *Radio includes:* Tornado (Nellie Award for Best Radio Drama), Sugarcane, White Sand, Thicket, A Big White Light, The Quickening. *Honours:* two Toronto Arts Awards, several Chalmer Awards, Canadian Author's Asscn B'nai Brith Award, Epilepsy Toronto Humanitarian Award. *Address:* Great North Artists' Management, Inc., 350 Dupont Street, Toronto, Ontario, M5R 1V9, Canada. *E-mail:* juditht@interlog.com.

THOMPSON, Kate, MA; British writer; b. 1956, Halifax, Yorkshire; d. of E. P. Thompson and Dorothy Thompson; pnr Conor Minogue; two d. *Education:* Univ. of Limerick, Ireland. *Career:* fmrly worked with racehorses; moved to Ireland 1981. *Publications:* There is Something (poems) 1992; novels for adults: Down Among the Gods 1997, Thin Air 1999, An Act of Worship 2000; novels for children: Switchers 1994, Midnight's Choice 1998, Wild Blood 1999, The Missing Link (aka Fourth World) 2000, Only Human 2001, The Beguilers (Irish Children's Book of the Year) 2001, The Alchemist's Apprentice (Irish Children's Book of the Year) 2002, Origins 2003, Annan Water (Irish Children's Book of the Year) 2004, The New Policeman (Whitbread Children's Book, Guardian Children's Fiction Prize, Dublin Airport Authority Children's Book of the Year) 2005, The Fourth Horseman 2006. *Literary Agent:* c/o Sophie Hicks, Ed Victor Ltd, 6 Bayley Street, Bedford Square, London, WC1B 3HE, England. *E-mail:* sophie@edvictor.com. *E-mail:* kate@katethompson.info. *Website:* www.katethompson.info.

THOMPSON, Samuel Richard Charles, BA, MA, PGCE; British teacher, poet and writer; *Teacher of English and Drama and Head of Year, Guernsey Grammar School;* b. 9 Feb. 1968, London, England; partner; two d. *Education:* Univ. of Manchester, Charlotte Mason Coll. of Educ., Univ. of Lancaster. *Career:* Head of English, Fyling Hall School, N Yorks. 1993–95; Head of English and Drama, Int. School at Sotogrande, Spain 1997–99; Teacher of English and Drama and Head of Year, Guernsey Grammar School 1999–; Ed. Muse magazine 1989, Que Me Cuentas 1997–99; Publishing Dir Sotogrande Press 2002–; mem. Univ. of Manchester Poetry Soc., Chair. 1990. *Poetry performances:* Ambleside 1991, Ulverstone 1992, Manchester 1996, Guernsey annually 2001–. *Radio broadcasts of poetry:* Radio Guernsey 2002. *Publications:* poetry: What Am I Doing Here 1996, Where Home Was (also CD, with guitar accompaniment by Martin Spoelstra) 2002, Church Poems 2007; contrib. to anthologies, including Crossing the Bridge 2003, Mish-Mash 2004; to journals, including Envoi, Exeter Flying Post, Fylingtales, Grammalogue, Guernsey Press, Hrafnhoh, In Touch, La Vista, Lynx, Ore, Canoe Focus. *Honours:* Thomas de Quincy Prize, Univ. of Manchester 1989. *Address:* Guernsey Grammar School, Les Varendes, St Andrew's, Guernsey, GY6 8TD, Channel Islands (office). *Telephone:* (1481) 256571 (office); (1481) 266379 (home). *Fax:* (1481) 251236 (office). *E-mail:* samthompson@cwgsy.net (home).

THOMSON, David; British film critic; b. 1941, London; m.; two s. *Career:* fmrly taught film studies, Dartmouth Coll.; film critic, living in California, contributing to Film Comment, Film Criticism, The Independent, Movieline, The New Republic, New York Times, Sight and Sound, and others. *Publications include:* fiction: Warren Beatty and Desert Eye, Suspects 1985, Silver Light 1990; non-fiction: A Biographical Dictionary of Film (fourth edn as The New Biographical Dictionary of Film) 1975, Showman: The Life of David O. Selznick (biog.) 1993, Rosebud: The Story of Orson Welles (biog.) 1996, Beneath Mulholland: Thoughts on Hollywood and its Ghosts 1998, In Nevada: The Land, The People, God and Chance 1999, Hollywood: A Celebration 2001, Marlon Brando (biog.) 2003, Cinema Year by Year (revised edn, co-author) 2004, The Whole Equation: A History of Hollywood 2004, Nicole Kidman (biog.) 2006. *Address:* c/o Random House, 1745 Broadway, New York, NY 10019, USA.

THOMSON, Derick Smith, (Ruaraidh MacThòmais), BA, MA, FBA, FRSE; British poet, writer and academic (retd); b. 5 Aug. 1921, Stornoway, Isle of Lewis, Scotland; m. Carol Galbraith 1952; five s. one d. *Education:* Univ. of Aberdeen, Emmanuel Coll., Cambridge. *Career:* Asst in Celtic, Univ. of Edinburgh 1948–49; Lecturer in Welsh, Univ. of Glasgow 1949–56, Prof. of Celtic 1963–91; Ed. Gairm Gaelic Literary Quarterly 1952–2002; Reader in Celtic, Univ. of Aberdeen 1956–63; mem. Glasgow Arts Club, Scottish Gaelic Texts Soc. (Hon. Pres.), Saltire Soc. (Hon. Pres. 1997), Scottish Poetry Library (Hon. Pres. 1999). *Publications:* An Dealbh Briste 1951, The Gaelic Sources of Macpherson's 'Ossian' 1952, Eadar Samhradh is Foghar 1967, An Rathad Cian 1970, The Far Road and Other Poems 1971, An Introduction to Gaelic Poetry 1974, Saorsa agus an Iolaire 1977, Creachadh na Clarsaich 1982, The Companion to Gaelic Scotland 1983, European Poetry in Gaelic Translation 1990, Smeur an Dochais 1992, Gaelic Poetry in the Eighteenth Century 1993, Meall Garbh/The Rugged Mountain 1995, Mac Mhaighstir Alasdair, Selected Poems 1996; contrib. to books, journals and magazines. *Honours:* Hon. DLitt (Wales) 1987, (Aberdeen) 1994; Scottish Arts Council Publication Awards 1971, 1992, FVS Foundation Ossian Prize, Hamburg 1974, Saltire Scottish Book of the Year Award 1983. *Address:* 15 Struan Road, Cathcart, Glasgow, G44 3AT, Scotland (home). *Telephone:* (141) 637-3704 (home).

THOMSON, Edward (see Tubb, Edwin Charles)

THOMSON, June Valerie, BA; British writer; b. 24 June 1930, Kent, England; m. (divorced); two s. *Education:* Bedford Coll., London Univ. *Career:* mem. CWA (cttee mem.), Detection Club. *Publications:* Not One of Us, 1972; Deadly Relations, 1979; Sound Evidence, 1984; No Flowers By Request, 1987; The Spoils of Time, 1989; The Secret Files of Sherlock Holmes, 1990; The

Secret Chronicles of Sherlock Holmes, 1992; Flowers for the Dead, 1992; The Secret Journals of Sherlock Holmes, 1993; A Study in Friendship, 1995; Burden of Innocence, 1996; The Secret Documents of Sherlock Holmes, 1997; The Unquiet Grave, 2000, Going Home 2006; contrib. several short stories to anthologies, including Ellery Queen Magazine, Winter's Crimes and CWA Anthology. *Honours:* Le Prix du Roman d'Aventures, 1983; Special Sherlock Award, 2000. *Address:* 177 Verulam Road, St Albans, Hertfordshire AL3 4DW, England.

THOMSON, Robert; Australian journalist and newspaper editor; *Editor, The Times;* b. 11 March 1961, Torrumbarry; m. Ping Wang; two s. *Career:* financial and gen. affairs reporter, then Sydney Corresp. The Herald, Melbourne 1979–83; sr feature writer Sydney Morning Herald 1983–85; corresp. for the Financial Times, Beijing 1985–89, Tokyo 1989–94, Foreign News Ed., London 1994–96, Asst Ed. Financial Times and Ed. Weekend FT 1996–98, US Man. Ed. Financial Times 1998–2002; Ed. The Times (UK) 2002–; mem. Knight-Bagehot Fellowship Bd, Columbia Univ.; Dir and Chair. Arts International 2000–02. *Television:* regular appearances on ABC News, CNN, Fox News Channel. *Publications:* The Judges – A Portrait of the Australian Judiciary, The Chinese Army, True Fiction (ed.). *Honours:* Business Journalist of the Year, The Journalist and Financial Reporting Group (TJFR) 2001. *Address:* The Times, 1 Pennington Street, Wapping, London, E98 1TT, England (office). *Telephone:* (20) 7782-5000 (office). *Fax:* (20) 7782-5142 (office). *E-mail:* janine.smith@thetimes.co.uk. *Website:* www .timesonline.co.uk (office).

THORNE, Ian (see May, Julian)

THORNE, Matt, MA, MLitt; British writer; b. 1974, Bristol, England; s. of David Thorne and Kaye Thorne; m. Lesley Thorne; one s. *Education:* Sidney Sussex Coll., Cambridge and St Andrews Univ. *Career:* reviewer, Independent, Independent on Sunday, Sunday Telegraph. *Publications:* Tourist 1998, Eight Minutes Idle (Encore Award 1999) 1999, Dreaming of Strangers 2000, All Hail the New Puritans (ed., anthology) 2000, Pictures of You 2001, Child Star 2003, Cherry 2004, Croatian Nights 2005; juvenile: Greengrove Castle 2004, Clearheart Castle 2005, The White Castle 2005. *Address:* 56A Windus Road, Stoke Newington, London, N16 6UP (home); c/o Weidenfeld & Nicholson, Orion House, 5 Upper St Martin's Lane, London, WC2H 9EA, England. *Telephone:* (20) 8442-4255 (home). *E-mail:* mdjthorne@aol.com (home).

THORNHILL, Arthur Horace, Jr, BA; American book publisher; b. 1 Jan. 1924, Boston, Mass.; s. of Arthur Horace Thornhill and Mary J. Peterson; m. Dorothy M. Matheis 1944; one s. one d. *Education:* Englewood School for Boys and Princeton Univ. *Career:* joined Little, Brown & Co. 1948, Vice-Pres. 1955–58, Exec. Vice Pres. 1958–62, Pres. and CEO 1962–86, Chair. of Bd 1970–87; Pres. Little, Brown & Co. (Canada) 1955–84; Vice-Pres. Time Inc. 1968–87; Dir Bantam Books Inc. 1965–67, Conrac Corpn 1972–87; Treas. and Trustee, Princeton Univ. Press 1971–86; Dir Asscn of American Publrs. 1978–81; Trustee Bennington Coll. 1969–76; Fellow Emer. Center for Creative Photography, Univ. of Ariz. *Honours:* Air Medal (USAF); Princeton Univ. Press Medal, Distinguished Alumnus Award, Dwight-Englewood School 1998. *Address:* 50 S School Street, Portsmouth, NH 03801, USA (home).

THORNTON, Margaret (see Poole, Margaret Barbara)

THORPE, Adam; British poet, novelist and dramatist; b. 1956, Paris, France; m.; three c. *Education:* Magdalen Coll., Oxford. *Career:* founder Equinox Travelling Theatre; fmr teacher of mime, drama and English literature, London; resides in France. *Plays:* for BBC Radio: The Fen Story 1991, Offa's Daughter 1993, An Envied Place 2002; stage play: Couch Grass and Ribbon 1996, Himmler's Boy 2004, Devastated Areas 2006. *Publications:* poetry: Mornings in the Baltic 1988, Meeting Montaigne 1990, From the Neanderthal 1999, Nine Lessons from the Dark 2003, Birds with a Broken Wing 2007; novels: Ulverton (Winifred Holtby Memorial Prize) 1992, Still 1995, Pieces of Light 1998, Nineteen Twenty-One 2001, No Telling 2003, The Rules of Perspective 2005, Between Each Breath 2007; short stories: Shifts 2000, Is This the Way You Said? 2006. *Honours:* Time Out Mime Street Entertainer of the Year 1984, Eric Gregory Award 1985. *Literary Agent:* c/o Lucy Luck Associates, 20 Cowper Road, London, W3 6PZ, England. *Telephone:* (20) 8992-6142. *E-mail:* lucy@lucyluck.com. *Website:* www.lucyluck.com.

THORPE, David Richard, BA, MA; British political biographer; b. (s. of Cyril Thorpe and Mary Thorpe (née Avision)), 12 March 1943, Huddersfield, England. *Education:* Selwyn Coll., Cambridge. *Career:* Archive Fellow, Churchill Coll., Cambridge 1986; apptd official biographer of Lord Home of the Hirsel 1990; new authorized biographer of Sir Anthony Eden 1996; Alistair Horne Fellow, St Antony's Coll., Oxford 1997–98; sr mem. Brasenose Coll., Oxford 1998–; mem. Johnson Club, Oxford and Cambridge Club. *Publications:* The Uncrowned Prime Ministers: A Study of Sir Austen Chamberlain, Lord Curzon and Lord Butler 1980, Selwyn Lloyd 1989, Alec Douglas-Home 1996, Eden: The Life and Times of Anthony Eden First Earl of Avon, 1897–1977 2003; contrib. to The Blackwell Biographical Dictionary of British Political Life in the 20th Century 1990, Telling Lives: From W. B. Yeats to Bruce Chatwin 2000, The Oxford Dictionary of National Biography 2004. *Address:* Brasenose College, Oxford, OX1 4AJ, England.

THORPE, Dobbin (see Disch, Thomas Michael)

THORPE, Marie Louise, BA, HDLS; South African writer and teacher; *Teacher in special education, Westridge High School*; b. 1 Oct. 1949, East London, South Africa; m. James Thorpe. *Education:* Univ. of Natal. *Career:* demonstrator, then lecturer 1973–74, librarian 1975, teacher for the handicapped 1980–82; Principal School for Street Children 1995–2001; tutor at writing school; teacher in special educ., Westridge High School 2005–. *Publications:* Write from the Beginning 1987, From Gladiators to Clowns 1988, Aesop's Fables Retold 1988, Lucy's Games 1992, Limbo Land 1996, also reading series The Wordwise Project (organized by Human Sciences Research Council). *Honours:* Merit Awards for Best Student in Philosophy 1970, 1971, 1972, Notcut Prize for Best Student in Philosophy 1973, Emma Smith Queens Scholarship 1974, Sonlan Award for Youth Literature 1992, SA Writers' Circle Quill Award 1993. *Address:* 201 Premier Court, 200 Umbilo Road, Durban, South Africa. *Telephone:* 2024875 (home).

THORUP, Kirsten; Danish writer; b. 9 Feb. 1942. *Career:* mem. State Foundation for the Arts (literary cttee 1993–), Danish PEN (bd mem. 1995–). *Publications:* I dagens anledning 1968, Love from Trieste (in trans.) 1969, Idag er det Daisy 1971, Baby 1973, Den lange sommer 1979, Himmel og helvede 1982, Romantica: Skuespil 1983, Den yderste grunse 1987, Elskede ukendte 1994, Projekt paradis: En trilogi 1997, Digte 1967–71 2000, Bonsai 2000. *Honours:* Lifetime Grant from Danish Art Foundation; Critics' Prize 1982, Danish Booksellers' Golden Laurels Award 1983, Danish Acad. Major Prize for Literature 2000. *Address:* c/o Curbstone Press, 321 Jackson Street, Willimantic, CT 06226-1738, USA. *E-mail:* info@curbstone.org. *Website:* www.curbstone.org.

THUBRON, Colin Gerald Dryden, CBE, FRSL; British writer; b. 14 June 1939, London; s. of Brig. Gerald Ernest Thubron and Evelyn Kate Dryden. *Education:* Eton Coll. *Career:* mem. Editorial Staff, Hutchinson & Co. Publishers Ltd 1959–62; freelance documentary film maker 1963–64; Production Ed., The Macmillan Co., USA 1964–65; freelance author 1965–; Vice-Pres. Royal Soc. of Literature. *Scenario:* The Prince of the Pagodas (ballet at The Royal Opera House, Covent Garden). *Publications:* Mirror to Damascus, The Hills of Adonis, Jerusalem, Journey into Cyprus, Among the Russians, Behind the Wall, The Lost Heart of Asia, In Siberia, Shadow of the Silk Road 2006; novels: The God in the Mountain, Emperor, A Cruel Madness, Falling, Turning Back the Sun, Distance, To the Last City. *Honours:* Hon. DLitt (Warwick) 2002; Silver Pen Award of PEN 1985, Thomas Cook Award 1988, Hawthornden Prize 1988, Mungo Park Medal, Royal Scottish Geographical Soc. 2000, Lawrence of Arabia Medal, Royal Soc. of Asian Affairs 2001. *Address:* 28 Upper Addison Gardens, London, W14 8AJ, England. *Telephone:* (20) 7602-2522.

THURLEY, Simon John, MA, PhD; British foundation executive and museum administrator; *Chief Executive, English Heritage*; b. 29 Aug. 1962, s. of the late Thomas Manley Thurley and Rachel Thurley (née House). *Education:* Kimbolton School, Bedford Coll., London, Courtauld Inst. *Career:* Insp. of Ancient Monuments, Crown Buildings and Monuments Group, English Heritage 1988–90; Curator Royal Historic Palaces 1990–97; Dir Museum of London 1997–2002; CEO English Heritage 2002–; Chair. Cttee Soc. for Court Studies 1996–; Pres. City of London Archaeological Soc. 1997–2002, Huntingdonshire Local History Soc.; Visiting Prof. of Medieval History and Hon. Fellow, Royal Holloway Coll., Univ. of London; mem. Council St Paul's Cathedral. *Publications:* Henry VIII: Images of a Tudor King (co-author) 1989, The Royal Palaces of Tudor England 1993, Whitehall Palace 2000, Lost Buildings of Britain 2004, Hampton Court 2004; frequent contribs to historical publs. *Honours:* Hon. Mem. RIBA . *Address:* English Heritage, 1 Waterhouse Square, 138–142 Holborn, London, EC1N 2ST, England (office). *Telephone:* (20) 7973-3000 (office). *E-mail:* chief.executive@english-heritage.org.uk. *Website:* www.english-heritage.org.uk (office).

THWAITE, Ann, MA, DLitt, FRSL; British writer; b. 4 Oct. 1932, London, England; d. of Angus Harrop and Hilda Harrop (née Valentine); m. Anthony Thwaite 1955; four d. *Education:* Univ. of Oxford. *Career:* Visiting Prof., Tokyo Women's Univ.; occasional named lectures at Univ. of Southern Mississippi, Toronto Public Library, Skidmore Coll.; Contributing Ed., Editorial Bd, Cricket Magazine (USA); mem. Soc. of Authors, PEN. *Publications:* Waiting for the Party: A Life of Frances Hodgson Burnett 1974, re-issued as Frances Hodgson Burnett: Beyond the Secret Garden 2007, Edmund Gosse: A Literary Landscape 1984, A. A. Milne: His Life 1990, Emily Tennyson: The Poet's Wife 1996, Glimpses of the Wonderful: The Life of Philip Henry Gosse 2002. *Honours:* Hon. Fellow, Univ. of Surrey 2001; Leverhulme, Churchill and Gladys Krieble Delmas (British Library) Fellowships; Duff Cooper Prize 1985, Whitbread Biography Award 1990. *Address:* The Mill House, Low Tharston, Norwich, Norfolk, NR15 2YN, England (home). *Telephone:* (1508) 489569 (home). *Fax:* (1508) 489221 (home).

THWAITE, Anthony Simon, OBE, MA, DLitt, FRSL, FSA; British writer and poet; b. 23 June 1930, Chester, Cheshire, England; s. of Hartley Thwaite and Alice Thwaite (née Mallinson); m. Ann Barbara Thwaite (née Harrop) 1955; four d. *Education:* Kingswood School, Bath, Christ Church, Oxford. *Career:* Visiting Lecturer in English Literature, Univ. of Tokyo 1955–57; radio producer BBC 1957–62; Literary Ed. The Listener 1962–65; Asst Prof. of English, Univ. of Libya, Benghazi 1965–67; Literary Ed. New Statesman 1968–72; Co-Ed. Encounter 1973–85; Editorial Dir, Editorial Consultant, André Deutsch 1986–95. *Publications:* poetry: Home Truths 1957, The Owl in the Tree 1963, The Stones of Emptiness 1967, Inscriptions 1973, New Confessions 1974, A Portion for Foxes 1977, Victorian Voices 1980, Poems 1953–1983 1984, revised edn as Poems 1953–1988 1989, Letter from Tokyo 1987, The Dust of the World 1994, Selected Poems 1956–1996 1997, A Different Country: New Poems 2000, A Move in the Weather 2003, The Ruins of Time (ed.) 2006, Collected Poems 2007; other: Contemporary English Poetry 1959, The Penguin Book of Japanese Verse (co-ed. with Geoffrey Bownas) 1964, Japan (with Roloff Beny) 1968, The Deserts of Hesperides 1969, Poetry Today 1973, The English Poets (co-ed. with Peter Porter) 1974, In Italy (with Roloff Beny and Peter Porter) 1974, New Poetry 4 (co-ed. with Fleur Adcock) 1978, Twentieth Century English Poetry 1978, Odyssey: Mirror of the Mediterranean (with Roloff Beny) 1981, Larkin at Sixty (ed.) 1982, Poetry 1945 to 1980 (co-ed. with John Mole) 1983, Six Centuries of Verse 1984, Philip Larkin: Collected Poems (ed.) 1988, Selected Letters of Philip Larkin (ed.) 1992, Philip Larkin: Further Requirements (ed.) 2001. *Honours:* Hon. Lay Canon, Norwich Cathedral 2005; Hon. DLitt (Hull) 1989; Richard Hillary Memorial Prize 1968, Cholmondeley Award 1983. *Address:* The Mill House, Low Tharston, Norwich, Norfolk, NR15 2YN, England (home). *Telephone:* (1508) 489569 (home). *Fax:* (1508) 489221 (home).

THWAITES, (Stephen) Dane, BA; Australian poet, publisher and bookseller; b. 15 June 1950, Inverell, NSW; m.; one s. *Education:* University of Nebraska, Armidale. *Publications:* Winter Light 1983, South China 1994; contrib. to various publications. *Honours:* co-winner, Mattara Prize 1987. *Address:* c/o Hobo Poetry Magazine, PO Box 166, Hazelbrook, NSW 2779, Australia.

TIBBER, Robert (see Friedman, (Eve) Rosemary)

TIBBER, Rosemary (see Friedman, (Eve) Rosemary)

TIELSCH, Ilse, DPhil; Austrian (b. Czechoslovakian) writer; b. 20 March 1929, Czechoslovakia; d. of Fritz Felzmann and Marianne Felzmann (née Zamanek); m. Herr Tielsch 1950; two s. two d. *Education:* Univ. of Vienna. *Career:* resident in Austria 1945–; studied journalism before becoming a writer of poetry and prose; Vice-Pres. Austrian PEN-Club. *Publications include:* novels and stories: Ein Elefant in unserer Straße, Erinnerung mit Bäumen, Die Ahnenpyramide (trilogy) 1980, 1982, 1988, Heimatsuchen, Fremder Strand, Die Früchte der Tränen, Der Solitär; poetry: In meinem Orangengarten, Anrufung des Mondes, Regenzeit, Nicht beweisbar, Zwischenbericht, Lob der Freundheit. *Honours:* Austrian Medal of Honour for Science and Art, Andreas Gryphius-Preis 1989, Anton Wildgans-Preis 1990, Goldenes Ehrenzeichen für Verdienste um das Land Wien 1999 and other awards. *Address:* St-Michael-Gasse 68, 1210 Vienna, Austria (home). *E-mail:* tielschilse@utanet.at (office).

TIFFANY, Carrie, MA; Australian writer; b. 1965, Yorkshire, England. *Education:* RMIT Univ., Melbourne and Latrobe Univ. *Career:* park ranger, Uluru, Kata Tjuta Nat. Park aged 19; writer, Dept of Natural Resources; freelance agricultural journalist 1996–. *Publications include:* Dr Darnell's Cure (short story) (Australian Book Review Short Fiction Award) 2002, Everyman's Rules for Scientific Living (novel) (Victorian Premier's Prize for an unpublished manuscript by an emerging Victorian writer 2003) 2005; contrib. short stories to Australian journals, including Overland, Ulittara, New Australian Writing (Beijing Univ., China), and to Penguin Summer Stories 2002. *Honours:* The Age short story award, University of Canberra short story award, Judah Waten short story award, HQ Flamingo short story award, Victorian Ministry of the Arts New Work Arts Development Grant 2000, Australia Council Literature Board Grant for an Emerging Writer 2001, Varuna Writers' Centre NSW Emerging Writers' Fellowship 2002. *Address:* c/o Publicity Department, Pan Macmillan Australia, Level 25, 1 Market Street, Sydney, NSW 2000, Australia. *E-mail:* panpublicity@macmillan.com.au.

TIGHE, Carl, BA, MA, PDESL, PhD; British writer and dramatist; b. 26 April 1950, Birmingham, England. *Education:* University College, Swansea, University of Leeds, University of Manchester. *Career:* mem. PEN, Welsh Acad., Writers Guild of Great Britain. *Publications:* Little Jack Horner 1985, Baku! 1986, Gdańsk: National Identity in the Polish-German Borderlands 1990, Rejoice! and Other Stories 1992, The Politics of Literature 1999, Pax: Variations 2000, Burning Worm 2001, KssssS 2004, Writing and Responsibility 2005; contrib. to anthologies, journals and radio broadcasts. *Honours:* Welsh Arts Council Literary Bursary 1983, All London Drama Prize 1987, British Council Travel Scholarship, Hungary 1990, City Life Writer of the Year 2000 Award, Authors' Club First Novel Award. *Address:* c/o Simon Trewin, PFD Agency, Drury House, 34–43 Russell Street, London WC2B 5HA, England. *Telephone:* (20) 7344-1000. *E-mail:* postmaster@pfd.co.uk.

TILLINGHAST, Richard Williford, BA, MA, PhD; American academic, poet and writer; b. 25 Nov. 1940, Memphis, TN; m. 1st Nancy Walton Pringle 1965 (divorced 1970); m. 2nd Mary Graves 1973; one s. one d. *Education:* University of the South, Harvard University. *Career:* Asst Prof. of English, University of California at Berkeley, 1968–73; Visiting Asst Prof., University of the South, 1979–80; Briggs-Copeland Lecturer, Harvard University, 1980–83; Assoc. Prof., 1983–92, Prof. of English, 1992–, University of Michigan at Ann Arbor; Assoc., Michigan Institute for the Humanities, 1989–90, 1993–94. *Publications:* Poetry: Sleep Watch, 1969; The Knife and Other Poems, 1980; Sewanee in Ruins, 1981; Fossils, Metal, and the Blue Limit, 1982; Our Flag Was Still There, 1984; The Stonecutter's Hand, 1994; Today in the Café Trieste, 1997; Six Mile Mountain, 2000. Other: A Quiet Pint in Kinvara, 1991; Robert

Lowell's Life and Work: Damaged Grandeur, 1995; A Visit to the Gallery: The University of Michigan Museum of Art (ed.), 1997. Contributions: newspapers, reviews, journals and magazines. *Honours:* National Endowment for the Humanities Grant, 1980; Bread Loaf Fellowship, 1982; Millay Colony Residency, 1985; Yaddo Writers' Retreat Residency, 1986; Amy Lowell Travel Fellowship, 1990–91; British Council Fellowship, 1992, and Travel Grant, 1994; Ann Stanford Prize for Poetry, University of Southern California at Los Angeles, 1992.

TILLMAN, Lynne; American writer, film-maker and academic; *Professor and Writer in Residence, Department of English, State University of New York at Albany*. *Career:* writer of novels, short stories and essays, dir of short and feature-length films; Co-Head Writing Dept, MFA Program, Bard Coll. 1993; Visiting Assoc. Prof. in Creative Writing, Brown Univ. 1998, Columbia Univ. 1999; Lecturer in Creative Writing, Princeton Univ. 1999–2001; Assoc. Prof. and Writer in Residence, The Univ. at Albany 2002–; Co-Ed. Paranoids Anonymous Newsletter 1976–79; Contributing Ed. Bomb, Nest, New Observations; mem. Voice Literary Supplement Bd 1988–90, Int. Advisory Bd Wexner Prize 1996–, Advisory Bd Fence magazine 2001–. *Films:* Earth Angel 1974, Gestures 1978, Committed (co-dir) 1984. *Publications include:* fiction: Living With Contradictions (with drawings by Jane Dickson) 1982, Weird Fucks 1982, Madame Realism (with drawings by Kiki Smith) 1984, Tagebuch einer Masochistin 1986, Haunted Houses 1987, Absence Makes The Heart 1990, Motion Sickness 1991, The Madame Realism Complex 1992, Cast in Doubt 1992, No Lease on Life 1998, Love Sentence 1999, This Is Not It 2002, American Genius: A Comedy 2006; non-fiction: Beyond Recognition: Representation, Power, Culture (co-ed.), 1992, The Velvet Years: Warhol and the Factory 1965–1967 (text by L. Tillman, photographs by Stephen Shore) 1996, The Broad Picture (essay collection) 1997, Bookstore: The Life and Times of Jeannette Watson and Books & Co. 1999; numerous articles and short stories in anthologies and magazines. *Honours:* Jerome Foundation Grant 1988, New York Foundation for the Arts Grant 1989, New York State Council on the Arts Grant 1989, MacDowell Fellow 1991, 1995–96, 1997, 1999, 2000, 2001. *Address:* c/o Joy Harris Literary Agency, 161 Fifth Avenue, Suite 617, New York, NY 10011 (office); Department of English, State University of New York at Albany, Humanities 350, 1400 Washington Avenue, Albany NY 12222; Peter Stuyvesant Station, POB 360, New York, NY 10009-0360, USA (home). *Telephone:* (212) 924-6269 (office); (518) 442-4097 (Albany); (212) 979-1739 (home). *E-mail:* Tillwhen@aol.com (home). *Website:* www.albany.edu/english.

TIMM, Uwe, DPhil; German writer; b. 1940, Hamburg. *Education:* Univ. of Munich, Univ. of Paris. *Publications include:* novels: Heisser Sommer 1974, Der Schlangenbaum 1980, Deutsche Kolonien 1981, Der Mann auf dem Hochrad 1984, The Train Mouse 1986, The Snake Tree 1988, Vogel, friss die Feige nicht 1989, Headhunter 1991, Kerbls Flucht 1991, The Invention of Curried Sausage 1993, Midsummer Night 1995, Johannisnacht 1996, Die Bubi Scholz story 1998, Nicht morgen, nicht gestern 1999, Eine Hand voll Gras 2000, Rot (trans. as Red) 2001, Morenga 2003, In My Brother's Shadow 2005, Der Freund und des Freunde 2005. *Honours:* Munich Literature Prize 1989, 2002, Grosser Literaturpreis der Bayerischen Akademie der Schönen Künste 2001, Jakob Wassermann Prize for Literature 2006. *Address:* Verlag Nagel & Kimche AG, V-Nr. 1320 506, Nordstr. 9, 8035 Zürich, Switzerland. *E-mail:* info@nagel-kimche.ch. *Website:* www.nagel-kimche.ch.

TINDALL, Gillian, MA, FRSL; British writer; b. 4 May 1938, London; d. of D.H. Tindall and U.M.D. Orange; m. Richard G. Lansdown 1963; one s. *Education:* Univ. of Oxford. *Career:* novelist, biographer, historian, freelance journalist, has worked on The Independent, The Times and other newspapers and periodicals and for BBC; JP, Inner London 1980–98; mem. Franco-British Council 1999–. *Publications:* novels: No Name in the Street 1959, The Water and the Sound 1961, The Edge of the Paper 1963, The Youngest 1967, Someone Else 1969, Fly Away Home (Somerset Maugham Award 1972) 1971, The Traveller and His Child 1975, The Intruder 1979, Looking Forward 1983, To The City 1987, Give Them All My Love 1989, Spirit Weddings 1992; short stories: Dances of Death 1973, The China Egg and Other Stories 1981, Journey of a Lifetime and Other Stories 1990; non-fiction: A Handbook on Witchcraft 1965, The Born Exile (biog. of George Gissing) 1974, The Fields Beneath 1977, City of Gold: The Biography of Bombay 1982, Rosamond Lehmann: An Appreciation 1985, Countries of the Mind: The Meaning of Places to Writers 1990, Célestine: Voices from a French Village (Franco-British Soc. Award 1995) 1995, The Journey of Martin Nadaud 1999, The Man Who Drew London (biog. of Wenceslaus Hollar) 2002, The House by the Thames and the People Who Lived There 2006. *Honours:* Chevalier des Arts et des Lettres 2001; Somerset Maugham Award 1972, Enid McLeod Prize 1985, Franco-British Soc. Award 1995. *Literary Agent:* Curtis Brown Ltd, 28–29 Haymarket, London, SW1Y 4SP, England. *Telephone:* (20) 7393-4400. *Fax:* (20) 7393-4401. *E-mail:* info@curtisbrown.co.uk. *Website:* www.curtisbrown.co.uk.

TIPTON, David John; British poet, writer, editor, translator and teacher; b. 28 April 1934, Birmingham, England; m. 1st Ena Hollis 1956; m. 2nd Glenys Tipton 1975; two s. three d. *Education:* Saltley Coll., Univ. of Essex. *Career:* Ed. Rivelin Press 1974–84, Redbeck Press 1984–. *Publications:* Peru: The New Poetry (trans.) 1970–76, Millstone Grit 1972, At Night the Cats, by Antonio Cisneros (trans.) 1985, Nomads and Settlers 1980, Wars of the Roses 1984, Crossing the Rimac 1995, Family Chronicle (poems) 1997, Path Through the Canefields (trans. of José Watanabe) 1997, Amulet Against the Evil Eye 1998, Paradise of Exiles (fiction) 1999, A Mountain Crowned by a Cemetery, by Tulio Mora (trans.) 2001, Nordic Barbarians (fiction) 2002, Medal for Malaya (fiction) 2002, A Sword in the Air (travel) 2003, Defying the Odds (poems) 2006, Blue Rondo (fiction) 2006; contrib. to various publs. *Address:* 24 Aireville Road, Frizinghall, Bradford, BD9 4HH, England (home).

TIWANA, Dalip Kaur, PhD; Indian academic and writer; *Life Fellow, Punjabi University, Patiala*; b. 4 May 1935, Vill-Rabbon, Punjab; d. of Kaka Singh and Chand Kaur Tiwana; m. Bhupinder Singh 1972; one s. *Education:* Mohindra Coll. (Patiala), Punjab Univ. *Career:* mem. Senate, Syndicate, Acad. Council and Bd of Studies in Punjabi, Punjabi Univ., Patiala, Head of Dept of Foreign Languages, Head Nawab Sher Mohammad Khan Inst. of Advanced Studies in Urdu, Persian, Arabic and Malerkotla, fmrly Dean Faculty of Languages, Prof. and Head Dept of Punjabi 1981–, currently Life Fellow; works translated into many languages, several adapted for TV; Pres. Punjab Sahit Acad. Chandigarh, mem. Punjab Arts Council (Chandigarh), Punjabi Bd Sahitya Acad. (New Delhi), Language Advisory Cttee (Bhartiya Jnanpith), Language Advisory Cttee, K.K. Birla Foundation Samman; mem. Advisory Bd North Zone Cultural Centre; fmr mem. Advisory Bd Doordarshan; Vice-Pres. Kendri Lekhak Sabha; presided over Int. Punjabi Conference, London 1980; participant Int. Writing Together, Scotland 1990, Women 20th Century Conference, Glasgow 1990; UGC Nat. Lectureship. *Publications include:* Sadhana (Govt of Punjab Award for Short Stories 1960–61) 1961, Ehu Hamar Jeevna (Sahitya Acad. Award) 1972, Panchaan Vich Parmesar (Ministry of Educ. and Social Welfare Award for Children's Short Stories) 1975, Peele Patian Di Dastan (Nanak Singh Award, Govt of Punjab) 1980, Nange Pairan Da Safar (Gurmukh Singh Musafir Award for Autobiography, Govt of Punjab) 1982, Katha Kuknus Di (Nanjanagudu Thirumalamba Award) 1994, Duni Suhava Bagh (Vagdevi Award 1998), Katha Kaho Urvashi (Sarswati Samman, KK Birla Foundation Award) 2001. *Honours:* Canadian Int. Asscn of Punjabi Authors and Artists Award 1985, Shiromani Sahitkai Award, Govt of Punjab 1987, Praman Patar Award 1989, Dhaliwal Award, Punjabi Acad. (Ludhiana) 1991, Best Novelist of the Decade 1980–90 1993, Mata Sahib Kaur Award 1999, Kartar Singh Dhaliwal Award 2000, Padma Shri 2004, Doordarshan Panj Pani Award 2005. *Address:* Punjabi University Campus, B-13, Patiala 147 002, India. *Telephone:* (175) 2282239; (175) 2281229 (home). *E-mail:* DKTiwana@yahoo.com.

TLILI, Mustapha; Tunisian writer, political philosopher and academic; *Senior Fellow, Remarque Institute and Research Scholar, New York University*; b. 17 Oct. 1947, Fériana; one d. *Education:* Sorbonne, Univ. of Paris. *Career:* numerous posts with UN, including Dir France Information Centre, Paris, Chief Namibia, Anti-Apartheid, Palestine and Decolonization programmes and Dir Communications Policy, Dept of Public Information, UN HQ, New York; fmr Sr Fellow and Dir UN Project, New School World Policy Inst.; fmr Adjunct Prof. of Int. Affairs, Columbia Univ.; currently Sr Fellow, Remarque Inst. and Research Scholar, New York Univ., Founder and Dir Dialogues, Islamic World–US –The West; adviser, Americans for Informed Democracy; mem. Human Rights Watch Middle East and North Africa Advisory Cttee; UNITAR Adley Stevenson Fellow. *Publications:* fiction: La Rage aux tripes 1975, Le Bruit dort 1978, Gloire des sables 1982, La Montagne du lion 1988; non-fiction: For Nelson Mandela (co-ed. with Jacques Derrida) 1987; contrib. to Sorbonne Revue de Métaphysique et de la Morale, World Policy Journal, The Philadelphia Inquirer. *Honours:* Chevalier, Ordre des Arts et des Lettres. *Address:* Dialogues: Islamic World–US –The West, Remarque Institute, New York University, 194 Mercer Street, Fourth Floor, New York, NY 10012, USA (office). *Telephone:* (212) 998-7638 (office). *Fax:* (212) 995-4091 (office). *E-mail:* tlili@islamuswest.org. *Website:* www.islamuswest.org.

TOBIA, Maguid, BSc; Egyptian writer; b. 25 March 1938, Minia. *Career:* teacher of math. 1960–68; mem. Higher Council of Arts and Literature 1969–78; mem. staff Ministry of Culture 1978–; mem. Writers' Union, Chamber of Cinema Industry, Soc. of Egyptian Film Critics, Fiction Cttee of Supreme Council of Culture. *Film scripts include:* Story of Our Country 1967, Sons of Silence 1974, Stars' Maker 1978, Harem Cage 1981. *Play:* International Laugh Bank 2001. *Television:* Friendly Visit (series) 1980. *Publications:* (collections of short stories): Vostock Reaches the Moon 1967, Five Unread Papers 1970, The Coming Days 1972, The Companion 1978, The Accident Which Happens 1987, 23 Short Stories 2001; (novels): Circles of Impossibility 1972, The They 1973, Sons of Silence 1974, The Strange Deeds of Kings and the Intrigues of Banks 1976, The Room of Floor Chances 1978, The Music Kiosk 1980, Hanan 1981, West Virgin 1986, The Emigration to the North Country of Hathoot's Tribe (3 vols: To the North Country 1987, To the South Country 1992, To the Lakes Country 2005), The Story of Beautiful Reem 1991, The Great History of Donkeys 1996, Amosis Case 2005; contribs to Al Ahram and several Arabic magazines. *Honours:* Medal of Science and Arts (First Class); several literary prizes. *Address:* 15 El-Lewaa Abd El Aziz Aly, Heliopolis 11361, Cairo, Egypt. *Telephone:* 2917801. *Fax:* 2917801.

TODD, Emmanuel, PhD; French historian, political scientist and writer; b. 16 May 1951, Saint-Germain-en-Laye; s. of Olivier Todd. *Education:* Institut de Etudes Politiques, Univ. of Cambridge. *Career:* research officer, Institut National d'Études Démographiques, Paris. *Publications:* La Chute final: essais sur la décomposition de la sphère soviétique 1976, Le Fou et le prolétaire 1979, L'Invention de la France (with Hervé Le Bras) 1981, La Troisième planète: structures familiales et système idéologiques 1983, L'Enfance du monde: structures familiales et développement 1984, La Nouvelle France 1988, L'Invention de l'Europe 1990, Le Destin des immigrés:

assimilation et ségrégation dans les démocraties occidentales 1994, L'Illusion économique: essai sur la stagnation des sociétés développées 1998, La Diversité du monde: structures familiales et modernité 1999, Après l'empire: essai sur la décomposition du système américain 2002. *Address:* Institut National d'Études Démographiques, 133 boulevard Davout, Paris 75980, France (office). *E-mail:* todd@ined.fr (office). *Website:* www.ined.fr (office).

TODD, Janet Margaret, BA, PhD; British academic, writer and editor; *Francis Hutcheson Professor of English, University of Glasgow*; b. 10 Sept. 1942, Llandrindod-Wells, Wales; m. 1st Aaron R. Todd 1966 (divorced 1984); one s. one d.; m. 2nd D. W. Hughes 2001. *Education:* Newnham College, Cambridge, University of Leeds, University of Florida. *Career:* Lecturer in African and English Literature, Mfantsipim and University of Cape Coast, Ghana, 1964–67; Asst Prof. of English, University of Puerto Rico, Mayaguez, 1972–74; Asst, Assoc. and full Prof. of English, Rutgers University, 1974–83; Visiting Prof., Jawaharlal Nehru University and University of Rajastan, 1980, University of Southampton, 1982–83; Fellow in English, Sidney Sussex College, Cambridge, 1983–90; Prof. of English, University of East Anglia, 1990–2000; Francis Hutcheson Prof. of English, University of Glasgow, 2000–; mem. Arts and Humanities Research Board, English panel, 1999–2003; British Society for Eighteenth-Century Studies, pres., 2000–02. *Publications:* In Adam's Garden: A Study of John Clare's Pre-Asylum Poetry, 1973; Mary Wollstonecraft: An Annotated Bibliography, 1976; Women's Friendship in Literature, 1980; English Congregational Hymns in the Eighteenth Century: Their Purpose and Design (co-author), 1983; Mary Wollstonecraft (with M. Ferguson), 1984; Sensibility: An Introduction, 1986; Feminist Literary History, 1988; The Sign of Angellica: Woman, Writing and Fiction 1660–1800, 1989; Gender, Art and Death, 1993; The Secret Life of Aphra Behn, 1996; The Critical Fortunes of Aphra Behn, 1998; Mary Wollstonecraft: A Revolutionary Life, 2000; Rebel Daughters: Ireland in Conflict 1798, 2003, Death and the Maidens: Fanny Wollstonecraft and the Shelley Circle 2007. Editor: Dictionary of British and American Women Writers 1660–1800, 1985; The Complete Works of Mary Wollstonecraft, seven vols, 1989; A Dicitonary of British Women Writers, 1989; The Complete Works of Aphra Behn, seven vols, 1992–96; Female Education in the Age of Enlightenment, six vols, 1996; Aphra Behn Studies, 1996; The Collected Letters of Mary Wollstonecraft, 2003. Contributions: scholarly books and journals. *Honours:* National Endowment for the Humanities Grant, 1977–79; ACLS Fellowship, 1978–79; Guggenheim Fellowship, 1981–82; Helen Bing Fellowship, Huntingdon Library, 1991; Leverhulme Institutional Grant, 1991–93; Folger Shakespeare Library Fellowship, 1993–94; Bye-Fellowship, Newnham College, Cambridge, 1998; Hon. Fellowship, Lucy Cavendish College, Cambridge, 1999–. *Address:* c/o Department of English, University of Glasgow, Glasgow G12 8QQ, Scotland.

TODD, Olivier René Louis, LèsL, MA; French writer; b. 19 June 1929, Neuilly; s. of Julius Oblatt and Helen Todd; m. 1st Anne-Marie Nizan 1948; m. 2nd France Huser 1982; two s. two d. *Education:* Sorbonne, Corpus Christi Coll., Cambridge. *Career:* teacher, Lycée Int. du Shape 1956–62; Univ. Asst, St-Cloud 1962–64; reporter, Nouvel Observateur 1964–69; Ed. TV Programme Panorama 1969–70; Asst Ed. Nouvel Observateur 1970–77; columnist and Man. Ed. L'Express 1977–81; worked for BBC (Europa, 24 Hours) and ORTF 1964–69. *Publications:* Une demi-campagne 1957, La traversée de la Manche 1960, Des trous dans le jardin 1969, L'année du Crabe 1972, Les canards de Ca Mao 1975, La marelle de Giscard 1977, Portraits 1979, Un fils rebelle 1981, Un cannibale très convenable 1982, Une légère gueule de bois 1983, La balade du chômeur 1986, Cruel Avril 1987, La négociation 1989, La Sanglière 1992, Albert Camus, une vie 1996, André Malraux, une vie 2001, Catre d'identités, souvenirs 2005. *Honours:* Chevalier, Légion d'honneur, Commdr, Ordre des Arts et des Lettres; Hon. PhD (Stirling, Bristol), Hon. DLitt (Edinburgh) 2005; Prix Cazes 1981, Prix France Télévision 1997, Prix du Mémorial 1997. *Address:* 21 rue de l'Odéon, 75006 Paris (home); 8 rue du Pin, 83310 La Garde Freinet, France. *Telephone:* 1-43-29-55-26 (home).

TOFFLER, Alvin, BA; American writer; b. 4 Oct. 1928, New York, NY; m. Adelaide Elizabeth (Heidi) Toffler (née Farrell) 1950; one d. *Education:* New York Univ. *Career:* Assoc. Ed., Fortune Magazine 1959–61; Visiting Scholar, Russell Sage Foundation 1969–70; Fellow, American Asscn for the Advancement of Science; mem. American Soc. of Journalists and Authors, Int. Inst. for Strategic Studies, World Future Studies Federation. *Publications:* The Schoolhouse in the City 1968, The Eco-Spasm Report 1975; with Heidi Toffler: The Culture Consumers 1964, Future Shock 1970, The Futurists (ed.) 1972, Learning for Tomorrow (ed.) 1973, The Third Wave 1980, Previews and Premises 1983, The Adaptive Corporation 1984, Power Shift 1990, War and Anti-War 1993, Creating a New Civilization 1994–95; contrib. to newspapers, journals and periodicals. *Honours:* hon. doctorates; American Soc. of Journalists and Authors Author of the Year, Prix de Meilleur Livre Étranger; Medal Pres. of Italy, Officer, Ordre des Arts et des Sciences. *Literary Agent:* Curtis Brown Ltd, 10 Astor Place, New York, NY 10003, USA.

TOFFLER, Adelaide Elizabeth (Heidi), BA; American writer; b. (Adelaide Elizabeth Farrell), 1 Aug. 1929, New York, NY; m. Alvin Toffler 1950; one d. *Education:* Long Island Univ. *Publications:* with Alvin Toffler: The Culture Consumers 1964, Future Shock 1970, The Futurists (ed.) 1972, Learning for Tomorrow (ed.) 1973, The Third Wave 1980, Previews and Premises 1983, The Adaptive Corporation 1984, Power Shift 1990, War and Anti-War 1993, Creating a New Civilization 1994–95; contrib. to newspapers, journals and periodicals. *Honours:* hon. doctorates; Pres. of Italy Medal. *Literary Agent:* Curtis Brown Ltd, 10 Astor Place, New York, NY 10003, USA.

TÓIBÍN, Colm; Irish journalist and writer; b. 1955, Enniscorthy, Co. Wexford; s. of Michéal Tóibín. *Education:* Christian Brothers School, Enniscorthy, Univ. Coll., Dublin. *Career:* in Spain 1975–78; Features Ed., In Dublin 1981–82; Ed. Magill (political and current affairs magazine) 1982–85; journalist and columnist, Dublin Sunday Independent 1985–. *Play:* Beauty in a Broken Place 2003. *Publications:* fiction: Infidelity (contrib.), The South (Irish Times First Novel Award 1991) 1990, The Heather Blazing (Encore Award) 1993, The Story of the Night 1996, The Blackwater Lightship 1999, Finbar's Hotel (contrib.) 1999, The Master (Int. IMPAC Dublin Literary Award 2006) 2004, Mothers and Sons 2006; non-fiction: Seeing is Believing: Moving Statues in Ireland 1985, Walking Along the Border (with T. O'Shea) 1987, Homage to Barcelona 1990, Dubliners 1990, The Trial of the Generals: Selected Journalism 1980–90 1990, Bad Blood 1994, Sign of the Cross 1994, The Kilfenora Teaboy 1997, The Irish Famine 1999, Love in a Dark Time 2001, Lady Gregory's Toothbrush 2002; editor: SOHO Square VI: New Writing from Ireland 1993, Enniscorthy: History & Heritage 1998, Penguin Book of Irish Fiction 1999, The Modern Library 1999, New Writing II 2002; contrib. articles. *Honours:* American Acad. of Arts and Letters E. M. Forster Award 1995, Center for Scholars and Writers Fellowship, New York Public Library, Soc. of Authors Travelling Scholarship 2004. *Literary Agent:* c/o A. P. Watt Ltd, 20 John Street, London, WC1N 2DR, England. *Telephone:* (20) 7405-6774. *Fax:* (20) 7831-2154. *E-mail:* apw@apwatt.co.uk. *Website:* www.apwatt.co.uk; www.colmtoibin.com.

TOKARCZUK, Olga; Polish writer; b. 1962, Sulechow. *Education:* Univ. of Warsaw. *Publications:* Podroz ludzi ksiegi (Journey of the People of the Book) 1993, E.E. 1995, Prawiek i inne czasy (Prawiek and Other Times) 1996, Szafa (The Wardrobe) 1997, Dom dzienny, dom nocny (House of Day, House of Night) 1998, Opowiesci wigilijne (Christmas Tales, with Jerzy Pilch and Andrzej Stasiuk) 2000, Lalka i perla (The Doll and the Pearl) 2001, Gra na wielu bebenkach (Playing on a Multitude of Drums, short stories) 2001, Ostatrie historie (The Lost Stories) 2004; contrib. to Granta journal. *Honours:* Polish Publishers' Asscn Prize, Koscielski Prize, three NIKE Readers' Prizes, Brücke Berlin Prize 2001. *Address:* c/o Granta, 2–3 Hanover Yard, Noel Road, London, N1 8BE, England (office).

TOLAND, John Willard, BA; American historian and author; b. 29 June 1912, La Crosse, WI; m. 1st; two d.; m. 2nd Toshiko Matsumura 1960; one d. *Education:* Williams College, Yale Drama School. *Career:* mem. Accademia del Mediterraneo; Authors' Guild; National Archives, advisory council; Western Front Asscn, hon. vice-pres. *Publications:* Non-Fiction: Ships in the Sky, 1957; Battle: The Story of the Bulge, 1959; But Not in Shame, 1961; The Dillinger Days, 1963; The Flying Tigers, 1963; The Last 100 Days, 1966; The Battle of the Bulge, 1966; The Rising Sun, 1970; Adolf Hitler, 1976; Hitler: The Pictorial Documentary of His Life, 1978; No Man's Land, 1980; Infamy, 1982; In Mortal Combat, 1991; Captured by History, 1997. Fiction: Gods of War, 1985; Occupation, 1987. *Honours:* Best Book on Foreign Affairs Award, Overseas Press Club, 1961, 1970, 1976; Pulitzer Prize for Non-Fiction, 1970; Van Wyck Brooks Award for Non-Fiction, 1970; Hon. doctorates.

TOLSTAYA, Tatyana Nikitichna; Russian writer; b. 3 May 1951, Leningrad (now St Petersburg); d. of Mikhail Lozinsky; great-grandniece of Leo Tolstoy and granddaughter of Alexei Tolstoy; m. Andrey V. Lebedev; two s. *Education:* Univ. of Leningrad. *Career:* Ed. of Eastern Literature Nauka Publishing, Moscow 1987–89; fmr Assoc. Prof. of English, Skidmore Coll., NJ, USA; co-host The School for Scandal TV interview show (Telekanal Kultura). *Publications:* On the Golden Porch (short story) 1983, Sleepwalker in a Fog 1992, Night 1995, Day 1997, Kys 1998, Two of Them 2001, The Slynx 2007. *Honours:* Triumph Prize 2001. *Address:* c/o Telekanal Kultura (Television Channel Culture), 123995 Moscow, ul. M. Nikitskaya 24, Russian Federation; c/o NYRB Classics, New York Review Books, 1755 Broadway, 5th Floor, New York, NY 10019, USA. (office). *Telephone:* (495) 238-22-15 (Moscow). *E-mail:* kultura@tvkultura.ru. *Website:* www.tvkultura.ru.

TOMALIN, Claire, MA, FRSL; British writer; b. 20 June 1933, London; d. of Emile Delavenay and Muriel Emily Herbert; m. 1st Nicholas Osborne Tomalin 1955 (died 1973); two s. three d. (one d. and one s. deceased); m. 2nd Michael Frayn (q.v.) 1993. *Education:* Hitchin Girls' Grammar School, Dartington Hall School, Newnham Coll., Cambridge. *Career:* publr's reader and Ed. 1955–67; Asst Literary Ed. New Statesman 1968–70, Literary Ed. 1974–77; Literary Ed. Sunday Times 1979–86; Vice-Pres. English PEN 1997, Royal Literary Fund 2000; mem. London Library Cttee 1997–2000, Advisory Cttee for the Arts, Humanities and Social Sciences, British Library 1997–2000, Council RSL 1997–2000; Trustee, Nat. Portrait Gallery 1992–2002, Wordsworth Trust 2004. *Exhibitions:* Mrs. Jordan, English Heritage Kenwood 1995, Hyenas in Petticoats: Mary Wollstonecraft and Mary Shelley, Wordsworth Trust and Nat. Portrait Gallery 1997–98. *Play:* The Winter Wife 1991. *Publications:* The Life and Death of Mary Wollstonecraft 1974, Shelley and his World 1980, Katherine Mansfield: A Secret Life 1987, The Invisible Woman 1990, The Winter Wife 1991, Mrs Jordan's Profession 1994, Jane Austen: A Life 1997, Maurice by Mary Shelley (ed.) 1998, Several Strangers: Writing from Three Decades 1999, Samuel Pepys: The Unequalled Self (Whitbread Awards for Book of the Year and Best Biog.) 2002, Thomas Hardy: The Time-Torn Man 2006, Selected Poems of Thomas Hardy 2006. *Honours:* Hon. Fellow, Lucy Cavendish Coll. Cambridge 2003, Newnham Coll. Cambridge 2003; Hon.

DLitt (East Anglia) 2005, (Birmingham) 2005, (Greenwich) 2006, (Cambridge) 2007; Whitbread Prize 1974, James Tait Black Prize 1990, NCR Book Award 1991, Hawthornden Prize 1991, Samuel Pepys Award 2003, Rose Mary Crawshay Prize 2003. *Literary Agent:* c/o David Godwin, 55 Monmouth Street, London, WC2H 9DG, England.

TOMAZOS, Criton Plato, DipArch; British architect, artist, poet and playwright, writer, journalist and critic; *Co-ordinating Director, Theatre for Mankind*; b. 13 April 1940, Larnaca, Cyprus; s. of Plato Tomazos and Thessalia Tomazos. *Education:* The Polytechnic, Regent Street (now Univ. of Westminster), Croydon Coll. of Fine Art and Technology, London Acad. of Film and TV. *Career:* various positions in pvt and public architectural offices 1960–74; co-founder, Co-ordinating Dir Environmental Forum 1970–94; founder, resident playwright, designer, then Chair. Prometheus Theatre Co. 1982–84; Founder-Dir Theatre for Mankind Voluntary Org. 1985–; Ed., journalist, letters and arts page, Parikiaki 1997–: currently Deputy Dir Gen. Int. Biographical Centre, Cambridge; mem. Writers' Guild, Poetry Soc., Writers' Forum, Theatre for Mankind, Theatre Writers' Union (Cttee mem.), New Playwrights' Trust (Man. Cttee mem.), Asscn of Greek Scientists/ Professional People, Acad. Maison Internationale des Intellectuelles 1993–94; Fellow, ABI Bd of Research, Millennium Awards. *Art:* many paintings, 3-D works; one of three artists representing UK in first Int. Arts Biennale of Malta 1991. *Plays:* Rehearsal, Maxim & Minnie, The Shark, Tickets to No-Man's Land, Not Suitable for the National; in Greek: Certificate for an Insignificant Woman; bilingual: libretto for Fedeas (people's opera). *Radio:* five monologues by poet Yiannis Ritsos, LGR (London Greek Radio) co-production. *Film scripts:* The Fraud, Daydreams Burn, Close Shave, Terra Incognita, Eyes Open at Midnight, A Spanish Tragedy. *Publications:* poetry: Lovepoem 1965, Monologue of the Ancient Hero 1970, Relationships 1975, Poems of 1960–61 1976, He Who Left His Fingerprints 1979, Factory Backyard 1980, Diaphanies (Transparencies) (first prize for poetry EDON Int. Youth Festival 1982) 1982, Letter to the Returning Astronaut 1982, The Song of Tefcros (first prize Eden Festival) 1983, Synora Mnemes (Boundaries of Memory) 1987–88, The Visit 1988, First Explorations 1989, Relationships, The Story of Water & Night March 1990, Tora (Now) 1994; prose: The Gospel of Contemporary Slavery (essay) 1977, Eugene Delacroix, the Painter, The Dramatic Work of Angelos Sikelianos, The Meaning of Work in Contemporary Society; contrib. to numerous anthologies, including Our Poems 2004, to magazines and journals. *Honours:* Dr hc (London Inst. of Applied Research), (Acad. des Sciences Universelles), (World Univ., Benson USA); Millennium Award for project Wake Up to Your Environment 2003. *Address:* c/o Theatre for Mankind, POB 671, Enfield, EN3 5DD (office); 2 Park Terrace, Bell Lane, Enfield, Middlesex EN3 5EU, England (home). *Telephone:* (20) 8443-4643. *E-mail:* enform2003@yahoo.co.uk (office).

TOMIOKA, Taeko; Japanese poet, novelist, critic, playwright and screenwriter; b. 1935, Ōsaka. *Education:* Ōsaka Women's Coll. *Career:* poetry debut 1957; turned to fiction 1970; author of novels, short stories, plays, screenplays, essays and criticism; has translated works of Gertrude Stein and Susan Sontag. *Films:* Shinjû: Ten no amijima (Double Suicide) 1969, Himiko 1974, Sakura no Mori no Mankai no Shita 1975, Yari no gonza (Gonza the Spearman) 1986. *Publications:* Oka ni mukatte hito wa narabu (Facing the Hills They Stand) 1971, Shokubutsusai (The Festival of Plants) (Tamura Toshiko Award) 1973, Meido no kazoku (Family in Hell) (Women Writers' Award) 1974, Tōsei bonjin den (Stories of Contemporary People) (Kawabata Yasunari Award) 1976, See You Soon: Poems of Taeko Tomioka 1979, Namiutsu tochi 1983, Taishuron: Taidan 1984, Saikaku no katari (Sakka no hoho) 1987, Hyogen no fukei, Fuji no koromo ni asa no fusuma, Ko iu jidai no shosetsu 1989, Shinkazoku: Jisen tanpenshu 1990, 'Katari' no chikei ('Genzai' to no taiwa) 1990, Towazugatari (Koten no tabi) 1990, Suijo teien (Shirizu 'monogatari no tanjo') 1991, Danryū bungakuron (co-author) (A Study of Male Literature) 1992, Naka Kansuke no koi (Naka Kansuke's Love) 1993, Nobuyoshi Araki: Akt-Tokyo: 1971–1991 (co-author) 1993, Shaku Choku noto 2000. *Address:* c/o Iwanami Shoten Publishers, 2-5-5, Hitotsubashi, Chiyoda-ku, Tokyo 101-8002, Japan (office). *Telephone:* (3) 5210-4000 (office). *Fax:* (3) 5210-4039 (office). *Website:* www.iwanami.co.jp (office).

TOMLINSON, (Alfred) Charles, CBE, BA, MA; British academic, poet and writer; *Professor Emeritus and Senior Research Fellow, University of Bristol*; b. 8 Jan. 1927, Stoke-on-Trent, Staffordshire, England; m. 1948; two d. *Education:* Queens' Coll., Cambridge. *Career:* Lecturer, Univ. of Bristol 1956–68, Reader 1968–82, Prof. of English 1982–92, Prof. Emer. 1992–, Sr Research Fellow 1996–; Visiting Prof., Univ. . of New Mexico, USA 1962–63; O'Connor Prof., Colgate Univ., New York 1967–68, 1989–90; Visiting Fellow of Humanities, Princeton Univ. 1981; Lamont Prof., Union Coll., New York 1987; mem. academic and literary orgs. *Publications:* poetry: Relations and Contraries 1951, The Necklace 1955, Seeing is Believing 1958, A Peopled Landscape 1963, American Scenes 1966, The Poem as Initiation 1968, The Way of a World 1969, Renga 1970, Written on Water 1972, The Way In 1974, The Shaft 1978, Selected Poems 1951–74 1978, The Flood 1981, Airborn: Hijos del aire 1981, Notes from New York 1984, Collected Poems 1985, The Return 1987, Nella pienezza del tempo 1987, Annunciations 1989, The Door in the Wall 1992, Poemas 1992, Gedichte 1994, La insistencia de las cosas 1994, In Italia 1995, Jubilation 1995, Portuguese Pieces 1996, The Fox Gallery 1996, Parole e Acqua 1997, Selected Poems 1955–97 1997, The Vineyard Above the Sea 1999, Luoghi Italiani 2000, Lugares y Relaciones 2003, Skywriting 2003, En la Plenitud del Tiempo 2005, Cracks in the Universe 2006; other: In Black and White 1976, The Oxford Book of Verse in English Translation (ed.) 1980, Some Americans: A Literary Memoir 1981, Poetry and Metamorphosis 1983, Eros Englished: Erotic Poems from the Greek and Latin (ed.) 1991, American Essays: Making it New 2001, Metamorphoses: Poetry and Translation 2003, John Dryden: Poems Selected by Charles Tomlinson 2003; contrib. to books, professional journals and other publs. *Honours:* Hon. Fellow, Queens' Coll., Cambridge 1976–, Royal Holloway Coll., London 1991, Modern Language Asscn 2003; Hon. Foreign Fellow, American Acad. of Arts and Sciences 1998; hon. doctorates; Bess Hokin Prize 1968, Oscar Blumenthal Prize 1960, Inez Boulton Prize 1964, Frank O'Hara Prize 1968, Cheltenham Poetry Prize 1976, Cholmondeley Poetry Award 1979, Wilbur Award for Poetic Achievement 1982, Premio Europeo di Cittadella, Italy 1991, Bennett Award for Poetry 1992, Premio Intenazionale Flaiano 2001, The New Criterion Poetry Prize 2003, Premio Internazionale di Poesia 'Attilio Bertolucci' 2004. *Address:* Department of English, 3–5 Woodland Road, University of Bristol, Bristol, BS8 1TB, England (office). *Telephone:* (117) 928-7787 (office). *Fax:* (117) 928-8860 (office). *Website:* www.bris.ac.uk/english (office).

TOMLINSON, Gerald Arthur, BA; American writer, editor and publisher; b. 24 Jan. 1933, Elmira, NY; m. Mary Alexis Usakowski 1967; two s. *Education:* Marietta Coll., OH, Columbia Law School, New York. *Career:* Assoc. Ed. Business and Professional Books, Prentice Hall 1960–63, School Dept, Harcourt Brace Jovanovich 1963–66; Sr Ed., English Dept, Holt, Rinehart and Winston 1966–69; Exec. Ed., K-12 English, Silver Burdett and Ginn 1969–82; Publisher, Home Run Press 1985–; mem. Authors' Guild, MWA, Soc. for American Baseball Research. *Publications:* On a Field of Black (novel) 1980, School Administrator's Complete Letter Book 1984, 2003, Speaker's Treasury of Sports Anecdotes, Stories and Humor 1990, Encyclopedia of Religious Quotations 1991, The New Jersey Book of Lists (co-author) 1992, Murdered in Jersey 1994, Fatal Tryst 1999, How to do Baseball Research (gen. ed.) 2000, Seven Jersey Murders 2003; contrib. to magazines and journals. *Honours:* Best Detective Stories of the Year 1976, MWA Annual Anthologies. *Address:* 19 Harbor Drive, Lake Hopatcong, NJ 07849, USA. *E-mail:* geraldtomlinson@hotmail.com.

TONG, Raymond, BSc, DipEd; British poet and writer; b. 20 Aug. 1922, Winchester, Hants., England; m. Mariana Apergis 1946. *Education:* Univ. of London. *Career:* Education Officer, Sr Educ. Officer, Nigeria 1949–58, Uganda 1958–61; British Council Admin., S America, India, Middle East, England 1961–82; mem. Poetry Soc. (Life mem.), West Country Writers' Asscn. *Publications:* Today the Sun 1947, Angry Decade 1950, African Helicon (anthology) 1954, Fabled City 1960, A Matter of History 1976, Crossing the Border 1978, Selected Poems 1994, Returning Home 1996, Necessary Words 2006; contrib. to many reviews, quarterlies and journals in England and overseas. *Address:* 1 Beaufort Road, Clifton, Bristol, BS8 2JT, England (home).

TOOMEY, Jeanne Elizabeth, BA; American animal welfare activist and writer; b. 22 Aug. 1921, New York, NY; m. Peter Terranova 1951 (died 1968); one s. one d. *Education:* Hofstra Univ., Fordham Univ. School of Law, Southampton Coll., Monmouth Coll. *Career:* staff, Brooklyn Daily Eagle 1943–52, King Features Syndicate 1953–55, New York Journal-American 1955–61, Associated Press 1963–64, News Tribune, Woodbridge, NJ 1976–86; Ed., Calexico Chronicle, CA 1987–88; Pres. and Dir, Last Post Animal Sanctuary, Falls Village, CT 1991–; mem. Newswomen's Club of New York, New York Press Club, Overseas Press Club, The Silurians, Vivisection Investigation League (pres. and dir), Millennium Guild; Head of 37-acre wildlife preserve and animal retirement home, Falls Village. *Publications:* How to Use Your Dreams to Solve Your Problems 1970, Murder in the Hamptons 1994, Assignment Homicide 1998; contrib. to various publications. *Honours:* New York Women's Press Club Woman of the Year 1960, Snowsheds of Nev. State Press Asscn Southern Pacific Award 1961. *Address:* 95 Belden Street, Falls Village, CT 06031, USA. *Telephone:* (860) 824-0831. *Fax:* (860) 824-5460.

TOPOL, Jáchym; Czech poet and writer; b. 4 Aug. 1962, Prague; s. of Josef Topol; m.; one d. *Career:* prevented from univ. educ. because of father's dissident activities; fmrly worked as stoker, stocker, construction worker, coalman; imprisoned several times for publishing activities; signatory to Charter 77 human rights declaration; wrote lyrics for brother's rock band, Psí Vojáci 1970s–1980s; co-f. of samizdat (clandestinely copied and printed) magazines, Violit 1982, Revolver Revue 1985 (Ed.-in-Chief –1993); took part in Velvet Revolution in Czechoslovakia 1989; wrote, ed. and published Informacní servis newsletter, which became investigative weekly magazine Respekt, reporter 1989–92; published first collection of poetry in samizdat 1988; residency Ledig House, New York (USA) 1995. *Song lyrics:* three albums by Monika Naceva: Monosti tu sou 1994, Nebe je rudý 1996, Mimoid 1998; album: Sestra: Jáchym Topol & Psí Vojáci. *Publications:* I Love You Madly (poems) (Tom Stoppard Prize for Unofficial Literature, Charter 77 Foundation, Stockholm) 1988, The War Will Be On Tuesday (poems) 1993; City Sister Silver (novel) (Egon Hostovský Prize for Czech Book of the Year) 1994, Andel (novella) 1995, Trnová divka (trans., collection of native American myths and legends) 1996; contrib. in English to anthologies and reviews. *Address:* c/o Catbird Press, 16 Windsor Road, North Haven, CT 06473, USA. *E-mail:* info@catbirdpress.com.

TOPOLSKI, Daniel, BA, MA, FRGS; British writer and broadcaster; b. 4 June 1945, London, England; m. Susan Gilbert; one s. two d. *Education:* New Coll.,

Oxford. *Career:* fmr BBC sports commentator, Olympic Games, World Rowing, Boat Race; Churchill Fellow; trustee, Topolski Memoir Ltd; mem. Leander Club, London Rowing Club. *Publications:* Muzungu: One Man's Africa 1976, Travels with my Father: South America 1983, Boat Race: The Oxford Revival 1985, True Blue: The Oxford Mutiny 1988, Henley: The Regatta 1989; contrib. to periodicals, radio and television. *Honours:* Sports Book of the Year 1990, Radio Travel Programme of the Year 1994. *Address:* 69 Randolph Avenue, London, W9 1DW, England. *Fax:* (20) 7266-1884. *E-mail:* dtopo35410@aol.com.

TORON, Steve (see Stebel, Sidney Leo)

TORRANCE, Lee (see Sadgrove, Sidney Henry)

TORRANCE, Very Rev. Thomas Forsyth, MBE, MA, DTheol, DD, DLitt, DSc, FBA, FRSE; British minister of religion and academic; b. 30 Aug. 1913, Chengtu, Szechuan, China; s. of Rev. Thomas Torrance and Annie Elizabeth Torrance (née Sharp); m. Margaret Edith Spear 1946; two s. one d. *Education:* Bellshill Acad., Univs of Edin., Basel and Oxford. *Career:* war service with Church of Scotland Huts and Canteens, Middle East and Italy 1943–45; Prof. of Systematic Theology, Auburn Theol. Seminary, USA 1938–39; Minister, Alyth Barony Parish, Church of Scotland 1940–47, Beechgrove Parish Aberdeen 1947–50; Prof. of Church History, Univ. of Edin. 1950–52, of Christian Dogmatics, also Head of Dept 1952–79; Cross of St Mark, Cross of Aksum, Protopresbyter of Greek Orthodox Church. *Publications:* The Doctrine of Grace in the Apostolic Fathers 1948, Calvin's Doctrine of Man 1949, Royal Priesthood 1955, Kingdom and Church 1956, Conflict and Agreement in the Church (two vols) 1959, 1960, Karl Barth: Introduction to his Early Theology 1962, Theology in Reconstruction 1965, Theological Science 1969, Space, Time and Incarnation 1969, God and Rationality 1971, Theology in Reconciliation 1975, Space, Time and Resurrection 1976, The Ground and Grammar of Theology 1980, The Incarnation (ed.) 1980, Belief in Science and in Christian Life (ed.) 1980, Christian Theology and Scientific Culture 1980, Divine and Contingent Order 1981, Reality and Evangelical Theology 1981, Juridical Law and Physical Law 1982, Transformation and Convergence in the Frame of Knowledge 1984, James Clerk Maxwell. A Dynamical Theory of the Electromagnetic Field (ed.) 1982, Reality and Scientific Theology 1985, The Mediation of Christ 1983, The Christian Frame of Mind 1985, The Trinitarian Faith 1988, The Hermeneutics of John Calvin 1988, Karl Barth, Biblical and Evangelical Theologian 1990, Trinitarian Perspectives 1994, Preaching Christ Today, The Gospel and Scientific Thinking 1994, Divine Meaning, Studies in Patristic Hermeneutics 1995, The Christian Doctrine of God, One Being, Three Persons 1996, Scottish Theology from John Knox to John McLeod Campbell 1996, A Passion for Christ (with J. B. and D. W. Torrance) 1999, The Soul and the Person of the Unborn Child 1999, The Person of Jesus Christ 1999, H. R. Mackintosh, Theologian of the Cross 2000. *Honours:* Hon. DD (Montreal, St Andrews, Edin. 1996); Hon. DTheol (Geneva, Faculté Libre Paris, Oslo, Debrecen 1988); Hon. DSc (Heriot-Watt Univ.) 1983; Collins Prize 1969, Templeton Prize 1978. *Address:* 37 Braid Farm Road, Edinburgh, EH10 6LE, Scotland (home). *Telephone:* (131) 447-3224 (home). *Fax:* (131) 447-3224 (home). *E-mail:* ttorr@globalnet.co.uk (home).

TOSCHES, Nick; American writer; b. 1949, Newark, NJ. *Career:* began writing in small music magazines; worked with Lester Bangs at Creem; has written liner notes for compilation albums by numerous artists, including Jerry Lee Lewis and Carl Perkins; collaborated with Hubert Selby, Jr; Contributing Ed., Vanity Fair. *Recordings:* albums: Blue Eyes and Exit Wounds (with Hubert Selby Jr) 1998, Nick & Homer (with Homer Henderson) 1998. *Publications include:* Country 1977, Hellfire (biog.) 1982, Unsung Heroes of Rock 'N' Roll 1984, Power on Earth 1986, Cut Numbers (novel) 1988, Dino: Living High in the Dirty Business of Dreams (Italian-American Literary Achievement Award for Distinction in Literature 1993) 1992, Trinities (novel) (New York Times Book Review Notable Book of the Year) 1994, Chaldea (poems) 1999, The Devil and Sonny Liston 2000, The Nick Tosches Reader (anthology) 2000, Where Dead Voices Gather 2001, The Last Opium Den 2002, In The Hand of Dante 2002, King of the Jews: The Arnold Rothstein Story 2006; contrib. poems to publications, including Contents, Esquire, GQ, Long Shot, Open City, Smokes Like a Fish. *E-mail:* webmaster@exitwounds.com. *Website:* www.nicktosches.com.

TÓTH, Krisztina; Hungarian poet and translator; b. 1967. *Career:* trans. of contemporary French literature. *Publications:* A beszélgetés fonala (The Thread of Conversation) 1994, Porhó (Snow) 2001, A Londoni mackók (London Teddy Bears) (Best Book of the Year award) 2003; contrib. to TLS, Hungarian Quarterly, crosspathculture.org. *Honours:* Graves Prize 1996, Déry Tibor Prize 1996, József Attila Prize 2000. *Address:* c/o Arc Publications, Nanholme Mill, Shaw Wood Road, Todmorden, Lancs. OL14 6DA, England.

TOURNIER, Michel, LèsL, LenD, DPhil; French writer; b. 19 Dec. 1924, Paris; s. of Alphonse Tournier and Marie-Madeleine (née Fournier) Tournier. *Education:* Saint-Germain-en-Laye and Univs of Paris (Sorbonne) and Tübingen (Germany). *Career:* radio and TV production 1949–54; press attaché, Europe No. 1 1955–58; head of literary services, Editions Plon 1958–68; contrib. to Le Monde, Le Figaro; mem. Acad. Goncourt 1972–. *Publications:* fiction: Vendredi, ou les limbes du Pacifique (trans. as Friday) 1967, Le Roi des Aulnes (trans. as The Ogre) (Acad. Française Grand Prix du Roman) 1970, Vendredi, ou la vie sauvage (trans. as Friday and Robinson: Life on Esperanza Island) 1971, Les Météores (Prix Goncourt) 1975, Le Coq de

bruyère 1978, Pierrot, ou les secrets de la nuit 1979, Gaspard, Melchior et Balthazar (trans. as The Four Wise Men) 1980, Gilles et Jeanne 1983, Le Vagabond immobile 1984, Journal de voyage au Canada 1984, La Goutte d'or (trans. as The Golden Droplet) 1986, Le Médianoche amoureux (trans. as The Midnight Love Feast) 1989, La Couleuvrine 1994, Eléazar, ou la source et le buisson 1996, Telling Tales (contrib. to charity anthology) 2004; non-fiction: Le Vent paraclet (trans. as The Wind Spirit: An Autobiography) 1977, Des clefs et des serrures 1979, Le Vol du vampire 1981, Le Tabor et le Sinaï 1989, Le Crépuscle des masques 1992, Le Miroir des idées 1994, Le Pied de la lettre 1994, Alaia (with Azzedine Alaia and Juan Gatty) 1998, Célebrations 1999. *Honours:* Dr hc (Univ. Coll. London) 1997; Goethe Medal 1993; Officier, Légion d'honneur, Commdr, Ordre nat. du Mérite. *Address:* Le Presbytère, Choisel, 78460 Chevreuse, France. *Telephone:* 1-30-52-05-29.

TOWNLEY, Roderick Carl, AB, PhD; American writer and poet; b. 7 June 1942, NJ; m. Wyatt Townley 1986; one s. one d. *Education:* Bard Coll., Rutgers Univ. *Career:* Prof. of English, Universidad de Concepcion, Chile 1978–79; Nat. Editorial Writer, TV Guide 1980–89; Sr Ed. US magazine 1989–90; Exec. Dir The Writers Place, Kansas City, Mo. 1995–96. *Publications:* poetry: Three Musicians 1978, Final Approach 1986; novels: Minor Gods 1977, The Great Good Thing 2001, Into the Labyrinth 2002, Sky 2004, The Constellation of Sylvie 2006, The Red Thread 2007; non-fiction: The Early Poetry of William Carlos Williams 1975, Night Errands: How Poets Use Dreams 1998; contrib. to newspapers, journals and anthologies. *Honours:* Acad. of American Poets Co-winner 1969, First Prize 1971, Fulbright Professorship, Chile 1978–79, Peregrine Prize in Short Fiction 1998, Kansas Arts Comm. Individual Artist grant 2000, Kansas Gov.'s Arts Award 2003, Thorpe Menn Award 2003. *Literary Agent:* c/o Writers House, 21 West 26 Street, New York, NY 10010, USA. *Telephone:* (212) 685-2405. *Address:* PO Box 13302, Shawnee Mission, KS 66282, USA (office). *E-mail:* rodericktownley@everestkc.net (office). *Website:* rodericktownley.com.

TOWNSEND, Susan (Sue) Lilian, FRSL; British writer; b. 2 April 1946, Leicester; m. (divorced); four c. *Career:* started writing professionally early 1980s; mem. Writers' Guild, PEN. *Plays:* Bazaar and Rummage 1984, Groping for Words 1984, Womberang 1984, The Great Celestial Cow 1985, Ten Tiny Fingers, Nine Tiny Toes 1990, The Secret Diary of Adrian Mole Aged 13¾ 1992, Dayroom, The Ghost of Daniel Lambert, Captain Christmas and the Evil Adults, Are You Sitting Comfortably?. *Television:* Think of England (writer, narrator and presenter) 1991. *Publications:* The Secret Diary of Adrian Mole Aged 13¾ 1982, The Growing Pains of Adrian Mole 1984, Rebuilding Coventry 1988, Mr Bevan's Dream 1989, True Confessions of Adrian Albert Mole, Margaret Hilda Roberts and Susan Lilian Townsend 1989, Adrian Mole from Minor to Major 1991, The Queen and I 1992, Adrian Mole: The Wilderness Years 1993, Adrian Mole, The Lost Years 1994, Ghost Children 1997, Adrian Mole, The Cappuccino Years 1999, The Public Confessions of a Middle-Aged Woman Aged 55¾ 2001, Number 10 2002, Adrian Mole and the Weapons of Mass Destruction 2004, Queen Camilla 2006; contribs to London Times, New Statesman, Observer, Sainsbury's Magazine. *Honours:* Hon. MA (Leicester) 1991. *Literary Agent:* The Sale Agency, 11 Jubilee Place, London, SW3 3TD; Curtis Brown Group Ltd, 28–29 Haymarket, London, SW1Y 4SP, England (office). *Address:* c/o Reed Books, Michelin House, 81 Fulham Road, London, SW3 6RB, England (office). *E-mail:* kate50@fsmail.net.

TOWNSEND, Thomas (Tom) L.; American novelist; b. 1 Jan. 1944, Waukegan, IL; m. Janet L. Simpson 1965. *Education:* Arkansas Military Acad. *Publications:* Texas Treasure Coast, 1978; Where the Pirates Are, 1985; Trader Wooly, 1987; Trader Wooly and the Terrorists, 1988; Queen of the Wind, 1989; Battle of Galveston, 1990; Trader Wooly and the Ghost in the Colonel's Jeep, 1991; The Holligans, 1991; Bubba's Truck, 1992; The Ghost Flyers, 1993; A Fair Wind to Glory, 1994. *Honours:* Friend of American Writers Award, 1986; Texas Blue Bonnet Master List, 1986; Silver Award, Best Children's Video, Houston International Film Festival, 1986.

TOYNBEE, Polly; British journalist and broadcaster; *President, Social Policy Association;* b. 27 Dec. 1946, d. of the late Philip Toynbee and of Anne Powell; m. Peter Jenkins 1970 (died 1992); three d. one s. *Education:* Badminton School, Bristol, Holland Park Comprehensive, London and St Anne's Coll., Oxford. *Career:* feature writer on The Observer newspaper (UK) 1968–70, 1971–77; Ed. The Washington Monthly, USA 1970–71; columnist on The Guardian newspaper 1977–88, 1998–; SDP Parl. Cand. for Lewisham E 1983; Social Affairs Ed. BBC 1989–95; Assoc. Ed., columnist on The Independent newspaper 1995–98; Gov. LSE 1988–99; mem. Dept of Health Advisory Cttee on the Ethics of Xenotransplantation 1996, Nat. Screening Cttee 1996–; Pres. Social Policy Asscn 2005–; Chair. Brighton Dome and Festival 2005–; Visiting Fellow, Nuffield Coll., Oxford 2005–. *Publications:* Leftovers 1966, A Working Life 1970, Lost Children 1985, Hospital 1987, The Way We Live Now 1987, Did Things Get Better? (with David Walker) 2001, Hard Work: Life in Low Pay Britain 2003, Better or Worse? Has Labour Delivered? (with David Walker) 2005. *Honours:* Catherine Pakenham Award 1976, British Press Awards 1977, 1982, Columnist of the Year 1986, BBC What the Papers Say Award 1996, Magazine Writer of the Year, PPA 1996, George Orwell Prize 1997. *Address:* The Guardian, 119 Farringdon Road, London, EC1R 3ER (office). *Telephone:* (20) 7278-2332 (office); (20) 7622-6492 (home). *E-mail:* p.toynbee@guardian.co.uk (office). *Website:* www.guardian.co.uk (office).

TRABOULSI, Yasmina; Lebanese writer; b. 1975. *Publication:* Les enfants de la Place (novel, title in trans.) 2003. *Address:* c/o Editions Mercure de France, 26 rue de Condé, 75006 Paris, France (office).

TRACY, James D., BA, MA, PhD; American academic, writer and editor; b. 14 Feb. 1938, St Louis, MO; m. Nancy Ann McBride 1968, two s. one d. *Education:* St Louis University, Johns Hopkins University, University of Notre Dame, Princeton University. *Career:* Instructor in History, University of Michigan, 1964–66; Assoc. Prof. of History, 1966–77, Prof. of History, 1977–, University of Minnesota; Man. Ed., Journal of Early Modern History, 1995–. *Publications:* Erasmus: The Growth of a Mind, 1972; Early Modern European History, 1500–1715 (ed.), 1976; The Politics of Erasmus: A Pacifist Intellectual and His Political Milieu, 1979; True Ocean Found: Paludanus's Letters on Dutch Voyages to the Kara Sea, 1595–1596, 1980; A Financial Revolution in the Habsburg Netherlands: Renten and Renteniers in the Country of Holland, 1515–1565, 1985; Holland Under Habsburg Rule, 1506–1566: The Formation of a Body Politic, 1990; The Rise of Merchant Empires: Long-Distance Trade in the Early Modern World, 1350–1750 (ed.), 1990; The Political Economy of Merchant Empires: State Power and World Trade, 1350–1750 (ed.), 1991; Handbook of European History, 1400–1600: Late Middle Ages, Renaissance, and Reformation (ed. with Thomas A. Brady and Heiko A. Oberman), 1996; Erasmus of the Low Countries, 1996; Europe's Reformations, 1450–1650, 1999; City Wall: The Urban Enceinte in Global Perspective (ed.), 2000. Contributions: scholarly books and learned journals. *E-mail:* tracy001@umn.edu.

TRANSTRÖMER, Tomas Gösta; Swedish poet and psychologist; b. 15 April 1931, Stockholm; m. Monica Blach 1958; two d. *Education:* University of Stockholm. *Career:* mem. Swedish Writers Union. *Publications:* In English: Twenty Poems, 1970; Night Vision, 1971; Windows and Stones: Selected Poems, 1972; Elegy: Some October Notes, 1973; Citoyens, 1974; Baltics, 1975; Truth Barriers: Poems by Tomas Transtromer, 1980; How the Late Autumn Night Novel Begins, 1980; Tomas Transtromer: Selected Poems, 1982; The Wild Marketplace, 1985; Selected Poems of Tomas Transtromer, 1954–1986, 1987; Collected Poems, 1987; For the Living and the Dead, 1995; The Sorrow Gondola, 1996. Contributions: periodicals. *Honours:* Aftonbladets Literary Prize, 1958; Bellman Prize, 1966; Swedish Award, International Poetry Forum, 1971; Oevralids Prize, 1975; Boklotteriets Prize, 1981; Petrarca Prize, 1981; Nordic Council Literary Prize, 1990.

TRAPIDO, Barbara Louise, DipEd, BA; British writer; b. 5 Nov. 1941, Cape Town, South Africa; m. Stanley Trapido 1963; one s. one d. *Education:* Univ. of Natal, Durban, S Africa, Univ. of London. *Career:* high school English teacher, London 1964–68, Lecturer in English Literature, Univ. of Durham 1968–70. *Publications:* Brother of the More Famous Jack 1982, Noah's Ark 1985, Temples of Delight 1990, Juggling 1994, The Travelling Horn Player 1998, Frankie and Stankie 2003; contrib. to Spectator, Sunday Telegraph, Sunday Times. *Honours:* Whitbread Award 1982. *Literary Agent:* c/o Victoria Hobbs, AM Heath and Co., 6 Warwick Court, London, WC1R 5DJ, England. *Address:* c/o Bloomsbury Books, 38 Soho Square, London, W1D 3HB, England (office). *Website:* www.bloomsbury.com (office).

TRAVIS, Aaron (see Saylor, Steven Warren)

TRAWICK, Leonard Moses, BA, MA, PhD; American academic, poet, writer and editor; b. 4 July 1933, Decatur, AL; m. Kerstin Ekfelt 1960, one s. one d. *Education:* University of the South, Sewanee, TN, University of Chicago, Harvard University. *Career:* Instructor to Asst Prof. of English, Columbia University, 1961–69; Assoc. Prof., 1969–72, Prof. of English, 1972–98, Prof. Emeritus, 1998–, Principal Ed., 1971–98, and Dir, 1990–92, Poetry Center, Cleveland State University; Founding Ed., 1980, Co-Ed., 1983–92, The Gamut journal. *Publications:* Poetry: Beast Forms, 1971; Severed Parts, 1981; Beastmorfs, 1994. Opera Librettos: Spinoza, by Julius Drossin, 1982; The Enchanted Garden, by Klaus G. Roy, 1983; Mary Stuart: A Queen Betrayed, by Bain Murray, 1991. Other: Backgrounds of Romanticism: English Philosophical Prose of the Eighteenth Century, 1967; World, Self, Poem (ed.), 1990; German Literature of the Romantic Era and the Age of Goethe (co-ed. and principal trans.), 1993. Contributions: scholarly books and journals, and to anthologies and magazines. *Honours:* Fulbright Scholarship, University of Dijon, 1956–57; Individual Artist Award, Ohio Arts Council, 1980; Award for Excellence in the Media, Northern Ohio Live, 1990; Co-Recipient, James P. Barry Ohioana Award for Editorial Excellence, 1991; Ohioana Poetry Award for Lifetime Achievement in Poetry, 1994.

TREANOR, Oliver, BA, PGCE, DipPhil, STB, STL, STD; Northern Irish writer, theologian, academic and priest; b. 1 May 1949, Warrenpoint. *Education:* Queen's University, Belfast, Pontifical Università Gregoriana, Rome, Italy. *Career:* ordained Roman Catholic Priest; Lecturer, Systematic Theology, Pontifical University, Maynooth, Ireland. *Publications:* Mother of the Redeemer, Mother of the Redeemed, 1988; Seven Bells to Bethlehem: The O Antiphons, 1995; This Is My Beloved Son: Aspects of The Passion, 1997; The God Who Loved Stories, 1999. Contributions: Priests and People, Durham, England; Osservatore Romano, Vatican City; Religious Life Review, Dublin; International Christian Digest, USA; The Furrow, Maynooth; Bible Alive, Stoke-on-Trent. *Address:* Maynooth College, Maynooth, Co. Kildare, Ireland. *Telephone:* (1) 7083600 (office).

TREGLOWN, Jeremy Dickinson, BLitt, MA, PhD, FRSL; British academic, writer and journalist; *Professor of English, University of Warwick;* b. 24 May 1946, Anglesey, N Wales; s. of late Rev. G. L. Treglown and of Beryl Treglown; m. 1st Rona Bower 1970 (divorced 1982); one s. two d.; m. 2nd Holly Eley (née Urquhart) 1984. *Education:* Bristol Grammar School, St Peter's Coll., Oxford. *Career:* Lecturer in English Literature, Lincoln Coll., Oxford 1973–76, Univ. Coll., London 1976–79; Asst Ed. The Times Literary Supplement 1979–81, Ed. 1982–90; Prof. of English, Univ. of Warwick 1993– (Chair. Dept of English and Comparative Literary Studies 1995–98); Chair. of Judges, Booker Prize 1991, Whitbread Book of the Year Award 1998; Co-ed. Liber, a European Review of Books 1989; Contributing Ed., Grand Street magazine, New York 1991–98; Visiting Fellow, All Souls Coll., Oxford 1986; Fellow Huntington Library 1988; Mellon Visiting Assoc., Calif. Inst. of Tech. 1988; Ferris Visiting Prof., Princeton Univ. 1992; Jackson Brothers Fellow, Beinecke Library, Yale Univ. 1999; Leverhulme Research Fellow 2001–03; Margaret and Herman Sokol Fellow, Cullman Center for Scholars and Writers, New York Public Library 2002–03. *Publications:* The Letters of John Wilmot, Earl of Rochester (ed.) 1980, Spirit of Wit: Reconsiderations of Rochester (ed.) 1982, Roald Dahl: A Biography 1994, Grub Street and the Ivory Tower: Literary Journalism, and Literary Scholarship from Fielding to the Internet (ed. with Bridget Bennett) 1998, Romancing: The Life and Work of Henry Green 2000, VS Pritchett: a Working Life 2004; contrib. introductions to recent edns of R. L. Stevenson's In the South Seas, Robert Louis Stevenson's The Lantern Bearers, the complete novels of Henry Green; contrib. various articles on poetry, drama and literary history. *Honours:* Hon. Research Fellow, Univ. Coll. London 1991–. *Address:* Gardens Cottage, Ditchley Park, Enstone, Oxfordshire, OX7 4EP; English and Comparative Literary Studies, Room H526, University of Warwick, Coventry, CV4 7AL, England (office). *Telephone:* (24) 7652-3323 (office). *Fax:* (24) 7652-4750 (office). *E-mail:* Jeremy.Treglown@warwick.ac.uk (office). *Website:* www2.warwick.ac.uk/fac/arts/english/staff/profjtreglown (office).

TREHEARNE, Elizabeth (see Maxwell, Patricia Anne)

TREISMAN, Deborah; British; *Fiction Editor, The New Yorker;* b. Oxford; m. Kenny Cummings. *Education:* Univ. of Berkeley, USA. *Career:* Fiction Ed., The New Yorker 2003–. *Literary Agent:* The Wylie Agency, 250 W 57th Street, New York, NY 10107, USA. *E-mail:* mail@wylieagency.com. *Website:* www.wylieagency.com.

TRELFORD, Donald Gilchrist, MA, FRSA; British journalist; b. 9 Nov. 1937, Coventry; s. of T. S. Trelford and Doris Gilchrist; m. 1st Janice Ingram 1963 (divorced 1978); two s. one d.; m. 2nd Katherine Louise Mark 1978 (divorced 1998); one d.; m. 3rd Claire Elizabeth Bishop 2001. *Education:* Bablake School, Coventry, Selwyn Coll., Cambridge. *Career:* pilot officer, RAF 1956–58; worked on newspapers in Coventry and Sheffield 1961–63; Ed. Times of Malawi and corresp. in Africa, The Times, Observer, BBC 1963–66; joined Observer as Deputy News Ed. 1966, Asst Man. Ed. 1968, Deputy Ed. 1969–75, Dir and Ed. 1975–93, CEO 1992–93; Dir Optomen Television 1988–97, Observer Films 1989–93, Cen. Observer TV 1990–93; Dir, Prof. Dept of Journalism Studies, Sheffield Univ. 1994–2000, Visiting Prof. 2001–; Chair. Soc. of Gentlemen, Lovers of Musick 1996–2002, London Press Club 2002–; mem. British Exec. Cttee, Int. Press Inst. 1976–, Asscn of British Eds 1984–, Guild of British Newspaper Eds 1985– (mem. Parl. and Legal Cttee 1987–91); Vice Pres. British Sports Trust 1988–2002; Ind. Assessor BBC TV Regional News 1997; mem. Council, Media Soc. 1981–2003 (Pres. 1999–2002), Judging Panel, British Press Awards 1981– (Chair. 2003–05), Scottish Press Awards 1985, Olivier Awards Cttee, SWET 1984–93, Defence, Press and Broadcasting Cttee 1986–93, Cttee, MCC 1988–91, Competition Comm.'s Newspaper Panel 1999–, Council Advertising Standards Authority 2002–; Vice-Pres. Newspaper Press Fund 1992– (Chair. Appeals Cttee 1991), Acting Ed. The Oldie 1994; Judge, Whitbread Literary Awards 1992, George Orwell Prize 1998; sports columnist Daily Telegraph 1993–; Dir St Cecilia Int. Festival of Music 1995–2002. *Radio:* presenter, LBC Breakfast News 1994; regular panellist, BBC Radio Five Live. *Television:* presenter sports and current affairs series, Channel 4 and BBC 2. *Publications:* Siege 1980, Snookered 1986, Child of Change (with Garry Kasparov) 1987, Saturday's Boys 1990, Fine Glances 1990; (contrib.) County Champions 1982, The Queen Observed 1986, Len Hutton Remembered 1992, World Chess Championships (with Daniel King) 1993, W. G. Grace 1998; Ed.: Sunday Best 1981, 1982, 1983, The Observer at 200 1992; contrib. to Animal Passions 1994. *Honours:* Freeman City of London 1988; Hon. DLitt (Sheffield); Granada Newspaper of the Year Award 1983, 1993; commended, Int. Ed. of the Year (World Press Review) 1984. *Address:* Flat 3, 6 River Terrace, Henley-on-Thames, RG9 1BG, England. *Telephone:* (7850) 131742 (mobile). *E-mail:* donaldtrelford@yahoo.co.uk (home).

TREMAIN, Rose, CBE, BA, FRSL; British writer; b. (Rosemary Jane Thomson), 2 Aug. 1943, London; d. of the late Keith Thomson and Viola Mabel Thomson; m. 1st Jon Tremain 1971; one d.; m. 2nd Jonathan Dudley 1982 (dissolved 1990); pnr Richard Holmes. *Education:* Sorbonne, Paris and Univ. of East Anglia. *Career:* novelist and playwright 1971–; part-time tutor Univ. of East Anglia 1988–95; mem. judging panel, Booker Prize 1988, 2000. *Plays for radio include:* Temporary Shelter 1985, Who Was Emily Davison? 1996, The End of Love 1999, One Night in Winter 2001. *Television:* A Room for the Winter 1979, Daylight Robbery 1982. *Publications:* fiction: Sadler's Birthday 1976, Letter to Sister Benedicta 1978, The Cupboard 1981, The Swimming Pool Season 1984, Restoration (Sunday Express Book of the Year Award) 1989, Sacred Country (James Tait Black Memorial Prize 1993, Prix Fémina Etranger 1994) 1992, The Way I Found Her 1997, Music and Silence (Whitbread Novel of the Year) 1999, The Colour 2003, The Road Home 2007;

for children: Journey to the Volcano 1985; short story collections: The Colonel's Daughter (Dylan Thomas Short Story Prize 1984) 1982, The Garden of the Villa Mollini 1988, Evangelista's Fan 1994, Collected Short Stories 1996, The Darkness of Wallis Simpson and Other Stories 2005; non-fiction: The Fight for Freedom for Women 1971, Stalin: An Illustrated Biography 1974. *Honours:* Hon. DLitt (East Anglia) 2001, (Essex) 2005; Univ. of Essex Fellowship 1979–80; one of Granta's Best Young British Novelists 1983, Giles Cooper Award 1985, Angel Literary Award 1986, Sony Award 1996. *Address:* 2 High House, South Avenue, Thorpe St Andrew, Norwich, NR7 0EZ, England (home). *Telephone:* (1603) 439682 (home). *Fax:* (1603) 434234 (home).

TREMAYNE, Peter (see Ellis, Peter Berresford)

TREMBLAY, Gail Elizabeth, BA, MFA; American poet, artist and teacher; b. 15 Dec. 1945, Buffalo, NY. *Education:* University of New Hampshire, University of Oregon. *Career:* Lecturer, Keene State College, NH; Asst Prof., University of Nebraska; Faculty, Evergreen State College, Olympia, Washington; mem. Indian Youth of America, pres.; International Asscn of Art, UNESCO, US National Committee board mem.; Native American Writers Circle of the Americas; Woman's Caucus for Art, board mem., pres. *Publications:* Night Gives Woman the Word, 1979; Talking to the Grandfathers, 1980; Indian Singing in 20th Century America, 1990. Contributions: reviews, quarterlies and journals. *Honours:* Alfred E. Richards Poetry Prize 1967.

TREMBLAY, Michel; Canadian writer; b. 25 June 1942, Montréal. *Education:* Graphic Arts Inst. of Québec. *Career:* worked as linotypist 1963–66. *Film scripts include:* Françoise Durocher, Waitress 1972, Il était une fois dans l'Est 1973, Parlez-nous d'amour 1976, Le Soleil se lève en retard 1977. *Plays include:* Les Belles sœurs 1968, En pièces detachées 1969, La Duchesse de Langeais 1969, Les Paons 1971, Hosanna 1973, Bonjour Là, bonjour 1974, Ste Carmen de la Main 1976, Damnée Manon, Sacrée Sandra 1977, L'Impromptu d'outremont 1980, Les Grandes vacances 1981, Les Anciennes odeurs 1981, Albertine en cinq temps 1984, Le Vrai monde? 1987, La Maison suspendue 1990, Nelligan (opera libretto, Opéra de Montréal) 1990, Marcel poursuivi par les chiens 1992, Messe solennelle pour une pleine lune d'été 1996, Encore une fois, si vous permettez 1998, L'État des lieux 2002, Le Passé antérieur 2003. *Radio plays include:* Le Cœur découvert 1986, Le Grand Jour 1988, Six Heures au plus tard 1988. *Television:* Le Cœur découvert 2000. *Publications:* Contes pour buveurs attardés 1966, La Cité dans l'oeuf 1969, C't'à ton tour, Laura Cadieux 1973, La Grosse femme d'à côté est enceinte 1973, Thérèse et Pierrette à l'école des Saints-Anges 1980, La Duchesse et le roturier 1982, Des Nouvelles d'Edouard 1984, Le Cœur découvert 1986, Le Premier quartier de la lune 1989, Les Vues animées 1991, Douze coups de théâtre 1992, Le Cœur éclaté 1995, Un Ange cornu avec des ailes de tôle 1996, L'Homme qui entendait siffler une bouilloire 2001, Bonbons assortis 2002, Le Cahier noir 2003, Le Cahier rouge 2004. *Honours:* Dr hc (Concordia, McGill, Stirling, Windsor); first prize for young writers sponsored by CBC (for play Le Train, written 1959) 1964, Gov.-Gen.'s Performing Arts Award 1999; Officier, Ordre des Arts et des Lettres, France. *Literary Agent:* Agence Goodwin, 839 Sherbrooke est, Suite 200, Montréal, QC H2L 1K6, Canada. *Telephone:* (514) 598-5252 (office). *Fax:* (514) 598-1878 (office). *E-mail:* artistes@goodwin.agent.ca (office). *Website:* www.agencegoodwin.com (office).

TREMLETT, George William, OBE; British author, journalist and bookseller; b. 5 Sept. 1939, England; m. Jane Mitchell 1971, three s. *Career:* mem. BBC Community Programme Unit, advisory panel, 1985–. *Publications:* 17 biographies of rock musicians 1974–77; Living Cities, 1979; Caitlin (with Mrs Caitlin Thomas), 1986; Clubmen, 1987; Homeless, Story of St Mungo's, 1989; Little Legs (with Roy Smith), 1989; Rock Gold, 1990; Dylan Thomas: Book: In the Mercy of His Means, 1991; Gadaffi: The Desert Mystic, 1993; David Bowie, 1994; The Death of Dylan Thomas (with James R. B. Nashold), 1997. Screenplay: The Map of Love, 1998.

TRENHAILE, John Stevens, BA, MA; British writer; b. 29 April 1949, Hertford, England. *Education:* Magdalen Coll., Oxford. *Career:* Ed. Taipei Review, Taiwan 1995–2001. *Publications:* Kyril 1981, A View from the Square 1983, Nocturne for the General 1985, The Mahjong Spies 1986, The Gates of Exquisite View 1987, The Scroll of Benevolence 1988, Kyrsalis 1989, Acts of Betrayal 1990, Blood Rules 1991, The Tiger of Desire 1992, A Means to Evil 1993, Against All Reason 1994. *Literary Agent:* Blake Friedman Literary Agents, Arlington Road, London, NW1 7HP, England.

TRETYAKOV, Vitaly Toviyevich; Russian journalist; b. 2 Jan. 1953, Moscow; m.; one s. *Education:* Moscow State Univ. *Career:* jr ed. to Ed. Press Agency Novosti (APN) 1976–88; reviewer, political reviewer, Deputy Ed.-in-Chief Moskovskiye Novosti (weekly) 1988–90; f. Nesavisimaya Gazeta (newspaper) 1990, Ed.-in-Chief 1990–2000; Dir-Gen. Indpendent Publishing Group 2001–; mem. Exec. Bd Council on Foreign and Defence Policy. *Publications include:* Philanthropy in Soviet Society 1989, Gorbachev, Ligachev, Yeltsin: Political Portraits on the Perestroika Background 1990, Titus of Sovietologists: Their Struggle for Power: Essays on Idiotism of Russian Policy 1996; numerous articles on political problems. *Address:* Independent Publishing Group, Moscow, Russia (office). *E-mail:* wt1t@narod.ru (office).

TREVELYAN, (Walter) Raleigh, FRSL; British writer; b. 6 July 1923, Port Blair, Andaman Islands; s. of Col W. R. F. Trevelyan and Olive Trevelyan (née Frost). *Education:* Winchester School. *Career:* publisher 1948–88; mem.

Anglo-Italian Soc. for the Protection of Animals (pres.), PEN (vice-pres.). *Publications:* The Fortress, 1956; A Hermit Disclosed, 1960; Italian Short Stories: Penguin Parallel Texts (ed.), 1965; The Big Tomato, 1966; Princes Under the Volcano, 1972; The Shadow of Vesuvius, 1976; A Pre-Raphaelite Circle, 1978; Rome '44, 1982; Shades of the Alhambra, 1984; The Golden Oriole, 1987; La Storia dei Whitaker, 1989; Grand Dukes and Diamonds: The Wernhers of Luton Hoo, 1991; A Clear Premonition, 1995; The Companion Guide to Sicily, 1996; Sir Walter Raleigh, 2002. Contributions: newspapers and journals. *Honours:* John Florio Prize for Trans. 1967. *Literary Agent:* A. M. Heath & Co Ltd, 79 St Martin's Lane, London WC2N 4RE, England. *Address:* 18 Hertford Street, London, W1J 7RT; St Cadix, St Veep, Lostwithiel, Cornwall, PL22 0PB, England. *Telephone:* (20) 7629-5879 (home). *Fax:* (20) 7629-5879 (home).

TREVOR, William, CLit, BA; Irish writer; b. 24 May 1928, Mitchelstown, Co. Cork; s. of James William Cox and Gertrude Cox; m. Jane Ryan 1952; two s. *Education:* St Columba's Coll., Dublin, Trinity Coll., Dublin. *Career:* mem. Irish Acad. of Letters. *Publications:* The Old Boys 1964, The Boarding House 1965, The Love Department 1966, The Day We Got Drunk on Cake 1967, Mrs Eckdorf in O'Neill's Hotel 1968, Miss Gomez and the Brethren 1969, The Ballroom of Romance 1970, Elizabeth Alone 1972, Angels at the Ritz 1973, The Children of Dynmouth 1977, Lovers of Their Time 1979, Other People's Worlds 1980, Beyond the Pale 1981, Fools of Fortune 1983, A Writer's Ireland: Landscape in Literature 1984, The News from Ireland 1986, Nights at the Alexandra 1987, The Silence in the Garden 1988, Family Sins and Other Stories 1989, The Oxford Book of Irish Short Stories (ed.) 1989, Two Lives 1991, William Trevor: The Collected Stories 1992, Juliet's Story 1992, Excursions in the Real World (essays) 1993, Felicia's Journey 1994, Ireland: Selected Stories 1995, After Rain 1996, Cocktails at Doney's and Other Stories 1996, Death in Summer 1998, The Hill Bachelors 2000, The Story of Lucy Gault 2002, A Bit on the Side (short stories) 2004, Cheating at Canasta 2007. *Honours:* Hawthornden Prize 1965, Royal Soc. of Literature Prize 1978, Whitbread Prize for Fiction 1978, Allied Irish Banks Award for Services to Literature 1978, Whitbread Prize for Fiction 1983, Whitbread Book of the Year 1994; Sunday Express Book of the Year Award 1994, David Cohen British Literature Prize 1999, PEN Prize for Short Stories 2001, Irish Times Prize for Irish Fiction 2001; Hon. DLitt (Exeter) 1984, (Dublin) 1986, (Queen's Univ., Belfast) 1989, (Nat. Univ. Cork) 1990; Hon. KBE 2002. *Literary Agent:* PFD, 34–43 Russell Street, London, WC2B 5HA, England.

TREWIN, Ion; British editor; *Chairman, Cheltenham Literary Festival*. *Career:* Literary Ed., The Times 1972–79; Editorial Dir, Hodder & Stoughton; Ed.-in-Chief, Weidenfeld & Nicolson –2006; London Ed., Publisher Weekly (USA); Ed., Drama Magazine; Chair. Booker Prize judging panel 1974, mem. Advisory Cttee 1989; Chair. Cheltenham Booker Prize, Cheltenham Literary Festival 1996–; Deputy Administrator of Man Booker Prize 2004–06, Administrator 2006–. *Publications:* Journalism 1975, Norfolk Cottage 1977, Diaries: Into Politics, by Alan Clark (ed.) 2000, The Last Diaries: In and Out of the Wilderness, by Alan Clark (ed.) 2002. *Address:* c/o Weidenfeld and Nicolson, 5 Upper St Martin's Lane, London, WC2H 9EA, England.

TRILLARD, Marc; French journalist and writer; b. 1955, Baden-Baden, Germany. *Education:* Conservatoire régional d'art dramatique, Toulouse. *Career:* freelance journalist 1987–94; writer for radio, TV and stage; founder and Dir Salon des littératures francophones, Balma. *Publications:* Un exil 1988, Tête de cheval 1992, Cabotage: à l'écoute du chant des îles Cap-Vert 1994, Eldorado 51 (Prix Interallié) 1994, Coup de lame (Prix Louis Guilloux) 1997, Avène: au coeur du haut pays d'Oc (with Alain Aigoin) 1997, Journal cochinchinois: de Saïgon à Camau 1997, Madagascar 1999, Cuba, en attendant l'année prochaine 1999, Si j'avais quatre dromadaires 2000, Campagne dernière 2001, Entre Fosses et Cages 2001, Le Maître et la mort 2003. *Address:* c/o Editions Phébus, 12 rue Grégoire de Tours, 75006 Paris, France.

TRILLIN, Calvin Marshall, BA; American journalist and writer; b. 5 Dec. 1935, Kansas City, MO; s. of Abe Trillin and Edyth Trillin; m. Alice Stewart 1965; two d. *Education:* Yale Univ. *Career:* fmrly served in the army; reporter, later writer, Time magazine 1960–63; staff writer, The New Yorker 1963–, including 'US Journal' series 1967–82, 'American Chronicles' series 1984–; columnist, The Nation 1978–, now contributing weekly comic verse; syndicated columnist with King Features Syndicate 1986–, including 'Uncivil Liberties' series. *Shows:* Calvin Trillin's Uncle Sam (American Place Theatre, New York) 1988, Calvin Trillin's Words, No Music (American Place Theatre, New York) 1990. *Publications:* An Education in Georgia: Charlayne Hunter, Hamilton Holmes and the Integration of the University of Georgia 1964, Barnett Frummer is an Unbloomed Flower and Other Adventures of Barnett Frummer, Rosalie Mondle, Roland Magruder and Their Friends 1969, US Journal 1971, American Fried: Adventures of a Happy Eater 1974, Runestruck (novel) 1977, Alice, Let's Eat: Further Adventures of a Happy Eater 1978, Floater (novel) 1980, Uncivil Liberties (collected columns) 1982, Third Helpings 1983, Killings 1984, With All Disrespect: More Uncivil Liberties (collected columns) 1985, If You Can't Say Something Nice (collected columns) 1987, Travels with Alice 1989, Enough's Enough and Other Rules of Life (collected columns) 1990, American Stories (non-fiction) 1991, Remembering Denny 1993, Deadline Poet: My Life as a Doggerelist (poems from The Nation) 1994, Too Soon to Tell 1995, Messages from Father 1996, Family Man 1998, Tepper's Not Going Out (novel) 2002, Obliviously on he Sails: The Bush Administration in Rhyme 2004, About Alice 2007. *Honours:* Dr hc (Beloit

Coll.), (Albertus Magnus Coll.); Books-Across-the-Sea Ambassador of Honor Citation, English-Speaking Union 1985. *Address:* c/o The Nation, 33 Irving Place, New York, NY 10003, USA.

TRIVERS, Robert L., BA, PhD; American sociobiologist; *Professor of Anthropology and Biological Sciences, Rutgers University*; b. 19 Feb. 1943, Washington, DC; s. of Howard Trivers and Mildred Trivers; m. 1st Lorna Staples 1974 (divorced 1988); three d. one s.; m. 2nd Debra Dixon 1997 (divorced 2004); one d. *Education:* Phillips Acad., Andover and Harvard Univ. *Career:* Instructor in Anthropology, Harvard Univ. 1971–72, Asst Prof. in Biology 1973–75, Assoc. Prof. of Biology 1975–78; Prof. of Biology, Univ. of California, Santa Cruz 1978–94; Prof. of Anthropology and Biological Sciences, Rutgers Univ. 1994–; Visiting Prof. of Psychology, Harvard Univ. 2005. *Publications:* Social Evolution 1985, Natural Selection and Social Theory: Selected Papers of Robert Trivers 2002, Genes in Conflict: The Biology of Selfish Genetic Elements (with Austin Burt) 2006; contrib. numerous papers to journals. *Address:* Department of Anthropology, Rutgers University, New Brunswick, NJ 08901-1414, USA (office). *E-mail:* trivers@rci .rutgers.edu (office). *Website:* anthro.rutgers.edu/faculty/trivers.shtml (office).

TROGDON, William Lewis (see Heat-Moon, William Least)

TROLLOPE, Joanna, (Caroline Harvey), OBE, MA, DL; British writer; b. 9 Dec. 1943, England; d. of Arthur Trollope and Rosemary Hodson; m. 1st David Potter 1966; two d.; m. 2nd Ian Curteis 1985 (divorced 2001); two step-s. *Education:* Reigate Co. School and St Hugh's Coll. Oxford. *Career:* Information and Research Dept Foreign Office 1965–67; various teaching posts, including Farnham Girl's Grammar School, Daneshill School 1967–79; Chair. Advisory Cttee on Nat. Reading Initiative, Dept of Nat. Heritage 1996–97; mem. Advisory Cttee on Nat. Year of Reading, Dept of Educ. 1998, Council of Soc. of Authors 1997–, Campaign Bd St Hugh's Coll., Oxford; Vice-Pres. Trollope Soc., West Country Writers' Asscn; Trustee Joanna Trollope Charitable Trust 1995–; Patron County of Glos. Community Foundation 1994–; apptd Deputy Lieutenant for Co. of Gloucestershire 2002. *Publications:* as Caroline Harvey: Eliza Stanhope 1978, Parson Harding's Daughter (aka Mistaken Virtues) 1979, Leaves from the Valley 1980, The City of Gems 1981, The Steps of the Sun 1983, The Taverners' Place 1986, Legacy of Love 1992, A Second Legacy 1993, A Castle in Italy 1993, The Brass Dolphin 1997; as Joanna Trollope: Britannia's Daughters: A Study of Women in the British Empire 1983, The Choir 1988, A Village Affair 1989, A Passionate Man 1990, The Rector's Wife 1991, The Men and the Girls 1992, A Spanish Lover 1992, The Best of Friends 1992, The Country Habit: An Anthology (ed.) 1993, Next of Kin 1996, Faith 1996, Other People's Children 1998, Marrying the Mistress 2000, Girl from the South 2002, Brother and Sister 2004, Second Honeymoon 2006, The Book Boy 2006, Britannia's Daughters 2007; contribs to newspapers and magazines. *Honours:* Romantic Historical Novel of the Year 1980. *Address:* PFD, Drury House, 34–43 Russell Street, London, WC2B 5HA, England. *E-mail:* joanna@joannatrollope.net. *Website:* www.joannatrollope .net.

TROUILLOT, Lyonel; Haitian writer, poet and journalist; *Secretary-General, Association des écrivains haïtiens*; b. 31 Dec. 1956, Port-au-Prince. *Career:* Prof. of Literature, Ecole normale supérieure; co-founder, ed. and contributor to journals, including Lakansyèl, Vivre en Haïti, Tèm, Langaj, Cahiers du Vendredi; Sec.-Gen. Association des écrivains haïtiens; appointed dir of the cabinet under the Sec. of State for Culture 2004–. *Publications:* novels: Depale (with Pierre Richard Narcisse) 1979, Zanj nan dlo 1995, Les fous de Saint-Antoine 1989, Le Livre de Marie 1993, Les dits du fou de l'île (novella) 1997, La Rue des pas perdus 1998, Thérèse en mille morceaux 2000, Les Enfants des héros 2002, Le Testament du mal de mer (short story in L'Odysée atlantique) 2002, Fait divers sur écran noir (short story in Paradis Brisé, nouvelles des Caraïbes) 2004, Bicentenaire 2004; poetry: La petite fille au regard d'île 1994, 'menm zwazo a mouri levi...' (poem in Conjonction 195, 54-5) July-Sept. 1992. *Address:* c/o Ministry of Culture, 4 rue Nagny, Port-au-Prince, Haiti.

TROUPE, Quincy Thomas, Jr, AA, BA; American poet, writer and university instructor; b. 23 July 1943, New York, NY; m. Margaret Porter, four c. *Education:* Gambling College, Los Angeles City College. *Career:* Instructor, various colleges and universities; Instructor in Creative Writing and American, African-American and Caribbean Literature, University of California at San Diego; many poetry readings; mem. Poetry Society of America. *Publications:* Watts Poets: A Book of New Poetry and Essays (ed.), 1968; Embryo Poems, 1967–1971, 1972; Giant Talk: An Anthology of Third World Writings (ed. with Rainer Schulte), 1975; The Inside Story of TV's 'Roots' (ed. with David L. Wolper), 1978; Snake-back Solos: Selected Poems, 1969–1977, 1978; Skulls Along the River (poems), 1984; Soundings, 1988; James Baldwin: The Legacy (ed.), 1989; Miles: The Autobiography (with Miles Davis), 1989; Weather Reports: New and Selected Poems, 1991; Avalanche: Poems, 1996; Choruses: Poems, 1999; Miles and Me, 2000. Contributions: periodicals. *Honours:* National Endowment for the Arts Award in Poetry, 1978; American Book Awards, 1980, 1990; New York Foundation for the Arts Fellowship in Poetry, 1987.

TROWBRIDGE, William, BA, MA, PhD; American poet, editor and academic; *Lecturer, University of Nebraska*; b. 9 May 1941, Chicago, IL; m. Waneta Sue Downing 1963; two s. one d. *Education:* Univ. of Missouri at Columbia, Vanderbilt Univ. *Career:* instructor, Univ. of Missouri at Columbia 1966, Vanderbilt Univ. 1968–70; Asst Prof. to Distinguished Univ. Prof., Northwest

Missouri State Univ. 1971–98, Distinguished Univ. Prof. Emer. 1998–; Co-Ed. The Laurel Review 1986–99, Assoc. Ed. 2001; Asst Ed. The Georgia Review 2000; Lecturer, Univ. of Missouri at Kansas City 2005; Lecturer, Low-Residency MFA Program, Univ. of Nebraska 2005–. *Publications:* The Book of Kong 1986, Enter Dark Stranger 1989, O Paradise 1995, Flickers 2000, The Four Seasons 2002, The Complete Book of Kong 2003, The Packing House Cantata 2006; contrib. to Poetry, Georgia Review, Kenyon Review, Southern Review, Gettysburg Review and many others. *Honours:* Acad. of American Poets Prize 1970, Bread Loaf Writers' Conf. Scholarship 1981, Yaddo Fellowship 1992, Camden Press Chapbook Prize 2005. *Address:* 224 SW Green Teal Street, Lee's Summit, MO 64082-4507, USA (home). *Telephone:* (816) 623-9036 (home). *E-mail:* willtrow@comcast.net (home).

TRUMAN, Jill, BA; British teacher, writer and dramatist; b. 12 June 1934, Enfield, Middx; m. Tony Truman 1956 (died 1975); one s. three d. *Career:* mem. Writers' Guild of GB. *Radio plays:* Letter to My Husband 1986, Gone Out-Back Soon 1988, Travels in West Africa 1990, For Lizzie 1994, Sounds of Silence 1998; plays for BBC Radio 4. *Theatre:* The Web (play) 1991, Flit (puppet play) 1992, Kings of the Night (musical) 1993; fringe theatre. *Publications:* Letter to My Husband 1988, On The Terrace (short story) 1998, Full Moon (short story) 1998, In the Supermarket (short story) 1998; also memoirs, contrib. to magazines. *Address:* 2 Ellesmere Road, Bow, London, E3 5QX, England. *Telephone:* (20) 8983-6414 (office). *E-mail:* jilltruman@freeuk .com (office).

TRUMAN, (Mary) Margaret, BA; American writer; b. 17 Feb. 1924, Independence, MO; m. E. Clifton Daniel Jr 1956 (died 2000); four s. *Education:* George Washington Univ. *Publications:* Fiction: Murder in the White House, 1980; Murder on Capitol Hill, 1981; Murder in the Supreme Court, 1982; Murder in the Smithsonian, 1983; Murder on Embassy Row, 1985; Murder at the FBI, 1985; Murder in Georgetown, 1986; Murder in the CIA, 1987; Murder at the Kennedy Center, 1989; Murder in the National Cathedral, 1990; Murder at the Pentagon, 1992; Murder on the Potomac, 1994; Murder in the National Gallery, 1996; Murder at the Watergate, 1998; Murder at the Library of Congress, 1999; Murder in Foggy Bottom, 2000. Non-Fiction: White House Pets, 1969; Harry S. Truman, 1973; Women of Courage, 1976; Letters from Father, 1981; Bess W. Truman, 1986; Where the Buck Stops: The Personal and Private Writings of Harry S. Truman (ed.), 1989; First Ladies, 1995. *Honours:* LHD, Wake Forest University, 1972; HHD, Rockhurst College, 1976. *Address:* c/o Harry S. Truman Library Institute for National and International Affairs, US 24 Highway and Delaware Street, Independence, MO 64050, USA.

TRUSS, Lynne, BA, FRSL; British writer and broadcaster; b. 31 May 1955, Kingston, Surrey. *Education:* Univ. Coll. London. *Career:* copy ed., Radio Times; Literary Ed., The Listener 1986–90; writer and teacher at Arvon Foundation; contributor and presenter, BBC Radio 4; book reviewer, The Sunday Times columnist, The Times, Woman's Journal; sports writer, The Times; Fellowship, Univ. Coll. London 2004. *Plays:* for BBC Radio 4: Acropolis Now (two series) 2000–01, A Certain Age 2002, Full Circle 2003, Inspector Steine 2007. *Publications:* novels: With One Lousy Free Packet of Seed 1994, Tennyson's Gift 1996, Going Loco 1999; non-fiction: Making the Cat Laugh 1995, Eats, Shoots and Leaves: The Zero Tolerance Approach to Punctuation (British Book Award Book of the Year 2004) 2003, Talk to the Hand 2005, A Certain Age: Twelve Monologues from the Classic Radio Series 2007. *Honours:* Dr hc (Brighton) 2005, (Open Univ., (New York School of Visual Arts) 2006. *Address:* c/o Profile Books, 3a Exmouth House, Pine Street, Exmouth Market, London, EC1R 0JH, England (office). *E-mail:* info@profilebooks.co.uk (office); info@lynnetruss.com (home). *Website:* www.profilebooks.co.uk (office); lynnetruss.com (home).

TSALOUMAS, Dimitris; Australian poet, editor and translator; b. 13 Oct. 1921, Leros, Greece; two s. two d. *Career:* teacher, Victoria schools 1958–82; writer-in-residence, University of Oxford, University of Melbourne, Queensland University, La Trobe University. *Publications:* Resurrection, 1967; Triptych for a Second Coming, 1974; Observations for a Hypochondriac, 1974; The House with the Eucalyptus, 1975; The Sick Barber and Other Characters, 1979; The Book of Epigrams, 1981; The Observatory: Selected Poems, 1983; Falcon Drinking: The English Poems, 1988; Portrait of a Dog, 1991; The Barge, 1993; Six Improvisations On the River, 1995; The Harbour, 1998; Stoneland Harvest, 1999; New and Selected Poems, 2000. *Honours:* Australia Council Grant and Fellowship; National Book Council Award, 1983; Wesley M. Wright Prize for Poetry, 1994; Patrick White Award, 1994; John Bray Poetry Award, Adelaide Festival, 2000; Australia Council Emeritus Award, 2002.

TSE, David K. S.; British playwright, actor and director; *Artistic Director, Yellow Earth Theatre*; b. 17 Nov. 1964, Hong Kong; s. of Tse Shin Kay and Tse Lai Oi Lin. *Education:* read law, trained as actor Rose Bruford Coll., as dir Leicester Haymarket, studied Beijing Opera movement with Lee Siu Wah and Jamie Guan. *Career:* Artistic Dir Yellow Earth touring theatre co. 1995–. *Plays as director:* for Yellow Earth: The Nightingale, Chinese Two-Step, Maritime Mysteries, 58, Lear's Daughters, Friends, The Butcher's Skin, Legend of Old Bawdy Town, Rashomon, Play to Win (Sainsbury's Checkout Award, with Soho Theatre), Behind the Takeaway, New Territories (Time Out Critics' Choice), Tibetan Inroads; at Leicester Haymarket: Dance and the Railroad, House of Sleeping Beauties, Pandavas in Leicester, The Pilgrims; other: Ballad of Mulan (NYMT), Kensuke's Kingdom (Polka Theatre). *Plays as* *actor:* Cross-mopolitan (Chung Ying, Hong Kong), Rashomon (YET), Whisper of a Leaf Falling (David Glass), New Territories (YET), Blue Remembered Hills (David Glass), Playstars (Soho), Cellarworks (LIFT/theatre-rites), The Tempest (Royal Nat. Theatre), The Changeling (Mark Rylance), The Magic Paintbrush (Polka Theatre), Yoshi and Teakettle (Fringe Award, Polka Theatre), Yellow Gentlemen (Sirius Arts), Under a Street Light (Royal Court). *Plays written:* for Yellow Earth: Play to Win 1997, New Territories 2000, The Nightingale; for Polka Theatre: The Snow Lion, The Magic Paintbrush. *Radio plays:* as actor: A Fire in the West, Breaking Jewel, The Searide Came out of a Van, Little Emperors, Tiananmen Square, Stream of Dragons, Nightwaves (BBC Radio 3), The Verb (BBC Radio 3), Trevor's World of Sport (BBC Radio 4); as presenter: Beyond the Takeaway (BBC Radio 4). *Radio plays as writer:* The Old Woman and the Beggar (BBC Radio 3). *Television appearances:* The Grid 2004, Down to Earth, Holby City, Hearts & Bones, Thieftakers, Cracker, Minder. *Film appearances:* Spy Game 2001, Tomb Raider 2001, Hermit of Amsterdam, Foreign Moon, Annnie 2, Soursweet. *Publication:* The Magic Paintbrush 1997. *Honours:* Sainsbury's Checkout Theatre Award 2000, Windrush Arts Achievement Award 2004, Pearl Creative Arts Award 2004. *Address:* c/o Yellow Earth Theatre, 18 Rupert Street, London, W1D 4TG, England (office). *Telephone:* (20) 7734-6165 (office). *Fax:* (20) 7287-3141 (office). *E-mail:* david@yellowearth.org (office). *Website:* www.yellowearth.org (office).

TSUJI, Hitonari, (Jinsei Tsuji); Japanese novelist, scriptwriter and musician; b. 4 Oct. 1959, Tokyo; m. Nakayama Miho. *Career:* fmr singer rock band, Echoes; solo artist 1993–. *Recordings include:* albums: with Echoes: Welcome to the Lost Child Club 1985, Heart Edge 1986, Goodbye Gentle Land 1987, Hurts 1988, Foolish Game 1988, The History of Echoes 1985–89 1989, Dear Friend 1989, Eggs 1990, Gold Water 1990, Silver Bullet 1991, No Kiddin' 1994; solo: The Best of Jinsei Songs 1993, New Wall 1996, Best Wishes 1997. *Film scripts:* Tenshi no wakemae 1994, Sennen tabito 1999, Hotoke 2001, Filament 2001, Calmi Cuori Appassionati 2001, Mokka no koibito 2002. *Publications:* novels: Pianishimo (Pianissimo) (Subaru Literature Prize) 1989, Kuraudi (Cloudy) 1989, Tabibito no ki (The Tree of the Traveller) 1992, Haha naru nagi to chichi naru shike (Motherly Calm, Fatherly Storm) 1993, Passajio 1994, Kaikyô no hikari (Lights in the Channel) (Akutagawa Prize) 1996, Hakubutsu (The White Buddha) (Prix Fémina Étranger 1999) 1997, Ai no Kumeni (Objective) 1997, Reisei to jônetsu no aida (with Ekuni Kaori) 2001, Antinoise 2005, Tokyo décibels 2005. *Address:* c/o Éditions Gallimard, 5, rue Sébastien-Bottin, 75328 Paris cedex 07, France.

TSURUMI, Shunsuke, BS; Japanese writer; b. 25 June 1922, Tokyo; s. of Yusuke Tsurumi and Aiko Tsurumi; m. Sadako Yokoyama 1960; one s. *Education:* Harvard Coll. *Career:* f. The Science of Thought (philosophical journal) 1946; Asst Prof., Univ. of Kyoto 1949, Tokyo Inst. of Tech. 1954; Prof., Doshisha Univ. 1960; freelance author 1970–; Visiting Prof., El Colegio de México 1972–73, McGill Univ. 1979–80. *Publications:* Collected Works (five vols) 1974, An Intellectual History of Wartime Japan 1986, A History of Mass Culture in Postwar Japan 1987, Collected Works (12 vols) 1992, Conversation (ten vols) 1996, Further Collected Works (five vols) 2000. *Honours:* Takano Chóei Prize 1976, Osaragi Jiro Prize 1982, Mystery Writers' Soc. Prize 1989, Asahi Prize 1994. *Address:* 230-99 Nagatanicho, Iwakura, Sakyōku, Kyoto, Japan (home).

TSUTSUI, Yasutaka, BA; Japanese novelist and actor; b. 24 Sept. 1934, Osaka. *Education:* Doshisha Univ. *Career:* writer of science fiction, renowned for experimental, post-modern approach to fiction; co-f. science fiction magazine, Null 1960; early short stories published in SF Magazine and Hoseki; refrained from publication as a protest against literary conservatism 1993–97, returned with novellas in Shincho and Bungaku-kai literary journals 1997; helped establish JALInet literary website 1996; publishes work online; mem. Science Fiction Writers' Asscn of Japan (exec. sec. 1980–83, pres. 1984–85), Japan PEN. *Film appearances:* Bungakusho satsujin jiken: Oinaru jyoso 1989, Kowagaru hitobito 1994, Otokotachi no kaita e 1996, Ki no ue no sogyo 1997, Sôseiji 1999, Hakuchi 1999, Shisha no gakuensai 2000, Stacy 2001, Eli, Eli, rema, sabachthani? 2005, Yokubô 2005. *Television:* Gensou Midnight (writer and actor, series), Nanase futatabi (writer and actor, series), Meguriai (actor, series) 1998, Gakkou no kaidan (actor) 2000, Hojo Tokimune (actor, series) 2001. *Publications:* novels: Tokaido Senso (The Tokyo–Osaka War) 1964, Vietnam Kanko Kosha (The Vietnam Tourist Bureau) 1967, Dasso to Tsuiseki no Samba (The Samba for Runaways and Chasers) 1972, Kazoku Hakkei (What the Maid Saw: Eight Psychic Tales) 1972, Kyojin-tachi (Fictional Characters) (Izumi Kyoka Award 1981), Yumenokizaka-Bunkiten (The Yumenokizaka Intersection) (Tanizaki Jun'ichiro Award 1987), Yoppa-dani eno Koka (A Descent into the Yoppa Valley) (Kawabata Yasunari Award 1989), 48-oku no Mousou (4,800 Million Delusions), Afurika no Bakudan (The African Bomb), Toki wo Kakeru Shoujo (The Little Girl who Conquered Time), Fugou Keiji (The Millionaire Detective), Kyoku Sendan (The Fictional Fleet), Watashi no Guranpa (My Grandpa), Bungaku-bu Tadano Kyoju (Hitoshi Tadano the Professor of Literary Studies) 1990, Asa no Gasuparu (Gaspard of the Morning) (Japan SF Award) 1992, Paprika 1993, Tabi no Ragosu 1994, Zanzou ni Kuchibeni wo 1995, Teki 1998, Kyojintachi 1998, Engattsuio Shireitou 2000, Gyoran Kannonki 2000; short stories: The Rumours About Me 1972, When the Shogun Awoke 1974, The Last of the Smokers 1974, How to Sleep 1979, The Wind 1984, The Dream Censor 1987, The Fish 1988, Standing Woman 1990,

Polar King 1990; non-fiction: Kyoufu 2001, Gyorankannonki 2003. *Honours:* Chevalier, Ordre des Arts et des Lettres 1997. *Website:* www.jali.or.jp/tti/.

TSVETKOV, Aleksey, PhD; Russian poet and critic; b. 2 Feb. 1947, Stanislaw (now Ivano-Frankivsk), Ukraine; s. of Petr Tsvetkov and Bella Tsvetkov (née Tsyganov); m. Olga Samilenko 1978. *Education:* Odessa and Moscow Univs, Univ. of Mich., USA. *Career:* journalist in Siberia and Kazakhstan; poetry recitals and participant in Volgin's Moscow Univ. literary soc. Luch 1970–75; emigrated to USA 1974; co-of Russkaya zhizn', San Francisco 1976–77; Prof. of Russian Language and Literature, Dickinson Coll., Pa 1981–85; broadcaster, Voice of America; poetry has appeared in Kontinent, Ekho, Vremya i my, Apollon, Glagol and elsewhere. *Publications include:* A Collection of Pieces for Life Solo 1978, Three Poets: Kuzminsky, Tsvetkov, Limonov, 1981, Dream State 1981, Eden 1985, Simply Voice 1991. *Honours:* Dr hc (Univ. of Mich.) 1977.

TUBB, Edwin Charles, (Chuck Adams, Jud Cary, J. F. Clarkson, James S. Farrow, James R. Fenner, Charles S. Graham, Charles Grey, Volsted Gridban, Alan Guthrie, George Holt, Gill Hunt, E. F. Jackson, Gregory Kern, King Lang, Mike Lantry, P. Lawrence, Chet Lawson, Arthur MacLean, Carl Maddox, M. L. Powers, Paul Schofield, Brian Shaw, Roy Sheldon, John Stevens, Edward Thomson, Douglas West, Eric Wilding); British writer; b. 15 Oct. 1919, London, England. *Publications include:* (under various pseudonyms) novels: Saturn Patrol 1951, Argentis 1952, Planetoid Disposals Ltd 1953, The Living World 1954, The Fighting Fury 1955, Alien Dust 1955, Scourge of the South 1956, The Space-Born 1956, Wagon Trail 1957, Touch of Evil 1959, Target Death 1961, Too Tough to Handle 1962, Airborne Commando 1963, Moon Base 1964, Death is a Dream 1967, COD Mars 1968, STAR Flight 1969, The Jester at Scar 1970, Lallia 1971, Century of the Manikin 1972, Mayenne 1973, Veruchia 1973, Zenya 1974, Atilus the Slave 1975, Jack of Swords 1976, Haven of Darkness 1977, Incident on Ath 1978, The Quillian Sector 1978, Web of Sand 1979, Iduna's Universe 1979, Stellar Assignment 1979, The Luck Machine 1980, The Terra Data 1980, World of Promise 1980, Nectar of Heaven 1981, The Terridae 1981, The Coming Event 1982, Earth is Heaven 1982, Melome 1983, Stardeath 1983, Angado 1984, Symbol of Terra 1984, The Temple of Truth 1985, Pandora's Box 1996, Temple of Death 1996, Assignment New York 1996, Kalgan the Golden 1996, The Return 1997, I Fight for Mars 1998, Death God's Doom 1999, The Wall 1999, The Sleeping City 1999, Earthfall 2002, Alien Seed 2002, Earthbound 2003, Mirror of the Night 2003, Best Science Fiction of E. C. Tubb 2003; short stories: Ten From Tomorrow 1966, Murder in Space 1997, Alien Life 1998; contrib. over 230 stories to magazines and journals. *Address:* 67 Houston Road, London, SE23 2RL, England.

TUCKER, Eva Marie, BA; German/British writer; b. 18 April 1929, Berlin, Germany; m. 1950 (died 1987); three d. *Education:* Univ. of London. *Career:* C. Day-Lewis Writing Fellow, Vauxhall Manor School, London 1978–79; Hawthornden Writing Fellowship 1991; mem. English PEN, Soc. of Authors. *Publications:* Contact (novel) 1966, Drowning (novel) 1969, Radetzkymarch by Joseph Roth (trans.) 1974, Dorothy Richardson: The Enchanted Guest of Spring and Summer, A Monograph 2003, Berlin Mosaic (novel) 2005; contrib. to BBC Radio 3 and 4, Encounter, London Magazine, Woman's Journal, Vogue, Harper's, Spectator, Listener, PEN International, TLS . *Address:* 63B Belsize Park Gardens, London, NW3 4JN, England (home). *Telephone:* (20) 7722-9010 (home). *E-mail:* eva.tucker@btinternet.vom (home).

TUCKER, Helen, BA; American writer; b. 1 Nov. 1926, Raleigh, NC; m. William Beckwith. *Education:* Wake Forest Univ., Columbia Univ. *Career:* newspaper reporter and writer for radio, Burlington, NC, Twin Falls and Boise, ID, Salt Lake City, UT, Raleigh, NC 1947–58; worked in editorial dept, Columbia Univ. Press 1959–60; Dir of Publs and Publicity, North Carolina Museum of Art, Raleigh 1967–70. *Publications:* The Sound of Summer Voices 1969, The Guilt of August Fielding 1972, No Need of Glory 1973, The Virgin of Lontano 1974, A Strange and Ill-Starred Marriage 1978, A Reason for Rivalry 1979, A Mistress to the Regent: An Infamous Attachment 1980, The Halverton Scandal 1980, A Wedding Day Deception 1981, The Double Dealers 1982, Season of Dishonor 1982, Ardent Vows 1983, Bound by Honor 1984, The Lady's Fancy 1991, Bold Impostor 1991; contrib. to Lady's Circle, Ellery Queen Mystery Magazine, Alfred Hitchcock Mystery Magazine, Ladies' Home Journal, Crescent Review, Montevallo Review, Redbook Magazine. *Honours:* Wake Forest Univ. Distinguished Alumni Award 1971, Franklin County Artist of the Year Award 1992. *Address:* 2930 Hostetler Street, Raleigh, NC 27609, USA.

TUCKER, (Allan) James, BA, MA; British writer; b. 15 Aug. 1929, Cardiff, Wales; m. Marian Roberta Craig 1954; three s., one d. *Education:* University of Wales, Cardiff. *Career:* mem. Authors' Guild, CWA, MWA. *Publications:* Equal Partners, 1960; The Alias Man, 1968; The Novels of Anthony Powell, 1976; The Lolita Man, 1986; Baby Talk, 1998; Lovely Mover, 1998; The Tattooed Detective, 1998; Bay City, 2000; Kill Me, 2000; Pay Days, 2001; Split, 2001; Double Jeopardy, 2002. Contributions: Punch; Spectator; New Statesman; New Review. *Literary Agent:* Curtis Brown Ltd, Haymarket House, 28–29 Haymarket, London, SW1Y 4SP, England. *Telephone:* (20) 7393-4400. *Fax:* (20) 7393-4401. *E-mail:* info@curtisbrown.co.uk. *Website:* www .curtisbrown.co.uk.

TUCKER, Martin, BA, MA, PhD; American academic, writer and poet; *Editor, Confrontation magazine;* b. 8 Feb. 1928, Philadelphia, PA. *Education:* New York Univ., Univ. of Arizona. *Career:* Faculty, Long Island Univ. 1956–96,

Prof. Emer. 1996–; Ed. Confrontation magazine 1970–; mem. African Literature Asscn, African Studies Asscn, Authors' Guild, Modern Language Asscn, Nat. Book Critics Circle, PEN (mem. Exec. Bd 1973–96), Poetry Soc. of America. *Publications:* Modern British Literature, Vols I–IV (ed.) 1967–76, Africa in Modern Literature 1967, The Critical Temper, Vols I–V (ed.) 1970–89, Joseph Conrad 1976, Homes of Locks and Mysteries (poems) 1982, Literary Exile in the United States 1991, Sam Shepard 1992, Attention Spans (poems) 1997, Modern American Literature (ed.) 1997, While There is Time (poems) 2005, Love Among the Squabbles (plays) 2006; contrib. to professional journals and general periodicals. *Honours:* Nat. Endowment for the Arts/Co-ordinating Council and Literary Magazine Awards for Editorial Distinction 1976, 1984, English-Speaking Union Award 1982. *Address:* Confrontation, English Department, C.W. Post of Long Island University, Brookville, NY 11548, USA (office). *Telephone:* (516) 299-2720 (office). *Fax:* (516) 299-2735 (office). *E-mail:* martin.tucker@liu.edu (office).

TUDGE, Colin; British science writer and journalist; b. 22 April 1943, London. *Education:* Peterhouse, Cambridge. *Career:* Features Ed., New Scientist magazine 1980–84; fmrly worked for the BBC on science programmes for BBC Radio (host, Spectrum); Visiting Research Fellow Centre for Philosophy, LSE 1995–; fmr council mem. The Zoological Soc. of London. *Publications:* Home Farm: Complete Food Self-Sufficiency 1977, The Famine Business 1977, Future Cook 1980, Food Crops for the Future: the Development of Plant Resources 1988, Global Ecology 1991, Last Animals at the Zoo 1991, The Engineer in the Garden 1993, The Day Before Yesterday (B. P. Conservation Book of the Year Award) 1995, The Food Connection: The BBC Guide to Healthy Eating 1995, Neanderthals, Bandits and Farmers: How Agriculture Really Began 1998, In Mendel's Footnotes 2000, The Second Creation: Dolly and the Age of Biological Control (with Keith Campbell and Ian Wilmut) 2000, The Variety of Life: A Survey and a Celebration of All the Creatures that Have Ever Lived 2000, So Shall We Reap 2003, The Secret Life of Trees 2005, Feeding People is Easy 2007; contrib. to newspapers and magazines, including The Independent, The Times, Natural History and New Statesman. *Honours:* Glaxo/ABSW Science Writer of the Year Award 1972, 1984, 1990. *Literary Agent:* Felicity Bryan, 2A North Parade, Banbury Road, Oxford, OX2 6LX, England. *Telephone:* (1865) 513816. *Fax:* (1865) 310055. *E-mail:* agency@felicitybryan.com. *Website:* www.felicitybryan.com.

TUDOR-CRAIG, Pamela Wynn, Lady Wedgwood, BA, PhD, FSA; British art historian and writer; b. 26 June 1928, London, England; m. 1st Algernon James Riccarton Tudor-Craig 1956 (died 1969); one d.; m. 2nd Sir John Wedgwood 1982 (died 1989). *Education:* Courtauld Inst. of Art, London. *Career:* lecturer at several US colls 1969–96; presenter, The Secret Life of Paintings television series 1986; mem. Cathedrals Advisory Commission 1975–90; mem. Architectural Advisory Panel, Westminster Abbey 1979–98; f. annual Harlaxton Symposium of English Medieval Studies 1984–, Cambridgeshire Historic Churches Trust 1982–; mem. English Speaking Union (cultural affairs cttee) 1990–98, Soc. of Antiquaries (council mem. 1989–92). *Publications:* Richard III 1973, The Secret Life of Paintings (with R. Foster) 1986, Bells Guide to Westminster Abbey (co-author) 1986, Exeter Cathedral (contrib.) 1991, Anglo-Saxon Wall Paintings 1991, The Regal Image of Richard II and the Wilton Diptych 1997, King Arthur's Round Table 2000, Old St Paul's: the Society of Antiquaries Diptych 1616 2004; contrib. to books, exhibition catalogues, journals and learned journals, including Church Times, History Today, radio and television. *Honours:* Hon. DH (William Jewell Coll.) 1983. *Address:* 9 St Anne's Crescent, Lewes, East Sussex BN7 1SB (home); Society of Antiquaries, Burlington House, Piccadilly, London, W1J 0BE, England (office). *Telephone:* (1273) 479564 (home).

TUENI, Ghassan, MA; Lebanese journalist, writer and publishing executive; *Chairman and CEO, An-Nahar newspaper*; b. 5 Jan. 1926, Beirut; s. of Gebran Tueni and Adèle Tueni (née Salem); m. 2nd Chadia El-Khazen; one s. *Education:* American Univ. of Beirut and Harvard Univ. *Career:* Lecturer in Political Science, American Univ. of Beirut 1947–48; Ed.-in-Chief An-Nahar daily newspaper 1948, Pres. . Annahar Daily –2000, Man. An-Nahar Publishing Co. (now Dar an-Nahar SAL) 1963–, Pres. Dar Annahar Publishing 'Les Editions Dar an-Nahar' SAL 2000–, Chair. and CEO An-Newspaper 2006–; Co-founder Lebanese Acad. of Law and Political Science 1951, Lecturer 1951–54; mem. Parl. for Beirut 1953–57, 2006; mem. Lebanese del. to UN Gen. Ass. 1957; f. Middle East Business Services and Research Corpn 1958, Chair. 1958–70; Founder, Chair. and Man.-Dir Press Co-operative, SAL 1960–; Deputy Prime Minister and Minister of Information and Nat. Educ. 1970–71; arrested Dec. 1973, appeared before mil. tribunal and then released in accordance with press laws; Minister for Social Affairs and Labour, Tourism, Industry and Oil 1975–76; Perm. Rep. to UN 1977–82; Founding Pres. Balamand Univ. 1990–93; Trustee Emer. American Univ. of Beirut. *Publications:* Peace-Keeping Lebanon 1979, Laissez vivre mon peuple! 1984, Une guerre pour les autres 1985, El Bourj (Place de la liberté et porte du Levant) 2000, Un siècle pour rien 2002, Trialogue (with Jean Lacouture and Gérard D. Khoury); several publs in Arabic and English on the Middle East, Palestine and the Lebanese wars 1952–. *Honours:* Détenteur des insignes d'Officier de la Légion d'honneur 2005; Hon. DHumLitt (American Univ. of Beirut) 2005. *Address:* An-Nahar Newspaper, PO Box 11-226, An-Nahar Building, Martyr Square, Beirut (office); Ras Kafra, Beit Mery, Lebanon (home). *Telephone:* (1) 963717 (office); (1) 994888 (office). *Fax:* (1) 970375 (office). *E-mail:* ghs@annahar.com.lb (office).

TULLI, Magdalena; Polish novelist; b. 1955; m.; two s. *Publications:* Sny i kamienie (Dreams and Stones) 1995, W czerwieni (In Red) 1998, Tryby (novel) 2003. *Honours:* Koscielski Foundation Prize 1995. *Address:* c/o W.A.B. Publishers, ul. Lowicka 31, 02-502 Warsaw, Poland.

TULLY, Sir (William) Mark, Kt, KBE, MA; British journalist; b. 24 Oct. 1935, Calcutta, India; s. of William S. C. Tully and Patience T. Tully; m. Frances M. Butler 1960; two s. two d. *Education:* Marlborough Coll., Trinity Hall, Cambridge. *Career:* Regional Dir Abbeyfield Soc. 1960–64; Personnel Officer BBC 1964–65, Asst Rep. then Rep. (a.i.), BBC, Delhi 1965–69, Hindi Programme Organizer BBC External Services, London 1969–70, Chief Talks Writer 1970–71, Chief of Bureau BBC, Delhi 1971–93, BBC South Asia Corresp. 1993–94; now freelance writer, broadcaster, journalist 1994–. *Radio:* series: Raj to Rajiv BBC 1987, Something Understood BBC 1995–. *Television:* series: Lives of Jesus BBC 1996. *Publications:* Amritsar: Mrs Gandhi's Last Battle (jtly) 1985, Raj to Rajiv (jtly) 1988, No Full Stops in India 1991, The Heart of India 1995, The Lives of Jesus 1996, India in Slow Motion (with Gillian Wright) 2002. *Honours:* Hon. Fellow Trinity Hall, Cambridge 1994; Hon. DLitt (Strathclyde) 1997; Dimbleby Award (BAFTA) 1984, Padma Shri (India) 1992, Padma Bhushan 2005. *Address:* 1 Nizamuddin East, Delhi 110013, India (office). *Telephone:* (11) 24359687; (11) 24352878. *Fax:* (11) 24359687. *E-mail:* tulwri@ndf.vsnl.net.in (office).

TUMWINE, James K.; Ugandan writer and paediatrician; b. Kabale. *Education:* Makerere Univ. *Career:* has worked in the UK and Zimbabwe; founder of African Health Sciences journal 2001–; Pres., Forum for African Medical Editors. *Publications include:* non-fiction: Drawers of Water: 30 Years of Change in Domestic Water Use and Environmental Health – Uganda County Case Study 2001. *Address:* African Health Sciences, Makerere University Medical School, PO Box 7072, Kampala, Uganda. *Telephone:* (41) 530020. *Fax:* (41) 530022. *E-mail:* pic@infocom.co.ug.

TUNNICLIFFE, Stephen, BA, MA, PGCE; British poet and writer; b. 22 May 1925, Wakefield, Yorks.; m. Hilary Katharine Routh 1949; three s. (one deceased). *Education:* Univ. of London, Inst. of Education. *Career:* mem. Soc. of Authors. *Publications:* English in Practice (with Geoffrey Summerfield) 1971, Reading and Discrimination (with Denys Thompson) 1979, Poetry Experience: Teaching and Writing Poetry in Secondary Schools 1984, Building and Other Poems 1993, Uneasy Souls: A Forgotten Genius (novel) 1999, Some Poems 2003, Discovering Shakespeare (new edn) 2003, Dangers I Had Passed (novel) 2003; other: Libretti for John Joubert: The Martyrdom of St Alban, The Raising of Lazarus, The Magus, The Prisoner, The Wayfarers, Wings of Faith, For Francis Routh: Circles; contrib. to reviews and journals. *Address:* Upper Clairmont, Kidd Lane, Clun, Shropshire, SY7 8LN, England (office). *Fax:* (1588) 640398 (office). *E-mail:* talent@clairmontpress.co.uk (office). *Website:* www.clairmontpress.co.uk (office).

TUOMEY, Nesta Catherine; Irish writer and dramatist; b. 21 Oct. 1941, Dublin; m. Laurence J. Tuomey; three s. one d. *Education:* Nat. Coll. of Art, Dublin. *Career:* mem. Soc. of Irish Playwrights (Chair. 1980–82), Irish PEN (Sec. 2005–06), Writers' Union. *Publications:* Up Up and Away 1995, Like One of the Family 1999; plays: The Same Again 1969, One of These Days 1977, Country Banking 1982, Whose Baby? 1996; 18 documentaries; contrib. to many magazines and journals. *Honours:* John Power Short Story at Listowel Award 1981, Image/Oil of Ulay Short Story 1994, O. Z. Whitehead Play Competition 1996. *Address:* Tully, Ballinteer Road, Dublin 16, Ireland. *E-mail:* nesta@nestatuomey.com. *Website:* www.nestatuomey.com.

TURK, Frances Mary; British novelist; b. 14 April 1915, Huntingdon, England. *Career:* mem. Romantic Novelists Asscn; many other professional organizations. *Publications:* Paddy O'Shea 1937, The Precious Hours 1938, Paradise Street 1939, Lovable Clown 1941, Angel Hill 1942, The Five Grey Geese 1944, Salutation 1949, The Small House at Ickley 1951, The Gentle Flowers 1952, The Dark Wood 1954, The Glory and the Dream 1955, Dinny Lightfoot 1956, No Through Road 1957, The White Swan 1958, A Temple of Fancy 1959, A Journey to Eternity 1960, A Time to Know 1960, The Secret Places, 1961, A Man Called Jeremy 1961, A Lamp From Murano 1963, The Guarded Heart 1964, The Sour-Sweet Days 1965, The Rectory at Hay 1966, Goddess of Threads 1966, Legacy of Love 1967, Lionel's Story 1967, The Flowering Field 1967, The Marion Window 1968, The Lesley Affair 1968, Fair Recompense 1969, Goddess of Threads 1975, A Visit to Marchmont 1977, Candle Corner 1986. Contributions: many periodicals. *Address:* 36 Church Street, Buckden, St Neots, PE19 5TP, England.

TURNER, Alberta Tucker; American academic, poet and writer; b. 22 Oct. 1919, New York, NY; m. William Arthur Turner 1943; one s. one d. *Education:* BA, Hunter College, CUNY, 1940; MA, Wellesley College, Massachusetts, 1941; PhD, Ohio State University, 1946. *Career:* Lecturer to Prof., 1964–90, Dir, Poetry Center, 1964–90, Prof. Emerita, 1990–, Cleveland State University; Assoc. Ed., Field, Contemporary Poetry and Poetics, 1970–; mem. Milton Society of America; PEN American Center. *Publications:* Poetry: Need, 1971; Learning to Count, 1974; Lid and Spoon, 1977; A Belfry of Knees, 1983; Beginning with Ane: New and Selected Poems, 1994. Other: 50 Contemporary Poets: The Creative Process (ed.), 1977; Poets Teaching (ed.), 1981; To Make a Poem, 1982; 45 Contemporary Poems: The Creative Process (ed.), 1985; Responses to Poetry, 1990; Tomorrow is a Tight Fist, 2001. Contributions: journals and magazines. *Honours:* MacDowell Colony Fellowship, 1985; Cleveland Arts Prize, 1985; Ohio Poetry Award, 1986; Ohio

Governor's Award for Arts in Education, 1988. *Address:* 482 Caskey Court, Oberlin, OH 44074, USA.

TURNER, Brian Lindsay; New Zealand poet and writer; b. 4 March 1944, Dunedin; one s. *Career:* fmrly customs officer, rabbiter, sawmiller, ed. for Oxford Univ. Press; Managing Ed., John McIndoe Ltd, Dunedin 1975–83, 1985–86; writer-in-residence, Univ. of Canterbury 1997; Te Mata Estate New Zealand Poet Laureate 2003–05; Robert Burns Fellow, Univ. of Otago 1984. *Publications:* poetry: Ladders of Rain (Commonwealth Poetry Prize) 1978, Ancestors 1981, Listening to the River 1983, Bones 1985, All That Blue Can Be 1989, Beyond (New Zealand Book Award for Poetry 1993) 1992, Taking Off 2001, Footfall 2005; other: Images of Coastal Otago 1982, New Zealand High Country: Four Seasons 1983, The Visitor's Guide to Fiordland, New Zealand 1983, Finger's Up? (play) (J.C. Reid Memorial Prize) 1985, Opening Up (with Glenn Turner) 1987, Lifting the Covers (with Glenn Turner) 1987, The Last River's Song 1989, Timeless Land (with Owen Marshall and Graham Sydney) 1992, The Guide to Trout Fishing in Otago 1994, On the Loose (biog., with Josh Kronfeld) 1998, New Zealand Photographers (with Scott Freeman) 2000, The Art of Grahame Sydney (essay contrib.) 2001, Meads (with Colin Meads) 2002, Somebodies and Nobodies (autobiog.) 2002, Inside (with Anton Oliver) 2005; contrib. to National Business Review, Independent, poetry anthologies, literary sports anthologies, columns, reviews and articles to daily and weekly newspapers; TV scripts. *Honours:* Scholarship in Letters 1994; New Zealand Journalists' Union Dulux Award for Sport Writing 1975, John Crowe Reid Memorial Prize 1985. *Address:* Main Road, Oturehua, Central Otago, New Zealand.

TURNER, Frederick, BA, MA, BLitt; British academic, writer and poet; *Founders Professor of Arts and Humanities, University of Texas at Dallas;* b. 19 Nov. 1943, East Haddon, Northamptonshire, England; m. Mei Lin Chang 1966; two s. *Education:* Univ. of Oxford. *Career:* Asst Prof. of English, Univ. of California, Santa Barbara 1967–72; Assoc. Prof. of English, Kenyon Coll. 1972–85; Ed., Kenyon Review 1978–83; Visiting Prof. of English, Univ. of Exeter 1984–85; Founders Prof. of Arts and Humanities, Univ. of Texas at Dallas, Richardson 1985–; mem. PEN. *Publications:* Shakespeare and the Nature of Time 1971, Between Two Lives 1972, The Return 1979, The New World 1985, The Garden 1985, Natural Classicism 1986, Genesis: An Epic Poem 1988, Rebirth of Value 1991, Tempest, Flute and Oz 1991, April Wind 1991, Beauty 1991, Foamy Sky: The Major Poems of Miklos Radnoti (trans. with Zsuzanna Ozsváth) 1992, The Culture of Hope 1995, The Ballad of the Good Cowboy 1997, Hadean Eclogues 1999, Shakespeare's Twenty-First Century Economics: The Morality of Love and Money 1999, The Iron-Blue Vault: Selected Poems of Attila József (trans. with Zsuzsanna Ozsváth) 1999; contrib. to journals and periodicals. *Honours:* Ohioana Prize for Editorial Excellence 1980, Djerassi Foundation Grant and Residency 1981, Levinson Poetry Prize 1983, Missouri Review Essay Prize 1986, PEN Golden Pen Award 1992, Milan Fust Prize 1996. *Address:* 2668 Aster Drive, Richardson, TX 75082, USA.

TURNER, George Reginald; Australian writer; b. 8 Oct. 1916, Melbourne, Vic. *Career:* mem. Australian Soc. of Authors. *Publications:* Young Man of Talent, 1959; A Stranger and Afraid, 1961; A Waste of Shame, 1965; The Lame Dog Man, 1967; Beloved Son, Transit of Cassidy, 1978; Vaneglory, 1982; Yesterday's Men, 1983; The Sea and Summer, 1987; A Pursuit of Miracles, 1990; The Destiny Makes, 1993. *Honours:* Miles Franklin Award 1962, Arthur C. Clarke Award 1987.

TURNER, Mary (see Lambot, Isobel Mary)

TUROW, Scott F., JD; American writer and lawyer; b. 12 April 1949, s. of David Turow and Rita Pastron; m. Annette Weisberg 1971; three c. *Education:* Amherst Coll. and Stanford and Harvard Univs. *Career:* mem. Bar, Ill. 1978, US Dist Court. Ill. 1978, US Court of Appeals (7th Circuit) 1979; Assoc. Suffolk Co. Dist Attorney, Boston 1977–78; Asst US Attorney, US Dist Court, Ill., Chicago 1978–86; partner Sonnenschein, Nath & Rosenthal, Chicago 1986–; mem. Chicago Council of Lawyers. *Publications:* One L.: An Inside Account of Life in the First Year at Harvard Law School 1977, Presumed Innocent 1987, The Burden of Proof 1990, Pleading Guilty 1993, The Laws of our Fathers 1996, Personal Injuries 1999, Reversible Errors 2002, Ultimate Punishment: A Lawyer's Reflections on Dealing with the Death Penalty 2003, Ordinary Heroes 2006, The Best American Mystery Stories (ed.) 2006, Limitations 2007; contribs to professional journals. *Address:* Sonnenschein, Nath & Rosenthal, Sears Tower, Suite 8000, 233 South Wacker Drive, Chicago, IL 60606, USA.

TUSIANI, Joseph, DLitt; American (b. Italian) poet, translator and fmr academic; b. 14 Jan. 1924, Foggia, Italy. *Education:* Univ. of Naples. *Career:* Chair Italian Dept, Coll. of Mount St Vincent 1948–71; Lecturer in Italian, Hunter Coll., CUNY 1950–62; Visiting Assoc. Prof., New York Univ. 1956–64; CUNY 1971–83; NDEA Visiting Prof. of Italian, Connecticut State Coll. 1962; Prof., Lehman Coll., CUNY 1971–83; mem. Catholic Poetry Soc. of America, Poetry Soc. of America. *Publications:* Dante in Licenza 1952, Two Critical Essays on Emily Dickinson 1952, Melos Cordis (poems in Latin) 1955, Odi Sacre: Poems 1958, The Complete Poems of Michelangelo 1960, Lust and Liberty: The Poems of Machiavelli 1963, Tasso's Jerusalem Delivered (verse trans.) 1970, Italian Poets of the Renaissance 1971, The Age of Dante 1973, Tasso's Creation of the World 1982, Rosa Rosarum (poems in Latin) 1984, In

Exilio Rerum (poems in Latin) 1985, La Parola Difficile (three vols) 1988, 1991, 1992, Carmina Latina 1994, Leopardi's Canti (trans.) 1994, Le Poesie Inglesi di G. A. Borgese 1995, Pulci's Morgante (verse trans.) 1998, Dante's Lyric Poems 1998, Radicitus (poems in Latin) 2000, Ethnicity 2000, Two Languages, Two Lands (proceedings of an int. convention on his work) 2000, Collected Poems 2004, Un Italiano in America (anthology) 2004, Le Lingue dell'Altrove 2004; contrib. to books and journals. *Honours:* Dr hc (Univ. of Foggia) 2004; Greenwood Prize for Poetry 1956, Leone di San Marco Award 1982, Joseph Tusiani Scholarship Fund founded in his honour, Lehman Coll., CUNY 1983, Congressional Medal of Merit 1984, Progresso Medal of Liberty 1986, American Asscn of Teachers of Italian Outstanding Teacher Award 1987, Renoir Literary Award 1988, Festschrift published in his honour 1995, Enrico Fermi Award 1995, Nat. Endowment for the Humanities Fellowship 1998, Fiorello La Guardia Award 1998, Governor's Award for Excellence 2000, Premio Puglia 2000, Premio Italiani nel Mondo 2004, fêted in Rome's Campidolglio 2004; Cavaliere Ufficiale, Italy 1973, Gold Medal from Gov. of Puglia 2004. *Address:* 308 E 72nd Street, New York, NY 10021, USA.

TUTTLE, Lisa, BA; American writer; b. 16 Sept. 1952, Houston, TX. *Education:* Syracuse Univ. *Publications:* Windhaven, 1981; Familiar Spirit, 1983; Catwitch, 1983; Children's Literary Houses, 1984; Encyclopedia of Feminism, 1986; A Spaceship Built of Stone and Other Stories, 1987; Heroines: Women Inspired by Women, 1988; Lost Futures, 1992; Memories of the Body, 1992; Panther in Argyll, 1996; The Pillow Friend, 1996. Contributions: Magazines. *Honours:* John W. Campbell Award 1974.

TWICHELL, Chase, BA, MFA; American poet, writer, teacher and publisher; b. 20 Aug. 1950, New Haven, CT; m. Russell Banks 1989. *Education:* Trinity College, University of Iowa. *Career:* Ed., Pennyroyal Press, 1976–85; Assoc. Prof., University of Alabama, 1985–88; Lecturer, Princeton University, 1990–2000; Assoc. Faculty, Goddard College, 1996–98, Warren Wilson College, 1999–; Ed., Ausable Press, 1999–. *Publications:* Northern Spy, 1981; The Odds, 1986; Perdido, 1991; The Practice of Poetry (co-ed.), 1992; The Ghost of Eden, 1995; The Snow Watcher, 1998. Contributions: Antaeus; Field; Georgia Review; Nation; New England Review; New Yorker; Ohio Review; Ontario Review; Paris Review; Ploughshares; Poetry Review; Southern Review; Yale Review. *Honours:* National Endowment for the Arts Fellowships, 1987, 1993; Guggenheim Fellowship, 1990; Artists Foundation Fellowship, Boston, 1990; New Jersey State Council on the Arts Fellowship, 1990; American Acad. of Arts and Letters Award, 1994; Alice Fay Di Castagnola Award, Poetry Society of America, 1997.

TYLDESLEY, Joyce Ann, BA, DPhil; British archaeologist and researcher; b. 25 Feb. 1960, Bolton, England; m. Steven Ralph Snape 1985; one s. one d. *Education:* Univ. of Liverpool, St Anne's Coll., Oxford, St Cross Coll., Oxford. *Career:* Lecturer in Archaeology of the Eastern Mediterranean 1986–87, Research Fellow, Inst. of Prehistoric Science and Archaeology 1987–91, Hon. Research Fellow, School of Archaeology, Classics and Oriental Studies 1993–, Univ. of Liverpool; mem. Egypt Exploration Soc. *Publications:* The Wolvercote Channel Handaxe Assemblage: A Comparative Study 1986, The Bout Coupe Biface: A Typological Problem 1987, Nazlet Tuna: An Archaeological Survey in Middle Egypt (co-author) 1988, Daughters of Isis: Women of Ancient Egypt 1994, Hatchepsut: The Female Pharaoh 1996, Nefertiti: The Sun Queen 1998, Pyramids: The Real Story Behind Egypt's Most Ancient Monuments 2003; contrib. articles and reviews to professional journals and popular magazines, including History Today, Focus, Popular Archaeology. *Honours:* British Acad. grant 1987. *Literary Agent:* Watson Little Ltd, Capo di Monte, Windmill Hill, London, NW3 6RJ, England. *Telephone:* (20) 7431-0770 (office). *Fax:* (20) 7341-7225 (office). *Address:* c/o Department of Archaeology, University of Liverpool, 14 Abercromby Square, Liverpool, L69 3BX, England (office).

TYLER, Anne, BA; American writer; b. 25 Oct. 1941, Minneapolis, Minn.; d. of Lloyd Parry Tyler and Phyllis (Mahon) Tyler; m. Taghi M. Modarressi 1963 (died 1997); two c. *Education:* Duke Univ., Columbia Univ. *Career:* mem. American Acad. of Arts and Letters, American Acad. of Arts and Sciences. *Publications:* If Morning Ever Comes 1964, The Tin Can Tree 1965, A Slipping-Down Life 1970, The Clock Winder 1972, Celestial Navigation 1974, Searching for Caleb 1976, Earthly Possessions 1977, Morgan's Passing 1980, Dinner at the Homesick Restaurant 1982, The Best American Short Stories (ed. with Shannon Ravenel) 1983, The Accidental Tourist (Nat. Book Critics Circle Award for Fiction) 1985, Breathing Lessons (Pulitzer Prize for Fiction 1989) 1988, Saint Maybe 1991, Tumble Tower (juvenile) 1993, Ladder of Years 1995, A Patchwork Planet 1998, Back When We Were Grown-ups 2001, The Amateur Marriage (Richard & Judy Book Club Choice 2005) 2004, Digging to America 2006; short stories in magazines. *Address:* 222 Tunbridge Road, Baltimore, MD 21212, USA. *E-mail:* atmBaltimore@aol.com (home).

TYSON, Harvey Wood; South African journalist; b. 27 Sept. 1928, Johannesburg; two s. one d. *Education:* Kingswood Coll., Rhodes Univ., Grahamstown. *Career:* Ed.-in-Chief The Star, Sunday Star, Johannesburg 1974–90; Dir Argus Holdings 1991–94, Argus Newspapers 1991–94, Sussens Mann Tyson Ogilvie & Mather, Omni Media Holdings 1994–. *Publication:* Editors Under Fire 1993. *Address:* c/o The Star, 47 Sauer Street, PO Box 1014, Johannesburg 2000, South Africa. *Telephone:* (11) 8867153. *Fax:* (11) 8867676.

U

UGLOW, Jenny, BA, BLitt; British publisher, biographer and writer; *Editorial Director, Chatto & Windus*; b. 28 March 1947, Cumbria; m. Steve Uglow; four c. *Education:* Cheltenham Ladies' Coll., St Anne's Coll., Oxford. *Career:* Ed. Macmillan Press; Editorial Dir Chatto and Windus 1996–. *Television:* historical consultant to classic serials: Tom Jones, Wives and Daughters, Vanity Fair, Daniel Deronda, The Way We Live Now, Bleak House, Sense and Sensibility, Diary of a Nobody. *Publications:* George Eliot 1987, Elizabeth Gaskell: A Habit of Stories (British Acad. Prize) 1993, Henry Fielding 1995, Hogarth: A Life and a World 1997, Dr Johnson, his Club and Other Friends 1998, In a Green Shade 2002, The Lunar Men: The Friends Who Made the Future (James Tait Black Memorial Prize for Biography 2003) 2002, A Little History of British Gardening 2004, Nature's Engraver: A Life of Thomas Bewick 2006; editor: The Macmillan Biographical Dictionary of Women (fourth edn) 2005, Cultural Babbage: Technology Time and Invention (with Francis Spufford) 1996; contribs to The Guardian, Times Literary Supplement, Independent on Sunday, Sunday Times. *Honours:* Dr hc (Univs of Kent, Birmingham, Aston, Staffordshire, Cen. England); PEN Int. Hessell-Tiltman Prize for History. *Literary Agent:* c/o Deborah Rogers, Rogers, Coleridge & White, 20 Powis Mews, London, W11 1JN, England. *Website:* www.jennyuglow.com.

UGREŠIC, Dubravka; Croatian novelist, essayist and literary scholar; b. 27 March 1949. *Career:* Lecturer Inst. for Theory of Literature, Univ. of Zagreb 1974–93; Visiting Lecturer Wesleyan Univ., USA 1989, 1992, Univ. of Amsterdam, The Netherlands 1996–99, UCLA, USA 2001, Harvard Univ., USA 2002, Frey Foundation Distinguished Visiting Prof. Univ. of N Carolina, USA 1998–99; lives in Amsterdam, The Netherlands. *Publications:* Mali plamen (juvenile) 1971, Filip i Srecica 1976, Poza za prozu (short stories) 1978, Nova ruska proza 1980, Stefica Cvek u raljama Zivota (short story, trans. as Steffie Speck in the Jaws of Life) 1981, Zivot je bajka (short stories) 1983, Forsiranje romana-reke (trans. as Fording the Stream of Consciousness) 1988, Kucni duhovi 1988, Mladinska knjiga 1990, Americki fikcionar (non-fiction, trans. as Have a Nice Day) 1993, Kultura lazi (non-fiction, trans. as The Culture of Lies) 1996, Muzej bezuvjetne predaje (novel, trans. as The Museum of Unconditional Surrender) 1996, Zabranjeno citanje (non-fiction, trans. as Thank You for Not Reading) 2001, Ministarstvo Boli (novel, trans. as The Ministry of Pain) (English PEN Writers in Translation Award 2005) 2004, Nikeg Nema Duma 2005. *Honours:* Prix Européen de l'Essai Charles Veillon (Switzerland) 1996, Verzetsprijs (The Netherlands) 1997, SWF-Bestenliste Literature Prize (Germany) 1998, State Prize for European Literature (Austria) 1999, Heinrich Mann Award (Germany) 2000, Premio Feronia (Italy) 2004, Samuel Fischer Fellowship, Frei Universität 2006; several grants. *Literary Agent:* The Susijn Agency Ltd, Third Floor, 64 Great Titchfield Street, London, W1W 7QH, England. *Telephone:* (20) 7580-6341. *Fax:* (20) 7580-8626. *E-mail:* info@thesusijnagency.com. *Website:* www.thesusijnagency.com.

UHDE, Milan, PhD; Czech politician, journalist and playwright; b. 28 July 1936, Brno; m.; two c. *Education:* Masaryk Univ., Brno. *Career:* Ed. of literary monthly A Guest Is Coming 1958–70; signed Charter 77; published essays in unofficial periodicals and abroad; Reader, Faculty of Philosophy, Masaryk Univ., Brno Dec. 1989–; Ed.-in-chief, Atlantis Publishing House, Brno March–June 1990; Minister of Culture, Czech Repub. 1990–92; Pres. of Foundation for Preservation of Cultural Monuments 1991–; mem. Civic Democratic Party (ODS) 1991–98, Unie Svobody 1998; Deputy to Czech Nat. Council June 1992–; mem. Presidium; Pres. of Parl., Czech Repub. 1992–96; Chair. Civic Democratic Party in Parl. 1996–97; mem. State Radio Council 1999–. *Plays include:* King Vávra 1964, The Tax-Collector 1965, Witnesses 1966, The Tart from the Town of Thebes 1967, The Gang 1969, A Dentist's Temptation 1976, Lord of the Flames 1977, The Hour of Defence 1978, The Blue Angel 1979. *Publications:* novels: Like Water off a Duck's Back 1961, A Mysterious Tower in B. 1967. *Honours:* Medal for Merit 2000; Czechoslovak Radio Prize 1966. *Address:* Barvičova 59, 602 00 Brno, Czech Republic. *Telephone:* (5) 43240201. *Fax:* (5) 43240201.

UHRMAN, Celia, PhD; American artist and poet; b. 14 May 1927, New London, Conn.; d. of the late David Aaron and Pauline (née Schwartz) Uhrman. *Education:* Brooklyn Coll., Univ. of Gdańsk, Poland, City Univ. of New York, Brooklyn Museum Art School, Columbia Univ. *Career:* teacher, New York 1948–82; Pnr Uhrman Studio 1973–83; solo exhibitions include Leffert Jr High School (Brooklyn) 1958, Connecticut Chamber of Commerce (New London) 1962, Flatbush Chamber of Commerce (New York) 1963; group exhibitions include Smithsonian Inst. (Washington, DC) 1958, Springfield Museum of Fine Arts (MA) 1959, Brooklyn Museum 1959, Old Mystic Art Center (CT) 1959, Carnegie Endowment Int. Center (New York) 1959, Lyman Allyn Museum (New London, CT) 1960, Palacio de la Virrelna (Barcelona, Spain) 1961, Soc. of 4 Arts (Palm Beach, FL) 1964, Premier Salon Int. (Charleroi, Belgium) 1968, Int. Arts Guild Shows (Monte Carlo) 1969–88, Dibiux-Joan Miró Premi Int. (Barcelona) 1970, Ovar Museum (Portugal) 1974; works in perm. collections of Brooklyn Coll. and Brooklyn Evangelical Church; Founding Fellow, World Literary Acad. and Int. Acad. of Poets 1985; Hon. Life mem. World Poetry Day Comm. Inc., Nat. Poetry Day Comm. 1977–. *Publications:* Poetic Ponderances 1969, A Pause for Poetry 1970, Poetic

Love Fancies 1970, A Pause for Poetry for Children 1973, The Chimps are Coming 1975, Love Fancies 1987. *Honours:* Order of Gandhi Award of Honour, Kt of Grand Cross 1972; George Washington Medal of Honor 1964, Diplôme d'Honneur, Palme d'Or des Beaux Arts Exhibition (Monaco) 1969, 1972, Gold Laurel Award, Exposition Int. d'Art Contemporain (Paris) 1974.

ULITSKAYA, Ludmila Yevgenyevna; Russian writer and screenwriter; b. 21 Feb. 1943, Davlekanovo, Bashkiria; m. Krasulin Andrei Nikolayevich; two s. *Education:* Moscow State Univ. *Career:* Head of Literary Div., Jewish Chamber Theatre 1979–89. *Publications include:* One Hundred Buttons (juvenile) 1983, Sonechka (short stories) 1992, Daughter of Bukhara 1993, Medea and her Children (novel) 1996, Merry Funerals 1998, It is Easy for Me 1999, Poor Relatives 1999, The Kukotsky Case (novel) 2000, The Funeral Party (novel) 2000; plays: Carmen, Jose and Death, My Grandchild Benjamin; film scripts: Sisters Liberty, A Woman for Everybody, It is Easy to Die 1999; contrib. short stories to anthologies. *Honours:* Medici Prize for Best Translated Novel 1995, Giuseppe Acerbi Prize, Moscow Pen Club Medal, PEN Club Prize (Italy) 1998, Smirnoff-Booker Prize 2001. *Address:* EKSMO Publishers, Narodnogo Opolcheniya str 38, 123298 Moscow, Russia. *Telephone:* (495) 950-48-10.

UNDERHILL, Charles (see Hill, Reginald Charles)

UNDERWOOD, Elizabeth (see McConchie, Lyn)

UNGER, Barbara, BA, MA; American fmr academic, poet and writer; b. 2 Oct. 1932, New York, NY; m. 1st; two c.; m. 2nd Theodore Kiichiro Sakano 1987. *Education:* City Coll., CUNY. *Career:* Prof. of English and Creative Writing, Rockland Community Coll., SUNY from 1969 (now retired), continues as Adjunct Prof.; mem. Poetry Soc. of America. *Publications:* Basement Poems 1959–1961 1975, The Man Who Burned Money (poems) 1976, Inside the Wind (poems) 1986, Learning to Foxtrot (poems) 1989, Dying for Uncle Ray and Other Stories 1990, Blue Depression Glass (poems) (Goodman Award 1989, Anna Davidson Rosenberg Award for Poems on the Jewish Experience 1990) 1991, Bronx Accent: A Literary and Pictorial History of the Borough (J. M. Kaplan Furthermore grant, New York Soc. Library Book Award for Borough History 2000) 2000, Bittersweet Legacy 2001. *Honours:* New York State Council on the Arts grant, NEA grant, Edna St Vincent Millay Colony for the Arts grant, Bread Loaf Scholar 1978, Nat. Poetry Competition Award 1982, Ragdale Foundation Fellowships 1985, 1986, Djerassi Foundation Literature Residency 1991, J. H. G. Roberts Writing Award in Poetry 1991. *Address:* c/o English Department, SUNY Rockland Community College, 145 College Road, Suffern, NY, USA.

UNGER, David, BA, MFA; Guatemalan writer, poet and translator; b. 6 Nov. 1950, Guatemala City; s. of the late Luis Unger and of Fortuna Unger; m. Anne Gilman; two d. one step-d. *Education:* Univ. of Massachusetts at Amherst, Columbia Univ., New York. *Career:* US co-ordinator, Guadalajara Int. Book Fair; Dir City Coll. Publishing Certificate Program. *Publications include:* Neither Caterpillar or Butterfly (poetry), The Girl in the Treehouse, Life in the Damn Tropics (novel) 2002, published in Spanish and Chinese trans.; translations: Antipoems: New and Selected, by Nicanor Parra 1985, Dead Leaves, by Bárbara Jacobs 1993, First Love and Look for my Obituary, by Elena Garro 1997, Popol Vuh, by Victor Montejo 1999, The Love You Promised Me, by Silvia Molina 1999, Girl from Chimel, by Rigoberta Menchu 2005, Letters to My Mother, by Teresa Cardenas 2006, others by Roque Dalton, Mario Benedetti, Sergio Ramirez, Luisa Valenzuela, José Agustin, Paco Igacio Taibo II, Vicente Aleixandre, Enrique Lihn. *Honours:* trans. grants from New York State Council on the Arts; Manhattan Borough Pres.'s Award for Excellence in the Arts 1991, Ivri-Nasawi Poetry Prize 1998. *Address:* Division of Humanities, NAC 5225, City College of New York, New York, NY 10031, USA (office). *Telephone:* (212) 650-7925 (office). *Fax:* (212) 650-7912 (office). *E-mail:* filny@aol.com (office).

UNGER, Michael Ronald; British newspaper editor and business executive; b. 8 Dec. 1943, Surrey; s. of Ronald Unger and Joan Stanbridge; m. 1st Eunice Dickens 1966 (divorced 1992); one s. one d. (deceased); m. 2nd Noorah Ahmed 1993. *Education:* Wirral Grammar School, Liverpool Polytechnic. *Career:* trainee journalist, Stockport 1963–65; Production Ed., Reading Evening Post 1965–67; News Ed., Perth, Australia 1967–71; Deputy Ed. Daily Post, Liverpool 1971–79, Ed. 1979–82; Ed. Liverpool Echo 1982–83; Ed. Manchester Evening News 1983–97; Dir Guardian Media Group 1983–97, Manchester Evening News PLC 1983–97; Gen. Man. Jazz FM 2000; Chair. The Lowry Centre 1996, Youth Charter for Sport 1996–2000; mem. Broadcasting Standards Comm. 1999–2000; Trustee Scott Trust 1986–97. *Publication:* The Memoirs of Bridget Hitler 1979. *Honours:* various newspaper awards including Newspaper Design 1980, 1981, 1982, 1994; Ed. of the Year 1988.

UNSWORTH, Barry; British writer; b. 10 Aug. 1930, Wingate, Co. Durham; s. of the late Michael Unsworth and Elsie Unsworth; m. 1st Valerie Irene Moore 1959 (divorced 1991); three d.; m. 2nd Aira Pohjanvaara-Buffa 1992. *Education:* Manchester Univ. *Career:* nat. service; taught English in France and at Univs. of Athens and Istanbul; Writer-in-Residence Ambleside, Cumbria 1979, Univ. of Liverpool 1985; Visiting Literary Fellow Univs. of

Durham and Newcastle 1982; moved to Helsinki 1987; now lives in Italy. *Publications:* The Partnership 1966, The Greeks Have A Word For It 1967, The Hide 1970, Mooncranker's Gift (winner Heinemann Fiction Prize) 1973, The Big Day 1976, Pascali's Island 1980, The Rage of the Vulture 1982, Stone Virgin 1985, Sugar and Rum 1988, Sacred Hunger 1992 (jt winner, Booker Prize 1992), Morality Play 1995, After Hannibal 1996, Losing Nelson 1999, The Songs of the Kings 2002, The Ruby in her Navel 2006. *Honours:* Hon. Litt. D. (Manchester) 1998. *Address:* c/o Giles Gordon, Curtis Brown, Haymarket House, 28–29 Haymarket, London, SW1Y 4SP, England; Casella Postale 24, 06060 Agello (PG), Italy (home). *Telephone:* (20) 7396-6600 (London). *Fax:* (20) 7396-0110 (London).

UPCHURCH, Michael, BA; American writer; *Book Critic, Seattle Times*; b. 5 Feb. 1954, Rahway, NJ; Partner John Hartl 1992. *Education:* Univ. of Exeter, UK. *Career:* Book Critic, Seattle Times 1998–; mem. Nat. Book Critics' Circle. *Publications:* fiction: Jamboree 1981, Air 1986, The Flame Forest 1989, Passive Intruder 1995; contribs to periodicals including New York Times Book Review, Chicago Tribune, American Scholar, Washington Post Book World, San Francisco Chronicle, Seattle Times, The Oregonian. *Address:* 9725 Sand Point Way, NE, Seattle, WA 98115, USA (office). *Telephone:* (206) 525-2268 (office). *Fax:* (206) 525-0350 (office). *E-mail:* michaelupchurch@comcast.net (office).

UPDIKE, John Hoyer, AB; American writer and poet; b. 18 March 1932, Shillington, Penn.; s. of Wesley R. Updike and Linda Grace Hoyer Updike; m. 1st Mary Pennington 1953 (divorced 1977); two s. two d.; m. 2nd Martha Bernhard 1977. *Education:* Shillington High School, Pennsylvania, Harvard Univ., Ruskin School of Drawing and Fine Art, Oxford. *Career:* reporter on the magazine New Yorker 1955–57, contributor 1955–; mem. Nat. Inst. of Arts and Letters, American Acad. of Arts and Sciences. *Publications:* The Carpentered Hen (poems) 1958, The Poorhouse Fair (novel) 1959, The Same Door (short stories) 1959, Rabbit, Run (novel) 1960, Pigeon Feathers and Other Stories 1962, The Centaur (novel) 1963, Telephone Poles and Other Poems 1963, Assorted Prose 1965, Of the Farm (novel) 1965, The Music School (short stories) 1966, Couples (novel), Midpoint and other poems 1969, Bech: A Book 1970, Rabbit Redux (novel) 1972, Seventy Poems 1972, Museums and Women and Other Stories 1972, Buchanan Dying (play) 1974, A Month of Sundays (novel) 1975, Picked-up Pieces 1976, Marry Me (novel) 1976, The Coup (novel) 1978, Tossing and Turning (poems) 1978, Sixteen Sonnets 1979, Problems (short stories) 1979, Your Lover Just Called 1980, Rabbit is Rich (novel) 1981, Bech is Back 1982, Hugging the Shore (essays and criticism) 1984, The Witches of Eastwick (novel) 1984, Facing Nature 1984, Jester's Dozen (poems) 1984, The Year's Best American Short Stories (ed.) 1985, Roger's Version (novel) 1986, Trust Me (short stories) 1987, S (novel) 1988, Self-Consciousness (autobiog.) 1989, Just Looking (essays) 1989, Rabbit at Rest 1990, Odd Jobs (essays and criticism) 1991, Memories of the Ford Administration (novel) 1992, Collected Poems 1953–1993 1993, Brazil (novel) 1993, The Afterlife and Other Stories 1994, In the Beauty of the Lilies 1996, Golf Dreams (writings on golf) 1996, Toward the End of Time 1997, A Century of Arts and Letters (ed.) 1998, Bech at Bay: A quasi-novel 1999, More Matter (essays and criticism) 1999, Gertrude and Claudius (novel) 2000, The Best American Short Stories of the Century (ed.) 2000, Americana and Other Poems 2001, Licks of Love 2001, Seek My Face 2002, The Early Stories 1953–1975 2003, Telling Tales (contrib. to charity anthology) 2004, Villages (novel) 2005, Still Looking: Essays on American Art (art criticism) 2006, Terrorist 2006. *Honours:* Dr hc (Harvard) 1992; Rosenthal Award, Nat. Inst. of Arts and Letters 1960, Nat. Book Award for Fiction 1966, Prix Médicis Etranger 1966, O. Henry Story Award 1967, 1991, MacDowell Medal for Literature 1981, US Nat. Book Critics Circle Award 1982, 1984, 1991, Pulitzer Prize 1982, 1991, PEN/Malamud Memorial Prize 1988, Nat. Medal of Arts 1989, Scanno Prize 1991, Harvard Arts Medal 1998, Nat. Book Foundation Award for Lifetime Achievement 1999, PEN/Faulkner Awarf 2004. *Address:* c/o Alfred A. Knopf Inc., 299 Park Avenue, New York, NY 10171 (office); Beverly Farms, MA 01915, USA.

UPTON, Andrew; Australian playwright, film-maker and director; m. Cate Blanchett 1997; two s. *Career:* Second Unit Dir, Big Sky (TV series); Dir, two Writers' Studios at the Australian Nat. Playwrights' Centre 1995–96. *Plays:* Hanging Man 2002, Cyrano de Bergerac (adaptation), Don Juan (adaptation). *Films:* Babe (asst ed.) 1995, Parklands (continuity) 1996, The Well 1997, Thank God he Met Lizzie 1997, A Little Bit of Soul 1998, Bangers (writer, prod., dir) 1999. *Literary Agent:* RGM Associates, PO Box 128, Surry Hills, NSW 2010, Australia. *Telephone:* (2) 9281-3911. *Fax:* (2) 9281-4705. *E-mail:* info@rgm.com.au. *Website:* www.rgm.com.au.

UPTON, Lee, BA, MFA, PhD; American academic, poet and writer; *Professor of English, Lafayette College*; b. 2 June 1953, St Johns, MI; m. Eric Jozef Ziolkowski 1989; two d. *Education:* Michigan State Univ., Univ. of Massachusetts at Amherst, State Univ. of New York at Binghamton. *Career:* Visiting Asst Prof., Lafayette Coll. 1986–87, Asst Prof. of English 1988–92, Assoc. Prof. of English 1992–98, Prof. of English and Writer-in-Residence 1998–; Asst Prof., Grand Valley State Univ. 1987–88; mem. Modern Language Asscn, Nat. Council of Teachers of English, Poetry Soc. of America. *Publications:* poetry: The Invention of Kindness 1984, Sudden Distances 1988, No Mercy 1989, Approximate Darling 1996, Civilian Histories 2000; criticism: Jean Garrigue: A Poetics of Plenitude 1991, Obsession and Release: Rereading the Poetry of Louise Bogan 1996, The Muse of Abandonment: Origin, Identity and Mastery in Five American Poets 1998, Defensive Measures 2005; contribs to numerous reviews, quarterlies, journals and periodicals. *Honours:* Pushcart Prize 1988, Georgia Contemporary Poetry Series Award 1996, 2000, The Writer/Emily Dickinson Award 2005, Lyric Poetry Award 2005. *Address:* Department of English, Lafayette College, Easton, PA 18042, USA (office). *Telephone:* (610) 330-5250 (office). *E-mail:* uptonlee@lafayette.edu (office).

URASAWA, Naoki; Japanese writer and illustrator; b. 2 Jan. 1960, Fuchu, Tokyo. *Education:* Meisei Univ. *Career:* creator of numerous manga comic series; professional debut with Beta!! 1984. *Publications:* manga comics: Yawara!: A Fashionable Judo Girl (29 vols) (Shogakukan Manga Award 1990) 1986–93, Pineapple Army (10 vols, illustrator) 1986–88, Dancing Policeman 1987, Master Keaton (18 vols) 1988–94, Happy! (23 vols) 1993–99, Monster (18 vols) (Media Arts Festival Award for Excellence 1997, Asahi Newspaper Tezuka Osamu Award 1999) 1994–2001, 20th Century Boys (21 vols) (Media Arts Festival Award for Excellence 2002) 1999–, Pluto (two vols) 2003–; short story collections: NASA 1988, Jigoro! 1994. *Honours:* Shogakukan New Manga Artist Award 1982. *Address:* c/o Shogakukan Inc., 2-3-1, Hitotsubashi, Chiyoda-ku, Tokyo 101-8001, Japan. *Website:* www.shogakukan.co.jp.

URBAN, Jerzy; Polish journalist; *President, URMA Company Ltd*; b. 3 Aug. 1933, Łódź; s. of Jan Urban and Maria Urban; m. 1st 1957; one d.; m. 3rd Małgorzata Daniszewska 1986. *Education:* Warsaw Univ. *Career:* staff writer, weekly Po Prostu, Warsaw 1955–57; head of home section, weekly Polityka, Warsaw 1960–63, 1968–81; columnist of satirical weekly Szpilki, articles written under pen-names including Jan Rem and Jerzy Kibic; Govt Press Spokesman 1981–89; Minister without portfolio, Head Cttee for Radio and Television April–Sept. 1989; Dir and Ed.-in-Chief, Nat. Workers' Agency Nov. 1989–90; Dir and Ed.-in-Chief Unia-Press Feb.–May 1990; Pres. Kier Co. Ltd 1990–; Pres. URMA Co. Ltd, Warsaw 1991–; Ed.-in-Chief, political weekly Nie Oct. 1990–; participant Round Table debates, mem. group for mass media Feb.–April 1990; mem. Journalists' Asscn of Polish People's Repub. 1982–, Polish Writers' Union. *Screenplays include:* Sekret, Otello. *Publications:* Kolekcja Jerzego Kibica 1972, Impertynencje: Felietony z lat 1969–72 1974, Wszystkie nasze ciemne sprawy 1974, Grzechy chodzą po ludziach 1975, Gorączka 1981, Romanse 1981, Robak w jabłku 1982, Na odlew 1983, Samosądy 1 1984, Felietony dla cudzych zon 1984, Samosądy 2 1984, Z pieprzem i solą 1986, Jakim prawem 1988, Rozkosze podglądania 1988, Cały Urban 1989, Alfabet Urbana 1990, Jajakobyły 1991, Prima aprilis towarzysze 1992, Klątwa Urbana 1995, Druga Klątwa Urbana 2000. *Honours:* Ztoty KrzyżZastTugi, KrzyżKomandorski Polonia Restituta; Victor Prize (TV) 1987. *Address:* URMA Co. Ltd, ul. Słoneczna 25, 00 789 Warsaw, Poland (office). *Telephone:* (22) 8485290 (office). *Fax:* (22) 8497258 (office). *E-mail:* NIE@redakcja.nie.com.pl (office); nie@redakcja.nie.com.pl (office).

URIAS, Alfonso Quijada; Salvadorean writer and poet; b. 8 Dec. 1940, Quezaltepeque. *Career:* fmr journalist. *Publications:* From Now On (co-author) 1968, Otras historias famosas (Nuevapal abra) 1976, They Come and Knock on the Door (in trans.) 1991, The Better to See You (contributor) 1994. *Address:* c/o Curbstone Press, 321 Jackson Street, Willimantic, CT 06226-1738, USA. *E-mail:* info@curbstone.org. *Website:* www.curbstone.org.

URQUHART, Jane, BA; Canadian writer; b. 21 June 1949, Gerladton, ON; d. of Walter Andrew and Marian (née Quinn) Carter; m. Tony Urquhart 1976; one d. *Education:* Havergal Coll. (Toronto) and Univ. of Guelph. *Career:* writer 1978–; Writer-in-Residence Univ. of Ottawa 1990–, Memorial Univ. of Newfoundland 1992–, Massey Coll., Univ. of Toronto 1997–; books have been published in Canada, UK, France, USA, Germany, Spain, Italy, Sweden and Norway; mem. Writer's Union of Canada, PEN Int., League of Canadian Poets; Canada Council and Ontario Arts Council Grants; Hon. LLD (Waterloo) 1997, (St Thomas) 1998, (Newfoundland) 1999, (Guelph) 1999, (Toronto) 1999; Govt of Ont. Trillium Award (with Margaret Atwood q.v.) 1993, Marian Engel Award 1994. *Publications:* False Shuffles 1981, I am Walking in the Garden of His Imaginary Palace 1981, The Little Flowers of Mme de Montespan (poetry) 1984, The Whirlpool (novel, aka Niagara) (Best Foreign Book Award, Paris 1992) 1986, Storm Glass (short stories) 1987, Changing Heaven (novel) 1990, Away (novel) 1993, The Underpainter (Gov.-Gen.'s Award) 1997, The Stone Carvers 2001, A Map of Glass 2005. *Address:* c/o POB 208, Wellesley, ON N0B 2T0, Canada. *Telephone:* (519) 656-2613.

URSELL, Geoffrey, BA, MA, PhD; Canadian writer, dramatist, poet and composer; b. 14 March 1943, Moose Jaw, SK; m. Barbara Sapergia 1967. *Education:* Univ. of Manitoba, Univ. of London. *Career:* Lecturer 1975–79, Special Asst Prof. in English 1980–81, 1982–83, Univ. of Regina; writer-in-residence, Saskatoon Public Library 1984–85; mem. Writers' Union of Canada, Asscn of Canadian Television and Radio Artists, Guild of Canadian Playwrights, Playwrights Canada. *Publications:* Number One Northern: Poetry from Saskatchewan (co-ed.) 1977, The Tenth Negative Pig (co-author) 1980, The Running of the Deer (play) (Clifford E. Lee Nat. Playwriting Award 1977) 1981, Saskatoon Pie! (Persephone Theatre Nat. Playwriting Award 1981) 1981, Black Powder (musical) 1982, Saskatchewan Gold (ed.) 1982, Trap Lines (poems) 1982, Perdue, or, How the West Was Lost (novel) (WHSmith/Books in Canada First Novel Award 1984) 1984, Sky High: Stories from Saskatchewan 1988, Way Out West (short stories) 1989, The Look-Out Tower (poems) 1989, Jumbo Gumbo (co-ed.) (Vicki Metcalfe Award 1990) 1990, Due West (ed.) 1996; various unpublished stage plays and radio plays; contrib. to periodicals. *Honours:* several prizes and awards. *Address:* c/o The Writers'

Union of Canada, 90 Richmond Street East, Suite 200, Toronto, ON M5C 1P1, Canada.

USHERWOOD, Elizabeth Ada; British writer and lecturer; b. 10 July 1923, London; d. of Walter Beavington and Annie Beavington (née Noonan); m. Stephen Usherwood 1970. *Career:* fmr Red Cross nurse; fmr int. banker; lectures on historical subjects. *Publications:* Visit Some London Catholic Churches (with Stephen Usherwood) 1982, The Counter-Armada 1596: The Journal of the 'Mary Rose' (with Stephen Usherwood) 1983, We Die for the Old Religion (with Stephen Usherwood) 1987, Women First 1989, A Saint in the Family (with Stephen Usherwood) 1992; contribs to periodicals. *Address:* 24 St Mary's Grove, Canonbury, London, N1 2NT, England. *Telephone:* (20) 7226-9813. *E-mail:* eau@waitrose.com (home).

UTAMI, Ayu; Indonesian writer; b. 21 Nov. 1968, Bogor. *Publications:* novels: Saman 1998, Larung 2001, Sex, Sketches and Stories (short stories) 2003; essays: Parasit Lajang—Seks, Sketsa, Cerita 2003. *Honours:* Best Novel, Jakarta Art Council 1998, Dutch Prince Clause Award 2000. *Address:* Jln. Utan Kayu, 68H, 13120 Jakarta, Indonesia (office). *Telephone:* (21) 8573388 (office). *Fax:* (21) 8573387 (office). *E-mail:* ayutami@isai.or.id (office).

UTLEY, Steven; American writer and poet; b. 10 Nov. 1948, Fort Knox, KY. *Education:* Middle Tennessee State Univ., Murfreesboro, TN. *Publications:* Lone Star Universe (ed. with Geo W. Proctor) 1976, Ghost Seas (short stories) 1997, This Impatient Ape (poems) 1998, Career Moves of the Gods (poems) 2000, The Beasts of Love (short stories) 2004, Where or When (short stories) 2005; contrib. to Aphelion, Asimov's Science Fiction, Bewildering Stories, Poetry Today, Cyclo-Flame, Galaxy, Liquid Ohio, Lone Star Stories, Shayol, New Dimensions, Bachy, Fly by Night, Cthulhu Calls, SumerMorn. *Address:* 113 Kentwell Drive, Smyrna, TN 37167, USA (home); c/o PS Publishing, Grosvenor House, 1 New Road, Hornsea, East Yorkshire HU18 1PG, England (office).

UTTAMCHANDANI, Sundri Assandas, MA; Indian writer; b. 28 Sept. 1924, Hyderabad, Sind (now Pakistan); d. of Doolaram Ichatanmal Narwani; m. Assandas Uttamchandani 1947; two d. *Education:* Univs in Pakistan and India. *Career:* has acted on stage and in one film; co-ed. SATHI (women's magazine) 1946; Pres. Sindhu Women's Org. *Publications:* two novels and eight short story collections including Bhuri, To Jineeji Tat Bardhan, Travelogue (essays); has published translations of several novels; magazine articles and works for TV and radio. *Honours:* numerous awards including Soviet Land Nehru Peace Prize, Hindi Directorate Award, Sahitya Acad. Award 1986, Akhil B. B. Sabha Prize. *Address:* B-9 Floreana, Miraway Society, ST Road, Mumbai 400 016, India. *Telephone:* (22) 4374136.

UYS, Pieter-Dirk, BA; South African playwright, performer and producer; b. 28 Sept. 1945, Cape Town; s. of Helga Bassel and Hannes Uys. *Education:* Univ. of Cape Town, London Film School, UK. *Career:* joined Space Theatre, Cape Town 1973; f. Syrkel Theatre Co.; Dir P. D. Uys Productions, Bapetikosweti Marketing Enterprises; produced and performed 30 plays in revues throughout SA and in UK, USA, Australia, Canada, Netherlands; several videos and TV films and documentaries. *Theatre:* cr. Mrs Evita Bezuidenhout – the most famous white woman in South Africa. *Television:* Evita Live and Dangerous, weekly talk/satire show 1999. *Publications:* Die van Aardes van Grootoor 1979, Paradise is Closing Down 1980, God's Forgotten 1981, Karnaval 1982, Selle ou storie 1983, Farce about Uys 1984, Appassionata 1985, Skote! 1986, Paradise is Closing Down and Other Plays 1989, No one's Died Laughing 1986, P.W. Botha: In His Own Words 1987, A Part Hate, A Part Love 1990, Funigalore 1995. *Honours:* Hon. DLitt (Rhodes Univ.) 1997. *Address:* Evita SE Perron Theatre/Cafe/Bar Darling Station, Darling 7345 (office); 17 Station Road, Darling 7345, South Africa. *Telephone:* (22) 4922831 (office); (22) 4923208 (home). *Fax:* (22) 4923208 (home). *E-mail:* evita@africa.com (office); evitadarling@hotmail.com (home). *Website:* millennia.co.za/evita (office).

V

VACHSS, Andrew Henry, BA, JD; American writer and attorney; b. 19 Oct. 1942, New York, NY; m. Alice Vachss. *Education:* Case Western Reserve University, New England School of Law. *Career:* bd of counselors, Child-trauma Acad.; Nat. Advisory Bd, Protect PAC; Contributing Ed., Parade Magazine; mem. PEN American Center, Writers' Guild of America. *Publications:* novels: Flood 1985, Strega 1987, Blue Belle 1988, Hard Candy 1989, Blossom 1990, Sacrifice 1991, Shella 1993, Down in the Zero 1994, Another Chance to Get it Right 1995, Footsteps of the Hawk 1995, Batman: The Ultimate Evil 1995, False Allegations 1996, Safe House 1998, Choice of Evil 1999, Dead and Gone 2000, Pain Management 2001, Only Child 2002, The Getaway Man 2003, Down Here 2004; graphic novels: Hard Looks: Adapted Stories 1992, Predator: Race War 1995; other: The Life-Style Violent Juvenile: The Secure Treatment Approach (non-fiction) 1979, Proving It (audio book) 2001, Born Bad: Stories 1994, Everybody Pays: Stories 1999. *Honours:* John Hay Whitney Foundation Fellow 1976–77, Grand Prix de Littérature Policière 1988, Falcon Award, Maltese Falcon Soc. of Japan 1988, Deutschen Krimi Preis from Die Jury des Bochumer Krimi Archivs 1989, Raymond Chandler Award 2000. *Address:* 420 Lexington Avenue, Suite 2860, New York, NY 10170, USA. *Website:* www.vachss.com.

VACULÍK, Ludvík; Czech writer, journalist and essayist; b. 23 July 1926, Brumov. *Career:* expelled from Communist Party 1967; publications banned by Communists 1969–89; signatory to Charter 77 human rights declaration; Ed. Literámí Noviny, Rude Pravo; publisher of samizdat (clandestinely copied and printed) series, Edice Petlice 1973–79; columnist Lidové Noviny. *Publications:* novels: Sekyra (trans. as The Axe) 1966, Morčata (trans. as The Guinea Pigs) 1970, Český Snář 1980, A Cup of Coffee with my Interrogator: The Prague Chronicles of Ludvík Vaculík 1987, Jak se dělá chlapec (trans. as How to Make a Boy) 1998, Nepaměti 1998, My Dear Classmates, Immemoirs, A Mountain Trip to Praděd, The Last Word 2002; non-fiction: Two Thousand Words (manifesto) 1968.

VAIZEY, Lady Marina, MA; British (b. American) art critic, lecturer and writer; b. 16 Jan. 1938; m. Lord Vaizey 1961 (died 1984); two s. one d. *Education:* Brearley School, New York, Putney School, Vermont, Radcliffe Coll., Harvard Univ. and Girton Coll., Cambridge, UK. *Career:* Art Critic, Financial Times 1970–74, Sunday Times 1974–92; Dance Critic Now! 1979–81; mem. Art Panel Arts Council 1973–79, Deputy Chair. 1976–79; mem. Paintings for Hosps 1974–; mem. Advisory Cttee Dept of Environment 1975–81, mem. Art Working Group on Nat. Curriculum, Dept of Educ. and Science 1990–91; mem. Cttee Contemporary Arts Soc. 1975–79, 1980–94; Exec. Dir Mitchell Prize for the History of Art 1976–87; mem. History of Art and Complementary Studies Bd, CNAA 1978–82, Photography Bd 1979–81, Fine Arts Bd 1980–83, Cttee 20th Century Soc. 1995–98; Trustee Nat. Museums and Galleries on Merseyside 1986–2001, Geffrye Museum, London 1990–, Imperial War Museum 1991–2003; mem. Fine Arts Advisory Cttee British Council 1987–, Crafts Council 1988–94, Int. Rescue Cttee UK 1998–; Editorial Dir Nat. Art Collections Fund 1991–94 (Consultant 1994–98); Gov. Camberwell Coll. of Arts and Crafts 1971–82, Bath Acad. of Art 1978–81, South Bank Centre 1993–2003, London Open House 1996–, Nat. Army Museum 2001–; touring exhbn Painter as Photographer 1982–85; Judge, Turner Prize 1997. *Publications:* 100 Masterpieces of Art 1979, Andrew Wyeth 1980, The Artist as Photographer 1982, Peter Blake 1985, Christiane Kubrick 1990, Christo 1990, Sorensen 1994, Picasso's Ladies 1998, Sutton Taylor 1999, Felim Egan 1999, Great Women Collectors (with Charlotte Gere) 1999, Art, the Critics' Choice (ed.) 1999, Magdalene Odundo 2001, Wendy Ramshaw 2004; articles in periodicals, anthologies and catalogues. *Address:* 24 Heathfield Terrace, London, W4 4JE, England. *Telephone:* (20) 8994-7994. *Fax:* (20) 8995-8057. *E-mail:* marina@vaizey.demon.co.uk.

VAKSBERG, Arkady Iosifovich, DJur; Russian writer, journalist and lawyer; b. 11 Nov. 1933, Novosibirsk; m.; one d. *Education:* Moscow State Univ. *Career:* barrister Moscow City Bd of Bar –1973; political observer in Paris, Literaturnaya Gazeta; Vice-Pres. Russian PEN Centre; mem. Russian Writer's Union, Journalist's Union, Union of Cinematography Workers, Int. Cttee of Writers in Prison. *Screenplays for films:* The Storm Warning, The Provincial Romance, In Broad Daylight. *Plays:* A Shot in the Dark, The Supreme Court, The Alarm. *TV work includes:* The Special Reporter (serial), A Dangerous Zone (actor and scriptwriter), Reprise (Grand-Prix and Best Screenplay, International Telefilm Festival). *Publications:* three books and numerous articles on copyright law; over 40 works of fiction, collections of essays, biogs. and memoirs. *Honours:* Grand-Prix, the Eurasian Teleforum (Moscow). *Address:* Krasnoarmeiskaya str. 23, Apt. 65, 125319 Moscow, Russia (home); 17 blvd Garibaldi, 75015 Paris, France. *Telephone:* (495) 151-33-69 (home); 1-45-66-45-31. *Fax:* 1-45-66-45-31. *E-mail:* vaksberg@noos.fr (home).

VALENTINE, Alana, BA; Australian playwright; b. Redfern, NSW. *Education:* Univ. of Sydney. *Radio plays:* Screamers, The Word Salon, Oysters at the Paragon, Swallowing Communion. *Screenplays:* Mother Love 1994, The Witnesses 1995, Reef Dreaming 1997. *Plays:* The Story of Anger Lee Bredenza 1989, Southern Belle 1994, Swimming the Globe 1996, The Conjurers 1997, Spool Time 1998, Ozone 1998, Savage Grace 2001, Row of Tents 2001, The Prospectors 2001, The Mapmaker's Brother 2002, Titania's Boy 2003, Run Rabbit Run 2004, The Prospectors 2004, Covenant 2005, Crossing the Mountains 2005, Butterfly Dandy 2005. *Honours:* AWGIE Award, NSW State Literary Award, Churchill Fellowship, Rodney Seaborne Playwright's Award, ANPC/New Dramatist's Award, NSW Writer's Fellowship 2003, Queensland Premier's Literary Award 2004. *Literary Agent:* RGM Associates, PO Box 128, Surry Hills, NSW 2010, Australia. *Telephone:* (2) 9281-3911. *Fax:* (2) 9281-4705. *E-mail:* info@rgm.com.au. *Website:* www.rgm.com.au.

VALENZUELA, Luisa; Argentine writer and journalist; b. 26 Nov. 1938, Buenos Aires; d. of Luisa Mercedes Levinson and Pablo F. Valenzuela; m. Théodore Marjak 1958 (divorced); one d. *Education:* Belgrano Girls' School, Colegio Nacional Vicente Lopez, Buenos Aires. *Career:* lived in Paris, writing for Argentinian newspapers and for the RTF 1958–61; Asst Ed. La Nación Sunday Supplement, Buenos Aires 1964–69; writer, lecturer, freelance journalist in USA, Mexico, France, Spain 1970–73, Buenos Aires 1973–79; taught in Writing Div., Columbia Univ., New York 1980–83; conducted writers' workshops, English Dept, New York Univ. and seminars, Writing Div. 1984–89; returned to Buenos Aires 1989; Fulbright Grant 1969–70; Guggenheim Fellow 1983; Fellow New York Inst. for the Humanities; mem. Acad. of Arts and Sciences, Puerto Rico. *Publications:* novels: Hay que sonreír 1966, El gato eficaz 1972, Como en la guerra 1977, Cambio de armas 1982, Cola de largartija 1983, Novela negra con argentinos 1990, Realidad Nacional desde la cama 1990; short stories: Los heréticos 1967, Aquí pasan cosas raras 1976, Libro que no muerde 1980, Donde viven las águilas 1983, Simetrías (Cuentos de Hades) 1993, Antología Personal 1998, Cuentos Completos y Uno Más 1999, La travesía 2001, Peligrosas palabras 2001. *Honours:* Dr. hc (Knox Coll., Ill., USA) 1991; Machado de Assis Medal, Brazilian Acad. of Letters 1997. *Address:* Artilleros 2130, 1428 Buenos Aires, Argentina. *Telephone:* (11) 4781-3593.

VALERY, Anne; British scriptwriter, novelist and playwright; b. (Anne Catherine Firth), 24 Feb. 1926, London, England. *Education:* South Hampstead High School, Badminton School. *Career:* lecturer in writing for TV; TV producer for overseas stations; has presented more than 500 programmes on TV; mem. PEN International, Fawcett Soc. *Plays:* more than 40 plays for TV; Tenko (series) (BAFTA Award 1984), Crown Court. *Publications:* Baron Von Kodak, Shirley Temple and Me 1973, The Edge of a Smile 1974, The Passing Out Parade (theatre) 1979, Tenko Reunion 1984, Talking About the War. . . (non-fiction) 1991; contrib. to A Stately Homo, Radio Times and other publs. *Honours:* Telegraph Book of the Month. *Address:* Flat 3, 28 Arkwright Road, London, NW3 6BH, England (home). *Telephone:* (20) 7435-8663 (home).

VALGARDSON, William Dempsey; Canadian writer, poet, dramatist and academic; b. 7 May 1939, Winnipeg, Manitoba; m. (divorced); one s. one d. *Education:* BA, United College, 1961; BEd, University of Manitoba, 1966; MFA, University of Iowa, 1969. *Career:* Assoc. Prof., 1970–74, Prof., 1974–, University of Victoria, BC; Fiction Ed., Canadian Author, 1996–. *Publications:* Bloodflowers, 1973; God is Not a Fish Inspector, 1975; In the Gutting Shed, 1976; Red Dust, 1978; Gentle Simmers, 1980; The Carpenter of Dreams, 1986; What Can't Be Changed Shouldn't Be Mourned, 1990; The Girl With the Botticelli Face, 1992; Thor, 1994; Sarah and the People of Sand River, 1996; Garbage Creek, 1997. Contributions: Magazines. *Honours:* Books in Canada First Novel Award, 1980; Ethel Wilson Literary Prize, 1992; Mr Christie Prize, 1995; Vicky Metcalf Short Story Award, 1998. *Address:* 1908 Waterloo Road, Victoria, BC V8P 1J3, Canada.

VALK, (Elizabeth) Lisa, BA, MBA; American publishing executive; b. 1951, Winston-Salem, NC. *Education:* Hollins Univ., Harvard Business School. *Career:* mem. circulation staff Time Inc. 1979, Circulation Dir Fortune Magazine 1982–84, Sports Illustrated 1984–85, Time 1985–86, Publr Life magazine (first woman publr at Time Inc.) 1986–88, Publr People magazine 1988–91, Publr Time magazine 1991–93, Pres. Time magazine 1993, then Exec. Vice Pres. Time Inc. –2001; mem. Bd of Dirs Steelcase Inc., J.M. Smucker Co., Jefferson Pilot Corpn; Chair. Bd of Trustees Hollins Univ. *Honours:* Matrix Women in Communications Award 1992. *Address:* c/o Board of Trustees, Hollins University, Roanoke, VA 24020, USA.

VALLBONA, Rima Gretel Rothe, (Rima de Vallbona), BS, MA, DML; Costa Rican/American academic and writer; *Professor Emerita of Spanish, University of St Thomas;* b. 15 March 1931, San José, Costa Rica; d. of the late Ferdinand Hermann and Emilia (née Strassburger) Rothe; m. Carlos Vallbona 1956; four c. *Education:* Colegio Superior de Señoritas, San José, Univ. of Costa Rica, Middlebury Coll., VT, Univ. of Paris (Sorbonne), France and Univ. of Salamanca, Spain. *Career:* Liceo J. J. Vargas Calvo, Costa Rica 1955–56; Faculty mem. specializing in Latin American Literature Univ. of St Thomas, Houston, TX 1964–, Head then Chair. Spanish Dept 1966–71, Prof. of Spanish 1978–95, Chair. Modern Languages Dept 1978–80, Cullen Foundation Prof. of Spanish 1989–95, Prof. Emer. 1995–; Visiting Prof. Univ. of Houston 1975–76, Madrid 1980, Rice Univ. and Univ. of Houston 1980–83, 1995; mem. American Asscn of Teachers of Spanish and Portuguese, Asociación de Literatura Femenina Hispánica, Instituto Internacional de Literatura Iberoamericana, Academia Norteamerican de la Lengua Española 1999–. *Publications:* literary studies: Yolanda Oreamuno 1971, La obra en prosa de Eunice Odio 1981, Vida i sucesos de la Monja Alférez 1992, La narrativa de Yolanda Oreamuno 1995; novels: Noche en vela 1968, Las sombras que perseguimos 1983, Mundo, demonio y mujer 1991; short stories: Polvo del camino 1973, La salamandra rosada 1979, Mujeres y agonias 1982, Baraja de soledades 1983, Cosecha de pecadores 1988, El arcángel del perdón 1990, Los infernos de la mujer y algo más... 1992, Flowering Inferno: Tales of Sinking Hearts 1992, Tormy, la gata prodigiosa de Donaldito (children's) 1997, Tejedoras de sueños versus realidad (short stories) 2003. *Honours:* El Lazo de Dama de la Orden del Mérito Civil, Spain 1989; Nat. Novel Prize, Costa Rica 1968, Jorge Luis Borges Short Story Prize, Fundación Givré, Argentina 1977, Agripina Montes del Valle Latin American Novel Prize, Colombia 1978, Prof. Lilia Ramos Children's Poetry Prize, Uruguay 1978, Constantin Foundation Research Grants, Univ. of St Thomas 1981, Southwest Conf. of Latin American Studies Literary Prize 1982, Ancora Award for Best Book, Costa Rica 1983–84, Hispanic Women Hall Award 1993, Bay Area Writers' League Prize 2003. *Address:* 3706 Lake Street, Houston, TX 77098, USA (home). *Telephone:* (713) 528-6137 (home). *E-mail:* rvallbona@aol.com (home).

VALLEJO, Fernando; Colombian writer, screenwriter and film director; b. 1942, Medellín. *Education:* studied film in Cinecittà, Italy. *Films:* Crónica roja (screenplay and dir) 1977, En la tormenta (screenplay and dir) 1980, Barrio de campeones (screenplay and dir) 1981. *Publications include:* Logoi (non-fiction) 1983, Los días azules (vol. one of autobiog., El río del tiempo) 1985, El fuego secreto (vol. two of autobiog., El río del tiempo) 1987, Los caminos a Roma (vol. three of autobiog., El río del tiempo) 1988, Años de indulgencia (vol. four of autobiog., El río del tiempo) 1989, El Mensajero (vol. five of autobiog., El río del tiempo) 1991, Entre fantasmas (vol. six of autobiog., El río del tiempo) 1993, La virgen de los sicarios (novel, trans. as Our Lady of the Assassins) 1994, La tautología darwinista 1998, El desbarrancadero (Premio Internacional de Novela Rómulo Gallegos 2003) 2002, La rambla paralela 2002, Almas en Pena, Chapolas Negras 2002, Mi hermano el alcalde 2003, Manualito de imposturología física 2005. *Address:* c/o Alfaguara, Calle Torrelaguna 60, 28043 Madrid, Spain (office). *E-mail:* alfaguara@santillana.es (office).

VALLGREN, Carl-Johan; Swedish writer and musician; b. 26 July 1964, Linköping. *Recordings:* albums: Klädpoker med Djävulen 1996, Easy listening för masochister 1998, Kärlek och andra katastrofer 2001, 2000 mil, 400 nätter 2003, I provinsen 2004. *Publications:* novels: Nomaderna 1987, Längta bort 1988, Fågelkvinnan 1991, Berättelser om sömn och vaka 1994, Dokument rörande Spelaren Rubashov 1996, För herr Bachmanns broschyr 1998, Berlin på 8 kapitel 1999, Den vidunderliga kärlekens historia (Augustpriset 2002) 2002. *Honours:* Årets bok-Månadens boks litterära pris 2002. *Address:* c/o Bonnier Books, PO Box 3159, 103 63 Stockholm, Sweden. *E-mail:* bonnierforlagen@bok.bonnier.se. *Website:* www.vallgren.nu.

VALLVEY, Ángela, BA; Spanish writer and poet; b. 1964, Ciudad Real. *Education:* Universidad de Granada. *Publications:* poetry: Capitales de tiniebla 1997, El tamaño del universo (Premio Jaén de Poesía) 1998, Extraños en el paraíso 2001; novels: Kippel y la mirada electrónica 1995, Donde todos somos John Wayne 1997, Vida sentimental de Bugs Bunny 1997, A la caza del último hombre salvaje 2000, Vías de extinción 2000, Los estados carenciales (Premio Nadal) 2002, No lo llames amor 2003, La ciudad del diablo 2005. *Address:* c/o Penguin Publicity, 80 Strand, London, WC2R 0RL, England.

VALTINOS, Thanassis; Greek writer; b. 16 Dec. 1932, Karatoula Kynourias; m.; one d. *Education:* Athens Univ. *Career:* Visiting Prof., War Research Inst., Frankfurt 1993–; Pres. Greek Soc. of Authors; mem. European Acad. of Sciences and Arts, Int. Inst. of Theatre, Greek Society of Playwriters. *Honours:* Scenario Award Cannes Festival 1984, Nat. Literary Award 1990. *Address:* 66 Astidamantos Street, 116 34 Athens, Greece. *Telephone:* 7218793.

VAN DE LAAR, Waltherus Antonius Bernardinus, (Stella Napels, Victor Vroomkoning), MA; Dutch poet and writer; b. 6 Oct. 1938, Boxtel; one s. one d. *Education:* degrees in philosophy, Dutch linguistics and literature. *Career:* teacher, Interstudie Teachers' Training Coll., Arnhem 1977–83; Co-Ed., Kritisch Literatuur Lexicon 1981–; mem. Lira. *Publications:* De einders tegemoet 1983, De laatste dingen 1983, Circuit des souvenirs 1984, Klein museum 1987, Groesbeek Tijdrit 1989, Echo van een echo 1990, Oud zeer 1993, Een zucht als vluchtig eerbetoon 1995, Boxtel 1995, Lippendienst 1997, Ysbeerbestaan 1999, Verloren Spraak 2000, Bij verstek 2002, Het format van waterland 2004, Stapelen 2005; contribs to magazines and periodicals. *Honours:* Pablo Neruda Prize 1983, Blanka Gyselen Prize 1995, Pieter Geert Buckinx Prize 2003, De Zilveren Kei 2004. *Address:* Aldenhof, 70-17, 6537 DZ Nijmegen, The Netherlands (home). *Telephone:* (24) 3441694 (home). *E-mail:* vroomkoning@planet.nl (home).

VAN DEN BOOGAARD, Oscar; Dutch writer and playwright; b. 1964. *Education:* Univs of Montpellier, Amsterdam and Brussels. *Career:* grew up in Suriname and the Netherlands; worked briefly in legal profession; full-time writer in Brussels 1990–. *Plays:* Verwantschappen (actor in theatre experiment) 2000, Lucia (writer) 2001, Nest (writer) 2004, Lucia Smelt 2004. *Publications:* Dentz 1990, Fremdkörper 1991, Bruno's optimisme 1993, De heerlijkheid van Julia 1995, Liefdesdood (trans. as Love's Death) 1999, Sensaties 2000, Een bed vol schuim 2002, Inspiration Point 2004, Het Verticale Strand 2005. *Address:* c/o Farrar, Straus and Giroux, 19 Union Square W, New York, NY 10003, USA. *E-mail:* oscarvdb@skynet.be. *Website:* www.oscarvandenboogaard.com.

VAN DER KISTE, John Patrick Guy; British author and library assistant; b. 15 Sept. 1954, Wendover, Bucks.; s. of the late Wing Commdr R.E.G. Van der Kiste; m. Kim Graham (née Geldard) 2003. *Education:* Ealing Tech. Coll. School of Librarianship. *Career:* Library Asst, Plymouth Coll. of Further Educ. (now City Coll., Plymouth) 1978–. *Publications:* Frederick III 1981, Dearest Affie (with Bee Jordaan) 1984, Queen Victoria's Children 1986, Windsor and Habsburg 1987, Edward VII's Children 1989, Beyond the Summertime (with Derek Wadeson) 1990, Princess Victoria Melita 1991, George V's Children 1991, George III's Children 1992, Crowns in a Changing World 1993, Kings of the Hellenes 1994, Childhood at Court 1995, Northern Crowns 1996, King George II & Queen Caroline 1997, The Romanovs 1818–1959 1998, Kaiser Wilhelm II 1999, The Georgian Princesses 2000, Gilbert and Sullivan's Christmas 2000, Dearest Vicky, Darling Fritz 2001, Royal Visits to Devon and Cornwall 2002, Once a Grand Duchess (with Coryne Hall) 2002, William & Mary 2003, The Man on the Moor 2004, Emperor Francis Joseph 2005, Sons, Servants and Statements 2006, Devon Murders 2006, Divided Kingdom 2007; contrib. to books, periodicals and CD booklets. *Address:* c/o Sutton Publishing Ltd, Phoenix Mill, Thrupp, Stroud, Glos., GL5 2BU, England.

VAN DER VALK, Sonja, PhD; Dutch drama critic and magazine editor; b. 8 Oct. 1952, Poeldijk; pnr Joost Sternheim (died 1992); two d. *Education:* Univ. of Utrecht. *Career:* theatre critic 1977–, writer for Toneel Teatraal, Serpentine (women's magazine), De groene Amsterdammer (weekly); apptd Ed. Toneel Theatraal 1990; teacher at theatre school, Amsterdam 1992–; Art Adviser to Amsterdamse Kunstraad 1992–. *Publications:* Theater Persona: Een Terugblik op Negen Jaar Theater Maken; contrib. articles on the theatre to magazines and newspapers. *Address:* Uithoornstraat 4, II, 1070 SX Amsterdam, Netherlands. *Telephone:* (20) 6648848. *Fax:* (20) 6648848.

VAN DER VAT, Dan, BA; British writer and journalist; b. 28 Oct. 1939, Alkmaar, Netherlands; m. Christine Mary Ellis 1962; two d. *Education:* Univ. of Durham. *Career:* mem. Campaign for Freedom of Information, Soc. of Authors, Amnesty International, Liberty. *Publications:* The Grand Scuttle 1982, The Last Corsair 1983, Gentlemen of War 1984, The Ship That Changed the World 1985, The Atlantic Campaign, 1939–45 1988, The Pacific Campaign, 1941–45 1991, Freedom Was Never Like This: A Winter's Journey in East Germany 1991, Stealth at Sea: History of the Submarine 1994, The Riddle of the Titanic (with Robin Gardiner) 1995, The Good Nazi: The Life and Lies of Albert Speer 1997, Standard of Power: The Royal Navy in the 20th Century 2000, Pearl Harbor: The Day of Infamy: An Illustrated History 2001, D-Day: The Greatest Invasion, a People's History 2004; contrib. to newspapers, magazines, radio and television. *Honours:* Yorkshire Post Best First Work Award 1982, King George's Fund for Sailors Best Book of the Sea Award 1983, Publisher's Weekly Book of the Year 1997. *Literary Agent:* c/o Curtis Brown Ltd, Haymarket House, 28–29 Haymarket, London, SW1Y 4SP, England. *Telephone:* (20) 7393-4400. *Fax:* (20) 7393-4401. *E-mail:* info@curtisbrown.co.uk. *Website:* www.curtisbrown.co.uk.

VAN DIS, Adriaan; Dutch writer; b. 16 Dec. 1946, Bergen. *Education:* Univ. of Amsterdam. *Career:* fmr Ed. NRC Handelsblad newspaper. *Television:* presenter Here is... Adriaan van Dis 1983–92. *Play:* Tropenjaren 1986. *Publications:* Nathan Sid (novel) (Gouden Ezelsoor Award) 1984, Casablanca (short stories) 1986, De rat van Arras 1986, Komedie om geld 1986, Zoen 1987, Een barbaar in China 1987, Zilver, of Het verlies van de onschuld 1988, Een uur in de wind 1989, Het beloofde land 1990, In Afrika 1991, Waar twee olifanten vechten 1992, Noord Zuid 1994, Indische duinen (novel) (Gouden Uil Literature Prize 1995, Trouw Public Award 1995) 1994, Wij, koningin 1995, Palmwijn 1996, Een waarze sat 1997, Totok 1998, Een deken van herinnering 1998, Dubbelliefde (novel) 1999, Op oorlogspad in Japan (novel) 2000, Familieziek (novel) 2002, De reisromans 2003, De karakterromans 2004, Onder het zink 2004. *Honours:* Nipkowschijf prize for tv show 1986. *Address:* c/o Uitgeverij Augustus, Herengracht 481, 1017 BT Amsterdam, The Netherlands. *Website:* www.adriaanvandis.nl.

VAN HENSBERGEN, Gijs; Dutch author and art critic. *Education:* trained as an architect. *Career:* lectures on architecture. *Publications:* A Taste of Castille (travel book, aka In the Kitchens of Castile) 1980, Art Deco 1986, Gaudí: A Biography 2001, Guernica: The Biography of a Twentieth-Century Icon 2004. *Literary Agent:* c/o Euan Thorneycroft, A.M. Heath & Company Ltd, 6 Warwick Court, Holborn, London, WC1R 5DJ, England. *Telephone:* (20) 7242-2811. *Fax:* (20) 242-2711.

VAN HERK, Aritha, FRSC, BA, MA; Canadian academic and writer; *Professor, University of Calgary*; b. 26 May 1954, Wetaskiwin, AB; m. Robert Sharp 1974. *Education:* Univ. of Alberta. *Career:* Asst Prof., Univ. of Calgary 1983–85, Assoc. Prof. 1985–91, Prof. 1991–. *Publications:* Judith 1978, More Stories from Western Canada (co-ed.) 1980, The Tent Peg 1981, West of Fiction (co-ed.) 1983, No Fixed Address 1986, Places Far From Ellesmere 1990, Alberta Rebound (ed.) 1990, In Visible Ink 1991, A Frozen Tongue 1992, Boundless Alberta (ed.) 1993, Due West 1996, Restlessness 1998, Mavericks: An Incorrigible History of Alberta 2001. *Honours:* Seal Books First Novel Award 1978, Alberta Achievement Award in Literature 1978, Grant MacEwan Award 2002. *Address:* Department of English, University of Calgary, Social Sciences Tower, 11th Floor, 2500 University Drive NW, Calgary, AB T2N 1N4, Canada (office). *Telephone:* (403) 220-5481 (office). *Fax:* (403) 289-1123 (office). *E-mail:* vanherk@ucalgary.ca (office). *Website:* www.english.ucalgary.ca (office).

VAN LUSTBADER, Eric, BA; American writer; b. 24 Dec. 1946, New York, NY; m. Victoria Lustbader. *Education:* Columbia Univ. *Publications:* The Sunset Warrior, 1977; Shallows of Night, 1978; Dai-San, 1978; Beneath an Opal Moon, 1980; The Ninja, 1980; Sirens, 1981; Black Heart, 1982; The Miko, 1984; Jian, 1985; Shan, 1987; Zero, 1988; French Kiss, 1988; White Ninja, 1989; Angel Eyes, 1991; Black Blade, 1993; The Keishe, 1993; Batman: The Last Angel, 1994; The Floating City, 1994, The Bourne Betrayal 2007. Contributions: Magazines. *Address:* c/o Henry Morrison Inc, Box 235, Bedford Hills, NY 10507, USA.

VAN WINCKEL, Nance, BA, MA; American poet, writer and academic; b. 24 Oct. 1951, Roanoke, VA, USA; m. Robert Fredrik Nelson 1985. *Education:* University of Wisconsin, Milwaukee, University of Denver. *Career:* Instructor in English, Marymount College, Salina, KS, 1976–79; Assoc. Prof. of English and Dir, Writing Program, Lake Forest College, IL, 1979–90; Assoc. Prof. to Prof. of English, Eastern Washington University, Cheney, 1990–; Faculty, Vermont College, 2000–. *Publications:* The Twenty-Four Doors: Advent Calendar Poems, 1985; Bad Girl, with Hawk (poems), 1988; Limited Lifetime Warranty (short stories), 1994; The Dirt (poems), 1994; Quake (short stories), 1997; After a Spell (poems), 1998; Curtain Creek Farm (short stories), 2000. Contributions: many periodicals. *Honours:* Illinois Arts Council Fellowships, 1983, 1985, 1987, 1989; National Endowment for the Arts Fellowships, 1988, 2001; Society of Midland Authors Poetry Award, 1989; Gordon Barber Award, Poetry Society of America, 1989; Northwest Institute Grants, 1991, 1993, 1994; Paterson Fiction Prize, 1998; Washington State Artists Trust Literary Award in Fiction, 1998; Washington State Gov.'s Award for Literature, 1999.

VAN WISSEN, Driek; Dutch poet; b. 12 July 1943, Groningen. *Education:* Rijksuniversiteit Groningen. *Career:* Dichter des Vaderlands (Dutch Poet Laureate) 2005–. *Publications include:* De match Luteijn Donner: een schaakcursus in twee maal twaalf sonnetten 1976, Het mooiste meisje van de klas 1978, Meisjesgenade 1980, De badman heeft gelijk 1982, Dartele dactylus: ollekebollekes nieuwste verzameling metrisch plezier 1984, Letterkundig verskwartet 1985, Gezichtsbedrog 1992, Een loopje met de tijd 1993, De hap van Adam 1999, Onverwoestbaar mooi, verzamelde gedichten 2003, De Dichter des Vaderlands. Zijn mooiste verzen 2005. *Honours:* Kees Stipprijs 1987. *Address:* c/o Stichting Schrijvers School Samenleving, Huddestraat 7, 1018 HB Amsterdam (office); c/o Nijgh & Van Ditmar, PO Box 3879, 1001 AR Amsterdam, The Netherlands (office). *E-mail:* info@sss.nl.

VANDERHAAR, Gerard Anthony, BA, STD; American academic and writer; b. 15 Aug. 1931, Louisville, KY; m. Janice Marie Searles 1969. *Education:* Providence Coll., Univ. of St Thomas, Rome. *Career:* faculty mem., St John's Univ., New York 1964–65, Providence Coll. 1965–68, Wesleyan Univ. 1968–69, Christian Brothers Univ. 1971–; mem. American Acad. of Religion, American Asscn of Univ. Profs, Pax Christi, Fellowship of Reconcilitation, War Registers League. *Publications:* A New Vision and a New Will for Memphis 1974, Christians and Nonviolence in the Nuclear Age 1982, Enemies and How to Love Them 1985, Way of Peace: A Guide to Nonviolence (co-ed.) 1987, The Philippines: Agony and Hope (co-author) 1989, Active Nonviolence: A Way of Personal Peace 1990, Why Good People Do Bad Things 1994, Beyond Violence 1998; booklets: Nonviolence, Theory and Practice 1980, Nonviolence in Christian Tradition 1983; contrib. to reference books and journals. *Honours:* Outstanding Educators of America 1971, UN Asscn Distinguished Service Award 1981, Catholic Press Asscn Book Award for Spirituality 1991, Tennessee Higher Education Commission Award for Community Service 1994, Pax Chisti Nat. Book Award 1998. *Address:* c/o Christian Brothers University, 650 East Parkway South, Memphis, TN 38104, USA (office).

VANDERHAEGHE, Guy Clarence, BA, MA, BEd; Canadian writer and playwright; b. 5 April 1951, Esterhazy, SK; s. of Clarence Earl Vanderhaeghe and Alma Beth Allen; m. Margaret Nagel 1972. *Education:* Univ. of Saskatchewan, Univ. of Regina. *Career:* Visiting Prof. of English, St Thomas More College, Univ. of Saskatchewan 1993–. *Publications:* novels: Man Descending (Gov. Gen. Literary Award for Fiction 1982, Geoffrey Faber Memorial Prize 1987) 1982, The Trouble With Heroes 1983, My Present Age 1984, Homesick (City of Toronto Book Award 1990) 1989, Things As They Are? 1992, The Englishman's Boy (Gov. Gen. Literary Award for Fiction) 1996, The Last Crossing 2004; plays: I Had a Job I Liked, Once (Canadian Authors' Asscn Award for Drama 1993) 1991, Dancock's Dance 1995. *Honours:* Hon. DLitt (Saskatchewan) 1997; Canadian Authors' Asscn Award for Drama 1996, Saskatchewan Book Award 1996. *Address:* c/o Department of English, St Thomas More College, University of Saskatchewan, Saskatoon, SK S7N OW0, Canada. *Address:* c/o McClelland and Stewart, 481 University Avenue, Toronto, ON M5G 2E9, Canada (office).

VANDERKAM, James Claire, AB, BD, PhD; American academic and writer; b. 15 Feb. 1946, Cadillac, MI; m. Mary Vander Molen 1967, two s. one d. *Education:* Calvin Coll., Calvin Theological Seminary, Harvard Univ. *Career:* Prof. of Theology, Univ. of Notre Dame. *Publications:* Textual and Historical Studies in the Book of Jubilees, 1977; Enoch and the Growth of Apocalyptic Tradition, 1984; The Book of Jubilees, 2 vols, 1989; The Dead Sea Scrolls Today, 1994; Enoch: A Man for All Generations, 1995; The Jewish Apocalyptic Heritage in Early Christianity (ed. with William Alder), 1996; Calenders in the Dead Sea Scrolls, 1998. *Honours:* Distinguished Research and Literary Publication Award, College of Humanities and Social Sciences, North Carolina State University, 1991; Biblical Archaeology Society Publication Award for Best Popular Book on Archaeology, 1995.

VANDO (HICKOK), Gloria, BA; American poet, publisher and editor; *Publisher and Editor, Helicon Nine Editions*; b. (Gloria Lucille Vando), 21 May 1936, New York, NY; d. of Erasmo Vando and Anita Velez-Mitchell; m. 1st Maurice Peress 1955; one s. two d.; m. 2nd William Harrison Hickok 1980. *Education:* Texas A & I Coll., Corpus Christi, Southampton Coll., Long Island Univ., NY. *Career:* Founding Publr and Ed. Helicon Nine Editions 1977–; Founder and Pres. Midwest Center for the Literary Arts, Inc. 1977– 96; Carolyn Benton Cockefair Chair, Univ. of Missouri-Kansas City (mem. Bd and Speakers Cttee) 1994–; Co-founder and mem. Bd The Writers' Place, Kansas City 1992–; Chair. Arts Cttee League of United Latin American Citizens 1987–90; Vice-Pres. Advisory Bd Missouri Center for the Book, State Library, Jefferson City, Mo. 1997–; mem. Bd Kansas City Arts Council 1984–86, Bd Soc. for Contemporary Photography 1985–87, Bd Educational Services Center 1986–88, Advisory Bd Midtown Arts Center, St Louis, Mo. 1993–98, Advisory Bd BkMk Press, Univ. of Missouri-Kansas City 1997–; mem. Alvin Ailey Dance Theatre, Judith Jamison Partners 1990–92, Council of Literary Magazines and Presses Literary Network 1993–; Founding mem. Nat. Museum of Women in the Arts 1985–90; mem. PEN Int., Poetry Soc. of America, Acad. of American Poets; Trustee N.W. Dible Foundation 1980–, Clearinghouse for Midcontinent Foundations 1985–. *Play:* Moving Targets: Three Interpretations of Murder, produced by MultiStages at Sackett Group's Women's Work Festival 1999. *Publications:* Caprichos 1987, Promesas: Geography of the Impossible 1993, Touching the Fire: Fifteen Poets of Today's Latino Renaissance (anthology) 1998, Spud Songs: An Anthology of Potato Poems (co-ed.) 1999, Shadows and Supposes: Poems 2002, Poetry on Record: 98 Poets Read Their Work, 1888–2006 2006, Chance of a Ghost (co-ed.) 2006; contrib. to Cottonwood Magazine (Gloria Vando Issue, Summer 1994), Kenyon Review, Western Humanities Review, Seattle Review, New Letters, Carolina Quarterly. *Honours:* Poetry Fellowship, Kansas Arts Comm. 1989–91, Grant from Money for Women/Barbara Deming Memorial Fund, Inc. 1989, Billee Murray Denny Prize 1989, Kansas Gov.'s Arts Award 1991, Thorpe Menn Book Award 1994, Second Place, River Styx Int. Poetry Award 1997, Alice Fay Di Castagnola Award, Poetry Soc. of America 1998, Latino Hall of Fame Best Poetry Book of the Year 2003, Torch Award for Excellence in Journalism, Greater Kansas City Women's Political Caucus 2004. *Address:* c/o Helicon Nine Editions, PO Box 22412, Kansas City, MO 64113, USA (office). *Telephone:* (816) 753-1095 (office). *Fax:* (816) 753-1016 (office). *E-mail:* vandog@heliconnine.com (office). *Website:* www.heliconnine.com (office).

VANE, Brett (see Kent, Arthur William Charles)

VANIČEK, Zdeněk, (Alois Bocek), MA, LLD, PhD; Czech diplomatist, academic, poet and writer; *Assistant Professor, Czech Technical University, Prague*; b. 24 June 1947, Chlumec nad Cidlinou; m. Nadya Jankovska; two s. one d. *Education:* Charles Univ., Prague, Diplomatic Acad., Prague. *Career:* mem. Czechoslovak diplomatic service 1972–91; journalist and diplomatic adviser 1991–93; Prof. of Int. Relations and Law, Cyprus 1993–95; Asst Prof. in Tech. Law, Czech Tech. Univ., Prague 1995–; Pres. Czech Asscn of Competitive Communications 1999–; mem. Poetry Soc. (UK), RSL; Fellow, American Biographical Inst. *Publications:* The Theory and the Practice of British Neo-Conservatism 1988, Amidst the Ruins of Memories 1990, To the Ends of the Earth 1992, On the Edge of Rain 1994, Under the Range of Mountains of Five Fingers 1996, Seven Thousand Years Chiselled in Limestone 1996, Amidst Memory's Ruins (mid-life poetry 1988–1998) 1999, Whereupon He Was Arrested (short stories) 2003, 2004, To the Four Corners of the Earth 2005, 2007, La Haute Société 2007; contrib. to newspapers and magazines. *Honours:* Pontifical Medal 1990, Greek Olympic Cttee Commemorative Medal 1990, Acad. of Arts Masaryk Award 1997, Karel Hynek Mácha Prize for Poetry 1998, Emperor Rudolf II Prize for Poetry 2002. *Telephone:* (2) 24152120. *Fax:* (2) 24152121. *E-mail:* cacc@cacc.cz (office). *Website:* www.cacc.cz (office).

VANNI, Carla, LLD; Italian journalist; *Editor-in-Chief, Grazia Magazine*; b. 18 Feb. 1936, Leghorn (Livorno); m. Vincenzo Nisivoccia; two c. *Education:* Univ. of Milan. *Career:* joined Mondadori Publrs, working on fashion desk of Grazia magazine 1959, Head fashion desk 1964, Jt Ed.-in-Chief 1974, Ed.-in-Chief 1978–, responsible for launch of Marie Claire magazine in Italy 1987, Publishing Dir Marie Claire until 2002 and Cento Cose-Energy 1987–99, Donna Moderna 1995–, Flair 2003–, Easy Shop 2004–; has created several new supplements of Grazia: Grazia Bricolage, Grazia Blu and Grazia Int., Grazia Accessori and Grazia Uomo, Grazia Profumi e Balocchi and introduced coverage of social problems; also Ed.-in-Chief Grazia Casa; mem. juries of several nat. and int. literary awards and many beauty competitions. *Honours:* Montenapoleone d'Oro (Best Journalist) 1970, The Oner (Journalist of the Year) 1987, Gullace (for coverage of women's interest issues) 1995, Letterario Castiglioncello costa degli Etruschi Award 2001, Milan Fashion Award 2003, Fondazione Marisa Bellisario Award 2003, Forte dei Marmi 'Dietro la bellezza' Award 2003, Premio Milano per la Moda 2003, Premio 'Dietro la bellezza', Ponte dei Nariù 2003, Premio Narisa Bellsario 2003. *Address:* c/o Grazia, Via Arnoldo Mondadori, 20090 Segrate, Milan, Italy (office). *Telephone:* (02) 754212390 (office). *Fax:* (02) 75422515 (office). *E-mail:* vanni@mondadori.it (office).

VANSITTART, Peter, FRSL; British novelist and historian; b. 27 Aug. 1920, Bedford; s. of Edwin Vansittart and Mignon Vansittart. *Education:* Haileybury Coll. and Worcester Coll. Oxford. *Career:* school teacher 1940–60; writer 1942–. *Publications include:* The Overseer 1948, The Game and the Ground 1955, The Friends of God 1963, The Story Teller 1968, Dictators 1973, The

Death of Robin Hood 1983, Paths from a White Horse 1985, London 1994, A Safe Conduct 1995, In the Fifties 1995, In Memory of England 1998, Survival Tactics 1998, Hermes in Paris 2000, John Paul Jones 2004, Secret Protocols 2006. *Honours:* Hon. Fellow, Worcester Coll. Oxford 1993. *Address:* Little Manor, Church Hill, Kersey, Ipswich, Suffolk, IP7 6DZ, England (home). *Telephone:* (1473) 823163 (home).

VARGAS, Fred; French novelist, historian and archaeologist; b. (Frédérique Audouin-Rouzeau), 1957, Paris; one s. *Career:* writes under pseudonym; currently archaeologist Inst. Pasteur. *Publications:* Les Jeux de l'amour et de la mort (Prix du festival de Cognac) 1986, Ceux qui vont mourir te saluent 1987, Debout les morts (Prix Mystère de la critique 1996) (trans. as The Three Evangelists) 1995, Un Peu plus loin sur la droite 1996, L'Homme aux cercles bleus 1996, Sans feu ni lieu 1997, L'Homme à l'envers (Grand Prix du roman noir de Cognac 2000) (trans. as Seeking Whom he May Devour) 1999, Les Quatre fleuves (Prix Alph-Art du meilleur scénario au festival d'Angoulême 2001) 2000, Pars vite et reviens tard (Prix des libraires 2001, Prix Européen des jeunes lecteurs 2005) (trans. as Have Mercy on Us All) 2001, Petit Traité de toutes vérités sur l'existence 2001, Coule la Seine (novellas) 2002, Salut et liberté 2004, Sous les vents de Neptune (trans. as Wash This Blood Clean from my Hand) 2004, La Vérité sur Césare Battisti 2004, Dans les bois éternels 2006. *Address:* c/o Institut Pasteur, 25–28 rue du Dr Roux, 75015 Paris, France.

VARGAS LLOSA, (Jorge) Mario Pedro, PhD; Peruvian/Spanish writer and journalist; b. 28 March 1936, Arequipa, Peru; s. of Ernesto Vargas Maldonado and Dora Llosa de Vargas; m. 1st Julia Urquidi 1955 (divorced 1964); m. 2nd Patricia Llosa Urquidi 1965; two s. one d. *Education:* Colegio La Salle, Lima, Peru, Leoncio Prado Military Acad., Lima, Colegio Nacional San Miguel, Piura, Universidad Nacional Mayor de San Marcos, Lima and Universidad Complutense de Madrid, Spain. *Career:* journalist on local newspapers, Piura, Peru 1951, for magazines Turismo and Cultura Peruana and for Sunday supplement of El Comercio 1955; News Ed. Radio Panamericana, Lima 1955; Spanish teacher, Berlitz School 1959; journalist, Agence-France Presse 1959; broadcaster, Latin American services of Radiodiffusion Télévision Française 1959; Lecturer in Latin American Literature, Queen Mary Coll., Univ. of London, UK 1967, Prof. King's Coll. 1969; trans. UNESCO 1967; Visiting Prof., Washington State Univ., USA 1968, Univ. de Puerto Rico 1969, Columbia Univ., USA 1975; Prof., Univ. of Cambridge, UK 1977, Harvard Univ., USA 1992, Princeton Univ., USA 1993, Georgetown Univ., USA 1994, 1999; Writer-in-Residence, Woodrow Wilson Int. Center for Scholars, Smithsonian Inst., Washington, DC, USA 1980; Prof. of Ibero-American Literature and Culture, Georgetown Univ., Washington, DC 2001–, Distinguished Writer-in-Residence 2003; Mentor, Literature Program of the Rolex Mentor and Protégé Arts Initative, Second Cycle 2004–05; Weidenfeld Visiting Prof. of European Comparative Literature, St Anne's Coll., Oxford, UK 2004; f. Movimiento Libertad political party and co-f. Frente Democrático (FREDEMO) coalition 1988; cand. for Pres. of Peru 1990; Pres. Jury, Iberoamerican Film Festival, Huelva, Spain 1995, San Sebastian Int. Film Festival 2004; mem. Jury, ECHO Television and Radio Awards 1998, Miguel de Cervantes Prize 1998; Pres. PEN Club Int. 1976–79; mem. Acad. Peruana de la Lengua 1975, Real Acad. Española 1994 (incorporation 1996), Int. Acad. of Humanism 1996, Cervantes Inst. Foundation 1998; Neil Gunn Int. Fellow, Scottish Arts Council 1986; Fellow Wissenschaftskolleg, Berlin 1991–92, Deutscher Akademischer Austauschdienst, Berlin 1997–98. *Films:* Co-Dir of film version of his novel Pantaleón y las visitadoras. *Television:* Dir La torre de Babel 1981. *Publications:* novels: La cuidad y los perros (Biblioteca Breve Prize) 1963, La casa verde (Premio Nacional de Novela, Peru 1967) 1966, Conversación en la catedral 1969, Pantaleón y las visitadoras 1973, La tía Julia y el escribidor (ILLA Prize, Italy 1982) 1977, La guerra del fin del mundo (Pablo Iglesias Literature Prize 1982) 1981, Historia de Mayta 1984, ¿Quién mató a Palomino Molero? 1986, El hablador 1987, Elogio de la madrastra 1988, Lituma en los Andes (Planeta Prize, Spain 1993, Archbishop Juan de San Clemente de Santiago de Compostella Literary Prize, Spain 1994, Int. Literary Prize, Chianti Ruffino Antico Fattore, Italy 1995) 1993, Los cuadernos de Don Rigoberto 1997, La fiesta del Chivo (first Book of the Year Prize, Union of Booksellers of Spain 2001, Readers of Crisol Libraries Prize, Spain 2001) 2000, El paraíso en la otra esquina (chosen for inclusion in "Books to Remember 2003" by cttee of librarians from The New York Public Library 2004) 2003; short stories: El desafío (Revue Française Prize) 1957, Los jefes (Leopoldo Alas Prize) 1959, Los cachorros 1967; anthologies: Contra viento y marea Vol. I (1962–72) 1986, Vol. II (1972–83) 1986, Vol. III (1983–90) 1990, Desafíos a la libertad 1994, Making Waves (Nat. Book Critics' Circle Award, New York 1998) 1996; plays: La huída del Inca 1952, La señorita de Tacna 1981, Kathie y el hipopótamo 1983, La Chunga 1986, El loco de los balcones 1993, Ojos bonitos, cuadros feos 1994, La verdad de las mentiras (II Bartolome March Prize for revised edn 2002) 1990; non-fiction: El pez en el agua (autobiog.) 1993, La orgía perpetua (criticism) 1975, La utopía arcaica 1978, Cartas a un joven novelista (literary essay) 1997, Nationalismus als neue Bedrohung (in German) 2000, El lenguaje de la pasión (selection of articles) 2001, L'Herne. Mario Vargas Llosa (essays etc.) 2003, Diario de Irak (essays) 2003, La tentación de lo imposible (essay on Les Miserables de Victor Hugo) 2004, Mario Vargas Llosa. Obras Completas, Vol. I Narraciones y novelas (1959–1967) and Vol. II, Novelas (1969–1977) 2004, Un demi-siècle avec Borges (interview and essays on Borges written between 1964 and 1999, in French) 2004; contrib. to El País (series Piedra de Toque), Letras Libres, Mexico (series Extemporaneos). *Honours:* Hon. Fellow, Hebrew Univ., Israel 1976, Modern Language Asscn of America 1986, American Acad. and Inst. of Arts and Letters 1986; Hon. Prof., Universidad de Ciencias Aplicadas, Lima 2001; Chevalier, Légion d'honneur, Commdr Ordre des Arts et des Lettres 1993, Medal Orden El Sol del Perú (Great Cross of Diamonds) 2001, Medalla de Honor en el Grado de Gran Cruz, Peru 2003; Hon. DHumLitt (Connecticut Coll., USA) 1991; Hon. DLitt (Warwick) 2004; Dr hc (Florida Int. Univ. of Miami) 1990, (Boston) 1992, (Geneva) 1992, (Dowling College (USA) 1993, (Universidad Francisco Marroquin (Guatemala) 1993, (Georgetown) 1994, (Yale) 1994, (Rennes II) 1994, (Murcia) 1995, (Valladolid) 1995, (Lima) 1997, (Universidad Nacional de San Agustin, Peru) 1997, (Ben Gurion) 1998, (Univ. Coll. London) 1998, (Harvard) 1999, (Universidad Nacional Mayor de San Marcos, Lima) 2001, (Rome Tor Vergata) 2001, (Pau) 2001, (Universidad Nacional San Antonio Abad del Cusco) 2002, (Univ. of French Polynesia) 2002, (La Trobe Univ., Melbourne) 2002, (Skidmore Coll., USA) 2002, (Universidad Nacional de Piura) 2002, (Universidad Nacional Pedro Ruiz Gallo) 2002, (Catholic Univ. of Louvain) 2003, (Universidad Nacional de Ingenieria, Lima) 2003, (Oxford) 2003, (Universidad Pedagogica Nacional Francisco Morazan, Tegucigalpa, Honduras) 2003, (Universidad Católica Santa María, Arequipa) 2004; Diploma de Honor, Universidad Nacional Mayor de San Marcos 2000; Crítica Española Prize 1966, Premio de la Crítica, Argentina 1981, Ritz Paris Hemingway Prize 1985, Príncipe de Asturias Prize, Spain 1986, Castiglione de Sicilia Prize, Italy 1990, Miguel de Cervantes Prize, Spain 1994, Jerusalem Prize, Israel 1995, Congressional Medal of Honour, Peru 1982, T.S. Eliot Prize, Ingersoll Foundation of The Rockford Institute, USA 1991, Golden Palm Award, INTAR Hispanic American Arts Center, New York 1992, Miguel de Cervantes Prize, Ministry of Culture (Spain) 1994, Jerusalem Prize 1995, Peace Prize, German Publishers, Frankfurt Book Fair 1996, Pluma de Oro Award, Spain 1997, Medal and Diploma of Honour, Univ. Católica de Santa María, Arequipa, Peru 1997, Medal of the Univ. of Calif. 1999, Jorge Isaacs Award, Int. Festival of Art, Cali, Colombia 1999, Medal "Patrimonio Cultural de la Humanidad", Municipalidad de Arequipa 2000, Certificate of Recognition, Colegio de Abogados 2001, Crystal Award, World Econ. Forum, Davos, Switzerland 2001, Americas Award, Americas Foundation 2001, Son Latinos Festival Prize, Tenerife, Spain 2001, Caonabo de Oro Prize, Dominican Asscn of Journalsits and Writers, 2002, Golden Medal, City of Genoa (Italy) 2002, PEN Nabokov Award 2002, Int. Prize of Letters, Cristobal Gabarron Foundation 2002, Premio Ateneo Americano, on Xth Anniversary of Casa de America 2002, Medal of Honour, City of Trujillo, Peru 2003, Roger-Caillois PEN Club Prize 2003, Budapest Prize 2003, Presidential Medal of Hofstra Univ., New York 2003, Grinzane Cavour Prize: "A Life for Literature International Prize", Turin 2004, Konex Foundation Prize 2004, Medal of the Centenary of Pablo Neruda, Govt of Chile 2004, Medal of Honor of Peruvian Culture, Nat. Inst.Inst. of Culture 2004. *Address:* Las Magnolias 295, 6° Piso, Barranco, Lima 4, Peru. *Telephone:* (1) 477-3868. *Fax:* (1) 477-3518.

VARMUS, Harold Eliot, MA, MD; American microbiologist and academic; *President and CEO, Memorial Sloan-Kettering Cancer Center*; b. 18 Dec. 1939, Oceanside, NY; s. of Frank Varmus and Beatrice (née Barasch) Varmus; m. Constance Louise Casey 1969; two s. *Education:* Amherst Coll., Harvard Univ., Columbia Univ. *Career:* physician, Presbyterian Hosp., New York 1966–68; Clinical Assoc., NIH, Bethesda, Md 1968–70; lecturer, Dept of Microbiology, Univ. of Calif. at San Francisco 1970–72, Asst Prof. 1972–74, Assoc. Prof. 1974–79, Prof. 1979–83, American Cancer Soc. Research Prof. 1984–93; Dir NIH 1993–99; Pres. and CEO Memorial Sloan-Kettering Cancer Center 2000–; Consultant, Chiron Corp., Emoryville, Calif.; Assoc. Ed. Cell Journal; mem. Editorial Bd Cancer Surveys; mem. American Soc. of Virology, American Soc. of Microbiology, AAAS. *Publications:* (ed.) Molecular Biology of Tumor Viruses 1982, 1985, Readings in Tumor Virology 1983. *Honours:* Calif. Acad. of Sciences Scientist of the Year 1982, Lasker Foundation Award 1982 (co-recipient), Passano Foundation Award 1983, Armand Hammer Cancer Prize 1984, Gen. Motors Alfred Sloan Award, Shubitz Cancer Prize (NAS) 1984, Nobel Prize 1989, Nat. Medal of Science 2001, Rave Award, Wired Magazine 2004. *Address:* Memorial Sloan-Kettering Cancer Center, 1275 York Avenue, New York, NY 10021, USA (office). *Telephone:* (212) 639-7317 (office); (212) 639-7227 (office). *Fax:* (212) 717-3125 (office). *E-mail:* varmus@mskcc.org (office). *Website:* www.mskcc.org (office).

VARRASSI, Lillian M., BA; American poet; b. 9 Aug. 1949, Queens, NY. *Education:* Inst. of Children's Literature, Queens Coll., CUNY. *Publications:* Soliloquoy 1991, Through a Glass Darkly 2000; contrib. to American Poetry Annual 1991, Visions and Beyond 1991, A View from the Edge 1992, Reflections 1992, Expectations 1992, Poetry Voices of America 1992, Beneath the Winter Sky 1998, Voices of the New Century 2000. *Honours:* Amherst Soc. Certificate of Poetic Achievement 1992, The Poetry Center Certificate of Poetic Accomplishment 1992. *Address:* 59-32 72nd Street, Maspeth, NY 11378, USA. *E-mail:* lvarrassi@aol.com.

VASILYEV, Boris Lvovich; Russian writer, dramatist and essayist; b. 21 May 1924, Smolensk; m. Zorya Albertovna Vasilyeva; two adopted s. *Education:* Mil. Acad. of Armoured Troops. *Career:* served in Red Army in World War II, seriously wounded; engineer with Acad. of Armoured Troops 1943–54; USSR People's Deputy 1989–91; mem. USSR Supreme Soviet 1991. *Publications include:* Dawns are Quiet Here 1969, Do Not Shoot the White Swans 1975, My Horses are Flying 1983, And Tomorrow was War (novel) 1984, The Burning Bush 1987, Regards from Baba Vera 1988, Absent from the Casualty List (novel) 1988, There was Evening, There was Morning 1989, The

Short Castling 1989, The Carnival (novel) 1990, The House Built by the Old Man 1991, Kahunk and Prince Prophetic Oleg (novel) 1996, Two Bananas in one Peel (novel) 1996, A Gambler and Rabid Duellist 1998; many screenplays. *Honours:* USSR State Prize 1975; Konstantin Simonov Prize; Dovzhenko Gold Medal. *Address:* Chasovaya Str. 58, Apt. 40, 125319 Moscow, Russia. *Telephone:* (495) 152-99-01.

VASILYEVA, Larisa Nikolayevna; Russian poet and writer; b. 23 Nov. 1935, Kharkov, Ukraine; d. of Nikolai Alekseyevich Kucherenko and Yekaterina Vasilievna Kucherenko; m. Oleg Vasiliyev 1957; one s. *Education:* Moscow Univ. *Career:* started publishing 1957; first collection of verse 1966; Sec. of Moscow Br. of Russian Union of Writers; Pres. Fed. of Russian Women Writers 1989–, Int. Publishing League Atlantida 1992–. *Publications include:* (stories, prose works) Albion and the Secret of Time 1978, Novel About My Father 1983, Cloud of Fire 1988, Selected Works (2 vols) 1989, The Kremlin Wives 1992, The Kremlin Children 1996, The Wives of the Russian Crown; (poetry) Fire-fly 1969, The Swan 1970, Blue Twilight 1970, Encounter 1974, A Rainbow of Snow 1974, Meadows 1975, Fire in the Window 1978, Russian Names 1980, Foliage 1980, Fireflower 1981, Selected Poetry 1981, Grove 1984, Mirror 1985, Moskovorechie 1985, Lantern 1985, Waiting For You In The Sky 1986, A Strange Virtue 1991. *Honours:* Moscow Komsomol Prize 1971. *Address:* Usiyevicha str. 8, Apt. 86, 125319 Moscow, Russia. *Telephone:* (495) 155-74-86.

VASSANJI, M.G., OC, BS, PhD; Canadian writer; b. 30 May 1950, Nairobi, Kenya; s. of Gulamhussein V. Nanji and Daulatkhanu V. Nanji; m. Nurjehan Vassanji (née Aziz) 1979; two s. *Education:* MIT and Univ. of Pennsylvania. *Career:* grew up in Dar es Salaam, Tanzania; Post-doctoral Fellow Atomic Energy of Canada Ltd 1978–80; Research Assoc., Univ. of Toronto 1980–89; first novel published 1989, full-time writer 1989–; Writer-in-Residence Int. Writing Program, Univ. of Iowa 1989. *Publications:* The Gunny Sack (novel) (Commonwealth First Novel Award, Africa Region 1990) 1989, No New Land (novel) 1991, Uhuru Street (short stories) 1991, The Book of Secrets (novel) 1994, Amriika (novel) 1999, The In-Between World of Vikram Lall (novel) 2003, When She Was Queen (short stories) 2005. *Honours:* Hon. DLitt (York) 2005, (McMaster) 2006; Giller Prize for Best Novel (Canada) 1994, 2003, Harbour Front Literary Award 1994, F. G. Bressani Award 1994. *Address:* 39 Woburn Avenue, Toronto, ON M5M 1K5, Canada (office).

VASSILIKOS, Vassilis; Greek writer; b. 18 Nov. 1934, Kavala; m. Vasso Papantoniou 1985; one d. *Education:* Univ. of Salonika Law School, Yale Drama School, School of Radio and Television, New York, USA. *Career:* Dir-Gen. of Greek TV (public) 1981–85; presenter of weekly TV show on books; Amb. to UNESCO 1996–2004; Pres. Hellenic Authors' Soc. 1999–2005. *Publications include:* (in English trans.): The Plant, The Well, The Angel 1963, Z 1968, The Harpoon Gun 1972, Outside the Walls 1973, The Photographs 1974, The Monarch 1976, The Coroner's Assistant 1986, ...And Dreams Are Dreams 1996, The Few Things I Know About Glafkos Thrassakis 2003. *Honours:* Commdr, Ordre des Arts et Lettres 1999. *Address:* Alkyonis 54, 17562 Athens, Greece (home). *Telephone:* (210) 3634868 (home). *Fax:* (210) 9858709 (home). *E-mail:* newopera@otenet.gr (home).

VATSUYEVA, Aset; Russian journalist; *Television Presenter and Co-Host Strana i Mir programme, NTV;* b. 1977, Grozny, Chechnya; one s. *Education:* St Petersburg Univ., Moscow State Univ. *Career:* corresp., Voice of the Chechen Repub. newspaper, Grozny 1997; fmr reporter, Obshaya Gazeta and Obyedinennaya Gazeta, Moscow; reporter, NTV Namedni 2002, Co-Host Strana i Mir (Russia and the World) programme, NTV 2003–. *Honours:* Honoured Cultural Artist of Ingushetia 2004. *Address:* c/o NTV Independent Television, ul. Akademika Koroleva 12, 127000 Moscow, Russia (office). *Telephone:* (495) 725-5389 (office). *Fax:* (495) 215-1888 (office). *E-mail:* avatsuyeva@ntv.ru (office). *Website:* www.ntv.ru (office).

VAUGHAN WILLIAMS, (Joan) Ursula Penton, FRCM; British writer; b. 15 March 1911, Valletta, Malta; m. 1st Michael Forrester Wood 1933 (died 1942); m. 2nd Ralph Vaughan Williams 1953 (died 1958). *Career:* writer of songs, song cycles, libretti for cantatas and opera libretti; cttees: RVW Ltd., Ralph Vaughan Williams Trust. *Publications:* No Other Choice 1941, Fall of Leaf 1944, Need for Speech 1948, Silence and Music 1959, Ralph Vaughan Williams (biog.) 1964, Aspects 1984, Paradise Remembered (autobiog.) 2002, Complete Poems 2003; seven vols of poems, three novels, two books of photographs of Ralph Vaughan Williams; libretti for operas and cantatas by various composers. *Honours:* Hon. FRAM, Hon. RNCM. *Address:* 66 Gloucester Crescent, London, NW1 7EG, England.

VELLIDIS, Katerina; Greek publisher; b. 1947, Thessaloniki; d. of Ioannis Vellidis and Anna Vellidis; m. (divorced); one d. *Education:* Univ. of Geneva and Sorbonne, Paris. *Career:* Pres. Bd and Man. Dir I. K. Vellidis Press Org. of Northern Greece (publrs of newspapers and magazines, including Thessaloníki) 1980–; Pres. Ioannis and Anna Vellidis Foundation. *Honours:* numerous awards including Silver Medal of Acad. of Athens. *Address:* c/o Thessaloníki, Odos Monastiriou 85, 546 27 Thessaloníki, Greece.

VENCLOVA, Tomas, PhD; American linguist, academic, writer and poet; *Professor of Slavic Languages and Literatures, Yale University;* b. 11 Sept. 1937, Klaipeda, Lithuania; m. Tanya Milovidova 1990; one s. one d. *Education:* Univ. of Vilnius, Yale Univ. *Career:* Lecturer in Literature, Linguistics and Semiotics, Univ. of Vilnius 1966–73; Jr Fellow, Inst. of History, Lithuanian Acad. of Sciences 1974–76; Regents Prof. in Slavic

Languages and Literatures, Univ. of California, Berkeley 1977; Lecturer in Slavic Languages and Literatures, UCLA 1977–80; Morton Prof. of Philosophy, Ohio Univ. 1978; Lecturer and Acting Instructor of Slavic Languages and Literatures, Yale Univ. 1980–85, Asst Prof. 1985–90, Assoc. Prof. 1990–93, Prof. 1993–; Fellow, New York Inst. for the Humanities 1981–84, Kennan Inst. for Advanced Russian Studies 1981; mem. Asscn for the Advancement of Baltic Studies (Pres. 1989–91), Int. PEN, PEN in Exile (mem. Exec. Bd 1982). *Publications:* poetry: Kalbos zenklas 1972, 98 eilerasciai 1977, Pasnekesys ziema (partial trans. as Winter Dialogue) 1991, Szesc wierszy 1991, Cistost soli 1991, Mondjatok meg Fortinbrasnak 1992, Reginys is alejos 1998, Rinktine 1999, Vor der Tür das Ende der Welt 2000; prose: Tekstai apie tekstus 1985, Neustoichivoe ravnovesie: vosem russkikh poeticheskikh tekstov 1986, Vilties formos: Eseistika ir publistisika (partial trans. as Forms of Hope) 1991, Aleksander Wat: Life and Art of an Iconoclast 1996, Sobesedniki na piru 1997, Manau, kad... 2000, Ligi Lietuvos 10.000 kilometru 2003; translations: many works by major writers into Lithuanian; contrib. to articles to professional journals, including International Journal of Slavic Linguistics and Poetics, Russian Literature, Russian Review, World Literature Today, Journal of Baltic Studies, Comparative Civilizations Review, UCLA Slavic Studies. *Honours:* Dr hc (Lublin) 1991, (Jagellonian Univ., Kraków) 2000; Vilenica Int. Literary Prize 1990, Lithuanian Nat. Prize 2000; 1956 Hungarian Revolution Memorial Award 2006. *Address:* Department of Slavic Languages and Literatures, Yale University, New Haven, CT 06520 (office); 100 York Street, Apt 12 S, New Haven, CT 06511, USA (home). *E-mail:* tomas.venclova@yale.edu (office).

VENDLER, Helen Hennessy, AB, PhD; American academic and literary critic; *A. Kingsley Porter University Professor, Department of English, Harvard University;* b. 30 April 1933, Boston, Mass.; d. of George Hennessy and Helen Conway; one s. *Education:* Emmanuel Coll. and Harvard Univ. *Career:* Instructor Cornell Univ. 1960–63; Lecturer, Swarthmore Coll., Pa and Haverford Coll., Pa 1963–64; Asst Prof. Smith Coll. Northampton, Mass. 1964–66; Assoc. Prof. Boston Univ. 1966–68, Prof. 1968–85; Visiting Prof. Harvard Univ. 1981–85, Kenan Prof. 1985–, Assoc. Acad. Dean 1987–92, A. Kingsley Porter Univ. Prof. 1990–; Sr Fellow, Harvard Soc. of Fellows 1981–92; poetry critic, New Yorker 1978–; mem. American Acad. of Arts and Sciences, Norwegian Acad., American Philosophical Soc., Educ. Advisory Bd Guggenheim Foundation, Pulitzer Prize Bd 1990–99; Fulbright Fellow 1954; A.A.U.W. Fellow 1959; Guggenheim Fellow 1971–72; American Council of Learned Socs. Fellow 1971–72; N.E.H. Fellow 1980, 1985, 1994; Wilson Fellow 1994; Fulbright Lecturer, Univ. of Bordeaux 1968–69; Overseas Fellow, Churchill Coll. Cambridge 1980; Parnell Fellow, Magdalene Coll. Cambridge 1996, Hon. Fellow 1996–. *Publications include:* Yeats's Vision and the Later Plays 1963, On Extended Wings: Wallace Stevens' Longer Poems 1969, The Poetry of George Herbert 1975, Part of Nature, Part of Us 1980, The Odes of John Keats 1983, Wallace Stevens: Words Chosen Out of Desire 1985, Harvard Book of Contemporary American Poetry 1985, The Music of What Happens 1988, The Given and the Made 1995, The Breaking of Style 1995, Soul Says 1995, Poems, Poets, Poetry 1996, The Art of Shakespeare's Sonnets 1997, Seamus Heaney 1998, Coming of Age as a Poet: Milton, Keats, Eliot, Plath 2003, Poets Thinking: Pope, Whitman, Dickinson, Yeats 2005. *Honours:* 17 hon. degrees; Lowell Prize 1969, Explicator Prize 1969, Nat. Inst. of Arts and Letters Award 1975, Nat. Book Critics Award 1980, Newton Arvin Award, Jefferson Medal. *Address:* Harvard University, Department of English, Barker Center 205, 12 Quincey Street, Cambridge, MA 02138 (office); 54 Trowbridge Street, Apt. B, Cambridge, MA 02138, USA. *Telephone:* (617) 496-6028 (office); (617) 547-9197 (home). *Fax:* (617) 496-8737 (office); (617) 496-8737 (office). *E-mail:* aperalta@fas.harvard.edu (office). *Website:* www.fas.harvard.edu/~english (office).

VENN, George Andrew Fyfe, BA, MFA; American academic, writer, poet and editor; *Professor Emeritus of English, Eastern Oregon University;* b. 12 Oct. 1943, Tacoma, WA; m. Elizabeth Cheney (divorced); one s. one d. *Education:* Coll. of Idaho, Univ. of Montana, Central Univ., Quito, Ecuador, Univ. of Salamanca, Spain, City Literary Inst., London. *Career:* Gen. Ed., Oregon Literature Series Vols I–VI 1989–; faculty mem., Eastern Oregon Univ., Prof. Emer. 2002–; Pres. Oregon Council of Teachers of English 2001–03; mem. Oregon Council of Teachers of English, PEN West, Nat. Council of Teachers of English. *Publications:* Sunday Afternoon: Grande Ronde 1975, Off the Main Road 1978, Marking the Magic Circle 1988, West of Paradise: New Poems 1999, Soldier to Advocate: C. E. S. Wood's 1877 Legacy 2006; contrib. to Oregon Humanities, Writer's Northwest Handbook, North West Review, Northwest Reprint Series, Poetry Northwest, Willow Springs, Clearwater Journal, Oregon East, Portland Review, Worldviews and the American West (book). *Honours:* Pushcart Prize 1980, Oregon Book Award 1988, Stewart Holbrook Award 1994, Northwest Writers Andres Berger Poetry Prize 1995, Eastern Oregon Univ. Distinguished Teaching Award 2002. *Address:* c/o Department of English, Eastern Oregon University, La Grande, OR 97850 (office); 706 B Avenue, La Grande, OR 97850, USA (home). *Telephone:* (541) 962-0380 (home). *Fax:* (541) 663-0920 (home). *Website:* www.georgevenn.com (office).

VENTURI, Robert, AB, MFA, FAIA; American architect; b. 25 June 1925, Philadelphia, Pa; s. of Robert C. Venturi and Vanna Lanzetta; m. Denise (Lakofski) Scott Brown 1967; one s. *Education:* Princeton Univ. *Career:* Designer, Oskar Stonorov 1950, Eero Saarinen & Assoc. 1950–53; Rome Prize Fellow, American Acad. in Rome 1954–56; Designer, Louis I. Kahn 1957;

Assoc. Prof., School of Fine Arts, Univ. of Pennsylvania 1957–65; Charlotte Shepherd Davenport Prof., Yale Univ. 1966–70; Prin., Venturi, Cope & Lippincott 1958–61, Venturi and Short 1961–64, Venturi and Rauch 1964–80, Venturi, Rauch and Scott Brown (architects and planners) 1980–89; Venturi, Scott Brown and Assocs June 1989–; Fellow American Acad. in Rome, Accademia Nazionale di San Luca, American Acad. of Arts and Sciences. *Works include:* Vanna Venturi House, Phila, Pa 1961, Guild House, Phila 1961, Franklin Court, Phila 1972, Allen Memorial Art Museum Addition, Oberlin, Ohio 1973, Inst. for Scientific Information Corpn HQ, Phila 1978, Gordon Wu Hall, Princeton Univ., NJ 1980, Seattle Art Museum, Seattle, Wash. 1984, Clinical Research Bldg, Univ. of Pa 1985 (with Payette Assocs.), Nat. Gallery, Sainsbury Wing, London, UK 1986, Fisher-Bendheim Hall, Princeton Univ. 1986, Charles P. Stevenson Library, Bard Coll. 1989, Regional Govt Bldg, Toulouse, France 1992, Kirifuri Resort facilities, Nikko, Japan 1992, Univ. of Del. Student Center, Newark, Del. 1992, Memorial Hall Restoration and Addition, Harvard Univ. 1992, The Barnes Foundation Restoration and Renovation, Merion, Pa 1993, Disney Celebration Bank, Celebration, Fla 1993, Irvine Auditorium, Perelman Quadrangle, Univ. of Pa 1995, Princeton Campus Center, Princeton Univ. 1996, Congress Avenue Building, Yale Univ. School of Medicine 1998, Master Plan and Bldgs for Univ. of Michigan 1997–. *Publications:* Complexity and Contradiction in Architecture 1966, Learning from Las Vegas (with Denise Scott Brown and Steven Izenour) 1972, A View from the Campidoglio: Selected Essays, 1953–1984 (with Denise Scott Brown) 1984, Iconography and Electronics upon a Generic Architecture 1996; numerous articles in professional journals. *Honours:* Hon. FRIBA; Hon. Fellow Royal Incorporation of Architects in Scotland, American Acad. and Inst. of Arts and Letters; Hon. DFA (Oberlin, Yale, Penn., Princeton, Phila Coll of Art); Hon. LHD (NJ Inst. of Tech.); Laurea hc (Univ. of Rome La Sapienza) 1994; Nat. Medal of Arts 1992 and numerous other awards. *Address:* Venturi, Scott Brown and Associates, 4236 Main Street, Philadelphia, PA 19127, USA (office). *Telephone:* (215) 487-0400 (office). *Fax:* (215) 487-2520 (office). *E-mail:* venturi@vsba.com (office). *Website:* www.vsba.com (office).

VERGHESE, Abraham; Ethiopian writer; b. 1955; m.; two c. *Education:* Madras Medical Coll. India, East Tennessee State Univ., Johnson City, USA. *Career:* specialist in HIV and AIDS research 1985–89; worked at Univ. of Iowa outpatient AIDS clinic 1990; currently Prof. of Medicine and Chief of Infectious Diseases, Texas Tech Health Sciences Center, El Paso, TX. *Publications:* My Own Country: A Doctor's Story of a Town and its People in the Age of AIDS 1994, Soundings: A Doctor's Life in the Age of AIDS 1994, The Tennis Partner: A Doctor's Story of Friendship and Loss 1998, Short Stories 1999; contrib. to The New Yorker, North American Review, Granta, Sports Illustrated, Story, numerous medical journals. *Address:* c/o HarperCollins Publishers Ltd, 77–85 Fulham Palace Road, London, W6 8JB, England. *Website:* www.harpercollins.co.uk.

VERMES, Geza, MA, DTheol, DLitt, FBA; British academic and writer; *Editor, Journal of Jewish Studies;* b. 22 June 1924, Mako, Hungary; m. 1st Pamela Hobson 1958 (died 1993); m. 2nd Margaret Unarska 1996. *Education:* Univ. of Budapest, Univ. of Louvain. *Career:* Licencié en Histoire et Philologie Orientales; Lecturer, later Senior Lecturer in Divinity, University of Newcastle 1957–65; Reader in Jewish Studies, University of Oxford 1965–89; Fellow, Wolfson Coll. 1965–91, Fellow Emer. 1991–, Prof. of Jewish Studies, Univ. of Oxford 1989–91, Prof. Emer. 1991–; Ed., Journal of Jewish Studies 1971–; Dir, Oxford Forum for Qumran Research, Oxford Centre for Hebrew and Jewish Studies 1991–; Inaugural Lecturer, Geza Vermes Lectures in the History of Religions, University of Leicester 1997; many visiting lectureships and professorships; mem. British Assen for Jewish Studies, pres. 1975, 1988; Pres. European Assen for Jewish Studies 1981–84; Fellow, European Acad. of Arts, Sciences and Humanities 2001. *Publications:* Les manuscrits du désert de Juda 1953, Discovery in the Judean Desert 1956, Scripture and Tradition in Judaism 1961, The Dead Sea Scrolls in English 1962, Jesus the Jew 1973, History of the Jewish People in the Age of Jesus Christ, by E. Schürer I–III (co-reviser with F. Millar and M. Goodman) 1973–87, Post-Biblical Jewish Studies 1975, The Dead Sea Scrolls: Qumran in Perspective (with Pamela Vermes) 1977, The Gospel of Jesus the Jew 1981, Essays in Honour of Y. Yadin (co-ed.) 1982, Jesus and the World of Judaism 1983, The Essenes According to the Classical Sources (with M. D. Goodman) 1989, The Religion of Jesus the Jew 1993, The Complete Dead Sea Scrolls in English 1997, Providential Accidents: An Autobiography 1998, Discoveries in the Judaean Desert XXVI: The Community Rule (with P. S. Alexander) 1998, An Introduction to the Complete Dead Sea Scrolls 1999, The Changing Faces of Jesus 2000, The Dead Sea Scrolls 2000, Jesus in His Jewish Context 2003, The Authentic Gospel of Jesus 2003, The Passion 2005, Who's Who in the Age of Jesus 2005; contrib. to scholarly books and journals. *Honours:* Hon. DD (Edinburgh) 1989, (Durham) 1990; Hon. DLitt (Sheffield) 1994; W. Bacher Medallist, Hungarian Acad. of Sciences 1996. *Address:* West Wood Cottage, Foxcombe Lane, Boars Hill, Oxford, OX1 5DH, England (home). *Telephone:* (1865) 735384 (office). *Fax:* (1865) 735034 (office). *E-mail:* geza.vermes@orinst.ox.ac.uk (office).

VERONESI, Sandro; Italian writer; b. 1959, Florence. *Publications include:* novels: Per dore parte questo treno allegro 1988, La forza del passato (trans. as The Force of the Past) 2000; contrib. to Cronache Italiene: Racconti 1992, Superalbo: Le storie complete 2002. *Honours:* Campiello Prize. *Address:* c/o

Ecco, 77–85 Fulham Palace Road, London, W6 8JB, England. *Website:* www.harpercollins.co.uk.

VICKERS, Hugo Ralph; British writer and lecturer; *Chairman, Jubilee Walkway Trust;* b. 12 Nov. 1951, London, England; s. of the late Ralph Cecil Vickers, MC and Dulcie Vickers; m. Elizabeth Anne Blyth Vickers 1995; two s. one d. *Education:* Eton Coll., Univ. of Strasbourg, France. *Career:* radio and TV broadcaster 1973–; Dir Burkes Peerage 1974–79; mem. Historic Houses Assen, RSL, Jubilee Walkway Trust (Trustee 2000–, Vice-Chair. 2001, Chair. 2002–); mem. Council of Man., Windsor Festival 1999–; Lay Steward, St George's Chapel, Windsor 1970–, Deputy Vice-Capt. Lay Stewards 1996–. *Publications:* We Want the Queen 1977, Gladys, Duchess of Marlborough 1979, Debretts Book of the Royal Wedding 1981, Cocktails and Laughter (ed.) 1983, Cecil Beaton: The Authorised Biography 1985, Vivien Leigh 1988, Loving Garbo 1994, Royal Orders 1994, The Private World of the Duke and Duchess of Windsor 1995, The Kiss 1996, Alice, Princess Andrew of Greece 2000, The Unexpurgated Beaton (ed.) 2002, Beaton in the Sixties (ed.) 2003, Alexis – The Memoirs of the Baron de Redé (ed.) 2005, Elizabeth the Queen Mother 2005; contrib. to books and periodicals. *Honours:* PEN Stern Prize for Non-Fiction 1996. *Literary Agent:* c/o Aitken Alexander Associates Ltd, 18–21 Cavaye Place, London, SW10 9PT, England. *Telephone:* (20) 7373-8672. *Fax:* (20) 7373-6002. *E-mail:* reception@aitkenalexander.co.uk. *Website:* www.aitkenalexander.co.uk. *Address:* Wyeford, Ramsdell, Hants., RG26 5QL, England (home).

VICKERS, Salley; British writer and psychologist; two c. *Career:* fmr university lecturer in English literature; analytical psychologist; lecturer on literature, psychology and religion. *Publications:* Miss Garnet's Angel 2000, Instances of the Number 3 2001, Mr Golightly's Holiday 2003, Nice 'N' Easy 2003, The Other Side of You 2006; contrib. to Quicksilver magazine, newspapers. *Address:* c/o Fourth Estate, 77–85 Fulham Palace Road, London W6 8JB, England. *E-mail:* reception@salleyvickers.com. *Website:* www.salleyvickers.com.

VICTOR, Edward (Ed), MLitt; British literary agent; b. 9 Sept. 1939, New York, USA; s. of the late Jack Victor and the late Lydia Victor; m. 1st Michelene Dinah Samuels 1963 (divorced); two s.; m. 2nd Carol Lois Ryan; one s. *Education:* Dartmouth Coll., USA, Pembroke Coll., Cambridge. *Career:* Arts Book Ed., then Editorial Dir Weidenfeld & Nicolson 1964–67; Editorial Dir Jonathan Cape Ltd 1967–71; Sr Ed. Alfred A. Knopf Inc., New York 1972–73, literary agent and Dir John Farquharson Ltd 1974–76; Founding Ed. Victor Agency 1977; mem. Council Aids Crisis Trust 1986–98; Vice-Chair. Almeida Theatre 1994–2002 (Dir 1993–2002); Trustee, The Arts Foundation 1991–2004. *Publications include:* The Obvious Diet 2001. *Address:* Ed Victor Ltd, 6 Bayley Street, Bedford Square, London, WC1B 3HB (office); 10 Cambridge Gate, Regents Park, London, NW1 4JX, England (home). *Telephone:* (20) 7304-4100 (office); (20) 7224-3030 (home). *Fax:* (20) 7304-4111 (office); (20) 7935-3096 (home). *E-mail:* ed@edvictor.com.

VIDA, Vendela; American writer; m. Dave Eggers 2003. *Education:* Columbia Univ. *Career:* Co-Ed., The Believer literary magazine. *Publications:* Girls on the Verge 1999, And Now You Can Go 2003, Let the Northern Lights Erase Your Name 2007. *Address:* 826 Valencia Street, San Francisco, CA 94110, USA. *E-mail:* letters@believermag.com. *Website:* www.believermag.com.

VIDAL, Gore; American writer; b. 3 Oct. 1925, West Point, New York; s. of Eugene L. Vidal and Nina Vidal (née Gore). *Education:* Phillips Acad., Exeter, NH. *Career:* served in US Army 1943–46; Drama Critic, Reporter (magazine) 1959, Democratic-Liberal Cand. for US Congress from New York 1960; mem. Pres. Kennedy's Advisory Council on the Arts 1961–63; Co-Chair. People's Party 1970–72; writes thrillers under pseudonym Edgar Box. *Film and television screenplays:* Wedding Breakfast, The Catered Affair 1956, The Left-Handed Gun 1958, I Accuse 1958, The Death of Billy the Kid (TV) 1958, Suddenly Last Summer 1959, The Best Man (Cannes Critics' Prize) 1964, Is Paris Burning? 1966, The Last of the Mobile Hotshots 1970, Dress Gray 1986. *Publications:* novels: Williwaw 1946, In a Yellow Wood 1947, The City and the Pillar 1948, The Season of Comfort 1949, A Search for the King 1950, Dark Green, Bright Red 1950, The Judgment of Paris 1952, Messiah 1954, Julian 1964, Washington, DC 1967, Myra Breckinridge 1968, Two Sisters 1970, Burr 1972, Myron 1974, 1876 1976, Kalki 1978, Creation (Prix Deauville) 1980, Duluth 1983, Lincoln 1984, Empire 1987, Hollywood 1990, Live from Golgotha 1992, With Honors 1994, Dark Green, Dark Red 1995, The Season of Conflict 1996, The Essential Vidal 1998, The Smithsonian Institution 1998, The Golden Age 2000; short stories: A Thirsty Evil 1956; plays: Visit to a Small Planet 1956, The Best Man 1960, Romulus 1962, Weekend 1968, An Evening with Richard Nixon 1972, Gore Vidal's Lincoln 1988, On the March to the Sea 2005; non-fiction: Rocking the Boat 1962, Reflections upon a Sinking Ship 1969, Homage to Daniel Shays 1972, Matters of Fact and Fiction 1977, The Second American Revolution 1982, Armageddon? 1987, At Home: Essays 1982–88 1988, A View from the Diners Club: Essays 1987–1991 1991, Screening History (memoir) 1992, United States: Essays 1952–1992 (Nat. Book Award) 1993, Palimpsest (memoir) 1995, Virgin Islands: A Dependency of United States Essays 1992–97 1997, The Last Empire: Essays 1992–2000 2001, Perpetual War for Perpetual Peace: How We Got So Hated 2002, Inventing a Nation: Washington, Adams, Jefferson 2003, Imperial America 2004, Point To Point Navigation (memoir) 2006; criticism in Partisan Review, The Nation, New York Review of Books, Times Literary Supplement.

Honours: Hon. Citizen, Ravello, Italy 1983; Chevalier, Ordre Nat. des Arts et des Lettres; Edgar Allan Poe Award for Television 1955. *Address:* c/o Doubleday Publicity Department, 1745 Broadway, New York, NY 10019, USA. *E-mail:* ddaypub@randomhouse.com.

VIEWEGH, Michal; Czech novelist and writer; b. 31 March 1931, Prague. *Education:* Charles Univ., Prague. *Career:* primary school teacher; Ed. Czech Writer publishing house 1993–95; Lecturer, Czech Acad. of Literature 1999–2004. *Publications:* Názory na vraždu 1990, Báječná léta pod psa (Jiří Orten Award 1993) 1992, Nápady laskavého čtenáře (parodies) 1993, Výchova dívek v Čechách (trans. as Bringing up Girls in Bohemia) 1994, Účastníci zájezdu 1996, Zapisovatelé otcovský lásky 1998, Povídky o manželství a sexu 1999, Nové nápady laskavého čtenáře (parodies) 2000, Román pro ženy 2001, Báječná léta s Klausem 2002, Případ nevěrné Kláry 2003, Vybíjená 2004, Tři v háji (co-author) 2004, Lekce tvůrčího psaní 2005, Báječný rok (diary) 2006, Andělé všedního dne (novella) 2007; contrib. to newspapers and magazines. *Literary Agent:* Dana Blatná Literary Agency, Jinačovice 3, 66434 Kuřim, Czech Republic. *E-mail:* dblatna@volny.cz.

VIGÉE, Claude André, MA, PhD; French writer and poet; b. (Claude Strauss), 3 Jan. 1921, Bischwiller (Bas-Rhin); s. of Robert Strauss and Germaine Meyer; m. Evelyne Meyer 1947; two c. *Education:* Strasbourg Univ., Ohio State Univ. *Publications:* poetry: Claude Vigée, la Corne du grand pardon 1954, L'Été indien 1957, Moisson de Canaan 1967, Le Soleil sous la mer 1972, Du bec à l'oreille 1977, Pâque de la Parole 1978, Les Orties noires flambent dans le vent 1984, Heimat des Hauches 1985, Wénderôwefir/Le Feu d'une nuit d'hiver 1989, Apprendre la nuit 1991, L'héritage du feu 1992, Aux portes du labyrinthe: poèmes du passage (1939–1996) 1996; essays: Les Artistes de la faim 1960, Révoltes et Louanges 1962, La Lune d'hiver 1970, Délivrance du souffle 1977, L'Art et le Démonique 1978, L'Extase et l'Errance 1982, Le Parfum et la Cendre, entretiens sur trois continents 1984, Une voix dans le défilé, vivre à Jérusalem 1985, La Manne et la Rosée, fête de la Tora 1986, La Faille du regard 1987, Aux sources de la littérature moderne 1989, Vision et silence dans la poésie juive 1999; translations: Mon printemps viendra, poèmes de D. Seter 1965, Les yeux dans le rocher, poèmes de David Rokéah 1968, L'Herbe du songe, poèmes d'Yvan Goll 1971, Le vent du retour, poèmes de R. M. Rilke 1989, Quatre Quatuors, poèmes de T. S. Eliot 1992, Un abri pour nos têtes, poésie de Shirley Kaufman 2003; autobiography: Un panier de houblon 1995. *Honours:* Officier, Légion d'honneur, Chevalier, Ordre Nat. du Mérite, Chevalier, Ordre des Palmes Académiques; Prix Pierre de Régnier de l' Acad. française 1972, Univ. of Basle Prix Jacob-Burckhardt 1977, Prix Fémina-Vacaresco 1979, Prix Johann-Peter Hebel 1984, Grand Prix de la poésie de la Soc. des gens de lettres 1987, Prix des arts, des lettres et des sciences de la Fondation du judaïsme français 1994, Grand Prix de poésie de l' Acad. française 1996. *Address:* c/o Editions Albin Michel, 22 rue Huyghens, 75014 Paris, France (office); 21 rue Radak, Jerusalem 92187, Israel (home). *E-mail:* abw@inter.net.il.

VILA-MATAS, Enrique; Spanish writer; b. 1948, Barcelona. *Career:* fmr journalist for Fotogramas magazine, Paris. *Publications include:* non-fiction: Al sur de los párpados 1980, Nunca voy al cine 1982, El viajero más lento 1992, Veneno en la boca, conversaciones con 18 escritores: Antón Castro 1994, Recuerdos inventados: primera antología personal 1994, El traje de los domingos 1995, Para acabar con los números redondos 1997, Desde la ciudad nerviosa 2000; fiction: La asesina ilustrada 1977, Impostura 1984, Historia abreviada de la literatura portátil 1985, Una casa para siempre 1988, Suicidios ejemplares 1991, Hijos sin hijos 1993, Lejos de Veracruz 1995, Extraña forma de vida 1997, El viaje vertical (Premio Rómulo Gallegos 2001) 1999, Bartleby y compañía 2000, El mal de Montano 2002, París no se acaba nunca 2003, Doctor Pasavento (Premio de la Real Academia Española 2006) 2005. *Honours:* Premio Ciudad de Barcelona 2000, Prix au meilleur livre étranger 2000, Premio de la Crítica 2002, Premio Herralde 2002, Prix Médicis 2003, Chevalier, Légion d'honneur 2006. *Address:* c/o Editorial Anagrama SA, Pedró de la Creu 58, 08034 Barcelona, Spain (office). *E-mail:* anagrama@anagrama-ed.es (office).

VILIKOVSKÝ, Pavel; Slovak writer and translator; b. 27 June 1941, Palúdzka. *Publications:* Citova vychova v marci 1965, Prva veta spanku 1983, Kon na poschodi, Slepec vo Vrabloch, Vecne je zeleny 1989, Eskalacia citu 1989, Slovensky Casanova, Okno po erotickych snoch 1991, Pesi pribeh 1992, Kruty strojvodca 1996, Okridlena klietka 1998. *Address:* POB 8, 90201 Pezinok, Slovakia.

VILLANUEVA, Tino; American writer, translator and poet; b. 11 Dec. 1941, San Marcos, TX. *Career:* founder, Imagine Publishers Inc; Ed., Imagine, International Chicano Poetry Journal; teacher, Boston Univ., MA. *Publications:* poetry: Shaking off the Dark 1984, Scene from the Movie GIANT 1993, Crónica de mis años peores (trans. as Chronicle of My Worst Years) 1994, La llaman América 1998, Primera Causa (trans. as First Cause) 1999. *Honours:* American Book Award, Before Columbus Foundation 1994. *Address:* c/o Curbstone Press, 321 Jackson Street, Willimantic, CT 06226-1738, USA. *E-mail:* info@curbstone.org. *Website:* www.curbstone.org.

VILLASEÑOR, Victor; American writer; b. 11 May 1940, Carlsbad, CA. *Publications:* Macho!, 1973; Jury: The People vs Juan Corona (non-fiction), 1977; Ballad of Gregorio Cortez (screenplay); Rain of Gold (memoir), 1991; Snow Goose: Global Thanksgiving (philosophy), 1993; Wild Steps of Heaven (memoir), 1996; Walking Stars (short stories), 1996; Thirteen Senses (memoir), 2001; nine novels and 65 short stories. *Literary Agent:* Margret

McBride Literary Agency, 7744 Fay Avenue, Suite 201, La Jolla, CA 92037, USA. *E-mail:* Victor@victorvillasenor.com. *Website:* www.victorvillasenor.com.

VILLENEUVE, Jeanne Madeleine; French journalist; b. 29 Jan. 1949, Paris; d. of Henry Villeneuve and Jacqueline Picq. *Education:* Inst. d'Etudes Politiques. *Career:* Financial Analyst, Banque Nat. de. Paris 1974–78; Chef de Service, Soc. Générale de Presse 1978–82, daily newspaper Libération 1982–86, weekly l'Express Feb.–Sept. 1986; Chief Reporter, l'Evènement du Jeudi 1986–91; Asst Ed. Parisien 1991–95; Ed. Libération 1996–97. *Publication:* Le mythe Tapie 1988. *Address:* c/o Journal Libération, 11 rue Béranger, 75003 Paris, France.

VILLORO, Juan; Mexican writer; b. 1956, Mexico City. *Education:* Universidad Autónoma Metropolitana, Mexico City. *Career:* fmr magazine production ed. Pauta; Programme Dir El lado oscuro de la luna 1977–81; Cultural Attaché Embassy of Mexico in Berlin, Germany 1981–84; Dir cultural supplement, La Jornada Semanal 1995–98. *Publications:* Vivir mata (screenplay), Madona de Guadalupe (short story), El mariscal de campo (short stories) 1978, La noche navegable (short stories) 1980, El cielo inferior (short stories) 1984, Las galosinas secretas (juvenile) 1985, Albercas (short stories) 1985, Tiempo transcurrido 1986, Las palmeras de la brisa rápida: un viaje a Yucatán (travel memoir) 1989, El disparo de Argón (novel) 1991, La alcoba dormida (short stories) 1992, El Profesor Ziper y la fabulosa guitarra eléctrica (juvenile) 1992, Los once de la Tribu (essay) 1995, Baterista numeroso (juvenile) 1997, Matéria dispuesta (novel) 1997, Autopista sanguijuela (juvenile) 1997, La casa pierde (short stories) (Premio Xavier Villarrutia) 1999, Efectos personales (essay) (Premio Mazatlán, Barcelona 2001) 2000, El té de tornillo del Profesor Ziper (juvenile) 2000, Entre amigos (short story) 2000, La voz del enemigo (short story) 2002, El testigo (novel) (Premio Herralde) 2004; contrib. to newspapers, including Uno más uno, Diorama de la Cultura, El Gallo Ilustrado, Sábado. *Honours:* Premio Cuauhtémoc de traducción 1988. *Address:* c/o La Jornada Semanal, Avda Cuauhtémoc 1236, Col. Santa Cruz Atoyac, Del. Benito Juárez, 03310 México DF, Mexico.

VINCENT, Rev. John James, DTheol; British theologian, broadcaster and writer; b. 29 Dec. 1929, Sunderland; s. of David Vincent and Beatrice Ethel Vincent (née Gadd); m. Grace Johnston Stafford 1958; two s. one d. *Education:* Manchester Grammar School, Richmond Coll., London Univ., Drew Univ., Madison, NJ, USA, Basel Univ., Switzerland. *Career:* ordained in Methodist Church 1956; Minister, Manchester and Salford Mission 1956–62; Supt Minister, Rochdale Mission 1962–69, Sheffield Inner City Ecumenical Mission 1970–77; Dir Urban Theology Unit, Sheffield 1969–97, Dir Emer. and Doctoral Supervisor 1997–; Pres. Methodist Conf. 1989–90; Visiting Prof. of Theology, Boston School of Theology, USA 1969, New York Theological Seminary 1970, Theological School, Drew Univ. 1977; elected mem. Studiorum Novi Testamenti Societas 1961; Sec. Regional Working Party, WCC Faith and Order 1958–63; mem. British Council of Churches Comm. on Defence and Disarmament 1963–65, 1969–72; NW Vice-Pres. Campaign for Nuclear Disarmament 1957–69; Founding mem. Methodist Renewal Group 1961–70; Founding mem. and Leader Ashram Community 1967–; Chair. Alliance of Radical Methodists 1971–74, Urban Mission Training Asscn of GB 1976–77, 1985–90; Co-ordinator, British Liberation Theology Project 1990–; mem. Bd Int. Urban Ministry Network 1991–; presented Petition of Distress from the Cities to HM the Queen 1993; mem. Ind. Human Rights Del. to Colombia 1994, Partnership Bd Burngreave New Deal for Communities 2001–; Chair. Methodist Report on The Cities 1997. *Publications:* Christ in a Nuclear World 1962, Christ and Methodism 1964, Here I Stand 1967, Secular Christ 1968, The Race Race 1970, The Jesus Thing 1973, Stirrings, Essays Christian and Radical 1975, Alternative Church 1976, Disciple and Lord 1976, Starting All Over Again 1981, Into the City 1982, O.K. Let's Be Methodists 1984, Radical Jesus 1986, Mark at Work 1986, Britain in the 90s 1989, Discipleship in the 90s 1991, Liberation Theology from the Inner City 1992, A Petition of Distress from the Cities 1993, A British Liberation Theology (ed.) 1995, The Cities: A Methodist Report 1997, Gospel from the City (ed.) 1997, Hope from the City 2000, Journey: Explorations in Discipleship 2001, Bible and Practice (ed.) 2001, Faithfulness in the City (ed.) 2003, Methodist and Radical (ed.) 2003, Outworkings: Gospel Practice and Interpretation 2005, Mark: Gospel of Action (ed.) 2006, Lifestyles of Sharing 2007. *Honours:* Hon. Lecturer, Biblical Studies Dept, Univ. of Sheffield 1990–, Theology Dept, Univ. of Birmingham 2003–; Fellow, St Deiniol's Library 2003; Centenary Achievement Award, Univ. of Sheffield 2005. *Address:* 178 Abbeyfield Road, Sheffield, S4 7AY, England (home). *Telephone:* (114) 243-5342 (office); (114) 243-6688 (home). *Fax:* (114) 243-5356.

VINCENZI, Penny; British writer; b. 10 April 1939, Bournemouth; m.; four c. *Career:* Sec., Vogue and Tatler magazines; staff, The Daily Mirror, Nova, Woman's Own; co-founder, Looking Good magazine; Contributing Ed., Cosmopolitan; Deputy Ed., Options. *Publications:* novels: Old Sins 1989, Free Sins 1990, Wicked Pleasures 1992, An Outrageous Affair 1993, Another Woman 1994, Forbidden Places 1995, The Dilemma 1996, The Glimpses 1996, Windfall 1997, Almost a Crime 1999, Into Temptation 2002, Sheer Abandon 2004, An Absolute Scandal 2007; non-fiction: The Compleat Liar 1977, Cosmopolitan Vital Health Guide 1982, There's One Born Every Minute: A Survival Guide for Parents 1984, Taking Stock: Over 75 Years of the Oxo Cube 1985. *Address:* c/o Orion Publishing Group Ltd, 5 Upper St Martin's Lane, London, WC2H 9EA, England. *Website:* www.penny-vincenzi.com.

VINE, Barbara (see Rendell of Babergh, Ruth Barbara)

VINER, Katharine; British editor; *Editor of Weekend magazine, The Guardian. Career:* fmrly feature writer, Deputy Women's Ed., The Guardian newspaper, then Ed. G2, Ed. The Guardian 'Weekend' magazine 1998–; fmrly worked on The Sunday Times, Cosmopolitan magazine; mem. of bd Royal Court Theatre, Women's Library. *Publications:* contrib. chapter, The personal is still political, to On the Move: Feminism for a New Generation. *Honours:* Newspaper Magazine Editor of the Year (twice). *Address:* c/o The Guardian, 119 Farringdon Road, London, EC1R 3ER, England.

VINEY, Ethna, BSc, BA; Irish writer, television and film producer and director; b. 17 Jan. 1933, West Cavan; m. Michael Viney 1965; one d. *Education:* College of Pharmacy, Dublin, University College, Dublin. *Career:* Independent Pharmacist, 1956–61; Television Producer, 1966–76; Freelance Journalist, 1964–; Independent Television Film Producer and Dir, 1990–. *Television documentaries:* Risen Women 1991, Shape of the Wind 1993, The Man Who Found léide 1995, Joclann na mBanta (series) 1997, Lé hecs an Tuath 1999, A Year's Turning (series) 2001. *Publications:* A Dozen Lips, 1994; Survival or Salvation, 1994; Dancing to Different Tunes, 1996, 1997; A Wildlife Narrative, 1999. *Honours:* Outstanding Academic Book of the Year, USA, 1997. *Address:* Thallabawn, Westport, County Mayo, Ireland.

VINGE, Vernor Steffen, BS, MA, PhD; American mathematician and writer; b. 2 Oct. 1944, Waukesha, WI. *Education:* Michigan State Univ., Univ. of California at San Diego. *Career:* faculty, Dept of Mathematics, San Diego State University, 1972–2000; mem. American Mathematical Soc., SFWA. *Publications:* Grimm's World, 1969; The Wilting, 1976; The Peace War, 1984; Marooned in Realtime, 1986; A Fire Upon the Deep, 1992; A Deepness in the Sky, 1999; True Names and the Opening of Cyberspace Frontier (with James Frenkel), 2001. Contributions: anthologies and periodicals. *Honours:* Hugo Award 1993.

VINKEN, Pierre; Dutch publishing executive (retd); b. 25 Nov. 1927, Heerlen. *Education:* Univs of Utrecht and Amsterdam. *Career:* consultant neurosurgeon, Univ. of Amsterdam 1964–71; Man. Dir Excerpta Medica Publishing Co. Amsterdam 1963–71, Elsevier Science Publrs, Amsterdam 1971–73; Chair. and CEO Elsevier NV, Amsterdam (now Reed/Elsevier PLC London) 1977–99, Chair. 1993–95. *Publications:* Handbook of Clinical Neurology (78 vols), The Shape of the Heart 2000; articles on medicine and art history in journals. *Honours:* hon. mem. various scientific asscns; Kt, Order of Netherlands Lion 1983, Commdr Order of Hipólito Unanul (Peru) 1984, Commdr, Order of Orange Nassau 1995; Dr hc (Paris). *Address:* 142 Bentveldsweg, 2111 EE, Aerdenhout, Netherlands (home). *Telephone:* (23) 5246342 (home). *Fax:* (23) 5246032 (home). *E-mail:* vinken@quicknet.nl (home).

VINKENOOG, Simon; Dutch poet and writer; b. 18 July 1928, Amsterdam. *Career:* Ed., anthology Atonaal 1951; helped found Poëzie in Carré theatre in Amsterdam 1966; Dichter des Vaderlands (Dutch Poet Laureate) 2004–05. *Publications include:* Wondkoorts 1950, Atonaal 1951, Land zonder nacht 1952, Heren Zeventien 1953, Zolang te water 1954, Lessen uit de nieuwe school van taboes 1955, Tweespraak 1956, Enkele reis Nederland 1957, Onder eigen dak 1957, Wij helden 1957, Drie staat tot één 1962, Spiegelschrift 1962, Het verhaal van Karel Appel 1963, Preambuul voor een nieuwe wereld 1963, Eerste gedichten 1949–1964 1965, Hoogseizoen 1965, Liefde. Zeventig dagen op ooghoogte 1965, Manifesten en manifestaties 1967, The Book of Grass 1967, Vogelvrij 1967, Weergaloos 1968, Leven en dood van Marcel Polak 1969, Het moederkruid 1970, Aan het daglicht 1971, Het hek van de dam 1971, Tussen wit en zwart - het ABC van de I Ching 1971, Wonder boven wonder 1971, To Timothy Leary, magiër 1972, Niet niets. De kunst van het sterven 1974, Mij best 1976, De andere wereld 1978, Het huiswerk van de dichter 1978, Levend licht 1978, Tegen de wet 1980, Voeten in de aarde en bergen verzetten 1982, Maandagavondgedichten 1985, Jarings jaren '60 1986, Stadsnatuur 1986, Op het eerste gehoor 1988, Brieven 1950–1956 1989, Louter genieten 1993, Bloemlezing uit de poëzie van Simon Vinkenoog 1994, Herem'ntijd 1998, Vreugdevuur 1998, De ware Adam, gedichten rond de eeuwwisseling 2000, Goede raad is vuur 2004; contrib. to numerous anthologies and journals. *Literary Agent:* Bas Pauw, Singel 464, 1017 Amsterdam, Netherlands. *Telephone:* (20) 620 62 61. *Fax:* (20) 620 71 79. *E-mail:* b.pauw@nlpvf.nl. *Website:* www.simonvinkenoog.nl.

VIRAG, Ibolya; Hungarian publisher, translator, editor and art consultant; *Publisher, Editions Ibolya Virag;* b. 7 Dec. 1950, Budapest; m. *Education:* Eötvös Coll., Eötvös Loránd Univ., Univ. of the Sorbonne, Paris. *Career:* interpreter, Kolinda Group (world music and literature) 1970s; went into exile, France 1980; cr. Cen. Europe Editorial Collection (publishes works of Cen. European writers in French, including Sandor Marai, Peter Esterhazy, Josef Hirsal, Lajos Grendel, Hanna Krall, Ivan Matousek, Istvan Bibo, Jenö Szücs, Karel Capek, Jaroslav Hasek, Jaroslav Durych, Gyula Krudy, Dezsö Kosztolanyi, Antal Szerb, Sandor Weöres, Béla Marko, Otto Tolnai, Imre Oravecz), Paris 1983; joined Albin Michel Publrs 1989; Founder and Publr Editions Ibolya Virag, Paris 1996–; art consultant for MAGYart (Year of Hungarian Culture in France) 1999–2001. *Honours:* Chevalier des Arts et des Lettres 1993, Officier 2003. *Address:* Editions Ibolya Virag, 28 avenue de la Porte de Choisy, 75013 Paris, France (office). *Telephone:* 1-76-67-09-23 (office). *E-mail:* virageditions@hotmail.com (office). *Website:* www.zazieweb.fr/site/editeur/pageediteurinfo.php?num=563 (office).

VIRGO, Seán, BA; Canadian writer and poet; b. 1940, Mtarfa, Malta. *Education:* University of Nottingham. *Career:* mem. League of Canadian Poets. *Publications:* Fiction: White Lies and Other Fictions, 1979; Through the Eyes of a Cat: Irish Stories, 1983; Selakhi, 1987; Wormwood, 1989; White Lies... Plus Two, 1990; Waking in Eden, 1990; The Scream of the Butterfly, 1996. Poetry: Sea Change, 1971; Pieces for the Old Earth Man, 1973; Island (with Paul and Lutia Lauzon), 1975; Kiskatinaw Songs (with Susan Musgrave), 1977; Deathwatch on Skidegate Narrows, 1979; Selected Poems, 1992.

VIRILIO, Paul; French writer and artist; *Editorial Director, Editions Galilee;* b. 1932, Paris. *Education:* Ecole des Metiers d'Art, Paris, Univ. of the Sorbonne, Paris. *Career:* worked as artist in stained glass alongside Matisse in various churches in Paris; untrained architect; Chair. and Dir Ecole Spéciale d'Architecture, Paris 1968–98, Prof. Emer. 1998–; Ed. Espace Critique, Editions Galilee, Paris 1973–; Co-Founder and Programme Dir Collège Int. de Philosophie 1990–; mem. French Comm. concerned with housing for the poor (HCLD) 1992–; fmr mem. Editorial Bds Esprit, Cause Commune, Critiques, Traverses; has worked with Fondation Cartier pour l'art contemporain on several exhbns including Bunker Archeology, Pompidou Centre 1975, Speed, Jouy-en-Josas 1991, Unknown Quantity, Paris 2002. *Publications include:* Bunker Archeologie 1975, L'Insecurité du territoire 1976, Speed and Politics 1977, Popular Defense and Ecological Struggles 1978, L'Esthetique de la disparition 1980, Pure War (with Sylvère Lotringer) 1983, War and Cinema: The Logistics of Perception 1984, L'Espace critique 1984, Polar Inertia 1990, The Art of the Motor 1995, Politics of the Very Worst 1996, Open Sky 1997, The Information Bomb 1998, The Strategy of Deception 1999, A Landscape of Events 2000, Ground Zero 2002, Negative Horizon 2005, The Original Accident 2007; numerous technical works. *Honours:* Grand Prix Nat. de la Critique 1987. *Address:* Editions Galilee, 9 rue de Linné, 75005 Paris, France (office). *Telephone:* 1-43-31-23-84 (office). *Fax:* 1-45-35-53-68 (office). *E-mail:* editions.galilee@free.fr (office).

VIRTUE, Noel; New Zealand author; b. 3 Jan. 1947, Wellington. *Education:* studied in New Zealand. *Publications:* The Redemption of Elsdon Bird 1987, Then Upon the Evil Season 1988, Among the Animals: A Zookeeper's Story (autobiog.) 1988, In the Country of Salvation 1990, Always the Islands of Memory 1991, The Eye of the Everlasting Angel 1993, Sandspit Crossing 1994, Once a Brethren Boy (autobiog.) 1995, Losing Alice 2000, Lady Jean 2001.

VITALE, Alberto; American publishing executive; b. 22 Dec. 1933, Vercelli, Piedmont, Italy; s. of Sergio Vitale and Elena Segre; m. Gemma G. Calori 1961; two s. *Education:* Turin Univ., IPSOA Business School and Wharton School, Univ. of Pa (Fulbright Scholar). *Career:* joined Olivetti 1958; moved to USA to assist in Olivetti's acquisition of Underwood 1959; Exec. IFI (Agnelli family holding co.) 1971; Exec. Vice-Pres. for Admin Bantam Books, New York 1975, Co-CEO 1985, sole CEO 1986; Pres. and CEO Bantam-Doubleday-Dell 1987; Chair., Pres. and CEO Random House 1989–96, Chair., CEO 1996–98; Chair. Supervisory Bd Random House Inc., New York 1998; mem. Bd of Dirs Transworld Publrs; mem. Bd of Trustees Mercy Coll. NY; mem. Nat. Advisory Council, Reading is Fundamental. *Honours:* Chevalier des Arts et Lettres 1996. *Address:* 135 Grace Trail, Palm Beach, FL 33480, USA (home).

VITIELLO, Justin, BA, MA, PhD; American academic, poet and writer; b. 14 Feb. 1941, New York, NY; one s. *Education:* Brown Univ., Univ. of Michigan, Univ. of Madrid, Spain. *Career:* Teaching Fellow in Spanish 1964–69, Distinguished Teaching Fellow 1967, Lecturer in Romance Languages 1969–70, Asst Prof., Comparative Literature and Spanish 1969–73, Head, Residential College's Comparative Literature Program, Univ. of Michigan; Asst Prof. 1974–80, Assoc. Prof. 1980–91, ATTIC Distinguished Teacher 1990, Prof. of Italian 1991–2006, Temple Univ., Philadelphia and Rome; mem. MLA; American Italian Historical Asscn; American Asscn for Italian Studies; life mem. MELUS. *Publications:* poetry: Vanzetti's Fish Cart 1991, Subway Home 1994, Subway Home in Italian 1998; other: Confessions of a Joe Rock 1992, Poetry and Literature of the Sicilian Diaspora: Studies in Oral History and Story Telling 1998, Labyrinths and Volcanoes: Windings Through Sicily 1999, Via Terra: Anthology of Neodialect Poetry 1999; Contributions: books and periodicals. *Honours:* Fulbright Scholar. *Address:* c/o Temple Roma, Lungotevere Arnaldo da Brescia 15, 00196 Rome, Italy.

VITIER, Cintio; Cuban poet and writer; b. 25 Sept. 1921, Key West, FL, USA; s. of Medardo Vitier; m. Fina García Marruz. *Education:* Univ. of Havana. *Career:* worked on Orígenes magazine 1944–56; Lecturer, Escuele Normal para Maestros, Havana, Universidad Cen. de las Villas; researcher, José Martí Nat. Library 1962–77; Pres. Centre of Martianos Studies. *Publications include:* poetry: Vísperas 1953, Testimonios 1968, La fecha al pie 1981, Nupcias 1993; fiction: De peña pobre 1980, Los papeles de Jacinto Finalé 1984, Rajando la leña está 1986; essays: Lo cubano en la poesía 1958, Temas Martianos (with Fina García Marruz) 1969, Crítica Sucesiva 1971, Ese sol del mundo moral 1975, Rescate de Zenea 1987, Crítica cubana 1988. *Honours:* Officier, Ordre des Arts et des Lettres; Dr hc (Univ. of Havana), (Universidad Cen. de las Villas), (Soka Univ., Japan); Nat. Literature Prize 1988, 30th Anniversary Medal, Acad. of Sciences, Order of José Martí 2002, Juan Rulfo Prize for Literature 2002. *Address:* c/o Editorial Letras Cubanas, Ediciones Unión, No. 4, esq. Tacón, Hababa Vieja, Havana, Cuba (office). *Website:* www.cubaliteraria.cu (office).

VITUKHNOVSKAYA, Alina Aleksandrovna; Russian poet, writer and journalist; b. 27 March 1973, Moscow. *Career:* first verses published late 1980s in periodicals; arrested on charge of drugs trafficking, freed Oct. 1995, arrested Nov. 1997; mem. Russian PEN Centre, Writers' Union; Pushkin Scholarship, Hamburg, Germany 1998. *Publications include:* Anomaly 1993, Children's Book of the Dead 1994, Pavlov's Dog (with K. Kedrov) 1996, The Last Old Woman Money-lender of Russian Literature (stories) 1996, Land of Zero 1996, Romance with Phenamine (novel) 1999, Day of Poetry (collaboration with French and Russian poets) 2001, Black Icon 2002. *Address:* Leningradskoye shosse 80, Apt. 89, 125565 Moscow, Russia. *Telephone:* (495) 452-15-31.

VIZENOR, Gerald Robert, BA; American author, poet and academic; *Professor of American Studies, University of New Mexico, Albuquerque;* b. 22 Oct. 1934, Minneapolis, Minn.; m. 1st Judith Helen Horns 1959 (divorced 1968); one s.; m. 2nd Laura Jane Hall 1981. *Education:* Univ. of Minnesota. *Career:* Lecturer, Univ. of California at Berkeley 1976–80, Prof. of Native American Literature 1990–, Richard and Rhoda Goldman Distinguished Prof. of American Studies 2000–02, Prof. Emer. of American Studies 1991–2005; Prof., Univ. of Minnesota, 1980–85, Univ. of California at Santa Cruz, 1987–90; Resident Scholar, School of American Research, Santa Fe 1985–86; David Burr Chair of Letters, Prof., Univ. of Oklahoma 1990–91; Prof. of American Studies, Univ. of New Mexico, Albuquerque 2005–. *Publications:* Thomas James White Hawk 1968, Summer in the Spring: Anishinaabe Lyric Poems and Stories 1970, The Everlasting Sky: New Voices from the People Named the Chippewa 1972, Tribal Scenes and Ceremonies 1976, revised edn as Crossbloods: Bone Courts, Bingo, and Other Reports 1990, Darkness in Saint Louis Bearheart (novel) 1978, revised edn as Bearheart: The Heirship Chronicles 1990, Wordarrows: Indians and Whites in the New Fur Trade 1978, Earthdivers: Tribal Narratives on Mixed Descent 1983, The People Named the Chippewa: Narrative Histories 1983, Matsushima: Pine Islands (collected haiku poems) 1984, Griever: An American Monkey King in China (novel) 1986, Touchwood: A Collection of Ojibway Prose (ed.) 1987, The Trickster of Liberty: Tribal Heirs to a Wild Baronage (novel) 1988, Narrative Chance: Postmodern Discourse on Native American Literatures (ed.) 1989, Interior Landscapes: Autobiographical Myths and Metaphors 1990, Landfill Meditation (short stories) 1991, The Heirs of Columbus (novel) 1991, Dead Voices: Natural Agonies in the New World (novel) 1993, Manifest Manners: Postindian Warriors of Survivance (critical essays) 1994, Shadow Distance: A Gerald Vizenor Reader 1994, Native American Literature (ed.) 1995, Hotline Healers: An Almost Browne Novel 1997, Fugitive Poses: Native American Indian Scenes of Absence and Presence 1998, Postindian Conversations 1999, Cranes Arise (haiku). 1999, Raising the Moon Vines (haiku) 1999, Chancers (novel) 2000, Hiroshima Bugi: Atomu 57 (novel) 2003, Bear Island: The War at Sugar Point (narrative poem) 2006, Almost Ashore (selected poems) 2006; contribs to numerous books, journals, and periodicals. *Honours:* New York Fiction Collective Award, 1986; American Book Award, 1988; California Arts Council Artists Fellowship in Literature, 1989; Josephine Miles Awards, PEN Oakland, 1990, 1996; Doctor of Humane Letters, Macalester College, 1999, Western Literature Distinguished Achievement Award 2005. *Address:* American Studies, 309 Ortega Hall, University of New Mexico, Albuquerque, NM 87131, USA (office). *Telephone:* (505) 255-4255 (home). *Fax:* (505) 277-7410 (office). *E-mail:* vizenor@unm.edu (home).

VIZINCZEY, Stephen; Canadian/British writer; b. 12 May 1933, Kaloz, Hungary; m. 1963; three d. *Education:* Univ. of Budapest, Acad. of Theatre Arts, Budapest. *Career:* Ed. Exchange Magazine 1960–61; Producer CBC 1962–65; mem. Soc. of Authors, Authors' Licensing and Collecting Soc. *Publications:* In Praise of Older Women 1965, The Rules of Chaos 1969, An Innocent Millionaire 1983, Truth and Lies in Literature 1986, The Man with the Magic Touch 1994, Be Faithful unto Death (trans.) 1995, One Life After Another 2005; contrib. to Currently, Los Angeles Times Book Review. *Honours:* Premio Letterario Isola d'Elba 2004. *Address:* 70 Coleherne Court, Old Brompton Road, London, SW5 0EF, England (home). *E-mail:* vizinczey@btinternet.com (home).

VLADISLAV, Jan; Czech poet, writer and translator; b. (Ladislav Bambásek), 1923, Hlohovec. *Career:* leading figure of Czech dissident movement, Charta 77. *Publications include:* Nedokončený obraz, Pařížský zápisník I, Portréty a autoportréty, Sny a malé básně v próze, Dar 1946, Hořící člověk 1948, Samomluvy 1950–60, Věty 1962–72, Fragmenty 1978–89, Kniha poezie 1991.

VOGEL, Paula Anne, BA; American dramatist and teacher; b. 18 Nov. 1951, Washington, DC. *Education:* Catholic Univ. of America, Washington, DC. *Career:* consultant on playwrighting and theatre arts; faculty mem., Brown Univ. *Plays:* The Long Christmas Ride Home, The Swan Song of Sir Henry 1974, Meg 1977, Apple-Brown Betty 1979, Desdemona, A Play About a Handkerchief 1979, The Last Pat Epstein Show Before the Reruns 1979, Bertha in Blue 1981, The Oldest Profession 1981, And Baby Makes Seven 1986, The Baltimore Waltz 1991, Hot 'n' Throbbing 1992, The Mineola Twins 1996, How I Learned to Drive 1997. *Honours:* NEA Fellowships 1980, 1991, AT&T Award 1992, Obie Award 1992, Fund for New American Plays 1994, Guggenheim Fellowship 1995, Pew Charitable Trust Sr Artist Residency 1995–97, Lucille Lortel Award 1997, Pulitzer Prize for Drama 1998. *Literary Agent:* William Morris Agency, 1325 Avenue of the Americas, New York, NY 10019, USA. *E-mail:* plays@wma.com.

VOGELSANG, Arthur, BA, MA, MFA; American poet and editor; b. 31 Jan. 1942, Baltimore, Md; m. Judith Ayers 1966. *Education:* Univ. of Maryland, Johns Hopkins Univ., Univ. of Iowa. *Career:* fmr Jt Ed. The American Poetry Review. *Publications:* A Planet 1983, Twentieth Century Women 1988, Cities and Towns 1996, The Body Electric: America's Best Poetry from The American Poetry Review (co-ed.) 2001, Left Wing of a Bird 2003. *Honours:* Nat. Endowment for the Arts Fellowships in Poetry 1976, 1985, 1995, California Arts Council Grant 1995, Juniper Prize 1995. *Address:* 1730 N Vista Street, Los Angeles, CA 90046, USA (home). *Telephone:* (323) 874-2220 (home). *Fax:* (323) 874-2221 (home). *E-mail:* arthurv123@aol.com (office).

VOIGT, Ellen Bryant, BA, MFA; American poet and teacher; b. 9 May 1943, Danville, VA; m. Francis G. W. Voigt 1965, one s. one d. *Education:* Converse College, Spartanburg, SC, University of Iowa. *Career:* Faculty, Iowa Wesleyan College, 1966–69, Goddard College, 1969–79, MIT, 1979–82, Warren Wilson College, 1981–. *Publications:* Claiming Kin, 1976; The Forces of Plenty, 1983; The Lotus Flowers, 1987; Two Trees, 1992; Kyrie, 1996; The Flexible Lyric, 2001; Shadow of Heaven, 2002. Contributions: Reviews, quarterlies, and journals. *Honours:* National Endowment for the Arts Fellowship, 1975; Guggenheim Fellowship, 1978; Pushcart Prizes, 1983, 1987; Honorable Mention, The Poets' Prize, 1987; Emily Clark Balch Award, 1987; Hon. Doctor of Letters, Converse College, 1989; Haines Award for Poetry, Fellowship of Southern Writers, 1993; Acad. of American Poets Fellowship, 2001; inducted, Fellowship of Southern Writers, 2003; elected Chancellor, Acad. of American Poets, 2003.

VOINOVICH, Vladimir Nikolayevich; Russian writer; b. 26 Sept. 1956, Dushanbe, Tajikistan; m.; one d. *Education:* Moscow Regional Pedagogical Inst. *Career:* active in dissident movt 1960s; freelance writer; mem. USSR Writers' Union, expelled 1974, expulsion revoked 1990; deprived of Soviet citizenship 1981, emigrated and lived in Germany 1980–92; Prof. Princeton Univ., USA; mem. Bavarian Acad. of Fine Arts. *Publications:* I Want to Be Honest (short story), We Live Here 1963, The Degree of Confidence 1972, Life and Extraordinary Adventures of the Soldier Ivan Chonkin, Hat, Ivankyada, By Mutual Correspondence, Moscow–2042, Monumental Propaganda 2005. *Honours:* Triumph Prize. *Address:* Russian Pen-Centre, Neglinnaya str. 18/1, Bldg 2, Moscow, Russia (office). *Telephone:* (495) 209-45-89 (office). *Fax:* (495) 200-02-93 (office).

VOLD, Jan Erik; Norwegian poet, novelist, translator and editor; b. 18 Oct. 1939, Oslo; s. of Ragnar Vold. *Publications:* poetry: Mellom speil og speil (Between Mirror and Mirror) (Tarjei Vesaas Debut Prize) 1965, Blikket (The Glance) 1966, Hekt 1966, Svingstang 1967, Mor Godhjertas glade versjon: ja 1968, Bo på Briskeby blues 1969, Kykelipi 1969, Spor, snø 1970, Bok 8: LIV 1970, S 1978, Sirkel sirkel: boken om prins Adrians reise 1979, Sorgen, Sangen, Veien 1987, En som het Abel Ek 1988, Elg 1989, IKKE: skillingstrykk fra nittitallet (Bragepris) 1993, En sirkel is 1993, Kalenderdikt 1995, Ikkje 1997, I vektens tegn 2000, Tolv meditasjoner (trans. as Twelve Meditations) 2002, Diktet minner om verden 2003, Utvidet utgave på Gyldendal forlag 2004, Drømmemakeren sa 2004; prose: Fra rom til rom: Sad and Crazy 1967, BusteR BrenneR 1976; also essays. *Honours:* Hon. PhD (Oslo) 2000; Bragepris 1997, Kulturrådets oversetterpris 1992, Aschehougprisen 1981, Gyldendalprisen 2000.

VOLK, Patricia, BFA; American writer; b. 16 July 1943, New York; d. of Cecil Sussman Volk and Audrey Elayne Morgen Volk; m. Andrew Blitzer 1969; one s. one d. *Education:* Syracuse Univ., Acad. de la Grande Chaumière, Paris, School of Visual Arts, The New School, Columbia Univ. *Career:* Art Dir Appelbaum and Curtis 1964–65, Seventeen Magazine 1967–68; copy-writer, Assoc. Creative Dir, Sr Vice-Pres. Doyle Dane Bernbach Inc. (DDB Needham Worldwide Inc.) 1969–88; Adjunct Instructor of Fiction, Yeshiva Coll. 1991; columnist, Newsday, NY 1995–96; mem. PEN Authors Guild; Yaddo Fellow; MacDowell Fellow. *Publications include:* The Yellow Banana 1985, White Light 1987, All It Takes 1990, Stuffed: Adventures of a Restaurant Family 2001; contribs to The New York Times Magazine, The Atlantic, Quarterly, Cosmopolitan, Family Circle, Mirabella, Playboy, 7 Days, Manhattan Inc., The New Yorker, New York Magazine, Red Book, Good Housekeeping, Allure; Anthologies: Stories About How Things Fall Apart and What's Left When They Do 1985, A Reader for Developing Writers 1990, Exploring Language 1992, Magazine and Feature Writing 1992, Hers 1993, Her Face in the Mirror 1994. *Honours:* Word Beat Fiction Book Award 1984 and numerous other awards. *Address:* c/o Gloria Loomis, 133 East 35th Street, New York, NY 10016, USA.

VOLKOV, Solomon; American musicologist; b. 17 April 1944, Ura-Tyube, Tajikistan. *Education:* Leningrad Conservatory. *Career:* Artistic Dir, Leningrad Experimental Studio of Chamber Opera 1965–70; staging of Fleischmann's Rothschild's Violin, completed by Shostakovich; research at Russian Inst., Columbia Univ. 1976. *Publications:* Young Composers of Leningrad 1971, Remembrance of the 'Leningrad Spring' 1974, Testimony: The Memoirs of Dmitri Shostakovich (ed.) 1979, Scissors and Music: Music Censorship in the Soviet Union 1983, Balanchine's Tchaikovsky 1985, Yevgeny Mravinsky, Leningrad's Master Builder 1988, From Russia to the West: the Musical Memoirs of Nathan Milstein (with N. Milstein) 1990, St Petersburg: A Cultural History 1995, Conversations with Joseph Brodsky 1998, Shostakovich and Stalin 2004; contrib. articles in journals and newspapers 1959–. *Address:* c/o Alfred A. Knopf, 1745 Broadway, New York, NY 10019, USA.

VOLLMANN, William T., BA; American writer; b. 28 July 1959, Santa Monica, CA; m.; one d. *Education:* Deep Springs Coll., Cornell Univ., Univ. of California at Berkeley. *Career:* Ella Lyman Cabot Trust Fellowship 1982, Regent's Fellow Univ. of California at Berkeley 1982–83. *Publications:* You Bright and Risen Angels (Whiting Writers' Award 1988) 1987, The Convict Bird: A Children's Poem 1987, The Tale of the Dying Lungs 1989, The Rainbow Stories 1989, Seven Dreams: A Book of North American Landscapes (seven vols, including so far The Ice Shirt 1990, Fathers and Crows 1992, The Rifles 1994, Argall: The True Story of Pocahontas and Captain John Smith 2001) 1990–, Whores for Gloria 1991, An Afghanistan Picture Show, or, How I Saved the World 1992, Thirteen Stories and Thirteen Epitaphs 1993, Butterfly Stories: A Novel 1993, The Atlas (PEN Center West Award 1997) 1996, The Students of Deep Springs College (with Michael A. Smith and L. Jackson Newell) 2000, The Royal Family (California Book Awards Silver Medal for Non-Fiction 2001) 2000, Expelled from Eden: A William T. Vollmann Reader 2003, Rising Up and Rising Down (seven vols) 2003, Europe Central (short stories) (Nat. Book Award for Fiction) 2005, Uncentering the Earth: Copernicus and the Revolutions of the Heavenly Spheres 2006, Poor People 2007; contrib. to The New Yorker, Esquire, Spin, Gear, Granta. *Honours:* Ludwig Vogelstein Award 1987, Shiva Naipaul Memorial Prize 1989. *Literary Agent:* Susan Golomb Literary Agency, 875 Avenue of the Americas, Suite 2302, New York, NY 10001, USA.

VOLPI, Jorge, LicenDer, DPhil; Mexican novelist and essayist; b. 1968, Mexico City, DF. *Education:* Universidad Nacional Autónoma de México, Universidad de Salamanca. *Career:* fmr lawyer and lawyer's sec.; fmrly Visiting Prof., Cornell Univ.; currently Dir, Centro Cultural Mexicano, Paris; Dir of public television channel, Canal 22, Mexico 2007–; mem. Sistema Nacional de Creadores de México. *Publications:* fiction: A pesar del oscuro silencio (novel) 1993, Días de ira (novella) 1994, La paz de los sepulcros (novel) 1995, El temperamento melancólico (novel) 1996, Sanar tu piel amarga (novella) 1997, En busca de Klingsor (first novel of 'Trilogía del siglo XX') (Premio Biblioteca Breve 1999, Prix Deux Océans Grinzane Cavour, France 1999, Instituto Cervantes de Roma prize for best translation 2002) 1999, El juego del Apocalipsis (novella) 2000, El fin de la locura (second novel of 'Trilogía del siglo XX') 2003; non-fiction: La guerra y las palabras: una historia del alzamiento zapatista (essay), La imaginación y el poder. Una historia intelectual de 1968 (essay) 1998, Día de muertos (non-fiction) 2001. *Honours:* Guggenheim Foundation Fellowship. *Address:* c/o Editorial Seix Barral, Avda Diagonal 662–664, 7°, Barcelona 08034, Spain. *E-mail:* editorial@seix-barral.es. *Website:* blogs.prisacom.com/volpi/?p=1.

VOM VENN, Hubert; German writer and publisher; b. 12 Oct. 1953, Monschau/Eifel; m. Ingrid Peinhardt-Franke, one d. *Education:* studied journalism. *Career:* journalist 1974–; gag author 1984–91; TV writer 1988–93; radio comedian 1980–2002; radio speaker 1985–98; Chief Ed. Radio Station 1998–99; Theatre Dir 1995–; mem. Int. Fed. of Journalists, Deutscher Journalisten Verband. *Publications:* Bundesstrasse 258 1990, Zum Drehen und Wenden 1991, Die Schlacht um Monschau 1992, Meine Sorgen möchte ich haben 1994, Wir sind'n Volk 1995, Und Sonst – Wie Sonst 1996, Die Hand im Moor 1999, Kaisermord 2000, Mein Jahr in der Eifel 2001, Alles für die Katz 2002; co-author: Hurra Deutschland 1991, Fritten fuer um hier zu essen (CD) 1997, Charly's Leute 1997, Der Tod klopft an 2000, Der Tod trifft ein 2001, Frühling, Sommer, Herbst und Mord 2003, The Best (CD) 2003. *Address:* Kalfstrasse 73A, Roetgen 52159, Germany. *E-mail:* hubert-vom-venn@t-online.de. *Website:* www.hubert-vom-venn.de.

VON DASSANOWSKY, Robert, (Robert Dassanowsky), BA, MA, PhD; American/Austrian writer, academic and film producer; *Professor of German and Film Studies and Chairman, University of Colorado at Colorado Springs*; b. 28 Jan. 1960, New York, NY. *Education:* American Acad. of Dramatic Arts, American Film Inst. Conservatory Program, Los Angeles, Univ. of California, Los Angeles. *Career:* Founding Ed. Rohwedder: International Magazine of Literature and Art 1986–93; Corresp. Ed. Rampike 1991–; Visiting Asst Prof. of German, UCLA 1992–93, Visiting Prof. of German 2007; Asst Prof. of German, Univ. of Colorado at Colorado Springs 1993–99, Assoc. Prof. of German and Film Studies 1999–2006, Prof. of German and Film Studies 2006–, Chair. Dept of Languages and Cultures 2001–, Interim Chair. Dept of Visual and Performing Arts 2001–02, Dir Film Studies; Co-Head, Belvedere Film 1999–; mem. Editorial Bd Osiris 1991–, Modern Austrian Literature 1997–2000, Poetry Salzbury Review 2002–; mem. Bd LA Flickapalooza film festival 2001–03, TIE The Int. Experimental Cinema Exposition 2002–, Denver British Film Festival 2003–; German Ed., The Adirondack Review 2002–04; columnist, Celluloid: The Austrian Film Magazine 2002–; Cinema Series Ed., University Press of the South 2004–; mem. Nominating Cttee, Rockefeller Foundation Media Arts Fellowships; consultant, Austrian Cultural Forum, New York; mem. Exec. Council Modern Austrian Literature and Culture Asscn 2006–; Founder and Vice-Pres. Int. Alexander Lernet-Holenia Soc. 1997–, Austrian American Film Asscn 1998–; mem. MLA, PEN/USA West, Austrian PEN, Poet and Writers, Asscn of Austrian Film Producers, Film Independent LA, Soc. for Cinema Studies, German Studies Asscn, Int. Asscn for Germanic Studies, Screen Actors' Guild, PEN Colorado (Founding Pres. 1994–99, 2001–02); mem. European Acad. of Arts and Sciences 2001. *Films as executive producer:* Semmelweis 2001, Epicure 2001, The Nightmare Stumbles Past 2002, Believe 2002, Wilson Chance 2005, The Archduke and Herbert Hinkel 2007. *Publications:* Phantom Empires: The Novels of Alexander Lernet-Holenia and the Question of Postimperial Austrian Identity 1996, Hans Raimund: Verses of a Marriage (trans.) 1996, Telegrams from the Metropole: Selected Poetry 1999, Alexander Lernet-Holenia: Mars in Aries (trans.) 2003, Austrian Cinema: A History 2005; other: several plays and TV scripts; contribs: Contributing Ed., Gale Encyclopedia of Multicultural America 1999; mem. Editorial Bd and contrib. to International Dictionary of Films and Film-makers 2000; numerous book chapters, and poetry and articles in periodicals and anthologies. *Honours:* Constantinian Order of St George, Order of Vitez (Hungary), Decoration of Honour in Silver (Austria); Academico hc (Academia Culturale d'Europa, Italy) 1989; Pres.'s Fund for the Humanities grants, Univ. of Colorado 1996, 2001, Outstanding Teaching Award, Univ. of Colorado at Colorado Springs 2001, Prof. of the Year for Colorado, Carnegie Foundation/CASE US 2004, Chancellor's Award, Univ. of Colorado at Colorado Springs 2006. *Address:* Department of Languages and Cultures, University of Colorado, Colorado Springs, CO 80933, USA (office). *Telephone:* (719) 262-3562 (office). *Fax:* (719) 262-3146 (office). *E-mail:* belvederefilm@yahoo.com (office). *Website:* www.belvederefilm.com (office).

VON DER GRUN, Max; German writer; b. 25 May 1926, Bayreuth; m. Elke Hüser, one s. one d. *Education:* commercial studies; bricklayer apprenticeship. *Career:* mem. PEN Club; Verband Deutscher Schriftsteller. *Publications:* Männer in zweifacher Nacht, 1962; Irrlicht und Feuer, 1963; Zwei Briefe an Pospischiel, 1968; Stellenweise Glatteis, 1973; Menschen in Deutschland, 1973; Leben im gelobten Land, 1975; Wenn der rote Rabe von Baum fällt, 1975; Vorstadtkrokodile, 1976; Wie war das eigentlich?: Kindheit und Jugend im Dritten Reich, 1979; Flächenbrand, 1979; Etwas ausserhalb der Legalität, 1980; Meine Fabrik, 1980; Klassengespräche, 1981; Späte Liebe, 1982; Friedrich und Friederlike, 1983; Die Lawine, 1986; Springflut, 1990; Die Saujagd und andere Vorstadtgeschichten, 1995. *Honours:* Grand Cultural Prize of the City of Nuremberg, 1974; Wilhelm Lubke Prize, 1979; Gerrit Engelke Prize, Hannover, 1985. *Address:* Bremsstrasse 40, 44239 Dortmund, Germany.

VON LUCIUS, Wulf D., Dr rer. pol; German scientific publisher; *Publisher and President, Lucius & Lucius Verlag*; b. 29 Nov. 1938, Jena; s. of the late Tankred R. von Lucius and of Annelise Fischer; m. Akka Achelis 1967; three s. *Education:* Heidelberg, Berlin and Freiburg. *Career:* mil. service 1958–60; Asst Inst. of Econometrics, Freiburg 1965–66; worked in several publishing houses and as public accountant 1966–69; partner and Man. Dir Gustav Fischer Verlag 1969–95; mem. Bd of Exec. Officers, German Publrs. Asscn (Börsenverein) 1976–86; mem. Bd C. Hanser Verlag 1984–; Publr and Pres. Lucius & Lucius Verlag, Stuttgart 1996–; Chair. Int. Publishers Copyright Council 1995–98, Asscn of Scientific Publrs in Germany 1994–2001; mem. Exec. Cttee Int. Publrs Asscn Geneva 1996–; Bd of the German Nat. Library 1981–. *Publications:* Bücherlust-Vom Sammeln 2000, Verlagswirtschaft 2005; numerous articles on publishing, copyright and book history. *Honours:* Friedrich-Perthes-Medaille 1999, Antiquaria Preis 2001, Ludwig Erhard Preis 2004. *Address:* Gerokstrasse 51, 70184 Stuttgart (office). *Telephone:* (711) 242060 (office). *Fax:* (711) 242088 (office). *E-mail:* lucius@luciusverlag.com (office). *Website:* luciusverlag.com (office).

VON STAHLENBERG, Elisabeth (see Freeman, Gillian)

VONARBURG, Elisabeth, BA, MA, PhD; French/Canadian writer and translator; b. 5 Aug. 1947, Paris, France; m. Jean-Joel Vonarburg 1969 (divorced 1990). *Education:* University of Dijon, Université de Laval. *Career:* Asst Lecturer in Literature, Université du Québec à Chicoutimi, 1973–81; Asst Lecturer in Literature and Creative Writing, Université du Québec à Rimouski, 1983–86; Teacher of Creative Writing in Science Fiction, Université Laval, 1990; Science Fiction Columnist, Radio-Canada, 1993–95; mem. Infini, France; International Asscn for the Fantastic in the Arts; SFWA; Science Fiction Canada; Science Fiction Research Asscn. *Publications:* L'Oeil de la nuit, 1980; Le Silence de la Cité, 1981, English trans. as The Silent City, 1990; Janus, 1984; Comment Escrire des Histoires: Guide de l'explorateur, 1986; Histoire de la Princesse et du Dragon, 1990; Ailleurs et au Japon, 1991; Chroniques de Pays des Meres, 1992, English trans. as In the Mother's Land, 1992; Les Voyageurs maigre eux, 1992, English trans. as Reluctant Voyagers, 1995; Les Contes de la Chatte Rouge, 1993; Contes et Légendes de Tyranael, 1994. *Honours:* several Canadian and French science fictions awards. *E-mail:* evarberg@royaume.com. *Website:* www.sfwa.org/members/vonarburg/.

VOS, Ida; Dutch author and poet; b. 13 Dec. 1931, Gröningen; m. Henk Vos 1956, two s. one d. *Education:* teacher training. *Career:* mem. Dutch Writers' Asscn. *Publications:* Wie niet weg is wordt Gezien, 1981, English trans. as Hide and Seek, 1991; Anna is er nog, 1986, English trans. as Anna Is Still There, 1993; Dansen op de brig can Avignon, 1989, English trans. as Dancing on the Bridge at Avignon, 1995; The Key is Lost, 2000. Other: several other books and poems in Dutch. Contributions: periodicals. *Honours:* many nat. literary prizes.

VOYNOVICH, Vladimir Nikolayevich; Russian author, playwright and film scriptwriter; b. 26 Sept. 1932, Stalinabad (now Dushanbe), Tajikistan; s. of Nikolai Pavlovich Voinovich and Rosa (née Goikhman) Voinovich; m. 1st Valentina Voinovich; one s. one d.; m. 2nd Irina Braude 1970; one d. *Career:* served in Soviet Army 1951–55; worked as carpenter 1956–57; studied Moscow Pedagogical Inst. 1958–59; started literary activity (and song-writing for Moscow Radio) 1960; various dissident activities 1966–80; expelled from USSR Writers' Union 1974; elected mem. French PEN Centre 1974; emigrated from USSR 1980; USSR citizenship restored 1990; mem. Bavarian Acad. of Fine Arts. *Publications include:* The Life and Unusual Adventures of Private

Ivan Chonkin (samizdat 1967) 1975 (English trans. 1977), Ivankiada 1976, By Way of Mutual Correspondence 1979, Pretender to the Throne 1981, Moscow–2042 1987, The Fur Hut 1989, The Zero Decision 1990, Case N3484 1992, The Conception 1994, Tales for Adults 1996.

VOZNESENSKY, Andrey Andreyevich; Russian poet; *Vice-President, Russian PEN Centre*; b. 12 May 1933, Moscow; s. of Andrey N. Voznesensky and Antonina S. Voznesensky; m. Zoya Boguslavskaya 1965; one s. *Education:* Moscow Architectural Inst. *Career:* mem. Union of Soviet Writers, mem. Bd 1967–; Vice-Pres. Soviet (now Russian) PEN Centre 1989–. *In English:* Selected Poems 1964, Anti-worlds 1966, Anti-worlds and the Fifth Ace 1967, Dogalypse 1972, Story under Full Sail 1974, Nostalgia for the Present 1978. *Publications:* poems: The Masters 1959, Forty Lyrical Digressions from a Triangular Pear 1962, Longjumeau 1963, Oza 1964, Story Under Full Sail 1970, Ice-69 1970, Queen of Clubs 1974, The Eternal Flesh 1978, Andrey Polisadov 1980, Unaccountable 1981, The Ditch 1981; collections: Parabola 1960, Mosaic 1960, Anti-Worlds 1964, Heart of Achilles 1966, Verses 1967, The Shadow of a Sound 1970, The Glance 1972, Let The Bird Free 1974, Violoncello Oak Leaf 1975, The Master of Stained Glass 1976, Temptation 1978, Metropol (poetry and prose, co-author with 22 others) 1979, Selected Poems 1979, Collected Works (Vols 1–3) 1984, Aksioma Samoiska 1990, Videomes 1992, Rossia-Casino 1997, On the Virtual Wind 2000. *Honours:* Hon. mem. American Acad. of Arts and Letters 1972, Bayerischen Kunst Akad., French Acad. Merimé; Int. Award for Distinguished Achievement in Poetry 1978, State Prize 1978. *Address:* Kotelnicheskaya nab. 1/15, korp. B., Apt. 62, Moscow 109240, Russia. *Telephone:* (495) 915-49-90.

VRBOVÁ, Alena Liberta, PhD, MuDr; Czech writer and neurologist; b. 3 Oct. 1919, Plzeň; d. of Jan. Tadeáš; and Albertina Vrba. *Education:* Univ. of Poitiers, France and Charles Univ., Prague. *Career:* began writing aged 11; asst, Acad. of Sciences, Prague 1942–44; nurse 1944–45; Neurologist State Sanitorium for Nervous Diseases, Mar Lázně 1951–77, Chair. 1963–77; mem. Syndicate of Czech Writers 1941–89; Founder-mem. Community of Czech Writers 1990–; mem. Cttee Corpn of Culture, Svatobor 1990–; has attended numerous int. confs for writers or medical specialists in Europe, USA, India, Mongolia etc. *Publications include:* poetry: River Voyage 1942, Contention 1946, Sounds and Songs 1963, Fountain di Trevi 1963, Antigony 1969, Time-Sorcery 1988; novels: We Are Two 1943, In Monte Rose Again 1971, Veneziana 1975, Departure Via Madras 1978, Indian Summer 1987; six collections of short stories 1964–88; two historical novel trilogies 1976–89–96; numerous scientific papers for professional journals. *Honours:* Hon. MA 1982; Rustavelli Medal 1958, Nezval Medal 1989, Franz Kafka Medal 1999. *Address:* Pohořelec 3, Hradčany, 118-00 Prague 1; Dm Experiment 599, 353-01 Mariánské Lázně, Czech Republic. *Telephone:* (2) 20515417.

VREELAND, Susan, BA, MA; American writer and teacher; b. 20 Jan. 1946, Racine, WI; m. Joseph C. Gray 1988. *Education:* San Diego State Univ. *Career:* taught English, San Diego City Schools 1969–99, and ceramics 1986–99; mem. California Asscn of Teachers of English. *Publications:* What Love Sees (novel) 1988, If I Had My Life to Live Over I Would Pick More Daisies (anthology) 1992, Family: A Celebration 1995, What English Teachers Want: A Student Handbook 1996, Generation to Generation 1998, Girl in Hyacinth Blue (novel) (Theodore Geisel Award Winner, Foreword Magazine Best Novel of the Year) 1999, The Passion of Artemisia (novel) (San Diego Book Awards Theodore Geisel Award, Best Novel of the Year) 2002, The Forest Lover (novel) 2004; contrib. to Missouri Review, Dominion Review, Confrontation, Alaska Quarterly Review, Calyx, Crescent Review, West Wind Review, Ambergris, So To Speak, Phoebe, New England Review. *Honours:* Women's National Book Asscn First Place in Short Fiction 1991, Dominion Review First Prize for Essay 1996, New Millennium First Prize for Essay 1996, Inkwell Magazine Grand Prize for Fiction 1999. *E-mail:* susan@svreeland.com. *Website:* www.svreeland.com.

VROOMKONING, Victor (see Van De Laar, Waltherus Antonius Bernardinus)

WA THIONG'O, Ngugi, (James Thiong'o Ngugi), BA; Kenyan writer, dramatist and critic; *Director of the International Center for Writing and Translation, University of California at Irvine*; b. 5 Jan. 1938, Limuru; m. 1st Nyambura 1961 (divorced 1982); m. 2nd Njeeri 1992; four s. two d. *Education:* Makerere Univ. Coll., Uganda and Univ. of Leeds, UK. *Career:* Lecturer in Literature, Univ. Nairobi 1967–69, Sr Lecturer, Assoc. Prof. and Chair Dept of Literature 1972–77; Fellow in Creative Writing, Makerere Univ. 1969–70; Visiting Assoc. Prof., Northwestern Univ., USA 1970–71; arrested and detained Dec. 1977, released Dec. 1978; in exile in London 1982–; Lecturer in Politics and Literature, Yale Univ.; Dir, Int. Center for Writing and Translation, Univ. of California at Irvine. *Publications:* The Black Hermit (play) 1962, Weep Not, Child (novel) 1964, The River Between (novel) 1965, A Grain of Wheat (novel) 1967, This Time Tomorrow: Three Plays 1970, Homecoming: Essays on African and Caribbean Literature, Culture and Politics 1972, Secret Lives and Other Stories 1973, The Trial of Dedan Kimathi (with Micere Githae-Mugo) 1976, Petals of Blood (novel) 1977, Mtawa Mweusi 1978, Caitaani mutharaba-ini (trans. as Devil on the Cross) 1980, Writers in Politics: Essays 1981, Detained: A Writer's Prison Diary 1981, Njamba Nene na mbaathi i mathagu (trans. as Njamba Nene and the Flying Bus) 1982, Ngaahika Ndeena: Ithaako ria Ngerekano (play with Ngugi wa Mirii), (trans. as I Will Marry When I Want) 1982, Barrel of a Pen: Resistance to Repression in Neo-Colonial Kenya 1983, Bathitoora va Njamba Nene, 1984, English trans. as Njamba Nene's Pistol 1986, Decolonising the Mind: The Politics of Language in African Literature 1986, Writing Against Neo-colonialism 1986, Matigari ma Ngirũũngi (trans. as Matigari) 1986, Njambas Nene no Chiubu King'ang'i 1986, Moving the Centre: The Struggle for Cultural Freedoms 1992, Wizard of the Crow 2006. *Honours:* Fonlon-Nicholas Award 1996. *Address:* International Center for Writing and Translation, School of Humanities, 172 Humanities Instruction Building, University of California at Irvine, Irvine, CA 92697-3380, USA.

WADDELL, Martin, (Catherine Sefton); Northern Irish children's writer; b. 10 April 1941, Belfast. *Publications:* Little Dracula's First Bite 1976, Little Dracula's Christmas 1976, Ernie's Chemistry Set 1978, Ernie's Flying Trousers 1978, Napper Goes for Goal 1981, The Great Green Mouse Disaster 1981, Napper Strikes Again 1981, Harriet (series) 1982–, Going West 1984, The Mystery Squad (series) 1984–, Big Bad Bertie 1984, The House Under the Stairs 1984, School Reporter's Notebook 1985, Budgie Said Grrr! 1985, The Day it Rained Elephants 1986, Alice the Artist 1988, Tales from the Shop That Never Shuts 1988, Fred the Angel 1989, Judy the Bad Fairy 1989, We Love Them 1990, Amy Said 1990, My Great Grandpa 1990, Our Wild Weekend 1990, Rosie's Babies (Best Book for Babies Award) 1992, The Happy Hedgehog Band 1993, The Toymaker 1993, Squeak-A-Lot 1993, Owl Babies 1994, The Pig in the Pond 1994, Sailor Bear 1994, Farmer Duck (British Book Award for Children's Illustrated Book of the Year, Smarties Book Prize) 1995, When the Teddy Bears Came 1996, The Big Big Sea 1996, The Hollyhock Wall 2000, Starry Night (Other Award) 2000, Frankie's Story 2001, The Beat of the Drum 2001, A Kitten Called Moonlight 2001, What Use is a Moose? 2001, Cup Final Kid 2001, Once There Were Giants 2001, Herbie Monkey 2001, Night Night, Cuddly Bear 2001, I'll Tell You a Story and Other Story Poems 2001, Sam Vole and his Brothers 2002, The Tough Princess 2002, Tom Rabbit 2002, Webster J. Duck 2002, The Park in the Dark (Kurt Maschler Award) 2002, Going Up! 2003, Cup Run 2003, Snow Bears 2003, Hi, Harry! 2004, Shooting Star 2004, Well Done, Little Bear 2005, You and Me, Little Bear 2005, Let's Go Home, Little Bear 2005, Can't You Sleep, Little Bear? (Smarties Book Prize) 2005, Tiny's Big Adventure 2005, Who Do You Love? 2005, It's Quacking Time! 2005, Star Striker Titch 2005, Ernie and the Fishface Gang 2006. *Address:* c/o Walker Books, 87 Vauxhall Walk, London, SE11 5HJ, England. *E-mail:* editorial@walker.co.uk.

WADDINGTON-FEATHER, John Joseph, BA, PGCE, FRSA; British writer, poet, Anglican priest and publisher; *Director, Feather Books*; b. 10 July 1933, Keighley, Yorkshire, England; m. Sheila Mary Booker 1960; three d. *Education:* Univs of Leeds and Keele. *Career:* ordained priest 1977; Co-Ed. Orbis 1971–80; teacher, Shrewsbury Sixth Form Coll. 1981–83, Khartoum Univ. 1984–85; Hon. Chaplain, HM Prisons 1977–; Chaplain, Prestfelde School 1985–96; Dir Feather Books; Ed. Poetry Church Magazine, Poetry Church Anthology 1997–; mem. Brontë Soc., Council mem. 1994–2000, Yorkshire Dialect Soc., J.B. Priestley Soc. (Chair. 1998–2004, Vice-Pres. 2004–). *Publications:* Collection of Verse 1964, Of Mills, Moors and Men 1966, Garlic Lane 1970, Easy Street 1971, One Man's Road 1977, Quill's Adventures in the Great Beyond 1980, Tall Tales from Yukon 1983, Khartoum Trilogy and Other Poems 1985, Quill's Adventures in Wasteland 1986, Quill's Adventures in Grozzieland 1988, Six Christian Monologues 1990, Six More Christian Poems 1994, Shropshire 1994, Feather's Foibles 1995, Wild Tales from the West 1999, The Museum Mystery 1999, The Bradshaw Mystery 2000, The Marcham Mystery 2002, Yorkshire Dialect 2002, Legends of Americada 2002, Grundy and Feather Hymn Series (Part I) 2002, The Lollipop Man 2002, Chance-Child (Part I) 2003, Chance-Child (Part II) 2003, Sermonettes and Essays (Part I) 2003, Quill's Adventures in Mereful 2003, Legend Land 2004, Grundy and Feather Hymns and Songs for Seasons and Occasions 2004, Sermonettes and Essays (Part II) 2004, Grundy and Feather Hymns form the Classics 2005, Illingworth House 2005, Quill's Adventures in Human folkland

2005, The Graveyard Mystery 2005; contrib. to journals and magazines. *Honours:* Brontë Soc. Prize 1966, Cyril Hodges Poetry Award 1974, Burton Prize 1999, William de Witt Romig Poetry Award 2002. *Address:* Fair View, Old Coppice, Lyth Bank, Shrewsbury, Shropshire, SY3 0BW (home); Feather Books, PO Box 438, Shewsbury, SY3 0WN, England (office). *Telephone:* (1743) 872177 (office). *Fax:* (1743) 872177 (office). *E-mail:* john@waddsyweb.freeuk.com (office).

WADE, David; British writer; b. 2 Dec. 1929, Edinburgh, Scotland; m.; one s. one d. *Education:* Queens' College, Cambridge. *Career:* Radio Critic, The Listener, 1965–67, The Times, 1967–89; mem. Society of Authors. *Publications:* Trying to Connect You; The Cooker; The Guthrie Process; The Gold Spinners; Three Blows in Anger; The Ogden File; The Carpet Maker of Samarkand; The Nightingale; Summer of 39; The Facts of Life; A Rather Nasty Crack; On Detachment; The Tree of Strife; Power of Attorney; Alexander. *Address:* Willow Cottage, Stockland Green Road, Southborough, Kent TN3 0TL, England.

WADE, Rebekah; British newspaper editor; *Editor, The Sun*; b. 27 May 1968, d. of the late Robert Wade and of Deborah Wade. *Education:* Appleton Hall, Cheshire and Univ. of the Sorbonne, Paris. *Career:* began career as Features Ed., later Assoc. Ed. and Deputy Ed. News of the World –1998, Ed. 2000–03; Deputy Ed. The Sun 1998–2000, Ed. 2003–; Founder-mem. and Pres. Women in Journalism. *Address:* The Sun, 1 Virginia Street, Wapping, London, E1 9XR, England (office). *Telephone:* (20) 7782-4001 (office). *E-mail:* news@the-sun.co.uk (office). *Website:* www.thesun.co.uk (office).

WADLEY, Veronica; British journalist and editor; *Editor, London Evening Standard*; b. 28 Feb. 1952, London; d. of Neville John Wadley and Anne Hawise Colleton (née Browning); m. Tom Bower 1985; one s. one d. *Education:* Francis Holland School, London, Benenden. *Career:* journalist Condé Nast Publs 1971–74, Sunday Telegraph Magazine 1978–81, Mail on Sunday 1982–86; Features Ed. Daily Telegraph 1986–89, Asst Ed. 1989–94, Deputy Ed. 1994–95; Assoc. Ed. Daily Mail 1995–98, Deputy Ed. (Features) 1998–2002; Ed. London Evening Standard 2002–. *Address:* The Evening Standard, Northcliffe House, 2 Derry Street, Kensington, London, W8 5EE, England (office). *Telephone:* (20) 7938-6000 (office). *Fax:* (20) 7937-2849 (office). *E-mail:* veronica.wadley@standard.co.uk (office).

WAGNER, Eliot; American writer; b. 19 Dec. 1917, New York, NY; m. Ethel Katell 1940, one d. *Career:* mem. Authors' Guild. *Publications:* fiction: Grand Concourse, 1954; Wedding March, 1961; Better Occasions, 1974; My America!, 1980; Princely Quest, 1985; Nullity Degree, 1991. Short Stories: Delightfully Different Deities, 1994. Contributions: Crisis; Chicago Jewish Forum; Commentary; Antioch Review; Opinion. *Honours:* Yaddo Fellowships, 1950, 1951, 1952, 1957; MacDowell Colony Fellowship, 1955.

WAGNER-MARTIN, Linda; American academic, poet and writer; b. 18 Aug. 1936, St Marys, Ohio. *Education:* BA, English, 1957, MA, English, 1959, PhD, English, 1963, Bowling Green State University. *Career:* Instructor and Asst Prof., Bowling Green State University, 1961–66; Asst Prof., Wayne State University, 1966–68; Asst Prof. to Prof., Michigan State University, 1968–87; Hanes Prof. of English and Comparative Literature, University of North Carolina at Chapel Hill, 1988–; mem. Ellen Glasgow Society, pres., 1982–87; Ernest Hemingway Foundation and Society, pres., 1993–96; MLA; Society for the Study of Midwestern Literature, pres., 1974–76; Society for the Study of Narrative Technique, pres., 1988–89. *Publications:* The Poems of William Carlos Williams: A Critical Study, 1964; Denise Levertov, 1967; Intaglios: Poems, 1967; The Prose of William Carlos Williams, 1970; Phyllis McGinley, 1971; Hemingway and Faulkner: Inventors/Masters, 1975; Ernest Hemingway: A Reference Guide, 1977; William Carlos Williams: A Reference Guide, 1978; Dos Passos: Artist as American, 1979; American Modern: Selected Essays in Fiction and Poetry, 1980; Songs for Isadora: Poems, 1981; Ellen Glasgow: Beyond Convention, 1982; Sylvia Plath: A Biography, 1987; The Modern American Novel, 1914–1945, 1989; Wharton's The House of Mirth: A Novel of Admonition, 1990; Plath's the Bell Jar: A Novel of the Fifties, 1992; Telling Women's Lives: The New Biography, 1994; 'Favored Strangers': Gertrude Stein and Her Family, 1995; Wharton's The Age of Innocence: A Novel of Ironic Nostalgia, 1996; The Mid-Century American Novel, 1935–1965, 1997; Sylvia Plath: A Literary Life, 1999. Editor: William Faulkner: Four Decades of Criticism, 1973; Ernest Hemingway: Five Decades of Criticism, 1974; T. S. Eliot, 1976; 'Speaking Straight Ahead': Interviews with William Carlos Williams, 1976; Robert Frost: The Critical Heritage, 1977; Denise Levertov: In Her Own Province, 1979; Joyce Carol Oates: Critical Essays, 1979; Sylvia Plath: Critical Essays, 1984; Ernest Hemingway: Six Decades of Criticism, 1987; New Essays on Hemingway's The Sun Also Rises, 1987; Sylvia Plath: The Critical Heritage, 1988; Anne Sexton: Critical Essays, 1989; Denise Levertov: Critical Essays, 1991; The Oxford Companion to Women's Writing in the United States (with Cathy N. Davidson), 1995; The Oxford Book of Women's Writing in the United States, 1995; New Essays to Faulkner's Go Down, Moses, 1996; Ernest Hemingway: Seven Decades of Criticism, 1998; Festchrift for Frederick Eckman (with David Adams), 1998; The Historical Guide to Ernest Hemingway, 1999. Contributions: scholarly books and journals. *Honours:* Guggenheim Fellowship, 1975–76; Bunting

Institute Fellow, 1975–76; Rockefeller Foundation Fellow, Bellagio, Italy, 1990; Fellow, Institute for the Arts and Humanities, University of North Carolina, 1992; National Endowment for the Humanities Senior Fellowship, 1992–93; Teacher-Scholar Award, College English Asscn, 1994; Visiting Distinguished Prof., Emory University, 1994; Citation for Exceptional Merit, House of Representatives, Ohio, 1994; Brackenridge Distinguished Prof., University of Texas at San Antonio, 1998. *Address:* c/o Dept of English, 3520 University of North Carolina at Chapel Hill, Chapel Hill, NC 27599, USA.

WAGONER, David Russell, MA; American writer and academic; *Professor Emeritus of English, University of Washington;* b. 5 June 1926, Massillon, Ohio; m. 1st Patricia Parrott 1961 (divorced 1982); m. 2nd Robin H. Seyfried 1982; two d. *Education:* Pennsylvania State Univ., Indiana Univ. *Career:* served in USN 1944–46; Instructor, DePauw Univ., Greencastle, Ind. 1949–50, Pennsylvania State Univ. 1950–54; Assoc. Prof., Univ. of Washington, Seattle 1954–66, Prof. of English 1966–2000, Prof. Emer. 2000–; Elliston Lecturer, Univ. of Cincinnati 1968; Ed. Poetry Northwest, Seattle 1966–, Ed. Princeton Univ. Press Contemporary Poetry Series 1977–81; Poetry Ed. Missouri Press 1983–; Guggenheim Fellowship 1956, Ford Fellowship 1964, American Acad. Grant 1967, Nat. Endowment for the Arts Grant 1969. *Short Stories:* Afternoon on the Ground 1978, Wild Goose Chase 1978, Mr. Wallender's Romance 1979, Cornet Solo 1979, The Water Strider 1979, Fly Boy 1980, The Bird Watcher 1980, Snake Hunt 1980. *Play:* An Eye for an Eye for an Eye 1973. *Verse:* Dry Sun, Dry Wind 1953, A Place to Stand 1958, Poems 1959, The Nesting Ground 1963, Five Poets of the Pacific Northwest (with others) 1964, Staying Alive 1966, New and Selected Poems 1969, Working Against Time 1970, Riverbed 1972, Sleeping in the Woods 1974, A Guide to Dungeness Spit 1975, Travelling Light 1976, Who Shall Be the Sun? Poems Based on the Lore, Legends and Myths of Northwest Coast and Plateau Indians 1978, In Broken Country 1979, Landfall 1981, First Light 1983, Through the Forest 1987, Walt Whitman Bathing 1996, Traveling Light: Collected and New Poems 1999, The House of Song 2002. *Novels:* The Man in the Middle 1955, Money, Money, Money 1955, Rock 1958, The Escape Artist 1965, Baby, Come On Inside 1968, Where is My Wandering Boy Tonight? 1970, The Road to Many a Wonder 1974, Tracker 1975, Whole Hog 1976, The Hanging Garden 1980. *Honours:* Morton Dauwen Zabel Prize (Poetry, Chicago) 1967, Ruth Lilly Prize 1991, Levinson Prize (Poetry, Chicago) 1994, Union League Prize (Poetry, Chicago) 1997; Pacific NW Booksellers Award 2000. *Address:* University of Washington, PO Box 354330, Seattle, WA 98105; 5416 154th Place, SW, Edmonds, WA 98026, USA (home). *Telephone:* (425) 745-6964. *E-mail:* renogawd@aol.com (home).

WAINAINA, Binyavanga; Kenyan writer and journalist; b. 1971. *Education:* Univ. of Transkei. *Career:* owner catering and food consultancy business, Amuka Investments; staff writer, G21 Africa (www.g21.net); f. and Ed., literary magazine, Kwani?; food and travel journalist. *Publications:* An Affair to Dismember (short story); Discovering Home (short story), 2001; Flights of My Fancy (novel), 2003. Contributions: Weekend Argus, Cape Town; Sunday Times, South Africa; Mail and Guardian; Y magazine; SL magazine; Pforward magazine; The Top of the Times (Cape Times weekend supplement); Adbusters, Canada; literary journals. *Honours:* Caine Prize for African Writing 2002. *Address:* c/o Kwela Books, PO Box 6525, Roggebaai 8012, South Africa. *E-mail:* editors@kwani.org. *Website:* www.kwani.org.

WAINWRIGHT, Geoffrey, MA, DD (Cantab.), DrThéol; British ecclesiastic and academic; *Robert Earl Cushman Professor of Christian Theology, Divinity School, Duke University;* b. 16 July 1939, Yorks.; s. of Willie Wainwright and Martha Burgess; m. Margaret H. Wiles 1965; one s. two d. *Education:* Gonville & Caius Coll. Cambridge and Univ. of Geneva. *Career:* Prof. of Dogmatics, Protestant Faculty of Theology, Yaoundé, Cameroon 1967–73; Lecturer in Bible and Systematic Theology, Queen's Coll. Birmingham 1973–79; Roosevelt Prof. of Systematic Theology, Union Theological Seminary, New York 1979–83; Robert Earl Cushman Prof. of Christian Theology, Duke Univ. 1983–; mem. Faith and Order Comm. WCC 1977–91; Pres. Soc. Liturgica 1985–87; Co-Chair. Jt Comm. between World Methodist Council and Roman Catholic Church 1986–; Sec. American Theological Soc. 1988–95, Pres. 1996–97; Leverhulme European Fellow 1966–67; Pew Evangelical Fellow 1996–97. *Publications include:* Christian Initiation 1969, Eucharist and Eschatology 1971, Doxology 1980, The Ecumenical Moment 1983, On Wesley and Calvin 1987, Methodists in Dialogue 1995, Worship With One Accord 1997, For Our Salvation: Two Approaches to the Work of Christ 1997, Is the Reformation Over? Protestants and Catholics at the Turn of the Millennia 2000, Lesslie Newbigin: A Theological Life 2000, Oxford History of Christian Worship 2005. *Honours:* Hon. DD (North Park Univ.) 2001; Berakah Award, N American Acad. of Liturgy 1999, Festschrift: 'Ecumenical Theology in Worship, Doctrine and Life: Essays Presented to Geoffrey Wainwright on his Sixtieth Birthday' (ed. David Cunningham and others), Oxford Univ. Press 1999, Outstanding Ecumenist Award, Washington Theological Consortium 2003. *Address:* The Divinity School, Box 90967, Duke University, Durham, NC 27708 (office); 4011 W Cornwallis Road, Durham, NC 27705, USA (home). *Telephone:* (919) 660-3460 (office); (919) 489-2795 (home). *Fax:* (919) 660-3473 (office). *E-mail:* gwainwright@div.duke.edu (office). *Website:* www.divinity.duke.edu/faculty/theological/wainwright (office).

WAINWRIGHT, Hilary, BA, BPhil; British journalist and editor; b. 1949, Leeds. *Education:* The Mount School, York, St Anne's Coll., Oxford and St Anthony's Coll., Oxford. *Career:* Research Asst Sociology Dept, Durham Univ. 1973–75, Research Fellow 1975–78; Social Science Council Research Fellow,

Open Univ. 1979–81; Founder, Asst Chief Econ. Advisor and Co-ordinator Popular Planning Unit, GLC (now GLA) 1982–86; freelance writer, lecturer and journalist, The New Statesman and The Guardian 1986–88; Fellow, Transnational Inst., Amsterdam 1988, now Research Dir New Politics Programme; Sr Simon Fellow, Sociology Dept, Univ. of Manchester 1989–90; Visiting Fellow, Center for Social Theory and Comparative History, UCLA 1991; Sr Research Fellow, Centre for Labour Studies, Univ. of Manchester 1992, now Hon. Fellow; Political Ed. Red Pepper Magazine 1994–95, Ed. 1995–; mem. Council Charter 88; frequent TV and radio appearances on UK discussion programmes including Question Time (BBC), Channel 4 News, Any Questions, Today Programme (BBC Radio 4) etc. *Publications:* The Workers' Report of Vickers (co-author) 1978, Beyond the Fragments (co-author) 1980, State Intervention in Industry: A Worker's Inquiry 1981, The Lucas Plan: A New Trades Unionism in the Making? 1982, A Taste of Power: The Politics of Local Economics (co-ed) 1986, Labour: A Tale of Two Parties 1987, After the Wall: Social Movements and Democratic Politics in the New Europe (ed) 1991, Arguments for a New Left: Answering the Free Market Right 1993, Reclaim the State: Adventures in Popular Democracy 2003; numerous essays and articles; regular articles in the Guardian. *Address:* Red Pepper Magazine, 1B Waterlow Road, London, N19 5NJ, England; c/o Transnational Institute, PO Box 14656, 1001 LD, Amsterdam, Netherlands. *Telephone:* (20) 7281-7024. *Fax:* (20) 7263-9345. *E-mail:* redpepper@redpepper.org.uk. *Website:* www.redpepper.org.uk; www.tni.org.

WAINWRIGHT, Jeffrey, BA, MA; British poet, dramatist, translator and academic; b. 19 Feb. 1944, Stoke on Trent, Staffs.; m. Judith Batt 1967; one s. one d. *Education:* Univ. of Leeds. *Career:* Asst Lecturer, Lecturer, Univ. of Wales 1967–72; Visiting Instructor, Long Island Univ. 1970–71; Sr Lecturer, Manchester Metropolitan Univ. 1972–99, Prof. 1999–; Northern Theatre Critic, The Independent 1988–99. *Publications:* poetry: The Important Man 1970, Heart's Desire 1978, Selected Poems 1985, The Red-Headed Pupil 1994, Out of the Air 1999; other: Poetry: The Basics (criticism) 2004, Acceptable Words: Essays on the Poetry of Geoffrey Hill (criticism) 2006, trans of various plays into English; contribs to various anthologies, BBC Radio and many periodicals. *Honours:* Judith E. Wilson Visiting Fellow 1985. *Address:* Department of English, Manchester Metropolitan University, Manchester, M15 6LL, England (office). *Telephone:* (161) 247-1724 (office). *E-mail:* j.wainwright@mmu.ac.uk (office); jeffwainwright@supanet.com (home). *Website:* www.mmu.ac.uk/english (office); www.jeffreywainright.co.uk (home).

WAITE, Peter Busby, OC, BA, MA, PhD, FRSC; Canadian academic and writer; *Professor of History Emeritus, Dalhousie University;* b. 12 July 1922, Toronto, ON; m. Masha Maria Gropuzzo 1958; two d. *Education:* Univ. of British Columbia, Univ. of Toronto. *Career:* Lecturer 1951–55, Asst Prof. 1955–60, Assoc. Prof. 1960–61, Prof. of History 1961–88, Prof. Emeritus 1988–, Dalhousie Univ.; mem. Canadian Historical Asscn (pres. 1968–69), Humanities Research Council (chair. 1968–70), Aid to Publications Cttee Social Science Federation (chair. 1987–89). *Publications:* The Life and Times of Confederation, 1864–1867 1962, Canada 1874–1896 1971, John A. Macdonald, His Life and World 1975, The Man from Halifax: Sir John Thompson, Prime Minister 1985, Lord of Point Grey: Larry MacKenzie of UBC 1987, Between Three Oceans: Challenges of a Continental Destiny, 1840–1900, Chapter IV Illustrated History of Canada 1988, The Loner: The Personal Life and Ideas of R. B. Bennett 1870–1947 1992, The Lives of Dalhousie University: Vol. I Lord Dalhousie's College, 1818–1925 1994, Vol. II The Old College Transformed, 1925–1980 1998; contrib. some 55 articles to numerous magazines and journals. *Honours:* Hon. LLD (Dalhousie Univ.) 1991, Hon. DLitt (Univ. of New Brunswick) 1991, (Memorial Univ. of Newfoundland) 1991, (Carleton Univ.) 1993; Lieutenant-Governor's Medal, BC 1987. *Address:* 960 Ritchie Drive, Halifax, NS B3H 3P5, Canada.

WAKEFIELD, Dan, BA; American writer and screenwriter; b. 21 May 1932, Indianapolis, IN. *Education:* Columbia University. *Career:* News Ed., Princeton Packet, NJ, 1955; Staff Writer, The Nation magazine, 1956–59; Staff, Bread Loaf Writers Conference, 1964, 1966, 1968, 1970, 1986; Visiting Lecturer, University of Massachusetts at Boston, 1965–66, University of Illinois, 1968; Contributing Ed., The Atlantic Monthly, 1969–80; Writer-in-Residence, Emerson College, 1989–92; Contributing Writer, GQ magazine, 1992–; Distinguished Visiting Writer, Florida International University, 1995–; mem. Authors' Guild of America; National Writers Union; Writers Guild of America. *Publications:* Island of the City: The World of Spanish Harlem, 1959; Revolt in the South, 1961; An Anthology, 1963; Between the Lines, 1966; Supernation at Peace and War, 1968; Going All the Way, 1970; Starting Over, 1973; All Her Children, 1976; Home Free, 1977; Under the Apple Tree, 1982; Selling Out, 1985; Returning: A Spiritual Journey, 1988; The Story of Your Life: Writing a Spiritual Autobiography, 1990; New York in the Fifties, 1992; Expect a Miracle, 1995; Creating from the Spirit, 1996; How Do We Know When It's God?, 1999. Editor: The Addict: An Anthology, 1963. Television: James at 15, 1977–78; The Seduction of Miss Leona, 1980; Heartbeat, 1988. *Honours:* Bernard DeVoto Fellow, Bread Loaf Writers Conference, 1957; Rockefeller Foundation Grant, 1968; Short Story Prize, National Council of the Arts, 1968. *Literary Agent:* Janklow & Nesbit Associates, 445 Park Avenue, New York, NY 10022, USA.

WAKELING, Edward, BSc, MSc; British writer and editor; b. 31 Aug. 1946, Sutton Scotney, Hants. *Education:* Bishop Otter Coll., Chichester, Hatfield

Polytechnic, Univ. of Oxford. *Career:* mem. Lewis Carroll Soc., Sec. 1976–79, Chair. 1982–85, Treas. 1986–89, Chair. Editorial Bd 1997–2002; organized first Int. Lewis Carroll Conf. 1989; contrib. to a variety of TV programmes. *Publications:* The Logic of Lewis Carroll 1978, The Cipher Alice 1990, Lewis Carroll's Games and Puzzles 1992, Lewis Carroll's Oxford Pamphlets 1993, Lewis Carroll's Diaries (ed.), nine vols 1993–2005, Rediscovered Lewis Carroll Puzzles 1995, Alice in Escherland 1998, Lewis Carroll, Photographer (with Roger Taylor) 2002, Lewis Carroll and His Illustrators (with Morton N. Cohen) 2003; contrib. to many reviews, quarterlies and journals. *Honours:* Hon. MA (Luton) 1996. *Address:* Yew Tree Cottage, Parks Road, Clifford, Herefords., HR3 5HQ, England (home). *E-mail:* edward@wakeling.demon.co.uk (home). *Website:* www.lewiscarroll-site.com (office).

WAKOSKI, Diane, BA; American poet and academic; *University Distinguished Professor, Department of English, Michigan State University*; b. 3 Aug. 1937, Whittier, Calif.; m. Robert J. Turney 1982. *Education:* Univ. of Calif. at Berkeley. *Career:* began writing poetry, New York 1960–73; worked as a book shop clerk, a jr high school teacher and by giving poetry readings on coll. campuses; Poet-in-Residence, Prof. of English Michigan State Univ. 1975–, Distinguished Prof. 1990–; mem. Authors' Guild, PEN, Poetry Soc. of America. *Publications:* Coins and Coffins 1962, Discrepancies and Apparitions 1966, The George Washington Poems 1967, Inside the Blood Factory 1968, The Magellanic Clouds 1970, The Motorcycle Betrayal Poems 1971, Smudging 1972, Dancing on the Grave of a Son of a Bitch 1973, Trilogy (reprint of first three collections) 1974, Virtuoso Literature for Two and Four Hands 1975, Waiting for the King of Spain 1976, The Man Who Shook Hands 1978, Cap of Darkness 1980, The Magician's Feastletters 1982, Norii Magellanici (collection of poems from various vols trans. into Romanian) 1982, The Collected Greed 1984, The Rings of Saturn 1986, Emerald Ice (selected poems 1962–87) 1988 (William Carlos Williams Prize 1989), The Archaeology of Movies and Books: Vol. I Medea The Sorceress 1991, Vol. II Jason The Sailor 1993, Vol. III The Emerald City of Las Vegas 1995, Vol. IV Argonaut Rose 1998, The Butcher's Apron: New and Selected Poems 2000; Towards A New Poetry (criticism) 1980. *Honours:* Cassandra Foundation Grant 1970, Guggenheim Fellowship 1972, Nat. Endowment for the Arts Grant 1973, Writer's Fulbright Award 1984, Mich. Arts Foundation Award 1989, Michigan Arts Foundation Distinguished Artist Award 1989, Michigan Library Asscn Author of the Year 2003. *Address:* 607 Division Street, East Lansing, MI 48823 (home); 205 Morrill Hall, East Lansing, MI 48824, USA (office). *Telephone:* (517) 355-0308 (office); (517) 332-3385 (home). *E-mail:* dwakoski@aol.com; wakoski@msu.edu (office). *Website:* www.english.msu.edu (office).

WALCOTT, Derek, OBE, BA, FRSL; Saint Lucia poet and playwright; b. 23 Jan. 1930, Castries; s. of Warwick Walcott and Alix Walcott; m. 1st Fay Moston 1954 (divorced 1959); one s.; m. 2nd Margaret R. Maillard 1962 (divorced); two d.; m. 3rd Norline Metivier 1982 (divorced 1993). *Education:* St Mary's Coll., Castries, Univ. of Wisconsin, Univ. of the West Indies, Jamaica. *Career:* teacher, St Mary's Coll., Castries 1947–50, 1954, Grenada Boys' Secondary School, St George's 1953–54, Jamaica Coll., Kingston 1955; feature writer, Public Opinion, Kingston 1956–57; founder-Dir, Little Carib Theatre Workshop, later Trinidad Theatre Workshop 1959–76; feature writer, Trinidad Guardian, Port-of-Spain 1960–62, drama critic 1963–68; Visiting Prof., Columbia Univ., USA 1981, Harvard Univ. 1982, 1987; Asst Prof. of Creative Writing, Brown Univ. 1981, Visiting Prof. 1985–; hon. mem. American Acad. of Arts and Letters; mem. Poetry Soc. (vice-pres.); Rockefeller Foundation grants 1957, 1966, and Fellowship 1958, Ingram Merrill Foundation grant 1962, Eugene O'Neill Foundation Fellowship 1969, Guggenheim Fellowship 1977, John D. and Catherine T. MacArthur Foundation Fellowship 1981. *Plays:* Cry for a Leader 1950, Henri Christophe: A Chronicle 1950, Robin and Andrea 1950, Senza Alcun Sospetto 1950, The Price of Mercy 1951, Three Assassins 1951, Harry Dernier 1952, The Charlatan 1954, Crossroads 1954, The Sea at Dauphin 1954, The Golden Lions 1956, The Wine of the Country 1956, Ione: A Play with Music 1957, Ti-Jear and his Brothers 1957, Drums and Colours 1958, Jourmard 1959, Malcochon 1959, Batai 1965, Dream on Monkey Mountain 1967, Franklin: A Tale of the Islands 1969, In a Fine Castle 1970, The Joker of Seville (with G. Mcdermott) 1974, O Babylon! 1976, Remembrance 1977, The Snow Queen 1977, Pantomime 1978, Marie Leveau (with G. Mcdermott) 1979, The Isle is Full of Noises 1982, Beef, No Chicken 1985, The Odyssey 1993, The Capeman (musical, jtly) 1997. *Publications:* poetry: 25 Poems 1948, Epitaph for the Young: XII Cantos 1949, Poems 1951, In a Green Night, Poems 1948–60 1962, Selected Poems 1964, The Castaway and Other Poems 1965, The Gulf and Other Poems 1969, Another Life 1973, Sea Grapes 1976, The Star-Apple Kingdom 1979, Selected Poetry 1981, The Fortunate Traveller 1981, The Caribbean Poetry of Derek Walcott, and the Art of Romare Bearden 1983, Midsummer 1984, Collected Poems 1948–1984 1986, The Arkansas Testament 1987, Omeros (epic poem) (WHSmith Literary Award 1991) 1989, Poems 1965–1980 1992, The Bounty 1997, Tiepolo's Hounds 2000, The Prodigal: A Poem 2005, Selected Poems 2007; non-fiction: The Antilles, Fragments of Epic Memory: The Nobel Lecture 1993, What the Twilight Says (essays) 1998, Homage to Robert Frost (jtly) 1998. *Honours:* Arts Advisory Council of Jamaica Prize 1960, Guinness Award 1961, Borestone Mountain Awards 1964, 1977, RSL Heinemann Awards 1966, 1983, Cholmondeley Award 1969, Gold Hummingbird Medal, Trinidad 1969, Obie Award 1971, Welsh Arts Council Int. Writers Prize 1980, Los Angeles Times Book Prize 1986, Queen's Gold Medal for Poetry 1988, Nobel Prize for Literature 1992. *Address:* PO Box GM 926, Castries, St Lucia, West Indies (home); c/o Faber & Faber, 3 Queen Square, London, WC1N 3AU, England (office). *Telephone:* 450-0559 (home). *Fax:* 450-0935 (home).

WALDEN, (Alastair) Brian; British broadcaster and journalist; b. 8 July 1932, s. of W. F. Walden; m. Hazel Downes; one s. (and three s. from fmr marriages). *Education:* West Bromwich Grammar School, Queen's Coll. and Nuffield Coll., Oxford. *Career:* univ. lecturer; MP (Labour) for Birmingham All Saints 1964–74, Birmingham Ladywood 1974–77; TV presenter, Weekend World (London Weekend TV) 1977–86; mem. W Midland Bd, Cen. Ind. TV 1982–84; columnist London Standard 1983–86, Thomson Regional Newspapers 1983–86, The Sunday Times; presenter, The Walden Interview (London Weekend TV for ITV network) 1988, 1989, 1990–94, Walden on Labour Leaders (BBC) 1997, Walden on Heroes (BBC) 1998, Walden on Villains 1999, A Point of View (BBC Radio 4) 2005–; Chair. Paragon 1994–, Ten Alps 2002–, Capital 2006–. *Publication:* The Walden Interviews 1990. *Honours:* Shell Int. Award 1982, BAFTA Richard Dimbleby Award 1985; Aims of Industry Special Free Enterprise Award 1990; ITV Personality of the Year 1991. *Address:* Landfall, Fort Road, St Peter Port, GY1 1ZU, Guernsey. *Telephone:* (1481) 722860. *E-mail:* walden@guernsey.net.

WALDMAN, Anne, BA; American poet, lecturer, performer and editor; b. 2 April 1945, Millville, NJ. *Education:* Bennington Coll. *Career:* Ed., Angel Hair Magazine, 1965–, The World, 1966–78; Asst Dir, Poetry Project, St Mark's Church In-the-Bowery, 1966–68; Dir, Poetry Project, New York City, 1968–78; Founder-Dir, Jack Kerouac School of Disembodied Poetics, Naropa Institute, Boulder, CO; Poetry readings and performance events world-wide; mem. Committee for International Poetry; PEN Poetry Society of America. *Publications:* Journals and Dreams, 1976; First Baby Poems, 1983; Makeup on Empty Space, 1984; Invention, 1985; Skin Meat Bones, 1985; Blue Mosque, 1987; The Romance Thing, 1987–88; Helping the Dreamer: New and Selected Poems, 1966–1988; Iovis, 1993; Troubairitz, Kill or Cure, 1994; Iovis, Book II, 1996. Editor: The World Anthology, 1969; Another World, 1971; Nice to See You: Homage to Ted Berrigan, 1991; In and Out of This World: An Anthology of the St Mark's Poetry Project, 1992; The Beat Book, 1996. Contributions: various publications. *Honours:* National Endowment for the Arts Grant, 1980; Achievement in Poetry Award, Bennington College Alumni, 1981. *Address:* c/o The Naropa Institute, 2130 Arapahoe Avenue, Boulder, CO 80302, USA.

WALDROP, Rosmarie, MA, PhD; German poet, writer, translator, editor and publisher; b. 24 Aug. 1935, Kitzingen-am-Main; m. Keith Waldrop 1959. *Education:* Univ. of Würzburg, Univ. of Aix-Marseille, France, Univ. of Freiburg, Univ. of Michigan, USA. *Career:* Wesleyan Univ., Middletown, Conn., USA 1964–70; Co-Ed. and Co-Publr (with Keith Waldrop), Burning Desk Press 1968–; Visiting Assoc. Prof., Brown Univ., Providence, RI, USA 1977–78, 1983, 1990–91; Visiting Lecturer, Tufts Univ., Boston, Mass, USA 1979–81; mem. PEN. *Publications:* poetry: The Aggressive Ways of the Casual Stranger 1972, The Road is Everywhere or Stop This Body 1978, When They Have Senses 1980, Nothing Has Changed 1981, Differences for Four Hands 1984, Streets Enough to Welcome Snow 1986, The Reproduction of Profiles 1987, Shorter American Memory 1988, Peculiar Motions 1990, Lawn of Excluded Middle 1993, A Key Into the Language of America 1994, Another Language: Selected Poems 1997, Split Infinites 1998, Reluctant Gravities 1999, Blindsight 2003, Love, like Pronouns 2003; fiction: The Hanky of Pippin's Daughter 1986, A Form/of Taking/it All 1990; essays: Against Language? 1971, The Ground is the Only Figure: Notebook Spring 1996, Lavish Absence: Recalling and Rereading Edmond Jabès 2002, Dissonance (If You are Interested): Collected Essays 2005, various poetry chapbooks and trans. *Honours:* Chevalier, Ordre des Arts et des Lettres 1999; Major Hopwood Award in Poetry 1963, Alexander von Humboldt Fellowships 1970–71, 1975–76, Howard Foundation Fellowship 1974–75, Trans. Center Award, Columbia Univ. 1978, Nat. Endowment for the Arts Fellowships 1980, 1984, Gov.'s Arts Award, RI 1988, Fund for Poetry Award 1990, PEN/Book-of-the-Month Club Citation in Trans. 1991, Deutscher Akademischer Austauschdienst Fellowship, Berlin 1993, Harold Morton Landon Trans. Award 1994, Lila Wallace-Reader's Digest Writer's Award 1999–2001, Foundation for Contemporary Performance Arts Award 2003. *Address:* 71 Elmgrove Avenue, Providence RI 02906, USA. *E-mail:* bernard_waldrop@brown.edu (home).

WALI, Najem, MA; Iraqi journalist and novelist; *Cultural Correspondent, Al-Hayat*; b. 1956, Al-Amarah. *Education:* Baghdad Univ. *Career:* emigrated to Hamburg, Germany at outbreak of Iran–Iraq war; lived in Madrid, Spain 1987–90, later returning to Hamburg; currently freelance journalist, Cultural Corresp. Al-Hayat newspaper. *Publications:* novels: War in the Destruction of Pleasure 1989, The Least Night to Mary 1995, Place Names Kumait 1997, Tel Al Leham (trans. as The Mountain of Meet) 2001; short story collections: There in the Strange City 1990, Waltzing Matilda 2001. *Address:* c/o Dar al-Mada, Damascus, Syria.

WALKER, Alice Malsenior, BA; American writer; b. 9 Feb. 1944, Eatonton, Ga; d. of Willie L. Walker and Minnie (née Grant) Walker; m. Melvyn R. Leventhal 1967 (divorced 1977); one d. *Education:* Sarah Lawrence Coll. *Publications:* Once 1968, The Third Life of George Copeland 1970, Five Poems 1972, In Love and Trouble 1973, Langston Hughes, American Poet 1973, Revolutionary Petunias 1974, Meridian 1976, I Love Myself When I am Laughing 1979, You Can't Keep a Good Woman Down 1981, Good Night Willi Lee, I'll See You in the Morning 1979, The Color Purple 1982, In Search of Our Mothers' Gardens 1983, Horses Make a Landscape Look More Beautiful 1984, To Hell with Dying 1988, Living By the Word 1988, The Temple of My

Familiar 1989, Her Blue Body Everything We Know: Earthling Poems (1965–90) 1991, Finding the Green Stone 1991, Possessing the Secret of Joy 1992, Warrior Marks (with Pratibha Parmar) 1993, Double Stitch: Black Women Write About Mothers and Daughters (jtly) 1993, Everyday Use 1994, By the Light of my Father's Smile 1998, Alice Walker Banned 1996, Everything We Love Can Be Saved 1997, The Same River Twice 1997, The Way Forward is with a Broken Heart (ed.) 2000, Absolute Trust in the Goodness of the Earth: New Poems 2003, The Third Life of Grange Copeland 2003, Now is the Time to Open Your Heart 2004, We Are the Ones We Have Been Waiting For (essays) 2007. *Honours:* Hon. PhD (Russell Sage Univ.) 1972; Hon. DHL (Univ. of Mass.) 1983; Bread Loaf Writers Conf. Scholar 1966, Ingram Merrill Foundation Fellowship 1967, McDowell Colony Fellowships 1967, 1977–78, Nat. Endowment for the Arts Grants 1969, 1977, Richard and Hinda Rosenthal Pound Award, American Acad. and Inst. of Arts and Letters 1974, Lillian Smith Award 1974, Rosenthal Award, Nat. Inst. of Arts and Letters 1973, Guggenheim Foundation Award 1979, American Book Award 1983, Pulitzer Prize 1983, O. Henry Award 1986, Nora Astorga Leadership Award 1989, Freedom to Write Award, PEN Center West 1990. *Literary Agent:* Wendy Weil Agency Inc, 232 Madison Avenue, Suite 1300, New York, NY 10016, USA.

WALKER, George Frederick; Canadian playwright; b. 23 Aug. 1947, Toronto, ON. *Education:* Riverdale Coll., Toronto. *Career:* resident playwright, New York Shakespeare Festival 1981. *Publications:* The Prince of Naples, 1971; Ambush at Tether's End, 1971; Sacktown Rag, 1972; Baghdad Saloon, 1973; Beyond Mozambique, 1974; Ramona and the White Slaves, 1976; Gossip, 1977; Zastrozzi: The Master of Discipline, 1977; Filthy Rich, 1979; Rumours of our Death (musical), 1980; Theatre of the Film Noir, 1981; Science and Madness, 1982; The Art of War: An Adventure, 1983; Criminals in Love, 1984; Better Living, 1986; Beautiful City, 1987; Nothing Sacred, after Turgenev, 1988; Love and Anger, 1990; Escape from Happiness, 1991; Shared Anxiety, 1994. *Honours:* Governor-General's Awards in Drama, 1985, 1988; Toronto Arts Award for Drama, 1994. *Literary Agent:* Great North Artists, Suite 500, 345 Adelaide Street West, Toronto, ON, Canada.

WALKER, Harry (see Waugh, Hillary Baldwin)

WALKER, Jeanne Murray, BA, MA, PhD; American academic, poet, dramatist and writer; *Professor of Poetry and Script Writing, University of Delaware*; b. 27 May 1944, Parkers Prairie, MN; m. E. Daniel Larkin 1983; one s. one d. *Education:* Wheaton Coll., Ill., Loyola Univ., Chicago, Univ. of Penn. *Career:* Asst Prof. of English, Haverford Coll., Penn.; currently Prof. of Poetry and Script Writing, Dept of English, Univ. of Delaware; mem. editorial bd Shenandoah 1994–; Poetry Ed. Christianity and Literature 1988–; mem. Dramatists' Guild, PEN, Poets and Writers. *Publications:* poetry: Nailing Up the Home Sweet Home 1980, Fugitive Angels 1985, Coming into History 1990, Stranger Than Fiction 1992, Gaining Time 1997, A Deed to the Light 2004; eight plays 1990–2001; poems appeared on trains and buses in association with Poetry in Motion, American Acad. of Poets; numerous reviews, quarterlies, journals and periodicals, including American Scholar, Arizona Quarterly, American Poetry Review, Aspen Anthology, Ariel, Poetry Miscellany, Jawbone, Carolina Quarterly, Chicago Tribune, Christian Science Monitor, Cimarron Review, Chariton Review, Critical Quarterly, Georgia Review, Southern Humanities Review, Iowa Review, Image, The Journal, Kenyon Review, Louisville Review, Lyric, Massachusetts Review, Milkweed Chronicle, Descant, Northwest Review, Christian Century, New England Review, Nantucket Review, Wascona Review, Poet and Critic, 2 Plus 2, Poetry Now, St Andrews Review, Pennsylvania Review, Kansas Quarterly, Seattle Review, Poetry, Shenandoah, Painted Bride Quarterly, Whetstone, Boulevard, Partisan Review, Prairie Schooner, The Nation. *Honours:* Delaware Humanities Council grant 1979, Delaware Arts Council grant 1981, six Pennsylvania Council on the Arts Fellowships 1983–2001, Prairie Schooner/Strousse Award 1988, winner Washington Nat. Theatre Competition 1990, Colladay Award for Poetry 1992, Fellow Center for Advanced Studies 1993, Nat. Endowment for the Arts Fellowship 1994, Brigham Young Theatre Lewis Prizes for New Plays 1995, 1997, Pew Fellow in the Arts Stagetime Award 1998. *Address:* Department of English, 131 Memorial Hall, University of Delaware, Newark, DE 19716, USA (office). *Telephone:* (610) 660-5230 (office). *E-mail:* jwalker@udel.edu (office). *Website:* www.english.udel.edu/jwalker (office).

WALKER, Lou Ann, BA; American writer; b. 9 Dec. 1952, Hartford City, IN; m. Speed Vogel 1986; one d. *Education:* Ball State University, University of Besançon, Harvard University. *Career:* reporter, Indianapolis News, 1976; Asst to Exec. Ed., New York (magazine), New York, 1976–77; Cosmopolitan, New York City, 1979–80; Asst Ed., Esquire Magazine, 1977–79; Assoc. Ed., Diversion (magazine), New York City, 1980–81; Ed., Direct (magazine), New York City, 1981–82; Sign Language Interpretor for New York Society for the Deaf; Consultant to Broadway's Theater Development Fund and sign language adviser on many Broadway shows, 1984–; Contributing Ed., New York Woman, 1990–92; mem. Authors' Guild. *Publications:* Amy: The Story of a Deaf Child, 1985; A Loss for Words: The Story of Deafness in a Family (autobiog.), 1986; Hand, Heart and Mind, 1994; Roy Lichtenstein: The Artist at Work, 1994. Contributions: New York Times Book Review; Chicago Sun-Times; Esquire; New York Times Magazine; New York Woman; Life. *Honours:* Rockefeller Foundation Humanities Fellowship, 1982–83; Christopher Award, 1987; National Endowment for the Arts Creative Writing Grant, 1988.

WALKER, Martin, MA; British journalist, writer and broadcaster; *Editor-in-Chief, United Press International*; b. 23 Jan. 1947, Durham, England; m. Julia Watson 1978. *Education:* Balliol Coll., Oxford, Harvard Univ. *Career:* staff Guardian, Manchester 1972–, Moscow Bureau Chief 1983–88, US Bureau Chief 1989–98; Ed.-in-Chief United Press Int. 2004–; numerous radio and TV broadcasts; many lectures; Congressional Fellow American Political Science Asscn 1970–71; Public Policy Fellow Woodrow Wilson Int. Center for Scholars 2000–01; Sr Fellow World Policy Inst., New School Univ., New York; mem. NUJ. *Television:* Martin Walker's Russia (BBC series) 1989. *Publications:* The National Front 1977, Daily Sketches: A History of Political Cartoons 1978, The Infiltrators (novel) 1978, A Mercenary Calling (novel) 1980, The Eastern Question (novel) 1981, Powers of the Press: A Comparative Study of the World's Leading Newspapers 1981, The Waking Giant: Gorbachev and Perestroika 1987, Martin Walker's Russia 1989, The Independent Traveller's Guide to the Soviet Union 1990, The Insight Guide to Washington, DC 1992, The Cold War: A History 1993, The President We Deserve: Bill Clinton: His Rise, Falls, and Comebacks 1996, America Reborn: A Twentieth-Century Narrative in Twenty-Six Lives 2000, The Iraq War 2003; contrib. to anthologies and periodicals. *Address:* United Press International, 1510 H Street, Washington, DC 20005, USA (office). *Telephone:* (202) 898-8141 (office). *E-mail:* mwalker@upi.com (office).

WALKER, Mary Willis, BA; American writer; b. 24 May 1942, Foxpoint, WI; m. (divorced); two d. *Education:* Duke Univ. *Career:* mem. Texas Inst. of Letters, MWA, Sisters in Crime. Int. Asscn of Crime Writers, Austin Writers' League. *Publications:* Zero at the Bone 1991, The Red Scream 1994, Under the Beetle's Cellar 1995, All the Dead Lie Down 1998, Mom's in Prison... Again (documentary script); contrib. essays to periodicals, including New York Times, Mostly Murder, book reviews to Mostly Murder, Austin American-Statesman. *Honours:* Agatha Award 1991, Mystery Readers Int. Macavity Award 1991, Int. Asscn of Crime Writers Hammett Award 1995, Anthony Award, Bouchercon 1995, MWA Edgar Award 1995. *Address:* POB 5612, Austin, TX 78763-5612 (office); Inkwell Management, 521 Fifth Avenue, New York, NY 10175, USA (office). *Fax:* (512) 323-0209 (office). *E-mail:* mwillis@austin.rr.com.

WALL, Ethan (see Holmes, Bryan John)

WALL, Geoffrey, (Geoffrey Chadwick), BA, BPhil; British academic, biographer and translator; *Reader in Modern French Literature, University of York*; b. 10 July 1950, Cheshire, England. *Education:* Univ. of Sussex, St Edmund Hall. *Career:* Lecturer, Dept of English and Related Literature, Univ. of York 1975–97, Sr Lecturer 1997–2002, Reader in Modern French Literature 2002–; Co-Ed. Cambridge Quarterly 1998; mem. Asscn of Univ. Teachers. *Publications:* translator: Madame Bovary, by Gustave Flaubert 1992, The Dictionary of Received Ideas, by Gustave Flaubert 1994, Selected Letters, by Gustave Flaubert 1997, Modern Times: Selected Writings, by Jean-Paul Sartre 1999, Flaubert: A Life 2001, Sentimental Education, by Gustave Flaubert 2004; contrib. to scholarly journals and newspapers. *Literary Agent:* David Higham Associates Ltd, 5–8 Lower John Street, Golden Square, London, W1F 9HA, England. *Telephone:* (20) 7434-5900. *Fax:* (20) 7437-1072. *E-mail:* dha@davidhigham.co.uk. *Website:* www.davidhigham.co.uk. *Address:* Department of English and Related Literature, University of York, Heslington, York, YO10 5DD, England (office). *E-mail:* gw2@york.ac.uk (office). *Website:* www.york.ac.uk.

WALL, William, BA; Irish novelist and poet; b. 1955, Cork; m.; two c. *Education:* Univ. Coll. Dublin. *Career:* school teacher for 25 years. *Publications:* novels: Alice Falling 2000, Minding Children 2001, The Map of Tenderness 2003, This is the Country 2005; poetry: Mathematics and Other Poems 1997, Fahrenheit Says Nothing To Me 2004; short stories: No Paradiso 2006; contrib. to The Irish Press, The Sunday Tribune, Phoenix Irish Short Stories, Southword, Carve magazine, Faber Book of Best Irish Short Stories, RTÉ Radio. *Honours:* Patrick Kavanagh Award for Poetry 1995, American Ireland Fund/Listowel Writers' Week Award (Poetry) 1996, 1997, (Short Story) 1998, Seán O'Faoláin Award (Short Story) 2003. *Literary Agent:* c/o Gill Coleridge, Rogers, Coleridge & White, 20 Powis Mews, London, WC11 1JN, England. *Telephone:* (20) 7221-3717. *Fax:* (20) 7229-9084. *E-mail:* GillC@rcwlitagency.co.uk. *Website:* www.rcwlitagency.co.uk. *E-mail:* kirwall@eircom.net. *Website:* homepage.eircom.net/~williamwall.

WALLACE, David Foster, AB, MFA; American writer and academic; *Associate Professor of English, Illinois State University*; b. 21 Feb. 1962, Ithaca, NY. *Education:* Amherst Coll., Univ. of Arizona. *Career:* Assoc. Prof. of English, Illinois State Univ. 1993–. *Publications:* The Broom of the System 1987, Girl With Curious Hair 1988, Signifying Rappers: Rap and Race in the Urban Present (with Mark Costello) 1990, Infinite Jest 1996, A Supposedly Fun Thing I'll Never Do Again: Essays and Arguments 1997, Oblivion: Stories 2004, Everything and More: A Compact History of Infinity 2005, Consider the Lobster: And Other Essays 2006; contrib. to various publications. *Honours:* Whiting Writers' Award 1987, Yaddo residencies 1987, 1989, Nat. Endowment for the Arts Fellowship 1989, Lannan Foundation Award for Literature 1996, John D. and Catherine T. MacArthur Foundation Fellowship 1997. *Address:* c/o Department of English, Illinois State University, Normal, IL 61790, USA.

WALLACE, Ian Robert; Canadian writer and illustrator; b. 31 March 1950, Niagara Falls, ON; m. Debra Wiedman. *Education:* Ontario College of Art. *Career:* mem. Canadian Children's Book Centre, Writer's Union of Canada. *Publications:* writer and illustrator: Julie News 1974, The Christmas Tree

House 1976, Chin Chiang and the Dragon's Dance 1984, The Sparrow's Song 1986, Morgan the Magnificent 1987, Mr Kneebone's New Digs 1991, A Winter's Tale 1997, Boy of the Deeps 1999, Duncan's Way 2000, The True Story of Trapper Jack's Left Big Toe 2002, The Naked Lady 2002, The Man Who Walked the Earth 2003; illustrator: Seven books 1986–96; other: The Sandwich (with A. Wood) 1974. *Honours:* A. F. Howard Gibbons Award, Canadian Library Asscn 1984, IODE Book Award 1985, IBBY Honour List 1986, 2000, Mr Christie Book Award 1990, Aesop Accolade List 1994, Smithsonian Best Books of the Year List 2000. *Address:* 184 Major Street, Toronto, ON M5S 2L3, Canada.

WALLACE, Naomi French, BA, MFA; American poet and playwright; b. 17 Aug. 1960, Kentucky; m. Bruce McLeod; three d. *Education:* Hampshire Coll., Univ. of Iowa. *Career:* plays have been performed at theatres in UK and USA; teacher of play writing, Univ. of Iowa 1990–93; Playwright-in-Residence, Ill. State Univ. 1994. *Plays include:* War Boys, In the Heart of America, Slaughter City (Mobil Prize) 1995, One Flea Spare (Obie Award for Best Play) 1997, Birdy 1997, Trestle at Pope Lick Creek 1999. *Film:* Lawn Dogs 1997 (writer). *Publications include:* To Dance a Stony Field (poems) 1995; contrib. to reviews, journals and magazines. *Honours:* Susan Smith Blackburn Award, The Nation/Discovery Award, Fellowship of Southern Writers Award. *Address:* c/o Rod Hall Agency, 6th Floor, Fairgate House, 78 New Oxford Street, London, WC1A 1HB, EnglandTelephone +44 Facsimile +44 (. *Telephone:* (20) 7079-7987. *Fax:* (845) 638-4094.

WALLACE, Ronald William, BA, MA, PhD; American poet and academic; *Felix Pollak Professor of Poetry, University of Wisconsin, Madison*; b. 18 Feb. 1945, Cedar Rapids, IA; m. Margaret Elizabeth McCreight 1968; two d. *Education:* Coll. of Wooster, Univ. of Michigan. *Career:* Dir of Creative Writing, Univ. of Wisconsin, Madison 1975–, Felix Pollak Prof. of Poetry 1982–; Series Ed., Brittingham Prize in Poetry 1985–; Dir, Wisconsin Inst. for Creative Writing 1986–; mem. Poets and Writers, Associated Writing Programs. *Publications:* Henry James and the Comic Form 1975, Installing the Bees 1977, Cucumbers 1977, The Last Laugh 1979, The Facts of Life 1979, Plums, Stones, Kisses and Hooks 1981, Tunes For Bears To Dance To 1983, God Be With the Clown 1984, The Owl in the Kitchen 1985, People and Dog in the Sun 1987, Vital Signs 1989, The Makings of Happiness 1991, Time's Fancy 1994, The Uses of Adversity 1998, Quick Bright Things 2000, Long for This World: New and Selected Poems 2003; contrib. to New Yorker, Atlantic, Nation, Poetry, Southern Review, Poetry Northwest. *Honours:* Hopwood Award for Poetry 1970, Council for Wisconsin Writers Awards 1978, 1979, 1984, 1985, 1986, 1988, Helen Bullis Prize in Poetry 1985, Robert E. Gard Award for Excellence in Poetry 1990, Posner Poetry Prize 1992, 2004, Gerald A. Bartell Award in the Arts 1994. *Address:* Department of English, 600 N Park Street, University of Wisconsin, Madison, WI 53706, USA (office). *Telephone:* (608) 263-3705 (office). *Fax:* (608) 263-3709 (office). *E-mail:* rwallace@wisc.edu (office).

WALLACE-CRABBE, Christopher Keith, MA, FAHA; Australian poet and critic; b. 6 May 1934, Melbourne; s. of Kenneth Eyre Inverell Wallace-Crabbe and Phyllis Vera May Wallace-Crabbe (née Cock); m. 1st Helen Margaret Wiltshire 1957; one s. one d.; m. 2nd Marianne Sophie Feil 1979; two s. *Education:* Melbourne Univ., Yale Univ., USA. *Career:* cadet metallurgist 1951–52; then journalist, clerk, schoolteacher; Lockie Fellow in Australian Literature, Univ. of Melbourne 1962; Harkness Fellow, Yale Univ. 1965–67; Sr Lecturer in English, Univ. of Melbourne 1967, Reader 1976, Prof. 1987–; Personal Chair. 1987–97; Prof. Emer. Australian Centre 1997–; Visiting Chair. in Australian Studies, Harvard Univ., USA 1987–88. *Publications:* The Music of Division 1959, Selected Poems 1974, Melbourne or the Bush 1974, The Emotions are not Skilled Workers 1980, Toil and Spin: Two Directions in Modern Poetry 1980, Splinters (novel) 1981, The Amorous Cannibal 1985, I'm Deadly Serious 1988, Sangue è l'Acqua 1989, For Crying out Loud 1990, Falling into Language 1990, Poetry and Belief 1990, From the Republic of Conscience 1992, Rungs of Time 1993, Selected Poems 1956–94 1995, Whirling 1998, By and Large 2001. *Honours:* Masefield Prize for Poetry 1957, Farmer's Poetry Prize 1964, Grace Leven Prize 1986, Dublin Prize 1987, Christopher Brennan Award 1990, Age Book of the Year Prize 1995, Philip Hodgins Memorial Medal 2002, Centenary Medal 2003. *Address:* Department of English, University of Melbourne, Parkville, Vic. 3052; Ca d'Oro, 2 Burchett Street, Brunswick, Vic. 3056, Australia. *Telephone:* (3) 9387-3662 (home); (3) 8344-6864. *E-mail:* ckwc@unimelb.edu.au (office). *Website:* www .hlc.unimelb.edu.au/cwc/ (office).

WALLENSTEIN, Barry, BA, MA, PhD; American poet and academic; b. 13 Feb. 1940, New York, NY; m. Lorna Harbus 1978, one s. one d. *Education:* New York University. *Career:* Prof. of English, City College, CUNY, 1965–; Exchange Prof., University of Paris, 1981, Polytechnic of North London, 1987–88; Writer-in-Residence, University of North Michigan, 1993; mem. Acad. of American Poets; Poets and Writers; Poets House. *Publications:* Poetry: Beast is a Wolf with Brown Fire, 1977; Roller Coaster Kid, 1982; Love and Crush, 1991; The Short Life of the Five Minute Dancer, 1993; A Measure of Conduct, 1999. Criticism: Visions and Revisions: An Approach to Poetry, 1971. Contributions: anthologies, reviews, quarterlies, and journals. *Honours:* CUNY Research Fund Grant; MacDowell Colony Residency Fellowship.

WALLER, Robert James; American writer and musician; b. 1 Aug. 1939, s. of Robert Waller Sr and Ruth Waller; m. Georgia A. Wiedemeier; one d. *Education:* Northern Iowa and Indiana Univs. *Career:* Prof. of Man. Univ. of N

Iowa 1968–91, Dean Business School 1979–85; singer; guitarist; flautist. *Album:* The Ballads of Madison County 1993. *Publications:* Just Beyond the Firelight 1988, One Good Road is Enough 1990, Iowa: Perspectives on Today and Tomorrow 1991, The Bridges of Madison County 1992, Slow Waltz at Cedar Bend 1994, Old Songs in a New Café 1994, Selected Essays 1994, Border Music 1995, Puerto-Vallarta Squeeze 1995. *Literary Agent:* Aaron Priest Literary Agency, 708 3rd Avenue, 23rd Floor, New York, NY 10017, USA.

WALLEY, Byron (see Card, Orson Scott)

WALLIN, Raimo S.; Finnish novelist, playwright, poet and publisher; m. Terttu Wallin 1972. *Career:* fmr teacher; f. publishing co, Kustannus Sokrates. *Publications:* 100 Vuotta Kansakoulutoimintaa Vanajassa (with Uolevi Nurminen), 1965; Alttari (play), 1967; Matkan Loppu (short stories), 1967; Persialaisella Matolla, 1972; Saul Ja Daavid, 1972; Luova Kirjoitus, 1973; Kansanruno-Kalevala (with Merja Totro, Terttu Wallin), 1979; Luova Kirjoitus 5, 1982; Minä, Muut, Maailma, 1982; Minä, Muut, Maailma, 1983; Vapaat Kahleet, 1986; Kaikki Tiet Käyvät Roomaan, 1997; Luova Kirjoitus ABCD, 1998. *Address:* c/o Kustannus Sokrates Ky, Ounasvaarantie 1 C 75, 00970 Helsinki, Finland.

WALLINGTON, Vivienne Elizabeth, (Elizabeth Duke); Australian writer; b. 8 Feb. 1937, Adelaide, SA; m. John Wallington 1959; one s. one d. *Education:* library registration. *Career:* mem. Romance Writers of America, Romance Writers of Australia, Fellowship of Australian Writers. *Publications:* Somewhere 1982, Butterfingers 1986, Names are Fun 1990, Outback Legacy 1993, Shattered Wedding 1994, To Catch a Playboy 1995, Heartless Stranger 1996, Takeover Engagement 1997, The Marriage Pact 1997, Look-alike Fiancée 1998, The Husband Dilemma 1998, The Parent Test 1999, Outback Affair 2000, Claiming his Bride 2001, Kindergarten Cupids 2002, In her Husband's Image 2004, The Last Time I Saw Venice 2005; contrib. to newspapers and magazines. *Address:* 38 Fuller Street, Mitcham, Vic. 3132, Australia (home). *Telephone:* (3) 9873-1446 (home). *Fax:* (3) 9874-7367 (home).

WALSER, Martin, DPhil; German writer, playwright and poet; b. 24 March 1927, Wasserburg, Bodensee; s. of Martin Walser and Augusta Schmid; m. Käthe Jehle 1950; four d. *Education:* Theologisch-Philosophische Hochschule, Regensburg and Univ. of Tübingen. *Career:* writer 1951–. *Publications:* novels: Ehen in Philippsburg 1957, Halbzeit 1960, Das Einhorn 1966, Fiction 1970, Die Gallistlische Krankheit 1972, Der Sturz 1973, Jenseits der Liebe 1976, Ein fliehendes Pferd 1978, Seelenarbeit 1979, Das Schwanenhaus 1980, Brief an Lord Liszt 1982, Brandung 1985, Dorle und Wolf 1987, Jagd 1988, Die Verteidigung der Kindheit 1991, Ohne einander 1993, Finks Krieg 1996, Ein springender Brunnen 1998, Der Lebenslauf der Liebe 2001, Tod eines Kritikers 2002, Der Augenblick der Liebe 2004; short stories: Ein Flugzeug über dem Haus 1955, Lügengeschichten 1964; plays: Der Abstecher 1961, Eiche und Angora 1962, Überlebensgross Herr Krott 1963, Der schwarze Schwan 1964, Die Zimmerschlacht 1967, Ein Kinderspiel 1970, Das Sauspiel 1975, In Goethe's Hand 1982, Die Ohrfeige 1986, Das Sofa 1992, Kaschmir in Parching 1995; essays: Beschreibung einer Form, Versuch über Franz Kafka 1961, Erfahrungen und Leseerfahrungen 1965, Heimatkunde 1968, Wie und wovon handelt Literatur 1973, Wer ist ein Schriftsteller 1978, Selbstbewusstsein und Ironie 1981, Messmers Gedanken 1985, Über Deutschland reden 1988, Vormittag eines Schriftstellers 1994, Messmers Reisen 2003; poetry: Der Grund zur Freude 1978, Die Verwaltung des Nichts 2004. *Honours:* Grosses Bundesverdienstkreuz mit Stern 1997; Group 47 Prize 1955, Hermann-Hesse Prize 1957, Gerhart-Hauptmann Prize 1962, Schiller Prize 1980, Büchner Prize 1981, Orden pour le mérite 1994, Friedenspreis des Deutschen Buchhandels 1998. *Address:* Zum Hecht 36, 88662 Überlingen-Nussdorf, Germany (home). *Telephone:* (7551) 4131 (home). *Fax:* (7551) 68494 (home). *E-mail:* nussdorf@t-online.de (home).

WALSH, (Mary) Noëlle, BA; British journalist; *Director, The Value for Money Co. Ltd*; b. 26 Dec. 1954, d. of Thomas Walsh and Mary Walsh (née Ferguson); m. David Heslam 1988; one s. one d. *Education:* Univ. of East Anglia. *Career:* Editorial Asst Public Relations Dept, St Dunstan's Org. for the War-Blinded 1977–79; News Ed. Cosmopolitan 1979–85; Ed. London Week 1985–86; freelance writer 1986–; Deputy Ed. Good Housekeeping 1986–87, Ed. 1987–91; Dir The Value For Money Co. Ltd 1992–. *Television:* Presenter, Consumer Issues, Channel 5 1998. *Publications:* Hot Lips, the Ultimate Kiss and Tell Guide 1985, Ragtime to Wartime: the best of Good Housekeeping 1922–39 1986, The Home Front: the best of Good Housekeeping 1939–45 (co-ed) 1987, The Christmas Book: the best of Good Housekeeping at Christmas 1922–62 (co-ed) 1988, Food Glorious Food: eating and drinking with Good Housekeeping 1922–42 1990, Things My Mother Should Have Told Me 1991, Childhood Memories 1991, The Good Deal Directory 1992–, The Home Shopping Handbook 1995, Baby on a Budget 1995, Wonderful Wedding That Won't Cost a Fortune 1996, The Good Mail Order Guide 1996, The Good Deal Directory (annual) 1994–. *Address:* PO Box 4, Lechlade, Glos., GL7 3YB, England (office). *Telephone:* (1367) 860017 (office). *Fax:* (1367) 860177 (office). *E-mail:* nheslam@aol.com (office). *Website:* www.gooddealdirectory.co.uk; www.gooddealhouse.com; www.ukgrandsales.co.uk.

WALSH, Sheila, (Sophie Leyton); British writer; b. 10 Oct. 1928, Birmingham, England. *Education:* Southport College of Art. *Career:* mem. Romantic Novelists' Asscn (vice-pres.), Soroptimist International of Southport. *Publications:* The Golden Songbird, 1975; The Sergeant Major's Daughter, 1977; A Fine Silk Purse, 1978; The Incomparable Miss Brady, 1980; The Rose Domino,

1981; A Highly Respectable Marriage, 1983; The Runaway Bride, 1984; Cousins of a Kind, 1985; The Incorrigible Rake, 1985; An Insubstantial Pageant, 1986; Bath Intrigue, 1986; Lady Aurelia's Bequest, 1987; Minerva's Marquis, 1988; The Nabob, 1989–90; A Woman of Little Importance, 1991; Until Tomorrow, 1993; Remember Me, 1994; A Perfect Bride, 1994; Kate and the Marquess, 1997. *Honours:* Best Romantic Novel of the Year 1983.

WALSHE, Aubrey Peter, BA, DPhil; British academic and writer; *Professor of Political Science, University of Notre Dame;* b. 12 Jan. 1934, Johannesburg, South Africa; m. Catherine Ann Pettifer 1957; one s. three d. *Education:* Wadham Coll., Oxford, St Antony's Coll., Oxford. *Career:* Lecturer, Univ. of Lesotho 1959–62; Prof. of Political Science, Univ. of Notre Dame, IN 1967–; Fellow Joan Kroc Inst. for Int. Peace Studies. *Publications:* The Rise of African Nationalism in South Africa 1971, Black Nationalism in South Africa 1974, Church Versus State in South Africa 1983, Prophetic Christianity and the Liberation Movement in South Africa 1996; contrib. to Cambridge History of Africa 1986, professional journals and newspapers. *Address:* c/o Department of Political Science, University of Notre Dame, Notre Dame, IN 46556, USA.

WALT, Stephen Martin, BA, MA, PhD; American academic; *Professor of International Affairs, John F. Kennedy School of Government, Harvard University;* b. 2 July 1955; m.; two c. *Education:* Stanford Univ., Univ. of Calif. *Career:* part-time mem. Professional Staff Center for Naval Analyses 1980–82; Research Fellow Center for Science and Int. Affairs, Harvard Univ. 1981–84, now Prof. of Int. Affairs, Academic Dean, John F. Kennedy School of Govt 2002–06; Asst Prof. Princeton Univ. 1984–89; Resident Assoc., Carnegie Endowment for Int. Peace 1986–87; Guest Scholar Brookings Inst. 1988; Assoc. Prof. Univ. of Chicago 1989–95, Prof. 1995–99, Master, Social Sciences Collegiate Div. and Deputy Dean, Div. of Social Sciences 1996–99; Visiting Prof. Nanyang Tech. Univ. Singapore 2000; mem. Editorial Bds Security Studies, Foreign Policy, Bulletin of the Atomic Scientists, Columbia Int. Affairs Online Service, Journal of Cold War Studies; Co-Ed. Cornell Studies in Security Affairs; mem. American Political Science Asscn, Int. Studies Asscn, Soc. of Historians of American Foreign Relations, IISS. *Publications:* The Origins of Alliances 1987, Revolution and War 1996, Taming American Power: The Global Response to US Primacy 2006; numerous articles and chapters in journals and books. *Address:* John F. Kennedy School of Government, Harvard University, 79 John F. Kennedy Street, Cambridge, MA 02138, USA (office). *Telephone:* (617) 495-5712 (office). *Fax:* (617) 495-8963 (office). *E-mail:* stephen_walt@harvard.edu (office). *Website:* ksghome.harvard.edu (office).

WALTERS, Minette, BA; British writer; b. 26 Sept. 1949, Bishops Stortford, England; m. Alexander Walters 1978; two s. *Education:* Univ. of Durham. *Publications:* The Ice House (CWA John Creasey Award for Best First Crime Novel) 1992, The Sculptress 1993, The Scold's Bridle (CWA Gold Dagger 1994) 1994, The Dark Room 1995, The Echo 1997, The Breaker 1998, The Tinder Box 1999, The Shape of Snakes (Pelle Rosekrantz Award, Denmark) 2000, Acid Row 2001, Fox Evil (CWA Gold Dagger 2003) 2002, Disordered Minds 2003, The Devil's Feather 2005, Chickenfeed 2006. *Honours:* Hon. DLitt (Bournemouth) 2005, (Southampton Solent) 2006; Macavity Award 1993, Edgar Allan Poe Award 1993, Pelle Rosenkrantz Prize 2000. *Literary Agent:* Gregory and Company Authors' Agents, 3 Barb Mews, London, W6 7PA, England. *Website:* www.minettewalters.net.

WALVIN, James, BA, MA; British academic and writer; b. 2 Jan. 1942, Manchester, England; m. Jennifer Walvin, two s. *Education:* University of Keele, McMaster University. *Career:* Prof. of History, University of York. *Publications:* A Jamaica Plantation: Worthy Park 1670–1870 (with M. Craton), 1970; The Black Presence: A Documentary of the Negro in Britain, 1971; Black and White: The Negro and English Society 1555–1945, 1973; The People's Game: A Social History of British Football, 1975; Slavery, Abolition, and Emancipation (co-ed.), 1976; Beside the Seaside: A Social History of the Popular Seaside Holiday, 1978; Leisure and Society 1830–1950, 1978; Abolition of the Atlantic Slave Trade (co-ed.), 1981; A Child's World: A Social History of English Childhood 1900–1914, 1982; Slavery and British Society 1776–1848 (ed.), 1982; English Radicals and Reformers 1776–1848 (with E. Royle), 1982; Slavery and the Slave Trade, 1983; Black Personalities: Africans in Britain in the Era of Slavery, 1983; Leisure in Britain Since 1800 (co-ed.), 1983; Urban England 1776–1851, 1984; Manliness and Morality (co-ed.), 1985; Football and the Decline of Britain, 1986; England, Slaves, and Freedom, 1776–1838, 1986; Victorian Values, 1987; Black Ivory: A History of British Slavery, 1992; Slaves and Slavery, 1992; The People's Game: The History of Football Revisited, 1994; The Life and Times of Henry Clarke of Jamaica, 1994; Questioning Slavery, 1996; Fruits of Empire: Exotic Produce and British Taste 1660–1800, 1997; The Quakers: Money and Morals, 1997; An African Life, 1998; Making the Black Atlantic, 2000; The Only Game, 2001, The Slavery Reader (ed. with Gad Heuman) 2003, The Trader, The Owner, The Slave 2007, A Short History of Slavery 2007. *Address:* c/o Department of History, University of York, Heslington, Yorkshire Y01 5DD, England.

WALWICZ, Ania, DipEd; Australian poet, dramatist, writer and artist; *Teacher, Royal Melbourne Institute of Technology;* b. 19 May 1951, Swidnica, Poland. *Education:* Univ. of Melbourne, Victorian Coll. of the Arts. *Career:* writer-in-residence, Deakin Univ. 1987–88, Murdoch Univ. 1988; teacher in creative writing, Victorian Coll. of the Arts, Melbourne Univ., Royal Melbourne Inst. of Tech. 1993–. *Composition:* Corruption (opera, commissioned by Ministry of Arts 2004, in development by Chamber Made Opera,

North Melbourne 2005–06). *Recording:* Body 1999. *Plays:* Girlboytalk 1986, Dissecting Mice 1989, Elegant 1990, Red Roses 1992, Telltale 1994, Scattergun Project (St Martin's Theatre, Melbourne). *Publications:* Writing 1982, Boat 1989; contrib. to over 100 anthologies. *Honours:* Australian Council Literature Board grants, and Fellowship 1990, Victorian Premier's Literary Awards New Writing Prize 1990. *Address:* Unit 40, 26 Victoria Street, Melbourne, Vic. 3065, Australia. *Telephone:* (3) 9416-1370.

WALZER, Michael, BA, PhD; American academic, editor and writer; *Professor of Social Science, School of Social Science, Institute for Advanced Study;* b. 3 March 1935, New York, NY; m. Judith Borodovko 1956; two d. *Education:* Brandeis and Harvard Univs, Univ. of Cambridge, UK. *Career:* Asst Prof. of Politics Princeton, NJ 1962–66; Assoc. Prof. Harvard Univ. 1966–68, Prof. of Govt 1968–80; Ed. Dissent 1964–; Prof. of Social Science, School of Social Science, Inst. for Advanced Study, Princeton, NJ 1980–; mem. Conf. on the Study of Political Thought, Soc. of Ethical and Legal Philosophy; mem. Editorial Bd Political Theory; Contributing Ed. The New Republic (weekly newsmagazine); mem. Bd of Govs Hebrew Univ. *Publications:* The Revolution of the Saints: A Study in the Origins of Radical Politics 1965, The Political Imagination in Literature (co-ed. with Philip Green) 1968, Obligations: Essays on Disobedience, War and Citizenship 1970, Political Action: A Practical Guide to Movement Politics 1971, Regicide and Revolution: Speeches at the Trial of Louis XVI (ed.) 1974, Just and Unjust Wars: A Moral Argument with Historical Illustrations 1977, Radical Principles: Reflections of an Unreconstructed Democrat 1977, Spheres of Justice: A Defense of Pluralism and Equality 1983, Exodus and Revolution 1985, Interpretation and Social Criticism 1987, The Company of Critics: Social Criticism and Political Commitment in the Twentieth Century 1988, Civil Society and American Democracy (selected essays in German) 1992, What it Means to be an American 1992, Thick and Thin: Moral Argument at Home and Abroad 1994, Pluralism, Justice and Equality (with David Miller) 1995, Toward a Global Civil Society (ed.) 1995, On Toleration 1997, Arguments from the Left (selected essays in Swedish) 1977, Pluralism and Democracy (selected essays in French) 1997, Reason, Politics and Pasion (The Horkheimer Lectures, in German) 1999, The Jewish Political Tradition, Vol. 1 Authority (co-ed with Menachem Lorberbaum, Noam Zohar and Yair Lorberbaum) 2000, Exilic Politics in the Hebrew Bible 2001, War, Politics, and Morality (selected essays in Spanish) 2001, The Thread of Politics: Democracy, Social Criticism, and World Government (selected essays in Italian) 2002, Erklärte Kriege— Kriegserklärungen (selected essays in German) 2003, Arguing About War (selected essays and articles) 2004, Politics and Passion 2004; contribs to professional journals. *Honours:* Dr hc (Lawrence Univ.) 1980, (Brandeis Univ.) 1981, (Georgetown Univ.) 1992, (Kalamazoo Coll.) 1994, (Tel-Aviv Univ.) 2003, Brandeis Univ. Doctorate Alumni Award 2001; Fulbright Fellow, Univ. of Cambridge 1956–57, Harbison Award 1971. *Address:* School of Social Science, Institute for Advanced Study, Einstein Drive, Princeton, NJ 08540, USA (office). *Telephone:* (609) 734-8256 (office). *Fax:* (609) 951-4434 (office). *E-mail:* walzer@ias.edu (office). *Website:* www.sss.ias.edu/home/walzer.html (office).

WAMBAUGH, Joseph, MA; American writer; b. 22 Jan. 1937, East Pittsburgh, PA; s. of Joseph A. Wambaugh and Anne Malloy; m. Dee Allsup 1955; two s. (one deceased) one d. *Education:* Calif. State Coll., Los Angeles. *Career:* served US Marine Corps 1954–57; police officer, LA 1960–74; creator, TV series, Police Story 1973. *Publications:* The New Centurions 1971, The Blue Knight 1972, The Onion Field 1973, The Choirboys 1975, The Black Marble 1978, The Glitter Dome 1981, The Delta Star 1983, Lines and Shadows 1984, The Secrets of Harry Bright 1985, Echoes in the Darkness 1987, The Blooding 1989, The Golden Orange 1990, Fugitive Nights 1992, Finnegan's Week 1993, Floaters 1996, Fire Lover: A True Story 2002, Hollywood Station 2007. *Honours:* MWA Edgar Allan Poe Award 1974, Int. Asscn of Crime Writers Rodolfo Walsh Prize 1989. *Address:* c/o William Morrow & Co, HarperCollins Publishers, 10 E 53rd Street, New York, NY 10022, USA.

WANDOR, Michelene Dinah, BA, LTCL, DipTCL, MA, MMus; British writer, poet, dramatist, critic and musician; b. 20 April 1940, London, England; m. Edward Victor 1963 (divorced); two s. *Education:* Newnham Coll., Cambridge, Univ. of Essex, Trinity Coll. of Music, London, Univ. of London. *Career:* Poetry Ed. Time Out Magazine 1971–82; Sr Lecturer in Creative Writing, London Metropolitan Univ. 1998–2006; Royal Literary Fund Fellowship 2004–07; mem. Soc. of Authors, RSL. *Play:* The Wandering Jew (Nat. Theatre) 1987. *Publications:* Cutlasses and Earrings (ed. and contrib.) 1977, Carry on Understudies 1981, Upbeat 1981, Touch Papers 1982, Five Plays 1984, Gardens of Eden 1984, Routledge 1986, Look Back in Gender 1987, Guests in the Body 1987, Drama 1970–1990 1993, Gardens of Eden Revisited 1999, Post-War British Drama: Looking Back in Gender 2000, False Relations 2004, Musica Transalpina (Poetry Book Soc. Recommendation) 2006, The Music of the Prophets 2007; contrib. to periodicals. *Honours:* Int. Emmy Award 1987. *Address:* 71 Belsize Lane, London, NW3 5AU, England. *Website:* www .mwandor.co.uk.

WANG, Anyi; Chinese writer; b. 1954, Tong'an, Fujian Prov. *Education:* Xiangming Middle School. *Career:* fmrly musician, Xuzhou Pref. Song and Dance Ensemble; Ed. Children's Time; Vice-Chair. Shanghai Writers Asscn. *Publications:* Song of Eternal Hatred (Mao Dun Prize for Literature), Xiaobao Village, The Love of a Small Town, The Story of a School Principal, Self-selected Works of Wang Anyi (six vols). *Address:* Shanghai Writers Association, Shanghai, People's Republic of China (office).

WANG, Chen, MScS; Chinese journalist and editor; *Editor-in-Chief, Renmin Ribao (People's Daily)*; b. 1950, Wen'an Co., Hebei Prov. *Education:* School of Postgraduate Studies, Chinese Acad. of Social Sciences, Beijing. *Career:* joined CCP CCP; fmr reporter, CCP Yijun Co. Cttee, CCP Yan'an Municipal Cttee, Shaanxi Prov.; reporter, Guangming Daily, then successively Ed., Dir Chief Ed.'s Office, Assoc. Chief Ed. 1982–95, Chief Ed. 1995–2000; Deputy Dir Dept of Propaganda, CCP Cen. Cttee 2000; Ed.-in-Chief Renmin Ribao (People's Daily) 2001–, Pres. 2002–; mem. CPPCC Nat. Cttee 1998–2003; mem. 16th CCP Cen. Cttee 2002–. *Address:* Renmin Ribao (People's Daily), 2 Jin Tai Xi Lu, Chao Yang Men Wai, Beijing 100733, People's Republic of China (office). *Telephone:* (10) 65092121 (office). *Fax:* (10) 65091982 (office). *E-mail:* rmrb@peopledaily.com.cn (office). *Website:* www.people.com.cn (office).

WANG, Shuo; Chinese writer; b. 1958, Nanjing. *Career:* spent four years in navy, then worked at various jobs before becoming a full-time writer 1983; first novel Air Stewardesses published 1984; collected works banned by authorities in China 1996; has written over 20 novels with 10 million copies in print, has written scripts for TV and films including work for American Zeotrope, USA. *Film:* script: The Trouble-Shooters 1989. *Publications include:* Playing for Thrills (translated to English 1997), Please Don't Call Me Human (translated to English 1998). *Address:* c/o No Exit Press, 16 Capitol Court, 128 School Lane, Didsbury, Manchester, M20 6LB, England (office). *Telephone:* (161) 445 6635 (office). *Website:* www.noexit.co.uk (office).

WARD, John Hood; British writer and poet; b. 16 Dec. 1915, Newcastle upon Tyne, England; m. Gladys Hilda Thorogood 1940, one s. two d. *Education:* Royal Grammar School, Newcastle. *Career:* Sr Principal, Dept of Health and Social Security –1978; mem. Manchester Poets; Society of Civil Service Authors. *Publications:* A Late Harvest, 1982; The Dark Sea, 1983; A Kind of Likeness, 1985; The Wrong Side of Glory, 1986; A Song at Twilight, 1989; Grandfather Best and the Protestant Work Ethic, 1991; Tales of Love and Hate, 1993; The Brilliance of Light, 1994; Winter Song, 1995; Selected Poems, 1968–95, 1996. Contributions: anthologies and periodicals. *Honours:* Imperial Service Order, 1977; Poetry Prize, City of Westminster Arts Council, 1977; Open Poetry Prize, Wharfedale Music Festival, 1978; Lancaster Festival Prizes, 1982, 1987, 1988, 1989, 1994, 1995; First Prize, Bury Open Poetry Competition, 1987; First Prizes, High Peak Open Competition, 1988, 1989; First Prize, May and Alfred Wilkins Memorial Prize, 1995.

WARD, Philip, FRGS, FRSA; British librarian and writer; b. 10 Feb. 1938, Harrow, England; m. 1964, two d. *Education:* University for Foreigners, Perugia, Coimbra University. *Career:* Hon. Ed. The Private Library 1958–64; Co-ordinator Library Services Tripoli, Libya 1963–71; Dir National Library Services 1973–74; mem. Private Libraries Asscn. *Publications:* The Oxford Companion to Spanish Literature 1978, A Dictionary of Common Fallacies 1978–80, Lost Songs 1981, A Lifetime's Reading 1983, Japanese Capitals 1985, Travels in Oman 1987, Sofia: Portrait of a City 1989, Wight Magic 1990, Bulgaria 1990, South India 1991, Western India 1991, Bulgarian Voices: Letting the People Speak. 1992, Bahrain 1993, Gujarat, Daman, Diu 1994, The Comfort of Women (novel) 2002, His Enamel Mug (poems) 2004. *Honours:* Guinness Poetry Award 1959, First Prize International Travel Writers Competition 1990. *Address:* c/o Oxford University Press, Great Clarendon Street, Oxford OX2 6DP, England.

WARDLE, (John) Irving, BA, ARCM; British drama critic and writer (retd); b. 20 July 1929, Bolton, Lancs.; m. 1st Joan Notkin 1958 (divorced); m. 2nd Fay Crowder 1963 (divorced); two s.; m. 3rd Elizabeth Grist 1975; one s. one d. *Education:* Wadham Coll., Oxford, Royal Coll. of Music, London. *Career:* sub-ed., Times Educational Supplement 1956; Deputy Theatre Critic, The Observer 1960; Drama Critic, The Times 1963–89; Ed. Gambit 1973–75; Theatre Critic, The Independent on Sunday 1989. *Play produced:* The Houseboy 1974. *Publications:* The Houseboy 1974, The Theatres of George Devine 1978, Theatre Criticism 1992. *Address:* 51 Richmond Road, New Barnet, Herts., EN5 1SF, England (home). *Telephone:* (20) 8440-3671 (home). *E-mail:* irving@ontheroad.demon.co.uk.uk (home).

WARE, Armytage (see Barnett, Paul le Page)

WARKENTIN, Juliet, BA; Canadian magazine editor; *Editorial Director, Redwood Publishing*; b. 10 May 1961; m. Andrew Lamb 1991. *Education:* Univ. of Toronto and London Coll. of Fashion (UK). *Career:* Ed. Toronto Life Fashion, Draper's Record, UK 1993–96, Marie Claire (UK) 1996–98; Man. Dir Marketing and Internet Devt Arcadia Group PLC 1998–2000; Partner The Fourth Room 2000–02; Editorial Dir Redwood Publishing 2002–. *Honours:* Nat. Magazine Award, Canada 1989, PPA Business Ed. of the Year 1994. *Address:* Redwood Publishing, 7 St Martin's Place, London, WC2N 4HA (office). *Fax:* (20) 7261-5277 (office).

WARNER, Alan, BA, MPhil; British novelist; b. 1964, Oban, Scotland; s. of Frank Warner and Patricia Bowman; m. Hollie Warner. *Education:* Oban High School, Ealing Coll., Univ. of Glasgow. *Film:* Morvern Callar (adaptation) 2003. *Publications:* Morvern Callar 1995, These Demented Lands 1997, The Sopranos 1998, The Man Who Walks 2002, The Worms Can Carry Me to Heaven 2006; contrib. to Children of Albion Rovers 1997, Disco Biscuits 1997. *Honours:* Somerset Maugham Award, Encore Award 1998, Saltire Prize. *Literary Agent:* David Godwin Associates, 55 Monmouth Street, London, WC2H 9DG, England.

WARNER, Francis, (Robert Le Plastrier), MA, DLitt; British poet, dramatist and tutor; *Fellow Emeritus, St Peter's College, Oxford*; b. 21 Oct. 1937, Bishopthorpe, Yorks.; m. 1st Mary Hall 1958 (divorced 1972); two d.; m. 2nd Penelope Anne Davis 1983; one s. one d. *Education:* Christ's Hosp., London Coll. of Music, St Catharine's Coll., Cambridge. *Career:* Supervisor in English, St Catharine's Coll., Cambridge 1959–65, Hon. Fellow Residential 1999–; Staff Tutor in English, Univ. of Cambridge Bd of Extra-Mural Studies 1963–65; Fellow and Tutor 1965–99, Fellow Librarian 1966–76, Dean of Degrees 1984–2006, Vice-Master 1987–89, Fellow Emer. 1999–, St Peter's Coll., Oxford; Univ. Lecturer, Univ. of Oxford 1966–99, Pro-Proctor 1989–90, 1996–97, 1999–2000; Founder Elgar Centenary Choir and Orchestra 1957; Foreign Academician Acad. of Letters and Arts, Portugal 1993. *Recording:* conducted Honegger's King David, King's Coll. Chapel, Cambridge 1958, issued as an historic Landmark Recording by OxRecs Digital 2004. *Publications:* poetry: Perennia 1962, Early Poems 1964, Experimental Sonnets 1965, Madrigals 1967, The Poetry of Francis Warner (USA) 1970, Lucca Quartet 1975, Morning Vespers 1980, Spring Harvest 1981, Epithalamium 1983, Collected Poems 1960–84 1985, Nightingales: Poems 1985–96 1997, Cambridge 2001, Oxford 2002, By the Cam and the Isis 2005; plays: Maquettes: A Trilogy of One-Act Plays 1972, Requiem: Part 1 Lying Figures 1972, Part 2 Killing Time 1976, Part 3 Meeting Ends 1974, A Conception of Love 1978, Light Shadows 1980, Moving Reflections 1983, Living Creation 1985, Healing Nature: The Athens of Pericles 1988, Byzantium 1990, Virgil and Caesar 1993, Agora: An Epic 1994, King Francis First 1995, Goethe's Weimar 1997, Rembrandt's Mirror 1999; editor: Eleven Poems by Edmund Blunden 1965, Garland 1968, Studies in the Arts 1968; contrib. to anthologies and journals. *Honours:* Benemerenti Silver Medal, Kts of St George, Constantinian Order, Italy 1990; Messing Int. Award for Literature 1972. *Telephone:* (1865) 511857 (home). *Address:* St Peter's College, Oxford, OX1 2DL (office); St Catharine's College, Cambridge, CB2 1RL, England. *Website:* www.colinsmythe.co.uk/authors (office).

WARNER, Malcolm, BA, PhD; British writer and educator; *Senior Curator, Kimbell Art Museum*; b. 17 May 1953, Aldershot, England; m. Sara Ryan 1988; one s. one d. *Education:* Courtauld Inst. of Art, London. *Career:* Lecturer, Lawrence Univ. of Wisconsin's London Centre 1979–87, Univ. of Chicago 1989, Univ. of California at San Diego 1993; Lecturer 1982–83, 1984–85, Visiting Asst Prof. 1984–85, Victoria Univ. of Manchester; Lecturer School 1988, Research Curator Dept of European Painting 1988–90, Art Inst. of Chicago; Curator, Prints and Drawings 1990–96, European Art 1992–96, San Diego Museum of Art; Ailsa Mellon Bruce Visiting Sr Fellowship, Center for Advanced Study in the Visual Arts, Nat. Gallery of Art 1994; Fellowship for Museum Professionals, Nat. Endowment for the Arts 1995; Sr Curator of Paintings and Sculpture, Yale Center for British Art 1996–2001; Assoc. Ed., New Dictionary of Nat. Biography 1997–; Sr Curator, Kimbell Art Museum 2002–; mem. Print Council of America, Historians of British Art. *Publications:* Portrait Painting 1979, The Phaidon Companion to Art and Artists in the British Isles (co-author) 1980, A Guide to European Painting (contrib.) 1980, James Tissot 1982, Rainy Days at Brig o'Turk: The Highland Sketchbooks of John Everett Millais, 1853 (co-ed.) 1983, The Image of London: Views by Travellers and Emigrés, 1550–1920 1987, The Art of the Print: Glossary 1991, The Prints of Harry Sternberg 1994, French and British Paintings from 1600 to 1800 in the Art Institute of Chicago: A Catalogue of the Collection (co-author) 1996, The Victorians: British Painting, 1837–1901 1997, Millais: Portraits (co-ed.) 1999, Great British Paintings from American Collections 2001, Stubbs and the Horse 2004; contrib. to exhibition catalogues, articles and reviews to periodicals, including Apollo, Burlington Magazine, TLS, Pre-Raphaelite Review, Journal of the RSA, Huntington Library Quarterly. *Address:* Kimbell Art Museum, 3333 Camp Bowie Blvd, Fort Worth, TX 76107, USA. *E-mail:* mwarner@kimbellmuseum.org.

WARNER, Marina Sarah, MA, FBA; British author; *Professor of Literature, University of Essex*; b. 9 Nov. 1946, London; d. of Esmond Warner and Emilia Terzulli; m. 1st William Shawcross 1971; one s.; m. 2nd John Dewe Mathews 1981. *Education:* St Mary's Convent, Ascot and Lady Margaret Hall, Univ. of Oxford. *Career:* Getty Scholar, Getty Centre for the History of Art and the Humanities 1987–88; Tinbergen Prof., Erasmus Univ., Rotterdam 1990–91; Visiting Prof., Queen Mary and Westfield Coll., Univ. of London 1994, Univ. of Ulster 1994, Univ. of York 1996–, Birkbeck Coll., London; Tanner Lecturer, Yale Univ. 1999; Clarendon Lecturer, Oxford 2001; Prof. of Literature, Univ. of Essex 2004–; Fellow Commonership, Trinity Coll. Cambridge 1998; Visiting Fellow, All Souls Coll. Oxford 2001, Univ. Paris XIII 2003; Fellow, Italian Acad., Columbia Univ., New York, 2003; Sr Fellow, Remarque Inst., New York Univ. 2006; mem. Exec. Cttee Charter 88 –1997, Literature Panel Arts Council of England –1997, Advisory Council British Library –1997, Man. Cttee Nat. Council for One-Parent Families, Bd Artangel, Cttee London Library, Cttee PEN. *Exhibitions include:* The Inner Eye (curator) 1996, Metamorphing: Transformation in Art, Science and Myth (curator) 2003, Only Make-Believe: Ways of Playing, Compton Verney 2005. *Radio:* short stories, criticism. *Publications:* Alone of All Her Sex: The Myth and the Cult of the Virgin Mary 1976, Joan of Arc 1982, Monuments and Maidens: The Allegory of the Female Form 1985, The Lost Father 1988, Indigo 1992, Mermaids in the Basement (short stories) 1993, Wonder Tales (ed.) 1994, Six Myths of Our Time – The 1994 Reith Lectures, From the Beast to the Blonde: On Fairy Tales and Their Tellers 1994, The Inner Eye: Art Beyond the Visible 1996, No Go the Bogeyman: On Scaring, Lulling and Making Mock 1998, The Leto Bundle 2001, Fantastic Metamorphoses, Other Worlds: The Clarendon Lectures 2002, Murderers I Have Known (short stories) 2002, Signs and Wonders: Essays on Literature and Culture 2003, Phantasmagoria: Spirit Visions, Metaphors, and

Media 2006. *Honours:* Chevalier des Arts et des Lettres 2000, Commendatore dell'Ordine della Stella di Solidareità 2005; Hon. DLitt (Exeter) 1998, (Univ. of East London) 1999, (Kent) 2005, (Leicester) 2006, Oxford (2006); Dr hc (Sheffield Hallam, York, N London, St Andrews) 1998, (RCA) 2004; Fawcett Prize 1986, Harvey Darton Award 1996, Mythopoeic Fantasy Award 1996, Katherine M. Briggs Award 1999, Rosemary Crawshay Prize, British Acad. 2000, Aby Warburg Prize 2004. *Literary Agent:* c/o Rogers, Coleridge & White, 20 Powis Mews, London, W11 1JN, England. *Telephone:* (20) 7221-3717. *Fax:* (20) 7229-9084. *Website:* www.rcwlitagency.co.uk. *Address:* LIFTS, University of Essex, Colchester, CO4 3SQ, England (office). *E-mail:* mswarner@essex.ac.uk (office). *Website:* www.marinawarner.com.

WARNER, Val, BA, FRSL; British writer and poet; b. 15 Jan. 1946, Middx, England. *Education:* Somerville Coll., Oxford. *Career:* Writer-in-Residence, Univ. Coll. of Swansea 1977–78, Univ. of Dundee 1979–81; mem. PEN. *Publications:* These Yellow Photos 1971, Under the Penthouse 1973, The Centenary Corbiere (trans.) 1975, The Collected Poems and Prose of Charlotte Mew (ed.) 1981, Before Lunch 1986, The Collected Poems and Selected Prose of Charlotte Mew (ed.) 1997, Tooting Idyll 1998; contrib. to many journals and periodicals. *Honours:* Gregory Award for Poetry 1975, Third Prize, Lincolnshire Literature Festival Poetry Competition 1995. *Address:* c/o Carcanet Press, Alliance House, Cross Street, Manchester, M2 7AQ, England. *E-mail:* valwarner@etce.freeserve.co.uk (home).

WARNOCK, Baroness (Life Peer), cr. 1985, of Weeke in the City of Winchester; **(Helen) Mary Warnock,** DBE, FCP, FRSM; British philosopher and university administrator; b. 14 April 1924, Winchester; d. of the late Archibald Edward Wilson and Ethel Schuster; m. Sir Geoffrey J. Warnock 1949 (died 1995); two s. three d. *Education:* St Swithun's, Winchester and Lady Margaret Hall, Oxford. *Career:* Tutor in Philosophy, St Hugh's Coll. Oxford 1949–66; Headmistress, Oxford High School 1966–72; Talbot Research Fellow, Lady Margaret Hall 1972–76; Sr Research Fellow, St Hugh's Coll. 1976–84; Mistress of Girton Coll. Cambridge 1985–91; Chair. Cttee of Inquiry into Special Educ. 1974–78, Advisory Cttee on Animal Experiments 1979–86, Cttee of Inquiry into Human Fertilization 1982–84, Educ. Cttee Girls' Day School Trust 1994–2001; mem. IBA 1973–81, Royal Comm. on Environmental Pollution 1979–84, Social Science Research Council 1981–85, UK Nat. Comm. for UNESCO 1981–85, Archbishop of Canterbury's Advisory Group on Medical Ethics 1992–; Chair. Planning Aid Trust 2002–; Fellow, Coll. of Teachers (fmrly Coll. of Preceptors). *Publications:* Ethics since 1900 1960, J.-P. Sartre 1963, Existentialist Ethics 1966, Existentialism 1970, Imagination 1976, Schools of Thought 1977, What Must We Teach? (with T. Devlin) 1977, Education: A Way Forward 1979, A Question of Life 1985, Teacher Teach Thyself (Dimbleby Lecture) 1985, Memory 1987, A Common Policy for Education 1989, Universities: Knowing Our Minds 1989, The Uses of Philosophy 1992, Imagination and Time 1994; Women Philosophers (ed.) 1996, An Intelligent Person's Guide to Ethics 1998, A Memoir: People and Places 2000, Making Babies 2002, Nature and Mortality 2003, Utilitariansim (ed.) 2003, Special Education: A New Look 2005. *Honours:* Hon. Master of the Bench, Gray's Inn 1986; Hon. Fellow, Imperial Coll. London 1986, Hertford Coll. Oxford 1997, Lady Margaret Hall Oxford, St Hugh's Coll. Oxford; Hon. FRCM; Hon. Fellow, Royal Soc. of Physicians, Scotland; Hon. FBA 2000; Hon. FRCP 2002; Hon. DUniv (Open Univ.) 1980, (St Andrews) 1992; Hon. LLD (Manchester) 1987, (Liverpool) 1991, (London) 1991; Hon. DLitt (Glasgow) 1988; Dr hc (Univ. of York) 1989; RSA Albert Medal 1998. *Address:* House of Lords, Westminster, London, SW1A 0PW (office); 60 Church Street, Great Bedwyn, Wilts., SN8 3PF, England (home). *Telephone:* (20) 7219-8619 (office); (1672) 870214 (home). *E-mail:* warnock@parliament.uk. *Website:* www.parliament.uk (office).

WARREN, Rosanna, BA, MA; American academic, poet and writer; *Emma Mactachlan Metcalf Professor of the Humanities, Boston University*; b. 27 July 1953, Fairfield, CT; m. Stephen Scully 1981; two d. one step-s. *Education:* Yale University, Johns Hopkins University. *Career:* Asst Prof., Vanderbilt University, 1981–82; Visiting Asst Prof., 1982–88, Asst Prof., 1989–95, Assoc. Prof. of English, 1995–99, Emma Mactachlan Metcalf Prof. of the Humanities 1999–, Boston University; Poetry Consultant and Contributing Ed., Partisan Review, 1985–97; Poet-in-Residence, Robert Frost Farm, 1990; mem. American Acad. of Arts and Sciences; Acad. of American Poets, board of chancellors, 1999–; MLA; American Literary Trans Asscn; Asscn of Literary Scholars and Critics; PEN. *Publications:* The Joey Story 1963, Snow Day 1981, Each Leaf Shines Separate 1984, The Art of Translation: Voices from the Field (ed.) 1989, Stained Glass 1993, Eugenio Montale's Cuttlefish Bones (ed.) 1993, Euripides' Suppliant Women (trans. with Stephen Scully) 1995, Eugenio Montale's Satura (ed.) 1998, Departure 2003. Contributions: many journals and magazines. *Honours:* National Discovery Award in Poetry, 92nd Street YMHA-YWCA, New York City, 1980; Yaddo Fellow, 1980; Ingram Merrill Foundation Grants, 1983, 1993; Guggenheim Fellowship, 1985–86; ACLS Grant, 1989–90; Lavan Younger Poets Prize, 1992, and Lamont Poetry Prize, 1993, Acad. of American Poets; Lila Wallace Writers' Fund Award, 1994; Witter Bynner Prize in Poetry, American Acad. of Arts and Letters, 1994; May Sarton Award, New England Poetry Club, 1995. *Address:* c/o University Profs Program, Boston University, 745 Commonwealth Avenue, Boston, MA 02215, USA.

WARSH, Lewis, BA, MA; American poet, writer, publisher and teacher; *Associate Professor, Long Island University*; b. 9 Nov. 1944, New York, NY; m. 1st Bernadette Mayer 1975; one s. two d.; m. 2nd Katt Lissard 2001. *Education:* City College, CUNY. *Career:* Co-Founder and Co-Ed., Angel Hair magazine and Angel Hair Books, New York City, 1966–77; Co-Ed., Boston Eagle, Massachusetts, 1973–75; Teacher, St Mark's in the Bowery Poetry Project, 1973–75; Co-Founder and Publisher, United Artists magazine and United Artists Books, New York, 1977–; Lecturer, Kerouac School of Disembodied Poetics, Boulder, CO, 1978, New England College, 1979–80, Queens College, CUNY, 1984–86, Farleigh Dickinson University, 1987–; Assoc. Prof., Long Island University, 1987–. *Publications:* poetry: Moving Through Air 1968, Dreaming as One 1971, Long Distance 1971, Today 1974, Blue Heaven 1978, Methods of Birth Control 1982, The Corset 1986, Information from the Surface of Venus 1987, Avenue of Escape 1995, The Origin of the World 2001, Debtor's Prison (with Julie Harrison) 2001, Inseparable 2007; fiction: Agnes and Sally 1984, A Free Man 1991, Money Under the Table 1998, Touch of the Whip 2001, Ted's Favorite Skirt 2002, A Place in the Sun 2007; other: Part of My History (autobiog.) 1972, The Maharajah's Son (autobiog.) 1977. *Honours:* Poet's Foundation Award 1972, Creative Artists Public Service Award in Fiction 1977, National Endowment for the Arts Grant in Poetry 1979, Co-ordinating Council of Literary Magazines Ed.'s Fellowship 1981, Fund for Poetry Award 1987, James Shestack Prize American Poetry Review 1994. *Address:* c/o Brooklyn Campus, Long Island University, 1 University Plaza, Brooklyn, NY 11201-8423 (office); 114 West 16th Street, 5C, New York, NY 10011, USA (home). *E-mail:* lwarsh4mindspring.com (home).

WASSMO, Herbjørg; Norwegian writer and poet; b. 6 Dec. 1942, Myre i Vesteralen. *Publications:* fiction: Huset med den blinde glassveranda, 1981, English trans. as The House With the Blind Glass Windows, 1987; Det stumme rommet, 1983; Hudlos himmel, 1986; Dinas bok, 1989, English trans. as Dina's Book, 1994; Lykkens sonn, 1992; Reiser: Fire Fortellinger, 1995. Poetry: Vingeslag, 1976; Flotid, 1977; Lite gront bilde i stor bla ramme, 1991. Contributions: periodicals. *Honours:* Norwegian Critics' Award 1982, Nordic Council Literature Prize 1987.

WATADA, Terry, BA, BEd, MA; Canadian writer, dramatist, poet, editor and musician; b. 6 July 1951, Toronto, ON; m. Tane Akamatsu 1989; one s. *Education:* Univ. of Toronto, York Univ. *Publications:* Asian Voices: Stories from Canada, Korea, China, Vietnam and Japan (ed.) 1992, The Tale of the Mask (play) 1995, Face Kao: Portraits of Japanese Canadians Interned During World War II (ed.) 1996, Bukkyo Tozen: A History of Jodo Shinshu Buddhism in Canada 1996, A Thousand Homes (poems) 1997, Daruma Days (short stories) 1997, Collected Voices: An Anthology of Asian North American Periodical Writing (ed.) 1997, Ten Thousand Views of Rain (poems) 2000; unpublished plays; contrib. to periodicals. *Honours:* City of Toronto William P. Hubbard Award for Race Relations 1991, League of Canadian Poets Gerald Lampert Memorial Award 1995, first prize in poetry Moon Rabbit Review Fiction and Poetry Contest 1996. *Address:* 6 Wildwood Crescent, Toronto, ON M4L 2K7, Canada (home). *E-mail:* tanea@sympatico.ca (home).

WATANABE, Tsuneo; Japanese newspaper executive; *President, CEO and Editor-in-Chief, Yomiuri Shimbun*; b. 1926. *Career:* began career with Yomiuri Shimbum newspaper as reporter 1950, fmr Washington DC corresp. USA, chief editorial writer, Pres. 1991–, currently Pres., CEO and Ed.-in-Chief, also Chair. Yomiuri Group. *Publications:* Memoirs of Tsuneo Watanabe 2000. *Address:* Yomiuri Shimbum, 1-7-1, Otemachi, Chiyoda-ku, Tokyo 100-8055, Japan (office). *Telephone:* (3) 3242-1111 (office). *E-mail:* webmaster@yomiuri.co.jp (office). *Website:* www.yomiuri.co.jp (office).

WATERHOUSE, Keith Spencer, CBE, FRSL; British writer; b. 6 Feb. 1929, Leeds; s. of Ernest Waterhouse and Elsie Edith Waterhouse; m. 2nd Stella Bingham 1984 (divorced 1989); one s. two d. by previous marriage. *Career:* journalist 1950–, columnist, Daily Mirror 1970–86, Daily Mail 1986–, contrib. to various periodicals; mem. Kingman Cttee on Teaching of the English Language 1987–88. *Films (with Willis Hall) include:* Billy Liar, Whistle Down the Wind, A Kind of Loving, Lock Up Your Daughters. *Plays:* Mr. and Mrs. Nobody 1986, Jeffrey Bernard is Unwell (Evening Standard Comedy of the Year 1990) 1989, Bookends 1990, Our Song 1992, Good Grief 1998, Bing-Bong 1999. *Plays (with Willis Hall) include:* Billy Liar 1960, Celebration 1961, All Things Bright and Beautiful 1963, Say Who You Are 1965, Whoops-a-Daisy 1968, Children's Day 1969, Who's Who 1972, The Card (musical) 1973, Saturday, Sunday, Monday (adapted from play by de Filippo) 1973, Filumena (adapted from de Filippo) 1977, Worzel Gummidge 1981, Budgie (musical) 1988. *TV series:* Budgie, Queenie's Castle, The Upper Crusts, Billy Liar, The Upchat Line, The Upchat Connection, Worzel Gummidge, West End Tales, The Happy Apple, Charters and Caldicott. *TV films:* Charlie Muffin 1983, This Office Life 1985, The Great Paperchase 1986. *Others:* Café Royal (with Guy Deghy) 1956, Writers' Theatre (ed.) 1967, The Passing of the Third-floor Buck 1974, Mondays, Thursdays 1976, Rhubarb, Rhubarb 1979, Fanny Peculiar 1983, Mrs Pooter's Diary 1983, Waterhouse At Large 1985, Collected Letters of a Nobody 1986, The Theory and Practice of Lunch 1986, The Theory and Practice of Travel 1988, Waterhouse on Newspaper Style 1989, English Our English 1991, Jeffrey Bernard is Unwell and Other Plays 1992, Sharon & Tracy and the Rest 1992, City Lights 1994, Streets Ahead 1995. *Publications:* (novels) There is a Happy Land 1957, Billy Liar 1959, Jubb 1963, The Bucket Shop 1968, Billy Liar on the Moon 1975, Office Life 1978, Maggie Muggins 1981, In the Mood 1983, Thinks 1984, Our Song 1984, Bimbo 1990, Unsweet Charity 1992, Good Grief 1997, Soho 2001, Palace Pier 2003. *Honours:* Granada Columnist of the Year Award 1970; IPC Descriptive Writer of the Year Award 1970; IPC Columnist of the Year Award 1973; British Press

Awards Columnist of the Year 1978, 1989; Granada Special Quarter Century Award 1982; Press Club Edgar Wallace Award 1996; Gerald Barry Lifetime Achievement Award 2000. *Address:* c/o Alexandra Cann Representation, 12 Abingdon Road, London, W8 6AF; 84 Coleherne Court, London, SW5 0EE, England.

WATERMAN, Andrew John, BA; British poet and academic (retd); b. 28 May 1940, London; m. (divorced); one s. *Education:* Univ. of Leicester, Worcester Coll., Oxford. *Career:* Lecturer, Univ. of Ulster, Coleraine, NI 1968–78, Sr Lecturer in English 1978–97. *Publications:* Living Room 1974, From the Other Country 1977, Over the Wall 1980, Out for the Elements 1981, The Poetry of Chess (ed.) 1981, Selected Poems 1986, In the Planetarium 1990, The End of the Pier Show 1995, Collected Poems 1959–1999 2000, The Captain's Swallow 2007; contrib. to anthologies, journals and periodicals. *Honours:* Poetry Book Soc. Choice 1974, and Recommendation 1981, Cholmondeley Award for Poetry 1977, Arvon Poetry Competition Prize 1981. *Address:* 5 Guernsey Road, Norwich, Norfolk, NR3 1JJ, England (home). *Telephone:* (1603) 762952 (home). *E-mail:* andrewwaterman@onetel.com (home). *Website:* www.andrewwaterman.co.uk.

WATERS, John Frederick, BS; American writer; b. 27 Oct. 1930, Somerville, MA. *Education:* Univ. of Massachusetts. *Career:* mem. Southeastern Massachusetts Creative Writers Club, Cape Cod Writers, 12 O'Clock Scholars, Society of Children's Book Writers, Authors' Guild. *Publications:* Marine Animal Collectors, 1969; The Crab From Yesterday, 1970; The Sea Farmers, 1970; What Does An Oceanographer Do?, 1970; Saltmarshes and Shifting Dunes, 1970; Turtles, 1971; Neighborhood Puddle, 1971; Some Mammals Live in the Sea, 1972; Green Turtle: Mysteries, 1972; The Royal Potwasher, 1972; Seal Harbour, 1973; Hungry Sharks, 1973; Giant Sea Creatures, 1973; The Mysterious Eel, 1973; Camels: Ships of the Desert, 1974; Carnivorous Plants, 1974; Exploring New England Shores, 1974; The Continental Shelves, 1975; Creatures of Darkness, 1975; Victory Chimes, 1976; Maritime Careers, 1977; Fishing, 1978; Summer of the Seals, 1978; The Hatchlings, 1979; Crime Labs, 1979; A Jellyfish is Not a Fish, 1979; Flood, 1991; Watching Whales, 1991; The Raindrop Journey, 1991; Deep Sea Vents, 1994; Night Raiders Along the Cape, 1996; Mystery of the Horse Phoenix, 1999; Murder on Seal Island, 2000; Who Killed the Whale?, 2001; Mystery of the Yellow Eyes, 2001. Contributions: Cape Cod Compass. *Honours:* Jr Literary Book Choice (twice), Outstanding Science Books for Children Award (seven times).

WATERS, Sarah, PhD; British writer; b. 1966, Neyland, Wales. *Education:* Univs of Kent, Lancaster and London. *Career:* fmr Assoc. Lecturer, Open Univ. *Publications:* Tipping the Velvet 1998, Affinity (Sunday Times Young Writer of the Year 2000, Somerset Maugham Award 2000,) 1999, Fingersmith 2002, The Night Watch 2006; contrib. of articles on lesbian and gay writing, cultural history. *Honours:* Betty Trask Award 1999, CWA Ellis Peters Historical Dagger 2002, British Book Award for Author of the Year 2002. *Literary Agent:* c/o Greene & Heaton (Authors' Agents) Ltd, 37 Goldhawk Road, London, W12 8QQ, England. *Telephone:* (20) 8749-0315. *Website:* www.sarahwaters.com.

WATKINS, Clive, BL; British poet; b. 1945, Sheffield, South Yorkshire; m.; three c. *Career:* teacher, headteacher. *Publications:* Jigsaw 2003. *Address:* c/o The Waywiser Press, 9 Woodstock Road, London, N4 3ET, England. *Website:* www.waywiser-press.com.

WATKINS, Floyd C.; American academic, writer and farmer; b. 19 April 1920, Cherokee County, GA; m. Anna E. Braziel 1942; one s. two d. *Education:* BS, Georgia Southern University, 1946; AM, Emory University, 1947; PhD, Vanderbilt University, 1952. *Career:* Instructor, 1949–61, Prof., 1961–80, Candler Prof. of American Literature, 1980–88, Prof. Emeritus, 1988–, Emory University; Visiting Prof., Southeastern University, Oklahoma, 1961, 1970, Texas A & M University, 1980. *Publications:* The Literature of the South (co-ed.), 1952; Thomas Wolfe's Characters, 1957; Old Times in the Faulkner Country (co-author), 1961; The Flesh and the Word, 1971; In Time and Place, 1977; Then and Now: The Personal Past in the Poetry of Robert Penn Warren, 1982; Some Poems and Some Talk About Poetry (co-author), 1985; Talking About William Faulkner (co-author), 1996.

WATKINS, Karen Christna, (Catrin Collier, Katherine John); British writer; b. 30 May 1948, Pontypridd, Wales; m. Trevor John Watkins 1968; two s. one d. *Education:* Swansea Coll. *Career:* mem. PEN, Soc. of Authors, CWA, Welsh Acad. *Publications:* Without Trace 1989, Hearts of Gold 1992, One Blue Moon 1993, Six Foot Under, A Silver Lining 1994, Murder of a Dead Man 1994, All That Glitters 1995, By Any Other Name 1995, Such Sweet Sorrow 1996, Past Remembering 1997, Broken Rainbows 1998, Winners and Losers 2004, Sinners and Shadows 2004, Midnight Murders 2006, Murder of a Dead Man 2006; as Catrin Collier: Tiger Bay Blues 2006. *Address:* c/o Random House UK Ltd, 20 Vauxhall Bridge Road, London, SW1V 2SA, England.

WATKINS, Paul, BA; American writer; b. 23 Feb. 1964, Redwood City, CA; m. Cath Watkins; one d. *Education:* Eton Coll., Yale Univ., Syracuse Univ. *Publications:* fiction: Night over Day over Night 1988, Calm at Sunset, Calm at Dawn 1989, In the Blue Light of African Dreams 1990, The Promise of Light 1992, Archangel 1995, The Story of My Disappearance 1998, The Forger 2000, Thunder God 2004, The Fellowship of Ghosts 2004, The Ice Soldier 2005; non-fiction: Stand Before Your God 1994. *Honours:* Encore Award 1989. *Address:*

c/o Faber and Faber Ltd, 3 Queen Square, London, WC1N 3AU, England. *Website:* www.paulwatkins.com.

WATMOUGH, David Arthur; Canadian writer and novelist; b. 17 Aug. 1926, London, England; s. of Gerald Arthur Watmough and Ethel Bassett Watmough. *Education:* King's Coll., London. *Career:* mem. Writers' Union of Canada, Fed. of British Columbia Writers. *Publications:* Ashes for Easter (short stories) 1972, Love and the Waiting Game (short stories) 1975, From a Cornish Landscape (short stories) 1975, No More into the Garden (novel) 1978, Fury (short stories) 1984, The Connecticut Countess (short stories) 1984, The Unlikely Pioneer (opera) 1985, Vibrations in Time (short stories) 1986, The Year of Fears (novel) 1987, Thy Mother's Glass (novel) 1992, The Time of the Kingfishers (novel) 1994, Hunting with Diana (short stories) 1996, The Moor is Dark Beneath the Moon (novel) 2002, Vancouver Voices (novel) 2005; contrib. to Encounter, Spectator, New York Times Book Review, Saturday Night (Canada), Canadian Literature, Dalhousie Review, Connoisseur (New York), Malahat Review, Vancouver Step. *Honours:* Canada Council Sr Literary Arts Awards 1976, 1986, Winner, Best Novel of Year Award, Giovanni's Room, Philadelphia 1979. *Address:* Kernow, 175–65B Street, Delta, BC V4L 1M9, Canada (home). *Telephone:* (604) 948-2561 (home). *E-mail:* dwatmough@dccnet.com (home).

WATSON, John Richard, BA, MA, PhD; British academic, writer and poet; b. 15 June 1934, Ipswich, England; m. Pauline Elizabeth Roberts 1962; one s. two d. *Education:* Magdalen Coll., Oxford, Univ. of Glasgow. *Career:* Asst, then Lecturer, Univ. of Glasgow 1962–66; Lecturer, then Sr Lecturer, Univ. of Leicester 1966–78; Prof. of English 1978–99, Public Orator 1989–99, Univ. of Durham; mem. Charles Wesley Soc., Int. Asscn of Univ. Profs of English (pres. 1995–98), MHRA, Charles Lamb Soc. (pres.). *Publications:* A Leicester Calendar 1976, Everyman's Book of Victorian Verse (ed.) 1982, Wordsworth's Vital Soul 1982, Wordsworth 1983, English Poetry of the Romantic Period 1789–1830 1985, The Poetry of Gerard Manley Hopkins 1986, Companion to Hymns and Psalms 1988, A Handbook to English Romanticism 1992, The English Hymn 1997, An Annotated Anthology of Hymns 2002, Romanticism and War 2003, Awake My Soul 2005; contrib. to scholarly and literary journals. *Honours:* Univ. of Oxford Matthew Arnold Memorial Prize 1961, Univ. of Glasgow Ewing Prize 1962, Stroud Festival Prize 1971, Suffolk Poetry Soc. Prize 1975. *Address:* Stoneyhurst, 27 Western Hill, Durham, DH1 4RL, England. *E-mail:* j.r.watson@durham.ac.uk.

WATSON, Larry, BA, MA, PhD; American writer and poet; b. 1947, Rugby, ND; m. Susan Watson; two d. *Education:* Univ. of North Dakota, Univ. of Utah. *Career:* fmr teacher of writing and literature Univ. of Wisconsin at Stevens Point; Visiting Prof. Marquette Univ. 2003–. *Publications:* In a Dark Time (novel) 1980, Leaving Dakota (poems) 1983, Montana 1948 (novel) 1993, Justice (short stories) 1995, White Crosses (novel) 1997, Laura (novel) 2000, Orchard (novel) 2003; contrib. to anthologies, including Essays for Contemporary Culture, Imagining Home, Off the Beaten Path, Baseball and the Game of Life, The Most Wonderful Books, These United States, Writing America; contrib. short stories and poems to Gettysburg Review, New England Review, North American Review, Mississippi Review and other journals, essays and book reviews to Los Angeles Times, Washington Post, Chicago Sun-Times, Milwaukee Journal-Sentinel and other periodicals. *Honours:* Hon. DLitt (Ripon Coll.), Nat. Education Asscn Creative Writing Fellowship 1987, NEA grants 1987, 2004, Wisconsin Arts Board grant; Milkweed Nat. Fiction Prize 1993. *Address:* c/o English Department, Marquette University, POB 1881, Milwaukee, WI 53201-1881, USA. *E-mail:* readermail@larry-watson.com. *Website:* www.larry-watson.com.

WATSON, Lyall, PhD, FZS, FLS; British writer and biologist; b. 12 April 1939, South Africa; m. 1st Vivienne Mawson 1961 (divorced 1966); m. 2nd Alice Coogan 2003. *Education:* Rondebosch Boys High School, Witwatersrand Univ. and Univs of Natal and London. *Career:* Dir Johannesburg Zoo 1964–65; Producer and Reporter, BBC TV 1966–67; Founder and Dir Biologic of London (Consultancy) 1968–; organizer and leader of numerous expeditions 1970–; Commr for Seychelles on Int. Whaling Comm. 1978–82; lives on ocean-going trawler 'Amazon' and in a cottage in West Cork, Ireland. *Television:* Documentary series for ITV and Discovery Channel. *Miscellaneous:* sailed single-handed across the Atlantic Ocean. *Publications:* Omnivore 1970, Supernature 1972, The Romeo Error 1974, Gifts of Unknown Things 1976, Lifetide 1978, Lightning Bird 1980, Whales of the World 1982, Heavens Breath 1984, Earthworks 1986, Beyond Supernature 1986, Supernature II 1986, The Water Planet 1987, Sumo 1988, Neophilia 1988, The Nature of Things 1990, Turtle Islands 1995, Dark Nature 1996, Monsoon 1996, Warriors, Warthogs and Wisdom 1997, Perfect Speed 1998, Jacobson's Organ 1999, Natural Mystery 2000, Elephantoms 2002, The Whole Hog: Exploring the Extraordinary Potential of Pigs 2004. *Honours:* Kt Order of Golden Ark, Netherlands 1983. *Address:* c/o BCM-Biologic, London, WC1N 3XX, England; Castle Mohigan, Goleen, Co. Cork, Ireland (home).

WATSON, Lynn, BA, MFA; American teacher, writer and poet; b. 5 June 1948, Woodland, CA. *Education:* Univ. of California at Berkeley, Sonoma State Univ., Univ. of Iowa. *Career:* teacher, Univ. of Iowa, Coll. of the Desert, Sonoma State Univ., Santa Rosa Jr Coll.; mem. California Poets-in-the-Schools. *Publications:* Alimony or Death of the Clock (novel) 1981, Amateur Blues (poems) 1990, Catching the Devil (poems) 1995; contrib. to journals and periodicals. *Honours:* first place Nat. Poetry Asscn 1990, honorable mention

World of Poetry Contest 1991. *Address:* PO Box 1253, Occidental, CA 95465, USA. *E-mail:* petalumapoet@hotmail.com.

WATSON, Mary, MA; South African writer; b. 1975, Cape Town. *Education:* Univ. of Cape Town, Univ. of Bristol. *Career:* Lecturer in Film Studies, Univ. of Cape Town. *Publications:* Moss (short stories) 2004, Jungfrau (short story) (Caine Prize for African Writing) 2006. *Address:* University of Cape Town, Private Bag, Rondebosch 7701, Cape Town, South Africa (office).

WATSON, Richard Allan, MA, PhD, MS, FAAS; American academic and writer; *Professor Emeritus of Philosophy, Washington University, St Louis*; b. 23 Feb. 1931, New Market, IA; m. Patty Jo Andersen 1955; one d. *Education:* Univ. of Iowa, Univ. of Minnesota. *Career:* 1st Lieutenant, USAF 1953–55; instructor Univ. of Michigan 1961–64; Asst Prof. Washington Univ., St Louis 1964–67, Assoc. Prof. 1967–74, Prof. of Philosophy 1974–2004, Prof. Emer. 2004–; Assoc. Philosophy Faculty Affiliate Univ. of Montana 2004–; Ed. Classics in Speleology 1968–73, Speleologia 1974–81, Cave Books 1980–2002, Journal of the History of Philosophy 1983 (bd of dirs 1982–2002, pres. 1990–95), Journal of the History of Philosophy Monograph Series 1985–96, Journal of the History of Philosophy Book Series 2002; ACLS Fellow 1967–68; Center for Advanced Study in the Behavioral Sciences Fellowships 1967–68, 1981–82, 1991–92; Center for Int. Studies Fellow Princeton, NJ 1975–76; Camargo Foundation Fellow 1995; Bogliasco Foundation Fellow 1998; mem. Int. Writers' Center (bd of dirs 1990–2002), Alpine Karst Foundation 2004–, American Asscn for the Advancement of Science, American Philosophical Asscn, Cave Research Foundation (bd of dirs 1965–74, pres. 1965–67), Authors' League of America, Nat. Parks and Conservation Asscn (trustee 1969–81). *Publications include:* The Mammoth Cave National Park Research Center (with Philip M. Smith) 1964, The Downfall of Cartesianism 1966, Man and Nature (with Patty Jo Watson) 1969, The Longest Cave (with Roger W. Brucker) 1976, Under Plowman's Floor (novel) 1978, The Runner (novel) 1981, The Philosopher's Diet (American Health Top 10 Book Award) 1985, The Breakdown of Cartesian Metaphysics 1987, The Philosopher's Joke 1990, Writing Philosophy 1992, Niagara (novel) 1993, Caving 1994, The Philosopher's Demise 1995, Representational Ideas From Plato to Patricia Churchland 1995, Good Teaching 1997, Cogito, Ergo Sum: The Life of René Descartes (NY Public Library 25 Books to Remember) 2002, In the Dark Cave (juvenile) 2005; contrib. to professional journals and literary quarterlies. *Honours:* hon. life mem. Spéléo Club de Paris, Nat. Speleological Soc.; Nat. Endowment for the Humanities grant 1975, Pushcart Prize 1990. *Address:* 2870 Solterra Lane, Missoula, MT 59803, USA (home). *Telephone:* (406) 327-0098 (home). *E-mail:* rawatson@artsci.wustl.edu (home).

WATSON, (Margaret) Sophia Laura, BA, PGCE; British writer; b. 20 June 1962, London, England; m. Julian Watson 1986 (divorced 2000); four d. *Education:* Univ. of Durham, Univ. of Exeter. *Career:* Asst Ed., Quartet Books, London 1983–84; Ed., Fisher Publishing, London 1984–85, Hamish Hamilton, London 1985–87; feature writer, Mail on Sunday, London 1987, Daily Mail, London 1988–90. *Publications:* Winning Women: The Price of Success in a Man's World 1989, Marina: The Story of a Princess 1994, Her Husband's Children 1995, Strange and Well Bred 1996, The Perfect Treasure 1998, Only Pretending 2000. *Address:* Royal Oak House, Church Street, Wiveliscombe, Somerset TA4 2LR, England. *E-mail:* sophiawatson@watson545.fsnet.co.uk.

WATT-EVANS, Lawrence; American writer; b. 26 July 1954, Arlington, MA; m. Julie F. McKenna 1977, one s. one d. *Education:* Princeton University. *Career:* mem. SFWA; Horror Writers Asscn. *Publications:* The Lure of the Basilisk, 1980; The Seven Altars of Düsarra, 1981; The Cyborg and the Sorcerers, 1982; The Sword of Bheleu, 1983; The Book of Silence, 1984; The Chromosomal Code, 1984; The Misenchanted Sword, 1985; Shining Steel, 1986; With a Single Spell, 1987; The Wizard and the War Machine, 1987; Denner's Wreck, 1988; Nightside City, 1989; The Unwilling Warlord, 1989; The Nightmare People, 1990; The Blood of a Dragon, 1991; The Rebirth of Wonder, 1992; Crosstime Traffic, 1992; Taking Flight, 1993; The Spell of the Black Dagger, 1993; Split Heirs (with Esther Friesner), 1993; Out of This World, 1994; In the Empire of Shadow, 1995; The Reign of the Brown Magician, 1996; Touched by the Gods, 1997; Dragon Weather, 1999; Night of Madness, 2000; The Dragon Society, 2001; The Wizard Lord, 2006; The Ninth Talisman, 2007. Contributions: journals and magazines. *Honours:* Isaac Asimov's Science Fiction Readers Poll Award, 1987; Science Fiction Achievement Award (Hugo) for Best Short Story of 1987, 1988. *Literary Agent:* c/o Scott Meredith Literary Agency, 200 West 57th Street, Suite 904, New York, NY 10019, USA. *E-mail:* lwe@sff.net (office). *Website:* www.watt-evans.com (office).

WATTAR, Tahir (see Ouettar, Tahar)

WATTS, Nigel John; British writer; b. 24 June 1957, Winchester, England; m. Sahera Chohan 1991. *Publications:* The Life Game, 1989; Billy Bayswater, 1990; We All Live in a House Called Innocence, 1992; Twenty Twenty, 1995. *Honours:* Betty Trask Award 1989.

WAUGH, Alexander Evelyn Michael, MusB, DipMus; British writer; b. 30 Dec. 1963, London, England; m. Eliza Chancellor; one s. two d. *Education:* Univ. of Manchester, Univ. of Surrey. *Career:* Dir, Manygate Management 1988–90; opera critic, Mail on Sunday 1990–91, Evening Standard 1991–96; founder and Chief Exec., Travelman Publishing 1997–. *Publications:* Opera on CD (with Julian Haylock) 1994, 1995, 1996, Classical Music on CD (with Julian Haylock) 1994, 1995, 1996, Classical Music, a New Way of Listening 1995, Opera, a New Way of Listening 1996, Time, from Microseconds to Millennia, a Search for the Right Time 1999, Bon Voyage! A Musical Farce (with Nathaniel Waugh) 2000, God: The Unauthorised Biography 2001, Fathers and Sons: The Autobiography of a Family 2004; contrib. to Literary Review, Spectator and others. *Honours:* Music Retailers Asscn Award 1994, Grand Prix du Disque 1995, Vivian Ellis Award for Best New Musical 1996, Design Council Millennium Award 2000. *Literary Agent:* Aitken Alexander Associates Ltd, 18–21 Cavaye Place, London, SW10 9PT, England. *Telephone:* (20) 7373-8672. *Fax:* (20) 7373-6002. *E-mail:* reception@aitkenalexander.co.uk. *Website:* www.aitkenalexander.co.uk.

WAUGH, Carol-Lynn Rössel, MA; American writer, artist and photographer; b. 5 Jan. 1947, Staten Island, NY; d. of Carl and Muriel (née Kiefer) Rössel; m. Charles Waugh 1967 (divorced 2001); one s. one d. *Education:* State Univ. of New York at Binghamton (Harpur Coll) and Kent State Univ. *Career:* Instructor in Art History Univ. of Maine 1977; freelance writer and artist 1973–; articles and lectures on teddy bears, dolls and antique toys; sculptor of original dolls 1973–; designer original teddy bears for House of Nisbet, UK 1987–, Effanbee Dolls 1989–, Ashton-Drake Galleries 1989–, Russ Berrie Ltd (USA and UK) 1991–; designer plates for Brimark Ltd 1986; numerous awards for watercolours, photography and designs; mem. Soc. of Children's Book Writers, Original Doll Artist Council of America, Mystery Writers of America, Maine Soc. of Doll and Bear Artists. *Publications include:* Petite Portraits 1982, My Friend Bear 1982, Teddy Bear Artists 1984, Contemporary Artist Dolls (jtly) 1986, The Official Guide to Antique and Modern Teddy Bears (jtly) 1990, Selling Your Dolls and Teddy Bears (jtly) 1996, Holmes for Christmas (jtly) 1996, Bear Making 101 1999, Heirloom Sewing for Teddy Bears and Dolls 2001; co-editor: The Twelve Crimes of Christmas 1981, Big Apple Mysteries 1982, Show Business Is Murder 1983, Murder on the Menu 1984, Manhattan Mysteries 1987, Hound Dunnit 1987, The Sport of Crime, Purr-fect Crime 1989, Senior Sleuths 1989, More Holmes for the Holidays 1999; contribs to professional magazines. *Address:* 17 Morrill Street, Winthrop, ME 04364, USA. *Telephone:* (207) 377-6769. *Fax:* (207) 377-4158. *E-mail:* CLWaugh@aol.com.

WAUGH, Hillary Baldwin, (Elissa Grandower, H. Baldwin Taylor, Harry Walker), BA; American writer; b. 22 June 1920, New Haven, CT; m. 1st Diana Taylor 1951 (divorced 1980); one s. two d.; m. 2nd Shannon O. Cork 1983 (divorced 1995). *Education:* Yale Univ. *Career:* mem. MWA, CWA. *Publications:* Madam Will Not Dine Tonight 1947, Hope to Die 1948, The Odds Run Out 1949, Last Seen Wearing... 1952, A Rag and a Bone 1954, The Case of the Missing Gardener 1954, Rich Man, Dead Man 1956, The Girl Who Cried Woolf 1958, The Eighth Mrs Bluebeard 1958, Sleep Long, My Love 1959, Road Block 1960, Murder on the Terrace 1961, That Night it Rained 1961, Born Victim 1962, The Late Mrs D 1962, Prisoner's Plea 1963, Death and Circumstance 1963, The Duplicate 1964, The Missing Man 1964, Girl on the Run 1965, End of a Party 1965, Pure Poison 1966, The Triumvirate 1966, The Trouble with Tycoons 1967, 30 Manhattan East 1968, The Con Game 1968, Run When I Say Go 1969, The Young Prey 1969, Finish Me Off 1970, The Shadow Guest 1971, Parrish for the Defense 1974, A Bride for Hampton House 1975, Seaview Manor 1976, The Summer at Raven's Roost 1976, The Secret Room of Morgate House 1977, Madman at My Door 1978, Blackbourne Hall 1979, Rivergate House 1980, The Glenna Powers Case 1980, The Billy Cantrell Case 1981, The Doria Rafe Case 1981, The Nerissa Claire Case 1983, The Veronica Dean Case 1984, The Priscilla Copperwaite Case 1985, Murder on Safari 1987, A Death in a Town 1988. *Honours:* Swedish Acad. of Detection Grand Master 1981, MWA Grand Master 1989. *Address:* c/o Mystery Writers of America, 17 E 47th Street, Sixth Floor, New York, NY 10017, USA.

WAUGH, Sylvia, BA; British writer; b. (Sylvia Richardson), m 1964; three c. *Education:* Univ. of Durham. *Career:* fmr teacher of English in local school; now writer of children's books. *Publications include:* The Mennyms (Guardian Children's Fiction Prize 1994) 1993, Mennyms in the Wilderness 1995, Mennyms Under Siege 1995, Mennyms Alive 1996, Mennyms Alone 1996, Space Race 2000, Earthborn 2002, Who Goes Home 2003. *Address:* c/o Publicity Department, Random House, 20 Vauxhall Bridge Road, London, SW1V 2SA, England.

WAUGH, Teresa Lorraine, BA; British writer; b. 26 Feb. 1940, London, England; m. Auberon Waugh 1961 (died 2001); two s. two d. *Education:* University of Exeter. *Publications:* The Travels of Marco Polo: A Modern Translation (trans.), 1984; Painting Water (novel), 1984; Waterloo, Waterloo (novel), 1986; The Entertaining Book (co-author), 1986; An Intolerable Burden (novel), 1988; A Song at Twilight (novel), 1989; Sylvia's Lot (novel), 1994; The Gossips (novel), 1995; A Friend Like Harvey (novel), 1998; Alphonse de Custine (trans.), 1999; The House (novel), 2002.

WAYMAN, Thomas (Tom) Ethan, BA, MFA; Canadian poet, fiction writer and essayist; *Associate Professor, University of Calgary*; b. 13 Aug. 1945, Hawkesbury, Ont. *Education:* Univ. of British Columbia, Univ. of California, Irvine. *Career:* Instructor, Colorado State Univ. 1968–69; Writer-in-Residence, Univ. of Windsor, Ont. 1975–76, Univ. of Alberta 1978–79, Simon Fraser Univ., Burnaby, BC 1983; Asst Prof., Wayne State Univ., Detroit 1976–77; Faculty, David Thompson Univ. Centre, Nelson, BC 1980–82, Banff School of Fine Arts, Alberta 1980, 1982, Kwantlen Coll., Surrey, BC 1983, 1988–89, 1998–2000, Kootenay School of Writing, Vancouver 1984–87; Prof., Okanagan Univ. Coll., Kelowna, BC 1990–91, 1993–95; Faculty, Kootenay

School of the Arts, Nelson, BC 1991–92, Co-Head, Writing Studio 1995–98; Presidential Writer-in-Residence, Univ. of Toronto 1996; Assoc. Prof., Univ. of Calgary 2002–; Fulbright Visiting Research Chair, Arizona State Univ. 2007; mem. Asscn of Writers and Writing Programs, Fed. of British Columbia Writers, Alberta Writers' Guild. *Publications:* poetry: Waiting for Wayman 1973, For and Against the Moon 1974, Money and Rain 1975, Free Time 1977, A Planet Mostly Sea 1979, Living on the Ground 1980, Introducing Tom Wayman: Selected Poems 1973–80 1980, The Nobel Prize Acceptance Speech 1981, Counting the Hours 1983, The Face of Jack Munro 1986, In a Small House on the Outskirts of Heaven 1989, Did I Miss Anything?: Selected Poems 1973–1993 1993, The Astonishing Weight of the Dead 1994, I'll Be Right Back: New & Selected Poems 1980–1996 1997, The Colours of the Forest 1999, My Father's Cup 2002, High Speed Through Shoaling Water 2007; non-fiction: Inside Job: Essays on the New Work Writing 1983, A Country Not Considered: Canada, Culture, Work 1993; short fiction: Boundary Country 2007; editor: Beaton Abbot's Got the Contract 1974, A Government Job at Last 1976, Going for Coffee 1981, East of Main: An Anthology of Poems from East Vancouver (with Calvin Wharton) 1989, Paperwork 1991, The Dominion of Love: An Anthology of Canadian Love Poems 2001; contrib. to anthologies and magazines. *Honours:* Michigan State Univ. A. J. M. Smith Prize 1976, first prize Nat. Bicentennial Poetry Awards, San Jose 1976, several Canada Council Sr Arts grants. *Address:* PO Box 163, Winlaw, BC V0G 2J0, Canada (home). *Telephone:* (403) 220-4662 (office). *E-mail:* appledor@netidea.com (office). *Website:* www.library.utoronto.ca/canpoetry/wayman.

WAYS, C. R. (see Blount, Roy Alton, Jr)

WEARNE, Alan Richard, BA, DipEd; Australian poet and novelist; *Senior Lecturer, University of Wollongong;* b. 23 July 1948, Melbourne, Vic. *Education:* Latrobe Univ. and Rusden. *Publications:* Public Relations 1972, New Devil, New Parish 1976, The Nightmarkets 1986, Out Here 1987, Kicking in Danger 1997, The Lovemakers, Book One 2001, The Lovemakers, Book Two 2004, The Australian Popular Songbook 2007. *Honours:* Nat. Book Council Award 1987, gold medal Asscn for the Study of Australian Literature 1987, New South Wales Premier's Prize for Poetry (Kenneth Slessor Award) 2002, New South Wales Premier's Prize Book of the Year 2002, Arts Queensland Judith Wright Calanthe Award for Australian Poetry 2002, Colin Roderick Award 2004. *Address:* POB 4399, University of Wollongong, Wollongong, NSW 2500, Australia (office). *Telephone:* (4) 2230-5780 (home); (2) 4221-4093 (office). *Fax:* (2) 4221-3301 (office). *E-mail:* awearne@uow.edu .au (office). *Website:* www.wikig.net.

WEBB, Phyllis, OC, BA; Canadian poet and writer; b. 8 April 1927, Victoria, BC; d. of Alfred and Mary (née Patton) Webb. *Education:* Univ. of BC and McGill Univ. *Career:* Teaching Asst Univ. of BC 1960; mem. Public Affairs Dept, CBC 1964; co-creator and Exec. Producer Ideas (radio programme) 1967; writer-in-residence Univ. of Alberta 1980–81; Adjunct Prof. Creative Writing Dept, Univ. of Victoria 1989–91; mem. Amnesty Int., League of Canadian Poets. *Publications:* poetry: Trio (with G. Turnbull and Eli Mandel) 1954, Even Your Right Eye 1956, The Sea is Also a Garden 1962, Selected Poems 1954–1965 1971, Naked Poems 1965, Wilson's Bowl 1980, Sunday Water: Thirteen Anti Ghazals 1982, The Vision Tree: Selected Poems (Gov-Gen's Award for Poetry) 1982, Water and Light: Ghazals and Anti Ghazals 1984, Hanging Fire 1990; other: Talking (essays) 1982, Nothing But Brush Strokes: Selected Prose 1995. *Address:* 167 Quarry Drive, Saltspring Island, BC V8K 1J2, Canada (home). *Telephone:* (250) 537-1934.

WEBER, Katharine; American critic and writer; *Lecturer, Yale University;* b. 12 Nov. 1955, New York, NY; m. Nicholas Fox Weber 1976, two d. *Education:* New School for Social Research, New York and Yale Univ. *Career:* columnist, Sunday New Haven Register, Conn. 1985–87; reviewer, Publishers Weekly 1988–92; Visiting Writer-in-Residence, Connecticut Coll. 1996–97; Visiting Lecturer, Yale Univ. 1997, Lecturer 1998–; Writer-in-Residence, Paris Writers Workshop 2004; mem. Authors' Guild, PEN, Nat. Book Critics Circle (Bd mem.). *Publications:* Objects in Mirror are Closer Than They Appear 1995, The Music Lesson 1999, The Little Women 2003; contrib. to numerous periodicals. *Honours:* Best Columnist of the Year, New England Women's Press Asscn 1986, Discovery Award, New England Booksellers Asscn 1995, Granta Best Young American Novelist 1996. *Address:* 108 Beacon Road, Bethany, CT 06524, USA. *E-mail:* katweber@snet.net. *Website:* www .katharineweber.com.

WEBSTER, Ernest; English writer (retd); b. 24 Oct. 1923, Habrough, England; m. 1942; two d. *Education:* studied history and economics in London. *Career:* fmr transport fleet man.; mem. Radio Soc. of Great Britain. *Publications:* The Friulan Plot 1980, Madonna of the Black Market 1981, Cossack Hide-Out 1981, Red Alert 1982, The Venetian Spy-Glass 1983, The Verratoli Inheritance 1983, Million-Dollar Stand-In 1983, The Watchers 1984. *Address:* 17 Chippendale Rise, Otley, West Yorkshire LS21 2BL, England. *Telephone:* (1943) 467814.

WEBSTER, John (Jack) Barron; British journalist and writer; b. 8 July 1931, Maud, Aberdeenshire; m. Eden Keith 1956; three s. *Education:* Peterhead Acad., Robert Gordon's Coll., Aberdeen. *Career:* reporter, Aberdeen Press and Journal 1950–60; feature writer, Scottish Daily Express 1960–80; columnist, Glasgow Herald 1986–2000. *Writing for television:* The Webster Trilogy 1992, John Brown: The Man Who Drew a Legend 1994, Walking Back to Happiness 1996. *Publications:* The Dons 1978, A Grain of Truth 1981, Gordon Strachan 1984, Another Grain of Truth 1988, Alistair MacLean: A Life

1991, Famous Ships of the Clyde 1993, The Flying Scots 1994, The Express Years 1994, In the Driving Seat 1996, The Herald Years 1996, Webster's World 1997, From Dalí to Burrell 1997, Reo Stakis (biog.) 1999, The Auld Hoose 2005. *Honours:* Hon. MUniv (Aberdeen) 2000; Bank of Scotland Columnist of the Year 1996, UK Speaker of the Year 1996, BAFTA Award 1996. *Address:* 58 Netherhill Avenue, Glasgow, G44 3XG, Scotland (home).

WEBSTER, Leonard (Len), BEd, MA, DipHigherEd; British poet and fiction writer; *Lecturer, Handsworth City College, Birmingham;* b. 6 July 1948, Birmingham, England; m. Emorn Puttalong 1985. *Education:* Univ. of Warwick, Univ. of Leicester, Univ. of Birmingham. *Career:* journalist, Birmingham Post and Mail 1965–68, Coventry Evening Telegraph 1973–74; teacher, Oldbury High School 1976–77, Tarsus American Coll., Turkey 1977–78, King Edward VI Grammar School, Handsworth, Birmingham 1978–84; Lecturer, Ministry of Education, Singapore 1984–87, 1988–94, City Coll., Handsworth, Birmingham 1996–; mem. Poetry Soc., Soc. of Authors. *Publications:* Behind the Painted Veil 1972, Beneath the Blue Moon 1992, Hell-Riders 1994, Flight From the Sibyl 1994. *Address:* c/o 48 Marshall Road, Warley, West Midlands B68 9ED, England. *Website:* www3 .shropshire–cc.gov.uk/webster.htm.

WEDDE, Ian, MA; New Zealand writer, poet, dramatist and translator; b. 17 Oct. 1946, Blenheim; m. Rosemary Beauchamp 1967, three s. *Education:* University of Auckland. *Career:* Poetry Reviewer, London magazine, 1970–71; Writer-in-Residence, Victoria University, Wellington, 1984; Art Critic, Wellington Evening Post, 1983–90. *Publications:* Fiction: Dick Seddon's Great Drive, 1976; The Shirt Factory and Other Stories, 1981; Symmes Hole, 1986; Survival Arts, 1988. Poetry: Homage to Matisse, 1971; Made Over, 1974; Pathway to the Sea, 1974; Earthly: Sonnets for Carlos, 1975; Don't Listen, 1977; Spells for Coming Out, 1977; Castaly, 1981; Tales of Gotham City, 1984; Georgicon, 1984; Driving Into the Storm: Selected Poems, 1988; Tendering, 1988; The Drummer, 1993; The Commonplace Odes, 2001. Plays: Stations, 1969; Pukeko, 1972; Eyeball, Eyeball, 1983; Double or Quit: The Life and Times of Percy TopLiss, 1984. Editor: The Penguin Book of New Zealand Verse (with Harvey McQueen), 1986; Now See Hear!: Art, Language, and Translation (with G. Burke), 1990.

WEDGWOOD, Lady (see Tudor-Craig, Pamela Wynn)

WEI HUI (see Zhou, Wei Hui)

WEI, Jun-Yi; Chinese writer; b. Oct. 1917, Beijing; d. of Wei Hang; m. Yuang Shu; three c. *Education:* Tsinghua Univ., Beijing. *Career:* apptd Ed. and Pres. Renmin Wenxue Chubunshe (People's Literature Publishing House) 1950. *Publication:* Mother and Son 1982. *Honours:* Nat. Award for writing 1983. *Address:* People's Literature Publishing House, 166 Chaoyangmen Nei Dajie, Beijing 100705, People's Republic of China (office). *Telephone:* (10) 5138394 (office).

WEIDENFELD, Baron (Life Peer), cr. 1976, of Chelsea in Greater London; **Arthur George Weidenfeld,** Kt; British publisher; b. 13 Sept. 1919, Vienna, Austria; s. of the late Max Weidenfeld and Rosa Weidenfeld; m. 1st Jane Sieff 1952; one d.; m. 2nd Barbara Skelton Connolly 1956 (divorced 1961); m. 3rd Sandra Payson Meyer 1966 (divorced 1976); m. 4th Annabelle Whitestone 1992. *Education:* Piaristen Gymnasium, Vienna, Univ. of Vienna and Konsular Akademie. *Career:* came to England 1938; BBC Monitoring Service 1939–42; BBC News Commentator on European Affairs on BBC Empire and N American service 1942–46; Foreign Affairs columnist, News Chronicle 1943–44; Political Adviser and Chief of Cabinet of Pres. Weizmann of Israel 1949–50; Founder of Contact Magazine 1945, George Weidenfeld & Nicolson Ltd 1948–; Chair. George Weidenfeld & Nicolson Ltd 1948–, Wheatland Corpn, New York 1985–90, Grove Press, New York 1985–90, Wheatland Foundation, San Francisco and New York 1985–92; Dir (non-exec.) Orion 1991–; Consultant Bertelsmann Foundation 1991–, Axel Springer AG Germany; Chair. Bd of Govs, Ben Gurion Univ. of the Negev 1996–; Gov. of Tel-Aviv Univ. 1980–, Weizmann Inst. of Science 1964–; Columnist Die Welt, Die Welt am Sonntag; mem., South Bank Bd 1986–99; mem. Bd ENO 1988–98, Herbert-Quandt-Foundation 1999–; Trustee Royal Opera House 1974–87, Nat. Portrait Gallery 1988–95, Potsdam Einstein Forum, Jerusalem Foundation; Chair. Cheyne Capital 2000–, Trialogue Educational Trust 1996–; mem. Governing Council, Inst. of Human Science, Vienna; Vice-Chair. Oxford Univ. Devt Programme 1994–99; Freeman City of London. *Publications:* The Goebbels Experiment 1943, Remembering My Good Friends 1994. *Honours:* Hon. Senator Bonn Univ. 1996; Hon. Fellow St Peter's Coll. Oxford 1992, St Anne's Coll. Oxford 1993; Golden Kt's Cross of Order of Merit (Austria) 1989; Chevalier, Légion d'honneur 1990; Kt Commdr's Cross (Badge and Star) of Order of Merit (Germany) 1991; Austrian Cross of Honour First Class for Arts and Science, Vienna 2003; Honour of City of Vienna 2003; Hon. MA (Oxon.) 1992; Hon. PhD (Ben Gurion Univ.); Hon. DLitt (Exeter) 2001; Charlemagne Medal 2000; London Book Fair/Trilogy Lifetime Achievement Award 2007. *Address:* Orion House, 5 Upper St Martin's Lane, London, WC2H 9EA (office); 9 Chelsea Embankment, London, SW3 4LE, England (home). *Telephone:* (20) 7520-4411 (office); (20) 7351-0042 (home). *Fax:* (20) 7379-1604 (office). *E-mail:* agw@orionbooks.co.uk (office).

WEIGEL, George, BA, MA; American theologian and writer; b. 17 April 1951, Baltimore, MD; m. Joan Balcombe 1975; one s. two d. *Education:* St Mary's Seminary and Univ., Baltimore, Univ. of St Michael's Coll., Toronto. *Career:* Fellow, Woodrow Wilson Int. Centre for Scholars 1984–85; Pres. Ethics and

Public Policy Center 1989–96 (Sr Fellow 1996–); mem. Editorial Bd First Things, Orbis; mem. Catholic Theological Soc. of America, Council on Foreign Relations. *Publications:* Tranquillitas Ordinis: The Present Failure and Future Promise of American Catholic Thought on War and Peace 1987, Catholicism and the Renewal of American Democracy 1989, American Interests, American Purpose: Moral Reasoning and US Foreign Policy 1989, Freedom and Its Discontents 1991, Just War and the Gulf War (co-author) 1991, The Final Revolution: The Resistance Church and the Collapse of Communism 1992, Idealism Without Illusions: US Foreign Policy in the 1990s 1994, Soul of the World: Notes on the Future of Public Catholicism 1995, Witness to Hope: The Biography of Pope John Paul II 1999, The Truth of Catholicism: Ten Controversies Explored 2001, The Courage To Be Catholic: Crisis, Reform, and the Future of the Church 2002, Letters to a Young Catholic 2004, The Cube and the Cathedral: Europe, America and Politics Without God 2005, God's Choice: Pope Benedict XVI and the Future of the Catholic Church 2005; contrib. to numerous publications. *Honours:* Papal Cross Pro Ecclesia et Pontifice 2000; several hon. doctorates; 'Gloria Artis' Gold Medal (Poland) 2006. *Literary Agent:* Loretta Barrett, 101 Fifth Avenue, New York, NY 10003, USA. *Address:* Ethics and Public Policy Center, 1015 15th Street NW, Suite 900, Washington, DC 20005, USA (office). *Telephone:* (202) 682-1200 (office). *Fax:* (202) 408-0632 (office).

WEIGL, Bruce, BA, MA, PhD; American academic, poet, writer, editor and translator; *Distinguished Professor, Lorain County Community College;* b. 27 Jan. 1949, Lorain, OH; m. Jean Kondo; one s. one d. *Education:* Oberlin Coll., Univ. of New Hampshire, Univ. of Utah. *Career:* instructor in English 1975–76, Distinguished Prof. 2000–, Lorain County Community Coll.; Asst Prof. of English, Univ. of Arkansas at Little Rock 1979–81, Old Dominion Univ., Norfolk 1981–86; Assoc. Prof. to Prof. of English, Pennsylvania State Univ. at Univ. Park 1986–2000. *Publications:* poetry: Like a Sack Full of Old Quarrels 1976, Executioner 1977, A Romance 1979, The Monkey Wars 1984, Song of Napalm 1988, What Saves Us 1992, Sweet Lorain 1996, Archeology of the Circle: New and Selected Poems 1999, After the Others, The Unravelling Strangeness, The Circle of Hanh: A Memoir 2000; editor: The Giver of Morning: On the Poetry of Dave Smith 1982, The Imagination as Glory: The Poetry of James Dickey (with T. R. Hummer) 1984, Charles Simic: Essays on the Poetry 1996, Writing Between the Lines: An Anthology on War and its Social Consequences (with Kevin Bowen) 1997, Mountain River: Vietnamese Poetry from the Wars, 1948–1993: A Bilingual Collection (with Kevin Bowen and Nguyan Ba Chung) 1998; other: Angel Riding the Beast (trans. from Romanian with author Lilliana Ursu), Poems from Captured Documents (trans. from Vietnamese with Nguyen); contrib. to anthologies, reviews, quarterlies and journals. *Honours:* Bronze Stud Vietnam Service 1967–68, American Acad. of Poets Prize 1979, Pushcart Prizes 1980, 1985, Bread Loaf Writers' Conference Fellowship 1981, Nat. Endowment for the Arts grant 1988. *Address:* 41 Glenhurst Drive, Oberlin, OH 44074, USA (home). *Telephone:* (440) 366-7141 (office); (440) 776-2041 (home). *E-mail:* BWeigl@lorainccc.edu.

WEIGLEY, Russell Frank; American academic and writer; b. 2 July 1930, Reading, PA; m. Emma Eleanor Seifrit 1963; one s. one d. *Education:* BA, Albright College, 1952; MA, 1953, PhD, 1956, University of Pennsylvania. *Career:* Instructor in History, 1956–58, Visiting Lecturer, 1958–63, University of Pennsylvania; Asst Prof. to Assoc. Prof. of History, Drexel Institute of Technology, 1958–62; Visiting Lecturer, Haverford College, 1961; Ed., Pennsylvania History, 1962–67; Assoc. Prof., 1962–64, Prof., 1964–85, Distinguished University Prof. of History, 1985–99, Prof. Emeritus, 1999–, Temple University; Visiting Prof., Dartmouth College, 1967–68, US Army War College, 1973–74; mem. American Historical Asscn; American Philosophical Society; Organization of American Historians; Society for Military History; Society of American Historians. *Publications:* Quartermaster General of the Union Army, 1959; Towards an American Army: Military Thought from Washington to Marshall, 1962; History of the United States Army, 1967; American Military (ed.), 1969; The Partisan War: The South Carolina Campaign of 1780–1782, 1970; The American Way of War: A History of American Military Strategy and Policy, 1973; The Draft and Its Enemies: A Documentary History, 1974; New Dimensions in Military History (ed.), 1977; Eisenhower's Lieutenants: The Campaign of France and Germany, 1944–1945, 1981; Philadelphia: A 300-Year History (ed.), 1982; The Age of Battles: The Quest for Decisive Warfare from Breitenfeld to Waterloo, 1991; A Great Civil War: A Military and Political History, 2000. Contributions: scholarly books and journals. *Honours:* Guggenheim Fellowship, 1969–70; Hon. DHL, Albright College, 1979; Samuel Eliot Morison Award, 1989; Outstanding Book Award, Society for Military History, 1992. *Address:* 327 S Smedley Street, Philadelphia, PA 19103, USA.

WEIN, Elizabeth Eve, (Elizabeth Gatland), BA, MA, PhD; American writer and folklorist; b. 2 Oct. 1964, New York, NY; d. of Norman Wein and Carol Flocken; m. Tim Gatland 1996; two c. *Education:* Yale Univ., Univ. of Pennsylvania. *Career:* mem. Authors' Guild, Science and Fiction Writers of America, Inc., Soc. of Children's Book Writers and Illustrators. *Publications:* The Winter Prince 1993, A Coalition of Lions 2003, The Sunbird 2004, The Mark of Solomon (in two parts, comprising Lion Hunter 2007 and The Empty Kingdom 2008); contrib. to anthologies and encyclopaedias. *Honours:* Jacob K. Javits Fellow 1988–92. *Literary Agent:* c/o Ginger Clark, Curtis Brown Ltd, 10 Astor Place, New York, NY 10003, USA. *Telephone:* (212) 473-5400. *Fax:* (212) 598-0917. *Website:* www.curtisbrown.com; www.elizabethwein.com.

WEINBERG, Gerhard Ludwig, BA, MA, PhD; American academic and writer; *Professor Emeritus of History, University of North Carolina at Chapel Hill;* b. 1 Jan. 1928, Hannover, Germany; m. Janet I. White 1989; one s. *Education:* New York State Coll. for Teachers, Univ. of Chicago. *Career:* Prof. Emer. of History, Univ. of N Carolina at Chapel Hill; mem. American Historical Asscn, Conf. Group for Cen. European History, German Studies Asscn, World War II Studies Asscn. *Publications:* Germany and the Soviet Union 1939–41 1954, Hitlers Zweites Buch 1961, The Foreign Policy of Hitler's Germany 1933–36 1970, The Foreign Policy of Hitler's Germany 1937–39 1980, World in the Balance: Behind the Scenes of World War II 1981, A World at Arms: A Global History of World War II 1994, Germany, Hitler and World War II 1995, Hitler's Second Book: The Unpublished Sequel to Mein Kampf 2003, Visions of Victory: The Hopes of Eight World War II Leaders 2005; contrib. to professional journals. *Honours:* Hon. LHD 1989; Hon. DPhil 2001; Beer Prizes, American Historical Asscn 1971, 1994, Halverson Prize, German Studies Asscn 1981. *Address:* 1416 Mt Willing Road, Efland, NC 27243, USA (office). *Telephone:* (919) 563-4224 (office). *E-mail:* gweinber@email.unc.edu.

WEINBERG, Steven, PhD; American physicist and academic; *Jack S. Josey-Welch Foundation Chair in Science and Regental Professor and Director, Theory Research Group, Department of Physics, University of Texas;* b. 3 May 1933, New York; s. of Fred Weinberg and Eva Weinberg; m. Louise Goldwasser 1954; one d. *Education:* Cornell Univ., Univ. of Copenhagen and Princeton Univ. *Career:* Columbia Univ. 1957–59; Lawrence Radiation Lab. 1959–60; Univ. of Calif. at Berkeley 1960–69; Prof. of Physics, MIT 1969–73; Higgins Prof. of Physics, Harvard Univ. 1973–83; Sr Scientist, Smithsonian Astrophysical Observatory 1973–83; Sr Consultant 1983–; Josey Chair and Regental Prof. of Science, Univ. of Texas, Austin 1982–, also Dir Theory Research Group; Co-Ed. Cambridge Univ. Press Monographs on Mathematical Physics 1978; Dir Jerusalem Winter School of Theoretical Physics 1983–, Headliners Foundation 1993–; mem. A.P. Sloan Foundation Science Book Cttee 1985–90, Einstein Archives Int. Advisory Bd 1988–, Scientific Policy Cttee, Supercollider Lab. 1989–93, American Acad. of Arts and Sciences 1968–, NAS 1972–, Council for Foreign Relations, President's Cttee on the Nat. Medal of Science 1979–80, Royal Soc. 1982–, American Philosophical Soc. 1983–; fmr mem. Council, American Physical Soc., Int. Astronomical Union, Philosophical Soc. of Tex. (Pres. 1994); Loeb Lecturer, Harvard Univ. and Visiting Prof. MIT 1966–69, Richtmeyer Lecturer of American Asscn of Physics Teachers 1974, Scott Lecturer, Cavendish Lab. 1975, Silliman Lecturer, Yale Univ. 1977, Lauritsen Lecturer, Calif. Inst. of Tech. 1979, Bethe Lecturer, Cornell Univ. 1979, Harris Lecturer, Northwestern Univ. 1982, Cherwell-Simon Lecturer, Oxford Univ. 1983, Bampton Lecturer, Columbia Univ. 1983, Hilldale Lecturer, Univ. of Wisconsin 1985, Brickweede Lecturer, Johns Hopkins Univ. 1986, Dirac Lecturer, Univ. of Cambridge 1986, Klein Lecturer, Univ. of Stockholm 1989, Sackler Lecturer, Univ. of Copenhagen 1994, Brittin Lecturer, Univ. of Colorado 1994, Gibbs Lecturer, American Math. Soc. 1996, Bochner Lecturer, Rice Univ. 1997, Sanchez Lecturer, Witherspoon Lecturer, Washington Univ. 2001. *Publications:* Gravitation and Cosmology 1972, The First Three Minutes 1977, The Discovery of Subatomic Particles 1982, Elementary Particles and the Laws of Physics (with R. P. Feynman) 1987, Dreams of a Final Theory 1993, The Quantum Theory of Fields (Vol. I) 1995, (Vol. II) 1996, (Vol. III) 2000, Facing Up 2001; and over 250 articles. *Honours:* Tex. A & M Int. Univ. 1998; Hon. DSc (Knox Coll.) 1978, (Chicago, Yale, Rochester) 1979, (City Univ., New York) 1980, (Clark Univ.) 1982, (Dartmouth) 1984, (Weizmann Inst.) 1985, (Columbia) 1990, (Salamanca) 1992, (Padua) 1992, (Barcelona) 1996, (Bates Coll.) 2002, (McGill Univ.) 2003; Hon. DLitt (Washington Coll.) 1985; J. R. Oppenheimer Prize 1973, Dannie Heinemann Mathematical Physics Prize 1977, American Inst. of Physics-U.S. Steel Foundation Science Writing Award 1977, Elliott Cresson Medal, Franklin Inst. 1979, Joint Winner, Nobel Prize for Physics 1979, James Madison Medal (Princeton) 1991, Nat. Medal of Science 1991, Andrew Gemant Award 1997, Piazzi Prize 1998, Lewis Thomas Prize Honoring the Scientist as Poet 1999, Benjamin Franklin Medal, American Philosophical Soc. 2004. *Address:* Department of Physics, University of Texas, Theory Group, RLM 5.208 C1608, Austin, TX 78712-1081, USA. *Telephone:* (512) 471-4394 (office). *Fax:* (512) 471-4888 (office). *E-mail:* weinberg@physics.utexas.edu (office). *Website:* www.ph.utexas.edu/~weintech/weinberg.html (office).

WEINFIELD, Henry Michael; Canadian academic, poet and writer; b. 3 Jan. 1949, Montréal, QC. *Education:* BA, City College, CUNY, 1970; MA, SUNY at Binghamton, 1973; PhD, CUNY, 1985. *Career:* Lecturer, SUNY at Binghamton, 1973–74; Adjunct Lecturer, Lehman College, 1974–77; Baruch College, 1979–81, City College, 1982–83, CUNY; Adjunct Lecturer, 1983–84, Special Lecturer, 1984–91, New Jersey Institute of Technology; Asst Prof., 1991–96, Assoc. Prof., 1996–2003, Prof., 2003–, in Liberal Studies, Univ. of Notre Dame. *Publications:* Poetry: The Carnival Cantata, 1971; In the Sweetness of New Time, 1980; Sonnets Elegiac and Satirical, 1982. Other: The Poet Without a Name: Gray's Elegy and the Problem of History, 1991; The Collected Poems of Stéphane Mallarmé, (trans. and commentator), 1995; The Sorrows of Eros and Other Poems, 1999. Contributions: articles, poems, trans in many publications. *Honours:* Co-ordinating Council of Literary Magazines Award, 1975; National Endowment for the Humanities Fellowship, 1989. *Address:* Program of Liberal Studies, University of Notre Dame, Notre Dame, IN 46556, USA.

WEINSTEIN, Michael Alan, BA, MA, PhD; American political philosopher, academic and writer; b. 24 Aug. 1942, New York, NY; m. Deena Schneiweiss 1964. *Education:* New York University, Western Reserve University. *Career:* Asst Prof., Western Reserve University, 1967, Virginia Polytechnic Institute, 1967–68, Purdue University, 1972–; Distinguished Prof. of Political Science, University of Wyoming, 1979. *Publications:* The Polarity of Mexican Thought: Instrumentalism and Finalism, 1976; The Tragic Sense of Political Life, 1977; Meaning and Appreciation: Time and Modern Political Life, 1978; The Structure of Human Life: A Vitalist Ontology, 1979; The Wilderness and the City: American Classical Philosophy as a Moral Quest, 1982; Unity and Variety in the Philosophy of Samuel Alexander, 1984; Finite Perfection: Reflections on Virtue, 1985; Culture Critique: Fernand Dumont and the New Quebec Sociology, 1985; Data Trash, 1994; Culture/Flesh: Explorations of Postcivilized Modernity, 1995. Contributions: Magazines and journals. *Honours:* Best Paper Prize, Midwest Political Science Asscn, 1969; Guggenheim Fellowship, 1974–75; Rockefeller Foundation Humanities Fellowship, 1976.

WEINTRAUB, Stanley, BS, MA, PhD; American academic, writer and editor; *Professor Emeritus of Arts and Humanities, Pennsylvania State University;* b. 17 April 1929, Philadelphia, Pa; m. Rodelle Horwitz 1954; two s. one d. *Education:* West Chester State College, PA, Temple Univ., Pennsylvania State Univ. *Career:* Instructor, Pennsylvania State Univ. 1953–59, Asst Prof. 1959–62, Assoc. Prof. 1962–65, Prof. of English 1965–70, Research Prof. 1970–86, Evan Pugh Prof. of Arts and Humanities 1986–2000, Prof. Emer. 2000–; Visiting Prof., UCLA 1963, Univ. of Hawaii 1973, Univ. of Malaya 1977, Nat. Univ. of Singapore 1982; mem. Authors' Guild, Nat. Book Critics Circle. *Publications:* Private Shaw and Public Shaw: A Dual Portrait of Lawrence of Arabia and George Bernard Shaw 1963, The War in the Wards: Korea's Forgotten Battle 1964, The Art of William Golding (with B. S. Oldsey) 1965, Reggie: A Portrait of Reginald Turner 1965, Beardsley: A Biography 1967, The Last Great Cause: The Intellectuals and the Spanish Civil War 1968, Evolution of a Revolt: Early Postwar Writings of T. E. Lawrence (with R. Weintraub) 1968, Journey to Heartbreak: The Crucible Years of Bernard Shaw 1914–1918 1971, Whistler: A Biography 1974, Lawrence of Arabia: The Literary Impulse (with R. Weintraub) 1975, Aubrey Beardsley: Imp of the Perverse 1976, Four Rossettis: A Victorian Biography 1977, The London Yankees: Portraits of American Writers and Artists in England 1894–1914 1979, The Unexpected Shaw: Biographical Approaches to G. B. Shaw and his Work 1982, A Stillness Heard Round the World: The End of the Great War 1985, Victoria: An Intimate Biography 1987, Long Day's Journey into War: December 7, 1941 1991, Bernard Shaw: A Guide to Research 1992, Disraeli: A Biography 1993, The Last Great Victory: The End of World War II, July/August 1945 1995, Shaw's People, Victoria to Churchill 1996, Albert, Uncrowned King 1997, MacArthur's War: Korea and the Undoing of an American Hero 2000, The Importance of Being Edward: King in Waiting, 1841–1901 2000, Silent Night: The Remarkable 1914 Christmas Truce 2001, Charlotte and Lionel: A Rothschild Love Story 2003, General Washington's Christmas Farewell: A Mount Vernon Homecoming 1783 2003, Iron Tears: America's Battle for Freedom, Britain's Quagmire: 1775–1783 2005; ed. of over 20 vols; contrib. to professional journals, Oxford Dictionary of National Biography 2004. *Honours:* Guggenheim Fellowship 1968–69, Pennsylvania Humanities Council Distinguished Humanist Award 1985. *Address:* 4 Winterfield Court, Beech Hill, Newark, DE 19711, USA. *E-mail:* sqw4@comcast.net.

WEIR, Anne, BA, MEd; American writer; b. 9 Feb. 1942, Boston, MA; three d. *Education:* Smith and Swarthmore Colleges, University of Maine. *Publications:* A Book of Certainties, 1992; Marlowe: Being in the Life of the Mind, 1996; The Color Book, 1998.

WEIR, Hugh William Lindsay, DLitt; Irish writer and publisher; *Managing Director, Weir Publishing Group;* b. 29 Aug. 1934; m. The Hon. Grania O'Brien 1973. *Education:* Trinity Coll., UIC, Trinity Coll., Dublin. *Career:* Managing Dir, Weir Publishing Group, Ballinakella Press and Bell'acards; mem. Irish Writers' Union. *Publications:* Hall Craig – Words on an Irish House, Ennis – 750 Facts, O'Brien People and Places, Houses of Clare, Ireland – A Thousand Kings, O'Connor People and Places, The Clare Young Environmentalists, One of Our Own: Memoirs of Change, Brian Boru: High King of Ireland, 941–1014; short stories, academic articles/essays and topographical/historical contributions made to various anthologies and books; contrib. to The Other Clare, The Clare Champion, The Church of Ireland Gazette, The Catholic Twin Circle, English Digest. *Honours:* Oidhreacht Award. *Address:* Ballinakella Lodge, Whitegate, County Clare, Ireland (office). *Telephone:* (61) 927030 (office); (61) 927030 (home). *Fax:* (61) 927418 (office). *E-mail:* weirgroup@hotmail.com (office).

WEISSBORT, Daniel, BA; British poet, translator, editor and academic; *Professor Emeritus, University of Iowa;* b. 1 May 1935, London. *Education:* Queens' Coll., Cambridge. *Career:* Co-founder (with Ted Hughes) Modern Poetry in Translation magazine 1966–83, Ed. relaunched version 1992–2004; Prof., Univ. of Iowa 1980, Prof. Emer. of the Translation Program. *Publications:* The Leaseholder 1971, In an Emergency 1972, Soundings 1977, Leaseholder: New and Collected Poems, 1965–85 1986, Inscription 1990, Lake 1993, Letters to Ted 2002, From Russia with Love 2004, Translation – Theory and Practice (co-author and co-ed.) 2006; editor: Far from Sodom: Selected Poems of Inna Lisnianskaya 2005, An Anthology of Russian Women Poets 2006, Selected Translations of Ted Hughes 2006; ed. and translator of Russian literature. *Honours:* Hon. Research Fellow, Dept of English, King's Coll., London; Hon. Prof., Centre for Translation and Comparative Cultural Studies, Univ. of Warwick 2003; Arts Council Literature Award 1984. *Address:* 3 Powis Gardens, London, NW11 8HH, England (home). *Telephone:* (20) 8632-9533 (office). *Fax:* (20) 8632-9533 (home). *E-mail:* weissbort@mpit.demon.co.uk (home).

WELCH, Liliane, BA, MA, PhD; Canadian academic, poet and writer; *Professor Emerita of French Literature, Mount Allison University;* b. 20 Oct. 1937, Luxembourg; m. Cyril Welch; one d. *Education:* Univ. of Montana, Pennsylvania State Univ. *Career:* Asst Prof. East Carolina Univ. 1965–66, Antioch Coll., Ohio 1966–67; Asst Prof. 1967–71, Assoc. Prof. 1971–72, Prof. of French Literature 1972–2003, Prof. Emer. 2003–; mem. Mount Allison Univ.; mem. Asscn of Italian-Canadian Poets, Federation of New Brunswick Writers, League of Canadian Poets, Letzebuerger Schrifttseller Verband; corresp. mem. Institut Grand Ducal de Luxembourg 1998. *Publications:* Emergence: Baudelaire, Mallarmé, Rimbaud 1973, Winter Songs 1973, Syntax of Ferment 1979, Assailing Beats 1979, October Winds 1980, Brush and Trunks 1981, From the Songs of the Artisans 1983, Manstoma 1985, Rest Unbound 1985, Word-House of a Grandchild 1987, Seismographs: Selected Essays and Reviews 1988, Fire to the Looms Below 1990, Life in Another Language 1992, Von Menschen und Orten 1992, Dream Museum 1995, Fidelities 1997, Frescoes: Travel Pieces 1998, The Rock's Stillness (poems) 1999, Unlearning Ice (poems) 2001, Untethered in Paradise (prose and poems) 2002, This Numinous Bond (poems) 2003, Dispensing Grace (poems) 2004; contrib. to professional and literary journals. *Honours:* Alfred Bailey Prize 1986, Bressani Prize 1992. *Address:* PO Box 1652, Sackville, NB E4L 1G6, Canada.

WELCH, Robert, BA, MA, PhD; Irish academic, writer, poet and editor; b. 25 Nov. 1947, Cork; m. Angela Welch 1970, three s. *Education:* National University of Ireland, University of Leeds. *Career:* Lecturer, University of Leeds, 1971–73, 1974–84, University of Ife, Nigeria, 1973–74; Visiting Lecturer, National University of Ireland, 1982; Prof. of English, 1984–, Head, Dept of English, Media and Theatre Studies, 1984–94, Dir, Centre for Irish Literature and Bibliography, 1994–, University of Ulster; Founder-General Ed., Ulster Editions and Monographs, 1988–. *Publications:* Irish Poetry from Moore to Yeats, 1980; The Way Back: George Moore's The Untilled Field and The Lake (ed.), 1982; A History of Verse from the Irish, 1789–1897, 1988; Literature and the Art of Creation: Essays in Honour of A. N. Jeffares (co-ed.), 1988; Muskerry (poems), 1991; Irish Writers and Religion (ed.), 1991; Changing States: Transformations in Modern Irish Writing, 1993; W. B. Yeats: Irish Folklore, Legend, and Myth (ed.), 1993; The Kilcolman Notebook (novel), 1994; The Oxford Companion to Irish Literature (ed.), 1996; Irish Myths, 1996; Patrick Falvin: New and Selected Poems (co-ed.), 1996; Groundwork (novel), 1997; Secret Societies (poems), 1997; Tearmann (novel), 1997; The Blue Formica Table (poems), 1998; A History of the Abbey Theatre, 1998; The Plays and Poems of J. M. Synge, 1999; The Concise Companion to Irish Literature, 2000. Contributions: books and periodicals. *Honours:* Visiting Fellow, St John's College, Oxford, 1986; Grants, Leverhulme Trust, 1989, Community Relations Council, 1990, British Acad., 1996; Critics Award, O'Reachtas, 1996.

WELDON, Fay, CBE, MA, FRSA; British author; b. 22 Sept. 1931, Alvechurch, Worcs.; d. of Frank T. Birkinshaw and Margaret J. Birkinshaw; m. 1st Ronald Weldon 1960 (divorced 1994); four s.; m. 2nd Nicholas Fox 1995. *Education:* Girls' High School, Christchurch, New Zealand, South Hampstead School for Girls and Univ. of St Andrews. *Career:* Chair. of Judges, Booker McConnell Prize 1983; Writer-in-Residence Savoy Hotel, London Oct.-Dec. 2002; Chair. of Creative Writing Brunel Univ. 2006–; fmr mem. Arts Council Literary Panel; mem. Video Censorship Appeals Cttee. *Theatre plays:* Words of Advice 1974, Friends 1975, Moving House 1976, Mr Director 1977, Action Replay 1979, I Love My Love 1981, Woodworm 1981, Jane Eyre 1986, The Hole in the Top of the World 1987, Jane Eyre (adaptation), Playhouse Theatre, London 1995, The Four Alice Bakers, Birmingham Repertory 1999, Breakfast with Emma, Lyric Hammersmith 2003; more than 30 television plays, dramatizations and radio plays. *Television:* Big Women (series), Channel 4 1999. *Publications:* novels: The Fat Woman's Joke (aka And the Wife Ran Away) 1967, Down Among the Women 1972, Female Friends 1975, Remember Me 1976, Little Sisters (aka Words of Advice) 1977, Praxis 1978, Puffball 1980, The President's Child 1982, The Life and Loves of a She-Devil 1984, The Shrapnel Academy 1986, The Heart of the Country 1987, The Hearts and Lives of Men 1987, The Rules of Life (novella) 1987, Leader of the Band 1988, The Cloning of Joanna May 1989, Darcy's Utopia 1990, Growing Rich 1992, Life Force 1992, Affliction (aka Trouble) 1994, Splitting 1995, Worst Fears 1996, Big Women 1997, Rhode Island Blues 2000, Bulgari Connection 2001, She May Not Leave 2005; children's books: Wolf the Mechanical Dog 1988, Party Puddle 1989, Nobody Likes Me! 1997; short story collections: Watching Me Watching You 1981, Polaris 1985, Moon Over Minneapolis 1991, Wicked Women 1995, Angel All Innocence and Other Stories 1995, A Hard Time to be a Father 1998, Nothing to Wear, Nowhere to Hide 2002; other: Letters to Alice 1984, Rebecca West 1985, Godless in Eden (essays) 2000, Auto da Fay (autobiog.) 2002, Mantrapped (autobiog.) 2004, What Makes Women Happy 2006. *Honours:* Fellow City of Bath Coll. 1999; Hon. DLitt (Bath) 1989, (St Andrews) 1992, (Birmingham); Women in Publishing Pandora Award 1997. *Literary Agent:* c/o Jonathan Lloyd, Curtis Brown, Haymarket House, 29 Haymarket, London, SW1Y 4SP, England.

WELLAND, Colin; British playwright and actor; b. (Colin Williams), 4 July 1934, Liverpool; s. of John Arthur Williams and Norah Williams; m. Patricia Sweeney 1962; one s. three d. *Education:* Newton-le-Willows Grammar School, Bretton Hall, Goldsmiths' Coll., London. *Career:* art teacher 1958–62; entered theatre 1962, Library Theatre, Manchester 1962–64; Fellow Goldsmiths Coll., Univ. of London 2001. *Stage roles:* Waiting for Godot 1987, The Churchill Play, Man of Magic, Say Goodnight to Grandma, Ubu Roi. *Plays written:* Roomful of Holes 1972, Say Goodnight to Grandma 1973, Roll on Four O'Clock 1981. *Film roles:* Kes (BAFTA Award for Best Supporting Actor), Villain, Straw Dogs, Sweeney, The Secret Life of Ian Fleming, Dancing through the Dark. *Screenplays:* Yanks 1978, Chariots of Fire 1980 (Acad. Award), Twice in a Lifetime 1986, A Dry White Season, War of the Buttons 1994. *Television appearances:* Blue Remembered Hills, The Fix, United Kingdom. *Television plays include:* Kisses at 50, Leeds United, Your Man from Six Counties, Bambino Mio, Slattery's Mounted Foot, Jack Point, The Hallelujah Handshake, Roll on Four O'Clock (BAFTA Award for Best TV Screenplay). *Literary Agent:* c/o PFD, Drury House, 34–43 Russell Street, London, WC2B 5HA, England. *Telephone:* (20) 7344-1000. *Website:* www.pfd .co.uk.

WELLS, Peter Frederick, (John Flint), MA, DPhil; British/New Zealand academic and writer; b. 28 Feb. 1918, Cardiff, Wales; m. 1st Jeanne Chiles 1945; three s.; m. 2nd Rita Davenport 1994. *Education:* University of Wales, University of Waikato, New Zealand. *Career:* migrated to New Zealand; Head Language Studies Dept, University of Waikato 1961–73; Dir Institute of Modern Languages, James Cook University of North Queensland 1974–84; mem. Founder Pres. New Zealand-Japan Society, Hamilton. *Publications:* Let's Learn French 1963, Les Quatre Saisons 1966, Let's Learn Japanese 1968, Nihongo no Kakikata 1971, A Description of Kalaw Kawaw Ya 1976; other: Anthology of Poems by Ishikawa Takuboku 1972, Phonetics and Orthography of French 1975, Three Loves and a Minesweeper 1998, Myra Migrating 1999; contrib. to Journal of Modern Languages and Literature, Bulletin de L'Asscn G. Budé, New Zealand Journal of French Studies, Education, LINQ, English Language and Literature Asscn. *Honours:* Order of the Sacred Treasure, Japan, Order of New Zealand. *Address:* 249 Bankwood Road, Chartwell, Hamilton, New Zealand.

WELLS, Robert; British poet and translator; b. 17 Aug. 1947, Oxford, England. *Education:* King's Coll., Cambridge. *Career:* teacher, Univ. of Leicester 1979–82. *Publications:* Shade Mariners (with Dick Davis and Clive Wilmer) 1970, The Winter's Task: Poems 1977, The Georgics, by Virgil (trans., four vols) 1981, Selected Poems 1986, The Idylls, by Theocritus (trans.) 1988, The Day and Other Poems 2006. *Address:* 6 Rue Albert Houdin, 41000, Blois, France (home).

WELLS, Roger, BA, DPhil; British academic and writer; b. 30 Jan. 1947, London, England; m. (divorced); one s. one d. *Education:* University of York. *Career:* Lecturer, University of Wales, 1972–73, University of Exeter, 1973–75, University of York, 1975–76; Senior Lecturer, University of Brighton, 1976–95; Prof. of History, Christ Church University College, Canterbury, 1995–; mem. Royal Historical Society. *Publications:* Dearth and Distress in Yorkshire, 1793–1801, 1977; Riot and Political Disaffection in Nottinghamshire in the Age of Revolutions 1776–1803, 1983; Insurrection: The British Experience 1795–1803, 1983; Wretched Faces: Famine in Wartime England, 1793–1801, 1988; Class, Conflict and Protest in the English Countryside (with M. Reed), 1700–1880, 1990; Victorian Village, 1992; Crime, Protest and Popular Politics in Southern England c. 1740–1850 (with J. Rule), 1997. Contributions: Social History; Rural History; Southern History; Northern History; Policing and Society; Journal of Peasant Studies; Journal of Historical Geography; Local Historian; English Historical Review; Agricultural History Review; London Journal; Labour History Bulletin; Journal of Social Policy. *Address:* Christ Church University College, Canterbury, Kent CT1 1QU, England. *E-mail:* r.wells@cant.ac.uk.

WELLS, Stanley William, CBE; British writer and editor; *Emeritus Professor, University of Birmingham. Career:* fmr Prof. of Shakespeare Studies, and Dir of the Shakespeare Institute, Univ. of Birmingham 1988–97, now Emeritus Prof.; currently Chair., Shakespeare Birthplace Trust, Stratford. *Publications:* Oxford Shakespeare Topics (gen. ed. with Peter Holland), Shakespeare: A Reading Guide 1969, Literature and Drama: With Special Reference to Shakespeare and his Contemporaries 1970, Shakespeare: Select Bibliographical Guides (ed.) 1974, Shakespeare: An Illustrated Dictionary (ed.) 1978, Royal Shakespeare: Four Major Productions at Stratford-upon-Avon 1977, Shakespeare 1978, Modernizing Shakespeare's Spelling: With Three Studies of the Text of Henry V (with Gary Taylor) 1979, Re-editing Shakespeare for the Modern Reader 1984, Twelfth Night: Critical Essays (ed.) 1986, The Cambridge Companion to Shakespeare (ed.) 1986, Shakespeare: A Bibliography 1989, Shakespeare and the Moving Image: The Plays on Film and Television (ed. with Anthony Davies) 1994, Shakespeare: A Dramatic Career 1994, Shakespeare – A Life in Drama 1995, Shakespeare in the Theatre: An Anthology of Criticism (ed.) 1997, Shakespeare: The Poet and His Plays 1997, Summerfolk: Essays Celebrating Shakespeare (ed.) 1997, A Dictionary of Shakespeare 1998, Shakespeare and Race (co-ed. with Catherine Alexander) 2000, Oxford Companion to Shakespeare (ed. with Michael Dobson) 2001, Shakespeare and Sexuality (ed. with Catherine M. S. Alexander) 2001, Shakespeare Surveys (ed. with others) 2002, Shakespeare: For All Time 2002, The Cambridge Companion to Shakespeare on Stage (ed. with Sarah Stanton) 2002, Shakespeare: An Oxford Guide (ed. with Lena

Cowen Orlin) 2003, Looking for Sex in Shakespeare 2004, Shakespeare's Sonnets (with Paul Edmondson) 2004, Shakespeare & Co 2006; gen. ed., co-ed., numerous editions, anthologies and collections of Shakespeare's plays. *Address:* c/o Shakespeare Birthplace Trust, Shakespeare Centre, Henley Street, Stratford-upon-Avon, Warwickshire CV37 6QW, England (office).

WELSH, Irvine, MBA; British writer; b. 1958, Edinburgh, Scotland. *Education:* Heriot-Watt Univ. *Career:* co-owner, 4 Way Productions film studio; Amb. for Unicef. *Publications:* Trainspotting (novel) 1993, The Acid House (short stories) 1994, Marabou Stork Nightmares: A Novel 1995, Ecstasy: Three Chemical Romances 1996, The Wedding (with Nick Wapling-ton) 1996, You'll Have Had Your Hole (play) 1997, Filth: A Novel 1998, Glue (novel) 2000, Porno (novel) 2002, Soul Crew (screenplay, also dir) 2003, Meat Trade (screenplay) 2004, The Bedroom Secrets of the Master Chefs (novel) 2006, Babylon Heights (with Dean Cavanagh) 2006, If You Liked School, You'll Love Work (short stories) 2007; contrib. to newspapers; contrib. to anthologies, including Children of Albion Rovers 1996, Disco Biscuits 1996, Ahead of its Time 1997, The Weekenders 2002, One City 2006; contrib. to Loaded, Guardian, Daily Telegraph. *Address:* c/o Jonathan Cape, 20 Vauxhall Bridge Road, London, SW1V 2SA, England.

WELSH, Louise, BA; British novelist; b. 1968, Edinburgh, Scotland. *Education:* Glasgow Univ., Univ. of Strathclyde. *Career:* bookshop owner. *Plays:* The Cutting Room (adaptation of novel) 2004. *Publications:* The Cutting Room 2002, Tamburlaine Must Die 2004, The Bullet Trick 2006. *Honours:* CWA John Creasey Memorial Dagger, Saltire First Book Award (jt winner). *Address:* c/o Canongate Books, 14 High Street, Edinburgh, EH1 1TE, Scotland.

WELTNER, Peter Nissen, BA, PhD; American academic and writer; b. 12 May 1942, Plainfield, NJ; pnr Atticus Carr. *Education:* Hamilton College, Indiana University. *Career:* Prof. of English, San Francisco State University, 1969–. *Publications:* Beachside Entries-Specific Ghosts, 1989; Identity and Difference, 1990; In a Time for Combat for the Angel, 1991; The Risk of His Music, 1997; How the Body Prays, 1999. *Honours:* O. Henry Prizes, 1993, 1998; Book of the Year Silver Award, ForeWord Magazine.

WELTON, Matthew; British poet and editor; b. 1969, Nottingham, England. *Career:* Ed., Stand Magazine; teacher of creative writing, Bolton Inst. *Publications:* Slag Heap, The Book of Matthew (Aldburgh Best First Collection Prize) 2003; contrib. to anthologies, including First Pressings, New Poetries 2. *Honours:* Eric Gregory Award 1997. *Address:* Editorial Office, Stand Magazine, School of English, Leeds University, Leeds, LS2 9JT, England (office).

WENDT, Albert; Samoan/New Zealand author; b. 1939, Apia; three c. *Career:* Prof. Head of English Dept, Auckland Univ. *Publications include:* novels: Pouliuli, Leaves of the Banyan Tree, Sons for the Return Home, Ola, Black Rainbow; short stories: Flying Fox in a Freedom Tree, The Best of Albert Wendt's Short Stories; poetry: Photographs. *Honours:* Hon. PhD (Univ. de Bourgogne, France) 1993; Order of Merit (Western Samoa). *Address:* Department of English, University of Auckland, Private Bag 92019, Auckland 1, New Zealand. *Telephone:* (9) 373-7999. *Fax:* (9) 373-7400. *Website:* www .auckland.ac.nz (office).

WENER, Louise; British singer, songwriter and writer; b. 1966, Ilford, Essex, England; pnr Andy MacLure; one d. *Education:* Manchester Univ. *Career:* lead singer, Sleeper 1993–98; numerous tours, festival appearances; mem. PRS, MU, PAMRA; writer 2002–. *Recordings include:* albums: Smart 1995, It Girl 1996, Pleased To Meet You 1997. *Publications:* novels: Goodnight Steve McQueen 2002, The Big Blind (aka The Perfect Play) 2003, The Half Life of Stars 2006. *Address:* c/o Hodder & Stoughton, 338 Euston Road, London, NW1 3BH, England.

WENNER, Jann S.; American publisher; *Editor and Publisher, Rolling Stone;* b. 7 Jan. 1946, New York, NY; m. Jane Schindelheim (divorced); three s. *Career:* founder, Ed. and Publisher, Rolling Stone magazine 1967–; TV appearances include Crime Story 1987–88; currently oversees Us and Men's Journal magazines; Chair., Wenner Media Inc. *Film appearances:* Up Your Legs Forever 1970, Perfect 1985, Jerry Maguire 1996, Almost Famous 2000. *Publications include:* Lennon Remembers (ed.) 1972, 20 Years of Rolling Stone: What a Long Strange Trip It's Been 1987, Rolling Stone Environmental Reader 1992. *Address:* Rolling Stone, Wenner Media Inc., 1290 Avenue of the Americas, New York, NY 10104-0298, USA (office). *Telephone:* (212) 484-1616 (office). *Website:* www.rollingstone.com (office).

WENTWORTH, Wendy (see Chaplin, Jenny)

WERBER, Bernard; French writer; b. Sept. 1961, Toulouse. *Education:* Ecole Supérieure de Journalisme de Paris. *Career:* scientific reviewer, Nouvel Observateur 1984–90. *Publications:* novels: The Ants 1991, The Day of the Ants 1992, The Secret Book of the Ants 1993, The Thanatonautes 1994, The Revolution of the Ants 1996, The Journey's Book 1997, The Father of our Fathers 1998. *Literary Agent:* Jacqueline Farvero, 22 rue Huygens, Paris 75014, France. *E-mail:* bwerber@free.fr. *Website:* www.bernardwerber.com.

WERTENBAKER, Timberlake, FRSL; British playwright; m. John Man; one d. *Career:* Resident Playwright, Royal Court Theatre 1984–85; Dir English Stage Co. 1991–99; mem. Exec. Cttee PEN 1999–2002; Royden B. Davis Visiting Prof. of Theatre, Georgetown Univ., Washington, DC 2005–06. *Plays include:* (for the Soho-Poly): Case to Answer 1980; (for the Women's

Theatre Group): New Anatomies 1982; (for the Royal Court): Abel's Sister 1984, The Grace of Mary Traverse 1985, Our Country's Good 1988, Three Birds Alighting on a Field 1991, Credible Witness 2001; (for Out of Joint): The Break of Day 1995; (for RSC): The Love of the Nightingale 1988; (for Hampstead Theatre): After Darwin 1998; (for Birmingham Rep.): The Ash Girl 2000; (for Theatre Royal, Bath): Galileo's Daughter 2004; (for RSC): trans. Arianne Mnouchkine's Mephisto, trans. Sophocles' Thebans; (for San Francisco ACT): trans. Euripides' Hecuba; (for Peter Hall Co.): trans. Eduardo de Filippo's Filumena (Piccadilly Theatre) 1998, (for Chichester) Jean Anouilh's Wild Orchards 2002; other trans. include Successful Strategies, False Admissions, La Dispute (Marivaux), Come tu mi vuoi (Pirandello), Pelleas and Mélisande (Maeterlinck). *Radio includes:* Credible Witness, Dianeira, Hecuba (trans. and adaptation), The H. File (adaptation of novel by Ismail Kadaré), Scenes of Seduction 2005, Divine Intervention 2006. *Television:* Belle and the Beast (BBC). *Films:* The Children (Channel 4), Do Not Disturb (BBC TV). *Publications:* Timberlake Wertenbaker: Plays 1996, The Break of Day 1996, After Darwin 1999, Filumena 1999, The Ash Girl 2000, Credible Witness 2001, Timberlake Wertenbaker: Plays 2 2002. *Honours:* Dr hc (Open Univ.); Guggenheim Fellowship 2004; Plays and Players Most Promising Playwright (for The Grace of Mary Traverse) 1985, Evening Standard Most Promising Playwright, Olivier Play of the Year (for Our Country's Good) 1988, Eileen Anderson Cen. Drama Award (for The Love of the Nightingale) 1989, Critics' Circle Best West End Play 1991, Writers' Guild Best West End Play, Susan Smith Blackburn Award (for Three Birds Alighting on a Field) 1992, Mrs Giles Whiting Award (for gen. body of work) 1989. *Address:* c/o Casarotto Ramsay, National House, 60–66 Wardour Street, London, W1V 4ND, England.

WESKER, Sir Arnold, Kt, FRSL; British playwright and director; b. 24 May 1932, Stepney, London; s. of Joseph Wesker and Leah Wesker (née Perlmutter); m. Doreen (Dusty) Cecile Bicker 1958; two s. one d. *Education:* mixed elementary schools and Upton House Central School, Hackney, London, London School of Film Technique. *Career:* left school 1948, worked as furniture maker's apprentice, carpenter's mate, bookseller's asst; RAF 1950–52 (ran drama group); plumber's mate, road labourer, farm labourer, seed sorter, kitchen porter and pastry-cook; Dir Centre 42 1961–70; Chair. British Centre of Int. Theatre Inst. 1978–82; Pres. Int. Cttee of Playwrights 1979–83; Arts Council Bursary 1959. *Film scripts:* The Master (free adaptation of An Unfortunate Incident by F. Dostoevsky) 1966, Madam Solario (from anonymous novel of same title) 1969, The Wesker Trilogy 1979, Lady Othello 1980, Homage to Catalonia (from George Orwell's autobiog.) 1991, Maudie (from Doris Lessing's novel Diary of a Good Neighbour) 1995, The Kitchen (for Italian film co.). *Opera libretto:* Caritas (music by Robert Saxton) 1988, Grief (one-woman opera commissioned by Shigeaki Saegusa) 2004. *Plays:* The Kitchen, Royal Court Theatre 1959, 1961, 1994, Chicken Soup with Barley, Roots, I'm Talking about Jerusalem (Trilogy), Belgrade Theatre, Coventry 1958–60, Royal Court Theatre 1960, Chips with Everything, Royal Court 1962, Vaudeville 1962, Broadway 1963, The Four Seasons, Belgrade Theatre and Saville 1965, Their Very Own and Golden City, Brussels and Royal Court 1966, The Friends (Stockholm and London) 1970, The Old Ones, Royal Court 1972, The Wedding Feast, Stockholm 1974, Leeds 1977, The Journalists, Coventry 1977, Germany 1981, The Merchant (later entitled Shylock), Stockholm and Århus 1976, Broadway 1977, Birmingham 1978, Love Letters on Blue Paper, Nat. Theatre 1978, Fatlips 1978, Caritas, Nat. Theatre 1981, Sullied Hand 1981, Edinburgh Festival and Finnish TV 1984, Four Portraits, Tokyo 1982, Edin. Festival 1984, Annie Wobbler, Birmingham 1983, Fortune Theatre 1984, New York 1986, One More Ride on the Merry-Go-Round, Leicester 1985, Yardsale, Edinburgh Festival and Stratford-on-Avon 1985, When God Wanted a Son 1986, Whatever Happened to Betty Lemon, Yardsale, London 1987, Little Old Lady, Sweden 1988, The Mistress 1988, Beorhtel's Hill, Towngate, Basildon 1989, Three Women Talking (now Men Die Women Survive) 1990, Chicago 1992, Letters to a Daughter 1990, Blood Libel 1991, Wild Spring 1992, Tokyo 1994, Denial, Bristol Old Vic 2000, Groupie 2001 (based on radio play), Longitude 2002 (adaptation of book by Dava Sobel), Letter To Myself 2004; 45-minute adaptations for Schools Shakespeare Festival of Much Ado About Nothing and Henry V 2006. *Own plays directed:* The Four Seasons, Cuba 1968, world première of The Friends at Stadsteatern, Stockholm 1970, London 1970, The Old Ones, Munich, Their Very Own and Golden City, Århus 1974, Love Letters on Blue Paper, Nat. Theatre 1978, Oslo 1980, Annie Wobbler, Birmingham 1983, London 1984, Yardsale and Whatever Happened to Betty Lemon, London 1987, Shylock (workshop production), London 1989, The Kitchen, Univ. of Wis. 1990, The Mistress, Rome 1991, The Wedding Feast, Denison Univ., Ohio 1995, Letter to a Daughter, Edin. Festival 1998; also Dir Osborne's The Entertainer, Theatre Clwyd 1983, The Merry Wives of Windsor, Oslo 1989. *Radio includes:* Bluey (Cologne Radio) 1985, (BBC) 1985, Groupie (commissioned by BBC) 2001, adaptation of Shylock (commissioned by BBC Radio 3) 2006. *Adaptations for TV:* Menace 1961, Thieves in the Night (Arthur Koestler) 1984–85, Diary of a Good Neighbour (Doris Lessing) 1989, Phoenix Phoenix Burning Bright (from own story, The Visit) 1992, Barabbas 2000. *Publications:* plays: The Kitchen 1957, Chicken Soup with Barley 1958, Roots 1959, I'm Talking About Jerusalem 1960, Chips with Everything 1962, The Four Seasons 1965, Their Very Own and Golden City 1966, The Old Ones 1970, The Friends 1970, The Journalists 1972, The Wedding Feast 1974, Shylock (previously The Merchant) 1976, Love Letters on Blue Paper (TV play) 1976, (stage play) 1977, Words – As Definitions of

Experience 1976, One More Ride on the Merry-Go-Round 1978, Fatlips 1980, Caritas 1980, Annie Wobbler 1982, Four Portraits – of Mothers 1982, Yardsale 1983, Cinders 1983, Bluey 1984, Whatever Happened to Betty Lemon 1986, When God Wanted a Son 1986, Badenheim 1939 1987, Shoeshine & Little Old Lady 1987, Lady Othello 1987, Beorhtel's Hill 1988, The Mistress 1988, Three Women Talking 1990, Letter to a Daughter 1990, Blood Libel 1991, Wild Spring 1992, Circles of Perception 1996, Break My Heart 1997, Denial 1997; essays, stories, etc.: Fears of Fragmentation 1971, Six Sundays in January 1971, Love Letters on Blue Paper 1974, Journey into Journalism 1977, Said the Old Man to the Young Man 1978, Distinctions 1985, As Much As I Dare (autobiog.) 1994, The Birth of Shylock and the Death of Zero Mostel (non-fiction) 1997, The King's Daughters 1998, The Wesker Trilogy 2001, One Woman Plays 2001; novels: Honey 2005, Longitude 2006. *Honours:* Hon. Fellow, Queen Mary Coll. London 1995; Hon. DLitt (Univ. of E Anglia) 1989; Hon. DHumLitt (Denison Univ., Ohio) 1997; Evening Standard Award for Most Promising Playwright (for Roots) 1959, third prize Encyclopaedia Britannica Competition (for The Kitchen) 1961, Premio Marzotto Drama Prize (for Their Very Own and Golden City) 1964, Gold Medal, Premios el Espectador y la Critica (for The Kitchen) 1973, (for Chicken Soup with Barley) 1979, The Goldie Award (for Roots) 1986, Last Frontier Award for Lifetime Achievement, Valdez, Alaska 1999, Royal Literary Fund annual pension and award for lifetime achievement 2003. *Address:* Hay on Wye, Hereford, HR3 5RJ, England (home). *Telephone:* (1497) 820473 (home). *Fax:* (1497) 821005 (home). *E-mail:* wesker@compuserve.com (home). *Website:* www.arnoldwesker.com (home).

WEST, Cornel Ronald, AB, MA, PhD; American academic and writer; b. 2 June 1953, Tulsa, Oklahoma; m. 1st (divorced); one s.; m. 2nd (divorced); m. 3rd Elleni West. *Education:* Harvard University, Princeton University. *Career:* Asst Prof. of the Philosophy of Religion, Union Theological Seminary, New York City, 1977–83, 1988; Assoc., Yale University Divinity School, 1984–87; University of Paris, 1987; Prof., Princeton University, 1989–94, 2002–, Harvard University, 1994–2002. *Publications:* Theology in the Americas: Detroit II Conference Papers (ed. with Caridad Guidote and Margaret Coakley), 1982; Prophesy Deliverance!: An Afro-American Revolutionary Christianity, 1982; Post-Analytic Philosophy (with John Rajchman), 1985; Prophetic Fragments, 1988; The American Evasion of Philosophy: A Genealogy of Pragmatism, 1989; Breaking Bread: Insurgent Black Intellectual Life (with Bell Hooks), 1991; The Ethical Dimensions of Marxist Thought, 1991; Out There: Marginalization and Contemporary Cultures (co-ed.), 1991; Race Matters, 1993; Keeping Faith: Philosophy and Race in America, 1993; Beyond Eurocentrism and Multiculturalism, 1993; The Cornel West Reader, 1999; The African American Century: How Black Americans Have Shaped Our Country (with Henry Louis Gates Jr), 2000. Contributions: newspapers and magazines. *Address:* c/o Harvard University, Cambridge, MA 02138, USA.

WEST, Douglas (see Tubb, Edwin Charles)

WEST, Ewan Donald, BA, MA, MBA, DPhil; British writer on music; b. 9 Aug. 1960, Cheltenham, Gloucestershire, England. *Education:* Exeter Coll., Oxford, Cranfield School of Management. *Career:* Lecturer on History of Music, Worcester Coll., Oxford 1986–94; Jr Research Fellow, Mansfield Coll., Oxford 1988–92; Dir of Studies in Music, Somerville Coll., Oxford 1989–94; mem. American Musicological Soc., Royal Musical Asscn. *Publications:* The Hamlyn Dictionary of Music 1982, The Oxford Dictionary of Opera (with John Warrack) 1992, The Concise Oxford Dictionary of Opera (third edn, with John Warrack) 1996; contrib. to Music and Letters, Austrian Studies. *Honours:* Univ. of Oxford James Ingham Halstead Scholar 1985–87. *Address:* 14 Moorhouse Road, London, W2 5DJ, England (office). *Telephone:* (20) 7221-6001 (home). *E-mail:* wean_west@hotmail.com (home).

WEST, Kathleene, BA, MA, PhD; American academic, poet and editor; b. 28 Dec. 1947, Genoa, NE. *Education:* University of Nebraska, University of Washington. *Career:* Assoc. Prof. of English, New Mexico State University, 1987–; Poetry Ed., Puerto del Sol, 1995–; mem. Associated Writing Programs; Barbara Pym Society; PEN. *Publications:* Land Bound, 1977; Water Witching, 1984; Plainswoman, 1985; The Farmer's Daughter, 1990. Contributions: reviews, quarterlies and journals. *Honours:* Fulbright Scholar, Iceland 1983–85.

WEST, Nigel; British writer; b. 8 Nov. 1951, London; m. 1979 (divorced 1996); one s. one d. *Education:* Univs of Grenoble and Lille, France and Univ. of London. *Career:* worked for BBC TV 1977–82. *Publications:* Spy 1980, A Matter of Trust: M15 1945–72 1982, Unreliable Witness 1984, Carbo M15 1981, M16 1983, GCHQ 1986, Molehunt 1986, The Friends 1987, Games of Intelligence 1990, Seven Spies Who Changed the World 1991, Secret War 1992, The Illegals 1993, Faber Book of Espionage 1993, Faber Book of Treachery 1995, Secret War for the Falklands 1997, Crown Jewels 1998, Counterfeit Spies 1998, Venona 1999, The Third Secret 2000, Mortal Crimes 2004, The Guy Liddell Diaries (ed.) 2005, Mask 2005; contrib. to The Times, Intelligence Quarterly. *Honours:* Observer The Expert's Expert 1989, US Asscn of Former Intelligence Officers' Lifetime Literature Award. *Address:* Westintel Research Ltd, PO Box 2, Goring on Thames, Berks., RG8 9SB, England (office). *E-mail:* nigel@westintel.co.uk (office). *Website:* www .nigelwest.com (office).

WEST, Owen (see Koontz, Dean Ray)

WEST, Paul, MA; American (b. British) author; b. 23 Feb. 1930, Eckington, Derbyshire, England; s. of Alfred West and Mildred Noden. *Education:* Univ. of Oxford, UK and Columbia Univ. *Career:* served with RAF 1954–57; Asst Prof. of English, Memorial Univ., Newfoundland 1957–58, Assoc. Prof. 1958–60; arrived in USA 1961, became naturalized 1971; contrib., Washington Post, New York Times 1962–95, also contributes to Harper's and GQ magazines, Paris Review; mem. of staff Pa State Univ. 1962–, Prof. of English and Comparative Literature 1968–1995, Prof. Emer. 1995–; Crawshaw Prof., Colgate Univ. 1972; Melvin Hill Distinguished Visiting Prof., Hobart and William Smith Colls 1973; Distinguished Writer-in-Residence, Wichita State Univ. 1982; Writer-in-Residence, Univ. of Arizona 1984; Visiting Prof. of English, Cornell Univ. 1986, Brown Univ. 1992; Guggenheim Fellow 1962–63; Nat. Endowment for Arts Creative Writing Fellow 1979, 1984; mem. Author's Guild. *Publications include:* Byron and the Spoiler's Art 1960, I, Said the Sparrow 1963, The Snow Leopard 1965, Tenement of Clay 1965, The Wine of Absurdity 1966, I'm Expecting to Live Quite Soon 1970, Words for a Deaf Daughter 1970, Caliban's Filibuster 1971, Bela Lugosi's White Christmas 1972, Colonel Mint 1973, Gala 1976, The Very Rich Hours of Count von Stauffenberg 1980, Out of My Depths: A Swimmer in the Universe and Other Fictions 1988, The Place in Flowers Where Pollen Rests 1988, Lord Byron's Doctor 1989, Portable People, The Women of Whitechapel and Jack the Ripper 1991, James Ensor 1991, Love's Mansion 1992, A Stroke of Genius 1995, Sporting with Amaryllis 1996, Terrestrials 1997, Life with Swan 1999, O.K.: The Corral 2000, The Earps 2000, Doc Holliday 2000, The Dry Danube: A Hitler Forgery 2000, The Secret Lives of Words 2000, A Fifth of November 2001, Master Class 2001, Portable People 2001. *Honours:* Chevalier, Ordre Arts et Lettres; Aga Khan Fiction Prize 1973, Hazlett Memorial Award for Excellence in Arts (Literature) 1981, Literature Award, American Acad. and Inst. of Arts and Letters 1985, Pushcart Prize 1987, 1991, Best American Essays Award 1990, Grand Prix Halpérine Kaminsky Award 1992, Lannan Fiction Award 1993, Teaching Award NE Asscn of Grad. Schools 1994, Art of Fact Prize, State Univ. of NY 2000; Outstanding Achievement Medal, Pa State Univ. 1991. *Address:* c/o Elaine Markson Agency, 44 Greenwich Avenue, Floor 3, New York, NY 10011, USA. *Telephone:* (212) 243-8480. *Fax:* (607) 257-0631.

WESTHEIMER, David, (Z. Z. Smith), BA; American writer and poet; b. 11 April 1917, Houston, TX; m. Doris Rothstein Kahn 1945; two s. *Education:* Rice Inst., Houston. *Career:* mem. California Writers' Club, Retd Officers' Asscn, Writers' Guild of America West. *Publications:* Summer on the Water 1948, The Magic Fallacy 1950, Watching Out for Dulie 1960, This Time Next Year 1963, Von Ryan's Express 1964, My Sweet Charlie 1965, Song of the Young Sentry 1968, Lighter Than a Feather 1971, Over the Edge 1972, Going Public 1973, The Aulia Gold 1974, The Olmec Head 1974, Von Ryan's Return 1980, Rider on the Wind 1984, Sitting it Out 1992, The Great Wounded Bird (poems) 2000, Delay en Route 2002. *Honours:* Texas Review Press Poetry Prize 2000. *Address:* 11722 Darlington Avenue, No. 2, Los Angeles, CA 90049, USA (home). *Fax:* (310) 826-6899 (home). *E-mail:* dwestheime@aol.com (home).

WESTLAKE, Donald Edwin, (John B. Allan, Curt Clark, Tucker Coe, Timothy J. Culver, Samuel Holt, Richard Stark); American writer; b. 12 July 1933, Brooklyn, NY; m. 3rd Abigail Adams; four s. *Education:* Champlain Coll., Plattsburgh, NY, Harpur Coll. (now the SUNY at Binghamton). *Publications:* The Mercenaries 1960, Killing Time 1961, 361 1962, Killy 1963, Pity Him Afterwards 1964, The Fugitive Pigeon 1964, The Busy Body 1966, The Spy in the Ointment 1966, God Save the Mark 1967, Philip (children's) 1967, Who Stole Sassi Manoon? 1968, The Curious Facts Preceding My Execution and Other Fictions 1968, Somebody Owes Me Money 1969, Up Your Banners 1969, Adios, Scheherazade 1970, The Hot Rock 1970, I Gave at the Office 1971, Under an English Heaven 1972, Cops and Robbers 1972, Bank Shot 1972, Gangway (with Brian Garfield) 1973, Help, I'm Being Held Prisoner 1974, Jimmy the Kid 1974, Two Much 1975, Brother's Keepers 1975, Dancing Aztecs 1976, Enough 1977, Nobody's Perfect 1977, Castle in the Air 1980, Kahawa 1982, Why Me? 1983, A Likely Story 1984, Levine (short stories) 1984, High Adventure 1985, Transylvania Station (with Abby Westlake) 1986, High Jinx (with Abby Westlake) 1986, Good Behaviour 1987, The Hood House Heist 1987, The Maltese Herring 1988, Way Out West 1988, Double Crossing 1988, Trust Me on This 1988, Sacred Monster 1989, Tomorrow's Crimes (short stories) 1989, Drowned Hopes 1990, Humans 1992, Don't Ask 1993, Baby Would I Lie? A Romance of the Ozarks 1994, Smoke 1995, The Ax 1997, What's the Worse that Could Happen? 1997, A Good Story and Other Stories 1999, Payback 1999, The Hook 2000, Bad News: A Dortmunder Novel 2001, Firebreak 2001, Put a Lid on it 2002, Money for Nothing 2003; as John B. Allan: Elizabeth Taylor: A Fascinating Story of America's Most Talented Actress and the World's Most Beautiful Woman 1961; as Curt Clark: Anarchaos 1966; as Tucker Coe: Kinds of Love, Kinds of Death 1966, Murder Among Children 1967, Wax Apple 1970, A Jade in Aries 1970, Don't Lie to Me 1972; as Timothy J. Culver: Ex Officio 1970; as Samuel Holt: One of us is Wrong 1986, I Know a Trick Worth Two of That 1986, What I Tell You Three Times is False 1987, The Fourth Dimension is Death 1989; as Richard Stark: The Hunter 1962, The Man with the Getaway Face 1963, The Outfit 1963, The Mourner 1963, The Score 1964, The Juggler 1965, The Seventh 1966, The Handle 1966, The Rare Coin Score 1967, The Green Eagle Score 1967, The Damsel 1967, The Black Ice Score 1968, The Sour Lemon Score 1969, The Dame 1969, The Blackbird 1969, Lemons Never Lie 1971, Deadly Edge 1971, Slayground 1971, Plunder Squad 1972, Butcher's Moon 1974, Child Heist 1974, Comeback 1998, Backflash 1998, Flashfire 2000, Breakout 2002, Ask the Parrot 2007; also screenplays, ed. of anthologies, contrib. to Alfred Hitchcock's Mystery Magazine. *Honours:* three MWA Edgar Awards, MWA Grand Master, Bouchercon Cttee Lifetime Achievement Award 1997. *Address:* c/o Author Mail, Warner Books, 1271 Avenue of the Americas, New York, NY 10020, USA. *Website:* www.donaldwestlake.com.

WESTÖ, Kjell; Finnish writer and poet; b. 1961. *Career:* writes in Swedish. *Publications:* Tango Orange (poems) 1986, Epitaf över Mr Nacht (poems) 1988, Avig-Bön (poems, as Anders Hed) 1989, Utslag och andra noveller (short stories) 1989, Fallet Bruus (short stories) 1992, Drakarna över Helsingfors (novel) 1996, Vådan av vara Skrake (novel) 2000, Lang 2002, Lugna favoriter 2004. *Honours:* Nat. Prize for Literature 1990, Young Finland Prize 1996, Thank You for the Book Medallion 1997, Shadow Finlandia Prize 2001, Helsinki Medallion 2002, Svenska kulturfondens kulturpris 2004. *Address:* c/o Harvill Press, Random House, 20 Vauxhall Bridge Road, London, SW1V 2SA, England.

WESTON, Helen Gray (see Daniels, Dorothy)

WEVILL, David Anthony, BA; Canadian academic and poet; b. 15 March 1935, Yokohama, Japan; m. Assia Gutman 1960. *Education:* Caius Coll., Cambridge. *Career:* Lecturer, Univ. of Texas, Austin. *Publications:* Penguin Modern Poets, 1963; Birth of a Spark, 1964; A Christ of the Ice Floes, 1966; Firebreak, 1971; Where the Arrow Falls, 1973; Other Names for the Heart: New and Selected Poems, 1964–84, 1985; Figures of Eight, 1987; Departures: Selected Poems, 2003; translations of Hungarian poetry.

WEYERGANS, François; Belgian writer and critic; b. 9 Dec. 1941, Etterbeek. *Education:* Jesuit school, Brussels and Institut des Hautes Études Cinématographiques, Paris. *Career:* fmr film dir; literary and film critic, contributing to Cahiers du cinéma. *Films:* Béjart (writer, dir) 1962, Hieronymus Bosch (writer, dir) 1963, Cinéma de notre temps: Robert Bresson - Ni vu, ni connu (TV film; dir) 1965, Beaudelaire est mort en été (dir) 1967, Aline (writer, dir) 1967, Un film sur quelqu'un (dir) 1972, Maladie mortelle (dir) 1977, Je t'aime, tu danses (writer, dir) 1977, Couleur chair (writer, dir) 1979, Une femme en Afrique (writer) 1985. *Publications:* novels: Le Pitre (Prix Roger Nimier) 1973, Berlin, mercredi 1979, Les Figurants (Prix de la Société des Gens de Lettres, Académie Royale de Langue et de Littérature françaises de Belgique Prix Sander Pierron) 1980, Macaire le Copte (Prix Rossel, Belgium, Prix des Deux Magots) 1981, Le Radeau de la méduse (Prix méridien des quatre jurys) 1983, La Vie d'un bébé 1986, Françaises, français 1988, Je suis écrivain 1989, Rire et pleurer 1990, La Démence du boxeur (Prix Renaudot) 1992, Franz et François (Grand prix de la langue française) 1997, Salomé 2005, Trois jours chez ma mère (Prix Goncourt) 2005. *Address:* c/o Éditions Grasset, 61 rue des Saints-Pères, 75006 Paris, France.

WEYMANN, Gert; German theatre director and playwright; b. 31 March 1919, Berlin; s. of Hans Weymann and Gertrud Israel. *Education:* Grammar School, Berlin and Berlin Univ. *Career:* asst dir, later dir Berlin theatre 1947–; worked as dir in several W German cities and New York; Lecturer in Drama Depts, American univs 1963, 1966; Lecturer, Goethe Inst., Berlin 1970–; perm. ind. mem. SFB (radio and TV plays). *Plays:* Generationen (Gerhart Hauptmann Prize 1954), Eh' die Brücken verbrennen, Der Ehrentag; TV plays: Das Liebesmahl eines Wucherers, Familie 1960; radio plays: Der Anhalter, Die Übergabe. *Address:* Karlsruher Strasse 7, 10711 Berlin, Germany. *Telephone:* (89) 11861.

WHALEN, Terry Anthony, BA, MA, PhD; Canadian academic, writer and editor; *Professor of English, St Mary's University;* b. 1 Feb. 1944, Halifax, NS; m. Maryann Antonia Walters, 30 Feb. 1966, two s. two d. *Education:* Saint Mary's University, University of Melbourne, University of Oxford, University of Ottawa. *Career:* Tutor, University of Sydney, 1966, University of Melbourne, 1967; Lecturer, 1968–70, Asst Prof., 1970–76, 1978–80, Assoc. Prof., 1981–85, Prof. of English, 1985–, St Mary's University; Teaching Fellow, University of Ottawa, 1976–77; Ed., Atlantic Provinces Book Review, 1980–90; Adjunct Graduate Prof. of English, Dalhousie University, 1996–; mem. Writers Federation of Nova Scotia; Asscn of Canadian University Teachers of English; Northeast MLA; MLA; Philip Larkin Society. *Publications:* Philip Larkin and English Poetry, 1986; Bliss Carman and His Works, 1983; The Atlantic Anthology: Criticism (ed.), 1985; Charles G. D. Roberts and His Works, 1989; Routledge Encyclopaedia of Post-Colonial Literature in English (contributor), 1994. Contributions: books, journals and periodicals. *Honours:* British Commonwealth Scholarship, 1966–68; Election to Council Mem. Status, Writers' Federation of Nova Scotia; numerous grants. *Address:* 26 Oceanview Drive, Purcells Cove, Halifax, NS B3P 2H3, Canada.

WHALLON, William, BA; American poet and writer; b. 24 Sept. 1928, Richmond, IN. *Education:* McGill University. *Career:* Fellow, Center for Hellenic Studies, 1962; Fulbright Prof. in Comparative Literature, University of Bayreuth, 1985. *Publications:* A Book of Time (poems), 1990; Giants in the Earth (ed.), 1991; The Oresteia/Apollo & Bacchus (scenarios), 1997.

WHEATCROFT, John Stewart, BA, MA, PhD; American academic, writer and poet; b. 24 July 1925, Philadelphia, PA; m. 1st Joan Mitchell Osborne 1952 (divorced 1974); two s. one d.; m. 2nd Katherine Whaley Warner 1992. *Education:* Bucknell Univ., Rutgers Univ. *Publications:* poetry: Death of a Clown 1963, Prodigal Son 1967, A Voice from the Hump 1977, Ordering Demons 1981, The Stare on the Donkey's Face 1990, Random Necessities 1997; fiction: Edie Tells 1975, Catherine, her Book 1983, Slow Exposures (short stories) 1986, The Beholder's Eye 1987, Killer Swan 1992, Mother of All

Loves 1994, Trio with Four Players 1995, The Education of Malcolm Palmer 1997; other: Our Other Voices (ed.) 1991; contrib. to New York Times, New York Times Book Review, Hartford Courant, Herald Tribune, Harper's Bazaar, Mademoiselle, Yankee, many literary magazines. *Honours:* Alcoa Playwriting Award 1966, Nat. Educational Television Award 1967, Yaddo Fellowships 1972, 1985, MacDowell Colony Fellowship 1973, Virginia Center for the Creative Arts Fellowships 1976, 1978, 1980, 1982. *Address:* 350 River Road, Lewisburg, PA 17837, USA.

WHEATCROFT, Patience; British journalist; *Editor, The Sunday Telegraph;* b. Chesterfield, Derbyshire; m.; three c. *Education:* Univ. of Birmingham. *Career:* fmrly launch Ed. Retail Week, and worked on the financial sections of The Daily Mail and The Sunday Times; Deputy City Ed. Mail on Sunday –1997; Business and City Ed. The Times 1997–2006; Ed. The Sunday Telegraph 2006–. *Honours:* London Press Club Business Journalist of the Year 2003. *Address:* The Sunday Telegraph, 111 Buckingham Palace Road, London, SW1W 0DT, England (office). *Telephone:* (20) 7931-2000 (office). *Website:* www.telegraph.co.uk (office).

WHEELER, Katherine (Kate) Frazier, BA, MA; American teacher and writer; b. 27 July 1955, Tulsa, OK. *Education:* Rice University, Stanford University. *Career:* ordained Buddhist nun, Mahasi Sasana Yeiktha, Rangoon 1988; teacher of meditation; mem. Insight Meditation Soc. (bd mem.). *Publications:* Lo Esperado y lo vivado (co-trans.), 1984; In This Very Life: The Liberation Teachings of the Buddha (ed.), 1992; Not Where I Started From (short stories), 1993; When Mountains Walked, 2000. Contributions: periodicals. *Honours:* O. Henry Awards, 1982, 1993; Pushcart Press Prize, 1983–84; Best American Short Stories Prize, Houghton Mifflin Co, 1992; National Education Assscn Grant, 1994; Whiting Foundation Award, 1994.

WHEELER, Sara, BA, MA, FRSL; British writer; pnr; two s. *Education:* Univ. of Oxford. *Career:* mem. Royal Soc. of Literature (council mem. 2000–05); Trustee London Library 2006–. *Publications:* Evia: An Island Apart 1992, Travels in a Thin Country: A Journey Through Chile 1995, Terra Incognita: Travels in Antarctica 1997, Dear Daniel: Letters from Antarctica 1997, Amazonian: Penguin Book of Women's New Travel Writing (co-ed. with Dea Birkett) 1998, Cherry: A Life of Apsley Cherry-Garrard 2001, Too Close to the Sun: The Life and Times of Denys Finch Hatton 2006; essays in various publs worldwide. *Address:* 8 South Hill Park, London, NW3 2SB, England (home). *E-mail:* sara@easynet.co.uk (office).

WHEELWRIGHT, Julie Diana, BA, MA; British writer and broadcaster; b. 2 June 1960, Farnborough, Kent, England. *Education:* University of British Columbia, University of Sussex. *Career:* reporter, Vancouver Sun, 1980; Pres., Canadian University Press, 1981; Consultant, Open University, 1991; mem. Writers' Guild. *Publications:* Amazons and Military Maids, 1989; The Fatal Lover, 1992. Contributions: newspapers and journals. *Honours:* hon. research fellow Inst. of Historical Research, Royal Holloway, London; Canada Council Non-Fiction Writers' Grants 1990–91, 1994–95.

WHELAN, Peter, BA; British playwright; b. 3 Oct. 1931, Newcastle-under-Lyme, England; two s. one d. *Education:* Univ. of Keele, Staffordshire. *Career:* advertising copywriter and Dir 1959–90. *Plays:* Double Edge (with Leslie Darbon, Vaudeville Theatre) 1975, Captain Swing (RSC) 1978, The Accrington Pals 1981, Clay 1982, The Bright and Bold Design 1991, The School of Night 1992, Shakespeare Country 1993, The Tinderbox 1994, Divine Right 1996, The Herbal Bed (West End and Broadway) 1996, Nativity (co-author) 1999, A Russian in the Woods (RSC) 2001, The Earthly Paradise (Almeida, London) 2004. *Honours:* Hon. Assoc. RSC 1995; Lloyds Private Banking Playwright of the Year 1996, TMA Regional Theatre Award for Best New Play 1996. *Literary Agent:* The Agency, 24 Pottery Lane, Holland Park, London, W11 4LZ, England. *Telephone:* (20) 7727-1346 (office).

WHICKER, Alan Donald, CBE, FRSA; British television broadcaster, journalist and author; b. 2 Aug. 1925, s. of the late Charles Henry Whicker and Anne Jane Cross. *Education:* Haberdashers' Aske's. *Career:* Dir Army Film and Photo Unit, with 8th Army and US 5th Army; war corresp., Korea; Foreign Corresp. Exchange Telegraph 1947–57, BBC TV 1957–68; Founder mem. Yorkshire TV 1968. *Radio includes:* Whicker's Wireless World (BBC Radio series) 1983; Around Whicker's World (six programmes for Radio 2) 1998, Whicker's New World (7 programmes for Radio 2) 1999, Whicker's World Down Under (6 programmes for Radio 2) 2000, Fabulous Fifties (4 programmes for Radio 2) 2000, It'll Never Last—The History of Television (6 programmes for Radio 2) 2001, Fifty Royal Years (6 programmes celebrating Queen's Golden Jubilee, Radio 2), Around Whicker's World (series of Radio 4 essays) 2002, Comedy Map of Britain (series of 12 Radio 2 programmes) 2007. *Television:* joined BBC TV 1957; regular appearances on 'Tonight' programme, then series Whicker's World 1959–60, Whicker Down Under 1961, Whicker in Sweden 1963, Whicker's World 1965–67; made 122 documentaries for Yorkshire TV including Whicker's New World Series, Whicker in Europe, World of Whicker; returned to BBC TV 1982; programmes include: Whicker's World – The First Million Miles! (four programmes) 1982, Whicker's World, A Fast Boat to China (four programmes) 1983, Whicker! (series talk shows) 1984, Whicker's World – Living with Uncle Sam (10 programmes) 1985, Whicker's World – Living with Waltzing Matilda (10 programmes) 1988, Whicker's World – Hong Kong (eight programmes) 1990, Whicker's World – A Taste of Spain (eight programmes) 1992, Around Whicker's World (four programmes, for ITV) 1992, Whicker's World – The Sultan of Brunei 1992, South Africa: Whicker's Miss World and Whicker's

World – The Sun King 1993, South-East Asia: Whicker's World Aboard the Real Orient Express, Whicker's World – Pavarotti in Paradise 1994, Travel Channel (26 programmes) 1996, Whicker's Week, BBC Choice 1999; Travel Amb. on the Internet for AOL 2000; One on One 2002, Whicker's War Series (Channel 4) 2004. *Publications:* Some Rise by Sin 1949, Away – With Alan Whicker 1963, Best of Everything 1980, Within Whicker's World (autobiog.) 1982, Whicker's Business Travellers Guide 1983, Whicker's New World 1985, Whicker's World Down Under 1988, Whicker's World – Take 2! 2000, Whicker's War 2005. *Honours:* various awards, including Guild of TV Producers and Dirs., Personality of the Year 1964, Silver Medal, Royal TV Soc., Dimbleby Award, BAFTA 1978, TV Times Special Award 1978, first to be named in Royal Television Soc.'s new Hall of Fame for outstanding creative contrib. to British TV 1993, Travel Writers' Special Award, for truly outstanding achievement in travel journalism 1998, BAFTA Grierson Documentary Tribute Award 2001, Nat. Film Theatre tribute, sixth Television Festival 2002. *Address:* Trinity, Jersey, JE3 5BA, Channel Islands.

WHITAKER, Mark Theis, BA, LLD; American journalist and magazine editor; *Editor, Newsweek;* b. 7 Sept. 1957, Lower Merion, PA; m. Alexis Lynn Gelber; one s. one d. *Education:* Harvard Univ., Univ. of Oxford, UK, Wheaton Coll. *Career:* Marshall Scholar, Balliol Coll., Oxford 1979–81; Assoc. Ed. Newsweek 1981–83, Gen. Ed. 1983, Sr Writer 1984–86, Sr Ed., Business Ed. 1987–91, Asst Man. Ed. 1991–95, Man. Ed. 1996–98, Ed. 1998–; mem. Nat. Asscn of Black Journalists, Bd Dirs American Soc. of Magazine Eds 1999– (Pres. 2004–), Council on Foreign Relations, Century Asscn. *Address:* Newsweek, 251 W 57th Street, New York, NY 10019-1802, USA (office).

WHITBOURN, John, BA; British writer; b. 23 March 1958, Godalming, Surrey, England; m. Elizabeth Caroline Gale 1982; one s. two d. *Education:* University College, Cardiff. *Publications:* Binscombe Tales, 1989; Rollover Night, 1990; A Dangerous Energy, 1992; Popes and Phantoms, 1993; To Build Jerusalem, 1995; The Binscombe Tales (two vols), 1998–99; The Royal Changeling, 1998; Downs-Lord Dawn, 1999; Downs-Lord Day, 2000; Downs-Lord Doomsday, 2002. *Honours:* BBC-Gollancz First Fantasy Novel Prize 1991. *E-mail:* JAW@telinco.co.uk. *Website:* www.btinternet.com/~john .whitbourn.

WHITE, Edmund Valentine, III, BA; American writer and academic; *Professor of Creative Writing in the University Center for the Creative and Performing Arts, Princeton University;* b. 13 Jan. 1940, Cincinnati, OH; s. of E.V. White and Delilah Teddlie. *Education:* Univ. of Michigan. *Career:* writer, Time-Life Books, New York 1962–70; Sr Ed., Saturday Review, New York 1972–73; Asst Prof. of Writing Seminars, Johns Hopkins Univ. 1977–79; Adjunct Prof., Columbia Univ. School of the Arts 1981–83; Exec. Dir, New York Inst. for the Humanities 1982–83; Prof. of English, Brown Univ., Providence, RI 1990–92; Prof. of Humanities, Princeton Univ. 1999, now Prof. of Creative Writing in the Univ. Center for the Creative and Performing Arts; Guggenheim Fellowship; mem. Acad. of Arts and Letters 1998. *Publications:* fiction: Forgetting Elena 1973, Nocturnes for the King of Naples 1978, A Boy's Own Story 1982, Aphrodisiac (with others) 1984, Caracole 1985, The Darker Proof: Stories from a Crisis (with Adam Mars-Jones) 1987, The Beautiful Room is Empty 1988, Skinned Alive 1995, The Farewell Symphony 1997, The Married Man 2000, Fanny: A Fiction 2003, Chaos 2007, Hotel de Dream 2007; non-fiction: The Joy of Gay Sex: An Intimate Guide for Gay Men to the Pleasures of a Gay Lifestyle (with Charles Silverstein) 1977, States of Desire: Travels in Gay America 1980, The Faber Book of Gay Short Fiction (ed.) 1991, Genet: A Biography 1993, The Selected Writings of Jean Genet (ed.) 1993, The Burning Library (essays) 1994, Sketches from Memory 1994, Our Paris 1995, Proust 1998, The Flâneur 2001, My Lives (autobiog.) 2005. *Honours:* Officier, Ordre des Arts et des Lettres 1999. *Literary Agent:* c/o Amanda Urban, ICM, 825 8th Avenue, New York, NY 10019; Room 224, 185 Nassau Street, Princeton, NJ 08544, USA. *Telephone:* (212) 556-5764; (609) 258-5099 (Princeton). *E-mail:* ewhite@princeton.edu. *Website:* www.princeton.edu/ ~visarts/cwr.

WHITE, Howard; Canadian writer, poet, editor and publisher; b. 18 April 1945, Abbotsford, BC; m.; two s. *Career:* founder, Ed., Publisher, Peninsula Voice 1969–74; Ed., Raincoast Chronicles 1972–; founder, Pres., Publisher, Harbour Publishing 1974–; mem. Asscn of Book Publishers of British Columbia (pres. 1988–90). *Publications:* Raincoast Chronicles (ed.) (five vols) 1975–94, A Hard Man to Beat: The Story of Bill White, Labour Leader, Historian, Shipyard Worker, Raconteur: An Oral History (co-author) 1983, The Men There Were Then 1983, The New Canadian Poets (ed.) 1985, Spilsbury's Coast: Pioneer Years in the Wet West (co-author) 1987, The Accidental Airline: Spilsbury's QCA 1988, Writing in the Rain (essays and poetry) 1990, The Ghost in the Gears 1993, The Sunshine Coast: From Gibsons to Powell River 1996; contrib. to periodicals. *Honours:* Hon. DJur (Univ. of Victoria) 2003; Eaton's British Columbia Book Award 1976, Career Award for Regional History, Canadian History Asscn 1989, Stephen Leacock Medal for Humour 1990, Roderick Haig Brown Award 1995, James Douglas BC Publisher of the Year Award 2002; Order of British Columbia 1997, Queen Elizabeth II 50th Jubilee Medal 2002. *Address:* PO Box 219, Madeira Park, BC V0N 2H0, Canada. *Website:* www.harbourpublishing.com.

WHITE, James Patrick, BA, MA; American academic, writer, poet, dramatist and editor and translator; *Professor, University of South Alabama;* b. 28 Sept. 1940, Wichita Falls, TX; m. Janice Lou Turner 1961; one s. *Education:* Univ. of Texas at Austin, Vanderbilt Univ., Brown Univ. *Career:* Asst Prof. 1973–74,

Assoc. Prof. 1974–77, Univ. of Texas of the Permian Basin at Odessa; Ed., Sands literary review 1974–78; Visiting Prof., Univ. of Texas at Dallas 1977–78; Founder-Ed., Texas Books in Review 1977–79; Dir, Masters in Professional Writing, Univ. of Southern California at Los Angeles 1979–82; mem. int. editorial bd, Translation Review 1980–; Dir of Creative Writing 1982–, Prof. 1987–, Univ. of South Alabama; mem. Alabama Writer's Forum, Associated Writing Programs, Christopher Isherwood Foundation (dir), Gulf Coast Asscn of Creative Writing Teachers (founder-pres. 1993), Texas Asscn of Creative Writing Teachers (founder-pres. 1974–78). *Publications:* fiction: Birdsong 1977, The Ninth Car (with Anne Rooth) 1978, The Persian Oven 1985, Two Novellas: The Persian Oven and California Exit 1987, Clara's Call (in two short novels, with R. V. Cassill) 1992; poetry: Poetry 1979, The Great Depression (with Walter Feldman) 1997; editor: Clarity: A Text on Writing (with Janice White) 1982, Where Joy Resides: A Christopher Isherwood Reader (with Don Bachardy) 1989, Black Alabama: An Anthology of Contemporary Black Alabama Fiction Writers 1998; contrib. to anthologies, reviews, quarterlies, journals, newspapers and magazines. *Honours:* Guggenheim Fellowship 1988–89, Dean's Lecturer, Univ. of South Alabama 1990. *Address:* c/o Creative Writing Department, University of South Alabama, 307 University Blvd, Mobile, AL 36688-0002; PO Box 428, Montrose, AL 36559, USA.

WHITE, John Austin, LVO, BA, FRSA; British ecclesiastic, writer and poet; *Vice-Dean of Windsor*; b. 27 June 1942, England. *Education:* Univ. of Hull, Coll. of the Resurrection, Mirfield. *Career:* Asst Curate, St Aidan's Church, Leeds 1966–69; Asst Chaplain, Univ. of Leeds 1969–73; Asst Dir Post Ordination Training, Dioceses of Ripon 1970–73; Chaplain, Northern Ordination Course 1973–82; Canon of Windsor 1982–, Vice-Dean 2004–; Warden St George's House 2000–03; European Deputy for the Diocese of Mexico of the Anglican Church of Mexico 2003–. *Publications:* A Necessary End: Attitudes to Death (with Julia Neuberger) 1991, Nicholas Ferrar: Materials for a Life (with L.R. Muir) 1997, Phoenix in Flight (with Thetis Blacker); contrib. to various publications. *Address:* 4 The Cloisters, Windsor Castle, Berks., SL4 1NJ, England. *Telephone:* (1753) 848787 (office). *Fax:* (1753) 848752 (office). *E-mail:* precentor@stgeorges-windsor.org (office). *Website:* www.stgeorges-windosr.org (office).

WHITE, Jon Ewbank Manchip, MA; British writer, poet and academic (retd); b. 22 June 1924, Cardiff, Glamorganshire, Wales; m. Valerie Leighton (deceased); two d. *Education:* St Catharine's Coll., Cambridge. *Career:* story ed. BBC TV, London 1950–51; Sr Exec. Officer British Foreign Service 1952–56; author 1956–67, including a period as screenwriter for Samuel Bronston Productions, Paris and Madrid 1960–64; Prof. of English Univ. of Texas, El Paso 1967–77; Lindsay Young Prof. of English Univ. of Tennessee, Knoxville 1977–94; mem. Texas Inst. of Letters, Welsh Acad. *Publications:* fiction: Mask of Dust 1953, Build Us a Dam 1955, The Girl from Indiana 1956, No Home But Heaven 1957, The Mercenaries 1958, Hour of the Rat 1962, The Rose in the Brandy Glass 1965, Nightclimber 1968, The Game of Troy 1971, The Garden Game 1973, Send for Mr Robinson 1974, The Moscow Papers 1979, Death by Dreaming 1981, The Last Grand Master 1985, Whistling Past the Churchyard 1992; poetry: Dragon and Other Poems 1943, Salamander and Other Poems 1945, The Rout of San Romano 1952, The Mountain Lion 1971; prose: Ancient Egypt 1952, Anthropology 1954, Marshal of France: The Life and Times of Maurice, Comte de Saxe 1962, Everyday Life in Ancient Egypt 1964, Diego Velázquez, Painter and Courtier 1969, The Land God Made in Anger: Reflections on a Journey Through South West Africa 1969, Cortés and the Downfall of the Aztec Empire 1971, A World Elsewhere: One Man's Fascination with the American Southwest 1975, Everyday Life of the North American Indians 1979, What to do When the Russians Come: A Survivors' Handbook (with Robert Conquest) 1984, The Journeying Boy: Scenes from a Welsh Childhood 1991, Whistling Past the Churchyard 1992, Echoes & Shadows 2003. *Address:* 5620 Pinellas Drive, Knoxville, TN 37919, USA (home). *Telephone:* (865) 558-8578 (home). *E-mail:* salamanderjmw@man.com (home).

WHITE, Kenneth, MA, DèsL; British poet and writer; b. 28 April 1936, Glasgow, Scotland; m. Marie Claude Charlut. *Education:* Univ. of Glasgow, Univ. of Munich, Germany, Univ. of Paris, France. *Career:* Lecturer in French, Univ. of Glasgow 1963–67; Lecturer in English, Univ. of Paris VII 1969–83; Prof. of 20th Century Poetics, Univ. of Paris-Sorbonne 1983–96. *Publications:* poetry: Wild Coal 1963, En Toute Candeur 1964, The Cold Wind of Dawn 1966, The Most Difficult Area 1968, A Walk Along the Shore 1977, Mahamudra 1979, Le Grand Rivage 1980, Terre de Diamant 1983, Atlantica: Mouvements et meditations 1986, The Bird Path: Collected Longer Poems 1989, Handbook for the Diamond Country: Collected Shorter Poems 1990, Les Rives du Silence 1997, Limites et Marges 2000, Open World; Collected Poems 2003; fiction: Letters from Gourgounel 1966, Les Limbes Incandescents 1978, Le Visage du Vent d'Est 1980, La Route Bleue 1983, Travels in the Drifting Dawn 1989, Pilgrim of the Void 1994, House of Tides 2000, Across the Territories 2004; essays: La Figure du Dehors 1982, L'Esprit Nomade 1987, Le Plateau de l'Albatros, an introduction to geopoetics 1994, On Scottish Ground 1998, The Wanderer and his Charts 2004; contrib. to various publs. *Honours:* Dr hc (Glasgow, Heriot-Watt, Open Univ.); Hon. mem. Royal Scottish Acad.; Prix Médicis Etranger 1983, Grand Prix du Rayonnement, French Acad. 1985. *Address:* Chemin du Goaquer, 22560 Trébeurden, France (home).

WHITE, Robert M., II, AB; American journalist; b. 6 April 1915, Mexico, Mo.; s. of L. Mitchell White and Maude White (née See); m. 1st Barbara Spurgeon 1948 (died 1983); one s. three d.; m. 3rd Linda Hess Grimsley 1992. *Education:* Missouri Military Acad. and Washington and Lee Univ. *Career:* with United Press 1939; Army service 1940–45; Pres., Ed. and Publr Mexico (Missouri) Ledger 1945–87, Ed. Emer. 1987–; Ed. and Pres. New York Herald Tribune 1959–61: Dir American Newspaper Publishers' Asscn 1955–63, Treas. 1962–63; Dir New York World's Fair 1964–65; fmr Chair. Associated Press Nominating Cttee; fmr Chair. and Pres., Inland Daily Press Asscn; Pres. See TV Co. 1965–81; Vice-Chair. American Cttee Int. Pres. Inst. 1968–71, 1981–91, Chair. 1982–86; Dir American Soc. of Newspaper Eds. 1968–70; Pres. Soc. of Professional Journalists 1967; Dir Stephen's Coll., Missouri Mil. Acad.; Visiting Prof., Univ. of Missouri 1968–69; mem. Pulitzer Prize Jury for Journalism 1964–66; Chair. American Soc. of Newspaper Eds. Freedom of Information Cttee 1970-72; Chair. Missouri Free Press-Fair Trial Cttee 1970–74; Pres. Missouri Press Asscn; Vice-Pres. Mo. Inst. for Justice 1978–82, Bd of Dirs. 1982–87; Vice-Pres. Gen. Douglas MacArthur Foundation 1979–81, Pres. 1981–; mem. Bd of Dirs. Associated Press 1971–80, Bd of Dirs. Washington Journalism Center 1972–84, State Historical Soc. of Missouri, Missouri Public Expenditure Survey 1980–85 (Pres. 1981–83), Bd of Dirs. Washington and Lee Univ. Alumni Inc. 1976–80, World Press Freedom Comm. 1984–; Dir Commerce Bank of Mexico 1971–85, Commerce Bancshares Inc. 1971–85; Dir Thomson Newspapers (Toronto) 1986–92; mem. Bd of Dirs. Int. Eye Foundation 1987–89. *Publications:* A Study of the Printing and Publishing Business in the Soviet Union (co-author), China Journey 1972, Second Journey To China 1977. *Honours:* Distinguished Service to Journalism Award, Univ. of Missouri 1967, Nat. Newspapers Asscn Pres. Award of Merit 1967. *Address:* Apartment 1037, 4000 Massachusetts Avenue, NW, Washington, DC 20016 (office); 4871 Glenbrook Road, NW, Washington DC 20016, USA.

WHITE, William Robinson, BA, MA; American writer and poet; b. 12 July 1928, Kodaikanal, South India; m. Marian Biesterfeld 1948 (died 1983); two s. one d. *Education:* Yale University, California State Polytechnic University. *Career:* Ed.-in-Chief, Per-Se International Quarterly, Stanford University Press, 1965–69; Instructor, Photojournalism, 1973, Dir, Creative Writing Seminar, 1984, Mendocino Art Center; Lecturer, Scripps College, 1984; Fiction Ed., West-word literary magazine, 1985–90; Instructor, University of California, Los Angeles, 1985–; Research Reader, The Huntington Library, 1985–86; Lecturer, Writing Programme and CompuWrite, California State Polytechnic University, 1985–93; Bread Loaf Fellow, Middlebury College, 1956; Stegner Creative Writing Fellow, Stanford University, 1956–57; mem. Authors' Guild; California State Poetry Society. *Publications:* House of Many Rooms, 1958; Elephant Hill, 1959; Men and Angels, 1961; Foreign Soil, 1962; All In Favor Say No, 1964; His Own Kind, 1967; Be Not Afraid, 1972; The Special Child, 1978; The Troll of Crazy Mule Camp, 1979; Moses the Man, 1981; The Winning Writer, 1997. Contributions: journals and magazines. *Honours:* Harper Prize, 1959; O. Henry Prize, 1960; Co-ordinating Council of Literary Magazines Award, 1968; Distinguished Achievement Award, Educational Press, 1974; Spring Harvest Poetry Awards, 1992, 1994, 1995; Ed.'s Choice Awards, Poetry, 1998, 2000; California State Polytechnic University Golden Leaves Award, 2000; New Century Writers Award, 2000. *Address:* 1940 Fletcher Avenue, South Pasadena, CA 91030, USA.

WHITEHOUSE, David, FRAS; British journalist; *Science Correspondent, BBC News Online*. *Career:* fmr space scientist and astronomer Mullard Space Science Lab. Univ. Coll., London and at Jodrell Bank radio observatory; currently Science Corresp. BBC, and Science Ed. BBC News Online; broadcasts regularly on TV and radio; presenter, science series (BBC TV); mem. Soc. for Popular Astronomy (fmr pres. *Publications:* non-fiction: The Moon: A Biography 2001, The Sun: A Biography 2004; contrib. regularly to leading newspapers and magazines. *Honours:* two Glaxo science writing awards, five European Netmedia awards, including European Internet Journalist of the Year 2002, European Online Journalism award for science reporting. *Address:* c/o BBC News website, Room 7540, BBC Television Centre, Wood Lane, London, W12 7RJ, England. *Website:* www.bbc.co.uk.

WHITEHOUSE, David Bryn, BA, MA, PhD; British writer and editor; *Executive Director, The Corning Museum of Glass*; b. 15 Oct. 1941, Worksop, England. *Education:* Univ. of Cambridge. *Career:* Chief Curator Corning Museum of Glass, NY 1984, Deputy Dir Collections 1988, Dir 1992, Exec. Dir 1999; Correspondent Archeologia Medievale; Ed. Journal of Glass Studies 1988–; Advisory Ed. American Early Medieval Studies 1991–; Advisory Bd Encyclopedia of Islamic Archaeology 1991; mem. Accademia Fiorentina delle Arti del Disegno, Int. Asscn for the History of Glass (pres. 1991–94), Keats-Shelley Memorial Asscn, Rome (pres. 1982–83), Pontificia Accademia Romana di Archeologia, RGS, Soc. of Antiquaries of London, Unione Internazionale degli Istituti di Archeologia, Storia e Storia dell'Arte in Roma (pres. 1980–81). *Publications:* Glass of the Roman Empire 1988, Glass: A Pocket Dictionary 1993, English Cameo Glass 1994, Roman Glass in the Corning Museum of Glass, Vol. 1 1997, Vol. 2 2001, Vol. 3 2003, Excavations at Ed-Dur, Vol. 1 The Glass Vessels 1998, The Corning Museum of Glass: A Decade of Glass Collecting 2000; co-author: Archaeological Atlas of the World 1975, Aspects of Medieval Lazio 1982, Mohammed, Charlemagne and the Origins of Europe 1983, Glass of the Caesars 1987, The Portland Vase 1990, Treasures from the Corning Museum of Glass 1992; contrib. to books, journals and other publications. *Address:* Corning Museum of Glass, One Museum Way, Corning, NY 14830-2253, USA (office). *Telephone:* (607) 974-8424 (office). *Fax:* (607) 974-8470 (office). *E-mail:* whitehoudb@cmog.org.

WHITEMAN, Robin, NDD, MA; British writer and filmmaker; b. 5 May 1944, King's Langley, Herts.; m.; three c. *Education:* City of Canterbury Coll. of Art and Royal Coll. of Art. *Career:* writer and Dir United Motion Pictures, London 1968–70; Dir and Prod. Video Tracks Ltd, Royal Leamington Spa 1980–85; writer and Partner, Talbot Whiteman, Royal Leamington Spa 1985–. *Publications:* The Cotswolds, 1987, Shakespeare's Avon: A Journey from Source to Severn 1989, The English Lakes 1989, Cadfael Country 1990, In the North of England: The Yorkshire Moors and Dales 1991, The Cadfael Companion 1991, The Benediction of Brother Cadfael 1992, The Heart of England 1992, The West Country 1993, Wessex 1994, The Garden of England: The Counties of Kent, Surrey and Sussex 1995, English Landscapes 1995, East Anglia and the Fens 1996, Brother Cadfael's Herb Garden 1996, The Peak District 1997, Lakeland Landscapes 1997, Northumbria: English Border Country 1998, Yorkshire Landscapes 1998, Cotswold Landscapes 1999, England 2000, Brother Cadfael's Book of Days 2000, A Family to Remember 2005. *Honours:* Gold Award, British Film and Video Festival 1984, Border TV Prize 1998. *Address:* c/o Weidenfeld and Nicolson, Orion House, 5 Upper St Martin's Lane, London, WC2H 9EA, England. *Telephone:* (20) 7240-3444. *Fax:* (20) 7240-4822. *Website:* www.orionbooks.co.uk.

WHITESIDE, Lesley, BA, DipEd, MA; Irish historian and writer; b. 13 May 1945, County Down; m. Robert Whiteside 1968; one s. two d. *Education:* Trinity Coll., Dublin, studied in Liverpool, Nat. Univ. of Ireland, Trinity Coll., Dublin. *Career:* Asst Keeper of Manuscripts, Trinity Coll., Dublin 1968–69; Archivist, The King's Hospital, Dublin 1969–. *Publications:* A History of The King's Hospital 1975, George Otto Simms: A Biography 1990, Through the Year with George Otto Simms (ed.) 1993, The Spirituality of St Patrick 1996, St Saviour's Church, Arklow 1997, In Search of Columba 1997, The Chapel of Trinity College, Dublin 1998, St Patrick in Stained Glass 1998, The Book of Saints 1998, The Stained Glass of Christ Church Cathedral, Dublin 1999, The Stained Glass of St Patrick's Cathedral, Dublin 2002, Music in the King's Hospital 1675–2003, Dublin 2003. *Address:* The Meadows, Marlinstown, Mullingar, County Westmeath, Ireland. *Telephone:* (353) 44-9342994.

WHITFIELD, Stephen Jack, BA, MA, PhD; American historian and academic; *Max Richter Chair of American Civilization, Brandeis University;* b. 3 Dec. 1942, Houston, Tex.; s. of Bert Whitfield and Joan Whitfield (née Schwarz); m. Lee Cone Hall 1984. *Education:* Tulane Univ., Yale Univ., Brandeis Univ. *Career:* instructor, Southern Univ. of New Orleans 1966–68; Asst Prof. 1972–75, Assoc. Prof. 1979–85, Prof. 1985–, Max Richter Chair of American Civilization, Dept of American Studies 1986–88, 1994–96, Brandeis Univ.; Fulbright Visiting Prof., Hebrew Univ. of Jerusalem 1983–84, Catholic Univ. of Louvain, Belgium 1993; Visiting Prof., Univ. of Paris IV 1994, 1998, Ludwig-Maximilian-Universität Munich 2004; mem. American Jewish Historical Soc. *Publications:* Scott Nearing: Apostle of American Radicalism 1974, Into the Dark: Hannah Arendt and Totalitarianism 1980, Voices of Jacob, Hands of Esau: Jews in American Life and Thought 1984, A Critical American: The Politics of Dwight Macdonald 1984, A Death in the Delta: The Story of Emmett Till 1988, American Space, Jewish Time 1988, The Culture of the Cold War 1991, In Search of American Jewish Culture 1999, A Companion to 20th Century America (ed.) 2004; contrib. to scholarly journals. *Honours:* Univ. of Colorado Kayden Prize 1981, Outstanding Academic Book Citation Choice 1985, Int. Center for Holocaust Studies of the Anti-Defamation League of B'nai B'rith Merit of Distinction 1987, Gustavus Myers Center for the Study of Human Rights Outstanding Book Citations 1989, 1992, Rockefeller Foundation Fellow, Bellagio, Italy 1991, Louis D. Brandeis Prize for Excellence in Teaching 1993. *Address:* Mailstop #005, Department of American Studies, Brandeis University, 415 South Street, Waltham, MA 02454-9110, USA (office). *Telephone:* (781) 736-3035 (office). *Fax:* (781) 736-3040 (office). *E-mail:* swhitfield@brandeis.edu (office).

WHITMAN, Ruth Bashein, BA, MA; American poet, editor, translator and teacher; b. 28 May 1922, New York, NY; m. 1st Cedric Whitman 1941 (divorced 1958); two d.; m. 2nd Firman Houghton 1959 (divorced 1964); one s.; m. 3rd Morton Sacks 1966. *Education:* Radcliffe College, Harvard University. *Career:* Editorial Asst, 1941–42, Educational Ed., 1944–45, Houghton Mifflin Co, Boston; Freelance Ed., Harvard University Press, 1945–60; Poetry Ed., Audience magazine, 1958–63; Dir, Poetry Workshop, Cambridge Center for Adult Education, 1964–68, Poetry in the Schools Program, Massachusetts Council on the Arts, 1970–73; Scholar-in-Residence, Radcliffe Institute, 1968–70; Instructor in Poetry, Radcliffe College, 1970–, Harvard University Writing Program, 1979–84; Writer-in-Residence and Visiting Lecturer at various colleges and universities; many poetry readings; mem. Authors' Guild; Authors League of America; New England Poetry Club; PEN; Poetry Society of America. *Publications:* Blood and Milk Poems, 1963; Alain Bosquet: Selected Poems (trans. with others), 1963; Isaac Bashevis Singer: The Seance (trans. with others), 1968; The Marriage Wig, and Other Poems, 1968; The Selected Poems of Jacob Glatstein (ed. and trans.), 1972; The Passion of Lizzie Borden: New and Selected Poems, 1973; Poetmaking: Poets in Classrooms (ed.), 1975; Tamsen Donner: A Woman's Journey, 1975; Permanent Address: New Poems, 1973–1980, 1980; Becoming a Poet: Source, Process, and Practice, 1982; The Testing of Hanna Senesh, 1986; The Fiddle Rose: Selected Poems of Abraham Sutzkever (trans.), 1989; Laughing Gas: Poems New and Selected, 1963–1990, 1991; Hatsheput, Speak to Me, 1992. Contributions: anthologies and periodicals. *Honours:* MacDowell Colony Fellowships, 1962, 1964, 1972–74, 1979, 1982; Kovner Award, Jewish Book Council of America, 1969; Guiness International Poetry Award, 1973; National Endowment for the Arts Grant,

1974–75; John Masefield Award, 1976; Senior Fulbright Fellowship, 1984–85; Urbanarts Award, 1987.

WHITNEY, Phyllis Ayame; American writer; b. 9 Sept. 1903, Yokohama, Japan; d. of Charles Whitney and Lillian Whitney (née Mandeville); m. 1st George Garner 1925; m. 2nd Lovell Jahnke 1950 (died 1973). *Education:* McKinley High School, Chicago. *Career:* Children's Book Ed. Chicago Sun 1942–46, Philadelphia Inquirer 1947–48; Instructor in writing juvenile fiction, New York Univ. 1947–58; fmrly writer of juvenile fiction, currently writes for adult market; mem. Mystery Writers of America. *Publications include:* A Place for Ann 1941, Red is for Murder 1943, The Silver Inkwell 1945, Writing Juvenile Fiction 1947, Linda's Homecoming 1950, Love Me, Love Me Not 1952, Mystery of the Black Diamonds 1954, The Fire and the Gold (Jr Literary Guild) 1956, Mystery of the Green Cat (Jr Literary Guild) 1957, Mystery of the Haunted Pool (Mystery Writers' Asscn Edgar award) 1961, Seven Tears for Apollo 1963, Sea Jade 1965, Hunter's Green 1968, The Vanishing Scarecrow 1971, The Turquoise Mask 1974, The Glass Flame 1978, Vermilion 1981, Guide to Fiction Writing 1982, Rainsong 1984, Dream of Orchids 1985, Flaming Tree 1986, Silversword 1987, Feather on the Moon 1988, Rainbow in the Mist 1989, The Singing Stones 1990, The Ebony Swan 1992, Star Flight 1993, Daughter of the Stars 1994, Amethyst Dreams 1997. *Honours:* Agatha Award Malice Domestic 1990, Rita award Romance Writers of America 1990. *Address:* c/o McIntosh and Otis, 353 Lexington Avenue, New York, NY 10016-0941, USA. *Website:* www.phyllisawhitney.com.

WHITTALL, Arnold, MA, PhD; British musicologist; b. 11 Nov. 1935, Shrewsbury, Shropshire. *Education:* Emmanuel Coll., Cambridge. *Career:* Lecturer, Univ. of Nottingham 1964–69; Sr Lecturer, Univ. Coll., Cardiff 1969–75; Reader, King's Coll., London 1976–81, Prof. of Musical Theory and Analysis 1981–96; Visiting Prof., Yale Univ. 1985. *Publications include:* Post-Twelve Note Analysis 1968, Stravinsky and Music Drama 1969, Schoenberg Chamber Music 1972, Music Since the First World War 1977, The Music of Britten and Tippett 1982, Romantic Music 1987, Wagner's Later Stage Works 1990, The Emancipation of Dissonance: Schoenberg and Stravinsky 1993, Musical Composition in the Twentieth Century 1999, Exploring Twentieth Century Music 2003.

WHITTAM SMITH, Andreas, CBE; British journalist; b. 13 June 1937, s. of Canon J. E. Smith; m. Valerie Catherine Sherry 1964; two s. *Education:* Keble Coll., Oxford. *Career:* with N. M. Rothschild 1960–62, Stock Exchange Gazette 1962–63, Financial Times 1963–64, The Times 1964–66; Deputy City Ed. The Telegraph 1966–69; City Ed. The Guardian 1969–70; Ed. Investors Chronicle, Stock Exchange Gazette and Dir Throgmorton Publs 1970–77; City Ed. Daily Telegraph 1977–85; Ed. The Independent 1986–94, Ed.-in-Chief Independent on Sunday 1991–94; Dir Newspaper Publishing PLC 1986–, CEO 1987–93, Chair. 1994–95; Chair. Publr Notting Hill 1995–, Sir Winston Churchill Archive Trust 1995–2000, Financial Ombudsman Service Ltd. 1999–2003; Pres. British Bd of Film Classification 1998–2002; First Church Estates Commr; Vice-Pres. Nat. Council for One Parent Families 1982–86, 1991–. *Honours:* Hon. Fellow Keble Coll., Oxford, UMIST 1989, Liverpool John Moores 2001; Hon. DLitt (St Andrew's, Salford) 1989; Wincott Award 1975; Journalist of the Year 1987. *Address:* 154 Campden Hill Road, London, W8 7AS, England.

WHITTEN, Leslie Hunter, Jr, BA; American writer, poet and journalist; b. 21 Feb. 1928, Jacksonville, FL; m. Phyllis Webber 1951; three s. one d. *Education:* Lehigh Univ. *Publications:* Progeny of the Adder 1965, Moon of the Wolf 1967, Pinion, The Golden Eagle 1968, The Abyss 1970, F. Lee Bailey 1971, The Alchemist 1973, Conflict of Interest 1976, Washington Cycle (poems) 1979, Sometimes a Hero 1979, A Killing Pace 1983, A Day Without Sunshine 1985, The Lost Disciple 1989, The Fangs of Morning 1994, Sad Madrigals 1997, Moses: The Lost Book of the Bible 1999; contrib. to newspapers and literary magazines. *Honours:* Hon. DHumLitt (Lehigh Univ.) 1989, journalistic awards, American Civil Liberties Union Edgerton Award. *Address:* 114 Eastmoor Drive, Silver Spring, MD 20901, USA.

WHITTINGTON, Peter (see Mackay, James Alexander)

WHYTE, Ken; Canadian journalist and editor; b. 1960, Winnipeg, Man.; m. Tina Leino-Whyte; one d. *Education:* Univ. of Alberta. *Career:* fmr janitor; Sports Reporter, Sherwood Park News; Staff Writer, then Exec. Ed. Alberta Report; Western Columnist, The Globe and Mail, Western Ed., then Ed. Saturday Night magazine; f. National Post 1998, Ed.-in-Chief 1998–2003. *Address:* c/o National Post, 1450 Don Mills Road, Suite 300, Don Mills, Ont., M3B 2X7, Canada (office). *Telephone:* (416) 510-6748 (office). *Fax:* (416) 510-6743 (office). *Website:* www.nationalpost.com (office).

WICHTERICH, Christa, Dr rer. pol; German journalist and writer; b. 4 March 1949, Brühl; m. Uwe Hoering 1979. *Education:* Univs of Bonn, Munich and Kassel. *Career:* Lecturer Univ. of Gilan, Rasht, Iran 1978–79, Jawaharlal Nehru Univ., New Delhi 1979–82; Guest Lecturer Univ. of Kassel 1983, Göttingen 1984, Münster 1986, Frankfurt/Main 1991, Bochum 1994; Foreign Corresp. for Africa for German newspapers and radio stations, Nairobi 1988–90; currently freelance journalist and writer; German Govt Award for Journalists working in the field of Devt Politics 1986. *Publications:* Stree Shakti, Frauen in Indien 1986, Kein Zustand dauert ewig, Afrika in den neunziger Jahren 1991, Die Erde bemuttern, Frauen und Ökologie nach dem Erdgipfel in Rio 1992, Menschen nach Maß, Bevölkerungspolitik in Nord und Süd 1994, Frauen der Welt, vom Fortschritt der Ungleichheit 1995, Wir sind das Wunder, Durch das wir Überleben, die Vierte Weltfrauenkonferenz in Peking 1996, The Globalised Woman 2000. *Address:* Schloßtr 2, 53115 Bonn, Germany. *Telephone:* (228) 265032. *Fax:* (228) 265033.

WICKER, Thomas (Tom) Grey, AB, DJur; American journalist (retd) and author; b. 18 June 1926, Hamlet, NC; s. of Delancey D. Wicker and Esta Cameron; m. 1st Neva J. McLean 1949 (divorced 1973); one s. one d.; m. 2nd Pamela A. Hill 1974. *Education:* Univ. of N Carolina. *Career:* Exec. Dir Southern Pines (NC) Chamber of Commerce 1948–49; Ed. Sandhill Citizen, Aberdeen, NC 1949; Man. Ed. The Robesonian, Lumberton, NC 1949–50; Public Information Dir NC Bd of Public Welfare 1950–51; copy-ed., Winston-Salem (NC) Journal 1951–52, Sports Ed. 1954–55, Sunday Feature Ed. 1955–56, Washington Corresp. 1957, editorial writer 1958–59; Nieman Fellow, Harvard Univ. 1957–58, Joan Shorenstein Barone Center on the Press, Politics and Public Policy 1993; Assoc. Ed. Nashville Tennessean 1959–60; mem. staff, Washington Bureau, New York Times 1960–71, Chief of Bureau 1964–68; Assoc. Ed. New York Times 1968–85; columnist 1966–91; Visiting Scholar, First Amendment Center, Nashville 1998; Visiting Prof. of Journalism, Davidson Coll. NC, Middle Tenn. State Univ. 1999, Univ. of Southern Calif. 1999. *Publications:* novels (under pseudonym Paul Connolly): Get Out of Town 1951, Tears Are for Angels 1952, So Fair, So Evil 1955; novels (under own name): The Kingpin 1953, The Devil Must 1957, The Judgment 1961, Facing the Lions 1963, Unto This Hour 1984, Donovan's Wife 1992, Easter Lilly 1998; non-fiction: Kennedy without Tears 1964, JFK and LBJ: The Influence of Personality Upon Politics 1968, A Time To Die 1975, On Press 1978, One of Us: Richard Nixon and the American Dream 1991, Tragic Failure: Racial Integration in America 1996, Keeping the Record 2001, Dwight D. Eisenhower 2002, George Herbert Walker Bush 2004, Shooting Star: The Brief Arc of Joe McCarthy 2006; book chapters, contribs to nat. magazines. *Address:* Austin Hill Farm, 688 Austin Hill Road, Rochester, VT 05767, USA (home). *Telephone:* (802) 767-4433 (home). *Fax:* (802) 767-3699 (home). *E-mail:* twicker@sover.net (home).

WICKS, Susan Jane, BA, DPhil; British writer and poet; *Director of the Centre for Creative Writing, University of Kent*; b. 24 Oct. 1947, Kent, England; m. John Collins 1973; two d. *Education:* Univ. of Hull, Univ. of Sussex. *Career:* Assoc. Lecturer in English, Univ. of Dijon 1974–76; Asst Lecturer in French, Univ. Coll., Dublin 1976–77; part-time Tutor in Comparative Literature, Univ. of Kent, Tonbridge 1983–2000, Lecturer, then Sr Lecturer in Creative Writing 2000–, currently Dir of the Centre for Creative Writing; mem. Soc. of Authors, Poetry Soc., Kent and Sussex Poetry Soc. *Publications:* Singing Underwater 1992, Open Diagnosis 1994, Driving My Father (prose) 1995, The Clever Daughter 1996, The Key (novel) 1997, Little Thing (novel) 1998, Night Toad 2003, De-iced 2007; contrib. to TLS, Observer, LRB, Poetry Review, London Magazine, The Rialto, Ambit, Poetry London, Poetry Wales, Poetry Ireland Review, Magma, Smith's Knoll, Poetry East, Southern Review, Women's Review of Books, The New Yorker. *Honours:* MacDowell Colony residencies 1997, 2005, Hedgebrook, Washington State residency 1991, Aldeburgh Poetry Festival Prize 1992, Ragdale residency, IL 1992, Virginia Centre for the Creative Arts residency 1994–2005, Villa Mont-Noir residency 1999, 2003. *Address:* School of English, Rutherford College, University of Kent, Canterbury, Kent CT2 7NX, England (office).

WIDDECOMBE, Rt Hon. Ann Noreen, PC, MA; British politician and writer; b. 4 Oct. 1947, Bath, Somerset; d. of the late James Murray Widdecombe and of Rita Noreen Plummer. *Education:* La Sainte Union Convent, Bath, Univ. of Birmingham, Lady Margaret Hall Oxford. *Career:* with Marketing Dept Unilever 1973–75; Sr Admin. Univ. of London 1975–87; contested Burnley 1979, Plymouth Devonport 1983; MP for Maidstone 1987–97, Maidstone and The Weald 1997–; Parl. Pvt. Sec. to Tristan Garel-Jones, MP 1990; Parl. Under-Sec. State Dept of Social Security 1990–93, Dept of Employment 1993–94; Minister for Employment 1994–95, Home Office 1995–97; Shadow Health Minister 1998–99, Shadow Home Sec. 1999–2001; Conservative. *Publications:* Layman's Guide to Defence 1984, Inspired and Outspoken 1999, The Clematis Tree (novel) 2000, An Act of Treachery 2001, An Act of Peace 2005, Father Figure 2005. *Honours:* Spectator/Highland Park Minister of the Year 1996, Despatch Box Best Front Bencher 1998, Talk Radio Straight Talker of the Year 1998. *Address:* House of Commons, Westminister, London, SW1A 0AA (office). *Telephone:* (20) 7219-5091 (office). *Fax:* (20) 7219-2413 (office). *E-mail:* WiddecombeA@parliament.uk (office). *Website:* www .annwiddecombemp.com (office).

WIDDICOMBE, Gillian, ARAM; British music critic and journalist; b. 11 June 1943, Aldham, Suffolk, England; m. Sir Jeremy Isaacs 1988. *Education:* Royal Acad. of Music, Gloucester Cathedral. *Career:* music division, BBC 1966; Glyndebourne Festival Opera 1969; critic and journalist on various publications, including Financial Times 1970–76, The Observer 1977–93; subtitles for television opera productions; Opera Consultant, Channel Four 1983–88; Arts Ed., The Observer 1988–93; Features Writer, The Independent 1993–95; Dir, Jeremy Isaacs Productions 1995–; Production Exec., Cold War 1998; Assoc. Prod., Millennium 1999; Prod., Artsworld TV Programmes, including Star Recitals with Paco Peña, Amanda Roocroft and Simon Preston 2000–; Poulenc, A Human Voice (for BBC 2). *Honours:* Prix Italia 1982, BP Award for Arts Journalism 1986. *Address:* 80 New Concordia Wharf, Mill Street, Bermondsey, London, SE1 2BB, England.

WIDEMAN, John Edgar, BA, BPhil; American writer; *Professor of English, University of Massachusetts at Amherst*; b. 14 June 1941, Washington, DC; m.;

three c. *Education:* Univ. of Pennsylvania, Univ. of Oxford, Univ. of Iowa. *Career:* Prof. of English, Univ. of Wyoming 1974–85, Univ. of Massachusetts, Amherst 1986–; mem. American Acad. of Arts and Sciences, American Acad. of Arts and Letters, American Asscn of Rhodes Scholars, MLA. *Publications:* A Glance Away 1967, Hurry Home 1969, The Lynchers 1973, Hiding Place 1981, Damballah 1981, Sent for You Yesterday 1983, Brothers and Keepers 1984, Reuben 1987, Fever 1989, Philadelphia Fire 1990, The Homewood Books 1992, The Stories of John Edgar Wideman 1992, All Stories Are True 1993, Fatheralong 1994, The Cattle Killing 1996, Hoop Roots 2001, God's Gym 2005; contrib. to professional journals and general periodicals. *Honours:* PEN/Faulkner Awards for Fiction 1984, 1991, John D. and Catherine T. MacArthur Foundation Fellowship 1993. *Address:* c/o Department of English, University of Massachusetts, Amherst, MA 01003, USA.

WIEBE, Rudy Henry, BA, MA, ThB; Canadian writer and academic; *Professor Emeritus of English and Creative Writing, University of Alberta*; b. 4 Oct. 1934, Fairholme, Sask.; m. Tena F. Isaak 1958, two s. one d. *Education:* Univ. of Alberta, Univ. of Tübingen, Mennonite Brethren Bible Coll., Univ. of Manitoba, Univ. of Iowa. *Career:* Asst and Assoc. Prof. of English, Goshen College, Ind. 1963–67; Asst Prof., Univ. of Alberta 1967–71, Assoc. Prof. 1971–77, Prof. of English and Creative Writing 1977–92, Prof. Emer. 1992–; mem. Writers Guild of Alberta (Founding Pres. 1980), Writers Union of Canada (Pres. 1986–87). *Publications:* Fiction: Peace Shall Destroy Many 1962, First and Vital Candle 1966, The Blue Mountains of China 1970, The Temptations of Big Bear 1973, Where is the Voice Coming From? 1974, The Scorched-Wood People 1977, Alberta: A Celebration 1979, The Mad Trapper 1980, The Angel of the Tar Sands and Other Stories 1982, My Lovely Enemy 1983, A Chinook Christmas 1992, A Discovery of Strangers 1994, River of Stone: Fictions and Memories 1995, Sweeter Than All the World 2001; Non-fiction (memoir): Of This Earth: A Mennonite Boyhood in the Boreal Forest 2006; Play: Far as the Eye Can See, 1977. Essays: A Voice in the Land, 1981; Playing Dead: A Contemplation Concerning the Arctic, 1989. Editor: The Story-Makers: A Selection of Modern Short Stories, 1970; Stories from Western Canada, 1971; Stories from Pacific and Arctic Canada (with Andreas Schroeder), 1974; Double Vision: Twentieth Century Stories in English, 1976; Getting Here, 1977; More Stories from Western Canada (with Aritha van Herk), 1980; West of Fiction (with Aritha van Herk and Leah Flater), 1983; numerous contribs to anthologies and periodicals. *Honours:* Hon. DLitt Univ. of Winnipeg 1986, Wilfred Laurier Univ. 1991, Brock Univ. 1991; Governor-General's Awards for Fiction, 1973, 1994, Lorne Pierce Medal, Royal Soc. of Canada, 1987, Charles Taylor Prize for Literary Non-fiction 2007. *Address:* c/o Department of English and Film Studies, University of Alberta, 3-5 Humanities Centre, Edmonton, Alberta T6G 2E5, Canada. *E-mail:* rudy .wiebe@shaw.ca. *Website:* www.humanities.ualberta.ca/english.

WIENER, Joel Howard, BA, PhD, FRHistS; American academic and writer; *Professor Emeritus of History, City University of New York*; b. 23 Aug. 1937, New York, NY; m. Suzanne Wolff 1961; one s. two d. *Education:* New York Univ., Univ. of Glasgow, Cornell Univ. *Career:* Asst Prof. of History Skidmore Coll. 1964–66; Assoc. Prof. 1966–76, Prof. of History 1977–2000, Prof. Emeritus of History 2000–, City Coll. and the Graduate School and Univ. Center, CUNY; mem. American Historical Asscn, American Journalism Historians Asscn, Conference on British Studies, Research Soc. for Victorian Periodicals (pres.). *Publications:* The War of the Unstamped 1969, A Descriptive Finding List of Unstamped British Periodicals: 1830–1836 1970, Great Britain: Foreign Policy and the Span of Empire 1689–1970 (ed., four vols) 1972, Great Britain: The Lion at Home (four vols) 1974, Radicalism and Freethought in 19th Century Britain 1983, Innovators and Preachers: The Role of the Editor in Victorian England (ed.) 1985, Papers for the Millions: The New Journalism in Britain c. 1850s–1914 (ed.) 1988, William Lovett 1989, Dictionary of National Biography (assoc. ed.) 1999–2004; contrib. to scholarly books and journals. *Address:* 267 Glen Court, Teaneck, NJ 07666, USA (home). *Telephone:* (201) 837-5452 (home). *Fax:* (201) 837-8658 (home). *E-mail:* jwiener267@aol.com (home).

WIENER, Valerie, MA; American politician, media executive, writer and publisher; *President and CEO, Wiener Communications Group*; b. 30 Oct. 1948, Las Vegas, Nev.; d. of Louis Wiener nd Tui Wiener (née Knight); m. 1972 (divorced 1979). *Education:* Univ. of Missouri, Univ. of Ill. and McGeorge School of Law. *Career:* Propr and Vice-Pres. Broadcast Assocs Inc. 1972–86; Public Affairs Dir First Ill. Cable TV 1973–74; Ed. Ill. State Register 1973–74; Producer KLVX-TV 1974–75; Account Exec. KBMI 1975–79; Exec. Vice-Pres. and Gen.-Man. KXKS and KKJY Stations 1980–81; Exec. Admin. KSET, KVEG, KFMS and KKJY 1981–83; Pres. and CEO Wiener Communications Group 1988–; Nev. State Senator 1996–2004, Senate Democratic Whip; mem. Nat. Asscn of Women Business Owners, Soc. for Professional Journalists, Nat. Fed. of Press Women. *Publications:* Power Communications 1994, Gang Free 1995, The Nesting Syndrome 1997, Winning the War Against Youth Gangs 1999, Power Positioning 2000, Advancing Yourself Through Media Relations 2000, Advancing Yourself Through Political Positioning 2000, Advancing Yourself Through Self-Promotion 2000, Advancing Yourself Through Expert-Client Relations 2005. *Honours:* winner 157 communications awards; Outstanding Woman Advocate for Education, Virginia Commonwealth Univ. 2000, Int. Community Service Award, Int. New Thought Alliance Award 2001. *Address:* Wiener Communications Group, 1500 Foremaster Lane, Suite 2, Las Vegas, NV 89101-1103; 3540 West Sahara Avenue, #352, Las Vegas, NV 89102, USA. *Telephone:* (702) 871-6536 (office); (702) 221-0068 (office). *Fax:*

(702) 221-9239 (office). *E-mail:* contact@valeriewiener.com (office). *Website:* www.valeriewiener.com.

WIER, Dara, (Phraz Barrois), BS, MFA; American poet and academic; *Professor, University of Massachusetts at Amherst;* b. 30 Dec. 1949, New Orleans, LA; one d. one s. *Education:* Louisiana State Univ., Longwood Coll., Bowling Green State Univ. *Career:* Instructor, Univ. of Pittsburgh 1974–75; Instructor 1975–76, Asst Prof. 1977–80, Hollins Coll.; Assoc. Prof. 1980–85, Dir of Graduate Studies 1980–82, Dir of Writing Program 1983–84, Univ. of Alabama at Tuscaloosa; Assoc. Prof. 1985–96, Prof. 1996–, Dir MFA programmes for writers and poets 1985–91, 1992–94, 1997–98, 2004–07, Univ. of Massachusetts at Amherst; visiting poet at various colls and univs; mem. Associated Writing Programs (pres. 1981–82), Authors' Guild, Authors' League of America, PEN, Poetry Soc. of America. *Publications:* Blood, Hook, and Eye 1977, The 8-Step Grapevine 1981, All You Have in Common 1984, The Book of Knowledge 1988, Blue for the Plough 1992, Our Master Plan 1997, Voyages in English 2001, Hat on a Pond 2002, Reverse Rapture (American Poetry Archives/Poetry Center Book Award 2005) 2005, Remnants of Hannah 2006; contrib. to anthologies and periodicals. *Honours:* Nat. Endowment for the Arts Fellowship 1980, Guggenheim Fellowship 1993–94, Jerome Shestack Award, American Poetry Review 2001, Pushcart Prize 2002. *Address:* 504 Montague Road, Amherst, MA 01002, USA. *Telephone:* (413) 549-1115 (home); (413) 545-0643 (office). *E-mail:* daraw@hfa.umass.edu (office).

WIESEL, Elie(zer), KBE; American author and academic; *University Professor, Andrew W. Mellon Professor in the Humanities and Professor of Philosophy and Religion, Boston University;* b. 30 Sept. 1928, Sighet, Romania; s. of Shlomo Wiesel and Sarah Wiesel (née Feig); m. Marion E. Wiesel 1969; one s. one step d. *Education:* Sorbonne, Paris. *Career:* naturalized US citizen 1963; Distinguished Prof., Coll. of City of New York 1972–76; Andrew Mellon Prof. in Humanities, Boston Univ. 1976–, Prof. of Philosophy and Religion 1988–; Founder The Elie Wiesel Foundation for Humanity 1986; mem. Bd Fund for the Holocaust 1997–; Founding Pres. Universal Acad. of Cultures, Paris 1993; mem. numerous bds of dirs, trustees, govs and advisers including Int. Rescue Cttee, American Jewish World Service, Yad Vashem, Mutual of America, AmeriCares, US Cttee for Refugees; mem. PEN, The Authors' Guild, Foreign Press Asscn, Writers and Artists for Peace in the Middle East, Council of Foreign Relations, American Acad. of Arts and Sciences, American Acad. of Arts and Letters (Dept of Literature), Jewish Acad. of Arts and Sciences, European Acad. of Arts, Sciences and Humanities, Royal Norwegian Soc. of Sciences and Letters. *Publications:* Night 1960, Dawn 1961, The Accident 1962, The Town Beyond the Wall 1964, The Gates of the Forest 1966, The Jews of Silence 1966, Legends of Our Time 1968, A Beggar in Jerusalem 1970, One Generation After 1971, Souls on Fire 1972, The Oath 1973, Ani Maamin, Cantata 1973, Zalmen or the Madness of God (play) 1975, Messengers of God 1976, A Jew Today 1978, Four Hasidic Masters 1978, The Trial of God 1979, One Generation After 1979, Le testament d'un poète juif assassiné 1980 (Prix Livre-Inter 1980, Prix des Bibliothéquaires 1981), The Testament 1980, Images from the Bible 1980, Five Biblical Portraits 1981, Somewhere a Master: Further Tales of the Hasidic Master 1982, Paroles d'étranger 1982, The Golem 1983, The Fifth Son (Grand Prix de la Littérature, Paris) 1985, Signes d'exode 1985, Against Silence 1985, A Song for Hope 1987, Job ou Dieu dans la tempête (with Josy Eisenberg) 1987, A Nobel Address 1987, Twilight (novel) 1988, The Six Days of Destruction (with Albert Friedlander) 1988, L'oublie 1989, Silences et mémoire d'hommes 1989, From the Kingdom of Memory, Reminiscences (essays) 1990, Evil and Exile 1990, A Journey of Faith 1990, Sages and Dreamers 1991, Célébration Talmudique 1991, The Forgotten 1992, A Passover Haggadah 1993, Se taire est impossible 1995, All Rivers Run to the Sea (Memoirs, Vol.I) 1995, Et la mer n'est pas remplie (Memoirs, Vol.II) 1996 (trans. as And the Sea Is Never Full 1999), Célébration prophétique 1998, King Solomon and His Magic Ring 2000, D'où viens-tu? 2001, The Judges 2002, After the Darkness 2002, Wise Men and Their Tales 2003, Et où vas-tu? 2004, The Time of the Uprooted 2005, Un Désir fou de Danser 2006, Confronting Anti-Semitism (with Kofi Annan) 2006. *Honours:* Grand Officer, Légion d'honneur, Grand Cross of the Order of the Southern Cross, Brazil 1987, Grand Cross of the Order of Rio Branco, Brazil 2001, Grand Officer, Order of the Star of Romania 2002, Commander's Cross, Order of Merit of Hungary 2004, King Hussein Award, Jordan 2005, Hon. KBE 2006; recipient of over 110 hon. degrees; Prix Rivarol 1964, Jewish Heritage Award 1965, Remembrance Award 1965, Prix Médicis 1968, Prix Bordin (Acad. Française) 1972, Eleanor Roosevelt Memorial Award 1972, American Liberties Medallion, American Jewish Comm. 1972, Martin Luther King Jr Award (Coll. of City of New York) 1973, Faculty Distinguished Scholar Award, Hofstra Univ. 1973–74, Congressional Gold Medal of Achievement 1985, Nobel Peace Prize 1986, Medal of Liberty Award 1986, Ellis Island Medal of Honor 1992, Presidential Medal of Freedom 1993, and numerous other awards. *Address:* Boston University, 147 Bay State Road, Boston, MA 02215, USA (office). *Telephone:* (617) 353-4561 (office). *Fax:* (617) 353-4024 (office). *E-mail:* rstrauss@bu.edu (office). *Website:* www.bu.edu/philo (office).

WIESENFARTH, Joseph John, BA, MA, PhD; American academic and writer; *Professor Emeritus, University of Wisconsin at Madison;* b. 20 Aug. 1933, Brooklyn, NY; m. Louise Halpin 1971; one s. *Education:* Catholic Univ. of America, Washington, DC, Univ. of Detroit. *Career:* Asst Prof., La Salle Coll., Philadelphia 1962–64; Asst Prof. 1964–67, Assoc. Prof. 1967–70,

Manhattan Coll., New York; Assoc. Prof. 1970–76, Prof. of English 1976–2000, Chair Dept of English 1983–86, 1989–92, Assoc. Dean Graduate School 1995–96, Assoc. Dean Coll. of Letters and Science 1997, Prof. Emeritus 2000–, Univ. of Wisconsin at Madison; Advisory Ed., George Eliot-George Henry Lewes Studies, Connotations, Renascence, Int. Ford Madox Ford Studies; Fellow Nat. Endowment for the Humanities 1967–68; Inst. for Research in Humanities Fellow 1975; Fulbright Fellow 1981–82; Fellow Istituto di Studi Avazati, Bologna 2004; mem. MLA, Jane Austen Soc. of N America, Henry James Soc., Katherine Anne Porter Soc., Ford Madox Ford Soc.; mem. Christian Gauss Prize Award Cttee 1986–88, 1989–90. *Publications:* Henry James and the Dramatic Analogy 1963, The Errand of Form: An Essay of Jane Austen's Art 1967, George Eliot's Mythmaking 1977, George Eliot: A Writer's Notebook 1854–1879 1981, Gothic Manners and the Classic English Novel 1988, Ford Madox Ford and the Arts 1989, Jane Austen's Jack and Alice 2001, History and Representation in Ford Madox Ford's Writings 2004, Jane Austen's The Three Sisters 2004, Ford Madox Ford and the Regiment of Women 2005; contrib. numerous articles on British and American Fiction. *Address:* 5401 Greening Lane, Madison, WI 53705-1252, USA. *Fax:* (608) 233-2295 (home). *E-mail:* jjwiesen@wisc.edu.

WIGGINS, Marianne; American writer and academic; b. 8 Sept. 1947, Lancaster, Pa; m. Salman Rushdie 1988 (divorced 1993). *Education:* Manheim Township High School, Lancaster, Pa. *Career:* Professor of English, Univ. of Southern Calif. 2005–. *Publications include:* Went South 1980, Separate Checks 1984, Herself in Love 1987, John Dollar 1989, Bet They'll Miss Us When We're Gone (short stories) 1991, Eveless Eden 1995, Almost Heaven 1998, Evidence of Things Unseen 2003, John Dollar (Janet Heidiger Kafka Prize 1990) 1989, Eveless Eden 1996, Almost Heaven, Evidence of Things Unseen (Commonwealth Club Prize Gold Medal 2004) 2003, The Shadow Catcher 2007; two short story collections. *Honours:* Whiting Award 1989, Janet Heidiger Kafka Prize 1990. *Address:* Department of English, THH 404, University of Southern California, 3551 Trousdale Parkway, Los Angeles, CA 90089-4012, USA (office). *Telephone:* (213) 740-2808 (office). *E-mail:* wigginsm@usc.edu (office). *Website:* www.usc.edu/schools/college/engl/home/index.shtml (office).

WIGNALL, Anne, (Alice Acland, Anne Marreco); British writer; b. 12 June 1912, London, England; m. 1st Francis Egerton Grosvenor, Fifth Baron of Ebury 1933 (divorced); two s.; m. 2nd Barton Wignall 1947 (deceased); one d.; m. 3rd Anthony Marreco 1961 (divorced). *Publications:* as Alice Acland: Caroline Norton (biog.) 1948, Templeford Park (novel) 1954, A Stormy Spring (novel) 1955, A Second Choice (novel) 1956, A Person of Discretion (novel) 1958, The Corsican Ladies (novel) 1974, The Secret Wife (novel) 1975, The Ruling Passion (novel) 1976; as Anne Marreco: The Charmer and the Charmed (novel) 1963, The Boat Boy (novel) 1964, The Rebel Countess (biog.) 1967. *Literary Agent:* Curtis Brown Ltd, Haymarket House, 28–29 Haymarket, London, SW1Y 4SP, England. *Telephone:* (20) 7393-4400. *Fax:* (20) 7393-4401. *E-mail:* info@curtisbrown.co.uk. *Website:* www.curtisbrown.co.uk.

WIKSTRÖM, Jan-Erik, BA; Swedish politician and publisher; b. 11 Sept. 1932, St Skedvi, Dalarna; s. of Börje Wikström and Essy (Lilja) Wikström; m. Rev. Cecilia Wikström 1995; three s. one d. *Education:* Gothenberg Univ. *Career:* Man. Dir Gummessons Bokförlag Publishing House 1961–76; mem. Municipal Council, Stockholm 1962–70; mem. Riksdag (Parl.) 1970–73, 1976–92; Minister of Educ. and Cultural Affairs 1976–82; Gov. of Uppsala 1992–97; mem. Folkpartiet (Liberal Party). *Publications:* Röd och gul och vit och svart 1950, Skall kyrkan skiljas från staten 1958, Storm över Kongo 1961, Indien vid korsvägen 1962, Inför Herrens ansikte 1962, Politik och kristen tro 1964, Skall samhället utbilda präster? 1966, Liberala positioner 1969, Med frisinnat förtecken 1970, En bättre skola 1973, Möten med Mästaren 1975, I väntan på befrielsen 1977, Friket Mångfald Kvalitet 1978, Liberalism med frisinnat förtecken 1981. *Address:* Domkyrkoplan 1, 753 10 Uppsala, Sweden.

WILBER, Ken; American writer, spiritualist and psychologist; b. 1949, Oklahoma City, OK. *Education:* Duke Univ. *Career:* founder, Integral Inst. 2000. *Publications include:* non-fiction: The Spectrum of Consciousness 1977, No Boundary: Eastern and Western Approaches to Personal Growth 1979, The Attman Project 1980, Up from Eden 1981, Holographic Paradigm and Other Paradoxes 1982, A Sociable God 1982, Eye to Eye: The Quest for the New Paradigm 1984, The Marriage of Sense and Soul 1988, Grace and Grit 1991, Sex, Ecology, Sprituality 1995, A Brief History of Everything 1995, The Eye of Spirit 1997, One Taste 1999, Integral Psychology: Consciousness Spirit, Psychology Therapy 2000, A Theory of Everything 2001, Boomeritis 2002, The Simple Feeling of Being 2004; editor: Quantum Questions: Mystical Writings of the World's Great Physicists 1984. *Address:* c/o Shambhala Publications, PO Box 308, Boston, MA 02117, USA. *Website:* www.shambhala.com.

WILBUR, Richard Purdy, MA; American poet and academic; b. 1 March 1921, New York City; s. of Lawrence L. Wilbur and Helen Purdy Wilbur; m. Charlotte Ward 1942; three s. one d. *Education:* Amherst Coll. and Harvard Univ. *Career:* Asst Prof. of English, Harvard Univ. 1950–54; Assoc. Prof. Wellesley Coll. 1954–57; Prof. Wesleyan Univ. 1957–77; Writer in Residence, Smith Coll., Northampton, Mass. 1977–86; mem. American Acad. of Arts and Sciences, Soc. of Fellows of Harvard Univ. 1947–50; Guggenheim Fellow 1952–53, 1963, Ford Fellow 1961; Chancellor, Acad. of American Poets 1961; Poet Laureate of USA 1987–88; mem. PEN; Pres. American Acad. of Arts and Letters 1974–76, Chancellor 1977–78; mem. Dramatists Guild. *Publications:*

The Beautiful Changes and Other Poems 1947, Ceremony and Other Poems 1950, A Bestiary (anthology, with Alexander Calder) 1955, The Misanthrope (trans. from Molière) 1955, Things of This World (poems) 1956, Poems 1943–1956 1957, Candide (comic opera, with Lillian Hellman and others) 1957, (edition of his poems with introduction and notes) 1959, Advice to a Prophet (poems) 1961, Tartuffe (trans. from Molière) 1963, The Poems of Richard Wilbur 1963, Loudmouse (for children) 1963, Poems of Shakespeare (with Alfred Harbage) 1966, Walking to Sleep (new poems and translations) 1969, School for Wives (trans. from Molière) 1971, Opposites (children's verse, illustrated by the author) 1973, The Mind-Reader 1976, Responses: Prose Pieces 1953–1976 1976, The Learned Ladies (trans. from Molière) 1978, Selected Poems of Witter Bynner (editor) 1978, Seven Poems 1981, Andromache (trans. from Racine) 1982, The Whale (translations) 1982, Molière: Four Comedies (contains 4 plays translated previously listed) 1982, Phaedra (trans. from Racine) 1986, Lying and Other Poems 1987, New and Collected Poems 1988, More Opposites 1991, School for Husbands (trans. from Molière) 1992, The Imaginary Cuckold (trans. from Molière) 1993, A Game of Catch 1994, Amphitryon (trans. from Molière) 1995, The Catbird's Song (prose pieces) 1997, The Disappearing Alphabet (for children and others) 1998, Bone Key and Other Poems 1998, Mayflies (poems) 2000, Don Juan (trans. from Molière) 2000, The Bungler (trans. from Molière) 2000, Opposites, More Opposites and Some Differences (for children) 2000, The Pig in the Spigot (for children) 2000, Collected Poems 1953–2004 2004. *Honours:* Hon. Fellow, Modern Language Asscn 1986; Chevalier, Ordre des Palmes Académiques 1984; Harriet Monroe Prize 1948, Oscar Blumenthal Prize 1950, Prix de Rome from American Acad. of Arts and Letters 1954–55, Edna St Vincent Millay Memorial Award 1956, Nat. Book Award, Pulitzer Prize 1957, co-recipient Bollingen Translation Prize 1963, co-recipient Bollingen Prize in Poetry 1971, Prix Henri Desfeuilles 1971, Brandeis Creative Arts Award 1971, Shelley Memorial Prize 1973, Harriet Monroe Poetry Award 1978, Drama Desk Award 1983, PEN Translation Prize 1983, St Botolph's Foundation Award 1983, Aiken Taylor Award 1988, L.A. Times Book Award 1988, Pulitzer Prize 1989, Gold Medal for Poetry, American Acad. of Arts and Letters 1991, MacDowell Medal 1992, Nat. Arts Club Medal of Honour for Literature 1994, PEN/Manheim Medal for Translation 1994, Nat. Medal of Arts 1994, Milton Center Prize 1995, Robert Frost Medal, Poetry Soc. of America 1996, T. S. Eliot Award 1996, Wallace Stevens Award 2003, Theater Hall of Fame 2003. *Address:* 87 Dodwells Road, Cummington, MA 01026; 715R Windsor Lane, Key West, FL 33040, USA. *Telephone:* (413) 634-2275; (305) 296-7499.

WILBY, Basil Leslie, (Gareth Knight), BA; British writer; b. 1930, Colchester, England. *Education:* Royal Holloway Coll., London, Sheffield Hallam Univ. *Publications:* A Practical Guide to Qabalistic Symbolism 1965, The New Dimensions Red Book 1968, The Practice of Ritual Magic 1969, Occult Exercises and Practices 1969, Meeting the Occult 1973, Experience of the Inner Worlds 1975, The Occult: An Introduction 1975, The Secret Tradition in Arthurian Legend 1983, The Rose Cross and the Goddess 1985, The Treasure House of Images 1986, The Magical World of the Inklings 1990, The Magical World of the Tarot 1991, Magic and the Western Mind 1991, Tarot and Magic 1991, Evoking the Goddess 1993, Dion Fortune's Magical Battle of Britain 1993, Introduction to Ritual Magic (with Dion Fortune) 1997, The Circuit of Force (with Dion Fortune) 1998, Magical Images and the Magical Imagination 1998, Principles of Hermetic Philosophy (with Dion Fortune) 1999, Merlin and the Grail Tradition 1999, Dion Fortune and the Inner Light 2000, Spiritualism and Occultism (with Dion Fortune) 2000, Pythoness, the Life and Work of Margaret Lumley Brown 2000, Esoteric Training in Everyday Life 2001, The Magical World of J. R. R. Tolkien 2001, The Magical World of C. S. Lewis 2001, The Magical World of Charles Williams 2002, The Magical World of Owen Barfield 2002, Practical Occultism (with Dion Fortune) 2002, The Abbey Papers 2002, Dion Fortune and the Threefold Way 2002, The Wells of Vision 2002, Granny's Magic Cards 2004, The Magical Fiction of Dion Fortune 2005, The Arthurian Formula (with Dion Fortune and Margaret Lumbley Brown) 2005; contrib. to Inner Light Journal 1993–. *Address:* c/o 38 Steeles Road, London, NW3 4RG, England. *Website:* www.angelfire.com/az/garethknight.

WILBY, Peter; British journalist; b. 7 Nov. 1944, Leicester; m. Sandra James; two s. *Education:* Univ. of Sussex. *Career:* reporter, The Observer 1968–72, Educ. Corresp. 1972–75; Educ. Corresp. The New Statesman 1975–77, Ed. 1998–2005, now writes weekly column on media; Educ. Corresp. The Sunday Times 1977–86; Educ. Ed. The Independent 1986–89, Home Ed. 1989–91, Deputy Ed. 1991–95; Ed. Independent on Sunday 1995–96. *Address:* c/o The New Statesman, 3rd Floor, 52 Grosvenor Gardens, London, SW1W 0AU, England (office). *Website:* www.newstatesman.com/writers/peter_wilby (office).

WILCOX, James, BA; American author; b. 4 April 1949, Hammond, LA. *Education:* Yale Univ. *Career:* mem. Authors' Guild, PEN. *Publications:* Modern Baptists 1983, North Gladiola 1985, Miss Undine's Living Room 1987, Sort of Rich 1989, Polite Sex 1991, Guest of a Sinner 1993, Plain and Normal 1998, Heavenly Days 2002; contrib. to periodicals. *Literary Agent:* International Creative Management, 40 W 57th Street, New York, NY 10019, USA.

WILD, Peter, BA, MA, MFA; American academic, poet and writer; b. 25 April 1940, Northampton, MA; m. 1st Sylvia Ortiz, 1966; m. 2nd Rosemary Harrold, 1981. *Education:* University of Arizona, University of California at Irvine. *Career:* Asst Prof., Sul Ross State University, Alpine, Texas, 1969–71; Asst Prof., 1971–73, Assoc. Prof., 1973–79, Prof. of English. 1979–, University of

Arizona; Contributing Ed., High Country News, 1974–; Consulting Ed., Diversions, 1983–. *Publications:* poetry: The Good Fox, 1967; Sonnets, 1967; The Afternoon in Dismay, 1968; Mica Mountain Poems, 1968; Joining Up and Other Poems, 1968; Mad Night with Sunflowers, 1968; Love Poems, 1969; Three Nights in the Chiricahuas, 1969; Poems, 1969; Fat Man Poems, 1970; Term and Renewals, 1970; Grace, 1971; Dilemma, 1971; Wild's Magical Book of Cranial Effusions, 1971; Peligros, 1972; New and Selected Poems, 1973; Cochise, 1973; The Cloning, 1974; Tumacacori, 1974; Health, 1974; Chihuahua, 1976; The Island Hunter, 1976; Pioneers, 1976; The Cavalryman, 1976; House Fires, 1977; Gold Mines, 1978; Barn Fires, 1978; Zuni Butte, 1978; The Lost Tribe, 1979; Jeanne d'Arc: A Collection of New Poems, 1980; Rainbow, 1980; Wilderness, 1980; Heretics, 1981; Bitteroots, 1982; The Peaceable Kingdom, 1983; Getting Ready for a Date, 1984; The Light on Little Mormon Lake, 1984; The Brides of Christ, 1991; Easy Victory, 1994. Other: Pioneer Conservationists of Western America, 2 vols, 1979, 1983; Enos Mills, 1979; Clarence King, 1981; James Welch, 1983; Barry Lopez, 1984; John Haines, 1985; John Nicholas, 1986; The Saguaro Forest, 1986; John C. Van Dyke: The Desert, 1988; Alvar Núñez Cabeza de Vaca, 1991; Ann Zwinger, 1993. Editor: New Poetry of the American West (with Frank Graziano), 1982. *Honours:* Writer's Digest Prize, 1964; Hart Crane and Alice Crane Williams Memorial Fund Grant, 1969; Ark River Review Prize, 1972; Ohio State University Pres.'s Prize, 1982.

WILDING, Eric (see Tubb, Edwin Charles)

WILDING, Michael, BA, MA, DLitt, FAHA; British academic and writer; *Emeritus Professor, University of Sydney*; b. 5 Jan. 1942, Worcester, England. *Education:* Univ. of Oxford, Univ. of Sydney. *Career:* Lecturer 1963–66, Sr Lecturer 1969–72, Reader 1972–92, Prof. 1993–2000, Emeritus Prof. 2001–, Univ. of Sydney; Lecturer, Univ. of Birmingham 1967–68; Visiting Prof., Univ. of California 1987. *Publications:* Aspects of the Dying Process 1972, Living Together 1974, Short Story Embassy 1975, West Midland Underground 1975, Scenic Drive 1976, The Phallic Forest 1978, Political Fictions 1980, Pacific Highway 1982, Reading the Signs 1984, The Paraguyan Experiment 1985, The Man of Slow Feeling 1985, Dragons Teeth 1987, Under Saturn 1988, Great Climate 1990, Social Visions 1993, The Radical Tradition, Lawson, Furphy, Stead 1993, This is for You 1994, Book of the Reading 1994, The Oxford Book of Australian Short Stories 1994, Somewhere New 1996, Studies in Classical Australian Fiction 1997, Wildest Dreams 1998, Raising Spirits, Making Gold and Swapping Wives: The True Adventures of Dr John Dee and Sir Edward Kelly 1999, Academia Nuts 2002. *Honours:* Australia Council Literature Bd Sr Fellowship 1978. *Address:* c/o Department of English, University of Sydney, Sydney, NSW 2006, Australia. *E-mail:* nswwc@ozemail .com.au.

WILENTZ, Robert Sean, BA, PhD; American historian and writer; b. 20 Feb. 1951, New York; m. Mary Christine Stansell 1980, one s. one d. *Education:* Columbia Coll., Univ. of Oxford, Yale Univ. *Career:* mem. Soc. of American Historians. *Publications:* Chants Democratic, 1984; Rites of Power, 1985; The Key of Liberty, 1993; The Kingdom of Matthias, 1994. Contributions: New Republic; Dissent. *Honours:* Beveridge Award 1984, Turner Award 1985.

WILFORD, John Noble, BS, MA; American journalist and writer; *Science Correspondent, New York Times*; b. 4 Oct. 1933, Murray, KY; m. Nancy Watts Paschall 1966; one d. *Education:* Univ. of Tennessee, Syracuse Univ., Columbia Univ. *Career:* science reporter 1965–73, 1979–, Asst Nat. Ed., New York Times 1973–75, Dir of Science News 1975–79, Science Correspondent 1979–; McGraw Distinguished Lecturer in Writing, Princeton Univ. 1985; Prof. of Science Journalism, Univ. of Tennessee 1989–90; American Acad. of Arts and Sciences Fellow 1998; mem. Century Club (New York), Nat. Asscn of Science Writers, American Geographical Soc. (council mem. 1994–). *Publications:* We Reach the Moon 1969, The Mapmakers 1981, The Riddle of the Dinosaur 1985, Mars Beckons 1990, The Mysterious History of Columbus 1991, Cosmic Dispatches 2000; contrib. to Nature, Wilson Quarterly, New York Times Magazine, Science Digest, Popular Science, National Geographic. *Honours:* Westinghouse-American Asscn for the Advancement of Science Writing Award 1983, Pulitzer Prizes for Nat. Reporting 1984, 1987 (jtly), American Soc. of Mechanical Engineers Ralph Coats Roe Medal 1995, American Geological Inst. Award for Outstanding Contributions to Public Understanding of Geosciences 2001, Mayor's Award for Excellence in Science and Technology, New York 2001. *Address:* New York Times, 229 W 43rd Street, New York, NY 10036, USA (office).

WILHELM, Hans; American children's writer and illustrator; b. 21 Sept. 1945, Bremen, Germany; m. Judy Henderson. *Career:* lived in Africa for many years. *Publications include:* Waldo series: Waldo, Waldo and the Desert Island Adventure, Waldo at the Zoo, Waldo, One, Two, Three, Waldo, Tell me about Christ, Waldo, Tell me about Christmas, Waldo, Tell me about Dying, Waldo, Tell me about God, Waldo, Tell me about Guardian Angels, Waldo, Tell me about Me, Waldo, Tell me Where's Grandpa, Waldo's Christmas Surprise; Dinofours series: Let Me Play, I'm the Winner, It's Snowing, My Seeds Won't Grow, It's Thanksgiving, It's Class Picture Day, Bind Up, Our Holiday Show, I'm Sorry! I'm Sorry!, We Love Mud!; A Christmas Journey, A Cool Kid Like Me, A New Home A New Friend, All For The Best, Anook The Snow Princess, Bingo, Bunny Trouble, More Bunny Trouble, Bad Bad Bunny Trouble, Buzz Said the Bee, Don't Cut My Hair!, Franklin and the Messy Pigs, Friends are Forever, Hello Sun, Hiccups for Elephant, I am Lost!, I Can Help, I Hate Bullies!, I Hate My Bow, I Lost my Tooth!, I Love Colors!, I Love my Shadow, I

Wouldn't Tell a Lie, I'll Always Love You, It's Too Windy!, Let's Be Friends Again, Mother Goose on the Loose, Never Lonely Again, No Kisses Please, Oh, What a Mess, Quacky Ducky's Easter Fun, Quacky Ducky's Easter Egg, Schnitzel is Lost, Schnitzel's First Christmas, Tales From the Land Under my Table, The Big Boasting Battle, The Boy Who Wasn't There, The Bremen Town Musicians, The Royal Raven, The Trapp Family Book, Tyrone the Horrible, Tyrone the Double Dirty Rotten Cheater, Tyrone and the Swamp Gang, Wake Up, Sun!, With Lots of Love. *Honours:* numerous int. awards. *Address:* PO Box 109, Westport, CT 06881, USA. *E-mail:* hans@hanswilhelm .com. *Website:* www.hanswilhelm.com.

WILKERSON, Cynthia (see Levinson, Leonard)

WILKINSON, Lisa Clare; Australian magazine editor; b. 19 Dec. 1958, Wollongong, NSW; d. of the late Raymond William and of Beryl Jean Wilkinson; m. Peter FitzSimons 1992. *Education:* Campbelltown High School (NSW). *Career:* Editorial Asst Dolly Magazine (magazine for girls) 1978, Asst Ed. 1979–80, apptd Ed. aged 21, youngest ever ed. of nat. women's magazine 1980, later Ed.-in-Chief, currently Consultant; apptd Ed. Cleo (women's lifestyle magazine) magazine 1985, Int. Ed.-in-Chief Cleo's Int. edns in NZ, Singapore, Malaysia and Thailand; consultant Australian Consolidated Press; currently Ed. Australian Women's Weekly. *Address:* The Australian Women's Weekly, GPO Box 4178, Sydney, NSW 1028, Australia.

WILL, Frederic, BA, PhD; American poet, academic and ; *Tutor in Philosophy, Instituto de Estudios Criticos;* b. 4 Dec. 1928, New Haven, CT; m. Umotejohwo Ogaga 1995; six c. *Education:* Indiana and Yale Univs. *Career:* Instructor in Classics, Dartmouth Coll. 1951–54; Asst Prof. of Classics, Pennsylvania State Univ. 1955–60, Univ. of Texas 1960–65; Assoc. Prof. of English and Comparative Literature 1964–66, Prof. of Comparative Literature 1966–71, Univ. of Iowa, Assoc. Dir Int. Writing Program 1983–85, Fellow, Inst. of Advanced Studies 1985–90; Prof. of Comparative Literature, Univ. of Massachusetts at Amherst 1971–83; Dir Bd of Overseers and Pres., Mellen Univ. 1991–2000; Fulbright Prof., Univ. of the Ivory Coast 2000–02; Prof. of American Studies, Hunan Normal Univ. 2003; Fulbright Sr Specialist, Univ. of N'djamena, Chad; Visiting Prof. of Greek, Deep Springs Coll. 2004–05; Professeur titulaire, École supérieure universitaire Robert de Sorbon 2004–06; Tutor en Filosofia, Instituto de Estudios Criticos, Mexico City 2007–; poetry and scholarly readings at major US univs; Founding Ed. (with William Arrowsmith) Arion: A Journal of Classical Culture 1962. *Publications:* Intelligible Beauty in Aesthetic Thought: From Winckelmann to Victor Cousin 1958, Mosaic and Other Poems 1959, A Wedge of Words (poems) 1962, Kostes Palamas: The Twelve Words of the Gypsy (trans.) 1964, Hereditas: Seven Essays on the Modern Experience of the Classical (ed.) 1964, Metaphrasis: An Anthology from the University of Iowa Trans. Workshop 1964–65 (ed.) 1965, Flumen Historicum: Victor Cousin's Aesthetic and Its Sources 1965, Literature Inside Out: Ten Speculative Essays 1966, Planets (poems) 1966, Kostes Palamas: The King's Flute (trans.) 1967, From a Year in Greece 1967, Archilochos 1969, Herondas 1972, Brandy in the Snow (poems) 1972, Theodor Adorno: The Jargon of Authenticity (trans. with Knut Tarnowski) 1973, The Knife in the Stone 1973, The Fact of Literature 1973, Guatemala 1973, Botulism (poems) 1975, The Generic Demands of Greek Literature 1976, Belphagor 1977, Epics of America (poems) 1977, Our Thousand Year Old Bodies: Selected Poems 1956–1976 1980, Shamans in Turtlenecks: Selected Essays 1984, The Sliced Dog 1984, Entering the Open Hole 1989, Recoveries 1993, Trips of the Psyche 1993, Textures, Spaces, Wonders 1993, Literature as Sheltering the Human 1993, Singing with Whitman's Thrush 1993, Adventure in Algiers 2002, Bill Ryerson's African Passion 2002, The Poppy Web 2002, By the Sweat of thy Brow 2002, Three North American Agricultural Communities 2002, Miroirs d'Eternité, une saison au Sahel 2002, Mellen University, Early Life and Times 2002, Flesh and the Color of Love 2002; contrib. of many poems and articles to various periodicals. *Honours:* Pfatteicher Prize 1946, Fulbright grants 1950–51, 1955, 1956–57, 1975–76, 1980–81, 2000–02, ACLS grant 1958, Texas Inst. of Letters Voertman Poetry Awards 1962, 1964, Bollingen Foundation grant 1963, Nat. Endowment for the Arts grant 1963, NEA and CCLM editorial grants 1965–73. *Address:* 617 7th Street NW, Mount Vernon, IA 52314, USA (home). *Telephone:* (319) 895-6159 (home). *Fax:* (319) 895-6399 (home). *E-mail:* samuelw981@aol.com (home).

WILL, George Frederick, BA, MA, PhD; American political columnist, broadcaster and writer; b. 4 May 1941, Champaign, IL. *Education:* Trinity College, Oxford, Princeton University. *Career:* Prof. of Political Philosophy, Michigan State University, 1967–68, University of Toronto, 1968–70; Ed., The National Review, 1973–76; Syndicated Political Columnist, The Washington Post, 1974–; Contributing Ed., Newsweek magazine, 1976–; Television News Analyst, ABC-TV, 1981–. *Publications:* The Pursuit of Happiness and Other Sobering Thoughts, 1979; The Pursuit of Virtue and Other Tory Notions, 1982; Statecraft as Soulcraft: What Government Does, 1983; The Morning After: American Successes and Excesses, 1986; The New Season: A Spectator's Guide to the 1988 Election, 1987; Men at Work, 1990; Suddenly: The American Idea at Home and Abroad, 1988–89, 1990; Restoration: Congress, Term Limits and the Recovery of Deliberate Democracy, 1992; The Leveling Wind: Politics, the Culture and Other News, 1994. *Honours:* Pulitzer Prize for Commentary 1977.

WILLIAMS, Charles Kenneth (C. K.), BA; American poet and academic; *Lecturer, Creative Writing, Department of Comparative Literature, Princeton University;* b. 4 Nov. 1936, Newark, NJ; s. of Paul Bernard and Dossie (née Kasdin) Williams; m. 1st Sarah Dean Jones 1966 (divorced 1975); one d.; m. 2nd Catherine Justine Mauger 1975; one s. *Education:* Univ. of Pennsylvania. *Career:* Visiting Prof. of Literature, Beaver Coll., Jenkintown, Pa 1975, Drexel Univ., Philadelphia 1976, Franklin and Marshall Coll., Pa 1977, Univ. of Calif. at Irvine 1978, Boston Univ. 1979–80, Brooklyn Coll., CUNY 1982–83; Prof. of Writing, Columbia Univ. NY 1981–85; Prof. of Literature, George Mason Univ., Fairfax Va 1982–95; Halloway Lecturer Univ. of Calif. at Berkeley 1986; Lecturer, Creative Writing, Dept of Comparative Literature, Princeton Univ. 1995–; contributing Ed. American Poetry Review 1972–; Fellow Guggenheim Foundation 1975–, Nat. Endowment for Arts 1985, 1993; mem. PEN, American Acad. of Arts and Sciences, American Acad. of Arts and Letters. *Publications:* A Day for Anne Frank 1968, Lies 1969, The Sensuous President 1972, I am the Bitter Name 1972, With Ignorance 1977, The Women of Trachis (co-trans.) 1978, The Lark, The Thrush, The Starling 1983, Tar 1983, Flesh and Blood 1987, Poems 1963–1983, 1988, The Bacchae of Euripides (trans.) 1990, Helen 1991, A Dream of Mind 1992, Selected Poems 1994, The Vigil 1997, Poetry and Consciousness (selected essays) 1998, Repair (poems) 1999, Misgivings: A Memoir 2000, Love About Love 2001, The Singing 2004, Pétain (1856–1951) 2005, Collected Poems 2006; contrib. to Akzent, Atlantic, Carleton Miscellany, Crazyhorse, Grand Street, Iowa Review, Madison Review, New England Review, New Yorker, Seneca Review, Transpacific Review, TriQuarterly, Yale Review, Threepenny Review. *Honours:* Pushcart Press Prizes 1982, 1983, 1987, Nat. Book Critics Circle Award for Poetry 1987, Morton Dauwen Zabel Prize, American Acad. of Arts and Letters 1989, Lila Wallace Writers Award 1993, Harriet Monroe Prize 1993, Berlin Prize, American Acad. in Berlin 1998, Voelcker Career Achievement Award, PEN 1998, Pulitzer Prize for Poetry 2000, LA Times Book Award 2000, Weathertop Prize 2000, Nat. Book Award 2003. *Address:* 71 Leigh Avenue, Princeton, NJ 08542, USA (home).

WILLIAMS, David Larry, BA, MA, PhD; Canadian writer and academic; *Professor of English, University of Manitoba;* b. 22 June 1945, Souris, Man.; m. Darlene Olinyk 1967; two s. *Education:* Briercrest Bible Inst., Saskatchewan, Univ. of Saskatchewan, Univ. of Massachusetts (Amherst). *Career:* Lecturer in English, Univ. of Manitoba, Winnipeg 1972–73; Asst Prof. 1973–77, Assoc. Prof. 1977–83, Prof. of English 1983–; mem. Editorial Bd Canadian Review of American Studies 1976–86, Canadian Literature 2006–; Guest Prof., Indian Asscn for Canadian Studies, MS Univ. of Baroda 1992; Woodrow Wilson Fellow 1968–69; Canada Council Fellow 1969–72; mem. Writers' Union of Canada, PEN Int., Asscn of Canadian Coll. and Univ. Teachers of English, Asscn for Canadian and Québec Literatures. *Publications:* The Burning Wood (novel) 1975, Faulkner's Women: The Myth and the Muse (criticism) 1977, The River Horsemen (novel) 1981, Eye of the Father (novel) 1985, To Run with Longboat: Twelve Stories of Indian Athletes in Canada (with Brenda Zeman) 1988, Confessional Fictions: A Portrait of the Artist in the Canadian Novel 1991, Imagined Nations: Reflections on Media in Canadian Fiction (criticism) (Asscn for Canadian and Québec Literatures Gabrielle Roy Prize) 2003; contrib. to books and professional journals. *Honours:* Canada Council Arts grant 'B' 1977–78, 1981–82, Touring Writer in Scandinavia for External Affairs, Canada 1981, RH Inst. Award for Research in Humanities 1987, Olive Beatrice Stanton Award for Excellence in Teaching 1992, UM-UM Student Union Certificate of Teaching Excellence 1994. *Address:* Department of English, St Paul's College, University of Manitoba, Winnipeg, MB R3T 2M6, Canada (office). *E-mail:* dwillms@cc.umanitoba.ca (office).

WILLIAMS, Gordon MacLean; British writer; b. 1934, Paisley, Renfrewshire, Scotland. *Career:* journalist, sportswriter. *Publications:* novels: The Last Day of Lincoln Charles 1965, The Camp 1966, The Man Who Had Power Over Women 1967, From Scenes Like These 1968, The Siege of Trencher's Farm (aka Straw Dogs) 1969, Upper Pleasure Garden 1970, Walk Don't Walk 1972, Big Morning Blues 1974, The Duellists 1977, The Microcolony 1979, Revolution of the Micronauts 1981, Pomeroy 1983, Pomeroy Unleashed 1986; co-writer of Hazell novels with Terry Venables. *Address:* c/o Bloomsbury Publishing PLC, 38 Soho Square, London, W1V 5DF, England. *Website:* www .bloomsbury.com.

WILLIAMS, Heathcote; British playwright and poet; b. 15 Nov. 1941, Helsby, Cheshire, England. *Career:* Assoc. Ed., Transatlantic Review, New York and London. *Publications:* The Local Stigmatic, 1967; AC/DC, 1970; Remember the Truth Dentist, 1974; The Speakers, 1974; Very Tasty: A Pantomime, 1975; An Invitation to the Official Lynching of Abdul Malik, 1975; Anatomy of a Space Rat, 1976; Hancock's Last Half-Hour, 1977; Playpen, 1977; The Immortalist, 1977; At It, 1982; Whales, 1986. Poetry: Whale Nation, 1988; Falling for a Dolphin, 1988; Sacred Elephant, 1989; Autogeddon, 1991. Other: The Speakers, 1964; Manifestoes, Manifestern, 1975; Severe Joy, 1979; Elephants, 1983. *Honours:* Evening Standard Award 1970. *Literary Agent:* Curtis Brown Ltd, Haymarket House, 28–29 Haymarket, London, SW1Y 4SP, England. *Telephone:* (20) 7393-4400. *Fax:* (20) 7393-4401. *E-mail:* info@ curtisbrown.co.uk. *Website:* www.curtisbrown.co.uk.

WILLIAMS, Herbert Lloyd; British writer, poet, dramatist and producer; b. 8 Sept. 1932, Aberystwyth, Wales; s. of Richard David Williams and Minnie Esther Williams; m. Dorothy Maud Edwards 1954; four s. one d. *Education:* Ardwyn Grammar School, Aberystwyth. *Career:* journalist with daily and weekly papers in Wales, England and Scotland; Editorial Officer, Wales Tourist Board; BBC radio producer; freelance writer of books, TV and radio plays and documentaries; part-time univ. tutor; Fellow, Welsh Acad.; mem.

Soc. of Authors. *Television:* Taff Acre 1981, A Welsh Rarebit 1982, A Solitary Mister 1983, Alone in a Crowd 1984, Land of Milk and Money 1986, Davies the Ocean 1987, Calvert in Camera 1990, The Great Powys 1994, Arouse All Wales 1996; script consultant for prize-winning adaptation of A Child's Christmas in Wales by Atlantis Films, Canada. *Radio:* A Lethal Kind of Love 1968, Dear Merthyr 1983, A Very Private View 1983, A Shropshire Lass 1984, Doing the Bard 1986, Bodyline 1991 A Child's Christmas in Wales (adaptation) 1994, The Citadel (adaptation) 1997. *Publications:* The Trophy 1967, A Lethal Kind of Love 1968, Battles in Wales 1975, Come Out Wherever You Are 1976, Stage Coaches in Wales 1977, The Welsh Quiz Book 1978, Railways in Wales 1981, The Pembrokeshire Coast National Park 1987, Stories of King Arthur 1990, Ghost Country 1991, Davies the Ocean 1991, The Stars in Their Courses 1992, John Cowper Powys 1997, Looking Through Time 1998, A Severe Case of Dandruff 1999, Voices of Wales 1999, The Woman in Back Row 2000, Punters 2002; contrib. to reviews and journals. *Honours:* Welsh Arts Council Short Story Prize 1972, and Bursary 1988, Aberystwyth Open Poetry Competition 1990, Hawthornden Poetry Fellowship 1992, Rhys Davies Short Story Award 1995, Harri Webb Poetry Award 2004. *Address:* 63 Bwlch Road, Fairwater, Cardiff, CF5 3BX, Wales (office). *Telephone:* (29) 2065-3211 (office); (7929) 828554 (mobile). *E-mail:* h.williams13@ntlworld.com (office). *Website:* www.herbert-williams.co.uk.

WILLIAMS, Hugo Mordaunt, FRSL; British poet and journalist; b. 20 Feb. 1942, Windsor, Berks.; m. Hermine Demoriane 1966; one d. *Education:* Eton Coll. *Career:* Asst Ed., London Magazine 1961–70; TV critic 1983–88, Poetry Ed. New Statesman 1984–93; Theatre Critic, Sunday Correspondent 1989–91, writer of the Freelance Column in TLS 1988–; Film Critic, Harpers & Queen 1993–98. *Publications:* poetry: Symptoms of Loss 1965, Sugar Daddy 1970, Some Sweet Day 1975, Love Life 1979, Writing Home 1985, Selected Poems 1989, Self-Portrait with a Slide 1990, Dock Leaves 1994, Billy's Rain 1999, Curtain Call: 101 Portraits in Verse (ed.) 2001, Collected Poems 2002, Dear Room 2006, John Betjeman: Selected Poems (ed.) 2006; non-fiction: All the Time in the World 1966, No Particular Place to Go 1981, Freelancing: Adventures of a Poet 1993; contrib. to newspapers and periodicals. *Honours:* Eric Gregory Award 1965, Cholmondeley Award 1970, Geoffrey Faber Memorial Prize 1979, T. S. Eliot Prize 1999, Queen's Gold Medal for Poetry 2004. *Address:* 3 Raleigh Street, London, N1 8NW, England (office). *Telephone:* (20) 7226-1655 (office).

WILLIAMS, J(eanne), (Megan Castell, Jeanne Crecy, Jeanne Foster, Kristin Michaels, Deirdre Rowan); American writer; b. 10 April 1930, Elkhart, KS. *Education:* Univ. of Oklahoma. *Career:* mem. Authors' Guild, Western Writers of America (pres. 1974–75). *Publications:* To Buy a Dream 1958, Promise of Tomorrow 1959, Coyote Winter 1965, Beasts with Music 1967, Oil Patch Partners 1968, New Medicine 1971, Trails of Tears 1972, Freedom Trail 1973, Winter Wheat 1975, A Lady Bought with Rifles 1977, A Woman Clothed in Sun 1978, Bride of Thunder 1978, Daughter of the Sword 1979, The Queen of a Lonely Country (as Megan Castell) 1980, The Valiant Women 1981, Harvest of Fury 1982, The Heaven Sword 1983, A Mating of Hawks 1984, The Care Dreamers 1985, So Many Kingdoms 1986, Texas Pride 1987, Lady of No Man's Land 1988, No Roof but Heaven 1990, Home Mountain 1990, The Island Harp 1991, The Longest Road 1993, Daughter of the Storm 1994, The Unplowed Sky 1994, Home Station 1995, Wind Water 1997, The Underground River (Beneath the Burning Ground trilogy book one) 2004, The Hidden Valley (Beneath the Burning Ground trilogy book two) 2004, The Trampled Fields (Beneath the Burning Ground trilogy book three) 2005; as J. R. Williams: Mission in Mexico 1960, The Horsetalker 1961, The Confederate Fiddle 1962, River Guns 1962, Oh Susanna 1963, Tame the Wild Stallion 1967; as Jeanne Crecy: Hands of Terror (aka Lady Gift, The Lightning Tree) 1972, My Face Beneath Stone 1975, The Winter-Keeper 1975, The Night Hunters 1975; as Deirdre Rowan: Dragon's Mount 1973, Silver Wood 1974, Shadow of the Volcano 1975, Time of the Burning Mask 1976, Ravensgate 1976; as Kristin Michaels: To Begin with Love 1976, Enchanted Journey 1977, Song of the Heart 1977, Make Believe Love 1978; as Jeanne Foster: Deborah Leigh 1981, Eden Richards 1982, Woman of Three Worlds 1984; contrib. to journals. *Honours:* Texas Inst. of Letters Best Children's Book 1958, Four Western Writers of America Spur Awards, Best Novel of the West 1981, 1990, Levi Strauss Golden Saddleman Award for Lifetime Achievement 1988. *Address:* PO Box 335, Portal, AZ 85632, USA. *Telephone:* (520) 558-2436 (home). *E-mail:* jeannewilliams30@hotmail.com. *Website:* www.jeannewilliams.net.

WILLIAMS, John Alfred, BA; American writer, journalist, poet and educator; b. 5 Dec. 1925, Jackson, MS; m. 1st Carolyn Clopton 1947 (divorced); two s.; m. 2nd Lorrain Isaac 1965, one s. *Education:* Syracuse University. *Career:* Ed. and Publisher, Negro Market Newsletter, 1956–57; Contributing Ed., Herald-Tribune Book Week, 1963–65, American Journal, 1972–74, Politicks, 1977, Journal of African Civilizations, 1980–88; Lecturer, College of the Virgin Islands, 1968, City College, CUNY, 1968–69; Visiting Prof., Macalester College, 1970, University of Hawaii, 1974, Boston University, 1978–79, University of Houston, 1994, Bard College, 1994–95; Regents Lecturer, University of California at Santa Barbara, 1972; Guest Writer, Sarah Lawrence College, 1972–73; Distinguished Prof., LaGuardia Community College, CUNY, 1973–79; Distinguished Visiting Prof., Cooper Union, 1974–75; Prof., Rutgers University, 1979–93; Exxon Visiting Prof., New York University, 1986–87; mem. Authors' Guild; Poets and Writers; PEN. *Publications:* Fiction: The Angry Ones, 1960, revised edn as One for New

York, 1975; Night Song, 1961; Sissie, 1963; The Man Who Cried I Am, 1967; Sons of Darkness, Sons of Light, 1969; Captain Blackman, 1972; Mothersill and the Foxes, 1975; The Junio Bachelor Society, 1976; !Click Song, 1982; The Berhama Account, 1985; Jacob's Ladder, 1987; Clifford's Blues, 1999. Libretto: Vanqui, premier, 1999. Poetry: Safari West, 1998. Non-Fiction: Africa: Her History, Lands and People, 1963; The Protectors, 1964; This Is My Country Too, 1965; The Most Native of Sons: A Biography of Richard Wright, 1970; The King God Didn't Save: Reflections on the Life and Death of Martin Luther King Jr., 1970; Flashbacks: A Twenty-Year Diary of Article Writing, 1973; Minorities in the City, 1975; If I Stop I'll Die: The Comedy and Tragedy of Richard Pryor (with Dennis A Williams), 1991. Editor or Co-Editor: The Angry Black, 1962, revised edn as Beyond the Angry Black, 1967; Amistad 1, 1970; Amistad 2, 1971; Y'Bird, 1978; Introduction to Literature, 1985; Street Guide to African Americans in Paris, 1992; Approaches to Literature, 1994; Bridges: Literature Across Cultures, 1994. Contributions: anthologies, journals, reviews, and magazines. *Honours:* National Institute of Arts and Letters Award, 1962; Centennial Medal, 1970, Hon. DLitt, 1995, Syracuse University; Richard Wright-Jacques Roumain Award, 1973; National Endowment for the Arts Award, 1977; Hon. Doctor of Literature, Southeastern Massachusetts University, 1978; American Book Awards, Before Columbus Foundation, 1983, 1998; New Jersey State Council on the Arts Award, 1985; Michael Award, New Jersey Literary Hall of Fame, 1987; Distinguished Writer Award, Middle Atlantic Writers, 1987; J. A. Williams Archive established, University of Rochester, 1987; Carter G. Woodson Award, Mercy College, 1989; National Literary Hall of Fame, 1998. *Address:* 693 Forest Avenue, Teaneck, NJ 07666, USA.

WILLIAMS, John Hartley, BA, MPhil; British poet and lecturer; b. 7 Feb. 1942, England; m. Gizella Horvat 1970; one d. *Education:* Univ. of Nottingham, Univ. of London, Univ. Coll. London. *Career:* Lecturer, Free Univ. of Berlin 1976–; mem. Poetry Soc. *Publications:* Hidden Identities 1982, Bright River Yonder 1987, Cornerless People 1990, Double 1994, Ignoble Sentiments 1995, Teach Yourself Writing Poetry (with Matthew Sweeney) 1997, Canada 1997, The Scar in the Stone (contributing trans. to poems from Serbo-Croatian) 1998, Spending Time with Walter 2001, Marin Soresa: Censored Poems (trans.) 2001, Mystery in Spiderville 2002, North Sea Improvisation, a fotopoem 2003, Blues 2004; contrib. to anthologies, reviews and journals. *Honours:* First Prize Arvon Int. Poetry Competition 1983, Poetry Book Recommendation 1987. *Address:* 18 Jenbacherweg, 12209 Berlin, Germany. *E-mail:* johnhartleywilliams@t-online.de. *Website:* www.johnhartleywilliams.de.

WILLIAMS, John Hoyt, BA, MA, PhD; American academic (retd) and writer; b. 26 Oct. 1940, Darien, CT; m. 1962; one s. one d. *Education:* University of Connecticut, University of Florida. *Career:* Asst Prof. of History, 1969–73, Assoc. Prof. of History, 1973–78, Prof. of History, 1978–2000, Indiana State University. *Publications:* Rise and Fall of the Paraguayan Republic 1800–1870, 1979; A Great and Shining Road, 1988; Sam Houston: A Biography of the Father of Texas, 1993. Contributions: Atlantic Monthly; Christian Century; Americas; National Defense; Current History; Hispanic American Historical Review. *Honours:* Distinguished Prof. of Arts and Sciences, 1996.

WILLIAMS, Joy, MA, MFA; American writer; b. 11 Feb. 1944, Chelmsford, MA; m. Rust Hills, one c. *Education:* Marietta College, University of Iowa. *Publications:* State of Grace 1973, The Changeling 1978, Taking Care 1982, The Florida Keys: A History and Guide 1986, Breaking and Entering 1988, Escapes 1990, The Quick and the Dead 2000, Ill Nature 2001, Honored Guest (short stories) 2004; contrib. to anthologies. *Honours:* National Endowment for the Arts Grant 1973, Guggenheim Fellowship 1974, National Magazine Award 1980, American Acad. of Arts and Letters Literature Citation 1989, and Straus Living Award 1993–97, Rea Award 1999. *Address:* c/o International Creative Management, 40 W 57th Street, New York, NY 10019, USA.

WILLIAMS, Malcolm David, CertEd; Welsh writer; b. 9 April 1939, South Wales; m. (deceased); one d. *Education:* Birmingham Univ. Inst. of Education. *Career:* Fellow World Literary Acad.; mem. Soc. of Authors, West Country Writers' Asscn, British Haiku Soc. *Publications:* Yesterday's Secret 1980, Poor Little Rich Girl 1981, Debt of Friendship 1981, Another Time, Another Place 1982, My Brother's Keeper 1982, The Stuart Affair 1983, The Cordillera Conspiracy 1983, The Girl from Derry's Bluff 1983, A Corner of Eden 1984, Sorrow's End 1984, A Stranger on Trust 1987, Shadows From the Past 1989, This Mask I Wear Today 1998, And the Dragons are Dead 2003; contrib. hundreds of serial stories, articles and short stories to numerous publications. *Honours:* first prizes in many short story and poetry competitions 1960–2005. *Address:* 17 Beaumont Road, Cheltenham, Gloucestershire GL51 0LP, England (home). *Telephone:* (1242) 519319 (home).

WILLIAMS, Merryn, BA, PhD; British writer and poet; *Editor, The Interpreter's House;* b. 9 July 1944, Devon, England; m. John Hemp 1973; one s. one d. *Education:* Univ. of Cambridge. *Career:* Lecturer, Open Univ. 1970–71; Ed., The Interpreter's House 1996–; Ed., Wilfred Owen Asscn newsletter; mem. Open Univ. Poets, Welsh Acad. *Publications:* The Bloodstream 1989, Selected Poems of Federico García Lorca 1992, Wilfred Owen 1993, The Sun's Yellow Eye 1997, The Latin Master's Story 2000, In the Spirit of Wilfred Owen (ed., anthology) 2002; contrib. to reviews, quarterlies, journals and magazines. *Address:* Wolfson College, Oxford, OX2 6UD, England (office). *E-mail:* hemp@cranfield.ac.uk (office).

WILLIAMS, Miller, BS, MS; American academic, writer and poet; *Professor, University of Arkansas*; b. 8 April 1930, Hoxie, AR; m. 1st Lucille Day 1951; one s. two d.; m. 2nd Jordan Hall 1969. *Education:* Arkansas State Coll., Univ. of Arkansas. *Career:* Founder-Ed. 1968–70, Advisory Ed. 1975–, New Orleans Review; Prof., Univ. of Arkansas 1971–; Dir, Univ. of Arkansas Press 1980–97. *Publications:* A Circle of Stone 1964, Southern Writing in the Sixties (with J. W. Corrington, two vols) 1966, So Long at the Fair 1968, Chile: An Anthology of New Writing 1968, The Achievement of John Ciardi 1968, The Only World There Is 1968, The Poetry of John Crowe Ransom 1971, Contemporary Poetry in America 1972, Halfway from Hoxie: New and Selected Poems 1973, How Does a Poem Mean? (with John Ciardi) 1974, Railroad (with James Alan McPherson) 1976, Why God Permits Evil 1977, A Roman Collection 1980, Distraction 1981, Ozark, Ozark: A Hillside Reader 1981, The Boys on Their Bony Mules 1983, Living on the Surface: New and Selected Poems 1989, Adjusting to the Light 1992, Points of Departure 1995, The Ways We Touch (poems) 1997, Some Jazz a While: Collected Poems 1999, The Lives of Kelvin Fletcher: Stories Mostly Short 2002; contrib. to various publications. *Honours:* Hon. DHum (Lander Coll.) 1983, Hon. LHD (Hendrix Coll.) 1995; Henry Bellaman Poetry Award 1957, Bread Loaf Fellowship in Poetry 1961, Fulbright Lecturer 1970, American Acad. of Arts and Letters Prix de Rome 1976, Nat. Poets Prize 1992, John William Corrington Award for Excellence in Literature, Centenary Coll., LA 1994, American Acad. of Arts and Letters Award 1995, Inaugural Poet, Presidential Inauguration 1997. *Address:* 1111 Valley View Drive, Fayetteville, AR 72701, USA (home). *Telephone:* (479) 521-2934 (home). *E-mail:* mwms1000@aol.com (home).

WILLIAMS, Nigel, MA; British writer and television producer; b. 20 Jan. 1948, Cheshire; s. of the late David Ffrancon Williams; m. Suzani Harrison 1973; three s. *Education:* Highgate School, Oriel Coll., Oxford. *Career:* trainee BBC 1969–73, Producer/Dir Arts Dept 1973–85, Ed. Bookmark 1985–92, Omnibus 1992–96, writer and presenter 1997–2000. *Television includes:* Double Talk, Talking Blues, Real Live Audience 1977, Baby Love 1981, Breaking Up 1986, The Last Romantics 1992, Skallagrig (BAFTA Award) 1994. *Stage plays include:* Class Enemy 1978 (Plays and Players Award for Most Promising Playwright 1978), Trial Run 1980, Line 'Em 1980, Sugar & Spice 1980, My Brother's Keeper 1985, Country Dancing 1986, Nativity 1989, Harry & Me 1995, The Last Romantics 1997. *Publications:* (novels) My Life Closed Twice 1977 (jt winner Somerset Maugham Award), Jack Be Nimble 1980, Star Turn 1985, Witchcraft 1987, The Wimbledon Poisoner 1990, They Came from SW19 1992, East of Wimbledon 1994, Scenes from a Poisoner's Life 1994, Stalking Fiona 1997, Fortysomething 1999; (travel) Wimbledon to Waco 1995. *Address:* c/o Judy Daish Associates, 2 St Charles Place, London, W10 6EG; 18 Holmbush Road, Putney, London, SW15 3LE, England (home). *Telephone:* (20) 8964-8811. *Fax:* (20) 8964-8966.

WILLIAMS, Peter Fredric, BA, MusB, MA, PhD, LittD; British musicologist, academic, writer, organist and harpsichordist; b. 14 May 1937, Wolverhampton, Staffordshire, England; m. Rosemary Seymour 1982; three s. one d. *Education:* Birmingham Inst., St John's Coll., Cambridge. *Career:* Lecturer 1962–72, Reader 1972–82, Prof. 1982–85, Dean 1984, Univ. of Edinburgh; Dir, Russell Coll. of Harpsichords, Edinburgh 1969; Founder-Ed., The Organ Yearbook 1969–; Arts and Sciences Distinguished Prof. 1985–95, Dir, Graduate Center for Performance Practice Studies 1990–96, Duke Univ., Durham, NC, USA; John Bird Prof., Univ. of Wales, Cardiff 1996–2002; mem. British Inst. of Organ Studies (chair.). *Publications:* The European Organ 1450–1850 1966, Figured Bass Accompaniment (two vols) 1970, Venta/Peeters the Organ of the Netherlands (trans.) 1971, Bach Organ Music 1972, A New History of the Organ From the Greeks to the Present Day 1980, The Organ Music of J. S. Bach (three vols) 1980–84, Bach, Handel and Scarlatti: Tercentenary Essays (ed.) 1985, Playing the Works of Bach 1986, The Organ 1988, Playing the Organ Music of Bach 1988, Mozart: Perspectives in Performance (ed. with L. Todd) 1991, The Organ in Western Culture 750–1250 1992, The King of Instruments: How Do Churches Come to Have Organs? 1993, The Chromatic Fourth During Four Centuries of Music 1995, Cambridge Studies in Performance Practice (series ed., four vols) 1995, Music to Hear, or Fears for Higher Music Study 2001, Bach: The Goldberg Variations 2001, The Life of Bach 2005 (expanded as JS Bach: A Life in Music 2007); several vols of keyboard music by Bach and Handel; contrib. to scholarly books and journals. *Honours:* Hon. Fellow, Royal Scottish Acad. of Art, Research Fellow, Cornell Univ., New York, Curt Sachs Award, American Musical Instrument Soc. 1996. *Address:* c/o Department of Music, Corbett Road, University of Wales, Cardiff, CF10 3EB, Wales.

WILLIAMS, Most Rev., Rt Hon. Rowan Douglas, MA, DPhil, DD, FRSL, FBA; British ecclesiastic and academic; *Archbishop of Canterbury*; b. 14 June 1950, Swansea; m. Jane Paul 1981; one s. one d. *Education:* Christ's Coll. Cambridge, Wadham Coll. Oxford. *Career:* tutor, Westcott House, Univ. of Cambridge 1977–80, Lecturer in Divinity 1980–1986, Dean and Chaplain, Clare Coll. 1984–1986; deacon 1977; priest 1978; Canon Theologian Leicester Cathedral 1981–82; Canon Residentiary, Christ Church, Oxford 1986–92; Lady Margaret Prof. of Theology, Oxford Univ. 1986–92; Bishop of Monmouth 1992–2002; Archbishop of Wales 2000–02; Archbishop of Canterbury Dec. 2002–; Fellow, British Acad. 1990. *Television:* Conversations with Rowan Williams 2003. *Publications include:* The Wound of Knowledge 1979, Resurrection 1982, The Truce of God 1983, Arius: Heresy and Tradition 1987, Teresa of Avila 1991, Open to Judgement: Sermons and Addresses 1994, A Ray of Darkness 1995, Christ on Trial: How the Gospel Unsettles our Judgement 2000, Lost Icons: Reflection on Cultural Bereavement 2000, On Christian Theology 2000, Ponder These Things: Praying With Icons of the Virgin 2002, Writing in the Dust: Reflections on 11th September and its Aftermath 2002, Silence and Honey Cakes 2003, The Dwelling of the Light 2003, Anglican Identities 2004, Love's Redeeming Work (ed.), Why Study the Past? 2005, Grace and Necessity 2006, Tokens of Trust: An Introduction to Christian Belief 2007, Living the Lord's Prayer (with Wendy Beckett) 2007; poetry: Poems of Rowan Williams 2002, Remembering Jerusalem, After Silent Centuries. *Honours:* Hon. Fellow, Univ. of Wales, Swansea, Newport, Aberystwyth, Cardiff, Clare Coll., Cambridge, Christ Church, Oxford, Wadham Coll., Oxford, Christ's Coll., Cambridge; Dr hc (Erlangen, Bonn, Nashoteh House, Exeter, Aberdeen, Wales, Open Univ., Roehampton, Cambridge, Oxford); Hon. Curate, St George, Chesterton, Cambridge 1980–1983, Hon. Fellow, Univ. of Wales, Bangor 2003. *Address:* Lambeth Palace, London, SE1 7JU, England. *Telephone:* (20) 7898-1200. *Fax:* (20) 7261-9836. *Website:* www.archbishopofcanterbury.org.

WILLIAMS, Roy; British playwright; b. 1968. *Education:* Rose Bruford Drama School. *Plays:* No Boys Cricket Club 1996, Starstruck 1997, Lift Off 1999, The Gift 2000, Clubland 2001, Sing Yer Heart Out for the Lads 2002, Fallout 2003, Days of Significance 2007. *Publications include:* Plays 1 2002, Plays 2004. *Honours:* TAPS Writer of the Year Award 1996, Alfred Fagon Award 1998, John Whiting Award for Best New Play 1998–99, Evening Standard Most Promising Playwright Award 2001. *Address:* c/o A & C Black Publishing Ltd, 38 Soho Square, London, W1D 3HB, England. *Telephone:* 20 7758 0200. *Fax:* 20 7758 0222. *Website:* www.acblack.com. *Address:* 45d Cambridge Gardens, London, W10 5UA, England.

WILLIAMS, Terry Tempest; American writer; b. Utah; m. Brooke Williams. *Career:* fmr naturalist-in-residence, Utah Museum of Natural History. *Publications:* Pieces of White Shell: A Journey to Navajoland 1984, Coyote's Canyon 1989, Refuge: An Unnatural History of Family and Place 1991, An Unspoken Hunger (essays) 1994, Desert Quartet: An Erotic Landscape 1995, Leap 2000, Red: Patience and Passion in the Desert 2001, The Open Space of Democracy 2004; children's books: The Secret Language of Snow (with Ted Major) 1984, Between Cattails 1985; other: Great and Peculiar Beauty: A Utah Centennial Reader (ed. with Thomas J. Lyon) 1995, Testimony: Writers of the West Speak on Behalf of Utah Wilderness (ed. with Stephen Trimble) 1996, New Genesis: a Mormon Reader on Land and Community (ed. with William B. Smart, Gibbs M. Smith) 1998; contrib. to anthologies, journals and newspapers, incl. New Yorker, The Nation, Outside, Audubon, Orion, Iowa Review, New England Review. *Honours:* Inductee, Rachel Carson Honor Roll; National Wildlife Federation Conservation Award for Special Achievement; Guggenheim Memorial Foundation fellow; Lannan Literary Fellowship in Creative Non-fiction. *Literary Agent:* Steven Barclay Agency, 12 Western Avenue, Petaluma, CA 94952, USA. *Telephone:* (707) 773-0654. *Fax:* (707) 778-1868. *Website:* www.barclayagency.com. *Address:* c/o Vintage Books, Random House, 1745 Broadway, Third Floor, New York, NY 10019, USA. *Website:* www.coyoteclan.com.

WILLIAMS-WITHERSPOON, Kimmika L. H., BA, MFA; American playwright, poet and performance artist; b. 7 Jan. 1959, PA; m. Darrell V. Witherspoon 1992, two d. *Education:* Howard University, Temple University. *Career:* Future Faculty Fellow, Anthropology Dept, Temple University; mem. Poets and Prophets; Poets and Writers. *Publications:* God Made Men Brown, 1982; It Ain't Easy To Be Different, 1986; Halley's Comet, 1988; Envisioning a Sea of Dry Bones, 1990; Epic Memory: Places and Spaces I've Been, 1995; Signs of the Times: Culture Gap, 1999. *Contributions:* Women's Words; Sunlight on the Moon. *Honours:* Playwrights Exchange Grants 1994, 1996.

WILLIAMSON, David Keith, AO, BE; Australian playwright and screenwriter; b. 24 Feb. 1942, Melbourne; s. of Edwin Keith David Williamson and Elvie May (née Armstrong) Williamson; m. Kristin Ingrid Lofven 1974; two s. one d. *Education:* Monash Univ., Melbourne Univ. *Career:* Design Engineer Gen. Motors-Holden's 1965; lecturer Swinbourne Tech. Coll. 1966–72; freelance writer 1972–. *Plays:* The Removalists 1972, Don's Party 1973, Three Plays 1974, The Department 1975, A Handful of Friends 1976, The Club 1977, Travelling North 1979, The Perfectionist 1981, Sons of Cain 1985, Emerald City 1987, Top Silk 1989, Siren 1990, Money and Friends 1992, Brilliant Lies 1993, Sanctuary 1994, Dead White Males 1995, Corporate Vibes 1999, Face to Face 1999, The Great Man 2000. *Screenplays:* Gallipoli 1981, Phar Lap 1983, The Year of Living Dangerously 1983, Travelling North 1986, Emerald City 1988, The Four Minute Mile (2-part TV series) 1988, A Dangerous Life (6-hour TV series) 1988, Top Silk 1989, Siren 1990, Money and Friends 1992, Dead White Males 1995, Heretic 1996, Third World Blues 1997, After the Ball 1997, Brilliant Lies 1996, On the Beach 2000. *Honours:* numerous writing, TV and cinema awards. *Address:* c/o Anthony Williams Management Pty Ltd, PO Box 1379, Darlinghurst, NSW 2010, Australia.

WILLIAMSON, Joel R., AB, MA, PhD; American writer and academic (retd); b. 27 Oct. 1929, Anderson County, SC; m. Betty Anne Woodson 1986; one s. two d. *Education:* Univ. of South Carolina, Univ. of California, Berkeley. *Career:* instructor 1960–64, Asst Prof. 1964–66, Assoc. Prof. 1966–69, Prof. 1969–85, Linberger Prof. in Humanities 1985–2003, Dept of History, Univ. of North Carolina, Chapel Hill; mem. Soc. of American Historians, Southern Historical Asscn, Organization of American Historians, Southern Asscn for Women Historians, American Historical Asscn. *Publications:* After Slavery: The Negro in South Carolina During Reconstruction 1965, Origins of Segregation

1968, New People: Miscegenation and Mulattoes in the United States 1980, The Crucible of Race 1984, A Rage for Order 1986, William Faulkner and Southern History 1993; contrib. to various publications. *Honours:* Parkman, Emerson, Owsley, Kennedy, Mayflower Awards 1985, Fellow Guggenheim Foundation 1970–71, Center for Advanced Study in Behavioral Sciences, Stanford, CA 1977–78, summer 1979, 1980, 1981, NEH 1987–88, Southern Fellow 1961–62, Charles Warren Center, Harvard Univ. 1981–82, Mayflower Cup 1994. *Address:* 211 Hillsborough Street, Chapel Hill, NC 27514, USA (home). *Telephone:* (919) 929-6613 (home). *E-mail:* william@email.unc.edu (home).

WILLIAMSON, Kristin Ingrid; Australian novelist and biographer; b. 16 Sept. 1940, Melbourne, Vic.; m. David Williamson 1974; three s. *Education:* BA, Latrobe University, 1981; Drama, Trinity College, London; TPTC. *Career:* Teacher of English, History and Drama, primary and high schools, Victoria, 1960–70; Lecturer in Drama, Melbourne State College, 1970–72; Freelance Journalist, 1973–79; Journalist, Columnist, National Times, Sydney, 1979–87; Writer, 1987–. *Publications:* The Last Bastion, 1984; Princess Kate (novel), 1988; Tanglewood (novel), 1992; The Jacaranda Years (novel), 1995; Brothers To Us (biog.), 1997; Treading on Dreams (novel), 1998; Women on the Rocks (novel), 2003. *Literary Agent:* Curtis Brown Pty, PO Box 19, Paddington, NSW 2021, Australia.

WILLIAMSON, Philip G., (Philip First, Joe Fish, Will Phillips); British writer; b. 4 Nov. 1955, Worcestershire, England. *Education:* Goldsmiths College, London. *Publications:* The Great Pervader, 1983; Paper Thin and Other Stories, 1986; Dark Night, 1986; Dinbig of Khimmur, 1991, The Legend of Shadd's Torment, 1993, From Enchantery, 1993; Moonblood, 1993; Heart of Shadows, 1994; Citadel, 1995; Enchantment's Edge, three vols, 1996–98; The Mates, 2003; Killing Time, 2003.

WILLIS, Meredith Sue, BA, MFA; American writer and educator; *Special Lecturer, New York University;* b. 31 May 1946, WV; m. Andrew B. Weinberger 1982; one s. *Education:* Barnard Coll., Columbia Univ. *Career:* currently Special Lecturer, New York Univ. *Publications:* A Space Apart 1979, Higher Ground 1981, Only Great Changes 1985, Personal Fiction Writing 1984, Quilt Pieces 1990, Blazing Pencils 1990, Deep Revision 1993, The Secret Super Power of Marco 1994, In the Mountains of America 1994, Marco's Monster 1996, Trespassers 1997, Oradell at Sunset 2002, Dwight's House and Other Stories 2004, The City Built of Starships 2005. *Honours:* Nat. Endowment for the Arts Fellowship 1978, New Jersey Arts Fellowship 1995, Honoree Emory and Henry Literary Festival 1995, Hon. DHumLitt (West Virginia) 2004. *Address:* 311 Prospect Street, South Orange, NJ 07079, USA. *E-mail:* msuewillis@aol.com. *Website:* www.meredithsuewillis.com.

WILLMOTT, Hedley Paul, BA, MA, PhD; British lecturer and writer; b. 26 Dec. 1945, Bristol, England; m. Pauline Anne Burton 1978; one s. one d. *Education:* University of Liverpool, University of London. *Career:* Military Writer and Lecturer, Royal Military Acad., Sandhurst, 1969–; Programme Writer, British Broadcasting Corporation World Service, 1986–92; Visiting Lecturer, Temple University, Philadelphia, 1989, Memphis State University, Tennessee, 1989–90, National War College, Dept of Defense, Washington, DC, 1992–. *Publications:* Warships, 1975; B-17 Flying Fortress, 1980; Sea Warfare: Weapons, Tactics and Strategy, 1981; Empires in the Balance: Japanese and Allied Pacific Strategies to April 1942, 1982; The Barrier and the Javelin: Japanese and Allied Pacific Strategies, February to June 1942, 1983; Pearl Harbor, 1983; Zero A6M, 1983; June 1944, 1984; The Great Crusade: A New Complete History of the Second World War, 1989; Grave of a Dozen Schemes: British Naval Planning and the War against Japan, 1943–1945, 1996. *Honours:* Leman Award 1984.

WILLOUGHBY, Cass (see Olsen, Theodore Victor)

WILLS, Garry, BA, MA, PhD; American writer, journalist and academic; *Professor of History Emeritus, Northwestern University;* b. 22 May 1934, Atlanta, GA; m. Natalie Cavallo 1959; two s. one d. *Education:* St Louis Univ., Xavier Univ., Cincinnati and Yale Univ. *Career:* Fellow Center for Hellenic Studies 1961–62; Assoc. Prof. of Classics 1962–67, Adjunct Prof. 1968–80, Johns Hopkins Univ.; Newspaper Columnist Universal Press Syndicate 1970–; Henry R. Luce Prof. of American Culture and Public Policy 1980–88, Adjunct Prof., later Prof. of History Emeritus 1988–, Northwestern Univ.; mem. American Philosophical Soc., American Acad. of Arts and Letters, American Acad. of Arts and Sciences. *Publications:* Chesterton 1961, Politics and Catholic Freedom 1964, Roman Culture 1966, Jack Ruby 1967, Second Civil War 1968, Nixon Agonistes 1970, Bare Ruined Choirs 1972, Inventing America 1978, At Button's 1979, Confessions of a Conservative 1979, Explaining America 1980, The Kennedy Imprisonment 1982, Lead Time 1983, Cincinnatus 1984, Reagan's America 1987, Under God 1990, Lincoln at Gettysburg (Nat. Book Critics Circle Award 1993, Pulitzer Prize for General Non-Fiction 1993) 1992, Certain Trumpets: The Call of Leaders 1994, Witches and Jesuits: Shakespeare's Macbeth 1994, John Wayne's America 1997, Saint Augustine 1999, A Necessary Evil: A History of American Distrust of Government 1999, Papal Sin: Structures of Deceit 2000, Saint Augustine's Childhood 2001, Why I Am a Catholic 2002, President 2003, Saint Augustine's Sin 2004, Saint Augustine's Conversion 2004, Bush's Fringe Government 2006. *Honours:* various hon. doctorates; Nat. Humanities Medal 1998. *Address:* c/o Department of History, Northwestern University, Evanston, IL 60201, USA (office).

WILLUMSEN, Dorrit; Danish writer; b. 31 Aug. 1940. *Publications:* novels: Neonhaven (trans. as Neon Park) 1976, Hvis det virk elig var en film 1978 (trans. as If It Really Were a Film 1982), Marie: A Novel about the Life of Madame Tussaud 1983, Umage par 1983, Suk hjerte 1986, Manden som påskud 1987, Glemslens forår (trans. as Seeds of Oblivion) 1988, Bang 1996, Koras stemme 2000. *Honours:* Nordic Council Prize for Literature 1997. *Address:* c/o Curbstone Press, 321 Jackson Street, Willimantic, CT 06226-1738, USA. *Website:* www.curbstone.org.

WILMER, Clive, BA, MA; British academic, writer, poet, translator and broadcaster; *Fellow in English, Sidney Sussex College Cambridge;* b. 10 Feb. 1945, Harrogate, Yorks.; m. Diane Redmond 1971 (divorced 1986); one s. one d. *Education:* King's Coll., Cambridge. *Career:* Visiting Instructor in Creative Writing, Univ. of California at Santa Barbara 1986; Ed. Numbers 1986–90; Presenter Poet of the Month series, BBC Radio 3 1989–92; Hon. Fellow, Anglia Polytechnic Univ. (now Anglia Ruskin Univ.) 1996–, Research Fellow and Poet-in-Residence 1998–; Assoc. Teaching Officer, Sidney Sussex and Fitzwilliam Colls, Cambridge 1999–, Fellow in English, Sidney Sussex Coll. 2005–; mem. Companion of the Guild of St George 1995–, Dir Guild of St George 2004–; Bye-Fellow, Fitzwilliam Coll., Cambridge 2004–. *Publications:* poetry: The Dwelling Place 1977, Devotions 1982, Of Earthly Paradise 1992, Selected Poems 1995, The Falls 2000, Stigmata 2005, The Mystery of Things 2006; trans.: Forced March, by Miklós Radnóti (with G. Gömöri) 1979 (revised edn 2003), Night Song of the Personal Shadow, by György Petri (with G. Gömöri) 1991, My Manifold City, by George Gömöri 1996, Eternal Monday by György Petri (with G. Gömöri) 1999; ed.: Thom Gunn: The Occasions of Poetry 1982, John Ruskin: Unto This Last and Other Writings 1985, Dante Gabriel Rossetti: Selected Poems and Translations 1991, William Morris: News From Nowhere and Other Writings 1993, Poets Talking: The 'Poet of the Month' Interviews from BBC Radio 3 1994, Cambridge Observed: An Anthology (ed. with Charles Moseley) 1998, Donald Davie: With the Grain 1998, The Life and Work of Miklós Radnóti: Essays (ed. with George Gömöri) 1999, Donald Davie: Modernist Essays 2004; contribs to many reviews, newspapers, quarterlies and journals. *Honours:* Hon. Sr Scholar, King's Coll. Cambridge 1967; Chancellor's Medal for an English Poem, Univ. of Cambridge 1967, Writer's Grant, Arts Council of GB 1979, Author's Foundation Grant 1993, Mikimoto Memorial Ruskin Lecturer, Univ. of Lancaster 1994, Hungarian PEN Club Memorial Medal for Trans. 1998, Hungarian Ministry of Culture Medal 'Pro Cultura Hungarica' 2005. *Literary Agent:* A.M. Heath & Co Ltd, 79 St Martin's Lane, London, WC2N 4RE, England. *Address:* 57 Norwich Street, Cambridge, CB2 1ND, England (home). *Telephone:* (1223) 511975 (home). *E-mail:* clive .wilmer@ntlworld.com (home); cw291@cam.ac.uk (office).

WILMERS, Mary-Kay; British editor; *Editor, London Review of Books;* two s. *Career:* Ed., London Review of Books 1992–. *Address:* London Review of Books, 28 Little Russell Street, London, WC1A 2HN, England. *Telephone:* (20) 7209-1101. *Fax:* (20) 7209-1102. *E-mail:* edit@lrb.co.uk. *Website:* www.lrb.co .uk.

WILOCH, Thomas, BA; American poet, writer and editor; b. 3 Feb. 1953, Detroit, Mich.; m. Denise Gottis 1981. *Education:* Wayne State Univ. *Career:* associated with Gale Group 1977–2004; columnist, Retrofuturism 1991–93, Photo Static 1993–94; book reviewer, Anti-Matter Magazine 1992–94, Green Man Review 2002–04; Assoc. Ed. Sidereality Magazine 2004–05; mem. Asscn of Literary Scholars and Critics, Nat. Asscn for Self-Employed. *Publications:* Stigmata Junction 1985, Paper Mask 1988, The Mannikin Cypher 1989, Tales of Lord Shantih 1990, Decoded Factories of the Heart 1991, Night Rain 1991, Narcotic Signature 1992, Lyrical Brandy 1993, Mr Templeton's Toyshop 1995, Neon Trance 1997, Crime: A Serious American Problem 2004, National Security 2005, Prisons and Jails 2005, Screaming in Code 2006; contrib. to more than 200 magazines. *Honours:* Schoolcraft Coll. Poet Hunt Award 1985, Scantle Magazine Prize 1986, Bohemian Chronicle Award 1994. *Address:* 42015 Ford Road, Suite #226, Canton, MI 48187, USA. *Fax:* (734) 468-0190. *E-mail:* twiloch@wowway.com (office).

WILSON, Andrew Norman (A. N.), MA, FRSL; British writer; b. 27 Oct. 1950, England; s. of the late N. Wilson and of Jean Dorothy Wilson (née Crowder); m. 1st Katherine Dorothea Duncan-Jones 1971 (divorced 1989); two d.; m. 2nd Ruth Guilding 1991; one d. *Education:* Rugby School and New Coll., Oxford. *Career:* Asst Master Merchant Taylors' School 1975–76; Lecturer St Hugh's Coll. and New Coll., Oxford 1976–81; Literary Ed. Spectator 1981–83, Evening Standard 1990–97. *Publications:* fiction: The Sweets of Pimlico 1977, Unguarded Hours 1978, Kindly Light 1979, The Healing Art (Somerset Maugham Award) 1980, Who Was Oswald Fish? 1981, Wise Virgin (WHSmith Award) 1982, Scandal 1983, Gentleman in England 1985, Love Unknown 1986, Stray 1987, Incline Our Hearts 1988, A Bottle in the Smoke 1990, Daughters of Albion 1991, The Vicar of Sorrows 1993, Hearing Voices 1995, A Watch in the Night 1996, Hazel the Guinea-pig (for children) 1997, Dream Children 1998, My Name is Legion 2004, A Jealous Ghost 2005; non-fiction: The Laird of Abbotsford 1980, A Life of John Milton 1983, Hilaire Belloc 1984, How Can We Know? An Essay on the Christian Religion 1985, The Church in Crisis (jtly) 1986, Landscape in France 1987, The Lion and the Honeycomb 1987, Penfriends from Porlock: Essays and Reviews 1977–86 1988, Tolstoy (Whitbread Award for Biography and Autobiography) 1988, Eminent Victorians 1989, John Henry Newman: prayers, poems, meditations (ed.) 1989, C. S. Lewis: A Biography 1990, Against Religion 1991, Jesus 1992, The Faber Book of Church and Clergy (ed.) 1992, The Rise and Fall of the House of Windsor 1993, The Faber Book of London (ed.) 1993, Paul: The Mind of the

Apostle 1997, God's Funeral 1999, The Victorians 2003, Beautiful Shadow: A Life of Patricia Highsmith 2003, Iris Murdoch as I Knew Her 2004, London: A Short History 2004, After the Victorians 2005, Betjeman (biog.) 2006. *Honours:* Hon. mem. American Acad. of Arts and Letters 1984; Chancellor's Essay Prize 1975, Ellerton Theological Prize 1975. *Address:* 5 Regent's Park Terrace, London, NW1 7EE, England.

WILSON, Charles; British journalist; b. 18 Aug. 1935, Glasgow, Scotland; s. of Adam Wilson and Ruth Wilson; m. 1st Anne Robinson 1968 (divorced 1973); one d.; m. 2nd Sally O'Sullivan 1980 (divorced 2001); one s. one d.; m. 3rd Rachel Pitkeathley 2001. *Education:* Eastbank Acad., Glasgow. *Career:* copy boy, The People 1951; later reporter with Bristol Evening World, News Chronicle and Daily Mail; Deputy Ed. Daily Mail (Manchester) 1971–74; Asst Ed. London Evening News 1974–76; Ed., Evening Times, Glasgow 1976; later Ed., Glasgow Herald; Ed. Sunday Standard, Glasgow 1981–82; Exec. Ed., The Times 1982, Jt Deputy Ed. 1984–85, Ed. 1985–90; Int. Devt Dir News Int. 1990–91; Ed.-in-Chief, Man. Dir The Sporting Life 1990–98; Editorial Dir Mirror Group Newspapers 1991–92, Group Man. Dir Mirror Group 1992–98; Acting Ed. The Independent 1995–96; Dir (non-exec.) Chelsea and Westminster Hosp.; mem. Newspaper Panel, Competition Comm. 1999–; mem. Jockey Club 1993–, Youth Justice Bd 1998–2004; Trustee World Wildlife Fund-UK 1997–2004, Royal Naval Museum 1999–. *Address:* Chairman's Office, Chelsea and Westminster Trust, 369 Fulham Road, London, SW10 9NH (office); 23 Campden Hill Square, London, W8 7JY, England. *Telephone:* (20) 7727-3366 (home). *Website:* www.competition-commission.org.uk (office).

WILSON, Christopher, PhD; British novelist and semiotician; b. 18 Nov. 1949, London. *Education:* LSE. *Career:* fmr Lecturer, Goldsmiths' Coll., London; currently semiotician. *Publications:* novels: Gallimauf's Gospel 1986, Baa: A Novel 1987, Bluegrass 1990, Mischief 1991, Fou 1992, The Wurd 1995, The Ballad of Lee Cotton (aka Cotton) 2005. *Address:* c/o Little, Brown Book Group, Brettenham House, Lancaster Place, London, WC2E 7EN, England. *E-mail:* Email.UK@twbg.co.uk.

WILSON, Colin Henry; British writer; b. 26 June 1931, Leicester; s. of Arthur Wilson and Annetta Jones; m. 1st Dorothy Troop 1951; one s.; m. 2nd Joy Stewart 1960; two s. one d. *Education:* Gateway Secondary Technical School, Leicester. *Career:* laboratory asst 1948–49, civil servant (taxes) 1949–50; RAF 1950, discharged on medical grounds 1950; then navvy, boot and shoe operative, dish washer, plastic moulder; lived Strasbourg 1950, Paris 1953; later factory hand and dish washer; writer 1956–; Writer in Residence, Hollins Coll., Virginia, USA 1966–67; Visiting Prof., Univ. of Washington 1967–68, Dowling Coll., Majorca 1969, Rutgers Univ., NJ 1974. *Publications include: philosophy:* The Outsider 1956, Religion and the Rebel 1957, The Age of Defeat 1958, The Strength to Dream 1961, Origins of the Sexual Impulse 1963, Beyond the Outsider 1965, Introduction to the New Existentialism 1966; *other non-fiction:* Encyclopaedia of Murder 1960, Rasputin and the Fall of the Romanovs 1964, Brandy of the Damned (music essays) 1965, Eagle and Earwig (literary essays) 1965, Sex and the Intelligent Teenager 1966, Voyage to a Beginning (autobiog.) 1968, Shaw: A Reassessment 1969, A Casebook of Murder 1969, Poetry and Mysticism 1970, The Strange Genius of David Lindsay (with E. H. Visiak) 1970, The Occult 1971, New Pathways in Psychology 1972, Strange Powers 1973, A Book of Booze 1974, The Craft of the Novel 1975, The Geller Phenomenon 1977, Mysteries 1978, Beyond The Occult 1988; *novels:* Ritual in the Dark 1960, Adrift in Soho 1961, The World of Violence 1963, Man Without a Shadow 1963, Necessary Doubt 1964, The Glass Cage 1966, The Mind Parasites 1967, The Philosopher's Stone 1969, The Killer 1970, The God of the Labyrinth 1970, The Black Room 1970, The Schoolgirl Murder Case 1974, The Space Vampires 1976, Men of Strange Powers 1976, Enigmas and Mysteries 1977; *other works include:* The Quest for Wilhelm Reich 1979, The War Against Sleep: the Philosophy of Gurdjieff 1980, Starseekers 1980, Frankenstein's Castle 1980, The Directory of Possibilities (ed. with John Grant) 1981, Poltergeist! 1981, Access to Inner Worlds 1983, Encyclopaedia of Modern Murder (with Donald Seaman) 1983, The Psychic Detectives 1984, The Janus Murder Case 1984, The Personality Surgeon 1984, A Criminal History of Mankind 1984, Encyclopaedia of Scandal (with Donald Seaman) 1985, Afterlife 1985, Rudolf Steiner 1985, Strindberg (play) 1970, Spiderworld—The Tower 1987, Encyclopaedia of Unsolved Mysteries (with Damon Wilson) 1987, Aleister Crowley: the nature of the beast 1987, The Misfits 1988, Spiderworld—The Delta 1988, Written in Blood 1989, The Serial Killers 1990, Mozart's Journey to Prague (play) 1991, Spider World: the Magician 1992, The Strange Life of P. D. Ouspensky 1993, From Atlantis to the Sphinx 1996, Atlas of Sacred Sites and Holy Places 1996, Alien Dawn 1998, The Books in My Life 1998, The Devil's Party 2000, Atlantis Blueprint (with Rand Fle'math) 2000, Spiderworld—Shadowland 2003, Dreaming to Some Purpose (autobiography) 2004, Crimes of Passion (with Damon Wilson) 2006, Atlantis and the Neanderthals 2006, The Angry Years 2007. *Address:* Tetherdown, Trewallock Lane, Gorran Haven, Cornwall, PL26 6NT, England. *Telephone:* (1726) 842708.

WILSON, Donald M.; American journalist and publishing executive; *Publisher, NJBIZ;* b. 27 June 1925; m. Susan M. Neuberger 1957; one s. two d. *Education:* Yale Univ. *Career:* USAAF navigator, Second World War; magazine assignments in 35 countries 1951–61; fmr Far Eastern Corresp., Life magazine, Chief Washington Correspondent 1957–61; Deputy Dir US Information Agency 1961–65; Gen. Man. Time-Life Int. 1965–68; Assoc. Publisher Life magazine 1968–69; Vice-Pres. Corp. and Public Affairs, Time Inc. 1969–81, Corp. Vice-Pres. Public Affairs Time Inc. 1981–89; Publr NJBIZ 1989–. *Address:* NJBIZ, 104 Church Street, New Brunswick, NJ 08901 (office); 4574 Province Line Road, Princeton, NJ 08540, USA (home).

WILSON, Edward Osborne, PhD; American academic and writer; *Pellegrino University Professor Emeritus, Department of Entomology, Museum of Comparative Zoology, Harvard University;* b. 10 June 1929, Birmingham, AL; s. of the late Edward Osborne Wilson Sr and Inez Freeman Huddleston; m. Irene Kelley 1955; one d. *Education:* Univ. of Alabama and Harvard Univ. *Career:* Jr Fellow, Soc. of Fellows, Harvard Univ. 1953–56, Prof. of Zoology 1964–76, F. B. Baird Prof. of Science 1976–94, Pellegrino Univ. Prof. 1994–97, Research Prof. 1997–2002, now Prof. Emer., Curator of Entomology, Museum of Comparative Zoology, 1974–97, Hon. Curator 1997–; Fellow, Guggenheim Foundation 1977–78, Advisory Bd 1979–90, mem. Selection Cttee 1982–90; mem. Bd of Dirs., World Wildlife Fund 1983–94, Org. for Tropical Studies 1984–91, American Museum of Natural History 1992–, American Acad. of Liberal Educ. 1993–2004, Nature Conservancy 1994–, Conservation Int. 1997–; Foreign mem. Royal Soc. 1990 and other orgs. *Publications:* The Theory of Island Biogeography (with R. H. MacArthur) 1967, The Insect Societies 1971, Sociobiology: The New Synthesis 1975, On Human Nature 1978, Caste and Ecology in the Social Insects (with G. F. Oster) 1978, Genes, Mind and Culture (with C. J. Lumsden) 1981, Promethean Fire (with C. J. Lumsden) 1983, Biophilia 1984, Biodiversity (ed.) 1988, The Ants (with Bert Hölldobler) 1990, Success and Dominance in Ecosystems 1990, The Diversity of Life 1991, Naturalist 1994, Journey to the Ants (with Bert Hölldobler) 1994, Consilience: The Unity of Knowledge 1998, Biological Diversity: The Oldest Human Heritage 1999, The Future of Life 2002, Pheidole in the New World: A Dominant, Hyperdiverse Ant Genus 2002, The Creation: An Appeal to Save Life on Earth 2006; numerous articles on evolutionary biology, entomology and conservation. *Honours:* Nat. Medal of Science 1976, Pulitzer Prize for Gen. Non-Fiction 1978, 1981, Tyler Prize for Environmental Achievement 1983, Ingersoll Foundation Weaver Award for Scholarly Letters 1989, Royal Swedish Acad. of Sciences Crafoord Prize 1990, Int. Prize for Biology, Govt of Japan 1993, Audubon Soc. Medal 1995, Los Angeles Times Book Prize for Science 1995, Schubert Prize (Germany) 1996, German Ecological Foundation Book Award 1998, American Philosophical Soc. Franklin Prize for Science 1999, Nonino Prize (Italy) 2000, King Faisal Int. Prize for Science (Saudi Arabia) 2000, Foundation for the Future Kistler Prize 2000, Silver Cross of Columbus (Dominican Republic) 2003, TED (Technology Entertainment Design) Prize (co-recipient) 2007, others. *Address:* Museum of Comparative Zoology, MCZ Labs Room 419, Harvard University, 26 Oxford Street, Cambridge, MA 02138-2902 (office); 1010 Waltham Street, Lexington, MA 02421, USA (home). *E-mail:* ewilson@oeb.harvard.edu (office). *Website:* www.mcz.harvard.edu/Departments/Entomology/index.cfm (office).

WILSON, Gina, MA; British children's writer and poet; b. 1 April 1943, Abergele, N Wales. *Education:* Univ. of Edinburgh, Mount Holyoke Coll., Mass, USA. *Career:* Asst Ed. Scottish Nat. Dictionary 1967–73, Dictionary of the Older Scottish Tongue 1972–73. *Publications:* Cora Ravenwing 1980, A Friendship of Equals 1981, The Whisper 1982, All Ends Up 1984, Family Feeling 1986, Just Us 1988, Polly Pipes Up 1989, I Hope You Know 1989, Jim Jam Pyjamas 1990, Wompus Galumpus 1990, Riding the Great White 1992, Prowlpuss 1994, Ignis 2001, Grandma's Bears 2004. *Honours:* Frogmore Poetry Prize 1997, Annual Lace Poetry Prize 1999. *Address:* 24 Beaumont Street, Oxford, OX1 2NP, England (home).

WILSON, Jacqueline, OBE; British writer; b. 17 Dec. 1945, Bath; d. of the late Harry Aitken and of Margaret Aitken (née Clibbons); m. William Millar Wilson 1965 (divorced 2004); one d. *Education:* Coombe Girls' School. *Career:* journalist D. C. Thomsons 1963–65; teenage magazine Jackie named after her; Amb. Reading is Fundamental, UK 1998–; mem. Cttee Children's Writers and Illustrators Group, Soc. of Authors 1997–; Advisory mem. Panel Whitbread Book Awards 1997–; Judge Rhône-Poulenc Prizes for Jr Science Books 1999; mem. Bd Children's Film and TV Foundation 2000–; Children's Laureate 2005–07. *Television:* novels Girls in Love, Girls Under Pressure, Girls Out Late and Girls in Tears adapted into 13-part TV series, Granada 2003; The Story of Tracy Beaker adapted into five series on BBC children's TV; The Illustrated Mum adapted for Channel 4 children's TV (two BAFTA Awards, one Emmy Award). *Publications include:* fiction: Hide and Seek 1972, Truth or Dare 1973, Snap 1974, Let's Pretend 1975, Making Hate 1977; juvenile fiction: Nobody's Perfect 1982, Waiting for the Sky to Fall 1983, The Other Side 1984, Amber 1986, The Power of the Shade 1987, Stevie Day Series 1987, This Girl 1988, Is There Anybody There? 1990, Deep Blue 1993, Take a Good Look 1990, The Story of Tracy Beaker 1991, The Suitcase Kid (Children's Book of the Year Award 1993) 1992, Video Rose 1992, The Mum-minder 1993, The Werepuppy 1993, The Bed and the Breakfast Star (The Young Telegraph/Fully Booked Award 1995) 1994, Mark Spark in the Dark 1994, Twin Trouble 1995, Glubbslyme 1995, Jimmy Jelly 1995, The Dinosaur's Packed Lunch 1995, Cliffhanger 1995, Double Act (Children's Book of the Year Award, Smarties Prize) 1995, My Brother Bernadette 1995, Werepuppy on Holiday 1995, Bad Girls 1996, Mr Cool 1996, Monster Story-teller 1997, The Lottie Project 1997, Girls in Love 1997, Connie and the Water Babies 1997, Buried Alive! 1998, Girls Under Pressure 1998, How to Survive Summer Camp 1998, The Illustrated Mum (Guardian Children's Book of the Year Award, Children's Book of the Year Award 1999) 1999, Girls Out Late 1999, Lizzie Zipmouth 1999, The Dare Game 2000, Vicky Angel 2000, The Cat Mummy 2001, Sleepovers 2001, Dustbin Baby 2001, Secrets 2002, Girls in Tears 2002, The Worry Website 2002, Lola Rose 2003, Midnight 2004, The Diamond Girls

2004, Clean Break 2005, Love Lessons 2005, Best Friends (Red House Children's Book Award) 2005, Candyfloss 2006, Starring Tracy Beaker 2006, Kiss 2007; other: Jacky Daydream (autobiog.) 2007. *Honours:* Hon. DEd (Kingston Univ.) 2001; Oak Tree Award 1992, Sheffield Children's Book Award, WHSmith Children's Book of the Year 2002, BT Childline Award 2004. *Literary Agent:* David Higham Associates, 5–8 Lower John Street, Golden Square, London, W1F 9HA, England. *Telephone:* (20) 7434-5900 (office). *Website:* www.jacquelinewilson.co.uk.

WILSON, Keith, BS, MA; American poet and writer; b. 26 Dec. 1927, Clovis, NM; m. Heloise Brigham 1958, one s. four d. *Education:* US Naval Acad., University of New Mexico. *Publications:* Homestead, 1969; Thantog: Songs of a Jaguar Priest, 1977; While Dancing Feet Shatter the Earth, 1977; The Streets of San Miguel, 1979; Retablos, 1981; Stone Roses: Poems from Transylvania, 1983; Meeting at Jal (with Theodore Enslin), 1985; Lion's Gate: Selected Poems 1963–1986, 1988; The Wind of Pentecost, 1991; Graves Registry, 1992; The Way of the Dove, 1994; Bosque Redoudo: The Enclosed Grove, 2000. Contributions: journals. *Honours:* National Endowment for the Arts Fellowship; Fulbright-Hays Fellowship; D. H. Lawrence Creative Writing Fellowship.

WILSON, Lanford; American dramatist and stage director; b. 13 April 1937, Lebanon, MO. *Education:* San Diego State College. *Career:* Resident Playwright and Dir, Circle Repertory Co, New York City, 1969–95; mem. Dramatists Guild. *Publications:* Balm in Gilead and Other Plays, 1966; The Rimers of Eldritch and Other Plays, 1968; The Gingham Dog, 1969; Lemon Sky, 1970; The Hotel Baltimore, 1973; The Mound Builders, 1976; Fifth of July, 1979; Talley's Folly, 1980; Angels Fall, 1983; Serenading Louie, 1985; Talley & Son, 1986; Burn This, 1988; Redwood Curtain, 1992; 21 Short Plays, 1994; By the Sea by the Beautiful Sea, 1996; Sympathetic Magic, 1998. *Honours:* Vernon Rice Award, 1966–67; Rockefeller Foundation Grants, 1967, 1973; ABC Yale Fellow, 1969; Guggenheim Fellowship, 1970; National Institute of Arts and Letters Award, 1970; Obie Awards, 1972, 1975, 1984; Outer Critics Circle Award, 1973; Drama Critics Circle Awards, 1973, 1980; Pulitzer Prize for Drama, 1980; Brandeis University Creative Arts Award, 1981; John Steinbeck Award, 1990; National Endowment for the Arts Grant, 1990; Edward Albee Last Frontier Award, 1994; American Acad. of Achievement Award, 1995; Hon. doctorates. *Address:* c/o Dramatists' Guild, 234 W 44th Street, New York, NY 10036, USA.

WILSON, Robert McLiam; British writer; b. 1964, Belfast, Northern Ireland; m. *Education:* Univ. of Cambridge. *Career:* several BBC TV documentaries. *Publications:* novels: Ripley Bogle 1989, Manfred's Pain 1992, Eureka Street 1996, The Extremists 2004; non-fiction: The Dispossessed 1992. *Honours:* Rooney Prize 1989, Hughes Prize 1989, Betty Trask Prize 1990, Irish Book Award 1990. *Address:* c/o Secker & Warburg, Random House, 20 Vauxhall Bridge Road, London SW1V 2SA, England.

WILSON, William Julius; American sociologist and academic; b. 20 Dec. 1935, Derry Township, Pennsylvania; m. 1st Mildred Marie Hood 1957; two d.; m. 2nd Beverly Ann Huebner 1970; one s. one d. *Education:* BA, Wilberforce University, 1958; MA, Bowling Green State University, 1961; PhD, Washington State University, 1966. *Career:* Asst Prof., 1965–69, Assoc. Prof. of Sociology, 1969–71, University of Massachusetts, Amherst; Visiting Assoc. Prof. and Research Scholar, 1971–72, Assoc. Prof. of Sociology, 1972–75, Prof. of Sociology, 1975–80, Lucy Flower Prof. of Urban Sociology, 1980–84, Lucy Flower Distinguished Service Prof., 1984–90, Lucy Flower University Prof. of Sociology and Public Policy, 1990–96, University of Chicago; Visiting Assoc. Prof., 1972, Malcolm Wiener Prof. of Social Policy, 1996–98, John F. Kennedy School of Government, Lewis P. and Linda L. Geyser University Prof., Harvard University, 1998–; Fellow, Center for Advanced Study in the Behavioral Sciences, Stanford, CA, 1981–82; Andrew Dixon White Prof.-at-Large, Cornell University, 1994–98; mem. A Philip Randolph Institute, national board, 1981–; American Acad. of Arts and Sciences, fellow; American Acad. of Political and Social Science, fellow; American Asscn for the Advancement of Science, fellow; American Philosophical Society; American Sociological Asscn, pres., 1989–90; Center for Urban Studies, exec. committee, 1974–; National Acad. of Education; National Acad. of Sciences; National Urban League, board of trustees, 1995–98; Russell Sage Foundation, board of dirs, chair, 1988–98, 1994–96; Sociological Research Asscn, pres., 1987–88. *Publications:* Power, Racism and Privilege: Race Relations in Theoretical and Sociohistorical Perspectives, 1973; Through Different Eyes: Black and White Perspectives on American Race Relations (ed. with Peter I Rose and Stanley Rothman), 1973; The Declining Significance of Race: Blacks and Changing American Institutions, 1978; The Truly Disadvantaged: The Inner City, the Underclass, and Public Policy, 1987; The Ghetto Underclass: Social Science Perspectives (ed.), 1989; Sociology and the Public Agenda (ed.), 1993; Poverty, Inequality and the Future of Social Policy: Western States in the New World Order (ed. with Katherine McFate and Roger Lawson), 1995; When Work Disappears: The World of the New Urban Poor, 1996; The Bridge Over the Racial Divide: Rising Inequality and Coalition Politics, 1999. Contributions: many scholarly books, journals, and reviews, and general periodicals. *Honours:* John D. and Catherine T. MacArthur Foundation Fellowship, 1987–92; New York Times Book Review Best Book Citations, 1987, 1996; Washington Monthly Annual Book Award, 1988; C. Wright Mills Award, Society for the Study of Social Problems, 1988; Dubois, Johnson, Frazier Award, American Sociological Asscn, 1990; Burton Gordon Feldman Award, Brandeis University, 1991; Frank E. Seidman Distinguished Award in

Political Economy, Rhodes College, Memphis, Tennessee, 1994; Martin Luther King Jr National Award, Southern Christian Leadership Council, Los Angeles, 1998; Lester F. Ward Distinguished Contributions to Applied Sociology Award, 1998; National Medal of Science, 1998; numerous hon. doctorates. *Address:* John F. Kennedy School of Government, Harvard University, 79 JFK Street, Cambridge, MA 02138, USA.

WILTON-JONES, Anni, (Áine an Caipín), DSRT, DSRR, BA, PGCE, MA, AMBDA; British performance poet and learning development officer; b. 8 April 1949, Bromborough; two s. five d. *Education:* School of Radiography, Southampton, Open Univ., Univ. of Wales, Newport. *Publications:* Bridges 1999, This is... Salem 1999, Fresh Voices for Younger Listeners 2000, Anam Cara (CD) 2001, Light Touch 2002; contrib. to newspapers and journals. *Address:* Ty Beirdd, 53 Church Street, Ebbw Vale, NP23 6BG, Wales (home). *E-mail:* annipoetry@lycos.co.uk (home).

WIMAN, Christian; American poet and essayist; *Editor, Poetry. Career:* Editor, Poetry magazine 2003–. *Publications:* The Long Home (Nicholas Roerich Prize) 1998, Ambition and Survival: Essays on Poetry 2004, Hard Night 2005; contrib. to journals, including At Length, Atlantic Monthly, Harper's, LRB. *Address:* Poetry, 1030 N Clark Street, Suite 420, Chicago, IL 60610, USA. *Telephone:* (312) 787-7070. *Fax:* (312) 787-6650. *Website:* www.poetrymagazine.org.

WINCH, Donald Norman, PhD, FBA, FRHistS; British academic; *Research Professor Emeritus, University of Sussex;* b. 15 April 1935, London; s. of Sidney Winch and Iris Winch; m. Doreen Lidster 1983. *Education:* Sutton Grammar School, London School of Econs, Princeton Univ. *Career:* Visiting Lecturer, Univ. of Calif., USA 1959–60; Lecturer in Econs, Univ. of Edin. 1960–63; Univ. of Sussex 1963–66, Reader 1966–69, Prof. History of Econs 1969–, now Research Prof. Emer., Dean School of Social Sciences 1968–74, Pro-Vice-Chancellor (Arts and Social Studies) 1986–89; Vice-Pres. British Acad. 1993–94; Visiting Fellow, School of Social Science, Inst. of Advanced Study, Princeton 1974–75; King's Coll., Cambridge 1983, History of Ideas Unit, ANU 1983, St Catharine's Coll., Cambridge 1989, All Souls Coll., Oxford 1994; Visiting Prof., Tulane Univ. 1984; Carlyle Lecturer, Univ. of Oxford 1995, Prof. Emer., School of Humanities; Publr Sec., Royal Econ. Soc. 1971–; Review Ed. The Economic Journal 1976–83. *Publications:* Classical Political Economy & Colonies 1965, James Mill, Selected Economic Writings 1966, Economics and Policy 1969, The Economic Advisory Council 1930–39 (with S. K. Howson) 1976, Adam Smith's Politics 1978, That Noble Science of Politics (with S. Collini and J. W. Burrow) 1983, Malthus 1987, Riches and Poverty 1996. *Address:* Arts B, University of Sussex, Brighton, BN1 9QN, England (office). *Telephone:* (1273) 678634 (office); (1273) 400635 (home). *E-mail:* d.winch@sussex.ac.uk (office). *Website:* www.economistspapers.org.uk (office).

WINCHESTER, Jack (see Freemantle, Brian Harry)

WINCHESTER, Simon; American writer; b. 1940. *Education:* Univ. of Oxford. *Publications:* Northern Ireland in Crisis 1975, American Heartbeat 1976, Their Noble Lordships 1978, Prison Diary, Argentina 1983, The Sun Never Sets: Travels to the Remaining Outposts of the British Empire 1986, The Rise and Fall of Travel 1989, Pacific Rising 1991, Pacific Nightmare: How Japan Starts World War III: A Future History 1992, The River at the Centre of the World 1996, The Surgeon of Crowthorne 1998, The Professor and the Madman 1998, The Fracture Zone: My Return to the Balkans 1999, The Map That Changed the World 2001, Tramping 2001, Outposts: Journeys to the Surviving Relics of the British Empire 2003, Krakatoa: The Day the World Exploded 2003, The Meaning of Everything: The Story of the Oxford English Dictionary 2003, Simon Winchester's Calcutta 2004, A Crack in the Edge of the World: The Great Earthquake of 1906 2005; co-author: Small World: A Global Photographic Project 1995, America's Idea of a Good Time 2001; contrib. to Stories of Empire: Buildings of the Raj 1983, Conde Nast Traveller, Smithsonian, National Geographic. *Address:* c/o Oxford University Press, Great Clarendon Street, Oxford, OX2 6DP, England. *Website:* www.simonwinchester.com.

WINDLEY, Carol; Canadian writer; b. 18 June 1947, Tofino, BC; m. Robert Windley 1971, one d. *Publications:* Visible Light, 1993; City of Ladies, 1998. Contributions: anthologies and periodicals. *Honours:* Bumbershoot-Weyerhauser Publication Award 1993, Canada Council B. grants 1995, 1997. *Address:* 5989 Tweedsmuir Crescent, Nanaimo, BC, Canada. *E-mail:* oolichan@mail.island.net.

WINDSOR, Patricia, (Colin Daniel, Katonah Summertree); American writer, poet and academic; b. 21 Sept. 1938, New York, NY; one s. one d. *Career:* faculty mem., Institute of Children's Literature, University of Maryland Writers Institute; Ed.-in-Chief, The Easterner, Washington, DC; Co-Dir, Wordspring Literary Consultants; Dir, Summertree Studios, Savannah; Instructor, Creative Writing, Armstrong Atlantic University, Savannah; mem. Authors' Guild; Children's Book Guild; International Writing Guild; MWA; Poetry Society of Georgia; Savannah Storytellers. *Publications:* The Summer Before, 1973; Something's Waiting for You, Baker D, 1974; Home is Where Your Feet Are Standing, 1975; Mad Martin, 1976; Killing Time, 1980; The Sandman's Eyes, 1985; The Hero, 1988; Just Like the Movies, 1990; The Christmas Killer, 1991; The Blooding, 1996; The House of Death, 1996. Contributions: anthologies and magazines. *Honours:* American Library Asscn Best Book Award, 1973; Outstanding Book for Young Adults Citation, New York Times, 1976; Edgar Allan Poe Award, MWA, 1986.

WINEGARTEN, Renee, BA, PhD; British literary critic and writer; b. 23 June 1922, London, England; m. Asher Winegarten (died 1946). *Education:* Girton Coll., Cambridge. *Career:* mem. George Sand Asscn, Soc. of Authors, Authors' Guild. *Publications:* French Lyric Poetry in the Age of Malherbe 1954, Writers and Revolution 1974, The Double Life of George Sand 1978, Madame de Staël 1985, Simone de Beauvoir: A Critical View 1988, Accursed Politics: Some French Women Writers and Political Life 1715–1850 2003; contrib. to journals. *Address:* 12 Heather Walk, Edgware, Middlesex HA8 9TS, England.

WINGATE, John Allan; British writer; b. 15 March 1920, Cornwall, England; one s. one d. *Career:* mem. Nautical Inst. *Publications:* Submariner Sinclair Series 1959–64, Sinclair Action Series 1968, 1969, 1971, HMS Belfast, In Trust for the Nation 1972, In the Blood 1973, Below the Horizon 1974, The Sea Above Them 1975, Oil Strike 1976, Black Tide 1976, Avalanche 1977, Red Mutiny 1977, Target Risk 1978, Seawaymen 1979, Frigate 1980, Carrier 1981, Submarine 1982, William the Conqueror 1984, Go Deep 1985, The Windship Race 1987, The Fighting Tenth 1990, The Man Called Mark 1996. *Honours:* Distinguished Service Cross 1943. *Address:* c/o Lloyd Bank Plc, Waterloo Place, Pall Mall, London, SW1Y 5NJ, England.

WINNER, Michael Robert, MA; British film producer and director and screenwriter; b. 30 Oct. 1935, London; s. of the late George Joseph Winner and Helen Winner. *Education:* Downing Coll. Cambridge. *Career:* Ed. and film critic of Cambridge Univ. paper; entered film industry as film critic and columnist for nat. newspapers and magazines 1951; wrote, produced and directed many documentary, TV and feature films for the Film Producers Guild, Anglo Amalgamated, United Artists 1955–61; Chair. Scimitar Films Ltd, Michael Winner Ltd, Motion Picture and Theatrical Investments Ltd 1957–; Columnist Sunday Times and News of the World; Chief Censorship Officer, Dirs. Guild of GB 1983, mem. Council and Trustee 1983–, Sr mem. 1991–; Founder and Chair. Police Memorial Trust 1984–; mem. Writers' Guild of Great Britain. *Films:* Play It Cool (dir) 1962, The Cool Mikado (dir, writer) 1962, West 11 (dir) 1963, The System (co-producer and dir) 1963–64, You Must Be Joking (producer, dir, writer) 1964–65, The Jokers (producer, dir, writer) 1966, I'll Never Forget What's 'is Name (producer, dir) 1967, Hannibal Brooks (producer, dir, writer) 1968, The Games (producer, dir) 1969, Lawman (producer, dir) 1970, The Nightcomers (producer, dir) 1971, Chato's Land (producer, dir) 1971, The Mechanic (dir) 1972, Scorpio (producer, dir) 1972, The Stone Killer (producer, dir) 1973, Death Wish (producer, dir) 1974, Won Ton Ton – The Dog Who Saved Hollywood (producer, dir) 1975, The Sentinel (producer, dir, writer) 1976, The Big Sleep (producer, dir, Writer) 1977, Firepower (producer, dir, writer) 1978, Death Wish II (producer, dir, writer) 1981, The Wicked Lady (producer, dir, writer) 1982, Scream For Help (producer, dir) 1983, Death Wish III (producer, dir) 1985, Appointment with Death (producer, dir, writer) 1988, A Chorus of Disapproval (producer, dir, co-writer) 1989, Bullseye! (producer, dir, co-writer) 1990, For the Greater Good (BBC film, actor, dir Danny Boyle) 1990, Decadence (actor, dir Steven Berkoff) 1993, Dirty Weekend (producer, jt screenplay writer) 1993, Parting Shots (producer, dir, writer) 1997. *Theatre:* The Silence of St Just (producer) 1971, The Tempest (producer) 1974, A Day in Hollywood, A Night in the Ukraine (producer) (Evening Standard Award for Best Comedy of the Year 1979). *Radio:* panellist, Any Questions (BBC Radio 4), The Flump (play) 2000. *Television appearances include:* Michael Winner's True Crimes (LWT), panellist, Question Time (BBC One), many variety show sketches, starring in and/or directing commercials for different cos 2003–. *Publications:* Winner's Dinners 1999, Winner Guide 2002, Winner Takes All: a Life of Sorts 2004; contrib. to Sunday Times, News of the World, Daily Mail. *Address:* 219 Kensington High Street, London, W8 6BD, England. *Telephone:* (20) 7734-8385. *Fax:* (20) 7602-9217.

WINNIFRITH, Thomas John, BA, MPhil, PhD; British writer; b. 5 April 1938, Dulwich, England; m. 1st Joanna Booker 1967; m. 2nd Helen Young 1988; one s. two d. *Education:* Christ Church, Oxford, Corpus Christi, Oxford, Univ. of Liverpool. *Career:* Asst Master Eton Coll. 1961–66, EK Chambers Student 1966–68, William Noble Fellow 1968–70; Lecturer, Sr Lecturer, Univ. of Warwick 1970–98; Visiting Fellow, All Souls Coll., Oxford 1984; Leverhulme Fellow Emer. 1999–2000. *Publications:* The Brontës and Their Background 1973, The Brontës 1977, Brontë Facts and Problems 1983, Nineteen Eighty Four and All's Well 1984, The Vlachs 1987, A New Life of Charlotte Brontë 1988, Charlotte and Emily Brontë 1989, Fallen Women in the Nineteenth Century Novel 1994, Shattered Eagles: Balkan Fragments 1996, Badlands Borderlands 2002. *Address:* 50 Sheep Street, Shipston on Stour, Warwicks., CV36 4AE, England (home). *Telephone:* (1608) 661244 (home). *Fax:* (1608) 661244 (home). *E-mail:* twinnifrith@fish.co.uk (home).

WINOCK, Michel, LèsL, DèsL; French historian, academic, writer and publisher; b. 19 March 1937, Paris; s. of Gaston Winock and Jeanne Winock (née Dussaule); m. Françoise Werner 1961; two s. *Education:* Sorbonne. *Career:* teacher, Lycée Joffre, Montpellier 1961–63, Lycée Hoche, Versailles 1963–66, Lycée Lakanal, Sceaux 1966–68; Lecturer, Sr Lecturer Univ. of Paris VIII-Vincennes à St-Denis 1968–78; Sr Lecturer, Institut d'Etudes politiques, Paris 1978–90, Prof. 1990–; Publr Editions du Seuil, Paris 1969–; radio producer, France-Inter 1983–85; Ed.-in-Chief L'Histoire magazine 1978–81, Editorial Adviser 1981–. *Publications:* Histoire politique de la revue esprit 1930–1950 1975, La république se meurt 1978, Les grandes crises politiques 1971–1968 1986, La Fière hexagonale 1986, Nationalisme, antisemitisme et fascisme en France 1990, Le socialisme en France et en Europe XIXe–XXe siècle 1992, Le siècle des intellectuels (essays) 1997, La guerre de 1914–1918 racontée aux enfants 1998, La France politique XIXe–XXe siècle 1999, Les Voix de la liberté 2001, Les écrivains engagés au XIXe siècle 2001, La France et les juifs (Prix Montaigne de Bordeaux 2005) 2004. *Address:* Institut d'Etudes politiques, 27 rue Saint-Guillaume, 75337 Paris Cedex 07, France. *Telephone:* 1-40-46-51-08. *Fax:* 1-40-46-51-75. *E-mail:* wimi@cybercable.fr; wimi@noos.fr.

WINSTON, Baron (Life Peer) cr. 1995, of Hammersmith in the London Borough of Hammersmith and Fulham; **Robert Maurice Lipson Winston,** MB, BS, DSc, FRCP, FRCOG, FMedSci, FRSA; British medical researcher; *Professor Emeritus of Reproductive Medicine, Imperial College London*; b. 15 July 1940, London, England; s. of the late Laurence Winston and of Ruth Winston-Fox; m. Lira Feigenbaum 1973; two s. one d. *Education:* St Paul's School, London and London Hosp. Medical Coll., Univ. of London. *Career:* Registrar and Sr Registrar, Hammersmith Hosp. 1970–74; Wellcome Research Sr Lecturer, Inst. of Obstetrics and Gynaecology 1974–78, Sr Lecturer 1978–81, Consultant Obstetrician and Gynaecologist 1978–2005; Prof. of Gynaecology, Univ. of Texas at San Antonio, USA 1980–81; Reader in Fertility Studies, Royal Postgraduate Medical School 1982–86, Prof. 1987–97; apptd Prof. of Fertility Studies, Imperial Coll. London 1997, now Prof. Emer. of Reproductive Medicine; Dir NHS Research and Devt, Hammersmith Hosps Trust 1998–2005; Chancellor Sheffield Hallam Univ. 2001–; Visiting Prof., Univ. of Leuven, Belgium 1976–77, Mount Sinai Hosp., New York, USA 1985; Chair. Select Cttee of Science and Tech., House of Lords 1999–2002; Vice-Chair. Parl. Office of Science and Tech. 2005–; Founder-mem. British Fertility Soc.; many other professional appointments. *Director:* Each in his Own Way (Pirandello), Edinburgh Festival 1969. *Television:* Presenter, Your Life In Their Hands (BBC) 1979–87, Making Babies 1996, The Human Body 1998, The Secret Life of Twins 1999, Child of our Time (BBC) 2000, Superhuman 2000, Human Instinct 2002, 2003, Threads of Life (BBC) 2003, The Human Mind (BBC) 2004, Story of God (BBC) 2005, Child Against All Odds (BBC) 2006. *Publications:* Reversibility of Sterilization 1978, Tubal Infertility (jtly) 1981, Infertility: A Sympathetic Approach 1987, Getting Pregnant 1989, Making Babies 1996, The IVF Revolution 1999, Superman 2000, Human Instinct 2002, The Human Mind 2003, What Makes Me, Me? (Aventis Jr Prize, Royal Soc. 2005) 2004, Human (BMA Award for Best Popular Medicine Book) 2005, The Story of God 2005, Body 2005, A Child Against All Odds 2006; about 300 scientific articles on reproduction. *Honours:* Hon. Fellow, Queen Mary and Westfield Coll. 1996; Hon. FRCSE; Hon. Fellow, Royal Coll. of Physicians and Surgeons (Glasg); Hon. FIBiol; 14 hon. doctorates at British univs, including: Hon. DSc (Cranfield) 2001, (UMIST) 2001, (Oxford Brookes) 2001; Victor Bonney Prize, Royal Coll. of Surgeons 1991–93, Chief Rabbinate Award for Contribution to Society 1992–93, Cedric Carter Medal, Clinical Genetics Soc. 1993, Gold Medal, Royal Soc. of Health 1998, Michael Faraday Award, Royal Soc. 1999, Wellcome Award for Science in the Media 2001, Edwin Stevens Medal, Royal Soc. of Medicine 2003, Gold Medal, North of England Zoological Soc. 2004, VLV Individual Award for Best contribs to UK Broadcasting 2004, Al Hammadi Medal, Royal Coll. of Surgeons, Edin. 2005. *Address:* The Hammersmith Hospital, Du Cane Road, London, W12 0HS (office); 11 Denman Drive, London, NW11 6RE, England (home). *Telephone:* (20) 8383-2183 (office); (20) 8455-7475 (home). *Fax:* (20) 8749-6973 (office); (20) 8458-4980 (home). *E-mail:* r.winston@imperial.ac.uk (office). *Website:* www.robertwinston.org.

WINSTON, Sarah; American writer; b. (Sarah E. Lorenz), 15 Dec. 1912, New York, NY; m. Keith Winston 1932, two s. *Education:* New York University, The Barnes Foundation. *Career:* mem. National League of American Pen Women. *Publications:* And Always Tomorrow, 1963; Everything Happens for the Best, 1969; Our Son, Ken, 1969; Not Yet Spring (poems), 1976; V-Mail: Letters of the World War II Combat Medic, 1985; Summer Conference, 1990; Of Apples and Oranges, 1993. Contributions: journals. *Honours:* first prize National League of American Pen Women 1972, 1974.

WINTERSON, Jeanette, OBE, BA; British writer; b. 27 Aug. 1959, Manchester. *Education:* Accrington Girls' Grammar School, St Catherine's Coll., Oxford. *Play:* The Power Book (Royal Nat. Theatre, London, Théâtre de Chaillot, Paris). *Screenplay:* Great Moments in Aviation 1992. *Television:* Oranges Are Not The Only Fruit (BBC) 1990 (BAFTA Award for Best Drama 1990, FIPA d'Argent Award for screenplay, Cannes Film Festival 1991), Orlando – Art That Shook the World (BBC) 2002, South Bank Show 2004. *Publications:* fiction: Oranges Are Not The Only Fruit (Whitbread Prize for Best First Novel 1985) 1985, Boating for Beginners 1985, Passion Fruit: Romantic Fiction with a Twist (ed.) 1986, The Passion 1987, Sexing the Cherry 1989, Written on the Body 1992, Art and Lies 1994, Gut Symmetries 1997, The World and Other Places (short stories) 1998, The Power Book 2000, The King of Capri (juvenile) 2003, Lighthousekeeping 2004, Weight: The Myth of Atlas and Heracles 2005, Tanglewreck (juvenile novel) 2006, The Stone Gods 2007; non-fiction: Fit for the Future 1986, Art Objects (essays) 1994. *Honours:* John Llewellyn Rhys Memorial Book Prize 1987, American Acad. of Arts and Letters E. M. Forster Award 1989, Golden Gate Award, San Francisco Int. Film Festival 1990, Best of Young British Novelists Award 1992, Int. Fiction Award, Festival Letteratura Mantua 1999. *Address:* William Morris Agency, Inc., 1325 Avenue of the Americas, New York, NY 10019, USA (office). *Website:* www.jeanettewinterson.com.

WINTON, Timothy John; Australian writer; b. 4 Aug. 1960, near Perth, WA; m. Denise Winton; two s. one d. *Education:* Western Australian Inst. of Technology. *Publications:* An Open Swimmer 1981, Shallows 1984, Scisson and Other Stories 1985, That Eye, The Sky 1986, Minimum of Two 1987, In the Winter Dark 1988, Jesse 1988, Lockie Leonard, Human Torpedo 1991, The Bugalugs Bum Thief 1991, Cloudstreet 1992, Lockie Leonard, Scumbuster 1993, Land's Edge (with Trish Ainslie and Roger Garwood) 1993, Local Colour: Travels in the Other Australia 1994, The Riders 1995, Blueback: A Contemporary Fable 1998, Dirt Music 2001, The Turning 2005. *Honours:* Vogel Literary Award 1981, Arts Management Miles Franklin Awards 1984, 1992, Deo Gloria Prize for Religious Writing 1991, Commonwealth Writers Prize 1995. *Literary Agent:* David Higham Associates, 5–8 Lower John Street, Golden Square, London, W1F 9HA, England. *Telephone:* (20) 7434-5900. *Fax:* (20) 7437-1072. *E-mail:* dha@davidhigham.co.uk. *Website:* www.davidhigham .co.uk.

WINTOUR, Anna; British editor; *Editor, Vogue;* b. 3 Nov. 1949, d. of the late Charles Wintour; m. David Shaffer 1984; one s. one d. *Education:* Queen's Coll. School, London and N London Collegiate School. *Career:* deputy fashion ed. Harpers & Queen 1970–76, Harper's Bazaar, New York 1976–77; fashion and beauty ed. Viva magazine 1977–78; contributing ed. for fashion and style, Savvy Magazine 1980–81; Sr Ed. New York Magazine 1981–83; Creative Dir US Vogue 1983–86; Ed.-in-Chief, UK Vogue 1986–87; Ed. House & Garden, New York 1987–88; Ed. US Vogue 1988–. *Address:* Vogue, 4 Times Square, New York, NY 10036, USA (office). *Telephone:* (212) 286-2860 (office). *Fax:* (212) 286-8169 (office). *Website:* www.style.com/vogue (office).

WISEMAN, Christopher Stephen, BA, MA, PhD; British academic (retd), poet and writer; b. 31 May 1936, Hull, Yorkshire, England; m. Jean Leytem, 1 Jan. 1963, two s. *Education:* University of Cambridge, University of Strathclyde. *Career:* Asst to Prof. of English, University of Calgary, 1969–97; mem. League of Canadian Poets; Writers Guild of Alberta. *Publications:* Waiting for the Barbarians, 1971; The Barbarian File, 1974; Beyond the Labyrinth: A Study of Edwin Muir's Poetry, 1978; The Upper Hand, 1981; An Ocean of Whispers, 1982; Postcards Home: Poems New and Selected, 1988; Missing Persons, 1989; Remembering Mr Fox, 1995; Crossing the Salt Flats, 1999. Contributions: reviews, quarterlies, journals and magazines. *Honours:* Writers Guild of Alberta Poetry Award, 1988; Alberta Achievement Award for Excellence in Writing, 1988; Alberta Poetry Awards, 1988, 1989. *E-mail:* christopher382@hotmail.com. *Website:* www.library .utoronto.ca/canpoetry/wiseman/index.htm.

WISSE, Ruth, BA, MA, PhD; American academic, writer, editor and translator; *College Professor, Harvard University;* b. 13 May 1936, Cernauti, Romania; m. Leonard Wisse 1957; two s. one d. *Education:* McGill Univ., Columbia Univ. *Career:* Asst Prof., McGill Univ. 1968–71, Assoc. Prof. 1975, Chair., Dept of Jewish Studies 1976–79, Prof. 1978–92, Montréal Jewish Community Chair in Jewish Studies 1986–92; Sr Lecturer, Univ. of Tel-Aviv and Hebrew Univ., Tel-Aviv 1971–73; Visiting Prof., YIVO Inst. for Jewish Research 1975, mem. Academic Advisory Bd 2000–; Martin Peretz Prof. of Yiddish Literature, Harvard Univ. 1993–2003, Dir Center for Jewish Studies 1993–96, College Prof. 2003–; mem. American Acad. for Jewish Research, Asscn for Jewish Studies (Pres. 1985–89), Bd of Academic Advisors Nat. Foundation for Jewish Culture 1979–82. *Publications:* The Schlemiel as Modern Hero 1970, A Shtetl and Other Yiddish Novellas (ed.) 1972, The Best of Sholem Aleichem (ed. with Irving Howe) 1979, The Penguin Book of Modern Yiddish Verse (ed. with Irving Howe and Khone Shmeruk) 1987, A Little Love in Big Manhattan 1988, The I. L. Peretz Reader (ed.) 1990, I. L. Peretz and the Making of Modern Jewish Culture 1991, If I Am Not for Myself: The Liberal Portrayal of the Jews 1992, The Modern Jewish Canon: A Journey Through Language and Culture 2000; contrib. to reference works and periodicals. *Honours:* Hon. DHumLitt (Yeshiva) 2004; J. I. Segal Awards for Literature 1971, 1989, Manger Prize for Yiddish Literature 1989, Moment Magazine Award in Jewish Scholarship 1989, Torch of Learning Award, Hebrew Univ., Tel-Aviv 1993, Maurice Stiller Prize, Baltimore Hebrew Univ. 1998, Jewish Cultural Achievement Award, Nat. Foundation for Jewish Culture 2001, Nat. Jewish Book Award 2001, Guardian of Zion Award of Rennert Center, Bar-Ilan Univ. 2003. *Address:* Department of Near Eastern Languages and Civilizations, Harvard University, Cambridge, MA 02138, USA (office). *E-mail:* wisse@fas.harvard.edu (office).

WITHEROW, John Moore; British journalist; *Editor, The Sunday Times;* b. 20 Jan. 1952, Johannesburg, S. Africa; s. of Cecil Witherow and Millicent Witherow; m. Sarah Linton 1985; two s. one d. *Education:* Bedford School, Univ. of York, Univ. of Cardiff. *Career:* two years' voluntary service in Namibia (then SW Africa) after school; posted to Madrid for Reuters; covered Falklands War for The Times 1982; joined The Sunday Times 1984, successively Defence and Diplomatic Corresp., Focus Ed., Foreign Ed., Man. Ed. (news), Acting Ed., The Sunday Times 1994, Ed. 1995–. *Publications:* The Winter War: The Falklands (with Patrick Bishop) 1982, The Gulf War 1993. *Address:* The Sunday Times, 1 Pennington Street, London, E1 9XW, England. *Telephone:* (20) 7782-5640. *Fax:* (20) 7782-5420. *Website:* www.sunday-times .co.uk.

WITT, Harold Vernon, BA, BLS, MA; American writer, poet and editor; b. 6 Feb. 1923, Santa Ana, CA; m. Beth Hewitt 1948, one s. two d. *Education:* University of California at Berkeley, University of Michigan. *Career:* Co-Ed., California State Poetry Quarterly, 1976, Blue Unicorn, 1977–; Consulting Ed., Poet Lore, 1976–91. *Publications:* The Death of Venus, 1958; Beasts in Clothes, 1961; Now Swim, 1974; Suprised by Others at Fort Cronkhite, 1975; Winesburg by the Sea, 1979; The Snow Prince, 1982; Flashbacks and Reruns,

1985; The Light at Newport, 1992; American Literature, 1994. Contributions: journals and periodicals. *Honours:* Hopwood Award, 1947; Phelan Award, 1960; First Prize, San Francisco Poetry Centre Poetic Drama Competition, 1963; Emily Dickinson Award, Poetry Society of America, 1972; various awards, World Order of Narrative Poets.

WITTICH, John Charles Bird, (Charles Bird), BA; British librarian (retd), writer and lecturer; b. 18 Feb. 1929, London, England; m. June Rose Taylor 1954, one s. one d. *Publications:* Off Beat Walks In London 1969, Curiosities of London 1973, London Villages 1976, Discovering London Street Names 1977, Discovering London's Parks and Squares 1981, Churches, Cathedrals and Chapels 1988, Hidden World of Regent's Park 1992, Exploring Cathedrals 1992, Curiosities of Surrey 1994, Spot-It Guide to London (for children) 1995, Walks Around Haunted London 1996, London Bus Top Tourist 1997, History and Guide: St Vedast's Church, City of London 1999; as Charles Bird: Curiosities of the Cities of London and Westminster 2003; contrib. to periodicals and journals. *Address:* 88 Woodlawn Street, Whitstable, Kent CT5 1HH, England.

WOESSNER, Warren Dexter, BA, PhD, JD; American attorney, editor, poet and writer; b. 31 May 1944, Brunswick, NJ; m. Iris Freeman 1990. *Education:* Cornell University, University of Wisconsin. *Career:* founder, Ed. and Publisher, Abraxas Magazine 1968–81, Sr Ed. 1981–; mem. of Bd of Dirs, Coffee House Press 1988–92, Pres. 1989–92; Contributing Ed., Pharmaceutical News. *Publications:* The Forest and the Trees, 1968; Landing, 1974; No Hiding Place, 1979; Storm Lines, 1987; Clear to Chukchi, 1996; Iris Rising, 1998; Chemistry, 2002. Contributions: anthologies, magazines and periodicals. *Honours:* National Endowment for the Arts Fellowship, 1974; Wisconsin Arts Board Fellowships, 1975, 1976; Loft-McKnight Fellow, 1985; Minnesota Voices, Competition for Poetry, 1986.

WOHMANN, Gabriele; German writer; b. 21 May 1932, Darmstadt; d. of Paul and Luise (née Lettermann) Guyot; m. Reiner Wohmann 1953. *Education:* Univ. of Frankfurt/Main. *Career:* Teacher 1953–56; Writer-in-Residence, Gutenberg-Museum, Mainz (Literature Prize Zweites Deutsches Fernsehen ZDF/Mainz) 1984; mem. Berlin Akad. der Künste, Deutsche Akad. für Sprache und Dichtung. *Publications include:* novels: Jetzt und nie 1958, Abschied für länger 1965, Ernste Absicht 1970, Paulinchen war allein zu Haus 1974 (also TV play 1981), Ausflug mit der Mutter 1976, Ach wie gut, daß niemand weiß 1980, Das Glücksspiel 1981, Der Flötenton 1987, Bitte nicht sterben 1993, Das Handicap 1996; short stories: Mit einem Messer 1958, Trinken ist das Herrlichste 1963, Gegenangriff 1972, Dorothea Wörth 1975, Alles zu seiner Zeit 1976, Streit 1978, Wir sind eine Familie 1980, Stolze Zeiten 1981, Einsamkeit 1982, Der Kirschbaum 1984, Ein russischer Sommer 1988, Kassensturz 1989, Das Salz, bitte! 1992, Die Schönste im ganzen Land 1995; poetry: Grund zur Aufregung 1978, Komm lieber Mai 1981, Passau-Gleis 3 1984, Das könnte ich sein 1989; radio plays: Komm Donnerstag 1964, Norwegian Wood 1967, Kurerfolg 1970, Tod in Basel 1972, Wanda Lords Gespenster 1978, Ein gehorsamer Diener 1987, Es geht mir gut, ihr Kinder 1988, Drück mir die Daumen 1991, Der Mann am Fenster 1994, Besser als Liegen ist tot sein 1996; TV plays: Große Liebe 1966, Die Witwen 1972, Heiratskandidaten 1975, Unterwegs 1985, Schreiben müssen 1990. *Honours:* Hon. Fellow American Asscn of Teachers of German 1994; Bundesverdienstkreuz (First Class) 1980; awards include Bremen Literature Prize 1971, Deutscher Schallplattenpreis 1981, J. H. Merck Honour, Darmstadt 1982, Adenauerpreis 1994. *Address:* Erbacher Str. 76A, Park Rosenhöhe, 64287 Darmstadt, Germany. *Telephone:* (6151) 46801.

WOIWODE, Larry Alfred; American writer and poet; b. 30 Oct. 1941, Carrington, ND; m. Carole Ann Peterson 1965, four c. *Education:* University of Illinois at Urbana-Champaign. *Career:* Writer-in-Residence, University of Wisconsin at Madison, 1973–74; Prof., Wheaton College, 1981, 1984; Visiting Prof., 1983–85, Prof. and Dir of the Creative Writing Program, 1985–88, SUNY at Binghamton; various workshops and readings at many colleges and universities. *Publications:* Fiction: What I'm Going to Do, I Think, 1969; Beyond the Bedroom Wall: A Family Album, 1975; Poppa John, 1981; Born Brothers, 1988; The Neumiller Stories, 1989; Indian Affairs: A Novel, 1992; Silent Passengers: Stories, 1993. Poetry: Even Tide, 1975. Non-Fiction: Acts, 1993; The Aristocrat of the West: Biography of Harold Schafer, 2000; What I Think I Did: A Season of Survival in Two Acts (autobiog.), 2000. Contributions: books, anthologies, reviews, periodicals, journals, etc. *Honours:* Notable Book Award, American Library Asscn, 1970; William Faulkner Foundation Award, 1970; Guggenheim Fellowship, 1971–72; Fiction Award, Friends of American Writers, 1976; Hon. doctorates, North Dakota State University, 1977, Geneva College, 1997; Fiction Award, 1980, Medal of Merit, 1995, American Acad. of Arts and Letters; Aga Khan Literary Prize, Paris Review, 1990; Book Award of Short Fiction, Louisiana State University/Southern Review, 1990; John Dos Passos Prize, 1991; Poet Laureate of North Dakota, 1995.

WOLF, Christa; German writer; b. 18 March 1929, Landsberg an der Warthe; m. Gerhard Wolf 1951; two d. *Education:* Univs of Jena and Leipzig. *Career:* mem. Deutsche Akademie für Sprache und Dichtung eV, Darmstadt, Freie Akademie der Künste, Hamburg. *Publications:* Moskauer Novelle 1961, Die geteilte Himmel (trans. as Divided Heaven: A Novel of Germany Today) 1963, Nachdenken über Christa T (trans. as The Quest for Christa T) 1968, Lesen und Schreiben: Aufsätze und Betrachtungen (trans. as The Reader the Writer: Essays, Sketches, Memories) 1972, Unter den Linden: Drei unwahrscheinliche Geschichten 1974, Kindheitsmuster (trans. as A Model Childhood) 1976, J'écris sur ce qui m'inquiète: Débat dans Sinn und Form sur don derneir roman 1977, Kein Ort. Nirgends (trans. as No Place on Earth) 1979, Fortgesetzter Versuch: Aufsätze, Gespräche, Essays 1979, Gesammelte Erzählungen 1980, Neue Lebensansichten eines Katers: Juninachmittag 1981, Kassandra: Vier Vorlesungen: Eine Erzählung (trans. as Cassandra: A Novel and Four Essays) 1983, Störfall: Nachrichten eines Tages (trans. as Accident: A Day's News) 1987, Die Dimension des Autors: Essays und Aufsätze, Reden und Gespräche 1959–86 (trans. as The Author's Dimension: Selected Essays) 1987, Sommerstück 1989, Was bleibt 1990, Im Dialog: Aktuelle Texte 1990, Sei gegrüsst und lebe!: Eine Freundschaft in Briefen 1964–73 1993, Akteneinsicht-Christa Wolf: Zerrspiegel und Dialog 1993, Auf dem Weg nach Tabou, Texte 1990–94 1994, Die Zeichen der Nuria Quevado 1994, Medea: Stimmen 1996, Hierzulande, Andernorts 2000, Telling Tales (contrib. to charity anthology) 2004. *Honours:* Art Prize, Halle 1961, Heinrich-Mann Prize 1963, Nationalpreis für Kunst und Literatur (GDR) 1964, 1987, Free Hanseatic City of Bremen Literature Prize 1972, Theodor Fontane Prize for Art and Literature 1972, Georg-Büchner Prize, Deutsche Akad. der Sprache und Dichtung 1980, Schiller Memorial Prize 1983, Austrian Prize for European Literature 1984, Mondello Literature Prize 1990, Rahel Varnhagen von Ense Medal 1994; Officier, Ordre des Arts et des Lettres 1990. *Address:* c/o Deutsche Akademie für Sprache und Dichtung eV, Alexandraweg 23, 64287 Darmstadt, Germany.

WOLF, Naomi, BA; American writer and feminist; b. 15 Nov. 1962, San Francisco, Calif.; d. of Leonard Wolf and Deborah Wolf; m. David Shipley 1993 (divorced 2005); one c. *Education:* Yale Univ., New Coll., Univ. of Oxford, UK. *Career:* Rhodes Scholar 1986; Co-founder Woodhull Inst. for Ethical Leadership 1997–, now Scholar in Residence and Woodhull Fellow; fmr columnist, George magazine; consultant, Al Gore Presidential campaign 2000. *Publications:* The Beauty Myth: How Images of Beauty Are Used Against Women 1990, Fire With Fire: The New Female Power and How It Will Change in the 21st Century 1993, Promiscuities: The Secret Struggle for Womanhood 1997, Misconceptions: Truth, Lies and the Unexpected on the Journey to Motherhood 2001, The Treehouse: Eccentric Wisdom from my Father on How to Live, Love and See 2006. *Address:* c/o The Woodhull Institute, 770 Broadway, 2nd Floor, New York, NY 10003; c/o Royce Carlton Inc., 866 UN Plaza, New York, NY 10017, USA. *Telephone:* (646) 495-6060 (Woodhull). *Fax:* (646) 495-6059 (Woodhull). *E-mail:* info@woodhull.org. *Website:* woodhull.org.

WOLFE, Christopher, BA, PhD; American academic and writer; *Professor of Political Science, Marquette University*; b. 11 March 1949, Boston, Mass; m. Anne McGowan 1972; five s. five d. *Education:* Univ. of Notre Dame, Ind., Boston Coll. *Career:* Instructor, Assumption Coll., Worcester, Mass 1975–78; Asst Prof., Marquette Univ., Milwaukee, Wis. 1978–84, Assoc. Prof. 1984–92, Prof. of Political Science 1992–; Founder and Pres. American Public Philosophy Inst. 1989; mem. American Political Science Asscn, Federalist Soc., Fellowship of Catholic Scholars. *Publications:* The Rise of Modern Judicial Review: From Constitutional Interpretation to Judge-Made Law 1986, Faith and Liberal Democracy 1987, Judicial Activism: Bulwark of Freedom or Precarious Security? 1991, Liberalism at the Crossroads (ed. with John Hittinger) 1994, How to Interpret the Constitution 1996, The Family, Civil Society and the State (ed.) 1998, Homosexuality and American Public Life (ed.) 1999, Natural Law and Public Reason (ed. with Robert George) 2000, Same-Sex Matters (ed.) 2000, That Eminent Tribunal: Judicial Supremacy and the Constitution (ed.) 2004; contrib. to professional journals and general periodicals. *Honours:* Woodrow Wilson Fellowship 1971, Inst. for Educational Affairs grants 1982, 1983, Bradley Foundation grant 1986, Nat. Endowment for the Humanities Fellowship 1994, Templeton Honor Roll for Educ. in a Free Society 1997. *Address:* Department of Political Science, Marquette University, Box 1881, Milwaukee, WI 53201, USA (office). *Telephone:* (414) 288-6841 (office). *E-mail:* christopher.wolfe@mu.edu (office).

WOLFE, Peter, BA, MA, PhD; American academic and writer; *Curator's Professor of English, University of Missouri at St Louis*; b. 25 Aug. 1933, New York, NY; m. 1st Marie Paley 1962 (divorced 1969); two s.; m. 2nd Retta Cardwell 1998. *Education:* City Coll., CUNY, Lehigh Univ., Univ. of Wisconsin. *Career:* currently Curator's Prof. of English, Univ. of Missouri at St Louis. *Publications:* Iris Murdoch 1966, Mary Renault 1969, Rebecca West 1971, Graham Greene 1972, John Fowles 1976, Ross Macdonald 1977, Jean Rhys 1980, Dashiell Hammett 1980, Laden Choirs: Patrick White 1983, Something More Than Night: Raymond Chandler 1985, John le Carré 1987, Yukio Mishima 1989, Alarms and Epitaphs: Eric Ambler 1993, In the Zone: Rod Serling's Twilight Vision 1997, A Vision of his Own: William Gaddis 1997, Alan Bennett 1999, August Wilson 1999, Penelope Fitzgerald 2004, James Ellroy 2005, Havoc in the Hub: A Reading of George V. Higgins 2006; contrib. to Weekend Australian, Sydney Morning Herald, New Zealand Listener, Calcutta Statesman, New York Times Book Review, Chicago Tribune. *Honours:* Fulbright Awards to India 1987, Poland 1991, Univ. of Missouri Pres.'s Award for Creativity and Research 1995. *Address:* Department of English, Office 465 Lucas, University of Missouri at St Louis, 8001 Natural Bridge Road, St Louis, MO 63121-4499, USA (office). *Telephone:* (314) 516-5617 (office). *Fax:* (314) 516-5781 (office). *E-mail:* spwolfe@umsl.edu (office).

WOLFE, Thomas (Tom) Kennerly, Jr, AB, PhD; American author and journalist; b. 2 March 1931, Richmond, Va; s. of Thomas Kennerly and Helen Hughes; m. Sheila Berger; one s. one d. *Education:* Washington and Lee, and Yale Univs. *Career:* reporter, Springfield (Mass) Union 1956–59; reporter, Latin American Corresp., Washington Post 1959–62; reporter, magazine writer, New York Herald Tribune 1962–66; magazine writer, New York World Journal Tribune 1966–67; Contributing Ed. New York magazine 1968–76, Esquire Magazine 1977–; Contributing Artist, Harper's magazine 1978–81; exhibited one-man show of drawings, Maynard Walker Gallery, New York 1965, Tunnel Gallery, New York 1974; mem. American Acad. of Arts and Letters 1999. *Publications:* The Kandy-Kolored Tangerine-Flake Streamline Baby 1965, The Electric Kool-Aid Acid Test 1968, The Pump House Gang 1968, Radical Chic and Mau-mauing the Flak Catchers 1970, The New Journalism 1973, The Painted Word 1975, Mauve Gloves and Madmen, Clutter and Vine 1976, The Right Stuff 1979, In Our Time 1980, From Bauhaus to Our House 1981, The Purple Decades: A Reader 1982, The Bonfire of the Vanities 1987, Ambush at Fort Bragg 1998, A Man in Full 1998, Hooking Up (short stories) 2000, I Am Charlotte Simmons 2004. *Honours:* Hon. DFA (Minneapolis Coll. of Art) 1971; Hon. LittD (Washington and Lee) 1974; Hon. LHD (Virginia Commonwealth Univ.) 1983, (Southampton Coll., NY) 1984; Front Page Awards for Humour and Foreign News Reporting, Washington Newspaper Guild 1961, Award of Excellence, Soc. of Magazine Writers 1970, Frank Luther Mott Research Award 1973, Virginia Laureate for Literature 1977, Harold D. Vursell Memorial Award, American Acad. and Inst. of Arts and Letters 1980, American Book Award for Gen. Non-Fiction 1980, Columbia Journalism Award 1980, Citation for Art History, Nat. Sculpture Soc. 1980, John Dos Passos Award 1984, Gari Melchers Medal 1986, Benjamin Pierce Cheney Medal (E Washington Univ.) 1986, Washington Irving Medal (St Nicholas Soc.) 1986, Theodore Roosevelt Medal 1990, St Louis Literary Award 1990, President's Humanities Medal 2001. *Website:* www.tomwolfe.com.

WOLFERS, Michael; British writer and translator; b. 28 Sept. 1938, London, England. *Education:* Wadham Coll., Oxford and South Bank Polytechnic. *Career:* journalist, The Times, London 1965–72; Visiting Sr Lecturer in African Politics and Government, Univ. of Juba 1979–82; mem. Royal Inst. of Int. Affairs, Gyosei Inst. of Management. *Publications:* Black Man's Burden Revisited 1974, Politics in the Organization of African Unity 1976, Luandino Vieira: The Real Life of Domingos Xavier 1978, Poems from Angola 1979, Samir Amin, Delinking: Towards a Polycentric World 1990, Hamlet and Cybernetics 1991, Thomas Hodgkin: Letters from Africa 2000, Thomas Hodgkin: Wandering Scholar 2007; contrib. to numerous publications. *Address:* 66 Roupell Street, London, SE1 8SS, England.

WOLFF, Christoph Johannes, PhD; German academic, writer and editor; *Adams University Professor, Harvard University*; b. 24 May 1940, Solingen; m. Barbara Mahrenholz 1964, three d. *Education:* University of Berlin, University of Freiburg im Breisgau, University of Erlangen. *Career:* Lecturer University of Erlangen 1966–69; Asst Prof. University of Toronto 1968–70; Assoc. Prof. 1970–73, Prof. of Musicology 1973–76, Columbia University; Visiting Prof. Princeton University 1973, 1975; Ed. Bach-Jahrbuch 1974–; Prof. of Musicology 1976–, Dept Chair. 1980–88, 1990–91, William Powell Mason Prof. 1985–, Acting Dir University Library 1991–92, Dean Graduate School of Arts and Sciences 1992–2000, Adams Univ. Prof. 2002–, Harvard University; Dir Bach Archive, Leipzig 2000–; mem. American Musicological Soc.; Gesellschaft für Musikforschung; International Musicological Soc., American Philosophical Soc. *Publications:* Der stile antico in der Musik Johann Sebastian Bachs 1968, The String Quartets of Haydn, Mozart, and Beethoven: Studies of the Autograph Manuscripts (ed.) 1980, Bach Compendium: Analytisch-bibliographisches Repertorium der Werke Johann Sebastian Bachs (ed. with H.-J. Schulze), seven vols 1986–89, Bach: Essays on His Life and Music 1991, Mozart's Requiem: Historical and Analytical Studies, Documents, Score 1993, Wereld van de Bach-cantatas: The World of the Bach Canatatas 1997, The New Bach Reader (ed.) 1998, Driven Into Paradise: The Musical Migration from Nazi Germany to the United States (ed. with R. Brinkmann) 1999, Johann Sebastian Bach: The Learned Musician 2000; other: critical edns of works by Scheidt, Buxtehude, Bach, Mozart and Hindemith; contrib. to scholarly books and journals. *Honours:* Hon. Prof. University of Freiburg im Breisgau 1990–, Fellow American Acad. of Arts and Sciences 1982–; Dent Medal Royal Musical Asscn, London 1978. *Address:* c/o Department of Music, Harvard University, Cambridge, MA 02138, USA.

WOLFF, Cynthia Griffin, BA, PhD; American academic and writer; b. 20 Aug. 1936, St Louis, MO; m. 1st Robert Paul Wolff 1962 (divorced 1986); two s.; m. 2nd Nicholas J. White 1988. *Education:* Radcliffe College, Harvard University. *Career:* Asst Prof. of English, Manhattanville College, Purchase, New York, 1968–70; Asst Prof., 1971–74, Assoc. Prof., 1974–76, Prof. of English, 1976–80, University of Massachusetts, Amherst; Prof. of Humanities, 1980–85, Class of 1922 Prof. of Literature and Writing, 1985–, MIT; mem. American Studies Asscn. *Publications:* Samuel Richardson, 1972; A Feast of Words: The Triumph of Edith Wharton, 1977; Emily Dickinson, 1986. Contributions: scholarly journals. *Honours:* National Endowment for the Humanities Grants, 1975–76, 1983–84; ACLS Grant, 1984–85.

WOLFF, Geoffrey Ansell, BA; American academic and author; b. 5 Nov. 1937, Los Angeles, CA; m. Priscilla Bradley Porter 1965, two s. *Education:* Eastbourne College, England, Princeton University, Churchill College, Cambridge. *Career:* Lecturer, Robert College, Istanbul, 1961–63, University of Istanbul, 1962–63, Maryland Institute and College of Art, 1965–69, Middlebury College, Vermont, 1976–78; Book Ed., Washington Post, 1964–69, Newsweek magazine, 1969–71, New Times magazine, 1974–79; Visiting Lecturer, 1970–71, Ferris Prof., 1980, 1992, Princeton University; Book Critic,

Esquire magazine, 1979–81; Visiting Lecturer, Columbia University, 1979, Boston University, 1981, Brown University, 1981, 1988; Writer-in-Residence, Brandeis University, 1982–95; Visiting Prof., Williams College, 1994; Prof. of English and Creative Writing, University of California at Irvine, 1995–; mem. PEN. *Publications:* Bad Debts, 1969; The Sightseer, 1974; Black Sun, 1976; Inklings, 1978; The Duke of Deception, 1979; Providence, 1986; Best American Essays (ed.), 1989; The Final Club, 1990; A Day at the Beach, 1992; The Age of Consent, 1995. Contributions: various publications. *Honours:* Woodrow Wilson Fellowship, 1961–62; Fulbright Fellowship, 1963–64; Guggenheim Fellowships, 1972–73, 1977–78; National Endowment for the Humanities Senior Fellowship, 1974–75; National Endowment for the Arts Fellowships, 1979–80, 1986–87; ACLS Fellowship, 1983–84; Governor's Arts Award, RI, 1992; Lila Wallace Writing Fellowship, 1992; American Acad. of Arts and Letters Award, 1994.

WOLFF, Tobias Jonathan Ansell, BA, MA; American writer; b. 19 June 1945, Birmingham, Ala; s. of Arthur S. Wolff and Rosemary Loftus; m. Catherine Dolores Spohn 1975; two s. one d. *Education:* The Hill School, Oxford Univ., (UK) and Stanford Univ. (Calif.). *Career:* served in US Army 1964–68; reporter, Washington Post 1972; Writing Fellow, Stanford Univ. 1975–78, Prof. of English and Creative Writing 1997–; Writer-in-Residence, Ariz. State Univ. 1978–80; Peck Prof. of English Syracuse Univ. 1980–97; Wallace Stegner Fellowship 1975–76, Nat. Endowment Fellow 1978, 1984; Arizona Council on the Arts and Humanities Fellowship 1980, Guggenheim Fellow 1983; mem. PEN. *Publications:* Ugly Rumours 1975, Hunters in the Snow 1981, The Barracks Thief (PEN/Faulkner Award for Fiction 1985) 1984, Back in the World 1985, A Doctor's Visit: The Short Stories of Anton Chekhov (ed.) 1987, The Stories of Tobias Wolff 1988, This Boy's Life 1989, The Picador Books of Contemporary American Stories (ed.) 1993, In Pharaoh's Army: Memories of a Lost War 1994, The Vintage Book of Contemporary American Short Stories 1994, The Best American Short Stories 1994, The Night in Question (stories) 1996, Writers Harvest 3 (ed.) 2000, Old School 2003. *Honours:* Hon. Fellow Hertford Coll., Oxford 2000; St Lawrence Award for Fiction 1982, Rea Award for Short Story 1989, Whiting Foundation Award 1989, LA Times Book Prize for Biography 1989, Ambassador Book Award 1990, Lila Wallace/Reader's Digest Award 1993, Lyndhurst Foundation Award 1994, Esquire-Volvo-Waterstones Award for Non-Fiction 1994, Award of Merit, American Acad. of Arts and Letters 2001. *Address:* English Department, Stanford University, Stanford, CA 94305, USA.

WOLINSKY, Leo, BA; American journalist and editor; *Deputy Managing Editor, Los Angeles Times;* b. 9 May 1949, Los Angeles, CA; m. Roberta Leith (née Wardle). *Education:* Univ. of Southern Calif. *Career:* with Los Angeles Times 1977–, positions included staff writer South Bay Bureau 1977–79, transportation and environment corresp. Orange Co. Edn 1979–82, City Co. Bureau 1982–85, Sacramento Bureau 1985–87, Asst Bureau Chief 1987–88, Asst City Ed. 1989–90, Calif. Political Ed. 1990–91, City Ed. 1991–93, Metropolitan Ed. 1994–97, Man. Ed. of News 1997–2000, Exec. Ed. Los Angeles Times 2000–01, Deputy Man. Ed. 2001–. *Honours:* Pulitzer Prize 1993, 1995, 1998. *Address:* Los Angeles Times, 202 W First Street, Los Angeles, CA 90012, USA (office). *E-mail:* Leo.Wolinsky@latimes.com (office). *Website:* www.latimes.com (office).

WOLKSTEIN, Diane, BA, MA; American writer and storyteller; b. 11 Nov. 1942, New York, NY; m. Benjamin Zucker 1969; one d. *Education:* Smith Coll., Bank Street Coll. of Education. *Career:* host of radio show Stories from Many Lands with Diane Wolkstein (WNYC-Radio), New York 1967–; Instructor, Bank Street Coll. 1970–; teacher, New York Univ. 1983–2003, Sarah Lawrence Coll. 1984, New School for Social Research, New York 1989; leader of many storytelling workshops; has performed world-wide, including at the British Museum, London, American Museum of Natural History and Avery Fisher Hall, New York, The Smithsonian Inst., Washington, DC, and in Australia; described as "The greatest storyteller in the western world" by Joseph Campbell. *Publications:* 8,000 Stones 1972, The Cool Ride in the Sky: A Black-American Folk Tale 1973, The Visit 1974, Squirrel's Song: A Hopi-Indian Story 1975, Lazy Stories 1976, The Red Lion: A Persian Sufi Tale 1977, The Magic Orange Tree and Other Haitian Folk Tales 1978, White Wave: A Tao Tale 1979, The Banza: A Haitian Folk Tale 1980, Inanna, Queen of Heaven and Earth: Her Stories and Hymns from Summer (with Samuel Noah Kramer) 1983, The Magic Wings: A Chinese Tale 1983, The Legend of Sleepy Hollow 1987, The First Love Stories 1991, Oom Razoom 1991, Little Mouse's Painting 1992, Step by Step 1994, Esther's Story 1996, White Wave 1996, Bouki Dances the Kokioko 1997, The Magic Orange Tree 1997, The Glass Mountain 1999, The Day Ocean Came to Visit 2001, Treasures of the Heart: Holiday Stories that Reveal the Soul of Judaism 2003, Sunmother Wakes the World 2004; contrib. to periodicals and recordings. *Honours:* several citations and awards. *Address:* 10 Patchin Place, New York, NY 10011, USA. *E-mail:* dianewolkstein@hotmail.com. *Website:* www.dianewolkstein.com.

WOLSTENCROFT, David; British writer. *Career:* writer and creator of 'Spooks' (BBC, on A&E Network as MI-5). *Publications:* novels: Good News, Bad News 2004, Contact Zero 2006. *Literary Agent:* c/o Jonny Geller, Curtis Brown Ltd, Haymarket House, 28–29 Haymarket, London, SW1Y 4SP, England. *Telephone:* (20) 7393-4400. *Fax:* (20) 7393-4401. *E-mail:* info@ curtisbrown.co.uk. *Website:* www.curtisbrown.co.uk. *E-mail:* david@ davidwolstencroft.com. *Website:* www.davidwolstencroft.com.

WOMACK, Peter, BA, PhD; British academic and writer; b. 27 Jan. 1952, Surrey, England. *Education:* University of Oxford, University of Edinburgh. *Career:* Lecturer, 1988–96, Senior Lecturer, 1996–, University of East Anglia. *Publications:* Ben Jonson, 1986; Improvement and Romance, 1989; English Drama: A Cultural History (with Simon Shepherd), 1996. Contributions: scholarly books and journals.

WOOD, Adrian John Bickersteth, CBE, MA, MPA, PhD; British economist; *Professor of International Development, University of Oxford;* b. 25 Jan. 1946, Woking; s. of the late John H. F. Wood and of Mary E. B. Brain (née Ottley); m. Joyce M. Teitz 1971; two d. *Education:* Bryanston School, King's Coll. Cambridge and Harvard Univ. *Career:* Fellow, King's Coll. Cambridge 1969–77; Asst Lecturer, Lecturer, Univ. of Cambridge 1973–77; Economist, Sr Economist, IBRD 1977–85; Professorial Fellow, Inst. of Devt Studies, Univ. of Sussex 1985–2000; Chief Economist Dept for Int. Devt 2000–05; Prof. of Int. Devt, Univ. of Oxford 2005–; Harkness Fellowship 1967–69. *Publications:* A Theory of Profits 1975, A Theory of Pay 1978, Poverty and Human Development (with others) 1981, China: Long-Term Development Issues and Options (with others) 1985, North-South Trade, Employment and Inequality 1994. *Address:* Queen Elizabeth House, 3 Mansfield Road, Oxford, OX1 3TB, England (office). *Telephone:* (1865) 281837 (office). *Fax:* (1865) 281801 (office). *E-mail:* adrian.wood@qeh.ox.ac.uk (office). *Website:* www.qeh .ox.ac.uk (office).

WOOD, Charles Gerald, FRSL; British playwright and scriptwriter; b. 6 Aug. 1932, St. Peter Port, Guernsey; s. of John Edward Wood and Catherine Mae Wood (née Harris); m. Valerie Elizabeth Newman 1954; one s. one d. *Education:* King Charles I School, Kidderminster and Birmingham Coll. of Art. *Career:* corporal, 17/21st Lancers 1950–55; factory worker 1955–57; Stage Man., scenic artist, cartoonist, advertising artist 1957–59; Bristol Evening Post 1959–62; mem. Drama Advisory Panel, South Western Arts 1972–73; consultant to Nat. Film Devt Fund 1980–82; mem. Council BAFTA 1991–93. *Plays include:* Prisoner and Escort, Spare, John Thomas 1963, Meals on Wheels 1965, Don't Make Me Laugh 1966, Fill the Stage with Happy Hours 1967, Dingo 1967, H 1969, Welfare 1971, Veterans 1972, Jingo 1975, Has 'Washington' Legs? 1978, Red Star 1984, Across from the Garden of Allah 1986; adapted Pirandello's Man, Beast and Virtue 1989, The Mountain Giants 1993, Alexandre Dumas's The Tower 1995. *TV plays include:* Prisoner and Escort, Drill Pig, A Bit of a Holiday, A Bit of an Adventure, Love Lies Bleeding, Dust to Dust. *Screenplays include:* The Knack 1965, Help! 1965, How I Won the War 1967, The Charge of the Light Brigade 1968, The Long Day's Dying 1969, Cuba 1980, Wagner 1983, Red Monarch 1983, Puccini 1984, Tumble-down 1988, Shooting the Hero 1991, An Awfully Big Adventure 1993, England my England (with John Osborne) 1995, The Ghost Road 1996, Mary Stuart 1996, Iris (with Richard Eyre) 1999, Snow White in New York 2001. *TV series:* Don't Forget to Write 1986, My Family and Other Animals 1987, The Settling of the Sun 1987, Sharpe's Company 1994, Sharpe's Regiment 1996, Mute of Malice (Kavanagh QC) 1997, Sharpe's Waterloo 1997, Monsignor Renard 1999. *Publications:* (plays): Cockade 1965, Fill the Stage with Happy Hours 1967, Dingo 1967, H 1970, Veterans 1972, Has 'Washington' Legs? 1978, Tumbledown 1987, Man, Beast and Virtue 1990, The Giants of the Mountain 1994, The Tower 1995, Iris 2002. *Honours:* Evening Standard Drama Award 1963 1972, Screenwriters Guild Award 1965, Royal TV Soc. Award 1988, BAFTA Award 1988, Prix Italia 1988, Humanitas Award 2002. *Address:* c/o Sue Rogers, ICM Ltd, Oxford House, 76 Oxford Street, London, W1P 1BS, England. *Telephone:* (20) 7636-6565. *E-mail:* charles@wood4760.fsnet.co.uk (home).

WOOD, Michael; British academic and writer; b. 19 Aug. 1936, Lincoln, England; m. Elena Uribe 1967; two s. one d. *Education:* BA, Modern and Medieval Languages, 1957, MA, 1961, PhD, 1962, St John's College, Cambridge. *Career:* Fellow in French, St John's College, Cambridge, 1961–64; Instructor, 1964–66, Asst Prof., 1968–71, Assoc. Prof., 1971–74, of English, Prof. of English and Comparative Literature, 1974–82, Columbia University; Visiting Prof., National University of Mexico, 1981–82; Prof. of English Literature, University of Exeter, 1982–95; Charles Barnwell Straut Prof. of English and Prof. of Comparative Literature, Princeton University, 1995–; Visitor, Institute for Advanced Study, Princeton, 2001–02. *Publications:* Stendahl, 1971; America in the Movies, 1975; García Márquez: One Hundred Years of Solitude, 1990; The Magician's Doubts: Nabokov and the Risks of Fiction, 1994; Children of Silence: On Contemporary Fiction, 1998; Franz Kafka, 1998; Belle de Jour, 2001; The Road to Delphi: The Life and Afterlife of Oracles, 2004. Contributions: Reviews, quarterlies and journals. *Honours:* Guggenheim Fellowship, 1972–73; National Endowment for the Humanities Fellowship, 1980–81; FRSL, 1992–; Leverhulme Trust Fellow, 1993; Fellow, New York Institute for the Humanities, 1994–; Senior Fellow, Society of Fellows, Princeton University, 1999–. *Address:* 26 Alexander Street, Princeton, NJ 08540, USA.

WOOD, Michael; British journalist, broadcaster, film-maker, historian and writer; b. Manchester, England; m.; two d. *Education:* Oriel Coll., Oxford. *Career:* writer and presenter, over 60 TV series and documentaries on history, travel, politics and cultural history. *Television:* Saddam's Killing Fields, Darshan, The Sacred Way, Great Railway Journeys of the World 1981, River Journeys 1985, In Search of the Trojan War (PBS) 1985, Art of the Western World 1989, Legacy: In Search of the Origins of Civilization 1992, In the Footsteps of Alexander the Great (BBC) 1997, Hitler's Search for the Holy Grail 1999, Conquistadors (BBC2) 2000, In Search of Shakespeare (BBC2)

2003, In Search of Myths and Heroes (BBC2) 2005. *Publications:* In Search of the Dark Ages 1981, Great Railway Journeys of the World 1981, In Search of the Trojan War 1985, World Atlas of Archaeology (ed.) 1985, Domesday: A Search for the Roots of England 1986, Legacy: A Search for the Origins of Civilization 1992, The Smile of Murugan: A South Indian Journey 1995, In the Footsteps of Alexander the Great: A Journey from Greece to Asia 1997, In Search of England 1999, Conquistadors 2000, In Search of Shakespeare 2003, In Search of Myths and Heroes 2005, India: An Epic Journey Across the Subcontinent 2007; contrib. reviews and articles in Daily Telegraph, Evening Standard, Literary Review, Times, Guardian, Daily Express, Independent, Daily Mail, Observer, Newsday, Dialogue magazine. *Address:* c/o BBC Worldwide Ltd, 80 Wood Lane, London, W12 0TT, England.

WOOD, Victoria, OBE, BA; British writer and comedian; b. 19 May 1953, d. of the late Stanley and of Helen Wood; m. Geoffrey Durham 1980; one d. one s. *Education:* Univ. of Birmingham. *Career:* singer and performer on TV and radio 1974–78; first play Talent, at Crucible Theatre, Sheffield 1978, TV production won three Nat. Drama Awards 1980; numerous tours. *TV includes:* Screenplay (writer) 1979, Talent 1979, Nearly a Happy Ending (writer) 1981, Happy Since I Met You 1981, Wood and Walters (series with Julie Walters) 1981–82, Victoria Wood As Seen on TV (first series, Broadcasting Press Guilds Award, BAFTA Award for Best Light Entertainment Programme and Performance Awards) 1985, (second series, BAFTA Award for Best Light Entertainment Programme Award) 1986, (Special, BAFTA Award for Best Light Entertainment Programme Award) 1987, Acorn Antiques 1986, An Audience With Victoria Wood (BAFTA Award for Best Light Entertainment Programme and Performance Awards) 1988, Victoria Wood 1989 (series), Julie Walters and Friends 1991, Victoria Wood's All Day Breakfast 1992, Victoria Wood Live in Your Own Home 1995, Pat and Margaret 1995, Dinnerladies (two series) (British Comedy Award for Best TV Comedy 2000, Montreux Festival Press Prize for first series) 1998–2000, Don't Panic! The Dad's Army Story 2000, Victoria Wood with All the Trimmings 2000, Big Fat Documentary 2004, Victoria Wood: Moonwalking 2004, Housewife, 49 (BAFTA Award for Best Actress 2007) 2006, Victoria's Empire 2007. *Stage appearances include:* Good Fun (writer, musical) 1980, Funny Turns 1982, Lucky Bag 1984, Victoria Wood 1987, Victoria Wood Up West 1990, Victoria Wood Live 1997, Victoria Wood – At It Again 2001, Acorn Antiques: The Musical, Haymarket 2005. *Film:* The Wind in the Willows. *Publications:* Victoria Wood Song Book 1984, Up to You, Porky 1985, Barmy 1987, Mens Sana in Thingummy Doodah 1990, Chunky 1996, Victoria on Victoria 2007. *Honours:* Hon. DLitt (Lancaster) 1989, (Sunderland) 1994, (Bolton) 1995, (Birmingham) 1996; Variety Club BBC Personality of the Year 1987; Top Female Comedy Performer, British Comedy Awards 1996. *Address:* c/o Phil McIntyre, 35 Soho Square, London, W1V 5DG, England. *Telephone:* (20) 7439-2270.

WOODCOCK, Joan; British poet, artist and genealogist; b. 6 Feb. 1908, Bournemouth, Dorset, England; m. Alexander Neville Woodcock 1937; two s. one d. *Career:* mem. British Haiku Society; Calne Writers' Circle; NFSPS, USA; Peterloo Poets; Poetry Society; various genealogical organizations. *Publications:* The Wandering Years, 1990; Borrowing From Time, 1992; Stabbed Awake, 1994. Contributions: anthologies and journals.

WOODEN, Rodney John; British playwright; b. 16 July 1945, London, England. *Career:* mem. PEN International. *Publications:* Woyzeck (adaptation of Büchner's play), 1990; Your Home in the West, 1991; Smoke, 1993; Moby Dick, 1993. *Honours:* First Prize, Mobil International Playwriting Competition, 1990; John Whiting Award, 1991; Mobil Writer-in-Residence Bursary, 1991–92. *Literary Agent:* Micheline Steinberg Associates, 104 Great Portland Street, London, W1W 6PE, England. *E-mail:* info@steinplays.com.

WOODFORD, Peggy, MA; British writer; b. 19 Sept. 1937, Assam, India; m. Walter Aylen 1967; three d. *Education:* St Anne's Coll., Oxford. *Career:* mem. Soc. of Authors, RSL. *Publications:* Abraham's Legacy 1963, Please Don't Go 1972, Mozart: His Life and Times 1977, Schubert: His Life and Times 1978, Rise of the Raj 1978, See You Tomorrow 1979, The Girl With a Voice 1981, Love Me, Love Rome 1984, Misfits 1984, Monster in Our Midst 1987, Out of the Sun 1990, Blood and Mortar 1994, Cupid's Tears 1995, On the Night 1997, Jane's Story 1998, One Son Is Enough 2005. *Address:* 24 Fairmount Road, London, SW2 2BL, England. *Website:* www.peggywoodford.com.

WOODRING, Carl Ray, BA, MA, PhD; American writer; b. 29 Aug. 1919, Terrell, TX; m. Mary Frances Ellis 1942 (died 2003). *Education:* Rice Univ., Harvard Univ. *Career:* Guggenheim Fellowship 1955; ACLS Fellow 1965; PKB Visiting Scholar 1974–75; Sr Mellon Fellow 1987–88; mem. American Acad. of Arts and Sciences, Int. Asscn of Univ. Profs of English, Grolier Club. *Publications:* Victorian Samplers 1952, Virginia Woolf 1966, Wordsworth 1965, Politics in English Romantic Poetry 1970, Nature into Art 1989, Table Talk of Samuel Taylor Coleridge 1990, Columbia History of British Poetry (ed.) 1993, Columbia Anthology of British Poetry (co-ed.) 1995, Literature: An Embattled Profession 1999, Lucky Thirteen: USS Hopkins, DD 249, DMS 13 (co-author) 2000; contrib. to Western Review, Virginia Quarterly Review, Keats-Shelley Journal, Comparative Drama. *Address:* 1034 Liberty Park Drive, Apt 105, Austin, TX 78746, USA. *Telephone:* (512) 328-7839 (office). *E-mail:* woodring@earthlink.net (office).

WOODS, P. F. (see Bayley, Barrington John)

WOODWARD, Robert (Bob) Upshur, BA; American journalist and writer; *Assistant Managing Editor, The Washington Post;* b. 26 March 1943, Geneva, IL; s. of Alfred Woodward and Jane Upshur; m. Elsa Walsh 1989; two c. *Education:* Yale Univ. *Career:* reporter, Montgomery Co. (MD) Sentinel 1970–71; reporter, Washington Post 1971–78; Metropolitan Ed. 1979–81, Asst Man. Ed. 1981–. *Publications:* All the President's Men (with Carl Bernstein) 1973, The Final Days (with Carl Bernstein) 1976, The Brethren (with Scott Armstrong) 1979, Wired 1984, Veil: The Secret Wars of the CIA 1987, The Commanders 1991, The Man Who Would Be President (with David S. Broder) 1991, The Agenda: Inside the Clinton White House 1994, The Choice 1996, Shadow: Five Presidents and the Legacy of Watergate 1999, Maestro, Greenspan's Fed and the American Boom 2000, Bush at War... Inside the Bush White House 2002, Plan of Attack 2004, The Secret Man 2005, State of Denial: Bush at War, Part III 2006. *Honours:* Pulitzer Prize citation 1972. *Address:* Washington Post Co., 1150 15th Street, NW, Washington, DC 20071, USA.

WOODWARD, Gerard, MA; British poet and writer; b. Dec. 1961, London. *Education:* LSE, Manchester Univ. *Career:* creative writing lecturer, Bath Spa Univ. 2004–. *Publications:* poetry: Householder 1991, After the Deafening 1994, Island to Island 1999, Healing Fountain 2003, We Were Pedestrians 2005; fiction: August 2001, I'll Go to Bed at Noon 2004, A Curious Earth 2007. *Honours:* Somerset Maugham Award 1992. *Address:* c/o Chatto & Windus Ltd, 20 Vauxhall Bridge Road, London, SW1V 2SA, England (office).

WOODWORTH, Steven Edward, BA, PhD; American academic and writer; b. 28 Jan. 1961, Akron, OH; m. Leah Dawn Bunke 1983, five s. *Education:* Southern Illinois University at Carbondale, University of Hamburg, Rice University. *Career:* Adjunct Instructor, Houston Community College, 1984–87; Instructor in History, Bartlesville Wesleyan College, Oklahoma, 1987–89; Asst Prof. of History, Toccoa Falls College, Georgia, 1989–97, Texas Christian University, 1997–; mem. Grady Mcwhiney Research Foundation, fellow; American Historical Asscn; Organization of American Historians; Southern Historical Asscn; Organization of Military Historians; Society of Civil War Historians. *Publications:* Jefferson Davis and His Generals: The Failure of Confederate Command in the West, 1990; The Essentials of United States History, 1841 to 1877: Westward Expansion and the Civil War, 1990; The Essentials of United States History, 1500 to 1789: From Colony to Republic, 1990; The Advanced Placement Examination in United States History, 1990; Davis and Lee at War, 1995; Leadership and Command in the American Civil War (ed.), Vol. I, 1995; The American Civil War: A Handbook of Literature and Research (ed.), 1996; Six Armies in Tennessee: The Chickamauga and Chattanooga Campaigns, 1998; Civil War Generals in Defeat (ed.), 1999; No Band of Brothers: Problems in the Rebel High Command, 1999; The Human Tradition in the Civil War and Reconstruction (ed.), 2000; Cultures in Conflict: The American Civil War, 2000; A Scythe of Fire: The Civil War Story of the Eighth Georgia Regiment, 2001; The Religious World of Civil War Soldiers, 2001. Contributions: books and professional journals. *Honours:* Fletcher Pratt Awards, 1991, 1996.

WORSLEY, Dale; American writer and dramatist; b. 3 Nov. 1948, Baton Rouge, LA; m. Elizabeth Fox 1991. *Education:* Southwestern Univ., Memphis. *Career:* mem. Dramatists' Guild. *Publications:* The Focus Changes of August Previco, 1980; The Art of Science Writing, 1989. Plays: Cold Harbor, 1983; The Last Living Newspaper, 1993. *Honours:* NEA Fellowship in Fiction 1986, NEAFellowship in Playwriting 1989.

WORSTHORNE, Sir Peregrine Gerard, Kt, MA; British journalist; b. 22 Dec. 1923, London; s. of Col A. Koch de Gooreynd and the late Baroness Norman; m. 1st Claudia Bertrand de Colasse 1950 (died 1990); one d. one step-s.; m. 2nd Lady Lucinda Lambton 1991. *Education:* Stowe School, Peterhouse, Cambridge and Magdalen Coll., Oxford. *Career:* mem. editorial staff, Glasgow Herald 1946–48; mem. editorial staff, The Times 1948–50, Washington corresp. 1950–52, leader writer 1952–55; leader writer, Daily Telegraph 1955–61; Deputy Ed. Sunday Telegraph 1961–76, Assoc. Ed. 1976–86, Ed. 1986–89, Ed. Comment Section 1989–91; columnist, The Spectator 1997–. *Publications:* The Socialist Myth 1972, Peregrinations 1980, By The Right 1987, Tricks of Memory (memoirs) 1993, In Defence of Aristocracy 2004. *Honours:* Granada TV Journalist of the Year 1981. *Address:* The Old Rectory, Hedgerley, Bucks., SL2 3UY, England (home). *Telephone:* (1753) 646167 (home). *Fax:* (1753) 646914 (home). *E-mail:* therectory.hedgerley@virgin.net (office).

WORTIS, Avi, (Avi), BA, MA, MS; American children's author; b. 23 Dec. 1937, New York, NY; m. 1st Joan Gabriner 1963 (divorced 1982); two s.; m. 2nd Coppelia Kahn 1983; one step-s. *Education:* University of Wisconsin at Madison, Columbia University. *Career:* Librarian, New York Public Library, 1962–70, Trenton State College, NJ, 1970–86; Conducted workshops and seminars with children, parents and educators; mem. Authors' Guild. *Publications:* Things That Sometimes Happen, 1970; Snail Tale, 1972; No More Magic, 1975; Captain Grey, 1977; Emily Upham's Revenge, 1978; Night Journeys, 1979; Man From the Sky, 1980; History of Helpless Harry, 1980; A Place Called Ugly, 1981; Who Stole the Wizard of Oz?, 1981; Sometimes I Think I Hear My Name, 1982; Shadrach's Crossing, 1983; Devil's Race, 1984; SOR Losers, 1984; The Fighting Ground, 1984; Bright Shadow, 1985; Wolf Rider, 1986; Romeo and Juliet (Together and Alive!) At Last, 1987; Something Upstairs, 1988; The Man Who Was Poe, 1989; True Confessions of Charlotte Doyle, 1990; Windcatcher, 1991; Nothing But the Truth, 1991; Blue Heron,

1992; Who Was That Masked Man, Anyway?, 1992; Punch With Judy, 1993; City of Light, City of Dark, 1993; The Bird, the Frog, and the Light, 1994; Smuggler's Island, 1994; The Barn, 1994; Tom, Babette & Simon, 1995; Poppy, 1995; Escape From Home, 1996; Finding Providence, 1996; Beyond the Western Sea, 1996; Something Upstairs: A Tale of Ghosts, 1997; What Do Fish Have to Do With Anything and Other Stories, 1997; Finding Providence: The Story of Roger Williams, 1997; Perloo the Bold, 1998; Poppy and Rye: A Tale from Dimwood Forest, 1998. Contributions: Library Journal. *Honours:* American Library Asscn Notable Book Awards, 1984, 1991, 1992, 1993, 1995, 1996; One of the Best Books of the Year Awards, Library of Congress, 1989, 1990; Newbery Honor Book Awards, 1991, 1992; many others. *Website:* www.avi-writer.com.

WOUK, Herman, AB; American writer and dramatist; b. 27 May 1915, New York, NY; s. of Abraham Isaac Wouk and Esther Levine; m. Betty Sarah Brown 1945; three s. (one deceased). *Education:* Columbia Univ. *Career:* radio scriptwriter for leading comedians, New York 1935–41; presidential consultant to US Treasury 1941; served in USNR 1942–46; Visiting Prof. of English, Yeshiva Univ., New York 1952–57; Trustee, Coll. of the Virgin Islands 1961–69; mem. Authors' Guild, USA, Authors' League, Center for Book Nat. Advisory Bd, Library of Congress, Advisory Council, Center for US –China Arts Exchange. *Publications:* fiction: The Man in the Trench Coat 1941, Aurora Dawn 1947, The City Boy 1948, Slattery's Hurricane 1949, The Caine Mutiny 1951, Marjorie Morningstar 1955, Slattery's Hurricane 1956, Youngblood Hawke 1961, Don't Stop the Carnival 1965, The Lomokome Papers 1968, The Winds of War (also TV screenplay) 1971, War and Remembrance (also TV screenplay) 1978, Inside, Outside 1985, The Hope 1993, The Glory 1994, A Hole in Texas 2004; plays: The Traitor 1949, Modern Primitive 1951, The Caine Mutiny Court-Martial 1953, Nature's Way 1957; non-fiction: This is My God: The Jewish Way of Life 1959, The Will to Live on: The Resurgence of Jewish Heritage 2000. *Honours:* Hon. LHD (Yeshiva Univ.); Hon. DLitt (Clark Univ.), (George Washington Univ.) 2001; Hon. DLitt (American Int. Coll.) 1979; Hon. PhD (Bar Ilan) 1990, (Hebrew Univ.) 1997; Hon. DST (Trinity Coll.) 1998; Pulitzer Prize for Fiction 1952, Columbia Univ. Medal for Excellence, Alexander Hamilton Medal, Columbia Univ. 1980, Ralph Waldo Emerson Award, Int. Platform Asscn 1981, Univ. of Calif., Berkeley Medal 1984, Yad Vashem Kazetnik Award 1990, USN Memorial Foundation Lone Sailor Award 1987, Washingtonian Book Award (for Inside, Outside) 1986, American Acad. of Achievement Golden Plate Award 1986, Bar Ilan Univ. Guardian of Zion Award 1998, Univ. of California at San Diego Medal 1998, Jewish Book Council Lifetime Literary Achievement Award 2000. *Literary Agent:* BSW Literary Agency, 303 Crestview Drive, Palm Springs, CA 92264, USA.

WRIGHT, Amos Jasper, III, BA, MLS; American medical librarian, writer and poet; b. 3 March 1952, Gadsden, AL; m. Margaret Dianne Vargo 1980; one s. one d. *Education:* Auburn University, University of Alabama. *Career:* Assoc. Prof., Univ. of Alabama at Birmingham School of Medicine; mem. Anaesthesia History Asscn, Medical Library Asscn. *Publications:* Frozen Fruit (poems), 1978; Right Now I Feel Like Robert Johnson (poems), 1981; Criminal Activity in the Deep South, 1800–1930, 1989. Contributions: Medical journals, anthologies, reviews, quarterlies, and magazines. *Address:* 119 Pintail Drive, Pelham, AL 35124, USA (home); University of Alabama at Birmingham School of Medicine, Department of Anesthesiology, Jefferson Tower 965, 619 South 19th Street, Birmingham, AL 35249-6810, USA (office). *E-mail:* ajwright@uab.edu. *Website:* www.anes.uab.edu/ajcv.htm.

WRIGHT, Anthony David, BA, MA, DPhil, FRHistS; British academic and writer; *Reader in Ecclesiastical History, University of Leeds*; b. 9 June 1947, Oxford, England. *Education:* Merton Coll., Oxford, British School, Rome, Brasenose Coll., Oxford. *Career:* Lecturer, Univ. of Leeds 1974–92, Sr Lecturer in History 1992–2001, Reader in Ecclesiastical History 2001–; Visiting Fellow, Univ. of Edinburgh 1983, Jesuit Historical Inst., Rome 2002; mem. Accad. di San Carlo, Ecclesiastical History Soc. *Publications:* The Counter-Reformation: Catholic Europe and the Non-Christian World 1982 (revised edn 2005), Baronio Storico e la Controriforma (with Romeo De Maio, L. Gulia, and A. Mazzacane) 1982, Catholicism and Spanish Society Under the Reign of Philip II, 1555–1598, and Philip III, 1598–1621 1991, The Early Modern Papacy: From the Council of Trent to the French Revolution 1564–1789 2000; contrib. to scholarly books and journals. *Address:* School of History, University of Leeds, Leeds, LS2 9JT, England (office). *Telephone:* (113) 343-3586 (office). *Fax:* (113) 234-2759 (office). *E-mail:* A.D.Wright@leeds .ac.uk (office). *Website:* www.leeds.ac.uk/history (office).

WRIGHT, Carolyn D., BA, MFA; American poet and academic; *Israel J. Kapstein Professor of English, Brown University;* b. 6 Jan. 1949, Mountain Home, AR; m. Forrest Gander 1983; one s. *Education:* Univ. of Memphis, Univ. of Arkansas. *Career:* Prof. of English and Creative Writing, Brown Univ. 1983–; State Poet of Rhode Island 1994–; mem. PEN, New England, Council Mem. *Publications:* Terrorism, 1979; Translations of the Gospel Back Into Tongues, 1981; Further Adventures with God, 1986; String Light, 1991; Just Whistle, 1993; The Lost Roads Project: A Walk-in Book of Arkansas, 1994; The Reader's Map of Arkansas, 1994; Tremble, 1996; Deepstep Come Shining, 1998; Steal Away: Selected and New Poems, 2002. Contributions: American Letters and Commentary; BRICK; Conjunctions; Sulfur. *Honours:* National Endowment for the Arts Fellowships, 1981, 1987; Witter Bynner Prize for Poetry, 1986; Guggenheim Fellowship, 1987; Mary Ingraham Bunting Fellowship, 1987; General Electric Award for Younger Writers, 1988; Whiting

Writers Award, 1989; Rhode Island Governor's Award for the Arts, 1990; Lila Wallace/Reader's Digest Writers Award, 1992; University of Arkansas Distinguished Alumni Award, 1998; Lannan Literary Award, 1999; Artist Award, Foundation for Contemporary Performance Art, 1999; Lange-Taylor Prize, Center for Documentary Studies, 2000. *Address:* 351 Nayatt Road, Barrington, RI 02806, USA. *E-mail:* carolyn_wright@brown.edu.

WRIGHT, Charles Penzel, BA, MFA; American poet, writer and teacher; b. 25 Aug. 1935, Pickwick Dam, TN; m. Holly McIntire 1969; one s. *Education:* Davidson Coll., Univ. of Iowa, Univ. of Rome. *Career:* Faculty, Univ. of California at Irvine 1966–83, Univ. of Virginia 1983–; mem. Acad. of American Poets (bd of chancellors 1999–2002), American Acad. of Arts and Letters, Fellowship of Southern Writers, American Acad. of Arts and Sciences, PEN American Centre. *Publications:* Grave of the Right Hand 1970, Hard Freight 1973, Bloodlines 1975, China Trace 1977, Southern Cross 1981, Country Music 1982, The Other Side of the River 1984, Zone Journals 1988, The World of the 10,000 Things 1990, Chickamauga 1995, Black Zodiac 1997, Appalachia 1998, Negative Blue: Selected Later Poems 2000, A Short History of the Shadow, Snake Eyes 2004; contrib. to numerous journals and magazines. *Honours:* Acad. of American Poets Edgar Allan Poe Award 1976, PEN Trans. Award 1979, Nat. Book Award for Poetry 1983, Brandeis Book Critics Circle Award 1998, Pulitzer Prize for Poetry 1998. *Address:* 940 Locust Avenue, Charlottesville, VA 22901, USA.

WRIGHT, Donald Richard, BA, MA, PhD; American historian and academic; *Distinguished Teaching Professor of History, State University of New York at Cortland;* b. 3 Aug. 1944, Richmond, IN; s. of Richard Marion Wright and Wilma Sprong Wright; m. 1st Olwen Twyman 1969 (divorced 1987); two s.; m. 2nd Marilou Briggs 1990 (died 1997); m. 3rd Doris DeLuca 2004. *Education:* De Pauw Univ., Indiana Univ., Bloomington. *Career:* served to Capt., USAF 1968–72; Editorial Asst, American Historical Review 1975–76; Asst Prof., State Univ. of NY (SUNY) at Cortland 1976–79, Assoc. Prof. 1979–84, Dept Head 1983–85, Prof. 1984–90, Distinguished Teaching Prof. of History 1990–; presenter summer workshops 1980–95; Collector, Curator, Nat. Museum of the Gambia, Banjul 1982; Lead Scholar, Alabama Humanities Foundation Inst. 1994; Visiting Lecturer, History Dept, Univ. of Witwatersrand, Johannesburg, S Africa 2000; Scholar-in-Residence, Rockefeller Foundation Study and Conf. Center, Bellagio, Italy 2003; Mark W. Clark Distinguished Visiting Chair of History, The Citadel 2005–06; mem. African Studies Asscn, American Historical Asscn, World History Asscn, Mande Studies Asscn; Fellow, Nat. Endowment for the Humanities 1982–83. *Publications:* The Early History of Niumi: Settlement and Foundation of a Mandinka State on the Gambia River 1977, Oral Traditions from the Gambia, Vol. I: Mandinka Griots 1979, Vol. II: Family Elders 1980, Muslim Peoples (contrib.) 1984, What to Teach about Africa: A Guide for Secondary Teachers 1990, African Americans in the Colonial Era: From African Origins through the American Revolution 1990, African Americans in the Early Republic, 1789–1831 1993, The World and a Very Small Place in Africa 1997, The Atlantic World: A History, 1400–1888 (co-author) 2007; contrib. to books, articles and reviews to journals, including Journal of American Ethnic History, American Heritage, Journal of General Education, African Economic History, Africana Journal, History in Africa, American Historical Review, Journal of Southern History. *Honours:* Air Force Commendation Medal, Fulbright Fellow 1974–75, SUNY Chancellor's Award for Excellence in Teaching 1989. *Address:* 4355 Locust Avenue, Homer, NY 13077-9476, USA. *E-mail:* wrightd@cortland.edu.

WRIGHT, George Thaddeus, BA, MA, PhD; American academic, writer and poet; *Regents' Professor Emeritus, University of Minnesota;* b. 17 Dec. 1925, Staten Island, NY; m. Jerry Honeywell 1955. *Education:* Columbia Coll., Columbia Univ., Univ. of Geneva, Univ. of California. *Career:* teaching asst 1954–55, Lecturer 1956–57, Univ. of California; Visiting Asst Prof., New Mexico Highlands Univ. 1957; Instructor-Asst Prof., Univ. of Kentucky 1957–60; Asst Prof., San Francisco State Coll. 1960–61; Assoc. Prof., Univ. of Tennessee 1961–68; Fulbright Lecturer, Univ. of Aix-Marseilles 1964–66, Univ. of Thessaloniki 1977–78; Visiting Lecturer, Univ. of Nice 1965; Prof. 1968–89, Chair English Dept 1974–77, Regents' Prof. 1989–93, Regents' Prof. Emeritus 1993–, Univ. of Minnesota; mem. Minnesota Humanities Comission 1985–88, MLA, Shakespeare Asscn of America. *Publications:* The Poet in the Poem: The Personae of Eliot, Yeats and Pound 1960, W. H. Auden 1969, Shakespeare's Metrical Art 1988, Aimless Life: Poems 1961–1995 1999, Hearing the Measures: Shakespearean and Other Inflections 2002; editor: Seven American Literary Stylists from Poe to Mailer: An Introduction 1973; contrib. articles, reviews, poems and translations in many periodicals and books. *Honours:* Guggenheim Fellowship 1981–82, Nat. Endowment for the Humanities Fellowship 1984–85, MLA William Riley Parker Prizes 1974, 1981, Robert Fitzgerald Prosody Award 2002. *Address:* 2617 W Crown King Drive, Tucson, AZ 85741, USA (home). *Telephone:* (520) 575-1130 (home). *E-mail:* twright@earthlink.net (home).

WRIGHT, Jay, MA; American poet and dramatist; b. 25 May 1934, Albuquerque, NM. *Education:* Univ. of California at Berkeley, Union Theological Seminary, New York, Rutgers Univ. *Career:* Hodder Fellow Princeton Univ. 1970; Joseph Compton Creatiave Writing Fellow Dundee Univ. 1972; Fellow American Acad. of Arts and Sciences. *Publications:* The Homecoming Singer 1971, Soothsayers and Omens 1976, Dimensions of History 1976, The Double Invention of Komo 1980, Explications/Interpretations 1984, Selected Poems of Jay Wright 1987, Elaine's Book 1988, Boleros 1991, Transfigurations: Collected Poems 2000. *Honours:* American Acad. and

Inst. of Arts and Letters Award, Guggenheim Fellowship, MacArthur Fellowship, Ingram Merrill Foundation Award, NEA grant, Acad. of American Poets Fellowship 1996, Lannan Literary Award for Poetry 2000, L. L. Winship/PEN Award 2001, Anisfield-Wolf Lifetime Achievement Award 2002, Bollingen Prize for American Poetry 2005. *Address:* PO Box 381, Bradford, VT 05033, USA.

WRIGHT, Karen Jocelyn, MA, MBA, FRSA; American editor and journalist; b. 15 Nov. 1950, New York; d. of Louis David Wile and Grace Carlin Wile; m. 1981; two d. *Education:* Brandeis Univ., Univ. of Cambridge and London Grad. School of Business Studies, UK. *Career:* Founder-Owner Hobson Gallery, Cambridge 1981–87; co-f. (with Peter Fuller) Modern Painters magazine 1987–, Ed. 1990–2006–Ed.-at-Large 2006–; co-f. (with David Bowie, Sir Timothy Sainsbury and Bernard Jacobson) 21 Publishing 1997–; mem. Asscn Int. des Critiques d'Art. *Publications:* The Penguin Book of Art Writing (co-ed.) 1998, Colour for Kosovo (ed.) 1999, The Grove Book of Art Writing 2000, Colour 2003; contrib. to Independent on Sunday. *Address:* 21 Publishing, Unit 204, Buspace Studios, Conlan Street, London, W10 5AP; c/o LTB Media (UK) Ltd, 72 Hammersmith Road, Crown House, Suite 420, London, W14 8TH; 39 Portland Road, London, W11 4LH, England (home). *Telephone:* (20) 8964-1113 (21 Publishing) (office). *Fax:* (20) 8964-9993 (21 Publishing). *E-mail:* info@21publishing.com. *Website:* www.21publishing.com; www .modernpainters.co.uk (office).

WRIGHT, Nicholas; British playwright; b. 5 July 1940, Cape Town, South Africa. *Education:* London Acad. of Music and Dramatic Art. *Career:* Literary Man. 1987, Assoc. Dir 1992, Nat. Theatre, London, England. *Publications:* Treetops 1978, The Gorky Brigade 1979, One Fine Day 1980, The Crimes of Vautrin (after Balzac) 1983, The Custom of the Country 1983, The Desert Air 1984, Six Characters in Search of an Author (after Pirandello) 1987, Mrs Klein 1988, Thérèse Raquin (after Zola) 1990, Essays 1992, Cressida 1999, Vincent in Brixton 2002, Changing Stages (with Richard Eyre) 2002, The Little Prince (libretto) 2003, His Dark Materials (after Philip Pullman) 2003, Three Sisters (after Chekhov) 2003, The Reporter 2006. *Address:* 2 St Charles Place, London, W10 6EG, England.

WRIGHT, Rt Rev. Nicholas Thomas, BA, MA, DPhil, DD; British theologian and Anglican bishop; *Bishop of Durham;* b. 1 Dec. 1948, Morpeth, Northumberland; s. of Nicholas Irwin Wright and Rosemary Wright (née Forman); m. Margaret Elizabeth Anne Fiske 1971; two s. two d. *Education:* Sedbergh School, Exeter Coll., Oxford, Wycliffe Hall, Oxford. *Career:* ordained deacon 1975, priest 1976; Jr Research Fellow, Merton Coll. Oxford 1975–78, Jr Chaplain 1976–78; Fellow and Chaplain Downing Coll. Cambridge 1978–81; Asst Prof. of New Testament Studies, McGill Univ., Montreal and Hon. Prof., Montreal Diocesan Theological Coll., Canada 1981–86; Lecturer in Theology, Univ. of Oxford and Fellow, Tutor and Chaplain, Worcester Coll. Oxford 1986–93; Dean of Lichfield 1994–99; Canon Theologian of Coventry Cathedral 1992–99; Canon Theologian of Westminster 2000–03; Bishop of Durham July 2003–; Fellow Inst. for Christian Studies, Toronto 1992–; mem. Doctrine Comm., Church of England 1979–81, 1989–95, Lambeth Comm. 2004; regular broadcasts on TV and radio. *Publications include:* Small Faith, Great God 1978, The Work of John Frith 1983, The Epistles of Paul to the Colossians and to Philemon 1987, The Glory of Christ in the New Testament (co-ed.) 1987, The Interpretation of the New Testament 1861–1986 (co-author) 1988, The Climax of the Covenant 1991, New Tasks for a Renewed Church 1992, The Crown and the Fire 1992, The New Testament and the People of God 1992, Who Was Jesus? 1992, Following Jesus 1994, Jesus and the Victory of God 1996, The Lord and His Prayer 1996, What Saint Paul Really Said 1997, For All God's Worth 1997, Reflecting the Glory 1998, The Meaning of Jesus (co-author) 1999, The Myth of the Millennium 1999, Romans and the People of God (co-ed.) 1999, Holy Communion for Amateurs 1999, The Challenge of Jesus 2000, Twelve Months of Sundays, Year C 2000, Easter Oratorio (co-author) 2000, Twelve Months of Sundays, Year A 2001, Luke for Everyone 2001, Mark for Everyone 2001, Paul for Everyone: Galatians and Thessalonians 2002, John for Everyone 2002, Twelve Months of Sundays, Year B 2002, New Interpreter's Bible, Vol. X (contrib.) 2002, The Contemporary Quest for Jesus 2002, Paul for Everyone (The Prison Letters) 2002, Matthew for Everyone 2002, Paul for Everyone (I Corinthians) 2003, Paul for Everyone (II Corinthians) 2003, Quiet Moments 2003, The Resurrection of the Son of God 2003, For All the Saints? 2003, Hebrews for Everyone 2003, Paul for Everyone (The Pastoral Letters) 2003, Paul for Everyone: Romans 2004, Scripture and the Authority of God 2005. *Honours:* Hon. Fellow Downing Coll. Cambridge 2003, Merton Coll. Oxford 2004; Hon. DD (Aberdeen) 2000; Hon. DHumLitt (Gordon Coll., Mass) 2003. *Address:* Bishop of Durham, Auckland Castle, Bishop Auckland, Co. Durham, DL14 7NR, England (office). *Telephone:* (1388) 602576 (office). *Fax:* (1388) 605264 (office). *E-mail:* bishops.office@durham .anglican.org (office). *Website:* www.durham.anglican.org (office).

WRIGHT, Richard Bruce, BA; Canadian writer; b. 4 March 1937, Midland, ON; m. Phyllis Mary Cotton; two s. *Education:* Ryerson Polytechnic Inst., Toronto, Trent Univ., Peterborough. *Career:* fmr teacher of English, Ridley Coll., St Catharines, ON (now retd). *Publications:* Andrew Tolliver 1965, The Weekend Man 1970, In the Middle of a Life 1973, Farthing's Fortunes 1976, Final Things 1980, The Teacher's Daughter 1982, Tourists 1984, Sunset Manor 1990, The Age of Longing 1995, Clara Callan 2001, Adultery 2004. *Honours:* Hon. DLitt (Brock Univ.) 2000, (Ryerson Univ.) 2002, (Trent Univ.) 2006; fellowships; City of Toronto Book Award 1973, Geoffrey Faber Memorial Prize, England 1975, Gov.-Gen.'s Award for Literature 2001, Giller Prize

2001, Trillium Award 2001. *Address:* 52 St Patrick Street, St Catharines, ON L2R 1K3 (home); c/o Harper Collins Publishers, 2 Bloor Street E, 20th Floor, Toronto, ON M4W 1A8, Canada (office).

WRIGHT, Ronald, MA; British/Canadian writer; b. 1948, Surrey, England. *Education:* Univ. of Cambridge. *Career:* mem. PEN Canada, Survival Int. *Publications:* Memoirs: Cut Stones and Crossroads: A Journey in Peru 1984, On Fiji Islands 1986, Time Among the Maya 1989, Stolen Continents (history) 1992, Home and Away (essays) 1993, A Scientific Romance (novel) 1997, Henderson's Spear (novel) 2001, A Short History of Progress (Massey Lectures) 2004; contrib. to journals, including TLS. *Honours:* Hon. LLD (Univ. of Calgary) 1996; Gordon Montador Award 1993, David Higham Prize for Fiction 1997, Libris Non-Fiction Book of the Year 2005. *Literary Agent:* Aitken Alexander Associates Ltd, 18–21 Cavaye Place, London, SW10 9PT, England. *Telephone:* (20) 7373-8672. *Fax:* (20) 7373-6002. *E-mail:* reception@ aitkenalexander.co.uk. *Website:* www.aitkenalexander.co.uk.

WU, Duncan, BA, DPhil; British academic and writer; b. 3 Nov. 1961, Woking, Surrey, England. *Education:* University of Oxford. *Career:* Postdoctoral Fellow, British Acad., 1991–94; Reader in English Literature, University of Glasgow, 1995–; Ed., Charles Lamb Bulletin; mem. Charles Lamb Society, council mem.; Keats-Shelley Memorial Asscn, committee mem. *Publications:* Wordsworth's Reading 1770–1799, 1993; Romanticism: An Anthology, 1994; William Wordsworth: A Selection, 1994; Six Contemporary Dramatists, 1994; Romanticism: A Critical Reader, 1995; Wordsworth's Reading, 1800–15, 1996; Romantic Women Poets: An Anthology, 1997; Wordsworth: An Inner Life, 2001. Contributions: journals and periodicals.

WUNSCH, Josephine McLean, BA; American writer; b. 3 Feb. 1914, Detroit, MI; m. Edward Seward Wunsch 1940, one s. two d. *Education:* Univ. of Michigan. *Publications:* Flying Skis, 1962; Passport to Russia, 1965; Summer of Decision, 1968; Lucky in Love, 1970; The Aerie (as J. Sloan McLean with Virginia Gillett), 1974; Girl in the Rough, 1981; Class Ring, 1983; Free as a Bird, 1984; Breaking Away, 1985; The Perfect Ten, 1986; Lucky in Love, 1987; Between Us, 1989.

WURLITZER, Rudolph; American author and screenwriter; b. 1937, Cincinnati, OH. *Education:* Columbia University, University of Aix-en-Provence. *Publications:* Nog, 1969; Flats, 1970; Two-Lane Blacktop (with Will Cory), 1971; Quake, 1972; Pat Garrett and Billy the Kid, 1973; Slow Fade, 1984; Walker, 1987; Hard Travels to Sacred Places, 1994. Other: several screenplays. Contributions: books and periodicals.

WURM, Franz, BA, MA; British writer; b. 16 March 1926, Prague, Czechoslovakia; s. of Josef Wurm and Regina Wurm (née Klatscher); m. Barbara M. Z'Graggen 1992. *Education:* Queen's Coll., Oxford. *Career:* Head of Third Program, German Swiss Radio, Zürich 1966–69; Dir, Feldenkrais Inst., Zürich 1974–; mem. Hölderlin Gesellschaft, Tübingen, Franz Kafka Soc., Prague. *Publications:* Anmeldung 1959, Vorgang 1962, Anker und Unruh 1964, Vier Gedichte 1965, Brehy v zádech 1974, Acht Gedichte in Faksimile 1975, Hundstage 1986, In diesem Fall 1989, Dirzulande 1990, Unter Anderen (play) 1992, Nachbemerkungen zu Feldenkrais 1995, Briefwechsel (with Paul Celan) 1995, 53 Gedichte 1996, König auf dem Dach 1997, Orangenblau 1998, Postscriptum 1998, Blaue Orangen 2004, Rozevrená fuga 2004, Schneetreiben im Zimmer 2005, Und woher 2006; trans. of: René Char 1963, Paul Valéry 1965, Moshé Feldenkrais 1968, 1977, 1985, 1989, Ludwig Wittgenstein 1991, Michael Hamburger 2000, Henri Michaux 2001, Vladimir Holan 2003; contrib. to Neue Zürcher Zeitung, Akzente, Neue Rundschau, Literatur und Kritik, Neue Deutsche Literatur, Das Nachtcafé, Text & Kritik, Revolver Revue. *Address:* Via Orelli 16, 6612 Ascona, Switzerland.

WURTS, Janny, BA; American writer; b. 10 Dec. 1953, Bryn Mawr, PA. *Education:* Hampshire College, Moore College of Art. *Publications:* Sorcerer's Legacy, 1982; Stormwarden, 1984; Daughter of the Empire (co-author), 1987; Keeper of the Keys, 1988; Shadowfane, 1988; Servant of the Empire (co-author), 1990; Mistress of the Empire (co-author), 1992; The Master of White Storm, 1992; The Curse of the Mistwraith, 1995; Ships of Merior, 1995; That Way Lies Camelot, 1996.

WYLIE, Andrew, BA; American literary agent; *President, The Wylie Agency;* b. 4 Nov. 1947; m. 1st Christina Meyer 1969; one s.; m. 2nd Camilla Carlini; two d. *Education:* St Paul's School, Harvard Coll. *Career:* founder and Pres. The Wylie Agency, New York 1980–, London 1996–, Madrid 1999–, with over 500 clients. *Address:* The Wylie Agency, 250 W 57th Street, Suite 2114, New York, NY 10107, USA. *Telephone:* (212) 246-0069. *Fax:* (212) 586-8953. *E-mail:* mail@wylieagency.com. *Website:* www.wylieagency.com.

WYLIE, Betty Jane, BA, MA; Canadian writer, dramatist and poet; b. 21 Feb. 1931, Winnipeg, MB; m. William Tennent Wylie, two s. two d. *Education:* University of Manitoba. *Career:* Bunting Fellow, Radcliffe College, 1989–90; Writer-in-Residence, Metro Toronto Library, York Branch, 2001; mem. Playwrights' Union of Canada; Writers' Union of Canada. *Publications:* over 35 books, many plays; contrib. to periodicals.

WYLIE, Laura (see Matthews, Patricia Anne)

WYNAND, Derk, BA, MA; Canadian academic, poet, writer, translator and editor; b. 12 June 1944, Bad Suderode, Germany; m. Eva Kortemme 1971. *Education:* Univ. of British Columbia. *Career:* Visiting Lecturer 1969–73, Asst Prof. to Prof. 1973–, Chair Dept of Creative Writing 1987–90, 1996–99, Univ. of Victoria; Ed., The Malahat Review (named Magazine of the Year 1995)

1992–98. *Publications:* Locus 1971, Snowscapes 1974, Pointwise 1979, One Cook, Once Dreaming 1980, Second Person 1983, Fetishistic 1984, Heatwaves 1988, Airborne 1994, Door Slowly Closing 1995, Closer to Home 1997, Dead Man's Float 2001. *Honours:* honourable mention bp Nichol Chapbook Award 1995. *Address:* c/o Department of Writing, University of Victoria, PO Box 3045, Victoria, BC V8W 3P4, Canada.

X

XENAKIS, Françoise Marguerite Claude; French journalist and writer; b. 27 Sept. 1930, Blois; d. of Robert and Suzanne (née Richard) Gargouil; m. Yannis Xenakis 1953; one c. *Career:* Journalist and literary critic on Le Matin de Paris and L'Express, Paris 1987–. *Publications:* Des dimanches et des dimanches 1977, Moi, j'aime pas la mer, Le temps usé, La natte coupée, Zut, on a encore oublié Madame Freud 1985, Mouche-toi Cléopâtre 1986, Elle lui dirait dans l'île (play) 1987, La vie exemplaire de Rita Capuchon 1988, Chéri, tu viens pour la photo 1990, Attends moi (Prix des Libraires) 1993, Désolée mais ça ne se fait pas 1996. *Address:* 9 rue Chaptal, 75009 Paris, France.

XINRAN, Xue; Chinese radio journalist, writer and columnist; b. 19 July 1958, Beijing; m. 1st (divorced); one s.; m. 2nd Toby Eady 2002. *Education:* First Mil. Univ. of PLA. *Career:* writer under name, Xinran; radio producer, presenter, Words on the Night Breeze programme, Henhan Broadcasting and Jiangsu Broadcasting 1989–97; moved to London 1997; teacher, SOAS, London; Founder The Mothers' Bridge of Love charitable org. 2003; columnist, The Guardian. *Publications:* The Good Women of China (non-fiction) 2002, Sky Burial (non-fiction) 2004, What the Chinese Don't Eat 2006, Miss Chopsticks (novel) 2007; contribs to Western and Chinese newspapers and broadcasting journals. *Literary Agent:* The Mothers' Bridge of Love, 9 Orme Court, London, W2 4RL, England. *Telephone:* (20) 7034-0686. *Fax:* (20) 7792-0879. *E-mail:* xinran@motherbridge.org. *Website:* www.motherbridge.org.

XONGERIN, Badai; Chinese Inner Mongolia administrator, writer and poet; b. 5 June 1930, Bayinguoltng Prefecture, Hejin Co., Xinjiang; s. of Honger Xongerin and Bayinchahan Xongerin; m. 1952; two s. two d. *Career:* Pres. Xinjiang Broadcasting and TV Univ. 1982–; Chair. Cttee of Xinjiang Uygur Autonomous Region of CPPCC 1989; mem. Standing Cttee CPPCC 1991. *Publications:* several books of prose, poetry and history in Mongol language and Chinese. *Address:* 15 South Beijing Road, Urumqi, Xinjiang, People's Republic of China. *Telephone:* (991) 2825701 (office); (991) 3839303 (home). *Fax:* (991) 2823443.

XU, Zhenshi; Chinese photographer, artist and publisher; b. 18 Aug. 1937, Songjiang Co., Shanghai; s. of Xu Weiqing and Jiang Wanying, step-s. of Cheng Shi-fa; m. Zhang Fuhe 1967; one d. *Education:* No. 1 High School, Songjiang Co., Zhejiang Acad. of Fine Arts. *Career:* moved to Beijing 1965; Ed. People's Fine Arts Publishing House 1965–86, Dir Picture Editorial Dept 1986–, Ed.-in-Chief 1992–; mem. China Artists' Asscn; Deputy Sec.-Gen. Spring Festival Pictures Research Centre, Publrs' Asscn of China; Deputy Sec.-Gen. and Assoc. Dir Photography Research Centre; mem. Selection Cttee 3rd, 4th and 5th Nat. Exhbns of Spring Festival Pictures and other exhbns; Assoc. Dir Standing Cttee Spring Festival Pictures; Sr Adviser, Office of East China–UN TIPS Nat. Exploit Bureau 1994–; exhbns in China, Japan, Korea, Hong Kong, Thailand; Vice-Ed.-in-Chief Gouache Vol. of Anthology of Contemporary Chinese Fine Arts 1996; Vice-Pres. Chinese Fan Art Soc. 1997; organized 1st Nat. Exhbn of Calligraphy and Paintings to Help the Poor 1998; Dir Foundation for Underdeveloped Regions in China 1998–; prepared 6th Nat. Exhbn of Spring Festival Pictures 1998; union art exhib., St Petersburg, Russia 2006. *Exhibitions include:* Taiyuan Shanxi Prov. 2003, Wei Fang Shandong Prov. 2004, Hangzhou 2005. *Publications:* China's Cultural Relics Unearthed during the Great Cultural Revolution 1973, Travel in China (four vols) 1979–80, Tibet 1981, Travel in Tibet 1981, Costumes of China's Minority Nationalities 1981, Travel in Guilin 1981, Travel Leisurely in China 1981, Travel in Yunnan 1982, China's Flowers in Four Seasons 1982, Poet Li Bai 1983, Native Places of Tang Dynasty Poems 1984, Travel along the Yangtse River 1985, Through the Moongate: A Guide to China's Famous Historical Sites 1986, Waters and Mountains in China 1986, Travel in Guangzhou 1986, China 1987, The Chinese Nation 1989, Poet Du Fu 1989, Selected Works of Xu Zhenshi 1990, 1993, Selected Paintings of Xu Zhenshi 1993, 1994, Boat on the Plateau 1998, Album of Xu Zhenshi's Sketches 1999, Love for China 2003; collection of Xu Zhenshi published in 2003, Love for China 2003. *Honours:* numerous awards including Bronze Medal for albums of photographs, Leipzig Int. Book Exhbn 1987, Nat. Award 1993, Model Ed. Nat. Press and Publs System 1997, 1998, State Prize for Spring Festival Pictures 2001, two 6th Nat. Exhbn of Spring Festival Pictures Prizes (China) 1998, Chinese Contemporary Art Achievement Prize, Hong Kong, State Prize of Spring Festival Pictures 2001, Prize of A Brilliant Contrib. 2001, Outstanding People's Artist Award. *Address:* People's Fine Arts Publishing House, No. 32 Beizongbu Hutong, Beijing, People's Republic of China (office). *Telephone:* (10) 65244901 (office); (10) 65246353 (home).

Y

YAAD, (Muhammad) Mansha, MA; Pakistani fiction writer and playwright; b. 5 Sept. 1937, small village nr Farukabad, Shiakhupura Dist; s. of Haji Nazir Ahmed. *Education:* Diploma in Civil Eng, Punjab Univ., Lahore. *Career:* Deputy Dir/Civil Engineer, Capital Devt Authority, Islamabad 1960–97; Founder Halqa-e Arbab-e Zauq Islamabad literary forum 1972; writes in Urdu and Punjabi; numerous plays for Radio Pakistan and Pakistan TV. *Television:* serials: Janoon, Bandhan, Rahain (PTV Nat. Award), Pooray Chand ki Raat. *Publications:* short story collections: Band Muthi Main Jugnu (Firefly in the Fist) 1975, Mass Aur Mitti (Flesh and Clay) 1980, Khala Andar Khala (Space Within Space) 1983, Waqt Samundar (Time the Ocean) 1986, Mansha Yad Ke Muntkhib Afsany (Selected Stories) 1986, Wagda Pani (Running Water) 1987, Darakhat Adami (Tree the Man) 1990, Door Ki Awaz (A Distant Voice) 1994, Mansha Yad Ke Behtreen Afsany (Best Short Stories) 1994, Mansha Yad Ke Tees Muntakhib Afsany (Thirty Selected Short Stories) 1997, Tamasha (The Show) 1998; novel: Tanwan Tanwan Tara (Sparsely a Star) 1997, Khawb Saraiy (Lodge of Dreams). *Honours:* Waris Shah Adabi Awards, Pakistan Acad. of Letters for Punjabi books, Pres.'s Award 'Pride of Performance' for Literature 2004. *Address:* House No. 8, Seventh Avenue, Sector G-7/4, Islamabad 44000, Pakistan (home). *E-mail:* manshayaad@hotmail.com (home); afsananigar@yahoo.com (home). *Website:* www.manshayaad.com; manshayaad.tripod.com.

YAFFE, James, BA; American academic, writer and dramatist; b. 31 March 1927, Chicago, IL; m. Elaine Gordon 1964; one s. two d. *Education:* Yale University. *Career:* Prof., 1968–, Dir, General Studies, 1981–, Colorado College; mem. American Asscn of University Profs; Authors' League; Dramatists' Guild; MWA; PEN. *Publications:* Poor Cousin Evelyn, 1951; The Good-for-Nothing, 1953; What's the Big Hurry?, 1954; Nothing But the Night, 1959; Mister Margolies, 1962; Nobody Does You Any Favors, 1966; The American Jews, 1968; The Voyage of the Franz Joseph, 1970; So Sue Me!, 1972; Saul and Morris, Worlds Apart, 1982; A Nice Murder for Mom, 1988; Mom Meets Her Maker, 1990; Mom Doth Murder Sleep, 1991; Mom Among the Liars, 1992; My Mother, the Detective, 1997. Plays: The Deadly Game, 1960; Ivory Tower (with Jerome Weidman), 1967; Cliffhanger, 1983. Other: Television plays. Contributions: various publications. *Honours:* National Arts Foundation Award, 1968.

YAGUELLO, Marina; French linguist and writer; b. 1944, Paris. *Career:* Prof., Université de Paris VII (Denis Diderot). *Publications include:* Les Mots et les femmes: essai dapproche socio-linguistique de la condition féminine 1978, Alice au pays du langage (trans. as Language Through the Looking-Glass) 1981, Les Fous du langage: des langues imaginaires et de leurs inventeurs (trans. as Lunatic Lovers of Language: Imaginary Languages and their Inventors) 1984, Le Sexe des mots 1988, Catalogue des idées reçues sur la langue 1988, Histoire de Lettres 1990, En écoutant parler la langue 1991, Grammaire exploratoire de l'anglais 1991, J'apprends le wolof, Damay jang wolof (with Jean-Léopold Diouf) 1991, T'ar ta gueule à la récré! (with Nestor Salas) 1991, La Planète des langues 1993, Subjecthood and Subjectivity: Status of the Subject in Linguistic Theory 1994, Petits Faits de langue 1998, Le Grand livre de la langue française (with Claire-Blanche Benveniste, Jean-Paul Colin, Françoise Gadet et al) 2003.

YAMADA, Amy (Eimi); Japanese writer; b. (Yamada Futaba), 8 Feb. 1959, Tokyo. *Career:* fmr cartoonist; novelist and short story writer 1980–. *Publications:* Beddo taimu aizu (Bedtime Eyes) (Kawade Literary Prize 1985, Bungei Prize for Literature 1987) 1985, Yubi no tawamure (Finger Play) 1986, Jeshii no sebone (Jessie's Spine) 1986, Chô-cho no tensoku (Binding the Butterfly's Feet) 1987, Harlem World 1987, Sôru myûjikku, rabaazu on rii (Soul Music: Lovers Only, novellas) (Naoki Prize) 1987, Fûsô no kyôshitsu (Classroom for the Abandoned Dead) (Hirabayashi Taiko Prize) 1988, Hôkago no kiinooto (After-School Music) 1989, Trash 1991, I Can't Study 1993, 120% Coool 1994, Animal Logic 1996, 4U 1997, Magnet 1999, A2Z 2003, Pay Day! 2003. *Address:* c/o Kodansha International Ltd, Otowa YK Building, 1-17-14 Otowa 1 chome, Bunkyo-ku, Tokyo 112-8652, Japan. *E-mail:* akaogi@kodansha-intl.co.jp.

YAMADA, Taichi; Japanese screenwriter, playwright and novelist; b. 1934, Tokyo. *Education:* Waseda Univ. *Career:* worked in Ofuna Studio Production Dept Shochiku Film Co. 1958–65. *Television writing includes:* Sorezore no Aki (Annual TV Award Grand Prize, Japan Screenwriters' Guild TV programme Award, New Talent Award) 1973, Kishibe no Arubamu 1977, Ensen Chizu 1979, Otoko tachi no Tabiji 1976, Omoide Zukuri 1981, Nagaraeba (Educ. Minister's Award) 1982, Fuzoroi no Ringo tachi 1983, Soushun Sukkechi-bukku 1983, Nihon no Omokage (Mukoda Kuniko Prize 1984, Kikuchi Kan Prize 1985) 1984, Omote dori e nukeru michi (Japanese Civilian Broadcasting Fed. Grand Prix Award) 1988, Kanashikute yarikirenai 1992, Aki no eki 1993, Setsunai Haru 1995, Shasin no ura 1995, Nara he ikumade 1998, Ichiban Kirei na toki 1999, And... Friend 2000, This Winter's Romance 2002, How to Walk a Maze 2002, The Fan of Hong Kong STAR 2002, The Following Days (Broadcasting Cultural Fund Award) 2004. *Plays include:* Rabu, Jyampu, Suna no Ue no Dansu, Kawa no Mukou de Hito ga Yobu, Yonaka ni Okiteiru no wa. *Film screenplay:* Shonen Jidai (scenario) (Mainichi Film Competition, Japan Acad. Award, Japan Writers' Asscn Scenario Award, Japan Broadcast Writers' Asscn, Japan Scenario Writers' Asscn Mems) 1991. *Publications:*

novels: Ai Yori Aoku, Owari ni Mita Machi, Ijintachi tono Natsu (Yamamoto Shugoro Prize), Tobu Yume wo Shibaraku Minai (Belgium Int. Film Festival Grand Prize), Mienai Kurayami, Koi no Shisei de, Minareta Machi ni Kaze ga Fuku, In Search of a Distant Voice 2006; novels serialized in newspapers: Kishibe no Arubamu, Oka no Ue no Himawari, Kimi Wo Miagete. *Address:* c/o Faber and Faber Ltd, 3 Queen Square, London, WC1N 3AU, England. *E-mail:* info@yamadataichi.com. *Website:* www.yamadataichi.com.

YAMAMOTO, Keith R., BSc, PhD; American writer, academic and scientist; *Editor-in-Chief, Molecular Biology of the Cell Education:* Iowa State Univ., Princeton Univ., Univ. of California San Francisco. *Career:* Asst Prof. of Biochemistry 1976–79, Assoc. Prof. of Biochemistry 1979–83, Prof. of Biochemistry 1983–, Vice-Chair 1985–94, Dept of Biochemistry and Biophysics, Univ. of California San Francisco; Dir of Biochemistry and Molecular Biology Program in Biological Sciences 1988–, Chair Dept of Cellular and Molecular Pharmacology 1994–2003, Univ. of California San Francisco; Ed.-in-Chief, Molecular Biology of the Cell; program mem., Univ. of California San Francisco Comprehensive Cancer; mem. Univ. of California San Francisco Biomedical Sciences Program; mem. Herbert Boyer Program in Biological Sciences. *Publications include:* co-author: Gene Wars: Military Control over the New Genetic Technologies 1988, Transcriptional Regulation: Monograph 22 1992; contrib. to numerous academic publications. *Address:* Molecular Biology of the Cell, American Society for Cell Biology, 8120 Woodmont Avenue, Suite 750, Bethesda, MD 20814-2762; Box 2280, University of California San Francisco, San Francisco, CA 94143-2280, USA. *E-mail:* yamamoto@cgl.ucsf.edu. *Website:* www.molbiolcell.org.

YAMASHITA, Karen Tei; American writer, dramatist and academic; b. 8 Jan. 1951, Oakland, CA; m. Ronaldo Yamashita; one s. one d. *Career:* Asst Prof., University of California at Santa Cruz, 1997–; mem. PEN Center West. *Publications:* Through the Arc of the Rain Forest, 1990; Brazil-Moru, 1992; Hannah Kusoh: An American Butoh, 1995; Tropic of Orange, 1997. Other: Short stories; Unpublished plays and screenplays. Contributions: anthologies and periodicals. *Honours:* Rockefeller Playwright-in-Residence Fellow, East West Players, Los Angeles, 1977–78; American Book Award, 1991; Janet Heidinger Kafka Award, 1992; City of Los Angeles Cultural Grant Award, 1992–93; Japan Foundation Artist Fellowship, 1997. *Address:* c/o University of California at Santa Cruz, Santa Cruz, CA 95064, USA.

YAN, Lianke; Chinese author; b. 1958, Henan province. *Publications include:* novels: Xia Riluo 1994, Shouhuo (Enjoyment) (Lao She Award) 2004, Serve the People 2005, The Dream of Ding Village 2006; also short stories. *Honours:* Lu Xun Award 2000. *Literary Agent:* The Susijn Agency Ltd, Third Floor, 64 Great Titchfield Street, London, W1W 7QH, England. *Telephone:* (20) 7580-6341. *Fax:* (20) 7580-8626.

YANCEY, Philip David, BA, MA; American writer and editor; b. 4 Nov. 1949, Atlanta, GA; m. Janet Norwood 1970. *Education:* Columbia Bible Coll., Wheaton Coll., Univ. of Chicago. *Career:* Ed., Campus Life 1971–77; Ed.-at-Large, Christianity Today 1980–. *Publications:* After the Wedding 1976, Where is God When It Hurts? 1977, Unhappy Secrets of the Christian Life (with Tim Stafford) 1979, Fearfully and Wonderfully Made (with Paul Brand) 1980, Open Windows 1982, In His Image (with Paul Brand) 1984, The Student Bible (with Tim Stafford) 1988, Disappointment With God: Questions Nobody Asks Aloud 1989, A Guided Tour of the Bible: Six Months of Daily Readings 1990, I Was Just Wondering 1990, Reality and the Vision 1990, Pain: The Gift Nobody Wants (with Paul Brand) 1993, Discovering God: A Devotional Journey Through the Bible 1993, Finding God in Unexpected Places 1995, The Jesus I Never Knew 1996, The Jesus I Never Knew Study Guide (with Brenda Quinn) 1997, What's So Amazing About Grace? 1997, Church, Why Bother?: My Personal Pilgrimage 1998, The Bible Jesus Read 1999, When Life Hurts: Understanding God's Place in Your Pain 1999, Meet the Bible: A Panorama of God's Word in 366 Readings and Reflections 2000, Reaching for the Invisible God: What Can We Expect to Find? 2000, Soul Survivor 2001, Rumors of Another World 2003, Prayer: Does It Make Any Difference? 2006; contrib. to numerous periodicals. *Honours:* many Evangelical Christian Publishers' Asscn Golden Medallion awards. *Address:* c/o Christianity Today, 465 Gundersen Drive, Carol Stream, IL 60188, USA.

YANG, Lian; New Zealand poet and writer; b. 22 Feb. 1955, Bern, Switzerland; m. Liu You Hong 1989. *Career:* began writing when sent to countryside in the 1970s; on return to Beijing was one of group of underground poets who published literary magazine Jintian; became poet in exile after Tiananmen massacre; writer Central Broadcasting 1977–88; Visiting Scholar Auckland Univ. 1989–90, Sydney Univ. 1992–93; numerous writer-in-residence posts, including Berlin 1990–91, Akademie Scloss Solitude, Germany 1994, Bellagio Center, USA 1996, Taipei City, Taiwan 2002, Cove Park, Scotland 2004–05; poet-in-residence Yaddo arts colony, USA 1992, 1994, 1997, Kustlerhaus Schloss, Germany 1997, M.E.E.T., St Nazaire, France 1998, Univ. of Auckland 2003; Visiting Prof. Bard Coll., USA 2003, European Grduate School, Switzerland 2005; Fellowship Amherst Coll., USA 1993–94; founder mem. Survivors Poetry Club; mem. Today Literature Research Soc. (councillor). *Publications:* in Chinese: Lihun (Ritualization of the Soul) 1985, Huanghun (Desolate Soul) 1986, Huang (Yellow) 1989, Ren de zijue (Man's

Self-Awakening) 1989, Mian ju yu e yu (trans. as Masks and Crocodile: A Contemporary Chinese Poet and his Poetry) 1990, Liu wang shi wo men huo de le shen me? (trans. as The Dead in Exile) 1990, Taiyang yu ren (The Sun and the People) 1991, Guihua (trans. as Ghostspeak) 1994, Ren jing – Guihua (Human Scene – Ghostspeak) 1994, Yi 1994, Da hai ting zhi zhi chu (trans. as Where the Sea Stands Still) (Poetry Book Soc. recommended translation 1999) 1995, Yang Lian zuopin 1982–1997 (Yang Lian's Works 1982–1997) 1998, Si shi ren de cheng (trans. as City of Dead Poets) 2000, Yue shi de qi ge ban ye (Seven Half-Nights of Lunar Eclipse) 2002, Yang Lian Xin Zuo 1998–2002 (Yang Lian's New Works) 2003, Notes of a Blissful Ghost 2005, Whaur the Deep Sea Devauls (Where the Sea Stands Still) 2005, Tong xin yuan (Concentric Circles) 2005, Unreal City 2006; contrib. to anthologies and books, journals and periodicals, including Representations, Goldbatt, Xinwen ziyou daoji, Orientierungen, Australian Journal of Chinese Affairs, Canadian Review of Comparartive Literature, Asian and African Studies, New Zealand Listener, PN Review, Renditions: A Chinese-English Translation Magazine, World Literature Today, Dushu, Zhongguo, TLS, New Left Review, Index on Censorship, The Guardian, Granta, Positions, Poetry London, OOTAL, Ezra Pound Magazine, Dove si ferma il mare, Kasel Documenta. *Honours:* Chinese Poetry Reader's Choice 1986, Flaiano Int. Poetry Prize, Italy 1999. *Address:* 22 Carlton Mansions, Holmleigh Road, London, N16 5PX, England (home). *Telephone:* (20) 7502-1821 (office). *Website:* www.yanglian.net (home).

YANG, Namu; Chinese singer and writer; b. 1966, Zuosuo, Yunnan Prov. *Education:* Shanghai Music Conservatory. *Career:* moved to Shanghai, later won singing competition and moved to Beijing 1982; performed in clubs and recorded six albums; went on to become music star and model; divides her time between Geneva, Beijing and San Francisco. *Television includes:* autobiographical documentary for Chinese TV. *Publications include:* Leaving the Kingdom of Daughters 1997, Leaving Mother Lake: A Girlhood at the Edge of the World (with Christine Mathieu) 2003. *Address:* c/o Author Mail, Little, Brown & Company, 1271 Avenue of the Americas, New York, NY 10020, USA.

YANKOWITZ, Susan, BA, MFA; American writer and dramatist; b. 20 Feb. 1941, Newark, NJ; m. Herbert Leibowitz 1978, one s. *Education:* Sarah Lawrence Coll., Yale Drama School. *Career:* mem. Authors' Guild, Dramatists' Guild, New Dramatists, PEN, Writers' Guild of America. *Plays* Slaughterhouse Play 1971, Boxes 1973, Terminal 1975, Alarms 1988, Night Sky 1992, The Revenge, A Knife in the Heart, Phaedra in Delirium 2003. *Film screenplay:* Portrait of a Scientist 1974. *Libretto:* Deronda (opera in three acts 1985–89, after George Eliot's Daniel Deronda). *Publications:* novel: Silent Witness 1977. *Honours:* Joseph Levine Fellowship in Screenwriting 1968, Vernon Rice Drama Desk Award for Most Promising Playwright 1969, Rockefeller Foundation grant 1973, and Award 1974, Guggenheim Fellowship 1975, MacDowell Colony Residencies 1975, 1984, 1987, 1990, NEA grants 1979, 1984, New York Foundation for the Arts grant 1989, McKnight Fellowship 1990. *E-mail:* susan@susanyankowitz.com; syankowitz@aol.com. *Website:* www.susanyankowitz.com.

YASUI, Kaoru, LLD; Japanese jurist and poet; b. 25 April 1907, Osaka; s. of Harumoto Yasui and Harue Yasui; m. Tazuko Kuki 1936; one s. one d. *Education:* Tokyo Univ. *Career:* Asst Prof., Tokyo Univ. 1932–42, Prof. 1942–48; Prof., Hosei Univ. 1952, Dean Faculty of Jurisprudence 1957–63, Dir 1963–66, Prof. Emer. 1978–; Leader (Chair. etc.) Japan Council Against Atomic and Hydrogen Bombs 1954–65; Pres. Japanese Inst. for World Peace 1965–; Dir Maruki Gallery for Hiroshima Panels 1968–; Chair. Japan–Korea (Democratic People's Repub.) Solidarity Cttee of Social Scientists 1972–; Dir-Gen. Int. Inst. of the Juche Idea 1978–; mem. Lenin Peace Prize Cttee. *Publications:* Outline of International Law 1939, Banning Weapons of Mass Destruction 1955, People and Peace 1955, Collection of Treaties 1960, My Way 1967, The Dialectical Method and the Science of International Law 1970, A Piece of Eternity (poems) 1977. *Honours:* Hon. mem. Japanese Asscn of Int. Law 1976–; Hon. DJur (San Gabriel Coll., USA); Lenin Peace Prize 1958; Gold Medal (Czechoslovakia) 1965. *Address:* Minami-Ogikubo 3-13-11, Suginami-ku, Tokyo, Japan.

YATROMANOLAKIS, Yoryis; Greek writer; b. 1940, Crete. *Career:* Prof. of Ancient Greek, Univ. of Athens. *Publications include:* novels: Leimonario (trans. as The Spiritual Meadow) 1974, The History of a Vendetta 1991, A Report of a Murder 1995, Eroticon 1998. *Honours:* First Greek National Prize for Literature, Nikos Kazantzakis Prize. *Address:* c/o Dedalus Ltd, Langford Lodge, St Judith's Lane, Sawtry, Cambridgeshire PE28 5XE, England. *Website:* www.dedalusbooks.com.

YAZGHI, Muhammad al-, LenD; Moroccan politician, lawyer and newspaper executive; *Minister of Territorial Administration, Water Resources and the Environment;* b. 28 Sept. 1935, Fez; m. Balafrej Souada 1972; two s. *Education:* Moulay Youssef Coll., Lycée Gouraud, Univ. of Rabat and Ecole Nat. d'Admin., Paris. *Career:* Dir of Budget, Ministry of Finance 1957–60; Dir Al-Moharir (daily paper) 1975–81, Liberation (daily paper) 1989–; First Sec. Moroccan Press Union 1977–93; Deputy to Parl. 1977–; mem. Political Bureau, Union Socialiste des Forces Populaires (USFP) 1975–91, Joint Vice-Sec. 1992–; Minister of Territorial Admin, the Environment, Urban Planning and Housing, then Minister of Territorial Administration, Water Resources and the Environment. *Publications:* articles in magazines and journals. *Address:* Ministry of Territorial Administration, Water Resources and the Environment, 36 ave el-Abtal, Agdal, Rabat (office); 5 rue Ibn Tofai, Les Orangers, Rabat, Morocco (home). *Telephone:* (3) 7772634 (office). *Fax:* (3) 7772756 (office). *E-mail:* info@minenv.gov.ma (office). *Website:* www.minenv.gov.ma (office).

YEH, Jane, MA, MFA; American writer and poet; b. 1971. *Education:* Manchester Metropolitan Univ., Univ. of Iowa Writers' Workshop, Harvard Univ. *Career:* researcher, writer and Asst Ed., Let's Go Travel Guides (UK and USA) 1992–93; Research Asst, Univ. of Iowa Spine Research Center 1995–96; Asst Ed., The Village Voice, New York 1996–2001; freelance journalist and poet on various English-language publications 2001–05; writer-in-residence, Kingston Univ. 2003–05, Lecturer in Creative Writing 2003–. *Publications:* Teen Spies (chapbook) 2003, Marabou 2005; contrib. to numerous journals and newspapers, including TLS, The Village Voice, Time Out New York, and to anthologies. *Honours:* Harvard Univ. Acad. of American Poets Prize 1993, Univ. of Iowa Graduate Research Fellowship 1994–96, Prairie Lights Poetry Prize 1995, Scholarship to Bread Loaf Summer Writers' Conference 1996, Grolier Poetry Prize 1996, New York Foundation for the Arts Poetry Fellowship 2001. *Address:* Holmwood House, Kingston University, Penrhyn Road, Kingston upon Thames, KT1 2EE, England. *E-mail:* jane.yeh@kingston.ac.uk. *Website:* janeyeh.mysite.wanadoo-members.co.uk.

YEHOSHUA, Abraham B., MA; Israeli writer and academic; *Professor of Comparative and Hebrew Literature, University of Haifa;* b. 9 Dec. 1936, Jerusalem; s. of Yakov Yehoshua and Malka Rosilio; m. Rivka Kirsninski 1960; two s. one d. *Career:* served in paratroopers unit 1954–57; Dir Israeli School in Paris 1964; Gen. Sec. World Union of Jewish Studies, Paris 1963–67; Dean of Students, Haifa Univ. 1967–72, Prof. of Comparative and Hebrew Literature 1972–; Visiting Prof., Harvard Univ., USA 1977, Univ. of Chicago 1988, 1997, 2000, Princeton Univ. 1992–; Co-Ed. Keshet 1965–72, Siman Kria 1973–, Tel Aviv Review 1987–; active mem. Israeli Peace Movt. *Film adaptations of novels and stories include:* The Lover, Facing the Forests, Continuing Silence, Mr Mani, Open Heart, A Voyage to the End of the Millennium, Early in the Summer of 1970. *Plays:* A Night in May 1969, Last Treatments 1973, Possessions 1992, The Night's Babies 1993. *Publications:* Death of the Old Man (short stories) 1963, Facing the Forest (short stories) 1968, Three Days and a Child (short stories) 1970, Early in the Summer of 1970 (novella) 1973, Two Plays 1975, The Lover (novel) 1977, Between Right and Right (essays) 1980, A Late Divorce (novel) (Flaiano Int. Poetry Prize, Italy 1996) 1982, Possessions 1986, Five Seasons (novel) (Nat. Jewish Book Award 1990, Cavour Prize, Italy 1994) 1988, The Wall and the Mountain (essays) 1988, Mister Mani (novel) (Israeli Booker Prize 1992, Nat. Jewish Book Award 1993, Wingate Prize, UK 1994) 1990, The Return from India 1994, Open Heart (novel) 1994, A Voyage to the End of the Millennium (novel) (Koret Prize) 1997, The Terrible Power of a Minor Guilt (essays) 1998, The Liberated Bride (novel) (Napoli Prize, Lampedusa Prize) 2001, The Mission of the Human Resource Man (novel) 2004, A Woman in Jerusalem 2006, Friendly Fire (novel) 2007. *Honours:* Dr hc (Hebrew Union Coll., Tel-Aviv Univ., Univ. of Turin, Bar Ilan Univ.); Brener Prize 1983, Alterman Prize 1986, Bialik Prize 1989, Booker Prize 1992, European B'nai B'rith Award 1993, Israel Prize 1995. *Address:* 33 Shoshanat Ha-Carmel, Haifa, 34322, Israel. *Telephone:* 4-8370001. *Fax:* 4-8375569. *E-mail:* bulli@research.haifa.ac.il (home).

YELLAND, David Ian, BA, AMP; British business executive and fmr journalist; *Partner, Brunswick Group LLP;* b. 14 May 1963, Harrogate; s. of John Michael Yelland and Patricia Ann McIntosh; m. Tania Farrell 1996 (divorced 2003, died 2006); one s. *Education:* Brigg Grammar School, Lincs., Univ. of Coventry, Harvard Business School, USA. *Career:* grad. trainee, Westminster Press 1985; trainee reporter, Buckinghamshire Advertiser 1985–87; industrial reporter, Northern Echo 1987–88; gen. news and business reporter, North West Times and Sunday Times 1988–89; city reporter, Thomson Regional Newspapers 1989–90; joined News Corpn 1990; city reporter, then City Ed. The Sun 1990–92, New York Corresp. 1992–93, Ed. 1998–2003; Deputy Business Ed. Business Ed., then Deputy Ed. New York Post 1993–98; Sr Vice-Pres. News Corpn, New York 2003–04; Vice-Pres. Weber Shandwick Worldwide (public relations consultancy) 2004–06; Partner, Brunswick Group LLP 2006–. *Address:* Brunswick Group LLP, 16 Lincoln's Inn Fields, London, WC2A 3ED, England (office). *Telephone:* (20) 7404-5959 (office). *Fax:* (20) 7936-7730 (office). *E-mail:* dyelland@brunswickgroup.com (office). *Website:* www.brunswickgroup.com (office).

YEN MAH, Adeline, MD; Chinese writer; b. 1937; m. Robert A. Mah; two c. *Career:* winner of int. playwriting competition aged 14; studied medicine at univ.; began career as anaesthetist; est. medical practice in Calif., USA; autobiog. Falling Leaves became global bestseller with one million copies sold 1997; gave up career in medicine to write full-time 1997; participant, Cheltenham Festival of Literature 2002. *Publications include:* Falling Leaves 1997, Chinese Cinderella (autobiog. for children), Watching the Tree, A Thousand Pieces of Gold 2002. *Address:* c/o Harper Collins, 77–85 Fulham Palace Road, Hammersmith, London, W6 8JB, England (office).

YERUSHALMI, Yosef Hayim, BA, MA, PhD; American academic and historian; *Salo Wittmayer Baron Professor of Jewish History, Culture and Society, Columbia University;* b. 20 May 1932, New York, NY; m. Ophra Pearly 1959; one s. *Education:* Yeshiva Univ., Jewish Theological Seminary of America, Columbia Univ. *Career:* Instructor, Rutgers Univ. 1963–66; Asst Prof. 1966–70, Prof. of Hebrew and Jewish History 1970–78, Jacob E. Safra Prof. of Jewish History and Sephardic Civilization, and Chair, Dept of Near Eastern Languages and Civilizations 1978–80, Harvard Univ.; Salo Wittmayer Baron Prof. of Jewish History, Culture and Society, and Dir, Center for Israel and Jewish Studies, Columbia Univ. 1980–; corresp. mem. Portuguese Acad. of History, Lisbon 1985. *Publications:* Biblioteca Española-Portugueza-Judaica (ed.), 1971; From Spanish Court to Italian Ghetto: Isaac Cardoso, A Study in Seventeenth-Century Marranism and Jewish Apologetics, 1971; History of the Origin and Establishment of the Inquisition in Portugal (ed.), 1972; Haggadah and History: A Panorama in Facsimile of Five Centuries of the Printed Haggadah from the Collections of Harvard University and the Jewish Theological Seminary of America, 1974; The Lisbon Massacre of 1506 and the Royal Image in the Shebet Yehudah, 1976; Assimilation and Racial Anti-Semitism, 1982; Zakhor: Jewish History and Jewish Memory, 1982; Spinoza on the Survival of the Jews, 1983; Usages de l'oubli, 1988; A Jewish Classic in the Portuguese Language: Samuel Usque's Consolacam as Tribulacoens de Israel, 1989; Freud's Moses: Judaism Terminable and Interminable, 1991; Ein Feld in Anatot: Versuche über Jüdische Geschichte, 1993; Diener von Königen und nicht Diener von Dienern: Einige Aspekte der politischen Geschichte der Juden, 1995; Sefardica: Essais sur l'histoire des Juifs, des Marranes, et des Nouveaux Chrétiens, d'origine Hispano-Portugaise, 1998. Contributions: many articles on Spanish and Portuguese history and history of psychoanalysis, to various publications. *Honours:* Hon. MA (Harvard) 1970, Hon. DHL (Jewish Theological Seminary of America) 1987, (Spertus Inst. of Jewish Studies Chicago) 2002, Hon. LHD (Hebrew Union Coll.) 1996, Hon. PhD (Haifa Israel) 1997, (Ludwig-Maximilians Munich) 1997, (Ecole Pratique des Hautes Etudes Sorbonne-Paris) 2003;Kent Fellow 1963, Fellow, American Acad. for Jewish Research 1972, Fellow, Nat. Endowment for the Humanities 1976, Rockefeller Fellow 1983–84, Fellow, American Acad. of Arts and Sciences 1986, Guggenheim Fellowship 1989–90, Fellow, Carl Friedrich von Siemens Stiftung, Munich 1996–97; Ansley Award, Columbia University Press 1968, Newman Medal, CUNY 1975, Nat. Jewish Book Award 1983, Gold Medal Portuguese Acad. of History, Lisbon 1989, Medal of the Nat. Foundation for Jewish Culture for Achievement in History 1995. *Literary Agent:* George Borchardt, 136 E 57th Street, New York, NY, USA. *Address:* 511 Fayerweather Hall, Columbia University, New York, NY 10027, USA. *E-mail:* yhyl@columbia.edu.

YESSENIN-VOLPIN, Alexander Sergeyevich; Russian mathematician, philosopher and poet; b. 5 Dec. 1924, Leningrad (now St Petersburg); s. of poet Sergey Esenin and Nadiezhda Volpina; m. 1st V. B. Volpina; m. 2nd I. G. Kristi; m. 3rd 1994; one c. *Career:* studied at Faculty of Math., Moscow Univ. 1941–46; arrested for his poetry and committed to mental asylum 1949; in exile Karaganda, Kazakh SSR 1950; amnestied 1953; wrote numerous articles on logic and math. and translated extensively; worked at USSR Acad. of Sciences Inst. of Scientific and Tech. Information 1961–72; dissident activity 1959–; emigrated 1972. *Publications include:* A Free Philosophical Treatise 1959, A Leaf of Spring 1959, 1961, Open Letter to Solzhenitsyn 1970, Report on Committee on Rights of Man 1971, On the Logic of Moral Sciences (in English) 1988; numerous articles in Western and Russian scientific journals (after 1990s). *Address:* 1513 North Shore Road, 2nd Floor, Revere, MA 02151, USA. *Telephone:* (781) 289-1072.

YEVTUSHENKO, Yevgeniy Aleksandrovich; Russian poet and writer; b. 18 July 1933, Zima, Irkutsk Region; m. 1st Bella Akhmadulina 1954 (divorced); m. 2nd Galina Sokol 1962; one s.; m. 3rd Jan Butler 1978; two s.; m. 4th Maria Novikova 1986; two s. *Education:* Moscow Literary Inst. *Career:* geological expeditions with father to Kazakhstan 1948, the Altai 1949–50; literary work 1949–; mem. Editorial Bd of Yunost magazine 1962–69; People's Deputy of the USSR 1989–91; Sec. USSR Writers' Union 1986–91; Vice-Pres. Soviet PEN Cttee; moved to Tulsa, Okla, USA in mid-1990s, now teaches at Univ. of Tulsa; sometime Prof. Pittsburgh Univ. USA, Univ., Autónoma de Santo Domingo, Dominican Rep. *Films directed include:* Kindergarten 1983, Stalin's Funeral 1987; acted in Ascent (film on Tsiolkovsky). *Publications include:* poetry: Scouts of the Future (collected verse) 1952, The Third Snow (lyric verse) 1955, The Highway of Enthusiasts 1956, Zima Junction 1956, The Promise (collected verse) 1960, Moscow Goods Station, The Nihilist, The Apple 1960–61, Do the Russians Want War?, Babi Yar 1961, The Heirs of Stalin, Fears 1962, A Sweep of the Arm 1962, Tenderness 1962, A Precocious Autobiography 1963, The City of Yes and the City of No, Bratskaya Hydro-Electric Power Station 1964, Letter to Yesenin 1965, Italian Tears, A Boat of Communication, Poems Chosen by the Author 1966, Collection of Verses Yelabuga Nail, Cemetery of Whales 1967, That's What Is Happening to Me 1968, It's Snowing White 1969, Kazan University 1971, I am of Siberian Stock 1971, The Singing Domba 1972, Stolen Apples 1972, Under the Skin of the Statue of Liberty (play) 1972, Intimate Lyrics 1973, A Father's Hearing 1975, 1978, From Desire to Desire 1976, Love Poems 1977, People of the Morning 1978, Winter Station 1978, A Dove in Santiago: A Novella in Verse 1978, Heavy Soils 1979, The Face Behind the Face 1979, Ivan the Terrible and Ivan the Fool 1979, Berries (novel) 1981, Ardabiola (short story) 1981, Almost at the End (prose and verse) 1985, A Wind of Tomorrow (essays) 1987, Fatal Half Measures 1989, The Collected Poems 1952–90 1991, Farewell to Red Banner 1992, Twentieth Century Russian Poetry (compiler) 1994, Don't Die Before You're Dead (novel) 1996, My Very, Very... (poetry) 1996; photography: Divided Twins: Alaska and Siberia, Invisible Threads, Shadows and Faces. *Honours:* USSR Cttee for Defence of Peace Award 1965, Order of Red Banner of Labour, Badge of Honour, USSR State Prize 1984. *Address:* Kutuzovski Prospekt 2/1, Apt. 101, 121248 Moscow, Russia. *Telephone:* (495) 243-37-69.

YI, Hoe-song (see Ri Kai-sei)

YING, Diane; Taiwanese journalist and publisher; b. Xian, People's Republic of China. *Education:* Univ. of Iowa, USA. *Career:* emigrated with family from mainland China to Taiwan 1949; fmr reporter, The Philadelphia Inquirer, USA, Taiwan corresp. at various times for Asian Wall Street Journal, New York Times and United Press Int.; Co-founder, Chief Ed. and Publr Commonwealth financial monthly 1981–; teaches journalism at Nat. Cheng-chi Univ.; Commr Nat. Unification Council. *Address:* 4th Floor, 87 Sungkiang Road, Taipei, Taiwan.

YOLEN, Jane, BA, MEd; American writer, poet, editor and storyteller; b. 11 Feb. 1939, New York, NY; m. David Wilber Stemple 1962; two s. one d. *Education:* Smith Coll., Univ. of Massachusetts. *Career:* mem. Authors' Guild, Children's Literature Asscn, MWA, SFWA (pres. 1986–88), Soc. of Children's Book Writers and Illustrators (bd of advisers 1970–). *Publications:* adult books: Briar Rose, Cards of Grief, One-Armed Queen, Sister, Light, Sister Dark, White Jenna, The Books of Great Alta, Among Angels (poems), Dragonfield, Merlin's Booke, The Radiation Sonnets, Storyteller Nesfa, Tales of Wonder, Sister Emily's Lightship and Other Stories, The Whitethorn Wood and Other Magicks (chapbook); children's poetry: Animal Fare, A Sip of Aesop, Best Witches, Bird Watch, Color Me a Rhyme, Dear Mother, Dear Daughter, Dinosaur Dances, Dragon Night, Horizons, How Beastly, O Jerusalem, Least Things, The Originals, Raining Cats & Dogs, Ring of Earth, Sacred Places, Sea Watch, Snow, Snow, Three Bears Holiday Rhyme Book, Three Bears Rhyme Book, Water Music, What Rhymes With Moon, Wild Wings; children's fiction: All in the Woodland Early, All Those Secrets of the World, An Invitation to the Butterfly Ball, Baby Bear's Bedtime Book, The Ballad of the Pirate Queens, Before the Storm, Beneath the Ghost Moon, Bird of Time, Boy Who Had Wings, Child of Faerie, Dove Isabeau, Eeny Meeny Miney Mole, Elfabet, Elsie's Bird, The Emperor & the Kite, Encounter, Fairy Holiday Book, Firebird, The Flying Witch, The Girl in the Golden Bower, The Girl Who Loved the Wind, Good Griselle, Grandad Bill's Song, Grandma's Hurrying Child, Greyling, Gwinellen: The Princess Who Could Not Sleep, Hands, Hannah Dreaming, Harvest Home, Honkers, Hoptoad, How Do Dinosaurs Get Well Soon?, How Do Dinosaurs Say Goodnight?, Isabel's Noel, It All Depends, King Longshanks, The Lady & the Merman, Letter From Phoenix Farm, Letting Swift River Go, Little Angel's Birthday, Little Mouse and Elephant, Little Spotted Fish, Longest Name on the Block, Meet the Monsters, Merlin & the Dragons, Milkweed Days, Minstrel & the Mountain, Miz Berlin Walks, Moonball, Mouse's Birthday, Musicians of Bremen, My Brothers' Flying Machine, My Uncle Emily, No Bath Tonight, Nocturne, Off We Go, Old Dame Counterpane, Owl Moon, Pegasus the Flying Horse, Picnic With Piggins, Piggins, Piggins & the Royal Wedding, Prince of Egypt, Rainbow Rider, Raising Yoder's Barn, Sea King, The Seeing Stick, See This Little Line, The Seventh Mandarin, The Simple Prince, Sky Dogs, Sleeping Beauty, Soft House, The Sultan's Perfect Tree, Tam Lin, Tea With an Old Dragon, Too Old For Naps, Traveler's Rose, Welcome to the Green House, Welcome to the Ice House, Welcome to the Sea of Sand, Welcome to the River of Grass, Where Have the Unicorns Gone?, Wings, The Witch Who Wasn't, Commander Toad in Space, Commander & the Big Black Hole, Commander Toad & the Intergalactic Spy, Commander Toad & the Space Pirates, Commander Toad & the Dis-Asteroid, Commander Toad & the Planet of the Grapes, Commander Toad & the Voyage Home, The Giants' Farm, The Giants Go Camping, Mice on Ice, Sleeping Ugly, Spider Jane, Spider Jane on the Move, Acorn Quest, Adventures of Eeka Mouse, And Twelve Chinese Acrobats, Boy Who Spoke Chimp, Boots & the Seven Leaguers, Disas-Tour, Brothers of the Wind, Hobo Toad & the Motorcycle Gang, Inway Investigators, The Magic Three of Solatia, The Mermaid's Three Wisdoms, Pay the Piper, Robot & Rebecca: The Case of the Code-Carrying Kids, Robot & Rebecca: The Mystery of the Missing Owser, The Seaman, Shirlick Holmes & The Case of the Wandering Wardrobe, Tartan Magic: The Pictish Child, Tartan Magic: The Wizard's Map, Tartan Magic: Bagpiper's Ghost, Transfigured Hart, Uncle Lemon's Spring, Wild Hunt, Wizard of Washington Square, Wizard's Hall, Young Heroes: Atalanta and The Arcadian Beast, Young Heroes: Hippolyta and the Curse of the Amazons, Young Heroes: Odysseus in the Serpent Maze, Young Heroes: Jason and the Gorgon's Blood, Passager, Hobby, Merlin, Armageddon Summer, Children of the Wolf, The Devil's Arithmetic, Dragon's Boy, The Gift of Sarah Barker, Dragon's Blood, Heart's Blood, A Sending of Dragons, Prince in the Heather, Queen's Own Fool, Rogue's Apprentice, Girl in a Cage, The Stone Silenus, Sword of the Rightful King, Trust a City Kid; non-fiction: Fairy Tale Feasts, Friend: The Story of George Fox & the Quakers, The Wolf Girls, Mary Celeste, Roanoke Colony, Salem Witch Trials, Amelia Earhart, House, House, My Brothers' Flying Machine, The Perfect Wizard: Hans Christian Andersen, Pirates in Petticoats, Ring Out: A Book of Bells, Simple Gifts: The Story of the Shakers, Wizard Islands, World on a String: The Story of Kites; other: short story collections, contrib. to anthologies, periodicals. *Honours:* Dr hc (Smith Coll., Northampton, MA), (Baypath Coll., Longmeadow, MA), (Keene State Coll., Keene, NH), (Our Lady of the Elms Coll., Chicopee, MA); Christopher Medals 1979, 2001, Mythopoeic Soc. Awards 1986, 1993, Smith Coll. Medal 1988, Caldecott Medal 1988, Regina Medal 1992, Keene State Coll. Children's Book Award 1995, Nebula Awards 1997, 1998, World Fantasy Award 1988. *Address:* Phoenix Farm, PO Box 27, Hatfield, MA 01038, USA. *E-mail:* janeyolen@aol.com (office). *Website:* www.janeyolen.com.

YOON, Prabda, BFA; Thai writer, artist and journalist; b. 1973, Bangkok. *Education:* Cooper Union School for the Advancement of Science and Art, New York. *Screenplays:* One Night Husband 2003, Last Life in the Universe 2003.

Publications: City of Right Angles (short story) 1999, Probability (short story) 2002, Unstill Pictures (non-fiction). *Honours:* SEA Write Award 2002.

YORK, Alison (see Nicole, Christopher (Robin))

YORK, Andrew (see Nicole, Christopher Robin)

YORKE, Margaret, (Margaret Beda Nicholson); British writer; b. 30 Jan. 1924, Surrey, England; m. Basil Nicholson 1945 (divorced 1957, deceased); one s. one d. *Career:* Asst Librarian St Hilda's Coll., Oxford 1959–60; Library Asst Christ Church, Oxford 1963–65; Chair. CWA 1979–80. *Publications:* Summer Flight 1957, Pray Love Remember 1958, Christopher 1959, Deceiving Mirror 1960, The China Doll 1961, Once a Stranger 1962, The Birthday 1963, Full Circle 1965, No Fury 1967, The Apricot Bed 1968, The Limbo Ladies 1969, Dead in the Morning 1970, Silent Witness 1972, Grave Matters 1973, No Medals for the Major 1974, Mortal Remains 1974, The Small Hours of the Morning 1975, Cast for Death 1976, The Cost of Silence 1977, The Point of Murder 1978, Death on Account 1979, The Scent of Fear 1980, The Hand of Death 1981, Devil's Work 1982, Find Me a Villain 1983, The Smooth Face of Evil 1984, Intimate Kill 1985, Safely to the Grave 1986, Evidence to Destroy 1987, Speak for the Dead 1988, Crime in Question 1989, Admit to Murder 1990, A Small Deceit 1991, Criminal Damage 1992, Dangerous to Know 1993, Almost the Truth 1994, Pieces of Justice 1994, Serious Intent 1995, A Question of Belief 1996, Act of Violence 1997, False Pretences 1998, The Price of Guilt 1999, A Case to Answer 2000, Cause for Concern 2001. *Honours:* Swedish Acad. of Detection Award 1982, CWA Cartier Diamond Dagger 1999. *Literary Agent:* Curtis Brown Ltd, Haymarket House, 28–29 Haymarket, London, SW1Y 4SP, England. *Telephone:* (20) 7393-4400. *Fax:* (20) 7393-4401. *E-mail:* info@curtisbrown.co.uk. *Website:* www.curtisbrown.co.uk.

YORONGAR, Ngarledjy; Chadian politician and editorial director; *Leader, Fédération Action pour le République;* m.; five c. *Education:* schools and univs in Chad, Canada and France. *Career:* civil servant and govt official; also worked for int. orgs including OECD, Science and Educ. Admin. and Financial Office in Zaire, Int. Insurance Inst. (IIA) in Cameroon; Cand. in Presidential Elections 1996, 2001; campaigner against human rights violations and corruption, arrested numerous occasions including 1996 and on winning 2001 elections, imprisoned 1998–99; currently Leader, Fédération Action pour le République (FAR); Fed. Exec. Co-ordinator of Federalist Party; Pres. of Foundation for the Respect of Law and Liberties (FORELLI); Editorial Dir of newspapers La Roue and Le Phare Républicain. *Address:* Fédération Action pour la République, BP 4197, N'Djamena, Chad (office). *Telephone:* 51-45-59. *Fax:* 51-45-59. *E-mail:* yorongar@intnet.td.

YOSHIMASU, Gozo, BA; Japanese poet, essayist and lecturer; b. 22 Feb. 1939, Tokyo; m. Marilia 1973. *Education:* Keio Univ. *Career:* Chief Ed., Sansai Finer Arts magazine 1964–69; Fulbright Visiting Writer, Univ. of Iowa 1970–71; poet-in-residence, Oakland Univ., Rochester, MI 1979–81; Lecturer, Tama Art Univ. 1984–; visiting lecturer at various institutions; many poetry readings around the world; mem. Japan PEN Club, Japan Writers' Asscn. *Publications include:* Shuppatsu (Departure) 1964, A Thousand Steps and More: Selected Poems and Prose, 1964–1984 (in English trans.) 1987; contrib. to anthologies and periodicals. *Honours:* Takami Jun Prize 1971, Rekitei Prize 1979, Hanatsubaki Modern Poetry Prize 1984, Japan Govt Purple Ribbon Award 2003. *Address:* c/o Japan Writers' Association, Shinkan 7F, Bungei-Shunju Building, 3-23, Kioi-Cho, Chiyoda-ku, Tokyo 102-8559, Japan.

YOSHIMOTO, Banana; Japanese writer; b. (Mahoko Yoshimoto), 24 July 1964, Tokyo; d. of Takaaki Yoshimoto. *Education:* Nihon Univ. *Career:* mem. Japan Writers' Asscn. *Publications:* Mūn raito shadou (Moonlight Shadow) 1986, Kicchen (Kitchen) (Izumi Kyoka Literary Prize 1986, Kaien Magazine New Writer Prize 1987) 1987, Tugumi (Goodbye Tsugumi) (Yamamoto Shugoro Literary Prize 1989) 1988, Pineapple Pudding, N.P. 1990, Fruit Basket, Tokage (Lizard) 1993, Amrita (Murasaki-shikibu Prize 1995) 1994, Furin to nanbei (Asleep) (Bunkamura Duet Magot Literary Prize 2000) 2000, Hardboiled/Hard Luck 2005. *Honours:* Minister of Educ. Award for New Artists 1988, Scanno Prize 1993, Fendissime Literary Prize 1996, Maschera d'argento Prize 1999. *E-mail:* admin@yoshimotobanana.com. *Website:* www.yoshimotobanana.com.

YOSHIMURA, Akira; Japanese writer; b. 1 May 1927, Tokyo. *Career:* mem. Japanese Writers' Union (pres.), Int. PEN. *Publications include:* (titles in translation) Shipwrecks 1970, Zero Fighter 1996, Battleship: Musashi: The Making & Sinking of the World's Biggest Battleship 1999, On Parole 2000, One Man's Justice 2001, Storm Rider 2004. *Honours:* Dazai Prize 1966. *Address:* c/o Canongate Books, 14 High Street, Edinburgh, EH1 1TE, Scotland.

YOUNG, Albert (Al) James, BA; American writer and poet; b. 31 May 1939, Ocean Springs, MS; m. Arline June Belch 1963, one s. *Education:* Univ. of Michigan, Stanford Univ., Univ. of California at Berkeley. *Career:* Edward B. Jones Lecturer in Creative Writing, Stanford Univ. 1969–76; writer-in-residence, Univ. of Washington, Seattle 1981–82; founder (with Ishmael Reed) and Ed., Quilt magazine 1981–; Mellon Distinguished Prof. of Humanities, Rice Univ. 1982; Lila Wallace-Readers Digest Fellowship Lecturer 1992–94; Woodrow Wilson Lecturer 1995–99; Rockefeller Distinguished Lecturer, Univ. of Arkansas at Pine Bluff 1995; Lurie Prof. of Creative Writing, San Jose State Univ. 2002; McGee Prof. in Writing, Davidson Coll., Davidson, NC 2003; Coffey Visiting Prof. of Creative Writing, Appalachian State Univ., Boone, NC 2003; bd mem., California Council on Humanities 1987–91, Squaw Valley

Community of Writers 1995–. *Screenplays:* Nigger 1972, Sparkle 1972, A Piece of the Action 1976, Bustin' Loose 1979, Personal Problems (TV pilot, with Ishmael Reed) 1982, The Stars and Their Courses 1983. *Publications:* poetry: Dancing 1969, The Song Turning Back into Itself 1971, Geography of the Near Past 1976, The Blues Don't Change: New and Selected Poems 1982, Heaven: Collected Poems 1956–1990 1992, Straight No Chaser (chapbook) 1994, Conjugal Visits (chapbook) 1996, The Sound of Dreams Remembered: Poems 1990–2000 (Before Columbus Foundation American Book Award, New York 2002) 2001; prose: Snakes (novel) (American Library Asscn Notable Book of the Year 1970) 1970, Yardbird Lives! (ed., with Ishmael Reed) 1972, Who is Angelina? (novel) 1976, Sitting Pretty (novel) 1976, Calafía: The California Poetry (co-ed.) 1979, Ask Me Now (novel) (New York Times Notable Book of the Year 1980) 1980, Bodies and Soul (musical memoir) (American Book Award 1982) 1981, Kinds of Blue (musical memoir) 1984, Things Ain't What They Used to Be (musical memoir) 1987, Seduction by Light (novel) 1988, Mingus/Mingus: Two Memoirs (with Janet Coleman) 1989, Drowning in the Sea of Love (musical memoir) (PEN/USA Award for Best Non-Fiction Book of the Year 1996) 1995, African American Literature: A Brief Introduction and Anthology (ed.) 1996, The Literature of California (vols I and II, co-ed.) 2000, 2002. *Honours:* Wallace Stegner Writing Fellowship 1966, Nat. Arts Council Award for Magazine Editing (for Loveletter) 1969, Joseph Henry Jackson Award for Poetry 1969, CCLM Award for Poetry 1969, NEA Special Projects grant 1970, Guggenheim Fellowship 1974, NEA Writing Fellowship for Fiction 1975, Pushcart Prizes 1976, 1980, Key to the City of Detroit 1982, Detroit Bd of Education Outstanding Achievement Citation 1982, Fulbright Fellowship, Yugoslavia 1984, Ploughshares Rita and Mel Cohen Award for Poetry 1987, San Francisco Arts Commission Outstanding Artist Award 1987, Peninsula Book Club of California Outstanding Writer 1990, PEN/Library of Congress Award for Short Fiction 1991, Univ. of Michigan Martin Luther King Jr/ César Chávez/ Rosa Parks Award 1993. *E-mail:* alyoung@alyoung.org. *Website:* www.alyoung.org.

YOUNG, Bertram Alfred, OBE; British writer; b. 20 Jan. 1912, London, England. *Career:* Asst Ed., 1949–62, Punch; Drama Critic 1962–64, Arts Ed. 1971–77, Financial Times; mem. Critics Circle, Soc. of Authors, Garrick Club. *Publications:* Tooth and Claw 1958, Bechuanaland 1966, Cabinet Pudding 1967, The Mirror Up to Nature 1982, The Rattigan Version 1986; contrib. to numerous professional journals and general magazines. *Address:* 1 Station Street, Cheltenham, Gloucester GL50 3LX, England.

YOUNG, Dean; American poet; b. 1955, Columbia, PA; m. Cornelia Nixon. *Career:* fmr teaching positions include Loyola Univ., St Mary's Coll., Warren Wilson Coll.; currently faculty mem., Iowa Writers' Workshop, Univ. of Iowa. *Publications:* Design with X 1988, Beloved Infidel 1992, Strike Anywhere (Colorado Poetry Prize) 1995, First Course in Turbulence 1999, Skid 2002; contrib. to anthologies, including The Best American Poetry, and to journals, including Ploughshares, The Threepenny Review, Fence, American Letters & Commentary. *Honours:* Fine Arts Work Center, Provincetown fellowship, Stanford Univ. Stegner fellowship, two Nat. Endowment for the Arts fellowships, Guggenheim Fellowship 2002. *Address:* Iowa Writers' Workshop, University of Iowa, 102 Dey House, Iowa City, Iowa 52242-1408, USA (office). *E-mail:* writersworkshop@uiowa.edu. *Website:* www.uiowa.edu/~iww/.

YOUNG, Ian George; British/Canadian poet, writer and editor; b. 5 Jan. 1945, London, England; s. of George Roland Young and Joan Margaret Patricia Young (née Morris); spouse: Wulf. *Career:* Dir Catalyst Press 1969–80, TMW Communications 1990–; Dir Ian Young Books 2001–. *Publications:* poetry: White Garland 1969, Year of the Quiet Sun 1969, Double Exposure 1970, Cool Fire 1970, Lions in the Stream 1971, Some Green Moths 1972, The Male Muse 1973, Invisible Words 1974, Common-or-Garden Gods 1976, The Son of the Male Muse 1983, Sex Magick 1986; fiction: On the Line 1981; non-fiction: The Male Homosexual in Literature 1975, Overlooked and Underrated 1981, Gay Resistance 1985, The AIDS Dissidents 1993, The Stonewall Experiment 1995, The AIDS Cult 1997, The AIDS Dissidents: A Supplement 2001, Autobibliography 2001, The Beginnings of Gay Liberation in Canada 2004, Out in Paperback: A Visual History of Gay Pulps 2007. *Honours:* several Canada Council and Ont. Arts Council Awards. *Address:* 2483 Gerrard Street E, Scarborough, ON M1N 1W7, Canada. *E-mail:* iyoung@arvotek.net (home). *Website:* www.ianyoungbooks.com.

YOUNG OF HORNSEY, Baroness (Life Peer), cr. 2004, of Hornsey in the London Borough of Haringey; **Margaret Omolola (Lola) Young,** OBE, DipArts, BA, PhD, FRSA; British arts and heritage consultant and fmr government official and fmr academic; *Chairwoman Arts Advisory Committee, British Council;* b. 1 June 1951; m. Barrie Birch 1984; one s. *Education:* Parliament Hill School for Girls, London, New Coll. of Speech and Drama, Middlesex Univ. *Career:* began career in arts devt promoting black arts and culture; residential social worker London Borough of Islington 1971–73; professional actor 1976–84; Co-Dir and Training and Devt Man. Haringey Arts Council 1985–89; freelance lecturer and arts consultant 1989–91; Lecturer in Media Studies Polytechnic of West London/Thames Valley Univ. 1990–92; Lecturer, Univ. of Middx, later Sr Principal Lecturer, Prof. of Cultural Studies 1992–2001; Head of Culture, GLA 2002–04; currently works with METAL (arts centre) London; Project Dir Nat. Museum and Archives of Black History and Culture (NMABHC) 1997–2001; Commissioner Royal Commission on Historical Manuscripts 2000–01; Chair. British Council Arts Advisory Cttee 2004–; mem. Bd Dirs Royal Nat. Theatre 2000–03, South

Bank Centre 2002–; numerous radio and television broadcasts. *Publication:* Fear of the Dark: Race, Gender and Sexuality in Cinema 1996; numerous newspaper articles. *Address:* Cultural Brokers, Building D, Unit 208, The Chocolate Factory, London, N22 6XJ, England (office). *Telephone:* (20) 8888-8797 (office). *Fax:* (20) 8888-8797 (office). *E-mail:* culturalbrokers@btconnect .com (office). *Website:* www.culturalbrokers.com (office).

YOUNG, Rose (see Harris, Marion Rose)

YOUNG, Wayland (see Kennet, 2nd Baron)

YOUNG-BRUEHL, Elisabeth, BA, MA, PhD; American academic, psychoanalyst and writer; b. 3 March 1946, Elkton, MD. *Education:* New School for Social Research, New York. *Career:* Prof. of Philosophy, Wesleyan Univ. 1974–91; Prof. of Psychology, Haverford Coll., PA 1991–99; mem. Authors' Guild. *Publications:* Freedom and Karl Jaspers' Philosophy 1981, Hannah Arendt: For Love of the World 1982, Vigil 1983, Anna Freud: A Biography 1988, Mind and the Body Politic 1989, Freud on Women 1990, Creative Characters 1991, Global Cultures 1994, The Anatomy of Prejudices 1996, Subject to Biography 1999, Cherishment 2000, Where Do We Fall When We Fall in Love? 2003, Why Hannah Arondt Matters 2006; contrib. to professional journals. *Honours:* Nat. Endowment for the Humanities Fellowship 1984–85, Guggenheim Fellowship 1986–87. *Address:* 240 E Houston Street, Suite 5D, New York, NY 10002, USA.

YOUNG-EISENDRATH, Polly, BA, MA, MSW, PhD; American psychologist, psychoanalyst and writer; *Clinical Associate Professor in Psychiatry, University of Vermont at Burlington*; b. 4 Feb. 1947, Akron, OH; m. Edward Epstein 1985; two s. one d. *Education:* Ohio Univ., Inst. de Touraine, France, Goddard Coll., Washington Univ., Inter-Regional Soc. of Jungian Analysts. *Career:* Chief Psychologist, Jungian analyst, Pres., Clinical Assocs West, P. C. Radnor 1986–94; independent practice as psychologist and Jungian analyst, Burlington, VT 1994–; Clinical Assoc. Prof. in Psychiatry, Medical Coll., Univ. of Vermont, Burlington 1996–, Clinical Assoc. Research Prof. in Psychology 2005–; Clinical Supervisor in Psychology, Norwich Univ. at Northfield 2005–; numerous lectures worldwide; mem. Int. Asscn for Analytical Psychology, American Psychological Asscn, Independent Soc. for Analytical Psychology (founding mem.). *Publications:* Jung's Self Psychology: A Constructivist Perspective 1991, You're Not What I Expected: Learning to Love the Opposite Sex 1993, The Gifts of Suffering: Finding Insight, Compassion and Renewal 1996, Gender and Desire: Uncursing Pandora 1997, A Cambridge Companion to Jung (co-ed.) 1997, Women and Desire: Beyond Wanting to be Wanted 1999, The Psychology of Mature Spirituality: Integrity, Wisdom, Transcendence 2000, Awakening and Insight: Zen Buddhism and Psychotherapy 2002, Subject to Change: Jung, Gender and Subjectivity in Psychoanalysis 2004, We Just Want You to Be Happy: Where American Parenting Went Wrong 2007; contrib. to professional journals. *Honours:* various fellowships, assistantships and awards. *Address:* 195 Calais Road, Worcester, VT 05682, USA (office). *Telephone:* (802) 223-6223 (office). *E-mail:* pollye@adelphia.net (office).

YOUSSEF, Samir al-; Palestinian writer, essayist and reviewer; b. 1965, Lebanon. *Career:* regular contrib. to major Arab periodicals and London-based Arabic news services. *Publications include:* Domestic Affairs (short stories) 1994, Gaza Blues (short stories, with Etgar Keret) 2004, The Illusion of Return (novel) 2007. *Address:* c/o Halban Publishers Ltd, 22 Golden Square, London, W1F 9JW, England.

YSÁS SOLANES, Pere, PhD; Spanish historian; *Faculty Professor, Autonomous University of Barcelona*; b. 1955, Rubi, Barcelona. *Education:* Universidad de Barcelona. *Career:* Prof., Dept of Modern and Contemporary History, Faculty of Philosophy and Literature, Autonomous Univ. of Barcelona 1986–, Dir Faculty of Political Science and Sociology 1986–98; mem. Grup de Recerca sobre l'Época Franquista, Arxiu Històric de la CONC (cttee mem.), Biografías Obreras investigative project (cttee mem.), Centre d'Estudis sobre les Epoques Franguista i Democratica (cttee mem.). *Publications:* L'oposició antifeixista a Catalunya 1939–1950 (with Carmen Molinero) 1981, 'Patria, Justicia y Pan'. Nivell de vida i condicions de treball a Catalunya 1939–1951 (with Carmen Molinero) 1985, Els industrials catalans durant el franquisme (with Carmen Molinero) 1991, El règim franquista. Feixisme, modernització i consens (with Carmen Molinero) 1992, Productores disciplinados y minorías subversivas. Clase obrera y conflictividad laboral en la España franquista (with Carmen Molinero) 1998, Catalunya durant el franquisme (with Carmen Molinero) 1999; contrib. chapters to numerous publications, articles to journals and newspapers, including Arraona, L'Avenç Revista d'Història, Avui, Ayer, Balma: Didàctica de les Ciencies Socials, Geografia i Historia, Cuadernos de Relaciones Laborales, Historia Contemporánea, Historia Social, Nous Horitzons, El País, Realitat, Revista de Historia Económica, Taula de Canvi, La Vanguardia, Veus Alternatives, Historia Politica de España 1939–2000 (with Carmen Molinero and Jose M. Marin) 2001, Disidencia y Subversión: La Lucha del Regimen Franquista por su Supervivencia 1960–75 2004. *Address:* Departamento de Historia Moderna y Contemporánea, Universitat Autònoma de Barcelona, Campus Universitari, 08193 Bellaterra, Barcelona (office); Calle Le Mola 3, 08912 Sant Quirze del Vallei, Barcelona, Spain (home). *Telephone:* (93) 5812318 (office). *Fax:* (93) 5812001 (office). *E-mail:* Pere.Ysas@uab.es (office).

YSTAD, Vigdis, DPhil; Norwegian academic; *Professor of Scandinavian Literature, University of Oslo*; b. 13 Jan. 1942, Verdal; d. of Ottar Ystad and Guri Todal; m. 1st Asbjørn Liland 1962; m. 2nd Daniel Haakonsen 1971; one s. one d. *Education:* Univs of Trondheim and Oslo. *Career:* lecturer, Univ. of Oslo 1974, Prof. of Scandinavian Literature 1979–, mem. Univ. Bd 1990–92; Chair. Council for Research in the Humanities 1985; Chair. Bd Centre for Advanced Study, Norwegian Acad. of Science and Letters 1992–93; Vice-Chair. Nat. Acad. of Dramatic Art 1993–96; mem. Norwegian Research Council 1979–85, Norwegian Govt Research Cttee 1982–84; mem. Norwegian Acad. of Science and Letters, Norwegian Acad. for Language and Literature, Royal Swedish Acad. of Letters, History and Antiquities 2004, Kungliga Vetenskaps-Societeten 2004; mem. Bd Nat. Acad. of Art 2000–02, Oslo Acad. of Art 2000–02, Nansenskolen, Lillehammer 2001–; Gen. Ed. Henrik Ibsens skrifter 1998–. *Publications:* Kristofer Uppdals Lyrikk 1978, Henrik Ibsens Dikt 1991, Sigrid Undsel: Et kvinneliv-'livets endeløse gåde' 1993, Ibsens dikt og drama 1996, Contemporary Approaches to Ibsen, Ibsen studies (ed.). *Address:* Centre for Ibsen Studies, Box 1116, Blindern, 0316 Oslo (office); Thomas Heftyes gt. 56b, 0267 Oslo, Norway (home). *Telephone:* 22-85-91-65 (office); 22-55-94-66 (home). *Fax:* 22-85-91-69 (office). *E-mail:* a.v.ystad@ibsen .uio.no (office).

YU, Guangzhong; Taiwanese academic, poet, critic, translator and essayist; b. 9 Sept. 1928, Nanjing City, Jiangsu Prov.; m. Wo Chun Fan 1956; four d. *Education:* Iowa Univ., USA. *Career:* Chief Ed. of Blue Stars and Modern Literature; Prof., Taiwan Normal Univ., Chinese Univ. of Hong Kong; Kuang Hua Chair. Prof. of English, Nat. Sun Yat-sen Univ. 1998–; Pres. Taipei Chinese Centre, PEN Int. 1990–99. *Publications:* Elegy of Boatman, Stalactite, Blue Plume, Sirius, White Jade Bitter Gourd, A Tug of War with Eternity, Dream and Geography, Selected Poetry of Yu Guangzhong Vols I and II, The Child of Dogwood–A Life of Yu Guangzhong 1999, The Old Man and the Sea (trans.), The Importance of being Earnest (trans.), Lust for Life (trans.) Bartleby the Scrivener (trans.), Modern English and American Poetry (trans.). *Honours:* Hon. Fellow Hong Kong Trans. Soc. 1991; Australian Cultural Award 1972; Best Books of the Year 1994, 1996, 1998, 2000 (Taiwan), 1998 (Hong Kong); Nat. Poetry Prize, Wu San-Lian Prose Prize and six others. *Address:* Foreign Literature Institute, Sun Yat-sen University, 135 Xingang Road, Guanzhou 510275, Guangdong Province, People's Republic of China. *Telephone:* (7) 5564908 (home); (20) 84112828. *Fax:* (20) 84039173. *E-mail:* adpo@zsu.edu.cn (office). *Website:* www.zsu.edu .cn (office).

YU, Hua, MA; Chinese writer; b. 1960, Gaotang, Shandong Prov. *Education:* Beijing Normal Univ. *Career:* worked as a dentist for five years; writer 1983–. *Publications:* To Live, Chronicle of a Blood Merchant, Shouting in the Drizzle, Events of the World Are Like Smoke, One Kind of Reality, Leaving Home for a Long Journey at Eighteen, An Incident, Mistake at Riverside. *Honours:* James Joyce Foundation Award 2002. *Address:* c/o National Human Resources Exchange Centre, Beijing, People's Republic of China (office).

YŪ, Miri; South Korean/Japanese writer, playwright and essayist; b. 22 June 1968, Kanagawa, Japan; one s. *Career:* fmr actress and Asst Dir Tokyo Kid Brothers theatre group; co-founder Seishun Gogetsu To (The May Youth Group) theatre group 1986–. *Plays:* Sakana no matsur (play, trans. as Fish Festival) 1993, Himawari no hitsugi (play, trans. as The Sunflowers' Coffin) 1993, Green Bench (play) 1993,. *Publications:* Ishi ni oyogu sakana (novel, trans. as Fish Swimming in Stone) 1994, Kazoku no hyōhon (essays, trans. as Family Disunity) 1995, Yū Miri no jisatsu (essays, trans. as Yū Miri's 'Suicide') 1995, Mado no aru shoten kara (essays, trans. as From the Bookshop with a Window) 1996, Full House (novel) 1996, Kazoku Shinema (novel, trans. as Family Cinema) (Akutegawa Prize) 1997, Mizube no yurikago 1997, Kaisetsu 1997, Kamen no kuni 1998, Gold Rush (novel) 1998, Inochi (memoir) 2000, Tamashii 2001, Ikiru 2001. *Honours:* Kishida Kunio Drama Prize, Izumi Kyoka Prize, Noma Bungei Newcomer Literature Prize. *Website:* www.yu -miri.com.

YU, Nick; Chinese playwright; b. 1971, Anhui Prov. *Career:* theatrical marketing man.; also part-time playwright; versions of his plays have been performed in Singapore, Japan and USA. *Plays:* The Mental Asylum is Next Door to Heaven, Last Winter 2000, www.com 2001. *Address:* c/o Shanghai People's Art Theatre, 284 Anfu Lu, Shanghai, People's Republic of China (office).

YU, Youxian; Chinese publisher; *Commissioner, National Copyright Administration of China*; b. 1937, Penglai Co., Shandong. *Career:* Vice-Gov. of Henan Prov. 1993–2000; Commr of State Admin of Press and Publs, 1999–; Commr, Nat. Copyright Admin of China 1999–; Chair. Asscn of Chinese Publrs. *Address:* c/o Press and Publications Administration, State Council, Beijing, People's Republic of China (office).

YUDKIN, Leon Israel, BA, MA, DLit; British academic and writer; b. 8 Sept. 1939, England; m. Meirah Goss 1967. *Education:* Univ. of London. *Career:* Asst Lecturer, Lecturer, Univ. of Manchester 1966–; Lecturer, Univ. Coll. London 1996; Visiting Prof., Univ. of Paris VIII 2000; Visiting Prof., Charles Univ., Prague, Univ. of N Carolina, USA, Univ. of Paris 8 2004–. *Publications:* Isaac Lamdan: A Study in Twentieth-Century Hebrew Poetry 1971, Meetings with the Angel (co-ed.) 1973, Escape into Siege 1974, U. Z. Greenberg: On the Anvil of Hebrew Poetry 1980, Jewish Writing and Identity in the Twentieth Century 1982, 1948 and After: Aspects of Israeli Fiction 1984, Modern Hebrew Literature in English Translation (ed.) 1986, Agnon: Texts and Contexts in English Translation (ed.) 1988, Else Lasker-Schüler: A Study in German-Jewish Literature 1990, Beyond Sequence: Current Israeli Fiction and its

Context 1992, The Israeli Writer and the Holocaust (ed.) 1993, The Other in Israeli Literature (ed.) 1993, A Home Within: Varities of Jewish Expression in Modern Fiction 1996, Public Crisis and Literary Response: Modern Jewish Literature 2001, Literature in the Wake of the Holocaust 2003, Israel: A Vision of a State and its Literature 2006; contrib. to various publications. *Address:* c/o Department of Hebrew Studies, University College London, Gower Street, London, WC1E 4BT, England (office). *E-mail:* l.yudkin@ucl.ac.uk.

YUSUF, Nova Riyanti; Indonesian novelist; b. 27 Nov. 1977. *Publications:* Mahadewa Mahadewi (trans. as God, Goddess) 2003. *Address:* c/o Pustaka Utma, Jalan Utan Kayu 68EFG, Utan Kayu Utara, Jakarta 13120, Indonesia.

Z

ZABALETA, Marta Raquel, (Martita Criolla), BSc, MA, DPhil; British/Argentine economist, researcher, poet and writer; *Honorary Senior Visiting Lecturer in Latin American Studies, Middlesex University*; b. 26 June 1937, Alcorta, Santa Fe, Argentina; d. of the late Roque Zabaleta and Catalina Gerlo de Zabaleta; one s. one d. *Education:* Univ. del Litoral (Argentina), ESCOLATINA, Univ. de Chile and Inst. of Development Studies, Univ. of Sussex. *Career:* Jr Fellow, CELADE UN, Chile 1965–66, ICIRA (FAO), Chile 1966–67; Assoc. Lecturer, then Prof., Univ. of Concepción, Chile 1968–73, Deputy Head, Dept of Econs 1973; expelled from Chile 1973; Researcher, Consejo Fed. de Inversiones, CFI Buenos Aires 1975; expelled from Argentina 1976; Lecturer, Univ. of Middx (fmrly Middx Polytechnic) 1989–92, Sr Lecturer in Spanish and Latin American Studies, Culture and Gender, and Philosophy, Psychology and Sociology in Spanish 1992–2002, currently Hon. Visiting Sr Lecturer in Latin American Studies; Adviser, Change International UK 1980–2005; Co-ordinator Working Group on Gender and Women Studies, CEISAL 2001– (mem. int. jury of CEISAL annual prize 2002–06); Founder and Co-ordinator Int. Network 'Women and Words in the World' 1995–; mem. Exec. Cttee Latin American Women Rights' Service, UK 2005–; organized several int. confs, simposia and round tables for Univ. of Middx, ICA and SLAS; corresp., FM Radio del Mar (Argentina) in London. *Television:* featured in video and film documentaries, including Daughters of de Beauvoir (BBC) 1989. *Publications:* Reclaim the Earth: Women Speak Out for Life on Earth (contrib.) 1983, Daughters of de Beauvoir (contrib.) 1989, Women in Argentina: Realities, Myths and Dreams 1810–1992 1993, An Analysis of the Speeches of Eva Perón 1994, Feminine Stereotypes and Roles in Theory and Practice in Argentina Before and After the First Lady Eva Perón 2000, The Body Matters (ed.) 2002; several book chapters and conf. papers, in English, Spanish, Portuguese and Polish. *Honours:* Govt of Argentina Presidential Decree of Recognition for work as Social Scientist 1973; grants from several insts., including British Acad., British Council, German Acad., Soc. for the Protection of Science and Learning, Inst. of Development Studies, and others. *Address:* University of Middlesex, Trent Park, London, England (office). *Telephone:* (20) 8411-5000 (office). *Fax:* (20) 8411-6878 (office). *E-mail:* m.zabaleta@mdx.ac.uk (office). *Website:* www.martazabaleta.com.

ZABUZHKO, Oksana, PhD; Ukrainian novelist and poet; b. 1961, Lutsk; m. Rostyslav Luzhetsky. *Education:* Taras Shevchenko Univ. of Kiev. *Career:* fmr Assoc., Inst. of Philosophy, Nat. Acad. of Arts and Sciences, Kiev; Writer-in-Residence, Pennsylvania State Univ., USA 1992; Fulbright Scholar, Harvard Univ. and Univ. of Pittsburgh, USA 1994. *Publications:* poetry: Travnevyj Inij (translatedas May Hoarfrost) 1985, Dyrygent Ostannyoji Svichky (translated as The Conductor of the Last Candle) 1990, Avtostop (translated as Hitchhiking) 1994, A Kingdom of Fallen Statues (poems and essays in trans.) 1996, Novyj Zakon Arkhimeda. Vybrani Virshi 1980–1998 (New Archimedes' Rule. Selected Poems 1980–1998) 2000, Druha Sproba (translated as The Second Try) 2005; fiction: Polyovi Doslidzhennia z Ukrajins'koho Seksu (novel, translated as Field Work in Ukrainian Sex) 1996, Kazka pro Kalynovu Sopilku (novella, translated as The Reedpipe Tale) 2000, Sestro, Sestro (short stories, translated as Sister, Sister) 2003; non-fiction: Shevchenkiv Mif Ukrajiny: Sproba Filosofs'koho Analizu (criticism, translated as Shevchenko's Myth of Ukraine: Toward a Philosophical Verification) 1997, Khroniky vid Fortinbrasa (translated as Chronicles of Fortinbras: the Selected Essays of the 1990s) 1999, Reportazh z 2000-ho Roku (essays, translated as News Report from the Year 2000) 2001, Let My People Go: 15 Textiv pro Ukrains'ku Revoliciju (Let My People Go: 15 Texts on Ukrainian Revolution) 2005, Notre Dame d'Ukraine: Ukrainka V Konflikti Mifolohij (criticism, translated as Notre Dame d'Ukraine: Ukrainka in the Clash of Mythologies) 2007; trans in fifteen countries; contrib. to Agni, Glas, Harvard Review, International Quarterly, Massachusetts Review, Mr Cogito, Nimrod, Partisan Review, Ploughshares, Poetry Miscellany, Slavic and East European Journal, Ukrainian Quarterly. *Honours:* Global Commitment Foundation Poetry Prize 1997, McArthur Grant 2002, The Most Important Ukrainian Book of the 15 Years of Independence Award 2006, Newsweek Ukraine's Top 100 Most Influential Ukrainians 2006. *Address:* Galina Dursthoff Literarische Agentur, Marsiliusstr. 70, 50937 Cologne, Germany. *Telephone:* (221) 444254. *Fax:* (221) 46 00053. *E-mail:* galina@dursthoff.de; gdursthoff@hotmail.com. *Website:* www.zabuzhko.com.

ZACHARIUS, Walter, BA; American publisher; *Chairman and CEO, Kensington Publishing Corporation*; b. 16 Oct. 1923, New York; s. of Abraham Zacharius and Sara Cohen; m. Alice Riesenberg 1948; one s. one d. *Education:* Coll. of City of New York School of Business, New York Univ., New School of Social Research, Empire State Univ. *Career:* served US Army 1942–45; circulation depts McFadden Publishing Inc. 1947–, Popular Library Inc. 1948–49, American Mercury Inc. 1949–51; Circulation Dir Ace News Co., New York 1951–61; Pres. Magnum Royal Publs Inc., New York 1961–; Pres., Chair. of Bd Magnum Communications, New York 1961; Pres. Lancer Books Inc., New York 1961–75, Walter Zacharius Assoc. 1964–; f. Kensington Publishing Corpn 1974; Pres. United Cerebral Palsy of Queens 1986–89; Chair. Bd Kensington Publishing Corpn Inc. 1976–. *Honours:* World War II Medal, American Service Medal; European-African-Middle Eastern Service Medal; Public Relations Award-United Cerebral Palsy of Queens 1970, Award of Honor, UJA Fed. Campaign 1987, UJA Fed.'s Distinguished Service Award

1992, Gallatin Div. of New York City Certificate of Distinction 1993. *Address:* Kensington Publishing Corporation, 850 3rd Avenue, New York, NY 10022 (office); 400 East 56th Street, New York, NY 10022, USA (home). *Telephone:* (877) 422-3665 (office). *E-mail:* wzacharius@kensingtonbooks.com (office). *Website:* www.kensingtonbooks.com.

ZAGAJEWSKI, Adam, BA, MA; Polish writer, poet and academic; *Associate Professor of English, Creative Writing Program, University of Houston*; b. 21 June 1945, Lvov; s. of Tadeusz Zagajewski and Ludwika Zagajewska; m. Maria Zagajewska. *Education:* Jagiellonian Univ., Kraków. *Career:* first published poetry and essays in literary reviews in 1960s; became well known as leading poet of "Generation of 1968"; first collection of poems 1972; lived in France and joined staff of Zeszyty Literackie 1982–2002; Assoc. Prof. of English, Creative Writing Program, Univ. of Houston, USA 1988–; mem. Polish Writers' Asscn, PEN Club; co-editor Zeszyty Literackie. *Publications include:* collections of poetry: Komunikat (Communique) 1972, (Sklepy miesne) Meat Shops 1975, Letter: An Ode to Multiplicity 1983, Jechac do Lwowa (Travelling to Lvov) 1985, Plotno (The Canvas) 1990, Ziemia ognista (The Fiery Land) 1994, Pragnienie (Desire) 2000, Powrót (Without End) 2003; novels: Cieplo, zimno (Warm and Cold) 1975, Cienka kreska (The Thin Line) 1983, Absolute Pitch (in German); short stories: Two Cities 1991; essays: Swiat nie przedstawiony (The Unpresented World, with Julian Kornhauser) 1974, Drugi oddech (Second Wind) 1978, Solidarnosc i samotnosc (Solidarity and Solitude) 1986, W cudzym pieknie (In the Beauty of Others) 1998, Obrona żarliwości (In Defence of Fervour) 2002. *Honours:* Koscielscy Foundation Award 1975, Andrzej Kijowski Award 1987, Alfred Jurzykowski Foundation Award 1989, Guggenheim Fellowship 1992, Int. Vilenica Prize (Slovenia) 1996, Tomas Transtromer Prize (Sweden) 2000. *Address:* University of Houston, Department of English, 234B, Houston, TX 77204-3012, USA (office). *Telephone:* (713) 743-3014 (office). *Fax:* (713) 743-3215 (office). *Website:* www.class.uh.edu/English (office).

ZAHIROVIĆ, Ajša Džemila; Bosnia and Herzegovina writer, poet and lawyer; b. 21 March 1948, Sarajevo; d. of Ago Zahirović and Džemila Haćam; one d. *Education:* Faculty of Law, Sarajevo. *Career:* Adviser and Chef de Cabinet Cen. Cttee of Communist Party, Bosnia and Herzegovina 1970–78; Cultural Adviser and Chef de Cabinet Presidency of Bosnia and Herzegovina 1978–84; writer and poet 1984–; has published 15 books of poetry, works included in seven anthologies of women's poetry and several other anthologies; Co-Ed. Skylark Int. journal of poetry, India; mem. World Acad. of Arts and Culture, World Congress of Poets, Int. Women's Writing Guild, USA, Int. Poets' Acad., Madras (now Chennai), India, World Poetry Research Inst. Council of Dirs (Repub. of Korea), Poet–India Editorial Bd, Writers' Asscn of Bosnia and Herzegovina; many other literary orgs. *Publications include:* The Porch 1981, By The White Eye 1983, Terra Mare Amore 1983, Sapno Ki Chaya Me 1985, Vedeshi Mallige 1985, Another Moment 1987, At the Verge of the Road 1987, The Bridge Has Eyes 1988, Ak Aur Bazghashat 1989, Under the Crown (Australia Day Medallion 1991) 1991, Selected Poems 1998, From Sarajevo to Ekashila 1998, Selected Poems 2002, Haiku From Sarajevo 2002; ed. of anthologies From Verse to Poem 1985, Special Yugoslav Women's Poetry Number of Skylark 1986, Special Bosnia and Herzegovina Poetry Number of Skylark 1987, Ombrela 1987, Pan Y Sueño – Anthologia de la Poesia Feminina Contemporanea Yugoslava 1989, Malaysia: Anthology of Contemporary Poetry 1990, The Poetic Voices of Women from all Meridians 1991, 1992; poems translated into languages including Italian, Hindi, English, Arabic, Urdu, Turkish, German, Greek, Spanish, Japanese, Punjabi, Bengali, French, Portuguese, Chinese, Malaysian, Thai, Korean, Gujrati, Telugu, Kashmiri, Tamil etc. *Honours:* Hon. mem. New Zealand PEN 1994; Hon. LittD (World Acad. of Arts and Culture) 1988; Int. Eminent Poet, Int. Poets' Acad., Madras, Robert Frost Award, Adult Literary Arts, San Mateo, USA 1990, World Award Gold Crown, World Poetry Research Inst. 1990, Silver Crown, Accad. Internazzionale di Pontzen, Italy 1991, Int. Prize for Poetry, Int. Soc. of Greek Writers 1994, Radio Corridor Golden Plate of Humanity, Sarajevo 1996, Poetry Day Australia Golden Medallion Dove in Peace 1996, Int. Poets' Acad. Poet of the Millennium, India –2000, World Acad. of Arts and Culture XX World Congress of Poets Prize, Thessaloniki, Greece 2000, World Award Mikis Theodorakis, Greece 2004, World Award Int. Asscn of Greek Writers and Int. Acad. of Literature and Arts Athens Goddess 2004, Int. Peace Prize 2005, United Cultural Convention 2005, and other awards. *Address:* Str. Kranjčevićeva 41/3, 71000 Sarajevo, Bosnia and Herzegovina (home). *Telephone:* (33) 667578 (home). *Fax:* (33) 667578 (home).

ZAHNISER, Edward (Ed) DeFrance, BA; American writer, poet and editor; *Editor and Senior Writer, US National Park Service Media Development Group*; b. 11 Dec. 1945, Washington, DC; m. Ruth Christine Hope Detwel 1968; two s. *Education:* Greenville Coll., IL, Defence Information School. *Career:* Poetry Ed., The Living Wilderness Magazine 1972–75; Founding Ed., Some of Us Press, Washington, DC 1972–75; Arts Ed., Good News Paper 1981–; Ed., Arts and Kulchur 1989–91; Assoc. Poetry Ed., Antietam Review 1992–; Ed. and Sr Writer, US Nat. Parks Service Media Devt Group 1995–; Woodrow Wilson Fellow 1967. *Publications:* The Ultimate Double Play (poems) 1974, I Live in a Small Town (with Justin Duewel-Zahniser) 1984, The Way to Heron Mountain (poems) 1986, Sheenjek and Denali (poems)

1990, Jonathan Edwards (artist book) 1991, Howard Zahniser: Where Wilderness Preservation Began: Adirondack Wilderness Writings (ed.) 1992, A Calendar of Worship and Other Poems 1995, Mall-Hopping with the Great I Am (poems) 2006; contrib. to anthologies and periodicals. *Honours:* first and second prize in Poetry West Virginia Writers' Annual Competitions 1989, 1991, 1992, 2004, second prize in Essay 1995. *Address:* c/o Atlantis Rising, PO Box 955, Shepherdstown, WV 25443-0955, USA. *Telephone:* (304) 876-2442.

ZAHRA, Trevor; Maltese writer and illustrator; b. 16 Dec. 1947, Zejtun; m. Stella Zahra (deceased); one s. one d. *Education:* Teachers' Coll. of Education. *Career:* mem. Maltese Acad. of Writers, Maltese Literary Soc. (sec. 1970–74). *Publications include:* Il-Pulena tad-Deheb 1971, Eden 1972, Il-Ghar tax-Xelter 1972, Dawra Durella 1972, Dwal fil-Fortizza 1973, Is-Surmast 1973, Il-Praspar ta' Kuncett u Marinton 1974, Il-Kaxxa taz-Ziju 1974, Taht il-Weraq tal-Palm 1974, Praspar Ohra ta' Kuncett u Marinton 1975, Hdejn in-Nixxiegha 1975, Grajjiet in-Nannu Cens 1975, Qamar Ahdar 1976, Villa Siko-Sao 1977, Hmistax-il Numru 1977, Meta Jaqa' c-Cpar 1978, Il-Miraklu tal-Gizirana 1981, It-Tmien Kontinent 1981, Trid Kukkarda Hamra f'GieH il-Biza'? 1982, Il-Praspar Kollha ta' Kuncett u Marinton 1983, Darba Kien Hemm Sultan 1984, LogHob Merill 1985, Qrempucu f'Belt il-Gobon 1985, Il-Ktieb tal-Fenek l-Ahmar 1986, Holm tal-Milied? 1987, Kliem ix-XiH 1988, Rigal tal-Milied 1989, Stella, Jien u HU 1990, Tlieta f'WieHed 1994, Is-Surmast 1994, Fuklar Qadim u Bnadar Imcarrta 1995, Is-Seba' TronGiet Mewwija 1995, Hanut tal-Helu 1995, Lubien 1996, TaHt Sema Kwiekeb 1997, Naqra Storja ZgHra 1997, Sib it-Tezor 1999, PassiGGata 1999, Mar id-Dawl 1999, Borma Minestra 1999, Koronata Traskurata 2000, Provenz 2000, Zvelajrin 2001, Mincott Hajt Iswed 2001, X'Tixtiequ JagHmel il-Fenek? 2002, Din l-Art u Kull ma Fiha 2002, Il-Kotba gHat-Tfal 2002, Kieku Kieku 2005, Sfidi 2005, Kemm Naf InpinGi 2005, Ojnk Ojnk 2005, Krispella 2005; numerous translations, workbooks. *Honours:* Medal for Services to the Republic, Malta 2004; first prize Book Club, Malta 1974, co-winner Rothmas Award 1975, Nat. Literary Award (seven times). *Address:* 23 Qrempuc Street, Marsaskala ZBR-11, Malta. *Telephone:* (621) 632944 (home). *E-mail:* trevor@orbit.net.mt (office); tezah@waldonet.net.mt (home). *Website:* www.trevorzahra.com.

ZAKARIA, Fareed, BA, PhD; American editor, academic and writer; *Editor, Newsweek International;* b. India; m.; one s. one d. *Education:* Yale and Harvard Univs. *Career:* Lecturer on Int. Politics and Econs, Harvard Univ., also Head of Project on the Changing Security Environment; Adjunct Prof., Columbia Univ., New York, Case Western Reserve Univ., Cleveland, OH; Man. Ed. Foreign Affairs journal 1992–2000; Ed. Newsweek Int. 2000–; columnist, Newsweek (USA), Newsweek Int., The Washington Post 2001–; Host and Man. Ed. Foreign Exchange with Fareed Zakaria (PBS Series); speaker at World Econ. Forum, Davos, Switzerland and various univs; political commentator, ABC News; wine columnist for Slate (webzine); mem. Bd Trilateral Comm., IISS, Shakespeare and Co., The Century Asscn. *Publications include:* From Wealth to Power: The Unusual Origins of America's World Role, The American Encounter: The United States and the Making of the Modern World (co-ed.), The Future of Freedom 2003; contrib. to publs including The New York Times, The New Yorker and The Wall Street Journal. *Honours:* Overseas Press Club Award, Deadline Club Award, Edwin Hood Award. *Address:* Newsweek International, Newsweek Building, 251 West 57th Street, New York, NY 10019-1894, USA (office). *E-mail:* editors@newsweek.com (office). *Website:* www.newsweek-int.com (office); www.fareedzakaria.com.

ZAKHAROV, Vladimir Evgenyevich, PhD; Russian physicist, mathematician and poet; *Scientific Supervisor, Laboratory of Nonlinear Wave Processes, Shirshov Institute of Oceanology;* b. 1 Aug. 1939, Kazan; m. Svetlana; three c. *Education:* Novosibirsk State Univ. *Career:* jr then sr researcher Inst. of Nuclear Physics, Siberian branch USSR (now Russian) Acad. of Sciences (RAN) 1966–73; joined Landau Inst. of Theoretical Physics, RAN 1974, Dir 1992–2003; scientific supervisor lab. of nonlinear wave processes, Shirshov Inst. of Oceanology, RAN 1985–; Chair. Scientific Council on Nonlinear Dynamics, RAN 1988–; Dir Int. Centre on Nonlinear Studies 1990–; Prof. of Math., Univ. of Arizona, Tucson, USA 1991–; Ed.-in-Chief Journal of Nonlinear Science 1991–; mem. USSR Acad. of Sciences (corresp. mem. 1984–91, full mem. 1991–). *Publications:* over 220 scientific works, including Theory of Solitons: The Method of the Inverse Scattering 1980, Kolmogorov Spectra of Wave Turbulence 1992; poetry: The Chorus in the Winter 1991, The Southern Autumn 1992; contrib. to numerous periodicals. *Honours:* Order of Honour 1989, Rank IV Order for Service to the Fatherland; USSR State Prize 1987, Russian Fed. State Prize 1993, Dirac Medal 2003. *Address:* c/o Shirshov Institute of Oceanology, Russian Academy of Sciences, Nakhimovsky prosp. 36, 117218 Moscow (office); ul. Profsoyuznaya 43/2, apt 479, 117420 Moscow, Russia (home). *Telephone:* (095) 1248538 (office); (095) 3315137 (home). *E-mail:* zakharov@itp.ac.ru (office).

ZALBEN, Jane Breskin, BA; American writer, artist and teacher; b. 21 April 1950, New York, NY; m. Steven Zalben 1969; two s. *Education:* Queens Coll., CUNY, Pratt Graphics Centre. *Career:* mem. Soc. of Children's Book Writers, Authors' Guild, PEN. *Publications:* Cecilia's Older Brother 1973, Lyle and Humus 1974, Basil and Hillary 1975, Penny and the Captain 1977, Norton's Nightime 1979, Will You Count the Stars Without Me 1979, All in the Woodland Early: An ABC by Jane Yolen 1979, Oliver and Alison's Week 1980, Oh Simple! 1981, Porcupine's Christmas Blues 1982, Maybe It Will Rain Tomorrow 1982, Here's Looking at You, Kid 1987, Water from the Moon 1987,

Beni's First Chanukah 1988, Earth to Andrew O. Blechman 1989, Happy Passover, Rosie 1989, Leo and Blossom's Sukkah 1990, Goldie's Purim 1991, The Fortune Teller in 5B 1991, Beni's Little Library 1991, Buster Gets Braces 1992, Inner Chimes: Poems on Poetry 1992, Happy New Year, Beni 1993, Papa's Latkes 1994, Beni's First Chanukah 1994, Miss Violet's Shining Day 1995, Pearl Plants a Tree 1995, Beni's Family Cookbook 1996, Unfinished Dreams 1996, Papa's Latkes 1996, Pearl's Marigolds for Grandpa 1997, Beni's First Wedding 1998, Beni's Family Teasury 1998, Pearl's Eight Days of Chanukah 1998, To Every Season: A Family Cookbook 1999, Don't Go 2001, The Magic Menorah: A Modern Chanukah Tale 2001, Pearl's Passover 2002, Let There Be Light: Poems for Repairing the World 2002, Saturday Night at the Beastro (with Steven Zalben) 2004, Baby Babka, the Gorgeous Genius 2004, Hey, Mama Goose 2005, Paths to Peace: People who Changed the World 2006, Leap 2007; contrib. to journals and magazines. *Honours:* Sydney Taylor Honour Award 1989, and Silver Medal 2003, New York Public Library Best Books Citation 1991, Int. Reading Assn Citation 1993, Parents' Choice Award 1995, ALA Notable Award 1996, CBC/Notable Social Studies Books 2003. *Address:* 70 South Road, Sands Point, NY 11050, USA. *E-mail:* janezalben@hotmail.com. *Website:* www.janebreskinzalben.com.

ZAMOYSKI, Adam, BA, MA, FSA, FRSA, FRSL; British/Polish historian and writer; b. 11 Jan. 1949, New York, NY, USA; s. of Count Stefan Zamoyski and Princess Elizabeth Czartoryska; m. Emma Sergeant 2001. *Education:* Univ. of Oxford. *Publications:* Chopin: A New Biography 1979, The Battle for the Marchlands 1981, Paderewski: A Biography 1982, The Polish Way 1987, The Last King of Poland 1992, The Forgotten Few 1995, Holy Madness 1999, Poland: A Traveller's Gazetteer 2001, 1812: Napoleon's Fatal March on Moscow 2004, Rites of Peace: The Fall of Napoleon and the Congress of Vienna 2007. *Literary Agent:* Aitken Alexander Associates, 18–21 Cavaye Place, London, SW10 9PT, England. *Telephone:* (20) 7373-8672. *Fax:* (20) 7373-6002. *E-mail:* reception@aitkenalexander.co.uk. *Website:* www.aitkenalexander.co.uk. *Address:* 12 Avenue Studios, Sydney Close, London, SW3 6HW, England (home). *E-mail:* adam@adamzamoyski.com. *Website:* www.adamzamoyski.com.

ZANCANELLA, Don, BS, MA, PhD; American academic and writer; b. 29 Oct. 1954, Rock Springs, WY; m. Dorene Kahl 1981; two c. *Education:* Univ. of Virginia, Univ. of Denver, Univ. of Missouri. *Career:* Assoc. Prof. of English Education, Univ. of New Mexico, Albuquerque 1988–, now also Co-Dir Secondary English Language Arts Program. *Publications:* Western Electric (short stories) (Iowa Writers' Workshop John Simmons Short Fiction Award 1996) 1996, The Chimpanzees of Wyoming Territory (short story) 1998; contrib. to English Journal, Prairie Schooner, Alaska Quarterly Review, New Letters, Mid-American Review. *Honours:* O. Henry Award 1998. *Address:* Hokona Hall 214, Department of Language, Literacy and Sociocultural Studies, University of New Mexico, Albuquerque, NM 87131-0001, USA. *E-mail:* zanc@unm.edu.

ZANGANA, Haifa; British novelist, journalist and painter; b. 1950, Iraq. *Career:* writes in Arabic and English; moved to London 1976. *Publications:* Halabja (collection of essays by Arab writers, ed.) 1989; Through the Vast Halls of Memory, 1991; Bayt al-Namal (The Ant's Nest), 1996; Beyond What the Eye Sees, 1997; The Presence of Others (short stories), 1999; Keys to the City, 2000; Women on a Journey, 2001; co-author: El Kalima; Aswat; Al Ightirab al Adabi. *Address:* c/o Exiled Writers Ink!, 31 Hallswelle Road, London NW11 0DH, England. *E-mail:* haifa_zangana@yahoo.co.uk.

ZARIÂB, Spôjmaï; Afghan writer; b. 1949, Kabul; d. of Abdul and Zabeida Raouf; m. Rahnaward Zariâb; three d. *Education:* Faculty of Literature and Fine Arts, Univ. of Kabul, Université Paul-Valéry, France. *Career:* began publishing stories in Dari (a variation of Persian) aged 17; trans., French Embassy in Kabul 1973–89; teacher of French and Dari languages, Kabul; published work in Iran, Pakistan and the Writer's Union (Afghanistan's only publisher and printer) during Soviet occupation; in exile, Montpellier, France 1991–. *Publications include:* Ringing the Bells (anthology of short stories) 1983, In Another Country 1988, Boots of Delirium (short story), Identity Card (short story), Portrait of a City on a Purple Background (adapted to theatre and performed at Avignon Off Festival 1991), These Walls That Listen to Us (novel) 2000, (adapted to theatre and performed at Avignon) 2003, The Plain of Cain (collection of short stories) 2001, Draw me a Rooster (short stories) 2003. *Honours:* Chevalier, Ordre des Arts et des Lettres 2001; Prix Literature, Germany 2003. *Address:* c/o Éditions de l'Aube, BP 32, Le Moulin du Château, 84240 La Tour d'Aignes (office); 5 cité du Labyrinthe, 75020 Paris, France (home). *Telephone:* (1) 43-49-05-71 (home). *E-mail:* spojmaizariab@hotmail.fr (home).

ZAVALA, Iris M., PhD; Puerto Rican academic and writer; *Professor Emerita, Faculteit der Letteren, Rijksuniversiteit te Utrecht;* b. 27 Dec. 1936, Puerto Rico; one c. *Education:* Univs of Puerto Rico and Salamanca (Spain). *Career:* Asst Prof. Univ. of Puerto Rico 1962–64, Visiting Prof. 1978, 1981; Research Fellow El Colegio de México 1964–65, Visiting Prof. 1979; Visiting Lecturer Queen's Coll., New York 1966; Asst Prof. Hunter Coll., New York 1968–69; Assoc. Prof. State Univ. of New York at Stony Brook 1969–71, Prof. 1971–83, Jt Prof. of Comparative Literature 1976–83; Chair. of Hispanic Literatures Rijksuniversiteit te Utrecht, Netherlands 1983–, Prof. Emer. 1997–; Visiting Prof. Univ. di Calabria, Italy 1985, Univ. de les Illes Balears, Mallorca, Spain 1989; mem. Editorial Bd numerous journals including Third Woman 1982–, Anales de la Narrativa Española Contemporánea 1977–, Diálogos Hispánicos

1986–, La Torre 1986–, Journal of Interdisciplinary Studies 1988–; mem. Soc. for Spanish-Portuguese Historical Studies, American Asscn of Teachers of Spanish and Portuguese; has lectured on culture, literature and history in N and S America, E and W Europe, etc; Fellow American Philosophical Soc. 1966; Guggenheim Foundation Fellowship 1966–67; Dr hc (Univ. of Puerto Rico) 1996; Encomienda Lazo de Damad. la Orden de Mérito (Spain) 1988. *Publications include:* Unamuno y su teatro de conciencia (Nat. Literary Prize of Puerto Rico 1964) 1963, La Revolución de 1868: historia, pensamiento, literatura (co-ed.) 1970, Ideología y política en la novela española del siglo XIX (Nat. Literary Prize of Puerto Rico 1972) 1971, Escritura destada (ed.) 1974, Historia social de la literatura española 1979, Que nadie muera sin amar el mar 1983, Nocturna mas no funesta (Finalist Premio Herralde) 1987, Rubén Darío bajo el signo del cisne (Nat. Literary Prize 1990) 1989, Teorías de la modernidad 1991, Historia feminista de la literatura española (ed.) 1992; numerous articles. *Address:* Rijksuniversiteit te Utrecht, Faculteit der Letteren, Kromme Nieuwegracht 29, 3512 KD Utrecht, Netherlands. *Telephone:* (30) 253-6537. *Fax:* (30) 253-6167. *Website:* www2.let.uu.nl/solis (office).

ZAWODNY, Janusz Kazimierz, BS, MA, PhD; American retd academic and writer; b. 11 Dec. 1921, Warsaw, Poland; m. LaRae Jean Koppit 1971; one s. *Education:* Univ. of Iowa, Stanford Univ. *Career:* instructor and Asst Prof., Princeton Univ. 1955–58; Fellow, Center for Advanced Study in the Behavioral Sciences, Stanford 1961–62; Assoc. Prof. 1962–63, Prof. of Political Science 1965–75, Univ. of Pennsylvania; Prof. of Political Science, Washington Univ., St Louis 1963–65; Research Assoc., Center for Int. Affairs, Harvard Univ. 1968; sr assoc. mem., St Antony's Coll., Oxford 1968–69; mem., Inst. for Advanced Study, Princeton 1971–72; Avery Prof. of Int. Relations, Claremont Graduate Univ. and Pomona Coll., CA 1975–82; consultant staff, Nat. Security Council, USA 1979–84. *Publications:* Death in the Forest: The Story of the Katyn Forest Massacre 1962, Guide to the Study of International Relations 1967, Man and International Relations: Contribution of the Social Sciences to the Study of Conflict and Integration (ed. and contrib., two vols) 1967, Nothing But Honour: The Story of the Uprising of Warsaw 1944 1978, Uczestnicy i Swiadkowie Powstania Warszawskiego 1994, Motyl na Sniegu 2004; contrib. to scholarly books and journals. *Honours:* Hon. MA (Univ. of Pennsylvania) 1965, (Univ. of Oxford) 1968; Literary Award, Kultura, Paris 1981, Jurzykowski Foundation Citation and Award 1982, Research Awards, Polish Scientific Soc., London 1982, 1989, Scientific Soc. Book of the Year Award, Univ. of Lublin, Poland 1988, History Award, J. Pilsudski Inst., New York 1997; Order of Virtuti Militari 1944, Order of Merit, Pres. of Poland 1994, Kustosz Pamieci Narodowej 2003. *Address:* 23703 NE Margaret Road, Brush Prairie, WA 98606, USA.

ZELDIN, Theodore; British essayist and historian; b. 1933; m. Deirdre Wilson. *Career:* fmr Fellow and Dean, St Anthony's Coll., Oxford; Assoc. Fellow, Templeton Coll., Oxford; Visiting Prof., Harvard Univ., Univ. of Southern California; Pres., The Oxford Muse; mem. European Acad., British Acad., Soc. of Authors, BBC Brains Trust. *Publications:* Conflicts in French Society (ed.) 1971, France 1848–1945: Ambition, Love and Politics 1973, Ambition and Love 1979, Politics and Anger 1979, Taste and Corruption 1980, Intellect and Pride 1980, Anxiety and Hypocrisy 1981, The French 1983, Happiness 1988, A History of French Passions: Intellect, Taste and Anxiety 1993, An Intimate History of Humanity 1994, Conversation: How Talk Can Change Our Lives 1998. *Honours:* Wolfson Prize.

ZELEZA, Paul Tiyambe, BA, MA, PhD; Malawi academic and writer; *Professor and Head, Department of African-American Studies, University of Illinois at Chicago*; b. 25 May 1955, Harare, Zimbabwe; m.; one d. *Education:* Univ. of Malawi, Univ. of London, Dalhousie Univ., Canada. *Career:* Lecturer, Univ. of Malawi 1976–77, Univ. of Nairobi 1977–80, Univ. of the West Indies 1982–84, Kenyatta Univ. 1984–89; fmr Ed. Odi journal, Umodzi magazine; Founder-mem. Malawian Writer's Series 1974; Assoc. Prof., Dept of History and Comparative Devt Studies, Trent Univ., Ont., Canada 1990–95, Prof. 1995, Acting Dir Trent Int. Program 1994–95, Prin. Lady Eaton Coll. 1994–95; Prof. of History and African Studies and Dir Center for African Studies, Univ. of Illinois at Urbana-Champaign 1995–2003, Prof. and Head, Dept of African-American Studies, Univ. of Illinois at Chicago 2007–; Prof. of African Studies and History, Pennsylvania State Univ. 2003–06. *Publications:* fiction: Night of Darkness and Other Stories 1976, Smouldering Charcoal 1992, The Joys of Exile (short stories) 1994; non-fiction: Rethinking Africa's Globalization, Vol. 1: The Intellectual Challenges 2003, Imperialism and Labour: The International Relations of the Kenyan Labour Movement 1987, Labour, Unionization and Women's Participation in Kenya 1965–1987 1988, A Modern Economic History of Africa, Vol. 1: The Nineteenth Century 1993, Vol. 2: The Twentieth Century, Maasai 1994, Akamba 1994, Mijikenda 1994, Manufacturing African Studies and Crises 1997; contrib. to numerous articles, chapters, reviews and short stories. *Honours:* Noma Award 1994, Special Commendation 1998. *Address:* Department of African-American Studies, Banner Dept: 2-363000, 1223 UH MC 069, 601 S Morgan Street, Chicago, IL 60607-7112, USA (office). *Telephone:* (312) 996-2950 (office). *Fax:* (312) 996-5799 (office). *E-mail:* zeleza@uic.edu (office). *Website:* www.zeleza.com.

ZELLER, Eva; German writer; b. 25 Jan. 1923, Eberswalde; d. of Franz-Maria and Elisabeth (née Bertrand) Feldhaus; m. Reimar Zeller 1951; one s. three d. *Education:* Secondary school in Droyssig bei Zeitz, Univs of Greifswald, Marburg and Berlin. *Career:* left GDR for FRG 1956; Guest Prof. of Poetry Univ. of Mainz 1987; mem. Deutsche Akad. für Sprache und Dichtung, Akad. der Wissenschaften und der Literatur zu Mainz. *Publications:* novels: Der Sprung über den Schatten, Lampenfieber, Die Hauptfrau, Solange ich denken kann 1980, Nein und Amen 1985, Ein Stein aus Davids Hirtentasche 1992, Das versiegelte manuskript 1998, Stiftsgarten, Tübingen 2002; short stories: Die magische Rechnung, Ein Morgen Ende Mai, Der Turmbau 1975, Tod der Singschwäne; poetry: Sage und schreibe, Fliehkraft, Auf dem Wasser gehn, Stellprobe 1989; editor: Dreißig deutsche Jahre: zum Generationsbruch heute; also radio plays, etc. *Honours:* Droste Preis 1975, Ida-Dehmel Preis 1986, Eichendorff-Preis 1991. *Address:* c/o Werderstr 17, 6900 Heidelberg 1, Germany.

ZELLER, Florian; French novelist and playwright; b. 1979. *Career:* currently Lecturer in Literature, Institut d'études politiques de Paris (Sciences Po), also regular contrib. to Paris Match and Vogue. *Plays:* L'Autre (Théatre des Mathurins, Paris), Le Manège (Petit Montparnasse, Paris) 2004. *Publications:* novels: Neiges artificielles (Prix de la Fondation Hachette) 2002, Les Amants du n'importe quoi (trans. as Lovers Or Something Like It) (Prix Prince Pierre de Monaco) 2003, La Fascination du pire (Prix Interallié) 2004, Julien Parme 2006. *Address:* c/o Pushkin Press, 12 Chester Terrace, London, NW1 4ND, England.

ZEPHANIAH, Benjamin Obadiah Iqbal; British poet, writer, dramatist, musician and singer; b. 15 April 1958, Birmingham. *Career:* writer-in-residence, Africa Arts Collective, Liverpool 1989, Hay-on-Wye Literature Festival 1991, Memphis State Univ., TN 1991–95; numerous radio performances, acting roles, appearances; mem. Musicians' Union, Equity, Performing Rights Soc., ALCS. *Recordings:* albums: Rasta 1983, Us and Dem 1990, Back To Our Roots 1995, Belly Of The Beast 1996, Heading For The Door 2000, Naked 2006; singles: Dub Ranting (EP) 1982, Big Boys Don't Make Girls Cry 1984, Free South Africa 1986, Crisis 1992, Naked 2004; contributor to: Dancing Tribes (single, with Back To Base) 1999, Illegal (with Swayzak) 2000. *Radio plays:* Hurricane Dub 1988, Our Teacher's Gone Crazy 1990, Listen To Your Parents 2000. *Television play:* Dread Poets Society 1991. *Publications:* fiction: Face 1999, Refugee Boy 2001; poetry: Pen Rhythm 1980, The Dread Affair 1985, Inna Liverpool 1988, Rasta Time in Palestine 1990, City Psalms 1992, Talking Turkeys 1994, Funky Chickens 1996, Propa Propaganda 1996, School's Out 1997, We Are Britain 2002, Too Black, Too Strong 2002, The Little Book of Vegan Poems 2002, Gangsta Rap 2004; plays: Playing the Right Tune 1985, Job Rocking 1987, Delirium 1987, Streetwise 1990, The Trial of Mickey Tekka 1991; contrib. to periodicals, radio, television and recordings. *Honours:* Dr hc (Univ. of North London) 1998, (Univ. of West of England) 1999, (Staffordshire Univ.) 2001, (Oxford Brookes Univ.) 2002, (South Bank Univ., London) 2002, (Univ. of East London) 2003, (Univ. Coll. Northampton) 2003, (Open Univ.) 2004, (Univ. of Central England) 2005, Hon. DLitt (Westminster Univ.) 2006; BBC Young Playwrights Festival Award 1988. *Literary Agent:* PFD, 34–43 Russell Street, London, WC2A 5HD, England. *Address:* PO Box 1153, Spalding, Lincs. PE11 9BN, England (office). *Telephone:* (20) 7344-1000 (office). *Website:* www.benjaminzephaniah.com.

ZERNOVA, Ruf Aleksandrovna; Russian writer, essayist and translator; b. (Ruf Zevina), 1919, Tiraspol, Moldavia; m. 1st (divorced); m. 2nd Ilya Z. Serman; one s. one d. *Education:* Leningrad Inst. of Philosophy, Literature and History, Leningrad State Univ. *Career:* translator, Navy Ministry, Moscow 1939–41; translator and ed., TASS press agency; imprisoned in labour camps 1949–54; reviewer and writer for journals, including Zvezda, Iunost, Ogonek; first short story published 1956; founder mem. Writers' Union 1954–. *Publications include:* Skorpionovy iagody (trans. as Scorpion Berries) 1961, Bakaloo (trans. as Baccalao) 1963, Svet i ten' (trans. as Light and Shadow) 1963, linnoe, dlinnoe leto (trans. as A Long, Long Summer) 1967, Rasskazy pro Antona (trans. as Stories About Anton) 1968, Solnechnaia storona (trans. as The Sunny Side) 1968, Nemye zvonki (Mute Phone Calls) 1974, Zhenskie rasskazy (trans. as Stories of Women) 1981, Eto bylo pri nas (trans. as It Was in Our Time) 1988, Izali i okresnosti (trans. as Israel and its Surroundings) 1990, Mute Phone Calls and Other Stories (in trans.) 1991; editor: Leningradtsy v Ispanii 1936–1939: Sbornik vospominanii (trans. as Leningraders in Spain 1936–1939: An Anthology of Recollections) 1967. *Address:* c/o New Brunswick Rutgers University Press, 100 Joyce Kilmer Avenue, Piscataway, NJ 08854, USA.

ZHANG, Husheng; Chinese journalist. *Career:* fmr Dir Int. Dept, People's Daily, Ed.-in-Chief Overseas Edn 1991–, Deputy Ed.-in-Chief People's Daily 1995–; Head of Information Bureau of 7th NPC Standing Cttee 1988–93. *Address:* People's Daily, 2 Jin Tai Xi Lu, Chao Yang Men Wai, Beijing 100733, People's Republic of China (office). *Telephone:* (10) 65092121. *Fax:* (10) 65091982.

ZHANG, Wei; Chinese writer; b. 1956, Longkou, Shangdong Province. *Education:* Yantai Normal Inst. *Career:* fmrly apptd Vice-Mayor of Longkou city 1987; mem. Shandong Writers' Asscn (fmr assoc. chair.), Young Writers' Asscn (Shandong Province) (fmr assoc. chair.), Chinese Writers' Asscn. *Publications include:* Visiting the Bugler (long poem), The Ancient Boat (novel), Blending into the Untamed Land (essay), Voice (short story) (Chinese Writers' Asscn Award 1982), A Pool of Clear Water (short story) (Chinese Writers' Asscn Award 1984), The Autumn of Wrath (novella) (Novella Magazine Award 1986), Selected Writings of Zhang Wei (Shangdong Province Award for Best Book 1997), September's Fable (novel) (Chinese Writers' Asscn and China News Best Novel Award 1998). *Address:* c/o Chinese Writers'

Association, No. 25 East Tucheng Road, Chaoyang District, Beijing 100013, People's Republic of China.

ZHANG, Xianliang; Chinese writer and poet; b. 1936, Jiangsu; m. Yan Huili; one d. *Career:* fmr teacher in Beijing and Ningxia; in political disgrace 1957–79; mem. editorial staff Shuofang literary magazine late 1970s; cttee mem. People's Consultative Conference 1983, People's Republic of China Writers' Asscn (vice-pres. 1986). *Publications:* Song of the Great Wind (poem) 1957, Soul and Flesh (aka A Herdsman's Story) 1981, Contemporary Chinese Short Stories (with Zhang Xian and others) 1984, Mimosa 1984, Prize-Winning Stories from China 1980–1981 (with others) 1985, Half of Man is Woman 1985, Yi Xiang Tian Kai (screenplay) 1986, Women Shi Shijie (screenplay) 1988, Getting Used to Dying 1989, Grass Soup 1992, My Bodhi Tree 1994. *Honours:* Best Novel of the Year Awards (China) 1981, 1983, 1984. *Address:* Ningxia Writers' Association, Yinchuan City, People's Republic of China (office).

ZHANG CHANGXIN, (Dongli Jiefu); Chinese writer; b. 30 Nov. 1940, Liaoning; m. Huang Fuju 1962; one s. one d. *Education:* China Siping Teachers' School. *Career:* mem. China Asscn of Writers, China Playwrights' Asscn. *Publications:* Changba Shan Hun, English trans. as Spirit of Changba Mountains, 1985; Aide San Yuan Se, English trans. as Three Colours of Love, 1987; East Madrid, 1989; Zni Zhi Qiu, English trans. as Enjoyment in Autumn, 1991; Qingxi Lanxi, English trans. as Black and Blue, 1994; Chaoji Ai Qing Siwang, English trans. as The Death of Super Love, 1995. *Address:* c/o Jilin Writers' Association, Bldg 9, 167 Renmin Street, Changchun, Jilin, 130021, People's Republic of China.

ZHAO, Jia-Zi; Chinese musicologist; b. 30 Aug. 1934, Jiang-Su; m. Xu Si-Jie 1959; one s. one d. *Education:* Shanghai Conservatory of Music. *Career:* Research Scholar, Music Univ. of New Dheli, The Indian Art Centre, Chennai Ethonomusicology Research Inst. 1986–88; Head of Inst. Music Research of Shanghai Conservatory of Music; full-time Supervisor, Shanghai Conservatory of Music; Deputy Dir, World Ethnomusicological Asscn, Oriental Music Asscn; mem. Indian Musicological Soc., Singapore Asscn for Asian Studies, Chinese Writers' Asscn, Chinese Musicians' Asscn. *Publications:* The Music of Asia, Ethnic Music of Asian Countries, Collection of Writings on the Music of Shen Zhi-Bai, Indian Music Around the Period of Sui and Tang Dynasty, Rabindranath Tagore and his Music, Gamelan Music in Java and Bali, Comparative Study of Indian and Chinese Ancient Music, Comparative Study of Wu Dan-Qi Shen and Qi Tiao Bei. *Address:* c/o Trinity College, University of Melbourne, Royal Parade, Parkville 3052, Vic., Australia.

ZHAOYAN, Ye; Chinese writer; b. 1957, Nanjing. *Publications:* Tale of the Jujube Tree 1988, Nanjing 1937 – A Love Story 1996. *Address:* c/o Faber and Faber Ltd, 3 Queen Square, London, WC1N 3AU, England. *Website:* www .faber.co.uk.

ZHOU, Wei Hui; Chinese writer; b. 1973, Ning Bo City. *Education:* Fudan Univ., Shanghai. *Career:* first year of coll. spent in mil. training; fifth novel Shanghai Baby banned in China 2001. *Publications include:* (titles in translation) The Shriek of the Butterfly, Virgin in the Water, Crazy Like Wei Hui, Desire Pistol, Shanghai Baby 1999, Marrying Buddha 2005. *Address:* c/o Joanne Wang, Constable & Robinson Ltd, 3 The Lanchester, 162 Fulham Road, London, W6 96R, England (office). *E-mail:* enquiries@ constablerobinson.com.

ZHU, Wen; Chinese writer, poet, film director and screenwriter. *Films:* Wu shan yun yu (writer) 1996, Guo nian hui jia (writer) 1999, Hai xian (writer and dir, translated as Seafood) 2001, Yun de nan fang (dir, translated as South of the Clouds) 2003. *Address:* c/o Ministry of Culture, 10 Chaoyangmen Bei Jie, Dongcheng Qu, Beijing 100020, People's Republic of China (office).

ZHU, Yinghuang, MA; Chinese journalist; *Professor of Journalism and Communications, Tsinghua University;* b. 28 Dec. 1943, Shanghai; m. Yao Xiang 1972; one d. *Education:* Stanford Univ., USA. *Career:* fmr Ed.-in-Chief China Daily, now Ed.-in-Chief Emer.; Prof. of Journalism and Communications, Tsinghua Univ.; Prof. of Communication, Univ. of China; mem. CPPCC. *Honours:* Outstanding Journalist of China 1984. *Address:* China Daily, 15 Huixin Dongjie, Chao Yang Qu, Beijing 100029, People's Republic of China (office). *Telephone:* (10) 64918248 (office), (10) 64280990 (home). *Fax:* (10) 64918377 (office). *E-mail:* yhzhu@chinadaily.com.cn (office). *Website:* www .chinadaily.com.cn (office).

ZIEGLER, Philip Sandeman, CVO, MA, FRHistS, FRSL; British writer; b. 24 Dec. 1929, Ringwood, Hants.; s. of Colin Louis Ziegler and Dora Ziegler (née Barnwell); m. 1st Sarah Collins 1960 (deceased); one s. one d.; m. 2nd Mary Clare Charrington 1971; one s. *Education:* Eton Coll., New Coll. Oxford. *Career:* joined Foreign Office 1952, served Vientiane, Paris, Pretoria, Bogotá; Editorial Dir Collins Publishers 1972, Ed.-in-Chief 1979–80, resgnd when apptd to write official biog. of the late Earl Mountbatten; Chair. London Library 1979–85, Soc. of Authors 1988–90, Public Lending Right Advisory Cttee 1993–96. *Publications include:* Duchess of Dino 1962, Addington 1965, The Black Death 1969, William IV 1971, Omdurman 1973, Melbourne 1976, Crown and People 1978, Diana Cooper 1981, Mountbatten 1985, Elizabeth's Britain 1926 to 1986 1986, The Sixth Great Power: Barings 1762–1929 1988, King Edward VIII, The Official Biography 1990, Wilson: The Authorized Life of Lord Wilson of Rievaulx 1993, London at War: 1939–45 1994, Osbert Sitwell 1998, Britain Then and Now 1999, Soldiers: Fighting Men's Lives 1901–2001 2001, Rupert Hart-Davis: Man of Letters 2004; editor: The Diaries of Lord

Louis Mountbatten 1920–1922 1987, Personal Diary of Admiral the Lord Louis Mountbatten 1943–1946 1988, From Shore to Shore: The Diaries of Earl Mountbatten of Burma 1953–1979 1989, Brooks's: A Social History (with Desmond Seward) 1991. *Honours:* Hon. DLitt (Westminster Coll., Mo., USA) 1987, (Univ. of Buckingham) 2000; Chancellor's Essay Prize 1950, Heinemann Award 1976. *Address:* 22 Cottesmore Gardens, London, W8 5PR, England. *Telephone:* (20) 7937-1903. *Fax:* (20) 7937-5458.

ZIFFRIN, Marilyn, BM, MA; American composer and writer; *Professor Emerita, New England College, Henniker;* b. 7 Aug. 1926, Moline, IL; d. of Harry B. and Betty S. Ziffrin. *Education:* Univ. of Wisconsin, Columbia Univ., Univ. of Chicago. *Career:* teacher, Chicago Public Schools 1952–56; Asst Prof. of Music Northeastern Ill. Univ. 1956–66; Assoc. Prof. of Music New England Coll., Henniker, NH 1957–83, Prof. Emer. 1983–; MacDowell Colony Fellowships 1961, 1963, 1971, 1977, 1980, 1989. *Compositions include:* solo: Theme and Variations for piano 1949, Suite for piano 1955, Toccata and Fugue for organ 1956, Three Songs for woman's voice 1957, Rhapsody for solo guitar 1958, Four Pieces for tuba 1973, Three Movements for guitar 1989, Themes and Variations for organ 1990, Three Songs of the Trobairitz 1991, Recurrences piano solo 1998, Moods piano solo 2003, Three Songs for D'Anna 2003, Piano Sonata 2005–06; chamber music: The Little Prince for clarinet and bassoon 1953, Make a Joyful Noise quintet for recorder 1966, In the Beginning for percussion ensemble 1968, XIII for chamber ensemble 1969, String Quartet 1970, Haiku for soprano, viola and harpsichord 1971, Movements for clarinet and percussion 1972, Sonata for organ and cello 1973, Trio for xylophone, soprano and tuba 1974, Trio for violin, cello and piano 1975, Quintet for oboe and string quartet 1976, Concerto for viola and woodwind quintet 1978, SONO for cello and piano 1980, White Lies (film score) 1983, Yankee Hooray piano duet 1984, Duo for alto recorders 1985, Conversations for double bass and harpsichord 1986, Tributum for clarinet, viola and double bass 1992, Flute Fun for two flutes 1995, Fantasy for two pianos 1995, Lines and Spaces for brass quintet 1996, For Love of Cynthia for baritone and classical accordion, or violin, horn and piano 1997, Two Songs for soprano, viola and piano 1998, String Quartet No. 2 1999, Two Movements for woodwind quintet 2000, Abbot's Duo for alto sax and violin 2001, Sonatina for trumpet and piano 2001, Trio for flute, clarinet and piano 2004, A Little Music for handbells 2006; choral: Jewish Prayer 1950, Death of Moses 1954, Prayer 1966, Drinking Song and Dance, from Captain Kidd 1971, Chorus from Alcestis 1990, Choruses from the Greeks 1992, New England Epitaphs 1994, Cantata for Freedom 2000, Almanack 1688 2002, Two Holiday Songs for chorus 2005; orchestral: Strings 1966, Soundscape 2000, Soundscape II 2002, Trio for flute, clarinet and piano 2004, Soundscape III 2005, Duo for Flute and Piano 2006. *Publications:* Carl Ruggles: Composer, Painter and Storyteller 1994; contrib. to The New Grove Dictionary of Music and Musicians 1980, The New Grove Dictionary of American Music 1986. *Honours:* Special Mention Delius Composition Competition 1971, first prize Delius Composition Competition 1972, ASCAP Awards 1981–2007, Virginia Center for the Creative Arts Residency 1987, Music Fix Prize 1996, New Hampshire MTA Composer of the Year 1997, Laureate mem. 2006. *Address:* PO Box 179, Bradford, NH 03221, USA.

ZIGAL, Thomas, BA, MA; American writer; b. 20 Oct. 1948, Galveston, Tex.; one s. *Education:* Univ. of Texas, Stanford Univ. *Career:* mem. Texas Inst. of Letters 1995–, Mystery Writers of America, Authors Guild. *Publications:* Playland 1982, Into Thin Air 1995, Hardrock Stiff 1996, Pariah 1999, The White League (Violet Crown Award 2005) 2005. *Literary Agent:* c/o Bill Contardi, Brandt and Hochman Literary Agents, 1501 Broadway, Suite 2310, New York, NY 10036, USA. *Website:* www.thomaszigal.com.

ZIMDAHL, Catherine; Australian playwright and screenwriter. *Education:* Australian Film, Television and Radio School. *Career:* writer of short features Sparks and Life on Earth as I Know It. *Plays:* Family Running for Mr Whippy 1995, Clark in Sarajevo 1998, The Wharf at Wooloomooloo, The Darling Loves 2005. *Honours:* Developing Writer's Grant, Literature Bd of the Australia Council; AFI Awards for Best Short Film, Best Short Screenplay 1990, Gold Plaque Award at the Chicago Int. Film Festival 1990, Le Prix Recherché at the Clermont Ferrand Film Festival 1990, Legal & General Umbrella Award for Best New Australian Writing 1998, Louis Esson Prize for Drama, Victorian Premier's Literary Awards 1999, ANPC/New Dramatists' Exchange to New York 1999. *Literary Agent:* RGM Associates, PO Box 128, Surry Hills, NSW 2010, Australia. *Telephone:* (2) 9281-3911. *Fax:* (2) 9281-4705. *E-mail:* info@ rgm.com.au. *Website:* www.rgm.com.au.

ZIMLER, Richard, BA, MA; American journalist and writer; b. 1 Jan. 1956, Manhasset, Long Island, NY. *Education:* Duke Univ., Stanford Univ. *Career:* journalist 1982–90; teacher of journalism in Oporto Portugal; reviewer for the LA Times and Literary Review. *Publications:* Unholy Ghosts 1996, The Last Kabbalist of Lisbon 1997, The Secret Life of Images by Al Berto (trans.) 1997, The Angelic Darkness 1998, Hunting Midnight 2003, Guardian of the Dawn 2005, The Search for Sana 2005, The Seventh Gate 2007. *Honours:* National Endowment of the Arts Fellowship in Fiction 1994; Herodotus Award. *Literary Agent:* Cynthia Cannell, 833 Madison Avenue, New York, NY 10021, USA. *Telephone:* (212) 396-9595. *Fax:* (212) 396-9797. *E-mail:* cynthiacannell@aol.com. *E-mail:* rczimler@hotmail.com. *Website:* www.zimler .com.

ZIMMER, Carl; American writer and journalist. *Publications:* At the Water's Edge 1998, Parasite Rex 2001, Evolution: The Triumph of an Idea: From

Darwin to DNA 2002, Soul Made Flesh 2004; contrib. to Newsweek, Science, Discover, Sunday Telegraph, Popular Science, New York Newsday; monthly columnist for Natural History. *Address:* c/o Random House UK Ltd, 20 Vauxhall Bridge Road, London, SW1V 2SA, England. *E-mail:* mail@carlzimmer.com. *Website:* www.carlzimmer.com.

ZIMMERMAN, Franklin B., BLitt, PhD, FACLS; American musician, conductor and musicologist; b. 20 June 1923, Wanneta, KS; m. 1988; one s. five d. *Education:* Univ. of Southern California, Univ. of Oxford, studied French Horn with Aubrey Brain, conducting with Ernest Read, orchestration with Leon Kirchner and Ingolf Dahl. *Career:* created Music SoundScapes, a three-dimensional, animated and colour-coded graphic musical notation; debut, London 1957; founder and Dir, Pennsylvania Pro Musica playing over 5,200 concerts; mem. AMS, IMS. *Recordings:* Handel L'Allegro ed Il Penseroso 1981. *Publications:* Henry Purcell: Analytical Catalog 1963, Henry Purcell: Life and Times 1967, Henry Purcell: Thematic Index 1973, Words to Music 1965, Facsimile Editions: An Introduction to the Skill of Musick by John Playford (12th edn, corrected and amended by Henry Purcell, with index, introduction and glossary) 1972, Henry Purcell: a Guide to Research 1989, Henry Purcell (1659–1695): Analytical Essays on his Music 2001, Visible Music Sound-Scapes: A New Approach to Musical Notation and Understanding, Purcellian Melodies Indexed: A Thematic Index to the Complete Work of Henry Purcell; contrib. numerous articles and monographs. *Honours:* Arnold Bax Medal for Musicology 1958. *Address:* Visible Music SoundScapes Inc., Suite 1A, 225 S 42nd Street, Philadelphia, PA 19104, USA. *E-mail:* musica@dca.net. *Website:* www.visiblemusics.com/new.

ZINN, Howard, BA, MA, PhD; American writer and academic; *Professor Emeritus of Political Science, Boston University*; b. 24 Aug. 1922, New York, NY; m. Roslyn Shechter 1944; one s. one d. *Education:* New York Univ., Columbia Univ. *Career:* instructor, Upsala Coll., East Orange, NJ 1953–56; Visiting Lecturer, Brooklyn Coll., CUNY 1955–56; Chair., Dept of History and Political Science, Spelman Coll., Atlanta 1956–63; Assoc. Prof. 1964–66, Prof. of Political Science 1966–88, Prof. Emeritus 1988–, Boston Univ.; Harvard Univ. Center for East Asian Studies Fellowship 1960–61; mem. PEN. *Publications:* LaGuardia in Congress 1959, SNCC: The New Abolitionists 1964, The Southern Mystique 1964, New Deal Thought (ed.) 1965, Vietnam: The Logic of Withdrawal 1967, Disobedience and Democracy 1968, The Politics of History 1970, Post-War America 1973, Justice in Everyday Life (ed.) 1974, A People's History of the United States 1980, Declarations of Independence 1990, You Can't Be Neutral on a Moving Train 1995, The Zinn Reader 1997, Marx in Soho 1999, On War 2001, On History 2001, Terrorism and War 2002, Voices of a People's History (jtly), Emma: A Play 2002; contrib. to professional journals and general periodicals, including The Progressive. *Honours:* American Historical Asscn Albert J. Beveridge Prize 1958, Thomas Merton Award 1991, Lannan Literary Award 1998. *Address:* 29 Fern Street, Auburndale, MA 02166, USA. *E-mail:* hzinnz@yahoo.com.

ZIOLKOWSKI, Theodore Joseph, BA, MA, PhD; American academic and writer; *Professor Emeritus of German and Comparative Literature, Princeton University*; b. 30 Sept. 1932, Birmingham, Ala; s. of Miecislaw Ziolkowski and Cecilia J. Ziolkowski; m. Yetta Bart Goldstein 1951; two s. one d. *Education:* Duke Univ., Univ. of Innsbruck, Yale Univ. *Career:* instructor to Asst Prof., Yale Univ. 1956–62; Assoc. Prof., Columbia Univ. 1962–64; Prof. of Germanic Languages and Literature, Princeton Univ. 1964–69, Class of 1900 Prof. of Modern Languages 1969–2001, Prof. of Comparative Literature 1975–2001, Dean, Grad. School 1979–92, Prof. Emer. of German and Comparative Literature 2001–; various visiting lectureships and professorships; Resident Fellow, Bellagio Study Centre, Italy 1993; mem. Acad. of Literary Studies, American Acad. of Arts and Sciences, American Philosophical Soc., American Asscn of Teachers of German (Hon. Life Mem.), Asscn of Grad. Schools (Pres. 1990–91), Authors' Guild, Modern Language Asscn (Pres. 1985), Asscn of Literary Scholars and Critics, Int. Asscn of Germanists, German-American Academic Council, Austrian Acad. of Sciences, Göttingen Acad. of Sciences, Deutsche Akad. für Sprache und Dichtung, Darmstadt. *Publications:* Hermann Broch 1964, The Novels of Hermann Hesse 1965, Hermann Hesse 1966, Dimensions of the Modern Novel 1969, Fictional Transfigurations of Jesus 1972, Disenchanted Images 1977, Der Schriftsteller Hermann Hesse 1979, The Classical German Elegy 1980, Varieties of Literary Thematics 1983, German Romanticism and its Institutions 1990, Virgil and the Moderns 1993, The Mirror of Justice 1997, The View from the Tower 1998, Das Wunderjahr in Jena 1998, The Sin of Knowledge 2000, Berlin: Aufstieg einer Kulturmetropole um 1810 2002, Hesitant Heroes 2004, Clio the Romantic Muse 2004, Ovid and the Moderns 2005, Vorboten der Moderne: Kulturgeschichte der Fruehromantik 2006, Modes of Faith: Secular Surrogates for Lost Religious Faith 2007; editor: Hermann Hesse: Autobiographical Writings 1972, Hermann Hesse: Stories of Five Decades 1972, Hesse: A Collection of Critical Essays 1972, Hermann Hesse: My Belief: Essays on Life and Art 1974, Hermann Hesse: Pictor's Metamorphoses and Other Fantasies 1982, Hermann Hesse: Soul of the Age: Selected Letters 1891–1962 1991, Friedrich Duerrenmatt: Selected Fiction 2006; contrib. to books and professional journals. *Honours:* Commdr's Cross, Order of Merit (Germany) 2000; Hon. DPhil (Greifswald) 2001; Fulbright Research Grant 1958–59, American Philosophical Soc. Grant 1959, Guggenheim Fellowship 1964–65, American Council of Learned Socs Fellowships 1972, 1976, James Russell Lowell Prize for Criticism 1972, Yale Univ. Wilbur Lucius Cross Medal 1982, Goethe Inst. Gold Medal 1987, Henry Allen Moe Prize in Humanities 1988, Jacob und

Wilhelm Grimm Prize 1998, Christian Gauss Award in Criticism 1998, Mellon Emer. Faculty Award 2004, Bannicelli Prize 2004, Robert Motherwell Award 2005. *Address:* 36 Bainbridge Street, Princeton, NJ 08540, USA (home). *Telephone:* (609) 430-0209 (office). *E-mail:* tjziol@aol.com (home).

ŽIVKOVIĆ, Zoran, BA, MA, PhD; Serbian writer; b. 5 Oct. 1948, Belgrade; m. Mia; two s. (twins). *Education:* Univ. of Belgrade. *Career:* founder of imprint, Polaris 1982; science-fiction writer and essayist. *Television:* Zvezdani ekran (The Starry Screen, series about sci-fi fiction cinema) 1984. *Publications:* fiction (titles in translation): The Fourth Circle (Milos Crnjanski Award 1994) 1993, Time Gifts 1997, The Writer 1998, The Book 1999, Impossible Encounters 2000, Seven Touches of Music 2001, The Library (World Fantasy Award for Best Novella 2003) 2002, Steps Through the Mist 2003, Hidden Camera 2003, Compartments 2004, Four Stories Till the End 2004, Twelve Collections and the Teashop 2005, The Bridge 2006. *E-mail:* j.jarrold@btopenworld.com *E-mail:* zz@zoranzivkovic.com. *Website:* www.zoranzivkovic.com.

ZOLOTOW, Charlotte Shapiro; American publishing executive and writer; b. 26 June 1915, Norfolk, VA; d. of Louis J. Shapiro and Ella Shapiro (née Bernstein); m. Maurice Zolotow 1938 (divorced 1969, died 1991); one s. one d. *Education:* Univ. of Wisconsin. *Career:* Editorial Dir Junior Books Dept, Harper and Row 1938–44, Sr Ed. 1962–70; Vice-Pres. and Assoc. Publr Harper Jr Books 1976–81; Publr Emer., Adviser to Harper-Collins Jr Books 1991–; Editorial Dir Charlotte Zolotow Books 1982–90; mem. PEN, Authors' League. *Publications include:* children's books: The Park Book 1944, The Storm Book 1952, Over and Over 1957, Do You Know What I'll Do? 1958, Big Brother 1960, The Three Funny Friends 1961, Mr Rabbit and the Lovely Present 1962, A Tiger Called Thomas 1963, The Quarreling Book 1963, The Sky Was Blue 1963, Someday (Outstanding Children's Book of 1964–65) 1965, When I Have a Little Girl 1965, Big Sister and Little Sister 1966, If It Weren't For You 1966, When I Have a Little Boy 1967, My Friend John 1968, The Hating Book 1969, A Father Like That 1971, Wake Up and Goodnight 1971, Hold My Hand 1972, William's Doll (Outstanding Children's Book of 1972) 1972, Janey 1973, The Summer Night 1974, My Grandson Lew (Christopher Award) 1974, The Unfriendly Book 1975, When the Wind Stops 1975, May I Visit? 1976, It's Not Fair 1976, Someone New 1978, If You Listen 1980, But Not Billy 1983, The Poodle Who Barked at the Wind 1987, A Rose, a Bridge and a Wild Black Horse 1987, Sleepy Book 1988, Something is Going to Happen, The Seashore Book 1992, Snippets 1992, This Quiet Lady 1992, The Moon was Best 1993, Peter and the Pigeons 1993, The Old Dog 1995, Who is Ben 1997; children's short stories: An Overpraised Season 1973, Early Sorrow 1986. *Honours:* Harper Gold Medal Award for Editorial Excellence 1974, Kerlan Award, Univ. of Minnesota 1986, Charlotte Zolotow Award cr. by Univ. of Wisconsin at Madison and given annually to honour the text of the previous year's most outstanding children's book. *Address:* 29 Elm Place, Hastings-on-Hudson, NY 10706, USA (home). *E-mail:* charlottesdaughter@charlottezolotow.com (home). *Website:* www.charlottezolotow.com.

ZOLYNAS, Algirdas (Al) Richard Johann, BA, MA, PhD; American academic, poet and writer; *Professor of English, Alliant International University*; b. 1 June 1945, Dornbirn, Austria; m. 24 June 1967. *Education:* Univ. of Illinois, Univ. of Utah. *Career:* fmrly Instructor, Asst Prof. and writer-in-residence, Southwest State Univ., Marshall, MN; Lecturer, Weber State Coll., Ogden, UT and San Diego State Univ.; currently Prof. of English in the Dept of Global Liberal Studies, Alliant Int. Univ.; mem. Poets and Writers. *Publications:* The New Physics 1979, 4 Petunia Avenue 1987, Men of Our Time: An Anthology of Male Poetry in Contemporary America (ed. with Fred Moramarco) 1992, Under Ideal Conditions 1994, The Same Air 1997. *Honours:* San Diego Book Award for Best Poetry 1994. *Address:* Alliant International University, 10455 Pomerado Road, San Diego, CA 92131, USA. *E-mail:* azolynas@alliant.edu; azolynas@usiu.edu.

ZORIN, Leonid Genrikhovich; Russian playwright and writer; b. 3 Nov. 1924, Baku, Azerbaijan; s. of Genrikh Zorin and Polina Zorin; m. 1st 1951 (deceased); m. 2nd Tatjana Pospelova 1985; one s. *Education:* Azerbaijan State Univ., M. Gorky Inst. of Literature in Moscow. *Career:* literary Baku Russian Drama Theatre; later freelance, mem. USSR Union of Writers 1941–; Int. PEN Club, Russian PEN Centre, Russian Acad. of Cinema, Science and the Arts. *Plays:* more than 49 produced in 16 countries, including Decembrists, Kind Men, The Coronation, The Deck, Warsaw Melody, The Copper Grandmother, The Quotation, The Perished Plot, The Infidelity, The Carnival, The Moscow Nest, Lusgan, The Warsaw Melody 1997, Tsar's Hunt, Roman Comedy, The Invisibles 1999, The Maniac 2000, The Misprint 2001, The Outcome 2002, The Detectives 2003. *Film scripts:* 15 including A Man from Nowhere, The Law, Peace to the Newcomer, Grandmaster, Transit, The Friends and the Years, Pokrovskye Gates, Tsar's Hunt, Hard Sand 2002. *Publications:* (novels and short stories) Old Manuscript 1983, Wanderer 1987, The Topic of the Day 1992, Proscenium 1997, The Plots 1998, The Teetotaller (Banner Prize, Apollon Grigorjev Prize) 2001, The Auction (collection of novels and stories) 2001, Whip (Banner Prize) 2002, Jupiter 2002, Oblivion 2004; numerous essays; Theatre Fantasy (collection of plays) 1974, Selected Plays (2 vols) 1986, The Green Notebooks (collection of essays etc.), The Curtain of the Millennium (collection of later plays) 2002, The Sansara (novel) 2004, The Will of Yzand (humorous book) 2005, The Prose (collection of novels and short stories) in two vols, The Parting March (humorous book) 2005, The National Idea 2006, The Letters from Petersburg 2006. *Honours:* Grand Prix for the best film script Grandmaster (Festival in Kranje, Yugoslavia), Golden Medal for filmscript Peace to the Newcomer, Venice Film Festival 1961, Prize of All-Union Contest of Playwrights Revival of Russia (for Moscow Nest) 1995, (for Lusgan) 1997, Laureate of Apollon Igoziev-Price 2003, Prize of the Russian Authors Org. 2006. *Address:* Krasnoarmeyskaya str. 21, Apt. 73, 125319 Moscow, Russia. *Telephone:* (495) 151-43-33 (home).

ZUCKERMAN, Mortimer (Mort) Benjamin, BA, LLM, MBA; American (b. Canadian) real estate developer, publisher and editor; *Chairman and Editor-in-Chief, US News and World Report, L.P.*; b. 4 June 1937, Montreal, Québec; s. of Abraham Zuckerman and Esther Zuckerman. *Education:* McGill Univ., Pennsylvania Univ., Harvard Univ. *Career:* Sr Vice-Pres. Cabot, Cabot and Forbes 1965–69; Lecturer, then Assoc. Prof., Harvard Univ. Grad. School of Design 1966–74; Visiting Lecturer, Yale Univ. 1967–69; Chair. Boston Properties Co. 1970–; Dir RET Income Foundation 1976–79, Property Capital Trust Co. 1979–80; Pres., Chair. Atlantic Monthly Co., Boston 1980–; Chair. and Ed.-in-Chief US News and World Report 1980–; Propr New York Daily News. *Address:* Boston Properties, 599 Lexington Avenue, Room 1800, New York, NY 10022; US News and World Report L.P., 1050 Thomas Jefferson Street, NW, Washington, DC 20007-3837, USA (office). *Telephone:* (202) 955-2000 (office). *Fax:* (202) 955-2685 (office). *Website:* www.usnews.com (office).

ZUCKERT, Catherine H., BA, MA, PhD; American political scientist and writer; *Nancy Reeves Dreux Professor, University of Notre Dame*; b. 20 Oct. 1942, Miami, FL; m. Michael Zuckert 1965, three d. *Education:* Cornell Univ. and Univ. of Chicago. *Career:* fmrly taught at Carleton Coll., St Olaf Coll., Cornell Univ., Claremont Colls, Fordham Univ. and Univ. of Michigan at Ann Arbor; currently Nancy Reeves Dreux Prof. in the Dept of Political Science, Univ. of Notre Dame; mem. American Political Science Asscn, Soc. for the Study of Greek Thought, Midwest Political Science Asscn. *Publications include:* Understanding the Political Spirit 1988, Natural Right and the American Imagination: Political Philosophy in Novel Form 1990, Postmodern Platos: Nietzsche, Heidegger, Gadamer, Strauss, Derrida 1996. *Address:* Department of Political Science, 217 O'Shaughnessy Hall, University of Notre Dame, Notre Dame, IN 46556, USA (office).

ZWICKY, (Julia) Fay, BA; Australian poet and editor; b. 4 July 1933, Melbourne, Vic.; m. 1st Karl Zwicky 1957; one s. one d.; m. 2nd James Mackie 1990. *Education:* Univ. of Melbourne. *Career:* Sr Lecturer in English, Univ. of Western Australia 1972–87; Assoc. Ed., Westerly 1973–95. *Publications:* Isaac Babel's Fiddle 1975, Quarry: A Selection of Western Australian Poetry (ed.) 1981, Kaddish and Other Poems 1982, Journeys: Poems by Judith Wright, Rosemary Dobson, Gwen Harwood, Dorothy Hewett (ed.) 1982, Hostages and Other Stories 1983, The Lyre in the Pawnshop: Essays on Literature and Survival, 1974–84 1986, Procession: Youngstreet Poets 3 (ed.) 1987, Ask Me 1990, Poems 1970–1992 1993, The Gatekeeper's Wife 1997, Picnic 2006. *Honours:* New South Wales Premier's Award 1982, Western Australian Premier's Awards 1987, 1991, 1999, Patrick White Literary Award 2005, Christopher Brennan Award for Poetry 2005. *Address:* 30 Goldsmith Road, Claremont, WA 6010, Australia.

ZWICKY, Jan, BA, MA, PhD; Canadian poet and philosopher; b. 10 May 1955, Calgary, AB. *Education:* Univ. of Calgary, Univ. of Toronto. *Career:* teacher, Univ. of Waterloo 1981, 1984, 1985, Princeton Univ. 1982, Univ. of Western Ontario 1989, Univ. of Alberta 1992, Univ. of New Brunswick 1994, 1995, Univ. of Victoria 1996–; Ed., Brick Books. *Publications:* Wittgenstein Elegies 1986, The New Room 1989, Lyric Philosophy 1992, Songs for Relinquishing the Earth 1998, Wisdom & Metaphor 2003, Robinson's Crossing 2004, Thirty-seven Small Songs and Thirteen Silences 2005. *Honours:* Gov.-Gen.'s Award for Poetry 1999, Dorothy Livesay Poetry Prize 2004. *Address:* c/o Department of Philosophy, University of Victoria, PO Box 3045, Victoria, BC V8W 3P4, Canada (office).

ZWINGER, Anne Haymond, MA; American natural history writer and illustrator; b. 12 March 1925, Muncie, IN; d. of William T. and Helen G. Haymond; m. Herman H. Zwinger 1952; three d. *Education:* Wellesley Coll., Indiana Univ. (Bloomington) and Radcliffe Coll. (Cambridge, MA). *Career:* freelance natural history writer and illustrator 1969–; Outdoor Consultant for various river cos since 1975; apptd Dir American Electric Power 1977; Adjunct Prof. Colorado Coll. since 1980; Trustee Nature Conservancy 1984; endowed Chair. Hulbert Center for Southwest Studies 1991; Dr hc (Colorado Coll) 1976, (Carleton Coll) 1984; Burroughs Medal for Natural History Writing 1976; Wellesley Coll. Alumnae Award 1977. *Publications:* Beyond the Aspen Grove 1970, Land Above the Trees 1972, Run, River Run 1975, Wind in the Rock 1978, A Desert Country Near the Sea 1983, The Mysterious Lands 1987; numerous further books and articles in magazines.

Directory

APPENDIX A: LITERARY AWARDS AND PRIZES

J. R. Ackerley Prize for Autobiography: English Centre of International PEN, Lancaster House, 33 Islington High Street, London, N1 9LH, England. *Telephone:* (20) 7713-0023. *Fax:* (20) 7013-0005. *E-mail:* enquiries@englishpen.org. *Website:* www.englishpen.org. Annual award for literary autobiography, written in English and published in the preceding year. Short-listed titles are chosen by the Literary Executors of J. R. Ackerley. Nominations are not accepted.

Jane Addams Children's Book Award: Jane Addams Peace Association, 777 United Nations Plaza, Sixth Floor, New York, NY 10017, USA. *Telephone:* (212) 682-8830. *Fax:* (212) 286-8211. *E-mail:* apa@igc.apc.org. *Website:* www.soemadison.wisc.edu/ccbc/public/jaddams.htm. f. 1953. Annual award, in association with the Women's International League for Peace and Freedom, for a picture book and a longer book for children that best combine literary merit with themes stressing peace, social justice, world community and the equality of the sexes and all races. Open to books for pre-school through to high school age, including translations or titles published in English in other countries. Books may be submitted by the publishers or requested by the committee.

Akutagawa Ryûnosuke Shô (Akutagawa Prize): Association for the Promotion of Japanese Literature, Bungei-Shunjû Bldg, 3 Kioi-cho, Chiyoda-ku, Tokyo 102, Japan. Japan's top literary award for young writers. f. 1935 by Kikuchi Kan, the editor of Bungei Shunjû magazine, in memory of novelist Akutagawa Ryûnosuke. Awarded twice a year, in January and July, to the best literary short story published in a newspaper or magazine by a new author.

Alexander Prize: Royal Historical Society, University College London, Gower Street, London, WC1E 6BT, England. *Telephone:* (20) 7387-7532. *Fax:* (20) 7387-7532. *E-mail:* royalhistsoc@ucl.ac.uk. *Website:* www.rhs.ac.uk. Offered for a paper based on original historical research. The paper must not exceed 8,000 words and can relate to any historical subject. Candidates must either be under 35 years of age or be registered for a higher degree (or have been registered for such a degree within the last three years).

Alice Literary Award: Society of Women Writers (Australia), PO Box 2621, Sydney, NSW 2001, Australia. Biennial award presented by the Society of Women Writers (Australia) for a distinguished and long-term contribution to literature by an Australian woman.

American Academy of Arts and Letters Gold Medal (Letters): American Academy of Arts and Letters, 633 West 155th Street, New York, NY 10032-5699, USA. *Telephone:* (212) 368-5900. A series of prestigious awards, which rotate between literary and artistic disciplines. Each discipline is awarded once every six years, with categories including poetry, belles lettres and criticism, history, drama, fiction, essays, music, and architecture.

Hans Christian Andersen Awards: International Board on Books for Young People (IBBY), Nonnenweg 12, Postfach, 4003 Basel, Switzerland. *Telephone:* (61) 272 29 17. *Fax:* (61) 272 27 57. *E-mail:* ibby@ibby.org. *Website:* www.ibby.org. f. 1956. Biennial awards to honour an author (Hans Christian Andersen Award for Writing), and an illustrator (Hans Christian Andersen Award for Illustration), whose work has made a lasting contribution to children's literature. Awards are open to living candidates from any country. Nominations are made by National Sections of IBBY.

Asham Award: Asham Literary Endowment Trust, The Town Hall, High Street, Lewes, East Sussex, BN7 2QS, England. *Website:* www.lewes.gov.uk/arts/asham.html. Biennial award, sponsored by Waterstone's, for short stories (up to 4,000 words) by new women writers. Open to women aged over 18, resident in the UK, who have not yet had a novel or collection of short stories published. The entries must be in English and previously unpublished.

Australian Literature Society Gold Medal: Association for the Study of Australian Literature (ASAL) Ltd, Australia. *Website:* www.asc.uq.edu.au/asal. Annual award for an outstanding Australian literary work published in the preceding year, or occasionally awarded for outstanding services to Australian literature. Award was inaugurated by the ALS, which was incorporated in the Association for the Study of Australian Literature in 1982. No direct application is accepted. No nominations are required; instead ASAL members are invited to propose potential winners to the judging panel.

The Australian/Vogel Literary Award: Allen & Unwin Publishers, POB 8500, St Leonards, NSW 1590, Australia. *Telephone:* (2) 8425-0100. *Fax:* (2) 9906-2218. *Website:* www.allanandunwin.com. f. 1980. Annual award for an original unpublished manuscript of Australian history, fiction or biography. Entrants must normally be residents of Australia aged under 35. Manuscripts must be between 30,000 and 100,000 words and must not be under offer to any other publisher or award.

Authors' Club Best First Novel Award: Authors' Club, 40 Dover Street, London, W1X 3RB, England. *Telephone:* (20) 7499-8581. *Fax:* (20) 7409-0913. *Website:* www.theartsclub.co.uk. f. 1954. Annual award to the most promising first full-length novel of the year, published in the UK by a British author. The winner is selected from entries submitted by publishers.

BA/Book Data Author of the Year Award: Minster House, 272 Vauxhall Bridge Road, London, SW1V 1BA, England. *Telephone:* (20) 7834-5477. *Fax:* (20) 7834-8812. *E-mail:* mail@booksellers.org.uk. *Website:* www.booksellers.org.uk. f. 1993. Annual award to the author judged to have had the most impact for booksellers in the year, as voted for by members of the Booksellers Association. The living author must be British or Irish.

Banipal Prize for Arabic Literary Translation: c/o The Banipal Trust, PO Box 22300, London, W13 8ZQ, England. *Telephone:* (20) 8568-9747. *E-mail:* info@banipaltrust.org. *Website:* www.banipaltrust.org.uk/prize. f. 2006. Annual award to the translator of a full-length imaginative and creative work of literary merit published in English. Aims to raise the profile of contemporary Arabic literature and honour the work of translators.

BBC FOUR Samuel Johnson Prize for Non-Fiction: c/o Colman Getty PR, Middlesex House, 34–42 Cleveland Street, London, W1T 4JE, England. *E-mail:* pr@colmangettypr.co.uk. *Website:* www.bbc.co.uk/bbcfour/books/features/samueljohnson. Formerly the AT&T Non-Fiction Award. Annual award to the best work of general non-fiction published by a British publisher in the previous year. Entries must be written in English by living writers from the British Commonwealth or the Republic of Ireland. Entries are submitted by publishers.

Benson Medal: Royal Society of Literature, Somerset House, Strand, London, WC2R 1LA, England. *Telephone:* (20) 7845-4676. *Fax:* (20) 7845-4679. *E-mail:* info@rslit.org. *Website:* www.rslit.org. f. 1916 by A. C. Benson, irregular periodical award recognizing works of poetry, fiction or biography. Submissions are not accepted.

David Berry Prize: Royal Historical Society, University College London, Gower Street, London, WC1E 6BT, England. *Telephone:* (20) 7387-7532. *Fax:* (20) 7387-7532. *E-mail:* royalhistsoc@ucl.ac.uk. *Website:* www.rhs.ac.uk. Annual award to the writer of the best essay on a subject dealing with Scottish history, of between 6,000 and 10,000 words. Previous winners may not reapply.

Besterman/McColvin Medals: The CILIP, 7 Ridgmount Street, London, WC1E 7AE, England. *Telephone:* (20) 7255-0650. *Fax:* (20) 7255-0501. *E-mail:* marketing@cilip.org.uk. *Website:* www.cilip.org.uk. Two medals are awarded annually for outstanding works of reference published in the UK: one for print and one for electronic formats. The awards are sponsored by Whitaker and judged by panels of reference librarians and members of the Society of Indexers.

James Tait Black Memorial Prizes: Department of English Literature, University of Edinburgh, David Hume Tower, George Square, Edinburgh, EH8 9JX, Scotland. *Telephone:* (131) 650-3619. *Fax:* (131) 650-6898. *E-mail:* s.strathdee@ed.ac.uk. *Website:* www.englit.ed.ac.uk/jtbinf.htm. f. 1918. Two annual awards for biographical and fictional work published in the preceding year. Works must be written in English and be published or co-published in the UK. Only publishers may apply.

Book of the Year Award: Welsh Academy, Third Floor, Mount Stuart House, Mount Stuart Square, Cardiff, CF10 5FQ, Wales. *Telephone:* (29) 2047-2266. *E-mail:* post@academi.org. f. 1992. Annual awards given for works of exceptional merit by Welsh authors (by birth or residence) published during the preceding year. Works may be in Welsh or in English, in the categories of poetry, fiction and creative non-fiction (including literary criticism, biography and autobiography). Non-fiction works must have subject matter that is concerned with Wales. Two First Prizes are given: one for works in Welsh, one in English.

Booker—Open Russia Prize: Khohlovsky per. 13/1, 109028 Moscow, Russia. *Telephone:* (495) 789 3179. *Fax:* (495) 789 3177. *E-mail:* info@openrussia.info. *Website:* www.russianbooker.ru. f. 1991, as the first independent literary prize in Russia, with the support of the British Booker Prize. In 2002 general sponsorship of the prize was taken over by the regional charitable organization, Open Russia. The prize is awarded each year for the best novel written in the Russian language; it aims to encourage the creativity of authors writing in Russian, to arouse interest in contemporary Russian literature, and to assist the renaissance of the publishing industry and of translations from Russian into other languages. Works considered for the prize are put forward by Russian and foreign nominators appointed by the Russian Booker Committee, as well as by Russian publishing houses. After screening for conformity with the rules of the competition, these works comprise the Long List which is then judged by a jury consisting of professional literary critics, authors and other leading cultural figures. The jury delivers its Short List of six finalists, before finally choosing the winner.

The Booker Prize: see Man Booker Prize for Fiction.

Boston Globe-Horn Book Award: Boston Globe, 135 William T. Morrissey Boulevard, Boston, MA 02125, USA. f. 1967 by The Boston Globe and The Horn Book Magazine. Annual award for books published in the USA within the previous year, in the categories of fiction, non-fiction and picture book.

BP Natural World Book Prize: Book Trust, 45 East Hill, London, SW18 2QZ, England. *Telephone:* (20) 8516-2972. *Website:* www.booktrust.org.uk/prizes/bp.htm. Award for environmental literature, amalgamating the former BP Conservation Book Prize and the Wildlife Trust Natural World Book of the Year Award. Only publishers may submit entries.

Bremen Literatur Förderungspreis (City of Bremen Literary Encouragement Prize): Bremen City Council, Herdentorsteinweg 7, 28195 Bremen, Germany. f. 1952 in honour of Rudolf Alexander Schröder, as the Literaturpreis der Freien Hansestadt Bremen. Annual award to a German-speaking writer or poet.

Bridport Prize: Bridport Arts Centre, South Street, Bridport, Dorset DT6 3NR, England. *Telephone:* (1398) 459444. *Fax:* (1308) 459166. *E-mail:* frances@bridport-arts.com. *Website:* www.bridportprize.org.uk. f. 1973 by Peggy Chapman-Andrews. Annual award for original poems of not more than 42 lines, and short stories between 1,000 and 5,000 words. Open to previously unpublished works, written in English, not entered in any other competition.

British Academy Book Prize: British Academy, 10 Carlton House Terrace, London, SW1Y 5AH, England. *Telephone:* (20) 7969-5263. *E-mail:* externalrelations@britac.ac.uk. f. 2001. Annual award to the best book published in social sciences and the humanities, in the preceding year. Nominations by publishers.

British Book Awards: Publishing News, 39 Store Street, London, WC1E 7DB, England. *Telephone:* (20) 7692-2900. *Fax:* (20) 7419-2111. *E-mail:* nibbies@mdla.co.uk. *Website:* www.publishingnews.co.uk. f. 1989. 21 annual awards, known as 'Nibbies', in a range of categories, with various awards sponsored by different companies. Categories include Editor, Publisher, Author, Independent Bookseller and Children's Book.

British Columbia Book Prizes: West Coast Book Prize Society, Suite 902, 207 West Hastings Street, Vancouver, BC V6B 1H7, Canada. *Telephone:* (604) 687-2405. *Fax:* (604) 669-3701. *E-mail:* info@rebuscreative.net. *Website:* www.harbour.sfu.ca/bcbook. f. 1985. Awards celebrating the achievements of British Columbian writers and publishers, presented in categories including fiction, non-fiction, poetry, regional writing, illustrated children's literature. Books must have been published during the preceding year; residency conditions for authors vary according to category.

British Fantasy Awards: British Fantasy Society, 201 Reddish Road, South Reddish, Stockport SK5 7HR, England. *E-mail:* info@britishfantasysociety.org.uk. *Website:* www.britishfantasysociety.org.uk. Set of awards presented by the British Fantasy Society at its annual conference, in categories including best novel (the August Derleth Award), best short story, and best anthology. The winners are selected by BFS members.

British Science Fiction Association Awards: British Science Fiction Association, 8 Century House, Armoury Road, London, SE8 4LH, England. *Telephone:* (20) 8469-3354. *E-mail:* awards@amaranth.aviators.net. *Website:* www.bsfa.co.uk. f. 1966 to promote the best British (and other) science fiction novel, story, artwork, etc. Entries must have been first published in the UK in that year. No applications are permitted.

Bruntwood Playwriting Competition: Royal Exchange Theatre, St Ann's Square, Manchester, M2 7DH, England. *Telephone:* (161) 615 6765. *E-mail:* bruntwood@royalexchange.co.uk. *Website:* www.royalexchange.co.uk/playwriting. f. 2005 by the Royal Exchange Theatre, Manchester. Annual competition to reward the best plays by writers across the UK and Ireland. Entries are judged anonymously and the competition is open to anyone over the age of 18 with a play not previously performed. The winner's play is staged at the Royal Exchange Theatre.

Georg-Büchner-Preis: Deutsche Akademie für Sprache und Dichtung, Alexandraweg 23, 64287 Darmstadt, Germany. *Telephone:* (6151) 40920. *Fax:* (6151) 409299. *Website:* www.deutscheakademie.de. f. 1951. Annual award in recognition of the winner's special status and contribution to contemporary German culture. Awarded to a novelist or poet writing in German.

Buckland Award: 24 Water Street, PO Box 760, Dunedin, New Zealand. Annual award for work of the highest literary merit by a New Zealand writer.

Caine Prize for African Writing: African Centre, 2 Drayson Mews, London, W8 4LY, England. *Telephone:* (20) 7376-0440. *Fax:* (20) 7603-3274. *E-mail:* info@caineprize.com. *Website:* www.caineprize.com. f. 2000. Annual award to a short story or narrative poem (between 3,000 and 10,000 words) by an African writer, published in English anywhere in the world in the previous five years. Submissions should be made by publishers.

Randolph Caldecott Medal: Association for Library Service to Children, 50 East Huron Street, Chicago, IL 70711, USA. *E-mail:* alsc@ala.org. *Website:* www.ala.org/alsc. Annual award to an illustrator of the most distinguished American picture book for children published in the preceding year.

James Cameron Memorial Award: Department of Journalism, City University, Northampton Square, London, EC1 0HB, England. Annual award for journalism to a reporter of any nationality working for the British media. Nominations are not accepted.

Canadian Authors' Association Literary Awards: 27 Doxsee Avenue North, PO Box 419, Campbellford, ON K0L 1L0, Canada. *Telephone:* (705) 653-0323. *Fax:* (705) 653-0593. *E-mail:* canauth@redden.on.ca. *Website:* www.canauthors.org. A series of annual awards from the Canadian Authors' Association and the Canada Council for the Arts, including fiction (CAA MOSAID Technology Inc. Award for Fiction), poetry (CAA Jack Chalmers Poetry Award), short story (CAA Jubilee Award for Short Stories), biography (CAA Birks Family Foundation Award for Biography), Canadian history (CAA Lela Common Award for Canadian History), drama (CAA Carol Bolt Drama Award), children's (CAA Children's Short Story Award), as well as a special award for a complete body of work. Awards are for full-length English-language literature by living writers who are Canadians or landed immigrants. All entries must have been first published during the preceding year, although publication may have taken place outside Canada. Previous winners are not eligible for awards they have won, but may be entered in the other categories.

Canadian Library Association Book of the Year for Children Award: Canadian Library Association, 328 Frank Street, Ottawa, ON K2P 0X8, Canada. *Telephone:* (613) 232-9625. *Fax:* (613) 563-9895. *E-mail:* info@cla.ca. *Website:* www.cla.ca. Annual award to an author of an outstanding children's book published in Canada during the previous year. The book must be suitable for children up to 14 years of age.

Carnegie Medal: The CILIP, 7 Ridgmount Street, London, WC1E 7AE, England. *Telephone:* (20) 7255-0650. *Fax:* (20) 7255-0501. *E-mail:* marketing@cilip.org.uk. *Website:* www.cilip.org.uk. Annual award for an outstanding book for children written in English and receiving its first publication in the UK during the preceding year.

Children's Book Award: The Federation of Children's Book Groups, 2 Bridge Wood View, Horsforth, Leeds, West Yorkshire LS18 5PE, England. *Telephone:* (1132) 588910. *Fax:* (1132) 588920. *E-mail:* info@fcbg.org.uk. *Website:* www.fcbg.org.uk. Annual award, sponsored by Red House, judged by children. The short-list is announced at the annual conference of the Federation of Children's Book Groups. The three categories are picture books, shorter novels and longer novels, all of which are then considered for the Best Book of the Year award.

Children's Laureate: Education Department, Book Trust, Book House, 45 East Hill, London, SW18 2QZ, England. *Website:* www.childrenslaureate.org. f. 1999. Biennial award to honour a writer or illustrator of children's books for lifetime achievement. Nominees must be UK-based, have a significant body of work, and have attracted critical and popular success.

Arthur C. Clarke Award for Science Fiction: 60 Bournemouth Road, Folkestone, Kent CT19 5AZ, England. *Telephone:* (1303) 252939. *E-mail:* arthurcclarkeaward@yahoo.co.uk. *Website:* www.clarkeaward.com. f. 1987 to encourage science fiction in the UK. Annual award to the best science fiction novel published in the UK in the preceding year. The award is jointly administered and judged by the British Science Fiction Association, Science Fiction Foundation and the Science Museum.

CNA Letterkkunde Toekenning (CNA Literary Award): Central News Agency Ltd, POB 9380, Johannesburg, South Africa. f. 1961. Annual literary award, the highest honour for South African literature, for books by South African residents or citizens in any of the following categories: novel, poetry, biography, drama, history and travel.

David Cohen British Literature Prize: Arts Council of England, Literature Department, 14 Great Peter Street, London, SW1P 3NQ, England. *Telephone:* (20) 7973-6442. *Fax:* (20) 7973-6520. *E-mail:* info.literature@artscouncil.org.uk. *Website:* www.artscouncil.org.uk. f. 1980. Biennial award recognizing lifetime achievement of a living novelist, short story writer, essayist, biographer, poet, dramatist, travel writer or writer in any other literary genre.

Commonwealth Writers' Prize: The Commonwealth Writers' Prize Administrator, Book Trust, Book House, 45 East Hill, London, SW18 2QZ, England. *Telephone:* (20) 8516-2972. *Fax:* (20) 8516-2978. *Website:* www.booktrust.org.uk. f. 1987. Annual award to reward excellence in Commonwealth literature; it is sponsored by the Commonwealth Foundation and administered by Booktrust. For the purposes of the award the Commonwealth is divided into four regions: Africa, the Caribbean and Canada, Eurasia (which includes the UK), and Southeast Asia and the South Pacific. A shortlist is drawn up with a best book and a best first book for each region. Each year the award ceremony is held in a different Commonwealth country. Open to any work of prose fiction (drama and poetry are excluded). The work must have been written by a living citizen of the Commonwealth, must be of a reasonable length and be in English. It must have been first published during the previous calendar year. To be eligible for the best first published book category the entry must be the first work of fiction that the author has published.

Thomas Cook Travel Book Awards: Thomas Cook Publishing, Coningsby Road, North Bretton, Peterborough PE3 8SB, England. *E-mail:* ipmc@freenet.co.uk. *Website:* www.thetravelbookaward.com. Annual award for best travel book published in the previous year.

Duff Cooper Prize: Artemis Cooper, 54 St Maur Road, London, SW6 4DP, England. *Telephone:* (20) 7736-3729. *Fax:* (20) 7731-7638. Annual award to a literary work in the field of history, biography, politics or poetry, published in the previous year.

Costa Book Awards: Booksellers' Association of the UK and Ireland, Minster House, 272 Vauxhall Bridge Road, London, SW1V 1BA, England. *Telephone:* (20) 7834-5477. *Fax:* (20) 7834-8812. *Website:* www .costabookawards.com. f. 1971 as the Whitbread Book Awards, changed sponsorship and name 2006. Annual awards to promote and increase good English literature in each of five categories: novel, first novel, biography, children's novel and poetry. Entries are submitted by publishers and the authors must have been resident in the UK or Republic of Ireland for at least three years. One category winner is then voted Book of the Year by the panel of judges.

Crime Writers' Association (CWA) Awards: Crime Writers' Association, PO Box 273, Borehamwood, Hertfordshire WD6 2XA, England. *E-mail:* secretary@thecwa.co.uk. *Website:* www.thecwa.co.uk. The CWA makes a series of annual awards for outstanding works in the field of crime literature: Cartier Diamond Dagger for Fiction (for outstanding contribution to the genre), Duncan Lawrie Dagger for Fiction (formerly the Gold Dagger for Fiction, awarded for the best crime fiction of the year), Silver Dagger for Fiction, Gold Dagger for Non-Fiction (for the best non-fiction crime book), Short Story Dagger (for the best short story in the crime genre), Ian Fleming Steel Dagger (for the best thriller, adventure novel or spy fiction novel), John Creasey Memorial Dagger (for the best first crime novel by an author), Ellis Peters Historical Dagger (for the best historical crime novel), Dagger in the Library (for the author whose work has given the most pleasure to readers, judged by librarians), Début Dagger (for an unpublished writer of crime fiction), Mystery and Thriller People's Choice Dagger (chosen by members of the book club).

Den Store Pris: Det Danske Akademi, Rungstedlund, Rungsted Strandvej 111, 2960 Rungsted Kyst, Denmark. *Telephone:* 33 13 11 12. *Fax:* 33 32 80 45. *E-mail:* lawoffice@philip.dk. *Website:* www.danskeakademi.dk. f. 1961 by the Ministry of Culture. Biennial award for a complete body of work, with the recipient chosen by members of the Danish Academy. Open only to Danish authors. No direct applications are accepted.

Deutscher Buchpreis: Börsenverein des Deutschen Buchhandels eV, Grosser Hirschgraben 17–21 Buchhändlerhaus, 60311 Frankfurt am Main, Germany. *Telephone:* (69) 13 06 0. *Fax:* (69) 13 06 201. *E-mail:* info@boev.de. *Website:* www.boersenverein.de. f. 2005 by the Börsenverein des Deutschen Buchhandels (German Publishers' & Booksellers' Association); annual award to promote literature written in German; open to any writer in German; the winner is announced at the Frankfurt Book Fair.

Encore Award: Society of Authors, 84 Drayton Gardens, London, SW10 9SB, England. *Telephone:* (20) 7373-6642. *Fax:* (20) 7373-5768. *E-mail:* info@ societyofauthors.org. *Website:* www.societyofauthors.org. f. 1990. Annual award for a second published novel.

Geoffrey Faber Memorial Prize: Faber and Faber Ltd, 3 Queen Square, London, WC1N 3AU, England. *Telephone:* (20) 7465-0045. *Fax:* (20) 7465-0043. *E-mail:* belinda.matthews@faber.co.uk. *Website:* www.faber.co.uk. f. 1963, in memory of the founder of the publishing firm Faber and Faber. Annual award, with prizes alternating between verse or fiction. Entrants must be under 40 years of age and a citizen of the UK and colonies, the Commonwealth, or the Republic of Ireland or South Africa. Entries must have been published in the two years preceding the year in which the award is given.

Eleanor Farjeon Award: . *E-mail:* contact@childrensbookcircle.org.uk. *Website:* www.childrensbookcircle.org.uk. Awarded by the Children's Book Circle for distinguished service to children's books, both in the UK and overseas. Recipients include librarians, publishers, booksellers and authors and are chosen from nominations from members of the Children's Book Circle.

Kathleen Fidler Award: c/o Book Trust Scotland, Scottish Book Centre, Fountainbridge Library, 137 Dundee Street, Edinburgh, EH11 1BG, Scotland. *Website:* www.scottishbooktrust.com. Annual award for an unpublished children's novel of no fewer than 25,000 words, for children aged 8–12. The author must not have had a novel published previously for this age group.

Sir Banister Fletcher Prize of the Authors' Club: Authors' Club, 40 Dover Street, London, W1X 3RB, England. *Telephone:* (20) 7499-8581. *Fax:* (20) 7409-0913. *Website:* www.theartsclub.co.uk. f. 1954 and named after the late Sir Banister Fletcher, a former President of both the Authors' Club and the Royal Institute of British Architects (RIBA), this annual prize is awarded for the most deserving book of the previous year on either architecture or the arts. Publishers only are invited to apply to the Club Secretary.

Miles Franklin Award: Permanent Trustee Co. Ltd, 35 Clarence Street, Sydney, NSW 2000, Australia. *Telephone:* (2) 8295 8100. *Fax:* (2) 8295 8659. *E-mail:* linda.ingaldo@permanentgroupcom.au. *Website:* www.permanentgroupcom .au. f. 1957. Annual award for a novel or play of high literary merit, presenting aspects of Australian life, published in the previous year.

Giller Prize: see The Scotiabank Giller Prize.

Glenfiddich Food and Drink Awards: 4 Bedford Square, London, WC1B 3RA, England. *Telephone:* (20) 7255-1100. *Fax:* (20) 7436-4164. *Website:* www .graylinggroup.com. f. 1970. Annual awards recognizing the excellence in writing, publishing and broadcasting on the subjects of food and drink. Categories include best food book, best drinks book, best newspaper cookery writer, restaurant critic of the year and best drinks writer. Entries are accepted from publishers only.

Goodman Fielder Wattie Book Award: PO Box 44-146, Auckland 2, New Zealand. Annual award for a book published in New Zealand in the previous year by a New Zealand author (including New Zealand residents and Pacific Island countries).

Governor-General's Literary Awards: Canada Council, 350 Albert Street, PO Box 1047, Ottawa, ON K1P 5V8, Canada. *Telephone:* (613) 566-4305. *Website:* www.canadacouncil.ca/prizes/ggla. f. 1937. Annual awards, given by the Canada Council for the Arts and the Bank of Montréal, for Canadian authors writing both in English and French. Categories are: adult fiction, poetry, drama, non-fiction, children's literature (text), children's literature (illustrated), translation. Prizes in each language.

Gradam Litrochta Cló Iar-Chonnachta (Cló Iar-Chonnachta Literary Award): Cló Iar-Chonnachta Teo, Indreabhán, Connemara, County Galway, Ireland. *Telephone:* (91) 593307. *Fax:* (91) 593362. *E-mail:* cic@iol.ie. *Website:* www.cic.ie. f. 1995 by Micheal o Conghaile, writer and founder of Irish-language publisher Cló Iar-Chonnachta, to encourage Irish language writing. Annual award for a newly-written and unpublished work in the Irish language, a different type of work each year, either poetry, drama, novel or short story.

Grand Prix de la Francophonie (Grand Francophony Prize): Académie Française, Institut de France, 23 quai de Conti, 75006 Paris, France. *Telephone:* 1 44 41 43 00. *Fax:* 1 43 29 47 45. *E-mail:* contact@academie -francaise.fr. *Website:* www.academie-francaise.fr. f. 1986 at the suggestion of the Canadian government, with support from the governments of France, Monaco and Morocco and several private sponsors. Administered by the Académie Française, this annual award aims to promote the influence of French-language literature. Open to living authors of all ages; only published works may be submitted, and they must have appeared during the preceding year.

Kate Greenaway Medal: The CILIP, 7 Ridgmount Street, London, WC1E 7AE, England. *Telephone:* (20) 7255-0650. *Fax:* (20) 7255-0501. *E-mail:* marketing@cilip.org.uk. *Website:* www.cilip.org.uk. Annual award for an outstanding book in terms of illustration for children, published in the UK in the preceding year.

Guardian Children's Fiction Award: The Guardian, 119 Farringdon Road, London, EC1R 3ER, England. Annual award for an outstanding work of fiction for children by a Commonwealth or British author, first published in the UK in the previous year, excluding picture books and previous winners.

Guardian First Book Award: The Guardian, 119 Farringdon Road, London, EC1R 3ER, England. Annual award for a work of fiction by a British, Irish or Commonwealth writer and published in the UK. Submissions are not accepted.

Hammett Awards: *E-mail:* jeremiahealy@earthlink.net. *Website:* jmc.ou .edu/AIEP/index.htm. Annual award given by the North American branch of the Asociación Internacional de Escritores Policiacos, or International Association of Crime Writers, to reward excellence in the genre of crime literature. Open to US or Canadian writers.

Hawthornden Prize: 42a Hays Mews, Berkeley Square, London, W1X 7RU, England. f. 1919. Annual award to a British writer for a work of imaginative literature, published during the previous year. No direct applications are accepted.

W. H. Heinemann Award: Royal Society of Literature, Somerset House, Strand, London, WC2R 1LA, England. *Telephone:* (20) 7845-4676. *Fax:* (20) 7845-4679. *E-mail:* info@rslit.org. *Website:* www.rslit.org. f. 1944. Annual award aiming to encourage contributions to literature, given to a work, usually non-fiction, judged to be of outstanding literary distinction. The book must be written in English, published in the previous year and submitted by publishers.

William Hill Sports Book of the Year: Greenside House, 50 Station Road, Wood Green, London, N22 4TP, England. *E-mail:* pressoffice@williamhill.co .uk. *Website:* www.williamhillmedia.com. Sponsored by bookmakers, William Hill. All books must be published in the UK during the previous year.

Historical Novel Prize in Memory of Georgette Heyer: The Bodley Head, Random Century, 20 Vauxhall Bridge Road, London, SW1V 2SA, England. Annual award for a full-length, previously unpublished, historical novel set before 1939.

P. C. Hooft-prijs voor Letterkunde (P. C. Hooft Prize for Literature): Postbus 90515, Prins Willem, Alexanderhof 5, 2595 LM, The Hague, The Netherlands. f. 1947. Annual award presented to a Dutch writer for lifetime achievement in literature. Works of prose, essay and poetry are all considered for the prize.

Richard Imison Memorial Award: Society of Authors, 84 Drayton Gardens, London, SW10 9SB, England. Designed to encourage talent and help maintain high standards, this award is given for the best work of radio drama, as judged by the Society of Authors Broadcasting Committee. Works must be original, the first dramatic work by the author(s) to be broadcast, and must be written specifically for radio (adaptations for works orginally intended for stage, film or television are not eligible).

Independent Foreign Fiction Prize: Literature Department, Arts Council England, 14 Great Peter Street, London, SW1P 3NQ, England. *Telephone:* (20) 7333-0100. *Fax:* (20) 7973-6590. *E-mail:* info.literature@artscouncil.org.uk. *Website:* www.artscouncil.org.uk. f. 1990. Open to works of fiction by a living author, which have been translated into English from any other language and published in the UK during the previous year. The prize is shared between author and translator.

Institute of Historical Research Prize—IHR Prize: Institute of Historical Research, Senate House, London, WC1E 7HU, England. *Telephone:* (20) 7862-8756. *Website:* www.history.ac.uk. f. 2000. Biennial award to enable professional historians to write their first book for a general readership. Entrants must be previously unpublished professional historians (not including monographs, university press publications or academic imprints).

International IMPAC Dublin Literary Award: Dublin City Library and Archive, 138–144 Pearse Street, Dublin 2, Ireland. *Telephone:* (1) 674-4802. *Fax:* (1) 674-4879. *E-mail:* literaryaward@dublincity.ie. *Website:* www.impacdublinaward.ie. f. 1995 by Dublin City Council, in partnership with IMPAC, a productivity improvement company that operates worldwide. Annual award for the best work of fiction written in or translated into English. Books are nominated by selected libraries in capital and major cities around the world.

Irish Times International Fiction Prize: Irish Times Ltd, 10–16 D'Olier Street, Dublin 2, Ireland. f. 1989. Biennial award to the author of a work of fiction written in English, published in Ireland, the UK or the USA in the previous two years. Nominations come from critics and editors. Submissions are not accepted.

Irish Times Irish Literature Prizes: Irish Times Ltd, 10–16 D'Olier Street, Dublin 2, Ireland. *Telephone:* (1) 679-2022. *Fax:* (1) 679-3910. f. 1988. Biennial awards for books in four categories: Irish fiction, Irish non-fiction, Irish poetry and Irish language. Authors must be born in Ireland or be an Irish citizen. Books are nominated by critics and editors. Submissions are not accepted.

Jerusalem Prize: Binyaney Ha'ooma, PO Box 6001, Jerusalem 91060, Israel. Biennial award to a writer whose work expresses the idea of the freedom of the individual in society.

Kalinga Prize: c/o UNESCO, 7 place de Fontenoy, 75352 Paris 07 SP, France. Annual award to popularizers of science with distinguished careers as writers, editors, lecturers, directors or producers. The winner is expected to have an understanding of science and technology and an awareness of the scientific work of the UN and UNESCO.

Keats–Shelley Prize: Keats–Shelley Memorial Association, 117 Cheyne Walk, London, SW10 0ES, England. *Fax:* (20) 7352-6705. *Website:* www.keats-shelley.com. f. 1998. Sponsored by the Esmée Fairbairn Foundation and the David Cohen Family Charitable Trust. Annual award for an essay or poem on any aspect of Keats' or Shelley's work or life. Essays and poems must be in English and must be original and unpublished work; they must not have been submitted to a previous competition. Entries should be of 2,000–3,000 words, including quotations.

Kiriyama Pacific Rim Book Prize: 650 Delancey Street, Suite 101, San Francisco, CA 94107-2082, USA. *Telephone:* (415) 777-1628. *Fax:* (415) 777-1646. *E-mail:* info@kiriyamaprize.org. *Website:* www.kiriyamaprize.org. f. 1996. Award in two categories, fiction and non-fiction, to promote books that will contribute to greater understanding and co-operation among the peoples and nations of the Pacific Rim.

John W. Kluge Prize: Office of Scholarly Programs, Library of Congress LJ 120, 101 Independence Avenue SE, Washington, DC 20540-4860, USA. *Telephone:* (202) 707-3302. *Fax:* (202) 707-3595. *E-mail:* scholarly@loc.gov. *Website:* www.loc.gov/loc/kluge/kluge-prize.html. f. 2003. Annual prize, endowed by Library of Congress benefactor, John W. Kluge. The prize recognizes lifetime achievement in the human sciences (a wide range of disciplines, including history, philosophy, politics, anthropology, sociology, religion, criticism in the arts and humanities, and linguistics). The recipient may be of any nationality, the writing in any language.

Lannan Literary Awards: Lannan Foundation, 313 Read Street, Santa Fe, NM 87501-2628, USA. *Telephone:* (505) 986-8160. *Fax:* (505) 986-8195. *E-mail:* info@calannan.org. *Website:* www.lannan.org. f. 1989. Annual awards to honour established and new writers whose work is of exceptional quality. Recipients are chosen by the Foundation's Literary Committee, on recommendation from anonymous nominators. Awards are made in the areas of fiction, non-fiction and poetry for a body of work.

Lloyds Private Banking Playwright of the Year Award: Tony Ball Association PLC, 174–78 North Gower Street, London, NW1 2NB, England. f. 1994. Award to encourage new and diverse writing for theatre, broadening support for the theatre and extending the links between Lloyds Private Banking and the arts. Playwrights should be British or Irish, whose new works have been performed in the UK or the Republic of Ireland for the first time in the previous year. Nominations by theatre critics form a short-list, with winners chosen by a panel of judges.

Longman/History Today Book of the Year Award: History Today, 20 Old Compton Street, London, W1V 5PE, England. Annual award, administered by History Today, for an author's first or second non-fiction book on an historical subject, written in English.

Los Angeles Times Book Prizes: Los Angeles Times, Times Mirror Square, Los Angeles, CA 90053, USA. f. 1980. Prizes in nine single-title categories: biography, current interest, fiction, first fiction (the Art Seidenbaum Award, named after the founder of the Book Prize programme), history, mystery/thriller, poetry, science and technology, and young-adult fiction. In addition, the Robert Kirsch Award (named after a novelist and editor who was book critic for the LA Times) recognizes the body of work by a writer living in and/or writing on the American West. Entries must have been first published in English in the USA between January and December of the previous year. Translations are eligible and authors may be of any nationality. They should be alive at the time of their book's qualifying US publication, although eligibility is also extended to significant new translations of the work of deceased writers.

The Lulu Blooker Prize: 8311 Brier Creek Parkway, Suite 105-374, Raleigh, NC 27617, USA. . *E-mail:* blookerprize@lulu.com. *Website:* www.lulublookerprize.com. f. 2006. Annual award, sponsored by Lulu, in three categories (fiction, non-fiction and comics) for 'blooks', or books with content originally in the form of a blog, web comic or website.

McKitterick Prize: Society of Authors, 84 Drayton Gardens, London, SW10 9SB, England. *Telephone:* (20) 7373-6642. *Fax:* (20) 7373-5768. *E-mail:* info@societyofauthors.org. *Website:* www.societyofauthors.org. Annual award for a full-length work written in English and first published in the UK or previously unpublished. Open to writers over 40 years old, who have had no previous work published other than that submitted.

Macmillan Writer's Prize for Africa: Macmillan Oxford, Between Towns Road, Oxford, OX4 3PP, England. *Telephone:* (1865) 405700. *Fax:* (1865) 405799. *E-mail:* writersprize@macmillan.co.uk. *Website:* www.write4africa.com. f. 2002. Biennial award for previously unpublished works of fiction in English, in three categories: Children's Literature (8–12 years old), Children's Literature (13–17 years old), and Most Promising New Children's Writer. Open to nationals or naturalized citizens of any African country.

Walter McRae Russell Award: *Website:* www.asc.uq.edu.au/asal. Biennial award by Association for the Study of Australian Literature for an outstanding work of literary scholarship on an Australian subject. No nominations are accepted.

Mail on Sunday/John Llewellyn Rhys Prize: Booktrust, Book House, 45 East Hill, London, SW18 2QZ, England. *Telephone:* (20) 8516-2972. *Fax:* (20) 8516-2978. *Website:* www.booktrust.org.uk. f. 1942. Annual award for works of fiction, non-fiction, drama or poetry written in English and published in the UK in the preceding calendar year. Writers must be under 35 years old at the time of publication, a citizen of the UK or Commonwealth. Previous winners are not eligible. Publishers are invited to submit entries.

The Man Booker International Prize: Colman Getty PR, Middlesex House, 34–42 Cleveland Street, London, W1T 4JE, England. *Telephone:* (20) 7631-2666. *Fax:* (20) 7631-2699. *E-mail:* pr@colmangettypr.co.uk. *Website:* www.manbookerinternational.com. f. 2005. Biennial award recognizing one writer's achievement in literature and their significant influence on writers and readers worldwide. It can be won by an author of any nationality, providing that his or her work is available in English.

The Man Booker International Prize for Translation: Colman Getty PR, Middlesex House, 34–42 Cleveland Street, London, W1T 4JE, England. *Telephone:* (20) 7631-2666. *Fax:* (20) 7631-2699. *E-mail:* pr@colmangettypr.co.uk. *Website:* www.manbookerinternational.com. f. 2005. Award recognizing the role of translators in bringing fiction to an international audience.

The Man Booker Prize for Fiction: Colman Getty PR, Middlesex House, 34–42 Cleveland Street, London, W1T 4JE, England. *Telephone:* (20) 7631-2666. *Fax:* (20) 7631-2699. *E-mail:* pr@colmangettypr.co.uk. *Website:* www.manbookerprize.com. Established 1968 by Booker Brothers (now Booker Prize Foundation) as The Booker Prize. It is judged by literary critics, editors, writers and academics: the judging panel changes every year and is selected by a management committee. The award is made to the judges' choice of the best novel of the year. Sponsored by Man Group, an alternative investment fund manager and broker. Writers must be citizens of the British Commonwealth or the Republic of Ireland. Only full-length novels written in English are considered. The prize may be awarded posthumously.

Marsh Award for Children's Literature in Translation: Authors' Club, 40 Dover Street, London, W1X 3RB, England. f. 1996. Biennial award to British translators of books for 4–16 year olds, published in the UK by a British publisher. The award is sponsored by the Marsh Christian Trust to encourage the translation of foreign children's books into English. No encyclopaedias, reference works or electronic books.

Marsh Biography Award: Authors' Club, 40 Dover Street, London, W1X 3RB, England. Formerly the Marsh Christian Trust Award. Biennial award for a significant biography by a British author, published in the UK in the two preceding years. Nominations are submitted by publishers.

Meyer-Whitworth Award: Drama Department, Arts Council England, 14 Great Peter Street, London, SW1P 3NQ, England. *E-mail:* info.drama@ artscouncil.org.uk. *Website:* www.artscouncil.org.uk. Established to commemorate the Shakespeare Memorial National Theatre Committee of 1908, where the movement for a National Theatre joined forces with the movement to create a monument to William Shakespeare. Awarded to a playwright whose work displays promise of new talent, whose writing is of individual quality and whose work 'reveals the truth about the relationships of human beings with each other and the world at large' (Geoffrey Whitworth). Plays must be written in English and have been produced in the UK in the previous year.

Milner Award: The Friends of the Atlanta Fulton Public Library, 1 Margaret Mitchell Square, Atlanta, GA 30303, USA. Award to a living American author of children's books.

The Mitchell Prize for Art History/The Eric Mitchell Prize: c/o The Burlington Magazine, 14–16 Duke's Road, London, WC1H 9SZ, England. The Mitchell Prize is awarded for a book that has made an outstanding and original contribution to the understanding of the visual arts. The Eric Mitchell Prize is awarded for the best exhibition catalogue. Both must be on western art, written in English and published in the previous two years.

Naoki Prize: Association for the Promotion of Japanese Literature, Bungei-Shunju Building, 3 Kioi-cho, Chiyoda-ku, Tokyo 102, Japan. f. 1935, along with the Akutagawa Prize, for a work of popular fiction written by a more established writer. Awarded twice a year, in January and July.

National Book Awards: National Book Foundation, 95 Madison Avenue, Suite 709, New York, NY 10016, USA. *Telephone:* (212) 685-0261. *Fax:* (212) 213-6570. *E-mail:* nationalbook@nationalbook.org. *Website:* www.nationalbook .org. f. 1950. Annual awards to living American writers in four categories (fiction, non-fiction, poetry and young people's literature), and the Medal for Distinguished Contribution to American Letters.

National Book Critics Circle Awards: National Book Critics Circle, 360 Park Avenue South, New York, NY 10010, USA. *Website:* www.bookcritics .org. Annual awards for excellence in works of fiction, general non-fiction, poetry, biography/autobiography and criticism by American authors, published for the first time in the previous year. Nominated by members. In addition the NBCC awards, the Ivan Sandrof Lifetime Achievement Award honours one member of the Circle with the Nona Balakian Citation for Excellence in Reviewing.

National Short Story Prize: Room 316, BBC Henry Wood House, 3 & 6 Langham Place, London, W1A 1AA, England. *Website:* www.theshortstory.org .uk. f. 2005. Annual award, funded by the National Endowment for Science, Technology and the Arts (NESTA), in association with BBC Radio 4, Prospect magazine, Booktrust and Scottish Book Trust. The prize aims to celebrate the finest writers of short stories. It is open to authors with a previous record of publication, who are either UK nationals or residents. Entries may be stories published during the previous year, or previously unpublished.

Nebula Awards: Science Fiction and Fantasy Writers of America Inc., PO Box 877, Chestertown, MD 21620, USA. *Fax:* (410) 778-3052. *E-mail:* info@ sfwa.org. *Website:* www.sfwa.org. f. 1965. Annual awards presented to the best science fiction novel, novella, novelette and short story.

Nestlé Smarties Book Prize: Book Trust, Book House, 45 East Hill, London, SW18 2QZ, England. *Telephone:* (20) 8516-2986. *Fax:* (20) 8516-2978. *Website:* www.booktrusted.com. f. 1985. Annual awards for children's books in three categories (Gold, Silver and Bronze in age categories of 5 and under, 6–8 and 9–11), written in English by a citizen of, or an author resident in the UK, and published in the UK.

Neustadt International Prize for Literature: World Literature Today, University of Oklahoma, 110 Monnet Hall, Norman, OK 73019-4033, USA. *Telephone:* (405) 325-4531. *Fax:* (405) 325-7495. *E-mail:* rcdavis@ou.edu. *Website:* www.ou.edu/worldlit. f. 1969. Biennial award recognizing outstanding achievement of a living author, in fiction, poetry or drama. No applications are accepted.

John Newbery Medal: Association for Library Service to Children, American Library Association, 50 East Huron Street, Chicago, IL 60611-2795, USA. *Telephone:* (312) 944-7671. *E-mail:* alsc@ala.org. *Website:* www .ala.org/alsc. Annual award to the author of the most distinguished contribution to literature for children, published in the USA during the preceding year. Writing of any form can be considered: fiction, non-fiction and poetry. The award may be made posthumously. Only original works are considered; reprints and compilations are not eligible. Authors must be citizens or residents of the USA and the work must not have been published originally outside the USA.

Nobelpriset i Litteratur (Nobel Prize in Literature): The Nobel Committee of the Swedish Academy, PO Box 2118, 103 13 Stockholm, Sweden. *Telephone:* (8) 555 125 54. *Fax:* (8) 555 125 49. *E-mail:* sekretariat@ svenskaakademien.se. *Website:* www.nobel.se. One of several annual prizes for outstanding achievement in various fields, founded by the chemist Alfred Nobel. The prize in the field of literature has been awarded annually since 1901 in recognition of the literary merit of a distinguished writer in world letters. The Literature laureate is chosen from writers nominated by members of literary academies, academics, presidents of societies of authors, professors of literature and languages, and previous prize-winners, via the Nobel Committee. It is not possible to propose oneself as a candidate.

Nordic Council Literary Prize: Riksdagen, 100 12 Stockholm, Sweden. *Website:* www.norden.org. Award to a work published in Danish, Norwegian or Swedish during the past two years, or other Nordic languages during the last four years.

Ondaatje Prize: Royal Society of Literature, Somerset House, Strand, London, WC2R 1LA, England. *Telephone:* (20) 7845-4676. *Fax:* (20) 7845-4679. *E-mail:* info@rslit.org. *Website:* www.rslit.org. f. 2003. Sponsored by Sir Christopher Ondaatje, replacing the Winifred Holtby Memorial Prize. Annual award to a work of fiction or non-fiction with a strong sense of a particular place. Entries must have been written in the English language (translations are not eligible) by a living citizen of the UK, Republic of Ireland or Commonwealth, and published in the year preceding the year in which the award is presented.

Orange Broadband Prize for Fiction: Book Trust, Book House, 45 East Hill, London, SW18 2QZ, England. *Telephone:* (20) 8516-2972. *Fax:* (20) 8516-2978. *Website:* www.orangeprize.co.uk. f. 1996. Annual award founded by leading women in the publishing industry to help promote and reward female writers. Awarded for a full-length novel written in English by a woman of any nationality, which has been published in the UK by a UK publisher.

Orwell Prize: f. 1993. Annual awards by George Orwell Memorial Fund to encourage writing about politics, political thinking or public policy. The two categories are: book or pamphlet and newspaper and/or periodical article, feature or column, or sustained reportage on a theme. Writing must be in English and published in the preceding year in the UK or Ireland.

Pandora Award: *E-mail:* contacts@wipub.org.uk. *Website:* www.wipub.org .uk. Annual award from the Women in Publishing organization.

Francis Parkman Prize: Society of American Historians, Columbia University, 603 Fayerweather Hall, New York, NY 10027, USA. Awarded by the Society of American Historians to the book which best represents the union of the historian and the artist.

PEN/Faulkner Award for Fiction: Folger Shakespeare Library, 201 East Capitol Street SE, Washington, DC 20003, USA. f. 1981. Annual award for the best work of fiction by an American citizen published in the preceding year.

A. A. Phillips Award: Association for the Study of Australian Literature, c/o Department of English, School of Humanities & Social Sciences, John Woolley Building A 20, University of Sydney, 2006 Sydney, Australia. *Website:* www .asc.uq.edu.au/asal. Occasional award to be made on the recommendation of the ASAL executive, when a work or the work of an author is considered to merit attention as an outstanding contribution to Australian literature or literary studies.

Edgar Allan Poe Awards: Mystery Writers of America, 17 East 47th Street, Sixth Floor, New York, NY 10017, USA. *Website:* www.mysterywriters.org. f. 1954. These awards, sponsored by The Mystery Writers of America, honour the best in mystery fiction and non-fiction produced the previous year. The awards, known as the Edgars, are awarded to authors of distinguished work in various categories. Categories include short stories, novels, critical studies, juvenile and young adult fiction, television and motion picture screenplays, first novels, paperback originals, fact crime, and critical/biographical work. A Grand Master Award is also presented for lifetime achievement.

Premio Camões (Camões Prize): Rua Rodrigues Sampaio, 113, 1150-279, Lisbon, Portugal. *Telephone:* (21) 3109100. *E-mail:* geral@instituto-camoes.pt. *Website:* www.instituto-camoes.pt. f. 1988 by the governments of Portugal and Brazil. Annual award by the governments of Portugal and Brazil for an author writing in Portuguese.

Premio Cervantes (Cervantes Prize): Dirección General del Libro y Bibliotecas, Ministerio de Cultura, Plaza del Rey, 28004 Madrid, Spain. f. 1974. Annual award for the entire body of an author's output in Spanish.

Premio Nadal: Ediciones Destino SA, Calle Provenza 260, 08008 Barcelona, Spain. *Website:* www.edestino.es/nadal.htm. The oldest literary prize in Spain. Awarded annually for unpublished novels in Spanish, which have not won any prize previously.

Premio Octavio Paz de Poesía y Ensayo (Octavio Paz Poetry and Essay Prize): Fundación Octavio Paz, Francisco Sosa 383, Col. Barrio de Santa Catarina, 04000 México, DF, Mexico. *Telephone:* (5) 659-5797. *Fax:* (5) 554-9705. *Website:* www.fundacionpaz.org.mx. Annual award for a poet or essayist with high artistic, intellectual and critical qualities, following in the modern tradition that Octavio Paz represented. Nominations are invited from official bodies and learned institutions.

Premio Planeta: Editorial Planeta, Córsega 273–79, 08008 Barcelona, Spain. *Website:* www.editorial.planeta.es. Annual award for the best unpublished and original novel in Spanish.

Premio Príncipe de Asturias (Prince of Asturias Award for Letters): Fundación Príncipe de Asturias, General Yague 2, 33004 Oviedo, Spain. *Website:* www.fpa.es/esp/index.html. The prize is one of eight awarded by the Foundation, which were granted for the first time in 1981. (The others include Social Communication and Humanities, Arts, Sciences, Scientific Research and Technical Co-operation.) The prize is presented to a person, institution or group whose work represents an important contribution to the fields of linguistics and literature.

Thomas Pringle Award: English Academy of Southern Africa, PO Box 124, Wits, 2050, South Africa. *Telephone:* (11) 717-9339. *Fax:* (11) 717-9339. *E-mail:* englishacademy@societies.wits.ac.za. *Website:* www.englishacademy .co.za. f. 1962. Annual award to honour achievements in five different categories: reviews, educational articles, literary articles, short stories or one act plays, and poetry. Three categories are honoured each year.

Prix Femina (Femina Prize): f. 1904 by 22 members of the periodical La Vie heureuse, in protest against the exclusion of women from the jury of the Prix Goncourt, the prize aims to encourage writing by women. It is awarded each year for a novel written in French by a woman. The winner is decided by an all-female jury. In 1986 the Prix Fémina Étranger, for foreign novels, was established, to provide an opportunity to recognize an outstanding work in the field of foreign novels.

Prix Goncourt (Goncourt Prize): Drouant, 18 Place Gaillon, 75002 Paris, France. *Telephone:* 1 45 20 27 21. *Website:* www.academie-goncourt.fr. The Académie (Société littéraire des Goncourt) was established in 1900, and comprises ten members, who hold a salon on the first Tuesday of every month above the restaurant Drouant in Paris. The first Prix Goncourt was awarded in 1903 and it has become regarded as France's most prestigious literary award. Prizes are awarded in the categories of novels, first novels, biography, children's book and poetry.

Prix Médicis (Médicis Prizes): 25 rue Dombasle, 75015 Paris, France. *Telephone:* 1 48 28 76 90. f. 1958. Annual awards in three categories: Prix Médicis (aims to reflect contemporary literary trends), Prix Médicis de l'Essai (awarded to an essay written in French), Prix Médicis Étranger (awarded to a novel which has been translated into French).

The Pulitzer Prizes: Columbia University, 709 Journalism Building, 2950 Broadway, New York, NY 10027, USA. *Telephone:* (212) 854-3841. *Fax:* (212) 854-3342. *E-mail:* pulitzer@pulitzer.org. *Website:* www.pulitzer.org. The Pulitzer Prizes were established in 1917 following a bequest from Joseph Pulitzer, a Hungarian-born journalist and pioneering publisher of American newspapers. The first Pulitzer Prizes were awarded as an incentive to excellence. There are now 21 prizes in total. In the category of 'Letters' (literature), awards are made in the fields of fiction, non-fiction and poetry, as well as biography/autobiography, drama and history. Entries must be published during the previous calendar year. Only US writers are considered except in the history category where author may be of any nationality as long as the book deals with American history. Fiction awards are made preferably to books dealing with American life.

Pushcart Prize: Best of the Small Presses: Pushcart Press, PO Box 380, Wainscott, NY 11975, USA. *Telephone:* (516) 324-9300. Annual award for work published by a small press or literary journal. Works are nominated by editors and then reviewed by judges. The winning works are published in a special anthology. Works of poetry, short fiction, essays, or self-contained extracts from books are eligible.

The Quill Book Awards: The Quills Literacy Foundation, 360 Park Avenue South, New York, NY 10010-1710, USA. *Telephone:* (646) 746-6447. *Fax:* (646) 746-6446. *Website:* www.thequills.org. f. 2005 to inspire reading and promote literacy; awards chosen by the public and by panels of experts in 15 categories: Book of the Year, Rookie of the Year, Book Club Award, Children's Book of the Year, Best Book to Film, Graphic Novel of the Year, Design, Literary Fiction, Suspense/Mystery or Thriller, Science Fiction/Fantasy or Horror, Romance, Biography/Memoir, Religion/Spirituality, Science, Health/Self Improvement, Sports, Business, History/Current Events/Politics.

Rea Award for the Short Story: Dungannon Foundation, 53 West Church Hill Road, Washington, CT 06794, USA. *Website:* www.reaaward.org. f. 1986 by Michael M. Rea. Annual award to a writer who has made a significant contribution to the short story genre. US and Canadian writers are eligible. No applications are accepted.

Theodore Roethke Memorial Foundation Triennial Poetry Prize: 11 West Hannum Boulevard, Saginaw, MI 48602, USA. Awarded for a book of poetry in English, not a collection. Selected by three judges, chosen by the Poet Laureate.

Romantic Novel of the Year: Romantic Novelists' Association, 36 Eastgate, Hallaton, Leicestershire LE16 8UB, England. *Telephone:* (1858) 555602. f. 1981. This annual award, administered by the Romantic Novelists' Association (RNA) is given to the best modern or historical (i.e. set before 1950) romantic novel of the year. Entries must be written in English and have been first published in the UK in the preceding year.

Rooney Prize for Irish Literature: Strathlin, Templecarrig, Delgany, County Wicklow, Ireland. A non-competitive prize to reward and encourage young Irish talent. Writers must be Irish, under 40 years of age, and their work must be written in Irish or English. No applications are accepted, recipients are chosen by a panel of judges. Special awards are given on rare occasions where deemed of merit.

Royal Society Prizes for Science Books: The Royal Society, 6 Carlton House Terrace, London, SW1Y 5AG, England. *Telephone:* (20) 7451-2500. *Fax:*

(20) 7930-2170. *E-mail:* info@royalsoc.ac.uk. *Website:* www.royalsoc.ac.uk. f. 1988 by COPUS—the Committee on the Public Understanding of Science of the Royal Society, the Royal Institution and the British Association for the Advancement of Science—and the Science Museum. Sponsored by the Aventis Foundation and known as the Aventis Prizes until 2006. General Prize and Junior Prize awarded to authors of popular non-fiction science or technology books, written in English, which are judged to contribute most to the public understanding of science.

Sagittarius Prize: Society of Authors, 84 Drayton Gardens, London, SW10 9SB, England. *Telephone:* (20) 7373-6642. *Fax:* (20) 7373-5768. *E-mail:* info@ societyofauthors.org. *Website:* www.societyofauthors.org. f. 1990. Award for a first published novel by an author over the age of 60.

Saltire Society Literary Awards: The Saltire Society, 9 Fountain Close, 22 High Street, Edinburgh, EH1 1TF, Scotland. *Telephone:* (131) 556-1836. *Fax:* (131) 557-1675. *E-mail:* saltire@saltiresociety.org. *Website:* www .saltiresociety.org.uk. f. 1936. Annual awards in four categories: Scottish Book of the Year (f. 1982), Scottish First Book of the Year (f. 1988), Scottish History Book of the Year (f. 1965), and Scottish Research Book of the Year. Open to any book by an author of Scottish descent or living in Scotland, or to any book which deals with the work or life of a Scot, or with a Scottish question, event or situation.

Saltire Society/Times Educational Supplement Scotland Prize for Educational Publications: The Saltire Society, 9 Fountain Close, 22 High Street, Edinburgh, EH1 1TF, Scotland. *Telephone:* (131) 556-1836. *Fax:* (131) 557-1675. *E-mail:* saltire@saltiresociety.org.uk. *Website:* www.saltiresociety .org.uk. f. 1992 to enhance the teaching and learning of an aspect or aspects of the Scottish curriculum. Annual award open to published works of non-fiction, which must be relevant to Scottish schoolchildren aged 5–18, although not necessarily the product of a Scottish author or publisher. To be eligible, a work has to be a book or a package, the bulk of which comprises written words. Non-written elements such as videotapes or computer software may be included but must make up no more than 25% of the package.

Olive Schreiner Prize: English Academy of Southern Africa, PO Box 124, Wits, 2050, South Africa. *Telephone:* (11) 717-9339. *Fax:* (11) 717-9339. *E-mail:* englishacademy@societies.wits.ac.za. *Website:* www.englishacademy .co.za. f. 1964. Annual award to honour new talent for excellence in prose, poetry and drama. Open to works written in English by Southern African writers, published in South Africa. Winners are chosen by a panel of experts.

The Scotiabank Giller Prize: c/o Elana Rabinovitch, 576 Davenport Road, Toronto, ON M5R 1K9, Canada. *Telephone:* (416) 934-0755. *E-mail:* contact@ scotiabankgillerprize.ca. *Website:* www.scotiabankgillerprize.ca. f. 1994 by Toronto businessman Jack Rabinovitch, in memory of his late wife, literary journalist Doris Giller. Annual award, co-sponsored by Scotiabank, for the best Canadian novel or short story collection published in English in the preceding year.

Scottish Arts Council Book of the Year Award: Scottish Arts Council, 12 Manor Place, Edinburgh, EH3 7DD, Scotland. *Telephone:* (131) 226-6051. *Website:* www.scottishbooktrust.com. f. 2002 to replace the former Scottish Arts Council Book Awards and Children's Book Awards. One winner is now chosen in each category of Adult and Children's Book of the Year. Authors should be Scottish, resident in Scotland or have written works of Scottish interest. Applications from publishers only.

Somerset Maugham Awards: Somerset Maugham Trust Fund, Society of Authors, 84 Drayton Gardens, London, SW10 9SB, England. *Telephone:* (20) 7373-6642. *Fax:* (20) 7373-5768. *E-mail:* info@societyofauthors.org. *Website:* www.societyofauthors.org. Awarded to a writer on the strength of a published work.

Stand Magazine Short Story Competition: Stand Magazine, School of English, Leeds University, Leeds, LS2 9JT, England. *Telephone:* (1132) 334794. *Fax:* (1132) 332791. *E-mail:* Stand@leeds.ac.uk. Awarded for an original story of no more than 8,000 words, written in English. Works must be previously unpublished and unbroadcast.

Sunday Times Award for Literary Excellence: The Sunday Times, 1 Pennington Street, London, E1 9XW, England. f. 1987. Annual award to fiction and non-fiction writers. The winner is chosen by a panel of judges consisting of Sunday Times critics and awarded at the discretion of the Literary Editor.

Sunday Times Young Writer of the Year Award: The Sunday Times, 1 Pennington Street, London, E1 9XW, England. f. 1987. Annual award to a published writer of fiction or non-fiction, under the age of 30. The winner is chosen by a panel of judges consisting of Sunday Times critics.

Texas Institute of Letters Awards: Texas Institute of Letters, Literary Awards, PO Box 935, St Edward's University, Houston House, 217 Wook Street, Austin, TX 78704, USA. *Telephone:* (512) 448-8702. *Website:* www .stedwards.edu/newc/marks/til. A series of annual awards presented by the Texas Institute of Letters. Awards include Jesse H. Jones Award for a novel, Best Book of Poetry Award, Natalie Ornish Poetry Award, Steven Turner Award for a novel, John Bloom Humor Award, Soeurette Diehl Fraser Translation Award, O. Henry Award, Brazos Bookstore Short Story Award. Open to authors who have lived in Texas for two consecutive years or non-residents whose work concerns Texas; entries must have been published in the previous year.

Dylan Thomas Prize: Dylan Thomas Centre, Ty Llen, Somerset Place, Swansea, SA1 1RR, Wales. *Telephone:* (1792) 474051. *E-mail:* info@ thedylanthomasprize.com. *Website:* www.thedylanthomasprize.com. f. 2004 (first award 2006); awarded to a piece of writing in English by an author under the age of 30, from anywhere in the world.

Tir na n-Og Awards: Welsh Books Council, Castell Brychan, Aberystwyth, SY23 2JB, Wales. *Telephone:* (1970) 624151. *Fax:* (1970) 625385. *E-mail:* castellbrychan@cllc.org.uk. *Website:* www.cllc.org.uk. Annual awards in three categories: Best Welsh-Language Fiction of the Year, Best Welsh-Language Non-Fiction Book of the Year, and Best English (Anglo-Welsh) Book of the Year.

Tom-Gallon Award: Society of Authors, 84 Drayton Gardens, London, SW10 9SB, England. *Telephone:* (20) 7373-6642. *Fax:* (20) 7373-5768. *E-mail:* info@ societyofauthors.org. *Website:* www.societyofauthors.org. Biennial award for writers of limited means who have had at least one short story published.

Translators' Association Translation Prizes: Translators' Association, 84 Drayton Gardens, London, SW10 9SB, England. *Telephone:* (20) 7373-6642. *Fax:* (20) 7373-5768. *E-mail:* info@societyofauthors.org. Nine awards: John Florio Prize (biennial award for the best translation of a full-length 20th-century Italian literary work into English, published in the UK); Calouste Gulbenkian Prize (triennial award for translations into English of works from any period by a Portuguese national; the prize is also open to unpublished translations of works by Portuguese nationals); Hellenic Foundation for Culture Prize (triennial award for the best translation into English from modern Greek of a full-length work of imaginative literature); Scott Moncrieff Prize (annual award for the best translation into English of a full-length French literary work of the last 150 years, published in the UK); Sasakawa Prize (triennial award for the best translation into English of a full-length Japanese literary work, published in the UK); Schlegel-Tieck Prize (annual award for the best translation into English of a full-length German literary work of the last 100 years, published in the UK); Bernard Shaw Prize (triennial award for the best translation into English of a full-length Swedish work, published in the UK); Premio Valle Inclán (for the best translation into English of a full-length Spanish work from any period, published in the UK); Vondel Translation Prize (for the best translation of a Dutch or Flemish literary work into English, published in the UK or the USA).

Betty Trask Prize: Society of Authors, 84 Drayton Gardens, London, SW10 9SB, England. *Telephone:* (20) 7373-6642. *Fax:* (20) 7373-5768. *E-mail:* info@ societyofauthors.org. *Website:* www.societyofauthors.org. Annual award for authors under 35 years old and Commonwealth citizens, for a first novel of a traditional or romantic nature.

Travelling Scholarship Fund: Society of Authors, 84 Drayton Gardens, London, SW10 9SB, England. *Telephone:* (20) 7373-6642. *Fax:* (20) 7373-5768. *E-mail:* info@societyofauthors.org. *Website:* www.societyofauthors.org. Non-competitive awards enabling British writers to travel abroad. No submissions accepted.

Whitbread Book Awards: see Costa Book Awards.

Whitfield Prize: Royal Historical Society, University College London, Gower Street, London, WC1E 6BT, England. Award for an author's first book on British history, published in the UK in the previous three years. The winner is announced at the Royal Historical Society annual reception in July.

John Whiting Award: Drama Department, Arts Council England, 14 Great Peter Street, London, SW1P 3NQ, England. *Telephone:* (20) 7973-6431. *Fax:* (20) 7973-6983. *E-mail:* info.drama@artscouncil.org.uk. *Website:* www .artscouncil.org.uk. f. 1965. Award to commemorate the contribution of playwright John Whiting (member of the Drama Panel of the Arts Council 1955–63) to British post-war theatre. Writers who have received an award offer from the Arts Council Theatre Writing Scheme are eligible, as are those who have had a commission or premiere from a theatre company funded by the Arts Council or a Regional Arts Board.

Whiting Writers' Awards: Mrs Giles Whiting Foundation, 1133 Avenue of the Americas, New York, NY 10036, USA. *Website:* www.whitingfoundation .org. Annual awards presented to emergent writers in recognition of their writing achievement and future promise in four categories: fiction, poetry, non-fiction and drama. By internal nomination; applications are not accepted.

WHSmith Awards: WHSmith PLC, Nations House, 103 Wigmore Street, London, W1U 1WH, England. *Telephone:* (20) 7409-3222. *Fax:* (20) 7514-9633. *Website:* www.whsmith.co.uk. Annual awards in eight categories: fiction, general knowledge, business, new talent, biography, travel, children's fiction, and home and leisure, and a literary award for an outstanding contribution to English literature in the year under review, to the author of a book written in English and published in the UK. Authors considered will be from the UK, the Commonwealth, or Ireland, but writers cannot submit work themselves. Voted for by the public.

WHSmith Thumping Good Read Award: WHSmith PLC, Nations House, 103 Wigmore Street, London, W1U 1WH, England. *Telephone:* (20) 7409-3222. *Fax:* (20) 7514-9633. *Website:* www.whsmith.co.uk. f. 1992. Concentrates on books more 'accessible' than 'literary'; genre fiction like murder mysteries, espionage thrillers, etc. is considered.

David T. K. Wong Prize for Short Fiction: International PEN, 9–10 Charterhouse Buildings, Goswell Road, London, EC1M 7AT, England. *Telephone:* (20) 7253-4308. *Fax:* (20) 7253-5711. *E-mail:* intpen@dircon.co .uk. *Website:* www.internatpen.org.uk. f. 2000. Biennial award to promote literary excellence in the form of the unpublished short story, written in English and incorporating one or more of the ideals of International PEN.

Yorkshire Post Book of the Year Award: c/o Margaret Brown, The Rectory, Ripley, Harrogate, North Yorkshire HG3 3AY, England. Annual award for a work of fiction or non-fiction by a British writer or one resident in the UK, published in the UK in the preceding year. Up to four books may be submitted by any one publisher for each imprint.

APPENDIX B: LITERARY ORGANIZATIONS

For organizations of particular interest to poets, please see Appendix C of the International Who's Who in Poetry.

Albania

Albanian PEN Centre: Rruga Ded Gjo Luli, Pallati 5, shk. 3/4, Tirana. *E-mail:* albania@aol2.albaniaonline.net.

Albanian Writers' and Artists' League: Rr. Kavajes Nr. 4, Tirana. *Telephone:* (42) 28229. *Fax:* (42) 27036.

Argentina

Argentine PEN Centre: Coronel Diaz 2089, 17°, 1425 Buenos Aires.

Salta PEN Centre: Biblioteca de Textos Universitarios, Universidad Católica de Salta, Pellegrini 790, Salta 4400.

Armenia

Armenian PEN Centre: Apt 8, 24 Papazian str., 375012 Yerevan. *E-mail:* armpen@arminco.com.

Australia

Australian Society of Authors: PO Box 1566, Strawberry Hills, NSW 2012. *Telephone:* (2) 9318 0877. *Fax:* (2) 9318 0530. *E-mail:* office@asauthors.org. *Website:* www.asauthors.org.

Australian Writers' Guild Ltd: 60 Kellett Street, Kings Cross, Sydney, NSW 2011. Professional association for writers in areas of television, radio, screen and stage to promote and protect professional interests.

Bibliographical Society of Australia and New Zealand: c/o Secretary/Treasurer, PO Box 1463, Wagga Wagga, NSW 2650. *Telephone:* (2) 6931-8669. *Fax:* (2) 6931-8669. *E-mail:* rsalmond@pobox.com. *Website:* www.csu.edu.au/community/BSANZ. Promotes research, largely through publishing, in all aspects of physical bibliography.

Canberra PEN Centre: PO Box 261, Dickson, ACT 2602. *Telephone:* (2) 6248-0912. *E-mail:* lawjs@ozemail.com.au. *Website:* www.pen.org.au.

Children's Book Council of Australia: (ACT Branch), PO Box 5548, Hughes, ACT 2605.

Melbourne PEN Centre: PO Box 2273, Caulfield Junction, Vic. 3161. *E-mail:* penmelbourne@optusnet.com.au. *Website:* www.pen.org.au.

PEN Australia North: PO Box 328, Annerley, Qld 4103. *Telephone:* (7) 3890-2089. *E-mail:* pen@plateaupress.com.au. *Website:* www.pen.org.au.

Perth PEN Centre: PO Box 1131, Subiaco, WA 6008. *Website:* www.pen.org.au.

Society of Editors: PO Box 176, Carlton South, Vic. 3053. Professional association of book editors. Organizes training seminars, monthly meetings and a newsletter.

Sydney PEN Centre: Faculty of Humanities and Social Sciences, University of Technology Sydney, PO Box 123, Broadway, NSW 2007. *Telephone:* (2) 9514-2738. *Fax:* (2) 9514-2778. *E-mail:* sydney@pen.org.au. *Website:* www.pen.org.au.

Austria

Austrian PEN Centre: Concordia Haus, Bankgasse 8, 1010 Vienna. *E-mail:* oepen.club@netway.at. *Website:* www.penclub.at.

Azerbaijan

Azerbaijani PEN Centre: ul. Bol'shaia Krepostnaia, 28, Baku.

Bangladesh

Bangladeshi PEN Centre: L'Espoir, 60/2, North Dhanmondi, Kalabagan, Dhaka-1205. *Telephone:* (2) 912-8965. *E-mail:* shajel123@hotmail.com.

Belarus

Belarusian PEN Centre: PO Box 218, Minsk 220050. *E-mail:* pen@pen.unibel.by. *Website:* www.pen.unibel.by.

Belgium

International PEN Club, Belgian Dutch-speaking Centre: Wiesbeek 25, 9255 Buggenhout. *E-mail:* penvl@skynet.be.

International PEN Club, Belgian French-speaking Centre: 10 avenue des Cerfs, 1950 Kraainem, Brussels. *E-mail:* huguette.db@skynet.be. Receptions of foreign writers, defence of the liberty of thought of all writers, participation at the worldwide congresses of PEN.

Koninklijke Vlaamse Academie van Belgie voor Wetenschappen en Kunsten (Royal Flemish Academy of Belgium for Science and the Arts): Paleis der Academien, Hertogsstraat 1, 1000 Brussels. *Telephone:* (2) 550-2323. *Fax:* (2) 550-2325. *E-mail:* info@kvab.be. *Website:* www.kvab.be.

Société de Langue et de Litterature Wallonnes: Université de Liège, 4000 Liège. Holds meetings, lectures, exhibitions, library, media, archives, publications.

Société Royale des Bibliophiles et Iconophiles de Belgique: 4 Boulevard de l'Empereur, 1000 Brussels. Publication of Le Livre et l'Estampe (Semestrial), exhibitions.

Society of Literary Writers: Rue du Prince Royal 87, 1050 Brussels. *Telephone:* (2) 551 0320. *Fax:* (2) 551 0325.

Benin

Benin PEN Centre: PO Box 03-2810, Cotonou.

Bolivia

Bolivian PEN Centre: PO Box 5920, Cochabamba. *E-mail:* gabyvall@supernet.com.bo.

Bosnia and Herzegovina

Association of Writers of Bosnia and Herzegovina: Ferhadija 19, 71000 Sarajevo.

PEN Centre of Bosnia and Herzegovina: Vrazova 1, Sarajevo 71 000. *E-mail:* krugpen@bih.net.ba.

Brazil

Academia Cearense de Letras: Palácio Senador Alencar, Rua São Paulo 51, 60000 Fortaleza CE. Cultivates and develops literature and scientific achievement. Meets monthly, annual publication.

Associação Brasileira de Imprensa (Brazilian Press Association): Rua Araújo Porto Alegre, 71 Centro, 20030, Rio de Janeiro, RJ. *Telephone:* (21) 2282-1292. *Website:* www.abi.org.br.

Brazilian PEN Centre: Praia do Flamengo 172, 11°, Rio de Janeiro, RJ.

Brazilian Translators' Union (SINTRA): Rua de Quitanda, 194 sala 1005, Centro, PO Box 20091, Rio de Janeiro, RJ.

Companhia Editora Nacional: Rua Joli 294, São Paulo, SP 03016-020.

Sindicato de Escritores de Rio de Janeiro: Avenida Heitor Beltrão 353, 20550, Rio de Janeiro, RJ.

Bulgaria

Bulgarian PEN Centre: Bull. Vassil Levsky 60, Sofia 1000. *E-mail:* alek@astratek.net.

Bulgarian Writers' Union: Anguel Kantchev 5, 1000 Sofia. *Telephone:* (2) 89 83 46.

Union of Bulgarian Writers: 2A Slaveikov Square, 1000 Sofia. *Telephone:* (2) 9880031.

Cameroon

Centre PEN du Cameroun (Cameroonian PEN Centre): PO Box 5329, Yaounde 1er.

Canada

Canada Council for the Arts—Conseil des Arts du Canada: 350 Albert Street, PO Box 1047, Ottawa, ON K1P 5V8. *Website:* www.canadacouncil.ca. Supports Canadian professional writers and book and magazine publishers to develop, produce and promote works of literary merit. Administers the annual Governor-General's Literary Awards.

Canadian Association of Journalists—L'Association Canadienne des Journalistes: Algonquin College, 1385 Woodroffe Avenue, B224, Ottawa, ON K2G 1V8. *Telephone:* (613) 526-8061. *Fax:* (613) 521-3904. *Website:* www.caj.ca.

Canadian Authors' Association: PO Box 419, Campbellford, ON K0L 1L0. *Telephone:* (705) 653-0323. *Fax:* (705) 653-0593. *E-mail:* info@canauthors.org. *Website:* www.canauthors.org. f. 1921.

Canadian PEN Centre: Suite 214, 24 Ryerson Avenue, Toronto, ON M5T 2P3. *E-mail:* pen@pencanada.ca. *Website:* www.pencanada.ca.

Canadian Science Writers' Association: PO Box 75, Station A, Toronto, ON M5W 2S9.